EDITOR & PUBLISHER

PUBLISHER
Mike Blinder
406-445-0000 ext. 1
mike@editorandpublisher.com

EDITOR-IN-CHIEF
Robin Blinder
406-445-0000 ext. 0
robin@editorandpublisher.com

INDUSTRY NEWS EDITOR
Cindy Durham
cdurham@newspapers.org

CONTRIBUTING EDITOR
Gretchen A. Peck
gretchenapeck@gmail.com

CONTRIBUTING WRITERS
Rob Tornoe, Doug Phares,
Richard E. Brown, Guy Tasaka

CHIEF REVENUE OFFICER
John Newby
815-326-9061
john@editorandpublisher.com

DIRECTOR OF ADVERTISING SALES
Peter Conti, Jr.
804-852-5663 (cell)
Peter@editoranpublisher.com

CHIEF MEDIA TECHNOLOGY EVANGELIST
Guy Tasaka
Guy@EditorandPublisher.com

BILLING AND ACCOUNTING
406-445-0000 ext. 0
office@editorandpublisher.com

MEDIA JOB BOARD
406-445-0000 ext. 4
jobs@editorandpublisher.com

SUBSCRIPTION SERVICES
406-445-0000 ext. 7
circ@editorandpublisher.com

DESIGN AND PRODUCTION
DESIGN2PRO
Howard Barbanel
516-860-7440
howard@design2pro.com
www.design2pro.com

BUSINESS MAILING ADDRESS
Editor & Publisher Magazine
1028 Crutcher Station Drive
Hendersonville, TN 37075-1457

www.editorandpublisher.com
406-445-0000

Editor & Publisher is printed in the U.S.A.

America's Oldest Journal
Covering the Newspaper Industry

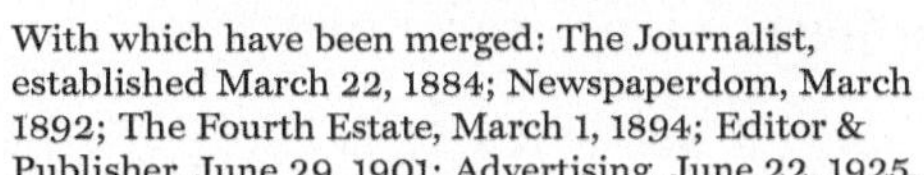

With which have been merged: The Journalist, established March 22, 1884; Newspaperdom, March 1892; The Fourth Estate, March 1, 1894; Editor & Publisher, June 29, 1901; Advertising, June 22, 1925.

Letter from the General Manager...

Welcome to "*2024 Editor & Publisher News Media DataBook.*" Inside, you will find a wealth of information about daily, community, niche, alternative newspapers, and many more categories related to the newspaper publishing industry in the U.S. and Canada.

And we are proud to announce that this is the 103rd anniversary of the DataBook. It contains nearly 1,000 pages of valuable industry information.

The listings in this directory are designed to give you all the essential information about these newspapers. Most include the names of key personnel, telephone numbers and emails, circulation, and other important information pertinent to industry research.

More and more DataBook users are now using our online DataBook for the most up-to-date information. E&P and even the newspapers themselves continuously update their information. Visit our website at editorandpublisher.com, and in the upper left corner of the homepage, you will find the link titled "DataBook" which will allow you to access the database.

You can purchase only the data you need or purchase a one-year subscription. Plus, the data will be fresh and up to date. The system allows any newspaper to update its information directly and securely online.

This DataBook is divided into three sections: Section I contains Daily Newspapers, Section II contains Community, Alternative and Niche publications and Section III contains Services and Organizations.

E&P considers a daily newspaper as one with a 90 percent paid circulation and is published seven days a week either online, in print, or a combination of both that equals seven days of publishing. Community newspapers are defined as newspapers publishing less than seven days a week, be it online and/or print.

As always, we welcome feedback from our subscribers and listees as we continue our efforts to supply the most useful and reliable information possible. Please continue to direct your DataBook comments, questions and suggestions to us at office@editorandpublisher.com.

Sincerely,

Peter Conti, Jr.
Director of Advertising Sales

Thank you to our partners for providing additional data for the E&P DataBook

Dirks, Van Essen & April

Dirks, Van Essen & April is the leading merger and acquisition firm in the U.S. newspapers industry and its top authority on transactions and valuations.

dirksvanessen.com

Section I

Daily Newspapers Published in the United States and Canada United States Dailies

Canada

Daily Canadian Newspapers

UNITED STATES DAILY NEWSPAPERS

ALABAMA

ALEXANDER CITY OUTLOOK

Street address 1: 548 Cherokee Road
Street address city: Alexander City
Street address state: AL
Zip/Postal code: 35010-2503
County: Tallapoosa
Country: USA
Mailing address: PO BOX 999
Mailing city: ALEXANDER CITY
Mailing state: AL
Mailing zip: 35011-0999
General Phone: (256) 234-4281
Advertising Phone: (256) 234-4281 ext.15
Editorial Phone: (256) 234-4281 ext.23
General/National Adv. E-mail: kenneth.boone@alexcityoutlook.com
Display Adv. E-mail: tippy.hunter@alexcityoutlook.com
Classified Adv. e-mail: linda.ewing@alexcityoutlook.com
Editorial e-mail: austin.nelson@alexcityoutlook.com ; editorgroup@alexcityoutlook.com
Primary Website: www.alexcityoutlook.com
Year Established: 1892
News Services: Landon Media Group.
Special Editions: Bridal (Apr); Back-to-School (Aug); Christmas Greetings (Dec); Parade (Feb); Home Town Business (Jan); FYI (Jul); Spring Fashion (Mar); Graduation (May); Gift Guide (Nov); Fall Fashion (Sept).
Special Weekly Sections: Lake Martin Fish Wrapper (Fri); Education (Thur); Automotive (Wed).
Syndicated Publications: Parade (S); American Profile (Weekly).
Delivery Methods: Mail`Newsstand`Carrier`Racks
Own Printing Facility?: Y
Commercial printers?: Y
Sat. Circulation Paid: 5300
Audit By: Sworn/Estimate/Non-Audited
Audit Date: 12.07.2019
Personnel: Kenneth Boone (Pub.); David Kendrick (Circ. Mgr); Mitch Sneed (Managing Ed); Tippy Hunter (Dir of Advert); Betsy Iler (Magazine Manag. Ed); Mia Osborn (Asst. Mag. Ed); Lee Champion (Prodn. Mgr.); Kim Morse (Market. Consultant); Doug Patterson (National Accts.); Robert Hudson (Sports Ed.); Cathy Higgins (Sports Ed.)
Parent company (for newspapers): Boone Newspapers, Inc.

ANDALUSIA STAR-NEWS

Street address 1: 207 Dunson St
Street address city: Andalusia
Street address state: AL
Zip/Postal code: 36420-3705
County: Covington
Country: USA
Mailing address: PO BOX 430
Mailing city: ANDALUSIA
Mailing state: AL
Mailing zip: 36420-1208
General Phone: (334) 222-2402
Editorial Phone: (334) 222-2402
General/National Adv. E-mail: ruck.ashworth@andalusiastarnews.com
Display Adv. E-mail: ruck.ashworth@andalusiastarnews.com
Classified Adv. e-mail: ruck.ashworth@andalusiastarnews.com
Editorial e-mail: michele.gerlach@andalusiastarnews.com
Primary Website: www.andalusiastarnews.com
Mthly Avg Views: 498200
Mthly Avg Unique Visitors: 3570
Year Established: 1939
News Services: NEA.
Special Editions: Baseball (Apr); Football (Aug); Progress (Feb); Chamber Guide (Jan); Pride In America (Jun); Home Improvement (Mar); Graduation (May);
Special Weekly Sections: Health Page (Fri); Business/Financial Page (Tues); Education (Tues); Education (Wed.).
Syndicated Publications: American Profile (Weekly).
Delivery Methods: Mail`Newsstand`Carrier`Racks
Sat. Circulation Paid: 3600
Audit By: Sworn/Estimate/Non-Audited
Audit Date: 12.07.2019
Personnel: Michele Gerlach (Pub./Ed); Ruck Ashworth (Adv. Mgr.); Chris Love (Prodn. Mgr.); Lisa Rainey (Office Mgr); Kendra Majors (Principal Designer/Magazine Ed); Josh Dutton (Sports Ed.)
Parent company (for newspapers): Boone Newspapers, Inc.

THE ANNISTON STAR

Street address 1: 4305 McClellan Blvd
Street address city: Anniston
Street address state: AL
Zip/Postal code: 36206-2812
County: Calhoun
Country: USA
Mailing address: PO BOX 189
Mailing city: ANNISTON
Mailing state: AL
Mailing zip: 36202-0189
General Phone: (256) 236-1551
Advertising Phone: (256) 235-9222
Editorial Phone: (256) 235-9556
General/National Adv. E-mail: mbergstresser@annistonstar.com
Display Adv. E-mail: mbergstresser@annistonstar.com
Classified Adv. e-mail: mbergstresser@annistonstar.com
Editorial e-mail: news@annistonstar.com
Primary Website: www.annistonstar.com
Year Established: 1883
News Services: NYT, Tribune
Special Editions: Healthy Living
Special Weekly Sections: TV Star (Fri)
Syndicated Publications: Parade (S). LongLeaf
Delivery Methods: Mail`Newsstand`Carrier`Racks
Areas Served - City/County or Portion Thereof, or Zip codes: East Alabama
Own Printing Facility?: Y
Commercial printers?: Y
Avg Free Circ: 613
Sat. Circulation Paid: 9983
Sat. Circulation Free: 613
Sun. Circulation Paid: 11344
Sun. Circulation Free: 483
Audit By: AAM
Audit Date: 31.03.2019
Personnel: H. Brandt Ayers (Chrmn./Pub.); Phillip A. Sanguinetti (Pres.); Robert Jackson (VP for Operations); Robert Jackson (V.P/ Sales & Mktg); Scott Calhoun (Office Manager); Ben Gilreath (Pro. Mgr.); Dennis Dunn (Circ. Mgr); Chris Pittman (Online Dir); Ben Cunningham (Mng. Ed.); Donnie Bowman (Circ. Mgr.); Lisa Davis (Features Ed.); Mandy Schlemminger (Customer Serv Mgr); George Smith (Columnist); Phillip Tutor (Commentary Ed.); Trent Penny (Photo Ed.); Bob Davis (Pub./Ed.)
Parent company (for newspapers): Consolidated Publishing Co.

THE NEWS-COURIER

Street address 1: 410 W Green St
Street address city: Athens
Street address state: AL
Zip/Postal code: 35611-2518
County: Limestone
Country: USA
Mailing address: PO BOX 670
Mailing city: ATHENS
Mailing state: AL
Mailing zip: 35612-0670
General Phone: (256) 232-2720
Advertising Phone: (256) 232-2720
Editorial Phone: (256) 232-2720
General/National Adv. E-mail: katherine@athensnews-courier.com
Display Adv. E-mail: katherine@athensnews-courier.com
Classified Adv. e-mail: classifieds@athensnews-courier.com
Editorial e-mail: nicolle@athensnews-courier.com
Primary Website: www.enewscourier.com
Mthly Avg Views: 568052
Mthly Avg Unique Visitors: 129014
Year Established: 1880
News Services: AP
Special Weekly Sections: TV Times (Thurs); Food Day (Wed)
Syndicated Publications: TV Tab (Thurs)
Delivery Methods: Mail`Newsstand`Racks
Areas Served - City/County or Portion Thereof, or Zip codes: Limestone County
Own Printing Facility?: N
Commercial printers?: N
Sat. Circulation Paid: 5051
Sat. Circulation Free: 1,25
Audit By: USPS
Audit Date: 29.09.2022
Personnel: Katherine Miller (Publisher); Carey Carter (Classified Adv Sales); Heather Casillas (Adv Sales); Angie Christopher (Adv Sales); Adam Dodson (Sports); Tom Mayer (Editor); Christy Patterson (Reporter); Teresa Masey (Customer Service/Circulation); J.R. Tidwell (Reporter); Angie McElyea (Adv Sales); Nicolle Sartain (Editor); Anna Moyers (Production); Adam Smith (Manag. Editor); Glenda Smith (Production); Taylor Lane (Reporter); Glenda Smith (Ad Production); Lora Scripps (News Editor); Jean Cole (Reporter); Kala Tatum (Audience Development Associate); Sarah Pavlik (reporter); Jeff Edwards (Sports); Jessica Barnett (reporter)
Parent company (for newspapers): CNHI, LLC

THE CLANTON ADVERTISER

Street address 1: 1109 7th St N
Street address city: Clanton
Street address state: AL
Zip/Postal code: 35045-2113
County: Chilton
Country: USA
Mailing address: PO BOX 1379
Mailing city: CLANTON
Mailing state: AL
Mailing zip: 35046-1379
General Phone: (205) 755-5747
Advertising Phone: (205)755-5747 ext 606 ; ext. 604
Editorial Phone: (205) 755-5747, ext. 610
General/National Adv. E-mail: zack.bates@clantonadvertiser.com ; brandy.clackley@clantonadvertiser.com
Display Adv. E-mail: zack.bates@clantonadvertiser.com ; brandy.clackley@clantonadvertiser.com
Classified Adv. e-mail: zack.bates@clantonadvertiser.com ; brandy.clackley@clantonadvertiser.com
Editorial e-mail: stephen.dawkins@clantonadvertiser.com
Primary Website: www.clantonadvertiser.com
Special Editions: Senior Scene (Apr); Football Preview (Aug); Christmas Greetings (Dec); Progress (Feb); Bridal Guide (Jan); Faces and Places (Jul); Peach Festival (Jun); Life in the South (Mar); Graduating Seniors (May); Christmas Songbook (Nov); Holiday Cookbook (Oct); H
Syndicated Publications: American Profile (Weekly).
Areas Served - City/County or Portion Thereof, or Zip codes: Chilton County
Sat. Circulation Paid: 5000
Sun. Circulation Paid: 5000
Audit By: Sworn/Estimate/Non-Audited
Audit Date: 12.07.2019
Personnel: Tim Prince (Pres/Publisher); Stephen Dawkins (Managing Editor); Jimmy Ruff (Prodn. Mgr.); Zack Bates (Marketing Consul); Scott Mims (Mailroom mgr); Laura Cleckley (Customer Service); Brandy Clackley (Marketing Consultant); Anthony Richards (Staff Writer); Emily Reed (Staff Writer)
Parent company (for newspapers): Boone Newspapers, Inc.

THE CULLMAN TIMES

Street address 1: 300 4th Ave SE
Street address city: Cullman
Street address state: AL
Zip/Postal code: 35055-3611
County: Cullman
Country: USA
Mailing address: 300 4TH AVE SE
Mailing city: CULLMAN
Mailing state: AL
Mailing zip: 35055-3699
General Phone: (256) 734-2131
Advertising Phone: (256) 734-2131
Editorial Phone: (256) 734-2131
General/National Adv. E-mail: karas@cullmantimes.com
Display Adv. E-mail: karas@cullmantimes.com
Classified Adv. e-mail: debbiem@cullmantimes.com ; ewilliams@cullmantimes.com
Editorial e-mail: editor@cullmantimes.com
Primary Website: www.cullmantimes.com
Year Established: 1901
News Services: AP.
Special Editions: Consumer How To Guide (Apr); Sound Off (Aug); Christmas Greetings (Dec); Bridal Guide (Feb); Prime Times (Jan); Prime Times (Jul); Reader's Choice Awards (Jun); Spring Fashion (Mar); Graduation (May); Alabama Auto Guide (Monthly); Thanksgiving Day (Nov);
Special Weekly Sections: Church Page (Fri); Opinion Page (S); Used Auto Buyers Guide (Sat); Nascar Page (Thur); Outdoors (Tues); Best Food Day-Farm Page (Wed).
Syndicated Publications: Relish (Monthly)American Profile (Weekly).
Areas Served - City/County or Portion Thereof, or Zip codes: Cullman (AL)
Sat. Circulation Paid: 10000
Sun. Circulation Paid: 10500
Audit By: Sworn/Estimate/Non-Audited
Audit Date: 12.07.2019
Personnel: Terry Connor (Pub.); David Palmer (Ed.); Debbie Miller (Classifieds); Pete Lewter (Bus. Mgr.); Laurie Chapman (Adv. Dir.); Sam Mazzara (Dir. of Audience Develp); Amanda Shavers-Davies (News Ed.); Trent Moore (Digital Ed.); Tiffeny Owens (Staff Writer); Jake Winfrey (Sports Ed.)
Parent company (for newspapers): CNHI, LLC

THE DECATUR DAILY

Street address 1: 201 1st Ave SE
Street address city: Decatur
Street address state: AL
Zip/Postal code: 35601-2333
County: Morgan
Country: USA
Mailing address: PO BOX 2213
Mailing city: DECATUR
Mailing state: AL
Mailing zip: 35609-2213
General Phone: (256)353-4612
Advertising Phone: (256)340-2362
Editorial Phone: (256)340-2430
General/National Adv. E-mail: news@decaturdaily.com
Display Adv. E-mail: Deborah.lemen@decaturdaily.com
Classified Adv. e-mail: classifieds@decaturdaily.com
Editorial e-mail: news@decaturdaily.com
Primary Website: www.decaturdaily.com
Mthly Avg Views: 1262222
Mthly Avg Unique Visitors: 554856
Year Established: 1912
News Services: AP, NYT, SHNS, TMS.
Special Weekly Sections: Agriculture (Mon); Business Page (S); Church Page (Sat); Building Page (Tues); Shopping Bag (Wed).
Syndicated Publications: Parade (S).
Delivery Methods: Carrier
Areas Served - City/County or Portion Thereof, or Zip codes: Decatur and the Tennessee Valley in North Alabama

Own Printing Facility?: Y
Commercial printers?: Y
Avg Free Circ: 823
Sat. Circulation Paid: 11823
Sat. Circulation Free: 823
Sun. Circulation Paid: 15436
Sun. Circulation Free: 479
Audit By: AAM
Audit Date: 31.12.2017
Personnel: Clint Shelton (Pub.); Scott Brown (Dir., Operations); Don Hudson (Exec. Ed.); Scott Brown (Op. Dir.); Craig Hatcher (Ad. Dir.); Bruce McLellan (Mng. Ed. (Online)); Barb McKillip (Circ. Mgr.); Eric Flerschauer (Bus. Writer); Bayne Hughes (Educ. Writer); Franklin Harris (Asst. Metro Ed.); John Godbey (Photo Dept. Ed.); Shelia Smith (Major Accts Mgr); Michael Wetzel (Asst. Sports Ed); Stephen Johnson (Art Dept Mgr.); Michael Hagen (Ad Sale Exec)
Parent company (for newspapers): Tennessee Valley Printing

THE DOTHAN EAGLE

Street address 1: 227 N Oates St
Street address city: Dothan
Street address state: AL
Zip/Postal code: 36303-4555
County: Houston
Country: USA
Mailing address: PO BOX 1968
Mailing city: DOTHAN
Mailing state: AL
Mailing zip: 36302-1968
General Phone: (334) 792-3141
Advertising Phone: (334)702-2600 ; (334) 702-6060 (classified)
Editorial Phone: (334) 792-3141
General/National Adv. E-mail: sales@dothaneagle.com; advertising@dothaneagle.com
Display Adv. E-mail: advertising@dothaneagle.com
Classified Adv. e-mail: classifieds@dothaneagle.com
Editorial e-mail: letters@dothaneagle.com
Primary Website: www.dothaneagle.com
Mthly Avg Views: 1000000
Year Established: 1903
News Services: AP, NEA.
Special Editions: Wire Grass Outdoors (Monthly); Football Weekend (Nov); Football Weekend (Oct); New Car (Quarterly); Football Weekend (Sept); Golf (Spring); Golf (Summer).
Special Weekly Sections: Home & Garden (Fri); Expanded Business Pages (S); Church Page (Sat); Food (Wed).
Syndicated Publications: Relish (Monthly); USA WEEKEND Magazine (S).
Delivery Methods: Newsstand`Carrier
Areas Served - City/County or Portion Thereof, or Zip codes: Houston, Covington, Henry, Barbour, Pike Counties (AL); Holmes, Jackson Counties (FL)
Own Printing Facility?: Y
Avg Free Circ: 1585
Sat. Circulation Paid: 15078
Sat. Circulation Free: 1585
Sun. Circulation Paid: 17011
Sun. Circulation Free: 1406
Audit By: AAM
Audit Date: 30.06.2018
Personnel: Steve Smith (Regional Publisher); William Perkins (Editorial Page Ed.); Jerry Morgan (Regional Sales Dir); Jon Johnson (Sports Ed.); Kendall Clinton (Managing Ed.); Stephanie Madden (Mgr., Mktg.); Christie Kulavich (News Ed.); Charlie Gibson (Prodn. Mgr.); Tim Slater (Prodn. Mgr., Pressroom)
Parent company (for newspapers): BH Media Group; Lee Enterprises, Incorporated

THE ENTERPRISE LEDGER

Street address 1: 1110 Boll Weevil Cir
Street address 2: Ste D
Street address city: Enterprise
Street address state: AL
Zip/Postal code: 36330-1390
County: Coffee
Country: USA
Mailing address: PO BOX 311130
Mailing city: ENTERPRISE
Mailing state: AL
Mailing zip: 36331-1130
General Phone: (334) 347-9533
Advertising Phone: (334) 347-9533
Editorial Phone: (334) 347-9533
General/National Adv. E-mail: news@eprisenow.com
Display Adv. E-mail: LAllgood@eprisenow.com
Classified Adv. e-mail: classifieds@eprisenow.com
Editorial e-mail: news@eprisenow.com
Primary Website: www.eprisenow.com
Year Established: 1898
Special Editions: Home & Garden (April); Fort Rucker Appreciation (May); Class of 20XX, 12 years later (May); Newcomers Guide (July)
Syndicated Publications: Real Estate (Monthly); Apartment Living (Quarterly).
Delivery Methods: Mail`Newsstand`Carrier`Racks
Areas Served - City/County or Portion Thereof, or Zip codes: Coffee County and parts of Dale, Geneva, and Covington counties
Sun. Circulation Paid: 7700
Audit By: Sworn/Estimate/Non-Audited
Audit Date: 12.07.2019
Personnel: Kyle Mooty (Gen. Mgr./Editor); Gwen Black (News Clerk); Laren Allgood (Account Exec.); Mable Ruttlen (Account Exec.); Josh Boutwell (Reporter); Courtney Gilley (Reporter); Ginger McClay (Receptionist)
Parent company (for newspapers): BH Media Group; Lee Enterprises, Incorporated

TIMES DAILY

Street address 1: 219 W. Tennessee Street
Street address city: Florence
Street address state: AL
Zip/Postal code: 35630-5440
County: Lauderdale
Country: USA
Mailing address: PO BOX 797
Mailing city: FLORENCE
Mailing state: AL
Mailing zip: 35631-0797
General Phone: (256) 766-3434
Advertising Phone: (256) 740-5815
Editorial Phone: (256) 740-4725
General/National Adv. E-mail: melody.bishop@timesdaily.com
Display Adv. E-mail: renita.jimmar@timesdaily.com
Classified Adv. e-mail: erica.mayfield@timesdaily.com
Editorial e-mail: mike.goens@timesdaily.com
Primary Website: www.timesdaily.com
Year Established: 1890
News Services: AP.
Special Editions: Explore the Shoals (Apr); High School Football (Aug); Progress (Feb); Money Matters (Jan); Living Here (Jul); Senior Living (Jun); Lawn and Garden (Mar); Graduation (May); High School Basketball (Nov); Readers Choice (Oct). Shoals Woman (every other month);Tennessee Valley Brides (annual);TNValleyHomefinder (monthly); TNValleyWheels (biweekly)
Special Weekly Sections: Currents (Fri); Best Food Day (Wed).
Syndicated Publications: Shoals Woman (Every other month); Shoals Magazine (Quarterly); USA Weekend (S)Explore the Shoals (AprProgress (Feb); Money Matters (Jan); Living Here (Jul); Senior Living (Jun); Tennessee Valley Brides (annual);TNValleyHomefinder (monthly); TNValleyWheels (biweekly)
Own Printing Facility?: Y
Commercial printers?: Y
Avg Free Circ: 1126
Sat. Circulation Paid: 15679
Sat. Circulation Free: 1126
Sun. Circulation Paid: 17899
Sun. Circulation Free: 426
Audit By: AAM
Audit Date: 30.06.2017
Personnel: Kevin Blurton (Prod. Dir.); Melody Bishop (Adv. Dir.); Renita Jimmar (Adv. Mgr., Display); Darrell R. Sandlin (Pub.); Gary Maitland (Exec. Ed.); Chris Giroir (Dir., ITS/Pre Press Serv.); Charlotte Ann Filloramo (Controller); Walter Goggins (TVPCO circ mgr); Sherhonda Allen (City Ed.); Teri T. Stepleton (Lifestyle Ed.); Valerie Sherer (News Asst.); Matthew T. McKean (Photo Ed.); Gregg Dewalt (Sports Ed.); Jeff McIntyre (Asst. Sports Ed.); Bruce McLellan (Online Ed); Lin Reynolds (Prodn. Mgr., Pre Press); Mike Roberts (Pressroom Mgr.); Leta Milstead (Office Mgr)
Parent company (for newspapers): Tennessee Valley Printing

THE TIMES-JOURNAL

Street address 1: 811 Greenhill Boulevard NW
Street address city: Fort Payne
Street address state: AL
Zip/Postal code: 35967
County: De Kalb
Country: USA
Mailing address: PO BOX 680349
Mailing city: FORT PAYNE
Mailing state: AL
Mailing zip: 35968-1604
General Phone: (256) 845-2550
Advertising Phone: (256) 304-0061
Editorial Phone: (256) 304-0053
General/National Adv. E-mail: lstiefel@times-journal.com
Display Adv. E-mail: composing@times-journal.com
Classified Adv. e-mail: classified@times-journal.com
Editorial e-mail: hbuckner@times-journal.com
Primary Website: www.times-journal.com
Year Established: 1878
Syndicated Publications: American Profile (Weekly), USA Weekend (Weekly), The EXTRA (Tues), The Sand Mountain Shopper's Guide(Tues)
Delivery Methods: Mail`Newsstand`Carrier`Racks
Areas Served - City/County or Portion Thereof, or Zip codes: DeKalb and Fort PayneCounty, Alabama
Own Printing Facility?: N
Commercial printers?: N
Avg Free Circ: 294
Sat. Circulation Paid: 2961
Sat. Circulation Free: 294
Audit By: AAM
Audit Date: 31.03.2017
Personnel: Tricia Clinton Dunne (Pres./Pub.); Linda Stiefel (Advertising Manager); Emily Tipton (Classified Representative); Connie Hughes (Circ. Mgr); Lew Gilliland (Ed.); Melissa Henry (Chief Photo); Bradley Roberts (Mng. Ed.)
Parent company (for newspapers): Southern Newspapers Inc.

THE GADSDEN TIMES

Street address 1: 401 Locust St
Street address city: Gadsden
Street address state: AL
Zip/Postal code: 35901-3737
County: Etowah
Country: USA
Mailing address: PO BOX 188
Mailing city: GADSDEN
Mailing state: AL
Mailing zip: 35902-0188
General Phone: (256) 549-2000
Advertising Phone: (256) 549-2071
Editorial Phone: (256) 399-9742
General/National Adv. E-mail: tina.peppers@gadsdentimes.com
Display Adv. E-mail: wes.williams@gadsdentimes.com
Classified Adv. e-mail: dana.brown@gadsdentimes.com
Editorial e-mail: ron.reaves@gadsdentimes.com
Primary Website: www.gadsdentimes.com
Mthly Avg Views: 2400000
Year Established: 1867
News Services: AP
Special Editions: Football (Aug); County Focus Editions (4) (Feb); Home & Garden (Mar); Graduation (May); Basketball (Nov).
Special Weekly Sections: Religious News (Fri); People (Mon); Real Estate (S); Health News (Thur); Home (Tues); Food (Wed).
Syndicated Publications: Parade (S).
Delivery Methods: Mail`Newsstand`Carrier`Racks
Areas Served - City/County or Portion Thereof, or Zip codes: 35901, 35903, 35904 35905, 35906, 35907, 35950, 35951, 35952, 35953, 35954, 35956, 35957, 35959, 35960, 35961, 35962, 35963, 35967, 35968, 35971, 35972, 35973, 35974, 35983, 35986, 35987, 35990, 36250, 36265, 36271, 36272, 36279
Own Printing Facility?: Y
Commercial printers?: N
Sat. Circulation Paid: 12597
Sun. Circulation Paid: 13609
Audit By: AAM
Audit Date: 31.03.2016
Personnel: Glen Porter (Pub.); Richard Davis (Finance Dir.); Willie King (District Mgr.); David Braggs (Adv. Mgr.); Greg Bailey (Assoc. Ed.); Kevin Taylor (MultiMedia Copy Ed.)
Parent company (for newspapers): Gannett; CherryRoad Media

DAILY MOUNTAIN EAGLE

Street address 1: P.O. Box 1469
Street address city: Jasper
Street address state: AL
Zip/Postal code: 35502
County: Walker
Country: USA
Mailing address: PO BOX 1469
Mailing city: JASPER
Mailing state: AL
Mailing zip: 35502-1469
General Phone: (205) 221-2840
Advertising Phone: (205) 221-2840
Editorial Phone: (205) 221-2840
General/National Adv. E-mail: jerry.geddings@mountaineagle.com
Display Adv. E-mail: jerry.geddings@mountaineagle.com
Classified Adv. e-mail: donna.hicks@mountaineagle.com
Editorial e-mail: ron.harris@mountaineagle.com
Primary Website: www.mountaineagle.com
Year Established: 1872
News Services: AP.
Special Editions: Atlanta Braves (Apr); Football (Aug); Letters to Santa (Dec); Progress (Feb); Senior Citizen (Jul); Home Folks (Jun); Graduation (May); Gift Guide (Nov); Women's World (Oct); Newcomer's Guide (Sept).
Syndicated Publications: TV Guide (Fri); USA WEEKEND Magazine (S); Business & Industrial Review (Tues); Best Food (Wed); American Profile (Weekly).
Areas Served - City/County or Portion Thereof, or Zip codes: 35501, 35503
Avg Free Circ: 458
Sat. Circulation Paid: 5406
Sat. Circulation Free: 458
Sun. Circulation Paid: 6054
Sun. Circulation Free: 157
Audit By: AAM
Audit Date: 31.12.2017
Personnel: James Phillips (Ed./Pub.); Jonathan Bentley (Sports Ed.); Charlotte Caterson (Office/Credit Mgr.); Sandra Lawson (Classified Ad Mgr.); Michael Keeton (Prod. Mgr); Tia Jones (Circ. Dir.); Jake Aaron (Adv. Dir.)
Parent company (for newspapers): Cleveland Newspapers, Inc.

THE VALLEY TIMES-NEWS

Street address 1: 220 N 12th St
Street address city: Lanett
Street address state: AL
Zip/Postal code: 36863-6422
County: Chambers
Country: USA
Mailing address: PO BOX 850
Mailing city: LANETT
Mailing state: AL
Mailing zip: 36863-0850
General Phone: (334) 644-8100
Advertising Phone: (334) 644-8100
Editorial Phone: (334) 644-8123
General/National Adv. E-mail: advertising@valleytimes-news.com
Display Adv. E-mail: advertising@valleytimes-news.com
Classified Adv. e-mail: classifieds@valleytimes-news.com
Editorial e-mail: news@valleytimes-news.com
Primary Website: www.valleytimes-news.com
Year Established: 1950
News Services: AP.
Special Editions: Christmas Greetings (Dec); Progress (Apr); Cookbook (Nov); Car Care (Oct); Football (Aug).
Special Weekly Sections: Food Section (Wed); Television (Fri). Extensive automobile and real estate advertising(Fri)
Delivery Methods: Mail`Newsstand`Carrier`Racks
Areas Served - City/County or Portion Thereof, or Zip codes: West Point, Georgią, & Lanett and Valley (AL)
Own Printing Facility?: N
Commercial printers?: N
Audit By: USPS
Audit Date: 01.10.2016
Personnel: Cy Wood (Ed.); Martha Milner (Classified Manager); Kathy Reeves (Graphics Ed.); Scott Sickler (Sports Ed.)
Parent company (for newspapers): The Valley Times-News; Boone Newspapers, Inc.

PRESS-REGISTER

Street address 1: 401 N. Water Street
Street address city: Mobile
Street address state: AL
Zip/Postal code: 36602

County: Mobile
Country: USA
Mailing address: PO BOX 2488
Mailing city: MOBILE
Mailing state: AL
Mailing zip: 36652-2488
General Phone: (251) 219-5400
Advertising Phone: (251) 219-5545
Editorial Phone: (251) 219-5632
General/National Adv. E-mail: adservices@press-register.com
Display Adv. E-mail: classnational@mobileregister.com
Editorial e-mail: news@press-register.com; newsroom@mobileregister.com
Primary Website: www.al.com/mobile
Mthly Avg Unique Visitors: 3902000
News Services: AP, LAT-WP, MCT, NEW, SHNS, Religious News, NYT.
Special Editions: Home Builders Association (Apr); Parade of Homes (Aug); Holiday Gift Guide (Dec); Home Builders Showcase (Feb); Better Business Bureau (Jan); Automotive Hot Sellers (Jul); Soil & Sea (Jun); Easter (Mar); Congratulations Graduates (May); Jr. League Christm
Special Weekly Sections: TV Supplement (Fri); Farm Page (Mon); Travel Page (S); Church Pages (Sat).
Syndicated Publications: Parade (S).
Sat. Circulation Paid: 3184
Sun. Circulation Paid: 43117
Audit By: AAM
Audit Date: 30.06.2018
Personnel: Vicki Catlett (Controller/Treasurer); Lee Stringfellow (Dir., HR); Britt Pickett (Adv. Mgr., Classified); Wanda Jacobs (Adv. Mgr., Nat'l); Steve Hall (Adv. Mgr., Retail); Randy Granger (Dir., Mktg./Promo.); George Markevicz (Circ. Dir.); Wayne Carrier (Circ. Mgr., Home Delivery); Bill Van Hook (Circ. Mgr., Opns.); Jim McKeel (Circ. Mgr., Single Copy); Michael Marshall (Vice Pres., News/Ed.); Dewey English (Mng. Ed.); K.A. Turner (Bus./Finance Ed.); Frances Coleman (Editorial Page Ed.); Ben Raines (Environmental Reporter); Charles Croft (Farm/Agriculture Ed.); Debbie Lord (Features Ed.); Thom Dudgeon (Graphics Ed.); Bill Finch (Growth/Environmental Ed.); Monique Curet (Health/Medical Reporter)
Parent company (for newspapers): Advance Publications, Inc.

MONTGOMERY ADVERTISER

Street address 1: 425 Molton Street
Street address city: Montgomery
Street address state: AL
Zip/Postal code: 36104
County: Montgomery
Country: USA
Mailing address: PO BOX 1000
Mailing city: MONTGOMERY
Mailing state: AL
Mailing zip: 36101-1000
General Phone: (334) 262-1611
Advertising Phone: (334) 264-3733
Editorial Phone: (334) 261-1524
Editorial e-mail: jearnhardt@gannett.com
Primary Website: www.montgomeryadvertiser.com
Year Established: 1829
News Services: AP, SHNS, MCT, GNS, PR Newswire.
Special Editions: Coupon Book (Apr); Game Day College (Aug); SEC Game Day (Dec); Health & Fitness (Feb); Coupon Book (Jan); Hyundai (Jul); Restaurant Guide (Jun); Gulf Coast Tab (Mar); Health & Fitness (May); Holiday Gift Guide (Nov); Coupon Book (Oct); First Methodist Ven
Special Weekly Sections: Religion (Fri); TV Week (S); Home & Garden (Sat); Go (weekly entertainment) (Thur); Health (Tues); Food (Wed).
Syndicated Publications: USA WEEKEND Magazine (S).
Areas Served - City/County or Portion Thereof, or Zip codes: Montgomery, Prattville and the River Region
Own Printing Facility?: Y
Avg Free Circ: 959
Sat. Circulation Paid: 11278
Sat. Circulation Free: 959
Sun. Circulation Paid: 14865
Sun. Circulation Free: 71
Audit By: AAM
Audit Date: 31.03.2019
Personnel: Brad Zimanek (Consumer Exper. Dir/Sports Ed); Steve Arnold (Content Strategist/Digital Ed.); Bro Krift (Exec. Ed.); Michael Galvin (Pres.); Debbie Goddard (Exec/ Asst.); Jim Broyles (Adv. Dir.)
Parent company (for newspapers): Gannett

OPELIKA-AUBURN NEWS

Street address 1: 2901 Society Hill Road
Street address city: Opelika
Street address state: AL
Zip/Postal code: 36804
County: Lee
Country: USA
Mailing address: PO BOX 2208
Mailing city: OPELIKA
Mailing state: AL
Mailing zip: 36803-2208
General Phone: (334) 749-6271
Advertising Phone: (334) 737-2488
Editorial Phone: (334) 749-6271
General/National Adv. E-mail: shaydel@oanow.com
Display Adv. E-mail: shaydel@oanow.com
Classified Adv. e-mail: oanewsclassifieds@oanow.com ; crussell@oanow.com
Editorial e-mail: pjohnston@oanow.com
Primary Website: www.oanow.com
Year Established: 1904
News Services: AP.
Special Weekly Sections: Best Automotive Days (Fri); Best Real Estate Days (S); Church Page (Sat); Business Pages (Thur); Business Pages (Tues); Living Pages (Wed).
Syndicated Publications: USA WEEKEND Magazine (S).
Delivery Methods: Mail
Areas Served - City/County or Portion Thereof, or Zip codes: Auburn, Auburn University, Opelika, Lee County and East Alabama
Avg Free Circ: 737
Sat. Circulation Paid: 8281
Sat. Circulation Free: 737
Sun. Circulation Paid: 9295
Sun. Circulation Free: 598
Audit By: AAM
Audit Date: 31.12.2018
Personnel: Rex Maynor (Pub); Patrick Johnston (Mng. Ed.); Dana Sulonen (Sports Ed); Sheila Haydel (Adv. Dir); Crystal Russell (Classified Adv. Mgr); Greg Curry (Creative Serv Mgr); John Gaddy (Circ. Dir); H. T. Bear (Prod. Dir)
Parent company (for newspapers): BH Media Group; Lee Enterprises, Incorporated

THE JACKSON COUNTY SENTINEL

Street address 1: 701 Veterans Drive
Street address city: Scottsboro
Street address state: AL
Zip/Postal code: 35768
County: Jackson
Country: USA
Mailing address: PO BOX 220
Mailing city: SCOTTSBORO
Mailing state: AL
Mailing zip: 35768-0220
General Phone: (256) 259-1020
General/National Adv. E-mail: nicole.rhoads@jcsentinel.com
Display Adv. E-mail: nicole.rhoads@jcsentinel.com
Classified Adv. e-mail: lynn.loy@jcsentinel.com
Editorial e-mail: dewayne.patterson@jcsentinel.com
Primary Website: www.thedailysentinel.com
Year Established: 1887
News Services: AP, TMS.
Delivery Methods: Mail`Newsstand`Carrier`Racks
Areas Served - City/County or Portion Thereof, or Zip codes: Jackson County (AL)
Own Printing Facility?: Y
Commercial printers?: Y
Avg Free Circ: 148
Sat. Circulation Paid: 2841
Sat. Circulation Free: 113
Audit By: CAC
Audit Date: 31.03.2017
Personnel: Brent Miller (Pub.); Nicole Rhoads (Adv.); Lynn Loy (Classified Sales); Brian Butler (Circ. Mgr.); Dewayne Patterson (Mng. Ed.); Jason Bowen (Sports Ed.)
Parent company (for newspapers): Southern Newspapers Inc.

THE SELMA TIMES-JOURNAL

Street address 1: 1018 Water Ave
Street address city: Selma
Street address state: AL
Zip/Postal code: 36701-4617
County: Dallas
Country: USA
Mailing address: PO BOX 611
Mailing city: SELMA
Mailing state: AL
Mailing zip: 36702-0611
General Phone: (334) 875-2110
General/National Adv. E-mail: ads@selmatimesjournal.com
Display Adv. E-mail: ads@selmatimesjournal.com
Classified Adv. e-mail: michelle.coleman@selmatimesjournal.com
Editorial e-mail: tim.reeves@selmatimesjournal.com
Primary Website: www.selmatimesjournal.com
Mthly Avg Views: 400000
Mthly Avg Unique Visitors: 47000
Year Established: 1827
News Services: AP
Special Editions: Battle of Selma (Apr); Kickoff-Football (Aug); Horizons-Progress (Feb); FYI-For Your Information (Jun); Graduation (May); Chamber of Commerce (Nov); Women in Business (Sept); Health & Fitness (Jan); Hoopla (Nov); Pilgrimage (Mar); Industry (Jun); Calender (Dec)
Syndicated Publications: Parade (S).
Delivery Methods: Mail`Newsstand`Carrier`Racks
Areas Served - City/County or Portion Thereof, or Zip codes: Dallas, Wilcox, Perry Counties
Own Printing Facility?: Y
Commercial printers?: Y
Avg Free Circ: 8000
Sat. Circulation Paid: 8500
Sun. Circulation Paid: 10000
Audit By: Sworn/Estimate/Non-Audited
Audit Date: 12.07.2019
Personnel: Dennis Palmer (Pub.); Jay Davis (VP/Bus. Mgr.); Tasha Tice (Audience Devt. Mgr); Justin Averette (Ed.); Fred Scott (Prodn. Mgr.); Tina Yelverton (Adv. Mgr.); Stephanie Reeves (Acct. Dept Mgr); Karen Lawler (Composition Mgr); Daniel Evans (News Ed.)
Parent company (for newspapers): Boone Newspapers, Inc.

THE DAILY HOME

Street address 1: 6 Sylacauga Hwy
Street address city: Talladega
Street address state: AL
Zip/Postal code: 35160
County: Talladega
Country: USA
Mailing address: PO BOX 977
Mailing city: TALLADEGA
Mailing state: AL
Mailing zip: 35161-0977
General Phone: (256) 362-1000
Advertising Phone: (256) 362-1000
Editorial Phone: (256) 362-1000
General/National Adv. E-mail: padamson@dailyhome.com
Display Adv. E-mail: padamson@dailyhome.com
Classified Adv. e-mail: chutto@dailyhome.com
Editorial e-mail: efowler@dailyhome.com
Primary Website: www.dailyhome.com
Year Established: 1867
News Services: AP.
Special Editions: Uppdate (February) Football (Aug); Spirit of Christmas (Dec); Vacation Drawing (Feb);Lakeside (monthly) Home & Garden (Mar); Graduation Tab (May); Christmas Gift Guide (Nov); Adopt A Pet Classified Promotion (Oct)
Special Weekly Sections: Religion Page (Sat); Food Page (Wed).
Syndicated Publications: Parade (S).
Delivery Methods: Mail`Newsstand`Carrier`Racks
Areas Served - City/County or Portion Thereof, or Zip codes: Talladega & St. Clair Counties
Own Printing Facility?: N
Commercial printers?: N
Sat. Circulation Paid: 9872
Sun. Circulation Paid: 9872
Audit By: Sworn/Estimate/Non-Audited
Audit Date: 12.07.2019
Personnel: Robert Jackson (Publisher); Jim Smothers (Webpage Coord.); Pam Adamson (Adv. Dir.); Janice Keith (Assoc. Ed.); Sandy Carden (Adv. Mgr., Retail Sales); Carrie Hutto (Classified Mgr.); Kandi Macy (Circ. Mgr.); LaVonte Young (Sports Ed.); Barbara Wilson (Business Mgr)
Parent company (for newspapers): Consolidated Publishing Co.

THE TROY MESSENGER

Street address 1: 918 S Brundidge St
Street address city: Troy
Street address state: AL
Zip/Postal code: 36081-3222
County: Pike
Country: USA
Mailing address: PO BOX 727
Mailing city: TROY
Mailing state: AL
Mailing zip: 36081-0727
General Phone: (334) 566-4270
Advertising Phone: (334) 670-6306
Editorial Phone: (334) 670-6323
General/National Adv. E-mail: travis.williams@troymessenger.com
Display Adv. E-mail: brittany.harrison@troymessenger.com
Classified Adv. e-mail: rachel.hicks@troymessenger.com
Editorial e-mail: robbyn.brooks@troymessenger.com
Primary Website: www.troymessenger.com
Year Established: 1866
News Services: NEA.
Syndicated Publications: American Profile (Weekly).
Areas Served - City/County or Portion Thereof, or Zip codes: Troy and Pike County
Sun. Circulation Paid: 2814
Audit By: Sworn/Estimate/Non-Audited
Audit Date: 12.07.2019
Personnel: Stacy Graning (Pub.); Jaine Treadwell (Features Ed.); Mike Hensley (Sports Writer); Scottie Brown (Staff Writer); Jessica Stuff (Class. Mgr and Bookkeeping); Travis Williams (Retail Advert); Rennie Raines (Distrb. Mgr)
Parent company (for newspapers): Boone Newspapers, Inc.

THE TUSCALOOSA NEWS

Street address 1: 315 28th Ave
Street address city: Tuscaloosa
Street address state: AL
Zip/Postal code: 35401-1022
County: Tuscaloosa
Country: USA
Mailing address: 315 28th Ave
Mailing city: Tuscaloosa
Mailing state: AL
Mailing zip: 35401-1022
General Phone: (205) 345-0505
Advertising Phone: (205) 722-0148
Editorial Phone: (866)400-8477
General/National Adv. E-mail: chris.powell@tuscaloosanews.com
Display Adv. E-mail: chris.powell@tuscaloosanews.com
Classified Adv. e-mail: chris.powell@tuscaloosanews.com
Editorial e-mail: michael.james@tuscaloosanews.com
Primary Website: www.tuscaloosanews.com
Mthly Avg Views: 2700000
Mthly Avg Unique Visitors: 428000
Year Established: 1818
News Services: AP, NYT.
Special Editions: University of Alabama Today (Aug); Fall Homes Decorating (Dec); Focus (Feb); Back-to-School (Jul); Family-owned Businesses (Jun); Focus (Mar); Outdoors (May); Parade of Homes (Oct); Outdoors (Sept).
Special Weekly Sections: Church Page (Fri); TV Click (S); Best Food Day (Wed).
Syndicated Publications: Parade (S).
Delivery Methods: Carrier`Racks
Areas Served - City/County or Portion Thereof, or Zip codes: West Alabama
Own Printing Facility?: Y
Commercial printers?: Y
Sat. Circulation Paid: 16744
Sun. Circulation Paid: 19642
Audit By: AAM
Audit Date: 31.03.2018
Personnel: Michael James (Exec. Ed.); Cecil Hurt (Sports Ed.); Ken Roberts (City Ed.); Amy Robinson (Chief Multimedia Copy Ed.); Kelcey Sexton (Multimedia Copy Ed.); Edwin Stanton (Exec. Sports Ed.); Terrin Waack (TideSports Ed.); Stephen Fowler (Production Mgr.); Michelle Boswell (District Sales Mgr.); Paige Davis (Multimedia Sales Exec.); Yaisa Jones (Classified

Account Exec.); Maci Lankford (MultiMedia Sales Exec.); Carolyn Durel (Senior GL Accountant); Carla Gillespie (Human Resources/Administrative); Bobby Rice (Gen. Mgr.)
Parent company (for newspapers): Gannett; CherryRoad Media

ALASKA

ALASKA DISPATCH NEWS

Street address 1: 300 W 31st Ave
Street address city: Anchorage
Street address state: AK
Zip/Postal code: 99503-3878
County: Anchorage
Country: USA
Mailing state: AK
General Phone: (907) 257-4200
Advertising Phone: (907) 257-4504
Editorial Phone: (907) 257-4303
General/National Adv. E-mail: advertising@alaskadispatch.com
Display Adv. E-mail: advertising@alaskadispatch.com
Classified Adv. e-mail: classifieds@alaskadispatch.com
Editorial e-mail: newstips@alaskadispatch.com
Primary Website: www.adn.com
Mthly Avg Views: 11547966
Mthly Avg Unique Visitors: 1528515
Year Established: 2014
News Services: NYT, LAT-WP, MCT, RN, CNS, DJ, TMS, UPI.
Special Editions: Best of Alaska (Jan); Iditarod (Feb); Back to School (Aug); Holiday Gift Guide (Nov)
Special Weekly Sections: We Alaskans (Sun); Alaska Life (Sun); Play (Fri)
Delivery Methods: Mail`Newsstand`Carrier`Racks
Areas Served - City/County or Portion Thereof, or Zip codes: Entire state of Alaska
Own Printing Facility?: Y
Commercial printers?: Y
Sat. Circulation Paid: 29110
Sun. Circulation Paid: 34908
Audit By: AAM
Audit Date: 30.06.2016
Personnel: Alice Rogoff (Pub.); David Hulen (Executive Ed.); Kea Cuaresma (Advertising Operations Director); Maia Nolan-Partnow (Director, Sales & Special Content); Margy Johnson (Executive Vice President); Roger Weinfurter (VP, Audience Engagement); Ken Carter (VP, Production)
Parent company (for newspapers): Alaska Dispatch Publishing LLC; Binkley Co.

ANCHORAGE DAILY NEWS

Street address 1: 300 W. 31st Avenue
Street address city: Anchorage
Street address state: AK
Zip/Postal code: 99503
County: Anchorage
Country: USA
Mailing address: 300 W. 31st Ave.
Mailing city: Anchorage
Mailing state: AK
Mailing zip: 99503
General Phone: (907) 257-4200
Advertising Phone: (907) 257-4200
Editorial Phone: (907) 257-4596
General/National Adv. E-mail: advertising@adn.com
Display Adv. E-mail: advertising@adn.com
Classified Adv. e-mail: classifieds@adn.com
Editorial e-mail: newstips@adn.com
Primary Website: www.adn.com
Year Established: 1946
Delivery Methods: Mail
Sun. Circulation Paid: 32395
Audit By: AAM
Audit Date: 30.06.2018
Personnel: Ryan Binkley (President & CEO); Andy Pennington (Pub.); David Hulen (Ed.); Kea Cuaresma (Director, Marketing Services); Roger Weinfurter (Weinfurter); Erin Austin (CFO)
Parent company (for newspapers): Arc Publishing; Binkley Co.

FAIRBANKS DAILY NEWS-MINER

Street address 1: 200 N Cushman St
Street address city: Fairbanks
Street address state: AK
Zip/Postal code: 99701-2832
County: Fairbanks North Star
Country: USA
Mailing address: PO BOX 70710
Mailing city: FAIRBANKS
Mailing state: AK
Mailing zip: 99707-0710
General Phone: (907) 456-6661
Advertising Phone: (907) 459-7548
Editorial Phone: (907) 459-7572
General/National Adv. E-mail: editor@newsminer.com
Display Adv. E-mail: ads@newsminer.com
Classified Adv. e-mail: ads@newsminer.com
Editorial e-mail: newsroom@newsminer.com
Primary Website: www.newsminer.com
Mthly Avg Views: 2700000
Mthly Avg Unique Visitors: 380000
Year Established: 1903
News Services: AP, NYT.
Special Editions: Building (Apr); Back-to-School (Aug); Christmas Greeter (Dec); Valentine's Day (Feb); Hunting (Jul); Visitor's Guide (Jun); Winter Carnival (Mar); Christmas Shopper (Nov); Winter Survival (Sept).
Special Weekly Sections: Health (Tue); Best Food Day (Wed); Outdoors, Religion Arts, Nightlife (Fri); Youth (Sat); TV, Business (Sun); Entertainment (Daily)
Syndicated Publications: Parade (S).
Delivery Methods: Mail`Newsstand`Carrier`Racks
Areas Served - City/County or Portion Thereof, or Zip codes: North & West Alaska
Own Printing Facility?: Y
Sat. Circulation Paid: 13356
Sun. Circulation Paid: 16022
Audit By: AAM
Audit Date: 30.09.2014
Personnel: Katherine Strle (Gen. Mgr.); Rod Boyce (Mng. Ed.); Julie Strcker (Online Ed.); Danita Swensson (MulitM Acc. Exec.); Fuller Cowell (Pub.)
Parent company (for newspapers): Helen E Snedded Foundation

JUNEAU EMPIRE

Street address 1: 3100 Channel Dr
Street address 2: Ste 1
Street address city: Juneau
Street address state: AK
Zip/Postal code: 99801-7837
County: Juneau
Country: USA
Mailing address: 3100 CHANNEL DR STE 1
Mailing city: JUNEAU
Mailing state: AK
Mailing zip: 99801-7837
General Phone: (907) 586-3740
Advertising Phone: (907)523-2290
Editorial Phone: (907) 523-2265
General/National Adv. E-mail: kathryn.nickerson@juneauempire.com
Display Adv. E-mail: kathryn.nickerson@juneauempire.com
Classified Adv. e-mail: kathryn.nickerson@juneauempire.com
Editorial e-mail: editor@juneauempire.com
Primary Website: www.juneauempire.com
Mthly Avg Views: 1100000
Mthly Avg Unique Visitors: 216000
Year Established: 1912
News Services: AP, MCT.
Special Editions: Salmon Derby (Aug); Christmas (Dec); George Washington's Birthday (Feb); Legislature (Jan); Juneau Guide (May); High School Basketball Preview (Nov); Lifestyles (Oct).
Special Weekly Sections: Neighbors (Fri); TV Week (S); Preview (Thur); Spotlight (Tues); Neighbors (Wed).
Syndicated Publications: Juneau Guide - tourism/travel
Delivery Methods: Newsstand`Carrier`Racks
Areas Served - City/County or Portion Thereof, or Zip codes: 99801
Own Printing Facility?: Y
Commercial printers?: Y
Avg Free Circ: 120
Audit By: Sworn/Estimate/Non-Audited
Audit Date: 12.07.2019
Personnel: Terry Ward (Pub./Pres.); Robert Monteith (Gen. Mgr.); Emily Russo Miller (Ed.); Shawn Miller (Pressroom Mgr.); Angelo Saggiomo (Digital Content Ed.)
Parent company (for newspapers): Black Press Group Ltd.

PENINSULA CLARION

Street address 1: 150 Trading Bay Rd
Street address 2: # 1
Street address city: Kenai
Street address state: AK
Zip/Postal code: 99611-7716
County: Kenai Peninsula
Country: USA
Mailing address: PO BOX 3009
Mailing city: KENAI
Mailing state: AK
Mailing zip: 99611-3009
General Phone: (907) 283-7551
Advertising Phone: (907)283-7551
Editorial Phone: (907) 335-1251
General/National Adv. E-mail: advertising@peninsulaclarion.com
Display Adv. E-mail: advertising@peninsulaclarion.com
Classified Adv. e-mail: advertising@peninsulaclarion.com
Editorial e-mail: will.morrow@peninsulaclarion.com
Primary Website: www.peninsulaclarion.com
Year Established: 1970
News Services: AP.
Special Editions: Mother's Day (Apr); Hunting (Aug); Greetings (Dec); Industry (Feb); Fathers' Day (Jun); Recreation Guide (May); Real Estate (Monthly); Coupon Book (Quarterly).
Special Weekly Sections: Community, Neighbors, Seniors (Mon); Schools, Pets (Tue); Grocery, Food (Wed); What's Happening, Entertainment, Business (Thur); Outdoors, Real Estate (Fri); Travel, Inside Alaska, Health, Nutrition, TV, Comics (Sun)
Delivery Methods: Mail`Newsstand`Carrier
Areas Served - City/County or Portion Thereof, or Zip codes: Central Peninsula
Sun. Circulation Paid: 5710
Audit By: Sworn/Estimate/Non-Audited
Audit Date: 12.07.2019
Personnel: Leslie Talent (Adv. Dir); Will Morrow (Mng. Ed.); Brian Smith (City Ed. Reporter); Stephanie Davidson (Adv. Rep.); Rashah McChesney (Reporter); Gregory Harrington (Adv. Rep); Annette Evans-Helle (Classified Adv.); Tom Janz (Circ.Mgr); Jane Rusell (HR.); Vitto Kleinschmidt (Pub.)
Parent company (for newspapers): Black Press Group Ltd.

KETCHIKAN DAILY NEWS

Street address 1: 501 Dock St
Street address city: Ketchikan
Street address state: AK
Zip/Postal code: 99901-6411
County: Ketchikan Gateway
Country: USA
Mailing address: PO BOX 7900
Mailing city: KETCHIKAN
Mailing state: AK
Mailing zip: 99901-2900
General Phone: (907) 225-3157
Advertising Phone: (907) 225-3157
Editorial Phone: (907) 225-3157
General/National Adv. E-mail: kdn@kpunet.net
Display Adv. E-mail: kdn@kpunet.net
Classified Adv. e-mail: classified@ketchikandailynews.com
Editorial e-mail: news@ketchikandailynews.com
Primary Website: www.ketchikandailynews.com
Year Established: 1934
News Services: AP.
Special Editions: Christmas Card Edition (Annually). Moonlight Madness. Tax-Free Day. Hunting. Fourth of July. Graduation. Mother's Day. Walking Tour (of Ketchikan). Fishing/Maritime.
Special Weekly Sections: Waterfront. Education. Business. Religion. People. First City Scene (entertainment).
Delivery Methods: Mail`Newsstand`Carrier`Racks
Areas Served - City/County or Portion Thereof, or Zip codes: Entire state of Alaska
Sat. Circulation Paid: 4117
Audit By: Sworn/Estimate/Non-Audited
Personnel: Lew Williams (Co-Pub.); Tena Williams (Co-Pub.); Scott Bowlen (Editor); Lecile Kiffer (Circ. Mgr.); Kathy Williams (Classified clerk); Terry Miller (Mng. Ed.)
Parent company (for newspapers): Pioneer Printing Co., Inc.

KODIAK DAILY MIRROR

Street address 1: 1419 Selig St
Street address city: Kodiak
Street address state: AK
Zip/Postal code: 99615-6450
County: Kodiak Island
Country: USA
Mailing address: 1419 SELIG ST
Mailing city: KODIAK
Mailing state: AK
Mailing zip: 99615-6450
General Phone: (907) 486-3227
Advertising Phone: (907) 486-3227 ext. 613; ext. 628
Editorial Phone: (907) 486-3227 ext. 622
General/National Adv. E-mail: advertising@kodiakdailymirror.com
Display Adv. E-mail: sales@kodiakdailymirror.com
Classified Adv. e-mail: classifieds@kodiakdailymirror.com
Editorial e-mail: editor@kodiakdailymirror.com
Primary Website: www.kodiakdailymirror.com
Mthly Avg Views: 130000
Mthly Avg Unique Visitors: 50000
Year Established: 1940
News Services: AP, CNS, TMS.
Special Editions: United States Coast Guard Supplement (Aug); Holiday Gift Guide (Dec); Bear Chronicles (Apr); Graduation (May); ComFish (Mar); Crab Festival (May); Summer Adventures (May); Getting Involved (Mar, Sep); Holiday Greetings (Dec); Joe Floyd Tournament Preview (Jan); Health & Fitness (Feb); Back to School (Aug).
Special Weekly Sections: Fisheries Wrap up (Mon); Gardengate (Mon); Outdoors (Tues).
Delivery Methods: Mail`Carrier`Racks
Areas Served - City/County or Portion Thereof, or Zip codes: 01001, 03048, 10021, 26301, 33431, 33630, 34610, 45309, 49038, 50325, 71913, 80202, 83854, 84037, 92116, 94553, 95222, 97007, 97324, 97365, 97365, 98188, 98195, 98199, 98370, 98607, 99337, 99501, 99503, 99504, 99506, 99508, 99515, 99517, 99519, 99521, 99550, 99565, 99577, 99603, 99615, 99619, 99624, 99643, 99644, 99664, 99669, 99685, 99686, 99697, 99701, 99775, 99811
Own Printing Facility?: Y
Commercial printers?: N
Audit By: Sworn/Estimate/Non-Audited
Audit Date: 12.07.2019
Personnel: Richard Harris (Publisher); Derek Clakston (Reporter); Janet Baker (Circulation); Michael McGee (Pressroom); Pam Reynolds (Business Manager); Julie Herrmann (Reporter); Nicole Klauss (Reporter); James Brooks (Editor); Dan Zeleznik (Office Manager); Nicole Clark (Advertising Sales)
Parent company (for newspapers): Helen E Snedded Foundation

DAILY SITKA SENTINEL

Street address 1: 112 Barracks St
Street address city: Sitka
Street address state: AK
Zip/Postal code: 99835-7532
County: Sitka
Country: USA
Mailing address: 112 BARRACKS ST
Mailing city: SITKA
Mailing state: AK
Mailing zip: 99835-7532
General Phone: (907) 747-3219
Advertising Phone: (907) 747-3219
Editorial Phone: (907) 747-3219
General/National Adv. E-mail: susan@sitkasentinel.com
Display Adv. E-mail: susan@sitkasentinel.com
Classified Adv. e-mail: cyndi@sitkasentinel.com
Editorial e-mail: thad@sitkasentinel.com
Primary Website: www.sitkasentinel.com
Year Established: 1940
News Services: AP.
Special Editions: Back-to-School (Aug); Christmas Greetings (Dec); Boat Show (Mar); Summer Visitors (May); Christmas Shopping Issue (Nov); Moonlight Madness (Oct).
Special Weekly Sections: Sitka Weekend (entertainment, TV schedules, feature stories)

Delivery Methods: Newsstand`Carrier
Areas Served - City/County or Portion Thereof, or Zip codes: Sitka
Own Printing Facility?: Y
Commercial printers?: Y
Audit By: Sworn/Estimate/Non-Audited
Audit Date: 12.07.2019
Personnel: Thad Poulson (Co-Pub.); Susan Mcfadden (Adv. Mgr.); Sandy Poulson (Ed.)
Parent company (for newspapers): Verstovia Corp.

ARIZONA

MOHAVE VALLEY DAILY NEWS

Street address 1: 2435 Miracle Mile
Street address city: Bullhead City
Street address state: AZ
Zip/Postal code: 86442-7311
County: Mohave
Country: USA
Mailing address: PO BOX 21209
Mailing city: BULLHEAD CITY
Mailing state: AZ
Mailing zip: 86439-1209
General Phone: 928-763-2505
Advertising Phone: (928) 763-2505 ext. 2221
Editorial Phone: (928) 763-2505 ext. 5144
General/National Adv. E-mail: national@nwppub.com
Display Adv. E-mail: national@nwppub.com
Classified Adv. e-mail: fastclassifieds@nwppub.com
Editorial e-mail: mjsmith@mohavedailynews.com
Primary Website: www.mohavedailynews.com
Mthly Avg Views: 365000
Mthly Avg Unique Visitors: 100000
Year Established: 1963
News Services: AP.
Special Editions: Resource Guide, January; Dining Out, February; Health & Wellness, March; River Run, April; May, Life on the Colorado; Best Of, June; Newcomer's Guide, October; Happy Holidays, November; Last Minute Gift Guide, December.
Special Weekly Sections: Laughlin Nevada Times (weekly) Needles Desert Star (weekly) Boosters (shoppers) Clippin' the River (TMC) Colorado River Real Estate Magazine (monthly) Desert Deals (monthly coupon book)
Syndicated Publications: American Profile (Tuesday)
Delivery Methods: Mail`Newsstand`Carrier`Racks
Areas Served - City/County or Portion Thereof, or Zip codes: Bullhead City, Fort Mojave, Mohave Valley, Topock, & Golden Shores (Ariz) ; Laughlin (Nev) ; Needles (Calif)
Own Printing Facility?: Y
Commercial printers?: Y
Avg Free Circ: 412
Sun. Circulation Paid: 7610
Sun. Circulation Free: 122
Audit By: Sworn/Estimate/Non-Audited
Audit Date: 12.07.2019
Personnel: Bill McMillen (City Editor); Daniel McKillop (Sports Ed.); Carlos Ruiz (CTP (Creo)); Larry Kendrick (Operations Director); Jamie MCorkle (Sales Manager); MJ Smith (Chief Editor); Wells Andrews (Sales and Circulation Director)
Parent company (for newspapers): Brehm Communications, Inc.

ARIZONA DAILY SUN, FLAGSTAFF

Street address 1: 1751 S Thompson St
Street address city: Flagstaff
Street address state: AZ
Zip/Postal code: 86001-8716
County: Coconino
Country: USA
Mailing address: 1751 S THOMPSON ST
Mailing city: FLAGSTAFF
Mailing state: AZ
Mailing zip: 86001-8716
General Phone: (928) 774-4545
Advertising Phone: (928) 774-4545
Editorial Phone: (928) 556-2241
General/National Adv. E-mail: drowley@azdailysun.com
Display Adv. E-mail: cbrady@azdailysun.com
Classified Adv. e-mail: lsmith@azdailysun.com
Editorial e-mail: news@azdailysun.com
Primary Website: www.azdailysun.com
Mthly Avg Views: 1230000
Mthly Avg Unique Visitors: 220139
Year Established: 1883
News Services: AP, MCT, TMS, CSM.
Special Editions: JANUARY: Lose to Win New Year's Special FEBRUARY: ValentineÂ£s Day Dining Club Card MARCH: St. Patrick's Day APRIL: Easter Dining Health Tabloid MAY: Mother's Day Memorial Day 99 Things JUNE: Father's Day Summer Tourist Guide Locally Owned JULY: Fourth of July Summer Tourist Guide AUGUST: Dining Club Card Back To School Summer Tourist Guide Welcome Back NAU SEPTEMBER: Festival of Science OCTOBER: Daily Sun Calendar Best of Flagstaff #1 NOVEMBER: Women in Business Thanksgiving Holiday Shopping DECEMBER: Best of Flagstaff #2 Letters to Santa Last Minute Shopping
Special Weekly Sections: SUNDAY: Health & Medicine Wednesday TV Book
Syndicated Publications: Athlon (Monthly);Relish (Monthly); Parade (S).
Delivery Methods: Mail`Newsstand`Carrier`Racks
Areas Served - City/County or Portion Thereof, or Zip codes: 86001,86004, 86015, 86017, 86018, 86040, 86045, 86046, 86047, 86351, 86033, 86023, 86339
Own Printing Facility?: Y
Commercial printers?: Y
Sat. Circulation Paid: 7212
Sun. Circulation Paid: 8250
Audit By: Sworn/Estimate/Non-Audited
Audit Date: 12.07.2019
Personnel: Randy Wilson (Editorial Page Ed.); William Smith (Prodn. Mgr., Pressroom); Colleen Brady (Ad Director); Chris Etling (Mng. Ed.)
Parent company (for newspapers): Dispatch-Argus; Lee Enterprises, Incorporated

KINGMAN DAILY MINER

Street address 1: 3015 N Stockton Hill Rd
Street address city: Kingman
Street address state: AZ
Zip/Postal code: 86401-4162
County: Mohave
Country: USA
Mailing address: 3015 N STOCKTON HILL RD
Mailing city: KINGMAN
Mailing state: AZ
Mailing zip: 86401-4162
General Phone: (928) 753-6397
Advertising Phone: (928) 753-6397
Editorial Phone: (928) 753-6397
General/National Adv. E-mail: advertising@kdminer.com
Display Adv. E-mail: advertising@kdminer.com
Classified Adv. e-mail: classified@kdminer.com
Editorial e-mail: editorial@kdminer.com
Primary Website: www.kdminer.com
Year Established: 1882
News Services: AP, Papert (Landon).
Special Editions: Business Showcase (Apr); Back-to-School (Aug); Last Minute Christmas (Dec); Top 10 Stories of the Year (Jan); Soap Box Derby (Jul); Welcome to Kingman (Jun); Home & Garden (Mar); Park & Recreation Book (May); Christmas Kick-Off (Nov); Destination Kingman
Special Weekly Sections: American (Mon);Business, Showcase (Wed); Entertainment (Thur); TV/ Entertainment, Religion, School, Homes (Fri); Business, Properties (Sun)
Syndicated Publications: Relish (Monthly); Parade (S); American Profile (Weekly).
Areas Served - City/County or Portion Thereof, or Zip codes: Kingman, Arizona, and Mohave County
Sun. Circulation Paid: 8172
Audit By: Sworn/Estimate/Non-Audited
Audit Date: 12.07.2019
Personnel: Debbie White-Hoel (Pub.); Shawn Byrne (Ed.); Claire Whitley (News Ed.)
Parent company (for newspapers): Western News&Info, Inc.

TODAY'S NEWS-HERALD

Street address 1: 2225 Acoma Blvd W
Street address city: Lake Havasu City
Street address state: AZ
Zip/Postal code: 86403-2907
County: Mohave
Country: USA
Mailing address: 2225 ACOMA BLVD W
Mailing city: LAKE HAVASU CITY
Mailing state: AZ
Mailing zip: 86403-2995
General Phone: (928) 453-4237
Advertising Phone: (928) 855-2197
Editorial Phone: (928) 453-4237
General/National Adv. E-mail: ads@havasunews.com
Display Adv. E-mail: ads@havasunews.com
Classified Adv. e-mail: classified@havasunews.com
Editorial e-mail: editor@havasunews.com
Primary Website: www.havasunews.com
Mthly Avg Views: 366048
Mthly Avg Unique Visitors: 74000
News Services: AP.
Special Editions: Holiday Shopping Guide (Dec); Winter Visitor's Guide (Feb); Meet Your Merchant (Mar); Summer Guide (May); Winter Visitor's Guide (Nov); London Bridge Days (Oct).
Special Weekly Sections: Sports (Mon); Business (Tue); Best Food (Wed); Health (Thur); Entertainment, Church (Fri); Real Estate, Comics, TV (Sun)
Syndicated Publications: American Profile (Weekly).
Delivery Methods: Mail`Newsstand`Carrier`Racks
Areas Served - City/County or Portion Thereof, or Zip codes: Lake Havasu, AZ
Own Printing Facility?: N
Commercial printers?: N
Avg Free Circ: 120
Sun. Circulation Paid: 8947
Sun. Circulation Free: 120
Audit By: VAC
Audit Date: 30.06.2017
Personnel: Michael E. Quinn (Pres/Pub); Sandy Stangifer (Controller); Christine Hammers (Adv. Dir.); Kevin Baird (Sports); Alexis Christensen (Circ. Mgr.); Shannon Engles (Bus. Mgr.); Cindy Taylor (Pro. Mgr.); Chris Walker (HR Mgr.); Gwen Girsdansky (Copy Ed); Brandon Bowers (Ed)
Parent company (for newspapers): Wick Communications; Western News&Info, Inc.

THE ARIZONA REPUBLIC

Street address 1: 200 E Van Buren St
Street address city: Phoenix
Street address state: AZ
Zip/Postal code: 85004-2238
County: Maricopa
Country: USA
Mailing address: PO BOX 1950
Mailing city: PHOENIX
Mailing state: AZ
Mailing zip: 85001-1950
General Phone: (602) 444-8000
Advertising Phone: (602) 444-4444
Editorial Phone: (602) 444-6397
Classified Adv. e-mail: classified@arizonarepublic.com
Editorial e-mail: newstips@arizonarepublic.com
Primary Website: www.azcentral.com
Mthly Avg Unique Visitors: 9236651
Year Established: 1890
News Services: AP, LAT-WP, NYT, SHNS, RN, MCT, HN, CSM, GNS, TMS.
Special Editions: Working (Apr); Football Extra Preview (Aug); Fiesta/College Bowl Preview (Dec); Spring Training/Baseball Preview (Feb); Phoenix Open (Jan); Mercury/WNBA Preview (Jun); Arizona Inc. (May); Working (Oct); Rep AZ Best (Sept).
Special Weekly Sections: Food (Wed); AZ Living, Things To Do (Thur); Preview (Fri); Travel (Sun)
Syndicated Publications: Vista (Fri); USA WEEKEND Magazine (S).
Delivery Methods: Mail`Newsstand`Carrier`Racks
Areas Served - City/County or Portion Thereof, or Zip codes: The Arizona Republic provides delivery to all zip codes in Maricopa, Pinal, Yavapai, Gila and Graham counties. Select zip codes in Coconino, Navajo, Apache, Greenlee, Cochise and Pima counties. Only small SCS delivery in Mohave, La Paz and Yuma counties.
Sat. Circulation Paid: 161643
Sun. Circulation Paid: 256654
Audit By: AAM
Audit Date: 31.12.2017
Personnel: Greg Burton (Exec. Ed.); John Adams (Sr. Dir.); Philip Boas (Ed. Dir.); Joanna Allhands (Ed.); Abe Kwok (Ed.); Kim Meader (Office Mgr.); Kimberly M. Torres (News Asst.); Rebecca Bartkowski (Features Dir.); Kim Bui (Director of Audience Innovation); Mark Faller (Sports Ed.); Mike Meister (Director of Visuals); Diana Payan (Video Strategist); Stacy Sullivan (Community Relations Director); Josh Susong (News Dir.); Kathy Tulumello (News Dir.); Dan Nowicki (National Politics Ed.); Wyatt Buchanan (Ed.)
Parent company (for newspapers): Gannett

THE DAILY COURIER

Street address 1: 8307 E. State Route 69
Street address city: Prescott Valley
Street address state: AZ
Zip/Postal code: 86314
County: Yavapai
Country: USA
Mailing address: 8307 E. State Route 69
Mailing city: Prescott Valley
Mailing state: AZ
Mailing zip: 86314
General Phone: (928) 445-3333
Advertising Phone: (928) 776-8122
Editorial Phone: (928) 445-3333
General/National Adv. E-mail: editorial@prescottaz.com
Display Adv. E-mail: msmith@prescottaz.com
Classified Adv. e-mail: classifieds@prescottaz.com
Editorial e-mail: editorial@prescottaz.com
Primary Website: www.dcourier.com
Mthly Avg Views: 2014719
Mthly Avg Unique Visitors: 235052
Year Established: 1882
News Services: Western Newspapers Inc..
Special Editions: Bride & Groom(Feb); Home Style-Home Improvement(March and Sept); Health Care Focus(April and Oct); Wildwest Frontier Days(June); Celebrations- holiday decorating and entertaining(Nov, Dec)
Special Weekly Sections: Real Estate (Fri); Business (S).
Syndicated Publications: Relish(1st Wed/month), Spry(2nd Wed/month), Parade(Sun), Athlon Sports(3rd Tues/month, counting from the first full week), American Profile(Thurs), and Comics(Sun)
Delivery Methods: Mail`Newsstand`Carrier`Racks
Areas Served - City/County or Portion Thereof, or Zip codes: Yavapai County(Prescott Valley, Chino Valley, and Camp Verde)
Own Printing Facility?: Y
Commercial printers?: Y
Avg Free Circ: 246
Sat. Circulation Paid: 12534
Sat. Circulation Free: 246
Sun. Circulation Paid: 13178
Sun. Circulation Free: 236
Audit By: VAC
Audit Date: 30.09.2015
Personnel: Kit K. Atwell (Pub.); Tim Wiederaenders (News/Sports Ed.); Doug Graham (Community Ed.); Les Stukenberg (Photo Ed.); Brian Bergner (News/ Sports Ed.); Megan Smith (Adv. Dir.); Jack Perkins (Audience Development Dir.)
Parent company (for newspapers): Western News&Info, Inc.

WICK COMMUNICATIONS - HERALD/REVIEW

Street address 1: 102 Fab Ave
Street address city: Sierra Vista
Street address state: AZ
Zip/Postal code: 85635-1741
County: Cochise
Country: USA
General Phone: (520) 458-9440
Advertising Phone: (520) 515-4630
Editorial Phone: (520) 515-4610
General/National Adv. E-mail: publisher@myheraldreview.com
Display Adv. E-mail: alycia.mccloud@myheraldreview.com
Classified Adv. e-mail: classified@myheraldreview.com
Editorial e-mail: editor@myheraldreview.com
Primary Website: www.myheraldreview.com
Mthly Avg Views: 1250000
Mthly Avg Unique Visitors: 120000
Year Established: 1955
News Services: AP, NYT
Special Editions: Nabur Magazine (Quarterly) Chamber Directory (Jan); Back-to-School (Jul); Life In Cochise (Feb); Douglas, Benson, Willcox, Tombstone and Bisbee annual directories, Tombstone Map, Imagine Cochise Calendar, Cochise County Hues postcards, Holiday Flavors (Nov), Best of Preps, Academic All-Stars, Cochise County's Most Influential
Special Weekly Sections: Religion Page (FRi); Business (Sun); Comics (S); Real Estate (Sun); Food (Wed); Entertainment (Fri),
Delivery Methods: Mail`Newsstand`Carrier`Racks

Areas Served - City/County or Portion Thereof, or Zip codes: Cochise County
Own Printing Facility?: Y
Commercial printers?: Y
Avg Free Circ: 130
Sun. Circulation Paid: 5809
Sun. Circulation Free: 130
Audit By: USPS
Audit Date: 30.09.2022
Personnel: Jennifer Sorenson (Publisher); Becky Bjork (Adv. Dir.); Joan Hancock (Bus. Mgr.); Matt Hickman (Managing Editor); Alycia McCloud (Marketing Team Manager); Eric Petermann (Opinions Ed.); Ken Bohl (Audience Development Director); Dean Kinney (Production Manager); Pat Wick (Asst. Gen. Mgr.); Fanny Weiland (Business Manager)
Parent company (for newspapers): Wick Communications

DAILY NEWS-SUN

Street address 1: 17220 N Boswell Blvd
Street address 2: Ste 101
Street address city: Sun City
Street address state: AZ
Zip/Postal code: 85373-2065
County: Maricopa
Country: USA
Mailing address: 17220 N BOSWELL BLVD STE 101
Mailing city: SUN CITY
Mailing state: AZ
Mailing zip: 85373-2065
General Phone: (623) 977-8351
Advertising Phone: (623)876-2566
Editorial Phone: (623) 876-2534
General/National Adv. E-mail: rcarlton@yourwestvalley.com
Display Adv. E-mail: rcarlton@yourwestvalley.com
Classified Adv. e-mail: trodgers@yourwestvalley.com
Editorial e-mail: dmccarthy@yourwestvalley.com
Primary Website: www.yourwestvalley.com
Mthly Avg Views: 165000
Mthly Avg Unique Visitors: 55000
Year Established: 1956
News Services: AP, DJ, ONS.
Special Editions: Choices (Apr); Funeral Planner (Jun); Spring Home Improvement (Mar); Senior Caregivers (May); Holiday Gift Guides (Nov); Fall Home Improvement (Oct).
Special Weekly Sections: Week's End/Business Review (Sat); Weekender/Entertainment (Thur); Food & Nutrition (Tues); Travel (Wed).
Syndicated Publications: TV/Entertainment (Fri); USA WEEKEND Magazine (Sat).
Delivery Methods: Mail`Newsstand`Carrier`Racks
Areas Served - City/County or Portion Thereof, or Zip codes: Sun City, Sun City West, Sun City Grand, El Mirage, Youngtown, and Surprise
Own Printing Facility?: Y
Commercial printers?: Y
Sat. Circulation Paid: 29275
Audit By: CAC
Audit Date: 30.06.2016
Personnel: Marji Ranes (Pub.); Robert Martin (Circulation. Dir.); Penny Bruns (Adv. Dir.); Dan McCarthy (Exec. Ed.); Rich Bolas (Sports Ed.); Michael Bergstrom (Op. Dir.); Louis Gobin (Bus. Mgr.); Cameron Carranza (Preprint/Warehouse)
Parent company (for newspapers): Independent Newsmedia Inc. USA

ARIZONA DAILY STAR

Street address 1: 4850 S. Park Avenue
Street address city: Tucson
Street address state: AZ
Zip/Postal code: 85714
County: Pima
Country: USA
Mailing address: 4850 S PARK AVE
Mailing city: TUCSON
Mailing state: AZ
Mailing zip: 85714-3395
General Phone: 520-573-4142
Advertising Phone: (520) 573-4366
Editorial Phone: (520) 573-4142
General/National Adv. E-mail: advertising@tucson.com
Display Adv. E-mail: advertising@tucson.com
Classified Adv. e-mail: advertising@tucson.com
Editorial e-mail: mparham@tucson.com
Primary Website: www.tucson.com
Mthly Avg Views: 12066635
Mthly Avg Unique Visitors: 1137934
Year Established: 1877
News Services: AP, NYT, MCT, SHNS, DJ, DF, TMS.
Special Weekly Sections: Caliente (entertainment) (Thurs); TV Week (S); Food & More (Wed).
Syndicated Publications: USA WEEKEND Magazine (Fri). ; Parade(Sun)
Delivery Methods: Mail`Newsstand`Racks
Areas Served - City/County or Portion Thereof, or Zip codes: Pima County, Cochise County, Santa Cruz County, Pinal County, Graham County
Sat. Circulation Paid: 57868
Sun. Circulation Paid: 78301
Audit By: AAM
Audit Date: 31.12.2017
Personnel: Jill Spitz (Ed.); Joel Rohlik (VP Finance); Alisha Owens (VP Adv. Sales & Mktg.); John Lundgren (Dir. Print Ops.); Rob Wisner (Dir. Digital Innovation); Darrell Durham (Mrktg. Dir.); Mike Facemire (Dir. IT); Mark Lolwing (Dir. Circ & Consumer Innovation); Hipolito R. Corella (Sr. Ed.); Debbie Kornmiller (Sr. Editor); George Campbell (Copy Chief); Ann Brown (Editorial Page Ed.); Maria Parham (Editorial Page Ed.); Phil Villarreal (Film Critic); Kristen Cook (Food/Home Ed.); Stephnie Innes (Health/Medical Ed.); John Bolton (Starnet Online Ed.); Ryan Finley (High School Sports Ed.); Jennin Corner (Sports Ed.); Norma Coile (Science/Technology Ed.); Elaine Raines (News/Research Servs. Dir.); Johnny Childs (Circ. Distrib. Spec); John D'Orlando (Pres./Pub.)
Parent company (for newspapers): Media News Group; Dispatch-Argus; Lee Enterprises, Incorporated

THE DAILY TERRITORIAL

Street address 1: 7225 N. Mona Lisa Rd.
Street address 2: #125
Street address city: Tucson
Street address state: AZ
Zip/Postal code: 85741
County: Pima
Country: USA
Mailing address: 7225 N. Mona Lisa Rd., #125
Mailing city: Tucson
Mailing state: AZ
Mailing zip: 85741
General Phone: (520) 797-4384
Advertising Phone: (520) 294-1200
Editorial Phone: (520) 294-1200
General/National Adv. E-mail: tucsoneditor@tucsonlocalmedia.com
Display Adv. E-mail: classifieds@tucsonlocalmedia.com
Classified Adv. e-mail: jahearn@azbiz.com
Editorial e-mail: tucsoneditor@tucsonlocalmedia.com
Primary Website: www.azbiz.com
Year Established: 1966
News Services: American Newspaper Representatives Inc..
Areas Served - City/County or Portion Thereof, or Zip codes: 856-857
Audit By: Sworn/Estimate/Non-Audited
Audit Date: 12.07.2019
Personnel: Jason Joseph (Pres./Pub.); Laura Horvath (Circulation Manager & Special Events Manager); Meredith Hansen (Sales Admin); Jim Nintzel (News Editor); Logan Burtch-Buus (Ed.); Casey Anderson (Art Dir./Associate Pub.); Pamela Laramie (Bookkeeping)
Parent company (for newspapers): Wick Communications

YUMA SUN

Street address 1: 2055 S. Arizona Avenue
Street address city: Yuma
Street address state: AZ
Zip/Postal code: 85364
County: Yuma
Country: USA
Mailing address: PO BOX 271
Mailing city: YUMA
Mailing state: AZ
Mailing zip: 85366-0271
General Phone: (928) 539-6800
Advertising Phone: (928)539-6829
Editorial Phone: (928) 539-6862
General/National Adv. E-mail: nationals@yumasun.com
Display Adv. E-mail: nationals@yumasun.com
Classified Adv. e-mail: classifieds@yumasun.com
Editorial e-mail: news@yumasun.com
Primary Website: www.yumasun.com
Year Established: 1872
News Services: AP.
Special Editions: Health Connections (Every other month, odd months); Raising Healthy Yuma Families (4x a year); Yuma's Best (Feb); Ag in Yuma (Mar.); Southwest Living (every other month); Dove Hunting (Aug. or Sept); Visiting in Yuma (Oct.); PAWS pet adoption (monthly). Military Publications-Desert Flightline and Outpost (Every Monday-the two publications alternate); Southwest Services (monthly)
Special Weekly Sections: Business/Financial (S); Religion (Sat); Food (Tues); Business/Financial (Wed).
Syndicated Publications: Parade
Delivery Methods: Mail`Carrier`Racks
Areas Served - City/County or Portion Thereof, or Zip codes: 85364, 85365, 92283, 85367, 85356, 85352, 85350, 85336, 85349
Own Printing Facility?: Y
Commercial printers?: Y
Avg Free Circ: 244
Sat. Circulation Paid: 8840
Sat. Circulation Free: 244
Sun. Circulation Paid: 9656
Sun. Circulation Free: 188
Audit By: CAC
Audit Date: 30.06.2018
Personnel: John Vaughn (Editor, Bajo El Sol); Randy Hoeft (Special Content Ed.); David Fornof (Production Dir.); Kathy White (Business Mgr.); Grady Garrett (Sports Ed.); Darlene F (Nationals Account Manager)
Parent company (for newspapers): Horizon Publications Inc.; RISN Operations Inc.

ARKANSAS

ARKADELPHIA SIFTINGS HERALD

Street address 1: 205 S 26th St
Street address city: Arkadelphia
Street address state: AR
Zip/Postal code: 71923-5423
County: Clark
Country: USA
Mailing address: PO BOX 10
Mailing city: ARKADELPHIA
Mailing state: AR
Mailing zip: 71923-0010
General Phone: (870) 246-5525
Advertising Phone: (870) 246-5525
Editorial Phone: (870) 246-5525
General/National Adv. E-mail: rhaycox@siftingsherald.com
Display Adv. E-mail: rhaycox@siftingsherald.com
Classified Adv. e-mail: jjones@siftingsherald.com
Editorial e-mail: wledbetter@siftingsherald.com
Primary Website: www.siftingsherald.com
Year Established: 1899
News Services: AP.
Syndicated Publications: American Profile (Weekly).
Delivery Methods: Mail`Newsstand`Carrier`Racks
Areas Served - City/County or Portion Thereof, or Zip codes: Arkadelphia, Clark County and the surrounding area
Own Printing Facility?: Y
Commercial printers?: Y
Audit By: Sworn/Estimate/Non-Audited
Audit Date: 12.07.2019
Personnel: Jennifer Allen (Pub.); Summer Benedict (Sales Rep.); Kendall Kegley (Classified Ads); Lewis Delavan (Online Ed.); Jeff Meek (Mng. Ed.)
Parent company (for newspapers): CherryRoad Media

BATESVILLE DAILY GUARD

Street address 1: 258 W Main St
Street address city: Batesville
Street address state: AR
Zip/Postal code: 72501-6711
County: Independence
Country: USA
Mailing address: PO BOX 2036
Mailing city: BATESVILLE
Mailing state: AR
Mailing zip: 72503-2036
General Phone: (870) 793-2383
Advertising Phone: (870) 793-2383
Editorial Phone: (870) 793-2383
General/National Adv. E-mail: advertising@guardonline.com
Display Adv. E-mail: advertising@guardonline.com
Classified Adv. e-mail: classifieds@guardonline.com
Editorial e-mail: news@guardonline.com
Primary Website: www.guardonline.com
Year Established: 1876
News Services: AP.
Special Editions: Batesville USA (Apr); Fair Time (Aug); Spirit of Christmas (Dec); Brides (Jan); Father's Day (Jun); Baseball (Mar); Graduation (May); Basketball (Nov); Hunting (Oct).
Special Weekly Sections: Education (Fri); Outdoors (Thur); Business (Tues); Agriculture (Wed).
Syndicated Publications: River Country Tab (Fri); American Profile (Weekly).
Delivery Methods: Mail`Newsstand`Carrier`Racks
Areas Served - City/County or Portion Thereof, or Zip codes: Batesville (AR) & surrounding area
Own Printing Facility?: Y
Commercial printers?: Y
Audit By: Sworn/Estimate/Non-Audited
Audit Date: 12.07.2019
Personnel: Ronnie Bell (Gen. Mgr.); Andrea Bruner (Mng. Ed.); Scott McDonald (Sports Ed.)
Parent company (for newspapers): Paxton Media Group

THE SALINE COURIER

Street address 1: 321 N Market St
Street address city: Benton
Street address state: AR
Zip/Postal code: 72015-3734
County: Saline
Country: USA
Mailing address: PO BOX 207
Mailing city: BENTON
Mailing state: AR
Mailing zip: 72018-0207
General Phone: (501) 315-8228
Advertising Phone: (501) 315-8228
Editorial Phone: (501) 315-8228
General/National Adv. E-mail: news@bentoncourier.com
Display Adv. E-mail: dwills@bentoncourier.com
Classified Adv. e-mail: class@bentoncourier.com
Editorial e-mail: news@bentoncourier.com; subscription@bentoncourier.com
Primary Website: www.bentoncourier.com
Mthly Avg Views: 90000
Mthly Avg Unique Visitors: 22000
Year Established: 1876
News Services: AP.
Special Editions: American Home Week/Home Improvement (Apr); Back-to-School (Aug); Christmas (Dec); Business Profile (Feb); Summer Recreation Guide (Jun); Fashion/Bridal (Mar); Spring Car Care (May); Cooking (Nov); Fall Car Care (Oct); Hunting (Sept).
Special Weekly Sections: Religion (Sat); Living (S); Neighbors (Lifestyle) (Thur); Business (Tues); Food & Good Health (Wed).
Syndicated Publications: TV Magazine (S); American Profile (Weekly).
Delivery Methods: Newsstand`Carrier`Racks
Areas Served - City/County or Portion Thereof, or Zip codes: 72015, 72019, 72022, 72002, 72011, 72103, 72167
Own Printing Facility?: Y
Commercial printers?: Y
Avg Free Circ: 10900
Sat. Circulation Paid: 65,2
Sun. Circulation Paid: 5700
Audit By: Sworn/Estimate/Non-Audited
Audit Date: 12.07.2019
Personnel: Patricia Stuckey (Composing Manager); Kelly Freudensprung (Pub.); Josh Briggs (Ed.); Ricky Walters (Press Room Mgr.)
Parent company (for newspapers): Horizon Publications Inc.

BLYTHEVILLE COURIER NEWS

Street address 1: 900 N Broadway St
Street address city: Blytheville
Street address state: AR
Zip/Postal code: 72315-1714
County: Mississippi
Country: USA
Mailing address: PO BOX 1108
Mailing city: BLYTHEVILLE
Mailing state: AR
Mailing zip: 72316-1108
General Phone: (870) 763-4461
Advertising Phone: (870) 763-4461
Editorial Phone: (870) 763-4461

General/National Adv. E-mail: sriley@couriernews.net
Display Adv. E-mail: sdelaney@couriernews.net
Classified Adv. e-mail: sdelaney@couriernews.net
Editorial e-mail: aweld@couriernews.net
Primary Website: www.couriernews.net
News Services: AP.
Special Editions: Income Tax (Jan).
Special Weekly Sections: Church Page (Fri); Senior Outlook (Mon); Kids Page (S); Business (Thur); Health & Environment (Tues); Best Food Day (Wed).
Syndicated Publications: TV Magazine (Fri); Relish (Monthly); Color Comics (S).
Delivery Methods: Mail`Racks
Areas Served - City/County or Portion Thereof, or Zip codes: Blytheville Community
Own Printing Facility?: Y
Commercial printers?: Y
Avg Free Circ: 0
Sun. Circulation Paid: 2290
Sun. Circulation Free: 0
Audit By: CAC
Audit Date: 30.09.2013
Personnel: David Tennyson (Pub.); Harry Dorby (Adv. Mgr.); Mark Brassfield (Mng. Ed.); Andy Weld (Ed.); Susie Robison (Prodn. Foreman, Pressroom); Aaron Fitzpatrick (Staff Writer)
Parent company (for newspapers): Rust Communications

CAMDEN NEWS

Street address 1: 113 Madison Ave NE
Street address city: Camden
Street address state: AR
Zip/Postal code: 71701-3514
County: Ouachita
Country: USA
Mailing address: PO BOX 798
Mailing city: CAMDEN
Mailing state: AR
Mailing zip: 71711-0798
General Phone: (870) 836-8192
Advertising Phone: (870) 836-8192
General/National Adv. E-mail: camnews@cablelynx.com
Display Adv. E-mail: advertising@camdenarknews.com
Editorial e-mail: sports@camdenarknews.com
Primary Website: www.camdenarknews.com
Year Established: 1920
News Services: AP.
Special Editions: Industrial Progress (Apr); Football (Aug); Bridal (Jan); Home, Lawn, & Garden (Mar); Cookbook (Oct); Fall Fashion (Sept).
Syndicated Publications: Relish (Monthly); Food (Tues); American Profile (Weekly).
Audit By: Sworn/Estimate/Non-Audited
Audit Date: 12.07.2019
Personnel: Walter E. Hussman (Pub.); Sue Silliman (Gen. Mgr.); Pam Hulse (Bus. Mgr.); Susan Silliman (Adv. Mgr.); LaDonna Foster (Circ. Mgr.); Jim Edwards (Mng. Ed.); Kelly Blair (Sports Ed.)
Parent company (for newspapers): WEHCO Media, Inc.

LOG CABIN DEMOCRAT

Street address 1: 1121 Front Street
Street address city: Conway
Street address state: AR
Zip/Postal code: 72032
County: Faulkner
Country: USA
Mailing address: 1121 Front Street
Mailing city: Conway
Mailing state: AR
Mailing zip: 72032
General Phone: (501) 327-6621
Advertising Phone: (501) 505-1227
Editorial Phone: (501) 505-1245
General/National Adv. E-mail: ads@thecabin.net
Display Adv. E-mail: ads@thecabin.net
Classified Adv. e-mail: classads@thecabin.net
Editorial e-mail: editorial@thecabin.net
Primary Website: www.thecabin.net
Year Established: 1879
News Services: AP, SHNS.
Special Editions: Toad Suck Daze (Apr); Football (Aug); Last Minute Gift Guide (Dec); Bridal Tab (Feb); Red Tag Sale (Jan); Newcomer's Guide (Jul); June Shopping Spree (Jun); Spring Fashion (Mar); Mother's Day Gift Guide (May); Christmas Gift Guide (Nov); Auto Car Care (Oct)
Special Weekly Sections: Church Directory (Fri); Business Page (S); Best Food Day (Tues); Education Page (Wed).
Syndicated Publications: USA WEEKEND Magazine (S); American Profile (Weekly).
Delivery Methods: Newsstand`Carrier`Racks
Areas Served - City/County or Portion Thereof, or Zip codes: 72032, 72033, 72034, 72039, 72047, 72058, 72061, 72106, 72173
Own Printing Facility?: N
Commercial printers?: N
Sat. Circulation Paid: 5653
Sun. Circulation Paid: 7319
Audit By: Sworn/Estimate/Non-Audited
Audit Date: 12.07.2019
Personnel: Kelly Sublett (Pub.); Lisa Licht (Adv. Dir.); Nick Stahl (Dir. of Ed./Prod. Online Services); Jay Prince (Adv. Production); Rob Hambuchen (Circ. Mgr.); Kelly Booy (Adv. Exec.); Crystal Geraldson (Adv. Exec.); Leigh Anne Gray (Adv. Exec.); Eliesha Wolverton (CSR)
Parent company (for newspapers): Paxton Media Group

EL DORADO NEWS-TIMES / SUNDAY NEWS

Street address 1: 111 N Madison Ave
Street address city: El Dorado
Street address state: AR
Zip/Postal code: 71730-6124
County: Union
Country: USA
Mailing address: PO BOX 912
Mailing city: EL DORADO
Mailing state: AR
Mailing zip: 71731-0912
General Phone: (870) 862-6611
Advertising Phone: (870) 862-6611
Editorial Phone: (870) 862-6611
General/National Adv. E-mail: editorial@eldoradonews.com
Display Adv. E-mail: advertising@eldoradonews.com
Classified Adv. e-mail: classifieds@eldoradonews.com
Editorial e-mail: editorial@eldoradonews.com
Primary Website: www.eldoradonews.com
Year Established: 1876
News Services: AP.
Special Editions: Spring Fashion (Apr); Back-to-School (Aug); Progress (Mar); Graduation (May); Senior Health (July); Veterans Section (Oct.); Christmas Catalogue (Nov); Fall Fashion (Sept). Bella Magazine (Feb., May, Oct,)
Special Weekly Sections: Education (Tue); Best Food (Wed); Real Estate (Fri); Religion (Sat); Living, Entertainment (Sun); Business, Finance (Mon)
Syndicated Publications: Relish (Monthly); USA WEEKEND Magazine (S);
Delivery Methods: Mail`Carrier`Racks
Areas Served - City/County or Portion Thereof, or Zip codes: 71730, 71759, 71750, 71765, 71762, 71749, 71758, 71768, 71724,
Own Printing Facility?: Y
Commercial printers?: Y
Avg Free Circ: 720
Sat. Circulation Paid: 4413
Sat. Circulation Free: 720
Sun. Circulation Paid: 4212
Sun. Circulation Free: 405
Audit By: AAM
Audit Date: 31.03.2018
Personnel: Nichole Patterson (Adv. Dir.); Danny Leftridge (Circ. Mgr.); Janice McIntire (Features Ed.); Tony Burns (Sports Ed.); Iva Gail Riser (Prodn. Mgr.); Paula Burson (Business Office Mgr.); Buddy King (VP); Randal Curtman (Managing Ed.); Kelsey Womack (Rep.); J.W. Misenheimer; Madeleine Leroux (Man. Ed.)
Parent company (for newspapers): WEHCO Media, Inc.

NORTHWEST ARKANSAS DEMOCRAT-GAZETTE

Street address 1: 212 N East Ave
Street address city: Fayetteville
Street address state: AR
Zip/Postal code: 72701-5225
County: Washington
Country: USA
Mailing address: PO BOX 1607
Mailing city: FAYETTEVILLE
Mailing state: AR
Mailing zip: 72702-1607
General Phone: (479) 442-1700
Advertising Phone: (866) 652-4373
General/National Adv. E-mail: keikenberry@nwadg.com
Primary Website: www.nwaonline.com
News Services: AP.
Delivery Methods: Mail`Newsstand`Carrier`Racks
Own Printing Facility?: Y
Commercial printers?: Y
Audit By: AAM
Audit Date: 30.09.2017
Personnel: Todd Nelson (Pres.); Crystal Costa (Adv./Mktg. Dir.); Kent Eikenberry (Adv. Mgr.); Vanessa Wrutz (Mktg. Mgr.)
Parent company (for newspapers): NAN LLC; WEHCO Media, Inc.

TIMES-HERALD

Street address 1: 222 N Izard St
Street address city: Forrest City
Street address state: AR
Zip/Postal code: 72335-3324
County: Saint Francis
Country: USA
Mailing address: PO BOX 1699
Mailing city: FORREST CITY
Mailing state: AR
Mailing zip: 72336-1699
General Phone: (870) 633-3130
General/National Adv. E-mail: publisher@thnews.com
Display Adv. E-mail: thnewsads@gmail.com
Classified Adv. e-mail: classifiedads@thnews.com
Editorial e-mail: publisher@thnews.com
Primary Website: www.thnews.com
Avg Free Circ: 8500
Audit By: Sworn/Estimate/Non-Audited
Audit Date: 12.09.2021
Personnel: Tamara Johnson (Pub.); Caleb Talley (Reporter. / Photographer); Amy Hale (Adv. Mgr.); Courtney Hunt (Class. Adv. Mgr.); Bonner McCollum (Pub. Emer.)
Parent company (for newspapers): Horizon Publications Inc.; Argent Arkansas News Media

TIMES RECORD

Street address 1: 3600 Wheeler Ave
Street address city: Fort Smith
Street address state: AR
Zip/Postal code: 72901-6621
County: Sebastian
Country: USA
Mailing address: PO BOX 1359
Mailing city: FORT SMITH
Mailing state: AR
Mailing zip: 72902-1359
General Phone: (479) 785-7700
Advertising Phone: (479) 785-7700
General/National Adv. E-mail: jnewman@swtimes.com
Display Adv. E-mail: jnewman@swtimes.com
Classified Adv. e-mail: jnewman@swtimes.com
Editorial e-mail: mtaylor@swtimes.com
Primary Website: www.swtimes.com
Mthly Avg Views: 900000
Mthly Avg Unique Visitors: 160000
Year Established: 1893
News Services: AP.
Special Weekly Sections: OnScreen
Syndicated Publications: USA Weekend
Delivery Methods: Mail`Newsstand`Carrier`Racks
Areas Served - City/County or Portion Thereof, or Zip codes: Crawford, Franklin, Johnson, Logan, Polk, Scott, and Sebastian counties in Arkansas; Haskell, LeFlore and Sequoyah counties in Oklahoma
Own Printing Facility?: N
Commercial printers?: Y
Avg Free Circ: 1270
Sat. Circulation Paid: 13718
Sat. Circulation Free: 1270
Sun. Circulation Paid: 18224
Sun. Circulation Free: 262
Audit By: AAM
Audit Date: 31.03.2019
Personnel: Julie Newman (Outside Sales Mgr.); Glen Hogue (Circ. Mgr.); Tara Lynch (Dig. Sales Mgr.); Brian Sanderford (Sports Ed.); Crystal Costa (Pub.); Steve Peterson (Feat. Ed.); Mardi Taylor (Exec. Ed.); Tara Lynch (Dig. Mgr.)
Parent company (for newspapers): Gannett; CherryRoad Media

HARRISON DAILY TIMES

Street address 1: 111 W Rush Ave
Street address city: Harrison
Street address state: AR
Zip/Postal code: 72601-4218
County: Boone
Country: USA
Mailing address: PO BOX 40
Mailing city: HARRISON
Mailing state: AR
Mailing zip: 72602-0040
General Phone: (870) 741-2325
Advertising Phone: (870)743-0624
Editorial Phone: (870)743-0601
General/National Adv. E-mail: dailytimes@harrisondaily.com
Display Adv. E-mail: jasono@harrisondaily.com
Classified Adv. e-mail: debbiel@harrisondaily.com
Editorial e-mail: news@harrisondaily.com
Primary Website: www.harrisondaily.com
Mthly Avg Views: 277368
Mthly Avg Unique Visitors: 44599
Year Established: 1876
News Services: AP.
Special Editions: Health, Fitness & Medical (Monthly). Progress, March, Full Market Coverage (Monthly), Thanksgiving / Black Friday
Special Weekly Sections: TV Magazine-Focus (Fri).
Syndicated Publications: USA WEEKEND Magazine (S).
Areas Served - City/County or Portion Thereof, or Zip codes: 72601, 72611, 72615, 72616, 72619, 72644, 72648, 72638, 72641, 72630, 72650, 72662, 72682, 72685, 72687
Own Printing Facility?: Y
Avg Free Circ: 112
Sat. Circulation Paid: 6529
Sat. Circulation Free: 41
Audit By: CVC
Audit Date: 31.12.2014
Personnel: Jim Perry (Pub.); Jason Overman (Gen. Mgr.); Donna Braymer (Bus./Finance Ed.); James White (City/Metro Ed.); Yvonne Cone (Fashion/Style Ed.); Jane Dunlap Christenson (Food Ed.); Lee Dunlap (Political/Gov't Ed.); Jeff Brasel (Mng. Ed.); Lynn Blevins (Managing Ed.); Jim Kennedy (Circ. Mgr); Todd Edwards (Advertising Manager)
Parent company (for newspapers): Community Publishers, Inc.; Phillips Media Group LLC

HOPE STAR

Street address 1: 522 W 3rd St
Street address city: Hope
Street address state: AR
Zip/Postal code: 71801-5001
County: Hempstead
Country: USA
Mailing address: PO BOX 648
Mailing city: HOPE
Mailing state: AR
Mailing zip: 71802-0648
General Phone: (870) 777-8841
General/National Adv. E-mail: hopestar71802@yahoo.com
Display Adv. E-mail: thaycox@hopestar.com
Editorial e-mail: kmclemore@hopestar.com
Primary Website: www.hopestar.com
Year Established: 1899
News Services: AP.
Special Editions: Watermelon Festival (Jul); Progress (Mar); Graduation (May).
Syndicated Publications: Star Time Entertainment (weekly TV section) (Fri); American Profile (Weekly).
Audit By: Sworn/Estimate/Non-Audited
Audit Date: 12.07.2019
Personnel: Donnie Hollis (Circ. Dir.); Shane Allen (Sr. Group Pub.); Marsha Hunt (Bus. Mgr.); Tim Haycox; Richard Kennedy (Ed.)
Parent company (for newspapers): CherryRoad Media

THE SENTINEL-RECORD

Street address 1: 300 Spring St
Street address city: Hot Springs National Park
Street address state: AR
Zip/Postal code: 71901-4148
County: Garland
Country: USA
Mailing address: PO BOX 580
Mailing city: HOT SPRINGS NATIONAL PARK
Mailing state: AR
Mailing zip: 71902-0580
General Phone: (501) 623-7711
General/National Adv. E-mail: debej@hotsr.com
Display Adv. E-mail: debej@hotsr.com

Classified Adv. e-mail: debbiel@hotsr.com
Editorial e-mail: editor@hotsr.com
Primary Website: www.hotspringssr.com
Year Established: 1877
News Services: AP.
Special Editions: Mail-it-Away (Feb); Spring Home Improvement (Mar); Come to Play, Come to Stay (Apr); Ladies' Night Out (Apr); Family Owned Business (May); Readers' Choice (Jun); Back to School (Jul); Senior Resource Guide (Aug); Football (Aug); Hot Springs Village Appreciation Days (Sep); Fall Home Improvement (Oct); Garland County Cares (Oct); Senior Scene (Monthly).
Special Weekly Sections: TV Magazine (S).
Syndicated Publications: Relish (Monthly); USA WEEKEND Magazine (Sat); American Profile (Weekly).
Delivery Methods: Mail`Newsstand`Carrier`Racks
Areas Served - City/County or Portion Thereof, or Zip codes: 71901, 71913, 71909, others
Avg Free Circ: 490
Sat. Circulation Paid: 7993
Sat. Circulation Free: 490
Sun. Circulation Paid: 8728
Sun. Circulation Free: 440
Audit By: AAM
Audit Date: 31.03.2019
Personnel: Walter E. Hussman (Pub.); Mark Gregory (Online Ed.); Richard Rasmussen (Photo Ed.); Alison Harbour (Photographer); Lynda Lampinen (Real Estate Ed.); Linda Arneson (Religion Ed.); Robert Wisener (Sports Ed.); Jimmy Robertson (Prodn. Mgr., Pre Press); Debe Johnson (Adv. Dir.); Glenn Waits (Circ. Dir.); Gary Troutman; Harry Porter (Gen. Mgr.)
Parent company (for newspapers): WEHCO Media, Inc.

THE JONESBORO SUN

Street address 1: 518 Carson St
Street address city: Jonesboro
Street address state: AR
Zip/Postal code: 72401-3128
County: Craighead
Country: USA
Mailing address: 518 CARSON ST
Mailing city: JONESBORO
Mailing state: AR
Mailing zip: 72401-3128
General Phone: (870) 935-5525
Display Adv. E-mail: llynn@jonesborosun.com
Classified Adv. e-mail: msmith@jonesborosun.com
Editorial e-mail: cwessel@jonesborosun.com
Primary Website: www.jonesborosun.com
Year Established: 1903
News Services: AP.
Special Editions: Farm Family, NEA Plants, Academic Allstars, ASU Campus Guide, High School Football/ Basketball, NEA District Fair, Chamber Leadership, Local Favorites, Sun Outdoors, NEA Harvest, Let's Eat Out, Susan G. Komen Cancer Awareness, Christmas Open House, Jonesboro Concierge Guide
Special Weekly Sections: Lifestyle (S); Church Page (Sat); Food (Wed). Entertainment (Thurs)
Syndicated Publications: TV Guide (S), Athlon Sports, Relish
Delivery Methods: Mail`Newsstand`Carrier`Racks
Areas Served - City/County or Portion Thereof, or Zip codes: 72005 72019 72031 72043 72067 72076 72101 72104 72112 72118 72143 72160 72183 72201 72206 72211 72313 72315 72320 72324 72330 72347 72350 72351 72354 72358 72365 72370 72377 72386 72387 72391 72395 72396 72401 72403 72404 72410 72411 72412 72413 72414 72415 72416 72417 72419 72421 72422 72425 72426 72427 72428 72429 72430 72431 72432 72433 72434 72435 72436 72437 72438 72440 72441 72442 72443 72444 72445 72447 72449 72450 72451 72453 72454 72455 72456 72457 72458 72459 72460 72461 72462 72464 72465 72466 72467 72469 72470 72471 72472 72473 72474 72475 72476 72478 72479 72482 72501 72503 72513 72519 72522 72529 72530 72532 72542 72543 72554 72560 72653 72654 72703 72756 72921 72956
Own Printing Facility?: Y
Commercial printers?: Y
Sat. Circulation Paid: 19830
Sun. Circulation Paid: 22564
Audit By: Sworn/Estimate/Non-Audited
Audit Date: 12.07.2019
Personnel: David Mosesso (Pub.); Lisa Lynn (Adv. Dir.); Kevin Turbeville (Sports Ed.); Roger Brumley (Production Manager, IT); Michael Shain (Controller); Lorri Householder (Circ. Director); Chris Wessel (Editor); Waylon Harris (Mng. Ed.)
Parent company (for newspapers): Paxton Media Group

ARKANSAS DEMOCRAT-GAZETTE

Street address 1: 121 East Capital
Street address city: Little Rock
Street address state: AR
Zip/Postal code: 72201
County: Pulaski
Country: USA
Mailing address: PO BOX 2221
Mailing city: LITTLE ROCK
Mailing state: AR
Mailing zip: 72203-2221
General Phone: (501) 378-3400
Advertising Phone: (501)378-3434
Editorial Phone: (501) 378-3485
General/National Adv. E-mail: dbrowning@arkansasonline.com
Display Adv. E-mail: dbrowning@arkansasonline.com
Classified Adv. e-mail: dbrowning@arkansasonline.com
Editorial e-mail: ffellone@arkansasonline.com
Primary Website: www.ardemgaz.com
Mthly Avg Unique Visitors: 928680
Year Established: 1991
Special Weekly Sections: Business, Farm, Style, Weather (Daily); Style (Tue/Sun); Active, Business, Technology (Mon); Best Food Day, Family (Wed); Arkansas Weekend (Thur); Movies (Fri); Home, Garden, Religion (Sat); Dear Abby, high Profile, TV, Real Estate, Book, Travel (Sun)
Delivery Methods: Mail`Newsstand`Carrier`Racks
Areas Served - City/County or Portion Thereof, or Zip codes: ARKANSAS
Own Printing Facility?: Y
Sat. Circulation Paid: 112086
Sun. Circulation Paid: 152652
Audit By: AAM
Audit Date: 31.03.2018
Personnel: Walter Hussman (Pub.); Lynn Hamilton (Pres./Gen. Mgr.); Scott Stine (VP, Adv./Mktg); Larry Graham (V.P./Circulation); Danny Shameer (City Ed.); Matthew Costa (Online Dir.); Heidi White (State Ed.); Sonny Albarado (Projects Ed.); Barry Arthur (Asst. Managing Ed.); John Sykes (Chief Photographer); Eric Gilreath (Info. Systems Mgr.); Conan Gallaty (Online Dir.); Nick Elliott (Vice Pres.); Kathy Faver (Vice Pres. of Finance)
Parent company (for newspapers): WEHCO Media, Inc.

BANNER-NEWS

Street address 1: 130 S Washington
Street address city: Magnolia
Street address state: AR
Zip/Postal code: 71753-3523
County: Columbia
Country: USA
Mailing address: PO BOX 100
Mailing city: MAGNOLIA
Mailing state: AR
Mailing zip: 71754-0100
General Phone: (870) 234-5130
Advertising Phone: (870) 234-5130
General/National Adv. E-mail: cmartin@bannernews.net
Display Adv. E-mail: advertising@bannernews.net
Editorial e-mail: news@bannernews.net
Primary Website: www.bannernews.net
Year Established: 1878
News Services: AP.
Special Editions: Blossom Festival (Apr); Bride (Jan); Progress (May);
Syndicated Publications: Relish (Monthly);
Delivery Methods: Mail`Newsstand`Carrier`Racks
Areas Served - City/County or Portion Thereof, or Zip codes: 71753
Own Printing Facility?: N
Commercial printers?: Y
Audit By: Sworn/Estimate/Non-Audited
Audit Date: 12.07.2019
Personnel: Walter E. Hussman (Pub.); Susan Gill (Gen. Mgr.); Stepahnie Scott (Circ. Mgr.); Dan Marsh (Mng. Ed.); Chris Gilliam (Sports Ed.)
Parent company (for newspapers): WEHCO Media, Inc.

MALVERN DAILY RECORD

Street address 1: 219 Locust St
Street address city: Malvern
Street address state: AR
Zip/Postal code: 72104-3721
County: Hot Spring
Country: USA
Mailing address: PO BOX 70
Mailing city: MALVERN
Mailing state: AR
Mailing zip: 72104-0070
General Phone: (501) 337-7523
Advertising Phone: (501) 337-1226 ext. 216
Editorial Phone: (501) 337-1226 ext. 215
General/National Adv. E-mail: advertising@malvern-online.com
Display Adv. E-mail: advertising@malvern-online.com
Classified Adv. e-mail: classifieds@malvern-online.com
Editorial e-mail: editor@malvern-online.com
Primary Website: www.malvern-online.com
Year Established: 1914
News Services: AP.
Special Editions: Christmas (Dec); Progress (Jan); Thanksgiving/Christmas Kick-off (Nov).
Syndicated Publications: Food Days (TUE); Consumer Review (Thur); Food Days (TUE); American Profile (SAT).
Delivery Methods: Mail`Newsstand`Carrier`Racks
Areas Served - City/County or Portion Thereof, or Zip codes: 72104, 71923, 71929, 71941, 72128, 72167, 71913
Own Printing Facility?: N
Commercial printers?: N
Avg Free Circ: 3740
Sat. Circulation Paid: 3200
Audit By: Sworn/Estimate/Non-Audited
Audit Date: 12.07.2019
Personnel: Kathi Ledbetter (Circ. Mgr.); Michelle Cummins (Adv. Dir.); Richard Folds (Pub.); Stephanie Rhea (Composition Mgr.); Kim Taber (Business Mgr.); Eric Moore (Sports Ed.); Josh Waddles (Gov. & City Reporter); Gretchen Ritchey (Lifestyles Ed.)
Parent company (for newspapers): Horizon Publications Inc.

THE EVENING TIMES

Street address 1: 1010 State Highway 77
Street address city: Marion
Street address state: AR
Zip/Postal code: 72364-9007
County: Crittenden
Country: USA
Mailing address: PO BOX 459
Mailing city: WEST MEMPHIS
Mailing state: AR
Mailing zip: 72303-0459
General Phone: (870) 735-1010
Advertising Phone: (870) 735-1010
Editorial Phone: (870) 735-1010
General/National Adv. E-mail: news@theeveningtimes.com
Display Adv. E-mail: retailadv@theeveningtimes.com
Classified Adv. e-mail: Classified@theeveningtimes.com
Editorial e-mail: news@theeveningtimes.com
Primary Website: www.theeveningtimes.com
Year Established: 1943
Special Editions: Pigskin Preview (Aug); Christmas Greetings (Dec); Farm Family (Aug.); Valentine Pages (Feb); Progress (March-April); Back-to-School Tab (Jul); Holiday Gift Guide
Syndicated Publications: American Profile (Weekly).
Delivery Methods: Mail`Carrier`Racks
Areas Served - City/County or Portion Thereof, or Zip codes: 72303, 72364, 72348, 72301
Own Printing Facility?: Y
Commercial printers?: Y
Audit By: Sworn/Estimate/Non-Audited
Audit Date: 12.07.2019
Personnel: Nick Coulter (Adv. Dir.); Mike Coulter; Alice Rains (Business manager); Alex Coulter (Pub.); Alice Raines (Office/Credit Mgr.); Gary Meece (Managing editor); Gail Clark (Circ. Mgr.)
Parent company (for newspapers): Crittenden Publishing Co.

THE BAXTER BULLETIN

Street address 1: 16 W 6th St
Street address city: Mountain Home
Street address state: AR
Zip/Postal code: 72653-3508
County: Baxter
Country: USA
Mailing address: PO BOX 1750
Mailing city: MOUNTAIN HOME
Mailing state: AR
Mailing zip: 72654-1750
General Phone: (870) 508-8000
Advertising Phone: (870) 508-8078
Editorial Phone: (870) 508-8064
General/National Adv. E-mail: advertising@baxterbulletin.com
Display Adv. E-mail: classads@baxterbulletin.com
Editorial e-mail: newsroom@baxterbulletin.com
Primary Website: www.baxterbulletin.com
Mthly Avg Views: 950000
Mthly Avg Unique Visitors: 126790
Year Established: 1901
News Services: AP, GNS.
Special Editions: Health (Apr); Back-to-School (Aug); Letters to Santa (Dec); Baxter County Fact Book (Feb); Chronology (Jan); Home Show (Mar); Twin Lakes Real Estate Guide (Monthly); Christmas Gift Guide (Nov); Baxter County Fair (Sept).
Special Weekly Sections: TV Book (Fri); Technology (Mon); Faith/Religion (Sat); Entertainment (Thur); Health/Fitness (Tues); Food (Wed).
Syndicated Publications: USA WEEKEND Magazine (Sat).
Areas Served - City/County or Portion Thereof, or Zip codes: 65655, 72519, 72531, 72537, 72538, 72544, 72566, 72583, 72585, 72619, 72623, 72626, 72634, 72635, 72642, 72651, 72653, 72658, 72677, 72661, 72687
Avg Free Circ: 277
Sat. Circulation Paid: 7219
Sat. Circulation Free: 206
Sun. Circulation Paid: 106
Audit By: AAM
Audit Date: 30.09.2017
Personnel: Clyde Anderson (Distribution/ Dock Supervisor); Tammy House (Composing Supervisor); Joanne Bratton (Features ed.); Sonny Elliott (Managing Editor); Thomas Garrett (Editorial page Ed.); Linda Masters (Online Ed. / Food Ed.); Adrianne Dunn (Adv. Dir.); Stormi Day (Ad. Acct. Relationship Specialist); Kendra Spencer (Advertising Acct. Relationship Specialist); Marsha Meissner (Ad. Clerk); Armando Rios; Paul Berry (Exec. Dir.); Allen Jones (Pres.); Scott Liles (Reporter); Billy Jean Louis (Health & Education Rep.)
Parent company (for newspapers): Gannett; Phillips Media Group LLC

PARAGOULD DAILY PRESS

Street address 1: 1401 W Hunt St
Street address city: Paragould
Street address state: AR
Zip/Postal code: 72450-3575
County: Greene
Country: USA
Mailing address: 1401 W HUNT ST
Mailing city: PARAGOULD
Mailing state: AR
Mailing zip: 72450-3575
General Phone: (870) 239-8562
Advertising Phone: (870)239-8562
Editorial Phone: (870)239-8562
General/National Adv. E-mail: bkeller@paragoulddailypress.com
Display Adv. E-mail: advertising@paragoulddailypress.com
Classified Adv. e-mail: advertising@paragoulddailypress.com
Editorial e-mail: editor@paragoulddailypress.com
Primary Website: www.paragoulddailypress.com
Mthly Avg Unique Visitors: 29131
News Services: AP.
Special Editions: Travel (Apr); Fall Fashions (Aug); Christmas (Dec); Loose Caboose Festival (Jul); Family-Owned Business (Jun); Spring Fashions (Mar); Thanksgiving (Nov); Outdoors (Oct); Football (Sept).
Special Weekly Sections: Entertainment (Fri); Weddings (S); Outdoors; Farm (Thur); Business (Tues); Food (Wed).
Areas Served - City/County or Portion Thereof, or Zip codes: 72450, 72443, 72436, 72474, 72412, 72439, 72461, 72425, 72454, 72476, 63829
Sun. Circulation Paid: 4200
Audit By: Sworn/Estimate/Non-Audited
Audit Date: 12.07.2019
Personnel: Mike McKinney (Sports Ed.); Brenda Keller (General Manager); Steve Gillespie (Editor)

Parent company (for newspapers): Paxton Media Group

PINE BLUFF COMMERCIAL

Street address 1: 300 S Beech St
Street address city: Pine Bluff
Street address state: AR
Zip/Postal code: 71601-4039
County: Jefferson
Country: USA
Mailing address: PO BOX 6469
Mailing city: PINE BLUFF
Mailing state: AR
Mailing zip: 71611-6469
General Phone: (870) 534-3400
Advertising Phone: (870) 543-1452
Editorial Phone: (870) 543-1456
General/National Adv. E-mail: kbrickey@pbcommercial.com
Display Adv. E-mail: pbcads@pbcommercial.com
Editorial e-mail: news@pbcommercial.com
Primary Website: www.pbcommercial.com
News Services: AP, MCT, NEA.
Special Editions: Good News Tab (Apr); Football Tab (Aug); Wedding Tab (Feb); FYI Community Information Tab (Jul); Garden & Home Improvement (Mar); Wrap It Up Early (Nov); Fall Hunting/Fishing Guide Tab (Sept).
Special Weekly Sections: Weekend Entertainment (Fri); Business News (S); TV (Sat); Business News (Wed).
Syndicated Publications: USA WEEKEND Magazine (S).
Avg Free Circ: 190
Sat. Circulation Paid: 5045
Sat. Circulation Free: 190
Sun. Circulation Paid: 5519
Sun. Circulation Free: 81
Audit By: CAC
Audit Date: 30.09.2018
Personnel: Jennifer Allen (Pub.); John Worthen (Mng. Ed.); Mae Washington (Circ. Mgr.); Betty Bishop (Business Mgr.)
Parent company (for newspapers): WEHCO Media, Inc.; CherryRoad Media

THE COURIER

Street address 1: 201 E 2nd St
Street address city: Russellville
Street address state: AR
Zip/Postal code: 72801-5102
County: Pope
Country: USA
Mailing address: 201 E 2ND ST
Mailing city: RUSSELLVILLE
Mailing state: AR
Mailing zip: 72801-5102
General Phone: (479) 968-5252
Advertising Phone: (479) 967-7355
General/National Adv. E-mail: michelle@couriernews.com
Display Adv. E-mail: michelle@couriernews.com
Classified Adv. e-mail: class1@couriernews.com
Editorial e-mail: info@couriernews.com
Primary Website: www.couriernews.com
Mthly Avg Views: 400000
Mthly Avg Unique Visitors: 65000
Year Established: 1875
News Services: AP,
Special Editions: Newcomer's Guide (Apr); Football (Aug); Active Lifestyles (Dec); RVL Magazine (Jan); RVL Magazine (Jul); RVL Magazine (Jun); Medical Directory (Mar); Salute to Area Business (May); Gift Guide (Nov); Progress (Oct);
Special Weekly Sections: Church Directory (Fri); Real Estate (S); Business Review (Tues); Best Food Day (Wed). TV Book (Sun)
Syndicated Publications: Relish - monthly (S). Athlon Sports
Delivery Methods: Mail`Newsstand`Carrier`Racks
Areas Served - City/County or Portion Thereof, or Zip codes: 72823, 72837, 72843, 72847, 72858, 72801, 72802, 72824, 72829, 72823, 72834,72842, 72853, 72857, 72830, 72845, 72846
Own Printing Facility?: Y
Commercial printers?: Y
Sat. Circulation Paid: 6000
Sun. Circulation Paid: 7000
Audit By: USPS
Audit Date: 15.10.2017
Personnel: David Meadows (Pub.); Michelle Harris (Adv. Dir.); David Weaver (Prod. Mgr.)

Parent company (for newspapers): Paxton Media Group

THE DAILY CITIZEN

Street address 1: 723 W Beebe Capps Expy
Street address city: Searcy
Street address state: AR
Zip/Postal code: 72143-6303
County: White
Country: USA
Mailing address: 723 W BEEBE CAPPS EXPY
Mailing city: SEARCY
Mailing state: AR
Mailing zip: 72143-6303
General Phone: (501) 268-8621
Advertising Phone: (501) 268-8621
General/National Adv. E-mail: bblack@thedailycitizen.com
Display Adv. E-mail: classifieds@thedailycitizen.com
Editorial e-mail: editor@thedailycitizen.com
Primary Website: www.thedailycitizen.com
Year Established: 1854
News Services: AP, NEA.
Special Weekly Sections: Weekend Review (Fri); Business Review (Mon); Business News (S); Business News (Thur); Merchant's Market (Tues); Best Food Day (Wed).
Syndicated Publications: Color Comics (S).
Sat. Circulation Paid: 5686
Sun. Circulation Paid: 5686
Audit By: Sworn/Estimate/Non-Audited
Audit Date: 12.07.2019
Personnel: Mike Murphy (Pub.); Pat Tullos (Adv. Dir.); Jessica Jackson (Circ. Mgr.); Jay Strasner (Ed.); Warren Watkins (Mng. Ed.); Wendy Waring (Community Ed.); Gabe Calzada (News Ed.); Quinton Bagley (Sports Ed.); Steve Watts (Ed.); Harrison Keegan (Sports Ed.)
Parent company (for newspapers): Paxton Media Group

STUTTGART DAILY LEADER

Street address 1: 111 W 6th St
Street address city: Stuttgart
Street address state: AR
Zip/Postal code: 72160-4243
County: Arkansas
Country: USA
Mailing address: 111 W 6TH ST
Mailing city: STUTTGART
Mailing state: AR
Mailing zip: 72160-4243
General Phone: (870) 673-8533
General/National Adv. E-mail: sales@stuttgartdailyleader.com
Display Adv. E-mail: sales@stuttgartdailyleader.com
Classified Adv. e-mail: sales@stuttgartdailyleader.com
Editorial e-mail: editor@stuttgartdailyleader.com
Primary Website: www.stuttgartdailyleader.com
News Services: AP, TMS.
Special Editions: Summer Baseball, City (June); Farm, Family, Real Estate (July); Back to School, Football, Home, harvest (Aug); Football, Real Estate, Pretty Baby, Home, Hunting Guide (Sept); Football, Homecoming, Red Ribbon Week, Home, Auto, Home Lawn (Oct); Duck Edition, Open House, Shopping, Hometown Holiday, Real Estate, Restaurant Guide (Nov); Countdown to Christmas, Lights Content, Last Minute Shopping, Hometown Holiday (Dec)
Special Weekly Sections: Civic Minded (Mon); Business, Bowling (Tue); Outdoors (Thur); Education, Church (Fri);
Syndicated Publications: TV (Every other week); Fifty-plus (Monthly); American Profile (Weekly).
Areas Served - City/County or Portion Thereof, or Zip codes: 72160 (Stuttgart), 72042 (Dewitt), 72003 (Almyra)
Own Printing Facility?: Y
Audit By: Sworn/Estimate/Non-Audited
Audit Date: 12.07.2019
Personnel: Stephanie Tiner (Business Mgr.); Willene Boehn (Circ. Mgr.); Stephanie Fischer (Managing Editor); John Tucker (Senior Publisher); April Scott (Composing Director); Dudley Raper (Press Manager); Mitch Bettis (Pub.); Danni Jo Bueker (Acct. Exec.)
Parent company (for newspapers): CherryRoad Media; CherryRoad Media

TEXARKANA GAZETTE

Street address 1: 101 E Broad St
Street address city: Texarkana
Street address state: AR
Zip/Postal code: 71854-5901
County: Miller
Country: USA
Mailing address: PO BOX 621
Mailing city: TEXARKANA
Mailing state: TX
Mailing zip: 75504-0621
General Phone: (870) 330-7550
Advertising Phone: (870)330-7611
Editorial Phone: (870)330-7652
General/National Adv. E-mail: jbright@texarkanagazette.com
Display Adv. E-mail: jbright@texarkanagazette.com
Classified Adv. e-mail: wshipp@texarkanagazette.com
Editorial e-mail: lminor@texarkanagazette.com
Primary Website: www.texarkanagazette.com
Mthly Avg Views: 3233128
Mthly Avg Unique Visitors: 331412
Year Established: 1875
News Services: AP, TMS, SHNS, CNS, Roll Call Report Syndicate.
Special Editions: Bridal, Super Bowl (Jan); Valentine (Feb); Home & Garden, Outdoors (Mar); Spring Fashion, Lawn, Garden (Apr); Mother's Day, Progress (May); Newcomer's Guide (Jun); Back to School, Football (Aug); Quality Section, Home Improvement, Race for the Cure (Oct); Holiday Cookbook, Thanksgiving (Nov); Santa's Helper (Dec)
Special Weekly Sections: Best Food Day (Wed); Religion (Sat);
Syndicated Publications: Relish (Monthly); USA WEEKEND Magazine (S); American Profile (Weekly).
Delivery Methods: Mail`Newsstand`Carrier`Racks
Areas Served - City/County or Portion Thereof, or Zip codes: 71753, 71801, 71822, 71826, 71832, 71833, 71834, 71836, 71837, 71838, 71839, 71840, 71842, 71845, 71846, 71851, 71852, 71853, 71854, 71855, 71857, 71859, 71860, 71862, 71865, 71866, 75426, 75455, 75501, 75503, 75551, 75554, 75555, 75556, 75559, 75560, 75561, 75563, 75566, 75567, 75568, 75569, 75570, 75571, 75572, 75573, 75574, 75638, 75656
Own Printing Facility?: Y
Avg Free Circ: 2712
Sat. Circulation Paid: 11168
Sat. Circulation Free: 2712
Sun. Circulation Paid: 11732
Sun. Circulation Free: 2711
Audit By: AAM
Audit Date: 31.03.2021
Personnel: Les Minor (Ed.); Rick Meredith (Adv. Sales Mgr.); Christy Busby (City Ed.); Russell McDermott (Editorial Page Ed.); Greg Bischof (Farm Reporter); James Bright (Gen. Mgr.); Evan Lewis (Photo Ed.)
Parent company (for newspapers): Texarkana Newspapers, Inc.

CALIFORNIA

THE ORANGE COUNTY REGISTER

Street address 1: 2190 S. Towne Centre Place
Street address city: Anaheim
Street address state: CA
Zip/Postal code: 92806
County: Orange
Country: USA
Mailing address: 2190 S. Towne Centre Place
Mailing city: Anaheim
Mailing state: CA
Mailing zip: 92806
General Phone: (714) 796-7000
Advertising Phone: (714) 796-3845
Editorial Phone: (714) 796-7984
General/National Adv. E-mail: chymovitz@scng.com
Display Adv. E-mail: chymovitz@scng.com
Classified Adv. e-mail: escimeca@ocregister.com
Editorial e-mail: local@ocregister.com
Primary Website: www.ocregister.com
Mthly Avg Unique Visitors: 3649055
Year Established: 1905
News Services: AP
Special Editions: LA Auto Show (Jan); Orange County Fair (Jul); Used Car/Auto Service (Jun); Home Beautiful (Mar); Best of Orange County (Sept).
Special Weekly Sections: Home & Garden (Sat); Commentary (S); Food(Thur); Health & Fitness (Wed).
Syndicated Publications: Parade (S).
Delivery Methods: Newsstand`Carrier`Racks
Areas Served - City/County or Portion Thereof, or Zip codes: Orange County, CA
Own Printing Facility?: Y
Commercial printers?: Y
Sat. Circulation Paid: 99838
Sun. Circulation Paid: 190565
Audit By: AAM
Audit Date: 31.03.2018
Personnel: Ron Hasse (Pres. & Pub.); Kyla Rodriguez (Sr. Vice Pres. of Adv.); Frank Pine (Exec. Ed.); Rosemaria Altieri (Vice Pres., H.R.); Bill Van Laningham (Vice Pres., Mkt.); Jon Merendino (VP, Op.); Dan Scofield (CFO); Kat Wang (Dir. of Circ.); Craig Hymovitz (VP of Adv.); Daniel Maynard (Automotive Adv.); Tom Bray (Local News Ed.); Todd Harmonson (Investigations, Politics, Business, Health and Environment); Kim Guimarin (Public Safety); Leo Smith (Local Ed.); Heather McRea (Local Ed.); Mark Evans (Crime and Public Safety Ed.); Steve Green (Crime and Public Safety Ed.); Jim Radcliffe (Crime and Public Safety Ed.); Frank Suraci (Investigations Ed.); Samantha Gowen (Bus. Ed.); Andre Mouchard (Politics Ed.); Jeffrey Miller (Features Ed.); Vanessa Franko (Features Ed.); Erik Pedersen (Features Ed.); Jerry Rice (Features Ed.); Tom Moore (Exec. Sports Ed.); Brian Martin (Deputy Sports Ed.); Todd Bailey (Sports Ed.); Brian Patterson (Sports Ed.)
Parent company (for newspapers): Digital First Media; MediaNews Group

AUBURN JOURNAL

Street address 1: 1030 High St
Street address city: Auburn
Street address state: CA
Zip/Postal code: 95603-4707
County: Placer
Country: USA
Mailing address: 188 CIRBY WAY
Mailing city: ROSEVILLE
Mailing state: CA
Mailing zip: 95678-6481
General Phone: (916) 774-7910
Advertising Phone: (530) 852-0225
Editorial Phone: (530) 885-6585 ext. 2
General/National Adv. E-mail: ajournal@goldcountrymedia.com
Display Adv. E-mail: mjh@goldcountrymedia.com
Classified Adv. e-mail: classifieds@goldcountrymedia.com
Editorial e-mail: ajournal@goldcountrymedia.com; derlcr@goldcountrymedia.com
Primary Website: www.auburnjournal.com
Year Established: 1872
News Services: AP, U.S. Suburban Press Inc., TMS, UPI.
Syndicated Publications: USA WEEKEND Magazine (S).
Delivery Methods: Mail`Newsstand`Carrier`Racks
Areas Served - City/County or Portion Thereof, or Zip codes: Placer County
Own Printing Facility?: Y
Commercial printers?: Y
Avg Free Circ: 0
Sun. Circulation Paid: 8163
Sun. Circulation Free: 0
Audit By: VAC
Audit Date: 31.12.2016
Personnel: Todd Frantz (Publisher); Kelly Leibold (Brehm Communications, Inc. Director of Circulations); Beth O'Brien (Advert Direct.)
Parent company (for newspapers): Brehm Communications, Inc.

THE BAKERSFIELD CALIFORNIAN

Street address 1: 3700 Pegasus Dr.
Street address city: Bakersfield
Street address state: CA
Zip/Postal code: 93308
County: Kern
Country: USA
Mailing address: PO BOX 440
Mailing city: BAKERSFIELD
Mailing state: CA
Mailing zip: 93302-0440
General Phone: (661) 395-7500
Advertising Phone: (661) 395-7500
Editorial Phone: (661) 395-7244
General/National Adv. E-mail: srockwell@bakersfield.com
Display Adv. E-mail: jwells@bakersfield.com
Classified Adv. e-mail: jwells@bakersfield.com
Editorial e-mail: JArthur@bakersfield.com
Primary Website: www.bakersfield.com

Year Established: 1866
News Services: AP, NYT, McClatchy, CSM.
Special Editions: Relay for Life ROP Pages (Apr); Holiday Worship (Dec); Wedding Planner (Feb); Kern Life (Jul); Best of Kern County (May); Focus on Living (Monthly); Harvest Home Show (Oct); Kern County Fair Guide (Sept).
Special Weekly Sections: Sports (Mon); Business (Tue); Business, garden, Home, Best Food (Wed); Business, Weekend, Entertainment (Thur); Movies (Fri); Religion, Auto, Homes (Sat); Real Estate, TV, Travel, Best Food (Sun)
Syndicated Publications: Parade (S); Latino Weekly Magazine (Weekly).
Delivery Methods: Mail`Newsstand`Carrier`Racks
Areas Served - City/County or Portion Thereof, or Zip codes: Kern County
Avg Free Circ: 23751
Sat. Circulation Paid: 24107
Sat. Circulation Free: 24220
Sun. Circulation Paid: 26193
Sun. Circulation Free: 26338
Audit By: AAM
Audit Date: 31.03.2018
Personnel: Ginger F. Moorhouse (Chrmn. of the Board/ Pub.); Michelle Chantry (Pres. & Chief Exec. Officer); Lois Henry (Asst. Mng. Ed.); Robert Price (Exec. Ed.); Virginia Cowenhoven (Assoc. Pub.); Jarrod Graham (Design Ed.); Jennifer Self (Lifestyles Ed.); Timothy Heinrichs (Copy/Layout Ed.); Zach Ewing (Sports Ed.); Benavente Christine (Prod. Dev. Director); Felix Adamo (Chief Photographer); Chris McCullah (S.r Video Producer)
Parent company (for newspapers): Horizon Publications Inc.; Sound Publishing

BENICIA HERALD

Street address 1: 820 1st St
Street address city: Benicia
Street address state: CA
Zip/Postal code: 94510-3216
County: Solano
Country: USA
Mailing address: PO BOX 65
Mailing city: BENICIA
Mailing state: CA
Mailing zip: 94510-0065
General Phone: (707) 745-0733
General/National Adv. E-mail: adsbenicia@yahoo.com
Display Adv. E-mail: adsbenicia@yahoo.com
Classified Adv. e-mail: adsbenicia@yahoo.com
Editorial e-mail: beniciaherald@gmail.com
Primary Website: www.beniciaheraldonline.com
Year Established: 1898
News Services: Papert (Landon), U.S. Suburban Press Inc..
Special Weekly Sections: Financial (Tue); Best Food (Wed); Seniors (Thur); Auto, Entertainment, Religion (fri); Real Estate (Sun);
Syndicated Publications: USA WEEKEND Magazine (S).
Sun. Circulation Paid: 2707
Audit By: Sworn/Estimate/Non-Audited
Audit Date: 12.07.2019
Personnel: Pam Poppe (Adv. Mgr.); Joe Smith (Circ. Mgr.); Marc Ethier (Ed.); David Payne (Pub.)
Parent company (for newspapers): McNaughton Newspapers; Gibson Radio & Publishing Co.

VENTURA COUNTY STAR

Street address 1: 550 Camarillo Center Drive
Street address city: Camarillo
Street address state: CA
Zip/Postal code: 93010
County: Ventura
Country: USA
Mailing address: PO BOX 6006
Mailing city: CAMARILLO
Mailing state: CA
Mailing zip: 93011-6006
General Phone: (805) 437-0000
Advertising Phone: (805) 437-0000
Editorial Phone: (805) 437-0000
General/National Adv. E-mail: feedback@vcstar.com
Display Adv. E-mail: shanna.cannon@vcstar.com
Editorial e-mail: news@vcstar.com
Primary Website: www.vcstar.com
Mthly Avg Views: 7000000
Mthly Avg Unique Visitors: 800000
Year Established: 1925
News Services: AP, NYT, McClatchy, SHNS, MCT, NEA, TMS.
Special Editions: Spelling Bee (March); Star Scholar Awards (April); Readers' Choice (May); Eldercare (July); Living Here (October) Pink (October)
Special Weekly Sections: Time Out (Fri); CARS (Sat).; Homes (Sun)
Syndicated Publications: Parade (S); Relish, Spry
Delivery Methods: Mail`Newsstand`Carrier`Racks
Areas Served - City/County or Portion Thereof, or Zip codes: Ventura County, Carpinteria
Own Printing Facility?: Y
Commercial printers?: Y
Sat. Circulation Paid: 37725
Sun. Circulation Paid: 46279
Audit By: AAM
Audit Date: 31.03.2017
Personnel: Denice Atcheson (Dir., Finance); Amy Aguilar (Digital Adv.); Monica White (Dir., Mktg.); John Rotter (Circ. Dir., Home Delivery); John Moore (Mng. Ed.); DeAnn Justesen (Asst. Mng. Ed.); Jim Medina (Bus. Ed.); Darrin Peschka (News Ed.); Ray Meese (Dig. Media); Shanna Cannon (Reg. Pub.); Natealine Judie (VP Adv.)
Parent company (for newspapers): Gannett

CHICO ENTERPRISE-RECORD

Street address 1: 400 E Park Ave
Street address city: Chico
Street address state: CA
Zip/Postal code: 95928-7127
County: Butte
Country: USA
Mailing address: PO BOX 9
Mailing city: CHICO
Mailing state: CA
Mailing zip: 95927-0009
General Phone: (530) 891-1234
Advertising Phone: (530) 896-7751
Editorial Phone: (530) 896-7754
General/National Adv. E-mail: chicoer@chicoer.com
Display Adv. E-mail: fcrosthwaite@chicoer.com
Classified Adv. e-mail: rridgell@chicoer.com
Editorial e-mail: dlittle@chicoer.com
Primary Website: www.chicoer.com
Year Established: 1853
News Services: AP, NEA, SHNS.
Special Editions: Home & Garden Issue (Apr); University (Aug); Last Minute Gift Guide (Dec); Chico Outlook (Feb); Salute to Agriculture Tab (Mar); Silver Dollar Fair Tab (May); Senior's Tab (Monthly); Christmas Opening (Nov); Health & Wellness Tab (Quarterly); Chico Expo (
Special Weekly Sections: Sports, Lifetsyle, Stock (Daily); Business (Wed/Sat); Best Food (Wed); Home & Garden (Fri); Entertainment (Thur); Church, TV (Sat); Farm news (Sun)
Syndicated Publications: Relish (Monthly); USA WEEKEND Magazine (S); TV Times (Sat).
Delivery Methods: Mail`Newsstand`Carrier`Racks
Areas Served - City/County or Portion Thereof, or Zip codes: 95926, 95928, 95973, 95938, 95966, 95965, 95969
Sat. Circulation Paid: 17502
Sun. Circulation Paid: 25379
Audit By: AAM
Audit Date: 30.09.2015
Personnel: Robert Gardner (Controller); Maureen Garrity (Dir., HR); Steve Schoonover (City Ed.); Michelle King (Ed.); Dave Davies (Sports Ed.); Fred Crosthwaite (Adv. Dir.); Ray Kirk (Systems Mgr.); Rene Ridgell (Classified Adv. Mgr.); Mazi Kavoosi (Circ. Dir.); Jim Gleim (Pub.)
Parent company (for newspapers): Digital First Media; MediaNews Group

DAILY PILOT

Street address 1: 1375 Sunflower Ave
Street address city: Costa Mesa
Street address state: CA
Zip/Postal code: 92626-1665
County: Orange
Country: USA
Mailing address: 1375 SUNFLOWER AVE
Mailing city: COSTA MESA
Mailing state: CA
Mailing zip: 92626-1665
General Phone: (714) 966-4600
Advertising Phone: (714) 966-5777
Editorial Phone: (714) 966-4600
General/National Adv. E-mail: dailypilot@latimes.com
Display Adv. E-mail: marissa.contreras-dominguez@latimes.com
Editorial e-mail: John.Canalis@latimes.com
Primary Website: www.dailypilot.com
Year Established: 1961
News Services: Papert (Landon), U.S. Suburban Press Inc..
Special Editions: Healthy, Wealthy & Wise (Apr); New Year (Dec); Annual Almanac (Feb); Healthy, Wealthy & Wise (Jan); Healthy, Wealthy & Wise (Jul); Menu Guide (Jun); Toshiba Senior Golf Classic (Mar); Student Design-an-Ad (May); Gift Guide (Nov); Top 103 (Sept).
Special Weekly Sections: Auto Pilot (Sat).
Syndicated Publications: Real Estate (Sat).
Areas Served - City/County or Portion Thereof, or Zip codes: Huntington Beach, Seal Beach, Laguna Beach, Newport Beach, Costa Mesa, Corona del Mar
Avg Free Circ: 14400
Sat. Circulation Paid: 29500
Sun. Circulation Paid: 29500
Audit By: Sworn/Estimate/Non-Audited
Audit Date: 12.07.2019
Personnel: John Canalis (Exec. Ed.); Rob Vardon (City Ed.); Ann Haley (Online Ed.); Don Leach (Photo Ed.); Steve Virgen (Sports Ed.); Debbie Zucco (Community Ed.)

IMPERIAL VALLEY PRESS

Street address 1: 205 N. 8th Street
Street address city: El Centro
Street address state: CA
Zip/Postal code: 92243
County: Imperial
Country: USA
Mailing address: PO BOX 2641
Mailing city: EL CENTRO
Mailing state: CA
Mailing zip: 92244-2641
General Phone: (760) 337-3400
Advertising Phone: (760) 337-3443
Editorial Phone: (760) 337-3453
General/National Adv. E-mail: circulation@ivpressonline.com
Display Adv. E-mail: advertising@ivpressonline.com
Classified Adv. e-mail: classified@ivpressonline.com
Editorial e-mail: rbrown@ivpressonline.com
Primary Website: www.ivpressonline.com
Year Established: 1901
News Services: AP.
Special Editions: Women of Imperial Valley (Aug); California Midwinter Fair (Feb); Inland Empire (Jan); County Progress (Jul); Graduation (Jun); Sweet Onion Festival (May); Business Journal (Monthly); Cattle Call Tab (Oct); Football Preview (Sept).
Special Weekly Sections: Church Page (Fri); Lifestyles (S); Youth Page (Sat); Farm Page (Thur); Food Page (Tues).
Syndicated Publications: Relish (Monthly); TV Plus (TV Guide) (S); American Profile (Tues).
Avg Free Circ: 251
Sat. Circulation Paid: 4193
Sat. Circulation Free: 251
Sun. Circulation Paid: 4288
Sun. Circulation Free: 894
Audit By: AAM
Audit Date: 31.03.2019
Personnel: Brad Jennings (Ed.); Mario Renteria (Sports Ed.); Sarah Malan (Copy Editor); Esteban Ortiz (Copy Ed); Vincenta Tamayo (Designer. Copy Ed); Norma Lira (Sales Mgr); Belinda Mills (Pub.); Tom Bodus (Editor-in-Chief); Julio Navarro (Single Copy and Home Delivery Manager)
Parent company (for newspapers): Horizon Publications Inc.; Imperial Valley News Media Inc.

LOS ANGELES TIMES

Street address 1: 2300 E. Imperial Highway
Street address city: El Segundo
Street address state: CA
Zip/Postal code: 90245
County: Los Angeles
Country: USA
Mailing address: 2300 E. Imperial Highway
Mailing city: El Segundo
Mailing state: CA
Mailing zip: 90245
General Phone: (213) 237-5000
Advertising Phone: (800) 528-4637 ext. 72769
Editorial Phone: (213) 237-7000
General/National Adv. E-mail: myad@latimes.com
Primary Website: www.latimes.com
Mthly Avg Views: 137500000
Mthly Avg Unique Visitors: 39000000
Year Established: 1881
Special Editions: Hoy (Spanish-language), The Envelope, Hot Property, DesignLA, Times Community News
Delivery Methods: Newsstand`Carrier`Racks
Areas Served - City/County or Portion Thereof, or Zip codes: Southern California (print edition), Worldwide (online & digital products & editions)
Own Printing Facility?: N
Commercial printers?: Y
Sat. Circulation Paid: 446593
Sun. Circulation Paid: 671924
Audit By: AAM
Audit Date: 31.03.2019
Personnel: Mike Kechichian (VP, Adv. Marketing); Dr. Patrick Soon-Shiong (Owner and Exec Chairman); Michael Whitley (Asst. Managing Ed.); Jeff Glasser (General Counsel); Bob Drogin (Deputy Bureau Chief, Washington D.C.); Scott Kraft (Managing Ed.); Allen Schaben (Staff Photographer); Nicholas Goldberg (Ed. of the Editorial Pages); John Myers (Sacramento Bureau Chief); Shelby Grad (Local & CA., Asst. Managing Ed.); Ben Welsh (Data Desk, Senior Dig. Ed.); James Angius (News Op., Exec. News Ed.); Chris Argentieri (Chief Operating Officer); Norman Pearlstine (Executive Ed.); Kimi Yoshino (Sr. Dep. Mgr. Ed.)
Parent company (for newspapers): NantMedia Holdings, LLC

TIMES-STANDARD

Street address 1: 930 6th St
Street address city: Eureka
Street address state: CA
Zip/Postal code: 95501-1112
County: Humboldt
Country: USA
Mailing address: PO BOX 3580
Mailing city: EUREKA
Mailing state: CA
Mailing zip: 95502-3580
General Phone: (707) 441-0500
Advertising Phone: (707) 441-0556
Editorial Phone: (707) 441-0507
General/National Adv. E-mail: ads@times-standard.com
Display Adv. E-mail: jmarchetti@times-standard.com
Classified Adv. e-mail: class@times-standard.com
Editorial e-mail: mvalles@times-standard.com
Primary Website: www.times-standard.com
Mthly Avg Views: 470627
Mthly Avg Unique Visitors: 162320
Year Established: 1854
News Services: AP.
Special Editions: North Coast 101 (May); Humboldt County Fair Tab (Aug); Gift Guide (Dec); Spring Bridal (May); Winter Bridal (Jan); Best Of (Mar); Women in Business Tab (Oct); Football Preview (Sept).
Special Weekly Sections: Business & Service Directory, Entertainment/TV Listings, Business, Style (Daily); Business, Seniors (Tue); Business, Food (Wed); Home & Garden (Thur); Business, Art (Fri); On the market, Religion (Sat); Business, Comics (Sun)
Delivery Methods: Mail`Newsstand`Carrier`Racks
Areas Served - City/County or Portion Thereof, or Zip codes: 95501 95503 95519 95521 95524 95525 95528 95531 95536 95540 95542 95546 95547 95548 95549 95551 95553 95555 95556 95560 95562 95563 95565 95567 95570 95571 95573
Own Printing Facility?: Y
Commercial printers?: Y
Sat. Circulation Paid: 8166
Sun. Circulation Paid: 9564
Audit By: Sworn/Estimate/Non-Audited
Audit Date: 12.07.2019
Personnel: Marc Valles (Mng. Ed.); Carmel Bonitatibus (Advertising Director/Production Director)
Parent company (for newspapers): Digital First Media; MediaNews Group

DAILY REPUBLIC

Street address 1: 1250 Texas Street
Street address city: Fairfield
Street address state: CA
Zip/Postal code: 94533
County: Solano
Country: USA
Mailing address: PO BOX 47
Mailing city: FAIRFIELD
Mailing state: CA
Mailing zip: 94533-0747
General Phone: (707) 425-4646
Advertising Phone: (707) 427-6937
Editorial Phone: (707) 427-6925

General/National Adv. E-mail: tbmcnaughton@dailyrepublic.net
Display Adv. E-mail: bkermoade@dailyrepublic.net
Classified Adv. e-mail: kmonroe@dailyrepublic.net
Editorial e-mail: gfaison@dailyrepublic.net
Primary Website: www.dailyrepublic.com
Year Established: 1855
News Services: AP, NYT, SHNS.
Special Editions: American Home Week (Apr); Annual Welcome (Aug); Thanksgiving Morning (Nov); Cookbook (Oct); Solano Seniors (Other); Solano Summer (Summer).
Special Weekly Sections: Automobiles (Fri); Religion (S); Religion (Sat); Best Food Day (Wed).
Syndicated Publications: Relish (Monthly); USA WEEKEND Magazine (S); Real Estate Magazine (Sat); American Profile (Weekly).
Areas Served - City/County or Portion Thereof, or Zip codes: 94533,94534, 94585
Avg Free Circ: 1349
Sat. Circulation Paid: 8979
Sat. Circulation Free: 1349
Sun. Circulation Paid: 9546
Sun. Circulation Free: 6272
Audit By: CAC
Audit Date: 30.06.2018
Personnel: Foy McNaughton (Pres./CEO/Pub.); Sharon Guy (Adv. Dir.); Brian Kermoade (Adv. Mgr., Nat'l); Nick DeCicco (Tailwind Ed.); Brian Arnold (Asst. Sports Ed.); Susan Winslow (Copy Ed.); Maureen Fissolo (Design Ed.); Shawn Miller (News Ed.); Kathleen L'Ecluse (Online/Projects Ed.); Brad Zweerink (Photo Ed.); Paul Farmer (Sports Ed.); Joe Boydston (IT Dir.); T. Burt McNaughton (Opns. Dir.); Larry Mammen (Prodn. Foreman, Pressroom)
Parent company (for newspapers): McNaughton Newspapers

THE FRESNO BEE

Street address 1: 1626 E St
Street address city: Fresno
Street address state: CA
Zip/Postal code: 93786-0001
County: Fresno
Country: USA
Mailing address: 1626 E ST
Mailing city: FRESNO
Mailing state: CA
Mailing zip: 93786-0002
General Phone: (559) 441-6111
Editorial Phone: (559) 441-6307
Editorial e-mail: jkieta@fresnobee.com
Primary Website: www.fresnobee.com
Mthly Avg Views: 7988637
Mthly Avg Unique Visitors: 1138974
Year Established: 1922
News Services: AFP, AP, NYT, LAT-WP, MCT, SHNS.
Special Weekly Sections: Best Food Day (Wed); Entertainment (Fri); Auto, Church, Home, Garden (Sat); Travel, Entertainment, TV, Cable Guide, Business (Sun)
Syndicated Publications: 7 Magazine (Fri); Color Comics (S).
Sat. Circulation Paid: 48888
Sun. Circulation Paid: 58968
Audit By: AAM
Audit Date: 31.12.2018
Personnel: Tim Ritchey (Pres. & Pub.); Cyndy Kutka (Asst. to Pres. & Pub.); Joe Kieta (Ed.); Mark Ochinero (Regional Human Resources Manager); Stan Diebert (Local Sales Dir.); John Rich (Managing Ed.); Matt Lloyd (Social Media Editor); Victor Patton (Enterprise News Ed.); Carey Norton (Ed.); Monica Stevens (Assistant Ed.); Cherie Arambel (Copy Editor/Page Designer); Kenny Lewis (Copy Editor/Page Designer); Michael Yparrea (Copy Editor/Page Designer)
Parent company (for newspapers): The McClatchy Company; Chatham Asset Management

THE UNION

Street address 1: 464 Sutton Way
Street address city: Grass Valley
Street address state: CA
Zip/Postal code: 95945
County: Nevada
Country: USA
Mailing address: 464 SUTTON WAY
Mailing city: GRASS VALLEY
Mailing state: CA
Mailing zip: 95945-4102
General Phone: (530) 273-9561
Advertising Phone: (530) 273-9567
Editorial Phone: (530) 477-4249
General/National Adv. E-mail: letters@theunion.com
Display Adv. E-mail: ads@theunion.com
Editorial e-mail: letters@theunion.com
Primary Website: www.theunion.com
Mthly Avg Views: 700000
Mthly Avg Unique Visitors: 100000
Year Established: 1864
News Services: AP.
Special Editions: Best of Nevada County (Apr); Fair (Aug); Bride (Jan); Home & Garden (Mar); Football (Sept).
Special Weekly Sections: Business (Mon); Home and Garden (Sat); Family (Thur); Health (Tues); Food (Wed).
Syndicated Publications: American Profile (Weekly).
Delivery Methods: Mail`Newsstand`Carrier`Racks
Areas Served - City/County or Portion Thereof, or Zip codes: 95959, 95945, 95949, 95946, 95602
Own Printing Facility?: Y
Commercial printers?: Y
Avg Free Circ: 430
Sat. Circulation Paid: 8041
Sat. Circulation Free: 430
Audit By: AAM
Audit Date: 31.12.2018
Personnel: Steve Schurkey (Circ. Dir.); Brian Hamilton (Ed.); Liz Kellar (City Editor); Walter Ford (Sports Ed.); Tom Harbert (Mgmt. Info Servs./Online Mgr.); Lee Brant (Prodn. Dir.); Julia Stidham (Adv. Mgr.); Elizabeth Baldwin (Circ. Dir.); Don Rogers (Pub.)
Parent company (for newspapers): Swift Communications, Inc.; Ogden Newspapers Inc.

THE SENTINEL

Street address 1: 300 W 6th St
Street address city: Hanford
Street address state: CA
Zip/Postal code: 93230-4518
County: Kings
Country: USA
Mailing address: PO BOX 9
Mailing city: HANFORD
Mailing state: CA
Mailing zip: 93232-0009
General Phone: (559) 582-0471
Advertising Phone: (559) 582-0471
Editorial Phone: (559) 582-0471
General/National Adv. E-mail: mlee@hanfordsentinel.com
Display Adv. E-mail: jvikjord@hanfordsentinel.com
Classified Adv. e-mail: jvikjord@HanfordSentinel.com
Editorial e-mail: editor@hanfordsentinel.com
Primary Website: www.hanfordsentinel.com
Year Established: 1886
News Services: AP.
Special Editions: Bridal Tab (Feb); Dairy (Jun); Home Improvement (Mar); Christmas Opening (Nov); Football (Sept); Living in The Valley (Sept); Our Towns (Quarterly)
Special Weekly Sections: Prime Time, Senior (Mon); Best Food Day (Tue); Real Estate (Fri); Church, Farm (Weekend)
Syndicated Publications: Relish (Monthly); USA WEEKEND Magazine (S); Parade (Weekly).
Areas Served - City/County or Portion Thereof, or Zip codes: 93230, 93245, 93202
Avg Free Circ: 641
Sat. Circulation Paid: 3908
Sat. Circulation Free: 619
Audit By: AAM
Audit Date: 31.03.2018
Personnel: Mark Eiman (City Ed.); Victoria Beierschmitt (Adv. Mgr.); Linda Green (Editor); Davis Taylor (Publisher)
Parent company (for newspapers): Horizon Publications Inc.; Lee Enterprises, Incorporated

LAKE COUNTY RECORD-BEE

Street address 1: 2150 S Main St
Street address city: Lakeport
Street address state: CA
Zip/Postal code: 95453-5620
County: Lake
Country: USA
Mailing address: 2150 S MAIN ST
Mailing city: LAKEPORT
Mailing state: CA
Mailing zip: 95453
General Phone: (707) 900-2016
Advertising Phone: (707) 900-2016
Editorial Phone: (707) 900-2016
General/National Adv. E-mail: ahansmith@record-bee.com
Display Adv. E-mail: ahansmith@record-bee.com
Classified Adv. e-mail: kpinkston@record-bee.com
Editorial e-mail: dfaries@record-bee.com
Primary Website: www.record-bee.com
Special Weekly Sections: Business (Tue); Health (Wed); Eat+Drink (Thur) Arts, Entertainment (Fri); Real Estate, Religion (Sat)
Delivery Methods: Mail`Newsstand`Carrier`Racks
Areas Served - City/County or Portion Thereof, or Zip codes: 95453, 95435, 95493, 95485, 95464, 95458, 95451, 95426, 95443, 95423, 95424, 95422, 95457, 95467, 95461
Sat. Circulation Paid: 4821
Audit By: AAM
Audit Date: 30.06.2017
Personnel: Kevin McConnell (Pub.); Ariel Carmona Jr. (Mng. Ed.); Brian Sumpter (Sports & Outdoors Ed.); Greg DeBoth (Circ. District Mgr.)
Parent company (for newspapers): Digital First Media; MediaNews Group

LODI NEWS-SENTINEL

Street address 1: 125 N Church St
Street address city: Lodi
Street address state: CA
Zip/Postal code: 95240-2102
County: San Joaquin
Country: USA
Mailing address: PO BOX 1360
Mailing city: LODI
Mailing state: CA
Mailing zip: 95241-1360
General Phone: (209) 369-2761
Advertising Phone: (209) 369-2761
Editorial Phone: (209) 369-7035
General/National Adv. E-mail: martw@lodinews.com
Display Adv. E-mail: ads@lodinews.com
Editorial e-mail: news@lodinews.com
Primary Website: www.lodinews.com
Year Established: 1881
News Services: AP, MCT
Special Editions: Senior services (Jan); Brides (Feb); Visitors Guide (May); Home Improvement Guide (Jun); How-To Guide (July); Grape & Wine Festival (Sept); Christmas (Dec).
Special Weekly Sections: Business/Stock Market (Fri); Church (Sat); Business/Stock Market (Thur); Business/ Stock Market (Tues); Best Food Day (Wed).
Syndicated Publications: USA WEEKEND Magazine (Sat).
Delivery Methods: Mail`Newsstand`Carrier`Racks
Areas Served - City/County or Portion Thereof, or Zip codes: 95220, 95227, 95237, 95240, 95242, 95253, 95258, 95632, 95686
Own Printing Facility?: Y
Commercial printers?: N
Avg Free Circ: 1930
Sat. Circulation Paid: 6858
Sat. Circulation Free: 1930
Audit By: AAM
Audit Date: 31.03.2019
Personnel: Stephanie Hiatt (Bookkeeper); Scott Howell (Newsroom Ed); Ahbeck Casson (Chief Photographer); Richard Hanner (Ed.); Chuck Barton (Pressroom Foreman); Steven Malkowich (Pub.); Glenn Stifflemire (Pub.)
Parent company (for newspapers): Horizon Publications Inc.; Central Valley News-Sentinel Inc.

PRESS-TELEGRAM

Street address 1: 727 Pine Ave
Street address city: Long Beach
Street address state: CA
Zip/Postal code: 90813-4321
County: Los Angeles
Country: USA
Mailing address: 5150 E. Pacific Coast Hwy, Suite 200
Mailing city: LONG BEACH
Mailing state: CA
Mailing zip: 90815
General Phone: (562) 435-1161
Advertising Phone: (562) 499-1243
Editorial Phone: (562) 499-1337
General/National Adv. E-mail: online@presstelegram.com; ptnews@presstelegram.com
Display Adv. E-mail: adertising@scng.com
Classified Adv. e-mail: advertising@scng.com
Editorial e-mail: ptnews@presstelegram.com
Primary Website: www.presstelegram.com
Mthly Avg Views: 507370
Mthly Avg Unique Visitors: 261337
Year Established: 1897
News Services: AP
Delivery Methods: Mail`Newsstand`Carrier`Racks
Areas Served - City/County or Portion Thereof, or Zip codes: Artesia, Bell, Bellflower, Carson, Cerritos, Compton, Cypress, Downey, Hawaiian Gardens, Huntington Park, La Mirada, Lakewood, Long Beach, Los Alamitos, Lynwood, Norwalk, Paramount, Pico Rivera, San Pedro, Santa Fe Springs, Seal Beach, Signal Hill, South Gate and Wilmington.
Own Printing Facility?: Y
Commercial printers?: Y
Sun. Circulation Paid: 29272
Audit By: AAM
Audit Date: 30.09.2022
Personnel: Ron Hasse (Pres. & Pub.); Frank Pine (Exec. Ed.); Kyla Rodriquez (SVP, Advertising); Bill VanLaningham (VP Mktg); Dan Scofield (Chief Fin Officer); Tom Bray (Sr. Ed.); Rosemaria Altieri (VP HR); Tom Taylor (Retail Sales Mgr.); Toni Sciacqua (Mng Digital Ed); Tom Moore (Exec Sports Ed); Brian Calle (Opinion Ed); Melene Alfonso (Vice President, Advertising)
Parent company (for newspapers): Southern California News Group; Digital First Media

LA OPINION

Street address 1: 915 Wilshire Blvd
Street address 2: Ste 800
Street address city: Los Angeles
Street address state: CA
Zip/Postal code: 90017-3488
County: Los Angeles
Country: USA
Mailing address: 915 WILSHIRE BLVD STE 800
Mailing city: LOS ANGELES
Mailing state: CA
Mailing zip: 90017-3488
General Phone: (213) 896-2150
Advertising Phone: (213) 896-2300
Editorial Phone: (213) 896-2333
General/National Adv. E-mail: lorena.torres@laopinion.com
Display Adv. E-mail: lorena.torres@laopinion.com
Editorial e-mail: editor@laopinion.com
Primary Website: www.laopinion.com
Year Established: 1926
News Services: AP, EFE, CNS, AFP, NOTIMEX, UPI, PR Newswire, PRWEB
Special Editions: Calendario Torneo (Jan); Calendario Torneo (March); Mujeres Destacadas (March); Dodgers Calendar (April); Angels Calendar (April); Mothers Day (May); Cinco de Mayo (May); MLB All Star (July); 4th of July Special (July); Mexican Soccer League (July); Back to School La Opinion (July/August); Back to School Contigo (August); Fiestas Patrias (Sept); Gift Ideas (Nov); Gift Ideas (Dec).
Special Weekly Sections: Entertainment, life, Style Sports, Business (Daily); Education, Small Business, Employment (Mon); Health, Personal Finance, Legal (Tue); Food, Morgage (wed); Entertainment, Technology, Real Estate (Thur); Auto, Community, marketing (Fri); Auto, Beauty, Fashion, Economy (Sat); Children, Travel, International Business (Sun)
Syndicated Publications: Main News (daily), Ciudad (daily), Negocios (daily), hola LA (Everyday except thurs.), La Vibra (Thursdays) Deportes (daily), Clasificados (daily)
Delivery Methods: Newsstand`Racks
Own Printing Facility?: N
Commercial printers?: Y
Sat. Circulation Paid: 29314
Sun. Circulation Paid: 33098
Audit By: AAM
Audit Date: 31.03.2016
Personnel: Monica Lozano (CEO/Pub.); Davan Maharaj (Ed. / Exec. Vice Pres.); Bob Mason (Dir. IT); Lorena Torres (Dir., Local Sales)
Parent company (for newspapers): impreMedia LLC

NEWS-PRESS

Street address 1: 202 W 1st St
Street address 2: Fl 2nd
Street address city: Los Angeles
Street address state: CA
Zip/Postal code: 90012-4299
County: Los Angeles
Country: USA
Mailing address: 202 W 1ST ST FL 2
Mailing city: LOS ANGELES

Mailing state: CA
Mailing zip: 90012-4299
General Phone: (818) 637-3200
Advertising Phone: (818) 637-3200
Editorial Phone: (818) 637-3200
General/National Adv. E-mail: lisa.cosenza@latimes.com
Display Adv. E-mail: Kim.Nguyen2@latimes.com
Classified Adv. e-mail: Josie.Flores@latimes.com
Editorial e-mail: gnp@latimes.com
Primary Website: www.glendalenewspress.com
Mthly Avg Views: 150000
Year Established: 1905
News Services: City News Services
Delivery Methods: Mail`Carrier`Racks
Areas Served - City/County or Portion Thereof, or Zip codes: Glendale, La Crescenta, Montrose, Verdugo City
Sat. Circulation Paid: 36159
Audit By: VAC
Audit Date: 21.03.2004
Personnel: Jeff Young (VP/Advertising); Lisa Consenza (Dir. Adv.); Dan Evans (Ed.); Mark Kellam (City Ed.); Grant Gordon (Sports Ed.); Sameea Kamal (Web Ed.); Steve Appleford (Feat. Ed.); Carol Cormaci (Mng. Ed.)
Parent company (for newspapers): Tribune Publishing, Inc.; Outlook Newspapers

MANTECA BULLETIN

Street address 1: 531 E Yosemite Ave
Street address city: Manteca
Street address state: CA
Zip/Postal code: 95336-5806
County: San Joaquin
Country: USA
Mailing address: PO BOX 1958
Mailing city: MANTECA
Mailing state: CA
Mailing zip: 95336-1156
General Phone: (209) 249-3500
Advertising Phone: (209) 249-3500
Editorial Phone: (209) 249-3500
Display Adv. E-mail: ads@mantecabulletin.com
Editorial e-mail: news@mantecabulletin.com
Primary Website: www.mantecabulletin.com
Year Established: 1908
News Services: AP; MNCC
Special Editions: HS Football Preview (Aug); Pumpkin Fair (Oct); Sidewalk Fair (Apr)
Special Weekly Sections: BulletinExtra On-the-Road (Fridays); Home Guide (Saturday);
Syndicated Publications: American Profile (Weekly); Relish (monthly); Spry (monthly)
Delivery Methods: Mail`Newsstand`Carrier`Racks
Areas Served - City/County or Portion Thereof, or Zip codes: 95336, 95337, 95330, 95366, 95231, 95206
Own Printing Facility?: Y
Commercial printers?: Y
Sat. Circulation Paid: 5350
Sun. Circulation Paid: 5350
Audit By: VAC
Audit Date: 01.06.2011
Personnel: Dennis Wyatt (Editorial Page Ed.); Kay Garcia (Composing Mgr.); Dave Winegarden (Group Publisher); Chuck Higgs (Advertising Director); Drew Savage (Circulation Director); Tamara Foreman (Business Manager); Howard Santiago (Pressroom Manager); Rose Albano-Risso (City Editor); Jonamar Jacinto (Sports Editor); Adam Wright (I.T. Manager); Teri Garcia (Adv. Mgr.); Amy Hitchcock (Circ. Mgr.); Hank Vander Veen (Group Pub.)
Parent company (for newspapers): Morris Multimedia, Inc.; Vander Veen Media

APPEAL DEMOCRAT

Street address 1: 1530 Ellis Lake Dr
Street address city: Marysville
Street address state: CA
Zip/Postal code: 95901-4258
County: Yuba
Country: USA
Mailing address: 1530 ELLIS LAKE DR
Mailing city: MARYSVILLE
Mailing state: CA
Mailing zip: 95901-4269
General Phone: (530) 741-4700
Advertising Phone: (530) 749-6556
Editorial Phone: (530) 749-6552
General/National Adv. E-mail: info@appealdemocrat.com
Display Adv. E-mail: info@appealdemocrat.com
Classified Adv. e-mail: adclass@appealdemocrat.com
Editorial e-mail: adnewsroom@appealdemocrat.com
Primary Website: www.appealdemocrat.com
Mthly Avg Views: 1529197
Mthly Avg Unique Visitors: 174360
Year Established: 1860
News Services: AP, MCT, TMS.
Special Editions: Explore (Jan); How To Guide (Apr); Medical Directory (Feb & Aug); New Neighbors (Feb); Brides (Jan); Business Card Directory (Mar); Y-S Fair (Jul); Graduation (Jun); Home Improvement (Mar); Spirit of Freedom (Nov); Inside the Locker Room (Aug); Friday Night Lights (Sep-Nov); Best of Yuba/Sutter (Sept); Pride (Oct); Christmas Kick-Off (Nov-Dec).
Special Weekly Sections: Life (S); Real Estate (Sat); Food (Wed). Entertainment (Thurs)
Syndicated Publications: Parade Magazine (Sunday)
Delivery Methods: Mail`Newsstand`Carrier`Racks
Areas Served - City/County or Portion Thereof, or Zip codes: Yuba County, Sutter County
Own Printing Facility?: Y
Commercial printers?: Y
Avg Free Circ: 342
Sat. Circulation Paid: 9158
Sat. Circulation Free: 342
Sun. Circulation Paid: 9444
Sun. Circulation Free: 152
Audit By: AAM
Audit Date: 30.09.2018
Personnel: Nancy Brown (Adv. Mgr., Classified); Donna Blair (Business Manager); Steve Miller (Editor); Glenn Stiffemire (Publisher); Jamie Keith (Sales & Marketing Director); Lori Wilson (Circulation Manager)
Parent company (for newspapers): Horizon Publications Inc.; VISTA California News Media. Inc.

MERCED SUN-STAR

Street address 1: 3033 North G Street
Street address city: Merced
Street address state: CA
Zip/Postal code: 95340
County: Merced
Country: USA
Mailing address: 3033 G ST
Mailing city: MERCED
Mailing state: CA
Mailing zip: 95340-2108
General Phone: (209) 722-1511
General/National Adv. E-mail: rperes@mercedsun-star.com
Display Adv. E-mail: rperes@mercedsun-star.com
Classified Adv. e-mail: mrocci@mercedsun-star.com
Editorial e-mail: editor@mercedsun-star.com
Primary Website: www.mercedsun-star.com
Mthly Avg Views: 2035479
Mthly Avg Unique Visitors: 401626
Year Established: 1869
News Services: AP.
Special Editions: Senior Scene (Monthly).
Special Weekly Sections: Diversity (Mon); Health, Fitness (Tue); Food, Flavor (Wed); Arts, Entertainment (Thur); Family (Fri); Auto, Church, Pets, Real Estate, TV, Technology, Travel (Sat); Business, Finance (Daily)
Syndicated Publications: Preview/Entertainment (Fri); UC Merced (Quarterly); Parade (S); TV Update (Sat).
Delivery Methods: Mail`Newsstand`Carrier`Racks
Areas Served - City/County or Portion Thereof, or Zip codes: Merced/Mariposa Counties and Chowchilla in northern Madera County
Own Printing Facility?: N
Commercial printers?: N
Avg Free Circ: 4102
Sat. Circulation Paid: 9728
Sat. Circulation Free: 5206
Audit By: AAM
Audit Date: 30.09.2017
Personnel: Ken Riddick (Pres./Pub.); Michelle Morgante (Mng. Ed.); Michael Rocci (Ops. Dir.); Brian Clark (Digital Ed.); Jim Silva (Digital Content Prod); Maria Ravera (VP Audience Dev)
Parent company (for newspapers): The McClatchy Company; Chatham Asset Management

THE MODESTO BEE

Street address 1: 1325 H St
Street address city: Modesto
Street address state: CA
Zip/Postal code: 95354-2427
County: Stanislaus
Country: USA
Mailing address: PO BOX 3928
Mailing city: MODESTO
Mailing state: CA
Mailing zip: 95352-3928
General Phone: (209) 578-2000
Advertising Phone: (209) 578-2040
Editorial Phone: (209) 578-2343
General/National Adv. E-mail: ejohnston@modbee.com
Display Adv. E-mail: tritchey@modbee.com
Classified Adv. e-mail: dwhitmore@modbee.com
Editorial e-mail: jfarrow@modbee.com
Primary Website: www.modbee.com
Mthly Avg Views: 5048509
Mthly Avg Unique Visitors: 729785
Year Established: 1884
News Services: AP, NYT, LAT-WP, MCT, MNS.
Special Weekly Sections: Health (Mon); Workpalce, Pets, Fun, Poker (Tue); Taste, Small Business, bowling, Fishing (Wed); Technology, Teens, High School Sports (Thur); Arts, Entertainment, Auto, Fantasy Sports (Fri); Recreation, Leisure, Home & Garden, Real Estate, Agriculture (Sat); Friends, Family, Comics, Finance, Consumer (Sun)
Syndicated Publications: Parade (S).
Delivery Methods: Newsstand`Carrier`Racks
Areas Served - City/County or Portion Thereof, or Zip codes: Counties: Stanislaus, San Joaquin, Calaveras, Tuolumne, Merced, Mariposa
Own Printing Facility?: Y
Commercial printers?: N
Sat. Circulation Paid: 33664
Sun. Circulation Paid: 42687
Audit By: AAM
Audit Date: 31.12.2017
Personnel: Walter E. Kletke (Dir., Finance); Tim Ritchey (Adv. Vice Pres.); Deanna Whitmore (Adv. Mgr., Inside Sales); Patty Tharp (Circ. Mgr., Acquisition); Craig Mackenzie (Circ. Mgr., Distr.); Joe Kieta (Exec. Ed.); Judy Sly (Editorial Page Ed.); Jim Lawrence (Graphics Dir.); Ken Carlson (Health/Medical Reporter); Debbie Noda (Chief Photographer); Peggy Luty (Nat'l Sales Coord.); Ken Riddick (Pres. & Pub.); Garth Stapley (Editorial Page Ed.)
Parent company (for newspapers): The McClatchy Company; Chatham Asset Management

SAN GABRIEL VALLEY TRIBUNE

Street address 1: 605 E Huntington Dr
Street address 2: Ste 100
Street address city: Monrovia
Street address state: CA
Zip/Postal code: 91016-6353
County: Los Angeles
Country: USA
Mailing address: 605 E HUNTINGTON DR STE 100
Mailing city: MONROVIA
Mailing state: CA
Mailing zip: 91016-6353
General Phone: (626) 962-8811
Advertising Phone: (626) 962-8811
Editorial Phone: (626) 544-0811
General/National Adv. E-mail: news.tribune@sgvn.com
Display Adv. E-mail: business@sgvn.com
Classified Adv. e-mail: carla.asmundson@sgvn.com
Editorial e-mail: steve.hunt@sgvn.com
Primary Website: www.sgvtribune.com
Year Established: 1955
News Services: AP, CNS, MCT, Scripps-McClatchy, BPI, DJ, TMS, NYT.
Special Editions: The Body (Apr); Local Business (Aug); The Rose Magazine (Dec); The Body (Jan); Seen Magazine (Jul); Health Beat (Jun); Health Beat (Mar); Water Awareness (May); Holiday Guide (Nov); The Body (Oct); College & Prep Football (Sept).
Special Weekly Sections: Career Site (S); Home Buyer (Sat).
Syndicated Publications: Relish (Monthly); U Magazine (mS) (Other); TV Magazine (S).
Sat. Circulation Paid: 22201
Sun. Circulation Paid: 31844
Audit By: AAM
Audit Date: 31.03.2015
Personnel: Joe Robidoux (Circu.Dir); Steve Hunt (Senior Ed.); Mark Welches; Mickie Sullivan (VP, Nat'l Sales/ Major Retail)
Parent company (for newspapers): Southern California News Group

THE WHITTIER DAILY NEWS

Street address 1: 605 E Huntington Dr
Street address 2: Ste 100
Street address city: Monrovia
Street address state: CA
Zip/Postal code: 91016-6353
County: Los Angeles
Country: USA
General Phone: (562) 698-0955
Advertising Phone: (626) 544-0888
Editorial Phone: (562) 567-7543
General/National Adv. E-mail: jon.merendino@langnews.com
Editorial e-mail: news.wdn@sgvn.com
Primary Website: www.whittierdailynews.com
News Services: AP, CNS, MCT, Scripps-McClatchy, BPI, DJ, NYT, United Media.
Special Editions: Prep Extra (Aug.); The Rose Magazine (Dec); Holiday Guide (Nov); Dining Guide (Sept).
Special Weekly Sections: Career Site (S); New Home Buyer (Sat).
Syndicated Publications: Relish (Monthly); TV Magazine (S).
Delivery Methods: Newsstand`Carrier`Racks
Own Printing Facility?: N
Sat. Circulation Paid: 9651
Sun. Circulation Paid: 13901
Audit By: AAM
Audit Date: 31.03.2015
Personnel: Steve Hunt (Mng. Ed.); Kevin Smith (Bus. Ed.); Daniel Tedford (City Editor); Mike Sprague (Reporter); Sandra Molina (Reporter); Peter Fullam; Venusse Navid (Clerk); Fred Robledo (Prep Editor); Mickie Sullivan (VP, Nat'l Sales/Major Retail)
Parent company (for newspapers): Southern California News Group

THE MONTEREY COUNTY HERALD

Street address 1: 2200 Garden Rd
Street address city: Monterey
Street address state: CA
Zip/Postal code: 93940-5329
County: Monterey
Country: USA
Mailing address: PO BOX 271
Mailing city: MONTEREY
Mailing state: CA
Mailing zip: 93942-0271
General Phone: (831) 372-3311
Advertising Phone: (831) 646-4308
Editorial Phone: (831) 646-4381
General/National Adv. E-mail: circservices@montereyherald.com
Display Adv. E-mail: dkrolczyk@montereyherald.com
Classified Adv. e-mail: openhouses@montereyherald.com
Editorial e-mail: mhcity@montereyherald.com
Primary Website: www.montereyherald.com
Year Established: 1922
News Services: AP, LAT-WP, NYT, MCT.
Special Editions: Classic Car Weekend (Aug); Holiday Gift Guide (Dec); Wedding Planner (Feb); AT&T Pro-Am Golf (Jan); California Rodeo Salinas (Jul); Discover Carmel Valley 1 (Jun); Senior 1 (Mar); Focus on Salinas (May); Discover Carmel Valley 2 (Nov); Cherry's Jubilee Ca
Special Weekly Sections: Senior, Go Calendar (Mon); Business (Tue); Best Food Day (Wed); Entertainment (Thur); Auto (Fri); Real Estate, Religion, Home & Garden (Sat); Leisure, TV, Health and Science (Sun)
Syndicated Publications: TV Week (S).
Avg Free Circ: 949
Sat. Circulation Paid: 12072
Sat. Circulation Free: 949
Sun. Circulation Paid: 13639
Sun. Circulation Free: 30595
Audit By: AAM
Audit Date: 30.09.2016
Personnel: Dana Arvig (Ad. Dir.); Mardi Browning (Circ. Dir.); David Kellog (Mng. Ed.); Vern Fisher (Dir. of Photography); Gary Omernick (Pub.)
Parent company (for newspapers): Digital First Media; MediaNews Group

NAPA VALLEY REGISTER

Street address 1: 1615 Soscol Avenue
Street address city: Napa
Street address state: CA
Zip/Postal code: 94559
County: Napa
Country: USA
General Phone: (707) 226-3711
Advertising Phone: (707) 257-3003
General/National Adv. E-mail: napaprod@napanews.com

Display Adv. E-mail: nkostecka@napanews.com
Classified Adv. e-mail: valleyclassifieds@napanews.com
Editorial e-mail: napaopinion@napanews.com
Primary Website: www.napavalleyregister.com
News Services: AP.
Special Editions: Once Upon A Time (Apr); Football (Aug); Wishbooks (Dec); Bridal (Feb); Healthwise (Jan); The Best Years (Jul); County Fair (Jun); Spring Home & Garden (Mar); Napa Solano Home & Garden (May); Auto Showcase (Nov); Transamerica Golf (Oct); Heirlooms (Sept).
Special Weekly Sections: Best Food (Tue); Auto (Fri); Home & Garden, Entertainment (sat); Real Estate (Sun); Business (Daily)
Syndicated Publications: Relish (Monthly); USA WEEKEND Magazine (S).
Own Printing Facility?: Y
Commercial printers?: Y
Avg Free Circ: 745
Sat. Circulation Paid: 8466
Sat. Circulation Free: 365
Sun. Circulation Paid: 8632
Sun. Circulation Free: 718
Audit By: AAM
Audit Date: 31.03.2018
Personnel: Norma Kostecka (Adv. Dir.); Sasha Paulsen (Features Ed.); Sean Scully (Ed.); Kevin Courtney (City Ed.); Rodolfo Schwanz (Class. Adv. Dir)
Parent company (for newspapers): Lee Enterprises, Incorporated

INLAND VALLEY DAILY BULLETIN

Street address 1: 3100 Guasti Rd.
Street address city: Ontario
Street address state: CA
Zip/Postal code: 91761
County:
Country:
Mailing address:
Mailing city:
Mailing state: CA
Mailing zip:
General Phone: (909) 987-6397
Advertising Phone: (909) 987-9200
Editorial Phone: (909) 987-6360
General/National Adv. E-mail: advertising@scng.com
Display Adv. E-mail: advertising@scng.com
Classified Adv. e-mail: advertising@scng.com
Editorial e-mail: inlandeditors@scng.com
Primary Website: www.dailybulletin.com
Mthly Avg Views: 456430
Mthly Avg Unique Visitors: 231483
Year Established: 1882
News Services: AP
Delivery Methods: Newsstand`Carrier`Racks
Areas Served - City/County or Portion Thereof, or Zip codes: Alta Loma, Chino, Chino Hills, Claremont, Corona, Diamond Bar, Fontana, Jurupa, La Verne, Montclair, Norco, Ontario, Pomona, Rancho Cucamonga, Rialto, San Dimas and Upland
Own Printing Facility?: Y
Commercial printers?: Y
Sun. Circulation Paid: 24749
Audit By: AAM
Audit Date: 30.09.2022
Personnel: Ron Hasse (President & Publisher); Jim Maurer (Adv. VP); Frank Pine (Exec. Ed.); Kimberly Guimarin (Senior Editor); Mike Cruz (City Editor)
Parent company (for newspapers): Southern California News Group

OROVILLE MERCURY - REGISTER

Street address 1: 2124 5th Ave
Street address city: Oroville
Street address state: CA
Zip/Postal code: 95965-5862
County: Butte
Country: USA
General Phone: (530) 896-7751
General/National Adv. E-mail: slehman@orovillemr.com
Primary Website: www.orovillemr.com
Areas Served - City/County or Portion Thereof, or Zip codes: Butte County
Sat. Circulation Paid: 2703
Audit By: AAM
Audit Date: 30.09.2015
Personnel: Steve Schoonover (Local News Editor); Sandra Lehman (Adv, Exec.); Fred Crosthwaite (Adv. Dir.)
Parent company (for newspapers): Media News Group

THE DESERT SUN

Street address 1: 750 N Gene Autry Trl
Street address city: Palm Springs
Street address state: CA
Zip/Postal code: 92262-5463
County: Riverside
Country: USA
Mailing address: PO BOX 2734
Mailing city: PALM SPRINGS
Mailing state: CA
Mailing zip: 92263-2734
General Phone: (760) 322-8889
Advertising Phone: (760) 322-8889
Editorial Phone: (760) 778-4637
Editorial e-mail: localnews@desertsun.com
Primary Website: www.thedesertsun.com
Year Established: 1927
News Services: AP, GNS.
Special Editions: Home Sweet Home (Apr); Football (Aug); Restaurant Guide (Dec); Riverside County Date Festival (Feb); Bob Hope Golf Classic (Jan); Newsweek & Evert Cup Tennis Championships (Mar); Keeping Cool & Summer Fun (May); Pure Gold Coupons (Monthly); Discover the C
Special Weekly Sections: Desert Living (Sun); Snapshots, Golf (Tue); Food & Drink (Wed); Healthy Living (Thur); Weekend Entertainment (Fri); TV, Home, Real Estate (Sat); Business, Bilingual (Monthly)
Syndicated Publications: Weekend Entertainment Guide (Fri); Desert Magazine (Monthly); TV Magazine (Sat).
Sat. Circulation Paid: 26544
Sun. Circulation Paid: 29308
Audit By: AAM
Audit Date: 31.03.2019
Personnel: Matt Solinsky (Sports Ed.); Chris Weddle (Prod.); Jose Bastidas (Prod.); Maire McCain (Prod.); Julie Makinen (Exec. Ed.)
Parent company (for newspapers): Gannett

ANTELOPE VALLEY PRESS

Street address 1: 37404 Sierra Hwy
Street address city: Palmdale
Street address state: CA
Zip/Postal code: 93550-9343
County: Los Angeles
Country: USA
Mailing address: PO BOX 4050
Mailing city: PALMDALE
Mailing state: CA
Mailing zip: 93590-4050
General Phone: (661) 273-2700
Advertising Phone: (661) 273-2700
Editorial Phone: (661)273-2700
General/National Adv. E-mail: email@avpress.com
Classified Adv. e-mail: classified@avpress.com
Editorial e-mail: sarnold@avpress.com
Primary Website: www.avpress.com
Year Established: 1915
News Services: Metro, AP, TMS, N YT, Bloomberg, CNS, CSM, MCT.
Special Editions: Annual Fair (Aug); Annual Future Leaders (Feb); Annual Welcome (Oct) Wedding(Jan) New Vehicles(Oct)
Special Weekly Sections: Automotive (Fri); Real Estate (S); Food (Wed). Business (M-Sun)
Syndicated Publications: Parade (Weekly).Relish monthly
Delivery Methods: Mail`Newsstand`Carrier`Racks
Areas Served - City/County or Portion Thereof, or Zip codes: 93536, 93551, 93534, 93535, 93550, 93560, 93552, 93543, 93505, 93510, 93501, 93591, 93532, 93553, 93561, 93523, 93516, 93544, 91355, 91390, 91351
Own Printing Facility?: Y
Commercial printers?: Y
Avg Free Circ: 31
Sat. Circulation Paid: 8746
Sat. Circulation Free: 31
Sun. Circulation Paid: 10865
Sun. Circulation Free: 2966
Audit By: VAC
Audit Date: 31.05.2017
Personnel: William C. Markham (Pub.); Cherie Bryant (Vice Pres./Gen. Mgr.); Charles Bostwick (Ed.); James Skeen (Bus./Finance Ed.); Ron Siddle (Photo Ed.); Karen Maeshiro (Special Sections Ed.); Dennis Birks (Prodn. Mgr., Opns.); Mike McMullin (Classified Adv. Dir.); Mark Sherwood (Adv. Dir.)
Parent company (for newspapers): Horizon Publications Inc.; Sound Publishing

THE PORTERVILLE RECORDER

Street address 1: 115 E Oak Ave
Street address city: Porterville
Street address state: CA
Zip/Postal code: 93257-3807
County: Tulare
Country: USA
Mailing address: PO BOX 151
Mailing city: PORTERVILLE
Mailing state: CA
Mailing zip: 93258-0151
General Phone: (559) 784-5000
Advertising Phone: (559) 784-5000 ext. 1061
Editorial Phone: (559) 784-5000 ext. 1040
General/National Adv. E-mail: recorderads@portervillerecorder.com
Editorial e-mail: recorder@portervillerecorder.com
Primary Website: www.portervillerecorder.com
Mthly Avg Views: 400000
Mthly Avg Unique Visitors: 60000
Year Established: 1909
News Services: AP, MCT, NEA, TMS.
Special Editions: Medical Directory (Feb); Bridal (Jan); Readers Choice (Jul); Porterville Fair (May); Holiday Gifts (Nov); Women in Business (Oct); Living Here (Sept); From the Fields (twice a year); Tulare County - In the Shadow of Giants(spring and fall).
Special Weekly Sections: Financial, Health and Fitness (Sat); Arts & Entertainment (Thur); Schools (Tues); Heritage (Weds.).
Syndicated Publications: Parade Magazine (Sat); The Buzz (Mon). American Profile (Mon) Relish (First Wed of month)
Delivery Methods: Mail`Newsstand`Carrier`Racks
Areas Served - City/County or Portion Thereof, or Zip codes: 93257, 93247, 93258, 93265, 93267, 93270
Own Printing Facility?: N
Commercial printers?: N
Sat. Circulation Paid: 6500
Audit By: Sworn/Estimate/Non-Audited
Audit Date: 12.07.2019
Personnel: Craig Dimmitt (Bus. Mgr.); Josie Chapman (Adv./Mktg. Dir.); Rick Elkins (Pub./Ed.); Alex Larson (Circ. Dir.); Terry Feagin (Asst. Circ. Mgr.); Brian Williams (Mng. Ed./ Asst. Pub.)
Parent company (for newspapers): Horizon Publications Inc.; Sound Publishing

DAILY NEWS

Street address 1: 728 Main St
Street address city: Red Bluff
Street address state: CA
Zip/Postal code: 96080-3342
County: Tehama
Country: USA
Mailing address: PO BOX 220
Mailing city: RED BLUFF
Mailing state: CA
Mailing zip: 96080-0220
General Phone: (530) 527-2151
Advertising Phone: (530) 737-5044
Editorial Phone: (530) 737-5042
General/National Adv. E-mail: geckels@redbluffdailynews.com
Display Adv. E-mail: geckels@redbluffdailynews.com
Editorial e-mail: editor@redbluffdailynews.com
Primary Website: www.redbluffdailynews.com
Year Established: 1885
News Services: AP, NYT, SHNS.
Special Editions: Rodeo (Apr); Back-To-School (Aug); Future Ad Designers (Dec); Red Bluff Today (Feb); Corning Today (Jan); Fourth of July (Jul); Health (Mar); Women (May); Farm/City (Nov); Antiques & Collectables (Oct); Tehama Dist. Fair (Sept).
Special Weekly Sections: Best Food Days, Senior Citizen (Tue); Business (Wed); Highlights, TV, Farm (Sat)
Syndicated Publications: Relish (Monthly); USA WEEKEND Magazine (Sat); American Profile (Weekly).
Areas Served - City/County or Portion Thereof, or Zip codes: Tehama County
Sat. Circulation Paid: 3419
Audit By: AAM
Audit Date: 30.09.2015
Personnel: Chip Thompson (Ed.); Julie Zeeb (Reporter); Jake Hutchison (Reporter); Kathy Hogan (Circ. Mgr.); Gayla Eckels (Multi-Media Account Exec.); Sandy Valdivia (Production Mgr.)
Parent company (for newspapers): MediaNews Group; Gannett

RECORD SEARCHLIGHT

Street address 1: 1101 Twin View Boulevard
Street address city: Redding
Street address state: CA
Zip/Postal code: 96049-2397
County: Shasta
Country: USA
Mailing address: PO BOX 492397
Mailing city: REDDING
Mailing state: CA
Mailing zip: 96049-2397
General Phone: 530-225-8250
Advertising Phone: (530) 225-8241
Editorial Phone: (530) 225-8211
General/National Adv. E-mail: Lynnette.Young@redding.com
Classified Adv. e-mail: RRSClassified@redding.com
Editorial e-mail: letters@redding.com
Primary Website: www.redding.com
Mthly Avg Unique Visitors: 771115
Year Established: 1938
News Services: AP, LAT-WP, McClatchy, SHNS, MCT, TMS.
Special Editions: Best of North State - Annual Health Care - Annual
Special Weekly Sections: Business (daily); Education, Computer Technology (Mon); Best Food (Wed); Entertainment, health, Fitness, Outdoors, Arts (Thur); Auto, Key Buys (Fri); Religion, Home & Garden (Sat); Real Estate (Sat/Sun); Travel, Outdoor (Sun)
Syndicated Publications: Parade (S).
Delivery Methods: Mail`Newsstand`Carrier`Racks
Own Printing Facility?: Y
Commercial printers?: Y
Avg Free Circ: 205
Sat. Circulation Paid: 14233
Sat. Circulation Free: 205
Sun. Circulation Paid: 16503
Sun. Circulation Free: 193
Audit By: AAM
Audit Date: 30.06.2018
Personnel: Carole Ferguson (Mng. Ed.); Damon Arthur (Multimedia Journalist); Andreas Fuhrmann (Photo.); Silas Lyons (Ed./VP of New Media Content); Ronnie Aldo (Sup. of Press Ops.)
Parent company (for newspapers): Gannett

THE FACTS (REDLANDS)

Street address 1: 1255 W. Colton Ave
Street address 2: Ste 102
Street address city: Redlands
Street address state: CA
Zip/Postal code: 92374
County: San Bernardino
Country: USA
General Phone: (909) 793-259-9315
Advertising Phone: (909) 793-3221
Editorial Phone: (909) 793-3221
General/National Adv. E-mail: advertising@scng.com
Display Adv. E-mail: advertising@scng.com
Classified Adv. e-mail: advertising@scng.com
Editorial e-mail: inlandeditors@scng.com
Primary Website: www.redlandsdailyfacts.com
Mthly Avg Views: 255823
Mthly Avg Unique Visitors: 197144
Year Established: 1890
News Services: AP
Delivery Methods: Newsstand`Carrier`Racks
Areas Served - City/County or Portion Thereof, or Zip codes: Highland, Loma Linda, Mentone, Redlands and Yucaipa.
Sun. Circulation Paid: 3123
Audit By: AAM
Audit Date: 30.09.2022
Personnel: Toni Sciacqua (Managing Editor, Digital Operations); Jessica Keating (City Editor); Ron Hasse (Pres./Pub.); Tom Moore (Exec. Sports Ed.); Frank Pine (Executive Editor)
Parent company (for newspapers): Southern California News Group

THE DAILY INDEPENDENT

Street address 1: PO Box 7
Street address city: Ridgecrest
Street address state: CA
Zip/Postal code: 93556-0007
County: Kern

Country: USA
Mailing address: PO BOX 7
Mailing city: RIDGECREST
Mailing state: CA
Mailing zip: 93556-0007
General Phone: (760) 375-4481
Advertising Phone: (760) 375-4880
Editorial Phone: (760) 375-4481
General/National Adv. E-mail: pmckay@ridgecrestca.com
Display Adv. E-mail: miueck@ridgecrestca.com
Classified Adv. e-mail: cbarrera@ridgecrestca.com
Primary Website: www.ridgecrestca.com
News Services: AP.
Special Editions: Christmas Carols & Greetings (Dec); Independent Babies (Jan); Graduation Congratulations (Jun); Home Show (Mar); Spring Car Care (May); Fall Home Improvement (Nov); New Car Buyers Guide (Oct); Fall Sports (Sept).
Special Weekly Sections: Real Estate (Fri); Business (S); Automotive (Thur); Automotive (Tues); Best Food Day (Wed).
Syndicated Publications: American Profile (Weekly).
Sat. Circulation Paid: 7900
Audit By: Sworn/Estimate/Non-Audited
Audit Date: 12.07.2019
Personnel: John Watkins (Pub.); Paula McKay (Display Adv. Mgr.); Rodney Connors (Classified Adv. Mgr.); Brian Voigt (Circ. Mgr.); Nathaniel Lidle (City Ed.); Cheeto Barrera (Sports Ed.); Anthony Gentile (Sports Ed.); Jack Barnwell (Mng. Ed.); Aaron Crutchfield (Mng. Ed.)
Parent company (for newspapers): John Watkins; CherryRoad Media

THE PRESS-ENTERPRISE

Street address 1: 1825 Chicago Ave
Street address 2: Ste 100
Street address city: Riverside
Street address state: CA
Zip/Postal code: 92507-2373
County: Riverside
Country: USA
Mailing address: PO BOX 792
Mailing city: RIVERSIDE
Mailing state: CA
Mailing zip: 92502-0792
General Phone: (951) 684-1200
Advertising Phone: (951) 368-9250
Editorial Phone: (951) 368-9460
General/National Adv. E-mail: adavis@pe.com
Display Adv. E-mail: adavis@pe.com
Classified Adv. e-mail: classifieds@pe.com
Editorial e-mail: penews@pe.com
Primary Website: www.pe.com
Mthly Avg Unique Visitors: 1199397
Year Established: 1878
News Services: AP, MCT, TMS
Special Editions: Readers' Choice, Summer Fun, Holiday Gift Guides (2)
Special Weekly Sections: Senior Lifestyles (Mon); The Guide (Fri); Homes (Sat); Real Estate, Business (Sun)
Delivery Methods: Newsstand`Carrier`Racks
Areas Served - City/County or Portion Thereof, or Zip codes: Many
Own Printing Facility?: Y
Commercial printers?: Y
Sat. Circulation Paid: 77878
Sun. Circulation Paid: 133042
Audit By: AAM
Audit Date: 31.03.2015
Personnel: Eric Vilchis (Photo-Visuals Ed.); ron hasse (Managing Ed.); Nikie Johnson (Ed.); Cassie MacDuff (Columnist); Roger Ruvolo (Asst. Managing Ed.); Mark Acosta (Metro Ed.); Frank Escobedo (Gen. Mgr./Hispanic Media); John Kerr (Dir. Multimedia Sales Dev.); Anita Davis (Adv. Dir.); Paul McAfee (Interactive Dev. Dir.); Mike Kreiser (Circ. Mgr., Home Del.); Richard Mirman (Pub.); Kimberly Guimarin (Sr. Ed.)
Parent company (for newspapers): MediaNews Group; Digital First Media

THE SACRAMENTO BEE

Street address 1: 2100 Q St
Street address city: Sacramento
Street address state: CA
Zip/Postal code: 95816-6816
County: Sacramento
Country: USA
Mailing address: PO BOX 15779
Mailing city: SACRAMENTO
Mailing state: CA
Mailing zip: 95852-0779
General Phone: (916) 321-1485
Advertising Phone: (916) 321-1465
Editorial Phone: (916) 321-1851
General/National Adv. E-mail: rmote@sacbee.com
Editorial e-mail: opinion@sacbee.com
Primary Website: www.sacbee.com
Mthly Avg Unique Visitors: 3343258
Year Established: 1857
News Services: AP, Bloomberg, CT, MCT, LAT-WP, NYT, SHNS, DJ, GNS, HN.
Special Weekly Sections: Friday's Ticket (Fri); Travel (S); Home & Garden (Sat); Food & Wine (Wed); Feast (Sunday).
Syndicated Publications: Parade (S).
Delivery Methods: Mail`Newsstand`Carrier`Racks
Areas Served - City/County or Portion Thereof, or Zip codes: Sacramento (CA) Sacramento County, Yolo County, Placer County, El Dorado County plus portions of surrounding counties.
Own Printing Facility?: Y
Commercial printers?: Y
Sat. Circulation Paid: 142046
Sun. Circulation Paid: 195495
Audit By: AAM
Audit Date: 31.12.2016
Personnel: Cheryl Dell (Pres./Pub.); Gary Strong (Sr. Vice Pres., Finance); Linda Brooks (Vice Pres., HR); Francesca Lewis (Adv. Sr. Vice Pres.); Darrell Kunken (Adv. Mgr., Market Analysis); Suzanne Deegan (Adv. Mgr., Nat'l); Maria Ravera (VP Audience Development); Mark Montgomery (Audience Admin & Operations Manager); Gary Pitts (New Business & Operations Manager); Robert Ford (Production Director); Pam Dinsmore (Director Community affairs); Stuart Leavenworth (Editorial Pages Editor); Joyce Terhaar (Executive Editor & Sr. VP News); Steve Howard (National/Key Account Manager); Ryan Mote (VP, Adv.)
Parent company (for newspapers): Chatham Asset Management; The McClatchy Company

THE SUN

Street address 1: 290 N D St
Street address 2: Ste 101
Street address city: San Bernardino
Street address state: CA
Zip/Postal code: 92401-1711
County: San Bernardino
Country: USA
Mailing address: 290 N D ST STE 100
Mailing city: SAN BERNARDINO
Mailing state: CA
Mailing zip: 92401-1711
General Phone: (909) 889-9666
Advertising Phone: (909) 386-3950
Editorial Phone: (909) 386-3991
General/National Adv. E-mail: voice@inlandnewspapers.com
Display Adv. E-mail: shawna.federoff@inlandnewspapers.com
Editorial e-mail: citydesk@sbsun.com
Primary Website: www.sbsun.com
Year Established: 1894
News Services: AP, MCT, GNS, SHNS, McClatchy, City News Service.
Special Editions: Nursing in the Inland Empire (Nov); Health & Fitness (5 times/yr) (Other); News of the City (Quarterly); Home & Garden (Semi-yearly); Route 66 (Sept).
Special Weekly Sections: Weekend (Fri); Business File (Mon); Business Sunday (S); Home Guide (Sat); Gardening (Tues); Food (Wed).
Syndicated Publications: Relish (Monthly); TV Week (S).
Delivery Methods: Mail`Newsstand`Carrier`Racks
Areas Served - City/County or Portion Thereof, or Zip codes: 91701 91730 91739 91786 92220 92223 92252 92277 92284 92301 92307 92308 92311 92313 92314 92315 92316 92320 92324 92325 92327 92335 92336 92337 92339 92342 92345 92346 92347 92352 92354 92358 92359 92371 92373 92374 92376 92377 92382 92392 92394 92397 92399 92401 92404 92405 92407 92408 92410 92411
Own Printing Facility?: Y
Commercial printers?: Y
Sat. Circulation Paid: 43254
Sun. Circulation Paid: 63041
Audit By: AAM
Audit Date: 30.09.2012
Personnel: Ron Hasse (Pres./Pub.); Frank Pine (Exec. Ed.); Shawna Federoff (Marketing Dir); Mickie Sullivan (VP, Nat'l Sales/Major Retail); Kimberly Guimarin (Sr. Ed.)
Parent company (for newspapers): Southern California News Group

THE SAN DIEGO UNION-TRIBUNE

Street address 1: P. O. Box 120191
Street address city: San Diego
Street address state: CA
Zip/Postal code: 92112
County: San Diego
Country: USA
Mailing address: PO BOX 120191
Mailing city: SAN DIEGO
Mailing state: CA
Mailing zip: 92112-0191
General Phone: (800) 533-8830
Advertising Phone: (619) 293-2335
Editorial Phone: (619) 293-1211
Editorial e-mail: letters@sduniontribune.com
Primary Website: www.sandiegouniontribune.com
Mthly Avg Views: 7000000
Mthly Avg Unique Visitors: 3800000
Year Established: 1868
News Services: Landon Media & Metro Suburbia, CNS, NYT, MCT, RN, DF, DJ, LAT-WP, NNS, SHNS, TMS.
Special Editions: San Diego's Best (Aug); Auto Show (Dec); Super Bowl (Feb); NFL Playoffs (Jan); Summer Adventures (Jul); Summer Adventures (Jun); SD Best Ballot (Mar); Passport (May); Holiday Gift Guide (Nov); Dining Guide (Oct); NFL Football Preview (Sept.)
Special Weekly Sections: Health (Tues); Food (Wed); Night & Day (Entertainment Guide) (Thur); Night+Day Weekend, RPM (Fri);Wheels, Home & Garden, New Homes (Sat); SD In-Depth, Arts & Culture, Military (Sun)
Syndicated Publications: Dining Around (Central) (Annually); SD Home (Every other month); SD Health (Other); Fashion Forward (Semi-yearly) Eldercare (annually); Vida Latina (weekly)
Delivery Methods: Mail`Newsstand`Carrier`Racks
Areas Served - City/County or Portion Thereof, or Zip codes: 92007, 92008, 92009, 92010, 92011, 92024, 92054, 92056, 92057, 92058, 92075, 92081, 92083, 92084, 92003, 92025, 92026, 92027, 92028, 92029, 92059, 92060, 92061, 92069, 92078, 92082, 91901, 91902, 91905, 91906, 91910, 91911, 91913, 91914, 91915, 91916, 91917, 91931, 91932, 91934, 91935, 91941, 91942, 91945, 91950, 91962, 91963, 91977, 91978, 91980, 92014, 92019, 92020, 92021, 92037, 92040, 92064, 92067, 92071, 92091, 92101, 92102, 92103, 92104, 92105, 92004, 92036, 92065, 92066, 92070, 92086, 92106, 92107, 92108, 92109, 92110, 92111, 92113, 92114, 92115, 92116, 92117, 92118, 92119, 92120, 92121, 92122, 92123, 92124, 92126, 92127, 92128, 92129, 92130, 92131, 92139, 92154, 92173, 92530, 92532, 92543, 92544, 92545, 92562, 92563, 92583, 92584, 92585, 92586, 92587, 92590, 92591, 92592, 92595, 92596, 92883
Own Printing Facility?: N
Commercial printers?: N
Sat. Circulation Paid: 119707
Sun. Circulation Paid: 207881
Audit By: AAM
Audit Date: 31.03.2023
Personnel: Jeff Light (Publisher and Editor in Chief); Lora Cicalo (Managing Editor); Matthew Hall (Editorial & Opinion Director)
Parent company (for newspapers): NantMedia Holdings, LLC; MediaNews Group

SAN FRANCISCO CHRONICLE

Street address 1: 901 Mission Street
Street address city: San Francisco
Street address state: CA
Zip/Postal code: 94103
County: San Francisco
Country: USA
Mailing address: 901 MISSION ST
Mailing city: SAN FRANCISCO
Mailing state: CA
Mailing zip: 94103-3067
General Phone: (415) 777-7000
Advertising Phone: (415) 777-7272
Editorial Phone: (415) 777-7100
General/National Adv. E-mail: advertise@sfchronicle.com
Display Adv. E-mail: advertise@sfchronicle.com
Classified Adv. e-mail: DFitzgibbon@sfchronicle.com
Editorial e-mail: metro@schronicle.com
Primary Website: www.sfchronicle.com
Mthly Avg Unique Visitors: 2800000
Year Established: 1865
News Services: AP, Bloomberg, Getty, MCT, NYT, WP
Special Editions: Weddings (Jan); SF Chronicle Wine Competition, Napa Valley (Feb); Spring Fashion (Mar); Rising Star Chefs, Top 100 Restaurants (Apr); Schools, Camps, and Activities Guide (May); Weekend Destinations (Jun); Travel (Jul); Fall Arts Preview, Wine Country Guide (Aug); Fall Fashion (Sept); Warriors Pre-Season, Bar Stars (Oct); Holiday Entertaining, Ski (Nov); Gift Guide (Dec)
Special Weekly Sections: Business, Finance, Art, Entertainment (Daily); Technology (Mon); Home & Garden (Wed); Weekend Datebook (Thur); Cars (Fri); New Homes (Sat); Real Estate, Travel, Hot Jobs, Style, Food+Home (Sun);
Syndicated Publications: Parade (S).
Delivery Methods: Newsstand`Carrier`Racks
Sat. Circulation Paid: 131578
Sun. Circulation Paid: 210880
Audit By: AAM
Audit Date: 30.09.2017
Personnel: Mick Cohen (VP of Cir.); Audrey Cooper (Editor in Chief); John Diaz (Editorial Page Ed); Alan Saracevic (Sports Ed.); Demian Bulwa (Deputy Metro Ed); Trapper Byrne (Metro Editor); Kat Duncan (Photo Ed); Suzanne Espinosa Solis (Assist. Metro Ed); Nicole Fruge (Photo Ed); Leba Hertz (Arts/Entertain. Ed); Spud Hilton (Travel Ed); Lois Kazakoff (Deputy Editorial Ed); Terry Robertson (Asst. Metro Ed); Michael Lerseth (Asst. Sports Ed); Mark Lundgren (Asst. Metro Ed); Tim O'Rourke (Asst. Mng. Ed.); Walter Addiego (Movie Ed./Copy Ed.); Michael Gray (Mng. Ed., Enterprise); Fernando Diaz (Mng. Ed., Digital); Owen Thomas (Business and Tech Ed); Sarah Cooney (VP Marketing); Bill Nagel (Pub. & CEO)
Parent company (for newspapers): Hearst Communications, Inc.

THE EXAMINER

Street address 1: 835 Market St Ste 550
Street address 2: Suite 550
Street address city: San Francisco
Street address state: CA
Zip/Postal code: 94103-1906
County: San Francisco
Country: USA
Mailing state: VA
Mailing zip: 94105
General Phone: (415) 728-4227
Advertising Phone: (415) 359-2704
Editorial Phone: (415) 728-4227
General/National Adv. E-mail: jcurran@sfmediaco.com
Display Adv. E-mail: gzuehls@sfmediaco.com
Classified Adv. e-mail: gzuehls@sfmediaco.com
Editorial e-mail: gzuehls@sfmediaco.com
Primary Website: www.sfexaminer.com
Mthly Avg Views: 1400000
Mthly Avg Unique Visitors: 490000
Year Established: 1865
Special Weekly Sections: Health, Art, Nightlife (Thur); Movies (Fri); Real Estate, Food (Sun)
Areas Served - City/County or Portion Thereof, or Zip codes: San Francisco county and San Mateo County
Own Printing Facility?: Y
Commercial printers?: Y
Avg Free Circ: 63196
Sat. Circulation Free: 155390
Sun. Circulation Free: 253712
Audit By: VAC
Audit Date: 30.09.2015
Personnel: J. Curran (Pub.); A. Barbero (Vice Pres. of Operations); K. Winston (Classified & Obituaries)
Parent company (for newspapers): Black Press Community News Media

THE MERCURY NEWS

Street address 1: 4 North 2nd Street
Street address 2: Ste 800
Street address city: San Jose
Street address state: CA
Zip/Postal code: 95113
County: Santa Clara
Country: USA
General Phone: 408-920-5000
General/National Adv. E-mail: mturpin@bayareanewsgroup.com
Classified Adv. e-mail: classads@bayareanewsgroup.com
Primary Website: www.mercurynews.com
Delivery Methods: Mail`Newsstand`Carrier`Racks

Own Printing Facility?: Y
Commercial printers?: Y
Sat. Circulation Paid: 96910
Sun. Circulation Paid: 161896
Audit By: AAM
Audit Date: 30.09.2018
Personnel: Sharon Ryan (Pres./Pub.); Lisa Buckingham (Sr. VP/CFO); Jason Cross (Sr. VP/Digital Adv.); Sandra Gonzales (City Ed.); Michael Turpin (Exec. VP Chief Revenue Officer); Dan Smith (Vice President/ Audience); Bert Robinson (Managing Editor/Content); Randall Keith (Managing Editor/Digital)
Parent company (for newspapers): Digital First Media; MediaNews Group

THE TRIBUNE

Street address 1: 3825 S Higuera St
Street address city: San Luis Obispo
Street address state: CA
Zip/Postal code: 93401-7438
County: San Luis Obispo
Country: USA
Mailing address: PO BOX 112
Mailing city: SAN LUIS OBISPO
Mailing state: CA
Mailing zip: 93406-0112
General Phone: (805) 781-7800
Advertising Phone: (805) 781-7831
Editorial Phone: (805) 781-7902
General/National Adv. E-mail: majoraccounts@thetribunenews.com
Display Adv. E-mail: majoraccounts@thetribunenews.com
Classified Adv. e-mail: classifiedsells@thetribunenews.com
Editorial e-mail: letters@thetribunenews.com
Primary Website: www.sanluisobispo.com
Mthly Avg Views: 5409521
Mthly Avg Unique Visitors: 1023458
Year Established: 1869
News Services: AP, Scripps-McClatchy Western Services, MCT, CNS, LAT-WP, NYT, TMS.
Special Editions: Vintages, Central Coast Beach Towns, Living Here
Special Weekly Sections: Home, Garden, (Wed); Ticket Entertainment (Thur); Real Estate Weekly (Sat); Showcase, Travel,. Arts, Books, Food & Wine, Comics, (Sun)
Syndicated Publications: TV Book, Parade (Sun).
Delivery Methods: Carrier`Racks
Areas Served - City/County or Portion Thereof, or Zip codes: 93452, 93428, 93430, 93442, 93402, 93401, 93405, 93451, 93465, 93426, 93446, 93461, 93422, 93432, 93453, 93424, 93449, 93433, 93420, 93445, 93444, 93454
Own Printing Facility?: N
Commercial printers?: N
Sat. Circulation Paid: 20358
Sun. Circulation Paid: 21078
Audit By: AAM
Audit Date: 30.09.2018
Personnel: Cathy Veley (Circulation Manager); Sergio Holguin (Local Sales Dir.); Joe Tarica (Digital Development Dir.); Dan Itel (Local News Ed.); Stephanie Finucane (Opinion Ed.); Sarah Linn (Ent. Ed.); Mari Wylie (Finance Mgr.); Tim Ritchey (Pres & Pub.)
Parent company (for newspapers): The McClatchy Company

SAN MATEO DAILY JOURNAL

Street address 1: 1900 Alameda De Las Pulgas
Street address 2: Ste 112
Street address city: San Mateo
Street address state: CA
Zip/Postal code: 94403-1295
County: San Mateo
Country: USA
Mailing address: 1900 ALAMEDA DE LAS PULGAS STE 112
Mailing city: SAN MATEO
Mailing state: CA
Mailing zip: 94403-1295
General Phone: (650) 344-5200
General/National Adv. E-mail: ads@smdailyjournal.com
Classified Adv. e-mail: classifieds@smdailyjournal.com
Editorial e-mail: news@smdailyjournal.com
Primary Website: www.smdailyjournal.com
Year Established: 2000
News Services: AP.
Special Editions: Easter (Apr); Summer Shopping (Aug); Post-Holiday Clearance (Dec); Valentine's Day (Feb); Post-Holiday Clearance (Jan); Summer Shopping (Jul); Summer Employment (Jun); St. Patrick's Day (Mar); Summer Employment (May); Holiday Gift Guide (Nov); Holiday Emp
Special Weekly Sections: Automotive (Fri); Automotive (Sat); Kids Korner (Thur); Health (Tues); Education Directory (Wed).
Syndicated Publications: Relish (Monthly).
Areas Served - City/County or Portion Thereof, or Zip codes: San Francisco Peninsula
Sat. Circulation Paid: 14800
Audit By: Sworn/Estimate/Non-Audited
Audit Date: 12.07.2019
Personnel: Jerry Lee (Pub.); Jon Mays (Ed.); Erik Oeverndiek (Copy Ed./Page Designer); Nicola Zeuzem (Prodn. Mgr.)
Parent company (for newspapers): Bigfoot Media, Inc.; SMDJ LLC

MARIN INDEPENDENT JOURNAL

Street address 1: 4000 Civic Center Dr
Street address 2: Ste 301
Street address city: San Rafael
Street address state: CA
Zip/Postal code: 94903-4129
County: Marin
Country: USA
General Phone: (415) 883-8600
Primary Website: marinij.com
Audit By: Sworn/Estimate/Non-Audited
Audit Date: 12.07.2019
Parent company (for newspapers): Media News Group; Digital First Media

SANTA BARBARA NEWS-PRESS

Street address 1: 715 Anacapa St
Street address city: Santa Barbara
Street address state: CA
Zip/Postal code: 93101-2203
County: Santa Barbara
Country: USA
Mailing address: PO BOX 1359
Mailing city: SANTA BARBARA
Mailing state: CA
Mailing zip: 93102-1359
General Phone: (805) 564-5200
Advertising Phone: (805) 564-5200
Editorial Phone: (805)564-5271
General/National Adv. E-mail: advertising@newspress.com
Display Adv. E-mail: advertising@newspress.com
Classified Adv. e-mail: classad@newspress.com
Editorial e-mail: news@newspress.com
Primary Website: www.newspress.com
Mthly Avg Unique Visitors: 116141
Year Established: 1868
News Services: AP, NYT, MCT, SHNS, DJ, TMS.
Special Editions: Home and Decorator (Apr); Back to School (Aug); Gift Guide (Dec); Weddings (Feb); Business Outlook (Jan); Fiesta (Jul); Fashion (Mar); Chefs (May); The Season Begins (Nov); Surf (Oct); Prep Football (Sept).
Special Weekly Sections: Business, Technology (Mon); Seniors (Tue); Healthy Living (Wed); Best Food (Thur); Entertainment, Arts, Culture, TV (Fri); Religion, Garden (Sat); Travel, Real Estate, Comics, Arts, Books, Perspective (Sun);
Syndicated Publications: USA WEEKEND Magazine (S).
Sat. Circulation Paid: 25199
Sun. Circulation Paid: 25439
Audit By: AAM
Audit Date: 30.09.2013
Personnel: Arthur Von Wiesenberger (Co-Pub.); Wendy Mccaw (Co-Pub.); Norman Colavincenzo (CFO/Dir., Opns.); Graham Brown (Dir., Community Rel.); Jacky Barnard (Customer Serv. Mgr.); Linda Strean (Mng. Ed.); Travis K. Armstrong (Editorial Page Ed.); Gary Robb (Features Ed.); Len Wood (Photo/Graphics Ed.); John Zant (Sports Columnist); Raul Gil (Dir., Systems); Rick Merrick (MIS Mgr.); Mary Beckman (Web Designer/Developer); Bob Yznaga (Prodn. Dir.); Sharon Moore (Prodn. Mgr., Publishing Servs.); Tony Peck (Editorial Page Assistant); Ray Rosenthal (Nat'l Adv. Sales Mgr.); Deborah Garcia (Ed. in chief)
Parent company (for newspapers): Ampersand Publishing

SANTA CLARITA VALLEY SIGNAL

Street address 1: 24000 Creekside Rd
Street address city: Santa Clarita
Street address state: CA
Zip/Postal code: 91355-1726
County: Los Angeles
Country: USA
Mailing address: 24000 CREEKSIDE RD
Mailing city: SANTA CLARITA
Mailing state: CA
Mailing zip: 91355-1726
General Phone: (661) 259-1234
General/National Adv. E-mail: info@the-signal.com
Primary Website: www.the-signal.com
Year Established: 1919
News Services: AP.
Special Weekly Sections: Entertainment (Fri); Valley Homes (S); Religion (Sat); Lifestyles/Features (Tues); Lifestyles/Features (Wed).
Own Printing Facility?: Y
Commercial printers?: Y
Avg Free Circ: 48
Sat. Circulation Paid: 10673
Sat. Circulation Free: 48
Audit By: VAC
Audit Date: 31.12.2016
Personnel: Russ Briley (Exec VP); Jason Schaff (Executive Editor); Lila Littlejohn (Editorial Ed.); Cary Osborne (Asst. Mng. Ed./Sports Ed.); Jim Holt (Senior Writer); Charles Champion (Pres./Pub.); Jana Adkins (Mng. Ed.)
Parent company (for newspapers): Paladin Multi-Media

SANTA CRUZ SENTINEL

Street address 1: 318 Encinal
Street address city: Santa Cruz
Street address state: CA
Zip/Postal code: 95060
County: Santa Cruz
Country: USA
Mailing state: CA
General Phone: (831) 423-4242
Advertising Phone: (831) 648-4301
Editorial Phone: (831)429-2427
General/National Adv. E-mail: newsroom@santacruzsentinel.com
Editorial e-mail: newsroom@santacruzsentinel.com
Primary Website: www.santacruzsentinel.com
Year Established: 1856
News Services: AP, McClatchy, NYT.
Special Editions: Back to School (Aug); Last Minute Gift Guide (Dec); Forecast (Feb); Bride & Groom (Jan); Wharf to Wharf Race (Jul); Antiques (Jun); Home & Garden (Mar); Holiday Gift Guide (Nov); Employment Digest (Oct); Santa Cruz County Fair (Sept).
Special Weekly Sections: Spotlight-Entertainment & Dining (Fri); Seniors (Mon); Education (S); Sports-Breaking Away (Thur); Best Food Day (Wed).
Syndicated Publications: Relish (Monthly); TV Magazine (S).
Sat. Circulation Paid: 17013
Sun. Circulation Paid: 18779
Audit By: AAM
Audit Date: 30.09.2018
Personnel: Melissa Murphy (Mng. Ed.); Mardi Browning (Circ. Mgr.); Steve Bennett (Adv. Dir.); Donald Fukui (Asst. City Ed.); Jim Seimas (Asst. Sports Ed.); Gary Omernick (Pub.); Julie Jag (Sports Ed.)
Parent company (for newspapers): Digital First Media; Media News Group

SANTA MARIA TIMES

Street address 1: 3200 Skyway Dr
Street address city: Santa Maria
Street address state: CA
Zip/Postal code: 93455-1824
County: Santa Barbara
Country: USA
Mailing address: PO BOX 400
Mailing city: SANTA MARIA
Mailing state: CA
Mailing zip: 93456-0400
General Phone: (805) 925-2691
Advertising Phone: (888) 422-8822
Editorial Phone: (805) 739-2143
General/National Adv. E-mail: cschur@santamariatimes.com
Display Adv. E-mail: sedwards@santamariatimes.com
Classified Adv. e-mail: bcunningham@santamariatimes.com
Editorial e-mail: mcooley@santamariatimes.com
Primary Website: www.santamariatimes.com
News Services: AP, GNS, MCT, NYT, SHNS, TMS.
Special Editions: Santa Maria Strawberry Festival (Apr); Readers' Choice (Aug); Last Minute Gift Guide (Dec); Farm & Agriculture (Feb); Wedding Guide (Jan); Mid-State Fair (Jul); Flower Festival (Jun); Personal Improvement (Mar); Fire Safety (May); Coupon Direct (Monthly);
Special Weekly Sections: Entertainment (Wed); Senior (Thur); best Food (Fri); Religion (Sat); Travel (Sun)
Syndicated Publications: Relish (Monthly); USA WEEKEND Magazine (S).
Avg Free Circ: 1287
Sat. Circulation Paid: 8965
Sat. Circulation Free: 432
Sun. Circulation Paid: 9517
Sun. Circulation Free: 5650
Audit By: AAM
Audit Date: 30.09.2015
Personnel: Cynthia Schur (Pres./Pub.); Rick Macke (Circ. Dir.); Tom Bolton (Exec. Ed.); Marga K. Cooley (Mng. Ed.); Len Wood (Asst. Mng. Ed.); Gary Robb (Online Ed.); Elliott Stern (Sports Ed.); Jose Aquino (Web Developer); George Fischer (Prodn. Mgr.); Draxton Carroll (Web Master); Sara Edwards (Retail Mgr.); Guillermo Tamayo (Circ. Mgr.)
Parent company (for newspapers): Dispatch-Argus; Horizon Publications Inc.; Lee Enterprises, Incorporated

SANTA MONICA DAILY PRESS

Street address 1: 1640 5th St Ste 218
Street address 2: Suite 218
Street address city: Santa Monica
Street address state: CA
Zip/Postal code: 90401-3325
County: Los Angeles
Country: USA
Mailing address: 1640 5TH ST STE 218
Mailing city: SANTA MONICA
Mailing state: CA
Mailing zip: 90401-3325
General Phone: 310-458-7737
Advertising Phone: (310) 573-8342
Editorial Phone: (310) 573-8350
General/National Adv. E-mail: daniela@smdp.com
Display Adv. E-mail: schwenker@smdp.com
Editorial e-mail: editor@smdp.com
Primary Website: www.smdp.com
Year Established: 2001
Sat. Circulation Paid: 12087
Audit By: Sworn/Estimate/Non-Audited
Audit Date: 12.07.2019
Personnel: Ross Furukawa (Pub); Matthew Hall (Editor-in-Chief); Kelsey Fowler (Staff Writer)
Parent company (for newspapers): David Danforth

THE PRESS DEMOCRAT

Street address 1: 427 Mendocino Ave
Street address city: Santa Rosa
Street address state: CA
Zip/Postal code: 95401-6313
County: Sonoma
Country: USA
Mailing address: PO BOX 569
Mailing city: SANTA ROSA
Mailing state: CA
Mailing zip: 95402-0569
General Phone: (707) 526-8570
Advertising Phone: (707) 526-8570
Editorial Phone: (707)521-5288
General/National Adv. E-mail: ken.jaggie@pressdemocrat.com
Display Adv. E-mail: ken.jaggie@pressdemocrat.com
Classified Adv. e-mail: jennifer.williams@pressdemocrat.com
Editorial e-mail: letters@pressdemo.com
Primary Website: www.pressdemocrat.com
Mthly Avg Unique Visitors: 551959
Year Established: 1857
News Services: NYT, AP, LAT-WP, McClatchy, TMS,
Special Weekly Sections: Technology (Mon); Lifestyle, Teen, Classified (Tue); Best Food & Wine Day (Wed); Time Out, Outdoor, Fitness, Wellness (Thur); Entertainment (Fri); Home and Garden, Auto (Sat); Forum, Travel, TV, Real Estate (Sun)
Syndicated Publications: Santa Rosa Magazine (Quarterly); TV Week (S);
Delivery Methods: Mail`Newsstand`Carrier`Racks
Areas Served - City/County or Portion Thereof, or Zip codes: 95425, 95482, 94508, 94515, 94562, 94567, 94573, 94574, 94576, 95449, 95469, 95470,

95490, 95422, 95443, 95451, 95453, 95457, 95468, 95461, 95467, 95464, 95485, 95493, 95410, 95420, 95421, 95432, 95437, 95445, 95450, 95456, 95459, 95460, 95468, 95480, 95494, 95497, 95423, 95424, 94928, 94931, 94951, 94952, 94954, 95401, 95403, 95404, 95405, 95407, 95409, 95416, 95431, 95433, 95439, 95448, 95472, 95476, 95487, 95492, 94922, 94923, 94929, 94971, 94972, 95419, 95430, 95436, 95441, 95442, 95444, 95446, 95452, 95462, 95465, 95471. 95486
Own Printing Facility?: Y
Commercial printers?: Y
Sat. Circulation Paid: 47803
Sun. Circulation Paid: 53389
Audit By: AAM
Audit Date: 30.09.2018
Personnel: Stephen Daniels (Controller); Carolyn McCulligh (Adv. Dir.); Don Wolff (Adv. Mgr., Nat'l); Cindy Butner (Dir., Mktg.); Dava Amador (Circ. Mgr.); Jennifer Williams (Digital Development Director); Catherine Barnett (Pub.); Robert Swofford (Mng. Ed.); George Millener (Sr. Ed., Presentation); Paul Gullixson (Editorial Page Ed.); Greg Retsinas (Digital Director); Emily DeBacker (HR Dir.); Sam Caddle (Production Dir.); Heather Irwin; Barbara Mitchel (Gen. Mgr.)
Parent company (for newspapers): Sonoma Media Investments LLC

THE UNION DEMOCRAT

Street address 1: 84 S Washington St
Street address city: Sonora
Street address state: CA
Zip/Postal code: 95370-4711
County: Tuolumne
Country: USA
Mailing address: 84 S WASHINGTON ST
Mailing city: SONORA
Mailing state: CA
Mailing zip: 95370-4797
General Phone: (209) 532-7151
Advertising Phone: (209) 588-4555
Editorial Phone: (209) 588-4525
General/National Adv. E-mail: ads@uniondemocrat.com
Display Adv. E-mail: ads@uniondemocrat.com
Classified Adv. e-mail: class@uniondemocrat.com
Editorial e-mail: newsroom@uniondemocrat.com; letters@uniondemocrat.com
Primary Website: www.uniondemocrat.com
Mthly Avg Views: 500000
Mthly Avg Unique Visitors: 40000
Year Established: 1854
News Services: AP.
Special Editions: MotherLode Fair (Jul); Know It All (Aug); Home & Garden (Apr); MotherLode Roundup (May);Christmas Countdown (Nov/Dec);Recreation Guide (Jan)
Special Weekly Sections: Health, Medicine (Mon); Food, Drink (Tue); Business (Wed); Sierra Living (Thur); Community (Fri)
Syndicated Publications: Parade (Fri)
Delivery Methods: Mail`Newsstand`Carrier`Racks
Areas Served - City/County or Portion Thereof, or Zip codes: 95370, 95327, 95383, 95346, 95310, 95321, 95372, 95373,95379
Own Printing Facility?: Y
Commercial printers?: Y
Avg Free Circ: 485
Sat. Circulation Paid: 6588
Sat. Circulation Free: 485
Audit By: AAM
Audit Date: 31.03.2018
Personnel: Lynne Fernandez (Bus. Mgr.); Peggy Pietrowicz (Adv. Mgr.); Margie Thompson (Mng. Ed., Features); Bill Rozak (Sports Ed.); Derek Rosen (Coord., Systems/Web); Yochanan Quillen (Prodn. Mgr., Opns./Press); Sharon Sharp (Circulation Manager); Kari Borgen (Interim Publisher); Gary Piech (Pub); Lyn Riddle (Editor); Wells Andrews (Pub.)
Parent company (for newspapers): Horizon Publications Inc.; Rhode Island Suburban Newspapers

TAHOE DAILY TRIBUNE

Street address 1: 3079 Harrison Ave
Street address city: South Lake Tahoe
Street address state: CA
Zip/Postal code: 96150-7976
County: El Dorado
Country: USA
Mailing address: 3079 HARRISON AVE
Mailing city: SOUTH LAKE TAHOE
Mailing state: CA
Mailing zip: 96150-7976
General Phone: (530) 541-3880
Display Adv. E-mail: classifieds@sierranevadamedia.com
Editorial e-mail: editor@tahoedailytribune.com
Primary Website: tahoedailytribune.com
Year Established: 1952
News Services: AP.
Special Editions: Almanac Series (Feb).
Special Weekly Sections: Entertainment (Fri). Real Estate (Sat)
Syndicated Publications: Tahoe Magazine (May and November) (Twice-Annually); Lake Tahoe Action (Thurs); Tahoe Tastes (February and August) (Twice-Annually); Best of Tahoe (July) (Annually)
Delivery Methods: Newsstand`Carrier`Racks
Areas Served - City/County or Portion Thereof, or Zip codes: 96150+
Own Printing Facility?: Y
Commercial printers?: Y
Sat. Circulation Paid: 469
Sat. Circulation Free: 7943
Audit By: Sworn/Estimate/Non-Audited
Audit Date: 10.06.2019
Personnel: Rob Galloway (Pub.); Carolan LaCroix (Sr. Bus. Dvp. Mgr.); Annemarie Prudente (Adv. Acct. Exec.); Justine Dhollande (Acct. Mgr.); Ryan Hoffman (Ed.); Bill Rozak (Sports Ed.)
Parent company (for newspapers): Swift Communications, Inc.; Ogden Newspapers Inc.; Ogden Newspapers

THE RECORD

Street address 1: 530 E Market St
Street address city: Stockton
Street address state: CA
Zip/Postal code: 95202-3009
County: San Joaquin
Country: USA
General Phone: (209) 943-6397
Advertising Phone: (209) 546-8200
Editorial Phone: (209) 546-8250
General/National Adv. E-mail: advertising@recordnet.com
Display Adv. E-mail: advertising@recordnet.com
Classified Adv. e-mail: advertising@recordnet.com
Editorial e-mail: newsroom@recordnet.com
Primary Website: www.recordnet.com
Mthly Avg Views: 1800000
Mthly Avg Unique Visitors: 400000
Year Established: 1895
News Services: AP, MCT.
Special Editions: Pinnacle (Annually); Outlook 1 (Feb); Holiday Guide (Nov); Best of San Joaquin (Oct).
Special Weekly Sections: Health & Fitness - Mondays; Home & Garden - Tuesdays; Food - Wednesdays; Entertainment - Thursdays; Automotive - Friday; Real Estate - Sat/Sun; Travel - Sunday;
Delivery Methods: Newsstand`Carrier`Racks
Areas Served - City/County or Portion Thereof, or Zip codes: San Joaquin County
Own Printing Facility?: Y
Commercial printers?: Y
Avg Free Circ: 226
Sat. Circulation Paid: 10733
Sat. Circulation Free: 226
Sun. Circulation Paid: 14189
Sun. Circulation Free: 318
Audit By: AAM
Audit Date: 31.03.2019
Personnel: Claudine Dunham (Credit Mgr.); Deitra Kenoly (Adv. Dir.); Mike Klocke (Editor); Donald W. Blount (Mng. Editor); Genette Brookshire (Online Editor); Bob Highfill (Sports Editor); Ken Damilano (Tech Servs. Mgr.); Jim Frankel (Safety, Environmental, Maintenance Mgr.); Charles Scott (CFO); Barbara Zumwalt (Metro Ed.); David Greenlee (Press Manager); Sandi Johnson (HR Director); Josh Harmon (New Media Dir.)
Parent company (for newspapers): Gannett; CherryRoad Media

TEHACHAPI NEWS

Street address 1: 411 N Mill St
Street address city: Tehachapi
Street address state: CA
Zip/Postal code: 93561-1351
County: Kern
Country: USA
Mailing address: 411 N MILL ST
Mailing city: TEHACHAPI
Mailing state: CA
Mailing zip: 93561-1351
General Phone: (661) 822-6828
General/National Adv. E-mail: advertise@tehachapinews.com
Display Adv. E-mail: classifieds@tehachapinews.com
Editorial e-mail: editorial@tehachapinews.com
Primary Website: www.tehachapinews.com
Year Established: 1899
Delivery Methods: Mail`Carrier`Racks
Areas Served - City/County or Portion Thereof, or Zip codes: 93561, 93531
Commercial printers?: Y
Avg Free Circ: 26338
Sat. Circulation Paid: 24107
Sat. Circulation Free: 24220
Sun. Circulation Paid: 26193
Sun. Circulation Free: 26338
Audit By: AAM
Audit Date: 31.03.2018
Personnel: Stephanie Ursua (Bus. Mgr)
Parent company (for newspapers): TBC Media

DAILY BREEZE

Street address 1: 21250 Hawthorne Blvd
Street address 2: Ste 170
Street address city: Torrance
Street address state: CA
Zip/Postal code: 90503-5514
County: Los Angeles
Country: USA
Mailing address: 21250 HAWTHORNE BLVD STE 170
Mailing city: TORRANCE
Mailing state: CA
Mailing zip: 90503-5514
General Phone: (310) 540-5511
Advertising Phone: (310) 540-5511
Editorial Phone: (310) 540-5511
General/National Adv. E-mail: tom.kelly@langnews.com
Display Adv. E-mail: tom.kelly@langnews.com
Classified Adv. e-mail: marilyn.james@dailybreeze.com
Editorial e-mail: newsroom@dailybreeze.com; calendar@dailybreeze.com
Primary Website: www.dailybreeze.com
Year Established: 1894
News Services: AP, City News Service, SHNS, Religion News Service
Delivery Methods: Mail`Newsstand`Carrier`Racks
Areas Served - City/County or Portion Thereof, or Zip codes: 90245, 90247, 90248, 90249, 90250, 90254, 90260, 90266, 90274, 90275, 90277, 90278, 90501, 90502, 90503, 90504, 90505, 90506, 90710, 90717, 90731, 90732, 90744, 90745, 90746, 90747
Own Printing Facility?: N
Commercial printers?: Y
Sat. Circulation Paid: 49144
Sun. Circulation Paid: 61294
Audit By: AAM
Audit Date: 31.03.2015
Personnel: Ron Hasse (Pres. & Pub.); Toni Sciacqua (Ed.); Frank Suraci (City Ed.); Frank Pine (Exec. Ed.); Daniel Tedford (Dig. News Dir.); Tom Moore (Exec. Sports Ed.); Tom Bray (Sr. Ed.)
Parent company (for newspapers): Southern California News Group; MediaNews Group

PASADENA STAR-NEWS

Street address 1: 21250 Hawthorne Blvd
Street address 2: Ste 170
Street address city: Torrance
Street address state: CA
Zip/Postal code: 90503-5514
County: Los Angeles
Country: USA
General Phone: (310) 543-6110
Advertising Phone: (310) 543-6110
Editorial Phone: (310) 543-6110
General/National Adv. E-mail: mickie.sullivan@langnews.com
Display Adv. E-mail: mickie.sullivan@langnews.com
Classified Adv. e-mail: carla.asmundson@sgvn.com
Editorial e-mail: news.star-news@sgvn.com
Primary Website: www.pasadenastarnews.com
News Services: AP, CNS, Scripps-McClatchey, DJ, NYT, TMS.
Special Editions: Earth Day (Apr); Pro Football Tab (Aug); The Rose Magazine (Dec); The Body (Jan); Hot Blues and Cool Jazz (Jul); Health Beat (Jun); Health Beat (Mar); Water Awareness (May); Holiday Guide (Nov); Rodeo Tab (Oct); Think Environmental (Sept).
Special Weekly Sections: Home Buyer (S); Home Buyer (Sat).
Syndicated Publications: Relish (Monthly); USA WEEKEND Magazine (S).
Sat. Circulation Paid: 22016
Sun. Circulation Paid: 36581
Audit By: AAM
Audit Date: 30.09.2012
Personnel: Gloria Arango (V.P./HR); Larry Wilson (Ed.); Kevin Smith (Bus. Ed.); Ron Hasse (Pres./Pub.); Frank Pine; Tom Moore (Exec. Sports Ed.)
Parent company (for newspapers): Southern California News Group

THE UKIAH DAILY JOURNAL

Street address 1: 415 Talmage Rd Suite A
Street address city: Ukiah
Street address state: CA
Zip/Postal code: 95482-4912
County: Mendocino
Country: USA
Mailing address: 415 Talmage Rd Suite A
Mailing city: UKIAH
Mailing state: CA
Mailing zip: 95482-4912
General Phone: (707) 468-3500
Advertising Phone: (707) 468-3500
Editorial Phone: (707) 468-3500
General/National Adv. E-mail: udjemily@ukiahdj.com
Display Adv. E-mail: udjemily@ukiahdj.com
Classified Adv. e-mail: advertising@record-bee.com
Editorial e-mail: udj@ukiahdj.com
Primary Website: www.ukiahdailyjournal.com
Mthly Avg Views: 600000
Mthly Avg Unique Visitors: 90000
Year Established: 1860
Special Editions: Home & Garden (Apr); Redwood Empire Fair Official Program (Aug); Christmas Songbook (Dec); Auto Show (Feb); Ukiah Lifestyles/ Almanac (Jul); Summer Fun Coupon Book (Jun); Holy Week Directory (Mar); Mother's Day Dining/Gift Guide (May); Homemakers School (O
Special Weekly Sections: Best Food Day, Health & Wellness (Tue); Business (Wed); Lifestyle, Arts, Entertainment (Thur); Real Estate, Community (Fri); Religion (Sat); This Was News, Photo, Weddings, Engagements, Births (Sun)
Syndicated Publications: Relish (Monthly); On TV (S); American Profile (Weekly).
Delivery Methods: Mail`Newsstand`Carrier`Racks
Own Printing Facility?: N
Commercial printers?: N
Sat. Circulation Paid: 5070
Sun. Circulation Paid: 5344
Audit By: AAM
Audit Date: 30.09.2014
Personnel: Kevin McConnell (Pub.); Jody Martinez (Asst. Ed.); K.C. Meadows (Online Ed.); Sarah McGrath (General Manager/Advertising Manager); Brittany Dashiell (Webpage Ed.); Gail McAlister (Lake Mendo Group Dig. Dir.)
Parent company (for newspapers): Digital First Media; MediaNews Group

THE REPORTER

Street address 1: 916 Cotting Ln
Street address city: Vacaville
Street address state: CA
Zip/Postal code: 95688-9338
County: Solano
Country: USA
Mailing address: 916 COTTING LN
Mailing city: VACAVILLE
Mailing state: CA
Mailing zip: 95688-9338
General Phone: (707) 448-6401
Advertising Phone: (707) 453-8109
Editorial Phone: (707) 448-2200
General/National Adv. E-mail: mhutt@thereporter.com
Display Adv. E-mail: mhutt@thereporter.com
Editorial e-mail: letters@thereporter.com
Primary Website: www.thereporter.com
Year Established: 1883
News Services: AP.
Special Weekly Sections: Auto (Fri); Home (S); Religion (Sat); Prime Time (Tues); Food (Wed).

Syndicated Publications: Relish (Monthly); USA WEEKEND Magazine (S); American Profile (Weekly).
Delivery Methods: Mail
Areas Served - City/County or Portion Thereof, or Zip codes: Solano County
Sat. Circulation Paid: 16195
Sun. Circulation Paid: 17569
Audit By: Sworn/Estimate/Non-Audited
Audit Date: 12.07.2019
Personnel: Jim Gleim (Pub.); Jerry Schoenberg (Circ. Mgr.); Marc Hutt (Adv. Dir.); Greg Trott (Features Ed.); Brent Dobbier (Prodn. Mgr.); Steffanie Jackson (HR Dir.); Matt Miller (Managing Ed.)
Parent company (for newspapers): Digital First Media; MediaNews Group

VALLEJO TIMES-HERALD

Street address 1: 420 Virginia St
Street address 2: Ste 2A
Street address city: Vallejo
Street address state: CA
Zip/Postal code: 94590-6018
County: Solano
Country: USA
Mailing address: 420 VIRGINIA ST STE 2A
Mailing city: VALLEJO
Mailing state: CA
Mailing zip: 94590-6018
General Phone: (707) 644-1141
Advertising Phone: (707) 453-8178
Editorial Phone: (707) 644-1141
General/National Adv. E-mail: sgilroy@timesheraldonline.com
Display Adv. E-mail: dsheely@bayareanewsgroup.com
Classified Adv. e-mail: sally@thereporter.com
Editorial e-mail: jbungart@timesheraldonline.com
Primary Website: www.timesheraldonline.com
Year Established: 1875
News Services: AP, SHNS, McClatchy, Bay City News.
Special Editions: Baseball Preview (Apr); I Do-Bridal (Feb); Super Bowl (Jan); Fremont Art & Wine Festival (Jul); Daytrips (May); California Home (Monthly); Grand National Rodeo-Cow Palace (Oct); NFL Preview (Sept).
Special Weekly Sections: Technology (Mon); Life (Tue); Food & Wine (Wed); Eye (Thur); Life (Fri); Home & Garden, Real Estate (Sat); Business, Lifestyle, Travel, TV (Sun)
Syndicated Publications: Relish (Monthly); USA WEEKEND Magazine (S); American Profile (Weekly).
Delivery Methods: Newsstand`Carrier`Racks
Areas Served - City/County or Portion Thereof, or Zip codes: 94590, 94591, 94510
Own Printing Facility?: Y
Commercial printers?: N
Sat. Circulation Paid: 13199
Sun. Circulation Paid: 13777
Audit By: AAM
Audit Date: 30.09.2009
Personnel: Jim Gleim (Pub.); Sally Schulz (Classified Mgr.); Matt Miller (Adv. Dir.); Richard Freedman (Community Ed.); Lisa Lerseth (Pre Press Mgr.); Hernan Ponce (VP, Sales); Jack Bungart (Mng. Ed.)
Parent company (for newspapers): Digital First Media; MediaNews Group

DAILY PRESS

Street address 1: 13891 Park Ave
Street address city: Victorville
Street address state: CA
Zip/Postal code: 92392-2435
County: San Bernardino
Country: USA
Mailing address: 13891 Park Ave
Mailing city: Victorville
Mailing state: CA
Mailing zip: 92392-2435
General Phone: (760) 241-7744
Advertising Phone: (760) 951-6288
Editorial Phone: (760) 951-6270
General/National Adv. E-mail: rlipscomb@vvdailypress.com
Display Adv. E-mail: acallahan@vvdailypress.com
Classified Adv. e-mail: acallahan@vvdailypress.com
Editorial e-mail: DKeck@vvdailypress.com
Primary Website: www.vvdailypress.com
Year Established: 1937
Avg Free Circ: 437
Sat. Circulation Paid: 8877
Sat. Circulation Free: 437
Sun. Circulation Paid: 10443
Sun. Circulation Free: 312
Audit By: AAM
Audit Date: 31.12.2018
Personnel: Steve Hunt (Pub.); Mario Mejia (Circ. Mgr.); Steve Nakutin (Interim Advertising Mgr.); Jason Vrtis (Ed.)
Parent company (for newspapers): CherryRoad Media

DESERT DISPATCH

Street address 1: 13891 Park Ave
Street address city: Victorville
Street address state: CA
Zip/Postal code: 92392-2435
County: San Bernardino
Country: USA
Mailing address: 13891 PARK AVE
Mailing city: VICTORVILLE
Mailing state: CA
Mailing zip: 92392-2435
General Phone: (760) 256-2257
Advertising Phone: (760) 951-6288
Editorial Phone: (760) 951-6270
Primary Website: www.desertdispatch.com
Year Established: 1910
News Services: AP.
Special Editions: Exploring Barstow (Apr); Main St. USA (Aug); Letters to Santa (Dec); Presidents' Day (Feb); Gettysburg Address (Jan); Declaration of Independence (Jul); Parade of Homes (Jun); Battle Colors (Mar); Memorial Day (May); Veterans Day (Nov); Parade of Homes (Oct)
Special Weekly Sections: Real Estate (Fri); Business Page (Mon); Food (Wed).
Syndicated Publications: Weekender Magazine (Fri); On TV (S).
Delivery Methods: Mail`Newsstand`Carrier`Racks
Areas Served - City/County or Portion Thereof, or Zip codes: Barstow
Own Printing Facility?: Y
Sat. Circulation Paid: 1862
Audit By: CAC
Audit Date: 31.03.2015
Personnel: Steve Hunt (Pub.); Scott Nordhues (City Ed.); Jason Vrtis (Weeklies Ed.); Steve Nakutin (Advertising Dir.); Tony Martin (Finance Mgr.); Mario Mejia (Circ. Mgr.)
Parent company (for newspapers): LMG National Publishing, Inc.; Gannett

TULARE ADVANCE-REGISTER

Street address 1: 330 N West St
Street address city: Visalia
Street address state: CA
Zip/Postal code: 93291-6010
County: Tulare
Country: USA
Mailing address: PO BOX 31
Mailing city: VISALIA
Mailing state: CA
Mailing zip: 93279-0031
General Phone: 559-735-3200
Advertising Phone: (559) 735-3231
Editorial Phone: (559) 735-3277
General/National Adv. E-mail: dygarcia@visaliatimesdelta.com
Display Adv. E-mail: dygarcia@visaliatimesdelta.com
Classified Adv. e-mail: dygarcia@visaliatimesdelta.com
Editorial e-mail: dhayes2@visaliatimesdelta.com
Primary Website: www.tulareadvanceregister.com
Year Established: 1882
Special Editions: Health & Fitness (Jan);World AG Expo (Feb); Job Fair (Apr); Health & Fitness (Apr); Living Here (May); Medical Directory (June); Health & Fitness (July); Tulare County Fair (Sept); Kids Fest (Nov); Get Fit (Dec); Real Estate Plus (Semi-monthly)
Special Weekly Sections: Health, Agriculture (Mon); Best Food, Grocery (Wed); Home (Thur); Choices, Entertainment, Auto (Fri); Real Estate, TV (Sat)
Delivery Methods: Mail`Newsstand`Carrier`Racks
Areas Served - City/County or Portion Thereof, or Zip codes: 93274, 93277
Commercial printers?: Y
Sat. Circulation Paid: 14935
Audit By: AAM
Audit Date: 30.09.2014
Personnel: Paula Goudreau (Pres./Pub.); Theresa Simpson (Circ. Mgr.); Karen Ferguson (Regional Publisher); Silas Lyons (Exec. Ed.)
Parent company (for newspapers): Gannett

VISALIA TIMES-DELTA

Street address 1: 330 N. West Street
Street address city: Visalia
Street address state: CA
Zip/Postal code: 93291
County: Tulare
Country: USA
Mailing address: PO BOX 31
Mailing city: VISALIA
Mailing state: CA
Mailing zip: 93279-0031
General Phone: (559) 735-3200
Advertising Phone: (559) 735-3231
Editorial Phone: (559) 735-3277
General/National Adv. E-mail: publisher@visaliatimesdelta.com
Display Adv. E-mail: retail@visaliatimesdelta.com
Classified Adv. e-mail: classified@visaliatimesdelta.com
Editorial e-mail: news@visaliatimesdelta.com
Primary Website: www.visaliatimesdelta.com
Mthly Avg Views: 1174358
Mthly Avg Unique Visitors: 188553
Year Established: 1859
News Services: AP, GNS, NYT, TMS.
Special Editions: Health & Fitness (Jan); Health & Fitness (Apr); Living Here (May); Medical Directory (June); Health & Fitness (July); Tulare County Fair (Sept); Real Estate Plus (Semi-monthly)
Special Weekly Sections: Health, Agriculture (Mon); Best Food, Grocery (Wed); Home (Thur); Choices, Entertainment, Auto (Fri); Real Estate, TV (Sat)
Syndicated Publications: Vista (Mon/1x month); USA Weekend(Sat).
Delivery Methods: Mail`Newsstand`Carrier`Racks
Areas Served - City/County or Portion Thereof, or Zip codes: 93291, 93292, 93277, 93274, 93235, 93221, 93223, 93227, 93247, 93271, 93272, 93286, 93618
Own Printing Facility?: Y
Commercial printers?: Y
Avg Free Circ: 386
Sat. Circulation Paid: 13120
Sat. Circulation Free: 1537
Sun. Circulation Paid: 211
Audit By: AAM
Audit Date: 31.03.2018
Personnel: Paula Goudreau (Pres./Pub.); Jim Houck (City Ed.); David Sutton (Prodn. Mgr., Opns.); Melinda Morales (Daily Ed.); Jimmy Fryar (Adv. Dir.); Michael Skrocki (Circ. Sales/Opns. Mgr.); Theresa Simpson (Media Group Rep.); Mari Benko Wylie (VP Finance); Karen Ferguson (Regional Publisher); Trey Dean (Advert Mgr); Eric Woomer (News Ed); Silas Lyons (Exec. Ed.)
Parent company (for newspapers): Gannett

EAST BAY TIMES

Street address 1: 175 Lennon Ln Ste 100
Street address 2: Suite 100
Street address city: Walnut Creek
Street address state: CA
Zip/Postal code: 94598-2466
County: Contra Costa
Country: USA
Mailing address: 175 LENNON LN STE 100
Mailing city: WALNUT CREEK
Mailing state: CA
Mailing zip: 94598-2466
General Phone: (925) 935-2525
Advertising Phone: (925) 779-7120
Editorial Phone: (925) 943-8235
General/National Adv. E-mail: ccnnewsrelease@bayareanewsgroup.com.
Display Adv. E-mail: rsimmonds@bayareanewsgroup.com
Classified Adv. e-mail: cctclassifieds@bayareanewsgroup.com
Editorial e-mail: dhatfield@bayareanewsgroup.com
Primary Website: www.eastbaytimes.com
Year Established: 2005
News Services: AP, LAT-WP, NYT, States News Service, McClatchy.
Syndicated Publications: Bloomberg Financial (S).
Delivery Methods: Mail`Carrier`Racks
Areas Served - City/County or Portion Thereof, or Zip codes: Eastern part of Contra Costa County: Antioch, Pittsburg, Brentwood, Oakley, Discovery Bay, Bay Point, Bryon, Rio Vista, Knightsen, and Bethel Island.
Own Printing Facility?: Y
Commercial printers?: Y
Sat. Circulation Paid: 88517
Sun. Circulation Paid: 138794
Audit By: AAM
Audit Date: 30.09.2018
Personnel: Sharon Ryan (Pres./Pub.); Neil Chase (Exec. Ed.); Keith Randall (Mng. Ed.); Theresa Martinez (Exec. Asst. to the Ed.); Veronia Vargas (Exec. Asst.); Sarah Dussault (AME, Visual Journalism)
Parent company (for newspapers): Digital First Media; MediaNews Group

REGISTER-PAJARONIAN

Street address 1: 100 Westridge Dr
Street address city: Watsonville
Street address state: CA
Zip/Postal code: 95076-6602
County: Santa Cruz
Country: USA
Mailing address: 100 WESTRIDGE DR
Mailing city: WATSONVILLE
Mailing state: CA
Mailing zip: 95076-6602
General Phone: (831) 761-7300
Advertising Phone: (831) 761-7351
Editorial Phone: (831) 761-7322
General/National Adv. E-mail: businessoffice@register-pajaronian.com
Display Adv. E-mail: advertising@register-pajaronian.com
Editorial e-mail: newsroom@register-pajaronian.com
Primary Website: www.register-pajaronian.com
Mthly Avg Views: 107596
Mthly Avg Unique Visitors: 34558
Year Established: 1868
News Services: AP, SHNS.
Special Editions: Home Improvement (Monthly); Progress (Oct).
Special Weekly Sections: Real Estate (Fri); Education (Sat); Business (Thur); Best Food Day (Tues).
Syndicated Publications: TV Weekly (Sat).
Delivery Methods: Mail`Newsstand`Racks
Areas Served - City/County or Portion Thereof, or Zip codes: 95076
Own Printing Facility?: N
Commercial printers?: N
Sat. Circulation Paid: 5603
Audit By: Sworn/Estimate/Non-Audited
Audit Date: 12.07.2019
Personnel: Michael Rand (Controller); John Bartlett (Pub.); Allison Stenberg (Ad. Sales); Erik Chaloub (Mng. Ed.); Amy Bartlett (General Manager); Jeanie Johnson (Pub.)
Parent company (for newspapers): San Luis Valley Publishing; Weeklys

THE DAILY DEMOCRAT

Street address 1: 711 Main St
Street address city: Woodland
Street address state: CA
Zip/Postal code: 95695-3406
County: Yolo
Country: USA
Mailing address: 711 MAIN ST
Mailing city: WOODLAND
Mailing state: CA
Mailing zip: 95695-3406
General Phone: (530) 662-5421
Advertising Phone: (707) 453-8138
Editorial Phone: (530) 406-6230
General/National Adv. E-mail: news@dailydemocrat.com
Display Adv. E-mail: aperkes@dailydemocrat.com
Classified Adv. e-mail: classifieds@dailydemocrat.com
Editorial e-mail: news@dailydemocrat.com
Primary Website: www.dailydemocrat.com
Year Established: 1857
News Services: AP, NYT, TMS.
Special Editions: Home & Garden (Apr); Childcare Directory (Aug); Christmas Express (Dec); Bridal Tab (Feb); Ad Packages (Jan); Made in Woodland (Jul); Class (Graduation) (Jun); National Ag Tab Sun (Mar); National Police (May); Holiday Gift (Nov); National Cosmetology Mont
Special Weekly Sections: Best Food Day (Wed); Farm, Goodlife, Arts (Thur); Real Estate, Business, Finance, Entertainment, Auto (Fri); Religion (Sat)
Syndicated Publications: Relish (Monthly); USA WEEKEND Magazine (S); American Profile (Weekly).
Sat. Circulation Paid: 6904
Sun. Circulation Paid: 7179

Audit By: AAM
Audit Date: 30.06.2015
Personnel: Jim Gleim (Pub.); Allison Perkes (Adv. Dir.); Jim Smith (Ed.); Bruce Burton (Sports Ed.); James Price (Internet Mgr.); Nancy Nusz (Pre Press Mgr.)
Parent company (for newspapers): Digital First Media; MediaNews Group

LOS ANGELES DAILY NEWS

Street address 1: 21860 Burbank Blvd
Street address 2: Ste 200
Street address city: Woodland Hills
Street address state: CA
Zip/Postal code: 91367-7439
County: Los Angeles
Country: USA
Mailing address: PO BOX 4200
Mailing city: WOODLAND HILLS
Mailing state: CA
Mailing zip: 91365-4200
General Phone: (818) 713-3000
Advertising Phone: (818) 713-3000
Editorial Phone: (818) 713-3639
General/National Adv. E-mail: paul.ingegneri@langnews.com
Display Adv. E-mail: melene.alfonso@dailynews.com
Classified Adv. e-mail: melene.alfonso@dailynews.com
Editorial e-mail: dnmetro@dailynews.com
Primary Website: www.dailynews.com
Year Established: 1911
News Services: AP, MCT, NYT, City News Service, McClatchy.
Special Weekly Sections: High School Football Special (in season) (Fri); So. Cal. Wheels (Mon); Real Estate (S); Real Estate (Sat); Best Food Day (Wed).
Syndicated Publications: Relish (Monthly); Access (S).
Areas Served - City/County or Portion Thereof, or Zip codes: 91367, 91364, 91306, 91311, 91316, 91324, 91344, 91352, 91360, 91361, 91407, 91411, 91601, 93063, 93536, 93551, 91355, 91201, 91501, 91401
Sat. Circulation Paid: 35792
Sun. Circulation Paid: 58530
Audit By: AAM
Audit Date: 31.03.2017
Personnel: Dan Scofield (CFO); Melene Alfonso (Adv. Vice Pres.); Bill Vanlaningham (Dir., Mktg./Pub. Rel.); Liz Hamm (Dir., Mktg. Research); Frank Pine (Exec. Ed.); Larry Lipson (Restaurant Critic); Dennis McCarthy (Columnist); Dean Musgrove (Photo Dir.); Robert Lowman (Entertainment/Book Ed.); Sharyn Betz (Features Ed.); Ron Hasse (Pres. & Pub.); Brian Harr (Exec News Ed); Tom Kelly (Chief Rev. Officer); Toni Sciacqua (Managing Ed., Digital Op.); Jessica Keating (Opinion Ed.); Tom Moore (Exec. Sports Ed.); Kimberly Guimarin (Asst. Managing Ed.); Gloria Arango (VP, HR); Jessica Davis (Dig. News Dir.)
Parent company (for newspapers): Southern California News Group; Digital First Media

SISKIYOU DAILY NEWS

Street address 1: 309 S Broadway St
Street address city: Yreka
Street address state: CA
Zip/Postal code: 96097-2905
County: Siskiyou
Country: USA
Mailing address: PO BOX 129
Mailing city: YREKA
Mailing state: CA
Mailing zip: 96097-0129
General Phone: (530) 842-5777
Advertising Phone: (530) 842-5777
Editorial Phone: (530) 842-5777
General/National Adv. E-mail: advertising@siskiyoudaily.com
Display Adv. E-mail: advertising@siskiyoudaily.com
Classified Adv. e-mail: cmurphy@siskiyoudaily.com
Editorial e-mail: editor@siskiyoudaily.com
Primary Website: www.siskiyoudaily.com
Year Established: 1859
News Services: AP.
Special Editions: Spring Car Care (Apr); Siskiyou Golden Fair (Aug); Year-End Review (Dec); Chamber Information Book (Jun); Progress (Mar); Holiday Gift Guide (Nov); Football Kick-off (Sept).
Special Weekly Sections: Best Food Day (Tue); TV (Wed)
Syndicated Publications: Siskiyou Spotlight Tab (Fri); Siskiyou County Properties (Real Estate) (Monthly); American Profile (Weekly).
Delivery Methods: Carrier
Areas Served - City/County or Portion Thereof, or Zip codes: Siskiyou County
Audit By: Sworn/Estimate/Non-Audited
Audit Date: 12.07.2019
Personnel: Matt Guthrie (Pub.); Pat Mills (Bookkeeper/Purchasing Agent); David Nelmes (Adv. Dir.); Jean Smith (Circ. Mgr.); Mike Slizewski (Mng. Ed.); Dan Murphy (Sports Ed.); David Smith (Managing Ed)
Parent company (for newspapers): CherryRoad Media

COLORADO

VALLEY COURIER

Street address 1: 2205 State Ave
Street address city: Alamosa
Street address state: CO
Zip/Postal code: 81101-3559
County: Alamosa
Country: USA
Mailing address: PO BOX 1099
Mailing city: ALAMOSA
Mailing state: CO
Mailing zip: 81101-1099
General Phone: (719) 589-2553
Advertising Phone: (719) 589-6573
Editorial Phone: (719) 589-6573
General/National Adv. E-mail: ads@alamosanews.com
Display Adv. E-mail: ads@alamosanews.com
Classified Adv. e-mail: wantads@alamosanews.com
Editorial e-mail: news@alamosanews.com
Primary Website: www.alamosanews.com
Mthly Avg Views: 600000
Mthly Avg Unique Visitors: 50000
Year Established: 1926
News Services: AP.
Special Editions: Home Improvement (Apr) (Sept); Back-to-School (Aug); Christmas (Dec); Rodeo (Jul); Summer Lifestyle (May); Ski (Nov); Hunting (Sept); others too numerous to mention.
Special Weekly Sections: Western Living: Outdoors and Agriculture (Thur).
Delivery Methods: Mail`Newsstand`Carrier`Racks
Areas Served - City/County or Portion Thereof, or Zip codes: 81101 81120 81123 81124 81125 81130 81131 81132 81133 81136 81140 81141 81144 81146 81148 81149 81151 81152 81154
Own Printing Facility?: Y
Commercial printers?: Y
Sat. Circulation Paid: 5500
Audit By: Sworn/Estimate/Non-Audited
Audit Date: 12.07.2019
Personnel: Keith R. Cerny (Publisher); Shasta Quintana (Circ. Mgr.); Ruth Heide (Editor); Vernon Trujillo (Prodn. Foreman, Pressroom); Stephen Jiron (Sports Editor); Debra Sowards-Cerny (Advertising Manager); Steven Willis (advertising sales); Marco Garmendia (Adv. sales)
Parent company (for newspapers): San Luis Valley Publishing

ASPEN DAILY NEWS

Street address 1: 625 E Main St Unit 204
Street address 2: 2nd Floor
Street address city: Aspen
Street address state: CO
Zip/Postal code: 81611-2154
County: Pitkin
Country: USA
Mailing address: 625 E. Main Suite #204
Mailing city: Aspen
Mailing state: CO
Mailing zip: 81611
General Phone: (970) 925-2220
Advertising Phone: (970) 925-2220
Editorial Phone: (970) 925-2220
General/National Adv. E-mail: david@aspendailynews.com
Display Adv. E-mail: david@aspendailynews.com
Classified Adv. e-mail: classifieds@aspendailynews.com
Editorial e-mail: letters@aspendailynews.com
Primary Website: www.aspendailynews.com
Mthly Avg Views: 165000
Mthly Avg Unique Visitors: 18000
Year Established: 1978
News Services: AP.
Special Editions: Winter Guide (Dec); Winterskol (Jan); Summer Guide (Jun); Winternational (Mar); Spruce Up for Spring (May); 24 Hours of Aspen (Nov).
Special Weekly Sections: Time Out (A&E, Thur)
Delivery Methods: Racks
Areas Served - City/County or Portion Thereof, or Zip codes: Roaring Fork Valley (CO)
Own Printing Facility?: Y
Commercial printers?: Y
Sat. Circulation Paid: 12500
Sun. Circulation Paid: 12500
Audit By: Sworn/Estimate/Non-Audited
Audit Date: 12.07.2019
Personnel: David N. Danforth (Owner); Dawn Manges (Bus. Mgr.); Lynn Chaffler (Adv. Dir.); Rafael Perez (Circ. Mgr.); Curtis Wackerle (Mng. Ed.); Carolyn Sackariason (Ed.); Damien Williamson (Web/Assoc. Special Sections Ed.)
Parent company (for newspapers): Silver News, LLC

THE ASPEN TIMES

Street address 1: 314 E Hyman Ave
Street address city: Aspen
Street address state: CO
Zip/Postal code: 81611-1918
County: Pitkin
Country: USA
Mailing address: 314 E HYMAN AVE
Mailing city: ASPEN
Mailing state: CO
Mailing zip: 81611-1918
General Phone: (970) 925-3414
Advertising Phone: (925) 925-9937
Editorial Phone: (970) 925-3414
General/National Adv. E-mail: gunilla@aspentimes.com
Display Adv. E-mail: ahewitt@aspentimes.com
Classified Adv. e-mail: classifieds@cmnm.org
Editorial e-mail: rcarroll@aspentimes.com
Primary Website: www.aspentimes.com
Mthly Avg Views: 3575778
Mthly Avg Unique Visitors: 1651360
Year Established: 1881
News Services: AP, LAT-WP, NYT.
Special Editions: Restaurant Guide (Dec); Style (Jun).
Syndicated Publications: Weekend (Fri).
Areas Served - City/County or Portion Thereof, or Zip codes: Pitkin County (CO)
Sat. Circulation Paid: 11000
Audit By: Sworn/Estimate/Non-Audited
Audit Date: 12.07.2019
Personnel: Jenna Weatherred (Pub.); Dottie Wolcott (Bus. Mgr.); Gunilla Asher (Adv. Dir.); Bob Lombardi (Circ. Mgr.); Rick Carroll (Mng. Ed.); Stewart Oksenhorn (Arts Ed.); Dale Strode (Sports Ed.); David Laughren (Ad. Dir.); Samantha Johnston (Gen. Mgr.)
Parent company (for newspapers): Swift Communications, Inc.; Ogden Newspapers Inc.; Ogden Newspapers

VAIL DAILY

Street address 1: 40780 US Hwy 6 & 24
Street address city: Avon
Street address state: CO
Zip/Postal code: 81620
County: Eagle
Country: USA
Mailing address: PO BOX 81
Mailing city: VAIL
Mailing state: CO
Mailing zip: 81658-0081
General Phone: (970) 949-0555
Advertising Phone: (970) 949-0555
Editorial Phone: (970) 949-0555
General/National Adv. E-mail: pconnolly@vaildaily.com
Display Adv. E-mail: pconnolly@vaildaily.com
Classified Adv. e-mail: classifieds@cmnm.org
Editorial e-mail: estoner@vaildaily.com
Primary Website: www.vaildaily.com
Mthly Avg Views: 3302480
Mthly Avg Unique Visitors: 2209634
Year Established: 1981
News Services: AP.
Special Editions: Taste of Vail (Apr); Rocky Mtn. Wedding Guide (Feb); Best of the Vail Valley (Jan); Eagle County Rodeo Program (Jul); High Country Homestyle (Jun); Vail Valley Summertime (May); Vail Valley Holiday Guide (Nov).
Special Weekly Sections: Mountain Homes & Properties Real Estate (S); Religion (Sat); Education (Thur); The Marketplace (Tues); Food & Wine (Wed).
Areas Served - City/County or Portion Thereof, or Zip codes: Vail, Lionshead, Beaver Creek, Arrowhead, Ski Cooper & surrounding communities
Sat. Circulation Paid: 10525
Sun. Circulation Paid: 9332
Audit By: Sworn/Estimate/Non-Audited
Audit Date: 12.07.2019
Personnel: Edward Stoner (Mng. Ed.); Mark Bricklin (Mktg. Dir.); Scott Miller (Bus. Ed.); Chris Freud (Sports Ed.); Jim Hemig (Prod. Mgr., Press); Tommy Kubitsky (Prodn. Mgr., Pre Press); Sandy Sandberg (Nat'l Acct. Mgr.); Patrick Connolly (Adv. Dir.); Wren Wertin (Circ. Mgr.)
Parent company (for newspapers): Swift Communications, Inc.; Ogden Newspapers Inc.; Ogden Newspapers

COLORADO DAILY

Street address 1: 2500 55th St
Street address 2: Ste. 210
Street address city: Boulder
Street address state: CO
Zip/Postal code: 80301
County: Boulder
Country: USA
Mailing address: 2500 55TH ST STE 210
Mailing city: BOULDER
Mailing state: CO
Mailing zip: 80301-5740
General Phone: (303) 473-1414
Advertising Phone: (303) 473-1414
Editorial Phone: (303) 473-1414
General/National Adv. E-mail: johnsonk@dailycamera.com
Display Adv. E-mail: johnsonk@dailycamera.com
Classified Adv. e-mail: johnsonk@dailycamera.com
Editorial e-mail: johnsonk@dailycamera.com
Primary Website: www.coloradodaily.com
Year Established: 1892
News Services: CSM, MCT, UPI.
Special Editions: Menu Guide (Apr); Welcome Back Fall (Aug); Graduation (Dec); CU & Boulder's Best (Feb); Welcome Back Spring (Jan); Boulder Summer (Jun); Graduation (May); Boulder Winter (Oct); Stadium Stampede (6 editions in Oct & Nov) (Other).
Special Weekly Sections: Real Estate, Entertainment (Fri); Our Town (Mon); Visitors' Edition (Other); Food & Drink (Thur); The Arts (Tues); Body & Soul (Wed).
Areas Served - City/County or Portion Thereof, or Zip codes: Boulder (CO)
Own Printing Facility?: Y
Commercial printers?: Y
Audit By: Sworn/Estimate/Non-Audited
Audit Date: 12.07.2019
Personnel: Kathy Johnson (Nat'l Adv. Rep.)
Parent company (for newspapers): Digital First Media; MediaNews Group

DAILY CAMERA

Street address 1: 2500 55th St
Street address 2: Ste 210
Street address city: Boulder
Street address state: CO
Zip/Postal code: 80301-5740
County: Boulder
Country: USA
Mailing address: PO BOX 591
Mailing city: BOULDER
Mailing state: CO
Mailing zip: 80306-0591
General Phone: (303) 442-1202
Advertising Phone: (303) 473-1400
Editorial Phone: (303) 473-1365
General/National Adv. E-mail: jstravolemos@prairiemountainmedia.com
Display Adv. E-mail: stravolemosj@dailycamera.com
Classified Adv. e-mail: jill@dailycamera.com
Editorial e-mail: kaufmank@dailycamera.com
Primary Website: www.dailycamera.com
Mthly Avg Views: 4000000
Mthly Avg Unique Visitors: 1478939
Year Established: 1890
News Services: AP, LAT-WP, NYT, SHNS.
Special Editions: Summer Camping (Apr); Back-to-School (Aug); Holiday Guide (Dec); Wedding Guides (Feb); Home & Garden/HGTV Mag. (Jul); Wedding Guides (Jun); Home & Gardens/HGTV Mag. (Mar); Bolder Boulder Race Guide (May); School Choice Guide (Nov); Voter's Guide (Oct).

Special Weekly Sections: Monday, Business Plus, Wednesday, Essentials, Friday, Friday Magazine and At Home, Sunday, Life and Style
Syndicated Publications: Parade (S).
Delivery Methods: Newsstand`Carrier`Racks
Areas Served - City/County or Portion Thereof, or Zip codes: Primarily Boulder County
Own Printing Facility?: N
Commercial printers?: Y
Sat. Circulation Paid: 20668
Sun. Circulation Paid: 21703
Audit By: AAM
Audit Date: 30.09.2016
Personnel: Al Manzi (Pub.); Jill Stravolemos (Mgr., Mktg./Promo./New Media); Kevin Kaufman (Exec. Ed.); Matt Sebastian (City Ed.)
Parent company (for newspapers): Digital First Media; MediaNews Group

THE CANON CITY DAILY RECORD

Street address 1: 1202 Royal Gorge Blvd
Street address city: Canon City
Street address state: CO
Zip/Postal code: 81212-3836
County: Fremont
Country: USA
General Phone: (719) 275-7565
Advertising Phone: (719) 275-5300
Editorial Phone: (719) 275-7565
General/National Adv. E-mail: kwurzbach@prairiemountainmedia.com
Display Adv. E-mail: dcoseboonf@prairiemountainmedia.com
Editorial e-mail: malcala@prairiemountainmedia.com
Primary Website: www.canoncitydailyrecord.com
Mthly Avg Views: 500000
Mthly Avg Unique Visitors: 70000
Year Established: 1873
News Services: AP.
Special Editions: Community Report (Progress Edition) (Apr); Bridal Guide (Feb); Real Estate Preview (Semi-monthly);
Special Weekly Sections: American Profile (Weekly).
Syndicated Publications: Relish (Monthly); USA WEEKEND Magazine (Sat); American Profile (Weekly).
Delivery Methods: Mail`Newsstand`Carrier
Areas Served - City/County or Portion Thereof, or Zip codes: 81212
Own Printing Facility?: Y
Commercial printers?: Y
Sat. Circulation Paid: 2800
Audit By: Sworn/Estimate/Non-Audited
Audit Date: 12.07.2019
Personnel: Michael Alcala (Ed.); Karl Wurzbach (Pub./Gen. Mgr.)
Parent company (for newspapers): Media News Group; Digital First Media

THE GAZETTE

Street address 1: 30 E. Pikes Peak Avenue, Suite 100
Street address city: Colorado Springs
Street address state: CO
Zip/Postal code: 80903-1504
County: El Paso
Country: USA
Mailing address: 30 E PIKES PEAK AVE
Mailing city: COLORADO SPRINGS
Mailing state: CO
Mailing zip: 80903-1504
General Phone: (719) 632-5511
Advertising Phone: (719) 636-0306
Editorial Phone: (719) 636-0266
General/National Adv. E-mail: nicole.raphael@gazette.com
Display Adv. E-mail: erik.carlson@gazette.com
Classified Adv. e-mail: julie.bland@gazette.com
Editorial e-mail: opinion@gazette.com
Primary Website: www.gazette.com
Mthly Avg Views: 4700000
Mthly Avg Unique Visitors: 148206
Year Established: 1872
News Services: AP, MCT/LAT-WP
Special Editions: Best of the Springs (Apr); Summer Fun (May), Homebuyers Guide, Prep Peak Performers, Dining Guide (Jun.), Parade of Homes, Football Preview (Aug); FYI Magazine (Sep.), Winter Fun and Celebrate Magazine (Nov.)
Special Weekly Sections: Family (Mon.), Health+Wellness (Tue.),Food (Wed.); Out There (Thu.); Go!, SpringsWheels (Fri.), Home+Garden, Real Estate (Sat.); Life+Travel, Springs Military Life, Your Career, Real Estate (Sun.)
Syndicated Publications: Parade (Sun.) Dash (monthly)
Delivery Methods: Carrier`Racks
Areas Served - City/County or Portion Thereof, or Zip codes: El Paso, Pueblo, Fremont, Elbert, Teller, Douglas, Fremont counties.
Own Printing Facility?: N
Sat. Circulation Paid: 38523
Sun. Circulation Paid: 51093
Audit By: AAM
Audit Date: 30.09.2018
Personnel: Chris Reen (Pub.); Vince Bzdek (Ed.); Traci Conrad (Real Estate Mgr.); Craig Barbic (Automotive Mgr.); Jim Broyles (V. P. Sales); Karen Hogan (Director of Advertising Operations/Marketing/Events); Traci Conrad (Retail Advertising Sales Mgr.); Vicki Cederholm (Dir. of Op.); Jerry Herman (Online News Dir.)
Parent company (for newspapers): Clarity Media

CRAIG DAILY PRESS

Street address 1: 466 Yampa Ave
Street address city: Craig
Street address state: CO
Zip/Postal code: 81625-2610
County: Moffat
Country: USA
Mailing address: PO BOX 5
Mailing city: CRAIG
Mailing state: CO
Mailing zip: 81626-0014
General Phone: (970) 824-7031
Advertising Phone: (970) 824-7031
Editorial Phone: (970) 824-7031
General/National Adv. E-mail: kbalfour@craigdailypress.com
Display Adv. E-mail: kbalfour@craigdailypress.com
Classified Adv. e-mail: veverard@SteamboatToday.com
Editorial e-mail: lschlichtman@SteamboatToday.com
Primary Website: www.craigdailypress.com
Year Established: 1891
News Services: AP.
Special Weekly Sections: Saturday Northwest (Sat).
Syndicated Publications: American Profile (Weekly).
Areas Served - City/County or Portion Thereof, or Zip codes: Craig, Moffat & Rio Blanco Counties (CO)
Sat. Circulation Paid: 9600
Audit By: Sworn/Estimate/Non-Audited
Audit Date: 12.07.2019
Personnel: Renee Campbell (Pub.); Amy Fontenot (Circ. Mgr.); Day Kelsey (Designer); Thomas Martinez (Ed.)
Parent company (for newspapers): Swift Communications, Inc.; Ogden Newspapers Inc.

THE DENVER POST

Street address 1: 101 West Colfax Avenue
Street address city: Denver
Street address state: CO
Zip/Postal code: 80202
County: Denver
Country: USA
Mailing address: 101 W COLFAX AVE
Mailing city: DENVER
Mailing state: CO
Mailing zip: 80202-5315
General Phone: (303) 954-1010
Advertising Phone: (303) 892-2525 (class.)
Editorial Phone: (303) 954-1201
General/National Adv. E-mail: jkittelson@denverpost.com
Display Adv. E-mail: jkittelson@denverpost.com
Classified Adv. e-mail: questions-comments@denverpost.com
Editorial e-mail: newsroom@denverpost.com
Primary Website: www.denverpost.com
Mthly Avg Views: 37825321
Mthly Avg Unique Visitors: 7167139
Year Established: 1892
News Services: AP, NYT, LAT-WP, Bloomberg, McClatchy.
Special Editions: The Deal Going Green National Western Stock Show Home Show Parade of Homes Komen Race for the Cure Denver Auto Show Ski Expo
Syndicated Publications: Parade (S) Color Comics (S) TV (S) USA Weekend (S)
Delivery Methods: Newsstand`Carrier
Areas Served - City/County or Portion Thereof, or Zip codes: Entire Colorado region
Own Printing Facility?: N
Commercial printers?: Y
Sat. Circulation Paid: 149828
Sun. Circulation Paid: 264422
Audit By: AAM
Audit Date: 31.03.2018
Personnel: Lee Ann Colacioppo (Ed.); Vicki Makings (Editorial Librarian); Kevin Dale (News Director); Linda Shapley (Dir., News Ops); J. Damon Cain (ME, Presentation); Tim Rasmussen (AME-Photography); Scott Monserud (Asst. Managing Ed. Sports); Larry Ryckman (Senior Ed. News); Dana Plewka; Geri Meireis; Jerry Grilly; William Reynolds (Sr. VP. of Circ.); Mac Tully (Pub. Chief Exec. Officer); Michael Henry (Senior VP of Finance and Chief Financial Officer); Christine Moser (VP of Adv.); Bill Reynolds (Senior VP Pres, Cir.); Missy Miller (Senior VP Pres., HR, Labor Relations); Bob Kinney (VP, Info. Tech. & Pre-Pub.); Reid Wicoff (VP Pres. of Dig. Sales); Megan Lyden (Senior Ed. for Photography & Multimedia); Jim Bates (Night Ed.); Megan Schrader (Ed. Pg. Ed.)
Parent company (for newspapers): Digital First Media; MediaNews Group

DURANGO HERALD

Street address 1: 1275 Main Ave
Street address city: Durango
Street address state: CO
Zip/Postal code: 81301-5137
County: La Plata
Country: USA
Mailing address: 1275 MAIN AVE
Mailing city: DURANGO
Mailing state: CO
Mailing zip: 81301-5137
General Phone: (970) 247-3504
Advertising Phone: (970) 247-3504
Editorial Phone: (970) 247-3504
General/National Adv. E-mail: sales@durangoherald.com
Display Adv. E-mail: sales@durangoherald.com
Classified Adv. e-mail: sales@durangoherald.com
Editorial e-mail: dlindley@durangoherald.com
Primary Website: www.durangoherald.com
Year Established: 1881
News Services: AP, NYT, CNS.
Special Editions: Southwest Summer (Apr); Focus on Business (Feb); County Fair (Jul); Newcomers (Jun); Christmas Gift Guide (Nov); Southwest Winter (Oct).
Special Weekly Sections: Religion (Fri); Arts & Entertainment (Mon); Business (S); Arts & Entertainment (Thur); TV (Tues); Education (Wed).
Syndicated Publications: USA WEEKEND Magazine (Sat); Cross Currents (Semi-monthly).
Areas Served - City/County or Portion Thereof, or Zip codes: Southwest Colorado
Avg Free Circ: 336
Sat. Circulation Paid: 6198
Sat. Circulation Free: 336
Sun. Circulation Paid: 6891
Sun. Circulation Free: 111
Audit By: AAM
Audit Date: 30.09.2015
Personnel: Richard G. Ballantine (Pub.); Sharon Hermes (Mktg/Promos); Mark Drudge (Dir., Adv./Mktg.); John Ellis (Circ. Mgr.); David Tabar (IT Mgr.)
Parent company (for newspapers): Ballantine Communications

THE COLORADOAN

Street address 1: 1300 Riverside Ave
Street address city: Fort Collins
Street address state: CO
Zip/Postal code: 80524-4353
County: Larimer
Country: USA
Mailing address: 1300 RIVERSIDE AVE
Mailing city: FORT COLLINS
Mailing state: CO
Mailing zip: 80524-4353
General Phone: (970) 493-6397
Editorial Phone: (970) 224-7730
General/National Adv. E-mail: tylerkidd@coloradoan.com
Display Adv. E-mail: tylerkidd@coloradoan.com
Classified Adv. e-mail: classifieds@colroadoan.com
Editorial e-mail: lgustus@reno.gannett.com
Primary Website: www.coloradoan.com
Year Established: 1873
News Services: AP, GNS, LAT-WP.
Special Weekly Sections: Xplore; Ticket; Real Estate Guide; TV Week
Syndicated Publications: Mind & Body, FYI, NOCO Health Directory
Delivery Methods: Mail`Newsstand`Carrier`Racks
Areas Served - City/County or Portion Thereof, or Zip codes: 80512, 80521, 80523, 80524, 80525, 80526, 80528, 80534, 80535, 80536, 80537, 80538, 80539, 80545, 80546, 80547, 80549, 80550, 80610, 80615, 80631, 80634
Own Printing Facility?: Y
Commercial printers?: N
Avg Free Circ: 277
Sat. Circulation Paid: 16557
Sat. Circulation Free: 277
Sun. Circulation Paid: 20516
Sun. Circulation Free: 263
Audit By: AAM
Audit Date: 30.09.2018
Personnel: Kathy Jack-Romero (Pres./Pub.); Josh Awtry (Exec. Ed.); Jared Bartels (Finance Dir., Controller); Rebecca Powell (Sr. Ed. for Platforms); Joseph Harmon (Digital Sales Mgr.)
Parent company (for newspapers): Gannett

SUMMIT DAILY NEWS

Street address 1: 331 W Main St
Street address city: Frisco
Street address state: CO
Zip/Postal code: 80443
County: Summit
Country: USA
Mailing address: PO BOX 329
Mailing city: FRISCO
Mailing state: CO
Mailing zip: 80443-0329
General Phone: (970) 668-3998
Advertising Phone: (970) 668-3998
Editorial Phone: (970) 668-3998
General/National Adv. E-mail: jwoodside@summitdaily.com
Display Adv. E-mail: mbutler@summitdaily.com
Classified Adv. e-mail: classifieds@cmnm.org
Editorial e-mail: news@summitdaily.com
Primary Website: www.summitdaily.com
Mthly Avg Views: 2826984
Mthly Avg Unique Visitors: 1388572
Year Established: 1989
News Services: AP.
Special Weekly Sections: Summit Scene (Fri); Summit Homes & Properties (Sat).
Areas Served - City/County or Portion Thereof, or Zip codes: Summit County & the Rocky Mountain Region (CO)
Avg Free Circ: 9600
Sat. Circulation Free: 10500
Sun. Circulation Free: 10000
Audit By: Sworn/Estimate/Non-Audited
Audit Date: 12.07.2019
Personnel: Matt Sandberg (Publisher); Ben Trollinger (Mng. Ed.); Shawn Butler (Circ. Dir.)
Parent company (for newspapers): Swift Communications, Inc.; Ogden Newspapers Inc.; Ogden Newspapers

GLENWOOD SPRINGS POST INDEPENDENT

Street address 1: 824 Grand Ave
Street address city: Glenwood Springs
Street address state: CO
Zip/Postal code: 81601-3557
County: Garfield
Country: USA
Mailing address: 824 GRAND AVE STE B
Mailing city: GLENWOOD SPRINGS
Mailing state: CO
Mailing zip: 81601-3557
General Phone: (970) 945-8515
Advertising Phone: (970) 945-8515
Editorial Phone: (970) 945-8515
General/National Adv. E-mail: glenwoodads@cmnm.org
Display Adv. E-mail: glenwoodads@cmnm.org
Classified Adv. e-mail: classifieds@cmnm.org
Editorial e-mail: ressex@postindependent.com
Primary Website: www.postindependent.com
Mthly Avg Views: 870000
Mthly Avg Unique Visitors: 150000
Year Established: 1889
News Services: AP.

Special Editions: Bicycling (March); Summer Recreation Guide (May); Locals' Choice (May); Hunting (Aug); Adventures in Aging (Oct.); Holiday Kick-off (Thanksgiving)
Special Weekly Sections: Church (Sat); Business (Mon); Go! (outdoors/entertainment, Fridays starting in April 2017)
Delivery Methods: Newsstand`Racks
Areas Served - City/County or Portion Thereof, or Zip codes: Glenwood Springs & Garfield County
Avg Free Circ: 9500
Sat. Circulation Free: 9000
Sun. Circulation Free: 9000
Audit By: Sworn/Estimate/Non-Audited
Audit Date: 12.07.2019
Personnel: Randy Essex (Publisher and Editor); Brad Howard (Advertising Director); Will Grandbois (Outdoors and entertainment editor); John Stroud (Reporter); Ryan Summerlin (Reporter); Amanda Cerveny (Advertising sales); Becky Levin (Advertising sales); Casey Weaver (Advertising sales); Chelsea Self (Visual journalist); Ariella Gintzler; Josh Carney (Sports editor)
Parent company (for newspapers): Swift Communications, Inc.; Ogden Newspapers Inc.; Ogden Newspapers

THE DAILY SENTINEL

Street address 1: 734 S 7th St
Street address city: Grand Junction
Street address state: CO
Zip/Postal code: 81501-7737
County: Mesa
Country: USA
Mailing address: PO BOX 668
Mailing city: GRAND JUNCTION
Mailing state: CO
Mailing zip: 81502-0668
General Phone: (970) 242-5050
Advertising Phone: (970) 242-5050
Editorial Phone: (970) 242-5050
General/National Adv. E-mail: robin.gavegan@gjsentinel.com
Display Adv. E-mail: robin.gavegan@gjsentinel.com
Classified Adv. e-mail: classified@gjsentinel.com
Primary Website: www.gjsentinel.com
Year Established: 1893
News Services: AP, NYT (Pony).
Special Editions: Food and Fitness (Apr); Grand Valley Values (Aug); Late Shopper's Guide (Dec); Grand Valley Values (Feb); Coupon Book (Jan); Home Improvement Directory (Jul); Grand Valley Values (Jun); Baseball (Mar); Coupon Book (May); Coupon Book (Nov); Grand Valley Va
Special Weekly Sections: Health & Wellness (Tue); Best Food Day, TMC (Wed); Outdoors (Fri); Home, Garden, Religion (Sat); Business, Real Estate, Employment (Sun)
Syndicated Publications: Parade (S). Dash
Delivery Methods: Mail`Newsstand`Carrier`Racks
Own Printing Facility?: Y
Commercial printers?: Y
Avg Free Circ: 3012
Sat. Circulation Paid: 17647
Sat. Circulation Free: 863
Sun. Circulation Paid: 20358
Sun. Circulation Free: 771
Audit By: AAM
Audit Date: 30.09.2018
Personnel: Jay Seaton (Pub.); Bud Winslow (Dir. of Op.); Sandra Rogers (HR); Bob Visotcky (Market Manager & CRO); Sam Black (CFO); Tracy Gibson (Circ. & Classified Dir.); Dale Shrull (Editorial/Managing Ed.)
Parent company (for newspapers): Seaton Publishing Company, Inc.

GREELEY DAILY TRIBUNE

Street address 1: 501 8th Ave
Street address city: Greeley
Street address state: CO
Zip/Postal code: 80631-3913
County: Weld
Country: USA
Mailing address: PO BOX 1690
Mailing city: GREELEY
Mailing state: CO
Mailing zip: 80632-1690
General Phone: (970) 352-0211
Advertising Phone: (970) 352-0211
Editorial Phone: (970) 352-0211
General/National Adv. E-mail: advertising@greeleytribune.com
Display Adv. E-mail: advertising@greeleytribune.com
Classified Adv. e-mail: classifieds@greeleytribune.com
Editorial e-mail: editorial@greeleytribune.com
Primary Website: www.greeleytribune.com
Year Established: 1870
News Services: LAT-WP, AP.
Special Editions: Stampede (Jul); Homes On Parade (May); Holiday Magazine (Nov); Click (Oct); Homes On Parade (Sept); #greality (monthly); MyWindsor (monthly);
Special Weekly Sections: Preview TV/Entertainment (Fri); People/Senior (S); Education (Sat); Outdoors (Thur); Family/Health (Wed).
Syndicated Publications: USA WEEKEND Magazine (S).
Areas Served - City/County or Portion Thereof, or Zip codes: Northern Colorado
Avg Free Circ: 1887
Sat. Circulation Paid: 11799
Sat. Circulation Free: 1887
Sun. Circulation Paid: 14446
Sun. Circulation Free: 1492
Audit By: CAC
Audit Date: 31.12.2018
Personnel: Bart Smith (Pub.); Joe Luethmers (Circ. Dir.); Randy Bangert (Ed.); Kelly Tracer (Mng. Ed.); Mike Peters (Action Line Ed.); Sharon Dunn (City Ed.); Donovan Henderson (Entertainment Ed.); Bill Jackson (Farm/Agriculture Ed.); Nate Miller (Sports Ed.); Jeff Kelly (Mgmt. Info Servs. Mgr.); Ron Heil (Prodn. Mgr., Mailroom); Robert Rodd (Prodn. Foreman, Pressroom); Dustin Bell (Prodn. Mgr., Pre Press); Kayla Cornett (Sports Rep.); Bryce Jacobson (Pub.)
Parent company (for newspapers): Media News Group; Swift Communications, Inc.

LA JUNTA TRIBUNE-DEMOCRAT

Street address 1: 422 Colorado Ave
Street address city: La Junta
Street address state: CO
Zip/Postal code: 81050-2336
County: Otero
Country: USA
Mailing address: PO BOX 500
Mailing city: LA JUNTA
Mailing state: CO
Mailing zip: 81050-0500
General Phone: (719) 384-1437
Advertising Phone: (719) 384-1437
Editorial Phone: (719) 384-1437
General/National Adv. E-mail: agsales@ljtdmail.com
Display Adv. E-mail: tara@ljtdmail.com
Classified Adv. e-mail: classifieds@ljtdmail.com
Editorial e-mail: publisher@ljtdmail.com
Primary Website: www.lajuntatribunedemocrat.com
News Services: AP.
Special Editions: Spring Fashion (Apr); Kids Rodeo (Aug); Progress (Jan); Christmas Shopping (Nov).
Special Weekly Sections: Agriculture (Fri); Best Food Day (Tues); Best Food Day (Wed).
Syndicated Publications: This Week in La Junta (Sat).
Areas Served - City/County or Portion Thereof, or Zip codes: La Junta (CO)
Audit By: Sworn/Estimate/Non-Audited
Audit Date: 12.07.2019
Personnel: Candi Hill (Ed.); Rita Ojeda (Class. Adv.); Jennifer Justice (Asst. Ed.); Jason Gallegos (Adv. Dir.)
Parent company (for newspapers): Gannett; CherryRoad Media; CherryRoad Media

LONGMONT TIMES-CALL

Street address 1: 1860 Industrial Cir
Street address city: Longmont
Street address state: CO
Zip/Postal code: 80501-6559
County: Boulder
Country: USA
Mailing address: PO BOX 299
Mailing city: LONGMONT
Mailing state: CO
Mailing zip: 80502-0299
General Phone: (303) 776-2244
Advertising Phone: (303) 776-2244
Editorial Phone: (303) 776-2244
General/National Adv. E-mail: labozanc@dailycamera.com
Display Adv. E-mail: labozanc@dailycamera.com
Classified Adv. e-mail: lambertk@dailycamera.com
Editorial e-mail: jvahlenkamp@times-call.com
Primary Website: www.timescall.com
Year Established: 1871
News Services: AP, U.S. Suburban Press Inc., The Newspaper Network (TNN).
Special Editions: Inside & Out (Apr); Longmont Magazine (Aug); Holiday Gifts (Dec); Bridal (Feb); Health Magazine (Jan); Fair & Rodeo (Jul); Health Directory (Jun); Progress (Mar); Graduation (May); Coupon Book (Monthly); Longmont Magazine (Nov); A Taste of Home (Oct); Boo
Special Weekly Sections: Best Food Day, Education (Wed); Religion, Health, Entertainment (Fri); Home, Design, Religion, Outdoor, Real Estate (Sat); Business, Travel (Sun)
Syndicated Publications: Relish (Monthly); USA WEEKEND Magazine (S); American Profile (Sat).
Areas Served - City/County or Portion Thereof, or Zip codes: Northern Colorado
Sat. Circulation Paid: 20800
Sun. Circulation Paid: 34029
Audit By: AAM
Audit Date: 30.09.2014
Personnel: Christine Labozan (Adv. Dir.); Cindy Piller (NIE Coord.); Maurice Elhart (Circ. Dir., Cor.); John Vahlenkamp (Mng. Ed.); Tony Kindelspire (Bus. Ed.); Quentin Young (Day Ed.); Richard Hackett (Chief Photographer); Travis Pryor; Albert Manzi (Pub.); Kathy Johnson (Major/Nat'l Acct. Rep.); Lori Cooper (Prod. Services Mgr.)
Parent company (for newspapers): Digital First Media; MediaNews Group

LOVELAND REPORTER-HERALD

Street address 1: 201 E 5th St
Street address city: Loveland
Street address state: CO
Zip/Postal code: 80537-5605
County: Larimer
Country: USA
Mailing address: PO BOX 59
Mailing city: LOVELAND
Mailing state: CO
Mailing zip: 80539-0059
General Phone: (970) 669-5050
Advertising Phone: (970) 635-3650
Editorial Phone: (970) 669-5050
General/National Adv. E-mail: advertising@reporter-herald.com
Display Adv. E-mail: advertising@reporter-herald.com
Classified Adv. e-mail: advertising@reporter-herald.com
Editorial e-mail: news@reporter-herald.com
Primary Website: www.reporterherald.com
Year Established: 1880
News Services: AP, LAT-WP, TMS.
Special Editions: Vacation Guide (Apr); Corn Roast (Aug); Community photo calendar (Dec); Making a Difference (Feb); Wedding (Jan); Loveland Snapshot (Jul); Tour of New Homes (Jun); Home and Garden How-To (Mar); Women in Business (May); Coupon Book (Monthly); Holiday Open
Special Weekly Sections: Food (Wed); Kids, Outdoors (Thur); Entertainment (Fri); Agriculture, Consumer, Home, Real Estate, Business (Sat); TV, Commentary, Stock, Travel (Sun)
Syndicated Publications: Health Line (Monthly); USA WEEKEND Magazine (S); American Profile (Sat).
Delivery Methods: Carrier`Racks
Areas Served - City/County or Portion Thereof, or Zip codes: 80537, 80513, 80534
Avg Free Circ: 3084
Sat. Circulation Paid: 10051
Sat. Circulation Free: 3084
Sun. Circulation Paid: 11240
Sun. Circulation Free: 5454
Audit By: AAM
Audit Date: 30.09.2016
Personnel: Edward Lehman (Pub.); Linda Story (Adv. Dir.); Marge Reiber (HR Coord.); Linda Larsen (Mgr., Mktg./Promo.); John Ellis (Circ. Mgr.); Jeff Stahla (Mng. Ed.); Kenneth J Amundson (Gen. Mgr./Ed.); Dean G. Lehman (Pres.); Linda Mitchell (Librarian); Mike Brohard (Sports Ed.); Bill Schmich (Online Mgr.); Dennis Book (Prodn. Creative Servs. Mgr.)
Parent company (for newspapers): Digital First Media; MediaNews Group

THE MONTROSE DAILY PRESS

Street address 1: 3684 N Townsend Ave
Street address city: Montrose
Street address state: CO
Zip/Postal code: 81401-5949
County: Montrose
Country: USA
General Phone: (970) 249-3444
Advertising Phone: (970) 249-3444
Editorial Phone: (970) 249-3444
General/National Adv. E-mail: ads@montrosepress.com
Display Adv. E-mail: ads@montrosepress.com
Classified Adv. e-mail: classified@montrosepress.com
Editorial e-mail: editor@montrosepress.com
Primary Website: www.montrosepress.com
Year Established: 1882
News Services: AP.
Special Editions: January Sun Year in review Sun Lifestyles February Thur Home, Garden, Business Expo Sat Answer Book March Sat Spring Sports Preview Sat Home & Garden w/Earth Day April Sun Destination Montrose Sun Lifestyles May Sat Graduation Tab Thur. Montrose County Fair Book June Outlook editions Tues Agriculture Wed Community Thurs Non-profits Fri Health Sat Industry Sun Photo Expo July Thur M. County Fair and Rodeo Sun Lifestyles August Thur Olathe Sweet Corn Sat Back to School Thur Fall Sports Preview September Sat Best of the Valley October Sat Energy Guide Sun Destination Montrose Sun Lifestyle November Thur Veterans Tab Sat Winter Sports Tab Sun Holiday Gift guide
Special Weekly Sections: Best Food Day (Wed); Scene, Entertainment, TV (Fri); Focus (Sun)
Delivery Methods: Newsstand`Carrier`Racks
Areas Served - City/County or Portion Thereof, or Zip codes: 81401, 81402, 81403, 81425, 81432
Own Printing Facility?: Y
Commercial printers?: Y
Sat. Circulation Paid: 4116
Sun. Circulation Paid: 4778
Audit By: Sworn/Estimate/Non-Audited
Audit Date: 12.07.2019
Personnel: Dennis Anderson (Adv. Dir.); Tisha McCombs (Circ. Dir.); Katharhynn Heidelberg (Senior writer); Denny Haulman (Prodn. Mgr., Mailroom); Francis Wick (Pub.); Monica Garcia (News editor); Andrew Kiser (Staff writer); Tonya Maddox (Publisher); Justin Tubbs (Managing editor)
Parent company (for newspapers): Wick Communications

THE PUEBLO CHIEFTAIN

Street address 1: 825 W. 6th Street
Street address city: Pueblo
Street address state: CO
Zip/Postal code: 81003-0036
County: Pueblo
Country: USA
Mailing address: PO BOX 36
Mailing city: PUEBLO
Mailing state: CO
Mailing zip: 81002-0036
General Phone: (719) 544-3520
Advertising Phone: (719) 544-3520
Editorial Phone: (719) 544-3520
General/National Adv. E-mail: msweeney@chieftain.com
Display Adv. E-mail: msweeney@chieftain.com
Classified Adv. e-mail: classads@chieftain.com
Editorial e-mail: city@chieftain.com
Primary Website: www.chieftain.com
Year Established: 1868
News Services: AP, MCT, TMS.
Special Editions: Colorado State Fair (Aug); Holiday Greetings (Dec); Graduation (Jun); Spring Home & Garden (Mar); Classroom Chieftain (May); Active Years, 50 & Above (Monthly); Winterfest (Nov); Generation X-tra (Quarterly); Fall Home Improvement (Sept).
Special Weekly Sections: Real Estate (Fri); Real Estate (S); Best Food Day (Wed).
Syndicated Publications: Relish (Monthly); Parade (S); TV Magazine (Sat).
Delivery Methods: Mail`Newsstand`Carrier`Racks
Areas Served - City/County or Portion Thereof, or Zip codes: Southern Colorado
Own Printing Facility?: Y
Commercial printers?: Y
Avg Free Circ: 1873
Sat. Circulation Paid: 23351
Sat. Circulation Free: 1873
Sun. Circulation Paid: 26205
Sun. Circulation Free: 792
Audit By: AAM
Audit Date: 30.09.2018
Personnel: Lee Bachlet (Pub.); Blake Fontenay (Editorial Page Ed.); Dennis Darrow (Bus. Ed.); Matt Forsyth

(Adv. Dir.); Monica Sweeney (Adv. Prod. Mgr.); Steve Henson (Ed.); Julie Fairman (Weekend Ed.); Jeff Letofsky (Preps Ed.); Karen Vigil (Night City Ed.); Amanda Bengston (Controller)
Parent company (for newspapers): Gannett; CherryRoad Media

ROCKY FORD DAILY GAZETTE

Street address 1: 912 Elm Ave
Street address city: Rocky Ford
Street address state: CO
Zip/Postal code: 81067-1249
County: Otero
Country: USA
Mailing address: PO BOX 430
Mailing city: ROCKY FORD
Mailing state: CO
Mailing zip: 81067-0430
General Phone: (719) 254-3351
Advertising Phone: (719) 254-3351
Editorial Phone: (719) 254-3351
General/National Adv. E-mail: sales@rockyforddailygazette.com
Display Adv. E-mail: sales@rockyforddailygazette.com
Classified Adv. e-mail: sales@rockyforddailygazette.com
Editorial e-mail: news@rockyforddailygazette.com
Primary Website: Doesn't have a website
Year Established: 1887
Special Weekly Sections: Best Food Days (Tue/Wed)
Syndicated Publications: Television (Fri).
Areas Served - City/County or Portion Thereof, or Zip codes: Otero & Crowley Counties (CO)
Audit By: Sworn/Estimate/Non-Audited
Audit Date: 12.07.2019
Personnel: J.R. Thompson (Pub./Ed./Bus. Mgr.); Laura Thompson (Adv. Mgr.); Jessica Tofoya (Circ. Dir.)
Parent company (for newspapers): Rocky Ford Publishing Company Inc.

THE MOUNTAIN MAIL

Street address 1: 125 E 2nd St
Street address city: Salida
Street address state: CO
Zip/Postal code: 81201-2114
County: Chaffee
Country: USA
Mailing address: PO BOX 189
Mailing city: SALIDA
Mailing state: CO
Mailing zip: 81201-0189
General Phone: (719) 539-6691
Advertising Phone: (719) 539-6691
Editorial Phone: (719) 539-6691
General/National Adv. E-mail: vickiesue@avpsalida.com
Display Adv. E-mail: vickiesue@avpsalida.com
Classified Adv. e-mail: classifieds@themountainmail.com
Editorial e-mail: pgoetz@themountainmail.com
Primary Website: www.themountainmail.com
Year Established: 1880
News Services: Papert (Landon).
Delivery Methods: Mail`Carrier`Racks
Areas Served - City/County or Portion Thereof, or Zip codes: Salida & Upper Arkansas Valley
Own Printing Facility?: Y
Commercial printers?: Y
Audit By: Sworn/Estimate/Non-Audited
Audit Date: 12.07.2019
Personnel: Merle Baranczyk (Pub.); Vicki Vigil (Adv. Mgr.); Sandra Christensen (Circ. Mgr.); Paul Goetz (Mng. Ed.); Joerge Hasselbrink (Online Mgr.); Holly Russell (Online Contact); Morris Christensen (Prodn. Mgr.); Shelley Mayer (Copy Ed.)
Parent company (for newspapers): Baranczyk Family

STEAMBOAT TODAY

Street address 1: 1901 Curve Plz
Street address city: Steamboat Springs
Street address state: CO
Zip/Postal code: 80487-4912
County: Routt
Country: USA
Mailing address: PO BOX 774827
Mailing city: STEAMBOAT SPRINGS
Mailing state: CO
Mailing zip: 80477-4827
General Phone: (970) 879-1502
Advertising Phone: (970) 879-1502
Editorial Phone: (970) 879-1502
General/National Adv. E-mail: advertising@steamboatToday.com
Display Adv. E-mail: advertising@SteamboatToday.com
Classified Adv. e-mail: qkaufhold@SteamboatToday.com
Editorial e-mail: news@SteamboatToday.com
Primary Website: www.steamboattoday.com
Year Established: 1884
News Services: AP.
Special Weekly Sections: 4 Points (Fri).
Syndicated Publications: At Home in Steamboat Springs Colorado Hunter Explore Steamboat
Delivery Methods: Racks
Areas Served - City/County or Portion Thereof, or Zip codes: 80477-80488
Own Printing Facility?: Y
Commercial printers?: Y
Avg Free Circ: 10500
Sat. Circulation Paid: 8563
Sat. Circulation Free: 9000
Sun. Circulation Paid: 5600
Audit By: Sworn/Estimate/Non-Audited
Audit Date: 12.07.2019
Personnel: Suzanne Schlicht (Pub.); Steve Balgenorth (Circ. Dir.); Scott Stanford (General Manager); Lisa Schlichtman (Ed.); Tyler Jacobs (Online Devel. Mgr.); Laura Tamucci (Adv. Dir.)
Parent company (for newspapers): Swift Communications, Inc.; Ogden Newspapers Inc.

JOURNAL-ADVOCATE

Street address 1: 504 N 3rd St
Street address city: Sterling
Street address state: CO
Zip/Postal code: 80751-3203
County: Logan
Country: USA
Mailing address: PO BOX 1272
Mailing city: STERLING
Mailing state: CO
Mailing zip: 80751-1272
General Phone: (970) 522-1990
Advertising Phone: (970) 526-9299
Editorial Phone: (970) 526-9310
General/National Adv. E-mail: dmcclain@journal-advocate.com
Display Adv. E-mail: ecpcadvertising@dailycamera.com
Editorial e-mail: swaite@journal-advocate.com
Primary Website: www.journal-advocate.com
Special Weekly Sections: Lifestyles (Mon); Business, Food (Tue); Agriculture (Thur); Religion (Fri)
Areas Served - City/County or Portion Thereof, or Zip codes: 80751
Own Printing Facility?: Y
Commercial printers?: Y
Avg Free Circ: 14500
Audit By: Sworn/Estimate/Non-Audited
Audit Date: 12.07.2019
Personnel: Julie Tonsing (Pub.); Sara Waite (Mng. Ed.); Duane Miles (Pre-press Mgr.); Michael Foster (Prodn. Dir.); Krista Kasten (Circ.)
Parent company (for newspapers): Digital First Media; MediaNews Group

THE FORT MORGAN TIMES

Street address 1: P.O. Box 495
Street address city: Sterling
Street address state: CO
Zip/Postal code: 80751
County: Morgan
Country: USA
Mailing address: P.O. Box 495
Mailing city: Sterling
Mailing state: CO
Mailing zip: 80751
General Phone: (970) 867-5651
Advertising Phone: (970) 867-5651
Editorial Phone: (970) 867-5651
General/National Adv. E-mail: bporter@prairiemountainmendia.com
Display Adv. E-mail: bporter@prairiemountainmendia.com
Classified Adv. e-mail: classifieds@prairiemountainmedia.com
Editorial e-mail: swaite@prairiemountainmedia.com
Primary Website: www.fortmorgantimes.com
Year Established: 1884
Special Editions: Senior Living (Apr); Back to School (Aug); Christmas Greetings/Letters to Santa (Dec); Income Tax Preparation Guide (Feb); Soil Conservation District Annual Meeting (Jan); Morgan County Fair (Jul); July 4th/Rodeo (Jun); Progress (Mar); Graduation (May); C
Special Weekly Sections: TV Schedule (Sat).
Syndicated Publications: American Profile (Weekly).
Areas Served - City/County or Portion Thereof, or Zip codes: Fort Morgan & Morgan County
Avg Free Circ: 3800
Sat. Circulation Paid: 3186
Audit By: Sworn/Estimate/Non-Audited
Audit Date: 01.10.2022
Personnel: Sherrie Hunter (Circ. Mgr.); Brian Porter (Publisher); Andrew Ohlson (Adv. Rep.); Sara Waite (Editor); Geoff Baumgartner (Ed.); Jenni Grubbs (Rep.); Kara Morgan (Rep.); Paul Dineen (Sports Ed.); Teresa Roberts (Adv. Rep.)
Parent company (for newspapers): Digital First Media; MediaNews Group

TELLURIDE DAILY PLANET; THE WATCH; THE NORWOOD POST

Street address 1: 307 E Colorado Ave
Street address city: Telluride
Street address state: CO
Zip/Postal code: 81435
County: San Miguel
Country: USA
Mailing address: PO BOX 2315
Mailing city: TELLURIDE
Mailing state: CO
Mailing zip: 81435-2315
General Phone: (970) 728-9788
Advertising Phone: (970) 728-9788
Editorial Phone: (970) 728-9788
General/National Adv. E-mail: maureen@telluridedailyplanet.com
Classified Adv. e-mail: classifieds@telluridenews.com
Editorial e-mail: editor@tellurideplanet.com
Primary Website: www.telluridenews.com
Year Established: 1898
Special Editions: Publishers of Telluride Style, Adventure Guide and Shelter magazines in the summer and winter.
Delivery Methods: Mail`Newsstand`Racks
Areas Served - City/County or Portion Thereof, or Zip codes: San Miguel, Ouray and Montrose Counties
Audit By: Sworn/Estimate/Non-Audited
Audit Date: 12.07.2019
Personnel: Andrew Mirrington (Pub.); Dusty Atherton (Assoc. Pub.); Maureen Pelisson (Adv. Mgr.); Shelly Kennett
Parent company (for newspapers): Telluride Newspapers; Thirteenth Street Media

THE CHRONICLE-NEWS

Street address 1: 200 Church St
Street address city: Trinidad
Street address state: CO
Zip/Postal code: 81082-2603
County: Las Animas
Country: USA
Mailing address: PO BOX 763
Mailing city: TRINIDAD
Mailing state: CO
Mailing zip: 81082-0763
General Phone: (719) 846-3311
Advertising Phone: (719) 846-3311
Editorial Phone: (719) 846-3311
General/National Adv. E-mail: news@trinidadchroniclenews.com
Display Adv. E-mail: tparker@trinidadchroniclenews.com
Classified Adv. e-mail: tparker@trinidadchroniclenews.com
Editorial e-mail: mhiesiger@trinidadchroniclenews.com
Primary Website: www.thechronicle-news.com
Year Established: 1877
News Services: AP.
Special Editions: Rodeo (Other).
Special Weekly Sections: TV Entertainment (Thur).
Syndicated Publications: Parade (Weekly).
Areas Served - City/County or Portion Thereof, or Zip codes: Southeastern Colorady & Northeastern New Mexico
Audit By: Sworn/Estimate/Non-Audited
Audit Date: 12.07.2019
Personnel: Aileen Hood (Pub.); Sheila Hamlan (Prodn. Mgr.); Eric John Monson (Editor); Allyson Sheumaker (Gen. Mgr.); Bruce Leonard (Ed.); Adam Sperandio (Ad.)
Parent company (for newspapers): Chronicle-News Media Group

CONNECTICUT

CONNECTICUT POST

Street address 1: 410 State St
Street address city: Bridgeport
Street address state: CT
Zip/Postal code: 06604-4501
County: Fairfield
Country: USA
Mailing address: 410 STATE ST
Mailing city: BRIDGEPORT
Mailing state: CT
Mailing zip: 06604-4560
General Phone: (203) 333-0161
Advertising Phone: (203) 330-6409
Editorial Phone: (203) 330-6233
General/National Adv. E-mail: ehuron@hearstmediact.com
Display Adv. E-mail: gdoucette@hearstmediact.com
Classified Adv. e-mail: classifieds@ctpost.com
Editorial e-mail: editorials@ctpost.com
Primary Website: www.ctpost.com
Mthly Avg Views: 22000000
Mthly Avg Unique Visitors: 885891
Year Established: 1883
News Services: AP, MCT, LAT-WP, CNS, NYT, SHNS, TMS.
Special Editions: Summer Education (Apr); Higher Education (Aug); Holiday Gift Guide 2 (Dec); Bact to School/College (Fall); President's Day Auto (Feb); Education (Jan); Retirement Options (Jul); Trumbull Day (Jun); New York Auto Show (Mar); Stratford Day (May); Christmas
Special Weekly Sections: Auto/Truck (Fri); Seniors (Mon); Arts/Theater (S); Religion (Sat); Preview (Thur).
Syndicated Publications: Preview/Entertainment Guide (Fri); Relish (Monthly); USA WEEKEND Magazine (S); Parade (Weekly).
Areas Served - City/County or Portion Thereof, or Zip codes: Greater Fairfield County
Sat. Circulation Paid: 21778
Sun. Circulation Paid: 33947
Audit By: AAM
Audit Date: 30.09.2017
Personnel: John Alcott (Mng. Ed.); Ralph Hohman (Assistant Mng. Ed.); Jim Shay (Digital News Ed.); Pat Quinn (Arts & Entertainment Ed.); Hugh Bailey (Editorial Page Ed.); Lee Steele (Features Ed.)
Parent company (for newspapers): Hearst Communications, Inc.

THE BRISTOL PRESS

Street address 1: 188 Main St
Street address city: Bristol
Street address state: CT
Zip/Postal code: 06010-6308
County: Hartford
Country: USA
Mailing address: 188 MAIN ST
Mailing city: BRISTOL
Mailing state: CT
Mailing zip: 06010-6308
General Phone: (860) 584-0501
Advertising Phone: (860) 583-2378
Editorial Phone: (860) 584-0501
General/National Adv. E-mail: gcurran@centralctcommunications.com
Display Adv. E-mail: gcurran@centralctcommunications.com
Classified Adv. e-mail: gcurran@centralctcommunications.com
Editorial e-mail: letters@centralctcommunications.com
Primary Website: www.bristolpress.com
Mthly Avg Views: 669000
Mthly Avg Unique Visitors: 78000
Year Established: 1871
News Services: AP.
Special Editions: Bridal (Jan); Bristol Home Show (Feb); Business & Industry Review (Jan); Home Improvement (Apr); Bridal (Jun); Back-to-School (Aug); Home Improvement (Oct); Gift Guide (Nov); Holiday Gift Guides (Nov-Dec).
Special Weekly Sections: Prime Time (Mon); Religion (Sat); Healthy Living (Tues); Weekend (Thurs); Food (Wed); Home & Garden (Fri).

Areas Served - City/County or Portion Thereof, or Zip codes: 06013, 06032, 06051, 06052, 06111, 06109, 06067, 06037, 06489, 06716, 06782, 06786, 06787
Own Printing Facility?: N
Commercial printers?: N
Avg Free Circ: 496
Sat. Circulation Paid: 4019
Sat. Circulation Free: 496
Audit By: AAM
Audit Date: 30.09.2015
Personnel: Michael Schroeder (Pub.); Gary Curran (Adv. Mgr.); Michael Orazzi (Chief Photographer); Paul Angilly (Sports Ed.); Michael Marciano (Editor); James Drzewiecki (Associate editor)
Parent company (for newspapers): Central Connecticut Communications LLC

THE NEWS-TIMES

Street address 1: 333 Main St
Street address city: Danbury
Street address state: CT
Zip/Postal code: 06810-5818
County: Fairfield
Country: USA
Mailing address: 333 MAIN ST
Mailing city: DANBURY
Mailing state: CT
Mailing zip: 06810-5868
General Phone: (203) 744-5100
Advertising Phone: (203) 744-5100
Editorial Phone: (203) 731-3347
General/National Adv. E-mail: ads@newstimes.com
Display Adv. E-mail: ads@newstimes.com
Classified Adv. e-mail: ads@newstimes.com
Editorial e-mail: editors@newstimes.com
Primary Website: www.newstimes.com
Year Established: 1883
News Services: AP, DJ, MCT, ONS.
Special Editions: Real Estate Showcase (Monthly); Inside Business (Quarterly).
Special Weekly Sections: Sports (Mon); Best Food (Wed); Business, Neighbors (Thur); Weekend, Entertainment (Fri); Religion (Sat); Travel, TV, Business, Stock (Sun)
Syndicated Publications: Relish (Monthly); Parade (S).
Delivery Methods: Newsstand`Carrier`Racks
Areas Served - City/County or Portion Thereof, or Zip codes: 06810, 06811, 06812, 06784, 06776, 06755, 06785, 06757, 06754, 06777, 06794, 06793, 06783, 06798, 06804, 06801, 06470, 06482, 06488, 06752, 06896, 06877, 12564, 12531, 12563, 10509, 10541, 10560, 10536, 10590, 10518, 10526, 10597, 10578, 10589, 10505, 10598, 10527, 10501, 10536
Own Printing Facility?: Y
Commercial printers?: Y
Sat. Circulation Paid: 9440
Sun. Circulation Paid: 12810
Audit By: AAM
Audit Date: 30.09.2017
Personnel: David Parks (Circ. Mgr.); Karen Geffert (Director of Human Resources); Linda Tuccio-Koonz (Features Ed.); Rich Joudy (IT Help Desk); John Alcott (Mng. Ed.); Ron Darr (Ops. Dir.); Jacqueline Smith (Editorial Page Editor); Sean Barker (Sports Ed.); Stephen Spinosa (Multimedia Sales Director); Nancy Mengler (Creative Services Manager); Lee Steele (Features Editor); Eugene Jackson (Nat'l Accts. Sales Dir.); Loraine Marshall (Adv. Sales Mgr.); Susan Tuz (Ed. Dept.)
Parent company (for newspapers): Hearst Communications, Inc.

THE HARTFORD COURANT

Street address 1: 285 Broad St
Street address city: Hartford
Street address state: CT
Zip/Postal code: 06105-3785
County: Hartford
Country: USA
Mailing address: 285 BROAD ST
Mailing city: HARTFORD
Mailing state: CT
Mailing zip: 06105-3719
General Phone: (860) 241-6200
Editorial Phone: (860) 241-3698
General/National Adv. E-mail: llatusek@courant.com
Display Adv. E-mail: ecom@tribune.com
Classified Adv. e-mail: mtingley@courant.com
Editorial e-mail: letters@courant.com.
Primary Website: www.courant.com
Mthly Avg Views: 24447578
Mthly Avg Unique Visitors: 2652406
Year Established: 1764
News Services: Reuters, WP-Bloomberg, MCT, RN Photo.
Special Editions: Scholastic Sports (Jan); President's Day Auto I (Feb); Guide To Education (Apr); Scholastic Sports (Apr); Travelers Championship Golf Tournament (June); Scholastic Sports (Jul); UConn Football Preview (Aug); Guide to Education (Aug); Breast Cancer Awareness (Oct); UConn Basketball Preview (Nov); Ski, Sun and Travel (Nov); Guide To Education (Dec);
Special Weekly Sections: TV Week (Sun.), Flavor (Thur.), At Home (Fri.),
Delivery Methods: Mail`Newsstand`Carrier`Racks
Areas Served - City/County or Portion Thereof, or Zip codes: Entire state of Connecticut
Own Printing Facility?: Y
Commercial printers?: Y
Sat. Circulation Paid: 90006
Sun. Circulation Paid: 139090
Audit By: AAM
Audit Date: 31.03.2018
Personnel: Mary Lou Stoneburner (VP Adv.); Susan Kerr (Circ. Dir.); Brian McEnery (Circ. Ops. Dir.); Andrew S. Julien (Publisher & Editor-in-Chief); Jennifer T. Humes (Dir. of Marketing and Communications); Thomas J. Anischik (Sr. VP Ops Admin.); Christine W. Taylor (VP/ Digital Platform); Michele Tingley (Adv. Dir.); Dana Bisconti (Finance Director)
Parent company (for newspapers): Alden Global Capital; Tribune Publishing, Inc.

JOURNAL INQUIRER

Street address 1: 306 Progress Dr
Street address city: Manchester
Street address state: CT
Zip/Postal code: 06042-9011
County: Hartford
Country: USA
Mailing address: PO BOX 510
Mailing city: MANCHESTER
Mailing state: CT
Mailing zip: 06045-0510
General Phone: (860) 646-0500
Advertising Phone: (860) 646-0500
Editorial Phone: (860) 646-0500
General/National Adv. E-mail: jiads@journalinquirer.com
Display Adv. E-mail: jiads@journalinquirer.com
Classified Adv. e-mail: jiads@journalinquirer.com
Editorial e-mail: news@journalinquirer.com
Primary Website: www.journalinquirer.com
Year Established: 1968
News Services: AP, NYT, SHNS.
Special Editions: Spring Home & Garden (Apr); Back-to-School (Aug); Washington's Birthday Auto (Feb); Super Sunday (Feb); Discovery (Jul); Fall Brides (Jun); Business Profiles (June); Dining Out Guide (May); Sleighbell (Nov); Inside Football (Oct); Fall Sports (Sept). UCONN Football (August). Uconn Basketball (Oct).
Special Weekly Sections: Parade (Weekend); Time Out (Thursday); Food Day (Wednesday). Homes Plus (Sat). Autos Plus (Sat).
Syndicated Publications: Parade (Weekend), Relish (Monthly), American Profile (Weekly).
Delivery Methods: Mail`Newsstand`Carrier`Racks
Areas Served - City/County or Portion Thereof, or Zip codes: 06231, 06232, 06278, 06043, 06016, 06237, 06238, 06026, 06118, 06108, 06088, 06029, 06082, 06033, 06248, 06040, 06042, 06045, 06250, 06071, 06074, 06075, 06076, 06077, 06078, 06084, 06066, 06093, 06279, 06095, 06096
Own Printing Facility?: N
Commercial printers?: N
Avg Free Circ: 2428
Sat. Circulation Paid: 20416
Sat. Circulation Free: 2571
Audit By: AAM
Audit Date: 31.03.2019
Personnel: Elizabeth S. Ellis (Publisher); Walter Rudewicz (Vice President for Finance); William K. Sybert (Vice President for Advertising); Gary Catania (Circulation Director); Chris Powell (Vice President for News and Managing Editor); Lee Giguere (Assistant Managing Editor for Production); Ralph W. Williams (Assistant Managing Editor for News); Chip LeClerc (Living Section Editor); Brian Coyne (Executive Sports Editor); Timothy Noon (Vice President for Production); Kimberly Philips (State Ed.)
Parent company (for newspapers): Journal Inquirer Publishing Company

RECORD-JOURNAL

Street address 1: 500 S Broad St
Street address 2: Ste 1
Street address city: Meriden
Street address state: CT
Zip/Postal code: 06450-6643
County: New Haven
Country: USA
Mailing address: 500 S BROAD ST STE 1
Mailing city: MERIDEN
Mailing state: CT
Mailing zip: 06450-6643
General Phone: (203) 235-1661
Advertising Phone: (203) 317-2407
Editorial Phone: (203) 317-2385
General/National Adv. E-mail: dpare@record-journal.com
Display Adv. E-mail: dpare@record-journal.com
Classified Adv. e-mail: classified@record-journal.com
Editorial e-mail: newsroom@record-journal.com
Primary Website: www.myrecordjournal.com
Year Established: 1867
News Services: AP, NYT, RNS.
Special Editions: Spring Home & Garden (Apr); Bus & Homeroom (Aug); Holiday Gift Pages (Dec); President's Day Auto (Feb); Weddings (Jan); Services Guide (Jul); Summertime (Jun); Design-An-Ad (Mar); Business & Industry (May); Holiday Shopping (Nov); Celebrate Wallingford (O
Special Weekly Sections: Health & Fitness (Fri); Front Porch (Mon); Neighbors (S); Enjoy! (Thur); Home (Tues); Great Taste (Wed).
Syndicated Publications: Parade (S)
Delivery Methods: Mail`Newsstand`Carrier`Racks
Areas Served - City/County or Portion Thereof, or Zip codes: Meridan, Wallingford, Southington & Cheshire (CT)
Own Printing Facility?: Y
Avg Free Circ: 0
Sat. Circulation Paid: 0
Sat. Circulation Free: 0
Sun. Circulation Paid: 12842
Sun. Circulation Free: 459
Audit By: VAC
Audit Date: 31.12.2015
Personnel: Eliot C. White (Pub.); Elizabeth White (VP/ Assist. to Pub.); Michael Killian (Sr. Vice Pres., Sales/ Mktg.); Tim Ryan (Sr. Vice Pres.); David Pare (Circ. Dir.); Ralph Tomaselli (Mng. Ed.); Eric Cotton (City Ed.); Michael Misarski (News Ed.); Chris Zajac (Chief Photographer); Jeffery Kurz (Sr. Writer); Bryant Carpenter (Asst. Sports Ed.); Doug Bevins (Copy Desk Chief); Carolyn Wallach; Richie Rathsack (Digital Content Editor); Alison W. Muschinsky
Parent company (for newspapers): The Record-Journal Publishing Co.

NEW BRITAIN HERALD

Street address 1: One Liberty Square
Street address 2: 3rd Floor
Street address city: New Britain
Street address state: CT
Zip/Postal code: 6050
County: Hartford
Country: USA
Mailing address: 1 COURT ST STE 404
Mailing city: NEW BRITAIN
Mailing state: CT
Mailing zip: 06051-2262
General Phone: (860) 225-4601
Advertising Phone: (860) 229-8687
Editorial Phone: (860) 225-4601
General/National Adv. E-mail: lfletcher@newbritainherald.com
Display Adv. E-mail: gcurran@newbritainherald.com
Classified Adv. e-mail: gcurran@newbritainherald.com
Editorial e-mail: mbatterson@newbritainherald.com
Primary Website: www.newbritainherald.com
Mthly Avg Views: 419000
Mthly Avg Unique Visitors: 63000
Year Established: 1880
News Services: AP.
Special Editions: Senior Citizens (Apr); Coupon Book (Aug); Christmas Song Book (Dec); Presidents' Sale (Feb); Health & Fitness (Jan); Crazy Days (Jul); Father's Day Co-op (Jun); Basketball (Mar); Mother's Day Dining (May); Homefinder (Monthly); Thanksgiving Dining (Nov);
Special Weekly Sections: Your Weekend (Fri); Property Transfers (Mon); Health and Tech (S); Rental Guide (Sat); Auto (Thur); Classroom (Tues); Best Food Day (Wed).
Syndicated Publications: USA WEEKEND Magazine (S).
Areas Served - City/County or Portion Thereof, or Zip codes: New Britain, Berlin, Plainville, Newington, Wethersfield & Southington (CT)
Avg Free Circ: 621
Sat. Circulation Paid: 4054
Sat. Circulation Free: 621
Sun. Circulation Paid: 7907
Sun. Circulation Free: 508
Audit By: AAM
Audit Date: 31.03.2015
Personnel: Michael E. Schroeder (Ed. & Pub); Matt Straub (Sports Ed.); Wayne DePaolo (Prepress Mgr.); Gary Curran (Adv. Mgr.); Brad Carroll (Mng. Ed.)
Parent company (for newspapers): Central Connecticut Communications LLC

NEW HAVEN REGISTER

Street address 1: 100 Gando Drive
Street address city: New Haven
Street address state: CT
Zip/Postal code: 6513
County: New Haven
Country: USA
Mailing address: 100 GANDO DR
Mailing city: NEW HAVEN
Mailing state: CT
Mailing zip: 06513-1014
General Phone: (203) 789-5200
Advertising Phone: (203) 789-5200
Editorial Phone: (203) 789-5708
General/National Adv. E-mail: pprovost@digitalfirstmedia.com
Display Adv. E-mail: pprovost@digitalfirstmedia.com
Classified Adv. e-mail: classified@nhregister.com
Editorial e-mail: letters@nhregister.com
Primary Website: www.nhregister.com
Mthly Avg Unique Visitors: 899392
Year Established: 1812
News Services: AP, SHNS, LAT-WP, MCT, NYT, TMS.
Special Editions: NCAA Section (Apr); Courses & Careers (Aug); Holiday Gift Guides (Dec); Internet Guide (Feb); Walter Camp Football Foundation (Jan); Menu Guide (Jul); International Festival Arts/Ideas (Jun); Home Show (Mar); Zoomers (May); Business Expo (Nov); Luxury Liv
Special Weekly Sections: Spirit, Finance, Business (Mon); Health, Science, Zone (Tue); Best Food (Wed); Lifestyle, Zone (Thur); Weekend, Gardening, Overdrive Auto (Fri); Home Furnishing, Home, Real Estate, Cars (Sat); Arts, Travel, TV, Living (Sun)
Syndicated Publications: USA WEEKEND Magazine (S); Parade (Weekly).
Delivery Methods: Mail`Newsstand`Carrier`Racks
Areas Served - City/County or Portion Thereof, or Zip codes: New Haven County
Sat. Circulation Paid: 21140
Sun. Circulation Paid: 37878
Audit By: AAM
Audit Date: 30.09.2017
Personnel: Paul Barbetta (Group Pub.); George Velezis (Controller); Helen Bennett Harvey (Exec. Ed.); Viktoria Sundqvist (Assistant Managing Ed.); Sean Barker (Sports Ed.); Al Santangelo (Night News Ed.); James Walker (Metro Ed.)
Parent company (for newspapers): Hearst Communications, Inc.

THE MIDDLETOWN PRESS

Street address 1: 100 Gando Drive
Street address city: New Haven
Street address state: CT
Zip/Postal code: 06513
County: New Haven
Country: USA
Mailing address: 100 Gando Drive
Mailing city: New Haven
Mailing state: CT
Mailing zip: 06513
General Phone: (860) 347-3331
Advertising Phone: (860) 347-3331
Editorial Phone: (860) 347-3331
General/National Adv. E-mail: jgallacher@registercitizen.com
Display Adv. E-mail: jpage@middletownpress.com
Classified Adv. e-mail: sam@middletownpress.com
Editorial e-mail: editor@middletownpress.com

Primary Website: www.middletownpress.com
Mthly Avg Unique Visitors: 1394520
Year Established: 1884
News Services: AP, NYT, LAT-WP.
Special Editions: Summer Entertaining (Apr); College Student's Guide (Aug); Last Minute Gift Guide (Dec); Valentine (Feb); Super Bowl (Jan); Hartford Open (Jul); Middlesex Summer (Jun); March Madness (Mar); Summer Preview (May); Coupon Book (Monthly); Thanksgiving (Nov); M
Special Weekly Sections: Auto (Fri); Seniors (Mon); Real Estate (Sat); Entertainer (Thur); Health (Tues); Food (Wed)
Syndicated Publications: Parade (Weekly).
Areas Served - City/County or Portion Thereof, or Zip codes: Middlesex County (CT)
Sat. Circulation Paid: 6114
Audit By: Sworn/Estimate/Non-Audited
Audit Date: 12.07.2019
Personnel: Paul Barbetta (Pub.); Helen Bennett (Exec. Ed.); Viktoria Sundqvist (Exec. Prod.); Cassandra Day (Mng. Ed.); Sean Barker (Sports Ed.)
Parent company (for newspapers): Hearst Communications, Inc.

THE DAY

Street address 1: 47 Eugene Oneill Dr
Street address city: New London
Street address state: CT
Zip/Postal code: 06320-6306
County: New London
Country: USA
Mailing address: PO BOX 1231
Mailing city: NEW LONDON
Mailing state: CT
Mailing zip: 06320-1231
General Phone: (860) 442-2200
Advertising Phone: (860) 701-4200
Editorial Phone: (860) 440-1000
General/National Adv. E-mail: b.briere@theday.com
Display Adv. E-mail: advertising1@theday.com
Classified Adv. e-mail: class@theday.com
Editorial e-mail: m.nadolny@theday.com
Primary Website: www.theday.com
Mthly Avg Views: 3500000
Mthly Avg Unique Visitors: 553000
Year Established: 1881
News Services: AP, CQ, NYT, MCT, New England News Service, TMS.
Special Editions: Education Guide (Bi-annually); DaySaver - Coupons (Monthly); Special Auto (Bi-annually); Dining (Annually); Song Book (Annually); Gift Guide (Annually)
Special Weekly Sections: Travel, Employment, Business, Marketplace, Daybreak (Sun); Education (Mon); Best Food, Recruitment (Wed); Night and Day (Thur); Real Estate, Home Court, Beliefs (Fri); Auto, Military, People (Sat)
Syndicated Publications: Mystic Country Magazine (Annually); Go Westerly Magazine (Annually), Grace Magazine (Bi-Monthly); Sound & Country Magazine (Quarterly)
Delivery Methods: Newsstand`Carrier`Racks
Areas Served - City/County or Portion Thereof, or Zip codes: Southeastern Connecticut
Own Printing Facility?: Y
Commercial printers?: Y
Sat. Circulation Paid: 22113
Sun. Circulation Paid: 23005
Audit By: AAM
Audit Date: 30.06.2018
Personnel: Bob Briere (Adv. Mgr.); Tim Cotter (Managing Editor); William Langman (Director of Operations); Daniel Williams (Director of Audience Development); Chris Cleaveland (Director of Information Technology); Michael Flaig (Commercial Print Sales Manager); Colleen Proctor (Product Manager); Timothy Tighe (Press Manager); Christine Brown (Advertising Services Manager); Bence Strickland (Classified Advertising Manager); David Gellar (Sales Development Manager); Sally Stapleton (Managing Editor/Multimedia); Carol McCarthy (Deputy Managing Editor/News Operations); Lisa McGinley (AME/Reporters); Mel Seeger (Purchasing Agent); Richard Zesk (Adv. Mgr., Classified); Roberta McLaughlin (Adv. Mgr., Classified/Telephone Sales); Shawn E. Palmer (Adv. Dir.); Diane Martin (Adv. Mgr., Retail); Mark L. Barry (Circ. Dir.); Janet M. Ballestrini (Circ. Mgr.); Gary Farrugia (Pub); Timothy Dwyer (Pres. & Pub.)
Parent company (for newspapers): The Day Publishing Co.; Day Publishing Company

THE HOUR

Street address 1: 301 Merritt 7
Street address 2: 4th Floor
Street address city: Norwalk
Street address state: CT
Zip/Postal code: 6851
County: Fairfield
Country: USA
Mailing address: 1 SELLECK ST FL 4
Mailing city: NORWALK
Mailing state: CT
Mailing zip: 06855-1117
General Phone: (203) 846-3281
Advertising Phone: (203) 354-1093
Editorial Phone: (203) 354-1062
General/National Adv. E-mail: jbrosz@thehour.com
Display Adv. E-mail: jreid@thehour.com
Classified Adv. e-mail: classified@thehour.com
Editorial e-mail: news@thehour.com
Primary Website: www.thehour.com
Mthly Avg Views: 1500000
Mthly Avg Unique Visitors: 205000
Year Established: 1871
News Services: AP, MCT.
Special Editions: The Stamford Times Wilton Villager
Special Weekly Sections: Health (Tues); Entertainment (Thur); Fitness (Tues)
Syndicated Publications: USA WEEKEND Magazine (S); American Profile (Weekly). Relish (Monthly), Spry (Monthly)
Delivery Methods: Mail`Newsstand`Carrier`Racks
Areas Served - City/County or Portion Thereof, or Zip codes: Norwalk & Surrounding areas
Own Printing Facility?: N
Commercial printers?: N
Avg Free Circ: 1454
Sat. Circulation Paid: 10935
Sat. Circulation Free: 1454
Sun. Circulation Paid: 12965
Sun. Circulation Free: 8878
Audit By: AAM
Audit Date: 31.12.2015
Personnel: Thane Grauel (Mng. Ed.); Jacky Smith (Editorial Page Ed.); Sean Barker (Sports Ed.); Lee Steele (Features Ed.); Patrick Quinn (GO! Section Ed.); Ned Gerard (Photo Ed.)
Parent company (for newspapers): Hearst Communications, Inc.

THE BULLETIN

Street address 1: 10 Railroad Place
Street address city: Norwich
Street address state: CT
Zip/Postal code: 6360
County: New London
Country: USA
Mailing address: 10 Railroad Place
Mailing city: Norwich
Mailing state: CT
Mailing zip: 06360-5829
General Phone: (860) 887-9211
Advertising Phone: (860) 887-9211
Editorial Phone: (860) 887-9211
General/National Adv. E-mail: ttergeoglou@norwichbulletin.com
Display Adv. E-mail: ttergeoglou@norwichbulletin.com
Classified Adv. e-mail: classifieds@norwichbulletin.com
Editorial e-mail: news@norwichbulletin.com
Primary Website: www.norwichbulletin.com
Year Established: 1791
News Services: AP, GNS.
Special Editions: Spring Home & Garden (Apr); Back-to-School (Aug); Holiday Gift Guides (Dec); Home Improvement (Feb); Job Fair (Jan); Back-to-School (Jul); Job Fair (Jun); Job Fair (Mar); Spring Home & Garden (May); Job Fair (Nov); Job Fair (Sept).
Special Weekly Sections: Best Food (Wed/Sun); Business (Mon); Healthy, Living, Technology (Tue); Entertainment, Home Improvement, Furnishing, Gardening (Thur); Auto (Sat); Society, Building, Business (Sun)
Syndicated Publications: USA WEEKEND Magazine (S).
Delivery Methods: Mail`Newsstand`Carrier`Racks
Areas Served - City/County or Portion Thereof, or Zip codes: Eastern Connecticut
Own Printing Facility?: Y
Commercial printers?: N
Avg Free Circ: 93
Sat. Circulation Paid: 9087
Sat. Circulation Free: 93
Sun. Circulation Paid: 12039
Sun. Circulation Free: 96
Audit By: AAM
Audit Date: 30.06.2018
Personnel: Nadine McBride (Pub.); Louvenia Brandt (Adv. Mgr.); Jim Konrad (Exec. Editor); Aaron Flaum (Multimedia Ed.); Anna Maria Della Costa (Op. Ed.); Robert Miller (Online Ed.)
Parent company (for newspapers): Gannett; CherryRoad Media

GREENWICH TIME

Street address 1: 1445 E Putnam Ave
Street address 2: Ste 6
Street address city: Old Greenwich
Street address state: CT
Zip/Postal code: 06870-1377
County: Fairfield
Country: USA
Mailing address: 1445 E PUTNAM AVE STE 6
Mailing city: OLD GREENWICH
Mailing state: CT
Mailing zip: 06870-1377
General Phone: (203) 625-4400
Advertising Phone: (203) 964-2428
Editorial Phone: (203) 964-2293
General/National Adv. E-mail: ehuron@hearstmediact.com
Display Adv. E-mail: twhite@hearstmediact.com
Classified Adv. e-mail: classified@scni.com
Editorial e-mail: editorials@scni.com
Primary Website: www.greenwichtime.com
Mthly Avg Views: 22000000
Mthly Avg Unique Visitors: 376537
Year Established: 1877
News Services: AP, LAT-WP, MCT.
Special Editions: New York Auto Show (Apr); Survey of Education (Aug); Great Gift Ideas (Dec); Cruise/Guide (Feb); Weddings (Jan); Travel (Jul); Water, Water, Water (Jun); Home (Mar); New England Vacations (May); Holiday Countdown (Nov); Kitchen & Bath (Oct); Bahamas Trave
Special Weekly Sections: Weekend (Fri); Family Room (Mon); Travel (S); Life & Style (Thur); Health (Tues); Food (Wed).
Syndicated Publications: Parade (S).
Delivery Methods: Mail`Newsstand`Carrier`Racks
Areas Served - City/County or Portion Thereof, or Zip codes: 06830, 06831, 06807, 06870, 06878
Own Printing Facility?: N
Commercial printers?: N
Avg Free Circ: 58
Sat. Circulation Paid: 3199
Sat. Circulation Free: 58
Sun. Circulation Paid: 3526
Sun. Circulation Free: 30
Audit By: AAM
Audit Date: 31.03.2019
Personnel: Michelle McAbee (Pub.); Barbara Roessner (Exec. Editor); Chris McNamee (Sports Editor); Mike Pignataro (Vice Pres. Operations); Dennis Tidrick (Prodn. Mgr., Pre Press); Henry B. Haitz III (Group Publisher and President); Stephanie Borise (Business Editior); Thomas Mellana (Mng. Ed.)
Parent company (for newspapers): Hearst Communications, Inc.

THE WESTERLY SUN

Street address 1: 99 Mechanic St
Street address city: Pawcatuck
Street address state: CT
Zip/Postal code: 06379-2187
County: New London
Country: USA
General Phone: (401) 348-1000
Display Adv. E-mail: ktremaine@thewesterlysun.com
Classified Adv. e-mail: classified@thewesterlysun.com
Editorial e-mail: editorial@thewesterlysun.com
Primary Website: www.thewesterlysun.com
Mthly Avg Views: 2,013
Mthly Avg Unique Visitors: 377346
Year Established: 1856
News Services: AP.
Special Editions: Christmas Gift Guide (Dec); Automobile (Feb); Year-in-Review (Jan); Schoolboy Football (Nov); Automobile (Oct); Home Improvement (Sept).
Special Weekly Sections: Places in the Sun (Fri); Business (S); Business (Sat); The Guide (Thur); Food (Wed).
Syndicated Publications: Relish (Monthly); USA WEEKEND Magazine (S); American Profile (Weekly).
Delivery Methods: Mail`Newsstand`Carrier`Racks
Areas Served - City/County or Portion Thereof, or Zip codes: Washington County & New London County (CT)
Own Printing Facility?: N
Commercial printers?: N
Avg Free Circ: 28
Sat. Circulation Paid: 6003
Sat. Circulation Free: 28
Sun. Circulation Paid: 6642
Sun. Circulation Free: 1991
Audit By: CAC
Audit Date: 30.09.2015
Personnel: David Tranchida (VP & Editor); John Layton (VP and Advertising director); Shawn Palmer (Sr. Vice Pres.); Dave Pare (Circ Dir); Corey Fyke (News & Digital Editor); Heather Caulkins (Digital Advertising Mgr); Karen Davis (Classified Adv. Mgr); Mike Souza (Assoc. Ed.); Mike Blais (Sales Dir); Kelly Tremaine (Associate Publisher)
Parent company (for newspapers): Rhode Island Suburban Newspapers

THE ADVOCATE

Street address 1: 9A Riverbend Dr S
Street address city: Stamford
Street address state: CT
Zip/Postal code: 06907-2524
County: Fairfield
Country: USA
Mailing address: PO BOX 9307
Mailing city: Stamford
Mailing state: CT
Mailing zip: 6907
General Phone: (203) 964-2200
Advertising Phone: (203) 964-2428
Editorial Phone: (203) 964-2293
General/National Adv. E-mail: scniads@scni.com
Display Adv. E-mail: scniads@scni.com
Classified Adv. e-mail: classified@scni.com
Editorial e-mail: editorials@scni.com
Primary Website: www.stamfordadvocate.com
Mthly Avg Views: 22000000
Mthly Avg Unique Visitors: 404362
Year Established: 1829
News Services: AP, LAT-WP, MCT.
Special Editions: Garden (Apr); Educational Outlook (Aug); Steppin Out New Years (Dec); Business & Economic Review (Feb); Educational Outlook (Jan); Healthy Connections (Jul); Summer Party Guide (Jun); NY Auto Show (Mar); Health & Wellness (May); Stamford Business Outlook
Special Weekly Sections: Family, Technology (Mon); Health, Fitness (Tue; Best Food (Wed); Weekend (Thur); Life, Real Estate, Auto (Fri); Religion (Sat); Arts, Travel, TV Times, Neighbors, Community, Comics (Sun)
Syndicated Publications: Color Comics (S).
Areas Served - City/County or Portion Thereof, or Zip codes: Stamford (IL)
Sat. Circulation Paid: 6620
Sun. Circulation Paid: 12267
Audit By: AAM
Audit Date: 30.09.2015
Personnel: Thomas Mellana (Mng. Ed.); Mike Pignataro (Asst. Mng. Ed.); John Breunig (Editorial Page Ed.); Sean Barker (Sports Ed.); Lee Steele (Features Ed.)
Parent company (for newspapers): Hearst Communications, Inc.

THE REGISTER CITIZEN

Street address 1: 59 Field St
Street address city: Torrington
Street address state: CT
Zip/Postal code: 06790-4942
County: Litchfield
Country: USA
Mailing address: 59 FIELD ST
Mailing city: TORRINGTON
Mailing state: CT
Mailing zip: 06790-4942
General Phone: (860) 489-3121
Advertising Phone: (860) 489-3121 ext. 312
Editorial Phone: (860) 489-3121
General/National Adv. E-mail: advertising@registercitizen.com
Display Adv. E-mail: advertising@registercitizen.com
Classified Adv. e-mail: classified@registercitizen.com

Editorial e-mail: editor@registercitizen.com
Primary Website: www.registercitizen.com
Mthly Avg Unique Visitors: 1394520
Year Established: 1874
News Services: AP.
Special Editions: Home Improvement (Apr); Fall Festivals (Aug); First Night (Dec); Progress (Feb); Bridal (Jan); Torrington (Jul); Graduation (Jun); Car Care (Mar); Memorial Day Activities (May); Christmas Gift Guide (Nov); Fall Car Care (Oct); Fall Bridal (Sept).
Special Weekly Sections: Senior (Mon); Health, Science (Tue); Religion (Wed); Arts, Entertainment (Thur); Food (Fri); Auto, Real Estate (Sat); Help Wanted, Home, Garden, Local History, Business, Wedding, Engagements (Sun)
Syndicated Publications: Comics (S).
Delivery Methods: Mail`Newsstand`Carrier`Racks
Areas Served - City/County or Portion Thereof, or Zip codes: Northwestern Connecticut
Sat. Circulation Paid: 2069
Sun. Circulation Paid: 2410
Audit By: AAM
Audit Date: 30.09.2015
Personnel: Paul Barbetta (Pub.); Helen Bennett (Exec. Ed.); Viktoria Sundqvist (Exec. Prod.); Emily Olson (Comm. Ed.)
Parent company (for newspapers): Hearst Communications, Inc.

REPUBLICAN-AMERICAN

Street address 1: 389 Meadow Street, P.O. Box 2090
Street address city: Waterbury
Street address state: CT
Zip/Postal code: 6722
County: New Haven
Country: USA
Mailing address: PO BOX 2090
Mailing city: WATERBURY
Mailing state: CT
Mailing zip: 06722-2090
General Phone: 203-574-3636
Advertising Phone: (203) 574-3636
Editorial Phone: (203) 574-3636
General/National Adv. E-mail: adres@rep-am.com
Display Adv. E-mail: adres@rep-am.com
Classified Adv. e-mail: classads@rep-am.com
Editorial e-mail: smacoy@rep-am.com
Primary Website: www.rep-am.com
Year Established: 1844
News Services: AP, MCT,
Special Editions: Coupon Madness (Jan thru Dec). President's Day Auto (Feb); Brides Guides (Feb & Oct); Home & Energy (Feb & Oct..); Health Matters (March & Sept); Homestyle (Apr & Sept); Main St Wtby (June, Nov. & Dec); Summer Lifestyles (May); Table of Tides (May): Graduation (June); College Bound (July); Litchfield Jazz (Aug); Autumn Lifestyles (Aug); Kitchen & Bath (Oct) Holidays on Magical Mile (Nov); HS Football (Nov); Holiday Gift Guide (Nov. & Dec.); Annual Calendars (Dec).
Special Weekly Sections: Real Estate/Home, Commentary, Travel/Leisure, Comics (Sun); Technology (Sat); Best Food Day (Wed); Country Life (Thur); Connecticut Weekend (Fri): Wheels Page (Sat); Lifestyle; Business (Daily)
Syndicated Publications: Parade (S). Dash (Monthly - Wed); Athlon Sports (Monthly - Wed)
Delivery Methods: Mail`Newsstand`Carrier`Racks
Areas Served - City/County or Portion Thereof, or Zip codes: 06010 to 06798
Own Printing Facility?: Y
Commercial printers?: Y
Avg Free Circ: 1661
Sat. Circulation Paid: 32780
Sat. Circulation Free: 1586
Sun. Circulation Paid: 39737
Sun. Circulation Free: 837
Audit By: AAM
Audit Date: 30.09.2016
Personnel: William J. Pape II (Publisher); Richard Welch (Nat'l Adv. Mgr.); Susan Sprano (Advertising Director); William B. Pape (President); Richard Stoll (Controller); Anne Karolyi (Managing Editor); Robert Lee (Human Resources Manager); Edward Winters (Vice President/ Circulation Director)
Parent company (for newspapers): American-Republican, Incorporated

THE CHRONICLE

Street address 1: 1 Chronicle Rd
Street address 2: PO Box 148
Street address city: Willimantic
Street address state: CT
Zip/Postal code: 06226-1932
County: Windham
Country: USA
Mailing address: PO BOX 148
Mailing city: WILLIMANTIC
Mailing state: CT
Mailing zip: 06226-0148
General Phone: (860) 423-8466
Editorial Phone: (860) 423-8466
General/National Adv. E-mail: advertising@thechronicle.com
Display Adv. E-mail: advertising@thechronicle.com
Classified Adv. e-mail: classified@thechronicle.com
Editorial e-mail: news@thechronicle.com
Primary Website: www.thechronicle.com
Year Established: 1877
News Services: Reuters, McClatchy Tribune News Services
Special Editions: Back-to-School (Aug); Gift Gallery (Dec); Bridal (Jan); Summer Guide (Jun); Spring Special (May); Christmas (Nov); Harvest Values (Oct); Sports (Sept).
Special Weekly Sections: Real Estate (Mon); Society/ Wedding (Sat); Arts (Thur); Food (Wed).
Syndicated Publications: Album (Sat); American Profile (Weekly).
Delivery Methods: Mail`Newsstand`Carrier`Racks
Areas Served - City/County or Portion Thereof, or Zip codes: 06226, 06257, 06242, 06278, 06279, 06269, 06268, 06238, 06232, 06248, 06237, 06249, 06254, 06264, 06247, 06235, 06250, 06256, 06280
Own Printing Facility?: Y
Commercial printers?: Y
Avg Free Circ: 664
Sat. Circulation Paid: 5859
Sat. Circulation Free: 514
Audit By: CAC
Audit Date: 31.12.2016
Personnel: Patrice Crosbie (Pub.); Charles Ryan (Ed.); Thomas Nevers (Adv. Dir.); Todd Charland (Circ. Dir.); Lynn Coleman (Prodn. Mgr.)
Parent company (for newspapers): Central Connecticut Communications LLC

DELAWARE

DELAWARE STATE NEWS

Street address 1: 110 Galaxy Dr
Street address city: Dover
Street address state: DE
Zip/Postal code: 19901-9262
County: Kent
Country: USA
Mailing address: 110 GALAXY DR
Mailing city: DOVER
Mailing state: DE
Mailing zip: 19901-9262
General Phone: (302) 674-3600
Advertising Phone: (302) 741-8200
Editorial Phone: (302) 741-8229
General/National Adv. E-mail: adsales@newszap.com
Display Adv. E-mail: adsales@newszap.com
Classified Adv. e-mail: classads@newszap.com
Editorial e-mail: newsroom@newszap.com
Primary Website: http://delawarestatenews.net
Mthly Avg Views: 207000
Mthly Avg Unique Visitors: 72000
Year Established: 1953
News Services: AP
Special Editions: Bridal (Feb/Oct); Black History (Feb); Holiday Gift Guide (Nov); NASCAR Race Tabs (May and Sept/Oct): Holiday Events & Celebrations (Nov/Dec); 100 Things to do this Summer (May); Summer Camp Guide (March)
Special Weekly Sections: Education (Tue); Best Food Day (Wed), Health & Wellness (Thurs); Entertainment (Fri); Religion (Sat); Real Estate, Auto (Sun); Business (Mon); NASCAR (Thurs)
Syndicated Publications: PARADE Magazine (Sunday); Select TV/Comics (Sunday)
Delivery Methods: Newsstand`Carrier`Racks
Areas Served - City/County or Portion Thereof, or Zip codes: 19709 Middletown 19711 Newark 19730 Odessa 19734 Townsend 19801 Wilmington 19901 Dover 19904 West Dover 19930 Bethany Beach 19933 Bridgeville 19934 Camden/Wyoming 19936 Cheswold 19938 Clayton 19939 Dagsboro 19940 Delmar 19941 Ellendale 19950 Farmington/ Greenwood 19943 Felton 19944 Fenwick Island 19945 Frankford 19946 Frederica 19947 Georgetown 19950 Greenwood 19951 Harbeson 19952 Harrington 19953 Hartly 19954 Houston 19955 Kenton 19956 Laurel 19958 Lewes 19960 Lincoln 19962 Magnolia 19963 Milford 19964 Marydel 19966 Millsboro/Long Neck/ Oak Orchard 19967 Millville 19968 Milton 19969 Nassau 19970 Ocean View/ Clarksville 19971 Rehoboth Beach 19973 Seaford 19975 Selbyville 19977 Smyrna 19979 Viola 19980 Woodside 21607 Barclay 21913 Cecilton 21617 Centreville 21620 Chestertown 21623 Church Hill 21628 Crumpton 21675 Delmar 21629 Denton 21632 Federalsburg 21635 Galena 21636 Goldsboro 21639 Greensboro 21640 Henderson 21645 Kennedyville 21649 Marydel 21651 Millington 21657 Queen Anne 21660 Ridgely 21661 Rock Hall 21667 Still Pond 21668 Sudlersville 21678 Worton
Own Printing Facility?: Y
Commercial printers?: Y
Avg Free Circ: 491
Sat. Circulation Paid: 8588
Sat. Circulation Free: 491
Sun. Circulation Paid: 10368
Sun. Circulation Free: 489
Audit By: AAM
Audit Date: 31.03.2019
Personnel: Darel LaPrade (Sr. VP New Media); Konrad La Prade (Promo. Mgr.); Andrew West (Mng. Ed.); Andy Walter (Sports Ed.); Rita Maier (Circ. Dir.); Tonda Parks (VP, Adv. Develop.); Ed Dulin (CEO/President); Tim Gary (Major Accounts Advertising Manager); Dianna Sellers (Classified Manager); Tom Byrd (Publisher); Tom Bugbee (Printing Plant - Operations Manager)
Parent company (for newspapers): Independent Newsmedia Inc. USA

THE NEWS JOURNAL

Street address 1: 950 W Basin Rd
Street address city: New Castle
Street address state: DE
Zip/Postal code: 19720-1008
County: New Castle
Country: USA
Mailing address: PO BOX 15505
Mailing city: WILMINGTON
Mailing state: DE
Mailing zip: 19850-5505
General Phone: (302) 324-2500
Advertising Phone: (302) 324-2631
Editorial Phone: (302) 324-2990
General/National Adv. E-mail: wjames@delawareonline.com
Editorial e-mail: jsweeny@delawareonline.com
Primary Website: www.delawareonline.com
Mthly Avg Views: 8493535
Mthly Avg Unique Visitors: 1197614
Year Established: 1919
News Services: AP, GNS, LAT-WP, Baltimore Sun.
Special Editions: Football (Aug); Shopping Guide (Nov & Dec); Academic All Stars (Jun); Camp Guide (Mar); Beach Guide (May)
Special Weekly Sections: 55 Hours (Fri); Arts (Fri); Family (Mon); Food & Drink (Wed); Auto (Sat); Crossroads (Thurs); Family Life (Tues); Education (Sun)
Syndicated Publications: USA WEEKEND Magazine (S).
Delivery Methods: Mail`Newsstand
Areas Served - City/County or Portion Thereof, or Zip codes: New Castle County, Sussex County, Kent County
Own Printing Facility?: Y
Sat. Circulation Paid: 63674
Sun. Circulation Paid: 78607
Audit By: AAM
Audit Date: 31.12.2015
Personnel: Mike Feeley (Executive Ed.); Phil Freedman (News Dir.); Robert Long (Consumer Experience Director); Betsy Price (Community Content/Features); Matthew Albright (Engagement Ed.)
Parent company (for newspapers): Gannett

DISTRICT OF COLUMBIA

THE WASHINGTON POST

Street address 1: 1301 K St NW
Street address city: Washington
Street address state: DC
Zip/Postal code: 20071-0004
County: District Of Columbia
Country: USA
Mailing state: DC
Mailing zip: 20071-0002
General Phone: (202) 334-6000
Advertising Phone: (202) 334-5299
Editorial Phone: (202) 334-7410
General/National Adv. E-mail: @washpost.com
Display Adv. E-mail: washingtonpostads@washpost.com
Classified Adv. e-mail: pokusab@washpost.com
Editorial e-mail: national@washpost.com
Primary Website: www.washingtonpost.com
Mthly Avg Views: 959000000
Mthly Avg Unique Visitors: 83000000
Year Established: 1877
News Services: AFP, AP, CT, DJ, MCT, NEA, NNS, RN.
Special Editions: Home & Design (Apr); Football Preview (Aug); Holiday Guide Feature (Dec); Cruise (Feb); Bridal Feature (Jan); Homes Showcase (Jul); Homes Showcase (Jun); Home Showcase (Mar); Outdoor Living Feature (May); Ski (Nov); Bermuda & the Bahamas (Oct); Fall Fashion
Special Weekly Sections: Health (Tue); Food (Wed); Local Living (Thur); Weekend (Fri); Real Estate (Sat); Travel, Outlook, Arts & Style (Sun)
Syndicated Publications: Washington Post Magazine
Delivery Methods: Mail`Newsstand`Carrier`Racks
Areas Served - City/County or Portion Thereof, or Zip codes: Entire United States
Own Printing Facility?: Y
Commercial printers?: Y
Sat. Circulation Paid: 260302
Sun. Circulation Paid: 437269
Audit By: AAM
Audit Date: 30.09.2018
Personnel: Jim Coley (Vice Pres., Prodn.); Rich Handloff (Director, Consumer Marketing); Gregg Fernandes (Vice President); Hugh Price (Dir. of Operations & Planning); Bryant Despeaux (Division Manager Commercial Sales $ Deli); Ethan Selzer (Director of Advertising, MAU); Sheila Daw (Account Manager, National Retail); Jared Farber (Director of Digital Marketing); Rebecca Haase (Director, Regional Sales); Jed Hartman (Chief Revenue Officer); Stephen Gibson (CFO/VP, Finance & Admin.); Beth Diaz (VP, Audience Develop.); Kristine Coratti (VP, Communications); Molly Urciolo (Partner Program Manager); Martin Baron (Editor); Fred Ryan (Publisher); Elite Truong; Joy Robbins (Chief Revenue Officer)
Parent company (for newspapers): Nash Holdings

THE WASHINGTON TIMES

Street address 1: 3600 New York Ave NE
Street address city: Washington
Street address state: DC
Zip/Postal code: 20002-1947
County: District Of Columbia
Country: USA
Mailing address: 3600 NEW YORK AVE NE
Mailing city: WASHINGTON
Mailing state: DC
Mailing zip: 20002-1996
General Phone: (202) 636-3000
Advertising Phone: (202) 636-3000
Editorial Phone: (202) 636-3000
General/National Adv. E-mail: nationaladvertising@washingtontimes.com
Display Adv. E-mail: acrofoot@washingtontimes.com
Classified Adv. e-mail: jalmond@washingtontimes.com
Editorial e-mail: yourletters@washingtontimes.com
Primary Website: www.washingtontimes.com
Mthly Avg Views: 14904284
Mthly Avg Unique Visitors: 5650000
Year Established: 1982
News Services: MCT, AP, RN, CNS, Bloomberg, AFP, SHNS, Cox News Service, UPI, CSM, London Daily Telegraph, Xinhua News Service, CN, NEA.
Special Editions: Farm Review & Forecast (Apr); Back-to-School (Aug); Christmas (Dec); Customer Appreciation (Jan); Progress (Jul); Basketball (Mar); Basketball (Nov); Sidewalk Sale Days (Sept).
Special Weekly Sections: Classifieds, Opinions (Daily); Home, Weekend, Auto (Fri)
Syndicated Publications: American Profile (Sat).
Delivery Methods: Mail`Newsstand`Carrier`Racks
Areas Served - City/County or Portion Thereof, or Zip codes: Washington, DC
Own Printing Facility?: Y
Commercial printers?: N
Sat. Circulation Paid: 8768

Sun. Circulation Paid: 45427
Audit By: Sworn/Estimate/Non-Audited
Audit Date: 12.07.2019
Personnel: Lisa Gray (Circ. Mgr., Systems); Maria Stainer (Asst. Mng. Ed, Universal Desk); Stephen Dinan (Politics Ed.); Valerie Richardson (Denver Bureau Chief); John Bourantas (Asst. Mng. Ed.); Christopher Dolan (Mng. Ed.); Adam VerCamman (Dir. Adv. & Sales); Larry Beasley (Pres. & CEO); Ian Bishop (Managing Ed. - Dig.)
Parent company (for newspapers): CNHI, LLC; The Washington Times

WASHINGTON POST

Street address 1: 1301 K St NW
Street address city: Washington
Street address state: DC
Zip/Postal code: 20071
Country: USA
General Phone: 202-740-5300
General/National Adv. E-mail: info@washpost.com
Display Adv. E-mail: advertising@washpost.com
Classified Adv. e-mail: listings@washpost.com
Primary Website: washingtonpost.com
Audit By: AAM
Audit Date: 30.09.2021
Personnel: Martin Baron (Exec. Ed.); Circulation Department (Circ. Dept)

WASHINGTON POST EXPRESS

Street address 1: 1150 15th St NW
Street address city: Washington
Street address state: DC
Zip/Postal code: 20071-0001
County: District Of Columbia
Country: USA
General Phone: (202) 334-6000
Advertising Phone: (202) 334-7642
General/National Adv. E-mail: Ronald.Ulrich@washpost.com
Display Adv. E-mail: Ronald.Ulrich@washpost.com
Editorial e-mail: Inbox@readexpress.com
Primary Website: www.expressnightout.com
Year Established: 2003
Delivery Methods: Mail`Newsstand`Racks
Audit By: CAC
Audit Date: 30.09.2018
Personnel: Ronald Ulrich (Adv)
Parent company (for newspapers): The Washington Post

FLORIDA

BRADENTON HERALD

Street address 1: 1111 3rd Avenue West
Street address city: Bradenton
Street address state: FL
Zip/Postal code: 34205
County: Manatee
Country: USA
Mailing address: PO BOX 921
Mailing city: BRADENTON
Mailing state: FL
Mailing zip: 34206-0921
General Phone: (941) 748-0411
General/National Adv. E-mail: dhaimer@bradenton.com
Display Adv. E-mail: dhaimer@bradenton.com
Classified Adv. e-mail: jpatterson@bradenton.com
Editorial e-mail: cwille@bradenton.com
Primary Website: www.bradenton.com
Mthly Avg Views: 4341445
Mthly Avg Unique Visitors: 939181
Year Established: 1922
Special Weekly Sections: Best Food (Wed); Travel, Arts, Entertainment (Sun); Health (Tue); Taste (Wed); Weekend (Thur); Neighbors (Fri); Religion, Real Estate (Sat)
Delivery Methods: Newsstand`Carrier
Areas Served - City/County or Portion Thereof, or Zip codes: 34201, 34202, 34203, 34205, 34207, 34208, 34209, 34210, 34211, 34212, 34215, 34216, 34217, 34218, 34219, 34221, 34222, 34243
Own Printing Facility?: N
Commercial printers?: N
Sat. Circulation Paid: 22068
Sun. Circulation Paid: 25555
Audit By: AAM
Audit Date: 31.03.2019
Personnel: Robert Turner (Pub.); Darren Haimer (Gen. Mgr./VP, Adv.); Jami Patterson (Display Advertising Manager); Jacqueline Middlemus (HR Mgr.)
Parent company (for newspapers): The McClatchy Company; Chatham Asset Management

CITRUS COUNTY CHRONICLE

Street address 1: 1624 N Meadowcrest Blvd
Street address city: Crystal River
Street address state: FL
Zip/Postal code: 34429-5760
County: Citrus
Country: USA
Mailing address: 1624 N MEADOWCREST BLVD
Mailing city: CRYSTAL RIVER
Mailing state: FL
Mailing zip: 34429-8751
General Phone: (352) 563-6363
Advertising Phone: (352) 563-5592
Editorial Phone: (352) 563-5660
General/National Adv. E-mail: advertising@chronicleonline.com
Display Adv. E-mail: advertising@chronicleonline.com
Classified Adv. e-mail: advertising@chronicleonline.com
Editorial e-mail: newsdesk@chronicleonline.com
Primary Website: www.chronicleonline.com
Mthly Avg Views: 474000
Mthly Avg Unique Visitors: 99000
Year Established: 1890
News Services: AP.
Special Editions: Home Improvement (Apr); Football (Aug); Gift Guide (Dec); Business Almanac (Feb); Income Tax Guide (Jan); Snowbird (Jul); Nature Coast (Jun); Fair Guide (Mar); Hurricane Tab (May); Seniors Illustrated (Monthly); Crystal River Merchants (Nov); Festival of
Special Weekly Sections: Commentary, Sports, Business, Real Estate, Stocks, Comics, Community (Sun); Sports, Community (Mon); Stocks, Health, Fitness, Auto (Tue); Stocks, Education, Community (Wed); Food, Stocks (Thur); Stocks, Entertainment (Fri); Religion (Sat)
Syndicated Publications: USA WEEKEND Magazine (S).
Delivery Methods: Mail`Newsstand`Carrier`Racks
Own Printing Facility?: Y
Commercial printers?: Y
Avg Free Circ: 825
Sat. Circulation Paid: 15567
Sat. Circulation Free: 825
Sun. Circulation Paid: 19895
Sun. Circulation Free: 833
Audit By: AAM
Audit Date: 31.12.2018
Personnel: Gerry Mulligan (Pub.); Matthew Beck (Photo Ed.); Mike Arnold (Mng. Ed.); Tom Feeney (Prodn. Mgr.); John Murphy (Classified Adv. Mgr.); Trina Murphy (Publisher)
Parent company (for newspapers): Paxton Media Group; Citrus Publishing Inc.; Paxton Media

DAYTONA BEACH NEWS-JOURNAL

Street address 1: 901 Sixth Street
Street address city: Daytona Beach
Street address state: FL
Zip/Postal code: 32117
County: Volusia
Country: USA
Mailing address: PO BOX 2831
Mailing city: DAYTONA BEACH
Mailing state: FL
Mailing zip: 32120-2831
General Phone: (386) 252-1511
Advertising Phone: (386) 681-2750
Editorial Phone: (386) 681-2220
General/National Adv. E-mail: bill.offill@news-jrnl.com
Display Adv. E-mail: adv@news-jrnl.com
Classified Adv. e-mail: debbie.keesee@news-jrnl.com
Editorial e-mail: njscoop@news-jrnl.com
Primary Website: www.news-journalonline.com
Mthly Avg Views: 4500000
Mthly Avg Unique Visitors: 469000
Year Established: 1883
News Services: AP
Special Editions: Palm Coast How to Guide (Apr); Football Preview (NFL) (Aug); Letters to Santa (Dec); Volusia County Schools Newsletter (Every other month); Bridal Guide (Feb); Prospectus (Jan); Speed (Jul); Disaster Guide (Jun); Garden & Leisure Lifestyle Show (Mar); Par
Special Weekly Sections: Business, Parimutuel News, TV Listings/Comics (Daily); At Your Service, Cold Case, Fresh Talk, Snapshots, To Your Health (Mon); Pet Connection, Chasing Rainbows, Heyville, Words from War (Tue); School Daze, Taking up Space, Married to the Movies, Gen Zgen, Game On, Supper Club or Lunch Brunch, Footnote, Campus Page (Wed); Police Beat, Pets of the Week, The Beat Goes On, Fresh Talk, At Home (Thur); Fishing News, Go Entertainment Section, Market News, Movies, Footnote (Fri); Faith, Market News, Movies, Religion, Footnote, Ask Martha, Earth Talk, Environmental News, Going Wild (Sat); Movies, Arts/Books, Travel News, Business News, Comics, Chatterbox, Cultural News, Deeds & Building Permits, Fun Coast Real Estate, Innovations, National Auto Racing, Political News, Travel News, TV Journal, USA Weekend, Amusement Section (Sun)
Syndicated Publications: Homes & Property (Monthly); TV Journal (S).
Delivery Methods: Mail`Newsstand`Carrier`Racks
Areas Served - City/County or Portion Thereof, or Zip codes: All of Volusia and Flagler counties
Own Printing Facility?: Y
Commercial printers?: Y
Sat. Circulation Paid: 45418
Sun. Circulation Paid: 56607
Audit By: AAM
Audit Date: 31.03.2018
Personnel: Brad Gordner (Mgr., Mktg. Devel.); Frank Fernandez (Mng. Ed./Bureau Chief); Lori Kopp (Mgr., Strategic Mktg.); John K. Shaw (Circ. Mgr.); Cory Lancaster (Mng. Ed.); Aaron London (Asst. Bureau Chief); Cal Massey (Deputy Mng. Ed., News); Derek Catron (Asst. Mng. Ed.); Bill Offill (Publisher); Pat Rice (Editor); Mike Baskin (Advertising Director); Marc L. Davidson (Chrmn. of the Board); David Kendall (CFO); Ellen Andrews (Mgr., Accounting); Kathy Tiller (Community Rel. Mgr.); Douglas R. Davis (Circ. Dir.); Larry Saffer (Circ. Sales/Mktg. Mgr.); Marc Davidson (Co-Ed.); Tony Briggs (Mng. Ed., Online); Nick Klasne (Assistant Managing Editor/Team Leader); David Wersinger; Rachael Smith (Ed.); Cynthia Cross (Retail Adv. Mgr.); Jane Katona (Advert Director)
Parent company (for newspapers): Gannett; CherryRoad Media

MIAMI HERALD

Street address 1: 3511 NW 91st Ave
Street address city: Doral
Street address state: FL
Zip/Postal code: 33172-1216
County: Miami-Dade
Country: USA
Mailing state: FL
General Phone: (800)766-2820
Advertising Phone: (866) 860-6000
Editorial Phone: (305) 376-2317
General/National Adv. E-mail: adinfo@miamiherald.com
Display Adv. E-mail: adinfo@miamiherald.com
Classified Adv. e-mail: adinfo@miamiherald.com
Editorial e-mail: AMarques@MiamiHerald.com
Primary Website: www.miamiherald.com
Mthly Avg Views: 45360278
Mthly Avg Unique Visitors: 18106861
Year Established: 1903
News Services: AP, DJ, MCT, LAT-WP, SOU, TV Data.
Special Editions: Special sections: Health Reports, Arts, Education, Sports, Hispanic
Special Weekly Sections: Travel, Home, Design, Employment, Issues, ideas, Comics, TV, Neighbors, Home, Design (Sun); Local, Sports, Business, Classified, Tropical (Daily); Business (Mon); Neighbors, Values (Thur); Weekend (Fri); Auto, Homes (Sat)
Syndicated Publications: Parade (S).
Delivery Methods: Mail`Newsstand`Carrier`Racks
Areas Served - City/County or Portion Thereof, or Zip codes: Miami-Dade and Broward Counties
Own Printing Facility?: Y
Commercial printers?: Y
Avg Free Circ: 1040
Sun. Circulation Paid: 6669
Sun. Circulation Free: 1040
Audit By: AAM
Audit Date: 31.03.2019
Personnel: Greg Curling (CFO & VP of Finance); Bernie Kosanke (Regional Dir. of Audience Development (Circulation)); Aminda Marques Gonzalez (Executive Editor); Rick Hirsch (Managing Editor); Dave Wilson (Senior Editor / Administration); Alexandra Villoch (Pres./Pub.); Lesley DeCanio (VP of Advertising)
Parent company (for newspapers): Hearst Communications, Inc.

ENGLEWOOD SUN

Street address 1: 120 W Dearborn St
Street address city: Englewood
Street address state: FL
Zip/Postal code: 34223-3237
County: Sarasota
Country: USA
General Phone: (941) 681-3000
General/National Adv. E-mail: cymoore@sun-herald.com
Primary Website: www.yoursun.com/csp/mediapool/sites/SunNews/Englewood/index.csp
Audit By: Sworn/Estimate/Non-Audited
Audit Date: 12.07.2019
Personnel: Carol Moore (Pub.)
Parent company (for newspapers): Sun Coast Media Group - APG; Adams Publishing Group, LLC

SOUTH FLORIDA SUN-SENTINEL

Street address 1: This Location Closed
Street address city: Fort Lauderdale
Street address state: FL
Zip/Postal code: 33394
County: Broward
Country: USA
Mailing address: 333 SW 12TH AVE
Mailing city: DEERFIELD BEACH
Mailing state: FL
Mailing zip: 33442-3196
General Phone: (954) 356-4000
Advertising Phone: (954) 425-1817
Editorial Phone: 954.356.4500
General/National Adv. E-mail: dscroggin@sun-sentinel.com
Display Adv. E-mail: dscroggin@sun-sentinel.com
Classified Adv. e-mail: dscroggin@sun-sentinel.com
Editorial e-mail: dbanker@sunsentinel.com
Primary Website: www.sun-sentinel.com
Mthly Avg Views: 18000000
Mthly Avg Unique Visitors: 4000000
Year Established: 1911
Special Editions: PRIME
Special Weekly Sections: Seminar Notices (Mon); Food, Shalom (Wed); Jewish journal, Inside Auto, Society, (Thur); Temple, Community, Marketplace, Showtime (Fri); Inside Real Estate, Auto (Sat); Travel, Lifestyle, Home and Garden, Employment, Comics, Community, Real Estate, Outlook, Sports (Sun)
Areas Served - City/County or Portion Thereof, or Zip codes: Broward County Palm Beach County
Own Printing Facility?: N
Commercial printers?: N
Sat. Circulation Paid: 109103
Sun. Circulation Paid: 169430
Audit By: AAM
Audit Date: 30.06.2018
Personnel: Doug Scroggin (Dir., Major Adv.); Howard Saltz (Ed.); Rob Cravaritis (Vice President Sales/Advertising); Joel Meyer (Manufacturing Director)
Parent company (for newspapers): Tribune Publishing, Inc.

THE NEWS-PRESS

Street address 1: 2442 Dr. Martin Luther King Jr. Blvd.
Street address city: Fort Myers
Street address state: FL
Zip/Postal code: 33901
County: Lee
Country: USA
Mailing address: 2442 Dr. Martin Luther King Jr. Blvd.
Mailing city: Fort Myers
Mailing state: FL
Mailing zip: 33901
General Phone: (239) 992-1345
Editorial Phone: (239) 335-0280
Editorial e-mail: cmcross@news-press.com
Primary Website: www.news-press.com
Year Established: 1884
Sat. Circulation Paid: 39458
Sun. Circulation Paid: 53126
Audit By: AAM
Audit Date: 31.03.2018

Personnel: Bill Barker (Pres./Pub.); Cindy McCurry-Ross (Exec. Ed.); Matt Petro (VP / Finance); Nancy Solliday (VP / Advertising Sales); Ed Reed (Regional Sports Ed.)
Parent company (for newspapers): Gannett - USA Today Network

NORTHWEST FLORIDA DAILY NEWS

Street address 1: 2 Eglin Pkwy NE
Street address city: Fort Walton Beach
Street address state: FL
Zip/Postal code: 32548-4915
County: Okaloosa
Country: USA
Mailing address: PO BOX 2949
Mailing city: FORT WALTON BEACH
Mailing state: FL
Mailing zip: 32549-2949
General Phone: (850) 863-1111
Advertising Phone: (850) 863-1111
Editorial Phone: (850) 863-1111
General/National Adv. E-mail: scollins@pcnh.com
Display Adv. E-mail: staylor@nwfdailynews.com
Classified Adv. e-mail: Jbranda@pcnh.com
Editorial e-mail: news@nwfdailynews.com
Primary Website: www.nwfdailynews.com
Mthly Avg Views: 1,7
Mthly Avg Unique Visitors: 242800
Year Established: 1946
News Services: AP
Special Editions: Football (Aug); Gift Guide (Dec); Home Improvement (Mar); Welcome Guide (May).
Special Weekly Sections: Showcase/Entertainment (Fri); Food (Wed).
Syndicated Publications: Parade (S).
Delivery Methods: Mail`Newsstand`Carrier`Racks
Areas Served - City/County or Portion Thereof, or Zip codes: 32531, 32536, 32539, 32541, 32542, 32547, 32548, 32549, 32564, 32544, 32567, 32569, 32578, 32588, 32579, 32580, 32563, 32583, 32566, 32433, 32435, 32439, 32550, 32434, 32538, 32455, 32459
Own Printing Facility?: N
Commercial printers?: Y
Avg Free Circ: 682
Sat. Circulation Paid: 25722
Sat. Circulation Free: 682
Sun. Circulation Paid: 28331
Sun. Circulation Free: 182
Audit By: AAM
Audit Date: 31.03.2019
Personnel: Jim Shoffner (Editorial Page Ed.); Brenda Shoffner (Ent. Ed.); Del Stone (Online Ed.); Noel Shauf (IT Dir.); Donna Talla; Diane Winnemuller (Publisher); Vickie Gainer (Regional Business Development and Marketing Director); Eleanor Hypes (Regional Human Resource Dir); Shawna Laethem; RJ Driskill; Roger Underwood; Wendy Victora
Parent company (for newspapers): Gannett; CherryRoad Media

THE GAINESVILLE SUN

Street address 1: 2700 SW 13th St
Street address city: Gainesville
Street address state: FL
Zip/Postal code: 32608-2015
County: Alachua
Country: USA
Mailing address: PO BOX 147147
Mailing city: GAINESVILLE
Mailing state: FL
Mailing zip: 32614-7147
General Phone: (352) 378-1411
Advertising Phone: (352) 374-5012
Editorial Phone: (352) 374-5075
General/National Adv. E-mail: online@gvillesun.com
Display Adv. E-mail: Lynda.strickland@gvillesun.com
Classified Adv. e-mail: classified@gvillesun.com
Editorial e-mail: doug.ray@gvillesun.com
Primary Website: www.gainesville.com
Mthly Avg Unique Visitors: 618591
Year Established: 1876
News Services: AP, NYT, LAT-WP, MCT, SHNS, TMS.
Special Editions: Gainesville Magazine (Apr); Gainesville Magazine (Aug); Gainesville Magazine (Dec); Gainesville Magazine (Feb); Wedding Book (Jan); Travel-Caribbean Value Season (Jul); Gainesville Magazine (Jun); Travel-Summer in Europe (Mar); Travel-USA & Canada (May);
Special Weekly Sections: BEst Food Day (Wed); Scene, House, Home, Wheels, Movies (Fri); Gardening, Church (Sat); Real Estate, Travel, Entertainment (Sun); Finance (Tue-Sun)
Syndicated Publications: Parade (S).
Avg Free Circ: 2551
Sat. Circulation Paid: 17263
Sat. Circulation Free: 950
Sun. Circulation Paid: 21837
Sun. Circulation Free: 979
Audit By: AAM
Audit Date: 31.03.2018
Personnel: James E. Doughton (Pub.); Jeffrey Pole (Controller); James Holmes (Bus. Devel. Mgr.); Craig Grant (Online Sales Mgr.); Jim Miller (Circ. Dir.); Jim Osteen (Exec. Ed.); Jacki Levine (Mng. Ed.); Anthony Clark (Bus. Ed.); Dave Schlenker (Amusements/ Entertainment Ed.); Ron Cunningham (Editorial Page Ed.); Nathan Crabbe (Editorial Page Ed.); Cindy Swirko (Educ. Writer, Lower); Diane Chun (Health Ed.); Jon Rabiroff (Metro Ed.); Lynda Strickland (Sr. Adv. Mgr.); Arnold Feliciano (Sports Ed.); Douglas K. Ray (Gen Mgr)
Parent company (for newspapers): Gannett; CherryRoad Media

THE INDEPENDENT FLORIDA ALLIGATOR

Street address 1: PO Box 14257
Street address city: Gainesville
Street address state: FL
Zip/Postal code: 32604-2257
County: Alachua
Country: USA
Mailing address: PO BOX 14257
Mailing city: GAINESVILLE
Mailing state: FL
Mailing zip: 32604-2257
General Phone: 352-376-4446
Advertising Phone: (352) 376-4482
Editorial Phone: (352) 376-4458
General/National Adv. E-mail: tcarey@alligator.org
Display Adv. E-mail: advertising @alligator.org
Classified Adv. e-mail: ellight@alligator.org
Editorial e-mail: editor@alligator.org
Primary Website: www.alligator.org
Year Established: 1906
Special Weekly Sections: Thursday Entertainment section
Delivery Methods: Racks
Areas Served - City/County or Portion Thereof, or Zip codes: uf campus, all og Gainesville
Own Printing Facility?: Y
Avg Free Circ: 30000
Audit By: Sworn/Estimate/Non-Audited
Audit Date: 12.07.2019
Personnel: Kristan Wiggins (Ed.); Colleen Wright (Mng. Ed. Print); Bakr Saliq (Mng. Ed. Online); Beatrice Dupuy (University Ed.); Rachel Crosby (Metro Ed.); Elliot Levy (Opinions Ed.)

THE FLORIDA TIMES-UNION

Street address 1: 1 Riverside Ave
Street address city: Jacksonville
Street address state: FL
Zip/Postal code: 32202-4917
County: Duval
Country: USA
Mailing address: 1 Riverside Ave
Mailing city: Jacksonville
Mailing state: FL
Mailing zip: 32202-4917
General Phone: (904) 359-4111
Advertising Phone: (904) 359-4318
Editorial Phone: (904) 359-4280
General/National Adv. E-mail: WeCanHelp@jacksonville.com
Display Adv. E-mail: WeCanHelp@jacksonville.com
Classified Adv. e-mail: WeCanHelp@jacksonville.com
Editorial e-mail: newstips@jacksonville.com
Primary Website: www.jacksonville.com
Mthly Avg Unique Visitors: 1800490
Year Established: 1864
News Services: AP
Special Editions: TPC (May), Fl/Ga (October) Football (August)
Special Weekly Sections: Home (Sat); Drive (Saturday) Religion (Saturday) Health (Wednesday) Taste (Thursday) Jack - weekly entertainment (Friday) Sholrelines (sat)
Syndicated Publications: Parade
Delivery Methods: Mail`Newsstand`Carrier`Racks
Areas Served - City/County or Portion Thereof, or Zip codes: 32202, 32206, 32208, 32209, 32218, 32219, 32226, 32227, 32233, 32250, 32266, 32211, 32225, 32277, 32224, 32246, 32256, 32207, 32216, 32217, 32223, 32257, 32258, 32204, 32205, 32220, 32221, 32234, 32254, 32210, 32212, 32222, 32244, 32003, 32043, 32065, 32068, 32073, 32079, 32033, 32084, 32096, 32080, 32081, 32082, 32092, 32095, 32259, 32009, 32034, 32097, 32011,
Own Printing Facility?: Y
Commercial printers?: Y
Sat. Circulation Paid: 45685
Sun. Circulation Paid: 67331
Audit By: AAM
Audit Date: 30.06.2018
Personnel: Mary Kelli Palka (Ed.); Liz Borten (Sales Dir.); Mike Clark (Editorial Page Ed.); Paul Runnestrand (News Ed.); Gary Mills (Digital Dir.); Joe Fenton (Metro Ed.); Scott Butler (Assistant Metro Ed.); Tom Szaroleta (Lifestyle Ed.)
Parent company (for newspapers): Gannett; CherryRoad Media

KEY WEST CITIZEN

Street address 1: 3420 Northside Dr
Street address city: Key West
Street address state: FL
Zip/Postal code: 33040-4254
County: Monroe
Country: USA
Mailing address: PO BOX 1800
Mailing city: KEY WEST
Mailing state: FL
Mailing zip: 33041-1800
General Phone: (305) 292-7777
Advertising Phone: (305) 292-7777
Editorial Phone: (305) 292-7777
Classified Adv. e-mail: classifieds@keysnews.com
Primary Website: www.keysnews.com
Mthly Avg Views: 223869
Year Established: 1876
News Services: AP.
Special Editions: Bridal Magazine(Jan); Taste of Key West (Apr); Hurricane Tab (May); Summer Fun (Jun); Your Pet (Sept); Fantasy Fest (Oct); Gift Guide (Nov); Keys Style: A Locals Guide (Monthly); Healthfile (Quarterly); Home Improvement (Quarterly); Menu Guide (Quarterly)
Special Weekly Sections: Business, Finance (Daily); Best Food (Wed); Arts, Entertainment (Thur); Religion (Fri); Health, Auto (Sat); Auto, Health, Home, Living, Real Estate, Business, Arts, Entertainment (Sun)
Syndicated Publications: Comics (S).
Delivery Methods: Mail`Newsstand`Carrier`Racks
Areas Served - City/County or Portion Thereof, or Zip codes: Monroe County
Own Printing Facility?: N
Commercial printers?: N
Sat. Circulation Paid: 7597
Sun. Circulation Paid: 7789
Audit By: Sworn/Estimate/Non-Audited
Audit Date: 12.07.2019
Personnel: Richard Tamborrino (Pub.); Kay Harris (Ed.); Ernistine Balin (Adv. Consult.)
Parent company (for newspapers): Adams Publishing Group, LLC

LAKE CITY REPORTER

Street address 1: 180 E Duval St
Street address city: Lake City
Street address state: FL
Zip/Postal code: 32055-4085
County: Columbia
Country: USA
Mailing address: PO BOX 1709
Mailing city: LAKE CITY
Mailing state: FL
Mailing zip: 32056-1709
General Phone: (386) 752-1293
Advertising Phone: (386) 755-5440
Editorial Phone: (386) 754-0428
General/National Adv. E-mail: twilson@lakecityreporter.com
Display Adv. E-mail: abutcher@lakecityreporter.com
Editorial e-mail: rbridges@lakecityreporter.com
Primary Website: www.lakecityreporter.com
Year Established: 1874
News Services: AP, SHNS.
Special Editions: Suwannee Valley Vacation Guide (Jan.); Rodeo magazine (March); North Florida Living (Apr); Football (Aug); Song Book (Dec); Physicians Directory (Jan); Columbia Style Biz (Jul); Best of the Best (May); Home for the Holidays (Nov); Guide to Columbia County (Oct); County Fair magazine (Oct.); Health & Nutrition (Sept).
Special Weekly Sections: Real Estate (Fri);
Syndicated Publications: Parade (S); American Profile (Weekly).
Delivery Methods: Mail`Newsstand`Carrier`Racks
Own Printing Facility?: Y
Commercial printers?: Y
Avg Free Circ: 10000
Sat. Circulation Paid: 8887
Sun. Circulation Paid: 8887
Audit By: Sworn/Estimate/Non-Audited
Audit Date: 12.07.2019
Personnel: Todd Wilson (Publisher); Sue Brannon (Controller); Tim Kirby (Sports Ed.); Dave Kimler (IT Mgr.); Ashley Butcher (Advertising Director); Robert Bridges (Editor); Mandy Brown (Circulation Director); Lynda Strickland (Adv. Dir.); Russell Waters (Circ. Dir.); Tom Mayer (Ed.); Jerry Spaeder (Mng. Ed.)
Parent company (for newspapers): Community Newspapers, Inc.

THE LEDGER

Street address 1: 300 W Lime St
Street address 2: 300 West Lime Street
Street address city: Lakeland
Street address state: FL
Zip/Postal code: 33815-4649
County: Polk
Country: USA
Mailing address: PO BOX 408
Mailing city: LAKELAND
Mailing state: FL
Mailing zip: 33802-0408
General Phone: (863) 802-7323
Advertising Phone: (863) 802-7381
Editorial Phone: (863) 802-7504
General/National Adv. E-mail: ron.moates@theledger.com
Display Adv. E-mail: ron.moates@theledger.com
Classified Adv. e-mail: kim.edwards@ledgermediagroup.com
Editorial e-mail: newstips@theledger.com
Primary Website: www.theledger.com
Mthly Avg Views: 10333000
Mthly Avg Unique Visitors: 907423
Year Established: 1924
News Services: AP, NYT, MCT, LAT-WP.
Special Editions: Back-to-School (Aug); Year In Review (Dec); Automotive (Jan); Football (Jul); Spring Health Care (Mar); Mayfaire-By-The-Lake (May); Today's Senior (Monthly); Reader's Choice (Nov); Parade of Homes (Oct); Fall Health Care (Sept).
Special Weekly Sections: Health (Tue); The Arts (Wed); Best Food Day, Entertainment (Thur); Religion, Real Estate (Sat); Senior (Sun)
Syndicated Publications: Parade (S).
Delivery Methods: Mail`Newsstand`Carrier`Racks
Areas Served - City/County or Portion Thereof, or Zip codes: 33565, 33566, 33567, 33801, 33803, 33805, 33809, 33810, 33811, 33812, 33813, 33815, 33823, 33827, 33830, 33834, 33835, 33837, 33896, 33897, 33838, 33839, 33841, 33843, 33844, 33850, 33851, 33853, 33859, 33855, 33856, 33860
Own Printing Facility?: Y
Commercial printers?: Y
Sat. Circulation Paid: 23133
Sun. Circulation Paid: 27302
Audit By: AAM
Audit Date: 31.12.2018
Personnel: Brian Burns (Pub.); Bill Thompson (Editorial Page Ed.); Bob Heist (Exec. Ed.); Patricia Martin (Adv. Dir.); Sharon Schackne (HR Dir.); Bruce Dube (Marketing Dir.); Amanda Trejbrowski (Senior Finance Mgr.); Jeff Amero (Circ. Mgr.)
Parent company (for newspapers): Gannett; CherryRoad Media

THE DAILY COMMERCIAL

Street address 1: 212 E Main St
Street address city: Leesburg
Street address state: FL
Zip/Postal code: 34748-5227
County: Lake
Country: USA
Mailing address: PO BOX 490007
Mailing city: LEESBURG
Mailing state: FL
Mailing zip: 34749-0007
General Phone: (352) 365-8200
Advertising Phone: (352) 365-8287
Editorial Phone: (357) 365-8266

General/National Adv. E-mail: news@dailycommercial.com
Display Adv. E-mail: kevinaustin@dailycommercial.com
Classified Adv. e-mail: linda@dailycommercial.com
Editorial e-mail: news@dailycommercial.com
Primary Website: www.dailycommercial.com
Year Established: 1875
News Services: AP, NYT.
Special Editions: Home Improvement (Apr); Women's Quarterly (Aug); Holiday Gift Guide (Dec); Women's Quarterly (Feb); Super Bowl Preview (Jan); For Your Health (Mar); Women's Quarterly (May); Women's Quarterly (Nov); Welcome Back (Oct).
Special Weekly Sections: Medicine in the News (Mon); Best Food (Wed); Health (Thur); Church, Real Estate (Sat); TV, (Sun); Explore Leesburg, Golden Triangle (Monthly)
Syndicated Publications: TV Week (offset) (S); USA WEEKEND Magazine (Thur).
Avg Free Circ: 1367
Sat. Circulation Paid: 8333
Sat. Circulation Free: 1367
Sun. Circulation Paid: 10182
Audit By: AAM
Audit Date: 31.03.2019
Personnel: Tom McNiff (Exec. Ed.); Paul Nikolai (Circ. Dir.); Sharon Schacknem (Human Resources Dir.); Eric Killen (Account Exec.), Whitney Lehnecker (Digital Ed.)
Parent company (for newspapers): Gannett; CherryRoad Media

JACKSON COUNTY FLORIDAN

Street address 1: 4403 Constitution Ln
Street address city: Marianna
Street address state: FL
Zip/Postal code: 32448-4472
County: Jackson
Country: USA
General Phone: (850) 526-3614
Advertising Phone: (850) 526-3614
Editorial Phone: (850) 526-3614
General/National Adv. E-mail: editorial@jcfloridan.com
Display Adv. E-mail: sales@jcfloridan.com
Classified Adv. e-mail: classifieds@jcfloridan.com
Editorial e-mail: editorial@jcfloridan.com
Primary Website: www.jcfloridan.com
Year Established: 1928
News Services: Associated Press
Special Editions: Senior Citizen (Apr); Football (Aug); Marianna Christmas Bucks (Dec); Visitor's Guide Supplement (Feb); Income Tax (Jan); Senior Citizen (Jul); Visitor's Guide Supplement (Jun); Home & Garden (Mar); Mother's Day (May); Farm City (Nov); Back To School (Sep
Special Weekly Sections: Business (Daily); Religion (Fri); Family, Real Estate (Sun)
Delivery Methods: Mail`Newsstand`Carrier`Racks
Areas Served - City/County or Portion Thereof, or Zip codes: 32420, 32423, 32426, 32431, 32432, 32440, 32442, 32443, 32431, 32445, 32446, 32447, 32448, 32460
Own Printing Facility?: N
Commercial printers?: N
Sat. Circulation Paid: 3690
Sun. Circulation Paid: 3733
Audit By: AAM
Audit Date: 31.03.2016
Personnel: Angie Cook (Editor); Valeria Roberts (Pub./Adv. Dir.); Dena Oberski (Circ. Mgr.); Deborah Buckhalter (Reporter); Mark Skinner (Photographer/Photo Ed.); Rolando Rosa (Sports Editor); Michael Becker (Ed.)
Parent company (for newspapers): BH Media Group; Lee Enterprises, Incorporated; Lee Enterprises

FLORIDA TODAY

Street address 1: P.O. Box 419000
Street address city: Melbourne
Street address state: FL
Zip/Postal code: 32941-9000
County: Brevard
Country: USA
Mailing address: PO BOX 419000
Mailing city: MELBOURNE
Mailing state: FL
Mailing zip: 32941-9000
General Phone: 1-877-424-0156
Advertising Phone: (321) 242-3765
Editorial Phone: (321) 242-3606
General/National Adv. E-mail: sshook@floridatoday.com
Display Adv. E-mail: jprice@floridatoday.com
Editorial e-mail: bstover@floridatoday.com
Primary Website: www.floridatoday.com
Year Established: 1966
News Services: AP, Gannett Content One
Special Editions: HealthSource; Health & Medicine; Brevard County Moms; Fact Book;
Special Weekly Sections: Money (Mon); Health, Fitness (Tue); Community (Wed); Best Food, Health, Style (Thur); TGIF (Fri); Spaces (Sat); Style, Comics, TV (Sun)
Syndicated Publications: USA Weekend (Sun)
Delivery Methods: Mail`Newsstand`Carrier`Racks
Areas Served - City/County or Portion Thereof, or Zip codes: Brevard County, FL
Own Printing Facility?: Y
Commercial printers?: Y
Sat. Circulation Paid: 31998
Sun. Circulation Paid: 45449
Audit By: AAM
Audit Date: 31.03.2018
Personnel: Mara Bellaby (Exec. Ed.); Bobby Block (Watchdog Ed.); John McCarthy (Investigations Ed.); Isadora Rangel (Engagement Ed.); Tim Thorsen (Planning Ed.); Laura Lemmon (Breaking News Ed.); Suzy Fleming Leonard (Food & Dining Ed.); Dave Berman (County Government Ed.); Britt Kennerly (Community Content Ed.); Leween Jones (Dir. of Adv.); John Vizzini (Distribution Dir.); Mike O'Leary (Regional Production Dir.)
Parent company (for newspapers): Gannett

NAPLES DAILY NEWS

Street address 1: 1100 Immokalee Road
Street address city: Naples
Street address state: FL
Zip/Postal code: 34110
County: Collier
Country: USA
Mailing address: 1100 IMMOKALEE RD
Mailing city: NAPLES
Mailing state: FL
Mailing zip: 34110-4810
General Phone: (239) 262-3161
Advertising Phone: (239) 262-3161 (display)
Editorial Phone: (239) 263-4863
General/National Adv. E-mail: info@naplesnews.com
Display Adv. E-mail: sales@naplesnews.com
Classified Adv. e-mail: classad@naplesnews.com
Primary Website: www.naplesnews.com
Mthly Avg Unique Visitors: 955407
News Services: AP, SHNS, NYT.
Special Editions: Newcomers (Apr); Back-to-School (Aug); Newcomers (Dec); Ambience (Feb); Newcomers (Jan); In Business (Jul); Parents & Kids (Jun); Newcomers (Mar); Parents & Kids (May); Real Estate Marketplace (Monthly); Homes for the Holidays (Nov); Portfolio of Homes (O
Special Weekly Sections: Business (Mon); Health (Tue); Food (Wed); Arts (Thur); Home (Fri); Gulf Life, Religion (Sat); Real Estate, Travel, Comics (Sun)
Syndicated Publications: Visitor's Guide (Other); Comics (S).
Areas Served - City/County or Portion Thereof, or Zip codes: South Lee County, Collier County
Own Printing Facility?: Y
Commercial printers?: Y
Sat. Circulation Paid: 38229
Sun. Circulation Paid: 44580
Audit By: AAM
Audit Date: 30.06.2018
Personnel: Trish Priller (Asst. Pub.); Allen Bartlett (City Ed.); Harriet Howard Heithaus (Homes/Ambience Ed.); Tim Aten (News Ed.); Greg Hardwig (Sports Ed.); Cathy Rodrick (Mgr., IS/Pre Press); Glenn Williams (Mgr., Packaging); Cassay Cote (Prodn. Mgr., Pressroom); Bill Barker (Pres./Pub.); Len Egdish (Nat'l Adv. Mgr.); Manny Garcia (Editor); Jigsha Desai (Digital Content Director); Robin Lankton (Director of Marketing); Shawna Devlin (Advertising Director)
Parent company (for newspapers): Gannett - USA Today Network

NORTH PORT SUN

Street address 1: 13487 Tamiami Trl
Street address city: North Port
Street address state: FL
Zip/Postal code: 34287-1211
County: Sarasota
Country: USA
General Phone: (941) 429-3000
General/National Adv. E-mail: cymoore@sun-herald.com
Primary Website: www.yoursun.com/northport/
Audit By: Sworn/Estimate/Non-Audited
Audit Date: 12.07.2019
Personnel: Mike Beatty (Pres.); Glen Nickerson (Pub.); Jim Gouvellis (Exec. Ed.); Garry Overbey (Ed.); Stacie Goldberg (Advertising Manager); Mark Yero (Circ. Dir.)
Parent company (for newspapers): Sun Coast Media Group - APG; Adams Publishing Group, LLC

OCALA STAR-BANNER

Street address 1: 2121 SW 19th Avenue Rd
Street address city: Ocala
Street address state: FL
Zip/Postal code: 34471-7752
County: Marion
Country: USA
Mailing address: 2121 SW 19TH AVENUE RD
Mailing city: OCALA
Mailing state: FL
Mailing zip: 34471-7704
General Phone: (352) 867-4010
Advertising Phone: (352) 867-4060
Editorial Phone: (352) 867-4013
General/National Adv. E-mail: online@starbanner.com
Display Adv. E-mail: steve.martin@starbanner.com
Classified Adv. e-mail: classified@starbanner.com
Editorial e-mail: doug.ray@gvillesun.com
Primary Website: www.ocala.com
Mthly Avg Views: 7814477
Mthly Avg Unique Visitors: 605052
Year Established: 1866
News Services: AP, NYT
Special Editions: Hurricane Guide, Living Here (area guide)
Special Weekly Sections: TV, Business, Sports, Entertainment Weather (Daily); Stock (Tue-Sat); Life (Mon-Wed); Entertainment, Best Food (Thur); Auto, TMC (Fri); Home, Real Estate, Religion (Sat); Arts, Entertainment, business, Travel (Sun)
Syndicated Publications: Real Estate Review (Sat); Parade (S);
Delivery Methods: Newsstand`Carrier`Racks
Own Printing Facility?: Y
Commercial printers?: Y
Sat. Circulation Paid: 23230
Sun. Circulation Paid: 28380
Audit By: AAM
Audit Date: 31.03.2017
Personnel: Melody Day (Adv. Mgr., Classified); Steve Martin (Adv. Mgr., Retail); Mary Baggs (Community Relations); Bill Hayter (Circ. Mgr.); Tom McNiff (Dir Edit); Jim Ross (Assistant Managing Editor); Alan Youngblood (Photo Editor); Andy Marks (Sports Ed.); Susan Pinder (Advertising Director); Jim Osteen (Executive Editor); Richard Anguiano (Online Community Editor); Brad Rogers (Editorial Page Ed.); Jim Doughton (Pub.); Bryce Abshier (Nat'l Adv. Acct. Exec.); Susan Leitgeb (Adv. Dir.); Douglas K. Ray (Exec Ed/Gen Mgr)
Parent company (for newspapers): Gannett; CherryRoad Media

ORLANDO SENTINEL

Street address 1: 633 North Orange Avenue
Street address 2: Lbby
Street address city: Orlando
Street address state: FL
Zip/Postal code: 32801-1349
County: Orange
Country: USA
Mailing address: PO BOX 2833
Mailing city: ORLANDO
Mailing state: FL
Mailing zip: 32802-2833
General Phone: (407) 420-5000
Advertising Phone: (407) 420-5100
Editorial Phone: (407) 420-5411
General/National Adv. E-mail: ecom@tronc.com
Classified Adv. e-mail: classified_ad@orlandosentinel.com
Editorial e-mail: insight@orlandosentinel.com
Primary Website: www.orlandosentinel.com
Mthly Avg Unique Visitors: 2907248
Year Established: 1876
News Services: NYT, MCT, LAT-WP, AP, Cox News Service, CQ, TMS.
Special Editions: Dealer's Choice (Apr); Football Preview (Aug); Holiday Dining (Dec); Lake County Spring Parade of Homes (Feb); Florida Forecast (Jan); Hot Cars (Jul); Career Builder Xtra (Jun); Bay Hill Invitational (Mar); Hurricane Survival Guide (May); Auto Show I (Nov
Special Weekly Sections: Business, Stock (Daily); Homes, Travel (Sun); Lifestyle, Entertainment (Mon-Sun); Business, Features (Mon); Good Eating (Wed); Drive (Thur); Calendar (Fri)
Syndicated Publications: Parade (S).
Areas Served - City/County or Portion Thereof, or Zip codes: 32801
Own Printing Facility?: Y
Commercial printers?: Y
Sat. Circulation Paid: 72017
Sun. Circulation Paid: 159732
Audit By: AAM
Audit Date: 31.03.2018
Personnel: Avido Khahaifa (Editor/SVP/Director of Content-Florida); Dyana Burke (Compensation/Commun. Mgr.); John D'Orlando (Adv. Vice Pres./Dir.); Jack Curtin (Adv. Sr. Mgr., Delivery); Rich Miller (Adv. Mgr., Bus.); Linda Schaible (Vice Pres., Interactive); Bert Ortiz (Circ. Vice Pres.); Dave Elder (Circ. Mgr., Subscriber Servs.); Charlotte H. Hall (Ed.); Mark Russell (Vice President, Editor, Webmaster); Gail Rayos (Assoc. Mng. Ed., Bus.); Kim Marcum (Assoc. Mng. Ed., Features); Bonita Miyagi (Assoc. Mng. Ed., Photo/Design/Visuals); Dana Eagles (Ed., Recruitment/Staff Devel.); Anne Dunlap (Arts/Entertainment Ed.); Bill Zimmerman (Bus. News Ed.); Lisa Cianci (City Ed.); Barry Glenn (Lifestyles Ed.); Chance Schlesman (Acct. Mgr.); Dana Wardeh (Nat'l Retail Dir.); Amy Moon; Michael Friedenberg (Pres.)
Parent company (for newspapers): Alden Global Capital; Tribune Publishing, Inc.

PALATKA DAILY NEWS

Street address 1: 1825 Saint Johns Ave
Street address city: Palatka
Street address state: FL
Zip/Postal code: 32177-4442
County: Putnam
Country: USA
Mailing address: PO BOX 777
Mailing city: PALATKA
Mailing state: FL
Mailing zip: 32178-0777
General Phone: (386) 312-5200
Advertising Phone: (386) 312-5210
General/National Adv. E-mail: mwells@palatkadailynews.com
Editorial e-mail: akrombach@palatkadailynews.com
Primary Website: www.palatkadailynews.com
Year Established: 1885
News Services: AP.
Special Editions: Back-to-School (Aug); Fact Book (Feb); Meet the Manager (Jan); Blue Crab Festival (May); Gift Guide (Nov); Create a Beautiful Home (Oct); Industry Appreciation (Sept).
Special Weekly Sections: Currents (Fri); Health and Fitness Page (Wed).
Sat. Circulation Paid: 13309
Audit By: Sworn/Estimate/Non-Audited
Audit Date: 12.07.2019
Personnel: Mary Kaye Wells (Adv. Dir.); John Allender (Circ. Dir.); Andy Hall (Sports Ed.); Wayne Knuckles (Pub.); Scott Bryan (Ed.)
Parent company (for newspapers): Community Newspapers, Inc.

PALM BEACH DAILY NEWS

Street address 1: 400 Royal Palm Way
Street address 2: Ste 100
Street address city: Palm Beach
Street address state: FL
Zip/Postal code: 33480-4117
County: Palm Beach
Country: USA
Mailing address: 400 ROYAL PALM WAY STE 100
Mailing city: PALM BEACH
Mailing state: FL
Mailing zip: 33480-4117
General Phone: (561) 820-3800
Advertising Phone: (561) 820-3815
Editorial Phone: (561) 820-3865
General/National Adv. E-mail: lgoings@pbdailynews.com
Display Adv. E-mail: lgoings@pbdailynews.com
Classified Adv. e-mail: lgoings@pbdailynews.com
Editorial e-mail: jreingold@pbdailynews.com
Primary Website: www.palmbeachdailynews.com
Year Established: 1897

Special Weekly Sections: Insider Society Section (Wed); Home, Real Estate (Fri); Business, Finance, Fashion (Sun)
Syndicated Publications: Palm Beach Life
Delivery Methods: Mail`Racks
Sat. Circulation Paid: 2746
Sun. Circulation Paid: 4057
Audit By: AAM
Audit Date: 30.06.2018
Personnel: Elizabeth Clarke (Ed.); Shelly Darby (Mng. Ed.)
Parent company (for newspapers): Gannett; CherryRoad Media

THE NEWS HERALD

Street address 1: 501 W 11th St
Street address city: Panama City
Street address state: FL
Zip/Postal code: 32401-2330
County: Bay
Country: USA
Mailing address: PO BOX 1940
Mailing city: PANAMA CITY
Mailing state: FL
Mailing zip: 32402-1940
General Phone: (850) 747-5000
Advertising Phone: (850) 747-5030
Editorial Phone: (850) 747-5070
General/National Adv. E-mail: news@pcnh.com
Display Adv. E-mail: lcarver@pcnh.com
Classified Adv. e-mail: jbullock@pcnh.com
Editorial e-mail: skent@pcnh.com
Primary Website: www.newsherald.com
Year Established: 1937
News Services: AP, MCT.
Special Weekly Sections: Lifestyle & Viewpoint (S); Religion (Sat); Outdoors (Thur); Food (Wed).
Syndicated Publications: Parade Magazine (S).
Delivery Methods: Mail`Newsstand`Carrier`Racks
Areas Served - City/County or Portion Thereof, or Zip codes: Bay, Gulf, Franklin, Jackson, Washington, Holmes and Walton Counties in Florida
Own Printing Facility?: Y
Commercial printers?: Y
Sat. Circulation Paid: 18446
Sun. Circulation Paid: 21923
Audit By: CAC
Audit Date: 31.03.2015
Personnel: Robert Delaney (Rgl.Controller); Lorraine Grimes (Rgl HR Dir.); Glenda Sullivan (Circ. Customer Service Mgr.); Joye McCormick (Adv. Services Mgr.); Mike Cazalas (Eastern Ed., Halifax NW Florida Group); Tony Simmons (Online Ed.); Pat McCann (Sports Ed.); Ron Smith (Rgl. Ops. Dir.); Sharon Heckler (Rgl. Circ. Dir.); Will Glover (Managing Ed.); Ray Glenn (Copy Desk Chief); Lori Ann Carver (Adv. Dir.); Tonya Clay (Adv. Mgr. - Digital); Wayne Kight (Retail Adv. Mgr.); Ron Bennett (Rgl. IT Dir.); Vickie Gainer (Rgl. Mktg. Dir.); Roger Underwood; Lee Knapp (Pub.); Tim Thompson (Publisher)
Parent company (for newspapers): Gannett; CherryRoad Media

PENSACOLA NEWS JOURNAL

Street address 1: 2 N Palafox St
Street address city: Pensacola
Street address state: FL
Zip/Postal code: 32502-5626
County: Escambia
Country: USA
Mailing address: PO BOX 12710
Mailing city: PENSACOLA
Mailing state: FL
Mailing zip: 32591-2710
General Phone: (850) 435-8500
Advertising Phone: (850) 435-8585
Editorial Phone: (850) 435-8542
General/National Adv. E-mail: jbell@pnj.com
Display Adv. E-mail: rboles@pnj.com
Classified Adv. e-mail: 1889
Editorial e-mail: news@pnj.com
Primary Website: www.pnj.com
Mthly Avg Unique Visitors: 505065
News Services: AP, GNS.
Special Editions: Football (Aug); Hurricane (May).
Special Weekly Sections: Business (Mon-Sat); Food & Wine, Moneysaver (Wed); Weekender (Fri); Coast Life, Homefinder, Cars, School (Sat); Business, Coast Life, Jobs, Health, Fitness, Travel, Military (Sun)
Syndicated Publications: USA WEEKEND Magazine (S).
Sat. Circulation Paid: 21426
Sun. Circulation Paid: 30843
Audit By: AAM
Audit Date: 31.12.2018
Personnel: Kevin Doyle (Pub./Pres.); Tom Hartley (Dir., Finance); Bobby Rice (Dir., Adv. Sales); Nadja Silvey (Adv. Mgr., Retail); Debora Lefort (Adv. Mgr., Inside Sales); Becca Boles (Dir., Market Devel.); Gregory L. Clay (Strategic Mktg. Mgr.); Pat Daugherty (Circ. Dir.); Richard Schneider (Exec. Ed.); Gray Biel (Mng. Ed.); Earl Melvin (Archives Mgr.); Julio Diaz (Community Content Editor); Carl Wernicke (Editorial Page Ed.); Mark Everett (Circ. Direc.); Lisa Reese (President & Publisher); Carolyn Campbell (Nat'l Sales Coord.); Rob Johnson (Content Coach/Watchdog); Jodi Bell (Director of Sales)
Parent company (for newspapers): Gannett

SUN COAST MEDIA GROUP - APG

Street address 1: 23170 Harborview Rd
Street address city: Port Charlotte
Street address state: FL
Zip/Postal code: 33980-2100
County: Charlotte
Country: USA
Mailing address: 23170 Harborview Road
Mailing city: Port Charlotte
Mailing state: FL
Mailing zip: 33980-2100
General Phone: (941) 206-1000
Advertising Phone: (941) 206-1214
Editorial Phone: (941) 206-1100
General/National Adv. E-mail: info@sun-herald.com
Display Adv. E-mail: gnickerson@sun-herald.com
Classified Adv. e-mail: jharrington@sun-herald.com
Editorial e-mail: editors@sun-herald.com
Primary Website: www.yoursun.com
Year Established: 1977
News Services: MCT, AP Limited, AP Photo Feed, Bloomberg-Washington Post, News Service of Florida, St. Petersburg Times
Special Editions: Charlotte Sun Englewood Sun North Port Sun Venice Gondolier Sun
Special Weekly Sections: Best Food Day (Wed); Fishing, Boating, Best Food (Thur); Auto, Entertainment, Travel (Fri); Real Estate, Furniture (Sat); TV, Business, Style (Sun)
Syndicated Publications: Harbor Style The Arcadian West Villages Sun Charlotte Sun Weekly North Port Sun Weekly Venice/Englewood Sun Weekly Welcome Home
Delivery Methods: Mail`Newsstand`Carrier`Racks
Areas Served - City/County or Portion Thereof, or Zip codes: 33834, 33873, 33890, 33921, 33946, 33947, 33948, 33950, 33952, 33953, 33954, 33955, 33980, 33981, 33982, 33983, 34223, 34224, 34229, 34266, 34269, 34275, 34285, 34286, 34287, 34288, 34289, 34291, 34292, 34293
Own Printing Facility?: Y
Commercial printers?: Y
Sat. Circulation Paid: 33627
Sun. Circulation Paid: 50351
Audit By: AAM
Audit Date: 31.03.2018
Personnel: David Dunn-Rankin (President/CEO/COO); Chris Porter (Exec. Ed.); Glen Nickerson (President/ News-Sun & Highlands Sun); Leslee Peth (Ad Director/ PGH); Mark Yero (Circ. Dir.); Jim Gouvellis (VP/Polk Operations Publisher/Heartland Newspapers); Jim Merchant (Systems Ed.); Chris Germann (Press Room Mgr.); Steve Sachkar (Publisher/North Port Sun); Mary Skaggs (Mgr., HR); Jim Gouvellis (Exec. Ed.); Carol Moore (Publisher, Englewood Sun); Joe Gallimore (Publisher, Arcadian); Joanne Hackney (Data Processing Mgr.); Cynthia Acevedo (Nat'l/Major Acct. Sales); Tim Smolarick (Publisher, Venice Gondolier Sun); Glen Nickerson (Publisher)
Parent company (for newspapers): Adams Publishing Group, LLC

ST. LUCIE NEWS TRIBUNE

Street address 1: 760 NW Enterprise Dr
Street address city: Port Saint Lucie
Street address state: FL
Zip/Postal code: 34986-2228
County: Saint Lucie
Country: USA
General Phone: (722) 337-5800
Advertising Phone: (772) 409-1361
Editorial e-mail: adam.neal@tcpalm.com
Primary Website: www.tcpalm.com
Sat. Circulation Paid: 40111
Sun. Circulation Paid: 53433
Audit By: AAM
Audit Date: 30.06.2018
Personnel: Adam Neal (Editor)
Parent company (for newspapers): Gannett

THE ST. AUGUSTINE RECORD

Street address 1: 1 News Pl
Street address city: Saint Augustine
Street address state: FL
Zip/Postal code: 32086-6520
County: Saint Johns
Country: USA
Mailing address: 1 NEWS PL
Mailing city: SAINT AUGUSTINE
Mailing state: FL
Mailing zip: 32086-6520
General Phone: (904) 829-6562
Advertising Phone: (904) 819-3475
General/National Adv. E-mail: ads@staugustinerecord.com
Editorial e-mail: editor@staugustinerecord.com
Primary Website: www.staugustine.com
News Services: AP, MCT, LAT-WP, Morris News Service.
Special Editions: Active Lifestyles (Apr); Back-to-School (Aug); Christmas Greetings (Dec); Bridal (Feb); Active Lifestyles (Jan); Active Lifestyles (Jul); Just Say No (Mar); Real Estate Today (May); Holiday Style & Fashion (Nov); Explore St. John's (Oct); Football (Sept).
Special Weekly Sections: Neighbors, Morning Brew, Club Life (Mon); Community (Tue); Coupons (Wed); Food, Health & Science (Thur); Arts, Entertainment, Religion, Driving, NASCAR, Neighbors (Fri); Seniors, Gardening, Business, Real Estate, Fashion (Sat); Lifestyles, TV, Travel, Youth, Education, Business, Job Finder (Sun);
Syndicated Publications: Relish (Monthly); USA WEEKEND Magazine (S).
Avg Free Circ: 1331
Sat. Circulation Paid: 10709
Sat. Circulation Free: 1171
Sun. Circulation Paid: 12762
Sun. Circulation Free: 2243
Audit By: AAM
Audit Date: 30.06.2018
Personnel: Paul Kennedy (Circ. Mgr.); Peter Guinta (Senior Writer); Renee Unsworth (Compass Ed.); Anne Heymen (Features Ed.); Shaun Ryan (Health Ed.); Steve Everberg (Prodn. Dir.); Gail Cumiskey (Special Projects Dir.); Delinda Fogel (Publisher); Austen Gregerson (Sports writer); Ron Davidson (Pub.); Tonya Clay (Adv. Dir.); Tiffany Lowe (Nat'l Coord.)
Parent company (for newspapers): Gannett; CherryRoad Media

SARASOTA HERALD-TRIBUNE

Street address 1: 1777 Main Street, 4th Floor
Street address city: Sarasota
Street address state: FL
Zip/Postal code: 34236
County: Sarasota
Country: USA
Mailing address: 1741 MAIN ST
Mailing city: SARASOTA
Mailing state: FL
Mailing zip: 34236-5812
General Phone: (941) 953-7755
Advertising Phone: (941) 361-4000
Editorial Phone: (941) 361-4800
General/National Adv. E-mail: carmen.cook@heraldtribune.com
Display Adv. E-mail: shari.brickley@heraldtribune.com
Classified Adv. e-mail: greg.trippel@heraldtribune.com
Editorial e-mail: advocate@heraldtribune.com
Primary Website: www.heraldtribune.com
Mthly Avg Unique Visitors: 1344419
Year Established: 1925
News Services: AP, LAT-WP, NYT.
Special Editions: Golf Guide (Apr); Year-End Auto Clearance (Aug); Auto Showcase (Dec); Dining Guide (Feb); Jubilee (Jan); Dining Guide (Jul); Suncoast Off-shore Program (Jun); Wine Fest (Mar); Hurricane (May); Holiday Gift Guide (Nov); Season (Oct); Clubs (Sept).
Special Weekly Sections: Business (Mon); Health, Fitness (Tue); Food, Wine (Wed); Entertainment (Thur); Home (Fri); Real Estate (Sat); Comics, Real Estate, Arts (Sun)
Syndicated Publications: Style Magazine (Luxury Lifestyle), 1st Sunday Monthly; Better Living (Senior Lifestyle), quarterly
Delivery Methods: Mail`Newsstand`Carrier`Racks
Areas Served - City/County or Portion Thereof, or Zip codes: 34203, 34205, 34207, 34208, 34209, 34210, 34215, 34217, 34221, 34222, 34201, 34202, 34211, 34212, 34219, 34243, 34251, 34228, 34229, 34231, 34232, 34233, 34234, 34235, 34236, 34237, 34238, 34239, 34240, 34241, 34242, 34275, 34285, 34292, 34293, 34286, 34287, 34288, 34289, 34291, 33921, 33946, 33947, 33953, 33981, 34223, 34224
Own Printing Facility?: Y
Commercial printers?: Y
Sat. Circulation Paid: 46283
Sun. Circulation Paid: 53766
Audit By: AAM
Audit Date: 31.12.2018
Personnel: Shari Brickley (Adv. Dir.); Jennifer Eichorn (Circ. Mgr.); Deborah Winsor (Asst. Mng. Ed.); Matt Sauer (Gen. Mgr.); David Grimes (Columnist); Tom Lyons (Columnist); Jay Handelman (Critic, Theater/ Television); Thomas Lee Tryon (Editorial Page Ed.); Kyle Booth (Front Page Ed.); Mike Lang (Photo Dir.); Cindy Allegretto (Web Ed.); Keisha Gray; Holly Ronnick (Nat'l Adv. Sales); Patrick E. Dorsey (Pub.); Robert Bolone
Parent company (for newspapers): CherryRoad Media; Gannett Company Inc.

HIGHLANDS NEWS-SUN

Street address 1: 321 N. Ridgewood Drive
Street address city: Sebring
Street address state: FL
Zip/Postal code: 33870
County: Highlands
Country: USA
Mailing address: 321 N. Ridgewood Drive
Mailing city: Sebring
Mailing state: FL
Mailing zip: 33870
General Phone: (863) 385-6155
General/National Adv. E-mail: cliff.yeazel@highlandsnewssun.com
Display Adv. E-mail: cliff.yeazel@highlandsnewssun.com
Classified Adv. e-mail: sandra.gillard@highlandsnewssun.com
Editorial e-mail: allen.moody@highlandsnewssun.com
Primary Website: yoursun.com/sebring/
Year Established: 1927
News Services: AP, TMS.
Special Editions: 101 Things to do in the Heartland (Jan); 12 Hours of Sebring Race Tab (Mar).
Special Weekly Sections: Business (S); Religion (Sat).
Syndicated Publications: USA WEEKEND Magazine (Fri); American Profile (Mon).
Delivery Methods: Mail`Newsstand`Carrier`Racks
Areas Served - City/County or Portion Thereof, or Zip codes: 33825, 33852, 33857, 33870, 33872, 33875, 33876
Own Printing Facility?: Y
Commercial printers?: Y
Sat. Circulation Paid: 16609
Sun. Circulation Paid: 16609
Audit By: Sworn/Estimate/Non-Audited
Audit Date: 12.07.2019
Personnel: David Dunn-Rankin (Pres.); Timothy Smolarick (D-R Media Group VP & Publisher); Ramona Washington (Corp. Exec. Ed.); Karen Klogston (Mng. Ed.); Allen Moody (Ed.); Sandra Gillard (Class/Circ.); Cliff Yeazel (Adv. Dir.)
Parent company (for newspapers): Sun Coast Media Group - APG

TAMPA BAY TIMES

Street address 1: 490 1st Ave S
Street address city: St Petersburg
Street address state: FL
Zip/Postal code: 33701-4204
County: Pinellas
Country: USA
Mailing address: PO BOX 1121
Mailing city: ST PETERSBURG
Mailing state: FL
Mailing zip: 33731-1121
General Phone: (727) 893-8289
Advertising Phone: (727) 894-1141
Editorial Phone: (727) 893-8215
General/National Adv. E-mail: mediakit@tampabay.com
Display Adv. E-mail: tbtadvertise@tbt.com
Classified Adv. e-mail: tbtadvertise@tbt.com
Editorial e-mail: local@tampabay.com
Primary Website: www.tampabay.com
Mthly Avg Views: 9296000

Mthly Avg Unique Visitors: 2011000
Year Established: 1884
News Services: AP, NYT, LAT-WP, SHNS, MCT.
Special Editions: Clearwater Fun 'n Sun (Apr); Football (Aug); Personal Best (Every other month); Hernando Profiles (Feb); School Search (Jan); Wedding Guides (Jul); West Virginia (Jun); Chasco Fiesta (Mar); Hurricane (May); Home Search (Monthly); Holiday Gift Guide (Nov);
Special Weekly Sections: Health (Tue); Best Food (Wed); Entertainment (Thur); Auto (Sat); Travel, Arts, Literature, Homes, Real Estate (Sun)
Syndicated Publications: Bay (Every other month); Sunday Comics (S).
Own Printing Facility?: Y
Commercial printers?: Y
Sat. Circulation Paid: 185938
Sun. Circulation Paid: 332296
Audit By: AAM
Audit Date: 31.12.2017
Personnel: Paul Tash (Chairman & CEO); Jana Jones (VP / CFO); Joe DeLuca (VP / Tampa Pub., TampaBay.com Pub.); Sebastian Dortch (HR Dir.); Andrew P. Corty (Vice Pres./Sec.); Mark Shurman (Adv. Mgr.); Michelle Mitchell (Adv. Mgr., Classified); Nancy Waclawek (Dir., Cor. Giving); Kerry O'Reilly (Marketing Dir.); Dave LaBell (Community/Events Mgr.); Jounice Nealy-Brown (Communications Dir.); Jim Booth (Sr. Ed.); Bill Stevens (Ed., North Suncoast); Ben Hayes (Op. Dir.); Jerry Haynes; Neil Brown (Ed. & VP); Debbie Doane; Bruce Faulmann (VP / Sales & Marketing); Gretchen Letterman (Dir., Editorial/Creative, Times Targeted Media); Kelly Spamer (Nat'l Sales); Monica Boyer (Sr. Adv. Mgr.); Mike Wilson (Mng. Ed., Enterprise); John Schlander (Digital General Mgr.); Amber McDonald; Joe Childs (Mng. Ed., Tampa Bay); Amy Hollyfield (Deputy Managing Ed./Politics, Business); Jeanne Grinstead (Deputy Managing Ed./Features, Lifestyles); Ed Nicholson (Chief Info. Officer); Mark Katches (Exec. Ed.); Carolyn Fox (Senior Deputy Editor); Ellen Clarke (Deputy Editor, Life & Culture); Kathleen McGrory (Deputy Editor, Investigations and Enterprise); Traci Johnson (Deputy Editor, Sports); Graham Brink (Editor of the Editorial Pages); Jennifer Orsi (Managing Ed.); Chris Davis (Deputy Managing Ed./Investigations); Ron Brackett (Deputy Managing Ed./tampabay.com, Presentation); Tim Nickens (Ed. of Editorials)
Parent company (for newspapers): Times Publishing Co

THE STUART NEWS

Street address 1: 1939 SE Federal Hwy
Street address city: Stuart
Street address state: FL
Zip/Postal code: 34994-3915
County: Martin
Country: USA
Mailing address: PO BOX 9009
Mailing city: STUART
Mailing state: FL
Mailing zip: 34995-9009
General Phone: (772) 287-1550
Editorial e-mail: feedback@tcpalm.com
Primary Website: www.tcpalm.com
Avg Free Circ: 367
Sat. Circulation Paid: 37734
Sat. Circulation Free: 364
Sun. Circulation Paid: 51118
Sun. Circulation Free: 361
Audit By: AAM
Audit Date: 30.06.2018
Personnel: Adam Neal (Mng. Ed.)
Parent company (for newspapers): Gannett

TALLAHASSEE DEMOCRAT

Street address 1: 277 N. Magnolia Drive
Street address city: Tallahassee
Street address state: FL
Zip/Postal code: 32301
County: Leon
Country: USA
Mailing address: PO BOX 990
Mailing city: TALLAHASSEE
Mailing state: FL
Mailing zip: 32302-0990
General Phone: (850) 599-2100
Advertising Phone: (850) 599-2189
Editorial Phone: (850) 599-2210
General/National Adv. E-mail: clevans@tallahassee.com
Display Adv. E-mail: clevans@tallahassee.com
Classified Adv. e-mail: khanselman@tallahassee.com
Editorial e-mail: letters@tallahassee.com
Primary Website: www.tallahassee.com
Year Established: 1905
News Services: MCT, AP, TMS, GNS.
Special Editions: Living Here (Aug); Home & Design (Every other month); College Football Preview (Fall); Business Outlook (Feb); North Florida Home Show (Jan); Chamber of Commerce (Jul); Legislature 2008 (Mar); Money Clip (Monthly); Holiday Planner (Nov); Physicians & Health; Your Health (monthly); Moms like Me (Monthly);
Special Weekly Sections: Family (Sun); Volunteer (Mon); Schools, Education (Tue); Health (Wed); Taste (Thur); My Nest, Limelight (Fri); Faith (Sat)
Syndicated Publications: USA WEEKEND Magazine (S).
Delivery Methods: Mail`Newsstand`Carrier`Racks
Areas Served - City/County or Portion Thereof, or Zip codes: 31792, 32301. 32302, 32303, 32304, 32305, 32306, 32308, 32309, 32310, 32311, 32312, 32317, 32320, 32321, 32322, 32323, 32324, 32327, 32328, 32330, 32331, 32332, 32333, 32334, 32337, 32340, 32343, 32344, 32346, 32347, 32348, 32351, 32352, 32355, 32358, 32361, 32399, 32421, 32424, 32425, 32428, 32446, 32447, 32448, 32456, 32460, 39817, 39819, 39827, 39828, 39897
Own Printing Facility?: Y
Commercial printers?: Y
Sat. Circulation Paid: 23763
Sun. Circulation Paid: 28815
Audit By: AAM
Audit Date: 30.09.2018
Personnel: Skip Foster (Pres.); Cari Evans (Adv. Dir.); Chet Noll (Distribution Director); Ryan Walthall (Controller)
Parent company (for newspapers): Gannett

THE VILLAGES DAILY SUN

Street address 1: 1100 Main St
Street address city: The Villages
Street address state: FL
Zip/Postal code: 32159-7719
County: Lake
Country: USA
General Phone: (352) 753-1119
Advertising Phone: (352) 753-1119
Editorial Phone: (352) 753-1119
General/National Adv. E-mail: advertising@thevillagesmedia.com
Display Adv. E-mail: advertising@thevillagesmedia.com
Classified Adv. e-mail: classifieds@thevillagesmedia.com
Editorial e-mail: larry.croom@thevillagesmedia.com
Primary Website: www.thevillagesdailysun.com
Mthly Avg Views: 1100000
Mthly Avg Unique Visitors: 24100
Year Established: 1997
News Services: AP.
Special Editions: Salute to Business (Apr); Football Preview (Aug); Paradise in Pictures (Feb); Social Security (Mar); Hurricane Preparedness Guide (May); Newcomers (Sept).
Special Weekly Sections: Wheels (Fri), Home & Garden (Sat), Travel (Sun), Next Door News (Sat.)
Syndicated Publications: Parade Magazine (S): Athlon Sports (Monthly);
Delivery Methods: Newsstand`Carrier`Racks
Areas Served - City/County or Portion Thereof, or Zip codes: 32162;32163;32159,32179;32195;32726;32757;32778;33513;33538;34420;34473;34481;34484;34491;34731;34748;34785;34788; 34471; 34472; 34474; 34476; 34480
Own Printing Facility?: Y
Commercial printers?: Y
Avg Free Circ: 1056
Sat. Circulation Paid: 45857
Sat. Circulation Free: 1166
Sun. Circulation Paid: 47842
Sun. Circulation Free: 1131
Audit By: AAM
Audit Date: 31.03.2024
Personnel: John Gagnon (Circ. Dir.); Wendy Crowther-Barnes (Customer Service Manager); Steven Infinger (Director of Operations); Larry Croom (Ombudsman); Bonita Miyagi (Vice President for Editorial Operations); Matt Fry (Managing Editor); Dan Sprung (Director, Marketing/Publishing); James Sprung (General Manager); Curt Hills (Managing Editor of Projects); Philip Markward (Pub.); William McNair (Printing & Distribution Manager)

INDIAN RIVER PRESS JOURNAL

Street address 1: 2066 14th Ave
Street address 2: Ste 200
Street address city: Vero Beach
Street address state: FL
Zip/Postal code: 32960-4420
County: Indian River
Country: USA
General Phone: (772) 287-1550
General/National Adv. E-mail: feedback@tcpalm.com
Primary Website: www.tcpalm.com
Avg Free Circ: 63
Sat. Circulation Paid: 15007
Sat. Circulation Free: 125
Sun. Circulation Paid: 17365
Sun. Circulation Free: 125
Audit By: AAM
Audit Date: 30.06.2018
Personnel: Adam Neal (Editor)
Parent company (for newspapers): Gannett

THE PALM BEACH POST

Street address 1: 2751 S. Dixie Highway
Street address city: West Palm Beach
Street address state: FL
Zip/Postal code: 33405
County: Palm Beach
Country: USA
Mailing address: PO BOX 24700
Mailing city: WEST PALM BEACH
Mailing state: FL
Mailing zip: 33416-4700
General Phone: (561) 820-4100
Advertising Phone: (561) 820-4300
Editorial Phone: (561) 820-4401
General/National Adv. E-mail: ablizzard@pbpost.com
Display Adv. E-mail: ablizzard@pbpost.com
Classified Adv. e-mail: tdiglio@pbpost.com
Editorial e-mail: pb_metro@pbpost.com; pb_sports@pbpost.com; pb_business@pbpost.com
Primary Website: www.pbpost.com
Mthly Avg Unique Visitors: 1244742
Year Established: 1908
News Services: AP, Bloomberg, LAT-WP, NYT, PR Newswire, Cox.
Special Editions: SunFest (Apr); Football (Aug); Holiday Gift Guide (Dec); Treasure Coast Fairs & Festivals (Feb); Super Bowl (Jan); Back To School (Jul); Palm Beach Medical Society Directory (Jun); Home & Garden (Mar); Discover Florida (May); Palm Beach Post Financial Sho
Special Weekly Sections: Local Business (Mon); Health, Living (Tue); Food, Dining, (Wed); Neighborhood Post/ Florida Pennysaver (zoned), Notables (in Accent May-September) (Thur); Religion/Church News, TGIF, Florida Home New Home (Fri); Neighborhoods (Sat); Book Reviews, Health, Accent, Comics, TV, Real Money (Sun)
Syndicated Publications: Color Comics (S).
Sat. Circulation Paid: 62179
Sun. Circulation Paid: 91464
Audit By: AAM
Audit Date: 30.06.2018
Personnel: Charles Gerardi (Vice Pres./Gen. Mgr.); Linda Murphy (Vice Pres., HR); Susan Meldonian (Credit Mgr.); Gregg Harr (Adv. Dir., Opns.); Steve Waxelbaum (Adv. Mgr., Retail, Bureau Offices); Laura Cunningham (Dir., Mktg. Servs.); Michelle Ruzgar (Internet Mktg. Mgr.); Suzanne Willcox (Mgr., Research/Sales Presentations); Barry Berg (Circ. Vice Pres.); Linda Campbell (Circ. Mgr., Admin. Servs.); Rich Schnars (Circ. Mgr., Opns.); Rick Christie (Editorial Page Ed.); Pete Cross (Asst. Mng. Ed., Photo); Bill Greer (Asst. Mng. Ed., Projects); Michelle Quigley (Data interactive editor); Christopher Caneles (VP Operations); Andy Blizzard (VP, Revenue Develop.)
Parent company (for newspapers): Gannett; CherryRoad Media

NEWS CHIEF

Street address 1: 455 6th St NW
Street address city: Winter Haven
Street address state: FL
Zip/Postal code: 33881-4061
County: Polk
Country: USA
Mailing address: 455 6TH ST NW
Mailing city: WINTER HAVEN
Mailing state: FL
Mailing zip: 33881-4061
General Phone: (863) 401-6900
Advertising Phone: (863) 401-6938
Editorial Phone: (863) 802-7504
General/National Adv. E-mail: jerome.ferson@theledger.com
Display Adv. E-mail: susan.gossett@newschief.com
Classified Adv. e-mail: leslie.colon@newschief.com
Editorial e-mail: news@newschief.com; features@newschief.com
Primary Website: www.newschief.com
Mthly Avg Views: 855000
Mthly Avg Unique Visitors: 83000
Year Established: 1911
News Services: AP, SHNS, DF, LAT-WP.
Special Editions: Citrus Exposition (Feb); Newcomer's Guide (Jan); Outlook (Mar).
Special Weekly Sections: Home Finder (Sat).
Syndicated Publications: Real Estate (Fri); Relish (Monthly); Retirement Living (Other); USA WEEKEND Magazine (S).
Delivery Methods: Newsstand`Carrier`Racks
Own Printing Facility?: N
Commercial printers?: Y
Avg Free Circ: 33
Sat. Circulation Paid: 597
Sat. Circulation Free: 33
Sun. Circulation Paid: 656
Sun. Circulation Free: 16
Audit By: AAM
Audit Date: 31.03.2019
Personnel: Bruce Baker (Bus. Mgr.); Jeff Amero (Circ. Dir.); Roger Ballas (Exec. Ed.); Dennis Wilkinson (Prodn. Dir.); Kevin Drake (Publisher); Ron Moates (Nat'l Adv. Mgr.); Scott Girouard (Digital Adv. Mgr.)
Parent company (for newspapers): CherryRoad Media

GEORGIA

AMERICUS TIMES-RECORDER

Street address 1: 101 Hwy 27 E
Street address city: Americus
Street address state: GA
Zip/Postal code: 31709
County: Sumter
Country: USA
Mailing address: PO BOX 1247
Mailing city: AMERICUS
Mailing state: GA
Mailing zip: 31709-1247
General Phone: (229) 924-2751
Advertising Phone: (229) 924-2751 ext. 1518
Editorial Phone: (229) 924-2751 ext. 1529
General/National Adv. E-mail: tom.overton@gaflnews.com
Display Adv. E-mail: joshua.burdick@gaflnews.com
Editorial e-mail: beth.alston@gaflnews.com
Primary Website: www.americustimesrecorder.com
Year Established: 1879
News Services: AP, TNN.
Special Editions: Car Care (Apr); Football (Aug); Holiday Cookbook (Dec); Business & Service Directory (Feb); Insurance Week (Jan); Christmas in July (Jul); Summer Recreation (Jun); Lawn & Garden (Mar); Mother's Day (May); ValueTown-Thanksgiving (Nov); Home-Owned Business
Special Weekly Sections: Church Briefs (Wed); Area Beat (Sun, Wed).
Syndicated Publications: South Georgia Rural Living (Monthly); Parade (S).
Delivery Methods: Mail`Newsstand`Carrier`Racks
Areas Served - City/County or Portion Thereof, or Zip codes: 31709
Sun. Circulation Paid: 6917
Audit By: Sworn/Estimate/Non-Audited
Audit Date: 12.07.2019
Personnel: Beth Alston (Ed. & Pub.); Nichole Buchanan (Bus. Dev. Mgr.); Ken Gustafson (Sports Ed.); Shawn Cavender (Mkt. Rep.)
Parent company (for newspapers): Boone Newspapers, Inc.

ATHENS BANNER-HERALD

Street address 1: One Press Place
Street address city: Athens
Street address state: GA
Zip/Postal code: 30601
County: Clarke
Country: USA
Mailing address: PO BOX 912
Mailing city: ATHENS

Mailing state: GA
Mailing zip: 30603-0912
General Phone: (706) 549-0123
Advertising Phone: (706) 208-2281
Editorial Phone: (706) 208-2227
General/National Adv. E-mail: tracy.traylor@onlineathens.com
Display Adv. E-mail: tracy.traylor@onlineathens.com
Classified Adv. e-mail: tracy.traylor@onlineathens.com
Editorial e-mail: scot.morrissey@onlineathens.com
Primary Website: www.onlineathens.com
Mthly Avg Views: 8000000
Mthly Avg Unique Visitors: 1350000
Year Established: 1832
News Services: AP, BPI, LAT-WP.
Special Editions: Golf Guide (Apr); College Football (Aug); Gift Guide (Dec); Spotlight 1 (Feb); Top Citizen (Jan); Locally Owned Business (Jun); Spotlight 2 (Mar); Twilight Criterium (May); New Car Intro (Nov); Gameday (Oct); Senior Living/Primetime (Quarterly); Gameday (
Special Weekly Sections: Health, Fitness (Tue); Best Food Day (Wed); Around Athens, Arts, Entertainment (Thur); Church, Auto (Sat); Business, Society, Family, Real Estate, Nat'l Coupons (Sun)
Syndicated Publications: Relish (Monthly); Homefront, USA Weekend (S); Marquee (Entertainment) (Thur).
Avg Free Circ: 7000
Sat. Circulation Paid: 10374
Sat. Circulation Free: 7000
Sun. Circulation Paid: 13192
Sun. Circulation Free: 7819
Audit By: AAM
Audit Date: 30.06.2017
Personnel: Greg Williamson (Controller, Division); Jordan Magness (VP of Ad Sales); Maeghan Pawley (Director of Mktg.); Linda Howard (Circ. Dir.); Donnie Fetter (Managing Ed.); Andre Gallant (Arts/Entertainment Ed.); Don Nelson (Bus./Finance Ed.); Jim Thompson (Editorial Page Ed.); Courtney Pomeroy (Features Ed.); Roger Nielsen (Metro Ed.); Wayne Ford (Oconee Ed.); John Curry (Photo Dir.); Dennis McCraven (Prodn. Dir.); Scott Morrissey (Pub.)
Parent company (for newspapers): CherryRoad Media; Gannett

ATLANTA JOURNAL-CONSTITUTION

Street address 1: 223 Perimeter Center Pkwy NE
Street address city: Atlanta
Street address state: GA
Zip/Postal code: 30346-1301
County: Dekalb
Country: USA
Mailing address: 223 PERIMETER CENTER PKWY NE
Mailing city: ATLANTA
Mailing state: GA
Mailing zip: 30346-1301
General Phone: (404) 526-7003
Advertising Phone: (404) 577-5775
Editorial Phone: (404) 526-2161
General/National Adv. E-mail: allen.dunstan@coxinc.com
Display Adv. E-mail: eric.myers@ajc.com
Classified Adv. e-mail: ajcclass@ajc.com
Editorial e-mail: newstips@ajc.com
Primary Website: www.ajc.com
Mthly Avg Unique Visitors: 4808000
Year Established: 1868
News Services: Cox News Service, AP, DJ, LAT-WP, NYT, MCT, CNS, CQ, NNS, PNS, SHNS, TMS.
Special Editions: Breast Cancer Education (Annually); Golf/Masters (Apr); Back to School (Aug); Holiday Gift Guides (Dec); Brides (Feb); Safety Vehicles (Jan); Peachtree Road Race (Jul); Executive Homes (Jun); Braves Baseball Preview (Mar); Fun in the Sun (May); Pulse (Mon
Special Weekly Sections: Food & Drink (Thur); Go Guide, Cars (Fri); AJC Cars (Sat); Homefinder, Business, Jobs (Sun)
Syndicated Publications: Color Comics (S).
Delivery Methods: Mail`Newsstand`Carrier`Racks
Areas Served - City/County or Portion Thereof, or Zip codes: 30002 30004 30005 30008 30009 30011 30012 30013 30014 30016 30017 30018 30019 30021 30022 30024 30025 30028 30030 30032 30033 30034 30035 30038 30039 30040 30041 30043 30044 30045 30046 30047 30052 30054 30055 30056 30058 30060 30062 30064 30066 30067 30068 30071 30075 30076 30078 30079 30080 30082 30083 30084 30087 30088 30092 30093 30094 30096 30097 30101 30102 30103 30104 30105 30106 30107 30108 30110 30113 30114 30115 30116 30117 30120 30121 30122 30124 30125 30126 30127 30132 30134 30135 30137 30141 30143 30144 30145 30147 30152 30153 30157 30161 30165 30168 30170 30171 30172 30173 30176 30178 30179 30180 30183 30184 30185 30187 30188 30189 30204 30213 30214 30215 30220 30223 30228 30229 30233 30236 30238 30248 30250 30252 30253 30259 30260 30263 30265 30268 30269 30272 30273 30274 30276 30277 30281 30288 30290 30291 30294 30295 30296 30297 30303 30305 30306 30307 30308 30309 30310 30311 30312 30313 30314 30315 30316 30317 30318 30319 30320 30322 30324 30326 30327 30328 30329 30331 30334 30336 30337 30338 30339 30340 30341 30342 30344 30345 30346 30349 30350 30354 30360 30361 30363 30501 30504 30506 30507 30510 30517 30518 30519 30523 30525 30527 30528 30529 30533 30534 30542 30548 30549 30554 30564 30566 30577 30601 30605 30606 30607 30620 30621 30622 30642 30655 30656 30666 30677 30680 30683 30701 30733 31024 31029 31030 31061 31088 31201
Own Printing Facility?: Y
Commercial printers?: N
Sat. Circulation Paid: 127777
Sun. Circulation Paid: 207476
Audit By: AAM
Audit Date: 30.06.2018
Personnel: Amy Chown (VP, Marketing); Laura Inman (Dir., Mktg. Devel.); Chris Hood (Mktg. Mgr., Classified/Territory); Amy Glennon (Pub.); Kevin Riley (Ed.); Eric Myers (VP, Adv. Sales); Allen Dunstan (Sr. Dir., Nat'l Accts.); Brian Cooper (Sr. VP, Finance & Business Op.); Mark Medici (Sr. VP, Audience & Group Lead for CMG Newspapers); Joe McKinnon (VP, Fulfillment)
Parent company (for newspapers): Cox Media Group

FULTON COUNTY DAILY REPORT

Street address 1: 190 Pryor St SW
Street address city: Atlanta
Street address state: GA
Zip/Postal code: 30303-3607
County: Fulton
Country: USA
Mailing address: 190 PRYOR ST SW
Mailing city: ATLANTA
Mailing state: GA
Mailing zip: 30303-3685
General Phone: (404) 521-1227
Advertising Phone: (404) 419-2870
General/National Adv. E-mail: lsimcoe@alm.com
Primary Website: www.dailyreportonline.com
Delivery Methods: Mail`Newsstand`Carrier`Racks
Own Printing Facility?: N
Commercial printers?: Y
Avg Free Circ: 225
Sat. Circulation Paid: 3095
Sat. Circulation Free: 225
Sun. Circulation Paid: 3095
Sun. Circulation Free: 225
Audit By: VAC
Audit Date: 31.12.2016
Personnel: Ed Bean (Editor); Wayne Curtis (Group Publisher); Scott Pitman (Systems Director); George Haj (Regional Editor-in-Chief); Jonathan Ringel (Mng. Ed.)
Parent company (for newspapers): ALM

THE AUGUSTA CHRONICLE

Street address 1: 725 Broad St
Street address city: Augusta
Street address state: GA
Zip/Postal code: 30901-1336
County: Richmond
Country: USA
Mailing address: PO BOX 1928
Mailing city: AUGUSTA
Mailing state: GA
Mailing zip: 30903-1928
General Phone: (706) 724-0851
Advertising Phone: (706) 823-3283
Editorial Phone: (706) 823-3430
General/National Adv. E-mail: newsroom@augustachronicle.com
Display Adv. E-mail: adsales@augustachronicle.com
Classified Adv. e-mail: advertising@augustachronicle.com
Editorial e-mail: letters@augustachronicle.com
Primary Website: www.chronicle.augusta.com/
Mthly Avg Views: 5019380
Mthly Avg Unique Visitors: 622408
Year Established: 1785
News Services: AP, MCT, Morris, SHNS,
Special Editions: Masters Golf (Apr); Back-to-School (Aug); Gift Guides (Dec); Brides (Jan); Graduation (May); Eat (December and June), Food and Fun Guide (April),
Special Weekly Sections: Applause (Fri); Today's Home (S); Religion (Sat); Food (Wed).
Syndicated Publications: Relish (Monthly); USA WEEKEND Magazine (S). Spry
Delivery Methods: Mail`Newsstand`Carrier`Racks
Areas Served - City/County or Portion Thereof, or Zip codes: 30802, 30809, 30813, 30814, 30815, 30901, 30904, 30906, 30907, 30909, 28941, 29860
Own Printing Facility?: Y
Commercial printers?: Y
Sat. Circulation Paid: 42831
Sun. Circulation Paid: 47814
Audit By: AAM
Audit Date: 31.03.2017
Personnel: William S. Morris III (Publisher); Ashlee Duren (Publisher, AUGUSTA MAGAZINE); David Enoch (VP of Circulation); Rick McKee (Editorial Cartoonist); Michael Ryan (Editorial Page Editor); John Gogick (Executive Editor); John Boyette (Sports Editor); Cynthia Spencer (HR Director); Pat McCue (Production Director); James Holmes (VP of Sales); Rachel Watson (Administrative Assistant to the President); Greg Williamson (Division Controller); Ashlee Edelen (Marketing Director); Stephen Wade (Pres.); Lisa Dorn (Advertising Director, AUGUSTA Magazine); Tim Rausch (Business Editor); Kim Luciani (Digital Product Development Director)
Parent company (for newspapers): CherryRoad Media; Gannett

THE BRUNSWICK NEWS

Street address 1: 3011 Altama Ave
Street address city: Brunswick
Street address state: GA
Zip/Postal code: 31520-4626
County: Glynn
Country: USA
Mailing address: PO BOX 1557
Mailing city: BRUNSWICK
Mailing state: GA
Mailing zip: 31521-1557
General Phone: (912) 265-8320
General/National Adv. E-mail: advertising@thebrunswicknews.com
Editorial e-mail: editor@thebrunswicknews.com; newsroom@thebrunswicknews.com
Primary Website: www.thebrunswicknews.com
Mthly Avg Views: 580000
Mthly Avg Unique Visitors: 60000
Year Established: 1902
News Services: AP, NEA.
Special Editions: Newcomers Guide (Apr); Football (Aug); Christmas Greetings (Dec); Wedding Bells (Feb); Outlook Glynn (Jan); Back to School (Jul); Hurricane Survival (Jun); Tour of Homes (Mar); Graduation (May); Holiday Gift Guide (Nov); Celebration (Oct); Health and Fitn
Special Weekly Sections: Health Section (Tue); Real Estate & Homes (Fri); Weekend Driver (Fri).
Syndicated Publications: Relish (Monthly; Spry (monthly); American Profile (Weekly); News & Advertiser (Weekly).
Delivery Methods: Newsstand`Carrier`Racks
Areas Served - City/County or Portion Thereof, or Zip codes: 31 520 315 213 152 200 000 000 000 000 000 000 000 000 000 000 000 000 000 000 000 000
Own Printing Facility?: Y
Commercial printers?: Y
Sat. Circulation Paid: 17800
Audit By: USPS
Audit Date: 27.09.2017
Personnel: Buff Leavy (President and Publisher); Ron Maulden (Vice President/General Manager); Frank Lane (Circulation Director); Buddy Hughes (Mng. Ed.); Amy Lee (Dir of Advert & Mktg); Tim O'Briant (Exec. Ed.)
Parent company (for newspapers): Leavy Family

BRUNSWICK NEWS, INC.

Street address 1: 3011 Altama Ave
Street address city: Brunswick
Street address state: GA
Zip/Postal code: 31520
County: Glynn
Country: USA
General Phone: (912) 265-8320
Display Adv. E-mail: nationaladvertising@brunswicknews.com
Primary Website: https://thebrunswicknews.com/
Year Established: 1902
Audit By: Sworn/Estimate/Non-Audited
Audit Date: 12.07.2019
Personnel: Eric Lawson (Co-Pub.)

CHEROKEE TRIBUNE

Street address 1: 521 E Main St
Street address city: Canton
Street address state: GA
Zip/Postal code: 30114-2805
County: Cherokee
Country: USA
Mailing address: 521 E MAIN ST
Mailing city: CANTON
Mailing state: GA
Mailing zip: 30114-2805
General Phone: (770) 479-1441
Advertising Phone: (770) 479-1441
Editorial Phone: (770) 479-1441
General/National Adv. E-mail: wstephens@mdjonline.com
Display Adv. E-mail: wstephens@mdjonline.com
Editorial e-mail: kfowler@cherokeetribune.com
Primary Website: www.cherokeetribune.com
News Services: AP.
Special Weekly Sections: Real Estate (S).
Syndicated Publications: USA WEEKEND Magazine (S).
Sat. Circulation Paid: 4238
Sun. Circulation Paid: 4449
Audit By: AAM
Audit Date: 31.12.2014
Personnel: Otis Brumby (CEO/Pub.); Kim Fowler (Adv. Mgr.); Matt Heck (Circ. Mgr.); Barbara Jacoby (Ed.); Wade Stephens (VP, Sales/Mktg); Lee Garrett (Gen. Mgr.); Dave Gossett (Circ. Mgr.); Joe Fernandez (VP, Productions)
Parent company (for newspapers): McNaughton Newspapers; Brumby Newspapers; Neighbor Newspapers; Times-Journal, Inc.

TIMES-GEORGIAN

Street address 1: 901 Hays Mill Rd
Street address city: Carrollton
Street address state: GA
Zip/Postal code: 30117-9576
County: Carroll
Country: USA
Mailing address: 901 HAYS MILL RD
Mailing city: CARROLLTON
Mailing state: GA
Mailing zip: 30117-9576
General Phone: (770) 834-6631
Advertising Phone: (770) 214-2285
Editorial Phone: (770) 214-2285
General/National Adv. E-mail: melissa@times-georgian.com
Classified Adv. e-mail: classifieds@times-georgian.com
Editorial e-mail: circulation@times-georgian.com
Primary Website: www.times-georgian.com
Mthly Avg Views: 239329
Mthly Avg Unique Visitors: 13595
Year Established: 1871
News Services: AP.
Delivery Methods: Mail`Newsstand`Carrier`Racks
Areas Served - City/County or Portion Thereof, or Zip codes: Carroll County, GA
Own Printing Facility?: Y
Commercial printers?: Y
Avg Free Circ: 18
Sun. Circulation Paid: 5092
Sun. Circulation Free: 18
Audit By: USPS
Audit Date: 28.09.2016
Personnel: Bruce Browning (Managing Ed.); Corey Cusick (Sports Ed.); Melissa Wilson (Reg. Adv. Dir.); Marvin Enderle (Pub.); Mark Golding (Cir. Dir.); Branyon Michael (Press Mgr.); Ricky Stilley (IT Mgr.)
Parent company (for newspapers): Paxton Media Group

THE DAILY TRIBUNE NEWS

Street address 1: 251 S Tennessee St
Street address city: Cartersville
Street address state: GA
Zip/Postal code: 30120-3605
County: Bartow
Country: USA
Mailing address: 251 S TENNESSEE ST

Mailing city: CARTERSVILLE
Mailing state: GA
Mailing zip: 30120-3605
General Phone: (770) 382-4545
General/National Adv. E-mail: advertising@daily-tribune.com
Display Adv. E-mail: jennifer.moates@daily-tribune.com
Classified Adv. e-mail: classifieds@daily-tribune.com
Editorial e-mail: jason.greenberg@daily-tribune.com
Primary Website: www.daily-tribune.com
Year Established: 1946
News Services: AP INAME, SNPA, SCAMA
Special Editions: Earth Day Tab (Apr); Christmas Greetings (Dec); Medical Tab (Feb); Chamber Tab (Jan); Progress (Jul); Graduation (Jun); Holiday Cookbook (Nov).
Special Weekly Sections: Best Food Day (Sun); Legal (Thur); Real Estate, Auto (Fri); Wedding, Select TV, Business, Arts, Entertainment, Consumer (Sun)
Syndicated Publications: Relish (Monthly); TV Outlook (S); American Profile (Weekly).
Delivery Methods: Mail`Carrier`Racks
Areas Served - City/County or Portion Thereof, or Zip codes: Bartow County
Own Printing Facility?: Y
Commercial printers?: N
Avg Free Circ: 242
Sat. Circulation Paid: 4615
Sat. Circulation Free: 242
Sun. Circulation Paid: 4805
Sun. Circulation Free: 250
Audit By: AAM
Audit Date: 6/31/2018
Personnel: Byron Pezzarossi (Prod. Dir., Pressroom); Jennifer Moates (Retail Adv. Dir.); Alan Davis (Pub.); Mindy Salaman (Office Mgr.)
Parent company (for newspapers): Cleveland Newspapers, Inc.

COLUMBUS LEDGER-ENQUIRER

Street address 1: 945 Broadway Ste 102
Street address 2: Suite 102
Street address city: Columbus
Street address state: GA
Zip/Postal code: 31901-2772
County: Muscogee
Country: USA
Mailing address: 945 BROADWAY STE 102
Mailing city: COLUMBUS
Mailing state: GA
Mailing zip: 31901-2772
General Phone: (706) 324-5526
Advertising Phone: (706) 320-4407
Editorial Phone: (706) 571-8565
General/National Adv. E-mail: rmcduffie@ledger-enquirer.com
Display Adv. E-mail: rmcduffie@ledger-enquirer.com
Classified Adv. e-mail: rmcduffie@ledger-enquirer.com
Editorial e-mail: dkholmes@ledger-enquirer.com
Primary Website: www.ledger-enquirer.com
Mthly Avg Views: 4100000
Mthly Avg Unique Visitors: 622000
Year Established: 1930
Special Weekly Sections: Best Food (Wed); Vacation, Travel, Living, Society, TV (Sun); Money, Business, Family (Mon); Health, Fitness (Tue); Community (Wed); Entertainment (Thur); Auto, Religion, Homes (Sat); Business (Tue-Sat)
Syndicated Publications: Parade (S).
Delivery Methods: Newsstand`Carrier
Avg Free Circ: 681
Sat. Circulation Paid: 13908
Sat. Circulation Free: 469
Sun. Circulation Paid: 18955
Sun. Circulation Free: 418
Audit By: AAM
Audit Date: 31.03.2018
Personnel: Wanda Howell (HR Manager); Pat Chitwood (Circ. Dir.); Dimon Kendrick-holmes (Exec. Ed.); Marcia McAllister (Assoc. Ed.); Tim Chitwood (Columnist); Brad Barnes (Entertainment Writer); Dawn Minty (Features Ed.); Larry Foley (News Ed.); Kevin Price (Sports Ed.); Jimmy Mann (Chief Technician); David Crute (Prodn. Foreman, Platemaking); Heather Williams (Circ. Mktg.); Valerie Canepa (Pres./Pub.); Bill Wall (Sr. Nat'l/Major Sales Rep.); Ross McDuffie (VP of Ads.)
Parent company (for newspapers): The McClatchy Company; Chatham Asset Management

THE DAILY CITIZEN

Street address 1: 308 S Thornton Ave
Street address city: Dalton
Street address state: GA
Zip/Postal code: 30720-8268
County: Whitfield
Country: USA
Mailing address: PO BOX 1167
Mailing city: DALTON
Mailing state: GA
Mailing zip: 30722-1167
General Phone: (706) 217-6397
Advertising Phone: (706) 272-7729
Editorial Phone: (706) 272-7714
General/National Adv. E-mail: internet@daltoncitizen.com
Display Adv. E-mail: jeffmutter@daltoncitizen.com
Editorial e-mail: internet@daltoncitizen.com
Primary Website: www.dailycitizen.news
News Services: AP, SHNS.
Special Editions: Progress (Mar).
Special Weekly Sections: Entertainment (Sat).
Syndicated Publications: Relish (Monthly); USA WEEKEND Magazine (S).
Sat. Circulation Paid: 11040
Sun. Circulation Paid: 10426
Audit By: Sworn/Estimate/Non-Audited
Audit Date: 12.07.2019
Personnel: Keith Barlow (Pub.); Jeff Mutter (Gen. Mgr.); Jamie Jones (Mng. Ed.); Leslie Hayes (Circ. Mgr.); Renee Reddix (Advertising Account Exec.); Susy Talley (Office/Classified Mgr.); Victor Miller (City Ed.); Daniel Bell (News Ed.); Emmalee Molay (Sports Ed.)
Parent company (for newspapers): CNHI, LLC

THE COURIER HERALD

Street address 1: 115 S Jefferson St
Street address city: Dublin
Street address state: GA
Zip/Postal code: 31021-5146
County: Laurens
Country: USA
Mailing address: PO BOX B
Mailing city: DUBLIN
Mailing state: GA
Mailing zip: 31040-2449
General Phone: (478) 272-5522
Advertising Phone: (478) 272-5522
General/National Adv. E-mail: advertising@courier-herald.com
Display Adv. E-mail: advertising@courier-herald.com
Classified Adv. e-mail: classifieds@courier-herald.com
Editorial e-mail: news@courier-herald.com
Primary Website: www.courier-herald.com
Year Established: 1876
News Services: AP.
Special Editions: Medical Directory (Jan); Bridal Guide (Feb); St. Patrick's Preview (Feb); Porter's Guide to Hunting & Fishing (Mar, Aug, Nov); Worship Tab (Apr); Home & Garden Tab (Apr); Graduation Year Book (May) Senior Citizens Guide (Jun); Back To School (Aug); Football Preview (Aug); Go Green (Sept); Relish Cooking School (Oct); Holiday Gift Guide (Nov); Christmas Greetings (Dec)
Special Weekly Sections: Best Food Day, Lifestyle (Wed); Business (Thur); Legal, Religion, Entertainment (Sat)
Syndicated Publications: USA WEEKEND Magazine (Sat).
Delivery Methods: Carrier`Racks
Own Printing Facility?: Y
Commercial printers?: Y
Avg Free Circ: 29
Sat. Circulation Paid: 7141
Sat. Circulation Free: 29
Audit By: AAM
Audit Date: 31.12.2018
Personnel: Pam Burney (Adv. Dir.); Prudence Price (Classified); Cheryl Gay (Circ. Mgr.); Jason Halcombe (Managing Ed.); Joey Wilson (Photo Ed.); Griffin Lovett (Pub.); Travis Ryan (Online Mgr.); Elizabeth Mimbs (Prodn. Mgr.); DuBose Porter (CEO)
Parent company (for newspapers): Herald Newspapers, Inc.

THE TIMES

Street address 1: 345 Green St NW
Street address city: Gainesville
Street address state: GA
Zip/Postal code: 30501-3370
County: Hall
Country: USA
Mailing address: PO BOX 838
Mailing city: GAINESVILLE
Mailing state: GA
Mailing zip: 30503-0838
General Phone: (770) 532-6338
General/National Adv. E-mail: lnelson@gainesvilletimes.com
Display Adv. E-mail: lnelson@gainesvilletimes.com
Editorial e-mail: news@gainesvilletimes.com
Primary Website: www.gainesvilletimes.com
Mthly Avg Views: 2040000
Mthly Avg Unique Visitors: 241000
Year Established: 1947
News Services: AP, AP Sportswire, AP Photo, AP Graphics,MCT
Special Editions: Back to School (Aug); Newcomers Guide (July); Health Watch (quarterly); Progress (Mar); ; Business Link (Monthly);
Special Weekly Sections: Church Page (Sat); Get Out (Thur); Food (Wed).
Syndicated Publications: Relish (monthly)
Delivery Methods: Newsstand`Carrier`Racks
Areas Served - City/County or Portion Thereof, or Zip codes: 30501 30502 30503 30504 30506 30542
Own Printing Facility?: Y
Commercial printers?: Y
Sat. Circulation Paid: 14000
Sun. Circulation Paid: 16000
Audit By: Sworn/Estimate/Non-Audited
Audit Date: 12.07.2019
Personnel: Norman Baggs (Gen. Mgr.); Keith Albertson (Exec. Ed.); Shannon Casas (EIC); Michael Beard (New Media Ed.); DeJuan Woodward (Mgmt. Info Servs. Mgr.); Mark Hall (Prodn. Dir.); Scott Whitworth (Circ. Dir.); Leah Nelson (Ad. Director)
Parent company (for newspapers): Morris Multimedia, Inc.

GRIFFIN DAILY NEWS

Street address 1: 1403 N Expressway
Street address 2: Ste J
Street address city: Griffin
Street address state: GA
Zip/Postal code: 30223-9015
County: Spalding
Country: USA
Mailing address: PO BOX M
Mailing city: GRIFFIN
Mailing state: GA
Mailing zip: 30224-0073
General Phone: (770) 227-3276
General/National Adv. E-mail: advertising@griffindailynews.com
Display Adv. E-mail: advertising@griffindailynews.com
Editorial e-mail: editor@griffindailynews.com
Primary Website: www.griffindailynews.com
News Services: AP.
Special Editions: Progress (Apr); Football (Aug); Valentines (Feb); Super Bowl (Jan); Vacation (Jun); Spring Fashion (Mar); Youth Sports (May); Newcomer's Guide (Sept).
Special Weekly Sections: TV Notes (S).
Syndicated Publications: USA WEEKEND Magazine (S).
Delivery Methods: Mail`Carrier`Racks
Own Printing Facility?: N
Commercial printers?: N
Sat. Circulation Paid: 6936
Sun. Circulation Paid: 6246
Audit By: Sworn/Estimate/Non-Audited
Audit Date: 12.07.2019
Personnel: Joy Gaddy (Pub./Adv. Dir.); Mark Golding (Circ. Dir.); Tim Daly (Mng. Ed.); Anthony Rhoades (Asst. Mng. Ed.)
Parent company (for newspapers): Paxton Media Group

CLAYTON NEWS DAILY

Street address 1: 138 Church St
Street address city: Jonesboro
Street address state: GA
Zip/Postal code: 30236-3514
County: Clayton
Country: USA
Mailing address: PO BOX 1286
Mailing city: LAWRENCEVILLE
Mailing state: GA
Mailing zip: 30046-1286
General Phone: (770) 478-5753
General/National Adv. E-mail: ccollier@news-daily.com
Display Adv. E-mail: ccollier@news-daily.com
Classified Adv. e-mail: ccollier@news-daily.com
Editorial e-mail: info@news-daily.com
Primary Website: www.news-daily.com
Year Established: 1970
News Services: AP.
Special Editions: Spring Tour of Homes (Apr); Football Kick-off (Aug); Christmas Gift Guide (Dec); Bride's Tour (Feb); Progress (Jan); Newcomer's Guide (Jul); Spring Car Care (Mar); Welcome Summer (May); Meet the Merchants (Oct); Introduction to New Cars (Sept).
Special Weekly Sections: Best Food Day (Wed); Real Estate (Last Fri/Month); Religion (Sat)
Syndicated Publications: Relish (Monthly); USA WEEKEND Magazine (Sat).
Avg Free Circ: 6673
Sat. Circulation Paid: 1600
Sat. Circulation Free: 6673
Audit By: CAC
Audit Date: 30.09.2012
Personnel: Donna Goodson (Office Mgr.); Luke Strickland (Sports Ed.); Rita Camp (Classified Adv. Mgr.); Alice Queen (Ed.)
Parent company (for newspapers): Southern Community Newspapers, Inc.

LAGRANGE DAILY NEWS

Street address 1: 105 Ashton St
Street address city: Lagrange
Street address state: GA
Zip/Postal code: 30240-3111
County: Troup
Country: USA
Mailing address: PO BOX 929
Mailing city: LAGRANGE
Mailing state: GA
Mailing zip: 30241-0117
General Phone: (706) 884-7311
Advertising Phone: (706) 884-7311 ext. 238
Editorial Phone: (706) 884-7311 x232
General/National Adv. E-mail: advertising@lagrangenews.com
Display Adv. E-mail: advertising@lagrangenews.com
Classified Adv. e-mail: advertising@lagrangenews.com
Editorial e-mail: editor@lagrangenews.com
Primary Website: www.lagrangenews.com
Mthly Avg Views: 500000
Mthly Avg Unique Visitors: 65000
Year Established: 1843
News Services: AP, NEA.
Special Weekly Sections: Best Food Day (Wed); Auto (Thur); Real Estate (Fri); Religion, Arts, Entertainment, Living (Sat); Art, Entertainment, Living (Sun)
Syndicated Publications: USA WEEKEND Magazine (S); American Profile (Weekly).
Delivery Methods: Mail`Newsstand`Carrier`Racks
Areas Served - City/County or Portion Thereof, or Zip codes: 30240
Own Printing Facility?: Y
Commercial printers?: Y
Sat. Circulation Paid: 13400
Sun. Circulation Paid: 13400
Audit By: Sworn/Estimate/Non-Audited
Audit Date: 12.07.2019
Personnel: Baker Ellis (Pub.); Ed Pugh (Circ. Mgr); Donna Ennis (Bus. Mgr.); Daniel Evans (Mng. Ed.); Kevin Eckleberry (Sports Ed.); Jennie Overfelt (Adv. Mgr.); Maggie Langford (CSR)
Parent company (for newspapers): Boone Newspapers, Inc.

THE TELEGRAPH

Street address 1: 1675 Montpelier Ave
Street address 2: Ste 100
Street address city: Macon
Street address state: GA
Zip/Postal code: 31201
County: Bibb
Country: USA
Mailing address: PO BOX 4167
Mailing city: MACON
Mailing state: GA
Mailing zip: 31208-4167
General Phone: (478) 744-4200
Advertising Phone: (478) 744-4359
Editorial Phone: (478) 744-4342

General/National Adv. E-mail: rmcduffie@ledger-enquirer.com
Display Adv. E-mail: rmcduffie@ledger-enquirer.com
Classified Adv. e-mail: rmcduffie@ledger-enquirer.com
Primary Website: www.macon.com
Mthly Avg Views: 6518872
Mthly Avg Unique Visitors: 844458
Year Established: 1826
News Services: AP, MCT, LAT-WP, HN, NYT, TMS.
Special Weekly Sections: Best Food Day (Wed); Health, Fitness (Mon); Bibb County TMC (Tue); Home, Garden (Thur); Entertainment (Fri); Spiritual Living (Sat); Homes, Travel (Sun)
Delivery Methods: Newsstand`Carrier`Racks
Areas Served - City/County or Portion Thereof, or Zip codes: 31201 31204 31206 31210 31211 31216 31217 31220 31052 31088 31093 & 98 31069 31047 31028 31005 31030 31008 31016, 31029, 31046, Part 31220, part 31210 31044, 31017, 31020, Part 31217 31032, 31033, Part 31217 part 31052, 31050, 31078, 31066 31061 31014 31023, 31077 31012, 31009, 31027, 31022, 31021 31036 31024 31031, 31054 31015, 31091, 31092, 31041, 31057, 31063, 31068, 31011, 31549, 31750, 31539, 31055, 31060, 31001, 31079 31096, 31002, 30445, 30474, 30457, 30411, 30642, 31038, 31064, 31087, 31089, 31082 30204, 30286, 31006 31016, 31029, 31046,31044, 31017, 31020,31032, 31033, 31052, 31050, 31078, 31066, 31217, 31061, 31014, 31023, 31077, 31012, 31009, 31027, 31022, 31021, 31036, 31024, 31031, 31054,31015, 30642 31201, 31204, 31206, 31210, 31211, 31216, 31217, 31220, 31052 31088, 31093, 31098, 31025, 31047, 31028, 31005, 31030, 31008
Own Printing Facility?: N
Commercial printers?: Y
Sat. Circulation Paid: 21726
Sun. Circulation Paid: 28456
Audit By: AAM
Audit Date: 30.06.2018
Personnel: Ross McDuffie (Gen. Mgr. & VP of Advertising); Tim Regan-Porter (South Region Editor); Sundra Hominik (Sr. Ed.); Lauren Gorla (Deputy Ed.); Crystal Ragan (Advertising Sales Mgr.); Susan Webster (Circ. Operations Mgr.); Sarah Young (Finance)
Parent company (for newspapers): The McClatchy Company; Chatham Asset Management

MARIETTA DAILY JOURNAL

Street address 1: 580 S Fairground St SE
Street address city: Marietta
Street address state: GA
Zip/Postal code: 30060-2751
County: Cobb
Country: USA
Mailing address: PO BOX 449
Mailing city: MARIETTA
Mailing state: GA
Mailing zip: 30061-0449
General Phone: (770) 428-9411
Advertising Phone: (770) 428-9411
Editorial Phone: (770) 428-9411 ext. 512
General/National Adv. E-mail: mdjnews@mdjonline.com
Display Adv. E-mail: advertising@mdjonline.com
Editorial e-mail: letters@mdjonline.com
Primary Website: www.mdjonline.com
Year Established: 1866
News Services: AP, SHNS, CNS, LAT-WP, TMS.
Special Editions: Lawn & Garden (Apr); Football Preview (Aug); Gift Guide (Dec); Progress (Feb); Year-in-Review (Jan); Fact Book (Jul); Father's Day (Jun); Brides (Mar); Spring Car Care (May); Thanksgiving (Nov); Fall Home & Garden (Sept).
Special Weekly Sections: Lifestyle, TV, Comics, Real Estate, Business, Coupons (Sun); Business (Mon); Food (Thur); Auto, Public Notices, Entertainment (Fri); Religion (Sat)
Syndicated Publications: Going Out (local entertainment) (Fri); USA WEEKEND Magazine (S).
Avg Free Circ: 376
Sat. Circulation Paid: 12571
Sat. Circulation Free: 376
Sun. Circulation Paid: 13410
Sun. Circulation Free: 238
Audit By: AAM
Audit Date: 31.12.2016
Personnel: Otis A. Brumby (CEO/Pub.); Jay Whorton (Assoc. Pub.); Joanne Shivley (Accounting Mgr.); Lee Garrett (Gen. Mgr.); Wade Stephens (VP, Sales/Mktg.); Billy Mitchell (Mng. Ed.); Bill Kinney (Columnist); Dick Yarbourgh (Columnist); Damion Guarnieri (Photo Dept. Mgr.); Zuriel Reyes (Online Mgr.); David Tallmadge (Prodn. Mgr.); Matt Heck (Circ. Dir.); Pat McClesky (Prodn. Mgr., Mailroom); Leigh Braddy (Prodn. Mgr., Pre Press); Alice Davis (Credit Mgr.); J. K. Murphy (Mng. Ed.)
Parent company (for newspapers): Times-Journal, Inc.; Brumby Newspapers

THE UNION-RECORDER

Street address 1: 165 Garrett Way NW
Street address city: Milledgeville
Street address state: GA
Zip/Postal code: 31061-2318
County: Baldwin
Country: USA
Mailing address: PO BOX 520
Mailing city: MILLEDGEVILLE
Mailing state: GA
Mailing zip: 31059-0520
General Phone: (478) 452-0567
Advertising Phone: (478) 453-1430
Editorial Phone: (478) 453-1450
Display Adv. E-mail: abudrys@unionrecorder.com
Classified Adv. e-mail: classifieds@unionrecorder.com
Editorial e-mail: newsroom@unionrecorder.com
Primary Website: www.unionrecorder.com
News Services: AP.
Special Editions: Football (Aug); Gift Ideas (Dec); Black History (Feb); Focus on Milledgeville (Jul); Home Improvement & Gardening (Mar); Graduation (May); Gift Guide (Nov); Historic Guide to Milledgeville (Oct).
Special Weekly Sections: Schools (Fri); Family (Sat); Health (Tues); Wedding Planner (Weekly).
Syndicated Publications: TV Magazine (Fri); Relish (Monthly); USA WEEKEND Magazine (Sat).
Sat. Circulation Paid: 7416
Audit By: Sworn/Estimate/Non-Audited
Audit Date: 12.07.2019
Personnel: Keith E. Barlow (Publisher); Keith Justice (Production Director); Lynda Jackson (Bus. Mgr.); Natalie Davis Linder (Editor); Erin Simmons (Adv. Dir.); Tiffany Jones (Business Manager); Michael Evans (Circ. Dir.); Natalie Davis (Mng. Ed.); Jonathan Jackson (City Ed.)
Parent company (for newspapers): CNHI, LLC

THE MOULTRIE OBSERVER

Street address 1: 25 N Main St
Street address city: Moultrie
Street address state: GA
Zip/Postal code: 31768-3861
County: Colquitt
Country: USA
Mailing address: PO BOX 2349
Mailing city: MOULTRIE
Mailing state: GA
Mailing zip: 31776-2349
General Phone: (229) 985-4545
Advertising Phone: (229) 985-4545
Editorial Phone: (229) 985-4545
General/National Adv. E-mail: laura.rogers@gaflnews.com
Display Adv. E-mail: chris.white@gaflnews.com
Editorial e-mail: dwain.walden@gaflnews.com
Primary Website: www.moultrieobserver.com
Year Established: 1894
News Services: AP.
Special Editions: Brides (Apr); Back-to-School (Aug); Progress (Jul); Colquitt Pride (Jun); Home, Lawn & Garden (Mar); Super Mom (May); Agricultural Exposition (Oct); New Car (Sept).
Special Weekly Sections: Real Estate, Business, Comics, Money, TV (Daily); Best Food (Wed); Church (Fri); Comics, TV, Entertainment, Wedding, Engagements (Sun)
Syndicated Publications: Chamber of Commerce Guide (Annually); Relish (Monthly); Parade (S).
Sat. Circulation Paid: 7198
Sun. Circulation Paid: 7198
Audit By: Sworn/Estimate/Non-Audited
Audit Date: 12.07.2019
Personnel: Jeff Masters (Pub.); Laurie Gay (Gen. Mgr./Adv.); Rachel Wainwright (Circ. Dir.); Kevin C. Hall (Mng. Ed.)
Parent company (for newspapers): CNHI, LLC

THE NEWNAN TIMES-HERALD

Street address 1: 16 Jefferson St
Street address city: Newnan
Street address state: GA
Zip/Postal code: 30263-1913
County: Coweta
Country: USA
Mailing address: PO BOX 1052
Mailing city: NEWNAN
Mailing state: GA
Mailing zip: 30264-1052
General Phone: (770) 253-1576
Advertising Phone: (770) 683-1707
Editorial Phone: 770-683-1723
General/National Adv. E-mail: colleen@newnan.com
Display Adv. E-mail: colleen@newnan.com
Classified Adv. e-mail: classifieds@newnan.com
Editorial e-mail: winston@newnan.com
Primary Website: www.times-herald.com
Mthly Avg Views: 400000
Mthly Avg Unique Visitors: 430000
Year Established: 1865
News Services: AP.
Special Editions: Back to School, 50 Things to Do, Vision, Year in Review, Bridal Planner, Football, Chamber Annual Report, Coweta Living
Special Weekly Sections: Community, Education, Religion, Sports, Health, Senior Living, See & Do
Delivery Methods: Newsstand`Carrier`Racks
Areas Served - City/County or Portion Thereof, or Zip codes: Newnan, Senoia, Moreland, Sharpsburg, Grantville, Palmetto
Own Printing Facility?: N
Commercial printers?: N
Sun. Circulation Paid: 9300
Audit By: USPS
Audit Date: 30.09.2016
Personnel: William W. Thomasson (Pres.); Marianne Thomasson (VP); Diana Shellabarger (Controller); Colleen Mitchell (Sales & Marketing Dir.); Winston Skinner (News Ed.); Kandice Bell (Reporter); Doug Gorman (Sports Editor); Neely Clay (Reporter); Sarah Campbell (Reporter); Jeff Armstrong (Sports Writer)
Parent company (for newspapers): The Newnan Times-Herald

ROME NEWS-TRIBUNE

Street address 1: 305 E 6th Ave
Street address city: Rome
Street address state: GA
Zip/Postal code: 30161-6007
County: Floyd
Country: USA
Mailing address: PO BOX 1633
Mailing city: ROME
Mailing state: GA
Mailing zip: 30162-1633
General Phone: (706) 291-6397
Advertising Phone: (706) 290-5220
Editorial Phone: (706) 290-5252
General/National Adv. E-mail: romenewstribune@rn-t.com
Primary Website: www.romenews-tribune.com
Mthly Avg Views: 2266978
Mthly Avg Unique Visitors: 199685
Year Established: 1843
News Services: NYT, AP, NEA, MCT.
Special Editions: Administrative Professionals (Apr); Harmon Football Forecast (Aug); Santas Letters (Dec); Prime Time (Every other month); Review and Forecast (Feb); Bride's World I (Jan); Rome Symphony (Jul); Medical (Jun); Review and Forecast (Mar); Memorial Classified
Special Weekly Sections: Roman Record (Mon); Roman Life (S); Tribune Viewers Guide (Sat); Young Romans (Tues); Best Food Guide (Wed).
Syndicated Publications: Business Tab (Mon); Parade (S); TV/Cable Program Magazine (Sat); Youth Tab (Tues).
Delivery Methods: Mail`Newsstand`Carrier`Racks
Areas Served - City/County or Portion Thereof, or Zip codes: Rome, Cedartown, Rockmart, Cartersville, Centre , Al, Sumerville
Own Printing Facility?: Y
Commercial printers?: Y
Sat. Circulation Paid: 14921
Sun. Circulation Paid: 15466
Audit By: Sworn/Estimate/Non-Audited
Audit Date: 12.07.2019
Personnel: Cecilia Crow (Adv. Dir.); Mike Colombo (Mng. Ed.); Jeremy Stewart (Sports Ed.); Tona Deaton (Prodn. Dir., Dispatch); Rob Broadway (Prodn. Mgr., Press); Burgett H. Mooney (Pub.); Dan Mozley
Parent company (for newspapers): Rome News-Tribune; Brumby Newspapers

SAVANNAH MORNING NEWS

Street address 1: 1375 Chatham Parkway, P.O. Box 1088
Street address 2: Fl 1
Street address city: Savannah
Street address state: GA
Zip/Postal code: 31405
County: Chatham
Country: USA
Mailing address: PO BOX 1088
Mailing city: SAVANNAH
Mailing state: GA
Mailing zip: 31402-1088
General Phone: (912) 236-9511
Advertising Phone: (912) 652-0241
Editorial Phone: (912) 652-0327
Primary Website: www.savannahnow.com
News Services: AP, NEA, MCT, LAT.
Special Weekly Sections: Accent, Exchange, TV, Homes, Real Estate (Sun); Best Food (Wed); Entertainment (Thur); Homes, Real Estate (Sat)
Syndicated Publications: Relish (Monthly); USA WEEKEND Magazine (S).
Avg Free Circ: 1822
Sat. Circulation Paid: 19229
Sat. Circulation Free: 1822
Sun. Circulation Paid: 25754
Sun. Circulation Free: 600
Audit By: AAM
Audit Date: 31.03.2018
Personnel: Michael Traynor (Pub.); Frankie Fort (HR Dir.); Randy Mooney (Adv. Dir.); Ken Boler (Adv. Mgr., Classified); Cynthia Barnes (Adv. Mgr., Display); Elena Mitchell (Acct. Mgr.); Stacy Jennings (Dir., Mktg./Promo.); Todd Timmons (Circ. Dir.); David Ellis (Circ. Mgr); Susan Catron (Exec. Ed.); Steve Corrigan (Community Ed.); Tom Barton (Editorial Page Ed.); Edward Fulford (Editorial Writer); Jenel Few (Educ. Reporter); Mary Landers (Environmental Reporter); Pamela E. Walck (Gov't/Bus. Ed.); Stephen Komives (News Planning Ed.); Steve Yelvington; Josh Rayburn; Tim Anderson (VP, Adv.); Kathy Harmon (Nat'l Acct. Rep.)
Parent company (for newspapers): CherryRoad Media; Gannett Company Inc.

STATESBORO HERALD

Street address 1: 1 Proctor St
Street address city: Statesboro
Street address state: GA
Zip/Postal code: 30458-1387
County: Bulloch
Country: USA
Mailing address: PO Box 888
Mailing city: Statesboro
Mailing state: GA
Mailing zip: 30459-0888
General Phone: (912) 764-9031
Advertising Phone: (912) 764-9031
Editorial Phone: (912) 489-9400
General/National Adv. E-mail: jmelton@statesboroherald.com
Display Adv. E-mail: jmelton@statesboroherald.com
Classified Adv. e-mail: ppollard@statesboroherald.com
Editorial e-mail: jwermers@statesboroherald.com
Primary Website: www.statesboroherald.com
Mthly Avg Views: 540000
Mthly Avg Unique Visitors: 85000
Year Established: 1937
News Services: AP, The Newspaper Network, SHNS.
Special Editions: Bridal (Apr); Community Pride (Feb); Newcomer's Guide (Jun); Home Improvement (Mar); Georgia Southern University New Student Guide (May); Healthy Living (Nov); Best
Special Weekly Sections: TV Tab (S); Community Voice (Thur); Business Tuesday (Tues).
Syndicated Publications: Parade (S); Relish; American Profile; Athlon Sports
Delivery Methods: Mail`Newsstand`Carrier`Racks
Areas Served - City/County or Portion Thereof, or Zip codes: 30458;30461
Own Printing Facility?: Y
Commercial printers?: Y
Sat. Circulation Paid: 6700
Sun. Circulation Paid: 7100
Audit By: USPS
Audit Date: 10.07.2014

Personnel: Jim Healy (Operations Manager); Jan Melton (Adv. Dir.); Darrell Elliott (Circ. Mgr.); Pamela Pollard (Adv. Mgr., Classified); Kelly Dailey (Print Adv. Mgr.); Eddie Ledbetter (Asst. Ed. / Prod.); Mike Anthony (Sports Ed.); DeWayne Grice (Bus. Ed.)
Parent company (for newspapers): Morris Multimedia, Inc.

THOMASVILLE TIMES-ENTERPRISE

Street address 1: 106 South St
Street address city: Thomasville
Street address state: GA
Zip/Postal code: 31792-6061
County: Thomas
Country: USA
Mailing address: PO BOX 650
Mailing city: THOMASVILLE
Mailing state: GA
Mailing zip: 31799-0650
General Phone: (229) 226-2400
General/National Adv. E-mail: laura.rogers@gaflnews.com
Display Adv. E-mail: andrew.wardle@gaflnews.com
Editorial e-mail: mark.lastinger@gaflnews.com
Primary Website: www.timesenterprise.com
Mthly Avg Views: 400000
Mthly Avg Unique Visitors: 75000
News Services: AP.
Special Editions: Rural Living (Monthly), Health Matters, Home Style, Bridal Scene, Rose City Run
Special Weekly Sections: Church Pages (Fri); Business (S); Weekend Page (Thur); Best Food Days (Tues); Best Food Days (Wed).
Syndicated Publications: Relish (Monthly); Color Comics (S).
Delivery Methods: Mail`Newsstand`Carrier`Racks
Own Printing Facility?: N
Commercial printers?: Y
Sat. Circulation Paid: 8293
Sun. Circulation Paid: 8291
Audit By: Sworn/Estimate/Non-Audited
Audit Date: 12.07.2019
Personnel: Chris White Mohr (Gen. Mgr./Adv. Dir.); Andrew Wardle (Circ. Dir.); Pat Donahue (Mng. Ed.); Theresa Westberry (Major/Nat. Adv. Mgr.)
Parent company (for newspapers): CNHI, LLC

THE TIFTON GAZETTE

Street address 1: 211 Tift Ave N
Street address city: Tifton
Street address state: GA
Zip/Postal code: 31794-4463
County: Tift
Country: USA
Mailing address: PO BOX 708
Mailing city: TIFTON
Mailing state: GA
Mailing zip: 31793-0708
General Phone: (229) 382-4321
Advertising Phone: (229) 382-4321
Editorial Phone: (229) 382-4321
General/National Adv. E-mail: ttg.editorial@gaflnews.com
Display Adv. E-mail: kitty.stone@gaflnews.com
Classified Adv. e-mail: kitty.stone@gaflnews.com
Editorial e-mail: ttg.editorial@gaflnews.com
Primary Website: www.tiftongazette.com
Year Established: 1888
News Services: AP.
Special Editions: Love Affair Tab (Apr); Back-to-School (Aug); Christmas Greetings (Dec); Love Lines (Feb); Health & Fitness (Jan); Home-owned Business (Jul); Home and Garden (Mar); Mother's Day (May); Holiday Gift Guide (Nov); Shop Early (Oct); Oktoberfest (Sept).
Special Weekly Sections: Entertainment (Sun); Education (Thur); Best Food Day (Wed).
Delivery Methods: Newsstand`Carrier`Racks
Own Printing Facility?: N
Commercial printers?: Y
Sat. Circulation Paid: 9046
Sun. Circulation Paid: 9046
Audit By: Sworn/Estimate/Non-Audited
Audit Date: 12.07.2019
Personnel: Dan Sutton (Pub/Adv. Dir); Jetty Tanner (Office Mgr.); Laura Rogers (Adv. Mgr.); Kitty Stone (Adv. Mgr., Retail Sales); Melody Cowart (Promo. Mgr.); Rachel Wainwright (Circ. Mgr.); Angye Morrison (Mng. Ed.); Becky Taylor (Sports Ed.)
Parent company (for newspapers): CNHI, LLC

VALDOSTA DAILY TIMES

Street address 1: 201 N Troup St
Street address city: Valdosta
Street address state: GA
Zip/Postal code: 31601-5774
County: Lowndes
Country: USA
Mailing address: PO BOX 968
Mailing city: VALDOSTA
Mailing state: GA
Mailing zip: 31603-0968
General Phone: (229) 244-1880
General/National Adv. E-mail: vdt.advertising@gaflnews.com
Classified Adv. e-mail: classified.marketplace@gaflnews.com
Editorial e-mail: vdt.newsroom@gaflnews.com
Primary Website: www.valdostadailytimes.com
Mthly Avg Views: 894677
Mthly Avg Unique Visitors: 253017
Year Established: 1867
News Services: AP, SHNS.
Special Editions: Football (Aug); Cookbook (Jun); Yearbook (Mar); Living Here (Nov).
Special Weekly Sections: Business Page (S); Church Page (Sat); Food Page (Tues).
Syndicated Publications: Relish (Monthly); Parade (S).
Delivery Methods: Mail`Newsstand`Carrier`Racks
Areas Served - City/County or Portion Thereof, or Zip codes: 31601, 31602, 31603, 31605, 31606, 31620, 31625, 31629, 31632, 31634, 31635, 31636, 31638, 31639, 31641, 31643, 31645, 31647, 31648, 31649, 31699
Own Printing Facility?: Y
Commercial printers?: Y
Sat. Circulation Paid: 10528
Sun. Circulation Paid: 12419
Audit By: Sworn/Estimate/Non-Audited
Audit Date: 12.07.2019
Personnel: Jim Zachary (Ed.); Andrew Wardle (VP Circ.); Laurie Gay (Advertising Director); Hubby Brooks (VP Technology); Vince Cribb (VP Prodn.); Jeff Masters (Adv. VP); Dan Friedman (Controller); Shan Miller (Business Mgr.); Theresa Westberry (Advertising Director)
Parent company (for newspapers): CNHI, LLC

WAYCROSS JOURNAL-HERALD

Street address 1: 400 Isabella St
Street address city: Waycross
Street address state: GA
Zip/Postal code: 31501-3637
County: Ware
Country: USA
Mailing address: PO BOX 219
Mailing city: WAYCROSS
Mailing state: GA
Mailing zip: 31502-0219
General Phone: (912) 283-2244
General/National Adv. E-mail: wjhnews@wjhnews.com
Display Adv. E-mail: ads.production@wjhnews.com
Editorial e-mail: newsroom@wjhnews.com
Primary Website: www.wjhnews.com
Year Established: 1875
News Services: AP
Special Editions: Football (Aug); Christmas (Dec); Bridal (Feb); Spring (Mar); Cookbook (Oct); Fair (Sept)
Delivery Methods: Carrier`Racks
Areas Served - City/County or Portion Thereof, or Zip codes: 3 150 131 510 315 160 000 000 000 000 000 000 000 000
Own Printing Facility?: Y
Commercial printers?: Y
Sat. Circulation Paid: 6475
Audit By: Sworn/Estimate/Non-Audited
Audit Date: 12.07.2019
Personnel: Roger L. Williams (Pub.); Van Carter (Adv. Mgr., Nat'l); Debbie Rowell (Adv. Mgr., Classified); Donnie Carter (Business/General Manager); Scott Cooper (Amusements Ed.); Gary Griffin (Film/Theater Ed.); Myra Thrift (Food/Garden Ed.); James Hooks (Photo Dept. Mgr.); Jack Williams (Vice President); Donna Cox (Circ. Mgr.)

HAWAII

HAWAII TRIBUNE-HERALD

Street address 1: 355 Kinoole St
Street address city: Hilo
Street address state: HI
Zip/Postal code: 96720-2945
County: Hawaii
Country: USA
Mailing address: PO BOX 767
Mailing city: HILO
Mailing state: HI
Mailing zip: 96721-0767
General Phone: (808) 935-6621
Advertising Phone: (808) 935-6622
Display Adv. E-mail: displayads@hawaiitribune-herald.com
Classified Adv. e-mail: classifieds@hawaiitribune-herald.com
Primary Website: www.hawaiitribune-herald.com
Delivery Methods: Newsstand`Carrier`Racks
Avg Free Circ: 1475
Sun. Circulation Paid: 14373
Sun. Circulation Free: 534
Audit By: AAM
Audit Date: 31.03.2018
Personnel: David Bock (Pub/Ed.); Dennis Francis (Pres.); Dave Kennedy (CRO); Jay Higa (Reg Adv Dir); Arlan Vierra (Sys Mgr); Matt Gerhart (Sports Ed); John Burnett (Police/Courts Reporter); Tom Callis (County/Govt Reporter); Kevin Jakahi (Sports Reporter); Stephanie Salmons (General Assignment Reporter); Hollyn Johnson (Photographer); Michael Brestovansky (General Assignment Reporter); Kirsten Johnson (General Assignment Reporter)
Parent company (for newspapers): Oahu Publications Inc.

HONOLULU STAR-ADVERTISER

Street address 1: 500 Ala Moana Boulevard, Suite 7-500
Street address 2: Ste 7-500
Street address city: Honolulu
Street address state: HI
Zip/Postal code: 96813-4930
County: Honolulu
Country: USA
General Phone: (808) 529-4700
Editorial Phone: (808) 529-4747
General/National Adv. E-mail: displayads@staradvertiser.com
Display Adv. E-mail: displayads@staradvertiser.com
Classified Adv. e-mail: classifieds@staradvertiser.com
Editorial e-mail: citydesk@staradvertiser.com
Primary Website: www.staradvertiser.com
Mthly Avg Views: 12659632
Mthly Avg Unique Visitors: 1695548
Year Established: 2010
Special Editions: Ala Moana (Mar, Jun, Nov) Career Expo (March & Aug) Chamber of Commerce Annual Directory (Dec) Community Support Guide (Oct) Credit Union (Oct) Earth Day (Apr) Easter (Apr) Football Fever (Aug-Jan) Hawaii's Best (Jun) Hawaii Talks (June, Sep, Dec) Holiday Gift Guides (Nov-Dec) Honolulu Pulse Awards (Aug) Keiki Day (May) Military Appreciation (Apr) Nurses Week (May) School Sections (Mar, Jun) Top Restaurants (Oct) University of Hawaii Sports (Aug-May) Young at Heart (Mar & Sep)
Special Weekly Sections: tgif (Fri), Dining Out (Sun), Hawaii Renovation (Sun), Crave (Wed)
Syndicated Publications: HILuxury, Pacific Journey, Go Kailua, Go Kapolei, Aulani (Disney Aulani Resort in-room magazine), Trump Hookipa (Trump International Hotel in-room magazine), Kahala Life, Aloha Hilton Hawaiian Village, Aloha Waikoloa Village, Castle Resorts Hoonanea, 101 Things To Do, Drive
Delivery Methods: Mail`Newsstand`Carrier`Racks
Areas Served - City/County or Portion Thereof, or Zip codes: All
Own Printing Facility?: Y
Commercial printers?: Y
Sat. Circulation Paid: 143811
Sun. Circulation Paid: 154944
Audit By: AAM
Audit Date: 31.12.2018
Personnel: Dennis Francis (Pres. & Pub.); Dave Kennedy (Chief Revenue Officer); Frank Bridgewater (VP/Ed.); Roger Forness (VP/Tech); Troy Fujimoto (VP/Digital Media); Rebecca Stolar (VP/HR); TC Gray (VP/Controller); Patrick Klein (VP/Advertising); Linda Woo (National Adv.); Aaron Kotarek (Sr Vp Audience and Operations); Jay Higa (VP/Bus. Dev. & Reg. Sales); Ed Lynch (Deputy Editor); Michael Rovner (Managing Ed./Design); Marsha McFadden (Managing Editor/News); E. Clarke Reilly (Managing Editor/Special Sections); Marty Black (VP/Prod.); Betty Shimabukuro (Managing Ed./Prod.)
Parent company (for newspapers): Oahu Publications Inc.

USA TODAY HAWAII EDITION

Street address 1: 500 Ala Moana Blvd
Street address 2: Ste 7-500
Street address city: Honolulu
Street address state: HI
Zip/Postal code: 96813-4930
County: Honolulu
Country: USA
Mailing address: 500 ALA MOANA BLVD STE 7-500
Mailing city: HONOLULU
Mailing state: HI
Mailing zip: 96813-4930
General Phone: (808) 529-4700
General/National Adv. E-mail: lwoo@staradvertiser.com
Year Established: 2012
Delivery Methods: Newsstand`Carrier`Racks
Areas Served - City/County or Portion Thereof, or Zip codes: All
Own Printing Facility?: Y
Audit By: AAM
Audit Date: 24.10.2018
Personnel: Dennis Francis (Pres. & Pub.); Dave Kennedy (CRO); Jay Higa (VP Business Development/Regional Sales); Aaron Kotarek (Sr VP Audience and Operations); Patrick Klein (VP of Advertising)
Parent company (for newspapers): Oahu Publications Inc.

WEST HAWAII TODAY

Street address 1: 75-5580 Kuakini Hwy
Street address city: Kailua Kona
Street address state: HI
Zip/Postal code: 96740-1647
County: Hawaii
Country: USA
Mailing address: PO BOX 789
Mailing city: KAILUA KONA
Mailing state: HI
Mailing zip: 96745-0789
General Phone: (808) 329-9311
Advertising Phone: (808) 329-2644
Display Adv. E-mail: displayads@westhawaiitoday.com
Classified Adv. e-mail: classifieds@westhawaiitoday.com
Primary Website: www.westhawaiitoday.com
Mthly Avg Views: 916483
Mthly Avg Unique Visitors: 151947
Year Established: 1968
Delivery Methods: Newsstand`Carrier`Racks
Own Printing Facility?: Y
Avg Free Circ: 699
Sun. Circulation Paid: 8520
Sun. Circulation Free: 644
Audit By: AAM
Audit Date: 31.03.2018
Personnel: Dennis Francis (President); Dave Kennedy (Chief Revenue Officer); Tom Hasslinger (Ed.); Jay Higa (Regional Advertising Director); Chelsea Jensen (Associate Editor); J.R. De Groote (Sports Editor); Nancy Cook-Lauer (County/Gov. Reporter); Max Dible (Enviro/Ag/Social Reporter); Cameron Miculka (Education, Health and Development Reporter); Rick Winters (Sports Reporter); Tiffany DeMasters (Police & Courts Reporter); Laura Ruminski (Photographer); Elizabeth Pitts (Arts & Entertainment Reporter)
Parent company (for newspapers): Oahu Publications Inc.

THE GARDEN ISLAND, KAUAI

Street address 1: 3-3137 Kuhio Hwy
Street address city: Lihue
Street address state: HI
Zip/Postal code: 96766-1141
County: Kauai
Country: USA
Mailing address: PO BOX 231
Mailing city: LIHUE
Mailing state: HI
Mailing zip: 96766-0231

General Phone: (808) 245-3681
Display Adv. E-mail: displayads@thegardenisland.com
Classified Adv. e-mail: tgiclassifieds@thegardenisland.com
Editorial e-mail: bbuley@thegardenisland.com
Primary Website: www.thegardenisland.com
Mthly Avg Views: 1654666
Mthly Avg Unique Visitors: 189544
Year Established: 1902
Delivery Methods: Mail`Newsstand`Carrier`Racks
Areas Served - City/County or Portion Thereof, or Zip codes: All
Own Printing Facility?: Y
Commercial printers?: Y
Avg Free Circ: 2631
Sun. Circulation Paid: 6867
Sun. Circulation Free: 2331
Audit By: AAM
Audit Date: 31.03.2016
Personnel: Dennis Francis (Pres.); Jay Higa (Adv. Dir.); Bill Mossman (Ed.); Dave Kennedy (CRO); Christopher Harm (Circ.); Darwin Rogers (Sales Mgr.); Aaron Kotarek (VP, Circ.)
Parent company (for newspapers): Oahu Publications Inc.

THE MAUI NEWS

Street address 1: 100 Mahalani St
Street address city: Wailuku
Street address state: HI
Zip/Postal code: 96793-2529
County: Maui
Country: USA
Mailing address: PO BOX 550
Mailing city: WAILUKU
Mailing state: HI
Mailing zip: 96793-0550
General Phone: (808) 244-3981
Advertising Phone: (808) 242-6363
Editorial Phone: (808) 242-6343
General/National Adv. E-mail: adsales@mauinews.com
Display Adv. E-mail: adsales@mauinews.com
Classified Adv. e-mail: class@mauinews.com
Editorial e-mail: letters@mauinews.com
Primary Website: www.mauinews.com
Year Established: 1900
News Services: AP,
Special Editions: Back-to-School (Aug);Best of Maui (Sept), Kahului Industrial Area, Christmas (Dec); Bridal Fair (Feb); Outlook (Economic Outlook Tab) (Jan); Maui Contractors Assoc.-Building & Materials Expo (Jun); Graduation (May); First Hawaiian Auto Show (Nov); Aloha Festivals (Oct); Maui Real Estate (Quarterly); Parade
Special Weekly Sections: Real Estate (Fri); Weekly TV Tab (S); Maui Scene (Thur); Super Market Ads (Tues)., Scene Magazine (Entertainment) Thurs.
Syndicated Publications: Parade (S).
Delivery Methods: Mail`Newsstand`Carrier`Racks
Areas Served - City/County or Portion Thereof, or Zip codes: 96793, 96732, 96753, 96761, 96708, 96714, 96790, 96748
Own Printing Facility?: Y
Commercial printers?: Y
Avg Free Circ: 83
Sat. Circulation Paid: 11271
Sat. Circulation Free: 83
Sun. Circulation Paid: 12843
Audit By: AAM
Audit Date: 31.03.2019
Personnel: Joe Bradley (Pub.); Dawne Miguel (Adv. Mgr., Retail); Chris Minford (Circ. Mgr.); Brian Perry (City Ed.); Lee Imada (News Ed.); Brad Sherman (Sports Ed.); Lehia Apana
Parent company (for newspapers): Ogden Newspapers Inc.

IDAHO

MORNING NEWS

Street address 1: 34 N Ash St
Street address city: Blackfoot
Street address state: ID
Zip/Postal code: 83221-2101
County: Bingham
Country: USA
Mailing address: PO BOX 70
Mailing city: BLACKFOOT
Mailing state: ID
Mailing zip: 83221-0070
General Phone: (208) 785-1100
Advertising Phone: (208) 785-1100
Editorial Phone: (208) 785-1100
General/National Adv. E-mail: jacquegraham@cableone.net
Display Adv. E-mail: wingram@cableone.net
Classified Adv. e-mail: class@cableone.net
Editorial e-mail: mnews@cableone.net
Primary Website: www.am-news.com
Mthly Avg Views: 102400
Mthly Avg Unique Visitors: 32000
Year Established: 1903
News Services: AP.
Special Editions: Progress (Mar); Outdoors (May/Aug); State Fair (Aug); Seniors (Jul/Nov).
Special Weekly Sections: Religion News (Fri); Agriculture (Sat); Food Day (Wed).
Syndicated Publications: American Profile (Weekly).
Delivery Methods: Mail`Newsstand`Carrier`Racks
Areas Served - City/County or Portion Thereof, or Zip codes: Blackfoot, Bingham County and Southeast Idaho
Own Printing Facility?: Y
Commercial printers?: Y
Sat. Circulation Paid: 3450
Audit By: Sworn/Estimate/Non-Audited
Audit Date: 12.07.2019
Personnel: Leonard Martin (Pub.); Wayne Ingram (Adv. Mgr.); Joe Kimbro (Circ. Mgr.); Robert Hudson (Ed.); Jason Ens (Sports Ed.); Kelly Koontz (Prodn. Mgr.)
Parent company (for newspapers): Horizon Publications Inc.; Adams Publishing Group, LLC

IDAHO STATESMAN

Street address 1: UPS Store 1116 S. Vista Ave. PMB 228
Street address city: Boise
Street address state: ID
Zip/Postal code: 83705
County: Ada
Country: USA
Mailing address: UPS Store 1116 S. Vista Ave. PMB 228
Mailing city: BOISE
Mailing state: ID
Mailing zip: 83705
General Phone: (208) 377-6400
Editorial Phone: (208) 377-6400
General/National Adv. E-mail: editor@idahostatesman.com
Display Adv. E-mail: mjenkins@thenewstribune.com
Editorial e-mail: newsroom@idahostatesman.com
Primary Website: www.idahostatesman.com
Year Established: 1864
Special Weekly Sections: Parade (Fri); Scene/Entertainment (Fri)
Delivery Methods: Mail`Carrier`Racks
Areas Served - City/County or Portion Thereof, or Zip codes: Ada and Canyon County
Own Printing Facility?: N
Commercial printers?: N
Sat. Circulation Paid: 34348
Sun. Circulation Paid: 43258
Audit By: AAM
Audit Date: 30.06.2018
Personnel: Rhonda Prast (Ed./VP); Chadd Cripe (Editor); Logan Osterman (Adv. Dir.)
Parent company (for newspapers): The McClatchy Company; Chatham Asset Management; McClatchy

COEUR D'ALENE PRESS

Street address 1: 215 N 2nd St
Street address city: Coeur D Alene
Street address state: ID
Zip/Postal code: 83814-2803
County: Kootenai
Country: USA
Mailing address: PO BOX 7000
Mailing city: COEUR D ALENE
Mailing state: ID
Mailing zip: 83816-1929
General Phone: (208) 664-8176
Advertising Phone: (208) 664-8176 ext. 3049
Editorial Phone: (208) 664-8176 ext. 2000
General/National Adv. E-mail: amurdock@cdapress.com
Display Adv. E-mail: kpacker@cdapress.com
Classified Adv. e-mail: classifieds@cdapress.com
Editorial e-mail: mpatrick@cdapress.com
Primary Website: www.cdapress.com
Mthly Avg Views: 1005279
Mthly Avg Unique Visitors: 246834
Year Established: 1887
News Services: AP, NEA.
Special Editions: Real Estate Digest. Live Well Magazine. Big Deals and Values. Living 50 Plus. Inland NW Bridal
Special Weekly Sections: Real Estate (S); Auto Plus (Sat). Health and Food (Wed). Entertainment (F). Outdoors (Thurs)
Syndicated Publications: CDA Magazine (Semi-yearly); American Profile (bi-weekly).
Delivery Methods: Mail`Newsstand`Carrier`Racks
Areas Served - City/County or Portion Thereof, or Zip codes: 83814, 83858, 83854, 83835, 83869
Own Printing Facility?: Y
Commercial printers?: Y
Sat. Circulation Paid: 21340
Sun. Circulation Paid: 28500
Audit By: Sworn/Estimate/Non-Audited
Audit Date: 12.07.2019
Personnel: Mike Patrick (Ed.); Aafke Murdock (National Ad. Director); Kattie George (Classified Adv. Dir.); Kari Packer (Sales Manager); Larry Riley (Pub.)
Parent company (for newspapers): Hagadone Corporation

POST REGISTER

Street address 1: 333 Northgate Mile
Street address city: Idaho Falls
Street address state: ID
Zip/Postal code: 83401-2529
County: Bonneville
Country: USA
Mailing address: PO BOX 1800
Mailing city: IDAHO FALLS
Mailing state: ID
Mailing zip: 83403-1800
General Phone: (208) 522-1800
Advertising Phone: (208) 542-6711
Editorial Phone: (208) 542-6795
General/National Adv. E-mail: dmills@postregister.com
Display Adv. E-mail: bacor@postregister.com
Classified Adv. e-mail: classifieds@postregister.com
Editorial e-mail: mlaorange@postregister.com
Primary Website: www.postregister.com
Mthly Avg Views: 481727
Mthly Avg Unique Visitors: 72031
Year Established: 1880
News Services: AP, SHNS, MCT.
Special Editions: Progress (Jan); Restaurant Guide (Jan); Health & Fitness (Feb); Home Improvement (Apr); Block by Block (Jul); Mayhem on the Middle Folk (Jun); Upset (May); Perfect Ending (May); 10 Peaks in 10 Weeks (May); In the Woods (Apr); Twice as Nice (Mar).
Special Weekly Sections: Community; Food & Home; Sports; Farm & Ranch.
Syndicated Publications: Parade (S).
Delivery Methods: Mail`Newsstand`Carrier`Racks
Areas Served - City/County or Portion Thereof, or Zip codes: Eastern Idaho
Own Printing Facility?: Y
Commercial printers?: Y
Avg Free Circ: 250
Sat. Circulation Paid: 18200
Sat. Circulation Free: 250
Sun. Circulation Paid: 19000
Sun. Circulation Free: 250
Audit By: Sworn/Estimate/Non-Audited
Audit Date: 12.07.2019
Personnel: Roger Plothow (Pub./Ed.); Brett Acor (Sales Dir.); Monte LaOrange (Asst. Mng. Ed.)
Parent company (for newspapers): Adams Publishing Group, LLC

LEWISTON MORNING TRIBUNE

Street address 1: 505 Capital St
Street address city: Lewiston
Street address state: ID
Zip/Postal code: 83501-1843
County: Nez Perce
Country: USA
Mailing address: PO BOX 957
Mailing city: LEWISTON
Mailing state: ID
Mailing zip: 83501-0957
General Phone: (208) 746-8742
Advertising Phone: (208) 848-2251
Editorial Phone: (208) 848-2269
General/National Adv. E-mail: kburner@lmtribune.com
Display Adv. E-mail: cmccollum@lmtribune.com
Classified Adv. e-mail: hposey@lmtribune.com
Editorial e-mail: dbauer@lmtribune.com
Primary Website: www.lmtribune.com
Year Established: 1892
News Services: AP, MCT.
Special Editions: Balance (Jul); Golden Times (Jul); Highway 12 (Jul); LC Valley Homes (May); Auto Finder (Apr); Students (Apr); Nez Perce Fair (Aug); Christmas Greeters (Dec); Explorations (Feb); Getting Married (Jan); Coupons (Jul); Health Beat (Jun); Spring Car Care (Mar); Agriculture (May); Getting Ready (Nov); At Home (Oct); From House to Home (Quarterly).
Special Weekly Sections: Arts & Entertainment (Fri); Agriculture (Mon); Business (S); Outdoors (Thur); Food (Wed).
Syndicated Publications: Parade (S).
Delivery Methods: Mail`Newsstand`Carrier
Areas Served - City/County or Portion Thereof, or Zip codes: 83501 83541 83524 83540 83545 83544 83520 83553 83546 83827 83539 53533 83554 83530 83522 82526 83549 83552 83525 83531 83832 83535 83843/844 83537 83871 83823 83855 83857 83834 83806 83872 83523 83543 83536 83555 99403 99401 99402 99347 99102 99111 99113 99130 66161 99163/164 99179
Own Printing Facility?: Y
Commercial printers?: Y
Avg Free Circ: 2777
Sat. Circulation Paid: 20626
Sat. Circulation Free: 2777
Sun. Circulation Paid: 21599
Sun. Circulation Free: 2718
Audit By: Sworn/Estimate/Non-Audited
Audit Date: 12.07.2019
Personnel: Nathan Alford (Pub./Ed.); Kim Burner (Adv. Mgr.); Fred Board (Gen. Mgr.); Doug Bauer (Mng. Ed.); Philip Charlo (Controller); Michael McBride (Circ. Dir.); Craig Clohessy (City Ed.); Marty Trillhause (Editorial Page Ed.); Eric Barker (Environmental Ed.); Jeanne DePaul (Garden Ed.); Brian Beesley (Graphics Ed./Art Dir.); Susan Engle (Health/Medical Ed.); Bill Furstenau (News Ed.); Jay Brown (Pressroom Manager); Phyllis Collins (Librarian)
Parent company (for newspapers): Verstovia Corp.; TPC Holdings Inc.

MOSCOW-PULLMAN DAILY NEWS

Street address 1: 220 E 5th St Rm 218
Street address 2: Rm 218
Street address city: Moscow
Street address state: ID
Zip/Postal code: 83843-2964
County: Latah
Country: USA
Mailing address: 220 E 5TH ST RM 218
Mailing city: MOSCOW
Mailing state: ID
Mailing zip: 83843-2964
General Phone: (208) 882-5561
Advertising Phone: (208) 882-5561
Editorial Phone: (208) 882-5561
General/National Adv. E-mail: ad@dnews.com
Display Adv. E-mail: ad@dnews.com
Classified Adv. e-mail: class@dnews.com
Editorial e-mail: editor@dnews.com
Primary Website: www.dnews.com
Year Established: 1911
News Services: AP, SHNS.
Special Editions: Tax Help (Apr); Fall Ag (Aug); Bridal (Feb); Brides (Jan); Agriculture (Mar); Mother's Day (May); Christmas Opening (Nov); Brides (Oct); Football (Sept).
Special Weekly Sections: Slice of Life (Sat); Arts & Entertainment (Thur); Business (Sat).
Syndicated Publications: USA Weekend (Weekly).
Delivery Methods: Mail`Newsstand`Carrier`Racks
Areas Served - City/County or Portion Thereof, or Zip codes: Latah County, Idaho, and Whitman County, Washington
Sat. Circulation Paid: 6500
Audit By: Sworn/Estimate/Non-Audited
Audit Date: 12.07.2019
Personnel: Nathan Alford (Pub./Ed.); Fred Board (Gen. Mgr.); Craig Staszkow (Adv. Mgr.); Mike McBride (Circ. Mgr.); Alan Solan (News Ed.); Michael-Shawn Dugar (Sports Editor); Geoff Crimmins (Photo Ed.); Lee Rozen (Managing Editor)

Parent company (for newspapers): Verstovia Corp.; TPC Holdings Inc.

IDAHO PRESS-TRIBUNE

Street address 1: 1618 N Midland Blvd
Street address city: Nampa
Street address state: ID
Zip/Postal code: 83651-1751
County: Canyon
Country: USA
Mailing address: PO BOX 9399
Mailing city: NAMPA
Mailing state: ID
Mailing zip: 83652-9399
General Phone: (208) 467-9251
Advertising Phone: (208) 465-8149
Editorial Phone: (208) 465-8124
General/National Adv. E-mail: asammons@idahopress.com
Display Adv. E-mail: svogel@idahopress.com
Classified Adv. e-mail: classifieds@idahopress.com
Editorial e-mail: vholbrook@idahopress.com
Primary Website: www.idahopress.com
Year Established: 1883
News Services: AP, SHNS.
Special Editions: Today's Woman (May); Snake River Stampede 2013 (Jul); Homemakers School (Apr); Caldwell Night Rodeo (Aug); Holiday Gift Guide (Dec); Cavalcade (Feb); Newcomer's Guide (Jul); Graduation (Jun); Mom of the Year (May); Holiday Delights (Nov); Get Ready for Winter (Oct); Healthy Living (Sept).
Special Weekly Sections: M.O.R.E. (Fri); Health Page (Mon); Family (S); Religion (Sat); Movie Review (Thur); People (Wed).
Syndicated Publications: Relish (Monthly); Parade (S).
Delivery Methods: Mail`Newsstand`Carrier`Racks
Areas Served - City/County or Portion Thereof, or Zip codes: Canyon County
Own Printing Facility?: Y
Commercial printers?: Y
Sat. Circulation Paid: 15404
Sun. Circulation Paid: 17794
Audit By: CAC
Audit Date: 30.06.2017
Personnel: Matt Davison (Pub.); Scott McIntosh (Mng. Ed.); Stacy Vogel (Adv. Dir.); Michelle Robinson (Adv. Mgr); Angela Sammons (Adv. Mgr.); Rhonda McMurtrie (Bus. Mgr.); Erik Franks (Advertising Manager); David Woosley (Asst. Mng. Ed.); Kaye Steffler (Community Ed.); Tom Fox (Sports Ed.); Joe Hansen (Prodn. Dir., Mailroom); Daniel Paris (Prodn. Dir., Press); Sean Evans (Advertising Director)
Parent company (for newspapers): Adams Publishing Group, LLC

SHOSHONE NEWS-PRESS

Street address 1: 620 E Mullan
Street address city: Osburn
Street address state: ID
Zip/Postal code: 83849
County: Shoshone
Country: USA
Mailing address: PO BOX 589
Mailing city: OSBURN
Mailing state: ID
Mailing zip: 83849-0589
General Phone: (208) 783-1107
Advertising Phone: (208) 783-1107
Editorial Phone: (208) 783-1107
General/National Adv. E-mail: kalexander@shoshonenewspress.com
Display Adv. E-mail: kalexander@shoshonenewspress.com
Classified Adv. e-mail: kalexander@shoshonenewspress.com
Editorial e-mail: ddrewry@shoshonenewspress.com
Primary Website: www.shoshonenewspress.com
Year Established: 1897
News Services: AP, NEA.
Special Editions: Progress (Other).
Special Weekly Sections: Best Food Days (Wed);
Syndicated Publications: Relish (Monthly); The North Idaho Advertiser (Other); Visitor's Guide Tab (Thur); American Profile (Weekly).
Delivery Methods: Mail`Newsstand`Carrier
Areas Served - City/County or Portion Thereof, or Zip codes: Shoshone County and Cataldo/Medimont areas in Kootenai County
Sat. Circulation Paid: 3315
Sun. Circulation Paid: 28500
Audit By: Sworn/Estimate/Non-Audited
Audit Date: 12.07.2019
Personnel: Linn Reese (Adv. Specialist); Amber Kitt (Assistant Adv. Dir.); Kelsey Saintz (Ed.); Zak Failla (Interim Ed.); Keri Alexander (Mgr./Adv. Dir.); Jennifer Smith (Marketing Consultant)
Parent company (for newspapers): Hagadone Corporation

IDAHO STATE JOURNAL

Street address 1: 305 S Arthur Ave
Street address city: Pocatello
Street address state: ID
Zip/Postal code: 83204-3306
County: Bannock
Country: USA
Mailing address: PO BOX 431
Mailing city: POCATELLO
Mailing state: ID
Mailing zip: 83204-0431
General Phone: (208) 232-4161
Advertising Phone: (208) 239-3151
Editorial Phone: (208) 239-3121
General/National Adv. E-mail: lshutes@journalnet.com
Display Adv. E-mail: kclements@journalnet.com
Classified Adv. e-mail: stubbs@journalnet.com
Editorial e-mail: ifennell@journalnet.com
Primary Website: www.journalnet.com
Year Established: 1890
News Services: AP, MCT, SHNS.
Special Editions: Summer Recreation (Jun); Yesteryear (Dec); Family Living (Monthly); Flourish (Monthly); Medical Guide (Apr); 101 Things to Do in Pocatello (Dec); Tis the Season (Nov); At Home (Apr); Bridal Guide 2013 (Jun); Park & Recreation (Apr).
Special Weekly Sections: Church (Fri); Youth Page (Mon); HomeLife (Sat); Escapes (Thur); Teen Page (Tues); Best Food Day (Wed).
Syndicated Publications: Parade (S); TV Journal (Sat).
Delivery Methods: Mail`Newsstand`Carrier`Racks
Areas Served - City/County or Portion Thereof, or Zip codes: Pocatello, American Falls, Blackfoot, Inkom, Chubbuck, Fort Hall, Lava Hot Springs, Downey, McCammon, Soda Springs, Malad, and Preston
Own Printing Facility?: Y
Commercial printers?: Y
Avg Free Circ: 1630
Sun. Circulation Paid: 12507
Sun. Circulation Free: 803
Audit By: CAC
Audit Date: 30.06.2017
Personnel: Andy Pennington (Pub.); Henry Johnson (Bus. Mgr.); Michele True (Adv. Dir.); Susie Tubbs (Classified Adv. Mgr.); Linda Shutes (General Sales Mgr.); Nathan Slater (Circ. Dir.); Matthew Plooster (Circ. Mgr., Newspapers in Educ./Sales); Ian Fennell (Mng. Ed.); John O'Connell (City Ed.); Jodeane Albright (Community Editor); Doug Lindley (Photo Ed.); Tim Flagstad (Sports Ed.); Justin Smith (Dir., Info Tech Servs.)
Parent company (for newspapers): Adams Publishing Group, LLC; Pioneer News Group

THE STANDARD-JOURNAL

Street address 1: 23 S 1st E
Street address city: Rexburg
Street address state: ID
Zip/Postal code: 83440-1901
County: Madison
Country: USA
Mailing address: PO BOX 10
Mailing city: REXBURG
Mailing state: ID
Mailing zip: 83440-0010
General Phone: (208) 356-5441
General/National Adv. E-mail: sanderson@uvsj.com
Display Adv. E-mail: sjads@uvsj.com
Classified Adv. e-mail: classifieds@uvsj.com
Editorial e-mail: editor@uvsj.com
Primary Website: www.uvsj.com
Year Established: 1881
News Services: AP
Special Weekly Sections: Parade; Food; Entertainment.
Delivery Methods: Mail`Newsstand`Carrier
Areas Served - City/County or Portion Thereof, or Zip codes: 83440, 83445
Own Printing Facility?: Y
Commercial printers?: Y
Avg Free Circ: 7700
Sat. Circulation Paid: 5000
Audit By: Sworn/Estimate/Non-Audited
Audit Date: 12.07.2019
Personnel: Travis Quast (Pub.); Jeremy Cooley (Gen. Mgr.); Koster Kennard (Sports Ed.)
Parent company (for newspapers): Adams Publishing Group; Adams Publishing Group, LLC

BONNER COUNTY DAILY BEE

Street address 1: 310 Church St
Street address city: Sandpoint
Street address state: ID
Zip/Postal code: 83864-1345
County: Bonner
Country: USA
Mailing address: PO BOX 159
Mailing city: SANDPOINT
Mailing state: ID
Mailing zip: 83864-0159
General Phone: (208) 263-9534
General/National Adv. E-mail: jmckiernan@bonnercountydailybee.com
Display Adv. E-mail: jmckiernan@bonnercountydailybee.com
Classified Adv. e-mail: ctraver@cdapress.com
Editorial e-mail: clobsinger@bonnercountydailybee.com
Primary Website: www.bonnercountydailybee.com
Mthly Avg Views: 211000
Mthly Avg Unique Visitors: 42600
Year Established: 1966
News Services: AP.
Special Editions: Progress (Apr); Neighbors (Monthly); Real Estate Guide (Monthly); Spring (Mar); Resource Guide (May); Chamber Directory (Sept) Winter Sports (Nov)
Syndicated Publications: Relish (Monthly); American Profile (Weekly).
Delivery Methods: Newsstand`Carrier`Racks
Areas Served - City/County or Portion Thereof, or Zip codes: Bonner County, Boundary County and Northern Idaho and Western Montana.
Own Printing Facility?: Y
Commercial printers?: Y
Sat. Circulation Paid: 5537
Sun. Circulation Paid: 28500
Audit By: USPS
Audit Date: 01.10.2015
Personnel: Keith Kinnaird (News Ed.); Caroline Lobsinger (News Room Ed.); Eric Plummer (Sports Ed.); Sheri Jones (Business Mgr.); Jim McKiernan (Publisher)
Parent company (for newspapers): Hagadone Corporation

THE TIMES-NEWS

Street address 1: 132 Fairfield St W
Street address city: Twin Falls
Street address state: ID
Zip/Postal code: 83301-5492
County: Twin Falls
Country: USA
Mailing address: PO BOX 548
Mailing city: TWIN FALLS
Mailing state: ID
Mailing zip: 83303-0548
General Phone: (208) 733-0931
General/National Adv. E-mail: clapp@magicvalley.com
Display Adv. E-mail: debi.perkins@magicvalley.com
Classified Adv. e-mail: apackham@magicvalley.com
Editorial e-mail: mchristensen@magicvalley.com
Primary Website: www.magicvalley.com
Mthly Avg Views: 2800000
Mthly Avg Unique Visitors: 575000
Year Established: 1904
News Services: AP, WP-Bloomberg
Special Editions: Football Tab (Aug) Readers Choice (Jun)
Special Weekly Sections: Entertainment (Fri); Business (Tues); Church Page (Sat); Outdoors (Thurs); Food (Wed); Ag (Mon)
Syndicated Publications: TV Magazine (Sun); Parade (Sun)
Delivery Methods: Mail`Newsstand`Carrier`Racks
Areas Served - City/County or Portion Thereof, or Zip codes: Southern Idaho / Magic Valley 8-county region
Own Printing Facility?: Y
Commercial printers?: Y
Avg Free Circ: 2793
Sat. Circulation Paid: 10164
Sat. Circulation Free: 2793
Sun. Circulation Paid: 13366
Sun. Circulation Free: 966
Audit By: AAM
Audit Date: 30.09.2017
Personnel: Matt Sandberg (Pub.); Russ Davis (Circ. Dir.); Alison Smith (Ed.); Debi Perkins (Adv. Dir.); Jerry Johns (Opt. Dir.)
Parent company (for newspapers): Lee Enterprises, Incorporated

ILLINOIS

THE TELEGRAPH

Street address 1: 111 E Broadway
Street address city: Alton
Street address state: IL
Zip/Postal code: 62002-6218
County: Madison
Country: USA
Mailing address: PO BOX 278
Mailing city: ALTON
Mailing state: IL
Mailing zip: 62002-0270
General Phone: (618) 463-2500
Advertising Phone: (618) 463-2527
Editorial Phone: (618) 463-2551
General/National Adv. E-mail: bmarkham@civitasmedia.com
Display Adv. E-mail: bmarkham@civitasmedia.com
Classified Adv. e-mail: juliejones@civitasmedia.com
Editorial e-mail: ngrimm@civitasmedia.com
Primary Website: www.thetelegraph.com
Mthly Avg Views: 1882352
Mthly Avg Unique Visitors: 308536
Year Established: 1836
News Services: AP, NEA, SHNS.
Special Editions: Senior Living (Apr); Back-to-School (Aug); Wrap it Up (Dec); Focus (Feb); Brides & Grooms (Jan); Bridal Guide (Jul); The Guide (Jun); Home Improvement (Mar); Heroes (May); Holiday Dining (Nov); Car Care (Oct); Fall Home Improvement (Sept).
Special Weekly Sections: Best Food Day (Wed); Entertainment (Thur); TV (Sun)
Syndicated Publications: Parade (S); American Profile (Weekly).
Delivery Methods: Mail`Newsstand`Carrier`Racks
Areas Served - City/County or Portion Thereof, or Zip codes: Madison, Jersey, Calhoun, Macoupin & Greene Counties (IL)
Own Printing Facility?: Y
Commercial printers?: N
Avg Free Circ: 234
Sat. Circulation Paid: 10663
Sat. Circulation Free: 234
Sun. Circulation Paid: 12486
Sun. Circulation Free: 106
Audit By: CAC
Audit Date: 30.09.2017
Personnel: Jill Moon (Special Sections Ed.); Kaci Beatty (Adv. Rep.); Julie Jones (Classifieds Rep.); Pete Hayes (Sports Ed.); Jill Sinkclear (Circ. Mgr.)
Parent company (for newspapers): Hearst Communications, Inc.

DAILY HERALD

Street address 1: 155 E Algonquin Rd
Street address city: Arlington Heights
Street address state: IL
Zip/Postal code: 60005-4617
County: Cook
Country: USA
Mailing address: PO BOX 280
Mailing city: ARLINGTON HEIGHTS
Mailing state: IL
Mailing zip: 60006-0280
General Phone: (847) 427-4300
Advertising Phone: (847) 427-4624
Editorial Phone: (847) 427-4642
General/National Adv. E-mail: sales@dailyherald.com
Display Adv. E-mail: sales@dailyherald.com
Classified Adv. e-mail: sales@dailyherald.com
Editorial e-mail: news@dailyherald.com
Primary Website: www.dailyherald.com
Mthly Avg Views: 5773664
Mthly Avg Unique Visitors: 2232534
Year Established: 1872
News Services: AP, CSM, RN, Bloomberg.
Delivery Methods: Mail`Newsstand`Carrier`Racks

Areas Served - City/County or Portion Thereof, or Zip codes: McHenry, Lake, Kane, DuPage, Cook and Will Counties (IL)
Own Printing Facility?: Y
Commercial printers?: Y
Sat. Circulation Paid: 56748
Sun. Circulation Paid: 66836
Audit By: AAM
Audit Date: 31.03.2018
Personnel: Daniel Baumann (Chairman Emeritus); Douglas K. Ray (Chairman/Pub./CEO); Robert Y. Paddock (Vice Chair/Exec. V.P./Admin); Colin O'Donnell (Sr. V.P., Dir. of Ops and Strat Initiatives); Kent Johnson (Sr. Vice Pres./CFO/Treasurer/Secretary); Heather Ritter (Vice Pres./Dir HR); Scott Stone (Pres/COO); M. Eileen Brown (VP/Dir Strat Mktg and Innovation); John Graham (Audience Analytics/Digital Ad Opts Mngr); John G. Janos (Circ Mngr); Wayne S. Gebis (Circ. Mgr., New Bus.); Joseph M. Marek (Circ Mgr, Single Copy Sales); Stuart Paddock (Sr. VP./Dir Dig/ Info Tech); Stefanie Anderson (Sr. VP / Gen Mgr / Southern Illinois Local Media Group); John Lampinen (Sr. Vice Pres./ Ed); Jim Baumann (VP/Mng Ed.); Peter Rosengren (VP/ Adv. Dir.); Ronald Salata (Dir. Display Adv.); Robert W. Smith (Major Retail Account Manager); Mark Stallings (Mgr Dig. Ops.); Kim Mikus (Sr. Bus. Ed.); Kelly Void (Dig. Ed. Engagement); Diane Dungey (Sr. Deputy Mng Ed.); Mike Evans (Dir. Local Adv.); Alan Musial (Adv. Operations Mgr.); Philippe Hall (Mgr. Dig Tech.); Jim Slusher (Deputy Mng Ed/Op Pg); Angela Pindel (Exec Asst to Exec VP/Vice Chairman); John McCarty (Build. Maint. Sup.); Greg Foster (Financial Ops Mgr.); Pete Nenni (Deputy Mng Ed / News); Renee Trappe (Group Ed / Southern Illinois Local Media Group); Travis Siebrass (Asst Mng Ed / Dig News); Neil Holdway (Asst Mng Ed / Copy Desk); Jeff Knox (Sr Dir of Visual Journalism); Kristine Wilson (Asst Corporate Secretary); Don Stamper (Dir of Prod); Mike Smith (Sports Ed.)
Parent company (for newspapers): Paddock Publications

DAILY SOUTHTOWN

Street address 1: 495 N Commons Dr
Street address city: Aurora
Street address state: IL
Zip/Postal code: 60504-8187
County: Dupage
Country: USA
General Phone: (708) 342-5646
Advertising Phone: (312) 283-7056
Editorial Phone: (708) 342-5646
General/National Adv. E-mail: CTMGSuburbanAdvertising@ctmg.com
Editorial e-mail: jbiesk@tribpub.com
Primary Website: www.dailysouthtown.com
Mthly Avg Views: 1200000
Year Established: 1906
News Services: AP
Special Weekly Sections: Sunday Rides, Wednesday Living, Thursday Homes,Friday Auto Mart, Friday Weekend Section
Delivery Methods: Newsstand`Carrier`Racks
Areas Served - City/County or Portion Thereof, or Zip codes: Chicago Southland
Own Printing Facility?: Y
Commercial printers?: Y
Sun. Circulation Paid: 20605
Audit By: AAM
Audit Date: 31.03.2017
Personnel: Jim Rotche (Gen. Mgr.); Joe Biesk (Ed.); Paul Eisenberg (News Ed.); Bill Scheibe (Sports Ed.)
Parent company (for newspapers): Tribune Publishing, Inc.

THE COURIER-NEWS

Street address 1: 495 N Commons Dr
Street address city: Aurora
Street address state: IL
Zip/Postal code: 60504-8187
County: Dupage
Country: USA
Mailing address: 495 N COMMONS DR
Mailing city: AURORA
Mailing state: IL
Mailing zip: 60504-8187
General Phone: (847) 696-6019
General/National Adv. E-mail: ahalston@tribpub.com
Display Adv. E-mail: jmcdermott@tribpub.com
Primary Website: www.chicagotribune.com/suburbs/elgin-courier-news
Year Established: 1875
Special Editions: Destination Spring Travel (Apr); Windfall of Homes (Aug); Readers Choice (Dec); Auto Show (Feb); Health Extra (Jan); Education Outlook (Jul); Health Extra (Jun); Education Outlook (Mar); Health Extra (Nov); Home Improvement (Oct); Health Extra (Sept).
Special Weekly Sections: Auto (Daily); Entertainment (Friday); New Homes (Friday)
Syndicated Publications: TV Week (Fri); USA WEEKEND Magazine (S).
Delivery Methods: Mail`Newsstand`Carrier`Racks
Areas Served - City/County or Portion Thereof, or Zip codes: Fox Valley (IL)
Own Printing Facility?: N
Commercial printers?: N
Sat. Circulation Paid: 1656
Audit By: AAM
Audit Date: 30.09.2018
Personnel: Pat Regan (Ed.); Robert Oswald (Metro Ed.); Bill Scheibe (Sports Ed.); Phil Jurik (Exec. Ed.); Jill McDermott (VP of Adv.)
Parent company (for newspapers): Alden Global Capital; CherryRoad Media

BELLEVILLE NEWS-DEMOCRAT

Street address 1: 120 S Illinois St
Street address city: Belleville
Street address state: IL
Zip/Postal code: 62220-2130
County: Saint Clair
Country: USA
Mailing address: PO BOX 427
Mailing city: BELLEVILLE
Mailing state: IL
Mailing zip: 62222-0427
General Phone: (618) 234-1000
Advertising Phone: (618) 239-2541
Editorial Phone: (618) 239-2500
General/National Adv. E-mail: mmason@bnd.com
Display Adv. E-mail: mmason@bnd.com
Classified Adv. e-mail: classified@bnd.com
Editorial e-mail: newsroom@bnd.com
Primary Website: www.bnd.com
Mthly Avg Views: 7750000
Mthly Avg Unique Visitors: 1369000
Year Established: 1858
News Services: NYT, AP, McClatchy, Tribune Media Services
Special Editions: Baseball (Apr); Home Builders' Show Tab (Feb); Auto Show Tab (Jan); MetroEast Living (Jul); Senior Citizens Tab (Jun); Home Improvement Tab (Mar);Auto Care Tab
Special Weekly Sections: Home/Fashion (Fri); Business (Mon); TV; Religion (Sat); Entertainment (Thur); Food (Tues); Shopping Guide (Fri)
Syndicated Publications: Parade (S).
Delivery Methods: Mail`Newsstand`Carrier`Racks
Areas Served - City/County or Portion Thereof, or Zip codes: St. Clair, Madison, Monroe, Clinton, Randolph & Washington Counties
Own Printing Facility?: Y
Commercial printers?: Y
Sat. Circulation Paid: 19475
Sun. Circulation Paid: 28334
Audit By: AAM
Audit Date: 31.12.2018
Personnel: Melissa Mason (VP Adv.); Stacy Richardson (VP Finance); Jeffrey Couch (Editor/VP); Don Bradley (Prod. Dir); Jay Tebbe (Pres./Pub.); Joe Ostermeier (Online Ed.); Gary Dotson (City Ed.); Michael Koziatek (Asst. City Ed.); Brian Brueggermann (Newsroom); Mike Fitzgerald (Newsroom); Jamie Forsythe (Newsroom); Beth Hundsdorfer (Newsroom); George Pawlaczyk (Newsroom); Carolyn Smith (Newsroom); Teri Maddox (Features); Roger Schueter (Features); Dean Criddle (Sports); Norm Sanders (Sports); Brad Weisenstein (Photo Ed.); Derik Holtmann (Photo); Steve Nagy (Photo); John Buese (Copy); Mary Cooley (Copy); Julie Ambry (Adv.); Sharon Peterson (Adv.); Darla Reynolds (Adv.); Erin Rinderer (Adv.); Tim Tucker (Adv.); Cathy White (Adv.); Michelle O'Leary; Debbie Buese; Donna Buckley; Sylvia Hammitt; Brian Keller; Joann Wymer; Eric Freeman; Dan Sliment; Bart Tate; Mark Watts; Tara Webster; Colleen Kleinschmidt; Greg Purcell; Bil Harrison; Kerry Wendler; Jerry Wilson; Joseph Bustos (Copy Editor); Garen Vartanian; Teresa Buelt; Pam Phelps; Ellen Gammill; Eschman Todd; David Wilhelm; Robyn Kirsch (Reporter); Casey Bischel (Copy Desk); Josh Connelly; Elizabeth O'Donnell; Stephanie Maher; Jarrod Beasley; Lucy Burton; Elizabeth Donald; Adam Evans; Jennifer Green; Hamner Robert; Jeff Hutchinson; Angie Hasamear; Jason Koch; Karen Latta; Becky Lemons; Jim Marks; Warren Mayes; Glenn McCoy; Dawn Peil; Jamie Phelps; Robin smith; Mike Strebel
Parent company (for newspapers): McClatchy; Chatham Asset Management

BENTON EVENING NEWS

Street address 1: 111 E Church St
Street address city: Benton
Street address state: IL
Zip/Postal code: 62812-2238
County: Franklin
Country: USA
Mailing address: PO BOX 877
Mailing city: BENTON
Mailing state: IL
Mailing zip: 62812-0877
General Phone: (618) 438-5611
General/National Adv. E-mail: jvitek@bentoneveningnews.com
Display Adv. E-mail: jarview@bentoneveningnews.com
Classified Adv. e-mail: mdarnell@bentoneveningnews.com
Editorial e-mail: newsroom@bentoneveningnews.com
Primary Website: www.bentoneveningnews.com
News Services: AP.
Special Editions:
Syndicated Publications: American Profile (Fri); USA WEEKEND Magazine (Sat).
Areas Served - City/County or Portion Thereof, or Zip codes: 62812, 62822
Sat. Circulation Paid: 3472
Audit By: Sworn/Estimate/Non-Audited
Audit Date: 12.07.2019
Personnel: Lynne Campbell (Pub.); Crystal Bullette (Classified Mgr.); Sam Waters (Circ. Dir.); Mona Sandefur (Reporter); Bruce Marsan (Sports Ed.); Jaime Reynolds (Sales Mgr.); Joe Vitek (Multi-Media Acct. Exec.); Kristen Reid (Digital Mktg. Specialist); Geoffery Ritter (Ed.)
Parent company (for newspapers): CherryRoad Media

THE PANTAGRAPH

Street address 1: 301 W. Washington Street
Street address city: Bloomington
Street address state: IL
Zip/Postal code: 61702-2907
County: McLean
Country: USA
Mailing address: PO BOX 2907
Mailing city: BLOOMINGTON
Mailing state: IL
Mailing zip: 61702-2907
General Phone: (309) 829-9000
Advertising Phone: (309) 829-9000
Editorial Phone: (309) 829-9000
General/National Adv. E-mail: advertising@pantagraph.com
Display Adv. E-mail: advertising@pantagraph.com
Classified Adv. e-mail: advertising@pantagraph.com
Editorial e-mail: newsroom@pantagraph.com
Primary Website: www.pantagraph.com
Mthly Avg Views: 6000000
Mthly Avg Unique Visitors: 500000
Year Established: 1837
News Services: AP, McClatchey.
Special Editions: Health and Fitness (Jan); Agribusiness (Feb); Home Show (March); Annual Report (March); Money Smart Week (April); Golf Guide (March); Spring Home and Garden (April); The Guide to Summer Fun and Entertainment (May); Campus Guide (August); Breast Cancer Awareness (Oct.); Calendar (Nov.) Hometown Holidays (Nov.) Readers Choice (July).
Special Weekly Sections: Business (Daily); Health, Fitness (Mon); Family (Tue); Food (Wed); Entertainment (Thur); Lifestyles, Real Estate (Fri); TV, Homes (Sat); Business, Viewpoint, Values (Sun)
Syndicated Publications: Relish (Monthly); Parade (S); American Profile (Wed).
Areas Served - City/County or Portion Thereof, or Zip codes: 61704, 61701, 61761
Own Printing Facility?: N
Commercial printers?: N
Sat. Circulation Paid: 22109
Sun. Circulation Paid: 28355
Audit By: AAM
Audit Date: 31.03.2018
Personnel: Michelle Pazar (President & Publisher); Barry L. Winterland (Gen. Mgr./Regional Finance Director); Mark Pickering (Ed.); Allison Petty (Regional Editor); Jim Thompson (Regional Circulation Director); Katie McShane (Circulation Services Manager); Todd Finch (Circulation Operations Director); Amanda Jones (Vice President of Sales); Hannah Craig (Social Media Manager); Taylor Hickson (Digital Fulfillment Specialist)
Parent company (for newspapers): Lee Enterprises, Incorporated

DAILY LEDGER

Street address 1: 53 W Elm St
Street address city: Canton
Street address state: IL
Zip/Postal code: 61520-2511
County: Fulton
Country: USA
Mailing address: PO BOX 540
Mailing city: CANTON
Mailing state: IL
Mailing zip: 61520-0540
General Phone: (309) 647-5100
General/National Adv. E-mail: mwhite@cantondalyledger.com
Display Adv. E-mail: ads@cantondailyledger.com
Classified Adv. e-mail: swelker@cantondailyledger.com
Editorial e-mail: editor@cantondailyledger.com
Primary Website: www.cantondailyledger.com
Year Established: 1849
News Services: AP.
Special Editions: Lawn & Garden (Apr); Agriculture (Aug); Christmas Wishbook (Dec); Agriculture (Feb); Income Tax (Jan); Bridal (Jul); Father's Day (Jun); Car Care (Mar); Home Improvement (May); Turkey Give-away (Nov); Home Improvement (Oct); Pre-Labor Day (Sept).
Syndicated Publications: Channel Guide (Fri); American Profile (Weekly).
Areas Served - City/County or Portion Thereof, or Zip codes: Fulton County (IL)
Sat. Circulation Paid: 3900
Audit By: Sworn/Estimate/Non-Audited
Audit Date: 12.07.2019
Personnel: Larry Eskridge (Reporter); Stephen Shank (Sports Ed.); Rick Bybee (Circ. Mgr.); Sandy Welker (Class.); Mary White (Adv. Mgr.); David Adams (Pub.); John Froehling (News Ed.); Deb Robinson (Ed.)
Parent company (for newspapers): Gannett; CherryRoad Media

THE SOUTHERN ILLINOISAN

Street address 1: 710 N Illinois Ave
Street address city: Carbondale
Street address state: IL
Zip/Postal code: 62901-1283
County: Jackson
Country: USA
Mailing address: 710 N ILLINOIS AVE
Mailing city: CARBONDALE
Mailing state: IL
Mailing zip: 62901-1283
General Phone: (618) 529-5454
Advertising Phone: (618) 351-5001
Editorial Phone: (618) 351-5090
General/National Adv. E-mail: lisa.giampaolo@thesouthern.com
Display Adv. E-mail: lyn.sargent@thesouthern.com
Classified Adv. e-mail: angela.oliver@thesouthern.com
Editorial e-mail: news@thesouthern.com
Primary Website: www.thesouthern.com
Mthly Avg Views: 1600000
Mthly Avg Unique Visitors: 325000
Year Established: 1878
News Services: AP, MCT, SHNS, TMS.
Special Editions: Spring Lawn & Garden (Apr); Football Preview (Aug); Holiday Wishes (Dec); Auto Racing (Feb); Southern Illinois Tourism Guide (Jan); Jackson City Visitor's Guide (Jul); Locally Owned Business (Jun); Spring Home Improvement (Mar); Southern Illinois Guide (M
Special Weekly Sections: Best Food Day (Wed); Health, Environment (Tue); Entertainment (Thur); Outdoors (Fri); Family, Religion (Sat); Technology, Auto (Daily); Parenting, TV, Finance, Real Estate, Home, Business, Outdoors (Sun_
Syndicated Publications: Parade (S); American Profile (Weekly).
Delivery Methods: Mail`Newsstand`Carrier`Racks
Areas Served - City/County or Portion Thereof, or Zip codes: Southern Illinois
Own Printing Facility?: Y
Commercial printers?: Y
Avg Free Circ: 662

Sat. Circulation Paid: 9675
Sat. Circulation Free: 486
Sun. Circulation Paid: 15609
Sun. Circulation Free: 946
Audit By: AAM
Audit Date: 30.09.2018
Personnel: Craig Rogers (Pub.); Tom English (Exec. Ed.); Les Winkeler (Sports Ed.); Alee Quick (Digital Editor); Byron Hetzler (Photo Ed.); Codell Rodriguez (Night Ed.)
Parent company (for newspapers): Lee Enterprises, Incorporated

THE CARMI TIMES

Street address 1: 323 E Main St
Street address city: Carmi
Street address state: IL
Zip/Postal code: 62821-1810
County: White
Country: USA
Mailing address: PO BOX 190
Mailing city: CARMI
Mailing state: IL
Mailing zip: 62821-0190
General Phone: (618) 382-4176
Advertising Phone: (618) 382-4176
Editorial Phone: (618) 382-4176
General/National Adv. E-mail: carmitimes@yourclearwave.com
Display Adv. E-mail: carmitimes@yourclearwave.com
Classified Adv. e-mail: carmitimes@yourclearwave.com
Editorial e-mail: editorial@carmitimes.com
Primary Website: www.carmitimes.com
Year Established: 1950
News Services: AP.
Special Weekly Sections: Best Food Day (Tue)
Delivery Methods: Mail`Newsstand
Areas Served - City/County or Portion Thereof, or Zip codes: Carmi and White County
Audit By: Sworn/Estimate/Non-Audited
Audit Date: 12.07.2019
Personnel: Kerry Kocher (Pub.); Duke Conover (Regional Ed.); Robert Beskow (Sports Ed.); Cheryl Trout (Adv. Mgr.); Rhonda Beason (Circ. Mgr.)
Parent company (for newspapers): Paxton Media Group; CherryRoad Media

MORNING SENTINEL

Street address 1: 232 E Broadway
Street address city: Centralia
Street address state: IL
Zip/Postal code: 62801-3251
County: Marion
Country: USA
Mailing city: Centralia
Mailing state: IL
Mailing zip: 62801-9110
General Phone: (618) 532-5604
Editorial Phone: (618) 532-5601
General/National Adv. E-mail: sentinelvip@charter.net
Display Adv. E-mail: sentinelvip@charter.net
Classified Adv. e-mail: classifieds@morningsentinel.com
Editorial e-mail: news@morningsentinel.com
Year Established: 1863
News Services: AP.
Special Weekly Sections: Gardening (Tues.); Education (Thurs.); Religion (Fri); Food (Sat.); Farm,, Comics, Feature (Sun); Local News, Sports, Stocks, Lifestyles, State, World News (Daily)
Syndicated Publications: Telly Times (Sat.); Comics (S).
Delivery Methods: Mail`Newsstand`Carrier`Racks
Areas Served - City/County or Portion Thereof, or Zip codes: We Cover Marion, Clinton, Jefferson, Marion and Washington Counties
Own Printing Facility?: Y
Avg Free Circ: 810
Sat. Circulation Paid: 12090
Sat. Circulation Free: 815
Sun. Circulation Paid: 12360
Sun. Circulation Free: 836
Audit By: CVC
Audit Date: 31.03.2016
Personnel: Julie Copple (Office Mgr.); John Perrine (Pub.); Daniel Nichols (Adv. Mgr.); Judith Joy (Farm Ed./Features Ed.); LuAnn Droege (Sr. Ed.); Terri Kelly (Prodn. Supvr., Composing)
Parent company (for newspapers): Centralia Press Ltd.

THE NEWS-GAZETTE

Street address 1: 2101 Fox Drive
Street address city: Champaign
Street address state: IL
Zip/Postal code: 61820
County: Champaign
Country: USA
Mailing address: PO BOX 677
Mailing city: CHAMPAIGN
Mailing state: IL
Mailing zip: 61824-0677
General Phone: (217) 351-5266
Advertising Phone: 217-351-5275
Editorial Phone: 217-393-8261
General/National Adv. E-mail: news@news-gazette.com
Display Adv. E-mail: advertising@news-gazette.com
Classified Adv. e-mail: advertising@news-gazette.com
Editorial e-mail: news@news-gazette.com
Primary Website: www.news-gazette.com
Year Established: 1852
News Services: AP, CNS, MCT
Special Editions: Farm Leader of the Year, Agribuisness, Ebertfest, High School Football, High School Graduation
Special Weekly Sections: Business, Technology, Entertainment (Mon); Best Food Day (Wed); Living, Spin Off (Thur); Entertainment, Health, Fitness (Fri); Home, Real Estate (Sat); Farm, Travel, Entertainment, Business (Sun)
Syndicated Publications: At Home, Central Illinois Business
Delivery Methods: Mail`Newsstand`Carrier`Racks
Areas Served - City/County or Portion Thereof, or Zip codes: Counties served: Champaign (primary), DeWitt, Douglas, Edgar, Ford, Iroquois, McLean, Piatt, Vermilion, Coles
Own Printing Facility?: Y
Commercial printers?: Y
Sat. Circulation Paid: 33291
Sun. Circulation Paid: 36877
Audit By: AAM
Audit Date: 30.09.2018
Personnel: Jeff D'Alessio (Editor); Mike Goebel (Mng. Ed.); Matt Daniels (Sports Ed.); Jim Dey (Opinions Ed.); Niko Dugan (Online Ed.); George Dobrik (Deputy Mng. Ed.); Joel Leizer (News Ed.); Robin Scholz (Photo Ed.)
Parent company (for newspapers): Community Media Group; News Gazette, Inc.

CHICAGO SUN-TIMES

Street address 1: 30 N. Racine Avenue
Street address 2: 3rd Floor
Street address city: Chicago
Street address state: IL
Zip/Postal code: 60654
County: Cook
Country: USA
Mailing address: 30 N. Racine Ave.
Mailing city: Chicago
Mailing state: IL
Mailing zip: 60607
General Phone: (312) 321-3000
Advertising Phone: (312) 321-2200
Editorial Phone: (312) 321-2522
General/National Adv. E-mail: nkirby@suntimes.com
Display Adv. E-mail: advertisinginfo@suntimes.com
Classified Adv. e-mail: garroyo@suntimes.com
Editorial e-mail: editors@suntimes.com
Primary Website: www.suntimes.com
Mthly Avg Views: 14317000
Mthly Avg Unique Visitors: 3291000
Year Established: 1844
News Services: AP, UPI, DJ, LAT-WP, RN, Chicago City News Bureau.
Special Editions: Baseball Preview (Apr); Education Guide (Aug); 10 Days & Counting (Dec); Black History Month (Feb); Bride & Groom (Jan); Bride & Groom (Jul); Education Guide (Mar); Mother's Day Greeting Ads (May); Holiday Gift Guide (Nov); Bulls/NBA Preview (Oct); Energy
Special Weekly Sections: Autotimes (Fri); Autotimes (Mon); TV Preview (S); Autotimes (Wed).
Syndicated Publications: USA WEEKEND Magazine (S).
Areas Served - City/County or Portion Thereof, or Zip codes: 60654
Sat. Circulation Paid: 91721
Sun. Circulation Paid: 116164
Audit By: AAM
Audit Date: 31.03.2018
Personnel: Nykia Wright (Interim CEO); Steve Warmbir (Managing Ed.); Gladys Arroyo (Adv. Vice Pres.); Jim Dyer (Adv. Vice Pres., Classified); David D. Ruiz (Adv. Dir., Art/Entertainment/Local Markets); Dean R. Spencer (Adv. Vice Pres., Cor. Accts.); Dave Sherman (Adv. Dir., Local); Willie Wilkov (Vice Pres., Mktg.); Michael Perrone (Circ. Dir., Distr.); Peter Belluomini (Circ. Dir., Opns.); Robert Edwards (Circ. Dir., Sales); Sandra Mather (Circ. Dir., Single Copy Sales); Toby Roberts (Asst. to Ed.); Polly Smith (Bus. Ed.); Jack Higgins (Editorial Cartoonist); Tom McNamee (Editorial Page Ed.); Chris Fusco (Ed. in Chief); Adam Shibla (Sr. Mgr. Retail Relationship); Chris De Luca (Deputy Managing Ed., News/Sports); Steve Warmbir (Dir of Dig. and Editorial Innovation); Tom McNamee (Editorial Page Ed.)
Parent company (for newspapers): ST Acquisition Holdings LLC

CHICAGO TRIBUNE

Street address 1: 160 N. Stetson Avenue
Street address city: Chicago
Street address state: IL
Zip/Postal code: 60601
County: Cook
Country: USA
General Phone: (312) 222-3232
Advertising Phone: (800) 974-7520
Editorial Phone: (312) 222-3540
General/National Adv. E-mail: ecom@tribune.com
Display Adv. E-mail: ecom@tribune.com
Classified Adv. e-mail: classadinfo@tribune.com
Editorial e-mail: metro@tribune.com; sports@tribune.com; sunday@tribune.com; business@tribune.com
Primary Website: www.chicagotribune.com
Mthly Avg Views: 37975000
Mthly Avg Unique Visitors: 5097000
Year Established: 1847
News Services: AP, RN, NYT, TMS, DJ, MCT.
Special Editions: Education Today-Summer (Apr); Fall Fashion (Aug); Year in Pictures (Dec); Cruise Planner (Feb); Winter Breaker (Jan); Golf (Jun); Education Today-Spring (Mar); Midwest Vacations (May); Ski Time (Nov); Follow the Sun (Oct); Fall/Winter Cruises (Sept).
Special Weekly Sections: Friday (Fri); Business Technology (Mon); Transportation (S); New Homes (Sat); Cars (Thur); Good Eating (Wed).
Syndicated Publications: Parade (S).
Sat. Circulation Paid: 415454
Sun. Circulation Paid: 764860
Audit By: AAM
Audit Date: 31.03.2017
Personnel: Tony Hunter (Pub.); Phil Doherty (Vice Pres., Finance/CFO); Janice Jacobs (Vice Pres., HR); Scott Tafelski (Dir., Technical Devel.); Sarp Uzkan (Dir., Technical Opns./Help Desk); Deepak Agarwal (Dir., Client Servs.); Robert Fleck (Adv. Sr. Vice Pres.); Joe Farrell (Adv. Vice Pres., Interactive); Barbara Swanson (Adv. Dir., Classified); Kathy Manilla (Adv. Dir., Devel.); Kelly Shannon (Dir., Brand Mktg.); Maggie Wartik (Gen. Mgr. of Suburban Weeklies); Stephen Rynkiewicz; Clarence Page; Colin McMahon (Assoc. Ed.); Mark Barrons; Peter Kendall (Mng. Ed.); Joycelynn Winnecke (Associate Manger, Editor of National News); John Gregorio (Director of Major Accounts); Gerould Ken (SVP Ed.); R. Bruce Dold (Pub./Ed.-in-Chief); Kester Alleyne-Morris (Asst. Subj. Ed., Nat.); Daniel Ellman (Ed. Designer)
Parent company (for newspapers): Alden Global Capital; Tribune Publishing, Inc.

THE BEACON NEWS

Street address 1: 350 N Orleans St
Street address city: Chicago
Street address state: IL
Zip/Postal code: 60654-1975
County: Cook
Country: USA
Mailing address: 350 N ORLEANS ST # 10
Mailing city: CHICAGO
Mailing state: IL
Mailing zip: 60654-1975
Advertising Phone: (866) 399-0537
General/National Adv. E-mail: ahalston@tribpub.com
Display Adv. E-mail: CTMGSuburbanAdvertising@ctmg.com
Primary Website: www.chicagotribune.com/suburbs/aurora-beacon-news
News Services: CNS, AP, NEA, NYT.
Special Editions: Destination Spring Travel (Apr); Windfall of Homes (Aug); Readers Choice Awards (Dec); Auto Show (Feb); Health Extra (Jan); Education Outlook (Jul); Wedding Planner (Jun); Education Outlook (Mar); Education Outlook (Nov); Home Improvement (Oct); Windfall
Special Weekly Sections: Religion (Fri); Real Estate Showcase (S); New Homes (Sat); Go (Thur); Food (Wed).
Syndicated Publications: TV Program Guide (S); USA WEEKEND Magazine (Sat).
Areas Served - City/County or Portion Thereof, or Zip codes: Fox Valley (IL)
Sun. Circulation Paid: 5684
Audit By: AAM
Audit Date: 31.03.2015
Personnel: Anne Halston (Ed.); Dan Cassidy (Metro Ed.); Phil Jurik (Exec. Ed.); Jill McDermott (VP of Adv.)

NORTHWEST HERALD

Street address 1: P.O. Box 250
Street address city: Crystal Lake
Street address state: IL
Zip/Postal code: 60039
County: McHenry
Country: USA
Mailing address: PO BOX 250
Mailing city: CRYSTAL LAKE
Mailing state: IL
Mailing zip: 60039-0250
General Phone: (815) 459-4040
Advertising Phone: (815) 459-4040
Editorial Phone: (800) 589-8910
General/National Adv. E-mail: advertising@nwherald.com
Display Adv. E-mail: advertising@nwherald.com
Classified Adv. e-mail: classified@nwherald.com
Editorial e-mail: tips@nwherald.com
Primary Website: www.nwherald.com
Mthly Avg Views: 3700000
Mthly Avg Unique Visitors: 610000
Year Established: 1851
News Services: AP, Gatehouse, Washington Post/ Bloomberg News Service, Illinois Statehouse News, Tribune Content Agency, New York Times Syndicate
Special Editions: Auto Show Preview (Feb), Everyday Heroes Progress Edition (Feb), Spring Home Improvement (Mar), Prep Football Guide (Aug), Best Under 40 (Oct), Hometown Holidays (Nov), Last Minute Gift (Dec)
Special Weekly Sections: Food (Wed), Real Estate (Thurs), Entertainment Pl@y (Thurs), Wheels (Fri), Business (Sun), Jobs (Sun)
Syndicated Publications: Relish; American Profile, Spry, Athlon Sports
Delivery Methods: Newsstand`Carrier`Racks
Areas Served - City/County or Portion Thereof, or Zip codes: McHenry County
Own Printing Facility?: N
Commercial printers?: Y
Avg Free Circ: 3689
Sat. Circulation Paid: 17182
Sat. Circulation Free: 3689
Sun. Circulation Paid: 19480
Sun. Circulation Free: 4041
Audit By: AAM
Audit Date: 31.03.2018
Personnel: Dan McCaleb (Executive Group Editor); Kevin Elder (VP/Production); Steve Sulouff (I.T. Director); Shelly Bissell (Classified Mgr.); Scott Helmchen (Features Ed.); Jason Schaumburg (Editor, Northwest Herald); Megan Hampton (Advertising Operations Director); Maureen Ringness (Group Sales Dir.); Rebecca Dienhart (Major/Nat'l Sales Coord.); Kate Weber (Publisher); Bob Edwards (Senior Circulation Director); Karla Ahr (Group H.R. Manager); Brad Hanahan (Group Classified Director); Jim Ringness (Gen. Mgr.); Kevin Lyons (Managing Ed.)
Parent company (for newspapers): Shaw Media

COMMERCIAL NEWS

Street address 1: 28 Logan Terrace Three
Street address city: Danville
Street address state: IL
Zip/Postal code: 61832-1651
County: Vermilion
Country: USA
Mailing address: PO BOX 787
Mailing city: DANVILLE
Mailing state: IL
Mailing zip: 61834-0787
General Phone: (217) 446-1000

Advertising Phone: (217) 447-5115
Editorial Phone: (217) 447-5155
General/National Adv. E-mail: info@dancomnews.com
Editorial e-mail: newsroom@dancomnews.com
Primary Website: www.commercial-news.com
Year Established: 1866
News Services: AP, SHNS.
Special Editions: Turn the Key (Monthly).
Special Weekly Sections: Farm Page (Fri); Home Place (Thur); Best Food Day (Wed).
Syndicated Publications: Teleview (Fri); USA WEEKEND Magazine (S).
Delivery Methods: Mail`Newsstand`Carrier`Racks
Areas Served - City/County or Portion Thereof, or Zip codes: Greater Danville, IL
Own Printing Facility?: N
Commercial printers?: N
Sat. Circulation Paid: 8681
Sun. Circulation Paid: 10361
Audit By: AAM
Audit Date: 30.09.2012
Personnel: Amy Winter (Pub.); Larry Smith (Ed.); Cindy Decker (Adv. Sales. Mgr.); Chad Dare (Sports Ed.); John Dowers (Office Mgr.)
Parent company (for newspapers): CNHI, LLC; CNHI, LLC

HERALD & REVIEW, DECATUR

Street address 1: 601 E William St
Street address city: Decatur
Street address state: IL
Zip/Postal code: 62523-1142
County: Macon
Country: USA
General Phone: (217) 429-5151
Advertising Phone: (217) 421-6920
Editorial Phone: (217) 421-6979
General/National Adv. E-mail: jfletcher@herald-review.com
Display Adv. E-mail: chittmeier@herald-review.com
Classified Adv. e-mail: lconnelly@herald-review.com
Editorial e-mail: ddawson@herald-review.com
Primary Website: www.herald-review.com
Mthly Avg Views: 1700000
Mthly Avg Unique Visitors: 240000
Year Established: 1873
News Services: AP, Metro Surburbia Inc..
Special Editions: Christmas Storybook (Other).
Special Weekly Sections: Entertainment (Fri); Business (S); Religion/Family (Sat); Teens (Thur); Food/Health (Wed).
Syndicated Publications: Parade (S).
Areas Served - City/County or Portion Thereof, or Zip codes: Decatur & Macon County
Sat. Circulation Paid: 18445
Sun. Circulation Paid: 22360
Audit By: AAM
Audit Date: 30.09.2018
Personnel: Scott Perry (Managing. Ed./ Print); Tim Cain (Audience Engagement Ed.); Mike Albright (Sports Ed.); Karen Woare (Data Processing Supvr.); Brad Marshall (Tech. Servs. Mgr.); Beth McCormick (Online Mgr.); Chuck Rutherford (Prodn. Mgr., Press); Mark Hall (Circulation Operations Manager); Chris Coates (Ed.); Allison Petty (Managing Ed./Digital); Shawna Lawrence (Adv. Dir.); Cayla Hittmeier (Dig. Adv. Sales Mgr.); Joel Fletcher (Gen. Mgr.); Jeana Matherly (Deputy Managing Ed. / Print); John Reidy (Deputy Managing Ed./Digital)
Parent company (for newspapers): Lee Enterprises, Incorporated

DAILY CHRONICLE

Street address 1: 1586 Barber Greene Rd
Street address city: Dekalb
Street address state: IL
Zip/Postal code: 60115-7900
County: Dekalb
Country: USA
General Phone: (815) 756-4841
General/National Adv. E-mail: kpletsch@shawmedia.com
Display Adv. E-mail: kpletsch@shawmedia.com
Classified Adv. e-mail: classified@shawsuburban.com
Editorial e-mail: news@daily-chronicle.com
Primary Website: www.daily-chronicle.com
Year Established: 1880
News Services: AP, TMS, Gatehouse News Service, Washington Post/Bloomberg
Special Editions: Progress (Apr); Back-to-School (Aug); Gift Guide (Dec); Farm Forecast (Jan); Spring Fashion (Mar); Home Improvement-Lawn & Garden (May); Christmas (Nov); Fall Farm (Oct); Fall Home Improvement (Sept).
Syndicated Publications: USA WEEKEND Magazine (Weekly), Relish (Monthly), American Profile (Weekly), Spry (Monthly), Athlon Sports (Monthly)
Delivery Methods: Newsstand`Carrier`Racks
Areas Served - City/County or Portion Thereof, or Zip codes: 60111 60112 60115 60135 60145 60146 60530 60531 60150 60151 60536 60537 60541 60545 61068 60548 60549 60550 60551 60552 60178 60556
Own Printing Facility?: N
Commercial printers?: N
Avg Free Circ: 1344
Sat. Circulation Paid: 5521
Sat. Circulation Free: 1344
Sun. Circulation Paid: 6053
Sun. Circulation Free: 1269
Audit By: AAM
Audit Date: 31.03.2019
Personnel: Eric Olson (Gen. Mgr.); Eddie Carifio (Sports Ed.); Inger Koch (Features Ed.); Mark Busch (Photo Ed.); J. Babbitt (Classifieds)
Parent company (for newspapers): Shaw Media

THE TELEGRAPH

Street address 1: 113 S Peoria Ave
Street address 2: Ste 1
Street address city: Dixon
Street address state: IL
Zip/Postal code: 61021-2905
County: Lee
Country: USA
Mailing address: 113 S PEORIA AVE STE 1
Mailing city: DIXON
Mailing state: IL
Mailing zip: 61021-2905
General Phone: (815) 284-2224
Advertising Phone: (815) 284-2224
Editorial Phone: (815) 284-2224
General/National Adv. E-mail: jbaratta@saukvalley.com
Display Adv. E-mail: jbaratta@saukvalley.com
Classified Adv. e-mail: jdiehl@saukvalley.com
Editorial e-mail: llough@saukvalley.com
Primary Website: www.saukvalley.com
Year Established: 1851
News Services: AP, CNS, SHNS.
Special Editions: Career Guide (Apr); Whiteside County Fair (Aug); Last Minute Gift Guide (Dec); Internet Directory (Feb); Health & Fitness (Jan); Dixon Sidewalk Sale (Jul); Dixon Petunia Festival (Jun); Home & Garden (Mar); Today's Farm (May); Senior Echo (Monthly); Baske
Special Weekly Sections: Celebrations (Bi-Weekly); Food (Wed); Real Estate, Entertainment (Thur); Auto, Recreation, Travel (Sat)
Areas Served - City/County or Portion Thereof, or Zip codes: 61021, 61081, 61071
Avg Free Circ: 165
Audit By: AAM
Audit Date: 30.09.2017
Personnel: Jennifer Baratta (Adv. Mgr.); Ed Bushman (Gen. Mgr.); Sheryl Gulbranson (Circ. Mgr.); Larry Lough (Exec. Ed); Will Larkin (Sports Ed.); Andrea Mills (Travel Ed.); Ernie Appleyard (Prodn. Mgr.); Sam Fisher (Pub.); Kim Weinstock (Customer Service); Nicole Bollman (Mktg. Mgr.); JoAnne Mills (Finance Dir.)
Parent company (for newspapers): Shaw Media

DU QUOIN EVENING CALL

Street address 1: 9 N Division St
Street address city: Du Quoin
Street address state: IL
Zip/Postal code: 62832-1405
County: Perry
Country: USA
Mailing address: PO BOX 184
Mailing city: DU QUOIN
Mailing state: IL
Mailing zip: 62832-0184
General Phone: (618) 542-2133
General/National Adv. E-mail: duquoin@frontier.com
Display Adv. E-mail: csmith@duquoin.com
Classified Adv. e-mail: amilam@duquoin.com
Editorial e-mail: jcroessman@duquoin.com
Primary Website: www.duquoin.com
Year Established: 1895
News Services: AP.
Special Editions: Spring Home Improvements (Apr); Du Quoin State Fair (Aug); Tax Guide Tab (Feb); Bridal Show (Jan); Progress (Mar); Christmas Preview (Nov); Fall Home Improvements (Oct).
Special Weekly Sections: American Weekend (Fri); Business (Sat).
Syndicated Publications: USA WEEKEND Magazine (Sat); American Profile (Weekly).
Delivery Methods: Mail`Newsstand`Carrier`Racks
Areas Served - City/County or Portion Thereof, or Zip codes: Perry, Franklin, Randolph and Jackson Counties in Southern Illinois
Own Printing Facility?: N
Commercial printers?: N
Audit By: Sworn/Estimate/Non-Audited
Audit Date: 12.07.2019
Personnel: Lynne Campbell (Pub.); Debra Burns (Office Mgr.); Patty Malinee (Circ. Mgr.); Doug Daniels (Sports Ed.); Kathy Kopshever (News Ed.); Craig Smith (Adv. Mgr.)
Parent company (for newspapers): Paddock Publications, Inc.; CherryRoad Media

DISPATCH-ARGUS

Street address 1: 1033 7th Street, Suite 101
Street address city: East Moline
Street address state: IL
Zip/Postal code: 61244
County: Rock Island
Country: USA
General Phone: (309) 764-4344
Advertising Phone: (309) 757-5019
Editorial Phone: (309) 757-4990
General/National Adv. E-mail: info@qconline.com
Display Adv. E-mail: advertising@qconline.com
Classified Adv. e-mail: classifieds@qconline.com
Editorial e-mail: press@qconline.com
Primary Website: www.qconline.com
Mthly Avg Views: 1583872
Mthly Avg Unique Visitors: 168199
News Services: MCT, NYT, AP, NEA, Bloomberg.
Special Editions: QC Q & A (Aug); Holiday Gift Guide (Dec); Home Builders Show (Feb); Home Improvement (Jan); Back to School (Jul); Lawn & Garden (Mar); Summer Events (May); Holiday Cookbook (Nov); Fall Home Improvement (Oct); Bridal Guide (Sept).
Special Weekly Sections: TV Week (S); Religion (Sat); Entertainment (Thur); Best Food Day (Wed).
Syndicated Publications: PARADE Magazine (S).
Delivery Methods: Mail`Newsstand`Carrier`Racks
Areas Served - City/County or Portion Thereof, or Zip codes: 61230, 61231, 61412, 61413, 61232, 61233, 61234, 61235, 61236, 61238, 61239, 61241, 61240, 61241, 61242, 61244, 61284, 61250, 61434, 61254, 61256, 61257, 61258, 61259, 61260, 61442, 61443, 61453, 61261, 61262, 61263, 61264, 61344, 61265, 61462, 61272, 61465, 61468, 61273, 61274, 61275, 61276, 61277, 61278, 61279, 61201, 61476, 61281, 61282, 61283, 61284, 61486, 61490, 52722, 52801, 52802, 52803, 52804, 52806, 52807
Own Printing Facility?: N
Commercial printers?: N
Avg Free Circ: 1608
Sat. Circulation Paid: 36730
Sat. Circulation Free: 300
Sun. Circulation Paid: 54172
Sun. Circulation Free: 2276
Audit By: AAM
Audit Date: 31.12.2018
Personnel: Deb Anslem (Pub.); Kenda Burrows (Editorial Page Ed.); John Marx (Columnist); Laura Yeater (News Data Admin); Laura Fraembs (Assoc. Mng. Ed.); Marc Nesseler (Info. Ed./Sports & Rec.); Todd Mizener (Info. Ed./Photo & Multi); Tom Biermann (Gen. Mgr.)
Parent company (for newspapers): Lee Enterprises, Incorporated

EDWARDSVILLE INTELLIGENCER

Street address 1: 117 N 2nd St
Street address city: Edwardsville
Street address state: IL
Zip/Postal code: 62025-1938
County: Madison
Country: USA
General Phone: (618) 656-4700
General/National Adv. E-mail: aschaake@edwpub.net
Display Adv. E-mail: aschaake@edwpub.net
Classified Adv. e-mail: newads@edwpub.net
Editorial e-mail: news@edwpub.net
Primary Website: www.theintelligencer.com/
Mthly Avg Views: 550000
Year Established: 1862
News Services: AP, HN.
Special Editions: Good News (Apr); Fall Sports (Aug); Christmas Greetings (Dec); Draw-an-Ad (Feb); Auto Show (Jan); Customer Appreciation (Jun); Spring Sports (Mar); Travel & Leisure (May); Veterans Day (Nov); Harvest Homefest (Oct); Answer Book/Madison Co. (Sept).
Special Weekly Sections: Real Estate (Fri); Family (Mon); Best Food Day (Sat).
Syndicated Publications: Weekender (Entertainment) (Sat).
Areas Served - City/County or Portion Thereof, or Zip codes: Edwardsville, Glen Carbon, Maryville, Collinsville, Troy, Worden, Alhambra & Hamel (IL)
Sat. Circulation Paid: 4288
Audit By: Sworn/Estimate/Non-Audited
Audit Date: 12.07.2019
Personnel: Denise Vonder Haar (Pub.); Schaake Amy (Adv. Mgr.); Bill Tucker (Editor); Ron Harris (Mgmt. Info Servs. Mgr.); Nick Tennyson (Prodn. Supvr., Mailroom); Jennifer Dyer (Adv. Design Mgr.); David White (Prodn. Foreman, Press/Camera); Rosemary Kebel (Opns. Mgr.); Bill Roseberry (Sports Ed.)
Parent company (for newspapers): Hearst Communications, Inc.

EFFINGHAM DAILY NEWS

Street address 1: 201 N Banker St
Street address city: Effingham
Street address state: IL
Zip/Postal code: 62401-2304
County: Effingham
Country: USA
Mailing address: PO BOX 370
Mailing city: EFFINGHAM
Mailing state: IL
Mailing zip: 62401-0370
General Phone: (217) 347-7151 x 112
Display Adv. E-mail: darrell.lewis@effinghamdailynews.com
Classified Adv. e-mail: carrie.wente@effinghamdailynews.com
Editorial e-mail: editor@effinghamdailynews.com
Primary Website: www.effinghamdailynews.com
Mthly Avg Views: 290000
Mthly Avg Unique Visitors: 74000
Year Established: 1935
News Services: AP.
Special Weekly Sections: Homes (Tue); Health (Wed); Farm, NASCAR (Thur); Church, Entertainment (Fri); Food (Sat)
Delivery Methods: Mail`Newsstand`Carrier`Racks
Areas Served - City/County or Portion Thereof, or Zip codes: Effingham & Surrounding areas
Own Printing Facility?: N
Commercial printers?: N
Sat. Circulation Paid: 8000
Audit By: Sworn/Estimate/Non-Audited
Audit Date: 12.07.2019
Personnel: Darrell Lewis (Pub./Adv. Dir.); Jeff Long (Ed.); Cathy Griffith (Mng. Ed.); Todd Buenker (Circ. Mgr.); Jane Herring (Bus. Mgr.); Linda Niebrugge (Composing Suprv.)
Parent company (for newspapers): CNHI, LLC; CNHI, LLC

THE JOURNAL-STANDARD

Street address 1: 50 W Douglas St
Street address 2: Fl 9th
Street address city: Freeport
Street address state: IL
Zip/Postal code: 61032-4129
County: Stephenson
Country: USA
Mailing address: 50 W DOUGLAS ST STE 900
Mailing city: FREEPORT
Mailing state: IL
Mailing zip: 61032-4141
General Phone: (815) 232-1171
Advertising Phone: (815) 232-2171
Editorial Phone: (815) 232-0166
General/National Adv. E-mail: ann.young@journalstandard.com
Display Adv. E-mail: ann.young@journalstandard.com
Classified Adv. e-mail: classifieds@journalstandard.com
Editorial e-mail: frontdoor@journalstandard.com
Primary Website: www.journalstandard.com
Year Established: 1847
News Services: AP, CNS, MCT.

Special Editions: Dream Homes (Apr); Football Tab (Aug); Homefront (Every other month); Home & Garden (Mar); Summer Calendar (May); Christmas Gift Guide (Nov).
Special Weekly Sections: Hometown Connections (Tue); Food, Fashion (Wed); Auto, Education, Faith (Thur); Arts, Books, Movies (Fri); Get Up & Go, Home, Garden (Sat); Business, careers, Travel, TV, Celebrations, Comics (Sun)
Syndicated Publications: Parade (S); American Profile (Weekly).
Areas Served - City/County or Portion Thereof, or Zip codes: Northwest Illinois
Avg Free Circ: 206
Sat. Circulation Paid: 3723
Sat. Circulation Free: 206
Sun. Circulation Paid: 4271
Sun. Circulation Free: 206
Audit By: AAM
Audit Date: 31.03.2019
Personnel: Paul Gaier (Pub.); Mark Baldwin (Exec. Ed.); Denny Lecher (Adv. Dir.)
Parent company (for newspapers): Gannett; CherryRoad Media

THE REGISTER-MAIL

Street address 1: 140 S Prairie St
Street address city: Galesburg
Street address state: IL
Zip/Postal code: 61401-4605
County: Knox
Country: USA
Mailing address: PO BOX 310
Mailing city: GALESBURG
Mailing state: IL
Mailing zip: 61402-0310
General Phone: (309) 343-7181
Advertising Phone: (309) 343-7181
Editorial Phone: (309) 343-7181
General/National Adv. E-mail: lcampbell@gatehousemedia.com
Display Adv. E-mail: lcampbell@gatehousemedia.com
Classified Adv. e-mail: cuhlmann@register-mail.com
Editorial e-mail: tmartin@register-mail.com
Primary Website: www.galesburg.com
News Services: AP.
Special Editions: Lawn & Garden (Apr); Football (Aug); Gift Ads (Dec); Bridal Tab (Feb); Senior Citizens (Jan); Knox Co. Fair (Jul); Farmers' Forecast (Jun); Ag Day (Mar); Real Estate (May); Basketball (Nov); Farmers' Forecast (Oct); Senior Citizens (Sept).
Special Weekly Sections: Kids, Family (Mon); Business, Agriculture, Personal Income, Stargazers (tue); Food, Recipes, health, Fitness, Cook's Corner (Wed); Entertainment, Meeting Place, Trends (Thur); Auto, Parenting, Education (Fri); Home, Garden, Business (Sat); Travel, Arts (Sun)
Syndicated Publications: Parade (S).
Areas Served - City/County or Portion Thereof, or Zip codes: 61401, 61430, 61448, 61488, 61410, 61462
Sat. Circulation Paid: 9194
Sun. Circulation Paid: 10362
Audit By: AAM
Audit Date: 30.09.2014
Personnel: Nathan Clark (Adv. Mgr.); Tom Martin (Ed.); Robert Buck (Local News Ed.); David Adams (Pub.); Mike Trueblood (Sports Ed.); John Bown (Prodn. Mgr.); Jan Blair; Tony Scott (Pub.)
Parent company (for newspapers): Gannett; CherryRoad Media

LAKE COUNTY NEWS-SUN

Street address 1: 1225 Tri State Pkwy Ste 570
Street address 2: Suite 570
Street address city: Gurnee
Street address state: IL
Zip/Postal code: 60031-9163
County: Lake
Country: USA
Mailing address: 1225 TRI STATE PKWY STE 570
Mailing city: GURNEE
Mailing state: IL
Mailing zip: 60031-9163
General Phone: (312) 222-2425
Advertising Phone: (312) 283-7056
Editorial Phone: (312) 222-2350
General/National Adv. E-mail: jbiesk@tribpub.com
Display Adv. E-mail: CTMGSuburbanAdvertising@ctmg.com
Editorial e-mail: jbiesk@tribpub.com
Primary Website: www.newssunonline.com
News Services: AP.
Special Weekly Sections: SEARCHchicagoautos (Fri).
Syndicated Publications: USA WEEKEND Magazine (Sat).
Areas Served - City/County or Portion Thereof, or Zip codes: 60085
Avg Free Circ: 104000
Audit By: Sworn/Estimate/Non-Audited
Audit Date: 12.07.2019
Personnel: Jon Rabiroff (Mng. Ed.); Dan Moran (News Ed.); Joe Biesk (Ed.); Phil Jurik (Exec. Ed.); Jill McDermott (VP of Adv.)

ELDORADO DAILY JOURNAL

Street address 1: 35 S Vine St
Street address city: Harrisburg
Street address state: IL
Zip/Postal code: 62946-1725
County: Saline
Country: USA
Mailing address: PO BOX 248
Mailing city: HARRISBURG
Mailing state: IL
Mailing zip: 62946-0248
General Phone: (618) 253-7146
General/National Adv. E-mail: crann@dailyregister.com
Classified Adv. e-mail: nhawkins@dailyregister.com
Editorial e-mail: bdeneal@dailyregsiter.com
Primary Website: www.dailyregister.com
Year Established: 1911
News Services: AP
Syndicated Publications: TV Guide (Fri); USA WEEKEND Magazine (Sat).
Delivery Methods: Mail`Newsstand`Carrier`Racks
Areas Served - City/County or Portion Thereof, or Zip codes: 62930, 62946, 62935. 62984, 62977
Own Printing Facility?: N
Commercial printers?: N
Audit By: Sworn/Estimate/Non-Audited
Audit Date: 12.07.2019
Personnel: Brian DeNeal (Prodn. Mgr.); Norma Riley (Circ. Mgr.); David Adams (Pub.); John Homan (Ed.)
Parent company (for newspapers): CherryRoad Media; Paddock Publications, Inc.

THE DAILY REGISTER

Street address 1: 35 S Vine St
Street address city: Harrisburg
Street address state: IL
Zip/Postal code: 62946-1725
County: Saline
Country: USA
Mailing address: PO BOX 248
Mailing city: HARRISBURG
Mailing state: IL
Mailing zip: 62946-0248
General Phone: (618) 253-7146
Advertising Phone: (618) 253-7146
Editorial Phone: (618) 253-7146
General/National Adv. E-mail: crann@dailyregister.com
Display Adv. E-mail: crann@dailyregister.com
Classified Adv. e-mail: nhawkins@dailyregister.com
Editorial e-mail: bdeneal@dailyregister.com
Primary Website: www.dailyregister.com
Year Established: 1869
News Services: AP.
Syndicated Publications: American Profile (Fri); USA WEEKEND Magazine (Sat).
Delivery Methods: Mail`Newsstand`Carrier`Racks
Areas Served - City/County or Portion Thereof, or Zip codes: 62946, 62930, 62917, 62931, 62919, 62934, 62935, 62938, 62947, 62965, 62977, 62979, 62984, 62987
Audit By: Sworn/Estimate/Non-Audited
Audit Date: 12.07.2019
Personnel: Kay Brandsasse (Bus. Mgr.); Gatha Moore (Prodn. Mgr.); Brian DeNeal (Managing Editor); Lynne Campbell (Pres. Pub.); Norma Riley (Circ Mgr); Michael Dann (Sports Ed); Tom Kane (Reporter)
Parent company (for newspapers): News Media Corporation; CherryRoad Media

JACKSONVILLE JOURNAL-COURIER

Street address 1: 235 W State St
Street address city: Jacksonville
Street address state: IL
Zip/Postal code: 62650-2001
County: Morgan
Country: USA
General Phone: (217) 245-6121
General/National Adv. E-mail: jjcnews@myjournalcourier.com
Display Adv. E-mail: vselby@myjournalcourier.com
Classified Adv. e-mail: pat.schneider@myjournalcourier.com
Editorial e-mail: jjcnews@myjournalcourier.com
Primary Website: www.myjournalcourier.com
Mthly Avg Views: 800
Mthly Avg Unique Visitors: 600000
Year Established: 1830
News Services: AP, MCT
Special Editions: Back-to-School (Aug); New Year's Eve (Dec); Fall Auto Care Tab (Fall); Valentine Idea (Feb); July $ Days (Jul); Father's Day (Jun); Tax Preparation (Mar); Graduation Tab (May); Modern Farmer (Other); Spring Auto Tab (Spring); Summer Bridal Tab (Summer).
Special Weekly Sections: Society (S); Homes (S); Food (Wed).
Delivery Methods: Mail`Newsstand`Carrier`Racks
Areas Served - City/County or Portion Thereof, or Zip codes: Morgan, Greene, Scott, Schuyler, Cass, Pike and Macoupin counties
Own Printing Facility?: Y
Commercial printers?: Y
Sat. Circulation Paid: 8136
Sun. Circulation Paid: 9859
Audit By: Sworn/Estimate/Non-Audited
Audit Date: 12.07.2019
Personnel: David C.L. Bauer (Editor and publisher); Dennis Mathes (Sports Ed.); Jeff Lonergan (Prodn. Mgr.); Vicki Selby (Advertising manager); Brian Pond (Circulation director); Darren Iozia (Associate editor); Angela Bauer (Lifestyles editor)
Parent company (for newspapers): Hearst Newspapers

THE HERALD NEWS

Street address 1: 2175 Oneida Street
Street address city: Joliet
Street address state: IL
Zip/Postal code: 60435
County: Will County
Country: USA
Mailing address: 2175 Oneida Street
Mailing city: Joliet
Mailing state: IL
Mailing zip: 60435
General Phone: (815) 280-4100
General/National Adv. E-mail: advertisinginfo@suntimes.com
Classified Adv. e-mail: classified@shawsuburban.com
Editorial e-mail: jhosey@shawmedia.com
Primary Website: www.theherald-news.com
Year Established: 1877
News Services: AP, CNS, NYT.
Special Editions: Destination Spring Travel (Apr); Windfall of Homes (Aug); Readers Choice Awards (Dec); New Homes Spring Buyers (Feb); Super Suburban Jobs (Jan); Education Outlook (Jul); Wedding Planner (Jun); Education Outlook (Mar); Education Outlook (Nov); Home Improve
Special Weekly Sections: Automotive (Fri); Community Calendar (Mon); Health (S); Church (Sat); Weekend (Thur); Consumer Page (Tues); Food Page (Wed).
Syndicated Publications: USA WEEKEND Magazine (S); TV Update (Sat).
Areas Served - City/County or Portion Thereof, or Zip codes: Joliet & Surrounding areas (IL)
Sun. Circulation Paid: 21028
Audit By: AAM
Audit Date: 31.03.2017
Personnel: Steve Vanisko (Pub.); Joe Hosey (Ed.)
Parent company (for newspapers): Shaw Media

THE HERALD-NEWS

Street address 1: 2175 Oneida St
Street address city: Joliet
Street address state: IL
Zip/Postal code: 60435-6560
County: Will
Country: USA
General Phone: (815) 280-4100
Advertising Phone: 815-280-4101
General/National Adv. E-mail: thnads@shawmedia.com
Classified Adv. e-mail: classified@shawsuburban.com
Editorial e-mail: news@theherald-news.com
Primary Website: theherald-news.com
Year Established: 1839
Sat. Circulation Paid: 17066
Sun. Circulation Paid: 21028
Audit By: Sworn/Estimate/Non-Audited
Audit Date: 12.07.2019
Personnel: Steve Vanisko (Gen. Mgr.); Jon Styf (Ed.)
Parent company (for newspapers): Shaw Media

THE DAILY JOURNAL

Street address 1: 8 Dearborn Sq
Street address city: Kankakee
Street address state: IL
Zip/Postal code: 60901-3909
County: Kankakee
Country: USA
Mailing address: 8 DEARBORN SQ
Mailing city: KANKAKEE
Mailing state: IL
Mailing zip: 60901-3945
General Phone: (815) 937-3300
Advertising Phone: (815) 937-3376
Editorial Phone: (815) 802-5144
General/National Adv. E-mail: advertise@daily-journal.com
Display Adv. E-mail: advertise@daily-journal.com
Classified Adv. e-mail: classified@daily-journal.com
Editorial e-mail: editors@daily-journal.com
Primary Website: www.daily-journal.com
Year Established: 1853
News Services: AP; Washington Post; Bloomberg; Tribune News Service
Special Editions: Farm (Mar); House & Garden (May); Medical Guide (June); Summertime Fun (May);Ask the Experts (June); Farmer's Market (Jul); Back To School (Aug); Breast Cancer Awareness (Sept); Sports (Aug/Nov); Veterans Day (Nov); All Wrapped Up In One (Dec); Weddings (Spring/Summer/Fall/Winter); Family First (Feb, May, July, Oct.); Health & Wellness (Jan); Chicago Bears Training Camp Program (Jul); Progress (Mar/Apr); Graduation (May); HomeFinder (Monthly); Homebuyers Guide (Aug); THRIVE (Sept); Home & Yard (Oct);Holiday Guides I & II (Nov/Dec)
Special Weekly Sections: TV Weekly (Sat)
Delivery Methods: Mail`Newsstand`Carrier`Racks
Areas Served - City/County or Portion Thereof, or Zip codes: 60910, 60913, 60914, 60915, 60917, 60935, 60940, 60941, 60901, 60950, 60954, 60956, 60958, 60961, 60964, 60969, 60911, 60912, 60922, 60924, 60927, 60928, 60930, 60931, 60938, 60945, 60951, 60953, 60955, 60966, 60968, 60970, 60920, 60929, 60420, 60401, 60408, 60418, 60442, 60449, 60468, 60481, 60918, 60919, 60946, 60959, 60416, 60424, 60474
Own Printing Facility?: Y
Commercial printers?: N
Avg Free Circ: 2333
Sat. Circulation Paid: 16868
Sat. Circulation Free: 1944
Audit By: CAC
Audit Date: 31.03.2018
Personnel: Mike Frey (Ed.); Kiera Allen (Junior Life Ed.); Terry Yohnka (Copy Ed.); Aryana Adkanian (Digital Media Manager)
Parent company (for newspapers): Small Newspaper Group

STAR-COURIER

Street address 1: 105 E Central Blvd
Street address city: Kewanee
Street address state: IL
Zip/Postal code: 61443-2245
County: Henry
Country: USA
Mailing address: PO BOX A
Mailing city: KEWANEE
Mailing state: IL
Mailing zip: 61443-0836
General Phone: (309) 852-2181
Advertising Phone: (309) 852-2181
Editorial Phone: (309) 852-2181
General/National Adv. E-mail: diane@starcourier.com
Display Adv. E-mail: diane@starcourier.com
Classified Adv. e-mail: classifieds@starcourier.com
Editorial e-mail: editor@starcourier.com
Primary Website: www.starcourier.com
Year Established: 1898
News Services: AP.
Special Editions: Home Improvement (Apr); Hogsmopolitan (Aug); Bridal (Jan); People Making a Difference (Jul); Fair Tab (Jun); 101 Things to do in Henry County (May); Farm Tab (Monthly).
Special Weekly Sections: Best Food Day (Wed); Farm (Tue/Thur); Outdoors (Tue); Business (Thur); TV, Everyday, Church (Fri)

Syndicated Publications: American Profile (Weekly).
Areas Served - City/County or Portion Thereof, or Zip codes: Kewanee (IL)
Sat. Circulation Paid: 4739
Audit By: Sworn/Estimate/Non-Audited
Audit Date: 12.07.2019
Personnel: David Adams (Pub.); Kathy Werderman (Classified Adv. Mgr.); Mike Helenthal (Ed.); Mike Berry (Assoc. Ed.); Genie Stanley (Classifieds); Rae Padilla (Ed.)
Parent company (for newspapers): CherryRoad Media; Gannett

NEWS-TRIBUNE

Street address 1: 426 2nd St
Street address city: La Salle
Street address state: IL
Zip/Postal code: 61301-2334
County: La Salle
Country: USA
General Phone: (815) 223-3200
Advertising Phone: (815) 220-6945
Editorial Phone: (815) 220-6940
General/National Adv. E-mail: vpsales@newstrib.com
Display Adv. E-mail: vpsales@newstrib.com
Classified Adv. e-mail: support@newstrib.com
Editorial e-mail: ntnews@newstrib.com
Primary Website: www.newstrib.com
Mthly Avg Views: 1130000
Mthly Avg Unique Visitors: 115000
Year Established: 1946
News Services: AP.
Special Editions: Monthly: engagements, home improvement, health, financial, niche publications (magazines) focused: Boomers; Home/Garden/Life, Parent; Dream Wedding; annual: business/community review
Syndicated Publications: American Profile Magazine (Sat)
Delivery Methods: Mail`Carrier`Racks
Areas Served - City/County or Portion Thereof, or Zip codes: LaSalle-Putnam-Bureau-Marshall counties, IL
Own Printing Facility?: Y
Commercial printers?: Y
Avg Free Circ: 1952
Sat. Circulation Paid: 22665
Sat. Circulation Free: 1952
Audit By: AAM
Audit Date: 31.03.2019
Personnel: Joyce McCullough (Pub.); Craig Baker (Cor. Accounting Mgr.); Scott Stavrakas (Adv. Dir.); Mike Miller (Circ. Dir.); Craig Sterrett (News Ed.); Linda Kleczewski (Online Ed.); Diane Seghers (Online Mgr.); Fort Miller (Prodn. Mgr., Mailroom); Joseph Zokal (Prodn. Mgr., Pre Press); Ernest Appleyard (Press Manager)
Parent company (for newspapers): Daily NewsTribune, Inc.

DAILY RECORD

Street address 1: 1209 State St
Street address city: Lawrenceville
Street address state: IL
Zip/Postal code: 62439-2332
County: Lawrence
Country: USA
Mailing address: PO BOX 559
Mailing city: LAWRENCEVILLE
Mailing state: IL
Mailing zip: 62439-0559
General Phone: (618) 943-2331
General/National Adv. E-mail: syoung@lawdailyrecord.com
Display Adv. E-mail: mlewsader@lawdailyrecord.com
Classified Adv. e-mail: classads@lawdailyrecord.com
Editorial e-mail: lawnews@lawdailyrecord.com
Primary Website: www.lawdailyrecord.com
Year Established: 1847
News Services: AP, CNS.
Special Editions: Kreative Kids (Apr); Back-to-School (Aug); Christmas Greetings (Dec); Tax Guide (Feb); Summer Savings (Jul); Senior Citizen Salute (Jun); Spring Ag Salute (Mar); American Home Week (May); Christmas Opening (Nov); Working Women (Oct); Fall Festival (Sept).
Special Weekly Sections: Business (1 & 3 Tue); Health & Fitness (2 & 4 Tue); Shop at Home (3 Tues); Kids (Tue); Entertainment (Wed); Restaurant (1 & 3 Thur); Farm (2 & 4 Fri); Church (Fri)
Syndicated Publications: TV Section (Fri).
Delivery Methods: Mail`Carrier`Racks
Areas Served - City/County or Portion Thereof, or Zip codes: Lawrence County (IL)
Audit By: Sworn/Estimate/Non-Audited
Audit Date: 12.07.2019
Personnel: Kathleen Lewis (Pub.); Michael Van Dorn (Mng. Ed.); Sandie Young (Adv. Dir.); Joyce Tredway (Circ. Mgr.); Bill Richardson (Sports Ed.); Beverly Johnson (Layout Mgr.)
Parent company (for newspapers): Lewis Newspapers

LINCOLN COURIER

Street address 1: 206 S Chicago St
Street address city: Lincoln
Street address state: IL
Zip/Postal code: 62656-2701
County: Logan
Country: USA
Mailing address: PO BOX 740
Mailing city: LINCOLN
Mailing state: IL
Mailing zip: 62656-0740
General Phone: (217) 732-2101
Advertising Phone: (217) 732-2101
Editorial Phone: (217) 732-2101
General/National Adv. E-mail: ted.wolf@lincolncourier.com
Display Adv. E-mail: advertise@lincolncourier.com
Classified Adv. e-mail: advertise@lincolncourier.com
Editorial e-mail: news@lincolncourier.com
Primary Website: www.lincolncourier.com
Year Established: 1856
News Services: AP, CNS, SHNS.
Special Editions: County Fair (Aug); Progress (Mar).
Special Weekly Sections: Finance, TV (Daily); Best Food, Agriculture (Wed); Agriculture (Thur); TV (Fri)
Syndicated Publications: American Profile (Weekly).
Delivery Methods: Mail`Newsstand`Racks
Areas Served - City/County or Portion Thereof, or Zip codes: Lincoln and Logan County
Own Printing Facility?: Y
Commercial printers?: N
Sat. Circulation Paid: 5813
Audit By: Sworn/Estimate/Non-Audited
Audit Date: 12.07.2019
Personnel: Jean Ann Miller (Mng. Ed.); Todd Sears (Pub.); Ted Wolf (Advertising Manager)
Parent company (for newspapers): CherryRoad Media; Gannett

NEWS-HERALD

Street address 1: 112 E Ryder St
Street address city: Litchfield
Street address state: IL
Zip/Postal code: 62056-2031
County: Montgomery
Country: USA
Mailing address: PO BOX 160
Mailing city: LITCHFIELD
Mailing state: IL
Mailing zip: 62056-0160
General Phone: (217) 324-2121
General/National Adv. E-mail: lfdnews@litchfieldil.com
Display Adv. E-mail: ads.lfdnews@yahoo.com
Primary Website: No website
Year Established: 1856
News Services: AP.
Special Editions: Dollar Day (Aug); Back-to-School (Fall); Dollar Day (Feb); Christmas (Nov); Great Outdoors (Spring).
Delivery Methods: Mail`Newsstand`Carrier`Racks
Areas Served - City/County or Portion Thereof, or Zip codes: 62056, 62033, 62069, 62560, 62533, 62572, 62049 and across the United States
Own Printing Facility?: Y
Commercial printers?: N
Audit By: Sworn/Estimate/Non-Audited
Audit Date: 12.07.2019
Personnel: John C. Hanafin (Pub.); Lisa Land (Admin. Exec. Asst. to Pub.); Michelle Romanus (Wire Ed.); James Keith (Prodn. Supt.)

THE MCDONOUGH COUNTY VOICE

Street address 1: 26 W Side Sq
Street address city: Macomb
Street address state: IL
Zip/Postal code: 61455-2219
County: McDonough
Country: USA
General Phone: (309) 833-2114
General/National Adv. E-mail: mringenberger@mcdonoughvoice.com
Display Adv. E-mail: mringenberger@mcdonoughvoice.com
Classified Adv. e-mail: ahousewright@mcdonoughvoice.com
Editorial e-mail: jsmith@mcdonoughvoice.com
Primary Website: www.mcdonoughvoice.com
News Services: AP, LAT-WP.
Special Editions: Restaurant Directory Business directory Central Illinois Family Magazine (Monthly) Western Illinois University Coupon book
Special Weekly Sections: Church (Fri); Seniors (Mon); Lifestyles (S); Entertainment (Happenings) (Thur); Agriculture (Tues);Health (Wed).Business (Sat)
Syndicated Publications: Parade (S); American Profile (Weekly).Relish (Tuesday) Spry (Tuesday) Central Illinois Family Magazine (First Wed. month)
Delivery Methods: Mail`Newsstand`Carrier`Racks
Areas Served - City/County or Portion Thereof, or Zip codes: 61455, 61422, 62326,61420, 61438,61450,62367
Own Printing Facility?: Y
Commercial printers?: Y
Sat. Circulation Paid: 5000
Audit By: Sworn/Estimate/Non-Audited
Audit Date: 12.07.2019
Personnel: David Adams (Pub.); Michelle Langhout (Interim Ed.); Scott Holland (Sports Ed.); Michelle Ringenberger (Adv. Mgr.); Dusty Vaughn (Circ. Mgr.)
Parent company (for newspapers): Gannett; CherryRoad Media

THE MARION DAILY REPUBLICAN

Street address 1: 502 W Jackson St
Street address city: Marion
Street address state: IL
Zip/Postal code: 62959-2355
County: Williamson
Country: USA
Mailing address: PO BOX 490
Mailing city: MARION
Mailing state: IL
Mailing zip: 62959-0490
General Phone: (618) 993-2626
Advertising Phone: (618) 993-2626
Editorial Phone: (618) 993-2626
General/National Adv. E-mail: ad_manager@dailyrepublicannews.com
Display Adv. E-mail: ad_manager@dailyrepublicannews.com
Classified Adv. e-mail: classified@dailyrepublicannews.com
Editorial e-mail: editor@dailyrepublicannews.com
Primary Website: www.dailyrepublicannews.com
News Services: AP.
Special Weekly Sections: Best Food Day (Mon)
Syndicated Publications: USA WEEKEND Magazine (Sat); American Profile (Weekly).
Sat. Circulation Paid: 3600
Audit By: Sworn/Estimate/Non-Audited
Audit Date: 12.07.2019
Personnel: John Homan (Mng. Ed.); Justin Walker (Sports Ed.)
Parent company (for newspapers): CherryRoad Media; Paddock Publications, Inc.

JOURNAL GAZETTE & TIMES-COURIER

Street address 1: 700 Broadway Ave E
Street address 2: Ste 9A
Street address city: Mattoon
Street address state: IL
Zip/Postal code: 61938-4617
County: Coles
Country: USA
Mailing address: 700 BROADWAY AVE E STE 9A
Mailing city: MATTOON
Mailing state: IL
Mailing zip: 61938-4500
General Phone: (217) 235-5656
Advertising Phone: (217) 235-5656
Editorial Phone: (217) 235-5656
General/National Adv. E-mail: steve.lahr@lee.net
Display Adv. E-mail: steve.lahr@lee.net
Classified Adv. e-mail: canderson@jg-tc.com
Editorial e-mail: cwalworth@jg-tc.com
Primary Website: www.jg-tc.com
Year Established: 1840
News Services: AP.
Special Editions: Farm (Jan); Bagelfest (Jul); Graduation (May); Thanksgiving Day (Nov); Automotive (Oct).
Special Weekly Sections: Best Food, Business, NIE, Kids (Mon); Community, Internet (Tue); Community (Wed); Farm Feature (Thur); Church, Outdoors (Fri); School, Sports, lifestyle, NASCAR (Sat); Wellness (1st Thur)
Syndicated Publications: USA WEEKEND Magazine (Sat).
Areas Served - City/County or Portion Thereof, or Zip codes: Mattoon & Charleston (IL)
Sat. Circulation Paid: 10845
Audit By: AAM
Audit Date: 30.09.2014
Personnel: Tammy Jordan (Adv. Dir.); Mark Hall (Oper. Dir.); Steve Lahr (Nat'l Adv. Mgr.); Penny Weaver (Editor)
Parent company (for newspapers): Dispatch-Argus

DAILY REVIEW ATLAS

Street address 1: 400 S Main St
Street address city: Monmouth
Street address state: IL
Zip/Postal code: 61462-2164
County: Warren
Country: USA
Mailing address: PO BOX 650
Mailing city: MONMOUTH
Mailing state: IL
Mailing zip: 61462-0650
General Phone: (309) 734-3176
General/National Adv. E-mail: jbolitho@reviewatlas.com
Display Adv. E-mail: jbolitho@reviewatlas.com
Classified Adv. e-mail: jbolitho@reviewatlas.com
Editorial e-mail: jbolitho@reviewatlas.com
Primary Website: www.reviewatlas.com
Year Established: 1890
News Services: AP.
Syndicated Publications: Senior Citizens Magazine (Monthly); Weekend Update (Sat); Channel Guide-Television Guide Section (Weekly).
Areas Served - City/County or Portion Thereof, or Zip codes: Monmouth (IL)
Sat. Circulation Paid: 3159
Audit By: Sworn/Estimate/Non-Audited
Audit Date: 12.07.2019
Personnel: Tony Scott (Gen. Mgr.); Brian Elliott (Circ. Mgr.); Marty Pouchette (Sports Ed.); Barb Simmons (Prodn. Mgr.); Jake Bolitho (Ed.)
Parent company (for newspapers): Gannett; CherryRoad Media

MOUNT CARMEL REGISTER

Street address 1: 115 E 4th St
Street address city: Mount Carmel
Street address state: IL
Zip/Postal code: 62863-2110
County: Wabash
Country: USA
Mailing address: PO BOX 550
Mailing city: MOUNT CARMEL
Mailing state: IL
Mailing zip: 62863-0550
General Phone: (618) 262-5144
General/National Adv. E-mail: news@mtcarmelregister.com
Display Adv. E-mail: creativeads@mtcarmelregister.com
Classified Adv. e-mail: swiseman@mtcarmelregister.com
Editorial e-mail: news@mtcarmelregister.com
Primary Website: www.mtcarmelregister.com
Mthly Avg Views: 964165
Mthly Avg Unique Visitors: 180539
Year Established: 1839
News Services: Associated Press
Special Editions: Bridal Fair, Healthy Lifestyles, Progress, Prom Expo (Jan); Soil & Water, Financial/Tax, FFA, Valentines, Savvy Lifestyles (Feb); Home & Garden, Kids & Family, Spring (Mar); Spring Car Care, Prom, Bridal, Easter (Apr); Mother's Day, Graduation, Memorial Day, Home Show, Savvy Lifestyles (May); Little League, Summer Coupon Book, Meet Your Merchants, Father's Day, Outstanding Student (Jun); 4th of July, Bridal, Ag Days, Various County Fairs, Christmas In July (Jul); 4-H, Guide to Edwards County, Fall Sports, Savvy Lifestyles, Back To School (Aug); Ribberfest, Labor Day, Parent & Child, Fall Home Improvement, Guide to Wabash County (Sep); Fall Coupon Book, Homecoming, Bridal, Firefighters Salute, Chamber of Commerce Annual (Oct); Holiday

Gift Guide #1, Holiday Gift Guide #2, Savvy Lifestyles (Nov); Holiday Gift Guide #3, Holiday Gift Guide #4, Holiday Gift Guide #5, Songbook, Winter Sports, and Wellness Guide
Syndicated Publications: American Profile (bi-monthly); Real Estate Homes (monthly) and TSM Outdoor Magazine (quarterly).
Delivery Methods: Mail`Newsstand`Carrier`Racks
Areas Served - City/County or Portion Thereof, or Zip codes: 62863, 62811, 62852, 62855, 62818, 62815, 62806, 62844, 62410, 62476 and mixed zips.
Own Printing Facility?: N
Commercial printers?: Y
Avg Free Circ: 9000
Audit By: Sworn/Estimate/Non-Audited
Audit Date: 12.07.2019
Personnel: Phil Summers (Publisher/President); Andrea Howe (Editor); Bob Tanquary (Accounting Clerk); Susan Wiseman (Classifieds); Sandra Higgins (Advertising Sales Manager); Joey Luecke (Advertising Consultant/Digital Director); Laurie Snidle (Advertising Consultant); Marcus Smith (News Editor); T.J. Hug (Sports Editor/General Reporter)
Parent company (for newspapers): Paxton Media Group

OLNEY DAILY MAIL

Street address 1: 206 S Whittle Ave
Street address city: Olney
Street address state: IL
Zip/Postal code: 62450-2251
County: Richland
Country: USA
Mailing address: PO BOX 340
Mailing city: OLNEY
Mailing state: IL
Mailing zip: 62450-0340
General Phone: (618) 393-2931
General/National Adv. E-mail: advertising@olneydailymail.com
Display Adv. E-mail: advertising@olneydailymail.com
Classified Adv. e-mail: classifieds@olneydailymail.com
Editorial e-mail: editor@olneydailymail.com
Primary Website: www.olneydailymail.com
Year Established: 1898
News Services: AP.
Special Editions: Its About Family; Richland County Shopper
Special Weekly Sections: Best Food Day (Mon); School Life (Tues).
Syndicated Publications: American Profile (Weekly); Spry (Monthly); USA Weekend (Weekly);
Delivery Methods: Carrier
Areas Served - City/County or Portion Thereof, or Zip codes: 62450, 62421, 62868, 62425, 62452, 62476
Own Printing Facility?: Y
Commercial printers?: Y
Audit By: Sworn/Estimate/Non-Audited
Audit Date: 12.07.2019
Personnel: Kerry Kocher (Pub.); Mark Roberson (Prodn. Supvr., Press)
Parent company (for newspapers): Paxton Media Group; CherryRoad Media

THE TIMES

Street address 1: 110 W. Jefferson Street
Street address city: Ottawa
Street address state: IL
Zip/Postal code: 61350
County: La Salle
Country: USA
Mailing address: PO BOX 618
Mailing city: OTTAWA
Mailing state: IL
Mailing zip: 61350-0618
General Phone: (815) 433-2000
Advertising Phone: (815) 433-2002
Editorial Phone: (815) 433-2004
General/National Adv. E-mail: classad@mywebtimes.com
Display Adv. E-mail: classad@mywebtimes.com
Classified Adv. e-mail: classad@mywebtimes.com
Editorial e-mail: newsroom@MyWebTimes.com
Primary Website: www.mywebtimes.com
News Services: NEA, AP, TMS.
Special Editions: Spring Lawn & Garden (Apr); Football Preview (Aug); Holiday Gift Guide (Dec); Spring Farm (Feb); Bridal Guide (Jan); Summer Farm (Jul); Dining & Entertainment (Jun); Home Improvement (Mar); Graduation (May); Real Estate/Realtor Guide (Monthly); Basketball
Special Weekly Sections: Back-n-Forth (Wed); Pulse (Tue); Food (Wed); Spotlight (Thur); Inside-n-Out (Fri); Hometowns (Sat)
Syndicated Publications: Parade (Weekly).
Areas Served - City/County or Portion Thereof, or Zip codes: La Salle County (IL)
Avg Free Circ: 1782
Sat. Circulation Paid: 9163
Sat. Circulation Free: 1782
Audit By: CAC
Audit Date: 30.06.2018
Personnel: John Newby (Pub.); Cindy Liptak (Bus. Mgr.); Sherry Patterson (Adv. Mgr.); Mindy Crouch (Adv. Supvr., Classified); Cynthia J. Liptak (Circ. Dir.); Dan Hrabel (Editorial Page Ed.); Lonny Cain (Online Ed.); Tom Sistak (Photo Ed.); Paul Carpenter (Wire Ed.); Jerry Batties (Mgr., Electronics); Richard Todd (Prodn. Foreman, Press); Art Dougherty (Prodn. Mgr., Mailroom); Lisa Gerding (Majors/Nat'l Accts. Mgr.); Mike Bertok (Adv. Dir.); Dan Churney (Other); Tammy Sloup (Managing Editor); Derek Barichello (News Editor); Stephanie Jaquins (Digital Editor); Julie Stroebel-Barichellow (Night Editor)
Parent company (for newspapers): Shaw Media

PEKIN DAILY TIMES

Street address 1: 306 Court St
Street address city: Pekin
Street address state: IL
Zip/Postal code: 61554-3104
County: Tazewell
Country: USA
Mailing address: PO BOX 430
Mailing city: PEKIN
Mailing state: IL
Mailing zip: 61555-0430
General Phone: (309) 346-1111
Advertising Phone: (309) 346-1111
Editorial Phone: (309) 346-1111
General/National Adv. E-mail: advertise@pekintimes.com
Display Adv. E-mail: advertise@pekintimes.com
Classified Adv. e-mail: tmont@pekintimes.com
Editorial e-mail: mteheux@pekintimes.com
Primary Website: www.pekintimes.com
Year Established: 1873
News Services: AP, TMS.
Special Weekly Sections: Farm (Tue); Photo (Thur); Senior Citizen, School, Religion, Lifestyles (Sat); Business, Photo, Features (Daily)
Syndicated Publications: American Profile (Sat); Parade (Weekly).
Delivery Methods: Mail`Carrier
Areas Served - City/County or Portion Thereof, or Zip codes: 61534, 61546, 61550, 61554, 61564, 61567, 61568, 61607, 61610, 61611, 61734, 61747, 61755, 617,59, 62644, 62664, 62682
Sat. Circulation Paid: 8637
Audit By: Sworn/Estimate/Non-Audited
Audit Date: 12.07.2019
Personnel: Amy Gehrt (Ed.); Barb Schisler (Production Mgr.); Mike Mehl (Sales Mgr.); Drew Veskauf (Mng. Ed.); Nick McMillion (Assoc. Ed.)
Parent company (for newspapers): Gannett; CherryRoad Media

JOURNAL STAR

Street address 1: One News Plaza
Street address city: Peoria
Street address state: IL
Zip/Postal code: 61643
County: Peoria
Country: USA
General Phone: (309) 686-3000
Advertising Phone: (309) 686-3035
Editorial Phone: (309) 686-3114
General/National Adv. E-mail: Lsutton@pjstar.com
Display Adv. E-mail: dmoore@pjstar.com
Classified Adv. e-mail: tkelling@pjstar.com
Editorial e-mail: news@pjstar.com
Primary Website: www.pjstar.com
Year Established: 1855
News Services: AP, LAT-WP, SNS, CNS, TMS.
Special Weekly Sections: Cue (Thurs), Real Estate Connection (Fri), Home & Garden (Sat)
Syndicated Publications: Parade (S); AThlon Sports;
Areas Served - City/County or Portion Thereof, or Zip codes: Peoria (IL) and Surrounding areas
Sat. Circulation Paid: 45628
Sun. Circulation Paid: 51973
Audit By: AAM
Audit Date: 31.12.2016
Personnel: Ken Mauser (Pub.); Brian Kier (Controller); Gene Clime (Asst. Gen. Mgr.); Joe Dunlap (Credit Mgr.); Phil Jordan (Mgr., Mktg./Pub. Affairs); Dennis Anderson (Exec. Ed.); Sally McKee (Asst. Mng. Ed., Sunday Features/Servs.); Steve Tarter (Bus. Ed.); Anthony Smith (City Ed., Night); Danielle Hatch (Entertainment Ed.); Judy Hicks (Head Librarian); Jennifer Davis (Lifestyles Ed.); Mike Cecil (Metro Ed.); Jennifer Tower (Neighbors Ed.); Angie Lyons
Parent company (for newspapers): Gannett; CherryRoad Media

THE DAILY LEADER

Street address 1: 318 N Main St
Street address city: Pontiac
Street address state: IL
Zip/Postal code: 61764-1930
County: Livingston
Country: USA
Mailing address: 318 N MAIN ST
Mailing city: PONTIAC
Mailing state: IL
Mailing zip: 61764
General Phone: 8158421153
Advertising Phone: (815) 842-1153
Editorial Phone: (815) 842-1153
General/National Adv. E-mail: lstiles@pontiacdailyleader.com
Display Adv. E-mail: lstiles@pontiacdailyleader.com
Classified Adv. e-mail: tmelvin@pontiacdailyleader.com
Editorial e-mail: lstiles@pontiacdailyleader.com
Primary Website: www.pontiacdailyleader.com
Year Established: 1880
News Services: AP.
Special Weekly Sections: Business Page (Wed); Agriculture Page (Thur)
Syndicated Publications: Parade (Sat); American Profile (Weekly).
Delivery Methods: Mail`Newsstand`Carrier`Racks
Areas Served - City/County or Portion Thereof, or Zip codes: Pontiac/Livingston County
Own Printing Facility?: N
Commercial printers?: N
Sat. Circulation Paid: 2750
Audit By: Sworn/Estimate/Non-Audited
Audit Date: 12.07.2019
Personnel: Linda Stiles (Gen Mgr/Adv Mgr); Erich Murphy (Mng. Ed.); David Adams (Pub.)
Parent company (for newspapers): CherryRoad Media; Gannett

THE QUINCY HERALD-WHIG

Street address 1: 130 S 5th St
Street address city: Quincy
Street address state: IL
Zip/Postal code: 62301-3916
County: Adams
Country: USA
Mailing address: 130 S 5TH ST
Mailing city: QUINCY
Mailing state: IL
Mailing zip: 62301-3916
General Phone: (217) 223-5100
Advertising Phone: (217) 231-3464
Editorial Phone: (217) 221-3361
General/National Adv. E-mail: tkelling@whig.com
Display Adv. E-mail: tkelling@whig.com
Classified Adv. e-mail: smcintee@whig.com
Editorial e-mail: mhilfrink@whig.com
Primary Website: www.whig.com
Year Established: 1926
News Services: AP, Scripps-Howard.
Special Editions: Home Improvement (Apr); Progress (Mar); Basketball (Nov); Car Care (Oct); Fast Forward (Quarterly); Football (Sept).
Special Weekly Sections: Business, Finance (Daily); Work, Farm, Arts, Entertainment, Living, Travel, Parenting, Home Decor (Sun); Food, Health, Fitness (Wed); Entertainment (Thur); TV, Religion, Real Estate (Sat)
Syndicated Publications: Parade (S); TV Week Mini Book (Sat).
Areas Served - City/County or Portion Thereof, or Zip codes: Counties in West-Central Illinois & Northeast Missouri
Avg Free Circ: 440
Sat. Circulation Paid: 14529
Sat. Circulation Free: 440
Sun. Circulation Paid: 16196
Sun. Circulation Free: 363
Audit By: AAM
Audit Date: 30.06.2018
Personnel: Thomas A. Oakley (Pub.); Michael B. Hilfrink (Gen. Mgr./Exec. Ed); Tom Kelling (Adv. Dir.); Don Crim (Mng. Ed.); Debbie Gurtz Husar (Farm Ed.); Kevin Murphy (Page 1 Ed.); Phil Carlson (Photo Ed.); Don O'Brien (Sports Ed.); Holly Wagner (Online Contact); Joe Genenbacher (Prodn. Dir., Opns.); Ron Wallace (Gen. Mgr.); Sophie McIntee (Classified Adv. Mgr.)
Parent company (for newspapers): Quincy Media, Inc.; Phillips Media Group LLC

DAILY NEWS

Street address 1: 302 S Cross St
Street address city: Robinson
Street address state: IL
Zip/Postal code: 62454-2137
County: Crawford
Country: USA
Mailing address: PO BOX 639
Mailing city: ROBINSON
Mailing state: IL
Mailing zip: 62454-0639
General Phone: (618) 544-2101
General/National Adv. E-mail: wpiper@robdailynews.com
Display Adv. E-mail: kjones@robdailynews.com
Classified Adv. e-mail: dcorder@robdailynews.com
Editorial e-mail: news@robdailynews.com
Primary Website: www.robdailynews.com
Year Established: 1919
News Services: AP.
Special Editions: American Homes (Apr); LTC (Aug); Tax Guide (Feb); 4-H Fair (Jul); Agriculture (Mar); Heath Toffee Festival (May); Veteran's Salute (Nov); Working Women (Oct); Robinson Fall Festival (Sept).
Sat. Circulation Paid: 5933
Audit By: Sworn/Estimate/Non-Audited
Audit Date: 12.07.2019
Personnel: Greg Bilbrey (Mng. Ed.); Tom Osborne (Copy & Online Ed.); Josh Brown (Sports Ed.); Winnie Piper (Adv. Mgr.)
Parent company (for newspapers): Lewis Newspapers

ROCKFORD REGISTER STAR

Street address 1: 99 East State Street
Street address city: Rockford
Street address state: IL
Zip/Postal code: 61104
County: Winnebago
Country: USA
General Phone: (815) 987-1200
Advertising Phone: (815) 987-1300
Editorial Phone: (815) 987-1350
General/National Adv. E-mail: dlecher@rrstar.com
Display Adv. E-mail: dlecher@rrstar.com
Classified Adv. e-mail: classified@rrstar.com
Editorial e-mail: mbaldwin@rrstar.com
Primary Website: www.rrstar.com
Mthly Avg Views: 3433757
Mthly Avg Unique Visitors: 555658
Year Established: 1840
News Services: AP, GNS, MCT, LAT-WP.
Special Editions: Real Estate Marketplace (Monthly).
Special Weekly Sections: Go (Friday); Real Estate (S);Weekly TMC (Wednesday)
Syndicated Publications: USA WEEKEND Magazine (S); American Profile (Weekly).
Delivery Methods: Mail`Newsstand`Carrier`Racks
Areas Served - City/County or Portion Thereof, or Zip codes: 61101, 61102, 61103, 61104, 61107, 61108, 61109, 61111, 61112, 61114, 61115, 61016, 61072, 61073, 61080, 61008, 61011, 61065
Own Printing Facility?: Y
Commercial printers?: Y
Sat. Circulation Paid: 25644
Sun. Circulation Paid: 34061
Audit By: AAM
Audit Date: 30.06.2017
Personnel: Paul Gaier (Publisher); Mark Baldwin (Exec. Ed.); Anna Derocher (Asst. Mng. Ed.); Mike Kreppert (Prodn. Dir.); Denny Lecher (Adv. Dir.)
Parent company (for newspapers): Gannett; CherryRoad Media

THE STATE JOURNAL-REGISTER

Street address 1: 1 Copley Plz
Street address city: Springfield
Street address state: IL
Zip/Postal code: 62701-1927

County: Sangamon
Country: USA
Mailing address: PO BOX 219
Mailing city: SPRINGFIELD
Mailing state: IL
Mailing zip: 62705-0219
General Phone: (217) 788-1300
Advertising Phone: (217) 788-1353
Editorial Phone: (217) 788-1513
General/National Adv. E-mail: advertise@sj-r.com
Classified Adv. e-mail: angela.stewart@sj-r.com
Editorial e-mail: sjr@sj-r.com
Primary Website: www.sj-r.com
Year Established: 1831
News Services: AP, MCT, GateHouse News Service
Special Editions: Fall Festival Guide (Aug); Mother's Day Gifts (May); Welcome to Your Health (Monthly); Holiday Events Calender (Nov); SO Magazine (Other); Fall Home Improvement (Sept)., Seniors (monthly), & Home & Garden (monthly)
Special Weekly Sections: Financial, TV (Daily); Health (Mon); Teen (Th); Food (Wed): Arts, Entertainment (Thur); Religion, TV (Sun)
Syndicated Publications: Parade (S)., Relish, Dash, & Athlon
Delivery Methods: Mail`Newsstand`Carrier`Racks
Areas Served - City/County or Portion Thereof, or Zip codes: 62705
Own Printing Facility?: N
Commercial printers?: N
Sat. Circulation Paid: 23622
Sun. Circulation Paid: 29365
Audit By: AAM
Audit Date: 30.09.2018
Personnel: Tim Landis (Bus. Ed.); Jason Piscia (Digital Mang. Ed.); Rich Saal (Photo Ed.); Ted Schurter (Asst. Photo Ed.); Bart Bolton; Angela Stewart (Classified Adv. Mgr.); Kate Schott (Editorial Ed.); Todd Adams (Sports Ed.); Eric Mayberry (VP of Adv.); Eugene Jackson (Gen. Mgr. & Dir. of Adv.)
Parent company (for newspapers): Gannett; CherryRoad Media

DAILY GAZETTE

Street address 1: 3200 E Lincolnway
Street address city: Sterling
Street address state: IL
Zip/Postal code: 61081-1773
County: Whiteside
Country: USA
Mailing address: PO BOX 498
Mailing city: STERLING
Mailing state: IL
Mailing zip: 61081-0498
General Phone: (815) 625-3600
General/National Adv. E-mail: jbaratta@saukvalley.com
Display Adv. E-mail: jbaratta@saukvalley.com
Classified Adv. e-mail: jdiehl@saukvalley.com
Editorial e-mail: llough@saukvalley.com
Primary Website: www.saukvalley.com
Year Established: 1854
News Services: AP, CNS, United Media Service, SHNS.
Special Editions: Career Guide (Apr); Today's Farm (Aug); Sterling Sights & Sounds (Dec); Internet Directory (Feb); Health & Fitness (Jan); Dixon Sidewalk Sale (Jul); Dixon Petunia Festival (Jun); Extra Circulation Sunday (Mar); Mother's Day (May); Senior Echo (Monthly); F
Syndicated Publications: TV Week (Fri); USA WEEKEND Magazine (S); Big E (Entertainment Guide) (Thur).
Areas Served - City/County or Portion Thereof, or Zip codes: Sauk Valley (IL)
Own Printing Facility?: Y
Commercial printers?: Y
Avg Free Circ: 755
Sat. Circulation Paid: 12753
Sat. Circulation Free: 2
Sun. Circulation Paid: 12753
Sun. Circulation Free: 2
Audit By: AAM
Audit Date: 30.09.2017
Personnel: Jennifer Baratta (Adv. Dir.); Sheryl Gulbranson (Circ. Dir.); Larry Lough (Exec. Ed.); Alex Paschal (Chief Photographer); Ernie Appleyard (Production Dir.); Joanne Doherty (Finance Dir.); Sam Fisher (Pub.)
Parent company (for newspapers): Shaw Media

BREEZE COURIER

Street address 1: 212 S Main St
Street address city: Taylorville
Street address state: IL
Zip/Postal code: 62568-2219
County: Christian
Country: USA
Mailing address: PO BOX 440
Mailing city: TAYLORVILLE
Mailing state: IL
Mailing zip: 62568-0440
General Phone: (217) 824-2233
General/National Adv. E-mail: breezecourier@breezecourier.com
Display Adv. E-mail: breezecourier@breezecourier.com
Classified Adv. e-mail: breezeclassifieds@breezecourier.com
Editorial e-mail: breezenews@breezecourier.com
Primary Website: www.breezecourier.com
Mthly Avg Views: 97776
Mthly Avg Unique Visitors: 54294
Year Established: 1864
News Services: AP
Special Editions: Home Improvement (Apr); Back-to-School (Aug); First Baby (Dec); Senior Citizens (Feb); Tax Tab (Jan); County Fair (Jul); Bridal (Jun); Agriculture (Mar); Winter Sports (Nov); Car Care (Oct); Fall Home Improvement (Sept).
Special Weekly Sections: TV Tab (T).
Syndicated Publications: American Profile (S).
Delivery Methods: Mail`Newsstand`Carrier`Racks
Areas Served - City/County or Portion Thereof, or Zip codes: 62568
Own Printing Facility?: Y
Commercial printers?: Y
Avg Free Circ: 4500
Sun. Circulation Paid: 5157
Audit By: Sworn/Estimate/Non-Audited
Audit Date: 12.07.2019
Personnel: Wilda Quinn Cooper (Exec. Vice Pres.); Marylee Rasar (Pub.); Jeff Nation (Prodn. Mgr.); Rhonda Wilson (Adv.); Ron Verardi (Adv.); Dee Carroll (Adv.); Laurie Sparling (Adv.); Tracy Marshall (Class./Commercial Printing); Andy Lasswell (News); Derek Parris (Sports Ed.); Jacob Griffin (News); Jamie Painter (News); Barb Profeta (Business); Owen Lasswell (Business); Ryan Myles (Production)
Parent company (for newspapers): Better Newspapers

TIMES-REPUBLIC

Street address 1: 1492 E Walnut St
Street address city: Watseka
Street address state: IL
Zip/Postal code: 60970-1806
County: Iroquois
Country: USA
Mailing address: 1492 E WALNUT ST
Mailing city: WATSEKA
Mailing state: IL
Mailing zip: 60970-1806
General Phone: (815) 432-5227
Advertising Phone: (815) 432-5227
Editorial Phone: (815) 432-5227
General/National Adv. E-mail: watsekasales@intranix.com
Display Adv. E-mail: watsekasales@intranix.com
Classified Adv. e-mail: classifieds@intranix.com
Editorial e-mail: cwaters@intranix.com
Primary Website: www.watsekatimesrepublic.com
Year Established: 1870
News Services: AP.
Special Editions: Twin State Farmer (Every other month); Bridal (Other); Twin State News & Views (Quarterly).
Areas Served - City/County or Portion Thereof, or Zip codes: Iroquois County (IL)
Audit By: Sworn/Estimate/Non-Audited
Audit Date: 12.07.2019
Personnel: Kevin Armold (Prod. Dir.); Don Hurd (Pub.); Carla Waters (Mng. Ed.); Roberta Kempen (Adv. Dir.)
Parent company (for newspapers): Community Media Group

THE DAILY AMERICAN

Street address 1: 111 S Emma St
Street address city: West Frankfort
Street address state: IL
Zip/Postal code: 62896-2729
County: Franklin
Country: USA
Mailing address: PO BOX 617
Mailing city: WEST FRANKFORT
Mailing state: IL
Mailing zip: 62896-0617
General Phone: (618) 932-2146
Advertising Phone: (814) 444-5900
Editorial Phone: (814) 444-5928
General/National Adv. E-mail: lashbrook@dailyamericannews.com
Display Adv. E-mail: wfadvertising2@dailyamericannews.com
Classified Adv. e-mail: wfclass@dailyamericannews.com
Editorial e-mail: editor@dailyamericannews.com
Primary Website: www.dailyamericannews.com
Year Established: 1920
News Services: AP, TMS.
Special Editions: Progress (Feb); Bridal (Jan); Fourth of July Celebration (Jun); Homes (Monthly); Home Improvement (Oct).
Syndicated Publications: USA WEEKEND Magazine (Fri); Sports Saturday (Sat); American Profile (Weekly).
Areas Served - City/County or Portion Thereof, or Zip codes: Somerset County (IL)
Sat. Circulation Paid: 3510
Audit By: Sworn/Estimate/Non-Audited
Audit Date: 12.07.2019
Personnel: Kevin Haezebroek (Reg. Pub.); Crystal Bullett (Adv. Mgr., Classified); Heather Little (Office/Circ. Mgr.)
Parent company (for newspapers): Gannett; CherryRoad Media

INDIANA

THE HERALD BULLETIN

Street address 1: 1133 Jackson St
Street address city: Anderson
Street address state: IN
Zip/Postal code: 46016-1433
County: Madison
Country: USA
Mailing address: PO BOX 1090
Mailing city: ANDERSON
Mailing state: IN
Mailing zip: 46015-1090
General Phone: (765) 622-1212
Advertising Phone: (765) 640-2312
Editorial Phone: (765) 622-1212
General/National Adv. E-mail: annette.burcharts@indianamediagroup.com
Display Adv. E-mail: annette.burcharts@indianamediagroup.com
Classified Adv. e-mail: annette.burcharts@indianamediagroup.com
Editorial e-mail: scott.underwood@heraldbulletin.com
Primary Website: www.theheraldbulletin.com
Year Established: 1868
News Services: AP.
Special Editions: Spring Auto Guide (Apr); Fall Football (Aug); Visitor's Guide (Dec); Winter Clearance (Feb); Active Times (Jan); USA Proud (Jul); Father's Day Pages (Jun); Visitor's Guide (Mar); Mother's Day Gift Guide (May); Gift Guide (Nov); Active Times (Oct).
Special Weekly Sections: Food (Mon); Homes (S).
Syndicated Publications: Parade (S).
Delivery Methods: Mail`Newsstand`Carrier`Racks
Areas Served - City/County or Portion Thereof, or Zip codes: Madison County
Own Printing Facility?: Y
Commercial printers?: Y
Sat. Circulation Paid: 18691
Sun. Circulation Paid: 20422
Audit By: Sworn/Estimate/Non-Audited
Audit Date: 12.07.2019
Personnel: Beverly Joyce (Pub.); Mark Elliott (Adv. Dir.); Annette Burcharts (Classifieds); Scott Underwood (Ed.); Amy Winter (Circ. Dir.); Peggy Crabtree (Accounting); Peg Melton (Adv. Graphics); Janis Bowling (Newsroom Coord.); Tammy Everitt (Editorial Asst.); Steve Dick (Asst. Ed.); John Cleary (Photo Ed.)
Parent company (for newspapers): CNHI, LLC; CNHI, LLC

THE HERALD REPUBLICAN

Street address 1: 45 S Public Sq
Street address city: Angola
Street address state: IN
Zip/Postal code: 46703-1926
County: Steuben
Country: USA
Mailing address: 45 S PUBLIC SQ
Mailing city: ANGOLA
Mailing state: IN
Mailing zip: 46703-1970
General Phone: (260) 665-3117
Advertising Phone: (260) 665-3117 ext. 110
Editorial Phone: (260) 665-3117 ext. 140
General/National Adv. E-mail: lconley@kpcmedia.com
Display Adv. E-mail: lconley@kpcmedia.com
Classified Adv. e-mail: asaggars@kpcmedia.com
Editorial e-mail: news@kpcmedia.com
Primary Website: www.kpcnews.com
Mthly Avg Views: 500000
Mthly Avg Unique Visitors: 100000
Year Established: 1857
News Services: AP, SHNS.
Special Editions: Wedding Planner (Feb); Steuben County Answer Book (Jan); Big Bang 4th of July Sale (Jul); All In The Family Business (Jun); Angola Chamber Guide (Mar); Summer in Northeast Indiana (May).
Special Weekly Sections: Outdoor Life (Fri); Homes To Own (S).
Syndicated Publications: USA WEEKEND Magazine (S).
Delivery Methods: Mail`Newsstand`Carrier`Racks
Areas Served - City/County or Portion Thereof, or Zip codes: 46703, 46705, 46737, 46742, 46747, 46776, 46779
Own Printing Facility?: Y
Commercial printers?: Y
Sat. Circulation Paid: 4070
Sun. Circulation Paid: 4230
Audit By: AAM
Audit Date: 31.12.2014
Personnel: Terry Housholder (Pres./CEO/Pub.); Michael Marturello (Ed.); Amy Oberlin (News Ed.); Ken Fillmore (Sports Ed.); Lynette Donley (Adv. Dir.); Marta Wysong (Acct. Exec.); Machele Waid (Acct. Exec.); Brian Glick (IT Mgr.)
Parent company (for newspapers): KPC Media Group, Inc.

THE STAR

Street address 1: 102 N Main St
Street address city: Auburn
Street address state: IN
Zip/Postal code: 46706-1857
County: De Kalb
Country: USA
Mailing address: 118 W 9TH ST
Mailing city: AUBURN
Mailing state: IN
Mailing zip: 46706-2225
General Phone: (260) 347-0400
Advertising Phone: (260) 347-0400
Editorial Phone: (260) 347-0400
General/National Adv. E-mail: jnewman@kpcmedia.com
Display Adv. E-mail: jnewman@kpcmedia.com
Classified Adv. e-mail: randymitchell@kpcmedia.com
Editorial e-mail: randymitchell@kpcmedia.com
Primary Website: www.kpcnews.com
Mthly Avg Views: 608581
Mthly Avg Unique Visitors: 172250
Year Established: 1871
News Services: AP.
Special Editions: Health & wellness (Jan); DeKalb Community Guide (Feb); Business Card Blowout (Mar); Go West (Jul); Parade of Homes (Aug); DeKalb Co. 4-H Scrapbook (Oct); Festival of Trees (Nov); Holiday Gift Guide (Dec). How-To Guide Oct. Senior Service Directory in April Hunting Guide in Oct.
Special Weekly Sections: Outdoor Life (Fri); Business Page (Other); Homes To Own (S); Agri-Business (Sat); Entertainment Page (Thur); Best Food Day (Wed).
Delivery Methods: Mail`Newsstand`Carrier`Racks
Areas Served - City/County or Portion Thereof, or Zip codes: 46706, 46705, 46721, 46730, 46738, 46710, 46763, 46785, 46788,46793
Own Printing Facility?: Y
Commercial printers?: Y
Avg Free Circ: 344
Sun. Circulation Paid: 3752
Sun. Circulation Free: 14
Audit By: AAM
Audit Date: 31.12.2018
Personnel: Terry Housholder (Pres./Pub./CEO); Dave Kurtz (Exec. Ed.); Christy Day (District Mgr.); Lynette Donley (Adv. Dir.); Lisa Myers (Account Exec.); Jonathan Anderson (Multimedia Sales Executive); Randy Mitchell (CEO)

Parent company (for newspapers): KPC Media Group, Inc.

THE TIMES-MAIL

Street address 1: 813 16th St
Street address city: Bedford
Street address state: IN
Zip/Postal code: 47421-3822
County: Lawrence
Country: USA
Mailing address: PO BOX 849
Mailing city: BEDFORD
Mailing state: IN
Mailing zip: 47421-0849
General Phone: (812) 275-3355
Advertising Phone: (812) 331-4292
Editorial Phone: (812) 277-7258
General/National Adv. E-mail: lragle@schurz.com
Display Adv. E-mail: cgiddens@schurz.com
Classified Adv. e-mail: lleahy@hoosiertimes.com
Editorial e-mail: mikel@tmnews.com
Primary Website: www.tmnews.com
Mthly Avg Views: 600000
Mthly Avg Unique Visitors: 40000
Year Established: 1884
News Services: AP.
Special Editions: Business Expo (Apr); Back-to-School (Aug); Holiday Gift Guide (Dec); Area Dining Guide (Feb); Financial Focus (Jan); City-Wide Sidewalk Sale (Jul); Women in Business (Jun); Kitchen, Bath and Furniture (Mar); Summer Fun (May); Prime Advantage (Monthly).
Special Weekly Sections: TV Week (Fri).
Syndicated Publications: Parade (S).
Delivery Methods: Mail`Newsstand`Carrier`Racks
Areas Served - City/County or Portion Thereof, or Zip codes: Lawrence County
Sat. Circulation Paid: 11218
Sun. Circulation Paid: 40171
Audit By: Sworn/Estimate/Non-Audited
Audit Date: 12.07.2019
Personnel: Stacey Brown (Prod. Mgr.); Laurie Ragle (Adv. Dir.); Tim D. Smith (Circ. Dir.); Rich Janzaruk (Photo Ed.); Todd Davidson (Digital Media Dir.); Chad Giddens (Sales Mgr.); Leah Leahy (Classified Ad. Mgr.); Sean Duncan (Sports Ed.); Steve Sallee (District Mgr.); Krystal Ragle (Managing Ed.)
Parent company (for newspapers): Schurz Communications Inc

THE HERALD TIMES

Street address 1: 1900 S Walnut St
Street address city: Bloomington
Street address state: IN
Zip/Postal code: 47401-7720
County: Monroe
Country: USA
Mailing address: PO BOX 909
Mailing city: BLOOMINGTON
Mailing state: IN
Mailing zip: 47402-0909
General Phone: (812) 332-4401
Advertising Phone: (812) 331-4281
Editorial Phone: (812) 331-4364
Editorial e-mail: jbnd@gannett.com
Primary Website: www.heraldtimesonline.com
Mthly Avg Views: 2200000
Mthly Avg Unique Visitors: 175000
Year Established: 1877
News Services: AP.
Syndicated Publications: Parade (S)
Delivery Methods: Mail`Newsstand`Carrier`Racks
Areas Served - City/County or Portion Thereof, or Zip codes: Monroe County
Sat. Circulation Paid: 28408
Sun. Circulation Paid: 40171
Audit By: Sworn/Estimate/Non-Audited
Audit Date: 31.10.2021
Personnel: Cory Bollinger (Pub.); Larry D. Hensley (Gen. Mgr.); Tim D. Smith (Circ. Dir.); Janice Rickert (News Ed.); Stephen Crane (Interim Ed.); Pat Beane (Sports Ed.); Jenny Porter Tilley (Arts Ed.); Brack Stacy (Adv. Dir.)
Parent company (for newspapers): Schurz Communications Inc; Gannett

NEWS-BANNER

Street address 1: 125 N Johnson St
Street address city: Bluffton
Street address state: IN
Zip/Postal code: 46714-1907
County: Wells
Country: USA
Mailing address: PO BOX 436
Mailing city: BLUFFTON
Mailing state: IN
Mailing zip: 46714-0436
General Phone: (260) 824-0224
Advertising Phone: (260) 824-0224
Editorial Phone: (260) 824-0224
General/National Adv. E-mail: jeanb@news-banner.com
Display Adv. E-mail: jeanb@news-banner.com
Classified Adv. e-mail: jeanb@news-banner.com
Editorial e-mail: daves@news-banner.com
Primary Website: www.news-banner.com
Year Established: 1892
News Services: AP.
Special Editions: Christmas Greetings (Dec); Progress (Jun); Senior Lifestyle (Quarterly).
Special Weekly Sections: Agri-Business, All About Health, Spotlight on Business (Tue); House & Home (Wed); Best Food Day, Racing (Thur); Church (Fri); Church Directory, Finance/Local Business News, Ent./TV Weekly (Sat)
Syndicated Publications: Relish (Sat).
Delivery Methods: Mail`Newsstand`Carrier`Racks
Areas Served - City/County or Portion Thereof, or Zip codes: 46714, 46777, 46759, 46778, 46766, 46781, 46731, 46770, 46791, 46799, 46798, 46792, 47359
Own Printing Facility?: Y
Commercial printers?: Y
Avg Free Circ: 0
Sat. Circulation Paid: 3862
Sat. Circulation Free: 0
Audit By: Sworn/Estimate/Non-Audited
Audit Date: 12.07.2019
Personnel: Mark F. Miller (Vice President, Opinion Page Editor); Martha Poling (Bus. Mgr.); Jean Bordner (Adv. Sales Mgr.); Dianne Witwer (Dir., Mktg, Treasurer); David Schultz (Asst. Ed.); Glen Werling (Mng. Ed.); Paul Beitler (Sports Ed.); Howard Jones (Prodn. Supt.); Patty Elwell (Classified Mgr.); Doug Brown (President & Publisher)
Parent company (for newspapers): KPC Media Group, Inc.

THE BRAZIL TIMES

Street address 1: 531 E National Ave
Street address city: Brazil
Street address state: IN
Zip/Postal code: 47834-2633
County: Clay
Country: USA
Mailing address: PO BOX 429
Mailing city: BRAZIL
Mailing state: IN
Mailing zip: 47834-0429
General Phone: (812) 446-2216
General/National Adv. E-mail: jeanneburris.braziltimes@gmail.com
Display Adv. E-mail: brazilads@yahoo.com
Classified Adv. e-mail: classifiedcallcenter@yahoo.com
Editorial e-mail: Frank.phillips@gmail.com
Primary Website: www.thebraziltimes.com
Mthly Avg Views: 363090
Mthly Avg Unique Visitors: 88830
Year Established: 1888
News Services: AP
Special Editions: Christmas Greetings (Dec); Football (Fall); New Year's Baby (Jan); Graduation (May); Business & Industry (Other).
Special Weekly Sections: Best Food Day (Mon); School News Page (Sat); Agri-Business (Tues).
Syndicated Publications: Relish (Monthly); Weekender (Sat).
Delivery Methods: Mail`Newsstand`Racks
Areas Served - City/County or Portion Thereof, or Zip codes: 47834 46171 47833 47837 47840 47841 47853 47857 47881
Own Printing Facility?: Y
Commercial printers?: Y
Sat. Circulation Paid: 4633
Audit By: Sworn/Estimate/Non-Audited
Audit Date: 12.07.2019
Personnel: Chris Pruett (Pub.); Jeanne Burris (Gen. Mgr.); Carey Fox (Sports Ed.); Christina Meyer (Marketing Consultant)

Parent company (for newspapers): Rust Communications

THE DAILY CLINTONIAN

Street address 1: 422 S Main St
Street address city: Clinton
Street address state: IN
Zip/Postal code: 47842-2414
County: Vermillion
Country: USA
Mailing address: PO BOX 309
Mailing city: CLINTON
Mailing state: IN
Mailing zip: 47842-0309
General Phone: (765) 832-2443
Advertising Phone: (765) 832-2443
Editorial Phone: (765) 832-2443
General/National Adv. E-mail: cccc@mikes.com
Display Adv. E-mail: cccc@mikes.com
Classified Adv. e-mail: cccc@mikes.com
Editorial e-mail: cccc@mikes.com
Primary Website: www.ccc-clintonian.com
Year Established: 1912 (Daily)r
News Services: AP
Special Editions: Il Bollettino, Labor Day Weekend Christmas Edition
Delivery Methods: Mail`Newsstand`Carrier
Areas Served - City/County or Portion Thereof, or Zip codes: Vermillion and Parke Counties
Own Printing Facility?: Y
Commercial printers?: Y
Audit By: USPS
Audit Date: 12.01.2017
Personnel: George B. Carey (Pres./Pub.)

THE POST & MAIL

Street address 1: 927 W Connexion Way
Street address city: Columbia City
Street address state: IN
Zip/Postal code: 46725-1031
County: Whitley
Country: USA
Mailing state: IN
General Phone: (260) 244-5153
Advertising Phone: (260) 244-5153
Editorial Phone: (260) 244-5153 ext. 202
General/National Adv. E-mail: postandmailadvertising@gmail.com
Display Adv. E-mail: postandmailadvertising@gmail.com
Classified Adv. e-mail: postandmailclassifieds@earthlink.com
Editorial e-mail: editor@thepostandmail.com
Primary Website: www.thepostandmail.com
Year Established: 2007
News Services: AP.
Special Editions: Day in the Life of Whitley County (Jul); Real Estate Guide (Jul); On the Lakes (Jun); Athletes of the Year (Jul); Home & Garden Tab (Apr); 4-H Tab (Aug); Progress (Feb); Taxes & Finances Tab (Jan); Old Settlers Day (Community Festival) Program (Jul); Car Care Tab (May); TV Monthly (Monthly); High School Sports Tab (Nov).
Syndicated Publications: USA WEEKEND Magazine (Sat); American Profile (Weekly).
Delivery Methods: Mail`Newsstand`Carrier`Racks
Areas Served - City/County or Portion Thereof, or Zip codes: Whitley County
Sat. Circulation Paid: 4058
Audit By: Sworn/Estimate/Non-Audited
Audit Date: 12.07.2019
Personnel: Rick Kreps (Pub.); Sally Ballard (Circ. Mgr.); Nicole Ott (Ed.)
Parent company (for newspapers): Horizon Publications Inc.

THE REPUBLIC

Street address 1: 333 2nd St
Street address city: Columbus
Street address state: IN
Zip/Postal code: 47201-6709
County: Bartholomew
Country: USA
Mailing address: 333 2ND ST
Mailing city: COLUMBUS
Mailing state: IN
Mailing zip: 47201-6795
General Phone: (812) 372-7811
Advertising Phone: (812) 379-5652
Editorial Phone: (812) 379-5665
General/National Adv. E-mail: shardin@therepublic.com
Display Adv. E-mail: advertise@therepublic.com
Classified Adv. e-mail: classifieds@therepublic.com
Editorial e-mail: editorial@therepublic.com
Primary Website: www.therepublic.com
Year Established: 1872
News Services: AP, NEA, SHNS, MCT.
Special Editions: Business Profiles (Apr); Education (Aug); Year-in-Review (Dec); Tourism (Feb); 4-H (Jul); Answer Book (Jun); Fashion (Mar); Garden (May); Gift Guide (Nov); Cookbook (Oct); Home Improvement (Sept).
Special Weekly Sections: Health (Fri); School (Mon); Kids Page (S); Auto (Sat); Entertainment (Thur).
Syndicated Publications: Sunday Color Comics Continental (Other); USA WEEKEND Magazine (S).
Delivery Methods: Mail`Newsstand`Carrier
Areas Served - City/County or Portion Thereof, or Zip codes: Bartholomew County
Avg Free Circ: 246
Sat. Circulation Paid: 14067
Sat. Circulation Free: 246
Sun. Circulation Paid: 14924
Sun. Circulation Free: 133
Audit By: CAC
Audit Date: 31.03.2016
Personnel: Cheryl Spurgeon (Circ. Mgr.); Scott Hardin (Digital Media Dir.); Tom Jekel (Ed.); Jane Peabody (Newsroom Coord.); Kirk Johannesen (Asst. Managing Ed.); Julie McClure (Asst. Managing Ed.); Andrew Laker (Chief Photographer); Jay Heater (Sports Ed.); Jenny Elig (Lifestyle Ed.); Brian Blair (Features Ed.); Mike Rossetti (Adv. Dir.); Kathy Burnett (Adv. Ops. Mgr.); Jaime Vemillion (Classified Adv. Mgr.); Randy Reeves (Press Supvr.); Sharon Shumate (Adv. Dir., Sales/Mktg.); Wally Veluzat (Prodn. Mgr., Post Press)
Parent company (for newspapers): AIM Media Indiana

CONNERSVILLE NEWS-EXAMINER

Street address 1: 406 N Central Ave
Street address city: Connersville
Street address state: IN
Zip/Postal code: 47331-1926
County: Fayette
Country: USA
Mailing address: 406 N CENTRAL AVE
Mailing city: CONNERSVILLE
Mailing state: IN
Mailing zip: 47331-1926
General Phone: (765) 825-0581
Advertising Phone: (765) 825-0581 ext. 247
Editorial Phone: (765) 825-0588 ext. 235
General/National Adv. E-mail: mspillers@newsexaminer.com
Display Adv. E-mail: mspillers@newsexaminer.com
Classified Adv. e-mail: mspillers@newsexaminer.com
Editorial e-mail: newsexaminer@newsexaminer.com
Primary Website: www.newsexaminer.com
Year Established: 1887
News Services: AP.
Special Editions: Progress (Mar); Home Improvement (Apr); County Fair (Aug); Christmas Greetings (Dec); Bridal (Jan); TV (Mar); Cookbook Magazine (Nov); Car Care (Oct).
Special Weekly Sections: Church (Fri); Best Food Day (Mon); Best Real Estate Days (Thur); School coverage (Wed)
Delivery Methods: Newsstand`Carrier`Racks
Areas Served - City/County or Portion Thereof, or Zip codes: Fayette, Franklin, Union and Western Wayne County in East Central Indiana
Own Printing Facility?: N
Commercial printers?: N
Sun. Circulation Paid: 4390
Audit By: Sworn/Estimate/Non-Audited
Audit Date: 12.07.2019
Personnel: Anna Pugsley (General Manager/Advertising); Bob Hansen (Ed.)
Parent company (for newspapers): Paxton Media Group

JOURNAL REVIEW

Street address 1: 119 N Green St
Street address city: Crawfordsville
Street address state: IN
Zip/Postal code: 47933-1708
County: Montgomery
Country: USA
Mailing address: PO BOX 512
Mailing city: CRAWFORDSVILLE

Mailing state: IN
Mailing zip: 47933-0512
General Phone: (765) 362-1200
Advertising Phone: (765) 362-1200 ext. 109
Editorial Phone: (765) 362-1200 ext. 119
General/National Adv. E-mail: shawn.storie@jrpress.com
Display Adv. E-mail: kmanlief@jrpress.com
Classified Adv. e-mail: suzanne@jrpress.com
Editorial e-mail: tmcgrady@jrpress.com
Primary Website: www.journalreview.com
Mthly Avg Views: 550000
Year Established: 1841
News Services: AP.
Special Editions: Home Improvement (Apr); Fall Sports Preview (Aug); Caroling Song Book (Dec); Wedding Planner (Jul); Strawberry Festival (Jun); Area Golf Guide (Mar); Indy 500 (May); Basketball (Nov); Home Improvement (Oct); Fall Activity Guide (Sept).
Special Weekly Sections: Business Page: Wednesday Health Page: Thursday Chalk Board: Friday
Syndicated Publications: Montgomery County Directory (Annually); Montgomery County Realty (Monthly); USA WEEKEND Magazine (Sat).
Delivery Methods: Mail`Newsstand`Carrier`Racks
Areas Served - City/County or Portion Thereof, or Zip codes: Montgomery County
Own Printing Facility?: N
Commercial printers?: Y
Avg Free Circ: 161
Sat. Circulation Paid: 4995
Sat. Circulation Free: 161
Audit By: CAC
Audit Date: 30.09.2017
Personnel: Shawn Storie (Group Mgr./Pub.); Tina McGrady (Ed.); Addie Cucore (Composing Mgr.); Kim Starnes (Adv. Mgr.); Carla Walters (Cir. Mgr.)
Parent company (for newspapers): PTS, Inc.

THE PAPER OF MONTGOMERY COUNTY

Street address 1: 127 E. Main St.
Street address city: Crawfordsville
Street address state: IN
Zip/Postal code: 47933-2804
County: Montgomery
Country: USA
Mailing address: PO BOX 272
Mailing city: CRAWFORDSVILLE
Mailing state: IN
Mailing zip: 47933-0272
General Phone: (765) 361-0100
General/National Adv. E-mail: ttimmons@thepaper24-7.com
Display Adv. E-mail: ttimmons@thepaper24-7.com
Classified Adv. e-mail: judi@thepaper24-7.com
Editorial e-mail: news@thepaper24-7.com
Primary Website: www.thepaper24-7.com
Mthly Avg Views: 120000
Mthly Avg Unique Visitors: 30000
Year Established: 2004
Special Editions: Readers' Choice (Jan); Agriculture; Spring Home; Spring Car; 4-H Fair (Jul); How-To Guide; Christmas Gift Guide (Dec); Last-Minute Gift Guide (Dec). Soil & Water
Delivery Methods: Mail`Newsstand`Racks
Areas Served - City/County or Portion Thereof, or Zip codes: 47933, 47916, 47940, 47954, 47955, 47965, 47967, 47968, 47989, 47990, 47994
Own Printing Facility?: N
Commercial printers?: N
Audit By: USPS
Personnel: Tim Timmons (Pub.); Kim VanMatre (Adv. Mgr.)
Parent company (for newspapers): Sagamore News Media

POST-TRIBUNE

Street address 1: 2100 N Main St Ste 212
Street address 2: Suite 212
Street address city: Crown Point
Street address state: IN
Zip/Postal code: 46307-1877
County: Lake
Country: USA
Mailing state: IN
General Phone: (219) 663-4212
Advertising Phone: (219) 455-2349
General/National Adv. E-mail: rcains@post-trib.com
Display Adv. E-mail: rcains@post-trib.com
Classified Adv. e-mail: classifieds@post-trib.com
Editorial e-mail: jbiesk@tribpub.com
Primary Website: www.chicagotribune.com/suburbs/post-tribune
Year Established: 1908
News Services: AP, MCT, LAT-WP.
Special Editions: Cancer, Lifetime of Health, Senior, Neonatal, New Health Developments, Heart, Progress, Innovations, Neighbors' Choice, TimeOut Sports
Special Weekly Sections: Weekend, Health, Business, Today's Homes
Syndicated Publications: USA WEEKEND Magazine (S).
Delivery Methods: Newsstand`Carrier
Areas Served - City/County or Portion Thereof, or Zip codes: Northwest Indiana
Own Printing Facility?: Y
Commercial printers?: Y
Sat. Circulation Paid: 16000
Sun. Circulation Paid: 40000
Audit By: AAM
Audit Date: 16.10.2013
Personnel: R. Bruce Dold (Publisher & Editor-in-Chief); John P. McCormick (Editorial Page Editor); Christine Taylor (Managing Editor, Audience); Peter Kendall (Managing Editor, Content)
Parent company (for newspapers): Chicago Tribune/Chicago Tribune Media Group

DECATUR DAILY DEMOCRAT

Street address 1: 141 S 2nd St
Street address city: Decatur
Street address state: IN
Zip/Postal code: 46733-1664
County: Adams
Country: USA
Mailing address: 141 S 2ND ST
Mailing city: DECATUR
Mailing state: IN
Mailing zip: 46733-1688
General Phone: (260) 724-2121
Advertising Phone: (260) 724-2121
Editorial Phone: (260) 724-2121
General/National Adv. E-mail: businessmanager@decaturdailydemocrat.com
Display Adv. E-mail: advertising@decaturdailydemocrat.com
Classified Adv. e-mail: classified@decaturdailydemocrat.com
Editorial e-mail: circulation@decaturdailydemocrat.com
Primary Website: www.decaturdailydemocrat.com
Year Established: 1857
News Services: AP.
Special Editions: Basketball (Feb); Christmas Opening (Nov); Callithumpian (Oct).
Special Weekly Sections: Business Working for You (Mon); Kids, (Tue); Health (Wed); Entertainment, Nascar (Thur); Church (Fri); Business (Sat)
Syndicated Publications: Weekly TV Section (Fri);
Delivery Methods: Newsstand`Carrier`Racks
Areas Served - City/County or Portion Thereof, or Zip codes: Adams County
Own Printing Facility?: Y
Commercial printers?: N
Sat. Circulation Paid: 4500
Audit By: Sworn/Estimate/Non-Audited
Audit Date: 12.07.2019
Personnel: Ronald Storey (Pub.); Jennifer Kaerh (Office/Bus. Mgr.); J. Swygart (Managing Ed.); Jannaya Andrews (Associate Ed./News Ed.); Pam Mohr (Circ. Mgr.); Karri Rice (Graphics); Nichole Perry (Classified Mgr.); Ashley Bailey (Reporter); Mike Lamm (Reporter)
Parent company (for newspapers): Horizon Publications Inc.

ELKHART TRUTH

Street address 1: 421 S 2nd St
Street address 2: Ste 100
Street address city: Elkhart
Street address state: IN
Zip/Postal code: 46516-3230
County: Elkhart
Country: USA
Mailing state: IN
General Phone: (574) 294-1661
Editorial Phone: (574) 296-5805
General/National Adv. E-mail: proos@elkharttruth.com
Display Adv. E-mail: proos@elkharttruth.com
Editorial e-mail: newsroom@elkharttruth.com
Primary Website: www.elkharttruth.com
Mthly Avg Views: 2383978
Mthly Avg Unique Visitors: 305400
Year Established: 1889
News Services: AP, SHNS, MCT
Special Editions: Spring Car Care (Apr); Healthy Living (May & October); Business & Industry (Feb); Brides (Jan); 4-H Fair (Jul); Best of Elkhart (March); Fall Home Improvement (Sept).
Special Weekly Sections: Weekend Projects (Fri); A&E (Thurs); Faith (Sat); Food (Mon.); Health & Fitness (Wed); TV (Fri)
Delivery Methods: Mail`Newsstand`Carrier`Racks
Areas Served - City/County or Portion Thereof, or Zip codes: 46514, 46516, 46517, 46526, 46528, 46507, 46540, 46565, 46543, 46567, 46553, 46550, 46573, 46544, 46545, 46530, 49112, 49130, 49099
Own Printing Facility?: N
Commercial printers?: N
Sat. Circulation Paid: 15250
Sun. Circulation Paid: 18550
Audit By: Sworn/Estimate/Non-Audited
Audit Date: 12.07.2019
Personnel: Pete Van Baalen (Pub.)
Parent company (for newspapers): Paxton Media Group

THE ELWOOD CALL-LEADER

Street address 1: 317 S Anderson St
Street address city: Elwood
Street address state: IN
Zip/Postal code: 46036-2018
County: Madison
Country: USA
Mailing address: PO BOX 85
Mailing city: ELWOOD
Mailing state: IN
Mailing zip: 46036-0085
General Phone: (765) 552-3355
Advertising Phone: (765) 552-3355
Editorial Phone: (765) 552-3355
General/National Adv. E-mail: elpub@elwoodpublishing.com
Display Adv. E-mail: elpub@elwoodpublishing.com
Classified Adv. e-mail: elpub@elwoodpublishing.com
Editorial e-mail: elpub@elwoodpublishing.com
Primary Website: www.elwoodpublishing.com
Year Established: 1891
News Services: AP.
Special Editions: Farm & Garden (Apr); Fair Wrap-up (Aug); Cookbook (Feb); Mature Years (Jan); Welcome to Elwood (Jun); Spring Opening (Mar); Spring Home Improvement (May); Christmas Opening (Nov); Fall Brides (Oct); Frankton Heritage Days Festival (Sept).
Special Weekly Sections: Best Food Day (Mon).
Syndicated Publications: What's On TV (Fri); The Mini-Page for Kids (Tues).
Delivery Methods: Mail`Newsstand`Carrier`Racks
Areas Served - City/County or Portion Thereof, or Zip codes: Madison and Tipton County
Sat. Circulation Paid: 2100
Audit By: Sworn/Estimate/Non-Audited
Audit Date: 12.07.2019
Personnel: Jack Barnes (Pres.); Robert L. Nash (Pub.); Sandy Burton (Mng. Ed.); Ed Hamilton (Sports Ed.); Chris Idlewine-Wesco (Circ. Mgr.); Randy Bayne (Prodn. Mgr.)
Parent company (for newspapers): Barnes Newspapers, Inc.; Ray Barnes Newspapers, Inc.

EVANSVILLE COURIER & PRESS

Street address 1: 300 E. Walnut Street
Street address city: Evansville
Street address state: IN
Zip/Postal code: 47702
County: Vanderburgh
Country: USA
Mailing address: PO BOX 268
Mailing city: EVANSVILLE
Mailing state: IN
Mailing zip: 47702-0268
General Phone: (812) 424-7711
Advertising Phone: (812) 424-7711
Editorial Phone: (812) 464-7430
General/National Adv. E-mail: stephensonm@courierpress.com
Display Adv. E-mail: haydent@courierpress.com
Classified Adv. e-mail: stephensonm@courierpress.com
Editorial e-mail: ethridget@courierpress.com
Primary Website: www.courierpress.com
Mthly Avg Unique Visitors: 712940
Year Established: 1846
News Services: AP, SHNS.
Special Editions: Education Guide (Fall 2013); Discover Evansville (Jun); Homes (Aug); Progress (Jul); Coupon Book (Mar); Visitor Guide "Discover" (Jun); Progress (Aug); Coupon Book (Monthly).
Special Weekly Sections: TV Book, West, Warrick
Syndicated Publications: Access (Fri); Parade (S).
Delivery Methods: Mail`Newsstand`Carrier`Racks
Areas Served - City/County or Portion Thereof, or Zip codes: 47711,42420, 47601
Own Printing Facility?: Y
Commercial printers?: Y
Sat. Circulation Paid: 32958
Sun. Circulation Paid: 46092
Audit By: AAM
Audit Date: 31.12.2017
Personnel: Kathryn Gieneart (Dir., Mktg.); Krista McDivitt (I.T. Director); Steve Traud (Dir./Circ. Sales); Ron Obermeier (Adv. Mgr., Retail Sales); Carolyn Franklin (Mgr., Mktg. Servs.); Chuck Leach (Editorial Page Ed.); Roseann Derk (Librarian); Tim Ethridge (Exec. Ed.); Tim Hayden (VP of Sales)
Parent company (for newspapers): Gannett

THE JOURNAL GAZETTE

Street address 1: 600 W. Main Street, .O. Box 100
Street address city: FORT WAYNE
Street address state: IN
Zip/Postal code: 46802
County: Allen
Country: USA
Mailing address: 600 W Main St
Mailing city: Fort Wayne
Mailing state: IN
Mailing zip: 46802
General Phone: (260) 461-8679
Advertising Phone: (260) 461-8671
Editorial Phone: (260) 461-8377
General/National Adv. E-mail: advertising@fwn.fortwayne.com
Display Adv. E-mail: advertising@fwn.fortwayne.com
Classified Adv. e-mail: classifieds@fwn.fortwayne.com
Editorial e-mail: jgnews@jg.net
Primary Website: www.journalgazette.net
Year Established: 1863
News Services: AP, Tribune News Services
Special Weekly Sections: Entertainment (Fri); Food/Best Food Day (Wed).
Delivery Methods: Mail`Newsstand`Carrier`Racks
Areas Served - City/County or Portion Thereof, or Zip codes: Allen County and Northeast Indiana / Northwest Ohio
Own Printing Facility?: Y
Commercial printers?: Y
Sat. Circulation Paid: 36730
Sat. Circulation Free: 300
Sun. Circulation Paid: 54172
Sun. Circulation Free: 2276
Audit By: AAM
Audit Date: 31.03.2024
Personnel: Julie Inskeep (Pres./Pub.); Jim Chapman (Metro editor); Jim Touvell (Editor); Tom Pellegrene Jr. (Web/Social Media Editor); Sherry Skufca (Publisher); Terri Richardson (Features Ed.); Julie Inskeep (President, Journal Gazette Co.); Mark Jaworski (Sports editor); Lisa Green (Managing editor); Fred McKissack (Editorial page editor); Jeff ` Merritt (News desk editor); Devan Filchak (Metro editor); Corey McMaken (Features/Engagement editor)
Parent company (for newspapers): Ogden Newspapers Inc.; The Journal Gazette Co.; Fort Wayne Newspapers

THE NEWS-SENTINEL

Street address 1: 600 W Main St
Street address city: Fort Wayne
Street address state: IN
Zip/Postal code: 46802-1408
County: Allen
Country: USA
Mailing address: PO BOX 102
Mailing city: FORT WAYNE
Mailing state: IN
Mailing zip: 46801-0102
General Phone: (260) 461-8449
Advertising Phone: (260) 461-8243
Editorial Phone: (260) 461-8239
General/National Adv. E-mail: dcuddihy@fortwayne.com
Display Adv. E-mail: dcuddihy@fortwayne.com
Classified Adv. e-mail: dcuddihy@fortwayne.com
Editorial e-mail: bsaleik@news-sentinel.com

Primary Website: www.news-sentinel.com
Mthly Avg Views: 450000
Mthly Avg Unique Visitors: 220000
Year Established: 1833
News Services: AP
Special Editions: Home & Lawn (Apr); Health Career Expo (Feb); Big Boys Tech & Toys Show (Jan); Back-to-School (Jul); Town & Country (Mar); Indy 500 (May); Holiday Shopping Guide (Nov); Diner's Guide (Oct); Parade of Homes (Sept).
Special Weekly Sections: Business (Mon); Features/ Food Section (Tues); Neighbors (Wed, Sat); Ticket!/ Entertainment (Thurs); TV listings (Sat).
Syndicated Publications: Summit City Savings (Sat).
Delivery Methods: Newsstand`Carrier`Racks
Own Printing Facility?: Y
Commercial printers?: Y
Sun. Circulation Paid: 80879
Audit By: AAM
Audit Date: 31.12.2015
Personnel: Michael J. Christman (CEO/Pres./Pub.); Kerry Hubartt (Sr. Ed.); Lisa Esquivel Long (Asst. Metro/Bus. Ed.); Laura Weston-Elchert (Multimedia Ed.); Tom Davis (Sports Ed.); Brad Saleik (Design Ed.); Kevin Kilbane (Features Ed.); Kevin Leininger (Reporter/ columnist); Dan Vance (Multimedia Specialist); Justin Kenny (Multimedia Specialist); Blake Sebring; Reggie Hayes
Parent company (for newspapers): Ogden Newspapers Inc.

THE TIMES

Street address 1: 211 N Jackson St
Street address city: Frankfort
Street address state: IN
Zip/Postal code: 46041-1936
County: Clinton
Country: USA
Mailing address: 211 N JACKSON ST
Mailing city: FRANKFORT
Mailing state: IN
Mailing zip: 46041-1936
General Phone: (765) 659-4622
Advertising Phone: (765) 659-4622
Editorial Phone: (765) 659-4622
General/National Adv. E-mail: advertising@ftimes.com
Display Adv. E-mail: advertising@ftimes.com
Classified Adv. e-mail: classified@ftimes.com
Editorial e-mail: news@ftimes.com
Primary Website: www.ftimes.com
Year Established: 1877
News Services: AP.
Special Editions: Back to School (Aug); Spring Home Improvement (Apr); Fall Home Improvement (Fall); Father's Day (Jun); Mother's Day (May); 4-H Tab (Other); Fall Farm (Sept); Fall Gridiron (Aug); Spring Farm (Spring).
Syndicated Publications: USA WEEKEND Magazine (Fri).
Delivery Methods: Mail`Newsstand`Carrier`Racks
Areas Served - City/County or Portion Thereof, or Zip codes: 46041, 46065, 46035, 46050, 46039, 46057, 46067, 46058
Own Printing Facility?: Y
Commercial printers?: Y
Sat. Circulation Paid: 4694
Audit By: Sworn/Estimate/Non-Audited
Audit Date: 12.07.2019
Personnel: Sharon Bardonner (Pub.); Amanda Marcel (Circ. Dir.); Linda Clark (Circ. Mgr.); Angie Hale (Classified/Retail Inside Sales); Joann Spaulding (Accounting Clerk); Thaya Sterrett (Adv. Dir.); Scott Cousins (Ed.); Brian Peloza (Mng. Ed.)
Parent company (for newspapers): Paxton Media Group

DAILY JOURNAL

Street address 1: 30 S Water St
Street address 2: Ste A
Street address city: Franklin
Street address state: IN
Zip/Postal code: 46131-2316
County: Johnson
Country: USA
Mailing address: PO BOX 699
Mailing city: FRANKLIN
Mailing state: IN
Mailing zip: 46131-0699
General Phone: (317) 736-7101
Advertising Phone: (317) 736-2730
Editorial Phone: (317) 736-2712
General/National Adv. E-mail: newstips@dailyjournal.net
Display Adv. E-mail: newstips@dailyjournal.net
Classified Adv. e-mail: cwarren@dailyjournal.net
Editorial e-mail: newstips@dailyjournal.net
Primary Website: www.dailyjournal.net
Year Established: 1963
News Services: AP, SHNS.
Special Editions: Chronologies (Jan); Boomers (Mar); Business Exchange (Jun); American Home Week (Apr); Back to School (Aug); Worship Directory (Dec); Wedding Planner (Jan); Johnson County 4-H Fair (Jul); Junior Journal (Mar); Salute (May); Coupons Plus (Monthly); Holiday Gift Guide (Nov); Health Guide (Oct); Family (Quarterly).
Special Weekly Sections: School Page (Mon); Business Pages (Sat); Best Food Day (Thursday).
Syndicated Publications: Parade (Sat).
Delivery Methods: Mail`Newsstand`Carrier`Racks
Areas Served - City/County or Portion Thereof, or Zip codes: Franklin, Greenwood, Center Grove, Whiteland, New Whiteland, Bargersville, Trafalgar, Edinburgh, Morgantown and southern Marion County
Own Printing Facility?: Y
Commercial printers?: Y
Sat. Circulation Paid: 12904
Audit By: CAC
Audit Date: 31.03.2014
Personnel: Christina Cosner (Adv. Dir.); Mike Brogdon (IT mgr.); Scarlett Syse (Group Ed.); Annie Goeller (Asst. Managing Ed., News); Nicole Bingham (Operations Coord.); Paul Hoffman (Special Publications Ed.); Cindy Warren; Michele Holtkamp (Ed.)
Parent company (for newspapers): AIM Media Indiana

THE GOSHEN NEWS

Street address 1: 114 S Main St
Street address city: Goshen
Street address state: IN
Zip/Postal code: 46526-3702
County: Elkhart
Country: USA
Mailing address: PO BOX 569
Mailing city: GOSHEN
Mailing state: IN
Mailing zip: 46527-0569
General Phone: (574) 533-2151
Advertising Phone: (574) 533-2151
Editorial Phone: (574) 533-2151
General/National Adv. E-mail: angie.kulczar@goshennews.com
Display Adv. E-mail: cara.norvell@goshennews.com
Classified Adv. e-mail: classifieds@goshennews.com
Editorial e-mail: news@goshennews.com
Primary Website: www.goshennews.com
Mthly Avg Views: 460000
Mthly Avg Unique Visitors: 206000
Year Established: 1837
News Services: AP.
Special Editions: Elkhart County Living - Six times annually - Magazine Reader's Choice - January Progress Magazine - February Living Spaces - March Lawn & Garden - April Fifty-Plus - May Graduation - June Generations - June Elkhart County Fair - July How To guide - August Hometown Heroes - September Power of Pink - October Holiday Gift Guide - November Bridal Guide - December
Special Weekly Sections: Food/Recipe (Mon); Health (Wed); Religion (Sat); Senior Focus, TV Spotlight (Sat.); Business (Mon-Sat.); Entertainment (Daily)
Syndicated Publications: Parade (S).
Delivery Methods: Mail`Newsstand`Racks
Areas Served - City/County or Portion Thereof, or Zip codes: 46526,46528,46540, 46550, 46565, 46543, 46553
Own Printing Facility?: N
Commercial printers?: N
Avg Free Circ: 1200
Sat. Circulation Paid: 8900
Sat. Circulation Free: 1200
Audit By: Sworn/Estimate/Non-Audited
Audit Date: 12.07.2019
Personnel: Brian Bloom (Pub.); Julie Beer (Ed.); Richard Leinbach (IT Dir.); Kris Erb (Accounting); Brenda Donat (Accounting); Angie Kulczar (Classified Mgr.); Roger Schneider (City Ed.); Sheila Selman (Regl. Ed.); Cara Norvell (Sales Manager); Derreck Stahley (Account Executive); Melissa Troxel (Account Executive); Sharon Hite (Account Executive); Valerie Kite (Out-bound Sales); Geoff Lesar (Reporter); John Kline (Reporter); Leandra Beabout (Reporter); Aimee Ambrose (Reporter); Ann Showalter (Lifestyles); Stephen Brooks (Sports Editor); Greg Keim (Sports reporter)
Parent company (for newspapers): CNHI, LLC; CNHI, LLC

BANNER-GRAPHIC

Street address 1: 100 N Jackson St
Street address city: Greencastle
Street address state: IN
Zip/Postal code: 46135-1240
County: Putnam
Country: USA
Mailing address: PO BOX 509
Mailing city: GREENCASTLE
Mailing state: IN
Mailing zip: 46135-0509
General Phone: (765) 653-5151
General/National Adv. E-mail: mpingleton@bannergraphic.com
Display Adv. E-mail: mpingleton@bannergraphic.com
Classified Adv. e-mail: clesko@bannergraphic.com
Editorial e-mail: ebernsee@bannergraphic.com
Primary Website: www.bannergraphic.com
Mthly Avg Views: 648660
Mthly Avg Unique Visitors: 147870
Year Established: 1843
News Services: AP.
Syndicated Publications: Relish (Monthly); USA WEEKEND Magazine (Sat); American Profile (Weekly).
Delivery Methods: Mail`Newsstand`Racks
Areas Served - City/County or Portion Thereof, or Zip codes: Greencastle, Bainbridge, Cloverdale, Coatesville, Fillmore, Reelsville, Roachdale, Russelville
Own Printing Facility?: Y
Commercial printers?: Y
Sat. Circulation Paid: 5403
Audit By: Sworn/Estimate/Non-Audited
Audit Date: 12.07.2019
Personnel: Daryl Taylor (Gen. Mgr.); Merlin Maltsberger (Adv. Mgr.); Eric Bernsee (Ed.); Jared Jernagan (Asst. Ed.); Chris Pruett (Pub.); Montica Pingleton (Marketing Consultant); Kandi Collins (Marketing Consultant); Tina Coltharp (Office Mgr.); Kristin Judy (Accounting); Cathy Lesko (Receptionist/Typist); June Leer (Circ./ NIE Asst.); Nick Wilson; Bennett Joey (Sports Editor); Modglin Chelsea (Reporter)
Parent company (for newspapers): Rust Communications

DAILY REPORTER

Street address 1: 22 W New Rd
Street address city: Greenfield
Street address state: IN
Zip/Postal code: 46140-1090
County: Hancock
Country: USA
Mailing city: Greenfield
Mailing state: IN
Mailing zip: 46140-0279
General Phone: (317) 462-5528
Advertising Phone: (317) 467-6001
Editorial Phone: (317) 467-6022
General/National Adv. E-mail: advert@greenfieldreporter.com
Display Adv. E-mail: advert@greenfieldreporter.com
Classified Adv. e-mail: class@greenfieldreporter.com
Editorial e-mail: editorial@greenfieldreporter.com
Primary Website: www.greenfieldreporter.com
Mthly Avg Views: 40000
Year Established: 1908
News Services: AP, NEA.
Special Editions: Senior Living (Feb); Sports Posters (Mar); Spring Home/Garden (Apr); Meet Your Merchants (Apr); 4-H Fair (May); HS Grad. (May); Dining Guide (Jun); Discover (Aug); Riley Festival (Sept); Spirit to Survive (Oct); Church Directory (Nov); Letters to Santa (Dec); Year in Review (Dec).
Special Weekly Sections: Religion (Sat); Business (Fri); Arts/Ent. (Thur); Education, opinion (Tues);
Syndicated Publications: Pendleton Times-Post (Wed); New Palestine Press (Wed); Fortville/McCordsville Reporter (Thur); Parade (Sat).
Delivery Methods: Mail`Carrier`Racks
Areas Served - City/County or Portion Thereof, or Zip codes: Hancock County
Own Printing Facility?: Y
Commercial printers?: Y
Sat. Circulation Paid: 8729
Audit By: Sworn/Estimate/Non-Audited
Audit Date: 10.10.2022
Personnel: John Senger (Circ. Mgr.); Chuck Wells (Pub.); Noelle Steele; Tom Russo (Photo Ed.); Scott Slade (Community Ed.); Debby Brooks (Admin. Mgr.); Anne Smith (Copy Ed.); Larry Ham (Prodn. Dir.); Jason Corgman (Tech. Support); Tammy Clifton (Adv. Mgr., Clas.); Karen Crawford (Mng. Ed.); Carrie Lacy (Commercial Print Coord.); Jim Steele (Production Pre-Press); Aaron Kennedy (Editor); Steve Swails; Jane Smith (Ed. Asst.); Holly Lewis (Circ. Clerk); Ron Richmond (Circ. District Mgr.); Beverly Dillback (Sales Mgr.); Erika Whittington (Sr. Adv. Rep.); Rich Torres (Sports Ed.); Alana Lashaway (Adv. Rep., Clas.); Paul Hart (Circ. Dir.)
Parent company (for newspapers): AIM Media Indiana

GREENSBURG DAILY NEWS

Street address 1: 135 S Franklin St
Street address city: Greensburg
Street address state: IN
Zip/Postal code: 47240-2023
County: Decatur
Country: USA
Mailing address: PO BOX 106
Mailing city: GREENSBURG
Mailing state: IN
Mailing zip: 47240-0106
General Phone: (812) 663-3111
Advertising Phone: (812) 663-3111 ext. 7017
Editorial Phone: (812) 663-3111 ext. 7003
General/National Adv. E-mail: keith.wells@indianamediagroup.com
Display Adv. E-mail: keith.wells@indianamediagroup.com
Classified Adv. e-mail: linda.siefert@greensburgdailynews.com
Editorial e-mail: news@greensburgdailynews.com
Primary Website: www.greensburgdailynews.com
Mthly Avg Views: 350000
Mthly Avg Unique Visitors: 60000
Year Established: 1894
News Services: AP.
Special Editions: Health & Wellness (Feb); Graduation (May); Summer Fun (Jun).
Special Weekly Sections: School News (Tues); Business News (Tues); Agri-News (Wed); Pastimes (Thur); Church News (Fri).
Syndicated Publications: Relish (Monthly); American Profile (Weekly).
Delivery Methods: Newsstand`Carrier`Racks
Areas Served - City/County or Portion Thereof, or Zip codes: Decatur and surrounding counties
Own Printing Facility?: N
Commercial printers?: N
Sat. Circulation Paid: 4350
Audit By: Sworn/Estimate/Non-Audited
Audit Date: 12.07.2019
Personnel: Melissa Conrad (Managing Ed.); Brent Brown (News Ed.); Natalie Acra (Operations Mgr.); Lisa Huff (Dir. Audience Dev.); Shelley Barton (HR/Accounting); Denver E. Sullivan (IT Dir.); Laura Welborn (Rgl. Pub.); Boris Ladwig (Staff Writer); Amanda Browning (Staff Writer); Eric Wohlford (Sports); Jeanie York (Acc. Exec.); Chrystal Bushorn (Acc. Exec.); Susan Peters (Expeditor)
Parent company (for newspapers): CNHI, LLC; CNHI, LLC

NEWS TIMES

Street address 1: 100 N Jefferson St
Street address city: Hartford City
Street address state: IN
Zip/Postal code: 47348-2201
County: Blackford
Country: USA
Mailing address: PO BOX 690
Mailing city: HARTFORD CITY
Mailing state: IN
Mailing zip: 47348-0690
General Phone: (765) 348-0110
Advertising Phone: (765) 348-0110
Editorial Phone: (765) 348-0110
General/National Adv. E-mail: ntoffice@comcast.net
Display Adv. E-mail: ntoffice@comcast.net
Classified Adv. e-mail: ntoffice@comcast.net
Editorial e-mail: newstimes@comcast.net
Primary Website: www.hartfordcitynewstimes.com
Year Established: 1885
News Services: AP.
Special Editions: Spring Car Care (Apr); Progress (Feb); 4-H (Jul); Home & Garden (Mar); Graduation (May); Christmas Tab (Nov); Fall Home Yard Garden (Oct); Sizzlin' Summer Clearances (Aug), Big Boy Toys (Jun);

Mother's Day (May); Spring Fling Specials (Apr); Black Friday (Nov); Give Thanks to Kids (Nov); Last Minute Gift Guide (Dec); Heartland (Quarterly); Seasons (Quarterly); Healthbeat (Quarterly).
Special Weekly Sections: Sports; Environment; Around Indiana.
Delivery Methods: Mail`Carrier`Racks
Areas Served - City/County or Portion Thereof, or Zip codes: Blackford County
Own Printing Facility?: Y
Commercial printers?: Y
Audit By: USPS
Audit Date: 30.09.2011
Personnel: Pat Hughes (Ed.); Valarie Ashley (Adv. Conslt.); Teresa Hargis (Adv. Conslt.)
Parent company (for newspapers): Community Media Group

HUNTINGTON HERALD-PRESS

Street address 1: 7 N Jefferson St
Street address city: Huntington
Street address state: IN
Zip/Postal code: 46750-2839
County: Huntington
Country: USA
Mailing address: 7 N JEFFERSON ST
Mailing city: HUNTINGTON
Mailing state: IN
Mailing zip: 46750-2839
General Phone: (260) 356-6700
Advertising Phone: (260) 356-6700
Editorial Phone: (260) 356-6700
General/National Adv. E-mail: ariggers@h-ponline.com
Display Adv. E-mail: hpads@h-ponline.com
Classified Adv. e-mail: hpclass@h-ponline.com
Editorial e-mail: hpnews@h-ponline.com
Primary Website: www.h-ponline.com
Mthly Avg Views: 100000
Mthly Avg Unique Visitors: 60000
Year Established: 1848
News Services: AP.
Special Editions: Spring Home & Garden II (Apr); Markle Wildcat Days (Aug); Gift Hang-Up (Dec); Huntington County Landmarks (Feb); Girl's Basketball Sectional (Jan); Andrews Summer Festival (Jul); Heritage Days (Jun); Farm (Mar); Golf Guide (May); Holiday Charm (Nov); Nati
Special Weekly Sections: Church Page (Fri); Best Food Days (S); Business (Thur); Business Page (Tues); Farm Page (Wed).
Syndicated Publications: Current Bargains (Mon); Comics (S).
Delivery Methods: Carrier`Racks
Areas Served - City/County or Portion Thereof, or Zip codes: 46702, 46750, 46770, 46783, 46792
Commercial printers?: Y
Avg Free Circ: 3000
Sun. Circulation Paid: 3564
Audit By: USPS
Audit Date: 12.10.2012
Personnel: Megan Greve (Ed.); Audra Riggers (Pub. Gen. Mgr.); John Dempsey (Sports Ed.); Brenda Ross (Adv. Mgr., Classified)
Parent company (for newspapers): Paxton Media Group

THE INDIANAPOLIS STAR

Street address 1: 130 S Meridian St
Street address city: Indianapolis
Street address state: IN
Zip/Postal code: 46225-1046
County: Marion
Country: USA
Mailing address: PO BOX 145
Mailing city: INDIANAPOLIS
Mailing state: IN
Mailing zip: 46206-0145
General Phone: (317) 444-4000
Advertising Phone: (317) 444-7000
Editorial Phone: (317) 444-6160
General/National Adv. E-mail: Kevin.Marshall@indystar.com
Display Adv. E-mail: andrew.insley@indystar.com
Editorial e-mail: jeff.taylor@indystar.com
Primary Website: www.indystar.com
Mthly Avg Views: 28500000
Year Established: 1903
News Services: AP.
Special Editions: Pro & College Football (Aug); Final Four (Mar); 500-Mile Auto Race Souvenir (May); Voter's Guide (Nov); Pro Basketball (Oct).
Special Weekly Sections: Arts, Entertainment, Health (Tue); Movies, Best Food Day (Fri); Garden, Home, Religion, Auto (Sat); Real Estate, Travel, Auto, Arts, Entertainment (Sun)
Syndicated Publications: USA WEEKEND Magazine (S).
Delivery Methods: Mail`Newsstand`Carrier`Racks
Areas Served - City/County or Portion Thereof, or Zip codes: Indiana
Own Printing Facility?: Y
Commercial printers?: Y
Sat. Circulation Paid: 93441
Sun. Circulation Paid: 153761
Audit By: AAM
Audit Date: 31.12.2017
Personnel: Patricia Miller (President, Gannett Indiana); Jeff Taylor (Vice Pres./Ed.); Ronnie Ramos (Executive Editor); Jenny Green (Sports Director); Amanda Kingsbury (News Director); Kim Mitchell (Exec. Admin. Asst.); Tim Swarens (Opinion Director); Steve Berta (Senior Content Coach); Alvie Lindsay (News Director); David Hakanson (Director of Key Accounts); Ann Gelfius (Client Services Director); Mitch Still (Regional Finance Director)
Parent company (for newspapers): Gannett

THE HERALD

Street address 1: 216 E 4th St
Street address city: Jasper
Street address state: IN
Zip/Postal code: 47546-3102
County: Dubois
Country: USA
Mailing address: PO BOX 31
Mailing city: JASPER
Mailing state: IN
Mailing zip: 47547-0031
General Phone: (812) 482-2424
Advertising Phone: (812) 482-2424
Editorial Phone: (812) 482-2626
General/National Adv. E-mail: ads@dcherald.com
Display Adv. E-mail: ads@dcherald.com
Classified Adv. e-mail: classads@dcherald.com
Editorial e-mail: news@dcherald.com
Primary Website: www.duboiscountyherald.com
Mthly Avg Views: 700000
Year Established: 1895
News Services: AP, CNS.
Special Editions: Home, Lawn & Garden (Mar); Christmas Greetings (Dec); Boys Basketball Sectional (Feb); Brides & Weddings (Jan);Spring Agriculture Salute (Mar); 4-H Fair Kick-off (Jul);Back to School (July): Senior Citizen Salute (Aug); Strassenfest (Aug); Graduation (May); Fall Home Improvement (Sept); Band Invitational (Oct) Christmas Shopping Guide (Nov); Car Care (Winter 2012); Newspaper in Education (Mar); Health & Fitness (April); Patoka Playground (May) Salute to Veterans (Nov)
Special Weekly Sections: Food (Tues); Religion (Fri); Science (Mon); Travel (Thur).
Delivery Methods: Mail`Newsstand`Carrier`Racks
Areas Served - City/County or Portion Thereof, or Zip codes: 47546, 47542, 47527, 47521, 47532, 47513, 47541, 47575, 47580, 47523, 47531, 47536, 47537, 47550, 47552, 47556, 47577, 47579, 47611, 47564, 47585, 47590, 47598,
Own Printing Facility?: Y
Commercial printers?: Y
Avg Free Circ: 95
Sat. Circulation Paid: 8191
Sat. Circulation Free: 95
Audit By: Sworn/Estimate/Non-Audited
Audit Date: 12.07.2019
Personnel: Dan E. Rumbach (Co-Pres/Co-Pub.); John A. Rumbach (Co-president; co-publisher; editor); Justin Rumbach (Mng. Ed.); Mark Fierst (Controller/Treasurer); Mike Mazur (Mgr., HR); Don Weisheit (Subscriber Services manager); Dawn Mazur (Wire Ed.); Dan Hoppenjans (Dist. Mgr.); Alan Baumeister (Single Copy Sales & Print Distribution Manager); Brenda Adams (Advertising Director); Tom Stephens (Adv. Dir.)
Parent company (for newspapers): Paxton Media Group; Jasper Herald Co.

NEWS AND TRIBUNE

Street address 1: 221 Spring St
Street address city: Jeffersonville
Street address state: IN
Zip/Postal code: 47130-3353
County: Clark
Country: USA
Mailing address: PO BOX 867
Mailing city: JEFFERSONVILLE
Mailing state: IN
Mailing zip: 47131-0867
General Phone: (812) 283-6636
Advertising Phone: (812) 206-2143
Editorial Phone: (812) 206-2130
General/National Adv. E-mail: duke.freeman@newsandtribune.com
Display Adv. E-mail: mary.tuttle@newsandtribune.com
Classified Adv. e-mail: classifieds@newsandtribune.com
Editorial e-mail: shea.vanhoy@newsandtribune.com
Primary Website: www.newsandtribune.com
Year Established: 1851
News Services: AP, NEA, Scripps Howard.
Special Editions: Bridal Guide, Medical Directory, Worship Guide, Life Planning, Visitors/Relocation Guide (Jan, Feb, Mar); Southern Indiana Progress, Spring Home & Garden (Apr, May, Jun); Art Walk Guide, Back to School, HS Football Preview, Clark County Readers' Choice, Harvest Homecoming Guide, GCCS NAFC School Directory (Jul, Aug, Sept); Floyd County Readers' Choice, Boys and Girls Basketball, Letters to Santa, Power of Pink (Oct, Nov, Dec)
Special Weekly Sections: TV Weekly (Sat).
Syndicated Publications: TV News/Golden Opportunity (Monthly).
Delivery Methods: Mail`Newsstand`Carrier`Racks
Areas Served - City/County or Portion Thereof, or Zip codes: Clark, Floyd County
Sat. Circulation Paid: 7152
Audit By: Sworn/Estimate/Non-Audited
Audit Date: 12.07.2019
Personnel: Bill Hanson (Pub.); Susan Duncan (Ed.); Bob Orlandini (News Ed.); Elizabeth DePompei (Digital Ed.); Craig Pearson (Sports Ed.); Stephen Allen (Marketing Dir.); Jeff Smith (Adv. Dir.)
Parent company (for newspapers): CNHI, LLC; CNHI, LLC

THE NEWS SUN

Street address 1: 102 N Main St
Street address city: Kendallville
Street address state: IN
Zip/Postal code: 46755-1714
County: Noble
Country: USA
Mailing address: 102 N MAIN ST
Mailing city: KENDALLVILLE
Mailing state: IN
Mailing zip: 46755-1714
General Phone: (260) 347-0400
Advertising Phone: (260) 347-0400
Editorial Phone: (260) 347-0400
General/National Adv. E-mail: ldonley@kpcmedia.com
Display Adv. E-mail: cmiller@kpcmedia.com
Classified Adv. e-mail: asaggars@kpcmedia.com
Editorial e-mail: dkurtz@kpcmedia.com
Primary Website: www.kpcnews.com
Mthly Avg Views: 500000
Mthly Avg Unique Visitors: 100000
Year Established: 1911
News Services: AP.
Special Editions: Look at Lagrange (Apr); Wedding Planner (Aug); Wedding Planner (Feb); Noble County Answer Book (Jan); Noble Co. 4-H Scrapbook (Jul); Sectional Basketball Preview (Mar); Graduation (May); Basketball Preview (Nov); Apple Festival (Oct); ACD Festival (Sept).
Special Weekly Sections: Church Page (Fri); Business Page (Other); Homes To Own (S); Agri-Business Page (Sat); Outdoor Life (Thur).
Syndicated Publications: USA WEEKEND Magazine (S); American Profile (Weekly).
Delivery Methods: Mail`Newsstand`Carrier`Racks
Areas Served - City/County or Portion Thereof, or Zip codes: 46565; 46701; 46730; 46732; 46746; 46747; 46755; 46760; 46761; 46763; 46767; 46771; 46784; 46794; 46795
Own Printing Facility?: Y
Commercial printers?: Y
Sat. Circulation Paid: 6004
Sun. Circulation Paid: 5518
Audit By: AAM
Audit Date: 31.12.2018
Personnel: Terry Housholder (Pres./CEO/Pub.); Bruce Hakala (Circ. Dir.); Barry Rochford (Managing Ed.); Mark Murdock (Night Ed.); Erin Doucette (Presentation Ed.); Jan Richardson (Life Ed.); Carol Ernsberger (Desk Ed.); Lynette Donley (Adv. Dir.); Cynthia Miller (Acct. Exec.); Terri Myers (Acct. Exec.); Gary Crager (Production Mgr.); Ann Saggers (Creative Mgr.)
Parent company (for newspapers): KPC Media Group, Inc.

KOKOMO TRIBUNE

Street address 1: 300 N Union St
Street address city: Kokomo
Street address state: IN
Zip/Postal code: 46901-4612
County: Howard
Country: USA
Mailing address: PO BOX 9014
Mailing city: KOKOMO
Mailing state: IN
Mailing zip: 46904-9014
General Phone: (765) 459-3121
Advertising Phone: (765) 459-3121 ext. 6717
Editorial Phone: (765) 454-8584
General/National Adv. E-mail: susan.mccauley@kokomotribune.com
Display Adv. E-mail: peggy.martino@kokomotribune.com
Classified Adv. e-mail: kristin.johnson@kokomotribune.com
Editorial e-mail: jeff.kovaleski@kokomotribune.com
Primary Website: www.kokomotribune.com
Year Established: 1850
News Services: AP.
Special Editions: Howard County 4H Fair 2013 (Jul); Women Today (Jul); Brides 2013 (Jan); Best of Kokomo (Jan).
Special Weekly Sections: TV Weekly (Sat).
Syndicated Publications: Relish (Monthly); TV Update (Other); Parade (S).
Delivery Methods: Mail`Carrier`Racks
Areas Served - City/County or Portion Thereof, or Zip codes: Howard County
Own Printing Facility?: Y
Commercial printers?: Y
Sat. Circulation Paid: 20100
Sun. Circulation Paid: 20544
Audit By: Sworn/Estimate/Non-Audited
Audit Date: 12.07.2019
Personnel: Tim Bath (Photo Ed.); Jeff Kovaleski (Ed./Op. Page Ed.); Jill Bond (Managing Ed.); Robert Burgess (City Ed.); Robin Harper (Reg. Circ. Dir.); Misty Whittaker (Customer Service Mgr.); Jessyka Betzner (Customer Serice Rep./NIE Coord.); Beverly Sams (Rgl. Adv. Dir.); Kristin Johnson (Reg. Digital Mgr.); Robyn McCloskey (Pub.)
Parent company (for newspapers): CNHI, LLC; CNHI, LLC

HERALD-ARGUS

Street address 1: 701 State St
Street address city: La Porte
Street address state: IN
Zip/Postal code: 46350-3328
County: La Porte
Country: USA
Mailing address: 701 STATE ST
Mailing city: LA PORTE
Mailing state: IN
Mailing zip: 46350-3328
General Phone: (219) 362-2161
Advertising Phone: (219) 326-3881
Editorial Phone: (219) 326-3858
General/National Adv. E-mail: breisig@heraldargus.com
Display Adv. E-mail: display@heraldargus.com
Classified Adv. e-mail: classified@heraldargus.com
Primary Website: www.heraldargus.com
Year Established: 1880
News Services: AP, SHNS.
Special Editions: Home Improvement/Gardening (Apr); Finance (Feb); Farm (Mar); Christmas (Nov); Car Care (Oct).
Special Weekly Sections: Senior (Fri); Best Food Day (Mon); Religion (Sat); Homes (Thur); Agriculture (Tues); Business/Industry (Wed).
Syndicated Publications: TV Viewer (Sat); American Profile (Weekly).
Delivery Methods: Mail`Newsstand`Carrier`Racks
Areas Served - City/County or Portion Thereof, or Zip codes: 46350
Sat. Circulation Paid: 5054
Audit By: AAM
Audit Date: 30.09.2014
Personnel: Bill Hackney (Pub.); Kim King (Mng. Ed.); Carolyn Smith (Acct. Exec.); Patty Bryant (Acct. Exec.); Amanda Haverstick (Lead News Ed.); Adam

Parkhouse (Managing Ed.); Matt Christy (News Ed.); Jessica Campbell (Reporter); Leslie Dean (District Sales Mgr.); Isis Cains (Advertising Dir.); Cathie Doria (Acc. Exec.)
Parent company (for newspapers): Paxton Media Group

JOURNAL AND COURIER

Street address 1: 823 East Park Boulevard
Street address 2: Ste C
Street address city: Lafayette
Street address state: IN
Zip/Postal code: 47905
County: Tippecanoe
Country: USA
Mailing address: 823 PARK EAST BLVD STE C
Mailing city: LAFAYETTE
Mailing state: IN
Mailing zip: 47905-0811
General Phone: (765) 423-5511
Advertising Phone: (765) 423-5272
Editorial Phone: (765) 420-5235
General/National Adv. E-mail: sdavis@journalandcourier.com
Display Adv. E-mail: jholm@journalandcourier.com
Classified Adv. e-mail: amecklenburg@journalandcourier.com
Editorial e-mail: jstafford@journalandcourier.com
Primary Website: www.jconline.com
Mthly Avg Views: 5775000
Mthly Avg Unique Visitors: 415500
Year Established: 1920
News Services: AP, GNS, LAT-WP.
Special Editions: Schools of Greater Lafayette (May); Bragging Rights (Apr); Community Connections (Aug); Builders Showcase (Bi-Monthly); Football Saturday (Fall); Grading Our Schools (Jan); Spring Home Improvement (Mar); Coupon Express (Monthly); Profiles (Oct).
Special Weekly Sections: TGIF (Fri); Food & Drink (Mon); Life (S); Homes (Sat); Diversion (Thur); Health & Fitness (Tues); Relate (Wed).
Syndicated Publications: USA WEEKEND Magazine (Sat).
Delivery Methods: Mail`Newsstand`Carrier`Racks
Areas Served - City/County or Portion Thereof, or Zip codes: Tippecanoe, Benton, Carroll, Clinton, Fountain, Jasper, Newton, Warren, and White County
Own Printing Facility?: Y
Commercial printers?: Y
Sat. Circulation Paid: 16969
Sun. Circulation Paid: 21996
Audit By: AAM
Audit Date: 31.03.2018
Personnel: Chris Deno (Controller); Becky Taylor (Adv. Mgr., Classified); Nancy Jo Trafton (Dir., Market Devel.); Brenda Rudd (Cashier/Customer Service Rep.); Bill Cannon (Regl. Digital Dir.); Ken Thompson (Planning Ed.); Julie McClure (Features Ed.); Carol Bangert (Content Strategist); Dave Bangert (Col.); George Spohr (Exec. Ed.); Mike Carmin (Sports Rep.)
Parent company (for newspapers): Gannett

THE REPORTER

Street address 1: 117 E Washington St
Street address city: Lebanon
Street address state: IN
Zip/Postal code: 46052-2209
County: Boone
Country: USA
Mailing address: 117 E WASHINGTON ST
Mailing city: LEBANON
Mailing state: IN
Mailing zip: 46052-2209
General Phone: (765) 482-4650
Advertising Phone: (765) 482-4650
Editorial Phone: (765) 482-4650 ext. 4
General/National Adv. E-mail: rick.whiteman@reporter.net
Display Adv. E-mail: mary.ball@reporter.net
Classified Adv. e-mail: rick.whiteman@reporter.net
Editorial e-mail: news@reporter.net
Primary Website: www.reporter.net
Mthly Avg Views: 30000
Mthly Avg Unique Visitors: 22000
Year Established: 1891
News Services: AP.
Special Editions: County 4-H Fair and Open Show (Jul); Home and Garden (April); Graduation sections (May)
Special Weekly Sections: Business Page (Fri); Farm Pages (Tues);
Syndicated Publications: TV Times (Sat); American Profile (Weekly).
Delivery Methods: Mail`Racks
Areas Served - City/County or Portion Thereof, or Zip codes: Boone County, Advance, Jamestown, Sheridan, Thorntown, Whitestown and Zionsville
Own Printing Facility?: N
Sat. Circulation Paid: 5264
Audit By: Sworn/Estimate/Non-Audited
Audit Date: 12.07.2019
Personnel: Marda Johnson (Mng. Ed.); Greta Sanderson (Pub.); Rod Rose (Farm Ed.); Andrea Badger (Copy Ed.); Will Willems (Sports Ed.); Mary Ball (Adv. Rep.); Tim Peters (Adv. Rep.); Julie Benavides (Classified Rep.); Diane Clemens (Circ. and Prod.); Kerry Luchetta (Office Mgr.); Jared Selch (Sales Dir.)
Parent company (for newspapers): Media News Group; CNHI, LLC

GREENE COUNTY DAILY WORLD

Street address 1: 79 S Main St
Street address city: Linton
Street address state: IN
Zip/Postal code: 47441-1818
County: Greene
Country: USA
Mailing address: PO BOX 129
Mailing city: LINTON
Mailing state: IN
Mailing zip: 47441-0129
General Phone: (812) 847-4487
Advertising Phone: (812) 847-4487
Editorial Phone: (812) 847-4487
General/National Adv. E-mail: greenecountyads@yahoo.com
Display Adv. E-mail: christy_lehman@hotmail.com
Classified Adv. e-mail: christy_lehman@hotmail.com
Editorial e-mail: westfallgcdw@gmail.com
Primary Website: www.gcdailyworld.com
Mthly Avg Views: 1102170
Mthly Avg Unique Visitors: 253800
Year Established: 1905
News Services: AP.
Delivery Methods: Mail`Newsstand`Racks
Areas Served - City/County or Portion Thereof, or Zip codes: Linton, Jasonville, Sandborn, Lyons, Switz City, Worthington, Coalmont, Midland, Dugger, Newberry, Solsberry, Owensburg, Scotland, Elnora, Springville, Bloomfield
Own Printing Facility?: Y
Commercial printers?: Y
Sat. Circulation Paid: 3500
Audit By: Sworn/Estimate/Non-Audited
Audit Date: 12.07.2019
Personnel: Chris Pruett (Publisher); Travis David (Sports Editor); Terry Schwinghammer (Sports Writer); Mike Miller (Pressman); Cory Anweiler (Pressman); Heidi Puckett (Ad rep); Tina Davis (Ad rep); Stockrahm Sabrina (Editor); Andrew Christman (Reporter); Patti Danner (Reporter); Kelly Slaven (Reporter)
Parent company (for newspapers): Rust Communications

PHAROS-TRIBUNE

Street address 1: 517 E Broadway
Street address city: Logansport
Street address state: IN
Zip/Postal code: 46947-3154
County: Cass
Country: USA
Mailing address: PO BOX 210
Mailing city: LOGANSPORT
Mailing state: IN
Mailing zip: 46947-0210
General Phone: (574) 722-5000
Advertising Phone: (574) 732-5156
Editorial Phone: (574) 732-5155
General/National Adv. E-mail: becky.kesler@pharostribune.com
Display Adv. E-mail: lori.thornton@pharostribune.com
Classified Adv. e-mail: jody.taylor@pharostribune.com
Editorial e-mail: kevin.burkett@pharostribune.com
Primary Website: www.pharostribune.com
Mthly Avg Views: 377903
Mthly Avg Unique Visitors: 85972
Year Established: 1844
News Services: AP, MCT.
Special Editions: Football (Aug); 4-H (Jul); Winter Sports (Nov).
Special Weekly Sections: Religion (S); TV Encore(F).
Syndicated Publications: Parade (S).
Delivery Methods: Mail`Newsstand`Carrier
Areas Served - City/County or Portion Thereof, or Zip codes: Cass County
Own Printing Facility?: Y
Commercial printers?: Y
Sat. Circulation Paid: 7200
Audit By: Sworn/Estimate/Non-Audited
Audit Date: 12.07.2019
Personnel: Beau Wicker (Sports Ed.); Sarah Einselen (News Ed.); Beverly Sams (Regl. Adv. Dir.); Renee LoCoco (Marketing Exec.); Robin Harper (Regional Director Audience Developement); Theresia Kuritz (Circ. Supervisor.); Kayanna Smith (Customer Service Rep.); Amy Newcom (Reg. Op. Mgr.); Kevin Burkett (Editor); Jessica Deitrich (HR/Finance); Robyn McCloskey (Regional Publisher/ Senior VP Operations CNHI); Jody Taylor (Classified / Expeditor)
Parent company (for newspapers): CNHI, LLC; CNHI, LLC

MADISON COURIER, INC.

Street address 1: 310 West St
Street address city: Madison
Street address state: IN
Zip/Postal code: 47250-3711
County: Jefferson
Country: USA
Mailing address: 310 WEST ST
Mailing city: MADISON
Mailing state: IN
Mailing zip: 47250-3711
General Phone: (812) 265-3641
Advertising Phone: (812) 265-3641 ext. 228
Editorial Phone: (812) 265-3641 ext. 230
General/National Adv. E-mail: cjacobs@madisoncourier.com
Display Adv. E-mail: addept@madisoncourier.com
Classified Adv. e-mail: classifieds@madisoncourier.com
Editorial e-mail: etompkin@madisoncourier.com
Primary Website: www.madisoncourier.com
Mthly Avg Views: 845900
Mthly Avg Unique Visitors: 324000
Year Established: 1837
News Services: AP, NEA.
Special Editions: Home and Car Improvement Tab (Apr); Year-End Tab (Dec); Tax Tab (Feb); Wedding Tab (Jan); 4-H Fair Tab (Jul); Lawn & Garden Tab (Mar); Graduation Tab (May); Health Mind & Body (quarterly); Chautauqua Tab (Sept).
Syndicated Publications: American Profile (Weekly).
Delivery Methods: Mail`Newsstand`Carrier`Racks
Areas Served - City/County or Portion Thereof, or Zip codes: Jefferson and Switzerland County, Indiana and Trimble and Carroll County, Kentucky.
Own Printing Facility?: Y
Commercial printers?: N
Sat. Circulation Paid: 6000
Audit By: USPS
Audit Date: 14.10.2017
Personnel: Mark McKee (Nt'l. Acc. and Job Listings); Curt Jacobs (Pub.); Mark Campbell (Sports Ed.); David Campbell (Sports Ed.); Robin Cull (New Media Dir.); Elliot Tompkin (Ed.); Dianne Colber (Inside Sales); Shawntale Tingle (Carrier Mgr.)
Parent company (for newspapers): Paxton Media Group

CHRONICLE-TRIBUNE

Street address 1: 610 S Adams St
Street address city: Marion
Street address state: IN
Zip/Postal code: 46953-2041
County: Grant
Country: USA
Mailing address: PO BOX 309
Mailing city: MARION
Mailing state: IN
Mailing zip: 46952-0309
General Phone: (765) 664-5111
Advertising Phone: (765) 671-2230
Editorial Phone: (765) 671-2250
General/National Adv. E-mail: lkelsay@chronicle-tribune.com
Display Adv. E-mail: showard@chronicle-tribune.com
Classified Adv. e-mail: showard@chronicle-tribune.com
Editorial e-mail: dpenticuff@chronicle-tribune.com
Primary Website: www.chronicle-tribune.com
Mthly Avg Views: 2000000
Mthly Avg Unique Visitors: 87000
Year Established: 1867
News Services: AP, GNS.
Special Editions: Football Preview (Aug); Medical Directory (Feb); Bridal Tab (Jan); Senior Citizens (Jul); Progress (Mar); Women's Expo (Oct); Crossword Puzzle (Semi-yearly).
Special Weekly Sections: Travel (Fri); Best Food Day (Mon); Business (S); Business (Sat); Home (Thur); Kids Zone (Tues); Relationships (Wed).
Syndicated Publications: Northern Neighbors (S).
Delivery Methods: Mail`Newsstand`Carrier`Racks
Areas Served - City/County or Portion Thereof, or Zip codes: Frankfort, Huntington, Peru, and Wabash
Own Printing Facility?: Y
Commercial printers?: Y
Sat. Circulation Paid: 12536
Sun. Circulation Paid: 14524
Audit By: AAM
Audit Date: 31.03.2014
Personnel: Linda Kelsay (President & Pub.); David Penticuff (Ed.); Stan Howard (Adv. Dir.); Heather Korporal (Circ. Mgr.); Time Stanley (Pressroom Mgr.); Tyler Juranovich (Managing Ed.); Neal Bartrum (Distr. Mgr.)
Parent company (for newspapers): Paxton Media Group

THE REPORTER TIMES

Street address 1: 60 S Jefferson St
Street address city: Martinsville
Street address state: IN
Zip/Postal code: 46151-1968
County: Morgan
Country: USA
Mailing address: 60 S JEFFERSON ST
Mailing city: Martinsville
Mailing state: IN
Mailing zip: 46151-1968
General Phone: (765) 342-3311
Advertising Phone: (812) 331-4291
Editorial Phone: (765) 342-3311
General/National Adv. E-mail: lhensley@gannett.com
Display Adv. E-mail: cgiddens@schurz.com
Primary Website: www.reporter-times.com
Mthly Avg Views: 200000
Mthly Avg Unique Visitors: 35000
Year Established: 1889
Delivery Methods: Mail`Newsstand`Carrier`Racks
Areas Served - City/County or Portion Thereof, or Zip codes: Martinsville and Morgan County
Sat. Circulation Paid: 4714
Sun. Circulation Paid: 40171
Audit By: Sworn/Estimate/Non-Audited
Audit Date: 12.07.2019
Personnel: Cory Bollinger (Pub.); Larry D. Hensley (Gen. Mgr.); Tim D. Smith (Circ. Dir.); Chad Giddens (Adv. Sales Mgr.); Stephen Crane (Mng. Ed.); Brack Stacy (Adv. Dir.); Angie Skaggs (Adv. Rep.); Julie Varnell (Sports Ed.); Jennifer Paul (Finance Mgr.)
Parent company (for newspapers): Schurz Communications Inc; Gannett

NEWS DISPATCH

Street address 1: 121 W Michigan Blvd
Street address city: Michigan City
Street address state: IN
Zip/Postal code: 46360-3274
County: La Porte
Country: USA
Mailing address: 121 W MICHIGAN BLVD
Mailing city: MICHIGAN CITY
Mailing state: IN
Mailing zip: 46360-3274
General Phone: (219) 874-7211
Advertising Phone: (219) 874-7211 ext. 400
Editorial Phone: (219) 874-7211 ext. 451
General/National Adv. E-mail: icains@thenewsdispatch.com
Display Adv. E-mail: ads@thenewsdispatch.com
Classified Adv. e-mail: classifieds@thenewsdispatch.com
Editorial e-mail: jmcclure@thenewsdispatch.com
Primary Website: www.thenewsdispatch.com
Year Established: 1938
News Services: AP.
Special Editions: Real Estate Guide (Monthly).
Special Weekly Sections: Book Review (Fri); Business (S); Real Estate (Sat); Best Food Day (Fri).
Syndicated Publications: USA WEEKEND Magazine (S); TV Listings (own, local newsprint) (Sat).
Delivery Methods: Mail`Newsstand`Carrier`Racks

Areas Served - City/County or Portion Thereof, or Zip codes: 46360
Own Printing Facility?: Y
Sat. Circulation Paid: 5586
Audit By: AAM
Audit Date: 30.09.2014
Personnel: Isis Cains (Adv. Dir.); Bill Hackney (Publisher); Adam Parkhouse (Managing Ed.); Andy Steinke (News Ed.); Carron Phillips (Asst. Sports Ed.); Aaron McKrell (Sports Ed.)
Parent company (for newspapers): Paxton Media Group

HERALD JOURNAL

Street address 1: 114 S Main St
Street address city: Monticello
Street address state: IN
Zip/Postal code: 47960-2328
County: White
Country: USA
Mailing address: PO BOX 409
Mailing city: MONTICELLO
Mailing state: IN
Mailing zip: 47960-0409
General Phone: (574) 583-5121
Advertising Phone: (574) 583-5121
Editorial Phone: (574) 583-5121
General/National Adv. E-mail: sales@thehj.com
Display Adv. E-mail: dcarlson@thehj.com
Classified Adv. e-mail: tspear@thehj.com
Editorial e-mail: wriggs@thehj.com
Primary Website: www.thehj.com
Year Established: 1862
News Services: AP.
Special Editions: 2014 Where
Special Weekly Sections: TV (Fri); Best Food Day (Thurs); Business & Financial (Sat); Best Food Day (Thur); Senior Citizens (Tues); Self Help (Wed).
Delivery Methods: Mail`Newsstand`Racks
Areas Served - City/County or Portion Thereof, or Zip codes: White County
Own Printing Facility?: Y
Commercial printers?: N
Sat. Circulation Paid: 3500
Audit By: Sworn/Estimate/Non-Audited
Audit Date: 12.07.2019
Personnel: Greg Perrotto (Circ. Dir.); Cyndi Grace (Circ. Dir.); Deb Carlson (Adv. Mgr.); Mark Hornung (Pub.); Tom Tiernan (Adv. Dir.); Kris Mills (Sports Ed.); Vicki Shore (Adv. Mgr.)
Parent company (for newspapers): CNHI, LLC

THE STAR PRESS

Street address 1: 345 S High St
Street address city: Muncie
Street address state: IN
Zip/Postal code: 47305-2326
County: Delaware
Country: USA
Mailing address: PO BOX 2408
Mailing city: MUNCIE
Mailing state: IN
Mailing zip: 47307-0408
General Phone: (765) 213-5701
Advertising Phone: (765) 213-5732
Editorial Phone: (765) 213-5732
General/National Adv. E-mail: clindus@muncie.gannett.com
Display Adv. E-mail: msheridan@muncie.gannett.com
Classified Adv. e-mail: treese@muncie.gannett.com
Editorial e-mail: gfallon@muncie.gannett.com
Primary Website: www.thestarpress.com
Year Established: 1899
News Services: AP, MCT, SHNS, GNS.
Special Weekly Sections: Best Food (S).
Syndicated Publications: TV Week (S).
Delivery Methods: Mail`Newsstand`Carrier`Racks
Areas Served - City/County or Portion Thereof, or Zip codes: Delaware County
Own Printing Facility?: Y
Commercial printers?: Y
Sat. Circulation Paid: 15638
Sun. Circulation Paid: 18889
Audit By: AAM
Audit Date: 30.09.2018
Personnel: Cheryl Lindus (Gen. Mgr./Adv. Dir.); Danyel Decker (Classified Sales Rep.); Josie James (Legal Adv. Clerk); Tammy Reese (Classified Supervisor); Jane Jakubiak (HR Coord./Exec. Asst.); Heather Ault (Marketing Coord.); Phil Beebe (Online Ed.); Greg Fallon (Managing Ed.); Chris Simons (Copy Ed.); Cortney Felton (Account Mgr.); Mark Sheridan (Retail Adv. Mgr.); Robin Webb (Adv. Sales Exec.); Mary Vannatta (Key Acct. Exec.); Jeff Ward (Community Conversation Ed.); Kathy Scott (Night News Ed.)
Parent company (for newspapers): Gannett

THE TIMES OF NORTHWEST INDIANA

Street address 1: 601 45th St
Street address city: Munster
Street address state: IN
Zip/Postal code: 46321-2875
County: Lake
Country: USA
Mailing address: 601 45TH AVE
Mailing city: MUNSTER
Mailing state: IN
Mailing zip: 46321-2819
General Phone: (219) 933-3200
Advertising Phone: (219) 852-3035
Editorial Phone: (219) 933-3223
General/National Adv. E-mail: roxanne.olejnik@nwi.com
Display Adv. E-mail: eric.horon@nwi.com
Classified Adv. e-mail: classified@nwi.com
Editorial e-mail: joe.hosey@nwi.com
Primary Website: www.nwi.com
Mthly Avg Views: 30658687
Mthly Avg Unique Visitors: 1411129
Year Established: 1906
News Services: AP, CNS
Special Editions: Christmas Gift Guide (Nov/Dec); Best of the Region (May); NWI Now (February/March)
Special Weekly Sections: A & E (Thursday); Forum (Sunday); Food (Wednesday); Homes (Saturday)
Syndicated Publications: BusINess (2x/yr); Color Comics (Sunday); Get Healthy (12x/yr); Medical Guide (September)
Delivery Methods: Mail`Newsstand`Carrier`Racks
Areas Served - City/County or Portion Thereof, or Zip codes: Lake and Porter County in Indiana, mainly; however, we also deliver to LaPorte, Newton, and Jasper counties
Own Printing Facility?: Y
Commercial printers?: Y
Avg Free Circ: 1513
Sat. Circulation Paid: 23786
Sat. Circulation Free: 1594
Sun. Circulation Paid: 31608
Sun. Circulation Free: 10051
Audit By: AAM
Audit Date: 31.03.2019
Personnel: Chris White (Pub.); Eric Horon (Adv. Ops. Mgr.); Joe Battistoni (Gen. Mgr.); Jim Pellegrini (Mktg. Mgr.); Roxanne Olejnik (Advertising Sales Manager); Joseph Hosey (Executive Editor); Marc Chase (Local News Ed.); Mina Nicholas (Human Resource Generalist); Tom Schager (President); Crista Zivanovic (News Ed.); Kristina Martin (Director of Distribution); Funk Lindsey (Regional Finance Director); Opat Daniel (Production Director); Tom Ambrosetti; Chris Mallonee (Dig. Oper. Mgr.); Lisa Vosburg (Reg. HR. Generalist); Scott Kitner (Reg. Circ. Dir.); John Gregorio (Adv. Dir.)
Parent company (for newspapers): Lee Enterprises, Incorporated

TRIBUNE

Street address 1: 318 Pearl St
Street address 2: Ste 100
Street address city: New Albany
Street address state: IN
Zip/Postal code: 47150-3450
County: Floyd
Country: USA
Mailing state: IN
General Phone: (812) 944-6481
Advertising Phone: (812) 206-2133
Editorial Phone: (812) 206-2130
General/National Adv. E-mail: duke.freeman@newsandtribune.com
Display Adv. E-mail: mary.tuttle@newsandtribune.com
Classified Adv. e-mail: classifieds@newsandtribune.com
Editorial e-mail: shea.vanhoy@newsandtribune.com
Primary Website: www.newsandtribune.com
Year Established: 1851
News Services: AP.
Special Editions: Bridal Guide, Medical Directory, Worship Guide, Life Planning, Visitors/Relocation Guide (Jan, Feb, Mar); Southern Indiana Progress, Spring Home & Garden (Apr, May, Jun); Art Walk Guide, Back to School, HS Football Preview, Clark County Readers' Choice, Harvest Homecoming Guide, GCCS NAFC School Directory (Jul, Aug, Sept); Floyd County Readers' Choice, Boys and Girls Basketball, Letters to Santa, Power of Pink (Oct, Nov, Dec)
Special Weekly Sections: TV Weekly (Sat).
Syndicated Publications: Color Comics (S).
Areas Served - City/County or Portion Thereof, or Zip codes: Clark, Floyd County
Sun. Circulation Paid: 9854
Audit By: Sworn/Estimate/Non-Audited
Audit Date: 12.07.2019
Personnel: Chris Morris (Asst. Ed.); Bill Hanson (Pub.); Janice Ashby (Business Mgr.); Mike Massek (Circ. Mgr.); Greg Mengelt (Sports Ed.); Mary Tuttle (Adv. Mgr.); Jason Thomas (Asst. Ed.); Stephen Allen (Prod. Mgr.); Susan Duncan (Ed.)
Parent company (for newspapers): CNHI, LLC

THE COURIER-TIMES

Street address 1: 201 S 14th St
Street address city: New Castle
Street address state: IN
Zip/Postal code: 47362-3328
County: Henry
Country: USA
Mailing address: 201 S 14TH ST
Mailing city: NEW CASTLE
Mailing state: IN
Mailing zip: 47362-3328
General Phone: (765) 529-1111
Advertising Phone: (765) 575-4634
Editorial Phone: (765) 575-4651
General/National Adv. E-mail: information@thecouriertimes.com
Display Adv. E-mail: information@thecouriertimes.com
Classified Adv. e-mail: information@thecouriertimes.com
Editorial e-mail: information@thecouriertimes.com
Primary Website: www.thecouriertimes.com
Year Established: 1841
News Services: AP.
Special Editions: Hope (good news) Edition, (Feb); Agriculture (March) Car Care (Mar); Graduation Tab (May); Football (Aug) Basketball (Nov); Her magazine (Quarterly March, June, Sept. Dec), Bargain Buddy coupon mag (monthly)
Special Weekly Sections: Neighbors (society) Sunday
Delivery Methods: Mail`Newsstand`Carrier`Racks
Areas Served - City/County or Portion Thereof, or Zip codes: Henry County
Own Printing Facility?: N
Commercial printers?: Y
Sun. Circulation Paid: 4500
Audit By: Sworn/Estimate/Non-Audited
Audit Date: 12.07.2019
Personnel: Donna Cronk (Neighbors Ed.); Bob Hansen (Pub.); Hope Stevens (Customer Service Specialist); Shaun Adkins (Home Delivery Mgr.); Jayson Nunn (Adv. Sales. Exec.); Katie Clontz (Editor); Belinda Wise (Adv. Sales Exec.); Stacie Wrightsman (Adv. Dir.)
Parent company (for newspapers): Paxton Media Group

THE TIMES

Street address 1: 54 N. 9th St.
Street address city: Noblesville
Street address state: IN
Zip/Postal code: 46060-2261
County: Hamilton
Country: USA
General Phone: (317) 773-9960
General/National Adv. E-mail: ttimmons@thetimes24-7.com
Display Adv. E-mail: ttimmons@thetimes24-7.com
Classified Adv. e-mail: judi@thetimes24-7.com
Editorial e-mail: news@thetimes24-7.com
Primary Website: www.thetimes24-7.com
Mthly Avg Views: 225000
Mthly Avg Unique Visitors: 50000
Year Established: 1904
Special Editions: Readers' Choice (Jan); Home Care (Spring); Car Care (Spring); Valentine's (Feb); Flag Day (Jul); 4-H Fair Preview and Results (Jul); Fall Festival Guide (Fall); Golf Guide; Christmas Gift Guide (Dec); Last-Minute Gift Guide (Dec).
Syndicated Publications: Hamilton County Sports Report
Delivery Methods: Mail`Newsstand`Racks
Areas Served - City/County or Portion Thereof, or Zip codes: 46030, 46031, 46032, 46033, 46034, 46037, 46038, 46060, 46061, 46062, 46069, 46074, 46082, 46085
Own Printing Facility?: N
Commercial printers?: N
Audit By: Sworn/Estimate/Non-Audited
Personnel: Melissa Meme (Advertising Director); Tim Timmons (Pub.); Kevin Thompkins (Managing Editor)
Parent company (for newspapers): Sagamore News Media

PERU TRIBUNE

Street address 1: 26 W 3rd St
Street address city: Peru
Street address state: IN
Zip/Postal code: 46970-2155
County: Miami
Country: USA
Mailing address: 26 W 3RD ST
Mailing city: PERU
Mailing state: IN
Mailing zip: 46970-2155
General Phone: (765) 473-6641
Advertising Phone: (765) 473-6641
Editorial Phone: (765) 473-6641
General/National Adv. E-mail: twest@perutribune.com
Display Adv. E-mail: twest@perutribune.com
Classified Adv. e-mail: classifieds@perutribune.com
Editorial e-mail: ptnews@perutribune.com
Primary Website: www.perutribune.com
Year Established: 1921
News Services: AP.
Special Editions: Business Expo (Apr); This is Miami County (Aug); Christmas Gift Guides (Dec); Girls Basketball (Feb); Soil & Water (Jan); Circus (Jul); Softball Pages (Jun); Spring Farm (Mar); Mother's Day (May); Christmas Opening (Nov); Shopping with Santa (Oct).
Special Weekly Sections: Business Page (Mon); Milestones (Weddings, Engagements) (Sat); Food Page (Thur); School Page (Wed).
Syndicated Publications: Calendar (Annually); Channel Changer (Sat).
Delivery Methods: Mail`Newsstand`Carrier`Racks
Areas Served - City/County or Portion Thereof, or Zip codes: Miami County
Avg Free Circ: 6000
Sat. Circulation Paid: 3600
Sat. Circulation Free: 0
Sun. Circulation Paid: 3600
Sun. Circulation Free: 6000
Audit By: Sworn/Estimate/Non-Audited
Audit Date: 12.07.2019
Personnel: Patricia Nelson (Bus. Mgr.); Misty Sharp (Adv. Dir.); Eric Steg (Circ. Supvr.); Aaron Turner (Mng. Ed.); Laurie Kietaber (News Ed.); Austan Kas (Sports Ed.); Tom Gray (Pub.); Derek Beigh (Ed.)
Parent company (for newspapers): Paxton Media Group

PILOT NEWS

Street address 1: 218 N.Michigan Street
Street address city: Plymouth
Street address state: IN
Zip/Postal code: 46563-2135
County: Marshall
Country: USA
Mailing address: PO BOX 220
Mailing city: PLYMOUTH
Mailing state: IN
Mailing zip: 46563-0220
General Phone: (574) 936-3101
Advertising Phone: (574) 936-3101
Editorial Phone: (574) 936-3101
General/National Adv. E-mail: cstockton@thepilotnews.com
Display Adv. E-mail: cstockton@thepilotnews.com
Classified Adv. e-mail: class@thepilotnews.com
Editorial e-mail: news@thepilotnews.com
Primary Website: www.thepilotnews.com
Year Established: 1851
News Services: AP, SHNS.
Special Weekly Sections: Entertainment; Sports; Pet ; Faces and Places
Delivery Methods: Mail`Newsstand`Carrier`Racks
Areas Served - City/County or Portion Thereof, or Zip codes: Marshall County
Commercial printers?: Y
Sat. Circulation Paid: 4150
Audit By: Sworn/Estimate/Non-Audited

Audit Date: 12.07.2019
Personnel: Greg Hildebrand (Managing Ed.); Michele Louderback (Accounting Mgr.); Cindy Stockton (Adv. Mgr., Mktg.); Jim Master; Rusty Nixon
Parent company (for newspapers): Horizon Publications Inc.; Heritage Publications (2003) Inc.

THE COMMERCIAL REVIEW

Street address 1: 309 W Main St
Street address city: Portland
Street address state: IN
Zip/Postal code: 47371-1803
County: Jay
Country: USA
Mailing address: PO BOX 1049
Mailing city: PORTLAND
Mailing state: IN
Mailing zip: 47371-3149
General Phone: (260) 726-8141
Advertising Phone: (260) 726-8144
General/National Adv. E-mail: news@thecr.com
Display Adv. E-mail: ads@thecr.com
Classified Adv. e-mail: classifieds@thecr.com
Editorial e-mail: news@thecr.com
Primary Website: www.thecr.com
Mthly Avg Views: 30000
Mthly Avg Unique Visitors: 10000
Year Established: 1871
News Services: AP.
Special Editions: Spring Sports (Apr); Engine and Tractor Show (Aug); Christmas Greetings (Dec); New Cars (Feb); Brides (Jan); Senior Citizens (Jun); Spring Home Improvement (Mar); Graduation (May); Harvest (Oct); Fall Home Improvement (Sept); Agriculture (Apr); Summer Festivals (May); Thanksgiving (Nov); Jay County Fair (Jul); Jay County Marching Patriots (July)
Special Weekly Sections: Best Food Days (Wed); Best Auto Day (Thur); Real Estate (Wed); Business (Sat); Church (Thur)
Delivery Methods: Mail`Newsstand`Carrier
Areas Served - City/County or Portion Thereof, or Zip codes: 47371, 47373, 47326, 47336, 47369, 47381
Own Printing Facility?: Y
Commercial printers?: Y
Sat. Circulation Paid: 3384
Audit By: Sworn/Estimate/Non-Audited
Audit Date: 29.09.2022
Personnel: Jeanne Lutz (Adv. Mgr., Promo.); Ray Cooney (Ed.); Jack Ronald (Pub.); Chris Schanz (Sports Ed.); Nathan Rubbelke (Reporter); Caleb Bauer (Reporter)
Parent company (for newspapers): Graphic Printing Co., Inc.

PRINCETON DAILY CLARION

Street address 1: 100 N Gibson St
Street address city: Princeton
Street address state: IN
Zip/Postal code: 47670-1855
County: Gibson
Country: USA
Mailing address: PO BOX 30
Mailing city: PRINCETON
Mailing state: IN
Mailing zip: 47670-0030
General Phone: (812) 385-2525
Advertising Phone: (812) 385-2525
Editorial Phone: (812) 385-2525
General/National Adv. E-mail: news@pdclarion.com
Display Adv. E-mail: admail@pdclarion.com
Classified Adv. e-mail: admail@pdclarion.com
Editorial e-mail: andrea@pdclarion.com
Primary Website: www.tristate-media.com
Mthly Avg Views: 1112422
Mthly Avg Unique Visitors: 173974
Year Established: 1846
News Services: AP.
Special Weekly Sections: Entertainment Page (Fri); Best Food Day (Mon); Business Page (Thur)
Syndicated Publications: Savvy lifestyle; Outdoor News (Hunting & Fishing).
Delivery Methods: Mail`Newsstand`Carrier`Racks
Areas Served - City/County or Portion Thereof, or Zip codes: 47670, 47666, 47640,47648,47649,47665,47660,
Own Printing Facility?: Y
Commercial printers?: Y
Audit By: Sworn/Estimate/Non-Audited
Audit Date: 12.07.2019
Personnel: Jeff Shumacher (Pub.); Andrea Howe (Ed.); Michael Caterina (Presentation Ed.); Pete Swanson (Sports Ed.); Marietta Nelson (Bus. Mgr.); Nancy Wilder (Accounting Mgr.); Lorri Rembe (Admin. Asst.); Maggie Armstrong (Class. Adv. Mgr.); Lori Martin (Adv. Mgr.); Mark Short (Prod. Specialist); Cindy Walton (Prod. Coord.); Rick Simmons (Circl. Mgr.); Joe Vessels (Distribution Mgr.); Amanda Cooper (Circ. Clerk); Jancey Smith (Creative Dept. Mgr.); Chad Phillips (Graphic Designer); Madonna Smith (Graphic Designer); Jason Hembree (Graphic Designer); Ryan Spear (Computer Specialist)
Parent company (for newspapers): Paxton Media Group

RENSSELAER REPUBLICAN

Street address 1: 117 N Van Rensselaer St
Street address city: Rensselaer
Street address state: IN
Zip/Postal code: 47978-2651
County: Jasper
Country: USA
Mailing state: IN
General Phone: (219) 866-5111
Advertising Phone: (219) 866-5111
Editorial Phone: (219) 866-5111
General/National Adv. E-mail: cindy@rensselaerrepublican.com
Display Adv. E-mail: cindy@rensselaerrepublican.com
Classified Adv. e-mail: classifieds@rensselaerrepublican.com
Editorial e-mail: editor@rensselaerrepublican.com
Primary Website: www.myrepublican.info
Year Established: 1866
News Services: AP.
Special Editions: Football Preview (Aug); Spring Bridal (Feb); Business Established (Jan); Progress (Jun); Ag Day (Mar); Auto News (Monthly); Christmas Tab (Nov); Fall Home Improvement (Sept).
Special Weekly Sections: Church Page (Fri); Youth on the Move (Mon); Farm (Sat); Best Food Day (Thur); Business News (Tues); Farm (Wed).
Syndicated Publications: Final Score (Monthly); Farm Focus (Other).
Delivery Methods: Mail`Newsstand`Carrier`Racks
Areas Served - City/County or Portion Thereof, or Zip codes: Jasper County
Sat. Circulation Paid: 2049
Audit By: Sworn/Estimate/Non-Audited
Audit Date: 12.07.2019
Personnel: Robert Blankenship (Pub.); Misty Longstreth (Graphics/Art); Harley Tomlinson (Sports Ed.); Anita Padgett (Adv. Acct. Rep.); Greg Perrotto (Gen. Mgr.); Cyndi Grace (Circ.); Ashley Lawrence (Front Desk/Class.)
Parent company (for newspapers): Community Media Group

PALLADIUM-ITEM

Street address 1: 1175 N. A Street
Street address city: Richmond
Street address state: IN
Zip/Postal code: 47374
County: Wayne
Country: USA
Mailing address: 1175 N A ST
Mailing city: RICHMOND
Mailing state: IN
Mailing zip: 47374-3226
General Phone: (765) 962-1575
Advertising Phone: (765) 973-4422
Editorial Phone: (765) 962-1575
General/National Adv. E-mail: sbrandle@richmond.gannett.com
Display Adv. E-mail: dbutler@richmond.gannett.com
Classified Adv. e-mail: bregister@pal-item.com
Editorial e-mail: bguth@pal-item.com
Primary Website: www.pal-item.com
Year Established: 1831
News Services: AP, GNS.
Special Editions: Progress (Apr); Newcomer's Community Guide (Aug); Bridal (Feb); Farm (Jan); Home Improvement (Jul); Home Improvement (Jun); Racing (May); Home Improvement (Sept).
Special Weekly Sections: Education (Mon); Automotive Sunday (S); Business (Sat); Entertainment (Thur); Farm (Wed).
Syndicated Publications: USA WEEKEND Magazine (S).
Delivery Methods: Mail`Newsstand`Carrier`Racks
Areas Served - City/County or Portion Thereof, or Zip codes: Wayne County
Own Printing Facility?: Y
Commercial printers?: Y
Avg Free Circ: 63
Sat. Circulation Paid: 7943
Sat. Circulation Free: 63
Sun. Circulation Paid: 11749
Sun. Circulation Free: 49
Audit By: AAM
Audit Date: 30.06.2017
Personnel: Barbara Gadd (Accounting Advertising Clerk); Ron Mason (District Mgr.)
Parent company (for newspapers): Gannett

THE ROCHESTER SENTINEL

Street address 1: 118 E 8th St
Street address city: Rochester
Street address state: IN
Zip/Postal code: 46975-1508
County: Fulton
Country: USA
Mailing address: PO BOX 260
Mailing city: ROCHESTER
Mailing state: IN
Mailing zip: 46975-0260
General Phone: (574) 223-2111
Advertising Phone: (574) 224-5323
Editorial Phone: (574) 224-5327
General/National Adv. E-mail: advertising@rochsent.com
Display Adv. E-mail: ads@rochsent.com
Classified Adv. e-mail: classads@rochsent.com
Editorial e-mail: christinas@rochsent.com
Primary Website: www.rochsent.com
Year Established: 1858
News Services: AP, CNS, TMS.
Special Editions: Agriculture (Jan); High School Football (Aug); Year-in-Review (Dec); Basketball (Feb); Taxes (Jan); 4-H Fair (Jul); Home, Lawn, Garden (Mar and Sept); Graduates (May); Christmas Shopping (Nov); Winter Car Care (Oct); Senior Lifestyle (Sept); Round Barn Festival (June); Chili Fest and Car Show (Oct).
Special Weekly Sections: TV Guide (Sat); Church Page.
Syndicated Publications: American Profile; Spry Living
Delivery Methods: Mail`Newsstand`Racks
Areas Served - City/County or Portion Thereof, or Zip codes: 46975, 46939, 46910, 46912, 46931, 46945,46922
Own Printing Facility?: N
Commercial printers?: N
Sat. Circulation Paid: 3800
Audit By: USPS
Audit Date: 01.10.2015
Personnel: Sarah O. Wilson (Pub.); Karen Vojtasek (Adv. Dir.); William S. Wilson (Exec. Ed.); Christina Seiler (Mng. Ed.); Michael Kenny (Photo Dept. Mgr.); Val Tsoutsouris (Sports Ed.)
Parent company (for newspapers): Paxton Media Group

THE TRIBUNE

Street address 1: 100 Saint Louis Ave
Street address city: Seymour
Street address state: IN
Zip/Postal code: 47274-2304
County: Jackson
Country: USA
Mailing address: PO BOX 447
Mailing city: SEYMOUR
Mailing state: IN
Mailing zip: 47274-0447
General Phone: (812) 522-4871
Advertising Phone: (812) 523-7052
Editorial Phone: (812) 523-7051
General/National Adv. E-mail: MBane@TribTown.com
Display Adv. E-mail: BWalters@TribTown.com
Classified Adv. e-mail: cotte@TribTown.com
Editorial e-mail: awoods@hnenewspapers.com
Primary Website: www.tribtown.com
Year Established: 1877
News Services: AP, Freedom Wire, Knight Ridder
Special Editions: Veteran's (Nov); Holidays (Dec)
Delivery Methods: Mail`Newsstand`Carrier`Racks
Areas Served - City/County or Portion Thereof, or Zip codes: Jackson County
Own Printing Facility?: Y
Commercial printers?: N
Sat. Circulation Paid: 8951
Audit By: Sworn/Estimate/Non-Audited
Audit Date: 10.10.2022
Personnel: Chuck Wells (Pub.); Zach Spicer (Sports Ed.); Barb Walters (Adv. Admin.); Tammy Smith (Bus. Mgr.); Aubrey Woods (Ed.); Melissa Bane (Adv. Dir.); Tracie Lane; Paul Hart (Circ. Dir.); Steve Swails (Circulation Director); Dan Davis (Ed.); Robin Sporleder; Joanne Persinger (Commun./Copy Ed.); Michael Brabley (Page Ed.); Anita Emigh (Sales Rep.); Jeremiah McCulley (Sales Rep.); Debbie Felix (Business Office); Gary McDonough (Ops. Mgr.)
Parent company (for newspapers): AIM Media Midwest

THE SHELBYVILLE NEWS

Street address 1: 123 E Washington St
Street address city: Shelbyville
Street address state: IN
Zip/Postal code: 46176-1463
County: Shelby
Country: USA
Mailing address: 123 E WASHINGTON ST
Mailing city: SHELBYVILLE
Mailing state: IN
Mailing zip: 46176-1477
General Phone: (317) 398-6631
Advertising Phone: (317) 398-1264
Editorial Phone: (317) 398-1270
General/National Adv. E-mail: rhonda@shelbynews.com
Display Adv. E-mail: rhonda@shelbynews.com
Classified Adv. e-mail: rhonda@shelbynews.com
Editorial e-mail: pgable@shelbynews.com
Primary Website: www.shelbynews.com
Year Established: 1947
News Services: AP Graphics, MCT, NEA, SHNS, AP.
Special Editions: Then & Now (Jul); Shelby County Fair (Jun); Class of 2013 (May); Home & Garden (Apr); Santa Letters and Coloring Book (Dec); Girls Sectional Preview (Feb); Health & Fitness (Jan); Back-to-School (Jul); Car Care (May); Holiday Gift Guide (Nov); Home Improvement (Oct); Shelby County Profiles (Sept).
Syndicated Publications: USA WEEKEND Magazine (Sat).
Delivery Methods: Mail`Newsstand`Carrier`Racks
Areas Served - City/County or Portion Thereof, or Zip codes: Shelby County
Sat. Circulation Paid: 8315
Audit By: Sworn/Estimate/Non-Audited
Audit Date: 12.07.2019
Personnel: Rachael Raney (Pub.); Jeff Brown (Sports Ed.); Kim Haggard (Customer Service Rep.); Paul Gable (Ed.); Rhonda Schwegman (Adv. Dir.); Melissa Smith (Adv. Acct. Exec.); Ashly Spurlock (Adv. Acct. Exec.); Jack Hutcheson (Circ. Dir.); Anna Tungate (Single Copy Mgr.)
Parent company (for newspapers): Paxton Media Group

SOUTH BEND TRIBUNE

Street address 1: 225 West Colfax Avenue
Street address city: South Bend
Street address state: IN
Zip/Postal code: 46626
County: St Joseph
Country: USA
Mailing address: 225 W COLFAX AVE
Mailing city: SOUTH BEND
Mailing state: IN
Mailing zip: 46626-1001
General Phone: (574) 235-6222
Advertising Phone: (574) 235-6221
Editorial Phone: (574) 235-6161
General/National Adv. E-mail: jherum@sbtinfo.com
Display Adv. E-mail: jherum@sbtinfo.com
Classified Adv. e-mail: classifieds@sbtinfo.com
Editorial e-mail: letters@sbtinfo.com
Primary Website: www.southbendtribune.com
Year Established: 1872
News Services: AP, SHNS, PR Newswire.
Special Editions: ND Insider (Fri)
Special Weekly Sections: Faith (Fri); Food Focus (Mon); Automotion (S); Farming (Sat); Family (Tues); Our Health (Wed).
Syndicated Publications: TV Magazine (S).
Delivery Methods: Mail`Newsstand`Carrier
Areas Served - City/County or Portion Thereof, or Zip codes: St. Joseph County, Cass, Lagrange, Elkhart, Marshall, Fulton, Pulaski, Starke, LaPorte, Berrien, Kosclusko
Avg Free Circ: 572
Sat. Circulation Paid: 36120
Sat. Circulation Free: 335
Sun. Circulation Paid: 43640
Sun. Circulation Free: 339
Audit By: AAM
Audit Date: 31.03.2018

Personnel: Kevin Shaw (VP, Operations); Alan Achkar (Exec. Ed.); Peggy Bassier (Local Adv. Agr.); Mary Zenor (Classified, Adv. Mgr.); Jennifer Ellis (INTHEBEND.COM Ed.); Ed Henry (HR BUSINESS PARTNER); Sally Brown (Sr. VP., Gen. Mgr.); Carol Shultz (Controller); Shelley Chakan (VP, Adv.)
Parent company (for newspapers): Gannett; CherryRoad Media

SPENCER EVENING WORLD

Street address 1: 114 E Franklin St
Street address city: Spencer
Street address state: IN
Zip/Postal code: 47460-1818
County: Owen
Country: USA
Mailing address: PO Box 226
Mailing city: Spencer
Mailing state: IN
Mailing zip: 47460-0226
General Phone: (812) 829-2255
General/National Adv. E-mail: kim@spencereveningworld.com
Display Adv. E-mail: editor@spencereveningworld.com
Classified Adv. e-mail: editor@spencereveningworld.com
Editorial e-mail: editor@spencereveningworld.com
Primary Website: www.spencereveningworld.com
Year Established: 1927
Delivery Methods: Mail`Newsstand`Carrier`Racks
Areas Served - City/County or Portion Thereof, or Zip codes: Owen County
Own Printing Facility?: Y
Commercial printers?: Y
Audit By: Sworn/Estimate/Non-Audited
Audit Date: 12.07.2019
Parent company (for newspapers): Spencer Evening World Publishing, Inc.

THE SULLIVAN DAILY TIMES

Street address 1: 115 W Jackson St
Street address city: Sullivan
Street address state: IN
Zip/Postal code: 47882-1505
County: Sullivan
Country: USA
Mailing address: PO BOX 130
Mailing city: SULLIVAN
Mailing state: IN
Mailing zip: 47882-0130
General Phone: (812) 268-6356
Advertising Phone: (812) 268-6356
Editorial Phone: (812) 268-6356
General/National Adv. E-mail: ads.sdt@gmail.com
Display Adv. E-mail: ads2.sdt@gmail.com
Classified Adv. e-mail: sdt.classifieds@gmail.com
Editorial e-mail: editor.sdt@gmail.com
Primary Website: www.sullivan-times.com
Year Established: 1854
News Services: AP.
Special Editions: Bridal (Jan); SWCD Report (Feb); Spring Home & Garden (Mar); Spring Car Care (Apr); Graduation (May); 4-H Fair Preview (Jul); Corn Festival Preview (Sept); Christmas Shopping (Nov); Letters to Santa (Dec)
Special Weekly Sections: Religion (Fri); Agriculture (Mon); Nostalgia (Thur); Business (Tues); Opinion (Wed).
Syndicated Publications: Senior (Citizen) Informant (Monthly); TV Times (Thur).
Delivery Methods: Newsstand`Carrier`Racks
Areas Served - City/County or Portion Thereof, or Zip codes: Sullivan County
Audit By: Sworn/Estimate/Non-Audited
Audit Date: 12.07.2019
Personnel: Patricia Morgan (Bus. Mgr.); Aaron Kennedy (Sports Ed.); Jamie Isbell (Classifieds); Sarah Smith (Adv. Rep.); Gillian Kelk (Adv. Rep.); Doug Smith (Graphic Artist/Composing); Darcy O'Dell (Circ., Local Happenings); Andrew Krull (Ed.); Gillan Kelk (Pub.)
Parent company (for newspapers): Pierce Publishing, Inc.; Kelk Publishing

THE TRIBUNE STAR

Street address 1: 222 S 7th St
Street address city: Terre Haute
Street address state: IN
Zip/Postal code: 47807-3601
County: Vigo
Country: USA
Mailing address: 222 S 7TH ST
Mailing city: TERRE HAUTE
Mailing state: IN
Mailing zip: 47807-3601
General Phone: (812) 231-4200
Advertising Phone: (812) 231-4226
Editorial Phone: (812) 231-4336
General/National Adv. E-mail: erin.powell@tribstar.com
Display Adv. E-mail: erin.powell@tribstar.com
Classified Adv. e-mail: amanda.davis@tribstar.com
Editorial e-mail: max.jones@tribstar.com
Primary Website: www.tribstar.com
Mthly Avg Views: 819702
Mthly Avg Unique Visitors: 183276
Year Established: 1983
News Services: AP, MCT.
Special Weekly Sections: Entertainment (Fri); Best Food Day (Mon); Religion (Sat); Education (Wed).
Syndicated Publications: Terre Haute Living (Bi-Monthly); Valley Homes Tab (Fri); Parade (S).
Delivery Methods: Mail`Newsstand`Carrier`Racks
Areas Served - City/County or Portion Thereof, or Zip codes: Vigo, Clay, Sullivan, Greene, Parke, and Vermillion in Indiana and Edgar, Clark, and Crawford in Illinois.
Own Printing Facility?: Y
Commercial printers?: Y
Avg Free Circ: 1512
Sat. Circulation Paid: 13827
Sat. Circulation Free: 1512
Sun. Circulation Paid: 17338
Sun. Circulation Free: 353
Audit By: AAM
Audit Date: 31.03.2016
Personnel: B.J. Riley (Pub.); Robert Miller (Adv. Dir.); Courtney Zellars (Mktg. Dir.); Kyle Poorman (Circ. Mgr., Single Copy); Max Jones (Ed.); Mark Bennett (Columnist); Susan Duncan (News Ed.); Sheila K. Ter Meer (Online Ed.); Todd Golden (Sports Ed.); Brian Lane (Prod. Dir.); Alicia Morgan (News/Digital Ed.); Joseph Garza (Chief Photographer); Erin Powell (Adv. Dir.); Amy Francis (Marketing Mgr.); Dianne Hadley (Marketing Mgr.); Nikki Robinson (Adv. Sales Exec.); Lynn Smith (Adv. Sales Exec.); Mike Sullivan (Adv. Sales Exec.); Courtney Zellers (Adv. Sales Exec.); Michelle Poorman (Customer Service Mgr.); Tad Wesley (District Mgr.); Vicki Woodcock (Credit Mgr.); Tony Sciotto (Prod. Mgr.); Jerry Bringle (Controller); Mark McGranahan (District Mgr.)
Parent company (for newspapers): CNHI, LLC; CNHI, LLC

TIPTON COUNTY TRIBUNE

Street address 1: 116 S Main St
Street address 2: Ste A
Street address city: Tipton
Street address state: IN
Zip/Postal code: 46072-1864
County: Tipton
Country: USA
Mailing address: PO BOX 248
Mailing city: TIPTON
Mailing state: IN
Mailing zip: 46072-0248
General Phone: (765) 675-2115
Advertising Phone: (765) 675-2115
Editorial Phone: (765) 675-2115
General/National Adv. E-mail: tiptontribune@elwoodpublishing.com
Display Adv. E-mail: tiptoneditor@elwoodpublishing.com
Classified Adv. e-mail: tiptoneditor@elwoodpublishing.com
Editorial e-mail: tiptoneditor@elwoodpublishing.com
Primary Website: www.elwoodpublishing.com
Year Established: 1825
News Services: AP.
Special Editions: Farm & Garden (Apr); Football Preview (Aug); Mature Years (Jan); Mature Years (Jul); Spring Brides (Mar); Spring Home Improvement (May); Christmas Opening (Nov); Fall Home Improvement (Oct).
Syndicated Publications: Kid's Scoop (Other).
Delivery Methods: Mail`Newsstand`Carrier`Racks
Areas Served - City/County or Portion Thereof, or Zip codes: 46072, 46076, 46036, 46047, 46068
Sat. Circulation Paid: 2816
Audit By: Sworn/Estimate/Non-Audited
Audit Date: 12.07.2019
Personnel: Robert L. Nash (Pub.); Jackie Henry (Managing Ed.); Michelle Garmon (Sports Ed.); Randy Bayne (Prod. Mgr.); Jack Barnes (Pres.); Tammy Boyer (Circ. Mgr.); Lori Nash (Adv. Mgr.)
Parent company (for newspapers): Barnes Newspapers, Inc.; Ray Barnes Newspapers, Inc.

VINCENNES SUN-COMMERCIAL

Street address 1: 702 Main St
Street address city: Vincennes
Street address state: IN
Zip/Postal code: 47591-2910
County: Knox
Country: USA
Mailing address: PO BOX 396
Mailing city: VINCENNES
Mailing state: IN
Mailing zip: 47591-0396
General Phone: (812) 886-9955
General/National Adv. E-mail: retail@suncommercial.com
Display Adv. E-mail: retail@suncommercial.com
Classified Adv. e-mail: classified@suncommercial.com
Editorial e-mail: grobbins@suncommercial.com
Primary Website: www.suncommercial.com
Year Established: 1804
News Services: AP.
Special Editions: Bridal Planner (Jan.) Farm Review (Feb) Spring Home & Garden (March) Dining Guide (April, August) Knox County Fair (July) Vincennes University Campus guide (Aug.) Readers Choice (Aug.) Progress (Oct.) Christmas Gift Guide (Nov.)
Special Weekly Sections: TV Guide (Sunday) Wabash Valley NOW (Wed)
Syndicated Publications: Spry, American Profile, USA Weekend, Antholon
Delivery Methods: Mail`Newsstand`Carrier`Racks
Areas Served - City/County or Portion Thereof, or Zip codes: Vincennes, IN/Knox County, IN/Lawrence County, IL
Own Printing Facility?: N
Commercial printers?: Y
Sat. Circulation Paid: 4867
Sun. Circulation Paid: 5387
Audit By: Sworn/Estimate/Non-Audited
Audit Date: 12.07.2019
Personnel: Gayle Robbins (Pub.); Kim Gordon (Adv. Dir.); Veronica Gordon (Acct. Exec.); Tom Graham (Sports); Rodney Lopez (Sports); David Adkins (Dis. Mgr.); Jess Cohen (Reporter)
Parent company (for newspapers): Paxton Media Group

WABASH PLAIN DEALER

Street address 1: 123 W Canal St
Street address city: Wabash
Street address state: IN
Zip/Postal code: 46992-3042
County: Wabash
Country: USA
Mailing address: 123 W CANAL ST
Mailing city: WABASH
Mailing state: IN
Mailing zip: 46992-3042
General Phone: 260.563.2131
Advertising Phone: (260) 225-4949
Editorial Phone: (260) 225-4602
General/National Adv. E-mail: kgretschmann@wabashplaindealer.com
Display Adv. E-mail: kgretschmann@wabashplaindealer.com
Classified Adv. e-mail: csmith@wabashplaindealer.com
Editorial e-mail: news@wabashplaindealer.com
Primary Website: www.wabashplaindealer.com
Mthly Avg Views: 99660
Year Established: 1859
News Services: AP
Special Editions: Spring Home Improvement (Mar); Valentine's Day (Feb); Spring Working the Land (Mar); Wabash County 4-H Fair (Jul); Bridal Guide (Feb); Fall Home Improvement (Sept); Fall Working the Land (Sept); Reader's Choice (May)
Special Weekly Sections: Entertainment (Tue), North Manchester (Wed), Food (Thu), Worship (Fri), Business and Milestones (Sun)
Delivery Methods: Mail`Newsstand`Carrier`Racks
Areas Served - City/County or Portion Thereof, or Zip codes: LaFontaine, Lagro, North Manchester, Roann, Urbana, Wabash, Somerset
Own Printing Facility?: Y
Commercial printers?: Y
Sun. Circulation Paid: 3000
Audit By: Sworn/Estimate/Non-Audited
Audit Date: 12.07.2019
Personnel: Kelly Gretschmann (General Sales Manager); Cindy Brown (Advertising Account Executive); Eric Seaman (Managing Editor); Christy Smith (Customer Service Rep/Legals Clerk); Makenzie Holland (Reporter); Mackenzi Klemann (Reporter); Jacob Rude (Sports Editor)
Parent company (for newspapers): Paxton Media Group

TIMES-UNION

Street address 1: P.O. Box 1448
Street address 2: Corner Market and Indiana St
Street address city: Warsaw
Street address state: IN
Zip/Postal code: 46581
County: Kosciusko
Country: USA
Mailing address: PO BOX 1448
Mailing city: WARSAW
Mailing state: IN
Mailing zip: 46581-1448
General Phone: (574) 267-3111
Advertising Phone: (574) 267-3111
Editorial Phone: (574) 267-3111
General/National Adv. E-mail: advertising@timesuniononline.com
Display Adv. E-mail: advertising@timesuniononline.com
Classified Adv. e-mail: classified@timesuniononline.com
Editorial e-mail: news@timesuniononline.com
Primary Website: www.timesuniononline.com
Mthly Avg Views: 237765
Mthly Avg Unique Visitors: 58786
Year Established: 1854
News Services: AP, AP Laserphoto, MCT, NEA, SHNS.
Special Editions: Home Improvement (Apr); Holiday Wrap-Up (Dec); Girls' Sectional Preview (Feb); Halftimes (Jan); Customer Appreciation Week (Jul); Holiday Gift Guide (Nov); Home Improvement (Sept).
Special Weekly Sections: Business (Sat); Home & Auto (Sat) Education Pages (Tue) Leisure (Thur); Farm Page (Wed).
Delivery Methods: Mail`Newsstand`Carrier`Racks
Areas Served - City/County or Portion Thereof, or Zip codes: 46502, 46508, 46510, 46524, 46538, 46539, 46542, 46555, 46562, 46566, 46567, 46580, 46581, 46582, 46590, 46982
Own Printing Facility?: Y
Commercial printers?: N
Avg Free Circ: 315
Sat. Circulation Paid: 6133
Sat. Circulation Free: 421
Audit By: AAM
Audit Date: 30.06.2018
Personnel: Gary Gerard (Gen. Mgr.); Laura Sowers (Classified Supervisor); David Hays (IT Dir./Circ. Mgr.); Gary Kunkle (Prod. Dir.); Jessica Rodriguez (Comptroller); Paul Smith (Advertising Manager)
Parent company (for newspapers): Times-Union

THE NEWS-GAZETTE

Street address 1: 224 W Franklin St
Street address city: Winchester
Street address state: IN
Zip/Postal code: 47394-1808
County: Randolph
Country: USA
Mailing address: PO BOX 429
Mailing city: WINCHESTER
Mailing state: IN
Mailing zip: 47394-0429
General Phone: (765) 584-4501
Advertising Phone: (765) 584-4501
Editorial Phone: (765) 584-4501
Display Adv. E-mail: ngadvertising@comcast.net
Classified Adv. e-mail: ngadvertising@comcast.net
Editorial e-mail: ngeditor@comcast.net
Primary Website: www.winchesternewsgazette.com
Year Established: 1873
News Services: AP.
Special Weekly Sections: Church (Fri); Farm (Sat); Business Salute (Tues).
Syndicated Publications: American Profile (Weekly).
Delivery Methods: Mail`Newsstand`Carrier`Racks
Areas Served - City/County or Portion Thereof, or Zip codes: Randolph County
Own Printing Facility?: Y

Commercial printers?: Y
Sat. Circulation Paid: 3700
Audit By: Sworn/Estimate/Non-Audited
Audit Date: 12.07.2019
Personnel: Diane Jackson (Circ. Mgr.); Lesa Hawkins (Prod. Mgr.); Rick Reed (Mng. Ed./Sports Ed.); Bill Richmond (City Ed.); Dale Byrd (Press Room Mgr.)
Parent company (for newspapers): Community Media Group

IOWA

AMES TRIBUNE

Street address 1: 317 5th St
Street address city: Ames
Street address state: IA
Zip/Postal code: 50010-6101
County: Story
Country: USA
Mailing address: PO BOX 380
Mailing city: AMES
Mailing state: IA
Mailing zip: 50010-0380
General Phone: (515) 232-2160
Advertising Phone: (515) 663-6947
Editorial Phone: (515) 663-6917
General/National Adv. E-mail: knelson@amestrib.com
Display Adv. E-mail: jgreving@amestrib.com
Classified Adv. e-mail: classifieds@amestrib.com
Editorial e-mail: mcrumb@amestrib.com
Primary Website: www.amestrib.com
Mthly Avg Views: 495000
Mthly Avg Unique Visitors: 93938
Year Established: 1868
News Services: AP, CNS, NYT, TMS, Washington Post Bloomberg
Special Editions: Game Day; University (May and Aug); Facets (Monthly); Ames Business Monthly (Monthly); Green Together (Quarterly).
Special Weekly Sections: Art and Culture plus TV (Sunday); Ames Out Loud (Thur); Taste(Wed) Business (Sunday); Life and Leisure (Saturday);
Syndicated Publications: Art & Culture Plus TV (S); Ames Out Loud (Thur); Taste(Wed); Business (S); Life & Leisure (Sat).
Delivery Methods: Mail`Newsstand`Carrier`Racks
Areas Served - City/County or Portion Thereof, or Zip codes: 50010, 50011, 50014, 50105, 50075, 50130, 50230, 50231, 50236, 50248, 50278, 50056, 50154, 50161, 50201, 50036, 50124, 50134, 50244, 50046, 50055
Own Printing Facility?: Y
Commercial printers?: N
Avg Free Circ: 5
Sat. Circulation Paid: 6387
Sat. Circulation Free: 19
Sun. Circulation Paid: 6510
Sun. Circulation Free: 1504
Audit By: VAC
Audit Date: 30.09.2016
Personnel: Scott Anderson (Pub.); Michael Crumb (Ed.); Travis Hines (Sports Ed.); Phillip Grothus (Production Mgr.); Becky Bjork (Adv. Dir.); Michael Lynch (Ops. Dir.); Shannon Andersen (HR/Accounting Coordinator); Randy Terwilliger (Circ. Dir.); Jon Hilario (Circ. Coordinator); Faith Rau (CSR)
Parent company (for newspapers): Gannett; CherryRoad Media

ATLANTIC NEWS TELEGRAPH

Street address 1: 410 Walnut St
Street address city: Atlantic
Street address state: IA
Zip/Postal code: 50022-1365
County: Cass
Country: USA
Mailing address: PO BOX 230
Mailing city: ATLANTIC
Mailing state: IA
Mailing zip: 50022-0230
General Phone: (712) 243-2624
Advertising Phone: (712) 243-2624
Editorial Phone: (712) 243-2624
General/National Adv. E-mail: ant@ant-news.com
Display Adv. E-mail: ant@ant-news.com
Classified Adv. e-mail: ant@ant-news.com
Editorial e-mail: jrlund@ant-news.com
Primary Website: www.atlanticnewstelegraph.com
Year Established: 1871
News Services: AP.
Special Editions: Beauty/Cosmetology (Annually); Wedding (Jun); Wedding (Jan); Graduation (May); Real Estate (Monthly); Health (Quarterly).
Special Weekly Sections: Entertainment (Thur); Shopper (Tues)
Syndicated Publications: Atlantic Farm (Monthly); American Profile (Weekly).
Delivery Methods: Mail`Carrier
Areas Served - City/County or Portion Thereof, or Zip codes: Southwest Iowa
Sat. Circulation Paid: 2800
Audit By: Sworn/Estimate/Non-Audited
Audit Date: 12.07.2019
Personnel: Jeff Lundquist (Pub./Gen Mgr.); Deb Baker (Circ. Dir.); Mike Ruddy (Adv. Mgr.); Nate Tenopir (Sports Ed.)
Parent company (for newspapers): Community Media Group

THE HAWK EYE

Street address 1: 800 S Main St
Street address city: Burlington
Street address state: IA
Zip/Postal code: 52601-5870
County: Des Moines
Country: USA
Mailing address: PO Box 10
Mailing city: Burlington
Mailing state: IA
Mailing zip: 52601-5870
General Phone: (319) 754-8461
Advertising Phone: (319) 758-8130
Editorial Phone: (319) 754-8461
General/National Adv. E-mail: cconrad@thehawkeye.com
Display Adv. E-mail: lengler@thehawkeye.com
Classified Adv. e-mail: classifieds@thehawkeye.com
Editorial e-mail: dalison@thehawkeye.com
Primary Website: www.thehawkeye.com
Year Established: 1833
News Services: AP.
Special Editions: Homeless Shelter Open House (Jul); The Downtowner (Jun); WasteWrap Summer 2013 (Jun); Progress (Feb); Progress (Mar); Guide to Hawk Eye Land (May).
Special Weekly Sections: Education (Mon); Mutual Funds & Stocks (S); Religion (Sat); Entertainment (Thur); Health (Tues); Best Food Day (Wed).
Syndicated Publications: Relish (Monthly); TV Section (S); Home Magazine (Sat); American Profile (Weekly).
Delivery Methods: Mail`Carrier`Racks
Areas Served - City/County or Portion Thereof, or Zip codes: 52601, 52655, 52565, 52620, 52627, 61425, 62330, 52624, 52625, 52626, 52632, 52637, 61450, 61454, 52637, 52638, 52639, 52640, 52641, 52645, 52646, 52648, 52649, 52627, 52650, 52657, 61480, 52656, 52658, 52659, 52660
Own Printing Facility?: Y
Commercial printers?: Y
Avg Free Circ: 0
Sat. Circulation Paid: 15247
Sat. Circulation Free: 0
Sun. Circulation Paid: 16105
Sun. Circulation Free: 0
Audit By: VAC
Audit Date: 30.09.2015
Personnel: Sean Lewis (Gen. Mgr. & Adv. Dir.); Steven Deggendorf (Pressroom/Packaging Mgr.); John Gaines (Mng. Ed.); John Bohnenkamp (Sports Ed.); Craig Neises (Features Ed.)
Parent company (for newspapers): CherryRoad Media; Gannett

CARROLL DAILY TIMES HERALD

Street address 1: 508 N Court St
Street address city: Carroll
Street address state: IA
Zip/Postal code: 51401-2747
County: Carroll
Country: USA
Mailing address: PO BOX 546
Mailing city: CARROLL
Mailing state: IA
Mailing zip: 51401-0546
General Phone: (712) 792-3573
Advertising Phone: (712) 792-3575 ext. 26
Editorial Phone: (712) 792-3573
General/National Adv. E-mail: m.jensen@carrollspaper.com
Display Adv. E-mail: t.burns@carrollspaper.com
Classified Adv. e-mail: j.rohe@carrollspaper.com
Editorial e-mail: newspaper@carrollspaper.com
Primary Website: www.carrollspaper.com
Year Established: 1868
News Services: AP.
Special Editions: Chamber (Other).
Syndicated Publications: TV Magazine (Fri); American Profile (Weekly).
Delivery Methods: Mail`Carrier
Audit By: Sworn/Estimate/Non-Audited
Audit Date: 12.07.2019
Personnel: Ann Wilson (Gen Mgr.); Tom Burns (Adv. Mgr., Retail); Daniel Haberl (Circ. Mgr.); Larry Devine (News Ed.); Douglas Burns (Co-owner/Online Ed.); Brett Christie (Sports Ed.); Tim Bohling (Prodn. Foreman, Press); Marty Ball (Asst. Sports Ed.)
Parent company (for newspapers): Wilson Family

THE GAZETTE

Street address 1: 501 2nd Ave SE
Street address city: Cedar Rapids
Street address state: IA
Zip/Postal code: 52401-1303
County: Linn
Country: USA
Mailing address: PO BOX 511
Mailing city: CEDAR RAPIDS
Mailing state: IA
Mailing zip: 52406-0511
General Phone: (319) 398-8333
Advertising Phone: (319) 398-8222
Editorial Phone: (319) 398-8313
General/National Adv. E-mail: advertise@gazcomm.com
Display Adv. E-mail: advertise@sourcemedia.net
Classified Adv. e-mail: classifieds@sourcemedia.net
Editorial e-mail: editorial@thegazette.com
Primary Website: www.thegazette.com
Mthly Avg Views: 1071630
Mthly Avg Unique Visitors: 196502
Year Established: 1883
News Services: AP, LAT-WP, MCT.
Special Editions: College/Pro & Prep Football Guide (Aug); New Baby News (Feb); Stocks & Business Review (Jan); Freedom Festival Guide (Jun); Spring Car Care (Mar); Explore (May); College Guide (Sept).
Special Weekly Sections: Community (Mon-Wed); Hoopla, Arts, Entertainment, Food (Thur); House, Decorations, Living, Religion, People, Places (Fri); TV, Health (Sat); Home, Farm, Finance, Real Estate, Books, Wedding, Engagements (Sun)
Syndicated Publications: Dash(Monthly); Parade (S);
Delivery Methods: Mail`Newsstand`Carrier`Racks
Areas Served - City/County or Portion Thereof, or Zip codes: Eastern Iowa
Own Printing Facility?: Y
Commercial printers?: Y
Avg Free Circ: 3127
Sat. Circulation Paid: 37345
Sat. Circulation Free: 2900
Sun. Circulation Paid: 39068
Sun. Circulation Free: 2763
Audit By: AAM
Audit Date: 30.06.2018
Personnel: Joe Hladky (Chrmn.); Chuck Peters (CEO/Pres.); Ken Slaughter (Vice Pres./Treasurer); Lyle Muller (Editor); Dave Rasdal (Columnist); Jeff Tecklenburg (Opinion Page Ed.); Tim McDougall (Publisher); Steve Lorenz (Product Director); Annette Schulte (Managing Editor); Todd Dorman (Columnist); Jennifer Hemmingsen (Columnist); Dave Storey (Pub./Vice Pres./Gen. Mgr., Gazette Communications); Elizabeth T. Barry (Sec.); Jeff Wolff (Dir., Market Research/Adv. Servs.); Ted Fries (Circ. Systems Admin.); Steve Buttry (Ed.); Tim Banse (Automotive Columnist); Mike Deupree (Columnist); Diana Nolen (Community Ed.); George Ford; Mary Sharp (Iowa Ed.); Kathy Alter (Online Ed.); Orlan Love (Outdoors Writer); Rollin Banderob (Picture Ed.); Chris Edwards (VP, Adv.); Elizabeth Schott
Parent company (for newspapers): The Gazette Company

AD-EXPRESS & DAILY IOWEGIAN

Street address 1: 201 N 13th St
Street address city: Centerville
Street address state: IA
Zip/Postal code: 52544-1748
County: Appanoose
Country: USA
Mailing address: PO BOX 610
Mailing city: CENTERVILLE
Mailing state: IA
Mailing zip: 52544-0610
General Phone: (641) 856-6336
Advertising Phone: (641) 856-6336
Editorial Phone: (641) 856-6336
General/National Adv. E-mail: cmbriggs@dailyiowegian.com
Display Adv. E-mail: bmaxwell@dailyiowegian.com
Classified Adv. e-mail: sselix@dailyiowegian.com
Editorial e-mail: kocker@dailyiowegian.com
Primary Website: www.dailyiowegian.com
Year Established: 1864
News Services: AP.
Special Editions: Farm (Apr); Progress (Feb); Outdoor Recreation (Jun); Fall-Winter Sports Tab (Nov); Farm (Oct); Fall-Winter Sports Tab (Sept).
Syndicated Publications: Relish (Monthly); American Profile (Weekly).
Delivery Methods: Mail`Newsstand`Carrier
Areas Served - City/County or Portion Thereof, or Zip codes: Appanoose and Wayne County
Own Printing Facility?: N
Commercial printers?: N
Audit By: Sworn/Estimate/Non-Audited
Audit Date: 12.07.2019
Personnel: Ron Gutierrez (Circ. Mgr.); Kristal Fowler (Society Ed.); Cindy Briggs (Bus. Mgr.); Kyle Ocker (Editor)
Parent company (for newspapers): CNHI, LLC; CNHI, LLC

CLINTON HERALD

Street address 1: 221 6th Ave S
Street address city: Clinton
Street address state: IA
Zip/Postal code: 52732-4305
County: Clinton
Country: USA
Mailing address: PO BOX 2961
Mailing city: CLINTON
Mailing state: IA
Mailing zip: 52733-2961
General Phone: (563) 242-7101
Advertising Phone: (563) 242-7142 ext. 141
Editorial Phone: (563) 242-7142 ext. 155
General/National Adv. E-mail: shanelle@clintonherald.com
Display Adv. E-mail: rgutierrez@cnhi.com
Classified Adv. e-mail: senright@clintonherald.com
Editorial e-mail: cbielema@clintonherald.com
Primary Website: www.clintonherald.com
Mthly Avg Views: 450000
Mthly Avg Unique Visitors: 95000
Year Established: 1855
News Services: AP.
Special Editions: Car Care (Apr); Wedding (Jan); Progress (Mar); Beef (May); Pre-Christmas (Nov); Car Care (Oct).
Special Weekly Sections: Church Page (Sat); Best Food Day (Tue).
Syndicated Publications: Parade Magazine (Sat); TV Tab (Mon); American Profile (Weekly).
Delivery Methods: Mail`Newsstand`Carrier`Racks
Areas Served - City/County or Portion Thereof, or Zip codes: Clinton and Camanche, Iowa Fulton,IL
Own Printing Facility?: N
Commercial printers?: Y
Sat. Circulation Paid: 6590
Audit By: Sworn/Estimate/Non-Audited
Audit Date: 12.07.2019
Personnel: Ron Gutierrez (Pub.); Sherri Enright (Adv. Mgr., Classified); Charlene Bielema (Ed.)
Parent company (for newspapers): CNHI, LLC; CNHI, LLC

THE DAILY NONPAREIL

Street address 1: 300 W Broadway
Street address 2: Ste 108
Street address city: Council Bluffs
Street address state: IA
Zip/Postal code: 51503
County: Pottawattamie
Country: USA
General Phone: (712) 328-1811
Advertising Phone: (712) 328-1811 option 5
Editorial Phone: (712) 325-5728
General/National Adv. E-mail: circulation@nonpareilonline.com

Display Adv. E-mail: advertising@nonpareilonline.com
Classified Adv. e-mail: classifieds@nonpareilonline.com
Editorial e-mail: news@nonpareilonline.com
Primary Website: www.nonpareilonline.com
Mthly Avg Views: 842900
Mthly Avg Unique Visitors: 124900
Year Established: 1849
News Services: AP.
Special Editions: Reader's Choice, Living in the Bluffs, College & Careers, Puzzle Book
Special Weekly Sections: Art & Faith (Fri)
Delivery Methods: Mail`Carrier
Areas Served - City/County or Portion Thereof, or Zip codes: Southwestern Iowa and outlying communities
Own Printing Facility?: Y
Commercial printers?: Y
Avg Free Circ: 30
Sat. Circulation Paid: 7094
Sat. Circulation Free: 726
Sun. Circulation Paid: 7486
Sun. Circulation Free: 345
Audit By: AAM
Audit Date: 30.06.2020
Personnel: Thomas Schmitt (Pub.); Melissa Vanek (Circ. Mgr.); Courtney Brummer-Clark (Mng. Ed.); Rachel George (Managing Editor); Krystal Sidzyik (Digital Ed.); Jessica Boucher (Inside Sales Manager); Tony Digilio (Local Retail Sales Manager); Pat Donohue (Special Sections Ed.); Jeannette Johnson (HR); Scott Carr (Vice President of Sales)
Parent company (for newspapers): BH Media Group; Lee Enterprises, Incorporated

CRESTON NEWS ADVERTISER

Street address 1: 503 W Adams St
Street address city: Creston
Street address state: IA
Zip/Postal code: 50801-3112
County: Union
Country: USA
Mailing address: PO BOX 126
Mailing city: CRESTON
Mailing state: IA
Mailing zip: 50801-0126
General Phone: (641) 782-2141
Advertising Phone: (641) 782-2141
Editorial Phone: (641) 782-2141
General/National Adv. E-mail: advertising@crestonnews.com
Display Adv. E-mail: cmittag@crestonnews.com
Classified Adv. e-mail: classified@crestonnews.com
Editorial e-mail: sfinley@crestonnews.com
Primary Website: www.crestonnewsadvertiser.com
Mthly Avg Views: 200000
Mthly Avg Unique Visitors: 30000
Year Established: 1879
News Services: AP.
Special Editions: Car Care (Apr); Wedding (Jan); Progress (Mar); Beef (May); Pre-Christmas (Nov); Car Care (Oct). Ag Mag, Living Sections
Special Weekly Sections: People (Tues); Farm & Business (Wed); Community, The Entertainer Channel Guide (Fri); TV & Entertainment (Fri); Church Page (Thur); Best Food Day (Tues); Farm Page (Wed)
Syndicated Publications: American Profile (Fri); Relish (Monthly).
Delivery Methods: Mail`Newsstand`Carrier`Racks
Areas Served - City/County or Portion Thereof, or Zip codes: Adair, Madison, Adams, Union, Clarke, Taylor, and Ringgold
Own Printing Facility?: Y
Commercial printers?: Y
Audit By: Sworn/Estimate/Non-Audited
Audit Date: 12.07.2019
Personnel: Rose Henry (Office Mgr.); Craig Mittag (Adv. Mgr.); Kevin Lindley (Prodn. Mgr.); Sandy Allison (Circ. Mgr.); Mark Spensley (Pub.); Scott Vicker (Mng., Ed.); Kelsey Haugen (Associate Ed.); Ryan Kronberg (Sports Ed.); Kaleb Carter (Sports Reporter)
Parent company (for newspapers): Shaw Media

QUAD-CITY TIMES

Street address 1: 500 E 3rd St
Street address city: Davenport
Street address state: IA
Zip/Postal code: 52801-1708
County: Scott
Country: USA
Mailing address: PO BOX 3828
Mailing city: DAVENPORT
Mailing state: IA
Mailing zip: 52808-3828
General Phone: (563) 383-2200
Advertising Phone: (563) 383-2483
Editorial Phone: (563) 383-2264
General/National Adv. E-mail: dmcallister@qctimes.com
Display Adv. E-mail: dmcallister@qctimes.com
Classified Adv. e-mail: qctimes@qctimes.com
Editorial e-mail: newsroom@qctimes.com
Primary Website: www.qctimes.com
Year Established: 1848
News Services: AP, CNA, Associations, Inc..
Special Editions: Answer Book (Other); Spring Fashion (Spring); Summer Fun (Summer).
Special Weekly Sections: Home & Garden, Celebrate (Sun); Best Food (Wed);
Syndicated Publications: Relish (Monthly); Parade (S).
Delivery Methods: Mail`Newsstand`Carrier`Racks
Areas Served - City/County or Portion Thereof, or Zip codes: Davenport, Bettendorf, Moline, Rock Island and the Quad Cities Area of Iowa and Illinois
Own Printing Facility?: Y
Commercial printers?: Y
Sat. Circulation Paid: 20225
Sun. Circulation Paid: 33921
Audit By: AAM
Audit Date: 31.03.2018
Personnel: Deborah Anselm (Pub.); Debbie McAllister (Nat'l Adv. Coord.); Autumn Phillips (Ed.); Mark Mosbrucker (Ops. Mgr.); Dan Bowerman (Asst. Managing Ed.); Brett Riley (Dir. Audience Development); Andrew Wall (Reg. Dir. HR); David Zorich (Controller); Jon Alexander (Editorial Page Ed.); Deborah Brasier (Bus. Ed.); Adam Soebbing (Sports Ed.); Ann Boyd (Adv. Sales Dir.); Jennifer Carter (Adv. Sales Mgr.); Jessica Daack (Adv. Sales Mgr); Jennifer Johnston (Exec. Admin. Asst.)
Parent company (for newspapers): Lee Enterprises, Incorporated

DENISON BULLETIN & REVIEW

Street address 1: 1410 Broadway
Street address city: Denison
Street address state: IA
Zip/Postal code: 51442-2053
County: Crawford
Country: USA
Mailing address: PO BOX 550
Mailing city: DENISON
Mailing state: IA
Mailing zip: 51442-0550
General Phone: (712) 263-2122
Advertising Phone: (712) 263-2122
Editorial Phone: (712) 263-2122
General/National Adv. E-mail: lori.wehle@bulletinreview.com
Display Adv. E-mail: lori.wehle@bulletinreview.com
Classified Adv. e-mail: eileen.mullin@bulletinreview.com
Editorial e-mail: gordon.wolf@bulletinreview.com
Primary Website: www.dbrnews.com
Year Established: 1867
Delivery Methods: Mail`Carrier
Areas Served - City/County or Portion Thereof, or Zip codes: Woodbury, Ida, Sac, Calhoun, Mohona, Crawford, Carroll, Greene, Harrison, Shelby, Audubon, Guthrie, Pottawattamie, Cass, and Adair
Own Printing Facility?: Y
Commercial printers?: N
Avg Free Circ: 37500
Audit By: Sworn/Estimate/Non-Audited
Audit Date: 12.07.2019
Personnel: Greg Wehle (Pub.); Jolene Stoelk (Circ. Mgr.); Gordon Wolf (Ed.); Bonnie Hill (Prodn. Mgr.); Todd Banner (Sports Ed.); Lori Wehle (Adv. Sales Rep.); Cathy Jacoby (Office Mgr.); Angele Boehm (Bookkeeper)
Parent company (for newspapers): Lee Enterprises, Incorporated; Tampa Media Group

THE DES MOINES REGISTER

Street address 1: 400 Locust St
Street address 2: Ste 500
Street address city: Des Moines
Street address state: IA
Zip/Postal code: 50309-2355
County: Polk
Country: USA
Mailing address: 400 LOCUST ST STE 500
Mailing city: DES MOINES
Mailing state: IA
Mailing zip: 50309-2355
General Phone: (515) 284-8000
Advertising Phone: (515) 284-8043
Editorial Phone: (515) 284-8201
General/National Adv. E-mail: mwurzer@registermedia.com
Display Adv. E-mail: mwurzer@registermedia.com
Classified Adv. e-mail: classifieds@dmreg.com
Editorial e-mail: letters@news.dmreg.com
Primary Website: www.desmoinesregister.com
Mthly Avg Views: 6957000
Mthly Avg Unique Visitors: 750000
Year Established: 1915
News Services: AP, LAT-WP, MCT, NYT, GNS, Bloomberg.
Special Editions: Fall Auto Preview (October), Spring Auto Preview (March), Vacation Iowa (May), Ultimate Guide to Des Moines (June), State Fair (August), College Guide (Sept), Top Workplaces Guide (Sept).
Special Weekly Sections: Business, Career (Mon); Community, Best Food (Tue); Young Reader (Wed); Datebook, Community (Thur); Marketplace, Real Estate, Community (Fri); Home, Garden, Auto (Sat); Main, Iowa Life, Business, Farm, TV, Travel, Opinion (Sun)
Syndicated Publications: USA WEEKEND Magazine (S).
Delivery Methods: Newsstand`Carrier`Racks
Areas Served - City/County or Portion Thereof, or Zip codes: Des Moines and Central Iowa
Own Printing Facility?: Y
Commercial printers?: Y
Sat. Circulation Paid: 67286
Sun. Circulation Paid: 104394
Audit By: AAM
Audit Date: 30.06.2018
Personnel: Julie Shaw (Gen. Mgr.); Julie Harvey (VP, Finance); Kevin Johnson (GM, Production Ops.); Phil Legler (VP, Info. Tech.); Orton Preikschat (Sr. Distribution Dir.); Mark Wurzer (VP, Adv.); Lynn Hicks (Engagement/Opinion Ed.); Kelli Brown (Sr. News Dir. Digital); Andrea Crowley (Comm. Content Specialist-Juice); Carol Hunter (Int. Exec. Ed.); Chad Leistikow (Univ. of Iowa Reporter); Mike Trautmann (Content Strategist); David Chivers (Pub. & Pres.); Lisa Rossi (Storytelling Coach); Jason Noble (Chief Political Reporter)
Parent company (for newspapers): Gannett

TELEGRAPH HERALD

Street address 1: 801 Bluff Street
Street address city: Dubuque
Street address state: IA
Zip/Postal code: 52004-0688
County: Dubuque
Country: USA
Mailing address: PO BOX 688
Mailing city: DUBUQUE
Mailing state: IA
Mailing zip: 52004-0688
General Phone: (563) 588-5611
Advertising Phone: (563) 588-5680
Editorial Phone: (563) 588-5663
General/National Adv. E-mail: mike.fortman@wcinet.com
Display Adv. E-mail: Luke.rodham@thmedia.com
Classified Adv. e-mail: tricia.nelson@thmedia.com
Editorial e-mail: amy.gilligan@thmedia.com
Primary Website: www.thonline.com
Year Established: 1836
News Services: AP, MCT.
Special Editions: Her Magazine; Senior Living (monthly) Home Builders Show (Feb); Super Jobs Sunday (varies); Healthy Lifestyle (Mar); Outdoor Living (Apr); Family Time (Apr); Dubuque Gives (Apr); Those We Remember (May); Gallery of Grads (May); Mother's Day (May); Honoring Tri-State Heroes (May); Flag Page (June); Breast Cancer Awareness (Oct); Vacationland (May, Sept.), GoFindMyHome real estate magazine (Monthly).
Special Weekly Sections: Health, Fitness (Mon); Biz Buzz, Around the House, Family, Nostalgia, Images, Fashion (Tue); Food, Auto (Wed); Arts, Entertainment, NASCAR, Alternative Teen (Thur); Arts, Entertainment, TV (Fri); Religion, Youth (Sat); Travel, Business, Technology, Agriculture, Home/Garden, Lifestyle, Family, Music (Sun)
Syndicated Publications:
Delivery Methods: Mail`Newsstand`Carrier`Racks
Own Printing Facility?: N
Commercial printers?: N
Avg Free Circ: 1440
Sat. Circulation Paid: 18349
Sat. Circulation Free: 2642
Sun. Circulation Paid: 22491
Sun. Circulation Free: 1767
Personnel: Monty Gilles (News Ed.); Gary Dura (Copy Ed.); Dave Kettering (Photo Mgr.); Brian Cooper (Editorial Page Ed.); Jim Leitner (Sports Ed.); Jim Swenson (Features Ed.); Luke Rodham (Adv. Sales Suprv.); Mike Fortman (Group Dir. of Adv.); Amy Gilligan (Mng. Dir.); Matt Connolly (Interactive Media/ Database Director); Jamie Bahl (Natl./Rgl. Acct. Rep.); Bob Woodward (Vice-President - Woodward Community Media Publisher, TH Media); Sara Cluff (Marketing Manager); Annette Johnson (Audience Development Manager); Cindi Olson (Clas. Dir.); Steve Fisher (Pub.)
Parent company (for newspapers): Woodward Communications, Inc.

THE FAIRFIELD LEDGER

Street address 1: 112 E Broadway Ave
Street address city: Fairfield
Street address state: IA
Zip/Postal code: 52556-3202
County: Jefferson
Country: USA
Mailing address: PO BOX 110
Mailing city: FAIRFIELD
Mailing state: IA
Mailing zip: 52556-0002
General Phone: (641) 472-4129
Advertising Phone: (641) 472-4130
Editorial Phone: (641) 472-2116
General/National Adv. E-mail: adv@ffledger.com
Display Adv. E-mail: adv@ffledger.com
Classified Adv. e-mail: classifieds@ffledger.com
Editorial e-mail: news@ffledger.com
Primary Website: www.ffledger.com
Year Established: 1849
News Services: AP.
Special Editions: Senior Lifestyles (June); Home Improvement (Apr); Back-to-School (Aug); Bridal (Feb); Fairfield InfoGuide (Jan); Progress (Jul); Conservation (Mar); Beef Month (May); Pork Month (Oct); Women in Business (Oct); Draw an Ad (Feb); Health (Dec)
Special Weekly Sections: Religion (Fri); Business (Mon); Opinion (Thurs)
Syndicated Publications: Relish; Spry; American Profile (Weekly).
Delivery Methods: Mail`Newsstand`Carrier`Racks
Areas Served - City/County or Portion Thereof, or Zip codes: Fairfield and Jefferson County
Own Printing Facility?: Y
Commercial printers?: Y
Audit By: Sworn/Estimate/Non-Audited
Audit Date: 12.07.2019
Personnel: Melanie Imhoff (Office Mgr.); Janice Shaw (Circ. Mgr.); Vicki Tillis (News Ed.); Sherry Jipp (Retail ad manager); Leann Nolte (ad sales); Beth Ruckman (Prodn. Mgr.); Amy Sparby (Publisher); Andy Hallman (Editor); Diane Vance (Reporter)
Parent company (for newspapers): The Gazette Company; Cedar Rapids Press

THE MESSENGER

Street address 1: 713 Central Ave
Street address city: Fort Dodge
Street address state: IA
Zip/Postal code: 50501-3813
County: Webster
Country: USA
Mailing address: PO BOX 659
Mailing city: FORT DODGE
Mailing state: IA
Mailing zip: 50501-0659
General Phone: (515) 573-2141
Advertising Phone: (515) 573-2141 ext. 416
Editorial Phone: (515) 573-2141 ext. 458
General/National Adv. E-mail: cbargfrede@messengernews.net
Display Adv. E-mail: cbargfrede@messengernews.net
Classified Adv. e-mail: jeanwarg@messengernews.net
Editorial e-mail: bshea@messengernews.net
Primary Website: www.messengernews.net
Mthly Avg Views: 815134
Mthly Avg Unique Visitors: 66264
Year Established: 1856
News Services: AP
Special Editions: Bridal Guide (Jan); Progress Edition (Feb); Crime Prevention (Feb); Home & Garden Show (Mar); Golf Directory (Apr); Visitors Guide (May); Hometown Pride (June); Wedding Planner (July); Little League (July); Girls Sate Softball Tournament (July); Football Preview (Aug); All About Home (Sept); Winter

Sports (Nov); Holiday Showcase (Dec); Sunday Value Pack (Monthly); Senior's Tab (Monthly); Business Review (Monthly); Real Estate Buyer's Guide (Monthly), Fort Dodge Today Magazine (monthly)
Special Weekly Sections: Education Page (Mon); Business (S); Religion (Sat); Best Food Day (Wed); Select TV (S)
Syndicated Publications: Parade (S)
Delivery Methods: Mail`Newsstand`Carrier`Racks
Areas Served - City/County or Portion Thereof, or Zip codes: 50501-50599, 50246, 50249, 51449, 50132, 50040, 51453
Own Printing Facility?: Y
Commercial printers?: N
Avg Free Circ: 328
Sat. Circulation Paid: 7898
Sat. Circulation Free: 328
Sun. Circulation Paid: 9639
Sun. Circulation Free: 294
Audit By: AAM
Audit Date: 31.03.2019
Personnel: Terry Christensen (Publisher); Jean Warg (Adv. Mgr., Class.); Grant Gibbons (Circ. Dir.); Terry Dwyer (Editorial Page Ed.); Krissan Nelson (Farm Ed.); Michelle Colshan (Prodn Sup); Eric Pratt (Sports Ed.); Rex Lee (Data Processing Mgr.); Regina Suhrbier (Multi-Media Sales Manager); Cory Bargfrede (Adv. Dir.); Bill Shea (City Editor); Melissa Wendland (Office Manager); Jane Curtis (Editor)
Parent company (for newspapers): Ogden Newspapers Inc.

FORT MADISON DAILY DEMOCRAT

Street address 1: 1226 Avenue H
Street address city: Fort Madison
Street address state: IA
Zip/Postal code: 52627-4544
County: Lee
Country: USA
Mailing address: PO BOX 160
Mailing city: FORT MADISON
Mailing state: IA
Mailing zip: 52627-0160
General Phone: (319) 372-6421
Advertising Phone: (319) 372-6421 ext. 234
Editorial Phone: (319) 372-6421
General/National Adv. E-mail: advertising@dailydem.com
Display Adv. E-mail: lvandenberg@dailydem.com
Classified Adv. e-mail: classified@dailydem.com
Editorial e-mail: editor@dailydem.com
Primary Website: www.dailydem.com
Mthly Avg Views: 334485
Mthly Avg Unique Visitors: 47360
Year Established: 1868
News Services: AP.
Special Editions: MV Living (Jan); Business Profiles (Feb); Dinner Theatre (Apr); Small Business Salute (May); Outdoor Adventures (Apr); Tri-State Rodeo (Aug); Bridal Planner (Jan); Fair Outdoor Adventures (Jul); Summer Outdoor Adventures (Jun); Dinner Guide (Sept); Healthy New You (Dec.); Last Minute Gift Guide (Dec).
Special Weekly Sections: Religion (Fri); Weekend Sports Wrap-Up (Mon); Entertainment (Thur); Farm Page (Tues); Business Page (Wed).
Syndicated Publications: American Profile (Mon).
Delivery Methods: Mail`Newsstand`Carrier`Racks
Areas Served - City/County or Portion Thereof, or Zip codes: Fort Madison, West Point, Donnellson, Montrose, Denmark, Wever, Farmington, Dallas City, Nauvoo, and Niota
Own Printing Facility?: Y
Commercial printers?: Y
Audit By: Sworn/Estimate/Non-Audited
Audit Date: 12.07.2019
Personnel: Mary Older (Bus. Mgr.); Robin Delaney (Mng. Ed.); Chris Faulkner (Sports Ed.); Jeff Hunt (Reporter); Lee Vandenberg (Ad. Dir.); Chuck Vandenberg (Pub.)
Parent company (for newspapers): Community Media Group

IOWA CITY PRESS-CITIZEN

Street address 1: 123 N. Linn Street, Suite 2E
Street address 2: Ste 2E
Street address city: Iowa City
Street address state: IA
Zip/Postal code: 52245-2147
County: Johnson
Country: USA
Mailing address: PO BOX 2480
Mailing city: IOWA CITY
Mailing state: IA
Mailing zip: 52244-2480
General Phone: (319) 337-3181
Advertising Phone: (319) 337-3181
Editorial Phone: (319) 337-3181
General/National Adv. E-mail: advertising@press-citizen.com
Display Adv. E-mail: advertising@press-citizen.com
Classified Adv. e-mail: classifieds@press-citizen.com
Editorial e-mail: newsroom@press-citizen.com
Primary Website: www.press-citizen.com
Year Established: 1920
News Services: AP, GNS
Special Editions: Key (Aug); Holiday Guide (Dec); Best of Area (Nov)
Special Weekly Sections: Taste (Wednesdays), Go - entertainment (Thursdays)
Delivery Methods: Mail`Newsstand`Carrier`Racks
Areas Served - City/County or Portion Thereof, or Zip codes: Johnson County, Iowa
Own Printing Facility?: N
Commercial printers?: N
Avg Free Circ: 207
Sat. Circulation Paid: 7378
Sat. Circulation Free: 22
Sun. Circulation Paid: 488
Audit By: AAM
Audit Date: 31.03.2019
Personnel: Tory Brecht (Ed.); Michael Vitti (Sales Manager); Zach Berg (Reporter); Aimee Breaux (Reporter); Hillary Ojeda (Reporter); Dargan Southard (Reporter)
Parent company (for newspapers): Gannett

DAILY GATE CITY

Street address 1: 1016 Main St
Street address city: Keokuk
Street address state: IA
Zip/Postal code: 52632-4656
County: Lee
Country: USA
Mailing address: PO BOX 430
Mailing city: KEOKUK
Mailing state: IA
Mailing zip: 52632-0430
General Phone: (319) 524-8300
Advertising Phone: (319) 524-8300
Editorial Phone: (319) 524-8300
General/National Adv. E-mail: admanager@dailygate.com
Display Adv. E-mail: advertising@dailygate.com
Classified Adv. e-mail: classified@dailygate.com
Editorial e-mail: dgceditor@dailygate.com
Primary Website: www.dailygate.com
Year Established: 1847
News Services: AP.
Special Editions: Clark County Pride 2013 (Jun); Senior Lifestyles 2013 (Apr); Lawn & Garden (Apr); Labor Day (Aug); Chronology (Dec); Progress (Feb); Bridal (Jan); Estate (Jun); Spring Car Care (Mar); Newcomers & Vacation (May); Winter Sports (Nov); Woman (Oct); Fall Home Improvement (Sept).
Syndicated Publications: TV Magazine (Fri); American Profile (Weekly).
Delivery Methods: Mail`Newsstand`Carrier`Racks
Areas Served - City/County or Portion Thereof, or Zip codes: Fort Madison, West Point, Donnellson, Montrose, Denmark, Wever, Farmington, Dallas City, Nauvoo, and Niota
Own Printing Facility?: Y
Commercial printers?: Y
Audit By: Sworn/Estimate/Non-Audited
Audit Date: 12.07.2019
Personnel: Steve Dunn (Mng. Ed.); Cindy Iutzi (Mng. Ed.); Amy Morgan (Ad. Mgr.); Deana Young (Circ.); Chuck Vandenberg (Pub.); Megan McNeill (Staff Writer)
Parent company (for newspapers): Community Media Group

LE MARS DAILY SENTINEL

Street address 1: 41 1st Ave NE
Street address city: Le Mars
Street address state: IA
Zip/Postal code: 51031-3535
County: Plymouth
Country: USA
Mailing address: 41 1ST AVE NE
Mailing city: LE MARS
Mailing state: IA
Mailing zip: 51031-3535
General Phone: (712) 546-7031
Advertising Phone: (712) 546-7031 ext. 21
Editorial Phone: (712) 546-7031 ext. 15
General/National Adv. E-mail: dcopenhaver@lemarssentinel.com
Display Adv. E-mail: pgrant@lemarssentinel.com
Classified Adv. e-mail: mjost@lemarssentinel.com
Editorial e-mail: dseditor@frontiernet.net
Primary Website: www.lemarssentinel.com
Year Established: 1870
News Services: AP.
Special Editions: Visitor's Guide (Apr); Back-to-School (Aug); Holiday (Dec); Pride in Plymouth Co. (Feb); Bridal (Jan); County Fair (Jul); Summer Sports (Jun); Homes n' Style (Mar); Grad Tab (May); Homes n' Style (Sept).
Special Weekly Sections: NASCAR (Fri); Agriculture (Thur); Cooking (Tues);
Syndicated Publications: Relish (Monthly); American Profile (Weekly). Athlon Sports (Monthly)
Delivery Methods: Mail`Carrier`Racks
Areas Served - City/County or Portion Thereof, or Zip codes: 51031, 51001, 51024, 1028, 51038, 51045, 51050, 51101-51008
Own Printing Facility?: Y
Commercial printers?: Y
Audit By: Sworn/Estimate/Non-Audited
Audit Date: 12.07.2019
Personnel: Randy List (Pub.); Joanne Glamm (Editor); Monte Jost (Mktg. Dir.); Beverly Van Buskirk (Lifestyles Ed.); Judy Barnable (Data Processing Mgr.); Shannon Jost (Account manager-Advertising); Magdalene Landegent (Contributing Editor); Amy Erickson (Staff Writer); Jay Bell (Sports Editor)
Parent company (for newspapers): Rust Communications

TIMES-REPUBLICAN

Street address 1: 135 W Main St
Street address city: Marshalltown
Street address state: IA
Zip/Postal code: 50158-5843
County: Marshall
Country: USA
Mailing address: PO Box 1300
Mailing city: Marshalltown
Mailing state: IA
Mailing zip: 50158-1300
General Phone: (641) 753-6611
General/National Adv. E-mail: tradv@timesrepublican.com
Display Adv. E-mail: tradv@timesrepublican.com
Classified Adv. e-mail: trclass@timesrepublican.com
Editorial e-mail: news@timesrepublican.com
Primary Website: www.timesrepublican.com
Year Established: 1856
News Services: AP.
Special Editions: Seniors Tab (Apr); Football Contest (Aug); Holiday Greetings (Dec); Agri-Business (Feb); Bridal Tab (Jan); Little League Review (Jul); Outdoors (Jun); Home Improvement (Mar); Health Tab (May); Business Magazine (Monthly); Christmas Countdown (Nov).
Special Weekly Sections: Business/Financial (Daily); Best Food Day (Wed); Auto, Entertainment (Thur); Real Estate, Religion (Sat)
Syndicated Publications: Parade (S).
Delivery Methods: Mail`Newsstand`Carrier`Racks
Areas Served - City/County or Portion Thereof, or Zip codes: 50005; 50051; 50056; 50078; 50106; 50112; 50120; 50122; 50141; 50142; 50148; 50158; 50163; 50173; 50234; 50239; 50247; 50258; 50269; 50278; 50609; 50621; 50627; 50632; 50635; 50637; 50638; 50680; 52339; 52342
Own Printing Facility?: Y
Commercial printers?: Y
Avg Free Circ: 156
Sat. Circulation Paid: 6523
Sat. Circulation Free: 156
Sun. Circulation Paid: 6715
Sun. Circulation Free: 160
Audit By: AAM
Audit Date: 30.06.2017
Personnel: Emily Barske (News Ed.); Stephanie Bowers (Copy Ed.); Kathy Beane (Asst. Copy Ed.); Mike Donahey (Reporter); Adam Sodders (Reporter); Sara Jordan-Heintz (IT Dir.); Ross Thede (Sports Ed.); Thorn Compton (Asst. Sports Ed.); Deanna Davis McGowan (Adv./Mar. Dir.); Colleen Ward (Accounting/Office Manager); Clayton Steil (Prod. Mgr.); Steven Plain (Creative Services Dir.); Abigail Pelzer (Pub.)
Parent company (for newspapers): Ogden Newspapers Inc.

GLOBE GAZETTE, MASON CITY

Street address 1: 300 N Washington Ave
Street address city: Mason City
Street address state: IA
Zip/Postal code: 50401-3222
County: Cerro Gordo
Country: USA
Mailing address: PO BOX 271
Mailing city: MASON CITY
Mailing state: IA
Mailing zip: 50402-0271
General Phone: (641) 421-0500
Advertising Phone: (641) 421-0546
Editorial Phone: (641) 421-0524
General/National Adv. E-mail: rose.walker@globegazette.com
Display Adv. E-mail: greg.wilderman@globegazette.com
Classified Adv. e-mail: olivia.stalker@globegazette.com
Editorial e-mail: howard.query@globegazette.com
Primary Website: www.globegazette.com
Year Established: 1862
News Services: AP.
Special Editions: Lawn & Garden (May); North Iowa Farmer (Monthly); High School Winter Sports (Nov); Builder's Tour (Apr); Fall Fashion Show (Aug); Gifts (Dec); All About Love (Feb); Health & Fitness (Jan); Economic Report (Jul); Grilling Made Easy (Jun); Do It Yourself (Mar).
Special Weekly Sections: Style, Business, Celebrations, TV (Sun); Taste (Tue); Health, Fitness (Wed); Entertainment (Thur); Home, Garden (Fri); Faith, Outdoor (Sat); Travel (1st Sunday)
Syndicated Publications: Relish (Monthly); Parade (S); American Profile (Weekly).
Delivery Methods: Mail`Newsstand`Carrier`Racks
Areas Served - City/County or Portion Thereof, or Zip codes: 50421, 50423, 50424, 50616, 50428, 50436, 50438, 50441, 50446, 50447, 50448, 50452, 50401, 50457, 50458, 50459, 50461, 50464, 50467, 50470, 50472, 50475, 50477, 50479, 50511, 50605, 50625
Own Printing Facility?: Y
Commercial printers?: Y
Avg Free Circ: 1101
Sat. Circulation Paid: 7341
Sat. Circulation Free: 1101
Sun. Circulation Paid: 8935
Sun. Circulation Free: 906
Audit By: AAM
Audit Date: 31.03.2019
Personnel: Linda Halfman (Financial Mgr.); Amy Stoeffler (Adv. Mgr., Classified); Greg Wilderman (Adv. Mgr., Display); Ruth Miller (Mktg. Mgr.); Jeff Binstock (Circ. Mgr.); Joe Buttweiler (Ed.); Jane Reynolds (City Ed.); Bob Steenson (Editorial Page Ed.); Tom Thomas (Editorial Page Ed.); Judy Delperdang (Librarian); Karen Jacobs (Lifestyle Ed.); Olivia Ostrander (Online Ed.); Jan Horgen (Reporter); Kirk Hard Castle (Sports Ed.); Terry Balek (Data Processing Mgr.); Lisa Ahrens (Prodn. Supvr., Pre Press); Rob Curly (Prodn. Supvr., Pressroom); Rose Walker (Nat'l Adv. Rep.); Roy Biondi (Pub.)
Parent company (for newspapers): Lee Enterprises, Incorporated

MT. PLEASANT NEWS

Street address 1: 215 W Monroe St
Street address city: Mount Pleasant
Street address state: IA
Zip/Postal code: 52641-2110
County: Henry
Country: USA
Mailing address: PO BOX 240
Mailing city: MOUNT PLEASANT
Mailing state: IA
Mailing zip: 52641-0240
General Phone: 319-385-3131
Advertising Phone: (319) 385-3131
Editorial Phone: (319) 986-5186
General/National Adv. E-mail: adv@mpnews.net
Display Adv. E-mail: adv@mpnews.net
Classified Adv. e-mail: adv@mpnews.net
Editorial e-mail: news@mpnews.net
Primary Website: www.mpnews.net
Year Established: 1878
News Services: AP.

Special Editions: Home Improvement (Apr); Senior Citizen (Aug); Basketball (Dec); Brides (Jan); Fair (Jul); Little League/Softball (Jun); Agriculture (Mar); Summer Fun (May); Christmas Showcase (Nov); Chamber of Commerce (Oct); Senior Lifestyle (Sept).
Special Weekly Sections: Entertainment (Fri); Business (Mon); Education (Thur); Agriculture (Tues); Editorial Page (Wed).
Syndicated Publications: American Profile (Mon).
Delivery Methods: Mail`Newsstand`Carrier`Racks
Areas Served - City/County or Portion Thereof, or Zip codes: Mt. Pleasant and Henry County
Own Printing Facility?: N
Commercial printers?: N
Audit By: Sworn/Estimate/Non-Audited
Audit Date: 12.07.2019
Personnel: Matt Bryant (Publisher); Brooks Taylor (News Editor); Kaci Lundsford (Advertising Manager); Bill Gray (Editor & Publisher)
Parent company (for newspapers): Cedar Rapids Press; Folience

MUSCATINE JOURNAL

Street address 1: 301 E 3rd St
Street address city: Muscatine
Street address state: IA
Zip/Postal code: 52761-4116
County: Muscatine
Country: USA
Mailing address: 301 E 3RD ST
Mailing city: MUSCATINE
Mailing state: IA
Mailing zip: 52761-4191
General Phone: (563) 262-0550
Advertising Phone: (563) 262-0543
Editorial Phone: (563) 262-0532
General/National Adv. E-mail: jweikert@muscatinejournal.com
Display Adv. E-mail: sales@muscatinejournal.com
Classified Adv. e-mail: becky.gray@muscatinejournal.com
Editorial e-mail: rusty.schrader@muscatinejournal.com
Primary Website: www.muscatinejournal.com
Mthly Avg Views: 1076000
Mthly Avg Unique Visitors: 102691
Year Established: 1840
News Services: AP, DF, TMS.
Special Editions: Best of Muscatine 2012 (Nov); Muscatine Journal Graduation 2013 (May); Spring Car Care (Apr); Back-to-School (Aug); Gift Guide (Dec); Answer Book (Jul); Little League (Jun); Gift Guide (Nov); Car Care (Oct); Find it in Muscatine (Sept).
Special Weekly Sections: Sports (Mon); Best Food Day (Tue); Outdoor (Tue); Family, Friends, Real Estate (Wed); Health, Lifestyles (Thur); Faith (Fri); TV, Work, Money, Business, Agriculture (Sat)
Syndicated Publications: Primetime (Thur).
Delivery Methods: Mail`Newsstand`Carrier`Racks
Areas Served - City/County or Portion Thereof, or Zip codes: 52761, 52653, 52720, 52738, 52747, 52749, 52752, 52754, 52760, 52766, 52776
Own Printing Facility?: Y
Commercial printers?: N
Sat. Circulation Paid: 2066
Audit By: AAM
Audit Date: 31.03.2016
Personnel: Rusty Schrader (News Ed.); Steve Jameson (Editor / Publisher); Nick Cusick (Sports Editor); Karla Pinner (Pub.)
Parent company (for newspapers): Dispatch-Argus; Lee Enterprises, Incorporated

NEWTON DAILY NEWS

Street address 1: 200 1st Ave E
Street address city: Newton
Street address state: IA
Zip/Postal code: 50208-3716
County: Jasper
Country: USA
Mailing address: PO BOX 967
Mailing city: NEWTON
Mailing state: IA
Mailing zip: 50208-0967
General Phone: (641) 792-3121
Advertising Phone: (641) 792-3121
Editorial Phone: (641) 792-3121
General/National Adv. E-mail: advertising@newtondailynews.com
Display Adv. E-mail: advertising@newtondailynews.com
Classified Adv. e-mail: jholschuh@newtondailynews.com
Editorial e-mail: beschliman@newtondailynews.com
Primary Website: www.newtondailynews.com
Year Established: 1902
News Services: AP, CNS, MCT, NEA, TMS.
Special Editions: Jasper County Fair (Jul); Alumni Weekend (Jun); Health & Medical Directory 2013 (Apr); Recycling Guide (Apr); Progress Edition (Feb); Spring Bridal (Jan); Business Showcase (Nov); Local Business Women (Oct); Fall Football (Sept).
Special Weekly Sections: TV Digest (Fri).
Syndicated Publications: Relish (Monthly); American Profile (Thur).
Delivery Methods: Mail`Newsstand`Carrier`Racks
Audit By: Sworn/Estimate/Non-Audited
Audit Date: 12.07.2019
Personnel: Dan Goetz (Pub.); Brenda Lamb (Bus. Mgr.); Jeff Holschuh (Adv. Mgr.); Bob Eschliman (Ed.); Kelly Vest (Prodn. Mgr.); Chris Basinger (Prodn. Mgr., Commercial Printing); Mari Jo DeGrado (Prodn. Supvr., Composing Room); Abigail Pelzer (Editor)
Parent company (for newspapers): Shaw Media

THE OELWEIN DAILY REGISTER

Street address 1: 25 1st St SE
Street address city: Oelwein
Street address state: IA
Zip/Postal code: 50662-2306
County: Fayette
Country: USA
Mailing address: PO BOX 511
Mailing city: OELWEIN
Mailing state: IA
Mailing zip: 50662-0511
General Phone: (319) 283-2144
Advertising Phone: (319) 283-2144
Editorial Phone: (319) 283-2144
General/National Adv. E-mail: tracy.cummings@oelweindailyregister.com
Display Adv. E-mail: ads@oelweindailyregister.com
Classified Adv. e-mail: classifieds@oelweindailyregister.com
Editorial e-mail: editor@oelweindailyregister.com
Primary Website: www.oelweindailyregister.com
Year Established: 1882
News Services: AP.
Special Editions: Husky (Apr); Pigskin Preview (Aug); Christmas Promotions (Dec); Soil Conservation (Feb); Bridal (Jan); Summer Sports (Jul); Father's Day (Jun); Update (Mar); Graduation (May); Christmas Open House (Nov); Fire Prevention (Oct); Fall-Tourism (Sept).
Special Weekly Sections: Weekly TV (Fri); Agriculture Edition (Wed).
Delivery Methods: Mail`Newsstand`Racks
Areas Served - City/County or Portion Thereof, or Zip codes: Northeast Iowa
Own Printing Facility?: Y
Commercial printers?: Y
Avg Free Circ: 10193
Sat. Circulation Paid: 2354
Audit By: Sworn/Estimate/Non-Audited
Audit Date: 12.07.2019
Personnel: Deb Weigel (Pub.); Jack Swanson (Mng. Ed.); Deb Kunkle (City Ed.); David Geihausen (Prodn. Mgr.); James Barbutes (Circ. Mgr.)
Parent company (for newspapers): Community Media Group

OSKALOOSA HERALD

Street address 1: 1901 A Ave W
Street address city: Oskaloosa
Street address state: IA
Zip/Postal code: 52577-1962
County: Mahaska
Country: USA
Mailing address: 1901 A AVE W
Mailing city: OSKALOOSA
Mailing state: IA
Mailing zip: 52577-1962
General Phone: (641) 672-2581 ext. 427
Advertising Phone: (641) 672-2581 ext. 413
Editorial Phone: (641) 672-2581 ext. 425
General/National Adv. E-mail: debve@oskyherald.com
Display Adv. E-mail: debve@oskyherald.com
Classified Adv. e-mail: oskyclass@oskyherald.com
Editorial e-mail: oskynews@oskyherald.com
Primary Website: www.oskaloosaherald.com
Year Established: 1850
News Services: NEA, INA, AP.
Special Editions: Progress (Mar).
Special Weekly Sections: Health, Outdoors (Mon); Business (Wed); School (Thur); Church (Fri); TV (Daily)
Syndicated Publications: Relish (Monthly); American Profile (Weekly).
Delivery Methods: Mail`Carrier
Audit By: Sworn/Estimate/Non-Audited
Audit Date: 12.07.2019
Personnel: Deb Van Engelenhoven (Pub./Adv. Sales./ Classified Adv. Mgr./Display Adv.)
Parent company (for newspapers): CNHI, LLC; CNHI, LLC

THE OTTUMWA COURIER

Street address 1: 213 E 2nd St
Street address city: Ottumwa
Street address state: IA
Zip/Postal code: 52501-2902
County: Wapello
Country: USA
Mailing address: 213 E 2ND ST
Mailing city: OTTUMWA
Mailing state: IA
Mailing zip: 52501-2940
General Phone: (641) 684-4611
Advertising Phone: (641) 683-5349
Editorial Phone: (641) 683-5365
General/National Adv. E-mail: dsylvester@ottumwacourier.com
Display Adv. E-mail: dsylvester@ottumwacourier.com
Classified Adv. e-mail: classmgr@ottumwacourier.com
Editorial e-mail: news@ottumwacourier.com
Primary Website: www.ottumwacourier.com
Mthly Avg Views: 400000
Mthly Avg Unique Visitors: 120000
Year Established: 1848
News Services: AP.
Special Editions: Spring Home Improvement (Apr); Bridal Tab (Feb); Home Expo (Mar); Salute to Graduates (May); Fall Sports Preview (Sept).
Special Weekly Sections: Lifestyle, Racing, Bowling (Tue); Learning, Health (Wed); Food, Entertainment, Remember When (Thur); TV, NASCAR (Fri); Religion, Outdoors (Sat)
Syndicated Publications: Relish (Monthly); American Profile (Weekly); Parade (Weekly)
Delivery Methods: Mail`Newsstand`Carrier
Areas Served - City/County or Portion Thereof, or Zip codes: Wapello and Southeast Iowa
Own Printing Facility?: Y
Commercial printers?: Y
Sat. Circulation Paid: 9168
Audit By: Sworn/Estimate/Non-Audited
Audit Date: 12.07.2019
Personnel: Wanda Moeller (Pub./Ed.); Traci Counterman (Audience Development Director); Dan Sylvester (Adv. Mgr.); Danielle Lunsford (Reporter); Erica Kenney (Classified Supervisor); Marcia Kamerick (Business Manager); Nick Workman (Production Director)
Parent company (for newspapers): CNHI, LLC; CNHI, LLC

SIOUX CITY JOURNAL

Street address 1: 515 Pavonia St
Street address city: Sioux City
Street address state: IA
Zip/Postal code: 51101-2245
County: Woodbury
Country: USA
Mailing address: PO BOX 118
Mailing city: SIOUX CITY
Mailing state: IA
Mailing zip: 51102-0118
General Phone: (712) 293-4250
Advertising Phone: (712) 293-4325
Editorial Phone: (712) 293-4224
General/National Adv. E-mail: adv@siouxcityjournal.com
Display Adv. E-mail: adv@siouxcityjournal.com
Classified Adv. e-mail: adv@siouxcityjournal.com
Editorial e-mail: bhayworth@siouxcityjournal.com
Primary Website: www.siouxcityjournal.com
Mthly Avg Views: 320730
Mthly Avg Unique Visitors: 216000
Year Established: 1864
News Services: AP.
Special Editions: Progress (Mar).
Special Weekly Sections: Best Food (Wed); Health (Fri); Auto, Expanded Sports (Sat); Business, Sports, Living, Entertainment
Syndicated Publications: Parade Magazine (S); American Profile (Weekly).
Delivery Methods: Mail`Newsstand`Carrier`Racks
Own Printing Facility?: Y
Commercial printers?: N
Avg Free Circ: 1900
Sat. Circulation Paid: 15997
Sat. Circulation Free: 1900
Sun. Circulation Paid: 18575
Sun. Circulation Free: 1849
Audit By: AAM
Audit Date: 30.09.2018
Personnel: Ron Peterson (Pub.); Sue Stusse (Controller); Mitch Pugh (Ed.); Jeff Tobin (Mng. Ed., Sports); Barbara Walker (City Ed.); Mike Gors (Opinion Ed.); Janet Lubsen (Librarian); Bruce Miller (Music Ed.); Jim Jenkins (News Ed., Night); Tim Hynds (Photo Dept. Mgr.); Tim Gallagher (Society/Women's Ed.); Terry Hersom (Sports Ed.); Mark Schmith (Mgmt. Info Servs. Mgr.); Rob Kritzer (Online Mgr.); Brad Christopherson (Prodn. Foreman, Mailroom); Beth Birdsell (Nat'l Adv. Mgr.); Tom Kuchera (Retail Adv. Dir.); Dave Dreeszen (Managing Editor/News); Daniel Walock (Cir. Dir.)
Parent company (for newspapers): Lee Enterprises, Incorporated

THE DAILY REPORTER

Street address 1: 22 E. 4th St.
Street address city: Spencer
Street address state: IA
Zip/Postal code: 51301-4569
County: Clay
Country: USA
Mailing address: PO BOX 197
Mailing city: SPENCER
Mailing state: IA
Mailing zip: 51301-0197
General Phone: (712) 262-6610
Advertising Phone: (712) 262-6610
Editorial Phone: (712) 262-6610
General/National Adv. E-mail: publisher@spencerdailyreporter.com
Display Adv. E-mail: publisher@spencerdailyreporter.com
Classified Adv. e-mail: tjmurphyr@spencerdailyreporter.com
Editorial e-mail: news@spencerdailyreporter.com
Primary Website: www.spencerdailyreporter.com
Mthly Avg Views: 35000
Mthly Avg Unique Visitors: 12000
Year Established: 1959
News Services: AP
Delivery Methods: Mail`Carrier
Sat. Circulation Paid: 3852
Audit By: Sworn/Estimate/Non-Audited
Audit Date: 30.09.2023
Personnel: Randy Cauthron (Ed.); Paula Buenger (Pub.); Brad Hicks (Publisher); Jason Lindsey (Adv. Dir.); TJ Murphy (Sales Representative); Zach Jevne (Sports Ed.); Seth Boyes (Staff Writer)
Parent company (for newspapers): Rust Communications; Enterprise Media, Inc.

THE WASHINGTON EVENING JOURNAL

Street address 1: 111 N Marion Ave
Street address city: Washington
Street address state: IA
Zip/Postal code: 52353-1728
County: Washington
Country: USA
Mailing address: 111 N MARION AVE
Mailing city: WASHINGTON
Mailing state: IA
Mailing zip: 52353-1748
General Phone: (319) 653-2191
Advertising Phone: (319) 653-2191
Editorial Phone: (319) 653-2191
General/National Adv. E-mail: sales@washjrnl.com
Display Adv. E-mail: adv@washjrnl.com
Classified Adv. e-mail: adv@washjrnl.com
Editorial e-mail: news@washjrnl.com
Primary Website: www.washjrnl.com
News Services: AP.
Special Editions: Christmas (Dec); Fall Opening (Fall); Beef Issue (May); Pork Production (Oct); Spring Opening (Spring).
Special Weekly Sections: Week in Review (Fri); Business (Mon); Farm Page (Thur); Best Food Day (Tues).
Syndicated Publications: American Profile (Mon); Relish (Monthly).
Delivery Methods: Mail`Newsstand`Carrier`Racks

Areas Served - City/County or Portion Thereof, or Zip codes: Washington County
Own Printing Facility?: Y
Commercial printers?: Y
Audit By: Sworn/Estimate/Non-Audited
Audit Date: 12.07.2019
Personnel: Kim Stout (Circ. Dir.); Darwin K. Sherman (President); Aaron Viner (Sports Ed.); Steve Dunbar (Prodn. Mgr.); Matt Bryant (Publisher)
Parent company (for newspapers): Cedar Rapids Press; Folience

THE COURIER

Street address 1: 100 E 4th St
Street address 2: PO Box 540
Street address city: Waterloo
Street address state: IA
Zip/Postal code: 50703-4714
County: Black Hawk
Country: USA
Mailing address: PO BOX 540
Mailing city: WATERLOO
Mailing state: IA
Mailing zip: 50704-0540
General Phone: (800) 798-1717
Advertising Phone: (319) 291-1497
Editorial Phone: (319) 291-1460
General/National Adv. E-mail: tara.seible@wcfcourier.com
Display Adv. E-mail: angela.dark@wcfcourier.com
Classified Adv. e-mail: classads@wcfcourier.com
Editorial e-mail: woo.newsroom@wcfcourier.com
Primary Website: www.wcfcourier.com
Mthly Avg Views: 3500000
Mthly Avg Unique Visitors: 372000
Year Established: 1858
News Services: AP.
Special Editions: Babies on Parade (Jan); Progress Editions (Feb); Spring Farm (Mar); Spring/Summer Activities Guide (Apr); Bid & Buy Auction (May); Boone Bash (Jun); Chamber Book (Jun); Our Hometown (Jul); Crazy Days (Jul); School Calendar (Aug); Faces In The Crowd (Sept); Ladies Night (Oct); Wacky Wednesday (Nov); Holiday Greetings (Dec).
Special Weekly Sections: Flavor (Tue); Best Food Day, Health (Wed); Entertainment (Thur); Arts, Auto, Business, Home, Living, Real Estate, Technology, Travel, Women (Sun)
Syndicated Publications: Cedar Valley Business (Monthly)
Delivery Methods: Mail`Newsstand`Carrier`Racks
Areas Served - City/County or Portion Thereof, or Zip codes: 50613, 50614, 50701-06, 50705, 50667, 50703, 50626, 50613, 50643, 50651, 50648, 50644, 52326, 50612, 52224, 50675, 52229, 50669, 50638, 50642, 50642, 50600, 50665, 50770, 50602, 50649, 50658, 50630, 50659, 52154, 50666, 50676, 50674, 50677, 50647, 50622, 50668.
Own Printing Facility?: N
Commercial printers?: Y
Sun. Circulation Paid: 30423
Audit By: AAM
Audit Date: 31.03.2018
Personnel: Roy Biondi (Pub.); Nancy Newhoff (Ed.); Catherine Kittrell (Community Editor/Obituaries); Meta Hemenway-Forbes (Lifestyles and Features Ed.); Melody Parker (Lifestyles & Features Ed.); Doug Newhoff (Sports Ed.); Adam Bolander (Circ. Dir.); Tara Seible (Adv. Dir.)
Parent company (for newspapers): Lee Enterprises, Incorporated

THE DAILY FREEMAN-JOURNAL

Street address 1: 720 2nd St
Street address city: Webster City
Street address state: IA
Zip/Postal code: 50595-1437
County: Hamilton
Country: USA
Mailing address: PO BOX 490
Mailing city: WEBSTER CITY
Mailing state: IA
Mailing zip: 50595-0490
General Phone: (515) 832-4350
Advertising Phone: (515) 832-4350
Editorial Phone: (515) 832-4350
General/National Adv. E-mail: cbargfrede@freemanjournal.net
Display Adv. E-mail: jlovelace@freemanjournal.net
Classified Adv. e-mail: advertising@freemanjournal.net
Editorial e-mail: editor@freemanjournal.net
Primary Website: www.freemanjournal.net
Mthly Avg Views: 150000
Mthly Avg Unique Visitors: 46650
Year Established: 1857
News Services: AP.
Special Editions: Babies on Parade (Jan); Progress Editions (Feb); Spring Farm (Mar); Spring/Summer Activities Guide (Apr); Bid & Buy Auction (May); Boone Bash (Jun); Chamber Book (Jun); Our Hometown (Jul); Crazy Days (Jul); School Calendar (Aug); Faces In The Crowd (Sept); Ladies Night (Oct); Wacky Wednesday (Nov); Holiday Greetings (Dec).
Special Weekly Sections: Comics, Sports, Lifestyles, Entertainment (Daily); Education (Mon); Best Food (Wed); Business (Thur/Sun); Religion (Sat); TV, Comics, Entertainment, Farm (Sun)
Delivery Methods: Mail`Newsstand`Carrier`Racks
Areas Served - City/County or Portion Thereof, or Zip codes: Wright, Webster, Franklin, and Hardin County
Own Printing Facility?: Y
Commercial printers?: Y
Avg Free Circ: 10
Audit By: AAM
Audit Date: 30.06.2017
Personnel: Terry Christensen (Gen. Mgr./Pub); Grant Gibbon (Circ. Dir.); Cory Bargfrede (Adv. Mgr.); Anne Blankenship (Mng. Ed.); Troy Banning (Sports Ed.); Lance Draeger (Adv. Consultant); Josh Lovelace (Adv. Mgr.); Cory Bargfrede (Adv. Dir.)
Parent company (for newspapers): Ogden Newspapers Inc.

KANSAS

ABILENE REFLECTOR-CHRONICLE

Street address 1: 305 N Cedar St
Street address city: Abilene
Street address state: KS
Zip/Postal code: 67410-2616
County: Dickinson
Country: USA
Mailing address: 305 N Cedar ST
Mailing city: ABILENE
Mailing state: KS
Mailing zip: 67410-2616
General Phone: (785) 263-1000
Advertising Phone: (785) 263-1000
Editorial Phone: (785) 263-1000
General/National Adv. E-mail: advertising@abilene-rc.com
Display Adv. E-mail: advertising@abilene-rc.com
Classified Adv. e-mail: advertising@abilene-rc.com
Editorial e-mail: editor@abilene-rc.com
Primary Website: www.abilene-rc.com
Mthly Avg Views: 126815
Mthly Avg Unique Visitors: 13733
Year Established: 1942
News Services: AP.
Special Editions: (Jan); DARE Coloring Contest (Jan); Outlook (Feb); Spring Sports (Mar); Flint Hills Guide (Jul); Fall Auto Care (Sept); Women in Business (Oct); Christmas (Dec); Fall Home Tour Tab (Fall); Graduation (May).
Special Weekly Sections: Church/Religion (Thur); Organization/Club (Thur); Home & Garden ; Arts/Books (Sat); Business TV Listings Thur Weddings/Engagements daily; School Youth Thurs(t); Health/Fitness ().
Syndicated Publications: American Profile (Fri).
Delivery Methods: Mail`Newsstand`Carrier`Racks
Areas Served - City/County or Portion Thereof, or Zip codes: Dickinson County
Own Printing Facility?: N
Commercial printers?: N
Avg Free Circ: 4400
Audit By: Sworn/Estimate/Non-Audited
Audit Date: 12.07.2019
Personnel: Ron Preston (Sports); Kathy Hageman (Interim News Ed.); Kim Maguire (Adv. Sales Rep.); Sonya Thompson (Front Desk); Susi Parker (Adv. Asst.); Ed Boice (Reporter); Mike Heronumus (Editor); Gale Parsons (Reporter)
Parent company (for newspapers): The White Corporation

THE ARKANSAS CITY TRAVELER

Street address 1: 200 E 5th Ave
Street address city: Arkansas City
Street address state: KS
Zip/Postal code: 67005-2606
County: Cowley
Country: USA
Mailing address: PO BOX 988
Mailing city: ARKANSAS CITY
Mailing state: KS
Mailing zip: 67005-0988
General Phone: (620) 442-4200
Advertising Phone: (620) 442-4200
Editorial Phone: (620) 442-4200
General/National Adv. E-mail: ads@arkcity.net
Display Adv. E-mail: adman@arkcity.net
Classified Adv. e-mail: classman@arkcity.net
Editorial e-mail: arkcity@arkcity.net
Primary Website: www.arkcity.net
Mthly Avg Views: 350351
Mthly Avg Unique Visitors: 127195
Year Established: 1870
News Services: AP.
Special Editions: Senior (Bi-monthly)
Special Weekly Sections: Food & Health (Wed); Education (Mon); Weddings/Engagements (Sat); Nature (Thur); Faith (Fri); Business (Tues).
Syndicated Publications: USA WEEKEND Magazine (Sat).
Delivery Methods: Mail`Newsstand`Racks
Areas Served - City/County or Portion Thereof, or Zip codes: Arkansas City, Kansas; Cowley County, Kay County, Oklahoma
Own Printing Facility?: Y
Commercial printers?: Y
Sat. Circulation Paid: 4832
Audit By: Sworn/Estimate/Non-Audited
Audit Date: 12.07.2019
Personnel: Dave Seaton (Pub.); Susie Kincaid (Bus. Mgr.); Andrew Lawson (Managing Ed.); Joey Sprinkle (Sports Ed.); Donita Clausen (Photographer/Videographer); Grant Urban (Lifestyle/Action Ed.); Kayleigh Lawson (Online Ed.); Arty Hicks (Ad Director); Suvanah Perdue (Assistant Ad Director); Tina Pride (Adv. Consultant); Marilyn Coury (Circulation Manager); Jennie Steelman; Lukas Young (Head Pressman); Jean Crowley (Society Ed.); Moody R. Alford (Adv. Consultant); Janet Darnall (Adv. Asst.); Amber Cook (Classified Mgr.); Kay Batdorf (Prodn. Mgr., Pre Press)
Parent company (for newspapers): Kansas Press Association; Seaton Group

THE CHANUTE TRIBUNE

Street address 1: 26 W Main St
Street address city: Chanute
Street address state: KS
Zip/Postal code: 66720-1701
County: Neosho
Country: USA
Mailing address: PO BOX 559
Mailing city: CHANUTE
Mailing state: KS
Mailing zip: 66720-0559
General Phone: (620) 431-4100
General/National Adv. E-mail: shanna@chanute.com
Display Adv. E-mail: brandi@chanute.com
Classified Adv. e-mail: classified@chanute.com
Editorial e-mail: stu@chanute.com
Primary Website: www.chanute.com
Year Established: 1892
News Services: AP.
Special Editions: Basketball (Apr); Back-to-School (Aug); Holiday Recipe (Dec); Tax Tab (Feb); Bridal Tab (Jan); Medical Tab (Jul); Summer Fun (Jun); Football (Sept).
Special Weekly Sections: Family (Fri); Social/Anniversaries (Sat); Education (Thur); Community News (Tues); Edit (Wed).
Delivery Methods: Mail`Newsstand`Carrier`Racks
Areas Served - City/County or Portion Thereof, or Zip codes: Chanute and the four-county area
Own Printing Facility?: Y
Commercial printers?: Y
Sat. Circulation Paid: 4359
Audit By: Sworn/Estimate/Non-Audited
Audit Date: 12.07.2019
Personnel: Shanna Guiot (Pub./Bus. Mgr.); Amy Jensen (Circ. Mgr.); Stu Butcher (Exec. Ed.)
Parent company (for newspapers): Kansas Newspapers, LLC

THE CLAY CENTER DISPATCH

Street address 1: 805 5th St
Street address city: Clay Center
Street address state: KS
Zip/Postal code: 67432-2502
County: Clay
Country: USA
Mailing address: PO BOX 519
Mailing city: CLAY CENTER
Mailing state: KS
Mailing zip: 67432-0519
General Phone: (785) 632-2127
Advertising Phone: (785) 632-2127
Editorial Phone: (785) 632-2127
General/National Adv. E-mail: dispatch@claycenter.com
Display Adv. E-mail: addesk@claycenter.com
Classified Adv. e-mail: addesk@claycenter.com
Editorial e-mail: news@claycenter.com
Primary Website: www.claycenter.com
Mthly Avg Views: 110000
Mthly Avg Unique Visitors: 1555
Year Established: 1871
News Services: AP. McClatchy
Special Editions: Home & Garden (Apr); Back-to-School (Aug); F.F.A. (Feb); Social Security/Tax (Jan); Fair Preview Tab (Jul); Car Care (Mar); Graduation (May); Christmas (Nov); Car Care (Oct); Rodeo (Sept).
Special Weekly Sections: Clay Center Saver
Delivery Methods: Mail`Newsstand`Carrier
Areas Served - City/County or Portion Thereof, or Zip codes: 67432, 67487, 67468, 67466, 66937, 66938, 66962, 66449, 66953, 67447, 66531, 67458, 67417
Own Printing Facility?: Y
Commercial printers?: N
Avg Free Circ: 4700
Audit By: Sworn/Estimate/Non-Audited
Audit Date: 12.07.2019
Personnel: Harry E. Valentine (Pres./Pub./Treasurer); Dave Berggren (Sports Ed.); Aaron Bull (Prodn. Supt./Foreman, Composing); Lori Reardon (Circulation); Alicia Morgison (Ad Director)
Parent company (for newspapers): Flint Hills Media Group

COLBY FREE PRESS

Street address 1: 155 W 5th St
Street address city: Colby
Street address state: KS
Zip/Postal code: 67701-2312
County: Thomas
Country: USA
General Phone: (785) 462-3963
General/National Adv. E-mail: sfriedlander@nwkansas.com
Display Adv. E-mail: sfriedlander @nwkansas.com
Classified Adv. e-mail: khunter@nwkansas.com
Editorial e-mail: colby.editor@nwkansas.com
Primary Website: www.nwkansas.com
Year Established: 1888
News Services: AP.
Special Weekly Sections: Business Directory
Delivery Methods: Mail`Newsstand`Carrier`Racks
Areas Served - City/County or Portion Thereof, or Zip codes: Thomas County
Own Printing Facility?: Y
Commercial printers?: Y
Audit By: Sworn/Estimate/Non-Audited
Audit Date: 12.07.2019
Personnel: Sharon Friedlander (Pub.); Kathryn Ballard (Adv. Rep.); Kylee Hunter (Classified/ Adv. Graphic Designer); Melissa Edmondson (Office Mgr.); Janene Woodall (sales)
Parent company (for newspapers): Haynes Publishing Co.

CONCORDIA BLADE-EMPIRE

Street address 1: 510 Washington St
Street address city: Concordia
Street address state: KS
Zip/Postal code: 66901-2117
County: Cloud
Country: USA
Mailing address: PO BOX 309
Mailing city: CONCORDIA
Mailing state: KS
Mailing zip: 66901-0309

General Phone: (785) 243-2424
Advertising Phone: (785) 243-2424
Editorial Phone: (785) 243-2424
General/National Adv. E-mail: bladeempire@nckcn.com
Display Adv. E-mail: dixiewinter@nckcn.com
Classified Adv. e-mail: deniselah@nckcn.com
Editorial e-mail: bladeempire@nckcn.com
Primary Website: www.bladeempire.com
Mthly Avg Views: 1821200
Mthly Avg Unique Visitors: 847300
Year Established: 1920
News Services: AP.
Delivery Methods: Mail`Newsstand`Carrier
Areas Served - City/County or Portion Thereof, or Zip codes: Cloud County and surrounding counties
Audit By: Sworn/Estimate/Non-Audited
Audit Date: 12.07.2019
Personnel: John Hamel (Bus. Mgr.); Brad Lowell (Ed./Pub.); Jim Lowell (Sports Ed./Managing Ed.); Sharon Coy (Social Ed.); Dixie Winter (Adv. Sales); Jessica Leduc (Adv. Sale/Photographer); Denise Lahodny (Classified Adv.); Jay Lowell (Online Ed./Photographer/Adv. Sales)

COUNCIL GROVE REPUBLICAN

Street address 1: 208 W Main St
Street address city: Council Grove
Street address state: KS
Zip/Postal code: 66846-1705
County: Morris
Country: USA
Mailing address: PO BOX 237
Mailing city: COUNCIL GROVE
Mailing state: KS
Mailing zip: 66846-0237
General Phone: (620) 767-5123
Advertising Phone: (620) 767-5123
Editorial Phone: (620) 767-5123
General/National Adv. E-mail: cgnews@cgtelco.net
Display Adv. E-mail: cgnews@cgtelco.net
Classified Adv. e-mail: cgnews@cgtelco.net
Editorial e-mail: cgnews@cgtelco.net
Primary Website: N/A
Year Established: 1872
News Services: AP.
Special Editions: Tourism (Apr); Bridal (Feb); Soil Conservation (Jan); County Fair (Jul); Historical Festival (June) (Jun).
Delivery Methods: Mail`Newsstand`Carrier
Areas Served - City/County or Portion Thereof, or Zip codes: Morris County and adjacent counties
Own Printing Facility?: N
Commercial printers?: N
Audit By: Sworn/Estimate/Non-Audited
Audit Date: 12.07.2019
Personnel: Craig A. McNeal (Pub./Ed.); Becky Evans (Adv. Dir.); Christy Jimerson (Circ. Mgr.); Kay Roberts
Parent company (for newspapers): Council Grove Publishing Company, Inc.

DODGE CITY DAILY GLOBE

Street address 1: 705 N 2nd Ave
Street address city: Dodge City
Street address state: KS
Zip/Postal code: 67801-4410
County: Ford
Country: USA
Mailing address: PO BOX 820
Mailing city: DODGE CITY
Mailing state: KS
Mailing zip: 67801-0820
General Phone: (620) 225-4151
Advertising Phone: (620) 408-9919
Editorial Phone: (620) 408-9913
General/National Adv. E-mail: ceasterday@dodgeglobe.com
Display Adv. E-mail: ndirks@dodgeglobe.com
Classified Adv. e-mail: rmyers@dodgeglobe.com
Editorial e-mail: emily.shultz@dodgeglobe.com
Primary Website: www.dodgeglobe.com
Mthly Avg Views: 263651
Mthly Avg Unique Visitors: 187263
Year Established: 1878
News Services: AP.
Special Editions: Progress (Feb); Bridal Tab (Jan); Bridal Tab (Jul); City Guide (Jun); Tourist Tab (Mar); Christmas Kick-Off (Thanksgiving Day) (Nov); Senior Citizens (Oct); Fall Fashion (Sept).
Special Weekly Sections: Youth (Fri); Seniors (Mon); Business (Sat); Health (Tues); Best Food Day (Wed).
Syndicated Publications: USA WEEKEND Magazine (Fri); Relish (Monthly).
Delivery Methods: Mail`Newsstand`Carrier
Areas Served - City/County or Portion Thereof, or Zip codes: Ford County
Sat. Circulation Paid: 9700
Audit By: Sworn/Estimate/Non-Audited
Audit Date: 12.07.2019
Personnel: Edward O'Neil (Production Foreman); Conrad Easterday (Gen. Mgr.); Robbin Myers (Classified Adv. Mgr.); Nicole Dirks (Retail Adv. Mgr.); John Curtis (Sports Editor); Kathy Runquist (Business Office)
Parent company (for newspapers): CherryRoad Media; CherryRoad Media

THE EMPORIA GAZETTE

Street address 1: 517 Merchant St
Street address 2: Frnt
Street address city: Emporia
Street address state: KS
Zip/Postal code: 66801-7215
County: Lyon
Country: USA
Mailing address: PO BOX C
Mailing city: EMPORIA
Mailing state: KS
Mailing zip: 66801-7342
General Phone: (620) 342-4800
Advertising Phone: (620) 342-4841 ext. 233
Editorial Phone: (620) 342-4805
General/National Adv. E-mail: sales13@emporiagazette.com
Display Adv. E-mail: sales20@emporiagazette.com
Classified Adv. e-mail: classifieds@emporiagazette.com
Editorial e-mail: news@emporia.com
Primary Website: www.emporiagazette.com
Mthly Avg Views: 177109
Mthly Avg Unique Visitors: 6291
Year Established: 1895
News Services: AP, NYT, Kansas Press Association
Special Editions: Healthy Living (Jan); Spring Home Improvement (Feb); Ads by Kids, Baseball/Softball (Mar); Reader's Choice, Mature Living (Apr); Discover (May); Summer Theatre, Bridal Tab (Jun); Back to School (Jul); Campus Life (Aug); Football, Mature Living (Sept); Breast Cancer Awareness (Oct); Veterans (Nov); Basketball (Dec);
Special Weekly Sections: Weekend Business (Sat).
Syndicated Publications: TV Week (Sat).
Delivery Methods: Mail`Carrier
Areas Served - City/County or Portion Thereof, or Zip codes: Admire, Cottonwood Falls, Hamilton, Olpe, Allen, Council Grove, Hartford, Osage City, Americus, Dunlap, Lebo, Reading, Burlington, Emporia, Madison, Strong City, Bushong, Gridley, and Neosho Rapids.
Own Printing Facility?: N
Sat. Circulation Paid: 5746
Audit By: AAM
Audit Date: 30.09.2012
Personnel: Paul David Walker (Pres.); Christopher White Walker (Pub./Ed.); Barbara White Walker (Travel Ed.); Brenda Armitage (Circ. Mgr.); Ray J. Beals (Gen. Mgr.); Jay Wilson (Adv. Mgr., Display/Nat'l); Melissa Heinitz (Circ. Mgr.); Gwen Larson (Mng. Ed.); Patrick S. Kelley (Editorial Page Ed.); Dallas Sedgwick (Prodn. Mgr.); Larry Leaver (Mgr., Distr.); Lori Hickey; Ronda Henery; Briana Julo (Adv. Mgr.); Mark Matthews
Parent company (for newspapers): Kansas Press Association; The White Corporation

THE FORT SCOTT TRIBUNE

Street address 1: PO Box 150
Street address 2: 6 N Main
Street address city: Fort Scott
Street address state: KS
Zip/Postal code: 66701-0150
County: Bourbon
Country: USA
Mailing address: PO BOX 150
Mailing city: FORT SCOTT
Mailing state: KS
Mailing zip: 66701-0150
General Phone: (620) 223-2110
Advertising Phone: (620) 223-2110
Editorial Phone: (620) 223-2110
General/National Adv. E-mail: advertising@fstribune.com
Display Adv. E-mail: advertising@fstribune.com
Classified Adv. e-mail: advertising@fstribune.com
Editorial e-mail: thelm@fstribune.com
Primary Website: www.fstribune.com
Mthly Avg Views: 292504
Mthly Avg Unique Visitors: 65923
Year Established: 1884
Delivery Methods: Mail`Carrier`Racks
Areas Served - City/County or Portion Thereof, or Zip codes: 66701
Own Printing Facility?: Y
Commercial printers?: N
Sat. Circulation Paid: 3289
Audit By: Sworn/Estimate/Non-Audited
Audit Date: 12.07.2019
Personnel: Floyd Jernigan (Pub.); Lorie Harter (Publisher); Teresa Klumpp (Adv. Mgr./Office Mgr.); Christi Allmond (Circ. Asst.); Sara Simonds (Composition Mgr.); Tammy Helm (Mng. Ed.); Scott Nuzum (Sports Ed.); Lorie Harter (Pub./Dir. of Adv.); Andrew LaSota (Adv. Consultant)
Parent company (for newspapers): Rust Communications

THE GARDEN CITY TELEGRAM

Street address 1: 310 N 7th St
Street address city: Garden City
Street address state: KS
Zip/Postal code: 67846-5521
County: Finney
Country: USA
Mailing address: PO BOX 958
Mailing city: GARDEN CITY
Mailing state: KS
Mailing zip: 67846-0958
General Phone: (620) 275-8500
Advertising Phone: (620) 276-6862 ext. 225
Editorial Phone: (620) 275-8500 ext. 201
General/National Adv. E-mail: advertising@gctelegram.com
Display Adv. E-mail: advertising@gctelegram.com
Classified Adv. e-mail: classifieds@gctelegram.com
Editorial e-mail: newsroom@gctelegram.com
Primary Website: www.gctelegram.com
Mthly Avg Views: 148000
Mthly Avg Unique Visitors: 51000
Year Established: 1906
News Services: AP, Harris News Service.
Special Editions: Health & Wellness (Summer 2013); Discover Southwest Kansas (2013); Southwest Kansas Agriculture (May); Graduation Class of 2013 (May); Head Over Heels (Feb).
Special Weekly Sections: Weddings/Engagements (Sat); Church News (Fri); Real Estate Guide (Fri); Agricultural News (Thur); Classtime (Wed); Best Food Day (Tues).
Syndicated Publications: USA WEEKEND Magazine (Sat).
Delivery Methods: Mail`Newsstand`Carrier`Racks
Areas Served - City/County or Portion Thereof, or Zip codes: Greeley, Wichita, Scott, Lane, Hamilton, Kearny, Finney, Stanton, Grant, Haskell, Gray, and Stevens County.
Own Printing Facility?: Y
Commercial printers?: Y
Sat. Circulation Paid: 7966
Audit By: Sworn/Estimate/Non-Audited
Audit Date: 12.07.2019
Personnel: Dena Sattler (Pub./Ed.); Jeremy Banwell (Circ. Mgr.); Brett Riggs (Mng. Ed.); Brad Nading (Photo Dept. Mgr.); Sharynn Bowman (Classifieds Mgr.)
Parent company (for newspapers): CherryRoad Media; CherryRoad Media

GREAT BEND TRIBUNE

Street address 1: 2012 Forest Ave
Street address city: Great Bend
Street address state: KS
Zip/Postal code: 67530-4014
County: Barton
Country: USA
Mailing address: 2012 FOREST AVE
Mailing city: GREAT BEND
Mailing state: KS
Mailing zip: 67530-4014
General Phone: (620) 792-1211
Advertising Phone: (620) 792-1211
Editorial Phone: (620) 792-1211
General/National Adv. E-mail: tmason@gbtribune.com
Display Adv. E-mail: tmason@gbtribune.com
Classified Adv. e-mail: classifieds@gbtribune.com
Editorial e-mail: dhogg@gbtribune.com
Primary Website: www.gbtribune.com
Year Established: 1876
News Services: AP.
Special Editions: Area Source Magazines; Glossy Special Publications, Inspire Health
Special Weekly Sections: Church Page (Fri); Health (S); 50+ (Thur); Food Day (Wed).
Delivery Methods: Mail`Newsstand`Carrier`Racks
Own Printing Facility?: Y
Commercial printers?: Y
Sun. Circulation Paid: 5977
Audit By: USPS
Audit Date: 30.09.2006
Personnel: Mary Hoisington (Pub.); Dale Hogg (Mng. Ed.); Karma Byers (Prodn. Mgr., Pre Press); James Audus (Press manager); Diane Lacy-Trostle (Advertising Director); Tammy Mason (Marketing Consultant); Shonita Swank (Circ. Dir.); Jeff LeRoy (Graphic Designer); Hugo Gonzalez (Digital Media/Innovative Projects Coord.); Gina Werth (Classifieds); LeeAnn Byers (Distributors Asst.); Amie Thompson (Planning Editor Print & Digital); Jennifer Sorenson (Advertising Director)
Parent company (for newspapers): Morris Multimedia, Inc.

THE HAYS DAILY NEWS

Street address 1: 507 Main St
Street address city: Hays
Street address state: KS
Zip/Postal code: 67601-4228
County: Ellis
Country: USA
Mailing address: 507 MAIN ST
Mailing city: HAYS
Mailing state: KS
Mailing zip: 67601-4239
General Phone: (785) 628-1081
Advertising Phone: (785) 628-1081 ext. 118
Editorial Phone: (785) 628-1081 ext. 164
General/National Adv. E-mail: kkeller-smith@cherryroad.com
Display Adv. E-mail: kkeller-smith#cherryroad.com
Classified Adv. e-mail: advertising@dailynews.net
Editorial e-mail: hchapman@cherryroad.com
Primary Website: www.hdnews.net
Mthly Avg Views: 380109
Mthly Avg Unique Visitors: 63975
Year Established: 1929
News Services: Cherryroad Media
Special Editions: College (Aug); Christmas & New Years Greetings (Dec); Bridal Fair (Feb); Sidewalk Bazaar (Jul); Wild West Festival (Jun); Travel & Tourism (May); Christmas (Nov); Area Football (Sept).
Delivery Methods: Mail`Newsstand`Carrier`Racks
Areas Served - City/County or Portion Thereof, or Zip codes: 67601, 67737, 67738, 67748, 67701, 67740, 67736,67752,67751, 67631, 67672, 67656, 67637, 67548, 67667, 67553, 67575, 67516, 67660, 67560, 67556, 67572, 67584, 67521, 67520, 67661, 67646, 67669, 67663, 67651, 67654, 67639, 67622, 67645, 66967, 67675, 67657, 67632, 67625, 67642, 67623, 67473, 67650, 67659, 67640, 67665, 67671, 67627
Own Printing Facility?: Y
Commercial printers?: N
Sun. Circulation Paid: 6500
Audit By: Sworn/Estimate/Non-Audited
Audit Date: 12.07.2019
Personnel: Kimberly Smith (Multi Media Sales Executive); Hailey Chapman (Editor); Mary Karst (Adv. Dir.); Nick McQueen (Sports Ed.); Jon Howard (IT Dir.)
Parent company (for newspapers): CherryRoad Media; CherryRoad Media

THE HUTCHINSON NEWS

Street address 1: 300 W 2nd Ave
Street address city: Hutchinson
Street address state: KS
Zip/Postal code: 67501-5211
County: Reno
Country: USA
Mailing address: 300 W 2ND AVE
Mailing city: HUTCHINSON
Mailing state: KS
Mailing zip: 67501-5211
General Phone: (620) 694-5700
General/National Adv. E-mail: astuckey@hutchnews.com
Display Adv. E-mail: astuckey@hutchnews.com
Classified Adv. e-mail: classifieds@hutchnews.com
Editorial e-mail: rsylvester@hutchnews.com
Primary Website: www.hutchnews.com
Mthly Avg Views: 1150000

Mthly Avg Unique Visitors: 220000
Year Established: 1872
News Services: AP, SHNS, TMS
Special Editions: Experience Pratt (Jul); Tech 2013 (Jul); Kansas Homes Guide (monthly); Progress (March); Dream Homes (Jun); Discover (May)
Special Weekly Sections: Business (S); Weddings & Engagements (S); Taste of Life (Wed); Entertainment (Thurs); Preview (Fri); Faith (Sat).
Syndicated Publications: Parade Magazine (S), Athlon Sports (Monthly), Spry (Monday), Relish (Monday).
Delivery Methods: Mail`Newsstand`Carrier`Racks
Areas Served - City/County or Portion Thereof, or Zip codes: Greeley, Wichita, Scott, Lane, Hamilton, Kearny, Finney, Stanton, Grant, Haskell, Gray, Stevens, Seward, Meade, Ness, Hodgeman, Ford, Clark, Rush, Pawnee, Edwards, Kiowa, Comanche, Barton, Stafford, Pratt, Barber, Ellsworth, Rice, Reno, Kingman, Harper, McPherson, Harvey and Marion County
Own Printing Facility?: Y
Commercial printers?: Y
Avg Free Circ: 0
Sat. Circulation Paid: 17605
Sat. Circulation Free: 0
Sun. Circulation Paid: 21393
Sun. Circulation Free: 0
Audit By: VAC
Audit Date: 9/31/2015
Personnel: Stephen Wade (Pub.); Mack Jarrett (Acct. Mgr.); Jona Thomas (HR Mgr.); Elizabeth Garwood (Sub. Srv. Mgr.); Theresa Gehring (Circ. Opt. Mgr.); Jeff Arenz (Sports Ed.)
Parent company (for newspapers): Gannett; CherryRoad Media

INDEPENDENCE DAILY REPORTER

Street address 1: 320 N 6th St
Street address city: Independence
Street address state: KS
Zip/Postal code: 67301-3129
County: Montgomery
Country: USA
Mailing address: PO BOX 869
Mailing city: INDEPENDENCE
Mailing state: KS
Mailing zip: 67301-0869
General Phone: (620) 331-3550
Advertising Phone: (620) 331-3550
Editorial Phone: (620) 331-3550
General/National Adv. E-mail: ads@dreporter.com
Display Adv. E-mail: ads@dreporter.com
Classified Adv. e-mail: ads@dreporter.com
Editorial e-mail: ads@dreporter.com
Primary Website: www.indydailyreporter.com
News Services: AP.
Delivery Methods: Mail`Newsstand
Areas Served - City/County or Portion Thereof, or Zip codes: Montgomery County
Own Printing Facility?: N
Commercial printers?: N
Sun. Circulation Paid: 6654
Audit By: Sworn/Estimate/Non-Audited
Audit Date: 12.07.2019
Personnel: Josh Umholtz (Pub.); Scott Wood; Scott Wesner; Steve McBride (Adv. Mgr.)
Parent company (for newspapers): Wesner Media

THE IOLA REGISTER

Street address 1: 302 S Washington Ave
Street address city: Iola
Street address state: KS
Zip/Postal code: 66749-3255
County: Allen
Country: USA
Mailing address: PO BOX 767
Mailing city: IOLA
Mailing state: KS
Mailing zip: 66749-0767
General Phone: (620) 365-2111
Advertising Phone: (620) 365-2111
Editorial Phone: (620) 365-2111
General/National Adv. E-mail: registerdisplay@gmail.com
Display Adv. E-mail: registerdisplay@gmail.com
Classified Adv. e-mail: classifieds@iolaregister.com
Editorial e-mail: editorial@iolaregister.com
Primary Website: www.iolaregister.com
Mthly Avg Views: 318308
Year Established: 1897
News Services: AP.
Special Editions: Fair (Aug); Sports Tab (Dec); Fair (Jun); Spring (Mar); Business & Professional Tab (Oct); Sports Tab (Sept).
Special Weekly Sections: Humboldt News, Grocery Day, Farm Page (Tues); Colony News (Wed); TV Guide (Thur); NASCAR, Weddings, Court Report (Sat);
Delivery Methods: Mail`Newsstand`Racks
Areas Served - City/County or Portion Thereof, or Zip codes: Allen County
Own Printing Facility?: Y
Commercial printers?: Y
Sat. Circulation Paid: 3750
Audit By: Sworn/Estimate/Non-Audited
Audit Date: 12.07.2019
Personnel: Susan Lynn (Pub./Ed.); Mark L. Hastings (Adv. Mgr.); Pam Holland (Adv. Mgr., Classified); Richard Luken (Sports Ed.); Sara Weide (Prod. Mgr.); Jenelle Johnson (Health/Medical Ed.); Bob Johnson (City Ed.); David Gilham (Online Ed.); Jocelyn Sheets (Photo Ed.); Sarah Stansbury (Adv. Rep.); Whitney Coblentz (Adv. Rep./Graphic Designer); Susan Locke (Circ. Mgr.); Sarah Gonzalez (Classified Adv.); Kevin Swepton (Commercial Printing)
Parent company (for newspapers): Kansas Press Association; The Iola Register Publishing Co.

THE DAILY UNION

Street address 1: 222 W 6th St
Street address city: Junction City
Street address state: KS
Zip/Postal code: 66441-5500
County: Geary
Country: USA
Mailing address: PO BOX 129
Mailing city: JUNCTION CITY
Mailing state: KS
Mailing zip: 66441-0129
General Phone: (785) 762-5000
Advertising Phone: (785) 762-5000
Editorial Phone: (785) 762-5000
General/National Adv. E-mail: m.tyson@thedailyunion.net
Display Adv. E-mail: du.adv@thedailyunion.net
Classified Adv. e-mail: du.adv@thedailyunion.net
Editorial e-mail: m.editor@thedailyunion.net
Primary Website: www.yourdu.net
Mthly Avg Views: 106800
Mthly Avg Unique Visitors: 9680
Year Established: 1861
News Services: AP, CNS, TMS.
Special Editions: A-Z Page (Aug); Christmas Greetings (Dec); Outlook (Feb); Bridal (Jan); JC Guide (Jul); Spring Home & Garden (Mar); Gift Guide (Nov); Design an Ad (Oct); Football (Sept).
Special Weekly Sections: Faith (Fri); Wedding Page (S); Lifestyle (Thur); Food (Tues).
Syndicated Publications: TV Channel Cues (local, newsprint) (S).
Delivery Methods: Mail`Newsstand`Racks
Areas Served - City/County or Portion Thereof, or Zip codes: 66441, 66442
Own Printing Facility?: Y
Commercial printers?: Y
Sat. Circulation Paid: 3092
Sat. Circulation Free: 27
Audit By: Sworn/Estimate/Non-Audited
Audit Date: 12.07.2019
Personnel: Shane Ersland (Ed.)
Parent company (for newspapers): Seaton Publishing Company, Inc.

LAWRENCE JOURNAL-WORLD

Street address 1: 1035 N. 3rd Street, Suite 101-B
Street address 2: 645 New Hampshire St
Street address city: Lawrence
Street address state: KS
Zip/Postal code: 66044-8597
County: Douglas
Country: USA
Mailing address: PO BOX 888
Mailing city: LAWRENCE
Mailing state: KS
Mailing zip: 66044-0888
General Phone: (785) 843-1000
Advertising Phone: (785) 832-6307
Editorial Phone: (785) 832-6361
General/National Adv. E-mail: sstanford@ljworld.com
Display Adv. E-mail: ads@ljworld.com
Classified Adv. e-mail: hstein@ljworld.com
Editorial e-mail: clawhorn@ljworld.com
Primary Website: www.ljworld.com
Mthly Avg Views: 1000000
Mthly Avg Unique Visitors: 477000
Year Established: 1891
News Services: AP
Special Editions: Only in Lawrence (Apr); Kansas University (Aug); KU Basketball (Oct); Holiday Gift Guide (Nov).
Special Weekly Sections: Hometown Lawrence (Real Estate); Go!
Syndicated Publications: USA WEEKEND Magazine (S); Spry (Mon); Relish (Wed); American Profile (Sat)
Delivery Methods: Mail`Newsstand`Carrier`Racks
Areas Served - City/County or Portion Thereof, or Zip codes: 66025, 66044, 66045, 66046, 66047, 66049, 66050, 66066
Own Printing Facility?: N
Commercial printers?: N
Avg Free Circ: 1807
Sat. Circulation Paid: 8751
Sat. Circulation Free: 1807
Sun. Circulation Paid: 9728
Sun. Circulation Free: 985
Audit By: AAM
Audit Date: 30.09.2018
Personnel: Tom Keegan (Sports Ed.); Chad Lawhorn (Pub.); Nick Gerik (Digital Ed.); Kathleen Johnson (Advertising Manager)
Parent company (for newspapers): Ogden Newspapers Inc.

THE LEAVENWORTH TIMES

Street address 1: 422 Seneca St
Street address city: Leavenworth
Street address state: KS
Zip/Postal code: 66048-1910
County: Leavenworth
Country: USA
Mailing address: 422 SENECA ST
Mailing city: LEAVENWORTH
Mailing state: KS
Mailing zip: 66048-1910
General Phone: (913) 682-0305
Advertising Phone: (913) 682-0305
Editorial Phone: (913) 682-0305
General/National Adv. E-mail: kfrey@leavenworthtimes.com
Display Adv. E-mail: kheptig@leavenworthtimes.com
Classified Adv. e-mail: bdaniels@leavenworthtimes.com
Editorial e-mail: jroberts@leavenworthtimes.com
Primary Website: www.leavenworthtimes.com
Year Established: 1857
News Services: AP. GateHouse Media News
Syndicated Publications: USA WEEKEND Magazine (S).
Delivery Methods: Mail`Newsstand`Carrier`Racks
Areas Served - City/County or Portion Thereof, or Zip codes: 66048
Own Printing Facility?: Y
Commercial printers?: N
Sat. Circulation Paid: 4100
Audit By: Sworn/Estimate/Non-Audited
Audit Date: 12.07.2019
Personnel: Barbara Daniels (Classifieds/Circ. Dir.); Sandy Hattock (Gen. Mgr./Adv. Dir.); Beckie Mitchell (Bus. Mgr.); Brent Lager (Sports Ed.); John Richemeier (Reporter); Tim Linn (Reporter); Kristi Vornholt (Classified Mgr.); Kristen Frey (Adv. Acct. Exec.); Kathy Heptig (Av. Acct. Exec.); Tammy Lawson (Adv. Acct. Exec.); Mark Rountree (Managing Editor); Rimsie McConiga (News Ed.); Sandy Hattock (Gen. Mgr./ Adv. Dir.)
Parent company (for newspapers): CherryRoad Media; CherryRoad Media

THE LEADER & TIMES

Street address 1: 16 S Kansas Ave
Street address city: Liberal
Street address state: KS
Zip/Postal code: 67901-3732
County: Seward
Country: USA
Mailing address: PO BOX 889
Mailing city: LIBERAL
Mailing state: KS
Mailing zip: 67905-0889
General Phone: (620) 626-0840
Advertising Phone: (620) 626-0840
Editorial Phone: (620) 626-0840
General/National Adv. E-mail: earl@hpleader.com
Display Adv. E-mail: ads@hpleader.com
Classified Adv. e-mail: denasa@hpleader.com
Editorial e-mail: news@hpleader.com
Primary Website: www.leaderandtimes.com
Year Established: 1987
News Services: AP.
Special Editions: Life & Times (Mar); Life & Times (Sept).
Special Weekly Sections: Entertainment (Fri); Leisure Times (S); Farm & Ranch (Thur); Business Day (Tues); Best Food Day (Wed).
Syndicated Publications: FYI (S).
Delivery Methods: Mail`Newsstand`Carrier`Racks
Areas Served - City/County or Portion Thereof, or Zip codes: Seward County
Sun. Circulation Paid: 4500
Audit By: Sworn/Estimate/Non-Audited
Audit Date: 12.07.2019
Personnel: Earl Watt (Pub.); Denasa Rice (Classified Adv. Mgr.); Jessica Crawford (News)
Parent company (for newspapers): Kansas Press Association

THE MANHATTAN MERCURY

Street address 1: 318 N 5th St
Street address city: Manhattan
Street address state: KS
Zip/Postal code: 66502-5910
County: Riley
Country: USA
Mailing address: PO BOX 787
Mailing city: MANHATTAN
Mailing state: KS
Mailing zip: 66505-0787
General Phone: (785) 776-2200
Advertising Phone: (785) 776-2200
Editorial Phone: (785) 776-2300
General/National Adv. E-mail: advertising@themercury.com
Display Adv. E-mail: advertising@themercury.com
Classified Adv. e-mail: classifieds@themercury.com
Editorial e-mail: news@themercury.com
Primary Website: www.themercury.com
Mthly Avg Views: 837000
Mthly Avg Unique Visitors: 386000
Year Established: 1909
News Services: AP, NYT, LAT-WP, SHNS.
Special Editions: Spring Fix-Up (Apr); KSU (Aug); Weddings/Brides (Feb); Financial Planning (Jan); Senior Citizens (Monthly); Homes (Quarterly); Guide to Manhattan (Sept).
Special Weekly Sections: Food & Health (Tue); Plan-A-Weekend (Thur); Family & Youth, Church, Automotive (Fri); Entertainment, Travel, Business, Ag, Education, Weddings, Military, Home & Garden (Sun)
Syndicated Publications: TV Preview (Fri); Parade (Sun)
Delivery Methods: Mail`Carrier
Areas Served - City/County or Portion Thereof, or Zip codes: Riley and Pottawatomie County
Sun. Circulation Paid: 9136
Audit By: CAC
Audit Date: 31.03.2015
Personnel: Ned M. Seaton (Pub./Ed. in Chief); Edward Seaton (Chairman); Walter Braun (Editorial Page Ed.); Josh Kinder (Sports Ed.); Megan Moser (Exec. Ed.); Mike Dendurent (Wire Ed.); Sarah Midgorden (Photographer); Steve Stallwitz (Adv./Prod. Dir.); Jemie Wataha (Office Mgr.); Tami Yeager (Adv. Rep.); Bonnie Raglin (Circ. Mgr.); Kari Wilson (Customer Service Supervisor); Jelani Yancey (Online Content Mgr.)
Parent company (for newspapers): Kansas Press Association; Seaton Group

MCPHERSON SENTINEL

Street address 1: 116 S Main St
Street address city: McPherson
Street address state: KS
Zip/Postal code: 67460-4852
County: McPherson
Country: USA
Mailing address: 116 S MAIN ST
Mailing city: MCPHERSON
Mailing state: KS
Mailing zip: 67460-4830
General Phone: (620) 241-2422
Classified Adv. e-mail: lborn@mcphersonsentinel.com
Editorial e-mail: news@mcphersonsentinel.com
Primary Website: www.mcphersonsentinel.com
Year Established: 1887
News Services: AP.
Special Editions: Football (Sept); Hunting (Oct); Back-to-School (Aug); Christmas (Dec); Soil Conservation (Jan); 4-H & County Fair (Jul)

Special Weekly Sections: This Week on TV (Fri); Space & Places (Real Estate)
Syndicated Publications: American Profile (Sat); Spry (Sat); Relish (Sat); McPherson County Guide (Yearly); Bridal (Jan)
Delivery Methods: Mail`Newsstand`Carrier`Racks
Areas Served - City/County or Portion Thereof, or Zip codes: 67460
Own Printing Facility?: N
Commercial printers?: Y
Sat. Circulation Paid: 3600
Audit By: Sworn/Estimate/Non-Audited
Audit Date: 12.07.2019
Personnel: Linda Born-Smith (Adv. Dir., Classified); Mindy Kepfield (Mng. Ed.); Brooke Haas (Staff Writer); Matt Cole (Circ. Mgr.)
Parent company (for newspapers): CherryRoad Media; CherryRoad Media

THE NEWTON KANSAN

Street address 1: 121 W 6th St
Street address city: Newton
Street address state: KS
Zip/Postal code: 67114-2117
County: Harvey
Country: USA
Mailing address: PO BOX 268
Mailing city: NEWTON
Mailing state: KS
Mailing zip: 67114-0268
General Phone: (316) 283-1500
Advertising Phone: (316) 283-1500 ext. 110
Editorial Phone: (316) 283-1500 ext. 105
General/National Adv. E-mail: cwallace@thekansan.com
Display Adv. E-mail: jnewman@andoveramerican.com
Classified Adv. e-mail: jgarnica@thekansan.com
Editorial e-mail: cfrey@thekansan.com
Primary Website: www.thekansan.com
Mthly Avg Views: 3813
Mthly Avg Unique Visitors: 260665
Year Established: 1872
News Services: AP.
Special Editions: Bridal Tab (Jan); Welcome to Harvey County (Jun); Home Improvement (Mar); Christmas Kick-Off (Nov); Holiday Creations-Including Cookbook (Oct); Living Well (Quarterly).
Special Weekly Sections: Religion (Fri); Business, Community Calendar (Sat); Farm (Thur).
Syndicated Publications: Relish (Monthly); USA WEEKEND Magazine (Sat).
Delivery Methods: Mail`Carrier`Racks
Areas Served - City/County or Portion Thereof, or Zip codes: Newton and Harvey County
Sat. Circulation Paid: 7513
Audit By: Sworn/Estimate/Non-Audited
Audit Date: 12.07.2019
Personnel: Chad Frey (Mng. Ed.); Shelly Drake (Controller/Business Dir.); Mark Schnabel (Sports Ed.); Connie Wallace (Multimedia Sales Exec.); Jenna Garnica (Classifieds Adv/); Verna Rowe (Business Asst.); Jamie Seger (Circ. Supervisor); Matt Janzen (Creative Design); Lee Bachlet (Pub.); Maria Lazcano (Recruitment)
Parent company (for newspapers): CherryRoad Media; CherryRoad Media

PARSONS SUN

Street address 1: 220 S 18th St
Street address 2: P. O. Box 836
Street address city: Parsons
Street address state: KS
Zip/Postal code: 67357-4218
County: Labette
Country: USA
Mailing address: PO BOX 836
Mailing city: PARSONS
Mailing state: KS
Mailing zip: 67357-0836
General Phone: (620) 421-2000
Advertising Phone: (620) 421-2000
Editorial Phone: (620) 421-2000
General/National Adv. E-mail: rnolting@parsonssun.com
Display Adv. E-mail: alissa@chanute.com
Classified Adv. e-mail: classified@chanute.com
Editorial e-mail: news@parsonssun.com
Primary Website: www.parsonssun.com
Year Established: 1871
News Services: AP
Special Editions: Spring Home Improvement (Apr); Back-to-School (Aug); Football (Aug.); Basketball (Dec); Community magazine (March); Fair mag (Jul); Outdoor Living (May).
Delivery Methods: Mail`Carrier`Racks
Areas Served - City/County or Portion Thereof, or Zip codes: Labette County, parts of Neosho County
Sat. Circulation Paid: 5420
Audit By: Sworn/Estimate/Non-Audited
Audit Date: 12.07.2019
Personnel: Peter J. Cook (Pub.); Amy Jensen (Circ. Mgr.); Ray Nolting (Mng. Ed.); Shanna Guiot (Bus. Mgr.); Michele Cave (Graphic Designer); Jamie Willey (Asst. Mng. Ed.); James Jenson (Production Mgr.); Jason Peake (Sports Ed.); Hailey Phillips; Colleen Williamson; Jan Strait (Display Adv. Sales); Sean Frye; Haley Wiford (Display Adv. Sales); Kim Root (Classified Adv. Sales); Cynthia Miller; Tylie Baumgardner; Heather Forshey; Emily Gudde (Graphic Desgner); Tina Freeberg (Circ. Clerk); Lori Luma (Circ. Clerk)
Parent company (for newspapers): Kansas Newspapers, LLC; Kansas Newspapers LLC

THE MORNING SUN

Street address 1: 701 N Locust St
Street address city: Pittsburg
Street address state: KS
Zip/Postal code: 66762-4038
County: Crawford
Country: USA
Mailing address: PO BOX H
Mailing city: PITTSBURG
Mailing state: KS
Mailing zip: 66762-0570
General Phone: (620) 231-2600
Advertising Phone: (620) 231-2600 ext. 105
Editorial Phone: (620) 231-2600 ext. 140
General/National Adv. E-mail: jryan@morningsun.net
Display Adv. E-mail: jsimon@morningsun.net
Classified Adv. e-mail: lbush@morningsun.net
Editorial e-mail: anash@morningsun.net
Primary Website: www.morningsun.net
Year Established: 1887
News Services: AP.
Special Weekly Sections: Business (Other); Bridal (S); Church (Sat); Best Food Day (Wed).
Syndicated Publications: Relish (Monthly); USA WEEKEND Magazine (S); American Profile (Sat).
Delivery Methods: Mail`Newsstand`Carrier`Racks
Areas Served - City/County or Portion Thereof, or Zip codes: 66762, 66712, 66763, 66743, 66781, 66701, 66734, 66724, 66711, 66756, 66769, 66773, 64832, 64762, 66760, 66782
Own Printing Facility?: Y
Commercial printers?: Y
Sat. Circulation Paid: 5900
Sun. Circulation Paid: 6000
Audit By: Sworn/Estimate/Non-Audited
Audit Date: 12.07.2019
Personnel: Joe Leong (Pub.); Patrick Richardson (Mng. Ed.); Dashuan Vereen (Sports Ed.); Tim Holder (Regional Advertising Director); Miranda Slankard (Classified Sales)
Parent company (for newspapers): Pittsburg Publishing Co.,LLC; CherryRoad Media

THE SALINA JOURNAL

Street address 1: 333 S 4th St
Street address city: Salina
Street address state: KS
Zip/Postal code: 67401-3903
County: Saline
Country: USA
Mailing address: 333 S 4TH ST
Mailing city: SALINA
Mailing state: KS
Mailing zip: 67401-3903
General Phone: (785) 823-6363
Advertising Phone: (785) 822-1446
Editorial Phone: (785) 822-1411
General/National Adv. E-mail: dgilchrist@salina.com
Display Adv. E-mail: kmalm@salina.com
Classified Adv. e-mail: dnelson@salina.com
Editorial e-mail: smontague@salina.com
Primary Website: www.salina.com
Year Established: 1871
News Services: AP, MCT, Tribune
Special Editions: Guide to Salina (Aug); Christmas Gift Guide (Dec); Progress (Feb); Bridal (Jan); Back-to-School (Jul); Progress (Mar); Travel (May); Christmas Gift Guide (Nov); Football (Sept).
Special Weekly Sections: Scene/Entertainment (Fri); Neighbors (Mon); Church (Sat); Home/Garden (Thur); Best Food Day (Wed).
Syndicated Publications: Dream Homes (Quarterly); USA WEEKEND Magazine (S); TV Week (TV Listings) (Sat).
Delivery Methods: Mail`Newsstand`Carrier`Racks
Areas Served - City/County or Portion Thereof, or Zip codes: North-central and northwest Kansas
Own Printing Facility?: Y
Commercial printers?: Y
Avg Free Circ: 0
Sat. Circulation Paid: 18365
Sat. Circulation Free: 0
Sun. Circulation Paid: 19317
Sun. Circulation Free: 0
Audit By: VAC
Audit Date: 31.12.2016
Personnel: M. Olaf Frandsen (Pub.); Kathy Malm (Adv. Mgr.); Mollie Purcell (Circ. Mgr.); Sharon Montague (Exec. Ed.); Tom Dorsey (Chief Photograher); Bob Davidson (Sports Ed.); Dave Gilchrist (Rgl. Adv. Dir.); Debbie Nelson (Classified Consultant); Sue Austin (Classified Consultant); Norbert Laue (Prod. Dir.); Roxy Belden (Business Office Mgr.)
Parent company (for newspapers): CherryRoad Media; Gannett

THE TOPEKA CAPITAL-JOURNAL

Street address 1: 616 SE Jefferson St
Street address city: Topeka
Street address state: KS
Zip/Postal code: 66607-1137
County: Shawnee
Country: USA
Mailing address: 616 SE JEFFERSON ST
Mailing city: TOPEKA
Mailing state: KS
Mailing zip: 66607-1120
General Phone: (785) 295-1111
Advertising Phone: (785) 295-1263
Editorial Phone: (785) 295-1212
General/National Adv. E-mail: susan.cantrell@cjonline.com
Display Adv. E-mail: susan.cantrell@cjonline.com
Classified Adv. e-mail: linda.girardin@cjonline.com
Editorial e-mail: tomari.quinn@cjonline.com
Primary Website: www.cjonline.com
Mthly Avg Views: 13890000
Mthly Avg Unique Visitors: 1459500
Year Established: 1858
News Services: SHNS, AP, LAT-WP.
Special Editions: Best of Topeka; Prime Time, Downtown Topeka, Momentum 2022
Special Weekly Sections: Real Estate (Sat); Religion (Sat); Food & Fun (Sun)
Syndicated Publications: Relish (Wednesday) Parade (Sunday)
Delivery Methods: Mail`Newsstand`Carrier`Racks
Areas Served - City/County or Portion Thereof, or Zip codes: Shawnee County
Own Printing Facility?: N
Commercial printers?: N
Avg Free Circ: 3595
Sat. Circulation Paid: 20273
Sat. Circulation Free: 3595
Sun. Circulation Paid: 25480
Sun. Circulation Free: 2850
Audit By: AAM
Audit Date: 30.06.2017
Personnel: Stephen Wade (Pub.); Terri Benson (Dir. of Digital Sales); Tomari Quinn (Ed. and VP audience); Tim Bisel (Ed.)
Parent company (for newspapers): Gannett; CherryRoad Media

THE WICHITA EAGLE

Street address 1: 330 N. Mead
Street address city: Wichita
Street address state: KS
Zip/Postal code: 67202
County: Sedgwick
Country: USA
General Phone: (316) 268-6000
Advertising Phone: (316) 269-6709
Editorial Phone: (316) 268-6351
General/National Adv. E-mail: wenews@wichitaeagle.com
Display Adv. E-mail: jsmith@wichitaeagle.com
Classified Adv. e-mail: classified@wichitaeagle.com
Editorial e-mail: mroehrman@wichitaeagle.com
Primary Website: www.kansas.com
Mthly Avg Views: 10500000
Mthly Avg Unique Visitors: 1700000
Year Established: 1872
News Services: AP, MCT, WP/BLOOM
Syndicated Publications: Parade (S)
Delivery Methods: Newsstand`Carrier`Racks
Areas Served - City/County or Portion Thereof, or Zip codes: Sedgwick County
Own Printing Facility?: Y
Commercial printers?: Y
Sat. Circulation Paid: 37947
Sun. Circulation Paid: 55259
Audit By: AAM
Audit Date: 30.06.2018
Personnel: Michael Roehrman (Ed.); Jean Hays (Investigations Ed.); Marcia Werts (Content Ed.); Jeff Rosen (Sports Ed.); Jaime Green (Video Ed.); Julie Mah (Social Media Ed.)
Parent company (for newspapers): The McClatchy Company; McClatchy Company

COWLEY COURIER TRAVELER

Street address 1: PO Box 543
Street address city: Winfield
Street address state: KS
Zip/Postal code: 67156-0543
County: Cowley
Country: USA
Mailing address: PO BOX 543
Mailing city: WINFIELD
Mailing state: KS
Mailing zip: 67156-0543
General Phone: (620) 221-1050
General/National Adv. E-mail: advertising1@ctnewsonline.com
Display Adv. E-mail: classified@ctnewsonline.com
Editorial e-mail: news1@ctnewsonline.com
Primary Website: ctnewsonline.com
Delivery Methods: Mail
Areas Served - City/County or Portion Thereof, or Zip codes: 67156 67024
Audit By: Sworn/Estimate/Non-Audited
Audit Date: 10.06.2019
Personnel: David A. Seaton (Pub.); Marsha Wesler (Dir. Sales/Mktg.); Arty Hicks
Parent company (for newspapers): Winfield Publishing Co., Inc.

WINFIELD DAILY COURIER

Street address 1: 201 E 9th Ave
Street address city: Winfield
Street address state: KS
Zip/Postal code: 67156-2817
County: Cowley
Country: USA
Mailing address: PO BOX 543
Mailing city: WINFIELD
Mailing state: KS
Mailing zip: 67156-0543
General Phone: (620) 221-1050
Advertising Phone: (620) 221-1050
Editorial Phone: (620) 221-1050
General/National Adv. E-mail: courier@winfieldcourier.com
Display Adv. E-mail: advertising@winfieldcourier.com
Classified Adv. e-mail: classified@winfieldcourier.com
Editorial e-mail: zaccaria@winfieldcourier.com
Primary Website: www.winfieldcourier.com
Year Established: 1873
News Services: AP, LAT-WP.
Special Editions: Health Care (Apr); Cowley County Fair (Aug); Achievement (Feb); Spring Clean Up Tab (Mar); Cowley County Farmer-Rancher (Monthly); Getting Ready for Winter (Oct); Football Tab (Sept).
Special Weekly Sections: Recipes Tab; Kids Today.
Syndicated Publications: USA WEEKEND Magazine (Sat).
Delivery Methods: Mail`Newsstand`Racks
Areas Served - City/County or Portion Thereof, or Zip codes: Cowley, Sumner, Butler, Elk, and Chautauqua County
Own Printing Facility?: Y
Commercial printers?: Y
Sat. Circulation Paid: 4522
Audit By: Sworn/Estimate/Non-Audited
Audit Date: 12.07.2019
Personnel: Lloyd Craig (Pub.); Marsha Wesseler (Adv. Dir.); Frederick D. Seaton (Editorial Page Ed.); Judy Zaccaria (Managing Ed.); Dave Seaton (Chairman); David A. Seaton (Pub.); Jennifer Harrison (Adv.

Sales); Diana Taylor (Adv. Sales); Beth Glantz (Circ. Mgr.); Janet Dolch (Office Mgr.); Thomas Carver (Webmaster); Stella Lankton (Composition); Terri Snow (Classified)
Parent company (for newspapers): Kansas Press Association

KENTUCKY

THE DAILY INDEPENDENT

Street address 1: 224 17th St
Street address city: Ashland
Street address state: KY
Zip/Postal code: 41101-7606
County: Boyd
Country: USA
Mailing address: PO BOX 311
Mailing city: ASHLAND
Mailing state: KY
Mailing zip: 41105-0311
General Phone: (606) 326-2600
Advertising Phone: (606) 326-2622
Editorial Phone: (606) 326-2664
General/National Adv. E-mail: lcallihan@dailyindependent.com
Display Adv. E-mail: adservices@dailyindependent.com
Classified Adv. e-mail: classified@dailyindependent.com
Editorial e-mail: asnyder@dailyindependent.com
Primary Website: www.dailyindependent.com
Mthly Avg Views: 998000
Mthly Avg Unique Visitors: 157000
Year Established: 1896
News Services: AP, CNHI, SHNS.
Special Editions: Girls Basketball (Dec); Parents & Kids (Feb); Taxes & Investing (Jan); Primetime (Jul); Carter County Salute (Jun); Entertainment (Mar); Boys Basketball (Nov); Insight (Oct);Progress (March)
Special Weekly Sections: Best Food Day (Wed).
Delivery Methods: Mail`Newsstand`Carrier`Racks
Areas Served - City/County or Portion Thereof, or Zip codes: Greenup County, Boyd County, Carter County, Lawrence County
Own Printing Facility?: Y
Commercial printers?: N
Avg Free Circ: 26
Sat. Circulation Paid: 8342
Sat. Circulation Free: 1004
Sun. Circulation Paid: 9172
Sun. Circulation Free: 240
Audit By: Sworn/Estimate/Non-Audited
Audit Date: 31.12.2017
Personnel: Aaron Snyder (Editor); Eddie Blakeley (Pub.); Lee Ward (Lifestyles Ed.); Gene Hallahan (Composing Mgr.); Lisa Callihan (Business Manager); Lisa Callihan (Publisher); Kim Harper (Advertising Manager); Michael Gelbman (Advertising Director); Mark Maynard (Editor); Bengy Barrett (Prodn. Mgr., Mailroom); Mary Goldy (Website Creative/Adv.); David Rigas (Audience Development Director); Adam Vankirk (Copy Desk Ed./Night Ed.); Jami Kelley (News Clerk)
Parent company (for newspapers): CNHI, LLC; CNHI, LLC

DAILY NEWS

Street address 1: 813 College St
Street address city: Bowling Green
Street address state: KY
Zip/Postal code: 42101-2132
County: Warren
Country: USA
Mailing address: PO BOX 90012
Mailing city: BOWLING GREEN
Mailing state: KY
Mailing zip: 42102-9012
General Phone: (270) 781-1700
Advertising Phone: (270) 783-3233
Editorial Phone: (270) 783-3269
General/National Adv. E-mail: mmahagan@bgdailynews.com
Display Adv. E-mail: mmahagan@bgdailynews.com
Classified Adv. e-mail: jdickens@bgdailynews.com
Editorial e-mail: sgaines@bgdailynews.com
Primary Website: www.bgdailynews.com
Year Established: 1854
News Services: AP.
Special Editions: Home & Garden Tab (Apr); Pets on Parade (Aug); Holiday Gift Guide (Dec); Financial Tab (Feb); Back to School Tab (Jul); Soap Box Derby Tab (May); High School Basketball Tab (Nov); Industry Appreciation Tab (Oct); House to Home (Quarterly); Better Health &
Special Weekly Sections: Comics (Sun); Education (Tue); Super Wednesday, Business, NIE Copies (Wed); Time Out, Entertainment (Thur); Faith (Friday); Wellness (Sat);
Syndicated Publications: Relish (Monthly); Parade (S); American Profile (Weekly).
Delivery Methods: Mail`Newsstand`Carrier`Racks
Areas Served - City/County or Portion Thereof, or Zip codes: South Central Kentucky
Own Printing Facility?: Y
Commercial printers?: N
Sat. Circulation Paid: 21620
Sun. Circulation Paid: 22785
Audit By: AAM
Audit Date: 30.09.2013
Personnel: Pipes Gaines (Pub./Pres.); Scott Gaines (Co-Pub.); Mark Mahagan (Adv. Mgr.); Julie Dickens (Adv. Mgr., Classified); Joanie Davis (Adv. Mgr., Nat'l); Troy Warren (Circ. Mgr.); Sharrye Noel (Mgr., Educ. Serv.); Andy Dennis (Managing Ed.); Daniel Pike (City Ed.); Steve Gaines (Editorial Page Ed.); Alyssa Harvey (Features Ed.); Joe Imel (Asst. Mgr./Photo Editor); Larry Simpson (Prodn. Mgr.); George Stewart (Packaging Mgr.); Glen Spear (Prodn. Mgr., Pressroom); Mary Gaines (Co-Owner); Kent O'Toole (Gen. Mgr.); Melissa Miller (Office Mgr.); Glenda Spear (Accountant); Shirleen Conrad (Office Asst.); Tommy Richards (Asst. Circ. Dir.); Paul Ford (Single Copy Mgr.); Robyn Minor (City Ed.); Debi Highland (News Ed.); Eugene Embry (Weekend Ed.); Scotty Hyde (Copy Ed.); Crystal Akers (Copy Ed.); Mary Ann Andrews (Copy Editor); Rob Herbst (Sports Ed.); Miranda Pederson (Chief Photographer); George Steward (Packaging Mgr.)
Parent company (for newspapers): Bowling Green news Publishing Co.; Gaines Family

TIMES-TRIBUNE

Street address 1: 201 N Kentucky Ave
Street address city: Corbin
Street address state: KY
Zip/Postal code: 40701-1529
County: Whitley
Country: USA
Mailing address: PO BOX 516
Mailing city: CORBIN
Mailing state: KY
Mailing zip: 40702-0516
General Phone: (606) 528-2464
Advertising Phone: (606) 528-7898 ext. 27
Editorial Phone: (606) 528-7898 ext. 37
General/National Adv. E-mail: kjones@sentinel-echo.com
Display Adv. E-mail: rconn@thetimestribune.com
Classified Adv. e-mail: rlawson@thetimestribune.com
Editorial e-mail: editor@thetimestribune.com
Primary Website: www.thetimestribune.com
Year Established: 1882
News Services: AP.
Special Weekly Sections: Church Page (Sat); Business (Tues); Best Food Day (Wed).
Syndicated Publications: TV Guide (Sat); American Profile (Weekly).
Delivery Methods: Mail
Areas Served - City/County or Portion Thereof, or Zip codes: Knox, Laurel & Whitley Counties (KY)
Sat. Circulation Paid: 6166
Audit By: Sworn/Estimate/Non-Audited
Audit Date: 12.07.2019
Personnel: Willie Sawyers (Pub.); Becky Killian (Ed.); Kathy Jones (Adv. Mgr.); Kristie Gray (Business Mgr.); Brenda House (Accounting Clerk); Rebecca Conn (Adv. Sales Asst.); Lisa Harrison (Adv. Rep.); Ruth Rose (Adv. Rep.); Patricia Humphrey (Adv. Clerk); Rhonda Lawson (Adv. Classified Clerk); Cathy Farris (Circ. Mgr.); Yolanda Couch (Circ. District Mgr.); Renee Smith (Circ. Clerk); Chris Parsons (Sports Ed.); Christina Bentley (Web/Special Pages Ed.); Brad Hall (Nighttime/Religion Page Ed.)
Parent company (for newspapers): CNHI, LLC; CNHI, LLC

THE ADVOCATE-MESSENGER

Street address 1: 330 S 4th St
Street address city: Danville
Street address state: KY
Zip/Postal code: 40422-2033
County: Boyle
Country: USA
Mailing address: 330 S 4TH ST
Mailing city: DANVILLE
Mailing state: KY
Mailing zip: 40422-2033
General Phone: (859) 236-2551
Advertising Phone: (859) 236-2551
Editorial Phone: (859) 236-2551
General/National Adv. E-mail: gprice@amnews.com
Display Adv. E-mail: gprice@amnews.com
Classified Adv. e-mail: cwarren@amnews.com
Editorial e-mail: johnn@amnews.com
Primary Website: www.amnews.com
Year Established: 1940
News Services: AP.
Special Editions: Football Preview (Aug); Season's Greetings (Dec); Brass Band Festival (Jun); Basketball Preview (Nov).
Special Weekly Sections: Church Page (Fri); Tec Know Page (Mon); Business Page (S); Country Life Page (Tues); Seasonings (Wed).
Syndicated Publications: Parade (S); American Profile (Weekly).
Delivery Methods: Carrier
Areas Served - City/County or Portion Thereof, or Zip codes: South central Kentucky, south of Lexington, with distribution primarily in Boyle, Lincoln, Casey, Mercer and Garrard counties
Sun. Circulation Paid: 9913
Audit By: Sworn/Estimate/Non-Audited
Audit Date: 12.07.2019
Personnel: Renita Cox (Controller); Brenda Townes (District Mgr.); John Nelson (Exec. Ed.); Vicki Stevens (Asst. Managing Ed.); Larry Vaught (Sports Ed.); James Morris (Info. Tech. Dir.); Larry Hensley (Pres./Pub./Ed.); Mark Walker (Circ. Mgr.); Candi Campbell (NIE Coord.); Geri Ray (Adv. Mgr.); Carol Warren (Classifieds Asst.); Bobbie Curd; Hal Morris (Asst. Sports Ed.); John Preston (Digital Mgr.); Gary Moyers; Jerry Dunn (Adv. Mgr., Nat'l)
Parent company (for newspapers): Boone Newspapers, Inc.

THE NEWS-ENTERPRISE

Street address 1: 200 Sycamore St.
Street address 2: Suite 134
Street address city: Elizabethtown
Street address state: KY
Zip/Postal code: 42701-2455
County: Hardin
Country: USA
Mailing address: 200 Sycamore St., Suite 134
Mailing city: ELIZABETHTOWN
Mailing state: KY
Mailing zip: 42701-2499
General Phone: (270) 769-1200
Advertising Phone: (270) 505-1411
Editorial Phone: (270) 505-1418
General/National Adv. E-mail: ne@thenewsenterprise.com
Display Adv. E-mail: vserra@thenewsenterprise.com
Classified Adv. e-mail: bchism@thenewsenterprise.com
Editorial e-mail: ne@thenewsenterprise.com
Primary Website: www.thenewsenterprise.com
Mthly Avg Views: 880000
Mthly Avg Unique Visitors: 120000
Year Established: 1974
News Services: AP.
Special Weekly Sections: Entertainment (Thu); Senior Living (Mon); Business Pages (T, Th, S); Best Food Day (Weekend); Real Estate (Fri); Features (daily).
Delivery Methods: Newsstand`Carrier`Racks
Areas Served - City/County or Portion Thereof, or Zip codes: Elizabethtown (KY), Hardin County & Surrouding areas
Own Printing Facility?: Y
Commercial printers?: Y
Sun. Circulation Paid: 10590
Sun. Circulation Free: 432
Audit By: AAM
Audit Date: 9/31/2018
Personnel: Chris Ordway (Pub.); Lydia Leasor (Graphic Design Mgr); Ben Sheroan (Publisher); Chuck Jones (Sports Ed.); Valerie Serra (Advertising Director); David Dickens (Production Mgr.); Gina Clear (Editor); Jenny Simpson (Circulation Director); Charles Love (Prodn. Press Team Leader); Lisa D'Alessio (Business Mgr.); Erin Hahn (Adv. Dir.); Tom Siemers (Circ. Mgr.)
Parent company (for newspapers): Paxton Media Group; Landmark Communications, Inc.

THE STATE JOURNAL

Street address 1: 1216 Wilkinson Blvd
Street address city: Frankfort
Street address state: KY
Zip/Postal code: 40601-1243
County: Franklin
Country: USA
Mailing address: PO BOX 368
Mailing city: FRANKFORT
Mailing state: KY
Mailing zip: 40602-0368
General Phone: (502) 227-4556
Advertising Phone: (502) 227-4556
Editorial Phone: (502) 227-4556
General/National Adv. E-mail: admaenza@state-journal.com
Display Adv. E-mail: llynch@state-journal.com
Classified Adv. e-mail: llynch@state-journal.com
Editorial e-mail: pcase@state-journal.com
Primary Website: www.state-journal.com
Year Established: 1902
News Services: AP, NYT.
Syndicated Publications: Main Street (S); American Profile (Weekly).
Delivery Methods: Mail`Newsstand`Carrier`Racks
Areas Served - City/County or Portion Thereof, or Zip codes: Franklin County, Lawrence County
Own Printing Facility?: Y
Sun. Circulation Paid: 7361
Audit By: CAC
Audit Date: 31.03.2015
Personnel: Steve Stewart (Pub.); Catherine Boone (Gen. Mgr.); Sheri Bunker (Customer Service Manager); Chanda Veno (Mng. Ed.); Jim Wainscott (CSR); Hannah Brown (Design Ed.)
Parent company (for newspapers): Boone Newspapers, Inc.

GLASGOW DAILY TIMES

Street address 1: 100 Commerce Dr
Street address city: Glasgow
Street address state: KY
Zip/Postal code: 42141-1153
County: Barren
Country: USA
Mailing address: 100 COMMERCE DR
Mailing city: GLASGOW
Mailing state: KY
Mailing zip: 42141-1153
General Phone: (270) 678-5171
Advertising Phone: (270) 678-5171 ext. 235
Editorial Phone: (270) 678-5171 ext. 234
General/National Adv. E-mail: kponder@glasgowdailytimes.com
Display Adv. E-mail: kponder@glasgowdailytimes.com
Classified Adv. e-mail: classified@glasgowdailytimes.com
Editorial e-mail: mthomas@glasgowdailytimes.com
Primary Website: www.glasgowdailytimes.com
Year Established: 1865
News Services: AP.
Special Weekly Sections: TV Screen (Sat); Church (S);
Syndicated Publications: Relish (Monthly); Parade (S).
Delivery Methods: Mail`Newsstand`Racks
Areas Served - City/County or Portion Thereof, or Zip codes: 42717; 42722; 42127; 42129; 42133; 42141; 42746; 42152; 42749; 42759; 42765; 42160; 42171; 42166; 42167
Own Printing Facility?: N
Commercial printers?: N
Sat. Circulation Paid: 6267
Sun. Circulation Paid: 6267
Audit By: AAM
Audit Date: 30.09.2014
Personnel: Bill Hanson (Pub.); Cindy Green (Business Mgr.); James Brown (Digital Ed.); Daniel Pike (Gen. Mgr.); Lisa Simpson Strange (News Ed.); Martha J. Thomas (Newsroom Clerk); Scott Wilson (Sports Ed.); Michelle Copass (Special Accounts Mgr.); Lori Decker (Acct. Exec.); Teresa Furlong; Teresa S. Nunn; Steven D. Wilson (Acct. Exec.); Janis Davis (Circ. Bookkeeper); Sherry Powell (Classified Sales Exec.); Chuck Roberts (Prodn. Dir.); Mary Pike (Circ. Dir.); Scotty Maxwell (General Manager); Amy Lee (Adv. Dir.); Katie Batey (Customer Service)

Parent company (for newspapers): CNHI, LLC; CNHI, LLC

THE HARLAN DAILY ENTERPRISE

Street address 1: 1548 S US Highway 421
Street address city: Harlan
Street address state: KY
Zip/Postal code: 40831-2501
County: Harlan
Country: USA
Mailing address: PO BOX 1155
Mailing city: HARLAN
Mailing state: KY
Mailing zip: 40831-1155
General Phone: (606) 573-4510
Advertising Phone: (606) 573-4510
Editorial Phone: (606) 573-4510
General/National Adv. E-mail: wminard@civitasmedia.com
Display Adv. E-mail: wminiard@civitasmedia.com
Classified Adv. e-mail: ebell@civitasmedia.com
Editorial e-mail: bmoore@civitasmedia.com
Primary Website: www.harlandaily.com
Year Established: 1928
News Services: Landon Media Group.
Special Editions: Home Improvement (Apr); Christmas Greetings (Dec); Harlan County Heritage Tab (Feb); Christmas Shopping Guide (Nov); Fall Car Care Tab (Oct); Home Improvement (Sept).
Syndicated Publications: USA WEEKEND Magazine (Sat); American Profile (Weekly).
Delivery Methods: Mail`Newsstand`Carrier`Racks
Areas Served - City/County or Portion Thereof, or Zip codes: Harlan County, Kentucky
Own Printing Facility?: N
Commercial printers?: N
Sat. Circulation Paid: 5000
Audit By: Sworn/Estimate/Non-Audited
Audit Date: 12.07.2019
Personnel: Debbie Caldwell (News Ed.); Eva Bell (Receptionist/Classifieds/Legals); Bethany Moore (Editorial Clerk); Nola Sizemore (Staff Writer); Cynthia Orr (Publisher); Pat Cheek (Rgl. Admin. Coord.); Wylene Miniard (Inside Sales Rep.); Bryan Key (Business Development Specialist); Kipper House (Rgl. Delivery Mgr.); John Henson (Sports Ed.); Anthony Cloud (Reg. Ed.)
Parent company (for newspapers): Boone Newspapers, Inc.

THE GLEANER

Street address 1: 455 Klutey Park Plaza Dr
Street address 2: Ste A
Street address city: Henderson
Street address state: KY
Zip/Postal code: 42420-5213
County: Henderson
Country: USA
Mailing address: PO BOX 4
Mailing city: HENDERSON
Mailing state: KY
Mailing zip: 42419-0004
General Phone: (270) 827-2000
Advertising Phone: (270) 827-2000
Editorial Phone: (270) 831-8333
General/National Adv. E-mail: PMaurice@TheGleaner.com
Display Adv. E-mail: PMaurice@TheGleaner.com
Classified Adv. e-mail: PMaurice@TheGleaner.com
Editorial e-mail: DDixon@TheGleaner.com
Primary Website: www.thegleaner.com
Mthly Avg Unique Visitors: 712940
Year Established: 1885
News Services: AP.
Special Editions: Do-It-Yourself (Apr); Football Tab (Aug); Fair (Jul); Lawn & Garden (Mar); Holiday Entertaining (Nov).
Special Weekly Sections: NASCAR (Fri); Business (S); Farm (Sat); Health (Thur); Gleaner Jr. (Tues).
Syndicated Publications: Parade (S).
Delivery Methods: Mail`Carrier
Areas Served - City/County or Portion Thereof, or Zip codes: Henderson (KY)
Avg Free Circ: 413
Sat. Circulation Paid: 4997
Sat. Circulation Free: 413
Sun. Circulation Paid: 6105
Sun. Circulation Free: 380
Audit By: AAM
Audit Date: 31.12.2017
Personnel: Jack Pate (Pub.); Lori Bush (Circ. Mgr.); David Dixon (Ed.); Mike Moore (Graphics Ed./Art Dir.); Judy Jenkins (Health/Medical Ed.); Donna Stinnett (Lifestyle Ed.); Doug White (News Ed.); Mike Lawrence (Photo Ed.); Frank Boyett (Religion Ed.); Chuck Stinnett (Science/Technology Ed.); Caroline Sexton (Sales Mgr.); Sharon Alvey (Classified Sales); Karen Cox (Customer Service Rep.)
Parent company (for newspapers): Gannett

KENTUCKY NEW ERA

Street address 1: 1618 E 9th St
Street address city: Hopkinsville
Street address state: KY
Zip/Postal code: 42240-4430
County: Christian
Country: USA
Mailing address: PO BOX 729
Mailing city: HOPKINSVILLE
Mailing state: KY
Mailing zip: 42241-0729
General Phone: (270) 886-4444
Advertising Phone: (270) 887-3278
Editorial Phone: (270) 887-3230
General/National Adv. E-mail: advertising@kentuckynewera.com
Display Adv. E-mail: advertising@kentuckynewera.com
Classified Adv. e-mail: classified@kentuckynewera.com
Editorial e-mail: editor@kentuckynewera.com
Primary Website: www.kentuckynewera.com
Year Established: 1869
News Services: AP, TMS.
Special Editions: Please call our advertising department for a full list of special sections published monthly and yearly.
Special Weekly Sections: University of Kentucky Sports Page (Fri); Tax Tips (weekly, Jan-Apr) (Other); Outdoor Page (Sat); Farm Page (Thur); Best Food Day (Wed); Homes and Building Tips (Apr.-Jan.) (Weekly).
Syndicated Publications: Relish (Monthly); USA WEEKEND Magazine (Sat); American Profile (Weekly), Spry (Monthly), Athlon Sports (Monthly)
Delivery Methods: Newsstand`Carrier`Racks
Areas Served - City/County or Portion Thereof, or Zip codes: 42240, 42262, 42234, 42286, 42223, 42211, 42220, 42221, 42236, 42241, 42254, 42266, 42445, 42280, 42220, 42204, 42216
Own Printing Facility?: Y
Sat. Circulation Paid: 7073
Audit By: AAM
Audit Date: 30.09.2015
Personnel: Taylor Wood Hayes (Pub.); Sheryl Ellis (VP and Gen. Mgr.); Ted Jatczak (Adv./Mktg. Mgr.); Nancy Reece (Classified Manager); Tony Henson (Circ. Dir.); Eli Pace (Ed.); Chris Hollis (Prod. Mgr.); Joe Wilson (Sports Editor); Dana Long (Photographer / Copy Desk Chief); Jennifer Brown (Opinion Ed.); Chris Jung (Sports Editor); Melissa Mollohan (Features Ed.); Richard Wimsatt (Adv. Rep.); Kristi Williams (Adv. Rep.); Jillian Weatherford (Adv. Rep.); Bernie Starr (Adv. Rep.); Traci Rodgers (Adv. Rep.); Cynthia Cunningham (Classified Adv. Sales); John Godsey (Webmaster); Chuck Henderson (Pres.); Cole Davis (Copy Ed.)
Parent company (for newspapers): Paxton Media Group

LEXINGTON HERALD-LEADER

Street address 1: 100 Midland Avenue
Street address city: Lexington
Street address state: KY
Zip/Postal code: 40508-1999
County: Fayette
Country: USA
Mailing address: 100 MIDLAND AVE
Mailing city: LEXINGTON
Mailing state: KY
Mailing zip: 40508-1999
General Phone: (859) 231-3100
Advertising Phone: (859) 231-3434
Editorial Phone: (859) 231-3446
General/National Adv. E-mail: kwoods@herald-leader.com
Display Adv. E-mail: kwoods@herald-leader.com
Classified Adv. e-mail: kwoods@herald-leader.com
Editorial e-mail: pbaniak@herald-leader.com
Primary Website: www.kentucky.com
Mthly Avg Views: 13932767
Mthly Avg Unique Visitors: 2063045
News Services: AP, NYT, MCT, WP.
Special Weekly Sections: Weekender (Fri); Business Monday (Mon);
Syndicated Publications: Parade (S).
Delivery Methods: Mail`Newsstand`Carrier`Racks
Areas Served - City/County or Portion Thereof, or Zip codes: Fayette, Bourbon, Clark, Montgomery, Powell, Estill, Madison, Garrard, Jessamine, Boyle, Mercer, Woodford, Anderson, Franklin, Scott, Harrison
Own Printing Facility?: N
Commercial printers?: Y
Sat. Circulation Paid: 47854
Sun. Circulation Paid: 63984
Audit By: AAM
Audit Date: 31.12.2017
Personnel: Peter Baniak (Gen. Mgr./Ed.); Janet Plechowski (Asst. to Gen. Mgr.); Heather McGinnis (Sales Dir.); Sarah Cannon (Data Coordinator/ Diagnostics); Bailey Vandiver (Editorial Asst.)
Parent company (for newspapers): McClatchy; Chatham Asset Management

THE COURIER-JOURNAL

Street address 1: 525 W Broadway
Street address city: Louisville
Street address state: KY
Zip/Postal code: 40202-2206
County: Jefferson
Country: USA
Mailing address: PO BOX 740031
Mailing city: LOUISVILLE
Mailing state: KY
Mailing zip: 40201-7431
General Phone: (502) 582-4011
Advertising Phone: (502) 582-4711
Editorial Phone: (502) 582-4691
General/National Adv. E-mail: erhelton@gannett.com
Display Adv. E-mail: erhelton@gannett.com
Classified Adv. e-mail: classifieds@courier-journal.com
Editorial e-mail: nbudde@courier-journal.com
Primary Website: www.courier-journal.com
Mthly Avg Views: 14700000
Mthly Avg Unique Visitors: 1537329
Year Established: 1868
News Services: AP, NYT, LAT-WP, GNS, Dow Jones.
Special Editions: Thunder Preview (Apr); Used Car Guide (Aug); Be Heathly Kentuckiana (Feb); Parent's Survival Guide (Jul); Savvy Home Buyer (Mar); Be Healthy Kentuckiana (May); Be Healthy Kentuckiana (Nov); Tour of Homes-2nd Edition (Oct); On Course (Sept).
Special Weekly Sections: Food (Wed); Health & Fitness (Fri); Home & Garden (Sat); Arts, Sunday Scene (Sun)
Syndicated Publications: Her Scene (Quarterly); TV Week & Cable Guide (S); USA WEEKEND Magazine (Sat).
Delivery Methods: Mail`Newsstand`Carrier`Racks
Areas Served - City/County or Portion Thereof, or Zip codes: Kentucky & Indiana
Own Printing Facility?: Y
Commercial printers?: Y
Sat. Circulation Paid: 78267
Sun. Circulation Paid: 110258
Audit By: AAM
Audit Date: 30.09.2018
Personnel: Arnold Garson (Pres./Pub.); Jere Downs (Food/Restaurants Editor); Mike Trautman (Metro Ed.); Jeffrey Puckett (Music Critic); James Kirchner (Op. News Mgr.); Keith Runyon (Opinion Pages Ed.); Peter Smith (Religion Writer); Harry Bryan (Sports Ed.); Veda Morgan (News Dir.); Jeff Faughender (Online Production Mgr.); Wesley Jackson (Pres./Pub.); Peter Bateman (VP, IT); Neil Budde (Exec. Ed./VP, News); Dan Blake (Exec. Producer); David Harrison (Photo Dir.); Kim Kolarik (Community Engagement Dir.)
Parent company (for newspapers): Gannett

THE MESSENGER

Street address 1: 221 S Main St
Street address city: Madisonville
Street address state: KY
Zip/Postal code: 42431-2557
County: Hopkins
Country: USA
Mailing address: PO BOX 529
Mailing city: MADISONVILLE
Mailing state: KY
Mailing zip: 42431-0010
General Phone: (270) 824-3300
Advertising Phone: (270) 824-3300
Editorial Phone: (270) 824-3221
General/National Adv. E-mail: newsroom@the-messenger.com
Display Adv. E-mail: rwelch@the-messenger.com
Classified Adv. e-mail: csr@messenger-inquirer.com
Editorial e-mail: letters@the-messenger.com
Primary Website: www.the-messenger.com
Mthly Avg Views: 2200000
Mthly Avg Unique Visitors: 72000
Year Established: 1917
News Services: AP.
Special Editions: Football (Aug); Christmas Sections (Dec); Bridal Tour (Jan); Fair Tab (Jul); Christmas Sections (Nov); Women in Business (Oct); Progress (Sept).
Special Weekly Sections: Pennyrile Plus News & Review (Wed).
Syndicated Publications: Parade Magazine (S). Athlon Sports, Spry, Relish American Profile (W)
Delivery Methods: Mail`Newsstand`Carrier`Racks
Areas Served - City/County or Portion Thereof, or Zip codes: 42431
Own Printing Facility?: N
Commercial printers?: Y
Sat. Circulation Paid: 5147
Sun. Circulation Paid: 5147
Audit By: USPS
Audit Date: 11.12.2017
Personnel: Rick Welch (Pub.); Deborah Littlepage (Adv. Dir.); Don Perryman (Ed.); Melanie Miller (Bus. Office); Tina Dillingham (Retail Acct. Exec.); Melanie Duncan (Retail Acct. Exec.); Barry Carden (Circ. Dir.)
Parent company (for newspapers): Paxton Media Group

THE LEDGER INDEPENDENT

Street address 1: 120 Limestone St
Street address city: Maysville
Street address state: KY
Zip/Postal code: 41056-1284
County: Mason
Country: USA
Mailing state: KY
General Phone: (606) 564-9091
Advertising Phone: (606) 564-9091
Editorial Phone: (606) 564-9091
General/National Adv. E-mail: jdonahue@cmpapers.com
Display Adv. E-mail: jdonahue@cmpapers.com
Classified Adv. e-mail: jdonahue@cmpapers.com
Editorial e-mail: choots@cmpapers.com
Primary Website: www.maysville-online.com
Mthly Avg Views: 215000
Mthly Avg Unique Visitors: 80000
Year Established: 1968
News Services: AP.
Special Editions: Fall Sports Preview (Aug); Winter Sports Preview (Jan); Grad section (Jun); Back-to-School (Aug); Christmas Greetings (Dec); Cookbook (Feb); Income Tax Guide (Jan); Dairy Month (Jun); Basketball (Mar); Homemakers (May); Basketball (Nov); 4-H (Oct); Car Care (Sept).
Special Weekly Sections: Food (Mon); Lifestyles/TV (Sat); Home and Garden (Thur); Food (Wed).
Delivery Methods: Mail`Carrier`Racks
Areas Served - City/County or Portion Thereof, or Zip codes: Seven-countys from Northern Kentucky and Southern Ohio
Own Printing Facility?: Y
Commercial printers?: Y
Sat. Circulation Paid: 5139
Sat. Circulation Free: 97
Audit By: USPS
Audit Date: 28.09.2022
Personnel: Jennifer Donahue (Publisher); Christy Hoots (Editor); Rachel Adkins (Assistant Editor); Daniel Miller (Sports Editor); Chad Shelton (Production Manager/IT); Rod Baker (Publisher); Mary Ann Kearns (Ed.); Evan Dennison (Sports Ed.)
Parent company (for newspapers): Champion Media

MIDDLESBORO DAILY NEWS

Street address 1: 1275 N 25th St
Street address city: Middlesboro
Street address state: KY
Zip/Postal code: 40965-1964
County: Bell
Country: USA
Mailing address: PO BOX 579
Mailing city: MIDDLESBORO
Mailing state: KY
Mailing zip: 40965-0579

General Phone: (606) 248-1010
Advertising Phone: (606) 248-1010 ext. 1131
Editorial Phone: (606) 248-1010 ext. 1123
General/National Adv. E-mail: pcheek@heartlandpublications.com
Display Adv. E-mail: wpaul@heartlandpublications.com
Classified Adv. e-mail: krhymer@heartlandpublications.com
Editorial e-mail: dcaldwell@civitasmedia.com
Primary Website: www.middlesborodailynews.com
Year Established: 1911
News Services: AP.
Special Editions: Chamber of Commerce Membership Directory (Apr); Football (Aug); Letters to Santa (Dec); Progress (Feb); I'm Proud to be an American (Jul); Like Father Like Son (Jun); Home Improvement (Mar); Graduation (May); Caroling Book (Nov); Fall Festival (Oct); Read
Special Weekly Sections: Religion Page (Fri); Business Page (Thur).
Syndicated Publications: USA WEEKEND Magazine (Sat); American Profile (Tues).
Delivery Methods: Mail`Newsstand`Carrier`Racks
Areas Served - City/County or Portion Thereof, or Zip codes: Tri-state Area
Sat. Circulation Paid: 5873
Audit By: Sworn/Estimate/Non-Audited
Audit Date: 12.07.2019
Personnel: Pat Cheek (Adv. Dir.); Debbie Caldwell (Reg. Ed.); Cynthia Orr (Pub.); Wanda Paul (Business Development Specialist); Aimee Brock (Business Development Specialist); Angela Wright (Trading Post Clerk); Bethany Moore (Editorial Clerk); Roger Kirk (Prod. mgr.)
Parent company (for newspapers): Boone Newspapers, Inc.

THE MURRAY LEDGER & TIMES

Street address 1: 1001 Whitnell Ave
Street address city: Murray
Street address state: KY
Zip/Postal code: 42071-2975
County: Calloway
Country: USA
Mailing address: PO BOX 1040
Mailing city: MURRAY
Mailing state: KY
Mailing zip: 42071-0018
General Phone: (270) 753-1916
Advertising Phone: (270) 753-1916
Editorial Phone: (270) 753-1916
General/National Adv. E-mail: mdavis@murrayledger.com
Display Adv. E-mail: ads@murrayledger.com
Classified Adv. e-mail: classified@murrayledger.com
Editorial e-mail: editor@murrayledger.com
Primary Website: www.murrayledger.com
Year Established: 1879
News Services: AP, TMS.
Special Editions: Home Improvement (Apr); Back-to-School (Aug); In Our Backyard Magazine (June & Dec); Brides (Jan); Brides (Jun); Car Care (May); Fall Home Improvement (Oct); Homecoming (Sept).
Special Weekly Sections: Church Page (Fri); Farm Page (Mon); Outdoor Page (Sat); Arts & Entertainment (Thur); Education Page (Tues); Best Food Day (Wed).
Syndicated Publications: In Our Backyard Published in June and December
Delivery Methods: Mail`Newsstand`Carrier`Racks
Areas Served - City/County or Portion Thereof, or Zip codes: 42071; 42066; 42049; 42040; 42025; 42048; 42076; 38251; 38222; 38242
Own Printing Facility?: Y
Commercial printers?: N
Avg Free Circ: 6500
Sat. Circulation Paid: 7100
Audit By: Sworn/Estimate/Non-Audited
Audit Date: 12.07.2019
Personnel: Greg Travis (Managing Ed.); Mike Davis (Pub.); Chris Woodall (Adv. Mgr.); Crystal Duvall (Adv. Rep.); Jeff Arenz (Sports Ed.); Nicki Peach (Classified Mgr.); John Wright (Ed.)
Parent company (for newspapers): Lancaster Management, Inc.

MESSENGER-INQUIRER

Street address 1: 1401 Frederica St
Street address city: Owensboro
Street address state: KY
Zip/Postal code: 42301-4804
County: Daviess
Country: USA
Mailing address: PO BOX 1480
Mailing city: OWENSBORO
Mailing state: KY
Mailing zip: 42302-1480
General Phone: 2706917285
Advertising Phone: (270) 691-7239
Editorial Phone: (270) 691-7292
General/National Adv. E-mail: mweafer@messenger-inquirer.com
Display Adv. E-mail: amayes@messenger-inquirer.com
Classified Adv. e-mail: lhenderson@messenger-inquirer.com
Editorial e-mail: mfrancis@messenger-inquirer.com
Primary Website: www.messenger-inquirer.com
Year Established: 1875
News Services: AP, MCT.
Special Editions: Spring Improvements (Apr); Holiday Greetings (Dec); Home & Garden Show (Feb); Coupon Quarterly (Jan); Made in our Backyard (Jul); Southern Living Cooking School (Jun); Prime (Mar); Bar-B-Q Festival (May); Holiday Entertainments & Gifts (Nov); Voter's Guid
Special Weekly Sections: Entertainment (Fri); Style (S); Sports Weekend (Sat); Health (Thur); Community (Tues); Education (Wed).
Syndicated Publications: USA WEEKEND Magazine (S). Parade
Delivery Methods: Carrier
Areas Served - City/County or Portion Thereof, or Zip codes: Daviess, Hancock, McLean, Muhlenberg & Ohio Counties
Own Printing Facility?: Y
Commercial printers?: Y
Sat. Circulation Paid: 20613
Sun. Circulation Paid: 23791
Audit By: AAM
Audit Date: 16.02.2018
Personnel: Barry Carden (Circ. Dir.); Matthew Francis (Mng. Ed.); Mary Kissel (Copy Ed.); Mike Weafer (Ops. Mgr.); Scott Hagerman (News Ed.); Sherri Heckel (Librarian); Robert Bruck (Photo Ed.); Bob Bruck (City Ed.); Shawn Rumsey (Asst. News Ed.); Jay Wear (Mailroom Mgr.)
Parent company (for newspapers): Paxton Media Group

THE PADUCAH SUN

Street address 1: 408 Kentucky Ave
Street address city: Paducah
Street address state: KY
Zip/Postal code: 42003-1550
County: McCracken
Country: USA
Mailing address: PO BOX 2300
Mailing city: PADUCAH
Mailing state: KY
Mailing zip: 42002-2300
General Phone: (270) 575-8600
Advertising Phone: (270) 575-8750
Editorial Phone: (270) 575-8650
General/National Adv. E-mail: craney@paducahsun.com
Display Adv. E-mail: craney@paducahsun.com
Classified Adv. e-mail: classifieds@paducahsun.com
Editorial e-mail: news@paducahsun.com
Primary Website: www.paducahsun.com
Year Established: 1896
News Services: AP, MCT.
Special Editions: Quilt Show (Apr); Newspapers in Education Advertising Kick-Off (Aug); Holiday Greetings (Dec); NASCAR (Feb); Brides (Jan); Fall Fashion (Jul); The Crimestopping Handbook (Jun); Spring Outdoors (Mar); Lakeland (May); House Call (Monthly); Holiday Gift Guid
Special Weekly Sections: Church (Fri); Health (Mon); Books (S); Outdoor (Sat); Food Day (Tues); Outdoor (Wed).
Syndicated Publications: USA WEEKEND Magazine (S); Posh (Semi-monthly).
Delivery Methods: Carrier
Areas Served - City/County or Portion Thereof, or Zip codes: Western Kentucky
Sat. Circulation Paid: 19618
Sun. Circulation Paid: 22473
Audit By: AAM
Audit Date: 30.09.2011
Personnel: Jamie Paxton (Controller); Gary Adkisson (Gen. Mgr.); Carolyn Raney (Adv. Dir.); Judy Lynch (Circ. Mgr.); Duke Conover (Mng. Ed.); Joe Walker (Bus./Finance Ed.); Mac Thrower (Editorial Page Ed.); C.D. Bradley (Entertainment/Amusements Ed.); Ron Clark (Farm/Agriculture Ed.); Leigh Landini Wright (Home Furnishings Ed.); Chris Ash (Nat'l Ed.); Mark Hultman (News Ed.); Crystal Shackelford (Online Ed.); Barkley Thielman (Photo Ed.); Bill Bartleman (Political/Gov't Ed.)
Parent company (for newspapers): Paxton Media Group

THE RICHMOND REGISTER

Street address 1: 380 Big Hill Ave
Street address city: Richmond
Street address state: KY
Zip/Postal code: 40475-2012
County: Madison
Country: USA
Mailing address: PO BOX 99
Mailing city: RICHMOND
Mailing state: KY
Mailing zip: 40476-0099
General Phone: (859) 623-1669
Advertising Phone: (859) 624-6681
Editorial Phone: (859) 623-1669
General/National Adv. E-mail: pstocker@richmondregister.com
Display Adv. E-mail: nwoodward@richmondregister.com
Classified Adv. e-mail: classifieds@richmondregister.com
Editorial e-mail: editor@richmondregister.com
Primary Website: www.richmondregister.com
Year Established: 1917
News Services: AP.
Special Weekly Sections: Real Estate (Fri); Health & Fitness (Sun); TV Supplement (Sat); Outdoors (Thur); Food (Wed).
Delivery Methods: Carrier`Racks
Areas Served - City/County or Portion Thereof, or Zip codes: Richmond, Berea & Madison Counties (KY)
Sat. Circulation Paid: 4060
Sun. Circulation Paid: 4423
Audit By: AAM
Audit Date: 31.03.2014
Personnel: Bill Robinson (Ed./News Ed.); Sherrie Hawn (Rgl. Sales Mgr.); Heather Petitjean (Circ. Mgr.); Nathan Hutchison (Sports Ed.); Carrie Curry (Features Ed.); Liz Denny (Page Designer); Nancy Woodward (Media Advisor); Perry Stocker (Media Consultant); Joyce Rose; Marilyn Stewart (Office Mgr.); Dave Eldridge (Publisher); Jonathan Greene (Editor)
Parent company (for newspapers): CNHI, LLC; CNHI, LLC

THE COMMONWEALTH-JOURNAL

Street address 1: 110-112 E. Mt. Vernon Street
Street address city: Somerset
Street address state: KY
Zip/Postal code: 42501-1411
County: Pulaski
Country: USA
Mailing address: 110-112 E. Mt. Vernon Street
Mailing city: Somerset
Mailing state: KY
Mailing zip: 42501-1411
General Phone: (606) 678-8191
Advertising Phone: (606) 451-4904
Editorial Phone: (606) 451-4920
General/National Adv. E-mail: apetercheff@somerset-kentucky.com
Display Adv. E-mail: apetercheff@somerset-kentucky.com
Classified Adv. e-mail: jgarth@somerset-kentucky.com
Editorial e-mail: jneal@somerset-kentucky.com
Primary Website: www.somerset-kentucky.com
Year Established: 1895
News Services: AP, NEA.
Special Editions: High School Football (Aug); Christmas Songbook (Dec); Winter Clearance (Feb); Chamber Annual Report (Jan); Back-to-School (Jul); Summer Clearance (Jun); Agriculture Week (Mar); Grads (May); Regional Basketball Preview (Nov); Professional
Special Weekly Sections: Business (S); Best Food Days (Wed).
Syndicated Publications: Relish (Monthly); Parade (S).
Delivery Methods: Carrier
Areas Served - City/County or Portion Thereof, or Zip codes: Pulaski County (KY)
Sat. Circulation Paid: 4200
Sun. Circulation Paid: 4764
Audit By: Sworn/Estimate/Non-Audited
Audit Date: 12.07.2019
Personnel: Bill Hanson (Pub.); Jeff Neal (Ed.); Steve Cornelius (Sports Ed.); Acey Petercheff (Sales Rep.); JaKaye Garth (Pub.); Mark Walker (Circ. Mgr./Dir. Aud. Dev.); Candance Vanhook (Circ. Asst.); Carol LaFavers (Circ. Clerk)
Parent company (for newspapers): CNHI, LLC; CNHI, LLC

THE WINCHESTER SUN

Street address 1: 20 Wall St
Street address city: Winchester
Street address state: KY
Zip/Postal code: 40391-1900
County: Clark
Country: USA
General Phone: (859) 744-3123
Advertising Phone: (859) 355-1239
Editorial Phone: (859) 355-1218
General/National Adv. E-mail: Jfoley@winchestersun.com
Display Adv. E-mail: Jfoley@winchestersun.com
Classified Adv. e-mail: Rbenton@winchestersun.com
Editorial e-mail: Dstone@winchestersun.com
Primary Website: www.winchestersun.com
Year Established: 1878
News Services: AP.
Special Editions: Back-to-School (Aug); Holiday Greetings (Dec); Parade of Babies (Jan); Year In Review (Jul); Kids Today (Jun); Spring Home Improvement (Mar); Seniors Graduation (May); Holiday Gift Guide (Nov); Holiday Bazaars (Oct); Literacy (Sept).
Special Weekly Sections: Health & Fitness (Mon); Church (Sat); Business (Wed).
Syndicated Publications: Relish (Monthly); American Profile (Weekly).
Delivery Methods: Mail`Newsstand`Carrier`Racks
Areas Served - City/County or Portion Thereof, or Zip codes: Clark County (KY)
Own Printing Facility?: Y
Commercial printers?: Y
Sat. Circulation Paid: 6000
Audit By: USPS
Audit Date: 01.10.2013
Personnel: Mike Caldwell (Pub.); Karen Combs (CSR); Whitney Leggett (Ed.); Lana Smith (Adv. Mgr.)
Parent company (for newspapers): Boone Newspapers, Inc.

LOUISIANA

ABBEVILLE MERIDIONAL

Street address 1: 318 N Main St
Street address city: Abbeville
Street address state: LA
Zip/Postal code: 70510-4608
County: Vermilion
Country: USA
Mailing address: 318 N MAIN ST
Mailing city: ABBEVILLE
Mailing state: LA
Mailing zip: 70510-4608
General Phone: (337) 893-4223
Advertising Phone: (337) 893-4223
Editorial Phone: (337) 893-4223
General/National Adv. E-mail: kathy.cormier@vermiliontoday.com
Display Adv. E-mail: kathy.cormier@vermiliontoday.com
Classified Adv. e-mail: ashley.bossley@vermiliontoday.com
Editorial e-mail: chris.rosa@vermiliontoday.com
Primary Website: www.vermiliontoday.com
Year Established: 1856
News Services: AP, NEA.
Special Editions: Progress (Apr); Football (Aug); Newcomer (Feb); Bridal (Jan); Back To School (Jul); Substance Abuse (Jun); Home Improvement (Mar); Graduation (May); Christmas Gift Guide (Nov); Giant Omelette Festival (Oct); Women's Tab (Sept).
Special Weekly Sections: Bridal (S).
Syndicated Publications: Parade (S).
Delivery Methods: Mail`Newsstand`Carrier`Racks
Areas Served - City/County or Portion Thereof, or Zip codes: Vermilion
Sun. Circulation Paid: 5379
Audit By: Sworn/Estimate/Non-Audited
Audit Date: 12.07.2019

Personnel: Kathy Cormier (Pub.); Cynthia Nicholas (Managing Ed.); Christopher Rosa (Managing Ed.); Shaun Hearen (News Ed.); Nikki Vidos (Lifestyles Ed.); Joseph Cunningham (Sports Ed.); Jessica Meaux (Adv. Sales Rep.); Emeral Hebert (Adv. Sales Rep.); Ashley Bossley (Classified Sales Rep.); Theresa Milliman (Business Mgr.)
Parent company (for newspapers): LSN Publishing Company LLC; Louisiana State Newspapers

THE TOWN TALK

Street address 1: 1201 3rd St
Street address city: Alexandria
Street address state: LA
Zip/Postal code: 71301-8246
County: Rapides
Country: USA
Mailing address: PO BOX 7558
Mailing city: ALEXANDRIA
Mailing state: LA
Mailing zip: 71306-0558
General Phone: (318) 487-6397
Advertising Phone: (318) 487-6388
Editorial Phone: (318) 487-6409
General/National Adv. E-mail: christina.pierce@thetowntalk.com
Display Adv. E-mail: christina.pierce@thetowntalk.com
Classified Adv. e-mail: legals@thetowntalk.com
Editorial e-mail: news@thetowntalk.com
Primary Website: thetowntalk.com
Year Established: 1883
News Services: AP, SHNS, GNS.
Special Editions: Football (Aug)
Special Weekly Sections: Weekend (Fri); Amusement Page (S); Church (Sat); Shopper's Marketplace (Wed).
Delivery Methods: Mail`Newsstand`Carrier`Racks
Areas Served - City/County or Portion Thereof, or Zip codes: Rapides Parish
Own Printing Facility?: Y
Commercial printers?: N
Avg Free Circ: 22
Sat. Circulation Paid: 15983
Sun. Circulation Paid: 21384
Audit By: AAM
Audit Date: 31.12.2018
Personnel: Jim Smilie (Engagement & Community Content Editor); Christina Pierce (Gen. Mgr./Adv. Dir.); Deborah Schulte (Distribution Mgr.)
Parent company (for newspapers): Gannett

BASTROP DAILY ENTERPRISE

Street address 1: 119 W Hickory Ave
Street address city: Bastrop
Street address state: LA
Zip/Postal code: 71220-4549
County: Morehouse
Country: USA
Mailing address: PO BOX 311
Mailing city: BASTROP
Mailing state: LA
Mailing zip: 71221-0311
General Phone: (318) 281-4421
Advertising Phone: (318) 281-4421
Editorial Phone: (318) 281-2691
General/National Adv. E-mail: sharrell@gatehousemedia.com
Display Adv. E-mail: advertising@bastropenterprise.com
Classified Adv. e-mail: tturner@bastropenterprise.com
Editorial e-mail: kstewart@bastropenterprise.com
Primary Website: www.bastropenterprise.com
Year Established: 1898
Special Editions: Pride (Apr); Bridal (Feb); Newcomer Guide (Jul); Graduation (May); Gift Guide (Nov); Quarterly (Oct); Gin Whistle (Sept).
Special Weekly Sections: Farm (Thur); Food (Wed).
Syndicated Publications: American Profile (Weekly).
Delivery Methods: Mail`Newsstand`Carrier`Racks
Areas Served - City/County or Portion Thereof, or Zip codes: Bastrop, Oak Ridge, Collinston, Jones, Bonita, Mer Rouge, Crossett
Sat. Circulation Paid: 4241
Audit By: Sworn/Estimate/Non-Audited
Audit Date: 12.07.2019
Personnel: Teresa Hicks (Regional Group Pub.); Angee Norman (Gen. Mgr.); Marq Mitcham (Sports Ed.); Toney Davis (Circ. Mgr.)
Parent company (for newspapers): Gannett; CherryRoad Media

THE ADVOCATE

Street address 1: P.O. Box 588
Street address city: Baton Rouge
Street address state: LA
Zip/Postal code: 70821-0588
County: East Baton Rouge
Country: USA
Mailing address: PO BOX 588
Mailing city: BATON ROUGE
Mailing state: LA
Mailing zip: 70821-0588
General Phone: (225) 383-1111
Advertising Phone: (225) 388-0262
Editorial Phone: (225) 388-0283
General/National Adv. E-mail: csettle@theadvocate.com
Display Adv. E-mail: srunnels@theadvocate.com
Classified Adv. e-mail: adelatorre@theadvocate.com
Editorial e-mail: fkalmbach@theadvocate.com
Primary Website: www.theadvocate.com
Mthly Avg Views: 12040700
Mthly Avg Unique Visitors: 1772500
Year Established: 1925
News Services: AP, MCT-LAT.
Special Editions: The New Orleans Advocate The Acadiana Advocate
Special Weekly Sections: Wheels (Fri); Entertainment RED (Fri); Business (Sun); Wheels (Sun); Homes (Sun)
Syndicated Publications: Parade (S)
Delivery Methods: Mail`Newsstand`Carrier`Racks
Areas Served - City/County or Portion Thereof, or Zip codes: West Feliciana, Pointe Coupee, West Baton Rouge, East Baton Rouge, East Feliciana, St. Helena, Livingston, Tangipahoa, Ascension, St. James, Assumption
Own Printing Facility?: Y
Commercial printers?: Y
Avg Free Circ: 3910
Sat. Circulation Paid: 83139
Sat. Circulation Free: 1200
Sun. Circulation Paid: 90118
Sun. Circulation Free: 1182
Audit By: AAM
Audit Date: 30.09.2017
Personnel: Vicki Ferstel (Night Metro Editor); John Ballance (Photo Dir.); Sterling Rabalais (VP of Production); John Georges (Pub./CEO); Karen Martin (Features Ed.); Dan Shea (Pres./COO); Sheila Runnels (VP, Adv.); Connie Settle (National Adv. Mgr.); Karen Marchand (Adv. Asst.); Charlene Robert (Marketing Dir.); Jennifer Brown (Exec. News Ed.); Dianne Guidry (Exec. Asst.); Danny Heitman (Editorial Page Ed.); Joseph Schiefelbein (Exec. Sports Ed.); Martha Carr (New Orleans Managing Ed.); Michael Wilson (VP, Digital Media); Jason Gele (Online Adv. Coord.); Lou Hudson (Retail Sales Dir.); Sara Barnard (Director of Sales/Marketing); Peter Kovacs (Editor); Fred Kalmbach (Managing Ed.); Mark Ballard (CNB Ed.); Lori Tucker (Special Sections Editor); Laura Maggi (Metro Editor); Ken Duhe (Online News Editor); Perryn Keys (Asst. Sports Editor); Pierce Huff (Online Sports Editor)
Parent company (for newspapers): Capital City Press; Georges Media

THE CROWLEY POST-SIGNAL

Street address 1: 602 N Parkerson Ave
Street address city: Crowley
Street address state: LA
Zip/Postal code: 70526-4354
County: Acadia
Country: USA
Mailing address: 602 N PARKERSON AVE
Mailing city: CROWLEY
Mailing state: LA
Mailing zip: 70526-4354
General Phone: (337) 783-3450
Advertising Phone: (337) 783-3450
Editorial Phone: (337) 783-3450
General/National Adv. E-mail: harold.gonzales@crowleytoday.com
Display Adv. E-mail: advertising@crowleytoday.com
Classified Adv. e-mail: classifieds@crowleytoday.com
Editorial e-mail: steve.bandy@crowleytoday.com
Primary Website: www.crowleypostsignal.com
Year Established: 1885
News Services: AP, NEA.
Special Editions: National DARE Day (Apr); Drive Safely Page (Aug); Acadia Parish First Baby (Dec); Vo-Tech Education Week (Feb); Honor Roll (Jan); Rice Field Day (Jul); Flag Day (Jun); Home Improvement (Mar); Iota Graduation Page (May); Pharmacy Week (Nov); National 4-H W
Special Weekly Sections: Business (Wed.); Agriculture (Thur); Devotional (Fri)
Syndicated Publications: Parade (S).
Delivery Methods: Mail`Newsstand`Carrier`Racks
Areas Served - City/County or Portion Thereof, or Zip codes: Acadia
Sun. Circulation Paid: 4476
Audit By: Sworn/Estimate/Non-Audited
Audit Date: 12.07.2019
Personnel: Harold Gonzales (Gen. Mgr.); Kathy Duncan (Production Mgr.); Steve Bandy (Managing Ed.); Jeannine LeJeune (Online Ed.); Saja Hoffpauir (Lifestyles Ed.); Howie Dennis (Ed.); Chris Quebedeaux (Sports Ed.); Janet Doucet (Adv. Mgr.); Becky LaFleur (Classifieds Adv.); Wendy Newman (Bookkeeping)
Parent company (for newspapers): LSN Publishing Company LLC

FRANKLIN BANNER-TRIBUNE

Street address 1: 115 Wilson St
Street address city: Franklin
Street address state: LA
Zip/Postal code: 70538-6149
County: Saint Mary
Country: USA
Mailing address: PO BOX 566
Mailing city: FRANKLIN
Mailing state: LA
Mailing zip: 70538-0566
General Phone: (337) 828-3706
Advertising Phone: (337) 828-3706
Editorial Phone: (337) 828-3706
General/National Adv. E-mail: admanager@banner-tribune.com
Display Adv. E-mail: admanager@banner-tribune.com
Classified Adv. e-mail: classifieds@banner-tribune.com
Editorial e-mail: webmaster@banner-tribune.com
Primary Website: www.stmarynow.com
Year Established: 1885
News Services: AP.
Special Editions: Profile (Apr); Football (Aug); Christmas (Dec); Bridal (Jan); Drug Free (Oct).
Delivery Methods: Mail`Newsstand`Carrier
Areas Served - City/County or Portion Thereof, or Zip codes: 70538;70514;70522;70540
Avg Free Circ: 1500
Audit By: USPS
Audit Date: 28.09.2012
Personnel: Debbie Von Werder (Adv. Mgr.); Judy Touchet (Accounting); Debbie Billiot (Circ. Mgr.); Michelle Baker (Lifestyles Ed.); Anthony Mitchell (Sports Ed.); Christine Duhon; Roger Stouff (Managing Ed.); Allan Von Werder (Pub.); Tanya Sonnier (Classifieds Adv. Mgr.); Angela Guckeen (Adv. Rep.)
Parent company (for newspapers): LSN Publishing Company LLC; Morgan City Newspapers LLC

THE DAILY STAR

Street address 1: 725 S Morrison Blvd
Street address city: Hammond
Street address state: LA
Zip/Postal code: 70403-5401
County: Tangipahoa
Country: USA
Mailing address: 725 S MORRISON BLVD
Mailing city: HAMMOND
Mailing state: LA
Mailing zip: 70403-5401
General Phone: (985) 254-7827
Advertising Phone: (985) 254-7827
Editorial Phone: (985) 254-7827
General/National Adv. E-mail: kgingles@hammondstar.com
Display Adv. E-mail: mgallo@hammondstar.com
Classified Adv. e-mail: classads@hammondstar.com
Editorial e-mail: editor@hammondstar.com
Primary Website: www.hammondstar.com
Year Established: 1959
News Services: AP.
Special Editions: Strawberry Festival (Apr); Football (Aug); Basketball Tourney (Dec); Profile Progress (Feb); Medical (Jul); Kids Beat (Mar).
Special Weekly Sections: Church (Fri); Business (S); Best Food Days (Wed).
Syndicated Publications: Bon Temps (Fri); USA WEEKEND Magazine (S).
Delivery Methods: Mail`Newsstand`Carrier`Racks
Areas Served - City/County or Portion Thereof, or Zip codes: Tangipahoa Parish
Own Printing Facility?: Y
Commercial printers?: Y
Sat. Circulation Paid: 9595
Sun. Circulation Paid: 11186
Audit By: Sworn/Estimate/Non-Audited
Audit Date: 12.07.2019
Personnel: Lillian K. Mirando (Exec. Ed.); A.M. Sheehan (News Ed.); Michelle Gallo (Adv. Dir.); William Calcutt (Circ. Dir.); Stanley Davis (Circ. District Mgr.); Mary Ann Giovingo (Mailroom Mgr.); Trudy Shockley (Asst. Bus. Mgr.); David Bordok (Pressroom Supervisor); James Summerlin (Sports Ed.); Catherine Massawe (Circ. District Mgr.)
Parent company (for newspapers): Paxton Media Group

THE COURIER

Street address 1: 3030 Barrow St
Street address city: Houma
Street address state: LA
Zip/Postal code: 70360-7641
County: Terrebonne
Country: USA
Mailing address: PO BOX 2717
Mailing city: HOUMA
Mailing state: LA
Mailing zip: 70361-2717
General Phone: (985) 850-1100
Advertising Phone: (985) 857-2270
Editorial Phone: (985) 857-2201
General/National Adv. E-mail: alan.rini@houmatoday.com
Display Adv. E-mail: robin.blanchard@houmatoday.com
Classified Adv. e-mail: robin.blanchard@houmatoday.com
Editorial e-mail: keith.magill@houmatoday.com
Primary Website: www.houmatoday.com
Mthly Avg Views: 5500000
Mthly Avg Unique Visitors: 352000
Year Established: 1878
News Services: AP
Special Editions: Bayou Gourmet Cookbook (Apr); Football Tab (Aug); Christmas Greetings (Dec); Mardi Gras Tab (Feb); Tax Guide (Jan); Graduation (May); Bridal (Oct); Oil & Industry (Sept).
Special Weekly Sections: Big Fun on the Bayou (Fri); Health & Fitness (Mon); Louisiana Style (S); Outdoors (Thur); Home & Family (Tues); Bon Appetit (Wed).
Syndicated Publications: Parade (S); Athlon Sports (TH)
Delivery Methods: Mail`Newsstand`Carrier`Racks
Areas Served - City/County or Portion Thereof, or Zip codes: 70361, 70360, 70363, 70364, 70301, 70394, 70395, 70374, 70343, 70344, 70345, 70353, 70354, 70356, 70357, 70359, 70377, 70397
Own Printing Facility?: Y
Commercial printers?: Y
Sat. Circulation Paid: 9378
Sun. Circulation Paid: 10632
Audit By: AAM
Audit Date: 31.12.2017
Personnel: Darlene Rodrigue (Finance Dir.); Keith Magill (Executive Editor); Lawrence Knoblock (Circ. Mgr.); Karen Dauzat (HR); Alan Rini (Adv. Sales); Pam Fahey (Adv. Sales); Peyvand Maghsoud (Adv. Sales); Karen Robichaux (Circ. Clerk); Mindy Thibodaux (Accountant); Patricia Cheavis (District Mgr.); Mike Hill (Night City Ed.); Brent St. Germain (Sports Ed.); Marian Long (Adv. Dir.); Lee Bachlet (Pub.)
Parent company (for newspapers): Gannett; CherryRoad Media

JENNINGS (LA) DAILY NEWS

Street address 1: 238 N Market St
Street address city: Jennings
Street address state: LA
Zip/Postal code: 70546-5862
County: Jefferson Davis
Country: USA
Mailing address: PO BOX 910
Mailing city: JENNINGS
Mailing state: LA
Mailing zip: 70546-0910
General Phone: (337) 824-3011
Advertising Phone: (337) 824-3011
Editorial Phone: (337) 824-3011
General/National Adv. E-mail: jdnpublisher@bellsouth.net
Display Adv. E-mail: jdngm@jenningsdailynews.net
Classified Adv. e-mail: jdngm@jenningsdailynews.net

Editorial e-mail: jenningsnews@bellsouth.net
Primary Website: www.jenningsdailynews.net
Year Established: 1896
News Services: AP.
Special Editions: Pride in Business (Apr); Football (Aug); Home Buyer's Guide (Every other month); Business Focus (Feb); Income Tax (Jan); Rice Harvest (Jul); Pride in Business (Jun); Spring Lawn & Garden (Mar); Pride in Business (May); Drug Awareness (Nov); Christmas Head
Syndicated Publications: Market Street Trader (Wed).
Delivery Methods: Mail`Newsstand`Carrier`Racks
Areas Served - City/County or Portion Thereof, or Zip codes: Jenninggs, Welsh, Roanoke, Lake Arthur, Elton, Evangeline & Iota, Fenton, Lacassine, Iowa, Mermentau
Sun. Circulation Paid: 4816
Audit By: Sworn/Estimate/Non-Audited
Audit Date: 12.07.2019
Personnel: Dona H. Smith (Pub.); Sandra Miller (Circ. Mgr.); Rebecca Chaisson (News/Family/Living Ed.); Paula Bonin (Gen. Mgr./Adv. Mgr.); Casey Smith (Prod. Mgr.); Sheila Smith (Asst. Ed.); Sandy Crochet (Bookkeeping); Brigette Boudreaux (Composing Mgr.); Kevin Bruchhaus (Sports)
Parent company (for newspapers): Fackelman Newspapers

THE DAILY ADVERTISER

Street address 1: 1100 Bertrand Dr
Street address city: Lafayette
Street address state: LA
Zip/Postal code: 70506-4110
County: Lafayette
Country: USA
Mailing address: PO BOX 5310
Mailing city: LAFAYETTE
Mailing state: LA
Mailing zip: 70502-5310
General Phone: (337) 289-6397
Advertising Phone: (337) 289-6397
Editorial Phone: (337) 289-6397
General/National Adv. E-mail: news@theadvertiser.com
Display Adv. E-mail: arichards1@theadvertiser.com
Classified Adv. e-mail: arichards1@theadvertiser.com
Editorial e-mail: editorial@theadvertiser.com
Primary Website: www.theadvertiser.com
Year Established: 1865
News Services: AP, NYT, GNS.
Special Editions: Homes by Design (Apr); Back-to-School/Fall Fashion (Aug); Launching a New Millenium (Dec); Mardi Gras Tab (Feb); Technology for the Millennium (Jul); 3rd Annual Cookbook (Jun); Bridal/Spring Fashion (Mar); Acadiana Yearbook (May); Holiday Giver's Guide (N
Special Weekly Sections: Wheels (S); TV Week (Sat); Church Page (Weekly).
Syndicated Publications: USA WEEKEND Magazine (S).
Areas Served - City/County or Portion Thereof, or Zip codes: Jefferson Parish
Sat. Circulation Paid: 18576
Sun. Circulation Paid: 25324
Audit By: AAM
Audit Date: 31.03.2017
Personnel: Bill Decker; Caitlin Jacob (Digital Programming Ed.); Cindy McCurry-Ross (Exec. Ed./Rgl. Ed.); Diane Pantaleo (Copy Ed.); Eric Narcisse (Asst. Sports Ed.); Heidi Venable (Online Ed.); Judy Bastien (Opinion Page Ed.); Ken Stickney (Metro Ed.); Kevin Foote (Sports Ed.); Margurite Shipley (News Clerk); Jared Bartels (Regional Finance Director); Judith Terzotis (Pres./Pub.); Kristin Askelson (News Dir./Content Strategist)
Parent company (for newspapers): Gannett

AMERICAN PRESS

Street address 1: 4900 Highway 90 E
Street address city: Lake Charles
Street address state: LA
Zip/Postal code: 70615-4037
County: Calcasieu
Country: USA
Mailing address: PO BOX 2893
Mailing city: LAKE CHARLES
Mailing state: LA
Mailing zip: 70602-2893
General Phone: (337) 433-3000
Advertising Phone: (337) 494-4097
Editorial Phone: (337) 494-4080
General/National Adv. E-mail: cstevenson@americanpress.com
Display Adv. E-mail: ayellott@americanpress.com.
Classified Adv. e-mail: ayellott@americanpress.com.
Editorial e-mail: news@americanpress.com
Primary Website: www.americanpress.com
Year Established: 1895
News Services: AP.
Special Editions: Home Improvement (Apr); Back-to-School (Aug); Brides (Feb); Mardi Gras (Jan); Contraband Days (May); Christmas Gift Guide (Nov); Football (Sept).
Special Weekly Sections: Marquee (Fri); Face to Face (Mon); Face to Face (Tues).
Syndicated Publications: Parade (S); Focus (Sat).
Delivery Methods: Mail`Newsstand`Carrier`Racks
Areas Served - City/County or Portion Thereof, or Zip codes: 70601-70663, Allen-Beauregard-Calcasieu-Cameron-Jeff Davis
Own Printing Facility?: Y
Commercial printers?: Y
Avg Free Circ: 17004
Sat. Circulation Paid: 16157
Sat. Circulation Free: 17004
Sun. Circulation Paid: 19172
Sun. Circulation Free: 19423
Audit By: AAM
Audit Date: 6/31/2018
Personnel: Scooter Hobbs (Sports Ed.); Ava Yellott (Adv. Dir.); Karen Cole (National Desk/Sr. Acct. Exec.); Jessika Sarver (Preprints/Acct. Exec.); Crystal Stevenson (Exec. Ed.); Andrew Perzo (Copy Ed.); Pamela Seal (Living Ed.); Jim Gazzolo (Managing Ed.)
Parent company (for newspapers): Shearman Corporation; Boone Newspapers, Inc.

MINDEN PRESS HERALD

Street address 1: 203 Gleason St
Street address city: Minden
Street address state: LA
Zip/Postal code: 71055-3455
County: Webster
Country: USA
Mailing address: PO BOX 1339
Mailing city: MINDEN
Mailing state: LA
Mailing zip: 71055
General Phone: (318) 377-1866
Advertising Phone: (318) 377-1866
Editorial Phone: (318) 377-1866
General/National Adv. E-mail: davidaspecht@gmail.com
Display Adv. E-mail: davidaspecht@gmail.com
Classified Adv. e-mail: davidaspecht@gmail.com
Editorial e-mail: newsroom@press-herald.com
Primary Website: www.press-herald.com
Mthly Avg Views: 68000
Mthly Avg Unique Visitors: 31000
Year Established: 1895
News Services: AP.
Special Editions: Car Care (Fall); Car Care (Spring). Profile (February)
Delivery Methods: Mail`Newsstand`Carrier`Racks
Areas Served - City/County or Portion Thereof, or Zip codes: Minden and Webster Parish
Own Printing Facility?: Y
Commercial printers?: Y
Audit By: Sworn/Estimate/Non-Audited
Audit Date: 12.07.2019
Personnel: Telina Worley (Adv. Dir.); Curtis Mays (Adv. Exec.); Tina Specht (Co-Publisher)
Parent company (for newspapers): Specht Newspapers Inc

THE NEWS-STAR

Street address 1: 411 N 4th St
Street address city: Monroe
Street address state: LA
Zip/Postal code: 71201-6743
County: Ouachita
Country: USA
Mailing address: PO BOX 1502
Mailing city: MONROE
Mailing state: LA
Mailing zip: 71210-1502
General Phone: (318) 322-5161
Advertising Phone: (318) 322-5161
Editorial Phone: (318) 322-5161
General/National Adv. E-mail: dpetty@monroe.gannett.com
Display Adv. E-mail: christina.pierce@monroe.gannett.com
Classified Adv. e-mail: christina.pierce@monroe.gannett.com
Editorial e-mail: kspurlock@monroe.gannett.com
Primary Website: www.thenewsstar.com
Year Established: 1890
News Services: AP, GNS, MCT, LAT-WP.
Special Weekly Sections: Auto (Fri); Travel (S); Best Food Edition (Wed).
Syndicated Publications: This Week (Fri); USA WEEKEND Magazine (S).
Delivery Methods: Mail`Newsstand`Carrier`Racks
Areas Served - City/County or Portion Thereof, or Zip codes: Ouachita Parish
Sat. Circulation Paid: 10757
Sun. Circulation Paid: 13186
Audit By: AAM
Audit Date: 31.12.2018
Personnel: David B. Petty (Pres./Pub.); Brad Lackey (Adv. Dir.); Debbie Coplen (Gen. Sales Mgr.); Ken Stickney (Mng. Ed.); Eleanor Rushing (Asst. Mng. Ed., Local); Nick Delso (Asst. Mng. Ed., Online/Sports); Hope Young (Accent Ed.); Fred Phillips (Multimedia Ed.); Mark Henderson (News Ed.); Margaret Croft (Photography Ed.); Doug Nobles (Prodn. Dir.); Kathy Spurlock (Exec. Ed.); Mike Romaguera (Adv. Sales Leader); Chad Eymard (Multi-media Acc. Exec.); Antoinette Holbrook (Classified Inside Sales)
Parent company (for newspapers): Gannett

THE DAILY REVIEW

Street address 1: 1014 Front St
Street address city: Morgan City
Street address state: LA
Zip/Postal code: 70380-3226
County: Saint Mary
Country: USA
Mailing address: PO BOX 948
Mailing city: MORGAN CITY
Mailing state: LA
Mailing zip: 70381-0948
General Phone: (985) 384-8370
Advertising Phone: (985) 384-8370
Editorial Phone: (985) 384-8370
General/National Adv. E-mail: news@daily-review.com
Display Adv. E-mail: advertising@daily-review.com
Classified Adv. e-mail: classified@daily-review.com
Editorial e-mail: news@daily-review.com
Primary Website: www.banner-tribune.com
Year Established: 1872
News Services: AP.
Special Editions: Progress (Apr); Energy Coastal (Dec); Chamber of Commerce (Jan); Dixie Youth-Little League Baseball (Jul); Drug Free Tab (Oct); Shrimp & Petroleum Festival-Oil/Seafood (Sept).
Special Weekly Sections: Real Estate (Fri).
Areas Served - City/County or Portion Thereof, or Zip codes: Morgan City/St. Mary/70380-70381
Audit By: Sworn/Estimate/Non-Audited
Audit Date: 12.07.2019
Personnel: Allan Von Werder (Pub.); Tom Coleman (Webmaster); Bill Decker (Managing Ed.)
Parent company (for newspapers): LSN Publishing Company LLC; Morgan City Newspapers LLC

THE DAILY IBERIAN

Street address 1: 926 E Main St
Street address city: New Iberia
Street address state: LA
Zip/Postal code: 70560-3866
County: Iberia
Country: USA
Mailing address: 926 E MAIN ST
Mailing city: NEW IBERIA
Mailing state: LA
Mailing zip: 70560-3866
General Phone: (333) 365-6773
Advertising Phone: (337) 365-6773
Editorial Phone: (337) 365-6773
General/National Adv. E-mail: dailyiberian@cox.net
Display Adv. E-mail: iberianads@cox.net
Classified Adv. e-mail: diclass@cox.net
Editorial e-mail: dailyiberian@cox.net
Primary Website: www.iberianet.com
Year Established: 1893
News Services: AP.
Special Editions: HS Graduation (Apr); Estate Planning (Aug); Gift Guide (Dec); Newcomer's Guide (Feb); Bridal (Jan); Focus on Women (Jul); Father's Day (Jun); Home & Garden (Mar); Mother's Day (May); Gift Guide (Nov); Farm (Oct); Cookbook (Sept).
Special Weekly Sections: Church Page (Fri); Business (S); Business News (Thur); Health News (Tues); Food (Wed).
Syndicated Publications: TV Listings (Fri); USA WEEKEND Magazine (S).
Delivery Methods: Mail`Newsstand
Areas Served - City/County or Portion Thereof, or Zip codes: Iberia Parish
Avg Free Circ: 0
Sun. Circulation Paid: 7758
Sun. Circulation Free: 0
Audit By: VAC
Audit Date: 30.06.2017
Personnel: Beth Renard (Admin. Secretary); Mandy Seneca (Bus. Mgr.); Jackie Babineaux (Bus. Asst.); Bill Heirtzler (Adv. Dir.); Jeff Zeringue (Ed.); Chris Landry (Sports Ed.); JP Poirier (Circ. Mgr.); Justin Bourque (District Mgr.); Jerry Sexton (Prodn. Mgr.); Christina Pierce (Pub.); Don Shoopman (Sr. News. Ed./Outdoor Ed.); Delores Houston (Classified Adv. Supv.)
Parent company (for newspapers): Wick Communications

RUSTON (LA) DAILY LEADER

Street address 1: 212 W Park Ave
Street address city: Ruston
Street address state: LA
Zip/Postal code: 71270-4314
County: Lincoln
Country: USA
Mailing address: PO BOX 520
Mailing city: RUSTON
Mailing state: LA
Mailing zip: 71273-0520
General Phone: (318) 255-4353
Advertising Phone: (318) 255-4353
Editorial Phone: (318) 255-4353
General/National Adv. E-mail: rick@rustonleader.com
Display Adv. E-mail: flint@rustonleader.com
Classified Adv. e-mail: flint@rustonleader.com
Editorial e-mail: buddy@rustonleader.com
Primary Website: www.rustonleader.com
Mthly Avg Views: 928000
Mthly Avg Unique Visitors: 573460
Year Established: 1894
News Services: AP.
Special Editions: Chamber Connection, Home Guide, Living Well, Progress Edition, Ruston USA (Jan); Business Card Directory, Chamber Connection, Medical Directory, Spring Bride (Feb); Home Guide, Redi Reference (Mar); Pride Edition, Living Well (April); Graduation Edition (May); Peach Fetival (June); Back to School Edition (Jul); Gridiron Glory, Dawtown (Aug); North Louisiana Outdoors (Sept); Chicken Festival, Ducks Unlimited, Tech Homecoming (Oct); Veterans, Thanksgiging, Downtown Open House (Nov); Last Minute Santa, Seasons Greetings, Holiday Shopping (Dec.)
Syndicated Publications: Parade (S), Living Well (S) quarterly
Delivery Methods: Mail`Newsstand`Carrier`Racks
Areas Served - City/County or Portion Thereof, or Zip codes: 71270, 71222, 71241, 71260, 71201, 71277, 71280, 71225, 71235, Lincoln Parish Police Jury, Lincoln Parish School Board, Lincoln Parish Sherriff's office and the municipalities of Ruston, Choudrant, Grambling, Simsboro and Vienna.
Own Printing Facility?: Y
Commercial printers?: Y
Avg Free Circ: 6000
Sun. Circulation Paid: 5268
Audit By: Sworn/Estimate/Non-Audited
Audit Date: 12.07.2019
Personnel: Jeanie McCartney (Adv. Mgr.); Rick Hohlt (Pub./Ed.); O.K. Davis (Sports Ed.); Cody Richard (Gen. Mgr.); Adam Hohlt (Asst. Adv. Mgr.); Caskey Schexnyder (Circ. Mgr.); Elizabeth DeGrie (News Ed.); Will Avery (Composing Mgr.); Flint Boyce (Adv. Sales Exec.); Tina Richard (Office Mgr.)
Parent company (for newspapers): Fackelman Newspapers

THE TIMES

Street address 1: 401 Market St
Street address 2: Ste 1600
Street address city: Shreveport
Street address state: LA
Zip/Postal code: 71101-6911
County: Caddo
Country: USA
Mailing address: 401 MARKET ST STE 1600
Mailing city: SHREVEPORT

Mailing state: LA
Mailing zip: 71101-6911
General Phone: (318) 459-3200
Advertising Phone: (318) 459-3200
Editorial Phone: (318) 459-3233
General/National Adv. E-mail: Richard.Rose@shreveporttimes.com
Display Adv. E-mail: Richard.Rose@shreveporttimes.com
Classified Adv. e-mail: Richard.Rose@shreveporttimes.com
Editorial e-mail: aenglish@gannett.com
Primary Website: www.shreveporttimes.com
Mthly Avg Views: 4500000
Mthly Avg Unique Visitors: 350000
Year Established: 1872
News Services: AP, GNS.
Special Editions: Independence Bowl (Dec); Home Products Show (Feb); Outlook (Jan); Parade of Homes (Jun); Red River Revel (Sept).
Special Weekly Sections: Preview (Entertainment) (Fri); Voices (W); Automotive (Sat); Food (Wed).
Syndicated Publications: USA WEEKEND Magazine (S).
Delivery Methods: Mail`Newsstand`Carrier`Racks
Areas Served - City/County or Portion Thereof, or Zip codes: 71001, 71003, 71006, 71007, 71009, 71018, 71019, 71023, 71024, 71027, 71028, 71030, 71032, 71033, 71037, 71038, 71039, 71040, 71044, 71047, 71049, 71051, 71052, 71055, 71060, 71061, 71063, 71064, 71065, 71067, 71068, 71071, 71072, 71073, 71075, 71078, 71082, 71101, 71103, 71104, 71105, 71106, 71107, 71108, 71109, 71110, 71111, 71112, 71115, 71118, 71119, 71129, 71251, 71270, 71411, 71419, 71429, 71449, 71457, 75633, 75639, 75670, 75672, 75692
Own Printing Facility?: Y
Commercial printers?: Y
Sat. Circulation Paid: 27186
Sun. Circulation Paid: 35017
Audit By: AAM
Audit Date: 31.12.2016
Personnel: Anton Kaufer (Adv. Dir.); Rick Rose (Territory Sales Mgr.); Kevin Welsh (Circ. Dir.); Michele Marcotte (Features Content Strategist); Scott Ferrell (Sports Planning Ed.); Alan English (Pres./Pub.); Jeff Gauger (Exec. Ed.); Keyle Cavalier (Digital Sales Mgr.); Ricky Duke (News Planning Ed.)
Parent company (for newspapers): Gannett

DAILY COMET

Street address 1: P.O. Box 5238
Street address city: Thibodaux
Street address state: LA
Zip/Postal code: 70302
County: Lafourche
Country: USA
Mailing address: PO BOX 5238
Mailing city: THIBODAUX
Mailing state: LA
Mailing zip: 70302-5238
General Phone: (985) 448-7600
Advertising Phone: (985) 857-2291
Editorial Phone: (985) 448-7612
General/National Adv. E-mail: marian.long@houmatoday.com
Display Adv. E-mail: marian.long@dailycomet.com
Classified Adv. e-mail: peyvand.maghsoud@houmatoday.com
Editorial e-mail: news@dailycomet.com
Primary Website: www.dailycomet.com
Mthly Avg Views: 1526000
Mthly Avg Unique Visitors: 176000
Year Established: 1889
News Services: AP, NYT.
Special Editions: Living Here (Jan); Graduation (May); Christmas Opening (Nov); Football (Aug);Oil & Gas Section
Special Weekly Sections: Religion Page (Fri); Bridal Announcements (Mon); Mes Amis (Thur); Health Page (Tues); Best Food Day (Wed).
Syndicated Publications: USA WEEKEND Magazine (Fri); Athlon Sports (Th)
Delivery Methods: Mail`Newsstand`Carrier`Racks
Areas Served - City/County or Portion Thereof, or Zip codes: 70301, 70359, 70394, 70374, 70354, 70357, 70359, 70390, 70372, 70090, 70086,70372
Own Printing Facility?: N
Commercial printers?: Y
Avg Free Circ: 515
Sat. Circulation Paid: 4461
Sat. Circulation Free: 515
Audit By: AAM
Audit Date: 31.12.2017
Personnel: Darlene Rodrigue (Finance Dir.); Keith Magill (Exec. Ed.); Mike Hill (City Ed.); Mike Gorman (Op. Ed.); Lee Bachlet (Pub.); Karen Robichaux (Circ. Clerk); Marian Long (Adv. Dir.); Lawrence Knoblock (Circ. Mgr.); Teddy Renois (Sports Writer); Gloria Lebouef (District Mgr.); Alysa Hebert (Digital Sales); Mindy Thibodaux (Acct.)
Parent company (for newspapers): Gannett; CherryRoad Media

MAINE

KENNEBEC JOURNAL

Street address 1: 36 Anthony Ave Ste 101
Street address 2: Suite 101
Street address city: Augusta
Street address state: ME
Zip/Postal code: 04330-7891
County: Kennebec
Country: USA
Mailing address: PO BOX 1052
Mailing city: AUGUSTA
Mailing state: ME
Mailing zip: 4332
General Phone: (207) 623-3811
Advertising Phone: (207) 623-3811
Editorial Phone: (207) 623-3811
General/National Adv. E-mail: kjcommunity@mainetoday.com
Display Adv. E-mail: kjcommunity@mainetoday.com
Classified Adv. e-mail: CMarcoux@mainetoday.com
Editorial e-mail: smonroe@mainetoday.com
Primary Website: www.centralmaine.com
Mthly Avg Unique Visitors: 243450
Year Established: 1825
News Services: AP, NYT, LAT-WP, SHNS.
Special Editions: Spring Scouting (Apr); College Bound (Aug); Winter Scouting (Dec); Baby Parade (Feb); Maine Manufacturing Housing (Jan); Old Hallowell Days (Jul); Winslow 4th of July (Jun); Medical Journal (Mar); Brides & Grooms (May); Winter in Maine (Nov); Old Hallowel
Special Weekly Sections: What's Happening (entertainment) (Fri); What's on TV (S).
Syndicated Publications: USA WEEKEND Magazine (S).
Delivery Methods: Mail`Newsstand`Carrier`Racks
Areas Served - City/County or Portion Thereof, or Zip codes: Kennebec County
Own Printing Facility?: Y
Commercial printers?: Y
Avg Free Circ: 52
Sat. Circulation Paid: 5592
Sat. Circulation Free: 52
Sun. Circulation Paid: 5592
Sun. Circulation Free: 52
Audit By: AAM
Audit Date: 31.03.2019
Personnel: Lisa DeSisto (CEO/Pub.); Vince Ciampi (Sales Group Vice President); Stefanie Manning (Group Vice President â€" Consumer Marketing); Stewart Wright (Group Vice President â€" IT, Facilities, Pre-Production); Matt Fulton (Vice President â€" Digital Development); Jim Costello Jr. (Vice President â€" Production); Andrew Scheetz (Director of Finance); Judith Meyer (Exec. Ed.); Scott Monroe (Mng. Ed.); Rob Montana (City Ed.); Bill Stewart (Exec. Sports Ed.)
Parent company (for newspapers): Maine Today Media Inc.

BANGOR DAILY NEWS

Street address 1: 1 Merchants Plaza
Street address 2: Suite 1
Street address city: Bangor
Street address state: ME
Zip/Postal code: 4401
County: Penobscot
Country: USA
Mailing address: PO BOX 1329
Mailing city: BANGOR
Mailing state: ME
Mailing zip: 04402-1329
General Phone: (207) 990-8000
Advertising Phone: (207) 990-8020
Editorial Phone: (207) 990-8175
General/National Adv. E-mail: advertising@bangordailynews.net
Display Adv. E-mail: aconstantine@bangordailynews.com
Classified Adv. e-mail: tmcleod@bangordailynews.com
Editorial e-mail: syoung@bangordailynews.com
Primary Website: www.bangordailynews.com
Mthly Avg Views: 12500000
Mthly Avg Unique Visitors: 2094593
Year Established: 1889
News Services: AP, LAT-WP.
Special Editions: Bangor Spring Home Show (Apr); Home Furnishings: Trends & Styles (Aug); High School Basketball (Dec); Eastern Agency On Aging-Life Times (Feb); Photographs of the Year: The Best From Our Pages (Jan); Planning Your Wedding (Jul); Experience Maine (Jun); Do
Special Weekly Sections: Maine Style (S).
Syndicated Publications: Color Comics (S); Food (Wed).
Delivery Methods: Mail`Newsstand`Carrier`Racks
Areas Served - City/County or Portion Thereof, or Zip codes: Penobscot County
Own Printing Facility?: N
Commercial printers?: N
Avg Free Circ: 586
Sat. Circulation Paid: 32338
Sat. Circulation Free: 591
Audit By: AAM
Audit Date: 30.09.2017
Personnel: Jennifer Holmes (Vice President); Richard J. Warren (Pub.); Micheal J. Dowd (Metro/Standards Ed.); Susan Young (Editorial Page Ed.); Todd Benoit (V.P./C.O.O.); Jeanne Luetjen (Exec. Asst.); Kimberly Gonzales (Finance Dir.); Kelly Donnelly (Events and Brand Coord.); Michele Madden (HR Asst.); Brian Cotlar (Sales and Marketing Dir.); Josh O'Donnell (Client Advocate Mgr.); Anthony Ronzio (Exec. Dir.); Judy Long (Universal Desk Ed.); Rick Levasseur (State Ed.); Joe McLaughlin (Sports Ed.); Jason Oliver (Audience Dev't Mgr.); Sarah Walker Caron (News/Features Ed.); Luis Azeredo (Production Dir., Post Press); Kurt Parent; Elizabeth Hansen (Dir., Mktg. Servs.); Eric Zelz (Graphics/Design Ed.); Christopher Burns (Copy Ed.); Kaylie Reese (Copy Ed.); Jennifer Austin (Project Coord.); Michael Prazma (Dir. of Circu.); fred Stewart (Circ. Customer Advocate Mgr.); James Hayes (Sr. Adv. Circ.); Carolyn Mowers (Chair, Board of Dir.); Lauren Abbate (Features Reporter)
Parent company (for newspapers): Bangor Publishing Company

JOURNAL-TRIBUNE

Street address 1: 457 Alfred St
Street address city: Biddeford
Street address state: ME
Zip/Postal code: 04005-9447
County: York
Country: USA
General Phone: (207) 282-1535
Advertising Phone: (207) 282-1535 ext. 341
Editorial Phone: (207) 282-1535 ext. 322
General/National Adv. E-mail: publisher@journaltribune.com
Display Adv. E-mail: publisher@journaltribune.com
Classified Adv. e-mail: Classifieds@journaltribune.com
Editorial e-mail: Editor@journaltribune.com
Primary Website: www.journaltribune.com
Year Established: 1884
News Services: AP, SHNS.
Special Weekly Sections: Business; Religion
Syndicated Publications: USA WEEKEND Magazine (Sat).
Delivery Methods: Newsstand`Carrier`Racks
Areas Served - City/County or Portion Thereof, or Zip codes: 04005, 04072, 04073, 04083, 04054, 04063, 04027, 04074, 03907, 04087, 04030, 04005, 04042, 04093, 04004, 04038, 04048, 04095, 04076, 04001, 03906, 04002, 04046, 04094, 04046, 04090, 04043, 04002, 04064, 04014, 04042, 04061, 04006
Own Printing Facility?: Y
Commercial printers?: N
Avg Free Circ: 24
Sat. Circulation Paid: 7476
Sat. Circulation Free: 24
Audit By: Sworn/Estimate/Non-Audited
Audit Date: 12.07.2019
Personnel: Ed Pierce (Executive Editor); Alex Sponseller (Assoc. Sports Ed.); Bruce Hardina (Pub.)
Parent company (for newspapers): MaineToday Media Inc.; RFB Enterprises

THE TIMES RECORD

Street address 1: 3 Business Pkwy
Street address 2: Ste 1
Street address city: Brunswick
Street address state: ME
Zip/Postal code: 04011-7390
County: Cumberland
Country: USA
Mailing address: PO BOX 10
Mailing city: BRUNSWICK
Mailing state: ME
Mailing zip: 04011-1302
General Phone: (207)729-3311
Advertising Phone: (207)504-8270
Editorial Phone: (207)729-3311
General/National Adv. E-mail: mlester@timesrecord.com
Display Adv. E-mail: mlester@timesrecord.com
Classified Adv. e-mail: mlester@timesrecord.com
Editorial e-mail: mlester@timesrecord.com
Primary Website: www.timesrecord.com
Mthly Avg Views: 207345
Mthly Avg Unique Visitors: 48532
Year Established: 1967
News Services: AP, NYT.
Special Editions: Spring Home Improvement (April), Summer Guide (May), Taste of the Midcoast (June), Summer Guide 2 (July), Best of the Midcoast (Aug), Fall Home Improvement (Sept), Veterans (Nov), Holiday Gift Guides (Nov/Dec). Monthly: Healthy Living
Special Weekly Sections: Ticket (Fri); Best Food Day (Fri); Sights & Sounds (Thur); Milestones (Weddings & Engagements) (Tues); Business (Wed).
Syndicated Publications: Real Estate Plus, biweekly on Fridays; Healthy Living, third Wednesday of each month
Delivery Methods: Newsstand`Carrier`Racks
Areas Served - City/County or Portion Thereof, or Zip codes: Cumberland and Mid-Coast Maine
Own Printing Facility?: N
Commercial printers?: N
Sun. Circulation Paid: 8500
Audit By: Sworn/Estimate/Non-Audited
Audit Date: 12.07.2019
Personnel: George Reichert (Subscriber Services Mgr.); Stacy Wight (Business Mgr.); John Swinconeck (Ed.)
Parent company (for newspapers): MaineToday Media Inc.; RFB Enterprises

SUN JOURNAL

Street address 1: 104 Park Street
Street address city: Lewiston
Street address state: ME
Zip/Postal code: 4140
County: Androscoggin
Country: USA
Mailing address: PO BOX 4400
Mailing city: LEWISTON
Mailing state: ME
Mailing zip: 04243-4400
General Phone: (207) 784-5411
Advertising Phone: (207) 784-5411
Editorial Phone: (207) 784-5411
General/National Adv. E-mail: jjalbert@sunjournal.com
Display Adv. E-mail: brioux@sunjournal.com
Classified Adv. e-mail: scostello@sunjournal.com
Editorial e-mail: editor@sunjournal.com
Primary Website: www.sunjournal.com
Mthly Avg Views: 730000
Mthly Avg Unique Visitors: 240000
Year Established: 1861
News Services: AP, CSM, MCT.
Special Editions: HEALTHY LIVING, CHAMBERS AWARDS, CATHOLIC SCHOOLS WEEKLY (Jan); SPRING WEDDING GUIDE, PRESIDENTS DAY (Feb); SPRING HOME IMPROVEMENT, WESTERN ME BUILDERS, SPRING CAR CARE, LIVING WELL, LEWISTON AUBURN FILM FESTIVAL (Mar); LANDSCAPE & GARDEN, COLLEGE BOUND, PROFILE (Apr); GRADUATION, SUMMER IN MAINE, RIVER VALLEY RALLEY RELAY FOR LIFE (May); ANDROSCOGGIN RELAY FOR LIFE, BUSINESS TO BUSINESS TRADE SHOW (Jun); MOXIE FESTIVAL, TD BANK 250 (Jul); OUR TOWN, BALLOON FESTIVAL, FALL WEDDING GUIDE (Aug); FALL SPORTS, PROSPER, FALL HOME IMPROVEMENT, FALL CAR CARE, TASTE OF HOME, COOKING SCHOOL (Sept); FAMILY, CREDIT UNION DAY (Oct); VETERANS DAY, SHRINER'S FESTIVAL OF TREES, WESTERN ME HOLIDAY SERIES, HOLIDAY SERIES-ALL EDITIONS (Nov); WINTER SPORTS,WINTER IN MAINE, BUSINESS REVIEW (Dec);
Special Weekly Sections: Economy/Business, Weddings, Ent. (Sun); TV Preview (Sat).
Syndicated Publications: Relish (Monthly); USA WEEKEND Magazine, PARADE Magazine (Sun); American Profile (Weekly); Spry (Monthly); Decathalon Sports (Monthly).
Delivery Methods: Mail`Newsstand`Carrier`Racks

Areas Served - City/County or Portion Thereof, or Zip codes: Androscoggin County and Western Maine
Own Printing Facility?: Y
Commercial printers?: Y
Avg Free Circ: 792
Sat. Circulation Paid: 15489
Sat. Circulation Free: 792
Sun. Circulation Paid: 16774
Sun. Circulation Free: 468
Audit By: CAC
Audit Date: 30.09.2017
Personnel: Stephen M. Costello (Vice Pres. Adv./Mktg.); Jody Jalbert (Adv. Mgr.); Mike Theriault (Circ. Dir.); Rex Rhoades (Exec. Ed.); Judith Meyer (Mng. Ed., Day); Peter Phelan (Mng. Ed., Night); Heather McCarthy (Sr. Design); Russell Dillingham (Chief Photographer); Scott Thistle (REGL. ED.); James A. Thornton (Vice Pres./Bus. Mgr.); Bruce Rioux (Major Acc. Mgr.); Larry Baril (Acc. Exec.); Mike Blanchet (Acc. Exec.); Brian Croteau (Acc. Exec.); Dan McManus (Acc. Exec.); Norman Moreau (Acc. Exec.); Kelly Wade (Acc. Exec.); Denise Scammon (Special Sections Ed.); Carl Natale (Web Ed.); Mark Mogensen (Business, News Ed.); Steve Sherlock (Web Content Ed./Regl. Ed.); Justin Pelletier (Sports Ed.); Karen Kerworuka (Copy Desk Chief); Mary Delamater (Copy Ed.); David Costello (VP, Technology); Maureen Wedge (Vice Pres., HR); Bill Anctil (Adv. Sales)
Parent company (for newspapers): Sun Media Group

PORTLAND PRESS HERALD / MAINE SUNDAY TELEGRAM

Street address 1: 1 City Ctr Stop 7
Street address 2: 5th Floor
Street address city: Portland
Street address state: ME
Zip/Postal code: 04101-4009
County: Cumberland
Country: USA
Mailing address: PO BOX 1460
Mailing city: PORTLAND
Mailing state: ME
Mailing zip: 04104-5009
General Phone: (207) 791-6650
Advertising Phone: (207) 791-6200
Editorial Phone: (207) 791-6320
General/National Adv. E-mail: amuhs@mainetoday.com
Display Adv. E-mail: sbryan@mainetoday.com
Classified Adv. e-mail: cmnclass@centralmaine.com
Editorial e-mail: cschechtman@mainetoday.com
Primary Website: www.pressherald.com
Mthly Avg Views: 4600000
Mthly Avg Unique Visitors: 1173434
Year Established: 1862
News Services: AP, LAT-WP, Tribune Media, Universal Press, King Features, United Media, CSM, CQ.
Special Editions: 50 Plus (Apr); Vacationland (Aug); National Engineers Week (Feb); Wedding Planner (Jan); People's Choice, Seniority (Jul); Vacationland (Jun); Death and Dying (Mar); Vacationland (May); Holiday Gift Guide (Nov); Home Furnishings (Oct); Home Improvement (Fall).
Special Weekly Sections: Business Friday (Fri); On Screen (S); Religion & Values (Sat); GO (Thur); Business (Tues); Food & Health (Wed).
Syndicated Publications: Parade (S); American Profile (Weekly).
Delivery Methods: Mail`Newsstand`Carrier`Racks
Areas Served - City/County or Portion Thereof, or Zip codes: Southern Maine
Own Printing Facility?: Y
Commercial printers?: Y
Sat. Circulation Paid: 38128
Sun. Circulation Paid: 54506
Audit By: AAM
Audit Date: 30.09.2017
Personnel: Keith Toothaker (Prodn. Mgr., Pressroom/ Distr.); Jennifer Sorenson (Classified Adv. Mgr.); Don Coulter (Deputy Mng. Ed., Opns./Sports); Dieter Bradbury (Deputy Managing Ed.); Cliff Schechtman (Exec. Ed.); Steve Greenlee (Managing Ed.); Katherine Lee (City Ed.); Chelsea Conaboy (Features Ed.); Lisa DeSisto (CEO/Publisher); Barbara Bock (VP/Adv.); John Moore (Dir. Digital Products); Maryann Kelly (VP/ Labor & Employee Relations); Stefanie Manning (VP/ Circ. & Marketing); Stewart Wright (Chief Information Officer)
Parent company (for newspapers): Maine Today Media Inc.

MORNING SENTINEL

Street address 1: 31 Front St
Street address city: Waterville
Street address state: ME
Zip/Postal code: 04901-6626
County: Kennebec
Country: USA
Mailing address: 31 FRONT ST
Mailing city: WATERVILLE
Mailing state: ME
Mailing zip: 04901-6648
General Phone: (207) 873-3341
Advertising Phone: (207) 873-3341
Editorial Phone: (207) 873-3341
General/National Adv. E-mail: sentinelnews@mainetoday.com
Display Adv. E-mail: mscommunity@mainetoday.com
Classified Adv. e-mail: cmnclass@centralmaine.com
Editorial e-mail: smonroe@mainetoday.com
Primary Website: www.onlinesentinel.com
Mthly Avg Unique Visitors: 243450
Year Established: 1904
News Services: AP, LAT-WP, SHNS.
Special Editions: Spring Scouting (Apr); Skowhegan Fair (Aug); Holiday Shopping Guide II (Dec); Family Expo (Feb); Bridal (Jan); Pre-Owned Autos/Trucks/ SUVs (Jul); Graduation (Jun); Maine Paper Expo (Mar); Start Your Engines (May); Holiday Shopping Guide I (Nov); Fall Home
Special Weekly Sections: What's Happening (entertainment) (Fri); What's on TV (S).
Syndicated Publications: USA WEEKEND Magazine (S).
Delivery Methods: Mail`Newsstand`Carrier`Racks
Areas Served - City/County or Portion Thereof, or Zip codes: Franklin, Kennebec, Penobscot, and Somerset County
Own Printing Facility?: Y
Commercial printers?: Y
Avg Free Circ: 3567
Sat. Circulation Paid: 9243
Sat. Circulation Free: 3567
Sun. Circulation Paid: 9746
Sun. Circulation Free: 3542
Audit By: AAM
Audit Date: 31.03.2017
Personnel: Scott Monroe (Managing Ed.); Maureen Milliken (News Ed.); Stacy Blanchet (Community News Ed.); Ben Bragdon (Editorial Page Ed.); Bill Stewart (Exec. Sports Ed.); Dave Leaming (Photographers); Drew Bonifant (Sports Writer); Amy Calder (Reporter)
Parent company (for newspapers): Maine Today Media Inc.

MARYLAND

THE CAPITAL

Street address 1: 888 Bestgate Rd Ste 104
Street address 2: Suite 104
Street address city: Annapolis
Street address state: MD
Zip/Postal code: 21401-2950
County: Anne Arundel
Country: USA
General Phone: (410) 268-5000
Advertising Phone: (410) 268-7000
Editorial Phone: (410) 268-5000
General/National Adv. E-mail: mpadden@capgaznews.com
Display Adv. E-mail: mpadden@capgaznews.com
Classified Adv. e-mail: classifieds@capgaznews.com
Editorial e-mail: rhutzell@capgaznews.com
Primary Website: www.capitalgazette.com
Mthly Avg Views: 3500000
Year Established: 1884
News Services: AP, tronc
Delivery Methods: Newsstand`Carrier`Racks
Areas Served - City/County or Portion Thereof, or Zip codes: Annapolis, Anne Arundel County and Kent Island, Maryland.
Own Printing Facility?: Y
Commercial printers?: Y
Avg Free Circ: 1388
Sat. Circulation Paid: 14994
Sat. Circulation Free: 712
Sun. Circulation Paid: 18358
Sun. Circulation Free: 3045
Audit By: AAM
Audit Date: 31.03.2019
Personnel: Gerald Fischman (Editorial Page Ed.); Martin Padden (Adv. Dir.); Rick Hutzell (Editor); Tim Thomas (Publisher); Rob Hiassen (Managing Editor)
Parent company (for newspapers): Alden Global Capital; Tribune Publishing, Inc.

THE BALTIMORE SUN

Street address 1: 501 N. Calvert Street
Street address city: Baltimore
Street address state: MD
Zip/Postal code: 21278
County: Baltimore City
Country: USA
Mailing address: PO BOX 1377
Mailing city: BALTIMORE
Mailing state: MD
Mailing zip: 21203-1377
General Phone: (410) 332-6000
Advertising Phone: (410) 332-6300
Editorial Phone: (410) 332-6221
General/National Adv. E-mail: advertise@baltsun.com
Display Adv. E-mail: advertise@baltsun.com
Classified Adv. e-mail: advertise@baltsun.com
Editorial e-mail: trif.alatzas@baltsun.com
Primary Website: www.baltimoresun.com
Mthly Avg Unique Visitors: 5029173
Year Established: 1837
News Services: Tribune Newspaper Network, RN, MCT, NYT, DJ, LAT-WP, AFP.
Special Editions: Preakness Wrap-Up (Apr); Our Future/ Carroll Schools (Aug); High Tech Education (Dec); Health Today (Every other month); College Goal Sunday Program (Feb); Career Builder XL II (Jan); Ravens Training Camp (Jul); A.A. Co. Residents Guide (Jun); Credit Union.
Special Weekly Sections: Business (Tue); Taste (Wed); Health & Style (Thur); Live! (Fri); At Home, Sports (Sat); Travel, Art, Entertainment, Real Estate, Sports (Sun);
Syndicated Publications: Parade (Sun); Sun Magazine (6 times annually); Howard Magazine (8 times annually); Harford Magazine (5 times annually); Maryland Family (10 times annually); Chesapeake Home (7 times annually)
Delivery Methods: Mail`Newsstand`Carrier
Areas Served - City/County or Portion Thereof, or Zip codes: All of Maryland
Own Printing Facility?: Y
Commercial printers?: Y
Sat. Circulation Paid: 148657
Sun. Circulation Paid: 210440
Audit By: AAM
Audit Date: 31.12.2017
Personnel: Triffon Alatzas (Pub./Ed. -in-Chief); Samuel Davis (Managing Ed.); Laura Smitherman (Asst. Managing Ed.); Peter Sweigard (Asst. Managing Ed. Digital); Patricia Carroll (SVP - targeted Media); Susan Duchin (Adv. Dir.); Matthew Brown (Enterprise Ed.); Jacques Kelly (Columnist); Ron Fritz (Sr. Ed. sports); Andrew Knobel (Deputy Sports Ed.); Ellen Fishel (Features Content Ed.); Lori Sears (Events Mgr.); Andrew Green (Editorial Page Ed.); Matt Bracken (Dir. Audience/Dev.); Adam Marton (Sr. Ed. Interactive Design); Jay Judge (Sr. Ed. visuals); Steve Young (News Ed.)
Parent company (for newspapers): Alden Global Capital; Tribune Publishing, Inc.

THE DAILY RECORD

Street address 1: 11 E Saratoga St
Street address city: Baltimore
Street address state: MD
Zip/Postal code: 21202-2115
County: Baltimore City
Country: USA
Mailing address: 11 E SARATOGA ST STE 1
Mailing city: BALTIMORE
Mailing state: MD
Mailing zip: 21202-2199
General Phone: (443) 524-8100
Advertising Phone: (443) 524-8100
Editorial Phone: (443) 524-8150
General/National Adv. E-mail: suzanne.huettner@thedailyrecord.com
Display Adv. E-mail: advertising@thedailyrecord.com
Classified Adv. e-mail: justin.carson@thedailyrecord.com
Editorial e-mail: tbaden@thedailyrecord.com
Primary Website: www.thedailyrecord.com
Year Established: 1888
Areas Served - City/County or Portion Thereof, or Zip codes: 21202-2115
Avg Free Circ: 384
Audit By: CVC
Audit Date: 12.07.2019
Personnel: Suzanne Fischer-Huettner (Publisher); Maria Kelly (Comptroller); Tracy Bumba (Audience Dev. Dir.); Shelby Carter (Admin. Asst.); Thomas Baden Jr. (Ed.); Jason Whong (Digital Ed.); Danny Jacobs (Legal Ed.); Maximilian Franz (Sr. Photographer); Jessica Gregg (Special Products Ed.); Darice Miller (Acc. Mgr.); Terri Thompson (Acc. Mgr.); Haley Poling (Mktg. and Event Coord.)
Parent company (for newspapers): The Dolan Company; Gannett

THE CUMBERLAND TIMES-NEWS

Street address 1: 19 Baltimore St
Street address city: Cumberland
Street address state: MD
Zip/Postal code: 21502-3023
County: Allegany
Country: USA
Mailing address: PO BOX 1662
Mailing city: CUMBERLAND
Mailing state: MD
Mailing zip: 21501-1662
General Phone: (301) 722-4600
Advertising Phone: (301) 722-2504
Editorial Phone: (301) 784-2517
General/National Adv. E-mail: ctn@times-news.com
Display Adv. E-mail: advertising@times-news.com
Classified Adv. e-mail: classified@times-news.com
Editorial e-mail: ctn@times-news.com
Primary Website: www.times-news.com
Mthly Avg Views: 650000
Mthly Avg Unique Visitors: 175000
Year Established: 1988
News Services: AP, CNHI
Special Editions: Back-to-School (Aug); Bridal Tab (Feb); Tax Tips Tab (Jan); Regional Outlook (March); Home Improvement (May); Car Care Tab (Oct); High School Football (Sept.) Home Improvement (Sept). Medical Journal (Monthly)
Special Weekly Sections: TV & Entertainment (Sat)
Syndicated Publications: Relish (Monthly); Parade (Sunday).
Delivery Methods: Mail`Newsstand`Carrier`Racks
Areas Served - City/County or Portion Thereof, or Zip codes: Cumberland and the surrounding areas of Allegany and Garrett counties in Maryland, and Mineral County in West Virginia.
Own Printing Facility?: Y
Commercial printers?: Y
Avg Free Circ: 796
Sat. Circulation Paid: 17314
Sat. Circulation Free: 796
Sun. Circulation Paid: 18735
Sun. Circulation Free: 506
Audit By: AAM
Audit Date: 30.09.2016
Personnel: Mark Harris (News Editor); Mike Burke (Sports Ed.); Teresa McMinn (Digital Ed.); Jim Goldsworthy (Editorial page editor); Debbie Haan (Community Editor); Debbie Meyer (Community Editor); John Smith (Managing Editor); Marisa Hammond (Copy Editor); Jeff Landes (Sports Editor); Mike Sawyers (Outdoor Editor); Alex Rychwalski (sports reporter); Lindsay Renner-Wood (Reporter); Watson Don (Advertising Director); Robert Forcey (Publisher); Sue Sheehan (Regional circulation director); Greg Larry (Reporter)
Parent company (for newspapers): CNHI, LLC; CNHI, LLC

THE STAR-DEMOCRAT

Street address 1: 29088 Airpark Dr
Street address city: Easton
Street address state: MD
Zip/Postal code: 21601-7000
County: Talbot
Country: USA
Mailing address: PO BOX 600
Mailing city: EASTON
Mailing state: MD
Mailing zip: 21601-0600
General Phone: (410) 822-1500
Advertising Phone: (410) 770-4040
Editorial Phone: (410) 770-4093
General/National Adv. E-mail: klaprade@chespub.com

Display Adv. E-mail: klaprade@chespub.com
Classified Adv. e-mail: sgarcia@chespub.com
Editorial e-mail: bsauers@chespub.com
Primary Website: www.stardem.com
Year Established: 1896
News Services: AP.
Special Editions: Healthy Living (Monthly); Chesapeake 360 (Quarterly); Business Ledger (Quarterly)
Special Weekly Sections: Church Page (Fri); Weekend (Fri); Family Page (Mon); Life on the Shore (S); Life on the Shore (Wed).
Syndicated Publications: Relish (Monthly); USA WEEKEND Magazine (S); American Profile (Weekly).
Delivery Methods: Mail`Newsstand`Carrier`Racks
Areas Served - City/County or Portion Thereof, or Zip codes: 21601
Own Printing Facility?: Y
Commercial printers?: Y
Sun. Circulation Paid: 16326
Audit By: Sworn/Estimate/Non-Audited
Audit Date: 12.07.2019
Personnel: David Fike (Pres./Pub.); Kevin A. Fike (Circ. Dir.); John Griep (Exec. Ed.); Mike Bowen (Rgl. Plant & Prod. Dir.); David Alltop (Rgl. IT Mgr.); Melodie Haufe (Rgl. Controller); Greg Maki (Deputy/Weekend Ed.); Josh Bollinger (News Ed.); William Haufe (Sports Ed.); Richard Polk (Business Ed.); Katie Willis (Community Ed.); Ayman Alam (Staff Writer); Chris Polk (Staff Writer); Connie Connolly (Reporter); David Insley (Staff Writer); Sarah Drury (Reporter); Brandon Silverstein (Adv. Dir.)
Parent company (for newspapers): Adams Publishing Group, LLC

THE FREDERICK NEWS-POST

Street address 1: 351 Ballenger Center Dr
Street address city: Frederick
Street address state: MD
Zip/Postal code: 21703-7095
County: Frederick
Country: USA
Mailing address: 351 BALLENGER CENTER DR
Mailing city: FREDERICK
Mailing state: MD
Mailing zip: 21703-7095
General Phone: (301) 662-1177
Advertising Phone: (301) 662-1162
Editorial Phone: (301) 662-1178
General/National Adv. E-mail: chastings@newspost.com
Display Adv. E-mail: wmillander@newspost.com
Classified Adv. e-mail: classifieds@fredericknewspost.com
Editorial e-mail: theadlee@newspost.com
Primary Website: www.fredericknewspost.com
Year Established: 1883
News Services: AP, SHNS, CNS, MCT, TMS.
Special Editions: Frederick Keys Orioles Supplement (Pullout) (Apr); Fall Football Guide (Aug); Holiday Gift Guide (Dec); Wedding Planner (Jan); Hello Frederick County (Jul); Progress (Mar); Spring Automotive (May); Holiday Magazine (Nov); Fall Automotive (Oct); Healthy Frederick (Dec).
Special Weekly Sections: Lifestyle (Fri); Farm (Mon); Religion & Ethics (Sat); Business (Mon); Comics (S); Auto (Sat); Home & Family (Thur); Health & Fitness (Tues); Food (Wed).
Syndicated Publications: Relish (Monthly); USA WEEKEND Magazine (S); TV Week (Sat); American Profile (Wed).
Delivery Methods: Mail`Newsstand`Carrier`Racks
Areas Served - City/County or Portion Thereof, or Zip codes: 21701, 21704, 21702, 21703, 21710, 21717, 21754, 21765, 21770, 21771, 21774, 21797, 21717, 21727, 21757, 21778, 21780, 21787, 21788, 21791, 21157, 21158, 21762, 21776, 21793, 21798, 20180, 21195, 21713, 21716, 21755, 21756, 21758, 21777, 21779, 21782, 21714, 21718, 21740, 21741, 21742, 21746, 21769, 21773, 21783, 20837, 20841, 20842, 20850, 20855
Own Printing Facility?: Y
Commercial printers?: Y
Sat. Circulation Paid: 22990
Sun. Circulation Paid: 24514
Audit By: AAM
Audit Date: 30.09.2017
Personnel: Myron W. Randall (Pres.); Geordie Wilson (Pub.); Connie Hastings (Adv. Mgr.); Terry Headlee (Mng. Ed.); Peter McCarthy (City Ed.); Will Randall (CEO); Patrick Pexton (Ed.); Brent Renken (Dir. Adv. & Mrktg.); Travis Pratt (Web Ed.); Karen James (Community News); Christopher Kinsler (Ed.)
Parent company (for newspapers): Ogden Newspapers Inc.

THE HERALD-MAIL

Street address 1: 100 Summit Ave
Street address city: Hagerstown
Street address state: MD
Zip/Postal code: 21740-5509
County: Washington
Country: USA
Mailing address: PO BOX 439
Mailing city: HAGERSTOWN
Mailing state: MD
Mailing zip: 21741-0439
General Phone: (301) 733-5131
Advertising Phone: (301) 733-5131
Editorial Phone: (301) 733-5131
General/National Adv. E-mail: brittneyh@herald-mail.com
Display Adv. E-mail: advertising@herald-mail.com
Classified Adv. e-mail: advertising@herald-mail.com
Editorial e-mail: billk@herald-mail.com
Primary Website: www.heraldmailmedia.com
Mthly Avg Views: 4000000
Mthly Avg Unique Visitors: 330000
Year Established: 1873
News Services: AP.
Special Weekly Sections: Money (S); Weekend (Thur); Farm Page (Tues); Food Pages & Recipes (Wed).
Syndicated Publications: Relish (Monthly); Parade (S).
Delivery Methods: Mail`Newsstand`Carrier`Racks
Areas Served - City/County or Portion Thereof, or Zip codes: Maryland, Pennsylvania and West Virginia
Sat. Circulation Paid: 23637
Sun. Circulation Paid: 28289
Audit By: AAM
Audit Date: 31.03.2014
Personnel: Andy Mason (Sports Ed.); Crystal Schelle (Lifestyle Ed.); Jake Womer (Exec. Ed.); Dan Kauffman (Asst. Sports Ed.); Terry Headlee (Managing Ed.)
Parent company (for newspapers): Gannett; Schurz Communications Inc

THE DAILY TIMES

Street address 1: 115 S. Division St
Street address city: Salisbury
Street address state: MD
Zip/Postal code: 21801
County: Wicomico
Country: USA
Mailing address: PO Box 1080
Mailing city: SALISBURY
Mailing state: MD
Mailing zip: 21802
General Phone: (410) 749-7171
General/National Adv. E-mail: niovacchini@gannett.com
Display Adv. E-mail: niovacchini@gannett.com
Classified Adv. e-mail: sbyclass@gannett.com
Editorial e-mail: lbenedic@dmg.gannett.com
Primary Website: www.delmarvanow.com
Year Established: 1886
News Services: AP, NEA.
Delivery Methods: Mail`Newsstand`Carrier`Racks
Areas Served - City/County or Portion Thereof, or Zip codes: Wicomico County, Worcester County, Somerset County.
Own Printing Facility?: N
Commercial printers?: N
Avg Free Circ: 0
Sat. Circulation Paid: 8543
Sat. Circulation Free: 47
Sun. Circulation Paid: 11063
Sun. Circulation Free: 52
Audit By: AAM
Audit Date: 31.03.2022
Personnel: Laura Benedict (Executive Editor); Ron Pousson (Adv. Dir.); Lou Hault (Circ. Dir.)
Parent company (for newspapers): Gannett

CARROLL COUNTY TIMES

Street address 1: 201 Railroad Ave
Street address city: Westminster
Street address state: MD
Zip/Postal code: 21157-4823
County: Carroll
Country: USA
Mailing address: PO Box 169
Mailing city: Westminster
Mailing state: MD
Mailing zip: 21158
General Phone: (410) 848-4400
Advertising Phone: (410) 848-4400
Editorial Phone: (410) 857-7878
General/National Adv. E-mail: marketing@carrollcountytimes.com
Display Adv. E-mail: erin.hahn@carrollcountytimes.com
Classified Adv. e-mail: classified@lcniofmd.com
Editorial e-mail: jim.lee@carrollcountytimes.com
Primary Website: www.carrollcountytimes.com
Mthly Avg Views: 1290000
Mthly Avg Unique Visitors: 100000
Year Established: 1911
News Services: AP, GNS, SHNS.
Special Editions: Bridal Guide (Jan); Home & Garden (Mar); Pet Guide (June); Carroll Living (June); Fall Sports (Aug); Fall Home Improvement (Oct); Wine Festival (Sept); Holiday Guide (Nov).
Special Weekly Sections: Prep Sports (Fri); Religion (Sat); Entertainment/Encore (Thur); Best Food Day (Wed).
Syndicated Publications: Relish (Monthly); Parade Magazine (S); American Profile (Weekly); Spry (Monthly)
Delivery Methods: Newsstand`Carrier`Racks
Areas Served - City/County or Portion Thereof, or Zip codes: 21048, 21074, 21102, 21104, 21117, 21136, 21155, 21157, 21158, 21757, 21765, 21771, 21776, 21784, 21787, 21791, 21797
Own Printing Facility?: Y
Commercial printers?: Y
Avg Free Circ: 379
Sat. Circulation Paid: 10201
Sat. Circulation Free: 379
Sun. Circulation Paid: 12535
Sun. Circulation Free: 2009
Audit By: AAM
Audit Date: 31.03.2019
Personnel: Bob Blubaugh (News Ed.); Adam Malat (Adv. Dir.); Pat Stoetzer (Sports Ed.); Brian Compere (Night Ed.); Jeff Bill (Photo Ed.)
Parent company (for newspapers): Landmark Media Enterprises, LLC; Alden Global Capital

MASSACHUSETTS

ATHOL DAILY NEWS

Street address 1: 225 Exchange St
Street address city: Athol
Street address state: MA
Zip/Postal code: 01331-1843
County: Worcester
Country: USA
Mailing address: PO BOX 1000
Mailing city: ATHOL
Mailing state: MA
Mailing zip: 01331-5000
General Phone: (978) 249-3535
Advertising Phone: (978) 249-3535 ext. 615
Editorial Phone: (978) 249-3535 ext. 658
General/National Adv. E-mail: advertising@atholdailynews.com
Display Adv. E-mail: advertising@atholdailynews.com
Classified Adv. e-mail: classified@atholdailynews.com
Editorial e-mail: newsroom@atholdailynews.com
Primary Website: www.atholdailynews.com
Year Established: 1934
News Services: AP.
Special Editions: River Rat Review (Apr); First Baby Contest (Dec); Boy Scout Page (Feb); Bridal Supplement (Jan); Graduation Pages (Jun); Graduation Pages (May); Thanksgiving Greetings (Nov); Fire Prevention (Oct); Football Pages (Sept). Back to School supplement (Aug)
Special Weekly Sections: Quabbin Times (Tues).
Delivery Methods: Mail`Newsstand`Carrier
Areas Served - City/County or Portion Thereof, or Zip codes: 01331, 01364, 01365, 01378, 01344, 01366, 01368, 01379, 01468
Own Printing Facility?: Y
Commercial printers?: Y
Sat. Circulation Paid: 4661
Audit By: Sworn/Estimate/Non-Audited
Audit Date: 12.07.2019
Personnel: Richard J. Chase (Pub.); Deborrah Porter (Ed.); Jacqueline Caron (Adv. Mgr.); Lisa Arnot (Office Mgr.); Brandy Nadeau (Circ. Mgr.); Josh Talbot (Sports Ed.); Dee Wheeler (Classified Adv.); Theresa Cody (Prod. Mgr.); Jared Robinson (Webmaster)
Parent company (for newspapers): Athol Press Inc.

THE SUN CHRONICLE

Street address 1: 34 S Main St
Street address city: Attleboro
Street address state: MA
Zip/Postal code: 02703-2920
County: Bristol
Country: USA
Mailing address: PO BOX 600
Mailing city: ATTLEBORO
Mailing state: MA
Mailing zip: 02703-0600
General Phone: (508) 222-7000
Advertising Phone: (508) 236-0309
Editorial Phone: (508) 236-0887
General/National Adv. E-mail: rlacaillade@thesunchronicle.com
Display Adv. E-mail: jcambridge@thesunchronicle.com
Classified Adv. e-mail: class@thesunchronicle.com
Editorial e-mail: cborges@thesunchronicle.com
Primary Website: www.thesunchronicle.com
Mthly Avg Views: 1568000
Mthly Avg Unique Visitors: 500000
Year Established: 1889
News Services: AP
Special Editions: Health & Fitness, Your Home, Super Bowl, Preschool, Kindergarten, Childcare (Jan); Valentines, Bridal, Auto (Feb); Coupons (Mar); Readers' Choice, Beautiful Homes & Gardens, Business Card (Apr); Mother's Day Dining, Summertime Golf (May); Parenting, Church Directory (June); Back-to-School, Bus Routes, Sales Tax, Wedding Expo (Aug); High School Football, Home Impreovement (Sept); Frequent Flyer, Pink October, Dining Guide (Oct); Holiday Gift Guide (Nov); Last Minute Gifts, Festive Foods, Holiday Viewers, Basketball, New Year's Dining (Dec)
Special Weekly Sections: Pets (Mon); Teens (Tues); Best Food Day (Wed), Entertainment (Thurs).
Syndicated Publications: Relish (Monthly); USA WEEKEND Magazine (S); American Profile (Weekly).
Delivery Methods: Mail`Newsstand`Carrier`Racks
Areas Served - City/County or Portion Thereof, or Zip codes: Attleboro and North Attleboro, Foxboro, Mansfield, Norfolk, Norton, Plainville, Rehoboth, Seekonk, and Wrentham
Own Printing Facility?: Y
Commercial printers?: Y
Avg Free Circ: 652
Sat. Circulation Paid: 10769
Sat. Circulation Free: 652
Sun. Circulation Paid: 11752
Sun. Circulation Free: 227
Audit By: AAM
Audit Date: 30.06.2016
Personnel: Mike Kirby (Ed.); Ken Ross (Asst. Mng. Ed., Features); Craig Borges (Business); Mark Flanagan (Editorial Page Ed.); Dale Ransom (Sports Ed.); Tom Reilly (Sunday Ed.); Jeff Peterson (Pub.); Emily O'Donnell; Kathy Powell (Circ. Sales Mgr.); David Kiely (IT /Digital Media Mgr.); Ken Lechtanski (Sports)
Parent company (for newspapers): Horizon Publications Inc.; Triboro Massachusetts News Media Inc.

THE SALEM NEWS

Street address 1: 32 Dunham Rd
Street address city: Beverly
Street address state: MA
Zip/Postal code: 01915-1844
County: Essex
Country: USA
Mailing address: 32 DUNHAM RD
Mailing city: BEVERLY
Mailing state: MA
Mailing zip: 01915-1895
General Phone: (978) 922-1234
Advertising Phone: (978) 338-2640
Editorial Phone: (978) 338-2531
General/National Adv. E-mail: btrefethen@salemnews.com
Display Adv. E-mail: btrefethen@salemnews.com
Classified Adv. e-mail: btrefethen@salemnews.com
Editorial e-mail: dolson@salemnews.com
Primary Website: www.salemnews.com
Mthly Avg Views: 2300000
Year Established: 1880

News Services: AP
Syndicated Publications: Marblehead Home & Style
Delivery Methods: Mail`Newsstand`Carrier`Racks
Areas Served - City/County or Portion Thereof, or Zip codes: Salem, Beverly, Danvers, Peabody, Ipswich, Hamilton, Wenham, Marblehead, Swampscott, Middleton, Topsfield, Boxford and Manchester
Own Printing Facility?: Y
Commercial printers?: Y
Avg Free Circ: 833
Sat. Circulation Paid: 13730
Sat. Circulation Free: 833
Audit By: AAM
Audit Date: 30.06.2017
Personnel: Karen Andreas (Pub.); David Olson (Ed.); Bill Trefethen (Retail Adv. Mgr.); Helen Gifford (Mng. Ed.); Phil Stacey (Sports Ed.); Dove Morissette (Night Ed.); Muriel Hoffacker (Community Ed.)
Parent company (for newspapers): CNHI, LLC

BOSTON HERALD

Street address 1: 70 Fargo St Ste 600
Street address 2: Seaport Center
Street address city: Boston
Street address state: MA
Zip/Postal code: 02210-2131
County: Suffolk
Country: USA
Mailing address: 70 FARGO ST
Mailing city: BOSTON
Mailing state: MA
Mailing zip: 02210-2142
General Phone: (617) 426-3000
Advertising Phone: (617) 619-6185
Editorial Phone: (617) 619-6515
General/National Adv. E-mail: advertising@bostonherald.com
Display Adv. E-mail: advertising@bostonherald.com
Classified Adv. e-mail: classifiedads@bostonherald.com
Editorial e-mail: citydesk@bostonherald.com
Primary Website: www.bostonherald.com
Mthly Avg Views: 35000000
Mthly Avg Unique Visitors: 4879000
Year Established: 1846
News Services: AP, RN, Business Wire, DJ, TMS.
Special Editions: Careers Extra (Monthly); Health (Semi-Yearly).
Special Weekly Sections: Scene (Fri); Business Extra (Mon); Sports Pull-Out (Sun); Super Saturday Classifieds (Sat); Travel (Thur); Tuesday Business(Tues); Food (Wed).
Delivery Methods: Mail`Newsstand`Carrier`Racks
Areas Served - City/County or Portion Thereof, or Zip codes: 02210
Own Printing Facility?: N
Commercial printers?: N
Sat. Circulation Paid: 75492
Sun. Circulation Paid: 79183
Audit By: AAM
Audit Date: 31.03.2018
Personnel: Kevin Corrado (Pub.); Joseph Sciacca (Ed. in Chief); Marc Grasso (Controller/CFO); Gerald Sher (Circ. Mgr., Home Delivery); John Palmer (Circ. Mgr., Single Copy Sales); Sandra Kent (Deputy Mgr. Ed., Features); Jen Miller (Exec. City Ed.); Jim Potter (Design/Prod. Ed.); Shelly Cohen (Editorial Page Ed.); Joseph O'Neill (Sr. Dir. Finance & Info Technology); Gwen Gage (VP/Promotion); Brian Cox (Vice Pres./ Display Advertising); Joseph LoPilato (Vice Pres./ Classified Advt.); John Nemerowski (Dir. of Display Adv.); Steve Bowden (Dir. of Information Systems); Duncan Suss (Dir. of Publishing Systems); Kimberly Atkins (Washington Ed.); Rachelle Cohen (Editorial Page Ed.); John Strahinich (Managing Editor); Joseph Dwinell (City Desk Ed.); Tom Shattuck (Producer Herald Radio); Fiona Molloy (Sunday Editor); Jules Crittenden (City Ed.); James Mahoney (Photo Ed.); Zuri Berry (Multimedia Ed.); Arthur Pollock (Asst.t Photo Ed.); Gustavo Leon (Art Dir.)
Parent company (for newspapers): Digital First Media; MediaNews Group

METRO BOSTON

Street address 1: 101 Arch Street
Street address 2: 8th floor
Street address city: Boston
Street address state: MA
Zip/Postal code: 2110
County: Suffolk
Country: USA
Mailing address: 234 CONGRESS ST FL 4TH
Mailing city: BOSTON
Mailing state: MA
Mailing zip: 02110-2470
General Phone: (617) 210-7905
Advertising Phone: (617) 532-0100
General/National Adv. E-mail: adsboston@metro.us
Display Adv. E-mail: adsboston@metro.us
Classified Adv. e-mail: adsboston@metro.us
Editorial e-mail: letters@metro.us
Primary Website: metro.us/boston
Mthly Avg Views: 4439165
Mthly Avg Unique Visitors: 1984744
Year Established: 2001
Delivery Methods: Racks
Areas Served - City/County or Portion Thereof, or Zip codes: Great Boston: Suffolk, Middlesex, Norfolk, Essex
Own Printing Facility?: N
Commercial printers?: N
Avg Free Circ: 57752
Audit By: CAC
Audit Date: 30.09.2018
Personnel: Brian Cox (Associate Publisher/ Executive Sales Director)
Parent company (for newspapers): Metro US

THE BOSTON GLOBE

Street address 1: 135 William T Morrissey Blvd
Street address city: Boston
Street address state: MA
Zip/Postal code: 02125-3310
County: Suffolk
Country: USA
Mailing address: PO BOX 55819
Mailing city: BOSTON
Mailing state: MA
Mailing zip: 02205-5819
General Phone: (617) 929-2000
Advertising Phone: (617) 929-2100
Editorial Phone: (617) 929-3059
General/National Adv. E-mail: advertising@globe.com
Display Adv. E-mail: p_andrews@globe.com
Classified Adv. e-mail: classified@globe.com
Editorial e-mail: mcgrory@globe.com
Primary Website: www.bostonglobe.com
Mthly Avg Views: 200000000
Mthly Avg Unique Visitors: 5500000
Year Established: 1872
News Services: AP, DJ, LAT-WP, MCT, RN.
Special Editions: Mother's Day Restaurants (May); Cape Cod Distinctive Homes (Apr); College Football Preview (Aug); Continuing Education (Dec); Florida (Feb); Valentine's Day Restaurants (Jan); NHIS NASCAR (Jul); Cape Cod Distinctive Shopping (Jun); Health and Hospitals (Mar).
Special Weekly Sections: Real Estate (S); Life At Home (Thur); Health/Science (Tues); Food (Wed).
Syndicated Publications: Parade (S).
Delivery Methods: Mail`Newsstand`Carrier`Racks
Areas Served - City/County or Portion Thereof, or Zip codes: Metropolitan Statistical Areas surrounding Boston (MSAs include Boston, Barnstable-Hyannis, Brockton, Fitchburg-Leominster, Lawrence, Lowell, New Bedford, Worcester, MA: Providence-Warwick, RI: Manchester, Nashua, Portsmouth-Rochester, NH)
Own Printing Facility?: Y
Commercial printers?: Y
Sat. Circulation Paid: 234063
Sun. Circulation Paid: 323630
Audit By: AAM
Audit Date: 01.04.2018
Personnel: Brian McGrory (Ed.); David Dahl (Dep. Mng. Ed. Print/Ops.); Marjorie Pritchard (Dep. Mng. Ed. Edit. Pg.); Jason Tuohey (Sr. Dep. Mng. Ed. Dig. and Aud. Mgmt.); Linda Corcoran (Deputy Ed.); Alan Wirzbicki (Sr. Edit. Writer)
Parent company (for newspapers): John W. Henry

THE ENTERPRISE

Street address 1: 1324 Belmont St Ste 102
Street address 2: Unit 102
Street address city: Brockton
Street address state: MA
Zip/Postal code: 02301-4435
County: Plymouth
Country: USA
Mailing address: 1324 BELMONT ST STE 102
Mailing city: BROCKTON
Mailing state: MA
Mailing zip: 02301-4435
General Phone: (508) 586-6200
Advertising Phone: (508) 638-5580
Editorial Phone: (508) 427-4054
General/National Adv. E-mail: salesteam@wickedlocal.com
Display Adv. E-mail: salesteam@wickedlocal.com
Classified Adv. e-mail: salesteam@wickedlocal.com
Editorial e-mail: newsroom@enterprisenews.com
Primary Website: www.enterprisenews.com
Year Established: 1880
News Services: AP, LAT-WP, SHNS.
Special Editions: Education (Apr); Coupon Book (Aug); Chronology Pages/Year in Review (Dec); Living Well (Every other month); Coupon Book (Feb); Golfers Corner (Jul); How to Guide (Jun); Progress (Mar); Professional Profiles (May); Gift Guide (Nov); Coupon Book (Oct); Foot
Special Weekly Sections: Style (Fri); Next (Mon); Travel (S); Family Life (Sat); Mind & Body (Thur); Mind & Body (Tues); Good Taste (Wed).
Syndicated Publications: USA WEEKEND Magazine (S).
Delivery Methods: Mail`Carrier
Areas Served - City/County or Portion Thereof, or Zip codes: 02048, 02072, 02301, 02302, 02322, 02324, 02330, 02333, 02338, 02339, 02341, 02343, 02346, 02347, 02351, 02356, 02359, 02360, 02364, 02367, 02368, 02370, 02375, 02379, 02382, 02571, 02718, 02766, 02767, 02779, 02780, 99999
Own Printing Facility?: Y
Commercial printers?: Y
Sat. Circulation Paid: 9212
Sun. Circulation Paid: 13933
Audit By: AAM
Audit Date: 31.12.2018
Personnel: Mark Torpey (Sports Ed.); Chazy Dowaliby (Ed.); Steven Damish (Managing Ed.); Joe Brosseau (Evening News Ed.); Ken Johnson (Online Ed.); Dana Barbuto (Features Ed.); Jen Wagner (Visuals Ed.); Lisa Strattan (Exec. Ed.)
Parent company (for newspapers): Gannett; CherryRoad Media

THE HERALD NEWS

Street address 1: 207 Pocasset St
Street address city: Fall River
Street address state: MA
Zip/Postal code: 02721-1532
County: Bristol
Country: USA
Mailing address: 207 POCASSET ST
Mailing city: FALL RIVER
Mailing state: MA
Mailing zip: 02721-1532
General Phone: (508) 676-8211
Advertising Phone: (508) 676-2560
Editorial Phone: (508) 676-2534
General/National Adv. E-mail: ads@heraldnews.com
Display Adv. E-mail: lrufener@heraldnews.com
Classified Adv. e-mail: lrufener@heraldnews.com
Editorial e-mail: lsullivan@heraldnews.com
Primary Website: www.heraldnews.com
Mthly Avg Views: 292685
Mthly Avg Unique Visitors: 55947
Year Established: 1892
News Services: AP.
Special Editions: Progress (Mar); Home & Garden (Apr); Home & Garden (May); Fall River Celebrates America (Aug); Hockey & Basketball Preview (Dec); Auto (Feb); Super Bowl (Jan); Business Review (Jul); Bridal (Jun); County Kids (Monthly); Christmas in Fall River (Nov).
Special Weekly Sections: Entertainment Guide (Fri); Lifestyle (S); Real Estate Guide (Sat); Wheels (Tues); Best Food Day (Wed).
Syndicated Publications: Comics (S).
Delivery Methods: Mail`Carrier
Own Printing Facility?: Y
Commercial printers?: Y
Avg Free Circ: 83
Sat. Circulation Paid: 5766
Sat. Circulation Free: 83
Sun. Circulation Paid: 6686
Sun. Circulation Free: 50
Audit By: AAM
Audit Date: 31.03.2019
Personnel: Lisa Strattan (Pub.); Thomas Amato (Circ. Dir.); Lynne Sullivan (Editor-in-Chief); Chris Avis (Sales Mgr.); Linda Murphy (Lifestyles Ed.); Jon Root (Content/Interactive Dir.); Will Richmond (City Ed.); Mike Thomas (Sports Ed.); Aaron Frechette (Editorial Page Ed.); Mark Olivieri (Pub.)
Parent company (for newspapers): Gannett; CherryRoad Media

SENTINEL & ENTERPRISE

Street address 1: 808 Main Street
Street address city: Fitchburg
Street address state: MA
Zip/Postal code: 1420
County: Worcester
Country: USA
Mailing address: PO BOX 730
Mailing city: FITCHBURG
Mailing state: MA
Mailing zip: 01420-0007
General Phone: (978) 343-6911
Advertising Phone: (978) 343-6911
Editorial Phone: (978) 343-6911
General/National Adv. E-mail: hconry@MediaOneNe.com
Display Adv. E-mail: hconry@MediaOneNe.com
Classified Adv. e-mail: hconry@MediaOneNe.com
Editorial e-mail: cstamand@sentinelandenterprise.com
Primary Website: www.sentinelandenterprise.com
Year Established: 1838
News Services: AP, SHNS, TMS.
Special Editions: Back-to-School (Aug); Holiday Gift Guides (Dec); Washington's Birthday (Feb); Bride & Groom (Jan); Longso Bike Race (Jul); Spring Home Improvement (Mar); Graduation (May); Thanksgiving Sports (Nov); Fall Car Care (Oct); Fall Home Improvement (Sept).
Special Weekly Sections: Auto (Thur); Gallery of Homes (Wed); TV Week (Weekly).
Syndicated Publications: USA WEEKEND Magazine (S).
Delivery Methods: Mail`Carrier
Areas Served - City/County or Portion Thereof, or Zip codes: 01430, 01431, 01420, 01444, 01523, 01453, 01412, 01364, 01464, 01469, 01473, 01475
Avg Free Circ: 884
Sat. Circulation Paid: 6283
Sat. Circulation Free: 884
Sun. Circulation Paid: 7772
Sun. Circulation Free: 1252
Audit By: AAM
Audit Date: 30.06.2017
Personnel: Charles St. Amand (Ed.); Ross Edwards (Sports Ed.); Dennis West (Circ. Mgr.); Andrea Mendes (Emerging Media Dir.); David Florence (Adv. Mgr.); Holly Conry (Adv. Admin.); Cliff Clark (City Ed.)
Parent company (for newspapers): Digital First Media; MediaNews Group

METROWEST DAILY NEWS

Street address 1: 1 Speen St.
Street address city: Framingham
Street address state: MA
Zip/Postal code: 1701
County: Middlesex
Country: USA
Mailing address: PO BOX 9149
Mailing city: FRAMINGHAM
Mailing state: MA
Mailing zip: 01701-9149
General Phone: 508-626-4412
Advertising Phone: (508) 626-3984
Editorial Phone: (508) 626-3871
General/National Adv. E-mail: metrowest@wickedlocal.com
Display Adv. E-mail: salesteam@wickedlocal.com
Editorial e-mail: rlodge@wickedlocal.com
Primary Website: www.metrowestdailynews.com
Year Established: 1897
News Services: AP, GateHouse News Service, State House News Service
Special Editions: Spring Home & Garden (Apr); Back-to-School/College (Aug); Last Minute Gift Guide (Dec); Presidents' Day (Feb); Weddings (Jan); Community Guides (Jul); MetroWest Community Guide (Jun); Business (Mar); Health & Lifestyles (May); Holiday Gift Guide (Nov).
Special Weekly Sections: Autoweekly (Fri); MetroWest Business Journal (Mon); Expanded Entertainment (S); Mutual Fund Listing (Sat); MetroWest Weekend (Thur); Health and Environment (Tues); Best Food Day (Wed).
Syndicated Publications: USA WEEKEND Magazine (S).
Delivery Methods: Mail`Newsstand`Carrier`Racks
Areas Served - City/County or Portion Thereof, or Zip codes: 01701
Own Printing Facility?: Y
Commercial printers?: Y
Avg Free Circ: 800

Sat. Circulation Paid: 5612
Sat. Circulation Free: 790
Sun. Circulation Paid: 8323
Sun. Circulation Free: 782
Audit By: AAM
Audit Date: 31.03.2019
Personnel: Anne Brennan (Reg. Dir. of News & Opt.); Phil Maddocks (Op. Ed.); Caitlyn Kelleher (Director of Multimedia); Nancy Olesin (Arts Ed.); Bob Tremblay (Bus. Ed.); Mike Bentle (Multimedia Sales Mgr.)
Parent company (for newspapers): Gannett; CherryRoad Media

THE GARDNER NEWS

Street address 1: 309 Central St
Street address city: Gardner
Street address state: MA
Zip/Postal code: 01440-3839
County: Worcester
Country: USA
Mailing address: PO BOX 340
Mailing city: GARDNER
Mailing state: MA
Mailing zip: 01440-0340
General Phone: (978) 632-8000
Advertising Phone: (978) 632-8000 ext. 33
Editorial Phone: (978) 632-8000 ext. 20
General/National Adv. E-mail: ablake@thegardnernews.com
Display Adv. E-mail: cholden@thegardnernews.com
Classified Adv. e-mail: lineclassified@thegardnernews.com
Editorial e-mail: editorial@thegardnernews.com
Primary Website: www.thegardnernews.com
Year Established: 1869
News Services: AP.
Special Weekly Sections: Lifestyle (Mon); Serial Stories (Mon); Business (Tues); Voice (Tues); Food (Wed); Interactive Kids Page (Sat).
Delivery Methods: Mail`Newsstand`Carrier`Racks
Areas Served - City/County or Portion Thereof, or Zip codes: 01440, 01430, 01452, 01468, 01473, 01475
Own Printing Facility?: Y
Commercial printers?: N
Avg Free Circ: 158
Sat. Circulation Paid: 4099
Sat. Circulation Free: 158
Audit By: AAM
Audit Date: 30.06.2016
Personnel: Gary Hutner (Gen. Mgr.); Debra Bilodeau (Advertising); Crystal Kingsbury (Circ. Mgr.); John Ballou (Sports Ed.); Matt Garay (Managing Ed.); Matthew Roy (Ed./Web Ed.); John Vincent (Evening Ed.)
Parent company (for newspapers): Gannett; CherryRoad Media

GLOUCESTER DAILY TIMES

Street address 1: 36 Whittemore St
Street address city: Gloucester
Street address state: MA
Zip/Postal code: 01930-2553
County: Essex
Country: USA
Mailing address: 36 WHITTEMORE ST
Mailing city: GLOUCESTER
Mailing state: MA
Mailing zip: 01930-2553
General Phone: (978) 283-7000
Advertising Phone: (978) 283-7000 ext. 3446
Editorial Phone: (978) 283-7000 ext. 3438
General/National Adv. E-mail: mzappala@gloucestertimes.com
Display Adv. E-mail: mzappala@gloucestertimes.com
Classified Adv. e-mail: mbcallahan@gloucestertimes.com
Editorial e-mail: rlamont@gloucestertimes.com
Primary Website: www.gloucestertimes.com
Mthly Avg Views: 1055319
Mthly Avg Unique Visitors: 146207
Year Established: 1888
News Services: AP, ONS.
Special Editions: Spring Home Improvement (Apr); Washington's Birthday Auto (Feb); Business Update (Jan); Guide to the North Shore (Jun); Spring Bride (Mar); Spring Real Estate Review (May); Fall Home & Garden (Oct); Fall Fashions (Sept).
Special Weekly Sections: Food (Wed).
Syndicated Publications: USA WEEKEND Magazine (Fri); Relish (Monthly).
Delivery Methods: Mail`Newsstand`Carrier`Racks
Areas Served - City/County or Portion Thereof, or Zip codes: 01929, 01930, 01944, 01966
Own Printing Facility?: Y
Commercial printers?: N
Avg Free Circ: 463
Sat. Circulation Paid: 4506
Sat. Circulation Free: 463
Audit By: AAM
Audit Date: 31.03.2019
Personnel: Karen Andreas (Pub.); Ray Lamont (City Issues Reporter); Andrea Holbrook (Managing Ed.); Nick Curcuru (Sports Ed.); Christina Parisi (Community News Ed.); Mark Zappala (VP, Adv.); Marybeth Callahan (Adv. Mgr.); David Olson (Ed.)
Parent company (for newspapers): CNHI, LLC; CNHI, LLC

ATHOL DAILY NEWS

Street address 1: 14 Hope Street
Street address 2: Suite 101
Street address city: Greenfield
Street address state: MA
Zip/Postal code: 01301
County: Worcester
Country: United States
Mailing address: PO Box 1367
Mailing city: Greenfield
Mailing state: MA
Mailing zip: 01302
General Phone: (413) 772-0261
Display Adv. E-mail: advertising@atholdailynews.com
Classified Adv. e-mail: classified@atholdailynews.com
Editorial e-mail: newsroom@atholdailynews.com
Primary Website: atholdailynews.com
Year Established: 1934
Delivery Methods: Mail`Newsstand
Areas Served - City/County or Portion Thereof, or Zip codes: 01331 01364 01366 01368
Own Printing Facility?: N
Commercial printers?: N
Audit By: Sworn/Estimate/Non-Audited
Personnel: Shawn Palmer (Publisher); Dan Crowley (Executive Editor); Max Bowen (Editor); Jeff Lajoie (Sports Editor); Mark Galat (Circulation Manager); Stephanie Hadley (Sales Operations Director); Colleen McGrath (Advertising Manager); Edwin O'Connor (Regional Controller)
Parent company (for newspapers): Newspapers of New England

GREENFIELD RECORDER

Street address 1: 14 Hope Sreet
Street address 2: Suite 101
Street address city: Greenfield
Street address state: MA
Zip/Postal code: 01301
County: Franklin
Country: United States
Mailing address: PO Box 1367
Mailing city: Greenfield
Mailing state: MA
Mailing zip: 01302
General Phone: (413) 772-0261
Display Adv. E-mail: advertising@recorder.com
Classified Adv. e-mail: classinfo@recorder.com
Editorial e-mail: news@recorder.com
Primary Website: recorder.com
Mthly Avg Views: 1000000
Mthly Avg Unique Visitors: 250000
Year Established: 1792
Delivery Methods: Mail`Newsstand`Carrier
Areas Served - City/County or Portion Thereof, or Zip codes: 01349 01344 01354 01301 01330 01337 01338 01339 01340 01342 01351 01379 01360 01370 01373 01376 01331 01341 01355 01364 01375 01378
Own Printing Facility?: N
Commercial printers?: N
Audit By: Sworn/Estimate/Non-Audited
Personnel: Dan Crowley (Executive Editor); Shelby Brock (Managing Editor); Jeff Lajoie (Sports Editor); Paul Franz (Photo Editor); Mark Galat (Circulation Manager); Stephanie Hadley (Sales Operations Director); Colleen McGrath (Advertising Manager); Shawn Palmer (Publisher); Edwin O'Connor (Regional Controller)
Parent company (for newspapers): Newspapers of New England

THE RECORDER

Street address 1: 115 Conz Street
Street address city: Greenfield
Street address state: MA
Zip/Postal code: 1342
County: Franklin
Country: USA
Mailing address: PO BOX 1367
Mailing city: GREENFIELD
Mailing state: MA
Mailing zip: 01302-1367
General Phone: (413) 772-0261
Advertising Phone: (413) 772-0261
Editorial Phone: (413) 772-0261
General/National Adv. E-mail: sales@recorder.com
Display Adv. E-mail: sales@recorder.com
Classified Adv. e-mail: clasinfo@recorder.com
Editorial e-mail: news@recorder.com
Primary Website: www.recorder.com
Mthly Avg Views: 650000
Mthly Avg Unique Visitors: 190000
Year Established: 1792
News Services: AP, LAT-WP.
Special Editions: Business (Apr); Back-to-School (Aug); Holiday Recipes (Dec); Finance (Feb); Bridal (Jan); Summer Tourism (Jun); First Snow (Nov); Winter Tourism (Oct); Fall Tourism (Sept).
Special Weekly Sections: Rental Property Page (Fri); Child Services (Mon); Home & Garden (Sat); Arts/Entertainment (Thur); Classes, Courses & Workshops (Tues).
Syndicated Publications: Relish (Monthly); USA WEEKEND Magazine (Sat); American Profile (Weekly).
Delivery Methods: Newsstand`Carrier
Areas Served - City/County or Portion Thereof, or Zip codes: 01301, 01302
Own Printing Facility?: Y
Commercial printers?: Y
Avg Free Circ: 347
Sat. Circulation Paid: 9027
Sat. Circulation Free: 347
Audit By: AAM
Audit Date: 30.06.2018
Personnel: Michael Rifanburg (Pub.); Sharon Cross (Adv. Mgr.); Suzanne Hunter (Classified Adv. Coord.); Kevin Lamagdelaine (Circ. Dir.); George Forcier (Ed. in chief)
Parent company (for newspapers): Newspapers of New England

CAPE COD TIMES

Street address 1: 319 Main St
Street address city: Hyannis
Street address state: MA
Zip/Postal code: 02601-4037
County: Barnstable
Country: USA
Mailing address: 319 MAIN ST
Mailing city: HYANNIS
Mailing state: MA
Mailing zip: 02601-4038
General Phone: (508) 775-1200
Advertising Phone: (508) 775-6201
Editorial Phone: (508) 862-1166
General/National Adv. E-mail: advertising@capecodonline.com
Display Adv. E-mail: advertising@capecodonline.com
Classified Adv. e-mail: classified@capecodonline.com
Editorial e-mail: news@capecodonline.com
Primary Website: www.capecodtimes.com
Mthly Avg Views: 4500000
Mthly Avg Unique Visitors: 1000000
Year Established: 1936
News Services: AP, DJ, ONS, NYT, LAT-WP.
Special Editions: Classroom Times, Spring Times, Beyond 50, Rising Stars, Summer Destination, Cape House, Holiday Guide
Special Weekly Sections: Outdoors (Fri); Golf (Mon); At Home (S); Arts & Entertainment (Sat); Health & Fitness (Thur); Health & Science (Tues); Food (Wed).
Syndicated Publications: CapeWeek Magazine (Fri); Prime Time (Quarterly); Parade (S).
Delivery Methods: Mail`Newsstand`Carrier`Racks
Areas Served - City/County or Portion Thereof, or Zip codes: 02360, 02532, 02534, 02536, 02537, 02538, 02540, 02540, 02543, 02553, 02556, 02558, 02559, 02561, 02562, 02563, 02565, 02571, 02574, 02576, 02601, 02630, 02631, 02632, 02633, 02635, 02637, 02638, 02639, 02641, 02642, 02643, 02644, 02645, 02646, 02647, 02648, 02649, 02650, 02651, 02652, 02653, 02655, 02657, 02659, 02660, 02661, 02662, 02663, 02664, 02666, 02667, 02668, 02669, 02670, 02671, 02672, 02673, 02675
Own Printing Facility?: N
Commercial printers?: Y
Avg Free Circ: 527
Sat. Circulation Paid: 15376
Sat. Circulation Free: 527
Sun. Circulation Paid: 8086
Sun. Circulation Free: 454
Audit By: AAM
Audit Date: 31.03.2019
Personnel: Peter D. Meyer (President & Publisher); Paul Pronovost (Ed.); David Hundt (Controller); Stacia Plumb (Mgr., HR); Molly Evans (Adv. Dir.); Chad Campbell (Circ. Dir.); Angela Bucar (Digital Sales Mgr.)
Parent company (for newspapers): CherryRoad Media; Gannett

THE SUN

Street address 1: 491 Dutton St Ste 2
Street address 2: Suite 2
Street address city: Lowell
Street address state: MA
Zip/Postal code: 01854-4292
County: Middlesex
Country: USA
Mailing address: 491 DUTTON ST STE 1
Mailing city: LOWELL
Mailing state: MA
Mailing zip: 01854-4292
General Phone: (978) 458-7100
Advertising Phone: (978) 458-7100
Editorial Phone: (978) 970-4621
General/National Adv. E-mail: advertising@lowellsun.com
Display Adv. E-mail: enajeeullah@mediaonene.com
Classified Adv. e-mail: rrudeen@mediaonene.com
Editorial e-mail: jcampanini@lowellsun.com
Primary Website: www.lowellsun.com
Mthly Avg Views: 4220212
Mthly Avg Unique Visitors: 629630
Year Established: 1878
News Services: AP, SHNS, NEA, MCT.
Special Editions: Bridal (Feb); Local Heroes (Jan); Home & Garden/Home Improvement (Apr); Summer Auto (Aug); Christmas Gift Guide (Dec); Folk Festival (Jul); Summer Living (Jun); Spring Auto (Mar); Women in Business (May); Holiday Happenings (Nov); Fall Auto (Oct).
Special Weekly Sections: Color Comics (S); Restaurant Guide (Sat); Stepping Out (Thur); Food (Wed).
Syndicated Publications: USA WEEKEND Magazine (S).
Delivery Methods: Mail`Newsstand`Carrier`Racks
Own Printing Facility?: Y
Commercial printers?: Y
Sat. Circulation Paid: 18735
Sun. Circulation Paid: 30839
Audit By: AAM
Audit Date: 30.06.2017
Personnel: Kevin Corrado (Pub.); Mike Sheehan (VP Circulation); Gary Wright (Circ. Op. Mgr.); Beverly Corum (Customer Service Mgr.); Tom Zuppa (Sr. Ed.); Kris Pisarik (Mng. Ed. Nights); Christopher Scott (Enterprise Ed.); Dennis Whitton (Sports Ed.); Eddie Najeeullah (Regional Dir. of Adv.)
Parent company (for newspapers): Digital First Media; MediaNews Group

THE DAILY ITEM

Street address 1: 85 Exchange St
Street address city: Lynn
Street address state: MA
Zip/Postal code: 01901
County: Essex
Country: USA
Mailing state: MA
General Phone: (781) 593-7700
Advertising Phone: 781-214-1897
Editorial Phone: (781) 593-7700 ext. 1349
General/National Adv. E-mail: ecarpenter@itemlive.com
Display Adv. E-mail: ecarpenter@itemlive.com
Classified Adv. e-mail: classified@itemlive.com
Editorial e-mail: tgrant@itemlive.com
Primary Website: www.itemlive.com
Mthly Avg Views: 1950000
Mthly Avg Unique Visitors: 420000
Year Established: 1877
News Services: AP, SHNS.
Special Editions: Spring Home Improvement (Apr); Back-to-School (Aug); Holiday Songbook (Dec); Washington's Birthday Auto (Feb); Brides Tab (Jan); House-To-Home; Senior Living (Jun); Progress (Mar); Spring Car Care (May); New Car Preview (Nov); Business & Professional Womem (

Special Weekly Sections: Health (Mon); Religion (Sat); On-The-Town (Fri); Business (Tues); Lynn Neighbors (Wed); Saugus Neighbors (Thurs.).
Delivery Methods: Mail`Newsstand`Carrier`Racks
Areas Served - City/County or Portion Thereof, or Zip codes: 01901, 01902, 01904, 01905, 01906, 01945, 01960, 01970, 01907, 01940, 01923, 01880, 01915
Own Printing Facility?: Y
Commercial printers?: N
Sat. Circulation Paid: 6469
Audit By: CAC
Audit Date: 04.06.2025
Personnel: Mike Shanahan (CEO); Gary Grossman (Pub.); Ted Grant (Editor in Chief); Len Machesic (Controller, HR); Ernie Carpenter (Director of Advertising & Business Development); Fred Scheller (Circ. Dir.); Patty Bennett (Adv. Dir.); David R. Hilliard (Managing Ed.); Joanne Arbogast (Features Ed.); Todd Stanford (Sports Ed.); Lori Seebold (Adv. Services Mgr.); Carla Treon (Classifieds)
Parent company (for newspapers): Hastings & Sons Publishing Co.; Essex Media Group

MILFORD DAILY NEWS

Street address 1: 197 Main St
Street address city: Milford
Street address state: MA
Zip/Postal code: 01757-2635
County: Worcester
Country: USA
Mailing address: 197 MAIN ST
Mailing city: MILFORD
Mailing state: MA
Mailing zip: 01757-3287
General Phone: (508) 634-7522
Advertising Phone: (508) 626-3984
Editorial Phone: (508) 626-3871
General/National Adv. E-mail: salesteam@wickedlocal.com
Display Adv. E-mail: salesteam@wickedlocal.com
Classified Adv. e-mail: crobinson@wickedlocal.com
Editorial e-mail: rlodge@wickedlocal.com
Primary Website: www.milforddailynews.com
Mthly Avg Views: 1100000
Mthly Avg Unique Visitors: 145000
Year Established: 1887
News Services: NYT, AP.
Special Editions: Summer Fun Tab (May); Secretaries' Week Pages (Apr); Pawtucket Red Sox Night (Aug); Christmas Cards (Dec); Spring Bridal Tab (Feb); Tax Column (Jan); Sidewalk Sale Days (Jul); Father's Day Page (Jun); Physical Fitness Page (Mar); Gift Spotter (Nov).
Special Weekly Sections: Bridal Registry (Mon).
Syndicated Publications: Sports Extra (Fri); USA Weekender (Sat).
Delivery Methods: Mail`Carrier
Own Printing Facility?: Y
Commercial printers?: Y
Avg Free Circ: 113
Sat. Circulation Paid: 2070
Sat. Circulation Free: 113
Sun. Circulation Paid: 2277
Sun. Circulation Free: 101
Audit By: AAM
Audit Date: 31.03.2019
Personnel: Anne Brennan (Reg. Dir. of News & Opt.); Caitlyn Kelleher (Director of Multimedia); Phil Maddocks (Op. Ed.); Nancy Olesin (Arts Ed.); Bob Tremblay (Bus. Ed.); John Walker (Chief Photographer); Mike Bentle (Multimedia Sales Mgr.)
Parent company (for newspapers): Gannett; CherryRoad Media

THE STANDARD-TIMES

Street address 1: 25 Elm St
Street address city: New Bedford
Street address state: MA
Zip/Postal code: 02740-6228
County: Bristol
Country: USA
Mailing address: PO BOX 5912
Mailing city: NEW BEDFORD
Mailing state: MA
Mailing zip: 02742-5912
General Phone: (508) 997-7411
Advertising Phone: (508) 997-0011
Editorial Phone: (508) 979-4450
General/National Adv. E-mail: advertising@s-t.com
Display Adv. E-mail: ekedzierski@s-t.com
Classified Adv. e-mail: ksilvia@s-t.com
Editorial e-mail: bperdue@s-t.com
Primary Website: www.southcoasttoday.com
Mthly Avg Views: 2600000
Mthly Avg Unique Visitors: 579000
Year Established: 1850
News Services: AP, NYT, DJ, ONS.
Special Editions: Spring Auto Service (Apr); Health & Medicine (Aug); Last Minute Gift Guide (Dec); Washington's Birthday Auto (Feb); Parenting (Jan); Parenting (Jul); Seniors (Jun); Spring Home & Garden (Mar); Seaside Summer Recreation (May); Holiday Planner (Nov); Fall A
Special Weekly Sections: Sports Monday (Mon); At Home (S); Real Estate Today (Sat); Coastin' Entertainment (Th); Auto Today (W)
Delivery Methods: Newsstand`Carrier
Areas Served - City/County or Portion Thereof, or Zip codes: 02743, 02719, 02745, 02746, 02740, 02744, 02747, 02748, 02790, 02739, 02738, 02770, 02717, 02702, 02558, 02571, 02576, 02538, 02532, 02346, 02347
Own Printing Facility?: N
Commercial printers?: Y
Avg Free Circ: 449
Sat. Circulation Paid: 7735
Sat. Circulation Free: 449
Sun. Circulation Paid: 9065
Sun. Circulation Free: 300
Audit By: AAM
Audit Date: 31.03.2019
Personnel: Chad Campbell (Regional Circ. Dir.); Jennifer Driscoll (News Ed.); Brendan Kurie (Digital Sports Ed.); Laurie Los (Sports Ed.)
Parent company (for newspapers): Gannett; CherryRoad Media

THE DAILY NEWS

Street address 1: 23 Liberty St
Street address city: Newburyport
Street address state: MA
Zip/Postal code: 01950-2750
County: Essex
Country: USA
Mailing address: 23 LIBERTY ST
Mailing city: NEWBURYPORT
Mailing state: MA
Mailing zip: 01950-2750
General Phone: (978) 462-6666
Advertising Phone: (978) 462-6666 ext. 3242
Editorial Phone: (978) 462-6666 ext. 3255
General/National Adv. E-mail: bmacdonald@newburyportnews.com
Display Adv. E-mail: btrefethen@newburyportnews.com
Classified Adv. e-mail: bmacdonald@newburyportnews.com
Editorial e-mail: jmacone@newburyportnews.com
Primary Website: www.newburyportnews.com
Year Established: 1887
News Services: AP, ONS.
Special Editions: Amesbury Guide (May); Yankee Homecoming (Jul); Auto Showcase (Apr); Back-to-School (Aug); Christmas Gift Guide (Dec); Presidents' Day (Feb); Pulse (Jan); Guides to The North Shore (May); Traditions (Nov); Year End Clearance (Oct); Fall Home Improvement (Sept).
Special Weekly Sections: Food (Wed).
Syndicated Publications: USA WEEKEND Magazine (Fri).
Delivery Methods: Mail`Carrier
Areas Served - City/County or Portion Thereof, or Zip codes: Seabrook, Merrimac, Amesbury, Salisbury, West Newbury, Newburyport, Byfield, Newbury, and Rowley.
Avg Free Circ: 506
Sat. Circulation Paid: 5991
Sat. Circulation Free: 506
Audit By: AAM
Audit Date: 31.03.2019
Personnel: Karen Andreas (Pub.); Merrily Buchs (Night Ed.); Dan Guttenplan (Sports Ed.); Ann Reily (Features Ed.); Bryan Eaton (Photo Ed.); Mark Zappala (VP, Adv.); Bill Trefethen (Adv. Mgr.); Richard Lodge (Managing Ed.); christine Greco (Home Delivery Mgr.)
Parent company (for newspapers): CNHI, LLC; CNHI, LLC

THE EAGLE-TRIBUNE

Street address 1: 100 Turnpike St
Street address city: North Andover
Street address state: MA
Zip/Postal code: 01845-5033
County: Essex
Country: USA
Mailing address: 100 TURNPIKE ST
Mailing city: NORTH ANDOVER
Mailing state: MA
Mailing zip: 01845-5096
General Phone: (978) 946-2000
Advertising Phone: (978) 946-2000
Editorial Phone: (978) 946-2000
General/National Adv. E-mail: mzappala@eagletribune.com
Display Adv. E-mail: mzappala@eagletribune.com
Classified Adv. e-mail: mzappala@eagletribune.com
Editorial e-mail: awhite@eagletribune.com
Primary Website: www.eagletribune.com
Mthly Avg Views: 3304000
Mthly Avg Unique Visitors: 1400000
Year Established: 1868
News Services: AP, SHNS.
Special Editions: Auto Weekend (Oct); Where we Live (Jun); Easter Church Pages (Apr); Health & Fitness (Aug); Parent! (Feb); Accent on Finance (Jan); Parent! (Jun); Real Estate Review (Mar); Real Estate Review (Nov); Columbus Day (Oct).
Special Weekly Sections: Entertainment
Syndicated Publications: USA WEEKEND Magazine (S).
Delivery Methods: Mail`Newsstand`Carrier`Racks
Areas Served - City/County or Portion Thereof, or Zip codes: 01810,01825,01830,01832,01833,01834,01835,01840,01841,01843,01844,01845,01850,01860,01864,01876,01887,01913,01921,01949,01950,01952,01985,03036,03038,03053,03076,03079,03087,03811,03819,03826,03827,03841,03842,03848,03858,03865,03873,03874,
Own Printing Facility?: Y
Commercial printers?: Y
Avg Free Circ: 2989
Sat. Circulation Paid: 14173
Sat. Circulation Free: 2989
Sun. Circulation Paid: 16601
Sun. Circulation Free: 1231
Audit By: AAM
Audit Date: 31.03.2019
Personnel: Karen Andreas (Pub.); Jim Falzone (Gen. Mgr.); David Joyner (Exec. Ed.); Tracey Rauh (Mng. Ed.); Ken Johnson (Metro Ed.); Rosemary Ford (New Hampshire Ed.); Bill Cantwell (Morning Ed.); Bill Burt (Sports Ed.); Alexandra Nicolas (Digital Ed.); Mark Zappala (VP of Adv.); Sean McKenna (Retail Adv. Dir.); Steve Milone (Circ. Dir.)
Parent company (for newspapers): CNHI, LLC; CNHI, LLC

DAILY HAMPSHIRE GAZETTE

Street address 1: 23 Service Center Road
Street address city: Northampton
Street address state: MA
Zip/Postal code: 01060
County: Hampshire
Country: USA
Mailing address: PO BOX 299
Mailing city: NORTHAMPTON
Mailing state: MA
Mailing zip: 01061-0299
General Phone: (413) 584-5000
Display Adv. E-mail: sales@gazettenet.com
Classified Adv. e-mail: classifieds@gazettenet.com
Editorial e-mail: newsroom@gazettenet.com
Primary Website: www.gazettenet.com
Mthly Avg Views: 1500000
Mthly Avg Unique Visitors: 450000
Year Established: 1786
News Services: AP, LAT-WP.
Delivery Methods: Mail`Carrier
Areas Served - City/County or Portion Thereof, or Zip codes: 01002 01007 01012 01026 01027 01032 01033 01035 01039 01040 01050 01053 01054 01060 01062 01070 01072 01073 01075 01088 01093 01096 01301 01351 01373 01375 01330 01341 01039
Own Printing Facility?: Y
Commercial printers?: Y
Sat. Circulation Paid: 13071
Sat. Circulation Free: 214
Audit By: Sworn/Estimate/Non-Audited
Personnel: Rita Turcotte (Adv. Prodn. Mgr.); Chad Cain (Managing Editor); Dan Crowley (Executive Editor); Debra Scherban (Mng. Ed., Features); Shawn Palmer (Publisher); Deb Oakley (Religion Ed.); Mark Galat (Circulation Manager); Chris Kostek (Prodn. Mgr., Distr. Ctr.); Stephanie Hadley (Sales Operations Director); John Raymer (Prodn. Mgr., Pressroom); Carol Lollis (Photo Editor); John Stafford (Adv. Sales); Michael Rifanburg (Pub.); Jeff Lajoie (Sports Editor); Jon Stafford (Adv. Dir.); Colleen McGrath (Advertising Sales Manager); Edwin O'Connor (Regional Controller); Sarah Crosby (Photographer); Amanda Drane (Reporter/Sunday Ed.); Mike Moran (Sports Ed.); Jordan Prickett (Commercial Printing Mgr.)
Parent company (for newspapers): Newspapers of New England; H.S Gere & Sons Inc.

THE BERKSHIRE EAGLE

Street address 1: 75 S Church St
Street address 2: Ste L1
Street address city: Pittsfield
Street address state: MA
Zip/Postal code: 01201-6140
County: Berkshire
Country: USA
General Phone: (413) 447-7311
General/National Adv. E-mail: kteutsch@berkshireeagle.com
Display Adv. E-mail: kteutsch@berkshireeagle.com
Classified Adv. e-mail: classifieds@berkshireeagle.com
Editorial e-mail: news@berkshireeagle.com
Primary Website: www.berkshireeagle.com
Year Established: 1891
News Services: AP, New York Times, Washington Post
Delivery Methods: Mail`Newsstand`Carrier`Racks
Areas Served - City/County or Portion Thereof, or Zip codes: 01220, 01247, 01267, 01343, 01367, 05352, 01225, 01237, 01256, 01270, 01011, 01223, 01226, 01235, 01243, 01201, 01254, 01262, 01266, 01029, 01238, 01240, 01242, 01253, 01260, 01264, 01222, 01229, 01230, 01236, 01244, 01245, 01252, 01255, 01257, 01258, 01259, 12017, 12166, 12029, 12060, 12125, 12168
Own Printing Facility?: Y
Commercial printers?: Y
Sat. Circulation Paid: 16827
Sun. Circulation Paid: 19065
Audit By: AAM
Audit Date: 30.06.2018
Personnel: Bill Macfarlane (Systems Director); Andy Swanton (VP, Ops); Catherine Wandrei (HR); Bill Everhart (Editorial Page Ed.); Tony Dobrowolski (Bus. Ed.); Jeffrey Borak (Ent. Ed.); Jennifer Huberdeau (Online Ed.); Erik Sokolowski (Digital News Ed.); Kevin Moran (Rgl. Pub.); Tom Tripicco (Managing Ed.); Warren C. Dews Jr. (VP, Audience Development, Sales, Mktg); Holly Hartman (Circ. Office. Mgr.); Alan English (Publisher); Samantha Wood (Managing Editor for News); Larry Parnass (Investigations Editor)
Parent company (for newspapers): Birdland Acquisition LLC.

THE PATRIOT LEDGER

Street address 1: 2 Adams Place
Street address city: Quincy
Street address state: MA
Zip/Postal code: 02169
County: Norfolk
Country: USA
Mailing address: 2 Adams Place
Mailing city: Quincy
Mailing state: MA
Mailing zip: 02169
General Phone: (617) 786-7026
Editorial Phone: (617) 786-7076
General/National Adv. E-mail: newsroom@patriotledger.com
Display Adv. E-mail: salesteam@wickedlocal.com
Classified Adv. e-mail: classifieds@wickedlocal.com
Editorial e-mail: editpage@patriotledger.com
Primary Website: www.patriotledger.com
Year Established: 1837
News Services: NYT, AP, SHNS, TMS.
Special Editions: Jobs & Education (Apr); Your Community (Aug); Jobs & Education (Dec); Coupon Book (Feb); Superbowl (Jan); Jobs & Education II (Jul); Advice for the Experts (Jun); South Shore Women II (Mar); Career Connection I (May)
Special Weekly Sections: Housing Extra (Real Estate Section) (Fri); Lifestyle (Mon); Home (Sat); Get Out (Thur); Health/Science (Tues); Food (Wed).
Syndicated Publications: USA WEEKEND Magazine (Sat).
Delivery Methods: Mail`Carrier
Areas Served - City/County or Portion Thereof, or Zip codes: 02021, 02025, 02026, 02035, 02043, 02045, 02047, 02050, 02061, 02062, 02066, 02067, 02072, 02081, 02090, 02111, 02122, 02124, 02125, 02127, 02136, 02169, 02170, 02171, 02184, 02186, 02188,

02189, 02190, 02191, 02301, 02302, 02322, 02324, 02330, 02332, 02333, 02338, 02339, 02341, 02343, 02346, 02351, 02359, 02360, 02364, 02367, 02368, 02370, 02379, 02382, 02563, 99999
Own Printing Facility?: N
Commercial printers?: N
Sat. Circulation Paid: 27075
Audit By: AAM
Audit Date: 31.12.2017
Personnel: Lisa Strattan (Vice Pres.); Dana Barbuto (Features Ed.); Ken Johnson (Managing Ed.); Jen Wagner (Copy Desk Chief); Linda Shepherd (City Ed.); Gregory Mathis (Executive Editor); Chris McDaniel (Regional Sports Editor); Mark Torpey (Sports Ed.)
Parent company (for newspapers): Gannett; Gannett Co., Inc.; CherryRoad Media

SOUTHBRIDGE EVENING NEWS

Street address 1: PO Box 90
Street address 2: 25 Elm St
Street address city: Southbridge
Street address state: MA
Zip/Postal code: 01550-0090
County: Worcester
Country: USA
Mailing address: PO BOX 90
Mailing city: SOUTHBRIDGE
Mailing state: MA
Mailing zip: 01550-0090
General Phone: (508) 764-4325
Advertising Phone: (508) 909-4104
Editorial Phone: (508) 764-4325
General/National Adv. E-mail: jashton@stonebridgepress.com
Display Adv. E-mail: jashton@stonebridgepress.com
Classified Adv. e-mail: classifieds@stonebridgepress.com
Editorial e-mail: aminor@stonebridgepress.com
Primary Website: www.stonebridgepress.com
Mthly Avg Unique Visitors: 50000
Year Established: 1923
News Services: AP.
Delivery Methods: Mail`Carrier
Areas Served - City/County or Portion Thereof, or Zip codes: 01550
Own Printing Facility?: Y
Commercial printers?: N
Audit By: Sworn/Estimate/Non-Audited
Audit Date: 12.07.2019
Personnel: Frank Chilinski (President & Publisher); Jean Ashton (Display Adv.); Adam Minor (Ed.); Kerri Peterson (Circc.); Nick Ethier (Sports Ed.)
Parent company (for newspapers): Stonebridge Press, Inc.

THE REPUBLICAN

Street address 1: 1860 Main St
Street address city: Springfield
Street address state: MA
Zip/Postal code: 01103-1000
County: Hampden
Country: USA
Mailing address: PO BOX 1329
Mailing city: SPRINGFIELD
Mailing state: MA
Mailing zip: 01102-1329
General Phone: (413) 788-1000
Advertising Phone: (413) 788-1250
Editorial Phone: (413) 788-1200
General/National Adv. E-mail: mfrench@repub.com
Display Adv. E-mail: fsmith@repub.com
Classified Adv. e-mail: mmooney@repub.com
Editorial e-mail: wphaneuf@repub.com
Primary Website: www.masslive.com/republican
Mthly Avg Views: 13000000
Mthly Avg Unique Visitors: 709000
Year Established: 1824
News Services: AP, NYT, LAT-WP, NNS.
Special Editions: Back-to-School (Aug); Presidents' Day Auto (Feb); Outlook (Jan); Home Show (Mar); Fall Home Improvement (Sept).
Special Weekly Sections: Movies (Fri); Parenting (Mon); TV Time (S); Weekend (Thur); Unlisted for Teens (Tues); Best Food Day (Wed).
Syndicated Publications: Leisure Time (S).
Delivery Methods: Mail`Newsstand`Carrier`Racks
Areas Served - City/County or Portion Thereof, or Zip codes: Western Massachusetts
Own Printing Facility?: Y
Commercial printers?: Y
Sat. Circulation Paid: 31208
Sun. Circulation Paid: 74226
Audit By: AAM
Audit Date: 31.03.2017
Personnel: Mark French (Adv. Dir.); Marysue Mooney (Adv. Mgr., Classified); Ray Kelly (Asst. Managing Ed., Ent.); Cynthia Simison (Managing Ed.); James Kinney (Bus. Ed.); Lu R. Feorino (City Ed., Night); Joe Deburro (Online); Wayne E. Phaneuf (Exec. Ed.); Robert Rizzuto (Asst. Online Ed.); Vernon Hill (Asst. Managing Ed., Sports); Anne Gerard-Flynn (Asst. Managing Ed., Lifestyles); Stephen D. Smith (City Ed, Days); Mark Murray (Chief Photographer); Carolyn Robbins (Editorial Page Ed.); John Mazzulli (Major Accts. Mgr.); Dave Kotfila (Digital Adv. Sales Mgr.); Fran Smith (Adv. Sales Mgr.); Aileen Casey (Sales/Retention Mgr.); Denise Browne (NIE); Judith C. Fraser (Dir., HR); Tom Sewall (Ops. Dir.); Allison Werder (Pres.); Sally Azar (Marketing Mgr.); Natalia Collins (HR Mgr.); Mike Curtin (Sales Mgr., Worcester); Ed. Kubosiak (Ed. in Chief); John Beattie (Dir. of Dig. Ops.); Michael Burnham (Sales Mgr.)
Parent company (for newspapers): Advance Publications, Inc.

TAUNTON DAILY GAZETTE

Street address 1: 5 Cohannet St
Street address city: Taunton
Street address state: MA
Zip/Postal code: 02780-3903
County: Bristol
Country: USA
Mailing address: PO BOX 111
Mailing city: TAUNTON
Mailing state: MA
Mailing zip: 02780-0111
General Phone: (508) 880-9000
Advertising Phone: (508) 967-3120
Editorial Phone: (508) 967-3141
General/National Adv. E-mail: ttalbot@tauntongazette.com
Display Adv. E-mail: ttalbot@tauntongazette.com
Classified Adv. e-mail: classified@tauntongazette.com
Editorial e-mail: lsullivan@heraldnews.com
Primary Website: www.tauntongazette.com
Mthly Avg Views: 1154957
Mthly Avg Unique Visitors: 244866
Year Established: 1848
News Services: AP.
Special Editions: Springs Looking Good (Apr); Back-to-School (Aug); Procrastinator's Guide (Dec); Presidents' Day (Feb); Bridal Guide (Jan); Best of Best (Jul); Cape Road (Jun); Winter Wipe Out (Mar); Design an Ad (May); Coupons (Monthly); Christmas Gift (Nov); Trick or Tr
Special Weekly Sections: Look at Area Business (Fri); Professional Directory (Mon); Real Estate (Sat); Look at Area Business (Tues); Food Page (Wed).
Syndicated Publications: Coupons Tab (Monthly); USA WEEKEND Magazine (S).
Delivery Methods: Mail`Carrier
Areas Served - City/County or Portion Thereof, or Zip codes: Taunton, Raynham, Dighton, Berkley, Rehoboth, Lakeville, Freetown, and Norton
Own Printing Facility?: Y
Commercial printers?: Y
Avg Free Circ: 210
Sat. Circulation Paid: 4105
Sat. Circulation Free: 210
Sun. Circulation Paid: 4470
Sun. Circulation Free: 130
Audit By: AAM
Audit Date: 31.12.2017
Personnel: Lisa Stratton (Pub.); Tom Amato (Circ. Dir.); Lynne Sullivan (Editor-in-Chief); Rory Schuler (Exec. City. Ed.); Jon Root (Content Dir.); Paige Webster (Adv. Dir.)
Parent company (for newspapers): Gannett; CherryRoad Media

WAKEFIELD DAILY ITEM

Street address 1: 26 Albion St
Street address city: Wakefield
Street address state: MA
Zip/Postal code: 01880-2803
County: Middlesex
Country: USA
Mailing address: 26 ALBION ST
Mailing city: WAKEFIELD
Mailing state: MA
Mailing zip: 01880-2803
General Phone: (781) 245-0080
Advertising Phone: (781) 245-0080
Editorial Phone: (781) 245-0080
General/National Adv. E-mail: ads@wakefielditem.com
Display Adv. E-mail: ads@wakefielditem.com
Classified Adv. e-mail: ads@wakefielditem.com
Editorial e-mail: news@wakefielditem.com
Primary Website: www.localheadlinenews.com
Year Established: 1894
News Services: AP.
Special Editions: Mother's Day Page (Apr); Back-to-School (Aug); New Baby (Dec); Valentine's Page (Feb); Bridal Supplement (Jan); 4th of July (Jul); Father's Day Page (Jun); Easter Page (Mar); Graduation Pages (May); Thanksgiving Day (Nov); Columbus Day (Sept).
Delivery Methods: Mail`Newsstand`Carrier`Racks
Areas Served - City/County or Portion Thereof, or Zip codes: 01880
Audit By: Sworn/Estimate/Non-Audited
Audit Date: 12.07.2019
Personnel: Glenn Dolbeare (Pub./Gen. Mgr.); Phil Simonson (Adv. Mgr.); Marcia Perry (Adv. Mgr., Classified); Thomas Tine (Circ. Mgr.); Peter Rossi (Ed.); Robert Burgess (Asst. Ed.); Gail Lowe (School Ed.); Jim Southmayd (Sports Ed.)
Parent company (for newspapers): The Wakefield Item Co.

THE WESTFIELD NEWS

Street address 1: 62 School St
Street address city: Westfield
Street address state: MA
Zip/Postal code: 01085-2835
County: Hampden
Country: USA
Mailing address: 62 SCHOOL ST
Mailing city: WESTFIELD
Mailing state: MA
Mailing zip: 01085-2890
General Phone: (413) 562-4181
Advertising Phone: (413) 562-4181 ext. 101
Editorial Phone: (413) 562-4181 ext. 116
General/National Adv. E-mail: sales@thewestfieldnewsgroup.com
Display Adv. E-mail: martybaillargeon@thewestfieldnewsgroup.com
Classified Adv. e-mail: classifieds@thewestfieldnews.com
Editorial e-mail: danmoriarty@thewestfieldnews.com
Primary Website: www.thewestfieldnews.com
Year Established: 1971
News Services: AP.
Special Weekly Sections: Around Town; Business; Health; Entertainment.
Delivery Methods: Mail`Newsstand`Carrier
Areas Served - City/County or Portion Thereof, or Zip codes: Westfield, Southwick, and the surrounding Hilltowns
Sat. Circulation Paid: 4600
Audit By: Sworn/Estimate/Non-Audited
Audit Date: 12.07.2019
Personnel: Patrick Berry (Pres.); Marie Brazee (Bus. Mgr.); Dan Moriarty (Ed.); Hope Tremblay (Longmeadow Ed.); Chris Putz (Sports Ed.); Melissa Hartman (Circ. Mgr.); Jim McKeever (Content Dir.); Flora Masciadrelli (Classifieds Sales Mgr.); Lorie Perry (Art Room Dir.); Fred Gore (Chief Photographer)
Parent company (for newspapers): The Westfield News Group LLC; Advance Newspapers

DAILY TIMES CHRONICLE

Street address 1: 1 Arrow Dr
Street address 2: Ste 1
Street address city: Woburn
Street address state: MA
Zip/Postal code: 01801-2090
County: Middlesex
Country: USA
Mailing address: 1 ARROW DR STE 1
Mailing city: WOBURN
Mailing state: MA
Mailing zip: 01801-2090
General Phone: (781) 933-3700
Advertising Phone: (781) 933-3700
Editorial Phone: (781) 933-3700
General/National Adv. E-mail: news@dailytimesinc.com
Display Adv. E-mail: advertising@dailytimesinc.com
Classified Adv. e-mail: woburnclass@rcn.com
Editorial e-mail: news@woburnonline.com
Primary Website: www.homenewshere.com
Mthly Avg Views: 100378
Mthly Avg Unique Visitors: 59300
Year Established: 1901
News Services: AP, NEA.
Special Editions: Spring Home Improvement (Apr); Pre-Season Football (Aug); Christmas (Dec); Your Health (Feb); Graduation (Jun); Social Security (Mar); Spring Home Improvement (May); Fall Home Improvement (Nov); Fall Home Improvement (Oct); Bridal (Sept).
Special Weekly Sections: Bridal Directory (Fri); Medical Directory (Mon); Business Guide (Thur); Business Guide (Tues); Medical Directory (Wed).
Syndicated Publications: Middlesex East (Wed).
Delivery Methods: Mail`Carrier
Areas Served - City/County or Portion Thereof, or Zip codes: 01801, 01890, 01803, 01867
Audit By: Sworn/Estimate/Non-Audited
Audit Date: 12.07.2019
Personnel: Peter M. Haggerty (Pres./Pub./Treasurer/Personnel Mgr.); Joel Haggerty (Office Mgr./Purchasing Agent); Christopher Campbell (Controller); Thomas Kirk (Adv. Dir.); Mark Haggerty (Mgr., Promo.); Peter Curran (Circ. Mgr.); Gordon Vincent (City Ed.); Michael Haggerty (Film/Theater Ed.); James Haggerty (Nat'l Ed.); James D. Haggerty (News Ed.); John White (News Ed., Burlington); Chris Connelly (News Ed., Winchester); Melissa Finn (Social Ed.); Steve Algeri (Sports Ed.); Jay M. Haggerty (Prodn. Mgr.); Lance Jonsson (Prodn. Mgr., Pressroom)
Parent company (for newspapers): Woburn Daily Times, Inc.

TELEGRAM & GAZETTE

Street address 1: 100 Front St Ste 500
Street address 2: PO Box 15012
Street address city: Worcester
Street address state: MA
Zip/Postal code: 01608-1440
County: Worcester
Country: USA
General Phone: (508) 793-9100
Advertising Phone: (508) 793-9200
Editorial Phone: (508) 793-9245
General/National Adv. E-mail: advertise@telegram.com
Display Adv. E-mail: advertise@telegram.com
Classified Adv. e-mail: advertise@telegram.com
Editorial e-mail: newstips@telegram.com
Primary Website: www.telegram.com
Mthly Avg Views: 5800000
Mthly Avg Unique Visitors: 1100000
Year Established: 1866
News Services: AP, NYT, Bloomberg.
Special Editions: President's Auto, Summer Book, Worcester Living quarterly magazine, Hometeam, Winter Book, Community Profiles
Special Weekly Sections: Business Matters, Sunday Living, Go! entertainment guide
Syndicated Publications: Parade magazine, Relish magazine, Spry magazine
Delivery Methods: Mail`Newsstand`Carrier`Racks
Areas Served - City/County or Portion Thereof, or Zip codes: Worcester County
Own Printing Facility?: N
Commercial printers?: N
Sat. Circulation Paid: 28441
Sun. Circulation Paid: 34780
Audit By: AAM
Audit Date: 31.12.2018
Personnel: Karen Webber (Exec. Ed.); Tony Simollardes (Editorial Page Editor); Paul Provost (Pub.); Christine Ortoleva (Finance Director); Michele Marquis (Chief Revenue Officer); Gregory Richards (Digital Solutions Director); Joseph Valencourt (Advertising Director)
Parent company (for newspapers): Gannett; CherryRoad Media

MICHIGAN

THE DAILY TELEGRAM

Street address 1: 133 N Winter St
Street address city: Adrian
Street address state: MI
Zip/Postal code: 49221-2042
County: Lenawee
Country: USA
Mailing address: 133 N WINTER ST
Mailing city: ADRIAN
Mailing state: MI
Mailing zip: 49221-2085

General Phone: (517) 265-5111
Advertising Phone: (517) 265-5111 ext. 226
Editorial Phone: (517) 265-5111 ext. 230
General/National Adv. E-mail: dwerner@telegramadvertising.com
Display Adv. E-mail: dwerner@telegramadvertising.com
Classified Adv. e-mail: cgoodlockproctor@lenconnect.com
Editorial e-mail: editor@lenconnect.com
Primary Website: www.lenconnect.com
Mthly Avg Views: 1230000
Mthly Avg Unique Visitors: 7950
Year Established: 1892
News Services: GateHouse Media, Inc.
Special Weekly Sections: Entertainment TV Log (Fri); Outdoor Page (S); Church Page (Sat). Life & Style (Sun)
Syndicated Publications: Parade (S).
Delivery Methods: Mail`Newsstand`Carrier`Racks
Areas Served - City/County or Portion Thereof, or Zip codes: 49220, 49221, 49228, 49229, 49230, 49233, 49235, 49236, 49238, 49247, 49248, 49253, 49256, 49265, 49268, 49276, 49279, 49282, 49286, 49287, 49288, 43533
Own Printing Facility?: Y
Commercial printers?: Y
Avg Free Circ: 1279
Sat. Circulation Paid: 9912
Sat. Circulation Free: 1279
Sun. Circulation Paid: 11092
Sun. Circulation Free: 1278
Audit By: AAM
Audit Date: 31.03.2018
Personnel: Amy Russell (Accounting Mgr.); Jeff Stahl (Circ. Dir.); Brenda Leonard (Adv. Mgr.); Ray Kisonas (Regional Ed.); David Panian (News Ed.); Royce Ohlinger (Prodn. Mgr., Pressroom)
Parent company (for newspapers): Gannett; CherryRoad Media

MORNING SUN

Street address 1: 311 E Superior St Ste A
Street address 2: Suite P
Street address city: Alma
Street address state: MI
Zip/Postal code: 48801-1832
County: Gratiot
Country: USA
Mailing address: 311 E SUPERIOR ST STE A
Mailing city: ALMA
Mailing state: MI
Mailing zip: 48801-1832
General Phone: (989) 779-6000
Advertising Phone: (989) 779-6110
Editorial Phone: (989) 779-6003
General/National Adv. E-mail: cturner@michigannewspapers.com
Display Adv. E-mail: cturner@michigannewspapers.com
Classified Adv. e-mail: classifieds@michigannewspapers.com
Editorial e-mail: rmills@michigannewspapers.com
Primary Website: www.themorningsun.com
Mthly Avg Views: 21000000
Mthly Avg Unique Visitors: 1860000
Year Established: 1977
News Services: AP.
Special Editions: Yard & Garden (Apr); Football Preview (Aug); Basketball Tab (Dec); Progress (Feb); Bridal Tab (Jan); Bridal Tab (Jul); Home Show (Mar); Highland Festival (May); Thanksgiving Day (Nov); Car Care (Oct); Fall Yard and Garden (Sept).
Special Weekly Sections: Dining (Fri); Health Lifestyles (Thur); Golf (Tues).
Syndicated Publications: Parade (S).
Delivery Methods: Carrier`Racks
Areas Served - City/County or Portion Thereof, or Zip codes: 48615, 48617, 48618, 48622, 48625, 48632, 48801, 48832, 48847, 48858, 48877, 48878, 78880, 48883, 48893, 49310, 49340
Own Printing Facility?: Y
Commercial printers?: Y
Avg Free Circ: 3309
Sat. Circulation Paid: 6685
Sat. Circulation Free: 3158
Sun. Circulation Paid: 7736
Sun. Circulation Free: 4090
Audit By: AAM
Audit Date: 30.09.2014
Personnel: Rick Mills (Ed.); Jim Lahde (Sports Ed.); Kullen Logsdon (Community Ed.); Cindy Terwilliger (Recruitment Specialist)

Parent company (for newspapers): Digital First Media

THE ALPENA NEWS

Street address 1: 130 Park Pl
Street address city: Alpena
Street address state: MI
Zip/Postal code: 49707-2828
County: Alpena
Country: USA
Mailing address: PO BOX 367
Mailing city: ALPENA
Mailing state: MI
Mailing zip: 49707-0367
General Phone: (989) 354-3111
General/National Adv. E-mail: cwerda@thealpenanews.com
Display Adv. E-mail: alpenaads@thealpenanews.com
Classified Adv. e-mail: classifieds@thealpenanews.com
Editorial e-mail: newsroom@thealpenanews.com
Primary Website: www.thealpenanews.com
Mthly Avg Views: 375000
Year Established: 1899
News Services: AP, NEA.
Special Editions: Graduation (May); Young At Heart (Jun); Bridal Tab (Feb); Proud to Be an American (Jul); Sunrise Side's Best of the Best (Apr); Back-to-School (Aug); Home Improvement (Mar); Deer Hunting (Oct)
Special Weekly Sections: Entertainment (Thur); Entertainment (Fri); Entertainment (Sat); Real Estate Section (Thur).
Delivery Methods: Mail`Newsstand`Carrier`Racks
Areas Served - City/County or Portion Thereof, or Zip codes: 49743, 49759, 49765, 49776, 49779, 49707, 49744, 49747, 49753, 49766, 49777, 49709, 49746, 48705, 48721, 48740, 48742, 48745, 48750, 48762
Own Printing Facility?: Y
Commercial printers?: Y
Avg Free Circ: 106
Sat. Circulation Paid: 6330
Audit By: AAM
Audit Date: 31.03.2019
Personnel: Bill Speer (Pub./Ed.); Christie Werda (Adv. Mgr.); Diane Speer (Lifestyles Ed.); Steve Murch (Managing Ed.); James Andersen (Sports Ed.); Kathryn Burton (Business Office Mgr.); Ken Pokorzynski (Circ. Mgr.)
Parent company (for newspapers): Ogden Newspapers Inc.

HURON DAILY TRIBUNE

Street address 1: 211 N Heisterman St
Street address city: Bad Axe
Street address state: MI
Zip/Postal code: 48413-1239
County: Huron
Country: USA
Mailing state: MI
Mailing zip: 48413
General Phone: 9892696461
Advertising Phone: (989) 269-6461
Editorial Phone: (989) 269-6461
General/National Adv. E-mail: rgolder@hearstnp.com
Display Adv. E-mail: rgolder@hearstnp.com
Classified Adv. e-mail: rgolder@hearstnp.com
Editorial e-mail: khessling@hearstnp.com
Primary Website: www.michiganstthumb.com
Year Established: 1876
News Services: AP.
Special Editions: Golf (Apr); Real Estate Guides (Aug); Holiday Gift Guide (Dec); Real Estate Guides (Feb); Progress (Jan); Real Estate Guides (Jul); Real Estate Guides (Jun); Traveler (May); Holiday Gift Guide (Nov); Home Improvement (Sept).
Delivery Methods: Mail`Carrier
Areas Served - City/County or Portion Thereof, or Zip codes: 48413, 48720, 48723, 48725, 48726, 48427, 48731, 48432, 48434, 48735, 48441, 48445, 48453, 48456, 48754, 48465, 48755, 48467, 48468, 48470, 48759, 48472, 48475, 48767
Own Printing Facility?: Y
Commercial printers?: Y
Sat. Circulation Paid: 4000
Audit By: Sworn/Estimate/Non-Audited
Audit Date: 12.07.2019
Personnel: Kate Hessling (Ed.); Gary Wamsley (Circ. Dir.); Paul Adams (Sports Ed.); Rebecca Watson (General Manager)

Parent company (for newspapers): Hearst Communications, Inc.

BATTLE CREEK ENQUIRER

Street address 1: 77 E. Michigan Avenue, Suite 101
Street address 2: Suite 101
Street address city: Battle Creek
Street address state: MI
Zip/Postal code: 49017-7033
County: Calhoun
Country: USA
Mailing address: 77 MICHIGAN AVE E STE 101
Mailing city: BATTLE CREEK
Mailing state: MI
Mailing zip: 49017-7033
General Phone: (269) 964-7161
Advertising Phone: (269) 966-0570
Editorial Phone: (269) 966-0672
General/National Adv. E-mail: bsours@battlecreekenquirer.com
Display Adv. E-mail: bsours@battlecreekenquirer.com
Classified Adv. e-mail: alyon@battlecreekenquirer.com
Editorial e-mail: mmccullo@battlecreekenquirer.com
Primary Website: www.battlecreekenquirer.com
Mthly Avg Views: 1058062
Mthly Avg Unique Visitors: 203605
Year Established: 1900
News Services: AP, GNS.
Special Editions: Wedding Planner (Jan); Senior Connections (Jan, Mar, May, Jul, Nov) Progress (Feb); Homezone (Mar); Homebuyer Guide (Mar); Golf (April); Outdoors (Apr, Sep); Travel (May); Airshow (June); Big Summer Deals (June); Grad section (June); Resident Resource (Jul); Back to School (Jul); Football (Aug); Kidvertising (Oct); Holiday (Nov); Basketball (Dec).
Special Weekly Sections: WOW (Fri).
Syndicated Publications: USA WEEKEND Magazine (Fri).
Delivery Methods: Mail`Newsstand`Carrier`Racks
Areas Served - City/County or Portion Thereof, or Zip codes: 49017; 49015; 49037; 49014; 49020; 49021; 49046; 49050; 49058; 49060; 49073;49076; 49096; 49033; 49068; 49224; 49245; 49092; 49011; 49028; 49029; 49036; 49040; 49051; 49082; 49089; 49094; 49012; 49034; 49053;
Own Printing Facility?: N
Avg Free Circ: 95
Sat. Circulation Paid: 7794
Sat. Circulation Free: 95
Sun. Circulation Paid: 11536
Sun. Circulation Free: 92
Audit By: AAM
Audit Date: 30.06.2018
Personnel: Merrie Shina (Op. Mgr.); Michael McCullough (Gen. Mgr. and Exec. Ed.); Bob Warner (News Ed.); John Grap (Photo Ed.); Bill Broderick (Sports Ed.); Charles Carlson (ASSISTANT MNG. ED.); Annie Kelley (Features Ed.); Steve Smith (Opinion Page Ed.)
Parent company (for newspapers): Gannett

THE BAY CITY TIMES

Street address 1: 311 5th St
Street address city: Bay City
Street address state: MI
Zip/Postal code: 48708-5802
County: Bay
Country: USA
General Phone: (989) 895-8551
Advertising Phone: (800) 446-5588
General/National Adv. E-mail: msharp@mlive.com
Display Adv. E-mail: cplaxton@mlive.com
Classified Adv. e-mail: mcovingt@mlive.com
Editorial e-mail: rclark2@mlive.com
Primary Website: http://www.mlive.com/bay-city
Mthly Avg Views: 18000000
Mthly Avg Unique Visitors: 1500000
Year Established: 1873
News Services: AP, LAT-WP, NNS.
Special Editions: Catching ZZZ's (Apr); Football Tab (Aug); Last Minute Gifts (Dec); Everyday Money (Feb); Weddings (Jan); Salute to Bay Area Business (Jul); For Your Wedding (Jun); Women's Expo (Mar); Health Care (May); Five Star Favorites (Nov); Fall Care Care (Sept).
Special Weekly Sections: Outdoor Pages (Fri); Food (Mon); Farm Pages (S); Anniversaries (Sat); Weekend Scene Magazine (Thur); Kids Pages (Tues); Homestyle (Wed).
Syndicated Publications: Parade (S).
Delivery Methods: Mail`Newsstand`Carrier`Racks

Areas Served - City/County or Portion Thereof, or Zip codes: 48706 48708 48732 48611 48650 48631 48634 48661 48658 48759 48624 48750 48703 48763 48747 48659 48730 48767 48642 48755 48739 48653 48733 48610 48701
Own Printing Facility?: Y
Commercial printers?: N
Avg Free Circ: 519
Sat. Circulation Paid: 712
Sun. Circulation Paid: 16496
Sun. Circulation Free: 1566
Audit By: AAM
Audit Date: 31.12.2018
Personnel: Dan Gaydou (Pres.); Steve Westphal (Sr. Dir. for National Accounts); Bob White (Dir. of Adv. Operations); Charity Plaxton (Chief Revenue Officer); Michael Assink (VP of Sales); Andy Boldryeff (Dir. of Real Estate & Careers Sales); John Hiner (VP of Content); Bill Emkow (Dir. of Sports News); Kelly Frick (Sr. Dir. for Journalism and Engagement); Colleen Stone (Sr. Dir. for Digital Culture and Innovation); Paul Keep (Exec. Ed. of Print); Khalida Cook (Automotive Dir.); Andrea Sipka (Small Business Dir.); Nick Dionne (Sr. Strategy Dir.); Brett Christie (Sr. Retail Dir.); Christy Keizer (Regional Sales Dir. of Detroit & Ann Arbor); Robert Graham (Regional Sales Dir. of Flint, Saginaw and Bay City); Jamie Dionne (Regional Sales Dir. of Grand Rapids & Muskegon); Laurel Champion (General Mgr.); Jeff Leitch (Agency Relations Dir.); Andrea Miller (Advertising Support Dir.); Marjory Raymer (Dir. of News); Jen Eyer (Dir. of Community Engagement); Angel Offredi (Rgl. Sales Dir.); Colleen Huff (Rgl. Sales Mgr.); Mark Hauptschein (Chief Digital Officer); Matt Sharp (VP, Sales and Marketing)
Parent company (for newspapers): Advance Publications, Inc.

THE PIONEER - BIG RAPIDS

Street address 1: 115 N Michigan Ave
Street address city: Big Rapids
Street address state: MI
Zip/Postal code: 49307-1401
County: Mecosta
Country: USA
Mailing address: 115 N MICHIGAN AVE
Mailing city: BIG RAPIDS
Mailing state: MI
Mailing zip: 49307-1401
General Phone: (231) 796-4831
Advertising Phone: (231) 592-8359
Editorial Phone: (231) 592-8360
General/National Adv. E-mail: advertising@pioneergroup.com
Display Adv. E-mail: advertising@pioneergroup.com
Classified Adv. e-mail: classified@pioneergroup.com
Editorial e-mail: editor@pioneergroup.com
Primary Website: www.bigrapidsnews.com
Mthly Avg Views: 130000
Mthly Avg Unique Visitors: 16000
Year Established: 1862
News Services: AP.
Special Editions: Recreation (Apr); Ferris State University Orientation Welcome (Aug); Songbook (Dec); Car Care Tab (Fall); Bridal Issue (Jan); Sidewalk Sales (Jul); Progress (Jun); Graduation (May); Christmas Gift Guide (Nov); Soil Conservation (Sept); Car Care Tab (Sprin
Special Weekly Sections: Eye on Entertainment (Sat).
Syndicated Publications: USA WEEKEND Magazine (Sat); American Profile (Tues).
Delivery Methods: Mail`Carrier
Areas Served - City/County or Portion Thereof, or Zip codes: Big Rapids, Mecosta, Osceola, and parts of Lake and Newaygo Counties.
Sat. Circulation Paid: 5221
Audit By: Sworn/Estimate/Non-Audited
Audit Date: 12.07.2019
Personnel: Sharon Doxee (CFO); John Norton (Pub.); Patti Wilson (HR Mgr.); Sharon Frederick (Adv. Mgr.); Zeke Jennings (Sports Ed.); Robert Kaminski (Press. Mgr.); Jim Crees (Ed.); Danette Doyle (Adv.); Jonathan Eppley (News Ed.)
Parent company (for newspapers): The Pioneer Group; Hearst Corp.

CADILLAC NEWS

Street address 1: 130 N Mitchell St
Street address city: Cadillac
Street address state: MI
Zip/Postal code: 49601-1856
County: Wexford
Country: USA

Mailing address: PO BOX 640
Mailing city: CADILLAC
Mailing state: MI
Mailing zip: 49601-0640
General Phone: (231) 775-6565
Advertising Phone: (231) 779-4138
Editorial Phone: (231) 779-4126
General/National Adv. E-mail: jbailey@cadillacnews.com
Display Adv. E-mail: jbailey@cadillacnews.com
Classified Adv. e-mail: customerservice@cadillacnews.com
Editorial e-mail: mseward@cadillacnews.com
Primary Website: www.cadillacnews.com
Mthly Avg Views: 500000
Mthly Avg Unique Visitors: 100000
News Services: AP.
Special Editions: Spring Home Improvement (Apr); Brides & Weddings (Aug); Christmas Gift Guide (Dec); Home Show (Feb); Generations (50+) (Jan); Summer Recreation II (Jun); Progress (Mar); Summer Recreation I (May); Hunting Guide (Nov); Generations (50+) (Oct); Fall Home Im
Special Weekly Sections: Church (Fri); Outdoors (Sat); Entertainment (Thur); Seniors (Tues); Family (Wed).
Delivery Methods: Mail`Carrier
Areas Served - City/County or Portion Thereof, or Zip codes: 49601, 49618, 49638, 49657, 49665, 49656, 49688, 49655, 49631, 49677, 49623, 49639, 49679, 79663, 49651, 49667, 49632, 49668, 49620, 49689, 49633, 49644, 49625, 49684, 49686
Own Printing Facility?: Y
Commercial printers?: Y
Sat. Circulation Paid: 7200
Audit By: USPS
Audit Date: 01.12.2021
Personnel: Christopher Huckle (Pub.); Matthew Seward (Ed.); Ken Koch (Prod. Mgr.); Josh Bailey (Circ./ Marketing Dir.)
Parent company (for newspapers): Huckle Family

CHEBOYGAN DAILY TRIBUNE

Street address 1: 308 N Main St
Street address city: Cheboygan
Street address state: MI
Zip/Postal code: 49721-1545
County: Cheboygan
Country: USA
Mailing address: 308 N MAIN ST
Mailing city: CHEBOYGAN
Mailing state: MI
Mailing zip: 49721-1545
General Phone: (231) 627-7144
Advertising Phone: (231) 627-7144
Editorial Phone: (231) 627-7144
General/National Adv. E-mail: nkidder@cheboygantribune.com
Display Adv. E-mail: cheryl.mercer@cheboygantribune.com
Classified Adv. e-mail: deedra@cheboygantribune.com
Editorial e-mail: richard@cheboygantribune.com
Primary Website: www.cheboygannews.com
Year Established: 1876
News Services: AP.
Special Editions: Home Improvement (Apr); Design an Ad (Feb); Home Improvement (Mar).
Special Weekly Sections: Real Estate (Fri); Schools (Mon); Food (Thur); Business (Tues); Weddings (Wed).
Syndicated Publications: American Profile (Weekly).
Delivery Methods: Mail`Carrier`Racks
Areas Served - City/County or Portion Thereof, or Zip codes: 49701, 49705, 49718, 49721, 49749, 49755, 49759, 49761, 49765, 49769, 49791, 49792, 49799
Audit By: Sworn/Estimate/Non-Audited
Audit Date: 12.07.2019
Personnel: Gary Lamberg (Pub.); Nancy Kidder (Adv. Mgr.); Mary Whaley (Circ. Mgr.); Richard Crofton (Pub.); Jerry Pond (Prod. Mgr., Pressroom); Janis Coryell (Business Mgr.); Patty Niester (Composition Mgr.)
Parent company (for newspapers): Gannett; CherryRoad Media

THE DAILY TRIBUNE

Street address 1: 19176 Hall Rd
Street address 2: Ste 200
Street address city: Clinton Township
Street address state: MI
Zip/Postal code: 48038-6914
County: Macomb
Country: USA
General Phone: (586) 469-4510
Advertising Phone: (586) 783-0315
Editorial Phone: (248) 745-4587
General/National Adv. E-mail: dave.swantek@gdnn.com
Display Adv. E-mail: nklomp@21st-centurymedia.com
Classified Adv. e-mail: nklomp@21st-centurymedia.com
Editorial e-mail: Ggilbert@21st-centurymedia.com
Primary Website: www.dailytribune.com
Mthly Avg Unique Visitors: 424924
Year Established: 1902
Special Weekly Sections: Best Food Day (Wed.); Entertainment (Thur); Real Estate (Fri); Real Estate, TV Time, Travel, Automotive (Sun)
Sun. Circulation Paid: 5455
Audit By: AAM
Audit Date: 30.09.2014
Personnel: Teresa Goodrich (Rgl. VP, Sales); Don Wyatt (VP, News); George Pohly (Sports Ed.); Noelle Klomp (Classifieds Dir.); Jeanine Parent (Pub.)
Parent company (for newspapers): 21st Century Media

THE MACOMB DAILY

Street address 1: 19176 Hall Rd Ste 200
Street address 2: 2nd Floor
Street address city: Clinton Township
Street address state: MI
Zip/Postal code: 48038-6914
County: Macomb
Country: USA
Mailing address: 19176 HALL RD STE 200
Mailing city: CLINTON TOWNSHIP
Mailing state: MI
Mailing zip: 48038-6914
General Phone: (586) 469-4510
Advertising Phone: (586) 783-0293
Editorial Phone: (586) 469-4510
General/National Adv. E-mail: onlineads@21stcenturynewspapers.com
Display Adv. E-mail: roger.hages@macombdaily.com
Classified Adv. e-mail: nklomp@21st-centurymedia.com
Editorial e-mail: ken.kish@macombdaily.com
Primary Website: www.macombdaily.com
Mthly Avg Unique Visitors: 513650
Year Established: 1841
News Services: AP
Special Editions: Brides & Grooms (Jan); Social Security (Jan); North American (Jan); Auto Show (Jan); WaterWays/Detroit Boat Show (Feb); Choices in Education (Mar); Macomb on the Move/Quality of Life (Mar); Macomb on the Move/Made in Michigan (Mar); Macomb on the Move/Education (Apr); Spring Golf (Apr); Macomb on the Move/Business & Industry (May); Travels (May); Best of the Best (Jun); Brides & Grooms (Jun); Macomb Preps (Aug); Waterways (Sept); Travels (Sept); Choices in Education (Oct); Holiday Ideas (Nov); Last Minute Gift Guide (Dec); Holiday Wrap (Dec); Holiday Greetings to the Troops (Dec)
Special Weekly Sections: Homes (S); Marquee/ Entertainment (Fri); Health (Tues); Lifelines (S) Homefront (S) Wheels (Thur & S)
Syndicated Publications: Parade (S).
Delivery Methods: Newsstand`Carrier`Racks
Areas Served - City/County or Portion Thereof, or Zip codes: 48065, 48005, 48062, 48095, 48094, 48096, 48050, 48048, 48316, 48317, 48314, 48315, 48313, 48312, 48310, 48089, 48088, 48091, 48092, 48093, 48015, 48026, 48021, 48080, 48081, 48082, 48035, 48036, 48038, 48043, 48045, 48042, 48044, 48051, 48047
Own Printing Facility?: N
Commercial printers?: Y
Sat. Circulation Paid: 18072
Sun. Circulation Paid: 36899
Audit By: AAM
Audit Date: 31.03.2018
Personnel: George Pohly (Sports Ed.); Jim O'Rourke (Pub.); Teresa Goodrich (Rgl. VP, Sales); Noelle Klomp (Classifieds); Don Wyatt (VP, News); Jeff Payne (Managing Ed.)
Parent company (for newspapers): Digital First Media; MediaNews Group

THE DAILY REPORTER

Street address 1: 15 W Pearl St
Street address city: Coldwater
Street address state: MI
Zip/Postal code: 49036-1912
County: Branch
Country: USA
Mailing address: 15 W PEARL ST
Mailing city: COLDWATER
Mailing state: MI
Mailing zip: 49036-1097
General Phone: (517) 278-2318
Advertising Phone: (517) 278-2318 ext. 15
Editorial Phone: (517) 278-2318 ext. 27
General/National Adv. E-mail: dferro@thedailyreporter.com
Display Adv. E-mail: dferro@thedailyreporter.com
Classified Adv. e-mail: dferro@thedailyreporter.com
Editorial e-mail: jbarrand@thedailyreporter.com
Primary Website: www.thedailyreporter.com
Year Established: 1895
News Services: AP, LAT-WP.
Special Weekly Sections: TV Listing (Sat); NASCAR (Thur).
Syndicated Publications: American Profile (Weekly).
Delivery Methods: Mail`Carrier
Areas Served - City/County or Portion Thereof, or Zip codes: 49036, 49028, 49082, 49094, 49092, 49089, 49274, 49011, 49245, 49029
Sat. Circulation Paid: 5316
Audit By: Sworn/Estimate/Non-Audited
Audit Date: 12.07.2019
Personnel: Candice Phelps (Reg. Mng. Ed.); Troy Tennyson (Sports Ed.); Karen Allard (Circ. Mgr.); Lisa Vickers (Gen. Mgr.)
Parent company (for newspapers): Gannett; CherryRoad Media

DETROIT FREE PRESS

Street address 1: 615 W. Lafayette Boulevard
Street address city: Detroit
Street address state: MI
Zip/Postal code: 48226
County: Wayne
Country: USA
Mailing address: 615 W LAFAYETTE BLVD
Mailing city: DETROIT
Mailing state: MI
Mailing zip: 48226-3124
General Phone: (313) 222-6400
Advertising Phone: (313) 222-2700
Editorial Phone: (313) 222-6600
General/National Adv. E-mail: lrudy@dnps.com
Display Adv. E-mail: jtaylor@dnps.com
Classified Adv. e-mail: ilanteigne@dnps.com
Editorial e-mail: letters@freepress.com
Primary Website: www.freep.com
Mthly Avg Views: 1100000
Mthly Avg Unique Visitors: 6022082
Year Established: 1831
News Services: AP, NYT, RN, DJ, GNS.
Special Editions: Tiger Baseball (Apr); Michiganians of the Year (May) ; Auto Show (Jan); Rosa Parks Scholars (Jun); NBA/Pistons (Nov); NHL/Red Wings (Oct); Prep Football (Aug); College football (Aug); NFL (Sept).
Special Weekly Sections: Life, Working, Your Money, Sports (Mon); Life, Arts & Style, Sports (Tues); Life, Business, Sports (Wed); Motor City, Drive, Food (Thur); Homestyle, Sports (Fri); Life, Business, Weekend, Sports (Sat); Main, Business, Entertainment, Life, Auto, Real Estate, Travel, News & Views, Sports, Jobs, Sports (Sun)
Syndicated Publications: USA WEEKEND Magazine (S).
Delivery Methods: Mail`Newsstand`Carrier`Racks
Areas Served - City/County or Portion Thereof, or Zip codes: Service to +650 zip codes in Metro and State
Own Printing Facility?: Y
Commercial printers?: Y
Sun. Circulation Paid: 241864
Audit By: AAM
Audit Date: 31.03.2018
Personnel: Grace Bennett (Admin. Mgr.); Jonathan Wolman (Editor and Publisher); Michael Brown (Asst. Managing Editor); Dale Parry (Deputy Mng. Ed.); Pam Shermeyer (Online Content Dir.); Jeff Taylor (Deputy Mng. Ed.); Julie Topping (Deputy Mng. Ed.); Chris Rizk (City Ed., Night); Joanna Firestone (Business Editor); Richard Epps (Presentation Editor); Nancy Laughlin (Asst. Mng. Ed., Web); Alan Derringer (Auto Editor); Ron Dzwonkowski (Editorial Page Ed.); Randy Essex (Bus. Ed.); Felecia Henderson (Asst. Managing Editor); Alex Cruden (Copy Desk Chief); Walter Middlebrook (Asst. Managing Editor); Nolan Finley (Editorial Page Editor); Alice Pepper (Library Dir); Gary Miles (Deputy Managing Editor); Jim Wilhelm (Metro Ed.); Phil Laciura (Sports Editor); Todd Spangler (Deputy Metro Ed.); Carl Feusse (Copy Ed.); Christopher Kirkpatrick (Dir. of Business and Local Enterprise); Aaron Velthoven (VP. of Marketing); Jewel Gopwani (Asst. Ed., Opinion); Joseph Amormino (TECHNICAL SERVICES DIR.); Dawn Buckner (Facilities Mgr.); Shawn Fox (Director, Retail Sales); David Kiehle (Sales Dir.); Rebecca Steckler (Sr. VP of Sales & Marketing); Joyce Jenereaux (Pub.)
Parent company (for newspapers): Gannett

THE DETROIT NEWS

Street address 1: 615 W. Lafayette Boulevard
Street address 2: Ste 300
Street address city: Detroit
Street address state: MI
Zip/Postal code: 48226
County: Wayne
Country: USA
General Phone: (313) 222-2300
Advertising Phone: (313) 222-2700
Editorial Phone: (313) 222-2292
General/National Adv. E-mail: tdgruber@michigan.com
Display Adv. E-mail: tdgruber@michigan.com
Classified Adv. e-mail: tdgruber@michigan.com
Editorial e-mail: newsroom@detroitnews.com - letters@detroitnews.com
Primary Website: www.detroitnews.com
Mthly Avg Views: 35059437
Mthly Avg Unique Visitors: 3946,591
Year Established: 1873
News Services: Associated Press, Bloomberg, MCT
Special Weekly Sections: Monday - Arts & Style Tuesday- Arts & Style Wednesday-Arts & Style Thursday â€"Think, Go, Eats and Drinks, Drive Friday - On Screen, Homestyle Saturday - Weekend
Delivery Methods: Newsstand`Carrier`Racks
Areas Served - City/County or Portion Thereof, or Zip codes: 48001 48002 48003 48005 48006 48009 48014 48015 48017 48021 48022 48023 48025 48026 48027 48028 48030 48032 48033 48034 48035 48036 48038 48039 48040 48041 48042 48043 48044 48045 48046 48047 48048 48049 48050 48051 48054 48059 48060 48062 48063 48064 48065 48066 48067 48069 48070 48071 48072 48073 48074 48075 48076 48079 48080 48081 48082 48083 48084 48085 48088 48089 48091 48092 48093 48094 48095 48096 48097 48098 48101 48103 48104 48105 48108 48109 48111 48114 48116 48117 48118 48120 48122 48124 48125 48126 48127 48128 48130 48131 48133 48134 48135 48137 48138 48139 48140 48141 48143 48144 48145 48146 48150 48152 48154 48157 48158 48159 48160 48161 48162 48164 48165 48166 48167 48168 48169 48170 48173 48174 48176 48178 48179 48180 48182 48183 48184 48185 48186 48187 48188 48189 48190 48191 48192 48193 48195 48197 48198 48201 48202 48203 48204 48205 48206 48207 48208 48209 48210 48211 48212 48213 48214 48215 48216 48217 48218 48219 48220 48221 48223 48224 48225 48226 48227 48228 48229 48230 48234 48235 48236 48237 48238 48239 48240 48242 48243 48301 48302 48304 48306 48307 48309 48310 48312 48313 48314 48315 48316 48317 48320 48322 48323 48324 48326 48327 48328 48329 48331 48334 48335 48336 48340 48341 48342 48343 48346 48348 48350 48353 48356 48357 48359 48360 48362 48363 48367 48370 48371 48374 48375 48377 48380 48381 48382 48383 48386 48390 48393 48401 48412 48413 48415 48416 48418 48419 48420 48421 48422 48423 48426 48427 48428 48429 48430 48433 48437 48438 48439 48441 48442 48444 48445 48446 48449 48450 48451 48453 48454 48455 48456 48457 48458 48460 48461 48462 48463 48465 48466 48467 48469 48471 48473 48502 48503 48504 48505 48506 48507 48509 48519 48529 48532 48551 48601 48602 48603 48604 48607 48609 48610 48611 48612 48615 48616 48617 48618 48619 48621 48622 48623 48624 48625 48626 48627 48628 48629 48630 48631 48632 48635 48636 48638 48640 48642 48647 48649 48650 48651 48653 48654 48656 48657 48658 48659 48661 48703 48706 48708 48720 48721 48722 48723 48725 48726 48729 48730 48731 48732 48734 48737 48738 48739 48740 48741 48742 48745 48746 48748 48750 48755 48756 48759 48761 48762 48763 48768 48770 48801 48808 48811 48813 48817 48818 48819 48820 48821 48822 48823 48824 48827 48831 48832 48835 48836 48837 48838 48840 48842 48843 48846 48847 48848 48849 48854 48855 48856 48858 48864 48866 48867 48871 48872 48873 48875 48876 48878 48879 48880 48881 48883 48892 48884 48886 48888 48890 48893 48894 48895 48906 48909 48910 48911 48912 48915 48917 48919 48924 48933

49001 49002 49004 49005 49006 49007 49008 49009 49010 49011 49012 49013 49014 49015 49017 49020 49021 49022 49024 49028 49029 49032 49036 49037 49038 49040 49041 49045 49046 49047 49048 49053 49055 49057 49058 49060 49065 49068 49071 49072 49073 49076 49078 49079 49080 49082 49083 49085 49087 49090 49091 49092 49093 49094 49096 49097 49098 49099 49127 49130 49201 49202 49203 49220 49221 49224 49228 49229 49230 49233 49234 49235 49236 49237 49240 49242 49245 49246 49247 49249 49250 49251 49252 49253 49254 49261 49262 49264 49265 49266 49267 49269 49270 49271 49274 49282 49283 49285 49286 49287 49301 49304 49305 49307 49311 49315 49316 49317 49319 49321 49327 49329 49331 49332 49333 49336 49337 49338 49340 49341 49346 49348 49401 49404 49406 49408 49409 49410 49411 49412 49415 49416 49417 49418 49420 49423 49424 49431 49426 49428 49436 49437 49440 49441 49442 49444 49445 49448 49449 49453 49454 49456 49457 49460 49461 49464 49503 49504 49505 49506 49507 49508 49509 49512 49519 49525 49534 49544 49546 49548 49601 49610 49612 49614 49615 49616 49617 49619 49621 49622 49623 49625 49627 49628 49629 49630 49631 49632 49633 49635 49636 49637 49638 49639 49640 49643 49644 49645 49646 49648 49649 49650 49651 49653 49654 49655 49657 49659 49660 49664 49665 49668 49670 49674 49675 49676 49677 49679 49682 49683 49684 49685 49686 49688 49689 49690 49696 49701 49706 49707 49709 49711 49712 49713 49715 49716 49718 49719 49720 49721 49722 49723 49725 49726 49727 49730 49733 49735 49736 49738 49740 49743 49745 49746 49747 49749 49751 49752 49753 49755 49756 49757 49759 49761 49765 49766 49769 49770 49774 49776 49777 49779 49780 49781 49782 49783 49788 49791 49795 49796 49797 49820 49855 49864 49908 49971

Own Printing Facility?: Y
Commercial printers?: Y
Sat. Circulation Paid: 80145
Audit By: AAM
Audit Date: 31.03.2018
Personnel: Gary Miles (Ed. & Pub.); Kelley Root (Mng. Ed.); Nolan Finley (Editorial Pg. Ed.); Leslie Crutchfield (Features Ed.); Pam Shermeyer (Multimedia & Online Ed.); Lauren Abdel-Razzaq (Digital News Ed.)
Parent company (for newspapers): Digital First Media; MediaNews Group

DAILY PRESS

Street address 1: 600 Ludington Street
Street address city: Escanaba
Street address state: MI
Zip/Postal code: 49829
County: Delta
Country: USA
Mailing address: PO BOX 828
Mailing city: ESCANABA
Mailing state: MI
Mailing zip: 49829-0828
General Phone: (906) 786-2021
Advertising Phone: (906) 786-2021
Editorial Phone: (906) 786-2021
General/National Adv. E-mail: cderoeck@dailypress.net
Display Adv. E-mail: tbelongie@dailypress.net
Classified Adv. e-mail: classified@dailypress.net
Editorial e-mail: news@dailypress.net
Primary Website: www.dailypress.net
Mthly Avg Views: 850000
Mthly Avg Unique Visitors: 125000
Year Established: 1909
News Services: AP.
Special Editions: Spring Fashion (Apr); Fall Back-to-School (Aug); Bride & Groom (Jan); Fashion (Sept).
Syndicated Publications: USA WEEKEND Magazine (Sat).
Delivery Methods: Mail`Newsstand`Carrier`Racks
Areas Served - City/County or Portion Thereof, or Zip codes: 49812, 49874, 49886, 49847, 49896, 49845, 49807, 49894, 49837, 49818, 49872, 49880, 49829, 49878, 49835, 49817, 49854, 49840
Own Printing Facility?: Y
Commercial printers?: Y
Avg Free Circ: 302
Sat. Circulation Paid: 5794
Sat. Circulation Free: 481
Audit By: AAM
Audit Date: 31.03.2018
Personnel: Brian Rowell (Political/Gov't Ed.); Jessica Koth (Prodn. Foreman, Pressroom); corky deroeck (Publisher)
Parent company (for newspapers): Ogden Newspapers Inc.

THE FLINT JOURNAL

Street address 1: 540 S Saginaw St Ste 101
Street address 2: Suite 101
Street address city: Flint
Street address state: MI
Zip/Postal code: 48502-1813
County: Genesee
Country: USA
General Phone: (810) 766-6100
Advertising Phone: (800) 446-5588
General/National Adv. E-mail: advertise@mlive.com
Display Adv. E-mail: advertise@mlive.com
Classified Adv. e-mail: advertise@mlive.com
Editorial e-mail: flnews@mlive.com
Primary Website: www.mlive.com/flint
Year Established: 1876
News Services: AP, NYT, LAT-WP, NNS.
Special Editions: Golf (Apr); HS Football Preview (Aug); Wrap (Dec); Black History Month (Feb); Weddings (Jan); Business Profiles (Jun); The Answer Book (Mar); Home & Yard (May); Wrap (Nov); Senior Health Expo (Oct); Life & Legacy (Sept).
Special Weekly Sections: The Entertainer (Fri); Technology-Tempo (Mon); Viewpoint (S); Religion (Sat); Wheels (Thur); Food-Tempo (Tues); Education (Wed).
Syndicated Publications: Color Comics (S); Coupon Books (Wed).
Delivery Methods: Mail`Newsstand`Carrier`Racks
Areas Served - City/County or Portion Thereof, or Zip codes: 48412-48867
Avg Free Circ: 2076
Sat. Circulation Free: 672
Sun. Circulation Paid: 26860
Sun. Circulation Free: 6463
Audit By: AAM
Audit Date: 31.12.2018
Personnel: Dan Gaydou (Pub.); Steve Westphal (Sr. Dir. for National Accounts); Bob White (Dir. of Adv. Operations); Charity Plaxton (Chief Revenue Officer); Michael Assink (VP of Sales); Colleen Huff (Sr. Platform Director); Andy Boldryeff (Dir. of Real Estate & Careers Sales); John Hiner (VP of Content); Bill Emkow (Dir. of Sports News); Kelly Frick (Sr. Dir. for Journalism and Engagement); Colleen Stone (Sr. Dir. for Digital Culture and Innovation); Paul Keep (Exec. Editor of Print); Andrea Sipka (Small Business Dir.); Khalida Cook (Automotive Dir.); Nick Dionne (Sr. Strategy Dir.); Brett Christie (Sr. Retail Dir.); Christy Keizer (Regional Sales Dir. of Detroit & Ann Arbor); Robert Graham (Regional Sales Dir. of Flint, Saginaw and Bay City); Jamie Dionne (Regional Sales Dir. of Grand Rapids & Muskegon); Laurel Champion (Gen. Mgr.); Andrea Miller (Agency Relations Dir.); Marjory Raymer (Dir. of News); Jen Eyer (Dir. of Community Engagement)
Parent company (for newspapers): Advance Publications, Inc.

GRAND HAVEN TRIBUNE

Street address 1: 101 N 3rd St
Street address city: Grand Haven
Street address state: MI
Zip/Postal code: 49417-1209
County: Ottawa
Country: USA
Mailing address: 101 N 3RD ST
Mailing city: GRAND HAVEN
Mailing state: MI
Mailing zip: 49417-1296
General Phone: (616) 842-6400
Advertising Phone: (616) 842-6400 ext. 241
Editorial Phone: (616) 842-6400 ext. 232
General/National Adv. E-mail: ads@grandhaventribune.com
Display Adv. E-mail: rfrancis@grandhaventribune.com
Classified Adv. e-mail: classifieds@grandhaventribune.com
Editorial e-mail: cwelch@grandhaventribune.com
Primary Website: www.grandhaventribune.com
Year Established: 1885
Special Weekly Sections: Living Local (Sat); Church (Sat); Business (Thur)
Syndicated Publications: USA WEEKEND Magazine (Sat); Athlon Sports; American Profile; Spry; Relish
Delivery Methods: Mail`Newsstand`Carrier`Racks
Areas Served - City/County or Portion Thereof, or Zip codes: 49417, 49456, 49460, 49415, 49404, 40448, 49409
Own Printing Facility?: Y
Commercial printers?: Y
Sat. Circulation Paid: 8813
Audit By: AAM
Audit Date: 30.09.2011
Personnel: Kevin Hook (Pub./VP); Rob Francis (Dir. of Rev. Dev.); Matt DeYoung (Content Dir. & Audience Dev't.); Jerry Grimminck (Press Foreman/Supvr.); Don Rogers (Dir. of Op. Support); Jen Hosman (Business Services Supervisor)
Parent company (for newspapers): Paxton Media Group

THE GRAND RAPIDS PRESS

Street address 1: 169 Monroe Ave NW Ste 100
Street address 2: Suite 100
Street address city: Grand Rapids
Street address state: MI
Zip/Postal code: 49503-2632
County: Kent
Country: USA
General Phone: (616) 222-5400
Advertising Phone: (800) 446-5588
General/National Adv. E-mail: advertise@mlive.com
Display Adv. E-mail: advertise@mlive.com
Classified Adv. e-mail: advertise@mlive.com
Editorial e-mail: grnews@mlive.com
Primary Website: www.mlive.com/grand-rapids
Mthly Avg Unique Visitors: 4584000
Year Established: 1892
News Services: AP, NYT, SHNS, NNS, TMS.
Special Editions: Golf (Apr); High School Football (Aug); Home Expo (Feb); International Auto Show (Jan); Lakeshore Living (Jun); Home & Garden (Mar); Parade of Homes (May); Lakeshore Holidays (Nov); Grand Rapids Griffins-IHL Hockey (Oct); On Stage-Entertainment/Arts (Sept
Special Weekly Sections: Home and Garden (S); Outdoors (Sat); Weekend (Thur).
Syndicated Publications: Parade (S).
Delivery Methods: Mail`Newsstand`Carrier`Racks
Areas Served - City/County or Portion Thereof, or Zip codes: 48809 through 49770
Sat. Circulation Paid: 34430
Sun. Circulation Paid: 114941
Audit By: AAM
Audit Date: 31.12.2018
Personnel: Dan Gaydou (Pres.); Jeannie Parent (Chief Revenue Officer); John Hiner (Vice President of Content); Andrea Miller (Vice President of Operations); Jamie Dionne (Sr. Sales Dir.); Kelly Frick (Senior Director of News); Chris Machniak (Chief Analyst)
Parent company (for newspapers): Advance Publications, Inc.

THE DAILY NEWS

Street address 1: 109 N Lafayette St
Street address city: Greenville
Street address state: MI
Zip/Postal code: 48838-1853
County: Montcalm
Country: USA
Mailing address: 109 N Lafayette St
Mailing city: Greenville
Mailing state: MI
Mailing zip: 48838-1853
General Phone: (616) 754-9301
Advertising Phone: (616) 754-9301
Editorial Phone: (616) 754-9301
General/National Adv. E-mail: info@staffordgroup.com
Display Adv. E-mail: info@staffordgroup.com
Classified Adv. e-mail: classifieds@staffordgroup.com
Editorial e-mail: dclark@staffordgroup.com
Primary Website: www.thedailynews.cc
Year Established: 1855
News Services: AP.
Special Weekly Sections: TV Guide (Fri); Business Page (Mon); Home (Sat); Leisure Page (Thur); Food Page (Tues); Agriculture Page (Wed).
Syndicated Publications: USA WEEKEND Magazine (Sat).
Delivery Methods: Mail`Carrier
Sat. Circulation Paid: 8406
Audit By: Sworn/Estimate/Non-Audited
Audit Date: 12.07.2019
Personnel: Darrin Clark (Mng. Ed.); Elisabeth Waldon (News Ed.); Ryan Schlehuber (Sports Ed.); Amber Rood (Dir. of Sales & Mrkt.)
Parent company (for newspapers): View Newspaper Group

HILLSDALE DAILY NEWS

Street address 1: 2764 W Carleton Rd
Street address city: Hillsdale
Street address state: MI
Zip/Postal code: 49242-9191
County: Hillsdale
Country: USA
Mailing address: 2764 W CARLETON RD
Mailing city: HILLSDALE
Mailing state: MI
Mailing zip: 49242-9191
General Phone: (517) 437-7351
Advertising Phone: (517) 437-7351
Editorial Phone: (517) 278-2318 ext. 27
General/National Adv. E-mail: david.ferro@hillsdale.net
Display Adv. E-mail: david.ferro@hillsdale.net
Classified Adv. e-mail: david.ferro@hillsdale.net
Editorial e-mail: editor@thedailyreporter.com
Primary Website: www.hillsdale.net
Year Established: 1846
News Services: AP.
Special Editions: Classified Promotion (Apr); Jonesville Sidewalk Sales (Aug); New Year's Baby Promotion (Dec); Valentine's Promotion (Feb); Progress (Jan); Hillsdale Sidewalk Days (Jul); Silver Salute Tab (Jun); Health & Fitness Tab (Mar); Memoriams (May); Pre-Christmas (
Special Weekly Sections: TV Key (Fri).
Syndicated Publications: Relish (Monthly); USA WEEKEND Magazine (Sat); American Profile (Weekly).
Delivery Methods: Mail`Carrier
Sat. Circulation Paid: 7285
Audit By: Sworn/Estimate/Non-Audited
Audit Date: 12.07.2019
Personnel: David Ferro (Pub./ Gen. Mgr.); RoxAnne Morgret (Circ. Mgr.); Jamie Barrand (Exec. Ed.); Amanda VanAuker (News Ed.); Ed Patino (Sports Ed.); Matthew Thompson (Night Desk Ed.); Andy Barrand (Managing Ed.)
Parent company (for newspapers): Gannett; CherryRoad Media

THE HOLLAND SENTINEL

Street address 1: 54 W 8th St
Street address city: Holland
Street address state: MI
Zip/Postal code: 49423-3104
County: Ottawa
Country: USA
General Phone: (616) 546-4200
Advertising Phone: (616) 546-4227
Editorial Phone: (616) 392-2314
Display Adv. E-mail: james.briggs@hollandsentinel.com
Classified Adv. e-mail: Haley.Kelley@hollandsentinel.com
Editorial e-mail: newsroom@hollandsentinel.com
Primary Website: www.hollandsentinel.com
Mthly Avg Views: 3000000
Mthly Avg Unique Visitors: 350000
Year Established: 1896
News Services: AP, MCT.
Delivery Methods: Mail`Newsstand`Carrier`Racks
Areas Served - City/County or Portion Thereof, or Zip codes: Ottawa and Allegan Counties
Own Printing Facility?: Y
Commercial printers?: Y
Avg Free Circ: 746
Sat. Circulation Paid: 6476
Sat. Circulation Free: 746
Sun. Circulation Paid: 8684
Sun. Circulation Free: 4692
Audit By: AAM
Audit Date: 31.03.2019
Personnel: Jerry Raab (Prodn. Mgr., Pre Press); Steve Kenemer (Circ. Dir.); Sarah Leach (Asst. Mng. Ed.); Brent Morris (Pres. and Pub.)
Parent company (for newspapers): Gannett; CherryRoad Media

THE DAILY MINING GAZETTE

Street address 1: 206 Shelden Ave
Street address city: Houghton
Street address state: MI
Zip/Postal code: 49931-2134
County: Houghton

Country: USA
Mailing address: PO BOX 368
Mailing city: HOUGHTON
Mailing state: MI
Mailing zip: 49931-0368
General Phone: (906) 482-1500
Advertising Phone: (906) 483-2220
Editorial Phone: (906) 482-1500
General/National Adv. E-mail: yrobillard@mininggazette.com
Display Adv. E-mail: yrobillard@mininggazette.com
Classified Adv. e-mail: gazetteadv@mininggazette.com
Editorial e-mail: cpeterson@mininggazette.com
Primary Website: www.mininggazette.com
Mthly Avg Views: 512000
Mthly Avg Unique Visitors: 240000
Year Established: 1859
News Services: AP, Nutting Newspapers Inc.
Syndicated Publications: Happenings/TV Book (Thur).
Delivery Methods: Mail`Newsstand`Carrier`Racks
Areas Served - City/County or Portion Thereof, or Zip codes: 49931; Michigan's Upper Peninsula: Baraga, Houghton, Keweenaw and Ontonagon.
Own Printing Facility?: Y
Commercial printers?: Y
Avg Free Circ: 70
Sat. Circulation Paid: 5619
Sat. Circulation Free: 32
Audit By: AAM
Audit Date: 31.03.2018
Personnel: Randy Cutright (Pub.); Craig Peterson (Mng. Ed.); Josh Vissers (Associate Ed.); Dave Karnosky (Sports Ed.); Yvonne Robillard (Adv. Mgr.); Jennifer Robinson (Circ. Mgr.); Cathy O'Connell Ricci (Accounting Mgr.)
Parent company (for newspapers): Ogden Newspapers Inc.

THE LIVINGSTON COUNTY DAILY PRESS & ARGUS

Street address 1: 323 E Grand River Ave
Street address city: Howell
Street address state: MI
Zip/Postal code: 48843-2322
County: Livingston
Country: USA
Mailing address: 323 E GRAND RIVER AVE
Mailing city: HOWELL
Mailing state: MI
Mailing zip: 48843-2393
General Phone: (517) 548-2000
Advertising Phone: (517) 548-2000
Editorial Phone: (517) 548-2000
General/National Adv. E-mail: lvernon@hometownlife.com
Display Adv. E-mail: lvernon@hometownlife.com
Classified Adv. e-mail: lvernon@hometownlife.com
Editorial e-mail: mmalott@gannett.com
Primary Website: www.livingstondaily.com
Mthly Avg Views: 1400000
Mthly Avg Unique Visitors: 475900
Year Established: 1843
News Services: AP.
Syndicated Publications: USA WEEKEND Magazine (S); American Profile (Weekly).
Delivery Methods: Mail`Carrier
Areas Served - City/County or Portion Thereof, or Zip codes: Livingston
Own Printing Facility?: Y
Commercial printers?: Y
Avg Free Circ: 30
Sat. Circulation Paid: 249
Sun. Circulation Paid: 7133
Audit By: AAM
Audit Date: 31.03.2019
Personnel: Bill Khan (Sports Ed.); Mike Malott (Managing Ed.); Lisa Vernon (Multimedia Sales Mgr.); Susan Rosiek (Pub./Gen. Mgr.); Matt Smith (Copy Desk Chief); Chris Nagy (Niche Products Ed.); Al Ward (Multimedia Ed.); Amanda Whitesell (Web Ed.); Brett Maynard (Digital Specialist)
Parent company (for newspapers): Gannett

IONIA SENTINEL-STANDARD

Street address 1: 114 N Depot St
Street address city: Ionia
Street address state: MI
Zip/Postal code: 48846-1602
County: Ionia
Country: USA
Mailing address: 114 N DEPOT ST
Mailing city: IONIA
Mailing state: MI
Mailing zip: 48846-1688
General Phone: (616) 527-2100
Advertising Phone: (616) 527-2100
Editorial Phone: (616) 527-2100 ext. 104
General/National Adv. E-mail: advertising@sentinel-standard.com
Display Adv. E-mail: advertising@sentinel-standard.com
Classified Adv. e-mail: classads@sentinel-standard.com
Editorial e-mail: sarah.leach@hollandsentinel.com
Primary Website: www.sentinel-standard.com
Year Established: 1866
News Services: AP/More Content Now
Special Editions: Senior Life Ionia Free Fair In the Locker Room Medical Guide
Syndicated Publications: American Profile (Weekly).
Delivery Methods: Mail`Newsstand`Carrier`Racks
Areas Served - City/County or Portion Thereof, or Zip codes: 48809, 48851, 48845, 48846, 48849, 48851, 48860, 48865, 48870, 48873, 48875, 48881, 48897, 49331
Sat. Circulation Paid: 2001
Sat. Circulation Free: 21200
Sun. Circulation Free: 0
Audit By: Sworn/Estimate/Non-Audited
Audit Date: 12.07.2019
Personnel: Orestes Baez (Pres./Pub.); Sarah Leach (Ed.); Kim Mathewson (Business Office Mgr.); Brian Vernellis (Digital Dir.)
Parent company (for newspapers): Gannett; CherryRoad Media

THE DAILY NEWS

Street address 1: 215 E Ludington St
Street address city: Iron Mountain
Street address state: MI
Zip/Postal code: 49801-2917
County: Dickinson
Country: USA
Mailing address: PO BOX 460
Mailing city: IRON MOUNTAIN
Mailing state: MI
Mailing zip: 49801-0460
General Phone: (906) 774-2772
Advertising Phone: (906) 774-2772 ext. 35
Editorial Phone: (906) 774-2772 ext. 40
General/National Adv. E-mail: advertising@ironmountaindailynews.com
Display Adv. E-mail: advertising@ironmountaindailynews.com
Classified Adv. e-mail: classified@ironmountaindailynews.com
Editorial e-mail: news@ironmountaindailynews.com
Primary Website: www.ironmountaindailynews.com
Mthly Avg Views: 732354
Mthly Avg Unique Visitors: 70523
Year Established: 1921
News Services: AP, TMS.
Special Editions: Book Reviews (Jul); Progress 2014 Education (Jun); Logging Today (Apr); Vacation Guide (Aug); Christmas (Dec); Ski Jumping (Feb); Bride (Jan); Rodeo (Jul); Vacation Guide (Jun); Baby (Mar); Graduation (May); Cookbook (Nov); Hunting (Oct); Drug Coloring Book (Other); Logging Today (Sept).
Special Weekly Sections: TV Preview (Fri); Food (Mon); Business (Sat); Health (Thur); Business (Tues).
Syndicated Publications: Weekly entertainment guide
Delivery Methods: Mail`Newsstand`Carrier`Racks
Areas Served - City/County or Portion Thereof, or Zip codes: 49801 49802 49807 49815 49831 49834 49847 49852 49870 49874 49876 49881 49892 49902 49903 49915 49920 49935 54103 54119 54120 54121 54125 54151 54156
Own Printing Facility?: Y
Commercial printers?: Y
Avg Free Circ: 299
Sat. Circulation Paid: 6319
Sat. Circulation Free: 251
Audit By: AAM
Audit Date: 31.03.2018
Personnel: Ray King (Adv. Mgr.); Marguerite Lanthier (Ent. Ed.); Terri Castelaz (Lifestyles Ed.); Jim Anderson (News Ed.); Maggie Lanthier (Online Mgr.); Sally Johnson (Prodn. Mgr., Mailroom); Jeff Schwaller (Prodn. Mgr., Pressroom); Joe Edlebeck (Prod. Supv., Graphics); Theresa Prpudfit (Photo Ed.); Kristen Erickson (Accounting Mgr.); Linda Lobeck (Business Ed.); Theresa Proudfit (Photo Ed.); Jennifer Flynn (Cir. Dir.); Diane Adams (NIE Coord.); Betsy Bloom (Ed.); Corky DeRoeck (Publisher)
Parent company (for newspapers): Ogden Newspapers Inc.

THE DAILY GLOBE

Street address 1: 118 E McLeod Ave
Street address city: Ironwood
Street address state: MI
Zip/Postal code: 49938-2120
County: Gogebic
Country: USA
Mailing address: PO BOX 548
Mailing city: IRONWOOD
Mailing state: MI
Mailing zip: 49938-0548
General Phone: (906) 932-2211
Advertising Phone: (906) 932-2211 ext. 129
Editorial Phone: (906) 932-4211
General/National Adv. E-mail: gpennington@yourdailyglobe.com
Display Adv. E-mail: gpennington@yourdailyglobe.com
Classified Adv. e-mail: classifieds@yourdailyglobe.com
Editorial e-mail: lholcombe@yourdailyglobe.com
Primary Website: www.yourdailyglobe.com
Year Established: 1919
News Services: AP, LAT-WP.
Special Editions: Business Card Directory (Jul); Forget No Soldier (Jun); Home Improvement (Apr & Oct); County Fair (Jul); Christmas Gift Guide (Dec); Progress (Feb); Winter Fun Guide (Jan); Home Builders (Mar); Summer Fun Guide (May); Senior Sentinel (Monthly); Deer Hunting (Nov); Summer Fun (May) Winter Fun Guide (Oct); Resource Guide (Aug).
Special Weekly Sections: Health (Tues), Home & Garden (Fri), Dining Guide (Thurs), Education (Mon)
Syndicated Publications: TV Entertainment (Fri); American Profile (Mon);
Delivery Methods: Mail`Carrier
Areas Served - City/County or Portion Thereof, or Zip codes: Michigan: Ironwood, Bessemer, Wakefield, Ontonagon, Watersmeet, Ewen, Bergland, Marenisco; Wisconsin: Hurley, Mercer, Montreal, Gile, Boulder Jct., Mellen, Manitowish Waters, Land O'Lakes.
Own Printing Facility?: Y
Commercial printers?: Y
Sat. Circulation Paid: 6498
Audit By: Sworn/Estimate/Non-Audited
Audit Date: 12.07.2019
Personnel: Larry Holcombe (Mng. Ed.); Sue Mizell (Pub.); Jenna Martilla (Exec. Asst.); Marissa Casari (Circulation Supervisor); Heidi Ofstad (Adv. Dir.)
Parent company (for newspapers): Stevenson Newspapers

THE JACKSON CITIZEN PATRIOT

Street address 1: 100 E Michigan Ave
Street address 2: Ste 100
Street address city: Jackson
Street address state: MI
Zip/Postal code: 49201-1403
County: Jackson
Country: USA
General Phone: (517) 787-2300
Advertising Phone: (800) 446-5588
General/National Adv. E-mail: advertise@mlive.com
Display Adv. E-mail: advertise@mlive.com
Classified Adv. e-mail: advertise@mlive.com
Editorial e-mail: janews@mlive.com
Primary Website: www.mlive.com/jackson
Year Established: 1865
News Services: AP, MCT
Special Weekly Sections: In Town & Around Entertainment guide, Thursdays; TV magazine, Friday
Syndicated Publications: Parade (S); TV Mag (Fri).
Delivery Methods: Mail`Newsstand`Carrier`Racks
Areas Served - City/County or Portion Thereof, or Zip codes: 49201, 49202, 49203, 49234, 49230
Own Printing Facility?: Y
Commercial printers?: N
Sat. Circulation Paid: 1712
Sun. Circulation Paid: 17669
Audit By: AAM
Audit Date: 31.12.2017
Personnel: Dan Gaydou (Pres.); Charity Plaxton (Chief Revenue Officer); Steve Westphal (Sr. Dir. for National Accounts); Bob White (Dir.of Adv. Operations); Michael Assink (VP of Sales); Colleen Huff (Sr. Platform Dir.); Andy Boldryeff (Dir. of Real Estate & Careers Sales); John Hiner (VP of Content); Bill Emkow (Dir. of Sports News); Kelly Frick (Sr. Dir. for Journalism and Engagement); Colleen Stone (Sr. Dir. for Digital Culture and Innovation); Paul Keep (Exec. Ed. of Print); Khalida Cook (Dir. of Automotive Sales); Andrea Sipka (Small Business Dir.); Nick Dionne (Sr. Strategy Dir.); Brett Christie (Sr. Retail Dir.); Christy Keizer (Regional Sales Dir. of Detroit & Ann Arbor); Robert Graham (Regional Sales Dir. of Flint, Saginaw and Bay City); Jamie Dionne (Regional Sales Dir. of Grand Rapids & Muskegon); Laurel Champion (Gen. Mgr.); Andrea Miller (Adv. Support Dir.); Marjory Raymer (Dir. of News); Jen Eyer (Dir. of Community Engagement)
Parent company (for newspapers): Advance Publications, Inc.

THE KALAMAZOO GAZETTE

Street address 1: 306 S Kalamazoo Mall
Street address city: Kalamazoo
Street address state: MI
Zip/Postal code: 49007-4807
County: Kalamazoo
Country: USA
General Phone: (269) 345-3511
Advertising Phone: (800) 446-5588
General/National Adv. E-mail: advertise@mlive.com
Display Adv. E-mail: advertise@mlive.com
Classified Adv. e-mail: advertise@mlive.com
Primary Website: www.mlive.com/kalamazoo
Year Established: 1834
Delivery Methods: Mail`Newsstand`Carrier`Racks
Areas Served - City/County or Portion Thereof, or Zip codes: 49001 through 49450
Sat. Circulation Paid: 3250
Sun. Circulation Paid: 34708
Audit By: AAM
Audit Date: 31.12.2017
Personnel: Dan Gaydou (Pres.); Charity Plaxton (Chief Revenue Officer); Steve Westphal (Sr. Dir. for National Accounts); Bob White (Dir. of Adv. Operations); Michael Assink (VP of Sales); Colleen Huff (Sr. Platform Dir.); Andy Boldyreff (Dir. of Real Estate & Careers Sales); John Hiner (VP of Content); Bill Emkow (Dir. of Sports News); Kelly Frick (Sr. Dir. of Journalism and Engagement); Colleen Stone (Sr. Dir. for Digital Culture and Innovation); Khalida Cook (Dir. of Automotive Sales); Andrea Sipka (Small Business Dir.); Brett Christie (Sr. Retail Dir.); Christy Keizer (Regional Sales Dir. of Detroit & Ann Arbor); Robert Graham (Regional Sales Dir. of Flint, Saginaw and Bay City); Jamie Dionne (Regional Sales Dir. of Grand Rapids & Muskegon); Laurel Champion (Gen. Mgr.); Jeff Leitch (Agency Relations Dir.); Andrea Miller (Adv. Support Dir.); Marjory Raymer (Dir. of News); Jen Eyer (Dir. of Community Engagement); Paul Keep (Exec. Ed. of Print)
Parent company (for newspapers): Advance Publications, Inc.

LANSING STATE JOURNAL

Street address 1: 120 E. Lenawee Street
Street address 2: Ste 300
Street address city: Lansing
Street address state: MI
Zip/Postal code: 48919
County: Ingham
Country: USA
Mailing address: 300 S. Washington Sq., Suite 300
Mailing city: Lansing
Mailing state: MI
Mailing zip: 48933
General Phone: 517-377-1001
Advertising Phone: 517-377-1001
Editorial Phone: (517) 377-1001
General/National Adv. E-mail: cschnepf@michigan.com
Display Adv. E-mail: sholmes@michigan.com
Classified Adv. e-mail: lkeiser@michigan.com
Editorial e-mail: sangel@lsj.com
Primary Website: www.lsj.com
Year Established: 1855
News Services: AP, GNS.
Special Weekly Sections: Business Monday (Mon); Sunday Real Estate Advertising (S); What's On (Thur); Greater Lansing Real Estate Weekly (Wed).
Syndicated Publications: Parade
Delivery Methods: Mail`Carrier`Racks
Areas Served - City/County or Portion Thereof, or Zip codes: 48801, 48806, 48807, 48808, 48811, 48813, 48817, 48818, 48819, 48820, 48821, 48822, 48823, 48824, 48827, 48831, 48835, 48837, 48838, 48840, 48842, 48845, 48846, 48847, 48848, 48849, 48851,

48854, 48857, 48858, 48860, 48861, 48864, 48866, 48867, 48871, 48872, 48873, 48875, 48876, 48879, 48880, 48883, 48884, 48888, 48892, 48893, 48894, 48895, 48897, 48906, 48908, 48910, 48911, 48912, 48915, 48917, 48933, 49021, 49050, 49058, 49073, 49076, 49096, 49251, 49264, 49284, 49285
Own Printing Facility?: N
Commercial printers?: Y
Sat. Circulation Paid: 26878
Sun. Circulation Paid: 36519
Audit By: AAM
Audit Date: 30.06.2018
Personnel: David Davies (Controller); Kathi Waters (Accts. Mgr.); Melissa Alford (Dir., HR); Kevin McFatridge (Dir., Market Devel.); Ramon Brown (Mktg. Mgr.); Linda Argue (Circ. Dir.); Stephanie Angel (Mng. Ed.); Jason Cody (Asst. City Ed.); David McClendum (Asst. City Ed., Night); Derek Melot (Editorial Page Ed); Mike Hughes (Entertainment Ed.); Robin Swartz (Features Ed.); Cindy Hudson (News Ed.); Suzanne Salay (Online News Ed.); Chris Andrews (Political/Gov't Ed.); Mark Meyer (Sports Ed.); Rick Wagoner (Prodn. Dir.); Elaine Kulhanek (Content Strategist); Rebecca Poynter (President)
Parent company (for newspapers): Gannett

LUDINGTON DAILY NEWS

Street address 1: 202 N Rath Ave
Street address city: Ludington
Street address state: MI
Zip/Postal code: 49431-1663
County: Mason
Country: USA
Mailing address: PO BOX 340
Mailing city: LUDINGTON
Mailing state: MI
Mailing zip: 49431-0340
General Phone: (231) 845-5181
Advertising Phone: (231) 845-5181 ext. 320
Editorial Phone: (231) 845-5182 ext. 326
General/National Adv. E-mail: Ray McGrew <rmcgrew@cmgms.com>
Display Adv. E-mail: Ray McGrew <rmcgrew@cmgms.com>
Classified Adv. e-mail: jsteiger@ludingtondailynews.com
Editorial e-mail: editor@ludingtondailynews.com
Primary Website: www.ludingtondailynews.com
Year Established: 1867
News Services: AP.
Special Editions: Local Sports (Apr); Back-to-School (Aug); Christmas Catalogue (Dec); Bridal (Feb); Graduation (Jun); Progress (Mar); Lake Winds (May); Christmas Opener (Nov); Home Care/Car Care (Oct); Local Sports (Sept).
Special Weekly Sections: TV Week (Fri); Best Food Day (Mon); Youth (Sat); Outdoor (Thur); Bridal (Tues); Business (Wed).
Syndicated Publications: American Profile (Weekly). Relish (weekly)
Delivery Methods: Mail`Newsstand`Carrier
Areas Served - City/County or Portion Thereof, or Zip codes: 49431, 49454, 49405, 49410, 49458, 49411
Own Printing Facility?: Y
Commercial printers?: Y
Sat. Circulation Paid: 6489
Audit By: Sworn/Estimate/Non-Audited
Audit Date: 01.11.2021
Personnel: David Bossick (Editor); Julie Payment (Circ. Mgr.); Ray McGrew (Gen. Mgr.); Patti Klevorn (Managing Ed.)
Parent company (for newspapers): Community Media Group

MANISTEE NEWS ADVOCATE

Street address 1: 75 Maple St
Street address city: Manistee
Street address state: MI
Zip/Postal code: 49660-1554
County: Manistee
Country: USA
Mailing address: PO BOX 317
Mailing city: MANISTEE
Mailing state: MI
Mailing zip: 49660-0317
General Phone: (231) 723-3592
Advertising Phone: (231) 398-3115
Editorial Phone: (231) 398-3106
General/National Adv. E-mail: mnainfo@pioneergroup.com
Display Adv. E-mail: advertisingmna@pioneergroup.com
Classified Adv. e-mail: classmna@pioneergroup.com
Editorial e-mail: editormna@pioneergroup.com
Primary Website: www.manisteenews.com
Year Established: 1898
News Services: AP.
Special Editions: Spring Sports (Apr); Christmas Opening (Dec); Forest Festival (Jun); Bridal (Mar); Hunting (Oct); Fall Sports (Sept).
Special Weekly Sections: Religion (Fri); Business (Mon); Seniors (Sat); Outdoors (Thur); Lifestyles (Tues).
Syndicated Publications: USA WEEKEND Magazine (Sat); American Profile (Weekly).
Delivery Methods: Mail`Carrier
Areas Served - City/County or Portion Thereof, or Zip codes: 49660
Sat. Circulation Paid: 4928
Audit By: Sworn/Estimate/Non-Audited
Audit Date: 12.07.2019
Personnel: Marilyn Barker (Pub.); Aaron Dekuiper (Circ. Mgr.); David Barber (Religion Ed.); Sheryl Rossen (Prodn. Mgr., Pressroom); Dylan Savela (Sports Ed.); Michelle Graves (Managing Ed.)
Parent company (for newspapers): Pioneer Group; Hearst Corp.; The Pioneer Group

THE MINING JOURNAL

Street address 1: 249 W Washington St
Street address city: Marquette
Street address state: MI
Zip/Postal code: 49855-4321
County: Marquette
Country: USA
Mailing address: PO BOX 430
Mailing city: MARQUETTE
Mailing state: MI
Mailing zip: 49855-0430
General Phone: (906) 228-2500
Advertising Phone: (906) 228-2500 ext. 258
Editorial Phone: (906) 228-2500 ext. 244
General/National Adv. E-mail: ldoyle@miningjournal.net
Display Adv. E-mail: ldoyle@miningjournal.net
Classified Adv. e-mail: sjohnson@miningjournal.net
Editorial e-mail: bsargent@miningjournal.net
Primary Website: www.miningjournal.net
Mthly Avg Unique Visitors: 110000
Year Established: 1846
News Services: AP,
Special Editions: Superiorland (Sept); Menu Guide (May); Progress (Mar); Readers' Choice Winners (Jun); Bridal (Feb); Spring Home Improvement (Mar); Lawn & Garden (May); Cookbook (Nov); Fall Car Care (Oct).
Special Weekly Sections: Your Money (Mon); Health (Tues); Learning (Wed); Boomers & Beyond (Thur); Outdoors (Fri); Weekend (Sat); Our Youth (Sun); Scene Magazine (Mon); House To Home (Thur); TV Guide (Sat); Church Page (Sat); Automotive (Sun).
Syndicated Publications: TV Week (Sat); Parade (S).
Delivery Methods: Mail`Newsstand`Carrier`Racks
Areas Served - City/County or Portion Thereof, or Zip codes: 49855, 49908, 49946, 49970, 49919, 49884, 49862, 49806, 49883, 49853, 49868, 49866, 49861, 49871, 49833, 49808, 49891, 49820, 49853
Own Printing Facility?: Y
Commercial printers?: Y
Avg Free Circ: 40
Sat. Circulation Paid: 7464
Sat. Circulation Free: 40
Sun. Circulation Paid: 8452
Sun. Circulation Free: 40
Audit By: AAM
Audit Date: 31.03.2019
Personnel: James A. Reevs (Pub.); Jerry Newhouse (Circ. Mgr.); Bud Sargent (Mng. Ed.); Larry Doyle (Retail Sales Dir.); Sharon Johnson (Classified Mgr.); Emily Xu (Accountant); David Bond (Graphics Mgr.); Steve Brownlee (Sports Editor); Justin Marietta; Glen Fisk (Press room manager)
Parent company (for newspapers): Ogden Newspapers Inc.

MIDLAND DAILY NEWS

Street address 1: 124 S McDonald St
Street address city: Midland
Street address state: MI
Zip/Postal code: 48640-5161
County: Midland
Country: USA
Mailing address: 124 S MCDONALD ST
Mailing city: MIDLAND
Mailing state: MI
Mailing zip: 48640-5161
General Phone: (989) 835-7171
Advertising Phone: (989) 839-4222
Editorial Phone: (989) 839-4254
General/National Adv. E-mail: mmellstead@mdn.net
Display Adv. E-mail: cbott@mdn.net
Classified Adv. e-mail: classified@mdn.net
Editorial e-mail: mdnletters@mdn.net
Primary Website: www.ourmidland.com
Mthly Avg Views: 120000
Mthly Avg Unique Visitors: 857841
Year Established: 1937
News Services: AP, NYT, HN.
Special Editions: Envision (Feb); Envision (Mar).
Special Weekly Sections: Midland Living & Entertainment (Fri); Best Food Day (Mon); Science Page (S); Church Page (Sat); Agriculture (Thur); Arts Page (Wed).
Syndicated Publications: Color Comics (S); USA WEEKEND Magazine (Sat).
Delivery Methods: Mail`Carrier
Areas Served - City/County or Portion Thereof, or Zip codes: 48624, 48652, 48620, 48612, 48618, 48628, 48657, 48883, 48640, 48642, 48611, 48706, 48615, 48637, 48623, 48626, 48617
Own Printing Facility?: Y
Commercial printers?: Y
Avg Free Circ: 744
Sat. Circulation Paid: 8192
Sat. Circulation Free: 537
Sun. Circulation Paid: 8192
Sun. Circulation Free: 537
Audit By: AAM
Audit Date: 30.09.2017
Personnel: Gary Wamsley (Circ. Dir.); Ralph E. Wirtz (Editorial Page Ed.); Lori Qualls (Accent Ed.); Chris Stevens (Sports Ed.); Tim Newman (Gen. Mgr.); Erik Barnard (Adv. Mgr., Online Sales); Ryan Wood (Photo Ed.); Jack Telfer (Ed.); Peter Ricker (Group Adv. Dir.)
Parent company (for newspapers): Hearst Communications, Inc.

THE MONROE NEWS

Street address 1: 20 W. 1st Street
Street address city: Monroe
Street address state: MI
Zip/Postal code: 48161
County: Monroe
Country: USA
Mailing address: PO BOX 1176
Mailing city: MONROE
Mailing state: MI
Mailing zip: 48161-6176
General Phone: (734) 242-1100
Advertising Phone: (734) 240-5025
Editorial Phone: (734) 240-5748
General/National Adv. E-mail: jbragg@monroenews.com
Display Adv. E-mail: jbragg@monroenews.com
Classified Adv. e-mail: kprater@monroenews.com
Editorial e-mail: jnevels-haun@monroenews.com
Primary Website: www.monroenews.com
Year Established: 1825
News Services: AP
Special Editions: Fair Premium Guide (Apr); Fall Sports (Aug); High School Basketball (Dec); Auto Showcase (Jan); Monroe County Fair (Jul); Business Profiles (Jun); Bedford Business Association (Mar); Medical Directory (May).
Special Weekly Sections: Farm (Fri); Best Food Day (Mon); Business (S); Living (Thur); Health (Tues).
Syndicated Publications: Relish (Monthly); Parade (S).
Delivery Methods: Mail`Newsstand`Carrier`Racks
Areas Served - City/County or Portion Thereof, or Zip codes: 48161, 48162, 48117, 48159, 48131, 48160, 49267, 49276, 48144, 48182, 48140, 49270, 48134, 48173, 48164, 48183, 48133, 48157, 48179, 48166, 48145
Own Printing Facility?: Y
Commercial printers?: Y
Avg Free Circ: 694
Sat. Circulation Paid: 11008
Sat. Circulation Free: 694
Sun. Circulation Paid: 13159
Sun. Circulation Free: 23394
Audit By: AAM
Audit Date: 31.12.2018
Personnel: Lonnie Peppler-Moyer (Publisher); Jay Hollon (CFO); Jeanine Bragg (Adv. Dir., Sales); David Zewicky (Circ. Mgr.); Trent Langton (Opns. Dir., Systems); John Rankin (District Mgr.); Kristi Prater (Classifieds); Barbara Krolak (City Ed.); Jill Nevels-Haun (Editor)
Parent company (for newspapers): Gannett; CherryRoad Media

THE MUSKEGON CHRONICLE

Street address 1: 379 W Western Ave Ste 100
Street address 2: Suite 100
Street address city: Muskegon
Street address state: MI
Zip/Postal code: 49440-1265
County: Muskegon
Country: USA
General Phone: (231) 722-3161
Advertising Phone: (800) 446-5588
General/National Adv. E-mail: advertise@mlive.com
Display Adv. E-mail: advertise@Mlive.com
Classified Adv. e-mail: advertise@mlive.com
Editorial e-mail: munews@mlive.com
Primary Website: www.mlive.com/muskegon
Year Established: 1857
News Services: AP, NYT, SHNS, NNS, TMS.
Special Editions: Spring Sports (Apr); Football (Aug); Winter Sports (Dec); Home Show (Feb); Living Here (Jan); Personal Safety (Jul); Senior Lifestyles (Jun); Today's Living (Mar); Pet Care (May); Home for the Holidays (Nov); Full Cruisin' (Oct); Parade of Homes (Sept).
Special Weekly Sections: Church Pages (Fri); Best Food Day (Mon); Stock Market (S); Kids Pages (Sat); Venture Outdoors (Thur); Wheels (Wed).
Syndicated Publications: Parade (S).
Delivery Methods: Mail`Newsstand`Carrier`Racks
Areas Served - City/County or Portion Thereof, or Zip codes: 49441 49442 49445 49444 49461 49456 49457 49417 49437 49415 49412 49451 49421 49455 49425 49420 49446 49448 49440 49452 49431 49436 49327 49449
Sat. Circulation Paid: 2191
Sun. Circulation Paid: 21439
Audit By: AAM
Audit Date: 31.12.2018
Personnel: Dan Gaydou (Pres.); Steve Westphal (Sr. Dir. for National Accounts); Bob White (Dir. of Adv. Operations); Charity Plaxton (Chief Revenue Officer); Michael Assink (VP of Sales); Colleen Huff (Sr. Platform Dir.); Andy Boldryeff (Dir. of Real Estate & Careers Sales); John Hiner (VP of Content); Bill Emkow (Dir. of Sports News); Kelly Frick (Sr. Dir. for Journalism and Engagement); Colleen Stone (Sr. Dir. for Digital Culture and Innovation); Paul Keep (Exec. Ed. of Print); Khalida Cook (Dir. of Automotive Sales); Andrea Sipka (Small Business Dir.); Nick Dionne (Sr. Strategy Dir.); Brett Christie (Sr. Retail Dir.); Christy Keizer (Regional Sales Director of Detroit & Ann Arbor); Robert Graham (Regional Sales Dir. of Flint, Saginaw and Bay City); Jamie Dionne (Regional Sales Dir. of Grand Rapids & Muskegon); Laurel Champion (Gen. Mgr.); Jeff Leitch (Agency Relations Dir.); Andrea Miller (Adv. Support Dir.); Marjory Raymer (Dir. of News); Jen Eyer (Dir. of Community Engagement)
Parent company (for newspapers): Advance Publications, Inc.

DOWAGIAC DAILY NEWS

Street address 1: 217 N 4th St
Street address city: Niles
Street address state: MI
Zip/Postal code: 49120-2301
County: Berrien
Country: USA
Mailing address: 217 N 4TH ST
Mailing city: NILES
Mailing state: MI
Mailing zip: 49120-2301
General Phone: 269-683-2100
Editorial Phone: (269) 687-7706
General/National Adv. E-mail: ambrosia.neldon@leaderpub.com
Display Adv. E-mail: phil.langer@leaderpub.com
Classified Adv. e-mail: donna.knight@leaderpub.com
Editorial e-mail: ambrosia.neldon@leaderpub.com
Primary Website: www.leaderpub.com
Mthly Avg Views: 450000
Mthly Avg Unique Visitors: 48000
Year Established: 1886
News Services:
Delivery Methods: Mail`Newsstand`Racks
Areas Served - City/County or Portion Thereof, or Zip codes: 49120-49121-49047
Own Printing Facility?: Y
Commercial printers?: Y
Audit By: Sworn/Estimate/Non-Audited
Audit Date: 12.07.2019

Personnel: Ted Yoakum (Community Ed.)
Parent company (for newspapers): Boone Newspapers, Inc.

NILES DAILY STAR

Street address 1: 217 N 4th St
Street address city: Niles
Street address state: MI
Zip/Postal code: 49120-2301
County: Berrien
Country: USA
Mailing address: 217 N 4TH ST
Mailing city: NILES
Mailing state: MI
Mailing zip: 49120-2399
General Phone: (269) 683-2100
Advertising Phone: (269) 687-7700
Editorial Phone: (269) 687-7720
General/National Adv. E-mail: mike.caldwell@leaderpub.com
Display Adv. E-mail: mike.caldwell@leaderpub.com
Classified Adv. e-mail: classifieds@leaderpub.com
Editorial e-mail: ambrosia.neldon@leaderpub.com
Primary Website: www.leaderpub.com
Mthly Avg Views: 450000
Mthly Avg Unique Visitors: 48000
Year Established: 1867
Special Editions: College Choices (Jan); Progress (Feb); Summer Fun (May); Home Improvement (Mar & Sep); Best of the Best (Apr); Answer Book (June)
Special Weekly Sections: Off The Water (A&E)
Syndicated Publications:
Delivery Methods: Mail`Newsstand`Racks
Areas Served - City/County or Portion Thereof, or Zip codes: 49120-49121
Own Printing Facility?: Y
Commercial printers?: Y
Audit By: Sworn/Estimate/Non-Audited
Audit Date: 12.07.2019
Personnel: Sarah Culton (Managing Ed.); Scott Novak (Sports Ed.); Ambrosia Neldon (Gen. Mgr.); Rhonda Rauen (Accounting Mgr.); Angie Marciniak (Distribution Mgr.); Donna Knight (Customer Service Rep.); Doug Sriver (Press Foreman)
Parent company (for newspapers): Boone Newspapers, Inc.

THE ARGUS-PRESS

Street address 1: 201 E Exchange St
Street address city: Owosso
Street address state: MI
Zip/Postal code: 48867-3009
County: Shiawassee
Country: USA
Mailing address: 201 E EXCHANGE ST
Mailing city: OWOSSO
Mailing state: MI
Mailing zip: 48867-3094
General Phone: (989) 725-5136
Advertising Phone: (989) 725-5136
Editorial Phone: (989) 725-5136
General/National Adv. E-mail: ccampbell@argus-press.com
Display Adv. E-mail: ccampbell@argus-press.com
Classified Adv. e-mail: classified@argus-press.com
Editorial e-mail: news@argus-press.com
Primary Website: www.argus-press.com
Mthly Avg Views: 399100
Mthly Avg Unique Visitors: 229806
Year Established: 1854
News Services: AP
Special Editions: Baby Faces (Jan.); Agriculture (Mar.); Social Security (Spring / Fall); Car Care (Fall); Football Preview (August); Best of Shiawassee (Annually); Christmas Gift Guide (Nov).
Special Weekly Sections: ViewFinder (TV listings magazine) Sunday
Delivery Methods: Mail`Newsstand`Carrier`Racks
Areas Served - City/County or Portion Thereof, or Zip codes: 48414, 48418, 48817, 48429, 48841, 48848, 48449, 48857, 48460, 48867, 48872, 48882, 48476, 48616, 48649, 48831, 48866, 48879, 48436, 48473, 48807
Own Printing Facility?: Y
Commercial printers?: Y
Avg Free Circ: 21000
Sat. Circulation Paid: 7150
Sun. Circulation Paid: 7150
Sun. Circulation Free: 18776
Audit By: Sworn/Estimate/Non-Audited
Audit Date: 28.09.2022
Personnel: Thomas E. Campbell (Pub.); Catherine Campbell (Adv. Dir.); Kirk Tobey (Circ. Mgr.); Dan Basso (Managing Ed.); Ryan Weiss (Managing Editor); Tim Rath (Weekend Ed.)
Parent company (for newspapers): Campbell Family

PETOSKEY NEWS-REVIEW

Street address 1: 319 State St
Street address city: Petoskey
Street address state: MI
Zip/Postal code: 49770-2746
County: Emmet
Country: USA
Mailing address: 319 STATE ST
Mailing city: PETOSKEY
Mailing state: MI
Mailing zip: 49770-2796
General Phone: (231) 347-2544
Advertising Phone: (231) 439-9329
Editorial Phone: (231) 439-9302
General/National Adv. E-mail: clyons@petoskeynews.com
Display Adv. E-mail: clyons@petoskeynews.com
Classified Adv. e-mail: haugust@petoskeynews.com
Editorial e-mail: petoskeynews@petoskeynews.com
Primary Website: www.petoskeynews.com
Year Established: 1875
News Services: AP, U.S. Suburban Press Inc.
Special Editions: Summer Guide (Apr); Football Preview (Aug); Christmas Time Memories (Dec); Parenting Awareness (Feb); East Jordan Snow Blast (Jan); Petoskey Sidewalk Sales (Jul); Welcome Back Resorters (Jun); Your Home (Mar); Dining Guide (May); Homes (Monthly); Winter Guide
Special Weekly Sections: Real Estate (Fri); Food (Mon); NASCAR (Thur); Health (Tues); Outdoor (Wed).
Syndicated Publications: Parade (Fri).
Delivery Methods: Mail`Carrier
Areas Served - City/County or Portion Thereof, or Zip codes: 49770
Audit By: Sworn/Estimate/Non-Audited
Audit Date: 12.07.2019
Personnel: Christy Lyons (Adv. Dir.); Debbie McGuiness (Goodlife Ed.); Larry Hensley (CFO); Hilary August (Classifieds); Doug Caldwell (Pres./Pub.); Craig Currier (Asst. Ed.); Jeremy Speer (Exec. Sports Ed.); Jeremy McBain (Exec. Ed.)
Parent company (for newspapers): Gannett; Schurz Communications Inc

TIMES HERALD

Street address 1: 911 Military Street
Street address 2: Fl 2
Street address city: Port Huron
Street address state: MI
Zip/Postal code: 48061-5009
County: Saint Clair
Country: USA
Mailing address: 911 MILITARY ST. 2nd Floor
Mailing city: PORT HURON
Mailing state: MI
Mailing zip: 48060
General Phone: (810) 985-7171
Advertising Phone: (810) 985-7171
Editorial Phone: (810) 989-6257
General/National Adv. E-mail: lgougeon@michigan.com
Primary Website: www.thetimesherald.com
Mthly Avg Views: 2844001
Mthly Avg Unique Visitors: 311620
Year Established: 1869
News Services: AP, GNS and Thinkstock
Special Editions: Savvy (Bi-Monthly); Bridal (January); Cars.com (Qtrly); Woman's Day Expo (February); In Bloom (March); Golf (April); Blue Water Summer Guide (May); Menu Guide (May); Graduation (May); Mackinac (July); Football (August); SeasonÂ€Â™s End (September); Election Guide (October); Blue Water Winter Guide (October); Business Expo (November).
Special Weekly Sections: Manufacturers' Coupons (M-S) Spin Magazine (Thur); Outdoors Column (Fri); Religion (Sat); Real Estate/Classified Section (S); Full Color Comics (S); TV listings(S); Wedding Announcements (S); Engagements/Anniversaries (S); The Mix (S); Automotive Listings (S).
Delivery Methods: Mail`Newsstand`Carrier
Areas Served - City/County or Portion Thereof, or Zip codes: St. Clair County
Own Printing Facility?: N
Commercial printers?: N
Avg Free Circ: 95
Sat. Circulation Paid: 11395
Sat. Circulation Free: 58
Sun. Circulation Paid: 15911
Sun. Circulation Free: 53
Audit By: AAM
Audit Date: 30.09.2018
Personnel: Michael Eckert (Ed.); Liz Shepard (Local Content Ed.); Jeremy Ervin (Reporter); Bob Gross (Reporter)
Parent company (for newspapers): Gannett

THE SAGINAW NEWS

Street address 1: 100 S Michigan Ave Ste 3
Street address 2: Suite 3
Street address city: Saginaw
Street address state: MI
Zip/Postal code: 48602-2054
County: Saginaw
Country: USA
General Phone: (989) 752-7171
Advertising Phone: (800) 446-5588
General/National Adv. E-mail: advertise@mlive.com
Display Adv. E-mail: advertise@mlive.com
Classified Adv. e-mail: advertise@mlive.com
Editorial e-mail: sanews@mlive.com
Primary Website: www.mlive.com/saginaw
Year Established: 1859
News Services: Metro Suburbia Inc./Newhouse Newspapers, NNA, AP.
Special Editions: Garden Pages (Apr); Frankenmuth Music Fest (Aug); NASCAR Tab (Feb); Shiver on the River (Jan); Golf Pages (Jul); Garden Pages (Jun); HBA (Mar); Garden Pages (May); Holiday Gift Catalogue (Nov); Fall Parade of Homes (Oct); Frankenmuth Octoberfest (Sept).
Special Weekly Sections: Dining & Entertainment Guide (Fri); Agriculture (Mon); Color Comics (S); Religion (Sat); Venture Outdoors (Thur); Family/Living (Tues); At Home/Living (Wed).
Syndicated Publications: Parade (S).
Delivery Methods: Mail`Newsstand`Carrier`Racks
Areas Served - City/County or Portion Thereof, or Zip codes: 48655 through 48880
Sat. Circulation Paid: 745
Sun. Circulation Paid: 20999
Audit By: AAM
Audit Date: 31.12.2018
Personnel: Dan Gaydou (Pres.); Bob White (Dir. of Adv. Operations); Charity Plaxton (VP of Sales); Michael Assink (VP of Sales); Colleen Huff (Sr. Platform Dir.); John Hiner (VP of Content); Bill Emkow (Dir. of Sports News); Kelly Frick (Sr. Dir. for Journalism and Engagement); Colleen Stone (Sr. Dir. for Digital Culture and Innovation); Paul Keep (Exec. Ed. of Print); Khalida Cook (Automotive Dir.); Nick Dionne (Sr. Strategy Dir.); Brett Christie (Sr. Retail Dir.); Steve Westphal (Senior Dir. for National Accounts); Andy Boldryeff (Dir. of Real Estate & Careers Sales); Christy Keizer (Regional Sales Dir. of Detroit & Ann Arbor); Robert Graham (Regional Sales Dir. of Flint, Saginaw and Bay City); Jamie Dionne (Regional Sales Dir. of Grand Rapids & Muskegon); Laurel Champion (Gen. Mgr.); Andrea Sipka (Adv. Support Dir.); Marjory Raymer (Dir. of News); Jen Eyer (Dir. of Community Engagement)
Parent company (for newspapers): Advance Publications, Inc.

THE HERALD-PALLADIUM

Street address 1: 3450 Hollywood Rd
Street address city: Saint Joseph
Street address state: MI
Zip/Postal code: 49085-9155
County: Berrien
Country: USA
Mailing address: PO BOX 128
Mailing city: SAINT JOSEPH
Mailing state: MI
Mailing zip: 49085-0128
General Phone: (269) 429-2400
Advertising Phone: (269) 429-2400
Editorial Phone: (269) 429-4298
General/National Adv. E-mail: advertising@theh-p.com
Display Adv. E-mail: advertising@theh-p.com
Classified Adv. e-mail: classifieds@theh-p.com
Editorial e-mail: dbrown@theh-p.com
Primary Website: www.theh-p.com
Year Established: 1868
News Services: AP, NEA, SHNS, LAT-WP.
Special Editions: Tour Guide (Apr); Berrien County Youth Fair (Aug); Basketball Preview (Dec); Spring Brides (Feb); Glad-Peach Festival (Jul); Golden Years (Jun); Spring Car Care (Mar); Graduation Tab (May); Living in the Southwest (Monthly); Holiday Recipe/Craft Guide (No
Special Weekly Sections: Weekend Entertainment (Thur).
Syndicated Publications: USA WEEKEND Magazine (Sat).
Delivery Methods: Mail`Newsstand`Carrier`Racks
Areas Served - City/County or Portion Thereof, or Zip codes: Southwest Michigan: Berrien, Cass, Van Buren, and Allegan
Own Printing Facility?: Y
Commercial printers?: Y
Sat. Circulation Paid: 11659
Sun. Circulation Paid: 14391
Audit By: AAM
Audit Date: 31.03.2014
Personnel: David Holgate (Pub.); Robert Estes (Controller); Dave Brown (Managing Ed.); Steve Jewell (News Ed.); Dale Brewer (Editorial Page Ed.); Katie Krawczak (Features Ed.); Jason Mitchell (Sports Ed.); Don Campbell (Photo Ed.); Jim Dalgleish (Asst. Local News Ed.); Julie Simpleman (Circ. Dir.)
Parent company (for newspapers): Paxton Media Group

SAULT STE. MARIE EVENING NEWS

Street address 1: 109 Arlington St
Street address city: Sault Sainte Marie
Street address state: MI
Zip/Postal code: 49783-1901
County: Chippewa
Country: USA
Mailing address: 109 ARLINGTON ST
Mailing city: SAULT SAINTE MARIE
Mailing state: MI
Mailing zip: 49783-1942
General Phone: (906) 632-2235
Advertising Phone: (906) 632-2235
Editorial Phone: (906) 632-2235
General/National Adv. E-mail: kmills@sooeveningnews.com
Display Adv. E-mail: kmills@sooeveningnews.com
Classified Adv. e-mail: cfritz@sooeveningnews.com
Editorial e-mail: brigotti@sooeveningnews.com
Primary Website: www.sooeveningnews.com
Year Established: 1903
News Services: AP.
Special Editions: Fall Sports (Aug); Christmas (Dec); Graduation (Jun); Vacation Guide (May); Christmas (Nov).
Special Weekly Sections: TV Listing (Fri); Health (Mon); People (Tue); Arts/Entertainment (Thur); Education (Fri); Business, Religion (Sun)
Syndicated Publications: American Profile (Weekly).
Delivery Methods: Mail`Newsstand`Carrier
Areas Served - City/County or Portion Thereof, or Zip codes: 49710, 49715, 49717, 49724, 49725, 49726, 49728, 49827, 49780, 49736, 49838, 49748, 49788, 49752, 49757, 49853, 49762, 49868, 49774, 49715, 49785, 49783, 49730, 49790, 49781, 49793
Own Printing Facility?: Y
Commercial printers?: Y
Sat. Circulation Paid: 3772
Audit By: Sworn/Estimate/Non-Audited
Audit Date: 12.07.2019
Personnel: David Zewicky (Pub.); Brenda Rigotti (Ed.); Melissa Mansfield (Circ. Mgr.); Rob Roos (Sports Ed.); Deedra Haselhuhn (Adv. Mgr.); Chelsea Fritz (Classifieds)
Parent company (for newspapers): Gannett; CherryRoad Media

STURGIS JOURNAL

Street address 1: 205 E Chicago Rd
Street address city: Sturgis
Street address state: MI
Zip/Postal code: 49091-1753
County: Saint Joseph
Country: USA
Mailing address: PO BOX 660
Mailing city: STURGIS
Mailing state: MI
Mailing zip: 49091-0660
General Phone: (269) 651-5407
Advertising Phone: (269) 651-5407
Editorial Phone: (269) 651-5407
General/National Adv. E-mail: lvickers@thedailyreporter.com
Display Adv. E-mail: lvickers@thedailyreporter.com

Classified Adv. e-mail: classifieds@sturgisjournal.com
Editorial e-mail: phelps@sturgisjournal.com
Primary Website: www.sturgisjournal.com
Mthly Avg Views: 379000
Mthly Avg Unique Visitors: 58000
Year Established: 1859
News Services: AP.
Special Weekly Sections: Best Food Day (Mon); Church Page (Sat); Dining & Entertainment (Thur).
Syndicated Publications: Shoreline Magazine, TV Times (Saturday); American Profile (Weekly).
Delivery Methods: Mail`Newsstand`Carrier`Racks
Areas Served - City/County or Portion Thereof, or Zip codes: 49091, 49028, 49030, 49032, 49040, 49042, 49066, 49072, 49075, 49093, 49089, 49099, 46746
Own Printing Facility?: N
Commercial printers?: Y
Sat. Circulation Paid: 5500
Audit By: Sworn/Estimate/Non-Audited
Audit Date: 12.07.2019
Personnel: Gwen Donmyer (Bus. Mgr.); Candice Phelps (Ed./Website Mgr.); Dennis Volkert (Feat. Ed.); Corky Emrick (Sports Ed.); Sandy Mielcarek (Prepress Mgr.)
Parent company (for newspapers): CherryRoad Media; Gannett

THREE RIVERS COMMERCIAL-NEWS

Street address 1: 124 N Main St
Street address city: Three Rivers
Street address state: MI
Zip/Postal code: 49093-1522
County: Saint Joseph
Country: USA
Mailing address: PO BOX 130
Mailing city: THREE RIVERS
Mailing state: MI
Mailing zip: 49093-0130
General Phone: (269) 279-7488
Advertising Phone: (269) 279-7488 ext. 20
Editorial Phone: (269) 279-7488 ext. 26
General/National Adv. E-mail: marnie@threeriversnews.com
Display Adv. E-mail: christina@threeriversnews.com
Classified Adv. e-mail: classified@threeriversnews.com
Editorial e-mail: publisher@threeriversnews.com
Primary Website: www.threeriversnews.com
Year Established: 1895
News Services: AP.
Special Editions: 2013 Graduation Keepsake (May); 2013 Bridal Guide (Jan); Spring Car Care (Apr); Football Preview (Aug); Gift Certificate Page (Dec); White Sale (Feb); The Way We Were (Jan); Michigan Medical Society (Jul); The Way We Were (Jun); NCAA Basketball (grid) (Mar); Graduation (May); Gift Guide (Nov).
Special Weekly Sections: Best Food Day, Lifestyles (Mon); Business (Tue); Entertainment (Thur); Seniors (Fri); Real Estate, Church, Farm News (Sat);
Syndicated Publications: American Profile (Weekly).
Delivery Methods: Mail`Carrier`Racks
Areas Served - City/County or Portion Thereof, or Zip codes: 49032, 49040, 49042, 49061, 49066, 49067, 49072, 49075, 49093, 49087, 49091, 49097, 49099
Sat. Circulation Paid: 3043
Sun. Circulation Free: 14700
Audit By: Sworn/Estimate/Non-Audited
Audit Date: 12.07.2019
Personnel: Dirk Milliman (Pub.); Barb England (Gen. Mgr.); Elena Hines (Managing Ed.); Marnie Apa (Adv. Sales); Scott Hassinger (Sports Ed.); Ashley Ware (Classifieds); Kricket Arevalo (Circ.)
Parent company (for newspapers): Surf New Media

TRAVERSE CITY RECORD-EAGLE

Street address 1: 120 W Front St
Street address city: Traverse City
Street address state: MI
Zip/Postal code: 49684-2202
County: Grand Traverse
Country: USA
Mailing address: 120 W FRONT ST
Mailing city: TRAVERSE CITY
Mailing state: MI
Mailing zip: 49684-2280
General Phone: (231) 946-2000
Advertising Phone: (231) 933-1465
Editorial Phone: (231) 933-1472
General/National Adv. E-mail: mzucco@record-eagle.com
Display Adv. E-mail: mzucco@record-eagle.com
Classified Adv. e-mail: classifieds@record-eagle.com
Editorial e-mail: mtyree@record-eagle.com
Primary Website: www.record-eagle.com
Mthly Avg Views: 1200000
Mthly Avg Unique Visitors: 283000
Year Established: 1858
News Services: AP, DJ, ONS, MCT, LAT-WP.
Special Editions: Spring Guide (Apr); Autumn Guide (Aug); Holiday Gift Guide (Dec); Winter Home (Jan); Mid Summer Home (Jul); Summer Guide (Jun); Bridal (Mar); Lawn & Garden (May); Coupon Savings (Monthly); Ski Directory (Nov); Autumn Guide (Oct); Wine (Other); Summer Guide (Jun).
Special Weekly Sections: Arts & Entertainment (Fri); Food (Mon); Business (S); Faith (Sat); Our Town (Thur); Education (Tues); Business (Wed).
Syndicated Publications: Parade (S).
Delivery Methods: Mail`Carrier
Areas Served - City/County or Portion Thereof, or Zip codes: Northern Michigan
Own Printing Facility?: Y
Commercial printers?: Y
Avg Free Circ: 535
Sat. Circulation Paid: 15060
Sat. Circulation Free: 214
Sun. Circulation Paid: 19562
Sun. Circulation Free: 202
Audit By: AAM
Audit Date: 31.12.2017
Personnel: Paul Heidbreder (Pub.); Rich Roxbury (Circ. Dir.); Dan Roach (Advertising Department); Maia Conway (Mktg. Dir.); Dave Miller (Editorial Page Ed.); Loraine Anderson (Regl. Ed.); Michelle Mulliner (Prodn. Dir.); Monica Stanley (Prodn. Mgr., Mailroom); Jan Burda (Single Copy Mgr.); Denny Chase (Sports Ed.); Chuck Staske (Home Delivery Sales Mgr.); Dan Nielsen (Business Ed.); Nathan Payne (Features Ed.); Brian Steele (Ed. in Chief); Andy Taylor (Associate Ed.); Shawn Winter (Adv. Dir.)
Parent company (for newspapers): CNHI, LLC; CNHI, LLC

THE OAKLAND PRESS

Street address 1: 2125 Butterfield Dr.
Street address 2: Suite 102N
Street address city: Troy
Street address state: MI
Zip/Postal code: 48084
County: Oakland
Country: USA
Mailing address: 2125 Butterfield Dr., Suite 102N
Mailing city: Troy
Mailing state: MI
Mailing zip: 48084
General Phone: (248) 332-8181
Advertising Phone: (248) 745-4595
Editorial Phone: (248) 745-4587
General/National Adv. E-mail: tgoodrich@digitalfirstmedia.com
Display Adv. E-mail: lrao-cheney@digitalfirstmedia.com
Classified Adv. e-mail: noelle.klomp@oakpress.com
Editorial e-mail: glenn.gilbert@oakpress.com
Primary Website: www.theoaklandpress.com
Mthly Avg Views: 2000000
Mthly Avg Unique Visitors: 157467
Year Established: 1844
News Services: AP, LAT-WP, SHNS, NYT, TMS.
Special Editions: Religious Directory (Apr); Salute to Business (Aug); Tis the Season (Dec); Senior Living (Feb); No Ordinary Sale (Jan); Concours d'Elegance (Jul); Senior Living (Jun); Spring Home & Garden/Cobo (Mar); MI Vacation Guide (May); Lagniappe (Nov); College Guid
Special Weekly Sections: Marquee Entertainment Tab (Fri); Food (Mon); Real Estate (S); Building (Sat); Health (Thur); Youth & Teen (Tues); Real Estate (Wed).
Syndicated Publications: Parade (S).
Delivery Methods: Mail`Carrier
Areas Served - City/County or Portion Thereof, or Zip codes: 48430, 48442, 48350, 48462, 48348, 48346, 48371, 48362, 48360, 48359, 48370, 48267, 48366, 48363, 48306, 48307, 48309, 48326, 48346, 48342, 48341, 48328, 48329, 48327, 48386, 48383, 48356, 48357, 48380, 48381, 48382, 48390, 48326, 48324, 48323, 48322, 48302, 48304, 48301, 48009, 48098, 48084, 48083, 48017, 48071, 48067, 48030, 48229, 48237, 48070, 48072, 48076, 48075, 48025, 48034, 48336, 48334, 48331, 48335, 48375, 48377, 48393, 48165, 48178, 48374, 48167
Own Printing Facility?: Y
Commercial printers?: Y
Sat. Circulation Paid: 22822
Sun. Circulation Paid: 37048
Audit By: AAM
Audit Date: 31.03.2017
Personnel: Jeannie Parent (Pub.); Teresa Goodrich (Rgl VP, Sales); Dwight Major (Circ. Mgr.); Julie Jacobson-Hines (Local News Ed.); Angel Offredi (Digital Dir.); Lee Dryden (Metro Ed.); Noelle Klomp (Classifieds Dir.); Joe Hildebrand (Promotions Mgr.); Don Wyatt (VP, News); Nicole Robertson (Ent. Ed.); Matt Myftiu (News Ed.); Kathy Blake (Business Ed.); Stephen Frye (Online Ed.); Monica Drake (Community Engagement Ed.); Tim Thompson (Photo Ed.); Jeff Keuhn (Sports Ed.)
Parent company (for newspapers): Digital First Media

MINNESOTA

ALBERT LEA TRIBUNE

Street address 1: 808 W Front St
Street address city: Albert Lea
Street address state: MN
Zip/Postal code: 56007-1947
County: Freeborn
Country: USA
Mailing address: 808 W FRONT ST
Mailing city: ALBERT LEA
Mailing state: MN
Mailing zip: 56007-1947
General Phone: (507) 373-1411
Advertising Phone: (507) 379-3428
Editorial Phone: (507) 379-3433
General/National Adv. E-mail: crystal.miller@albertleatribune.com
Display Adv. E-mail: amanda.nelson@albertleatribune.com
Classified Adv. e-mail: michelle.daveiga@albertleatribune.com
Editorial e-mail: sarah.stultz@albertleatribune.com
Primary Website: www.albertleatribune.com
Mthly Avg Views: 400000
Mthly Avg Unique Visitors: 90000
Year Established: 1897
News Services: AP.
Special Editions: Sports (Apr); Fair (Aug); Progress (Feb); Pork (Jan); Albert Lea Guide (Jun); Health/Wellness (Mar); Wedding (May); Sports (Nov); Car Care (Oct); Seniors (Quarterly).
Delivery Methods: Mail`Newsstand`Carrier`Racks
Areas Served - City/County or Portion Thereof, or Zip codes: 56007
Own Printing Facility?: Y
Commercial printers?: Y
Sun. Circulation Paid: 6415
Sun. Circulation Free: 6022
Audit By: USPS
Audit Date: 27.09.2022
Personnel: Crystal Miller (Publisher); Tim Engstrom (Ed.); Sarah Stultz (Asst. Ed.); Terry Thissen (Production Dir.); Lisa Foley (Acct. Mgr.); Catherine Buboltz (Adv. Dir.); Melissa Goodwin (Circ. Rep.); Kathy Johnson (Creative Dir.); Rich Mirelli (Mailroom Mgr.); Micah Bader (Sports Ed.); Colleen Harrison (Community Ed.); Hannah Dillon (Special Sections Ed.)
Parent company (for newspapers): Boone Newspapers, Inc.

AUSTIN DAILY HERALD

Street address 1: 310 2nd St NE
Street address city: Austin
Street address state: MN
Zip/Postal code: 55912-3436
County: Mower
Country: USA
Mailing address: 310 2ND ST NE
Mailing city: Austin
Mailing state: MN
Mailing zip: 55912-3487
General Phone: (507) 433-8851
Advertising Phone: (507) 434-2220
Editorial Phone: (507) 434-2231
General/National Adv. E-mail: ben.ankeny@austindailyherald.com
Display Adv. E-mail: ben.ankeny@austindailyherald.com
Classified Adv. e-mail: classifieds@austindailyherald.com
Editorial e-mail: newsroom@austindailyherald.com
Primary Website: www.austindailyherald.com
Year Established: 1891
News Services: AP.
Special Editions: Freedom Fest (Jul); Picnic Patrol; Jump Start (2012-2013); Austin Living Magazine (Summer 2013); The Best of Mower County; Wedding Showcase; Discover Summer; Progress 2013; Southern Exposure
Special Weekly Sections: Lifestyles (S).
Syndicated Publications: Relish (Monthly); Parade (S); Southern MN Magazine (Quarterly).
Delivery Methods: Mail`Carrier
Areas Served - City/County or Portion Thereof, or Zip codes: 55912, 55918, 55909, 55917, 55926, 55933, 56007
Own Printing Facility?: Y
Commercial printers?: Y
Sun. Circulation Paid: 5280
Audit By: Sworn/Estimate/Non-Audited
Audit Date: 12.07.2019
Personnel: Jana Norman (Pub.); Heather Ryks (Sales & Mkt. Mgr.); Eric Johnson (Ed. / Photographer); Rocky Hulne (Sports Ed.); Mike Delhanty (Marketing Consultant); Heather Biwer (Classifieds); Trina Miller (Home Delivery Mgr.)
Parent company (for newspapers): Boone Newspapers, Inc.

THE BEMIDJI PIONEER

Street address 1: 1320 Neilson Ave SE
Street address city: Bemidji
Street address state: MN
Zip/Postal code: 56601-5406
County: Beltrami
Country: USA
Mailing address: PO BOX 455
Mailing city: BEMIDJI
Mailing state: MN
Mailing zip: 56619-0455
General Phone: (218) 333-9200
Advertising Phone: (218) 333-9778
Editorial Phone: (218) 333-9200
General/National Adv. E-mail: tkeute@bemidjipioneer.com
Display Adv. E-mail: tkeute@bemidjipioneer.com
Classified Adv. e-mail: classifieds@bemidjipioneer.com
Editorial e-mail: mcory@bemidjipioneer.com
Primary Website: www.bemidjipioneer.com
Mthly Avg Views: 500000
Mthly Avg Unique Visitors: 100000
Year Established: 1896
News Services: NEA.
Special Editions: FYI Bemidji Magazine, InMagazine, Meet Your Bemidji Business People
Special Weekly Sections: Living, Entertainment, Comics (Sun); Downtown Weekly (Tue); Outdoors (Fri.), Faith (Thur);
Syndicated Publications: Relish (Monthly); Parade (S).
Delivery Methods: Mail`Carrier`Racks
Areas Served - City/County or Portion Thereof, or Zip codes: 56601, 56630, 56650, 56667, 56621, 56676, 56678, 56663, 56633, 56647, 56683, 56661
Own Printing Facility?: N
Commercial printers?: N
Avg Free Circ: 47
Sat. Circulation Paid: 5119
Sat. Circulation Free: 46
Sun. Circulation Paid: 6089
Sun. Circulation Free: 46
Audit By: VAC
Audit Date: 30.09.2016
Personnel: Dennis Doeden (Pub.); Miles Kastella (Distribution Mgr.); Matt Cory (Ed.); Tammie Brooks (Controller); Tim Webb (Home Delivery Mgr.); Todd Keute (Advertising Director)
Parent company (for newspapers): Forum Communications Co.

BRAINERD DISPATCH

Street address 1: 506 James Street,
Street address city: Brainerd
Street address state: MN
Zip/Postal code: 56401
County: Crow Wing
Country: USA
Mailing address: PO BOX 974
Mailing city: BRAINERD
Mailing state: MN
Mailing zip: 56401-0974
General Phone: (218) 829-4705
Advertising Phone: (218) 855-5835
Editorial Phone: (218) 855-5860

General/National Adv. E-mail: susie.alters@brainerddispatch.com
Display Adv. E-mail: susie.alters@brainerddispatch.com
Classified Adv. e-mail: susie.alters@brainerddispatch.com
Editorial e-mail: Matt.Erickson@brainerddispatch.com
Primary Website: www.brainerddispatch.com
Year Established: 1881
News Services: AP, LAT-WP.
Special Editions: Golf Guide (Apr); Senior Class (Monthly); Weddings North (Feb); Up North Autos; Christmas Catalog (Nov); Her Voice (Quarterly): Health Watch (Quarterly); Outdoors Traditions (Quarterly); We are 181 (Spring & Fall)
Special Weekly Sections: Housing Page (Fri); TV Week, Outdoors, Business, Money (Sun); Auto, Dining, Food, Entertainment (Thur); Neighbors (Wed).
Syndicated Publications: Relish (Monthly); USA WEEKEND; Parade Magazine (S); American Profile (Weekly).
Delivery Methods: Mail`Newsstand`Carrier`Racks
Areas Served - City/County or Portion Thereof, or Zip codes: 56338, 56345, 56364, 56401, 56431, 56435, 56441, 56442, 56443, 56444, 56447, 56448, 56449, 56450, 56452, 56456, 56459, 56465, 56466, 56468, 56472, 56473, 56474, 56479, 56481, 56482, 56484, 56662, 56438, 56359, 56469, 56475
Own Printing Facility?: Y
Commercial printers?: Y
Sun. Circulation Paid: 13577
Sun. Circulation Free: 2748
Audit By: AAM
Audit Date: 31.03.2019
Personnel: Pete Mohs (Pub.); Matt Erickson (Ed.); Renee Richardson (Mng. Ed.); Jeremy Millsop (Sports Ed.); Jason Allord (Op. Mgr.); Dianna Blanck (Circ. Mgr.); Kari Lake (Controller/HR Dir.); Susie Alters (Adv. Dir.)
Parent company (for newspapers): Forum Communications Co.

CROOKSTON DAILY TIMES

Street address 1: 124 S Broadway
Street address city: Crookston
Street address state: MN
Zip/Postal code: 56716-1955
County: Polk
Country: USA
Mailing address: 124 S BROADWAY
Mailing city: CROOKSTON
Mailing state: MN
Mailing zip: 56716-1955
General Phone: (218) 281-2730
Advertising Phone: (218) 281-2730
Editorial Phone: (218) 281-2730
General/National Adv. E-mail: canderson@crookstontimes.com
Display Adv. E-mail: canderson@crookstontimes.com
Classified Adv. e-mail: sherberg@crookstontimes.com
Editorial e-mail: mchristopherson@crookstontimes.com
Primary Website: www.crookstontimes.com
Year Established: 1885
News Services: AP.
Special Editions: Religion Directory (Jul); Super Service Directory (Jul).
Special Weekly Sections: Best Foods (Tue)
Syndicated Publications: American Profile (Weekly).
Delivery Methods: Mail`Carrier
Areas Served - City/County or Portion Thereof, or Zip codes: 55101, 55102, 55108, 55126, 55330, 55371, 55415, 55424, 55811, 56379, 56401, 56510, 56517, 56523, 56535, 56540, 56542, 56548, 56556, 56560, 56562, 56581, 56592, 56601, 56716, 56722, 56723, 56750, 56762, 57201, 58078, 58201, 58203, 58208, 60197, 62914, 63501, 66601, 77479, 85021, 94583, 95822, 97070, 99326
Sat. Circulation Free: 8800
Audit By: Sworn/Estimate/Non-Audited
Audit Date: 12.07.2019
Personnel: Mike Christopherson (Mng. Ed.); Calvin Anderson (Adv. Mgr.); Carl Melbye (Circ. Mgr); Derek Martin (Sports Ed.); Samantha Herberg (Classifieds)
Parent company (for newspapers): CherryRoad Media

DULUTH NEWS TRIBUNE

Street address 1: 424 W 1st St
Street address city: Duluth
Street address state: MN
Zip/Postal code: 55802-1596
County: Saint Louis
Country: USA
Mailing address: 424 W 1ST ST
Mailing city: DULUTH
Mailing state: MN
Mailing zip: 55802-1596
General Phone: (218) 723-5252
Advertising Phone: (218) 723-5225
Editorial Phone: (218) 723-5300
General/National Adv. E-mail: customerservice@duluthnews.com
Display Adv. E-mail: advertising@duluthnews.com
Classified Adv. e-mail: classifieds@classifiedsFCC.com
Editorial e-mail: news@duluthnews.com
Primary Website: www.duluthnewstribune.com
Mthly Avg Views: 3310815
Mthly Avg Unique Visitors: 611259
Year Established: 1869
News Services: Forum News Service, MCT, LAT-WP.
Special Editions: Back to School (Aug); Gift Guide (Dec); Boat, Sports and Travel (Feb); Hockey Preview (Nov.)
Syndicated Publications: Parade (S); Dash (Monthly)
Delivery Methods: Mail`Newsstand`Carrier`Racks
Areas Served - City/County or Portion Thereof, or Zip codes: 55802, 55811
Own Printing Facility?: Y
Commercial printers?: Y
Avg Free Circ: 0
Sat. Circulation Paid: 22342
Sat. Circulation Free: 93
Sun. Circulation Paid: 31533
Sun. Circulation Free: 62
Audit By: VAC
Audit Date: 30.09.2021
Personnel: Rick Lubbers (Editor); Megan Keller (Advertising Director); Neal Ronquist (Publisher); Rich Roxbury (Circulation Director)
Parent company (for newspapers): Forum Communications Co.

SENTINEL

Street address 1: 64 Downtown Plaza
Street address city: Fairmont
Street address state: MN
Zip/Postal code: 56031
County: Martin
Country: USA
Mailing address: PO BOX 681
Mailing city: FAIRMONT
Mailing state: MN
Mailing zip: 56031-0681
General Phone: (507) 235-3303
Advertising Phone: (507) 235-3303
Editorial Phone: (507) 235-3303
General/National Adv. E-mail: ads@fairmontsentinel.com
Display Adv. E-mail: ads@fairmontsentinel.com
Classified Adv. e-mail: classified@fairmontsentinel.com
Editorial e-mail: news@fairmontsentinel.com
Primary Website: www.fairmontsentinel.com
Year Established: 1874
News Services: AP.
Special Editions: Golf Directory; Hometown Youth; Medical Directory; Bridal Tab; Visitor Guide.
Special Weekly Sections: Best Food (Mon); TV Book (Fri).
Syndicated Publications: USA WEEKEND Magazine (Sat).
Delivery Methods: Mail`Carrier
Areas Served - City/County or Portion Thereof, or Zip codes: 56031, 56075, 56039, 56060, 56062, 56088, 56181, 50514, 50517, 50522, 50581, 51334, 50539, 50559, 50578, 50590, 56010, 56013, 56023, 56025, 56047, 56001, 56002, 56003, 56006, 56097, 560898, 56014, 50424, 56027, 56033, 56051, 50451, 50556, 50465, 50480, 56121, 56127, 56171, 56176, 56111, 56118, 56120, 56143, 56159, 56160, 56162, 56081, 56101
Own Printing Facility?: Y
Commercial printers?: Y
Sat. Circulation Paid: 3556
Audit By: AAM
Audit Date: 31.03.2019
Personnel: Gary Andersen (Pub.); Kathy Ratcliff (Adv. Dir.); Amy Miller (Office Mgr.); Lee Smith (Ed.); Lisa Thate (Composition Supvr.)
Parent company (for newspapers): Ogden Newspapers Inc.

FARIBAULT DAILY NEWS

Street address 1: 514 Central Ave N
Street address city: Faribault
Street address state: MN
Zip/Postal code: 55021-4304
County: Rice
Country: USA
Mailing address: 514 CENTRAL AVE N
Mailing city: FARIBAULT
Mailing state: MN
Mailing zip: 56071
General Phone: (507) 333-3111
Advertising Phone: (507) 333-3108
Editorial Phone: (507) 333-3134
General/National Adv. E-mail: kfavro@faribault.com
Display Adv. E-mail: suzyrook@gmail.com
Classified Adv. e-mail: bnguyen@owatonna.com
Editorial e-mail: suzyrook@gmail.com
Primary Website: www.faribault.com
Year Established: 1914
News Services: AP.
Special Editions: Spring Sports (Apr); Christmas Song Book (Dec); Brides (Jan); Rice County Fair (Jul); Heritage Festival (Jun); Community Profile (Mar); Senior Lifestyles (May); Winter Sports Preview (Nov); Home & Garden (Sept).
Special Weekly Sections: Business (Tue); Seniors (Wed); Entertainment (Thur); Religion (Fri); Education (Sat)
Delivery Methods: Mail`Newsstand`Carrier`Racks
Areas Served - City/County or Portion Thereof, or Zip codes: 55021, 55018, 55019, 55946, 56069, 55052.
Own Printing Facility?: Y
Commercial printers?: Y
Avg Free Circ: 9946
Sat. Circulation Paid: 6687
Sat. Circulation Free: 14177
Audit By: CAC
Audit Date: 12.12.2017
Personnel: Sam Gett (Ed./Pub.); Mark Nelson (Adv. Team Leader); Suzanne Rook (Regional Managing Editor); Stacy Murphy (Reader Services)
Parent company (for newspapers): Adams Publishing Group, LLC

THE FERGUS FALLS DAILY JOURNAL

Street address 1: 914 E Channing Ave
Street address city: Fergus Falls
Street address state: MN
Zip/Postal code: 56537-3738
County: Otter Tail
Country: USA
Mailing address: 914 E CHANNING AVE
Mailing city: FERGUS FALLS
Mailing state: MN
Mailing zip: 56537-3738
General Phone: (218) 736-7511
Advertising Phone: (218) 205-8435
Editorial Phone: (218) 739-7023
General/National Adv. E-mail: adassist@fergusfallsjournal.com
Display Adv. E-mail: dave.churchill@austindailyherald.com
Classified Adv. e-mail: linda.reese@fergusfallsjournal.com
Editorial e-mail: joel.myhre@fergusfallsjournal.com
Primary Website: www.fergusfallsjournal.com
Year Established: 1873
News Services: AP.
Special Editions: Resorter (Aug); Christmas Gift Guide 3 (Dec); Profile (Feb); Chamber Tab (Jan); Crazy Days (Jul); Summer Fun Guide (Jun); Home & Health (Mar); Resorter (May); Christmas Gift Guide 1 (Nov); BPW (Oct); F.Y.I. (Sept).
Special Weekly Sections: Best Food (Wed); Business (Mon); Education, Outdoors (Tue); Real Estate (Wed); Church, Entertainment (Thur); Farm, Auto, Real Estate (Fri); Lifestyles, Home (Sun);
Syndicated Publications: USA WEEKEND Magazine (Sat); TV Journal (Thur).
Delivery Methods: Mail`Carrier
Sun. Circulation Paid: 8414
Audit By: Sworn/Estimate/Non-Audited
Audit Date: 12.07.2019
Personnel: Mitzi Moe (Pub.); Connie Knapp (Audience Development Mgr.); Zach Stich (Ed.); Mary Sieling (Assistant Adv. Mgr.); Anna Anderson (Classified Specialist)
Parent company (for newspapers): Wick Communications

HIBBING DAILY TRIBUNE

Street address 1: 2142 1st Ave
Street address city: Hibbing
Street address state: MN
Zip/Postal code: 55746-3759
County: Saint Louis
Country: USA
Mailing address: PO BOX 38
Mailing city: HIBBING
Mailing state: MN
Mailing zip: 55746-0038
General Phone: (218) 262-1011
Editorial Phone: (218) 262-1014
General/National Adv. E-mail: taune@hibbingdailytribune.net
Display Adv. E-mail: jodegaard@hibbingdailytribune.net
Classified Adv. e-mail: mferris@hibbingdailytribune.net
Editorial e-mail: kgrinsteinner@hibbingdailytribune.net
Primary Website: www.hibbingmn.com
Year Established: 1893
News Services: AP.
Special Editions: Home Improvement (Apr); Back-to-School (Aug); Progress (Feb); Bridal (Jan); Christmas (Nov); Car Fix-up (Sept).
Special Weekly Sections: TV Week (S); Churches (Sat).
Syndicated Publications: Relish (Monthly); American Profile (S).
Delivery Methods: Mail`Carrier
Own Printing Facility?: N
Commercial printers?: N
Sat. Circulation Paid: 4519
Sun. Circulation Paid: 4973
Audit By: Sworn/Estimate/Non-Audited
Audit Date: 12.07.2019
Personnel: Kelly Grinsteinner (Pub.); Sue Hancock (Family Ed.); Gary Giombetti (Sports Ed.)
Parent company (for newspapers): Adams Publishing Group, LLC

THE FREE PRESS

Street address 1: 418 S 2nd St
Street address city: Mankato
Street address state: MN
Zip/Postal code: 56001-3727
County: Blue Earth
Country: USA
Mailing address:
Mailing city:
Mailing state: MN
General Phone: (507) 625-4451
Advertising Phone: (507) 344-6364
Editorial Phone: (507) 344-6397
General/National Adv. E-mail: advertising@mankatofreepress.com
Display Adv. E-mail: mfpads@mankatofreepress.com
Classified Adv. e-mail: classified@mankatofreepress.com
Editorial e-mail: editor@mankatofreepress.com
Primary Website: www.mankatofreepress.com
Mthly Avg Views: 1500000
Mthly Avg Unique Visitors: 187535
Year Established: 1887
News Services: AP.
Delivery Methods: Mail`Carrier
Areas Served - City/County or Portion Thereof, or Zip codes: Nicollet, Blue Earth and Waseca Counties in Minnesota.
Avg Free Circ: 0
Sat. Circulation Paid: 20481
Sun. Circulation Paid: 20512
Audit By: Sworn/Estimate/Non-Audited
Audit Date: 31.05.2024
Personnel: Joe Spear (Mng. Ed.); Robb Murray (Features Editor); Kathy Vos (News Ed., Day); Glen Asleson (Prodn. Dir.); Steve Jameson (Publisher); Denise Zernechel (Circ. Dir.); Jim Rueda (Sports Ed.); Lon Youngerberg (Prodn. Foreman, Pressroom); Brooke High (Bus. Mgr.); Ginny Bergerson (Adv. Dir.)
Parent company (for newspapers): CNHI, LLC; CNHI, LLC

INDEPENDENT

Street address 1: 508 West Main Street
Street address 2: 508 W Main St
Street address city: Marshall
Street address state: MN
Zip/Postal code: 56258
County: Lyon
Country: USA
Mailing address: PO BOX 411
Mailing city: MARSHALL
Mailing state: MN
Mailing zip: 56258-0411
General Phone: (507) 537-1551

Advertising Phone: (507) 537-1551 ext. 116
Editorial Phone: (507) 537-1551 ext. 126
General/National Adv. E-mail: tbrandl@marshallindependent.com
Display Adv. E-mail: adcomp@marshallindependent.com
Classified Adv. e-mail: rstaeffler@marshallindependent.com
Editorial e-mail: phpeterson@marshallindependent.com
Primary Website: www.marshallindependent.com
Mthly Avg Views: 116821
Mthly Avg Unique Visitors: 36079
Year Established: 1874
News Services: AP.
Special Editions: Lawn & Garden (Apr); Back-to-School (Aug); Spring Bridal (Feb); Pork Products Tab (Jan); Crazy Days (Jul); Graduation (May); Cookbook (Nov); Fall Car Care (Oct).
Special Weekly Sections: Church News (Fri); Business (Mon); Weddings (Sat); Farm Focus (Thur); Best Food Day (Wed).
Delivery Methods: Mail`Newsstand`Carrier`Racks
Areas Served - City/County or Portion Thereof, or Zip codes: 56258,56115,56229,56130,56132,56239,56157,56264,56169,56291,56175,56113,56136,56142,56149,56178,56139,56170,56123,56214,56255,56263,56218,56292,56293,56180,56220,56223,56237,56241,56245,56280,56232,56297,56172.56152,56283.56151,56183,56164
Own Printing Facility?: N
Commercial printers?: Y
Avg Free Circ: 191
Sat. Circulation Paid: 3841
Sat. Circulation Free: 28
Audit By: AAM
Audit Date: 31.03.2019
Personnel: Greg Orear (Pub./Gen. Mgr.); Mike Lamb (News Ed.); Sam Thiel (Sports Ed.); Tara Brandl (Adv. Mgr.); Rob Purrington (Circ. Mgr.); Ruth Staeffler (Classified Ad Mgr.)
Parent company (for newspapers): Ogden Newspapers Inc.

STAR TRIBUNE

Street address 1: 650 3rd Avenue S
Street address city: Minneapolis
Street address state: MN
Zip/Postal code: 55488
County: Hennepin
Country: USA
Mailing address: 425 PORTLAND AVE
Mailing city: MINNEAPOLIS
Mailing state: MN
Mailing zip: 55488-0002
General Phone: (612) 673-4000
Advertising Phone: (612) 673-7777
Editorial Phone: (612) 673-7937
General/National Adv. E-mail: advertisinginformation@startribune.com
Display Adv. E-mail: paul.kasbohm@startribune.com
Classified Adv. e-mail: Linda.Thies@startribune.com
Editorial e-mail: nancyb@startribune.com
Primary Website: www.startribune.com
Mthly Avg Views: 80800000
Mthly Avg Unique Visitors: 7300000
Year Established: 1867
News Services: Associated Press, New York Times Service, McClatchy Tribune Information Service, Washington Post/Bloomberg Service, Scripps Howard News Service, Bloomberg, Dow Jones Information Service
Special Editions: Balance (Jan); MN Explorer (Mar, Aug, Nov); Golden Gavel (Mar, Sep); The Good Life (Mar, Apr, Aug, Sep); Drive (Spring/Fall); Top Workplaces (Jun); State Fair Preview (Aug); College Fair Guide (Oct); Charitable Giving Guide (Nov); Holiday Gift Guide (Nov); Homes Magazine (Monthly).
Special Weekly Sections: Business + Money (Sun); Travel, Opinion Exchange, Sunday Comics, Twin Cities + Life (Sun); Dakota County (Sun); StribExpress (Sun); Business Insider (Mon); Variety H+G, West Extra, South Extra (Wed); Vita.mn: Entertainment, Taste (Thur); Twin Cities Values (Sat).
Syndicated Publications: Parade (Sun.); TV Week Lite (Fri. Single Copy); DASH (Monthly)
Delivery Methods: Mail`Newsstand`Carrier`Racks
Areas Served - City/County or Portion Thereof, or Zip codes: 612, 651, 763, 952 (MN), 715, 534 (WI)
Own Printing Facility?: Y
Commercial printers?: Y
Sat. Circulation Paid: 239682
Sun. Circulation Paid: 420456
Audit By: AAM
Audit Date: 31.03.2018
Personnel: Michael Klingensmith (Pub./CEO); Kevin Desmond (Sr. VP, Op.); Steven H. Alexander (Sr. VP, Circ.); Chuck Brown (Sr. VP, CFO); Paul Kasbohm (CFO); Jane Messenger (Creative Director); Dave Gundersen (Dir., Sales Mktg./Research); Cindy Doege (Circ. Vice Pres.); Nancy Barnes (Ed./Sr. Vice Pres.); Scott Gillespie (Ed. Editorial Pages); Rene Sanchez (Ed. & Sr. VP); Cory Powell (Mng. Ed., Presentation/Innovation); Bob Schafer (Asst. Mng. Ed., Admin.); Terry Sauer (Asst. Mng. Ed., Continuous News); Steve Yaeger (VP and Chief Marketing Officer); Jeff Griffing (Chief Revenue Officer); Rob Gursha (VP, Consumer Marketing); Duchesne Drew (Managing Editor, Operations); Jim Bernard (Sr. VP, Digital); Randy Lebedoff (Sr. V.P. & Gen. Counsel); Ray Faust (VP, National & Emerging Media); Adrienne Sirany (Sr. VP, HR); Joe Allen; Derek Simmons (Asst. Managing Ed., Visuals); Drew Duchesne; John Hoeft (Associate VP, Digital Sales); James Byrd (Director, Digital Yield); Jason Cole (Services Sales Supervisor); Nicholas Gusmano (Retail Marketing Analyst); Jeff Sebesta (Retail Marketing Manager); Andrew Reinhardt (Retail Marketing Specialist); Jennifer Beckman (Sales Supervisor); Arden Dickey (Sr. VP, Cir.); Jason Erdahl (Exec. Dir., Digital); Brad Larson; Katherine Kohls (Preprint Sales Mgr.); Nicole Shannon; Sean Haley (Director, Sales Development); Todd Molldrem; Patricia Lopez (Ed.)
Parent company (for newspapers): Star Tribune

THE JOURNAL

Street address 1: PO Box 487
Street address 2: 303 N Minnesota St # 487
Street address city: New Ulm
Street address state: MN
Zip/Postal code: 56073-0487
County: Brown
Country: USA
Mailing address: PO Box 487
Mailing city: New Ulm
Mailing state: MN
Mailing zip: 56073-0487
General Phone: (507) 359-2911
Advertising Phone: (507) 359-2911
Editorial Phone: (507) 359-2911
General/National Adv. E-mail: ads@nujournal.com
Display Adv. E-mail: tbabel@nujournal.com
Classified Adv. e-mail: classads@nujournal.com
Editorial e-mail: ksweeney@nujournal.com
Primary Website: www.nujournal.com
Year Established: 1898
News Services: AP.
Special Editions: Tax Guide (Jan); Bridal Booklet (Jan); Visitor Guide (Jan); Progress (Feb); Health (Feb); Home Improvement (Mar); Spring Real Estate Guide (Apr); Medical Directory (Annually); Fall Car Care (Fall); Presidents' Day Coupon (Feb); January Thaw (Jan); Shamrock Days (Mar); Graduation Tab (May); Christmas Kick-Off (Nov); Spring Car Care (Spring); Winter Sports (Winter).
Special Weekly Sections: Best Food (Tue); Agribusiness (Fri); Church (Sat); Lifestyle, TV Time, Comics (Sun)
Syndicated Publications: Parade (S).
Delivery Methods: Mail`Newsstand`Carrier`Racks
Areas Served - City/County or Portion Thereof, or Zip codes: 56073
Own Printing Facility?: N
Commercial printers?: N
Avg Free Circ: 411
Sat. Circulation Paid: 10279
Sat. Circulation Free: 411
Sun. Circulation Paid: 11780
Sun. Circulation Free: 256
Audit By: AAM
Audit Date: 31.12.2017
Personnel: Greg Orear (Pub.); Kevin Sweeney (Ed.); Steve Grosam (Circ. Mgr.); Tim Babel (Adv. Dir.); D. Dubberly (Office Mgr.)
Parent company (for newspapers): Ogden Newspapers Inc.

OWATONNA PEOPLE'S PRESS

Street address 1: 135 W Pearl St
Street address city: Owatonna
Street address state: MN
Zip/Postal code: 55060-2316
County: Steele
Country: USA
Mailing address: PO BOX 346
Mailing city: OWATONNA
Mailing state: MN
Mailing zip: 55060-0346
General Phone: (507) 451-2840
Advertising Phone: (507) 444-2389
Editorial Phone: (507) 444-2370
General/National Adv. E-mail: gbergerson@owatonna.com
Display Adv. E-mail: gbergerson@owatonna.com
Classified Adv. e-mail: classified@owatonna.com
Editorial e-mail: jjackson@owatonna.com
Primary Website: www.owatonna.com
Mthly Avg Views: 370000
Year Established: 1874
News Services: AP.
Special Editions: Spring Sports (Apr); Steele County Fair (Aug); Park & Rec (Feb); Bridal (Jan); Park & Rec (Jul); Bridal (Jun); Portraits (Mar); Graduation (May); Christmas Kick-Off (Nov); Welcome Guide (May, Oct); Home & Garden (Sept).
Special Weekly Sections: Seniors (Wed); Entertainment (Thur); Trends (Fri); Religion, Real Estate (Sat)
Syndicated Publications: American Profile (Weekly);
Delivery Methods: Mail`Newsstand`Carrier`Racks
Areas Served - City/County or Portion Thereof, or Zip codes: 55060, 55049, 55924, 55917,56026, 55927
Own Printing Facility?: Y
Commercial printers?: Y
Avg Free Circ: 784
Sat. Circulation Paid: 5104
Sat. Circulation Free: 9316
Audit By: CAC
Audit Date: 31.12.2015
Personnel: Carol Harvey (Circ. Mgr.); Jeffrey Jackson (Mng. Ed.); Roger Stolley (Prodn. Mgr.); Ginny Bergerson (Advertising Director); Julie Frazier (Publisher); Ronald Ensley (Pub./Ed.); Debbie Ensley (Adv. Dir.)
Parent company (for newspapers): Adams Publishing Group, LLC

POST-BULLETIN

Street address 1: 18 1st Ave SE
Street address city: Rochester
Street address state: MN
Zip/Postal code: 55904-3722
County: Olmsted
Country: USA
Mailing address: PO BOX 6118
Mailing city: ROCHESTER
Mailing state: MN
Mailing zip: 55903-6118
General Phone: (507) 285-7600
Advertising Phone: (507) 285-7783
Editorial Phone: (507) 285-7700
General/National Adv. E-mail: mbarebo@postbulletin.com
Display Adv. E-mail: advertising@postbulletin.com
Classified Adv. e-mail: slovejoy@postbulletin.com
Editorial e-mail: letters@postbulletin.com
Primary Website: www.postbulletin.com
Mthly Avg Views: 558280
Mthly Avg Unique Visitors: 326420
Year Established: 1916
News Services: AP, NYT, MCT.
Special Editions: Pets (May); Dairy 2013 (Jun); Boomer (Apr); Education (Aug); Last Minute Gift Catalog (Dec); Rochester Area Builders Home Show (Feb); Weddings (Jan); Honor Roll (Jul); Rochesterfest (Jun); Employment (Mar); Spring Home & Garden (May); Home for the Holidays (Nov); Drive Magazine (Oct).
Special Weekly Sections: Real Estate Marketplace (Fri); Seniors (Mon); Travel (Sat); Prevue (Thur); Teen Beat (Tues); Food (Wed).
Syndicated Publications: Homefinder (Monthly); USA WEEKEND Magazine (Sat); American Profile (Weekly).
Delivery Methods: Mail`Carrier
Areas Served - City/County or Portion Thereof, or Zip codes: southeastern Minnesota
Own Printing Facility?: Y
Commercial printers?: Y
Avg Free Circ: 469
Sat. Circulation Paid: 29714
Sat. Circulation Free: 374
Audit By: CAC
Audit Date: 31.03.2018
Personnel: Christy Blade (Interim Pub.); Ken Henry (Advertising Dir.); Brian Sander (News Ed.); Jeff Pieters (News & Life Ed.)
Parent company (for newspapers): Forum Communications Co.

ST. CLOUD TIMES

Street address 1: 3000 7th St N
Street address city: Saint Cloud
Street address state: MN
Zip/Postal code: 56303-3108
County: Stearns
Country: USA
Mailing address: PO BOX 768
Mailing city: SAINT CLOUD
Mailing state: MN
Mailing zip: 56302-0768
General Phone: (320) 255-8700
Advertising Phone: (320) 255-8793
Editorial Phone: (320) 255-8776
General/National Adv. E-mail: mbirkland@stcloud.gannett.com
Display Adv. E-mail: jschlaghec@stcloud.gannett.com
Classified Adv. e-mail: classifieds@stcloudtimes.com
Editorial e-mail: rkrebs@stcloud.gannett.com
Primary Website: www.sctimes.com
Mthly Avg Views: 4695000
Mthly Avg Unique Visitors: 489000
Year Established: 1861
News Services: AP, GNS, Forum,
Special Editions: Christmas Gift Guide (Dec); Bridal (Jan); Bridal (Jul); Home Times (Semi-monthly); Football (Sept), Extra Helpings (Thanksgiving), Rocori Times (10x/year), Festival Guide (May), Progress Edition (Sept.), Quarterly Business Report, Whitney Times (4x/year), Prep Football (August), Auto Preview (Jan),
Special Weekly Sections: Travel Page (S); Weddings/Engagements (Sat); Up Next (Thur), Auto (Friday), Homes (Saturday); D'Lish (Wed), Business (7 days/week), Citizen Times (Monday)
Syndicated Publications: USA WEEKEND Magazine (Fri)
Delivery Methods: Mail`Newsstand`Carrier`Racks
Own Printing Facility?: Y
Commercial printers?: N
Avg Free Circ: 193
Sat. Circulation Paid: 18716
Sat. Circulation Free: 156
Sun. Circulation Paid: 19842
Sun. Circulation Free: 156
Audit By: AAM
Audit Date: 31.03.2018
Personnel: John L. Bodette (Exec. Ed.); Julie Schlagheck (Adv. Mgr., Online Devel.); Marilyn Birkland (Adv. Mgr., Territory Retail Sales); Tom Steve (Circ. Sales Mgr.); Mike Knaak (Asst. Mng. Ed.); Randy Krebs (Ed. Page Ed.); David Schwarz (Photo Dept. Mgr.); Melinda Vonderahe (President/Publisher)
Parent company (for newspapers): Gannett

ST. PAUL PIONEER PRESS

Street address 1: 10 River Park Plz
Street address 2: Ste 700
Street address city: Saint Paul
Street address state: MN
Zip/Postal code: 55107-1223
County: Ramsey
Country: USA
Mailing address: 10 RIVER PARK PLZ STE 700
Mailing city: SAINT PAUL
Mailing state: MN
Mailing zip: 55107-1223
General Phone: (651) 222-1111
Advertising Phone: (651) 228-5365
Editorial Phone: (651) 228-5490
General/National Adv. E-mail: gmazanec@pioneerpress.com
Display Adv. E-mail: gmazanec@pioneerpress.com
Classified Adv. e-mail: dmccants@pioneerpress.com
Editorial e-mail: letters@pioneerpress.com
Primary Website: www.twincities.com
Mthly Avg Views: 20000000
Mthly Avg Unique Visitors: 1995608
Year Established: 1849
News Services: AP, MCT, LAT-WP, The Newspaper Network (TNN).
Special Editions: Fall Gardening (Sep, Oct); Travel Guides (Mar, Aug); Live to Age Well (Mar, Aug, Nov); Worship Directory (Apr, Dec); Higher Education (Jul, Dec); State Fair (Aug); Vikings Season Preview (Sep); Arts previews (Mar, Sep, Nov); Breast Cancer Awareness (Oct); Non Profit Giving Guide (Nov); Golf

Guide (Apr); Home & Lifestyle (Aug); Ski (Dec); Winter Carnival (Jan); Home & Lifestyle (Jul); Summer Fun Guide (Jun); Summer Camp for Kids (Mar); Home & Lifestyle (Oct).
Special Weekly Sections: Eat (Thur); Wheels (Fri/Sat); TV Weekly, Real Estate, Business (Sun)
Syndicated Publications: Parade (S).
Delivery Methods: Mail`Newsstand`Carrier`Racks
Areas Served - City/County or Portion Thereof, or Zip codes: 55001 to 56750
Own Printing Facility?: Y
Commercial printers?: Y
Sat. Circulation Paid: 89793
Sun. Circulation Paid: 220963
Audit By: AAM
Audit Date: 31.12.2017
Personnel: Guy Gilmore (Publisher); Mike Burbach (Ed.); Pat Effenberger (Commun. Mgr.); Greg Mazanec (Vice Pres., Adv.); Dee Mccants (Adv. Dir., Classified); Andrew Mok (Vice Pres., Circ.); Lori Swanson (Dir., Mktg.); Jean Pearson (Dir., Market Research/Info.); Kevin Garris (VP, Production); Neil Mullen (CFO); Michael Garyantes; Hal Davis
Parent company (for newspapers): Digital First Media; MediaNews Group

MESABI DAILY NEWS

Street address 1: 704 S 7th Ave
Street address city: Virginia
Street address state: MN
Zip/Postal code: 55792-3086
County: Saint Louis
Country: USA
Mailing address: PO BOX 956
Mailing city: VIRGINIA
Mailing state: MN
Mailing zip: 55792-0956
General Phone: (218) 741-5544
Advertising Phone: (218) 741-5544
Editorial Phone: (218) 741-5544
General/National Adv. E-mail: cknight@mesabidailynews.net
Display Adv. E-mail: cknight@mesabidailynews.net
Classified Adv. e-mail: klaugen@mesabidailynews.net
Editorial e-mail: bhanna@mesabidailynews.net
Primary Website: www.virginiamn.com
Year Established: 1893
News Services: AP, NEA, TMS.
Special Editions: Our Schools (May); Business & Industry (Mar); Business & Industry (Feb).
Special Weekly Sections: Food (Wed); Business, Teen (Sat); Church, Outdoor, TV News (Sun)
Syndicated Publications: Relish (Monthly); USA WEEKEND Magazine (S); American Profile (Weekly).
Delivery Methods: Mail`Carrier
Sat. Circulation Paid: 9143
Sun. Circulation Paid: 10488
Audit By: Sworn/Estimate/Non-Audited
Audit Date: 12.07.2019
Personnel: Christopher Knight (Reg. Opt./Gen. Mgr./Adv. Dir.); Jerry Burnes (Ed.); Jim Romsaas (Sports Ed.); Vince Cleveland (Circ. Dir.)
Parent company (for newspapers): Adams Publishing Group, LLC

WEST CENTRAL TRIBUNE

Street address 1: 2208 Trott Ave SW
Street address city: Willmar
Street address state: MN
Zip/Postal code: 56201-2723
County: Kandiyohi
Country: USA
Mailing address: PO BOX 839
Mailing city: WILLMAR
Mailing state: MN
Mailing zip: 56201-0839
General Phone: (320) 235-1150
Advertising Phone: (320) 235-1150
Editorial Phone: (320) 235-1150
General/National Adv. E-mail: news@wctrib.com
Display Adv. E-mail: wctads@wctrib.com
Classified Adv. e-mail: wctads@wctrib.com
Editorial e-mail: SLunneborg@wctrib.com
Primary Website: www.wctrib.com
Year Established: 1895
News Services: Forum News Service
Special Editions: Earth Day (Apr); Fall Football Preview (Aug); Holiday (Dec); Bridal I (Feb); Willmar Mid Summer (Jul); City Festival (Jun); Agriculture (Mar); Mother's Day (May); Holiday Greetings (Nov); Health Services Directory (Oct); Fall Home Improvement (Sept).
Special Weekly Sections: Best Food Days, Health (Mon); Business (Tue); Arts/Entertainment, Auto (Thur); Church, Real Estate, TV (Fri); Farm, Outdoors, Travel, Technology (Sat)
Syndicated Publications: Parade (S).
Delivery Methods: Mail`Carrier
Own Printing Facility?: Y
Commercial printers?: Y
Avg Free Circ: 54
Sat. Circulation Paid: 9827
Sat. Circulation Free: 54
Audit By: VAC
Audit Date: 30.09.2017
Personnel: Steve Ammerman (Publisher); Kelly Boldan (Editor); Sharon Bomstad (Features Ed.); Susan Lunneborg (News Ed.); Nate Schueller (Circulation Manager); Christie Steffel (Advert. Mgr.)
Parent company (for newspapers): Forum Communications Co.

WINONA DAILY NEWS

Street address 1: 279 E 3rd St
Street address 2: Ste 110
Street address city: Winona
Street address state: MN
Zip/Postal code: 55897
County: Winona
Country: USA
Mailing address: 902 E 2ND ST STE 110
Mailing city: WINONA
Mailing state: MN
Mailing zip: 55987-6512
General Phone: (507) 453-3500
Advertising Phone: (507) 453-3561
Editorial Phone: (507) 453-3510
General/National Adv. E-mail: sales@winonadailynews.com
Display Adv. E-mail: stacia.king@lee.net
Classified Adv. e-mail: classifieds@winonadailynews.com
Editorial e-mail: letters@winonadailynews.com
Primary Website: www.winonadailynews.com
Mthly Avg Views: 987168
Mthly Avg Unique Visitors: 159968
Year Established: 1855
News Services: AP, Lee National Sales Group.
Special Editions: Kid's Korner (Jul); Home Buyers Guide (Jun); Real Estate Resource (Jun); Business Report (May); River Valley (May); Bike Trail (Apr); Bridal Showcase (Jan); Home Improvement (Mar, May, Aug, Oct); Farm Outlook (Mar, Sept) Golf Guide; Bike Guide (Apr); Back-to-School/Campus (Aug); Christmas (Dec).
Special Weekly Sections: Connections, Outdoors, Comics (Sun); Business (Mon); Best Food, Business Card (Wed); Preps, Live! (Thur); NASCAR, NFL, Real Estate (Fri); Neighbors (Sat)
Syndicated Publications: Parade (S); American Profile (Weekly).
Delivery Methods: Mail`Newsstand`Carrier
Areas Served - City/County or Portion Thereof, or Zip codes: 55987; 55981; 55979; 55974; 55972; 55971; 55969; 55962; 55959; 55952; 55947; 55943; 55925; 55921; 55910; 54773; 54756; 54747; 54661; 54630; 54629; 54625; 54622; 54612; 54610
Own Printing Facility?: N
Commercial printers?: Y
Avg Free Circ: 522
Sat. Circulation Paid: 6253
Sat. Circulation Free: 422
Sun. Circulation Paid: 6287
Sun. Circulation Free: 548
Audit By: AAM
Audit Date: 31.03.2018
Personnel: Josh Trust (River Valley Media Group Publisher); Jessica Peters (Regional Finance Dir.); John Casper Jr. (Ed.); Adam Watts (Sports Ed.); Lisa Faulkner (Advertising Mgr.)
Parent company (for newspapers): Lee Enterprises, Incorporated

WORTHINGTON DAILY GLOBE

Street address 1: 300 11th St
Street address city: Worthington
Street address state: MN
Zip/Postal code: 56187-2451
County: Nobles
Country: USA
Mailing address: PO BOX 639
Mailing city: WORTHINGTON
Mailing state: MN
Mailing zip: 56187-0639
General Phone: (507) 376-9711
Advertising Phone: (507) 376-9711
Editorial Phone: (507) 376-9711
General/National Adv. E-mail: dellerbroek@dglobe.com
Display Adv. E-mail: ccarlson@dglobe.com
Classified Adv. e-mail: dgclassified@dglobe.com
Editorial e-mail: rmcgaughey@dglobe.com
Primary Website: www.dglobe.com
Year Established: 1872
News Services: AP.
Special Editions: Home Improvement (Apr); Real Estate Guide (Every other month); Builders (Fall); Bridal Tab (Jan); Bridal Tab (Jun); Progress Annual Report (Mar); Active Life (Quarterly); Builders (Spring).
Special Weekly Sections: Best Food Days, Business (Mon); Agriculture, Home (Tue); Health (Wed); Religion (Thur); Dining, Entertainment, Outdoors (Fri); People, Education (Sat)
Syndicated Publications: TV Pre-Vu (Fri); Relish (Monthly); Parade (S); American Profile (Sat).
Delivery Methods: Mail`Carrier
Areas Served - City/County or Portion Thereof, or Zip codes: 56170, 56139, 56164, 56186, 56135, 56140, 56177, 56128, 56123, 56125, 56151, 56133, 56172, 56114, 56122, 56141, 56131, 56183, 56174, 56145, 56101, 56159, 56118, 56144, 56134, 56156, 56116, 56158, 56138, 56173, 56147, 56153, 56126, 56155, 56185, 56165, 56119, 56110, 56168, 56187, 56129, 56117, 56167, 56184, 56137, 56161, 56150, 56143, 51242, 51246, 51243, 51230, 51237, 51235, 51249, 51394, 51345, 51232, 51350, 51347, 51360, 51363, 51355, 51331, 51351, 51364, 51247, 51239, 51234, 51201, 51248, 51346, 51340, 51301
Own Printing Facility?: Y
Avg Free Circ: 53
Sat. Circulation Paid: 5830
Sat. Circulation Free: 53
Audit By: VAC
Audit Date: 30.09.2016
Personnel: Joni Harms (Pub.); Aaron Hagen (Sports Ed.); Beth Rickers (Features Ed); Rob Muck (Prodn. Mgr.); Ryan McGaughey (Mng. Ed.); Anita J Holmes (Business Mgr.)
Parent company (for newspapers): Forum Communications Co.

MISSISSIPPI

DAILY LEADER

Street address 1: 128 N Railroad Ave
Street address city: Brookhaven
Street address state: MS
Zip/Postal code: 39601-3043
County: Lincoln
Country: USA
Mailing address: PO BOX 551
Mailing city: BROOKHAVEN
Mailing state: MS
Mailing zip: 39602-0551
General Phone: (601) 833-6961
Advertising Phone: (601) 833-6961
Editorial Phone: (601) 833-6961
General/National Adv. E-mail: carol.teasley@dailyleader.com
Display Adv. E-mail: zane.brown@dailyleader.com
Classified Adv. e-mail: anna.montgomery@dailyleader.com
Editorial e-mail: rachel.eide@dailyleader.com
Primary Website: www.dailyleader.com
Year Established: 1883
News Services: AP.
Special Editions: FOCUS Magazine - quarterly Brides Magazine - annually Gridiron Magazine - annually
Special Weekly Sections: Business, Agriculture, Health (Tue); Food, Community, School (Wed); Faith (Fri); Business, Outdoor (Sun)
Syndicated Publications: Parade (S). Relish (m)
Delivery Methods: Mail`Carrier`Racks
Areas Served - City/County or Portion Thereof, or Zip codes: 3 960 139 629 396 620 000 000 000 000 000 000 000 000 000 000 000 000 000
Own Printing Facility?: Y
Commercial printers?: Y
Sun. Circulation Paid: 5384
Audit By: AAM
Audit Date: 30.09.2012
Personnel: Amy A. Jacobs (Exec. Vice Pres./Sec./Treasurer); Rick Reynolds (Pub.); Rachel Eide (Ed. / Gen. Mgr.); Tom Goetz (Sports Ed.); Malcom Stewart (Prodn. Mgr., Pressroom)
Parent company (for newspapers): Boone Newspapers, Inc.

THE BOLIVAR COMMERCIAL

Street address 1: 821 N Chrisman Ave
Street address city: Cleveland
Street address state: MS
Zip/Postal code: 38732-2110
County: Bolivar
Country: USA
Mailing address: PO BOX 1050
Mailing city: CLEVELAND
Mailing state: MS
Mailing zip: 38732-1050
General Phone: (662) 843-4241
Advertising Phone: (662) 843-4241 ext. 25
Editorial Phone: (662) 843-4241 ext. 34
General/National Adv. E-mail: advertising@bolivarcommercial.com
Display Adv. E-mail: advertising@bolivarcommercial.com
Classified Adv. e-mail: classifieds@bolivarcommercial.com
Editorial e-mail: news@bolivarcommercial.com
Primary Website: www.bolivarcom.com
Year Established: 1969
News Services: AP.
Special Editions: Crosstie Arts Festival (Apr); Football (Aug); Christmas Gift Guide (Dec); Valentine (Feb); Delta Agriculture Expo (Jan); Back-to-School (Jul); Summer/Outdoor (Jun); Italian Festival of Mississippi (Mar); Nurses' Week (May); Light Up Your Holidays (Nov); B
Special Weekly Sections: Food (Wed); Business, Religion (Fri); Sports, Mini-page (Sun)
Syndicated Publications: American Profile (Weekly).
Delivery Methods: Mail`Carrier
Audit By: Sworn/Estimate/Non-Audited
Audit Date: 12.07.2019
Personnel: Mark Williams (Pub.); David Laster (Adv. Mgr.); Denise Strub (Mng. Ed.); Andy Collier (Sports Ed.); Sharon Clinton (Prodn. Mgr.); Spencer Haywood (Head Pressman)
Parent company (for newspapers): Cleveland Newspapers, Inc.

THE COMMERCIAL DISPATCH

Street address 1: 516 Main St
Street address city: Columbus
Street address state: MS
Zip/Postal code: 39701-5734
County: Lowndes
Country: USA
Mailing address: PO BOX 511
Mailing city: COLUMBUS
Mailing state: MS
Mailing zip: 39703-0511
General Phone: (662) 328-2424
Advertising Phone: (662) 328-2424
Editorial Phone: (662) 328-2424
General/National Adv. E-mail: support@cdispatch.com
Display Adv. E-mail: bproffitt@cdispatch.com
Classified Adv. e-mail: classifieds@cdispatch.com
Editorial e-mail: news@cdispatch.com
Primary Website: www.cdispatch.com
Mthly Avg Views: 562000
Mthly Avg Unique Visitors: 164000
Year Established: 1879
News Services: AP, LAT-WP.
Special Editions: Catfish Alley magazine (quarterly); Football Preview (Aug); Health & Fitness (Feb); Money & Taxes (Jan); FYI (Jun); Home & Garden (Mar); Salute to Family Owned Business (May); Back to School (Sept).
Special Weekly Sections: Education (Mon); Food (Wed); Business (Thur); Religion (Fri/Sun)
Delivery Methods: Mail`Carrier
Areas Served - City/County or Portion Thereof, or Zip codes: Lowndes County, Oktibbeha County, Clay County, Noxubee County
Own Printing Facility?: Y
Commercial printers?: Y
Sun. Circulation Paid: 13997
Audit By: Sworn/Estimate/Non-Audited
Audit Date: 12.07.2019

Personnel: Peter Imes (Publisher); Birney Imes (Pub.); Beth Proffitt (Adv. Dir.); Tina Perry (Prepress Mgr.); Slim Smith (Reporter & Columnist); Mike Floyd (Circ. & Production Mgr.); Debbie Foster (Acct. Clerk); Zack Plair (Managing Editor); Stacy Clark (Catfish Alley Ed.); Adam Minichino (Sports Ed.)
Parent company (for newspapers): Commercial Dispatch, Inc.

THE DAILY CORINTHIAN

Street address 1: 1607 S Harper Rd
Street address city: Corinth
Street address state: MS
Zip/Postal code: 38834-6653
County: Alcorn
Country: USA
Mailing address: PO BOX 1800
Mailing city: CORINTH
Mailing state: MS
Mailing zip: 38835-1800
General Phone: (662) 287-6111
Advertising Phone: (662) 287-6111 ext. 339
General/National Adv. E-mail: advertising@dailycorinthian.com
Display Adv. E-mail: advertising@dailycorinthian.com
Classified Adv. e-mail: classad@dailycorinthian.com
Editorial e-mail: news@dailycorinthian.com
Primary Website: www.dailycorinthian.com
Year Established: 1895
News Services: AP.
Special Editions: Crossroads Magazine monthly
Special Weekly Sections: Church Page (Fri).
Syndicated Publications: USA WEEKEND Magazine (S).
Delivery Methods: Newsstand`Carrier`Racks
Areas Served - City/County or Portion Thereof, or Zip codes: 3 823 638 339 383 570 000 000 000 000 000 000 000 000 000 000 000 000 000
Own Printing Facility?: Y
Commercial printers?: Y
Sat. Circulation Paid: 6113
Sun. Circulation Paid: 6186
Audit By: Sworn/Estimate/Non-Audited
Audit Date: 12.07.2019
Personnel: Reese Terry (Pub.); Wille Walker (Circ. Dir.); Mark Boehler (Ed.); Fallon Hunt (Adv. Mgr.)
Parent company (for newspapers): Paxton Media Group

DELTA DEMOCRAT TIMES

Street address 1: 988 N Broadway St
Street address city: Greenville
Street address state: MS
Zip/Postal code: 38701-2349
County: Washington
Country: USA
Mailing address: PO BOX 1618
Mailing city: GREENVILLE
Mailing state: MS
Mailing zip: 38702-1618
General Phone: (662) 335-1155
Advertising Phone: (662) 378-0745
Editorial Phone: (662) 378-0711
General/National Adv. E-mail: suetriplett@ddtonline.com
Display Adv. E-mail: keithwilliams@ddtonline.com
Classified Adv. e-mail: cathybramuchi@ddtonline.com
Editorial e-mail: lauarsmith@ddtonline.com
Primary Website: www.ddtonline.com
Year Established: 1938
News Services: AP.
Special Editions: Fall Football (Aug); Bridal (Feb); Back-to-School (Jul); Our Town (Mar); Holiday Shopping Guide (Nov).
Special Weekly Sections: Food (Wed); Entertainment (Thur); Church (Fri); Comics, TV (Sun)
Syndicated Publications: USA Weekend, Color Comics (S)
Delivery Methods: Mail`Carrier`Racks
Avg Free Circ: 370
Sun. Circulation Paid: 5458
Sun. Circulation Free: 816
Audit By: AAM
Audit Date: 30.09.2016
Personnel: Jon Alverson (Ed./Pub.); Jeri Borst (Mng. Ed.); LeAnne Hughes (Prod. Mgr.)
Parent company (for newspapers): 1976

THE GREENWOOD COMMONWEALTH

Street address 1: 329 Highway 82 W
Street address city: Greenwood
Street address state: MS
Zip/Postal code: 38930-6538
County: Leflore
Country: USA
Mailing address: PO BOX 8050
Mailing city: GREENWOOD
Mailing state: MS
Mailing zip: 38935-8050
General Phone: (662) 453-5312
Advertising Phone: (662) 581-7230
Editorial Phone: (662) 581-7243
General/National Adv. E-mail: commonwealth@gwcommonwealth.com
Display Adv. E-mail: lalderman@gwcommonwealth.com
Classified Adv. e-mail: kturner@gwcommonwealth.com
Editorial e-mail: tkalich@gwcommonwealth.com
Primary Website: www.gwcommonwealth.com
Mthly Avg Views: 295194
Mthly Avg Unique Visitors: 36743
Year Established: 1896
News Services: AP.
Special Editions: Football (Aug); Health and Fitness (Sept); People's Choice (Oct); Christmas Gift Guide (Nov); Christmas Greetings (Dec); Profile (Feb); Top 30 Under 40 (March every other year); Top 30 Places to Work (March every other year); Farming (May)
Special Weekly Sections: Food (Tue); Religion (Fri); Lifestyles, Outdoors, Farm, Business (Sun)
Syndicated Publications: Parade (S)
Delivery Methods: Mail`Newsstand`Carrier`Racks
Own Printing Facility?: Y
Commercial printers?: Y
Avg Free Circ: 128
Sun. Circulation Paid: 3345
Sun. Circulation Free: 38
Audit By: AAM
Audit Date: 31.03.2019
Personnel: Tim Kalich (Pub./Ed.); Eddie Ray (Bus. Mgr.); Larry Alderman (Adv. Mgr.); Shirley Cooper (Circ. Mgr.); Charles Corder (Mng. Ed.); Bill Burrus (Sports Ed.)
Parent company (for newspapers): Commonwealth Publishing, Inc.; Emmerich Newspaper Group

THE SUN HERALD

Street address 1: 205 Debuys Rd
Street address city: Gulfport
Street address state: MS
Zip/Postal code: 39507-2838
County: Harrison
Country: USA
Mailing address: PO BOX 4567
Mailing city: BILOXI
Mailing state: MS
Mailing zip: 39535-4567
General Phone: (228) 896-2100
Advertising Phone: (228) 896-2490
Editorial Phone: (228) 896-2301
General/National Adv. E-mail: dladnerl@sunherald.com
Display Adv. E-mail: dladnerl@sunherald.com
Classified Adv. e-mail: sellit@sunherald.com
Editorial e-mail: letters@sunherald.com
Primary Website: www.sunherald.com
Mthly Avg Unique Visitors: 526614
Year Established: 1884
News Services: AP, MCT, SHNS.
Special Editions: Guide to Gulf Coast Living (Apr); Football (Aug); Attractions (Feb); Annual Progress (Jan); Wellness/Healthcare Directory (Jul); Nike Classic (Mar); Home & Products Show (May); Auto Showroom (Nov); Annual Salute to the Military (Oct); NIE Literacy (Sept).
Special Weekly Sections: Soundoff (Mon); Casinos (Tue); Food (Wed); Health, Marquee (Thur); Faith, Neighbors (Fri); Home & Garden (Sat); Arts, Travel, TV (Sun)
Syndicated Publications: Parade (S).
Delivery Methods: Mail`Carrier
Avg Free Circ: 225
Sat. Circulation Paid: 15684
Sat. Circulation Free: 158
Sun. Circulation Paid: 18497
Sun. Circulation Free: 167
Audit By: AAM
Audit Date: 31.12.2018
Personnel: Blake Kaplan (Exec. Ed./Gen. Mgr.); Lauren Walck (Sr. News/Visual Ed.); Justin Mitchell (Reg. Growth Ed.)
Parent company (for newspapers): The McClatchy Company; Chatham Asset Management

THE CLARION-LEDGER

Street address 1: 201 S Congress St
Street address city: Jackson
Street address state: MS
Zip/Postal code: 39201-4202
County: Hinds
Country: USA
Mailing address: PO BOX 40
Mailing city: JACKSON
Mailing state: MS
Mailing zip: 39205-0040
General Phone: (601) 961-7000
Advertising Phone: (601) 961-7143
Editorial Phone: (601) 961-7101
General/National Adv. E-mail: adunn@localiq.com
Display Adv. E-mail: adunn@localiq.com
Classified Adv. e-mail: adunn@localiq.com
Editorial e-mail: srhall@jackson.gannett.com
Primary Website: www.clarionledger.com
Mthly Avg Views: 8134213
Mthly Avg Unique Visitors: 1132687
Year Established: 1837
News Services: AP, GNS,
Special Editions: College Football (Aug); Discovery (Jun); Week on the Water (May); Tour of Homes (Oct); Tis the Season Holiday Gift Guide (Nov & Dec.)
Special Weekly Sections: Business, Real Estate, Sports, Outdoors, Arts (Sun); Health (Tue); Food (Wed); Community, Entertainment (Thur); Autos, Homes, Home & Garden (Fri); Religion (Sat);
Syndicated Publications: USA WEEKEND Magazine (S)
Delivery Methods: Mail`Carrier`Racks
Areas Served - City/County or Portion Thereof, or Zip codes: 39201; 39157; 39110; 39046
Own Printing Facility?: Y
Commercial printers?: Y
Sat. Circulation Paid: 35169
Sun. Circulation Paid: 41194
Audit By: AAM
Audit Date: 30.09.2017
Personnel: Sam R. Hall (Executive Ed.); Adrianne Dunn (Sales Dir.); Vera Bridges (Distribution Dir./ Circ.); Joe Williams (Finance Dir.)
Parent company (for newspapers): Gannett

ENTERPRISE-JOURNAL

Street address 1: 112 Oliver Emmerich Dr
Street address city: McComb
Street address state: MS
Zip/Postal code: 39648-6330
County: Pike
Country: USA
Mailing address: PO BOX 2009
Mailing city: MCCOMB
Mailing state: MS
Mailing zip: 39649-2009
General Phone: (601) 684-2421
Advertising Phone: (601) 684-2421 ext. 229
Editorial Phone: (601) 684-2421 ext. 217
General/National Adv. E-mail: advertising@enterprise-journal.com
Display Adv. E-mail: advertising@enterprise-journal.com
Classified Adv. e-mail: classifieds@enterprise-journal.com
Editorial e-mail: publisher@enterprise-journal.com
Primary Website: www.enterprise-journal.com
Mthly Avg Views: 200000
Mthly Avg Unique Visitors: 10000
Year Established: 1889
News Services: AP.
Special Editions: Graduation (Apr); Football (Aug); Christmas Greetings (Dec); Back-to-School (Jul); Perspective (Mar); Recipe (Sept); Adventure (Oct).
Syndicated Publications: Parade (S).
Delivery Methods: Mail`Carrier`Racks
Areas Served - City/County or Portion Thereof, or Zip codes: McComb/Pike/39648
Own Printing Facility?: Y
Commercial printers?: Y
Avg Free Circ: 122
Sun. Circulation Paid: 7523
Sun. Circulation Free: 121
Audit By: AAM
Audit Date: 30.06.2017
Personnel: Jack Ryan (Pub./Ed./ Gen. Mgr.); Vicky Deere (Adv. Mgr.); Matt Williamson (Managing Ed.); Margie Williams (Classifieds Adv. Mgr.); Kim Golden (Business Mgr.)
Parent company (for newspapers): 1976

THE MERIDIAN STAR

Street address 1: 814 22nd Ave
Street address city: Meridian
Street address state: MS
Zip/Postal code: 39301-5023
County: Lauderdale
Country: USA
Mailing address: PO BOX 1591
Mailing city: MERIDIAN
Mailing state: MS
Mailing zip: 39302-1591
General Phone: (601) 693-1551
Advertising Phone: (601) 693-1551 ext. 3257
Editorial Phone: (601) 693-1551 ext. 3213
General/National Adv. E-mail: advertising@themeridianstar.com
Display Adv. E-mail: advertising@themeridianstar.com
Classified Adv. e-mail: jwilliams@themeidianstar.com
Editorial e-mail: editor@themeridianstar.com
Primary Website: www.meridianstar.com
Year Established: 1898
News Services: AP.
Special Editions: EMCC Salute (Apr); Bands & Cheerleaders (Aug); Christmas Greetings (Dec); Profile (Feb); Tanning Page (Jan); FYI (Jul); State Games Tab (Jun); Spring Lawn & Garden (Mar); Jimmie Rogers Days (May); Christmas Early Bird Buys (Nov); Who's The Best (Oct); Fal
Special Weekly Sections: Food (Wed); Religion (Sat); Business, Finance (Sun)
Syndicated Publications: Relish (Monthly); Parade (S); American Profile (Weekly).
Delivery Methods: Carrier
Areas Served - City/County or Portion Thereof, or Zip codes: 30301, 30305
Own Printing Facility?: Y
Commercial printers?: N
Avg Free Circ: 398
Sat. Circulation Paid: 7295
Sat. Circulation Free: 398
Sun. Circulation Paid: 8615
Sun. Circulation Free: 130
Audit By: AAM
Audit Date: 30.09.2014
Personnel: Paula Merritt (Photo Dept. Mgr.); Ida Brown (Staff Writer); Elizabeth Ryan (Church Pages & Bus. Review); Alexander Gould (Pub.); Dave Bohrer (Ed.)
Parent company (for newspapers): CNHI, LLC; CNHI, LLC

THE NATCHEZ DEMOCRAT

Street address 1: 503 N Canal St
Street address city: Natchez
Street address state: MS
Zip/Postal code: 39120-2902
County: Adams
Country: USA
Mailing address: PO BOX 1447
Mailing city: NATCHEZ
Mailing state: MS
Mailing zip: 39121-1447
General Phone: (601) 442-9101
Advertising Phone: (601) 445-3634
Editorial Phone: (601) 445-3539
General/National Adv. E-mail: newsroom@natchezdemocrat.com
Display Adv. E-mail: sue.hicks@natchezdemocrat.com
Classified Adv. e-mail: sue.hicks@natchezdemocrat.com
Editorial e-mail: julie.cooper@natchezdemocrat.com
Primary Website: www.natchezdemocrat.com
Year Established: 1865
News Services: AP.
Special Editions: Profile (Feb); Natchez & Its Neighbors (Jul); Spring Pilgrimage (Mar); Fall Pilgrimage (Oct).
Special Weekly Sections: People (Wed/Sun); Religion (Sat); Business, Finance (Sun);
Syndicated Publications: USA WEEKEND Magazine (S). Natchez the Magazine (bi-monthly)
Delivery Methods: Newsstand`Carrier`Racks
Areas Served - City/County or Portion Thereof, or Zip codes: 39120, 39669, 39661, 39069, 71326, 71334, 71343, 71354, 71373, 71375
Own Printing Facility?: Y
Commercial printers?: Y

Sat. Circulation Paid: 8428
Sun. Circulation Paid: 8536
Audit By: Sworn/Estimate/Non-Audited
Audit Date: 12.07.2019
Personnel: Kevin Cooper (Pub.); Ryan Richardson (Marketing Coord.); Julie Cooper (Managing Ed.); Sam King (Circ. Mgr.)
Parent company (for newspapers): Boone Newspapers, Inc.

THE OXFORD EAGLE

Street address 1: 4 Private Road 2050
Street address city: Oxford
Street address state: MS
Zip/Postal code: 38655-8887
County: Lafayette
Country: USA
Mailing address: PO BOX 866
Mailing city: OXFORD
Mailing state: MS
Mailing zip: 38655-0866
General Phone: (662) 234-4331
Advertising Phone: (662) 234-4331
Editorial Phone: (662) 234-4331
General/National Adv. E-mail: addirector@oxfordeagle.com
Display Adv. E-mail: addirector@oxfordeagle.com
Classified Adv. e-mail: classifieds@oxfordeagle.com
Editorial e-mail: news@oxfordeagle.com
Primary Website: www.oxfordeagle.com
Year Established: 1867
News Services: AP.
Special Editions: Brides 2013 (Jan); Best of Oxford 2013 (Feb); Home Market Guide; Lease on Living (Mar); Senior Living Magazine (Apr); Graduation (May); Spring 2013; Welcome Back Rebels (Aug).
Special Weekly Sections: Business, Finance (Mon); Education (Tue); Lifestyle, Best Food Day (Wed); Health (Thur); Living, Weekend, Church (Fri)
Syndicated Publications: American Profile (Weekly).
Delivery Methods: Mail`Carrier
Audit By: Sworn/Estimate/Non-Audited
Audit Date: 12.07.2019
Personnel: Belinda Jones (Circ. Mgr.); Bruce Newman (Photo Ed.); Eddie Lance (Head Pressman); Delia Childers (Adv. Dir.); Davis Potter (Sports Ed.); Alex McDaniel (Ed.)
Parent company (for newspapers): Boone Newspapers, Inc.

STARKVILLE DAILY NEWS

Street address 1: 304 E Lampkin St
Street address city: Starkville
Street address state: MS
Zip/Postal code: 39759-2910
County: Oktibbeha
Country: USA
Mailing address: PO BOX 1068
Mailing city: STARKVILLE
Mailing state: MS
Mailing zip: 39760-1068
General Phone: (662) 323-1642
Advertising Phone: (662) 323-1642
Editorial Phone: (662) 324-8092
General/National Adv. E-mail: ads@starkvilledailynews.com
Display Adv. E-mail: ads@starkvilledailynews.com
Classified Adv. e-mail: classified@starkvilledailynews.com
Editorial e-mail: news@starkvilledailynews.com
Primary Website: www.starkvilledailynews.com
Year Established: 1875
News Services: AP.
Special Editions: Bulldog Weekend (Apr); Welcome Back Miss. State (Aug); Progress (Feb); Christmas Gift Guide (Nov).
Special Weekly Sections: Education (Mon); Local Roundup (Tue); Best Food, Entertainment (Wed); Weekend Roundup (Fri); Religion (Sat); Lifestyle, Wedding (Sun)
Syndicated Publications: American Profile (S).
Delivery Methods: Mail`Carrier
Sat. Circulation Paid: 7071
Sun. Circulation Paid: 7071
Audit By: Sworn/Estimate/Non-Audited
Audit Date: 12.07.2019
Personnel: Don Norman (Pub.); Mona Howell (Bus. Mgr.); Byron Norman (Circ. Mgr.); Larry Bost (Creative Dir.); Shea Staskowski (Educ. Ed.); Brian Hawkins (Ed.)
Parent company (for newspapers): Horizon Publications Inc.

NORTHEAST MS DAILY JOURNAL

Street address 1: 1242 S Green St
Street address city: Tupelo
Street address state: MS
Zip/Postal code: 38804-6301
County: Lee
Country: USA
Mailing address: PO BOX 909
Mailing city: TUPELO
Mailing state: MS
Mailing zip: 38802-0909
General Phone: (662) 842-2611
Advertising Phone: (662) 842-2614
Editorial Phone: (662) 842-2612
General/National Adv. E-mail: ads@journalinc.com
Display Adv. E-mail: ads@journalinc.com
Classified Adv. e-mail: classifieds@journalinc.com
Editorial e-mail: editor@journalinc.com
Primary Website: www.djournal.com
Mthly Avg Unique Visitors: 250000
Year Established: 1872
News Services: AP, MCT.
Special Editions: Business Journal (Monthly); Healthly Living (Jan); North MS Health Journal Magazine (Mar & Aug); Spring Fashion (Mar); Blue Suede Cruise (Apr); Gum Tree Writing (May); The Source Magazine (May); Memorial Day (May); Graduation (May); Young at Heart (June); How To Guide (June); Election tab (July); Back to School (July); Traveler Magazine (Aug); High School Football (Aug); Fall Brides (Aug); College Football (Aug); Fall Home Improvement (Sept); Fall Fashion (Sept); Marching Band Festival (Oct); Breast Cancer Awareness (Oct); Women at Work (Oct); Taste of the Season Cookbook (Nov); Holiday Gift Guide (Nov)
Special Weekly Sections: Education (Mon); NASCAR, Food (Wed); Neighbors (Thur); Health & Fitness, Auto, Home & Garden (Fri); Faith, Auto (Sat); Comics, Real Estate, Employment, Coupons (Sun)
Syndicated Publications: Relish (Monthly); Parade (S)
Delivery Methods: Mail`Newsstand`Carrier`Racks
Areas Served - City/County or Portion Thereof, or Zip codes: 38603 to 38915
Own Printing Facility?: Y
Commercial printers?: Y
Avg Free Circ: 594
Sat. Circulation Paid: 17555
Sat. Circulation Free: 586
Sun. Circulation Paid: 19162
Sun. Circulation Free: 481
Audit By: AAM
Audit Date: 31.03.2019
Personnel: William H. Bronson III (Pub./CEO); Charlotte Wolfe (Circulation Director); Rosemary Jarrell (CFO); Richard Crenshaw (Adv. & Marketing Dir.); Leslie Criss (Lifestyles Ed.); Michael King (Circ. Mgr.); Eddie Blakley (COO/VP Production); Elizabeth Walters (Daily Ed. & Dig. Ed.); Chris Kieffer (Op. Ed.)
Parent company (for newspapers): Journal Publishing Company

THE VICKSBURG POST

Street address 1: 1601F N Frontage Rd
Street address city: Vicksburg
Street address state: MS
Zip/Postal code: 39180-5149
County: Warren
Country: USA
Mailing address: PO BOX 821668
Mailing city: VICKSBURG
Mailing state: MS
Mailing zip: 39182-1668
General Phone: (601) 636-4545
Advertising Phone: (601) 636-4545
Editorial Phone: (601) 636-4545
General/National Adv. E-mail: ads@vicksburgpost.com
Display Adv. E-mail: bpartridge@vicksburgpost.com
Classified Adv. e-mail: classifieds@vicksburgpost.com
Editorial e-mail: kgamble@vicksburgpost.com
Primary Website: www.vicksburgpost.com
Year Established: 1883
News Services: AP.
Special Editions: Home Improvement (Apr); High School Football (Aug); Last Minute Gift Guide (Dec); African American History (Feb); Brides (Jan); Family-Owned Business (Jun); Industry (Mar); Car Care (May); Health Services Directory (Nov); Home Improvement (Oct); College F
Special Weekly Sections: Best Food Day (Wed); Business (Mon-Sun); Comics (Sun);
Syndicated Publications: Parade (S).
Delivery Methods: Mail`Carrier
Avg Free Circ: 7
Sat. Circulation Paid: 9811
Sat. Circulation Free: 7
Sun. Circulation Paid: 10300
Sun. Circulation Free: 7
Audit By: VAC
Audit Date: 31.03.2013
Personnel: Jimmy Clark (Gen. Mgr.); Barney Partridge (Adv. Dir.); Jimmy Mullen (Prod. Mgr); Tim Reeves (President/Publisher); Charles D. Mitchell (Exec. Ed.); Misty McDermitt (Asst. Mng. Ed., News); Brian Loden (Asst. Mng. Ed., Photo); Steve Wilson (Asst. Mng. Ed., Sports); Mary Kittrell (Presentation Ed.); Timothy Reeves (Publisher); Paul Barry (Mng. Ed.); Jan Griffey (Ed.)
Parent company (for newspapers): Boone Newspapers, Inc.

DAILY TIMES LEADER

Street address 1: 26463 E Main St
Street address city: West Point
Street address state: MS
Zip/Postal code: 39773-7995
County: Clay
Country: USA
Mailing address: PO BOX 1176
Mailing city: WEST POINT
Mailing state: MS
Mailing zip: 39773-1176
General Phone: (662) 494-1422
Advertising Phone: (662) 494-1422
Editorial Phone: (662) 494-1353
General/National Adv. E-mail: ads@dailytimesleader.com
Display Adv. E-mail: ads@dailytimesleader.com
Classified Adv. e-mail: class@dailytimesleader.com
Editorial e-mail: editor@dailytimesleader.com
Primary Website: www.dailytimesleader.com
Year Established: 1867
News Services: AP.
Special Editions: Progress (Feb); Gift Guide (Nov); Prairie Arts Festival (Sept); Best of West Point (2013); Community Profile; Graduation 2013
Special Weekly Sections: Business (Tue); Food (Wed); School (Thur); Home, Health (Fri); People (Sun)
Syndicated Publications: TeleVisions; Tuned In (S); American Profile (Weekly).
Delivery Methods: Mail`Carrier
Sun. Circulation Paid: 2758
Audit By: Sworn/Estimate/Non-Audited
Audit Date: 12.07.2019
Personnel: Don Norman (Pub.); Natasha Watson (Circ. Clerk); Byron Norman (Circ. Mgr.); Mandy Stewart (Gen. Mgr./Adv. Dir.); Brandon Walker (Managing Ed.)
Parent company (for newspapers): Horizon Publications Inc.

MISSOURI

LAKE SUN LEADER

Street address 1: 918 N Business Route 5
Street address city: Camdenton
Street address state: MO
Zip/Postal code: 65020-2648
County: Camden
Country: USA
Mailing address: 918 N Business Route 5
Mailing city: Camdenton
Mailing state: MO
Mailing zip: 65020-2648
General Phone: (573) 346-2132
Advertising Phone: (573) 346-2132
Editorial Phone: (573) 346-2132
General/National Adv. E-mail: business@lakesunleader.com
Display Adv. E-mail: michele.harris@lakesunonline.com
Classified Adv. e-mail: classifieds@lakesunonline.com
Editorial e-mail: newsroom@lakesunonline.com
Primary Website: www.lakenewsonline.com
Year Established: 1879
News Services: AP.
Special Weekly Sections: Travel, Sports (Mon); Business, School (Tue); Food (Wed); Upcoming Events (Thur); Real Estate, Entertainment (Fri)
Syndicated Publications: American Profile (Weekly).
Avg Free Circ: 28855
Audit By: Sworn/Estimate/Non-Audited
Audit Date: 12.07.2019
Personnel: Dave Cuddihy (Pub.); Joyce Miller (Circ./Ed. Dir); Becky Moos (Bus. Mgr.); Lisa Miller (Adv. Rep.); Charis Patires (Ed.); Amy Wilson (Mng. Ed.); Mike Losch (Sports Ed.)
Parent company (for newspapers): Vernon Publishing, Inc; CherryRoad Media

SOUTHEAST MISSOURIAN

Street address 1: 301 Broadway St
Street address city: Cape Girardeau
Street address state: MO
Zip/Postal code: 63701-7330
County: Cape Girardeau
Country: USA
Mailing address: PO BOX 699
Mailing city: CAPE GIRARDEAU
Mailing state: MO
Mailing zip: 63702-0699
General Phone: (573) 335-6611
Advertising Phone: (573) 338-2751
Editorial Phone: (573) 388-3625
General/National Adv. E-mail: advertising@semissourian.com
Display Adv. E-mail: ddenson@semissourian.com
Classified Adv. e-mail: ddenson@semissourian.com
Editorial e-mail: bmiller@semissourian.com
Primary Website: www.semissourian.com
Year Established: 1904
News Services: AP.
Special Editions: University Tab (Apr); Back-to-School (Aug); Traditional Christmas (Dec); Progress (Feb); Bridal (Jan); Vacations (Jun); Lawn & Garden (Mar); Vacations (May); Best of the Season (Nov); Newcomer's Guide (Oct); Fall Home Improvement & Decorating (Sept).
Special Weekly Sections: Business (Mon); Learning (Tue); Food (Wed); Health (Thur); Arts (Fri); Lifestyle, Travel, Real Estate (Sun);
Syndicated Publications: 1st Sunday (Monthly); Parade (S).
Avg Free Circ: 19130
Sun. Circulation Paid: 12416
Sun. Circulation Free: 265
Audit By: CAC
Audit Date: 31.03.2015
Personnel: Jon K. Rust (Pub.); Mark Kneer (Gen. Mgr.); Bob Miller (Ed.); Matt Sanders (Mng. Ed.); John Renaud (Prodn. Coord.); Danielle Smith (National Account Coord.); David Guay
Parent company (for newspapers): Rust Communications

CONSTITUTION-TRIBUNE

Street address 1: 818 Washington St
Street address city: Chillicothe
Street address state: MO
Zip/Postal code: 64601-2232
County: Livingston
Country: USA
Mailing address: PO BOX 707
Mailing city: CHILLICOTHE
Mailing state: MO
Mailing zip: 64601-0707
General Phone: (660) 646-2411
Advertising Phone: (660) 646-2411
Editorial Phone: (660) 646-2411
General/National Adv. E-mail: advertising@chillicothenews.com
Display Adv. E-mail: andrea@chillicothe.townnews.com
Classified Adv. e-mail: advertising@chillicothenews.com
Editorial e-mail: ctnews@chillicothenews.com
Primary Website: www.chillicothenews.com
Year Established: 1860
News Services: AP.
Special Weekly Sections: Agriculture (Tue); Best Food Day (Wed);
Delivery Methods: Mail`Newsstand`Carrier`Racks
Areas Served - City/County or Portion Thereof, or Zip codes: Livingston County
Avg Free Circ: 13220
Audit By: Sworn/Estimate/Non-Audited
Audit Date: 12.07.2019

Personnel: Rod Dixon (Pub./Purchasing Agent); Andrea Graves (Adv. Dir.); Jenetta Cramner (Circ. Mgr.); Catherine Ripley (Political/Gov't Ed.); Paul Sturm (Sports Ed.); Connie Jones (Classified Ads Mgr.)
Parent company (for newspapers): CherryRoad Media; CherryRoad Media

THE CLINTON DAILY DEMOCRAT

Street address 1: 212 S Washington St
Street address city: Clinton
Street address state: MO
Zip/Postal code: 64735-2073
County: Henry
Country: USA
Mailing address: PO BOX 586
Mailing city: Clinton
Mailing state: MO
Mailing zip: 64735-0586
General Phone: (660) 885-2281
General/National Adv. E-mail: dailydemocrat@embarqmail.com
Display Adv. E-mail: democrat.ads@embarqmail.com
Classified Adv. e-mail: dem.subscription@embarqmail.com
Editorial e-mail: dailydemocrat@embarqmail.com
Primary Website: www.clintondailydemocrat.com
Year Established: 1868
News Services: NEA.
Special Weekly Sections: Church News (Fri); Conservation/Outdoors (Thur).
Delivery Methods: Mail`Carrier
Areas Served - City/County or Portion Thereof, or Zip codes: Henry County Missouri
Own Printing Facility?: Y
Avg Free Circ: 17187
Audit By: Sworn/Estimate/Non-Audited
Audit Date: 12.07.2019
Personnel: Daniel B. Miles (Pub.); Jim Lawson (Sports Ed.); Mike Gregory (Prodn. Mgr.); Denise Smith (Associate Ed.)
Parent company (for newspapers): Democrat Publishing Co., Inc.

COLUMBIA DAILY TRIBUNE

Street address 1: 313 East Ash Street
Street address city: Columbia
Street address state: MO
Zip/Postal code: 65201
County: Boone
Country: USA
Mailing address: PO BOX 798
Mailing city: COLUMBIA
Mailing state: MO
Mailing zip: 65205-0798
General Phone: (573) 815-1600
Advertising Phone: (573) 815-1800
Editorial Phone: (573) 815-1700
General/National Adv. E-mail: display@columbiatribune.com
Display Adv. E-mail: display@columbiatribune.com
Classified Adv. e-mail: classifieds@columbiatribune.com
Editorial e-mail: editor@columbiatribune.com
Primary Website: www.columbiatribune.com
Year Established: 1901
News Services: AP, TMS, ABC, MPA, NAA
Special Weekly Sections: Food (Wed); Business (Mon-Fri); Entertainment, TV (Thur); Church, (Sat); Home, Travel, Weddings (Sun);
Delivery Methods: Mail`Newsstand`Carrier`Racks
Areas Served - City/County or Portion Thereof, or Zip codes: 65203, 65202, 65201, 65010, 65240, 65255, 65233, 65251, 65270, 65279, 65248, 65265, 65284, 65256, 65039, 65254, 65243, 65274, 65231, 65230, 65259, 65287, 65262, 65043, 65211, 65278, 65216, 65250, 65285, 65109, 65101, 65063
Own Printing Facility?: Y
Commercial printers?: Y
Avg Free Circ: 699
Sat. Circulation Paid: 12665
Sat. Circulation Free: 699
Sun. Circulation Paid: 14872
Sun. Circulation Free: 151
Audit By: AAM
Audit Date: 31.12.2017
Personnel: Terri Leifeste (Pub.); Aaron Consalvi (Adv. Dir.); Marva Miles (Human Resources Manager); Charles Westmoreland (Mng. Ed.); Rudi Keller (News Ed.); Jardyn Angell (Dig. Ed.); Garrick Hodge (Sports Ed.)
Parent company (for newspapers): Gannett; CherryRoad Media

COLUMBIA MISSOURIAN

Street address 1: 221 S 8th St
Street address city: Columbia
Street address state: MO
Zip/Postal code: 65201-4868
County: Boone
Country: USA
Mailing address: PO BOX 917
Mailing city: COLUMBIA
Mailing state: MO
Mailing zip: 65205-0917
General Phone: (573) 882-5700
Advertising Phone: (573) 882-5748
Editorial Phone: (573) 882-5720
General/National Adv. E-mail: advertising@columbiamissourian.com
Display Adv. E-mail: advertising@columbiamissourian.com
Classified Adv. e-mail: advertising@columbiamissourian.com
Editorial e-mail: editor@columbiamissourian.com
Primary Website: www.columbiamissourian.com
Year Established: 1908
News Services: AP
Special Editions: Progress (Growth of Columbia); Tourism (State of MO); Collegetown; Welcome Back; Tiger Kickoffs (Mizzou Football); Homecoming (Mizzou Tigers); Tiger Tipoffs (Mizzou Basketball)
Special Weekly Sections: Vox (Thur.)
Syndicated Publications: Parade (S)
Delivery Methods: Mail`Newsstand`Carrier`Racks
Areas Served - City/County or Portion Thereof, or Zip codes: 65010, 65201, 65202, 65203, 65211, 65212, 65215, 65039, 65240, 65251, 65255, 65256
Own Printing Facility?: N
Sun. Circulation Paid: 6010
Audit By: Sworn/Estimate/Non-Audited
Audit Date: 12.07.2019
Personnel: Dan Potter (Gen. Mgr.); Jeanne Abbott (Managing Ed.); Brian Kratzer (Photo Dir.); Bryan Chester (Adv. Dir.)
Parent company (for newspapers): Missouri Press Association; University of Missouri

THE DAILY STATESMAN

Street address 1: 133 S Walnut St
Street address city: Dexter
Street address state: MO
Zip/Postal code: 63841-2141
County: Stoddard
Country: USA
Mailing address: PO BOX 579
Mailing city: DEXTER
Mailing state: MO
Mailing zip: 63841-0579
General Phone: (573) 624-4545
Advertising Phone: (573) 624-4545
Editorial Phone: (573) 624-4545
General/National Adv. E-mail: mharmon@dailystatesman.com
Display Adv. E-mail: dglenn@dailystatesman.com
Classified Adv. e-mail: dlovins@dailystatesman.com
Editorial e-mail: nhyslop@dailystatesman.com
Primary Website: www.dailystatesman.com
Year Established: 1879
News Services: AP, NEA.
Special Editions: Spring Fashion (Apr); Progress (Feb); Fall Fashion (Sept).
Special Weekly Sections: Food (Wed); Farm, Entertainment (Thur); Church (Fri); Real Estate (Sun)
Syndicated Publications: Farm Monthly (Feb-Nov) (Monthly); Southeast Missouri Farmer (Feb-Nov) (Other); Parade (S).
Delivery Methods: Mail`Carrier`Racks
Own Printing Facility?: Y
Avg Free Circ: 0
Sun. Circulation Paid: 3150
Audit By: Sworn/Estimate/Non-Audited
Audit Date: 12.07.2019
Personnel: Noreen Hyslop (Gen/Manag Ed)
Parent company (for newspapers): Rust Communications

THE FULTON SUN

Street address 1: 115 E 5th St
Street address city: Fulton
Street address state: MO
Zip/Postal code: 65251-1714
County: Callaway
Country: USA
Mailing address: PO BOX 550
Mailing city: FULTON
Mailing state: MO
Mailing zip: 65251-0550
General Phone: (573) 642-7272
Advertising Phone: (573) 826-2415
Editorial Phone: (573) 826-2417
General/National Adv. E-mail: pmcdonald@fultonsun.com
Display Adv. E-mail: display@fultonsun.com
Classified Adv. e-mail: class@fultonsun.com
Editorial e-mail: news@fultonsun.com
Primary Website: www.fultonsun.com
Year Established: 1875
News Services: AP.
Special Editions: Customer Appreciation (Apr); Christmas Greetings (Dec); Women in Business (Jun); Graduation (May); Favorite Recipes (Oct); Senior Style (Quarterly); Sports Preview (Semi-yearly).
Special Weekly Sections: Farm, Health, Food (Wed); TV, Arts, Church (Fri)
Syndicated Publications: Parade (S).
Delivery Methods: Mail`Newsstand`Carrier`Racks
Areas Served - City/County or Portion Thereof, or Zip codes: Callaway County
Avg Free Circ: 9000
Sun. Circulation Paid: 4300
Audit By: Sworn/Estimate/Non-Audited
Audit Date: 12.07.2019
Personnel: Karen Atkins (Ed.); Ryan Boland (Sports Ed.); Pati McDonald (Marketing Manager); Dean Asher (Coord.)
Parent company (for newspapers): WEHCO Media, Inc.

HANNIBAL COURIER-POST

Street address 1: 200 N 3rd St
Street address city: Hannibal
Street address state: MO
Zip/Postal code: 63401-3504
County: Marion
Country: USA
Mailing address: PO BOX A
Mailing city: HANNIBAL
Mailing state: MO
Mailing zip: 63401-0780
General Phone: (573) 221-2800
Advertising Phone: (573) 221-2800
Editorial Phone: (573) 248-2757
General/National Adv. E-mail: jreynolds@gatehousemedia.com
Classified Adv. e-mail: classifieds@courierpost.com
Editorial e-mail: newsroom@courierpost.com
Primary Website: www.hannibal.net
Year Established: 1838
News Services: AP
Special Weekly Sections: Business (Tue); Health, Community (Wed); Education, Auctions (Thur); Religion, Weddings, Community Clubs (Sat)
Syndicated Publications: Relish (Monthly); USA WEEKEND Magazine (Sat); American Profile (Tues).
Delivery Methods: Mail`Newsstand`Carrier
Areas Served - City/County or Portion Thereof, or Zip codes: 63401
Own Printing Facility?: N
Commercial printers?: Y
Avg Free Circ: 70
Sat. Circulation Paid: 4432
Sat. Circulation Free: 38
Audit By: Sworn/Estimate/Non-Audited
Audit Date: 12.07.2019
Personnel: Terri Leifeste (Senior Group Publisher); Jaime Reynolds (Reg. Ad. Dir); Leslie Vanstrien (Bus. Mgr.)
Parent company (for newspapers): Phillips Media Group LLC; CherryRoad Media

THE EXAMINER / EXAMINER WEEKEND

Street address 1: 410 S Liberty St
Street address city: Independence
Street address state: MO
Zip/Postal code: 64050-3805
County: Jackson
Country: USA
Mailing address: 410 S LIBERTY ST
Mailing city: INDEPENDENCE
Mailing state: MO
Mailing zip: 64050-3805
General Phone: (816) 254-8600
Advertising Phone: (816) 350-6383
Editorial Phone: (816) 350-6365
General/National Adv. E-mail: displayads@examiner.net
Display Adv. E-mail: displayads@examiner.net
Classified Adv. e-mail: chris.goff@examiner.net
Editorial e-mail: sheila.davis@examiner.net
Primary Website: www.examiner.net
Year Established: 1898
News Services: AP, SHNS.
Special Editions: Spring Car Care (Apr); Senior Citizens (Aug); Holiday Gift Guide (Dec); Review & Forecast (Feb); Tourist Guide (Jan); Guide to Independence (Jun); Health & Fitness (Mar); Spring Parade of Homes (May); Christmas Opening (Nov); Car Care (Oct); Fall Parade o
Special Weekly Sections: Best Food Day (Wed); Home Life, Family (Tue); Arts, Outdoors (Thur); Education (Fri); Religion, Lifestyles (Sat)
Syndicated Publications: Relish (Monthly); USA WEEKEND Magazine (Sat).
Delivery Methods: Mail`Carrier
Sat. Circulation Paid: 6210
Audit By: VAC
Audit Date: 30.09.2017
Personnel: Deneane Hyde (Bus. Mgr.); Sheila Davis (Exec. Ed.); Karl Zinke (Mng. Ed.); Ryan Kedzierski (Pub.); Tonya Maddox (Adv. Dir.); Julie Moreno (Pub.)
Parent company (for newspapers): CherryRoad Media

NEWS TRIBUNE

Street address 1: 210 Monroe Street
Street address city: Jefferson City
Street address state: MO
Zip/Postal code: 65102
County: Cole
Country: USA
Mailing address: PO BOX 420
Mailing city: JEFFERSON CITY
Mailing state: MO
Mailing zip: 65102-0420
General Phone: (573) 636-3131
Advertising Phone: (573) 761-0228
Editorial Phone: (573) 761-0240
General/National Adv. E-mail: display@newstribune.com
Display Adv. E-mail: display@newstribune.com
Classified Adv. e-mail: class@newstribune.com
Editorial e-mail: editor@newstribune.com
Primary Website: www.newstribune.com
Mthly Avg Views: 1000000
Year Established: 1865
News Services: AP.
Special Editions: Active Times (monthly); Escape (Thursday); Styles (Sunday); Health (Tuesday); Flavors (Wednesday); TV Week (Friday); Church Page (Friday); Real Estate (Friday); Home Living (semi-annual); HER Magazine (bi-monthly)
Special Weekly Sections: Health, Minipage (Tue); Flavor (Wed); Escape (Thur); Church, TV (Fri); Garden (Sun)
Syndicated Publications: Parade (S); HER Magazine (bi-monthly); Home Living (quarterly)
Delivery Methods: Mail`Newsstand`Carrier
Areas Served - City/County or Portion Thereof, or Zip codes: 65001, 65010, 65013, 65014, 65016, 65018, 65023, 65024, 65026, 65032, 65035, 65039, 65043, 65046, 65048, 65049, 65051, 65053, 65054, 65058, 65059, 65061, 65063, 65066, 65074, 65075, 65076, 65080, 65081, 65082, 65084, 65085, 65101, 65109, 65251, 65086, 65582
Own Printing Facility?: Y
Commercial printers?: Y
Avg Free Circ: 346
Sat. Circulation Paid: 11446
Sat. Circulation Free: 346
Sun. Circulation Paid: 14675
Sun. Circulation Free: 191
Audit By: AAM
Audit Date: 30.09.2017
Personnel: Walter E. Hussman (Pub.); Jane Haslag (Adv. Mgr.); Gary Castor (Mng. Ed.); Tom Rackers (Sports Ed.); Michael Johns (Circ. Mgr.); Terri Leifeste (Gen. Mgr.); Mike Johns (Circ. Mgr.)
Parent company (for newspapers): WEHCO Media, Inc.

THE JOPLIN GLOBE

Street address 1: 117 E 4th St
Street address city: Joplin
Street address state: MO
Zip/Postal code: 64801-2302

County: Jasper
Country: USA
Mailing address: 117 E 4th St
Mailing city: Joplin
Mailing state: MO
Mailing zip: 64801-2302
General Phone: (417) 623-3480
Advertising Phone: (417) 781-5500
Editorial Phone: (417) 627-7281
General/National Adv. E-mail: publisher@joplinglobe.com
Display Adv. E-mail: jcombs@joplinglobe.com
Classified Adv. e-mail: sfitzjohn@joplinglobe.com
Editorial e-mail: aostmeyer@joplinglobe.com
Primary Website: www.joplinglobe.com
Mthly Avg Views: 1334695
Mthly Avg Unique Visitors: 301356
Year Established: 1896
News Services: AP.
Special Editions: Silver Enquirer (Monthly);
Special Weekly Sections: Best Food Day (Wed); Health & Family (Thur); Real Estate, Comics, Etc Entertainment (Sat)
Syndicated Publications: Parade (S).
Delivery Methods: Mail`Newsstand`Carrier`Racks
Areas Served - City/County or Portion Thereof, or Zip codes: Jasper, Newton, McDonald, Lawrence, Barton, Vernon Counties in Missouri. Crawford and Cherokee Counties in Kansas. Ottawa and Delaware Counties in Oklahoma
Avg Free Circ: 2060
Sat. Circulation Paid: 13014
Sat. Circulation Free: 698
Sun. Circulation Paid: 17768
Sun. Circulation Free: 372
Audit By: Sworn/Estimate/Non-Audited
Personnel: Andy Ostmeyer (Editor); Frank Leto (Pub.); Carol Stark (Ed.); Michael Stair (Night Ed.); Joe Hadsall (Dig. Ed.); Jim Henry (Sports Ed.); Jack Kaminsky (Director of Production); Kevin McClintock (Features Ed.); Jamie Strickland (Advertising Director); Dale Brendel (Publisher); Daniel Kuhns (Director of Audience Development); Bob Barth (Adv. Dir.); Dave Starchman (Prod. Dir.)
Parent company (for newspapers): CNHI, LLC; CNHI, LLC; Community Newspaper Holdings, Inc.

THE KANSAS CITY STAR

Street address 1: 1729 Grand Blvd
Street address city: Kansas City
Street address state: MO
Zip/Postal code: 64108-1413
County: Jackson
Country: USA
Mailing address: 1729 GRAND BLVD
Mailing city: KANSAS CITY
Mailing state: MO
Mailing zip: 64108-1458
General Phone: (816) 234-4636
Advertising Phone: (816) 234-4636
Editorial Phone: (816) 234-4900
General/National Adv. E-mail: mjolles@kcstar.com
Display Adv. E-mail: mjolles@kcstar.com
Classified Adv. e-mail: classfeedback@kcstar.com
Editorial e-mail: tberg@kcstar.com
Primary Website: www.kansascity.com
Mthly Avg Views: 30000000
Mthly Avg Unique Visitors: 4000000
Year Established: 1880
News Services: AP, MCT, NYT.
Special Editions: Lawn, Garden & Home (Apr); Diaper Days II (Aug); Holiday Religion (Dec); Remodeling & Decorating Expo (Feb); American Heart Association (Jan); Active Times (Jul); Progress (Jun); Recycling (Mar); Lawn, Garden & Home (May); The Star Gift Guide I (Nov); The
Special Weekly Sections: Sports (Mon); Business (Tue); Auto, Food, Neighborhood News (Wed); Entertainment (Thur); FYI (Fri); Auto, Faith, Neighborhood News (Sat); Travel, Home, Arts, Outdoor, Comics, Real Estate (Sun)
Syndicated Publications: Parade (S).
Delivery Methods: Mail`Newsstand`Carrier`Racks
Own Printing Facility?: Y
Commercial printers?: Y
Sat. Circulation Paid: 95302
Sun. Circulation Paid: 142283
Audit By: AAM
Audit Date: 30.06.2018

Personnel: Bryan Harbison (Vice President, Finance); Mike Fannin (Ed.); Lee Judge (Cartoonist); Joe Coleman (Prod. Dev. Dir.); Isaac Hindle (Marketing Analyst); Tony Berg (Pres./Pub.); Greg Farmer (Mng. Ed.)
Parent company (for newspapers): The McClatchy Company; Chatham Asset Management

THE DAILY DUNKLIN DEMOCRAT

Street address 1: 203 1st St
Street address city: Kennett
Street address state: MO
Zip/Postal code: 63857-2052
County: Dunklin
Country: USA
Mailing address: PO BOX 669
Mailing city: KENNETT
Mailing state: MO
Mailing zip: 63857-0669
General Phone: (573) 888-4505
Advertising Phone: (573) 888-4505
Editorial Phone: (573) 888-4505
General/National Adv. E-mail: awright@dddnews.com
Display Adv. E-mail: tcoleman@dddnews.com
Classified Adv. e-mail: cfolkes@dddnews.com
Editorial e-mail: mrasberry@dddnews.com
Primary Website: www.dddnews.com
Year Established: 1888
News Services: AP.
Special Editions: Progress (Mar). Newcomer's (Jul)
Special Weekly Sections: Food (Wed); School (Tue/Thur); Religion, Real Estate (Fri); Seniors (Thur)
Syndicated Publications: Relish (Monthly); Parade (S); American Profile (Weekly).
Delivery Methods: Mail`Newsstand`Carrier`Racks
Avg Free Circ: 5250
Sun. Circulation Paid: 3600
Audit By: Sworn/Estimate/Non-Audited
Audit Date: 12.07.2019
Personnel: Debbie Wright (Office Mgr.); Michelle Rasberry (Interim Ed.); Terri Coleman (Adv. Mgr.); Dustin Ward (Sports Ed.); Ron Kemp (Pub.); George Anderson (Managing Ed.); Regina Lee (Circ. Mgr.); Cody Tucker (Office Mgr.)
Parent company (for newspapers): Rust Communications

KIRKSVILLE DAILY EXPRESS

Street address 1: 110 E McPherson St
Street address city: Kirksville
Street address state: MO
Zip/Postal code: 63501-3506
County: Adair
Country: USA
Mailing address: PO BOX 809
Mailing city: KIRKSVILLE
Mailing state: MO
Mailing zip: 63501-0809
General Phone: (660) 665-2808
Advertising Phone: (660) 665-2808
Editorial Phone: (660) 665-2808
General/National Adv. E-mail: gwriedt@kirksvilledailyexpress.com
Display Adv. E-mail: ads@kirksvilledailyexpress.com
Classified Adv. e-mail: ads@kirksvilledailyexpress.com
Editorial e-mail: dailyexpresseditor@gmail.com
Primary Website: www.kirksvilledailyexpress.com
Year Established: 1901
News Services: AP.
Special Editions: Progress (Jul).
Special Weekly Sections: Entertainment (Thur); Religion (Fri); Business, Finance, Real Estate, Home, Living, Food (Sun)
Syndicated Publications: American Profile (S).
Delivery Methods: Mail`Newsstand`Carrier
Areas Served - City/County or Portion Thereof, or Zip codes: Adair County
Avg Free Circ: 14000
Sun. Circulation Paid: 4263
Audit By: Sworn/Estimate/Non-Audited
Audit Date: 12.07.2019
Personnel: Larry W. Freels (Pub./Bus. Mgr.); George Wriedt (Adv. Mgr.); Carole Murphy (Classified Ads. Mgr.); Jason Hunsicker (Ed.)
Parent company (for newspapers): Phillips Media Group LLC; CherryRoad Media

THE LEBANON DAILY RECORD

Street address 1: 100 E Commercial St
Street address city: Lebanon
Street address state: MO
Zip/Postal code: 65536-3257
County: Laclede
Country: USA
Mailing address: PO BOX 192
Mailing city: LEBANON
Mailing state: MO
Mailing zip: 65536-0192
General Phone: (417) 532-9131
Advertising Phone: (417) 532-9131
Editorial Phone: (417) 532-9131
General/National Adv. E-mail: jennifer@lebanondailyrecord.com
Display Adv. E-mail: jennifer@lebanondailyrecord.com
Classified Adv. e-mail: jennifer@lebanondailyrecord.com
Editorial e-mail: fmassey@lebanondailyrecord.com
Primary Website: www.lebanondailyrecord.com
Mthly Avg Views: 151170
Mthly Avg Unique Visitors: 46000
Year Established: 1934
News Services: AP.
Special Editions: Back-to-School (Aug); Progress (Feb); Fair Tab (Jul); Welcome to Lebanon (Jul); Welcome to Bennett Sring (Dec); Senior Living (Monthly); Winter Sports (Nov).
Special Weekly Sections: Agriculture (Tue); Food (Wed); Religion (Fri)
Syndicated Publications: Senior Living (Monthly); American Profile (Weekly); Relish (Monthly).
Delivery Methods: Mail`Newsstand`Carrier`Racks
Areas Served - City/County or Portion Thereof, or Zip codes: 65536, 65622, 65632, 65667, 65662, 65590, 65722, 65556, 65567
Own Printing Facility?: N
Commercial printers?: Y
Avg Free Circ: 2000
Sat. Circulation Paid: 4300
Audit By: Sworn/Estimate/Non-Audited
Audit Date: 12.07.2019
Personnel: Dalton C. Wright (Pres./Pub.); Julie Turner (Ed.); Rene Barker (Adv. Mgr.)
Parent company (for newspapers): Lebanon Publishing Co.

THE MARSHALL DEMOCRAT-NEWS

Street address 1: 121 N Lafayette Ave
Street address city: Marshall
Street address state: MO
Zip/Postal code: 65340-1747
County: Saline
Country: USA
Mailing address: PO BOX 100
Mailing city: MARSHALL
Mailing state: MO
Mailing zip: 65340-0100
General Phone: (660) 886-2233
Advertising Phone: (660) 886-2233
Editorial Phone: (660) 815-0258
General/National Adv. E-mail: mdavis@marshallnews.com
Display Adv. E-mail: mdavis@marshallnews.com
Classified Adv. e-mail: stevis@marshallnews.com
Editorial e-mail: ecrump@marshallnews.com
Primary Website: www.marshallnews.com
Year Established: 1879
News Services: AP.
Special Weekly Sections: Agriculture, Health, Food (Tue); Business, NIE (Thur); Weddings, Church (Fri)
Syndicated Publications: TV Preview (Fri); Relish (Monthly).
Delivery Methods: Mail`Racks
Avg Free Circ: 8586
Audit By: Sworn/Estimate/Non-Audited
Audit Date: 12.07.2019
Personnel: Dave Phillips (Pub.); Mike Davis (Adv. Mgr.); Pat Morrow (Circ. Mgr.); Eric Crump (Ed.); Chris Allen (Sports Ed.)
Parent company (for newspapers): Rust Communications

THE MARYVILLE DAILY FORUM

Street address 1: 111 E Jenkins St
Street address city: Maryville
Street address state: MO
Zip/Postal code: 64468-2318
County: Nodaway
Country: USA
Mailing address: PO BOX 188
Mailing city: MARYVILLE
Mailing state: MO
Mailing zip: 64468-0188
General Phone: (660) 562-2424
Advertising Phone: (660) 562-2424
Editorial Phone: (660) 562-2424
General/National Adv. E-mail: kholtman@maryvilledailyforum.com
Display Adv. E-mail: kholtman@maryvilledailyforum.com
Classified Adv. e-mail: rpiveral@maryvilledailyforum.com
Editorial e-mail: skyep@maryvilledailyforum.com
Primary Website: www.maryvilledailyforum.com
Mthly Avg Views: 270000
Mthly Avg Unique Visitors: 75000
Year Established: 1869
News Services: AP.
Special Editions: Real Estate (Aug); Holiday Gift Guide (Dec); Progress (Jan); Newcomers (Jul); Fair (Jun); Spring Home Improvement (Mar); Real Estate (May); Fall Sports (Football) (Sept).
Special Weekly Sections: Agriculture, high school, community life
Syndicated Publications: American Profile (S); TV Forum (Thur).
Delivery Methods: Mail`Newsstand`Racks
Areas Served - City/County or Portion Thereof, or Zip codes: 64468
Own Printing Facility?: N
Commercial printers?: N
Avg Free Circ: 18500
Audit By: Sworn/Estimate/Non-Audited
Audit Date: 12.07.2019
Personnel: Phil Cobb (Pub.); Lana Cobb (Business Mgr)
Parent company (for newspapers): Cobb Publishing, LLC

MEXICO LEDGER

Street address 1: 300 N Washington St
Street address city: Mexico
Street address state: MO
Zip/Postal code: 65265-2756
County: Audrain
Country: USA
Mailing address: PO BOX 8
Mailing city: MEXICO
Mailing state: MO
Mailing zip: 65265-0008
General Phone: (573) 581-1111
Advertising Phone: (573) 581-1111
Editorial Phone: (573) 581-1111
General/National Adv. E-mail: mkeller@mexicoledger.com
Display Adv. E-mail: display@mexicoledger.com
Classified Adv. e-mail: bfike@socket.net
Editorial e-mail: news@mexicoledger.com
Primary Website: www.mexicoledger.com
Year Established: 1855
News Services: AP, SHNS.
Special Editions: Home Improvement (Apr); Football (Aug); Progress (Feb); Hometown (Jun); Car Care (Mar); Christmas Kick-Off (Nov); Back-to-School (Oct).
Special Weekly Sections: Food (Tue/Wed); Entertainment, Amusement, Business, Finance (Daily); Church (Fri);
Syndicated Publications: Relish (Monthly); American Profile (Sat).
Delivery Methods: Mail`Carrier`Racks
Areas Served - City/County or Portion Thereof, or Zip codes: Audrain County
Avg Free Circ: 10820
Audit By: Sworn/Estimate/Non-Audited
Audit Date: 12.07.2019
Personnel: Janeen Sims (Ed.); Brenda Fike (News Ed.); Jim Stanley (Sports Ed.); Martin Keller (Adv. Mgr.); Joe May (Pub.)
Parent company (for newspapers): Westplex Media Group; CherryRoad Media

THE MOBERLY MONITOR-INDEX

Street address 1: 218 N Williams St
Street address city: Moberly
Street address state: MO
Zip/Postal code: 65270-1534
County: Randolph
Country: USA
General Phone: (660) 263-4123
Advertising Phone: (660) 263-4123
Editorial Phone: (660) 263-4123
General/National Adv. E-mail: advertising@moberlymonitor.com
Display Adv. E-mail: advertising@moberlymonitor.com

Classified Adv. e-mail: nbartolacci@moberlymonitor.com
Editorial e-mail: alindley@moberlymonitor.com
Primary Website: www.moberlymonitor.com
Year Established: 1869
News Services: AP, NEA, TMS.
Special Editions: Chamber Tab (Apr); Back-to-School (Aug); Christmas Greetings (Dec); Valentine Hearts (Feb); Bridal (Jan); County Fairs (Jul); Spring Bridal (Jun); Progress (Mar); Graduation (May); Cookbook (Nov); Fall Fashion (Sept).
Special Weekly Sections: Food, Coupon (Tue); Dining (Wed); Business, Church (Thur); TV Spotlight (Fri)
Syndicated Publications: Business Review (Fri); 50 Something (Monthly); American Profile (S); Youth Today (Tues).
Avg Free Circ: 700
Sun. Circulation Paid: 5342
Audit By: Sworn/Estimate/Non-Audited
Audit Date: 12.07.2019
Personnel: Terri Leifeste (Reg. Pub.); Allen Fennewald (Regional News Ed.); Nancy Bartolacci (Classified Ads)
Parent company (for newspapers): CherryRoad Media; Westplex Media Group

THE MONETT TIMES

Street address 1: 505 E Broadway St
Street address city: Monett
Street address state: MO
Zip/Postal code: 65708-2333
County: Barry
Country: USA
Mailing address: PO BOX 40
Mailing city: MONETT
Mailing state: MO
Mailing zip: 65708-0040
General Phone: (417) 235-3135
General/National Adv. E-mail: community@monett-times.com
Display Adv. E-mail: community@monett-times.com
Classified Adv. e-mail: classifieds@monett-times.com
Editorial e-mail: editor@monett-times.com
Primary Website: www.monett-times.com
Year Established: 1908
News Services: AP
Special Editions: Christmas (Dec); Progress (Feb); Football (Oct); Basketball (Other).
Special Weekly Sections: Auctions (Wed)
Syndicated Publications: American Profile (Weekly).
Delivery Methods: Mail`Racks
Avg Free Circ: 7400
Audit By: Sworn/Estimate/Non-Audited
Audit Date: 12.07.2019
Personnel: Murray Bishoff (Mng. Ed.); Kyle Troutman (Ed.)
Parent company (for newspapers): Rust Communications

NEOSHO DAILY NEWS

Street address 1: 1000 W Harmony St
Street address city: Neosho
Street address state: MO
Zip/Postal code: 64850-1631
County: Newton
Country: USA
Mailing address: PO BOX 848
Mailing city: NEOSHO
Mailing state: MO
Mailing zip: 64850-0848
General Phone: (417) 451-1520
Advertising Phone: (417) 451-1520
Editorial Phone: (417) 451-1520
General/National Adv. E-mail: rburtis@gatehousemedia.com
Display Adv. E-mail: rburtis@gatehousemedia.com
Classified Adv. e-mail: ndnclassifieds@sbcglobal.net
Editorial e-mail: editor@neoshodailynews.com
Primary Website: www.neoshodailynews.com
Year Established: 1905
News Services: AP
Special Editions: City-Wide Garage Sale (Apr); Back-to-School (Aug); Christmas Greetings (Dec); Year of Progress (Feb); Babies of Last Year (Jan); Fair Tabs (Jul); Lawn & Garden (Mar); Graduation (May); Holiday Gift Guide (Nov); Our Town (Oct).
Special Weekly Sections: Education (Wed); Religion (Fri); Seniors (Sun); Business (Sun)
Syndicated Publications: American Profile (Weekly).
Delivery Methods: Mail`Newsstand`Carrier`Racks
Own Printing Facility?: Y
Commercial printers?: Y
Audit By: Sworn/Estimate/Non-Audited
Audit Date: 12.07.2019
Personnel: Patrick Richardson (Ed.); Tim Holder (Reg. Adv. Dir.); Brock Sisney (Sports Ed.); Joe Leong (Pub.); Koni Tyler (Adv.); Lauren Busteed (Office Mgr.)
Parent company (for newspapers): CherryRoad Media; Sexton Media Group

THE NEVADA DAILY MAIL

Street address 1: 131 S Cedar St
Street address city: Nevada
Street address state: MO
Zip/Postal code: 64772-3309
County: Vernon
Country: USA
Mailing address: PO BOX 247
Mailing city: NEVADA
Mailing state: MO
Mailing zip: 64772-0247
General Phone: (417) 667-3344
Advertising Phone: (417) 667-3344
Editorial Phone: (417) 667-3344
General/National Adv. E-mail: advertising@nevadadailymail.com
Display Adv. E-mail: advertising@nevadadailymail.com
Classified Adv. e-mail: advertising@nevadadailymail.com
Editorial e-mail: editorial@nevadadailymail.com
Primary Website: www.nevadadailymail.com
Year Established: 1883
News Services: AP, NEA.
Special Editions: Back-to-School (Aug); Christmas Shoppers (Dec); Brides (Jan); Home Improvement (Mar); Graduation (May); Puzzle Pages (Monthly); Home Improvement (Oct).
Special Weekly Sections: Menus (Wed); Church, Senior (Fri)
Syndicated Publications: SHE; AGELESS
Delivery Methods: Mail`Newsstand`Racks
Own Printing Facility?: Y
Commercial printers?: Y
Avg Free Circ: 17000
Audit By: Sworn/Estimate/Non-Audited
Audit Date: 12.07.2019
Personnel: Sharon Knight (Pub.); Lorie Harter (Adv. Dir.); Lynn Wade (Ed.); Sharyon Duke (Lifestyles Ed.); Chris Jones (Prodn. Mgr.); Shirley Johnson (Circ. Supvr.)
Parent company (for newspapers): Rust Communications

DAILY JOURNAL, PARK HILLS

Street address 1: 1513 S Saint Joe Dr
Street address city: Park Hills
Street address state: MO
Zip/Postal code: 63601-2402
County: Saint Francois
Country: USA
Mailing address: PO BOX 9
Mailing city: PARK HILLS
Mailing state: MO
Mailing zip: 63601-0009
General Phone: (573) 431-2010
Advertising Phone: (573) 431-2010
Editorial Phone: (573) 518-3615
General/National Adv. E-mail: lstarkey@dailyjournalonline.com
Display Adv. E-mail: advertising@dailyjournalonline.com
Classified Adv. e-mail: lmaize@dailyjournalonline.com
Editorial e-mail: editorial@dailyjournalonline.com
Primary Website: www.dailyjournalonline.com
Mthly Avg Views: 2242184
Mthly Avg Unique Visitors: 240169
Year Established: 1935
News Services: NEA, AP, TMS.
Special Editions: Family Disaster Preparedness; Family Owned Business; Memorial Day, Camping Guide, Spring Body and More; Automotive Service Guide; New Year New You; Info Guide, Life Planning Guide, Business Card Directory
Special Weekly Sections: Daily Journal Weekly Real Estate
Delivery Methods: Mail`Newsstand`Carrier`Racks
Areas Served - City/County or Portion Thereof, or Zip codes: St. Francois County, MO and portions of adjacent counties
Own Printing Facility?: N
Commercial printers?: N
Avg Free Circ: 165
Sat. Circulation Paid: 4978
Sat. Circulation Free: 49
Audit By: AAM
Audit Date: 30.09.2014
Personnel: Gary Berblinger (Pub.); Doug Smith (Managing Ed.); Donn Adamson (Sports Ed.); Angel King (Circulation Manager); Jamila Khalil (Advertising Director); Teresa Ressel (Ed.)
Parent company (for newspapers): Dispatch-Argus; Lee Enterprises, Incorporated

DAILY AMERICAN REPUBLIC

Street address 1: PO Box 7
Street address city: Poplar Bluff
Street address state: MO
Zip/Postal code: 63902-0007
County: Butler
Country: USA
Mailing address: PO BOX 7
Mailing city: POPLAR BLUFF
Mailing state: MO
Mailing zip: 63902-0007
General Phone: (573) 785-1414
Advertising Phone: (573) 785-1414
Editorial Phone: (573) 785-1414
General/National Adv. E-mail: ads@darnews.com
Display Adv. E-mail: cpierce@darnews.com
Classified Adv. e-mail: cpierce@darnews.com
Editorial e-mail: sberry@darnews.com
Primary Website: www.darnews.com
Year Established: 1869
News Services: AP, NYT.
Special Weekly Sections: Regional (Mon); Education (Tue); Food, Business (Wed); Outdoors (Thur); TV, Religion (Fri); Lifestyles (Sun)
Syndicated Publications: USA Weekend, Parade (Sun).
Delivery Methods: Mail`Newsstand`Carrier`Racks
Areas Served - City/County or Portion Thereof, or Zip codes: Butler County
Own Printing Facility?: Y
Commercial printers?: Y
Sat. Circulation Paid: 7653
Sun. Circulation Paid: 8824
Sun. Circulation Free: 0
Audit By: CAC
Audit Date: 31.03.2014
Personnel: Don Schrieber (Publisher); Rachel Coleman (Bus. Mgr./Controller); Stan Berry (Editor); Barbara Horton (News Ed.); Brian Rosener (Sports Ed.); Randy Graves (Prodn. Foreman, Pressroom); Christy Pierce (Advertising Director); Joe Jordan (Adv. Dir.); Gary Richard (Circ. Dir.); Michele Friedrich (Lifestyle Ed.); Dorothy Carlson (Religion Ed.)
Parent company (for newspapers): Rust Communications

ROLLA DAILY NEWS

Street address 1: 101 W 7th St
Street address city: Rolla
Street address state: MO
Zip/Postal code: 65401-3243
County: Phelps
Country: USA
Mailing address: PO BOX 808
Mailing city: ROLLA
Mailing state: MO
Mailing zip: 65402-0808
General Phone: (573) 364-2468
Advertising Phone: (573) 364-2468
Editorial Phone: (573) 364-2468
General/National Adv. E-mail: mburns@therolladailynews.com
Display Adv. E-mail: mpence@gatehousemedia.com
Classified Adv. e-mail: mpence@gatehousemedia.com
Editorial e-mail: LynnBrennan@therolladailynews.com
Primary Website: www.therolladailynews.com
Year Established: 1880
News Services: AP.
Special Editions: Fashion (Apr); Back-to-School (Aug); Car Care (Dec); Newcomers (Feb); Bridal (Jan); Progress (Jul); Lawn & Garden (Mar); Christmas (Nov); Car Care (Oct); Welcome Back Students (College) (Sept).
Syndicated Publications: Best Food Days (Tue/Thur); Health, TV (Fri); Comics (Daily)
Areas Served - City/County or Portion Thereof, or Zip codes: Rolla, St. James Newburg, Doolittle, Edgar Springs, Phelps County
Avg Free Circ: 15600
Sat. Circulation Paid: 4875
Audit By: Sworn/Estimate/Non-Audited
Audit Date: 12.07.2019
Personnel: Lynn Brennan (Ed.); Paul Hackbarth (Managing Ed.); Marcia Burns (Adv. Dir.); Dave Roberts (Sports Ed.); Melissa Pence (Nat'l Adv. Rep.)
Parent company (for newspapers): Phillips Media Group LLC; CherryRoad Media

ST. CHARLES COUNTY BUSINESS RECORD

Street address 1: 125 N Main St
Street address city: Saint Charles
Street address state: MO
Zip/Postal code: 63301-2800
County: Saint Charles
Country: USA
Mailing address: 125 N. Main St. St. Charles, MO 63301
Mailing city: SAINT CHARLES
Mailing state: MO
Mailing zip: 63301
General Phone: (636) 949-6928
Advertising Phone: (314) 558-3257
Editorial Phone: (314) 558-3221
General/National Adv. E-mail: johnny.aguirre@molawyersmedia.com
Display Adv. E-mail: johnny.aguirre@molawyersmedia.com
Editorial e-mail: fred.ehrlich@molawyersmedia.com
Delivery Methods: Mail`Newsstand
Areas Served - City/County or Portion Thereof, or Zip codes: 63301
Commercial printers?: Y
Avg Free Circ: 150
Audit By: Sworn/Estimate/Non-Audited
Audit Date: 12.07.2019
Personnel: Liz Irwin (Pub); Fred Ehrlich (Ed); John Reno (Produ Mgr); Johnny Aguirre (Advt Dir); Amanda Passmore (Bus Mgr); Karie Clark (Public Notice Mgr)
Parent company (for newspapers): CherryRoad Media

ST. JOSEPH NEWS-PRESS

Street address 1: 825 Edmond St
Street address city: Saint Joseph
Street address state: MO
Zip/Postal code: 64501-2737
County: Buchanan
Country: USA
Mailing address: PO BOX 29
Mailing city: SAINT JOSEPH
Mailing state: MO
Mailing zip: 64502-0029
General Phone: (816) 271-8500
Advertising Phone: (816) 271-8666
Editorial Phone: (816) 271-8550
General/National Adv. E-mail: susan.white@newspressnow.com
Display Adv. E-mail: tim.weddle@newspressnow.com
Classified Adv. e-mail: classified@newspressnow.com
Editorial e-mail: dennis.ellsworth@newspressnow.com
Primary Website: www.newspressnow.com
Year Established: 1845
News Services: AP, MCT.
Special Editions: Bridal (Jan); Progress Edition (Mar); Foodball (Aug/Sept); Gift Guide (Nov/Dec)
Special Weekly Sections: Health (Tue); Business, Finance (Tue-Sun); Best Food Day, Employment (Wed); Entertainment (Fri); Auto (Sat); Employment (Sun)
Syndicated Publications: Parade (S).
Delivery Methods: Mail`Newsstand`Carrier`Racks
Own Printing Facility?: Y
Commercial printers?: Y
Avg Free Circ: 1441
Sat. Circulation Paid: 18319
Sat. Circulation Free: 1441
Sun. Circulation Paid: 21126
Sun. Circulation Free: 335
Audit By: AAM
Audit Date: 31.03.2018
Personnel: Dennis Ellsworth (Exec. Ed.); Tim Weddle (Adv. Dir.); Ross Martin (Sports Ed.); Dan Dozar (News Dir.); Stacey Hill (Dir of Adv/Sales); Lee M. Sawyer (Gen. Mgr.); David Bradley (Pub.); Susan White (Nat'l Adv. Mgr.); Tony Luke (Retail Adv. Mgr.)
Parent company (for newspapers): News-Press & Gazette Co.

ST. LOUIS POST-DISPATCH

Street address 1: 900 N Tucker Blvd
Street address city: Saint Louis
Street address state: MO
Zip/Postal code: 63101-1069

County: Saint Louis City
Country: USA
Mailing address: 900 N TUCKER BLVD
Mailing city: SAINT LOUIS
Mailing state: MO
Mailing zip: 63101-1099
General Phone: (314) 340-8000
Advertising Phone: (314) 340-8500
Editorial Phone: (314) 340-8387
General/National Adv. E-mail: dbischoff@post-dispatch.com
Display Adv. E-mail: dbischoff@post-dispatch.com
Classified Adv. e-mail: dbischoff@post-dispatch.com
Editorial e-mail: gbailon@post-dispatch.com
Primary Website: www.stltoday.com
Mthly Avg Views: 63671939
Mthly Avg Unique Visitors: 7744856
Year Established: 1878
News Services: AP, MCT, LAT-WP, NYT, RN, SHNS.
Special Editions: Top 100 Restaurants, Baseball Preview, Golf Preview, GO! List, Summer Fun, Hockey Preview, Holiday Gift Guide
Special Weekly Sections: STL Life (Sunday) Let's Eat (Wednesday), GO! (Friday)
Syndicated Publications: Parade
Delivery Methods: Mail`Newsstand`Carrier`Racks
Areas Served - City/County or Portion Thereof, or Zip codes: 62001 62002 62010 62012 62014 62018 62020 62021 62022 62024 62025 62026 62028 62034 62035 62037 62040 62046 62048 62052 62058 62060 62061 62062 62067 62074 62084 62087 62088 62090 62093 62095 62097 62201 62203 62204 62205 62206 62207 62208 62215 62216 62218 62219 62220 62221 62223 62225 62226 62230 62231 62232 62234 62236 62239 62240 62243 62244 62245 62248 62249 62250 62253 62254 62255 62257 62258 62260 62264 62265 62269 62278 62281 62282 62285 62289 62293 62294 62295 62298 63005 63010 63011 63012 63013 63015 63016 63017 63019 63020 63021 63023 63025 63026 63028 63030 63031 63033 63034 63037 63038 63039 63040 63041 63042 63043 63044 63045 63048 63049 63050 63051 63052 63055 63056 63068 63069 63070 63072 63073 63074 63077 63080 63084 63088 63089 63090 63101 63102 63103 63104 63105 63106 63107 63108 63109 63110 63111 63112 63113 63114 63115 63116 63117 63118 63119 63120 63121 63122 63123 63124 63125 63126 63127 63128 63129 63130 63131 63132 63133 63134 63135 63136 63137 63138 63139 63140 63141 63143 63144 63145 63146 63147 63301 63303 63304 63332 63338 63341 63343 63346 63347 63348 63349 63357 63362 63365 63366 63367 63368 63369 63373 63376 63379 63380 63383 63385 63386 63389 63390
Own Printing Facility?: Y
Commercial printers?: Y
Sat. Circulation Paid: 103796
Sun. Circulation Paid: 103796
Audit By: AAM
Audit Date: 30.09.2018
Personnel: Gilbert Bailon (Editor); Teresa Griffin (Digital Sales Director); Susan Eckert (Director of Major & National Adv.); Donna Bischoff (VP, Advertising); Gary Hairlson (Multimedia Director); Lisa Brown (Business Editor); Marcia Koenig (Metro Editor); Tod Robberson (Editorial Page Editor); Christopher Ave (Political and National Editor); Roger Hensley (Sports Editor); Amy Bertrand (Features Editor); Lisa Clark (VP of Market Development (Marketing, Research, PR & Media Relations))
Parent company (for newspapers): Lee Enterprises, Incorporated

THE SEDALIA DEMOCRAT

Street address 1: 700 S Massachusetts Ave
Street address city: Sedalia
Street address state: MO
Zip/Postal code: 65301-4548
County: Pettis
Country: USA
Mailing address: PO BOX 848
Mailing city: SEDALIA
Mailing state: MO
Mailing zip: 65302-0848
General Phone: (660) 826-1000
Advertising Phone: (660) 826-1000
Editorial Phone: (660) 826-1000
General/National Adv. E-mail: news@sedaliademocrat.com
Display Adv. E-mail: advertising@sedaliademocrat.com
Classified Adv. e-mail: theclassifieds@sedaliademocrat.com
Editorial e-mail: editor@sedaliademocrat.com
Primary Website: www.sedaliademocrat.com
Year Established: 1868
News Services: AP.
Special Editions: Back-to-School (Aug); Progress (Feb); Tax Guide (Jan); Newcomers (Jun); Farm (Mar).
Special Weekly Sections: Education (Mon); Editorial (Wed); Religion (Thur); Entertainment, Arts (Fri); High School Sport, Rural life, Weddings, Seniors, Editorial, Engagements (Sat)
Syndicated Publications: Relish (Monthly); TV Week Magazine (S); American Profile (Weekly).
Delivery Methods: Mail`Newsstand`Carrier`Racks
Avg Free Circ: 511
Sat. Circulation Paid: 5786
Sat. Circulation Free: 208
Audit By: CAC
Audit Date: 30.09.2014
Personnel: Denny Koenders (Publisher); Bob Satnan (Ed.); Kyle Smith (Sports Ed.); Richard Desort (Webmaster/Data Processing Mgr.); Dave Mullies (Prodn., Commercial Sales); Henry Holtzclaw (Prodn. Mgr., Mailroom); Will Weibert (Pub.); Nicole Cooke (Ed.)
Parent company (for newspapers): Phillips Media Group LLC

STANDARD DEMOCRAT

Street address 1: 205 S New Madrid St
Street address city: Sikeston
Street address state: MO
Zip/Postal code: 63801-2953
County: Scott
Country: USA
Mailing address: 205 S NEW MADRID ST
Mailing city: SIKESTON
Mailing state: MO
Mailing zip: 63801-2953
General Phone: (573) 471-1137
Advertising Phone: (573) 471-4141
Editorial Phone: (800) 675-6980
General/National Adv. E-mail: donc@standard-democrat.com
Display Adv. E-mail: dnelson@standard-democrat.com
Classified Adv. e-mail: class@standard-democrat.com
Editorial e-mail: news@standard-democrat.com
Primary Website: www.standard-democrat.com
Year Established: 1913
News Services: AP.
Special Editions: Real Estate Guide (Jun); YMCA (Spring 2013); Bright Holiday Wishes (2012); Veterans Day; About Us (2012)
Special Weekly Sections: Best Food Day (Wed); Real Estate, Church (Fri); Business, Finance, Dining, Wedding, Engagements (Sun)
Syndicated Publications: Parade (S).
Delivery Methods: Mail`Newsstand`Carrier`Racks
Areas Served - City/County or Portion Thereof, or Zip codes: Scott County
Sun. Circulation Paid: 4748
Audit By: CAC
Audit Date: 30.09.2014
Personnel: Don Culbertson (CEO); Michael L. Jensen (Pub.); Gary Rust (Co-Owner); DeAnna Nelson (Gen. Mgr.); Merlin Hagy (Circ. Mgr.); Jill Bock (News Ed.); Shawn Crawford (Classified Mgr.)
Parent company (for newspapers): Rust Communications

SPRINGFIELD NEWS-LEADER

Street address 1: 651 N Boonville Ave
Street address city: Springfield
Street address state: MO
Zip/Postal code: 65806-1005
County: Greene
Country: USA
Mailing address: PO BOX 798
Mailing city: SPRINGFIELD
Mailing state: MO
Mailing zip: 65801-0798
General Phone: (417) 836-1100
Advertising Phone: (417) 836-1108
Editorial Phone: (417) 836-1199
General/National Adv. E-mail: NationalAdManager@news-leader.com
Display Adv. E-mail: AdDirector@news-leader.com
Classified Adv. e-mail: ClassifiedManager@news-leader.com
Editorial e-mail: Letters@news-leader.com
Primary Website: www.news-leader.com
Year Established: 1867
News Services: AP, GNS, NYT, TMS, LAT-WP.
Special Editions: Garden (Apr); Progress (Feb); New Contruction (Jan); New Construction (Jul); Destinations (May); Coupon Clippers (Monthly); Holiday Gift Guide (Nov); New Construction (Oct); Progress (Sept).
Special Weekly Sections: E-Commerce (Mon); Health (Tue); Best Food Day, Auto (Wed); Outdoors (Thur); Weekend, Auto (Fri); Church, Real Estate (Sat); Travel, TV, Home (Sun)
Syndicated Publications: USA WEEKEND Magazine (S).
Delivery Methods: Mail`Newsstand`Carrier`Racks
Own Printing Facility?: Y
Commercial printers?: Y
Avg Free Circ: 140
Sat. Circulation Paid: 13940
Sat. Circulation Free: 140
Sun. Circulation Paid: 20877
Sun. Circulation Free: 186
Audit By: AAM
Audit Date: 31.03.2019
Personnel: Cheryl Whitsitt (News Ed.); Amos Bridges (Ed.); Stephen Herzog (Ed.); Matt Peterson (Ed.); Laura Johnson (Weekend Ed. & Prod.)
Parent company (for newspapers): Gannett

TRENTON REPUBLICAN-TIMES

Street address 1: 122 E 8th St
Street address city: Trenton
Street address state: MO
Zip/Postal code: 64683-2183
County: Grundy
Country: USA
Mailing address: PO BOX 548
Mailing city: TRENTON
Mailing state: MO
Mailing zip: 64683-0548
General Phone: (660) 359-2212
Advertising Phone: (660) 359-2212
Editorial Phone: (660) 359-2212
General/National Adv. E-mail: rtimes@lyn.net
Display Adv. E-mail: rtimes@lyn.net
Classified Adv. e-mail: rtimes@lyn.net
Editorial e-mail: rtimes@lyn.net
Primary Website: www.republican-times.com
Mthly Avg Views: 81690
Year Established: 1864
News Services: AP.
Special Editions: Home Improvement (Apr); Fall Sports (Aug); Graduation (May); Missouri Day Festival (Oct). Fall Outdoors (Nov.)
Special Weekly Sections: TV Guide (Thur).
Delivery Methods: Mail`Newsstand`Carrier
Areas Served - City/County or Portion Thereof, or Zip codes: 64683, 64641, 64652, 64679, 64673, 64661, 64648, 64642
Own Printing Facility?: N
Commercial printers?: N
Avg Free Circ: 12226
Audit By: Sworn/Estimate/Non-Audited
Audit Date: 12.07.2019
Personnel: Wendell Lenhart (Pub.); Diane Lowrey (Ed.); Angela Dugan (Adv. Mgr.)
Parent company (for newspapers): W.B. Rogers Printing Co., Inc.

THE DAILY STAR-JOURNAL

Street address 1: 135 E Market St
Street address city: Warrensburg
Street address state: MO
Zip/Postal code: 64093-1817
County: Johnson
Country: USA
Mailing address: PO BOX 68
Mailing city: WARRENSBURG
Mailing state: MO
Mailing zip: 64093-0068
General Phone: (660) 747-8123
Advertising Phone: (660) 747-8123 ext. 105
Editorial Phone: (660) 747-8123 ext. 110
General/National Adv. E-mail: Joani.Dittrich@npgco.com
Display Adv. E-mail: Joani.Dittrich@npgco.com
Classified Adv. e-mail: dsjclassifieds@npgco.com
Editorial e-mail: jack.miles@npgco.com
Primary Website: www.dailystarjournal.com
Mthly Avg Views: 298000
Mthly Avg Unique Visitors: 115000
Year Established: 1865
News Services: AP.
Special Editions: Best of the Berg Living 50 Plus DRIVE Dining Guide Resource Guide Sports Previews Veterans Tribute
Delivery Methods: Mail`Racks
Areas Served - City/County or Portion Thereof, or Zip codes: Johnson County, MO
Own Printing Facility?: Y
Commercial printers?: N
Avg Free Circ: 18323
Audit By: Sworn/Estimate/Non-Audited
Audit Date: 12.07.2019
Personnel: Joe Warren (Pub.); Jack Miles (Ed.); Brian Burton (Advertising Director)
Parent company (for newspapers): NPG Newspapers

DAILY GUIDE

Street address 1: 108 Hull Dr
Street address city: Waynesville
Street address state: MO
Zip/Postal code: 65583-2364
County: Pulaski
Country: USA
Mailing address: PO BOX 578
Mailing city: WAYNESVILLE
Mailing state: MO
Mailing zip: 65583-0578
General Phone: (573) 336-3711
Advertising Phone: (573) 336-3711
Editorial Phone: (573) 336-3711
General/National Adv. E-mail: advertising@waynesvilledailyguide.com
Display Adv. E-mail: advertising@waynesvilledailyguide.com
Classified Adv. e-mail: classified@waynesvilledailyguide.com
Editorial e-mail: editor@waynesvilledailyguide.com
Primary Website: www.waynesvilledailyguide.com
Year Established: 1967
News Services: AP.
Special Editions: Profiles (Jul).
Special Weekly Sections: Best Food Day (Wed); Church (Fri)
Syndicated Publications: Own Newsprint Mag (Fri).
Delivery Methods: Mail`Newsstand`Carrier`Racks
Areas Served - City/County or Portion Thereof, or Zip codes: Crocker, Dixon, Laquey, Fort Leonard Wood, Richland, St. Robert and Waynesville
Own Printing Facility?: Y
Commercial printers?: Y
Avg Free Circ: 8600
Sat. Circulation Paid: 892
Audit By: Sworn/Estimate/Non-Audited
Audit Date: 12.07.2019
Personnel: Floyd Jernigan (Pub.); Mike Valko (Circ. Mgr.); Dave Roberts (Sports Ed.); Katy Quigley (Ads Rep.)
Parent company (for newspapers): CherryRoad Media

WEST PLAINS DAILY QUILL

Street address 1: 205 Washington Ave
Street address city: West Plains
Street address state: MO
Zip/Postal code: 65775-3439
County: Howell
Country: USA
Mailing address: PO BOX 110
Mailing city: WEST PLAINS
Mailing state: MO
Mailing zip: 65775-0110
General Phone: (417) 256-9191
Advertising Phone: (417) 256-9191
Editorial Phone: (417) 256-9191
General/National Adv. E-mail: ads@wpdailyquill.net
Display Adv. E-mail: ads@wpdailyquill.net
Classified Adv. e-mail: classifieds@wpdailyquill.net
Editorial e-mail: editor@wpdailyquill.net
Primary Website: www.westplainsdailyquill.net
Mthly Avg Views: 246582
Mthly Avg Unique Visitors: 84072
Year Established: 1903
News Services: AP.
Special Editions: Tax Tips; Bridal (Jan.)Spring Church Directory;Spring Sports; Home Improvement;Doctor's Day (Mar): Valentine's Day;FFA Insert (Feb): Graduation Insert;Mother's Day;Older American Month;Memorial Day (May):Old Time Music Festival;Father's Day(June): Fair insert (July): Back-To-School;Fall Sports (Aug.): Grandparents Day;Fall Sports (Sept.): Breast Cancer Awareness(Oct.):Christmas Open House/Shop Locally;Black Friday (Nov.): Christmas Shopping Guide; Christmas Songbook; Christmas Greetings (Dec.)

Special Weekly Sections: People, Sports, Amusement (Daily); Outdoors (Fri); Food, Dining (Wed); Farm & Garden (Thu); Business, Finance (Thu); Auto, TV, Religion, Auctions, Real Estate (Fri); Color Comics (Sat); National Coupons (Sat)
Syndicated Publications: TV Week (Television Listings and Local Events Guide) (Sat); Smart Source (Sat); Parade (Sat); American Profile (Sat).
Delivery Methods: Mail`Racks
Areas Served - City/County or Portion Thereof, or Zip codes: 65775, 65793,65548, 65688, 65777, 65626, 65788, 65789, 65790, 65606, 65791, 65692, 65690, 65778, 65466, 65588, 65438, 65483, 65689, 65571, 65711, 65768, 65608, 65638, 65637, 65655, 65609, 65760, 65766, 65784, 72576, 72583, 72538, 72653, 72554
Own Printing Facility?: Y
Commercial printers?: Y
Avg Free Circ: 0
Sat. Circulation Paid: 5520
Sat. Circulation Free: 0
Audit By: USPS
Audit Date: 01.10.2016
Personnel: Jim Perry (Publisher); Mary Frazier (Production Manager / Digital Services); Allison Wilson (Managing Editor); Cody Sanders (Sports Editor); Vicki Johnson (Advertising Manager); Katie Dudden (Web Services, Pagination, Digital Print); Darla Evins (Customer Service Representative); Mary Ewers (General Assignment Reporter); Abby R Hess (Editorial Assistant, Senior Reporter); Lisa Lonon (Customer Service Representative); Monty C Reynolds (Commercial Printing); Vicky Rutter (Customer Service Representative); Cheryl Thompson (Customer Service Representative); Ron Woolman (Police/Courts Reporter); Regina Mozingo (News Editor)
Parent company (for newspapers): Phillips Media Group LLC

MONTANA

BILLINGS GAZETTE

Street address 1: 401 N 28th St
Street address city: Billings
Street address state: MT
Zip/Postal code: 59101-1243
County: Yellowstone
Country: USA
Mailing address: PO BOX 36300
Mailing city: BILLINGS
Mailing state: MT
Mailing zip: 59107-6300
General Phone: (406) 657-1200
Advertising Phone: (406) 657-1370
Editorial Phone: (406) 657-1241
General/National Adv. E-mail: citynews@billingsgazette.com
Display Adv. E-mail: dworstell@billingsgazette.com
Classified Adv. e-mail: dworstell@billingsgazette.com
Editorial e-mail: citynews@billingsgazette.com
Primary Website: www.billingsgazette.com
Mthly Avg Views: 10000000
Mthly Avg Unique Visitors: 940000
Year Established: 1885
News Services: AP, CNS, MCT, TMS.
Special Editions: First Res ponders (Oct) Readers' Choice Awards (Oct); ; Holiday Food and Gift Festival (Nov); Brawl of the Wild (Nov); Community of Giving (Dec); 40 under Forty (Feb); Home Improvement (May); Big Sky State Games (Jul); Parade of Homes (September); Nurses Appreciation (May)
Special Weekly Sections: Auto Plus (Fri); Your Home (S); Outdoors (Thur); Business Sections (S); Employment (S); Good Life (S); Health (Wed); Your Faith (Sat).
Syndicated Publications: Entertainment (Fri); Relish (Monthly); Parade (S); TV Book (Fri);
Delivery Methods: Mail`Newsstand`Carrier
Sat. Circulation Paid: 16255
Sun. Circulation Paid: 80105
Audit Date: 30.06.2018
Personnel: Shelli Scott (Retail Advertising Manager); Dave Worstell (Pub.); James Gaasterland (Human Resources Dir.); Ryan Brosseau (Adv. Dir.); Sondra Arnold (Controller); Chris Jorgensen (City Ed.); Darrell Ehrlick (Ed.); Pat Bellinghausen (Op. Ed.); Erica Doornek (Night Ed.); Barry Cronk (Circ. Dir.); Brett French (Ed.); Jeff Welsch (Executive Sports Ed.); Alyssa Small (City Ed.); John Letasky (Deputy Sports Ed.); Lindsay Rossmiller (Digital Sports Ed.); Larry Mayer (Photo Ed.); Chase Doak (Digital Ed.)
Parent company (for newspapers): Dispatch-Argus; Lee Enterprises, Incorporated; Lee Enterprises

BOZEMAN DAILY CHRONICLE

Street address 1: 2820 W. College Street
Street address city: Bozeman
Street address state: MT
Zip/Postal code: 59718
County: Gallatin
Country: USA
Mailing address: PO BOX 1190
Mailing city: BOZEMAN
Mailing state: MT
Mailing zip: 59771-1190
General Phone: (406) 587-4491
General/National Adv. E-mail: national@dailychronicle.com
Classified Adv. e-mail: classifieds@dailychronicle.com
Editorial e-mail: citydesk@dailychronicle.com
Primary Website: www.bozemandailychronicle.com
Mthly Avg Views: 1159000
Mthly Avg Unique Visitors: 231000
Year Established: 1883
News Services: AP, LAT-WP.
Special Editions: Football (Aug); Christmas Cheer (Dec); Spring Home Improvement (Feb); Montana Winter Fair (Jan); Gallatin County Summer Fair (Jul); The Hatch is On (Jun); VISTA (Mar); Explore Yellowstone (May); Christmas Gift Catalog (Nov); Hunting (Oct); Home Improvemen
Special Weekly Sections: Health (Mon); Economy (S); Outdoors (Thur); Lifestyle (Wed).
Syndicated Publications: This Week (newsprint) (Fri); Parade (S).
Delivery Methods: Mail`Newsstand`Carrier`Racks
Areas Served - City/County or Portion Thereof, or Zip codes: City/county
Own Printing Facility?: Y
Commercial printers?: Y
Avg Free Circ: 1079
Sat. Circulation Paid: 9321
Sat. Circulation Free: 1079
Sun. Circulation Paid: 10704
Sun. Circulation Free: 1000
Audit By: AAM
Audit Date: 31.12.2017
Personnel: Nick Ehli (Mng. Ed.); Ted Sullivan (Asst. Mng. Ed.); Michael Wright (City Ed.); Colton Pool (Sports Ed.); Rachel Hergette (Ruckus Arts & Culture Ed.); Cindy Sease (Adv. Dir.)
Parent company (for newspapers): Adams Publishing Group, LLC

THE MONTANA STANDARD

Street address 1: 25 W Granite St
Street address city: Butte
Street address state: MT
Zip/Postal code: 59701-9213
County: Silver Bow
Country: USA
Mailing address: PO BOX 627
Mailing city: BUTTE
Mailing state: MT
Mailing zip: 59703-0627
General Phone: (406) 496-5500
Advertising Phone: (406) 496-5583
Editorial Phone: (406) 496-5510
General/National Adv. E-mail: sales@mtstandard.com
Display Adv. E-mail: sales@mtstandard.com
Classified Adv. e-mail: classified@mtstandard.com
Editorial e-mail: editors@mtstandard.com
Primary Website: www.mtstandard.com
Year Established: 1876
News Services: AP, SHNS, MCT, TMS.
Special Editions: Fall Sports (Aug); Bridal Tab (Jan); Travel Guide (May); In Business (Quarterly); Hunting Tab (Sept).
Special Weekly Sections: Best Food Days (Wed); Religion, Entertainment, Tabloid (Sat); Business, Women's Section, Lifestyle (Sun)
Syndicated Publications: Big Sky View (S); Time Out (Sat).
Areas Served - City/County or Portion Thereof, or Zip codes: Southwest Montana
Avg Free Circ: 914
Sat. Circulation Paid: 6727
Sat. Circulation Free: 914
Sun. Circulation Paid: 6773
Sun. Circulation Free: 1552
Audit By: AAM
Audit Date: 31.03.2019
Personnel: Lynn Lloyd (Gen. Mgr.); Jenean Salle (Retail Adv. Mgr.); Steve Biere (Circ. Mgr.); Carmen Winslow (Mng. Ed.); Kristie Constantine (Lead Copy Ed.); Walter Hinick (Photo Ed.); David McCumber (Ed.); Tyler Miller (Publisher)
Parent company (for newspapers): Lee Enterprises, Incorporated

GREAT FALLS TRIBUNE

Street address 1: 205 River Drive South
Street address city: Great Falls
Street address state: MT
Zip/Postal code: 59403-5468
County: Cascade
Country: USA
Mailing address: PO BOX 5468
Mailing city: GREAT FALLS
Mailing state: MT
Mailing zip: 59403-5468
General Phone: (406) 791-1444
Advertising Phone: (406) 791-1440
Editorial Phone: (406) 791-1460
General/National Adv. E-mail: advertising@greatfallstribune.com
Display Adv. E-mail: msmith@greatfalltribune.com
Classified Adv. e-mail: gbebee@greatfallstribune.com
Editorial e-mail: tribcity@greatfallstribune.com
Primary Website: www.greatfallstribune.com
Year Established: 1884
News Services: AP, GNS.
Special Editions: Jan: Bridal Guide, What Women Want (WWW)magazine. Feb: Ag Outlook, Healthy MT magazine, Outlook 20xx. Mar: Western Art Roundup, What Women Want, College 101, Guide to Great Falls, Home and Garden Show. Apr:Newcomers Guide May:Draw Your Mom, Visit Great Falls,Glacier Gateway, WWW mag., Healthy MT. June:101 Things to Do in Montana, Draw Your Dad July: Visit Great Falls, State Fair Preview, WWW mag.,Back to School. Aug:Healthy MT, Pet Idol, Ag Outlook, Football Preview. Sept: College 101, Visit Great Falls, Fall Home Guide, WWW mag. Oct:WWW Expo Guide, Your Health Medical Directory. Nov:Visit Great Falls, WWW mag., Ag Outlook, Holiday Gift Guides, Healthy MT. Dec:Visit Great Falls. also Great Falls Business 6X/yr, fusion 12X/yr, Your Health 12X/yr,Military Retirees Appreciation 2X/yr,
Special Weekly Sections: Best Food Day (Wed); Health, Technology (Tue); Outdoors (Thur); Entertainment, Auto (Fri); Home, Living, Religion (Sat); Business/Agriculture, Travel, Family, Real Estate (Sun)
Syndicated Publications: USA WEEKEND Magazine (S).,relish (T), Spry (T). Glossy: What Women Want Magazine Healthy MT College 101
Delivery Methods: Mail`Newsstand`Carrier`Racks
Own Printing Facility?: Y
Commercial printers?: Y
Sat. Circulation Paid: 17755
Sun. Circulation Paid: 18487
Audit By: AAM
Audit Date: 30.09.2018
Personnel: James Strauss (Pres./Pub./Ed.); Viv Hunter (Acct. Mgr.); Mike Grafe (Production Operations Dir.); Gene Hieb (Production Mgr., Mailroom); Terry Oyhamburu (Dir. of Business Development & Marketing); Amie Thompson (Specialty Publication Editor); Jo Dee Black (Business Editor); Scott Mansch (Sports Editor); Lou Dewaele (Circ. Sales and Retention Mgr.); Lolly Hader (Literacy Outreach Coordinator); Grant Bebee (Adv. Mgr., Classified)
Parent company (for newspapers): Gannett

RAVALLI REPUBLIC

Street address 1: 232 W Main St
Street address city: Hamilton
Street address state: MT
Zip/Postal code: 59840-2552
County: Ravalli
Country: USA
Mailing address: 232 W MAIN ST
Mailing city: HAMILTON
Mailing state: MT
Mailing zip: 59840-2552
General Phone: (406) 363-3300
Advertising Phone: (406) 363-3300
Editorial Phone: (406) 363-3300
General/National Adv. E-mail: jodi.lopez@ravallirepublic.com
Classified Adv. e-mail: lacey.davis@ravallirepublic.com
Editorial e-mail: editor@ravallirepublic.com
Primary Website: www.ravallirepublic.com
Mthly Avg Views: 400000
Mthly Avg Unique Visitors: 70000
Year Established: 1897
News Services: AP.
Special Editions: Uncover Bitterroot (Sept); Agri-Business (Mar, Jun, Sept); Valley Vista (Tourism Publication) (March); Christmas Editions (Nov); Hunting and Outdoors (Oct).
Special Weekly Sections: Food, Health (Wed); Opinion, Business (Thur); TV, Entertainment (Fri); Outdoors (Sat); Opinion, Life in the Bitterroot (Sun)
Delivery Methods: Carrier`Racks
Areas Served - City/County or Portion Thereof, or Zip codes: Ravalli County, Montana
Own Printing Facility?: N
Commercial printers?: N
Avg Free Circ: 131
Sat. Circulation Paid: 1111
Sat. Circulation Free: 131
Sun. Circulation Paid: 1529
Sun. Circulation Free: 138
Audit By: AAM
Audit Date: 30.09.2018
Personnel: Mike Gulledge (Pub.); Kathy Best (Ed.); Linda Pollard (Bus. Mgr.); Jodi Lopez (Sales Mgr.)
Parent company (for newspapers): Lee Enterprises, Incorporated

THE HAVRE DAILY NEWS

Street address 1: 119 2nd St
Street address city: Havre
Street address state: MT
Zip/Postal code: 59501-3507
County: Hill
Country: USA
Mailing address: PO BOX 431
Mailing city: HAVRE
Mailing state: MT
Mailing zip: 59501-0431
General Phone: (406) 265-6795
Advertising Phone: (406) 265-6795
Editorial Phone: (406) 265-6795
General/National Adv. E-mail: mgilman@havredailynews.com
Display Adv. E-mail: adsales1@havredailynews.com
Classified Adv. e-mail: adsales2@havredailynews.com
Editorial e-mail: news@havredailynews.com
Primary Website: www.havredailynews.com
Year Established: 1914
News Services: AP.
Special Editions: Home & Car Care (Apr); Fair (Aug); Christmas Greetings (Dec); Senior Citizens (Feb); Tax Guide (Jan); Senior Citizens (Jul); Senior Citizens (Jun); Who's Who in Northern Montana (Mar); Tourist Guide (May); Thanksgiving (Nov); Hunting & Fishing Guide (Oct)
Special Weekly Sections: Food (Tue); Agriculture (Wed); Business (Thur); Church, Society, Real Estate (Fri)
Syndicated Publications: American Profile (Weekly).
Areas Served - City/County or Portion Thereof, or Zip codes: 59501, 59520, 59521, 59523, 59525, 59528, 59532, 59540
Audit By: Sworn/Estimate/Non-Audited
Audit Date: 12.07.2019
Personnel: Stacy Mantle (Pub./Adv. Mgr.); Craig Otterstrom (Circ. Dir.); Scott Anderson (Prodn. Mgr.); Jenn Thompson (Adv. Dir.); Hannah Somers (Adv. Consultant); Crystal Faldalen (Classified Adv. Mgr.); Tim Leeds
Parent company (for newspapers): Stevenson Newspapers

HELENA INDEPENDENT RECORD

Street address 1: 317 N Cruse Ave
Street address city: Helena
Street address state: MT
Zip/Postal code: 59601-5003
County: Lewis And Clark
Country: USA
Mailing address: PO BOX 4249
Mailing city: HELENA
Mailing state: MT
Mailing zip: 59604-4249
General Phone: (406) 447-4000
Advertising Phone: (406) 447-4011
Editorial Phone: (406) 444-5120
General/National Adv. E-mail: tonda.meyer@helenair.com

Display Adv. E-mail: tonda.meyer@helenair.com
Classified Adv. e-mail: rebecca.bruno@helenair.com
Editorial e-mail: irstaff@helenair.com
Primary Website: www.helenair.com
Mthly Avg Views: 2000000
Mthly Avg Unique Visitors: 240000
Year Established: 1867
News Services: AP, NYT, States News Service, Cox News Service.
Special Weekly Sections: Health, Fitness, Food (Wed); Entertainment, TV, Outdoors (Thur); Religion (Sat); Business, Travel (Sun)
Syndicated Publications: TV Guide (Fri); Parade (S); American Profile (Weekly).
Delivery Methods: Mail`Carrier`Racks
Own Printing Facility?: Y
Commercial printers?: Y
Avg Free Circ: 1027
Sat. Circulation Paid: 9065
Sat. Circulation Free: 1027
Sun. Circulation Paid: 9534
Sun. Circulation Free: 1115
Audit By: AAM
Audit Date: 30.09.2018
Personnel: Tyler Miller (Pub.); Karen Rickman (National Adv. Coord.); Jim Rickman (Adv. Mgr.); James DeHaven (Reporter); Jesse Chaney (Ed.)
Parent company (for newspapers): Lee Enterprises, Incorporated

DAILY INTER LAKE

Street address 1: 727 E. Idaho Street
Street address city: Kalispell
Street address state: MT
Zip/Postal code: 59901
County: Flathead
Country: USA
Mailing address: PO BOX 7610
Mailing city: KALISPELL
Mailing state: MT
Mailing zip: 59904-0610
General Phone: (406) 755-7000
Advertising Phone: (406) 755-7000
Editorial Phone: (406) 755-7000
General/National Adv. E-mail: wspencer@dailyinterlake.com
Display Adv. E-mail: wspencer@dailyinterlake.com
Classified Adv. e-mail: smiller@dailyinterlake.com
Editorial e-mail: edit@dailyinterlake.com
Primary Website: www.dailyinterlake.com
Mthly Avg Views: 825000
Mthly Avg Unique Visitors: 278302
Year Established: 1888
News Services: AP, LAT-WP.
Special Editions: Homes & Real Estate (Monthly); 101 Things To Do (Spring).Flathead Business Journal, Parade of Homes
Special Weekly Sections: Montana Life (S); Outdoors (Thur); Active Seniors (Tues); Food (Wed). This Week in the Flathead (Thurs)
Syndicated Publications: TV Listings Magazine (Fri); Parade (S); American Profile (Weekly).
Delivery Methods: Mail`Newsstand`Carrier`Racks
Areas Served - City/County or Portion Thereof, or Zip codes: Flathead County, Lake County, Lincoln County
Own Printing Facility?: Y
Commercial printers?: Y
Sat. Circulation Paid: 12307
Sun. Circulation Paid: 13306
Audit By: CAC
Audit Date: 31.03.2018
Personnel: Dorothy Glencross (Bus. Mgr.); Lynnette Hintze (Features Ed.); Frank Miele (Managing Ed.); Dave Lesnick (Sports Ed.); Ken Varga (Circulation Director); Rick Weaver (Publisher); Lisa Fleming (Collections); Matt Baldwin (Regional Ed.)
Parent company (for newspapers): Hagadone Corporation

THE LIVINGSTON ENTERPRISE

Street address 1: 401 S Main St
Street address city: Livingston
Street address state: MT
Zip/Postal code: 59047-3418
County: Park
Country: USA
Mailing address: PO BOX 2000
Mailing city: LIVINGSTON
Mailing state: MT
Mailing zip: 59047-4706
General Phone: (406) 222-2000
Advertising Phone: (800) 345-8412
Editorial Phone: (406) 222-2000
General/National Adv. E-mail: jdurfey@livent.net
Display Adv. E-mail: jdurfey@livent.net
Classified Adv. e-mail: classifieds@livent.net
Editorial e-mail: news@livent.net
Primary Website: www.livingstonenterprise.com
Year Established: 1883
News Services: AP.
Special Editions: Home & Garden (Apr); Back-to-School (Aug); Christmas Eve (Dec); Fall Sports (Fall); Presidential History Tab (Feb); Bridal Tab (Other); Car Care (Spring); Winter Sport (Winter).
Special Weekly Sections: Best Food Day (Wed)
Syndicated Publications: American Profile (Weekly).
Delivery Methods: Mail`Newsstand`Carrier`Racks
Areas Served - City/County or Portion Thereof, or Zip codes: 59047,59018,59030,59027, 59065, 59082,59086
Own Printing Facility?: Y
Commercial printers?: Y
Avg Free Circ: 73
Audit By: Sworn/Estimate/Non-Audited
Audit Date: 12.07.2019
Personnel: John Sullivan (Pub.); Scott Squillace (Controller); James Durfey (Adv. Dir.); David Campbell (Circ. Dir); Justin Post (Managing Editor); Dwight Harriman (News Ed.); Thomas Watson (Sports Editor); Luke Miller (Press Foreman); Alan Bublitz (Production Mgr.)
Parent company (for newspapers): Yellowstone Communications

MILES CITY STAR

Street address 1: 818 Main St
Street address city: Miles City
Street address state: MT
Zip/Postal code: 59301-3221
County: Custer
Country: USA
Mailing address: PO BOX 1216
Mailing city: MILES CITY
Mailing state: MT
Mailing zip: 59301-1216
General Phone: (406) 234-0450
Advertising Phone: (406) 234-0450
Editorial Phone: (406) 234-0450
General/National Adv. E-mail: advsales@midrivers.com
Display Adv. E-mail: advsales@midrivers.com
Classified Adv. e-mail: mcclassads@midrivers.com
Editorial e-mail: mceditor@midrivers.com
Primary Website: www.milescitystar.com
Year Established: 1911
News Services: AP.
Special Weekly Sections: Best Food Day (Tue); Livestock, Agriculture (Thur); Society, Entertainment (Wed); Society, Weekend (Fri)
Syndicated Publications: American Profile (Weekly).
Delivery Methods: Mail`Newsstand`Carrier
Areas Served - City/County or Portion Thereof, or Zip codes: Custer County (MT)
Commercial printers?: Y
Avg Free Circ: 29
Audit By: Sworn/Estimate/Non-Audited
Audit Date: 12.07.2019
Personnel: Dan Killoy (Pub.); Alan Hauge (Adv. Mgr.); Marla Prell (Ed.); Elaine Forman (News Ed.); Josh Samuelson (Sports Ed.); Sharon Cline (Data Processing Mgr.); Karen Hawkinson (Mgr., Commercial Printing)
Parent company (for newspapers): Yellowstone Communications

MISSOULIAN

Street address 1: 500 S Higgins Ave
Street address city: Missoula
Street address state: MT
Zip/Postal code: 59801-2736
County: Missoula
Country: USA
Mailing address: PO BOX 8029
Mailing city: MISSOULA
Mailing state: MT
Mailing zip: 59807-8029
General Phone: (406) 523-5200
Advertising Phone: (406) 523-5223
Editorial Phone: (406) 523-5240
General/National Adv. E-mail: advertising@missoulian.com
Classified Adv. e-mail: classified@missoulian.com
Editorial e-mail: oped@missoulian.com
Primary Website: www.missoulian.com
Mthly Avg Views: 4351563
Mthly Avg Unique Visitors: 536904
Year Established: 1905
News Services: AP, NYT.
Special Editions: Health Fair Tab (January), Missoula's Choice (January), Living Well (Bi-Monthly), Newspapers in Education (March), Montana's Cultural Treasures (March), Uncover Missoula (March), Spring Fasion (April), Montana Designs (April), International Wildlife Film Festival Program/Tab (April/May), Lawn & Garden (April), Graduation (June), Explore the Bitterroot (June), Hot Spots (June), HomeStyle (July), Montana Lyric Opera (July), Chamber of Commerce Directory (July), Missoula Relocation Guide (July), Western Montana Fair (August), MCPS Calendar (August), River City Roots Festival (August), Bear Necessities (August), Grizzly Game Day (Weekly beginning August through College football season), Montana Designs II (September),Fall Fashion (September), Hunting Journal (October), MT CINE International Film Festival (October), Health Resource Guide (October), Brawl of the Wild (November), Holiday Gift Guide (November), Faith Tab (December), Beer & Wine Journal (December), Montana Economic Report (December), Brides & Grooms (December)
Special Weekly Sections: Health (Tue); Food (Wed); Outdoors (Thur); Entertainment (Fri); Engagements, Business (Sun);
Syndicated Publications: Parade (Sunday), Missoula Magazine (Quarterly), Athlon Sports (Third Tuesday of the Month), Corridor (Monthly),
Delivery Methods: Mail`Newsstand`Carrier`Racks
Areas Served - City/County or Portion Thereof, or Zip codes: Western Montana
Avg Free Circ: 5429
Sat. Circulation Paid: 11158
Sat. Circulation Free: 5429
Sun. Circulation Paid: 12948
Sun. Circulation Free: 5186
Audit By: AAM
Audit Date: 30.09.2018
Personnel: Jim Strauss (Pub.); Gwen Florio (Acting Ed.); Tyler Christensen (Opinion Ed.); Anne Cruikshank (Dig. Ed.); Bob Meseroll (Asst. News Ed.); Tandy Neighbor (Office Mgr.); Jeff Welsch (Exec. Sports Ed.)
Parent company (for newspapers): Lee Enterprises, Incorporated

NEBRASKA

ALLIANCE TIMES-HERALD

Street address 1: 114 E 4th St
Street address 2: P O Box G
Street address city: Alliance
Street address state: NE
Zip/Postal code: 69301-3402
County: Box Butte
Country: USA
Mailing address: 114 E 4TH ST
Mailing city: ALLIANCE
Mailing state: NE
Mailing zip: 69301-3402
General Phone: (308) 762-3060
Advertising Phone: (308) 762-3060
Editorial Phone: (308) 762-3060
General/National Adv. E-mail: cassie@alliancetimes.com
Display Adv. E-mail: erica@alliancetimes.com
Classified Adv. e-mail: classified@alliancetimes.com
Editorial e-mail: athnews@alliancetimes.com
Primary Website: www.alliancetimes.com
Mthly Avg Views: 90000
Mthly Avg Unique Visitors: 75000
Year Established: 1887
News Services: AP.
Special Editions: Spring Home & Garden (Recycling) (Apr); Fair Section-Results (Aug); Letters to Santa and Christmas Greetings (Dec); Business & Industry (Feb); Tax (Jan); Heritage Days Festival (Jul); Spring Ag & Ranch (Mar); Beef (May); Winter Sports (Nov); Fall Ag (Oct)
Special Weekly Sections: Business Page (Other); Farm & Ranch (Thur); Food (Wed).
Delivery Methods: Mail`Newsstand`Carrier`Racks
Areas Served - City/County or Portion Thereof, or Zip codes: 69301
Own Printing Facility?: Y
Commercial printers?: N
Sat. Circulation Paid: 3025
Audit By: Sworn/Estimate/Non-Audited
Audit Date: 12.07.2019
Personnel: Tom Shaal (Director of Operations); Shaun Friedrichsen (News Dir.); Amanda Mittan (Ad Dir.)
Parent company (for newspapers): Seaton Group

BEATRICE DAILY SUN

Street address 1: 110 S 6th St
Street address city: Beatrice
Street address state: NE
Zip/Postal code: 68310-3912
County: Gage
Country: USA
Mailing address: 110 S 6TH ST
Mailing city: BEATRICE
Mailing state: NE
Mailing zip: 68310-3912
General Phone: (402) 223-5233
Advertising Phone: (402) 223-5233
Editorial Phone: (402) 223-5233
General/National Adv. E-mail: astokebrand@beatricedailysun.com
Display Adv. E-mail: astokebrand@beatricedailysun.com
Editorial e-mail: news@beatricedailysun.com
Primary Website: www.beatricedailysun.com
Mthly Avg Views: 1300000
Mthly Avg Unique Visitors: 40000
Year Established: 1902
News Services: AP, NEA.
Special Editions: Clean-up (Apr); Back-to-School (Aug); Senior Citizens (Feb); County Fair (Jul); Homestead Days (Jun); Family Business (Mar); Graduation (May); Sports (Nov); 4-H (Oct); Hunting (Sept).
Special Weekly Sections: Farm Page (Fri); Youth (Sat); Religion (Thur); Cooking (Wed).
Syndicated Publications: Relish (Monthly); USA WEEKEND Magazine (Sat); American Profile (Weekly).
Delivery Methods: Mail`Newsstand`Carrier`Racks
Areas Served - City/County or Portion Thereof, or Zip codes: Southeast Nebraska
Own Printing Facility?: Y
Commercial printers?: Y
Avg Free Circ: 249
Sat. Circulation Paid: 4239
Sat. Circulation Free: 194
Audit By: Sworn/Estimate/Non-Audited
Audit Date: 12.07.2019
Personnel: Patrick Ethridge (Regl. Pub.); Becky Reedy (Composing Mgr.); Amy Stokebrand (Sales TL)
Parent company (for newspapers): Dispatch-Argus; Lee Enterprises, Incorporated

THE COLUMBUS TELEGRAM

Street address 1: 1254 27th Ave
Street address city: Columbus
Street address state: NE
Zip/Postal code: 68601-5656
County: Platte
Country: USA
Mailing address: 1254 27th Ave
Mailing city: Columbus
Mailing state: NE
Mailing zip: 68601-5656
General Phone: (402) 564-2741
Advertising Phone: (402) 564-2741
Editorial Phone: (402) 564-2741
General/National Adv. E-mail: amy.bell@lee.net
Display Adv. E-mail: amy.bell@lee.net
Editorial e-mail: jdean@columbustelegram.com
Primary Website: www.columbustelegram.com
Mthly Avg Views: 700000
Year Established: 1879
News Services: AP, MCT, NEA.
Special Editions: Senior Salute (Apr); Columbus Day (Aug); Last Minute Gift Idea (Dec); Columbus Home Show (Feb); Bridal (Jan); Farm & Fair (Jul); Father's Day (Jun); Chamber of Commerce (Mar); Ag/Almanac/ Beef (May); Christmas Opening (Nov); Power and Progress (Oct); Colle
Special Weekly Sections: Sports, Lifestyles, Business, Precious Memories (Sun); Sports, Farm (Mon); Sports, Food, Health (Tue); Sports, Youth, Business (Wed); Sports, Dining, Entertainment, Home, Garden (Thur); Sports, Religion, Senior (Fri)
Syndicated Publications: Relish (Monthly); USA WEEKEND Magazine (S); American Profile (Wed).

Areas Served - City/County or Portion Thereof, or Zip codes: Boone, Butler, Colfax, Merrick, Nance, Platte & Polk Counties (NE)
Avg Free Circ: 840
Sun. Circulation Paid: 6910
Sun. Circulation Free: 901
Audit By: AAM
Audit Date: 30.09.2014
Personnel: Vincent Laboy (Reg. Pub.); Matt Lindberg (Mng. Ed.); Sam Pimper (News Ed.); Kelly Muchmore (Sales Exec.)
Parent company (for newspapers): Lee Enterprises, Incorporated

FREMONT TRIBUNE

Street address 1: 135 N Main St
Street address city: Fremont
Street address state: NE
Zip/Postal code: 68025-5673
County: Dodge
Country: USA
Mailing address: PO BOX 9
Mailing city: FREMONT
Mailing state: NE
Mailing zip: 68026-0009
General Phone: (402) 721-5000
Advertising Phone: (402) 941-1446
Editorial Phone: (402) 941-1433
General/National Adv. E-mail: julie.veskerna@lee.net
Display Adv. E-mail: julie.veskerna@lee.net
Editorial e-mail: fremont.newsroom@lee.net
Primary Website: www.fremonttribune.com
Mthly Avg Views: 1000000
Year Established: 1868
News Services: AP, Lee National Sales Group.
Special Editions: Bridal Tab (Other).
Special Weekly Sections: Fremont Living (Fri); Church Page (Sat); Agricultural Day (Thur); Business Day (Tues).
Syndicated Publications: Relish (Monthly); USA WEEKEND Magazine (Sat); TV Week (Weekly).
Areas Served - City/County or Portion Thereof, or Zip codes: Burt, Colfax, Cuming, Dodge, Douglas, Saunders and Washington counties
Avg Free Circ: 720
Sat. Circulation Paid: 5373
Sat. Circulation Free: 796
Audit By: AAM
Audit Date: 30.09.2014
Personnel: Amy Bill (Controller); Jessica Noel (Credit Mgr.); Vincent Laboy (Adv. Mgr.); Greg Pehrson (Circ. Dir.); Tracy Buffington (Exec. Ed.); Tammy McKeighan (News Ed.); Brent Wasenius (Sports Ed.); Janelle Prehal (Prodn. Mgr.); Joe Gaver (Prodn. Mgr., Press); Tony Gray (News Ed.)
Parent company (for newspapers): Dispatch-Argus; Lee Enterprises, Incorporated

THE GRAND ISLAND INDEPENDENT

Street address 1: 422 W 1st St
Street address city: Grand Island
Street address state: NE
Zip/Postal code: 68801-5802
County: Hall
Country: USA
Mailing address: PO BOX 1208
Mailing city: GRAND ISLAND
Mailing state: NE
Mailing zip: 68802-1208
General Phone: (308) 382-1000
Advertising Phone: (308) 382-1000
Editorial Phone: (308) 382-1000
General/National Adv. E-mail: patricia.bell@theindependent.com
Display Adv. E-mail: kimberly.sweetser@theindependent.com
Classified Adv. e-mail: patricia.bell@theindependent.com
Editorial e-mail: newsdesk@theindependent.com
Primary Website: www.theindependent.com
News Services: AP, SHNS.
Special Editions: Back-to-School (Aug); Progress and Bridal (Jan); Cooking Show (March) Farm (Mar); Graduation (May); Home Improvement (Monthly); Nebraska State Fair (Aug.); Senior EXPO (Sept); Salute to Women (Oct); Farm (Sept).Christmas Opening (Nov);
Special Weekly Sections: Entertainment (Fri); Building Page (Mon); Weddings/Engagements (S); Weekend Sports (Sat); Club Calendar (Thur); City Council (Tues); Lifelines (Wed).
Syndicated Publications: Relish (Monthly); TV Week (S); American Profile (Weekly).
Delivery Methods: Mail`Newsstand`Carrier`Racks
Areas Served - City/County or Portion Thereof, or Zip codes: Central Nebraska
Own Printing Facility?: Y
Commercial printers?: Y
Avg Free Circ: 693
Sat. Circulation Paid: 13254
Sat. Circulation Free: 693
Sun. Circulation Paid: 14259
Sun. Circulation Free: 333
Audit By: CAC
Audit Date: 30.06.2018
Personnel: Donald S. Smith (Pub./Pres.); Molly Holcher (HR Mgr.); Pat Bell (Adv. Dir.); Kim Sweetser (Adv. Mgr., Retail); Pete Letheby (Assoc. Ed.); Jim Faddis (Mng. Ed.); Lora Ruzicka (Prepress Prod. Supervisor); Barrett Stinson (Photo Ed.); Bob Hamar (Sports Ed.); Terri Hahn (Women's Ed.); John Lilly (Prodn. Dir., Opns.); Pat Brown (Circ. Dir.); Jack Schiefelbein (Controller); Carrie Colburn (New Media Dir.); RJ Post (Asst. Mng. Ed.); Bill Parten (Class. Mgr.); Stephanie Romanski (Web/Social Media Ed.); Terrie Baker (Gen. Mgr.)
Parent company (for newspapers): BH Media Group

HASTINGS TRIBUNE

Street address 1: 908 W. Second Street
Street address city: Hastings
Street address state: NE
Zip/Postal code: 68902
County: Adams
Country: USA
Mailing address: PO BOX 788
Mailing city: HASTINGS
Mailing state: NE
Mailing zip: 68902-0788
General Phone: (402) 462-2131
Advertising Phone: (402) 461-1242
Editorial Phone: (402) 462-2131
General/National Adv. E-mail: legals@hastingstribune.com
Display Adv. E-mail: class@hastingstribune.com
Classified Adv. e-mail: class@hastingstribune.com
Editorial e-mail: apaiser@hastingstribune.com
Primary Website: www.hastingstribune.com
Year Established: 1905
News Services: AP, NEA, SHNS, TMS.
Special Editions: Business Outlook (Feb.); Tax & Financial Planning (Feb.); Ag Outlook (March); Home & Garden (March); Parenting (March); Medical News (May); Bridal (June); Back To School (August); College Bound (September); Auto Guide (October); Health & Wellness (Dec.)
Special Weekly Sections: Reader Scrapbook Page (Monday); Food (Tuesday); Senior/Health Page (Wednesday); NASCAR (Thursday); Agri/Biz (Saturday)
Syndicated Publications: Happenings (Sat); American Profile (Weekly).
Delivery Methods: Mail`Carrier`Racks
Areas Served - City/County or Portion Thereof, or Zip codes: 68901, 68925, 68933, 68935, 68938, 68939, 68370, 68930, 68322, 68335, 68340, 68361, 68436, 68452, 68832, 688883, 68928, 68932, 68933, 68934, 68941, 68942, 68944, 68945, 68950, 68952, 68954, 68955, 68956, 68957, 68959, 68961, 68970, 68972, 68973, 68974, 68975, 68978, 68979, 68980, 68981
Own Printing Facility?: Y
Commercial printers?: N
Avg Free Circ: 161
Sat. Circulation Paid: 6052
Sat. Circulation Free: 161
Audit By: AAM
Audit Date: 31.03.2019
Personnel: Donald R. Seaton (Owner/President); Donald L. Kissler (Bus. Mgr./Credit Mgr.); Deb Bunde (Director of Marketing); Carla Carda (Mktg. Dir.); Darran Fowler (Pub.); Scott Carstens (Produ. Mgr.); Doug Edwards (Webmaster)
Parent company (for newspapers): Seaton Group

HOLDREGE DAILY CITIZEN

Street address 1: 418 Garfield St
Street address city: Holdrege
Street address state: NE
Zip/Postal code: 68949-2219
County: Phelps
Country: USA
Mailing address: PO BOX 344
Mailing city: HOLDREGE
Mailing state: NE
Mailing zip: 68949-0344
General Phone: (308) 995-4441
Advertising Phone: (308) 995-4441
Editorial Phone: (308) 995-4441
General/National Adv. E-mail: holdregecitizenads@yahoo.com
Display Adv. E-mail: holdregecitizenads@yahoo.com
Classified Adv. e-mail: holdregecitizenads@yahoo.com
News Services: AP.
Special Weekly Sections: Farm (Mon); Church (Thur); Best Food Day (Wed).
Audit By: Sworn/Estimate/Non-Audited
Audit Date: 12.07.2019
Personnel: Ruth E. King (Vice Pres.); Barbara Penrod (Mgr., Mktg./Promo.); Julie Horn (Circ. Mgr.); Robert D. King (Pub.); Tunney Price (Science Ed.); Daniel Jordan (Prodn. Mgr.); Linda Boyll (Adv. Mgr.)
Parent company (for newspapers): King Family

KEARNEY HUB

Street address 1: 13 E. 22nd Street
Street address city: Kearney
Street address state: NE
Zip/Postal code: 68847
County: Buffalo
Country: USA
Mailing address: PO BOX 1988
Mailing city: KEARNEY
Mailing state: NE
Mailing zip: 68848-1988
General Phone: (308) 237-2152
Advertising Phone: (308) 233-9701
Editorial Phone: (308) 237-2152
General/National Adv. E-mail: lori.guthard@kearneyhub.com
Display Adv. E-mail: lori.guthard@kearneyhub.com
Classified Adv. e-mail: jill.green@kearneyhub.com
Editorial e-mail: mike.konz@kearneyhub.com
Primary Website: www.kearneyhub.com
Mthly Avg Views: 1500000
Mthly Avg Unique Visitors: 300000
Year Established: 1888
News Services: AP, SHNS.
Special Editions: Home & Decor (Apr); Fair Results (Aug); Home & Decor (Dec); Valentines (Feb); Bridal (Jan); Prime Magazine (Jul); Discover Kearney (Jun); Home & Decor (Mar); Rodeo Nebraska (May); Home & Decor (Nov); Business Profiles (Oct); A Home of Your Own (Sept).
Special Weekly Sections: Sports, Public Record, Editorial Opinions, Comics, Markets (Daily); Senior Citizen (Mon); Lifestyles, Best Food Day (Tue); Lifestyles (Wed); Entertainment, Youth (Thur); Health, Cooking, Engagements, Weddings, Church, Business, Farm, Entertainment, Home Improvement, Real Estate, Auto (Sat)
Syndicated Publications: Relish (Monthly); USA WEEKEND Magazine (Sat); TV Plus (Thur); American Profile (Weekly).
Areas Served - City/County or Portion Thereof, or Zip codes: Kearney (NB)
Avg Free Circ: 536
Sat. Circulation Paid: 7945
Sat. Circulation Free: 338
Audit By: CAC
Audit Date: 30.06.2018
Personnel: Shon Barenklau (Pub.); Mike Konz (Enterprise Ed.); Erika Pritchard (Regional/Image Ed.); Ana Salazar (Video Ed.); Buck Mahoney (Sports Ed.); Courtney Louis (Copy Ed.)
Parent company (for newspapers): BH Media Group; Lee Enterprises, Incorporated

LINCOLN JOURNAL STAR

Street address 1: 926 P Street
Street address city: Lincoln
Street address state: NE
Zip/Postal code: 68508
County: Lancaster
Country: USA
Mailing address: PO BOX 81689
Mailing city: LINCOLN
Mailing state: NE
Mailing zip: 68501-1689
General Phone: (402) 475-4200
Advertising Phone: (402) 473-7450
Editorial Phone: (402) 473-7306
General/National Adv. E-mail: advertising@journalstar.com
Display Adv. E-mail: advertising@journalstar.com
Classified Adv. e-mail: classified@journalstar.com
Editorial e-mail: citydesk@journalstar.com
Primary Website: www.journalstar.com
Mthly Avg Views: 9091065
Mthly Avg Unique Visitors: 1204163
Year Established: 1867
News Services: AP, LAT-WP, MCT.
Special Editions: Lincoln Living (Apr); Ultimate Campus Guide (Aug); Last Minute Gift Ideas (Dec); Weddings (Jan); Salute to Lincoln Business (Jul); Lincoln Living (Jun); Girls Basketball (Mar); Lincoln Living (May); Gift Guide (Nov); Lincoln Living (Oct); Inside Football; Bridal Guide (Jan), Seniors/Prime Time (Feb, March, July, Sept); Medical Guide (March)
Special Weekly Sections: Entertainment Pages (Fri); Garden/Home (S);
Syndicated Publications: L Magazine; Star City Sports
Delivery Methods: Mail`Racks
Areas Served - City/County or Portion Thereof, or Zip codes: Lancaster
Own Printing Facility?: Y
Commercial printers?: Y
Sat. Circulation Paid: 40367
Sun. Circulation Paid: 48973
Audit By: AAM
Audit Date: 31.03.2019
Personnel: Dave Bundy (Ed.); Linda Sackshewsky (Controller); Ava Thomas (Pub); Brady Svendgard (Operations Dir.); Matt Kasik (Pkg. Mgr.); Dick Piersol (Bus. Editor); Todd Henrichs (City Ed.); Patty Beutler (Focus Ed.); Shelly Kulhanek (Asst. City Ed.); Gordon Winters (Editorial Page Ed.); L. Kent Wolgamott (Entertainment Reporter); Jeff Korbelik (Features Editor); Erin Andersen (Families/Schools/Kids Reporter); Art Hovey (Farm/Agribus. Reporter)
Parent company (for newspapers): Lee Enterprises, Incorporated

MCCOOK DAILY GAZETTE

Street address 1: W First & E Sts
Street address city: Mc Cook
Street address state: NE
Zip/Postal code: 69001
County: Red Willow
Country: USA
Mailing address: PO BOX 1268
Mailing city: MC COOK
Mailing state: NE
Mailing zip: 69001-1268
General Phone: (308) 345-4500
Advertising Phone: (308) 345-4500 ext. 101
Editorial Phone: (308) 345-4500 ext. 120
General/National Adv. E-mail: adsales5@mccookgazette.com
Display Adv. E-mail: adsales5@mccookgazette.com
Classified Adv. e-mail: classifieds@mccookgazette.com
Editorial e-mail: editor@mccookgazette.com
Primary Website: www.mccookgazette.com
Mthly Avg Views: 363000
Mthly Avg Unique Visitors: 49000
Year Established: 1911
News Services: AP.
Special Weekly Sections: TV Week (Fri); Farm (Thur); Grocery (Tues).
Syndicated Publications: Relish (Monthly); American Profile (Weekly).
Delivery Methods: Mail`Newsstand`Carrier`Racks
Areas Served - City/County or Portion Thereof, or Zip codes: 69001
Own Printing Facility?: Y
Audit By: Sworn/Estimate/Non-Audited
Audit Date: 12.07.2019
Personnel: Sharyn Skiles (Pub.); Marybeth Roschewski (Circ. Mgr.); Connie Jo Discoe (Regional Ed.); Steve Kodov (Sports Ed.); Bruce Crosby (Ed.); Dave Mefford (Press Foreman); Lloyd Shields (Prodn. Mgr., Pre Press); Brenda Gillen (Bus. Mgr.); Jeremy Blomstedt (Assoc. Ed.)
Parent company (for newspapers): Rust Communications

NORFOLK DAILY NEWS

Street address 1: 525 W. Norfolk Avenue
Street address city: Norfolk
Street address state: NE
Zip/Postal code: 68701
County: Madison
Country: USA
Mailing address: PO BOX 977
Mailing city: NORFOLK
Mailing state: NE

Mailing zip: 68702-0977
General Phone: (402) 371-1020
Advertising Phone: (402) 371-1020
Editorial Phone: (402) 371-1020
General/National Adv. E-mail: ads@norfolkdailynews.com
Display Adv. E-mail: ads@norfolkdailynews.com
Classified Adv. e-mail: lmcgill@norfolkdailynews.com
Editorial e-mail: editor@norfolkdailynews.com
Primary Website: www.norfolkdailynews.com
Mthly Avg Views: 1400000
Mthly Avg Unique Visitors: 210000
Year Established: 1887
News Services: AP, SHNS.
Special Editions: Agriculture (Apr); Back-to-School (Aug); Christmas Greetings (Dec); Insight (Progress) (Feb); All About Norfolk (Jul); Spring Car Care (Mar); Car Care (Nov); Restaurant (Oct).
Special Weekly Sections: TV Tab (Fri); Farm Pages (Thur); Youth Pages (Tues); Food Pages (Wed).
Syndicated Publications: USA WEEKEND Magazine (Sat).
Areas Served - City/County or Portion Thereof, or Zip codes: Madison County
Avg Free Circ: 1986
Sat. Circulation Paid: 11096
Sat. Circulation Free: 1986
Audit By: AAM
Audit Date: 31.03.2018
Personnel: Jerry Huse (Pres./Pub.); Les Mann (Gen. Mgr.); Deb Warneke (Bus. Mgr.); Cristina Anderson (Circ. Mgr.); Kent Warneke (Ed.); Grace Petersen (City Ed.); Mary Pat Finn-Hoag (Farm Ed.); Greg Wees (Regl. Ed.); Jay Prauner (Sports Ed.); Mike Jones (Prodn. Mgr.); Jeff Jones (Prodn. Foreman, Pressroom); Jason Feddern (Prodn. Foreman, Mailroom); Vickie Hrabanek (Adv. Dir.); Pam Zoucha (Retail Mgr.); Sarah Noel (E-Media Sales Mgr.); Jerry Guenther (Reg. Ed.); Tim Pearson (News Ed.); Tom Behmer (Asst. Sports Ed.); Nick Benes (Asst. Sports Ed.); Mary Hoag (Agriculture/Youth Ed.); Ashley Fortkamp (Ed. Asst.); Sheryl Schmeckpeper (Living Page Ed.); Dennis Meyer (Photo Mgr./Online Ed.); Darin Epperly (Photo Chief); Isaiah May (News Ed.); Chris Avery (Gatekeeper/News Ed.); Tyler Eisenbraun (Prod. Mgr.); Matt Petersen (Systems Mgr.); Kathryn Harris (Online News Ed.)
Parent company (for newspapers): Huse Publishing

THE NORTH PLATTE TELEGRAPH

Street address 1: 621 N Chestnut St
Street address city: North Platte
Street address state: NE
Zip/Postal code: 69101-4131
County: Lincoln
Country: USA
Mailing address: PO BOX 370
Mailing city: NORTH PLATTE
Mailing state: NE
Mailing zip: 69103-0370
General Phone: (308) 532-6000
Advertising Phone: (308) 532-6000
Editorial Phone: (308) 532-6000
General/National Adv. E-mail: cal.petersen@nptelegraph.com
Display Adv. E-mail: advertising@nptelegraph.com
Classified Adv. e-mail: advertising@nptelegraph.com
Editorial e-mail: editor@nptelegraph.com
Primary Website: www.nptelegraph.com
Year Established: 1881
News Services: AP.
Special Editions: Real Estate Guide (Monthly).
Special Weekly Sections: TV Week (S).
Syndicated Publications: Relish (Monthly); Parade (S); American Profile (Weekly).
Areas Served - City/County or Portion Thereof, or Zip codes: North Platte (NE)
Avg Free Circ: 442
Sat. Circulation Paid: 6655
Sat. Circulation Free: 442
Sun. Circulation Paid: 6754
Sun. Circulation Free: 366
Audit By: CAC
Audit Date: 30.06.2018
Personnel: Holli Synder (Bus. Mgr.); Dee Klein (Dir., Sales (NPC)); Joe Volcek (Circ. Dir.); Sage Merritt (News Ed.); John Bates (Prodn. Mgr.); Andrew Bottrell (Sports Ed.); Deb Egenberger (Asst. Mng. Ed.); Aly Rinehart (Copy Ed.); Mikayla Wiseman (Copy Ed.); Claudia Cable (Dist. Mgr., Circ.); Peg Kruger (Dist. Mgr., Circ.); Rob Hampton (Prod. Mgr.); Terrie Baker (Pub.); Joan Von Kampen (Managing Ed.)
Parent company (for newspapers): BH Media Group

OMAHA WORLD-HERALD

Street address 1: 1314 Douglas Street
Street address 2: Ste 800
Street address city: Omaha
Street address state: NE
Zip/Postal code: 68102
County: Douglas
Country: USA
Mailing address: 1314 DOUGLAS ST STE 800
Mailing city: OMAHA
Mailing state: NE
Mailing zip: 68102-1848
General Phone: (402) 444-1000
Advertising Phone: (402) 444-1420
Editorial Phone: (402) 444-1304
General/National Adv. E-mail: tsears@owh.com
Display Adv. E-mail: brett.snead@owh.com
Classified Adv. e-mail: debbie.mcchesney@owh.com
Editorial e-mail: news@owh.com
Primary Website: www.omaha.com
Mthly Avg Views: 17000000
Mthly Avg Unique Visitors: 2417167
Year Established: 1885
News Services: AP, Washington Post News Service with Bloomberg, Tribune News Service (formerly MCT)
Special Editions: Auto Show Outlook Kids Camp ACEC Engineers Colon Cancer Auction Block Omahaâ€™s Choice Awards (ballot) NCAA Basketball Preview + Sports wraps Better Business Bureau Worship â€“ Easter Lawn, Garden & Home (Saturday Living) Omaha Chamber â€“ Business Hall of Fame Golf Wrap (Sports) Spring Outdoors (Sports) Small Business Week (pop-out) Spring & Summer Travel/RV Lifestyle Berkshire Hathaway Best Places to Work World-Herald Scholars Parenting by Momaha Super Go! Summer Events & Attractions Go! Taste of Omaha College World Series + Sports wraps Omahaâ€™s Choice Awards (winners) Football Preview â€“ High School Football Preview â€“ College Metro Guide Septemberfest (pop-out) Arts Preview Fall Hunting (Sports) Aksarben Coronation We Donâ€™t Coast â€“ Omaha Chamber Automotive Year Review Architecture Basketball Preview â€“ College Smart Energy Talks The Holiday Book Small Business Saturday (pop-out) Worship â€“ Holiday Welcome Visitors (quarterly) College & Careers (spring & fall) Parade of Homes
Special Weekly Sections: Food Express (Wednesday), GO! Entertainment (Thursday), Home Guide (Friday), Autos (Saturday), HOMES (Sunday)
Syndicated Publications: Parade (Sunday)
Delivery Methods: Mail`Newsstand`Carrier`Racks
Areas Served - City/County or Portion Thereof, or Zip codes: 50020, 50022, 50025, 50076, 50801, 50833, 50841, 50848, 50849, 50851, 50853, 50864, 51034, 51040, 51063, 51104, 51105, 5110651401, 51430, 51442, 51445, 51446, 51454, 51455, 51461, 51463, 51465, 51467, 51501, 51503, 51510, 51521, 51525, 51526, 51527, 51528, 51529, 51530, 51531, 51532, 51533, 51534, 51535, 51536, 51537, 51540, 51541, 51542, 51544, 51545, 51546, 51548, 51549, 51551, 51553, 51555, 51556, 51557, 51559, 51560, 51561, 51562, 51563, 51564,51565, 51566, 51570, 51571, 51573, 51575, 51576, 51577, 51579, 51601, 51631, 51632, 51638, 51639, 51640, 51646, 51649, 51650, 51652, 51653, 51654, 64446, 64482, 68002, 68003, 68004, 68005, 68007, 68008, 68010, 68015, 68016, 68017, 68018, 68019, 68020, 68022, 68023, 68025,68028, 68029, 68031, 68033, 68034, 68036, 68037, 68038, 68041, 68044, 68045, 68046, 68047, 68048, 68050, 68055, 68057, 68058, 68059, 68061, 68063, 68064, 68065, 68066, 68067, 68068, 68069, 68070, 68071, 68072, 68073,68102, 68104, 68105, 68106, 68107, 68108, 68110, 68111, 68112, 68113, 68114, 68116, 68117, 68118, 68122, 68123, 68124, 68127, 68128, 68130, 68131, 68132, 68133, 68134, 68135, 68136, 68137, 68138, 68142, 68144, 68147, 68154, 68157, 68164, 68183, 69198, 68305, 68310, 68320, 68333, 68337, 68347, 68349, 68352, 68355, 68359, 68361, 68366, 68370, 68371, 68376, 68378, 68405, 68407, 68409, 68410, 68413, 68420, 68421, 68434, 68442, 68446, 68447, 68448, 68450, 68455, 68456, 68463, 68465, 68466, 68467, 68501, 68502, 68503, 68504, 68505, 68506, 68507, 68508, 68509, 68510, 68512, 68516, 68520, 68521, 68522, 68524, 68526, 68528, 68542, 68601, 68620, 68621, 68624, 68626, 68627, 68629, 68632, 68633, 68634, 68636, 68638, 68640, 68641, 68642, 68643, 68644, 68647, 68648, 68649, 68651, 68652, 68653, 68654, 68658, 68660, 68661, 68662, 68663, 68664, 68665, 68666, 68669, 68701, 68714, 68715, 68716, 68720, 68726, 68731, 68733, 68739, 68745, 68748, 68756, 68757, 68758, 68764, 68765, 68767, 68768, 68769, 68770, 68771, 68774, 68776, 68779, 68780, 68781, 68784, 68787, 68788, 68790, 68791, 68801, 68803, 68818, 68824, 68826, 68836, 68840, 68845, 68847, 68866, 68869, 68873, 68876, 68883, 68901, 68924, 68927, 68933, 68944, 68949, 68955, 68956, 68959, 68961, 68978, 68982, 69101
Own Printing Facility?: Y
Commercial printers?: Y
Sat. Circulation Paid: 90260
Sun. Circulation Paid: 110899
Audit By: AAM
Audit Date: 31.12.2018
Personnel: Jeff Carney (Dir., Dig Development); Mike Kirk (Finance Dir./Controller); Brett Snead (Dir of Local Sales); Tam Webb (Adv. Mgr., Cust Pub/Events); Deb McChesney (Dir of Class, Cust Pub, Real Estate); Sue Violi (Dir of Comm Rel); Melissa Matczak (Exec Ed); Todd Sears (Pres & Pub); Lowell Miller (Dir of Local Key Acc); Sam Kirkwood (Dir of Adv Oper); Rich Warren (Dir of Mkt); Rick Thornton (Vice Pres. of News)
Parent company (for newspapers): BH Media Group; Lee Enterprises, Incorporated

STAR-HERALD

Street address 1: 1405 Broadway
Street address city: Scottsbluff
Street address state: NE
Zip/Postal code: 69361
County: Scotts Bluff
Country: USA
Mailing address: PO BOX 1709
Mailing city: SCOTTSBLUFF
Mailing state: NE
Mailing zip: 69363-1709
General Phone: (308) 632-9000
Advertising Phone: (308) 632-9020
Editorial Phone: (308) 632-9040
General/National Adv. E-mail: starherald@starherald.com
Display Adv. E-mail: doug.southard@starherald.com
Classified Adv. e-mail: class@starherald.com
Editorial e-mail: news@starherald.com
Primary Website: www.starherald.com
Year Established: 1912
News Services: AP.
Special Weekly Sections: Farm & Ranch (S); TV Week (Sat); Motor News (Wed).
Syndicated Publications: Entertainment (Fri); Parade (S); Church & Religious (Sat); Health & Science (Thur); Business News (Tues); Best Food Day (Wed); American Profile (Weekly).
Avg Free Circ: 404
Sat. Circulation Paid: 8287
Sat. Circulation Free: 404
Sun. Circulation Paid: 8569
Sun. Circulation Free: 352
Audit By: CAC
Audit Date: 30.06.2018
Personnel: Debbie Flowers (Dir., Bus./Personnel Servs.); Doug Southard (Adv. Dir.); Steve Frederick (Ed.); Jeff Fielder (Sports Ed.); Jim Mortimore (Online Mgr.); Roger Tollefson (Gen. Mgr.); Richard Knott (Prodn. Mgr., Distr.); Kelly Zwetzig (Mktg. & Dig. Med. Mgr.); Maunette Loeks (New Med. Dir.)
Parent company (for newspapers): BH Media Group; Lee Enterprises, Incorporated

YORK NEWS-TIMES

Street address 1: 327 N Platte Ave
Street address city: York
Street address state: NE
Zip/Postal code: 68467-3547
County: York
Country: USA
Mailing address: PO BOX 279
Mailing city: YORK
Mailing state: NE
Mailing zip: 68467-0279
General Phone: (402) 362-4478
Advertising Phone: (402) 362-4478
Editorial Phone: (402) 362-4478
General/National Adv. E-mail: kathy.larson@yorknewstimes.com
Display Adv. E-mail: garrett.schwarz@yorknewstimes.com
Classified Adv. e-mail: cheri.knoell@yorknewstimes.com
Editorial e-mail: steve.moseley@yorknewstimes.com
Primary Website: www.yorknewstimes.com
Year Established: 1867
News Services: AP.
Special Weekly Sections: Church Directory/Religion Page (Fri); Regional News (Mon); Prime Time TV Tab (Thur); Best Food Day (Tues); Senior Citizens (Wed).
Syndicated Publications: Relish (Monthly); USA WEEKEND Magazine (Sat).
Delivery Methods: Mail`Newsstand`Carrier`Racks
Areas Served - City/County or Portion Thereof, or Zip codes: 68467, 68460,48456,68666,68434,684 36,68654,68651,68406,68401,68371,68843,6836 7,68365,68361,68359,68354,68351,68330,68319, 68316,68313,
Own Printing Facility?: Y
Commercial printers?: N
Sat. Circulation Paid: 3589
Audit By: Sworn/Estimate/Non-Audited
Audit Date: 12.07.2019
Personnel: Kathy Larson (Adv. Sales Mgr.); Steve Moseley (Ed.); Eric Eckert (Online Ed.); Ken Kush (Sports Ed.); Kerri Pankratz (Copy Ed./Layout/Obits.); Caitlyn Parker (Copy Ed./Layout); Carrie Colburn (Pub.)
Parent company (for newspapers): BH Media Group

NEVADA

NEVADA APPEAL

Street address 1: 580 Mallory Way Ste. #200
Street address city: Carson City
Street address state: NV
Zip/Postal code: 89701
County: Carson City
Country: USA
Mailing address: 580 MALLORY WAY
Mailing city: CARSON CITY
Mailing state: NV
Mailing zip: 89701-5360
General Phone: (775) 882-2111
Advertising Phone: (775) 881-7653
Editorial Phone: (775) 882-2111
General/National Adv. E-mail: mraher@sierranevadamedia.com
Display Adv. E-mail: jtreece@sierranevadamedia.com
Classified Adv. e-mail: classifieds@sierranevadamedia.com
Editorial e-mail: editor@nevadaappeal.com
Primary Website: www.nevadaappeal.com
Mthly Avg Views: 343840
Mthly Avg Unique Visitors: 169592
Year Established: 1865
News Services: AP.
Special Editions: Deadline Home Improvement (Apr); Deadline Primary Election (Aug); Last Minute Appeal Bonus (Dec); Deadline Customer Appreciation Appeal (Jul); Deadline Father's Day Bonus (Jun); Carson Country (Mar); Deadline Mother's Day Bonus (May); Thanksgiving Gift (N
Special Weekly Sections: Real Estate (Fri); TV Log (S); On the Road (Sat); Food (Wed).
Syndicated Publications: Sierra Magazine/Seniors (Monthly); TV Mag (S); American Profile (Weekly).
Delivery Methods: Mail`Newsstand`Carrier`Racks
Areas Served - City/County or Portion Thereof, or Zip codes: 89403, 89410, 89423, 89429, 89447, 89701, 89703, 89704, 89705, 89706
Own Printing Facility?: Y
Commercial printers?: Y
Avg Free Circ: 611
Sat. Circulation Paid: 7039
Sat. Circulation Free: 611
Sun. Circulation Paid: 10315
Sun. Circulation Free: 772
Audit By: CAC
Audit Date: 31.12.2017
Personnel: Rob Galloway (Pub.); Brad Bancroft (Publishing Operations Manager); Robert Glenn (Sr. Business Development Manager); Adam Trumble (Ed.); Ryan Shepherd (Bus. Dev. Mgr.); Brooke Warner (Gen. Mgr.); Charles Whisnand (City Ed.)
Parent company (for newspapers): Swift Communications, Inc.; Pacific Publishing Company

ELKO DAILY FREE PRESS

Street address 1: 3720 E Idaho St
Street address city: Elko
Street address state: NV
Zip/Postal code: 89801-4611
County: Elko
Country: USA
General Phone: (775) 738-3118

General/National Adv. E-mail: advertising@elkodaily.com
Display Adv. E-mail: advertising@elkodaily.com
Classified Adv. e-mail: classified@elkodaily.com
Editorial e-mail: editor@elkodaily.com
Primary Website: www.elkodaily.com
Mthly Avg Views: 1000000
Mthly Avg Unique Visitors: 7900
Year Established: 1883
News Services: AP, TMS.
Special Editions: Mining Quarterly (March, June, September, December); Fall Sports Preview (Aug); Christmas Gift Guide (Dec); Cowboy Poetry Gathering (Jan) Mining Expo (Jun); Newspapers in Education (Mar);
Special Weekly Sections: Entertainment (Fri); Society/Events/Business (Sat); Best Food Day (Tues).
Syndicated Publications: PARADE Magazine (Sat).
Areas Served - City/County or Portion Thereof, or Zip codes: all of Elko county
Own Printing Facility?: N
Commercial printers?: Y
Sat. Circulation Paid: 4983
Sun. Circulation Paid: 5122
Audit By: CAC
Audit Date: 30.09.2014
Personnel: Travis Quast (Pub.); Jeff Mullens (Ed.); Nancy Streets (Adv. Dir.); Robert Cooper (Cir.)
Parent company (for newspapers): Lee Enterprises, Incorporated; Dispatch-Argus

LAS VEGAS SUN

Street address 1: 2275 Corporate Cir
Street address 2: Ste 300
Street address city: Henderson
Street address state: NV
Zip/Postal code: 89074-7745
County: Clark
Country: USA
Mailing address: 2275 CORPORATE CIR STE 300
Mailing city: HENDERSON
Mailing state: NV
Mailing zip: 89074-7745
General Phone: (702) 385-3111
Advertising Phone: (702) 383-0388
Editorial Phone: (702) 385-3111
General/National Adv. E-mail: rebecca@lasvegassun.com
Display Adv. E-mail: brian@lasvegassun.com
Classified Adv. e-mail: brian@lasvegassun.com
Editorial e-mail: letters@lasvegassun.com
Primary Website: www.lasvegassun.com
Mthly Avg Views: 8200000
Mthly Avg Unique Visitors: 1500000
Year Established: 1950
News Services: AP, NYT, SHNS, DJ, GNS.
Delivery Methods: Mail`Newsstand`Carrier`Racks
Areas Served - City/County or Portion Thereof, or Zip codes: Las Vegas, Henderson, North Las Vegas, Boulder City/Clark County
Own Printing Facility?: N
Commercial printers?: N
Sat. Circulation Paid: 120573
Sun. Circulation Paid: 138209
Audit By: AAM
Audit Date: 31.03.2014
Personnel: Brian Greenspun (CEO/Pub./Ed.); Ric Anderson (Managing Ed.); John Frtiz (Deputy Managing Editor/Digital); Ray Brewer (Senior Editor/Sports); Nadine Guy (Office Coordinator); Robert Cauthorn (COO); Dave Mondt (The Sunday Managing Ed.); Cy Ryan (Carson City Bureau Chief); Craig Peterson (Special Pub. Ed.); Wade McAferty (Web Ed.); Elizabeth Brown (Assoc. Creative Dir.); LeAnn Elias (Designer); Jamie Genter (Copy Ed.); Marvin Lucas (Designer)
Parent company (for newspapers): Greenspun Family

LAS VEGAS REVIEW-JOURNAL

Street address 1: 1111 W. Bonanza Road
Street address city: Las Vegas
Street address state: NV
Zip/Postal code: 89106-3545
County: Clark
Country: USA
Mailing address: PO BOX 70
Mailing city: LAS VEGAS
Mailing state: NV
Mailing zip: 89125-0070
General Phone: (702) 383-0211
Advertising Phone: (702) 383-0388
Editorial Phone: (702) 383-0264
General/National Adv. E-mail: kparker@reviewjournal.com
Display Adv. E-mail: adhelp@reviewjournal.com
Classified Adv. e-mail: kdavis@reviewjournal.com
Editorial e-mail: gcook@reviewjournal.com
Primary Website: www.reviewjournal.com
Mthly Avg Views: 12000000
Mthly Avg Unique Visitors: 1626961
Year Established: 1905
News Services: AP, LAT-WP, MCT.
Special Editions: Guide to Pool & Patio (Apr); Football Preview (Aug); National Finals Rodeo (Dec); Dining Guide (Feb); Super Bowl (Jan); Guide to Pool & Patio (Jul); Dining Guide (Jun); Home and Garden (Mar); Home Furnishings (May); National Family Week (Nov); Las Vegas I
Special Weekly Sections: Travel, Living, Entertainment, Business, Sun Opinions (Sun); Neighborhood (Tue); Taste (Wed); Home, Furniture (Thur); Entertainment (Fri); Real Estate (Sat)
Syndicated Publications: USA Weekend, PARADE Magazine, TV Magazine (S).
Delivery Methods: Mail`Newsstand`Carrier`Racks
Own Printing Facility?: Y
Commercial printers?: Y
Sat. Circulation Paid: 89034
Sun. Circulation Paid: 112997
Audit By: AAM
Audit Date: 30.06.2018
Personnel: K.M. Cannon (Asst. Dir. of Photo); Patricia Rice (Office Mgr.); Craig Moon (Pub.); J. Keith Moyer (Ed. in Chief); Glenn Cook (Mng. Ed.)
Parent company (for newspapers): Las Vegas Review-Journal, Inc.; Adelson Family

RENO GAZETTE-JOURNAL

Street address 1: 955 Kuenzli Street
Street address city: Reno
Street address state: NV
Zip/Postal code: 89502-1160
County: Washoe
Country: USA
Mailing address: 955 KUENZLI ST
Mailing city: RENO
Mailing state: NV
Mailing zip: 89502-1179
General Phone: (775) 788-6397
Advertising Phone: (775) 788-7355
Editorial Phone: (775) 788-6397
General/National Adv. E-mail: ngladys@rgj.com
Display Adv. E-mail: ngladys@rgj.com
Classified Adv. e-mail: ngladys@rgj.com
Editorial e-mail: letters@rgj.com
Primary Website: www.rgj.com
Mthly Avg Views: 11000000
Mthly Avg Unique Visitors: 1000000
Year Established: 1870
News Services: AP, GNS, LAT-WP, Knight Ridder.
Special Editions: Nevada Living (Apr); Football (Aug); Super Bowl (Jan); Hot August Nights (Jul); Reno Rodeo (Jun); Dining Guide (May); Dining Guide (Nov); Health Source (Oct); National Air Races (Sept).
Special Weekly Sections: Sierra Living (seasonal) (Fri); Technology (Mon); TV Week (S); Homefinder (Sat); Best Bets (Thur); Auto Finder (Wed).
Syndicated Publications: USA WEEKEND Magazine (S).
Delivery Methods: Mail`Racks
Areas Served - City/County or Portion Thereof, or Zip codes: Metro area
Own Printing Facility?: Y
Commercial printers?: Y
Avg Free Circ: 123
Sat. Circulation Paid: 575
Sun. Circulation Paid: 9270
Sun. Circulation Free: 107
Audit By: AAM
Audit Date: 31.03.2018
Personnel: Peggy Santoro (Senior Content Ed.); Brian Duggan (Ed.); Johanna Huybers (Sports Ed.); Robert Galloway (Key Accnt. Sales Mgr.); Danielle Lacombe (Bus. Dev. Sales Mgr.); Ryan Kedzierski (Pres.); Conrad Velin (Controller); Craig Moon (Pub.); Keith Moyer (Ed.)
Parent company (for newspapers): Gannett

NEW HAMPSHIRE

EAGLE TIMES

Street address 1: 45 Crescent St
Street address city: Claremont
Street address state: NH
Zip/Postal code: 03743-2220
County: Sullivan
Country: USA
Mailing address: 45 Crescent St
Mailing city: Claremont
Mailing state: NH
Mailing zip: 03743-2220
General Phone: (603) 543-3100
General/National Adv. E-mail: cheri@eagletimes.com
Display Adv. E-mail: cheri@eagletimes.com
Classified Adv. e-mail: classi@eagletimes.com
Editorial e-mail: news@eagletimes.com
Primary Website: www.eagletimes.com
Year Established: 1970
News Services: AP, TMS, Washington Post.
Special Weekly Sections: Religion Page (Fri); Sports (S); Entertainment (Thur); Best Food Day (Wed).
Syndicated Publications: Color Comics (S); American Profile (Weekly).
Delivery Methods: Mail`Newsstand`Carrier`Racks
Areas Served - City/County or Portion Thereof, or Zip codes: Sullivan
Own Printing Facility?: Y
Commercial printers?: Y
Sun. Circulation Paid: 8016
Audit By: Sworn/Estimate/Non-Audited
Audit Date: 12.07.2019
Personnel: George Sample (Pub.); Frank Amato (Associate Pub.); Bill Chaisson (Ed.); Kameron Towle (Sports Ed.); Jason Guyer (Prod.); Emily Deane (Classified Adv.); Donna Oliver (Circ.)
Parent company (for newspapers): Sample News Group LLC; Eagle Printing & Publishing LLC

CONCORD MONITOR

Street address 1: 1 Monitor Dr
Street address city: Concord
Street address state: NH
Zip/Postal code: 03301-1834
County: Merrimack
Country: USA
Mailing address: PO BOX 1177
Mailing city: CONCORD
Mailing state: NH
Mailing zip: 03302-1177
General Phone: (603) 224-5301
Advertising Phone: (603) 224-5301
Editorial Phone: (603) 224-5301
General/National Adv. E-mail: ads@cmonitor.com
Display Adv. E-mail: ads@cmonitor.com
Classified Adv. e-mail: classifieds@cmonitor.com
Editorial e-mail: news@cmonitor.com
Primary Website: www.concordmonitor.com
Mthly Avg Views: 1500000
Mthly Avg Unique Visitors: 320000
Year Established: 1809
News Services: AP, CSM, LAT-WP.
Special Editions: Speedway Parade (Apr); Belknap County Fair (Aug); Gift Guide (Dec); Auto (Feb); Wedding (Jan); Market Days (Jul); Summer Directory (Jun); Town Meeting (Mar); Gift Guide (Nov); Fall Recreation (Oct); Business Profiles (Sept).
Special Weekly Sections: Entertainment (S); Auctions (Sat); Auctions (Thur); Business (Tues); Food (Wed).
Syndicated Publications: USA WEEKEND Magazine (S).
Delivery Methods: Mail`Newsstand`Racks
Areas Served - City/County or Portion Thereof, or Zip codes: 03301, 03304, 03303, 03275, 03268, 03224, 03046, 03045, 03307, 03237, 03837, 03229, 03281, 03216, 03230, 03235, 03276, 03269, 03244, 03440, 03280, 03242, 03106, 03101, 03281, 03244, 03278, 03257, 03260, 03273, 03287, 03221, 03255, 03773, 03272, 03218, 03225, 03037, 03234, 03261, 03884, 03263, 03258, 03246, 03249, 03256, 03217, 03220, 03253, 03222, 03243, 03223, 03245, 03894, 03809, 03254, 03801
Avg Free Circ: 1368
Sat. Circulation Paid: 11513
Sat. Circulation Free: 1368
Sun. Circulation Paid: 13395
Sun. Circulation Free: 613
Audit By: CAC
Audit Date: 30.06.2016
Personnel: Sandy Bourque (Controller); David Sangiorgio (Pub.); Ralph Jimenez (Opinion Ed.); Ben Allen (Tech. Servs. Mgr.); Sean McKenna (Adv. Dir.); Deb Sanborn (Sales Dir.); Thomas Ahearn (Dist. Mgr.); Keith Testa (Ed., The Concord Insider); Jon Bodell (Copy Ed.); Julie Byrd-Jenkins (Copy Ed.); Susan Doucett (Comm. Ed.); Jana Ford (Day Ed.); Khela McGann (Night Ed.); Jeff Novotny (Asst. Sports Ed.); Sandra Smith (Sports Ed.); Jennifer VanPelt (LiveWell Ed.); Clay Wirestone (Features Ed.); Dana Wormald (Ideas & Opinion Ed.); Harry Green Jr. (Press/Camera Mgr.)
Parent company (for newspapers): Newspapers of New England

FOSTER'S DAILY DEMOCRAT

Street address 1: 150 Venture Dr
Street address city: Dover
Street address state: NH
Zip/Postal code: 03820-5913
County: Strafford
Country: USA
Mailing state: NH
General Phone: (603) 742-4455
Advertising Phone: (603) 516-2969
General/National Adv. E-mail: news@fosters.com
Display Adv. E-mail: dispatch@fosters.com
Classified Adv. e-mail: fddads@fosters.com
Editorial e-mail: news@fosters.com
Primary Website: www.fosters.com
Mthly Avg Views: 42846
Mthly Avg Unique Visitors: 35000
Year Established: 1873
News Services: AP, NYT.
Syndicated Publications: USA WEEKEND Magazine (S)
Delivery Methods: Mail`Newsstand`Carrier`Racks
Areas Served - City/County or Portion Thereof, or Zip codes: Tri-City, Seacoast & Southern Maine region
Own Printing Facility?: Y
Commercial printers?: N
Sat. Circulation Paid: 6210
Audit By: AAM
Audit Date: 31.12.2018
Personnel: James Russell (Cir. Dir.); Simeon Broughton (IT Dir.); Mary Rowland (Mng. Ed.); Paul Dietterle (Ed. Rep.); Mike Whaley (Sports Ed.); John Huff (Chief Photo.); Howard Altschiller (Ex. Ed.); John Tabor (Pres. & Pub.)
Parent company (for newspapers): Gannett; CherryRoad Media

THE KEENE SENTINEL

Street address 1: 60 West St
Street address city: Keene
Street address state: NH
Zip/Postal code: 03431-3373
County: Cheshire
Country: USA
Mailing address: PO BOX 546
Mailing city: KEENE
Mailing state: NH
Mailing zip: 03431-0546
General Phone: (603) 352-1234
Advertising Phone: (603) 352-1234 ext 1220
Editorial Phone: (603) 352-1234 ext. 1400
General/National Adv. E-mail: adassist@keenesentinel.com
Display Adv. E-mail: advertising@keenesentinel.com
Classified Adv. e-mail: classified@keenesentinel.com
Editorial e-mail: news@keenesentinel.com
Primary Website: www.sentinelsource.com
Year Established: 1799
News Services: AP, CNS, LAT-WP, TMS.
Special Editions: Business Monadnock/Economic Outlook (Jan.); Brides (Feb.); Business Monadnock/Trendsetters (Mar.); Answer Book (Mar.); Home & Garden (Apr.); Reader's Choice Awards (May); Vows (Jun.); Monadnock Summer (Jun.); Extraordinary Women (Jul.); Monadnock Mid-Summer (Jul.); Keene State College City Guide (Aug.); Home & Hearth (Sep.); Monadnock Autumn (Oct.) Holiday Ideas (Nov.); Last Minute Holiday Ideas (Dec.)
Special Weekly Sections: Religion (Sat); ELF (Thur).
Syndicated Publications: Parade Magazine (S); Dash (1st Wed. Each Month)
Delivery Methods: Mail`Newsstand`Carrier`Racks
Own Printing Facility?: Y
Avg Free Circ: 201
Sat. Circulation Paid: 7190
Sat. Circulation Free: 97
Sun. Circulation Paid: 7190
Sun. Circulation Free: 97

Audit By: AAM
Audit Date: 31.03.2019
Personnel: Terry Williams (Pres./COO); Thomas M. Ewing (Own & Pub.); Linda Flagg (Bus. & HR Mgr.); Lorraine Ellis (Adv. Mgr., Classified); Paul A. Miller (Exec. Ed.); David Lanier (Sports Ed.); Cecily Weisburgh (Dig. Content Ed.); Chris Carreira (IT Dir.); Gregory Walker (Press Frmn); Robert Farnsworth (Graph. & Prod. Mgr.); Jessica Garcia (Inter. Media Dir.); Paul Miller (Executive Editor)
Parent company (for newspapers): Keene Publishing Corp.

THE LACONIA DAILY SUN

Street address 1: 1127 Union Ave
Street address 2: Ste 1
Street address city: Laconia
Street address state: NH
Zip/Postal code: 03246-2126
County: Belknap
Country: USA
General Phone: (603) 737-2030
Advertising Phone: (603) 737-2020
Editorial Phone: (603) 737-2026
General/National Adv. E-mail: ads@laconiadailysun.com
Display Adv. E-mail: ads@laconiadailysun.com
Classified Adv. e-mail: ads@laconiadailysun.com
Editorial e-mail: news@laconiadailysun.com
Primary Website: www.laconiadailysun.com
Mthly Avg Views: 300000
Mthly Avg Unique Visitors: 150000
Year Established: 2000
Special Editions: Wedding Guide 25,000 copies Publishes in March Summer Fun Guide 50,000 copies Publishes in May Fall Fun Guide 40,000 copies Publishes in August Holiday Gift Guide 8 weeks, November-December Thanksgiving pull-out section Wednesday before Thanksgiving Spring and Fall Home Improvement sections April-May; Sept-Oct Boating Special Section - end of June-October Saturday Weekend editions - Special features July-October NH Pumpkin Festival Special Section - second weekend in October
Special Weekly Sections: Tuesday - Business Wednesday - Health & Wellness Thursday - Lakestyle: Arts & Entertainment Friday - Outdoors Saturday - History and Feature Cover Stories
Delivery Methods: Newsstand`Carrier`Racks
Areas Served - City/County or Portion Thereof, or Zip codes: Laconia, Gilford, Meredith, Weirs Beach, Center Harbor, Belmont, Moultonborough, Winnisquam, Sanbornton, Tilton, Gilmanton, Alton, New Hampton, Plymouth, Bristol, Ashland, Holderness, Northfield, Franklin, Loudon, Wolfeboro
Own Printing Facility?: N
Commercial printers?: Y
Avg Free Circ: 18000
Sat. Circulation Free: 18000
Sun. Circulation Free: 18000
Audit By: Sworn/Estimate/Non-Audited
Audit Date: 12.07.2019
Personnel: Adam Hirshan (Publisher); Adam Hirshan (Pub.); Ginger Kozlowski (Managing Ed.); Elaine Hirshan (Advertising Manager); Edward Engler (Pres)
Parent company (for newspapers): Engler Group

THE TELEGRAPH

Street address 1: 110 Main St
Street address 2: Ste 1
Street address city: Nashua
Street address state: NH
Zip/Postal code: 03060-2723
County: Hillsborough
Country: USA
Mailing address: 110 MAIN ST # 1
Mailing city: NASHUA
Mailing state: NH
Mailing zip: 03060-2723
General Phone: (603) 882-2741
Advertising Phone: (603) 594-6555
Editorial Phone: (603) 594-6467
General/National Adv. E-mail: mgorman@nashuatelegraph.com
Display Adv. E-mail: adsales@nashuatlegraph.com
Classified Adv. e-mail: getclassifieds@nashuatelegraph.com
Editorial e-mail: news@nashuatelegraph.com
Primary Website: www.nashuatelegraph.com
Mthly Avg Views: 1600000
Mthly Avg Unique Visitors: 450000
Year Established: 1832
News Services: AP, LAT-WP.
Special Editions: Colossal Classified (Apr); Progress (March); Spring Home & Garden (April); Mothers Day (May); Summer Guide (May); Graduation (June); Community Guide (July); Back to Class (August); Fall Home & Garden (September); Holiday Gift Guide (November); Celebrate New Year's Eve (Dec); Valentine's Day (Feb); Celebrating Women (Oct).
Special Weekly Sections: Faith Pages (Sat); Encore -- Arts - Entertainment - Food (Thur); Food (Wed).
Syndicated Publications: USA WEEKEND Magazine (S).
Delivery Methods: Mail`Newsstand`Carrier`Racks
Areas Served - City/County or Portion Thereof, or Zip codes: In NH: Nashua, Hudson, Merrimack, Hollis, Brookline, Milford, Amherst, Litchfield, Londonderry Lyndeborough, Wilton, Mason, Greenville. In MA: Dunstable; Tyngsborough.
Own Printing Facility?: N
Commercial printers?: Y
Avg Free Circ: 409
Sat. Circulation Paid: 11815
Sat. Circulation Free: 409
Sun. Circulation Paid: 16105
Sun. Circulation Free: 198
Audit By: AAM
Audit Date: 30.06.2016
Personnel: George Pelletier (Bureau Chief); Matt Burdette (Editor in Chief); Casey Junkins (City Ed.); Alan Greenwood (Sports Ed.); Terry Foster (Community News Ed.); Lynda Vallatini (Adv. Dir.); Shawn Paulus (Circ. Dir.)
Parent company (for newspapers): Ogden Newspapers Inc.

THE CONWAY DAILY SUN

Street address 1: 64 Seavey St
Street address city: North Conway
Street address state: NH
Zip/Postal code: 03860-5355
County: Carroll
Country: USA
Mailing address: PO BOX 1940
Mailing city: NORTH CONWAY
Mailing state: NH
Mailing zip: 03860-1940
General Phone: (603) 356-3456
Advertising Phone: (603) 733-5808
Editorial Phone: (603) 356-8360
General/National Adv. E-mail: joyce@conwaydailysun.com
Display Adv. E-mail: Rick@conwaydailysun.com
Classified Adv. e-mail: Classifieds@conwaydailysun.com
Primary Website: www.conwaydailysun.com
Year Established: 1989
News Services: AP, RN.
Special Editions: Sports Preview (Apr); Dining Guide (Dec); Economic Review (Feb); Dining Guide (Jul); Sports Preview (May).
Special Weekly Sections: Education (Mon); Real Estate (Sat); Sports (Tues); Business (Wed).
Syndicated Publications: Cool News (Fri).
Delivery Methods: Mail`Newsstand`Carrier`Racks
Areas Served - City/County or Portion Thereof, or Zip codes: 03818, 03812, 03813 (Ctr. Conway), 03813 (Chatham), 03817, 03818, 03832, 03836, 03838, 03845, 03846, 03847, 04051, 03849, 03860, 03875, 03886, 03864, 04037, 03894, 03254
Own Printing Facility?: Y
Commercial printers?: Y
Avg Free Circ: 17100
Sat. Circulation Paid: 16100
Sat. Circulation Free: 17100
Audit By: Sworn/Estimate/Non-Audited
Audit Date: 12.07.2019
Personnel: David N. Danforth (Pres.); Mark Guerringue (Pub.); Joyce Brothers (Office Mgr.); Bart Bachman (Comm. Ed.); Jamie Gemmiti (Photography Ed.); Lloyd Jones (Sports Ed.); Alec Kerr (Wire/Entertainment Ed.); Frank Haddy (Sen. Press.); Terry Leavitt (Op-Ed. Ed); Darcy Gautreau (Graphics Mgr.); Margaret McKenzie (Mng. Ed.); Joyce Brothers (Op. Mgr. / Adv. Sls Mgr.)
Parent company (for newspapers): Mark Guerringue

PORTSMOUTH HERALD

Street address 1: 111 NH Ave
Street address city: Portsmouth
Street address state: NH
Zip/Postal code: 03801-2864
County: Rockingham
Country: USA
Mailing address: 111 NH AVE
Mailing city: PORTSMOUTH
Mailing state: NH
Mailing zip: 03801-3772
General Phone: (800) 439-0303
Advertising Phone: (603) 436-1800
Editorial Phone: (603) 570-2129
General/National Adv. E-mail: sales@seacoastonline.com
Display Adv. E-mail: scnadvertising@seacoastonline.com
Classified Adv. e-mail: classads@seacoastonline.com
Editorial e-mail: news@seacoastonline.com
Primary Website: www.seacoastonline.com
Year Established: 1884
News Services: AP.
Special Editions: Spring Lawn/Garden (Apr); Healthy Living (Aug); Last Minute Gift (Dec); Pres. Auto (Feb); Bridal (Jan); Summer Ports of Call (Jun); St. Pat's Auto (Mar); Mother's Day (May); N.E. Holidays (Nov); Harvest (Oct); Menu Guide (Sept).
Special Weekly Sections: Spotlight Weekly Magazine (Thur); Best Food Day (Wed).
Syndicated Publications: R.E. Guide (Monthly); Commercial Real Estate Guide (Quarterly); TV Times (S); Value Zone (Sat); Spotlight Magazine (Thur).
Areas Served - City/County or Portion Thereof, or Zip codes: Seacoast Region
Avg Free Circ: 1762
Sat. Circulation Paid: 5491
Sat. Circulation Free: 1762
Sun. Circulation Paid: 14147
Sun. Circulation Free: 1810
Audit By: AAM
Audit Date: 31.12.2018
Personnel: John Tabor (Pub.); Sandra Titus (Adv. Mgr., Classified/Sales); Dennis Thompson (Circ. Dir.); Howard Altschiller (Exec. Ed.); Rick Fabrizio (Mng. Ed.); Andrew Chernoff (Ad. Dir.); Therese SanSoucie (Graphics Sup.)
Parent company (for newspapers): Gannett; CherryRoad Media

VALLEY NEWS

Street address 1: 24 Interchange Dr
Street address city: West Lebanon
Street address state: NH
Zip/Postal code: 03784-2003
County: Grafton
Country: USA
Mailing address: PO BOX 877
Mailing city: WHITE RIVER JUNCTION
Mailing state: VT
Mailing zip: 05001-0877
General Phone: (603) 298-8711
Advertising Phone: (603) 298-6082
Editorial Phone: (603) 727-3217
General/National Adv. E-mail: advertising@vnews.com
Display Adv. E-mail: advertising@vnews.com
Classified Adv. e-mail: classified@vnews.com
Editorial e-mail: newseditor@vnews.com
Primary Website: www.vnews.com
Mthly Avg Views: 1008520
Mthly Avg Unique Visitors: 229865
Year Established: 1952
News Services: AP, LAT-WP, New England Wire Service.
Special Editions: Golf Guide (April); Readers Choice (October); Valley Parents (Quarterly); Enterprise (Monthly Business); Upper Valley Holidays (November);
Special Weekly Sections: Religion(Fri); Science & Technology (Mon); Movies (Sat); Arts (Thur); Education (Tues); Food & Garden (Wed); Real Estate (Sat)
Syndicated Publications: Valley Television (Sat);
Delivery Methods: Newsstand`Carrier`Racks
Areas Served - City/County or Portion Thereof, or Zip codes: Grafton
Own Printing Facility?: Y
Commercial printers?: Y
Avg Free Circ: 850
Sat. Circulation Paid: 11751
Sat. Circulation Free: 850
Sun. Circulation Paid: 12329
Sun. Circulation Free: 190
Audit By: AAM
Audit Date: 30.06.2018
Personnel: Daniel D. McClory (Pub.); Rich Wallace (Gen. Mgr.); Matt Clary (Editor); James Carey (Circ. Dir.); Geoff Hansen (Managing Editor); Terri Rieman (News/ Engagement Editor); Ernie Kohlsaat (Sunday and Bus. News Ed.); Bob Mathewson (Operations); Alex Hanson (Feat., Ed.); Dan Mackie (Editorial Page Ed.); Greg Fennell (Sports Ed.); John Gregg (News Editor); Maggie Cassidy (Web Editor)
Parent company (for newspapers): Newspapers of New England

NEW JERSEY

THE COURIER-POST

Street address 1: 301 Cuthbert Blvd
Street address city: Cherry Hill
Street address state: NJ
Zip/Postal code: 08002-2905
County: Camden
Country: USA
Mailing address: PO BOX 5300
Mailing city: CHERRY HILL
Mailing state: NJ
Mailing zip: 08034-0430
General Phone: (856) 663-6000
Advertising Phone: (856) 486-2503
Editorial Phone: (856) 486-2402
General/National Adv. E-mail: info@courierpostonline.com
Display Adv. E-mail: mbettner@gannett.com
Classified Adv. e-mail: classifiedads@courierpostonline.com
Editorial e-mail: cpedit@courierpostonline.com
Primary Website: www.courierpostonline.com
Year Established: 1875
News Services: AP, GNS.
Special Editions: Pic-a-Home Real Estate Magazine (); Cookbook (Apr); Labor Day Recipe Pages (Aug); End of Month Values (Dec); South Jersey Unlimited (Feb); Luxury Living (Jan); End of Month Values (Jul); Luxury Living (Jun); Luxury Living (Mar); UMD (May); End of Month Va
Special Weekly Sections: Business (Daily); Living, Family, Sports, (Mon); Our Towns (Tue); Taste, Living, Sports (Wed); Sports (Thur); Arts, Entertainment, Living, Real Estate Sports (Fri); Business, Family Fun, Home, Gardens, High School Sports (Sat); Books, Health, Food, Travel, Business, Real Estate, TV, Comics, Sports (Sun);
Syndicated Publications: USA WEEKEND Magazine (S).
Sat. Circulation Paid: 22810
Sun. Circulation Paid: 30376
Audit By: AAM
Audit Date: 31.12.2018
Personnel: Jean Wysocki (Controller); M.J. Fine (Regional Comm. Ed.); Sheri Berkery (Reg. Prod.); Karen Morgan (Regional Prod); Tammy Paolino (Reg. Engagement Ed.); Janice Linneman (Admin Assist.); Jerry Staas Haught (Cont. Strategist); Chris LaChall (Photo/Video); Tom McGurk (Reg. Sports Strategist/ Editor); Jason Alt (Regional Ed.); Craig Connolly (Dir., Info Servs.); Chris Silvestri (Reg. Plan.); Joseph Calchi (Pres. & Pub.); Leslie Emma (Asst. Cont.); Bonnie Still (HR Mgr.)
Parent company (for newspapers): Gannett

SOUTH JERSEY TIMES

Street address 1: 161 Bridgeton Pike
Street address 2: Ste E
Street address city: Mullica Hill
Street address state: NJ
Zip/Postal code: 08062-2669
County: Gloucester
Country: USA
Mailing state: NJ
General Phone: 856-754-7100
Advertising Phone: (856) 754-7152
Editorial Phone: (856) 754-7151
General/National Adv. E-mail: sjadvertising@njadvancemedia.com
Display Adv. E-mail: tdrummond@njadvancemedia.com
Classified Adv. e-mail: sjtclassifieds@njadvancemedia.com
Editorial e-mail: sjnews@njadvancemedia.com
Primary Website: www.nj.com/southjerseytimes
Mthly Avg Views: 71000000
Mthly Avg Unique Visitors: 14200000
News Services: AP, U.S. Suburban Press Inc..
Special Weekly Sections: Washington Township Times (Fridays) Indulge (Fridays)
Syndicated Publications: Parade (S).
Delivery Methods: Mail`Newsstand`Carrier`Racks
Areas Served - City/County or Portion Thereof, or Zip codes: Cumberland, Gloucester and Salem Counties, NJ

Own Printing Facility?: N
Commercial printers?: N
Avg Free Circ: 339
Sun. Circulation Paid: 11707
Sun. Circulation Free: 6308
Audit By: AAM
Audit Date: 30.06.2015
Personnel: Rhonda Barlow (VP Sales & Pub.); Jessica Beym (Community Editor)
Parent company (for newspapers): Advance Publications, Inc.

ASBURY PARK PRESS

Street address 1: 3600 Highway 66
Street address city: Neptune
Street address state: NJ
Zip/Postal code: 7754
County: Monmouth
Country: USA
Mailing address: PO BOX 1550
Mailing city: NEPTUNE
Mailing state: NJ
Mailing zip: 07754-1550
General Phone: (800) 822-9770
Advertising Phone: (732) 643-3703
Editorial Phone: (732) 922-6000
General/National Adv. E-mail: applegals@gannett.com
Display Adv. E-mail: bditty@njpressmedia.com
Classified Adv. e-mail: appclass@gannett.com
Editorial e-mail: yourviews@app.com
Primary Website: www.app.com
Mthly Avg Unique Visitors: 1743605
Year Established: 1879
Delivery Methods: Mail`Newsstand`Carrier`Racks
Areas Served - City/County or Portion Thereof, or Zip codes: Monmouth & Ocean Counties (NJ)
Sat. Circulation Paid: 53561
Sun. Circulation Paid: 80916
Audit By: AAM
Audit Date: 30.09.2018
Personnel: Hollis Towns (Exec. Ed. & Vice Pres./News); Thomas Donavan (Pres. & Pub.); Karen Guarasi (Regional VP/Adv.); Jack Roth (VP/Prod.); Wayne Peragallo (VP, Information Systems); Jane Pettigrew (VP/Circ.); Erik Statler (VP/Fin.); Paul D'Ambrosio (News & Invest. Dir.)
Parent company (for newspapers): Gannett

ASBURY PARK PRESS

Street address 1: 3600 Hwy 66
Street address city: Neptune
Street address state: NJ
Zip/Postal code: 7754-
County: Monmouth
Country: USA
Mailing address: PO Box 1550
Mailing city: Neptune
Mailing state: NJ
Mailing zip: 07754-1550
General Phone: (732) 922-6000
Primary Website: www.app.com
Personnel: Paul D'Ambrosio (Executive Editor)
Parent company (for newspapers): Gannett Co Inc.

THE BEACON

Street address 1: 3601 State Route 66
Street address 2: A Publication of the Press
Street address city: Neptune
Street address state: NJ
Zip/Postal code: 07753-2604
County: Ocean
Country: USA
Mailing address: 3601 State Route 66
Mailing city: Neptune
Mailing state: NJ
Mailing zip: 07753-2604
General Phone: (732) 922-6000
Editorial Phone: (800) 822-9770 ext 4110
General/National Adv. E-mail: tbeacon@app.com
Editorial e-mail: htowns@gannettnj.com
Primary Website: www.app.com
Delivery Methods: Newsstand`Carrier`Racks
Areas Served - City/County or Portion Thereof, or Zip codes: southern Ocean County NJ
Sat. Circulation Paid: 53561
Sun. Circulation Paid: 80916
Audit By: AAM
Audit Date: 30.09.2018
Personnel: Tom Donovan (Publisher); Linda Reddington (Editor)
Parent company (for newspapers): Gannett

THE STAR-LEDGER

Street address 1: 1 Gateway Center, Suite 1100
Street address city: Newark
Street address state: NJ
Zip/Postal code: 07102-1243
County: Essex
Country: USA
Mailing address: 1 STAR LEDGER PLZ STE 1
Mailing city: NEWARK
Mailing state: NJ
Mailing zip: 07102-1227
General Phone: (888) 782-7533
Advertising Phone: (973) 392-5894
Editorial Phone: (973) 392-4040
General/National Adv. E-mail: imest@njadvancemedia.com
Display Adv. E-mail: mhays@njadvancemedia.com
Editorial e-mail: metro@starledger.com
Primary Website: www.nj.com/starledger
Mthly Avg Unique Visitors: 6088000
News Services: Metro Suburbia Inc./Newhouse Newspapers, NNS, LAT-WP, DJ, RN, PR Newswire, MCT.
Special Weekly Sections: Real Estate Marketplace (Fri); Education (S); Home & Garden (Thur); Body Shop (Tues); Savor (Wed).
Syndicated Publications: Parade (S). Inside Jersey (mthly)
Delivery Methods: Mail`Newsstand`Carrier`Racks
Own Printing Facility?: Y
Commercial printers?: Y
Sat. Circulation Paid: 104607
Sun. Circulation Paid: 204915
Audit By: AAM
Audit Date: 30.06.2018
Personnel: Richard Vezza (Pub.); John F. Dennan (Gen. Mgr.); Brian Pfeifer (National Advertising Manager); Robert C. Provost (Director of Marketing.); Dennis Carletta (Circ. Dir.); David Tucker (Mng. Ed.); Tom Curran (Assoc. Ed.); Tom Moran (Editorial Page Ed.); Daniel Murphy (Deputy Editorial Page Ed.); Louis Stancampiano (Advertising Director); Bob Gray (Dir. Adv.); Robert Jarrach; Patricia Wells; Frances Eiss; Randi Ungar (Director); Steve Alessi (VP of Advertising)
Parent company (for newspapers): Advance Publications, Inc.

NEW JERSEY HERALD

Street address 1: 2 Spring St
Street address city: Newton
Street address state: NJ
Zip/Postal code: 07860-2077
County: Sussex
Country: USA
Mailing address: PO BOX 10
Mailing city: NEWTON
Mailing state: NJ
Mailing zip: 07860-0010
General Phone: (973) 383-1500
Advertising Phone: (973) 383-1500 option 2
Editorial Phone: (973) 383-1500 ext. 31899
General/National Adv. E-mail: advertising@njherald.com
Display Adv. E-mail: kflinn@njherald.com
Classified Adv. e-mail: classified@njherald.com
Editorial e-mail: newsroom@njherald.com
Primary Website: www.njherald.com
Year Established: 1829
News Services: AP, TMS.
Special Editions: Home and Garden (Apr); Back-to-School (Aug); Christmas Gift Guides (Dec); Progress (Feb); White Sale (Jan); Newton Sidewalk Sale (Jul); New Jersey Cardinals (Jun); Expo (Mar); Home & Garden (May); Human Resources (Nov); New Car (Oct); Fall Home Improvemen
Special Weekly Sections: Entertainment (Fri); Business (Mon); Food (S); Best Food Day (Wed).
Syndicated Publications: TV Week (S); American Profile (Weekly).
Delivery Methods: Mail`Newsstand`Carrier`Racks
Areas Served - City/County or Portion Thereof, or Zip codes: 07860 07422
Own Printing Facility?: Y
Commercial printers?: Y
Avg Free Circ: 643
Sun. Circulation Paid: 11925
Sun. Circulation Free: 307
Audit By: AAM
Audit Date: 31.03.2019
Personnel: Lee Williams (Promo./Special Projects Mgr.); Bruce Tomlinson (Exec. Ed.); Kathy Stevens (News Ed.); Jaime Kerr (Tech Mgr.); Keith Flinn (Pub.); John Kopec (Auto. Category Mgr.); Mara Clingingsmith (Class. Mgr.); Amy Paterson (Int. Dir.); Jesse Kryscio (Copy Ed.); Daniel Freel (Senior Photo.); Carl Barbati (Sports Ed.); Robin Fichter (HR & Admin. Ass.); Jay Gillispie (Cir. Dir.)
Parent company (for newspapers): CherryRoad Media

DAILY RECORD

Street address 1: 6 Century Drive
Street address 2: Ste 3
Street address city: Parsippany
Street address state: NJ
Zip/Postal code: 7054
County: Morris
Country: USA
Mailing address: PO BOX 217
Mailing city: PARSIPPANY
Mailing state: NJ
Mailing zip: 07054-0217
General Phone: (973) 428-6200
Advertising Phone: (973) 428-6551
Editorial Phone: (973) 428-6610
General/National Adv. E-mail: jungaro@gannettnjcom
Display Adv. E-mail: kguarasi@gannettnj.com
Classified Adv. e-mail: drclass@gannett.com
Editorial e-mail: jungaro@gannettnj.com
Primary Website: www.dailyrecord.com
Mthly Avg Views: 2300000
Mthly Avg Unique Visitors: 325000
Year Established: 1900
News Services: AP, GNS, Bloomberg, CNS, TMS.
Special Editions: Creative Homes (Apr); Family (Aug); Last Minute Gifts (Dec); Bridal (Feb); Coupon Clippers (Jan); Seniors (Jun); Fashion (Mar); Home Improvement (May); Going Shopping (Nov); Coupon Clippers (Oct); High School Football (Sept).
Special Weekly Sections: Real Estate (Fri); Technology (Mon); Real Estate (S); On The Row (Sat); Parisppany Plus (Thur); Business (Tues); Denville/Rockaway Plus (Wed).
Syndicated Publications: USA Weekend (S).
Areas Served - City/County or Portion Thereof, or Zip codes: Morris County (NJ)
Avg Free Circ: 681
Sat. Circulation Paid: 8629
Sat. Circulation Free: 681
Sun. Circulation Paid: 10448
Sun. Circulation Free: 81
Audit By: AAM
Audit Date: 31.12.2018
Personnel: Karen Guarasi (Reg. VP Adv.); Joe Ungaro (General Manager/Editor)
Parent company (for newspapers): Gannett

THE PRESS OF ATLANTIC CITY

Street address 1: 1000 W Washington Ave
Street address city: Pleasantville
Street address state: NJ
Zip/Postal code: 08232-3861
County: Atlantic
Country: USA
Mailing address: PO BOX 3100
Mailing city: PLEASANTVILLE
Mailing state: NJ
Mailing zip: 08232-0039
General Phone: (609) 272-7000
Advertising Phone: (609) 272-7000
Editorial Phone: (609) 272-7267
General/National Adv. E-mail: MRice@pressofac.com
Classified Adv. e-mail: JCompton@pressofac.com
Editorial e-mail: letters@pressofac.com
Primary Website: www.pressofatlanticcity.com
Mthly Avg Views: 4000000
Mthly Avg Unique Visitors: 500000
Year Established: 1872
News Services: AP, MCT, TMS
Special Editions: Clips Monthly Coupon Digest, Health Quarterly Magazine, Bliss Bridal Magazine, Jersey Strong, Fore Golf Digest, Atlantic County Living, Cape May County Living, Indulge Dining Magazine, Summer Family Fun Guide, Fall Fun Guide, Best of Press Readers Choice Awards, Brendan Borek, (Sept); NACAC Education Guide, Big Book Holiday Guide, High School Sports Best of Fall
Special Weekly Sections: Wellness (Mon); Life (M, T, W, F, Sa); At The Shore (Th) Entertainment Guide; Movies (Fri); Travel, E-Life, Pets, Taste, Real Estate, Marketplace, Auto (Sun), Business (T-Sat)
Syndicated Publications: Parade (S). Dash (monthly)
Delivery Methods: Mail`Newsstand`Carrier`Racks
Areas Served - City/County or Portion Thereof, or Zip codes: Atlantic, Cape May, Cumberland & South Ocean Counties (NJ)
Own Printing Facility?: N
Commercial printers?: N
Avg Free Circ: 4482
Sat. Circulation Paid: 27775
Sat. Circulation Free: 3278
Sun. Circulation Paid: 32787
Sun. Circulation Free: 3258
Audit By: AAM
Audit Date: 30.09.2018
Personnel: Kris Worrell (VP. News); Kevin Post (Local Content Producer/Business); Michelle Rice (VP. of Sales / Mktg.); Scott Cronick (At The Shore Ed. / AC Weekly); Steve Cronin (Local Content Producer/ Features); Mark Melhorn (Sports); Blum Mark (Pub); Mike Dellavecchia (Digital Mgr.); Alison Leonard (Adv. Sys. Mgr.); Vernon Ogrodnek (Multi. Media Ed.)
Parent company (for newspapers): BH Media Group

HERALD NEWS

Street address 1: 100 Commons Way
Street address city: Rockaway
Street address state: NJ
Zip/Postal code: 07866-2038
County: Morris
Country: USA
Mailing address: PO BOX 471
Mailing city: WOODLAND PARK
Mailing state: NJ
Mailing zip: 07424-0471
General Phone: (973) 569-7000
Advertising Phone: (973) 905-4023
Editorial Phone: (973) 569-7100
General/National Adv. E-mail: bartholomew@northjersey.com
Display Adv. E-mail: advertising@northjersey.com
Classified Adv. e-mail: classified@northjersey.com
Editorial e-mail: newsroom@northjersey.com
Primary Website: www.northjersey.com
Year Established: 1872
News Services: AP, McClatchy, Washington Post, Bloomberg, Christian Science Monitor, Religion News Service, Scripps
Special Editions: Health Quarterly (Feb., May., Aug., Sep.); Education (Mar., Oct.); Consumer Guide (Mar., Apr.); Holiday Dining (Monthly); High School Sports (Sept.); Breast Cancer Awareness (Oct.); Dine Out Guide (Nov.); Holiday Gift Guide (Dec.)
Syndicated Publications: TV Book (S).
Delivery Methods: Mail`Newsstand`Carrier
Areas Served - City/County or Portion Thereof, or Zip codes: 07603, 07601, 07606, 07010, 07410, 07407, 07663, 07026, 07057, 07604, 07644, 07607, 07662, 07075, 07020, 07024, 07452, 07605, 07643, 07624, 07627, 07640, 07641, 07647, 07648, 07675, 0720, 07626, 07631, 07632, 07670, 07630, 07642, 07645, 07656, 07675, 07676, 07677, 07660, 07072, 07073, 07071, 07032, 07070, 07450, 07417, 07436, 07432, 07481, 07430, 07446, 07463, 07666, 07410, 07423, 07458, 07649, 07652, 07661, 07621, 07628, 07646, 07450, 07403, 07011, 07012, 07013, 07014, 07508, 07420, 07506, 07421, 07424, 07508, 07055, 07501, 07502, 07503, 07504, 07505, 07509, 07510, 07513, 07514, 07522, 07524, 07442, 07456, 07512, 07465, 07470, 07435 & 07480
Own Printing Facility?: Y
Commercial printers?: Y
Sat. Circulation Paid: 7034
Sun. Circulation Paid: 7285
Audit By: AAM
Audit Date: 31.12.2017
Personnel: Deirdre Sykes (Sr. Dir.); Doug Clancy (Exec. Ed.); Alfred Doblin (Editorial Ed.); John Balkun (Dir. Sports); Elizabeth Houlton (Dir. News & Production); Jon Naso (Dir. Photography); Yuri Demidov (VP Internet Technology); Bob Konig (VP Operations); Jennifer A. Borg (VP/Corp Secretary & General Counsel); Sean Oates (Web Ed.); Thomas Heffernan (CEO); Martin Gottlieb (VP Ed.); Maggie Grande (Dir. Marketing); Greg Hoffmann (Dir. Information Technology); Mara Clingingsmith (Classified Mgr.); Richard Colandrea (Dir. Corporate & National Adv.); Marc McGuigan (Director of Internet Sales); Nick Maltezos (Dig. Ad. Ops. Mgr.); Kathy Batemarco (HR Man.)

Parent company (for newspapers): Gannett - USA Today Network

THE JERSEY JOURNAL

Street address 1: 1 Harmon Plz
Street address 2: Ste 1010
Street address city: Secaucus
Street address state: NJ
Zip/Postal code: 07094-2804
County: Hudson
Country: USA
Mailing state: NJ
General Phone: (201) 653-1000
Advertising Phone: (201) 217-2537
Editorial Phone: (201) 217-2500
General/National Adv. E-mail: pmagnani@jjournal.com
Display Adv. E-mail: bbartholomew@jjournal.com
Classified Adv. e-mail: classifieds@jjournal.com
Editorial e-mail: jjletters@jjournal.com
Primary Website: www.nj.com/jjournal
Year Established: 1867
News Services: AP, MCT, NNS.
Special Editions: Home Sweet Homes Tab (Apr); Women in Business (Aug); Letters to Santa (Dec); President's Pages I & II (Feb); School Guide Pages (Jan); Kids Tab (Jun); Women in Business (Mar); Mother's Day Tab (May); Thanksgiving Day Dine-Out I & II (Nov); Home Improvemen
Special Weekly Sections: Friday Entertainment Guide (Fri); Senior (Thur); Health (Wed).
Syndicated Publications: Parade (Sat).
Areas Served - City/County or Portion Thereof, or Zip codes: Hudson County (NJ)
Avg Free Circ: 1633
Sat. Circulation Paid: 9936
Sat. Circulation Free: 6339
Audit By: AAM
Audit Date: 30.09.2017
Personnel: Kenneth Whitfield (Pub.); Fran Donovan (Exec. Asst. to Pub.); Denise Copeland (Oper. Dir.); Sharon Ambis (Mktg. Dir.); S.I. Newhouse (Gen. Mgr.); John O'Shaughnessy (Acct. Dept. Mgr.); Tom Pritchard (Adv. Mgr., Retail); Steven Newhouse (Ed. in Chief); Judith Locorriere (Ed.); Margaret Schmidt (VP & Ed.); Agustin Torres (News Ed.); Ron Zeitlinger (Sports Ed.); Andy Savva (Mgmt. Info Servs. Mgr.); Gwen Ramsey (Prodn. Mgr., Pre Press); Kendrick Ross (PUBLISHER)
Parent company (for newspapers): Advance Publications, Inc.

COURIER NEWS

Street address 1: 92 East Main Street
Street address 2: Ste 202
Street address city: Somerville
Street address state: NJ
Zip/Postal code: 8876
County: Somerset
Country: USA
Mailing address: 92 E MAIN ST STE 202
Mailing city: SOMERVILLE
Mailing state: NJ
Mailing zip: 08876-2319
General Phone: 908-243-6600
Advertising Phone: (732) 643-3926
Editorial Phone: (908) 243-6600
General/National Adv. E-mail: www.gannettnj.com
Display Adv. E-mail: www.gannettnj.com
Classified Adv. e-mail: CNclass@gannett.com
Editorial e-mail: cnmetro@mycentraljersey.com
Primary Website: mycentraljersey.com
Year Established: 1883
News Services: USA TODAY NETWORK, AP
Special Weekly Sections: Kicks (Friday entertainment section)
Delivery Methods: Mail`Newsstand`Racks
Areas Served - City/County or Portion Thereof, or Zip codes: Somerset County
Own Printing Facility?: N
Commercial printers?: N
Avg Free Circ: 216
Sat. Circulation Paid: 6914
Sat. Circulation Free: 216
Sun. Circulation Paid: 8953
Sun. Circulation Free: 91
Audit By: AAM
Audit Date: 31.03.2018
Personnel: Paul Grzella (Gen. Mgr./Ed.); Jay Jefferson Cooke (Sen. Rep.); Keith Ryzewicz (Comm. Ed.); Thomas M. Donovan (President/Publisher)
Parent company (for newspapers): Gannett

HOME NEWS TRIBUNE

Street address 1: 92 E Main St
Street address city: Somerville
Street address state: NJ
Zip/Postal code: 08876-2319
County: Somerset
Country: USA
General Phone: 908-243-6600
Advertising Phone: 732-643-3926
Editorial Phone: 908-243-6600
General/National Adv. E-mail: www.gannettnj.com
Display Adv. E-mail: www.gannettnj.com
Classified Adv. e-mail: HNTclass@gannett.com
Editorial e-mail: hntletters@mycentraljersey.com
Primary Website: www.mycentraljersey.com
Year Established: 1879
News Services: USA TODAY, AP, Bloomberg.
Special Weekly Sections: Pulse Weekend Preview(Fri)
Delivery Methods: Mail
Areas Served - City/County or Portion Thereof, or Zip codes: Middlesex County
Own Printing Facility?: N
Commercial printers?: N
Sat. Circulation Paid: 13016
Sun. Circulation Paid: 15257
Audit By: AAM
Audit Date: 30.09.2018
Personnel: Paul Grzella (General Manager/Editor); Thomas M. Donovan (President/Publisher); Hollis Towns (Exec Ed. & VP News); Steve Feitl (Sports Ed.); Bill Canacci (Reg. Feat. Coord.); Wayne L. Peragallo (Sr. Dir. IT)
Parent company (for newspapers): Gannett

THE TIMES

Street address 1: 413 River View Plz
Street address city: Trenton
Street address state: NJ
Zip/Postal code: 08611-3420
County: Mercer
Country: USA
Mailing address: 413 RIVER VIEW PLZ
Mailing city: TRENTON
Mailing state: NJ
Mailing zip: 08611-3420
General Phone: (609) 989-5454
Advertising Phone: (609) 989-5452
Editorial Phone: (609) 989-5679
General/National Adv. E-mail: jmason@njtimes.com
Display Adv. E-mail: retail@njtimes.com
Classified Adv. e-mail: classify@njtimes.com
Editorial e-mail: letters@njtimes.com
Primary Website: www.nj.com/times/
News Services: AP, LAT-WP, NYT, NNS.
Special Editions: Spring Dining Guide (Apr); Fall Special Occasion Planner (Aug); Holiday Dining (Dec); Spring Wedding (Feb); Outlook (Jan); Summer Dining Guide (Jul); Parenting (Jun); Retirement Planning/ Nature Living (Mar); Spring Auto (May); Benchmarks (Monthly); Race f
Special Weekly Sections: Best Food Day (Wed); Home (Thur); Entertainment (Fri); Travel, Business, Entertainment, TV (Sun); Business (Daily)
Syndicated Publications: Parade (S).
Avg Free Circ: 4129
Sat. Circulation Paid: 20960
Sat. Circulation Free: 409
Sun. Circulation Paid: 22829
Sun. Circulation Free: 2339
Audit By: AAM
Audit Date: 30.06.2017
Personnel: Matt Dowling (News Ed.); Joan Mason (Pub.); Kevin Shea (Mng. Prod / Comm. Ed.); Nick Santise (Adv. Mgr.)
Parent company (for newspapers): Advance Publications, Inc.

THE TRENTONIAN

Street address 1: 600 Perry St
Street address city: Trenton
Street address state: NJ
Zip/Postal code: 08618-3934
County: Mercer
Country: USA
Mailing address: 600 PERRY ST
Mailing city: TRENTON
Mailing state: NJ
Mailing zip: 08618-3934
General Phone: (609) 989-7800
Advertising Phone: (609) 345-1706
Editorial Phone: (609) 349-7442
General/National Adv. E-mail: paadvertising@digitalfirstmedia.com
Display Adv. E-mail: bmurray@trentonian.com
Classified Adv. e-mail: classified@trentonian.com
Editorial e-mail: letters@trentonian.com
Primary Website: www.trentonian.com
Mthly Avg Unique Visitors: 467742
Year Established: 1946
News Services: AP, SNS, MCT.
Special Editions: Trenton Thunder (Apr); NFL Preview (Aug); Gift Guides I, II & III (Dec); Today's Health Care (Feb); Progress (Jan); Family Living (Jul); The Entrepreneurs (Jun); Spring Fashion (Mar); Mother's Day (May); Election Tab (Nov); Women's Health (Oct); Bucks Cou
Special Weekly Sections: Entertainment (Fri); Entertainment (S); Auto (Sat); Best Food Days (Wed).
Syndicated Publications: USA WEEKEND Magazine (S).
Avg Free Circ: 1419
Sat. Circulation Paid: 6538
Sat. Circulation Free: 1419
Sun. Circulation Paid: 12476
Sun. Circulation Free: 3483
Audit By: AAM
Audit Date: 31.03.2019
Personnel: John Berry (Ed.); Maggie Ashley (Adv. Dir.); Gregg Slaboda (Photo Ed.); Philip Metz (Cir. Dir.); Bill Murray (Adv. Mgr.); Edward Condra
Parent company (for newspapers): Digital First Media

THE DAILY JOURNAL

Street address 1: 891 E Oak Rd
Street address 2: Unit A
Street address city: Vineland
Street address state: NJ
Zip/Postal code: 08360-2311
County: Cumberland
Country: USA
Mailing address: 891 E OAK RD UNIT A
Mailing city: VINELAND
Mailing state: NJ
Mailing zip: 08360-2396
General Phone: (856) 691-5000
Advertising Phone: (732) 643-3703
Editorial Phone: (856) 691-5000
General/National Adv. E-mail: jcalchi@gannett.com
Display Adv. E-mail: jcalchi@gannett.com
Classified Adv. e-mail: classified@thedailyjournal.com
Editorial e-mail: djopinon@thedailyjournal.com
Primary Website: www.thedailyjournal.com
Year Established: 1875
News Services: AP, GNS.
Special Weekly Sections: Best Food Day (Wed); Real Estate (Fri); TV, School, Teen (Sat)
Syndicated Publications: TV Journal (Sat).
Areas Served - City/County or Portion Thereof, or Zip codes: Vineland, Millville & Greater Cumberland Counties (NJ)
Sat. Circulation Paid: 9518
Sun. Circulation Paid: 66
Audit By: AAM
Audit Date: 31.12.2017
Personnel: Joseph Calchi (Pres. & Pub.); Les Olson (Circ. Ops. Mgr.); John Garrahan (Plan. Ed.); Jason Alt (Reg. Ed.); Jerry Staas-Haught (Reg. Cont. Strategist)
Parent company (for newspapers): Gannett

BURLINGTON COUNTY TIMES

Street address 1: 4284 Route 130
Street address city: Willingboro
Street address state: NJ
Zip/Postal code: 08046-2027
County: Burlington
Country: USA
Mailing address: 4284 ROUTE 130
Mailing city: WILLINGBORO
Mailing state: NJ
Mailing zip: 08046-2080
General Phone: (609) 871-8000
Advertising Phone: (215) 949-4825
Editorial Phone: (609) 871-8143
General/National Adv. E-mail: feedback@thebct.com
Display Adv. E-mail: epursley@thebct.com
Classified Adv. e-mail: classifieds@thebct.com
Editorial e-mail: sfitzgerald@thebct.com
Primary Website: www.burlingtoncountytimes.com
Mthly Avg Unique Visitors: 800000
Year Established: 1958
News Services: AP, NEA.
Special Editions: Discover Burlington (May); Best of Burlington (Sep); HS Fall Sports (Sep); Holiday Gift Guide (Dec).
Special Weekly Sections: To Do (Fri);
Delivery Methods: Newsstand`Carrier`Racks
Areas Served - City/County or Portion Thereof, or Zip codes: All of Burlington County, New Jersey
Own Printing Facility?: Y
Commercial printers?: Y
Sun. Circulation Paid: 19533
Audit By: AAM
Audit Date: 30.06.2018
Personnel: Martha Esposito (Feat. Ed.); Audrey Harvin (Managing Editor); Shane Fitzgerald (Executive Editor)
Parent company (for newspapers): CherryRoad Media

THE RECORD

Street address 1: 1 Garret Mountain Plaza
Street address 2: Ste 201
Street address city: Woodland Park
Street address state: NJ
Zip/Postal code: 7424
County: Passaic
Country: USA
Mailing address: PO BOX 471
Mailing city: WOODLAND PARK
Mailing state: NJ
Mailing zip: 07424-0471
General Phone: (973) 569-7000
Advertising Phone: (973) 569-7434
Editorial Phone: (973) 569-7100
General/National Adv. E-mail: bartholomew@northjersey.com
Display Adv. E-mail: szollar@northjersey.com
Classified Adv. e-mail: classifieds@northjersey.com
Editorial e-mail: letterstotheeditor@northjersey.com
Primary Website: www.northjersey.com
Mthly Avg Unique Visitors: 6795911
Year Established: 1930
Sat. Circulation Paid: 85269
Sun. Circulation Paid: 101638
Audit By: AAM
Audit Date: 31.12.2017
Personnel: Malcom Borg (Chairman); Susan Beard (VP / HR); Robert Konig (VP / Cir. & Mfg.); Maggie Grande (Dir. of Marketing); Nancy Meyer (Pres.); Mark Szollar (Adv. Dir.); Deirdre Sykes; Kathy Batemarco (HR. Mgr.)
Parent company (for newspapers): Gannett

NEW MEXICO

ALAMOGORDO DAILY NEWS

Street address 1: 518 24th Street
Street address city: Alamogordo
Street address state: NM
Zip/Postal code: 88310
County: Otero
Country: USA
Mailing address: 518 24TH ST
Mailing city: ALAMOGORDO
Mailing state: NM
Mailing zip: 88310-6198
General Phone: (877) 301-0013
Advertising Phone: (575) 437-7120 ext. 7134
Editorial Phone: (575) 437-7120 ext. 7134
General/National Adv. E-mail: leudy@alamogordonews.com
Display Adv. E-mail: eduran@alamogordonews.com
Classified Adv. e-mail: bnajar@alamogordonews.com
Editorial e-mail: dbarbati@alamogordonews.com
Primary Website: www.alamogordonews.com
Mthly Avg Views: 413000
Mthly Avg Unique Visitors: 120000
Year Established: 1898
News Services: AP, CNS.
Special Editions: Back-to-School (Jul);Women of Merit (Mar); Holiday Gift Guide (Nov); Graduation (May)
Syndicated Publications: Relish (Monthly); USA WEEKEND Magazine (S);
Delivery Methods: Mail`Newsstand`Racks
Areas Served - City/County or Portion Thereof, or Zip codes: Otero County
Own Printing Facility?: N
Commercial printers?: N
Avg Free Circ: 745
Sat. Circulation Paid: 2724

Sat. Circulation Free: 745
Sun. Circulation Paid: 2978
Sun. Circulation Free: 88
Audit By: AAM
Audit Date: 30.06.2018
Personnel: Jessica Onsurez (News Director); Ken Wright (District Manager); Rynni Henderson (Regional Sales Director); Anthony Davis (Operations Coordinator)
Parent company (for newspapers): Gannett

ALBUQUERQUE JOURNAL

Street address 1: 7777 Jefferson Street NE
Street address city: Albuquerque
Street address state: NM
Zip/Postal code: 87109
County: Bernalillo
Country: USA
Mailing address: 7777 JEFFERSON ST NE
Mailing city: ALBUQUERQUE
Mailing state: NM
Mailing zip: 87109-4360
General Phone: 505-823-7777
Advertising Phone: (505) 823-3300
Editorial Phone: (505) 823-3800
General/National Adv. E-mail: sfriedes@abqpubco.com
Display Adv. E-mail: advertising@abqpubco.com
Classified Adv. e-mail: sgutierrez@abqpubco.com
Editorial e-mail: journal@abqjournal.com
Primary Website: www.abqjournal.com
Mthly Avg Unique Visitors: 679091
Year Established: 1880
News Services: AP, LAT-WP, CSM, MCT, RN.
Special Editions: At Home & Garden (Mar); American Home Week (Apr); Summer Guide (May); Green NM (Jun); Back to School, Native American Art NM (Aug); State Fair (Sept); Balloon Fiesta (Oct); Winter Guide (Nov); Holiday Gift Guide (Nov); Holiday Gift Ideas, Last Minute Gift Guide (Dec)
Special Weekly Sections: Business (Mon); Food (Wed); Venue (Fri); Entertainment (Sat); Travel, Leisure, Real Estate (Sun)
Syndicated Publications: Relish (Monthly); Parade (Sun); American Profile (Tue);Athlon Sports (Monthly)
Delivery Methods: Mail`Newsstand`Carrier`Racks
Areas Served - City/County or Portion Thereof, or Zip codes: New Mexico
Own Printing Facility?: Y
Commercial printers?: Y
Sat. Circulation Paid: 75319
Sun. Circulation Paid: 98824
Audit By: AAM
Audit Date: 31.12.2018
Personnel: William P. Lang (Pres./CEO); Lowell A. Hare (VP/CFO); Kent Walz (Ed-in-Chief); Karen Moses (Mng. Ed.); Charlie Moore (Bus. Ed.); Donn Friedman (Asst. Mng. Ed., Online); Adrian Gomez (Journal Arts & Entertain. Editor); Joe Kirby (Asst. Mng. Ed.); Sandy O'Dell (Office Mgr.); Isabel Sanchez (Asst. City Ed.); Nick Pappas (City Ed.); Ellen Marks (Asst. Bus. Ed.); Terry Feld (Bus. Edit. Asst.); Dan Herrera (Ed. Pg. Ed.); Stephen Williams (Asst. Poli. Ed.); Helen Taylor (Special Sec./Feat. Ed.); Ed Johnson (Journal Asst. Sports Ed.); Randy Harrison (Journal Sports Ed.); Mark Smith (Journal Asst. Sports Ed.); Robert Browman (Crime & Breaking News Ed., Onl.); Greg Peretti (Web Devel., Prod.); Morgan Petroski (Photo Ed.); Greg Sorber (Asst. Photo Ed.); Robyn Smith (Copy Ed.); Nancy Tipton (ABQJournal.com); Michael Coleman (Journal Wash. Bureau)
Parent company (for newspapers): Albuquerque Publishing Company

ARTESIA DAILY PRESS, INC.

Street address 1: 503 W Main St
Street address city: Artesia
Street address state: NM
Zip/Postal code: 88210-2067
County: Eddy
Country: USA
Mailing address: PO BOX 190
Mailing city: ARTESIA
Mailing state: NM
Mailing zip: 88211-0190
General Phone: (575) 746-3524
General/National Adv. E-mail: display@artesianews.com
Classified Adv. e-mail: classifieds@artesianews.com
Editorial e-mail: editor@artesianews.com
Primary Website: www.artesianews.com
Mthly Avg Views: 11000
Mthly Avg Unique Visitors: 11000
Year Established: 1954
News Services: ap
Special Editions: Business Review- January Tax Edition-February Spring Edition- March Health & Fitness- April Graduation- May County Fair- July Football Preview- August Oil & Soil Edition- September Best of Artesia- October Christmas Greetings- December
Delivery Methods: Mail`Newsstand`Carrier`Racks
Own Printing Facility?: Y
Commercial printers?: N
Sun. Circulation Paid: 3500
Audit By: USPS
Audit Date: 27.09.2012
Personnel: Danny Scott (Pub.); Latisha Romine (Admin.)
Parent company (for newspapers): Artesia Daily Press, Inc.

CURRENT-ARGUS

Street address 1: 620 S Main St
Street address city: Carlsbad
Street address state: NM
Zip/Postal code: 88220-6243
County: Eddy
Country: USA
Mailing address: PO BOX 1629
Mailing city: CARLSBAD
Mailing state: NM
Mailing zip: 88221-1629
General Phone: (575) 887-5501
Editorial Phone: (575) 628-5531
General/National Adv. E-mail: lanaya@currentargus.com
Display Adv. E-mail: carredondo@currentargus.com
Classified Adv. e-mail: daortiz@currentargus.com
Editorial e-mail: jonsurez@currentargus.com
Primary Website: www.currentargus.com
Mthly Avg Views: 750000
Mthly Avg Unique Visitors: 90000
Year Established: 1889
News Services: AP.
Special Editions: The Spring (Apr); Back-to-School (Aug); Christmas Greetings (Dec); Valentine's Love Photos (Feb); Chronology (Jan); Western Days (Jul); Our Town (Mar); Newspapers in Schools/Design-An-Ad (May); Christmas Gift Guide (Nov); Retirement (Oct); Football (Sept)
Special Weekly Sections: Best Real Estate Days (Fri); Best Real Estate Days (S); Best Food Day (Wed).
Syndicated Publications: TV Spotlight (Fri); USA WEEKEND Magazine (S); American Profile (Weekly).
Areas Served - City/County or Portion Thereof, or Zip codes: Carlsbad, Artesia, Loving & Eddy Counties (NM)
Avg Free Circ: 722
Sat. Circulation Paid: 3065
Sat. Circulation Free: 722
Sun. Circulation Paid: 3237
Sun. Circulation Free: 83
Audit By: AAM
Audit Date: 30.06.2018
Personnel: Cynthia Arredondo (Multi. Med. Cons.); Matt Hollinshead (Sports Editor); Shirley Maxwell (Acct. Crk.); Danny Fletcher (Gen. Mgr.); Judi Freisinger (Cir. Dist. Mgr.); Anthony Ortiz (Class. Rep.); Jessica Onsurez (Mng. Ed.); David R. Stringer (Pub.)
Parent company (for newspapers): Gannett

DEMING HEADLIGHT

Street address 1: 219 E Maple St
Street address city: Deming
Street address state: NM
Zip/Postal code: 88030-4267
County: Luna
Country: USA
Mailing address: 219 E MAPLE ST
Mailing city: DEMING
Mailing state: NM
Mailing zip: 88030-4267
General Phone: (575) 546-2611
Advertising Phone: (915) 541-5433
Editorial Phone: (575) 546-2611 ext. 2626
General/National Adv. E-mail: jngutierre@lcsun-news.com
Classified Adv. e-mail: gwebb@demingheadlight.com
Editorial e-mail: barmendariz@demingheadlight.com
Primary Website: www.demingheadlight.com
Year Established: 1881
News Services: AP.
Special Editions: Duck Race (Aug); Christmas Greetings (Dec); Community Guide (Feb); Life Off the Land (Jul); Medical Tab (Jun); Horizons (Mar); Senior (May); Christmas (Nov); Southwestern Fair (Oct); Mimbres Paguime Connection (Sept).
Syndicated Publications: American Profile (Weekly).
Areas Served - City/County or Portion Thereof, or Zip codes: Deming & Luna County (NM)
Audit By: Sworn/Estimate/Non-Audited
Audit Date: 12.07.2019
Personnel: Rynni Henderson (Pres.); Bill Armendariz (Ed.); Jared Hamilton (Gen. Mgr.); Joseph Gutierrez (Multi. Med. Acct. Exec.); Debbie Seats (Off. Admin.); Jesse Moya (Rep.); Larry Higgs (Circ. Mgr.)
Parent company (for newspapers): Gannett

THE DAILY TIMES

Street address 1: 203 W Main St
Street address 2: Ste 101
Street address city: Farmington
Street address state: NM
Zip/Postal code: 87401-6209
County: San Juan
Country: USA
Mailing address: 203 W MAIN ST STE 101
Mailing city: FARMINGTON
Mailing state: NM
Mailing zip: 87401-6209
General Phone: (505) 325-4545
Advertising Phone: (505) 325-4540
Editorial Phone: (505) 325-4545
General/National Adv. E-mail: chill@daily-times.com
Display Adv. E-mail: gjohnson@daily-times.com
Classified Adv. e-mail: megonzalez@daily-times.com
Editorial e-mail: croberts@daily-times.com
Primary Website: www.daily-times.com
Mthly Avg Unique Visitors: 121725
News Services: AP, NYT.
Special Editions: Reader's Choice (Apr); Connie Mack (Aug); Christmas (Dec); Home Expo (Feb); National High School Rodeo (Jul); Freedom Days (Jun); San Juan County Fair (May); Travel Guide (Nov); Parade of Homes (Oct); Health Living (Quarterly); Shiprock Fair (Sept).
Special Weekly Sections: Automotive (Fri); Business (Mon); Lifestyles (S); Explore (Thur); Lifestyles (Wed).
Syndicated Publications: Relish (Monthly); USA WEEKEND Magazine (S); American Profile (Weekly).
Delivery Methods: Mail`Newsstand`Carrier`Racks
Areas Served - City/County or Portion Thereof, or Zip codes: San Juan County
Own Printing Facility?: Y
Avg Free Circ: 2458
Sat. Circulation Paid: 5007
Sat. Circulation Free: 2458
Sun. Circulation Paid: 5338
Sun. Circulation Free: 100
Audit By: AAM
Audit Date: 31.03.2019
Personnel: Chris Roberts (Ed.); Chris Hill (Adv. Coord.); Julie Gambell (Dist. Cir. Sup.); Rueben Acosta (Cir. Dist. Mgr.); Penni Curtis (Admin. Asst.); Sammy Lopez (Pres.)
Parent company (for newspapers): Gannett

GALLUP INDEPENDENT

Street address 1: 500 N Ninth St
Street address city: Gallup
Street address state: NM
Zip/Postal code: 87301-5379
County: McKinley
Country: USA
Mailing address: PO BOX 1210
Mailing city: GALLUP
Mailing state: NM
Mailing zip: 87305-1210
General Phone: (505) 863-6811
Advertising Phone: (505) 863-6811 ext. 233
Editorial Phone: (505) 863-6811 ext. 213
General/National Adv. E-mail: ads1@gallupindependent.com
Classified Adv. e-mail: gaindep.class@gmail.com
Editorial e-mail: letters@gallupindependent.com
Primary Website: www.gallupindependent.com
Mthly Avg Views: 4500
Year Established: 1904
News Services: AP, NYT.
Special Editions: Off the Beaten Path (May, Sept.) Ceremonial (Aug.)
Syndicated Publications: American Profile (bi-weekly Sat.).
Delivery Methods: Newsstand`Carrier`Racks
Areas Served - City/County or Portion Thereof, or Zip codes: Northwestern NM, Northeastern AZ & Navajo Nation
Own Printing Facility?: Y
Commercial printers?: Y
Avg Free Circ: 81
Sat. Circulation Paid: 11358
Sat. Circulation Free: 81
Audit By: AAM
Audit Date: 31.12.2017
Personnel: Robert C. Zollinger (Vice Pres./Pub.); Barry Heifner (Mng. Ed.); Bill Donavan (Cops/courts); Alan Authur (Sports Ed.); Cecil Rodriguez (Prod. Ed.); Deborah Ramirez (Adv.); Leona Torrivio (Circ.); Cable Hoover (Chief Photo.); Richard Reyes (City Ed.)
Parent company (for newspapers): Gallup Independent; Zollinger Family

MESSENGER

Street address 1: 500 N Ninth St
Street address city: Gallup
Street address state: NM
Zip/Postal code: 87301-5379
County: McKinley
Country: USA
Mailing address: PO Box 1210
Mailing city: Gallup
Mailing state: NM
Mailing zip: 87305-1210
General Phone: (505) 863-6811
Areas Served - City/County or Portion Thereof, or Zip codes: 87305
Own Printing Facility?: Y
Audit By: Sworn/Estimate/Non-Audited
Audit Date: 12.07.2019
Personnel: Robert C. Zollinger (Pub.); Valda Brown (Circ. Mgr.)

HOBBS NEWS-SUN

Street address 1: 201 N. Thorp Street
Street address city: Hobbs
Street address state: NM
Zip/Postal code: 88240
County: Lea
Country: USA
Mailing address: PO BOX 850
Mailing city: HOBBS
Mailing state: NM
Mailing zip: 88241-0850
General Phone: (575) 393-2123
Advertising Phone: (575) 391-5404
Editorial Phone: (575) 393-2123
General/National Adv. E-mail: hnsads@hobbsnews.com
Display Adv. E-mail: advertise@hobbsnews.com
Classified Adv. e-mail: classifieds@hobbsnews.com
Editorial e-mail: editor@hobbsnews.com
Primary Website: www.hobbsnews.com
Year Established: 1928
News Services: AP, MCT
Special Editions: Back-to-School (Aug); Progress Issue (Mar); High School & College Graduation (May); Christmas Gift Guide (Nov); Energy (Oct)
Special Weekly Sections: Religion (Sat); Entertainment (Thur). Education (Fri)
Syndicated Publications: Relish (Monthly); Parade (Sun); American Profile (Sat).
Areas Served - City/County or Portion Thereof, or Zip codes: Lea County & Southeast NM
Own Printing Facility?: Y
Commercial printers?: N
Avg Free Circ: 1016
Sat. Circulation Paid: 5052
Sat. Circulation Free: 1016
Sun. Circulation Paid: 5321
Sun. Circulation Free: 337
Audit By: AAM
Audit Date: 31.12.2018
Personnel: Thomas B. Shearman (Vice Pres.); Scott Jones (Design Ed.); Daniel Russell (Pub.); Clayton Jones (Sports Ed.); Levi Hill (Mng. Ed.); Todd Bailey (Ed.)
Parent company (for newspapers): New Mexico Press Association; Shearman Corporation

LAS CRUCES SUN-NEWS

Street address 1: 256 Las Cruces Avenue
Street address city: Las Cruces
Street address state: NM

Zip/Postal code: 88005
County: Dona Ana
Country: USA
Mailing address: PO BOX 1749
Mailing city: LAS CRUCES
Mailing state: NM
Mailing zip: 88004-1749
General Phone: (575) 541-5400
Advertising Phone: (575) 541-6200
Editorial Phone: (575) 541-5438
General/National Adv. E-mail: bmills@lcsun-news.com
Display Adv. E-mail: agoins@lcsun-news.com
Classified Adv. e-mail: lcclassgeneral@lcsun-news.com
Editorial e-mail: sulloa@lcsun-news.com
Primary Website: www.lcsun-news.com
Mthly Avg Views: 14000000
Mthly Avg Unique Visitors: 300000
Year Established: 1881
News Services: AP, LAT-WP.
Special Editions: Back to School (July); Football (Aug); Tough Enough to Wear Pink (Oct.); Holiday Preview (Dec); Basketball (Jan); Reader Choices (Jun); Business & Industry (Mar); Discover Greater Las Cruces (May); Mariachi Conference Publication (Oct); Game Day (Sept).
Special Weekly Sections: Business Weekly (Mon); Pulse (Thurs); My Las Cruces (Sun);
Syndicated Publications: USA WEEKEND Magazine (S); American Profile (Weekly).
Delivery Methods: Mail`Newsstand`Carrier`Racks
Areas Served - City/County or Portion Thereof, or Zip codes: Southeast New Mexico
Sat. Circulation Paid: 7988
Sun. Circulation Paid: 10265
Audit By: AAM
Audit Date: 31.03.2019
Personnel: Rynni Henderson (Reg. Sales Dir.); Lucas Peerman (News Dir.); Jason Groves (Sports Ed.); Sylvia Soto (Cust. Serv. Sup.)
Parent company (for newspapers): Gannett

LOS ALAMOS MONITOR

Street address 1: 256 Dp Rd
Street address city: Los Alamos
Street address state: NM
Zip/Postal code: 87544-3233
County: Los Alamos
Country: USA
Mailing address: 256 DP RD
Mailing city: LOS ALAMOS
Mailing state: NM
Mailing zip: 87544-3233
General Phone: (505) 662-4185
General/National Adv. E-mail: laads@lamonitor.com
Display Adv. E-mail: info@lamonitor.com
Classified Adv. e-mail: laclassifieds@lamonitor.com
Editorial e-mail: laeditor@lamonitor.com
Primary Website: www.lamonitor.com
Mthly Avg Views: 190000
Mthly Avg Unique Visitors: 35000
Year Established: 1963
News Services: AP.
Special Editions: Call for details on special sections throughout the year.
Special Weekly Sections: Religion (Fri); Business (S); Diversions (Thur).
Syndicated Publications: Relish (Monthly); American Profile (S).
Delivery Methods: Newsstand`Carrier`Racks
Areas Served - City/County or Portion Thereof, or Zip codes: 87544
Own Printing Facility?: Y
Commercial printers?: Y
Sun. Circulation Paid: 4200
Audit By: Sworn/Estimate/Non-Audited
Audit Date: 12.07.2019
Personnel: Jill McLaughlin (Ed.); Jan Montoya (Adv. Dir.); Aries Margiotta (Classified Sales/Circ. Admin.)
Parent company (for newspapers): Landmark Communications, Inc.

ROSWELL DAILY RECORD

Street address 1: 2301 N Main St
Street address city: Roswell
Street address state: NM
Zip/Postal code: 88201-6452
County: Chaves
Country: USA
Mailing address: PO BOX 1897
Mailing city: ROSWELL
Mailing state: NM
Mailing zip: 88202-1897
General Phone: (575) 622-7710
Advertising Phone: (575) 622-7710
Editorial Phone: (575) 622-7710
General/National Adv. E-mail: hr@rdrnews.com
Display Adv. E-mail: addirector@rdrnews.com
Classified Adv. e-mail: classifieds@rdnews.com
Editorial e-mail: editor@rdrnews.com
Primary Website: www.rdrnews.com
Year Established: 1891
News Services: AP.
Special Editions: Sports Tab (Aug); Christmas Time Page (Dec); Valentine's Specials (Feb);(Jan); Pet Tab (Jul); Summer Specials (Jun); Mother's Day (May); Pre-Christmas Coupon Book (Nov); Fair Days (Oct); Car Care Tab (Sept).
Special Weekly Sections: Screens (Fri).
Syndicated Publications: Vision Magazine (Monthly); USA WEEKEND Magazine (S); American Profile (Weekly).
Delivery Methods: Mail`Newsstand`Carrier`Racks
Areas Served - City/County or Portion Thereof, or Zip codes: Roswell, Chaves County Dexter, Chaves County Hagerman, Chaves County Artesia, Eddy County Capitan, Lincoln County
Own Printing Facility?: Y
Commercial printers?: N
Sat. Circulation Paid: 9000
Sun. Circulation Paid: 10200
Audit By: Sworn/Estimate/Non-Audited
Audit Date: 12.07.2019
Personnel: Robert H. Beck (Pres.); Andrew Poertner (Ed.); Dana Beck (Pub.); Sara Fajardo (General Manager); Jim Dish (Cir. Dir.); Kim Gordon (Adv. Dir.); Barbara Beck (Publisher)
Parent company (for newspapers): New Mexico Press Association; Beck Family

THE SANTA FE NEW MEXICAN

Street address 1: 202 E Marcy St
Street address city: Santa Fe
Street address state: NM
Zip/Postal code: 87501-2021
County: Santa Fe
Country: USA
Mailing address: PO BOX 2048
Mailing city: SANTA FE
Mailing state: NM
Mailing zip: 87504-2048
General Phone: (505) 983-3303
Advertising Phone: (505) 986-3007
Editorial Phone: (505) 986-3035
General/National Adv. E-mail: advertising@sfnewmexican.com
Display Adv. E-mail: wortega@sfnewmexican.com
Classified Adv. e-mail: classad@sfnewmexican.com
Editorial e-mail: letters@sfnewmexican.com
Primary Website: www.santafenewmexican.com
Mthly Avg Views: 1700000
Mthly Avg Unique Visitors: 332000
Year Established: 1849
News Services: AP, NYT, LAT-WP, MCT.
Special Editions: SF Winter Fiesta (Jan), Health Directory (Feb), NM Restaurant Week (Feb), Basketball State Tourney (Mar), Kids Summer (Apr), Golf (Apr), Bienvenidos (May), Native Treasures (May), North Stars (Jun), Buckaroo Ball (Jun), International Folk Art (Jun), Spanish Market (Jul), SOFA (Jul), Indian Market (Aug), Fiesta (Aug), Winterlife (Oct), Feliz Navidad (Nov)
Special Weekly Sections: Teen Page (Fri); Health & Science (Mon); Comics (S); Religion (Sat); Outdoors (Thur); Business (Tues);
Syndicated Publications: Pasatiempo-Weekend Art & Entertainment Magazine (Fri); Parade (S); TV Book (Sat).
Delivery Methods: Mail`Newsstand`Carrier`Racks
Areas Served - City/County or Portion Thereof, or Zip codes: Santa Fe County (NM)
Own Printing Facility?: Y
Commercial printers?: Y
Avg Free Circ: 1833
Sat. Circulation Paid: 15911
Sat. Circulation Free: 1833
Sun. Circulation Paid: 17417
Sun. Circulation Free: 418
Audit By: AAM
Audit Date: 31.12.2017
Personnel: Mike Reichard (Cir. Dir.); Howard Houghton (City Ed.); Tom Cross (Pub.); Robin Martin (Owner); Cynthia Miller (News Ed./Copy Chief); James Barron (Sports Ed.); Madeleine Nicklin (Asst. Ed.); Tim Cramer (Director of Production); Phill Casaus (Editor); Susan Cahoon (HR Director)
Parent company (for newspapers): The New Mexican, Inc.

SILVER CITY SUN-NEWS

Street address 1: 208 W Broadway St
Street address city: Silver City
Street address state: NM
Zip/Postal code: 88061-5353
County: Grant
Country: USA
Mailing address: 208 W BROADWAY ST
Mailing city: SILVER CITY
Mailing state: NM
Mailing zip: 88061-5353
General Phone: (575) 538-5893
Advertising Phone: (538) 5893 ext. 5808
Editorial Phone: (538) 5893 ext. 5802
General/National Adv. E-mail: dborde@scsun-news.com
Display Adv. E-mail: bmills@lcsun-news.com
Editorial e-mail: editor@scsun-news.com
Primary Website: www.scsun-news.com
Delivery Methods: Mail`Racks
Areas Served - City/County or Portion Thereof, or Zip codes: Silver City, Grant County, Gila Region, Mimbres Valley & Mining District
Audit By: Sworn/Estimate/Non-Audited
Audit Date: 12.07.2019
Personnel: Lucas Peerman (News Dir.); Brock Chacon (Circ. Mgr.); Rynni Henderson (Regional Sales Mgr.)
Parent company (for newspapers): Gannett

NEW YORK

TIMES UNION

Street address 1: News Plaza, P.O. Box 15000
Street address city: Albany
Street address state: NY
Zip/Postal code: 12212
County: Albany
Country: USA
Mailing address: PO BOX 15000
Mailing city: ALBANY
Mailing state: NY
Mailing zip: 12212-5000
General Phone: (518) 454-5694
Advertising Phone: (518) 454-5588
Editorial Phone: (518) 454-5323
Editorial e-mail: tuletters@timesunion.com
Primary Website: www.timesunion.com
Mthly Avg Views: 26671689
Mthly Avg Unique Visitors: 1909672
Year Established: 1856
News Services: AP, Hearst Newspapers, NYT, MCT
Special Weekly Sections: Preview (Thur)
Syndicated Publications: 518 Life; Woman @ Work
Delivery Methods: Newsstand`Carrier`Racks
Areas Served - City/County or Portion Thereof, or Zip codes: Albany, Schenectady, Rensselaer, Saratoga, Schoharie counties
Own Printing Facility?: Y
Commercial printers?: Y
Sat. Circulation Paid: 37796
Sun. Circulation Paid: 88420
Audit By: AAM
Audit Date: 30.09.2017
Personnel: George R. Hearst (Pub./CEO); Rex Smith (Ed.); Todd Peterson (VP Circ.); Tom Eason (VP Adv.)
Parent company (for newspapers): Hearst

THE RECORDER

Street address 1: 1 Venner Rd
Street address city: Amsterdam
Street address state: NY
Zip/Postal code: 12010-5617
County: Montgomery
Country: USA
Mailing address: 1 VENNER RD
Mailing city: AMSTERDAM
Mailing state: NY
Mailing zip: 12010-5695
General Phone: (518) 843-1100
Advertising Phone: (518) 843-1100
Editorial Phone: (518) 843-1100
General/National Adv. E-mail: sales@recordernews.com
Display Adv. E-mail: sales@recordernews.com
Classified Adv. e-mail: sales2@recordernews.com
Editorial e-mail: news@recordernews.com
Primary Website: www.recordernews.com
News Services: LAT-WP, AP, MCT.
Special Editions: Pro Baseball Preview (Apr); Summer Projects (Aug); Christmas Gift Guide II (Dec); Year Outlook (Feb); Bridal Book I (Jan); Saratoga Horse Racing (Jul); Bridal Book II (Jun); Cooking Contest (Mar); Christmas Gift Guide I (Nov); Fall Car Care (Oct); Autumn
Special Weekly Sections: Business (Mon); Senior Citizens (S); Best Food Days (Wed).
Syndicated Publications: Silver Lining (Monthly); Currents-Arts (S).
Areas Served - City/County or Portion Thereof, or Zip codes: Amsterdam & Montgomery Counties (NY)
Sat. Circulation Paid: 8116
Sun. Circulation Paid: 8305
Audit By: Sworn/Estimate/Non-Audited
Audit Date: 12.07.2019
Personnel: Kevin McClary (Pub.); Brian Krohn (Gen. Mgr.); Geoff Dylong (Assoc. Pub.); Paul Antonelli (Sports Ed.); Rich Kretser (Circ.)
Parent company (for newspapers): Hume Family

THE CITIZEN, AUBURN

Street address 1: 25 Dill St
Street address city: Auburn
Street address state: NY
Zip/Postal code: 13021-3605
County: Cayuga
Country: USA
General Phone: (315) 253-5311
Advertising Phone: (315) 255-2241
Editorial Phone: (315) 282-2231
General/National Adv. E-mail: jeffrey.weigand@lee.net
Display Adv. E-mail: jeffrey.weigand@lee.net
Classified Adv. e-mail: jeffrey.weigand@lee.net
Editorial e-mail: jeremy.boyer@lee.net
Primary Website: www.auburnpub.com
Mthly Avg Views: 1800000
Mthly Avg Unique Visitors: 300000
Year Established: 1816
News Services: AP.
Special Editions: Golf (Apr); Brides (Feb); Health (Jan); (Mar); Finger Lake Summer Travel Guide (May); Holiday Gift Guide (Nov); Tomato Fest (Sept).
Special Weekly Sections: Family Matters (Fri); Food (Mon); Community and Family Features (S); Arts & Entertainment (Thur); Price Busters Tab (Tues); Home (Wed).
Syndicated Publications: Color Comics (S).
Delivery Methods: Mail`Newsstand`Carrier`Racks
Areas Served - City/County or Portion Thereof, or Zip codes: 13021 plus
Own Printing Facility?: Y
Commercial printers?: Y
Avg Free Circ: 1127
Sat. Circulation Paid: 5794
Sat. Circulation Free: 706
Sun. Circulation Paid: 7166
Sun. Circulation Free: 764
Audit By: AAM
Audit Date: 30.06.2016
Personnel: Jeremy Boyer (Exec. Ed.); Michael Dowd (Mng. Ed.); Robert Forcey (Pres./Pub.)
Parent company (for newspapers): Dispatch-Argus; Lee Enterprises, Incorporated

THE DAILY NEWS

Street address 1: 2 Apollo Dr
Street address city: Batavia
Street address state: NY
Zip/Postal code: 14020-3002
County: Genesee
Country: USA
Mailing address: 2 APOLLO DR
Mailing city: BATAVIA
Mailing state: NY
Mailing zip: 14020-3094
General Phone: (585) 343-8000
Advertising Phone: (585) 343-8000
Editorial Phone: (585) 343-8000
General/National Adv. E-mail: adsales@batavianews.com
Display Adv. E-mail: adsales@batavianews.com

Classified Adv. e-mail: classified@batavianews.com
Editorial e-mail: news@batavianews.com
Primary Website: www.thedailynewsonline.com
Mthly Avg Views: 1269931
Mthly Avg Unique Visitors: 179998
Year Established: 1831
News Services: AP, TMS.
Special Editions: Spring Sports (Apr); Back To School (Aug); Christmas Greetings (Dec); Business Outlook (Feb); Bridal Guide (Jan); Genesee County Fair (Jul); Dairy Month (Jun); Jaycees Home Show (Mar); Mother's Day (May); Christmas Gift Guide (Nov); Fall Car Care (Oct); F
Special Weekly Sections: Entertainment (Thurs.-Fri); Business (Mon); Religion (Sat); Entertainment (Thur); Agriculture (Tues); Recreation (summer) (Wed).
Syndicated Publications: USA WEEKEND Magazine (Sat); American Profile (Wed).
Delivery Methods: Newsstand`Carrier`Racks
Areas Served - City/County or Portion Thereof, or Zip codes: 14005, 14011, 14013, 14020, 14036, 14040, 14054, 14058, 14103, 14125, 14143, 14167, 14411, 14416, 14422, 14427, 14470, 14482, 14525, 14530, 14550, 14569, 14591
Own Printing Facility?: Y
Commercial printers?: N
Avg Free Circ: 141
Sat. Circulation Paid: 12036
Sat. Circulation Free: 140
Audit By: CVC
Audit Date: 19.12.2017
Personnel: Michael Messerly (BNC Pub. / JNC Dig. Dir.); John Anderson (Managing Editor); John Johnson (CEO / Co-Pub.); Harold B. Johnson (Pres.); Gary Durawa (Circulation Director); Jeanette Hardy (HR VP); Jennifer Zambito (Advert. Dir.)
Parent company (for newspapers): Johnson Newspaper Corp.

PRESS & SUN-BULLETIN

Street address 1: P.O. Box 1270
Street address 2: Ste 9
Street address city: Binghamton
Street address state: NY
Zip/Postal code: 13902
County: Broome
Country: USA
Mailing state: NY
General Phone: (607) 798-1234
Advertising Phone: (607) 798-1131
Editorial Phone: (607) 798-1151
General/National Adv. E-mail: rscott@pressconnects.com
Display Adv. E-mail: swinelan@binghamt.gannett.com
Classified Adv. e-mail: jgilmore@binghamt.gannett.com
Editorial e-mail: bgm-letters@gannett.com
Primary Website: www.pressconnects.com
Year Established: 1904
Syndicated Publications: Good Times (Thur); Home Marketplace (Sat.)
Areas Served - City/County or Portion Thereof, or Zip codes: Broome, Tioga, Chenango, Delaware & Otsego Counties (NY); Susquehanna County (PA)
Own Printing Facility?: Y
Commercial printers?: Y
Avg Free Circ: 172
Sat. Circulation Paid: 17215
Sat. Circulation Free: 172
Sun. Circulation Paid: 25209
Sun. Circulation Free: 172
Audit By: AAM
Audit Date: 30.09.2018
Personnel: Thomas Claybaugh (Pub.); Neill Borowski (Exec. Ed.); Robb Scott (Adv. Dir.); Kevin Crane (Gen. Mgr. / Gannett Pub. Serv.); George Troyano (Pres.)
Parent company (for newspapers): Gannett

EL DIARIO LA PRENSA

Street address 1: 1 Metrotech Ctr
Street address 2: Fl 18
Street address city: Brooklyn
Street address state: NY
Zip/Postal code: 11201-3948
County: Kings
Country: USA
Mailing address: 1 METROTECH CTR FL 18
Mailing city: BROOKLYN
Mailing state: NY
Mailing zip: 11201-3949
General Phone: (212) 807-4785
Advertising Phone: (212) 807-4600
Editorial Phone: (212) 807-4725
General/National Adv. E-mail: jorge.ayala@eldiariony.com
Display Adv. E-mail: mack.hood@eldiariony.com
Classified Adv. e-mail: mack.hood@eldiariony.com
Primary Website: www.eldiariony.com
Year Established: 1913
News Services: AP.
Special Editions: Dominican Independence, Charter Schools, Health, Education, Cinco de Mayo, Puerto Rican Heritage,World Cup,Colombian Independence, Peruvian Independence, Dominican Restoration, Mexican Independence, Hispanic Heritage, Holiday Gift Guide, El Awards, Mujeres Descatadas
Special Weekly Sections: Education, Health; Legal, Immigration, Food; Entertainment
Syndicated Publications: ESPN Deportes
Delivery Methods: Newsstand
Areas Served - City/County or Portion Thereof, or Zip codes: NYDMA
Own Printing Facility?: N
Avg Free Circ: 1085
Sat. Circulation Paid: 19762
Sat. Circulation Free: 1083
Sun. Circulation Paid: 16818
Sun. Circulation Free: 150
Audit By: Sworn/Estimate/Non-Audited
Audit Date: 12.07.2019
Personnel: Jorge Ayala (VP, Adv.); Mack Hood (Retail Dir.)
Parent company (for newspapers): impreMedia LLC; El Clasificado

NEW YORK DAILY CHALLENGE

Street address 1: 1195 Atlantic Ave
Street address 2: Fl 2
Street address city: Brooklyn
Street address state: NY
Zip/Postal code: 11216-2709
County: Kings
Country: USA
Mailing address: 1195 ATLANTIC AVE
Mailing city: BROOKLYN
Mailing state: NY
Mailing zip: 11216-2709
General Phone: (718) 636-9500
Advertising Phone: (718) 636-9500
Editorial Phone: (718) 636-9500
General/National Adv. E-mail: challengegroup@yahoo.com
Display Adv. E-mail: challengegroup@gmail.com
Classified Adv. e-mail: challengegroup@yahoo.com
Editorial e-mail: challengegroup@yahoo.com
Primary Website: facebook.com/Daily-Challenge-151449094871154
Year Established: 1972
Delivery Methods: Mail`Newsstand`Racks
Areas Served - City/County or Portion Thereof, or Zip codes: 11216
Audit By: Sworn/Estimate/Non-Audited
Audit Date: 12.07.2019
Personnel: Thomas H. Watkins (Pub.); T.J. Watkins (Assoc. Pub.); Dale Watkins (Marketing Director); Gary Brown (Ed.)

THE BUFFALO NEWS

Street address 1: P.O. Box 100
Street address 2: P.O. Box 100
Street address city: Buffalo
Street address state: NY
Zip/Postal code: 14240
County: Erie
Country: USA
Mailing address: PO BOX 100
Mailing city: BUFFALO
Mailing state: NY
Mailing zip: 14240-0100
General Phone: (716) 849-4444
Advertising Phone: (716) 856-5555
Editorial Phone: (716) 849-4444
General/National Adv. E-mail: adops@buffnews.com
Display Adv. E-mail: adops@buffnews.com
Classified Adv. e-mail: sdeaton-callahan@buffnews.com
Editorial e-mail: editor@buffnews.com
Primary Website: www.buffalonews.com
Year Established: 1880
News Services: AP, MCT, LAT-WP, RN.
Special Editions: First Sunday (Apr); Today's Education (Aug); Menus (Dec); Auto Show (Feb); Weddings (Jan); First Sunday (Jul); Horizons (Jun); Buffalo Home Show (Mar); WNY Nurses Assoc. (May); First Sunday (Nov); Bridal Planner (Oct); NFL Preview (Sept).
Special Weekly Sections: MoneySmart (Mon); Health, Sports (Tue); Best Food Day (Wed); Home, Garden, Entertainment (Fri); Real Estate (Sat); TV, Comics, Travel (Sun)
Syndicated Publications: Gusto (entertainment tab) (Fri); Monday Sports (tab) (Mon); Metro Comics (S); Home Finder (Sat); NEXT (young teens' tab) (Tues).
Avg Free Circ: 4942
Sat. Circulation Paid: 101562
Sat. Circulation Free: 3286
Sun. Circulation Paid: 152577
Sun. Circulation Free: 3401
Audit By: AAM
Audit Date: 30.06.2018
Personnel: Warren T. Colville (Pres./Pub.); Warren E. Buffett (Chairman); Mike Connelly (Ed.); Brian Connolly (Mng. Ed.); Stan Evans (Deputy Mng. Ed.); Margaret Kenny (Asst. Mng. Ed.); John Neville (Editorial Page Ed.); Vince Chiaramonte (Design Dir.)
Parent company (for newspapers): BH Media Group; Lee Enterprises, Incorporated

DAILY MESSENGER

Street address 1: 73 Buffalo St
Street address city: Canandaigua
Street address state: NY
Zip/Postal code: 14424-1001
County: Ontario
Country: USA
Mailing address: 73 BUFFALO ST
Mailing city: CANANDAIGUA
Mailing state: NY
Mailing zip: 14424-1085
General Phone: (585) 394-0770
Advertising Phone: (585) 394-0770
Editorial Phone: (585) 394-0770
General/National Adv. E-mail: bkesel@messengerpostmedia.com
Display Adv. E-mail: bkesel@messengerpostmedia.com
Classified Adv. e-mail: classifieds@messengerpostmedia.com
Editorial e-mail: bkesel@messengerpostmedia.com
Primary Website: www.mpnnow.com
Year Established: 1776
News Services: AP, SHNS, LAT-WP.
Special Editions: Homes & Landscapes (Apr); Rx For Good Health (Aug); Holiday Gift Guide (Dec); Interiors (Feb); Wedding Guide (Jan); Summer Homes (Jul); Summer Dining Guide (Jun); Salute to Seniors (Mar); Vacation Guide (May); Holiday Gift Guide (Nov); Rx for Good Health
Special Weekly Sections: Real Estate (Fri); Weddings and Engagements (Mon); Business/Consumer Page (Mon-fri); Stock Page (S); Farm Page (Thur); Seniors Page (Tues); Religion (Wed).
Syndicated Publications: Accent on Homes (Fri); TV Viewer (S); Steppin' Out (Thur).
Areas Served - City/County or Portion Thereof, or Zip codes: Ontario, Wayne & Northern Yates Counties (NY)
Sun. Circulation Paid: 9325
Audit By: Sworn/Estimate/Non-Audited
Audit Date: 12.07.2019
Personnel: Beth Kesel (Gen. Mng./Adv. Dir.); Sean McCrory (Exec. Ed.); Mike Murphy (Local Ed.); Jennifer Reed (Digital Pub. Ed.); Cathy Busker (Cir. Mgr.); Brian Doane (Pres. / Pub.)
Parent company (for newspapers): Gannett; CherryRoad Media

THE LEADER

Street address 1: 34 W Pulteney St
Street address city: Corning
Street address state: NY
Zip/Postal code: 14830-2211
County: Steuben
Country: USA
Mailing address: PO BOX 1017
Mailing city: CORNING
Mailing state: NY
Mailing zip: 14830-0817
General Phone: (607) 936-4651
Advertising Phone: (607) 936-4651
Editorial Phone: (607) 936-4651
General/National Adv. E-mail: amingos@the-leader.com
Display Adv. E-mail: amingos@the-leader.com
Classified Adv. e-mail: amingos@the-leader.com
Editorial e-mail: sdupree@the-leader.com
Primary Website: www.the-leader.com
Mthly Avg Views: 801000
Mthly Avg Unique Visitors: 200500
Year Established: 1854
News Services: AP.
Special Editions: Home Improvement (Apr); September Finger Lakes Fun Book (Aug); Gift Certificates (Dec); Valentine's Day Gifts (Feb); At Home (Jan); August Finger Lakes Fun Book (Jul); July Finger Lakes Fun Book (Jun); People Who Make a Difference (Mar); Corning Classic S
Special Weekly Sections: Flag to Flag Motorsports (Fri); Food (S); Entertainment (Thur).
Syndicated Publications: Parade (S); Weekend (Thur).
Delivery Methods: Newsstand`Carrier`Racks
Own Printing Facility?: N
Commercial printers?: Y
Sat. Circulation Paid: 9500
Sun. Circulation Paid: 10200
Audit By: Sworn/Estimate/Non-Audited
Audit Date: 12.07.2019
Personnel: Rick Emanuel (Pub.); Shawn Vargo (News Ed.); Heather Falkey (Classified/Display Adv. Mgr.); Breenna Hilton (Circ. Mgr.); Becky Jenkins (Bus. Office Mgr.)
Parent company (for newspapers): Gannett; CherryRoad Media

CORTLAND STANDARD

Street address 1: 110 Main St
Street address city: Cortland
Street address state: NY
Zip/Postal code: 13045-6600
County: Cortland
Country: USA
Mailing address: PO BOX 5548
Mailing city: CORTLAND
Mailing state: NY
Mailing zip: 13045-5548
General Phone: (607) 756-5665
Advertising Phone: (607) 756-5665
General/National Adv. E-mail: manderson@cortlandstandard.net
Display Adv. E-mail: advertising@cortlandstandard.net
Classified Adv. e-mail: classified@cortlandstandard.net
Editorial e-mail: news@cortlandstandard.net
Primary Website: www.cortlandstandard.net
Year Established: 1867
News Services: AP
Special Editions: Bridal (Jan); Outlook/Progess (Feb); Business Showcase (Mar); 50 Plus (Apr/May); Summer Guide (May); Dairy Edition (May/Jun); Graduation (Jun); NY Jets Training Camp (Jul); College (Aug); Autumn Guide (Sept); Driver's Guide (Oct); Gift Guides (Nov/Dec); Healthwise (Quarterly)
Special Weekly Sections: Best Food (Sat); Money/ Financial (Sat); Business Pages (Mon-Fri); Home & Garden (Wed); Consumer News (Mon); Real Estate (Bi-Weekly Thurs)
Delivery Methods: Mail`Newsstand`Carrier`Racks
Areas Served - City/County or Portion Thereof, or Zip codes: 13077, 13087, 13141, 13159, 13052, 13158, 13045, 13118, 13092, 13073, 13068, 13101, 13053, 13040, 13863, 13803, 13738
Own Printing Facility?: Y
Commercial printers?: N
Sat. Circulation Paid: 8240
Audit By: Sworn/Estimate/Non-Audited
Audit Date: 12.07.2019
Personnel: Kevin R. Howe (President); Kevin Conlon (Mng. Ed.); Thomas Shattuck (Adv. Mgr., Classified); Katie Hall (Society/Women's Ed.); Evan Geibel (Publisher); Michael J. Anderson (Adv. Mgr., Retail); Guy C. Ussery (Circ. Dir.); Sherwood W. Chapman (Exec. Ed.); Michael Wells (News Ed.); Al Butler (Sports Ed.); Stanley Carruthers (Prodn. Foreman, Composing); Raymond Marsh (Prodn. Foreman, Pressroom); Stephen Clark (Business Manager)
Parent company (for newspapers): New York Newspaper Advertising Service, Inc.; Geibel & Howe Family

THE OBSERVER

Street address 1: 10 E 2nd St
Street address city: Dunkirk
Street address state: NY
Zip/Postal code: 14048-1602
County: Chautauqua
Country: USA
Mailing address: PO BOX 391

Mailing city: DUNKIRK
Mailing state: NY
Mailing zip: 14048-0391
General Phone: (716) 366-3000
Advertising Phone: (716) 366-3000
Editorial Phone: (716) 366-3000
General/National Adv. E-mail: advertising@observertoday.com
Display Adv. E-mail: advertising@observertoday.com
Classified Adv. e-mail: classified@observertoday.com
Editorial e-mail: editorial@observertoday.com
Primary Website: www.observertoday.com
Year Established: 1882
News Services: Associated Press
Syndicated Publications: TV Magazine (Fri); Senior Scene Tab (Monthly); USA WEEKEND Magazine (S).
Areas Served - City/County or Portion Thereof, or Zip codes: 14048, 14063, 14062, 14081, 14006, 14027, 14716. 14718, 14723, 14034, 14035, 14041, 14061, 14070, 14047, 14750, 14091. 14752, 14757, 14129, 14769, 14135, 14136, 14782, 14138, 14784, 14166, 14787
Own Printing Facility?: Y
Avg Free Circ: 152
Sat. Circulation Paid: 6824
Sat. Circulation Free: 152
Sun. Circulation Paid: 7221
Sun. Circulation Free: 143
Audit By: Sworn/Estimate/Non-Audited
Audit Date: 12.07.2019
Personnel: John D'Agostino (Pub.); Meredith V. Patton (Adv. Dir.); Gregory Bacon (Managing Editor); Shawn Paulus (Circ. Mgr.); Jamie Ribbing (Bus. Mgr.); Gib Snyder (Lifestyles coordinator); Craig Harvey (News editor); Sheila Mcwillson (Classified coordinator); Nicole Gugino (City editor)
Parent company (for newspapers): Ogden Newspapers Inc.

STAR-GAZETTE

Street address 1: 310 E Church St
Street address city: Elmira
Street address state: NY
Zip/Postal code: 14901-2704
County: Chemung
Country: USA
Mailing address: PO BOX 285
Mailing city: ELMIRA
Mailing state: NY
Mailing zip: 14902-0285
General Phone: (607) 734-5151
Advertising Phone: (607) 271-8474
Editorial Phone: (607) 734-5158
General/National Adv. E-mail: jzych@binghamt.gannett.com
Display Adv. E-mail: jzych@binghamt.gannett.com
Classified Adv. e-mail: CNY-classified@gannett.com
Editorial e-mail: sgletters@gannett.com
Primary Website: www.stargazette.com
Year Established: 1828
News Services: AP, GNS
Special Editions: Outlook (Feb); Home & Garden (spring/fall) Bridal tab (spring); Guide to the Twin Tiers (fall)
Special Weekly Sections: Twin Tiers Homes (Sat); Entertainment (Thurs.)
Syndicated Publications: Full-Color Comics (S); Time Out (Thur).
Areas Served - City/County or Portion Thereof, or Zip codes: Chemung, Steuben & Schuyler Counties (NY); Bradford County (PA)
Avg Free Circ: 94
Sat. Circulation Paid: 11915
Sat. Circulation Free: 94
Sun. Circulation Paid: 18622
Sun. Circulation Free: 93
Audit By: AAM
Audit Date: 30.03.2016
Personnel: George Troyano (Pres.); Neill Borowski (Exec. Ed.); Robb Scott (Adv. Dir.); Joe Darrow (Adv. Mgr.); Christopher Kocher (Engagement Ed.)
Parent company (for newspapers): Gannett

FINGER LAKES TIMES

Street address 1: 218 Genesee St
Street address city: Geneva
Street address state: NY
Zip/Postal code: 14456-2323
County: Ontario
Country: USA
Mailing state: NY
General Phone: (315) 789-3333
Advertising Phone: (315) 789-3333 ext. 263
Editorial Phone: (315) 789-3333
General/National Adv. E-mail: nneabel@fltimes.com
Display Adv. E-mail: dduval@fltimes.com
Classified Adv. e-mail: classads@fltimes.com
Editorial e-mail: opinion@fltimes.com
Primary Website: www.fltimes.com
Year Established: 1895
News Services: SHNS, AP, LAT-WP.
Special Editions: Business Directory (Jan) ; Tax Guide & Money Management (Feb); Bridal Magazine (Feb); Vacation Guide (May), Graduation (Jun); Car Care/Home Improvement (Oct); High School Football (Aug); Empire Farm Days (Aug); Indulge (Sept); Bridal Magazine (Oct); Christmas Gift Guide (Nov); Last Minute Gift Guide (Dec); Year in Review (Dec)
Special Weekly Sections: Best Food Day, Inserts, Business, Stocks, health, Travel, Taste, Seniors, Entertainment (Sun); Farm (Mon); School (Tue); Pets (Wed); Finance, Business (Thur); Home, Garden, NASCAR, Religion, Real Estate (Fri)
Syndicated Publications: Automotion (Every other Wednesday); Jumpstart Entertainment (Thur); TV Times (Sun)
Delivery Methods: Mail`Newsstand`Carrier`Racks
Areas Served - City/County or Portion Thereof, or Zip codes: Ontario, Seneca, Wayne & Yates Counties (NY)
Own Printing Facility?: Y
Commercial printers?: Y
Avg Free Circ: 81
Sun. Circulation Paid: 11832
Sun. Circulation Free: 74
Audit By: CAC
Audit Date: 30.09.2016
Personnel: Paul M Barrett (Pub.); Diane Lahr-Smith (Business Mgr.); Maurice Barcomb (Circ. Dir.); Chuck Schading (Managing Ed.); Jesse P. Bond (Production Mgr.); Michael J. Cutillo (Exec. Ed.); R. Nicholas Neabel (Adv. Dir.); Ethan Fogg (Circ. Mktg. Dir.)
Parent company (for newspapers): Community Media Group

THE POST-STAR

Street address 1: 76 Lawrence St
Street address city: Glens Falls
Street address state: NY
Zip/Postal code: 12801-3741
County: WarrenÂ
Country: USA
Mailing address: PO BOX 2157
Mailing city: GLENS FALLS
Mailing state: NY
Mailing zip: 12801-2157
General Phone: (518) 792-3131
Advertising Phone: (518) 742-3304
Editorial Phone: (518) 792-3131
General/National Adv. E-mail: ads@poststar.com
Display Adv. E-mail: mrice@poststar.com
Classified Adv. e-mail: dmorehouse@poststar.com
Editorial e-mail: emanuel@poststar.com
Primary Website: www.poststar.com
Mthly Avg Views: 4700000
Mthly Avg Unique Visitors: 341000
Year Established: 1895
News Services: AP, MCT, TMS.
Special Editions: Hockey (Oct); Football (Sept); Business Outlook (Feb.)
Syndicated Publications: Relish (Monthly); USA WEEKEND Magazine (S).
Areas Served - City/County or Portion Thereof, or Zip codes: Upstate New York
Own Printing Facility?: Y
Commercial printers?: Y
Avg Free Circ: 3434
Sat. Circulation Paid: 14331
Sat. Circulation Free: 2853
Sun. Circulation Paid: 17733
Sun. Circulation Free: 3117
Audit By: AAM
Audit Date: 30.06.2018
Personnel: Robert Forcey (Pub.); Brian Corcoran (Controller); Michelle Giorgianni (Circ. Dir.); Caren Kuhle (Production Dir.); Ken Tingley (Ed.); Bob Condon (City Ed.); Will Doolittle (Projects Dir.); Adam Colver (Online Ed.)
Parent company (for newspapers): Lee Enterprises, Incorporated

THE LEADER-HERALD

Street address 1: 8 E Fulton St
Street address city: Gloversville
Street address state: NY
Zip/Postal code: 12078-3227
County: Fulton
Country: USA
Mailing address: 8 E Fulton St
Mailing city: Gloversville
Mailing state: NY
Mailing zip: 12078-3283
General Phone: (518) 725-8616
Advertising Phone: (518) 725-8616
Editorial Phone: (518) 725-8616
General/National Adv. E-mail: advertising@leaderherald.com
Display Adv. E-mail: advertising@leaderherald.com
Classified Adv. e-mail: classifieds@leaderherald.com
Editorial e-mail: tfonda@leaderherald.com
Primary Website: www.leaderherald.com
Mthly Avg Views: 1100000
Year Established: 1887
News Services: AP.
Special Editions: Spring Home Improvement & Garden Time (Apr); Lake Country (Aug); Portraits (Feb); Lake Country (Jul); Lake Country (Jun); Spring Car Care (Mar); Spring & Summer Vacation Guide (May); Real Estate (Monthly); Christmas Gift Guide (Nov); Fall Car Care (Oct);
Special Weekly Sections: Business-Stocks (S); Church News (Sat); Best Food (Wed).
Syndicated Publications: Parade (S).
Delivery Methods: Mail`Newsstand`Carrier`Racks
Areas Served - City/County or Portion Thereof, or Zip codes: Fulton, Hamilton & Montgomery Counties (NY)
Own Printing Facility?: Y
Commercial printers?: Y
Avg Free Circ: 361
Sat. Circulation Paid: 5603
Sat. Circulation Free: 361
Sun. Circulation Paid: 7938
Sun. Circulation Free: 414
Audit By: AAM
Audit Date: 31.12.2017
Personnel: Brenda Anich (Circ. Mgr.); Stephen Hansen; Cindy Reuben (Classifieds Rep.); Tim VanAernam (Prodn. Mgr., Mailroom); Patricia Older (Mng. Ed.); Paul Wager (Sports Ed.); Trevor Evans (Pub.); James Cornell (Bus. Mgr.); Chad Fleck (Mgmt. Info Servs. Mgr.)
Parent company (for newspapers): Ogden Newspapers Inc.; Hume Family

THE HERKIMER TELEGRAM

Street address 1: 111 Green St
Street address city: Herkimer
Street address state: NY
Zip/Postal code: 13350-1914
County: Herkimer
Country: USA
Mailing state: NY
General Phone: (315) 866-2220
Advertising Phone: (315) 866-2220
Editorial Phone: (315) 866-2220
General/National Adv. E-mail: bethadv@herkimertelegram.com
Display Adv. E-mail: jshaffer@timestelegram.com
Classified Adv. e-mail: bethadv@herkimertelegram.com
Editorial e-mail: tdewan@littlefallstimes.com
Primary Website: www.herkimertelegram.com
Year Established: 1898
News Services: AP.
Special Editions: Our Children (Apr); NASCAR (Feb); Who, What, Where (Jul); Spring Preview (May); Winter Sports Preview (Nov); Senior Life (Sept).
Special Weekly Sections: Food, Bride (Sat); Entertainment (Thur); Senior Lifestyle (Tues); Senior Lifestyle (Wed)
Syndicated Publications: TV Guide Weekly (Sat); American Profile (Weekly).
Sat. Circulation Paid: 6657
Audit By: Sworn/Estimate/Non-Audited
Audit Date: 12.07.2019
Personnel: Beth Brewer (Pub./Adv. Mgr.); Donna Thompson (Trends Ed.); Jon Rathbun (Sports Ed.); Robert Gall (Cir. Dir.); Rob Juteau (Mng. Ed.)
Parent company (for newspapers): CherryRoad Media

THE EVENING TRIBUNE

Street address 1: 32 Broadway Mall
Street address city: Hornell
Street address state: NY
Zip/Postal code: 14843-1920
County: Steuben
Country: USA
Mailing state: NY
General Phone: (607) 324-1425
Advertising Phone: (607) 324-1425
Editorial Phone: (607) 324-1425 ext. 205
General/National Adv. E-mail: advertising@eveningtribune.com
Display Adv. E-mail: kellyschecter@eveningtribune.com
Classified Adv. e-mail: bethhults@eveningtribune.com
Editorial e-mail: news@eveningtribune.com
Primary Website: www.eveningtribune.com
Year Established: 1872
News Services: AP.
Special Editions: Chistmas (Dec); Interstate 86 Travel Guide (Fall); Interstate 86 Travel Guide (Spring).
Special Weekly Sections: Food, Travel, Real Estate (Sun)
Syndicated Publications: Parade (S).
Delivery Methods: Mail`Newsstand`Carrier`Racks
Areas Served - City/County or Portion Thereof, or Zip codes: 14843
Own Printing Facility?: Y
Commercial printers?: Y
Sun. Circulation Paid: 7800
Audit By: Sworn/Estimate/Non-Audited
Audit Date: 12.07.2019
Personnel: Rick Emanuel (Regional Group Pub.); Chris Potter (Regional Ed.); Neal Simon (City Ed.); Heather Falkey (Advertising Dir.); Abigail Wilcox (Circ. Mgr.); Sandy Eveland (Accounting Mgr.)
Parent company (for newspapers): Gannett; CherryRoad Media

REGISTER-STAR

Street address 1: 1 Hudson City Ctr
Street address 2: Ste 202
Street address city: Hudson
Street address state: NY
Zip/Postal code: 12534-2355
County: Columbia
Country: USA
Mailing address: 1 HUDSON CITY CTR STE 202
Mailing city: HUDSON
Mailing state: NY
Mailing zip: 12534-2355
General Phone: (518) 828-1616
Advertising Phone: (518) 828-1616 ext. 2463
Editorial Phone: (518) 828-1616 ext. 2490
General/National Adv. E-mail: advertising@registerstar.com
Display Adv. E-mail: advertising@registerstar.com
Classified Adv. e-mail: classifieds@registerstar.com
Editorial e-mail: editorial@registerstar.com
Primary Website: www.hudsonvalley360.com
Mthly Avg Views: 1048368
Mthly Avg Unique Visitors: 162011
Year Established: 1785
News Services: AP.
Special Editions: Car Care (Apr/Oct); Holiday (Nov./Dec); Progress Edition (April); Bridal (Jan/June); Holiday (Nov/Dec); Home Improvement (Sept./May) We'll create special editions for your special events
Special Weekly Sections: Best Food Days (S); Best Food Days (Wed).
Syndicated Publications: USA Weekend, Parade Magazine, every week. Relish, Spry monthly.
Delivery Methods: Mail`Newsstand`Carrier`Racks
Areas Served - City/County or Portion Thereof, or Zip codes: All Columbia County, Greene County,
Own Printing Facility?: N
Commercial printers?: N
Avg Free Circ: 12
Sat. Circulation Paid: 3847
Sat. Circulation Free: 18
Audit By: AAM
Audit Date: 30.09.2016
Personnel: Mark Vinciguerra (Pub.); Tammi Ullrich (HR/Business Mgr.); Gregory Appel (Exec. Ed.); Susan Chasney (Ed.); Gregory Appel (Advertising Director)
Parent company (for newspapers): Johnson Newspaper Corp.

THE DAILY MAIL

Street address 1: 1 Hudson City Ctr
Street address 2: Ste 202
Street address city: Hudson
Street address state: NY
Zip/Postal code: 12534-2355
County: Columbia
Country: USA

Mailing state: NY
Mailing zip: 12534
General Phone: 5188281616
Advertising Phone: (518) 828-1616
Editorial Phone: (518) 828-1616
General/National Adv. E-mail: Tammiullrich@gmail.com
Display Adv. E-mail: Tammiullrich@gmail.com
Classified Adv. e-mail: Tammiullrich@gmail.com
Editorial e-mail: Tammiullrich@gmail.com
Primary Website: www.hudsonvalley360.com
Mthly Avg Views: 1048368
Mthly Avg Unique Visitors: 162011
Year Established: 1792
News Services: AP.
Special Editions: Car Care (Apr); Christmas Gift Guide (Dec); Progress Report (April); Bridal (Jan); Home Improvement (Mar); Christmas Gift Guide (Nov); Car Care (Oct); Home Improvement (Sept). destinations (May)
Special Weekly Sections: TV (Sat).On The Scene / entertainment guide (Fridays) Living Today (Saturday)
Syndicated Publications: Parade magazine (weekly);American Profile (Weekly); Spry (monthly); Relish (monthly)
Delivery Methods: Mail`Newsstand`Carrier
Areas Served - City/County or Portion Thereof, or Zip codes: Columbia and Greene Counties in NYS
Own Printing Facility?: N
Commercial printers?: N
Avg Free Circ: 14
Sat. Circulation Paid: 2259
Audit By: AAM
Audit Date: 30.09.2016
Personnel: Ray Pignone (Ed.); Tammi Ullrich (Admin./Asst.to the Pub.); Mark Vinciguerra (Pub./Gen. Mgr.); Gregory Appel (Advertising Director); Mary Dempsey (Executive Editor)
Parent company (for newspapers): Johnson Newspaper Corp.

THE ITHACA JOURNAL

Street address 1: 123 W State St
Street address city: Ithaca
Street address state: NY
Zip/Postal code: 14850-5427
County: Tompkins
Country: USA
Mailing address: 123 W STATE ST
Mailing city: ITHACA
Mailing state: NY
Mailing zip: 14850-5427
General Phone: (607) 272-2321
Advertising Phone: (607) 798-1131
Editorial Phone: (607) 272-2321
General/National Adv. E-mail: jriesbec@ithacajournal.com
Display Adv. E-mail: jriesbec@ithacajournal.com
Editorial e-mail: nborowski@gannett.com
Primary Website: www.ithacajournal.com
News Services: AP, GNS,
Syndicated Publications: The Real Estate Journal (Wed.) Ticket (Thurs.)
Own Printing Facility?: Y
Commercial printers?: Y
Avg Free Circ: 222
Sat. Circulation Paid: 9086
Sat. Circulation Free: 175
Sun. Circulation Paid: 180
Audit By: AAM
Audit Date: 30.06.2018
Personnel: Thomas Claybaugh (Pres./Pub.); Donna Bell (HR); Neill A. Borowski (Exec. Ed.); Kevin Crane (Gen. Mgr.)
Parent company (for newspapers): Gannett

THE POST-JOURNAL

Street address 1: 15 W 2nd St
Street address city: Jamestown
Street address state: NY
Zip/Postal code: 14701-5215
County: Chautauqua
Country: USA
Mailing address: PO BOX 3386
Mailing city: JAMESTOWN
Mailing state: NY
Mailing zip: 14702-3386
General Phone: (716) 487-1111
Advertising Phone: (716) 487-1111
Editorial Phone: (716) 487-1111
General/National Adv. E-mail: advertising@post-journal.com
Display Adv. E-mail: advertising@post-journal.com
Classified Adv. e-mail: adsales@post-journal.com
Editorial e-mail: editorial@post-journal.com
Primary Website: www.post-journal.com
Mthly Avg Views: 318888
Mthly Avg Unique Visitors: 109198
Year Established: 1826
News Services: AP.
Special Editions: Community Directory (Jan); Medical Directory & Weddings (Feb); Chatauqua Profiles (Mar); Golf Guide, Spring Car Care, Camping Guide (Apr); Vacation Guide, Lawn & Garden Care, Discover Erie (May); Chautauqua Book (Jun); Cautauqua Lake, Wine Time, Chautauqua Fair, Readers Choice, 101 Things to Do (Jul); Youth Soccer, NFL Preview, Gridiron (Aug); Chautauqua Chamber Tab, Buffalo Bills & Sabres Schedules, Back to School, Fall sports (Sept); Survivors, Fall Brides, Gas Giveaway (Oct); Experience Winter, Best Gifts (Nov); Holidy Gift Guide, Wrapping Paper, Song Book (Dec)
Special Weekly Sections: Best Food Day (Sat)
Syndicated Publications: TV Book (Fri); Community Marketplace
Areas Served - City/County or Portion Thereof, or Zip codes: Southern Chautauqua County (NY)
Sat. Circulation Paid: 10783
Sun. Circulation Paid: 11828
Audit By: AAM
Audit Date: 30.06.2018
Personnel: Micheal Bird (Pub.); Debra Brunner (Adv. Dir.); Kirsten Johnson (Mktg./Promo.); Andy Gee (Circ. Dir.); Dennis Phillips (Bus./Finance Ed.); John Whittaker (Ed.); Aimee Frederick (Features Ed.); Linda Carlson (Librarian); Brigetta Overcash (Magazine Ed.); Matt Spielman (News Ed.); Chris Kinsler (Regl. Ed.); Scott Kindberg (Sports Ed.); Peter C. Elofson (Prodn. Mgr., Pre Press); Andrew Cavaretta
Parent company (for newspapers): Ogden Newspapers Inc.

DAILY FREEMAN

Street address 1: 79 Hurley Ave
Street address city: Kingston
Street address state: NY
Zip/Postal code: 12401-2832
County: Ulster
Country: USA
General Phone: (845) 331-5000
Advertising Phone: (845) 331-5000 Ext. 01099
Editorial Phone: (845) 331-5000
General/National Adv. E-mail: ttergeoglou@freemanonline.com
Display Adv. E-mail: ttergeoglou@freemanonline.com
Classified Adv. e-mail: classified@freemanonline.com
Editorial e-mail: letters@freemanonline.com
Primary Website: www.dailyfreeman.com
Mthly Avg Views: 3500000
Mthly Avg Unique Visitors: 519977
Year Established: 1871
News Services: AP, TMS.
Special Editions: Kingston Classic (Apr); Spotlight on the Arts (Aug); Last Minute Gift Guide (Dec); Internet Directory (Feb); Brides (Jan); Parenting (Jul); Graduation (Jun); Housing Solutions (Mar); Summer Car Care (May); Winter Lifestyles (Nov); Women's View
Special Weekly Sections: Entertainment (Fri); Financial (S); Best Food Edition (Wed).
Syndicated Publications: Preview Tab (Fri); People & Events Magazine (S).
Delivery Methods: Mail`Newsstand`Carrier`Racks
Areas Served - City/County or Portion Thereof, or Zip codes: Ulster County/NY
Own Printing Facility?: N
Commercial printers?: N
Avg Free Circ: 1005
Sat. Circulation Paid: 6618
Sat. Circulation Free: 1010
Sun. Circulation Paid: 11027
Sun. Circulation Free: 3498
Audit By: AAM
Audit Date: 30.06.2018
Personnel: Kevin Corrado (Pub.); Timothy J. Tergeoglou (Adv. Dir.); Joe Sciacca (Reg. Ed.); Ivan Lajara (Senior Ed.); Jeremy Schiffres (City Ed.); Mike Sheehan (Circ. Dir.); Tony Sakellariou (Controller)
Parent company (for newspapers): Media News Group; Digital First Media

LOCKPORT UNION-SUN & JOURNAL

Street address 1: 135 Main Street
Street address 2: Ste 1
Street address city: Lockport
Street address state: NY
Zip/Postal code: 14094
County: Niagara
Country: USA
Mailing state: NY
General Phone: (716) 439-9222
Advertising Phone: (716) 439-1234
Editorial Phone: (716) 439-9222
General/National Adv. E-mail: ann.fisherbale@lockportjournal.com
Display Adv. E-mail: dan.tronolone@lockportjournal.com
Classified Adv. e-mail: leann.belfield@lockportjournal.com
Editorial e-mail: joyce.miles@lockportjournal.com
Primary Website: www.lockportjournal.com
Year Established: 1821
News Services: AP.
Special Editions: Spring Fashion (Apr); Farm Home (Aug); Car Care (Jun); Impact (Mar); Gift Guide (Nov); Better Homes (Oct); Women's World (Sept).
Special Weekly Sections: Best Food Day (Mon)
Areas Served - City/County or Portion Thereof, or Zip codes: Niagara County (NY)
Avg Free Circ: 308
Sat. Circulation Paid: 4282
Sat. Circulation Free: 308
Sun. Circulation Paid: 4037
Sun. Circulation Free: 218
Audit By: AAM
Audit Date: 31.12.2018
Personnel: John D'Onofrio (Sports Ed.); Joyce Miles (Mng. Ed.); John Celestino (Pub.); Rob Kaiser (Exec. Ed.); Ken Skryp (Cir.)
Parent company (for newspapers): CNHI, LLC; CNHI, LLC

THE MALONE TELEGRAM

Street address 1: 469 E Main St
Street address 2: Ste 4
Street address city: Malone
Street address state: NY
Zip/Postal code: 12953-2128
County: Franklin
Country: USA
Mailing address: 469 E MAIN ST STE 4
Mailing city: MALONE
Mailing state: NY
Mailing zip: 12953-2128
General Phone: (518) 483-4700
Advertising Phone: (518) 483-4720
Editorial Phone: (518) 483-2000
General/National Adv. E-mail: ads@mtelegram.com
Display Adv. E-mail: kcarre@mtelegram.com
Classified Adv. e-mail: classified@mtelegram.com
Editorial e-mail: news@mtelegram.com
Primary Website: www.mymalonetelegram.com
Year Established: 1905
News Services: AP.
Special Editions: Fair Tab (Aug); Bridal Tab (Feb); Winter Carnival (Jan); Meet the Merchants (Jun); Spring Tab (Mar); Summer Visitor (May); Christmas Gift Guide (Nov).
Special Weekly Sections: Home (Mon); Arts, Entertainment, Real Estate (Tue); Religion (Fri); Best Food Day, Business (Sat);
Delivery Methods: Mail`Newsstand`Carrier`Racks
Areas Served - City/County or Portion Thereof, or Zip codes: Northern Franklin County, NY
Own Printing Facility?: N
Commercial printers?: Y
Sat. Circulation Paid: 4721
Audit By: Sworn/Estimate/Non-Audited
Audit Date: 12.07.2019
Personnel: Betsy McGivney (Bus. Mgr.); Karen Carre (Adv. Mgr.); Ej Conzola (Ed.)
Parent company (for newspapers): Johnson Newspaper Corp.

DAILY COURIER-OBSERVER/ ADVANCE NEWS

Street address 1: 1 Harrowgate Cmns
Street address city: Massena
Street address state: NY
Zip/Postal code: 13662-2201
County: Saint Lawrence
Country: USA
Mailing address: 1 HARROWGATE CMNS
Mailing city: MASSENA
Mailing state: NY
Mailing zip: 13662-2201
General Phone: (315) 769-2451
Advertising Phone: (315) 661-2512
Editorial Phone: (315) 661-2532
General/National Adv. E-mail: nbellinger@ogd.com
Display Adv. E-mail: tmackin@ogd.com
Classified Adv. e-mail: class@ogd.com
Editorial e-mail: rmartin@ogd.com
Primary Website: www.mpcourier.com/
Delivery Methods: Mail`Racks
Avg Free Circ: 1900
Sat. Circulation Paid: 5900
Sat. Circulation Free: 1900
Audit By: Sworn/Estimate/Non-Audited
Audit Date: 12.07.2019
Personnel: Pery White (Ed.); John Johnson (Chief Exec. Off. / Co-Pub.); Harold Johnson (Pres. / Co-Pub.); Jeanette Hardy (HR VP); Gary Valik (Sales / Mktg. VP); Amber Bogart (Cir. CSR); Nathan Bellinger (Adv. Acct. Exec.)

NEWSDAY

Street address 1: 6 Corporate Center Drive
Street address city: Melville
Street address state: NY
Zip/Postal code: 11747
County: Suffolk
Country: USA
Mailing address: 235 PINELAWN RD
Mailing city: MELVILLE
Mailing state: NY
Mailing zip: 11747-4250
General Phone: (800) 639-7329
Advertising Phone: (631) 843-7653
Editorial Phone: (631) 843-7653
General/National Adv. E-mail: advertising@newsday.com
Display Adv. E-mail: advertising@newsday.com
Classified Adv. e-mail: ads.classified@newsday.com
Editorial e-mail: letters@newsday.com
Primary Website: www.newsday.com
Mthly Avg Views: 31500000
Mthly Avg Unique Visitors: 2463000
Year Established: 1940
News Services: AP, CSM, DJ, LAT-WP, NNS, RN, SHNS.
Special Editions: Caribbean American Chamber (Apr); Back-to-School (Aug); Holiday Gift Guide (Dec); President's Forum (Feb); Bridal (Jan); Auto Leasing (Jul); Dads & Grads (Jun); Tax Advice-Your Financial Checklist (Mar); Home, Lawn & Garden II (May); Holiday Almanac (Nov)
Special Weekly Sections: Business (Mon-Fri); Technology, Style (Mon); Health (Tue); Style, Kids (Wed); Food (Thur); Arts, Movies (Fri); Travel, Life (Sun)
Syndicated Publications: USA WEEKEND Magazine (Sat).
Own Printing Facility?: Y
Commercial printers?: N
Sat. Circulation Paid: 250643
Sun. Circulation Paid: 296251
Audit By: AAM
Audit Date: 30.09.2018
Personnel: Debby Krenek (Co-Pub.); Mary Ann Skinner (Asst. Mng. Ed., Admin.); Chris Gennario (Adv. Administrator, Newsday.com Bus.); Robert Keane (Vice Pres./Mng. Ed.); Richard Galant (Mng. Ed., News); Peter Bengelsdorf (Dir., Publishing Devel.); Michael Gatta (MGR Information Systems); James Rosenfeld; Chris Tobia (Director, Major Retail Sales); Lauren Andrich; Gordon McLeod (Pub.); Stefani Angeli (Senior Director National Sales); Edward Bushey (Co-Pub.); Deborah Henley (Ed.)
Parent company (for newspapers): Newsday

THE TIMES HERALD-RECORD

Street address 1: 40 Mulberry St
Street address city: Middletown
Street address state: NY
Zip/Postal code: 10940-6302
County: Orange
Country: USA
Mailing address: PO BOX 2046
Mailing city: MIDDLETOWN
Mailing state: NY
Mailing zip: 10940-0558
General Phone: 1-866-620-1700
Advertising Phone: (845) 341-1100 ext. 2094
Editorial Phone: (845) 346-3170
General/National Adv. E-mail: amcfarlane@recordonline.com

Display Adv. E-mail: amcfarlane@recordonline.com
Classified Adv. e-mail: kwalsh@th-record.com
Editorial e-mail: letters@th-record.com
Primary Website: www.recordonline.com
Mthly Avg Views: 5200000
Mthly Avg Unique Visitors: 38500
Year Established: 1960
News Services: AP, NewsCore
Special Editions: NY Auto Show (Apr); Back-to-School (Aug); Wish Book (Dec); Bridal (Feb); Progress (Jan); Star Spangled (Jul); Family Focus (Mar); Summer Guide (May); Inside Health (Monthly); Gift Guide (Nov); New Car (Oct); Family Focus (Sept).
Special Weekly Sections: Auto (Tue); Best Food Day (Wed); Entertainment (Fri); Home, Real Estate (Sun)
Syndicated Publications: Go Plus (Fri); Relish (Monthly); Sunday Magazine (S); Auto Plus (Tues).
Delivery Methods: Newsstand`Carrier`Racks
Areas Served - City/County or Portion Thereof, or Zip codes: Orange, Sullivan & Ulster Counties (NY), Pike County (PA), Sussex County (NJ)
Own Printing Facility?: Y
Commercial printers?: Y
Avg Free Circ: 3362
Sat. Circulation Paid: 25542
Sat. Circulation Free: 2691
Sun. Circulation Paid: 33681
Sun. Circulation Free: 2091
Audit By: AAM
Audit Date: 31.12.2018
Personnel: Joe Vanderhoof (Pres./Pub.); Stanton Frederick (Commercial Printing); Barry Lewis (Ed.); Anthony Mcfarlane (regional Ad Direcor)
Parent company (for newspapers): Gannett Company Inc.; CherryRoad Media

AMNEW YORK

Street address 1: 240 W 35th St
Street address 2: Fl 9th
Street address city: New York
Street address state: NY
Zip/Postal code: 10001-2506
County: New York
Country: USA
Mailing address: 240 W 35th St, Fl 9
Mailing city: New York
Mailing state: NY
Mailing zip: 10001-2506
General Phone: (646) 293-9499
Advertising Phone: (646) 293-9499
General/National Adv. E-mail: amnyMarketing@am-ny.com
Display Adv. E-mail: amnyMarketing@am-ny.com
Classified Adv. e-mail: Jneknez@newsday.com
Editorial e-mail: thoughts@amny.com
Primary Website: www.amny.com
Year Established: 2003
Special Weekly Sections: Education, Careers (Mon); Style (Tue); Travel (Tue); Dining, Health (Wed); City Living, Real Estate (Thur); Weekend (Fri)
Avg Free Circ: 4916
Audit By: CAC
Audit Date: 30.09.2018
Personnel: Donna Chibaro (Bus. Mgr.); Bill Praz (Cir. Dir); Nannette Fevola (National Sales Mktg Dir.); Debby Krenek (Co-Pub.); Edward Bushey (Co-Pub.); Jason Neknez (Class.); Polly Higgins (Ed. in Chief)
Parent company (for newspapers): Schneps Media; Newsday Media Group

METRO NEW YORK

Street address 1: 120 Broadway
Street address 2: 6th Floor
Street address city: New York
Street address state: NY
Zip/Postal code: 10271-0002
County: New York
Country: USA
General Phone: (212) 457-7790
Advertising Phone: (212) 457-7735
General/National Adv. E-mail: advertising@metro.us
Display Adv. E-mail: advertising@metro.us
Classified Adv. e-mail: newyorkclassifieds@metro.us
Editorial e-mail: letters@metro.us
Primary Website: metro.us
Mthly Avg Views: 4987057
Mthly Avg Unique Visitors: 2001409
Year Established: 2004
Special Weekly Sections: Education & Job (Mon), Health & Wellbeing (Mon-Fri), Travel & Finance (Tue), Style, home, real estate (Wed), Going out & weekend (Thu & Fri)
Delivery Methods: Racks
Areas Served - City/County or Portion Thereof, or Zip codes: New York DMA, Boston DMA, Philadelphia DMA
Own Printing Facility?: N
Commercial printers?: N
Avg Free Circ: 186185
Audit By: CAC
Audit Date: 30.09.2018
Personnel: Ed Abrams (Metro US Exec./National Sales Dir. & Associate Publisher Metro New York); Yggers Mortenson (CEO & Publisher); Wilf Maunoir (US Mktg. Dir.); Joe Lauletta (US Circ. Dir.)
Parent company (for newspapers): SB New York; Schneps Media

NEW YORK DAILY NEWS

Street address 1: 4 New York Plz Fl 6
Street address 2: Floor 6
Street address city: New York
Street address state: NY
Zip/Postal code: 10004-2473
County: New York
Country: USA
Mailing address: 4 NEW YORK PLZ FL 6
Mailing city: NEW YORK
Mailing state: NY
Mailing zip: 10004-2828
General Phone: (212) 210-2100
Advertising Phone: (212) 210-2004
Editorial Phone: (212) 210-6397
General/National Adv. E-mail: LBrancato@nydailynews.com
Classified Adv. e-mail: classifiedads@nydailynews.com
Editorial e-mail: voicers@nydailynews.com
Primary Website: www.nydailynews.com
Mthly Avg Unique Visitors: 42832510
Year Established: 1919
News Services: AP, MCT, TMS.
Special Weekly Sections: Friday (Weekend Entertainment Guide) (Fri); City Lights (S); Style (Thur); Food (Wed).
Syndicated Publications: Relish (Monthly); Sunday Gravure (S).
Delivery Methods: Mail`Newsstand`Carrier
Areas Served - City/County or Portion Thereof, or Zip codes: Tri-State Area
Sat. Circulation Paid: 145684
Sun. Circulation Paid: 199032
Audit By: AAM
Audit Date: 31.03.2019
Personnel: Mortimer B. Zuckerman (Chrmn./Pub.); Thomas H. Peck (CFO); James Brill (Sr. Vice Pres., Circ./Distr.); Rudy Zaccagno (VP, Adv.); Linda Brancato (VP Pres. Adv.); Joann Dinapoli (Retail Adv. Dir.); Rich Harknett (Circ. Vice Pres.); John Polizano (Sr. VP, Adv Dir.); Lenny Brown (Dir. Class. Adv. Sales); Sindy Speelman (Sales Mgr, Natl. Retail & Preprints); Colin Myler (Pres., Editor-in-chief); Kristen Lee (Dir., Digital Development); Zach Haberman (Deputy Managing Ed., Digital); Cristina Everett (Deputy Managing Ed., Digital Ent.); Christine Roberts (Ed., Mobile); Colleen Noonan (VP, Mktg); Tom Grosso (Pressroom); Kathy O'Dea (Mgr., Classified Tel. Sales); Kevin O'Brien (Dir., Nat. Adv.); Joe Anzalone (Dir. of Multi-Cultural Retail Sales Mgr.); Bianka Ratzmann (Sales Mgr.); Lisa Netcher (Adv. Dir., Ed., Health & Hosp.); Gina Rebelo (Sales Mgr., Real Estate & Travel); Douglas Fletcher (Acct. Mgr. Sup.); Dana Wynkoop (Account Exec., Financial); Marc Horowitz (Mgr., Motion Pic.); Alex Jones (Mng. Ed.)
Parent company (for newspapers): New York Daily News; Alden Global Capital

NEW YORK POST

Street address 1: 1185 Avenue of the Americas
Street address 2: Ste 900A
Street address city: New York
Street address state: NY
Zip/Postal code: 10036
County: New York
Country: USA
Mailing address: 1211 AVENUE OF THE AMERICAS STE 900A
Mailing city: NEW YORK
Mailing state: NY
Mailing zip: 10036-8701
General Phone: (212) 930-8000
Advertising Phone: (212) 930-5753
Editorial Phone: (212) 930-8288
General/National Adv. E-mail: slareau@nypost.com
Classified Adv. e-mail: clloyd@nypost.com
Editorial e-mail: letters@nypost.com
Primary Website: www.nypost.com
Year Established: 1801
News Services: AP, LAT-WP.
Special Editions: Mexico (Apr); Ski Vacations (Dec); Alaska (Jan); Summer Get-Aways (Jun); Spring & Summer Cruises (Mar); Catskills (May); Mexico (Nov); Follow the Sun (Oct); Autumn Travel (Sept).
Special Weekly Sections: Travel (Tues).
Syndicated Publications: Page Six (Quarterly); Parade (S).
Sat. Circulation Paid: 389967
Sun. Circulation Paid: 403013
Audit By: AAM
Audit Date: 30.09.2018
Personnel: Ken Kiczales (Adv. Mgr., Nat'l); Caitlin Lloyd (Advertising); David Rentas (Ed. Dept./Photo); Emily Smith (Ed. Dept./Page Six); Chris Shaw (Ed. Dept./ Sports); Richard Wilner (Ed. Dept./Business); Brad Feldman (Post Studios & Creative Services); Jesse Angelo (Pub. / CEO); Neil Nagraj (Ed.)
Parent company (for newspapers): News Corporation

THE NEW YORK TIMES

Street address 1: 620 8th Ave
Street address city: New York
Street address state: NY
Zip/Postal code: 10018-1618
County: New York
Country: USA
Mailing address: 620 8TH AVE
Mailing city: NEW YORK
Mailing state: NY
Mailing zip: 10018-1618
General Phone: (212) 556-1234
Advertising Phone: (212) 556-7777
Editorial Phone: (800) 698-4637
General/National Adv. E-mail: advertising@nytimes.com
Display Adv. E-mail: advertising@nytimes.com
Classified Adv. e-mail: classifiedadtrans.help@nytimes.com
Editorial e-mail: editorial@nytimes.com; letters@nytimes.com
Primary Website: www.nytimes.com
Mthly Avg Unique Visitors: 29817000
Year Established: 1851
News Services: AP, RN, PR Newswire, DJ, Tass.
Special Editions: Business Travel (Apr); PGA Tour (Aug); Circuits (Dec); Business of Green (Feb); Deal Book (Mar); Wealth/Personal Finance (May); Giving (Nov); Retirement (Oct); Well (Children's Health) (Sept).
Special Weekly Sections: Weekend Arts (Fri); Arts & Leisure (S); ThursdayStyles (Thur); Science Times (Tues); Dining In/Dining Out (Wed).
Syndicated Publications: T (Other); The New York Times Magazine (S); Real Estate (S); Key (Semi-yearly).
Avg Free Circ: 54090
Sat. Circulation Paid: 543728
Sat. Circulation Free: 19880
Sun. Circulation Paid: 989823
Sun. Circulation Free: 20796
Audit By: AAM
Audit Date: 30.09.2018
Personnel: Scott H. Heekin-Canedy (Pres./Gen. Mgr.); Cristian L. Edwards (Pres., News Servs.); Joseph Seibert (CIO); Dennis L. Stern (Sr. Vice Pres./Deputy Gen. Mgr.); Thomas K. Carley (Sr. Vice Pres., Planning); Denise F. Warren (Sr. Vice Pres./Chief Adv. Officer); Roland A. Caputo (Sr. Vice Pres./CFO); Michael Valentine (Vice Pres., HR); Terry L. Hayes (Vice Pres., Labor Rel.); Virginia French (Grp. Vice Pres.); Alexis Buryk (Adv. Sr. Vice Pres.); Thomas Helling (Adv. Vice Pres.); Mark W. Herlyn (Adv. Vice Pres.); Paul Smurl (Adv. Vice Pres.); Guy D. Holliday (Adv. Vice Pres., Sales); Seth Rogin (Adv. Vice Pres., Sales); Andy Wright (Senior VP, Adv. & Pub.); Yasmin Namini (Sr. Vice Pres., Mktg./Circ.); Diane McNulty (Dir., Community Affairs); Carol D'Andrea; Nick D'Andrea; Josh Williams; Todd Socia; Raymond Pearce (VP, Circulation & Reader Applications); James Dao; Aidan McNulty; Sebastian Tomich (VP, Ad Product & Plan. Senior VP, Adv.); Anthony Benten; Michael Golden (Vice Chairman); Alex MacCallum (Audience Expansion and Engagement Editor); Mark Thompson (CEO); Kinsey Wilson (Ed., Innovation & Strategy); Mat Yurow; Piper Rosenshein; Margaret Sullivan (Public Ed.); Arthur Sulzberger Jr. (Chairman & Pub.); David Perpich (Senior VP, Product); Michael Zimbalist (Senior VP, Ad Products & Research & Dev.); Kerrie Gillis (VP, Adv. & Sales Op.); Daphne Schwab (VP, Sales Dev.); Laura Sonnenfeld (VP, Adv.); Meredith Kopit Levien (Chief Rev. Officer); James Bennet (Editorial Ed.); Joseph Kahn (Mng. Ed.); Clifford Levy (Met. Ed.)
Parent company (for newspapers): The New York Times Co.

THE WALL STREET JOURNAL

Street address 1: 1211 Avenue of the Americas
Street address 2: Lowr C3
Street address city: New York
Street address state: NY
Zip/Postal code: 10036-8701
County: New York
Country: USA
Mailing address: 1211 AVENUE OF THE AMERICAS LOWR C3
Mailing city: NEW YORK
Mailing state: NY
Mailing zip: 10036-0003
General Phone: (800) 568-7625
Advertising Phone: (312) 750-4235
Editorial Phone: (800) 568-7625
General/National Adv. E-mail: gloria.hauter@wsj.com
Display Adv. E-mail: meri.westcott@wsj.com
Classified Adv. e-mail: luke.bahrenburg@wsj.com
Editorial e-mail: wsj.ltrs@wsj.com
Primary Website: www.wsj.com
Mthly Avg Views: 133370000
Mthly Avg Unique Visitors: 13971000
Year Established: 1889
News Services: AP, DJ.
Special Editions: Golf (Apr); Business Insight (Aug); Business Insight (Dec); Encore/Retirement Guide (Feb); Trend Report (Jan); Your Money Matters-Guide to Personal Finance (Jul); 401K (Jun); NCAA Men's Basketball (Mar); Best On The Street Analysts (May); Monthly Mutual F
Special Weekly Sections: Weekend Journal (Fri); Personal Journal (Thur); Personal Journal (Tues); Personal Journal (Wed).
Avg Free Circ: 36484
Sat. Circulation Paid: 1145230
Sat. Circulation Free: 21240
Sun. Circulation Paid: 1145230
Sun. Circulation Free: 21240
Audit By: AAM
Audit Date: 30.09.2017
Personnel: Todd H. Larsen (Sr. Vice Pres./COO); Rupert Murdoch (Exec. Chairman); Robert Thomson (CEO, News Group); Gerard Baker (Editor in Chief); William Lewis (CEO & Publisher); Rebecca Blumenstein (Deputy Editor in Chief); Matthew Murray (Exec. Ed.); Michael W. Miller (Senior Deputy); Michael F. Rooney (Chief Revenue Officer); F. James Pensiero (Vice Pres., News Projects); Daniel Bernard (Gen. Mgr., WSJ.com); Judy Barry (Adv. Sr. Vice Pres.); David Forgione (Adv. Vice Pres., Bus. Grp.); Walter Hodge (District Sales Mgr.); Imtiaz Patel (Vice Pres., Mktg. Strategy); Lynne K. Brennen (Vice Pres., Circ. Mktg.); Deborah Brewster (Deputy Mng. Ed.); Alix M. Freedman (Deputy Mng. Ed.); Gerald F. Seib (Asst. Mng. Ed./Exec. Washington Ed.); Colleen Schwartz (VP, President of Communications); Robert Rose (Bureau Chief, Atlanta); Kevin Helliker (Bureau Chief, Chicago); Paula Keve (Head of Corp. Comm.); Ashley Huston (Head of Corporate Communication); David Biderman (Director); Thom San Filippo (VP President, Customer Service); Jennifer Budig (Gen. Adv., Sales Dir.); Nancy McDonald (Gen. Adv., Sales Dir.); Alberto Apodaca (Lux. Adv., Sales Dir.); Paul V. Carlucci (Greater N.Y. Sec., Sales Dir.); Marti Gallardo (Class. Adv., VP Vertical Markets)
Parent company (for newspapers): Dow Jones & Company; News Corporation

NIAGARA GAZETTE

Street address 1: 473 Third Street
Street address city: Niagara Falls
Street address state: NY
Zip/Postal code: 14301
County: Niagara
Country: USA
Mailing address: 473 3RD ST STE 201
Mailing city: NIAGARA FALLS
Mailing state: NY
Mailing zip: 14301-1500
General Phone: (716) 282-2311
General/National Adv. E-mail: John Celestino <john.celestino@niagara-gazette.com>
Display Adv. E-mail: classads@gnnewspapers.com

Classified Adv. e-mail: Kevin Krisnosky <kevin.krisnosky@niagara-gazette.com>
Editorial e-mail: matt.winterhalter@niagara-gazette.com
Primary Website: www.niagara-gazette.com
Mthly Avg Views: 405250
Mthly Avg Unique Visitors: 287936
Year Established: 1854
News Services: AP, GNS.
Special Editions: Senior Guide (Apr); Back-to-School (Aug); Holiday Greetings (Dec); Progress (Feb); Health & Wellness (Jan); Added Value Certificates (Jul); Dining Guide (Jun); Home Improvement (Mar); Summer Events (May); Holiday Gift Guide (Nov); Fall Dining Guide (Oct);
Special Weekly Sections: Home & Garden (Fri); Food (Mon); Comics (S); Religion (Sat).
Own Printing Facility?: Y
Commercial printers?: Y
Sat. Circulation Paid: 8055
Sun. Circulation Paid: 7751
Audit By: AAM
Audit Date: 31.12.2018
Personnel: John Celestino (Pub.); Staci Cook (Circ.); Matt Winterhalter (Mng. Ed.); Mark Scheer (Reg. News Dir.)
Parent company (for newspapers): CNHI, LLC; CNHI, LLC

THE EVENING SUN

Street address 1: 29 Lackawanna Ave
Street address city: Norwich
Street address state: NY
Zip/Postal code: 13815-1404
County: Chenango
Country: USA
Mailing address: PO BOX 151
Mailing city: NORWICH
Mailing state: NY
Mailing zip: 13815-0151
General Phone: (607) 334-3276
Advertising Phone: (607) 334-3276
Editorial Phone: (607) 334-3276
General/National Adv. E-mail: rfoote@pennysaveronline.com
Display Adv. E-mail: bcarpenter@evesun.com
Editorial e-mail: news@evesun.com
Primary Website: www.evesun.com
Year Established: 1891
News Services: AP.
Special Weekly Sections: The Weekend Sun (Fri); Sports (Mon); Lifestyle (Thur); Health (Tues); Farm (Wed).
Delivery Methods: Newsstand`Carrier`Racks
Areas Served - City/County or Portion Thereof, or Zip codes: Norwich Chenango Count NY 13815
Own Printing Facility?: Y
Commercial printers?: Y
Audit By: Sworn/Estimate/Non-Audited
Audit Date: 12.07.2019
Personnel: Richard Snyder (Pres.); Russ Foote (Adv. Mgr.); Marty Conklin (General Manager Print Facility); Alshey Babbitt (Managing Editor)
Parent company (for newspapers): Snyder Communications

OGDENSBURG JOURNAL/ADVANCE NEWS

Street address 1: 230 Caroline St
Street address 2: Ste 1
Street address city: Ogdensburg
Street address state: NY
Zip/Postal code: 13669-1629
County: Saint Lawrence
Country: USA
Mailing state: NY
General Phone: 315-393-1003
Advertising Phone: (315) 661-2512
Editorial Phone: (315) 393-1003
General/National Adv. E-mail: bward@ogd.com
Display Adv. E-mail: arivera@ogd.com
Classified Adv. e-mail: dpeters@ogd.com
Editorial e-mail: egraham@wdt.net
Primary Website: www.ogd.com
Year Established: 1830
Delivery Methods: Mail`Racks
Areas Served - City/County or Portion Thereof, or Zip codes: St. Lawrence County (NY)
Sat. Circulation Paid: 4000
Sun. Circulation Paid: 8500
Audit By: Sworn/Estimate/Non-Audited
Audit Date: 12.07.2019
Personnel: Gary Valik (Corp VP Sales & Mktg.); Amber Bogart (Cir. CSR); Eileen Kast (HR/Purch.); Tom Graser (Ed.); Barbara Ward (Adv. Mgr.); Debra Petersen (Class.); John Johnson (CEO / Co-Pub.); Harold Johnson (Pres. / Co-Pub.)
Parent company (for newspapers): Johnson Newspaper Corp.

OLEAN TIMES HERALD

Street address 1: 639 Norton Drive
Street address city: Olean
Street address state: NY
Zip/Postal code: 14760
County: Cattaraugus
Country: USA
Mailing address: 639 W NORTON DR
Mailing city: OLEAN
Mailing state: NY
Mailing zip: 14760-1498
General Phone: (716) 372-3121
Advertising Phone: (716) 372-3121 ext. 208
Editorial Phone: (716) 372-3121 ext. 231
General/National Adv. E-mail: adcomp@oleantimesherald.com
Display Adv. E-mail: jkeim@oleantimesherald.com
Classified Adv. e-mail: cpowley@oleantimesherald.con
Editorial e-mail: news@oleantimesherald.com
Primary Website: www.oleantimesherald.com
Year Established: 2000
News Services: AP, NEA, SHNS, CNS.
Special Editions: Golf Tab (Apr); Christmas Stories (Dec); Tax Tab (Feb); Bridal (Jan); Frozen Food (Mar); Christmas (Nov); Hunting (Oct); Consumer Electronics (Sept); Spring Buyer Tab (Spring).
Special Weekly Sections: Best Food Days (Mon); TV (Sun);
Syndicated Publications: Olean Review (Other); USA WEEKEND Magazine (S).
Avg Free Circ: 61
Sat. Circulation Paid: 8113
Sat. Circulation Free: 61
Sun. Circulation Paid: 8824
Sun. Circulation Free: 60
Audit By: AAM
Audit Date: 30.06.2018
Personnel: Jim Bonn (Pub.); Jim Eckstrom (Mng. Ed.); Chuck Pollock (Sports Ed.); Nichole Finnerty (Cir. Mgr.)
Parent company (for newspapers): Community Media Group; Bradford Publishing Company

THE DAILY STAR

Street address 1: 102 Chestnut St
Street address city: Oneonta
Street address state: NY
Zip/Postal code: 13820-2584
County: Otsego
Country: USA
Mailing address: PO BOX 250
Mailing city: ONEONTA
Mailing state: NY
Mailing zip: 13820-0250
General Phone: (607) 432-1000
Editorial Phone: (607) 432-1000
General/National Adv. E-mail: mneighbour@thedailystar.com
Display Adv. E-mail: mneighbour@thedailystar.com
Classified Adv. e-mail: cbenson@thedailystar.com
Editorial e-mail: letters@thedailystar.com
Primary Website: www.thedailystar.com
Mthly Avg Views: 800000
Mthly Avg Unique Visitors: 125000
Year Established: 1890
News Services: AP, DJ, ONS, LAT-WP, TMS.
Syndicated Publications: Relish (Monthly); Parade (Weekly).
Delivery Methods: Mail`Newsstand`Carrier`Racks
Own Printing Facility?: Y
Commercial printers?: Y
Avg Free Circ: 475
Sat. Circulation Paid: 7491
Sat. Circulation Free: 475
Audit By: AAM
Audit Date: 31.12.2017
Personnel: Sam Pollak (Ed.); Denise Richardson (News Ed.); Julie Lewis (Photo Dept. Mgr.); Dean Russin (Sports Ed.); Fred Scheller (Pub.)
Parent company (for newspapers): CNHI, LLC; CNHI, LLC

THE PALLADIUM-TIMES

Street address 1: 140 W 1st St
Street address city: Oswego
Street address state: NY
Zip/Postal code: 13126-1514
County: Oswego
Country: USA
Mailing address: 140 W 1ST ST
Mailing city: OSWEGO
Mailing state: NY
Mailing zip: 13126-1597
General Phone: (315) 343-3800
Advertising Phone: (315) 343-3800
Editorial Phone: (315) 343-3800
General/National Adv. E-mail: kpercival@palltimes.com
Display Adv. E-mail: kpercival@palltimes.com
Classified Adv. e-mail: classifieds@palltimes.com
Editorial e-mail: smccrobie@palltimes.com
Primary Website: www.palltimes.com
Year Established: 1845
News Services: AP, SHNS.
Special Editions: Newcomer's Guide (Aug); Christmas Shopping (Dec); Welcome Back SUNY Tab (Feb); Weather (Jan); Auto Racing (Jul); Father's Day (Jun); Progress (Mar); Mother's Day (May); Historic (Monthly); Fall Sports (Oct); Bridal (Sept).
Special Weekly Sections: Health (Fri); Food (Mon); Entertainment (Thur); Business Pages (Tues).
Syndicated Publications: USA WEEKEND Magazine (Sat).
Sat. Circulation Paid: 8507
Audit By: Sworn/Estimate/Non-Audited
Audit Date: 12.07.2019
Personnel: Jon Spaulding (Pub.); Virginia DeCare (Accountant); Debra Robillard (Mng. Ed.); Michael LeBoeuf (Sports Ed.); Chrissy Mitchelson (Circ. Mgr.)
Parent company (for newspapers): Sample News Group LLC

PRESS-REPUBLICAN

Street address 1: 170 Margaret Street
Street address city: Plattsburgh
Street address state: NY
Zip/Postal code: 12901
County: Clinton
Country: USA
Mailing address: PO BOX 459
Mailing city: PLATTSBURGH
Mailing state: NY
Mailing zip: 12901-0459
General Phone: (518) 561-2300
Advertising Phone: (518) 561-2300
Editorial Phone: (518) 565-4131
General/National Adv. E-mail: grock@pressrepublican.com
Display Adv. E-mail: grock@pressrepublican.com
Classified Adv. e-mail: classifieds@pressrepublican.com
Editorial e-mail: news@pressrepublican.com
Primary Website: www.pressrepublican.com
Mthly Avg Views: 2000000
Year Established: 1942
News Services: AP, SHNS.
Special Editions: Senior Sentinel, (monthly); Jill Magazine for Women, (monthly); Newcomer News, (monthly); Clinton County Fair, (July); Holiday Bears, (November and December); Celebrations, (November); Gift Guide, (November).
Special Weekly Sections: Best Food Day (Saturday).
Syndicated Publications: Relish (monthly); Parade (Sundays); American Profile (weekly); Althon Sports, (monthly); Grandparenting Today (monthly).
Delivery Methods: Mail`Newsstand`Carrier`Racks
Areas Served - City/County or Portion Thereof, or Zip codes: 12836, 12855, 12870, 12883, 12901, 12903, 12910, 12911, 12912, 12913, 12914, 12915, 12916, 12917, 12918, 12919, 12920, 12921, 12923, 12924, 12926, 12928, 12929, 12930, 12930, 12932, 12933, 12934, 12935, 12936, 12937, 12939, 12941, 12942, 12943, 12944, 12945, 12946, 12950, 12952, 12953, 12955, 12956, 12957, 12958, 12959, 12960, 12961, 12962, 12964, 12966, 12969, 12970, 12972, 12974, 12975, 12977, 12978, 12979, 12980, 12981, 12983, 12985, 12986, 12987, 12989, 12992, 12993, 12994, 12995, 12996, 12997, 12998, 13655
Own Printing Facility?: Y
Commercial printers?: Y
Avg Free Circ: 579
Sat. Circulation Paid: 11623
Sat. Circulation Free: 579
Sun. Circulation Paid: 12531
Sun. Circulation Free: 341
Audit By: AAM
Audit Date: 30.06.2017
Personnel: Lois Clermont (Editor); Nathan Ovalle (Feat. Ed.); Suzanne Moore (News Editor); Kevin Hidook (Press Room Supervisor); Brad Bailey (Publisher); Ben Rowe (Night Editor); Ricky St. Clair (Sports Editor)
Parent company (for newspapers): CNHI, LLC; CNHI, LLC

POUGHKEEPSIE JOURNAL

Street address 1: 85 Civic Center Plz
Street address city: Poughkeepsie
Street address state: NY
Zip/Postal code: 12601-2498
County: Dutchess
Country: USA
Mailing address: PO BOX 1231
Mailing city: POUGHKEEPSIE
Mailing state: NY
Mailing zip: 12602-1231
General Phone: (845) 454-2000
Advertising Phone: (845) 437-4789
Editorial Phone: (845) 437-4800
General/National Adv. E-mail: jdewey@poughkeepsiejournal.com
Display Adv. E-mail: jdewey@poughkeepsiejournal.com
Classified Adv. e-mail: jdewey@poughkeepsiejournal.com
Editorial e-mail: newsroom@poughkeepsiejournal.com
Primary Website: www.poughkeepsiejournal.com
Year Established: 1785
News Services: AP, GNS
Special Editions: Spring Home & Gardens (Apr); Luxury Auto (Aug); Songbook (Dec); Menus (Feb); Bridal (Jan);
Special Weekly Sections: Business (Daily); Food (Wed); Entertainment, Auto (Fri); Business, Senior Citizens, Baby Boomers, Auto (Sun)
Areas Served - City/County or Portion Thereof, or Zip codes: Dutchess County
Own Printing Facility?: N
Commercial printers?: N
Sat. Circulation Paid: 18844
Sun. Circulation Paid: 24956
Audit By: AAM
Audit Date: 31.03.2017
Personnel: Traci Bauer (Exec. Ed.); Jim Fogler (Pres.); John Czarnecki (Circ. Mgr.); Nora Pietrafesa (HR partner); Barbara Gallo Farrell (Community Content Ed.)
Parent company (for newspapers): Gannett

DEMOCRAT AND CHRONICLE

Street address 1: 55 Exchange Boulevard
Street address city: Rochester
Street address state: NY
Zip/Postal code: 14614
County: Monroe
Country: USA
Mailing address: 245 E MAIN ST
Mailing city: ROCHESTER
Mailing state: NY
Mailing zip: 14604-2103
General Phone: (585) 232-7100
Advertising Phone: (585) 258-2552
Editorial Phone: (585) 258-2214
General/National Adv. E-mail: solutions@democratandchronicle .com
Display Adv. E-mail: solutions@ democratandchronicle .com
Classified Adv. e-mail: classified@democrat&chronicle.com
Editorial e-mail: editor@democratandchronicle.com
Primary Website: www.democratandchronicle.com
Mthly Avg Unique Visitors: 1294228
Year Established: 1833
News Services: AP, GNS, MCT, Bloomberg, National Weather Service, TMS.
Special Editions: Living Here (Apr); HOME: Design for Rochester (Every other month); Auto Show (Feb); College Guide (Jan); Rochester Music Fest (Jul); Jazz Fest (Jun); March Madness (Mar); NACAC College Fair (May); Day In The Life (Monthly); Rochester's Choice Winners (Nov
Special Weekly Sections: Inserts, Garden, Travel (Sun); Business (Mon); Editorial, Best Food Days (Tue); Health (Wed); Entertainment (Thur); Our Towns (Fri); Real Estate, Auto (Sat)

Syndicated Publications: Comics (S); Weekend Magazine (Thur).
Areas Served - City/County or Portion Thereof, or Zip codes: Rochester-area (NY)
Sat. Circulation Paid: 82308
Sun. Circulation Paid: 91623
Audit By: AAM
Audit Date: 30.09.2018
Personnel: Mike W. Kilian (Democrat and Chronicle Ed.); Cynthia Benjamin (Community Content Ed.); Steve Bradley (Content Strategist); Virginia Butler (Studio Dir.); Len LaCara (Content Strategy Analyst); Mark Liu (Custom Content Ed.); Scott Norris (Gen. Mgr., Specialty Publications); Julie Philipp (Senior Engagement Ed.); Sheila Rayam (Community Engagement Ed.); David Andreatta (Columnist & Reporter); Erica Bryant (Columnist); Leo Roth (Sports Columnist); Tamra Springer (Executive Asst.)
Parent company (for newspapers): Gannett

THE DAILY RECORD

Street address 1: 16 W Main St Ste 341
Street address 2: Suite 341
Street address city: Rochester
Street address state: NY
Zip/Postal code: 14614-1604
County: Monroe
Country: USA
General Phone: (585) 232-6920
Advertising Phone: (585) 232-6920
Editorial Phone: (585) 232-6922
General/National Adv. E-mail: karla.thomas@nydailyrecord.com
Classified Adv. e-mail: karla.esley@nydailyrecord.com
Editorial e-mail: bjacobs@nydailyrecord.com
Primary Website: www.nydailyrecord.com
Year Established: 1908
Audit By: Sworn/Estimate/Non-Audited
Audit Date: 12.07.2019
Personnel: Shappelle Thompson (Acct. Mgr.); Leo Roth (Ed.); Suzanne Fischer-Huettner (Pub.); Karla Esley (Admin. / Class.)
Parent company (for newspapers): Gannett

DAILY SENTINEL

Street address 1: 333 W. Dominick Street
Street address city: Rome
Street address state: NY
Zip/Postal code: 13440-5701
County: Oneida
Country: USA
Mailing address: PO BOX 471
Mailing city: ROME
Mailing state: NY
Mailing zip: 13442-0471
General Phone: (315) 337-4000
Advertising Phone: (315) 337-4000
General/National Adv. E-mail: bwaters@rny.com
Display Adv. E-mail: bwaters@rny.com
Classified Adv. e-mail: classad@rny.com
Editorial e-mail: camred@rny.com
Primary Website: www.romesentinel.com
Year Established: 1821
News Services: AP, TMS.
Special Editions: Spring Fashion (Easter) (Apr); Back-to-School (Aug); Christmas Coupon (Dec); Know Your Retailer (Jan); Graduation (Jun); Bridal Planner (May); Senior Citizens Tab (Primetime) (Monthly); Santa's Tour (Nov); Fall Fashion (Oct); Recipe (Sept).
Special Weekly Sections: Best Food (Sun); Arts, Auto, Business, Finance, Entertainment, Family, Fashion, Health, Home, Living, Real Estate, Religion, Technology, Travel, Women (Daily)
Syndicated Publications: TV Guide (S).
Delivery Methods: Mail`Newsstand`Carrier`Racks
Areas Served - City/County or Portion Thereof, or Zip codes: 13440, 13316, 13309, 13471, 13363, 13478, 13308, 13354, 13424, 13303, 13490, 13486, 13489, 13162, 13438, 13323, 13476, 13502, 13442, 13421, 13492, 13304, 13461, 13401, 13338, 13042, 13054, 13469, 13157, 13368, 13403, 13501
Own Printing Facility?: Y
Commercial printers?: N
Avg Free Circ: 143
Sat. Circulation Paid: 7801
Sat. Circulation Free: 143
Audit By: AAM
Audit Date: 31.12.2017
Personnel: Stephen B. Waters (Pub.); Joseph Silkowski (Sports Ed.); Richard Miller (Community Ed.); Daniel P. Bronson (IT Mgr.); Linda Karsten (Production Mgr.); Bradley Waters (Adv. Dir.)
Parent company (for newspapers): Rome Sentinel Company; Seaton Publishing Company, Inc.

ADIRONDACK DAILY ENTERPRISE

Street address 1: 54 Broadway
Street address city: Saranac Lake
Street address state: NY
Zip/Postal code: 12983-1704
County: Franklin
Country: USA
Mailing address: PO BOX 318
Mailing city: SARANAC LAKE
Mailing state: NY
Mailing zip: 12983-0318
General Phone: (518) 891-2600
Advertising Phone: (518) 891-2600
Editorial Phone: (518) 891-2600
General/National Adv. E-mail: ads@adirondackdailyenterprise.com
Display Adv. E-mail: ads@adirondackdailyenterprise.com
Classified Adv. e-mail: classifieds@adirondackdailyenterprise.com
Editorial e-mail: adenews@adirondackdailyenterprise.com
Primary Website: www.adirondackdailyenterprise.com
Mthly Avg Views: 578778
Mthly Avg Unique Visitors: 95473
Year Established: 1894
News Services: AP.
Special Editions: Back-to-School (Aug); Seasons Greetings (Dec); Bridal (Feb); July 4th Blast (Jul); Adirondack Summer Guide (Jun); Human Services (Mar); Adirondack Living Real Estate Guide (Monthly); Christmas Gift Guide (Nov); North Country Dining Guide (Other); Bridal (
Special Weekly Sections: Weekender
Delivery Methods: Mail`Newsstand`Carrier`Racks
Areas Served - City/County or Portion Thereof, or Zip codes: Saranac Lake, Tupper Lake, Lake Placid, New York, Essex and Franklin County
Own Printing Facility?: Y
Commercial printers?: Y
Sat. Circulation Paid: 3600
Audit By: USPS
Audit Date: 01.10.2016
Personnel: Catherine Moore (Pub.); Peter Crowley (Mng. Ed.); Steve Bradley (Prodn. Mgr.); Rick Burman (Pressroom Foreman); Morgan Ryan (Sports Ed.); Alec Bieber (Circ. Mgr.); Brittany Proulx (City editor)
Parent company (for newspapers): Ogden Newspapers Inc.

THE SARATOGIAN

Street address 1: 20 Lake Ave
Street address city: Saratoga Springs
Street address state: NY
Zip/Postal code: 12866-2314
County: Saratoga
Country: USA
Mailing address: 20 LAKE AVE
Mailing city: SARATOGA SPRINGS
Mailing state: NY
Mailing zip: 12866-2314
General Phone: (518) 584-4242
Advertising Phone: (518) 584-4242
Editorial Phone: (518) 584-2101
General/National Adv. E-mail: bfignar@21st-centurymedia.com
Display Adv. E-mail: lkilbara@saratogian.com
Classified Adv. e-mail: classified@saratogian.com
Editorial e-mail: news@saratogian.com
Primary Website: www.saratogian.com
Mthly Avg Unique Visitors: 437065
News Services: AP, MCT.
Special Editions: Thoroughbred Racing-Daily (Aug); Business Review (Jan); Summer Magazines (Jul); Summer Magazines (Jun); New Car Preview (Oct).
Special Weekly Sections: Property Transaction, Health, Business (Mon); Society, Athletes of the Week, Horse Racing (Tue); Popular Columnist (Wed); Local Entertainment (Thur); High School Sports, Entertainment (Fri); Auto, Real Estate (Sat); Music, Education, Travel, Real Estate, Business (Sun)
Syndicated Publications: USA WEEKEND Magazine (S).
Avg Free Circ: 367
Sat. Circulation Paid: 2158
Sat. Circulation Free: 367
Sun. Circulation Paid: 2997
Sun. Circulation Free: 1519
Audit By: AAM
Audit Date: 30.12.2018
Personnel: Bob O'Leary (Pub.); Joe Anderson (Circulation District Mgr.); Timothy Tergeoglou (Reg. Adv. Dir.); Louise Kilbara (Asst. Digital First Sales Mgr); Jaclyn Grady (Multi Media Account Exec.); Jake Loeb (Regional Digital Dir); Jordyn Moulton (Multi-Media Account Exec.); Ashley Schaal (Classified Adv. Inside Sales/Customer Service); Charlie Kraebel (Managing Ed.); David Johnson (Sports Ed.); Tom Cleary (Controller)
Parent company (for newspapers): Digital First Media; MediaNews Group

THE DAILY GAZETTE

Street address 1: 2345 Maxon Rd Ext
Street address city: Schenectady
Street address state: NY
Zip/Postal code: 12308-1105
County: Schenectady
Country: USA
Mailing address: 2345 Maxon Road Extension
Mailing city: Schenectady
Mailing state: NY
Mailing zip: 12301
General Phone: (518) 374-4141
Advertising Phone: (518) 395-3020
Editorial Phone: (518) 395-3140
General/National Adv. E-mail: boleary@dailygazette.net
Display Adv. E-mail: boleary@dailygazette.net
Classified Adv. e-mail: classified@dailygazette.net
Editorial e-mail: news@dailygazette.net
Primary Website: www.dailygazette.com
Mthly Avg Unique Visitors: 313714
Year Established: 1894
News Services: AP, LAT-WP, CSM.
Special Editions: Football (Aug-Jan); Ski (Nov-Apr); Golf (Apr-Sept)
Special Weekly Sections: Best Food Day (Wed); Outdoors (Thur); Arts, Entertainment (Thur/Fri); Business, Travel, Lifestyle, Education, Regional (Sun);
Syndicated Publications: Relish (Monthly); USA WEEKEND Magazine (S).
Delivery Methods: Newsstand`Carrier`Racks
Areas Served - City/County or Portion Thereof, or Zip codes: 12008, 12009, 12010, 12019, 12020, 12025, 12027, 12032, 12035, 12043, 12047, 12053, 12056, 12065, 12066, 12068, 12070, 12072, 12074, 12078, 12084, 12086, 12092, 12095, 12110, 12117, 12118, 12122, 12134, 12137, 12148, 12149, 12150, 12151, 12157, 12158, 12159, 12160, 12166, 12170, 12177, 12180, 12186, 12187, 12188, 12203, 12205, 12208, 12301, 12302, 12303, 12304, 12305, 12306, 12307, 12308, 12309, 12803, 12822, 12831, 12833, 12835, 12850, 12859, 12863, 12866, 13317, 13339, 13428, 13452, 13459
Own Printing Facility?: Y
Sat. Circulation Paid: 48220
Sun. Circulation Paid: 54849
Audit By: AAM
Audit Date: 31.12.2017
Personnel: Dawn Behuniak (Adv. Major Acct. Mgr.); Elizabeth Hume Lind (Chrwmn of the Board); Bill Finelli (News Ed.); Mark Mahoney; Miles Reed (Mng. Ed.)
Parent company (for newspapers): Daily Gazette Co.; Hume Family

STATEN ISLAND ADVANCE

Street address 1: 950 Fingerboard Road
Street address city: Staten Island
Street address state: NY
Zip/Postal code: 10305-1495
County: Richmond
Country: USA
Mailing address: 950 W FINGERBOARD RD
Mailing city: STATEN ISLAND
Mailing state: NY
Mailing zip: 10305-1495
General Phone: (718) 981-1234
Advertising Phone: (718) 816-2804
Editorial Phone: (718) 981-1594
General/National Adv. E-mail: danryan@siadvance.com
Display Adv. E-mail: danryan@siadvance.com
Classified Adv. e-mail: valenti@siadvance.com
Editorial e-mail: tips@siadvance.com
Primary Website: www.silive.com
Mthly Avg Unique Visitors: 869000
Year Established: 1886
News Services: AP, TNS, LAT-WP.
Special Editions: Readers Choice - Jan Bride & Groom - Feb Cookbook Preview - March Home - April Cookbook - April Women of Achievement - April SI Guide - June Bride & Groom - Aug SI Foodie - Sept Harvest Guide - Weekly pub Sept - Nov Holiday Guide - Nov Top Doc's/ Health - Dec Building Awards - Dec
Special Weekly Sections: Health (Mon); Food (Wed); AWE Entertainment (Thurs); Home (Thurs); Real Estate (Fri); Arts & Ideas (Sun)
Delivery Methods: Newsstand`Carrier
Areas Served - City/County or Portion Thereof, or Zip codes: Staten Island
Own Printing Facility?: Y
Commercial printers?: Y
Sat. Circulation Paid: 18880
Sun. Circulation Paid: 32886
Audit By: AAM
Audit Date: 31.12.2017
Personnel: Caroline D Harrison (Pub.); Arthur Silverstein (Controller); Brian Laline (Ed.); John Giustiniani (Production Director); Robert Walters
Parent company (for newspapers): Advance Publications, Inc.

THE POST-STANDARD

Street address 1: 220 S Warren St
Street address city: Syracuse
Street address state: NY
Zip/Postal code: 13202-1676
County: Onondaga
Country: USA
Mailing address: 220 S WARREN ST
Mailing city: SYRACUSE
Mailing state: NY
Mailing zip: 13202-1676
General Phone: (315) 470-0011
Advertising Phone: (315) 470-0032
Editorial Phone: (315) 470-0011
General/National Adv. E-mail: kbrill@advancemediany.com
Display Adv. E-mail: kbrill@advancemediany.com
Classified Adv. e-mail: gcarroll@advancemediany.com
Editorial e-mail: letters@syracuse.com
Primary Website: www.syracuse.com
Mthly Avg Views: 49400000
Mthly Avg Unique Visitors: 4700000
Year Established: 1829
News Services: NNS, NYT, LAT-WP, AP, MCT, CSM.
Special Editions: Spotlight on Auto (Feb); Home & Garden (Mar) Holiday Shopper (Dec);Parade of Homes (Jun); NCAA Hoops (Mar); Holiday Guide (Nov)
Special Weekly Sections: Neighbors, Weekend Entertainment (Thur); Travel, Entertainment, Real Estate, Employment, Auto, Comics (Sun)
Syndicated Publications: Parade (Sun)
Delivery Methods: Newsstand`Carrier
Areas Served - City/County or Portion Thereof, or Zip codes: Central New York
Own Printing Facility?: Y
Commercial printers?: Y
Sat. Circulation Paid: 31037
Sun. Circulation Paid: 108197
Audit By: AAM
Audit Date: 30.06.2017
Personnel: Tim Kennedy (President); Kellie Caimano (Executive Assistant); Stephen Rogers (Chairman); Bill Allison (VP, Sales); Michele Sardinia (VP Digital Solutions); Ken Brill (Sales Director); Annette Peters (VP Marketing)
Parent company (for newspapers): Advance Publications, Inc.

THE RECORD

Street address 1: 270 River Triangle Suite 202B
Street address city: Troy
Street address state: NY
Zip/Postal code: 12180
County: Rensselaer
Country: USA
Mailing address: 270 River Triangle Suite 202B
Mailing city: TROY
Mailing state: NY
Mailing zip: 12180
General Phone: (518) 270-1200
Advertising Phone: (518) 272-2255
Editorial Phone: (518) 270-1276
General/National Adv. E-mail: retailmgr@troyrecord.com
Display Adv. E-mail: retailmgr@troyrecord.com
Classified Adv. e-mail: class@troyrecord.com
Editorial e-mail: newsroom@troyrecord.com
Primary Website: www.troyrecord.com
Mthly Avg Views: 1677636

Mthly Avg Unique Visitors: 360846
Year Established: 1896
News Services: AP, MCT.
Special Editions: Spring Car Care (Apr); Truck Tab (Aug); Last Minute Gift Ideas (Dec); Baby Album (Feb); New Car Preview (Jan); Saratoga Life (Jul); Father's Day (Jun); Medical Physicians Guide (Mar); Mature Living (May); Christmas Gift Guide (Nov); Apple Fest (Oct); Heal
Special Weekly Sections: Health, Computers, Science (Mon); Money (Tue); Food, Stocks (Wed); Entertainment, Stocks (Thur); Education (Fri); Religion (Sat); TV (Sun); Real Estate (Monthly)
Syndicated Publications: Home Front (Monthly); Health Notes (Quarterly); TV & Cable quarter-fold magazine (S); Steppin' Out (Thur).
Areas Served - City/County or Portion Thereof, or Zip codes: Rensselaer, Albany & Saratoga Counties (NY)
Avg Free Circ: 279
Sat. Circulation Paid: 4120
Sat. Circulation Free: 279
Sun. Circulation Paid: 4565
Sun. Circulation Free: 344
Audit By: AAM
Audit Date: 30.06.2015
Personnel: Charlie Krabel (Ed.); Mike McMahon (Chief Photographer); Charlie Krabel (Managing Ed.); Timothy Tergeoglou (Reg. Adv. Dir.)
Parent company (for newspapers): Digital First Media

THE OBSERVER-DISPATCH

Street address 1: 221 Oriskany St E
Street address city: Utica
Street address state: NY
Zip/Postal code: 13501-1201
County: Oneida
Country: USA
Mailing address: 221 ORISKANY ST E
Mailing city: UTICA
Mailing state: NY
Mailing zip: 13501-1274
General Phone: (315) 792-5000
Advertising Phone: (315) 792-5107
Editorial Phone: (315) 792-5005
General/National Adv. E-mail: srosenburgh@uticaod.com
Display Adv. E-mail: srosenburgh@uticaod.com
Classified Adv. e-mail: pzehr@uticaod.com
Editorial e-mail: news@uticaod.com
Primary Website: www.uticaod.com
Mthly Avg Views: 2640000
Mthly Avg Unique Visitors: 382023
Year Established: 1817
News Services: AP, Tribune, GateHouse, Washington Post
Special Editions: Gift Guide (Dec); Business Review (Feb); Bridal (Jan); Teen All-Stars (May); Boilermaker Sections (Jul); Football Preview (Sept.); Comets Preview (Oct.) Coupons (Monthly); Thanksgiving Day (Nov); Basketball Preview (Dec.)
Special Weekly Sections: Scene Entertainment (Thursdays); TV Guide (Sundays)
Delivery Methods: Mail`Newsstand`Carrier`Racks
Areas Served - City/County or Portion Thereof, or Zip codes: Oneida County, Herkimer County, Madison County
Own Printing Facility?: N
Commercial printers?: Y
Avg Free Circ: 1294
Sat. Circulation Paid: 18083
Sat. Circulation Free: 1294
Sun. Circulation Paid: 23956
Sun. Circulation Free: 1059
Audit By: AAM
Audit Date: 30.09.2018
Personnel: Theresa Swider (Controller); Dave Dudajek (Opinion Page Ed.); Fran Perritano (Sports Ed.); Terry Cascioli (Pub.); Ron Johns (Managing Ed.); Robert Gall (Circ. Dir.); Scott Rosenburgh
Parent company (for newspapers): CherryRoad Media; Gannett Company Inc.

WATERTOWN DAILY TIMES

Street address 1: 260 Washington St
Street address city: Watertown
Street address state: NY
Zip/Postal code: 13601-4669
County: Jefferson
Country: USA
General Phone: (315) 782-1000
Advertising Phone: (315) 661-2422
Editorial Phone: (315) 661-2359
General/National Adv. E-mail: relias@wdt
Display Adv. E-mail: mbowers@wdt.net
Classified Adv. e-mail: gvalik@wdt.net
Editorial e-mail: news@wdt.net
Primary Website: www.watertowndailytimes.com
Mthly Avg Views: 1750000
Mthly Avg Unique Visitors: 350000
Year Established: 1861
News Services: NYT, LAT-WP, MCT, Bloomberg, WAPO
Special Weekly Sections: Best Food Day (Tues).
Syndicated Publications: Relish (Monthly); Parade (S); Farm & Garden Tab (newsprint) (Sat); American Profile (Weekly).
Delivery Methods: Mail`Newsstand`Carrier`Racks
Areas Served - City/County or Portion Thereof, or Zip codes: Three County Region
Own Printing Facility?: Y
Commercial printers?: Y
Sat. Circulation Paid: 14197
Sun. Circulation Paid: 17652
Audit By: AAM
Audit Date: 31.12.2017
Personnel: John Johnson (CEO & Co-Pub.); Cathie Egan (Asst. Feat. Ed.); Ray Weston (VP Finance); Gregory Gay (Sports Ed.); Mary Kaskan (Sunday Ed.); Jill VanHoesen (CIO); Dale Cronk (Prod. Mgr.); Gerald Moore (Editorial Page Ed.); Harold Johnson (Pres. & Co-publisher); Tim Farkas (VP News Ops.); Perry White (Managing Ed.)
Parent company (for newspapers): Johnson Newspaper Corp.

WELLSVILLE DAILY REPORTER

Street address 1: 159 N Main St
Street address city: Wellsville
Street address state: NY
Zip/Postal code: 14895-1149
County: Allegany
Country: USA
Mailing address: 159 N MAIN ST
Mailing city: WELLSVILLE
Mailing state: NY
Mailing zip: 14895-1158
General Phone: (585) 593-5300
Advertising Phone: (585) 593-5300
Editorial Phone: (585) 593-5300
General/National Adv. E-mail: wellsvillereader@aol.com
Display Adv. E-mail: wellsvillereader@aol.com
Classified Adv. e-mail: wellsvillereader@aol.com
Editorial e-mail: editor@wellsvilledaily.com
Primary Website: www.wellsvilledaily.com
Year Established: 1880
News Services: AP.
Special Editions: Medical-Health Guide (Aug); Bride's Guide (Jan); Balloon Rally Guide (Jul); Graduation (Jun); Spring Outdoor (Mar); Christmas (Nov); Annual Fall Outdoor Guide (Sept).
Sun. Circulation Paid: 10390
Audit By: Sworn/Estimate/Non-Audited
Audit Date: 12.07.2019
Personnel: Oak Duke (Adv. Dir.); Robert Polley (Circ. Mgr.); John Anderson (Regional Ed.); Melissa VanSkiver (Adv. Dir.)
Parent company (for newspapers): Gannett; CherryRoad Media

THE JOURNAL NEWS

Street address 1: 1133 Westchester Ave
Street address 2: Ste N-110
Street address city: White Plains
Street address state: NY
Zip/Postal code: 10604-3511
County: Westchester
Country: USA
Mailing address: 1133 WESTCHESTER AVE STE N-100
Mailing city: WHITE PLAINS
Mailing state: NY
Mailing zip: 10604-3543
General Phone: (914) 694-9300
Advertising Phone: (914) 694-5158
Editorial Phone: (914) 694-5077
General/National Adv. E-mail: ezaccagn@lohud.com
Display Adv. E-mail: sbaker@lohud.com
Editorial e-mail: letters@lohud.com
Primary Website: www.lohud.com
Mthly Avg Views: 10311784
Mthly Avg Unique Visitors: 1448635
Year Established: 1829
News Services: AP, GNS, LAT-WP.
Special Editions: Suburban Golf (Apr); Back-to-School (Aug); Holiday Food (Dec); Spring Bridal (Feb); Suburban Golf (Jul); Summer Dine Out Guide (Jun); Spring Home Design (Mar); Suburban Golf (May); Holiday Gift Guide (Nov); Fall Home Design (Oct); In the City (Quarterly);
Special Weekly Sections: Wheels (Fri); Tech E (Mon); Real Estate (S); The Line (Thur).
Syndicated Publications: USA WEEKEND Magazine (S).
Areas Served - City/County or Portion Thereof, or Zip codes: Lower Hudson Valley
Sat. Circulation Paid: 38755
Sun. Circulation Paid: 43263
Audit By: AAM
Audit Date: 31.12.2018
Personnel: Mike Fisch (Pres./Pub.); Anthony Simmons (Vice Pres., Circ.); Mauro Ferrotta (Circ. Mgr., Single Copy); Henry Freeman (Vice Pres./Exec. News Ed.); Cynthia Royle Lambert (Sr. Mng. Ed.); Robert Rodriguez (Design Dir.); Herb Pinder (Editorial Page Ed.); Mary Dolan (Lifestyles Ed.); Hai Do (Photo Ed.); Mark Faller (Sports Ed., Days); Mary Susan Arth (Asst. Sports Ed.); Kathy McClusky (Travel Ed.); Nat Hogan (Prodn. Dir.); Ed Forbes (Digital Team Leader); Liz Johnson
Parent company (for newspapers): Gannett

NORTH CAROLINA

THE COURIER-TRIBUNE

Street address 1: 500 Sunset Avenue
Street address city: Asheboro
Street address state: NC
Zip/Postal code: 27204
County: Randolph
Country: USA
Mailing address: PO BOX 340
Mailing city: ASHEBORO
Mailing state: NC
Mailing zip: 27204-0340
General Phone: (336) 625-2101
Advertising Phone: (336) 626-6114
Editorial Phone: (336) 626-6140
General/National Adv. E-mail: ads@courier-tribune.com
Display Adv. E-mail: ads@courier-tribune.com
Classified Adv. e-mail: classifieds@courier-tribune.com
Editorial e-mail: news@courier-tribune.com
Primary Website: www.courier-tribune.com
Mthly Avg Views: 425000
Year Established: 1876
News Services: AP, MCT, SHNS.
Special Editions: Back-to-School (Aug); Progress (Jan); Lawn & Garden (Mar); Graduation (May); Textile (Oct).
Special Weekly Sections: Church (Fri); Children's Page (S); Business (Wed).
Syndicated Publications: USA WEEKEND Magazine (S); Food (Wed).
Areas Served - City/County or Portion Thereof, or Zip codes: Asheboro & Randolph counties
Avg Free Circ: 302
Sat. Circulation Paid: 6653
Sat. Circulation Free: 302
Sun. Circulation Paid: 7891
Sun. Circulation Free: 516
Audit By: CAC
Audit Date: 31.03.2018
Personnel: Gary Lockhart (Circ. Dir.); Annette Jordan (Ed.); Dennis Garcia (Sports Ed.); Hazel Saunders (Prodn. Mgr.); Ben Kane (Prodn. Mgr., Pressroom); Leslie Green (Digital Ed./News Ed.)
Parent company (for newspapers): CherryRoad Media; Gannett Company Inc.

THE ASHEVILLE CITIZEN-TIMES

Street address 1: 14 Ohenry Ave
Street address city: Asheville
Street address state: NC
Zip/Postal code: 28801-2604
County: Buncombe
Country: USA
Mailing address: PO BOX 2090
Mailing city: ASHEVILLE
Mailing state: NC
Mailing zip: 28802-0716
General Phone: (828) 252-5610
Advertising Phone: (828) 232-5989
Editorial Phone: (828) 252-5611
General/National Adv. E-mail: scoghlin@citizen-times.com
Display Adv. E-mail: ehdugas@citizen-times.com
Classified Adv. e-mail: tcalloway1@citizen-times.com
Editorial e-mail: cterrell@citizen-times.com
Primary Website: www.citizen-times.com
Mthly Avg Views: 3500000
Mthly Avg Unique Visitors: 575000
Year Established: 1870
News Services: AP, GNS, NNS.
Special Editions: Mountain Travel Guide (Apr); Football (Aug); Agenda (Feb); Best of (Jun); Campus Connection (Oct); West Asheville (Quarterly); Mountain Travel Guide (Sept).
Special Weekly Sections: Take Five (Fri); Health & Fitness (Mon); Travel (S); Family (Thur); Computers & Technology (Tues); Food (Wed).
Syndicated Publications: USA WEEKEND Magazine (S).
Delivery Methods: Carrier`Racks
Own Printing Facility?: N
Commercial printers?: N
Sat. Circulation Paid: 21900
Sun. Circulation Paid: 29532
Audit By: AAM
Audit Date: 31.12.2018
Personnel: Casey Swaney (Digital Producer); Katie Wadington (News Dir.); Bruce Steele (Planning Ed.); Brian Ponder (Writing Coach); Joe Castle (Digital Prod.); Vicki Harrison (Operations Mgr.); Todd Runkle (Strategist/Analyst); Paul Clark (Ed.); Vivian Murciano (Dir. Adv.); Tom Claybaugh (Pres.)
Parent company (for newspapers): Gannett

HIGH COUNTRY PRESS

Street address 1: 1600 Highway 105
Street address city: Boone
Street address state: NC
Zip/Postal code: 28607-8731
County: Watauga
Country: USA
Mailing address: PO BOX 152
Mailing city: BOONE
Mailing state: NC
Mailing zip: 28607-0152
General Phone: (828) 264-2262
Advertising Phone: (828) 264-2262
Editorial Phone: (828) 264-2262
General/National Adv. E-mail: ads@highcountrypress.com
Display Adv. E-mail: ads@highcountrypress.com
Classified Adv. e-mail: ads@highcountrypress.com
Editorial e-mail: ken@highcountrypress.com
Primary Website: www.hcpress.com
Year Established: 2005
Delivery Methods: Mail`Newsstand
Audit By: Sworn/Estimate/Non-Audited
Audit Date: 12.07.2019
Personnel: Debbie Carter (Ad. Director); Ken Ketchie (Pub./Ed.); Jesse Wood (News. Ed.); Amanda Giles (Office Mgr.)

TIMES-NEWS

Street address 1: 707 S. Main Street
Street address city: Burlington
Street address state: NC
Zip/Postal code: 27215
County: Alamance
Country: USA
Mailing address: PO BOX 481
Mailing city: BURLINGTON
Mailing state: NC
Mailing zip: 27216-0481
General Phone: (336) 227-0131
Advertising Phone: (336) 227-0131
Editorial Phone: (336) 506-3040
General/National Adv. E-mail: sbowman@thetimesnews.com
Display Adv. E-mail: Burl-ADV@thetimesnews.com
Classified Adv. e-mail: dshue@thetimesnews.com
Editorial e-mail: mtaylor@thetimesnews.com
Primary Website: www.thetimesnews.com
Mthly Avg Views: 3300000
Mthly Avg Unique Visitors: 250000
Year Established: 1887
News Services: AP, McClatchy Tribune
Special Editions: Lawn & Garden/Home Improvement (Apr & Sept); Prep Ball Preview (Aug); Gift Guide (Dec); Racing Tab (Feb); Awards of Excellence(Apr))Holiday Lifestyles (Nov); Medical Reference Guide (June); Builders Parade(Oct); Living Here (Aug)Bridal Expo (Feb) Taste of Home (Oct) Alamance Health (quarterly)

Business card directory (Jan) Super Bowl (Feb)Behind the Scenes (March)How-To Guide (May) Breast Cancer Awareness (Oct) Design an Ad (Nov) Back to School (July) Monster Job Fair (Apr)
Special Weekly Sections: Scene (Entertainment) (Thurs); Teens & Twenties (Mon); Homes Front (Sat); Mini Page (Fri). TV Guide (Sat) Food (Wed.) Accent (Sun.)
Syndicated Publications: Parade Magazine (S); American Profile (Tues). Athlon Sports, Relish (Food)
Delivery Methods: Mail`Newsstand`Carrier`Racks
Areas Served - City/County or Portion Thereof, or Zip codes: 27215, 27217, 27244, 27249, 27253, 27258, 27302
Own Printing Facility?: Y
Commercial printers?: Y
Avg Free Circ: 436
Sat. Circulation Paid: 8785
Sat. Circulation Free: 436
Sun. Circulation Paid: 9953
Sun. Circulation Free: 258
Audit By: Sworn/Estimate/Non-Audited
Audit Date: 12.07.2019
Personnel: Serena Bowman (Sales Mgr.); Michele Terry (Mgr., Mktg./Promo.); Charity Apple (Features Ed.); Tom Jones (City Ed.); Bob Sutton (Sports Ed.); Joyce Thompson (HR Dir.); Sherwood Bland (Production Director); Sam Roberts (Chief Photog.); Paul Mauney (Publisher); Regina Howard-Glaspie (Audience Development Director); Michael Russo (Digital Director)
Parent company (for newspapers): CherryRoad Media; Lee Enterprises, Incorporated

THE CHARLOTTE OBSERVER

Street address 1: 550 S Caldwell St Ste 760
Street address 2: 10th Floor
Street address city: Charlotte
Street address state: NC
Zip/Postal code: 28202-2636
County: Mecklenburg
Country: USA
Mailing address: 550 S CALDWELL ST STE 760
Mailing city: CHARLOTTE
Mailing state: NC
Mailing zip: 28202-2636
General Phone: (704) 358-5000
Advertising Phone: (704) 358-5400
Editorial Phone: (704) 358-5040
General/National Adv. E-mail: drgordon@charlotteobserver.com
Display Adv. E-mail: pweber@charlotteobserver.com
Classified Adv. e-mail: chadmartin@charlotteobserver.com
Editorial e-mail: opinion@charlotteobserver.com
Primary Website: www.charlotteobserver.com
Mthly Avg Views: 45008400
Mthly Avg Unique Visitors: 6335602
Year Established: 1886
News Services: AP, Washington Post, Bloomberg News, NYT, Getty
Special Editions: Road Trips (Spring&Fall); Living Here Lake Norman (May); Living Here (Sept); Panthers/NFL Preview (Sept); Arts Preview (Sept)
Special Weekly Sections: CLT (Fri); Carolina Living (Arts, Style, Travel) (S); Your Weekend (Faith, Garden Home)(Sat); Food&Drink (Wed), Wheels(Fri); Home|Design(Sat)
Syndicated Publications: Parade (S), Dash
Delivery Methods: Mail`Newsstand`Carrier`Racks
Areas Served - City/County or Portion Thereof, or Zip codes: North and South Carolina's
Own Printing Facility?: Y
Commercial printers?: Y
Sat. Circulation Paid: 76838
Sun. Circulation Paid: 104355
Audit By: AAM
Audit Date: 31.12.2018
Personnel: Rodney Mahone (Pub.); Bernie Heller (VP, Advertising/Chief Revenue Officer); Adam Bell (Local News Ed.); Taylor Batten (Ed. of Editorial Pages); Peter St. Onge (Associate Ed.); Kevin Siers (Editorial Cartoonist); Ronnie Glassberg (Metro Ed.); Doug Miller (North Carolina High-Impact Ed.); Katy Petiford (Day News Ed.); Matt Walsh (Visuals Ed.)
Parent company (for newspapers): The McClatchy Company; Chatham Asset Management

THE SAMPSON INDEPENDENT

Street address 1: 109 W Main St
Street address city: Clinton
Street address state: NC
Zip/Postal code: 28328-4046
County: Sampson
Country: USA
Mailing address: 109 W MAIN ST
Mailing city: CLINTON
Mailing state: NC
Mailing zip: 28328-4046
General Phone: (910) 592-8137
Advertising Phone: (910) 592-8137
Editorial Phone: (910) 592-8137
General/National Adv. E-mail: smatthews@heartlandpublications.com
Display Adv. E-mail: gpate@heartlandpublications.com
Classified Adv. e-mail: gpate@heartlandpublications.com
Editorial e-mail: smatthews@heartlandpublications.com
Primary Website: www.clintonnc.com
Year Established: 1924
News Services: AP.
Special Editions: Spring Fashion (Apr); Back-to-School (Aug); Xmas Gift Guide (Dec); Insight (Feb); Tobacco (Jul); Bridal (May); Cookbook (Nov); Fall Car Care (Oct); Fall Fashion (Sept).
Syndicated Publications: Parade (S).
Areas Served - City/County or Portion Thereof, or Zip codes: Sampson County (NC)
Sat. Circulation Paid: 7962
Sun. Circulation Paid: 8100
Audit By: Sworn/Estimate/Non-Audited
Audit Date: 12.07.2019
Personnel: Sherry Matthews (Publisher/Editor); Brenda McCullen (Adv. Dir., Classified); Aothey Sampson (Adv. Dir., Retail); Alissa Bradford (Circ. Dir.); Doug Clark (Asst. Ed.); Shannon Best (Media Dir.)
Parent company (for newspapers): Champion Media

THE DAILY RECORD

Street address 1: 99 W Broad St
Street address city: Dunn
Street address state: NC
Zip/Postal code: 28334-6031
County: Harnett
Country: USA
Mailing address: PO BOX 1448
Mailing city: DUNN
Mailing state: NC
Mailing zip: 28335-1448
General Phone: (910) 891-1234
General/National Adv. E-mail: traffic.io@mydailyrecord.com
Display Adv. E-mail: retailads@mydailyrecord.com
Classified Adv. e-mail: classifieds@mydailyrecord.com
Editorial e-mail: news@mydailyrecord.com
Primary Website: www.mydailyrecord.com
Mthly Avg Views: 400000
Mthly Avg Unique Visitors: 18000
Year Established: 1950
Special Editions: Community Yearbook(Feb); Advertiser Appreciation (Aug); Christmas Greetings (Dec); Best of Harnett County (Jul);; Physicians Directory (Oct); Veteran's Salute (Nov);
Special Weekly Sections: Weekend (Fri); Best Food Day (Tues).
Delivery Methods: Mail`Racks
Areas Served - City/County or Portion Thereof, or Zip codes: 28334, 28339, 28342, 27524, 27526, 28344, 27543, 27546, 28356, 27552, 28366, 28368, 28382, 28390, 28395
Own Printing Facility?: Y
Commercial printers?: Y
Avg Free Circ: 300
Audit By: USPS
Audit Date: 23.09.2022
Personnel: Maria House (Publisher); Bart Adams (Owner); Emily Weaver (Managing editor); Emily Weaver (Managing Editor); Mellicent Adams (VP/Sec./Treas.); Maria House (Publisher, Marketing Director); Lisa Farmer (Online Ed.); Laura Patterson (Assistant managing editor); Wendy Gregory (Prodn. Mgr., Post Press)
Parent company (for newspapers): Record Publishing; Record Publishing Company; Record Publishing Co.; Record Publishing

THE HERALD-SUN

Street address 1: 1530 N Gregson St
Street address 2: Ste 2A
Street address city: Durham
Street address state: NC
Zip/Postal code: 27701-1164
County: Durham
Country: USA
Mailing address: 1530 N Gregson St, Ste 2A
Mailing city: Durham
Mailing state: NC
Mailing zip: 27701-1164
General Phone: (919) 419-6500
Advertising Phone: (919) 419-6700
Editorial Phone: (919) 419-6684
Display Adv. E-mail: drogers@newsobserver.com
Classified Adv. e-mail: classifieds@heraldsun.com
Editorial e-mail: news@heraldsun.com
Primary Website: www.heraldsun.com
Mthly Avg Views: 860690
Mthly Avg Unique Visitors: 337685
Year Established: 1889
News Services: AP
Special Editions: Reader's Choice, Senior Times, ACC Basketball Preview,ACC Basketball tournament review, ACC Football Preview, Everything Durham, Everything Orange
Syndicated Publications: WE ARE DURHAM Magazine (Other); USA WEEKEND Magazine (S).
Delivery Methods: Mail`Newsstand`Carrier`Racks
Own Printing Facility?: N
Commercial printers?: N
Avg Free Circ: 1479
Sat. Circulation Paid: 6679
Sat. Circulation Free: 1479
Sun. Circulation Paid: 8195
Sun. Circulation Free: 146
Audit By: Sworn/Estimate/Non-Audited
Audit Date: 12.07.2019
Personnel: Robyn Tomlin (Exec. Ed./Regional Ed.); Jane Elizabeth (Mng. Ed.); Thad Ogburn (Metro Ed.); Sarah Nagem (Breaking News / Public Safety Ed.); Jordan Schrader (State Politics Ed.); Mary Cornatzer (Business / Growth Ed.); Jessica Banov (Features Ed.); Steve Ruinsky (Sports Ed.); Scott Sharpe (Multimedia Ed.)
Parent company (for newspapers): The McClatchy Company; Chatham Asset Management

THE DAILY ADVANCE

Street address 1: 215 S Water St
Street address city: Elizabeth City
Street address state: NC
Zip/Postal code: 27909-4844
County: Pasquotank
Country: USA
Mailing address: PO BOX 588
Mailing city: ELIZABETH CITY
Mailing state: NC
Mailing zip: 27907-0588
General Phone: (252) 335-8076
Advertising Phone: (252) 335-8082
Editorial Phone: (252) 335-8110
General/National Adv. E-mail: sobrien@dailyadvance.com
Display Adv. E-mail: sobrien@dailyadvance.com
Classified Adv. e-mail: sharris@dailyadvance.com
Editorial e-mail: elizabethcity@dailyadvance.com
Primary Website: www.dailyadvance.com
Year Established: 1911
News Services: AP.
Special Editions: Medical Directory (Jan.), Albemarle Magazine (quarterly), Coast Guard Anniversary Tab (July), Senior Living (April.), Holiday Recipe/Songbook (Dec.)
Special Weekly Sections: Albemarle Life (Wed.-Sun.), Shelter pets (Mon.), School Page (Tues); Business Page (Sun.).
Syndicated Publications: Parade (S).
Delivery Methods: Mail`Newsstand`Carrier`Racks
Own Printing Facility?: Y
Commercial printers?: Y
Avg Free Circ: 689
Sat. Circulation Paid: 7840
Sat. Circulation Free: 689
Sun. Circulation Paid: 8182
Sun. Circulation Free: 86
Audit By: AAM
Audit Date: 30.09.2014
Personnel: Chuck Edwards (Circ. Mgr.); Robert Kelly-Goss (Albemarle Life Ed.); Mike Goodman (Editor/Editorial Page Editor); Julian Eure (News Ed.); Chris Day (Asst. News Ed.); Brian Gray (Creative Services Manager); Susan Harris (Customer Service/Classified Mgr.); Maureen Brinson (Financial/Accounting Manager); Lynne Watkins (IS Manager); Sean O'Brien (Director of Advertising Sales and Marketing)
Parent company (for newspapers): Adams Publishing Group, LLC

THE FAYETTEVILLE OBSERVER

Street address 1: 458 Whitfield St
Street address city: Fayetteville
Street address state: NC
Zip/Postal code: 28306-1614
County: Cumberland
Country: USA
Mailing address: PO BOX 849
Mailing city: FAYETTEVILLE
Mailing state: NC
Mailing zip: 28302-0849
General Phone: (910) 323-4848
Advertising Phone: (910) 486-2786
Editorial Phone: (910) 486-3500
General/National Adv. E-mail: advertise@fayobserver.com
Display Adv. E-mail: advertise@fayobserver.com
Classified Adv. e-mail: peikerb@fayobserver.com
Editorial e-mail: eletters@fayobserver.com
Primary Website: www.fayobserver.com
Mthly Avg Views: 5861074
Mthly Avg Unique Visitors: 515671
Year Established: 1816
News Services: AP, LAT-WP.
Special Editions: Wildcats (Apr); Discover Fayetteville (Aug); Holiday Gift Guide (Dec); Honor Roll (Feb); Cumberland Parent (Jan); Back-to-School (Jul); Storm Watch (Jun); Military Appreciation (May); Cumberland Parent (Nov); Motor Sports (Oct); Reader's Choice (Sept).
Special Weekly Sections: Faith (Fri); Health (Mon); Business (S); Real Estate Marketplace (Sat); Business (Thur); Business (Tues); Business (Wed).
Syndicated Publications: Relish (Monthly); Parade (S); TV Week (Sat).
Avg Free Circ: 1531
Sat. Circulation Paid: 20303
Sat. Circulation Free: 901
Sun. Circulation Paid: 24491
Sun. Circulation Free: 888
Audit By: AAM
Audit Date: 31.12.2018
Personnel: Robert Gruber (Publisher); Mike Adams (Exec. Ed.); Matt Leclercq (Exec. Ed.); Lynnie Guzman (Adv. Dir.); Jill Koonce (Credit Mgr.); Timothy White (Editorial Page Ed.); Rodger Mullen (Columnist); Alissa Melvin (Circ. Dir.)
Parent company (for newspapers): Gannett; CherryRoad Media

THE GASTON GAZETTE

Street address 1: 1893 Remount Rd
Street address city: Gastonia
Street address state: NC
Zip/Postal code: 28054-7413
County: Gaston
Country: USA
Mailing address: PO BOX 1538
Mailing city: GASTONIA
Mailing state: NC
Mailing zip: 28053-1538
General Phone: (704) 869-1700
Advertising Phone: (704) 869-1735
Editorial Phone: (704) 869-1812
General/National Adv. E-mail: scherry@gastongazette.com
Display Adv. E-mail: nsaunders@gastongazette.com
Editorial e-mail: gastongazette@gastongazette.com
Primary Website: www.gastongazette.com
Mthly Avg Views: 3000000
Mthly Avg Unique Visitors: 600000
Year Established: 1880
News Services: AP, SHNS, NYT, NEA.
Special Editions: Stress (Apr); Senior Living (Aug); Church Directory (Dec); Senior Living (Feb); Bridal Tab (Jan); Christmas in July (Jul); Legal Guide (Jun); Home & Garden (Mar); Senior Living (May); Senior Living (Nov); New Car Show (Oct); Travel (Sept).
Special Weekly Sections: Business Spotlight (Tues).
Syndicated Publications: Home Magazine (Fri); Gaston Seasons (Quarterly); USA WEEKEND Magazine (S); Lake Novman Gazette (Weekly).
Delivery Methods: Mail`Newsstand`Carrier`Racks
Own Printing Facility?: Y
Commercial printers?: Y
Sat. Circulation Paid: 13238
Sun. Circulation Paid: 15664
Audit By: AAM

Audit Date: 31.12.2017
Personnel: Lucy Talley (Pub.); Konrad LaPrade (Adv. Dir.); Will MacDonald (Health/Medical Ed.); Keith Raffone (Gen. Mgr./Finance Dir.); Natasha Alexander (Ad manager); Nancy Hogshead (Classified manager); Stephany Cherry (Major accounts); Kevin Ellis (Managing Editor)
Parent company (for newspapers): Gannett; CherryRoad Media

GOLDSBORO NEWS-ARGUS

Street address 1: 310 N Berkeley Blvd
Street address city: Goldsboro
Street address state: NC
Zip/Postal code: 27534-4326
County: Wayne
Country: USA
Mailing address: PO BOX 10629
Mailing city: GOLDSBORO
Mailing state: NC
Mailing zip: 27532-0629
General Phone: (919) 778-2211
Advertising Phone: (919) 778-2000
Editorial Phone: (919) 739-7791
General/National Adv. E-mail: retailads@newsargus.com
Display Adv. E-mail: displayads@newsargus.com
Classified Adv. e-mail: classads@newsargus.com
Editorial e-mail: news@newsargus.com
Primary Website: www.newsargus.com
Mthly Avg Views: 906600
Mthly Avg Unique Visitors: 70100
Year Established: 1885
News Services: AP.
Special Editions: Wedding Guide (Jan); Progress (Feb); Batter Up & Home & Garden (Mar); Pickle Festival (Apr); Destination Summer (May); Business Card Directory & Healthy Living (Jun); Back to School and Football (Aug); Readers Choice (Sept); Health Care Directory (Oct); Holiday Planner (Nov); Last Minute Gift Guide & Spirit of the Season (Dec).
Special Weekly Sections: Food (Wed); Farm (Wed); Health (Thur); Church (Fri); Travel (Sun); Military (Sun); Features (Sun); Real Estate (Sun); Auto Review (Sun); Business (Daily); Entertainment (Daily).
Syndicated Publications: Parade (S).
Delivery Methods: Mail`Newsstand`Carrier`Racks
Areas Served - City/County or Portion Thereof, or Zip codes: Wayne, Johnston, Lenoir, Greene, Duplin & Sampson counties
Own Printing Facility?: Y
Commercial printers?: Y
Avg Free Circ: 441
Sun. Circulation Paid: 14054
Sun. Circulation Free: 121
Audit By: AAM
Audit Date: 31.12.2016
Personnel: Hal H. Tanner (Publisher); Debbie M. Pennell (Mgr., HR); Georgia Gurley (Adv. Mgr., Nat'l); Dennis Hill (Mng. Ed.); Matt Whittle (Amusements Ed./Books Ed.); Renee Carey (Editor); Phyllis Moore (Educ./Health Ed.); Keith Taylor (Online Ed.); Becky Barclay (Society/Women's Ed.); Rudy Coggins (Sports Ed.); David Rouse (Mgmt. Info Servs. Mgr.); Rochelle Moore (Reporter)
Parent company (for newspapers): Paxton Media Group

NEWS & RECORD

Street address 1: 3001 S. Elm-Eugene Street
Street address city: Greensboro
Street address state: NC
Zip/Postal code: 27406
County: Guilford
Country: USA
Mailing city: GREENSBORO
Mailing state: NC
General Phone: (336) 373-7000
Advertising Phone: (336) 373-7150
Editorial Phone: (336) 373-7064
General/National Adv. E-mail: people@greensboro.com
Display Adv. E-mail: kmurphy@wsjournal.com
Classified Adv. e-mail: kmurphy@wsjournal.com
Editorial e-mail: edpage@greenboro.com
Primary Website: www.greensboro.com
Mthly Avg Views: 4100000
Mthly Avg Unique Visitors: 403710
Year Established: 1890
News Services: AP, Tribune
Special Editions: Discover the Triad (spring); Veterans (Nov); 7 Over Seventy (Aug); Inspire Women's Awards (June)
Special Weekly Sections: Food (Wed), A&E (Thu).
Delivery Methods: Newsstand`Carrier`Racks
Areas Served - City/County or Portion Thereof, or Zip codes: Guilford, Rockingham & Randolph counties (NC)
Own Printing Facility?: Y
Commercial printers?: Y
Sat. Circulation Paid: 33081
Sun. Circulation Paid: 43872
Audit By: AAM
Audit Date: 30.09.2022
Personnel: Alton Brown (Pub.); Jennifer Fernandez (Managing editor); Cindy Loman (Mng. Ed.); Katie Murphy (Advertising director); Carrie Benoit (Regional Human Resources Manager); Terry Mink (Sales Mgr.); Dimon Kendrick-Holmes (Executive editor (as of Oct. 2022)); Bob Scott (Circ. Dir.); Cindy Loman (Special sections editor); Melanie Armino (Classified Sales Mgr.); Eddie Wooten (Sports Ed.); David Stanfield (Controller)
Parent company (for newspapers): BH Media Group; Lee Enterprises, Incorporated

THE DAILY REFLECTOR

Street address 1: 1150 Sugg Pkwy
Street address city: Greenville
Street address state: NC
Zip/Postal code: 27834-9077
County: Pitt
Country: USA
Mailing address: PO BOX 1967
Mailing city: GREENVILLE
Mailing state: NC
Mailing zip: 27835-1967
General Phone: (252) 329-9500
Advertising Phone: (252) 329-9503
Editorial Phone: (252) 329-9560
General/National Adv. E-mail: dsingleton@reflector.com
Display Adv. E-mail: dsingleton@reflector.com
Editorial e-mail: baburns@reflector.com
Primary Website: www.reflector.com
Mthly Avg Views: 5000000
Mthly Avg Unique Visitors: 200000
Year Established: 1882
News Services: AP, NYT, LAT-WP.
Special Editions: Parade of Homes (Apr); Back to School (Aug); College Football Bowl Preview (Dec); Home Expo (Feb); Bridal Planner (Jan); Design an Ad (Mar); Graduation (May); Holiday Show (Nov); Medical Directory (Oct); Community Business (Sept); Greenville Magazine
Special Weekly Sections: Workweek (Mon); Best Food Day (Wed); Real Estate, Church (Sat); Travel (Sun); Business, AP Stock, Lifestyles (Daily)
Syndicated Publications: Pirate Gameday (during football season) (Sat); Her Magazine (monthly), Mixer Magazine (monthly).
Delivery Methods: Mail`Newsstand`Carrier`Racks
Areas Served - City/County or Portion Thereof, or Zip codes: 28530, 28513, 28590, 27858, 27837, 27834, 27828, 27829, 27834, 27871, 27892, 28580
Own Printing Facility?: Y
Commercial printers?: Y
Avg Free Circ: 3884
Sat. Circulation Paid: 14939
Sat. Circulation Free: 3884
Sun. Circulation Paid: 16160
Sun. Circulation Free: 872
Audit By: AAM
Audit Date: 12.12.2017
Personnel: John Cooke (Pub.); J. Tim Holt (Chief Operating Officer); Mariann McQueen (CFO); David Adams (Circ. Dir.); Donna Allen (HR Dir.); Betty Williams (Display Adv. Dir.); Elizabeth Semple (Dir., Mktg./Bus. Devel./Customer Care); Cherie Speller (Asst. Mng. Ed.); Mike Grizzard (Bus. Ed.); Steve Cagle (Features Ed.); Bobby Burns (Exec. Ed.); Rhett Butler (Photo Ed.); Jim Gentry (Sports Ed.); Dan Mastin (Dir., Ops.); Dawn Newton (Creative Servs. Mgr.); James Webb (Facilities Mgr.); Regina Lytle (Pre-Press Mgr.); David Adams (Circulation Dir.)
Parent company (for newspapers): Adams Publishing Group, LLC

DAILY DISPATCH

Street address 1: 304 S Chestnut St
Street address city: Henderson
Street address state: NC
Zip/Postal code: 27536-4225
County: Vance
Country: USA
Mailing address: 304 S CHESTNUT ST
Mailing city: HENDERSON
Mailing state: NC
Mailing zip: 27536-4225
General Phone: (252) 436-2800
Advertising Phone: (252) 436-2812
Editorial Phone: (252) 436-2831
General/National Adv. E-mail: dtuck@hendersondispatch.com
Display Adv. E-mail: dtuck@hendersondispatch.com
Classified Adv. e-mail: dtuck@hendersondispatch.com
Editorial e-mail: news@hendersondispatch.com
Primary Website: www.hendersondispatch.com
Year Established: 1914
News Services: AP.
Special Editions: Spring Home & Garden (Apr); Fall Sports (Aug); Christmas Greetings (Dec); Best of Vance County (Feb); Bridal (Jan); Funeral & Estate Planning (Jul); Graduation (Jun); Spring Fashion (Mar); Trade Show (May); Christmas Gift Guide (Nov); Football Contest (Se
Special Weekly Sections: Best Food Day (Wed). Faith (Sat). Showcase (Sun).
Syndicated Publications: USA WEEKEND Magazine (S). Spry. American Profile. Relish. Athlon Sports.
Delivery Methods: Mail`Newsstand`Carrier`Racks
Areas Served - City/County or Portion Thereof, or Zip codes: 23927, 27507, 27536, 27537, 27544, 27549, 27551, 27553, 27556, 27563, 27565, 27582, 27589
Own Printing Facility?: Y
Commercial printers?: Y
Avg Free Circ: 19050
Sat. Circulation Paid: 6000
Sun. Circulation Paid: 6500
Audit By: Sworn/Estimate/Non-Audited
Audit Date: 12.07.2019
Personnel: Nancy Wykle (Pub./Ed.); Matthew Murray (Circ. Mgr.); Ray Gronberg (Mng. Ed.); Brandon White (Sports Ed.); Desiree Brooks (Adv. Dir.)
Parent company (for newspapers): Paxton Media Group

TIMES-NEWS

Street address 1: 106 Henderson Crossing Plz
Street address city: Hendersonville
Street address state: NC
Zip/Postal code: 28792-2879
County: Henderson
Country: USA
Mailing address: 106 Henderson Crossing Plz
Mailing city: Hendersonville
Mailing state: NC
Mailing zip: 28792-2879
General Phone: (828) 692-0505
General/National Adv. E-mail: Wanda.Edney@blueridgenow.com
Display Adv. E-mail: tnads@blueridgenow.com
Classified Adv. e-mail: debbie.owen@blueridgenow.com
Editorial e-mail: tnletters@blueridgenow.com
Primary Website: www.blueridgenow.com
Mthly Avg Views: 2000000
Mthly Avg Unique Visitors: 200000
Year Established: 1881
News Services: AP, NYT.
Special Editions: Football (Aug); Apple Festival (Sep); Last Minute Gift Guide (Dec); Almanac (Feb); Medical Directory (Mar); Holiday Gift Guide (Nov); Motorama (Oct).
Special Weekly Sections: Weekend (Fri); Blue Ridge Living (S); Church Directory (Sat); Best Food Day (Wed).
Delivery Methods: Carrier`Racks
Areas Served - City/County or Portion Thereof, or Zip codes: Henderson, Polk & Transylvania Counties (NC)
Own Printing Facility?: Y
Avg Free Circ: 471
Sat. Circulation Paid: 10937
Sat. Circulation Free: 471
Sun. Circulation Paid: 11778
Sun. Circulation Free: 296
Audit By: AAM
Audit Date: 30.09.2014
Personnel: Jennifer Heaslip (Mng. Ed.); Heather Staton (Regional Adv. Mgr.); Patrick Sullivan (Chief Photographer); Dean Hensley (Sports Ed.)
Parent company (for newspapers): CherryRoad Media; Gannett

THE HICKORY DAILY RECORD

Street address 1: 1100 11th Ave. Blvd. SE
Street address city: Hickory
Street address state: NC
Zip/Postal code: 28602
County: Catawba
Country: USA
Mailing address: PO BOX 968
Mailing city: HICKORY
Mailing state: NC
Mailing zip: 28603-0968
General Phone: (828) 322-4510
Advertising Phone: (828) 322-4510
Editorial Phone: (828) 322-4510
General/National Adv. E-mail: advertising@hickoryrecord.com
Display Adv. E-mail: advertising@hickoryrecord.com
Classified Adv. e-mail: classified@carolinaclassifiedmarketplace.com
Editorial e-mail: news@hickoryrecord.com
Primary Website: www.hickoryrecord.com
Mthly Avg Views: 176307
Mthly Avg Unique Visitors: 8709
News Services: AP.
Special Editions: Hickory Hops (Apr); Hickory Heritage (Aug); Christmas (Dec); Health & Fitness (Feb); Visitor Guide (Jun); Taste of Hickory (Mar); Hickory Smoke (May); Christmas (Nov); Cultural Arts (Oct); Active Seniors (Quarterly); Best of Catawba (Sept).
Special Weekly Sections: Business, Best Food (Wed); Pastimes, Arts, Entertainment (Thur); Business, Learning (Fri); Building, Home, Garden, Living, Real Estate, Religion (Sat); Family (Sun)
Syndicated Publications: USA WEEKEND Magazine (S).
Delivery Methods: Mail`Newsstand`Carrier`Racks
Areas Served - City/County or Portion Thereof, or Zip codes: Catawba County
Avg Free Circ: 303
Sat. Circulation Paid: 8330
Sat. Circulation Free: 303
Sun. Circulation Paid: 9959
Sun. Circulation Free: 147
Audit By: AAM
Audit Date: 31.03.2019
Personnel: Tim Dearman (Reg. Pub.); John Miller (Mng. Ed.); David Eggers (Circ. Dir.); Jim Lillagore (Prodn. Mgr.); John Dayberry (Bus. Ed.); Patrick Jean (City Ed.); Josh LaFontaine (Editor); Michelle L. Bloomfield (News Ed.); Larry Clark (Interim Editor); Chris Hobbs (Sports Ed.); Vicki Hayes (Major Accounts Mgr.); Melanie Armino; Scott Bryan (Editor)
Parent company (for newspapers): BH Media Group; Lee Enterprises, Incorporated

HIGH POINT ENTERPRISE

Street address 1: 213 Woodbine St
Street address city: High Point
Street address state: NC
Zip/Postal code: 27260-8339
County: Guilford
Country: USA
Mailing address: 213 WOODBINE ST
Mailing city: HIGH POINT
Mailing state: NC
Mailing zip: 27260-8339
General Phone: (336) 888-3500
Advertising Phone: (336) 885-3555 (class)
Editorial Phone: (336) 888-3500
General/National Adv. E-mail: jmcclure@hpenews.com
Display Adv. E-mail: jmcclure@hpenews.com
Classified Adv. e-mail: classified@hpenews.com
Editorial e-mail: news@hpenews.com
Primary Website: www.hpenews.com/
Mthly Avg Views: 436000
Mthly Avg Unique Visitors: 168500
Year Established: 1883
News Services: AP, MCT, CNS, SHNS, TMS.
Special Editions: Everything High Point
Special Weekly Sections: Food (Wed); Dining, Entertainment (Thur); Travel, Real Estate (Sun); Business (Daily)
Syndicated Publications: American Profile (weekly); Athlon, Spry (1 a month)
Delivery Methods: Mail`Newsstand`Carrier`Racks
Areas Served - City/County or Portion Thereof, or Zip codes: Guilford, Davidson, Randolph, Forsyth counties (NC)
Own Printing Facility?: Y

Commercial printers?: Y
Avg Free Circ: 33000
Sat. Circulation Paid: 10200
Sun. Circulation Paid: 12200
Audit By: Sworn/Estimate/Non-Audited
Audit Date: 12.07.2019
Personnel: Rick Bean (Pub.); Nancy Baker (Controller); John McClure (Adv. Dir.)
Parent company (for newspapers): Paxton Media Group

THE DAILY NEWS

Street address 1: P.O. Box 196
Street address city: Jacksonville
Street address state: NC
Zip/Postal code: 28541
County: Onslow
Country: USA
Mailing address: PO BOX 196
Mailing city: JACKSONVILLE
Mailing state: NC
Mailing zip: 28541-0196
General Phone: (910) 353-1171
Advertising Phone: (910) 353-1171
Editorial Phone: (910) 353-1171
General/National Adv. E-mail: matt.holbrook@kinston.com
Display Adv. E-mail: Rachelle.Trout@JDNews.com
Classified Adv. e-mail: Lynnell.Burch@JDNews.com
Editorial e-mail: editor@jdnews.com
Primary Website: www.jdnews.com
Mthly Avg Views: 1400000
News Services: AP.
Special Editions: Spring Car Care (Apr); Answer Book (Aug); Christmas Color Book (Dec); NASCAR Preview (Feb); Super Bowl (Jan); Celebrate the Fourth (Jul); June Bride (Jun); Spring Gardening (Mar); Graduation (May); Coupon Book (Monthly); Cookbook (Nov); Swansboros Mullet
Special Weekly Sections: Business Page (Mon); Visions (S); Business Spotlights (Tues); Food (Wed).
Syndicated Publications: American Profile (Every other week); USA WEEKEND Magazine (S); Max Magazine (Thur).
Areas Served - City/County or Portion Thereof, or Zip codes: Jacksonville, Camp Lejeune, Onslow County and surrounding areas
Avg Free Circ: 582
Sat. Circulation Paid: 9736
Sat. Circulation Free: 582
Sun. Circulation Paid: 10890
Sun. Circulation Free: 143
Audit By: CAC
Audit Date: 31.12.2017
Personnel: Michael Distelhorst (Pub.); Amanda Humphrey (Ed.); Amanda Thames (City Ed.); Ken Warren (Adv. Dir.); Don Wilson (Circ. Mgr.)
Parent company (for newspapers): Gannett; CherryRoad Media

THE KINSTON FREE PRESS

Street address 1: 2103 N Queen St
Street address city: Kinston
Street address state: NC
Zip/Postal code: 28501-1622
County: Lenoir
Country: USA
Mailing address: 2103 N QUEEN ST
Mailing city: KINSTON
Mailing state: NC
Mailing zip: 28501-1695
General Phone: (252) 527-3191
Advertising Phone: (252) 527-3191
Editorial Phone: (252) 527-3191
General/National Adv. E-mail: matt.holbrook@kinston.com
Display Adv. E-mail: matt.holbrook@kinston.com
Classified Adv. e-mail: billy_moore@link.freedom.com
Primary Website: www.kinston.com
Year Established: 1882
News Services: AP.
Special Weekly Sections: School (Tue); Food (Wed); Auto (Fri); Real Estate (Sat);
Syndicated Publications: Homes Magazine (Every other month); USA WEEKEND Magazine (S); American Profile (Weekly).
Avg Free Circ: 208
Sat. Circulation Paid: 4031
Sat. Circulation Free: 208
Sun. Circulation Paid: 4716
Sun. Circulation Free: 50
Audit By: AAM
Audit Date: 31.03.2019
Personnel: Mike Distelhorst (Pub.); Chris Segal (Ed.); Darrell Moore (District Mgr.)
Parent company (for newspapers): Gannett; CherryRoad Media

THE LAURINBURG EXCHANGE

Street address 1: 211 W Cronly St
Street address city: Laurinburg
Street address state: NC
Zip/Postal code: 28352-3637
County: Scotland
Country: USA
Mailing address: 211 W CRONLY ST
Mailing city: LAURINBURG
Mailing state: NC
Mailing zip: 28352-3637
General Phone: (910) 276-2311
Advertising Phone: (910) 276-2311
Editorial Phone: (910) 276-2311
General/National Adv. E-mail: dperkins@civitasmedia.com
Display Adv. E-mail: asimpson@civitasmedia.com
Classified Adv. e-mail: lexclassifieds@heartlandpublications.com
Editorial e-mail: dperkins@civitasmedia.com
Primary Website: www.laurinburgexchange.com
Mthly Avg Unique Visitors: 30000
Year Established: 1882
News Services: AP.
Special Weekly Sections: Food (Wed); TV, Real Estate, Religion (Fri)
Syndicated Publications: American Profile (Weekly).
Sat. Circulation Paid: 8200
Audit By: Sworn/Estimate/Non-Audited
Audit Date: 12.07.2019
Personnel: Scott Witten (Ed.); Sharon Burke (Circ. Mgr.); Susie Smith (Bus. Off. Mgr.); Althea Simpson (Bus. Devp. Mgr.); Amy McNeill (Classified)
Parent company (for newspapers): Champion Media

NEWS-TOPIC

Street address 1: 123 Pennton Ave NW
Street address city: Lenoir
Street address state: NC
Zip/Postal code: 28645-4313
County: Caldwell
Country: USA
General Phone: (828) 758-7381
Advertising Phone: (828) 610-8718
Editorial Phone: (828) 610-8737
Classified Adv. e-mail: classads@newstopicnews.com
Editorial e-mail: news@newstopicnews.com
Primary Website: www.newstopicnews.com
Mthly Avg Views: 214000
Mthly Avg Unique Visitors: 29000
Year Established: 1875
News Services: AP,
Special Editions: Sports Tab (Aug.,Nov and March). Caldwell Book, May; Everything Caldwell, Feb
Special Weekly Sections: Church News (Fri).
Syndicated Publications: TV/Sunday Relish/Spry/Athlon Sports Thursday
Delivery Methods: Mail`Newsstand`Carrier`Racks
Areas Served - City/County or Portion Thereof, or Zip codes: 28645, 28630, 28638,
Own Printing Facility?: N
Commercial printers?: N
Avg Free Circ: 75
Sun. Circulation Paid: 5335
Sun. Circulation Free: 75
Audit By: Sworn/Estimate/Non-Audited
Audit Date: 12.07.2019
Personnel: Mike Lambert (Circ. Mgr.); Guy Lucas (Ed.); Melissa Haire (District Mgr.); Bryant Lilley (Sports Ed.)
Parent company (for newspapers): Paxton Media Group

THE DISPATCH

Street address 1: 30 E 1st Ave
Street address city: Lexington
Street address state: NC
Zip/Postal code: 27292-3302
County: Davidson
Country: USA
Mailing address: PO BOX 908
Mailing city: LEXINGTON
Mailing state: NC
Mailing zip: 27293-0908
General Phone: (336) 249-3981
Advertising Phone: (336) 249-1637
Editorial Phone: (336) 249-3981
General/National Adv. E-mail: tammie.wright@the-dispatch.com
Display Adv. E-mail: tammie.wright@the-dispatch.com
Classified Adv. e-mail: tammie.wright@the-dispatch.com
Editorial e-mail: news@the-dispatch.com
Primary Website: www.the-dispatch.com
Year Established: 1882
News Services: AP, NYT.
Special Weekly Sections: Business, Food (Wed); Religion (Sat)
Syndicated Publications: USA WEEKEND Magazine (Sat).
Delivery Methods: Mail`Newsstand`Carrier`Racks
Own Printing Facility?: Y
Commercial printers?: N
Avg Free Circ: 416
Sat. Circulation Paid: 5045
Sat. Circulation Free: 416
Audit By: AAM
Audit Date: 31.12.2017
Personnel: Steve Skaggs (Pub.); Stephanie Sprayberry (Asst. Controller); Tammie Wright (Adv. Mgr.); Vikki Hodges (Bus. Ed.); Donnie Roberts (Chief Photographer); Mike Duprez (Sports Ed.); Lindsay Hedrick (IT Mgr.); Julia Hudgins
Parent company (for newspapers): Gannett; CherryRoad Media

THE ROBESONIAN

Street address 1: 2175 N Roberts Ave
Street address city: Lumberton
Street address state: NC
Zip/Postal code: 28358-2867
County: Robeson
Country: USA
Mailing address: 2175 N ROBERTS AVE
Mailing city: LUMBERTON
Mailing state: NC
Mailing zip: 28358-2867
General Phone: (910) 739-4322
Advertising Phone: (910) 416-5668
Editorial Phone: (910) 416-5649
General/National Adv. E-mail: rwalker@heartlandpublications.com
Display Adv. E-mail: dmckenzie@heartlandpublications.com
Classified Adv. e-mail: obesonianclass@robesonian.com
Editorial e-mail: ddouglas@civitasmedia.com
Primary Website: www.robesonian.com
Year Established: 1870
News Services: AP, CN, CNS, NYT, SHNS, LAT-WP.
Special Editions: Tobacco Market (Other).
Special Weekly Sections: Health, Entertainment (Tue); Food, Education, Lifestyles, Entertainment (Wed); Agriculture, Entertainment (Thur); Auto, Religion, TV Spotlight (Fri); Education, Brides, Stock, Business, Lifestyles, Comics (Sun)
Syndicated Publications: Parade (S).
Areas Served - City/County or Portion Thereof, or Zip codes: Robeson County (NC)
Sat. Circulation Paid: 12562
Sun. Circulation Paid: 15108
Audit By: Sworn/Estimate/Non-Audited
Audit Date: 12.07.2019
Personnel: Sarah Willets (Managing Ed.); Scott Witten (Bus. Ed.); Donnie Douglas (Ed.); Knight Chamberlain (Educ. Ed.); Michael Jaenicke (Lifestyle Ed.); T.C. Hunter (Online Ed.); Steve Humbert (Photo Dept. Mgr.); Jaymie Baxley (Features Ed.); Rick Thomason (Pub.); Tammy Britt (Circ. Dir.)
Parent company (for newspapers): Champion Media

THE MCDOWELL NEWS

Street address 1: 136 Logan Street
Street address city: Marion
Street address state: NC
Zip/Postal code: 28752
County: McDowell
Country: USA
Mailing address: PO BOX 610
Mailing city: MARION
Mailing state: NC
Mailing zip: 28752-0610
General Phone: (828) 652-3313
Advertising Phone: (828) 559-4045
Editorial Phone: (828) 559-4051
General/National Adv. E-mail: ehorn@bhmginc.com
Display Adv. E-mail: jlinens@morganton.com
Classified Adv. e-mail: classified@mcdowellnews.com
Editorial e-mail: news@mcdowellnews.com
Primary Website: www.mcdowellnews.com
Mthly Avg Views: 438886
Mthly Avg Unique Visitors: 79640
News Services: AP.
Special Weekly Sections: Business (Tue); Entertainment (Wed); Promotions, Specials (Monthly); Comics, Religion (Fri)
Syndicated Publications: American Profile (Weekly); USA WEEKEND Magazine (Weekly).
Areas Served - City/County or Portion Thereof, or Zip codes: McDowell County (NC)
Own Printing Facility?: N
Commercial printers?: N
Avg Free Circ: 149
Sun. Circulation Paid: 2872
Sun. Circulation Free: 85
Audit By: AAM
Audit Date: 31.12.2018
Personnel: Lamar Smitherman (Pub.); Scott Hollifield (Ed.); Nina Linens (Adv. Dir.); Linda Early (Adv. Asst./Circ.)
Parent company (for newspapers): BH Media Group

THE NEWS HERALD

Street address 1: 301 Collett Street
Street address city: Morganton
Street address state: NC
Zip/Postal code: 28655
County: Burke
Country: USA
Mailing address: PO BOX 280
Mailing city: MORGANTON
Mailing state: NC
Mailing zip: 28680-0280
General Phone: (828) 437-2161
Advertising Phone: (828) 437-2161
Editorial Phone: (828) 437-2161
General/National Adv. E-mail: advertising@morganton.com
Display Adv. E-mail: advertising@morganton.com
Classified Adv. e-mail: classified@morganton.com
Editorial e-mail: news@morganton.com
Primary Website: www.morganton.com
Mthly Avg Views: 1404518
Mthly Avg Unique Visitors: 123564
News Services: AP.
Special Editions: Home & Garden (Apr); Football (Aug); Last Minute Gift Ideas (Dec); Valentine's Gift Ideas (Feb); % Off Sale (Jan); % Off Sale (Jul); Father's Day Gift Guide (Jun); Review & Forecast (Mar); Mother's Day Gift Guide (May); Christmas Around Burke (Nov); Hallo
Special Weekly Sections: Food (Wed); Entertainment, TV; Church (Fri); Business, Social, Living, Women (Sun)
Syndicated Publications: TV Herald (Fri); American Profile (Weekly).
Areas Served - City/County or Portion Thereof, or Zip codes: Burke County, NC
Own Printing Facility?: N
Commercial printers?: N
Avg Free Circ: 391
Sun. Circulation Paid: 4896
Sun. Circulation Free: 392
Audit By: AAM
Audit Date: 31.12.2018
Personnel: Lisa Wall (Ed.); Paul Schenkel (Sports Ed.); Lisa Butler (Circ. Mgr.); Nina Linens (Adv. Dir.); Justin Epley (Sports Editor)
Parent company (for newspapers): BH Media Group; Lee Enterprises, Incorporated

MOUNT AIRY NEWS

Street address 1: 319 N Renfro St
Street address city: Mount Airy
Street address state: NC
Zip/Postal code: 27030-3838
County: Surry
Country: USA
General Phone: (336) 786-4141
General/National Adv. E-mail: shurley@civitasmedia.com
Display Adv. E-mail: shurley@heartlandpublications.com
Classified Adv. e-mail: mtaclassifieds@mtairynews.com
Editorial e-mail: jpeters@civitasmedia.com

Primary Website: www.mtairynews.com
Mthly Avg Views: 600000
Mthly Avg Unique Visitors: 78000
Year Established: 1880
News Services: AP.
Special Editions: Simple Pleasures (Apr); Simple Pleasures (Aug); Simple Pleasures (Jul); Simple Pleasures (Jun); Progress (Mar); Simple Pleasures (May); Foothill Farmer (Monthly); Simple Pleasures (Oct); Simple Pleasures (Sept).
Special Weekly Sections: Best Food Day (Wed); Religion, Auto (Fri); Entertainment, TV, Real Estate (Sun)
Syndicated Publications: USA WEEKEND Magazine (S); American Profile (Weekly).
Areas Served - City/County or Portion Thereof, or Zip codes: Surry County (NC)
Own Printing Facility?: Y
Avg Free Circ: 12000
Sun. Circulation Paid: 11221
Audit By: Sworn/Estimate/Non-Audited
Audit Date: 12.07.2019
Personnel: Nikki Hawks (Adv. Mgr.); John Peters (Ed.); David Perkins (Nat'l Acct. Mgr.); Nathan DiBagno (Rgl. Local Bus. Develop. Mgr.); Ferris Simpson (Bus./Circ Mgr.); Thomas Smith (Sports Ed.); Sandra Hurley (Regional Publisher); Jeff Linville (Assistant Editor); Ron Clausen (Pub.)
Parent company (for newspapers): Adams Publishing Group, LLC; Champion Media

THE SUN JOURNAL

Street address 1: 3200 Wellons Boulevard
Street address city: New Bern
Street address state: NC
Zip/Postal code: 28562
County: Craven
Country: USA
Mailing address: 3200 WELLONS BLVD
Mailing city: NEW BERN
Mailing state: NC
Mailing zip: 28562-5234
General Phone: (252) 638-8101
Advertising Phone: (252) 638-8101
Editorial Phone: (252) 638-8101
General/National Adv. E-mail: Scott.Embry@NewBernSJ.com
Display Adv. E-mail: nbsjads@freedomenc.com
Classified Adv. e-mail: encclassifieds@jdnews.com
Editorial e-mail: sjnewsroom@newbernsj.com
Primary Website: www.newbernsj.com
Mthly Avg Views: 1400000
Year Established: 1783
News Services: AP, NEA.
Special Editions: Back-to-School (Aug); Brides (Feb); Shriners (Jan); Hurricane Awareness (Jul); Home and Garden (Mar); Christmas Catalog (Nov); Fall Home Improvement (Sept).
Special Weekly Sections: Health; Food (Wed); Farm (Thur); Entertainment (Fri); Church (Sat); TV, Business (Sun);
Syndicated Publications: Real Estate (Monthly); Healthy Living (Quarterly); USA WEEKEND Magazine (S); American Profile (Weekly).
Delivery Methods: Mail`Newsstand`Carrier`Racks
Avg Free Circ: 259
Sat. Circulation Paid: 8801
Sat. Circulation Free: 259
Sun. Circulation Paid: 10075
Sun. Circulation Free: 6
Audit By: CAC
Audit Date: 31.12.2017
Personnel: Randy Foster (Ed.); Sheila Meadows (Circ. Dir.); Terry Tokie (Adv. Dir.); Adam Thompson (Sports Ed.); Mike Distelhorst (Pub.)
Parent company (for newspapers): Gannett; CherryRoad Media

THE OBSERVER NEWS ENTERPRISE

Street address 1: 309 N College Ave
Street address city: Newton
Street address state: NC
Zip/Postal code: 28658-3255
County: Catawba
Country: USA
Mailing address: PO BOX 48
Mailing city: NEWTON
Mailing state: NC
Mailing zip: 28658-0048
General Phone: (828) 464-0221
General/National Adv. E-mail: admanager@observernewsonline.com
Display Adv. E-mail: admanager@observernewsonline.com
Classified Adv. e-mail: oneclassifieds@observernewsonline.com
Editorial e-mail: onenews@observernewsonline.com
Primary Website: www.observernewsonline.com
Year Established: 1879
News Services: AP.
Special Editions: Friday Magazine (Monthly).
Special Weekly Sections: Education (Tue); Business (Wed); Education, Health, Arts, Entertainment, Food, Family, Travel (Thur); Lifestyles, Religion (Sat); Real Estate (Upon Request)
Syndicated Publications: American Profile (Fri).
Areas Served - City/County or Portion Thereof, or Zip codes: Catawba County (NC)
Sat. Circulation Paid: 2303
Audit By: Sworn/Estimate/Non-Audited
Audit Date: 12.07.2019
Personnel: Yerby Ray (Mng. Ed.); Cindy Hull (Circ. Dir.); Adams Houston (Sports Ed.); Philip Rogers (Prodn. Mgr.); Richard Patton (Prodn. Foreman, Pressroom); Seth Mabry (Pub./Ed.); Greg Bailes (Bus. Office)
Parent company (for newspapers): Horizon Publications Inc.

THE NEWS & OBSERVER

Street address 1: 215 S McDowell St
Street address city: Raleigh
Street address state: NC
Zip/Postal code: 27601-1331
County: Wake
Country: USA
Mailing address: PO BOX 191
Mailing city: RALEIGH
Mailing state: NC
Mailing zip: 27602-9150
General Phone: (919) 829-4500
Advertising Phone: (919) 836-5600
Editorial Phone: (919) 829-4564
General/National Adv. E-mail: placeads@newsobserver.com.
Display Adv. E-mail: placeads@newsobserver.com.
Classified Adv. e-mail: placeads@newsobserver.com
Editorial e-mail: forum@newsobserver.com
Primary Website: www.newsobserver.com
Mthly Avg Views: 15000000
Mthly Avg Unique Visitors: 2224619
Year Established: 1894
News Services: AP, Bloomberg, CT, MCT, LAT-WP, NYT.
Special Editions: Business Expo (Apr); Fall Style (Aug); What's Up/1st Night (Dec); Taxes Work & Money (Feb); Economic Outlook (Jan); The N&O 100 (State's Public Companies) (Jun); Spring Style (Mar); Nurses Association (May); Expanded What's Up for the Holidays (Nov); Scho
Special Weekly Sections: Sports, Entertainment, Money, Travel, Comics (Sun); Sports, Life (Mon); Business, Stocks (Tue); Food (Wed); (Faith, What's Up (Fri); Home, Channels (Sat)
Syndicated Publications: Parade (S).
Areas Served - City/County or Portion Thereof, or Zip codes: Raleigh (NC)
Sat. Circulation Paid: 82637
Sun. Circulation Paid: 106327
Audit By: AAM
Audit Date: 30.06.2018
Personnel: Sara Glines (Pres./Pub.); John Drescher (Opinions & Solutions Ed.); Jim Puryear (Vice Pres. of Audience Development); Caroline Willingham (Vice. Pres. Finance); Bernie Heller (VP Advertising / Chief Revenue Officer); Robyn Tomlin (Exec. Ed./Regional Ed.); Jane Elizabeth (Mng. Ed.)
Parent company (for newspapers): The McClatchy Company

THE EDEN DAILY NEWS

Street address 1: 1921 Vance St
Street address city: Reidsville
Street address state: NC
Zip/Postal code: 27320-3254
County: Rockingham
Country: USA
Mailing address: PO BOX 2157
Mailing city: REIDSVILLE
Mailing state: NC
Mailing zip: 27323-2157
General Phone: 336-349-4331
Advertising Phone: (434) 385-5505
Editorial Phone: (336) 349-4331
General/National Adv. E-mail: pdurham@reidsvillereview.com
Display Adv. E-mail: legalads@registerbee.com
Classified Adv. e-mail: pdurham@reidsvillereview.com
Editorial e-mail: alehmert@reidsvillereview.com
Primary Website: www.newsadvance.com
News Services: AP, Universal Press Syndicate, NEA.
Special Weekly Sections: Food (Wed); Entertainment, Auto (Fri); Health (Thur); Home (Sat)
Syndicated Publications: USA WEEKEND Magazine (S).
Sun. Circulation Paid: 3961
Audit By: Sworn/Estimate/Non-Audited
Audit Date: 12.07.2019
Personnel: Alton Brown (Pub.); Dreama Armstrong (Office Mgr.); Pam Durham (Retail Adv. Dir.); Amanda K Lehmert (Grp. Ed.); Mary Thurman Terry Goad (Circ. Mgr.); Amanda Lehmert (Ed.)
Parent company (for newspapers): North Carolina Press Service, Inc.; BH Media Group; Media General, Inc. (OOB)

DAILY HERALD

Street address 1: 916 Roanoke Ave
Street address city: Roanoke Rapids
Street address state: NC
Zip/Postal code: 27870-2720
County: Halifax
Country: USA
Mailing address: 916 Roanoke Ave
Mailing city: Roanoke Rapids
Mailing state: NC
Mailing zip: 27870-2720
General Phone: (252) 537-2505
Advertising Phone: (252) 537-2505
Editorial Phone: (252) 537-2505
General/National Adv. E-mail: pwhite@rrdailyherald.com
Display Adv. E-mail: sconger@rrdailyherald.com
Classified Adv. e-mail: lindafoster@rrdailyherald.com
Editorial e-mail: shemelt@rrdailyherald.com
Primary Website: www.rrdailyherald.com
Year Established: 1914
News Services: AP.
Special Editions: Football Kick-off Tab (Aug); Christmas Greetings (Dec); Bride & Groom (Feb); Honor Roll of Business (Jan); July 4th Sales (Jul); Home & Garden (Mar); Progress Tab (May); Christmas Gift Guide (Nov); Businesswomen's Week (Oct); Fall Opening (Sept).
Special Weekly Sections: NIE (Tue); Food (Wed); Religion (Fri); Comics, Outdoor, Family, Senior (Sun)
Syndicated Publications: USA WEEKEND Magazine (S).
Areas Served - City/County or Portion Thereof, or Zip codes: Halifax & Northampton Counties (NC), Brunswick & Greensville Counties (VA)
Sun. Circulation Paid: 6793
Audit By: VAC
Audit Date: 30.06.2015
Personnel: Nancy Wykle (Pub.); Tia Bedwell (Ed.); Kristal Murphy (Circ. Dir.); Desiree Brooks (Adv. Dir.); Carolyn Harmon (News Ed.); Rhonda Irby (Account Exec.); Leslie Davis (Account Exec.)
Parent company (for newspapers): Paxton Media Group

RICHMOND COUNTY DAILY JOURNAL

Street address 1: 105 E Washington St
Street address city: Rockingham
Street address state: NC
Zip/Postal code: 28379-3639
County: Richmond
Country: USA
Mailing address: PO BOX 190
Mailing city: ROCKINGHAM
Mailing state: NC
Mailing zip: 28380-0190
General Phone: (910) 997-3111
Advertising Phone: (910) 997-3111
Editorial Phone: (910) 997-3111
General/National Adv. E-mail: rbacon@heartlandpublications.com
Display Adv. E-mail: Rbacon@heartlandpublications.com
Classified Adv. e-mail: rdjclassifieds@civitasmedia.com
Editorial e-mail: Jrobbins@heartlandpublications.com
Primary Website: www.yourdailyjournal.com
Mthly Avg Views: 500000
Mthly Avg Unique Visitors: 150000
Year Established: 1931
News Services: AP.
Special Editions: Raider Football Review (Aug);
Special Weekly Sections: Food (Wed); Entertainment, Auto (Fri); Health (Thur); Home (Sat)
Syndicated Publications: Relish (Monthly); American Profile (S).
Delivery Methods: Newsstand`Carrier`Racks
Areas Served - City/County or Portion Thereof, or Zip codes: Richmond County (NC)
Own Printing Facility?: Y
Commercial printers?: N
Avg Free Circ: 100
Sat. Circulation Paid: 7000
Audit By: Sworn/Estimate/Non-Audited
Audit Date: 12.07.2019
Personnel: Jimmy Herring (Circ. Mgr.); Shawn Stinson (Managing Editor/Sports Editor); Amanda Vaness (Prodn. Supvr.); Corey Friedman (Ed./Content Manager); David Spencer (Business Dev. Manager); Corey Friedman (Ed); Scott Ricardi (Advertising Director and General Manager)
Parent company (for newspapers): Champion Media

ROCKY MOUNT TELEGRAM

Street address 1: 1000 Hunter Hill Rd
Street address city: Rocky Mount
Street address state: NC
Zip/Postal code: 27804-1727
County: Nash
Country: USA
Mailing address: PO BOX 1080
Mailing city: ROCKY MOUNT
Mailing state: NC
Mailing zip: 27802-1080
General Phone: (252) 446-5161
Advertising Phone: (252)407-9927
Editorial Phone: (252)407-9943
General/National Adv. E-mail: jmbrown@rmtelegram.com
Display Adv. E-mail: jmbrown@rmtelegram.com
Classified Adv. e-mail: qmcneal@rmtelegram.com
Editorial e-mail: jherrin@rmtelegram.com
Primary Website: www.rockymounttelegram.com
Mthly Avg Views: 3200000
Mthly Avg Unique Visitors: 120000
Year Established: 1910
News Services: AP.
Special Editions: Super Sunday (Jan), Brides (Feb), Carolina Charm (Mar), Home & Garden, Brew Scene (May), Medical Directory (June), Shop Local (July), Carolina Charm, Forever Young, Football Preview (Aug), Readers Choice, Welcome Home, Fall Car (Sep), United Way (Oct), Holiday Gift Guide, Brew Scene; Forever Young (Nov) Letters to Santa, Last Minute Gift Guide (Dec)
Special Weekly Sections: Religion (Fri); School (Mon); Technology (S); TV Magazine (Sun); Entertainment (Thur); Church Fri. News (Fri); Best Food Day (Wed).
Syndicated Publications: Local Color Comics (S).
Delivery Methods: Mail`Newsstand`Carrier`Racks
Areas Served - City/County or Portion Thereof, or Zip codes: 27801, 27802, 27803, 27804, 27809, 27816, 27822, 27823, 27844, 27852, 27856, 27864, 27868, 27874, 27878, 27882, 27886, 27891
Own Printing Facility?: N
Commercial printers?: Y
Avg Free Circ: 2095
Sat. Circulation Paid: 9193
Sun. Circulation Paid: 11094
Sun. Circulation Free: 54
Audit By: AAM
Audit Date: 10.10.2017
Personnel: Jeff Herrin (Editor); Gwen Davis (Mgr., HR); Mark Wilson (Pub.); Quasha McNeal (Classified Adv. Mgr.); Gene Metrick (Online/Print Ed.); Ross Chandler (Features Ed.); Jenny White (Online Ed.); Heidi Hibbert (Cir. Mgr.)
Parent company (for newspapers): Adams Publishing Group, LLC

THE DAILY COURIER

Street address 1: 162 N Main St
Street address city: Rutherfordton
Street address state: NC
Zip/Postal code: 28139
County: Rutherford
Country: USA
Mailing address: 162 N Main Street
Mailing city: Rutherfordton
Mailing state: NC
Mailing zip: 28139

General Phone: (828) 245-6431
Advertising Phone: (828) 202-2924
Editorial Phone: (828) 202-2927
General/National Adv. E-mail: lspurling@thedigitalcourier.com
Display Adv. E-mail: imccain@thedigitalcourier.com
Classified Adv. e-mail: imccain@thedigitalcourier.com
Editorial e-mail: vyoung@thedigitalcourier.com
Primary Website: www.thedigitalcourier.com
Year Established: 1969
News Services: AP.
Special Editions: Home Improvement (Apr); Christmas Gift Guide (Dec); Income Tax (Jan); Back-to-School (Aug); Fall Sports (Aug); Hot Nights Cool Rides (Aug) Health-Fitness (Jun); Everything Rutherford (Oct); Graduation (May); Outdoors (Sept).
Special Weekly Sections: Television (S).
Syndicated Publications: USA WEEKEND Magazine (S); Spry (S); American Profile (S)
Delivery Methods: Mail`Newsstand`Carrier`Racks
Areas Served - City/County or Portion Thereof, or Zip codes: 28018, 28020, 28040, 28043, 28114, 28139, 28160, 28167, 28746, 28752, 28756, 28761
Own Printing Facility?: Y
Commercial printers?: N
Sat. Circulation Paid: 7200
Sun. Circulation Paid: 7200
Audit By: Sworn/Estimate/Non-Audited
Audit Date: 01.10.2023
Personnel: Lori Spurling (Pub.); Jean Gordon (Ed.); Imani McCain (Sales manager); Denise Downs (Circulation -CSR); Erica Meyer (Adv. Mgr.); Scott Carpenter (Reporter); Pam Dixon (Circ. Dir.); Victoria McGuinn Young (Editor); Ethan Benefield (Sports Writer); Garrett Byer (Photographer); Ritchie Starnes (Editor); Jeff Rollins (sports reporter)
Parent company (for newspapers): Paxton Media Group

SALISBURY POST

Street address 1: 131 W Innes St
Street address city: Salisbury
Street address state: NC
Zip/Postal code: 28144-4338
County: Rowan
Country: USA
Mailing address: 131 W INNES ST
Mailing city: SALISBURY
Mailing state: NC
Mailing zip: 28144-4338
General Phone: (704) 633-8950
Advertising Phone: (704) 797-4241
Editorial Phone: (704)797-4250
General/National Adv. E-mail: displayads@Salisburypost.com
Display Adv. E-mail: displayads@Salisburypost.com
Classified Adv. e-mail: classads@Salisburypost.com
Editorial e-mail: letters@Salisburypost.com
Primary Website: www.salisburypost.com
Year Established: 1905
News Services: Papert (Landon), AP, NEA, SHNS, LAT-WP.
Special Editions: Nat'l Sportscasters & Sportswriters Association (Apr); Explorer (Aug); Christmas Carol Book (Dec); Bridal (Feb); Tax (Jan); A Day in the Life (Jul); Graduation (Jun); Explorer (Mar); Summer Fun (May); Hometown Heroes (Nov); October Tour (Oct); Fall Home I
Special Weekly Sections: Food (Wed); Time Out, TV (Thur); Youth, Senior (Fri); Real Estate, Church, Stocks (Sat); Business, Travel, Insight (Sun)
Syndicated Publications: Relish (Monthly); USA WEEKEND Magazine (S); American Profile (Weekly).
Areas Served - City/County or Portion Thereof, or Zip codes: Rowan, Davie & Cabaruss counties (NC)
Sat. Circulation Paid: 15086
Sun. Circulation Paid: 15902
Audit By: AAM
Audit Date: 30.09.2014
Personnel: Greg Anderson (Pub); Chris Ratliff (Dir., Sales/Mktg.); Ron Brooks (Circ. Dir.); Deirdre Parker Smith (Books Ed.); Chris Verner (Editorial Page Ed.); Holly Lee (Educ. Ed.); Wayne Hinshaw (Photo Dept. Mgr.); Mark Wineka (Political Ed.); Katie Olson (Religion Ed.); Michael J. Bella (Prodn. Vice Pres., Opns.); Ronnie Gallagher (Sports Ed.); Katie Scarvey (Teen-Age/Youth Ed.); Sharon Jackson (Prodn. Mgr., Post Press); Jon Lakey; David Putrell (New City and Business Reporter)
Parent company (for newspapers): Boone Newspapers, Inc.

HERALD-SANFORD

Street address 1: 208 Saint Clair Ct
Street address city: Sanford
Street address state: NC
Zip/Postal code: 27330-3916
County: Lee
Country: USA
Mailing address: 208 SAINT CLAIR CT
Mailing city: SANFORD
Mailing state: NC
Mailing zip: 27330-3916
General Phone: (919) 708-9000
Advertising Phone: (919) 718-1203
Editorial Phone: (919) 718-1226
General/National Adv. E-mail: adsales@sanfordherald.com
Display Adv. E-mail: adsales@sanfordherald.com
Classified Adv. e-mail: classified@sanfordherald.com
Editorial e-mail: news@sanfordherald.com
Primary Website: www.sanfordherald.com
Year Established: 1930
News Services: AP.
Special Editions: Car Care (Apr); Football (Aug); Christmas Gift Guide (Dec); IRS (Feb); Summer Lifestyle (Jun); Small Business Expo (May); Fair (Sept).
Special Weekly Sections: Food (Wed); Entertainment, Farm (Thur); Real Estate, Religion (Fri); Auto (Sat); Business, Free Time, Health, Travel, Women (Sun)
Syndicated Publications: TV Preview (Fri); USA WEEKEND Magazine (S).
Sat. Circulation Paid: 7978
Sun. Circulation Paid: 7901
Audit By: Sworn/Estimate/Non-Audited
Audit Date: 12.07.2019
Personnel: Bill Horner (Mgr., Mktg./Promo., Pub.); Jeff Ayers (Circ. Dir.); Dave Shabaz (Advertising Dir.); Jennifer Gentile (News Ed.); Judy McNeil (News Clerk)
Parent company (for newspapers): Paxton Media Group

THE STAR

Street address 1: 315 E Graham St
Street address city: Shelby
Street address state: NC
Zip/Postal code: 28150-5452
County: Cleveland
Country: USA
Mailing address: PO BOX 48
Mailing city: SHELBY
Mailing state: NC
Mailing zip: 28151-0048
General Phone: (704) 669-3300
Advertising Phone: (704) 669-3366
Editorial Phone: (704) 669-3333
General/National Adv. E-mail: klaprade@gastongazette.com
Display Adv. E-mail: klaprade@gastongazette.com
Classified Adv. e-mail: classifieds@gastongazette.com
Editorial e-mail: kellis@gastongazette.com
Primary Website: www.shelbystar.com
Mthly Avg Views: 1800000
Mthly Avg Unique Visitors: 155000
Year Established: 1894
News Services: AP, SHNS.
Special Editions: Your Health (Apr); Senior Living (Aug); Christmas Gift Guide (Dec); Senior Living (Feb); Your Health (Jan); Your Health (Jul); Cleveland Now (Mar); Senior Living (May); Real Estate (Lincoln & Cleveland counties) (Monthly); Senior Living (Nov); Your Health
Special Weekly Sections: Health (Tue); Food (Wed); Entertainment (Thur); Faith (Fri); Wedding, Real Estate, TV, Comics (Sun)
Syndicated Publications: USA WEEKEND Magazine (S).
Delivery Methods: Carrier
Areas Served - City/County or Portion Thereof, or Zip codes: Cleveland County (NC)
Commercial printers?: Y
Sat. Circulation Paid: 14164
Sun. Circulation Paid: 14389
Audit By: Sworn/Estimate/Non-Audited
Audit Date: 12.07.2019
Personnel: Wade Allen (lifestyles reporter); Frankie Rice (Prodn. Dir., Mailroom); Barry Croucher (Prodn. Mgr., Pressroom); Konrad LaPrade (Adv. Dir.); Keith Raffone (Gen. Mgr./Finance Dir.); Lucy Talley (Pub.); Michelle Owens (Newsroom Clerk); Diane Turbyfill (managing editor); Joyce Orlando (reporter); Brittany Randolph (photographer)
Parent company (for newspapers): CherryRoad Media; Gannett

STATESVILLE RECORD & LANDMARK

Street address 1: 222 E. Broad Street
Street address city: Statesville
Street address state: NC
Zip/Postal code: 28677
County: Iredell
Country: USA
Mailing address: 222 E BROAD ST
Mailing city: STATESVILLE
Mailing state: NC
Mailing zip: 28677-5325
General Phone: (704) 873-1451
Advertising Phone: (704) 761-2927
Editorial Phone: (704) 873-1451
General/National Adv. E-mail: advertising@statesville.com
Display Adv. E-mail: advertising@statesville.com
Classified Adv. e-mail: classified@statesville.com
Editorial e-mail: dibach@statesville.com
Primary Website: www.statesville.com
Year Established: 1874
Special Weekly Sections: Education (Tue); Food (Wed); TV, Entertainment (Sun); Business (Daily)
Delivery Methods: Mail`Newsstand`Carrier`Racks
Areas Served - City/County or Portion Thereof, or Zip codes: 28677, 28625, 28115, 28117, 28634, 28689, 28678, 28166
Own Printing Facility?: Y
Commercial printers?: Y
Avg Free Circ: 266
Sat. Circulation Paid: 5728
Sat. Circulation Free: 266
Sun. Circulation Paid: 7498
Sun. Circulation Free: 100
Audit By: AAM
Audit Date: 31.03.2019
Personnel: Tim Dearman (Pub.); Dave Ibach (Ed.); LeAnna Dunlap (Adv. Dir.); Bud Welch (Circ. Mgr.); Lisa Guy (Business Mgr.); Eric Millsaps
Parent company (for newspapers): BH Media Group; Lee Enterprises, Incorporated

TRYON DAILY BULLETIN

Street address 1: 16 N Trade St
Street address city: Tryon
Street address state: NC
Zip/Postal code: 28782-6656
County: Polk
Country: USA
General Phone: (828) 859-9151
General/National Adv. E-mail: news@tryondailybulletin.com
Display Adv. E-mail: advertising@tryondailybulletin.com
Classified Adv. e-mail: classifieds@tryondailybulletin.com
Editorial e-mail: news@tryondailybulletin.com
Primary Website: www.tryondailybulletin.com
Mthly Avg Unique Visitors: 30000
Year Established: 1928
Special Editions: Progress (Feb); Steeplechase (Apr), Graduation (May), Fall Sports (Aug); Business Card Directory (Oct); Holiday Gift Guide (Nov)
Syndicated Publications: Foothills Magazine, Visitors Bulletin
Delivery Methods: Mail`Newsstand`Racks
Areas Served - City/County or Portion Thereof, or Zip codes: 28782, 28773, 28756, 28750, 29356, 28722, 29322
Own Printing Facility?: Y
Audit By: Sworn/Estimate/Non-Audited
Audit Date: 12.07.2019
Personnel: Claire Sachse (Managing Ed.); Jeff Allison (Press Room Mgr.); Kevin Powell (Gen. Mgr.)
Parent company (for newspapers): Boone Newspapers, Inc.

WASHINGTON DAILY NEWS

Street address 1: 217 N Market St
Street address city: Washington
Street address state: NC
Zip/Postal code: 27889-4949
County: Beaufort
Country: USA
Mailing address: PO BOX 1788
Mailing city: WASHINGTON
Mailing state: NC
Mailing zip: 27889-1788
General Phone: (252) 946-2144
Advertising Phone: (252) 946-2144
Editorial Phone: (252) 946-2144
General/National Adv. E-mail: kathryn.powell@thewashingtondailynews.com
Display Adv. E-mail: kathryn.powell@thewashingtondailynews.com
Classified Adv. e-mail: ronnie.daw@thewashingtondailynews.com
Editorial e-mail: news@thewashingtondailynews.com
Primary Website: www.wdnweb.com
Year Established: 1909
News Services: AP.
Special Editions: Visitor's Tourist Guide Tab (Apr); Football Tab (Aug); Basketball Tab (Dec); Tax Tab (Jan); Summer Festival (Jul); Lawn and Garden Tab (Mar); Graduation Tab (May).
Special Weekly Sections: Society (Tue); Food (Wed); Farm (Thur); Channel, Church (Fri); Food, Society (Sun)
Syndicated Publications: Parade (S).
Sat. Circulation Paid: 8644
Sun. Circulation Paid: 8829
Audit By: Sworn/Estimate/Non-Audited
Audit Date: 12.07.2019
Personnel: Ashley B. Futrell (Pres./Pub.); Susan B. Futrell (Vice Pres.); Rachel F. Futrell (Treasurer); Addie B. Laney (Controller); Ray McKeithen (Adv. Dir.); Brenda Foster (Adv. Mgr., Classified); Mike Voss (Ed.); Brenda Watters (Society Ed.); Kevin Travis (Sports Ed.); Jerry Cox (Prodn. Foreman, Mailroom); Vance Bell (Prodn. Foreman, Pressroom); Ashley Vansant (Publisher)
Parent company (for newspapers): Boone Newspapers, Inc.

STARNEWS

Street address 1: 1003 S 17th St
Street address city: Wilmington
Street address state: NC
Zip/Postal code: 28401-8023
County: New Hanover
Country: USA
General Phone: (910) 343-2000
General/National Adv. E-mail: cheryl.whitaker@starnewsonline.com
Display Adv. E-mail: dave.cuddihy@starnewsonline.com
Primary Website: starnewsonline.com
Avg Free Circ: 1457
Sat. Circulation Paid: 18378
Sat. Circulation Free: 791
Sun. Circulation Paid: 21271
Sun. Circulation Free: 723
Audit By: AAM
Audit Date: 31.03.2019
Personnel: Mike Distelhorst (Pub.); Dave Cuddihy (Adv. Dir.); Cheryl Whitaker (Office Mgr.); Sheila Meadows (Circ. Dir.); Randy Foster (Ed.)
Parent company (for newspapers): Gannett; CherryRoad Media

THE WILSON TIMES

Street address 1: 126 Nash St NE
Street address city: Wilson
Street address state: NC
Zip/Postal code: 27893-4013
County: Wilson
Country: USA
Mailing address: PO BOX 2447
Mailing city: WILSON
Mailing state: NC
Mailing zip: 27894-2447
General Phone: (252) 243-5151
Advertising Phone: (252) 243-5151
Editorial Phone: (252) 243-5151
General/National Adv. E-mail: ads@wilsontimes.com
Display Adv. E-mail: ads@wilsontimes.com
Classified Adv. e-mail: classads@wilsontimes.com
Editorial e-mail: editor@wilsontimes.com
Primary Website: www.wilsontimes.com
Mthly Avg Views: 1000000
Mthly Avg Unique Visitors: 180000
Year Established: 1896
News Services: AP,

Special Editions: Wilson Woman; Medical Directory; Wilson Wellness; Readers Choice; Eyes on Main St.; Southern Parent; Graduation; My Wilson; United Way; Dining Guide; Football Preview; Veteran's Day; Letters to Santa; Whirligig Park
Special Weekly Sections: Weddings; Tabletop; Mind & Body; At Home; Schools; Real Estate; Wide Awake Wilson; Milestones; Family Life
Delivery Methods: Mail`Newsstand`Carrier`Racks
Areas Served - City/County or Portion Thereof, or Zip codes: Wilson, Nash, Edgecombe, pitt, Greene, Wayne & Johnston Counties (NC)
Own Printing Facility?: N
Commercial printers?: Y
Sat. Circulation Paid: 10762
Sat. Circulation Free: 288
Audit By: Sworn/Estimate/Non-Audited
Audit Date: 31.12.2016
Personnel: Lisa Batts (Mng. Ed.); Paul Durham (Sports Ed.); Shana Hoover (Dir. Mktg & Adv); Keven Zepezauer (Pres. & Pub.); Morgan Dickerman (Pub); Brie Handgraaf (Staff Writer); Debbie Boykin (Controller); Kelsey Padgett (Paginator); Sean O'Brien (VP Sales & Marketing); Chris Coley (Circ Mngr); Corey Friedman (Executive Editor); Joseph Conner (Regional Circulation Manager); Cynthia Collins (Ad Rep); Beth Robbins (Ad Rep); Lisa Pearson (Ad Rep); Petina Garcia (Ad Sales Asst.)
Parent company (for newspapers): Restoration NewsMedia

WINSTON-SALEM JOURNAL

Street address 1: 418 N Marshall St
Street address city: Winston Salem
Street address state: NC
Zip/Postal code: 27101-2815
County: Forsyth
Country: USA
Mailing address: PO BOX 3159
Mailing city: WINSTON SALEM
Mailing state: NC
Mailing zip: 27102-3159
General Phone: (336) 727-7211
Advertising Phone: (336) 727-7492
Editorial Phone: (336) 727-7359
General/National Adv. E-mail: wbuschmann@wsjournal.com
Display Adv. E-mail: gwhiting@wsjournal.com
Classified Adv. e-mail: myclassifiedad@wsjournal.com
Editorial e-mail: letters@wsjournal.com
Primary Website: www.journalnow.com
Mthly Avg Unique Visitors: 710000
Year Established: 1897
News Services: AP, NYT, LAT-WP., TNS,
Special Editions: Winston-Salem Monthly Magazine, SPARK Magazine, Carolina Weddings Magazine, City Guide, WSWorks Magazine, Physicians Directory, Calendar,
Special Weekly Sections: Business(daily); Food (Wed); Journal West (Wed); Relish (Thurs);
Syndicated Publications: Parade (S).
Delivery Methods: Newsstand`Carrier`Racks
Areas Served - City/County or Portion Thereof, or Zip codes: Winston-Salem, Forsyth Counties (NC)
Own Printing Facility?: Y
Commercial printers?: Y
Avg Free Circ: 1357
Sat. Circulation Paid: 36145
Sat. Circulation Free: 1088
Sun. Circulation Paid: 43625
Sun. Circulation Free: 1013
Audit By: AAM
Audit Date: 30.09.2018
Personnel: Alton Brown (Pub.); Andy Morrissey (Managing Ed.); Mick Scott (Editorial Page Ed.); David Stanfield (Controller); Fred Greer (Circ. Dir.); Frank Clayton (Production Plant Manager); Carrie Benoit (HR Dir.); Kenwyn Caranna (Digital Content Ed.); Ragan Robinson (Digital Editor); Walt D. Unks (Photo Ed.); D. Jereoldene Young (City Ed.); Jennifer M. Young (Night Ed.)
Parent company (for newspapers): BH Media Group; Lee Enterprises, Incorporated

NORTH DAKOTA

THE BISMARCK TRIBUNE

Street address 1: 707 E Front Ave
Street address city: Bismarck
Street address state: ND
Zip/Postal code: 58504-5646
County: Burleigh
Country: USA
Mailing address: PO BOX 5516
Mailing city: BISMARCK
Mailing state: ND
Mailing zip: 58506-5516
General Phone: (701) 223-2500
Advertising Phone: (701) 250-8205
Editorial Phone: (701) 250-8247
General/National Adv. E-mail: brad.peltz@bismarcktribune.com
Display Adv. E-mail: brad.peltz@bismarcktribune.com
Classified Adv. e-mail: lisa.weisz@bismarcktribune.com
Editorial e-mail: news@bismarktribune.com
Primary Website: www.bismarcktribune.com
Mthly Avg Views: 5000000
Year Established: 1873
News Services: AP, LAT-WP, NEA.
Special Editions: Solutions (Quarterly).
Special Weekly Sections: Voices (Mon); Business Page (S); Religion Page (Thur); Business Page (Tues); Best Food Day (Wed).
Syndicated Publications: Parade Magazine (S).
Delivery Methods: Mail`Newsstand`Carrier`Racks
Areas Served - City/County or Portion Thereof, or Zip codes: Burleigh County
Own Printing Facility?: Y
Commercial printers?: Y
Sat. Circulation Paid: 21019
Sun. Circulation Paid: 25690
Audit By: AAM
Audit Date: 30.09.2018
Personnel: Libby Simes (Pub); Stacey Lang (Mktg. Mgr.); Chad Kourajian (HR Mgr.); Ken Bohl (Circ. Dir.); Vicky Weiss (Librarian); Steve Wallick (News Ed.); Mike McCleary (Photographer); Karen Herzog (Religion Reporter); Terry Alveshere; Duane Crabbe (Retail Ad. Mgr., Sales Mgr., The Finder); Keith Darnay (Online Mgr.); Stace Gooding (Systems Admin.); Robert Reidell (Sports Reporter); David Braton (Pub.)
Parent company (for newspapers): Dispatch-Argus; Lee Enterprises, Incorporated

DEVILS LAKE JOURNAL

Street address 1: 516 4th St NE
Street address city: Devils Lake
Street address state: ND
Zip/Postal code: 58301-2502
County: Ramsey
Country: USA
Mailing address: PO BOX 1200
Mailing city: DEVILS LAKE
Mailing state: ND
Mailing zip: 58301-1200
General Phone: (701) 662-2127
Advertising Phone: (701) 662-2127
Editorial Phone: (701) 662-2127
General/National Adv. E-mail: advertising@devilslakejournal.com
Display Adv. E-mail: advertising@devilslakejournal.com
Classified Adv. e-mail: classifieds@devilslakejournal.com
Editorial e-mail: news@devilslakejournal.com
Primary Website: www.devilslakejournal.com
Mthly Avg Views: 4727202
Year Established: 1906
News Services: AP.
Syndicated Publications: TV Preview (Fri); Golden Opportunities (Monthly); American Profile (Weekly).
Areas Served - City/County or Portion Thereof, or Zip codes: Devils Lake (ND)
Own Printing Facility?: Y
Audit By: Sworn/Estimate/Non-Audited
Audit Date: 12.07.2019
Personnel: Louise Oleson (Mng. Ed.); Patty Schwab (Class. Ad. Mgr.); Melinda Bennes (Circ. Mgr.); J. Reed Anderson (G.M.)
Parent company (for newspapers): CherryRoad Media; Gannett

THE DICKINSON PRESS

Street address 1: 1815 1st St W
Street address city: Dickinson
Street address state: ND
Zip/Postal code: 58601-2463
County: Stark
Country: USA
Mailing address: 1815 1ST ST W
Mailing city: DICKINSON
Mailing state: ND
Mailing zip: 58601-2463
General Phone: 701-225-8111
Advertising Phone: (701) 456-1220
Editorial Phone: (701) 456-1205
General/National Adv. E-mail: bcarruth@thedickinsonpress.com
Display Adv. E-mail: bcarruth@thedickinsonpress.com
Editorial e-mail: DMonke@thedickinsonpress.com
Primary Website: www.thedickinsonpress.com
Avg Free Circ: 169
Sun. Circulation Paid: 5599
Sun. Circulation Free: 169
Audit By: VAC
Audit Date: 30.09.2016
Personnel: Harvey Brock (Publisher); Bob Carruth (Adv. Dir); Joy Schoch (Bus. Mgr.); John Hodges (Cir. Mgr); Dustin Monke (Mng. Ed.); Linda Sailer (Lifestyles Ed.); Jeremy Kadrmas (Prod. Mgr); Colton Pool (Sports Ed.)
Parent company (for newspapers): Forum Communications

INFORUM

Street address 1: 101 5th St N
Street address city: Fargo
Street address state: ND
Zip/Postal code: 58102-4826
County: Cass
Country: USA
Mailing address: 101 5TH ST N
Mailing city: FARGO
Mailing state: ND
Mailing zip: 58102-4826
General Phone: (701) 235-7311
Advertising Phone: (701) 241-5431
Editorial Phone: (701) 235-7311
General/National Adv. E-mail: advsales@forumcomm.com
Display Adv. E-mail: natladv@forumcomm.com
Classified Adv. e-mail: classifieds@forumcomm.com
Editorial e-mail: letters@forumcomm.com
Primary Website: www.inforum.com
Year Established: 1891
News Services: AP, LAT-WP.
Special Editions: Auto Care (Apr); Generations (+55) (Aug); Celebrate Christmas (Dec); Generations (+55) (Jan); Father's Day (Jun); Generations (+55) (May); Generations (+55) (Nov); Auto Care (Oct).
Special Weekly Sections: Farmers Forum (Fri); Sports (Mon); Travel (S); TV Forum (Sat); Financial (Tues); Food (Wed).
Syndicated Publications: Relish (Monthly); Parade (S).
Own Printing Facility?: Y
Sat. Circulation Paid: 32135
Sun. Circulation Paid: 32386
Audit By: AAM
Audit Date: 31.03.2019
Personnel: William C. Marcil (Publisher/COO/Executive Vice President); Matthew Von Pinnon (Ed.); Amy Fredrickson (Adv. Dir.); Lloyd Case (Pres./COO); John Hajostek (CFO); Kate Freimanis (HR Dir.); Kerri Kava (Circ. Coord., Newspapers in Educ.); Jack Zaleski (Editorial Page Ed.); John Lamb (Features Ed.); Mark Merck (Page Des.); Mike Vosburg (Photo Ed.); Jay Ulku (News Ed., Bus.); Rob Beer (Online Ed.); Jaclyn Hollands (Multi-Media Sales Mgr.); Scott Schmeltzer (Dir. of Adv.); Wendy Reuer (Asst. Ed., W.F. Pioneer); Sherri Richards (Features/Business Editor); Dave Roepke (News Dir.); Kevin Schnepf (Sports Ed.); Heidi Tetzman (Asst. Feautures Ed.); Heidi Shaffer (Deputy Editor)
Parent company (for newspapers): Forum Communications Co.

GRAND FORKS HERALD

Street address 1: 375 2nd Ave N
Street address city: Grand Forks
Street address state: ND
Zip/Postal code: 58203-3707
County: Grand Forks
Country: USA
Mailing address: PO BOX 6008
Mailing city: GRAND FORKS
Mailing state: ND
Mailing zip: 58203
General Phone: (701) 780-1160
Advertising Phone: (701) 780-1156
Editorial Phone: (701) 780-1100
General/National Adv. E-mail: slord@gfherald.com
Display Adv. E-mail: slord@gfherald.com
Classified Adv. e-mail: msorensen@gfherald.com
Editorial e-mail: kstromsodt@gfherald.com
Primary Website: www.grandforksherald.com
Mthly Avg Views: 4199638
Mthly Avg Unique Visitors: 549687
Year Established: 1879
News Services: Forum News Service
Special Editions: Home and Garden (April); Bride & Groom (Dec); Progress (Jan); East Grand Forks Pride (Jul); Senior Lifestyles (Jun); Coupon Book (Mar); Chamber of Commerce (May); Senior Lifestyles (Nov); Fall Home Improvement (Oct); College (Sept).
Special Weekly Sections: Expanded Sports (Mon);Business (Sat); Outdoors (Sunday)
Syndicated Publications: Relish (Monthly); Parade (S).
Delivery Methods: Mail`Newsstand`Carrier`Racks
Areas Served - City/County or Portion Thereof, or Zip codes: 582 and 567 inclusive
Own Printing Facility?: Y
Commercial printers?: Y
Avg Free Circ: 27
Sun. Circulation Paid: 20992
Sun. Circulation Free: 27
Audit By: VAC
Audit Date: 30.09.2016
Personnel: Anita Geffre (Cont.); Kirsten Stromsodt (Assigning Ed.); Tom Dennis (Editorial Page Ed.); Wayne Nelson (Sports Ed.); Mark Young (IT Dir.); Keith Haus (Prodn. Mgr., Pressroom); Korrie Wenzel (Pub.); Staci Lord (Adv. Dir.); Beth Bohlman (circulation director)
Parent company (for newspapers): Forum Communications Co.

THE JAMESTOWN SUN

Street address 1: 121 3rd St NW
Street address city: Jamestown
Street address state: ND
Zip/Postal code: 58401-3127
County: Stutsman
Country: USA
Mailing address: PO BOX 1760
Mailing city: JAMESTOWN
Mailing state: ND
Mailing zip: 58402-1760
General Phone: (701) 252-3120
Advertising Phone: (701) 252-3120
Editorial Phone: (701) 252-3120
General/National Adv. E-mail: rkeller@jamestownsun.com
Display Adv. E-mail: jsadvertising@daktel.com
Classified Adv. e-mail: rmcdonald@jamestownsun.com
Editorial e-mail: ksteiner@jamestownsun.com
Primary Website: www.jamestownsun.com
News Services: AP.
Special Editions: Auto Show (Apr); Sport and Home (Feb); Progress (Mar); Fire Prevention (Oct).
Special Weekly Sections: Outdoors (Fri); Food (Sat); TV & Entertainment (Thur); Bridal (Wed).
Syndicated Publications: Relish (Monthly); Parade (S).
Delivery Methods: Mail`Newsstand`Carrier`Racks
Areas Served - City/County or Portion Thereof, or Zip codes: Jamestown & Stutsman Counties (ND)
Own Printing Facility?: N
Commercial printers?: N
Sat. Circulation Paid: 4168
Sat. Circulation Free: 0
Audit By: VAC
Audit Date: 30.09.2017
Personnel: John M. Steiner (Picture Ed.); Kathy Steiner (Mng. Ed.); Boyd Anderson (Press Foreman); Masaki Ova (Asst. Ed.); John Steiner (Chief Photo.); Dave Selvig (Sports Ed.); Tom LaVenture (Assignment Reporter); Kathy Hilgeman (Office manager)
Parent company (for newspapers): Forum Communications Co.

MINOT DAILY NEWS

Street address 1: 301 4th Street SE
Street address city: Minot
Street address state: ND
Zip/Postal code: 58701
County: Ward
Country: USA
Mailing address: PO BOX 1150
Mailing city: MINOT
Mailing state: ND
Mailing zip: 58702-1150
General Phone: (701) 857-1900
Advertising Phone: (701) 857-1963

Editorial Phone: (701) 857-1950
General/National Adv. E-mail: jhart@minotdailynews.com
Display Adv. E-mail: jhart@minotdailynews.com
Classified Adv. e-mail: classads@minotdailynews.com
Editorial e-mail: editor@minotdailynews.com
Primary Website: www.minotdailynews.com
Mthly Avg Views: 655138
Mthly Avg Unique Visitors: 158755
News Services: AP.
Special Editions: Year in Review (Jan);; Senior Scene (Qterly), Inside Ag (Qrterly), Coupon Book (Jan) (Mar); Progress (Apr); Destination Minot (May); Inside Energy (June/Dec), Booming Basin (Monthly, Graduation (May); State Fair (Jun); Football Preview(Aug); Hometown (Sept); Norsk Fest (Oct); Pulse (Nov); Readers' Choice (December)
Special Weekly Sections: Agriculture (Mon); Outdoor (S); Agriculture (Sat); Best Automotive Day (Thur); Best Food Day (Wed). Machinery Row (Sat)
Syndicated Publications: Parade (S).
Delivery Methods: Mail`Newsstand`Carrier`Racks
Areas Served - City/County or Portion Thereof, or Zip codes: 58701
Own Printing Facility?: Y
Commercial printers?: Y
Avg Free Circ: 221
Sat. Circulation Paid: 11004
Sat. Circulation Free: 221
Sun. Circulation Paid: 11824
Sun. Circulation Free: 120
Audit By: AAM
Audit Date: 31.03.2018
Personnel: Jim Hart; Mike Sasser (Editor); Kolby Jensen; Garrick Hodge; Dan McDonald (Publisher)
Parent company (for newspapers): Ogden Newspapers Inc.

VALLEY CITY TIMES-RECORD

Street address 1: 146 3rd St NE
Street address city: Valley City
Street address state: ND
Zip/Postal code: 58072-3047
County: Barnes
Country: USA
Mailing address: PO BOX 697
Mailing city: VALLEY CITY
Mailing state: ND
Mailing zip: 58072-0697
General Phone: (701) 845-0463
Advertising Phone: (701) 845-0463
Editorial Phone: (701) 845-0463
General/National Adv. E-mail: trads.dave@gmail.com
Display Adv. E-mail: trads.pam@gmail.com
Classified Adv. e-mail: trclass@times-online.com
Editorial e-mail: treditor@times-online.com
Primary Website: www.times-online.com
Year Established: 1879
News Services: AP, NEA.
Special Editions: Car Care Tab (Apr); Back-to-School (Aug); Last Minute Gift Guide (Dec); Valentines (Feb); First Baby of the Year Tab (Jan); Progress (Jul); Senior Scene Tab (Jun); Girl Scouts (Mar); Graduation Tab (May); Holiday Preview (Nov); Fire Prevention Tab (Oct);
Special Weekly Sections: Church Directory (Fri); Business Page (Mon-fri); TV (Thur); Ag Page (Wed); Super Service Directory (Weekly).
Syndicated Publications: T-R Shopper (Other); American Profile (Weekly).
Delivery Methods: Mail`Racks
Areas Served - City/County or Portion Thereof, or Zip codes: Barnes County (ND)
Own Printing Facility?: Y
Commercial printers?: Y
Audit By: Sworn/Estimate/Non-Audited
Audit Date: 12.07.2019
Personnel: Brenda Tompt (Office Mgr.); Pam Stark (Sales); Paul Riemerman (Ed.); Tina Olson (Prod. Mgr.); Bill Parsons (Publisher)
Parent company (for newspapers): Horizon Publications Inc.

THE DAILY NEWS

Street address 1: 601 Dakota Ave
Street address city: Wahpeton
Street address state: ND
Zip/Postal code: 58075-4325
County: Richland
Country: USA
Mailing address: PO BOX 760
Mailing city: WAHPETON
Mailing state: ND
Mailing zip: 58074-0760
General Phone: (701) 642-8585
Advertising Phone: (701) 642-8585
Editorial Phone: (701) 642-8585
General/National Adv. E-mail: ads@wahpetondailynews.com
Display Adv. E-mail: ads@wahpetondailynews.com
Classified Adv. e-mail: ads@wahpetondailynews.com
Editorial e-mail: editor@wahpetondailynews.com
Primary Website: www.wahpetondailynews.com
News Services: AP.
Special Editions: Progress Issue (Annually); School Activities Issue (Fall); News in Review (Jan); Voter's Guide (election years) (Nov); Bridal Issue (Other).
Syndicated Publications: Channeling (TV Section) (Fri); American Profile (Weekly).
Delivery Methods: Mail`Newsstand`Carrier`Racks
Areas Served - City/County or Portion Thereof, or Zip codes: Richland & Wahpeton Counties (ND) and Wilkin County (MN), Breckenridge (MN)
Own Printing Facility?: Y
Commercial printers?: Y
Avg Free Circ: 17
Sun. Circulation Paid: 2216
Audit By: Sworn/Estimate/Non-Audited
Audit Date: 12.07.2019
Personnel: Tara Klostreich (Pub.); Kathy Leinen (Mng. Ed.); Turner Blaufuss (Sports Ed.); Candace Engstrom (Prod. Mgr.); Janine Berg (Circ. Clerk); Carrie McDermott (Asst. Mng. Ed.); Frank Stanko (Reporter); Diana Hermes (Multi-Media Sales Rep); Patty Fugleberg (Business Office Manager)
Parent company (for newspapers): Wick Communications

WILLISTON DAILY HERALD

Street address 1: PO Box 1447
Street address city: Williston
Street address state: ND
Zip/Postal code: 58802-1447
County: Williams
Country: USA
Mailing state: ND
Mailing zip: 58781-4006
General Phone: (701) 572-2165
Advertising Phone: (701) 572-2165
Editorial Phone: (701) 572-2165
General/National Adv. E-mail: advertising@willistonherald.com
Display Adv. E-mail: advertising@willistonherald.com
Classified Adv. e-mail: classified@willistonherald.com
Editorial e-mail: editor@willistonherald.com
Primary Website: www.willistonherald.com
Mthly Avg Views: 58000
Mthly Avg Unique Visitors: 56264
Year Established: 1911
News Services: AP, Forum
Special Weekly Sections: TV Guide
Delivery Methods: Mail`Newsstand`Carrier`Racks
Areas Served - City/County or Portion Thereof, or Zip codes: Northwest ND & Northeast MT
Own Printing Facility?: Y
Commercial printers?: Y
Avg Free Circ: 0
Sat. Circulation Paid: 2834
Sat. Circulation Free: 0
Sun. Circulation Paid: 2834
Sun. Circulation Free: 0
Audit By: VAC
Audit Date: 30.09.2016
Personnel: Aaron Hanson (Comp. Dir.); Leah-Ann Kleber (Ret. Sales Mgr.); Tara Klostreich (Pub.); Jamie Kelly (Managing Ed.); Kathy Evenson (Circ. Mgr.)
Parent company (for newspapers): Wick Communications

OHIO

AKRON BEACON JOURNAL

Street address 1: 388 S Main St., Suite 720
Street address city: Akron
Street address state: OH
Zip/Postal code: 44308-1510
County: Summit
Country: USA
Mailing address: PO BOX 640
Mailing city: AKRON
Mailing state: OH
Mailing zip: 44309-0640
General Phone: (330) 996-3000
Advertising Phone: (330) 996-3410
Editorial Phone: (330) 996-3512
General/National Adv. E-mail: lcarver@thebeaconjournal.com
Display Adv. E-mail: lcarver@thebeaconjournal.com
Classified Adv. e-mail: lcarver@thebeaconjournal.com
Editorial e-mail: bjnews@thebeaconjournal.com
Primary Website: www.ohio.com
Mthly Avg Views: 7718024
Mthly Avg Unique Visitors: 1469315
Year Established: 1839
News Services: AP, MCT, RN.
Special Editions: New Year, New Career (Jan), Super Bowl; Summer Camp Guide; Beacon's Best; Envision; Auto Show; Home & Flower Show (Feb), New Baby News; Greater Akron Chamber (Mar), Great Places to Work; Beacon's Best Results(April), Star Students; Nurses Week; Summer Fun Guide; Green Chamber (May), Bridgestone Fan Guide; Boston Mills Artfest; Cavs Finals; Cavs Championship (June), High School Preview (Aug), Autumn Adventures (Sep), Halloween Happenings (Oct), Holiday Gift Guide; Veteran's Day; Beacon Savings Book (Nov), Holiday Gift Guide (Dec)
Special Weekly Sections: American Profile (Mon); Your Health (Tue); Food (Wed); Auto, Entertainment (Thur); Real Estate (Fri); Home, Saturday Lifestyle, Savvy Shopper, Relish, Spry (Sat); Life, Job Source (Sun)
Areas Served - City/County or Portion Thereof, or Zip codes: Summit, Medina, Stark, Portage, Wayne and parts of Cuyahoga Counties (OH)
Own Printing Facility?: N
Commercial printers?: N
Avg Free Circ: 1506
Sat. Circulation Paid: 56778
Sat. Circulation Free: 571
Sun. Circulation Paid: 59990
Sun. Circulation Free: 566
Audit By: AAM
Audit Date: 31.03.2019
Personnel: Tim Betz (Controller); Mark Cohen (Publisher); Bruce Winges (Night Mng. Ed.); Shaun Schweitzer (VP/Circulation); Dawn Bonfiglio (IT Director); Lori Carver (VP/Advertising); Jay Hunter (HR and Labor Relations Director); Cheryl Powell (Mng. Ed.)
Parent company (for newspapers): Gannett; CherryRoad Media

THE REVIEW

Street address 1: 40 S. Linden Avenue
Street address city: Alliance
Street address state: OH
Zip/Postal code: 44601
County: Stark
Country: USA
Mailing address: 40 S LINDEN AVE
Mailing city: ALLIANCE
Mailing state: OH
Mailing zip: 44601-2447
General Phone: (330) 821-1200
Advertising Phone: (330) 821-1200
Editorial Phone: (330) 821-1300
General/National Adv. E-mail: reviewads@the-review.com
Display Adv. E-mail: reviewads@the-review.com
Classified Adv. e-mail: classifieds@the-review.com
Editorial e-mail: reviewedit@the-review.com
Primary Website: www.the-review.com
Year Established: 1888
News Services: AP, CNS, DF, DJ, NYT, SHNS, TMS.
Special Editions: Year in Review (Jan).
Special Weekly Sections: Real Estate (Fri); Church Page (Sat); Entertainment-Let's Go (Thur); Business Page (Wed).
Syndicated Publications: TV Magazine (Fri); American Profile (Weekly).
Areas Served - City/County or Portion Thereof, or Zip codes: Alliance (OH) and Surrounding areas
Avg Free Circ: 323
Sat. Circulation Paid: 9409
Sat. Circulation Free: 258
Audit By: CAC
Audit Date: 30.06.2017
Personnel: Laura Kessel (Ed.); Jim Porter (Gen. Mgr.); Ron Hurst (Circ. Dir.); Patti Cochran (Accounts Dir.); Mindy Cannon (Adv. Dir.); Missy Beadnell (District Mgr.); Sue Fryfogle (CSR); Robert Todor (Sports Ed.)
Parent company (for newspapers): CherryRoad Media; Gannett Company Inc.

ASHLAND TIMES-GAZETTE

Street address 1: 40 East Second Street
Street address city: Ashland
Street address state: OH
Zip/Postal code: 44805
County: Ashland
Country: USA
Mailing address: 40 E 2ND ST
Mailing city: ASHLAND
Mailing state: OH
Mailing zip: 44805-2398
General Phone: (419) 281-0581
Advertising Phone: (419) 281-0581
Editorial Phone: (419) 281-0581 ext. 211
General/National Adv. E-mail: mkraker@times-gazette.com
Display Adv. E-mail: internetadvertising@dixcom.com
Classified Adv. e-mail: classified@times-gazette.com
Editorial e-mail: letters@times-gazette.com
Primary Website: www.times-gazette.com
Year Established: 1850
News Services: AP.
Special Editions: Auto Tab (Apr); Football Preview (Aug); Christmas Songbook (Dec); Senior Citizens (Feb); Bridal Tab (Jan); Senior Citizens (Jul); Balloon Fest (Jun); Spring Home Improvement (Mar); Hospital Nursing (May); Holiday Cookbook (Nov); Health Focus (Oct); Fair (
Special Weekly Sections: Clip2Save (Mon); Health, Teen (Tue); Business (Wed/Fri); Food (Wed); Real Estate, Religion (Fri); Agricultural (Sat)
Syndicated Publications: TV Weekly (Sat).
Delivery Methods: Mail`Newsstand`Carrier`Racks
Areas Served - City/County or Portion Thereof, or Zip codes: Ashland County
Own Printing Facility?: Y
Commercial printers?: N
Avg Free Circ: 633
Sat. Circulation Paid: 7746
Sat. Circulation Free: 633
Audit By: AAM
Audit Date: 31.03.2018
Personnel: Bill Albrecht (Pub.); Ted Daniels (Ed.); Aaron Bass (Adv. Dir./Gen. Mgr.); Bill Lally (Circ. Dir.); Jarred Opatz (Ed.); Mike Plant (Sports Ed.)
Parent company (for newspapers): CherryRoad Media; Gannett Company Inc.

STAR BEACON

Street address 1: 4626 Park Ave
Street address city: Ashtabula
Street address state: OH
Zip/Postal code: 44004-6933
County: Ashtabula
Country: USA
Mailing address: PO BOX 2100
Mailing city: ASHTABULA
Mailing state: OH
Mailing zip: 44005-2100
General Phone: (440) 998-2323
Advertising Phone: (440) 998-2323 Ext. 102
Editorial Phone: (440) 994-2323
General/National Adv. E-mail: marketplace@starbeacon.com
Display Adv. E-mail: marketplace@starbeacon.com
Classified Adv. e-mail: marketplace@starbeacon.com
Editorial e-mail: mhutton@starbeacon.com
Primary Website: www.starbeacon.com
Year Established: 1888
News Services: AP.
Special Editions: Football Features (Aug); Christmas (Dec); Bridal (Jan); Dog Days (Jul); Ashtabula County Almanac (Jun); Washington's Birthday (Mar); Health Care (May); Family Life (Monthly); Women in Business (Nov); Covered Bridge (Oct); Progress (Sept).
Special Weekly Sections: Entertainment (Fri); Best Food Day (Mon); Best Food Day (S); Church News (Sat).
Syndicated Publications: Relish (Monthly); TV Scene Magazine (S); American Profile (Weekly).
Areas Served - City/County or Portion Thereof, or Zip codes: Ashtabula, Lake, Geauga, Trumbull, Crawford, Erie Counties (OH)
Avg Free Circ: 580
Sat. Circulation Paid: 7525
Sat. Circulation Free: 580
Sun. Circulation Paid: 8810
Sun. Circulation Free: 325

Audit By: AAM
Audit Date: 31.12.2017
Personnel: Jamie Beacom (Pub. / Adv. Dir.); Warren Dillaway (Staff Writ. / Photo.); Matt Hutton (Ed.); Lisa Kondik (Bus. Mgr.); Pam Harper (CS Mgr.); Steve Traud (Dir. of Aud. Dev. (Cir.)); Shelley Lipps (Adv. Acct. Exec.)
Parent company (for newspapers): CNHI, LLC; CNHI, LLC

THE ATHENS MESSENGER

Street address 1: 9300 Johnson Hollow Rd
Street address city: Athens
Street address state: OH
Zip/Postal code: 45701-9028
County: Athens
Country: USA
Mailing address: PO BOX 4210
Mailing city: ATHENS
Mailing state: OH
Mailing zip: 45701-4210
General Phone: (740) 592-6612
Advertising Phone: (740) 592-6612 ext. 209
Editorial Phone: (740) 592-6612 Ext. 224
General/National Adv. E-mail: jbunch@athensmessenger.com
Display Adv. E-mail: gchristensen@athensmessenger.com
Classified Adv. e-mail: pdennis@athensmessenger.com
Editorial e-mail: jhiggins@athensmessenger.com
Primary Website: www.athensohiotoday.com
Year Established: 1848
News Services: AP, SHNS.
Special Editions: New Babies (Apr); Football Tab (Aug); Wedding Guide (Feb); County Fair (Jul); Fashion (Mar); Spring/Summer Car Care (May); Basketball Tab (Nov); Fall Car Care (Oct).
Special Weekly Sections: Church Page (Fri); Home & Garden (S).
Syndicated Publications: Color Comics (S); American Profile (Weekly).
Delivery Methods: Newsstand`Carrier`Racks
Areas Served - City/County or Portion Thereof, or Zip codes: Athens County (OH)
Sat. Circulation Paid: 11272
Sun. Circulation Paid: 11375
Audit By: Sworn/Estimate/Non-Audited
Audit Date: 12.07.2019
Personnel: Mark Cohen (Pub.); Tyler Buchanan (Ed.); Amanda Montgomery (Regional Advertising Dir.); Kevin Wiseman (Sports Ed.); Kathy Kerr (Community Ed.)
Parent company (for newspapers): Adams Publishing Group, LLC

BELLEFONTAINE EXAMINER

Street address 1: 127 E Chillicothe Ave
Street address city: Bellefontaine
Street address state: OH
Zip/Postal code: 43311-1957
County: Logan
Country: USA
Mailing address: PO BOX 40
Mailing city: BELLEFONTAINE
Mailing state: OH
Mailing zip: 43311-0040
General Phone: (937) 592-3060
Advertising Phone: (937) 651-2125
Editorial Phone: (937) 651-1124
General/National Adv. E-mail: ads@examiner.org
Display Adv. E-mail: bchampman@examiner.org
Classified Adv. e-mail: classifieds@examiner.org
Editorial e-mail: news@examiner.org
Primary Website: www.examiner.org
Mthly Avg Views: 175000
Year Established: 1891
News Services: AP.
Special Editions: Real Estate Tab (Apr); Sale Days (Aug); Christmas Greetings (Dec); Home Maintenance (Fall); Sale Days (Feb); Real Estate Tab (Jul); Bridal (Jun); Indian Lake Resort Tab (May); Real Estate Tab (Sept); Home Maintenance (Spring).
Areas Served - City/County or Portion Thereof, or Zip codes: Logan County (OH)
Own Printing Facility?: Y
Commercial printers?: N
Sat. Circulation Paid: 9130
Audit By: Sworn/Estimate/Non-Audited
Audit Date: 12.07.2019
Personnel: Janet K. Hubbard (Pub.); Jon B. Hubbard (Vice Pres.); Bob Chapman (Adv. Mgr.); Jill Thomas (Circ. Mgr.); Miriam Baier (Ed.); Matt Hammond (Sports Ed.); TJ Hubbarb (Asst. Gen. Mgr.); Mandy Loehr (Staff Writ.); Diane Lewis (Class.); Jim Strzalka (Adv. Sales. Rep.)
Parent company (for newspapers): Hubbard Publishing

SENTINEL-TRIBUNE

Street address 1: 300 E Poe Rd
Street address city: Bowling Green
Street address state: OH
Zip/Postal code: 43402-1329
County: Wood
Country: USA
Mailing address: PO BOX 88
Mailing city: BOWLING GREEN
Mailing state: OH
Mailing zip: 43402-0088
General Phone: (419) 352-4611
Advertising Phone: (419) 352-4611
Editorial Phone: (419) 352-4611
General/National Adv. E-mail: ads@sentinel-tribune.com
Display Adv. E-mail: ads@sentinel-tribune.com
Classified Adv. e-mail: ads@sentinel-tribune.com
Editorial e-mail: letters@sentinel-tribune.com
Primary Website: www.sent-trib.com
Year Established: 1867
News Services: AP.
Special Editions: Art Walk (Apr); Back-to-College (Aug); Bride & Groom (Sep); Baby (Jan); Fair (Jun); Travel & Recreation (May); Christmas Gifts (Nov); Health & Fitness (Semi-yearly).
Special Weekly Sections: Church Page (Fri); Best Food Day (Thur); Auto Section (Mon); Real Estate (Thur)
Syndicated Publications: USA WEEKEND Magazine (Fri).
Delivery Methods: Mail`Newsstand`Carrier`Racks
Areas Served - City/County or Portion Thereof, or Zip codes: 43402, 43403, 43551, 44817, 43406, 43511, 43413, 43525, 43437, 43443, 43447, 45872, 43619, 43450, 43451, 43457, 43460, 43462, 43565, 43465, 43466, 43569
Own Printing Facility?: Y
Commercial printers?: Y
Avg Free Circ: 178
Sat. Circulation Paid: 5392
Sat. Circulation Free: 178
Audit By: AAM
Audit Date: 31.03.2019
Personnel: T.M. Haswell (President); Kathryn A. Haswell (Sec./Treasurer); Randy Machan (Cir. Mgr.); Karmen Concannon (Pub.); Banks Dishmon (Adv. Dir.); Debbie Rodgers (Ed.)
Parent company (for newspapers): AIM Media Indiana

THE PLAIN DEALER

Street address 1: 4800 Tiedeman Rd
Street address city: Brooklyn
Street address state: OH
Zip/Postal code: 44144-2336
County: Cuyahoga
Country: USA
Mailing address: 4800 Tiedeman Rd
Mailing city: Brooklyn
Mailing state: OH
Mailing zip: 44144-2336
General Phone: (216) 999-5000
Editorial Phone: (216) 999-4825
Editorial e-mail: grodrigue@plaind.com
Primary Website: www.plaindealer.com
Mthly Avg Unique Visitors: 3168000
Year Established: 1842
News Services: AP, Washington Post, Tribune News Service, Bloomberg
Special Editions: Greater Cleveland Auto Show (Feb.); Cleveland Indians preview (April); A-List Dining Guide (April); Top Workplaces (June); High School Football preview (Aug.); Ohio State/College Football preview (Aug.); Cleveland Browns/NFL preview (Sept.); Cleveland Cavaliers/NBA preview (Oct.)
Special Weekly Sections: Taste (Wed); Friday Magazine (Entertainment) (Fri). Arts & Life (Sun), Travel (Sun) Seasonal: Varsity-High School football (Sat), Buckeye Extra-OSU/college football (Sun), Browns Extra-Pro football (Mon)
Delivery Methods: Mail`Newsstand`Carrier`Racks
Own Printing Facility?: Y
Commercial printers?: Y
Sat. Circulation Paid: 138375
Sun. Circulation Paid: 245320
Audit By: Sworn/Estimate/Non-Audited
Audit Date: 12.07.2019
Personnel: Bryan Schneider (Dir. Circ Distribution & Transportation); Joseph Bowman (VP of Operations); Damon Borom (Prodn. Mgr., Machinists/Engineers); Nick Vangelos (Prodn. Tech. Service Mgr.); Brian Ritchie (IT Prod System Mgr); Kathryn A. Kroll (Director of Print Operations); George Rodrigue (President & Editor); Tim Warsinskey (Managing Editor); Paul Cavanagh (Dir Labor & Empl Relations); Jennifer Szucs (Bus. Sol. Mgr., IT)
Parent company (for newspapers): Advance Publications, Inc.

THE BRYAN TIMES

Street address 1: 127 S Walnut St
Street address city: Bryan
Street address state: OH
Zip/Postal code: 43506-1718
County: Williams
Country: USA
Mailing address: 127 S WALNUT ST
Mailing city: BRYAN
Mailing state: OH
Mailing zip: 43506-1718
General Phone: (419) 636-1111
Advertising Phone: (419) 636-1111
Editorial Phone: (419) 636-1111
General/National Adv. E-mail: ads@bryantimes.com
Display Adv. E-mail: ads@bryantimes.com
Classified Adv. e-mail: classifieds@bryantimes.com
Editorial e-mail: editor@bryantimes.com
Primary Website: www.bryantimes.com
Year Established: 1949
News Services: AP, CT, CNS, CSM, TMS.
Special Editions: Car Care (Apr); Back to School (Aug); Gift Guide Tab (Dec); Personal Tax & Finance Guide (Feb); News Review (Jan); Fair Tab (Jul); Eye Care/Vision (Mar); Summer Guide (May); Christmas Opening (Nov); Your Health Tab (Oct); Fall Home Improvement Tab (Sept).
Special Weekly Sections: Business (Wed); Farm (Wed); Church (Fri); Football (In Season); Real Estate (Fri)
Syndicated Publications: Relish (Monthly); USA WEEKEND Magazine (Sat); American Profile (Weekly).
Areas Served - City/County or Portion Thereof, or Zip codes: 43501, 43505, 43506, 43517, 43518, 43531, 43543, 43554, 43557, 43570, 43502, 43521, 43553
Avg Free Circ: 117
Sat. Circulation Paid: 7995
Sat. Circulation Free: 117
Audit By: AAM
Audit Date: 30.09.2014
Personnel: Christopher Cullis (Chrmn./Pres./Pub.); Shelley Davis (Adv.); Sally Heaston (Gen. Mgr.); Mark J. Keller (Cir. Mgr.); Sharon Patten (Soc. Ed.); Max Reinhart (Asst. Ed.); Amy Thompson (Class. Adv. Mgr.); Don Koralewski (Ed.)
Parent company (for newspapers): Bryan Publishing Co.

THE DAILY JEFFERSONIAN

Street address 1: 831 Wheeling Avenue
Street address city: Cambridge
Street address state: OH
Zip/Postal code: 43725
County: Guernsey
Country: USA
Mailing address: PO BOX 10
Mailing city: CAMBRIDGE
Mailing state: OH
Mailing zip: 43725-0010
General Phone: (740) 439-3531
Advertising Phone: (740) 439-3532
Editorial Phone: (740) 439-3531
General/National Adv. E-mail: ads@daily-jeff.com
Display Adv. E-mail: ads@daily-jeff.com
Classified Adv. e-mail: kim@daily-jeff.com
Editorial e-mail: newsroom@daily-jeff.com
Primary Website: www.daily-jeff.com
Year Established: 1824
News Services: AP, Dixewire.
Special Editions: Babies (Apr); Back-to-School (Aug); Elected Officials Greetings (Dec); Health & Fitness (Feb); Tax Guide (Jan); Ohio Hills Folk Fest (Jul); Father's Day (Jun); Lawn & Garden (Mar); In Memoriam (May); Yuletide Gift Guide & Cash Give-away (Nov); Auto Care (
Special Weekly Sections: Best Food (Mon); Business, Engagements (Wed); Farm, Garden (Thur); Entertainment (Fri); Real Estate, Best Food Day, Stock, Market, Comics, Wedding, TV (Sun)
Syndicated Publications: Parade (S).
Avg Free Circ: 656
Sun. Circulation Paid: 8684
Sun. Circulation Free: 203
Audit By: AAM
Audit Date: 30.06.2017
Personnel: Andrew S. Dix (Pub.); Joyce Yontz (Controller); Chris Cryder (Cir. Dir.); Ray H. Booth (Exec. Ed.); Jeff Harrison (Sports Ed.); Ray Booth (Prodn. Mgr.); Kim Brenning (Adv. Dir.)
Parent company (for newspapers): CherryRoad Media; Gannett

THE REPOSITORY

Street address 1: 500 Market Ave S
Street address city: Canton
Street address state: OH
Zip/Postal code: 44702-2112
County: Stark
Country: USA
Mailing address: 500 Market Ave S
Mailing city: Canton
Mailing state: OH
Mailing zip: 44702-2112
General Phone: (330) 580-8500
Advertising Phone: (330) 580-8401
Editorial Phone: (330) 580-8300
General/National Adv. E-mail: joey.barlow@cantonrep.com
Display Adv. E-mail: sheila.casler@cantonrep.com
Classified Adv. e-mail: classconnect@cantonrep.com
Editorial e-mail: scott.brown@cantonrep.com
Primary Website: www.cantonrep.com
News Services: AP, CNS, LAT-WP.
Special Editions: Home and Garden (Apr); HS Football (Aug); Christmas Gift Guide (Dec); Weddings by Design (Jan); Professional Football Hall of Fame Tab (Jul); Senior Living (Jun); Spring Truck & Van (Mar); Summer Fun (May); Pizzazz (Monthly); Christmas Gift Guide (Nov); W
Special Weekly Sections: Best Food Day (Wed); Weekend Entertainment, Garden (Fri); Real Estate (Sat); Travel, Wheels, Medicine, Books, Education, Finance (Sun)
Syndicated Publications: Comics (S).
Areas Served - City/County or Portion Thereof, or Zip codes: 44702 and surrounding areas
Avg Free Circ: 6336
Sat. Circulation Paid: 31230
Sat. Circulation Free: 2190
Sun. Circulation Paid: 46498
Sun. Circulation Free: 21082
Audit By: AAM
Audit Date: 31.12.2017
Personnel: Jim Porter (Pub.); Rich Desrosiers (Exec. Ed.); Anita Dunn (Cir. Dir.); Sheila Casler (Advertising Sales Mgr.); Cam Denbrock (Single Copy Mgr.); Robin Foss (Home Delivery Mgr.); Pam Bittaker (Customer Service Mgr.); Chris Beaven (Sports Ed.); Joe Giampietro (Print News Ed.); Dan Kane (Ent. Ed.); Dwight Kier (Online News Ed.)
Parent company (for newspapers): Gannett; CherryRoad Media

THE DAILY STANDARD

Street address 1: 123 E Market St
Street address city: Celina
Street address state: OH
Zip/Postal code: 45822-1730
County: Mercer
Country: USA
Mailing address: PO BOX 140
Mailing city: CELINA
Mailing state: OH
Mailing zip: 45822-0140
General Phone: (419) 586-2371
Advertising Phone: (419) 584-1961
General/National Adv. E-mail: asnyder@dailystandard.com
Display Adv. E-mail: mpleiman@dailystandard.com
Classified Adv. e-mail: classad@dailystandard.com
Editorial e-mail: newsroom@dailystandard.com
Primary Website: www.dailystandard.com
Mthly Avg Views: 727000
Mthly Avg Unique Visitors: 58000
Year Established: 1848
News Services: AP, NYT, TNS.
Special Editions: Fall Sports (Aug); Christmas Greetings (Dec); Christmas Opening (Nov); Fall Opening (Sept).
Special Weekly Sections: State Line Farmer (Tues).

Areas Served - City/County or Portion Thereof, or Zip codes: Mercer & Auglaize Counties (OH)
Avg Free Circ: 0
Sat. Circulation Paid: 10000
Audit By: Sworn/Estimate/Non-Audited
Audit Date: 12.07.2019
Personnel: Dave Hoying (Bus. Mgr.); Aaron Snyder (Gen Manager); Frank Snyder (Publisher); Diane Buening (Circ. Mgr.); Pat Royse (Mng. Ed.); Betty Lawrence (Society/Women's Ed.); Ryan Hines (Sports Ed.); Kelly Braun (Wire Ed.); Larry Smelser (Prodn. Supt.)
Parent company (for newspapers): Snyder family

CHILLICOTHE GAZETTE

Street address 1: 50 W Main St
Street address city: Chillicothe
Street address state: OH
Zip/Postal code: 45601-3103
County: Ross
Country: USA
Mailing address: 50 W Main St.
Mailing city: Chillicothe
Mailing state: OH
Mailing zip: 45601-3103
General Phone: (740) 773-2111
Advertising Phone: (740) 775-7355
Editorial Phone: (740) 772-9368
General/National Adv. E-mail: cgoadv@nncogannett.com
Display Adv. E-mail: mrager@chillicothegazette.com
Classified Adv. e-mail: ksargent@mncogannett.com
Editorial e-mail: gaznews@nncogannett.com
Primary Website: www.chillicothegazette.com
Year Established: 1800
News Services: AP, LAT-WP.
Special Editions: Bridal/Weddings (Jan); Medical Directory (Feb) Ross County Fair (Aug); My Scioto Valley (Feb); Baby (Jun); Graduation (May); Holiday Gift Guide (Nov); Football Preview (August).
Special Weekly Sections: Transportation (Thur); Homes
Delivery Methods: Newsstand`Carrier`Racks
Areas Served - City/County or Portion Thereof, or Zip codes: Ross and Pike counties
Own Printing Facility?: N
Commercial printers?: N
Avg Free Circ: 50
Sat. Circulation Paid: 5130
Sat. Circulation Free: 50
Sun. Circulation Paid: 5589
Sun. Circulation Free: 50
Audit By: AAM
Audit Date: 31.03.2019
Personnel: Tonya Shipley (Planning Ed.); Jessie Balmert (State Government Rep.); Chris Balusik (Content Strategist); Toria Barnhart (Rep.); Jona Ison (Enterprise Rep.); David Wysong (Sports Rep.); Heather Bright (Oper. Mgr.)
Parent company (for newspapers): Gannett

THE CINCINNATI ENQUIRER

Street address 1: 312 Elm St
Street address city: Cincinnati
Street address state: OH
Zip/Postal code: 45202-2739
County: Hamilton
Country: USA
General Phone: (513) 721-2700
Advertising Phone: (513) 768-8404
Editorial Phone: (513) 768-8600
General/National Adv. E-mail: abaston@enquirer.com
Display Adv. E-mail: abaston@enquirer.com
Classified Adv. e-mail: abaston@enquirer.com
Editorial e-mail: ltrujillo@cincinnati.com
Primary Website: www.cincinnati.com; www.enquirermedia.com
Mthly Avg Views: 5200000
Mthly Avg Unique Visitors: 3300000
Year Established: 1841
News Services: AP, NYT, MCT, GNS.
Special Editions: Summer Vacations-Travel (Apr); Tennis Championships (Aug); Holiday Home Gift Guides (Dec); National Cruise Month Celebration (Feb); Warm Weather Travel Destinations (Jan); Regional Adventures (Jul); Homearama (Jun); Family Vacations (May); Holiday Gift Gu
Special Weekly Sections: Weather, Sports (Daily); Business, Sunday Forum, Good News, (Sun); Food, Classifieds (Wed); Healthy Living, Hometown (Thur); Weekend, Business (Fri); Home, Style, Hometown (Sat)
Syndicated Publications: USA WEEKEND Magazine (S).
Sat. Circulation Paid: 84430
Sun. Circulation Paid: 133477
Audit By: AAM
Audit Date: 31.03.2018
Personnel: Michael McCarter (Interim Editor); Denette Pfaffenberger (Group Dir/Home Delivery); Kate McGinty (Dir of News Content); Joe Powell (Dir. of Print Prod); Chris Strong (VP of Sales); Peter Bhatia (Ed. & VP of Audience Engagement); Jeff Lawson (Market Sales & Distribution Director); Libby Korosec (Client Strategy Director); John Berry (Major Sales & Marketing Manager)
Parent company (for newspapers): Gannett

THE CIRCLEVILLE HERALD

Street address 1: 401 E Main St
Street address city: Circleville
Street address state: OH
Zip/Postal code: 43113-1843
County: Pickaway
Country: USA
Mailing address: PO BOX 970
Mailing city: CIRCLEVILLE
Mailing state: OH
Mailing zip: 43113-0970
General Phone: (740) 474-3131
Advertising Phone: (740) 474-3131
Editorial Phone: (740) 474-3131
General/National Adv. E-mail: mklinebriel@circlevilleherald.com
Display Adv. E-mail: tmaynard@circlevilleherald.com
Classified Adv. e-mail: lhedrick@circlevilleherald.com
Editorial e-mail: news@circlevilleherald.com
Primary Website: www.circlevilleherald.com
Year Established: 1817
News Services: AP, U.S. Suburban Press Inc..
Special Editions: Real Estate (Apr); Football Review (Aug); Christmas Greetings (Dec); Progress (Feb); Graduation (Jun); 4-H (Mar); Basketball Preview (Nov); Pumpkin Show (Oct).
Special Weekly Sections: Best Food Days (Wed);
Syndicated Publications: USA WEEKEND Magazine (Sat); American Profile (Weekly).
Delivery Methods: Mail`Newsstand`Carrier`Racks
Areas Served - City/County or Portion Thereof, or Zip codes: Pickaway County (OH)
Commercial printers?: Y
Sat. Circulation Paid: 3837
Audit By: Sworn/Estimate/Non-Audited
Audit Date: 12.07.2019
Personnel: Nancy Radcliff (Photographer); Jennifer Bahney (Asst. Ed.); Brad Morris (Sports Ed.); Teresa Maynard (Pub.); Michelle Klinebriel (Acct. Exec.); Jeramiah Faulkner (Cir. Mgr.); Steven Collins (Reporter); Pennie McCain (Advertising Executive)
Parent company (for newspapers): Adams Publishing Group, LLC

THE COLUMBUS DISPATCH

Street address 1: 62 E Broad St
Street address city: Columbus
Street address state: OH
Zip/Postal code: 43215-3500
County: Franklin
Country: USA
Mailing address: 62 E BROAD ST
Mailing city: COLUMBUS
Mailing state: OH
Mailing zip: 43215-3500
General Phone: (614) 461-5000
Advertising Phone: (614) 888-8888
Editorial Phone: (614) 461-5200
General/National Adv. E-mail: cpettograsso@dispatch.com
Classified Adv. e-mail: lhammett@dispatch.com
Editorial e-mail: letters@dispatch.com
Primary Website: www.dispatch.com
Mthly Avg Unique Visitors: 306000
Year Established: 1871
News Services: AP, MCT, LAT-WP, NYT, RN.
Special Editions: Showcase of Remodelers (Apr); High School Sports (Aug); Last-Minute Gift Guide (Dec); Valentine's Greetings (Feb); From House to Home (Jan); Employment (Jul); Parade of Homes Program (Jun); Delicious Deals (Mar); Memorial Daily 2 (May); Bonus Package (Nov
Special Weekly Sections: Life & Arts (Mon, Tue); Food & Life (Wed); Weekender (Thur); Faith (Fri); Auto (Sat); Travel, Arts, Home, Real Estate, Health (Sun)
Syndicated Publications: USA WEEKEND Magazine (Sat).
Areas Served - City/County or Portion Thereof, or Zip codes: Central Ohio
Sat. Circulation Paid: 110858
Sun. Circulation Paid: 155000
Audit By: AAM
Audit Date: 31.03.2018
Personnel: Phil Pikelny (Vice Pres./New Media); Mary Plageman (Managing Ed. / Features); Alan Miller (Ed.); Bob LeBoeuf (Gen. Mgr.); Laura Hammett (Class. Sales Mgr.); Nikhil Hunshikatti (Mktg. Dir.)
Parent company (for newspapers): Gannett; CherryRoad Media

THE COSHOCTON TRIBUNE

Street address 1: 550 Main St
Street address city: Coshocton
Street address state: OH
Zip/Postal code: 43812-1612
County: Coshocton
Country: USA
Mailing address: 550 MAIN ST
Mailing city: COSHOCTON
Mailing state: OH
Mailing zip: 43812-1658
General Phone: (740) 622-1122
Advertising Phone: (740) 295-3450
Editorial Phone: (740) 295-3417
General/National Adv. E-mail: atrabitz@gannett.com
Display Adv. E-mail: mwilson3@mncogannett.com
Classified Adv. e-mail: ksargent@gannett.com
Editorial e-mail: psjames@gannett.com
Primary Website: www.coshoctontribune.com
Year Established: 1909
News Services: AP, GNS.
Special Editions: Showcase of Homes (Other).
Special Weekly Sections: Best Food Days (Mon/Sun); TV Today (Weekly); Health, Science (Thur); Farm News (Sat); Entertainment, Comics, Lifestyles, Business (Sun); Homes (Monthly)
Syndicated Publications: USA WEEKEND Magazine (S).
Areas Served - City/County or Portion Thereof, or Zip codes: Coshocton County (OH)
Avg Free Circ: 60
Sat. Circulation Paid: 1909
Sat. Circulation Free: 20
Sun. Circulation Paid: 2305
Sun. Circulation Free: 20
Audit By: AAM
Audit Date: 31.03.2019
Personnel: John Merriweather (Ops. Dir.); Pam James (Ed.); Adam Trabitz (Sales Dir.); Tonya Shipley (Class. Sales Ctr. Mgr.)
Parent company (for newspapers): Gannett

MIDDLETOWN JOURNAL

Street address 1: 1611 S Main Street
Street address city: Dayton
Street address state: OH
Zip/Postal code: 45409
County: Montgomery
Country: USA
Mailing address: 1611 S Main Street
Mailing city: Dayton
Mailing state: OH
Mailing zip: 45409
General Phone: (877) 267-0018
Advertising Phone: (513) 705-2860
Editorial Phone: (513) 705-2525
General/National Adv. E-mail: bruce.karlson@coxinc.com
Display Adv. E-mail: bruce.karlson@coxinc.com
Classified Adv. e-mail: bruce.karlson@coxinc.com
Editorial e-mail: news@coxohio.com
Primary Website: www.middletownjournal.com
Year Established: 1857
News Services: AP.
Special Editions: Home Improvement (Apr); Football (Aug); Progress (Feb); Bridal (Jan); Health & Fitness (Jul); Tax Guide (Mar); Outdoor Living (May); Christmas Gift Guide (Nov); Fall Car Care (Oct); Home Improvement (Sept).
Special Weekly Sections: Arts, Family, Food, Health, Home, Living, Real Estate (Monthly)
Syndicated Publications: TV Journal (S).
Sat. Circulation Paid: 12429
Sun. Circulation Paid: 13534
Audit By: AAM
Audit Date: 30.09.2013
Personnel: Tom Archdeacon (Sports/City Ed.); Lucy Baker (Sr. Copy Ed.); Jim Bebbington (Sr. Ed.); Greg Billing (Sports Ed.); Laura Bischoff (Rep.); Nick Blizzard (Rep.); Jackie Borchardt (Govt. Rep.); Sharahn D. Boykin (Govt. Rep.); John Boyle (Sr. Ed.)
Parent company (for newspapers): Cox Media Group

THE CRESCENT-NEWS

Street address 1: 624 W 2nd St
Street address city: Defiance
Street address state: OH
Zip/Postal code: 43512-2105
County: Defiance
Country: USA
Mailing address: PO BOX 249
Mailing city: DEFIANCE
Mailing state: OH
Mailing zip: 43512-0249
General Phone: (419) 784-5441
General/National Adv. E-mail: advertising@crescent-news.com
Display Adv. E-mail: advertising@crescent-news.com
Classified Adv. e-mail: classifieds@crescent-news.com
Editorial e-mail: crescent@crescent-news.com
Primary Website: www.crescent-news.com
Mthly Avg Views: 745000
Mthly Avg Unique Visitors: 69000
Year Established: 1888
News Services: AP, SHNS.
Special Editions: Tax & Finance (Feb); Bridal (Feb, Jun); Farm Review (Feb, Sept); Brag Book (Mar); Lawn & Garden (Apr, May, Jun); Car Care (Apr, Oct); Health & Fitness (Apr); Graduation (May); Summer Entertainment (Jun); Defiance County Fair (Jul); Senior Lifestyle (Jul); Back To School (Aug); Reader's Choice (Aug); Football Preview (Aug); Home Improvement (Sept, Oct); Business & Industry (Sept); Family Health (Oct); Recipes (Nov); Veteran's (Nov); Basketball Preview (Nov); Holiday Gift Guide (Nov, Dec); Christmas Greetings (Dec); Year End Review (Dec)
Special Weekly Sections: NASCAR, Outdoor (Thur); Farm, Church (Fri); Business, TV, Home, Garden, Health (Sun)
Syndicated Publications: American Profile (Weekly), Parade (Sun)
Delivery Methods: Mail`Newsstand`Carrier`Racks
Areas Served - City/County or Portion Thereof, or Zip codes: All of Defiance, Paulding, and Henry Counties and portions of Putnam, Fulton and Williams Counties
Own Printing Facility?: N
Commercial printers?: N
Avg Free Circ: 560
Sun. Circulation Paid: 13966
Sun. Circulation Free: 734
Audit By: AAM
Audit Date: 30.06.2017
Personnel: Jenny Derringer (Educ. Ed.); Mark Froelich (Features Ed.); Darlene Prince (Health/Med. Ed.); Todd Helberg (Political/Gov. Ed.); Lynn Groll; Chris Van Scoder (Adv. Mgr.); Greg Meyers (Circ. Mgr)
Parent company (for newspapers): Adams Publishing Group, LLC

THE DELAWARE GAZETTE

Street address 1: 40 N Sandusky St
Street address 2: Ste 202
Street address city: Delaware
Street address state: OH
Zip/Postal code: 43015-1973
County: Delaware
Country: USA
Mailing address: 40 N SANDUSKY ST STE 202
Mailing city: DELAWARE
Mailing state: OH
Mailing zip: 43015-1973
General Phone: (740) 363-1161
Advertising Phone: (740) 413-0893
Editorial Phone: (740) 413-0900
General/National Adv. E-mail: addept@delgazette.com
Display Adv. E-mail: addept@delgazette.com
Classified Adv. e-mail: classifieds@delgazette.com
Editorial e-mail: newsroom@delgazette.com
Primary Website: www.delgazette.com
Mthly Avg Views: 160000
Mthly Avg Unique Visitors: 22000
Year Established: 1818
News Services: AP, U.S. Suburban Press Inc..
Special Editions: Baby Bulletin (Jan); 4-H Focus, Progress Edition (Feb); Home & Garden (Mar); Lawn, Feature (Apr); Graduation (May); Council, Summer

Festival (June); Summer (Jul); Back to School, Fall (Aug); Sunday Fair, Fall Home Improvement (Sept); Fair in Review, Voters (Oct); Winter, Holiday (Nov); Holiday Gift Guide (Dec)
Special Weekly Sections: Best Food, Home (Mon); Auto (Tue); Business (Wed); NASCAR, Health (Thur); Church (Fri); Youth, Farm (Sat);
Delivery Methods: Mail`Newsstand`Carrier`Racks
Areas Served - City/County or Portion Thereof, or Zip codes: Delaware County (OH)
Own Printing Facility?: N
Commercial printers?: Y
Sat. Circulation Paid: 6000
Audit By: Sworn/Estimate/Non-Audited
Audit Date: 12.07.2019
Personnel: Denise Hill (Adv. Dir./Mkt. Mgr.); Joshua Keeran (Ed.); Jeanne DeWeese (Classifieds & Legal Adv.); Ben Stroup (Sports Ed.); Gary Budzak (News Ed.)
Parent company (for newspapers): AIM Media Texas

DELPHOS DAILY HERALD

Street address 1: 405 N Main St
Street address city: Delphos
Street address state: OH
Zip/Postal code: 45833-1577
County: Allen
Country: USA
Mailing address: 405 N MAIN ST
Mailing city: DELPHOS
Mailing state: OH
Mailing zip: 45833-1598
General Phone: (419) 695-0015
Advertising Phone: (419) 695-0015 ext. 138
Editorial Phone: (419) 695-0015 ext. 134
General/National Adv. E-mail: dthornberry@delphosherald.com
Display Adv. E-mail: mhoffman@delphosherald.com
Classified Adv. e-mail: classifieds@delphosherald.com
Editorial e-mail: nspencer@delphosherald.com
Primary Website: www.delphosherald.com
Year Established: 1869
News Services: AP.
Special Editions: National Secretaries Week (Apr); Football Tab (Aug); New Year Baby (Dec); Cooking School (Feb); 2 Dollar Days (Jan); 2 Dollar Days (Jul); 4-H Tab (Mar); Bride Tab (May); Senior Scenes (Monthly); Christmas Opening (Nov); Get Ready for Winter Tab (Oct); Old
Special Weekly Sections: Engagements, Weddings (Mon); Business (Wed); Farm (Thur); Church (Fri); Business Journal (Monthly)
Syndicated Publications: American Profile (Weekly).
Areas Served - City/County or Portion Thereof, or Zip codes: 45833, 45887, 45893, 45863, 45809, 45844, 45876, 45807, 45853, 45894, 45827, 45891, 45830
Own Printing Facility?: Y
Commercial printers?: N
Avg Free Circ: 10998
Audit By: Sworn/Estimate/Non-Audited
Audit Date: 12.07.2019
Personnel: Murray Cohen (Pub.); Ray Geary (Gen. Mgr.); Nancy Spencer (Ed.); Jim Metcalfe (Sports Ed.); Denny Klausing (Prod. Mgr.); David Thornberry (Adv.); Lori Silette (Cir. / Class.)
Parent company (for newspapers): Delphos Herald, Inc.

THE REVIEW

Street address 1: 210 E 4th St
Street address city: East Liverpool
Street address state: OH
Zip/Postal code: 43920-3144
County: Columbiana
Country: USA
Mailing address: 210 E 4TH ST
Mailing city: EAST LIVERPOOL
Mailing state: OH
Mailing zip: 43920-3144
General Phone: (330) 385-4545
Advertising Phone: (330) 385-4545
Editorial Phone: (330) 385-4545
General/National Adv. E-mail: lludovici@reviewonline.com
Display Adv. E-mail: retailadv@reviewonline.com
Classified Adv. e-mail: classified@reviewonline.com
Editorial e-mail: newsroom@reviewonline.com
Primary Website: www.reviewonline.com
Mthly Avg Views: 1020000
Mthly Avg Unique Visitors: 62500
Year Established: 1879
News Services: AP.
Special Editions: Business Profile Edition (Apr); Football (Aug); Basketball (Dec); Thanksgiving Day (Nov); Home Improvement (Apr/Oct)
Special Weekly Sections: Health, Travel, Arts, Entertainment (Sun); Entertainment (Fri); Religion (Sat)
Syndicated Publications: Parade (S); TV Review (Entertainment TV) (S)
Delivery Methods: Mail`Newsstand`Carrier`Racks
Areas Served - City/County or Portion Thereof, or Zip codes: 43920, 43932,43945,43961,43964,43968,44432,44441,44445,44492,26034,26050,26047,15059,15050,15043
Own Printing Facility?: Y
Commercial printers?: N
Avg Free Circ: 75
Sat. Circulation Paid: 5787
Sat. Circulation Free: 75
Sun. Circulation Paid: 5834
Sun. Circulation Free: 40
Audit By: AAM
Audit Date: 30.09.2014
Personnel: Tammie McIntosh (Pub.); Lisa Ludovici (Adv. Dir.); Kevin Fenton (Cir. Mgr.); Jim Mackey (Ed.)
Parent company (for newspapers): Ogden Newspapers Inc.

CHRONICLE-TELEGRAM

Street address 1: 225 East Avenue
Street address city: Elyria
Street address state: OH
Zip/Postal code: 44035
County: Lorain
Country: USA
Mailing address: 225 EAST AVE
Mailing city: ELYRIA
Mailing state: OH
Mailing zip: 44035-5639
General Phone: (440) 329-7000
Advertising Phone: (440) 329-7216
Editorial Phone: (440) 329-7111
General/National Adv. E-mail: jpfeiffer@chroniclet.com
Display Adv. E-mail: chama@chroniclet.com
Classified Adv. e-mail: classified@chroniclet.com
Editorial e-mail: letters@chroniclet.com
Primary Website: www.chroniclet.com
Year Established: 1829
News Services: Papert (Landon), MCT, SHNS.
Special Editions: Earth Day (Apr); Melon Festival (Aug); Letters to Santa (Dec); Health & Fitness (Feb); Midway Mall Auto Show (Jan); Medical Society (Jul); International Festival Guide (Jun); Car Care (Mar); Ohio Edison Parade of Homes (May); Holiday Planning Guide (Nov);
Special Weekly Sections: Best Food (Sun/Mon); Entertainment, TV Book (Fri); Homes, Real Estate (Sun)
Syndicated Publications: TV Weekly Booklet (Fri); Parade (S); American Profile (Weekly).
Areas Served - City/County or Portion Thereof, or Zip codes: Lorain County (OH)
Avg Free Circ: 2236
Sat. Circulation Paid: 14515
Sat. Circulation Free: 2236
Sun. Circulation Paid: 15505
Sun. Circulation Free: 311
Audit By: AAM
Audit Date: 31.03.2019
Personnel: Paul Martin (Pres.); Andy Young (Ed.); Carla Hama (Adv. Sales Mgr.); Jeff Pfeiffer (Adv. Mgr. /Nt'l Sales); Julie Wallace (Mng. Ed.)
Parent company (for newspapers): Lorain County Printing & Publishing Co.

THE COURIER

Street address 1: 701 W Sandusky St
Street address city: Findlay
Street address state: OH
Zip/Postal code: 45840-2325
County: Hancock
Country: USA
Mailing address: PO BOX 609
Mailing city: FINDLAY
Mailing state: OH
Mailing zip: 45839-0609
General Phone: (419) 422-5151
General/National Adv. E-mail: karifaulkner@thecourier.com
Display Adv. E-mail: karifaulkner@thecourier.com
Classified Adv. e-mail: karizellner@thecourier.com
Editorial e-mail: news@thecourier.com
Primary Website: www.thecourier.com
Mthly Avg Views: 950000
Mthly Avg Unique Visitors: 50732
Year Established: 1836
News Services: AP, WP, TMS
Special Editions: Progress (Feb); , Agriculture (Mar); Golf, Home Improvement, Bride (Apr); Seniors, Mother's Day, Downtown Findlay (May); Fathers Day (Jun); Pets (Jul); Balloon Fest, Back to School, High School/College Football (Aug); Spirit, Home Improvement, Susan Komen, Downtown Findlay (Sept); Brides, Halloween (Oct); Pets, Veterans Day, Basketball (Nov); Holiday Greetings (Dec)
Special Weekly Sections: Weekend (Sat); Celebrations (Tues).
Syndicated Publications: Parade (Fri), American Profile (Mon.) Dash, Athalon Sports, Relish
Delivery Methods: Mail`Newsstand`Carrier`Racks
Areas Served - City/County or Portion Thereof, or Zip codes: Findlay & Northwest Ohio
Own Printing Facility?: Y
Commercial printers?: Y
Avg Free Circ: 578
Sat. Circulation Paid: 18350
Sat. Circulation Free: 578
Audit By: CAC
Audit Date: 31.12.2018
Personnel: Karl L. Heminger (Pres./Pub.); David P. Glass (VP/Broadcast Commun.); Kurt F. Heminger (VP, CIO); Kari Faulkner (Adv. Mgr.); Kim Wilhelm (Readership and Audience Dev. Dir.); Rob Jenney (Circ. Mgr.); Kurt Leonard (City Ed.); Brenna Grietman (Family Ed.); James Harrold (News Ed.); Randy Roberts (Photo Ed.); Charles Lightner (Digital Design Manager)
Parent company (for newspapers): Ogden Newspapers Inc.; Findlay Publishing Co.

THE REVIEW TIMES

Street address 1: 113 E Center St
Street address city: Fostoria
Street address state: OH
Zip/Postal code: 44830-2905
County: Seneca
Country: USA
Mailing address: 113 E CENTER ST
Mailing city: FOSTORIA
Mailing state: OH
Mailing zip: 44830-2905
General Phone: (419) 435-6641
Advertising Phone: (419) 435-6641
General/National Adv. E-mail: advertising@reviewtimes.com
Display Adv. E-mail: advertising@reviewtimes.com
Editorial e-mail: rtnews@reviewtimes.com
Primary Website: www.reviewtimes.com
News Services: AP, LAT-WP.
Special Editions: Super Bowl (Jan); Community (Feb); Healthy Living (Mar); Home Improvement, Bridal (Apr); Graduation, Police Week (May); Fostorian, Relay for Life (Jun); Flag (Jul); High School Football, School (Aug); Shape Up, Health and Safety (Sept); Election, Bridal (Oct); Christmas Gift Guide (Nov); Basketball & Christmas Gift Guide (Dec)
Special Weekly Sections: Best Food Days (Sat); Church (Fri); Weekend, Education (Sat)
Syndicated Publications: Parade Athalon Sports American Profile
Delivery Methods: Mail`Newsstand`Carrier`Racks
Areas Served - City/County or Portion Thereof, or Zip codes: Seneca County (OH)
Own Printing Facility?: N
Commercial printers?: N
Sat. Circulation Paid: 3000
Audit By: USPS
Audit Date: 01.10.2017
Personnel: Karl L. Heminger (Pres.); Linda Woodland (News Ed.); Scott Scherf (Gen. Mgr.); Rob Jenney (Circ. Dir.)
Parent company (for newspapers): Ogden Newspapers Inc.; Findlay Publishing Co.

DAYTON DAILY NEWS

Street address 1: 5000 Commerce Center Dr
Street address city: Franklin
Street address state: OH
Zip/Postal code: 45005-7200
County: Warren
Country: USA
Mailing address: 1611 S MAIN ST
Mailing city: DAYTON
Mailing state: OH
Mailing zip: 45409-2547
General Phone: (937) 225-2000
Editorial Phone: (937) 222-5700
General/National Adv. E-mail: bruce.karlson@coxinc.com
Display Adv. E-mail: bruce.karlson@coxinc.com
Classified Adv. e-mail: bruce.karlson@coxinc.com
Editorial e-mail: newsdesk@cmgohio.com
Primary Website: www.daytondailynews.com
Mthly Avg Views: 15800000
Mthly Avg Unique Visitors: 157000
Year Established: 1898
News Services: Cox News Service, SHNS, AP, NYT, MCT, TV Data.
Special Editions: Pink Paper; Insight Section; various marketing milestones
Special Weekly Sections: Arts, Family, Food, Health, Home, Living, Real Estate (Mon)
Syndicated Publications: Parade (S).
Delivery Methods: Mail`Newsstand`Carrier`Racks
Areas Served - City/County or Portion Thereof, or Zip codes: 43072, 43078, 43128, 43160, 43215, 43228, 43311, 43318, 43324, 43331, 43343, 43348, 43357, 45004, 45032, 45036, 45044, 45050, 45054, 45056, 55066, 45067, 45068, 45113, 45169, 45177, 45302, 45303, 45304, 45305, 45306, 45308, 45309, 45310, 45311, 45312, 45314, 45315, 45317, 45318, 45320, 45321, 45322, 45323, 45324, 45325, 45326, 45327, 45328, 45330, 45331, 45333, 45334, 45335, 45337, 45338, 45339, 45341, 45342, 45344, 45345, 45346, 45347, 45358, 45350, 45351, 45354, 45356, 45358, 45359, 45361, 45362, 45363, 45365, 45370, 45371, 45373, 45377, 45378, 45380, 45381, 45382, 45383, 45384, 45385, 45387, 45388, 45389, 45390, 45401, 45402, 45403, 45404, 45405, 45406, 45408, 45409, 45410, 45414, 45415, 45416, 45417, 45418, 45420, 45422, 45424, 45426, 45427, 45428, 45429, 45430, 45431, 45432, 45433. 45434. 45435. 45439, 45440, 45449, 45458, 45459, 45469. 45502, 45503, 45504, 45505, 45822, 45826, 45828, 45845, 45846, 45860, 45865, 45869, 45871, 45883, 45885, 45895
Own Printing Facility?: Y
Commercial printers?: Y
Sat. Circulation Paid: 57641
Sun. Circulation Paid: 90621
Audit By: AAM
Audit Date: 30.06.2018
Personnel: Terry Bouquot (Sr. Director, Sales); Phonda Gamble (Sr. Director, Product Delivery); Julia Wallace (Market Vice President); Rob Rohr (Senior Vice President & General Manager); Jana Collier (Editor in Chief); Ron Rollins (Associate Editor); Mike Goheen (Director, Copy Desks); John Erickson (Senior Editor); Bruce Karlson (Sales Manager - National/Major); Suzanne Klopfenstein (Senior Director, Local & Major Accounts); Connie Post (Director of Organizational Development & Editorial Support); John Boyle (Sports Editor); Jim Bebbington (Shared Content Editor); Quindelda McElroy (Senior Director, Digital); James Cosby (VP of Sales); Nick Roberts (VP of Marketing); Toni Mitchell (Director of Human Resources); Larry Powell (Senior Director, Production & Operations); Dave Thomas (Senior Director, Technology & Operations); Robert Zikias (Vice President & CFO); Kathy Eagle (General Sales Manager - Radio); John Condit (General Sales Manager - TV); Chip Beale (General Sales Manager - Digital)
Parent company (for newspapers): Cox Media Group Ohio

NEWS HERALD

Street address 1: 1800 E State St
Street address 2: Ste B
Street address city: Fremont
Street address state: OH
Zip/Postal code: 43420-4083
County: Sandusky
Country: USA
Mailing address: 1800 E. State St., Suite B
Mailing city: FREMONT
Mailing state: OH
Mailing zip: 43420
General Phone: (419) 332-5511
Advertising Phone: 419-332-1069
Editorial Phone: (419) 734-1059
General/National Adv. E-mail: JCoppler@nncogannett.com
Display Adv. E-mail: mcruz@fremont.gannett.com
Classified Adv. e-mail: ksargent@nncogannett.com
Editorial e-mail: dyonke@gannett.com
Primary Website: www.portclintonnewsherald.com
News Services: AP.
Special Editions: Football (Aug); County Fair (Jul); Basketball (Nov).
Special Weekly Sections: Real Estate, Business (Wed); Entertainment (Thur); Religion (Sat)

Delivery Methods: Newsstand`Carrier`Racks
Areas Served - City/County or Portion Thereof, or Zip codes: Sandusky County (OH); Ottawa County (OH)
Own Printing Facility?: N
Avg Free Circ: 26
Sat. Circulation Paid: 1079
Sat. Circulation Free: 21
Sun. Circulation Paid: 41
Audit By: AAM
Audit Date: 31.03.2019
Personnel: David Yonke (Ed.); Doug Hillis (Dist. Mgr.)
Parent company (for newspapers): Gannett

THE NEWS-MESSENGER

Street address 1: 1800 E State St
Street address 2: Ste B
Street address city: Fremont
Street address state: OH
Zip/Postal code: 43420-4083
County: Sandusky
Country: USA
Mailing address: 1800 E STATE ST STE B
Mailing city: FREMONT
Mailing state: OH
Mailing zip: 43420-4083
General Phone: (419) 332-5511
Advertising Phone: (419) 334-1069
Editorial Phone: (419) 334-1059
General/National Adv. E-mail: scourson@gannett.com
Display Adv. E-mail: JCoppler@nncogannett.com
Editorial e-mail: dyonke@gannett.com
Primary Website: www.thenews-messenger.com
News Services: AP, GNS.
Special Editions: Home Week (Apr); Fair (Aug); Gift Guide (Dec); Progress (Feb); Bridal (Jan); Wellness (Jun); Accent on Agriculture (Mar); Graduation (May); Winter Sports (Nov); Fall Home Improvement (Oct); Business Showcase (Sept).
Special Weekly Sections: Neighbor (Mon); Real Estate (Wed); Weekly (Thur); Religion (Sat)
Delivery Methods: Newsstand`Carrier`Racks
Areas Served - City/County or Portion Thereof, or Zip codes: Sandusky County (OH); Ottawa County (OH)
Own Printing Facility?: N
Avg Free Circ: 77
Sat. Circulation Paid: 4803
Sat. Circulation Free: 71
Sun. Circulation Paid: 143
Audit By: AAM
Audit Date: 30.09.2017
Personnel: Jeff Coppler (Sales Mgr.); Doug Hillis (Cir. Dist. Mgr.); David Yonke (Ed.)
Parent company (for newspapers): Gannett

GALLIPOLIS DAILY TRIBUNE

Street address 1: 825 3rd Ave
Street address city: Gallipolis
Street address state: OH
Zip/Postal code: 45631-1624
County: Gallia
Country: USA
General Phone: (740) 446-2342
Advertising Phone: (740) 446-2342 ext. 11. or ext. 29
Editorial Phone: (740) 446-2342 ext 18
General/National Adv. E-mail: jschultz@civitasmedia.com
Display Adv. E-mail: jschultz@civitasmedia.com
Classified Adv. e-mail: kcade@civitasmedia.com
Editorial e-mail: michaeljohnson@civitasmedia.com
Primary Website: www.mydailytribune.com
News Services: AP.
Special Weekly Sections: TV Times (Fri); Best Food Day (S); Best Food Day (Wed).
Syndicated Publications: USA WEEKEND Magazine (S).
Delivery Methods: Mail`Newsstand`Carrier`Racks
Areas Served - City/County or Portion Thereof, or Zip codes: Gallipolis, Gallia County
Own Printing Facility?: Y
Commercial printers?: Y
Sun. Circulation Paid: 9068
Audit By: Sworn/Estimate/Non-Audited
Audit Date: 12.07.2019
Personnel: Bud Hunt (Pub.); Beth Sergent (Ed.); Matt Rodgers (Adv. Dir.); Patricia Wamsley (CSR); Bryan Walters (Sports. Ed.)
Parent company (for newspapers): AIM Media Indiana

DAILY ADVOCATE

Street address 1: 428 S Broadway St
Street address city: Greenville
Street address state: OH
Zip/Postal code: 45331-1926
County: Darke
Country: USA
Mailing address: PO BOX 220
Mailing city: GREENVILLE
Mailing state: OH
Mailing zip: 45331-0220
General Phone: (937) 548-3151
Advertising Phone: (937) 548-3151
Editorial Phone: (937) 548-3151
General/National Adv. E-mail: advertising@dailyadvocate.com
Display Adv. E-mail: mbevins@dailyadvocate.com
Classified Adv. e-mail: crandall@dailyadvocate.com
Editorial e-mail: cchalmers@dailyadvocate.com
Primary Website: www.dailyadvocate.com
Year Established: 1883
News Services: AP, NEA.
Special Weekly Sections: Next Generation (Mon); Religion Page, Senior (Fri); Prime Time (Wed).
Syndicated Publications: Cooks Corner (Mon); USA WEEKEND Magazine (Sat); Darke County Farmer Page (Tues); American Profile (Weekly).
Delivery Methods: Mail`Newsstand`Racks
Areas Served - City/County or Portion Thereof, or Zip codes: Darke County
Sat. Circulation Paid: 6468
Audit By: Sworn/Estimate/Non-Audited
Audit Date: 12.07.2019
Personnel: Christie Randall (Adv. Mgr.); Linda Moody (Rep.); Kyle Shaner (Sports Ed.); Christina Chalmers (Ed.); Teresa Ketring (Cust. Sales / Serv. Rep.); Diana Sleppy (Cust. Sales / Serv. Rep.)
Parent company (for newspapers): AIM Media Indiana

JOURNALNEWS

Street address 1: 228 Court St
Street address city: Hamilton
Street address state: OH
Zip/Postal code: 45011-2820
County: Butler
Country: USA
Mailing address: PO BOX 298
Mailing city: HAMILTON
Mailing state: OH
Mailing zip: 45012
General Phone: (513) 863-8200
Editorial Phone: (513) 705-2506
Primary Website: www.journal-news.com
Year Established: 1818
News Services: AP.
Special Editions: Perfect Wedding (Apr); Back to School (Aug); Progress (Feb); Perfect Wedding (Jan); Butler County Fair (Jul); NCAA (Mar); Explore Summer (May); Basketball Tip-Off (Nov); Fall Home Improvement (Sept).
Special Weekly Sections: Journal News (Mon); Test Drive (Sat).
Syndicated Publications: TV Update (S).
Avg Free Circ: 246
Sat. Circulation Paid: 22638
Sat. Circulation Free: 56
Sun. Circulation Paid: 26246
Sun. Circulation Free: 63
Audit By: AAM
Audit Date: 30.06.2015
Personnel: Karen Lehman (Controller); Rob Rohr (Sr. Vice President Slaes); Mike Stephens (Circ. Mgr.); Kira Lisa Warren (Ed.); Mike Wallace (Deputy Mng. Ed.); Rich Gillette (City Ed.); Mike Williams (Editorial Page Ed.); Mandy Gambrell (Lifestyle Ed.); Greg Lynch (Photo Ed.); Peggy McCracken (Religion Ed.); John Boyle (Sports Ed.); Carl Borsani (Mgmt. Info Servs. Mgr.)
Parent company (for newspapers): Cox Media Group

HILLSBORO TIMES-GAZETTE

Street address 1: 108 Governor Trimble Pl
Street address city: Hillsboro
Street address state: OH
Zip/Postal code: 45133-1145
County: Highland
Country: USA
Mailing address: 108 GOVERNOR TRIMBLE PL STE 101
Mailing city: HILLSBORO
Mailing state: OH
Mailing zip: 45133-1064
General Phone: (937) 393-3456
Advertising Phone: (937) 393-3456 ext. 1673
Editorial Phone: (937) 393-3456 ext. 1677
General/National Adv. E-mail: shughes@aimmediamidwest.com
Display Adv. E-mail: shughes@aimmediamidwest.com
Editorial e-mail: jgilliland@aimmediamidwest.com
Primary Website: www.timesgazette.com
Year Established: 1818
News Services: AP.
Special Editions: Christmas Tab (Dec); Fall Festival of Leaves Tab (Fall); Basketball Tab (Other); Spring Tab (Spring); Summer Tab (Summer).
Special Weekly Sections: Church Page (Fri); Farm Page (Mon).
Syndicated Publications: USA WEEKEND Magazine (Sat); American Profile (Weekly).
Areas Served - City/County or Portion Thereof, or Zip codes: Highland County (OH)
Sat. Circulation Paid: 4500
Audit By: Sworn/Estimate/Non-Audited
Audit Date: 12.07.2019
Personnel: Bud Hunt (Pub.); Sharon Hughes (Media Sales Dir.); Chuck Miller (Media Sales Consultant); Tracie Guisinger (Med. Sales Consultant); Jeff Gilliland (Ed.); David Wright (Med. Sales Cons.); Ryan Applegate (Sports Ed.); Tim Colliver (Reporter); Brenda Earley (Circ. Mgr.); Ann Runyon-Elam (Customer Service Rep.)
Parent company (for newspapers): AIM Media Indiana

THE IRONTON TRIBUNE

Street address 1: 2903 S 5th St
Street address city: Ironton
Street address state: OH
Zip/Postal code: 45638-2866
County: Lawrence
Country: USA
Mailing address: PO BOX 647
Mailing city: IRONTON
Mailing state: OH
Mailing zip: 45638-0647
General Phone: (740) 532-1441
Advertising Phone: (740) 532-1445
Editorial Phone: (740) 532-1445
General/National Adv. E-mail: shawn.randolph@irontontribune.com
Display Adv. E-mail: advertising@irontontribune.com
Classified Adv. e-mail: bonita.creger@irontontribune.com
Editorial e-mail: mike.caldwell@irontontribune.com
Primary Website: www.irontontribune.com
Year Established: 1928
News Services: AP, MCT.
Special Editions: Football Tab (Aug); Christmas (Dec); Profile (Feb); Bridal (Jan); Newcomer's Guide (Jul); Thanksgiving Day (Nov); Senior Citizen Guide (Sept).
Special Weekly Sections: Religion (Fri); Neighbors (S); Best Food Day (Wed).
Syndicated Publications: Parade (S).
Areas Served - City/County or Portion Thereof, or Zip codes: 45638
Sun. Circulation Paid: 7228
Audit By: Sworn/Estimate/Non-Audited
Audit Date: 12.07.2019
Personnel: Michael Caldwell (Pres./Pub.); Shawn Randolph (Mktg. / Adv. Dir.); Josh Morrison (Gen. Mgr. / Circ. Dir.); James Walker (Sports Ed.); Bo Elliott (Prod. Mgr. / Pres. Fore.); Bonita Creger (Class. Mktg. Rep.); Cindy Staton (Cir. Clerk / CSR)
Parent company (for newspapers): Boone Newspapers, Inc.

RECORD-COURIER

Street address 1: 1050 W. Main St.
Street address city: Kent
Street address state: OH
Zip/Postal code: 44240
County: Portage
Country: USA
Mailing address: 1050 W MAIN ST
Mailing city: KENT
Mailing state: OH
Mailing zip: 44240-2006
General Phone: (330) 541-9400
Advertising Phone: (330) 298-2012
Editorial Phone: (330) 298-1124
General/National Adv. E-mail: kcontini@recordpub.com
Display Adv. E-mail: advertising@recordpub.com
Classified Adv. e-mail: class@recordpub.com
Editorial e-mail: editor@recordpub.com
Primary Website: www.recordpub.com
Mthly Avg Views: 1000000
Mthly Avg Unique Visitors: 150000
Year Established: 1830
News Services: AP, SHNS.
Special Editions: Home Improvement (Apr); Football & Fall Sports (Aug); Gift Guide (Dec); Progress (Feb); Bridal Tab (Jan); Bridal Tab (Jun); Car Care (Mar); Summer Lifestyles (May); Gift Guide (Nov); Car Care (Sept).
Special Weekly Sections: Entertainment (Thur); Best Food Day (Tues).
Syndicated Publications: USA WEEKEND Magazine (S).
Areas Served - City/County or Portion Thereof, or Zip codes: Portage County (OH)
Avg Free Circ: 2938
Sat. Circulation Paid: 8454
Sat. Circulation Free: 2938
Sun. Circulation Paid: 9358
Sun. Circulation Free: 2555
Audit By: AAM
Audit Date: 30.06.2018
Personnel: Heather Rainone (Mng. Ed.); Jim Williams (General Manager/Advertising Director); Gary Hurst (Cir. Mgr.); Michael Shearer (Editor & General Manager)
Parent company (for newspapers): Gannett; CherryRoad Media

THE KENTON TIMES

Street address 1: 201 E Columbus St
Street address city: Kenton
Street address state: OH
Zip/Postal code: 43326-1583
County: Hardin
Country: USA
Mailing address: PO BOX 230
Mailing city: KENTON
Mailing state: OH
Mailing zip: 43326-0230
General Phone: (419) 674-4066
Advertising Phone: (419) 674-4066 ext. 221
Editorial Phone: (419) 674-4066 ext. 232
General/National Adv. E-mail: dvanbuskirk@kentontimes.com
Display Adv. E-mail: lheacock@kentontimes.com
Classified Adv. e-mail: dvanbuskirk@kentontimes.com
Editorial e-mail: kteditor@kentontimes.com
Primary Website: www.kentontimes.com
News Services: AP.
Special Editions: Car Care (Apr); Pre-Fair (Aug); First Baby Sections (Dec); Presidents' Day Promotion (Feb); Baby Times (Jan); Fair Premium (Jul); Moonlight Madness Promotion (Jun); 4-H (Mar); Graduation (May); Christmas Shopping Kick-off (Nov); Moonlight Madness Promotio
Syndicated Publications: American Profile (Weekly).
Areas Served - City/County or Portion Thereof, or Zip codes: Hardin County (OH)
Sat. Circulation Paid: 7200
Audit By: Sworn/Estimate/Non-Audited
Audit Date: 12.07.2019
Personnel: Jeff Barnes (Pub.); Lesa Heacock (Adv. Sales Mgr.); Kendrick Jesionowski (Staff Writ.); Timothy Thomas (News Ed.); Curt Mullholland (Prod. Mgr. / Web. Admin.)
Parent company (for newspapers): Barnes Newspapers, Inc.; Ray Barnes Newspapers, Inc.

LANCASTER EAGLE-GAZETTE

Street address 1: 138 W Chestnut St
Street address city: Lancaster
Street address state: OH
Zip/Postal code: 43130-4308
County: Fairfield
Country: USA
Mailing address: 138 W CHESTNUT ST
Mailing city: LANCASTER
Mailing state: OH
Mailing zip: 43130-4300
General Phone: (740) 654-1321
Advertising Phone: (877) 513-7355
Editorial Phone: (740) 681-4344
General/National Adv. E-mail: dnase@gannett.com
Display Adv. E-mail: mrager@gannett.com
Classified Adv. e-mail: ksargent@nncogannett.com
Editorial e-mail: jsabin@nncogannett.com
Primary Website: www.lancastereaglegazette.com
Year Established: 1807
News Services: AP, GNS.

Special Editions: Spring Car Care (Apr); Fall Sports Preview (Aug); Chamber Tab (Jan); Lancaster Festival (Jul); Pictorial Review (Jun); Home & Garden (Mar);
Special Weekly Sections: Color Comics (Sun); Entertainment (Thur); Best Food Day (Wed); Life Styles (Sun)
Syndicated Publications: USA WEEKEND Magazine (S).
Areas Served - City/County or Portion Thereof, or Zip codes: Fairfield County (OH)
Avg Free Circ: 103
Sat. Circulation Paid: 4364
Sat. Circulation Free: 68
Sun. Circulation Paid: 5172
Sun. Circulation Free: 68
Audit By: AAM
Audit Date: 31.03.2019
Personnel: Rick Szabrak (Group Publisher); Heather Bright (Ops. Mgr.); Jim Sabin (Editorial Page Ed.); Mark Rager (Sales. Mgr.); Tonya Shipley (Class. Mgr.)
Parent company (for newspapers): Gannett

THE LIMA NEWS

Street address 1: 3515 Elida Rd
Street address city: Lima
Street address state: OH
Zip/Postal code: 45807-1538
County: Allen
Country: USA
Mailing address: 3515 ELIDA RD
Mailing city: LIMA
Mailing state: OH
Mailing zip: 45807-1538
General Phone: (419) 223-1010
Advertising Phone: (419) 993-2040
Editorial Phone: (419) 222-6397
General/National Adv. E-mail: bstaples@civitasmedia.com
Display Adv. E-mail: jholtsberry@limanews.com
Classified Adv. e-mail: classifieds@limanews.com
Editorial e-mail: info@limanews.com
Primary Website: www.limaohio.com
Mthly Avg Views: 1560000
Mthly Avg Unique Visitors: 133000
Year Established: 1885
News Services: AP, CT, Freedom Wire, MCT, TMS.
Special Editions: Spring Car Care (Apr); Regional Football Preview (Aug); Christmas Gift Sections (Dec); Regional Prep Basketball Tournament Preview (Feb); Health & Fitness (Jan); Best of the Lima Region (Jul); Regional Salute to Graduates (Jun); Celebrating Our Spirit (Ma
Special Weekly Sections: 360 Entertainment Tab & Drivers Seat (Fri); Best Food Day (Mon); Agri-Business, Family, Consumer (S); Lifestyle Feature , Religion & High School Sports (Sat); Home & Fashion (Thur); Health (Tues); Lifestyle Feature, Reminisce & Antiques (Wed).
Syndicated Publications: 360 Entertainment Tab TV listings (Fri); Color Comics (S).
Areas Served - City/County or Portion Thereof, or Zip codes: Allen, Auglaize, Hancock, Hardin, Logan, Mercer, Putnam, Shelby, Van Wert Counties (OH)
Avg Free Circ: 1295
Sat. Circulation Paid: 17330
Sat. Circulation Free: 668
Sun. Circulation Paid: 20807
Sun. Circulation Free: 556
Audit By: AAM
Audit Date: 30.09.2018
Personnel: Doug Olsson (Pub.); Jim Krumel (Ed.); Dick Fuller (Circ. Dir.); Barbara Staples (Adv. Mgr.); Leila Osting (Dir., HR); David Trinko (Mng. Ed.); Craig Orosz (Photo Ed.); Adrienne McGee Sterrett (Ed.); Craig Kelly (Night Ed.); JosÃ© Nogueras (Sports Ed.)
Parent company (for newspapers): AIM Media Indiana

MORNING JOURNAL

Street address 1: 308 Maple Street
Street address city: Lisbon
Street address state: OH
Zip/Postal code: 44432
County: Columbiana
Country: USA
Mailing address: 308 MAPLE ST
Mailing city: LISBON
Mailing state: OH
Mailing zip: 44432-1205
General Phone: (330) 424-9541
Advertising Phone: (330) 424-9541 ext. 257
Editorial Phone: (330) 424-9541 ext. 297
General/National Adv. E-mail: lmcintosh@mojonews.com
Display Adv. E-mail: mspencer@mojonews.com
Classified Adv. e-mail: lmcintosh@mojonews.com
Editorial e-mail: news@mojonews.com
Primary Website: www.morningjournalnews.com
News Services: AP.
Special Editions: Lawn & Garden (Apr); Fall Home Improvement (Aug); Songbook (Dec); Fact Book (Feb); Christmas in July (Jul); Car Care (Mar); Fun in the Sun (May); Christmas Gift Catalog (Nov); Car Care (Oct).
Special Weekly Sections: Dining Guide (Fri); TV Journal (S); Football (Sat); Entertainment (Thur); Roasts & Toasts (Tues); Farm (Wed).
Syndicated Publications: USA WEEKEND Magazine (S).
Delivery Methods: Mail`Newsstand`Carrier`Racks
Areas Served - City/County or Portion Thereof, or Zip codes: Columbiana & Southern Mahoning County
Avg Free Circ: 240
Sat. Circulation Paid: 6346
Sat. Circulation Free: 240
Sun. Circulation Paid: 6239
Sun. Circulation Free: 196
Audit By: AAM
Audit Date: 30.09.2018
Personnel: Larry Dorschner (Pub.); Heidi Grimm (Circ. Dir.); Dorma Tolson (Ed.); Dennis Spalvieri (Asst. Ed.); Ron Flaviano (Mgmt. Info Servs. Mgr.); Mike Sweeney (Prodn. Mgr., Press)
Parent company (for newspapers): Media News Group; Ogden Newspapers Inc.

LOGAN DAILY NEWS

Street address 1: 72 E Main St
Street address city: Logan
Street address state: OH
Zip/Postal code: 43138-1221
County: Hocking
Country: USA
Mailing address: PO BOX 758
Mailing city: LOGAN
Mailing state: OH
Mailing zip: 43138-0758
General Phone: (740) 385-2107
General/National Adv. E-mail: tmaynard@logandaily.com
Display Adv. E-mail: tmaynard@logandaily.com
Classified Adv. e-mail: lburcham@logandaily.com
Editorial e-mail: dtobin@logandaily.com
Primary Website: www.logandaily.com
Year Established: 1842
News Services: Tribune News Service
Syndicated Publications: American Profile (Weekly).
Delivery Methods: Mail`Newsstand`Carrier`Racks
Areas Served - City/County or Portion Thereof, or Zip codes: Buchtel, Carbon Hill, Laurelville, Logan, Nelsonville, New Straitsville, Rockbridge, Shawnee, South Bloomingville, Union Furnace (OH)
Sat. Circulation Paid: 3000
Audit By: Sworn/Estimate/Non-Audited
Audit Date: 12.07.2019
Personnel: Lucy Burcham (Bus. Mgr.)
Parent company (for newspapers): Adams Publishing Group, LLC

THE MADISON PRESS

Street address 1: 55 W High St
Street address city: London
Street address state: OH
Zip/Postal code: 43140-1074
County: Madison
Country: USA
Mailing address: 55 W HIGH ST
Mailing city: LONDON
Mailing state: OH
Mailing zip: 43140-1074
General Phone: (740) 852-1616
Advertising Phone: (740) 852-1616 ext. 1623
Editorial Phone: (740) 852-1616 ext. 1619
Editorial e-mail: editor@madison-press.com
Primary Website: www.madison-press.com
Year Established: 1842
News Services: AP.
Special Editions: Antique (Apr); Summer Tab (Jun); Farm & Garden Tab (Mar); Home Improvement Tab (May); Car Tab (Oct); Variety (Sept).
Special Weekly Sections: Farm Page (Fri); Food Page (Mon); Outdoor Page (Thur); Kids Page (Wed).
Syndicated Publications: American Profile (Weekly).
Delivery Methods: Mail`Newsstand`Carrier`Racks
Areas Served - City/County or Portion Thereof, or Zip codes: 43140, 43162, 43064, 43143
Own Printing Facility?: Y
Commercial printers?: Y
Avg Free Circ: 4695
Sat. Circulation Paid: 4259
Audit By: Sworn/Estimate/Non-Audited
Audit Date: 12.07.2019
Personnel: Andrea Chaffin (Ed.); Madison Press; Sandra Oiler (Cir. Mgr.); Diana Shaw (Ed. Asst.); Jason Roby (Pub.); Jessica Henry (Adv. Mgr.); Sandi Powers (Class.); Tara Renner (Acct. Exec.)
Parent company (for newspapers): AIM Media Texas

THE MORNING JOURNAL

Street address 1: 1657 Broadway
Street address city: Lorain
Street address state: OH
Zip/Postal code: 44052-3439
County: Lorain
Country: USA
Mailing address: 1657 BROADWAY
Mailing city: LORAIN
Mailing state: OH
Mailing zip: 44052-3439
General Phone: (440) 245-6901
Advertising Phone: (440) 245-6901
Editorial Phone: (440) 245-6901 Ext. 90723
General/National Adv. E-mail: rbeal@morningjournal.com
Display Adv. E-mail: lbarker@morningjournal.com
Classified Adv. e-mail: legals@morningjournal.com
Editorial e-mail: letters@morningjournal.com
Primary Website: www.morningjournal.com
Mthly Avg Unique Visitors: 479756
News Services: AP, NYT, MCT.
Special Editions: Golf I (Apr); Tour of Homes (Aug); Truck I & II Tab (Dec); Finance/Tax (Feb); Town Crier (Jan); Truck I Tab (Jul); International Festival (Jun); BIA Home Craft Show (Mar); Lorain Pride (May); Early Holiday Gift Guide (Nov); BIA Home Tab (Oct); Country Liv
Special Weekly Sections: Arcade/Entertaiment (Fri); Real Estate (S); Real Estate (Sat).
Syndicated Publications: The Edge (sports edition) (Fri); Today's Woman (Mon); Job Digest (Other); TV Journal (S); Color Comics (6 pages) (Sat).
Sat. Circulation Paid: 11703
Sun. Circulation Paid: 14226
Audit By: AAM
Audit Date: 30.03.2017
Personnel: Ron Beal (Adv. Dir. / Gen. Mgr.); Tom Skoch (Ed.); Jeff Schell (Pub.); Douglas Fuller (Cir. Dir.); Darlene Smith (Sales Mgr.); Paula Velazquez (Leg. Adv.); Ron Adams (CFO)
Parent company (for newspapers): Media News Group; Digital First Media

NEWS JOURNAL

Street address 1: 70 W. Fourth Street
Street address city: Mansfield
Street address state: OH
Zip/Postal code: 44902
County: Richland
Country: USA
Mailing address: 70 W 4TH ST
Mailing city: MANSFIELD
Mailing state: OH
Mailing zip: 44903-1676
General Phone: (419) 522-3311
Advertising Phone: (419) 521-7343
Editorial Phone: (419) 521-7213
General/National Adv. E-mail: atrabitz@gannett.com
Display Adv. E-mail: dordiway@gannett.com
Classified Adv. e-mail: ksargent@nncogannett.com
Editorial e-mail: tbrennan@gannett.com
Primary Website: www.mansfieldnewsjournal.com
Mthly Avg Views: 3789695
Mthly Avg Unique Visitors: 381796
Year Established: 1930
News Services: AP, GNS.
Special Editions: He Is Risen (Apr); OSU Football (Aug); Share the Faith (Dec); Progress (Feb); Bridal Guide (Jan); Real Estate Today (Monthly); High School Football (Aug); Living Here
Special Weekly Sections: Health, Fitness (Mon); Best Food (Wed); Entertainment (Thur); Education, TV (Fri); Religion (Sat); Neighbors (Sun)
Syndicated Publications: USA WEEKEND Magazine (Sat).
Areas Served - City/County or Portion Thereof, or Zip codes: Richland County & Surrounding areas (OH)
Own Printing Facility?: N
Commercial printers?: N
Avg Free Circ: 1361
Sat. Circulation Paid: 9227
Sat. Circulation Free: 159
Sun. Circulation Paid: 12632
Sun. Circulation Free: 129
Audit By: AAM
Audit Date: 31.03.2019
Personnel: Ida Hanning (Cir. Mgr.); Brandie Davisson (Reg. Sales Mgr.); Jessie Balmert (State Government Rep.); Jason Molyet (Photographer/Videographer)
Parent company (for newspapers): Gannett; AIM Media Midwest

TELEGRAPH-FORUM

Street address 1: PO Box 25
Street address city: Mansfield
Street address state: OH
Zip/Postal code: 44901-0025
County: Richland
Country: USA
Mailing address: PO BOX 25
Mailing city: MANSFIELD
Mailing state: OH
Mailing zip: 44901-0025
General Phone: (419) 562-3333
Advertising Phone: (419) 562-3333
Editorial Phone: (419) 563-9227
General/National Adv. E-mail: atrabitz@gannett.com
Display Adv. E-mail: abass@gannett.com
Classified Adv. e-mail: classified@nncogannett.com
Editorial e-mail: jcoble@nncogannett.com
Primary Website: www.bucyrustelegraphforum.com
News Services: AP, GNS, UPI.
Special Weekly Sections: Best Food (Mon, Tue, Sat); Home (Tue); Religion (Fri); Travel (Sat)
Delivery Methods: Mail`Newsstand`Carrier
Areas Served - City/County or Portion Thereof, or Zip codes: Crawford County (OH)
Avg Free Circ: 33
Sat. Circulation Paid: 3416
Sat. Circulation Free: 46
Sun. Circulation Paid: 99
Audit By: AAM
Audit Date: 30.09.2017
Personnel: Ida Hanning (Cir. Mgr.); Adam Trabitz (Adv. Sales Dir.)
Parent company (for newspapers): Gannett

THE MARIETTA TIMES

Street address 1: 700 Channel Ln
Street address city: Marietta
Street address state: OH
Zip/Postal code: 45750-2342
County: Washington
Country: USA
Mailing address: 700 CHANNEL LN
Mailing city: MARIETTA
Mailing state: OH
Mailing zip: 45750-2300
General Phone: (740) 373-2121
Advertising Phone: (740) 373-2121 ext. 508
Editorial Phone: (740) 373-2121 ext. 536
General/National Adv. E-mail: advertising@mariettatimes.com
Display Adv. E-mail: lnorthcraft@mariettatimes.com
Classified Adv. e-mail: classifieds@mariettatimes.com
Editorial e-mail: letters@mariettatimes.com
Primary Website: www.mariettatimes.com
Mthly Avg Views: 850000
Mthly Avg Unique Visitors: 85000
Year Established: 1864
News Services: AP, GNS, GNS.
Special Weekly Sections: Life Pages (Daily); World of Wonder, NIE (Tue); Youth Sports (Thur); Sport (Fri); Comics, Lifestyle (Sat);Home (Monthly); Value Shopper (Bi-Monthly); Health, Travel (Quarterly); Live Green (Bi-Yearly)
Syndicated Publications: TV Weekly, USA WEEKEND Magazine (Sat).
Delivery Methods: Mail`Newsstand`Carrier`Racks
Areas Served - City/County or Portion Thereof, or Zip codes: Marietta (OH)
Own Printing Facility?: Y
Commercial printers?: Y
Avg Free Circ: 68
Sat. Circulation Paid: 7442

Sat. Circulation Free: 603
Audit By: AAM
Audit Date: 31.03.2018
Personnel: Patti Patton (Office Mgr.); Joseph Tranquill (Cir. Dir.); Jim Bartholow (Sr. Copy Ed.); Claire Hogue-Heiby (Copy Ed.); Art Smith (Online Mgr.); Russ Ryan (Info. Systems Mgr.); Jenny Houtman (Pub.); Lisa Kehl (Class.); Kate York (Ed.)
Parent company (for newspapers): Ogden Newspapers Inc.

THE MARION STAR

Street address 1: 163 E Center St
Street address 2: Ste 100
Street address city: Marion
Street address state: OH
Zip/Postal code: 43302-3813
County: Marion
Country: USA
Mailing address: 163 E CENTER ST STE 100
Mailing city: MARION
Mailing state: OH
Mailing zip: 43302-3093
General Phone: (740) 387-0400
Advertising Phone: (740) 375-5133
Editorial Phone: (740) 375-5107
General/National Adv. E-mail: scourson@gannett.com
Display Adv. E-mail: atrabitz@gannett.com
Classified Adv. e-mail: ksargent@nncogannett.com
Editorial e-mail: twilliams7@gannett.com
Primary Website: www.marionstar.com
Year Established: 1877
News Services: AP.
Special Editions: Drum Corps Championships (Aug); Christmas Greetings (Dec); Bride (Jan); Progress (Mar); Christmas Gifts (Nov); Popcorn Festival (Sept).
Special Weekly Sections: Best Food, Business, Farm (Sun); Real Estate (Sat)
Syndicated Publications: Golden Opportunities (Senior Citizen) (Monthly); USA WEEKEND Magazine (S); Reflections (Wed).
Areas Served - City/County or Portion Thereof, or Zip codes: Maroin County & Surrounding areas
Avg Free Circ: 132
Sat. Circulation Paid: 3469
Sat. Circulation Free: 132
Sun. Circulation Paid: 4216
Sun. Circulation Free: 43
Audit By: AAM
Audit Date: 31.03.2019
Personnel: Tom Brennan (Pub.); Jeff Coppler (Adv. Dir.); Ida Hanning (Dis. Mgr.); Henry Conte (Sports Ed.); Ryan Cook (Cons. Exp. Dir.); Benjamin Lanka (Enterprise Ed.); Adam Trabitz (Adv. Sales Dir.); Sharon Courson (Nat'l Sales Coord.); Aaron Bass (Sales Mgr.); Tonya Shipley (Class. Sales Ctr. Mgr.); Tom Williams (Ed.)
Parent company (for newspapers): Gannett

THE TIMES LEADER

Street address 1: 200 S 4th St
Street address city: Martins Ferry
Street address state: OH
Zip/Postal code: 43935-1312
County: Belmont
Country: USA
Mailing address: 200 S 4TH ST
Mailing city: MARTINS FERRY
Mailing state: OH
Mailing zip: 43935-1312
General Phone: (740) 633-1131
Advertising Phone: (740) 633-1131
Editorial Phone: (740) 633-1131
General/National Adv. E-mail: abutler@timesleaderonline.com
Display Adv. E-mail: bglenn@timesleaderonline.com
Classified Adv. e-mail: shiggins@timesleaderonline.com
Editorial e-mail: jcompston@timesleaderonline.com
Primary Website: www.timesleaderonline.com
Mthly Avg Unique Visitors: 1700
Year Established: 1891
News Services: AP.
Special Editions: Home Improvement (Apr); Auto Racing Quarterly (Aug); Drunk Driving Page (Dec); National Children's Health Month (Feb); Tax & Investment Guide (Jan); Jamboree In The Hills (Jul); Vacation Guide (Jun); National Poison Prevention (Mar); Auto Racing Quarterly; Indulge magazine quarterly; Prime Times (seniors) monthly;
Special Weekly Sections: Entertainment, Business, Finance, Arts, Living, Auto (Daily); Style, Local, Sports, Real Estate, Help Wanted (Daily/Sun); Best Food (Sun/Wed); Consumer, Money (Mon); Health (Tue); Health (Wed); Family/Kids (Thur); Entertainment, Weekend (Fri); Religion, Travel (Sat); Travel, People (Sun)
Syndicated Publications: TV Times/TV Magazine (S); USA WEEKEND Magazine (Sat).
Delivery Methods: Mail`Newsstand`Carrier`Racks
Areas Served - City/County or Portion Thereof, or Zip codes: Belmont County (OH) Monroe County (OH) Harrison County (OH) Parts of Jefferson County (OH)
Own Printing Facility?: Y
Commercial printers?: Y
Avg Free Circ: 28
Sat. Circulation Paid: 8833
Sat. Circulation Free: 28
Sun. Circulation Paid: 11573
Sun. Circulation Free: 98
Audit By: AAM
Audit Date: 31.03.2017
Personnel: Robert Kapral (Exec. Sports Ed.); Seth R. Staskey (Sports Ed.); Jennifer Compston-Strough (Mng. Ed.); Shelley Hanson (Staff Writer/Lifestyles); Miranda Sebroski (Staff Writer); Adam Tychonski (Staff Writer); Rick Thorp (Sports Writer); Kim North (Sports Writer); Pam Bennett (Advertising Director); Amy Butler (Advertising Sales Manager); Brad Glenn (Sales Rep)
Parent company (for newspapers): Ogden Newspapers Inc.

MARYSVILLE JOURNAL-TRIBUNE

Street address 1: 207 N Main St
Street address city: Marysville
Street address state: OH
Zip/Postal code: 43040-1161
County: Union
Country: USA
Mailing address: PO BOX 226
Mailing city: MARYSVILLE
Mailing state: OH
Mailing zip: 43040-0226
General Phone: (937) 644-9111
Advertising Phone: (937) 642-5656
Editorial Phone: (937) 642-6397
Display Adv. E-mail: jtads@marysvillejt.com
Primary Website: www.marysvillejt.com
Mthly Avg Views: 6000000
Mthly Avg Unique Visitors: 1000000
Year Established: 1849
News Services: AP
Special Editions: Football Opener (Aug); Christmas Greetings (Dec); 4-H Clubs (Mar); Christmas Shopping Guide (Nov); Home Improvement (Spring);
Special Weekly Sections: TV
Syndicated Publications: TV (Tue); American Profile (Tues).
Delivery Methods: Mail`Newsstand`Carrier`Racks
Areas Served - City/County or Portion Thereof, or Zip codes: 43040, 43344, 43045, 43060, 43067
Own Printing Facility?: N
Commercial printers?: Y
Sat. Circulation Paid: 7000
Audit By: USPS
Audit Date: 01.10.2017
Personnel: Chad Williamson (Managing Ed.); Marie Woodford (Adv. Dir.); Daniel E. Behrens (Pub.); Kevin Behrens (Gen. Mgr.)
Parent company (for newspapers): Behrens Family

THE INDEPENDENT

Street address 1: 729 Lincoln Way E
Street address city: Massillon
Street address state: OH
Zip/Postal code: 44646-6829
County: Stark
Country: USA
Mailing state: OH
General Phone: (330) 833-2631
Advertising Phone: (330) 833-2631
Editorial Phone: (330) 775-1125
General/National Adv. E-mail: jim.williams@cantonrep.com
Display Adv. E-mail: stan.sidaway@indeonline.com
Classified Adv. e-mail: gail.valli@cantonrep.com
Editorial e-mail: veronica.vandress@indeonline.com
Primary Website: www.indeonline.com
Year Established: 1863
News Services: AP, CNS, DF, SHNS, TMS.
Special Editions: Home & Garden (Apr); Football Contest (Aug); Gift Ideas (Dec); Valentine (Feb); Hall of Fame (Jul); Fun In The sun (Jun); Holy Week & Easter Church Guide (Mar); College Guide (May); Christmas Countdown (Nov); How To (Oct); Community Guide (Sept).
Special Weekly Sections: Business, Industry, Senior (Tue); Cuisine, Food, Restaurant (Wed); Community (Tue, Bi-monthly)
Syndicated Publications: TV Times (entertainment tab) (S).
Delivery Methods: Newsstand`Carrier`Racks
Areas Served - City/County or Portion Thereof, or Zip codes: Western Stark County (OH)
Avg Free Circ: 1540
Sat. Circulation Paid: 5365
Sat. Circulation Free: 1540
Audit By: AAM
Audit Date: 31.12.2017
Personnel: Jim Porter (Pub.); Sheila Casler (Cir. Dir.); Amy Knapp (Reporter); Chris Easterling (Sports Ed.); Chris Beaven (Gen. Mgr.); Sharon Ackerman (Adv. Dir.); Veronica Van Dress (Editor); Christina McCune (Reporter); Joe Mitchin (Sports Writer); Steven Grazier (Reporter); Kevin Whitlock (Photographer)
Parent company (for newspapers): Gannett; CherryRoad Media

THE MEDINA COUNTY GAZETTE

Street address 1: 885 W Liberty St
Street address city: Medina
Street address state: OH
Zip/Postal code: 44256-1312
County: Medina
Country: USA
Mailing address: 885 W LIBERTY ST
Mailing city: MEDINA
Mailing state: OH
Mailing zip: 44256-1396
General Phone: (800) 633-4623
Advertising Phone: (330) 721-4002
Editorial Phone: (440) 329-7152
General/National Adv. E-mail: jgwinnup@medina-gazette.com
Display Adv. E-mail: abarnes@medina-gazette.com
Classified Adv. e-mail: kfraley@medina-gazette.com
Editorial e-mail: letters@medina-gazette.com
Primary Website: www.medina-gazette.com
Year Established: 1832
News Services: AP.
Special Editions: Spring Time Showcase (Apr); Back-to-School (Aug); Last Minute Holiday Shopping Guide (Dec); Your Heart's Desire (Feb); Health & Fitness (Jan); Wheels Ii (Jul); Academic Excellence (Jun); Spring Home & Flower Tab (Mar); Wheels (May); Golden Guide (Monthly)
Special Weekly Sections: Best Food (Mon/Tue); Accent, Auto (Tue); Business, Cover Story (Wed); Auto, Entertainment (Thur); Real Estate, TV (Fri); Accent, Auto, Church (Sat); Farm, Garden (Weekly)
Syndicated Publications: Miscellaneous (Sat); American Profile (Weekly).
Areas Served - City/County or Portion Thereof, or Zip codes: Medina County
Avg Free Circ: 579
Sat. Circulation Paid: 6773
Sat. Circulation Free: 579
Audit By: AAM
Audit Date: 31.03.2019
Personnel: George D. Hudnutt (Pub.); Betty Szudlo (Sports Ed.); Gary Cozart (Cir. Mgr.); Lawrence Pantages (Mng. Ed.); Jason Gwinnup (Ret. Adv. Mgr.); Amy Barnes (Acct. Exec.)
Parent company (for newspapers): Lorain Publishing & Printing Co.; Medina County Publications, Inc.

MOUNT VERNON NEWS

Street address 1: 18 E Vine St
Street address city: Mount Vernon
Street address state: OH
Zip/Postal code: 43050-3226
County: Knox
Country: USA
Mailing address: PO BOX 791
Mailing city: MOUNT VERNON
Mailing state: OH
Mailing zip: 43050-0791
General Phone: (740) 397-5333
Advertising Phone: (740) 397-5333 ext. 240
Editorial Phone: (740) 397-5333 ext. 248
General/National Adv. E-mail: cwise@mountvernonnews.com
Display Adv. E-mail: emily.butler@mountvernonnews.com
Classified Adv. e-mail: kim@mountvernonnews.com
Editorial e-mail: samantha.scoles@mountvernonnews.com
Primary Website: www.mountvernonnews.com
Mthly Avg Views: 480000
News Services: AP.
Special Weekly Sections: Best Food Day (Wed); Farm (Sat);
Areas Served - City/County or Portion Thereof, or Zip codes: Knox County (OH)
Own Printing Facility?: Y
Commercial printers?: Y
Sat. Circulation Paid: 9099
Audit By: Sworn/Estimate/Non-Audited
Audit Date: 12.07.2019
Personnel: Kay H. Culbertson (Pub.); Elizabeth Lutwick (Asst. Pub.); Samantha Scoles (Mng. Ed.); Corby Wise (Adv. Mgr.); Kim Schwarz (Class. Mgr.); Michelle Hartman (Coor.); Fred Main (City Ed.); Bill Davis (Sports Ed.); Sheryl Shannon (Rec.)
Parent company (for newspapers): Ohio Newspaper Services, Inc.; Metric Media

NORTHWEST SIGNAL

Street address 1: 595 E Riverview Ave
Street address city: Napoleon
Street address state: OH
Zip/Postal code: 43545-1865
County: Henry
Country: USA
Mailing address: 595 E RIVERVIEW AVE
Mailing city: NAPOLEON
Mailing state: OH
Mailing zip: 43545-1865
General Phone: (419) 592-5055
Advertising Phone: (419) 592-5055
Editorial Phone: (419) 592-5055
General/National Adv. E-mail: ads@northwestsignal.net
Display Adv. E-mail: ads@northwestsignal.net
Classified Adv. e-mail: classifieds@northwestsignal.net
Editorial e-mail: briank@northwestsignal.net
Primary Website: www.northwestsignal.net
Year Established: 1852
News Services: AP.
Special Editions: Pigskin Preview (Aug); Greetings (Dec); Bride/Groom (Feb); First Baby (Jan); Community Salute (Jul); Automotive (Mar); Christmas (Nov).
Special Weekly Sections: Education (Mon); Health, Business (Tue); Business, Food (Wed); Farm (Thur); Church, Food (Sat)
Syndicated Publications: Relish (Monthly); American Profile (Weekly).
Areas Served - City/County or Portion Thereof, or Zip codes: Henry County (OH)
Sat. Circulation Paid: 4454
Audit By: Sworn/Estimate/Non-Audited
Audit Date: 12.07.2019
Personnel: Christopher Cullis (Pres./Pub.); Sally Heaston (VP, Adv./Mktg. Dir./Gen. Mgr.); Jeffrey Ratliff (Sports Ed.); Kim Imm (Asst. Pub. / Asst. Gen. Mgr.); Heather Marr (Adv.); Kim Cordes (Adv.)
Parent company (for newspapers): Bryan Publishing Co.

THE TIMES-REPORTER

Street address 1: 629 Wabash Ave NW
Street address city: New Philadelphia
Street address state: OH
Zip/Postal code: 44663-4145
County: Tuscarawas
Country: USA
Mailing address: PO BOX 667
Mailing city: NEW PHILADELPHIA
Mailing state: OH
Mailing zip: 44663-0667
General Phone: (330) 364-5577
Advertising Phone: (330) 364-8321
Editorial Phone: (330) 364-8407
General/National Adv. E-mail: advertising@TimesReporter.com
Display Adv. E-mail: advertising@timesreporter.com
Classified Adv. e-mail: classified@TimesReporter.com
Editorial e-mail: news@timesreporter.com
Primary Website: www.timesreporter.com
News Services: AP, MCT, SHNS.

Special Editions: Medical Booklet (Apr); Italian Festival (Aug); Gift Guide (Dec); Bridal (Feb); Progress (Jan); Christmas in July (Jul); Father's Day (Jun); Home & Garden (Mar); Lawn & Garden (May); Home Digest (Nov); Interior Design (Oct); Swiss Festival (Sept).
Special Weekly Sections: Arts & Leisure (Fri); Best Food Day, Health (Mon); Automotive Showcase (Sun/Thu); Religion, Engagement/Bridal, Real Estate (Sat); Senior Citizen (Wed)
Syndicated Publications: Parade (S).
Avg Free Circ: 1234
Sat. Circulation Paid: 12591
Sat. Circulation Free: 1234
Sun. Circulation Paid: 13005
Sun. Circulation Free: 1308
Audit By: AAM
Audit Date: 31.12.2016
Personnel: Paul Reynolds (Gen. Mgr.); Ann Blunt (Adv. Dir.); Hank Keathley (Local News Ed.); Melissa Griffy Seeton (Ed.); Robert Miller (Adv. Mgr.); Denise Milhoan (Cir. Dir.); Cam Denbrock (Ops. VP)
Parent company (for newspapers): CherryRoad Media; Gannett

THE ADVOCATE

Street address 1: 22 N 1st St
Street address city: Newark
Street address state: OH
Zip/Postal code: 43055-5608
County: Licking
Country: USA
Mailing address: 22 N 1ST ST
Mailing city: NEWARK
Mailing state: OH
Mailing zip: 43055-5624
General Phone: (740) 345-4053
Advertising Phone: (740) 328-8533
Editorial Phone: (740) 328-8821
General/National Adv. E-mail: scourson@gannett.com
Display Adv. E-mail: atrabitz@gannett.com
Classified Adv. e-mail: ksargent@nncogannett.com
Editorial e-mail: advocate@newarkadvocate.com
Primary Website: www.newarkadvocate.com
Year Established: 1820
News Services: AP.
Special Editions: Football (Aug); Various Christmas Sections (Dec); Bridal Guide (Jan); Annual Progress (Mar); Crossroads (Monthly);
Special Weekly Sections: Best Food Days (Mon/Wed); Society (Mon); Business (Tue); Farm (Wed); Real Estate (Sat); Stocks (Sun); Senior, Auto, Business, Health, Fitness, Home (Monthly)
Syndicated Publications: Color Comics (S); Real Estate Magazine (Sat).
Delivery Methods: Carrier`Racks
Areas Served - City/County or Portion Thereof, or Zip codes: Licking County (OH)
Own Printing Facility?: Y
Commercial printers?: N
Avg Free Circ: 158
Sat. Circulation Paid: 6779
Sat. Circulation Free: 158
Sun. Circulation Paid: 7922
Sun. Circulation Free: 106
Audit By: AAM
Audit Date: 31.03.2019
Personnel: Adam Trabitz (Sales Leader); Sharon Courson (Nat'l Sales Coord); John Merriweather (Ops. Mgr.); Tonya Shipley (Class. Sales Ctr. Mgr.)
Parent company (for newspapers): Gannett

NORWALK REFLECTOR

Street address 1: 61 E Monroe St
Street address city: Norwalk
Street address state: OH
Zip/Postal code: 44857-1532
County: Huron
Country: USA
Mailing address: PO BOX 71
Mailing city: NORWALK
Mailing state: OH
Mailing zip: 44857-0071
General Phone: (419) 668-3771
Advertising Phone: (419) 625-5500
Editorial Phone: (419) 668-3771 ext. 3
General/National Adv. E-mail: ashleypitts@norwalkreflector.com
Display Adv. E-mail: crystalmatter@norwalkreflector.com
Classified Adv. e-mail: markyocum@tandemnetwork.com
Editorial e-mail: news@norwalkreflector.com
Primary Website: www.norwalkreflector.com
Year Established: 1830
News Services: AP.
Special Editions: Home and Garden (Apr); Firelands Factbook (Mar); Christmas Gift Guide (Nov); Car Care (Apr/Oct).
Special Weekly Sections: Best Food Days (Mon/Wed)
Syndicated Publications: USA WEEKEND Magazine (Fri); American Profile (Weekly).
Areas Served - City/County or Portion Thereof, or Zip codes: 44807, 44811, 44814, 44826, 44837, 44846, 44847, 44851, 44855, 44857, 44850, 44865, 44889, 44890
Avg Free Circ: 919
Sat. Circulation Paid: 6494
Sat. Circulation Free: 919
Audit By: AAM
Audit Date: 31.03.2016
Personnel: Andy Prutsok (Pub.); Ashley Pitts (Adv. Traffic Coor.); Matt Roche (News Ed.); Emily Andrews (Dir. of Dig. Mktg); Ron Simpson (Asst. Cir. Mgr.); Joe Centers (Mng. Ed.)
Parent company (for newspapers): Ogden Newspapers Inc.; Sandusky Newspapers, Inc.

PIQUA DAILY CALL

Street address 1: 101 E High St
Street address city: Piqua
Street address state: OH
Zip/Postal code: 45356-2307
County: Miami
Country: USA
Mailing address: 101 E HIGH ST
Mailing city: PIQUA
Mailing state: OH
Mailing zip: 45356-2307
General Phone: (937) 773-2721
Advertising Phone: (937) 440-5252
Editorial Phone: (937) 773-2721
General/National Adv. E-mail: bsmith@civitasmedia.com
Display Adv. E-mail: sblack@civitasmedia.com
Classified Adv. e-mail: adillow@civitasmedia.com
Editorial e-mail: pdceditorial@civitasmedia.com
Primary Website: www.dailycall.com
Year Established: 1883
News Services: AP.
Special Weekly Sections: Neighbors, Local (Mon); Health, School News (Tue); Seniors, Food (Wed); Church, Sports (Thur); Business, Parenting, NASCAR, TV (Fri); Lifestyles, Neighbors, Transactions (Sat)
Syndicated Publications: USA WEEKEND Magazine (Sat); American Profile (Weekly); Relish (Monthly); Spry (Monthly); Athlon Sports (Monthly); SCORE (Quarterly).
Delivery Methods: Mail`Newsstand`Carrier`Racks
Areas Served - City/County or Portion Thereof, or Zip codes: 45356, 45365, 45333, 45380, 45318, 45308, 45326, 45317, 43072, 45373, 45359.
Own Printing Facility?: Y
Commercial printers?: Y
Avg Free Circ: 7802
Sat. Circulation Paid: 7100
Audit By: Sworn/Estimate/Non-Audited
Audit Date: 12.07.2019
Personnel: Melody Vallieu (Ed.); Jami Young (Cir. Dir.); Karen Brown; Becky Smith (Adv. Mgr.); Tammy Patrick (Dist. Mgr.)
Parent company (for newspapers): AIM Media Texas

THE DAILY SENTINEL

Street address 1: 109 W 2nd St
Street address city: Pomeroy
Street address state: OH
Zip/Postal code: 45769-1035
County: Meigs
Country: USA
Mailing address: 109 W 2ND ST
Mailing city: POMEROY
Mailing state: OH
Mailing zip: 45769-1035
General Phone: (740) 992-2156
Advertising Phone: (740) 992-2155
Editorial Phone: (740) 992-2342 ext. 2102
General/National Adv. E-mail: bdavis@civitasmedia.com
Display Adv. E-mail: sthompson@civitasmedia.com
Classified Adv. e-mail: sthompson@civitasmedia.com
Editorial e-mail: sfilson@civitasmedia.com
Primary Website: www.mydailysentinel.com
News Services: AP.
Special Editions: Senior Quarterly (Quarterly); Spring Home (Spring); Health Mind & Body (Quarterly)
Special Weekly Sections: TV Times (Fri); Farm Page (S); Best Food Day (Wed).
Areas Served - City/County or Portion Thereof, or Zip codes: Meigs County
Sun. Circulation Paid: 9068
Audit By: Sworn/Estimate/Non-Audited
Audit Date: 12.07.2019
Personnel: Matt Rodgers (Adv. Dir.); Beth Sergent (Ed.); Sarah Hawley (Mng. Ed.); Bryan Walters (Sports Ed.)
Parent company (for newspapers): AIM Media Texas; Cox Enterprises

THE PORTSMOUTH DAILY TIMES

Street address 1: 637 6th St
Street address city: Portsmouth
Street address state: OH
Zip/Postal code: 45662-3924
County: Scioto
Country: USA
Mailing address: PO BOX 581
Mailing city: PORTSMOUTH
Mailing state: OH
Mailing zip: 45662-0581
General Phone: (740) 353-3101
Advertising Phone: (740) 353-3101 ext. 4181
Editorial Phone: (740) 353-3101 ext. 4182
General/National Adv. E-mail: tison@civitasmedia.com
Display Adv. E-mail: hadkins@civitasmedia.com
Classified Adv. e-mail: pdtclassifieds@civitasmedia.com
Editorial e-mail: pdtnews@civitasmedia.com
Primary Website: www.portsmouth-dailytimes.com
Year Established: 1852
News Services: AP.
Special Editions: Back-to-School (Aug); Bridal (Jan); Home & Garden (Jun); Car Care (Mar); Christmas Preview (Nov); Car Care (Oct).
Special Weekly Sections: Education (Wed); Entertainment (Thur); Religion (Sat); Business, Agriculture, Food (Sun)
Delivery Methods: Mail`Newsstand`Carrier`Racks
Areas Served - City/County or Portion Thereof, or Zip codes: Scioto, Pike, Adams, Jackson & Lawrence Counties (OH); Greenup & Lewis Counties (KY)
Own Printing Facility?: N
Commercial printers?: N
Sat. Circulation Paid: 12447
Sun. Circulation Paid: 11631
Audit By: Sworn/Estimate/Non-Audited
Audit Date: 12.07.2019
Personnel: Ed Litteral (Cir. Mgr.); Hope Comer (Pub.); Chris Slone (Ed.)
Parent company (for newspapers): AIM Media Indiana

THE EVENING LEADER

Street address 1: 102 E Spring St
Street address city: Saint Marys
Street address state: OH
Zip/Postal code: 45885-2310
County: Auglaize
Country: USA
Mailing address: 102 E SPRING ST
Mailing city: SAINT MARYS
Mailing state: OH
Mailing zip: 45885-2300
General Phone: (419) 394-7414
Advertising Phone: (419) 394-7414
Editorial Phone: (419) 394-7414
General/National Adv. E-mail: retailadv@wapakwdn.com
Display Adv. E-mail: ads@theeveningleader.com
Classified Adv. e-mail: classifieds@theeveningleader.com
Editorial e-mail: editor@theeveningleader.com
Primary Website: www.theeveningleader.com
Year Established: 1905
News Services: AP.
Special Weekly Sections: Best Foods, Agriculture (Mon); Minipage, Life (Tue); County Life (Wed); Arts, TV (Thur); Faith, NASCAR (Fri); Business, Celebrations, Weddings, Engagements (Sat)
Syndicated Publications: The Source, TV Listing (Thur); American Profile (Tues).
Delivery Methods: Mail`Newsstand`Carrier`Racks
Areas Served - City/County or Portion Thereof, or Zip codes: Greater St. Mary's Ohio area
Own Printing Facility?: Y
Commercial printers?: N
Sat. Circulation Paid: 4470
Audit By: Sworn/Estimate/Non-Audited
Audit Date: 12.07.2019
Personnel: Mike Burkholder (Mng. Ed.); Gayle Masonbrink (Pub./Mktg. Mgr.); Amy Godinho (Bus. Mgr.); Amy Zwez (Cir. Mgr.)
Parent company (for newspapers): Horizon Publications Inc.

SALEM NEWS

Street address 1: 161 N Lincoln Ave
Street address city: Salem
Street address state: OH
Zip/Postal code: 44460-2903
County: Columbiana
Country: USA
Mailing address: PO BOX 268
Mailing city: SALEM
Mailing state: OH
Mailing zip: 44460-0268
General Phone: (330) 332-4601
Advertising Phone: (330) 332-4601
Editorial Phone: (330) 322-4601
General/National Adv. E-mail: advertising@salemnews.net
Display Adv. E-mail: kpope@salemnews.net
Classified Adv. e-mail: lflowers@salemnews.net
Editorial e-mail: salemnews@salemnews.net
Primary Website: www.salemnews.net
Year Established: 1889
News Services: AP.
Special Editions: Spring Home Improvement (Apr); Fair (Aug); Christmas Gift Savings (Dec); Progress (Feb); Bridal (Jan); Jubilee (Jul); Family Business (Jun); Car Care (Mar); Health (Monthly); Thanksgiving (Nov); Cookbook (Oct); Football (Sept).
Special Weekly Sections: Arts, Food, Health, Travel, Entertainment (Sun); Arts, Entertainment (Tue); Religion (Sat)
Syndicated Publications: Parade (S);
Delivery Methods: Mail`Newsstand`Carrier`Racks
Areas Served - City/County or Portion Thereof, or Zip codes: Columbiana County (OH)
Own Printing Facility?: Y
Commercial printers?: N
Avg Free Circ: 87
Sat. Circulation Paid: 3892
Sat. Circulation Free: 87
Sun. Circulation Paid: 3968
Sun. Circulation Free: 52
Audit By: AAM
Audit Date: 30.09.2014
Personnel: Beth Volosin (Pub.); J.D. Creer (Exec. Ed.); Kevin Smith (Cir. Mgr.); Laurie Flowers (Class.)
Parent company (for newspapers): Ogden Newspapers Inc.

SANDUSKY REGISTER

Street address 1: 314 W Market St
Street address city: Sandusky
Street address state: OH
Zip/Postal code: 44870-2410
County: Erie
Country: USA
General Phone: (419) 625-5500
Advertising Phone: (419) 502-2121
Editorial Phone: (419) 502-2160
General/National Adv. E-mail: advertising@sanduskyregister.com
Classified Adv. e-mail: classified@sanduskyregister.com
Editorial e-mail: mattwesterhold@sanduskyregister.com
Primary Website: www.sanduskyregister.com
Mthly Avg Views: 13000000
Mthly Avg Unique Visitors: 598135
Year Established: 1822
News Services: AP, SHNS, Capitol Wire.
Special Editions: Progress (Apr); Football (Aug); Home Improvement (Mar); Thanksgiving Day Gift Guide (Nov); Fall Car Care (Oct).
Special Weekly Sections: At Home (Wed); Religion (Sat)
Syndicated Publications: USA WEEKEND Magazine (Sat); American Profile (Weekly).
Areas Served - City/County or Portion Thereof, or Zip codes: 44870, 44824, 44846, 44839
Own Printing Facility?: Y
Commercial printers?: Y
Avg Free Circ: 1585
Sat. Circulation Paid: 18762
Sat. Circulation Free: 1585
Sun. Circulation Paid: 22215

Sun. Circulation Free: 556
Audit By: AAM
Audit Date: 31.03.2017
Personnel: Ron Waite (Pub.); Matt Westerhold (Mng. Ed.); William Ney (Circ. Dir.); Bob Rapp (Ntnl Sales Mgr); Ric Miller (Foreman); Denise Martinez (Staff Acct.)
Parent company (for newspapers): Sandusky Newspapers, Inc.; Ogden Newspapers Inc.

DAILY GLOBE

Street address 1: 37 W Main St
Street address city: Shelby
Street address state: OH
Zip/Postal code: 44875-1238
County: Richland
Country: USA
Mailing address: PO BOX 647
Mailing city: SHELBY
Mailing state: OH
Mailing zip: 44875-0647
General Phone: (419) 342-4276
Advertising Phone: (419) 342-4276
Editorial Phone: (419) 342-3261
General/National Adv. E-mail: globe@sdgnewsgroup.com
Display Adv. E-mail: globe@sdgnewsgroup.com
Classified Adv. e-mail: globe@sdgnewsgroup.com
Editorial e-mail: globe@sdgnewsgroup.com
Primary Website: www.sdgnewsgroup.com
Year Established: 1900
News Services: AP.
Special Editions: Home Improvement (Apr); Progress (Feb); Health & Fitness (Mar); Christmas Gift Guide (Nov); Car Care (Oct); City Directory (Sept).
Special Weekly Sections: Best Food Day (Mon); Farm Page (Thur).
Delivery Methods: Mail`Newsstand`Carrier`Racks
Areas Served - City/County or Portion Thereof, or Zip codes: Richland County
Own Printing Facility?: Y
Commercial printers?: Y
Sat. Circulation Paid: 2770
Audit By: Sworn/Estimate/Non-Audited
Audit Date: 12.07.2019
Personnel: Scott M. Gove (Pres./Pub.); Chuck Ridenour (Sports Ed.); Trent Gove (Assoc. Pub.)
Parent company (for newspapers): Horizon Publications Inc.

THE SIDNEY DAILY NEWS

Street address 1: 1451 N Vandemark Rd
Street address city: Sidney
Street address state: OH
Zip/Postal code: 45365-3547
County: Shelby
Country: USA
Mailing address: 1451 N VANDEMARK RD
Mailing city: SIDNEY
Mailing state: OH
Mailing zip: 45365-3547
General Phone: (937) 498-8088
Advertising Phone: (937) 498-5915
Editorial Phone: (937) 538-4822
General/National Adv. E-mail: cpierce@aimmediamidwest.com
Display Adv. E-mail: cpierce@aimmediamidwest.com
Classified Adv. e-mail: cking@aimmediamidwest.com
Editorial e-mail: mspeicher@aimmediamidwest.com
Primary Website: www.sidneydailynews.com
Year Established: 1891
News Services: AP.
Special Editions: Home Improvement (Apr); Fall Sports (Aug); Gifts & Greeting (Dec); Bride (Feb); Progress (Jan); Fair (Jul); Spring Sports (Mar); Graduation (May); Cookbook (Nov); Home Improvement (Sept).
Special Weekly Sections: Farm, Agriculture (Mon); Youth, Senior (Wed); Religion, NASCAR (Thur); Business (Sat)
Syndicated Publications: USA WEEKEND Magazine (Sat); American Profile (Weekly). Relish (Monthly), Athlon Sports (monthly); Spry (monthly);
Delivery Methods: Mail`Newsstand`Carrier`Racks
Areas Served - City/County or Portion Thereof, or Zip codes: 45365, 45356, 45333, 45383, 45768, 45845, 45388, 45351, 45865, 45869, 45885, 45871, 45337, 45306, 45334, 45360, 45302, 45340, 45353, 43318, 43343, 43070.
Own Printing Facility?: Y
Commercial printers?: Y
Avg Free Circ: 1657
Sat. Circulation Paid: 11500
Audit By: Sworn/Estimate/Non-Audited
Audit Date: 12.07.2019
Personnel: Natalie Buzzard (Gen. Mgr. / Med. Dir.); Melanie Speicher (News Ed.); Bryant Billing (Sports Ed.); Patricia Ann Speelman (Local Life Ed.); Carol Pierce (Media Sales Consultant); Suki Kaur (CSR)
Parent company (for newspapers): AIM Media Texas

SPRINGFIELD NEWS-SUN

Street address 1: 202 N Limestone St
Street address city: Springfield
Street address state: OH
Zip/Postal code: 45503-4246
County: Clark
Country: USA
Mailing address: 1 S LIMESTONE ST STE 1010
Mailing city: SPRINGFIELD
Mailing state: OH
Mailing zip: 45502-1294
General Phone: (937) 328-0300
Advertising Phone: (937) 328-0241
Editorial Phone: (937) 328-0342
General/National Adv. E-mail: bruce.karlson@coxinc.com
Display Adv. E-mail: bruce.karlson@coxinc.com
Classified Adv. e-mail: bruce.karlson@coxinc.com
Editorial e-mail: newssuneditor@coxohio.com
Primary Website: www.springfieldnewssun.com
Year Established: 1817
News Services: AP, MCT, LAT-WP, NYT, Cox News Service.
Special Editions: Arts, Family, Food, Health, Home, Living, Real Estate (Monthly)
Special Weekly Sections: Sports (Fri); Financial (S); Entertainment (Sat); Entertainment (Thur); Finances (Tues); Best Food Day (Wed).
Syndicated Publications: Channels-TV Book (S).
Avg Free Circ: 191
Sat. Circulation Paid: 15252
Sat. Circulation Free: 121
Sun. Circulation Paid: 20794
Sun. Circulation Free: 129
Audit By: AAM
Audit Date: 30.06.2015
Personnel: Steve Sidlo (Pub.); Emily Chambers (Dir., HR); Robert Mercer (Adv. Dir.); Don Jordan (Circ. Dir.); Jim Bebbington (Ed.); Tim Bucey (Bus. Ed.); Keith Streitenberger (Editorial Page Ed.); Steve Cooper (Film/Theater Ed.); Tom Hawkins (Graphics Ed./Art Dir.); Marshall Gorby (Photo Ed.); Kermit Rowe (Sports Ed.); Tom Stafford (Women's Ed.); Jerry Maurer (Prodn. Supvr., Bldg.); Brian Cooper (COO); Rob Rohr (Sr. VP, Adv. / Gen. Mgr.)
Parent company (for newspapers): Cox Media Group

HERALD-STAR

Street address 1: 401 Herald Sq
Street address city: Steubenville
Street address state: OH
Zip/Postal code: 43952-2059
County: Jefferson
Country: USA
Mailing address: 401 HERALD SQ
Mailing city: STEUBENVILLE
Mailing state: OH
Mailing zip: 43952-2090
General Phone: (740) 283-4711
Advertising Phone: (740) 283-4711
Editorial Phone: (740) 283-4711
General/National Adv. E-mail: jhale@heraldstaronline.com
Display Adv. E-mail: pbennett@theintelligencer.net
Classified Adv. e-mail: shiggins@theintelligencer.net
Editorial e-mail: rgallabrese@heraldstaronline.com
Primary Website: www.heraldstaronline.com
Year Established: 1806
News Services: AP.
Special Editions: Football (Aug); Basketball (Dec); Progress (Feb); Gift Guide (Nov)
Special Weekly Sections: Best Food Days (Wed/Sun); Building (Sun)
Delivery Methods: Mail`Newsstand`Carrier`Racks
Areas Served - City/County or Portion Thereof, or Zip codes: Jefferson County Ohio, Brooke and Hancock County West Virginia
Own Printing Facility?: Y
Commercial printers?: Y
Avg Free Circ: 156
Sat. Circulation Paid: 7059
Sat. Circulation Free: 156
Sun. Circulation Paid: 8550
Sun. Circulation Free: 130
Audit By: AAM
Audit Date: 22.12.2020
Personnel: John Hale (Publisher); Ross Gallabrese (Executive Ed.); Joe Catullo (Sports Ed.); Mike McElwain (News Ed.); Pam Bennett (Advertising Director); Mike Mathison (City Ed.); Ian Hicks (News Ed.); Michael D. McElwain (Director/Online Ed.); Denise Delatore (Retail Advertising Mgr.)
Parent company (for newspapers): Ogden Newspapers Inc.

WEIRTON DAILY TIMES

Street address 1: 401 Herald Sq
Street address city: Steubenville
Street address state: OH
Zip/Postal code: 43952-2059
County: Jefferson
Country: USA
Mailing address: 401 HERALD SQ
Mailing city: STEUBENVILLE
Mailing state: OH
Mailing zip: 43952-2059
General Phone: (740) 283-4711
Advertising Phone: (740) 283-4711
Editorial Phone: (740) 283-4711
General/National Adv. E-mail: jhale@heraldstaronline.com
Display Adv. E-mail: pbennett@theintelligencer.net
Classified Adv. e-mail: shiggins@theintelligencer.net
Editorial e-mail: news@heraldstaronline.com
Primary Website: www.weirtondailytimes.com
Year Established: 1928
Special Weekly Sections: Best Food Days (Wed/Sun); Building (Sun)
Delivery Methods: Mail`Newsstand`Carrier`Racks
Areas Served - City/County or Portion Thereof, or Zip codes: 26 062 260 472 603 500 000
Own Printing Facility?: Y
Commercial printers?: Y
Avg Free Circ: 142
Sat. Circulation Paid: 2521
Sat. Circulation Free: 142
Sun. Circulation Paid: 2521
Sun. Circulation Free: 142
Audit By: AAM
Audit Date: 31.03.2023
Personnel: John Hale (Pub.); Denise Delatore (Adv. Dir.); Ross Gallabrese (Executive Ed.); Craig Howell (Managing Ed.); Michael D. McElwain (Director/Online Ed.); Pam Bennett (Ad Director); Joe Catullo (Sports Ed.); Ian Hicks (News Ed.)
Parent company (for newspapers): Ogden Newspapers Inc.

THE ADVERTISER-TRIBUNE

Street address 1: 320 Nelson St
Street address city: Tiffin
Street address state: OH
Zip/Postal code: 44883-8956
County: Seneca
Country: USA
Mailing address: PO BOX 778
Mailing city: TIFFIN
Mailing state: OH
Mailing zip: 44883-0778
General Phone: (419) 448-3200
Advertising Phone: (419) 448-3238
Editorial Phone: (419) 448-3240
General/National Adv. E-mail: advertising@advertiser-tribune.com
Display Adv. E-mail: jsigler@advertiser-tribune.com
Classified Adv. e-mail: classified@advertiser-tribune.com
Editorial e-mail: newsroom@advertiser-tribune.com
Primary Website: www.advertiser-tribune.com
Mthly Avg Views: 222000
Mthly Avg Unique Visitors: 75000
News Services: AP.
Special Editions: Fall Sports Tab (Aug); Winter Sports Tab (Dec); Fair Tab (Jul); Home Improvement (Mar); Spring Car Care Tab (May); Cooking Contest (Nov); Home Improvement (Oct); Heritage Festival Tab (Sept).
Special Weekly Sections: Auto (Mon); Home Front (Wed); Auto, Real Estate (Thur); Auto (Sat); Real Estate, Business (Sun); Food (Sun/Mon)
Syndicated Publications: USA WEEKEND Magazine (S).
Areas Served - City/County or Portion Thereof, or Zip codes: Seneca County (OH)
Avg Free Circ: 108
Sat. Circulation Paid: 6105
Sat. Circulation Free: 108
Sun. Circulation Paid: 6684
Audit By: AAM
Audit Date: 30.09.2016
Personnel: Chris Dixon (Pub.); Rob Weaver (Ed.); Mary Huss (Bus. Mgr.); MJ McVay (Ed.); Kathy Sussang (Nat'l Adv. Mgr.); Rick Smith (Cir. Ops. Mgr.); Mary Martin (Cir. CS)
Parent company (for newspapers): Ogden Newspapers Inc.

THE BLADE

Street address 1: 541 N Superior St
Street address city: Toledo
Street address state: OH
Zip/Postal code: 43660-1000
County: Lucas
Country: USA
Mailing address: 541 N Superior St
Mailing city: Toledo
Mailing state: OH
Mailing zip: 43660-0001
General Phone: (419) 724-6000
Advertising Phone: (419) 724-6350
Editorial Phone: (419) 724-6050
General/National Adv. E-mail: info@toledoblade.com
Display Adv. E-mail: natadv@toledoblade.com
Editorial e-mail: webeditor@toledoblade.com
Primary Website: www.toledoblade.com
Mthly Avg Unique Visitors: 1525714
Year Established: 1835
News Services: AP, RN, LAT-WP, MCT, CSM, NYT, SHNS, Bloomberg, TMS.
Special Editions: Campus Connections (qtrly); TADA Auto Show, Golf Tab, Engineer's Week, HBA House & Home Show (Feb); Toledo PRO Home Show, Special Interest Camps, Pet Idol (Mar); Earth Day, Recreational Camping, Celebration of Artchitecture (Apr); Nurse's Week, National Teacher's Day, Senior Expo, BCSN Rewind, Credit Union (May); Top Honors, Family Owned Business (Jun); African American, Marathon LPGA, Exclaim! (Jul); German-American Festival, High School Football (Aug); Labor on Parade, HBA Parade of Homes, Season of the Arts, Little Darlings, Education 2014 (Sep); Walleye Opener, Credit Union, Caregivers Awards, Business Profiles (Oct); Social Security, Hot Holiday gifts (Nov); Winter Sports (Dec)
Special Weekly Sections: Real Estate (S); Peach Weekender (Th).
Syndicated Publications: Comics (S).
Delivery Methods: Mail`Newsstand`Carrier`Racks
Areas Served - City/County or Portion Thereof, or Zip codes: 75 zip codes served
Own Printing Facility?: N
Avg Free Circ: 8464
Sat. Circulation Paid: 52344
Sat. Circulation Free: 2775
Sun. Circulation Paid: 72947
Sun. Circulation Free: 17398
Audit By: AAM
Audit Date: 30.09.2017
Personnel: Joseph H. Zerbey (Gen. Mgr.); William Nolan (Dir. of HR.); Michael Mori (Sales Dir.); Richard Fuller (Circ. Dir.); Brad Schwanbeck (Circ. Mgr., Distr.); John Robinson Block (Ed. in Chief); John Crisp (VP of New Media); William Southern (Director of Finance and IT); Kurt Franck (Executive Editor); Brad Vriezelaar (New Media Director); Dave Murray (Managing Ed.); Luann Sharp (Asst. Managing Ed.); Greg Braknis (Web News Ed.); Kim Bates (City Ed.); Frank Corsoe (Sports Ed.); Tom Zeller (Audience Development and Customer Service Mgr.); Joe Bialorucki (Circulation Manager, Operations); Bettyann Cole (Sr. IT Manager); Heather Foor (Advertising Dir.); Kim Johns (Asst. to Pres.); Isabel Sloan (Exec. Asst.); Dr. Christine Smallman (Newspaper In Education Coordinator); Tony Durham (News Ed.); Doug Koerner (News Editor - Sunday/ Projects); Jim Provance (Columbus Bureau Chief); Steve Dolley (Controller); Angie Fredericksen (IT Support Mgr); John Fedderke (Dir. of Mktg.); Ken Burkett (PrePress Mgr); Tom Sutherland (Advert. Sales Mgr/PrePress Sup)
Parent company (for newspapers): Block Communications, Inc.

TROY DAILY NEWS

Street address 1: 224 S Market St
Street address city: Troy
Street address state: OH
Zip/Postal code: 45373-3327
County: Miami

Country: USA
Mailing address: 224 S MARKET ST
Mailing city: TROY
Mailing state: OH
Mailing zip: 45373-3300
General Phone: (937) 335-5634
Advertising Phone: (937) 552-2291 ext. 1639
Editorial Phone: (937) 552-2131
General/National Adv. E-mail: bsmith@aimmediamidwest.com
Display Adv. E-mail: bsmith@aimmediamidwest.com
Editorial e-mail: mvallieu@aimmediamidwest.com
Primary Website: www.troydailynews.com
Year Established: 1909
News Services: AP,
Special Editions: Car Care (Fall); Bridal (Jan); Miami County Community Guide (May); Thanksgiving (Nov); Car Care (Spring).
Special Weekly Sections: Health, Fitness, NIE (Mon); Money, IN-75 (Wed); Food (Thur); Arts, Entertainment (Fri); Church, NASCAR (Sat); TV, Business, Community, Stock, Comics, Home, Garden, Real Estate, Travel, Senior Citizen, Parenting, Coupons (Sun)
Syndicated Publications: Color Comics (Other); USA WEEKEND Magazine (S); American Profile (Weekly) Spry (Monthly); Relish (Monthly); Athlon Sports (Monthly); SCORE Magazine (quarterly).
Delivery Methods: Mail`Newsstand`Carrier`Racks
Areas Served - City/County or Portion Thereof, or Zip codes: 45373, 45371, 45383, 45337, 45339, 45359, 45312, 45389, 45356, 45318, 45326, 45317, 43072, 45326.
Own Printing Facility?: Y
Commercial printers?: Y
Avg Free Circ: 15146
Sat. Circulation Paid: 7918
Sun. Circulation Paid: 9827
Audit By: Sworn/Estimate/Non-Audited
Audit Date: 12.07.2019
Personnel: Tom Hutson (Pub.); Becky Smith (Adv. Dir.); Melody Vallieu (Ed.); Tammy Patrick (Cir. Mgr.)
Parent company (for newspapers): AIM Media Texas

THE DAILY CHIEF-UNION

Street address 1: 111 W Wyandot Ave
Street address city: Upper Sandusky
Street address state: OH
Zip/Postal code: 43351-1348
County: Wyandot
Country: USA
Mailing address: PO BOX 180
Mailing city: UPPER SANDUSKY
Mailing state: OH
Mailing zip: 43351-0180
General Phone: (419) 294-2332
Advertising Phone: (419) 294-2332 ext. 27
Editorial Phone: (419) 294-2331
General/National Adv. E-mail: dcuads@dailychiefunion.com
Display Adv. E-mail: dcuads@dailychiefunion.com
Classified Adv. e-mail: dcuads@dailychiefunion.com
Editorial e-mail: dcueditor@dailychiefunion.com
Primary Website: www.dailychiefunion.com
News Services: AP.
Special Editions: Christmas Greeting (Dec); Football (Fall); Presidents' Sale (Feb); January Sale (Jan); June Dairy (Jun); Memorial Day (May); Christmas Kick-Off (Nov); Boy and Girl Scouts (Other).
Special Weekly Sections: Best Food (Mon); Farm (Tue); Business (Wed); Entertainment (Thur)
Syndicated Publications: Business Cards (Other); American Profile (Weekly).
Sat. Circulation Paid: 3822
Audit By: Sworn/Estimate/Non-Audited
Audit Date: 12.07.2019
Personnel: Jeff Barnes (Pub.); Lonnie McMillan (Sports Ed.); David Barnes (Adv. Mgr.); Kelli Paugh (Cir. Mgr.); Alissa Paolella (City Ed.)
Parent company (for newspapers): Hardin County Publishing Co.; Ray Barnes Newspapers, Inc.

URBANA DAILY CITIZEN

Street address 1: 1637 E US Highway 36
Street address city: Urbana
Street address state: OH
Zip/Postal code: 43078-9156
County: Champaign
Country: USA
General Phone: (937) 652-1331
Advertising Phone: (937) 652-1331
Editorial Phone: (937) 508-2301
General/National Adv. E-mail: cherring@aimmediamidwest.com
Display Adv. E-mail: cherring@aimmediamidwest.com
Classified Adv. e-mail: cherring@aimmediamidwest.com
Editorial e-mail: bburns@aimmediamidwest.com
Primary Website: www.urbanacitizen.com
Mthly Avg Views: 210000
Mthly Avg Unique Visitors: 33500
Year Established: 1838
News Services: AP.
Special Editions: Christmas Greetings (Dec); Bride (Feb); County Fair (Aug); Health & Fitness (Jun); House and Home (Mar); Progress (May)
Delivery Methods: Mail`Newsstand`Carrier`Racks
Areas Served - City/County or Portion Thereof, or Zip codes: City/County
Own Printing Facility?: Y
Commercial printers?: Y
Sat. Circulation Paid: 4600
Audit By: Sworn/Estimate/Non-Audited
Audit Date: 01.10.2023
Personnel: Lane Moon (Publisher); Brenda Amlin (Bus. Mgr./Circ); Brenda Burns (Editor); Jason Roby (Sales Mgr.)
Parent company (for newspapers): AIM Media Texas

THE TIMES BULLETIN

Street address 1: 1167 Westwood Drive
Street address 2: Suite 101
Street address city: Van Wert
Street address state: OH
Zip/Postal code: 45891
County: Van Wert
Country: USA
Mailing address: P.O. Box 271
Mailing city: Van Wert
Mailing state: OH
Mailing zip: 45891-0271
General Phone: (419) 238-2285
Advertising Phone: (419) 238-2285
Editorial Phone: (419) 238-2285
General/National Adv. E-mail: info@timesbulletin.com
Display Adv. E-mail: nswaney@timesbulletin.com
Classified Adv. e-mail: nswaney@timesbulletin.com
Editorial e-mail: editor@timesbulletin.com
Primary Website: www.timesbulletin.com
Mthly Avg Views: 362782
Mthly Avg Unique Visitors: 78299
Year Established: 1844
Special Editions: Spring Sports Magazine (Apr); Fall Sports Magazine (Aug); Christmas Greetings (Dec); Progress (Jan); Weddings II (Jun); Agriculture Almanac (Mar); Graduation (May); Holiday Traditions (Nov); Weddings III (Oct); PrimeTime (Quarterly); Home Improvement (Sep
Special Weekly Sections: Local/State, Van Wert County, Arts & Entertainment, Health, Business, Sports, Opinion
Delivery Methods: Mail`Newsstand`Carrier`Racks
Areas Served - City/County or Portion Thereof, or Zip codes: 45874, 45891, 45894, 45898, 45899, 45832, 45863, 45833, 45838, 45886, 45882, 45862, 45822, 45828, 45879, 45851, 45849, 45880, 45855, 45844, 45827
Own Printing Facility?: Y
Commercial printers?: Y
Sat. Circulation Paid: 5500
Sat. Circulation Free: 7100
Audit By: Sworn/Estimate/Non-Audited
Audit Date: 06.10.2021
Personnel: Ray Geary (COO); Kirsten Barnhart (News Ed.); Nikki Swaney (Advertising Representative); Chris Howell (Sports Editor); Mike Marchek (Cir. Mgr.); Robin Pennell (Editor); Karrie Macke (Graphics)
Parent company (for newspapers): Delphos Herald, Inc.

WAPAKONETA DAILY NEWS

Street address 1: 520 Industrial Dr
Street address city: Wapakoneta
Street address state: OH
Zip/Postal code: 45895-9200
County: Auglaize
Country: USA
Mailing address: 520 INDUSTRIAL DR
Mailing city: WAPAKONETA
Mailing state: OH
Mailing zip: 45895-9200
General Phone: (419) 738-2128
Advertising Phone: (419) 300-1076
Editorial Phone: (419) 739-3515
General/National Adv. E-mail: marketingetc@wapakwdn.com
Display Adv. E-mail: marketingetc@wapakwdn.com
Classified Adv. e-mail: classified@wapakwdn.com
Editorial e-mail: editor@wapakwdn.com
Primary Website: www.wapakdailynews.com
Year Established: 1905
News Services: AP.
Special Editions: Home Improvement (Apr); Personal Image (Aug); Gift Guide (Dec); Progress (Feb); Bridal (Jan); Fair (Jul); Newspapers in Education (Mar); Graduation (May); Christmas Kick-Off (Nov); Car Care (Oct); Indian Summerfest (Sept).
Special Weekly Sections: Best Food Day (Mon); Farm News (Sat); Entertainment (Thur); Business (Tues).
Syndicated Publications: Homes/Real Estate (Monthly); American Profile (Weekly).
Delivery Methods: Mail`Newsstand`Carrier`Racks
Areas Served - City/County or Portion Thereof, or Zip codes: Wapakoneta, OH; 45895; Auglaize County
Own Printing Facility?: Y
Commercial printers?: Y
Avg Free Circ: 10000
Sat. Circulation Paid: 3000
Audit By: Sworn/Estimate/Non-Audited
Audit Date: 12.07.2019
Personnel: Deborah Zwez (Pub.); Gayle Masonbrink (Adv. Mgr.); Tom Wehrhahn
Parent company (for newspapers): Horizon Publications Inc.

THE TRIBUNE CHRONICLE

Street address 1: 240 Franklin St SE
Street address city: Warren
Street address state: OH
Zip/Postal code: 44483-5711
County: Trumbull
Country: USA
Mailing address: 240 FRANKLIN ST SE
Mailing city: WARREN
Mailing state: OH
Mailing zip: 44483-5761
General Phone: (330) 841-1600
Advertising Phone: (330) 841-1621
Editorial Phone: (330) 841-1600
General/National Adv. E-mail: hnewman@tribtoday.com
Display Adv. E-mail: hnewman@tribtoday.com
Classified Adv. e-mail: classified@tribtoday.com
Editorial e-mail: blinert@tribtoday.com
Primary Website: www.tribtoday.com
Mthly Avg Views: 412000
Mthly Avg Unique Visitors: 133000
Year Established: 1812
News Services: AP.
Special Weekly Sections: Health (Tue); Best Food Day (Wed); Entertainment, Auto (Thur); Senior Citizen (Fri); Real Estate (Sat); Comics, TV (Sun)
Delivery Methods: Mail`Newsstand`Carrier`Racks
Areas Served - City/County or Portion Thereof, or Zip codes: Trumbull County, Ohio
Own Printing Facility?: Y
Commercial printers?: Y
Avg Free Circ: 203
Sat. Circulation Paid: 14893
Sat. Circulation Free: 203
Sun. Circulation Paid: 17821
Sun. Circulation Free: 13439
Audit By: AAM
Audit Date: 31.03.2019
Personnel: Charles Jarvis (Pub.); F. Len Blose (Gen. Mgr.); Andy Gray (Ent. /Amusements Reporter); Scott Gee (Prod. Mgr., Mailroom); Brenda Linert (Ed.); Bill Waugaman (Cir. Dir.); Mandy Miles (Ad Prod. Mgr.)
Parent company (for newspapers): Ogden Newspapers Inc.

THE VINDICATOR

Street address 1: 240 Franklin St SE
Street address city: Warren
Street address state: OH
Zip/Postal code: 44483-5711
County: Trumbull
Country: USA
Mailing state: OH
General Phone: (330) 841-1600
Advertising Phone: (330) 841-1701
Editorial Phone: (330) 841-1600
General/National Adv. E-mail: tsnyder@tribtoday.com
Display Adv. E-mail: retailadv@tribtoday.com
Classified Adv. e-mail: classified@tribtoday.com
Editorial e-mail: editorial@tribtoday.com
Primary Website: www.vindy.com
Mthly Avg Views: 1800000
Mthly Avg Unique Visitors: 174400
Year Established: 1869
News Services: AP
Special Weekly Sections: Valley Grows(Mon), Fitness & Health(Tue), Hobbies & Food(Wed), Ticket(Thu), Prime Time(Fri)
Syndicated Publications: Parade (S)
Delivery Methods: Mail`Newsstand`Carrier`Racks
Areas Served - City/County or Portion Thereof, or Zip codes: Mahoning Valley Mahoning County, Trumbull County, Columbiana County (partial)
Own Printing Facility?: Y
Commercial printers?: Y
Avg Free Circ: 9
Sat. Circulation Paid: 28592
Sat. Circulation Free: 716
Sun. Circulation Paid: 30699
Sun. Circulation Free: 711
Audit By: AAM
Audit Date: 31.03.2019
Personnel: Charles R. Jarvis (Publisher); Ted Snyder (General Manager); Larry Kovach (Business Manager); Brenda Linert (Editor); Harry Newman (Director of Advertising); Scott Gee (Director of Circulation); Betty H. Brown Jagnow (Pub.); (Gen. Mgr.); Ted E. Suffolk (Asst. Gen. Mgr.); Robert Wiseman (HR Dir.); Mark Sweetwood (Mng. Ed.); Robert McFerren (Graphics Ed./Art Dir.); Todd Franko (Ed.); Barbara Staples (Adv. Mgr.)
Parent company (for newspapers): Vindicator Printing Company; Eastern Ohio Newspapers, Inc.

RECORD HERALD

Street address 1: 757 W Elm St
Street address city: Washington Court House
Street address state: OH
Zip/Postal code: 43160-2428
County: Fayette
Country: USA
Mailing address: 757 W ELM ST
Mailing city: WASHINGTON COURT HOUSE
Mailing state: OH
Mailing zip: 43160-2294
General Phone: (740) 335-3611
Advertising Phone: (740) 313-0347
Editorial Phone: (740) 335-0352
General/National Adv. E-mail: admanager@recordherald.com
Display Adv. E-mail: ssattler@recordherald.com
Classified Adv. e-mail: classifieds@recordherald.com
Editorial e-mail: ryancarter@civitasmedia.com
Primary Website: www.recordherald.com
Year Established: 1941
News Services: AP.
Special Editions: In Your Prime (Quarterly); Acres (Monthly)
Special Weekly Sections: Best Food (Wed); Local (Mon); Health (Tue); Business (Wed); Food, Outdoors, Generations (Thur); Religion (Fri); Entertainment (Sat)
Areas Served - City/County or Portion Thereof, or Zip codes: South Central Ohio
Sat. Circulation Paid: 5235
Audit By: Sworn/Estimate/Non-Audited
Audit Date: 12.07.2019
Personnel: Ryan Carter (Ed.); Kim Penwell (Med. Sales Cons.); Julie Howell (Adv. Sales Coor.)
Parent company (for newspapers): AIM Media Texas

THE NEWS-HERALD

Street address 1: 7085 Mentor Ave
Street address city: Willoughby
Street address state: OH
Zip/Postal code: 44094-7948
County: Lake
Country: USA
Mailing address: 7085 MENTOR AVE
Mailing city: WILLOUGHBY
Mailing state: OH
Mailing zip: 44094-7900
General Phone: (440) 951-0000
Advertising Phone: (440) 951-0000
Editorial Phone: (440) 951-0000
General/National Adv. E-mail: vlinhart@news-herald.com
Display Adv. E-mail: advertising@news-herald.com
Classified Adv. e-mail: classifieds@news-herald.com
Editorial e-mail: editor@news-herald.com

Primary Website: www.news-herald.com
Mthly Avg Unique Visitors: 736918
Year Established: 1879
News Services: AP, MCT, CNS, SHNS.
Special Editions: Golf (Apr); Most Beautiful Babies (Aug); Last Minute Gifts (Dec); Income Tax Guide (Feb); Chronology (Jan); Careers and Education (Jul); Graduation (Jun); Spring Lawn & Garden (Mar); Home Improvement (May); Elections (Nov); Fall Car Care (Oct); Fall Fashi
Special Weekly Sections: Technology, Video Games (Tue); Best Food Day (Wed); Entertainment (Fri); Religion (Sat); TV, Community, Real Estate, Travel (Sun)
Syndicated Publications: Coupon Book (Monthly); USA WEEKEND Magazine (Sat); Homes Alamanac (Semi-monthly); LIFE Magazine (Fri)
Delivery Methods: Mail`Newsstand`Carrier`Racks
Areas Served - City/County or Portion Thereof, or Zip codes: Lake & Geauga Counties (OH)
Own Printing Facility?: Y
Commercial printers?: Y
Avg Free Circ: 1287
Sat. Circulation Paid: 20834
Sat. Circulation Free: 1287
Sun. Circulation Paid: 25576
Sun. Circulation Free: 1564
Audit By: AAM
Audit Date: 31.03.2017
Personnel: Ron Adams (Controller); Jeff Schell (Adv. Dir.); Tricia Ambrose (Exec. Ed.); John Bertosa (Mng. Ed.); Mark Meszoros (Asst. Mng. Ed. / Feat.); Cheryl Sadler (Mobile/Digit. Ed.); Douglas Fuller (Cir. Dir.)
Parent company (for newspapers): Media News Group; Digital First Media

WILMINGTON NEWS JOURNAL

Street address 1: 1547 Rombach Ave
Street address city: Wilmington
Street address state: OH
Zip/Postal code: 45177-2517
County: Clinton
Country: USA
General Phone: (937) 382-2574
Advertising Phone: (937) 382-2574
Editorial Phone: (937) 382-2574
General/National Adv. E-mail: ehuber@aimmediamidwest.com
Editorial e-mail: rcarter@aimmediamidwest.com
Primary Website: www.wnewsj.com
Mthly Avg Views: 300000
Mthly Avg Unique Visitors: 110000
Year Established: 1838
News Services: AP.
Special Editions: Salt Magazine (Quarterly), Prep Sports (Fall); Prep Sports (Spring); Prep Sports (Winter). Clinton County Proud (yearly)
Delivery Methods: Mail`Newsstand`Carrier`Racks
Areas Served - City/County or Portion Thereof, or Zip codes: 45177 WILMINGTON 45107 BLANCHESTER 45169 SABINA 45113 CLARKSVILLE 45114 CUBA 45135 LEESBURG 45138 LEES CREEK 45142 LYNCHBURG 45146 MARTINSVILLE 45148 MIDLAND 45159 NEW VIENNA 45164 PORT WILLIAM 45166 REESVILLE 45335 JAMESTOWN
Own Printing Facility?: Y
Commercial printers?: Y
Sat. Circulation Paid: 6400
Audit By: Sworn/Estimate/Non-Audited
Audit Date: 01.10.2023
Personnel: Lane Moon (VP/Group Pub.); Elizabeth Mattingly (Media Sales Dir.); Mark Huber (Sports Ed.); Dawn Gunkel (Cir. Mgr); Ryan Carter (Editor); Tom Barr (Ed.)
Parent company (for newspapers): Gannett; AIM Media Midwest

THE DAILY RECORD

Street address 1: 212 E Liberty St
Street address city: Wooster
Street address state: OH
Zip/Postal code: 44691-4348
County: Wayne
Country: USA
Mailing address: PO BOX 918
Mailing city: WOOSTER
Mailing state: OH
Mailing zip: 44691-0918
General Phone: (330) 264-1125
Advertising Phone: (330) 264-1125
Editorial Phone: (330) 264-1125
General/National Adv. E-mail: adv@the-daily-record.com
Display Adv. E-mail: kgearhart@the-daily-record.com
Classified Adv. e-mail: classified@the-daily-record.com
Editorial e-mail: letters@the-daily-record.com
Primary Website: www.the-daily-record.com
News Services: AP.
Special Editions: Home & Garden (Apr); Wayne County Fair (Aug); Holiday Greetings (Dec); Bridal Showcase (Feb); Bridal Showcase (Jun); Builders (Mar); Senior Memories (May); Cost Cutter (Monthly); Christmas Kick-Off (Nov); At Home (Oct); Football Preview (Sept).
Special Weekly Sections: Farm (Tue); Religion, Health (Fri); Youth, Education, Business (Sun);
Syndicated Publications: TV News (printed in plant) (S); American Profile (Weekly).
Delivery Methods: Carrier
Areas Served - City/County or Portion Thereof, or Zip codes: Wayne & Holmes Counties (OH)
Own Printing Facility?: Y
Commercial printers?: Y
Avg Free Circ: 484
Sat. Circulation Paid: 16486
Sat. Circulation Free: 484
Sun. Circulation Paid: 17440
Sun. Circulation Free: 281
Audit By: AAM
Audit Date: 31.03.2018
Personnel: Randy Wilson (Nat'l Adv. Sales); Lance White (Mng. Ed.); Aaron Dorksen (Sports Ed.); Elizabeth Miles (Off. Mgr.); Bill Albrecht (Pub.)
Parent company (for newspapers): Gannett; CherryRoad Media

FAIRBORN DAILY HERALD

Street address 1: 1836 W Park Sq
Street address city: Xenia
Street address state: OH
Zip/Postal code: 45385-2668
County: Greene
Country: USA
Mailing address: 1836 W PARK SQ
Mailing city: XENIA
Mailing state: OH
Mailing zip: 45385-2668
General Phone: (937) 372-3993
Advertising Phone: (937) 372-4444 ext 200
Editorial Phone: (937) 878-3993 ext. 134
General/National Adv. E-mail: bvandeventer@civitasmedia.com
Display Adv. E-mail: cchambliss@civitasmedia.com
Classified Adv. e-mail: ttootle@civitasmedia.com
Editorial e-mail: editor@xeniagazette.com
Primary Website: www.fairborndailyherald.com
News Services: AP, U.S. Suburban Press Inc..
Special Editions: Private Property (Apr); Sidewalk Days (Jul); Business Directory (Mar); Car Care (May); Christmas Kick-Off (Nov); Home Improvement (Oct).
Syndicated Publications: USA WEEKEND Magazine (Sat).
Areas Served - City/County or Portion Thereof, or Zip codes: Fairborn, Enon & Yellow Springs (OH)
Sat. Circulation Paid: 3999
Audit By: Sworn/Estimate/Non-Audited
Audit Date: 12.07.2019
Personnel: Randy Graf (Pub.); Barb Vandeventer (Gen. Mgr.); MerriLee Embs (Managing Ed.); Cathy Chambliss (Adv.); Linda Skinner (Cir. Bus. Mgr.)
Parent company (for newspapers): AIM Media Indiana

XENIA DAILY GAZETTE

Street address 1: 1836 W Park Sq
Street address city: Xenia
Street address state: OH
Zip/Postal code: 45385-2668
County: Greene
Country: USA
Mailing address: 1836 W PARK SQ
Mailing city: XENIA
Mailing state: OH
Mailing zip: 45385-2668
General Phone: (937) 372-4444
Advertising Phone: (937) 372-4444 ext. 200
Editorial Phone: (937) 372-4444
General/National Adv. E-mail: nlebeau@civitasmedia.com
Display Adv. E-mail: nlebeau@civitasmedia.com
Classified Adv. e-mail: nlebeau@civitasmedia.com
Editorial e-mail: editor@xeniagazette.com
Primary Website: www.xeniagazette.com
Year Established: 1868
News Services: AP
Delivery Methods: Mail`Newsstand`Carrier
Areas Served - City/County or Portion Thereof, or Zip codes: Xenia (OH)
Own Printing Facility?: N
Commercial printers?: Y
Sat. Circulation Paid: 6000
Audit By: Sworn/Estimate/Non-Audited
Audit Date: 12.07.2019
Personnel: Barbara Vandeventer (Gen. Mgr.); Carol Kahle (Classified Sales); Scott Halasz (Ed./Rep.); John Bombatch (Sports Ed.)
Parent company (for newspapers): AIM Media Texas

TIMES RECORDER

Street address 1: 921 Linden Ave.
Street address city: Zanesville
Street address state: OH
Zip/Postal code: 43701
County: Muskingum
Country: USA
Mailing city: ZANESVILLE
Mailing state: OH
Mailing zip: 43701
General Phone: (740) 450-6700
Advertising Phone: (740) 452-4561
Editorial Phone: (740) 450-6750
General/National Adv. E-mail: scourson@gannett.com
Display Adv. E-mail: atrabitz@gannett.com
Classified Adv. e-mail: ksargent@nncogannett.com
Editorial e-mail: psjames@nncogannett.com
Primary Website: www.zanesvilletimesrecorder.com
Year Established: 1852
News Services: Landon Media Group, Newspapers Now, Gannett, NEA, TMS, GNS.
Syndicated Publications: USA WEEKEND Magazine (S).
Areas Served - City/County or Portion Thereof, or Zip codes: Muskingum County & Surrounding areas
Avg Free Circ: 840
Sat. Circulation Paid: 6071
Sat. Circulation Free: 840
Sun. Circulation Paid: 6976
Sun. Circulation Free: 278
Audit By: AAM
Audit Date: 31.03.2019
Personnel: Pam James (Ed.); Adam Trabitz (Adv. Sales Dir.); Sharon Courson (Nat'l Adv. Coord.); John Merriweather (Cir. Ops. Mgr.); Tonya Shipley (Class. Sales Ctr. Mgr.)
Parent company (for newspapers): Gannett

OKLAHOMA

THE ADA NEWS

Street address 1: 116 N Broadway Ave
Street address city: Ada
Street address state: OK
Zip/Postal code: 74820-5004
County: Pontotoc
Country: USA
Mailing address: PO BOX 489
Mailing city: ADA
Mailing state: OK
Mailing zip: 74821-0489
General Phone: (580) 332-4433
Advertising Phone: (580) 310-7502
Editorial Phone: (580) 310-7550
General/National Adv. E-mail: adanewsadvertising@cableone.net
Display Adv. E-mail: adanewsadvertising@cableone.net
Classified Adv. e-mail: mwise@theadanews.com
Editorial e-mail: adanewseditor@cableone.net
Primary Website: www.theadanews.com
News Services: AP.
Special Editions: Christmas (Dec); Football (Fall); Newcomer's Guide (Other).
Special Weekly Sections: Business, Services (Daily); NIE (Tue); Restaurant, Stocks, Commodities (Wed); Religion, Church (Fri); Sports, Lifestyle, Wedding, Engagements, Finance, Stocks, Real Estate (Sun)
Syndicated Publications: Sunday Comics (S).
Sun. Circulation Paid: 7879
Audit By: Sworn/Estimate/Non-Audited
Audit Date: 12.07.2019
Personnel: Dawn Keathley (Cir. Mgr.); Jeff Cali (Sports Ed.); Maurisa Nelson (Adv. Mgr.); Amy Johns (Pub.); Monica Wise (Class.); Glenn Puit (Exec. Ed.); Randy Mitchell (Mng. Ed.)
Parent company (for newspapers): CNHI, LLC; CNHI, LLC

ALTUS TIMES

Street address 1: 218 W Commerce St
Street address city: Altus
Street address state: OK
Zip/Postal code: 73521-3810
County: Jackson
Country: USA
Mailing address: PO BOX 578
Mailing city: ALTUS
Mailing state: OK
Mailing zip: 73522-0578
General Phone: (580) 482-1221
Advertising Phone: (580) 482-1221 ext. 2080
Editorial Phone: (580) 482-1221 ext. 2072
General/National Adv. E-mail: advertising@altustimes.com
Display Adv. E-mail: advertising@altustimes.com
Classified Adv. e-mail: advertising@altustimes.com
Editorial e-mail: esteinkopff@civitasmedia.com
Primary Website: www.altustimes.com
Year Established: 1900
News Services: AP.
Special Weekly Sections: Best Food Day (Wed); Church (Fri); TV (Sun)
Syndicated Publications: USA WEEKEND Magazine (Fri); American Profile (Weekly).
Delivery Methods: Mail`Newsstand`Carrier`Racks
Own Printing Facility?: Y
Commercial printers?: Y
Sun. Circulation Paid: 4591
Audit By: Sworn/Estimate/Non-Audited
Audit Date: 12.07.2019
Personnel: Stephanie Bogart (Adv. Sales Rep.); Rick Carpenter (Pub./Ed.); Ryan Lewis (Sports Ed.); Katrina Goforth (Rep.); Jeri Cox (Office Mgr.)
Parent company (for newspapers): Graystone Media Group LLC

THE ANADARKO DAILY NEWS

Street address 1: 117 E Broadway St
Street address city: Anadarko
Street address state: OK
Zip/Postal code: 73005-2823
County: Caddo
Country: USA
Mailing address: PO BOX 548
Mailing city: ANADARKO
Mailing state: OK
Mailing zip: 73005-0548
General Phone: (405) 247-3331
Advertising Phone: (405) 247-3331
Editorial Phone: (405) 247-3331
General/National Adv. E-mail: news@anadarko-news.com
Display Adv. E-mail: news@anadarko-news.com
Classified Adv. e-mail: news@anadarko-news.com
Editorial e-mail: news@anadarko-news.com
Year Established: 1901
News Services: AP
Special Weekly Sections: Best Food (Wed); TV (Fri)
Delivery Methods: Mail`Newsstand`Carrier`Racks
Areas Served - City/County or Portion Thereof, or Zip codes: 73005
Own Printing Facility?: Y
Commercial printers?: Y
Sat. Circulation Paid: 3000
Audit By: Sworn/Estimate/Non-Audited
Audit Date: 12.07.2019
Personnel: Joe W. McBride (Ed.); Carla McBride-Alexander (Mktg./Promo.); Philip Gomez (Circ. Mgr.); Carolyn N. McBride (Pub.)

THE ARDMOREITE

Street address 1: 117 W Broadway St
Street address city: Ardmore
Street address state: OK
Zip/Postal code: 73401-6226
County: Carter
Country: USA
Mailing address: PO BOX 1328
Mailing city: ARDMORE
Mailing state: OK
Mailing zip: 73402-1328

General Phone: (580) 223-2200
Advertising Phone: (580) 221-6501
Editorial Phone: (580) 221-6593
General/National Adv. E-mail: katherine.smith@ardmoreite.com
Display Adv. E-mail: katherine.smith@ardmoreite.com
Classified Adv. e-mail: classmanager@ardmoreite.com
Editorial e-mail: yournews@ardmoreite.com
Primary Website: www.ardmoreite.com
Mthly Avg Views: 500000
Year Established: 1893
News Services: AP.
Special Editions: Best of the Best Q1 - Fashion (Spring). Football tab (Fall), Gift Guide (Christmas), Home Improvemet (Spring and Fall), Restaurant Guide (spring) Blue Ribbon Scholars (June)
Special Weekly Sections: Children, Best Food (Wed); Spotlight (Thur); Religion, Entertainment (Fri); TV, Business, Education, Weddings, Engagements, Agriculture (Sun); Real Estate (Daily)
Syndicated Publications: Relish (Monthly); Carousel (local, newsprint) (S); American Profile (Weekly). Athlon sports, Relish (monthly)
Delivery Methods: Mail`Newsstand`Carrier`Racks
Areas Served - City/County or Portion Thereof, or Zip codes: 73401, 73443, 73456, 73463, 73438, 73030,73086,73460,73446
Own Printing Facility?: Y
Commercial printers?: Y
Sun. Circulation Paid: 5648
Audit By: VAC
Audit Date: 30.06.2017
Personnel: Kim Benedict (Pub.); Marsha Miller (News Ed.); Kathy Worley (Business Manager); Eddie Hunter (Adv. Dir.); Catherine Norvell (Class. Sales); Mary Butler (Cir. Dist. Mgr.); Robbie Short (Mng. Ed.)
Parent company (for newspapers): Gannett; CherryRoad Media

EXAMINER-ENTERPRISE

Street address 1: 4125 Nowata Rd
Street address city: Bartlesville
Street address state: OK
Zip/Postal code: 74006-5120
County: Washington
Country: USA
Mailing state: OK
General Phone: (918) 335-8200
Advertising Phone: (918) 335-8231
Editorial Phone: (918) 335-8246
General/National Adv. E-mail: ads@examiner-enterprise.com
Display Adv. E-mail: ads@examiner-enterprise.com
Classified Adv. e-mail: classads@examiner-enterprise.com
Editorial e-mail: cday@examiner-enterprise.com
Primary Website: www.examiner-enterprise.com
Mthly Avg Views: 300000
Mthly Avg Unique Visitors: 50000
News Services: AP.
Special Editions: Tourism Guide (Apr); Christmas (Dec); Customer Appreciation (Jan); OK Mozart (Jun); Progress (Mar); Christmas (Nov); Our Hometown (Oct).
Special Weekly Sections: Community, Computer, Real Estate, Travel, TV (Sun); Business (Sun/Wed); Food, Health (Wed); Golf, NASCAR (Thur); Agriculture, Church, InterUrbal (Fri)
Syndicated Publications: USA WEEKEND Magazine (S); American Profile (Weekly).
Delivery Methods: Carrier
Areas Served - City/County or Portion Thereof, or Zip codes: Bartesville (OK)
Own Printing Facility?: Y
Commercial printers?: Y
Avg Free Circ: 36
Sun. Circulation Paid: 6519
Sun. Circulation Free: 36
Audit By: AAM
Audit Date: 31.03.2016
Personnel: Janet Robinson (Cust. Rep.); Mike Tupa (Sports Ed.); Robert Dye (Cir. Mgr.); Tammy Green (Off. Mgr.); Matthew Tranquill (Pub.)
Parent company (for newspapers): CherryRoad Media

THE EXPRESS-STAR

Street address 1: 411 W Chickasha Ave
Street address 2: Ste 100
Street address city: Chickasha
Street address state: OK
Zip/Postal code: 73018-2472
County: Grady
Country: USA
Mailing address: PO BOX E
Mailing city: CHICKASHA
Mailing state: OK
Mailing zip: 73023-0835
General Phone: (405) 224-2600
Advertising Phone: (405) 224-2600
Editorial Phone: (405) 224-2600
General/National Adv. E-mail: advertising@chickashanews.com
Display Adv. E-mail: advertising@chickashanews.com
Classified Adv. e-mail: classifieds@chickashanews.com
Editorial e-mail: editor@chickashanews.com
Primary Website: www.chickashanews.com
Year Established: 1892
News Services: AP.
Special Editions: Fall Fashion (Aug); Progress (Feb); Christmas Gift Guides (Nov).
Special Weekly Sections: Best Food Day (wed); TV, Entertainment, Health (Sun); Business, Church (Fri)
Syndicated Publications: Relish (Monthly); TV Marquee (S).
Areas Served - City/County or Portion Thereof, or Zip codes: Grady County (OK)
Sun. Circulation Paid: 6300
Audit By: Sworn/Estimate/Non-Audited
Audit Date: 12.07.2019
Personnel: Vonnie Clark (Circ. Mgr.); Robin Rogers (Mailroom Supvr.); Kathy Black (Business Mgr.); Debi DeSilver (Managing Ed.); James Bright (Pub.)
Parent company (for newspapers): CNHI, LLC; CNHI, LLC

THE CLAREMORE DAILY PROGRESS

Street address 1: 315 W Will Rogers Blvd
Street address city: Claremore
Street address state: OK
Zip/Postal code: 74017-7021
County: Rogers
Country: USA
Mailing address: PO BOX 248
Mailing city: CLAREMORE
Mailing state: OK
Mailing zip: 74018-0248
General Phone: (918) 341-1101
Advertising Phone: (918) 341-1101 ext. 224
Editorial Phone: (918) 341-1101
General/National Adv. E-mail: ads@claremoreprogress.com
Display Adv. E-mail: ads@claremoreprogress.com
Classified Adv. e-mail: classifieds@claremoreprogress.com
Editorial e-mail: jdilmore@claremoreprogress.com
Primary Website: www.claremoreprogress.com
Year Established: 1893
News Services: AP, NEA, TMS.
Special Weekly Sections: Best Food (Wed); Family (Thur); Church (Fri); Health, Entertainment (Sun)
Syndicated Publications: Relish (Monthly); American Profile (S).
Delivery Methods: Mail`Newsstand`Carrier`Racks
Areas Served - City/County or Portion Thereof, or Zip codes: 74015-74019, 74031, 74036, 74053, 74055, 74080
Own Printing Facility?: Y
Commercial printers?: Y
Sun. Circulation Paid: 6500
Audit By: Sworn/Estimate/Non-Audited
Audit Date: 12.07.2019
Personnel: John Dillmore (Ed. / Pub.); Tom Fink (Staff Writer); Amy Walsh (Bus. Mgr.); Sheila Knight (HR Mgr.)
Parent company (for newspapers): CNHI, LLC; CNHI, LLC

THE CLINTON DAILY NEWS

Street address 1: 522 Avant Ave
Street address city: Clinton
Street address state: OK
Zip/Postal code: 73601-3436
County: Custer
Country: USA
Mailing address: 522 AVANT AVE
Mailing city: CLINTON
Mailing state: OK
Mailing zip: 73601-3436
General Phone: (580) 323-5151
General/National Adv. E-mail: cdnads@swbell.net
Display Adv. E-mail: cdnads@swbell.net
Classified Adv. e-mail: cdnclass@swbell.net
Editorial e-mail: cdnews@swbell.net
Primary Website: www.clintondailynews.com
Mthly Avg Views: 7696
Mthly Avg Unique Visitors: 4789
Year Established: 1903
Special Editions: Health Care in February Rt 66 Magazine in May Saluting our Veterans in July Senior Lifestyles in September Saluting our Local Heroes in October Holiday Magazine the first week of November
Special Weekly Sections: House of the Week (Tue); Oil, Gas (Wed); Entertainment, Legal, Farm, Food (Thur); Religion (Fri)
Delivery Methods: Mail`Newsstand`Racks
Areas Served - City/County or Portion Thereof, or Zip codes: 73601, 73620, 73622, 73624, 73625, 73632, 73639, 73647, 73669, 73096
Own Printing Facility?: Y
Commercial printers?: N
Sat. Circulation Paid: 3212
Audit By: Sworn/Estimate/Non-Audited
Audit Date: 12.07.2019
Personnel: Carol Sander (Vice Pres.); Cindy Gagne (Circ. Mgr.); Rod Serfoss (Pub./Ed.); Robert Bryan (Pho.); Sean Stephens (Nat. Adv. Mgr.); Eric Hunter (Prodn. Supv.)
Parent company (for newspapers): Engleman Family

THE DUNCAN BANNER

Street address 1: 1001 W Elm Ave
Street address city: Duncan
Street address state: OK
Zip/Postal code: 73533-4746
County: Stephens
Country: USA
Mailing address: PO BOX 1268
Mailing city: DUNCAN
Mailing state: OK
Mailing zip: 73534-1268
General Phone: (580) 255-5354
Advertising Phone: (580) 255-5354
Editorial Phone: (580) 255-5354
General/National Adv. E-mail: dana.boyles@duncanbanner.com
Display Adv. E-mail: dana.boyles@duncanbanner.com
Classified Adv. e-mail: classifieds@duncanbanner.com
Editorial e-mail: editor@duncanbanner.com
Primary Website: www.duncanbanner.com
Year Established: 1892
News Services: AP, NEA.
Special Weekly Sections: Best Food Day (Wed); Entertainment (Thur); Religion (Fri); TV (Sun)
Syndicated Publications: Relish (Monthly); American Profile (S).
Delivery Methods: Mail`Racks
Areas Served - City/County or Portion Thereof, or Zip codes: Stephens County (OK)
Own Printing Facility?: N
Commercial printers?: N
Sun. Circulation Paid: 6000
Audit By: Sworn/Estimate/Non-Audited
Audit Date: 12.07.2019
Personnel: Dana Boyles (Adv. Mgr.); Paula Blair (Adv. Mgr., Classified); Mike McCormack (Prodn. Mgr., Mailroom); Linda Rice (Business Mgr.); James Bright (Publisher)
Parent company (for newspapers): CNHI, LLC; CNHI, LLC

DURANT DEMOCRAT

Street address 1: 200 W Beech St
Street address city: Durant
Street address state: OK
Zip/Postal code: 74701-4316
County: Bryan
Country: USA
Mailing address: PO BOX 250
Mailing city: DURANT
Mailing state: OK
Mailing zip: 74702-0250
General Phone: (580) 924-4388
Advertising Phone: (580) 634-2157
Editorial Phone: (580) 634-2161
General/National Adv. E-mail: esmith@civitasmedia.com
Display Adv. E-mail: esmith@civitasmedia.com
Classified Adv. e-mail: bpollard@civitasmedia.com
Primary Website: www.durantdemocrat.com
Mthly Avg Unique Visitors: 28000
Year Established: 1901
News Services: AP, NEA.
Special Editions: Christmas Greetings (Dec); Chamber of Commerce (Feb); Space Clearance (Jan); Graduation (May); Christmas Promotion (Nov); Basketball Opening (Oct); Football Opening (Sept).
Special Weekly Sections: County Style (Tue); Best Food, Dining, Entertainment (Wed); Church (Fri); Home, Real Estate (Sun); Weather (Daily)
Syndicated Publications: USA WEEKEND Magazine (Fri); Entertainment Showcase (local entertainment & TV listings) (S); American Profile (Weekly).
Delivery Methods: Mail`Newsstand`Carrier`Racks
Own Printing Facility?: Y
Commercial printers?: Y
Sun. Circulation Paid: 5647
Audit By: Sworn/Estimate/Non-Audited
Audit Date: 12.07.2019
Personnel: Karen Brown (Adv. Mgr.); Matt Swearengin (Mng. Ed.); Michael Clements (Ed.); Kay Allen (Bus. Mgr.)
Parent company (for newspapers): Graystone Media Group LLC

ELK CITY DAILY NEWS

Street address 1: 206 W Broadway Ave
Street address city: Elk City
Street address state: OK
Zip/Postal code: 73644-4742
County: Beckham
Country: USA
Mailing address: 206 W BROADWAY AVE
Mailing city: ELK CITY
Mailing state: OK
Mailing zip: 73644-4736
General Phone: (580) 225-3000
Advertising Phone: (580) 225-3000
Editorial Phone: (580) 225-3000
General/National Adv. E-mail: ads@ecdailynews.com
Display Adv. E-mail: ads@ecdailynews.com
Classified Adv. e-mail: classifieds@ecdailynews.com
Editorial e-mail: news@ecdailynews.com
Primary Website: www.ecdailynews.com
Year Established: 1901
News Services: AP.
Special Editions: Graduation, Football Preview, Outdoor & Hunting, Basketball Preview, Last Minute Christmas Gift Guide, Back to School, Health Awareness, Spring Sports Preview
Special Weekly Sections: Best Food Days (Wed/Sun); Church (Thur); Living, Religion (Fri); Fashion, Health, Home, Women, TV (Sun)
Delivery Methods: Mail`Newsstand`Carrier`Racks
Areas Served - City/County or Portion Thereof, or Zip codes: Elk City (OK)
Sun. Circulation Paid: 4200
Audit By: Sworn/Estimate/Non-Audited
Audit Date: 12.07.2019
Personnel: Robert Fisher (Mng. Ed.); Kathy James (Circ. Mgr.); Blake Colston (Sports Ed.); Lorissa Graham (News reporter); Cheryl Overstreet (Community Ed.); Elizabeth Perkinson (Owner/Pres./Pub.); Jim Nicholas; Nancy McFarlin (Sales)
Parent company (for newspapers): The Elk City Daily News, Inc.

ENID NEWS & EAGLE

Street address 1: 227 W Broadway Ave
Street address city: Enid
Street address state: OK
Zip/Postal code: 73701-4017
County: Garfield
Country: USA
Mailing address: PO BOX 1192
Mailing city: ENID
Mailing state: OK
Mailing zip: 73702-1192
General Phone: (580) 233-6600
Advertising Phone: (580) 548-8136
Editorial Phone: (580) 548-8140
General/National Adv. E-mail: sales@enidnews.com
Display Adv. E-mail: sales@enidnews.com
Classified Adv. e-mail: classified@enidnews.com
Editorial e-mail: editor@enidnews.com
Primary Website: www.enidnews.com
Mthly Avg Views: 995508
Mthly Avg Unique Visitors: 209563
Year Established: 1893
News Services: Associated Press, CNHI News Service

Special Weekly Sections: Amusement, Weekend, Entertainment (Daily); Best Food Day (Wed/Sun); Entertainment (Fri); Farm, Business, Homes, Lifestyle (Weekly); Home Improvement, Progress, Cookbook, Back to School, Christmas Gift Guide (Annually)
Delivery Methods: Mail`Carrier`Racks
Areas Served - City/County or Portion Thereof, or Zip codes: Northwest Oklahoma All or parts of these counties:
Own Printing Facility?: Y
Commercial printers?: Y
Avg Free Circ: 650
Sat. Circulation Paid: 8187
Sat. Circulation Free: 650
Sun. Circulation Paid: 8781
Sun. Circulation Free: 194
Audit By: AAM
Audit Date: 30.06.2018
Personnel: Jeff Funk (Pres./Pub.); Margie Campbell (Major Acct. Rep.); Dee McCants (Adv. Dir.); Brad Nulph (Director of Audience Development (circulation)); Rob Collins (Executive Editor); Kellan Hohmann (Business manager); Frank Baker (Marketing Director); Violet Hassler (Digital Director); Mr. Kary Randles (Prepress Mgr); Tony Tolle (Pressroom Mgr)
Parent company (for newspapers): CNHI, LLC; CNHI, LLC

GUYMON DAILY HERALD

Street address 1: 515 N Ellison St
Street address city: Guymon
Street address state: OK
Zip/Postal code: 73942-4311
County: Texas
Country: USA
Mailing address: PO BOX 19
Mailing city: GUYMON
Mailing state: OK
Mailing zip: 73942-0019
General Phone: (580) 338-3355
Advertising Phone: (580) 338-3355
Editorial Phone: (580) 338-3355
General/National Adv. E-mail: dailyheraldads@gmail.com
Display Adv. E-mail: dailyheraldads@gmail.com
Classified Adv. e-mail: admanager@guymondailyherald.com
Editorial e-mail: guymondailyeditor@gmail.com
Primary Website: www.guymondailyherald.com
Year Established: 1886
News Services: AP.
Special Editions: Pioneer Days (Apr); Christmas Greetings (Dec); Progress (Feb); Graduation (May); Christmas Gift Guide (Nov); Texas County Fair (Sept).
Special Weekly Sections: Best Food (Wed); Agriculture, Business (Thur); Real Estate, Religion (Fri); Entertainment, Health (Sat)
Syndicated Publications: TV Guide Tab (Fri); American Profile (Sat).
Areas Served - City/County or Portion Thereof, or Zip codes: Entire Oklahoma region
Sat. Circulation Paid: 2332
Audit By: Sworn/Estimate/Non-Audited
Audit Date: 12.07.2019
Personnel: Myrna Campbell (Off. Mgr.); Alison Gipe (Adv. Dir. / Gen. Mgr.); Peggy Martinez (Cir. Mgr.); Kitie Matire (Mng. Ed.); Shawn Yorks (Sports Ed.)
Parent company (for newspapers): Horizon Publications Inc.

MCCURTAIN DAILY GAZETTE

Street address 1: 107 S Central Ave
Street address city: Idabel
Street address state: OK
Zip/Postal code: 74745-4847
County: McCurtain
Country: USA
Mailing address: PO BOX 179
Mailing city: IDABEL
Mailing state: OK
Mailing zip: 74745-0179
General Phone: (580) 286-3321
Advertising Phone: (580) 286-3321
Editorial Phone: (580) 286-3321
General/National Adv. E-mail: ads@mccurtain.com
Display Adv. E-mail: ads@mccurtain.com
Classified Adv. e-mail: ads@mccurtain.com
Editorial e-mail: paper@mccurtain.com
Year Established: 1905
News Services: AP.
Special Editions: Health (Jan); Home,Garden (Feb); Readers' Choice (Mar); Progress (Apr); Owa-Chito Celebration (Jun); back to School, Football (Aug); County Fair (Sept); Community, Hunter's (Oct); Holiday (Nov); Christmas (Dec)
Special Weekly Sections: TV, Comic, Society, Sports, farm, Wildlife (Sun); Comic, Society, Sports (Daily)
Syndicated Publications: Sunday Showcase Entertainment Tab (S); American Profile (Weekly).
Areas Served - City/County or Portion Thereof, or Zip codes: McCurtain County (OK)
Sun. Circulation Paid: 7800
Audit By: Sworn/Estimate/Non-Audited
Audit Date: 12.07.2019
Personnel: Gwen Willingham (Vice Pres. / Off. Mgr.); Shelly Davis (Adv. Dir.); Bruce Willingham (Pub. Ed.); Chris Willingham (Reporter); Hallee Deramus (Adv. Dir.)

THE LAWTON CONSTITUTION

Street address 1: 102 SW 3rd St
Street address city: Lawton
Street address state: OK
Zip/Postal code: 73501-4031
County: Comanche
Country: USA
Mailing address: PO BOX 2069
Mailing city: LAWTON
Mailing state: OK
Mailing zip: 73502-2069
General Phone: (580) 585-5000
Advertising Phone: (580) 585-5115
Editorial Phone: (580) 585-5000
General/National Adv. E-mail: support@swoknews.com
Display Adv. E-mail: ads@swoknews.com
Classified Adv. e-mail: djung@swoknews.com
Editorial e-mail: letters@swoknews.com
Primary Website: www.swoknews.com
Mthly Avg Views: 501507
Mthly Avg Unique Visitors: 87885
Year Established: 1910
News Services: AP, CNS.
Special Weekly Sections: Best Food (Wed); Home, Garden, Military (Thur); Entertainment (Fri); Religion (Fri); TV, Business, Real Estate, Auto (Sun)
Delivery Methods: Mail`Newsstand`Carrier`Racks
Areas Served - City/County or Portion Thereof, or Zip codes: Southwest Oklahoma
Own Printing Facility?: Y
Commercial printers?: N
Avg Free Circ: 368
Sat. Circulation Paid: 8628
Sat. Circulation Free: 368
Sun. Circulation Paid: 10239
Sun. Circulation Free: 244
Audit By: AAM
Audit Date: 9/31/2021
Personnel: Mike Owensby (Gen. Mgr.); Dee Ann Patterson (News Ed.); Larry Toth (Cir. Dir.); David Stringer (Publisher); Steve Metzer (City Ed.); David Hale (Managing Ed.); Kim Dodds (Adv. Dir.); Patty Entler (Nat'l Adv. Mgr.); JoAnn Robinson (Class.)
Parent company (for newspapers): Southern Newspapers Inc.

MCALESTER NEWS-CAPITAL

Street address 1: 500 S 2nd St
Street address city: McAlester
Street address state: OK
Zip/Postal code: 74501-5812
County: Pittsburg
Country: USA
Mailing address: PO BOX 987
Mailing city: MCALESTER
Mailing state: OK
Mailing zip: 74502-0987
General Phone: (918) 423-1700
Advertising Phone: (918) 421-2006
Editorial Phone: (918) 421-2023
General/National Adv. E-mail: advertising@mcalesternews.com
Display Adv. E-mail: advertising@mcalesternews.com
Classified Adv. e-mail: class@mcalesternews.com
Editorial e-mail: jbeaty@mcalesternews.com
Primary Website: www.mcalesternews.com
Year Established: 1896
News Services: AP, NEA.
Special Weekly Sections: Local, National News (Mon); Family (Tue); Best Food (Wed); Business (Thur); Religion (Fri); Real Estate, business, Milestone, Education, Health (Sun); Sports, Classifieds (Daily)
Syndicated Publications: Relish (Monthly); USA WEEKEND Magazine (S).
Areas Served - City/County or Portion Thereof, or Zip codes: Southeast Oklahoma
Sun. Circulation Paid: 10046
Audit By: Sworn/Estimate/Non-Audited
Audit Date: 12.07.2019
Personnel: James Beaty (Mng. Ed.); Debra Durbin (Prod. Mgr.); Reina Owens (Adv. Dir.); Glenn Puit (Exec. Ed.); Pat Hessdorfer (Bus. Mgr.); Ed Choate (Pub., Ed.)
Parent company (for newspapers): CNHI, LLC; CNHI, LLC

MIAMI NEWS-RECORD

Street address 1: 14 1st Ave NW
Street address city: Miami
Street address state: OK
Zip/Postal code: 74354-6224
County: Ottawa
Country: USA
Mailing address: PO BOX 940
Mailing city: MIAMI
Mailing state: OK
Mailing zip: 74355-0940
General Phone: (918) 542-5533
Advertising Phone: (918) 542-5533
Editorial Phone: (918) 542-5533
General/National Adv. E-mail: advertising@miaminewsrecord.com
Display Adv. E-mail: advertising@miaminewsrecord.com
Classified Adv. e-mail: classifieds@miaminewsrecord.com
Editorial e-mail: news@miaminewsrecord.com
Primary Website: www.miaminewsrecord.com
Year Established: 1890
News Services: AP.
Special Editions: Football (Aug); Christmas Greetings (Dec); Tax Tips (Feb); NEO Tournament (Jan); Sidewalk (Jul); Brides (Jun); Health (Mar); Graduation (May); Car Care (Nov); Community Visitor's Guide (Oct); Active Times (Quarterly); Hello Fall (Sept).
Special Weekly Sections: Best Food Day (Wed)
Syndicated Publications: TV Record (S).
Delivery Methods: Mail`Newsstand`Carrier`Racks
Areas Served - City/County or Portion Thereof, or Zip codes: Ottawa County (OK)
Own Printing Facility?: Y
Commercial printers?: N
Sun. Circulation Paid: 4000
Audit By: Sworn/Estimate/Non-Audited
Audit Date: 12.07.2019
Personnel: Joe Leong (Pub.); Bob Markham (Pagination Dir.); Susi Yount (Multi-Media Sales Exec.); Beckie Branham (Circ. Dir.); Patrick Richardson (Reg. Ed.)
Parent company (for newspapers): Reid Newspapers; CherryRoad Media

MUSKOGEE PHOENIX

Street address 1: 214 Wall St
Street address city: Muskogee
Street address state: OK
Zip/Postal code: 74401-6644
County: Muskogee
Country: USA
Mailing address: PO BOX 1968
Mailing city: MUSKOGEE
Mailing state: OK
Mailing zip: 74402-1968
General Phone: (918) 684-2828
Advertising Phone: (918) 684-2804
Editorial Phone: (918) 684-2933
General/National Adv. E-mail: phxads@muskogeephoenix.com
Display Adv. E-mail: troachell@muskogeephoenix.com/
Classified Adv. e-mail: khight@muskogeephoenix.com
Editorial e-mail: news@muskogeephoenix.com
Primary Website: www.muskogeephoenix.com
Year Established: 1888
News Services: AP, GNS.
Special Editions: Christmas Gift Guide (Annually); Visitors Guide (Semi-yearly).
Special Weekly Sections: Education, Parenting (Mon); Business, Health (Tue); Best Food (Wed); At Home (Thur); Entertainment (Fri); Auto, Religion (Sat); TV, Generations (Sun)
Syndicated Publications: USA WEEKEND Magazine (S).
Areas Served - City/County or Portion Thereof, or Zip codes: Northeast Oklahoma
Avg Free Circ: 204
Sat. Circulation Paid: 9195
Sat. Circulation Free: 204
Sun. Circulation Paid: 10500
Sun. Circulation Free: 153
Audit By: AAM
Audit Date: 30.09.2014
Personnel: Dale Brendel (Pub.); Elizabeth Ridenour (Executive Ed.); Mike Kays (Sports Ed.); Kevin Kizzia (Circ. Mgr.); Marci Apple (Advertising Dir.); Debbie Sherwood (Classifieds Mgr.)
Parent company (for newspapers): CNHI, LLC; CNHI, LLC

NORMAN TRANSCRIPT

Street address 1: 215 E Comanche St
Street address city: Norman
Street address state: OK
Zip/Postal code: 73069-6007
County: Cleveland
Country: USA
Mailing address: PO BOX 1058
Mailing city: NORMAN
Mailing state: OK
Mailing zip: 73070-1058
General Phone: (405) 321-1800
Advertising Phone: (405) 366-3587
Editorial Phone: (405) 366-3542
General/National Adv. E-mail: rebekah@normantranscript.com
Display Adv. E-mail: ads@normantranscript.com
Classified Adv. e-mail: jan@normantranscript.com
Editorial e-mail: editor@normantranscript.com
Primary Website: www.normantranscript.com
Year Established: 1889
News Services: AP, MCT, NEA.
Special Editions: Garden Guide (Apr); Greetings (Dec); Salute to Business (Feb); Tax Guide (Jan); Gift Guide (Nov); Home Improvement (Oct); Football (Sept).
Special Weekly Sections: Senior (Tue); Food, Family (Wed); Church, Entertainment (Fri); Real Estate (Sat); Business, Society, TV (Sun)
Syndicated Publications: USA WEEKEND Magazine (S).
Areas Served - City/County or Portion Thereof, or Zip codes: Norman, Cleveland & McClain Counties (OK)
Avg Free Circ: 466
Sat. Circulation Paid: 6395
Sat. Circulation Free: 466
Sun. Circulation Paid: 6736
Sun. Circulation Free: 178
Audit By: AAM
Audit Date: 30.09.2018
Personnel: Rebekah Collins (Adv. Mgr.); Jan Giza (Class. Sales Exec.); Mark Millsap (Pub.); Caleb Slinkard (Ed.); Vonnie Clark (Reg. Cir. Dir.); Tammy Griffis (Bus. Mgr.)
Parent company (for newspapers): CNHI, LLC; CNHI, LLC

THE NORMAN TRANSCRIPT

Street address 1: 215 E Comanche St
Street address city: Norman
Street address state: OK
Zip/Postal code: 73069-6007
County: Cleveland
Country: USA
Mailing address: PO BOX 1058
Mailing city: NORMAN
Mailing state: OK
Mailing zip: 73070-1058
General Phone: (405) 321-1800
Advertising Phone: (405) 366-3503
Editorial Phone: (405) 366-3543
General/National Adv. E-mail: kmiller@normantranscript.com
Display Adv. E-mail: kmiller@normantranscript.com
Classified Adv. e-mail: jtrowbridge@normantranscript.com
Editorial e-mail: editor@normantranscript.com
Primary Website: normantranscript.com
Mthly Avg Views: 710241
Mthly Avg Unique Visitors: 337659
Year Established: 1889
Areas Served - City/County or Portion Thereof, or Zip codes: Cleveland County
Audit By: USPS
Audit Date: 21.10.2023
Personnel: Katherine Miller (Publisher); Rob Rasor (Production Director); Beau Simmons (Editor); Jessica Trowbridge (Customer Service Manager); Kelly Senne (Circulation Senior District Manager); Paxson Haws (Assistant Editor); Chris Hartman (Prepress Manager); Tarik Masri (Sports Reporter); Andrea Hancock

(Reporter); Kyle Phillips (Photographer); Greta Samwel (Nationals/Special Projects Coordinator); Mark Millsap (Pub); Shana Adkisson (Ed); Vonnie Clark (Circ. Dir.); Tammy Griffis (Bus. Mgr.); Rob Rasor (Prod. Mgr.)
Parent company (for newspapers): CNHI, LLC

THE OKLAHOMAN

Street address 1: P.O. Box 25125
Street address 2: Suite 100
Street address city: Oklahoma City
Street address state: OK
Zip/Postal code: 73125-0125
County: Oklahoma
Country: USA
Mailing address: PO BOX 25125
Mailing city: OKLAHOMA CITY
Mailing state: OK
Mailing zip: 73125-0125
General Phone: (405) 475-3380
Advertising Phone: (405) 475-3380
Editorial Phone: (405) 475-3920
General/National Adv. E-mail: dvillanueva@oklahoman.com
Display Adv. E-mail: dvillanueva@oklahoman.com
Classified Adv. e-mail: dvillanueva@oklahoman.com
Editorial e-mail: kfry@oklahoman.com
Primary Website: www.newsok.com
Mthly Avg Views: 18050225
Mthly Avg Unique Visitors: 2795788
Year Established: 1903
News Services: Newspapers First, CT, DJ, CNS, MCT, SHNS, TMS.
Special Editions: Call 405-475-3380 for information
Special Weekly Sections: Business, Sports (daily); Culture , Fashion, Pop, Lifestyles, People, Society (Sun); Life, Health, Science, Technology (Tue); Life, Food (Wed); Life, Style (Thur); Weekend Life, Entertainment (Fri); Religion, Ethics, Values (Sat); Sunday Life, Spiritual, Travel, Society, Entertainment (Sun)
Syndicated Publications: Parade (S).
Delivery Methods: Mail`Newsstand`Carrier`Racks
Areas Served - City/County or Portion Thereof, or Zip codes: Entire Oklahoma region
Own Printing Facility?: N
Commercial printers?: Y
Sat. Circulation Paid: 74519
Sun. Circulation Paid: 106905
Audit By: AAM
Audit Date: 30.09.2018
Personnel: Christopher Reen (Pres. & Pub.); Scott Briggs (VP, Admin.); Kent Treadwell (Financial Mgr.); Tom Hite (Adv. Mgr., Classified); Mike Shannon (Mng. Ed.); Robby Trammell (Asst. Mng. Ed.); Clytie Bunyan (Bus. Ed.); Kelly Dyer Fry (Pub.); Derek Villanueva (National and Majors Sales Manager)
Parent company (for newspapers): Gannett; CherryRoad Media

OKMULGEE DAILY TIMES

Street address 1: 320 W 6th St
Street address city: Okmulgee
Street address state: OK
Zip/Postal code: 74447-5018
County: Okmulgee
Country: USA
Mailing address: 320 W 6TH ST
Mailing city: OKMULGEE
Mailing state: OK
Mailing zip: 74447-5018
General Phone: (918) 756-3600
Advertising Phone: (918) 756-3691
Editorial Phone: (918) 756-3693
General/National Adv. E-mail: carrie@bigbasinllc.com
Display Adv. E-mail: carrie@bigbasinllc.com
Classified Adv. e-mail: katina@bigbasinllc.com
Editorial e-mail: herman@bigbasinllc.com
Primary Website: www.okmulgeecountynewssource.com
News Services: AP.
Special Editions: Okmulgee Trade Show (Other).
Special Weekly Sections: Best Food Day (Wed); TV, Real Estate (Sun)
Syndicated Publications: Entertainment Times (television section) (S); American Profile (Weekly).
Sun. Circulation Paid: 6547
Audit By: Sworn/Estimate/Non-Audited
Audit Date: 12.07.2019
Personnel: Jeff Mayo (Pub.); Anthony Nieto (Gen. Mgr.); Carrie Carberry (Adv. Mgr.); Patrick Ford (Ed.); Katrina Holland (Legals/Classifieds); Larry Owen (Sports Ed.)

THE PERRY DAILY JOURNAL

Street address 1: 714 Delaware St
Street address city: Perry
Street address state: OK
Zip/Postal code: 73077-6425
County: Noble
Country: USA
Mailing address: PO BOX 311
Mailing city: PERRY
Mailing state: OK
Mailing zip: 73077-0311
General Phone: (580) 336-2222
Advertising Phone: (580) 336-2222
Editorial Phone: (580) 336-2222
General/National Adv. E-mail: mariapdj@yahoo.com
Display Adv. E-mail: mcvaypdj@yahoo.com
Classified Adv. e-mail: circclasspdjnews@yahoo.com
Editorial e-mail: pdjnews@yahoo.com
Primary Website: www.pdjnews.com
Year Established: 1893
Special Editions: High School Graduation and Speical Edition in conjunction with Cherokee Strip Celebratioin
Special Weekly Sections: Best Food (Wed)
Delivery Methods: Mail`Racks
Own Printing Facility?: Y
Sat. Circulation Paid: 3250
Audit By: Sworn/Estimate/Non-Audited
Audit Date: 12.07.2019
Personnel: Phillip Reid (Owner/Pub.); Lori Battles (Legal / Bill.); Bruce Atkinson (Cir. Mgr.); Gloria G. Brown (Managing Ed.); Stefani Nichols (Class. / Cir.)

THE PONCA CITY NEWS

Street address 1: 300 N 3rd St
Street address city: Ponca City
Street address state: OK
Zip/Postal code: 74601-4336
County: Kay
Country: USA
Mailing address: PO BOX 191
Mailing city: PONCA CITY
Mailing state: OK
Mailing zip: 74602-0191
General Phone: (580) 765-3311
Advertising Phone: (580) 765-3311
Editorial Phone: (580) 765-3311
General/National Adv. E-mail: ads@poncacitynews.com
Display Adv. E-mail: ads@poncacitynews.com
Classified Adv. e-mail: classified@poncacitynews.com
Editorial e-mail: letters@poncacitynews.com
Primary Website: www.poncacitynews.com
Year Established: 1893
News Services: AP.
Special Editions: Spring Home Improvement (Mar); Oklahoma Football (Aug); Christmas Greetings (Dec); Brides (Feb); Income Tax Guide (Jan);Welcome Neighbors (May); Medical Guide (Jul); Spring Car Care (Mar); Back to School (Jul); Holiday Gift Guide (Nov);
Special Weekly Sections: Garden (Mon); Business, Finance, Cooking (Tue); Best Food, Women (Wed); Entertainment (Thur); Religion, Education (Fri); TV, Family, Real Estate (Sun)
Syndicated Publications: TV Week (S).
Delivery Methods: Mail`Newsstand`Carrier`Racks
Areas Served - City/County or Portion Thereof, or Zip codes: 74604
Own Printing Facility?: Y
Commercial printers?: N
Sun. Circulation Paid: 8838
Audit By: AAM
Audit Date: 30.09.2011
Personnel: Michael Ellis (Controller); Pat Jordan (Adv. Mgr.); Tom Muchmore (Ed. / Pub.); Kristie Hayes (Mng. Ed); David Miller (Sports reporter); Fred Hilton (Sports Ed.); Jerry Helems (Prodn. Mgr.); Robyn Ryan (Retail Adv. Mgr.)

POTEAU DAILY NEWS

Street address 1: 804 N Broadway St
Street address 2: Ste A
Street address city: Poteau
Street address state: OK
Zip/Postal code: 74953-3503
County: Le Flore
Country: USA
Mailing address: PO BOX 1237
Mailing city: POTEAU
Mailing state: OK
Mailing zip: 74953-1237
General Phone: (918) 647-3188
Advertising Phone: (918) 647-3188
Editorial Phone: (918) 647-3188
General/National Adv. E-mail: publisher@poteaudailynews.com
Display Adv. E-mail: nmckimmey.pdn@gmail.com
Classified Adv. e-mail: classifieds.pdn@gmail.com
Editorial e-mail: editor@poteaudailynews.com
Primary Website: www.poteaudailynews.com
Year Established: 1895
News Services: AP.
Special Editions: Progress (Feb); Fact Book (Jul).
Special Weekly Sections: History (Tue); Agriculture (Wed); Education (Thur); Area Events (Fri); Celebrations (Sat)
Syndicated Publications: American Profile (Weekly).
Delivery Methods: Mail`Newsstand`Carrier`Racks
Areas Served - City/County or Portion Thereof, or Zip codes: LeFlore County
Own Printing Facility?: N
Commercial printers?: N
Sat. Circulation Paid: 3100
Audit By: Sworn/Estimate/Non-Audited
Audit Date: 12.07.2019
Personnel: David McKimmey (General Manager/ Circulation Director)
Parent company (for newspapers): Horizon Publications Inc.

SAPULPA DAILY HERALD

Street address 1: 16 S Park St
Street address city: Sapulpa
Street address state: OK
Zip/Postal code: 74066-4220
County: Creek
Country: USA
Mailing address: PO BOX 1370
Mailing city: SAPULPA
Mailing state: OK
Mailing zip: 74067-1370
General Phone: (918) 224-5185
Advertising Phone: (918) 224-5185 ext. 103
Editorial Phone: (918) 224-5185
General/National Adv. E-mail: admanager@sapulpadailyherald.com
Display Adv. E-mail: advertising1@sapulpadailyherald.com
Classified Adv. e-mail: classifieds@sapulpaheraldonline.com
Editorial e-mail: editor@sapulpaheraldonline.com
Year Established: 1914
News Services: AP.
Special Weekly Sections: Sports, Lifestyles (Daily); Best Food (Wed); Church (Fri); Business, TV (Sun)
Syndicated Publications: Relish (Monthly); TV Today (entertainment tab) (S); American Profile (Weekly).
Areas Served - City/County or Portion Thereof, or Zip codes: Sapulpa and surrounding communities (OK)
Sun. Circulation Paid: 4501
Audit By: Sworn/Estimate/Non-Audited
Audit Date: 12.07.2019
Personnel: Darren D. Sumner (Pub.); Teresa Cooper (Prodn. Mgr.); Chris Swafford (Adv. Mgr.); Connie Jones (Cir. Mgr.); John Brock (Ed.)
Parent company (for newspapers): CNHI, LLC

THE SEMINOLE PRODUCER

Street address 1: 121 N Main St
Street address city: Seminole
Street address state: OK
Zip/Postal code: 74868-4627
County: Seminole
Country: USA
Mailing address: PO BOX 431
Mailing city: SEMINOLE
Mailing state: OK
Mailing zip: 74818-0431
General Phone: (405) 382-1100
Advertising Phone: (405) 382-1100
Editorial Phone: (405) 382-1100
General/National Adv. E-mail: ads@seminoleproducer.com
Display Adv. E-mail: ads@seminoleproducer.com
Classified Adv. e-mail: ads@seminoleproducer.com
Editorial e-mail: news@seminoleproducer.com
Primary Website: www.seminoleproducer.com
Year Established: 1927
News Services: CNS, NEA, Capitol Press Report.
Special Weekly Sections: Best Foods (Wed)
Delivery Methods: Mail`Carrier`Racks
Areas Served - City/County or Portion Thereof, or Zip codes: Seminole County (OK)
Own Printing Facility?: Y
Commercial printers?: N
Sun. Circulation Paid: 5600
Audit By: Sworn/Estimate/Non-Audited
Audit Date: 12.07.2019
Personnel: Mike Gifford (Adv. Dir.); Cheryl Phillips (Entertainment/Amusements Ed.); Stu Phillips (Ed. / Pub.); Cody Phillips (Teen-Age/Youth Ed.); John Lewis (Prod. / Cir. Dir.); Ken Childers

SHAWNEE NEWS-STAR

Street address 1: 215 N Bell Ave
Street address city: Shawnee
Street address state: OK
Zip/Postal code: 74801-6913
County: Pottawatomie
Country: USA
Mailing address: PO BOX 1688
Mailing city: SHAWNEE
Mailing state: OK
Mailing zip: 74802-1688
General Phone: (405) 273-4200
Advertising Phone: (405) 214-3941
Editorial Phone: (405) 214-3922
General/National Adv. E-mail: orvena.gregory@news-star.com
Display Adv. E-mail: maria.flanagan@news-star.com
Classified Adv. e-mail: wanda.westerman@news-star.com
Editorial e-mail: kimberly.morava@news-star.com
Primary Website: www.news-star.com
Year Established: 1894
News Services: AP.
Special Editions: School (Aug); Christmas (Dec); Bridal (Jan); Lawn and Garden (Mar); Gift Guide (Nov); Home Improvement (Sept).
Special Weekly Sections: Education (Tue); Best Food, Gardening (Wed); Pets (Thur); Weekend, Entertainment (Fri); Religion, Agriculture (Sat); TV, Business, Weddings, Health (Sun)
Syndicated Publications: Relish (Monthly); Color Comics (Other); USA WEEKEND Magazine (S).
Sat. Circulation Paid: 7175
Sun. Circulation Paid: 8334
Audit By: Sworn/Estimate/Non-Audited
Audit Date: 12.07.2019
Personnel: Kent Bush (Pub.); Reita Easley (Operation Mgr.); Kim Morava (Ed.); Adam Ewing (Sports Ed.); Robby Parsons (Production Mgr.)
Parent company (for newspapers): Gannett; CherryRoad Media

STILLWATER NEWS PRESS

Street address 1: 211 W 9th Ave
Street address city: Stillwater
Street address state: OK
Zip/Postal code: 74074-4406
County: Payne
Country: USA
Mailing address: PO BOX 2288
Mailing city: STILLWATER
Mailing state: OK
Mailing zip: 74076-2288
General Phone: (405) 372-5000
General/National Adv. E-mail: advmgr@stwnewspress.com
Display Adv. E-mail: advmgr@stwnewspress.com
Classified Adv. e-mail: classifieds@stwnewspress.com
Editorial e-mail: editor@stwnewspress.com
Primary Website: www.stwnewspress.com
Mthly Avg Views: 130000
Mthly Avg Unique Visitors: 85000
Year Established: 1900
News Services: Associated Press, CNHINS
Special Editions: Medical Directory (Feb and Aug); Oklahoma State University Game Days (Fridays during Fall football season); Last Minute Gift Guide (Dec); Bridal (Jan); Payne County Fair (Jul); Progress (Jun); Apartment Guide (Sept. & Feb.); Graduation (May); Christmas Gift Guide (Nov); Dining Guide (Aug); Home Improvement (Sept, April).
Special Weekly Sections: Real Estate Weekly (Fri); Agriculture (S); TV Spotlight (Sun); Food (Wed).
Syndicated Publications: Parade (Fri.); Athlon Sports (monthly); Spry (Monthly); Comics (S).
Delivery Methods: Mail`Newsstand`Carrier`Racks

Areas Served - City/County or Portion Thereof, or Zip codes: Payne County and parts of surrounding counties in Oklahoma
Own Printing Facility?: N
Commercial printers?: N
Sat. Circulation Paid: 5200
Sun. Circulation Paid: 5800
Audit By: Sworn/Estimate/Non-Audited
Audit Date: 12.07.2019
Personnel: Jill Hunt (Adv. Mgr.); Dale Brendel (Pub.); Joe Toth (Dir. of Audience Dev.); Beau Simmons (Ed.)
Parent company (for newspapers): CNHI, LLC; CNHI, LLC

TAHLEQUAH DAILY PRESS

Street address 1: 106 W 2nd St
Street address city: Tahlequah
Street address state: OK
Zip/Postal code: 74464-4724
County: Cherokee
Country: USA
Mailing address: PO BOX 888
Mailing city: TAHLEQUAH
Mailing state: OK
Mailing zip: 74464
General Phone: 9184568833
Advertising Phone: (918) 456-8833
Editorial Phone: (918) 456-8833
General/National Adv. E-mail: s.elswick@muskogeephoenix.com
Display Adv. E-mail: hruotolo@tahlequahdailypress.com
Classified Adv. e-mail: hruotolo@tahlequahdailypress.com
Editorial e-mail: kpoindexter@cnhi.com
Primary Website: www.tahlequahdailypress.com
Mthly Avg Views: 30000
Year Established: 1844
News Services: AP.
Special Editions: Tahlequah - Green Country Tourism (Jan.); Progress (Feb.); HealthWatch (Mar., June, Sept., Dec.); Football Preview (Aug.); Lakes & River (May, June, July, Aug., Sept., Dec.)
Special Weekly Sections: Arts & Entertainment (Fri.); Church (Wed); Business & Farm (Sun).
Syndicated Publications: Relish (Monthly); USA WEEKEND Magazine (S); American Profile (Weekly). 911 @Play (S)
Delivery Methods: Mail`Newsstand`Racks
Areas Served - City/County or Portion Thereof, or Zip codes: Tahlequah & Cherokee County (OK)
Own Printing Facility?: N
Commercial printers?: N
Sun. Circulation Paid: 3500
Audit By: Sworn/Estimate/Non-Audited
Audit Date: 12.07.2019
Personnel: Kim Poindexter (Exec. Ed.); Sheri Gourd (Mult. Media Ed.); Byron Beers (sports editor); Tes Jackson (courts & crime reporter); Sean Rowley (news editor); Grant Crawford (general assignment reporter)
Parent company (for newspapers): CNHI, LLC; CNHI, LLC

TULSA WORLD

Street address 1: 315 S. Boulder Avenue
Street address city: Tulsa
Street address state: OK
Zip/Postal code: 74103
County: Tulsa
Country: USA
Mailing address: PO BOX 1770
Mailing city: TULSA
Mailing state: OK
Mailing zip: 74102-1770
General Phone: (918) 583-2161
Advertising Phone: (918) 581-8510
Editorial Phone: (918) 581-8330
General/National Adv. E-mail: advertising@tulsaworld.com
Display Adv. E-mail: advertising@tulsaworld.com
Classified Adv. e-mail: classad@tulsaworld.com
Editorial e-mail: letters@tulsaworld.com
Primary Website: www.tulsaworld.com
Mthly Avg Unique Visitors: 2490557
Year Established: 1905
News Services: AP, LAT-WP, MCT, GNS.
Special Editions: Football Preview (Aug); Christmas Gift Guide (Dec).
Special Weekly Sections: Entertainment (Thu); World of Homes (Sat); Fashion (Thur); Best Food Day (Wed).
Syndicated Publications: USA WEEKEND Magazine (S).
Delivery Methods: Mail`Carrier`Racks
Areas Served - City/County or Portion Thereof, or Zip codes: 74103 - plus
Own Printing Facility?: Y
Commercial printers?: Y
Sat. Circulation Paid: 52618
Sun. Circulation Paid: 64587
Audit By: AAM
Audit Date: 31.03.2018
Personnel: Susan Ellerbach (Exec. Ed.); Gloria Fletcher (Pres. & Pub.); Jennifer Carthel (Advertising Director); Mark Appleby (Audience Growth and Distribution Director); Angela Springer (Regional Human Resources Director)
Parent company (for newspapers): BH Media Group; Lee Enterprises, Incorporated

THE VINITA DAILY JOURNAL

Street address 1: 140 S Wilson St
Street address city: Vinita
Street address state: OK
Zip/Postal code: 74301-3730
County: Craig
Country: USA
Mailing address: PO BOX 328
Mailing city: VINITA
Mailing state: OK
Mailing zip: 74301-0328
General Phone: (918) 256-6422
Advertising Phone: (918) 639-8921
Editorial Phone: (918) 256-6422
General/National Adv. E-mail: vdj@cableone.net
Display Adv. E-mail: vdjproduction@cableone.net
Classified Adv. e-mail: classifieds@vinitanews.com
Editorial e-mail: vdj@cableone.net
Primary Website: www.vdjonline.com
Year Established: 1907
News Services: AP, NEA.
Special Editions: Home Improvement (Apr); Rodeo Pioneer (Aug); Christmas (Dec); Business Profiles (Jul); Christmas (Nov); Almanac (Oct); Calf Fry (Sept).
Special Weekly Sections: Best Food Days (Wed)
Syndicated Publications: Vinita Viewer (Fri).
Areas Served - City/County or Portion Thereof, or Zip codes: Vinita, Craig County, Grand Lake & Northeast Oklahoma
Audit By: Sworn/Estimate/Non-Audited
Audit Date: 12.07.2019
Personnel: Phillip R. Reid (Pub.); David Burgess (Mng. Ed.); Michelle Milner (Adv.)

WEATHERFORD DAILY NEWS

Street address 1: 118 S Broadway St
Street address city: Weatherford
Street address state: OK
Zip/Postal code: 73096-4924
County: Custer
Country: USA
Mailing address: PO BOX 191
Mailing city: WEATHERFORD
Mailing state: OK
Mailing zip: 73096-0191
General Phone: (580) 772-3301
Advertising Phone: (580) 772-3301
Editorial Phone: (580) 772-3301
General/National Adv. E-mail: wdn@wdnonline.com
Display Adv. E-mail: wdn@wdnonline.com
Classified Adv. e-mail: wdn@wdnonline.com
Editorial e-mail: wdn@wdnonline.com
Primary Website: www.wdnonline.com
Year Established: 1898
News Services: AP, CNS, NYT, TMS.
Special Editions: Parade of Homes (Apr); Koupon Kraze (Aug); Christmas Greetings (Dec); Valentine's Promo (Feb); Health Quarterly (Jan); Summer Clearance (Jul); Father's Day Gift Guide (Jun); Spring Home Improvement Tab (Mar); Sidewalk Sales (May); Gift Guide (Nov);
Special Weekly Sections: Best Food (Wed/Sun); Church, Real Estate (Fri); Fashion, Entertainment, Health, Real Estate (Sun);
Syndicated Publications: TV Entertainment Tab (S).
Areas Served - City/County or Portion Thereof, or Zip codes: Weatherford (OK)
Sat. Circulation Paid: 4464
Audit By: Sworn/Estimate/Non-Audited
Audit Date: 12.07.2019
Personnel: Phillip R. Reid (Pub.); Robyn England (Mktg. Rep.); Sarah Ryan (Class. Adv. Mgr.)

WOODWARD NEWS

Street address 1: 904 Oklahoma Ave
Street address city: Woodward
Street address state: OK
Zip/Postal code: 73801-4660
County: Woodward
Country: USA
Mailing address: PO BOX 1046
Mailing city: WOODWARD
Mailing state: OK
Mailing zip: 73802-1046
General Phone: (580) 256-2200
Advertising Phone: (580) 256-2200
Editorial Phone: (580) 256-2200
General/National Adv. E-mail: cthornton@woodwardnews.net
Display Adv. E-mail: mray@woodwardnews.net
Classified Adv. e-mail: classified@woodwardnews.net
Editorial e-mail: editor@woodwardnews.net
Primary Website: www.woodwardnews.net
News Services: AP.
Special Editions: Fall Sports (Aug); Spring Sports (Jan); Back-to-School (Jul); Progress (Mar).
Special Weekly Sections: Farm & Ranch (Tue); Best Food Day (Tue/Wed); Church, TV, Lap by Lap (Sat); Senior Scene (Sun)
Syndicated Publications: Relish (Monthly); American Profile (Weekly).
Delivery Methods: Mail`Racks
Areas Served - City/County or Portion Thereof, or Zip codes: Ellis, Harper, Dewey, Woodward & parts of Woods & Major Counties (OK)
Own Printing Facility?: Y
Commercial printers?: N
Avg Free Circ: 4350
Sat. Circulation Paid: 3600
Sun. Circulation Paid: 3700
Audit By: Sworn/Estimate/Non-Audited
Audit Date: 12.07.2019
Personnel: Sheila Gay (Pub. / Ad Mgr.); Johnny McMahan (Ed. / Sports Ed.); Anita Roach (Cir.); Carlinda Thornton (Adv.)
Parent company (for newspapers): CNHI, LLC

OREGON

ALBANY DEMOCRAT-HERALD

Street address 1: 600 Lyon St S
Street address city: Albany
Street address state: OR
Zip/Postal code: 97321-2919
County: Linn
Country: USA
Mailing address: PO BOX 130
Mailing city: ALBANY
Mailing state: OR
Mailing zip: 97321-0041
General Phone: (541) 926-2211
Advertising Phone: (541) 812-6073
Editorial Phone: (541) 812-6095
General/National Adv. E-mail: ads@dhonline.com
Display Adv. E-mail: ads@dhonline.com
Classified Adv. e-mail: ads@dhonline.com
Editorial e-mail: news@dhonline.com
Primary Website: www.democratherald.com
Mthly Avg Views: 1300000
Mthly Avg Unique Visitors: 234000
Year Established: 1865
News Services: AP
Special Weekly Sections: Business (Mon); People (Tue); Best Food, This Week, People (Wed); People, Young Voices (Thur); Religion, Entertainer, TV, Movies, Events, Arts, Dining (Fri); Home, Garden, Lifestyles (Sun);
Syndicated Publications: Relish (Monthly); Parade Magazine (S).
Delivery Methods: Mail`Newsstand`Carrier`Racks
Areas Served - City/County or Portion Thereof, or Zip codes: Albany & Linn County (OR)
Own Printing Facility?: Y
Commercial printers?: Y
Avg Free Circ: 637
Sat. Circulation Paid: 6954
Sat. Circulation Free: 637
Sun. Circulation Paid: 7165
Sun. Circulation Free: 848
Audit By: AAM
Audit Date: 31.03.2019
Personnel: Jeff Precourt (Pub.); Mike McInally (Mng. Ed.); Crystal Harris (Display Advertising Mgr.); Steve Gress (Sports Ed.); Cyndi Sprinkel-Hart (Advertising Account Mgr.)
Parent company (for newspapers): Dispatch-Argus; Lee Enterprises, Incorporated

THE DAILY ASTORIAN

Street address 1: 949 Exchange St
Street address city: Astoria
Street address state: OR
Zip/Postal code: 97103-4605
County: Clatsop
Country: USA
Mailing address: PO BOX 210
Mailing city: ASTORIA
Mailing state: OR
Mailing zip: 97103-0210
General Phone: (503) 325-3211
Advertising Phone: (503) 325-3211
Editorial Phone: (503) 325-3211
General/National Adv. E-mail: ads@dailyastorian.com
Display Adv. E-mail: ads@dailyastorian.com
Classified Adv. e-mail: classifieds@dailyastorian.com
Editorial e-mail: news@dailyastorian.com
Primary Website: www.dailyastorian.com
Mthly Avg Views: 330000
Mthly Avg Unique Visitors: 110000
Year Established: 1873
News Services: AP, NYT.
Special Editions: Bridal Planner (Feb); Our Coast magazine (Feb.); Good Health Directory (Mar); Spring Sports Tab (Mar); Crab, Seafood & Wine Festival (Apr.), Coastal Menu Guide (Jun); Scandinavian Festival (Jun); Car Care (Jun); Clatsop County Fair (July); At Home (July); Astoria Regatta (Aug); Who's Who in Clatsop Cty (Aug); Fall Sports Tab (Sept); Women In Business (Sept); Liberty Theater Presents (sept); Astor Street Opry (Oct); Home For the Holidays (Nov); Winter Sports Tab (Nov) & Property Lines (Jan, Mar, May, July, Sept., & Nov)
Special Weekly Sections: Marketplace (Tue); Observer, TV (Wed); Local Business, Entertainment (Thur); Religion, Community, Real Estate (Fri)
Syndicated Publications: Coast Weekend (Thur). Our Coast (February)
Delivery Methods: Mail`Newsstand`Carrier`Racks
Areas Served - City/County or Portion Thereof, or Zip codes: 97102, 97103, 97110, 98614, 97016, 97138, 97121, 98624, 98631, 97130, 98637, 98638, 97131, 98640, 98641, 97138, 98644, 97145, 97146, 97016, 97147
Own Printing Facility?: Y
Commercial printers?: Y
Avg Free Circ: 358
Audit By: AAM
Audit Date: 30.06.2017
Personnel: Kari Borgen (Publisher); Betty Smith (Adv. Mgr.); Derrick DePledge; Cridalyn Lyster (Digital Development Director); John Bruijin (Prodn. Mgr., Systems); Jim Stanovich (Pressroom Supervisor); Laura Sellers (Managing Editor); Heather Ramsdell (Circulation Manager); Carl Earl (Corporate Systems Manager); Debby Bloom; David Pero (Publisher and Editor)
Parent company (for newspapers): EO Media Group

THE BULLETIN

Street address 1: 320 SW Upper Terrace Dr. Suite #200
Street address city: Bend
Street address state: OR
Zip/Postal code: 97702
County: Deschutes
Country: USA
Mailing address: PO BOX 6020
Mailing city: BEND
Mailing state: OR
Mailing zip: 97708-6020
General Phone: (541) 382-1811
Advertising Phone: (541) 385-5809
Editorial Phone: (541) 383-0367
General/National Adv. E-mail: addrop@bendbulletin.com
Display Adv. E-mail: dderose@bendbulletin.com
Classified Adv. e-mail: dderose@bendbulletin.com
Editorial e-mail: elukens@bendbulletin.com
Primary Website: www.bendbulletin.com
Year Established: 1903
News Services: AP, LAT-WP, MCT, NYT.

Special Editions: PULSE Health Magazine (4x annually); Public School Directory (Aug); Sisters Magazine (Every other month); Sportsman's Show Guide (Feb); Baby Book (Jan); Deschutes County Fair (Jul); Graduation (Jun); Tee to Green: Golf Guide (May); Tour of Homes (July) PRCA Rodeo Guide (Nov); Fall Home Show Guide (Oct); Central Ore. U Magazine: Women's Mag. 4x annually). New Home Living (4x annually) Picture Your Home: Monthly Real Estate Magazine. Bid N Buy Advertiser Auctions 2x annually. Ageless (Senior Magazine) 4x annually.
Special Weekly Sections: GO! Magazine, Family (Fri); Green, Community, Life, Comics (Mon); At Home, Best Food Day, Comics (Tue); Outdoors (Wed); Health, Fitness (Thur); Entertainment, TV (Sat); Weddings, Engagements, Travel, Business (Sun); Community, Life (Daily)
Syndicated Publications: U Magazine (Every other month); Picture Your Home (Monthly); Pulse (Quarterly); Parade (S).
Delivery Methods: Mail`Newsstand`Carrier`Racks
Areas Served - City/County or Portion Thereof, or Zip codes: 20
Own Printing Facility?: Y
Commercial printers?: Y
Avg Free Circ: 3075
Sat. Circulation Paid: 18887
Sat. Circulation Free: 2260
Sun. Circulation Paid: 19428
Sun. Circulation Free: 2124
Audit By: AAM
Audit Date: 31.12.2017
Personnel: John Costa (Publisher); Denise Costa (Associate editor); Dean Guernsey (Photo Ed.); Bill Bigelow (Sports Ed.); Steve Hoffmann (IT Director); Alan Nelson (Prodn. Supvr.); Erik Lukens (Editor); dena derose (advertising director); mike hryko (circulation director)
Parent company (for newspapers): EO Media Group

THE WORLD

Street address 1: 350 Commercial Ave
Street address city: Coos Bay
Street address state: OR
Zip/Postal code: 97420-2269
County: Coos
Country: USA
Mailing address: PO BOX 1840
Mailing city: COOS BAY
Mailing state: OR
Mailing zip: 97420-0147
General Phone: (541) 269-1222
Advertising Phone: (541) 269-1222
Editorial Phone: (541) 269-1222
General/National Adv. E-mail: chris.rush@theworldlink.com
Display Adv. E-mail: dieter.kuhn@theworldlink.com
Classified Adv. e-mail: mike.hrycko@theworldlink.com
Editorial e-mail: larry.campbell@theworldlink.com
Primary Website: www.theworldlink.com
Year Established: 1878
News Services: Associated Press
Special Weekly Sections: Auto (Fri); Outdoor (Sat); Best Food Day (Tues); Gardening (Wed).
Syndicated Publications: Color Comics (Sat); American Profile (Sat).
Delivery Methods: Mail`Newsstand`Carrier`Racks
Areas Served - City/County or Portion Thereof, or Zip codes: Coos Bay, North Bend, Charleston, Coquille, Myrtle Point, Powers, Bandon & Reedstport (OR)
Own Printing Facility?: Y
Commercial printers?: Y
Avg Free Circ: 610
Sat. Circulation Paid: 3424
Sat. Circulation Free: 895
Audit By: AAM
Audit Date: 31.03.2019
Personnel: Dan Gordon (Prod. Supv.); Chris Rush (Pub.); Mike Hrycko (Cir. Dir.); Larry Campbell (Exec. Ed.); Dan Gordon (Press Foreman); Andris Jaunzems (Prod. Mgr.)
Parent company (for newspapers): Lee Enterprises, Incorporated

CORVALLIS GAZETTE-TIMES

Street address 1: 1835 NW Circle Blvd
Street address city: Corvallis
Street address state: OR
Zip/Postal code: 97330-1310
County: Benton
Country: USA
Mailing address: PO BOX 368
Mailing city: CORVALLIS
Mailing state: OR
Mailing zip: 97339-0368
General Phone: (541) 753-2641
Advertising Phone: (541) 812-6073
Editorial Phone: (541) 753-2641
General/National Adv. E-mail: cyndi.sprinkel-hart@lee.net
Display Adv. E-mail: cyndi.sprinkel-hart@lee.net
Classified Adv. e-mail: cyndi.sprinkel-hart@lee.net
Editorial e-mail: mike.mcinally@lee.net
Primary Website: www.gazettetimes.com
Mthly Avg Views: 1250000
Mthly Avg Unique Visitors: 182655
Year Established: 1862
News Services: AP, MCT.
Special Editions: Baby Book (April); Summer Guide (May); Our Town (Sept).
Special Weekly Sections: Food (Wed); Business, Stock (Tue-Sun); Best Food (Wed); Entertainment, Arts (Thu); Church (Sat); TV (Wed); People (Sat)
Syndicated Publications: Relish (Monthly);
Areas Served - City/County or Portion Thereof, or Zip codes: Corvallis & Benton County (OR)
Own Printing Facility?: Y
Commercial printers?: Y
Avg Free Circ: 873
Sat. Circulation Paid: 6453
Sat. Circulation Free: 873
Sun. Circulation Paid: 6398
Sun. Circulation Free: 848
Audit By: AAM
Audit Date: 31.03.2019
Personnel: Mike McInally (Ed.); Jeff Precourt (Publisher); Doug Byers (General manager)
Parent company (for newspapers): Lee Enterprises, Incorporated

THE REGISTER-GUARD

Street address 1: 3500 Chad Dr
Street address city: Eugene
Street address state: OR
Zip/Postal code: 97408-7426
County: Lane
Country: USA
Mailing address: 3500 CHAD DR
Mailing city: EUGENE
Mailing state: OR
Mailing zip: 97408-7426
General Phone: (541) 485-1234
Advertising Phone: (541) 342-1212
Editorial Phone: (541) 485-1234
General/National Adv. E-mail: kelly.grant@registerguard.com
Display Adv. E-mail: bob.saltz@registerguard.com
Classified Adv. e-mail: bob.saltz@registerguard.com
Editorial e-mail: dave.baker@registerguard.com
Primary Website: www.registerguard.com
Year Established: 1867
News Services: AP, NYT, LAT-WP, TMS.
Special Editions: College Football (Aug); Cycle Life (Jun); Fishing (Mar); Discovery Magazine (May); Home & Garden (Monthly); Holiday Gift Guide (Nov); Tastings (Quarterly); The Wedding Guide (Semi-yearly); Golf (Summer).
Special Weekly Sections: Health, Fitness (Mon); Outdoors (Tue); Food (Wed); Arts (Thur); Entertainment (Fri); Real Estate (Sat); Books, Travel, Wedding (Sun)
Syndicated Publications: blue chip (business)
Areas Served - City/County or Portion Thereof, or Zip codes: Lane County (OR)
Sat. Circulation Paid: 45542
Sun. Circulation Paid: 47286
Audit By: AAM
Audit Date: 31.03.2018
Personnel: Shanna Cannon (Pub.); Ken Clements (Adv. Dir.); Marty Kaye (Dir. of Finance); Mark Ogle (Circ. Dir.); Alison Bath (Ed.); Michelle Maxwell (Mng. Ed.); Rob Romig (Sr. Ed.)
Parent company (for newspapers): Gannett; CherryRoad Media

DAILY COURIER

Street address 1: 409 SE 7th St
Street address city: Grants Pass
Street address state: OR
Zip/Postal code: 97526-3003
County: Josephine
Country: USA
Mailing address: PO BOX 1468
Mailing city: GRANTS PASS
Mailing state: OR
Mailing zip: 97528-0330
General Phone: (541) 474-3700
Advertising Phone: (541) 474-3807
Editorial Phone: (541) 474-3823
General/National Adv. E-mail: display@thedailycourier.com
Display Adv. E-mail: display@thedailycourier.com
Classified Adv. e-mail: classified@thedailycourier.com
Editorial e-mail: news@thedailycourier.com
Primary Website: www.thedailycourier.com
Mthly Avg Views: 1000000
Mthly Avg Unique Visitors: 80000
Year Established: 1885
News Services: AP.
Special Editions: A-Z in Josephine (Jan.); All About Pets (Feb.); Business Pulse (Feb.); Home & Garden (March-July); The Good Life (March); Health & Wellness (April, July, Oct.); Wheels (June, Oct.) Back to the 50s (July); Home & Family (Aug.-Sept.); Back to School (Aug.); Beer, Wine & Dine (Sept.); Home for the Holidays (Nov. - Dec.); Josephine County Fair Program (Aug); Holiday Gift Guide (Dec); Prime Time (Sept.); Charitable Giving Guide (Dec.)
Special Weekly Sections: Churches (Fri); Color Gardening (Sun); Best Food Day (Tues)
Delivery Methods: Mail`Newsstand`Carrier`Racks
Areas Served - City/County or Portion Thereof, or Zip codes: Josephine County
Own Printing Facility?: Y
Avg Free Circ: 551
Sun. Circulation Paid: 10088
Sun. Circulation Free: 308
Audit By: AAM
Audit Date: 31.03.2019
Personnel: Debbie Thomas (Adv. Dir.); Scott Stoddard (Editor); Bill Parker (Purchasing Agent); Eileen Widdison (Circ. Mgr.)
Parent company (for newspapers): Western News & Info

HERALD AND NEWS

Street address 1: 2701 Foothills Boulevard
Street address city: Klamath Falls
Street address state: OR
Zip/Postal code: 97603
County: Klamath
Country: USA
Mailing address: PO BOX 788
Mailing city: KLAMATH FALLS
Mailing state: OR
Mailing zip: 97601-0320
General Phone: (541) 885-4410
Advertising Phone: (541) 885-4410
Editorial Phone: (541) 885-4410
General/National Adv. E-mail: bkenfield@heraldandnews.com
Display Adv. E-mail: bkenfield@heraldandnews.com
Classified Adv. e-mail: sfry@heraldandnews.com
Editorial e-mail: news@heraldandnews.com
Primary Website: www.heraldandnews.com
Year Established: 1906
News Services: AP.
Special Weekly Sections: Taste (Tue); Home, Garden, Kids (Wed); Agriculture, Diversions, Limelighter (Thur); Faith, TV (Fri); Connections (Sat); Living Well, Business, Focus (Sun); Sports (Daily)
Syndicated Publications: Relish (Monthly); Parade (S); American Profile (Weekly).
Delivery Methods: Mail`Racks
Areas Served - City/County or Portion Thereof, or Zip codes: Klamath Falls (OR)
Sun. Circulation Paid: 8660
Audit By: AAM
Audit Date: 30.09.2018
Personnel: Gerro O'Brien (Ed.); Jeanine Day (Bus. Mgr.); Dusty Metsker (Circ. Dir.); Gerry O'Brien (Editor); Pat Bushey (Opinion Ed.); Benjamin Kenfield (Adv. Dir.); Mark Dobie (Pres./Pub.)
Parent company (for newspapers): Adams Publishing Group, LLC

MAIL TRIBUNE

Street address 1: P.O. Box 1108
Street address city: Medford
Street address state: OR
Zip/Postal code: 97501
County: Jackson
Country: USA
Mailing address: PO BOX 1108
Mailing city: MEDFORD
Mailing state: OR
Mailing zip: 97501-0229
General Phone: (541) 776-4426
Advertising Phone: (541) 776-4422
Editorial Phone: (541) 776-4477
General/National Adv. E-mail: nsmith@mailtribune.com
Display Adv. E-mail: nsmith@mailtribune.com
Classified Adv. e-mail: class@mailtribune.com
Editorial e-mail: news@mailtribune.com
Primary Website: www.mailtribune.com
Year Established: 1906
News Services: AP, DJ, LAT-WP.
Special Editions: Real Estate Review (Apr); Football (Aug); Classroom Tribune (Dec); Tax & Financial Planning (Jan); Regional Recreation Guide (Jul); Our Valley (Mar); Pets (May); Ashland Festival of Lights (Nov); Fall Real Estate (Oct); Hunting (Sept).
Special Weekly Sections: Healthy (Tue); Best Food (Wed); Outdoors (Thur); TV, Religion, Out There (Fri); Home, Religion (Sat); Business, Music, Arts, Local, Seniors, Comics (Sun)
Syndicated Publications: Tempo (Fri); Relish (Monthly); Parade (S); American Profile (Weekly).
Areas Served - City/County or Portion Thereof, or Zip codes: Southern Oregon
Avg Free Circ: 409
Sat. Circulation Paid: 14523
Sat. Circulation Free: 298
Sun. Circulation Paid: 17154
Sun. Circulation Free: 525
Audit By: AAM
Audit Date: 31.12.2016
Personnel: James Grady Singletary (Pub.); Angela Fraley (Adv. Mgr., Classified/Phone Sales); John Mahalyo (Circ. Dir.); Robert Hunter (Ed.); Greg Stiles (Bus. Ed.); Paul Fattig (Columnist); Gary Nelson (Editorial Page Ed.); Cathy Noah (Features Ed.); Sarah Lemon (Food/Garden Ed.); Pam Sieg (Librarian); Bill Varble (Music Ed.); Rob Galvin (News Ed.); Julie Worth (Online Ed.); Mark Freeman (Outdoors Ed.); Bob Pennell (Photo Ed.); Richard Moeschel (Radio/Television Ed.); Tim Trower (Sports Ed.); Nicholas Morgan; Dena DeRose (Adv. Dir.)
Parent company (for newspapers): Rosebud Media; CherryRoad Media

THE ASHLAND DAILY TIDINGS

Street address 1: 111 N Fir St
Street address city: Medford
Street address state: OR
Zip/Postal code: 97501-2772
County: Jackson
Country: USA
Mailing address: PO BOX 1108
Mailing city: MEDFORD
Mailing state: OR
Mailing zip: 97501-0229
General Phone: (541)776-4411
Advertising Phone: (541) 776-4422
Editorial Phone: (541) 776-4477
General/National Adv. E-mail: nsmith@mailtribune.com
Display Adv. E-mail: nsmith@mailtribune.com
Classified Adv. e-mail: class@mailtribune.com
Editorial e-mail: news@mailtribune.com
Primary Website: www.dailytidings.com
Year Established: 1876
News Services: AP.
Special Weekly Sections: Healthy Living (Tue); Food, Entertainment (Wed); Medford Nickel (Thur); TV, Entertainment (Fri)
Syndicated Publications: Revels/On Television (Entertainment) (Thur).
Delivery Methods: Newsstand`Carrier`Racks
Areas Served - City/County or Portion Thereof, or Zip codes: Ashland
Own Printing Facility?: Y
Commercial printers?: Y
Avg Free Circ: 137
Sat. Circulation Paid: 1323
Sat. Circulation Free: 78
Audit By: AAM
Audit Date: 31.03.2015
Personnel: James Grady Singletary (Pub.); Dena DeRose (Adv. Dir.); Myles Murphy (City Ed.); Ed Rose (Operations Director); Bert Etling (Ed.); Danny Penza (Sports Ed.)
Parent company (for newspapers): Rosebud Media; CherryRoad Media

ARGUS OBSERVER

Street address 1: 1160 SW 4th St
Street address city: Ontario

Street address state: OR
Zip/Postal code: 97914-4365
County: Malheur
Country: USA
Mailing address: 1160 SW 4TH ST
Mailing city: ONTARIO
Mailing state: OR
Mailing zip: 97914-4365
General Phone: (541) 889-5387
Advertising Phone: (541) 889-5387
Editorial Phone: (541) 889-5387
General/National Adv. E-mail: kellyj@argusobserver.com
Display Adv. E-mail: kellyj@argusobserver.com
Classified Adv. e-mail: tonyaw@argusobserver.com
Editorial e-mail: editor@argusobserver.com
Primary Website: www.argusobserver.com
Mthly Avg Views: 265000
Mthly Avg Unique Visitors: 75000
Year Established: 1896
News Services: AP.
Special Weekly Sections: Best Food Day (Tue); Church (Fri); Outdoor, Amusement, TV, (Sun); Farm (Mon)
Syndicated Publications: Parade (S).
Delivery Methods: Mail`Newsstand`Carrier`Racks
Areas Served - City/County or Portion Thereof, or Zip codes: 97914, 97913, 97918, 97901, 97907, 83661, 83619, 83655, 83672, 83612, 83660
Own Printing Facility?: Y
Commercial printers?: Y
Avg Free Circ: 9
Audit By: VAC
Audit Date: 30.06.2016
Personnel: John Dillon (Pub./Adv. Dir.); Scott McIntosh (Ed.); Andy Shimojima (Adv. Mgr., Retail); Wade Cordes (Prodn. Mgr.); Dee Lee (Bus Mgr.)
Parent company (for newspapers): Wick Communications

EAST OREGONIAN

Street address 1: 211 SE Byers Ave
Street address city: Pendleton
Street address state: OR
Zip/Postal code: 97801-2346
County: Umatilla
Country: USA
General Phone: (541) 276-2211
Advertising Phone: (541) 278-2669
Editorial Phone: (541) 966-0835
General/National Adv. E-mail: info@eastoregonian.com
Display Adv. E-mail: ads@eastoregonian.com
Classified Adv. e-mail: classifieds@eastoregonian.com
Editorial e-mail: news@eastoregonian.com
Primary Website: www.eastoregonian.com
Mthly Avg Views: 425632
Mthly Avg Unique Visitors: 225205
Year Established: 1875
Special Editions: Umatilla County Fair Farm-City Pro Rodeo Pendleton Round-Up Health & Wellness Guide Graduation Discover Eastern Oregon Fall Sports Winter Sports Spring Sports Home Improvement & Car Care Holly Jolly Who's Who in Eastern Oregon Progress Edition Salute to Police Firefighters Salute Spring Home & Garden Wedding Planner Giving Guide
Special Weekly Sections: GO! (regional arts and entertainment)
Delivery Methods: Mail`Newsstand`Racks
Areas Served - City/County or Portion Thereof, or Zip codes: Northeastern Oregon: Umatilla County includes Pendleton, Hermiston, Umatilla, Stanfield, Echo, Pilot Rock, Helix, Adams, Athena, Weston and Milton-Freewater Morrow County includes Boardman, Irrigon, Heppner, Ione and Lexington
Own Printing Facility?: Y
Commercial printers?: Y
Avg Free Circ: 222
Sat. Circulation Paid: 4155
Sat. Circulation Free: 222
Audit By: AAM
Audit Date: 31.03.2019
Personnel: Kathryn B. Brown (Owner); Daniel Wattenburger (Managing Editor); Andrew Cutler (Regional Editor & Publisher); Phil Wright (Managing Editor); Mike Jensen (Production Manager); Christopher Rush (Regional Publisher & Revenue Director); Bonny Tuller (Circulation/Marketing Manager); Angela Treadwell (Retail Sales Manager)
Parent company (for newspapers): EO Media Group

THE OREGONIAN

Street address 1: 1500 SW 1st Avenue
Street address 2: Ste 500
Street address city: Portland
Street address state: OR
Zip/Postal code: 97201
County: Multnomah
Country: USA
Mailing state: OR
General Phone: (503) 221-8327
Advertising Phone: (503) 221-8000
Editorial Phone: (503) 221-8100
General/National Adv. E-mail: advertise@oregonian.com
Display Adv. E-mail: advertise@oregonian.com
Classified Adv. e-mail: advertise@oregonian.com
Editorial e-mail: newsroom@oregonian.com
Primary Website: www.oregonlive.com
Mthly Avg Views: 40938526
Mthly Avg Unique Visitors: 6732064
Year Established: 1850
Delivery Methods: Carrier
Areas Served - City/County or Portion Thereof, or Zip codes: Entire state of Oregon
Sat. Circulation Paid: 84766
Sun. Circulation Paid: 135040
Audit By: AAM
Audit Date: 30.09.2023
Personnel: Therese Bottomly (VP of Content); John Maher (Pres.); Jessica Denney (Vice President, Sales); Greg Thompson (Dir. Local Retail); Debi Walery (Adv. Dir.); Amy Lewin (Vice President, Brand & Strategic Partnerships/Here is Oregon); Kevin Denny (VP and General Manager); Steve Alberts (Circulation Operations Director); Jodie Krueger (Circ. Mgr., Opns.); Neal Burke (Circ. Mgr., Single Copy); Mike Burns (Chief Revenue Officer); Ed Rose (Dir. Cir. Audience)
Parent company (for newspapers): Advance Publications, Inc.

THE NEWS-REVIEW

Street address 1: 345 N.E. Winchester
Street address city: Roseburg
Street address state: OR
Zip/Postal code: 97470
County: Douglas
Country: USA
Mailing address: 345 NE WINCHESTER ST
Mailing city: ROSEBURG
Mailing state: OR
Mailing zip: 97470-3352
General Phone: (541) 672-3321
Advertising Phone: (541) 957-4250
Editorial Phone: (541) 957-4203
General/National Adv. E-mail: tsmith@nrtoday.com
Display Adv. E-mail: tsmith@nrtoday.com
Classified Adv. e-mail: classifieds@nrtoday.com
Editorial e-mail: creed@nrtoday.com
Primary Website: www.nrtoday.com
Mthly Avg Views: 340000
Mthly Avg Unique Visitors: 38530
Year Established: 1867
News Services: AP.
Special Editions: Recreational Vehicles (Apr); Blackberry Festival (Aug); Seasons Greetings (Dec); Readers Choice (Jan); Graffiti (Jul); All in the Family (Jun); How To Tab (Mar); Home & Garden (May); Encore (Monthly); Holiday Guide (Nov); DC Cou
Special Weekly Sections: Money (Mon); Tasty Tuesday (Tue); Health (Wed); Arts, Entertainment (Thur); Auto (Fri); Real Estate (Sun)
Syndicated Publications: Relish (Monthly); Parade (S); American Profile (Weekly).
Delivery Methods: Mail`Newsstand`Carrier`Racks
Areas Served - City/County or Portion Thereof, or Zip codes: 97417, 97429, 97432, 97435, 97436, 97443, 97447, 97457, 97462, 97469, 97470, 97471, 97473, 97479, 97484, 97486, 97495, 97496, 97499, 97481, 97416
Own Printing Facility?: Y
Commercial printers?: Y
Avg Free Circ: 815
Sat. Circulation Paid: 19246
Sat. Circulation Free: 815
Sun. Circulation Paid: 20136
Sun. Circulation Free: 511
Audit By: CAC
Audit Date: 31.12.2017
Personnel: Rachelle Carter (Gen. Mgr.); Analee Wulff (National Adv.); Victoria Batshon (Classifieds Sales); Ian Campbell (Mng. Ed.); Mike Henneke (News Ed.); Erica Welch (Special Sections Ed.); Tom Eggers (Sports Ed.); Brenda Fischer (Finance Dir.); Becca Weaver (Marketing Dir.); Katie Dargavell (Circ. Mgr.)
Parent company (for newspapers): Swift Communications, Inc.; Lotus Media Group

STATESMAN JOURNAL

Street address 1: 280 Church Street NE
Street address city: Salem
Street address state: OR
Zip/Postal code: 97301
County: Marion
Country: USA
Mailing address: 280 CHURCH ST NE
Mailing city: SALEM
Mailing state: OR
Mailing zip: 97301-3762
General Phone: (503) 399-6611
Advertising Phone: (503) 399-6648
Editorial Phone: (503) 399-6611
General/National Adv. E-mail: golocal@statesmanjournal.com
Display Adv. E-mail: golocal@statesmanjournal.com
Classified Adv. e-mail: ads@statesmanjournal.com
Editorial e-mail: letters@statesmanjournal.com
Primary Website: www.statesmanjournal.com
Year Established: 1851
News Services: AP, GNS.
Special Editions: State Fair (Aug); Gift Guides (Nov); Home Show (Feb); Tour of Homes (Jun);
Special Weekly Sections: Life (Mon, Tue); Best Food Day (Wed); Recreation, Weekend (Thur); Real Living, Home, Life (Fri); Auto, Life (Sat); Arts, Travel, Business, Career (Sun)
Syndicated Publications: Comics (S).
Delivery Methods: Mail`Newsstand`Carrier`Racks
Areas Served - City/County or Portion Thereof, or Zip codes: Salem & Keizer area (OR)
Sat. Circulation Paid: 26141
Sun. Circulation Paid: 32991
Audit By: AAM
Audit Date: 31.03.2017
Personnel: Michael Davis (Exec. Ed.); Ryan Kedzierski (Adv. Dir.); Valerie Thorne (Class. Mgr.); Jerry Scobie (CFO); Don Currie (Bus./Finance Ed.); Amy Read (Digital Ed.); Dick Hughes (Editorial Page Ed.); Dan Bender (Metro Ed.); Diane Stevenson (Photo Ed.); Michelle Maxwell (Senior Ed.); Victor Panichkul (Senior Ed.); James Day (Sports Ed.); Kelly Williams Brown (Theater/Music Ed.); Kristina Salaz (IT Mgr.); John Witherspoon (Prodn. Mgr., Distr.); Lisa Reese (Pub.); Neil Potter (Acct. Mgr.); Patrick Bruce (Auto Mgr.); Terry Horne (Pub.)
Parent company (for newspapers): Gannett

THE DALLES DAILY CHRONICLE

Street address 1: 315 Federal St
Street address city: The Dalles
Street address state: OR
Zip/Postal code: 97058-2115
County: Wasco
Country: USA
Mailing address: PO BOX 1910
Mailing city: THE DALLES
Mailing state: OR
Mailing zip: 97058-8010
General Phone: (541) 296-2141
Advertising Phone: (541) 296-2141
Editorial Phone: (541) 296-2141
General/National Adv. E-mail: cmarr@thedalleschronicle.com
Display Adv. E-mail: cmarr@thedalleschronicle.com
Classified Adv. e-mail: cmarr@thedalleschronicle.com
Editorial e-mail: mgibson@thedalleschronicle.com
Primary Website: www.thedalleschronicle.com
Year Established: 1890
News Services: AP.
Special Editions: Progress (Feb); Visit the Gorge (May).
Special Weekly Sections: Best Food Day (Tue)
Syndicated Publications: American Profile (Weekly).
Sun. Circulation Paid: 5468
Audit By: Sworn/Estimate/Non-Audited
Audit Date: 12.07.2019
Personnel: Marilyn Roth (Pub.); Tonya Flory (Adv. Dir.); Kathy Ursprung (Exec. Ed.); Nick Deleon (Class. Mgr.); Kathy Gray (Managing Ed.); Cece Fix (Office Mgr./ Bookkeeper)
Parent company (for newspapers): Eagle Newspapers, Inc.

PENNSYLVANIA

THE MORNING CALL

Street address 1: 101 N 6th St
Street address 2: PO Box 1260
Street address city: Allentown
Street address state: PA
Zip/Postal code: 18101-1403
County: Lehigh
Country: USA
Mailing address: PO BOX 1260
Mailing city: ALLENTOWN
Mailing state: PA
Mailing zip: 18105-1260
General Phone: (610) 820-6500
Advertising Phone: (610) 820-6633
Editorial Phone: (610) 820-6500
General/National Adv. E-mail: ccampbell@mcall.com
Display Adv. E-mail: ccampbell@mcall.com
Classified Adv. e-mail: classified@mcall.com
Editorial e-mail: news@mcall.com
Primary Website: www.mcall.com
Mthly Avg Views: 15200000
Mthly Avg Unique Visitors: 1074410
Year Established: 1883
Special Weekly Sections: Best Food Day, Golf (Wed/ Sun); Health, Fitness (Mon); Business, Family (Tue); Entertainment (Thur); Entertainment, Home, Fashion, Trends, Pets, Movies (Fri); Travel, Home, Real Estate, Business (Sun);
Sat. Circulation Paid: 74122
Sun. Circulation Paid: 103548
Audit By: AAM
Audit Date: 31.12.2017
Personnel: Timothy Ryan (Publisher, President and CEO); David Erdman (Vice President /Editor); Jim Feher (VP, Adv.); Linda McDonald (Circ. Dir.); Daniel Sarko (Digital/Interactive Manager); Elizabeth Bartolai (Digital/ Interactive Manager); Veronica Walter; Adrienne Tunke (Nat'l Adv. Mgr.); Omar Zucco (Dir. Major Accts./Nat'l Adv.); Robert York (Pub./Ed.-in-chief)
Parent company (for newspapers): Alden Global Capital; Tribune Publishing, Inc.

ALTOONA MIRROR

Street address 1: 301 Cayuga Avenue
Street address city: Altoona
Street address state: PA
Zip/Postal code: 16602
County: Blair
Country: USA
Mailing address: PO BOX 2008
Mailing city: ALTOONA
Mailing state: PA
Mailing zip: 16603-2008
General Phone: (814) 946-7411
Advertising Phone: (814) 946-7411
Editorial Phone: (814) 946-7441
General/National Adv. E-mail: jhancock@altoonamirror.com
Display Adv. E-mail: displayads@altoonamirror.com
Classified Adv. e-mail: classifieds@altoonamirror.com
Editorial e-mail: news@altoonamirror.com
Primary Website: www.altoonamirror.com
Mthly Avg Views: 1750000
Mthly Avg Unique Visitors: 275000
Year Established: 1876
News Services: AP.
Special Editions: Allegheníes Adventure glossy, Bridal glossy, Health & Wellness newsprint (Jan); Mirror Moms glossy (Feb); Blair Living glossy (finance focus), People & Progress newsprint (largest edition of the year) (Mar); Central PA Pets glossy, Inside Pitch newsprint baseball preview, Tee It Up gold guide newsprint (Apr); Mirror Moms glossy, Born to Ride motorcycle glossy, On the Go special travel section newsprint (May); Blair Living glossy (summer bridal focus), Graduation community section newsprint (Jun); Alleghenies Adventure glossy, Here's My Card glossy booklet, Blitz high school football glossy (Jul); Mirror Moms glossy, Football preview (hs/college/ NFL) newsprint (Aug); Blair Living glossy (medical focus), Health & Wellness newsprint, Penn State Gameday weekly newsprint (Sept); Central PA Pets

glossy, Fall Home Improvement newsprint (Oct); Mirror Moms glossy, Thanksgiving Day newsprint wraps, Thanksgiving Day poly bag sponsorship (Nov); Blair Living (Hometown Favorites focus), Shop Local newsprint section/contest, Winter Heat sports preview newsprint. (Dec)
Special Weekly Sections: Kids (Mon); Jobs (Tue); Food (Wed); Entertainment, Religion (Fri); TV (Sat); Business, Travel (Sun)
Syndicated Publications: Blair Living (quarterly glossy); Mirror Moms (quarterly glossy); Alleghenies Adventure (quarterly glossy); Born to Ride (annual glossy); Taste of the Alleghenies (annual glossy); Central PA Pets (annual glossy). Bridal Bliss (annual Glossy)
Delivery Methods: Mail`Newsstand`Carrier`Racks
Areas Served - City/County or Portion Thereof, or Zip codes: 16601, 16602, 16648, 16635, 16625, 16637, 16673, 16662, 16693, 16686, 16617, 16655, 15521, 16627, 15522, 16664, 16659, 16695, 16650, 16679, 16678, 16657, 16647, 16652, 16611, 16683, 16680, 16616, 16627, 16639, 16636, 16640, 16668, 16646, 15722, 16643, 15940, 16641, 16630, 15931, 15938, 15946, 15955, 15963,
Own Printing Facility?: Y
Commercial printers?: Y
Avg Free Circ: 573
Sat. Circulation Paid: 19037
Sat. Circulation Free: 573
Sun. Circulation Paid: 24838
Sun. Circulation Free: 1235
Audit By: AAM
Audit Date: 31.12.2018
Personnel: Ed Kruger (Pub.); Ray Eckenrode (Gen. Mgr. Adv.); Dan Slep (Circ. Dir.); Beth Claar (Circ. Mgr., Office); Steve Carpenter (Assist. Managing Ed.); J.D. Cavrich (Photo Ed.); Buck Frank (Sports Ed.); Barbara Cowan (Women's Ed.); Rick Bacza (Prodn. Mgr.); Neil Rudel (Managing Ed.); Luann Ulicne (Nat'l/Classifieds Adv. Mgr.); Amy Hanna (Marketing Mgr.)
Parent company (for newspapers): Ogden Newspapers Inc.

BEAVER COUNTY TIMES

Street address 1: 400 Fair Avenue
Street address city: Beaver
Street address state: PA
Zip/Postal code: 15009
County: Beaver
Country: USA
Mailing address: 400 FAIR AVE
Mailing city: BEAVER
Mailing state: PA
Mailing zip: 15009-1998
General Phone: (724) 775-3200
Advertising Phone: (724) 775-3200 x 141
Editorial Phone: (724) 775-3200 x 156
General/National Adv. E-mail: kmccracken@timesonline.com
Display Adv. E-mail: crager@timesonline.com
Classified Adv. e-mail: timesclassifieds@timesonline.com.
Editorial e-mail: timesnews@timesonline.com
Primary Website: www.timesonline.com
Mthly Avg Views: 2568968
Year Established: 1851
News Services: AP, GateHouse, More Content Now, Washington Post, Bloomberg News
Special Editions: Bridal (Jan.); Progress (Feb.); Big Knob Fair (July); Hookstown Fair (Aug.); Football Preview (Aug.); Basketball (Dec); Best of the Valley (May); Gift Guide (Nov); Car Care (Sept).
Special Weekly Sections: Weekend (entertainment, Thurs.)
Delivery Methods: Mail`Newsstand`Carrier`Racks
Areas Served - City/County or Portion Thereof, or Zip codes: Beaver County, western Allegheny and southern Lawrence counties
Own Printing Facility?: N
Commercial printers?: N
Sun. Circulation Paid: 27153
Audit By: Sworn/Estimate/Non-Audited
Audit Date: 12.07.2019
Personnel: Tina Bequeath (Publisher, Controller); Debbie Hays (Credit Mgr.); Mark Zuchelli (Circ. Mgr., Home Delivery); Vaughn Vacar (Circ. Mktg./Single Copy Mgr.); Tom Bickert (Editorial Page Editor; Ellwood City Ledger manager); Jody Schwartz (Dir., Adv. Sales); Patrick O'Shea (Ellwood City Ledger editor); Katie McCracken (Classifieds mgr.); Dan Hink (Digital sales mgr.); Nick Hink (Retail sales mgr.); Kevin Lorenzi (Chief photographer); Gwen Titley (Videographer); Lisa Micco (Executive editor, managing editor); Eric Arbore (Digital content coordinator); Vince Townley (Sports editor); Jim Pane (Multi-media content editor); Steve Hughes (Multi-media content editor); Bryan Heraghty (Multi-media content editor)
Parent company (for newspapers): Gannett Company Inc.; CherryRoad Media

THE BEDFORD GAZETTE

Street address 1: 424 W Penn St
Street address city: Bedford
Street address state: PA
Zip/Postal code: 15522-1230
County: Bedford
Country: USA
Mailing address: PO BOX 671
Mailing city: BEDFORD
Mailing state: PA
Mailing zip: 15522-0671
General Phone: (814) 623-1151
Editorial Phone: (800) 242-4250
General/National Adv. E-mail: sgrowden@bedfordgazette.com
Display Adv. E-mail: advertise@bedfordgazette.com
Classified Adv. e-mail: classifieds@bedfordgazette.com
Editorial e-mail: acarr@bedfordgazette.com
Primary Website: www.bedfordgazette.com
Year Established: 1805
News Services: AP.
Special Editions: Home & Garden (Apr); Back-to-School (Aug); Christmas 3 (Dec); Boy Scout Week Pages (Feb); Jaycee Week Pages (Jan); Bedford County Fair (Jul); Dairy Farm (Jun); Bridal & Spring Fashion (Mar); Graduation & Careers (May); Golden Years (Monthly); Christmas Ed
Special Weekly Sections: Village Crier (Fri); Lifestyles (Mon); Church Page (Sat); Lifestyles (Thur); Lifestyles (Tues); Best Food Day (Wed).
Syndicated Publications: American Profile (Weekly).
Areas Served - City/County or Portion Thereof, or Zip codes: 15521, 17211, 15522, 15533, 15534, 16625, 15535, 16631, 15536, 16633, 16637, 15537, 15539, 16650, 15545, 16655, 16659, 15550, 16662, 15553, 16664, 15554, 16667, 16670, 16672, 16673, 16678, 15559, 16679, 16691, 16695
Sat. Circulation Paid: 9837
Audit By: Sworn/Estimate/Non-Audited
Audit Date: 12.07.2019
Personnel: George Sample (Pres.); Joseph Beegle (Pub.); Elizabeth Coyle (Mng. Ed.); Andrew Carr (Ass. Ed.); Rebecca Smith (Bus. Mgr.); Susan Maybury (Cir.); Sherri Growden (Adv. Dir.); Stacy Bollman (Class.)
Parent company (for newspapers): Sample News Group LLC

PRESS ENTERPRISE, INC.

Street address 1: 3185 Lackawanna Avenue
Street address city: Bloomsburg
Street address state: PA
Zip/Postal code: 17815
County: Columbia
Country: USA
Mailing address: 3185 LACKAWANNA AVE
Mailing city: BLOOMSBURG
Mailing state: PA
Mailing zip: 17815-3398
General Phone: (570) 784-2121
Advertising Phone: (570) 387-1234 ext. 1210
Editorial Phone: (570) 784-2121 ext. 1305
General/National Adv. E-mail: adv@pressenterprise.net
Display Adv. E-mail: adv@pressenterprise.net
Classified Adv. e-mail: class@pressenterprise.net
Editorial e-mail: news@pressenterprise.net
Primary Website: www.pressenterpriseonline.com
Year Established: 1902
News Services: AP.
Special Editions: Your Home (Apr); Back-to-School (Aug); Gift Guide (Dec); Progress (Feb); Bridal (Jan); FYI (Jul); Recreation (Jun); MenuTabs (Mar); Senior Citizen (May); Gift Guide (Nov); New Autos (Oct); Fair (Sept).
Special Weekly Sections: Business (Mon); Health (Tue); Best Food Day (Wed); Auto, Business, School (Thur); American Profile (Sat); Stock (Sun)
Syndicated Publications: Color Comics (S); American Profile (Weekly); USA Weekend (Sun)
Areas Served - City/County or Portion Thereof, or Zip codes: Columbia, Montour, and Luzerne Counties; including Bloomsburg, Danville, Berwick, Benton, Millville, Catawissa and Elysburg.
Own Printing Facility?: Y
Commercial printers?: Y
Avg Free Circ: 428
Sat. Circulation Paid: 16678
Sat. Circulation Free: 428
Sun. Circulation Paid: 17508
Sun. Circulation Free: 427
Audit By: AAM
Audit Date: 31.12.2018
Personnel: Paul R. Eyerly (Pres.); James T. Micklow (Treasurer); Brandon R. Eyerly (Pub.); Dennis Ashenfelder (Bus. Office Mgr.); Sandra Sterner (Adv. Dir.); Pam Taylor (Circ. Mgr.); Dean Kashner (Mng. Ed., News); James Sachetti (Ed.); Lori Getty (Graphics Ed./ Art Dir.); Bill Hughes (Photo Ed.); Jeff Cragle (Mgmt. Info Servs. Mgr.); Julie Neitz (Prodn. Mgr., Bindery/ Post Press); Bill Bason (Prodn. Mgr., Opns.); Robert Temple (Prodn. Mgr., PM); Brad Conklin (Prodn. Mgr., Press); Carin Wharton (Classifieds Adv. Mg.); Bill Pitcavage (Bus. Office Mgr.); Paula Ream (Customer Service Mgr.)
Parent company (for newspapers): Freedom Communications, Inc.; Press Enterprise, Inc.

THE BRADFORD ERA

Street address 1: 43 Main St
Street address city: Bradford
Street address state: PA
Zip/Postal code: 16701-2019
County: McKean
Country: USA
Mailing address: PO BOX 365
Mailing city: BRADFORD
Mailing state: PA
Mailing zip: 16701-0365
General Phone: (814) 368-3173
Advertising Phone: (814) 369-3173
Editorial Phone: (814) 362-6531
General/National Adv. E-mail: news@bradfordera.com
Display Adv. E-mail: display@bradfordera.com
Classified Adv. e-mail: a.hayden@bradfordera.com
Editorial e-mail: news@bradfordera.com
Primary Website: www.bradfordera.com
Year Established: 1824
News Services: AP.
Special Editions: Univ. of Pittsburgh at Bradford (Aug); Progress (Jan); Zippo Days (Jul); Summer Guide, Sun 'n Fun (Jun); Brides (Mar); Design-an-Ad (May); Christmas Guide (Nov); Hunting Guide (Oct).
Syndicated Publications: USA WEEKEND Magazine (Sat).
Delivery Methods: Mail`Newsstand`Carrier`Racks
Areas Served - City/County or Portion Thereof, or Zip codes: Mckean, Elk, Potter, Cameron Counties
Own Printing Facility?: Y
Commercial printers?: Y
Avg Free Circ: 37
Sat. Circulation Paid: 7942
Sat. Circulation Free: 37
Audit By: VAC
Audit Date: 30.09.2015
Personnel: Jim Eckstrom (Grp Ed.); Gretchen Gallagher (Purchasing Agent); Jill Henry (Adv. Mgr.); John H. Satterwhite (Pub. Ed.); Marty Robacker Wilder (Mng. Ed.); Rick Kautz (Prodn. Mgr., Mailroom/Post Press); Linda Cardamone (Commercial Printing); Don Watts (Cir. Mng.); Mark Brahaney
Parent company (for newspapers): Community Media Group; Bradford Publishing Co.

BUTLER EAGLE

Street address 1: P.O. Box 271
Street address city: Butler
Street address state: PA
Zip/Postal code: 16003
County: Butler
Country: USA
Mailing address: PO BOX 271
Mailing city: BUTLER
Mailing state: PA
Mailing zip: 16003-0271
General Phone: (724) 282-8000
General/National Adv. E-mail: kgraham@butlereagle.com
Display Adv. E-mail: kgraham@butlereagle.com
Classified Adv. e-mail: classified@butlereagle.com
Editorial e-mail: letters@butlereagle.com
Primary Website: www.butlereagle.com
Year Established: 1895
News Services: AP.
Special Editions: Summer Car Care (Apr); Football (Aug); Christmas Photos of Children (Dec); Funeral Directors (Feb); Family Health Guide (Jan); Farm Show (Jul); Father's Day (Jun); Progress (Mar); Christmas (Nov); Diner's Guide (Oct); Ethnic Festival (Sept).
Special Weekly Sections: Best Food, TV, Weekend (Fri)
Syndicated Publications: USA WEEKEND Magazine (S).
Delivery Methods: Mail`Newsstand`Carrier
Avg Free Circ: 845
Sun. Circulation Paid: 20382
Sun. Circulation Free: 369
Audit By: AAM
Audit Date: 30.06.2018
Personnel: Keith Graham (Retail Sales Manager); Nedra Sutch (Adv. Mgr., Classified); Alice Lunn (Cir. Dir.); John Laing Wise (Ed.); Joseph Kaspryzk (Editorial Writer.); David Heastings (News Ed.); Justin Guido (Photo Ed.); John Enrietto (Sports Ed.); Chris Morelli (Mng. Ed.)
Parent company (for newspapers): Eagle Media; Wise Family

THE SENTINEL

Street address 1: 327 B Street
Street address city: Carlisle
Street address state: PA
Zip/Postal code: 17013
County: Cumberland
Country: USA
Mailing address: 327 B Street
Mailing city: CARLISLE
Mailing state: PA
Mailing zip: 17013
General Phone: (717) 243-2611
Advertising Phone: (717) 240-7114
Editorial Phone: (717) 240-7125
General/National Adv. E-mail: ads@cumberlink.com
Editorial e-mail: frontdoor@cumberlink.com
Primary Website: www.cumberlink.com
Mthly Avg Views: 1900000
Mthly Avg Unique Visitors: 290000
Year Established: 1860
News Services: AP.
Special Weekly Sections: History (Mon); Thrive (Tue); Cuisine (Wed); Scene (Thur); Family (Fri); Business, Homes (Sat)
Syndicated Publications: Parade Magazine (S)
Delivery Methods: Mail`Newsstand`Carrier
Areas Served - City/County or Portion Thereof, or Zip codes: Central and western Cumberland County from Mechanicsburg to slightly beyond Newville; Gardners and Idaville in Adams County; York Springs in York County; and central and western Perry County.
Own Printing Facility?: N
Commercial printers?: N
Sat. Circulation Paid: 9000
Audit By: Sworn/Estimate/Non-Audited
Audit Date: 12.07.2019
Personnel: Kim Kamowski (Pub./Adv. Dir.); Jeff Pratt (Exec. Ed.); Kevin Woodward (Circ. Mgr.); Naomi Creason (Mng. Ed.); Jeff Brown (Night Ed.); Pam Hedrick (Advertising Operations Manager); Jake Adams (Sports Ed.)
Parent company (for newspapers): Lee Enterprises, Incorporated

PUBLIC OPINION

Street address 1: 77 N. Third Street
Street address city: Chambersburg
Street address state: PA
Zip/Postal code: 17201
County: Franklin
Country: USA
Mailing address: PO BOX 499
Mailing city: CHAMBERSBURG
Mailing state: PA
Mailing zip: 17201-0499
General Phone: (717) 264-6161
Advertising Phone: (717) 262-4720
Editorial Phone: (717) 262-4764
General/National Adv. E-mail: gharriger@mediaonespa.com
Display Adv. E-mail: gharriger@mediaonespa.com
Classified Adv. e-mail: gharriger@mediaonespa.com
Editorial e-mail: bebennett@publicopinion.com
Primary Website: www.publicopiniononline.com
Mthly Avg Views: 8137364
Mthly Avg Unique Visitors: 1603024
Year Established: 1869
News Services: AP

Special Editions: Baby Book (Feb), Builders Show (Mar), Golf Preview (Apr), Living in the Valley (Jul), Football Preview (Aug), Holiday Songbook (Dec)
Special Weekly Sections: Food (Wed); Religion, Auto, Weekender (thur); Real Estate (Fri); Business, Religion (Sat); Food, Outdoor, TV (Sun)
Syndicated Publications: USA WEEKEND Magazine (Sun).
Delivery Methods: Mail`Newsstand`Carrier`Racks
Areas Served - City/County or Portion Thereof, or Zip codes: 17201 and surrounding in Franklin county, PA
Own Printing Facility?: Y
Commercial printers?: N
Avg Free Circ: 3150
Sat. Circulation Paid: 7899
Sat. Circulation Free: 3150
Sun. Circulation Paid: 10918
Sun. Circulation Free: 541
Audit By: AAM
Audit Date: 30.06.2018
Personnel: Caron Decker (Controller); Ginny Harriger (Adv. Dir.); Becky Bennett (Ed.); George Fuller (Circ. Dir.); Dave Myers (Production Dir.); Andrea Wretch (City Ed.); Ed Gotwals (Sports Ed.); Patty Clugston (Prodn. Mgr., Composing/Camera); Nancy Ramer (Circ. Asst. Mgr.); Sara Glines (Pub.)
Parent company (for newspapers): Gannett

THE PROGRESS

Street address 1: PO Box 952
Street address 2: PO Box 291
Street address city: Clearfield
Street address state: PA
Zip/Postal code: 16830-0952
County: Clearfield
Country: USA
Mailing address: PO BOX 952
Mailing city: CLEARFIELD
Mailing state: PA
Mailing zip: 16830-0952
General Phone: (814) 765-5581
Advertising Phone: (814) 765-9495
Editorial Phone: (814) 765-7813
General/National Adv. E-mail: display@theprogressnews.com
Display Adv. E-mail: display@theprogressnews.com
Classified Adv. e-mail: classified@theprogressnews.com
Editorial e-mail: news@theprogressnews.com
Primary Website: www.theprogressnews.com
Mthly Avg Views: 925235
Mthly Avg Unique Visitors: 32973
Year Established: 1913
News Services: AP,
Special Editions: Home & Garden (Apr); Football Tab (Aug); Bridal (Feb); Health & Fitness (Jan); County Fair (Jul); Summer Activities (May); Senior Lifestyles (Monthly); Hunting (Nov); Business (Oct); Holiday (Nov)
Special Weekly Sections: Postscript TV (Fri); Food (Fri).
Syndicated Publications: USA WEEKEND Magazine (Fri).
Delivery Methods: Mail`Newsstand`Carrier`Racks
Areas Served - City/County or Portion Thereof, or Zip codes: Clearfield, Curwensville, Philipsburg, and Moshannon Valley
Own Printing Facility?: Y
Commercial printers?: N
Avg Free Circ: 152
Sat. Circulation Paid: 8649
Sat. Circulation Free: 152
Audit By: CAC
Audit Date: 31.03.2014
Personnel: Margaret Krebs (Pres.); Linda Schultz (Treasurer/Controller); Ann K. Law (Credit Mgr./Purchasing Agent); Rebecca Johnson (Asst. Pub./Bus. Mgr.); Jeannine Barger (Adv. Mgr., Display); Cindy Aughenbaugh (Circ. Mgr.); Jill Golden (Ed.); Jaclyn Yingling (Sports Ed.); Steve Heichel (Prodn. Supt., Plant); Liza Miller (Assistant Editor); Shirley Rowles (Classified Advertising Manager)
Parent company (for newspapers): Community Media Group

PITTSBURGH POST-GAZETTE

Street address 1: 2201 Sweeney Dr
Street address city: Clinton
Street address state: PA
Zip/Postal code: 15026-1818
County: Beaver
Country: USA
Mailing address: 358 N SHORE DR
Mailing city: PITTSBURGH
Mailing state: PA
Mailing zip: 15212-5870
General Phone: (412) 263-1100
Advertising Phone: (412) 263-1201 (class)
Editorial Phone: (412) 263-1601
General/National Adv. E-mail: advertising@post-gazette.com
Primary Website: www.post-gazette.com
Mthly Avg Views: 20965374
Mthly Avg Unique Visitors: 4400000
Year Established: 1786
News Services: AP, NYT, NEA, WP, TCA, Bloomberg
Special Editions: See PG Media Kit: http://pgmediakit.com/
Special Weekly Sections: Food; PowerSource; Local Xtra News, Sports Varsity Xtra; Weekend, Home and Garden; Forum; Travel; Comics; Real Estate
Syndicated Publications: Parade (S).
Delivery Methods: Mail`Newsstand`Carrier`Racks
Areas Served - City/County or Portion Thereof, or Zip codes: Greater Pittsburgh Metropolitan Area
Own Printing Facility?: Y
Commercial printers?: Y
Sat. Circulation Paid: 119326
Sun. Circulation Paid: 164599
Audit By: AAM
Audit Date: 31.03.2018
Personnel: John Robinson Block (Chairman, Publisher & Editor-in-Chief); Stephen Spolar (Human Resources); Tracey DeAngelo (Director of Marketing and Audience); Jeffrey Malone (Home Delivery Distribution Opns. Mgr.); Matt Kennedy (Asst. Mng. Ed., Content); David Shribman (Exec. Ed. & VP); Jerry Micco (Sr. Managing Editor/NewsSlide); Mary Thomas (Arts Critic); Bill Southern (Director of Finance); Joe Cronin (Special Projects & Senior IT Manager); Lisa Hurm (General Manager); Rob Weber (Director of Operations); Adam Bush (Director of Advertising & Digital Initiatives); Robert Morgan (Retail Advertising Manager); Tim Wirth (Advertising Operation/System Manager); Steve Posti (Research Mgr.); Troy Piekarski (Manager Revenue Development, Classified); Deb Hansen (Classified Real Estate Mgr.); Benjamin Eisenhardt (Customer Service Supervisor); Sally Stapleton (Managing Editor); Jim Iovino (Deputy Managing Editor); Keith Burris (Exec. Ed.); Allan Block (Chairman, BCI)
Parent company (for newspapers): Block Communications, Inc.

DAILY COURIER

Street address 1: 127 W Apple St
Street address city: Connellsville
Street address state: PA
Zip/Postal code: 15425-3132
County: Fayette
Country: USA
Mailing address: 127 W APPLE ST
Mailing city: CONNELLSVILLE
Mailing state: PA
Mailing zip: 15425-3196
General Phone: (724) 628-2000
Advertising Phone: (724) 628-2000
Editorial Phone: (724) 628-2000
General/National Adv. E-mail: cwhipley@dailycourier.com
Display Adv. E-mail: cwhipley@dailycourier.com
Classified Adv. e-mail: rfurman@dailycourier.com
Editorial e-mail: newsroom@dailycourier.com
Primary Website: www.dailycourier.com
Year Established: 1879
News Services: AP.
Special Editions: Football Preview (Aug); Year in Review (Dec); Bridal (Jan); Fayette County Fair (Jul); Bridal (Jun); Progress (Mar).
Special Weekly Sections: Society (Mon); Best Food Day (Wed/Sun); Entertainment, Neighborhood (Thur); Home, Garden (Sat); Travel, Real Estate (Sun)
Avg Free Circ: 99
Sat. Circulation Paid: 4958
Sat. Circulation Free: 80
Sun. Circulation Paid: 901
Audit By: AAM
Audit Date: 30.09.2014
Personnel: Karen Strickland (Cir. Mgr.); Roxanne Abramowitz (Mng. Ed.); Jason Black (Sports Ed.); Dave Boden (Pub.); Marsha Shaffer (Rec. / Class.)

Parent company (for newspapers): Sample Media Group

CORRY JOURNAL

Street address 1: 28 W South St
Street address city: Corry
Street address state: PA
Zip/Postal code: 16407-1810
County: Erie
Country: USA
Mailing address: 28 W SOUTH ST
Mailing city: CORRY
Mailing state: PA
Mailing zip: 16407-1810
General Phone: (814) 665-8291
Advertising Phone: (814) 665-8291 ext. 21, ext. 22
Editorial Phone: (814) 665-8291 ext. 31
General/National Adv. E-mail: tim@thecorryjournal.com
Display Adv. E-mail: corryjournal@tbscc.com
Classified Adv. e-mail: corryjournal@tbscc.com
Editorial e-mail: bwilliams@thecorryjournal.com
Primary Website: www.thecorryjournal.com
News Services: AP.
Special Weekly Sections: Best Food Day (Sat)
Syndicated Publications: American Profile (Weekly).
Sat. Circulation Paid: 3512
Audit By: Sworn/Estimate/Non-Audited
Audit Date: 12.07.2019
Personnel: Bob Williams (Pub.); Erin Passinger (Mng. Ed.); Tim Joncas (Adv. Sales Mgr.); Terri Malek (Cir. Mgr.); Angie Burlew
Parent company (for newspapers): Sample News Group LLC

THE INTELLIGENCER

Street address 1: 333 N Broad St
Street address city: Doylestown
Street address state: PA
Zip/Postal code: 18901-3407
County: Bucks
Country: USA
Mailing address: PO BOX 858
Mailing city: DOYLESTOWN
Mailing state: PA
Mailing zip: 18901-0858
General Phone: (215) 345-3000
Advertising Phone: (215) 345-3080
Editorial Phone: (215) 345-3050
General/National Adv. E-mail: komalley@calkins.com
Display Adv. E-mail: komalley@calkins.com
Classified Adv. e-mail: classifieds@calkins.com
Editorial e-mail: news@calkins.com
Primary Website: www.theintell.com
Year Established: 1804
News Services: AP.
Special Editions: Newspapers in Education (Apr); Savings (Jan); Auto (Oct).
Special Weekly Sections: At Home (Sat).
Syndicated Publications: Parade (S).
Areas Served - City/County or Portion Thereof, or Zip codes: Central Bucks County, Upper Bucks County and Eastern Montgomery County
Avg Free Circ: 2498
Sun. Circulation Paid: 21129
Sun. Circulation Free: 2483
Audit By: AAM
Audit Date: 30.06.2018
Personnel: Jake Volcsko (Gen. Mgr.); Carol Schramm (Finance Dir.); Kevin Oâ€™Malley (Advertising Sales Mgr.); Steve Todd (Regional Distribution Dir.); Amy Maitland (Classified Mgr.); Shane Fitzgerald (Exec. Ed.); Audrey Harvin (Mng. Ed.); Danielle Camilli (News Dir.); Crissa Shoemaker DeBree (Enterprise/Investigative Ed.); Bob Braun (Operations Dir.)
Parent company (for newspapers): CherryRoad Media

THE COURIER EXPRESS

Street address 1: 500 Jeffers St
Street address city: Du Bois
Street address state: PA
Zip/Postal code: 15801-2430
County: Clearfield
Country: USA
Mailing address: PO BOX 407
Mailing city: DU BOIS
Mailing state: PA
Mailing zip: 15801-0407
General Phone: (814) 371-4200
Advertising Phone: (814)503-8877
Editorial Phone: (814)503-8863
General/National Adv. E-mail: ads@thecourierexpress.com
Display Adv. E-mail: ads@thecourierexpress.com
Classified Adv. e-mail: classified@thecourierexpress.com
Editorial e-mail: letters@thecourierexpress.com
Primary Website: www.thecourierexpress.com
Year Established: 1872
News Services: AP, SHNS.
Special Editions: Homes and Gardens (Apr); Fall Sports (Aug); Christmas Greetings (Dec); Cooking (Feb); Bridal (Jan); Little League All-Star (Jul); Vacation Close to Home (Jun); Easter Dining (Mar); Graduation and Careers (May); Christmas Kick-Off (Nov); Hunting (Oct); Fal
Special Weekly Sections: Snapshots Photo Page (Fri); Business Pages (S); Business Pages (Thur); Outdoors (Wed).
Syndicated Publications: Comics (S). TV (S)
Delivery Methods: Mail`Newsstand`Carrier`Racks
Areas Served - City/County or Portion Thereof, or Zip codes: 15801, 15825, 15851, 15711, 15860, 15829, 15840, 15767, 15860, 15715, 15824, 168938, 15828, 16830, 15829, 16833, 15860, 15848, 15849, 15847, 15860, 15863
Own Printing Facility?: Y
Commercial printers?: Y
Sun. Circulation Paid: 14002
Audit By: AAM
Audit Date: 30.09.2012
Personnel: S.W. Kronenwetter (Controller); Linda L. Smith (Adv. Dir., Nat'l); Dory Ferra (Adv. Mgr., Classified); Jim Nestlerode (Circ. Mgr.); Nick Hoffman (Mng. Ed.); Dena Bosak (Copy Ed.); Alice Bish Sylvis (News Ed.); Scott Shindledecker (Sports Ed.); Joy Norwood (Sunday Ed.); Pat Patterson (Pub.)
Parent company (for newspapers): Community Media Group

THE EXPRESS-TIMES

Street address 1: 30 N 4th St
Street address city: Easton
Street address state: PA
Zip/Postal code: 18042-3528
County: Northampton
Country: USA
Mailing address: 30 N 4TH ST
Mailing city: EASTON
Mailing state: PA
Mailing zip: 18042-3528
General Phone: (610)258-7171
Advertising Phone: (610)258-7171
Editorial Phone: (610)258-7171
General/National Adv. E-mail: advertising@express-times.com
Display Adv. E-mail: expresstimesads@lehighvalleytimes.com
Classified Adv. e-mail: expresstimeads@lehighvalleytimes.com
Editorial e-mail: news@express-times.com
Primary Website: www.lehighvalleylive.com
News Services: AP, Metro Suburbia Inc., LAT-WP, NNS.
Special Weekly Sections: Exposed, Entertainment Guide (Fri); Building & Real Estate Guide (Sun);
Syndicated Publications: Relish (Monthly); TV Update (quarterfold) (S).
Delivery Methods: Newsstand`Carrier`Racks
Areas Served - City/County or Portion Thereof, or Zip codes: 08865, 07823,07825, 07844, 07829, 07832, 07833, 07838, 07863, 07882, 08808, 07840, 07865, 08826, 08827, 07830, 08829, 08809, 08886, 08822, 08833, 08888, 08825, 08802, 08801, 08804, 08867, 08848, 18360, 18014, 18045, 18040, 18020, 18055, 18063, 18013, 18343, 1835, 18072, 18091, 18353, 18042, 18077, 18972, 18109, 18067, 18064, 18083, 18085, 18015, 18017, 18018
Sat. Circulation Paid: 12639
Sun. Circulation Paid: 24909
Audit By: AAM
Audit Date: 30.06.2018
Personnel: Al Kratzer (President and Publisher); Nick Falsone (Managing Prod.); Jim Flagg (Opinion Ed.); Kyle Craig (Sports Managing Prod.)
Parent company (for newspapers): Advance Publications, Inc.

ELLWOOD CITY LEDGER

Street address 1: 501 Lawrence Ave
Street address city: Ellwood City
Street address state: PA
Zip/Postal code: 16117-1927

County: Lawrence
Country: USA
Mailing address: 501 LAWRENCE AVE
Mailing city: ELLWOOD CITY
Mailing state: PA
Mailing zip: 16117-1927
General Phone: (724) 758-5573
Advertising Phone: (724)846-6300
Editorial Phone: (724) 758-5573
General/National Adv. E-mail: ads@ellwoodcityledger.com
Display Adv. E-mail: ads@ellwoodcityledger.com
Classified Adv. e-mail: ads@ellwood cityledger.com
Editorial e-mail: eclnews@ellwoodcityledger.com
Primary Website: www.ellwoodcityledger.com
Year Established: 1920
News Services: AP, U.S. Suburban Press Inc..
Special Editions: Annual Progress (Apr); Fall Bridal (Aug); Arts, Crafts & Food Festival (Jul); Visitor's Guide (Jun); Lawn & Garden (Mar); Car Care (May); Homefinders (Monthly); Health Care (Oct); Home Improvement (Sept).
Special Weekly Sections: Food Day (Mon); Food Day (Sat); Food Day (Wed).
Sat. Circulation Paid: 3425
Audit By: Sworn/Estimate/Non-Audited
Audit Date: 12.07.2019
Personnel: Patrick Oâ€™Shea (Ed.); Tom Bickert (Operations)
Parent company (for newspapers): Gannett; CherryRoad Media

ERIE TIMES-NEWS

Street address 1: 205 W. 12th Street
Street address city: Erie
Street address state: PA
Zip/Postal code: 16534-0001
County: Erie
Country: USA
Mailing address: 205 W 12TH ST
Mailing city: ERIE
Mailing state: PA
Mailing zip: 16534-0001
General Phone: (814) 870-1600
Advertising Phone: (814) 878-1642
Editorial Phone: (814) 870-1715
General/National Adv. E-mail: susan.schreiner@timesnews.com
Display Adv. E-mail: kate.weber@timesnews.com
Classified Adv. e-mail: classify@timesnews.com
Editorial e-mail: letters@timesnews.com
Primary Website: www.goerie.com
Year Established: 1888
News Services: AP, LAT-WP, MCT.
Special Editions: Spring Car Care (Apr); New Year's Dining Guide (Dec); Home Remodeling (Feb); Bridal (Jan); Senior Lifestyle (Jul); Graduation (Jun); Easter Dining (Mar); Golf (May); Thanksgiving Dining Guide (Nov); Fall Car Care (Oct); Progress (Quarterly); Bridal (Sept)
Special Weekly Sections: Health, Learning (Mon); Home, Garden, Business (Tue); Food, Business (Wed); Entertainment, Family (Thur); Business, Weekend (Fri); Home (Sat); Business, Comics, Religion, Sunday Living (Sun)
Syndicated Publications: Parade, TV Schedule (Sun); Her Times; Lake Erie Lifestyle
Delivery Methods: Mail`Newsstand`Carrier`Racks
Own Printing Facility?: N
Commercial printers?: N
Sat. Circulation Paid: 28891
Sun. Circulation Paid: 38531
Audit By: AAM
Audit Date: 30.09.2018
Personnel: Pat Howard (Mng. Ed.); Matt Martin (Online News Ed.); Rich Frosgren (CTO); David Stolar (Opns. Dir.); Kenneth Nelson (Pub.)
Parent company (for newspapers): Gannett; CherryRoad Media

GETTYSBURG TIMES

Street address 1: 1570 Fairfield Rd
Street address city: Gettysburg
Street address state: PA
Zip/Postal code: 17325-7252
County: Adams
Country: USA
Mailing address: PO BOX 3669
Mailing city: GETTYSBURG
Mailing state: PA
Mailing zip: 17325-0669
General Phone: (717) 334-1131
Advertising Phone: (717) 253-9403
Editorial Phone: (717) 253-9413
General/National Adv. E-mail: npritt@gettysburgtimes.com
Display Adv. E-mail: npritt@gettysburgtimes.com
Classified Adv. e-mail: class@gettysburgtimes.com
Editorial e-mail: ahayes@gettysburgtimes.com
Primary Website: www.gettysburgtimes.com
Mthly Avg Views: 1654701
Mthly Avg Unique Visitors: 109628
Year Established: 1802
News Services: AP, DF, MCT, SHNS, TMS, Washington Post News Group.
Special Editions: Spring Lawn & Garden (Apr); Football Preview (Fall); Bridal Faire (Feb); Medical/Wellness Guide (Jul); Community Fact Book (Jun); Spring Automotive (Mar); Holiday Songbook (Nov); Bridal Tab (Quarterly); Spring Home Improvement (Spring); Winter Sports Prev
Special Weekly Sections: LifeStyles Feature (Wed); Arts & Leisure Feature (Thurs); Food For Thought Feature (Thurs); HomeStyle Section (Fri); Religion Feature (Sat)
Syndicated Publications: Parade (Sat).
Delivery Methods: Mail`Newsstand`Carrier`Racks
Areas Served - City/County or Portion Thereof, or Zip codes: 17325, 17307, 17320, 17353, 17310, 17306, 17331, 17340, 17372, 17344, 17350, 17304
Own Printing Facility?: Y
Commercial printers?: N
Sat. Circulation Paid: 11605
Audit By: USPS
Audit Date: 31.03.2013
Personnel: Harry Hartman (Pub.); Alex Hayes (Mng. Ed.); Josh Martin (Sports Ed.); Kristy Allen (Webmaster); Nancy Pritt (Sales Mgr.); Debi Orndoff (Class.)
Parent company (for newspapers): Sample News Group LLC

TRIBUNE-REVIEW

Street address 1: 622 Cabin Hill Dr
Street address city: Greensburg
Street address state: PA
Zip/Postal code: 15601-1657
County: Westmoreland
Country: USA
Mailing address: 622 CABIN HILL DR
Mailing city: GREENSBURG
Mailing state: PA
Mailing zip: 15601-1692
General Phone: (724) 838-5124
Advertising Phone: (724) 779-6959
Editorial Phone: (412) 321-6460
General/National Adv. E-mail: info@tribweb.com
Display Adv. E-mail: golvido@tribweb.com
Classified Adv. e-mail: golvido@tribweb.com
Editorial e-mail: tribcity@tribweb.com
Primary Website: www.triblive.com
Mthly Avg Unique Visitors: 4737075
News Services: AP, CNS, MCT, LAT-WP.
Special Editions: College Football (Aug); RV Show (Dec); Enterprise (Feb); Bridal (Jan); Steeler Training Camp (Jul); Medical Directory (Mar); Summer Fun (May); Gift Guide (Nov); Quest for the Best (Oct); Pro Football (Sept).
Special Weekly Sections: Society (Mon); Best Food Day (Wed, Sun); Entertainment, Neighborhood (Thur); Home, Garden (Sat); Travel, Real Estate (Sun)
Syndicated Publications: Ticket (Fri); Relish (Monthly); USA WEEKEND Magazine (S); American Profile (Weekly).
Areas Served - City/County or Portion Thereof, or Zip codes: Westmoreland, Armstrong, Fayette and Indiana Counties
Sat. Circulation Paid: 62786
Sun. Circulation Paid: 86682
Audit By: AAM
Audit Date: 31.03.2017
Personnel: Susan K. McFarland (Exec. Ed.); Jerry DeFlitch (Executive Managing Editor); Kevin Smith (Sports Ed.); Jonna Miller (Features Ed.); Lori Falce (Community Engagement Ed.)
Parent company (for newspapers): Trib Total Media, Inc.

HAZLETON STANDARD-SPEAKER

Street address 1: 21 N Wyoming St
Street address city: Hazleton
Street address state: PA
Zip/Postal code: 18201-6068
County: Luzerne
Country: USA
Mailing address: PO BOX 578
Mailing city: HAZLETON
Mailing state: PA
Mailing zip: 18201-0578
General Phone: (570) 455-3636
Advertising Phone: (570) 455-3636
Editorial Phone: (570) 455-3636 ext. 3615
General/National Adv. E-mail: sales@standardspeaker.com
Display Adv. E-mail: sales@standardspeaker.com
Classified Adv. e-mail: sales@standardspeaker.com
Editorial e-mail: editorial@standardspeaker.com
Primary Website: www.standardspeaker.com
Mthly Avg Views: 1000000
Mthly Avg Unique Visitors: 140000
Year Established: 1866
News Services: AP.
Special Editions: Home Improvement (Apr); Football Preview (Aug); Christmas Greetings (Dec); Bridal (Feb); Bridal II (Jul); Progress (Jun); Create An Ad (Mar); Senior Citizen (May); Holiday Gift Guide (Nov); Dining Guides (Oct); FunFest (Sept).
Special Weekly Sections: Best Food Day (Wed); Business (Mon); Health, Science, School (Tue); Food (Wed); Business, Golf (Thur); Sports, NASCAR (Fri); Real Estate, Travel (Sat); TV, Home, Arts, Outdoors, Travel, Business (Sun)
Syndicated Publications: TV Showtime (S); Best Food Days (Sat); Best Food Days (Wed); American Profile (Weekly).
Delivery Methods: Newsstand`Carrier`Racks
Own Printing Facility?: Y
Avg Free Circ: 1642
Sat. Circulation Paid: 9681
Sat. Circulation Free: 1642
Sun. Circulation Paid: 11099
Sun. Circulation Free: 5554
Audit By: AAM
Audit Date: 31.03.2019
Personnel: Scott Lynett (Pres./Pub./CEO); Paul Ross (Adv. Dir.); John Patton (Ops. Mgr.); Gary Klinger (Circ. Mgr., Distr.); Mildred Rubinote (Lifestyle Ed.); Carl Christopher (News Ed.); Babe Conroy (Sports Ed.); James R. Seybert (Prodn. Mgr.); David Steiner (Prodn. Supt., Composing); Matthew Haggerty (Pub.); Don Farley (Gen. Mgr.); Mark Katchur (Ed.)
Parent company (for newspapers): Times-Shamrock Communications

THE WAYNE INDEPENDENT

Street address 1: 220 8th St
Street address city: Honesdale
Street address state: PA
Zip/Postal code: 18431-1854
County: Wayne
Country: USA
Mailing address: 220 8th Street
Mailing city: Honesdale
Mailing state: PA
Mailing zip: 18431-1854
General Phone: (570) 253-3055 ext 301
Advertising Phone: (570) 253-3055 ext. 301
Editorial Phone: (570) 253-3055 ext. 329
General/National Adv. E-mail: mfleece@wayneindependent.com
Display Adv. E-mail: mfleece@wayneindependent.com
Classified Adv. e-mail: pjordan@wayneindependent.com
Editorial e-mail: mleet@wayneindependent.com
Primary Website: www.wayneindependent.com
Mthly Avg Views: 148912
Mthly Avg Unique Visitors: 32177
Year Established: 1878
News Services: AP.
Special Editions: Bridal Guide; Progress Edition; Home Improvement; Wayne County Fair/Jr Livestock Edition; Health; Family Magazine; Real Estate Guide; Restaurant/Dining
Special Weekly Sections: Business (Daily); Health, Home, Entertainment (Sat)
Syndicated Publications: American Profile (Weekly), Spry, Relish and Athlon (Monthly), Parade, TV Week
Delivery Methods: Mail`Newsstand`Racks
Areas Served - City/County or Portion Thereof, or Zip codes: 18431, 18473, 18428, 18464, 18426, 18445, 18427, 18444, 18436, 18438, 18459, 18472, 18407, 18456, 18421, 18462, 18405, 18469, 18445, 18415, 18847, 18455, 18461, 18439, 18453, 18437, 18417, 13783, 12723, 12764, 18460, 18451, 18462, 18458, 18407, 18465
Own Printing Facility?: N
Commercial printers?: N
Sat. Circulation Paid: 2618
Audit By: USPS
Audit Date: 01.10.2016
Personnel: Kevin Edwards (Group Sports Editor); Michelle Fleece (Pub./Adv. Dir.); Melissa Lee (Managing Editor)
Parent company (for newspapers): CherryRoad Media; Gannett

THE HUNTINGDON DAILY NEWS

Street address 1: 325 Penn St
Street address 2: Ste 1
Street address city: Huntingdon
Street address state: PA
Zip/Postal code: 16652-1470
County: Huntingdon
Country: USA
Mailing address: PO BOX 384
Mailing city: HUNTINGDON
Mailing state: PA
Mailing zip: 16652-0384
General Phone: (814) 643-4040
Advertising Phone: (814)643-4040
Editorial Phone: (814)643-4040
General/National Adv. E-mail: dnewsads@huntingdailynews.com
Display Adv. E-mail: dnewsads@huntingdondailynews.com
Classified Adv. e-mail: classifieds@huntingdondailynews.com
Editorial e-mail: dnews@huntingdondailynews.com
Primary Website: www.huntingdondailynews.com
Year Established: 1922
News Services: AP.
Special Editions: Bridal (Feb); Spring Sports, Home and Garden (Mar); Hunting (Apr); Leisure (Summer); Firemen's Booklet (July); Back to School, Medical Directory (Aug); Football, Fall Home, Energy (Sept); Business Directory (Oct); Christmas Greeting (Dec)
Special Weekly Sections: Editorial, TV (Mon-Fri); Healthy Living (Tue); Best Food Days (Wed/Sat); Farm (Thur); Real Estate (Fri, Monthly); Minipage (Sat);
Syndicated Publications: American Profile (Weekly).
Sat. Circulation Paid: 9258
Audit By: Sworn/Estimate/Non-Audited
Audit Date: 12.07.2019
Personnel: Kenneth J. Smith (Purchasing Agent); Carol A. Cutshall (Adv. Dir.); Heather Lohr (Circ. Mgr.); George Germann (Editorial Page Ed.); Polly McMullen (News Ed.); Terry Bowser (Sports Ed.); Robert Dietz (Prodn. Mgr.); Lori Stevens (Bus. Mng.); John Cook (Pub); Michelle Carolus; Joseph F. Biddle II (Assoc. Pub.); Brenda Hoover (Circ. Mgr.)
Parent company (for newspapers): Sample News Group LLC

THE INDIANA GAZETTE

Street address 1: 899 Water St
Street address city: Indiana
Street address state: PA
Zip/Postal code: 15701-1705
County: Indiana
Country: USA
Mailing address: PO BOX 10
Mailing city: INDIANA
Mailing state: PA
Mailing zip: 15701-0010
General Phone: (724) 465-5555
Advertising Phone: (724) 465-5555
Editorial Phone: (724) 465-5555
General/National Adv. E-mail: jlash@indianagazette.net
Display Adv. E-mail: awilliams@indianagazette.net
Classified Adv. e-mail: bnichol@indianagazette.net
Editorial e-mail: eebeling@indianagazette.net
Primary Website: www.indianagazette.com
Year Established: 1890
News Services: AP, NEA, NYT. Scripps-Howard
Special Editions: Lawn & Garden (Apr); Football (Aug); Winter Sports (Dec); Financial Fitness (Feb); Bridal (Jan); Arts Festival (Jul); Car Care (Jun); Homebuilders Real Estate (Mar); Summer Recreation (May); Holiday Gift Guide (Nov); Car Care (Oct); Resource Directory (Sept).
Special Weekly Sections: Health (Tue); Best Food (Wed/Sun); Religion (Sat); Business, Stock, TV (Sun)
Syndicated Publications: USA WEEKEND Magazine (S).
Delivery Methods: Mail`Carrier`Racks
Areas Served - City/County or Portion Thereof, or Zip codes: 15701, 15748, 15717, 15681, 15714, 15742, 15759
Own Printing Facility?: Y

Commercial printers?: Y
Avg Free Circ: 2765
Sat. Circulation Paid: 8762
Sat. Circulation Free: 2765
Sun. Circulation Paid: 9258
Sun. Circulation Free: 447
Audit By: AAM
Audit Date: 31.03.2019
Personnel: Michael J. Donnelly (Pres./Pub.); Hastie D. Kinter (News In Edu. Coordinator); Joseph L. Geary (Gen. Mgr.); Robert W. Kanick (Controller); Cathy Reed (Adv. Dir.); Eric Ebeling (Exec. Ed.); Michael Peterson (Editorial Page Ed.); Tom Peel (Chief Photo.); Tony Coccagna (Sports Ed.); Donna Rethi (Prodn. Mgr.); Jason Levan (News Ed.); Chauncey Ross; Jarrod Lash (Adv. / Mrkt. Dir.)
Parent company (for newspapers): Indiana Printing & Publishing Co.; Sample News Group LLC

THE TRIBUNE-DEMOCRAT

Street address 1: 425 Locust St
Street address city: Johnstown
Street address state: PA
Zip/Postal code: 15901-1817
County: Cambria
Country: USA
Mailing address: PO BOX 340
Mailing city: JOHNSTOWN
Mailing state: PA
Mailing zip: 15907-0340
General Phone: (814) 532-5199
Advertising Phone: (814) 532-5150
Editorial Phone: (814) 532-5050
General/National Adv. E-mail: tpritt@tribdem.com
Display Adv. E-mail: marizzo@tribdem.com
Classified Adv. e-mail: tribads@lenzlink.net
Primary Website: www.tribune-democrat.com
Year Established: 1853
News Services: AP, NNS, GNS.
Special Editions: Spring Outdoor Guide (Apr); Simply the Best (Aug); Holiday Gift Guides (Dec); Progress (Feb); Bridal Guide (Jan); Bridal Guide (Jul); Real Estate (Mar); Summer Lifestyle (May); Holiday Gift Guides (Nov); Kitchen & Bath (Oct); Simply the Best (Sept).
Special Weekly Sections: Weekend, Entertainment (Fri); Best Food Days, Travel, Home, Auto, TV (Sun)
Syndicated Publications: Relish (Monthly); Parade (S).
Sat. Circulation Paid: 23423
Sun. Circulation Paid: 26135
Audit By: AAM
Audit Date: 31.03.2017
Personnel: Robin Quillon (Pub.); Louis Gjurich (Controller); Joan Hunter (Personnel Mgr.); Julie Fox-Arnott (Circ. Dir.); Bruce Wissinger (Editorial Page Ed.); Eric Knopsnyder (Sports Ed.); Renee Carthew (Style Ed.); Steve Sindleri (Prodn. Dir.); Tina Pritt (Major/ Nat'l. Sales); Mary Anne Rizzo (Director Adv.); Robert Forcey (Pub.)
Parent company (for newspapers): CNHI, LLC; CNHI, LLC

LEADER TIMES

Street address 1: 1270 N Water St
Street address 2: Ste E
Street address city: Kittanning
Street address state: PA
Zip/Postal code: 16201-1055
County: Armstrong
Country: USA
Mailing address: 460 RODI RD
Mailing city: PITTSBURGH
Mailing state: PA
Mailing zip: 15235-4547
General Phone: (724) 543-1303
Advertising Phone: (724) 779-6959
Editorial Phone: (724) 543-1303
General/National Adv. E-mail: advertising@leadertimes.com
Display Adv. E-mail: advertising@leadertimes.com
Classified Adv. e-mail: classified@leadertimes.com
Editorial e-mail: newsroom@leadertimes
Primary Website: www.leadertimes.com
News Services: AP.
Special Weekly Sections: Society (Mon); Best Food Day (Wed/Sun); Entertainment, Neighborhood (Thur); Home and Garden (Sat); Travel, Real Estate (Sun)
Areas Served - City/County or Portion Thereof, or Zip codes: Armstrong County
Avg Free Circ: 243
Sat. Circulation Paid: 5968
Sat. Circulation Free: 143
Sun. Circulation Paid: 704
Audit By: AAM
Audit Date: 30.09.2014
Personnel: A.J. Panian (Mng. Ed.); Joe Rhoades (Sports Ed.); Keith Mangus (Circ. Mgr.); Tammy Bish (Office Mgr.)
Parent company (for newspapers): Sample Media Group

LNP

Street address 1: 8 W King St
Street address city: Lancaster
Street address state: PA
Zip/Postal code: 17603-3824
County: Lancaster
Country: USA
Mailing address: PO BOX 1328
Mailing city: LANCASTER
Mailing state: PA
Mailing zip: 17608-1328
General Phone: (717) 291-8811
Advertising Phone: (717) 291-8711
Editorial Phone: (717) 291-8622
General/National Adv. E-mail: lnp@lnpnews.com
Display Adv. E-mail: advertising@lnpnews.com
Classified Adv. e-mail: class@lnpnews.com
Editorial e-mail: editorialdepartment@LNPnews.com
Primary Website: www.lancasteronline.com
Mthly Avg Views: 7500849
Mthly Avg Unique Visitors: 3028171
Year Established: 1764
News Services: AP, NYT, MCT, LAT-WP, States News Service, NEA.
Special Editions: (Feb) Always Lancaster; Summer Kids;I Do Bridal (Mar) NIE Week Design an Ad; (Apr) Visiting Lancaster; (May) Mother's Day; Senior Living (Aug) Readers Choice Awards;High School Football Preview (Sep) Fall Home Pages; Grandparent's Day Lancaster Chamber Business Expo (Nov)College Night Guide Book;Holiday Gifts and Livestyle Holiday Showcase; Small Business Saturday (Dec)Dear Santa;last Minute Gifts
Special Weekly Sections: Church (Sat); Entertainment (Thur); Food (Wed) Food (Sun)
Syndicated Publications: Parade (S)
Delivery Methods: Mail`Newsstand`Carrier`Racks
Areas Served - City/County or Portion Thereof, or Zip codes: 17501,19501,19310,17502,19310,17502,17503,17504,17505,17506,17507,17508,17566,17509,19330,17512,17516,17517,17518,17519,17520,17022,17522,17521,17527,17528,17529,17532,19344,17533,17534,17535,17536,17537,17601,17602,17603,17604,17605,17606,17607,17608,17538,17540,17543,17545,17547,17549,17550,17551,17552,17554,17555,17557,17560,19362,19363,17562,19365,17563,17564,17565,17566,17567,17568,17569,17572,17575,17576,17577,17578,17579,17580,17581,17582,17583,17584,17585
Own Printing Facility?: N
Commercial printers?: N
Sat. Circulation Paid: 51374
Sun. Circulation Paid: 75777
Audit By: AAM
Audit Date: 31.03.2019
Personnel: Barbara Hough Roda (Community Liaison); Robert Krasne (Publisher and Chairman); Tom Murse (Managing Editor); Jeff Twilley (Director, Technical Services); Connie Solon (Production Manager); Christine Stahl (Dir. Client Solutions); Caroline Muraro (Pres.); Ted Sickler (Mng. Ed.); Ralph Martin (Ex. V.P.)
Parent company (for newspapers): LNP Media Group

THE REPORTER

Street address 1: 307 Derstine Ave
Street address city: Lansdale
Street address state: PA
Zip/Postal code: 19446-3532
County: Montgomery
Country: USA
Mailing address: 307 DERSTINE AVE
Mailing city: LANSDALE
Mailing state: PA
Mailing zip: 19446-3558
General Phone: (215) 855-8440
Advertising Phone: (215) 855-8440
Editorial Phone: (215) 361-8820
General/National Adv. E-mail: advertising@thereporteronline.com
Display Adv. E-mail: econdra@journalregister.com
Classified Adv. e-mail: classifieds@thereporteronline.com
Editorial e-mail: citydesk@thereporteronline.com
Primary Website: www.thereporteronline.com
Mthly Avg Views: 1050922
Mthly Avg Unique Visitors: 271009
Year Established: 1870
News Services: AP, U.S. Suburban Press Inc., Robert Hitchings & Co..
Special Editions: Garden (Apr); Fall Sports (Aug); Gift Guide (Dec); Business Outlook (Feb); Community Guide Book (Jul); Health & Fitness (Mar); Gift Guide (Nov); New Cars (Oct); Bridal (Quarterly).
Special Weekly Sections: Celebrations, Stocks, Business Coverage, Region News, State News, World News, Daily Movie, Cable Listings (Daily); Sports, Employment, Kids, Business (Mon); Kids, Athletes of the Week, High School Sports (Tue); Food, Features, Recipes (Wed); Weekend Entertainment (Thur); Teen, high School Sports (Fri); Religions, Real Estate, high School Sports (Sat); Comics, Engagements, Stock Summary, Jobs (Sun)
Syndicated Publications: Parade Magazine (Sun)
Avg Free Circ: 534
Sat. Circulation Paid: 2584
Sat. Circulation Free: 342
Audit By: AAM
Audit Date: 31.03.2019
Personnel: Bernard DeAngelis (Controller/Purchasing Agent); Aixa Torregrosa (Lifestyles Ed.); Evelyn Short (Night Ed.); Geoff Patton (Online Ed.); Ann Cornell (Ed.); Holly Hill (Nat'l. Adv. Coord.); Edward Condra (Adv. Dir.)
Parent company (for newspapers): Media News Group; Digital First Media

THE TIMES HERALD

Street address 1: 307 Derstine Ave
Street address city: Lansdale
Street address state: PA
Zip/Postal code: 19446-3532
County: Montgomery
Country: USA
Mailing address: 307 DERSTINE AVE
Mailing city: LANSDALE
Mailing state: PA
Mailing zip: 19446-3532
General Phone: (610) 272-2500
Advertising Phone: (610) 272-3830
Editorial Phone: (610) 272-2501
General/National Adv. E-mail: advertising@timesherald.com
Display Adv. E-mail: advertising@timesherald.com
Classified Adv. e-mail: advertising@timesherald.com
Editorial e-mail: editors@timesherald.com
Primary Website: www.timesherald.com
Mthly Avg Views: 1000000
Mthly Avg Unique Visitors: 250000
Year Established: 1799
News Services: AP, SHNS.
Special Editions: Senior Lifestyles (Apr); Football (Aug); Song Book (Dec); Parenting (Feb); Super Sale (Jan); Fall Education (Jul); Children's Guide (Jun); Coupon Book (Mar); Coupon Book (May); Holiday Season Preview (Nov); Car Care (Oct); Fall Bridal (Sept).
Special Weekly Sections: TV Showcase, Travel, Comics, Auto, Real Estate, Recruitment, Coupons, Jobs (Sun); Best Food (Wed); Auto, Church (Thur); Welcome Home, Real Estate (Fri)
Syndicated Publications: USA WEEKEND Magazine (S).
Delivery Methods: Mail`Newsstand`Carrier`Racks
Areas Served - City/County or Portion Thereof, or Zip codes: Montgomery County, PA
Own Printing Facility?: Y
Commercial printers?: Y
Avg Free Circ: 427
Sat. Circulation Paid: 2837
Sat. Circulation Free: 427
Sun. Circulation Paid: 11572
Sun. Circulation Free: 4879
Audit By: AAM
Audit Date: 31.03.2019
Personnel: Shelley Meenan (Pub.); Amy Bernstiel (Asst. to Pub.); Stan Huskey (Ed.); Cheryl Kehoe Rodgers (City Ed.)
Parent company (for newspapers): MediaNews Group

THE LATROBE BULLETIN

Street address 1: 1211 Ligonier St
Street address city: Latrobe
Street address state: PA
Zip/Postal code: 15650-1921
County: Westmoreland
Country: USA
Mailing address: PO BOX 111
Mailing city: LATROBE
Mailing state: PA
Mailing zip: 15650-0111
General Phone: (724)537-3351
Advertising Phone: (724)537-3551 ext. 24
Editorial Phone: (724) 537-3351 ext. 27
General/National Adv. E-mail: latbull@gmail.com
Display Adv. E-mail: latbull@gmail.com
Classified Adv. e-mail: lb.class@verizon.net
Editorial e-mail: lb.editor@verizon.net
Primary Website: www.latrobebulletin.com
News Services: AP, SHNS, TMS.
Special Editions: Spring Car Care (Apr); Fall Bridal (Aug); Ligonier Greetings (Dec); Spring Bridal (Feb); Ligonier's Art About Town-Sidewalk Days (Jul); Spring Home Improvement (Mar); Mother's Day (May); Senior Citizen (Nov); Fort Ligonier Days (Oct); Fall Home Improvemen
Syndicated Publications: American Profile (Weekly). Parade
Delivery Methods: Newsstand`Carrier`Racks
Own Printing Facility?: Y
Commercial printers?: Y
Sat. Circulation Paid: 7767
Audit By: Sworn/Estimate/Non-Audited
Audit Date: 12.07.2019
Personnel: Jamie Knechtel (Office Mgr.); Gary Siegel (Pub., Adv. Dir.); Steve Kittey (Ed.); Randy Skubek (Sports Ed.); Louise F. Fritz (Women's Ed.); Mike Feltes (Prodn. Mgr., Pressroom); Brittany Keeton (Cir. Dir.)
Parent company (for newspapers): Sample News Group LLC

THE LEBANON DAILY NEWS

Street address 1: 718 Poplar St
Street address city: Lebanon
Street address state: PA
Zip/Postal code: 17042-6755
County: Lebanon
Country: USA
Mailing address: 718 POPLAR ST
Mailing city: LEBANON
Mailing state: PA
Mailing zip: 17042-6755
General Phone: (717) 272-5611
Advertising Phone: (717) 272-5611
Editorial Phone: (717) 272-5611
General/National Adv. E-mail: cbrewer@mediaonepa.com
Display Adv. E-mail: cbrewer@mediaonepa.com
Classified Adv. e-mail: advertising@mediaonemarketplace.com
Editorial e-mail: andrearich@ldnews.com
Primary Website: www.ldnews.com
Mthly Avg Views: 1000000
Mthly Avg Unique Visitors: 200000
Year Established: 1872
News Services: AP, NYT, TMS.
Special Editions: Valley Profiles (Progress)
Special Weekly Sections: Best Food Day (Wed); Church (Sat); Business (Sun)
Syndicated Publications: USA WEEKEND Magazine (S).
Own Printing Facility?: N
Commercial printers?: N
Avg Free Circ: 1059
Sat. Circulation Paid: 6278
Sat. Circulation Free: 1059
Sun. Circulation Paid: 7523
Sun. Circulation Free: 98
Audit By: AAM
Audit Date: 31.03.2019
Personnel: Karol Gress (City Ed.); Earl Brightbill (Photo Ed.); Andrea Rich (Managing Ed); Rahn Forney (Editorial Page Ed.); Jeff Clouser (Weekend Ed.); Scott Downs (Pub.); Kevin Madden (Controller); Jean Taylor (HR); Joe Clark (Circ. Mgr.); Rich Canazaro (Adv. Mgr.); Andrea Gillhoolley (Community Engagement Team Leader); Pat Bywater (Exec. Ed.); Michelle Brown; Michael Waterloo (Features Ed.)
Parent company (for newspapers): Gannett

TIMES NEWS

Street address 1: 594 Blakeslee Boulevard Drive West
Street address city: Lehighton
Street address state: PA
Zip/Postal code: 18235
County: Carbon
Country: USA
Mailing address: PO BOX 239
Mailing city: LEHIGHTON

Mailing state: PA
Mailing zip: 18235-0239
General Phone: (610) 377-2051
Advertising Phone: (610) 377-2051
Editorial Phone: (610) 377-2051
General/National Adv. E-mail: tnonline@postoffice.ptd.net
Display Adv. E-mail: khardy@tnonline.com
Classified Adv. e-mail: khardy@tnonline.com
Editorial e-mail: tneditor@tnonline.com
Primary Website: www.tnonline.com
Year Established: 1883
News Services: AP, Papert (Landon).
Special Editions: Home Improvement (Apr); Spring Bridal (Jan); Pocono 500 (Jun); Spring Car Care (May); Christmas Shopping (Nov); Fall Car Care (Oct); Football (Sept).
Special Weekly Sections: Best Food Day (Mon?Sat); Entertainment (Fri/Sat/Tue);
Syndicated Publications: USA WEEKEND Magazine (Sat); American Profile (Weekly).
Areas Served - City/County or Portion Thereof, or Zip codes: Carbon County, Schuylkill County, part of Monroe County, Part of North Hampton County, Part of Lehigh County
Avg Free Circ: 607
Sat. Circulation Paid: 11037
Sat. Circulation Free: 607
Audit By: AAM
Audit Date: 30.09.2017
Personnel: Fred L. Masenheimer (Pub.); Scott A. Masenheimer (VP, Ops.); Donald Reese (Adv. Dir., Mktg.); Kathy Carpenter (Circ. Mgr.); Ron Gower (Entertainment Ed.); Karen Cimms (Lifestyle Ed.); George Taylor (New Media Ed.); Ed Hedes (Sports Ed.); Jim Zbick (Wire Ed.); Will Schawb (Digital/Interactive Manager); David Helmer (Prodn. Dir.); Leonard Alabovitz (Prodn. Mgr., Pressroom); Bob Miller (Dir. of Pre-Press Operations); Tanya Pecha (Marketing Assistant); Rebecca Wraight (Mktg.); Donna Hall (Adv. Nat'l. Rep.); Kevin Hardy (Rgl. Adv. Mgr.)
Parent company (for newspapers): Pencor Services Inc.

BUCKS COUNTY COURIER TIMES

Street address 1: 8400 Bristol Pike
Street address city: Levittown
Street address state: PA
Zip/Postal code: 19057-5117
County: Bucks
Country: USA
Mailing address: 8400 BRISTOL PIKE
Mailing city: LEVITTOWN
Mailing state: PA
Mailing zip: 19057-5198
General Phone: (215) 949-4000
Advertising Phone: (215) 949-4125
Editorial Phone: (215) 949-4162
General/National Adv. E-mail: bgropper@calkins.com
Display Adv. E-mail: nstuski@calkins.com
Classified Adv. e-mail: classifieds@calkins.com
Editorial e-mail: newstips@calkins.com
Primary Website: www.buckscountycouriertimes.com
Year Established: 1954
News Services: AP, NEA, SHNS, TMS.
Special Editions: Investment Fair (Apr); Back-to-School (Aug); Bucks County Holiday (Dec); Job Fair (Feb); Mature Lifestyles (Jan); Mature Lifestyles (Jul); Internet Fair (Jun); Spring Home & Garden (Mar); Voter's Guide (May); Coupon Booklets (Monthly); Holiday Gift Guide
Special Weekly Sections: Focus On Newtown (Thur).
Syndicated Publications: Enjoy (entertainment magazine) (Fri); Parade (S).
Own Printing Facility?: Y
Commercial printers?: Y
Avg Free Circ: 16877
Sun. Circulation Paid: 25192
Sun. Circulation Free: 27022
Audit By: AAM
Audit Date: 30.06.2018
Personnel: Jake Volcsko (Gen. Mgr.); Carol Schramm (Finance Dir.); Kevin Oâ€™Malley (Advertising Sales Mgr.); Steve Todd (Circ. Dir.); Amy Maitland (Classified Mgr.); Shane Fitzgerald (Regional Exec. Ed.); Audrey Harvin (Mng. Ed.)
Parent company (for newspapers): CherryRoad Media

THE SENTINEL

Street address 1: 352 6th St
Street address city: Lewistown
Street address state: PA
Zip/Postal code: 17044-1213
County: Mifflin
Country: USA
Mailing address: 352 6TH ST
Mailing city: LEWISTOWN
Mailing state: PA
Mailing zip: 17044-1213
General Phone: (717) 248-6741
General/National Adv. E-mail: news@lewistownsentinel.com
Display Adv. E-mail: mbolich@lewistownsentinel.com
Classified Adv. e-mail: tunger@lewistownsentinel.com
Editorial e-mail: news@lewistownsentinel.com
Primary Website: www.lewistownsentinel.com
Year Established: 1903
News Services: AP.
Special Editions: Home & Garden (Apr); Hall of Fame (Aug); Happy Holidays (Dec); Juniata Valley (Feb); Brides (Jan); Get to Know Us (Jul); Brides (Jun); Agriculture (Mar); Low-Fat Cookbook (May); Holiday Gift Guide (Nov); Winter Car Care (Oct); Goose Day (Sept).
Special Weekly Sections: Agriculture, Lifestyle (Mon); Senior (Tue); BEst Food (Wed); Entertainment, Outdoors (Thur); Schools, Health, Real Estate, TV (Fri); Cars, Religion, Business, Connections (Sat)
Areas Served - City/County or Portion Thereof, or Zip codes: Mifflin County, Juniata County, portion of Snyder County, portion of Huntingdon County, portion of Perry County
Avg Free Circ: 43
Sat. Circulation Paid: 9144
Audit By: AAM
Audit Date: 31.03.2018
Personnel: Ruth Eddy (Pub.); Matt Bolich (Adv. Dir.); Ed Williams (Circ. Mgr.); Brian Cox (Managing Ed.)
Parent company (for newspapers): Ogden Newspapers Inc.

THE MEADVILLE TRIBUNE

Street address 1: 947 Federal Ct
Street address city: Meadville
Street address state: PA
Zip/Postal code: 16335-3234
County: Crawford
Country: USA
Mailing address: 947 FEDERAL CT
Mailing city: MEADVILLE
Mailing state: PA
Mailing zip: 16335-3286
General Phone: (814) 724-6370
Advertising Phone: (814)724-6370 ext. 258
Editorial Phone: (814) 724-6370 ext. 267
General/National Adv. E-mail: hgebhardt@meadvilletribune.com
Display Adv. E-mail: hgebhardt@meadvilletribune.com
Classified Adv. e-mail: wendieb@meadvilletribune.com
Editorial e-mail: rgreen@meadvilletribune.com
Primary Website: www.meadvilletribune.com
News Services: AP.
Special Editions: Home Improvement (Apr); Back-to-School (Aug); Winter Sports (Dec); Report to People (Feb); Bridal (Jan); Heritage Days (Jul); Hot Air Balloons (Jun); AG Day (Mar); Country Living (Monthly); Christmas Opening (Nov); Cookbook (Oct); Outdoor (Sept).
Special Weekly Sections: Faith, Values (Sat); Bridal (Wed); Entertainment (Thur); TV, Bridal (Sun)
Syndicated Publications: Relish (Monthly); USA WEEKEND Magazine (S).
Delivery Methods: Mail`Newsstand`Carrier`Racks
Areas Served - City/County or Portion Thereof, or Zip codes: 16335
Avg Free Circ: 1092
Sat. Circulation Paid: 7954
Sat. Circulation Free: 1092
Sun. Circulation Paid: 8050
Sun. Circulation Free: 189
Audit By: AAM
Audit Date: 30.06.2018
Personnel: Sharon Sorg; Michelle Brown (Bus. Mgr.); Allen Lyon (Prodn. Mgr.); Heidi Gebhardt (Adv. Dir.); Wendie Bergendahl (Classifieds Adv. Mgr.); Rick Green (Exec. Ed.); Pete Chiodo (Sports Ed.); Devon Stout (Circ. Dir.)
Parent company (for newspapers): CNHI, LLC; CNHI, LLC

THE STANDARD-JOURNAL

Street address 1: 21 N Arch St
Street address city: Milton
Street address state: PA
Zip/Postal code: 17847-1211
County: Northumberland
Country: USA
Mailing address: 21 N ARCH ST
Mailing city: MILTON
Mailing state: PA
Mailing zip: 17847-1211
General Phone: (570) 742-9671
Advertising Phone: (570) 742-9671
Editorial Phone: (570) 742-9671
General/National Adv. E-mail: amym@standard-journal.com
Display Adv. E-mail: amym@standard-journal.com
Classified Adv. e-mail: amym@standard-journal.com
Editorial e-mail: newsroom@standard-journal.com
Primary Website: www.standard-journal.com
News Services: AP.
Special Editions: Progress (Feb).
Special Weekly Sections: Best Food (Wed); Entertainment (Thur); Bridal (Sat)
Syndicated Publications: Relocation (Oct) (Annually).
Sat. Circulation Paid: 1418
Audit By: Sworn/Estimate/Non-Audited
Audit Date: 12.07.2019
Personnel: Karen Hendricks (Bus. Mgr.); Amy Moyer (Adv. Mgr.); Kevin Mertz (Circ. Dir.); Kevin Koch (Prodn. Mgr.)
Parent company (for newspapers): Sample News Group LLC

THE MON VALLEY INDEPENDENT

Street address 1: 996 Donner Ave
Street address city: Monessen
Street address state: PA
Zip/Postal code: 15062-1001
County: Westmoreland
Country: USA
General Phone: (714) 314-0030
General/National Adv. E-mail: Lbyron@yourmvi.com
Primary Website: monvalleyindependent.com
Audit By: Sworn/Estimate/Non-Audited
Audit Date: 12.07.2019
Personnel: Laurie Byron (Adv. Mgr.)

NEW CASTLE NEWS

Street address 1: 27 N Mercer St
Street address city: New Castle
Street address state: PA
Zip/Postal code: 16101-3806
County: Lawrence
Country: USA
Mailing address: PO BOX 60
Mailing city: NEW CASTLE
Mailing state: PA
Mailing zip: 16103-0060
General Phone: (724) 654-6651
Advertising Phone: (724) 654-6651 ext. 657
Editorial Phone: (724)654-6651 ext. 614
General/National Adv. E-mail: ssorg@ncnewsonline.com
Display Adv. E-mail: display@ncnewsonline.com
Classified Adv. e-mail: cdespraspro@ncnewsonline.com
Editorial e-mail: nceditor@ncnewsonline.com
Primary Website: www.ncnewsonline.com
News Services: AP, SHNS.
Special Editions: Car Care (Apr); Football (Aug); First Baby (Dec); Business-Industrial Review (Feb); Brides (Jan); Senior Citizens (Jul); Summer Fun (Jun); Home Improvement (Mar); Mother's Day (May); Car Care (Oct); Home Improvement (Sept).
Special Weekly Sections: Best Food Day (Wed/Sat); Family, parenting (Mon); Business (Tue); Education (Wed); Entertainment (Thur); religion, TV (Fri)
Syndicated Publications: Children's Mini Page (Fri); USA WEEKEND Magazine (Sat).
Avg Free Circ: 0
Sat. Circulation Paid: 8635
Sat. Circulation Free: 529
Audit Date: 30.06.2018
Personnel: Tom Covert (Mgr., Computer Serv.); Dan Irwin (Religion Ed.); Debbie Wachter Morris (Reporter); Matt Kingman (Mgr., Educ. Serv.); Rick Work (Adv. Mgr., Retail); Sharon Sorg (Pub.); Vanessa Koper (Advertising Director); DuWayne Nelson (Circ. Mgr.); Mitch Olszak (Mng. Ed.); Pete Sirianni (Editor); Lugene Hudson (Educ. Rep.); Brant Sappington (Audience Director); Patrick Litowitz (News Ed.); John K. Manna (Political Ed.); Kayleen Cubbal (Sports Ed.); Tim Kolodziej (Television/Film Ed.); Larry Corvi
Parent company (for newspapers): CNHI, LLC; CNHI, LLC

THE NEWS-HERALD/THE DERRICK

Street address 1: 1510 W 1st St
Street address city: Oil City
Street address state: PA
Zip/Postal code: 16301-3211
County: Venango
Country: USA
Mailing address: PO BOX 928
Mailing city: OIL CITY
Mailing state: PA
Mailing zip: 16301-0928
General Phone: (814) 676-7444
Advertising Phone: (814)677-8300
Editorial Phone: (814)677-8367
General/National Adv. E-mail: info.thederrick@gmail.com
Display Adv. E-mail: info.thederrick@gmail.com
Classified Adv. e-mail: classifieds.thederrick@gmail.com
Editorial e-mail: lukakrneta.thederrick@gmail.com
Primary Website: www.thederrick.com
News Services: AP.
Special Editions: Spring Car Care (Apr); Football (Aug); First Baby (Dec); Insurance (Feb); Senior Living (Jul); Today's Bride (Mar); Outdoor Living (May); Basketball (Nov); Cookbook I (Oct); Fall Car Care (Sept).
Special Weekly Sections: Best Food Day (Mon/Wed); Entertainment (Thur)
Syndicated Publications: American Profile (Weekly).
Sat. Circulation Paid: 7373
Audit By: Sworn/Estimate/Non-Audited
Audit Date: 12.07.2019
Personnel: Paul Hess (Display Advertising Manager); Joyce Lindsay (Vice Pres./Controller); Diane Cartwright (Online Advertising); Randy Bartley (Reporter); Luka Krneta (News Ed.); Mark Oliver (City Ed.); Edward Brannon (Sports Ed.)
Parent company (for newspapers): Boyle Family

METRO PHILADELPHIA

Street address 1: 2401 Walnut Street
Street address 2: Suite 102
Street address city: Philadelphia
Street address state: PA
Zip/Postal code: 19103
County: Philadelphia
Country: USA
General Phone: (215) 717-2600
Advertising Phone: (215) 717-2695
General/National Adv. E-mail: adsphilly@metro.us
Display Adv. E-mail: susan.peiffer@metro.us
Classified Adv. e-mail: phillyclassifieds@metro.us
Editorial e-mail: letters@metro.us
Primary Website: www.metro.us/philadelphia
Mthly Avg Views: 4439165
Mthly Avg Unique Visitors: 1984744
Year Established: 2000
Special Weekly Sections: News, Entertainment, Sports, Games (Daily); Careers, Education (Mon); Well Being, Health (Tue); Home (Wed); Going out, Travel (Thur); Weekend (Fri)
Delivery Methods: Newsstand`Racks
Areas Served - City/County or Portion Thereof, or Zip codes: Greater Philadelphia
Own Printing Facility?: N
Commercial printers?: N
Avg Free Circ: 71165
Audit By: CAC
Audit Date: 30.06.2018
Personnel: Susan Peiffer (Assoc. Pub.); Joseph Lauletta (Circ. Dir.); Wilf Maunoir (Marketing Dir.)
Parent company (for newspapers): Metro US; Schneps Media

PHILADELPHIA INQUIRER, DAILY NEWS & PHILLY.COM

Street address 1: 801 Market Street
Street address 2: Ste. 300
Street address city: Philadelphia
Street address state: PA
Zip/Postal code: 19107-3126
County: Philadelphia
Country: USA
Mailing address: 801 MARKET ST STE 300
Mailing city: PHILADELPHIA
Mailing state: PA
Mailing zip: 19107-3183

General Phone: 215 854 2000
Advertising Phone: (215) 854-5450
Editorial Phone: (215) 854-4531
General/National Adv. E-mail: advertisingrequests@phillynews.com
Display Adv. E-mail: advertisingrequests@phillynews.com
Classified Adv. e-mail: advertisingrequests@phillynews.com
Primary Website: www.philly.com
Mthly Avg Unique Visitors: 7963604
Year Established: 1829
News Services: AP, DJ, MCT, LAT-WP, RN.
Delivery Methods: Newsstand`Carrier`Racks
Areas Served - City/County or Portion Thereof, or Zip codes: Philadelphia, PA
Own Printing Facility?: Y
Commercial printers?: N
Sat. Circulation Paid: 195967
Sun. Circulation Paid: 322509
Audit By: AAM
Audit Date: 31.03.2018
Personnel: Elizabeth Robertson (Staff Photographer); Stan Wischnowski (Executive Editor); Harold Jackson (Editorial Page Editor); Donna Yannessa; Pat McElwee; Barbara Sadler (Advertising Director); Fred Lehman; Gabriel Escobar (Managing Ed., Features/Operations/Digital); Terrance C.Z. Egger (Publisher and CEO)
Parent company (for newspapers): Philadelphia Media Network; Nonprofit News Agency

THE MERCURY

Street address 1: 24 N Hanover St
Street address city: Pottstown
Street address state: PA
Zip/Postal code: 19464-5410
County: Montgomery
Country: USA
Mailing address: 24 N HANOVER ST
Mailing city: POTTSTOWN
Mailing state: PA
Mailing zip: 19464-5410
General Phone: (610) 323-3000
Advertising Phone: (610) 323-3000
Editorial Phone: (610) 970-4455
General/National Adv. E-mail: paadvertising@digitalfirstmedia.com
Display Adv. E-mail: paadvertising@digitalfirstmedia.com
Classified Adv. e-mail: paadvertising@digitalfirstmedia.com
Editorial e-mail: shuskey@21-centurymedia.com
Primary Website: www.pottsmerc.com
Mthly Avg Unique Visitors: 477882
Year Established: 1931
News Services: AP, Robert Hitchings & Co..
Special Editions: Lawn & Garden (Apr); Back-to-School (Aug); Last Minute Gift Guide (Dec); Washington's Birthday Auto (Feb); Education Outlook (Jan); Financial (Jul); Senior Lifestyles (Jun); Home Improvement (Mar); Racer's Edge (May); Automotive Today (Monthly); Pre-Holid
Special Weekly Sections: Health (Mon); Generations, Business (Tue); Best Food Days (Wed); Time Out, Auto (Thur); Schools, Auctions (Fri); Church, Auto (Sat); Real Estate, Recruitment, Jobs, Food, Auto, Wedding, Engagements, Travel, TV (Sun); Business (Daily)
Syndicated Publications: USA WEEKEND Magazine (S); US Express (Sat); Market Place (Wed).
Avg Free Circ: 627
Sat. Circulation Paid: 5830
Sat. Circulation Free: 212
Sun. Circulation Paid: 9987
Sun. Circulation Free: 2643
Audit By: AAM
Audit Date: 31.03.2019
Personnel: Thomas Abbot (Pub.); Patricia McKelvey (Controller); Steve Batten (Adv. Dir.); Mary Ann Matalavage (Adv. Mgr., Classified); Cindy Eisenhauer (Mgr., Penny Pincher); Nancy March (Ed.); Tony Phyrillas (ity Editor/Opinion Page Editor/Columnist/Blogger); Pat Sommers (Features Ed.); Don Seeley (Sports Ed.); Eileen Faust (Online Ed.); Jerry Fuhrmeister (Retail Adv. Mgr.); Joe Frost (Circ. Dir.)
Parent company (for newspapers): MediaNews Group

THE REPUBLICAN-HERALD

Street address 1: 111 Mahantongo St
Street address city: Pottsville
Street address state: PA
Zip/Postal code: 17901-3071
County: Schuylkill
Country: USA
Mailing address: 111 MAHANTONGO ST
Mailing city: POTTSVILLE
Mailing state: PA
Mailing zip: 17901-3071
General Phone: (570) 622-3456
Advertising Phone: (570) 628-6060
Editorial Phone: (570) 622-3456
General/National Adv. E-mail: mjoyce@republicanherald.com
Display Adv. E-mail: mjoyce@republicanherald.com
Classified Adv. e-mail: classifieds@republicanherald.com
Editorial e-mail: editorial@republicanherald.com
Primary Website: www.republicanherald.com
Mthly Avg Views: 1415000
Mthly Avg Unique Visitors: 251000
Year Established: 1884
News Services: AP
Special Editions: Wedding Guides - January, April, June Business Review - February Home Improvement / Lawn & Garden - March, April, August, October Senior Living - <arch, May, July, September, November Business Card Directory - March Reader's Choice - May Graduation - May Football - August Church Directory - September Education Guide - November Christmas Gifts - November, December
Special Weekly Sections: Best Food Day (Wed); Business Extra (Mon); Health (Tues) Entertainment (Fri)
Syndicated Publications: Relish (Monthly); Parade Magazine (S); American Profile (Sat); Mini-Page (Tues).
Delivery Methods: Mail`Newsstand`Carrier`Racks
Areas Served - City/County or Portion Thereof, or Zip codes: Schuylkill County, Pa
Own Printing Facility?: N
Commercial printers?: Y
Avg Free Circ: 1584
Sat. Circulation Paid: 16488
Sat. Circulation Free: 612
Sun. Circulation Paid: 17245
Sun. Circulation Free: 5780
Audit By: AAM
Audit Date: 31.03.2019
Personnel: Mike Joyce (Pub.); Andy Heintzelman (Mng. Ed.); Tina Heintzelman (Lifestyles Ed.); Eric Peddigree (News Ed.); Brian Smith (City Ed.); Stephanie Kunstek (Office Mgr.); Neal O'Brien (Circ. Mgr.)
Parent company (for newspapers): Times-Shamrock Communications

THE PUNXSUTAWNEY SPIRIT

Street address 1: 510 Pine St
Street address city: Punxsutawney
Street address state: PA
Zip/Postal code: 15767-1404
County: Jefferson
Country: USA
Mailing address: PO BOX 444
Mailing city: PUNXSUTAWNEY
Mailing state: PA
Mailing zip: 15767-0444
General Phone: (814) 938-8740
Advertising Phone: (814) 938-8740
Editorial Phone: (814) 938-8740
General/National Adv. E-mail: tlsmith@punxsutawneyspirit.com
Display Adv. E-mail: tlsmith@punxsutawneyspirit.com
Classified Adv. e-mail: tlsmith@punxsutawneyspirit.com
Editorial e-mail: tchapin@punxsutawneyspirit.com
Primary Website: www.punxsutawneyspirit.com
Year Established: 1873
News Services: AP.
Special Editions: Home & Garden (Apr); Fall Sports (Aug); Senior Citizen (Feb); Spring Home Improvement (Mar); Home & Garden (May); Outdoors (Nov); Senior Citizen (Sept).
Special Weekly Sections: Best Food Day (Wed);
Syndicated Publications: American Profile (Tues).
Delivery Methods: Mail`Newsstand`Carrier`Racks
Own Printing Facility?: Y
Commercial printers?: Y
Sat. Circulation Paid: 5545
Sat. Circulation Free: 2560
Audit By: Sworn/Estimate/Non-Audited
Audit Date: 12.07.2019
Personnel: Candice Shirley (Adv. Mgr., Classified); Zak Lantz (Editor); Dan Walk (Sports Ed.); Karen Petroff (Prodn. Supvr., Composing); Tracy Smith (Pub./Adv. Dir.); Susan Humble (Business Mgr.); Cindy Covatch (Circ. Mgr.)
Parent company (for newspapers): Horizon Publications Inc.

READING EAGLE

Street address 1: 345 Penn Street
Street address city: Reading
Street address state: PA
Zip/Postal code: 19601
County: Berks
Country: USA
Mailing address: PO BOX 582
Mailing city: READING
Mailing state: PA
Mailing zip: 19603-0582
General Phone: (610) 371-5000
Advertising Phone: (610) 371-5100
Editorial Phone: (610) 371-5010
General/National Adv. E-mail: sflank@readingeagle.com
Display Adv. E-mail: advertising@readingeagle.com
Classified Adv. e-mail: Classified@readingeagle.com
Editorial e-mail: news@readingeagle.com
Primary Website: www.readingeagle.com
Mthly Avg Views: 2836764
Mthly Avg Unique Visitors: 575394
Year Established: 1868
News Services: AP, LAT-WP, SHNS.
Special Editions: Clip-it Coupons (monthly); Health & Wellness (monthly, except December); Home & Garden (Feb., Apr, Sept.); 50+ (Feb., Apr, June, Aug, Oct, Dec.); Bridal (Feb., July); Berks Jazz Fest Guide (March); Readers Choice (July, Aug., Sept.) Holiday Gift guides (Nov., Dec.)
Special Weekly Sections: Garden Pages (Apr-Sept) (Mon); Home & Building/Real Estate (Sunday); Church (Sat); Restaurant & Entertainment (Thur); Best Food Day (Wed); Berks Country (Wed); Business Weekly (Tues) Classified Jobs (Sunday)
Syndicated Publications: Parade Magazine
Delivery Methods: Mail`Newsstand`Carrier`Racks
Areas Served - City/County or Portion Thereof, or Zip codes: Reading-Berks County Pottstown-Montgomery County South Schuylkill County
Own Printing Facility?: Y
Commercial printers?: Y
Sat. Circulation Paid: 38729
Sun. Circulation Paid: 54298
Audit By: AAM
Audit Date: 31.12.2017
Personnel: Peter Barbey (Pres.CEO); William S. Flippin (Chairman, Publisher); Anne T. Chubb (COO); Dave Kline (Exec. Dir of Circ & Promotions); David Mowery (Mng. Ed.); Mark Nemirow (Editorial Page Ed.); Keith Mayer (Asst. News Ed.); Joe Hainthaler (Asst. New Ed.); Sherry Jacobs (Classified Mgr); Eric Schaeffer (Senior Information Technology Director); Kevin Lawrence (Information Technology Director); Brandi Swenson (Web Designer); William J. Lobb (Circulation Sales Director); Connie Andrews (Senior Dir of Mktg); Albert A. Stallone (Packaging/Distr. Dir.); Steve Flank (General Sales Director); Denice Schaeffer (Multimedia Sales Manager); Chris D'Angelo (Sr. Director of Production); Shawn Moliatu (CFO); Garry Lenton (Editor)
Parent company (for newspapers): MediaNews Group

THE RIDGWAY RECORD

Street address 1: 325 Main St
Street address 2: Ste A
Street address city: Ridgway
Street address state: PA
Zip/Postal code: 15853-8019
County: Elk
Country: USA
Mailing address: 325 MAIN ST STE A
Mailing city: RIDGWAY
Mailing state: PA
Mailing zip: 15853-8099
General Phone: (814) 773-3161
Editorial Phone: (814) 773-3151
General/National Adv. E-mail: sales@ridgwayrecord.com
Display Adv. E-mail: sales@ridgwayrecord.com
Classified Adv. e-mail: sales@ridgwayrecord.com
Editorial e-mail: ridgwayrecord@shop-right.com
Primary Website: www.ridgwayrecord.com
News Services: AP.
Special Weekly Sections: Best Food Days (Sat);
Syndicated Publications: TV Section (Sat); American Profile (Weekly).
Delivery Methods: Mail`Newsstand`Carrier`Racks
Own Printing Facility?: Y
Commercial printers?: Y
Sat. Circulation Paid: 2656
Audit By: Sworn/Estimate/Non-Audited
Audit Date: 12.07.2019
Personnel: Christie Gardner (Pub.); Joseph Bell (Ed.); Karen Kilhoffer (Bus. Mgr.); Brandon Laiphner (Circ. Mgr.); Mike Tucker (Production Mgr.); Harlan Beagley
Parent company (for newspapers): Horizon Publications Inc.

THE DAILY PRESS

Street address 1: 245 Brusselles St
Street address city: Saint Marys
Street address state: PA
Zip/Postal code: 15857-1501
County: Elk
Country: USA
Mailing address: 245 BRUSSELLES ST
Mailing city: SAINT MARYS
Mailing state: PA
Mailing zip: 15857-1501
General Phone: (814) 781-1596
Advertising Phone: (814)781-1596
Editorial Phone: (814) 781-1539
General/National Adv. E-mail: sales@zitomedia.net
Display Adv. E-mail: sales@zitomedia.net
Classified Adv. e-mail: classifieds@smdailypress.com
Editorial e-mail: editor3@zitomedia.net
Primary Website: www.smdailypress.com
Mthly Avg Views: 62000
News Services: AP.
Special Editions: Progress (Apr); Football (Aug); Elk Haven Greetings (Dec); Boy Scouts (Feb); Pet Parade (Jul); Spring Home Improvement (May); Holiday Gift Guide (Nov); Octoberfest (Oct); Hometown Festival (Sept).
Special Weekly Sections: Best Food Days (Mon/Tue); Senior (Other); Weekender TV (Sat).
Syndicated Publications: American Profile (Weekly).
Delivery Methods: Mail`Newsstand`Carrier`Racks
Own Printing Facility?: N
Sat. Circulation Paid: 4891
Audit By: Sworn/Estimate/Non-Audited
Audit Date: 12.07.2019
Personnel: Christie Gardner (Pub.); Krista Zameroski (Adv. Mgr.); Grace Kriegisch (Group Ed.); James R. Bauer (Bus. Mgr.); Billie Kunes (Adv. Mgr., Classified); James Mulcahy (Sports Ed.)
Parent company (for newspapers): Horizon Publications Inc.

MORNING TIMES

Street address 1: 201 N Lehigh Ave
Street address city: Sayre
Street address state: PA
Zip/Postal code: 18840-2246
County: Bradford
Country: USA
Mailing address: 201 N LEHIGH AVE
Mailing city: SAYRE
Mailing state: PA
Mailing zip: 18840-2246
General Phone: (570) 888-9643
General/National Adv. E-mail: ads@morning-times.com
Display Adv. E-mail: ads@morning-times.com
Classified Adv. e-mail: classifieds@morning-times.com
Editorial e-mail: whoweler@morning-times.com
Primary Website: www.morning-times.com
Mthly Avg Views: 258180
Mthly Avg Unique Visitors: 90450
Year Established: 1890
News Services: AP.
Special Editions: Multiple
Special Weekly Sections: Times Extra TMC
Delivery Methods: Mail`Newsstand`Carrier`Racks
Areas Served - City/County or Portion Thereof, or Zip codes: 18840, 18810, 14892, 18850, 18848, 18837, 18831, 18817, 14889, 14833, 14895, 14825, 13827, 13812, 13734
Own Printing Facility?: N
Commercial printers?: Y
Sat. Circulation Paid: 5400
Audit By: Sworn/Estimate/Non-Audited
Audit Date: 12.07.2019
Personnel: Kelly Luvison (Pub., Purchasing Agent); Warren Howeler (Mng. Ed.); Dave Post (Sports Ed.); Ashley Moore (Adv. Dir.); Bill Kurtz (Circulation Director); Kirk Luvison (Production manager)

Parent company (for newspapers): Sample News Group LLC

THE TIMES-TRIBUNE

Street address 1: 149 Penn Avenue
Street address 2: Ofc
Street address city: Scranton
Street address state: PA
Zip/Postal code: 18503
County: Lackawanna
Country: USA
Mailing address: 149 PENN AVE OFC
Mailing city: SCRANTON
Mailing state: PA
Mailing zip: 18503-2056
General Phone: (570) 348-9100
Advertising Phone: (570) 348-9100 ext. 5202
General/National Adv. E-mail: cdemas@timesshamrock.com
Display Adv. E-mail: ads@timesshamrock.com
Classified Adv. e-mail: ads@timesshamrock.com
Editorial e-mail: newsroom@timesshamrock.com
Primary Website: www.thetimes-tribune.com
Mthly Avg Views: 4000000
Mthly Avg Unique Visitors: 660000
Year Established: 1895
News Services: AP, NYT, MCT.
Special Editions: Easter Dining Guide (Apr); Football Tab (Aug); Christmas Songbook (Dec); Home Builders Expo (Feb); Good Times (Jan); Good Times (Jul); Bridal Tab (Jun); Good Times (Mar); Good Times (May); Good Times (Nov); United Way Tab (Oct); Fall Home Improvement Tab
Special Weekly Sections: Amusements, Comics, Finance, Stocks, Neighbors, TV (Daily); Best Food (Wed); Business, Real Estate, Weekend, Entertainment (Thur); Travel, Entertainment, Business, Finance, Comics, Real Estate, Stocks, Veterans, People, Arts (Sun)
Syndicated Publications: Relish (Monthly); USA WEEKEND Magazine (Sat); Electric City (Thur); American Profile (Weekly).
Delivery Methods: Carrier
Avg Free Circ: 2431
Sat. Circulation Paid: 26941
Sat. Circulation Free: 2431
Sun. Circulation Paid: 33316
Sun. Circulation Free: 865
Audit By: AAM
Audit Date: 31.03.2019
Personnel: Mathew E. Haggerty (Pub.); Robert J. Lynett (Pub.); William R. Lynett (Ed./Pub.); Carolyn Timlin (Credit Mgr.); Alan Buntz (Controller/Purchasing Agent); William P. Nish (Dir., HR); Amy Lutheran (Adv. Mgr.); Renee Puchalski (Adv. Mgr., Nat'l); Cathy Labori (Dir., Mktg./Promo.); Jim Phillips (Circ. Dir.); Larry Beaupre (Mng. Ed.); Larry Holeva (Mng. Ed.); John Murphy (Asst. Mng. Ed.); Ted Geltner (Automotive Ed.); Jessica Mathews (Bus./Finance Ed.); John Cole (Cartoonist); Patrick J. McKenna (Editorial Page Ed.); Terry Bonifanti (Features Ed.); Stephanie Toffey; Jason Jones (Adv. Mgr.); John McAndrew (Production Director); James E. Towner (Gen. Mgr.); Carol Demas (Nat'l. Adv. Mgr.)
Parent company (for newspapers): Times-Shamrock Communications

THE NEWS-ITEM

Street address 1: 707 N Rock St
Street address city: Shamokin
Street address state: PA
Zip/Postal code: 17872-4930
County: Northumberland
Country: USA
Mailing address: 707 N ROCK ST
Mailing city: SHAMOKIN
Mailing state: PA
Mailing zip: 17872-4956
General Phone: (570) 644-6397
Advertising Phone: (570)644-6397 ext 4
Editorial Phone: (570) 644-6397 ext. 1341
General/National Adv. E-mail: jessica_w@newsitem.com
Display Adv. E-mail: jessica_w@newsitem.com
Classified Adv. e-mail: classifieds@newsitem.com
Editorial e-mail: editorial@newsitem.com
Primary Website: www.newsitem.com
Year Established: 1891
News Services: AP.
Special Editions: Car Care (Apr); Back-to-School (Aug); Xmas Gift Guide (Dec); Progress/Economic Review (Feb); Bridal (Jan); Christmas Gift Guide (Nov); Christmas Lay-Away (Oct); Fall Football Preview (Sept).
Special Weekly Sections: Area Schools Page (Fri); Church Pages (Sat); Outdoors Sports Page (Thur); Wedding and Engagement Pages (Tues); Business World Page (Wed); food and drink page.
Syndicated Publications: American Profile (Weekly). Parade magazine. Spry
Delivery Methods: Mail`Newsstand`Carrier`Racks
Areas Served - City/County or Portion Thereof, or Zip codes: Northumberland, Columbia and Schuylkill counties
Own Printing Facility?: N
Commercial printers?: Y
Avg Free Circ: 687
Sat. Circulation Paid: 6798
Sat. Circulation Free: 374
Sun. Circulation Paid: 6959
Sun. Circulation Free: 389
Audit By: Sworn/Estimate/Non-Audited
Audit Date: 12.07.2019
Personnel: Amy Moyer (General manager); David Sickle (Dir., Circ.); Andrew Heintzelman (Exec. Ed.); Charlie Rotch (Sports Ed.); Glenn Knarr (Systems Mgr.); Glenn A. Knarr (Prodn. Foreman, Composing); David Barry (Rgl. Adv. Dir.)
Parent company (for newspapers): Sample Media

THE HERALD

Street address 1: 52 S Dock St
Street address city: Sharon
Street address state: PA
Zip/Postal code: 16146-1808
County: Mercer
Country: USA
Mailing address: PO BOX 51
Mailing city: SHARON
Mailing state: PA
Mailing zip: 16146-0051
General Phone: (724) 981-6100
Advertising Phone: (724)981-6100
Editorial Phone: (724)981-6100
General/National Adv. E-mail: ssorg@sharonherald.com
Display Adv. E-mail: vkoper@sharonherald.com
Classified Adv. e-mail: bveres@sharonherald.com
Editorial e-mail: newsroom@sharonherald.com
Primary Website: www.sharonherald.com
Year Established: 1864
News Services: AP, ONS.
Special Editions: Lawn & Garden (Apr); Football Magazine (Aug); Outlook (Feb); Summer Fun (Jun); Car Care (Mar); Golf Guide (May); Holiday Gift Guide (Nov); Women's World (Oct); National Fuel (Sept).
Special Weekly Sections: Best Food Day (Wed); Entertainment (Thur); Real Estate (Fri); Religion (Sat); Business, Health, Living Travel (Sun);
Syndicated Publications:
Areas Served - City/County or Portion Thereof, or Zip codes: 16146, 16148, 16150, 16125, 44403, 44425, 16121, 16143, 16159
Sat. Circulation Paid: 10262
Sun. Circulation Paid: 12591
Audit Date: 31.12.2018
Personnel: Kelly Cummings (Controller); Sharon Sorg (Pub.); Renee Carey (Ed.); Devon Stout (Dir of Audience Development); Michael Roknick (Bus. Ed.); Richard Work (Adv. Sales Dir.); John Zavinski (Online Ed.); Vanessa Koper (Advertising Director); Eric Poole (Editor); Nancy Ash (Living/Lifestyle Ed.); Sarah Adams (News Ed.); Jeff Turk (Religion Ed.); Lynn Saternow (Sports Ed.); Richard Young (Travel Ed.); Laurie Doyle (Adv. Mgr.)
Parent company (for newspapers): CNHI, LLC; CNHI, LLC

DAILY AMERICAN

Street address 1: 334 W Main St
Street address city: Somerset
Street address state: PA
Zip/Postal code: 15501-1508
County: Somerset
Country: USA
Mailing address: PO BOX 638
Mailing city: SOMERSET
Mailing state: PA
Mailing zip: 15501-0638
General Phone: (814) 444-5900
Advertising Phone: (814) 444-5922
Editorial Phone: (814) 444-5928
General/National Adv. E-mail: adcopy@dailyamerican.com
Display Adv. E-mail: adcopy@dailyamerican.com
Classified Adv. e-mail: patf@dailyamerican.com
Editorial e-mail: news@dailyamerican.com
Primary Website: www.dailyamerican.com
Mthly Avg Views: 700000
Mthly Avg Unique Visitors: 160000
Year Established: 1929
News Services: AP.
Special Editions: Outdoor ().
Special Weekly Sections: Best Food (Wed/Sat); Auto (Thur); Entertainment (Fri); Business, Finance, Real Estate, Religion (Sat)
Syndicated Publications: USA WEEKEND Magazine (Sat).
Delivery Methods: Mail`Newsstand`Carrier`Racks
Areas Served - City/County or Portion Thereof, or Zip codes: Somerset and Cambria Counties, PA.
Own Printing Facility?: N
Commercial printers?: Y
Sat. Circulation Paid: 11412
Audit By: AAM
Audit Date: 30.09.2014
Personnel: Andy Bruns (Pub.); Karen Thomas (Office Mgr.); Tom Koppenhofer (Adv. Mgr.); Pat Foley (Adv. Mgr., Classified); Brian Whipkey (Editorial Page Ed.); Madolin Edwards (Lifestyles Ed.); Ronald Pritts (Sports Ed.); Rebecca Flyte (Gen. Mgr.)
Parent company (for newspapers): Gannett; Schurz Communications Inc

THE DAILY PRESS

Street address 1: 245 Brusselles St/
Street address city: St.Marys
Street address state: PA
Zip/Postal code: 15857
County: Elk
Country: USA
Mailing address: 245 Brusselles St.
Mailing city: St.Marys
Mailing state: PA
Mailing zip: 15857
General Phone: 814-781-1596
General/National Adv. E-mail: sales@ridgwayrecord.com
Display Adv. E-mail: dpsales@zitomedia.net
Classified Adv. e-mail: classifieds@ridgwayrecord.com
Editorial e-mail: editor3@zitomedia.net
Primary Website: www.smdailypress.com
Year Established: 1910
News Services: AP.
Special Editions: Big Buck Edition Elk County Fair Elk Expo Elk County on Display Best of Contest
Special Weekly Sections: Best Food Days (Mon/Sat); Dining Out, Entertainment (Fri)
Syndicated Publications: American Profile (Weekly).
Sat. Circulation Paid: 1996
Audit By: Sworn/Estimate/Non-Audited
Audit Date: 30.09.2023
Personnel: Christie Gardner (Publisher); Joseph Bell (Ed.); Cindy Hulings (Circulation/Business Manager); Julie Barrett (Adv.Dir.)
Parent company (for newspapers): Horizon Publications Inc.

CENTRE DAILY TIMES

Street address 1: 3400 E. College Avenue
Street address city: State College
Street address state: PA
Zip/Postal code: 16801
County: Centre
Country: USA
Mailing address: 3400 E COLLEGE AVE
Mailing city: STATE COLLEGE
Mailing state: PA
Mailing zip: 16801-7528
General Phone: (814) 238-5000
Advertising Phone: (814) 231-4651
Editorial Phone: (814) 238-5000
General/National Adv. E-mail: adtransfer@centredaily.com
Display Adv. E-mail: dbrown@centredaily.com
Classified Adv. e-mail: dbrown2@centredaily.com
Editorial e-mail: cdtnewstips@centredaily.com
Primary Website: www.centredaily.com
Mthly Avg Views: 4464091
Mthly Avg Unique Visitors: 750000
Year Established: 1898
News Services: AP, MCT.
Special Editions: Active Life (Apr); This is Penn State (Aug); Gift Guide Two (Dec); The Wedding Album (Feb); Business Outlook (Jan); Art Festival Magazine (Jul); Newspapers in Education (Mar); Home Improvement (May); Real Estate Buyers Guide (Monthly); Gift Guide One (Nov
Special Weekly Sections: Health, Science (Mon); Local (Tue); Best Food (Wed); Outdoors, Teen, Auto (Thur); Entertainment, Penn State Campus (Fri); Religion (Sat); Travel, Books, Business, Careers, Homes, Real Estate (Sun)
Syndicated Publications: Parade (S).
Own Printing Facility?: Y
Commercial printers?: Y
Sat. Circulation Paid: 12594
Sun. Circulation Paid: 15849
Audit By: AAM
Audit Date: 30.06.2018
Personnel: Erik Brown (Controller); Candy Butterworth (Cir. Ops. Mgr.); Adam Smeltz (Exec. Ed.)
Parent company (for newspapers): The McClatchy Company; Chatham Asset Management

POCONO RECORD

Street address 1: 511 Lenox St
Street address city: Stroudsburg
Street address state: PA
Zip/Postal code: 18360-1516
County: Monroe
Country: USA
Mailing address: 511 LENOX ST
Mailing city: STROUDSBURG
Mailing state: PA
Mailing zip: 18360-1599
General Phone: (570) 421-3000
Advertising Phone: (570) 421-3000 (Display)
Editorial Phone: (570) 421-3000
General/National Adv. E-mail: advertising@poconorecord.com
Display Adv. E-mail: advertising@poconorecord.com
Classified Adv. e-mail: kmcfall@poconorecord.com
Editorial e-mail: newsroom@poconorecord.com
Primary Website: www.poconorecord.com
Mthly Avg Views: 2450000
Mthly Avg Unique Visitors: 28900
Year Established: 1894
News Services: AP.
Special Editions: Spring Home & Garden (Apr); Medical Directory (Aug); Gift Guide (Dec); Medical Directory (Feb); Pocono Summer (Jul); Pocono Raceway (Jun); Pocono Summer (May); Gift Guide (Nov);
Special Weekly Sections: Best Food Days (Sun/Wed); Entertainment (Fri); Real Estate, Religion (Sat); Auto, Arts (Sun)
Syndicated Publications: Pocono Property Showcase (Monthly); Pocono Summer (May, July, Aug) (Other); TV Week (S); American Profile (Weekly).
Delivery Methods: Newsstand`Carrier`Racks
Areas Served - City/County or Portion Thereof, or Zip codes: Monroe and Pike Counties
Own Printing Facility?: N
Commercial printers?: N
Avg Free Circ: 1087
Sat. Circulation Paid: 6715
Sat. Circulation Free: 877
Sun. Circulation Paid: 10070
Sun. Circulation Free: 888
Audit By: AAM
Audit Date: 31.12.2017
Personnel: Joe Vanderhoof (President); Mike Kuhns (Interim Executive Ed.); Lou Tufano (Circulation Operations Mgr.)
Parent company (for newspapers): Gannett; CherryRoad Media

THE DAILY ITEM

Street address 1: 200 Market St
Street address city: Sunbury
Street address state: PA
Zip/Postal code: 17801-3402
County: Northumberland
Country: USA
Mailing address: PO BOX 607
Mailing city: SUNBURY
Mailing state: PA
Mailing zip: 17801-0607
General Phone: (570) 286-5671
Advertising Phone: (570) 286-5671
Editorial Phone: (570) 286-5671
General/National Adv. E-mail: pbennett@dailyitem.com

Display Adv. E-mail: pbennett@dailyitem.com
Classified Adv. e-mail: pbennett@dailyitem.com
Editorial e-mail: news@dailyitem.com
Primary Website: www.dailyitem.com
Mthly Avg Views: 750000
Mthly Avg Unique Visitors: 275589
Year Established: 1937
News Services: AP, ONS, MCT, TMS.
Special Editions: Real Estate Guide (Monthly); Today's Woman (Quarterly).
Special Weekly Sections: Lifetyle, Business, Home, Real Estate (Sun); Schools (Mon); Health (Tue); Auto, Entertainment (Thur); Religion, TV (Sat)
Syndicated Publications: Relish (Monthly); Parade (S); American Profile (Weekly).
Delivery Methods: Mail`Newsstand`Carrier`Racks
Own Printing Facility?: Y
Commercial printers?: Y
Avg Free Circ: 6039
Sat. Circulation Paid: 12381
Sat. Circulation Free: 1092
Sun. Circulation Paid: 14283
Sun. Circulation Free: 1039
Audit By: AAM
Audit Date: 31.03.2019
Personnel: Frank Leto (Pub.); Patty Bennett (Sr. Adv. Dir.); Norman Sinclair (Audience Dir); Dennis Lyons (Ed.); David Hillard (Managing Ed./Online News); John Zaktansky (Managing /Features); Bill Bowman (Ed. City Editor); Todd Stanford; Eric Pehowic (News Ed./ Weekend Ed.); Emma Ginader (Reporter); Eric Scicchitano (Reporter); Francis Scarcella (Reporter); Joe Sylvester (Reporter); Justin Strawser (Reporter); Karen Blackledge (Reporter); Marcia Moore (Reporter); Rick Dandes (Reporter); Carla Treon (Classified Advertising); Brett Neidig (Prodn. Mgr., Distr.); Thomas Hosey (Prodn. Mgr., Pressroom); Lori Seebold (Production Mgr.); Scott Dudinksie (Sports Reporter); Todd Hummel (Sports Reporter)
Parent company (for newspapers): CNHI, LLC

DELAWARE COUNTY DAILY TIMES

Street address 1: 639 S. Chester Road
Street address city: Swarthmore
Street address state: PA
Zip/Postal code: 19081
County: Delaware
Country: USA
Mailing address: 639 S CHESTER RD
Mailing city: SWARTHMORE
Mailing state: PA
Mailing zip: 19081-2315
General Phone: (610) 622-8800
Advertising Phone: (610) 622-8860
Editorial Phone: (610) 622-8810
General/National Adv. E-mail: paadvertising@digitalfirstmedia.com
Display Adv. E-mail: paadvertising@digitalfirstmedia.com
Classified Adv. e-mail: classifieds@delcotimes.com
Editorial e-mail: editor@delcotimes.com
Primary Website: www.delcotimes.com
Mthly Avg Unique Visitors: 670774
Year Established: 1876
News Services: AP, Robert Hitchings & Co., U.S. Suburban Press Inc..
Special Editions: Easter Dine Out (Apr); Back-to-School (Aug); Great Gifting (Dec); Swimsuit Guide (Feb); Super Bowl Auto (Jan); 55 & Up (Jul); Father's Day Gift Pages (Jun); Prom Guide (Mar); Mother's Day Gift Guide (May); Where to Dine Thanksgiving (Nov); Energy & Home I
Special Weekly Sections: Business (Daily); Auto (Mon); Restaurant Reviews (Wed); Auto, Entertainment, Church (Fri); Travel, Food, Real Estate (Sun)
Syndicated Publications: USA WEEKEND Magazine (S).
Avg Free Circ: 3291
Sat. Circulation Paid: 5615
Sat. Circulation Free: 1890
Sun. Circulation Paid: 16012
Sun. Circulation Free: 2525
Audit By: AAM
Audit Date: 31.03.2019
Personnel: Phil Heron (Ed.); Rob Parent (Sports Ed.); Edward Condra (Sr. Pub.); Joseph Forst (Cir. Dir.); Richard L. Crowe (Adv. Mgr.)
Parent company (for newspapers): MediaNews Group

THE TITUSVILLE HERALD

Street address 1: 209 W Spring St
Street address 2: Ste B
Street address city: Titusville
Street address state: PA
Zip/Postal code: 16354-1687
County: Crawford
Country: USA
Mailing address: 209 W SPRING ST STE B
Mailing city: TITUSVILLE
Mailing state: PA
Mailing zip: 16354-1687
General Phone: (814) 827-3634
General/National Adv. E-mail: advertising@titusvilleherald.com
Display Adv. E-mail: advertising@titusvilleherald.com
Classified Adv. e-mail: advertising@titusvilleherald.com
Editorial e-mail: news@titusvilleherald.com
Primary Website: www.titusvilleherald.com
Year Established: 1865
News Services: AP.
Special Editions: The Golden Years (Apr); Football (Aug); Recipe Book (Dec); Growth & Progress (Feb); Coupons (Jan); Oil Heritage Week (Jul); Graduation (Jun); Spring Preview & Bridal (Mar); Discover (May); Thanksgiving (Nov); Auto Promo (Oct); Spartansburg Fair (Sept).
Special Weekly Sections: Business, Finance, Entertainment (Daily); Best Food (Wed); Religion (Fri); Home, Family (Sat)
Delivery Methods: Mail`Newsstand`Carrier`Racks
Areas Served - City/County or Portion Thereof, or Zip codes: 16354 16404 16341
Own Printing Facility?: Y
Sat. Circulation Paid: 4000
Audit By: Sworn/Estimate/Non-Audited
Audit Date: 12.07.2019
Personnel: Karol Hartley (Office Mgr.); Michael Sample (Pub./Adv. Dir.); Dave Ohmer (Graphic Coord.); Stella Ruggiero (Mng. Ed.); Tom Boyle (Reporter); Mary Hill (Reporter); Paula Vandervort (Prodn. Mgr., Mailroom)
Parent company (for newspapers): The Titusville Herald

THE DAILY REVIEW

Street address 1: 116 Main St
Street address city: Towanda
Street address state: PA
Zip/Postal code: 18848-1832
County: Bradford
Country: USA
Mailing address: 116 MAIN ST
Mailing city: TOWANDA
Mailing state: PA
Mailing zip: 18848-1832
General Phone: (570) 265-2151
Advertising Phone: (570) 265-2151
Editorial Phone: (570) 265-2151
General/National Adv. E-mail: reviewads@thedailyreview.com
Display Adv. E-mail: reviewads@thedailyreview.com
Classified Adv. e-mail: srought@thedailyreview.com
Editorial e-mail: reviewnews@thedailyreview.com
Primary Website: www.thedailyreview.com
Year Established: 1879
News Services: AP, Washington Post
Special Editions: Spring Home Improvement II (Apr); Medical Directory (Aug); Winter Sports Profile (Dec); Women In Business (Feb); Bridal (Jan); Troy Fair (Jul); Graduation (Jun); Spring Tour Guide (Mar); Human Services (May); Our Schools (Monthly); Senior Style II (Nov);
Special Weekly Sections: Best Food Days (Wed/Sun); Nascar (Fri); Senior's Column (S).
Syndicated Publications: Relish (Monthly); (Sat); American Profile (Weekly), Parade (Weekly).
Delivery Methods: Mail`Newsstand`Carrier`Racks
Areas Served - City/County or Portion Thereof, or Zip codes: 13812, 13827, 14892, 16901, 16910, 16914, 16925, 12626, 16232, 16933, 16936, 16945, 16947, 17101, 17701, 17724, 17735, 17765, 18614, 18616, 18623, 18626, 18628, 18629, 18630, 18632, 18657, 18801, 18810, 18814, 18815, 18817, 18818, 18828, 18829, 18830, 18831, 18832, 18833, 18837, 18839, 18840, 18845, 18846, 18848, 18850, 18851, 18853, 18854
Own Printing Facility?: Y
Commercial printers?: Y
Sat. Circulation Paid: 7356
Sun. Circulation Paid: 8774
Audit By: CAC
Audit Date: 30.09.2017
Personnel: Debbie Bump (Circulation Supervisor); Brian Schlosser (Regional Director of Production); Kelly Andrus (Managing Editor); Sue Rought (Classified Advertising Manager); Matt Hicks (Editor-in-Chief); Dave Barry (General Manager); Kelly Luvison (Owner/ Publisher); Bill Kurtz (Circulation Director)
Parent company (for newspapers): Sample Media Group

THE DAILY HERALD

Street address 1: 1067 Pennsylvania Ave
Street address city: Tyrone
Street address state: PA
Zip/Postal code: 16686-1513
County: Blair
Country: USA
Mailing address: PO BOX 246
Mailing city: TYRONE
Mailing state: PA
Mailing zip: 16686-0246
General Phone: (814) 684-4000
Advertising Phone: (814)684-4000
Editorial Phone: (814)684-4000
General/National Adv. E-mail: ads@thedailyherald.net
Display Adv. E-mail: ads@thedailyherald.net
Classified Adv. e-mail: classifieds@thedailyherald.net
Editorial e-mail: astine@thedailyherald.net
Primary Website: www.thedailyherald.net
Year Established: 1867
News Services: Landon Media Group.
Special Editions: Home & Garden (Aug); Christmas Opening (Dec); Wedding (Feb); Business Direct (May); Home & Gardening (Sept).
Special Weekly Sections: TV Week (Fri).
Delivery Methods: Mail`Newsstand`Carrier`Racks
Own Printing Facility?: Y
Sat. Circulation Paid: 1737
Audit By: Sworn/Estimate/Non-Audited
Audit Date: 12.07.2019
Personnel: George R. Sample (Pres./Pub.); John Cook (VP & Gen Mgr.); Julie White (Ed.); Baretta Taylor (Adv. Dir.); Linda Daniels (Adv. Sales Mgr.); Joyce Alley (Circ. Mgr.); Mark Palmer; Neal Pattison
Parent company (for newspapers): Sample News Group LLC

HERALD-STANDARD

Street address 1: 8 East Church Street
Street address 2: # 18
Street address city: Uniontown
Street address state: PA
Zip/Postal code: 15401
County: Fayette
Country: USA
Mailing address: PO BOX 848
Mailing city: UNIONTOWN
Mailing state: PA
Mailing zip: 15401-0848
General Phone: (724) 439-7500
Advertising Phone: (724) 439-7520
Editorial Phone: (724) 439-7555
General/National Adv. E-mail: swallach@heraldstandard.com
Display Adv. E-mail: swallach@heraldstandard.com
Classified Adv. e-mail: swallach@heraldstandard.com
Editorial e-mail: jgarofalo@heraldstandard.com
Primary Website: www.heraldstandard.com
News Services: AP, SHNS.
Special Weekly Sections: Health (Mon); Food (Wed);, Entertainment (Thurs); Real Estate (Fri); Outdoors (Fri.), Education (Sun);
Delivery Methods: Newsstand`Carrier`Racks
Areas Served - City/County or Portion Thereof, or Zip codes: Uniontown/Fayette/15401
Own Printing Facility?: N
Commercial printers?: N
Avg Free Circ: 3169
Sun. Circulation Paid: 13802
Sun. Circulation Free: 4568
Audit By: AAM
Audit Date: 31.03.2019
Personnel: Bob Pinarski (Pub.)
Parent company (for newspapers): Ogden Newspapers Inc.

TIMES OBSERVER

Street address 1: 205 Pennsylvania Avenue West
Street address city: Warren
Street address state: PA
Zip/Postal code: 16365
County: Warren
Country: USA
Mailing address: PO BOX 188
Mailing city: WARREN
Mailing state: PA
Mailing zip: 16365-0188
General Phone: (814) 723-8200
Advertising Phone: (814) 723-1400
Editorial Phone: (814) 723-8200
General/National Adv. E-mail: advertising@timeobserver.com
Display Adv. E-mail: advertising@timesobserver.com
Classified Adv. e-mail: classified@timesobserver.com
Editorial e-mail: editorial@timesobserver.com
Primary Website: www.timesobserver.com
Mthly Avg Views: 742993
Mthly Avg Unique Visitors: 63009
News Services: AP.
Special Editions: Coupon Books (Quarterly).
Special Weekly Sections: TV Times (Fri); Best Food Day (Sat); Spotlite (Thur) Living Page (Mon); Food, Spotlight Entertainment Guide, Movies, Theatre, Music, Outdoors, Books, Automotive (Thurs); TV Times (Fri); Food, Automotive (Sat).
Syndicated Publications: USA WEEKEND Magazine (Sat).
Delivery Methods: Mail`Newsstand`Carrier`Racks
Own Printing Facility?: N
Avg Free Circ: 32
Sat. Circulation Paid: 6843
Sat. Circulation Free: 25
Audit By: AAM
Audit Date: 30.06.2018
Personnel: Jack Albaugh (Adv. Mgr., Classified); Bob Patchen (Publisher - Circulation Director); Eric Paddock (Managing Editor); Diana Paddock (Food Ed.); Tom Schultz (City Editor); Jon Sitler (Sports Ed.)
Parent company (for newspapers): Ogden Newspapers Inc.

OBSERVER-REPORTER

Street address 1: 122 S Main St
Street address city: Washington
Street address state: PA
Zip/Postal code: 15301-4904
County: Washington
Country: USA
Mailing address: 122 S MAIN ST
Mailing city: WASHINGTON
Mailing state: PA
Mailing zip: 15301-4904
General Phone: (724) 222-2200
Advertising Phone: (724) 222-2200
Editorial Phone: (724) 222-2200
General/National Adv. E-mail: sales@observer-reporter.com
Display Adv. E-mail: mtalerico@observer-reporter.com
Classified Adv. e-mail: mtmiller@observer-reporter.com
Editorial e-mail: newsroom@observer-reporter.com
Primary Website: www.observer-reporter.com
Year Established: 1808
News Services: AP, NYT.
Special Editions: Health & Fitness (Apr); College & Pro Football (Aug); Monthly Planner (Dec); Spring Home Improvement (Mar); Christmas Gift Guide (Nov); Fall Home Improvements (Sept).
Special Weekly Sections: Weekend Entertainment, Religion (Fri); Home Section (Sun); Business, Financial (Mon-Sat)
Syndicated Publications: USA WEEKEND Magazine (S); American Profile, Spry, (Weekly); Total Health, Southpointe Today, Energy Report (Monthly); Living in Washington County, South Hills Living, Greene County Living (bimonthly).
Delivery Methods: Mail`Newsstand`Carrier`Racks
Areas Served - City/County or Portion Thereof, or Zip codes: 15301
Own Printing Facility?: Y
Commercial printers?: N
Avg Free Circ: 605
Sat. Circulation Paid: 19289
Sat. Circulation Free: 605
Sun. Circulation Paid: 22587
Sun. Circulation Free: 345
Audit By: AAM
Audit Date: 31.03.2019
Personnel: Thomas P. Northrop (Pres./Pub.); David F. Lyle (CFO); Lucy S. Northrop (Director of News); Matt Miller (Adv. Dir.); Matt Talerico (Retail Sales Mgr.); Bridget Vilencia (Circ. Dir.); Park Burroughs (Mng. Ed.); Mike Bradwell (Bus. Ed.); Elizabeth Rogers (City/Metro Ed.); Denise Bachman (Entertainment/Amusements Ed.); Brant Newman (Asst. News Ed.); Chris Dugan (Sports Ed.); Dan Fennell (Systems Mgr.); Gerald

Hickman (Prodn. Mgr., Mailroom); James Helicke (Prodn. Mgr./Foreman, Pressroom); Rob Anders (National Accounts); Bess Dunlevy; Lucy Corwin; Nancy Milinovich
Parent company (for newspapers): Ogden Newspapers Inc.

THE RECORD HERALD

Street address 1: 30 Walnut St
Street address city: Waynesboro
Street address state: PA
Zip/Postal code: 17268-1644
County: Franklin
Country: USA
Mailing address: PO BOX 271
Mailing city: WAYNESBORO
Mailing state: PA
Mailing zip: 17268-0271
General Phone: (717) 762-2151
Advertising Phone: (717) 762-2151
Editorial Phone: (717) 762-2151
General/National Adv. E-mail: denise@therecordherald.com
Display Adv. E-mail: advertising@therecordherald.com
Classified Adv. e-mail: classified@therecordherald.com
Editorial e-mail: news@therecordherald.com
Primary Website: www.therecordherald.com
Year Established: 1824
News Services: AP.
Special Editions: Home Improvement No. 1 (Apr); Back-to-School (Aug); Gift Guides (3 times) (Dec); Progress No. 1 (Feb); Bridal No. 1 (Jan); Spotlight Newcomers (Jul); Golden Years (Mar); Bridal No. 2 (May); Gift Guides (3 times) (Nov); Financial (Oct); Home Improvement No
Special Weekly Sections: Best Food Day (Wed); TV (Sat).
Syndicated Publications: Relish (Monthly); American Profile (Weekly).
Sat. Circulation Paid: 8005
Audit By: Sworn/Estimate/Non-Audited
Audit Date: 12.07.2019
Personnel: Ken Browall (Pub.); Ben Destefan (News Ed.); Andrea Rose (Asst. Ed.); Dawn Friedman; Jay Wetzel (Prodn. Mgr.)
Parent company (for newspapers): Gannett; CherryRoad Media

DAILY LOCAL NEWS

Street address 1: 250 N Bradford Ave
Street address city: West Chester
Street address state: PA
Zip/Postal code: 19382-1912
County: Chester
Country: USA
General Phone: (610) 696-1775
Advertising Phone: (610) 430-1134
Editorial Phone: (610) 430-1130
General/National Adv. E-mail: paadvertising@digitalfirstmedia.com
Display Adv. E-mail: jbatog@dailylocal.com
Classified Adv. e-mail: mdenatale@21st-centurymedia.com
Editorial e-mail: tmurray@dailylocal.com
Primary Website: www.dailylocal.com
Mthly Avg Views: 4000000
Mthly Avg Unique Visitors: 503592
News Services: AP.
Special Editions: Fitness/Summer Fun (Apr); Back-to-School (Aug); Last Minute Gift Guide (Dec); Cutest Baby (Feb); Education Guide (Jan); Chester County Guide (Jul); Father's Day (Jun); Design-an-Ad (Mar); MADD Poster Contest (May); Employment Monthly (Monthly); Mature Lif
Special Weekly Sections: Best Food Days (Wed); Religion, Entertainment, Real Estate (Fri); Travel, Tabloid, TV (Sun); Business (Weekly); Women's Health (Monthly); Senior Citizen (Bi-Monthly)
Syndicated Publications: USA WEEKEND Magazine (Sat).
Delivery Methods: Mail`Newsstand`Carrier`Racks
Own Printing Facility?: Y
Avg Free Circ: 580
Sat. Circulation Paid: 5848
Sat. Circulation Free: 505
Sun. Circulation Paid: 12172
Sun. Circulation Free: 3496
Audit By: AAM
Audit Date: 31.03.2019
Personnel: Edward Condra (Pub.); Joseph Forst (Cir. Dir.); Jen Batog (Adv. Mgr.); Mary DeNatale (Class. Supv.); Andy Hachadorian (Ed.)
Parent company (for newspapers): MediaNews Group

THE CITIZENS' VOICE

Street address 1: 75 N Washington St
Street address city: Wilkes Barre
Street address state: PA
Zip/Postal code: 18701-3109
County: Luzerne
Country: USA
Mailing address: 75 N WASHINGTON ST
Mailing city: WILKES BARRE
Mailing state: PA
Mailing zip: 18701-3109
General Phone: (570) 821-2000
Advertising Phone: (570) 821-2030
Editorial Phone: (570) 821-2056
General/National Adv. E-mail: maltavilla@citizensvoice.com
Display Adv. E-mail: szremba@citizensvoice.com
Classified Adv. e-mail: classified@timesshamrock.com
Editorial e-mail: citydesk@citizensvoice.com
Primary Website: www.citizensvoice.com
Mthly Avg Views: 4000000
Mthly Avg Unique Visitors: 487410
News Services: AP, Papert (Landon).
Special Editions: Home & Improvement (Apr); Pigskin Preview (Aug); Christmas Shopping Guide (Dec); Bridal (Feb); Super Bowl Preview (Jan); Estate Planning (Jul); Graduation (Jun); Today's Woman (Mar); Who's Who in Wyoming Valley (May); Thanksgiving Holiday Shopping Guide (
Special Weekly Sections: Weekend (Fri); Regional (S); Best Food Day (Sat).
Syndicated Publications: Relish (Monthly); USA WEEKEND Magazine (S); American Profile (Weekly).
Delivery Methods: Mail`Newsstand`Carrier`Racks
Own Printing Facility?: Y
Commercial printers?: Y
Avg Free Circ: 2132
Sat. Circulation Paid: 16885
Sat. Circulation Free: 2132
Sun. Circulation Paid: 19575
Sun. Circulation Free: 890
Audit By: AAM
Audit Date: 31.03.2019
Personnel: W. Scott Lynett (Pub.); Danial Haggerty (Pub.); Mark Altavilla (Adv. Dir.); Judi Shaver (Coord.); Joe Neaoon (Asst. Circ. Dir.); Larry Holeva (Executive Editor); Jim Gittens (Editorial Page Ed.); Shanon Rushton (Web Ed.); Leonarda Bilbow (News Ed.); Neil Corbett (Sports Ed.); Michael McGlynn (Wire Ed.); Mark Moran (Photo Ed.); Dennis Briggs (Mgmt. Info Servs. Mgr.); John McGurk (Prodn. Mgr., Mailroom)
Parent company (for newspapers): Times-Shamrock Communications

TIMES LEADER

Street address 1: 15 N Main St
Street address city: Wilkes Barre
Street address state: PA
Zip/Postal code: 18701-2604
County: Luzerne
Country: USA
Mailing address: 15 N MAIN ST
Mailing city: WILKES BARRE
Mailing state: PA
Mailing zip: 18701-2690
General Phone: (570) 704-3953
Advertising Phone: (570) 829-7130
Editorial Phone: (570) 829-7242
General/National Adv. E-mail: lbyrnes@civitasmedia.com
Primary Website: www.timesleader.com
Mthly Avg Unique Visitors: 538857
News Services: AP, MCT, DF, DJ, NYT.
Special Editions: Profile (Apr); Football (Aug); Gift Guide (Dec); Bride & Groom (Feb); How to Guide (Jul); Best of Times (Jun); Spring Home Improvement (Mar); Best & Brightest (May); Focus on Women (Nov); Fall Home Improvement (Oct).
Special Weekly Sections: The Guide (Fri); Consumer (Mon); Travel (S); Health (Tues); Food (Wed). Entertainment, Business/Financial, Arts, Living, Automotive (Daily); Style, Local, Sports, Real Estate, Help Wanted (Daily & Sun); Best Food Day (Sun & Wed); Family/Kids (Thurs); Entertainment, Weekend guide (Fri); Religion, Travel (Sat); Travel, People, Grocer PP Day (Sun)
Syndicated Publications: Parade (S).
Avg Free Circ: 1420
Sat. Circulation Paid: 12825
Sat. Circulation Free: 620
Sun. Circulation Paid: 15896
Sun. Circulation Free: 605
Audit By: AAM
Audit Date: 31.03.2019
Personnel: Richard L. Connor (Ed./Pub.); Allison Uhrin (Vice Pres./CFO); Kim Dudick (Adv./Mktg. Vice Pres.); Dick Dehavan (Circ. Vice Pres.); George Spohr (Executive Editor); Rich Connor (Ed.); Joe Healey (Night Ed.); Dan Burnett (News Editor); Shelly Mccann (Prodn. Mgr., Pre Press)
Parent company (for newspapers): Civitas Media, LLC; Avant Publications

WILLIAMSPORT SUN-GAZETTE/ LOCK HAVEN EXPRESS

Street address 1: 252 West Fourth Street
Street address city: Williamsport
Street address state: PA
Zip/Postal code: 17701-0728
County: Lycoming
Country: USA
Mailing address: 252 West Fourth Street
Mailing city: Williamsport
Mailing state: PA
Mailing zip: 17701-0728
General Phone: (570) 326-1551
Advertising Phone: (570) 326-1551
Editorial Phone: (570) 326-1551
Editorial e-mail: news@sungazette.com
Primary Website: www.sungazette.com
Year Established: 1801
News Services: AP.
Special Editions: Insurance (Apr); Back-to-School (Aug); Year in Review (Dec); Winter Bridal (Feb); Winter Furniture (Jan); Summer Furniture (Jul); Graduation (Jun); Women in Business (Mar); Outdoor Lifestyle (May); Christmas Opener (Nov); Fall Car Care (Oct); Fall Home Im
Special Weekly Sections: TV Magazine (S); Religion (Sat); Entertainment (Thur); Best Food Day (Wed). Education (Mon); Health (Tues); Best Food Day (Wed); Religion (Sat); Business, Travel, Technology, Outdoors, Lifestyles (Sun)
Syndicated Publications: TV Week (S).
Delivery Methods: Mail`Newsstand`Carrier`Racks
Own Printing Facility?: Y
Commercial printers?: Y
Avg Free Circ: 837
Sat. Circulation Paid: 13318
Sat. Circulation Free: 837
Sun. Circulation Paid: 15799
Sun. Circulation Free: 141
Audit By: AAM
Audit Date: 31.03.2019
Personnel: L. Lee Janssen (Editor-In-Chief); Mike Maneval (City Ed.); Dave Troisi (Opinion Page Ed.); Tim Wertz (Design Ed.); Seth Nolan (Associate Ed.); Jay Hahn (Associate Ed.); Jon Gerardi (Sports Ed.); Courtney Hayden (Life & Education Ed.); Nick Seitzer (Arts & Entertainment Ed., West Branch Life Ed.); Robert O. Rolley (Pub.)
Parent company (for newspapers): Ogden Newspapers Inc.

THE YORK DISPATCH

Street address 1: 205 N George St
Street address city: York
Street address state: PA
Zip/Postal code: 17401-1107
County: York
Country: USA
Mailing address: 1891 LOUCKS RD
Mailing city: YORK
Mailing state: PA
Mailing zip: 17408-9708
General Phone: (717) 854-1575
Advertising Phone: (717) 767-6397
General/National Adv. E-mail: news@yorkdispatch.com
Editorial e-mail: news@yorkdispatch.com
Primary Website: www.yorkdispatch.com
Mthly Avg Views: 8137364
Mthly Avg Unique Visitors: 1603024
News Services: NYT, LAT-WP, AP, MNS, NEA, SHNS.
Special Weekly Sections: Best Food (Wed); Entertainment, Flipside (Thur); Entertainment (Fri); Business, Finance, Style, Local, Sports, Auto, Real Estate, Help Wanted (Daily);
Audit By: AAM
Audit Date: 30.09.2017
Personnel: Phil Buckner (Owner); Teresa Hoover (Bus. Mgr.); Mark Franklin (Mng. Ed.); Gayle Eubank (City Ed.); Patrick Delany (Ed.); Mel Barber (Entertainment/ Weekend Ed.); John Sincoe (News/Design Ed.); Steve Heiser (Sports Ed.); Melissa Barber (Style Ed.); Charles Burkhardt (Data Processing Mgr.); Scott Miller (Mgmt. Info Servs./Online Mgr.); Fred Uffelman (Pres./Pub.); Bryan Kelley (VP, Sales/Marketing)
Parent company (for newspapers): Gannett - USA Today Network; Buckner News Alliance

YORK DAILY RECORD/YORK SUNDAY NEWS

Street address 1: 1891 Loucks Road
Street address city: York
Street address state: PA
Zip/Postal code: 17408
County: York
Country: USA
Mailing address: 1891 LOUCKS RD
Mailing city: YORK
Mailing state: PA
Mailing zip: 17408-9708
General Phone: (717) 767-6397
Advertising Phone: (717) 767-3554
Editorial Phone: (717) 771-2000
Display Adv. E-mail: mbodani@LocaliQ.com
Classified Adv. e-mail: advertising@mediaonemarketplace.com
Editorial e-mail: news@ydr.com
Primary Website: www.ydr.com
Mthly Avg Views: 7200000
Mthly Avg Unique Visitors: 900000
Year Established: 1796
News Services: AP
Special Weekly Sections: Flipside (Thurs)
Delivery Methods: Mail`Newsstand`Carrier`Racks
Areas Served - City/County or Portion Thereof, or Zip codes: York and Adams Counties
Own Printing Facility?: N
Commercial printers?: N
Avg Free Circ: 215
Sat. Circulation Paid: 18207
Sat. Circulation Free: 215
Sun. Circulation Paid: 33519
Sun. Circulation Free: 350
Audit By: AAM
Audit Date: 30.09.2018
Personnel: Donna Mandl (Exec. Asst. to Pub.); Susan Martin (Asst. Mng. Ed., Metro); Randy Parker (News Dir.); Scott Fisher (Edit. Ed/Engage. Ed); Matt Eyer (Consumer Experience Director); Shelly Stallsmith (Digital Planning Editor)
Parent company (for newspapers): Gannett - USA Today Network; Gannett

RHODE ISLAND

THE NEWPORT DAILY NEWS

Street address 1: 101 Malbone Rd
Street address city: Newport
Street address state: RI
Zip/Postal code: 02840-1340
County: Newport
Country: USA
Mailing address: PO BOX 420
Mailing city: NEWPORT
Mailing state: RI
Mailing zip: 02840-0936
General Phone: (401) 849-3300
Advertising Phone: (401) 849-3300
General/National Adv. E-mail: Abrams@NewportRI.com
Display Adv. E-mail: Abrams@NewportRI.com
Classified Adv. e-mail: ndnadvertising@newportri.com
Editorial e-mail: editor@newportri.com
Primary Website: www.newportdailynews.com
Mthly Avg Views: 284068
Mthly Avg Unique Visitors: 42146
Year Established: 1846
News Services: AP, McClatchy.
Special Editions: Health and Fitness, Newport County Chamber of Commerce Quarterly, Winter Festival, 50 Plus, Spring Home and Garden, Spring Dining Guide,

Summer Activity Guide, Newport Flower Show, Tennis Hall of Fame Championships, Back to School, Fall Sports Preview, F all Home and Garden, Fall Dining Guide, Holiday Gift Guide, Last Minute Gift Guide
Delivery Methods: Carrier
Areas Served - City/County or Portion Thereof, or Zip codes: Aquidneck Island - Newport, Middletown, Portsmouth, Tiverton
Own Printing Facility?: Y
Commercial printers?: Y
Avg Free Circ: 2517
Sat. Circulation Paid: 12738
Sat. Circulation Free: 2517
Audit By: CAC
Audit Date: 31.03.2015
Personnel: William F. Lucey (Publisher); M. Catherine Callahan (City Ed.); Harvey B. Peters (News Ed.); Scott P. Barrett (Sports Ed.); Kevin F. Schoen (Operations Mgr.); Joanthan Zins (Editor); Lynn Abrams (Advertising Director)
Parent company (for newspapers): CherryRoad Media

THE TIMES

Street address 1: 23 Exchange St
Street address city: Pawtucket
Street address state: RI
Zip/Postal code: 02860-2026
County: Providence
Country: USA
Mailing address: PO BOX 307
Mailing city: PAWTUCKET
Mailing state: RI
Mailing zip: 02862-0307
General Phone: (401) 722-4000
Advertising Phone: (401) 722-4000
Editorial Phone: (401) 722-4000
General/National Adv. E-mail: mlbosiak@woonsocketcall.com
Display Adv. E-mail: advertising@pawtuckettimes.com
Classified Adv. e-mail: classified@woonsocketcall.com
Editorial e-mail: editor@pawtuckettimes.com
Primary Website: www.pawtuckettimes.com
Mthly Avg Views: 122000
Mthly Avg Unique Visitors: 57000
Year Established: 1885
News Services: AP.
Special Editions: Spring Car Care (Apr); Bus Schedule (Aug); Holiday Gift Guide I & II (Dec); Business Profile (Feb); Bridal Showcase (Jan); Who's the Best-Ballot (Jul); Business Review (Jun); Profile-Massachusetts (Mar); Momentum (May); Monthly Kid's Tab (Monthly); Holida
Special Weekly Sections: Homes, TV, Religion (Sat); Health (Tues); Food (Wed).
Syndicated Publications: USA WEEKEND Magazine (Sat).
Delivery Methods: Carrier`Racks
Areas Served - City/County or Portion Thereof, or Zip codes: East Providence etc.
Own Printing Facility?: N
Commercial printers?: N
Avg Free Circ: 73
Sat. Circulation Paid: 3322
Sat. Circulation Free: 48
Audit By: AAM
Audit Date: 31.03.2018
Personnel: Kathleen Kneeham (Controller); Diane Ames (Adv. Mgr., Classified); Bianca Pavoncello (Exec. Ed.); David Pepin (Managing Ed./News Ed.); Eric Benevides (Sports Ed.); Donna Kirwan (Asst. Ed.); Marylynn Bosiak (Adv. Dir./Gen. Mgr./Pub.)
Parent company (for newspapers): The Times Inc.

THE PROVIDENCE JOURNAL

Street address 1: 75 Fountain St
Street address city: Providence
Street address state: RI
Zip/Postal code: 02902-0050
County: Providence
Country: USA
General Phone: (401) 277-7000
Editorial Phone: (401) 277-7303
General/National Adv. E-mail: letters@providencejournal.com
Editorial e-mail: pjnews@providencejournal.com
Primary Website: www.providencejournal.com
Mthly Avg Unique Visitors: 1155752
Year Established: 1829
News Services: AP, LAT-WP, MCT, SHNS, TMS, CQ, DJ.
Special Editions: Family Fun (February); Summer Guide (May); Summer Food (June); Fall Guide (September); Student/Athlete Honor Roll (July); CVS Charity Classic (June);
Special Weekly Sections: Thrive (health and fitness), Monday; Connect (music, TV, technology gadgets), Tuesday; Food, Wednesday; Go! (things to do), Thursday; Movies, Friday; Decor (home and gardening), Saturday; Real Estate, Saturday; Homes, Sunday; Consumer, (personal finance), Sunday; The Rhode Islander, Sunday; All About You (fashion, self-care, relationships); Cars, Wednesday, Saturday and Sunday.
Syndicated Publications: Parade (S).
Delivery Methods: Mail`Newsstand`Racks
Areas Served - City/County or Portion Thereof, or Zip codes: The entire state of Rhode Island and southeastern Massachusetts
Own Printing Facility?: Y
Commercial printers?: Y
Sat. Circulation Paid: 68587
Sun. Circulation Paid: 75666
Audit By: AAM
Audit Date: 30.06.2017
Personnel: Janet Hasson (Pres. & Pub.); Alan Rosenberg (Exec. Ed.); Edward C. Achorn (Vice Pres. & Editorial Pages Ed.); Michael Ivancic (Vice Pres. of Op.); Jason Weiner (Adv. Dir.); Michael McDermott (Mng. Ed.)
Parent company (for newspapers): Gannett; CherryRoad Media

KENT COUNTY DAILY TIMES

Street address 1: 1353 Main Street
Street address city: West Warwick
Street address state: RI
Zip/Postal code: 2893
County: Kent
Country: USA
Mailing address: PO BOX 277
Mailing city: WEST WARWICK
Mailing state: RI
Mailing zip: 02893-0277
General Phone: (401) 821-7400
Advertising Phone: (401) 789-9744
Editorial Phone: (401) 789-9744 ext. 209
General/National Adv. E-mail: jboucher@ricentral.com
Display Adv. E-mail: jboucher@ricentral.com
Classified Adv. e-mail: jboucher@ricentral.com
Editorial e-mail: kceditor@ricentral.com
Primary Website: www.ricentral.com
Year Established: 1892
Special Weekly Sections: Wedding, Anniversary (Mon); Senior (Tue); Best Food (Wed); Arts, Entertainment, Fashion, Health (Thur); Home (Fri); Religion (Sat)
Delivery Methods: Newsstand`Carrier`Racks
Areas Served - City/County or Portion Thereof, or Zip codes: 02893, 02896, 02886,, 02817, 02818, 02827, 02831
Own Printing Facility?: Y
Commercial printers?: N
Avg Free Circ: 60
Sat. Circulation Paid: 862
Sat. Circulation Free: 55
Audit By: AAM
Audit Date: 31.03.2019
Personnel: Jody Boucher (Reg. Pub.); Phil Rowell (Cir. Dir.); Seth Bromley (Exec. Ed.); Gabrielle Falletta (Mng. Ed.); Esther Diggins (Advertising Coordinator)
Parent company (for newspapers): Horizon Publications Inc.; Southern Rhode Island Newspapers

THE CALL

Street address 1: 75 Main St
Street address city: Woonsocket
Street address state: RI
Zip/Postal code: 02895-4312
County: Providence
Country: USA
Mailing address: 75 MAIN ST
Mailing city: WOONSOCKET
Mailing state: RI
Mailing zip: 02895-4363
General Phone: (401) 762-3000
Advertising Phone: (401) 767-8505
Editorial Phone: (401) 767-8550
General/National Adv. E-mail: dbenjamin@woonsocketcall.com
Display Adv. E-mail: ads@WoonsocketCall.com
Classified Adv. e-mail: classified@woonsocketcall.com
Editorial e-mail: editor@woonsocketcall.com
Primary Website: www.woonsocketcall.com
Mthly Avg Views: 253000
Mthly Avg Unique Visitors: 113000
Year Established: 1892
News Services: AP.
Special Editions: Chamber of Commerce Annual Report (Jan).
Special Weekly Sections: Pets(Mon); Health(Tue); Food(Wed); Entertainment (Thur); Auto (Fri); Real Estate (Sat); TV, Then and Now (Sun);
Syndicated Publications: USA WEEKEND Magazine (S).
Delivery Methods: Newsstand`Carrier
Areas Served - City/County or Portion Thereof, or Zip codes: Providence County
Own Printing Facility?: N
Commercial printers?: Y
Avg Free Circ: 39
Sat. Circulation Paid: 2748
Sat. Circulation Free: 39
Sun. Circulation Paid: 3821
Sun. Circulation Free: 39
Audit By: AAM
Audit Date: 31.03.2019
Personnel: Kathie Needham (Controller); Jody Boucher (Pub.); Paul Palange (Gen. Mgr.); Seth Bromley (Ed.); Jorge Londono (Dist. Mgr.); Denise Benjamin (Nat. / Preprint Mgr.); Diane Ames (Adv. Mgr.); Christina Bevilacqua (Class. Adv.)
Parent company (for newspapers): Horizon Publications Inc.; RISN Operations Inc.

SOUTH CAROLINA

EVENING POST INDUSTRIES' AIKEN COMMUNICATIONS

Street address 1: 326 Rutland Dr NW
Street address city: Aiken
Street address state: SC
Zip/Postal code: 29801-4010
County: Aiken
Country: USA
Mailing state: SC
Mailing zip: 29801
General Phone: 803648-2311
Advertising Phone: (803) 644-2369
Editorial Phone: (803) 648-2311
General/National Adv. E-mail: dbell@aikenstandard.com
Display Adv. E-mail: dbell@aikenstandard.com
Classified Adv. e-mail: ddaniell@aikenstandard.com
Editorial e-mail: mystory@aikenstandard.com
Primary Website: www.aikenstandard.com
Mthly Avg Views: 1179650
Mthly Avg Unique Visitors: 162731
Year Established: 1867
News Services: AP, MCT.
Special Editions: Masters Golf Tournament (Apr); Football (Aug); Brides Book (Jan); Horse Industry (Mar); Christmas Gift Guide (Nov); Medical Directory (June); Discover Aiken (Sept).
Special Weekly Sections: Religious Page (Fri); Home Hunter (S); Auto (Sat); Entertainment (Thur); Health (Wed).
Delivery Methods: Mail`Newsstand`Carrier`Racks
Areas Served - City/County or Portion Thereof, or Zip codes: Aiken County
Own Printing Facility?: Y
Commercial printers?: Y
Avg Free Circ: 1037
Sat. Circulation Paid: 10112
Sat. Circulation Free: 1037
Sun. Circulation Paid: 11122
Sun. Circulation Free: 689
Audit By: Sworn/Estimate/Non-Audited
Audit Date: 12.07.2019
Personnel: Rhonda Overby (Pub./Adv. Dir.); Diane Daniell (Sales and Special Projects Man.); Mike Harris (Man ed.)
Parent company (for newspapers): Evening Post Publishing Newspaper Group

ANDERSON INDEPENDENT-MAIL

Street address 1: 1000 Williamston Road
Street address city: Anderson
Street address state: SC
Zip/Postal code: 29621
County: Anderson
Country: USA
General Phone: (864) 224-4321
Advertising Phone: (864) 260-1204
Editorial Phone: (864) 260-1244
General/National Adv. E-mail: beckt@independentmail.com
Display Adv. E-mail: beckt@independentmail.com
Classified Adv. e-mail: classifiedads@independentmail.com
Editorial e-mail: newsroom@independentmail.com
Primary Website: www.independentmail.com
Mthly Avg Unique Visitors: 476989
Year Established: 1899
News Services: AP, The Newspaper Network, NYT, SHNS, NEA.
Special Editions: Home Decorating (Apr); College Football Preview (Aug); HGTV Winter (Dec); NASCAR Preview (Feb); Homebuilders Tab (Jan); YMCA (Jul); South Carolina Factbook (Jun); HGTV Spring (Mar); High School Graduation Tab (May); Food Network Holiday Guide (Nov); YMCA
Special Weekly Sections: Automotive (Fri); Business (S); Automotive (Sat); Be (Thur); Food (Wed).
Syndicated Publications: Parade (S).
Delivery Methods: Carrier
Areas Served - City/County or Portion Thereof, or Zip codes: Anderson, pickens, upstate south carolina
Avg Free Circ: 1849
Sat. Circulation Paid: 12876
Sat. Circulation Free: 1849
Sun. Circulation Paid: 19707
Sun. Circulation Free: 1444
Audit By: AAM
Audit Date: 31.12.2017
Personnel: Susan Kelly-Gilbert (Pub. & CRO); Steve Mullins (Exec. Ed.); Alison Newton (Content Editor); Willie Mattress (Ed., HomeTown People); Mike Alexieff (City Ed.); Colleen Cozak (Night Ed.); Bill Bussey (IT Mgr.); Beck Tyrrell (Sales Support & Pagination); Kathy Nelson (Dir. Digital Media); Pete Barend (Dir. Circulation Sales); Chase Heatherly (Mktg. Mgr.)
Parent company (for newspapers): Gannett; Journal Media Group

THE BEAUFORT GAZETTE

Street address 1: 10 Buck Island Rd
Street address city: Bluffton
Street address state: SC
Zip/Postal code: 29910-5937
County: Beaufort
Country: USA
Mailing address: PO BOX 5727
Mailing city: HILTON HEAD
Mailing state: SC
Mailing zip: 29938-5727
General Phone: (843) 524-3183
Advertising Phone: (843) 706-8202
Editorial Phone: (843) 524-3183
General/National Adv. E-mail: bosborn@islandpack.com
Display Adv. E-mail: bosborn@islandpack.com
Classified Adv. e-mail: bosborn@islandpack.com
Editorial e-mail: sborton@islandpack.com
Primary Website: www.beaufortgazette.com
News Services: AP.
Special Editions: Garden & Home Improvement (Apr); Football (Aug); Coupon Pages (Dec); Income Tax (Feb); Bridal (Jan); Water Festival (Jul); Hurricane (Jun); Spring Tour of Homes (Mar); Gullah Festival (May); Cookbook/Gift Guide (Nov); Fall Tour of Homes (Oct); Coupon Page
Special Weekly Sections: Health, Sports (Mon); Neighbors (Tue);; Sports, Neighbors (Wed); Military, The Guide (Fri); Auto, Religion (Sat); Travel, Book, Art, Home, Real Estate, Brides, Sports, TV (Sun); Business, Stocks, Finance (Daily)
Syndicated Publications: TV Week, Wall St. Journal, Parade (S).
Avg Free Circ: 818
Sat. Circulation Paid: 4642
Sat. Circulation Free: 818
Sun. Circulation Paid: 5026
Sun. Circulation Free: 808
Audit By: AAM
Audit Date: 30.09.2017
Personnel: Sara Johnson Borton (Pres./Pub.); Sandy Gilles (Adv. Dir.); Jeff Kidd (Ed.); Tom Robinette (Features Ed.); Bob Sofaly (Photographer); Lance Hanlin (Sports Ed.); William King (Prodn. Dir.); Lorrie Anderson (Nat'l Adv. Dir); Brian Tolley (Exec. Ed.)

Parent company (for newspapers): The McClatchy Company

THE ISLAND PACKET

Street address 1: 10 Buck Island Rd
Street address city: Bluffton
Street address state: SC
Zip/Postal code: 29910-5937
County: Beaufort
Country: USA
Mailing address: PO BOX 5727
Mailing city: HILTON HEAD
Mailing state: SC
Mailing zip: 29938-5727
General Phone: (843) 706-8100
Advertising Phone: (843) 706-8100
Editorial Phone: (843) 706-8111
General/National Adv. E-mail: ads@islandpacket.com
Display Adv. E-mail: ads@islandpacket.com
Classified Adv. e-mail: arobbins@islandpacket.com
Editorial e-mail: newsroom@islandpacket.com
Primary Website: www.islandpacket.com
Mthly Avg Views: 1795182
Mthly Avg Unique Visitors: 260356
Year Established: 1970
News Services: AP, MCT, NYT, Pony Wire, SHNS.
Special Editions: Health & Fitness, Hilton Head Happenings (May); Hurricane, Readers' Choice (June); Newcomers Packet (July); Back to School (Aug); Woman (Sept); Holiday Gift Guide (Nov); Health Care Directory (Dec)
Special Weekly Sections: Schools, Education, sports, Lowcountry Life (Mon); Health, Fitness, Sports, business (Tue); Food (Wed); Military (Thur); The Guide, Sports, Business, Life (Fri); Auto, Faith, Values (Sat); Book, Social, Homes, Sports (Sun)
Syndicated Publications: Parade (S).
Delivery Methods: Mail`Newsstand`Carrier`Racks
Own Printing Facility?: Y
Commercial printers?: Y
Avg Free Circ: 2112
Sat. Circulation Paid: 14026
Sat. Circulation Free: 2112
Sun. Circulation Paid: 15637
Sun. Circulation Free: 2119
Audit By: AAM
Audit Date: 31.03.2018
Personnel: Rodney Mahone (Pub.); Brian Tolley (Exec. Ed.); Michelle Long (Advertising); Kimberly Gary (H. R.); Liz Farrell (Columnist/Senior Ed.); David Lauderdale (Columnist/Senior Ed.); Drew Martin (Multimedia Ed.); Mandy Matney (Real-Time News Ed.)
Parent company (for newspapers): The McClatchy Company; Chatham Asset Management

THE POST AND COURIER

Street address 1: 148 Williman
Street address city: Charleston
Street address state: SC
Zip/Postal code: 29403-4809
County: Charleston
Country: USA
Mailing state: SC
General Phone: (843) 577-7111
Advertising Phone: (843) 937-5468
Editorial Phone: (843) 937-5527
General/National Adv. E-mail: bbaulch@postandcourier.com
Display Adv. E-mail: akellner@postandcourier.com
Classified Adv. e-mail: asutton@postandcourier.com
Editorial e-mail: aphilips@postandcourier.com
Primary Website: www.postandcourier.com
Mthly Avg Views: 10000000
Mthly Avg Unique Visitors: 2300000
Year Established: 1803
News Services: AP, NYT.
Special Editions: Southeastern Wildlife; Komen Race for the Cure; Cooper River Bridge Run; Volvo Cup Open; Spoleto; My Charleston Visitor Guide, My Charleston Holiday; Boat Parade; Holocaust; Progress SC; Pigskin Preview
Special Weekly Sections: Business (Mon); Automotive (Fri); Real Estate (Sat); Health (Mon); Food (Weds); Entertainment (Thurs); Home & Real Estate, Arts & Culture (Sun); People, Real Estate (Sat); Faith and Values (Sat)
Syndicated Publications: Parade
Delivery Methods: Mail`Newsstand`Carrier`Racks
Areas Served - City/County or Portion Thereof, or Zip codes: Tri-County Area (Berkeley, Dorchester and Charleston Counties) plus out-lying areas such as Colleton County, Clarendon, Beaufort and Orangeburg, Columbia, Greenville and Myrtle Beach
Own Printing Facility?: Y
Commercial printers?: Y
Sat. Circulation Paid: 48332
Sun. Circulation Paid: 55319
Audit By: CVC
Audit Date: 31.07.2021
Personnel: Pamela (PJ) Browning (Publisher); Kurt Knapek (Dir., Audience Development); Robie Scott (Communications and Community Relations Mgr.); Becky Baulch (Assist. to Pub); Charles Rowe (Editorial Page Ed.); Rick Nelson (Managing Ed.); John McDermott (Bus. and Tech. Ed.); Lisa Rule (Transportation/Distrb. Mgr.); Chris Zoeller (Strategic Mktg. Dir.); Mitch Pugh (Executive Editor); Brad Boggs (Senior Director, Interactive Sales); Alex Kellner (Advertising Director); Ron Cartledge (President of Shared Services); Jamie Drolet (Retail Advert.); Betsy Miller (News Prod. Ed.); Elsa McDowell (Assoc. Ed.); Andy Morgan (Sales and Mktg. Mgr); John Posluszny (VP of Audience Development for Evening Post Industries); Lynn McLamb (VP of Evening Post Publishing Newspaper Group); Theresa Taylor (Feature's Ed.); Scott Embry (Adv. Dir.)
Parent company (for newspapers): Evening Post Publishing Newspaper Group

THE STATE

Street address 1: 1401 Shop Rd
Street address city: Columbia
Street address state: SC
Zip/Postal code: 29201-4843
County: Richland
Country: USA
Mailing address: 1401 SHOP RD
Mailing city: COLUMBIA
Mailing state: SC
Mailing zip: 29201-4814
General Phone: (800) 888-5353
Advertising Phone: (803) 771-8450
Editorial Phone: (803) 771-8451
General/National Adv. E-mail: bheller@thestate.com
Display Adv. E-mail: llibet@thestate.com
Classified Adv. e-mail: stateclassified@thestate.com
Editorial e-mail: sbrook@thestate.com
Primary Website: www.thestate.com
Mthly Avg Views: 12000000
Mthly Avg Unique Visitors: 1700000
Year Established: 1891
News Services: AP, LAT-WP, NYT, MCT.
Special Editions: Summer Fun (Apr); Welcome Back USC (Aug); A New Year, A New You (Dec); Body, Health & More (Feb); 20 Under 40 (Jan); CBJ Book of Lists (Jul); Readers Choice (Jun); Rooms & Blooms (Mar); Living Here (May); Faith Guide (Nov); Midlands Health (Oct); CareerBu
Special Weekly Sections: The Extra [TMC] (Wed); Weekend Section (Fri); TV Weekly (Sun)
Syndicated Publications: Weekend (Fri); Lake Murray Columbia Magazine (Monthly); Go Gamecocks (Other); Sunday Comics (S); Wedding Book (Semi-yearly).
Delivery Methods: Mail`Carrier
Areas Served - City/County or Portion Thereof, or Zip codes: The State circulates in 26 of 43 counties in South Carolina. Richland, Lexington and southern Kershaw counties make up the core market. The city of Columbia is in Richland County and contains the South Carolina State Capitol, The University of South Carolina and the U.S. Army's Fort Jackson. The city of Lexington is located in Lexington County.
Own Printing Facility?: Y
Commercial printers?: Y
Sat. Circulation Paid: 42467
Sun. Circulation Paid: 52674
Audit By: AAM
Audit Date: 31.12.2018
Personnel: Brian Tolley (Exec. Ed); Steve Brook (Mng. Ed.); Gary Ward (Managing Ed. for Online); Dawn Kujawa (Asst. Metro Ed.); Cindi Scoppe (Assoc. Ed.); Warren Bolton (Assoc. Ed.); Eileen Waddell (Asst. Mng. Ed.); Derek Lawson (Info Systems Site Mgr.); Diane Frea (Vice Pres., HR); Richard Curtis (Single Copy Mgr.); Sara Johnson Borton (Pres./Pub.)
Parent company (for newspapers): The McClatchy Company; Chatham Asset Management

MORNING NEWS

Street address 1: 310 S. Dargan Street
Street address city: Florence
Street address state: SC
Zip/Postal code: 29501
County: Florence
Country: USA
Mailing address: PO BOX 100528
Mailing city: FLORENCE
Mailing state: SC
Mailing zip: 29502-0528
General Phone: (843) 317-6397
Advertising Phone: (843) 317-7257
General/National Adv. E-mail: pgray@florencenews.com
Display Adv. E-mail: pgray@florencenews.com
Classified Adv. e-mail: clloyd@florencenews.com
Editorial e-mail: cnews@florencenews.com
Primary Website: www.scnow.com
Mthly Avg Unique Visitors: 900000
News Services: AP, SHNS.
Special Editions: Car Care Directory (Apr); Back-To-School (Aug); Christmas Guide (Dec); Furniture Selection (Feb); Super Bowl Preview (Jan); Grilling Made Easy (Jul); Summer Daze (Jun); Speed-Darlington Race (Mar); Mother's Day Gift Guide (May); Chamberlink (Monthly); Bas
Special Weekly Sections: Best Food Days (Wed/Sun);
Syndicated Publications: USA WEEKEND Magazine (S).
Avg Free Circ: 1174
Sat. Circulation Paid: 10027
Sat. Circulation Free: 1174
Sun. Circulation Paid: 12501
Sun. Circulation Free: 921
Audit By: AAM
Audit Date: 31.03.2019
Personnel: Bailey Dabney (Regional Pub.); William Calcutt (Regional Circ. Dir.); Don Kausler (Regional Ed.); John Rains (News Ed.); Jane Comfort (Regional Ad Dir.)
Parent company (for newspapers): BH Media Group; Lee Enterprises, Incorporated

THE GREENVILLE NEWS

Street address 1: 305 S Main St
Street address city: Greenville
Street address state: SC
Zip/Postal code: 29601-2605
County: Greenville
Country: USA
Mailing address: PO BOX 1688
Mailing city: GREENVILLE
Mailing state: SC
Mailing zip: 29602-1688
General Phone: (864) 298-4100
Advertising Phone: (864) 298-4216
Editorial Phone: (864) 298-4321
General/National Adv. E-mail: krogers@greenvillenews.com
Display Adv. E-mail: krogers@greenvillenews.com
Editorial e-mail: localnews@greenvillenews.com
Primary Website: www.greenvilleonline.com
Year Established: 1874
News Services: AP, LAT-WP, MCT, SHNS, TMS, GNS.
Special Editions: Guide to Greenville (Apr); High School Football (Aug); Late Christmas Gift Guide (Dec); Southern Home & Garden (Feb); Spring Bride (Jan); Best of the Upstate (Jul); Early Christmas Gift Guide (Nov); Progress (Oct).
Special Weekly Sections: TV, Community, Sports, Business, Lifestyle (Daily); Technology, Health, Lifestyle (Tue); City, Lifestyle, Food (Wed); Kids, NASCAR, Fashion, Lifestyle (Thur); Weekend, Entertainment (Fri); Auto, Religion (Sat); TV, Home, Business, Careers, Comics, Lifestyles, Art, Travel (Sun)
Syndicated Publications: USA WEEKEND Magazine (S).
Sat. Circulation Paid: 38572
Sun. Circulation Paid: 53426
Audit By: AAM
Audit Date: 30.09.2017
Personnel: Beth Padgett (Editorial Page Ed.); Wanda Owings (Food Ed.); Bill Fox (Mng. Ed.); David Dykes (Reporter); Susan Schwartzkopf (VP Market Devl and New Media); Donna Walker (City people writer); Susan Schwartzkopf-Deanne (VP, Marketing); Orestes Baez (VP, Sales, General Mgr.); Dave Hennigan (Content Strategist); Katrice Hardy (Exec. Ed.)
Parent company (for newspapers): Gannett

THE INDEX-JOURNAL

Street address 1: 610 Phoenix St
Street address city: Greenwood
Street address state: SC
Zip/Postal code: 29646-3253
County: Greenwood
Country: USA
Mailing address: PO BOX 1018
Mailing city: GREENWOOD
Mailing state: SC
Mailing zip: 29648-1018
General Phone: (864) 223-1411
Advertising Phone: (864) 943-2509
Editorial Phone: (864) 223-1811
General/National Adv. E-mail: bduncan@indexjournal.com
Display Adv. E-mail: bduncan@indexjournal.com
Classified Adv. e-mail: bduncan@indexjournal.com
Editorial e-mail: rwhiting@indexjournal.com
Primary Website: www.indexjournal.com
Year Established: 1919
News Services: AP, NEA.
Special Editions: Parents Magazine (Spring & Fall) School Children ages 1-5 (Monthly)
Special Weekly Sections: Best Food Day (Wed);
Syndicated Publications: Parade (S).
Delivery Methods: Carrier`Racks
Areas Served - City/County or Portion Thereof, or Zip codes: Counties of: Greenwood, Abbeville, McCormick,
Own Printing Facility?: Y
Commercial printers?: Y
Avg Free Circ: 52
Sat. Circulation Paid: 9814
Sat. Circulation Free: 52
Sun. Circulation Paid: 11364
Sun. Circulation Free: 55
Audit By: AAM
Audit Date: 30.09.2017
Personnel: Judith M. Burns (CEO/Pres./Pub.); Richard Whiting (Exec. News Ed.); Bob Simmonds (Web Page Ed.); Kevin Coleman (Prodn. Foreman, Mailroom); Albert Ashley (Circ. Mgr.); Nichole Varnum (Business Mgr.); Ed Gunderson (Advertising Director)
Parent company (for newspapers): Index Journal Co.

THE SUN NEWS

Street address 1: 1012 38th Avenue N - 3rd Floor
Street address city: Myrtle Beach
Street address state: SC
Zip/Postal code: 29577
County: Horry
Country: USA
Mailing address: 914 Frontage Rd E
Mailing city: Myrtle Beach
Mailing state: SC
Mailing zip: 29577-6700
General Phone: (843) 626-8555
Advertising Phone: (843) 626-0240
Editorial Phone: (843) 626-0319
General/National Adv. E-mail: display@thesunnews.com
Display Adv. E-mail: display@thesunnews.com
Classified Adv. e-mail: classifieds@thesunnews.com
Editorial e-mail: spedersen@thesunnews.com
Primary Website: www.myrtlebeachonline.com
Mthly Avg Views: 11100000
Mthly Avg Unique Visitors: 578953
Year Established: 1936
News Services: AP, NYT, MCT.
Special Editions: Home Improvement (Apr); Community Resource Guide (Aug); NASCAR (Feb); Volunteer of the Year (Jan); Health-Themed 2 (Jun); Myrtle Beach Hospitality Job Fair (Mar); Graduation (May); Design An Ad (Nov); Health-Themed 3 (Oct); Finance (Sept).
Special Weekly Sections: Best Food, Health, Dining Out (Wed); Neighbors (Thur); Entertainment (Fri); Homes, Gardens (Sat); Travel, Real Estate, People, Arts, Books, TV (Sun); Money, Business (Tue-Sun);
Syndicated Publications: Parade (S).
Delivery Methods: Mail`Newsstand`Carrier`Racks
Areas Served - City/County or Portion Thereof, or Zip codes: Horry County
Sat. Circulation Paid: 24426
Sun. Circulation Paid: 29533
Audit By: AAM
Audit Date: 30.09.2018
Personnel: Rich Canazaro (Gen. Mgr.); Fred Benson (VP, Adv.); Carolyn Murray (Ed.); Lynette Dudley (Op. Mgr.); Jake Gervin (Audience Dev. Dir.); Audrey Hudson (Ed.)
Parent company (for newspapers): The McClatchy Company; Chatham Asset Management

THE TIMES AND DEMOCRAT

Street address 1: 1010 Broughton St

Street address city: Orangeburg
Street address state: SC
Zip/Postal code: 29115-5962
County: Orangeburg
Country: USA
Mailing address: PO BOX 1766
Mailing city: ORANGEBURG
Mailing state: SC
Mailing zip: 29116-1766
General Phone: (803) 533-5500
Advertising Phone: (803) 534-3352
Editorial Phone: (803) 534-1060
General/National Adv. E-mail: kfraser@timesanddemocrat.com
Display Adv. E-mail: kfraser@timesanddemocrat.com
Editorial e-mail: lharter@timesanddemocrat.com
Primary Website: www.theTandD.com
Mthly Avg Views: 1700000
Mthly Avg Unique Visitors: 220000
Year Established: 1881
News Services: AP.
Special Editions: Home Improvement (Apr); Football (Aug); Greetings (Dec); Progress (Feb); Bridal (Jan); Car Care (Jun); Spring Fashion (Mar); Health & Fitness (May); Gift Guide (Nov); Car Care (Oct).
Special Weekly Sections: Sports, Local, Classifieds (Daily); Farm, Garden, Events (Mon); Business, NIE, Marketplace, Health (Tue); Best Food Day, Business, Markets (Wed); Business, Arts, Leisure, Community, Markets (Thur); Church, Markets, Religion (Fri); Classifieds, Real Estate, Sports, Outdoors, TV, Comics, Weddings, Home Decor, Special Sections, Local, Kids (Sun)
Syndicated Publications: Relish (Monthly); USA WEEKEND Magazine (S); American Profile (Weekly).
Delivery Methods: Mail`Newsstand`Carrier`Racks
Own Printing Facility?: Y
Commercial printers?: N
Avg Free Circ: 1701
Sat. Circulation Paid: 7911
Sat. Circulation Free: 1701
Sun. Circulation Paid: 8773
Sun. Circulation Free: 493
Audit By: AAM
Audit Date: 31.03.2016
Personnel: Cathy C. Hughes (Pub./Adv. Dir.); Barbara Beach (Controller); Kayla Wiser (Adv. Dir.); Carla Hall (Mktg./Promo.); Jeanne Crader (City Ed.); Lee Harter (Editorial Page Ed.); Wendy Crader (Features Ed.); Larry Hardy (Photographer); Carol Barker (Regl. Ed.); Brian Linder (Sports Ed.); Georgianne Walton (Asst. Pub.); Jerry Harvill (Mgmt. Info Servs. Mgr.); Jim Spears (Prodn. Mgr.); Barbara West-Ravenell (Prodn. Mgr., Distr.); Russell Cain (Prodn. Foreman, Pressroom); Missy Hutto (Nat'l Adv. Mgr.)
Parent company (for newspapers): Dispatch-Argus; Lee Enterprises, Incorporated

THE HERALD

Street address 1: 132 W Main St
Street address city: Rock Hill
Street address state: SC
Zip/Postal code: 29730-4430
County: York
Country: USA
Mailing address: 132 W Main St
Mailing city: Rock Hill
Mailing state: SC
Mailing zip: 29730-4430
General Phone: (803) 329-4000
Advertising Phone: (803) 329-4322
Editorial Phone: (803) 329-4073
General/National Adv. E-mail: webmaster@heraldonline.com
Display Adv. E-mail: mpettus@heraldonline.com
Classified Adv. e-mail: ssancickle@heraldonline.com
Editorial e-mail: posmundson@heraldonline.com
Primary Website: www.heraldonline.com
Mthly Avg Views: 3000000
Mthly Avg Unique Visitors: 500000
Year Established: 1872
News Services: AP, LAT-WP, McClatchy, DF, SHNS, NYT.
Special Editions: Come See Me (Apr); Back-to-School (Aug); Last Minute Gift Guide (Dec); York County Magazine (Feb); Health Horizons (Jan); Health Horizons (Jun); Newspapers in Education Student Stories (Mar); Emergency Medical Services (May); Wrap-up Christmas Early (Nov)
Special Weekly Sections: Automotive (Fri); TV Herald (S); Home & Real Estate (Sat); Star Watch (Wed).
Syndicated Publications: Parade (Fri).
Delivery Methods: Mail`Newsstand`Carrier`Racks
Areas Served - City/County or Portion Thereof, or Zip codes: York, Chester, Lancaster, South Carolina
Own Printing Facility?: N
Commercial printers?: Y
Sat. Circulation Paid: 10262
Sun. Circulation Paid: 12591
Audit By: AAM
Audit Date: 31.12.2018
Personnel: Cliff Harrington (Ed.); Andrew Dys (Rep.); Amanda Harris (Rep.); Hannah Smoot (Rep.); Tracy Kimball (Photographer/Videographer); Bret McCormick (Sports Ed.); Catherine Muccigrosso (Asst. Ed.); Greg DePaoli (Home Delivery Mgr.); Allan Johnson (Single Copy Mgr.); Meredith Straub (Consumer Sales Mgr.)
Parent company (for newspapers): The McClatchy Company

DAILY JOURNAL/MESSENGER

Street address 1: 210 W North 1st St
Street address city: Seneca
Street address state: SC
Zip/Postal code: 29678-3250
County: Oconee
Country: USA
Mailing address: PO BOX 547
Mailing city: SENECA
Mailing state: SC
Mailing zip: 29679-0547
General Phone: (864) 882-2375
Primary Website: www.upstatetoday.com
News Services: AP, DF, DJ.
Syndicated Publications: American Profile (Weekly).
Delivery Methods: Newsstand`Carrier`Racks
Own Printing Facility?: Y
Commercial printers?: Y
Sat. Circulation Paid: 9676
Audit By: Sworn/Estimate/Non-Audited
Audit Date: 12.07.2019
Personnel: Jerry Edwards (Owner); Linda Garren (Office Mgr.); Scott Nickels (Circ. Dir.); Vicki Tymon (Graphics Coord.); Steven Bradley (Sports Ed.); Michael Watts (Pressroom Mgr.); Hal Welch (Pub.); Pierce Sandra (Adv. Dir.)
Parent company (for newspapers): Edwards Publications

HERALD-JOURNAL

Street address 1: 189 W. Main Street
Street address city: Spartanburg
Street address state: SC
Zip/Postal code: 29306
County: Spartanburg
Country: USA
Mailing address: PO BOX 1657
Mailing city: SPARTANBURG
Mailing state: SC
Mailing zip: 29304-1657
General Phone: 864-562-7470
Advertising Phone: (864) 582-4511
Editorial Phone: (864) 582-4511 ext. 7210
General/National Adv. E-mail: caralyn.bess@shj.com
Display Adv. E-mail: caralyn.bess@shj.com
Classified Adv. e-mail: nancy.hogsed@shj.com
Editorial e-mail: chris.horeth@shj.com
Primary Website: www.goupstate.com
Mthly Avg Views: 4300000
Mthly Avg Unique Visitors: 499512
Year Established: 1842
News Services: AP, NYT, MCT.
Special Editions: Football (3) Prep, College, Band (Aug); Stroller Cookbook (Oct) Gift Guide (Dec); Auto Racing (Feb); Prime Time (Jun); Lawn & Garden/ Home Improvement (Mar); Showcase of Homes (May); Automotive Showcase (Nov); Arts Council (Sept).
Special Weekly Sections: Best Food (Wed); Financial (Tue-Sun); Entertainment (Thur); Real Estate, Lifestyle (Fri); Religion (Sat); Travel (Sun)
Delivery Methods: Mail`Newsstand`Carrier`Racks
Areas Served - City/County or Portion Thereof, or Zip codes: Spartanburg, Cherokee & Union Counties
Own Printing Facility?: N
Commercial printers?: N
Avg Free Circ: 861
Sat. Circulation Paid: 13458
Sat. Circulation Free: 861
Sun. Circulation Paid: 16481
Sun. Circulation Free: 361
Audit By: AAM
Audit Date: 9/31/2018
Personnel: Michael Smith (Exec. Ed.); Jason Spencer (Digital Assigning Ed.); Dan Sullivan (News Ed.); Robert Walton (Multimedia Copy Ed.); Linda Conley (Features Ed.); Robert W. Dalton (Sports Ed.); Ashley Dill (Community News Ed.)
Parent company (for newspapers): Gannett; CherryRoad Media

THE SUMTER ITEM

Street address 1: 20 N Magnolia St
Street address city: Sumter
Street address state: SC
Zip/Postal code: 29150-4940
County: Sumter
Country: USA
Mailing address: PO BOX 1677
Mailing city: SUMTER
Mailing state: SC
Mailing zip: 29151-1677
General Phone: (803) 774-1200
Advertising Phone: (803) 774-1256
Editorial Phone: (803) 774-1226
General/National Adv. E-mail: angela@theitem.com
Display Adv. E-mail: Jack@theitem.com
Classified Adv. e-mail: Kathy@theitem.com
Editorial e-mail: news@theitem.com
Primary Website: www.theitem.com
Mthly Avg Views: 1000000
Mthly Avg Unique Visitors: 100000
Year Established: 1894
News Services: AP, SC Press
Special Editions: Gift Guide (Dec); Bride & Groom (Jan); Weddings (Jun); Home & Gardens (Mar); Readers Choice (June);Summertime (May); Parade of Shops (Nov); Extraordinary Women (Oct);Life is Good (Jan); Chamber Guide (July); Meet the Professionals (September); Football Guide (Aug)
Special Weekly Sections: Local Events & Activities (Fri); The Mini Page (Mon); History/Community (S); Religion (Thursday); Kids Scoop (Thur); Career Connection (Tues); Recipes & Ideas (Wed). Clarendon Sun (Thurs)
Syndicated Publications: Parade (S); Relish, Spree, Athlon Sports
Delivery Methods: Mail`Newsstand`Carrier`Racks
Areas Served - City/County or Portion Thereof, or Zip codes: Sumter County, Clarendon County, Lee County
Own Printing Facility?: N
Commercial printers?: Y
Avg Free Circ: 5
Sat. Circulation Paid: 10113
Sat. Circulation Free: 5
Sun. Circulation Paid: 11307
Sun. Circulation Free: 5
Audit By: VAC
Audit Date: 30.06.2016
Personnel: Graham Osteen (Co-Pres.); Jack Osteen (Ed. & Pub./VP); Larry Miller (CEO); Kyle Osteen (Co-Pres.); Hubert D. Osteen (Chairman); Ivy Moore (Feat. Ed.); Rhonda Barrick (Univ. Desk Mgr.); Rick Carpenter (Managing Ed.); Dennis Brunson (Sports Ed.); Jeff West
Parent company (for newspapers): Creative Circle Media Solutions; Osteen Publishing Company; The Iris Digital Agency

UNION DAILY TIMES

Street address 1: 201 N Herndon St
Street address city: Union
Street address state: SC
Zip/Postal code: 29379-2210
County: Union
Country: USA
Mailing address: PO BOX 749
Mailing city: UNION
Mailing state: SC
Mailing zip: 29379-0749
General Phone: (864) 427-1234
Advertising Phone: (864) 427-1234
Editorial Phone: (864) 427-1234
General/National Adv. E-mail: dmcmurray@civitasmedia.com
Display Adv. E-mail: dmcmurray@civitasmedia.com
Editorial e-mail: pedwards@civitasmedia.com
Primary Website: www.uniondailytimes.com
Mthly Avg Views: 119450
Mthly Avg Unique Visitors: 23408
Year Established: 1850
News Services: NEA, AP.
Special Editions: Gardening (Apr); Football (Aug); Christmas (Dec); FYI-For Your Information (Jan); Graduation (May); Uniquely Union Festival (Oct); NASCAR Prime Time (Seniors) (Quarterly).
Syndicated Publications: American Profile (Sat).
Delivery Methods: Mail
Areas Served - City/County or Portion Thereof, or Zip codes: Union County
Own Printing Facility?: Y
Commercial printers?: N
Sat. Circulation Paid: 6409
Audit By: Sworn/Estimate/Non-Audited
Audit Date: 12.07.2019
Personnel: Charles Warner (Mng. Ed.)
Parent company (for newspapers): Champion Media

SOUTH DAKOTA

ABERDEEN AMERICAN NEWS

Street address 1: 124 S 2nd St
Street address city: Aberdeen
Street address state: SD
Zip/Postal code: 57401-4010
County: Brown
Country: USA
Mailing address: PO BOX 4430
Mailing city: ABERDEEN
Mailing state: SD
Mailing zip: 57402-4430
General Phone: (605) 225-5555
Editorial Phone: (605) 622-2300
General/National Adv. E-mail: corwig@aberdeennews.com
Display Adv. E-mail: corwig@aberdeennews.com
Classified Adv. e-mail: classified@aberdeennews.com
Editorial e-mail: swaltman@aberdeennews.com
Primary Website: www.aberdeennews.com
Year Established: 1885
News Services: AP, MCT.
Special Editions: Back-to-School (Aug); Christmas Gift Guide (Dec); Dakota Decades (Other); Spring Car Care (Spring).
Special Weekly Sections: Scrapbook, Education, Humor (Mon); College Sports, American Profile (Tue); Taste (Wed); Out and About, Entertainment, Prep Sports (Thur); Farm, Outdoors (Fri) Church (Sat); Comics, Dakota Living (Sun)
Syndicated Publications: Relish (Monthly); USA Weekend (Sat); Parade (S); American Profile (Weekly).
Avg Free Circ: 39
Sat. Circulation Paid: 11485
Sat. Circulation Free: 39
Sun. Circulation Paid: 12801
Sun. Circulation Free: 37
Audit By: CAC
Audit Date: 30.09.2013
Personnel: Lori Salfrank (Dir., Finance); Amy Jones (Dir., HR); Christy Orwig (Adv. Dir.); David Nelson (Circ. Dir.); John Papendick (Sports Ed.); Jeff Bahr (Women's Ed.); Marcia Sebert (Management Info Service Mgr.); Terry Salfrank (Prod. Mgr.); Cory Bollinger (Pub.); Dee McKibben (Adv. Sales Mgr.)
Parent company (for newspapers): Schurz Communications Inc

BROOKINGS REGISTER

Street address 1: 312 5th St
Street address city: Brookings
Street address state: SD
Zip/Postal code: 57006-1924
County: Brookings
Country: USA
Mailing address: PO BOX 177
Mailing city: BROOKINGS
Mailing state: SD
Mailing zip: 57006-0177
General Phone: (605) 692-6271
General/National Adv. E-mail: registeradvertising@brookingsregister.com
Display Adv. E-mail: registeradvertising@brookingsregister.com
Classified Adv. e-mail: registeradvertising@brookingsregister.com
Primary Website: www.brookingsregister.com
Year Established: 1882
News Services: AP.
Special Editions: Our Town (Aug); Business People (Jun); Progress (Mar).

Special Weekly Sections: Local, Community, Regional, national, World, Sports, Editorial, Opinion, Classifieds, Public Notices (Daily); Best ood (Mon); Business, Celebrations (Tue); Agriculture (Wed); Religion (Thur); Outdoor (Fri); TV (Sat)
Syndicated Publications: American Profile (Weekly).
Sat. Circulation Paid: 4263
Audit By: Sworn/Estimate/Non-Audited
Audit Date: 12.07.2019
Personnel: Kendra Deibert (Mgr.); William McMacken (Adv. Dir.); Doug Kott (News Ed.); Ken Curley (Managing Ed.); Steve Kleinsasser (Circ. Mgr.)
Parent company (for newspapers): San Luis Valley Publishing

THE DAILY PLAINSMAN

Street address 1: 49 3rd St SE
Street address city: Huron
Street address state: SD
Zip/Postal code: 57350-2015
County: Beadle
Country: USA
Mailing address: PO BOX 1278
Mailing city: HURON
Mailing state: SD
Mailing zip: 57350-1278
General Phone: (605) 352-6401
Advertising Phone: (605) 353-7421
Editorial Phone: (605) 353-7425
General/National Adv. E-mail: medemail@aol.com
Display Adv. E-mail: medemail@aol.com
Classified Adv. e-mail: classifieds.plainsman@midconetwork.com
Editorial e-mail: editor.plainsman@midconetwork.com
Primary Website: www.plainsman.com
News Services: AP.
Special Editions: Hunting (Oct); How to Guide (July); Real Estate Guide (Quarterly);
Special Weekly Sections: Best Food (Wed)
Syndicated Publications: Parade (S).
Delivery Methods: Mail`Newsstand`Carrier`Racks
Own Printing Facility?: Y
Commercial printers?: Y
Sat. Circulation Paid: 5377
Sun. Circulation Paid: 5740
Audit By: Sworn/Estimate/Non-Audited
Audit Date: 12.07.2019
Personnel: Mark Davis (Pub./Adv. Dir.); Roger Larsen (Political Ed.); Crystal Pugsley (Regl. Ed.); Mike Carroll (Sports Ed.); Sean Kelley (Ed.); Kimberly Davis (Circ. Mgr./Marketing Mgr.)
Parent company (for newspapers): Metro Newspaper Advertising Services, Inc.-OOB; San Luis Valley Publishing

THE MADISON DAILY LEADER

Street address 1: 214 S Egan Ave
Street address city: Madison
Street address state: SD
Zip/Postal code: 57042-2911
County: Lake
Country: USA
Mailing address: PO BOX 348
Mailing city: MADISON
Mailing state: SD
Mailing zip: 57042-0348
General Phone: (605) 256-4555
General/National Adv. E-mail: ads@madisondailyleader.com
Display Adv. E-mail: ads@madisondailyleader.com
Classified Adv. e-mail: classifieds@madisondailyleader.com
Editorial e-mail: news@madisondailyleader.com
Primary Website: www.DailyLeaderExtra.com
Year Established: 1880
News Services: AP, South Dakota Newspaper Association
Special Editions: Prairie Village Jamboree (Aug); Business Review & Forecast (Feb); Bridal Guide (Jan); Homeland Garden (May); Senior Scene (Oct).
Special Weekly Sections: Business (Mon); Best Food (Tue); Agriculture, Health, Fitness (Wed); Real Estate (Fri)
Delivery Methods: Mail`Newsstand`Carrier`Racks
Areas Served - City/County or Portion Thereof, or Zip codes: Lake County, Miner County, Moody County, Kingsbury County, Brookings County, McCook County and Minnehaha County.
Own Printing Facility?: Y
Commercial printers?: Y
Audit By: Sworn/Estimate/Non-Audited
Audit Date: 12.07.2019
Personnel: Melissa Hegg (Marketing Mgr.); Chuck Clement (City Reporter); Jon M. Hunter (Pub.); Larry Leeds (Sports Ed.); Marcia Schoeberl (Managing Ed.); Jeff Boldt (Tech. Manager); Alysia Sly (Classifieds); Jane Utecht (Reporter)

THE DAILY REPUBLIC

Street address 1: 120 S Lawler St
Street address city: Mitchell
Street address state: SD
Zip/Postal code: 57301-3443
County: Davison
Country: USA
Mailing address: PO BOX 1288
Mailing city: MITCHELL
Mailing state: SD
Mailing zip: 57301-7288
General Phone: (605) 996-5514
Advertising Phone: (605) 996-5515
Editorial Phone: (605) 996-5516
General/National Adv. E-mail: dailyads@mitchellrepublic.com
Display Adv. E-mail: dailyads@mitchellrepublic.com
Classified Adv. e-mail: dailyclass@mitchellrepublic.com
Editorial e-mail: dailynews@mitchellrepublic.com
Primary Website: www.mitchellrepublic.com
News Services: AP.
Special Editions: Car Care Series (Apr); Progress (Aug); Farm & Ranch (Feb); Bridal (Jan); Rodeo (Jul); Bridal (Jun); Home Improvement Series (Mar); Lawn & Garden (May); Christmas Preview (Nov); Hunting Guide (Oct); Fall Home Improvement Series (Sept).
Special Weekly Sections: Best Food Day (Tues)
Syndicated Publications: Relish (Monthly); Parade (S).
Avg Free Circ: 47
Sat. Circulation Paid: 9453
Sat. Circulation Free: 47
Audit By: VAC
Audit Date: 30.09.2015
Personnel: Annette Kroger (Bus. Mgr.); Korrie Wenzel (Pub.); Seth Tupper (Asst. Ed.); Leah Rado (Sports Ed.); Jessy Stroud (Internet/Systems Mgr.); Richard Popejoy (Prod. Foreman, Press-room); Lorie Hasen (Adv. Dir.); Adam Kaus (Circ. Mgr.)
Parent company (for newspapers): Forum Communications Co.

CAPITAL JOURNAL

Street address 1: 333 W Dakota Ave
Street address city: Pierre
Street address state: SD
Zip/Postal code: 57501-4512
County: Hughes
Country: USA
Mailing address: PO BOX 878
Mailing city: PIERRE
Mailing state: SD
Mailing zip: 57501-0878
General Phone: (605) 224-7301
General/National Adv. E-mail: julie.furchner@capjournal.com
Display Adv. E-mail: audrey.lucas@capjournal.com
Classified Adv. e-mail: jennifer.bieser@capjournal.com
Editorial e-mail: nick.lowrey@capjournal.com
Primary Website: www.capjournal.com
Year Established: 1889
News Services: AP.
Special Editions: 4-H Finals Rodeo Booklet (Aug); Bridal Tab (Feb); Legislative (Jan); Crazy Days Downtown (Jul); Fourth of July Rodeo (Jun); Home & Garden/Real Estate Tab (Mar); Graduation Brochure (May); Chamber Brochure (Nov); Fire Prevention Tab (Oct); Hunting Guide Bo
Special Weekly Sections: Best Food Day (Tue); Entertainment, TV, Auto, Real Estate (Fri)
Syndicated Publications: Reminder Plus (Wed).
Avg Free Circ: 21000
Audit By: Sworn/Estimate/Non-Audited
Audit Date: 12.07.2019
Personnel: Lance Nixon (Managing Ed.); Ray Pfeffer (Productions Mgr.); Nick Lowrey (Asst. Managing Ed.); Gidal Kaiser (Sports Ed); Ray Taylor (Circ Mgr); Laura Fischbach (Adv Consultant); Julie Furchner (Adv. Consultant); April Schroeder (Adv Consultant)
Parent company (for newspapers): Wick Communications

RAPID CITY JOURNAL

Street address 1: 507 Main St
Street address city: Rapid City
Street address state: SD
Zip/Postal code: 57701-2733
County: Pennington
Country: USA
Mailing address: PO BOX 450
Mailing city: RAPID CITY
Mailing state: SD
Mailing zip: 57709-0450
General Phone: (605) 394-8300
Advertising Phone: (605) 394-8331
Editorial Phone: (605) 394-8314
General/National Adv. E-mail: news@rapidcityjournal.com
Display Adv. E-mail: brandyn.crawford@rapidcityjournal.com
Classified Adv. e-mail: brandyn.crawford@rapidcityjournal.com
Editorial e-mail: bart.pfankuch@rapidcityjournal.com
Primary Website: www.rapidcityjournal.com
Mthly Avg Views: 6141454
Mthly Avg Unique Visitors: 1637855
Year Established: 1878
News Services: AP, LAT-WP, SHNS.
Special Weekly Sections: Black Hills Weekend (Fri); Health & Fitness (Mon); Living (S); Religion (Sat); Home & Garden (Thur); Sports (Tues); Food (Wed).
Syndicated Publications: Relish (Monthly); Parade (S); Athlon Sports (Monthly).
Delivery Methods: Mail`Carrier
Areas Served - City/County or Portion Thereof, or Zip codes: Western SD, Eastern WY, Northern NE
Commercial printers?: Y
Avg Free Circ: 391
Sat. Circulation Paid: 13270
Sat. Circulation Free: 391
Sun. Circulation Paid: 16697
Sun. Circulation Free: 670
Audit By: AAM
Audit Date: 31.03.2018
Personnel: Matthew Tranquill (Pub.); Brad Casto (Vice President of Advertising and Marketing); Josh Hart (Circ. Dir.); Lon Massingale (Sales Mgr.); Pat Butler (Mng. Ed.); Candy DenOuden (Online Ed.); Richard Anderson (Sports Ed.); Mark Andersen (Opinion Page Ed.); Holly Edmiston (Copy Ed.); Laura Schmidt (CSR)
Parent company (for newspapers): Lee Enterprises, Incorporated

ARGUS LEADER

Street address 1: 200 S Minnesota Ave
Street address city: Sioux Falls
Street address state: SD
Zip/Postal code: 57104-6314
County: Minnehaha
Country: USA
Mailing address: PO BOX 5034
Mailing city: SIOUX FALLS
Mailing state: SD
Mailing zip: 57117-5034
General Phone: (605) 331-2200
Advertising Phone: (605) 331-2355
Editorial Phone: (605) 331-2332
General/National Adv. E-mail: editor@argusleader.com
Display Adv. E-mail: allegals@argusleader.com
Classified Adv. e-mail: Classifieds@argusleader.com
Editorial e-mail: editor@argusleader.com
Primary Website: www.argusleader.com
Mthly Avg Views: 4800000
Mthly Avg Unique Visitors: 550000
Year Established: 1881
News Services: AP, GNS, MCT.
Delivery Methods: Mail`Newsstand`Carrier`Racks
Areas Served - City/County or Portion Thereof, or Zip codes: Minnehaha, Lincoln, Turner, McCook
Avg Free Circ: 615
Sat. Circulation Paid: 12641
Sat. Circulation Free: 615
Sun. Circulation Paid: 19644
Sun. Circulation Free: 400
Audit By: AAM
Audit Date: 31.03.2019
Personnel: Randell Beck (Pres./Pub.); Greg Robinson (Dir., Admin./Controller); Jean Healy (Principal HR Business Partner); Kelly Redfearn (Advertising Director); Maricarrol Kueter (Executive Editor); Patrick Lalley (Managing Editor); Cory Myers (Consumer Exp. Dir./News); Stu Whitney (Sports Editor); Owen Hotvet (Circulation Director); Sherry Szadziewicz (Marketing Director); Allen Jungels (Production Manager); Mike Golden (IT Manager); Kristi Grooms (Adv. Mgr., Retail)
Parent company (for newspapers): Gannett

BLACK HILLS PIONEER

Street address 1: 315 Seaton Cir
Street address city: Spearfish
Street address state: SD
Zip/Postal code: 57783-3212
County: Lawrence
Country: USA
Mailing address: PO BOX 7
Mailing city: SPEARFISH
Mailing state: SD
Mailing zip: 57783-0007
General Phone: (605) 642-2761
Advertising Phone: (605) 642-2761
Editorial Phone: (605) 642-2761
General/National Adv. E-mail: dru@bhpioneer.com
Display Adv. E-mail: dru@bhpioneer.com
Classified Adv. e-mail: classifieds@bhpioneer.com
Editorial e-mail: news@bhpioneer.com
Primary Website: www.bhpioneer.com
Year Established: 1876
News Services: AP.
Special Editions: Home Improvement (Apr); Deadwood Rodeo (Aug); Valentine's Day (Feb); New Year's Eve (Jan); 4th of July (Jul); Belle Fourche All Car Rally (Jun); St. Patrick's Day (Mar); Mother's Day (May); Christmas Greetings (Nov); Halloween (Oct); Football Contest (Sep
Special Weekly Sections: Best Food Day (Tue); Real Estate (Wed); Entertainment (Thur); Kids, Lifestyles (Fri); Black Hills State University (Sat)
Syndicated Publications: American Profile (Weekly).
Areas Served - City/County or Portion Thereof, or Zip codes: 57783, 57754, 57732, 57793, 57785, 57779, 57717
Sat. Circulation Paid: 4300
Audit By: Sworn/Estimate/Non-Audited
Audit Date: 12.07.2019
Personnel: Scott Lister (Circ. Mgr.); Letitia Lister (Pub.); Mark Watson (Ed.); Dru Thomas (Adv. Sales); Kari King (Classifieds Adv. Mgr.)
Parent company (for newspapers): Seaton Group

WATERTOWN PUBLIC OPINION

Street address 1: 120 3rd Ave NW
Street address city: Watertown
Street address state: SD
Zip/Postal code: 57201-2311
County: Codington
Country: USA
Mailing address: PO BOX 10
Mailing city: WATERTOWN
Mailing state: SD
Mailing zip: 57201-0010
General Phone: (605) 886-6901
Display Adv. E-mail: advertise@thepublicopinion.com
Editorial e-mail: news@thepublicopinion.com
Primary Website: www.thepublicopinion.com
Mthly Avg Views: 300000
Mthly Avg Unique Visitors: 100000
Year Established: 1887
News Services: AP.
Special Editions: Home & Garden (Apr); Family Resource (Aug); Sports (Aug), Sports (Dec); Farm Show (Feb); Bridal Showcase (Jan); Senior Focus (Jul); Health Tab (Jun); Health Tab (Mar); Winter Car Care (Oct); Fall Sportsman (Sept)
Special Weekly Sections: GoTV Guide, Business Spotlight (Tues); Real Estate Guide, Travel and Events, Good Health, Wedding Page (Weds); Outdoors, Church, Engagements and Anniversaries, Discover Downtown Watertown, Here'â€™s My Card, NFL, NASCAR (Thurs); Farm, Focus on Business, Casino Directory, Coupon Page (Fri); Home Builders (Sat)
Syndicated Publications: Parade (Sat)., Relish (1st Wed of the month)
Delivery Methods: Mail`Newsstand`Carrier`Racks
Areas Served - City/County or Portion Thereof, or Zip codes: 57201- Codington County Clark County, Day County, Deuel County, Grant County, Hamlin County, Kingsbury County, Roberts County, Big Stone (MN) County, Lac Qui Parle (MN) County, Traverse (MN) County, Yellow Medicine (MN)
Own Printing Facility?: Y
Commercial printers?: Y
Avg Free Circ: 437
Sat. Circulation Paid: 8603
Sat. Circulation Free: 230
Audit By: AAM
Audit Date: 30.06.2018

Personnel: Kevin Shaw (Pub.); Roger Whittle (Managing Ed.); Lana Holland (Sales & Mkt. Dir.); Jon Louder (DMG Logistics and Circulation); J.T. Fey (Online Ed.); Roger Merriam (Sports Ed.)
Parent company (for newspapers): CherryRoad Media

YANKTON DAILY PRESS & DAKOTAN

Street address 1: 319 Walnut St
Street address 2: Ste 2
Street address city: Yankton
Street address state: SD
Zip/Postal code: 57078-4344
County: Yankton
Country: USA
Mailing address: 319 WALNUT ST STE 2
Mailing city: YANKTON
Mailing state: SD
Mailing zip: 57078-4344
General Phone: (605) 665-7811
Advertising Phone: (605) 665-7811
Editorial Phone: (605) 665-7811
General/National Adv. E-mail: micki.schievelbein@yankton.net
Display Adv. E-mail: jim.gevens@yankton.net
Classified Adv. e-mail: tera.schmidt@yankton.net
Editorial e-mail: kelly.hurtz@yankton.net
Primary Website: www.yankton.net
Mthly Avg Views: 1028000
Mthly Avg Unique Visitors: 126000
Year Established: 1861
News Services: AP.
Special Editions: Spring Fashion Tab (Apr); Back-to-School Tab (Aug); Christmas Gift Ideas (Dec); Yankton Health (Feb); Progress (Jun); Weeder's Digest (Mar); Graduation Tab (May); Turkey Give-Away (Nov); Fall Fashion Tab (Oct); Fall Football (Sept). Her Voice Womens Magazine (6x year)
Special Weekly Sections: Business (Mon); Dining & Entertainmeng (Tues); Dining & Entertainment (Thurs); Food, Religion, TV & Entertainment (Fri); Outdoors, Agriculture (Sat)
Syndicated Publications: Relish (Monthly); USA WEEKEND Magazine (Sat); American Profile (Weekly).
Delivery Methods: Mail`Carrier`Racks
Areas Served - City/County or Portion Thereof, or Zip codes: Yankton County, Clay County, Bon Homme county, Hutchinson county, Turner County, and various parts of Nebraska
Own Printing Facility?: Y
Sat. Circulation Paid: 8600
Audit By: Sworn/Estimate/Non-Audited
Audit Date: 12.07.2019
Personnel: Gary Wood (Ed./Pub.); Tonya Schild (Bus. Mgr.); Micki Schievelbein (Adv. Dir.); Kelly Hertz (Mng. Ed.); Randy Dockendorf (Regional Ed.); James Cimburek (Sports Ed.); Beth Rye (New Media Director)
Parent company (for newspapers): Yankton Media Inc.

TENNESSEE

THE DAILY POST-ATHENIAN

Street address 1: 320 S Jackson St
Street address city: Athens
Street address state: TN
Zip/Postal code: 37303-4715
County: McMinn
Country: USA
Mailing address: PO BOX 340
Mailing city: ATHENS
Mailing state: TN
Mailing zip: 37371-0340
General Phone: (423) 745-5664
General/National Adv. E-mail: sheila.watson@dailypostathenian.com
Display Adv. E-mail: sheila.watson@dailypostathenian.com
Classified Adv. e-mail: patricia.mckenzie@dailypostathenian.com
Editorial e-mail: autumn.hughes@dailypostathenian.com
Primary Website: www.dailypostathenian.com
Year Established: 1848
News Services: AP.
Special Editions: Health & Fitness (Apr); Football Contest Pages (Aug); Friendly Fellow Greetings (Dec); Boy Scout Salute (Feb); Income Tax Guide (Jan); Crime Prevention (Jul); Dairy Salute (Jun); Farming Salute (Mar); Keepsake (May); Holiday Cookbook (Nov); Car Care Guide
Special Weekly Sections: Best Food, Education (Wed); Business (Thur); TV, Religion, Weekend (Fri)
Syndicated Publications: Entertainment (Fri).
Delivery Methods: Newsstand`Carrier`Racks
Areas Served - City/County or Portion Thereof, or Zip codes: 37371
Own Printing Facility?: Y
Commercial printers?: N
Audit By: Sworn/Estimate/Non-Audited
Audit Date: 12.07.2019
Personnel: Jeff Schumacher (Pub./Adv. Dir.); Dewey Morgan (Ed.); Patrick Helms; Larry Blackmon (District Mgr.)
Parent company (for newspapers): Adams Publishing Group, LLC

CHATTANOOGA TIMES FREE PRESS

Street address 1: 400 E. 11th Street
Street address city: Chattanooga
Street address state: TN
Zip/Postal code: 37403
County: Hamilton
Country: USA
Mailing address: PO BOX 1447
Mailing city: CHATTANOOGA
Mailing state: TN
Mailing zip: 37401-1447
General Phone: (423) 756-6900
Advertising Phone: (423)757-6517
Editorial Phone: (423) 757-6357
General/National Adv. E-mail: lkahana@timesfreepress.com
Display Adv. E-mail: lkahana@timesfreepress.com
Classified Adv. e-mail: dfarmer@timesfreepress.com
Editorial e-mail: agerber@timesfreepress.com
Primary Website: www.timesfreepress.com
Mthly Avg Views: 11133826
Mthly Avg Unique Visitors: 1613539
Year Established: 1869
News Services: AP, CNS, DF, NYT, SHNS.
Special Editions: Home Improvements (Apr); Football (Aug); Progress (Feb); Products & Services (Jul); Gift Guide (Nov); Health Trends (Oct); Home Improvements (Sept).
Special Weekly Sections: Chatanooga Weekend (Fri); Lifestyle (Mon); Arts & Travel (S); Lifestyle (Sat); Health & Fitness (Thur); Lifestyle (Wed).
Syndicated Publications: Relish (Monthly); Parade (S).
Delivery Methods: Mail`Newsstand`Carrier`Racks
Areas Served - City/County or Portion Thereof, or Zip codes: Chattanooga, Nashville, Myrtle Beach, Atlanta, Dalton, Cleveland
Own Printing Facility?: Y
Sat. Circulation Paid: 41664
Sun. Circulation Paid: 53443
Audit By: AAM
Audit Date: 30.06.2018
Personnel: Jeff DeLoach (Pres.); Paul Abraham (Controller); Leslie Kahana (Advertising Director); Alison Gerber (Ed. & Dir of Content); Mark Jones (Dir. of Strategic Marketing & Audience Dev.); Carroll Duckworth (Circ. Dir.); Alex Chambliss (Region Ed.); Clint Cooper (Free Press Page Ed.); Ed Bourn (Digital Dir.); Gary Webb (Production Dir.); Dennis Parker (Major & National Account Executive); Frank Maier (Dir of Circ Ops)
Parent company (for newspapers): WEHCO Media, Inc.

THE LEAF-CHRONICLE

Street address 1: 200 Commerce St
Street address city: Clarksville
Street address state: TN
Zip/Postal code: 37040-5101
County: Montgomery
Country: USA
Mailing address: PO BOX 31029
Mailing city: CLARKSVILLE
Mailing state: TN
Mailing zip: 37040-0018
General Phone: (931) 552-1808
Advertising Phone: (931) 245-0275
Editorial Phone: (931) 245-0282
Editorial e-mail: cssmith@gannett.com
Primary Website: www.theleafchronicle.com
Mthly Avg Views: 3700000
Mthly Avg Unique Visitors: 302800
Year Established: 1808
News Services: AP.
Special Editions: Football (Aug);Fact Book (Aug); Salute to Fort Campbell (Jun); Vacation/Outdoors (May); Christmas Gift Guide (Nov); Higher Education Guide (Sept) Health (monthly)
Special Weekly Sections: Go-Weekly Entertainment (Fri); Food Days (Mon, Wed); Living Well (Wed) Sunday Living (Sun)
Syndicated Publications: USA WEEKEND Magazine (S).
Delivery Methods: Mail`Newsstand`Carrier`Racks
Areas Served - City/County or Portion Thereof, or Zip codes: 37040, 37043, 37042, 37171, 37010, 37191, 37079, 37061, 42223
Own Printing Facility?: Y
Commercial printers?: Y
Avg Free Circ: 421
Sat. Circulation Paid: 7387
Sat. Circulation Free: 421
Sun. Circulation Paid: 10754
Sun. Circulation Free: 5575
Audit By: AAM
Audit Date: 30.06.2018
Personnel: Richard Stevens (Ed./Gen. Mgr.); Jimmy Settle (Bus. Ed.); Alane Megna (Sr. Ed./Digital); Chris Smith (Sr. Ed./News); Carol Daniels (Sales/Marketing Dir.)
Parent company (for newspapers): Gannett

CLEVELAND DAILY BANNER

Street address 1: 2075 N Ocoee St
Street address 2: Ste B
Street address city: Cleveland
Street address state: TN
Zip/Postal code: 37311
County: Bradley
Country: USA
General Phone: (423) 472-5041
Advertising Phone: (423) 472-5041
Editorial Phone: 423-749-1827
General/National Adv. E-mail: advertising@clevelandbanner.com
Display Adv. E-mail: advertising@clevelandbanner.com; classifieds@clevelandbanner.com
Classified Adv. e-mail: classifieds@clevelandbanner.com
Editorial e-mail: news@clevelandbanner.com; sports@clevelandbanner.com; lifestyles@clevelandbanner.com
Primary Website: www.clevelandbanner.com
Mthly Avg Views: 700000
Mthly Avg Unique Visitors: 80000
Year Established: 1854
News Services: AP, Tribune
Special Editions: Weddings (Jan); Money Matters (Jan); Progress (Feb); Spring Car Care (May); Spring Home Improvement (Apr); Thanksgiving (Nov); Fall Home Improvement (Oct); Football (Aug); Health and Fitness (Mar); Ocoee Regional Builders Association (Mar); Graduation (May); Mother's Day Special (May); Readers' Choice(July); Medical Journal (July); Senior Expo (Sep); 20 under 40 (Oct); Apple Festival (Oct); Breast Cancer Awareness (Oct); Winter Sports (Nov); Holiday Gift Guide (Nov); Christmas Greetings (Dec)
Special Weekly Sections: People(Sat); Church News (Thur); Business News (Sat)
Delivery Methods: Mail`Newsstand`Carrier`Racks
Areas Served - City/County or Portion Thereof, or Zip codes: Cleveland & Bradley Co, Polk County
Own Printing Facility?: Y
Commercial printers?: N
Avg Free Circ: 200
Sun. Circulation Paid: 10364
Sun. Circulation Free: 1333
Audit By: USPS
Audit Date: 30.09.2023
Personnel: Joyce Taylor (Credit Mgr.); Carrie Pettit (Prodn. Mgr., Pre Press); Patty Hawkins; Trena Bailey; Autumn Hughes (Editor); Tim Siniard (City Editor); Joe Cannon (Sports Editor); Kathy Payne (Advertising Sales Lead); Jack Bennett (Dir., Adv./Promo.); Stephen Crass (Ed.); Gwen Swiger (Assoc. Ed.); Mary Matthews (Librarian); Richard Roberts (Sports Ed.); Bettie Marlowe (Women's Ed.); Jim Bryant (Online Mgr.); Richard Yarber (Prodn. Foreman, Pressroom)
Parent company (for newspapers): Cleveland Newspapers, Inc.; Paxton Media Group

COLUMBIA DAILY HERALD

Street address 1: 1115 S Main St
Street address city: Columbia
Street address state: TN
Zip/Postal code: 38401-3733
County: Maury
Country: USA
Mailing address: PO BOX 1425
Mailing city: COLUMBIA
Mailing state: TN
Mailing zip: 38402-1425
General Phone: (931) 388-6464
Display Adv. E-mail: cduncan@c-dh.net
Editorial e-mail: newsroomc@c-dh.net
Primary Website: www.columbiadailyherald.com
Mthly Avg Views: 412000
Mthly Avg Unique Visitors: 68000
Year Established: 1848
News Services: AP, NEA.
Special Editions: Spring Fashion (Apr); Football (Aug); Christmas Greetings (Dec); Bridal (Jun); Graduation (May); Christmas Gift Guide (Nov); Fall Fashion (Sept); Healthy Living (monthly).
Special Weekly Sections: Church Page (Fri); Showtime TV Guide (S); Best Food Day (Wed).
Syndicated Publications: USA WEEKEND Magazine (S).
Delivery Methods: Mail`Newsstand`Carrier`Racks
Areas Served - City/County or Portion Thereof, or Zip codes: 38401; 38402,38482,38483,38474,38461, 8451,37174,37179,38462,38483,38472,37091,37034
Own Printing Facility?: Y
Commercial printers?: Y
Avg Free Circ: 389
Sun. Circulation Paid: 6482
Sun. Circulation Free: 96
Audit By: CAC
Audit Date: 31.03.2018
Personnel: Keith Ponder (Pub.); Anthony Dezarn (Circ. Mgr.); James Bennett (Ed.); Aaron Walther (News Ed.); Maurice Patton (Sports Ed.)
Parent company (for newspapers): Gannett; CherryRoad Media

HERALD-CITIZEN

Street address 1: 1300 Neal St
Street address city: Cookeville
Street address state: TN
Zip/Postal code: 38501-4330
County: Putnam
Country: USA
Mailing address: PO BOX 2729
Mailing city: COOKEVILLE
Mailing state: TN
Mailing zip: 38502-2729
General Phone: (931) 526-9715
General/National Adv. E-mail: advertising@herald-citizen.com
Display Adv. E-mail: advertising@herald-citizen.com
Classified Adv. e-mail: classified@herald-citizen.com
Editorial e-mail: editor@herald-citizen.com
Primary Website: www.herald-citizen.com
News Services: AP.
Special Editions: Cookeville Cookoff Community Festival (Aug); Home Show (Feb); Progress (Jan); Venture Tourist Magazine (May); Holidays in Upper Cumberland (Nov).
Special Weekly Sections: Best Food Day (Mon); Local School (Thur); Church, Religious (Fri); Auto (Fri/Sun); Real Estate, Stage, Studio, news, Weddings, Engagements, Farm, Business, News (Sun)
Syndicated Publications: Relish (Monthly); Focus TV Tab (S).
Sun. Circulation Paid: 11173
Audit By: AAM
Audit Date: 30.09.2011
Personnel: David Shelton (Adv. Mgr.); Keith McCormick (Circ. Mgr.); Bob McMillan (Wire Ed.); Mike DeLapp (Prodn. Mgr.)
Parent company (for newspapers): Cleveland Newspapers, Inc.

STATE GAZETTE

Street address 1: 294 US Highway 51 Byp N
Street address city: Dyersburg
Street address state: TN
Zip/Postal code: 38024-3659
County: Dyer
Country: USA
Mailing address: PO BOX 808
Mailing city: DYERSBURG
Mailing state: TN
Mailing zip: 38025-0808
General Phone: (731) 285-4091
Advertising Phone: (731) 285-4091 ext. 116
Editorial Phone: (731) 285-4091 x111
General/National Adv. E-mail: krambo@stategazette.com

Display Adv. E-mail: krambo@stategazette.com
Classified Adv. e-mail: krambo@stategazette.com
Editorial e-mail: srouse@stategazette.com
Primary Website: www.stategazette.com
Mthly Avg Views: 254000
Mthly Avg Unique Visitors: 18000
Year Established: 1865
News Services: AP.
Special Editions: Home Improvement (Apr); Family Business (Aug); Home for the Holidays (Dec); Progress (Feb); NASCAR (Jan); Kitchen & Bath (Jul); Seniors Tab (Jun); Lawn & Garden (Mar); Spring Fashion (May); Holiday Shopping Guide (Nov); Newspaper Week Tab (Oct); Newcomers
Special Weekly Sections: Food (Fri); TV Entertainer (S); Food (Wed).
Syndicated Publications: Relish (Monthly); Parade (S); American Profile (Weekly).
Delivery Methods: Mail
Areas Served - City/County or Portion Thereof, or Zip codes: Dyer County
Sun. Circulation Paid: 7900
Audit By: Sworn/Estimate/Non-Audited
Audit Date: 12.07.2019
Personnel: Shelia Rouse (Publisher); Jina Jeffries (Bus. Mgr.); Terry Brock (Circ. Dir.); Mike Smith (Mng. Ed.); Robert Pollard (Pressroom Mgr.)
Parent company (for newspapers): Rust Communications

ELIZABETHTON STAR

Street address 1: 300 N Sycamore St
Street address city: Elizabethton
Street address state: TN
Zip/Postal code: 37643-2742
County: Carter
Country: USA
Mailing address: PO BOX 1960
Mailing city: ELIZABETHTON
Mailing state: TN
Mailing zip: 37644-1960
General Phone: (423) 542-4151
Advertising Phone: (423) 542-4151
Editorial Phone: (423) 297-9064
General/National Adv. E-mail: delaney,scalf@elizabethton.com
Display Adv. E-mail: delaney.scalf@elizabethton,com
Classified Adv. e-mail: kathy.scalf@elizabethton.com
Editorial e-mail: rozella.hardin@elizabethton.com
Primary Website: www.elizabethton.com
Year Established: 1926
News Services: AP, Papert (Landon).
Special Editions: Christmas Gift Guide (Other).
Sun. Circulation Paid: 9366
Audit By: Sworn/Estimate/Non-Audited
Audit Date: 12.07.2019
Personnel: Delaney Scalf (Gen. Mgr.); Lynn Richardson (Pub.); Kathy Scalf (Circ. Mgr.); Shirley Nave (Adv. Mgr.); Rozella Hardin (Ed.); Patsy Johnson (Asst. to Pub.); Bill Parsons (Adv. Dir.)
Parent company (for newspapers): Boone Newspapers, Inc.

THE GREENEVILLE SUN

Street address 1: 121 W Summer St
Street address city: Greeneville
Street address state: TN
Zip/Postal code: 37743-4923
County: Greene
Country: USA
Mailing address: 121 W Summer St
Mailing city: GREENEVILLE
Mailing state: TN
Mailing zip: 37744-1630
General Phone: (423) 638-4181
Advertising Phone: (423) 638-4185
General/National Adv. E-mail: richard.clark@greenvillesun.com
Display Adv. E-mail: richard.clark@greenvillesun.com
Classified Adv. e-mail: richard.clark@greenvillesun.com
Editorial e-mail: scott.jenkins@greenevillesun.com
Primary Website: www.greenevillesun.com
Mthly Avg Views: 390000
Mthly Avg Unique Visitors: 101524
Year Established: 1897
News Services: AP.
Special Editions: Administrative Professionals Week (Apr); Greene Co. Guidebook (Aug); Christmas Greetings (Dec); Ladies Classic Basketball Tournament (Dec); Calendar Girls (Jan); Bridal Edition (Jan); Benchmarks (Mar); TN Greene (May); Salute To Industry (Oct; Pigskin Preview (Aug); Basketball (Nov); Car Care (Oct); Cheerleaders & Bands (Sept); People's Choice Awards (Nov); Greene County Partnership Directory (Jan).
Special Weekly Sections: Health (Mon); TV Week (Sat); Business (Thur); Maturity (Seniors) (Tues); Agriculture (Wed); Faith (Fri); Education (Wed).
Syndicated Publications: Athlon Sports, American Profile.
Delivery Methods: Mail`Newsstand`Carrier`Racks
Areas Served - City/County or Portion Thereof, or Zip codes: 37743, 37745, 37616, 37641, 37681, 37711, 37809, 37810, 37818, 37656.
Own Printing Facility?: Y
Commercial printers?: Y
Sat. Circulation Paid: 10500
Audit By: USPS
Audit Date: 26.09.2022
Personnel: Gregg K. Jones (Pub.); Brian Cutshall (Dir. Online Opp.); Dale Long (Circ/Prod. Mgr.); Paul Mauney (Gen. Mgr.); Arthur D. Wehenkel (Adv. Dir.); Sarah Gregory (Lifestyle Ed.); Clark Richard (Ad Director); Scott Jenkins (Editor); Michael Reneau (Ed.); Kristen Early (Assoc. Ed.)
Parent company (for newspapers): Adams Publishing Group, LLC

THE JACKSON SUN

Street address 1: 245 W Lafayette St
Street address city: Jackson
Street address state: TN
Zip/Postal code: 38301-6126
County: Madison
Country: USA
Mailing address: PO BOX 1059
Mailing city: JACKSON
Mailing state: TN
Mailing zip: 38302-1059
General Phone: (731) 427-3333
Advertising Phone: (731) 425-9610
Editorial Phone: (731) 425-9686
General/National Adv. E-mail: contactus@jacksonsun.com
Primary Website: www.jacksonsun.com
Year Established: 1879
News Services: AP, GNS.
Special Editions: Football (Aug); Fact Book (Feb); How To (Jan); Back-to-School (Jul); NAIA (Mar); Apple (Monthly); Home Builders (Nov); Design An Ad (Oct).
Special Weekly Sections: Health, Fitness, Technology (Mon); Family, Parenting (Tue); Best Food (Wed); Entertainment, Magazine, Education (Thur); Home, Garden (Fri); Expanded Sports, Automotive, Religion (Sat); Business, Finance, TV, Amusement, Comics, Travel, Living, Real Estate, NFL (Sun); Business, Your Town (Daily)
Syndicated Publications: TV Week (own, newsprint) (S); Weekend Plus (Thur).
Delivery Methods: Mail`Newsstand`Carrier`Racks
Own Printing Facility?: Y
Commercial printers?: Y
Avg Free Circ: 127
Sat. Circulation Paid: 9012
Sat. Circulation Free: 127
Sun. Circulation Paid: 15702
Sun. Circulation Free: 108
Audit By: AAM
Audit Date: 31.03.2018
Personnel: Roy Heatherly (Pub./Pres.); Tammy Gilliam (Finance Mgr.); Betty Allen (Credit Mgr.); Ron Prince (Adv. Dir.); Sarah Scott (Adv. Mgr., Display); Cathy Garrett (Dir., Market Devel.); Alice Sellers (Circ. Mgr.); Steve Coffman (Exec. Ed.); Brandon Shields (Ed.); Kelly South (Chief Content Ed.); Martin Jelinek (Online Mgr.); Brad Isaacs (Prodn. Servs. Mgr.); Beth Walker (Prodn. Mgr., Commercial Print Shop); Andy Curtis (Prodn. Mgr., Bldg.); Leesa Raines (Nat'l Adv. Rep.); Steve Coughman (Exec. Ed.)
Parent company (for newspapers): Gannett

JOHNSON CITY PRESS

Street address 1: 204 W. Main Street
Street address city: Johnson City
Street address state: TN
Zip/Postal code: 37601
County: Washington
Country: USA
Mailing address: PO BOX 1717
Mailing city: JOHNSON CITY
Mailing state: TN
Mailing zip: 37605-1717
General Phone: (423) 929-3111
Advertising Phone: (423) 929-3111
Editorial Phone: (423) 929-3111
General/National Adv. E-mail: adsales@johnsoncitypress.com
Display Adv. E-mail: adsales@johnsoncitypress.com
Classified Adv. e-mail: adsales@johnsoncitypress.com
Editorial e-mail: newsroom@johnsoncitypress.com
Primary Website: www.johnsoncitypress.com
Year Established: 1934
News Services: AP, NYT.
Special Editions: Bristol Motor Speedway Tab-Ford City 500 (Apr); Bristol Motor Speedway Tab-Sharpie 500 (Aug); Christmas Gifts (Dec); Children's Valentines (Feb); Wedding Guide (Jan); Progress (Mar); Outdoor Recreation (May); Thanksgiving (Nov); Car Care (Oct); School (Se
Special Weekly Sections: Best Food (Wed/Sat); TV, Entertainment (Daily); Stocks (Tue-Sat); TV (Fri); Church, Mutual Funds, Classifieds, Auto (Sat); Tempo, Business, Sports, Travel (Sun)
Syndicated Publications: Parade (S).
Delivery Methods: Newsstand`Carrier`Racks
Areas Served - City/County or Portion Thereof, or Zip codes: 37605, 37615, 37604
Own Printing Facility?: Y
Commercial printers?: N
Avg Free Circ: 2613
Sat. Circulation Paid: 16131
Sat. Circulation Free: 2613
Sun. Circulation Paid: 18173
Sun. Circulation Free: 3133
Audit By: AAM
Audit Date: 30.06.2018
Personnel: Rick Thompson (Pub.); Bill Cummings (Adv. Sales Mgr.); Phil Hensley (Circ. Dir.); John Molley (Mng. Ed.); Robert Houk (Editorial Page Ed.); Sam Watson (Educ./School Ed.); Lee Talbert (Photo Dept. Mgr.); Robert Pierce (Religion Ed.); Kelly Hodge (Sports Ed.); Jan Hearn (Travel Ed.); Sue Legg; Alan Broyles; Sharon Salyers; Richard Clark (Sales/Mktg Dir.)
Parent company (for newspapers): Johnson City Publishing Corp; Six Rivers Media, LLC

KINGSPORT TIMES-NEWS

Street address 1: 701 Lynn Garden Dr
Street address city: Kingsport
Street address state: TN
Zip/Postal code: 37660-5607
County: Sullivan
Country: USA
General Phone: (423) 246-8121
Advertising Phone: (423) 392-1328 (Retail)
Editorial Phone: (423) 392-1322
General/National Adv. E-mail: gcoleman@timesnews.net
Display Adv. E-mail: retail@timesnews.net
Classified Adv. e-mail: classifieds@timesnews.net
Editorial e-mail: news@timesnews.net
Primary Website: www.timesnews.net
Mthly Avg Views: 4556884
Mthly Avg Unique Visitors: 306826
Year Established: 1916
News Services: AP, MCT, CQ.
Special Editions: American Home & Garden (Apr); Football Preview (Aug); Christmas Gallery of Gifts (3 times) (Dec); Chamber Annual Report (Feb); Celebrating Diversity (Jan); Readers Choice V (Jun); Progress (Mar); Spring Tune-Up (May); 100+ Things to Do (March & Sept.); Sullivan County Fact Book (Dec.)
Special Weekly Sections: Best Food (Wed/Sun); Entertainment (Thur); Religion (Fri); Business, Travel, Technology (Sun)
Syndicated Publications: Relish; Parade
Delivery Methods: Mail`Newsstand`Carrier`Racks
Areas Served - City/County or Portion Thereof, or Zip codes: 37660, 24251, 37642, 37645, 37617, 37659,37601,24244,24290
Own Printing Facility?: Y
Commercial printers?: Y
Sat. Circulation Paid: 22761
Sun. Circulation Paid: 24544
Audit By: AAM
Audit Date: 20.09.2021
Personnel: Debbie Salyers (VP Finance); Stephanie McLellan (City Ed.); Dan Strickler (IT); Billy Kirk (VP of Advertising); Clark Richard (Vice President, Sales); Lynn Brooks (Nat'l Adv. Mgr.); Rick Thomason (Publisher); Ben Conkin (Digital Director)
Parent company (for newspapers): Sandusky Newspapers, Inc.; Six Rivers Media, LLC; Six Rivers Media

KNOXVILLE NEWS SENTINEL

Street address 1: 2332 News Sentinel Drive
Street address city: Knoxville
Street address state: TN
Zip/Postal code: 37921
County: Knox
Country: USA
Mailing address: 2332 NEWS SENTINEL DR
Mailing city: KNOXVILLE
Mailing state: TN
Mailing zip: 37921-5766
General Phone: (865) 521-8181
Advertising Phone: (865)342-6453
Editorial Phone: (865) 342-6300
General/National Adv. E-mail: kns@knoxnews.com
Display Adv. E-mail: ads@knoxnews.com
Editorial e-mail: jack.mcelroy@knoxnews.com
Primary Website: www.knoxnews.com
Mthly Avg Views: 8110967
Mthly Avg Unique Visitors: 1319705
Year Established: 1888
News Services: AP, SHNS, NEA, LAT-WP, INS Bizwire, PR Newswire.
Special Editions: Employer Spotlight (Apr); Prep Football (Aug); Fox 43 Winter Adventures (Dec); Childrens' Miracle Network Radiothon (Feb); Employer Spotlight (Jan); Employer Spotlight (Jul); Lenoir City Arts & Crafts Festival (Jun); Home Show (Mar); A Day in the Life (Ma
Special Weekly Sections: Preview (Fri); Science (Mon); Real Estate (S); Faith & Family (Sat); Style (Thur); Schools (Tues); Food (Wed).
Syndicated Publications: Parade (S).
Delivery Methods: Mail`Carrier
Areas Served - City/County or Portion Thereof, or Zip codes: East Tennessee
Own Printing Facility?: Y
Commercial printers?: Y
Sat. Circulation Paid: 55223
Sun. Circulation Paid: 71187
Audit By: AAM
Audit Date: 30.06.2018
Personnel: Patrick Birmingham (Pres./Pub.); Paul Abraham (Dir., Finance); Debi Welch (Dir., HR); Nancy Nabors (Adv. Mgr., Retail); Brenda Crisp (Classified Adv. Mgr.); Lisa Duncan (Mktg. Dir.); Jack McElroy (Ed.); Wade Saye (Ed., Special Publications); Tom Chester (Deputy Mng. Ed.); Michael Apuan (Asst. Mng. Ed., Graphics); David Keim (Bus. Ed.); Sam Venable (Columnist); Hoyt Canady (Editorial Page Ed.); Jan Avent (Asst. Editorial Page Ed.); Chuck Campbell (Entertainment Ed.); Betsy Pickle (Film Ed.); Susan Alexander (Home Furnishings Ed.); James Gill (Librarian); Bruce Hartmann; Heather Price (Senior Director, Circulation Sales)
Parent company (for newspapers): Gannett - USA Today Network

THE LEBANON DEMOCRAT

Street address 1: 115 N.Castle Heights Ave.
Street address 2: Suite 206
Street address city: Lebanon
Street address state: TN
Zip/Postal code: 37087-2306
County: Wilson
Country: USA
Mailing city: LEBANON
Mailing state: TN
Mailing zip: 37087-2306
General Phone: (615) 444-3952
General/National Adv. E-mail: news@lebanondemocrat.com
Display Adv. E-mail: rking@lebanondemocrat.com
Classified Adv. e-mail: rking@lebanondemocrat.com
Editorial e-mail: news@lebanondemocrat.com
Primary Website: www.lebanondemocrat.com
Mthly Avg Views: 750000
Mthly Avg Unique Visitors: 130000
Year Established: 1888
News Services: NEA, AP.
Delivery Methods: Mail`Newsstand`Carrier`Racks
Areas Served - City/County or Portion Thereof, or Zip codes: Lebanon/Wilson County/37087 Mt. Juliet/Wilson County/37121 Watertown/Wilson County/37184
Own Printing Facility?: Y
Commercial printers?: Y

Sat. Circulation Paid: 7236
Audit By: USPS
Audit Date: 01.10.2021
Personnel: Shelagh Mason (Mgr., Accounting); Andy Reed (Sports Ed.); Mark Rodgers (Prod. Mgr.); Richard Knowles (Prodn. Foreman, Pressroom); George Coleman (Publisher); Jared Felkins (Editor); Wes Ritter (Advertising Director)
Parent company (for newspapers): Paxton Media Group

THE DAILY TIMES

Street address 1: 307 E Harper Ave
Street address city: Maryville
Street address state: TN
Zip/Postal code: 37804-5724
County: Blount
Country: USA
Mailing address: 307 E HARPER AVE
Mailing city: MARYVILLE
Mailing state: TN
Mailing zip: 37804-5724
General Phone: (865) 981-1100
Advertising Phone: (865) 981-1150
Editorial Phone: (865) 981-1143
General/National Adv. E-mail: evelyn.sandlin@thedailytimes.com
Display Adv. E-mail: evelyn.sandlin@thedailytimes.com
Classified Adv. e-mail: classifieds@thedailytimes.com
Editorial e-mail: frank.trexler@thedailytimes.com
Primary Website: www.thedailytimes.com
Mthly Avg Views: 750000
Mthly Avg Unique Visitors: 100000
Year Established: 1883
News Services: AP.
Special Editions: Townsend Traveler (Apr); Football Round-up (Aug); Progress (Feb); Father's Day (Jun); Home Improvement (Mar); Brides (May); Car Care (Oct); Fall Home Improvement (Sept).
Special Weekly Sections: Real Estate (Wed); TV Times (Mon); Religious News (Sat); Food (Wed).Weekend Entertainment (Thu)
Syndicated Publications: USA WEEKEND Magazine (S), Relish, Athlon Sports
Delivery Methods: Mail`Newsstand`Carrier`Racks
Areas Served - City/County or Portion Thereof, or Zip codes: Blount County
Own Printing Facility?: N
Commercial printers?: N
Avg Free Circ: 1257
Sat. Circulation Paid: 15861
Sat. Circulation Free: 1257
Sun. Circulation Paid: 17731
Sun. Circulation Free: 74
Audit By: AAM
Audit Date: 31.03.2015
Personnel: Evelyn Sandlin (Adv. Dir.); Bryan Sandmeier (Circulation Director); Frank Trexler (Mng. Ed.); Bob Norris (City/Metro Ed.); Dean Stone (Editorial Page Ed.); Steven Wildsmith (Entertainment/Amusements Ed.); Melanie Tucker (Features Ed.); Richard Dodson (News Ed.); Marcus Fitzsimmons (Sports Ed.); Tim Malone (IT Director); Carl Esposito (Publisher); Amanda Greever (Asst. Mng. Ed.); David Ledford (Prodn. Mgr., Pre Press); Buzz Trexler
Parent company (for newspapers): Adams Publishing Group, LLC

THE COMMERCIAL APPEAL

Street address 1: 495 Union Ave
Street address city: Memphis
Street address state: TN
Zip/Postal code: 38103-3217
County: Shelby
Country: USA
Mailing address: 495 Union Ave.
Mailing city: Memphis
Mailing state: TN
Mailing zip: 38103
General Phone: (901) 529-2211
Advertising Phone: (901) 529-2251
Primary Website: www.commercialappeal.com
Mthly Avg Views: 7500000
Mthly Avg Unique Visitors: 785380
Year Established: 1840
News Services: GNS, AP
Special Editions: Memphis Most (Sept.)
Delivery Methods: Mail`Newsstand`Carrier`Racks
Areas Served - City/County or Portion Thereof, or Zip codes: Memphis TN & Surrounding communities
Own Printing Facility?: N
Commercial printers?: Y
Sat. Circulation Paid: 44773
Sun. Circulation Paid: 74398
Audit By: AAM
Audit Date: 30.09.2018
Personnel: Mike Jung (President); Mark Russell (Editor); Tommy Ewing (Advertising Sales Director); Ken McCloud (Circulation Director); Michelle Thompson (Sales Manager-Territories); Darlene Hardy (Adv. Sales Manager); Ann-Marie Johnson (Advertising Sales Director, Automotive); Jordan Tucker (Client Strategy Manager); Ehren Lowers (Sr. Manager, Newspaper Production); Keith Powers (Consumer Sales Manager); Danny Bowen (Site Director); Glenn Edwards (Executive Administrator)
Parent company (for newspapers): Gannett

THE DAILY NEWS

Street address 1: 193 Jefferson Ave
Street address city: Memphis
Street address state: TN
Zip/Postal code: 38103-2322
County: Shelby
Country: USA
Mailing address: 193 JEFFERSON AVE
Mailing city: MEMPHIS
Mailing state: TN
Mailing zip: 38103-2339
General Phone: (901) 523-1561
Advertising Phone: (901) 528-5283
Editorial Phone: (901) 523-8501
General/National Adv. E-mail: jjenkins@memphisdailynews.com
Display Adv. E-mail: jjenkins@memphisdailynews.com
Classified Adv. e-mail: jjenkins@memphisdailynews.com
Editorial e-mail: releases@memphisdailynews.com
Primary Website: www.memphisdailynews.com
Mthly Avg Views: 300000
Mthly Avg Unique Visitors: 100000
Year Established: 1886
News Services: CNS
Delivery Methods: Mail
Areas Served - City/County or Portion Thereof, or Zip codes: Madison, Tipton, Fayette, Shelby
Avg Free Circ: 2000
Audit By: Sworn/Estimate/Non-Audited
Audit Date: 12.07.2019
Personnel: Don Fancher (Public Notices); Janice Jenkins (Adv. Dir.); Terry Hollahan (Associate Publisher/ Exec. Ed.)
Parent company (for newspapers): The Daily News Publishing Co.

CITIZEN TRIBUNE

Street address 1: 1609 W. 1st North Street
Street address city: Morristown
Street address state: TN
Zip/Postal code: 37814
County: Hamblen
Country: USA
Mailing address: PO BOX 625
Mailing city: MORRISTOWN
Mailing state: TN
Mailing zip: 37815-0625
General Phone: (423) 581-5630
General/National Adv. E-mail: ads@citizentribune.com
Display Adv. E-mail: ads@citizentribune.com
Classified Adv. e-mail: ads@citizentribune.com
Primary Website: www.citizentribune.com
Mthly Avg Views: 500000
Mthly Avg Unique Visitors: 80000
Year Established: 1966
News Services: AP, U.S. Suburban Press Inc..
Special Editions: Christmas, Graduation, 50th Anniversary Edition
Special Weekly Sections: Entertainment, TV (Daily); Best Food (Wed); Church (Fri); Lakeway Living, Entertainment, Business, Sports (Sun)
Syndicated Publications: Relish (Monthly); Parade (S).
Delivery Methods: Mail`Newsstand`Carrier`Racks
Areas Served - City/County or Portion Thereof, or Zip codes: Morristown, Hamblen County, Jefferson County, Cocke County, Greene County, Hawkins County, Hancock County, Grainger County, Claiborne County.
Own Printing Facility?: Y
Commercial printers?: Y
Avg Free Circ: 1692
Sun. Circulation Paid: 20338
Sun. Circulation Free: 1854
Audit By: AAM
Audit Date: 31.03.2019
Personnel: R. Jack Fishman (President); John Gullion (Mng. Ed.); Stan Johnson (Features Ed.); Bob Moore (Health/Medical Ed.); Denise Williams (Travel Ed.); Ricky Ball (Prodn. Mgr.); Mike Walker (Sales/Mktg Dir.); Mike Fishman (Publisher); Phil Hensley (Circ. Dir.)
Parent company (for newspapers): Lakeway Publishers, Inc.

THE DAILY NEWS JOURNAL

Street address 1: 201 E Main St
Street address 2: Ste 400
Street address city: Murfreesboro
Street address state: TN
Zip/Postal code: 37130-3753
County: Rutherford
Country: USA
Mailing address: 201 E MAIN ST STE 400
Mailing city: MURFREESBORO
Mailing state: TN
Mailing zip: 37130-3753
General Phone: (615) 893-5860
Advertising Phone: (615) 893-5860
Editorial Phone: (615) 893-5860
General/National Adv. E-mail: slupton@tennessean.com
Display Adv. E-mail: adcopy@dnj.com
Editorial e-mail: mragland@dnj.com
Primary Website: www.dnj.com
Mthly Avg Views: 2500000
Mthly Avg Unique Visitors: 350000
Year Established: 1849
News Services: AP, U.S. Suburban Press Inc..
Special Editions: R.County Murfreesboro Magazine Readers Choice
Special Weekly Sections: Movie Review (Fri); Job Solutions (Mon); Sports (S); Public Record (Sat); Health & Fitness (Thur); Seniors (Tues); Best Food Day (Wed).
Syndicated Publications: Parade
Delivery Methods: Newsstand`Carrier`Racks
Own Printing Facility?: Y
Commercial printers?: Y
Avg Free Circ: 80
Sat. Circulation Paid: 5025
Sat. Circulation Free: 80
Sun. Circulation Paid: 6954
Sun. Circulation Free: 80
Audit By: AAM
Audit Date: 31.03.2019
Personnel: Tom Kreager (Sports Ed.); Sean Lupton (Nat'l Adv. Mgr.); Mealand Ragland (News Dir.)
Parent company (for newspapers): Gannett

THE TENNESSEAN

Street address 1: 1100 Broadway
Street address city: Nashville
Street address state: TN
Zip/Postal code: 37203-3116
County: Davidson
Country: USA
General Phone: (615) 259-8000
Advertising Phone: (615) 259-8818
Editorial Phone: (615) 259-8095
General/National Adv. E-mail: rateinfo@tennessean.com
Display Adv. E-mail: adv@tennessean.com
Classified Adv. e-mail: slupton@tennessean.com
Editorial e-mail: manastasi@gannett.com
Primary Website: www.tennessean.com
Mthly Avg Views: 20000000
Mthly Avg Unique Visitors: 4000000
Year Established: 1812
News Services: NYT, LAT-WP, MCT, SHNS, GNS.
Special Editions: Football(sept), Hockey(sept), FYI Magazine (Sept), Toast of Music City (July)
Special Weekly Sections: Best Food, Living, Food (Mon); Living, Health (Tue); Shopping (Wed); Metro Mix (Thur); Movies, Living, Style (Fri); Religion (Sat); Travel, Life, Home, Sports, Business, Comics (Sun)
Syndicated Publications: PARADE Magazine
Delivery Methods: Mail`Newsstand`Carrier`Racks
Areas Served - City/County or Portion Thereof, or Zip codes: Middle Tennessee
Own Printing Facility?: Y
Commercial printers?: Y
Sat. Circulation Paid: 59725
Sun. Circulation Paid: 95613
Audit By: AAM
Audit Date: 30.09.2018
Personnel: Bob Engel (Regional Finance Director); Thom Gregory (Gen. Mgr. GPS Production Nashville); Laura Hollingsworth (Pres./Pub.); Jay Winkler (Vice Pres., Circ.); Lance Williams (Consumer Exper. Dir.); Maria De Varenne (Director of News & Editor); Helen Jacobs (Sr. HR Business Partner); Sean Lupton (Manager, National/Major Accounts); Duane Gang (Content Strategist); Daphne Lowell; Juli Thanki (Music Reporter); Shelley Mays (Photographer); Shelley Davis (Director of Sales); ???? ????; Dan Douglas (Regional Sales Manager); Kimberly Hood (Key Accounts Mgr.); John Ward (VP, Sales); Peter Cooper (Music Writer); Frank Sutherland; David Anesta (Consumer Experience Director); Peter Antone
Parent company (for newspapers): Gannett

THE OAK RIDGER

Street address 1: 785 Oak Ridge Tpke
Street address city: Oak Ridge
Street address state: TN
Zip/Postal code: 37830-7076
County: Anderson
Country: USA
Mailing address: 575 OAK RIDGE TPKE STE 100
Mailing city: OAK RIDGE
Mailing state: TN
Mailing zip: 37830-7173
General Phone: (865) 482-1021
Advertising Phone: (865) 482-7355
Editorial Phone: (865) 220-5502
General/National Adv. E-mail: advertising@oakridger.com
Display Adv. E-mail: advertising@oakridger.com
Classified Adv. e-mail: advertising@oakridger.com
Editorial e-mail: editor@oakridger.com
Primary Website: www.oakridger.com
Year Established: 1949
News Services: AP.
Special Editions: Women in Business (Apr); Football (Aug); Greetings (Dec); Progress (Feb); Bride (Jan); Bride (Jun); Gardening (Mar); Outdoor (May); Cooking (Oct); Silver Salute (Sept).
Special Weekly Sections: Weekend Sports, Local (Mon); Business, American Profile (Tue); Best Food, Health (Wed); Garden, Weekend Entertainment (Thur); Real Estate, Weddings, Religion (Fri); Daily TV (Mon-Fri)
Syndicated Publications: USA WEEKEND Magazine (Fri); Relish (Monthly); American Profile (Weekly).
Audit By: Sworn/Estimate/Non-Audited
Audit Date: 12.07.2019
Personnel: Carol Skyberg (Major Acct.); Steve Traud (Circ. Dir.); Darrell G. Richardson (Publisher); Tank Johnston (News Ed.); Scott Fraker (Photographer)
Parent company (for newspapers): Gannett; CherryRoad Media

THE PARIS POST-INTELLIGENCER

Street address 1: 205 N. Market St
Street address city: Paris
Street address state: TN
Zip/Postal code: 38242
County: Henry
Country: USA
Mailing address: PO BOX 310
Mailing city: PARIS
Mailing state: TN
Mailing zip: 38242-0310
General Phone: (731) 642-1162
General/National Adv. E-mail: news@parispi.net
Display Adv. E-mail: advertising@parispi.net
Classified Adv. e-mail: advertising@parispi.net
Editorial e-mail: mwilliams@parispi.net
Primary Website: www.parispi.net
Mthly Avg Views: 100000
Mthly Avg Unique Visitors: 58250
Year Established: 1866
News Services: NEA, KFS, Universal Press.
Special Editions: Pets (Jan); Future Farmers (Feb); Home/lawn/garden (Mar); Cooking school (Mar); Tourism (Apr); Paris in the Spring (Apr); Graduation (May); Tennessee River Jam (May); Readers' Choice (Jul); Football (Aug); Fair (Aug); Business Anniversary (Sep); 4-H (Oct); Factbook (Oct); Basketball (Nov); Holiday Gifts (Nov); Last-minute gifts (Dec); Year in review (Dec)
Special Weekly Sections: Best Food, Gardening, Lifestyles, Opinions, Farm, Business, Outdoors, Sports
Delivery Methods: Mail`Carrier`Racks
Areas Served - City/County or Portion Thereof, or Zip codes: Henry County, TN
Own Printing Facility?: N

Commercial printers?: N
Audit By: Sworn/Estimate/Non-Audited
Audit Date: 01.10.2024
Personnel: Michael Williams (Editor); Michael Williams (Pub./Ed.); Tim Forrest (Circ. Mgr.); Glenn Tanner (News Ed.); Steve McCadams (Outdoors Ed.); Tommy Priddy (Sports Ed.); Jimmy Williams (Prodn. Supt.); Daniel Williams (Office Mgr.); Adam Barker (Advertising sales)
Parent company (for newspapers): Bill Williams (Paris Publishing Co.); Paris Publishing Co., Inc.

THE MOUNTAIN PRESS

Street address 1: 119 River Bend Dr
Street address city: Sevierville
Street address state: TN
Zip/Postal code: 37876-1943
County: Sevier
Country: USA
General Phone: (865) 428-0746
Advertising Phone: (865) 428-0748
Editorial Phone: (865) 428-0748
General/National Adv. E-mail: editor@themountainpress.com
Display Adv. E-mail: mrobertson@themountainpress.com
Classified Adv. e-mail: mrobertson@themountainpress.com
Editorial e-mail: editor@themountainpress.com
Primary Website: www.themountainpress.com
Mthly Avg Views: 225325
Mthly Avg Unique Visitors: 49285
Year Established: 1882
News Services: AP.
Special Editions: Football (Aug); Medical Directory (Mar), Eat Local (Jan); Newcomer's Guide (Jul); Graduation (May); Reader's Choice (Oct); Breast Cancer Awareness (Oct.).
Delivery Methods: Mail`Newsstand`Carrier`Racks
Areas Served - City/County or Portion Thereof, or Zip codes: Sevier County
Own Printing Facility?: Y
Commercial printers?: Y
Avg Free Circ: 15300
Sat. Circulation Paid: 5077
Sun. Circulation Paid: 5463
Audit By: Sworn/Estimate/Non-Audited
Audit Date: 09.09.2023
Personnel: Jana M. Thomasson (Pub.); Tammy McGaha (Circulation Sales Manager); Joi Whaley (Adv. Dir.); Robertson Michelle (Advertising Director); Cindy Simpson (Editor); R. Thomas McCarter (Production Dir.); Chadd Cripe; Rhonda Bietner (Editor)
Parent company (for newspapers): Paxton Media Group

SHELBYVILLE TIMES-GAZETTE

Street address 1: 323 E Depot St
Street address city: Shelbyville
Street address state: TN
Zip/Postal code: 37160-4027
County: Bedford
Country: USA
Mailing address: PO Box 380
Mailing city: Shelbyville
Mailing state: TN
Mailing zip: 37162-0380
General Phone: (931) 684-1200
Editorial Phone: (931) 684-1200 ext. 218
General/National Adv. E-mail: ssmith@t-g.com
Display Adv. E-mail: ssmith@t-g.com
Classified Adv. e-mail: classified@t-g.com
Editorial e-mail: sfowler@t-g.com
Primary Website: www.t-g.com
Year Established: 1948
News Services: AP, NEA,
Special Editions: Private Property (Apr); Back-to-School (Aug); Fashion (Fall); Jaycees (Jan); Dairy (Jun); Farm (Mar); Bride (May); Sports (Monthly); Gift Guide (Nov).
Special Weekly Sections: American Profile, Horse,Farm, Questions Answered (Tue); Business (Wed); Entertainment (Thur); Faith, Garden, Sports (Fri); Life, Leisure, Foods, Family, Parenting, TV, Comics (Sun); TV (Tue-Fri,Sun)
Syndicated Publications: Relish (Monthly); Parade (S); American Profile (Weekly).
Delivery Methods: Mail`Newsstand`Carrier`Racks
Areas Served - City/County or Portion Thereof, or Zip codes: 37060
Own Printing Facility?: Y
Commercial printers?: Y
Sun. Circulation Paid: 6566
Audit By: Sworn/Estimate/Non-Audited
Audit Date: 12.07.2019
Personnel: John I. Carney (Ed.); David Melson (Copy Ed.); Chris Siers (Sports Ed.); Diandra Womble (Adv. Dir.); Becky McBee (Bus. Mgr.)
Parent company (for newspapers): Rust Communications

THE MESSENGER

Street address 1: 613 E Jackson St
Street address city: Union City
Street address state: TN
Zip/Postal code: 38261-5239
County: Obion
Country: USA
Mailing address: PO BOX 430
Mailing city: UNION CITY
Mailing state: TN
Mailing zip: 38281-0430
General Phone: (731) 885-0744
General/National Adv. E-mail: advertising@ucmessenger.com
Display Adv. E-mail: advertising@ucmessenger.com
Classified Adv. e-mail: ucclass@ucmessenger.com
Editorial e-mail: dcritch@ucmessenger.com
Primary Website: www.nwtntoday.com
News Services: AP.
Special Weekly Sections: Business (Mon); Church (Thur); Farm (Tues); Food (Wed).
Delivery Methods: Mail`Newsstand`Carrier`Racks
Own Printing Facility?: Y
Commercial printers?: Y
Audit By: Sworn/Estimate/Non-Audited
Audit Date: 12.07.2019
Personnel: David Critchlow (Pres./Pub.); F. Scott Critchlow (Vice Pres./Office Mgr.); Penelia Davis (Bus. Mgr.); Glenda Langford (Adv. Mgr., Classified); Gloria Chesteen (Adv. Mgr., Retail); Donna Ryder (Farm Ed.); Mike Hutchens (Sports Ed.); Darlene Hayes (Women's Ed.); Jeremy Leckey (Online Mgr.); Rob Smith (Prodn. Mgr., Pressroom); John Travatham (Prodn. Mgr., Mailroom/Post Press); David Fuzzell (Prodn. Mgr., Pre Press)
Parent company (for newspapers): Paxton Media Group

TEXAS

ABILENE REPORTER-NEWS

Street address 1: 101 Cypress Street
Street address city: Abilene
Street address state: TX
Zip/Postal code: 79601
County: Taylor
Country: USA
Mailing address: PO BOX 30
Mailing city: ABILENE
Mailing state: TX
Mailing zip: 79604-0030
General Phone: (325) 673-4271
Advertising Phone: (325) 670-5280
Editorial Phone: (325) 676-6764
General/National Adv. E-mail: advertising@reporternews.com
Display Adv. E-mail: advertising@reporternews.com
Classified Adv. e-mail: classifieds@reporternews.com
Editorial e-mail: doug.williamson@reporternews.com
Primary Website: www.reporternews.com
Mthly Avg Views: 1206959
Mthly Avg Unique Visitors: 277311
Year Established: 1881
News Services: AP, NYT, SHNS.
Special Editions: Kickoff (Aug); Big Country Farm and Ranch Show (Feb); Reader's Choice Awards (Jul); Ft. Griffin Fandangle (Jun); Rattlesnake Round-up (Mar); Western Heritage Classic (May); City Sidewalks (Nov); Health Source Directory (July)
Special Weekly Sections: TMC (Wed); Leisure Life (Thur); Spiritual (Fri); Family, Real Estate, Home (Sat); Travel, TV, Auto (Sun); News, Life, Business, Sports, Classified, Local (Daily)
Syndicated Publications: Abilene Magazine (Other); Parade (S).
Delivery Methods: Mail`Newsstand`Carrier`Racks
Own Printing Facility?: Y
Commercial printers?: Y
Avg Free Circ: 146
Sat. Circulation Paid: 10133
Sat. Circulation Free: 41
Sun. Circulation Paid: 10133
Sun. Circulation Free: 41
Audit By: AAM
Audit Date: 31.03.2019
Personnel: Carla Draper (CFO); David Rowe (Circ. Dir.); Barton Cromeens (Ed.); Sidney Levesque (Editorial Page Ed.); Dann Reagan (Online Dir.); Mike Hall (Prodn. Dir., Opns.); Christian Wells (Prodn. Mgr.); Scott Pentecost (Prodn. Mgr., Mailroom (Nights)); David Nunez (Prodn. Mgr., Pressroom); Doug Williamson (Ed.); Dave Hedge (Ad. Director); David J. Hedges (Pub./VP, Sales & Mktg); Tim Ritter (Circ. Sales Dir.)
Parent company (for newspapers): Gannett; Journal Media Group

AMARILLO GLOBE-NEWS

Street address 1: 900 S. Harrison Street
Street address city: Amarillo
Street address state: TX
Zip/Postal code: 79101
County: Potter
Country: USA
Mailing address: PO BOX 2091
Mailing city: AMARILLO
Mailing state: TX
Mailing zip: 79166-0001
General Phone: (806) 376-4488
Advertising Phone: (806) 345-3231
Editorial Phone: (806) 345-3358
General/National Adv. E-mail: cindy.brown@amarillo.com
Display Adv. E-mail: cindy.brown@amarillo.com
Classified Adv. e-mail: cindy.ledesma@amarillo.com
Editorial e-mail: michele.mcaffrey@amarillo.com
Primary Website: www.amarillo.com
Mthly Avg Views: 4500000
Mthly Avg Unique Visitors: 480000
Year Established: 1909
News Services: AP, MCT, LAT-WP, DF.
Special Editions: Best of Amarillo, Discover Amarillo, Pigskin Preview
Special Weekly Sections: Best Food Day (Wed); Religion (Sat); Farm, Oil, Rea Estate, Business, Arts, Entertainment (Sun)
Syndicated Publications: Amarillo Magazine (Monthly); Parade (S); Relish (Monthly); Athlon (Monthly)
Delivery Methods: Mail`Newsstand`Carrier`Racks
Areas Served - City/County or Portion Thereof, or Zip codes: 79101 and beyond
Avg Free Circ: 2058
Sat. Circulation Paid: 10127
Sat. Circulation Free: 2058
Sun. Circulation Paid: 12819
Sun. Circulation Free: 1910
Audit By: AAM
Audit Date: 31.03.2019
Personnel: Robert Granfeldt (Pub.); Doug Hensley (Reg. Associate Ed./Dir. of Commentary); Jill Nevels-Haun (Exec. Ed.); Terry Parker (Accountant)
Parent company (for newspapers): Gannett; CherryRoad Media

ATHENS DAILY REVIEW

Street address 1: 201 S Prairieville St
Street address city: Athens
Street address state: TX
Zip/Postal code: 75751-2541
County: Henderson
Country: USA
Mailing address: PO BOX 32
Mailing city: ATHENS
Mailing state: TX
Mailing zip: 75751-0032
General Phone: (903) 675-5626
Advertising Phone: (903) 675-5626
Editorial Phone: (903) 675-5626
General/National Adv. E-mail: publisher@athensreview.com
Display Adv. E-mail: publisher@athensreview.com
Classified Adv. e-mail: publisher@athensreview.com
Editorial e-mail: editor@athensreview.com
Primary Website: www.athensreview.com
Year Established: 1901
News Services: AP.
Special Editions: Feb: Bridal March: Business Card Dir., Livestock Show Edition May: Graduation Edition, Backyard Vacations Aug: Football Preview Sept: Business Card Directory, How-to-Guide Oct: Outdoor Guide, Recipe Guide Nov: Veterans, Medical Directory
Special Weekly Sections: Best Food Days (Sat/Tue);
Syndicated Publications: Greater Athens Magazine - Monthly
Delivery Methods: Mail`Racks
Areas Served - City/County or Portion Thereof, or Zip codes: 75751,,75752, 75124, 75143, 75148, 75147, 75156, 75163, 75756, 75778, 75770,
Sun. Circulation Paid: 4600
Audit By: Sworn/Estimate/Non-Audited
Audit Date: 01.10.2023
Personnel: Lange Svehlak (Pub.); Andi Green (Nat'lAdv. Dir.); Ginger McDaniel (Circ. Mgr.); Jayson Larson (Ed.); Benny Rogers (Sports Ed.); Jeff Riggs (Ed.); Nita Sawicki (Classified Adv. Mgr.)
Parent company (for newspapers): CNHI, LLC; CNHI, LLC

AUSTIN AMERICAN-STATESMAN

Street address 1: 305 S. Congress Avenue
Street address city: Austin
Street address state: TX
Zip/Postal code: 78704
County: Travis
Country: USA
Mailing address: PO BOX 670
Mailing city: AUSTIN
Mailing state: TX
Mailing zip: 78767-0670
General Phone: (512) 445-3500
Advertising Phone: (512) 445-3742
Editorial Phone: (512) 445-3851
General/National Adv. E-mail: national@statesman.com
Display Adv. E-mail: shary.garza@coxinc.com
Classified Adv. e-mail: shary.garza@coxinc.com
Editorial e-mail: news@statesman.com
Primary Website: www.statesman.com
Mthly Avg Unique Visitors: 2256161
Year Established: 1871
News Services: AP, Cox News Service, MCT, LAT-WP, NNS, NYT, TMS.
Special Editions: High School & College Football (Aug); Gift Guide (Dec); Healthcare (Jan); This is Austin (Jul); SXSW (Mar); Diversity (Nov); Pro Football Preview (Oct); Austin City Limits Music Festival (Sept).
Special Weekly Sections: Food (Wed); Technology (Mon);Entertainment, Auto (Thur); Entertainment, Health (Fri); Auto, Weekly, Real Estate (Sun); Business, Living, Arts (Daily)
Syndicated Publications: Parade (S); Vista (Sat).
Delivery Methods: Carrier`Racks
Areas Served - City/County or Portion Thereof, or Zip codes: All of Central Texas
Sat. Circulation Paid: 80879
Sun. Circulation Paid: 111234
Audit By: AAM
Audit Date: 31.12.2017
Personnel: Eddie Burns (Vice Pres./CFO); Harry Davis (Vice Pres., Fulfillment/Group Lead); Jana Dobson (Circ. Dir.); Arnold Garcia (Editorial Page Ed.); Zach Ryall (Photo Dir.); Craig Wohlfort (Controller); Colleen Brewer (Adv. Dir.); Patrick E. Dorsey (Pub.); John Bridges (Exec. Ed.); Bill Church (Sr. Vice Pres., E.I.C.)
Parent company (for newspapers): CherryRoad Media; Gannett

THE BAYTOWN SUN

Street address 1: 1301 Memorial Drive
Street address city: Baytown
Street address state: TX
Zip/Postal code: 77520
County: Harris
Country: USA
Mailing address: PO BOX 90
Mailing city: BAYTOWN
Mailing state: TX
Mailing zip: 77522-0090
General Phone: (281) 422-8302
Advertising Phone: (281) 425-8036
Editorial Phone: (281) 425-8013
General/National Adv. E-mail: carol.skewes@baytownsun.com
Display Adv. E-mail: carol.skewes@baytownsun.com
Classified Adv. e-mail: jessica.rodriguez@baytownsun.com
Editorial e-mail: janie.gray@baytownsun.com
Primary Website: www.baytownsun.com
Year Established: 1922
News Services: AP, NEA, CNS, TMS.
Special Editions: Forecast (Feb); Back-to-School (Jul); Coastal Views (Jun); Forecast (Mar); Outdoors (Sept).

Special Weekly Sections: Arts & Entertainment (Fri); TV Guide (S); Religious (Sat); Business (Tues); Best Food Days (Wed).
Syndicated Publications: USA WEEKEND Magazine (S); American Profile (Weekly).
Delivery Methods: Mail`Newsstand`Carrier`Racks
Own Printing Facility?: Y
Commercial printers?: N
Avg Free Circ: 2016
Sun. Circulation Paid: 3746
Sun. Circulation Free: 1912
Audit By: AAM
Audit Date: 31.03.2019
Personnel: Joshua Hart (Circ. Mgr.); Sandy Denson (Business Manager/HR); Janie Gray (Ed. / Pub.); Gordon Gallatin (Adv. Mgr.); David Bloom (Mng. Ed.); Dave Rogers (Sports Ed.)
Parent company (for newspapers): Southern Newspapers Inc.

THE BEAUMONT ENTERPRISE

Street address 1: 380 Main St
Street address city: Beaumont
Street address state: TX
Zip/Postal code: 77701-2331
County: Jefferson
Country: USA
Mailing address: PO BOX 3071
Mailing city: BEAUMONT
Mailing state: TX
Mailing zip: 77704-3071
General Phone: (409) 880-0773
Advertising Phone: (409) 838-2819
Editorial Phone: (409) 838-2802
General/National Adv. E-mail: dvalentine@beaumontenterprise.com
Display Adv. E-mail: dvalentine@beaumontenterprise.com
Classified Adv. e-mail: chatcher@hearstnp.com
Editorial e-mail: tkelly@hearstnp.com
Primary Website: www.beaumontenterprise.com
Mthly Avg Views: 6000000
Mthly Avg Unique Visitors: 250000
Year Established: 1880
News Services: HN, NYT, AP.
Special Editions: Football Glossy Magazine(Aug); Readers Choice awards (April), Everything Book (Oct)
Special Weekly Sections: Health Plus (Wed.), CAT5-arts/entertainment (Thurs.), Food (Tues.), Auto (Fri.), Real Estate (Sunday), extra!(Sunday), Hardin County News (Wed.)Jasper News Boy (Wed.)
Delivery Methods: Mail`Newsstand`Carrier`Racks
Areas Served - City/County or Portion Thereof, or Zip codes: Beaumont/Port Arthur (Jefferson County) Orange/Vidor (Orange County) Lumberton (Hardin County) Jasper (Jasper County)
Own Printing Facility?: Y
Commercial printers?: N
Avg Free Circ: 169
Sat. Circulation Paid: 10417
Sat. Circulation Free: 169
Sun. Circulation Paid: 15054
Sun. Circulation Free: 179
Audit By: AAM
Audit Date: 30.06.2018
Personnel: Jeffrey Reedy (Circ. Dir., Opns.); Timothy M. Kelly (Ed.); Tom Taschinger (Editorial Page Ed.); Ashley Sanders (Managing Editor); Freddie Campbell (Mgmt. Info Servs. Mgr.); Mark Adkins (Publisher); Paul Banister (Circulation Director); Craig Hatcher (Chief Revenue Officer); Donna Valentine (Advertising Director)
Parent company (for newspapers): Hearst Communications, Inc.

BIG SPRING HERALD

Street address 1: PO Box 1431
Street address city: Big Spring
Street address state: TX
Zip/Postal code: 79721-1431
County: Howard
Country: USA
Mailing address: PO BOX 1431
Mailing city: BIG SPRING
Mailing state: TX
Mailing zip: 79721-1431
General Phone: (432) 263-7331
General/National Adv. E-mail: advertising@bigspringherald.com
Display Adv. E-mail: advertising@bigspringherald.com
Classified Adv. e-mail: advertising@bigspringherald.com
Editorial e-mail: editor@bigspringherald.com
Primary Website: www.bigspringherald.com
Mthly Avg Views: 700000
Year Established: 1904
News Services: AP.
Special Editions: Football (Aug); Year In Review (Jan); Community Guide (Jul); Rodeo (Jun); Progress (Mar); Christmas Shopping Guide (Nov).
Special Weekly Sections: Health, Medical (Mon); Food, Entertainment (Wed); Youth (Tue); Church, Civic (Fri); Business, TV (Sun)
Syndicated Publications: TV-Leisure (newsprint) (Other); American Profile (S).
Delivery Methods: Mail`Newsstand`Carrier`Racks
Areas Served - City/County or Portion Thereof, or Zip codes: 79720 plus
Own Printing Facility?: Y
Commercial printers?: Y
Sun. Circulation Paid: 5364
Audit By: Sworn/Estimate/Non-Audited
Audit Date: 12.07.2019
Personnel: Glenn Stifflemire (Pub.); Rachael Martinez (Bookkeeper); Rick Nunez (Adv. Mgr., Retail); Robert Smith (Circ. Mgr.); Bill McClellan (News Ed.); Tony Hernandez (Prodn. Mgr.)
Parent company (for newspapers): Horizon Publications Inc.

BORGER NEWS-HERALD

Street address 1: 207 S Main St
Street address city: Borger
Street address state: TX
Zip/Postal code: 79007-4715
County: Hutchinson
Country: USA
Mailing address: PO BOX 5130
Mailing city: BORGER
Mailing state: TX
Mailing zip: 79008-5130
General Phone: (806) 273-5611
Advertising Phone: (806) 273-2552
Editorial Phone: (806) 273-2552
General/National Adv. E-mail: publisher@borgernewsherald.com
Display Adv. E-mail: publisher@borgernewsherald.com
Classified Adv. e-mail: classifieds@borgernewsherald.com
Editorial e-mail: editor@borgernewsherald.com
Primary Website: www.borgernewsherald.com
Mthly Avg Views: 40000
Year Established: 1926
News Services: AP
Special Editions: County Livestock Show (Feb.) Tourism Guide (Apr.) Graduate (May) Best of the Best (July) HOPE Gala (Aug.) Patriots (Sep.) Education (Sep.) Cancer Awareness (Oct.) Veteran's Day (Nov.) Holiday Shopping Guide (Dec.)
Special Weekly Sections: Church (Fri); TV (Sun); Business (Daily)
Syndicated Publications: Relish (Monthly); TV tab (S); American Profile (Bi-Weekly).
Delivery Methods: Mail`Newsstand`Carrier`Racks
Areas Served - City/County or Portion Thereof, or Zip codes: Hutchinson County, TX.
Own Printing Facility?: Y
Commercial printers?: Y
Sun. Circulation Paid: 3000
Audit By: Sworn/Estimate/Non-Audited
Audit Date: 12.07.2019
Personnel: Rick Nunez (Publisher); Tom Hinde (Publisher)
Parent company (for newspapers): Horizon Publications Inc.

BRENHAM BANNER-PRESS

Street address 1: 2430 S Chappell Hill St
Street address city: Brenham
Street address state: TX
Zip/Postal code: 77833-6098
County: Washington
Country: USA
Mailing address: PO BOX 585
Mailing city: BRENHAM
Mailing state: TX
Mailing zip: 77834-0585
General Phone: (979) 836-7956
Advertising Phone: (979) 836-7956
General/National Adv. E-mail: mmueck@brenhambanner.com
Display Adv. E-mail: retail@brenhambanner.com
Classified Adv. e-mail: classified@brenhambanner.com
Editorial e-mail: edit@brenhambanner.com
Primary Website: www.brenhambanner.com
Mthly Avg Views: 1311312
Mthly Avg Unique Visitors: 483706
Year Established: 1866
News Services: AP, NEA.
Special Editions: Visitor's Guide (Apr); Back-to-School (Aug); Gift Guide (Dec); Progress (Jan); Real Estate Guide (Mar); Graduation (May); Cookbook (Nov); Businesswomen (Oct); Visitor's Guide (Sept); Spring Sports Recap (June); Dining Guide (June)
Special Weekly Sections: Food (Tue); Church (Fri);
Syndicated Publications: Relish (Monthly); TV Guide/Scene (S)
Delivery Methods: Mail`Newsstand`Carrier`Racks
Areas Served - City/County or Portion Thereof, or Zip codes: Brenham, Burton, Washington, Chappell Hill, Round Top, Carmine
Own Printing Facility?: Y
Commercial printers?: Y
Avg Free Circ: 295
Sun. Circulation Paid: 5860
Sun. Circulation Free: 295
Audit By: CVC
Audit Date: 30.06.2015
Personnel: Jay Strasner (Ed. & Pub.); Annell Meyer (Office Mgr.); Arthur Hahn (Mng. Ed.); Natalie Frels (News Ed.); Joe Alberico (Sports Ed.)
Parent company (for newspapers): Hartman Newspapers LP

THE BROWNSVILLE HERALD

Street address 1: 1135 E Van Buren St
Street address city: Brownsville
Street address state: TX
Zip/Postal code: 78520-7055
County: Cameron
Country: USA
Mailing address: 1135 E VAN BUREN ST
Mailing city: BROWNSVILLE
Mailing state: TX
Mailing zip: 78520-7099
General Phone: (956) 542-4301
Advertising Phone: (956) 982-6651
Editorial Phone: (956) 982-6628
General/National Adv. E-mail: lmedrano@brownsvilleherald.com
Display Adv. E-mail: lmedrano@brownsvilleherald.com
Classified Adv. e-mail: lmedrano@brownsvilleherald.com
Editorial e-mail: rhenry@brownsvilleherald.com
Primary Website: www.brownsvilleherald.com
News Services: AP, MCT.
Special Editions: Mother's Day (Apr); Back-to-School (Aug); Christmas Gift Guide (Dec); Golden Years (Feb); Health & Fitness (Jan); Today's Women (Jul); Home & Garden (Mar); Spring Car Care (May); Welcome Winter Texans (Nov); National Car Care (Oct); Fall Fashion (Sept).
Special Weekly Sections: El Extra (Fri); Business (S); Education Extra (Wed).
Syndicated Publications: Parade (S).
Delivery Methods: Newsstand`Carrier`Racks
Sat. Circulation Paid: 7025
Sun. Circulation Paid: 9514
Audit By: AAM
Audit Date: 31.03.2017
Personnel: Frank Escobedo (Pub.); Melva Juarez (Business Manager); Linda Medrano (Advertising Director); Ryan Henry (Editor); Gonzalez Abe (Circulation Director); Odie Carden (IT Systems Manager); Dr. Sandy McGehee (Education Services Director)
Parent company (for newspapers): AIM Media Texas

THE EAGLE

Street address 1: 1729 Briarcrest Dr
Street address city: Bryan
Street address state: TX
Zip/Postal code: 77802-2712
County: Brazos
Country: USA
Mailing address: PO BOX 3000
Mailing city: BRYAN
Mailing state: TX
Mailing zip: 77805-3000
General Phone: (979) 776-4444
Advertising Phone: (979) 776-4444 ext. 300
Editorial Phone: (979) 776-4444 ext. 401
General/National Adv. E-mail: news@theeagle.com
Display Adv. E-mail: advertising@theeagle.com
Editorial e-mail: news@theeagle.com
Primary Website: www.theeagle.com
Mthly Avg Views: 2531143
Mthly Avg Unique Visitors: 504463
Year Established: 1889
News Services: AP.
Special Editions: Back-to-School (Aug); Bridal Showcase (Jan); Senior Adults (Jun); Lawn & Garden (Mar); Holiday on the Brazos (Nov); Home Builders (Oct).
Special Weekly Sections: Business (S); Religion Pages (Sat); Entertainment (Thur); Best Food Days (Wed).
Syndicated Publications: Parade (S); American Profile (Weekly); Athlon (Weekly); Relish (M (monthly)
Delivery Methods: Mail`Newsstand`Carrier`Racks
Areas Served - City/County or Portion Thereof, or Zip codes: 77845, 77801, 77802, 77803, 77807, 77808, 77850,77840, 77837, 77856, 77868, 77836, 77864, 77871
Own Printing Facility?: Y
Commercial printers?: Y
Avg Free Circ: 2163
Sat. Circulation Paid: 10785
Sat. Circulation Free: 2163
Sun. Circulation Paid: 12426
Sun. Circulation Free: 1724
Audit By: AAM
Audit Date: 31.03.2018
Personnel: Crystal Dupre (Pub.); Rod Armstrong (Finance Dir.); Greg Parker (Circ. Dir.); Wayne Nedbalek (Dir. Mail Mgr.); Kelly Brown (Exec. Ed.); Robert C. Borden (Ed. Page Ed.); Darren Benson (News Ed.); Robert Cessna (Sports Ed.); Ben Tedrick (Mgmt. Info Servs. Mgr.); Mark Manning (Prod. Dir.); Donald Crawford (Mailroom Mgr.); Tammy Zimmerman (Pre Press Mgr.)
Parent company (for newspapers): BH Media Group; Lee Enterprises, Incorporated

CLEBURNE TIMES-REVIEW

Street address 1: 108 S Anglin St
Street address city: Cleburne
Street address state: TX
Zip/Postal code: 76031-5602
County: Johnson
Country: USA
Mailing address: 108 S ANGLIN ST
Mailing city: CLEBURNE
Mailing state: TX
Mailing zip: 76031-5602
General Phone: 817-645-2441
Advertising Phone: (817)645-2441
Editorial Phone: (817)645-2441
General/National Adv. E-mail: ralexander@trcle.com
Display Adv. E-mail: ralexander@trcle.com
Classified Adv. e-mail: tslade@trele.com
Editorial e-mail: dgosser@trcle.com
Primary Website: www.cleburnetimesreview.com
Mthly Avg Views: 350000
Mthly Avg Unique Visitors: 82000
Year Established: 1904
News Services: AP.
Special Editions: Football (Aug); Whistle Stop Christmas (Dec); Chamber of Commerce (monthly); Cleburne This Is Texas (Jan)
Special Weekly Sections: Best Food Days (T)
Syndicated Publications: Relish (Monthly); USA WEEKEND Magazine (S); American Profile (Weekly).
Delivery Methods: Mail`Newsstand`Racks
Areas Served - City/County or Portion Thereof, or Zip codes: 76031 76033 76009 76028 76058 76059 76044 76050 76093 76036
Own Printing Facility?: N
Commercial printers?: N
Sat. Circulation Paid: 2700
Audit By: Sworn/Estimate/Non-Audited
Audit Date: 12.07.2019
Personnel: Lisa Chappell (Pub.); Dale Gosser (Managing Ed.); Monica Faram (News Ed.); A.J. Crisp (Sports Ed.); Renae Alexander (Adv. Mgr.); Toscha Vaughan (Circ.)
Parent company (for newspapers): CNHI, LLC; CNHI, LLC

THE FACTS

Street address 1: 720 S Main St
Street address city: Clute
Street address state: TX
Zip/Postal code: 77531-5411
County: Brazoria

Country: USA
Mailing address: PO BOX 549
Mailing city: CLUTE
Mailing state: TX
Mailing zip: 77531-0549
General Phone: (979) 265-7411
Advertising Phone: (979)265-7411
Editorial Phone: (979)265-7411
General/National Adv. E-mail: cindy.cornette@thefacts.com
Display Adv. E-mail: cindy.cornette@thefacts.com
Classified Adv. e-mail: classifieds@thefacts.com
Editorial e-mail: michael.morris@thefacts.com
Primary Website: www.thefacts.com
Mthly Avg Views: 2517502
Mthly Avg Unique Visitors: 718935
Year Established: 1913
News Services: AP, NEA.
Special Editions: Fishing (Apr); Fashion (Aug); Chamber of Commerce (Feb); Bridal (Jan); Profile/Progress (Jul); Fishing Fiesta (Jun); Spring Fashion (Mar); Brazoria County Fair (Oct); Football (Sept).
Special Weekly Sections: Best Food Day (Wed); Entertainment (Fri); Religion (Sat); Lifestyle (Wed/Sun); Outdoor (Thur/Sun); Business, Sports (Daily)
Syndicated Publications: USA WEEKEND Magazine (S).
Delivery Methods: Mail`Newsstand`Carrier`Racks
Own Printing Facility?: Y
Commercial printers?: Y
Avg Free Circ: 1674
Sat. Circulation Paid: 12457
Sat. Circulation Free: 1674
Sun. Circulation Paid: 13498
Sun. Circulation Free: 2201
Audit By: AAM
Audit Date: 30.03.2015
Personnel: Bill Cornwell (Pub./Ed.); Judy Starnes (Gen. Mgr.); Cindy Cornette (Adv. Dir.); Yvonne Mintz (Managing Ed.); Waylon Smart (Info Servs./Online Mgr.); Frankie Ramirez (Prodn. Mgr.); Glenn Blount (Prodn. Mgr., Mailroom); Gloria Ashworth (Business Mgr.); Beth Swintek (Circ. Mgr.)
Parent company (for newspapers): Southern Newspapers Inc.

THE COURIER OF MONTGOMERY COUNTY

Street address 1: 100 Avenue A
Street address city: Conroe
Street address state: TX
Zip/Postal code: 77301-2946
County: Montgomery
Country: USA
Mailing address: 100 AVENUE A
Mailing city: CONROE
Mailing state: TX
Mailing zip: 77301-2946
General Phone: (281) 378-1950
Advertising Phone: (281) 378-1950
Editorial Phone: (281) 378-1950
General/National Adv. E-mail: bmiller-fergerson@hcnonline.com
Display Adv. E-mail: tlegg@hcnonline.com
Classified Adv. e-mail: ejames@hcnonline.com
Editorial e-mail: adubois@hcnonline.com
Primary Website: www.yourconroenews.com
Mthly Avg Views: 2700000
Mthly Avg Unique Visitors: 900000
Year Established: 1892
News Services: U.S. Suburban Press Inc., AP.
Special Editions: Back-to-School (Aug); Last Minute Gifts (Dec); Progress (Feb); Bridal (Jan); Montgomery County Magazine (Jul); Montgomery County Fair (Mar); Mother's Day (May); Holiday Cookbook (Nov); Answer Book (Oct); High School Football (Sept).
Special Weekly Sections: Best Food Days (Wed/Sun)
Syndicated Publications: USA WEEKEND Magazine (S).
Delivery Methods: Carrier`Racks
Areas Served - City/County or Portion Thereof, or Zip codes: Montgomery County
Own Printing Facility?: N
Commercial printers?: N
Avg Free Circ: 10936
Sat. Circulation Paid: 8430
Sun. Circulation Paid: 8532
Audit By: AAM
Audit Date: 15.03.2015
Personnel: Andy DuBois (Exec. Ed.); Brenda Miller-Fergerson (Pub.); Jim Fredricks (Grp. Pub.); Corey Turner (Gen. Sales Mgr.); Charles Lee (Adv. Dir.); Karen Maurmann (Adv. Mgr.); Rod Mcfarland (Circ. Dir.); Nancy Flake (City Ed.); Sandra Bosse (Features Ed.); Mike Jones (Sports Ed.); Ann Toppel (Mgmt. Info Servs. Mgr.); Kelly Lawson (Asst. Opns. Mgr.); Jason Joseph (Pub.); Tom Legg (Major/Nat'l Sr. Acct. Mgr.)
Parent company (for newspapers): Hearst Communications, Inc.

CORPUS CHRISTI CALLER-TIMES

Street address 1: 820 N. Lower Broadway
Street address city: Corpus Christi
Street address state: TX
Zip/Postal code: 78401-9136
County: Nueces
Country: USA
Mailing address: PO BOX 9136
Mailing city: CORPUS CHRISTI
Mailing state: TX
Mailing zip: 78469-9136
General Phone: (361) 884-2011
Advertising Phone: (361) 886-4301
Editorial Phone: (361) 886-3787
General/National Adv. E-mail: hornc@caller.com
Display Adv. E-mail: hornc@caller.com
Classified Adv. e-mail: classifieds@caller.com
Primary Website: www.caller.com
Mthly Avg Unique Visitors: 502082
Year Established: 1883
News Services: AP, NYT, MCT, SHNS.
Special Editions: South Texas Football (Aug); Best of Best (Dec); Horizons (Jan); Mi Vida (Monthly); Best of Best (Sept).
Special Weekly Sections: Health (Mon); Ladies Only (Tue); Best Food (Wed); Arts (Thur); Weekend (Fri); Home, Garden (Sat); Homes,Travel, Business, Hola (Sun)
Syndicated Publications: Parade (S).
Avg Free Circ: 288
Sat. Circulation Paid: 18198
Sat. Circulation Free: 288
Sun. Circulation Paid: 25435
Sun. Circulation Free: 284
Audit By: AAM
Audit Date: 31.03.2018
Personnel: Arthur Acuna (Vice Pres., HR); Libby Averyt (Pub./CRO); Michelle Koesema (CFO); Sylvia Perez (Exec. Sec.); Debra Villarreal (Credit Mgr.); Steve Arnold (Mktg. Dir.); Jeff Deloach (Circ. Vice Pres.); Bob Gage (Circ. Opns. Mgr.); Shane Fitzgerald (Ed.); Sandy Moorhead (Editorial Page Ed.); Cynthia Wilson (Features Ed.); Allison Ehrlich (Librarian); Tom Whitehurst (Bus. Ed.); Allison Pollan (Asst. Metro Ed.); Jen Deselms (News Ed.); John Allen (Sports Ed.); Tina Vasquez (Television Ed.); Darrell Coleman (Pres./Pub.); Chris Horn (Nat'l Sales Mgr.)
Parent company (for newspapers): Gannett - USA Today Network

CORSICANA DAILY SUN

Street address 1: 405 E Collin St
Street address city: Corsicana
Street address state: TX
Zip/Postal code: 75110-5325
County: Navarro
Country: USA
Mailing address: PO BOX 622
Mailing city: CORSICANA
Mailing state: TX
Mailing zip: 75151-9006
General Phone: (903) 872-3931
Advertising Phone: (903) 872-3931
Editorial Phone: (903) 872-3931
General/National Adv. E-mail: advertising@corsicanadailysun.com
Display Adv. E-mail: advertising@corsicanadailysun.com
Classified Adv. e-mail: advertising@corsicanadailysun.com
Editorial e-mail: dailysun@corsicanadailysun.com
Primary Website: www.corsicanadailysun.com
Mthly Avg Views: 500000
Mthly Avg Unique Visitors: 75000
Year Established: 1895
News Services: AP.
Special Editions: Football (Aug); Progress (Jun); Newcomers (Sept).
Special Weekly Sections: Best Food Fay, Business (Tue); Church (Fri); Business (Thur); Farm, Business, Living, Minipage, Entertainment (Sun)
Syndicated Publications: Relish (Monthly); USA WEEKEND Magazine (S).
Delivery Methods: Mail
Own Printing Facility?: N
Commercial printers?: Y
Sat. Circulation Paid: 5690
Sun. Circulation Paid: 6544
Audit By: Sworn/Estimate/Non-Audited
Audit Date: 12.07.2019
Personnel: David Smith (Circ. Mgr.); Chris Smith (Photo Ed.); Deana Pawlowski (Data Processing Mgr.); Karen Davis (Adv. Dir.); Terri Anderson (Acct. Exec.); Jake Mienk (Publisher); Sharon Brown (Bus. Mgr.); Thomas MartÃnez (Ed.)
Parent company (for newspapers): CNHI, LLC; CNHI, LLC

THE DALLAS MORNING NEWS

Street address 1: 1954 Commerce Street
Street address city: Dallas
Street address state: TX
Zip/Postal code: 75201
County: Dallas
Country: USA
Mailing address: 1954 Commerce Street
Mailing city: Dallas
Mailing state: TX
Mailing zip: 75201
General Phone: (214) 977-8222
Editorial Phone: (214) 977-8205
General/National Adv. E-mail: rj.flowers@belomediagroup.com
Display Adv. E-mail: rj.flowers@belomediagroup.com
Classified Adv. e-mail: alex.barnishin@belomediagroup.com
Editorial e-mail: asktheeditor@dallasnews.com
Primary Website: www.dallasnews.com
Year Established: 1885
News Services: AP, NYT, Washington Post, Tribune News Service, Getty
Special Weekly Sections: Guide (Fri); Travel (Sun); Points (Sun); Comics.
Syndicated Publications: Parade (Sun).
Delivery Methods: Mail`Newsstand`Carrier`Racks
Own Printing Facility?: Y
Commercial printers?: Y
Avg Free Circ: 60000
Sun. Circulation Paid: 272572
Sun. Circulation Free: 400000
Audit By: AAM
Audit Date: 31.03.2018
Personnel: Gene Chavez (Circ. Dir.); Tom Huang (Asst. Mng. Ed./Feat & Comm Engmt); Bill May (VP Prod); Grant Moise (EVP & Gen Mgr, Dallas Morning News); Mike Wilson (Ed); Alison Draper (Pres, BMG); Keith Campbell (Dep Mng Ed: News & Bus.); Mark Konradi (Dir. of News Oper.); Gary Leavell (Asst. Mng Ed/Sports); Marcia Allert (Dir of Photography); Denise Bieber (Ed/The Daily); Brendan Miniter (VP, Ed of Editorials); Susan Kerr (VP, Audience Development); Dan Sherlock (Vice Pres - Dig)
Parent company (for newspapers): A.H. Belo Corporation

DEL RIO NEWS-HERALD

Street address 1: 2205 N Bedell Ave
Street address city: Del Rio
Street address state: TX
Zip/Postal code: 78840-8007
County: Val Verde
Country: USA
Mailing address: 2205 N BEDELL AVE
Mailing city: DEL RIO
Mailing state: TX
Mailing zip: 78840-8007
General Phone: (830) 775-1551
Advertising Phone: (830) 775-1551
Editorial Phone: (830) 775-1551
General/National Adv. E-mail: claudia.deleon@delrionewsherald.com
Display Adv. E-mail: claudia.deleon@delrionewsherald.com
Classified Adv. e-mail: claudia.deleon@delrionewsherald.com
Editorial e-mail: claudia.deleon@delrionewsherald.com
Primary Website: www.delrionewsherald.com
Mthly Avg Views: 10000
Year Established: 1929
News Services: AP, NEA.
Special Weekly Sections: Best Food Days (Tue/Sun)
Syndicated Publications: Parade (S).
Delivery Methods: Mail`Newsstand`Carrier`Racks
Areas Served - City/County or Portion Thereof, or Zip codes: Del Rio Val Verde 78840
Own Printing Facility?: Y
Commercial printers?: Y
Avg Free Circ: 306
Sun. Circulation Paid: 2515
Sun. Circulation Free: 263
Audit By: CAC
Audit Date: 31.03.2017
Personnel: Brian Argabright (Managing Ed.); Josie Garcia (AR rep)
Parent company (for newspapers): Metro Newspaper Advertising Services, Inc.-OOB; Southern Newspapers Inc.

DENTON RECORD-CHRONICLE

Street address 1: 314 E Hickory St
Street address city: Denton
Street address state: TX
Zip/Postal code: 76201-4272
County: Denton
Country: USA
Mailing address: PO BOX 369
Mailing city: DENTON
Mailing state: TX
Mailing zip: 76202-0369
General Phone: (940) 387-3811
Advertising Phone: (940) 566-6858
Editorial Phone: (940) 566-6879
General/National Adv. E-mail: skelley@dentonrc.com
Display Adv. E-mail: drcretailad@dentonrc.comâ€‹
Classified Adv. e-mail: Classads@dentonrc.comâ€‹
Editorial e-mail: drc@dentonrcâ€‹.com
Primary Website: www.dentonrc.com
Mthly Avg Views: 1272407
Mthly Avg Unique Visitors: 188009
Year Established: 1903
News Services: AP.
Special Editions: Denton Time, Kid Life, Denton Business Chronicle, RealEstate, DealFinder, The A Train
Special Weekly Sections: Entertainment Chronicle (Thur).
Syndicated Publications: Parade (Sunday)
Delivery Methods: Carrier
Areas Served - City/County or Portion Thereof, or Zip codes: Northern Denton County including the city of Denton, TXâ€‹
Own Printing Facility?: N
Commercial printers?: N
Avg Free Circ: 2756
Sat. Circulation Paid: 7310
Sat. Circulation Free: 126
Sun. Circulation Paid: 9945
Sun. Circulation Free: 126
Audit By: AAM
Audit Date: 31.03.2015
Personnel: Bill Patterson (Pub.); Lucinda Breeding (Features Ed.); Sandra Hammond (Ad. Director)
Parent company (for newspapers): A.H. Belo Corporation

FOCUS DAILY NEWS

Street address 1: 1337 Marilyn Avenue
Street address city: DeSoto
Street address state: TX
Zip/Postal code: 75115
County: Dallas
Country: USA
Mailing address: P O Box 1714
Mailing city: DeSoto
Mailing state: TX
Mailing zip: 75123
General Phone: 972-223-9175
Advertising Phone: 972-223-9175
Editorial Phone: 972-223-9175
General/National Adv. E-mail: focusnews@wans.net
Display Adv. E-mail: focusnews@wans.net
Classified Adv. e-mail: focusnews@wans.net
Editorial e-mail: editor@focusdailynews.com
Primary Website: www.focusdailynews.com
Mthly Avg Views: 165000
Mthly Avg Unique Visitors: 165000
Year Established: 1987
Special Editions: Automotive, Readers Choice, Football, various holidays
Special Weekly Sections: Automotive
Delivery Methods: Newsstand`Carrier`Racks
Areas Served - City/County or Portion Thereof, or Zip codes: Cedar Hill, DeSoto, Duncanville, Lancaster, Glenn Heights, Grand Prairie, Red Oak, Waxahachie, Ovilla Texas
Own Printing Facility?: Y
Commercial printers?: Y

Avg Free Circ: 0
Sun. Circulation Paid: 49890
Audit By: USPS
Audit Date: 26.
Personnel: Marlon Hanson (Pub.); Joshua Johnson (Ed.); Alex Hanson (Prodn. Mgr.); Ginger Bolton (Circ. Mgr.); Kristin Barclay (Digital Operations Director)
Parent company (for newspapers): Marlin Hanson

EL PASO TIMES

Street address 1: 500 W. Overland Avenue, Suite #150
Street address 2: Ste 150
Street address city: El Paso
Street address state: TX
Zip/Postal code: 79901-1108
County: El Paso
Country: USA
General Phone: (915) 546-6100
Advertising Phone: (915) 546-6250
Editorial Phone: (915) 546-6124
General/National Adv. E-mail: advertising@elpasotimes.com
Display Adv. E-mail: advertising@elpasotimes.com
Classified Adv. e-mail: advertising@elpasotimes.com
Editorial e-mail: news@elpasotimes.com
Primary Website: www.elpasotimes.com
Mthly Avg Views: 3505161
Mthly Avg Unique Visitors: 640785
Year Established: 1881
News Services: AP, GNS, LAT-WP, Thunderdome
Special Editions: Healthcare Directory (Apr); Football (Aug); Last Minute Gift Guide (Dec); Legal Directory (Feb); Women in Business (Jan); Career Tab + Expo (Jul); Family-Owned Business (Jun); Sport Utility Vehicles (Mar); Career Tab + Expo (May); Early Christmas Gift Gui
Special Weekly Sections: Living (Mon-Fri); Best Food Day (Wed); Entertainment (Fri); Real Estate, Travel, TV, Living (Sun); Business (Tues - Sun)
Syndicated Publications: Eastside Reporter (Fri); USA WEEKEND Magazine (S). Relish Magazine.
Delivery Methods: Mail`Newsstand`Carrier`Racks
Own Printing Facility?: Y
Commercial printers?: Y
Sat. Circulation Paid: 19238
Sun. Circulation Paid: 95895
Audit By: Sworn/Estimate/Non-Audited
Audit Date: 12.07.2019
Personnel: Malena Field (Dir., HR); Randy Waldrop (Circ. Mgr., Transportation); Patsy Hernandez (VP of Production); Robert Moore (Executive Editor); Victor Kolenc; Lilia Jones (President); Salvador Hernandez (Sales Director)
Parent company (for newspapers): Gannett

THE ENNIS DAILY NEWS

Street address 1: 213 N Dallas St
Street address city: Ennis
Street address state: TX
Zip/Postal code: 75119-4011
County: Ellis
Country: USA
Mailing address: PO BOX 100
Mailing city: ENNIS
Mailing state: TX
Mailing zip: 75120-0100
General Phone: (972) 875-3801
Advertising Phone: (972) 875-3801
Editorial Phone: (972) 875-3801
General/National Adv. E-mail: keven@ennisdailynews.com
Display Adv. E-mail: advertising@ennisdailynews.com
Classified Adv. e-mail: classifieds@ennisdailynews.com
Editorial e-mail: editor@ennisdailynews.com
Primary Website: www.ennisdailynews.com
Mthly Avg Views: 100000
Mthly Avg Unique Visitors: 30000
Year Established: 1891
News Services: AP
Special Editions: Football program (July-August); Discover (September-October); Holiday Hometown (October-November);Thanksgiving (November); Christmas (December); Family Guide (January); Medical Guide (February); Hometown Living (glossy) 6x per year.
Delivery Methods: Newsstand`Carrier`Racks
Areas Served - City/County or Portion Thereof, or Zip codes: Ellis County
Own Printing Facility?: Y
Commercial printers?: Y
Sun. Circulation Paid: 3214
Audit By: Sworn/Estimate/Non-Audited
Audit Date: 12.07.2019
Personnel: Nikki Cohan (Gen. Mgr.); Deb Thompson (Bus./Sales Mgr.); Mark Warde (Sports Ed.)
Parent company (for newspapers): Fackelman Newspapers

FORT WORTH STAR-TELEGRAM

Street address 1: 307 W 7th St Ste 600
Street address city: Fort Worth
Street address state: TX
Zip/Postal code: 76102
County: Tarrant
Country: USA
Mailing address: PO BOX 1870
Mailing city: FORT WORTH
Mailing state: TX
Mailing zip: 76101-1870
General Phone: (817) 390-7400
Advertising Phone: (817) 390-7765
Editorial Phone: (817) 390-7150
General/National Adv. E-mail: marketguidefeedback@star-telegram.com
Display Adv. E-mail: mediakit@star-telegram.com
Classified Adv. e-mail: mediakit@star-telegram.com
Editorial e-mail: jwilley@star-telegram.com
Primary Website: www.star-telegram.com
Mthly Avg Unique Visitors: 2190375
Year Established: 1906
News Services: Newspapers First, MCT, LAT-WP, SHNS, DJ (Dow Jones).
Special Editions: Summer Vacation (Apr); Football (Aug); Gift Guide III (Dec); Texas Golf & Resort (Feb); Stock Show I (Jan); Education (Jul); Primetime (Jun); Primetime (Mar); Top 25 (May); Healthcare (Monthly); Primetime (Nov); The Answer Book (Oct); Fall Home & Garden S
Special Weekly Sections: TV (Daily); Best Food Day (Wed); Weekend (Fri); Religion, TV Supplement (Sat); Travel (Sun)
Syndicated Publications: StarTime (Fri); Tarrant Business (Mon); Relish (Monthly); TV Star (weekly TV Guide) (S).
Sat. Circulation Paid: 69030
Sun. Circulation Paid: 126333
Audit By: AAM
Audit Date: 31.03.2018
Personnel: Gary Wortel (Pres./Pub.); Roger Provost (Vice Pres./CFO); Michael J. Winter (Sr. Vice Pres., Adv.); Dolan Stidom (Circ. Vice Pres.); Terry Foley (Circ. Dir., Arlington); Lonna Hoffman (Circ. Dir., Sales/Training); Jim Witt (Sr. Vice Pres./Exec. Ed.); Bob Ray Sanders (Vice Pres./Assoc. Ed.); Kathy Vetter (Mng. Ed., Enterprise); Lois Norder (Mng. Ed., Investigations); Steve Kaskovich (Asst. Mng. Ed., Bus.); Catherine Mallette (Asst. Mng. Ed., Features); John Gravois (Asst. Mng. Ed., Gov't Affairs); Celeste Williams (Mng. Ed., Sports); James Burda (Majors/Nat'l Sales Dir.); Craig Diebel (VP); Charean Williams (Editorial Dept); Lee Williams (Mng. Ed./News); Christian Lee (VP of Audience Dev. Cir.)
Parent company (for newspapers): The McClatchy Company; Chatham Asset Management

THE GALVESTON COUNTY DAILY NEWS

Street address 1: 8522 Teichman Rd
Street address city: Galveston
Street address state: TX
Zip/Postal code: 77554-9119
County: Galveston
Country: USA
Mailing address: 8522 Teichman Road
Mailing city: GALVESTON
Mailing state: TX
Mailing zip: 77554
General Phone: (409) 683-5200
Advertising Phone: (409) 683-5224
Editorial Phone: (409) 683-5239
General/National Adv. E-mail: advertising@galvnews.com
Display Adv. E-mail: advertising@galvnews.com
Classified Adv. e-mail: advertising@galvnews.com
Editorial e-mail: newsroom@galvnews.com
Primary Website: www.galvnews.com
Mthly Avg Views: 2000000
Mthly Avg Unique Visitors: 350000
Year Established: 1842
News Services: AP.
Special Editions: Readers' Choice, 40 Under 40, Years of Excellence, Rememberances, Living, Live/Work/Play Galveston, etc.
Special Weekly Sections: Sports, TV Page, Business, Entertainment, Auto, Our County, Real Estate (Daily); Best Food, lifestyle (Wed); Entertainment (Fri); Auto, Our Faith, Real Estate (Sat); Lifestyle, Travel, Real Estate, Jobs (Sun)
Delivery Methods: Mail`Newsstand`Carrier`Racks
Areas Served - City/County or Portion Thereof, or Zip codes: 77550, 77551, 77554, 77568, 77590, 77591, 77563
Own Printing Facility?: Y
Commercial printers?: Y
Avg Free Circ: 750
Sat. Circulation Paid: 15007
Sat. Circulation Free: 932
Sun. Circulation Paid: 16216
Sun. Circulation Free: 225
Audit By: USPS
Audit Date: 31.10.2023
Personnel: Yvonne Mascorro (Audience and Circulation Director); D'Lorah Collier (Bus. Mgr.); Debbie Keith (Adv. Mgr., Retail); Michael A. Smith (Assoc. Ed.); Melissa Rivera (Creative Services Director); Heber Taylor (Ed.); Leonard Woolsey (Pub.); Michelle Robinson (Chief Revenue Officer); Jennifer Reynolds (Photo Editor); Angela Taylor (Community News Editor); Greg Mefford (Online Ed.); Brett Baker (Prodn. Foreman, Pressroom); Jordan Gordwin (Sports Editor); Scott Moon (Advertising Director); Michael Smith (Lifestyle Ed.); Joshua Buckley (Sports Ed.); John Flowers (Ad. Director)
Parent company (for newspapers): Southern Newspapers Inc.

HERALD-BANNER

Street address 1: 2305 King St
Street address city: Greenville
Street address state: TX
Zip/Postal code: 75401-3257
County: Hunt
Country: USA
Mailing address: PO BOX 6000
Mailing city: GREENVILLE
Mailing state: TX
Mailing zip: 75403-6000
General Phone: (903) 455-4220
Advertising Phone: (903)455-4220
Editorial Phone: (903) 455-4220
General/National Adv. E-mail: publisher@heraldbanner.com
Display Adv. E-mail: advertising@heraldbanner.com
Classified Adv. e-mail: classifieds@heraldbanner.com
Editorial e-mail: editor@heraldbanner.com
Primary Website: www.heraldbanner.com
Mthly Avg Views: 19000
Year Established: 1869
News Services: AP.
Special Weekly Sections: TV Tabloid (S).
Syndicated Publications: Relish (Monthly); USA WEEKEND Magazine (S).
Delivery Methods: Carrier`Racks
Areas Served - City/County or Portion Thereof, or Zip codes: Hunt County
Sat. Circulation Paid: 7945
Sun. Circulation Paid: 8621
Audit By: Sworn/Estimate/Non-Audited
Audit Date: 12.07.2019
Personnel: Lisa Chappell (Pub.); Mary Standfield (Bus. Mgr.); Leslie McMannis (Adv. Dir.); Robert Spillers (Circ. Dir.); Daniel Walker (Ed.); Warren Morrison (Mng. Ed.); Carol Ferguson (Features Ed.); David Claybourn (Sports Ed.); David Benini (Prodn. Mgr.); Derek Price
Parent company (for newspapers): CNHI, LLC; CNHI, LLC

VALLEY MORNING STAR

Street address 1: 1310 S. Commerce Street, P.O. Box 511
Street address city: Harlingen
Street address state: TX
Zip/Postal code: 78550
County: Cameron
Country: USA
Mailing address: 1310 S COMMERCE ST
Mailing city: HARLINGEN
Mailing state: TX
Mailing zip: 78550-7711
General Phone: (956) 430-6200
General/National Adv. E-mail: bmendell@rgvmedianetwork.com
Display Adv. E-mail: ccastillo@valleystar.com
Classified Adv. e-mail: ccastillo@valleystar.com
Editorial e-mail: lseiser@valleystar.com
Primary Website: www.valleymorningstar.com
Mthly Avg Views: 720000
Mthly Avg Unique Visitors: 250000
Year Established: 1911
News Services: AP, MCT, TMS.
Special Weekly Sections: Thursday Health & Wellness
Syndicated Publications: Parade, Relish, Athlon Sports, USA
Delivery Methods: Newsstand`Carrier`Racks
Areas Served - City/County or Portion Thereof, or Zip codes: Cameron & Willacy Counties
Own Printing Facility?: Y
Commercial printers?: Y
Sat. Circulation Paid: 10405
Sun. Circulation Paid: 11838
Audit By: AAM
Audit Date: 31.03.2017
Personnel: Melva Juarez (Acct. Mgr.); Peggy Elder (Adv. Ops. Mgr.); Rusty Hall (Circ. Dir.); Dave Favila (Sports Ed.); Lilia Castillo Jones (Pub./AD Dir.); Christina Castillo (Adv. Dir.); Lisa Seiser (Ed.)
Parent company (for newspapers): AIM Media Texas

HOUSTON CHRONICLE

Street address 1: 4747 Southwest Freeway
Street address city: Houston
Street address state: TX
Zip/Postal code: 77027
County: Harris
Country: USA
Mailing address: P.O. Box 4260
Mailing city: HOUSTON
Mailing state: TX
Mailing zip: 77210
General Phone: (713) 362-7211
General/National Adv. E-mail: help@chron.com
Editorial e-mail: news@chron.com
Primary Website: www.chron.com
Mthly Avg Views: 132527944
Mthly Avg Unique Visitors: 27911552
Year Established: 1901
News Services: AP, MCT, HN, NYT, CQ, Bloomberg, EFE, Getty Images, Sports Network, Financial Content.
Special Editions: Baseball (Apr); Football (Aug); Super Bowl (Feb); How-To Guide (Jul); Houston Open (Mar); Chronicle Top 100 (May); Health (Monthly); Holiday Guide (Nov); NBA Preview (Oct).
Special Weekly Sections: Houston Belief (Fri); InMotion (Other); Color Comics (S); New Homes (Sat); Preview/Dining Guide (Thur); Flavor (Wed).
Syndicated Publications: Zest (ROP) (S).
Delivery Methods: Mail`Newsstand`Carrier`Racks
Areas Served - City/County or Portion Thereof, or Zip codes: Austin, Brazoria, Chambers, Fort Bend, Galveston, Harris, Liberty, Montgomery, San Jacinto, Waller
Sat. Circulation Paid: 145918
Sun. Circulation Paid: 271040
Audit By: AAM
Audit Date: 30.09.2018
Personnel: John Perdigao (Chief Financial Officer); Michael C. LaBonia (Executive VP/Multi-Market Advertising); Mario Barson (Vice President, Recruitment Advertising); Michael Gorman (Vice President, Consumer Sales & Services); Michael H. Sacks (Vice President, Operations); Linda Schaible (Vice President, Audience Development & Planning); Veronica Flores-Panlagua (Outlook Editor); Rob Cravaritis (Executive Vice President/Sales); Nancy Barnes (Editor, Executive Vice President/News); Steve Proctor (Managing Editor); Andrea G. Mooney (Executive Producer/Director, Digital Content); Greg Cox (Director); Jeff Cohen (Editor); Maria Carrillo (Senior Ed.); Paul Barbetta (Chief Operating Officer); Jack Sweeney (Pub./Pres.); Mark Medici (Pres.)
Parent company (for newspapers): Hearst Communications, Inc.

THE HUNTSVILLE ITEM

Street address 1: 1409 10th St
Street address city: Huntsville
Street address state: TX
Zip/Postal code: 77320-3805
County: Walker
Country: USA
Mailing address: PO BOX 539
Mailing city: HUNTSVILLE
Mailing state: TX
Mailing zip: 77342-0539

General Phone: (936) 295-5407
General/National Adv. E-mail: huntsvilleitem@gmail.com
Display Adv. E-mail: rhaldeman@itemonline.com
Editorial e-mail: huntsvilleitem@gmail.com
Primary Website: www.itemonline.com
Mthly Avg Views: 225000
Mthly Avg Unique Visitors: 88800
Year Established: 1850
News Services: AP.
Special Editions: Walker County Proud (Progress Edition - February); Rodeo Tab (March); Fair Winners (April), Reader's Choice (May); Newcomer's Guide (June); Football Preview (August); (September); Breast Cancer Awareness (October); Inspiring Women in Business (October); Holiday Wrap,(November); Veterans Day Section (November); Moments & Memories Magazine (November); Holiday Coloring Book (December)
Special Weekly Sections: Teleview (S).
Syndicated Publications: Texas Dept. Corrections News Roundup (Monthly); USA WEEKEND Magazine (S); American Profile (Weekly);Magazine (Monthly).
Delivery Methods: Mail`Newsstand`Carrier`Racks
Areas Served - City/County or Portion Thereof, or Zip codes: 77320, 77340, 77342, 77358, 77334, 77873, 77367, 77876, 75862, 77864, 77359, 77364, 77831, 77852
Own Printing Facility?: Y
Commercial printers?: Y
Avg Free Circ: 20000
Sat. Circulation Paid: 3800
Sun. Circulation Paid: 4000
Audit By: Sworn/Estimate/Non-Audited
Audit Date: 12.07.2019
Personnel: Polly Johnson (Director of Audience Development); Tom Waddill (Editor); Christina Blount (Mailroom Mgr.); Rita Haldeman (Pub./Adv. Dir.)
Parent company (for newspapers): CNHI, LLC; CNHI, LLC

KERRVILLE DAILY TIMES

Street address 1: 429 Jefferson Street
Street address city: Kerrville
Street address state: TX
Zip/Postal code: 78028
County: Kerr
Country: USA
Mailing address: PO BOX 291428
Mailing city: KERRVILLE
Mailing state: TX
Mailing zip: 78029-1428
General Phone: (830) 896-7000
Advertising Phone: (830)896-7000
Editorial Phone: (830)896-7000
General/National Adv. E-mail: advertising@dailytimes.com
Display Adv. E-mail: advertising@dailytimes.com
Classified Adv. e-mail: advertising@dailytimes.com
Editorial e-mail: niece.bell@dailytimes.com
Primary Website: www.dailytimes.com
Year Established: 1910
News Services: AP.
Special Editions: Football (Aug); Christmas (Dec); Brides (Mar); Graduation (May); Hunting & Wild Game Guide (Nov); New Car (Oct).
Special Weekly Sections: Women in Business (Mon); Best Food Day (Wed); Business in Review, Entertainment (Thur); Religion (Fri); Business (Sun)
Syndicated Publications: Real Estate (Monthly); Parade (S); American Profile (Weekly).
Avg Free Circ: 609
Sun. Circulation Paid: 6636
Sun. Circulation Free: 577
Audit By: AAM
Audit Date: 31.03.2017
Personnel: Carlina Villalpando (Pub.); Travis Webb (Mng. Ed.); Jeanette Nash (Assistant Mng. Ed.); Sean Batura (News Ed.); Jonathan Toye (Sports Ed.); Travis O'Bryan (Commercial Printing/Press Mgr.)
Parent company (for newspapers): Southern Newspapers Inc.

KILLEEN DAILY HERALD

Street address 1: 1809 Florence Road, P.O. Box 1300
Street address city: Killeen
Street address state: TX
Zip/Postal code: 76540
County: Bell
Country: USA
Mailing address: PO BOX 1300
Mailing city: KILLEEN
Mailing state: TX
Mailing zip: 76540-1300
General Phone: (254) 634-2125
Advertising Phone: (254) 501-7500
Editorial Phone: (254) 501-7540
General/National Adv. E-mail: nationals@kdhnews.com
Display Adv. E-mail: aedwards@kdhnews.com
Classified Adv. e-mail: aedwards@kdhnews.com
Editorial e-mail: news@kdhnews.com
Primary Website: www.kdhnews.com
Mthly Avg Views: 88000
Year Established: 1890
News Services: AP, Landon Media Group.
Special Editions: Car Care (Apr); UMHB Sports (Aug); Wrap it Up 2 (Dec); Progressive (Feb); Boat Show (Jan); Mile Maker (Jul); 100 Best (Jun); Design An Ad (Mar); Festival of Flags (May); UCT Birthday (Nov); AUSA (Oct); Medical Directory (Sept).
Special Weekly Sections: Weekender (Fri); TV Book (S); Dollar Saver (Wed).
Syndicated Publications: Parade, Athlon sports
Delivery Methods: Mail`Newsstand`Carrier`Racks
Areas Served - City/County or Portion Thereof, or Zip codes: Killeen, Florence, Nolanville, Ft. Hood, Copperas Cove, Gatesville, Harker Heights and Belton
Own Printing Facility?: Y
Commercial printers?: Y
Avg Free Circ: 1991
Sat. Circulation Paid: 9350
Sat. Circulation Free: 1991
Sun. Circulation Paid: 12501
Sun. Circulation Free: 66
Audit By: AAM
Audit Date: 31.03.2018
Personnel: Sue Mayborn (Pub.); Terry E. Gandy (Gen. Mgr.); Rodney Sparks (Bus. Mgr.); Tiffany Muller (Adv. Mgr.); Olga Pena (Mng. Ed.); David Miller (Asst. Mng. Ed.); Mark Miller (Sports Ed.); Jason Browne (Coord., Telecommun.)
Parent company (for newspapers): Frank Mayborn Enterprises, Inc.

LAREDO MORNING TIMES

Street address 1: 111 Esperanza Drive
Street address city: Laredo
Street address state: TX
Zip/Postal code: 78041
County: Webb
Country: USA
Mailing address: PO BOX 2129
Mailing city: LAREDO
Mailing state: TX
Mailing zip: 78044-2129
General Phone: (956) 728-2500
Advertising Phone: (956) 728-2512
Editorial Phone: (956) 728-2563
General/National Adv. E-mail: bill@lmtonline.com
Display Adv. E-mail: ads@lmtonline.com
Editorial e-mail: ngeorgiou@lmtonline.com
Primary Website: www.lmtonline.com
Year Established: 1881
News Services: AP, LAT-WP, NYT, MCT, HN, CNS.
Special Editions: Fall Fashion (Aug); Washington's Birthday (Feb); Border Olympics (Spring); Border Olympics (Summer).
Special Weekly Sections: Business (Mon); Best Food Day, La Familia, El Mercadito Shopper, Comics (Wed); Youth, Campus (Thur); Entertainment (Fri); Fashion, Society, Art of Living (Sun); El Tiempo de Laredo (Daily)
Syndicated Publications: USA WEEKEND Magazine (S); American Profile (Weekly).
Delivery Methods: Mail`Newsstand`Carrier
Own Printing Facility?: N
Avg Free Circ: 130
Sat. Circulation Paid: 9041
Sat. Circulation Free: 130
Sun. Circulation Paid: 10411
Sun. Circulation Free: 27
Audit By: AAM
Audit Date: 31.12.2017
Personnel: William B. Green (Pub.); Joe Vied (Controller); Adriana Devally (Adv. Dir.); Cuate Santos (Photo Dept. Mgr.); Odie Arambula (Sunday Ed.); Diana Fuentes (Ed.)
Parent company (for newspapers): Hearst Communications, Inc.

LONGVIEW NEWS-JOURNAL

Street address 1: 320 E Methvin St
Street address city: Longview
Street address state: TX
Zip/Postal code: 75601-7323
County: Gregg
Country: USA
Mailing address: PO BOX 1792
Mailing city: LONGVIEW
Mailing state: TX
Mailing zip: 75606-1792
General Phone: (903) 237-7744
Advertising Phone: (903) 237-7736
Editorial Phone: (903) 237-7744
General/National Adv. E-mail: ljobe@news-journal.com
Display Adv. E-mail: cdean@news-journal.com
Classified Adv. e-mail: hchatelain@news-journal.com
Editorial e-mail: rbrack@news-journal.com
Primary Website: www.news-journal.com
Mthly Avg Views: 1750000
Mthly Avg Unique Visitors: 425000
Year Established: 1871
News Services: AP, NYT
Special Editions: Progress (March-April), AlleyFest (May), Great Texas Balloon Race (July), The Zone (August)
Special Weekly Sections: Religion (Sat), Business (Sun), Lifestyles (Sun), Health (Th), Taste (Wed), REW (Fri), @Play (Th)
Syndicated Publications: USA Weekend (Sun), American Profile (Mon), Relish (monthly Tuesday), Spry (monthly Thur), Athlon Sports (monthly Sun)
Delivery Methods: Mail`Newsstand`Carrier`Racks
Areas Served - City/County or Portion Thereof, or Zip codes: 75455 75563 75571 75601 75602 75603 75604 75605 75606 75607 75630 75631 75633 75638 75640 75644 75645 75647 75650 75651 75652 75654 75656 75657 75661 75662 75668 75670 75672 75683 75684 75686 75691 75692 75693 75755 75765
Own Printing Facility?: Y
Commercial printers?: Y
Sat. Circulation Paid: 13632
Sun. Circulation Paid: 15704
Audit By: AAM
Audit Date: 30.06.2018
Personnel: Stephen McHaney (Pub.); Jack Stallard (Sports Ed.); Kevin Green (Chief Photographer); Janet Owens (Prodn. Mgr.); Terresa Garrison (Bindery Mgr.); Josh Hart (Circ. Dir.); Pat Kinney (HR Dir.); Dana Morton; Denise Lytle (Chief Financial Officer); Ric Brack (Ed. Dlr.); Jerry Pye (Reg. Pub.); Debbi Knoll (Adv. Mgr.); Larry Jobe (Adv. Dir.)
Parent company (for newspapers): Victoria Advocate Publishing Co.; Texas Community Media Group

LUBBOCK AVALANCHE-JOURNAL

Street address 1: 710 Avenue J, P.O. Box 491
Street address city: Lubbock
Street address state: TX
Zip/Postal code: 79408
County: Lubbock
Country: USA
Mailing address: PO BOX 491
Mailing city: LUBBOCK
Mailing state: TX
Mailing zip: 79408-0491
General Phone: (806) 762-8844
Advertising Phone: (806) 766-8616
Editorial Phone: (806) 766-8701
General/National Adv. E-mail: robin.morse@lubbockonline.com
Display Adv. E-mail: shoni.wiseman@lubbockonline.com
Classified Adv. e-mail: robin.morse@lubbockonline.com
Editorial e-mail: stephen.beasley@lubbockonline.com
Primary Website: www.lubbockonline.com
Year Established: 1900
News Services: AP, MCT, LAT-WP.
Special Editions: Medical Directory (Aug); 50 Plus (Fall); Best of Lubbock (Jul); Life in Lubbock (Jun); 50 Plus (Spring); Sharing The Season (Winter).
Special Weekly Sections: Business, Industrial Review (Mon); Best Food Day (Wed); Entertainment (Fri); Special Section Calendar, Religion, Creative Living, TV, Real Estate (Sat); Entertainment, Agriculture, Local Daily News, Travel, Business (Sun)
Syndicated Publications: Relish (Monthly); USA WEEKEND Magazine (S).
Avg Free Circ: 18664
Sat. Circulation Paid: 10606
Sat. Circulation Free: 17971
Sun. Circulation Paid: 13671
Sun. Circulation Free: 18106
Audit By: AAM
Audit Date: 31.03.2019
Personnel: Robert Granfeldt (Regional Pub.); Jill Nevels-Haun (Regional Executive Ed.); Doug Hensley (Regional Associate Editor/Director of Commentary); Carlos Silva Jr. (Sports Ed.); Leanda Staebner (Digital Copy Ed.); Robert Bauwens (Production Mgr.); David Morel (Regional Distribution Dir.); Shoni Wiseman (Advertising Mgr.); Robin Morse (Classified Mgr.)
Parent company (for newspapers): Gannett; CherryRoad Media

THE LUFKIN DAILY NEWS

Street address 1: P O Box 1089
Street address city: Lufkin
Street address state: TX
Zip/Postal code: 75901
County: Angelina
Country: USA
Mailing address: PO BOX 1089
Mailing city: LUFKIN
Mailing state: TX
Mailing zip: 75902-1089
General Phone: (936) 632-6631
Advertising Phone: (936) 631-2630
Editorial Phone: (936) 631-2623
General/National Adv. E-mail: tkedrowicz@lufkindailynews.com
Display Adv. E-mail: tkedrowicz@lufkindailynews.com
Classified Adv. e-mail: sdoyle@lufkindailynews.com
Editorial e-mail: aadams@lufkindailynews.com
Primary Website: www.lufkindailynews.com
Mthly Avg Views: 805000
Mthly Avg Unique Visitors: 9700
Year Established: 1907
News Services: AP.
Special Editions: Parade of Homes (Annually); Back-to-School (Aug); Christmas Shopping Guide (Dec); Progress (Feb); Graduation (May).
Special Weekly Sections: Travel (Fri); Technology (Mon); Lifestyle (S); NASCAR (Sat); Food (Wed).
Syndicated Publications: USA Weekend (S); American Profile (Weekly); Athon Sports (Weekly); Relish (Monthly); Spry (Monthly)
Delivery Methods: Mail`Newsstand`Carrier`Racks
Areas Served - City/County or Portion Thereof, or Zip codes: 7 590 175 904 759 410 000 000 000 000 000 000 000 000 000 000 000 000 000 000 000 000 000 000,00
Own Printing Facility?: Y
Commercial printers?: Y
Avg Free Circ: 898
Sat. Circulation Paid: 7125
Sat. Circulation Free: 898
Sun. Circulation Paid: 8730
Sun. Circulation Free: 276
Audit By: AAM
Audit Date: 31.03.2017
Personnel: Greg Shrader (Pub.); Tammy Kedrowicz (Adv. Dir.); Jennifer Ricks (Circ. Dir.); Andy Adams (Ed.); Beverly Johnson (Lifestyles Ed.); Jeff Pownall (News Ed.); Joel Andrews (Photo Ed.); Josh Havard (Sports Ed.); Renee Guajardo (Data Processing Mgr.); Billy Ricks (Production. Mgr., Mailroom); Robin Nevills (Prodn. Mgr., Pre Press); Steve Reed (Prodn. Foreman, Pressroom); Jennifer Bess (Business Manager); Staci Hodges (Nacogdoches Adv. Mgr.)
Parent company (for newspapers): Southern Newspapers Inc.

MARSHALL NEWS MESSENGER

Street address 1: 309 E Austin St
Street address city: Marshall
Street address state: TX
Zip/Postal code: 75670-3475
County: Harrison
Country: USA
Mailing address: PO BOX 730
Mailing city: MARSHALL
Mailing state: TX
Mailing zip: 75671-0730
General Phone: (903)903-7914
Advertising Phone: (903) 927-5973
Editorial Phone: (903) 935-7914
General/National Adv. E-mail: awalker@news-journal.com
Display Adv. E-mail: dgray@news-journal.com
Classified Adv. e-mail: dgray@news-journal.com
Editorial e-mail: cshields@marshallnewsmessenger.com
Primary Website: www.marshallnewsmessenger.com

Year Established: 1877
News Services: AP.
Special Weekly Sections: Generations (Tue); Food, Education (Wed); Weekend (Thur); Religion, NASCAR (Sat); Business, Books (Sun)
Syndicated Publications: Parade (S); American Profile (Weekly).
Sat. Circulation Paid: 4517
Sun. Circulation Paid: 4713
Audit By: AAM
Audit Date: 31.03.2014
Personnel: Dana Morton (Bus. Mgr.); Chris Kundtson (District Mgr.); Phil Latham (Ed.); D.D. Turner (Asst. News Ed.); Robin Richardson (Features Ed.); Bethany Dean (Adv. Sales Exec.); Andrew Walker (Adv. Dir.); Josh Hart (Circ. Dir.); Jerry Pye (Pub.); Johnnie Fancher (Adv. Sales Exec.)
Parent company (for newspapers): Cox Media Group; Victoria Advocate Publishing Co.; Texas Community Media Group

THE MONITOR

Street address 1: 1400 E Nolana Ave
Street address city: McAllen
Street address state: TX
Zip/Postal code: 78504-6111
County: Hidalgo
Country: USA
Mailing address: PO BOX 3267
Mailing city: MCALLEN
Mailing state: TX
Mailing zip: 78502-3267
General Phone: (956) 686-4343
Advertising Phone: (956) 683-4113
Editorial Phone: (956) 683-4400
General/National Adv. E-mail: bmendell@themonitormgt.com
Display Adv. E-mail: Bmendell@themonitormgt.com
Classified Adv. e-mail: Bmendell@themonitormgt.com
Editorial e-mail: Swingert@themonitormgt.com
Primary Website: MyRGV.com
Mthly Avg Views: 1600000
Mthly Avg Unique Visitors: 260000
Year Established: 1909
News Services: AP.
Special Editions: B-T-S, HS Football (Aug); Business Directory (Apr), Hurricane (Jun.);
Special Weekly Sections: Religious Directory (Fri); Festiva
Delivery Methods: Mail`Newsstand`Carrier`Racks
Areas Served - City/County or Portion Thereof, or Zip codes: Hidalgo County,
Own Printing Facility?: Y
Commercial printers?: Y
Avg Free Circ: 1000
Sat. Circulation Paid: 14922
Sat. Circulation Free: 1625
Sun. Circulation Paid: 18526
Sun. Circulation Free: 1545
Audit By: AAM
Audit Date: 31.12.2018
Personnel: Stephan Wingert (Pub.); Debbie Grant (Dir., Finance & Controller); Armando Martinez (Rgl. HR Dir.); Benita Mendell (Gen. Mgr./Rgl. Adv. Mgr. RGV Media); Walt Bartlick (Commercial Print Director); Carlos Sanchez (Editor); Doug Fullerton (Regional Director of Information Technology); Ernie Cortez (Regional Production Director); Robert Levrier (Circ. Dir.); Dan Silva (Contact Center Manager); Bob Early (Advertising Director)
Parent company (for newspapers): AIM Media Texas

MIDLAND REPORTER-TELEGRAM

Street address 1: 201 E. Illinois Avenue
Street address city: Midland
Street address state: TX
Zip/Postal code: 79701
County: Midland
Country: USA
Mailing address: 201 E Illinois Ave
Mailing city: Midland
Mailing state: TX
Mailing zip: 79701-4852
General Phone: (432) 687-8813
Advertising Phone: (432) 687-8894
Editorial Phone: (432) 687-8855
General/National Adv. E-mail: jhouston@mrt.com
Display Adv. E-mail: jhouston@mrt.com
Classified Adv. e-mail: mrtclassified@mrt.com
Editorial e-mail: news@mrt.com
Primary Website: www.mrt.com
Mthly Avg Views: 2000000
Mthly Avg Unique Visitors: 310000
Year Established: 1929
News Services: AP, HN, NYT. MCT, Bloomberg
Special Editions: Youth Services (Apr); Back-to-School (Aug); Christmas Gift Guide (Dec); Primetime (Every other month); Outlook (Feb); Best of Midland (Jul); Senior Directory (Jun); Spring Home & Garden (Mar); Family Health (Nov); Oil (Oct); Fall Home & Garden (Sept); Football pre-view (Aug.)
Special Weekly Sections: Education (Tuesday), Health (Wednesday); Products, Services (Tue); Best Food Day, (Wed); Weekender (Thur); Religion, Lifestyle (Fri); Oil and Gas, Arts, Entertainment (Sun)
Syndicated Publications: Relish (Monthly); American Profile (Weekly).
Delivery Methods: Mail`Newsstand`Carrier`Racks
Areas Served - City/County or Portion Thereof, or Zip codes: Midland, Odessa, Permian Basin
Own Printing Facility?: Y
Commercial printers?: Y
Avg Free Circ: 1534
Sat. Circulation Paid: 7767
Sat. Circulation Free: 1534
Sun. Circulation Paid: 8921
Sun. Circulation Free: 198
Audit By: AAM
Audit Date: 31.03.2019
Personnel: Jeffery Shabram (Pub.); David Robbins (Vice President of Advertising and Marketing); Sharon Heckler (Circ. Dir.); Stewart Doreen (Ed.)
Parent company (for newspapers): Hearst Communications, Inc.

MINERAL WELLS INDEX

Street address 1: 300 SE 1st St
Street address city: Mineral Wells
Street address state: TX
Zip/Postal code: 76067-5331
County: Palo Pinto
Country: USA
Mailing address: 300 SE 1ST ST
Mailing city: MINERAL WELLS
Mailing state: TX
Mailing zip: 76067-5331
General Phone: (940) 325-4465
Advertising Phone: (940) 325-4465
Editorial Phone: (940) 325-4465 ext. 3416
General/National Adv. E-mail: adv@mineralwellsindex.com
Display Adv. E-mail: adv@mineralwellsindex.com
Classified Adv. e-mail: adv@mineralwellsindex.com
Editorial e-mail: editor@mineralwellsindex.com
Primary Website: www.mineralwellsindex.com
Year Established: 1900
News Services: AP.
Special Editions: Back-to-School (Aug); Christmas Gift Guide (Dec); Rodeo (May); Economic Development (Oct); Best of Mineral Wells (Sept).
Syndicated Publications: Relish (Monthly); TV Book (S); American Profile (Weekly).
Sun. Circulation Paid: 3500
Audit By: Sworn/Estimate/Non-Audited
Audit Date: 12.07.2019
Personnel: David May (General Manager & Editor)
Parent company (for newspapers): CNHI, LLC; CNHI, LLC

MOUNT PLEASANT DAILY TRIBUNE

Street address 1: 210 S Van Buren Ave
Street address city: Mount Pleasant
Street address state: TX
Zip/Postal code: 75455-4440
County: Titus
Country: USA
Mailing address: PO BOX 1177
Mailing city: MOUNT PLEASANT
Mailing state: TX
Mailing zip: 75456-1177
General Phone: (903) 572-1705
Advertising Phone: (903) 237-8863
Editorial Phone: (903)237-8863
General/National Adv. E-mail: kdaffern@tribnow.com
Display Adv. E-mail: kdaffern@tribnow.com
Classified Adv. e-mail: kdaffern@tribnow.com
Editorial e-mail: valerie.reddell@tribnow.com
Primary Website: www.dailytribune.net
Year Established: 1941
News Services: AP, NEA.
Special Editions: Progress (Jan); Rodeo (Jun); Graduation (May); Women in Business (Oct); Modern Living (Quarterly); Football (Sept).
Special Weekly Sections: Real Estate, Sports (Daily); Religion (Fri); Agriculture, Business, Lifestyles (Sun)
Syndicated Publications: TV Viewing (Fri); Color Comics (S); American Profile (Weekly).
Areas Served - City/County or Portion Thereof, or Zip codes: 75455
Own Printing Facility?: N
Commercial printers?: N
Sat. Circulation Paid: 3100
Sun. Circulation Paid: 4988
Audit By: Sworn/Estimate/Non-Audited
Audit Date: 12.07.2019
Parent company (for newspapers): Fenice Community Media

THE DAILY SENTINEL

Street address 1: 129 Sundown Drive
Street address city: Nacogdoches
Street address state: TX
Zip/Postal code: 75964
County: Nacogdoches
Country: USA
Mailing address: PO Box 630068
Mailing city: Nacogdoches
Mailing state: TX
Mailing zip: 75963
General Phone: 1,18176E+11
Advertising Phone: 19365583200
Editorial Phone: 19365583201
General/National Adv. E-mail: rick.craig@dailysentinel.com
Display Adv. E-mail: anne.long@dailysentinel.com
Classified Adv. e-mail: classifieds@dailysentinel.com
Editorial e-mail: josh.edwards@dailysentinel.com
Primary Website: www.dailysentinel.com
Mthly Avg Views: 350000
Mthly Avg Unique Visitors: 20000
Year Established: 1958
News Services: AP
Special Editions: Best of Nac (June) Senior Expo (October
Delivery Methods: Mail`Newsstand`Carrier`Racks
Areas Served - City/County or Portion Thereof, or Zip codes: Nacogdoches, County, Texas as primary.
Own Printing Facility?: N
Commercial printers?: Y
Avg Free Circ: 150
Sat. Circulation Paid: 4326
Sat. Circulation Free: 918
Sun. Circulation Paid: 5163
Sun. Circulation Free: 403
Audit By: USPS
Audit Date: 29.04.2023
Personnel: Rick Craig (Publisher); Kevin Gore (Sports); Josh Edwards (Managing Editor); Paul Bryant (City Editor)
Parent company (for newspapers): Southern Newspapers Inc.; Southern Newspapers, Inc.; Cox Media Group

NEW BRAUNFELS HERALD-ZEITUNG

Street address 1: 549 Landa Street
Street address city: New Braunfels
Street address state: TX
Zip/Postal code: 78130
County: Comal
Country: USA
Mailing address: PO BOX 311328
Mailing city: NEW BRAUNFELS
Mailing state: TX
Mailing zip: 78131-1328
General Phone: (830) 625-9144
Editorial Phone: (830) 625-9144 ext. 220
General/National Adv. E-mail: advertising@herald-zeitung.com
Display Adv. E-mail: david.compton@herald-zeitung.com
Classified Adv. e-mail: classifieds@herald-zeitung.com
Editorial e-mail: editorial@herald-zeitung.com
Primary Website: www.herald-zeitung.com
Year Established: 1852
News Services: AP.
Special Editions: Medical Tab (Apr); Visitors' Guide (Aug); Babies on Parade (Feb); Chamber Tab (Jan); Visitors' Guide (Jul); Visitors' Guide (Jun); Visitors' Guide (Mar); Small Business (May); Wurstfest Guide (Oct).
Special Weekly Sections: TV Listings, Food, Home, Sports, Planner, Comics, Weather Classifieds (Daily); Entertainment (Thur); Church (Sat); Wedding, Engagements (Sun)
Syndicated Publications: American Profile, Spry
Delivery Methods: Mail`Newsstand`Carrier`Racks
Areas Served - City/County or Portion Thereof, or Zip codes: Comal County, TX
Own Printing Facility?: Y
Commercial printers?: Y
Avg Free Circ: 603
Sat. Circulation Paid: 5711
Sat. Circulation Free: 603
Sun. Circulation Paid: 6483
Sun. Circulation Free: 182
Audit By: AAM
Audit Date: 31.03.2019
Personnel: Henry Coello (Prodn. Mgr.); Joe Hayden (Circ. Dir.); David Compton (Pub.); Jennifer Leal (Bus. Mgr.); Keith Domke (Managing Editor); Lee Stahle (Circ. Asst. Mgr.); Chris Lykins (Managing Ed.); Gerard MacCrossan (Mng. Ed.); Autumn Phillips (News Ed.); Chris Hossman (Sports Ed.); Gus Eibel (Pressroom Supvr.); Neice Bell (Pub.); David Burck (Adv. Dir.); Rosie Willingham (Business Mgr.)
Parent company (for newspapers): Southern Newspapers Inc.

ODESSA AMERICAN

Street address 1: 700 N. Grant, Suite 800
Street address city: Odessa
Street address state: TX
Zip/Postal code: 79761-5122
County: Ector
Country: USA
Mailing address: PO BOX 2952
Mailing city: ODESSA
Mailing state: TX
Mailing zip: 79760-2952
General Phone: (432)337-4661
Advertising Phone: (432) 333-7602
Editorial Phone: (432) 333-7764
General/National Adv. E-mail: sreeves@oaoa.com
Display Adv. E-mail: ckerley@oaoa.com
Classified Adv. e-mail: oaclassified@oaoa.com
Editorial e-mail: ldennis@oaoa.com
Primary Website: www.oaoa.com
Mthly Avg Views: 1300000
Mthly Avg Unique Visitors: 300000
Year Established: 1927
News Services: AP, MCT.
Special Editions: Graduation (June); Football (Aug); Oil Show (Oct - every other year); Holiday Happenings (Dec).
Special Weekly Sections: Best Food Day (Wed); Auto, Real Estate (Thur); Weekly, Entertainment (Fri); Church (Sat); Business, Oil & Gas, Finance (Sun)
Syndicated Publications: Parade (S), Relish, Spry, American Profile
Delivery Methods: Mail`Newsstand`Carrier`Racks
Areas Served - City/County or Portion Thereof, or Zip codes: Ector, Midland, Andrews, Crane, Pecos, Reeves, Upton, Ward and Winkler counties.
Own Printing Facility?: Y
Commercial printers?: Y
Sun. Circulation Paid: 10178
Audit By: AAM
Audit Date: 31.03.2017
Personnel: Laura Dennis (Editor); Gary Hesson (Prod. Foreman, Mail room); Coye Kerley (Director of Advertising & Marketing); Stacey Reeves (Nat'l Adv. Coord.)
Parent company (for newspapers): AIM Media Texas

PALESTINE HERALD-PRESS

Street address 1: 519 N Elm St
Street address city: Palestine
Street address state: TX
Zip/Postal code: 75801-2927
County: Anderson
Country: USA
Mailing address: PO BOX 379
Mailing city: PALESTINE
Mailing state: TX
Mailing zip: 75802-0379
General Phone: (903) 729-0281
General/National Adv. E-mail: jmienk@palestineherald.com
Display Adv. E-mail: jmienk@palestineherald.com
Classified Adv. e-mail: cveretto@palestineherald.com
Editorial e-mail: jmienk@palestineherald.com

Primary Website: www.palestineherald.com
Year Established: 1849
News Services: AP.
Special Editions: Graduation - May Holiday Gift Guide - November OctoberFest -October
Special Weekly Sections: Entertainment (Fri); Community (S); Weekend (Sat); Best Food Day (Tues); Community (Wed).
Syndicated Publications: American Profile (Weekly). Parade
Delivery Methods: Mail
Areas Served - City/County or Portion Thereof, or Zip codes: Anderson County
Own Printing Facility?: Y
Commercial printers?: Y
Sun. Circulation Paid: 6200
Sun. Circulation Free: 5013
Audit By: Sworn/Estimate/Non-Audited
Audit Date: 12.07.2019
Personnel: Liz Falesch (Bus. Mgr.); Candy Facklaeo (Circ. Mgr.); Angie Alvardo (Mng. Ed.); Cheril Vermon (Features Ed.); Scott Tyler (Sports Ed.); Jim Buckley (Prodn. Mgr.); Jake Mienk (Publisher); Thomas MartÃ-nez (Ed.)
Parent company (for newspapers): CNHI, LLC; CNHI, LLC

THE PAMPA NEWS

Street address 1: 403 W Atchison Ave
Street address city: Pampa
Street address state: TX
Zip/Postal code: 79065-6303
County: Gray
Country: USA
Mailing address: PO BOX 2198
Mailing city: PAMPA
Mailing state: TX
Mailing zip: 79066-2198
General Phone: (806) 669-2525
Advertising Phone: (806) 669-2525
Editorial Phone: (806) 669-2525
General/National Adv. E-mail: rwoods@thepampanews.com
Display Adv. E-mail: rwoods@thepampanews.com
Classified Adv. e-mail: classified1@thepampanews.com
Editorial e-mail: jclee@thepampanews.com
Primary Website: www.thepampanews.com
Year Established: 1906
News Services: AP.
Special Editions: Christmas Greetings/Letters to Santa Gray County Visitor's Guide Pride and Progress Football Guide Area Dining Guide Gray County Church Directory
Special Weekly Sections: Church (Wed); Women (Sat)
Syndicated Publications: Gray County Visitor's Guide (Annually).
Delivery Methods: Mail`Newsstand`Racks
Areas Served - City/County or Portion Thereof, or Zip codes: 79065
Own Printing Facility?: Y
Commercial printers?: Y
Sat. Circulation Paid: 4100
Audit By: Sworn/Estimate/Non-Audited
Audit Date: 12.07.2019
Personnel: Sue Pribble (Circ. Mgr.); ReDonn Woods (Pub./Adv. Mgr.); Beverly Taylor (Classified Mgr.); John Lee (Editor); Timothy Howsare (Ed.); Marcus Elkins (Production Mgr.)

THE PARIS NEWS

Street address 1: 5050 S. E. Loop 286
Street address city: Paris
Street address state: TX
Zip/Postal code: 75461
County: Lamar
Country: USA
Mailing address: PO BOX 1078
Mailing city: PARIS
Mailing state: TX
Mailing zip: 75461-1078
General Phone: (903) 785-8744
Advertising Phone: (903) 785-8744
Editorial Phone: (903) 785-8744
General/National Adv. E-mail: bren.garrett@theparisnews.com
Display Adv. E-mail: bren.garrett@theparisnews.com
Classified Adv. e-mail: myriah.nance@theparisnews.com
Editorial e-mail: editor@theparisnews.com
Primary Website: www.theparisnews.com
Year Established: 1869
News Services: AP.
Special Editions: Brides (Apr); Newcomer's Guide (Aug); Greetings (Dec); Home Furnishings (Feb); Quarterly Farm & Ranch Review (Jun); Quarterly Farm & Ranch Review (Mar); Progress (May); Car Care (Nov); New Car (Oct); Football (Sept).
Special Weekly Sections: Business & Industry (Mon); NASCAR (Tue); Outdoors, Spotlight on Business (Thur); Religion, Entertainment Weekly (Fri); Business, lifestyle (Sun); Senior (First Sunday); Farm, Ranch, Lifestyles (Quarterly)
Syndicated Publications: TV & Entertainment Guide (Fri); Parade (S).
Delivery Methods: Mail`Newsstand`Carrier`Racks
Own Printing Facility?: Y
Commercial printers?: Y
Avg Free Circ: 134
Sun. Circulation Paid: 4764
Sun. Circulation Free: 29
Audit By: AAM
Audit Date: 31.03.2019
Personnel: Relan Walker (Bus. Mgr.); Mel Parker (Adv. Dir.); Scott Baendy (Circ. Mgr.); Mary Madewell (Online Ed.); Van Hilburn (Sports Ed.); Tammy Barnes (Prodn. Mgr., Mailroom); Fred Downs (Prodn. Mgr., Pressroom); JD Davidson (Pub.); Sheryl Smith (Adv. Sales Rep.); Connie Beard (Managing Ed.)
Parent company (for newspapers): Southern Newspapers Inc.

PLAINVIEW HERALD

Street address 1: 820 Broadway St
Street address city: Plainview
Street address state: TX
Zip/Postal code: 79072-7316
County: Hale
Country: USA
Mailing address: 820 BROADWAY ST
Mailing city: PLAINVIEW
Mailing state: TX
Mailing zip: 79072-7316
General Phone: (806) 296-1340
Advertising Phone: (806) 296-1320
Editorial Phone: (806) 296-1353
General/National Adv. E-mail: cortega@hearstnp.com
Display Adv. E-mail: cortega@hearstnp.com
Classified Adv. e-mail: cmcgill@hearstnp.com
Editorial e-mail: william.carroll@hearstnp.com
Primary Website: www.myplainview.com
Year Established: 1889
News Services: AP, HN, NYT.
Special Editions: Back-to-School (Aug); Honor Roll (Mar).
Special Weekly Sections: Agriculture (Wed, Sun); Best Food Day (Thur); Church, Religion (Fri); Agriculture, Business (Sun)
Syndicated Publications: Relish (Monthly); Parade (S); American Profile (Weekly).
Delivery Methods: Mail`Newsstand`Carrier`Racks
Areas Served - City/County or Portion Thereof, or Zip codes: Hale County, Swisher County, Briscoe County, Lamb County, Floyd County, Castro County (Texas)
Own Printing Facility?: N
Commercial printers?: N
Sun. Circulation Paid: 6000
Audit By: Sworn/Estimate/Non-Audited
Audit Date: 12.07.2019
Personnel: Ellysa Harris (Ed.); Carmen Ortega (Adv. Dir.)
Parent company (for newspapers): Hearst Communications, Inc.

PORT ARTHUR NEWS

Street address 1: 2349 Memorial Blvd
Street address city: Port Arthur
Street address state: TX
Zip/Postal code: 77640-2822
County: Jefferson
Country: USA
Mailing address: PO BOX 789
Mailing city: PORT ARTHUR
Mailing state: TX
Mailing zip: 77641-0789
General Phone: (409) 721-2417
Editorial Phone: (409) 721-2431
General/National Adv. E-mail: ed.kestler@panews.com
Display Adv. E-mail: ed.kestler@panews.com
Classified Adv. e-mail: classads@panews.com
Editorial e-mail: panews@panews.com
Primary Website: www.panews.com
Year Established: 1897
News Services: AP.
Special Editions: Family-Owned Business (Jan); Visitor's Guide (May); Cav-oil-cade (Oct).
Special Weekly Sections: Best Food Day (Wed); Entertainment (Fri)
Syndicated Publications: American Profile (Fri); Relish (Monthly); USA WEEKEND Magazine (S).
Delivery Methods: Mail`Newsstand`Carrier`Racks
Own Printing Facility?: Y
Commercial printers?: Y
Sat. Circulation Paid: 8138
Sun. Circulation Paid: 9000
Audit By: AAM
Audit Date: 31.03.2017
Personnel: Rich Macke (Publisher); Roger Cowles (Editorial Page Ed.)
Parent company (for newspapers): Boone Newspapers, Inc.

LETTERS FROM NORTH AMERICA

Street address 1: 2002 N Greens Blvd
Street address city: Richmond
Street address state: TX
Zip/Postal code: 77406-6673
County: FORT BEND
Country: USA
Mailing address: 2002 N. Greens Blvd
Mailing city: Richmond
Mailing state: TX
Mailing zip: 77406
General Phone: (512) 653-8545
General/National Adv. E-mail: pperry@pearyperry.com
Primary Website: www.pearyperry.com
Mthly Avg Views: 5000
Mthly Avg Unique Visitors: 1000
Year Established: 1993
Avg Free Circ: 1000
Audit By: USPS
Personnel: Peary Perry (Self-Synd/Columnist)
Parent company (for newspapers): P.PERRY&ASSOCIATES

FORT BEND HERALD

Street address 1: 1902 4th St
Street address city: Rosenberg
Street address state: TX
Zip/Postal code: 77471-5140
County: Fort Bend
Country: USA
Mailing address: PO BOX 1088
Mailing city: ROSENBERG
Mailing state: TX
Mailing zip: 77471-1088
General Phone: 281-342-4474
General/National Adv. E-mail: leehart@herald-coaster.com
Display Adv. E-mail: leehart@fbherald.com
Classified Adv. e-mail: classad@fbherald.com
Editorial e-mail: swilley@fbherald.com
Primary Website: www.fbherald.com
Year Established: 1892
News Services: AP.
Special Weekly Sections: Sports, Comics, Classifieds, Editorial (Daily); Business (Wed); Entertainment, TV, Religion, Church, Weddings, Engagements (Sun)
Syndicated Publications: Relish (Monthly); American Profile (Weekly).
Delivery Methods: Mail`Newsstand`Carrier`Racks
Areas Served - City/County or Portion Thereof, or Zip codes: HOUSTON--GALVESTON--BRAZORIA, TX CMSA
Own Printing Facility?: Y
Commercial printers?: Y
Avg Free Circ: 179
Sun. Circulation Paid: 7450
Sun. Circulation Free: 254
Audit By: CVC
Audit Date: 30.06.2009
Personnel: Clyde C. King (Pres.); Lee Hartman (Gen. Mgr.); Gary Martin (Sports Ed.); Stephanie Welch (Prodn. Mgr.); Scott Reese Willey (Managing Ed.); Bill Shannon (Circ. Dir.); Dennis Garrison (Adv. Dir.)
Parent company (for newspapers): Hartman Newspapers LP

SAN ANGELO STANDARD-TIMES

Street address 1: 34 W. Harris Avenue
Street address city: San Angelo
Street address state: TX
Zip/Postal code: 76903
County: Tom Green
Country: USA
Mailing address: 34 W HARRIS AVE
Mailing city: SAN ANGELO
Mailing state: TX
Mailing zip: 76903-5838
General Phone: (325) 659-8201
Advertising Phone: (325) 659-8209
Editorial Phone: (325)659-8249
General/National Adv. E-mail: kate.rushing@gosanangelo.com
Display Adv. E-mail: kate.rushing@gosanangelo.com
Classified Adv. e-mail: kate.rushing@gosanangelo.com
Editorial e-mail: mike.kelly@gosanangelo.com
Primary Website: www.gosanangelo.com
Mthly Avg Unique Visitors: 323047
Year Established: 1884
News Services: AP, SHNS.
Special Editions: San Angelo Living (annual); Blitz football preview (Fridays during football season); San Angelo Stockshow and Rodeo (annual)
Special Weekly Sections: Business (Mon); Alternate Health, Education (Tue); Best Food (Wed); Viewpoints (Thur); Arts, Entertainment (Fri); Religion, Auto (Sat); TV (Sun);
Syndicated Publications: My San Angelo (local news weekly, broadsheet) (Other); Parade (S); Hunting (annual); Senior Sourcebook (annual)
Delivery Methods: Mail`Carrier`Racks
Areas Served - City/County or Portion Thereof, or Zip codes: 76821, 76825, 76837, 76849, 76856, 76859, 76861, 76866, 76875, 76886, 76901, 76903, 76904, 76905, 76908, 76930, 76932, 76933, 76934, 76935, 76936, 76937, 76941, 76943, 76945, 76950, 76951, 76957, 76958, 78624, 79567, 79739
Avg Free Circ: 404
Sat. Circulation Paid: 11355
Sat. Circulation Free: 404
Sun. Circulation Paid: 12378
Sun. Circulation Free: 322
Audit By: AAM
Audit Date: 31.12.2017
Personnel: Monty Stanley (HR Dir.); Tim Archuleta (Ed.); Rick Smith (Columnist); Jeff DeLoach (Pub./Adv. Dir.); Pam Hammer (Adv. Dir.); Kate Rushing (Nat'l Acct. Exec.); Jimmy Baugh (Circ. Sales Mgr.)
Parent company (for newspapers): Gannett - USA Today Network

SAN ANTONIO EXPRESS-NEWS

Street address 1: 301 Avenue E
Street address city: San Antonio
Street address state: TX
Zip/Postal code: 78297
County: Bexar
Country: USA
Mailing address: PO BOX 2171
Mailing city: SAN ANTONIO
Mailing state: TX
Mailing zip: 78297-2171
General Phone: (210) 250-3000
Advertising Phone: (210) 250-2500
Editorial Phone: (210) 250-3171
General/National Adv. E-mail: rmccutcheon@express-news.net
Display Adv. E-mail: rmccutcheon@express-news.net
Classified Adv. e-mail: murias@express-news.net
Editorial e-mail: mleary@express-news.net
Primary Website: www.mySA.com
Mthly Avg Views: 60000000
Mthly Avg Unique Visitors: 3335707
Year Established: 1865
News Services: AP, NYT, LAT-WP, Bloomberg, MCT, GNS.
Special Editions: Higher Education Handbook, Rodeo, Readers Choice, Guide to San Antonio, Spurs Nation
Special Weekly Sections: Health, Fitness, Elders, Business (Mon); Mom's, Business, Kids, Family, Animals, Pets (Tues), Stock (Tues-Sat), Live Music, TV (Wed), Style (Thurs), Entertainment, Auto (Fri), Religion, Drive, Trends (Sat), Real Estate, Technology, Travel, Arts, Comics, Taste, Home (Sun)
Areas Served - City/County or Portion Thereof, or Zip codes: 78238, 78229, 78240, 78251, 78253, 78250, 78254, 78006, 78023, 78249, 78255, 78256, 78015, 78257, 78228,78201, 78212, 78216, 78209, 78213, 78230, 78234, 78217, 78202, 78205, 78208, 78215, 78231, 78248, 78258, 78259, 78260, 78232, 78247, 78261, 78218, 78219, 78233, 78239, 78109, 78244, 78108, 78148, 78154, 78266, 78203, 78204, 78210, 78220, 78214, 78221, 78224, 78222, 78223, 78235, 78245, 78207, 78211, 78225, 78226, 78237, 78227, 78236, 78242, 78002, 78101, 78112, 78152, 78069, 78073, 78252, 78263, 78264
Sat. Circulation Paid: 76682

Sun. Circulation Paid: 129878
Audit By: AAM
Audit Date: 31.12.2017
Personnel: Raymond McCutcheon (EVP, Advertising and Marketing); Susan Lynch Pape (Publisher); Jamie Stockwell (Managing Editor); Cory Heikkila (Executive Digital Media Producer); Joseph Braunschweig (VP of Circulation); Mark Duvoisin (Ed. & VP)
Parent company (for newspapers): Hearst Communications, Inc.

SAN MARCOS DAILY RECORD

Street address 1: 1910 S Interstate 35
Street address city: San Marcos
Street address state: TX
Zip/Postal code: 78666-5901
County: Hays
Country: USA
Mailing address: PO BOX 1109
Mailing city: SAN MARCOS
Mailing state: TX
Mailing zip: 78667-1109
General Phone: (512) 392-2458
Advertising Phone: (512)392-2458
Editorial Phone: (512) 392-2458
General/National Adv. E-mail: mholt@sanmarcosrecord.com
Display Adv. E-mail: mholt@sanmarcosrecord.com
Classified Adv. e-mail: mholt@sanmarcosrecord.com
Editorial e-mail: dsweat@wimberleyview.com
Primary Website: www.sanmarcosrecord.com
Year Established: 1912
News Services: AP.
Special Editions: Back-to-School (Aug); Progress (Feb).
Special Weekly Sections: Best Food Day (Wed); Wellness, Grocery Ads (Tue); Living (Wed); Cultural Arts (Thur); Earth Talks (Fri)
Syndicated Publications: USA WEEKEND Magazine (S); American Profile (Weekly).
Delivery Methods: Newsstand`Carrier`Racks
Areas Served - City/County or Portion Thereof, or Zip codes: San Marcos, Hays, 78666
Own Printing Facility?: Y
Commercial printers?: Y
Avg Free Circ: 10000
Sun. Circulation Paid: 4100
Audit By: USPS
Audit Date: 01.10.2017
Personnel: Karen George (Circ. Dir.); Anita Miller (News Ed.); Joe Vozzelli (Sports Editor); Karen Ray (Prodn. Supvr.); Don Moore (Pub.); Marcy Holt (Adv. Dir.); David Short (Exec. Ed.); Chris Urbanovsky (Production Dir.)
Parent company (for newspapers): Moser Community Media

THE SEGUIN GAZETTE

Street address 1: 1012 Schriewer Road
Street address city: Seguin
Street address state: TX
Zip/Postal code: 78155
County: Guadalupe
Country: USA
Mailing address: PO BOX 1200
Mailing city: SEGUIN
Mailing state: TX
Mailing zip: 78156-1200
General Phone: (830) 379-5402
General/National Adv. E-mail: elizabeth.engelhardt@seguingazette.com
Display Adv. E-mail: elizabeth.engelhardt@seguingazette.com
Classified Adv. e-mail: classifieds@seguingazette.com
Editorial e-mail: editor@seguingazette.com
Primary Website: www.seguingazette.com
Mthly Avg Views: 500000
Mthly Avg Unique Visitors: 150000
Year Established: 1888
News Services: AP
Special Weekly Sections: Sports, TV, Comics, health, Education, Seniors (Daily); Real Estate, Auto (Tue, Wed, Thur, Sun); Agriculture, Health, TV, Weddings, Engagements, Outdoor, Business, Lifestyle, Opinions, Entertainment (Sun); Senior (Tue); Business, Lifestyle, Opinions (Wed); Entertainment, Garden, Agriculture, Best Food Day (Thur); Church, lifestyle, Opinions (Fri)
Syndicated Publications: Weekly TV Guide (S); American Profile (S); USA Weekend (F); Relish; Spry
Delivery Methods: Mail`Newsstand`Carrier`Racks
Areas Served - City/County or Portion Thereof, or Zip codes: City of Seguin; Guadalupe and Comal counties
Own Printing Facility?: N
Commercial printers?: N
Avg Free Circ: 1025
Sun. Circulation Paid: 3363
Sun. Circulation Free: 1814
Audit By: CAC
Audit Date: 31.03.2017
Personnel: Maggie Clarkson (Business Manager); Travis Webb (Managing Editor); Jeff Fowler (President, Editor & Publisher); Elizabeth Engelhardt (Advertising Director); Brenda Mrazek (Circulation Director); Hannah Ruiz (Creative Director)
Parent company (for newspapers): Southern Newspapers Inc.; The Seguin Gazette-Enterprise

HERALD DEMOCRAT

Street address 1: 603 S. Sam Rayburn Freeway
Street address city: Sherman
Street address state: TX
Zip/Postal code: 75090
County: Grayson
Country: USA
Mailing address: PO BOX 1128
Mailing city: SHERMAN
Mailing state: TX
Mailing zip: 75091-1128
General Phone: (903) 893-8181
General/National Adv. E-mail: advertising@heralddemocrat.com
Display Adv. E-mail: advertising@heralddemocrat.com
Classified Adv. e-mail: classified@heralddemocrat.com
Editorial e-mail: news@heralddemocrat.com
Primary Website: www.heralddemocrat.com
Year Established: 1879
News Services: AP, SHNS.
Special Editions: Home Improvement (Apr); Home Improvement (Aug); Christmas Greetings (Dec); Home Improvement (Jul); Car Care (Jun); Chamber of Commerce Industrial Review (Mar); Brides (May); Christmas Gift Guide (Nov); Car Care (Oct); Football (Sept).
Special Weekly Sections: Best Food Day (Wed); Business (Daily); Religion (Fri)
Syndicated Publications: Relish (Monthly); USA WEEKEND Magazine (S).
Delivery Methods: Mail`Newsstand`Carrier`Racks
Areas Served - City/County or Portion Thereof, or Zip codes: 75090, 75091, 75092, 75020, 75021
Own Printing Facility?: Y
Commercial printers?: Y
Avg Free Circ: 857
Sat. Circulation Paid: 7882
Sat. Circulation Free: 857
Sun. Circulation Paid: 8059
Sun. Circulation Free: 114
Audit By: AAM
Audit Date: 31.12.2018
Personnel: John P. Wright (Pub.); Dianne Harp (Credit Mgr.); Jennifer Parker (Adv. Mgr., Classified); Wes King (Adv. Dir./Nat'l Dir.); Mike Brezina (Circ. Dir.); Darrell McCorstin (News/Wire Ed.); Bill Spinks (Sports Ed.); Raymond Hodge (Mailroom Supvr.); Teresa Redd (Prodn. Mgr., Composing); Mike Harkey (Prodn. Mgr., Pressroom); Jonathan Cannon (Ed.)
Parent company (for newspapers): Gannett; CherryRoad Media

SNYDER DAILY NEWS

Street address 1: 3600 College Ave
Street address city: Snyder
Street address state: TX
Zip/Postal code: 79549-4637
County: Scurry
Country: USA
Mailing address: PO BOX 949
Mailing city: SNYDER
Mailing state: TX
Mailing zip: 79550-0949
General Phone: (325) 573-5486
General/National Adv. E-mail: advertising@snyderdailynews.com
Display Adv. E-mail: advertising@snyderdailynews.com
Classified Adv. e-mail: classified@snyderdailynews.com
Editorial e-mail: barkley@snyderdailynews.com
Primary Website: www.snyderdailynews.com
Mthly Avg Views: 120000
Mthly Avg Unique Visitors: 450
Year Established: 1950
News Services: Associated Press
Special Editions: Christmas Greetings (Dec); Football (Aug.); Graduation (May); various others.
Special Weekly Sections: Best Food Day (Tue); Oil, Farm (Thurs)
Delivery Methods: Mail`Newsstand`Carrier`Racks
Areas Served - City/County or Portion Thereof, or Zip codes: 79549+
Own Printing Facility?: Y
Commercial printers?: Y
Sun. Circulation Paid: 3400
Audit By: Sworn/Estimate/Non-Audited
Audit Date: 12.07.2019
Personnel: Wade Warren (Asst. Pub.); Donna Browning (Adv. Mgr., Classified); Larry McCarthy (Sports Ed.); Bill Crist (Pub.); Christie Adams (Business Mgr.); Ben Barkley (Ed.)
Parent company (for newspapers): Roberts Group

STEPHENVILLE EMPIRE-TRIBUNE

Street address 1: 702 E South Loop
Street address city: Stephenville
Street address state: TX
Zip/Postal code: 76401-5314
County: Erath
Country: USA
Mailing address: PO BOX 958
Mailing city: STEPHENVILLE
Mailing state: TX
Mailing zip: 76401-0009
General Phone: (254) 965-3124
Advertising Phone: (254) 965-3124
Editorial Phone: (254) 965-3124
General/National Adv. E-mail: ssimmons@empiretribune.com
Display Adv. E-mail: ssimmons@empiretribune.com
Classified Adv. e-mail: swoods@empiretribune.com
Editorial e-mail: svandenberge@empiretribune.com
Primary Website: www.yourstephenvilletx.com
Year Established: 1900
News Services: AP, General Media.
Special Editions: Progress (Feb); Mature Time (Monthly).
Special Weekly Sections: Best Food day (Tue); Religion (Fri); Lifestyles, Wedding, Engagements, Agriculture, 4-H, TV, Comics, Real Estate, Outdoors, Business, Movie, Entertainment (Sun)
Syndicated Publications: American Profile (S). SPRY, Atholon Sports
Delivery Methods: Mail`Newsstand`Carrier`Racks
Areas Served - City/County or Portion Thereof, or Zip codes: 76401
Own Printing Facility?: N
Commercial printers?: N
Sun. Circulation Paid: 4500
Audit By: Sworn/Estimate/Non-Audited
Audit Date: 12.07.2019
Personnel: Jerry Pye (Pub.); Judy Terry (Co-Pub.); Jimmy Gelvan (Managing Ed.); Jessie Frausto (Circ. Mgr.)
Parent company (for newspapers): Gannett; CherryRoad Media

SULPHUR SPRINGS NEWS-TELEGRAM

Street address 1: 401 Church St
Street address city: Sulphur Springs
Street address state: TX
Zip/Postal code: 75482-2681
County: Hopkins
Country: USA
Mailing address: PO BOX 596
Mailing city: SULPHUR SPRINGS
Mailing state: TX
Mailing zip: 75483-0596
General Phone: (903) 885-8663
General/National Adv. E-mail: angie@ssecho.com
Display Adv. E-mail: ashley@ssecho.com
Classified Adv. e-mail: classified-ads@ssecho.com
Editorial e-mail: editor@ssecho.com
Primary Website: www.myssnews.com
News Services: AP.
Special Weekly Sections: Best Food Day (Tue); Business (Thur); TV (Fri); Variety, Real Estate (Sun)
Areas Served - City/County or Portion Thereof, or Zip codes: 75482, 75478, 75471, 75420, 75433, 75481, 75431, 75437, 75497, 75494, 75440
Sun. Circulation Paid: 6118
Audit By: Sworn/Estimate/Non-Audited
Audit Date: 12.07.2019
Personnel: Scott Keys (Pres./Pub.); Jim Butler (Vice Pres.); Carolyn Keys (Sec./Treasurer); Butch Burney (Gen. Mgr.); Kristi Hayes (Circ. Mgr.); Faith Huffman (News Ed.); Bobby Burney (Sports Ed.); Davy Moseley (MIS Mgr./Websmaster); Leslie McCullough (Adv. Dir.); JR Foreman (Adv. Sales); Jeremy Reynolds (Adv. Sales Rep.); Sara Cessna (Classified Sales)
Parent company (for newspapers): Echo Publishing Co., Inc.

SWEETWATER REPORTER

Street address 1: 112 W 3rd St
Street address city: Sweetwater
Street address state: TX
Zip/Postal code: 79556-4430
County: Nolan
Country: USA
Mailing address: PO BOX 750
Mailing city: SWEETWATER
Mailing state: TX
Mailing zip: 79556-0750
General Phone: (325) 236-6677
Advertising Phone: (325)236-6677
Editorial Phone: (325)236-6677
General/National Adv. E-mail: business@sweetwaterreporter.com
Display Adv. E-mail: business@sweetwaterreporter.com
Classified Adv. e-mail: business@sweetwaterreporter.com
Editorial e-mail: publisher@sweetwaterreporter.com
Primary Website: www.sweetwaterreporter.com
Year Established: 1881
News Services: AP.
Special Editions: AJRA National Finals Tab (Jul); Rattlesnake Tab (Mar) Hometown Heroes(Sep)
Special Weekly Sections: Church News (Fri); Business (S); Grocery Inserts (Tues).
Syndicated Publications: American Profile (Weekly).
Delivery Methods: Mail`Carrier`Racks
Areas Served - City/County or Portion Thereof, or Zip codes: 79506, 79512, 79526, 79535, 79536, 79537, 79543, 79545, 79546, 79556
Own Printing Facility?: Y
Sun. Circulation Paid: 4176
Audit By: Sworn/Estimate/Non-Audited
Audit Date: 12.07.2019
Personnel: Sharon Friedlander (Pub.); Danica Hickson (Bus. Mgr.); Brenda Morales (Adv. Sales Mgr.); Justin Ramirez (Adv. Sales Mgr.); Pablo Rodriguez (Composing Mgr.); Bleu Reyes (Prodn. Mgr., Pressroom); Tatiana Rodriguez (Ed.); Rick Nunez (Ad Dir.); Zela Armstrong (Gen. Mgr. / Adv. Dir.)
Parent company (for newspapers): Horizon Publications Inc.

TEMPLE DAILY TELEGRAM

Street address 1: 10 South Third Street
Street address city: Temple
Street address state: TX
Zip/Postal code: 76501
County: Bell
Country: USA
Mailing address: PO BOX 6114
Mailing city: TEMPLE
Mailing state: TX
Mailing zip: 76503-6114
General Phone: (254) 778-4444
Advertising Phone: (254) 778-4444
General/National Adv. E-mail: advertiz@tdtnews.com
Display Adv. E-mail: advertiz@tdtnews.com
Classified Adv. e-mail: tdtads@tdnews.com
Editorial e-mail: tdt@tdtnews.com
Primary Website: www.tdtnews.com
Mthly Avg Views: 606000
Mthly Avg Unique Visitors: 138000
Year Established: 1907
News Services: AP.
Special Editions: Tex Appeal Bridal (Jan); Day For Women (Feb.); TABA Home and Garden Expo (Feb.); Roll of Honor (Feb.); Home and Garden (Mar.); Parade of Homes (Apr.); Family Owned Business (Apr.); Tex Appeal Women in Business (May); Community Guide (June); Tex Appeal Brides (July); Football Preview (Aug.); Tex Appeal Medical (Sept.); Readers Choice (Nov.); Holiday Gift Guide (Nov.); Holiday Favorite Finds (Dec.).
Special Weekly Sections: Farm (Mon); Business (Tue); Best Food (Wed); Auto, Entertainment (Thur); Auto (Fri); Church, Auto, Employment, Real Estate (Sat); Best Food, Arts, Entertainment, Employment, Real Estate (Sun); Editorials, Comics, TV (Daily)
Syndicated Publications: Parade (S); Relish (monthly); Athlon Sports (monthly)
Delivery Methods: Mail`Newsstand`Carrier`Racks

Areas Served - City/County or Portion Thereof, or Zip codes: 76501 Temple 76502 Temple 76504 Temple 76508 Temple 76511 Bartlett 76513 Belton 76518 Buckholts 76519 Burlington 76520 Cameron 76522 Copperas Cove 76527 Florence 76528 Eddy-Gatesville 76530 Granger 76534 Holland 76537 Jarrell 76539 Kempner 76541 Killeen 76542 Killeen 76543 Harker Heights/Killeen 76544 Fort Hood 76548 Harker Heights 76549 Killeen 76550 Lampasas 76554 Little River Academy 76557 Moody 76559 Nolanville 76567 Rockdale 76569 Rogers 76570 Rosebud 76571 Salado 76579 Troy 76656 Lott
Own Printing Facility?: Y
Commercial printers?: Y
Avg Free Circ: 1086
Sat. Circulation Paid: 11431
Sat. Circulation Free: 1086
Sun. Circulation Paid: 13625
Sun. Circulation Free: 331
Audit By: AAM
Audit Date: 31.03.2018
Personnel: Dan Cooper (Gen. Mgr.); Lauren Ballard (Adv. Dir.); Gary Garner (Retail Adv. Mgr.); Sue Mayborn (Editor and Publisher); Jerry Prickett (Assistant Managing Editor)
Parent company (for newspapers): Frank Mayborn Enterprises, Inc.

TYLER MORNING TELEGRAPH

Street address 1: 410 W Erwin St
Street address city: Tyler
Street address state: TX
Zip/Postal code: 75702-7133
County: Smith
Country: USA
Mailing address: 410 W ERWIN ST
Mailing city: TYLER
Mailing state: TX
Mailing zip: 75702-7133
General Phone: (903) 597-8111
Advertising Phone: (903) 597-8111
Editorial Phone: (903) 597-8111
General/National Adv. E-mail: advertising@tylerpaper.com
Display Adv. E-mail: advertising@tylerpaper.com
Classified Adv. e-mail: classifieds@tylerpaper.com
Editorial e-mail: apollan@tylerpaper.com
Primary Website: www.tylerpaper.com
Year Established: 1929
News Services: AP, SHNS.
Special Editions: Business & Industry (Apr); Football (Aug); Christmas Greetings (Dec); Engineer's Week (Feb); Pillars of Progress (Jan); Parade of Homes (Jul); Senior Citizens (Jun); TALC (Mar); Discover Summer (May); Rose Festival (Oct); Clubs & Organizations (Sept).
Special Weekly Sections: Business (Mon); Best Food Days (Wed/Sun); SAG (Thur)
Syndicated Publications: Parade (S).
Areas Served - City/County or Portion Thereof, or Zip codes: Smith, Henderson, Anderson, Cherokee, Rusk, Gregg, Wood, and Van Zandt counties
Sat. Circulation Paid: 13957
Sun. Circulation Paid: 16660
Audit By: AAM
Audit Date: 30.09.2017
Personnel: Nelson Clyde (Pub.); Thomas Clyde (CFO); Art McClelland (Vice Pres., Sales/Mktg.); Robin Land (Adv. Mgr., Nat'l); Jasper Curtis (Adv. Mgr., Ops.); Jerry Rives (Circ. Dir.); Jim Giametta (Exec. Ed.); Dave Berry (Mng. Ed.); Richard Loomis (Asst. Mng. Ed.); Danny Mogle (Asst. Mng. Ed.); Greg Junek (Bus. Ed.); Joyce Turner (Community Ed.); Betty Waters (Educ. Ed.); Diane May (Librarian); Patrick Butler (Religion Ed.); Phil Hicks (Sports Ed.); Terry Cannon (Travel Ed.); David R. Stringer (Adv. Dir.); Matt Milling (Prod. & Dist. Dir.); Carlina Villalpando (Editor); Mary Suits (Circ. Mgr.)
Parent company (for newspapers): M. Roberts Media; Victoria Advocate Publishing Co.

THE VERNON DAILY RECORD

Street address 1: 3214 Wilbarger St
Street address city: Vernon
Street address state: TX
Zip/Postal code: 76384-7927
County: Wilbarger
Country: USA
Mailing address: 3214 WILBARGER ST
Mailing city: VERNON
Mailing state: TX
Mailing zip: 76384-7927
General Phone: (940) 552-5454
Advertising Phone: (940)552-5454
Editorial Phone: (940)552-5454
General/National Adv. E-mail: advertising@vernonrecord.com
Display Adv. E-mail: advertising@vernonrecord.com
Classified Adv. e-mail: classified@vernonrecord.com
Editorial e-mail: publisher@vernonrecord.com
Primary Website: www.vernonrecord.com
Year Established: 1908
News Services: AP.
Special Weekly Sections: Best Food Day (Tue)
Delivery Methods: Newsstand`Carrier`Racks
Areas Served - City/County or Portion Thereof, or Zip codes: 76384, 76385, 79252, 79225, 79227
Own Printing Facility?: Y
Commercial printers?: Y
Sun. Circulation Paid: 2500
Audit By: Sworn/Estimate/Non-Audited
Audit Date: 12.07.2019
Personnel: Keith McCormick (Treasurer); Charles Ashley (Prodn. Mgr.); Bret McCormick (Pres./Pub.); Teri McCormick (Classified & New Media Dir.); Payton McCormick (Ed.); Daniel Walker (Managing Editor); Shelby McCormick (Advertising Director); Joyce Ashley (Lifestyle editor); Chance Baskerville (Sports Editor)
Parent company (for newspapers): Vernon Record, Inc.

VICTORIA ADVOCATE

Street address 1: 311 E Constitution St
Street address city: Victoria
Street address state: TX
Zip/Postal code: 77901-8140
County: Victoria
Country: USA
Mailing address: PO BOX 1518
Mailing city: VICTORIA
Mailing state: TX
Mailing zip: 77902-1518
General Phone: (361) 580-6557
Advertising Phone: (361) 574-1241
Editorial Phone: (361) 574-1222
General/National Adv. E-mail: tbonner@vicad.com
Display Adv. E-mail: tbonner@vicad.com
Classified Adv. e-mail: tbonner@vicad.com
Editorial e-mail: newsroom@vicad.com
Primary Website: www.victoriaadvocate.com
Year Established: 1846
News Services: AP, NYT.
Special Editions: Looking Good, Feeling Food (Aug); Holiday Inspirations (Dec); Livestock (Feb); Home Product Show (Mar); Meet Your Local Merchants (May); All In Good Taste (Nov); Farm & Ranch (Oct).
Special Weekly Sections: Good Living, Big Wed (Wed); Seniors, Entertainment (Thur); Home,Garden, Travel (Fri); Church, Auto (Sat); Farm, Oil & Gas, Lifestyles, Money (Sun)
Syndicated Publications: Parade (S).
Areas Served - City/County or Portion Thereof, or Zip codes: 78648, 78682, 78959, 78629, 78614, 78677, 78159, 78956, 78935, 78962, 77442, 77434, 77435, 77485, 77441, 77488, 77461, 77406, 77469, 77420, 77417, 77406, 77494, 77407, 77498, 77479, 77469, 77430, 77486, 77422, 77975, 77984, 77995, 77964, 77994, 77954, 78164, 78141, 77963, 77905, 77904, 77901, 77968, 77951, 78340, 78393, 78377, 77990, 77979, 77983, 77957, 77962, 77971, 77455, 77437, 77432, 77458, 77419, 77465, 77456, 77440, 77468, 77482, 78102, 78389, 78387, 78370, 78390, 78374, 78362, 78336, 78382, 78982
Avg Free Circ: 445
Sat. Circulation Paid: 15728
Sat. Circulation Free: 445
Sun. Circulation Paid: 17426
Sun. Circulation Free: 354
Audit By: AAM
Audit Date: 30.09.2018
Personnel: Catherine McHaney (Sec./Treasurer); Stephen McHaney (VP); Chris Cobler (Pub.); Becky Cooper (Other); John M. Roberts (Pres.); Frank Tilley (Photo Ed.); Ortega J.R. (Feat. Ed. and Diversity Reporter); Thomas Bonner (Nat'l Adv. Mgr.); Kevin Thaete (Cir. Dir.)
Parent company (for newspapers): Victoria Advocate Publishing Co.

WACO TRIBUNE-HERALD

Street address 1: 900 Franklin Avenue
Street address city: Waco
Street address state: TX
Zip/Postal code: 76701-1906
County: McLennan
Country: USA
Mailing address: PO BOX 2588
Mailing city: WACO
Mailing state: TX
Mailing zip: 76702-2588
General Phone: (254) 757-5788
Advertising Phone: (254) 757-5830
Editorial Phone: (254) 757-5701
General/National Adv. E-mail: rprince@wacotrib.com
Display Adv. E-mail: rprince@wacotrib.com
Classified Adv. e-mail: classifieds@wacotrib.com
Editorial e-mail: letters@wacotrib.com
Primary Website: www.wacotrib.com
Mthly Avg Views: 4255000
Mthly Avg Unique Visitors: 400000
Year Established: 1892
News Services: AP, NYT
Special Editions: Garden & Landscape (Apr); Back-to-School (Aug); Christmas Gift Guide (Dec); Spring Fashion (Feb); Bridal (Jan); This is Central Texas (Jul); Business & Industry (May); Seniors (Monthly); Health Directory (Nov); New Cars (Oct); Home Furnishings (Sept).
Special Weekly Sections: Business in Review (Mon); Health, Fitness (Tue); Best Food Day (Wed); Home, Entertainment (Thur); Movies (Fri); Religion, Auto (Sat); Focus, Neighbor, Farm, Ranch, Business, Real Estate, Travel, Books, Family, Wedding, Announcements, TV (Sun);
Syndicated Publications: Waco Today (Monthly); Startime (local TV supplement) (S).
Delivery Methods: Mail`Newsstand`Carrier`Racks
Areas Served - City/County or Portion Thereof, or Zip codes: 76621, 76622, 76624, 76513, 76626, 76629, 76630, 76520, 76632, 76633, 76634, 76635, 75110, 76637, 76638, 76639, 76524, 76640, 75840, 76641, 76528, 76642, 76531, 76643, 76645, 76648, 76055, 76538, 76653, 76654, 76655, 76656, 76656, 76660, 76661, 76664, 76657, 76665, 76667, 76557, 76671, 76673, 76561, 76676, 76678, 76680, 76682, 76570, 75860, 76501, 76687, 76579, 76689, 76701, 76704, 76705, 76706, 76707, 76708, 76710, 76711, 76712, 76691, 76692, 76693
Own Printing Facility?: N
Commercial printers?: N
Avg Free Circ: 1469
Sat. Circulation Paid: 19507
Sat. Circulation Free: 236
Sun. Circulation Paid: 22878
Sun. Circulation Free: 1072
Audit By: AAM
Audit Date: 30.06.2018
Personnel: Mike Copeland (Bus./Finance Ed.); Bill Whitaker (City Ed.); Rod Aydelotte (Chief Photographer); Chris Oliver (Radio/Television Ed.); Freida Jackson (Systems Ed.); Jim Wilson (Pub); Kristy Ferlet-Helton (Nat'l Sales Rep.); Ana Lozano-Harper (Adv. Sales Mgr.); Steve Boggs (Editor)
Parent company (for newspapers): BH Media Group; Lee Enterprises, Incorporated

WAXAHACHIE DAILY LIGHT

Street address 1: 200 W Marvin Ave
Street address city: Waxahachie
Street address state: TX
Zip/Postal code: 75165-3040
County: Ellis
Country: USA
Mailing address: PO BOX 877
Mailing city: WAXAHACHIE
Mailing state: TX
Mailing zip: 75168-0877
General Phone: (972) 937-3310
General/National Adv. E-mail: sbrooks@waxahachietx.com
Display Adv. E-mail: sbrooks@waxahachietx.com
Classified Adv. e-mail: srexrode@waxahachietx.com
Editorial e-mail: tsmith@waxahachietx.com
Primary Website: www.waxahachieTX.com
Year Established: 1867
News Services: AP.
Special Editions: Profile (Feb); Newcomers (Jul); Gingerbread Trail (Jun); Football (Sept).
Special Weekly Sections: School Zone (Tue); Best Food Days (Wed/Sun); Business, Finance, Entertainment (Thur); Auto, Health, Religion (Fri); Real Estate, Employment (Sun)
Syndicated Publications: American Profile (Weekly). Parade Magazine
Delivery Methods: Mail`Newsstand`Carrier`Racks
Areas Served - City/County or Portion Thereof, or Zip codes: 75165, 75167,75125, 75152, 75154, 76064, 76065, 76651
Own Printing Facility?: Y
Commercial printers?: Y
Sun. Circulation Paid: 5200
Audit By: Sworn/Estimate/Non-Audited
Audit Date: 12.07.2019
Parent company (for newspapers): Gannett; CherryRoad Media

THE WEATHERFORD DEMOCRAT

Street address 1: 512 Palo Pinto St
Street address city: Weatherford
Street address state: TX
Zip/Postal code: 76086-4128
County: Parker
Country: USA
Mailing address: 512 PALO PINTO ST
Mailing city: WEATHERFORD
Mailing state: TX
Mailing zip: 76086-4197
General Phone: (817) 594-7447
Advertising Phone: (817) 594-7447 ext. 213
Editorial Phone: (817) 594-7447 ext. 234
General/National Adv. E-mail: jthompson@weatherforddemocrat.com
Display Adv. E-mail: jthompson@weatherforddemocrat.com
Classified Adv. e-mail: classad@trcle.com
Editorial e-mail: editor@weatherforddemocrat.com
Primary Website: www.weatherforddemocrat.com
Year Established: 1895
News Services: AP.
Special Editions: Christmas Gift Guides (Dec); Chamber of Commerce (Feb); Frontier Days (Jul); Christmas Gift Guides (Nov); Football (Sept).
Special Weekly Sections: Best Food Day (Wed); Church, Outdoors (Fri); Lifestyle, Business, Seniors, School (Sun)
Syndicated Publications: Relish (Monthly); USA WEEKEND Magazine (S); American Profile (Weekly).
Delivery Methods: Mail`Carrier
Areas Served - City/County or Portion Thereof, or Zip codes: 76086, 76087, 76088, 76085, 76066, 76008, 76082, 76487
Avg Free Circ: 300
Sun. Circulation Paid: 4122
Sun. Circulation Free: 300
Audit By: AAM
Audit Date: 30.09.2014
Personnel: Sharon George (Bus. Mgr.); Janette Fant (Circ. Mgr.); Gregg Webb (Sports Ed.); Julie Killion (Pub.); Margarita Venegas (Ed.); Tamara Smart (Adv. Dir.); Jeff Smith (Pub.); Keith Hansen (Pub.)
Parent company (for newspapers): CNHI, LLC; CNHI, LLC

WICHITA FALLS TIMES RECORD NEWS

Street address 1: 1301 Lamar St
Street address city: Wichita Falls
Street address state: TX
Zip/Postal code: 76301-7032
County: Wichita
Country: USA
Mailing address: PO BOX 120
Mailing city: WICHITA FALLS
Mailing state: TX
Mailing zip: 76307-0120
General Phone: (940) 720-3491
Advertising Phone: (940) 720-3418
Editorial Phone: (940) 767-8341
General/National Adv. E-mail: tracyk@timesrecordnews.com
Display Adv. E-mail: stew@wtr.com
Primary Website: www.timesrecordnews.com
Mthly Avg Unique Visitors: 207521
Year Established: 1907
News Services: AP.
Special Weekly Sections: What's Cookin' (Wed); Business (Tue/Thur); Entertainment, Air Force Base (Fri); Religion (Sat); Arts, Living, Technology, Women (Sun)
Syndicated Publications: Parade (S). Relish Athalon
Avg Free Circ: 1175
Sat. Circulation Paid: 13417
Sat. Circulation Free: 1175
Sun. Circulation Paid: 15070
Sun. Circulation Free: 1144
Audit By: AAM

Audit Date: 31.12.2017
Personnel: Jackie Riley (Mktg./Promo. Dir.); Don Boyd (Circ. Dir.); Angel Riggs (Bus./Oil Ed.); Jill Sexton (Librarian); Lana Sweeten Shults (Radio/Television Ed.); Suzanne Moore (Regl. Ed.); Bill Lindemann (Dir., Information Systems); Darrell Coleman (Pub.); Kathy Tracy (Nat'l Accts. Mgr.); Stewart Swartz (Retail Adv. Mgr.); Swayne Bivona (Pub.); Dwayne Bivona (Publisher); Richard Carlson (Circ. Sales Dir.); Deanna Watson (Ed.)
Parent company (for newspapers): Gannett - USA Today Network

UTAH

THE HERALD JOURNAL

Street address 1: 75 W 300 N
Street address city: Logan
Street address state: UT
Zip/Postal code: 84321-3971
County: Cache
Country: USA
Mailing address: PO BOX 487
Mailing city: LOGAN
Mailing state: UT
Mailing zip: 84323-0487
General Phone: (435) 752-2121
Advertising Phone: (435) 752-2121 x 351
Editorial Phone: (435)752-2121 ext. 320
General/National Adv. E-mail: cliechty@hjnews.com
Display Adv. E-mail: cliechty@hjnews.com
Classified Adv. e-mail: hjclass@hjnews.com
Editorial e-mail: cmcollum@hjnews.com
Primary Website: www.hjnews.com
Mthly Avg Views: 1117273
Mthly Avg Unique Visitors: 259000
Year Established: 1930
News Services: AP, CSM.
Special Editions: Home & Garden (Apr); Football (Aug); Sidewalk Days (Jul); Customer Appreciation Days (Jun); Progress (Mar); Tourist (May); Basketball (Nov); Hunter's Guide (Sept).
Special Weekly Sections: Food (Tue); Technology (Wed); Faith (Thur); Cache Magazine, Outdoors (Fri); Enterprise (Sun);
Syndicated Publications: Parade (S).
Delivery Methods: Mail`Newsstand`Carrier`Racks
Own Printing Facility?: N
Avg Free Circ: 2625
Sat. Circulation Paid: 9331
Sat. Circulation Free: 2625
Sun. Circulation Paid: 10127
Sun. Circulation Free: 1351
Audit By: AAM
Audit Date: 31.03.2018
Personnel: Tyler Ricks (City Ed.); Charles McCollum (Managing Ed.); Chuck Nunn (News Editor); Shawn Harrison (Sports Ed.); Michael Starn (Pub.); Kyle Ashby (Adv. Dir.); Jason McNeely (Circ. Mgr.)
Parent company (for newspapers): Adams Publishing Group, LLC; Cache Valley Publishing LLC

STANDARD-EXAMINER

Street address 1: 332 Standard Way
Street address city: Ogden
Street address state: UT
Zip/Postal code: 84404
County: Weber
Country: USA
Mailing address: PO BOX 12790
Mailing city: OGDEN
Mailing state: UT
Mailing zip: 84412-2790
General Phone: (801) 625-4400
Advertising Phone: (801) 625-4333
Editorial Phone: (801) 625-4544
General/National Adv. E-mail: advertise@standard.net
Display Adv. E-mail: advertise@standard.net
Classified Adv. e-mail: dnewman@standard.net
Editorial e-mail: news@standard.net
Primary Website: www.standard.net
Mthly Avg Views: 3500000
Mthly Avg Unique Visitors: 400000
Year Established: 1888
News Services: AP, MCT, SHNS, DJ, LAT-WP.
Special Editions: Parade of Homes (Aug); Neighborhoods (Dec); Bride & Groom (Jan); Pioneer Days (Jul); Home & Garden (Mar); Coupon Power (Monthly); Auto Guide (Nov); Car Care (Oct); Health & Fitness (Quarterly); Homemaker's School (Sept).
Special Weekly Sections: TMC (Mon); Outdoor (Wed); Military (Thur); Classifieds, Auto, Entertainment (Fri); Religion, Real Estate, Entertainment (Sat);Best Food Day, Life Styles, Travel, Business, Help Wanted (Sun); Seniors, Women, Outdoors (Monthly);
Syndicated Publications: Relish (Monthly); USA WEEKEND Magazine (S); American Profile (Weekly).
Delivery Methods: Mail`Newsstand`Carrier`Racks
Own Printing Facility?: Y
Commercial printers?: Y
Sat. Circulation Paid: 28338
Sun. Circulation Paid: 31968
Audit By: AAM
Audit Date: 30.09.2017
Personnel: David Newman (Adv. Mgr., Classified); Jared Bird (Retail Adv. Mgr.); Julie Hartman (Adv. Mgr., Major/Nat'l); Karie Gardner (Adv. Supvr., Classified Telephone Sales); Brad Roghaar (Mgr., Creative); Ron Thornburg (Circ. Dir.); Vanessa Zimmer (Features Ed.); Andy Howell (Graphics Ed.); Cuba Tucker; Karla Woodward (Mrkting Dir.); Brandon Erlacher (Pub.); Jordan Carroll (Exec. Ed.)
Parent company (for newspapers): Ogden Newspapers Inc.

DAILY HERALD

Street address 1: 86 N. University Avenue, Suite 300
Street address 2: Ste 300
Street address city: Provo
Street address state: UT
Zip/Postal code: 84601-4474
County: Utah
Country: USA
Mailing address: PO BOX 717
Mailing city: PROVO
Mailing state: UT
Mailing zip: 84603-0717
General Phone: (801) 373-5050
Advertising Phone: (801) 344-2957
Editorial Phone: (801) 344-2935
General/National Adv. E-mail: tfrantz@heraldextra.com
Display Adv. E-mail: tfrantz@heraldextra.com
Classified Adv. e-mail: tfrantz@heraldextra.com
Editorial e-mail: stitrington@heraldextra.com
Primary Website: www.heraldextra.com
Mthly Avg Views: 305003
Mthly Avg Unique Visitors: 19631
Year Established: 1873
News Services: AP, CNS, MCT, TMS.
Special Editions: Summer Recreation & Travel (Apr); Football (Aug); Gift Guide (Dec); Valentine's Day (Feb); Father's Day (Jun); Progress (Mar); Provo Open (May); Home Interiors (Oct); Best of Utah Valley (Sept).
Special Weekly Sections: Wheels (Fri); TV Magazine (Sat); UV-Utah Valley's Weekly Entertainment Guide (Thur); Best Food Day (Tues).
Syndicated Publications: Relish (Monthly) Parade
Areas Served - City/County or Portion Thereof, or Zip codes: Utah County
Own Printing Facility?: N
Commercial printers?: N
Avg Free Circ: 1159
Sat. Circulation Paid: 9700
Sat. Circulation Free: 423
Sun. Circulation Paid: 13330
Sun. Circulation Free: 19245
Audit By: AAM
Audit Date: 30.09.2017
Personnel: Rhett Long (Circ. Dir.); Jordan Carroll (Exec. Ed.); Craig Conover (Retail Manager); Kurt Hanson (City Ed.); Stacy Johnson (Online Ed.); Ryan Olson (Night/Weekend Ed.); Phillip Morgan (Sports Ed.); Doug Fox (Features and Entertainment Ed.)
Parent company (for newspapers): Ogden Newspapers Inc.

THE SPECTRUM

Street address 1: 275 E Saint George Blvd
Street address city: Saint George
Street address state: UT
Zip/Postal code: 84770-2954
County: Washington
Country: USA
Mailing address: 275 E SAINT GEORGE BLVD
Mailing city: SAINT GEORGE
Mailing state: UT
Mailing zip: 84770-2986
General Phone: (435) 674-6200
Advertising Phone: (435) 674-6261
Editorial Phone: (435) 674-6286
General/National Adv. E-mail: advertising@thespectrum.com
Display Adv. E-mail: advertising@thespectrum.com
Classified Adv. e-mail: classifieds@thespectrum.com
Editorial e-mail: skiggins@thespectrum.com
Primary Website: www.thespectrum.com
Year Established: 1963
News Services: AP, GNS, LAT-WP.
Special Editions: Spring Home & Garden (Apr); Iron County Parade of Homes (Aug); Last Minute Gifts (Dec); St. George Parade of Homes (Feb); Bridal Fair (Jan); Washington County Fair (Jul); Tuacahn Tabloid (Jun); Getting in the Spirit (Nov); Complete Health (Oct); Kids Toda
Special Weekly Sections: Career Builder (Mon); Southwest Living, Technology, Food, Home (Tue/ Wed); Auto (Thur); Outdoors, Entertainment (Fri);Real Estate (Sat); Business, Finance, Religion, Living, TV (Sun); Dear Abby , Community, Weather, Stocks, Entertainment, Public Forum (Daily)
Syndicated Publications: Where It's @ (Fri); USA WEEKEND Magazine (S).
Avg Free Circ: 107
Sat. Circulation Paid: 10570
Sat. Circulation Free: 107
Sun. Circulation Paid: 12770
Sun. Circulation Free: 92
Audit By: AAM
Audit Date: 31.12.2017
Personnel: Todd Seifert (Online Ed.); Jackie Hermans (Online Mgr.); Brent Bowden (Nat'l/Major Acct. Exec.); Stacy Johnson (Pres./Pub.); Conrad Velin (Reg. Fin. Dir.); Jeremy Browning (Adv. Mgr.); David DeMille (Ed.)
Parent company (for newspapers): Gannett

DESERET NEWS

Street address 1: 55 N 300 W
Street address city: Salt Lake City
Street address state: UT
Zip/Postal code: 84101-3502
County: Salt Lake
Country: USA
Mailing address: PO BOX 1257
Mailing city: SALT LAKE CITY
Mailing state: UT
Mailing zip: 84110-1257
General Phone: (801) 236-6000
Advertising Phone: (801) 204-6300
Editorial Phone: (801) 237-2100
General/National Adv. E-mail: service@mediaoneutah.com
Display Adv. E-mail: advertising@mediaoneutah.com
Classified Adv. e-mail: service@mediaoneutah.com
Editorial e-mail: dwilks@deseretnews.com
Primary Website: www.deseretnews.com
Mthly Avg Views: 33183470
Mthly Avg Unique Visitors: 5449751
Year Established: 1850
News Services: AP, CSM, CT, LAT-WP, NNS, NYT.
Special Editions: Education Week, LDS General Conference, Mormons in America, Olympics, Outdoor Retailer, Rugby, Sports Picks, Sundance Film Festival, Utah Blaze, Utah Grizzlies
Special Weekly Sections: Family (Mon); Sports (Mon-Sun); Health, Science, Education (Tue); Religion, Real Estate (Sat); Lifestyles, Society, Arts, Travel, TV Comics, Employment (Sun); Business (Tue-Sun); Food (Wed); Recreation (Thur); Auto, Entertainment (Fri)
Syndicated Publications: Parade (S).
Delivery Methods: Mail`Newsstand`Carrier`Racks
Own Printing Facility?: Y
Commercial printers?: Y
Avg Free Circ: 2384
Sat. Circulation Paid: 43852
Sat. Circulation Free: 314
Sun. Circulation Paid: 113840
Sun. Circulation Free: 4398
Audit By: Sworn/Estimate/Non-Audited
Audit Date: 12.07.2019
Personnel: Michael Todd (CFO); Christine Rappleye (Features Editor); Chuck Wing (Photo Ed.); Kent Condon (Sports Ed.); Sarah Weaver (Church News Ed.); Brian West (News Director)
Parent company (for newspapers): Deseret News; Newspaper Agency Corporation

THE SALT LAKE TRIBUNE, INC

Street address 1: 90 S 400 W
Street address 2: Ste 700
Street address city: Salt Lake City
Street address state: UT
Zip/Postal code: 84101-1431
County: Salt Lake
Country: USA
Mailing address: 90 S 400 W STE 700
Mailing city: SALT LAKE CITY
Mailing state: UT
Mailing zip: 84101-1431
General Phone: (801) 257-8742
Advertising Phone: (801) 237-2815
Editorial Phone: (801) 257-8742
General/National Adv. E-mail: advertising@sltrib.com
Display Adv. E-mail: advertising@sltrib.com
Classified Adv. e-mail: classifieds@sltrib.com
Editorial e-mail: editor@sltrib.com
Primary Website: www.sltrib.com
Mthly Avg Views: 26092548
Mthly Avg Unique Visitors: 2838700
Year Established: 1871
News Services: AP, GNS, MCT, LAT-WP, CQ, Scripps McClatchy, West Wire, Religious News Service.
Special Editions: Yard & Home (Apr); Football (Aug); Christmas Gift (Dec); Wedding (Feb); Health & Fitness (Jan); Franklin Quest Golf (Jul); Father's Day (Jun); Progress (Mar); Seniors I (May); Early Bird Gift (Nov); Home & Garden (Oct); Focus on Business (Sept).
Special Weekly Sections: Business Pages (Fri); TV Book (S); Business Pages (Sat); Business Pages (Thur); Recreation Pages (Tues); Business Pages (Wed).
Syndicated Publications: Parade (S).
Delivery Methods: Mail`Newsstand`Carrier`Racks
Own Printing Facility?: N
Sun. Circulation Paid: 91879
Audit By: AAM
Audit Date: 30.09.2016
Personnel: Paul Huntsman (Pub./Owner); Jennifer Napier-Pearce; Matt Canham (Sr. Mng. Ed.); Tim Fitzpatrick (Exec. VP); Sheila R. McCann (Mng. Ed.); David Noyce (Mng. Ed.); Joe Baird (Sports Ed.); Ana Daraban (Office Mgr.)
Parent company (for newspapers): The Salt Lake Tribune, Inc; Huntsman Family Investments

VERMONT

THE TIMES ARGUS

Street address 1: 47 N Main St
Street address 2: Ste 200
Street address city: Barre
Street address state: VT
Zip/Postal code: 05641-4168
County: Washington
Country: USA
Mailing address: 47 N MAIN ST STE 200
Mailing city: BARRE
Mailing state: VT
Mailing zip: 05641-4168
General Phone: (802) 479-0191
Advertising Phone: (802) 479-0191
Editorial Phone: (802) 479-0191
General/National Adv. E-mail: colleen.flanagan@timesargus.com
Display Adv. E-mail: colleen.flanagan@timesargus.com
Editorial e-mail: steven.pappas@timesargus.com
Primary Website: www.timesargus.com
Mthly Avg Views: 948899
Mthly Avg Unique Visitors: 5592
Year Established: 1806
News Services: AP, NYT, McLatchy.
Special Editions: Christmas Gift Guide (Nov).
Special Weekly Sections: Real Estate (Wed); Real Estate, Business (Thur); Art, Entertainment (Fri); Church, Real Estate (Sat); Auto, Business, Agriculture, Living, Health (Sun)
Syndicated Publications: Relish (Monthly); Vermont Sunday Magazine (S).
Sat. Circulation Paid: 5796
Sun. Circulation Paid: 6276
Audit By: AAM
Audit Date: 30.09.2013
Personnel: Shawn Stabell (Circ. Dir.); Deborah Morse (Pub.); Mac Slivka (Exec. Asst.); Steven Pappas (Ed.)

Parent company (for newspapers): Sample News Group LLC

BENNINGTON BANNER

Street address 1: 425 Main St
Street address city: Bennington
Street address state: VT
Zip/Postal code: 05201-2141
County: Bennington
Country: USA
General Phone: (802) 442-7567
Advertising Phone: (800) 245-0254
Editorial Phone: (802)447-7567 ext. 115
General/National Adv. E-mail: rmorin@benningtonbanner.com
Display Adv. E-mail: rmorin@benningtonbanner.com
Classified Adv. e-mail: msinopoli@benningtonbanner.com
Editorial e-mail: kwhitcomb@benningtonbanner.com
Primary Website: www.benningtonbanner.com
Year Established: 1905
News Services: AP.
Special Editions: Spring Home & Garden (Apr); Business & Industry (Feb); Christmas Gift Guide (Nov); Fall Home Improvement (Oct); Bennington Antique Car Show (Sept).
Special Weekly Sections: Best Food Day (Mon/Thur); Business, Sports, Pet (Mon); Education (Tue); Health, Fitness (Wed); Entertainment (Thur)
Syndicated Publications: USA WEEKEND Magazine (Sat); American Profile (Weekly).
Own Printing Facility?: Y
Commercial printers?: Y
Avg Free Circ: 540
Sat. Circulation Paid: 3920
Sat. Circulation Free: 506
Audit By: AAM
Audit Date: 30.06.2017
Personnel: Dave LaChance (News Ed.); Mark Rondeau (Night News Ed.); Adam Samrov (Sports Ed.); Evan Pringle (Circ. Mgr.); Rebecca Grande (Customer Service Mgr.); Susan Plaisance (Adv. Sales Mgr.); Melodie Sinopoli (Classified Advertising Manager)
Parent company (for newspapers): Birdland Acquisition LLC.; Vermont News and Media

BRATTLEBORO REFORMER

Street address 1: 62 Black Mountain Rd
Street address city: Brattleboro
Street address state: VT
Zip/Postal code: 05301-9241
County: Windham
Country: USA
General Phone: (802) 254-2311
General/National Adv. E-mail: news@reformer.com
Display Adv. E-mail: advertising@reformer.com
Classified Adv. e-mail: classifieds@reformer.com
Editorial e-mail: news@reformer.com
Primary Website: www.reformer.com
Year Established: 1913
News Services: AP.
Special Weekly Sections: Business (Mon); Education, Home Improvement (Tue); Health (Wed); Entertainment (Thur); Food (Thur/Sat); Real Estate, Auto (Fri/Sat); TV (Sat); Employment (Sat/Mon)
Syndicated Publications: USA WEEKEND Magazine (Sat); American Profile (Weekly).
Delivery Methods: Mail`Newsstand`Carrier`Racks
Own Printing Facility?: Y
Commercial printers?: Y
Avg Free Circ: 591
Sat. Circulation Paid: 4598
Sat. Circulation Free: 465
Sun. Circulation Paid: 4598
Sun. Circulation Free: 465
Audit By: AAM
Audit Date: 31.03.2018
Personnel: Melanie Winters (News Ed.); Bill LeConey (Night News Ed.); Shane Covey (Sports Ed.); Noah Hoffenberg (Digital Ed.); Tia Wells (Circ. Mgr.); Jonathan Stafford (Advertising Mgr.); Melodie Sinopoli (Classified Advertising Mgr.); Fredrick Rutberg (Pres./Pub.); Kevin Moran (Executive Editor, Chief Content Officer)
Parent company (for newspapers): Birdland Acquisition LLC.; Paul Belogour

VERMONT NEWS AND MEDIA

Street address 1: 70 Landmark Hill drive
Street address city: Brattleboro
Street address state: VT
Zip/Postal code: 05301
County: Windham
Mailing state: MA
General Phone: 802-254-2311
Advertising Phone: 802-254-2311
Editorial Phone: 802-254-2311
General/National Adv. E-mail: publisher@reformer.com
Year Established: 2020
Avg Free Circ: 26000
Audit By: AAM

THE BURLINGTON FREE PRESS

Street address 1: 100 Bank St Ste 700
Street address 2: Suite 700
Street address city: Burlington
Street address state: VT
Zip/Postal code: 05401-4946
County: Chittenden
Country: USA
Mailing address: PO BOX 10
Mailing city: BURLINGTON
Mailing state: VT
Mailing zip: 05402-0010
General Phone: (802) 863-3441
Advertising Phone: (802) 660-1819
Editorial Phone: (802) 865-0940
General/National Adv. E-mail: tamjohnson@burlingtonfreepress.com
Display Adv. E-mail: tamjohnson@burlingtonfreepress.com
Classified Adv. e-mail: BFPclass@gannett.com
Editorial e-mail: estigliani@.burlingtonfreepress.com
Primary Website: www.burlingtonfreepress.com
Year Established: 1827
News Services: AP, GNS, LAT-WP, NYT.
Special Editions: Discover Jazz Festival (April); Gift Guides (Dec); Bridal (Jan); Food Festival (Jun); Festival of Fools (July); Maritime Festival (July) Marathon (May); Summer Fun Guide (May); Vermont House & Home (Monthly); Fall Fun Guide (September); Giving Season (Nov); Vermont Skier (Oct);
Special Weekly Sections: Innovate- Business (Thursday); Weekend (Thursday); Food & Wine (Friday); Wheels (Fri); Outdoor (Sat); Home (Sat); BTV Arts (Sun); Green Life (Sunday)
Syndicated Publications: USA WEEKEND Magazine (S).
Delivery Methods: Newsstand`Carrier`Racks
Own Printing Facility?: Y
Commercial printers?: Y
Avg Free Circ: 143
Sat. Circulation Paid: 10266
Sat. Circulation Free: 143
Sun. Circulation Paid: 13284
Sun. Circulation Free: 114
Audit By: AAM
Audit Date: 31.03.2019
Personnel: Tammy Shannon (Adv. Dir.); Aki Soga (Editorial Page Ed.); Trevor Chase (Dir., IT); Marianne Green (Media Specialist - National Sales); Adam Silverman (Content Strategist); Denis Finley (Executive Editor)
Parent company (for newspapers): Gannett

THE NEWPORT DAILY EXPRESS

Street address 1: 178 Hill St
Street address city: Newport
Street address state: VT
Zip/Postal code: 05855-9430
County: Orleans
Country: USA
Mailing address: PO BOX 347
Mailing city: NEWPORT
Mailing state: VT
Mailing zip: 05855-0347
General Phone: (802) 334-6568
Advertising Phone: (802)334-6568
Editorial Phone: (802)334-6568
General/National Adv. E-mail: advertising@newportvermontdailyexpress.com
Display Adv. E-mail: advertising@newportvermontdailyexpress.com
Classified Adv. e-mail: classified@newportvermontdailyexpress.com
Editorial e-mail: editor@newportvermontdailyexpress.com
Primary Website: www.newportvermontdailyexpress.com
Year Established: 1936
News Services: AP.
Special Editions: Spring Home Improvement (Apr); Gardening (May); June Dearie and Vacation Guide (June); Bridal (Feb); Menu Guide (July); Progress (Sept); Car Care(Oct).
Special Weekly Sections: Best Food Days (Mon); Arts, Entertainment, Travel (Wed); Auto, Travel (Thur); Health, Real Estate, Religion, Best Food Day (Fri); Home, Living, Women (Daily)
Syndicated Publications: American Profile (Weekly). SmartSource (Friday)
Delivery Methods: Mail`Newsstand`Carrier`Racks
Areas Served - City/County or Portion Thereof, or Zip codes: Greensboro, Holland, Irasburg, Jay, Lowell, Morgan, Newport City, Newport Town, North Troy, Orleans, Troy, Westfield, Westmare
Own Printing Facility?: Y
Commercial printers?: Y
Audit By: Sworn/Estimate/Non-Audited
Audit Date: 12.07.2019
Personnel: Roland L. McBride (CFO); Marilyn Gardyne (Adv. Dir.); Sadie Watters (Circ. Mgr.); Steve Blake (Mng. Ed.); David Radler (Pres., Opns.); Karen Bartleson (Prodn. Mgr.); Carol Temple (Circ. Mgr.); Patricia Sears (Pub.)
Parent company (for newspapers): Horizon Publications Inc.

RUTLAND HERALD

Street address 1: PO Box 668
Street address city: Rutland
Street address state: VT
Zip/Postal code: 05702-0668
County: Rutland
Country: USA
Mailing address: PO BOX 668
Mailing city: RUTLAND
Mailing state: VT
Mailing zip: 05702-0668
General Phone: (800) 498-4296
Advertising Phone: (802) 747-6126
Editorial Phone: (802) 747-6133
Display Adv. E-mail: ads@rutlandherald.com
Editorial e-mail: letters@rutlandherald.com
Primary Website: www.rutlandherald.com
Mthly Avg Views: 1437912
Mthly Avg Unique Visitors: 172888
Year Established: 1794
News Services: AP, NYT, MCT.
Special Editions: Spring Car Care (Apr);Summer Camp Guide, Sping Sports, Vermont State Fair (Aug); Best fthe Best Readers Choice, Graduation (Jun); Business Outlook (Mar); VT Home and Properties (Monthly); Gift Guide (Nov); Fall Vermont
Special Weekly Sections: TV (Daily); Best Food, Business (Mon); Weekend (Fri); Weekly TV (Sat); Vermont, Comics (Sun)
Syndicated Publications: Relish (Monthly); Parade Magazine (S).
Delivery Methods: Mail`Newsstand`Carrier`Racks
Areas Served - City/County or Portion Thereof, or Zip codes: Rutland County and Southern Vermont
Own Printing Facility?: Y
Sat. Circulation Paid: 11200
Sun. Circulation Paid: 12609
Audit By: AAM
Audit Date: 30.09.2013
Personnel: Deborah Morse (Bus. Office Mgr.); Shawn Stabell (Circ. Dir.); Duguay Tim (Adv. Sales Mgr.); Rich Alcott (Content Ed.)
Parent company (for newspapers): Sample News Group LLC

ST. ALBANS MESSENGER

Street address 1: 281 N Main St
Street address city: Saint Albans
Street address state: VT
Zip/Postal code: 05478-2503
County: Franklin
Country: USA
Mailing address: 281 N MAIN ST
Mailing city: SAINT ALBANS
Mailing state: VT
Mailing zip: 05478-2503
General Phone: (802) 524-9771
Advertising Phone: (802)524-9771 ext. 104
Editorial Phone: (802)524-9771 ext. 108
General/National Adv. E-mail: ads@samessenger.com
Display Adv. E-mail: ads@samessenger.com
Classified Adv. e-mail: classifieds@samessenger.com
Editorial e-mail: news@samessenger.com
Primary Website: www.samessenger.com
Mthly Avg Views: 52000
Year Established: 1861
News Services: AP.
Special Editions: Energy (Fall); Dairy (Jun); Meet Your Business and Professional Communities (May); Christmas (Nov); Home Improvements (Spring); Sports (Winter).
Special Weekly Sections: Best Business (Mon): Health (Tue); Travel, Entertainment (Thur); Auto (Fri); Food, TV (Sat)
Areas Served - City/County or Portion Thereof, or Zip codes: St. Albans, Franklin County
Sat. Circulation Paid: 5930
Audit By: Sworn/Estimate/Non-Audited
Audit Date: 12.07.2019
Personnel: Suzanne Lynn (Gen. Mgr.); Jeremy Read (Adv. Dir.); Gary Rutkowski (Ed.); Emerson Lynn (Pub.); Josh Kaufmann (Sports Ed.); Lynne Fletcher (Prodn. Mgr.); Alex Domina (Press Mgr.)
Parent company (for newspapers): Jim Oâ€™Rourke; O'Rourke Media Group

THE CALEDONIAN-RECORD

Street address 1: 190 Federal St
Street address 2: PO Box 8
Street address city: Saint Johnsbury
Street address state: VT
Zip/Postal code: 05819-5616
County: Caledonia
Country: USA
Mailing address: PO BOX 8
Mailing city: SAINT JOHNSBURY
Mailing state: VT
Mailing zip: 05819-0008
General Phone: (802) 748-8121
Advertising Phone: (802) 748-8121
Editorial Phone: (802) 748-8121
General/National Adv. E-mail: news@caledonian-record.com
Display Adv. E-mail: adv@caledonian-record.com
Classified Adv. e-mail: adv@caledonian-record.com
Editorial e-mail: news@caledonian-record.com
Primary Website: www.caledonianrecord.com
Mthly Avg Views: 1250000
Mthly Avg Unique Visitors: 240000
Year Established: 1837
News Services: AP.
Special Editions: Business Recognition (Jan); Bridal (Jan); Presidents' Day Auto (Feb); Real Estate/Home Improvement (Apr); Summer Guide (Jun); Sports Year in Review (Jun); Car Care (Sept); Winter Guide (Oct); Christmas Gift Guide (Nov);
Special Weekly Sections: School (Mon); Business (Sat); Health Beat (Thur); Family Page (Wed)., Entertainment (Fri), Youth Sports (Tue)
Delivery Methods: Mail`Newsstand`Carrier`Racks
Areas Served - City/County or Portion Thereof, or Zip codes: Vermont Counties: Caledonia, Essex, Orleans NH Counties: Grafton, Coos
Own Printing Facility?: N
Commercial printers?: Y
Avg Free Circ: 1840
Sat. Circulation Paid: 6694
Sat. Circulation Free: 1840
Audit By: Sworn/Estimate/Non-Audited
Audit Date: 12.07.2019
Personnel: Todd Smith (Publisher); Todd Smith (Pub./VP); Judy Burke (Bookkeeper); Dana Gray (Exec. Ed.); Andrew McGregor (City/Metro Ed.); Todd M. Smith (Pub.); Rosie Smith (Educ. Services Dir.); Peter Lynch (Picture Ed.); Michael Beniash (Sports Ed.); Michael Gonyaw (Adv. Dir./Online Mgr.); Glen Jardine (Dig. Services Dir.)
Parent company (for newspapers): The Caledonian-Record

VIRGINIA

BRISTOL HERALD COURIER

Street address 1: 410 Morrison Boulevard, P.O Box 609
Street address city: Bristol
Street address state: VA
Zip/Postal code: 24201-3812
County: Bristol City
Country: USA
Mailing address: PO BOX 609
Mailing city: BRISTOL

Mailing state: VA
Mailing zip: 24203-0609
General Phone: (276) 669-2181
Advertising Phone: (276) 645-2525
Editorial Phone: (276) 645-2534
Display Adv. E-mail: amanda.shell@lee.net
Classified Adv. e-mail: classifieds@bristolnews.com
Editorial e-mail: letters@bristolnews.com
Primary Website: www.heraldcourier.com
Mthly Avg Views: 2100000
Mthly Avg Unique Visitors: 450000
Year Established: 1870
News Services: AP, SHNS.
Special Editions: NASCAR (April & August) Football (Aug)Bristol Magazine (Quarterly)
Delivery Methods: Mail`Newsstand`Carrier`Racks
Areas Served - City/County or Portion Thereof, or Zip codes: Bristol, Tennessee 37620 Bristol, Virginia 24201
Own Printing Facility?: Y
Commercial printers?: Y
Avg Free Circ: 13346
Sat. Circulation Paid: 12560
Sat. Circulation Free: 13346
Sun. Circulation Paid: 14185
Sun. Circulation Free: 14509
Audit Date: 31.03.2019
Personnel: Rob Walters (Mng. Ed.); David McGee (News Editor)
Parent company (for newspapers): BH Media Group; Lee Enterprises, Incorporated

THE DAILY PROGRESS

Street address 1: 685 Rio Rd W
Street address city: Charlottesville
Street address state: VA
Zip/Postal code: 22901-1413
County: Albemarle
Country: USA
Mailing address: PO BOX 9030
Mailing city: CHARLOTTESVILLE
Mailing state: VA
Mailing zip: 22906-9030
General Phone: (434) 978-7200
Advertising Phone: (434) 978-7209
Editorial Phone: (434) 978-7240
General/National Adv. E-mail: fdubec@dailyprogress.com
Display Adv. E-mail: fdubec@dailyprogress.com
Classified Adv. e-mail: classfied@dailyprogress.com
Editorial e-mail: rjiranek@dailyprogress.com; whester@dailyprogress.com
Primary Website: www.dailyprogress.com
Mthly Avg Views: 1432758
Mthly Avg Unique Visitors: 309135
Year Established: 1892
News Services: AP, LAT-WP.
Special Editions: Homestyle; Silver Linings (Every other month); Charlotetsville Women; Graduation (May); How To Guide (May); Reader's Choice (July); Welcome Guide (Aug); Enterprise (Quarterly); Creative Home (Oct)
Special Weekly Sections: Best Food Day (S); Best Food Day (Wed); Select TV (Sat)
Syndicated Publications: USA WEEKEND Magazine (S).
Delivery Methods: Mail`Newsstand`Carrier`Racks
Areas Served - City/County or Portion Thereof, or Zip codes: Albemarle County
Own Printing Facility?: N
Commercial printers?: N
Avg Free Circ: 1092
Sat. Circulation Paid: 12523
Sat. Circulation Free: 1092
Sun. Circulation Paid: 14577
Sun. Circulation Free: 922
Audit By: AAM
Audit Date: 30.09.2018
Personnel: Peter Yates (Pub.); Aaron Richardson (Ed.); Jenny Rector (City Ed.); Mark Newton (Night Ed.); Anita Shelburne (Editorial Page Ed.); Jane Dunlap Sathe (Features Ed.); John Shifflett (Sports Ed.); Brandon Barfield (Circ. Dir.); Dave Massey (Adv. Dir.); Vincent Zorn (Digital Adv. Mgr.); Karla Hernandez (HR)
Parent company (for newspapers): BH Media Group

CULPEPER STAR-EXPONENT

Street address 1: 122 W Spencer St
Street address city: Culpeper
Street address state: VA
Zip/Postal code: 22701-2628
County: Culpeper
Country: USA
Mailing address: 122 W SPENCER ST
Mailing city: CULPEPER
Mailing state: VA
Mailing zip: 22701-2628
General Phone: (540) 825-0771
Advertising Phone: (540) 825-0771 ext. 4100
Editorial Phone: (540) 825-0771 ext. 4125
General/National Adv. E-mail: lgore@dailyprogress.com
Display Adv. E-mail: lgore@dailyprogress.com
Classified Adv. e-mail: classifieds@dailyprogress.com
Editorial e-mail: mmckenna@starexponent.com
Primary Website: www.dailyprogress.com
Avg Free Circ: 294
Sun. Circulation Paid: 3447
Sun. Circulation Free: 162
Audit By: AAM
Audit Date: 31.03.2018
Personnel: Lynn Gore (Adv. Mgr.)
Parent company (for newspapers): BH Media Group; Lee Enterprises, Incorporated

DANVILLE REGISTER & BEE

Street address 1: 700 Monument Street
Street address city: Danville
Street address state: VA
Zip/Postal code: 24541
County: Danville City
Country: USA
Mailing address: 700 MONUMENT ST
Mailing city: DANVILLE
Mailing state: VA
Mailing zip: 24541-1512
General Phone: (434) 793-2311
Advertising Phone: (434)791-7926
Editorial Phone: (434)791-7990
General/National Adv. E-mail: jrandell@registerbee.com
Display Adv. E-mail: jrandell@registerbee.com
Classified Adv. e-mail: classifieds@newsadvance.com
Editorial e-mail: rbenson@registerbee.com
Primary Website: www.godanriver.com
News Services: AP.
Special Editions: Chamber of Commerce Tab (Monthly); Postive Parenting (Quarterly).
Special Weekly Sections: Best Food Days (Wed/Sun)
Syndicated Publications: USA WEEKEND Magazine (S).
Avg Free Circ: 92
Sat. Circulation Paid: 9934
Sat. Circulation Free: 92
Sun. Circulation Paid: 12930
Sun. Circulation Free: 59
Audit By: AAM
Audit Date: 31.03.2017
Personnel: Kelly E. Mirt (Pub.); Keven Todd (Gen. Mgr./ Adv. Dir.); Mike Owens (Mng. Ed.)
Parent company (for newspapers): BH Media Group; Lee Enterprises, Incorporated; World Media Enterprises, Inc.

THE FREE LANCE-STAR

Street address 1: 616 Amelia St
Street address city: Fredericksburg
Street address state: VA
Zip/Postal code: 22401-3887
County: Fredericksburg City
Country: USA
Mailing address: 616 AMELIA ST
Mailing city: FREDERICKSBURG
Mailing state: VA
Mailing zip: 22401-3887
General Phone: (540) 374-5000
Advertising Phone: (540) 374-5460
Editorial Phone: (540) 374-5400
General/National Adv. E-mail: information@freelancestar.com
Display Adv. E-mail: advertising@freelancestar.com
Classified Adv. e-mail: classifieds@freelancestar.com
Editorial e-mail: newsroom@freelancestar.com
Primary Website: www.freelancestar.com
Mthly Avg Views: 560000
Mthly Avg Unique Visitors: 60000
Year Established: 1885
News Services: AP, MCT.
Special Editions: Bride & Groom (Feb); Parenting(Feb; Horse Scene(Mar); Garden Week (Apr); Spring Home Guide (May); Wedding Guide (Jun); Guide To Living (July) ; Back To School (Aug); High School Football (Aug); Holiday Gift Guide (Nov); Holiday Trimming (Dec);.
Special Weekly Sections: House & Home (Fri); Viewpoints (Sun); Town & Country (Tues); Weekender (Thur); Food & Life (Wed); Stars & Stripes (Fri)Farm & Garden 1st Friday each month; Living Well 3rd Friday each month.
Delivery Methods: Mail`Newsstand`Carrier`Racks
Areas Served - City/County or Portion Thereof, or Zip codes: NDM-22401, 22405, 22406, 22407, 22408, 22412, 22427, 22448, 22485, 22501, 22514, 22534, 22535, 22538, 22546, 22551, 22553, 22554, 22556, 22565, 22580
Own Printing Facility?: Y
Commercial printers?: Y
Avg Free Circ: 1427
Sat. Circulation Paid: 23267
Sat. Circulation Free: 1266
Sun. Circulation Paid: 26007
Sun. Circulation Free: 1188
Audit By: AAM
Audit Date: 30.09.2018
Personnel: Phil Jenkins (Editor); Samantha Ashley (Executive Assistant/HR Generalist); Gayle P Yanez (HR Dir.); Karen Harris (Bus. Mgr.); William P. Smith (Adv. Dir.); Betty Snider (Managing Editor); Katherine Shapleigh (Life Ed.); Timothy Krier (Circulation Director); Opal Curtis (Classified Call Ctr. Sales Mgr.); Catherine Davis (Graphics/Design Dir.); James Toler (Editorial Page Editor); Dale Lachniet (Pub.); Gary Snider (Ops. Dir.)
Parent company (for newspapers): BH Media Group; Lee Enterprises, Incorporated

DAILY NEWS-RECORD

Street address 1: 231 S. Liberty St
Street address city: Harrisonburg
Street address state: VA
Zip/Postal code: 22801-3621
County: Harrisonburg City
Country: USA
Mailing address: 231 S. Liberty St
Mailing city: Harrisonburg
Mailing state: VA
Mailing zip: 22801-3621
General Phone: (540) 574-6200
Advertising Phone: (540) 574-6220
General/National Adv. E-mail: ads@dnronline.com
Display Adv. E-mail: addirector@dnronline.com
Editorial e-mail: jsacco@dnronline.com
Primary Website: www.dnronline.com
Mthly Avg Views: 750000
Mthly Avg Unique Visitors: 220000
Year Established: 1913
News Services: AP.
Special Editions: Spring Car and Motorcycle Care (Apr); Community Guide (Aug); First Night (Dec); Valentines Day (Feb); Honor Roll of Business (Jan); Flag Insert (Jul); Graduation (Jun); Home & Garden (Mar); Our Valley (May); Real Estate Showcase (Monthly); Yuletide Gift G
Special Weekly Sections: TV Week (Fri);
Delivery Methods: Mail`Newsstand`Carrier`Racks
Areas Served - City/County or Portion Thereof, or Zip codes: City of Harrisonburg and Counties of Rockingham, Shenandoah, Page, and Augusta in Virginia plus Hardy and Pendleton Counties in W.VA
Own Printing Facility?: Y
Commercial printers?: Y
Avg Free Circ: 220
Sat. Circulation Paid: 21034
Sat. Circulation Free: 214
Audit By: AAM
Audit Date: 31.03.2021
Personnel: Craig Bartoldson (Pub.); Clarissa Cottrill (Ed.); Jeremy Hunt (City Ed.); Jim Sacco (Sports Ed.); Rhonda McNeal (Advertising Dir.); Mark Golding (Circ. Mgr.)
Parent company (for newspapers): Ogden Newspapers Inc.

THE NEWS & ADVANCE

Street address 1: 101 Wyndale Dr
Street address city: Lynchburg
Street address state: VA
Zip/Postal code: 24501-6710
County: Lynchburg City
Country: USA
Mailing address: 101 WYNDALE DR
Mailing city: LYNCHBURG
Mailing state: VA
Mailing zip: 24501-6710
General Phone: (434) 385-5400
Advertising Phone: (434) 385-5450
Editorial Phone: (434) 385-5555
General/National Adv. E-mail: ads@newsadvance.com
Display Adv. E-mail: ads@newsadvance.com
Classified Adv. e-mail: classifiedads@newsadvance.com
Editorial e-mail: cglickman@newsadvance.com
Primary Website: www.newsadvance.com
Year Established: 1866
News Services: AP, NYT.
Special Editions: Greater Lynchburg Chamber of Commerce Report (); Garden Week (Apr); Kaleidoscope (Aug); Last Minute Gifts (Dec); Best of Health (Every other month); Progress (Feb); Bride & Groom (Jan); How-To-Guide (Jul); Summer Living (Jun); Who's Who in Construction (M
Special Weekly Sections: Best Food, Arts (Wed/ Sun); Community (Tue/Thur); TV, Entertainment, Auto (Fri); Religion, Auto (Sat); Auto, Real Estate, Travel, Business, Health, Technology (Sun)
Areas Served - City/County or Portion Thereof, or Zip codes: Lynchburg City, Campbell County, Amherst County, Appomattox County, Bedford County
Own Printing Facility?: Y
Commercial printers?: Y
Avg Free Circ: 1350
Sat. Circulation Paid: 12867
Sat. Circulation Free: 1350
Sun. Circulation Paid: 15452
Sun. Circulation Free: 907
Audit By: AAM
Audit Date: 31.03.2019
Personnel: Caroline Glickman (Managing Editor); Logan Anderson (Editorial Page/Opinion. Ed.); Chris Morris (Sports Ed.); Sue Scruggs (Sales Support); Dean Smith (Digital Sales); Ronald McBride (Adv. Dir.); Stephanie Eubank (Circ. Dir.); Kevin Smith (Regional Ad Director)
Parent company (for newspapers): BH Media Group; Lee Enterprises, Incorporated

MARTINSVILLE BULLETIN

Street address 1: 204 Broad Street
Street address city: Martinsville
Street address state: VA
Zip/Postal code: 24112
County: Martinsville City
Country: USA
Mailing address: PO BOX 3711
Mailing city: MARTINSVILLE
Mailing state: VA
Mailing zip: 24115-3711
General Phone: (276) 638-8801
General/National Adv. E-mail: advertising@martinsvillebulletin.com
Display Adv. E-mail: advertising@martinsvillebulletin.com
Classified Adv. e-mail: classified@martinsvillebulletin.com
Editorial e-mail: info@martinsvillebulletin.com
Primary Website: www.martinsvillebulletin.com
Year Established: 1889
News Services: NEA, AP.
Special Editions: Race (Apr); Football (Aug); Christmas Greetings (Dec); Brides (Feb); Health & Fitness (Jan); Graduation (Jun); Spring (Mar); Real Estate (May); Christmas Shopping (Nov);Pastor's Appreciation (Oct); Medicine and Health (July)
Special Weekly Sections: Best Food Day (Wed); Entertainment (Fri); Business (Sun)
Syndicated Publications: Parade (S).
Delivery Methods: Mail`Newsstand`Carrier`Racks
Own Printing Facility?: N
Commercial printers?: Y
Avg Free Circ: 85
Sun. Circulation Paid: 9630
Sun. Circulation Free: 79
Audit By: AAM
Audit Date: 31.12.2018
Personnel: Antoinette M. Haskell (Chrmn. of the Bd.); Robert H. Haskell (Pres./Pub.); George H. Harris (Vice Pres./Gen. Mgr.); Elizabeth H. Haskell (Vice Pres.); Tammy Foster (Bus. Mgr.); Tammy Jones (Adv. Mgr.); Matthew Dishman (Circ. Mgr.); Amanda Buck (Mng. Ed.); Ginny Wray (Editorial Writer); Holly Kozelski (Food/Women's Ed.); Sue Carter (Librarian); Mike Wray (Photo Ed.); George Harris (Prodn. Mgr.); Brian Carlton (Ed.)
Parent company (for newspapers): BH Media Group; Lee Enterprises, Incorporated

USA TODAY

Street address 1: 7950 Jones Branch Drive
Street address 2: Ste 100

Street address city: McLean
Street address state: VA
Zip/Postal code: 22108
County: Fairfax
Country: USA
Mailing address: 7950 Jones Branch Dr, Ste 100
Mailing city: McLean
Mailing state: VA
Mailing zip: 22108-0003
General Phone: (703)854-3400
Advertising Phone: (703) 854-6000
Editorial Phone: (703)854-6000
General/National Adv. E-mail: advertising@usatoday.com
Display Adv. E-mail: advertising@usatoday.com
Editorial e-mail: editor@usatoday.com
Primary Website: www.usatoday.com
Year Established: 1982
News Services: Crain Communications, AP, GNS, RN, AFP, DJ, UPI.
Delivery Methods: Mail`Newsstand`Carrier`Racks
Own Printing Facility?: Y
Commercial printers?: Y
Sat. Circulation Paid: 925515
Sun. Circulation Paid: 957337
Audit By: AAM
Audit Date: 31.12.2017
Personnel: Joanne Lipman (Chief Content Officer); John Zidich (President & Publisher); Patty Michalski (Editor in Chief); Beryl Love (Executive Editor); Susan Motiff (General Manager); Bill Sternberg (Editor, Editorial Page); Brent Jones (Standards & Ethics Ed.); Kevin Gentzel (Chief Revenue Officer); Daniel Bernard (Chief Product Officer); David Morgan (Pres, Sports Media Group); Tom Miller (VP Marketing); Nicole Carroll (EIC)
Parent company (for newspapers): Gannett - USA Today Network

DAILY PRESS

Street address 1: 703 Mariners Row
Street address city: Newport News
Street address state: VA
Zip/Postal code: 23606-4432
County: Newport News City
Country: USA
General Phone: (757) 247-4600
Advertising Phone: (757) 247-4678
Editorial Phone: (757) 247-4730
General/National Adv. E-mail: jalger@dailypress.com
Display Adv. E-mail: jalger@dailypress.com
Classified Adv. e-mail: classified@dailypress.com
Editorial e-mail: news@dailypress.com
Primary Website: www.dailypress.com
Mthly Avg Views: 7500000
Mthly Avg Unique Visitors: 715320
Year Established: 1896
News Services: AP, MCT, TMS.
Special Editions: H.S. All Stars (Apr); H.S. Football (Aug); H.S. All Stars (Dec); Home Expo (Feb); H.S. All Stars (Jul); Prime Time (Jun); New Cars-Trucks-Vans (Mar); Guide to Pre-Owned Vehicles (May); College Basketball (Nov); New Cars (Oct); Arts Calendar (Quarterly); P
Special Weekly Sections: Entertainment (Mon); Shopping, Deals (Tue); Best Food Day (Wed); Home, Garden, Town Square (Thur); Entertainment, Auto (Fri); Auto, Entertainment, Religion, Real Estate, Health (Sat); Arts, Home, Travel, Real Estate (Sun); Business, Finance, Local, National (Daily)
Syndicated Publications: Hampton Roads Mom & Me (Monthly); MyTime for Hampton Roads Women (Other); TV Hampton Roads Magazine (S).
Delivery Methods: Mail`Newsstand`Carrier
Areas Served - City/County or Portion Thereof, or Zip codes: Tidewater
Own Printing Facility?: N
Commercial printers?: N
Sat. Circulation Paid: 24037
Sun. Circulation Paid: 72549
Audit By: AAM
Audit Date: 31.12.2018
Personnel: Keith Potts (HR Dir.); David Messick (Dir., Consumer Mktg.); Todd Hubbard (Circ. Mgr.); Marisa Porto (Pub.); Cindy Laraway (Admin./Planning Mgr.); Karen Morgan (Features Ed.); Dave Hendrickson; Amy Powers (VP, Adv.); Jerry E. Alger (Dir., Adv. Sales)
Parent company (for newspapers): Alden Global Capital; Tribune Publishing, Inc.

THE VIRGINIAN-PILOT

Street address 1: 150 W Brambleton Ave
Street address city: Norfolk
Street address state: VA
Zip/Postal code: 23510-2018
County: Norfolk City
Country: USA
Mailing address: 150 W Brambleton Ave
Mailing city: Norfolk
Mailing state: VA
Mailing zip: 23510-2075
General Phone: (757) 446-2983
Advertising Phone: (757) 662-1455
Editorial Phone: (757) 446-9000
General/National Adv. E-mail: kelly.till@pilotonline.com
Display Adv. E-mail: kelly.till@pilotonline.com
Classified Adv. e-mail: kelly.till@pilotonline.com
Editorial e-mail: steve.gunn@pilotonline.com
Primary Website: www.pilotonline.com
Mthly Avg Views: 12259378
Mthly Avg Unique Visitors: 1659758
Year Established: 1866
News Services: AP, MCT, LAT-WP, Landmark News Service.
Special Editions: Career Day (Apr); Hurricane Alert (Aug); Technical Career Banners (Feb); African American Today (Feb); Forecast (Jan); Discover Hampton Roads (Jul); Scholastic Achievement (Jun); Discover the Albemarle (Mar); Spring Outer Banks Vacation Guide (May); Auto Show (Nov); Career Day (Oct);
Special Weekly Sections: Your Business (Mon); Best Food (Wed/Sun); Auto, Pulse, Entertainment, Arts (Fri); Home, Real Estate (Sat); Gracious Living (Sun)
Syndicated Publications: Parade (S); dash (1st Wed)
Delivery Methods: Mail`Newsstand`Carrier`Racks
Areas Served - City/County or Portion Thereof, or Zip codes: South Hampton Roads, NE North Carolina
Own Printing Facility?: Y
Commercial printers?: Y
Sat. Circulation Paid: 78789
Sun. Circulation Paid: 118228
Audit By: AAM
Audit Date: 31.12.2018
Personnel: Ryan Gilchrest (Mng. Ed.); Jeff Reece (Sr. Ed.); Erica A. Smith (Online Ed. & Dir. of Digital Strategy); Eric Hartley; Jami Frankenberry (Sports Ed.); Jamesetta M. Walker (Features Ed.); C.W. Johnson (Editorial Page Ed.)
Parent company (for newspapers): Alden Global Capital; Tribune Publishing, Inc.

THE PROGRESS-INDEX

Street address 1: 15 Franklin St
Street address city: Petersburg
Street address state: VA
Zip/Postal code: 23803-4503
County: Petersburg City
Country: USA
Mailing address: 15 FRANKLIN ST
Mailing city: PETERSBURG
Mailing state: VA
Mailing zip: 23803-4503
General Phone: (804) 722-5137
Advertising Phone: (804) 732-3456
Editorial Phone: (804) 732-3456
General/National Adv. E-mail: acoleman@progress-index.com
Display Adv. E-mail: acoleman@progress-index.com
Classified Adv. e-mail: ads@progress-index.com
Editorial e-mail: bcouturier@progress-index.com
Primary Website: www.progress-index.com
News Services: Associated Press, McClathy, NYT
Special Editions: Spring Fix-up (Apr); Cruisin' (Aug); Dear Santa (Dec); Life Underwriters (Feb); First Aid (Jan); Customer Appreciation (Jul); School's Out-Summer Fun Guide (Jun); Progress (Mar); Dining Guide (May); Holiday Happenings (Nov); Fall Fix-up (Oct); Literacy Ta
Special Weekly Sections: Home, Garden (Mon); Best Food Day (Tue); NASCAR (Wed); Arts, Entertainment (Thur); Auto (Fri); Technology (Sat); Science, Health (Sun)
Syndicated Publications: Relish (Monthly); USA WEEKEND Magazine (S); American Profile (Weekly).
Commercial printers?: Y
Avg Free Circ: 425
Sat. Circulation Paid: 4489
Sat. Circulation Free: 425
Sun. Circulation Paid: 5557
Sun. Circulation Free: 543
Audit By: AAM
Audit Date: 31.03.2019
Personnel: Peggy Simon (Mgr., Accounting); Bob Seals (Circ. Dir.); Patrick Kane (Photo Dept. Mgr.,); Tom Dozier (Sports Ed.); Cathy Ballou (Wire Ed.); Ron Shifflet (Prodn. Mgr., Pressroom); Brian Couturier (Managing Ed.); Brian Courtier (Sunday Ed.); Baretta Taylor (Adv. Dir.); Lauren Andrews (Online Adv. Exec.); Craig Richards (Pub); Alice Coleman (Adv. Sales Asst.)
Parent company (for newspapers): Gannett; CherryRoad Media

THE SOUTHWEST TIMES (PULASKI, VA)

Street address 1: 34 5th St NE
Street address city: Pulaski
Street address state: VA
Zip/Postal code: 24301-4608
County: Pulaski
Country: USA
Mailing address: PO BOX 391
Mailing city: PULASKI
Mailing state: VA
Mailing zip: 24301-0391
General Phone: (540) 980-5220
Advertising Phone: (540)980-5220 ext. 316
Editorial Phone: (540)980-5220 ext. 312
General/National Adv. E-mail: brenda@southwesttimes.com
Display Adv. E-mail: brenda@southwesttimes.com
Classified Adv. e-mail: classified@southwesttimes.com
Editorial e-mail: editor@southwesttimes.com
Primary Website: www.southwesttimes.com
Year Established: 1906
News Services: AP.
Special Editions: Football (Aug); Fair (Jul); Pulaski County tourism (May); Graduation (May); quarterly quality-of-life magazine
Special Weekly Sections: Religion (Fri); Best Food Day (S); Best Food Day (Wed).
Delivery Methods: Mail`Newsstand`Racks
Areas Served - City/County or Portion Thereof, or Zip codes: 24301, 24084, 24141, 24312, 24382, 24347
Own Printing Facility?: N
Commercial printers?: N
Sun. Circulation Paid: 5500
Audit By: Sworn/Estimate/Non-Audited
Audit Date: 12.07.2019
Personnel: Brenda Adams (Pub.); Lynn Adams (Managing Editor)
Parent company (for newspapers): Fackelman Newspapers

RICHMOND TIMES-DISPATCH

Street address 1: 300 E. Franklin Street
Street address city: Richmond
Street address state: VA
Zip/Postal code: 23219
County: Richmond City
Country: USA
Mailing address: 300 E FRANKLIN ST
Mailing city: RICHMOND
Mailing state: VA
Mailing zip: 23219-2214
General Phone: (804) 649-6000
Advertising Phone: (804) 649-6251
Editorial Phone: (804) 649-6305
General/National Adv. E-mail: addispatch@timesdispatch.com
Display Adv. E-mail: addispatch@timesdispatch.com
Classified Adv. e-mail: addispatch@timesdispatch.com
Editorial e-mail: pmudd@timesdispatch.com
Primary Website: www.timesdispatch.com
Mthly Avg Unique Visitors: 1301601
Year Established: 1850
News Services: AP, Business Wire, LAT-WP, Media General News, NYT, SHNS, Bloomberg, MCT.
Special Editions: Monument Avenue 10K (Apr); Discover Richmond (Aug); Holiday Books (Dec); Super Bowl (Feb); Year-End Stock Report (Jan); New Homes (Mar); Race Week (Sun) (May); UVA-Tech Game (Nov); Medical Jobs (Oct); Race Week (Sun) (Sept).
Special Weekly Sections: Best Food (Wed); Metro Business (Mon); Weekend (Thur); Home, Garden, Auto (Fri); Real Estate, Home, Garden (Sat); Real Estate, Travel (Sun)
Syndicated Publications: Parade (S).
Sat. Circulation Paid: 83845
Sun. Circulation Paid: 99197
Audit By: AAM
Audit Date: 31.03.2018
Personnel: Thomas A. Silvestri (Pres./Pub.); Sam Hightower (Hand over production plant); Raymond McDowell (Controller); Karen Dillon (Mgr., Pre Press Design Servs.); Scott Christino (Classified Adv. Mgr.); Terry Hall (Telephone Sales Mgr.); David B. Kirkman (Vice Pres., Circ.); Thomas C. Smith (Circ. Mgr., Metro); John W. Kelly (VP, Revenue & Business Development); Erin Brooks (Regional Sales Director); LaJuan Lewis (Major/Nat'l Acct. Mgr.); Scott Payne (Delivery Mgr.); Nicole McMullin (Online Brand Director); Pamela Stallsmith (Opinions Ed.)
Parent company (for newspapers): BH Media Group; Lee Enterprises, Incorporated

THE ROANOKE TIMES

Street address 1: 201 Campbell Ave SW
Street address city: Roanoke
Street address state: VA
Zip/Postal code: 24011-1105
County: Roanoke City
Country: USA
General Phone: (540) 981-3211
Advertising Phone: (540) 981-3145
Editorial Phone: (540) 981-3113
General/National Adv. E-mail: mary.whelchel@roanoke.com
Display Adv. E-mail: adinfo@roanoke.com
Classified Adv. e-mail: classified@roanoke.com
Editorial e-mail: editor@roanoke.com
Primary Website: www.roanoke.com
Mthly Avg Views: 6000000
Mthly Avg Unique Visitors: 1500
Year Established: 1886
News Services: AP, Washington Post News Service
Special Weekly Sections: Sunday Business, TV Weekly (Friday). New River Valley (Part Run, Friday/Sunday), Laker Weekly (part run, Wednesday)
Delivery Methods: Mail`Newsstand`Carrier`Racks
Areas Served - City/County or Portion Thereof, or Zip codes: Roanoke and New River Valley's MSAs
Own Printing Facility?: Y
Commercial printers?: Y
Sat. Circulation Paid: 40328
Sun. Circulation Paid: 47532
Audit By: AAM
Audit Date: 30.06.2018
Personnel: Mary Whelchel (National and Majors Director); Dwayne Yancey (Editorial Page Editor); Liz Hock (Editor I); Lawrence McConnell (Executive Editor); Terry Jamerson (Publisher); Andrew Svec (Design and Presentation Editor); Karla Hernandez (Regional H/R Director); David Weaver (Business Manager); Lee Wolverton (Managing Editor); Emily Wood (Controller); Jamie Kinnaird (VP of Advertising); Linnie Pride (Regional Circulation Director)
Parent company (for newspapers): BH Media Group; Lee Enterprises, Incorporated

THE NEWS LEADER

Street address 1: 11 N Central Ave
Street address city: Staunton
Street address state: VA
Zip/Postal code: 24401-4212
County: Staunton City
Country: USA
Mailing address: 11 N CENTRAL AVE
Mailing city: STAUNTON
Mailing state: VA
Mailing zip: 24401-4212
General Phone: (540) 213-9199
Advertising Phone: (540) 213-9199
Editorial Phone: (540) 213-9128
General/National Adv. E-mail: ads@newsleader.com
Display Adv. E-mail: ads@newsleader.com
Classified Adv. e-mail: ads@newsleader.com
Editorial e-mail: news@newsleader.com
Primary Website: www.newsleader.com
Year Established: 1904
News Services: GNS, AP, LAT-WP.
Special Editions: Home & Garden (Apr); Football (Aug); Bride's World (Feb); America's Birthday (Jun); Fact Book (Mar); Graduation (May).
Special Weekly Sections: Weather, TV (Daily); NASCAR (Thur); Faith, Value (Fri); History (Sat); Lifestyles, Home, Real Estate (Sun)
Syndicated Publications: USA WEEKEND Magazine (S).
Avg Free Circ: 172
Sat. Circulation Paid: 7934
Sat. Circulation Free: 172
Sun. Circulation Paid: 9133
Sun. Circulation Free: 79
Audit By: AAM
Audit Date: 31.03.2019
Personnel: Roger Watson (Pub.); Wilma Raybin (Controller); Susan Armstong (Admin., HR); Tricia

Bryant (Adv. Mgr.); Mark Chamberlin (Adv. Mgr., Retail); Amy Smith (Adv. Servs. Mgr.); Kathy Myers (Circ. Dir.); David Fritz (Exec. Ed.); Hubert Grim (Sports Ed.); Chris Beard (Online Content Developer); Bryce Connelly (Prodn. Dir.); Jim McCloskey (Major Accts. Rep.); Jean Wysocki (Reg. Controller)
Parent company (for newspapers): Gannett

NORTHERN VIRGINIA DAILY

Street address 1: 152 N. Holliday Street, P.O. Box 69
Street address city: Strasburg
Street address state: VA
Zip/Postal code: 22657-2143
County: Shenandoah
Country: USA
General Phone: (540) 465-5137
Advertising Phone: (540) 465-5137
Editorial Phone: (540) 456-5137
General/National Adv. E-mail: mgochenour@nvdaily.com
Display Adv. E-mail: classifieds@nvdaily.com
Classified Adv. e-mail: classifieds@nvdaily.com
Editorial e-mail: news@nvdaily.com
Primary Website: www.nvdaily.com
Mthly Avg Views: 900000
Mthly Avg Unique Visitors: 175000
Year Established: 1932
News Services: AP, SHNS.
Special Editions: Discover the Valley/Tourism (Apr); Football (Aug); Bridal (Jan); Winchester County Guide (Jul); Farm & Home (Mar); Warren County Guide (May); Restaurants & Recipes (Nov); Winterize Home & Auto (Oct); Outdoors (Sept).
Special Weekly Sections: Wedding & Engagements (Mon); Real Estate/Home (Sat); Weekend + More (Thur); NASCAR (Wed).
Syndicated Publications: American Profile (Mon); USA WEEKEND Magazine (Sat).
Delivery Methods: Mail`Newsstand`Carrier`Racks
Areas Served - City/County or Portion Thereof, or Zip codes: Counties of: Shenandoah, Warren, Frederick, Clarke, Paige in Virginia. Hampshire, Hardy West Viriginia.
Own Printing Facility?: N
Commercial printers?: N
Avg Free Circ: 372
Sat. Circulation Paid: 7905
Sat. Circulation Free: 285
Audit By: AAM
Audit Date: 31.03.2019
Personnel: Beverly George (Preprint Adv.); Mike Gochenour (Pub./Gen Mgr.); Linda Ash (Ed.); Will Alsworth (District Sales Mgr.)
Parent company (for newspapers): Ogden Newspapers Inc.

SUFFOLK NEWS-HERALD

Street address 1: 130 S Saratoga St
Street address city: Suffolk
Street address state: VA
Zip/Postal code: 23434-5323
County: Suffolk City
Country: USA
Mailing address: PO BOX 1220
Mailing city: SUFFOLK
Mailing state: VA
Mailing zip: 23439-1220
General Phone: (757) 539-3437
Advertising Phone: (757) 539-3437
Editorial Phone: (757) 539-3437
General/National Adv. E-mail: dana.snow@suffolknewsherald.com
Display Adv. E-mail: dana.snow@suffolknewsherald.com
Classified Adv. e-mail: hope.rose@suffolknewsherald.com
Editorial e-mail: res.spears@suffolknewsherald.com
Primary Website: www.suffolknewsherald.com
Year Established: 1873
Special Editions: The Great Outdoors (Apr); Football (Aug); Christmas Greetings (Dec); Progress (Feb); Year in Review (Jan); Summer Lifestyles (Jul); June Bride (Jun); Home Improvement (Mar); Senior Citizens (May); Buckle Up for Safety Coloring Book (Nov); Peanut Festival
Special Weekly Sections: Food (Tue); Home, Garden (Wed); Military (Thur); Business (Fri); Religion (Sat); Leisure (Sun);
Delivery Methods: Mail`Newsstand`Carrier`Racks
Areas Served - City/County or Portion Thereof, or Zip codes: SUFFOLK Chesapeake Isle of Wight County
Own Printing Facility?: N
Commercial printers?: N
Avg Free Circ: 12119
Sat. Circulation Paid: 101
Sat. Circulation Free: 10787
Sun. Circulation Paid: 100
Sun. Circulation Free: 12649
Audit By: Sworn/Estimate/Non-Audited
Audit Date: 12.07.2019
Personnel: John Carr (Pub.); Tracy Agnew (Ed.); Cathy Daughtrey (Office Mgr.); Kandyce Kirkland (Marketing Consultant); Hope Rose (Classified Adv. Rep.)
Parent company (for newspapers): Boone Newspapers, Inc.

THE NEWS VIRGINIAN

Street address 1: 201 C Rosser Avenue
Street address city: Waynesboro
Street address state: VA
Zip/Postal code: 22980-2414
County: Waynesboro City
Country: USA
Mailing address: PO BOX 1027
Mailing city: WAYNESBORO
Mailing state: VA
Mailing zip: 22980-0747
General Phone: (540) 949-8213
Advertising Phone: (540) 949-8213
Editorial Phone: (540) 949-8216
General/National Adv. E-mail: mgads@newsvirginian.com
Display Adv. E-mail: mgads@newsvirginian.com
Classified Adv. e-mail: mgads@newsvirginian.com
Editorial e-mail: nvnews@newsvirginian.com
Primary Website: www.newsvirginian.com
News Services: AP, NEA, TMS, Media General News Service.
Special Editions: Tourist Guide (Fall); Bridal Guide (Jan); Senior Lifestyles (Jun); Home & Garden (Mar); Hunting (Oct); Tourist Guide (Spring); Tourist Guide (Summer).
Special Weekly Sections: Best Food Days (Wed/Sun); Real Estate (Thur)
Syndicated Publications: USA WEEKEND Magazine (S); TV Time (Sat).
Avg Free Circ: 317
Sat. Circulation Paid: 3362
Sat. Circulation Free: 317
Sun. Circulation Paid: 3580
Sun. Circulation Free: 210
Audit By: AAM
Audit Date: 30.09.2018
Personnel: Lawrence McConnell (Interim Pub.); Denise Carter (Bus. Mgr.); Sherry Suggs (Adv. Dir.); Paul Wash (Circ. Dir.); Jim Sacco (Sports Ed.); James Stratton (Pub.); Patti Butler (Bus. Develop sales Rep.); Stephanie Twitty (Classifieds Adv. Mgr.); Rob Longley (Mng. Ed.)
Parent company (for newspapers): BH Media Group; Lee Enterprises, Incorporated

THE WINCHESTER STAR

Street address 1: 2 N Kent St
Street address city: Winchester
Street address state: VA
Zip/Postal code: 22601-5038
County: Winchester City
Country: USA
Mailing address: 2 N KENT ST
Mailing city: WINCHESTER
Mailing state: VA
Mailing zip: 22601-5098
General Phone: (540) 667-3200
Advertising Phone: (540) 665-4950
Editorial Phone: (540) 665-4941
General/National Adv. E-mail: ads@winchesterstar.com
Display Adv. E-mail: ads@winchesterstar.com
Classified Adv. e-mail: ads@winchesterstar.com
Editorial e-mail: news@winchesterstar.com
Primary Website: www.winchesterstar.com
Year Established: 1896
News Services: AP, Washington Post
Special Editions: Christmas Gifts (Dec); Bridal (Feb); Our Community (Gov't) (Jan); Planting (Mar); Graduation (May); Real Estate Guide (Monthly); College & Pro Football (Sept).
Special Weekly Sections: Best Food Days (Wed/Sat); Business (Tue/Thur); Weekend, Church (Fri); Stocks (Sat)
Syndicated Publications: PARADE Magazine (Sat). American Profile (Wed) Athlon Sports (monthly)
Delivery Methods: Mail`Newsstand`Carrier`Racks
Own Printing Facility?: Y
Avg Free Circ: 873
Sat. Circulation Paid: 18433
Sat. Circulation Free: 390
Audit By: AAM
Audit Date: 30.09.2017
Personnel: Thomas W. Byrd (Gen. Mgr.); Bill Green (Circ. Mgr.); Maria Montgomery (Mng. Ed.); Bobby Ford (Online Ed.); Adrian O'Connor (Editorial Page Ed.); Glen Stickel (Prodn. Foreman, Pressroom); Joyce Williams (Systems Mgr.); Chrissy Hill (Adv. Manager); Kristen Colebank (Production Mgr)
Parent company (for newspapers): Ogden Newspapers Inc.

WASHINGTON

THE BELLINGHAM HERALD

Street address 1: 1155 N State St
Street address 2: Ste 200
Street address city: Bellingham
Street address state: WA
Zip/Postal code: 98225-5024
County: Whatcom
Country: USA
Mailing address: 1155 N STATE ST STE 200
Mailing city: BELLINGHAM
Mailing state: WA
Mailing zip: 98225-5086
General Phone: (360) 676-2600
Advertising Phone: (360) 676-2660
Editorial Phone: (360) 676-2660
General/National Adv. E-mail: advertising@bellinghamherald.com
Display Adv. E-mail: advertising@bellinghamherald.com
Classified Adv. e-mail: classifieds@bellinghamherald.com
Editorial e-mail: newsroom@bellinghamherald.com
Primary Website: www.bellinghamherald.com
Mthly Avg Unique Visitors: 648000
Year Established: 1890
News Services: AP, MCT, NYT, WaPo, McClatchy
Special Editions: Prime Time (Jan, March, May, July, Sept, Nov); Bellingham Families (March, May, Sept, Nov); Whatcom Weddings (Jan); Ski to Sea (May); Northwest Washington Fair Program (Aug); Whatcom Health Magazine (May); Northwest Homes (Bi Weekly); Photo Calendar (Dec); BIA Homeshow Program (Feb)
Special Weekly Sections: Best Food (Tue); Entertainment (Thur); TV, Major Dept. Store Adv. (Sun)
Syndicated Publications: Parade (Sun); Relish (Monthly)
Delivery Methods: Mail`Newsstand`Carrier`Racks
Areas Served - City/County or Portion Thereof, or Zip codes: 98220, 98225, 98226, 98227, 98229, 98239, 98231, 98240, 98244, 98247, 98248, 98262, 98264, 98266, 98281, 98295, 98276
Own Printing Facility?: N
Commercial printers?: N
Sat. Circulation Paid: 12146
Sun. Circulation Paid: 15646
Audit By: AAM
Audit Date: 31.03.2018
Parent company (for newspapers): The McClatchy Company; Chatham Asset Management

KITSAP SUN

Street address 1: 545 5th Street
Street address city: Bremerton
Street address state: WA
Zip/Postal code: 98337
County: Kitsap
Country: USA
Mailing address: PO BOX 259
Mailing city: BREMERTON
Mailing state: WA
Mailing zip: 98337-0053
General Phone: (360) 377-3711
Advertising Phone: (360) 377-9210
Editorial Phone: (360) 415-2679
General/National Adv. E-mail: ad-support@kitsapsun.com
Display Adv. E-mail: ad-support@kitsapsun.com
Classified Adv. e-mail: classifieds@kitsapsun.com
Editorial e-mail: David.Nelson@kitsapsun.com
Primary Website: www.kitsapsunmedia.com
Year Established: 1935
News Services: AP, SHNS.
Special Editions: Visitor's Guide (Apr); 5 Days til Christmas (Dec); Home & Garden (May); Festival of Trees (Nov); Football (Oct).
Special Weekly Sections: News, Sports (Mon); Business (Tue); Food (Wed); Business, Home, Garden, Sports (Thur); Arts, Entertainment, Seniors, Auto, Business, Military (Fri); Auto, Business, Health, Real Estate (Sat); Business, Employment, Travel, TV, News, Real Estate, Family (Sun); Weather (Daily)
Syndicated Publications: USA WEEKEND Magazine (S).
Avg Free Circ: 105
Sat. Circulation Paid: 8270
Sat. Circulation Free: 105
Sun. Circulation Paid: 9832
Sun. Circulation Free: 105
Audit By: AAM
Audit Date: 31.03.2019
Personnel: Robin Alexander (Credit Mgr.); Mike Stevens (Dir., Adv./Mktg.); Don Dosa (Nat'l Adv. Mgr.); Charles Horton (Pres./Pub.); David Nelson (Ed.); Michael Moore (Entertainment Writer); Christopher Dunagan (Environmental/Tech. Writer); Chuck Stark (Sports Ed.); Jim Campbell (Submitted Content Ed.); Ron Muhleman (Opns. Dir.); Randi Watson (Pre Press Mgr.); Barry Weaver (Classified Adv. Mgr.); Hugh Hirata (Circ. Dir.)
Parent company (for newspapers): Gannett - USA Today Network

DAILY RECORD

Street address 1: 401 N Main St
Street address city: Ellensburg
Street address state: WA
Zip/Postal code: 98926-3107
County: Kittitas
Country: USA
Mailing address: 401 N MAIN ST
Mailing city: ELLENSBURG
Mailing state: WA
Mailing zip: 98926-3107
General Phone: (509) 925-1414
Advertising Phone: (509)925-1414
Editorial Phone: (509)925-1414
General/National Adv. E-mail: rsmith@kvnews.com
Display Adv. E-mail: rsmith@kvnews.com
Classified Adv. e-mail: classified2@kvnews.com
Editorial e-mail: jmarkell@kvnews.com
Primary Website: www.kvnews.com
Year Established: 1883
News Services: AP.
Special Editions: Conservation/Agriculture (Apr); Fair Guide (Aug); Spring Visitor's Guide (May); Holiday Gift Guide (Nov); Rodeo (Sept); KV Living (April, July, Jan, Oct);
Special Weekly Sections: Religion (Sat); Business (Thurs), Food (Tues), Entertainment (Thurs), Outdoors (Fri)
Syndicated Publications: American Profile (Fri); Relish (Monthly); Parade (S).
Delivery Methods: Mail`Newsstand`Carrier`Racks
Own Printing Facility?: N
Commercial printers?: N
Sat. Circulation Paid: 5523
Audit By: Sworn/Estimate/Non-Audited
Audit Date: 12.07.2019
Personnel: Joanna Markell (Editor/General Manager); Richard Dalton (Telecom Mgr.); Robyn Smith (Advertising sales manager); Pam Shuart (Advertising process manager/national accts); Josh Crawford (Circulation director)
Parent company (for newspapers): Adams Publishing Group, LLC

THE DAILY HERALD

Street address 1: 1800 41st Street S-300
Street address city: Everett
Street address state: WA
Zip/Postal code: 98203
County: Snohomish
Country: USA
Mailing address: PO BOX 930
Mailing city: EVERETT
Mailing state: WA
Mailing zip: 98206-0930
General Phone: (425) 339-3000
Advertising Phone: (425) 339-3030
Editorial Phone: (425) 339-3400
General/National Adv. E-mail: advertising@heraldnet.com
Display Adv. E-mail: advertising@heraldnet.com

Classified Adv. e-mail: classified@heraldnet.com
Editorial e-mail: editor@heraldnet.com
Primary Website: www.heraldnet.com
Year Established: 1901
News Services: AP, LAT-WP, Scripps McClatchy News Service.
Special Editions: Herald Health (Quarterly);
Special Weekly Sections: Business (Mon); Health (Tue); Best Food (Wed); Home and Garden (Thur); Arts, Entertainment, Automotive (Fri); Travel (Sat); Money, Real Estate (Sun)
Syndicated Publications: Relish (Monthly); Access (S).
Delivery Methods: Newsstand`Carrier`Racks
Areas Served - City/County or Portion Thereof, or Zip codes: 98011, 98012, 98019, 98020, 98021, 98026, 98036, 98037, 98043, 98072, 98087, 98133, 98155, 98201, 98203, 98204, 98205, 98208, 98223, 98236, 98239, 98241, 98249, 98251, 98252, 98253, 98256, 98258, 98260, 98270, 98271, 98272, 98273, 98274, 98275, 98277, 98282, 98290, 98292, 98294, 98296
Own Printing Facility?: Y
Commercial printers?: Y
Sat. Circulation Paid: 28621
Sun. Circulation Paid: 33253
Audit By: AAM
Audit Date: 31.03.2018
Personnel: Jere Grubb (Circ. Opns. Mgr.); Neal Pattison (Exec. Ed.); Jim Davis (Herald Business Journal Editor); Melanie Munk (Features/Food Ed.); Bill Pedigo (Librarian/TV Ed.); Kevin Brown (Sports Ed.); Josh O'Connor; Robert Frank (City Ed.); Diane Shaver; David Dadisman (Pub.); Pilar Linares (Adv. Dir.); Carrie Radcliff (Retail Adv. Mgr.); Stephen Barrett (Dir., Nat'l and Regional Sales)
Parent company (for newspapers): Sound Publishing, Inc.

TRI-CITY HERALD

Street address 1: 4253 W 24th Ave Ste 20
Street address city: Kennewick
Street address state: WA
Zip/Postal code: 99338
County: Benton
Country: USA
Mailing address: PO BOX 2608
Mailing city: TRI CITIES
Mailing state: WA
Mailing zip: 99302-2608
General Phone: (509) 582-1500
Advertising Phone: (509) 582-1460
Editorial Phone: (509) 582-1523
General/National Adv. E-mail: ads@tricityherald.com
Display Adv. E-mail: ads@tricityherald.com
Classified Adv. e-mail: ads@tricityherald.com
Editorial e-mail: news@tricityherald.com
Primary Website: www.tricityherald.com
Mthly Avg Views: 3233688
Mthly Avg Unique Visitors: 493812
Year Established: 1947
News Services: Metro Suburbia Inc./Newhouse Newspapers, LAT-WP, MCT, NYT, McClatchy.
Special Editions: Healthy Living (Quarterly); Wine Press Northwest (Quarterly); Living TC (Quarterly)
Special Weekly Sections: Trends, Leisure (Mon); Family, Friends (Tue); Food, Nutrition (Wed); health, Fitness (Thur); Entertainment, Arts (Fri); Outdoors, Auto, Religion (Sat); Desert Living, Real Estate, Travel, Voices, TV, Business (Sun); Business, Sports, Mid-Columbia (Daily)
Syndicated Publications: Parade (S).
Delivery Methods: Mail`Newsstand`Carrier`Racks
Own Printing Facility?: N
Commercial printers?: N
Sat. Circulation Paid: 19449
Sun. Circulation Paid: 23629
Audit By: AAM
Audit Date: 31.12.2017
Personnel: Laurie Williams (Exec. Ed.); Lori Lancaster (Ed.); Cecilia Rexus (Ed.)
Parent company (for newspapers): McClatchy; Chatham Asset Management

THE DAILY NEWS

Street address 1: 770 11th Ave
Street address city: Longview
Street address state: WA
Zip/Postal code: 98632-2412
County: Cowlitz
Country: USA
Mailing address: PO BOX 189
Mailing city: LONGVIEW
Mailing state: WA
Mailing zip: 98632-7118
General Phone: (360) 577-2500
Advertising Phone: (360) 577-2500
Editorial Phone: (360) 577-2500
General/National Adv. E-mail: squaife@tdn.com
Display Adv. E-mail: squaife@tdn.com
Classified Adv. e-mail: ahurse@tdn.com
Editorial e-mail: andre@tdn.com
Primary Website: www.tdn.com
Year Established: 1923
News Services: AP, LAT-WP.
Special Editions: Thanksgiving (Other).
Special Weekly Sections: Business (Daily); Health, Lifestyle, Neighbors (Tue); Sasquatch, Best Food (Wed); Entertainment (Thur); Outdoor, TV (Fri); Religious. Auto (Sat); Travel, Real Estate, TV (Sun)
Syndicated Publications: Real Estate (Monthly); Parade (S).
Avg Free Circ: 5205
Sat. Circulation Paid: 8544
Sat. Circulation Free: 5205
Sun. Circulation Paid: 9074
Sun. Circulation Free: 2106
Audit By: AAM
Audit Date: 31.03.2019
Personnel: David Thornberry (Pub.); Steve Quaife (Adv. Mgr.); Nicholas Babineau (Circ. Dir.); Deziray Weikum (Accounting Clerk); Andre Stepankowsky (City Ed.); Nancy A. Edwards (Features Ed.); Shari Phiel (Online Ed.)
Parent company (for newspapers): Dispatch-Argus; Lee Enterprises, Incorporated

COLUMBIA BASIN HERALD/ HAGADONE MEDIA WASHINGTON

Street address 1: 813 West Third Ave
Street address city: Moses Lake
Street address state: WA
Zip/Postal code: 98837
County: Grant
Country: United States
General Phone: 509-765-4561
Advertising Phone: 509-765-4561
Editorial Phone: 509-765-4561
Display Adv. E-mail: jrountree@columbiabasinherald.com
Classified Adv. e-mail: lherbert@columbiabasinherald.com
Editorial e-mail: editor@columbiabasinherald.com
Primary Website: columbiabasinherald.com
Mthly Avg Views: 285000
Mthly Avg Unique Visitors: 90000
Year Established: 1941
Special Editions: Moses Lake Magazine Grant County Magazine Adams County Magazine Tourism Magazine Year in Review Potato Conference Columbia Basin Resource Guide Moses Lake Map Home Buyers Guide The Strength of the Columbia Basin Grant County Fair Adams County Fair Health & Wellness Puzzle Books
Special Weekly Sections: Home & Garden Local News/ Local Life
Delivery Methods: Mail`Newsstand`Carrier`Racks
Areas Served - City/County or Portion Thereof, or Zip codes: Grant & Adams County
Own Printing Facility?: Y
Commercial printers?: Y
Avg Free Circ: 2000
Audit By: Sworn/Estimate/Non-Audited
Audit Date: 12.[illegible]
Personnel: Denise Lembcke (Bus. Mgr.); Caralyn Bess (Regional Publisher); Joyce McLanahan (Nat'l Adv. Mgr.); Dave Burgess (Managing Editor); Curt Weaver (Prodn. Supt.); Bob Richardson (Advertising Director Columbia Basin Herald/Publisher Basin Business Journal); Dana Moreno (Marketing/ Audience Development Director); Rosalie Black (Sales Manager); Emily Thornton (Assistant Managing Editor); Tom Hinde (Circ. Dir.); Bill Stevenson (Mng. Ed.); Karyll Van Ness (Circulation District Manager); Sheri Jones (HR/Business Manager)
Parent company (for newspapers): Hagadone Corporation; Hagadone Media

SKAGIT VALLEY HERALD

Street address 1: 1215 Anderson Road
Street address city: Mount Vernon
Street address state: WA
Zip/Postal code: 98274
County: Skagit
Country: USA
Mailing address: PO BOX 578
Mailing city: MOUNT VERNON
Mailing state: WA
Mailing zip: 98273-0578
General Phone: (360) 424-3251
Advertising Phone: (360) 416-2128
Editorial Phone: (360) 416-2160
General/National Adv. E-mail: dpetit@skagitpublishing.com
Display Adv. E-mail: dpetit@skagitpublishing.com
Classified Adv. e-mail: dpetit@skagitpublishing.com
Editorial e-mail: editor@skagitpublishing.com
Primary Website: www.goskagit.com
Year Established: 1884
News Services: AP, MCT, LAT-WP.
Special Editions: Builders Assoc. Home Show (Apr); Anacortes Arts & Crafts (Aug); Bridal (Feb); Highland Games (Jul); Spring Home & Garden (Mar); Holiday Gift Guide (Nov); Swan (Woman of the Year) (Oct);
Special Weekly Sections: Business (Tue); best Food Day (Wed); Entertainment (Thur); Home & Garden (Fri); Religion (Sat); Skagit Living (Sun)
Syndicated Publications: TV Week Magazine (Weekly)
Delivery Methods: Mail`Newsstand`Carrier`Racks
Own Printing Facility?: Y
Commercial printers?: Y
Avg Free Circ: 383
Sat. Circulation Paid: 9311
Sat. Circulation Free: 383
Sun. Circulation Paid: 9700
Sun. Circulation Free: 58
Audit By: AAM
Audit Date: 31.03.2019
Personnel: Colette Weeks (Dir. of Content); Dan Ruthemeyer (Assignment Ed.); Scott Terrell (Photo Ed.); Marianne Graff (Assistant Assignment Ed.); Greg Fiscus (Lead Copy Ed.); Ben Davis (Copy Ed.); Duby Petit (Advertising and Marketing Dir.); Manny Nevarez (Circ. Dir.)
Parent company (for newspapers): Adams Publishing Group, LLC

THE OLYMPIAN

Street address 1: 111 Bethel St NE
Street address city: Olympia
Street address state: WA
Zip/Postal code: 98506-4365
County: Thurston
Country: USA
Mailing address: 111 BETHEL ST NE
Mailing city: OLYMPIA
Mailing state: WA
Mailing zip: 98506-4365
General Phone: (360) 754-5400
Advertising Phone: (360) 754-5457
Editorial Phone: (360) 754-5420
General/National Adv. E-mail: jdzaran@theolympian.com
Display Adv. E-mail: jdzaran@theolympian.com
Editorial e-mail: news@theolympian.com
Primary Website: www.theolympian.com
Mthly Avg Views: 2872129
Mthly Avg Unique Visitors: 468509
Year Established: 1889
News Services: AP, MCT, LAT-WP, NYT, Bloomberg
Special Editions: After Christmas Sale (Dec); Tour of Homes (Jul); Source Book (Jun); Holiday Gift Guide (Nov); Best of South Sound (Oct)
Special Weekly Sections: TV Week (S); Weekend (Fri)
Syndicated Publications: Parade (S).
Delivery Methods: Mail`Newsstand`Carrier`Racks
Areas Served - City/County or Portion Thereof, or Zip codes: 98501-98597, 98433
Own Printing Facility?: N
Commercial printers?: N
Sat. Circulation Paid: 13454
Sun. Circulation Paid: 16178
Audit By: AAM
Audit Date: 31.12.2018
Personnel: Phil Schroder (VP Circ.); Dusti Demarest (Features Ed.); Jerre Redecker (Sr. Ed.); Tammy McGee (Online Producer); Jennifer Matts-Sprague (VP Finance); John Dzaran (Adv. Dir.); Norine Mullen (HR Dir.)
Parent company (for newspapers): The McClatchy Company; Chatham Asset Management

PENINSULA DAILY NEWS

Street address 1: 305 W 1st St
Street address city: Port Angeles
Street address state: WA
Zip/Postal code: 98362-2205
County: Clallam
Country: USA
Mailing address: PO BOX 1330
Mailing city: PORT ANGELES
Mailing state: WA
Mailing zip: 98362-0246
General Phone: (360) 452-2345
Advertising Phone: (360) 417-3540
Editorial Phone: (360) 417-3531
General/National Adv. E-mail: sbarrett@soundpublishing.com
Display Adv. E-mail: sperry@peninsuladailynews.com
Classified Adv. e-mail: sperry@peninsuladailynews.com
Editorial e-mail: news@peninsuladailynews.com
Primary Website: www.peninsuladailynews.com
Mthly Avg Views: 1200000
Mthly Avg Unique Visitors: 270000
Year Established: 1916
News Services: AP. New York Times News Service.
Special Editions: Spring/Summer Viz Guide (May); Fairs (Aug); Christmas Gift Guide (Dec); Health and Welness (quarterly); Spring Home (Mar); Travel (May); New Cars (Nov); Fall-Winter Visitors Guide (Oct).
Special Weekly Sections: Best Food Day (Wed); Entertainment, Real Estate (Fri); Women, Real Estate (Sun)
Syndicated Publications: Relish (monthly) and Spry (monthly)
Delivery Methods: Mail`Carrier`Racks
Areas Served - City/County or Portion Thereof, or Zip codes: 98362, 98363, 98365, 98368, 98382, 98331, 98305, 98320, 98324,98325, 98326, 98334, 98339, 98343, 98350, 98357, 98365, 98376, 98381, 98399
Own Printing Facility?: N
Commercial printers?: N
Avg Free Circ: 134
Sun. Circulation Paid: 11159
Sun. Circulation Free: 24
Audit By: AAM
Audit Date: 31.03.2019
Personnel: Terry Ward (Pub.); Leah Leach (Ed.)
Parent company (for newspapers): Black Press Ltd.; Sound Publishing, Inc.

SEATTLE DAILY JOURNAL OF COMMERCE

Street address 1: 83 Columbia St
Street address city: Seattle
Street address state: WA
Zip/Postal code: 98104-1432
County: King
Country: USA
Mailing address: PO BOX 11050
Mailing city: SEATTLE
Mailing state: WA
Mailing zip: 98111-9050
General Phone: (206) 622-8272
Advertising Phone: (206)622-8272
Editorial Phone: (206)622-8272
General/National Adv. E-mail: advertising@djc.com
Display Adv. E-mail: advertising@djc.com
Classified Adv. e-mail: classifieds@djc.com
Editorial e-mail: editor@djc.com
Primary Website: www.djc.com
Year Established: 1893
News Services: AP, Business Wire.
Special Weekly Sections: Travel (Fri); Heavy Equipment (Mon); Plan Bulletin (Sat); Real Estate (Thur); Environment (Tues); Architecture & Engineering (Wed).
Delivery Methods: Mail`Newsstand
Own Printing Facility?: Y
Commercial printers?: N
Sat. Circulation Paid: 4500
Audit By: Sworn/Estimate/Non-Audited
Audit Date: 12.07.2019
Personnel: Phil Brown (Pub.); Jeff Mosely (Adv. Mgr.); Val Valdez (Circ. Mgr.); Laura Heberlein (Ed.); Trista Allen (Asst. Ed.); Maude Scott (Mng. Ed.); Ben Minnick (Construction Ed.); Lynn Porter (Real Estate Ed.); John Silver (Travel Ed.); John Elliott (IT Dir.); Nancy Slaney (Prodn. Mgr.); David Elleby (Prodn. Foreman, Pressroom)

THE SEATTLE TIMES

Street address 1: 1000 Denny Way
Street address city: Seattle
Street address state: WA
Zip/Postal code: 98109-5323
County: King

Country: USA
Mailing address: PO BOX 70
Mailing city: SEATTLE
Mailing state: WA
Mailing zip: 98111-0070
General Phone: (206) 464-2988
Advertising Phone: (206)464-2400
Editorial Phone: (206)464-8284
General/National Adv. E-mail: advertising@seattletimes.com
Display Adv. E-mail: advertising@seattletimes.com
Classified Adv. e-mail: advertising@seattletimes.com
Editorial e-mail: dshelton@seattletimes.com
Primary Website: www.seattletimes.com
Mthly Avg Views: 47800204
Mthly Avg Unique Visitors: 7916375
Year Established: 1896
Special Weekly Sections: NW Sunday, Real Estate, NW Traveler, Pacific NW (Sun); Best Food (Wed); Gardening (Thur); Weekend Plus, Homes (Sat)
Delivery Methods: Mail`Newsstand`Carrier`Racks
Own Printing Facility?: Y
Commercial printers?: Y
Sat. Circulation Paid: 185876
Sun. Circulation Paid: 273061
Audit By: AAM
Audit Date: 31.03.2018
Personnel: Michele Matassa Flores (Managing Ed.); Lynn Jacobson (Deputy Mng. Ed.); Don Shelton (Exec. Ed.); Ray Rivera (Deputy Managing Editor)
Parent company (for newspapers): Seattle Times

THE SPOKESMAN-REVIEW

Street address 1: 999 W Riverside Ave
Street address city: Spokane
Street address state: WA
Zip/Postal code: 99201-1005
County: Spokane
Country: USA
Mailing address: PO BOX 2160
Mailing city: SPOKANE
Mailing state: WA
Mailing zip: 99210-2160
General Phone: (509) 459-5000
Advertising Phone: (509) 459-5095
Editorial Phone: (509) 459-5400
General/National Adv. E-mail: MikeD@spokesman.com
Display Adv. E-mail: MikeD@spokesman.com
Classified Adv. e-mail: ScottB@spokesman.com
Editorial e-mail: robc@spokesman.com
Primary Website: www.spokesman.com
Mthly Avg Views: 3354242
Mthly Avg Unique Visitors: 679685
Year Established: 1883
News Services: Associated Press, MCT
Special Editions: Fishing (April); Golf Tab (June); Activities Guide (May); Holiday Shopping (Nov); Live Well (April/Oct) Fair Guide (August/Sept)
Special Weekly Sections: TV Week (Sun); Automotive (Sat); Food in Today Section (Wed); 7 Entertainment (Fri); Real Estate and Jobs (Sun); LiveWell (Tue); Boomer (Mon); Outdoors (Thu); Pinch (Sun); Pinch (Wed)
Syndicated Publications: Parade (Sun); Athlon Sports (Thu -1x per month); Dash (Wed - 1x per month)
Delivery Methods: Newsstand`Carrier`Racks
Areas Served - City/County or Portion Thereof, or Zip codes: 83801-99344
Own Printing Facility?: Y
Commercial printers?: N
Sat. Circulation Paid: 61655
Sun. Circulation Paid: 75640
Audit By: AAM
Audit Date: 31.03.2018
Personnel: Gary Graham (Editor); Addy Hatch (City Editor); Laurie Lunzer (Dir. Production/IT); Geoff Pinnock (Senior Editor); Kathleen Coleman (Dir., Sales and Mktg.); Connie Bantz (Mgr., HR); Lenny Kerstetter (Prodn. Mgr., Packaging Ctr.); Steve Heidal (Prodn. Mgr., Pressroom); Jim Groh (Prod.. Mgr.. Prepress); Michael Dixon (Director of Advertising); Rob Curley
Parent company (for newspapers): Cowles Publishing Co.

SUNNYSIDE SUN

Street address 1: 600 S 6th St
Street address city: Sunnyside
Street address state: WA
Zip/Postal code: 98944-2111
County: Yakima
Country: USA
Mailing address: PO BOX 878
Mailing city: SUNNYSIDE
Mailing state: WA
Mailing zip: 98944-0878
General Phone: (509) 837-4500
Advertising Phone: (509) 837-4500
Editorial Phone: (509) 837-4500
General/National Adv. E-mail: info@sunnysidesun.com
Display Adv. E-mail: ads@sunnysidesun.com
Classified Adv. e-mail: classifieds@sunnysidesun.com
Editorial e-mail: news@sunnysidesun.com
Primary Website: www.sunnysidesun.com
Mthly Avg Views: 78000
Mthly Avg Unique Visitors: 21000
Year Established: 1901
Special Editions: January: Reflections, Babies; February: Babies, Salute to FFA, Spring Sports Review; March: Business Card Directory, Valley Farmer; April: Health Choices; May: Cinco de Mayo; June: Salute to Dairy, Graduation; July: Who's Who; August: Fall Sports Review; September: Football Forecast, Pride of the Valley, Calendar; October: Women in Business; November: Salute to Heroes, Winter Sports Review; December: Christmas in the Valley, Letters to Santa
Audit By: Sworn/Estimate/Non-Audited
Audit Date: 12.07.2019
Personnel: Job Wise (Co-owner, General Manager); Debbie Guerrero (Office Manager); Patrick Shelby (News Ed.); Ileana Martinez (Co-owner, Media Director)
Parent company (for newspapers): Eagle Newspapers, Inc.; Sunnyside Media Group LLC

THE NEWS TRIBUNE

Street address 1: 1950 S State St
Street address city: Tacoma
Street address state: WA
Zip/Postal code: 98405-2817
County: Pierce
Country: USA
General Phone: (253) 597-8742
Advertising Phone: (253) 597-8487
Editorial Phone: (253) 597-8686
General/National Adv. E-mail: john.dzaran@thenewstribune.com
Display Adv. E-mail: john.dzaran@thenewstribune.com
Classified Adv. e-mail: john.dzaran@thenewstribune.com
Editorial e-mail: newstips@thenewstribune.com
Primary Website: www.thenewstribune.com
Mthly Avg Unique Visitors: 1260980
Year Established: 1880
News Services: AP, LAT-WP, MCT, McClatchy, Bloomberg, NYT
Special Weekly Sections: Go (Fri); 50+ (Monthly); SouthSound TV (S); Adventure (S).
Syndicated Publications: Parade (S).
Delivery Methods: Mail`Newsstand`Carrier`Racks
Own Printing Facility?: Y
Commercial printers?: N
Sat. Circulation Paid: 39754
Sun. Circulation Paid: 50322
Audit By: AAM
Audit Date: 30.06.2018
Personnel: Karen Peterson (Exec. Ed.); Dale Phelps (Mng. Ed.); Randy McCarthy (Crime/Breaking News Team Leader); Matt Misterek (Editorial Page Editor); Wes Corey (Production Manager); John Dzaran (VP Advertising); Ian Swenson (Asst. Mng. Ed., Online); Rebecca Poynter (Pub.)
Parent company (for newspapers): The McClatchy Company; Chatham Asset Management

THE PENINSULA GATEWAY

Street address 1: 1950 South State Street
Street address city: Tacoma
Street address state: WA
Zip/Postal code: 98405
County: Pierce
Country: USA
Mailing address: 1950 South State Street
Mailing city: Tacoma
Mailing state: WA
Mailing zip: 98405
General Phone: (253) 597-8742
General/National Adv. E-mail: dawn.leibold@thenewstribune.com
Display Adv. E-mail: dawn.leibold@thenewstribune.com
Editorial e-mail: dale.phelps@thenewstribune.com
Primary Website: thenewstribune.com
Year Established: 1917
Delivery Methods: Mail
Areas Served - City/County or Portion Thereof, or Zip codes: Pierce County
Sat. Circulation Paid: 39754
Sun. Circulation Paid: 50322
Audit By: AAM
Audit Date: 30.06.2018
Personnel: Rebecca Poynter (Pres./Pub.); Dawn Leibold (NW Dir. Sales); Dale Phillips (Ed./VP News)
Parent company (for newspapers): The McClatchy Company

THE COLUMBIAN

Street address 1: 701 West 8th Street
Street address city: Vancouver
Street address state: WA
Zip/Postal code: 98660
County: Clark
Country: USA
Mailing address: PO BOX 180
Mailing city: VANCOUVER
Mailing state: WA
Mailing zip: 98666-0180
General Phone: (360) 694-3391
Advertising Phone: (360) 735-4497
Editorial Phone: (360) 735-4569
General/National Adv. E-mail: metrodesk@columbian.com
Display Adv. E-mail: advertising@columbian.com
Classified Adv. e-mail: classified@columbian.com
Editorial e-mail: letters@columbian.com
Primary Website: www.columbian.com
Mthly Avg Views: 2460700
Mthly Avg Unique Visitors: 652000
Year Established: 1890
News Services: AP, CNS, MCT - LAT, WP - Bloomberg.
Special Editions: Jan: Economic forecast. Feb: Profiles. March: HS Football. Apr: family/summer camps. June: best of Clark Co. July: Clark Co. Fair. Sept. Parade of Homes. Resource Guide.Oct. Brest Cancer Awareness. Nov. Home for the Holidays I. Dec. Home for the Holidays II
Special Weekly Sections: Weekend (Fri); Cruise Control (Sat) Real Estate, Recruitment (Sun)
Syndicated Publications: Parade (S)
Delivery Methods: Mail`Newsstand`Carrier`Racks
Areas Served - City/County or Portion Thereof, or Zip codes: 98601, 98604, 98606, 98607, 98629, 98642, 98660, 98661, 98662, 98663, 98664, 98665, 98671, 98674, 98675, 98682, 98683, 98684, 98685, 98686
Own Printing Facility?: Y
Commercial printers?: Y
Sat. Circulation Paid: 23239
Sun. Circulation Paid: 27631
Audit By: AAM
Audit Date: 31.03.2018
Personnel: Scott Campbell (Pub.); Brandon Zarzana (CFO); Denise Sandvig (HR Dir.); Teresa Keplinger (Adv. Dir.); Rachel Rose (Circ. Mgr., Promo./Sales); Peter Geloff (Circ. Mgr., Single Copy); Craig Brown (Ed); Mark Bowder (Metro Ed.); Micah Rice (Sports Ed.); Laura Wenrick (Adv. Sales Mgr.); Greg Hartgrave (Circ.Systems Admin.); Greg Jayne (Editorial Page Ed.); Jody Campbell (Dir. of Community Outreach); Merridee Hanson (News Ed.); Tony Myers (Home Delivery Mgr.); Ben Campbell (Circulation Manager); Brian MacKay (IT Director); Cris Matta (Production Director); Amanda Cowan (Photo Editor); Kristeen Millett (Digital Marketing Manager); Amy Libby (Online Editor); Allan Brettman (Business Editor); John Hill (Metro Team Editor)
Parent company (for newspapers): Columbian Publishing Co.

WALLA WALLA UNION-BULLETIN

Street address 1: 112 S 1st Ave
Street address city: Walla Walla
Street address state: WA
Zip/Postal code: 99362-3011
County: Walla Walla
Country: USA
Mailing address: PO BOX 1358
Mailing city: WALLA WALLA
Mailing state: WA
Mailing zip: 99362-0306
General Phone: (509) 525-3300
Advertising Phone: (509) 525-3304
Editorial Phone: (509) 525-3303
General/National Adv. E-mail: advertising@wwub.com
Display Adv. E-mail: advertising@wwub.com
Classified Adv. e-mail: advertising@wwub.com
Editorial e-mail: letters@wwub.com
Primary Website: www.union-bulletin.com
Year Established: 1869
News Services: AP.
Special Editions: On the Grow (Oct); The Lifesyle (monthly); Visitors Guide (Mar); Family Forum (Quarterly)
Special Weekly Sections: TV (Mon); Best Food (Tue); Enterprise, Business, Outdoor (Wed); Entertainment (Thur); Religion, Perspective, Panorama (Sun)
Syndicated Publications: Parade (S).
Delivery Methods: Mail`Newsstand`Carrier`Racks
Areas Served - City/County or Portion Thereof, or Zip codes: 99323, 99324, 99328, 99329, 99347, 99348, 99359, 99360, 99361, 99362, 97813, 97862, 97886
Own Printing Facility?: Y
Commercial printers?: N
Avg Free Circ: 2627
Sun. Circulation Paid: 10395
Sun. Circulation Free: 475
Audit By: AAM
Audit Date: 30.09.2015
Personnel: Bill Thyken (Controller); Jay Brodt (Adv. Dir.); Michael Cibart (Circ. Mgr.); Rick Doyle (Ed.); Rick Eskil (Editorial Page Ed.); Alasdair Stewart (Asst. News Ed.); Andy Porter (Political Ed.); Jim Buchan (Sports Ed.); Catherine Hicks (Wire Ed.); Josh Gesler (Systems Specialist); Rob Blethen (Pub.); Kandi Suckow (Nat'l Adv. Rep.); Brian Hunt (Publisher); Steven Butcher (HR Mgr); James Blethen (Prod. Supervisor)
Parent company (for newspapers): The Seattle Times

THE WENATCHEE WORLD

Street address 1: 14 N Mission St
Street address city: Wenatchee
Street address state: WA
Zip/Postal code: 98801-2250
County: Chelan
Country: USA
Mailing address: PO BOX 1511
Mailing city: WENATCHEE
Mailing state: WA
Mailing zip: 98807-1511
General Phone: (509) 663-5161
Advertising Phone: (509) 664-7130
Editorial Phone: (509) 661-6391
General/National Adv. E-mail: newsroom@wenatcheeworld.com
Display Adv. E-mail: advertising@wenatcheeworld.com
Classified Adv. e-mail: advertising@wenatcheeworld.com
Editorial e-mail: newsroom@wenatcheeworld.com
Primary Website: www.wenatcheeworld.com
Year Established: 1905
News Services: Reuters, McClatchy
Special Editions: World's Best (annual); Visitors' Guide (annual); Progress Edition (annual)
Delivery Methods: Mail`Newsstand`Carrier
Areas Served - City/County or Portion Thereof, or Zip codes: 98801, 98802, 98826, 98815, 98816
Own Printing Facility?: Y
Commercial printers?: Y
Sun. Circulation Paid: 16841
Audit By: USPS
Audit Date: 30.09.2021
Personnel: Russ Hemphill (Managing Editor); Wilfred R. Woods (Chairman emeritus); Cal Fitzsimmons (Ed.); Marco Martinez (Features editor, Foothills magazine editor); Nevonne McDaniels (Business editor, Business World editor); Don Seabrook (Photo editor); Kelli Scott (Editorial Page Ed.); Sean Flaherty (Publisher); David Anderson (Advertising Sales manager); Marco Martinez (Features Ed.); Jeff Jones (Business manager, Circulation director); Don Seabrook; Joe Pitt; Gretchen Woods (Personnel Manager); Wyatt Gardiner (Circulation and Production Director); Rob Torbett (Controller); Michael Everson (Director of Technology and Communications); Andrea Andrus
Parent company (for newspapers): Wick Communications

YAKIMA HERALD-REPUBLIC

Street address 1: 114 N 4th St
Street address city: Yakima
Street address state: WA
Zip/Postal code: 98901-2707
County: Yakima
Country: USA
Mailing address: PO BOX 9668
Mailing city: YAKIMA

Mailing state: WA
Mailing zip: 98909-0668
General Phone: (509) 248-1251
Advertising Phone: (509) 452-7355
Editorial Phone: 509.577.7724
General/National Adv. E-mail: advertising@yakimaherald.com
Display Adv. E-mail: advertising@yakimaherald.com
Classified Adv. e-mail: classads@yakimaherald.com
Editorial e-mail: opinion@yakimaherald.com
Primary Website: www.yakimaherald.com
Mthly Avg Views: 4120000
Mthly Avg Unique Visitors: 331159
Year Established: 1889
News Services: AP, MCT, LAT-WP, NEA, TMS.
Special Editions: 509HomeFinder (Monthly) 509Autos (Biweekly) Childrenâ€™s Yearbook (Jan) How To Guide (Feb) College Bound (Apr) Spring Home & Garden (Apr) Graduates (May) Central Washington Sports Hall of Fame (Jun) Readersâ€™ Choice Guide (Jul, Sept) Prep Football (Aug) Breast Cancer Awareness (Oct) Women in Business (Oct) Holiday Gift Guide (Nov) Veterans Day (Nov)
Special Weekly Sections: Business Outdoors Auto Faith Home Garden
Delivery Methods: Mail`Newsstand`Carrier`Racks
Areas Served - City/County or Portion Thereof, or Zip codes: 98901 98902 98903 98908 98920 98921 98922 98923 98926 98930 98932 98933 98934 98935 98936 98937 98938 98939 98940 98941 98942 98944 98947 98948 98951 98952 98953 99350
Own Printing Facility?: Y
Commercial printers?: Y
Sat. Circulation Paid: 21661
Sun. Circulation Paid: 24410
Audit By: AAM
Audit Date: 31.12.2016
Personnel: Robert Crider (Pub); Maria Barajas (HR Dir.); Jennine Perkinson (Adv. Dir.); Alison Bath (Mng. Ed.); Roger Stanley (Op. Dir.); Paul Crawford (Digital Content Director); Tammy Fahsholtz (Senior Circulation Manager); Bill Thyken (Finance Director); Gloria Ibanez (Editor, El Sol de Yakima)
Parent company (for newspapers): The Seattle Times

WEST VIRGINIA

THE REGISTER HERALD

Street address 1: 801 N Kanawha St
Street address city: Beckley
Street address state: WV
Zip/Postal code: 25801-3822
County: Raleigh
Country: USA
Mailing address: PO BOX 2398
Mailing city: BECKLEY
Mailing state: WV
Mailing zip: 25802-2398
General Phone: (304) 255-4400
Advertising Phone: (304) 255-4425
Editorial Phone: (304) 255-4462
General/National Adv. E-mail: tharris@registerherald.com
Display Adv. E-mail: tharris@register-herald.com
Classified Adv. e-mail: dslone@register-herald.com
Editorial e-mail: dcain@register-herald.com
Primary Website: www.register-herald.com
Year Established: 1981
News Services: AP.
Special Weekly Sections: Entertainment, TV, Life (Daily); Childrens (Mon); Best Food (Wed); TV, Track (Fri); Church (Sat); Outdoor (Sun)
Syndicated Publications: Relish (Monthly); Parade (S).
Avg Free Circ: 1421
Sat. Circulation Paid: 15414
Sun. Circulation Paid: 17069
Sun. Circulation Free: 523
Audit By: AAM
Audit Date: 30.09.2014
Personnel: Frank Wood (Pub.); Drema Radford (Bus. Dir.); Diana Slone (Adv. Mgr., Classified); Charles Jessup (Adv. Mgr., Retail); Randy Taylor (Circ. Dir.); Mark Bowling (Circ. Dir., Single Copy Sales); Butch Antolini (Ed.); Mary Spillwell (Online Ed.); Rick Barbero (Chief Photographer); Pat Hanna (Regl. Ed.); David Morrison (Sports Ed.); Judy Karbonit (Vice Special Editions Ed.); Bev Davis (Women's Ed.); John Hart (Systems Mgr.); Richard Kelley (Ed.); Tammy Harris (Adv. Dir.); Wendy Holdren (Mng. Ed.)
Parent company (for newspapers): CNHI, LLC; CNHI, LLC

BLUEFIELD DAILY TELEGRAPH

Street address 1: 928 Bluefield Ave
Street address city: Bluefield
Street address state: WV
Zip/Postal code: 24701-2744
County: Mercer
Country: USA
Mailing address: PO BOX 1599
Mailing city: BLUEFIELD
Mailing state: WV
Mailing zip: 24701-1599
General Phone: (304) 327-2800
Advertising Phone: (304) 327-2816
Editorial Phone: (304) 327-2811
General/National Adv. E-mail: thale@bdtonline.com
Display Adv. E-mail: thale@bdtonline.com
Classified Adv. e-mail: @bdtonline.com
Editorial e-mail: sperry@bdtonline.com
Primary Website: www.bdtonline.com
Mthly Avg Views: 1781832
Mthly Avg Unique Visitors: 260000
Year Established: 1896
News Services: AP, Scripps Howard News Digest.
Special Editions: Bluefield Chamber (Apr); Football (Aug); Holiday Cookbook (Dec); Senior Citizens (Feb); Super Bowl (Jan); Business Profiles (Jul); Bridal (Jun); Lawn & Garden (Mar); Mt. Festival (May); Holiday Lifestyles (Nov); Women in the Area (Oct); Home Improvement (
Special Weekly Sections: Best Food (Wed/Sun); TV, Weekend (Fri); Business (Sun)
Syndicated Publications: Parade (S).
Delivery Methods: Mail`Newsstand`Carrier`Racks
Own Printing Facility?: Y
Commercial printers?: Y
Avg Free Circ: 701
Sat. Circulation Paid: 6818
Sat. Circulation Free: 701
Sun. Circulation Paid: 7892
Sun. Circulation Free: 385
Audit By: AAM
Audit Date: 30.06.2018
Personnel: Terri Hale (Adv. Dir.); Tom Colley (Exec. Ed.); Samantha Perry (Mng. Ed.); Fred Schmidt; Darryl Hudson (Pub.); Natalie Fanning (Retail Adv. Mgr.)
Parent company (for newspapers): CNHI, LLC; CNHI, LLC

THE CHARLESTON GAZETTE-MAIL

Street address 1: 1001 Virginia St E
Street address city: Charleston
Street address state: WV
Zip/Postal code: 25301-2816
County: Kanawha
Country: USA
Mailing address: 1001 VIRGINIA ST E
Mailing city: CHARLESTON
Mailing state: WV
Mailing zip: 25301-2895
General Phone: (304) 348-4800
Advertising Phone: (304) 348-4860
Editorial Phone: (304) 348-5100
General/National Adv. E-mail: gazette@wvgazettemail.com
Display Adv. E-mail: michael.moncada@cnpapers.com
Classified Adv. e-mail: jamie@cnpapers.com
Editorial e-mail: robbyers@wvgazettemail.com
Primary Website: www.wvgazettemail.com
Mthly Avg Views: 3958273
Mthly Avg Unique Visitors: 816356
Year Established: 1873
News Services: AP, MCT.
Special Editions: Home & Garden (Apr); Dance (Aug); Outlook (Feb); Bridal (Jan); WV Home Show (Mar); Fall Home Improvement (Oct); Hunting (Sept).
Special Weekly Sections: Auto, Religion (Sat); Best Food Day, Entertainment, Travel (Sun)
Syndicated Publications: PARADE (Sun)
Delivery Methods: Mail`Newsstand`Carrier`Racks
Areas Served - City/County or Portion Thereof, or Zip codes: The State Newspaper
Own Printing Facility?: Y
Commercial printers?: N
Sat. Circulation Paid: 36935
Sun. Circulation Paid: 45387
Audit By: AAM
Audit Date: 30.09.2017
Personnel: John McGucken (Major/Nat'l Accts.); Lisa Skeens (Nat'l Adv. Mgr.); Dawn Miller (Editorial Page Ed.)
Parent company (for newspapers): HD Media Company LLC

THE EXPONENT TELEGRAM

Street address 1: 324 Hewes Ave
Street address city: Clarksburg
Street address state: WV
Zip/Postal code: 26301-2744
County: Harrison
Country: USA
Mailing address: PO BOX 2000
Mailing city: CLARKSBURG
Mailing state: WV
Mailing zip: 26302-2000
General Phone: (304) 626-1400
Advertising Phone: (304) 626-1430
Editorial Phone: (304) 626-1473
General/National Adv. E-mail: advertising@wvnews.com
Display Adv. E-mail: advertising@wvnews.com
Classified Adv. e-mail: classified@wvnews.com
Editorial e-mail: news@wvnews.com
Primary Website: www.wvnews.com
Mthly Avg Views: 4200000
Mthly Avg Unique Visitors: 2100000
Year Established: 1927
News Services: AP.
Special Weekly Sections: Best Food Day (Wed)
Delivery Methods: Mail`Newsstand`Carrier`Racks
Areas Served - City/County or Portion Thereof, or Zip codes: Harrison, Marion, Lewis, Doddridge, Taylor, Upshur and Barbour Counties
Own Printing Facility?: Y
Commercial printers?: Y
Avg Free Circ: 893
Sat. Circulation Paid: 12966
Sat. Circulation Free: 1202
Sun. Circulation Paid: 16706
Sun. Circulation Free: 1837
Audit By: Sworn/Estimate/Non-Audited
Audit Date: 25.09.2023
Personnel: Robert Gaston (Operations Director); John Miller (Executive Editor); Brian Jarvis (President); Andy Kniceley (Publisher); Mia Biafore (Key Account Manager); Steve Ball (Business Manager); Crystal Eifert (Business Manager); Tammy Heitz (Advertising Director); Chad Everson (Digital Director)
Parent company (for newspapers): WV News

THE INTER-MOUNTAIN

Street address 1: 520 Railroad Ave
Street address city: Elkins
Street address state: WV
Zip/Postal code: 26241-3861
County: Randolph
Country: USA
Mailing address: PO BOX 1339
Mailing city: ELKINS
Mailing state: WV
Mailing zip: 26241-1339
General Phone: (304) 636-2121
Advertising Phone: (304) 636-2127
Editorial Phone: (304) 636-2124
General/National Adv. E-mail: publisher@theintermountain.com
Display Adv. E-mail: addirector@theintermountain.com
Classified Adv. e-mail: classifieds@theintermountain.com
Editorial e-mail: newsroom@theintermountain.com
Primary Website: www.theintermountain.com
Mthly Avg Views: 214863
Mthly Avg Unique Visitors: 26412
Year Established: 1892
News Services: AP.
Special Editions: The semi-annual Dining Guide, Visitors Guide and more. We also offer annual sports books for fall, winter and spring.
Special Weekly Sections: Inter-Tainment, a TV and local entertainment supplement
Delivery Methods: Mail`Newsstand`Carrier`Racks
Areas Served - City/County or Portion Thereof, or Zip codes: 24915 24920 24927 24934 24944 24954 26209 26264 26273 26282 26291 26294 26201 26210 26215 26218 26222 26228 26234 26236 26237 26343 26372 26452 26238 26250 26275 26405 26416 26224 26230 26241 26253 26254 26257 26259 26263 26267 26270 26273 26276 26278 26280 26283 26285 26293 26296 26260 26269 26271 26287 26289 26292 26804 26807 26814 26818 26836 26847 26855 26866 26884 26886
Own Printing Facility?: Y
Commercial printers?: Y
Avg Free Circ: 358
Sat. Circulation Paid: 4804
Sat. Circulation Free: 80
Audit By: AAM
Audit Date: 31.03.2019
Personnel: Steve Herron (Pub.); Marcia Myers (Bus. Office Mgr.); Brad Johnson (Exec. Ed.); Joey Kittle (Sports Ed.)
Parent company (for newspapers): Ogden Newspapers Inc.

TIMES WEST VIRGINIAN

Street address 1: 300 Quincy St
Street address city: Fairmont
Street address state: WV
Zip/Postal code: 26554-3136
County: Marion
Country: USA
Mailing address: PO BOX 2530
Mailing city: FAIRMONT
Mailing state: WV
Mailing zip: 26555-2530
General Phone: (304) 367-2500
Advertising Phone: (304) 367-2515
Editorial Phone: (304)367-2523
General/National Adv. E-mail: timeswv@timeswv.com
Display Adv. E-mail: bevmiller@timeswv.com
Classified Adv. e-mail: classified@timeswv.com
Editorial e-mail: ecravet@timeswv.com
Primary Website: www.timeswv.com
Mthly Avg Views: 359000
Mthly Avg Unique Visitors: 26960
Year Established: 1976
News Services: AP.
Special Editions: Year in Review, Bridal Tab, Three Rivers Festival (May); Business Review, Back to School, Hs Football Tab, College Football (Aug); Christmas Catalog, December Last Minute Gift Guide (Dec)
Syndicated Publications: Parade (S).
Delivery Methods: Carrier
Areas Served - City/County or Portion Thereof, or Zip codes: Marion Co. WV
Own Printing Facility?: Y
Commercial printers?: Y
Avg Free Circ: 530
Sat. Circulation Paid: 6590
Sat. Circulation Free: 730
Sun. Circulation Paid: 7245
Sun. Circulation Free: 312
Audit By: Sworn/Estimate/Non-Audited
Audit Date: 20.06.2021
Personnel: Titus Workman (Pub.); Eric Cravey (Ed.); Jerry Ferguson (Circ. Dir.); Cathy Morrison (Adv.)
Parent company (for newspapers): CNHI, LLC; CNHI, LLC

THE HERALD-DISPATCH

Street address 1: 946 5th Ave
Street address city: Huntington
Street address state: WV
Zip/Postal code: 25701-2004
County: Cabell
Country: USA
Mailing address: PO BOX 2017
Mailing city: HUNTINGTON
Mailing state: WV
Mailing zip: 25720-2017
General Phone: (304) 526-4002
Advertising Phone: (304) 526-6696
Editorial Phone: (304) 526-2787
General/National Adv. E-mail: cjessup@herald-dispatch.com
Display Adv. E-mail: cjessup@herald-dispatch.com
Classified Adv. e-mail: lwaddell@herald-dispatch.com
Editorial e-mail: editor@herald-dispatch.com
Primary Website: www.herald-dispatch.com
Year Established: 1909
News Services: AP
Special Editions: Progress (Mar);
Special Weekly Sections: Best Food (Wed/Sun); Entertainment (Thur); Style, Leisure (Sun);
Syndicated Publications: USA WEEKEND Magazine (S).

Delivery Methods: Mail`Newsstand`Carrier`Racks
Areas Served - City/County or Portion Thereof, or Zip codes: 25502, 25503, 25504, 25506, 25507, 25510, 25514, 25515, 25520, 25526, 25530, 25535, 25537, 25541, 25545, 25550, 25555, 25557, 25559, 25560, 25570, 25571, 25701, 25702, 25703, 25704, 25705, 41101 41102, 41129, 41230, 45619, 45623, 45638, 45669, 45678, 45680
Own Printing Facility?: Y
Commercial printers?: Y
Sat. Circulation Paid: 16619
Sun. Circulation Paid: 20188
Audit By: AAM
Audit Date: 31.12.2018
Personnel: Les Smith (Ed.); Lauren McGill (News Assignment Ed.); Rachel Bledsoe (Features Ed.); Nicole Fields (Night City Ed.); Rick McCann (Sports Ed.); Andrea Copley-Smith (Online Ed.); Charles Jessup (Adv. Dir.); Misty Deere (Circ. Mgr.); Judi Reed (HR); Georgetta Thevenin (Controller)
Parent company (for newspapers): HD Media Company LLC

MINERAL DAILY NEWS & TRIBUNE

Street address 1: 455 S. Mineral St.
Street address city: Keyser
Street address state: WV
Zip/Postal code: 26726-6012
County: Mineral
Country: USA
Mailing state: WV
General Phone: (304) 788-3333
Advertising Phone: (304) 788-3333
Editorial Phone: 304-788-3333
General/National Adv. E-mail: ebeavers@wvnews.com
Display Adv. E-mail: bshillingburg@wvnews.com
Classified Adv. e-mail: classified@mineralwvnews.com
Editorial e-mail: ebeavers@wvnews.com
Primary Website: www.wvnews.com
Year Established: 1885
News Services: AP.
Special Editions: Mineral County Chamber Directory Mineral County Fair Apple Harvest Festival High School Football Preview
Delivery Methods: Mail`Newsstand`Carrier`Racks
Areas Served - City/County or Portion Thereof, or Zip codes: 26726, 21562, 26750, 26710, 26717, 26753, 26719, 21557
Own Printing Facility?: N
Commercial printers?: N
Sat. Circulation Paid: 4064
Audit By: Sworn/Estimate/Non-Audited
Audit Date: 12.07.2019
Personnel: Liz Beavers (Managing Ed.); Kelly Miller (Pub); Barbara High (Staff Writer); Billie Jo Shillingburg (Advertising Manager); Mary Lou Weaver; Jessica Evans; Tracy Bean (Multi-Media Ad Exec); Nick Carroll (Sports Editor); Sandy Canfield (Staff)
Parent company (for newspapers): CherryRoad Media; Gannett; Clarksburg Publishing Company

WEST VIRGINIA DAILY NEWS

Street address 1: 188 Foster St
Street address city: Lewisburg
Street address state: WV
Zip/Postal code: 24901-2099
County: Greenbrier
Country: USA
Mailing address: PO BOX 471
Mailing city: LEWISBURG
Mailing state: WV
Mailing zip: 24901-0471
General Phone: (304) 645-1206
Advertising Phone: (304) 645-1206
Editorial Phone: (304) 645-1206
General/National Adv. E-mail: dailynewsad@suddenlinkmail.com
Display Adv. E-mail: dailynewsad@suddenlinkmail.com
Classified Adv. e-mail: dailynewsad@suddenlinkmail.com
Editorial e-mail: wvdailynews@suddenlinkmail.com
Primary Website: www.wvdailynews.net
Year Established: 1969
News Services: NEA, TMS.
Special Editions: Home Improvement (Apr); State Fair (Aug); Bridal (Jan); Christmas Gift Guide (Nov); Home Improvement (Sept).
Delivery Methods: Mail`Newsstand`Carrier`Racks
Own Printing Facility?: Y
Commercial printers?: Y
Audit By: Sworn/Estimate/Non-Audited
Audit Date: 12.07.2019
Personnel: Judy Steele (Pub.); Barbara Cordial (Adv. Dir.); Bill Frye (Ed.); Peggey Weikle (Prodn. Mgr., Camera); Susan Wade (Prodn. Mgr., Mailroom); Lea Ballard (Prodn. Mgr., Pressroom)
Parent company (for newspapers): Moffitt Newspapers; WV News

THE LOGAN BANNER

Street address 1: 435 Stratton St
Street address city: Logan
Street address state: WV
Zip/Postal code: 25601-3913
County: Logan
Country: USA
Mailing address: PO BOX 720
Mailing city: LOGAN
Mailing state: WV
Mailing zip: 25601-0720
General Phone: (304) 752-6950
Advertising Phone: (304)752-6950 ext. 305
General/National Adv. E-mail: rrichards@civitasmedia.com
Display Adv. E-mail: rrichards@civitasmedia.com
Classified Adv. e-mail: rrichards@civitasmedia.com
Editorial e-mail: msparks@civitasmedia
Primary Website: www.loganbanner.com
Year Established: 1888
News Services: AP.
Special Editions: Home Improvement (Apr); Football Signature Pages (Aug); Christmas Songbook (Dec); Basketball Pages (Feb); A-Z (Jul); Father's Day Photos (Jun); Girl Scout Page (Mar); Mother's Day Photos (May); Veteran's Day Page (Nov); Hunting (Oct); Football Pages (Sept
Special Weekly Sections: Entertainment (Daily); Best Food (Mon, Wed, Sun); Religion (Fri); Auto (Fri/Sun); Church, TV, Real Estate (Sun)
Syndicated Publications: Parade (S).
Areas Served - City/County or Portion Thereof, or Zip codes: Logan, Mingo, Boon, Wyoming
Sun. Circulation Paid: 9751
Audit By: Sworn/Estimate/Non-Audited
Audit Date: 12.07.2019
Personnel: Lee Davis (Mgr.); Dylan Vidovich (News Reporter); Melissa Blair (Adv. Mgr.); Judi Reed (HR); Georgetta Thevenin (Controller)
Parent company (for newspapers): HD Media Company LLC

THE JOURNAL

Street address 1: 207 W King St
Street address city: Martinsburg
Street address state: WV
Zip/Postal code: 25401-3211
County: Berkeley
Country: USA
Mailing address: 207 W King St
Mailing city: Martinsburg
Mailing state: WV
Mailing zip: 25401-3211
General Phone: (304) 263-8931
Advertising Phone: (304) 263-8931 ext 110
Editorial Phone: (304) 263-3381
General/National Adv. E-mail: jgelestor@journal-news.net
Display Adv. E-mail: bbarnes@journal-news.net
Classified Adv. e-mail: sphillips@journal-news.net
Editorial e-mail: mheath@journal-news.net
Primary Website: www.journal-news.net
Mthly Avg Views: 725000
Mthly Avg Unique Visitors: 110103
Year Established: 1907
News Services: AP.
Special Editions: Home Show (Apr); Fall Sports Tab (Aug); Christmas Songbook (Dec); Welcome Home (Feb); Bridal (Jan); Welcome Home (Jul); Welcome Home (Jun); Spring Sports Tab (Mar); Mother's Day Tab (May); Welcome Home (Nov); Halloween Safety (Oct); Welcome Home (Sept).
Special Weekly Sections: Health (Mon); Kids (Tue); Food, Recipes (Wed); Entertainment, Weekend (Thur); Home, Garden, Real Estate (Fri); Religion (Sat); Business (Sun); Neighborhood (Daily)
Syndicated Publications: Parade (S).
Delivery Methods: Newsstand`Carrier`Racks
Areas Served - City/County or Portion Thereof, or Zip codes: Berkeley, Jefferson and Morgan County WV
Own Printing Facility?: Y
Commercial printers?: Y
Avg Free Circ: 411
Sat. Circulation Paid: 10279
Sat. Circulation Free: 411
Sun. Circulation Paid: 11780
Sun. Circulation Free: 256
Audit By: AAM
Audit Date: 31.03.2017
Personnel: Judy Gelestor (Adv. Dir./Pub.); Mary Heath (Ed.); Eric Jones (News Ed.); Rick Kozlowski (Sports Ed.); Tiffany Niebauer (Office Mgr.)
Parent company (for newspapers): Ogden Newspapers Inc.

THE DOMINION POST

Street address 1: 1251 Earl L Core Rd
Street address city: Morgantown
Street address state: WV
Zip/Postal code: 26505-6298
County: Monongalia
Country: USA
Mailing address: 1251 EARL L CORE RD
Mailing city: Morgantown
Mailing state: WV
Mailing zip: 26505-6298
General Phone: (304) 292-6301
Advertising Phone: (304) 291-9449
Editorial Phone: (304) 291-9425
General/National Adv. E-mail: ads@dominionpost.com
Display Adv. E-mail: ads@dominionpost.com
Classified Adv. e-mail: ddavis@dominionpost.com
Editorial e-mail: newsroom@dominionpost.com
Primary Website: www.dominionpost.com
Year Established: 1923
News Services: AP, MCT, NEA.
Special Editions: Auto Care (Tab) (Apr); College Football (Aug); Xmas Gift Guide (3 times) (Dec); Health Fair (Tab) (Feb); Chamber of Commerce (Tab) (Jan); West Virginia's Birthday Party (Tab) (Jun); Progress (Mar); Summer Fun (May); Basketball (Nov); Goal Post (Oct); Buck
Special Weekly Sections: Best Food Days (Wed/Sun); Entertainment (Thur); Travel, Auto, Real Estate (Sun)
Syndicated Publications: Parade (S).
Delivery Methods: Mail`Newsstand`Carrier`Racks
Areas Served - City/County or Portion Thereof, or Zip codes: Marion, Monongalia, Preston
Own Printing Facility?: Y
Commercial printers?: Y
Avg Free Circ: 1788
Sat. Circulation Paid: 10855
Sat. Circulation Free: 1788
Sun. Circulation Paid: 12933
Sun. Circulation Free: 1423
Audit By: AAM
Audit Date: 31.03.2019
Personnel: David Raese (Pub.); Joe Duley (Operations Mgr.); Rich Goodwin (Home Delivery Mgr.); Pam Queen (Mng. Ed.); Amanda DeProspero (Asst. Mng. Ed.); Kathy Plum (Regional News Ed.); Brad Pennington (Sales Mgr.); Elise Coleman (Dig. Mrkt. Spec.); Brian D. Cole (Controller); Debbie Headley (Human Resources/ Accounts Payable); Chris Halterman (Prodn. Dir.)
Parent company (for newspapers): WV Newspaper Publishing Company, Inc.

MOUNDSVILLE DAILY ECHO

Street address 1: 713 Lafayette Ave
Street address city: Moundsville
Street address state: WV
Zip/Postal code: 26041-2143
County: Marshall
Country: USA
Mailing address: PO BOX 369
Mailing city: MOUNDSVILLE
Mailing state: WV
Mailing zip: 26041-0369
General Phone: (304) 845-2660
Advertising Phone: (304) 845-2660
Editorial Phone: (304) 845-2660
General/National Adv. E-mail: mdsvecho@gmail.com
Display Adv. E-mail: mdsvecho@gmail.com
Classified Adv. e-mail: mdsvecho@gmail.com
Editorial e-mail: mdsvecho@gmail.com
Year Established: 1891
News Services: AP.
Special Weekly Sections: Best Food Day (Wed)
Delivery Methods: Mail`Newsstand`Carrier`Racks
Areas Served - City/County or Portion Thereof, or Zip codes: 26038, 15370, 20151, 23060, 27106, 29464, 32127, 33803, 43747, 43947, 43950, 44450, 15143, 26155, 25305, 26101, 26170, 26505, 26003, 26031, 26041, 26033, 26039, 26055, 26041
Own Printing Facility?: Y
Commercial printers?: N
Audit By: Sworn/Estimate/Non-Audited
Audit Date: 12.07.2019
Personnel: Charlie Walton (Pub./Gen. Mgr.); Melanie Murdock (Adv. Rep.)
Parent company (for newspapers): Charles Walton

PARKERSBURG NEWS & SENTINEL

Street address 1: 519 Juliana St
Street address city: Parkersburg
Street address state: WV
Zip/Postal code: 26101-5135
County: Wood
Country: USA
Mailing address: PO BOX 1787
Mailing city: PARKERSBURG
Mailing state: WV
Mailing zip: 26102-1787
General Phone: (304) 485-1891
Advertising Phone: (304) 485-1891
Editorial Phone: (304) 485-1891
General/National Adv. E-mail: advertising@newsandsentinel.com
Display Adv. E-mail: advertising@newsandsentinel.com
Classified Adv. e-mail: classified@newsandsentinel.com
Editorial e-mail: editorial@newsandsentinel.com
Primary Website: www.newsandsentinel.com
Mthly Avg Views: 1400000
Mthly Avg Unique Visitors: 140000
News Services: AP.
Special Editions: Seniors (Monthly).
Special Weekly Sections: Food (Thur); Religion (Sat); TV, Food (Sun)
Syndicated Publications: Free Time (Entertainment) (Fri); Parade (S); Religion Tab (Sat).
Delivery Methods: Mail`Newsstand`Carrier`Racks
Own Printing Facility?: Y
Avg Free Circ: 120
Sat. Circulation Paid: 13729
Sat. Circulation Free: 63
Sun. Circulation Paid: 17158
Sun. Circulation Free: 527
Audit By: AAM
Audit Date: 31.12.2018
Personnel: James T. Spanner (Pub.); Joe Tranquill (Circ. Dir.); James Smith (Exec. Ed.); Paul LaPann (Mng. Ed.); Jess Mancini (City Ed.); Larry Cox (Editorial Page Ed.); Brett Dunlap (Film/Theater Ed.); Dave Poe (Sports Ed.); Chris Smith (Opns. Mgr.); Art Smith; Jim Spanner (Pub.); Kim Geibel (Nat'l Adv. Mgr.); Jason Rollins (Ad. Mgr.); Matthew Tranquill (Adv. Dir.)
Parent company (for newspapers): Ogden Newspapers Inc.

POINT PLEASANT REGISTER

Street address 1: 200 Main St
Street address city: Point Pleasant
Street address state: WV
Zip/Postal code: 25550-1030
County: Mason
Country: USA
Mailing address: 200 MAIN ST
Mailing city: POINT PLEASANT
Mailing state: WV
Mailing zip: 25550-1030
General Phone: (304) 675-1333
Advertising Phone: (304) 675-1333
Editorial Phone: (304) 675-1333
General/National Adv. E-mail: jschultz@civitasmedia.com
Display Adv. E-mail: jschultz@civitasmedia.com
Classified Adv. e-mail: pprclassified@civitasmedia.com
Editorial e-mail: news@mydailyregister.com
Primary Website: www.mydailyregister.com
Mthly Avg Views: 169000
Mthly Avg Unique Visitors: 25000
News Services: AP.
Special Weekly Sections: Church Page (Fri); Farm Page (Sun)
Delivery Methods: Mail`Newsstand`Carrier`Racks
Own Printing Facility?: Y
Sat. Circulation Paid: 3918
Audit By: Sworn/Estimate/Non-Audited
Audit Date: 12.07.2019
Personnel: David Lucas (Circ. Mgr.); Larry Crum (Sports Ed.); Sammy Lopez (Pub.); Julia Schultz (Adv. Mgr.); Beth Sergent (Ed.); Bud Hunt (Reg. Dir.)

Parent company (for newspapers): AIM Media Texas

THE INTELLIGENCER

Street address 1: 1500 Main St
Street address city: Wheeling
Street address state: WV
Zip/Postal code: 26003-2826
County: Ohio
Country: USA
Mailing address: 1500 MAIN ST
Mailing city: WHEELING
Mailing state: WV
Mailing zip: 26003-2851
General Phone: (304) 233-0100
Advertising Phone: (304) 233-0100
Editorial Phone: (304) 233-0100
General/National Adv. E-mail: pbennett@theintelligencer.net
Display Adv. E-mail: pbennett@theintelligencer.net
Classified Adv. e-mail: shiggins@theintelligencer.net
Editorial e-mail: Jmccabe@theintelligencer.net
Primary Website: www.theintelligencer.net
Mthly Avg Views: 1021969
Mthly Avg Unique Visitors: 128436
Year Established: 1852
News Services: AP.
Special Editions: Progress Edition (Feb.) Shale Play (Bi-Monthly) Football Preview (Aug.) Boomers & Beyond (Monthly) OV Parent (Monthly) Ohio Valley Real Estate (Monthly)
Special Weekly Sections: Entertainment (Fri); NFL Report (Mon); Best Food Day (Tue); Chalk Talk (Football Season (Thur); Faith (Sat)
Syndicated Publications: TV Book (own, local, newsprint) (S).
Delivery Methods: Newsstand`Carrier`Racks
Areas Served - City/County or Portion Thereof, or Zip codes: 26003
Own Printing Facility?: Y
Commercial printers?: Y
Avg Free Circ: 389
Sat. Circulation Paid: 12572
Sat. Circulation Free: 405
Audit By: AAM
Audit Date: 31.03.2019
Personnel: G. Ogden Nutting (Pub.); Perry A. Nardo (Gen. Mgr.); Charles Deremer (Controller); Shelly Higgins (Adv. Mgr., Classified); Pam Bennett (Adv. Dir.); Dave Kahkbaugh (Circ. Dir.); John McCabe (Bus./Finance Ed.); Heather Ziegler (City Ed., News-Register); J. Michael Myer (Editorial Page Ed., News-Register); Betsy Bethel (Entertainment Ed.); Linda Comins (Features Ed.); Phyllis Sigal (Food/Women's Ed.); Jennifer Compston (News Ed., Intelligencer)
Parent company (for newspapers): Gannett; Ogden Newspapers Inc.

WILLIAMSON DAILY NEWS

Street address 1: 38 West Second Avenue
Street address city: Williamson
Street address state: WV
Zip/Postal code: 25661-3500
County: Mingo
Country: USA
Mailing address: PO BOX 1660
Mailing city: WILLIAMSON
Mailing state: WV
Mailing zip: 25661-1660
General Phone: (304) 235-4242
Advertising Phone: (304) 235-4242
Editorial Phone: (304) 235-4242
General/National Adv. E-mail: wdn.ads@heartlandpublications.com
Display Adv. E-mail: wdn.ads@heartlandpublications.com
Classified Adv. e-mail: wdn.classified@heartlandpublications.com
Editorial e-mail: jbyers@heartlandpublications.com
Primary Website: www.williamsondailynews.com
Year Established: 1912
News Services: AP.
Special Editions: Visitor's Guide (Jun); Golden News (Monthly); Red Ribbon Salute (Oct); Bride's Guide (Semi-yearly).
Special Weekly Sections: Best Food Day (Wed); Church (Sat); Auto (Sun)
Syndicated Publications: Golden News (Monthly); Parade (S).
Sat. Circulation Paid: 8028
Sun. Circulation Paid: 8028
Audit By: Sworn/Estimate/Non-Audited
Audit Date: 12.07.2019
Personnel: Melissa Blair (Adv. Mgr.); Linda Waddell (Classified Adv.); Dave Hamilton (Prod. Dir.); Judi Reed (HR Dir.); Georgetta Thevenin (Controller); Lee Davis (Mgr.)
Parent company (for newspapers): HD Media Company LLC

WISCONSIN

ANTIGO DAILY JOURNAL

Street address 1: 612 Superior St
Street address city: Antigo
Street address state: WI
Zip/Postal code: 54409-2049
County: Langlade
Country: USA
Mailing address: 612 SUPERIOR ST
Mailing city: ANTIGO
Mailing state: WI
Mailing zip: 54409-2086
General Phone: (715) 623-4191
Advertising Phone: (715) 623-4191
Editorial Phone: (715) 623-4191
General/National Adv. E-mail: adj@dwave.net
Display Adv. E-mail: adj@dwave.net
Classified Adv. e-mail: adj@dwave.net
Editorial e-mail: adj@dwave.net
Primary Website: www.antigodailyjournal.com
Year Established: 1905
News Services: AP
Special Editions: Fitness & Health (Jan.); Bridal Guide (Feb.); Getting to Know You (March); Spring Home & Garden (April); Graduation (May); 4-H Youth Fair Days (July); Back to Back-to-School (Aug.); Northwoods Recreation (Sept.); Holiday Recipes (Nov.); Christmas Magazine (Nov.)
Special Weekly Sections: Local (Daily); Best Food (Mon); Around Town (Thur); TV (Sat)
Delivery Methods: Mail`Newsstand`Carrier`Racks
Own Printing Facility?: Y
Commercial printers?: N
Sat. Circulation Paid: 5760
Audit By: Sworn/Estimate/Non-Audited
Audit Date: 12.07.2019
Personnel: Fred A. Berner (Pub./Ed./Adv. Dir.); Debbie Igl (Reporter); Lisa Haefs (Teen-Age/Youth Ed.); Allan Gelhausen (Pressman); Sue Blahnik (Classifieds Adv. Mgr.); Cathy Wallace (Adv. Sales Consultant); Laura Harvey
Parent company (for newspapers): Adams Publishing Group, LLC

POST-CRESCENT

Street address 1: 306 W. Washington Street
Street address city: Appleton
Street address state: WI
Zip/Postal code: 54911
County: Outagamie
Country: USA
Mailing address: PO BOX 59
Mailing city: APPLETON
Mailing state: WI
Mailing zip: 54912-0059
General Phone: (920) 993-1000
Advertising Phone: (920) 996-7224
Editorial Phone: (920) 993-7155
General/National Adv. E-mail: pcads@appleton.gannett.com
Display Adv. E-mail: pcads@appleton.gannett.com
Classified Adv. e-mail: classified@wisinfo.com
Editorial e-mail: pcnews@postcrescent.com
Primary Website: www.postcrescent.com
Mthly Avg Views: 3785989
Mthly Avg Unique Visitors: 543900
Year Established: 1853
News Services: MCT, Landon Media Group, AP, Gannett.
Special Editions: Homes and More Magazine (monthly), Employment features (quarterly) Best of the Valley (Sept. & Oct.) Spring Home and Garden (April) Fall Home and Garden (Sept.) Prep football preview (Aug) Prep basketball preview (Nov)
Special Weekly Sections: Sports, Outdoor, Business, Travel (Sun); Business (Mon/Sun); Best Food (Wed); Entertainment (Thur); Home (Sat)
Syndicated Publications: USA WEEKEND Magazine (S).
Delivery Methods: Newsstand`Carrier`Racks
Areas Served - City/County or Portion Thereof, or Zip codes: 54911, 54913, 54914, 54915, 54190, 54136, 54140, 53014, 53061, 54106, 54110, 54113, 54129, 54131, 54165, 54170, 54929, 54981, 54940, 54942, 54944, 54945, 54947, 54949, 54952, 54956, 54961, 54981, 54983
Own Printing Facility?: Y
Commercial printers?: Y
Sat. Circulation Paid: 30444
Sun. Circulation Paid: 39339
Audit By: AAM
Audit Date: 31.03.2018
Personnel: Genia Lovett (Pres./Pub.); Mike Seeber (Vice Pres., Finance); Jason Adrians (News Director); Larry Gallup (Editor/Opinion); Ed Berthiaume (Editor/Sports & Features); Terry Lipshetz (Consumer Experience Director); Denise Wagner (Newsroom assistant); Steve Broas (Adv. Dir.); Joel Christopher (Editor/Digital); Jim Collar (Reporter/Fox Cities); Andy Thompson (Editor/Local enterprise); Amy Leitzke (Senior Director/Distribution-Wisconsin); Mark Johnson (Distribution Director); Steve Teofilo (Digital Manager); Steven Broas (VP/Adv. Dir./Interim Pub.); Ray Stevens (Nat'l Sales); James Fitzhenry; Pamela Henson
Parent company (for newspapers): Gannett

THE ASHLAND DAILY PRESS

Street address 1: 122 3rd St W
Street address city: Ashland
Street address state: WI
Zip/Postal code: 54806-1661
County: Ashland
Country: USA
Mailing address: 122 3RD ST W
Mailing city: ASHLAND
Mailing state: WI
Mailing zip: 54806-1661
General Phone: (715) 682-2313
Advertising Phone: (715)682-2313
Editorial Phone: (715) 685-4510
General/National Adv. E-mail: bnorth@ashlanddailypress.net
Display Adv. E-mail: bnorth@ashlanddailypress.net
Classified Adv. e-mail: hjuoni@ashlanddailypress.net
Editorial e-mail: lservinsky@ashlanddailypress.net
Primary Website: www.apg-wi.com
News Services: Tribune News Service
Special Editions: Spring Car Care & Home Improvement (Apr); Bayfield County Fair Tab (Aug); Football Preview section (Aug), Red Clay Classic (Sept. Oct.) Whitetail Section (Nov.) Basketball Preview section (Dec) Songs of Christmas/Gift Guide & Holiday Greetings (Dec); Valentine's Day Gift Tab (Feb); Father's Day Gifts (Jun); Graduation Gift Guides (May)
Delivery Methods: Mail`Newsstand`Carrier`Racks
Own Printing Facility?: Y
Sat. Circulation Paid: 6153
Audit By: Sworn/Estimate/Non-Audited
Audit Date: 12.07.2019
Personnel: David LaPorte (Managing Editor); Larry Servinsky (Editor); Garett Greenwald (Sports Editor); Rick Olivo (Staff Writer); Heidi Westerlund (Advertising); Sara Chase (Reporter); Karen Petras (Legals); Jake Brown (Sports Reporter)
Parent company (for newspapers): Adams Publishing Group, LLC

BARABOO NEWS REPUBLIC

Street address 1: 714 Matts Ferry Rd
Street address city: Baraboo
Street address state: WI
Zip/Postal code: 53913-3152
County: Sauk
Country: USA
Mailing address: 714 MATTS FERRY RD
Mailing city: BARABOO
Mailing state: WI
Mailing zip: 53913-3152
General Phone: (608) 356-4808
Advertising Phone: (608) 745-3800
General/National Adv. E-mail: bnr-news@capitalnewspapers.com
Display Adv. E-mail: mmeyers@capitalnewspapers.com
Classified Adv. e-mail: mmeyers@capitalnewspapers.com
Primary Website: www.wiscnews.com/bnr
News Services: AP.
Special Weekly Sections: Business, Society, Sports (Daily); Technology (Mon); Recreation (Wed); Entertainment (Thur); Entertainment, Home, Travel, TV, Food (Sat)
Syndicated Publications: Relish (Monthly); Parade (Sat); American Profile (Weekly).
Delivery Methods: Mail`Newsstand`Racks
Areas Served - City/County or Portion Thereof, or Zip codes: Sauk County
Own Printing Facility?: Y
Commercial printers?: N
Avg Free Circ: 181
Sat. Circulation Paid: 2647
Sat. Circulation Free: 88
Audit By: AAM
Audit Date: 30.06.2017
Personnel: Todd Krysiak (Ed.); Matt Meyers (Pub.); Teresa Klinger (Circ. Dir.); Andrew Analore (Asst. Ed.); Ben Bromley (Feature Ed.); Pete Watson (Sports Ed.); Nancy Preston (Prodn. Mgr., Mailroom); Jon Denk (Adv. Dir.)
Parent company (for newspapers): Dispatch-Argus; Lee Enterprises, Incorporated; Capital Newspapers

DAILY CITIZEN, BEAVER DAM

Street address 1: 805 Park Ave
Street address city: Beaver Dam
Street address state: WI
Zip/Postal code: 53916-2205
County: Dodge
Country: USA
Mailing address: PO BOX 558
Mailing city: BEAVER DAM
Mailing state: WI
Mailing zip: 53916-0558
General Phone: (920) 887-0321
Advertising Phone: (920) 887-0321
Editorial Phone: (920) 887-0321
General/National Adv. E-mail: szeinemann@capitalnewspapers.com
Display Adv. E-mail: dc-ads@capitalnewspapers.com
Classified Adv. e-mail: dc-ads@capitalnewspapers.com
Editorial e-mail: dc-news@capitalnewspapers.com
Primary Website: www.wiscnews.com
News Services: AP, NYT.
Special Weekly Sections: Entertainment, Family (Wed, Thur); Religion (Fri); Arts, Entertainment, Family, Food, Health, Living, Travel (Sat); Business, Financial (Mon-Sat); Home (3rd Sat); Bridal (1st/3rd Sat)
Syndicated Publications: Relish (Monthly); USA WEEKEND Magazine (Sat); American Profile (Weekly).
Avg Free Circ: 296
Sat. Circulation Paid: 4443
Sat. Circulation Free: 256
Audit By: AAM
Audit Date: 31.03.2019
Personnel: Scott Zeinemann (Gen. Mgr.); Teresa Klinger (Circ. Dir.); Aaron Holbrook (Ed.); James Kelsh (Pub.); Jim Kelsh (Editorial Page Ed.)
Parent company (for newspapers): Lee Enterprises, Incorporated

BELOIT DAILY NEWS

Street address 1: 149 State St
Street address city: Beloit
Street address state: WI
Zip/Postal code: 53511-6251
County: Rock
Country: USA
Mailing address: 149 STATE ST
Mailing city: BELOIT
Mailing state: WI
Mailing zip: 53511-6299
General Phone: (608) 365-8811
Advertising Phone: (608)364-9235
General/National Adv. E-mail: advertising@beloitdailynews.com
Display Adv. E-mail: tcolling@beloitdailynews.com
Classified Adv. e-mail: kboreen@beloitdailynews.com
Editorial e-mail: bbarth@beloitdailynews.com
Primary Website: www.beloitdailynews.com
Year Established: 1848
News Services: AP, United Media Service.
Special Editions: MDA Tub Run, Summer Bridal Tab, 2013 Tourism, 2013 Source Book, Savvy, Yearbook, Legends of Sports, Adopt a Pet, Bridal Directory, Home Improvement
Special Weekly Sections: Best Food (Sat/Wed); Business (Tue); Weekend Entertainment, Real Estate, Health, TV (Fri)
Delivery Methods: Mail`Newsstand`Carrier`Racks
Areas Served - City/County or Portion Thereof, or Zip codes: 53511, 53525, 61080, 61072, 61073
Own Printing Facility?: Y

Commercial printers?: Y
Avg Free Circ: 20
Audit By: Sworn/Estimate/Non-Audited
Audit Date: 12.07.2019
Personnel: Kent D. Eymann (Pub.); Clint Wolf (City Ed.); Bill Barth (Editorial Page Ed.); James Franz (Sports Ed.); Dave Shaw (Prodn. Mgr., Post Press); Tim Sager (Prodn. Mgr., Pressroom); Angie Meade (Business Manager); Todd Colling (Director of Business Development)
Parent company (for newspapers): Adams Publishing Group, LLC

THE CHIPPEWA HERALD

Street address 1: 321 Frenette Dr
Street address city: Chippewa Falls
Street address state: WI
Zip/Postal code: 54729-3372
County: Chippewa
Country: USA
Mailing address: PO BOX 69
Mailing city: CHIPPEWA FALLS
Mailing state: WI
Mailing zip: 54729-0069
General Phone: (715) 723-5515
Advertising Phone: (715) 723-5515
Editorial Phone: (715) 723-5515
General/National Adv. E-mail: publisher@chippewa.com
Display Adv. E-mail: advertising@chippewa.com
Editorial e-mail: news@chippewa.com
Primary Website: www.chippewa.com; www.chippewavalleynewspapers.com
Mthly Avg Views: 1031169
Mthly Avg Unique Visitors: 149863
Year Established: 1870
News Services: AP, DJ, TMS.
Special Editions: Chippewa Valley Business Report (Quarterly).
Special Weekly Sections: Dining, Entertainment (Thur); Real Estate (Sat); Best Food, Auto, Business, TV, Travel (Sun)
Syndicated Publications: Parade (S).
Areas Served - City/County or Portion Thereof, or Zip codes: Chippewa County, Wisocnsin
Avg Free Circ: 570
Sat. Circulation Paid: 3578
Sat. Circulation Free: 570
Sun. Circulation Paid: 3568
Sun. Circulation Free: 413
Audit By: AAM
Audit Date: 31.03.2016
Personnel: Adam Polden (Circ. District Mgr.); Ross Evavold (Editor); Bill Lenardson (Circ Dir); Stacia King (Adv. Dir. & Gen. Mgr.)
Parent company (for newspapers): Dispatch-Argus; Lee Enterprises, Incorporated

LEADER-TELEGRAM

Street address 1: 701 S Farwell St
Street address city: Eau Claire
Street address state: WI
Zip/Postal code: 54701-3831
County: Eau Claire
Country: USA
Mailing address: PO BOX 570
Mailing city: EAU CLAIRE
Mailing state: WI
Mailing zip: 54702-0570
General Phone: (715) 833-9200
Advertising Phone: (715) 833-7420
Editorial Phone: (715) 833-9203
General/National Adv. E-mail: dan.graaskamp@ecpc.com
Display Adv. E-mail: dan.graaskamp@ecpc.com
Classified Adv. e-mail: dan.graaskamp@ecpc.com
Editorial e-mail: gary.johnson@ecpc.com
Primary Website: www.leadertelegram.com
Year Established: 1912
News Services: AP, SHNS, MCT.
Special Editions: Impressions (Quarterly).
Special Weekly Sections: Business (Tue); Health, Business (Wed); Entertainment, Business (Thur); Outdoors, Business (Fri); Real Estate, Home, Religion (Sat); Entertainment, Travel, Lifestyles, Moments in Life, Business, Sports, Main News, Comics (Sun)
Syndicated Publications: USA WEEKEND Magazine (Sat).
Sat. Circulation Paid: 19006
Sun. Circulation Paid: 21241
Audit By: AAM
Audit Date: 31.03.2017
Personnel: Pieter Graaskamp (Pres./CEO); Daniel Graaskamp (VP); Kathy Hayden (Sales Dir.); Mike Carlson (Circ. Dir.); Don Huebscher (Ed.); Blythe Wachter (Food Ed.); Gary Johnson (Local News Ed.); Brian Sandy (Mktg. / Promo Mgr.)
Parent company (for newspapers): Eau Claire Press Co.; Adams Publishing Group, LLC

THE FOND DU LAC REPORTER

Street address 1: N6637 Rolling Meadows Dr
Street address city: Fond Du Lac
Street address state: WI
Zip/Postal code: 54937-9471
County: Fond Du Lac
Country: USA
Mailing address: PO BOX 1955
Mailing city: FOND DU LAC
Mailing state: WI
Mailing zip: 54936-1955
General Phone: (920) 922-4600
Advertising Phone: (920)922-4600
Editorial Phone: (920)922-4600
General/National Adv. E-mail: advertising@fdlreporter.com
Display Adv. E-mail: advertising@fdlreporter.com
Classified Adv. e-mail: advertising@fdlreporter.com
Editorial e-mail: treporter@fdlreporter.com
Primary Website: www.fdlreporter.com
Year Established: 1856
News Services: AP, GNS.
Special Editions: Answer Book (Oct).
Special Weekly Sections: Weather, Community/State, Nation/World, Opinion, Community, Records, Waupun News Daily, Obituaries, Entertainment, Travel, Comics, Sports (Daily); Business, Home Town, Advice, Farm, Outdoor, Home & Garden, Driving/Destinations, Color Comics, TV Book, Real Estate (Sun); Great Community Photo Page, Advice (Mon); Business, Seniors, Technology (Tue); Home, Garden, Food, Best Food Day, NIE (Wed); Business, Advice, GOLF, Entertainment, Women (Thur); Business, Church, NASCAR (Fri)
Syndicated Publications: USA WEEKEND Magazine (S).
Delivery Methods: Mail`Newsstand`Carrier
Own Printing Facility?: N
Commercial printers?: Y
Avg Free Circ: 178
Sat. Circulation Paid: 840
Sun. Circulation Paid: 11081
Sun. Circulation Free: 160
Audit By: AAM
Audit Date: 31.03.2016
Personnel: Pat Flood (Photo Dept. Mgr.); Paul Keup (Sports Ed.); Bill Hackney (Pub.); Karen Befus (Adv. Dir.)
Parent company (for newspapers): Gannett

DAILY JEFFERSON COUNTY UNION

Street address 1: 28 Milwaukee Ave W
Street address city: Fort Atkinson
Street address state: WI
Zip/Postal code: 53538-2018
County: Jefferson
Country: USA
Mailing address: PO BOX 801
Mailing city: FORT ATKINSON
Mailing state: WI
Mailing zip: 53549
General Phone: (920) 563-5553
Advertising Phone: (920) 563-5553
Editorial Phone: (920) 563-5553
General/National Adv. E-mail: advertising@dailyunion.com
Display Adv. E-mail: rgrindstaff@dailyunion.com
Classified Adv. e-mail: classifieds@dailyunion.com
Editorial e-mail: Cspangler@dailyunion.com
Primary Website: www.dailyunion.com
Mthly Avg Views: 400000
Mthly Avg Unique Visitors: 60000
Year Established: 1870
News Services: AP.
Special Editions: Home Improvement (Apr); Health (Monthly); Christmas (Dec); Money Matters (Jan); Bridal (Mar); Car Care (Oct); Home Improvement (Sept).
Special Weekly Sections: Union Extra shopper (Wed); Business (Tue); Best Food (Wed); Senior Citizen (Fri)
Delivery Methods: Mail`Newsstand`Carrier`Racks
Areas Served - City/County or Portion Thereof, or Zip codes: 53538, 53549, 53190, 53038, 53523, 53551, 53178, 53156
Own Printing Facility?: N
Commercial printers?: Y
Audit By: USPS
Audit Date: 28.09.2018
Personnel: ROBB GRINDSTAFF (Gen. Mgr.); Christine Spangler (Mng. Ed.); Robb Grindstaff (Adv. Mgr./Bus. Mgr.); Brian Knox II (Circ. Dir.)
Parent company (for newspapers): Adams Publishing Group, LLC

GREEN BAY PRESS-GAZETTE

Street address 1: 435 E. Walnut Street
Street address city: Green Bay
Street address state: WI
Zip/Postal code: 54301-5001
County: Brown
Country: USA
Mailing address: PO BOX 23430
Mailing city: GREEN BAY
Mailing state: WI
Mailing zip: 54305-3430
General Phone: (920) 435-4411
Advertising Phone: (920) 431-8293
Editorial Phone: (920) 431-8400
General/National Adv. E-mail: online@greenbaypressgazette.com
Display Adv. E-mail: prepress@greenbaypressgazette.com
Classified Adv. e-mail: classified@wisinfo.com
Editorial e-mail: localnews@greenbaypressgazette.com
Primary Website: www.greenbaypressgazette.com
Mthly Avg Views: 6023000
Mthly Avg Unique Visitors: 637000
Year Established: 1915
News Services: MCT, AP, GNS.
Special Editions: Design an Ad (Apr); Menu Guide (Aug); Last Minute Gifts (Dec); Bridal (Feb); Home & Garden (Jan); Home & Garden (Jul); Bridal (Jun); Home & Garden (Mar); Health First (Monthly); Home & Garden (Nov); Coupon Book (Oct); Coupon Book (Semi-monthly); Home & Ga
Special Weekly Sections: Finally Friday (Fri); Careers (S); On the Road and Off (Sat); Weekend (Thur); Careers (Wed).
Syndicated Publications: USA WEEKEND Magazine (S).
Delivery Methods: Mail`Carrier`Racks
Own Printing Facility?: Y
Sat. Circulation Paid: 34895
Sun. Circulation Paid: 47510
Audit By: AAM
Audit Date: 31.03.2018
Personnel: Peter Frank (News Ed.); Scott Daily (Circ. Dir.); Scott Johnson (President & Publisher); Tom Ricci (Controller); Phil Legler (IT Dir.); Robert Zizzo (Exec Editor); Karl Ebert (Content Coash); Peter Frank (Community Engagement Editor)
Parent company (for newspapers): Gannett

THE JANESVILLE GAZETTE - GAZETTEXTRA

Street address 1: 1 S Parker Dr
Street address city: Janesville
Street address state: WI
Zip/Postal code: 53545-3928
County: Rock
Country: USA
Mailing address: PO BOX 5001
Mailing city: JANESVILLE
Mailing state: WI
Mailing zip: 53547-5001
General Phone: (608) 754-3311
Advertising Phone: (608)755-8344
Editorial Phone: (608)755-8293
General/National Adv. E-mail: retailad@gazettextra.com
Display Adv. E-mail: retailad@gazettextra.com
Classified Adv. e-mail: classads@gazettextra.com
Editorial e-mail: newsroom@gazetteextra.com
Primary Website: www.gazetteextra.com
Year Established: 1845
News Services: AP, MCT.
Special Editions: Home & Garden (Apr); Football (Aug); Bride's (Feb); Progress Week (Jan); 4-H Fair (Jul); Spring Car Care (Mar); Summer Fun Vacation Tab (May); Building & Remodeling (Monthly); Xmas Opener (Nov); Auto Show (Oct); Parade of Homes (Sept).
Special Weekly Sections: Best Food (Wed/Sun); Entertainment (Thur); Travel (Sun); Real Estate, Coupon (Monthly)
Syndicated Publications: USA WEEKEND Magazine (S).
Delivery Methods: Newsstand`Carrier`Racks
Own Printing Facility?: Y
Avg Free Circ: 335
Sat. Circulation Paid: 13713
Sat. Circulation Free: 335
Sun. Circulation Paid: 16895
Sun. Circulation Free: 76
Audit By: AAM
Audit Date: 31.03.2019
Personnel: Sidney H. Bliss (CEO/Pub.); Jennifer Revels (Benefits Mgr.); Pam Milheiser (Sec.); Tom Bradley (Adv. Mgr., Retail); Lon Haneal (Director of Circulation); Sid Schwartz (Ed.); James Leute (Bus. Ed.); Shelly Birkelo (Community Living Ed.); Andrew Beaumont (Design Ed.); Greg Peck (Editorial Page Ed.); Frank Schultz (Educ. Reporter); Ann Fiore (Asst. Features Ed.); Tony DiNicola (Graphics Ed./Art Dir.); David Wedeward (Sports Ed.); Bill Olmsted (Photo Ed.); Rochelle Birkelo (Women's Ed.); Jonathan Lindquist (Dir., Online Services); Dan White (Adv. Dir.); Mary Jo Villa
Parent company (for newspapers): Adams Publishing Group, LLC

KENOSHA NEWS

Street address 1: 6535 Green Bay Road
Street address city: Kenosha
Street address state: WI
Zip/Postal code: 53142
County: Kenosha
Country: USA
Mailing address: 5800 7TH AVE
Mailing city: KENOSHA
Mailing state: WI
Mailing zip: 53140-4194
General Phone: (262) 657-1000
Advertising Phone: (262) 657-1500
Editorial Phone: (262) 656-6279
General/National Adv. E-mail: ads@kenoshanews.com
Classified Adv. e-mail: classad@kenoshanews.com
Editorial e-mail: newsroom@kenoshanews.com
Primary Website: www.kenoshanews.com
Year Established: 1894
News Services: AP, LAT-WP, SHNS.
Special Editions: Lawn & Garden (Apr); Bridal (Aug); Tax (Feb); Bridal (Jan); Home Improvement (Mar); New Car (Nov); Fall Car Care (Oct); Home Improvement (Sept), Gift Guide (Nov./Dec.), Best of Tab, Graduation Tab
Special Weekly Sections: Get Out (Fri); Color Comics (S).
Syndicated Publications: Spry, Parade (S).
Delivery Methods: Newsstand`Carrier`Racks
Areas Served - City/County or Portion Thereof, or Zip codes: 53104, 53105, 53109, 53128, 53139, 53140, 53142, 53143, 53144, 53147, 53157, 53158, 53159, 53168, 53170, 53177, 53179, 53181, 53182, 53192, 53402, 53403, 53404, 53405, 53406, 60002, 60031, 60046, 60048, 60083, 60087, 60096, 60099
Own Printing Facility?: N
Commercial printers?: Y
Avg Free Circ: 1281
Sat. Circulation Paid: 15810
Sat. Circulation Free: 1281
Sun. Circulation Paid: 19596
Sun. Circulation Free: 835
Audit By: AAM
Audit Date: 30.09.2018
Personnel: Mark Lewis (Pres. & Pub.); Donna Mueller (Regional Advertising Dir.); Jay Emmett (Advertising Sales Mgr.); Sandra Johnsrud (Circ. Mgr.); Bob Heisse (Exec. Ed.); Colleen Myers (Marketing Mgr.); Michael Johnson (Sports Ed.); David Walter (City Ed.)
Parent company (for newspapers): Lee Enterprises, Incorporated

LA CROSSE TRIBUNE

Street address 1: 1407 St Andrew St Suite 100
Street address city: La Crosse
Street address state: WI
Zip/Postal code: 54601
County: La Crosse
Country: USA
Mailing address: 401 3RD ST N
Mailing city: LA CROSSE
Mailing state: WI
Mailing zip: 54601-3281
General Phone: (608) 782-9710
Advertising Phone: (608) 791-8213
Editorial Phone: (608) 782-9710
General/National Adv. E-mail: ads@lacrossetribune.com
Display Adv. E-mail: ads@lacrossetribune.com

Classified Adv. e-mail: ads@lacrossetribune.com
Editorial e-mail: rusty.cunningham@lee.net
Primary Website: www.lacrossetribune.com
Mthly Avg Views: 4008251
Mthly Avg Unique Visitors: 586000
Year Established: 1902
News Services: AP, MCT, Metro Suburbia, Inc./ Newhouse Newspapers.
Special Editions: Football (Aug); Gift Guide (Dec); Winter Getaway (Feb); Winter Getaway (Jan); Graduation (May); Coupon Book (Monthly); Christmas Opening (Nov); Credit Unions (Oct); Ourtime (Quarterly); Super Saver Coupons (Semi-monthly); Kids Fest (Sept).
Special Weekly Sections: Best Food, Travel, Family, Real Estate, Auto, Home, Business, Family (Sun); A+ Achievers (Tue); Health (Wed); Outdoors, Entertainment, Auto (Thur); Religion, TV (Sat)
Syndicated Publications: Relish (Monthly); Parade (S).
Areas Served - City/County or Portion Thereof, or Zip codes: 52151, 52160, 52172, 53821, 53929, 54601, 54603, 54612, 54614, 54615, 54616, 54618, 54619, 54621, 54623, 54624, 54626, 54627, 54629, 54630, 54632, 54634, 54636, 54639, 54642, 54644, 54648, 54650, 54651, 54653, 54656, 54658, 54660, 54661, 54665, 54666, 54667, 54669, 54670, 54747, 54773, 55919, 55921, 55925, 55941, 55943, 55947, 55971, 55974, 55987
Own Printing Facility?: Y
Commercial printers?: Y
Sat. Circulation Paid: 22655
Sun. Circulation Paid: 24634
Audit By: AAM
Audit Date: 31.03.2018
Personnel: Michael Burns (Group Publisher); Mark Wehrs (Editorial Page Ed.); Marc Wehrs (Online Ed.); Jeff Brown (Sports Ed.); Bill Lenardson (Cir. Dir.); Robin Noth; Stacia King (Adv. Dir. / Gen. Mgr.)
Parent company (for newspapers): Lee Enterprises, Incorporated

WISCONSIN STATE JOURNAL, MADISON

Street address 1: 1901 Fish Hatchery Road
Street address city: Madison
Street address state: WI
Zip/Postal code: 53713
County: Dane
Country: USA
Mailing address: PO BOX 8058
Mailing city: MADISON
Mailing state: WI
Mailing zip: 53708-8058
General Phone: (608) 252-6100
Advertising Phone: (608) 252-6000
Editorial Phone: (608) 252-6200
General/National Adv. E-mail: jschroeter@madison.com
Display Adv. E-mail: jschroeter@madison.com
Classified Adv. e-mail: swheeler@madison.com
Editorial e-mail: cnpress@madison.com
Primary Website: https://madison.com/wsj/
Year Established: 1839
News Services: Metro Suburbia Inc./Newhouse Newspapers, NYT, MCT.
Special Weekly Sections: Work, Career (Thur); Taste, Food (Fri); Business (Sat); Arts, Entertainment, Lifestyle, Travel, Recreation, Books, Home, Garden, Outdoors (Sun)
Syndicated Publications: Comics (S).
Delivery Methods: Mail`Newsstand`Carrier`Racks
Own Printing Facility?: Y
Sat. Circulation Paid: 54744
Sun. Circulation Paid: 73380
Audit By: AAM
Audit Date: 31.03.2018
Personnel: Tom Wiley (Pub.); Nick Zizzo (Sports Copy Ed.); Beth Williams (Features & Business Ed.); Howard Thomas (Sports Copy Ed.); Greg Sprout (Sports Ed.); Reed Southmayd (Assistant Sports Ed.); John Smalley (Ed.); Julie Shirley, (Night Ed.); Scott Milfred (Editorial Page Ed.); Jason Klein (Visuals/Multimedia Ed.); Teryl Franklin (Senior Editor for Audience Development); Bill Dowlding (News Copy Ed.); Matthew DeFour (Assistant City Ed.); Sandy Cullen (Night City Ed.); Phil Brinkman (City Ed.)
Parent company (for newspapers): Lee Enterprises, Incorporated

HERALD TIMES REPORTER

Street address 1: 902 Franklin Street
Street address city: Manitowoc
Street address state: WI
Zip/Postal code: 54220
County: Manitowoc
Country: USA
Mailing address: 902 FRANKLIN ST
Mailing city: MANITOWOC
Mailing state: WI
Mailing zip: 54220-4514
General Phone: (920) 684-4433
Advertising Phone: (920)684-4433
Editorial Phone: (920)686-2130
General/National Adv. E-mail: MantyAds@smgpo.gannett.com
Display Adv. E-mail: MantyAds@smgpo.gannett.com
Classified Adv. e-mail: classified@wisinfo.com
Editorial e-mail: htrnews@htrnews.com
Primary Website: www.htrnews.com
Year Established: 1898
News Services: AP, NEA, SHNS, GNS.
Special Editions: Annual Business Issue (March) 50+ (monthly)
Special Weekly Sections: Sports, Business, Classified, Opinion, TV, Advice, Comics (Sun); Health, Sports (Mon), Lifestyle (Tue); Food, Sports (Wed); Lifestyle, Arts, Entertainment, Sports, Dining (Thur); Lifestyle, Religion, Sports, Youth (Fri); Sports, Lifestyle (Sat)
Syndicated Publications: USA WEEKEND Magazine (S).
Delivery Methods: Carrier
Areas Served - City/County or Portion Thereof, or Zip codes: 54220, 54221
Own Printing Facility?: N
Avg Free Circ: 164
Sat. Circulation Paid: 7284
Sat. Circulation Free: 164
Sun. Circulation Paid: 8523
Sun. Circulation Free: 91
Audit By: AAM
Audit Date: 31.03.2018
Personnel: Lowell Johnson (Adv. Dir.); Charles Matthews (Business, City of Manitowoc); Mike Knuth (Ed.); Bill Hackney (Gen. Mgr.); Mike Seeber (VP Finance); Scott Johnson (Pub)
Parent company (for newspapers): Gannett

EAGLEHERALD - EHEXTRA.COM

Street address 1: 1809 Dunlap Ave
Street address city: Marinette
Street address state: WI
Zip/Postal code: 54143-1706
County: Marinette
Country: USA
Mailing address: PO BOX 77
Mailing city: MARINETTE
Mailing state: WI
Mailing zip: 54143-0077
General Phone: (715) 735-6611
Advertising Phone: (715)735-6611 ext. 114
Editorial Phone: (715) 735-6611 ext. 155
General/National Adv. E-mail: khofer@eagleherald.com
Display Adv. E-mail: khofer@eagleherald.com
Classified Adv. e-mail: mmacdonald@eagleherald.com
Editorial e-mail: news@eagleherald.com
Primary Website: www.ehextra.com
Year Established: 1867
News Services: AP.
Special Editions: Football Preview (Aug); Christmas Gift Guide (Dec); People Making A Difference (Dec.); Menominee County Fair (Jul); Home Improvement (Mar); Graduation (May); Insights (Oct); Home Improvement (Sept).
Special Weekly Sections: From the Past (Mon); Health (Wed); Boomers & Beyond (Thur); Outdoors (Fri); Business (Sat)
Syndicated Publications: American Profile Spry
Own Printing Facility?: Y
Sat. Circulation Paid: 7589
Audit By: Sworn/Estimate/Non-Audited
Audit Date: 12.07.2019
Personnel: Dan Kitkowski (Editor); Jody Korch (Sports Ed.); Roger Zink (Prodn. Mgr., Press); Dan White (Gen. Mgr.); Kathy Springberg (Business manager); Kelly Hofer (Ad manager); Tim Greenwood (associate night editor); Penny Mullins (news and online editor); Lisa Reed (staff writer); Rick Gebhard (photographer); Melissa Kowalczyk (Page designer)
Parent company (for newspapers): Adams Publishing Group, LLC

MARSHFIELD NEWS-HERALD MEDIA

Street address 1: 144 N. Central Avenue
Street address city: Marshfield
Street address state: WI
Zip/Postal code: 54449
County: Wood
Country: USA
Mailing address: 144 N CENTRAL AVE
Mailing city: MARSHFIELD
Mailing state: WI
Mailing zip: 54449-2107
General Phone: (715) 384-3131
Advertising Phone: (715)898-7004
Editorial Phone: (715)845-0655
General/National Adv. E-mail: taramondloch@marshfieldnewsherald.com
Display Adv. E-mail: taramondloch@marshfieldnewsherald.com
Classified Adv. e-mail: classified@wisinfo.com
Editorial e-mail: mtreinen@gannett.com
Primary Website: www.marshfieldnewsherald.com
Year Established: 1927
News Services: AP.
Special Editions: Fairs (Aug); Basketball (Nov); Valentine's (Feb); Taxes (Jan); Hub City Days (Jul); Spring Builders & Auto (Mar); Dairyfest (May); Deer Hunting (Nov); Fall Auto (Oct); Fall Home Improvements (Sept)., Made in Central Wisconson (Sept); Academic All-Stars (April); Holiday Gift Guide (Dec); Home and Garden (April-Sept)
Special Weekly Sections: TV Listings (Mon-Fri); Food Recipes (Wed); Entertainment Page (Thur); Healthy Lifestyle (Mon); Homeroom Page (Sat); Home (Sat)
Delivery Methods: Carrier`Racks
Areas Served - City/County or Portion Thereof, or Zip codes: Portions of Clark, Marathon, Taylor and Wood counties
Own Printing Facility?: N
Commercial printers?: N
Avg Free Circ: 96
Sat. Circulation Paid: 4041
Sat. Circulation Free: 96
Sun. Circulation Paid: 368
Audit By: AAM
Audit Date: 31.03.2019
Personnel: Jim Fitzhenry (VP/News); Mark Treinen (News Director); Timothy Langton (Central Wisconsin Planning Editor); Robert Mentzer (Storytelling Content Coach)
Parent company (for newspapers): Gannett

MILWAUKEE JOURNAL SENTINEL

Street address 1: 333 West State Street
Street address city: Milwaukee
Street address state: WI
Zip/Postal code: 53203-1306
County: Milwaukee
Country: USA
Mailing address: PO BOX 371
Mailing city: MILWAUKEE
Mailing state: WI
Mailing zip: 53201-0371
General Phone: (414) 224-2000
Advertising Phone: (414) 224-2498
Editorial Phone: (414) 224-2047
General/National Adv. E-mail: btschacher@journalsentinel.com
Display Adv. E-mail: btschacher@journalsentinel.com
Classified Adv. e-mail: btschacher@journalsentinel.com
Editorial e-mail: jsedit@journalsentinel.com
Primary Website: www.jsonline.com
Mthly Avg Views: 20562000
Mthly Avg Unique Visitors: 1659000
Year Established: 1882
News Services: LA Times Sportswire, AP, MCT, LAT-WP, NYT, Entertainment News Service, Bloomberg.
Special Editions: Adult Education-Reinvention (Jan); Martin Luther King (Jan); Milwaukee NARI (Feb); College & Career Guide (Feb); Auto Show (1) (Feb); Auto Show (2) (Feb); Sports Show (March); Baseball Preview (Mar); Beer Week (April); CN Home Garden and Landscape (April); Nurse of the Year (April); Summer Getaways(May); Great Milwaukee Summer (May); Top Workplaces(May); Patio Dining (June); Summerfest (June); Adult Education-Reinvention (2) (July); State Fair (July); Make-A-Wish (Aug); Arts Season Preview (Aug); Packers Preview (Sept); Milwaukee NARI (2) (Sept); Martin Luther King (2) (Sept); College & Career Guide (2); Carol Deptolla's Top 30 Dining (Sept); Milwaukee Film (Sept); Think Pink (Sept); Wine and Dine (Nov); Holiday Lights (Nov); Winter Getaways (Nov)
Special Weekly Sections: Sports, TV, Business, Entertainment (Daily); Food (Wed); Wheels (Sat); Art, Books, Music, Travel, Entree, Sports, Business, Classified, Comics, TV, Employment, Real Estate (Sun)
Syndicated Publications: Holiday (Nov) (Other); USA WEEKEND Magazine (S).
Delivery Methods: Mail`Newsstand`Carrier`Racks
Areas Served - City/County or Portion Thereof, or Zip codes: Waukesha County
Sat. Circulation Paid: 105915
Sun. Circulation Paid: 176710
Audit By: AAM
Audit Date: 31.03.2018
Personnel: George Stanley (Ed. & Sr. V.P.); James Nelson (Business Editor); Jen Steele (Business Deputy Ed.)
Parent company (for newspapers): Gannett - USA Today Network

THE MONROE TIMES

Street address 1: 1065 4th Ave W
Street address city: Monroe
Street address state: WI
Zip/Postal code: 53566-1318
County: Green
Country: USA
Mailing address: 1065 4TH AVE W
Mailing city: MONROE
Mailing state: WI
Mailing zip: 53566-1318
General Phone: (608) 328-4202
Advertising Phone: (608) 328-4202
Editorial Phone: (608) 328-4202
General/National Adv. E-mail: lhughes@themonroetimes.com
Display Adv. E-mail: lhughes@themonroetimes.com
Classified Adv. e-mail: lhughes@themonroetimes.com
Editorial e-mail: editor@themonroetimes.com
Primary Website: www.themonroetimes.com
Mthly Avg Views: 760186
Mthly Avg Unique Visitors: 59513
Year Established: 1898
News Services: AP.
Special Editions: Home (Feb)Ag Week (March)Sports preview (March)Source (May) Graduation (May)Dairy Month (June) Fair(July)Sports Preview (August) Sports Preview (Nov)Holiday (Nov)
Special Weekly Sections: On Entertainment (Thursday)
Syndicated Publications: Spry (Monthly); American Profile (Sat).
Delivery Methods: Mail
Areas Served - City/County or Portion Thereof, or Zip codes: 53566, 53522, 53550, 53502 53520, 53570, 53574, 53508, 61060, 61089, 61087, 53587, 53599, 53541, 53504, 53516, 53530, 53586
Own Printing Facility?: N
Commercial printers?: N
Avg Free Circ: 0
Sat. Circulation Paid: 3100
Sat. Circulation Free: 0
Audit By: CVC
Audit Date: 30.09.2018
Personnel: Matt Johnson (Pub.); Kathy Pierce (Bus. Mgr.); Emily Massingill (Ed.); Tina Curran (Circ. Mgr.); Laura Hughes (Adv. Sales Mgr.)

OSHKOSH NORTHWESTERN

Street address 1: 224 State Street
Street address city: Oshkosh
Street address state: WI
Zip/Postal code: 54901
County: Winnebago
Country: USA
Mailing address: 224 STATE ST
Mailing city: OSHKOSH
Mailing state: WI
Mailing zip: 54901-4868
General Phone: (920) 235-7700
Advertising Phone: (920) 426-6639
Editorial Phone: (920) 426-6687
General/National Adv. E-mail: oshkoshad@thenorthwestern.com
Display Adv. E-mail: oshkoshad@thenorthwestern.com
Classified Adv. e-mail: oshkoshad@thenorthwestern.com
Editorial e-mail: oshkoshnews@thenorthwestern.com
Primary Website: www.thenorthwestern.com
News Services: AP, GNS, MCT.

Special Editions: Lawn-Garden-Home (Apr); Football (Aug); Holiday Greetings (Dec); Bridal (Jan); Experimental Aircraft (Jul); Parade of Homes (Jun); Mid-WI Fun Guide (May); Basketball (Nov); Home Interiors (Oct); Answer Book (Sept).
Special Weekly Sections: Main, Local, Lifestyle, Sports, Classified, Business (Daily); Best Food (Sat); Stocks, Outdoors, Building, Business, Travel, TV (Sun)
Syndicated Publications: USA WEEKEND Magazine (S).
Avg Free Circ: 359
Sat. Circulation Paid: 10218
Sat. Circulation Free: 359
Sun. Circulation Paid: 14609
Sun. Circulation Free: 144
Audit By: AAM
Audit Date: 31.03.2016
Personnel: Jim Fitzhenry (VP/News); Ed Berthiaume (News Dir.); Nathaniel Shuda (Ed.)
Parent company (for newspapers): Gannett

DAILY REGISTER

Street address 1: 1640 La Dawn Dr
Street address city: Portage
Street address state: WI
Zip/Postal code: 53901-8822
County: Columbia
Country: USA
Mailing address: PO BOX 470
Mailing city: PORTAGE
Mailing state: WI
Mailing zip: 53901-0470
General Phone: (608) 745-3500
Advertising Phone: (608) 745-3571
Editorial Phone: (608) 745-3511
General/National Adv. E-mail: pdr-news@capitalnewspapers.com
Display Adv. E-mail: mmeyers@madison.com
Classified Adv. e-mail: mmeyers@madison.com
Primary Website: www.portagedailyregister.com
Year Established: 1886
News Services: AP.
Special Weekly Sections: Best Food Day (Wed); Entertainment (Fri)
Syndicated Publications: Best Time (Monthly); Parade (Sat); American Profile (Weekly).
Delivery Methods: Mail`Newsstand`Carrier`Racks
Areas Served - City/County or Portion Thereof, or Zip codes: Columbia County
Own Printing Facility?: Y
Commercial printers?: Y
Avg Free Circ: 292
Sat. Circulation Paid: 2951
Sat. Circulation Free: 72
Audit By: AAM
Audit Date: 30.06.2017
Personnel: Teresa Klinger (Circ. Dir); Travis Houslet (Sports Ed.); Todd Krysiak (Regional Ed.)
Parent company (for newspapers): Lee Enterprises, Incorporated

THE JOURNAL TIMES

Street address 1: 212 4th St
Street address city: Racine
Street address state: WI
Zip/Postal code: 53403-1005
County: Racine
Country: USA
Mailing address: 212 4TH ST
Mailing city: RACINE
Mailing state: WI
Mailing zip: 53403-1066
General Phone: (262) 634-3322
Advertising Phone: (262) 634-3322
Editorial Phone: (262) 634-3322
General/National Adv. E-mail: donna.mueller@lee.net
Display Adv. E-mail: donna.mueller@lee.net
Classified Adv. e-mail: donna.mueller@lee.net
Editorial e-mail: stephanie.jones@lee.net
Primary Website: www.journaltimes.com
News Services: AP, MCT.
Special Weekly Sections: Best Food Day (Mon); Health (Wed); Entertainment (Thur/Sun); Home & Garden (Fri); Religion (Sat); Travel (Sun)
Syndicated Publications: Relish (Monthly); Parade (S); American Profile (Weekly).
Avg Free Circ: 820
Sat. Circulation Paid: 14744
Sat. Circulation Free: 820
Sun. Circulation Paid: 16844
Sun. Circulation Free: 1109
Audit By: AAM
Audit Date: 30.09.2018
Personnel: Mark Lewis (Pub.); Heidi Ward (Major/Nat'l Accts. Rep.); Mathew Johnsrud (Circ. Mgr.); Arne Arnold (Circ. Mgr., Pennysaver); Tom Farley (News Ed.); Heather Gascoigne (Asst. News Ed.); Mark Hertzberg (Photo Dir.); Jeffrey Wilford (Reporter); Susan Shemanske (Sports Ed.); Carl Simon (Prodn. Supvr., Pressroom); Donna Melby (Adv. Dir.); Donna Mueller (Adv. Dir.); Steve Lovejoy (Ed.)
Parent company (for newspapers): Lee Enterprises, Incorporated

THE NORTHWOODS RIVER NEWS

Street address 1: 232 S Courtney St
Street address 2: Stop 14
Street address city: Rhinelander
Street address state: WI
Zip/Postal code: 54501-3319
County: Oneida
Country: USA
Mailing address: 232 S COURTNEY ST STOP 14
Mailing city: RHINELANDER
Mailing state: WI
Mailing zip: 54501-3319
General Phone: (715) 365-6397
Advertising Phone: (715) 365-6397
Editorial Phone: (262) 306-5043
General/National Adv. E-mail: advertising@rivernewsonline.com
Display Adv. E-mail: advertising@rivernewsonline.com
Classified Adv. e-mail: classified@rivernewonline.com
Editorial e-mail: news@rivernewsonline.com
Primary Website: www.rivernewsonline.com
Mthly Avg Views: 112524
Mthly Avg Unique Visitors: 607352
Year Established: 1882
News Services: AP.
Special Editions: Spring Home Improvement Guide (Apr); Fall Home Improvement Guide (Aug); Christmas Church Service (Dec); Valentine's Day (Feb); Financial Planning & Tax Time Feature (Jan); Customer Appreciation Sale (Jul); Father's Day Gift Guide (Jun); Progress (Mar); Mo
Special Weekly Sections: UP NORTH (Fri).
Syndicated Publications: Best Years (Monthly); Parade (S).
Delivery Methods: Mail`Newsstand`Carrier
Areas Served - City/County or Portion Thereof, or Zip codes: Oneida County
Own Printing Facility?: N
Commercial printers?: N
Sun. Circulation Paid: 5302
Audit By: Sworn/Estimate/Non-Audited
Audit Date: 12.07.2019
Personnel: Gregg Walker (Pub./Ed.); Heather Schaefer (Assoc. Ed.); Jan Juedes (Adv. Dir.); Wendi Ell (Gen. Mgr.); Corey Richter (Circ. Mgr.); Jeremy Mayo (Sports Ed.); Susan Taves (Subscriptions)
Parent company (for newspapers): Walker Communications LLC; Northwoods Media LLC

SHAWANO LEADER

Street address 1: 1464 E Green Bay St
Street address city: Shawano
Street address state: WI
Zip/Postal code: 54166-2258
County: Shawano
Country: USA
Mailing address: 1464 E GREEN BAY ST
Mailing city: SHAWANO
Mailing state: WI
Mailing zip: 54166-2258
General Phone: (715) 526-2121
Advertising Phone: (715) 526-7012
Editorial Phone: (715) 526-7019
General/National Adv. E-mail: ckennedy@wolfrivermedia.com
Display Adv. E-mail: ckennedy@wolfrivermedia.com
Classified Adv. e-mail: classifieds@wolfrivermedia.com
Editorial e-mail: gmellis@wolfrivermedia.com
Primary Website: www.shawanoleader.com
Year Established: 1881
News Services: AP.
Special Editions: Sports (Aug); Packer Pre-Game (Fall); Finance (Jan); Dairy (Jun); Home Improvement (Mar); Vacation (May); Seniors (Monthly); Christmas Opener (Nov).
Special Weekly Sections: Education (Wed); Business (Thur); Religion, Entertainment (Fri); Weekend, Lifestyle, Engagements, Entertainment, Home, Health, Science, Outdoor, Auto (Sat)
Syndicated Publications: Parade (Weekly).
Delivery Methods: Mail`Newsstand`Carrier`Racks
Areas Served - City/County or Portion Thereof, or Zip codes: shawano, okono falls, ect.
Own Printing Facility?: Y
Commercial printers?: Y
Sun. Circulation Paid: 6906
Audit By: Sworn/Estimate/Non-Audited
Audit Date: 12.07.2019
Personnel: Paul Seveska (CEO/Pres./Pub.); Berni Hollinger (Group Controller); Roger Bartel (Editorial Director); Bob Perini (vice president production); Chris Kennedy (Regional Advertising Director)
Parent company (for newspapers): Wolf River Media/ division of BlueLine Media Holdings; Metro Suburbia, Inc./Newhouse Newspapers; BlueLine Media Holdings

THE SHEBOYGAN PRESS

Street address 1: 632 Center Ave
Street address city: Sheboygan
Street address state: WI
Zip/Postal code: 53081-4621
County: Sheboygan
Country: USA
Mailing address: 632 CENTER AVE
Mailing city: SHEBOYGAN
Mailing state: WI
Mailing zip: 53081-4621
General Phone: (920) 457-7711
Advertising Phone: (920) 453-5120
Editorial Phone: (920) 457-7711
General/National Adv. E-mail: news@sheboyganpress.com
Display Adv. E-mail: ads@sheboyganpress.com
Classified Adv. e-mail: classified@wisinfo.com
Editorial e-mail: editor@sheboyganpress.com
Primary Website: www.sheboyganpress.com
Year Established: 1907
News Services: AP, GNS.
Special Editions: Newspapers in Education (Apr); Football (Aug); Packers (Dec); Bridal Showcase (Jan); Graduation (Jun); Basketball (Nov); Fall Building (Oct); You (Mag.) (Quarterly); Packers (Sept).; Moxy (Monthly); Lake Shore Living (Monthly)
Special Weekly Sections: Food (Tue); Home, Garden, Entertainment, Weekend, Conservation (Thur); Beliefs, Religion (Fri); Beliefs, Travel, Outdoors (Sun)
Syndicated Publications: USA WEEKEND Magazine (S).
Delivery Methods: Mail`Newsstand`Carrier`Racks
Own Printing Facility?: N
Commercial printers?: Y
Avg Free Circ: 481
Sat. Circulation Paid: 10488
Sat. Circulation Free: 481
Sun. Circulation Paid: 13047
Sun. Circulation Free: 314
Audit By: AAM
Audit Date: 31.03.2018
Personnel: David Liebelt (Retail Adv. Mgr.); Dan Benson (Ed.); Bob Petrie (City Gov't); Jennifer Kuszynski (Community Ed.); Joe Gulig (Editorial Page Ed.); Bruce Halmo (Photo Lab); Robert Farina (Presentation Ed.); Allen Burgard (Transportation Supvr.); Brandon Reid (Sports Ed.)
Parent company (for newspapers): Gannett

STEVENS POINT JOURNAL

Street address 1: 1200 3rd Court
Street address city: Stevens Point
Street address state: WI
Zip/Postal code: 54481
County: Portage
Country: USA
Mailing address: 1200 3RD ST
Mailing city: STEVENS POINT
Mailing state: WI
Mailing zip: 54481-2835
General Phone: (715) 344-6100
Advertising Phone: (888)774-7744
Editorial Phone: (715)744-0655
General/National Adv. E-mail: lbolle@gannett.com
Display Adv. E-mail: lbolle@gannett.com
Classified Adv. e-mail: classified@wisinfo.com
Editorial e-mail: mtreinen@gannett.com
Primary Website: www.stevenspointjournal.com
News Services: AP, GNS.
Special Editions: Packer Final (Fall).
Special Weekly Sections: Stocks (Mon-Sat); High School Highlights (Mon); Parent & Child (Tue); Arts (Wed); Dining, Entertainment, TV Listings, Health, Auto (Thur); Real Estate, Area Church (Fri); Best Food Day, Church, Home, Food Kids (Sat)
Avg Free Circ: 192
Sat. Circulation Paid: 5224
Sat. Circulation Free: 192
Sun. Circulation Paid: 321
Audit By: AAM
Audit Date: 30.06.2018
Personnel: Mark Baldwin (Gen. Mgr.); Barb Soik (Adv. Mgr., Classified); Lisa Nellessen-Lara (Editorial Page Ed.); Jamie Jung (Lifestyles Ed.); Harold Goodridge (News Ed.); Doug Wojcik (Picture Ed.); Scott Williams (Sports Ed.); Kevin Kusava (Prodn. Mgr.); Robin Spindler (Prodn. Mgr., Pre Press); Gary Moyer (Prodn. Supt., Pressroom); Sari Lesk (News Reporter); Mary Jo Johnson (Adv. Dir.); Janie Hytry (Adv. Services Mgr.); Laurie Bolle (Gen. Mgr. / Dir. of Sales)
Parent company (for newspapers): Gannett

WATERTOWN DAILY TIMES

Street address 1: 113 W Main St
Street address city: Watertown
Street address state: WI
Zip/Postal code: 53094-7623
County: Jefferson
Country: USA
Mailing address: PO BOX 140
Mailing city: WATERTOWN
Mailing state: WI
Mailing zip: 53094-0140
General Phone: (920) 261-4949
Advertising Phone: (920)261-4949
Editorial Phone: (920) 261-5161
General/National Adv. E-mail: judyk@wdtimes.com
Display Adv. E-mail: judyk@wdtimes.com
Classified Adv. e-mail: classified@wdtimes.com
Editorial e-mail: news1@wdtimes.com
Primary Website: www.wdtimes.com
Year Established: 1895
News Services: AP.
Special Editions: Earth Day (Apr); Child Care/Back to School (Aug); Christmas Greetings (Dec); Financial (Feb); Bridal Section (Jan & June); Senior Style (May); Spring Home Improvement (Mar); Summer Life Styles (May); Christmas Open (Nov); Fall Tune Up (Oct); Health and Fitness (Jan); Games and Activities (Feb); Design and Ad (April); Graduation (May)'; June Dairy (June); Hunting (Aug)
Special Weekly Sections: Best Food Day (Mon); Commerce, Children's, American Profile (Tue); Agriculture, Business (Wed); Dining, Entertainment, Outdoors (Thur); Real Estate (Fri); Auto (Sat)
Syndicated Publications: USA WEEKEND Magazine (Sat); American Profile (Weekly); Spry (Monthly); Relish (Monthly)
Delivery Methods: Mail`Newsstand`Carrier`Racks
Own Printing Facility?: N
Commercial printers?: Y
Sat. Circulation Paid: 9287
Audit By: Sworn/Estimate/Non-Audited
Audit Date: 12.07.2019
Personnel: Patricia L. Clifford (Vice Pres.); Margaret A. Krueger (Sec.); Ralph H. Krueger (Treasurer/Bus. Mgr.); Kevin Clifford (Gen. Mgr.); Judy A. Kluetzmann (Adv. Dir., Retail/Nat'l); Mark Shingler (Adv. Mgr., Classified); Mark D. Kuehl (Circ. Dir.); James M. Clifford (Ed.); Thomas L. Schultz (Editorial Page Ed.); John Hart (Photo Ed.); Kevin Wilson (Sports Ed.); Gregory J. Thrams (Prodn. Mgr.)
Parent company (for newspapers): Adams Publishing Group, LLC

THE FREEMAN

Street address 1: PO Box 7
Street address 2: 801 N Barstow St
Street address city: Waukesha
Street address state: WI
Zip/Postal code: 53187-0007
County: Waukesha
Country: USA
Mailing address: PO BOX 7
Mailing city: WAUKESHA
Mailing state: WI
Mailing zip: 53187-0007
General Phone: (262) 542-2500
Advertising Phone: (262) 513-2621
Editorial Phone: (262) 513-2671
General/National Adv. E-mail: jbaumgart@conleynet.com

Display Adv. E-mail: jbaumgart@conleynet.com
Classified Adv. e-mail: jbaumgart@conleynet.com
Editorial e-mail: byorth@conleynet.com
Primary Website: www.gmtoday.com
Year Established: 1858
News Services: AP.
Special Editions: Tax Directory (Apr); Health/Medical Directory (Aug); Holiday Fun (Dec); Tax Directory (Feb); License Plate Contest (Jan); Antique Directory (Jul); Sidewalk Sale (Jun); National Women's History Month (Mar); National Home Decorating Month (May); Coupon Book
Special Weekly Sections: Best Food (Wed); Home, Real Estate, Leisure, Auto (Thur); Brides, TV, Auto (Sat); Easy Living, Health (Monthly); Resources, Summer Fun, Fall (Annually)
Syndicated Publications: Relish (Monthly); USA WEEKEND Magazine (Sat); American Profile (Weekly).
Delivery Methods: Mail`Newsstand`Carrier`Racks
Areas Served - City/County or Portion Thereof, or Zip codes: MILWAUKEE--RACINE, WI CMSA
Own Printing Facility?: Y
Commercial printers?: Y
Avg Free Circ: 256
Sat. Circulation Paid: 10649
Sat. Circulation Free: 3948
Audit By: CVC
Audit Date: 31.03.2017
Personnel: Jim Baumgart (Adv. Mgr.); Tom Badger (Circ. Mgr., Mktg./Promo.); Bill Yorth (Publisher & Ed. in Chief); Mary Carlson (Automotive Ed.); Hays Goodman (Online/Mgmt. Info Servs. Mgr.); Joe Rocha (Prodn. Coord., Mailroom); Tim Haffemann (Dist. Circ. Director); Shana Duffy (Editorial Page Ed.); Patricia Scheel (Prepress Mgr.)
Parent company (for newspapers): Conley Media LLC

THE WAUSAU DAILY HERALD

Street address 1: 800 Scott St
Street address city: Wausau
Street address state: WI
Zip/Postal code: 54403-4951
County: Marathon
Country: USA
Mailing address: PO BOX 1286
Mailing city: WAUSAU
Mailing state: WI
Mailing zip: 54402-1286
General Phone: (715) 842-2101
Advertising Phone: (715) 845-0754
Editorial Phone: (715) 845-0661
General/National Adv. E-mail: opinions@wausaudailyherald.com
Display Adv. E-mail: shehir@gannett.com
Classified Adv. e-mail: classified@wisinfo.com
Editorial e-mail: mbaldwin@wausau.gannett.com
Primary Website: www.wausaudailyherald.com
Year Established: 1907
News Services: AP, GNS.
Special Editions: Career Choices (Apr); Prep Football (Aug); Sidewalk Sale (Jul); Summer Events (May); Real Estate Guide (Monthly); Thanksgiving (Nov); Forest Forever (Oct); Escape (May and Sept); You Magazine (Bi-Monthly); Thirteen for Thirteen (Monthly); Hmong Connections (Quarterly); Senior Living (Quarterly); Pets (March); Academic Excellence (Oct-May); Volunteer (April); Made in Central Wisconsin (Sept); Online Auction (April & Oct); Reader's Choice Awards (March-May); Athletes of the Year (May); Graduation (June)
Special Weekly Sections: News, Sports, Business, Classifieds (Daily); Travel, Stock, Outdoors (Sun); Health, Fitness, Follow-ups (Mon); Lifestyle, Senior, Technology (Tue); Best Food day, Nutrition, Diet, Youth Sports (Wed); Family, Outdoors, Weekend, Entertainment (Thur); Religion, Xpressions (Fri); Homestyle, Real Estate Guide (sat)
Syndicated Publications: HomeStyle (Every other month); CW Business (Monthly); USA WEEKEND Magazine (S).
Delivery Methods: Mail`Newsstand`Carrier`Racks
Own Printing Facility?: Y
Commercial printers?: N
Avg Free Circ: 213
Sat. Circulation Paid: 9619
Sat. Circulation Free: 213
Sun. Circulation Paid: 24730
Sun. Circulation Free: 333
Audit By: AAM
Audit Date: 30.06.2018
Personnel: Jim Fitzhenry (VP/News); Mark Treinen (News Dir.); Larry Gallup (Content Experience Dir.); Timothy Langton (Central Wisconsin Planning Ed.); Robert Mentzer (Community Engagement Ed.); Jamie Rokus (Community Engagement Ed.)
Parent company (for newspapers): Gannett

THE WASHINGTON COUNTY DAILY NEWS

Street address 1: 100 S 6th Ave
Street address city: West Bend
Street address state: WI
Zip/Postal code: 53095-3309
County: Washington
Country: USA
Mailing address: 100 S 6TH AVE
Mailing city: WEST BEND
Mailing state: WI
Mailing zip: 53095-3309
General Phone: (262) 306-5000
Advertising Phone: 262-306-5011
Editorial Phone: (262) 306-5000
General/National Adv. E-mail: jdenk@conleynet.com
Display Adv. E-mail: jdenk@conleynet.com
Classified Adv. e-mail: sjerdee@conleynet.com
Editorial e-mail: dailynews@conleynet.com
Primary Website: www.gmtoday.com
Mthly Avg Views: 516000
Mthly Avg Unique Visitors: 147445
Year Established: 1995
News Services: AP, NYT.
Special Editions: Home & Garden, Holiday, etc. Call for additional sections
Special Weekly Sections: Call for current weekly sections
Syndicated Publications: Redplum (Sat) SmartSource (Sat)
Delivery Methods: Mail`Newsstand
Areas Served - City/County or Portion Thereof, or Zip codes: Washington County
Own Printing Facility?: Y
Commercial printers?: Y
Sat. Circulation Paid: 7776
Audit By: CVC
Audit Date: 31.03.2019
Personnel: Tim Haffemann (Circ. Dir.); Jon Denk (General Manager); Heather Rogge (Pub. /Adv. Mgr.)
Parent company (for newspapers): Conley Media LLC

DAILY TRIBUNE

Street address 1: 101 W. Riverview Expressway, Suite 131
Street address city: Wisconsin Rapids
Street address state: WI
Zip/Postal code: 54495-4154
County: Wood
Country: USA
Mailing address: 101 W RIVERVIEW EXPY STE 131
Mailing city: WISCONSIN RAPIDS
Mailing state: WI
Mailing zip: 54495-3367
General Phone: (715) 423-7200
Advertising Phone: (715) 422-6716
Editorial Phone: (715) 422-6723
General/National Adv. E-mail: tmondloch@marshfieldnewsherald.com
Display Adv. E-mail: tmondloch@marshfieldnewsherald.com
Classified Adv. e-mail: classified@marshfieldnewsherald.com
Editorial e-mail: editor@wisconsinrapidstribune.com
Primary Website: www.wisconsinrapidstribune.com
News Services: AP.
Special Editions: Boating Guide (Apr); Rivercities Fun Fest (Aug); Sports (Dec); Health Pages (Every other month); Badger State Games (Feb); Bridal Tab (Jan); Water Ski Tourney (Jul); Father's Day Honor Roll (Jun); Boating Guide (Mar); Graduation Tab (May); Sports (Nov); R
Special Weekly Sections: Best Food Day (Tue); Weekend Sports (Mon); Business, Stock (Tue-Sat); Agriculture (Wed); Dining, Entertainment, Outdoor (Thur); TV, Travel, Church, Religion (Fri); Seniors (Sat)
Avg Free Circ: 50
Sat. Circulation Paid: 4549
Sat. Circulation Free: 50
Sun. Circulation Paid: 480
Audit By: AAM
Audit Date: 31.03.2019
Personnel: Allen Hicks (Exec. Ed.); Tom Loucks (Photo Chief); Jamie Jung (Religion Ed.); Jery Rhoden (Sports Ed.); Matt Wolk (Gen. Mgr.); Mike Seeber (VP Finance); Noelle Klomp (Adv. Dir.)
Parent company (for newspapers): Gannett

WYOMING

CASPER STAR-TRIBUNE

Street address 1: 170 Star Lane
Street address city: Casper
Street address state: WY
Zip/Postal code: 82604
County: Natrona
Country: USA
Mailing address: PO BOX 80
Mailing city: CASPER
Mailing state: WY
Mailing zip: 82602-0080
General Phone: (307) 266-0500
Advertising Phone: (307) 266-0588
Editorial Phone: (307) 266-0575
General/National Adv. E-mail: janet.johnson@trib.com
Display Adv. E-mail: janet.johnson@trib.com
Classified Adv. e-mail: janet.johnson@trib.com
Editorial e-mail: editors@trib.com
Primary Website: www.trib.com
Mthly Avg Views: 2100347
Mthly Avg Unique Visitors: 398355
News Services: AP, NYT.
Special Editions: Football (Aug); Bridal Guide (Jan); College National Finals Rodeo (Jun); Growing Tomorrows (Mar); Discover Casper (May); Holiday Guide (Nov).
Special Weekly Sections: Science, Technology (Mon); Health (Tue); Enjoy!, Food (Wed); Open Spaces, Business (Thur); Family, Weekender (Fri); Religion, NASCAR (Sat); Home, Garden (Sun)
Syndicated Publications: Relish (Monthly); Sunday Comics (S); American Profile (Weekly).
Sat. Circulation Paid: 15701
Sun. Circulation Paid: 17108
Audit By: AAM
Audit Date: 30.09.2018
Personnel: Tom Biermann (Pub); Marvin Rone (Outside Sales Rep); Janet Johnson (Ad Dir); Nicole Ott (Marketing & Digital Dir); Jeff Hansen (Controller); Dale Bohren (Exec. Ed.); Ross Jacobsen (Sports Ed.); Mandy Burton (Ed)
Parent company (for newspapers): Dispatch-Argus; Lee Enterprises, Incorporated

WYOMING TRIBUNE-EAGLE

Street address 1: 702 W Lincolnway
Street address city: Cheyenne
Street address state: WY
Zip/Postal code: 82001-4359
County: Laramie
Country: USA
Mailing address: 702 W LINCOLNWAY
Mailing city: CHEYENNE
Mailing state: WY
Mailing zip: 82001-4397
General Phone: (307) 634-3361
Advertising Phone: (307) 633-3151
Editorial Phone: (307) 634-3361
General/National Adv. E-mail: wlopez@wyomingnews.com
Display Adv. E-mail: wlopez@wyomingnews.com
Classified Adv. e-mail: class1@wyomingnews.com
Editorial e-mail: bmartin@wyomingnews.com
Primary Website: www.wyomingnews.com
Year Established: 1894
News Services: NEA, AP, MCT.
Special Editions: Football (Aug); Estate Planning (Feb); Cheyenne Frontier Days (Jul); Investing (Jun); Entrepreneurs (May); Home Improvement (Sept).
Special Weekly Sections: Finance (Mon); Religion (Sat); Family, Milestones, Schools, Travel, Science (Sun)
Syndicated Publications: USA WEEKEND Magazine (Sat).
Delivery Methods: Mail`Newsstand`Carrier`Racks
Own Printing Facility?: Y
Commercial printers?: Y
Sat. Circulation Paid: 13864
Sun. Circulation Paid: 14901
Audit By: AAM
Audit Date: 30.09.2012
Personnel: L. Michael McCraken (Pres./Pub.); Ronald M. Brown (Vice Pres./Sec.); Larry D. Catalano (Treasurer/Controller); Scott P. Walker (Adv. Dir.); Lashay Hernandez (Adv. Mgr., Classified); Cynthia M. Marek (Adv. Mgr., Nat'l); Gina Larsen (Circ. Dir.); D. Reed Eckhardt (Mng. Ed.); Scott W. Smith (Editorial Page Ed.); C.J. Putnam (Features Ed.); Robert Gagliardi (Sports Ed.); James K. Thompson (Prodn. Dir.); Joyce Girardin (Prodn. Mgr., Mailroom); Larry E. Bechtholdt (Prodn. Foreman, Pressroom)
Parent company (for newspapers): Adams Publishing Group, LLC

THE NEWS-RECORD

Street address 1: 1201 W 2nd St
Street address city: Gillette
Street address state: WY
Zip/Postal code: 82716-3301
County: Campbell
Country: USA
Mailing address: PO BOX 3006
Mailing city: GILLETTE
Mailing state: WY
Mailing zip: 82717-3006
General Phone: (307) 682-9306
Advertising Phone: (307) 682-9306 ext. 217
Editorial Phone: (307) 686-9306
General/National Adv. E-mail: newsad@vcn.com
Display Adv. E-mail: newsad@vcn.com
Classified Adv. e-mail: classified@gillettenewsrecord.com
Editorial e-mail: news@gillettenewsrecord.com
Primary Website: www.gillettenewsrecord.com
Year Established: 1904
News Services: AP.
Special Editions: Health and Fitness(Jan);Do you wanna get away(Feb); Your Money(Jan) Hometown Business(Feb); Living 50+ (March); Here's my card(March); Spring on the road (April); Think Green (Earth Day); Home&Garden (May); Summer Guide (June) Energy Update (June); Health&Fitness (July) Hunting Guide(Booklet) (August); Parenting Guide/Cooler Days (Sept); Health&Fitness (Oct); Holiday Gift Guide (Nov); Home for the Holidays (Dec) Letters to Santa (Dec); Winter sports/Fall Sports/Christmas Greetings (Dec); Hunting Guide (Fall) Bridal Guide (April); Big Boys Toys (June); Home and Garden Issue(May)
Special Weekly Sections: Best Food (Tue); Business Section, Living, TV, Food (Sun)
Syndicated Publications: Health & Fitness Tab (Monthly); What's On (local entertainment and TV) (S); American Profile (Weekly).
Delivery Methods: Mail
Areas Served - City/County or Portion Thereof, or Zip codes: Campbell County
Own Printing Facility?: Y
Commercial printers?: Y
Sun. Circulation Paid: 6479
Audit By: Sworn/Estimate/Non-Audited
Audit Date: 12.07.2019
Personnel: Betty Kennedy (Pres.); Valerie Kettrey (Bus. Mgr.); Deb Holbert Sutton (Mng. Ed.); Ann Franscell (Editorial Page Ed.); Kathy Brown (Sports Ed.); Mike Urlaub (Prodn. Mgr.); Ann Turner; Mandi Gideon (Adv. Mgr.); Shauna Glasser (Circ. Mgr.); Ann Kennedy-Turner (Pub./Ed.)
Parent company (for newspapers): Gillete News-Record Co.

LARAMIE BOOMERANG

Street address 1: 320 E Grand Ave
Street address city: Laramie
Street address state: WY
Zip/Postal code: 82070-3712
County: Albany
Country: USA
Mailing address: 320 E GRAND AVE
Mailing city: LARAMIE
Mailing state: WY
Mailing zip: 82070-3712
General Phone: (307) 742-2176
Advertising Phone: (307) 742-2176
Editorial Phone: (307) 742-2176
General/National Adv. E-mail: sarah@laramieboomerang.com
Display Adv. E-mail: sarah@laramieboomerang.com
Classified Adv. e-mail: classads@laramieboomerang.com
Editorial e-mail: news@laramieboomerang.com
Primary Website: www.laramieboomerang.com

Year Established: 1881
News Services: AP.
Special Editions: Cute Pets (Jan); Bridal (Feb); Laramie Map (Feb); Home Improvement (Mar); Healthpro (Apr); Detour: Travel & Rec (May); High School Graduation (May); Senior Living (Jun); Halloween (Oct); Cowboy Basketball (Nov); Seasons Greetings (Dec).
Special Weekly Sections: Entertainment/TV Listings
Syndicated Publications: Parade (S).
Delivery Methods: Mail`Newsstand`Carrier`Racks
Areas Served - City/County or Portion Thereof, or Zip codes: Laramie County
Own Printing Facility?: Y
Commercial printers?: Y
Avg Free Circ: 7000
Sat. Circulation Paid: 5233
Sun. Circulation Paid: 5233
Audit By: Sworn/Estimate/Non-Audited
Audit Date: 12.07.2019
Personnel: Dianne Gallatin (Bus. Office Mgr.); Robert Hammond (Sports Ed.); Darcie Hoffland (Adv. Mgr.); Brandon Crago (Graphic Design Mgr.)
Parent company (for newspapers): Adams Publishing Group, LLC

THE RIVERTON RANGER

Street address 1: 421 E Main St
Street address city: Riverton
Street address state: WY
Zip/Postal code: 82501-4438
County: Fremont
Country: USA
Mailing address: PO BOX 993
Mailing city: RIVERTON
Mailing state: WY
Mailing zip: 82501-0118
General Phone: (307) 856-2244
Advertising Phone: (307) 856-2244
Editorial Phone: (307) 856-2244
General/National Adv. E-mail: rangerads@wyoming.com
Display Adv. E-mail: rangerads@wyoming.com
Classified Adv. e-mail: classified@dailyranger.com
Editorial e-mail: fremontnews@wyoming.com
Primary Website: www.dailyranger.com
Year Established: 1953
News Services: AP, MCT.
Special Editions: Fair and Rodeo (Aug); Christmas (Dec); Bridal (Jan); Rendezvous-Balloon Rally (Jul); State Mining (Jun); Community Roots (Mar); Election; Agriculture (Nov); Fire Prevents (Oct); Hunt-Fish (Sept).
Special Weekly Sections: Best Food (Wed); Business (Thur); Entertainment (Fri)
Syndicated Publications: American Profile (S); Entertainment, TV Area-wide Schedule (Tues).
Delivery Methods: Mail`Newsstand`Carrier`Racks
Areas Served - City/County or Portion Thereof, or Zip codes: 82501, 82510, 82512. 82513. 82514, 82515, 82516, 82520, 82523, 82524, 82310, 82604, 82649, 82443
Own Printing Facility?: Y
Commercial printers?: Y
Sun. Circulation Paid: 10400
Audit By: USPS
Audit Date: 01.10.2017
Personnel: Steven R. Peck (Ed./Pub.); Bruce Tippetts (Sports Ed.); Jamie Drendel (Copy Editor); Tracy Coston (Office Mgr.); Ruth Urbigikeit (Adv. Coord.); Luanne Luther (Classifieds Adv. Mgr.)
Parent company (for newspapers): Rivertown Times-Review Publishing Co.

ROCKET-MINER

Street address 1: 215 D St
Street address city: Rock Springs
Street address state: WY
Zip/Postal code: 82901-6234
County: Sweetwater
Country: USA
Mailing address: PO BOX 98
Mailing city: ROCK SPRINGS
Mailing state: WY
Mailing zip: 82902-0098
General Phone: (307) 362-3736
General/National Adv. E-mail: jades@rocketminer.com
Display Adv. E-mail: jades@rocketminer.com
Classified Adv. e-mail: publisher@rocketminer.com
Editorial e-mail: editor@rocketminer.com
Primary Website: www.rocketminer.com
Year Established: 1883
News Services: AP, NEA, TMS, Wyoming Press Association.
Special Editions: Election (Aug); Christmas (Dec); Bridal (Feb); Western Wyoming Review of Progress (Mar); Western Wyoming Vacation (May);Hunting (Sept);Veterans (Nov); Winter Sports (Dec); Fall Sports (Aug); Fair (July) Graduation (May); Gift Guide (Dec.); Letters to Santa (Dec.)
Special Weekly Sections: Best Food Day (Wed); Religion (Sun); Business, Finance, Entertainment (Daily)
Syndicated Publications: Parade Spry
Delivery Methods: Mail`Newsstand`Carrier`Racks
Areas Served - City/County or Portion Thereof, or Zip codes: Southwest Wyoming
Own Printing Facility?: Y
Commercial printers?: Y
Sat. Circulation Paid: 6500
Sun. Circulation Paid: 6500
Audit By: USPS
Audit Date: 30.09.2011
Personnel: Deb Sutton (Gen. Mgr./Ed.); Jeff Robertson (Group Pub.); Pam Haynes (Circ. Mgr.); Jade Stevenson (Adv. Dir.); Emily Nash (Office Mgr.)
Parent company (for newspapers): Adams Publishing Group, LLC

THE SHERIDAN PRESS

Street address 1: 144 E Grinnell Plz
Street address city: Sheridan
Street address state: WY
Zip/Postal code: 82801-3933
County: Sheridan
Country: USA
Mailing address: PO BOX 2006
Mailing city: SHERIDAN
Mailing state: WY
Mailing zip: 82801-2006
General Phone: (307) 672-2431
Advertising Phone: (307) 672-2431
Editorial Phone: (307)672-2431
General/National Adv. E-mail: beth@thesheridanpress.com
Display Adv. E-mail: beth@thesheridanpress.com
Classified Adv. e-mail: classified@thesheridanpress.com
Editorial e-mail: editor@thesheridanpress.com
Primary Website: www.thesheridanpress.com
Year Established: 1887
News Services: AP, MCT, NEA, TMS.
Special Editions: Bridal Issue (Feb); Senior Health & Leisure (Jan); Sheridan-WY Rodeo (Jun); Home Improvement (Mar); Big Horn Mountain Tourist and Recreation Guide (May); Christmas (Nov); Hunting (Sept).
Special Weekly Sections: Best Food (Tue); Youth (Wed); Outdoor (Thur); Smart Living, Entertainment (Fri); Church, Business, Options, Entertainment (Sat)
Syndicated Publications: American Profile (Sat).
Avg Free Circ: 28
Sat. Circulation Paid: 3362
Sat. Circulation Free: 24
Audit By: VAC
Audit Date: 30.06.2014
Personnel: Kristen Czaban (Pub.); Ashleigh Fox (Mng. Ed.); Chad Riegler (Production Mgr.); Caitlin Addlesperger (Director of Special Projects); Janea LaMeres (Lead Marketing Specialist)
Parent company (for newspapers): Seaton Group

NORTHERN WYOMING DAILY NEWS

Street address 1: 201 N 8th St
Street address city: Worland
Street address state: WY
Zip/Postal code: 82401-2614
County: Washakie
Country: USA
Mailing address: PO BOX 508
Mailing city: WORLAND
Mailing state: WY
Mailing zip: 82401-0508
General Phone: (307) 347-3241
Advertising Phone: (307) 347-3241
Editorial Phone: (307)347-3241
General/National Adv. E-mail: editor@wyodaily.com
Display Adv. E-mail: adsales@wyodaily.com
Classified Adv. e-mail: classads@wyodaily.com
Editorial e-mail: editor@wyodaily.com
Primary Website: www.wyodaily.com
Year Established: 1905
News Services: AP.
Special Editions: Health and Wellness (Jan); FFA (Feb); Graduation edition (May); Big Horn Basin (June); Harvest Agriculture (October); Hunting (Oct); Christmas (Dec)
Delivery Methods: Mail
Areas Served - City/County or Portion Thereof, or Zip codes: Washakie County, Hot Springs County, South Big Horn County; Mails out of state.
Own Printing Facility?: Y
Sat. Circulation Paid: 3468
Audit By: Sworn/Estimate/Non-Audited
Audit Date: 12.07.2019
Personnel: Jane Elliott (Production manager); Dustin Fuller (Adv. Mgr.); Mindy Shaw (Circulation Manager/ Bookkeeper); Lee Lockhart (Pub.); Alex Kuhn (Sports Editor); Karla Pomeroy (General Manager/Editor); Dennis Koch (Office Mgr./Circ. Mgr.); Christine Weber (People Page Ed.); Susan Lockhart (Special Projects Ed.); John Elliott (Prodn. Supt.)
Parent company (for newspapers): Stevenson Newspapers; Grand Teton News

DAILY CANADIAN NEWSPAPER

ALBERTA

CALGARY HERALD

Street address 1: 215 16 St. S.E
Street address city: Calgary
Street address province or territory: AB
Postal code: T2E 7P5
Country: Canada
Mailing address: PO Box 2400, Station M
Mailing city: Calgary
Mailing province or territory: AB
Mailing code: T2P 0W8
General Phone: (403) 235-7100
General Fax: (403) 235-7379
Advertising Phone: (403) 235-7168
Advertising Fax: (403) 235-8647
Editorial Phone: (403) 235-7546
Editorial Fax: (403) 235-7379
General/National Adv. E-mail: submit@calgaryherald.com
Display Adv. E-mail: advertising@calgaryherald.com
Classified Adv. e-mail: www.calgaryherald.com/placeanad
Editorial e-mail: Letters@calgaryherald.com
Primary Website: www.calgaryherald.com
Published: Mon`Tues`Wed`Thur`Fri`Sat
Avg Paid Circ: 36273
Avg Free Circ: 1890
Audit By: AAM
Audit Date: 30.09.2018
Personnel: Guy Huntingford (Publisher); Ed Huculak (Dir. of Sales); Chad Moore (Adv. Mgr., Classified); Lorne Motley (Ed. in Chief); Monica Zurowski (Exec. Producer); David Marsden (Editorial Page Ed.); Tom Babin (Tablet Senior Prod.); Paul Harvey (Print. Ed.); Gerry Turgeon (Dist. Mgr.); Bill Eshleman (Adv. Sales & Operations Mgr.); Laura Linnell (Adv. Sales Mgr.); Caroline Noseworthy (Adv. Exec. Asst.); Debi Tetz (Local Ad. Service Team Leader)

CALGARY SUN

Street address 1: 932 72 Ave NE
Street address city: Calgary
Street address province or territory: AB
Postal code: T2E 8V9
Country: Canada
Mailing address: 365 Bloor St E, Toronto, ON
Mailing city: Toronto
Mailing province or territory: ON
Mailing code: M4W 3L4
General Phone: (403) 235 7100
Advertising Phone: (403) 235 7423
Editorial Phone: (403) 235 7433
Editorial Fax: (403) 235 7379
General/National Adv. E-mail: submit@calgaryherald.com
Classified Adv. e-mail: www.postmediasolutions.com/
Editorial e-mail: submit@calgaryherald.com
Primary Website: www.calgarysun.com
Published: Mon`Tues`Wed`Thur`Fri`Sat`Sun
Avg Paid Circ: 15000
Avg Free Circ: 18000
Audit By: CCAB
Audit Date: 30.09.2021
Personnel: Martin Hutson (Mng. Ed.); Lorne Motley (Vice president Editorial, West Region); Monica Zurowski (Dep. Ed.); Michelle Jarvie (Ent. and Life Ed.); Myke Thomas (Homes Ed.); Greg Adams (Local Marketing Specialist)

METRO CALGARY

Street address 1: 3030 3 Avenue N.E., Suite 110
Street address city: Calgary
Street address province or territory: AB
Postal code: T2A 6T7
Country: Canada
Mailing address: 3030 3 Ave N.E., Suite 110
Mailing city: Calgary
Mailing province or territory: AB
Mailing code: T2A 6T7
General Phone: 403-444-0136
Advertising Phone: (403)444-0136
Editorial Phone: (403)444-0136
General/National Adv. E-mail: Adinfocalgary@metronews.ca
Display Adv. E-mail: Adinfocalgary@metronews.ca
Classified Adv. e-mail: classified@metronews.ca
Editorial e-mail: calgaryletters@metronews.ca
Primary Website: www.readmetro.com/en/canada/calgary
Published: Mon`Tues`Wed`Thur`Fri`Sat`Sun
Avg Free Circ: 60810
Audit By: CCAB
Audit Date: 30.09.2015

PARENT COMPANY (FOR NEWSPAPERS):»»»EDMONTON JOURNAL

Street address 1: 10006 - 101 St.
Street address city: Edmonton
Street address province or territory: AB
Postal code: T5J 0S1
Country: Canada
Mailing address: 10006 - 101 St.
Mailing city: Edmonton
Mailing province or territory: AB
Mailing code: T5J 0S1
General Phone: (780) 429-5100
General Fax: (780) 429-5500
Advertising Phone: (780) 429-5400
Advertising Fax: (780) 498-5602
Editorial Phone: (780) 429-5386
Editorial Fax: (780) 429-5500
General/National Adv. E-mail: rpaterson@postmedia.com
Display Adv. E-mail: rpaterson@postmedia.com
Classified Adv. e-mail: classifieds@edmontonjournal.com
Editorial e-mail: miype@postmedia.com
Primary Website: www.edmontonjournal.com
Published: Mon`Tues`Wed`Thur`Fri`Sat
Avg Paid Circ: 62734
Audit By: AAM
Audit Date: 30.09.2018
Personnel: Joseph Wuest (Adv. Mgr., Classified); Gordon Deeks (Adv. Mgr., Sales Planning/Nat'l Sales); Barb Wilkinson (Deputy Ed., Readership/Features); Keri Sweetman (Culture Ed.); David Becker (Vice Pres., Finance); Ken Wickenberg (Vice Pres., HR); David Marshall (Credit Mgr.); Ian Newman (Adv. Mgr., Retail Multi-Market Sales); Patricia Hutchison (Vice Pres., Mktg.); Cindy Mah (Mktg. Research Mgr.); Douglas Wass (Circ. Vice Pres., Reader Servs.); Chris Standring (At Home/Look Ed.); Janice Fehr (Digital Ad. Delivery Tech.); Mark Goodhand (Ed.-in-Chief); Louise Lozeau (Special Feat.); Lyn Propp (Adv. Services & Digital Mgr.); Stephanie Coombs (Managing Editor); John Caputo (Regional Vice-President Sales Prairie Region); Sandra Marocco (Director of Integrated Programs and Strategy)

THE EDMONTON SUN

Street address 1: 10006 101 St
Street address city: Edmonton
Street address province or territory: AB
Postal code: T5J 0S1
Country: Canada
Mailing address: 10006 101 St
Mailing city: Edmonton
Mailing province or territory: AB
Mailing code: TSJ 0S1
General Phone: (780) 468-0100
General Fax: (780) 468-0139
Advertising Phone: (780) 468-0114
Advertising Fax: (780) 468-0128
Editorial Phone: (780) 468-0281
Editorial Fax: (780) 468-0139
General/National Adv. E-mail: ted.dakin@sunmedia.ca
Display Adv. E-mail: ted.dakin@sunmedia.ca
Editorial e-mail: edm-mailbag@sunmedia.ca
Primary Website: www.edmontonsun.com
Published: Mon`Tues`Wed`Thur`Fri`Sat`Sun
Avg Paid Circ: 23321
Avg Free Circ: 9705
Audit By: CCAB
Audit Date: 30.09.2016
Personnel: David Black (Pub. & CEO); Gunther Motsch (Controller); Bob Paterson (Adv. Dir.); Nigel Wainwright (Circ. Dir.); Steve Serviss (Ed. in Chief); Nicole Bergot (City Ed.); Mike Jenkinson (Editorial Page Ed.); Tony Saloway (News Ed.); Tom Baraid (Photo Dept. Mgr.); Glenn Kaiser (Info. Serv. Mgr.); Will Stephani (Prodn. Dir.); Dave Breakenridge (Ed.-in-Chief); John Caputo (Pub.); Ted Dakin (Asst. Adv. Director & Distribution); Jean Figeat (Retail Adv. Mgr.); Craig Martin (VP of Operations, Western Canada); Gordon Norrie (Pub.); Gord Schwinghamer (Adv. Dir.); Catherine Stokes (Mgr., Customer Contact Centre); Dru Warwick (Prod. Mgr.)

FORT MCMURRAY TODAY

Street address 1: 8223 Manning Ave.
Street address city: Fort McMurray
Street address province or territory: AB
Postal code: T9H 1V8
Country: Canada
Mailing address: 8223 Manning Ave
Mailing city: Fort McMurray
Mailing province or territory: AB
Mailing code: T9H 1V8
General Phone: (780) 743-8186
General Fax: (780) 468-0139
Advertising Phone: (780) 743-8186 ext. 733245
Advertising Fax: (866) 485-8461
Editorial Phone: (780) 743-8186 ext. 733243
Editorial Fax: (780) 715-3820
General/National Adv. E-mail: wsomerville@postmedia.com
Display Adv. E-mail: wsomerville@postmedia.com
Classified Adv. e-mail: rhonda.kaiser@sunmedia.ca
Editorial e-mail: olivia.condon@sunmedia.ca
Primary Website: www.fortmcmurraytoday.com
Published: Mon`Tues`Wed`Thur`Fri
Avg Paid Circ: 1577
Audit By: AAM
Audit Date: 31.03.2016
Personnel: Mary-Ann Kostiuk (Pub.); Megan Kerton (Adv. Mgr.); Sonya Lacroixe (Circ. Mgr.); Erika Beauchesne (Acting Mng. Ed.); Amy Avery (Circ. Mgr.); Erika Beauchesme (Mng. Ed.)

DAILY HERALD-TRIBUNE

Street address 1: 10604 100 St.
Street address city: Grande Prairie
Street address province or territory: AB
Postal code: T8V 6V4
Country: Canada
Mailing address: 10604 100 St.
Mailing city: Grande Prairie
Mailing province or territory: AB
Mailing code: T8V 6V4
General Phone: (780) 532-1110
General Fax: (780) 532-2120
Advertising Phone: (780) 513-3991
Advertising Fax: (866) 485-8461
Editorial Phone: (780) 513-3995 ext. 726251
Editorial Fax: (780) 532-2120
General/National Adv. E-mail: peter.meyerhoffer@sunmedia.ca
Display Adv. E-mail: jane.mcrae@sunmedia.ca
Classified Adv. e-mail: selfserveclassifieds@postmedia.com
Editorial e-mail: lclow@postmedia.com
Primary Website: www.dailyheraldtribune.com
Published: Mon`Tues`Wed`Thur`Fri
Avg Paid Circ: 2733
Audit By: AAM
Audit Date: 2/31/2016
Personnel: Peter Meyerhoffer (Publisher/Plant Manager); Margaret Steele (Office Mgr.); Fern Hickson (Adv. Mgr., Nat'l); Diana Rinne (Ed.); Terry Farrell (Sports Ed.); Fred Rinne (Reg. Mng. Ed.)

THE LETHBRIDGE HERALD

Street address 1: 504 7th St. S.
Street address city: Lethbridge
Street address province or territory: AB
Postal code: T1J 2H1
Country: Canada
Mailing address: 504 7th Street South
Mailing city: Lethbridge
Mailing province or territory: AB
Mailing code: T1J 2H1
General Phone: (403) 328-4411
General Fax: (403) 328-4536
Advertising Phone: (430) 328-4410
Advertising Fax: (430) 329-8089
Editorial Phone: (403) 328-4418
Editorial Fax: (403) 329-9355
General/National Adv. E-mail: bhancock@lethbridgeherald.com
Display Adv. E-mail: bhancock@lethbridgeherald.com
Classified Adv. e-mail: nvaneden@lethbridgeherald.com
Editorial e-mail: editor@lethbridgeherald.com
Primary Website: www.lethbridgeherald.com
Published: Tues`Wed`Thur`Fri`Sat
Avg Paid Circ: 12000
Audit By: Sworn/Estimate/Non-Audited
Audit Date: 01.08.2021
Personnel: Don Winkler (Prodn. Mgr., Commercial Print); Randy Jensen (News Desk Ed.); Brian Hancock (Retail Sales Mgr.); Chris Tunke (Multi-Market/National Adv. Sales); Ryan Turner (Prod. & Systems Mgr.); Mike Hertz (Senior VP & Group Pub.)

LETHBRIDGE SUN TIMES

Street address 1: 504 - 7th Street S
Street address city: Lethrbidge
Street address province or territory: AB
Postal code: T1J 2G8
Country: Canada
Mailing address: 504 - 7th Street S
Mailing city: Lethrbidge
Mailing province or territory: AB
Mailing code: T1J 2G8
General Phone: (403) 328-4433
General Fax: (403) 329-9355
Advertising Fax:»Editorial Phone:»Editorial Fax:»General/National Adv. E-mail: suntimes@lethbridgeherald.com
Classified Adv. e-mail:»Editorial e-mail: ccampbell@abnewsgroup.com
Primary Website: www.lethsuntimes.com
Published: Mon`Tues`Wed`Thur`Fri`Sat`Sun
Avg Paid Circ: 19864
Audit By: AAM
Audit Date: 30.09.2017
Personnel: Coleen Campbell (Pub.)

MEDICINE HAT NEWS

Street address 1: 3257 Dunmore Rd S.E.
Street address city: Medicine Hat
Street address province or territory: AB
Postal code: T1A 7E6
Country: Canada
Mailing address: 3257 Dunmore Rd S.E.
Mailing city: Medicine Hat
Mailing province or territory: AB
Mailing code: T1A 7E6
General Phone: (403) 527-1101
General Fax: (403) 528-5696
Advertising Phone: (403) 527-1101
Advertising Fax: (403) 527-0737
Editorial Phone: (403)528-5691
Editorial Fax: (403) 527-1244
General/National Adv. E-mail: lgove@medicinehatnews.com
Display Adv. E-mail: lgove@medicinehatnews.com
Classified Adv. e-mail: dmattson@medicinehatnews.com
Editorial e-mail: ksandford@medicinehatnews.com
Primary Website: www.medicinehatnews.com
Published: Mon`Tues`Wed`Thur`Fri`Sat
Avg Paid Circ: 6967
Avg Free Circ: 3753
Audit By: AAM
Audit Date: 31.03.2019

Personnel: Michael Hertz (Pub.); Gordon Waterhouse (Circ. Dir.); Kerri Hamel (City Ed.); Sean Rooney (Sports Ed.); Tom Peterson (Prod. Mgr.); Kerri Sanford (Mng. Ed.); Chris Tunke (National & Multi-Market Sales)

RED DEER ADVOCATE

Street address 1: 2950 Bremner Ave.
Street address city: Red Deer
Street address province or territory: AB
Postal code: T4R 1M9
Country: Canada
Mailing address: 2950 Bremner Ave
Mailing city: Red Deer
Mailing province or territory: AB
Mailing code: T4R 1M9
General Phone: (403) 343-2400
General Fax: (403) 341-4772
Advertising Phone: (403) 314-4343
Advertising Fax: (403) 342-4051
Editorial Phone: (403) 314-4333
Editorial Fax: (403) 341-6560
General/National Adv. E-mail: advertising@reddeeradvocate.com
Display Adv. E-mail: advertising@reddeeradvocate.com
Classified Adv. e-mail: classified@reddeeradvocate.com
Editorial e-mail: editorial@reddeeradvocate.com
Primary Website: www.reddeeradvocate.com
Published: Mon`Tues`Wed`Thur`Fri`Sat
Avg Paid Circ: 6741
Avg Free Circ: 689
Audit By: AAM
Audit Date: 31.03.2019
Personnel: Fred Gorman (Pub.); Dan Relkow (Bus. Mgr.); Callum Scott (Adv. Dir.); Patricia Stamm (Adv. Mgr., Classified); Richard Smalley (Adv. Mgr., Major Accts.); Allan Melbourne (Circ. Mgr.); Joe McLaughlin (Mng. Ed.); Scott Williamson (Prodn. Mgr.); Randy Holt (Insert Mgr.); John Stewart (Mng. Ed.)

BRITISH COLUMBIA

THE DAILY COURIER

Street address 1: 550 Doyle Ave.
Street address city: Kelowna
Street address province or territory: BC
Postal code: V1Y 7V1
Country: Canada
Mailing address: 550 Doyle Ave.
Mailing city: Kelowna
Mailing province or territory: BC
Mailing code: V1Y 7V1
General Phone: (250) 762-4445
General Fax: (250) 762-3866
Advertising Phone: (250) 470-0761
Editorial Phone: (250) 470-0741
Editorial Fax: (250) 762-3866
General/National Adv. E-mail: krista.frasz@ok.bc.ca
Display Adv. E-mail: krista.frasz@ok.bc.ca
Classified Adv. e-mail: krista.frasz@ok.bc.ca
Editorial e-mail: Letters@ok.bc.ca
Primary Website: www.kelownadailycourier.ca
Published: Mon`Tues`Wed`Thur`Fri`Sat`Sun
Avg Paid Circ: 5982
Avg Free Circ: 1801
Audit By: CCAB
Audit Date: 16.11.2017
Personnel: Terry Armstrong (Pub.); Krista Frasz (Adv. Dir.); Steve MacNaull (Bus. Ed.); Dave Trifunov (Sports Ed.)

DAWSON CREEK MIRROR

Street address 1: 901-100th Ave.
Street address city: Dawson Creek
Street address province or territory: BC
Postal code: V1G 1W2
Country: Canada
Mailing address: 901-100th Ave.
Mailing city: Dawson Creek
Mailing province or territory: BC
Mailing code: V1G 1W2
General Phone: (250) 782-4888
General Fax: (250) 782-6300
Advertising Phone: (250) 782-4888
Advertising Fax: (250) 782-6300
Editorial Phone: (250) 782-4888
Editorial Fax: (250) 782-6300
General/National Adv. E-mail: jkmet@dcdn.ca
Display Adv. E-mail: jkmet@dcdn.ca
Classified Adv. e-mail: npalfy@dcdn.ca
Editorial e-mail: editor@dcdn.ca
Primary Website: www.dawsoncreekmirror.ca
Published: Thur
Avg Free Circ: 8000
Audit By: Sworn/Estimate/Non-Audited
Audit Date: 12.07.2022
Personnel: Nicole Palfy (Adv. Dir./Assoc. Pub.); Margot Owens (Circ. Mgr.); Alison McMeans (Mng. Ed.); Travis Hind (Prodn. Mgr., Pre Press); William Julian (Reg. Mgr.)

ALASKA HIGHWAY NEWS

Street address 1: 9916 98th St.
Street address city: Fort Saint John
Street address province or territory: BC
Postal code: V1J 3T8
Country: Canada
Mailing address: 9916 98th St.
Mailing city: Fort Saint John
Mailing province or territory: BC
Mailing code: V1J 3T8
General Phone: (250) 785-5631
General Fax: (250) 785-3522
Advertising Phone: (250) 785-5631
Advertising Fax: (250) 785-3522
Editorial Phone: (250) 785-5631
Editorial Fax: (250) 785-3522
General/National Adv. E-mail: rwallace@ahnfsj.ca
Display Adv. E-mail: rwallace@ahnfsj.ca
Classified Adv. e-mail: bpiper@ahnfsj.ca
Editorial e-mail: editor@ahnfsj.ca
Primary Website: www.alaskahighwaynews.ca
Published: Mon`Tues`Wed`Thur`Fri
Avg Paid Circ: 3790
Audit By: Sworn/Estimate/Non-Audited
Audit Date: 12.07.2019
Personnel: William Julian (Reg. Mgr.); Ryan Wallace (Adv. Mgr.); Alison McMeans (Mng. Ed.)

PENTICTON HERALD

Street address 1: 186 Nanaimo Ave W #101
Street address city: Penticton
Street address province or territory: BC
Postal code: V2A 1N4
Country: Canada
Mailing address: 186 Nanaimo Ave W #101
Mailing city: Penticton
Mailing province or territory: BC
Mailing code: V2A 1N4
General Phone: (250) 492-4002
General Fax: (250) 492-2403
Advertising Phone: (250) 490-0880 ext. 120
Advertising Fax: (250) 490-4829
Editorial Phone: (250) 490-0880 ext. 300
Editorial Fax: (250) 492-2403
General/National Adv. E-mail: accounting@pentictonherald.ca
Display Adv. E-mail: accounting@pentictonherald.ca
Classified Adv. e-mail: accounting@pentictonherald.ca
Editorial e-mail: editor@pentictonherald.ca
Primary Website: www.pentictonherald.ca
Published: Mon`Tues`Wed`Thur`Fri`Sat`Sun
Avg Paid Circ: 3668
Avg Free Circ: 582
Audit By: CCAB
Audit Date: 23.11.2017
Personnel: Ed Kennedy (Sales Mgr.); Shannon Haggard (Circ. Mgr.); James Millerjames (Mng. Ed.); Dave Crompton (Sports Ed.); Andre Martin (GM); Paul Varga (Mng. Ed.)

THE PRINCE GEORGE CITIZEN

Street address 1: 150 Brunswick St.
Street address city: Prince George
Street address province or territory: BC
Postal code: V2L 2B3
Country: Canada
Mailing address: 150 Brunswick St.
Mailing city: Prince George
Mailing province or territory: BC
Mailing code: V2L 2B3
General Phone: (250) 562-2441
General Fax: (250) 562-9201
Advertising Phone: (250) 960-2757
Advertising Fax: (250) 562-9201
Editorial Phone: (250) 562-2441
Editorial Fax: (250) 562-9201
General/National Adv. E-mail: ads@pgcitizen.ca
Display Adv. E-mail: ads@pgcitizen.ca
Classified Adv. e-mail: cls@pgcitizen.ca
Editorial e-mail: news@pgcitizen.ca
Primary Website: www.princegeorgecitizen.com
Published: Mon`Tues`Wed`Thur`Fri`Sat
Avg Paid Circ: 6236
Audit By: AAM
Audit Date: 31.12.2017
Personnel: Hugh Nicholson (Pub.); Lu Verticchio (Sales Mgr.); Colleen Sparrow (Pub.); Jim Swanson (Sports Ed.); George Lesniewicz (Prodn. Mgr., Mailroom/Pressroom); Kevin Eikum (Prodn. Foreman, Pressroom); Neil Godbout (Ed.); Alan Ramsay (Circ. Mgr.); Dave Smith (Adv. Mgr.)

DESIBUZZZCANADA

Street address 1: 16318 - 113B Avenue
Street address city: Surrey
Street address province or territory: BC
Postal code: V4N 5A2
Country: Canada
Mailing city:»Mailing province or territory:»Mailing code:»General Phone: 16048803463
Advertising Phone: 1604-880-3463
Editorial Phone: 16047104945
General/National Adv. E-mail: news@desibuzzbc.com
Display Adv. E-mail: editorpd@hotmail.com
Classified Adv. e-mail: classifieds@desibuzzbc.com
Editorial e-mail: editor@desibuzzbc.com
Primary Website: www.desibuzzbc.com
Published: Mon`Tues`Wed`Thur`Fri`Sat`Sun`Other
Avg Paid Circ: 1000
Avg Free Circ: 18000

TRAIL DAILY TIMES

Street address 1: 1136 Cedar Ave
Street address city: Trail
Street address province or territory: BC
Postal code: V1R 4B8
Country: Canada
Mailing address: 1163 Cedar Ave.
Mailing city: Trail
Mailing province or territory: BC
Mailing code: V1R 4B8
General Phone: (250) 368-8551
General Fax: (250) 368-8550
Advertising Phone: (250) 364-1416
Advertising Fax: (250) 368-8550
Editorial Phone: (250) 364-1242
General/National Adv. E-mail: nationals@trailtimes.ca
Display Adv. E-mail: l.hart@trailtimes.ca
Classified Adv. e-mail: nationals@trailtimes.ca
Editorial e-mail: editor@trailtimes.ca
Primary Website: www.trailtimes.ca
Published: Tues`Wed`Thur`Fri
Avg Paid Circ: 1335
Avg Free Circ: 5
Audit By: VAC
Audit Date: 28.02.2016
Personnel: Michelle Bedford (Circ. Mgr.); Guy Bertrand (Editor); Jeanine Margoreeth (classifieds); Dave Dykstra (sales); Eric Lawson (Group Publisher)

THE PROVINCE

Street address 1: #400 - 2985 Virtual Way
Street address city: Vancouver
Street address province or territory: BC
Postal code: V5M 4X7
Country: Canada
Mailing city:»Mailing province or territory: BC
General Phone: (604) 605-2000
Advertising Phone: 1 (877) 699-8222
Advertising Fax: (604) 605-2206
Editorial Phone: 1-877-979-9901
Editorial Fax: (604) 605-2323
General/National Adv. E-mail: adinquiries@sunprovince.com
Display Adv. E-mail: adinquiries@sunprovince.com
Classified Adv. e-mail: adinquiries@sunprovince.com
Editorial e-mail: vantips@postmedia.com
Primary Website: www.theprovince.com
Published: Mon`Tues`Wed`Thur`Fri`Sun
Avg Paid Circ: 75637
Audit By: AAM
Audit Date: 31.12.2018
Personnel: Paul Chapman (Deputy Editor); Hardip Johal (Weekend Editor); Harold Munro (Editor-in-Chief); Valerie Casselton (Managing Editor); Cassidy Olivier (City Editor); Gordon Clark (Editorial Page Editor)

THE VANCOUVER SUN

Street address 1: #400 - 2985 Virtual Way
Street address city: Vancouver
Street address province or territory: BC
Postal code: V5M 4X7
Country: Canada
Mailing city:»Mailing province or territory:»Mailing code:»General Phone: (604) 605-2000
General Fax: (604) 605-2443
Advertising Phone: 604-605-7355
Advertising Fax: (604) 605-2206
Editorial Phone: (604) 605-2030
Editorial Fax: (604) 605-2323
General/National Adv. E-mail: bkeller@postmedia.com
Display Adv. E-mail: tcopeman@postmedia.com
Classified Adv. e-mail: adinquiries@sunprovince.com
Editorial e-mail: vantips@postmedia.com
Primary Website: www.vancouversun.com
Published: Mon`Tues`Wed`Thur`Fri`Sat
Avg Paid Circ: 99079
Audit By: AAM
Audit Date: 31.12.2018
Personnel: Harold Munro (Ed. in Chief); Valerie Casselton (Mng. Ed.); Paul Chapman (Deputy Editor)

VICTORIA TIMES COLONIST

Street address 1: 2621 Douglas St.
Street address city: Victoria
Street address province or territory: BC
Postal code: V8T 4M2
Country: Canada
Mailing address: 2621 Douglas St
Mailing city: Victoria
Mailing province or territory: BC
Mailing code: V8T 4M2
General Phone: (250) 380-5211
General Fax: (250) 380-5353
Advertising Phone: (250) 380-5289
Advertising Fax: (250) 380-5253
Editorial Phone: (250) 380-5201
Editorial Fax: (250) 380-5353
General/National Adv. E-mail: pmiranda@timescolonist.com
Display Adv. E-mail: jscriven@timescolonist.com
Classified Adv. e-mail: classified@timescolonist.com
Editorial e-mail: letters@timescolonist.com
Primary Website: www.timescolonist.com
Published: Tues`Wed`Thur`Fri`Sat`Sun
Avg Paid Circ: 33719
Avg Free Circ: 37064
Audit By: AAM
Audit Date: 31.03.2019
Personnel: Catherine McConnell (Dir., Finance); David Whitman (Dir. Adv.); Bruce Cousins (Circ. Mgr., Distr./Mktg.); Dave Obee (Ed. in Chief)

MANITOBA

BRANDON SUN

Street address 1: 501 Rosser Ave.
Street address city: Brandon
Street address province or territory: MB
Postal code: R7A 0K4
Country: Canada
Mailing address: 501 Rosser Ave.
Mailing city: Brandon
Mailing province or territory: MB
Mailing code: R7A 0K4
General Phone: (204) 727-2451
General Fax: (204) 725-0976
Advertising Phone: (204)571-7424
Advertising Fax: (204)725-0976
Editorial Phone: (204) 571-7430
Editorial Fax: (204) 727-0385
General/National Adv. E-mail: ads@brandonsun.com+
Display Adv. E-mail: gparker@brandonsun.com
Classified Adv. e-mail: class@brandonsun.com
Editorial e-mail: mgoerzen@brandonsun.com
Primary Website: www.brandonsun.com
Published: Mon`Tues`Wed`Thur`Fri`Sat
Avg Paid Circ: 5599

Avg Free Circ: 6500
Audit By: AAM
Audit Date: 31.03.2019
Personnel: Jim Mihaly (Publisher); Glen Parker (Sales and Marketing Manager); James O'Connor (Mng. Ed.); Ernie Cameron (Distribution); Matt Goerzen (Ed.)

THE DAILY GRAPHIC

Street address 1: 1941 Saskatchewan Ave. W.
Street address city: Portage la Prairie
Street address province or territory: MB
Postal code: R1N 0R7
Country: Canada
Mailing address: 1941 Saskatchewan Ave W.
Mailing city: Portage la Prairie
Mailing province or territory: MB
Mailing code: R1N 0R7
General Phone: (204) 857-3427
General Fax: (204) 239-1270
Advertising Phone: (204) 857-3427
Advertising Fax: (204) 239-1270
Editorial Phone: (204) 857-3427
Editorial Fax: (204) 239-1270
General/National Adv. E-mail: cindy.makarchuk@sunmedia.ca
Display Adv. E-mail: cindy.makarchuk@sunmedia.ca
Classified Adv. e-mail: portagedailygraphic.classifieds@sunmedia.ca
Editorial e-mail: mdumont@postmedia.com
Primary Website: www.portagedailygraphic.com
Published: Mon`Tues`Wed`Thur`Fri`Sat
Avg Paid Circ: 2382
Audit By: Sworn/Estimate/Non-Audited
Audit Date: 12.07.2019
Personnel: Terrie Todd (Columnist)

THE WINNIPEG SUN

Street address 1: 1700 Church Ave.
Street address city: Winnipeg
Street address province or territory: MB
Postal code: R2X 3A2
Country: Canada
Mailing address: 1700 Church Ave.
Mailing city: Winnipeg
Mailing province or territory: MB
Mailing code: R2X 3A2
General Phone: (204) 694-2022
General Fax: (204)694-2347
Advertising Phone: (204) 632-2722
Advertising Fax: (204) 632-8709
Editorial Phone: (204) 632-2774
Editorial Fax: (204) 697-0759
General/National Adv. E-mail: wpgsun.classified@sunmedia.ca
Display Adv. E-mail: wpgsun.classified@sunmedia.ca
Classified Adv. e-mail: wpgsun.classified@sunmedia.ca
Editorial e-mail: mihamm@postmedia.com
Primary Website: www.winnipegsun.com
Published: Mon`Tues`Wed`Thur`Fri`Sat`Sun
Avg Paid Circ: 14110
Avg Free Circ: 22072
Audit By: CCAB
Audit Date: 30.09.2015
Personnel: Tom Brodbeck (City Columnist); Mark Hamm (Ed.); Paul Friesen (Senior Columnist); Ted Wyman (Sports Ed.); Kevin King (Reporter); Daria Zmiyiwsky (Director of Advertising)

WINNIPEG FREE PRESS

Street address 1: 1355 Mountain Ave.
Street address city: Winnipeg
Street address province or territory: MB
Postal code: R2X 3B6
Country: Canada
Mailing address: 1355 Mountain Ave.
Mailing city: Winnipeg
Mailing province or territory: MB
Mailing code: R2X 3B6
General Phone: (204) 697-7122
General Fax: (204) 697-7370
Advertising Phone: (204) 697-7332
Advertising Fax: (204) 697-7370
Editorial Phone: (204) 697-7301
Editorial Fax: (204) 697-7412
General/National Adv. E-mail: advertis@freepress.mb.ca
Display Adv. E-mail: fp.advertising@freepress.mb.ca
Classified Adv. e-mail: wfpclass@freepress.mb.ca
Editorial e-mail: letters@freepress.mb.ca
Primary Website: www.winnipegfreepress.com
Published: Mon`Tues`Wed`Thur`Fri`Sat
Avg Paid Circ: 91452
Audit By: AAM
Audit Date: 31.03.2019
Personnel: Laurie Finley (VP Sales and Marketing); Bob Cox (Publisher); Christine Fehler (Creative Services Manager); John Hill (Assistant Credit Manager); Sandra Kukreja (VP Digital Media); Paul Samyn (Editor); Debbie Thompson (Pre-press Supervisor); Kim Warburton (Director of National Sales); John Sullivan (Director of Online Editorial Operations)

NEW BRUNSWICK

L'ACADIE NOUVELLE

Street address 1: 476 St-Pierre O
Street address city: Caraquet
Street address province or territory: NB
Postal code: E1W 1B7
Country: Canada
Mailing address: 476 St-Pierre O
Mailing city: Caraquet
Mailing province or territory: NB
Mailing code: E1W 1B7
General Phone: (506) 727-4444
General Fax: (506) 727-0530
Advertising Phone: (506) 383-7433
Advertising Fax: (506) 383-7440
Editorial Phone: (506) 727-0502
Editorial Fax: (506) 727-7620
General/National Adv. E-mail: jean-michel.godin@acadiemedia.com
Display Adv. E-mail: jean-michel.godin@acadiemedia.com
Classified Adv. e-mail: charline.godin-landry@acadiemedia.com
Editorial e-mail: gaetan.chiasson@acadienouvelle.com
Primary Website: www.acadienouvelle.com
Published: Mon`Tues`Wed`Thur`Fri`Sat
Avg Paid Circ: 20152
Audit By: Sworn/Estimate/Non-Audited
Audit Date: 12.07.2019

THE DAILY GLEANER

Street address 1: 984 Prospect St
Street address city: Fredericton
Street address province or territory: NB
Postal code: E3B 2T5
Country: Canada
Mailing address: PO Box 3370
Mailing city: Fredericton
Mailing province or territory: NB
Mailing code: E3B 2T5
General Phone: (506) 458-6435
General Fax: (506) 452-7405
Advertising Phone: (506)859-4945
Advertising Fax: (506) 452-7405
Editorial Phone: (506) 452-6671
Editorial Fax: (506) 452-7405
General/National Adv. E-mail: nationaladvertising@brunswicknews.com
Display Adv. E-mail: nationaladvertising@brunswicknews.com
Classified Adv. e-mail: nationaladvertising@brunswicknews.com
Primary Website: www.telegraphjournal.com
Published: Mon`Tues`Wed`Thur`Fri`Sat
Avg Paid Circ: 16050
Avg Free Circ: 52
Audit By: CMCA
Audit Date: 30.06.2014
Personnel: Amanda Bona (National Customer Service Coordinator); Terra Coates (NB Distributor); Lois-Anne McGregor (NB Distributor); Kelly Madden (Director of National Sales); Carrie Moore (Interactive Advertising Manager)

TIMES & TRANSCRIPT

Street address 1: 939 Main St.
Street address city: Moncton
Street address province or territory: NB
Postal code: E1C 8P3
Country: Canada
Mailing address: Box 1001
Mailing city: Moncton
Mailing province or territory: NB
Mailing code: E1C 8P3
General Phone: (506) 859-4945
General Fax: (506) 859-4975
Advertising Phone: (506) 859-4900
Advertising Fax: (506) 859-4899
Editorial Phone: (506) 859-4901
Editorial Fax: (506) 859-4904
General/National Adv. E-mail: nationaladvertising@timestranscript.com
Display Adv. E-mail: bona.amanda@brunswicknews.com
Classified Adv. e-mail: bona.amanda@brunswicknews.com
Editorial e-mail: news@timestranscript.com
Primary Website: www.telegraphjournal.com
Published: Mon`Tues`Wed`Thur`Fri`Sat
Avg Paid Circ: 28812
Avg Free Circ: 76
Audit By: CMCA
Audit Date: 30.06.2014
Personnel: Terra Coates (NB Distributor); Amanda Leblanc (National Service Coordinator); Lois-Anne McGregor (NB Distributor); Kelly Madden (National Sales Director); Ashley McDavid (NB Distributor)

NEW BRUNSWICK TELEGRAPH-JOURNAL

Street address 1: 210 Crown St.
Street address city: Saint John
Street address province or territory: NB
Postal code: E2L 3V8
Country: Canada
Mailing address: PO Box 2350
Mailing city: Saint John
Mailing province or territory: NB
Mailing code: E2L 3V8
General Phone: 1 (506) 632-8888
General Fax: 1 (506) 645-3295
Advertising Phone: 1 (888) 443-2459
Advertising Fax: 1 (506) 645-3295
Editorial Phone: 1 (506) 632-8888
Editorial Fax: 1 (506) 645-3295
General/National Adv. E-mail: cressman.mark@brunswicknews.com
Display Adv. E-mail: tobon.johnl@brunswicknews.com
Classified Adv. e-mail: classified@brunswicknews.com
Editorial e-mail: TJnewsroom@brunswicknews.com
Primary Website: www.telegraphjournal.com
Published: Mon`Tues`Wed`Thur`Fri`Sat
Avg Paid Circ: 26863
Avg Free Circ: 94
Audit By: Sworn/Estimate/Non-Audited
Audit Date: 12.07.2019
Personnel: James C. Irving (VP & Publisher); Kevin Curnock (General Manager); Sean Watson (Sr. Director of Distribution & Logistics); Wendy Metcalfe (Editor in Chief); Mark Cressman (Head of Sales); Eric Falkjar (Director of IT); Sylvie Robichaud (Creative Director); Michael Horncastle (Adv. Mgr.); David Spragg (Editor - Administration); David Stonehouse (Bus. Ed.); Eric Mark (Editorial Page Ed.); James Cole (Prod. Mgr.)

NORTHWEST TERRITORIES

THE WESTERN STAR

Street address 1: 106 West St.
Street address city: Corner Brook
Street address province or territory: NL
Postal code: A2H 6E7
Country: Canada
Mailing address: P.O. Box 460
Mailing city: Corner Brook
Mailing province or territory: NL
Mailing code: A2H 6E7
General Phone: (709) 634-4348
General Fax: (709) 637-4675
Advertising Phone: (709) 637-4652
Advertising Fax: (709) 637-4675
Editorial Phone: (709) 634-4669
Editorial Fax: (709) 634-9824
General/National Adv. E-mail: advertising@thewesternstar.com
Display Adv. E-mail: advertising@thewesternstar.com
Classified Adv. e-mail: advertising@thewesternstar.com
Editorial e-mail: newsroom@thewesternstar.com
Primary Website: www.thewesternstar.com
Published: Mon`Tues`Wed`Thur`Fri`Sat
Avg Paid Circ: 3043
Avg Free Circ: 70
Audit By: CCAB
Audit Date: 23.11.2017
Personnel: Troy Turner (Mng. Ed.); Gladys Leonard (Bus. Mgr./Accountant); Ray Sweetapple (Editorial Page Ed.); David Kearsey (Sports Ed.); Ken Bennett (Prodn. Foreman); Bill Boland (IT/Prod. Supervisor); Gloria Hunt (Sales Mgr.)

THE TELEGRAM

Street address 1: 430 Topsail Rd
Street address city: Saint John's
Street address province or territory: NL
Postal code: A1E 4N1
Country: Canada
Mailing address: PO Box 86
Mailing city: Saint John's
Mailing province or territory: NL
Mailing code: A1E 4N1
General Phone: (709) 364-6300
General Fax: (709) 364-9333
Advertising Phone: (709) 748-0829
Advertising Fax: (709) 364-9333
Editorial Phone: (709) 364-2323
Editorial Fax: (709) 364-3939
General/National Adv. E-mail: sales@thetelegram.com
Display Adv. E-mail: sales@thetelegram.com
Classified Adv. e-mail: class@thetelegram.com
Editorial e-mail: telegram@thetelegram.com
Primary Website: www.thetelegram.com
Published: Mon`Tues`Wed`Thur`Fri`Sat
Avg Paid Circ: 9901
Avg Free Circ: 7482
Audit By: CCAB
Audit Date: 23.11.2017
Personnel: Keith Gover (Controller); Keith Connolly (Interim Pub./Adv. Mgr.); Kerry Hann (Mng. Ed.); Pam Frampton (Assoc. Ed.); Ian Kirby (Prod. Mgr.); Russell Wangersky (News Ed.); Robin Short (Sports Ed.); Don Mackey (Prodn. Mgr., Mailroom); Dean Jacobs (Circ. Mgr., Home Delivery Sales); Gerry Carew (Digital Dir.); Joann Chaulk (National Adv. Sales); Todd Foote (Multimedia Retail Adv. Mgr.); Leo Gosse (Reader Sales and Mktg. Mgr.)

NOVA SCOTIA

THE CHRONICLE HERALD

Street address 1: 2717 Joseph Howe Dr
Street address city: Halifax
Street address province or territory: NS
Postal code: B3J 2T2
Country: Canada
Mailing address: 2717 Joseph Howe Dr
Mailing city: Halifax
Mailing province or territory: NS
Mailing code: B3J 2T2
General Phone: (902) 426-2811
General Fax: (902) 426-1170
Advertising Phone: (902) 426-2811
Advertising Fax: (902) 426-1170
Editorial Phone: (902) 426-2811
Editorial Fax: (902) 426-1158
General/National Adv. E-mail: advertising@herald.ca
Display Adv. E-mail: advertising@herald.ca
Classified Adv. e-mail: classified@herald.ca
Editorial e-mail: newsroom@herald.ca
Primary Website: www.thechronicleherald.ca
Published: Mon`Tues`Wed`Thur`Fri`Sat`Sun
Avg Paid Circ: 49888
Avg Free Circ: 22541
Audit By: CCAB
Audit Date: 22.11.2017
Personnel: G.W. Dennis (Pub.); Sarah Dennis (Pub./CEO/Vice Pres.); Mary Lou Croft (Dir., Cor. Admin.); Theresa Williams (HR Mgr.); Ken Jennex (Purchasing); Paul Jacquart (Adv. Mgr., Retail Sales); Pam Nauss-Redden (Mktg. Mgr.); Tracey King (Research Analyst/ROP Specialist); Jim LaPierre (Dir., Dist. and Log.); Terry O'Neil (Dir., News Admin.); Dan Leger (Dir., News Content); John Howitt (Asst. Dir., Design); Frank De

Palma (Asst. Dir., Newsroom); Brian Ward (Assignment Ed., Day); Eva Hoare (Assignment Ed., Night); Christine Soucie (Books Ed.); Robert Howse (Editorial Page Ed.); Greg Guy (Entertainment Ed.); Margaret MacKay (Lifestyle Ed.); Barry Saunders (Director of Sales); Bruce MacCormack (Vice Pres., Bus. Devel.); Nancy Cook (Sales Dir.); Alex Liot (Mgr., Bus. Devel.); Claire McIlveen (Ed.); Jennifer Punch (Senior Mktg. Mgr.); Ian Scott (VP Operations); Shawn Woodford (Dir., Mktg. and Prod. Devel.)

THE NEWS

Street address 1: 352 E. River Rd.
Street address city: New Glasgow
Street address province or territory: NS
Postal code: B2H 5E2
Country: Canada
Mailing address: PO Box 159
Mailing city: New Glasgow
Mailing province or territory: NS
Mailing code: B2H 5E2
General Phone: (902) 752-3000
General Fax: (902) 752-1945
Advertising Phone: (902) 752-3000
Advertising Fax: (902) 928-1515
Editorial Phone: (902) 752-3000
General/National Adv. E-mail: news@ngnews.ca
Classified Adv. e-mail:»Editorial e-mail: news@ngnews.ca
Primary Website: www.ngnews.ca
Published: Mon`Tues`Wed`Thur`Fri`Sat
Avg Paid Circ: 4495
Avg Free Circ: 827
Audit By: CMCA
Audit Date: 31.12.2013
Personnel: Richard Russell (Pub.); Bernadine Hyson (Controller); Paul MacDonald (Circ. Dir.); Dave Glenen (Ed.); Inez Forbes (Sales Mgr.); Nancy Samson (Prod. Mgr.)

THE CAPE BRETON POST

Street address 1: 255 George St.
Street address city: Sydney
Street address province or territory: NS
Postal code: B1P 6K6
Country: Canada
Mailing address: PO Box 1500
Mailing city: Sydney
Mailing province or territory: NS
Mailing code: B1P 6K6
General Phone: (902) 564-5451
General Fax: (902) 562-7077
Advertising Phone: (902) 563-3873
Advertising Fax: (902) 564-6280
Editorial Phone: (902) 563-3838
Editorial Fax: (902) 562-7077
General/National Adv. E-mail: news@cbpost.com
Display Adv. E-mail: news@cbpost.com
Editorial e-mail: news@cbpost.com
Primary Website: www.capebretonpost.com
Published: Mon`Tues`Wed`Thur`Fri`Sat
Avg Paid Circ: 12497
Avg Free Circ: 1084
Audit By: CCAB
Audit Date: 30.12.2017
Personnel: Shaw Robinson (Bus. Mgr.); Robert Edshaw (Adv. Dir., Serv.); Helen Mccoy (Adv. Mgr., Classified); Rob EdShaw (Adv. Mgr.); Matt Dawson (Circ. Mgr., Promotional); Fred Jackson (Mng. Ed.); Doug McGee (Editorial Page Ed.); Steve Macinnis (News Ed.); Bob Duchemin (Sports Ed.); Heather MacKenzie (Online Mgr.); Paul Bruce (Prodn. Mgr.); Paul King (Prodn. Mgr., Pressroom); Tom Ayers (Ed. Dir.); Anita Delazzer (Pub.); Helen MacCoy (Dir., Reader Sales and Dist.); Scott MacQuarrie (Retail Sales Mgr.); Vernon O'Quinn (IT/ Systems Mgr.); Robert Redshaw (Dir., Sales & Mktg.)

THE DAILY NEWS

Street address 1: 6 Louise St.
Street address city: Truro
Street address province or territory: NS
Postal code: B2N 5C3
Country: Canada
Mailing address: PO Box 220
Mailing city: Truro
Mailing province or territory: NS
Mailing code: B2N 5C3
General Phone: (902) 893-9405
General Fax: (902) 893-0518
Advertising Phone: (902) 893-9405
Advertising Fax: (902) 895-6104
Editorial Phone: (902) 893-9405
Editorial Fax: (902) 893-0518
General/National Adv. E-mail: news@trurodaily.com
Display Adv. E-mail: bpearson@trurodaily.com
Editorial e-mail: cfleming@trurodaily.com
Primary Website: www.trurodaily.com
Published: Mon`Tues`Wed`Thur`Fri`Sat
Avg Paid Circ: 4378
Avg Free Circ: 502
Audit By: CMCA
Audit Date: 31.12.2013
Personnel: Richard Russell (Pub.); Bernadine Hyson (Office Mgr.); Bruce Pearson (Adv. Mgr.); Paul MacDonald (Circ. Mgr.); Dave Glennen (Mng. Ed.); Frank Cassidy (Assignment Ed.); Dave Conrad (Prodn. Mgr.); Sherry Martell (Newsroom Mgr.)

ONTARIO

THE WINDSOR STAR

Street address 1: 3000 Starway Ave.
Street address city: Windsor
Street address province or territory: ON
Postal code: N8W 5E5
Country: Canada
Mailing city:»Mailing province or territory: ON
General Phone: (519) 255-5555
General Fax: (519) 255-5250
Advertising Phone: (519) 255-5555
Advertising Fax: (519) 255-5778
Editorial Phone: (519) 255-5500
General/National Adv. E-mail: adinquiries@windsorstar.com
Display Adv. E-mail: adinquiries@windsorstar.com
Classified Adv. e-mail: www.windsorstar.com/placeanad
Editorial e-mail: cpearson@postmedia.com
Primary Website: www.windsorstar.com
Published: Tues`Wed`Thur`Fri`Sat
Avg Paid Circ: 35510
Audit By: AAM
Audit Date: 31.03.2019
Personnel: Craig Pearson (Managing Editor); Doug Shillington (Dir., Mfg.); Louise Veres (Personnel Mgr.); Ken Stewart (Dir. of Adv.); Maggie Saunders (Adv. Mgr., Classified); Beverly Becker (Dir. Digital sales & Mktg.); John Coleman (Editorial Page Ed.); Ted Shaw (Entertainment Ed.); Jim Potter (Metro Ed.); Mark Falkner (Sports Ed.); Bob Thwaites (Dir., Audience Development/Customer Service)

BELLEVILLE INTELLIGENCER

Street address 1: 199 Front St. Ste 535
Street address city: Belleville
Street address province or territory: ON
Postal code: K8N 5H5
Country: Canada
Mailing address: 199 Front St. Ste 535
Mailing city: Belleville
Mailing province or territory: ON
Mailing code: K8N 5H5
General Phone: (613) 962-9171
General Fax: (613) 962-9652
Advertising Phone: (613) 962-9171
Advertising Fax: (613) 962-9652
Editorial Phone: (613) 962-9171
Editorial Fax: (613) 962-9652
General/National Adv. E-mail: gerry.drage@postmedia.com
Display Adv. E-mail: gerry.drage@sunmedia.ca
Classified Adv. e-mail: intelligencer.classifieds@postmedia.com
Editorial e-mail: bmcvicar@postmedia.com
Primary Website: www.intelligencer.ca
Published: Mon`Tues`Wed`Thur`Fri`Sat
Avg Paid Circ: 5907
Avg Free Circ: 159
Audit By: CCAB
Audit Date: 30.09.2015
Personnel: John Knowles (Pres.); Bill Glisky (Mng. Ed.); Lisa Grills (Adv. Dir.); Tim Devine (Circ. Mgr.); Christopher Malette (City Ed.); Linda O'Connor (Lifestyles Ed.); Ady Vos (Sports Ed.); Jason Hawley (Dist. Mgr.)

BRANDTFORD EXPOSITOR

Street address 1: 195 Henry St. Bld 4, Unit 1
Street address city: Brantford
Street address province or territory: ON
Postal code: N3S 5C9
Country: Canada
Mailing address: 195 Henry St. Bld 4, Unit 1
Mailing city: Brantford
Mailing province or territory: ON
Mailing code: N3S 5C9
General Phone: (519) 756-2020
General Fax: (519) 756-3285
Advertising Phone: (519) 756-2020
Advertising Fax: (519) 756-3285
Editorial Phone: (519) 756-2020
Editorial Fax: (519) 756-3285
General/National Adv. E-mail: adam.giles@sunmedia.ca
Display Adv. E-mail: adam.giles@sunmedia.ca
Classified Adv. e-m ail: brandtfordexpositor.classifieds@sunmedia.ca
Editorial e-mail: knovak@postmedia.com
Primary Website: www.brantfordexpositor.ca
Published: Mon`Tues`Wed`Thur`Fri`Sat
Avg Paid Circ: 11288
Avg Free Circ: 6912
Audit By: CCAB
Audit Date: 30.09.2015
Personnel: Ken Koyama (Pub.); Jeff Dertinger (Mng. Ed.); Adam Giles (Adv. Dir.); Andrea Foster (Circ. Dir.); Kyle Butler (Prod. Mgr.)

THE BROCKVILLE RECORDER AND TIMES

Street address 1: 2479 Parkedale Ave.
Street address city: Brockville
Street address province or territory: ON
Postal code: K6V 3H2
Country: Canada
Mailing address: 2479 Parkedale Ave.
Mailing city: Brockville
Mailing province or territory: ON
Mailing code: K6V 3H2
General Phone: (613) 342-4441
General Fax: (613) 342-4456
Advertising Phone: (613)342-4441 ext. 500251
Advertising Fax: (613) 342-4542
Editorial Phone: (613) 342-4441 ext. 500107
Editorial Fax: (613) 342-4542
General/National Adv. E-mail: ksammon@postmedia.com
Display Adv. E-mail: ksammon@postmedia.com
Classified Adv. e-mail: ksammon@postmedia.com
Editorial e-mail: rzajac@postmedia.com
Primary Website: www.recorder.ca
Published: Mon`Tues`Wed`Thur`Fri
Avg Paid Circ: 9615
Audit By: CMCA
Audit Date: 31.12.2013
Personnel: Lesley Longchamps (Dist. Mgr.); Ron Zajac (Ed.); Kerry Sammon (Adv.)

THE CHATHAM DAILY NEWS

Street address 1: 138 King St. West
Street address city: Chatham
Street address province or territory: ON
Postal code: N7M 1E3
Country: Canada
Mailing address: 138 King St. West
Mailing city: Chatham
Mailing province or territory: ON
Mailing code: N7M 1E3
General Phone: (519) 354-2000
General Fax: (519) 354-3448
Advertising Phone: (519) 354-2000
Advertising Fax: (519) 354-3448
Editorial Phone: (519) 354-2000
Editorial Fax: (519) 354-3448
General/National Adv. E-mail: arodrigues@postmedia.com
Display Adv. E-mail: arodrigues@postmedia.com
Classified Adv. e-mail: chathamdailynews.classifieds@sunmedia.ca
Editorial e-mail: pepp@postmedia.com
Primary Website: www.chathamdailynews.ca
Published: Mon`Tues`Wed`Thur`Fri`Sat
Avg Paid Circ: 4658
Avg Free Circ: 118
Audit By: CCAB
Audit Date: 30.09.2015
Personnel: Dean Muharrem (Pub./Adv. Mgr.); Rod Hilts (Mng. Ed.)

CORNWALL STANDARD-FREEHOLDER

Street address 1: 1150 Montreal Rd.
Street address city: Cornwall
Street address province or territory: ON
Postal code: K6H 1E2
Country: Canada
Mailing address: 1150 Montreal Rd.
Mailing city: Cornwall
Mailing province or territory: ON
Mailing code: K6H 1E2
General Phone: (613) 933-3160
Advertising Phone: (613) 933-3160
Editorial Phone: (613) 933-3160
General/National Adv. E-mail: ksammon@postmedia.com
Display Adv. E-mail: ksammon@postmedia.com
Classified Adv. e-mail: csf.classifieds@sunmedia.ca
Editorial e-mail: hrodrigues@postmedia.com
Primary Website: www.standard-freeholder.com
Published: Mon`Tues`Wed`Thur`Fri`Sat
Avg Paid Circ: 5000
Avg Free Circ: 106
Audit By: Sworn/Estimate/Non-Audited
Audit Date: 12.07.2019
Parent company (for newspapers): Postmedia Network Inc.»»

THE STANDARD (ELLIOT LAKE)

Street address 1: 14 Hillside Dr. S.
Street address city: Elliot Lake
Street address province or territory: ON
Postal code: P5A 1M6
Country: Canada
Mailing address: 14 Hillside Dr. S.
Mailing city: Elliot Lake
Mailing province or territory: ON
Mailing code: P5A 1M6
General Phone: (705) 848-7195
General Fax: (705) 848-0249
Advertising Phone: (705) 848-7195
Advertising Fax: (866) 485-8461
Editorial Phone: (705) 848-7195
Editorial Fax: (705) 848-0249
General/National Adv. E-mail: kjohansen@postmedia.com
Display Adv. E-mail: kjohansen@postmedia.com
Classified Adv. e-mail: elliotlakestandard.classifieds@sunmedia.ca
Editorial e-mail: kmcsheffrey@postmedia.com
Primary Website: www.elliotlakestandard.ca
Published: Mon`Tues`Wed`Thur`Fri`Sat
Avg Paid Circ: 2743
Avg Free Circ: 4567
Audit By: Sworn/Estimate/Non-Audited
Audit Date: 12.07.2019
Personnel: Kevin McSheffrey (Man. Ed.); Karsten Johansen (General Manager); Lolene Patterson (Circulation Manager)

FORT FRANCES DAILY TIMES

Street address 1: 116 First St. E.
Street address city: Fort Frances
Street address province or territory: ON
Postal code: P9A 3M7
Country: Canada
Mailing address: 116 First St. E.
Mailing city: Fort Frances
Mailing province or territory: ON
Mailing code: P9A 3M7
General Phone: (807) 274-5373
General Fax: (807) 274-7286
Advertising Phone: (807) 274-5373
Advertising Fax: (807) 274-7286
Editorial Phone: (807) 274-5373
Editorial Fax: (807) 274-7286
General/National Adv. E-mail: jpierce@fortfrances.com
Display Adv. E-mail: jpierce@fortfrances.com
Classified Adv. e-mail: ads@fortfrances.com

Editorial e-mail: mbehan@fortfrances.com
Primary Website: www.fftimes.com
Published: Mon`Tues`Thur`Fri
Avg Paid Circ: 2500
Audit By: Sworn/Estimate/Non-Audited
Audit Date: 12.07.2019
Personnel: James R. Cumming (Pub.); Debbie Ballard (Adv. Mgr.); Pam Munn (Circ. Mgr.); Michael Behan (Ed.); Corey Westover (Online Mgr.); Don Cumming (Prodn. Mgr.); Debbie Logan (Adv. Mgr.)

THE GUELPH MERCURY TRIBUNE

Street address 1: 367 Woodland Road
Street address 2: Unit 1
Street address city: Guelph
Street address province or territory: ON
Postal code: N1H 7K9
Country: Canada
Mailing address: 367 Woodlawn Rd., Unit 1
Mailing city: Guelph
Mailing province or territory: ON
Mailing code: N1H 7K9
General Phone: (519) 822-4310
General Fax: (519) 767-1681
Advertising Phone: (519) 823-6010
Advertising Fax: (519) 822-4272
Editorial Phone: (519) 823-6060
Editorial Fax: (519) 767-1681
General/National Adv. E-mail: hdunbar@guelphmercurytribune.com
Display Adv. E-mail: hdunbar@guelphmercurytribune.com
Classified Adv. e-mail: classifieds@metroland.com
Editorial e-mail: editor@guelphmercurytribune.com
Primary Website: www.guelphmercury.com
Published: Mon`Tues`Wed`Thur`Fri`Sat
Avg Paid Circ: 8410
Avg Free Circ: 1000
Audit By: CCAB
Audit Date: 31.12.2013
Personnel: Phil Andrews (Mng. Ed.); Peter Hill (Circ. Mgr.); Daryl Warner (Prodn. Mgr.); Steven Cowley (Prodn. Foreman, Mailroom); C David Kruse (Adv. Dir./Gen. Mgr.); Paul McCuaig (Pub.)

THE HAMILTON SPECTATOR

Street address 1: 44 Frid St.
Street address city: Hamilton
Street address province or territory: ON
Postal code: L8N 3G3
Country: Canada
Mailing address: 44 Frid St.
Mailing city: Hamilton
Mailing province or territory: ON
Mailing code: L8N 3G3
General Phone: (905) 526-3333
General Fax: (905) 526-1696
Advertising Phone: (905) 526-3438
Advertising Fax: (905) 522-1696
Editorial Phone: (905) 526-3420
Editorial Fax: (905) 526-1395
General/National Adv. E-mail: sazzopardi@thespec.com
Display Adv. E-mail: sazzopardi@thespec.com
Classified Adv. e-mail: classifieds@metroland.com
Editorial e-mail: letters@thespec.com
Primary Website: www.thespec.com
Published: Mon`Tues`Wed`Thur`Fri`Sat
Avg Paid Circ: 60434
Avg Free Circ: 41571
Audit By: CCAB
Audit Date: 22.11.2017
Personnel: Neil Oliver (Pub.); Paul Berton (Ed. in Chief); Derek Fleming (Vice Pres., Bus. Admin.); Jamie Poehlman (Dir., HR); Susan Azzopardi (Dir. of Digital); Kelly Montague (Adv. Vice Pres.); Bill Repath (Director of Operations); Pauline Lewis (Adv. Mgr., Retail Sales); Cathryn Easterbrook (Adv. Mgr., Class.); Cathy Burse (Circ. Mgr., Home Delivery); Jackie Dekar; Patricia Allen (Dist. Mgr.); Gary Myers (VP, Circ. & Mktg.); Dean Zavarise (VP Prod.)

KENORA DAILY MINER & NEWS

Street address 1: 33 Main St. S.
Street address city: Kenora
Street address province or territory: ON
Postal code: P9N 3X7
Country: Canada
Mailing address: 33 Main St. South
Mailing city: Kenora
Mailing province or territory: ON
Mailing code: P9N 3X7
General Phone: (807) 468-5555
General Fax: (807) 468-4318
Advertising Phone: (807) 468-5555 ext. 226
Advertising Fax: (807)468-4318
Editorial Phone: (807)468-5555 ext. 243
Editorial Fax: (807)468-4318
General/National Adv. E-mail: candice.withers@sunmedia.ca
Display Adv. E-mail: candice.withers@sunmedia.ca
Classified Adv. e-mail: kenora.classifieds@sunmedia.ca
Editorial e-mail: lloyd.mack@sunmedia.ca
Primary Website: www.kenoradailyminerandnews.com
Published: Mon`Tues`Wed`Fri
Avg Paid Circ: 2700
Audit By: Sworn/Estimate/Non-Audited
Audit Date: 12.07.2019
Personnel: Lloyd Mack (Ed.); Alicia McLeod (Circ. Mgr.); Daria Zmiyiwsky (Pub.)

THE KINGSTON WHIG-STANDARD

Street address 1: 6 Cataraqui St.
Street address city: Kingston
Street address province or territory: ON
Postal code: K7L 4Z7
Country: Canada
Mailing address: 6 Cataraqui St.
Mailing city: Kingston
Mailing province or territory: ON
Mailing code: K7L 4Z7
General Phone: (613) 544-5000
General Fax: (613) 530-4122
Advertising Phone: (613) 544-5000
Advertising Fax: (613) 530-4121 (Class)
Editorial Phone: (613) 544-5000
Editorial Fax: (613) 530-4122
General/National Adv. E-mail: aalmeida@postmedia.com
Display Adv. E-mail: aalmeida@postmedia.com
Classified Adv. e-mail: thewhig.classifieds@sunmedia.ca
Editorial e-mail: steve.serviss@sunmedia.ca
Primary Website: www.thewhig.com
Published: Mon`Tues`Wed`Thur`Fri`Sat
Avg Paid Circ: 9942
Avg Free Circ: 283
Audit By: AAM
Audit Date: 31.03.2019
Personnel: Liza Nelson (Pub./Adv. Dir.); Mike Healey (Ntn'l Sales); Derek Shelly (Mng. Ed.); Sean Daly (Prod. Mgr.); Mike Beaudin (Ed.); Jeff Lundy (Regional Dir., Circ. & Dist.)

THE RECORD

Street address 1: 160 King St. East
Street address city: Kitchener
Street address province or territory: ON
Postal code: N2G 4E5
Country: Canada
Mailing address: 160 King St. East
Mailing city: Kitchener
Mailing province or territory: ON
Mailing code: N2G 4E5
General Phone: (519) 895-5552
General Fax: (519) 894-3912
Advertising Phone: (519) 894-1500 (Class)
Advertising Fax: (519) 894-1258
Editorial Phone: (519) 895-5602
Editorial Fax: (519) 894-3829
General/National Adv. E-mail: cschmidt@therecord.com
Display Adv. E-mail: cschmidt@therecord.com
Classified Adv. e-mail: classifieds@metroland.com
Editorial e-mail: mmarks@therecord.com
Primary Website: www.therecord.com
Published: Mon`Tues`Wed`Thur`Fri`Sat
Avg Paid Circ: 49167
Avg Free Circ: 11527
Audit By: BPA
Audit Date: 31.12.2013
Personnel: Paul McCuaig (Pub.); Lynn Haddrall (Ed-in-Chief); Donna Luelo (Dir. Adv. & Circ.); Paul McKeon (Dir. Prod. and Dist.); Sandra Lennox (Class. Mgr.); Melinda Marks (Mng. Ed.); Mike Handfield (Mailroom Mgr.); Ron DeRuyter (Bus. Ed.); Neil Ballantyne (City Ed.); John Roe (Editorial Page Ed.); Johanna Neufeld (Librarian); Karlo Berkovich (Online Ed.); Cathy Weisbrod (National Adv./Admin. Supervisor)

THE LONDON FREE PRESS

Street address 1: 369 York St.
Street address city: London
Street address province or territory: ON
Postal code: N6A 4G1
Country: Canada
Mailing address: 369 York St.
Mailing city: London
Mailing province or territory: ON
Mailing code: N6A 4G1
General Phone: (519) 679-1111
General Fax: (519) 667-4523
Advertising Phone: (519) 679-1111
Advertising Fax: (519) 667-4523
Editorial Phone: (519) 679-1111
Editorial Fax: (519) 667-4620
General/National Adv. E-mail: carolyn.johnson@sunmedia.ca
Display Adv. E-mail: carolyn.johnson@sunmedia.ca
Classified Adv. e-mail: lfpress.classifieds@sunmedia.ca
Editorial e-mail: joe.ruscitti@sunmedia.ca
Primary Website: www.lfpress.com
Published: Mon`Tues`Wed`Thur`Fri`Sat
Avg Paid Circ: 34452
Avg Free Circ: 13264
Audit By: AAM
Audit Date: 30.06.2018
Personnel: Susan Muszak (Pub./CEO, Digital & Print); Lisa Catania Chiaramida (Adv. Dir.); Jerry Pilkey (Adv. Mgr., Retail); Chris Kubinski (Adv. Mgr., Auto/Real Estate); Jim Heaven (Adv. Mgr., Digital); Sherri Scott (Circ. Dir., Reader Sales/Serv./Mktg.); Joe Ruscitti (Ed.-in-Chief); Howard Burns (News Ed.); Glen Besley (Mgmt. Info Servs. Mgr.); John Pacitto (Dir., Operations); Sherri Walker (Dir., Reader Sales, Service & Mktg.)

NIAGARA FALLS REVIEW

Street address 1: 4424 Queen St
Street address city: Niagara Falls
Street address province or territory: ON
Postal code: L2E 2L3
Country: Canada
Mailing address: 4424 Queen St.
Mailing city: Niagara Falls
Mailing province or territory: ON
Mailing code: L2E 2L3
General Phone: (905) 358-5711
General Fax: (905)356-0785
Advertising Phone: (905) 358-5711
Advertising Fax: (905)356-0785
Editorial Phone: (905) 358-5711
Editorial Fax: (905) 374-0461
General/National Adv. E-mail: jumacdonald@postmedia.com
Display Adv. E-mail: jumacdonald@postmedia.com
Classified Adv. e-mail: niagarafallsreview.classifieds@sunmedia.com
Editorial e-mail: ascott@postmedia.com
Primary Website: www.niagarafallsreview.ca
Published: Mon`Tues`Wed`Thur`Fri`Sat
Avg Paid Circ: 7090
Avg Free Circ: 5864
Audit By: CCAB
Audit Date: 30.09.2015
Personnel: Michael Cressman (Pub.); Mark Smith (Adv. Mgr.); Steven Gallagher (Ed. in Chief); Cory Larocque (Mng. Ed.); Judy Bullis (Senior Group Pub.); Peter Conradi (Mng. Ed.)

NORTH BAY NUGGET

Street address 1: 259 Worthington St. W.
Street address city: North Bay
Street address province or territory: ON
Postal code: P1B 3B5
Country: Canada
Mailing address: 259 Worthington St. West
Mailing city: North Bay
Mailing province or territory: ON
Mailing code: P1B 3B5
General Phone: (705) 472-3200
General Fax: (705) 472-1438
Advertising Phone: (705) 472-3200
Advertising Fax: (705) 472-1438
Editorial Phone: (705) 472-3200
Editorial Fax: (705) 472-1438
General/National Adv. E-mail: rdawson@postmedia.com
Display Adv. E-mail: rdawson@postmedia.com
Classified Adv. e-mail: nugget.classifieds@sunmedia.ca
Editorial e-mail: msandford@postmedia.com
Primary Website: www.nugget.ca
Published: Mon`Tues`Wed`Thur`Fri`Sat
Avg Paid Circ: 7189
Avg Free Circ: 280
Audit By: CCAB
Audit Date: 30.09.2015
Personnel: Dan Johnson (Pub.); Bruce Cowan (Mng. Ed.); Steve Page (Adv. Dir.); Paul Chapman (Prodn. Mgr., Post Press); Steve Hevenor (Prodn. Foreman, Pressroom)

LE DROIT

Street address 1: 47 Rue Clarence, Bureau 222
Street address city: Ottawa
Street address province or territory: ON
Postal code: K1G 3J9
Country: Canada
Mailing address: C.P. 8860, Succ. T., 47 Rue Clarence, Bureau 222
Mailing city: Ottawa
Mailing province or territory: ON
Mailing code: K1G 9K1
General Phone: (613) 562-0111
General Fax: (613) 562-7572
Advertising Phone: (514) 285-6884
Advertising Fax: (613) 562-7539
Editorial Phone: (613) 562-0111
Editorial Fax: (613) 562-7539
General/National Adv. E-mail: production@ledroit.com
Display Adv. E-mail: production@ledroit.com
Classified Adv. e-mail: petitesannonces@ledroit.com
Editorial e-mail: tirage@ledroit.com
Primary Website: www.lapresse.ca/le-droit
Published: Mon`Tues`Wed`Thur`Fri`Sat
Avg Paid Circ: 27903
Avg Free Circ: 7334
Audit By: AAM
Audit Date: 31.03.2016
Personnel: Eric Brousseau (Sales & Mktg. Dir.); Pierre-Paul Noreau; Patrice Gaudreault (Editor-in-chief); Sylvie Charrette (Special Projects)

THE OTTAWA CITIZEN

Street address 1: 1101 Baxter Rd.
Street address city: Ottawa
Street address province or territory: ON
Postal code: K2C 3M4
Country: Canada
Mailing address: PO Box 5020
Mailing city: Ottawa
Mailing province or territory: ON
Mailing code: K2C 3M4
General Phone: (613) 829-9100
General Fax: (613) 726-5852
Advertising Phone: (613) 596-3590
Advertising Fax: (613) 726-5895
Editorial Phone: (613) 596-3664
Editorial Fax: (613) 726-1198
General/National Adv. E-mail: adinquiries@ottawacitizen.com
Display Adv. E-mail: adinquiries@ottawacitizen.com
Classified Adv. e-mail: ottawacitizen.com/placeanad
Editorial e-mail: copydesk@ottawacitizen.com
Primary Website: www.ottawacitizen.com
Published: Mon`Tues`Wed`Thur`Fri`Sat
Avg Paid Circ: 81103
Audit By: AAM
Audit Date: 31.03.2018
Personnel: Michelle Richardson (Ed.); Keith Bonnell (Dep. Ed.); Chris Aung-Thwin (Dep. Ed.); Drake Fenton (City Ed.); Christina Spencer (Ed. Page Ed.); Michelle Walters (Arts & Life Ed.); Patrick Brennan (SVP, Manufacturing); Shirley Tam (Dir. of Finance)

THE OTTAWA SUN

Street address 1: 1101 Baxter Road
Street address city: Ottawa
Street address province or territory: ON
Postal code: K2H 5B1
Country: Canada
Mailing city: Ottawa
Mailing province or territory: ON

General Phone: (613) 829-9100
Advertising Phone:»Advertising Fax:»Editorial Phone:»Editorial Fax:»General/National Adv. E-mail: jstewart@postmedia.com
Display Adv. E-mail: jstewart@postmedia.com
Classified Adv. e-mail: ottawasun.classifieds@sunmedia.ca
Editorial e-mail: mirichardson@postmedia.com
Primary Website: www.ottawasun.com
Published: Mon`Tues`Wed`Thur`Fri`Sat`Sun
Avg Paid Circ: 25923
Avg Free Circ: 8215
Audit By: CCAB
Audit Date: 30.11.2018
Personnel: Keith Bonnell (Editor); Michelle Richardson; Michelle Walters (Breaking News Editor); Drake Fenton (City Editor); Chris Aung-Thwin (Deputy Editor, Digital); Christina Spencer (Editorial Pages Editor)

OWENSOUND SUN TIMES

Street address 1: 290 9th St., East
Street address city: Owen Sound
Street address province or territory: ON
Postal code: N4K 5P2
Country: Canada
Mailing address: 290 9th St., East
Mailing city: Owen Sound
Mailing province or territory: ON
Mailing code: N4K 5P2
General Phone: (519) 376-2250
General Fax: (519) 372-1861
Advertising Phone: (519) 376-2250
Advertising Fax: (519) 372-1861
Editorial Phone: (519) 376-2250
Editorial Fax: (519) 372-1861
General/National Adv. E-mail: lkazarian@postmedia.com
Display Adv. E-mail: lkazarian@postmedia.com
Classified Adv. e-mail: owensoundsuntimes.classifieds@sunmedia.ca
Editorial e-mail: doug.edgar@sunmedia.ca
Primary Website: www.owensoundsuntimes.com
Published: Mon`Tues`Wed`Thur`Sat
Avg Paid Circ: 12884
Audit By: CMCA
Audit Date: 31.12.2013
Personnel: Cheryl McMenemy (Pub.); Louise Kazarian-Hodder (Adv. Dir.); Brent Radbourne (Circ. Mgr.); Doug Edgar (Mng. Ed.); Marie David (Grey Bruce Group Pub.)

OBSERVER & NEWS (PEMBROKE)

Street address 1: 186 Alexander Street
Street address city: Pembroke
Street address province or territory: ON
Postal code: K8A 4L9
Country: Canada
Mailing address: P.O. Box 190
Mailing city: Pembroke
Mailing province or territory: ON
Mailing code: K8A 4L9
General Phone: (613) 732-3691
General Fax: (613) 732-1022
Advertising Phone: (613) 732-3691
Advertising Fax: (613) 732-2645
Editorial Phone: (613) 732-3691
Editorial Fax: (613)732-1022
Display Adv. E-mail:»Classified Adv. e-mail:»Editorial e-mail: pem.editorial@sunmedia.ca
Primary Website: www.thedailyobserver.ca
Published: Tues`Wed`Thur`Fri`Sat
Avg Paid Circ: 4179
Avg Free Circ: 517
Audit By: BPA
Audit Date: 31.12.2012
Personnel: David Bell (Circ. Mgr.); Peter Lapinskie (Editorial Page Ed.); Lisa Bell (Prodn. Mgr., Mailroom); Jim Kwiatkowski (Pub./Adv. Mgr.)

THE PETERBOROUGH EXAMINER

Street address 1: 60 Hunter St., East
Street address city: Peterborough
Street address province or territory: ON
Postal code: K9H 1G5
Country: Canada
Mailing address: 60 Hunter St. East
Mailing city: Peterborough
Mailing province or territory: ON
Mailing code: K9H 1G5
General Phone: (705) 745-4641
General Fax: (705) 745-3361
Advertising Phone: (705) 745-4641
Advertising Fax: (705) 745-3361
Editorial Phone: (705) 745-4641
Editorial Fax: (705) 741-3217
General/National Adv. E-mail: dmurphy@postmedia.com
Display Adv. E-mail: dmurphy@postmedia.com
Classified Adv. e-mail: thepeterboroughexaminer.classifieds@sunmedia.ca
Editorial e-mail: kmgordon@postmedia.com
Primary Website: www.thepeterboroughexaminer.com
Published: Mon`Tues`Wed`Thur`Fri`Sat
Avg Paid Circ: 8642
Avg Free Circ: 7934
Audit By: CCAB
Audit Date: 30.09.2015
Personnel: Darren Murphy (Pub.); Jim Hendry (Mng. Ed.); Gerry Drage (Adv. Mgr.); Marg Knot (Circ. Mgr.); Stefanie Lynch (Buss. Mgr.); Cindy Jacobs (Class.); Wayne Willis (Prod. Supervisor)

ST. CATHARINES STANDARD

Street address 1: 10-1 St. Paul St.
Street address city: Saint Catharine's
Street address province or territory: ON
Postal code: L2R 7L4
Country: Canada
Mailing address: 10-1 St. Paul St.
Mailing city: Saint Catharine's
Mailing province or territory: ON
Mailing code: L2R 7L4
General Phone: (905) 684-7251
General Fax: (905) 684-6032
Advertising Phone: (905) 684-7251
Advertising Fax: (905) 684-6032
Editorial Phone: (905) 684-7251
Editorial Fax: (905) 684-6032
General/National Adv. E-mail: john.tobon@sunmedia.ca
Display Adv. E-mail: john.tobon@sunmedia.ca
Classified Adv. e-mail: classifieds@stcatharinesstandard.ca
Editorial e-mail: ascott@postmedia.com
Primary Website: www.stcatharinesstandard.ca
Published: Mon`Tues`Wed`Thur`Fri`Sat
Avg Paid Circ: 10425
Avg Free Circ: 9640
Audit By: AAM
Audit Date: 30.06.2016
Personnel: Mark Cressman (Pub.); Mike Thompson (Adv. Mgr.); Peter Conradi (Ed. in Chief); Erica Bajer (Mng. Ed.); Keith Matheson (Prodn. Mgr., Mailroom); Daria Zmiyiwsky (Reg. Promo. & Comm. Relations Dir.)

ST. THOMAS TIMES-JOURNAL

Street address 1: 16 Hincks St.
Street address city: Saint Thomas
Street address province or territory: ON
Postal code: N5R 5Z2
Country: Canada
Mailing address: 16 Hincks St.
Mailing city: Saint Thomas
Mailing province or territory: ON
Mailing code: N5R 5Z2
General Phone: (519) 631-2790
General Fax: (519) 631-5653
Advertising Phone: (519) 631-2790
Advertising Fax: (519) 631-5653
Editorial Phone: (519) 631-2790
Editorial Fax: (519) 631-5653
General/National Adv. E-mail: linda.leblanc@sunmedia.ca
Display Adv. E-mail: linda.leblanc@sunmedia.ca
Classified Adv. e-mail: st.thomastj.class@sunmedia.ca
Editorial e-mail: don.biggs@sunmedia.ca
Primary Website: www.stthomastimesjournal.com
Published: Mon`Tues`Wed`Thur`Fri`Sat
Avg Paid Circ: 4165
Avg Free Circ: 4694
Audit By: BPA
Audit Date: 30.12.2010
Personnel: Bev Ponton (Pub./Adv. Mgr.); Ian McCallum (Page Ed.); Linda LeBlanc (Pub./Adv. Mgr.); Julie Tapsell (Office Mgr.); Joe Belanger (Ed.); Mia Stainsby (Ed.); Stephen Tipper (Ed.)

THE OBSERVER (SARNIA)

Street address 1: 140 South Front St.
Street address city: Sarnia
Street address province or territory: ON
Postal code: N7T 7M8
Country: Canada
Mailing address: 140 South Front St.
Mailing city: Sarnia
Mailing province or territory: ON
Mailing code: N7T 7M8
General Phone: (519) 344-3641
General Fax: (519) 322-2961
Advertising Phone: (519) 344-3641
Advertising Fax: (519)322-2961
Editorial Phone: (519) 344-3641
Editorial Fax: (519) 332-2951
General/National Adv. E-mail: linda.leblanc@sunmedia.ca
Display Adv. E-mail: linda.leblanc@sunmedia.ca
Classified Adv. e-mail: theobserver.classifieds@sunmedia.ca
Editorial e-mail: pepp@postmedia.com
Primary Website: www.theobserver.ca
Published: Mon`Tues`Wed`Thur`Fri`Sat
Avg Paid Circ: 10501
Avg Free Circ: 118
Audit By: CCAB
Audit Date: 31.12.2013
Personnel: Linda Leblanc (Pub./Sales Dir.); Rod Hilts (Mng. Ed.); Barb Mcbride (Office Mgr.); Marc Roberts (Circ.); Gary Squire (Prod. Mgr.)

THE SAULT STAR

Street address 1: 145 Old Garden River Rd.
Street address city: Sault Sainte Marie
Street address province or territory: ON
Postal code: P6A 5M5
Country: Canada
Mailing address: 145 Old Garden River Road
Mailing city: Sault Sainte Marie
Mailing province or territory: ON
Mailing code: P6A 5M5
General Phone: (705) 759-3030
General Fax: (705) 759-5947
Advertising Phone: (705) 759-3030
Advertising Fax: (705) 759-5947
Editorial Phone: (705) 759-3030
Editorial Fax: (705) 759-5947
General/National Adv. E-mail: mkennedy@postmedia.com
Display Adv. E-mail: mkennedy@postmedia.com
Classified Adv. e-mail: saultstar.classifieds@sunmedia.ca
Editorial e-mail: frupnik@postmedia.com
Primary Website: www.saultstar.com
Published: Mon`Tues`Wed`Thur`Fri`Sat
Avg Paid Circ: 7569
Avg Free Circ: 266
Audit By: CCAB
Audit Date: 30.09.2015
Personnel: Lou Maulucci (Pres./Pub.); Frank Rupnik (Ed.); Jackie DePasquale (Mgr., Admin.); Mike Kennedy (Adv. Mgr.); Bruno Vit (Dir., Reader Sales/Serv.); Jeff Ougler (City Ed.); Steve Shooks (Data Processing Mgr.); Kevin Caron (Prodn. Mgr.); Gary Graham (Prodn. Foreman, Pressroom)

SIMCOE REFORMER

Street address 1: 50 Gilbertson Dr.
Street address city: Simcoe
Street address province or territory: ON
Postal code: N3Y 4L2
Country: Canada
Mailing address: 50 Gilbertson Dr.
Mailing city: Simcoe
Mailing province or territory: ON
Mailing code: N3Y 4L2
General Phone: (519) 426-5710
General Fax: (519) 426-9255
Advertising Phone: (519) 426-5710
Advertising Fax: (519) 426-9255
Editorial Phone: (519) 426-5710
Editorial Fax: (519) 426-9255
General/National Adv. E-mail: sdowns@bowesnet.com
Display Adv. E-mail: sdowns@bowesnet.com
Classified Adv. e-mail: simcoereformer.classifieds@sunmedia.ca
Editorial e-mail: knovak@postmedia.com
Primary Website: www.simcoereformer.ca
Published: Mon`Tues`Wed`Thur`Fri
Avg Paid Circ: 8950
Audit By: Sworn/Estimate/Non-Audited
Audit Date: 12.07.2019
Personnel: Ken Koyoma (Pub.); Kim Novak (Mng. Ed.); Sue Downs (Adv. Mgr.); Andrew Kiss (Circ. Mgr.); Andrew Foster (Circ.); Deb Campbell (Prod. Mgr.)

THE STRATFORD BEACON HERALD

Street address 1: 789 Eerie St.
Street address city: Stratford
Street address province or territory: ON
Postal code: N4Z 1A1
Country: Canada
Mailing address: 789 Eerie St.
Mailing city: Stratford
Mailing province or territory: ON
Mailing code: N4Z 1A1
General Phone: (519) 271-2222
General Fax: (519) 271-1026
Advertising Phone: (519) 271-2222
Advertising Fax: (519) 271-1031
Editorial Phone: (519) 271-2222
Editorial Fax: (519)271-1026
General/National Adv. E-mail: carmstrong@postmedia.com
Display Adv. E-mail: carmstrong@postmedia.com
Editorial e-mail: burquhart@postmedia.com
Primary Website: www.stratfordbeaconherald.com
Published: Mon`Tues`Wed`Thur`Fri`Sat
Avg Paid Circ: 6643
Avg Free Circ: 214
Audit By: Sworn/Estimate/Non-Audited
Audit Date: 12.07.2019
Personnel: Bruce Urquhart (Mng. Ed.); Barb Boyne (Circ. Mgr.); Janice Humphrey (Credit Mgr.); Leigh McCann (Prodn. Mgr.); Galen Simmons (Reporter); Cory Smith (Sports Editor); Terry Bridge; Jonathan Juha (Reporter); Curtis Armstrong (Advertising Director)

THE SUDBURY STAR

Street address 1: 128 Pine Street Suite 201
Street address city: Sudbury
Street address province or territory: ON
Postal code: P3C 1X3
Country: Canada
Mailing address: 128 Pine St., Suite 201
Mailing city: Sudbury
Mailing province or territory: ON
Mailing code: P3C 1X3
General Phone: (705) 674-5271
General Fax: (705) 674-0624
Advertising Phone: (705) 674-5271 ext. 505250
Advertising Fax: (705)674-0624
Editorial Phone: (705)674-5271 ext. 505232
Editorial Fax: (705)674-0624
General/National Adv. E-mail: kjohansen@postmedia.com
Display Adv. E-mail: kjohansen@postmedia.com
Classified Adv. e-mail: thesudburystar.classifieds@sunmedia.com
Editorial e-mail: dmacdonald@postmedia.com
Primary Website: www.thesudburystar.com
Published: Mon`Tues`Wed`Thur`Fri`Sat
Avg Paid Circ: 8399
Avg Free Circ: 175
Audit By: CCAB
Audit Date: 30.09.2015
Personnel: Karsten Johansen (Publisher / Ad Director); Dave Pacquett (Circ. Mgr.); Mary Valade (Office Mgr.); Don MacDonald (City Ed.); Andrew Low (News Ed.); Bruce Heidman (Sports Ed.); ???? ????; David Kilgour (Pub./Adv. Dir.)

THE CHRONICLE-JOURNAL

Street address 1: 75 S. Cumberland St.
Street address city: Thunder Bay
Street address province or territory: ON
Postal code: P7B 1A3
Country: Canada
Mailing address: 75 S. Cumberland St.
Mailing city: Thunder Bay
Mailing province or territory: ON
Mailing code: P7B 1A3
General Phone: (807) 343-6200
General Fax: (807) 345-5991
Advertising Phone: (807) 343 6219
Advertising Fax: (807) 345-3582
Editorial Phone: (807) 343-6215
Editorial Fax: (807) 343-9409
General/National Adv. E-mail: skabir@chroniclejournal.com
Display Adv. E-mail: skabir@chroniclejournal.com

Classified Adv. e-mail: classifieds@chroniclejournal.com
Editorial e-mail: editor@chroniclejournal.com
Primary Website: www.chroniclejournal.com
Published: Mon`Tues`Wed`Thur`Fri`Sat`Sun
Avg Paid Circ: 13672
Avg Free Circ: 4648
Audit By: AAM
Audit Date: 30.06.2018
Personnel: Colin J. Bruce (Pub.); Greg Giddens (Managing Ed.); Hilda Caverly (Dir., Finance); Clint Harris (Pub./GM); Harry Brown (Circ. Dir.); Ian Pattison (Editorial Page Ed.); Joanne Kushnier (News Ed.); John Nagy (Sports Ed.); Dave Wadson (Systems/Traffic Mgr.); Joe St. Lawrence (Prodn. Foreman, Pressroom); Julio Gomes (Mng. Ed.); Steve Benoit (Mgr., Adv.)

THE TIMMINS DAILY PRESS

Street address 1: Virtual/Remote
Street address city: Timmins
Street address province or territory: ON
Postal code: P4N 7G1
Country: Canada
Mailing address: 187 Cedar St. South
Mailing city: Timmins
Mailing province or territory: ON
Mailing code: P4N 7G1
General Phone: (705) 268-5050
General Fax: (705) 268-7373
Advertising Phone: (705) 268-5050
Advertising Fax: (705) 268-7373
Editorial Phone: (705) 268-5050
Editorial Fax: (705) 268-7373
General/National Adv. E-mail: tdp.advertising@sunmedia.ca
Display Adv. E-mail: tdp.advertising@sunmedia.ca
Classified Adv. e-mail: timminspress.classifieds@sunmedia.ca
Editorial e-mail: tperry@postmedia.com
Primary Website: www.timminspress.com
Published: Tues`Thur`Sat
Avg Paid Circ: 6634
Avg Free Circ: 481
Audit By: BPA
Audit Date: 30.12.2010
Personnel: Lisa Wilson (Pub.); Thomas Perry (Mng. Ed.); Wayne Snider (City Ed.); Gio Crispo (Circ. Mgr.); Anne Laferriere (Adv. Mgr.); Dean Lessard (Circ. Mgr.)

NATIONAL POST

Street address 1: 365 Bloor St East
Street address city: Toronto
Street address province or territory: ON
Postal code: M4W3L4
Country: Canada
Mailing city: Toronto
Mailing province or territory: ON
General Phone: (416) 383-2300
General Fax: (416) 442-2209
Advertising Phone: (800) 668-5617
Advertising Fax: (416) 386-2696
Editorial Phone: (416) 383-2300
Editorial Fax: (416) 383-2443
General/National Adv. E-mail: queries@nationalpost.com
Display Adv. E-mail: advqueries@nationalpost.com
Editorial e-mail:»Primary Website: www.nationalpost.com
Published: Mon`Tues`Wed`Thur`Fri`Sat
Avg Paid Circ: 125674
Audit By: AAM
Audit Date: 30.09.2018
Personnel: Anne Marie Owens (Editor); Craig Barnard (SVP, Community Publishing Group + Reader Sales + Service); Gerry Nott (Senior VP, National Post); Paula Festas (Chief Revenue Officer); Gordon Fisher (President)

THE EPOCH TIMES

Street address 1: 344 Consumers Rd
Street address city: Toronto
Street address province or territory: ON
Postal code: M2J 1P8
Country: Canada
Mailing address: 344 Consumers Rd.
Mailing city: Toronto
Mailing province or territory: ON
Mailing code: M2J 1P8
General Phone: (416) 298-1933
General Fax: (416) 298-1299
Advertising Phone: (416) 986-3525
Advertising Fax: (416) 298-1299
Editorial Phone: (416) 298-1933
Editorial Fax: (416) 298-1299
General/National Adv. E-mail: canada_ads@epochtimes.com
Display Adv. E-mail: canada_ads@epochtimes.com
Classified Adv. e-mail: ethan.guo@epochtimes.com
Editorial e-mail: newsdesk@epochtimes.com
Primary Website: www.theepochtimes.com/#ca
Published: Mon`Tues`Wed`Thur`Fri`Sat`Sun
Avg Paid Circ: 0
Avg Free Circ: 15889
Audit By: CCAB
Audit Date: 20.12.2017
Personnel: Leah Lan (Senior Director of Sales Development)

THE GLOBE AND MAIL

Street address 1: 351 King St. E.
Street address 2: Suite 1600
Street address city: Toronto
Street address province or territory: ON
Postal code: M5A 0N1
Country: Canada
Mailing address: 351 King St. E. Suite 1600
Mailing city: Toronto
Mailing province or territory: ON
Mailing code: M5A 0N1
General Phone: (416) 585-5000
General Fax: (416) 585-5698
Advertising Phone: 416-585-5600
Advertising Fax: 888-391-0122
Editorial Fax:»General/National Adv. E-mail: advertising@globeandmail.com
Classified Adv. e-mail:»Editorial e-mail: newsroom@globeandmail.com
Primary Website: www.theglobeandmail.com
Published: Mon`Tues`Wed`Thur`Fri`Sat
Avg Paid Circ: 119426
Avg Free Circ: 1817
Audit By: AAM
Audit Date: 30.09.2021
Personnel: Sylvia Stead (Public Ed.); Natasha Hassan (Commentary Ed.); Andrew Gorham (Globe Review Ed.); David Walmsley (Ed.-in-Chief); Sean Humphrey (VP, Mktg.); Moe Doiron (Photo Ed.); Andrew Saunders (CRO); Michael Babad (Report on Bus. Ed.); Perry Nixdorf (VP, Operations)

TORONTO STAR

Street address 1: 1 Yonge St.
Street address city: Toronto
Street address province or territory: ON
Postal code: M5E 1E6
Country: Canada
Mailing address: 1 Yonge St.reet
Mailing city: Toronto
Mailing province or territory: ON
Mailing code: M5E 1E6
General Phone: (416) 367-2000
General Fax: (416) 869-4328
Advertising Phone: (416) 777-7777
Advertising Fax: 416-814-3270
Editorial Phone: (416) 869-4300
Editorial Fax: (416) 869-4328
General/National Adv. E-mail: adinfo@thestar.ca
Display Adv. E-mail: adinfo@thestar.ca
Classified Adv. e-mail: starad@thestar.ca
Editorial e-mail: lgentle@thestar.ca
Primary Website: www.thestar.com/?redirect=true
Published: Mon`Tues`Wed`Thur`Fri`Sat`Sun
Avg Paid Circ: 119943
Avg Free Circ: 116827
Audit By: CCAB
Audit Date: 24.11.2017
Personnel: John Cruickshank (Pub.); Michael Cooke (Ed. in Chief); Irene Gentle (Managing Ed.); Paula Sinclair (CIO, Metroland & Star Media Group, Group IT, Torstar Corporation); Peter Bishop (VP & CFO); Sandy Muir (VP, Adv.); Norm Laing (Adv. Grp. Dir., Home/Automotive/Sports/Entertainment); Carolyn Sadler (Adv. Grp. Dir., Nat'l/Technology); Jim Fahey (Adv. Mgr., Mktg. Research/Info); Robin Graham (Adv. Mgr., Syndicate); Sandy MacLeod (Vice Pres., Mktg.); Terry Willows (Dir. Cir.); Brenda Yarwood (Circ. Mgr., Home Delivery); Dean Zavarise (EVP-Torstar Printing Group); John Ferri (Asst. Mng. Ed., Entertainment/Life); Lorne Silver (Dir., Creative Mktg.); Jane Davenport (Mng. Ed.)

TORONTO SUN

Street address 1: 365 Bloor St. E., 6th Floor
Street address city: Toronto
Street address province or territory: ON
Postal code: M4W 3L4
Country: Canada
Mailing address: 365 Bloor St. E., 6th Floor
Mailing city: Toronto
Mailing province or territory: ON
Mailing code: M4W 3L4
General Phone: (416) 947-2222
General Fax: (416) 368-0374
Advertising Phone: (416) 947-2333
Advertising Fax: (416) 947-3139
Editorial Phone: (416) 947-2211
Editorial Fax: (416) 947-1664
General/National Adv. E-mail: torsun.retail@sunmedia.ca
Display Adv. E-mail: torsun.retail@sunmedia.ca
Classified Adv. e-mail: torontosun.classifieds@sunmedia.ca
Editorial e-mail: torsun.citydesk@sunmedia.ca
Primary Website: www.torontosun.com
Published: Mon`Tues`Wed`Thur`Fri`Sat`Sun
Avg Paid Circ: 86462
Avg Free Circ: 32869
Audit By: CCAB
Audit Date: 30.09.2015
Personnel: Kevin Hann (Deputy Editor); Chris Krygiel (Cor. Dir., HR); Lorrie Goldstein (Sr. Assoc. Ed.); Andrew Donato (Cartoonist); Robin Robinson (Travel Ed.); Bill Pierce (Sports Ed.); Kevin Williamson (Corporate Entertainment Editor); Rita DeMontis (Lifestyle/Food Ed.); Julie Kirsh (News Research Dept.); Richard Roy (VP & CIO, Info Serv.); Darren Murphy (Vice President, Advertising Sales); Lesley Annett (Sales Director/Director of Promotion); Piero Menicucci (Vice President, Finance); Christina Fleming (Executive Assistant to the Publisher); Adrienne Batra (Comment Editor); Mike Power (Pub.); Steve Angelevski (Corporate VP, Reader Sales & Services); Bill Bratt (Adv. Dir.)

WELLAND TRIBUNE

Street address 1: 228 East Main St.
Street address city: Welland
Street address province or territory: ON
Postal code: L3B 5P5
Country: Canada
Mailing address: P.O. Box 278
Mailing city: Welland
Mailing province or territory: ON
Mailing code: L3B 5P5
General Phone: (905) 732-2411
General Fax: (905) 732-4883
Advertising Phone: (905) 732-2411
Advertising Fax: (905) 732-0965
Editorial Phone: (905) 732-2411
Editorial Fax: (905) 732-3660
General/National Adv. E-mail: aldo.donofrio@sunmedia.ca
Display Adv. E-mail: aldo.donofrio@sunmedia.ca
Classified Adv. e-mail: placeit.sun@sunmedia.ca
Editorial e-mail: ascott@postmedia.com
Primary Website: www.wellandtribune.ca
Published: Mon`Tues`Wed`Thur`Fri`Sat
Avg Paid Circ: 8347
Avg Free Circ: 7308
Audit By: CCAB
Audit Date: 31.12.2013
Personnel: John Tobon (Pub.); Julia Coles (Adv. Dir.); Dan Dakin (Mng. Ed.); Karin Vanderzee (Circ. Mgr.); Bernd Frank (Sports Ed.); Judy Bullis (Senior Group Pub.); Lydia Kinos (Prod. Mgr.)

WOODSTOCK SENTINEL-REVIEW

Street address 1: 1269 Commerce Way, Unit 4
Street address city: Woodstock
Street address province or territory: ON
Postal code: N4V 0A2
Country: Canada
Mailing address: 1269 Commerce Way, Unit 4
Mailing city: Woodstock
Mailing province or territory: ON
Mailing code: N4V 0A2
General Phone: (519) 537-2341
General Fax: (519) 537-8542
Advertising Phone: (519) 537-2341
Advertising Fax: (519) 537-8542
Editorial Phone: (519) 537-2341
Editorial Fax: (519) 537-8542
General/National Adv. E-mail: burquhart@postmedia.com
Display Adv. E-mail: www.postmediasolutions.com/contact-us/
Classified Adv. e-mail: www.postmediasolutions.com/contact-us/
Editorial e-mail: burquhart@postmedia.com
Primary Website: www.woodstocksentinelreview.com
Published: Tues`Thur`Fri
Avg Paid Circ: 6000
Avg Free Circ: 31000
Audit By: Sworn/Estimate/Non-Audited
Audit Date: 12.07.2019
Personnel: Andrea Demeer (Pub.); Bruce Urquhart (Ed.); Rosaline Bruyns (Adv. Mgr.); Cory Smith (Sports Ed.); Debbie Campbell (Prodn. Mgr.); Mike Sissing (Circ. Mgr)

PRINCE EDWARD ISLAND

THE GUARDIAN

Street address 1: 165 Prince St.
Street address city: Charlottetown
Street address province or territory: PE
Postal code: C1A 4R7
Country: Canada
Mailing address: PO Box 760
Mailing city: Charlottetown
Mailing province or territory: PE
Mailing code: C1A 4R7
General Phone: (902) 629-6000
General Fax: (902) 566-3808
Advertising Phone: (902) 629-6068
Advertising Fax: (902) 566-9830
Editorial Phone: (902) 629-6039
Editorial Fax: (902) 566-3808
General/National Adv. E-mail: twilson@theguardian.pe.ca√É¬É£√É¬Ç√Ç¬†
Display Adv. E-mail: twilson@theguardian.pe.ca
Classified Adv. e-mail: class@theguardian.pe.ca
Editorial e-mail: newsroom@theguardian.pe.ca
Primary Website: www.theguardian.pe.ca
Published: Mon`Tues`Wed`Thur`Fri`Sat
Avg Paid Circ: 11672
Avg Free Circ: 251
Audit By: CCAB
Audit Date: 20.12.2017
Personnel: Don Brander (Pub.); Ron Kelly (Bus. Mgr.); Heather Tedford (Adv. Dir.); Ron Lund (Dir., Reader Sales & Dist.); Gary J. MacDougall (Mng. Ed.); Bill McGuire (Editorial Page Ed.); Carolyn Drake (Features Ed.); Wayne Thibodeau (News Ed.); Jason Malloy (Sports Ed.)

THE JOURNAL PIONEER

Street address 1: 316 Water St.
Street address city: Summerside
Street address province or territory: PE
Postal code: C1N 4K5
Country: Canada
Mailing address: PO Box 2480
Mailing city: Summerside
Mailing province or territory: PE
Mailing code: C1N 4K5
General Phone: (902) 436-2121
General Fax: (902) 436-3027
Advertising Phone: (902) 432-8238
Advertising Fax: (902) 436-0784
Editorial Phone: (902) 432-8216
Editorial Fax: (902) 436-3027
General/National Adv. E-mail: newsroom@journalpioneer.com
Display Adv. E-mail: newsroom@journalpioneer.com
Classified Adv. e-mail: newsroom@journalpioneer.com
Editorial e-mail: bworks@journalpioneer.com
Primary Website: www.journalpioneer.com
Published: Mon`Tues`Wed`Thur`Fri`Sat
Avg Paid Circ: 4211
Avg Free Circ: 27

Audit By: CCAB
Audit Date: 30.12.2017
Personnel: Sandy Rundle (Pub./GM); Paul Ramsay (Adv. Mgr.); Ron Lund (Dir., Reader Sales/Serv.); Jason Simmonds (Sports Ed.); Brad Works (Managing Editor); Ed Kennedy (Circ. Dir.); Jason Matheson (Prod. Supervisor); Mike Turner (Mng. Ed.)

QUEBEC

LA PRESSE

Street address 1: 750 boul. St-Laurent
Street address city: Montreal
Street address province or territory: QC
Postal code: H2Y 1K9
Country: Canada
Mailing address: 7 Rue St. Jacques
Mailing city: Montreal
Mailing province or territory: QC
Mailing code: H2Y 2Z4
General Phone: (514) 285-7000
Advertising Phone: (514) 285-6874
Editorial Phone: (514) 285-7070
General/National Adv. E-mail: communication@lapresse.ca
Classified Adv. e-mail:»Editorial e-mail: forum@lapresse.ca
Primary Website: www.lapresse.ca
Published: Mon`Tues`Wed`Thur`Fri`Sat`Sun
Avg Free Circ: 263624
Audit By: AAM
Audit Date: 31.12.2018
Personnel: Guy Crevier (Pub.); Jacques Tousignant (Vice Pres., Personnel/Labor Rel.); Caroline Jamet (Vice Pres., Commun.); Philippe-Denis Richard (Asst. to Pres./Legal Counsel); Robert Julien (Controller); Yves Lalonde (Adv. Dir., Retail); Jean Durocher (Vice Pres., Mktg.); Christiane Dube (Dir., Promo.); Jocelyn Godbout (Circ. Dir.); Philippe Cantin (Vice Pres./Ed.); Eric Trottier (Mng. Ed.); Jocelyne Lepage (Books Ed.); Andre Pratte (Editorial Dir.); Marie Allard (Educ. Ed.); Jon Sebastian Gagmom (Finance Ed.); Claude Gingras (Music Ed., Classical); Alain Brunet (Music Ed., Pop); Gilles Toupin (Ottawa Bureau); Benoit Giguere (Photo Ed.)

LE DEVOIR

Street address 1: 1265 Berri, 8th Floor
Street address city: Montreal
Street address province or territory: QC
Postal code: H2K 4X4
Country: Canada
Mailing address: 1265 Berri, 8th Floor
Mailing city: Montreal
Mailing province or territory: QC
Mailing code: H2X 4X4
General Phone: (514) 985-3333
General Fax: (514) 985-3360
Advertising Phone: (514) 985-3399
Advertising Fax: (514) 985-3390
Editorial Phone: (514)985-3333
Editorial Fax: (514) 985-3360
General/National Adv. E-mail: lmillette@ledevoir.com
Display Adv. E-mail: lmillette@ledevoir.com
Classified Adv. e-mail: petitesannonces@ledevoir.com
Editorial e-mail: redaction@ledevoir.com
Primary Website: www.ledevoir.com
Published: Mon`Tues`Wed`Thur`Fri`Sat`Sun
Avg Paid Circ: 8996
Audit By: AAM
Audit Date: 31.03.2019
Personnel: Bernard Descoteaux (Pub.); Catherine Laberge (Vice Pres., Bus./Finance); Jose Chriffaro (Dir., Promo.); Carolyn Simard (Circ. Dir.); Josee Boileau (Ed. in Chief); Gerard Berube (Economics Ed.); Michel Belair (Cultural Pages); Christian Goulet (Prodn. Dir.); Roland-Yves Carignan (Info. Mgr.); Lise Millette (VP, Adv. Sales); Vincent Spiridigliozzi (Asst. Sales Mgr.)

LE JOURNAL DE MONTREAL

Street address 1: 4545 Rue Frontenac
Street address city: Montreal
Street address province or territory: QC
Postal code: H2H 2R7
Country: Canada
Mailing address: 4545 Rue Frontenac
Mailing city: Montreal
Mailing province or territory: QC
Mailing code: H2H 2R7
General Phone: (514) 521-4545
General Fax: (514) 521-4416
Advertising Phone: (514) 521-4545
Advertising Fax: (514)521-4416
Editorial Phone: (514) 521-4545
Editorial Fax: (514)521-4416
General/National Adv. E-mail: Marc.Couture@quebecormedia.com
Display Adv. E-mail: Marc.Couture@quebecormedia.com
Classified Adv. e-mail: classees@quebecoremedia.com
Editorial e-mail: jdq-scoop@quebecormedia.com
Primary Website: www.journaldemontreal.com
Published: Mon`Tues`Wed`Thur`Fri`Sat`Sun
Avg Paid Circ: 158423
Avg Free Circ: 74585
Audit By: CCAB
Audit Date: 30.09.2015
Personnel: Lyne Robipaille (Pres./Pub.); Gilles Lamoureux (Adv. Mgr.); Denise Lareau (VP, Comm. & Promo.); Christianne Benjamin (Circ. Mgr.); Dany Doucet (Ed.-in-Chief); Serge LaBrosse (News Ed.); Denis Poissant (Sports Ed.); Luc Trudel (Data Processing Mgr.); Marie Andre Lessard (Audiotex Mgr., Servs.); Denis Tetrault (VP, Prodn.); Marc Bourassa (VP, Sales); Andre Phaneuf (Dir., Research & Mktg.)

MONTREAL GAZETTE

Street address 1: 1010 Sainte-Catherine St. W.
Street address 2: Suite 200
Street address city: Montreal
Street address province or territory: QC
Postal code: H3B 5L1
Country: Canada
Mailing city:»Mailing province or territory:»Mailing code:»General Phone: (514) 987-2222
General Fax: (514) 987-2270
Advertising Phone: (514) 987-2350
Advertising Fax: (514) 987-2380
Editorial Fax:»General/National Adv. E-mail: gazadv@montrealgazette.com
Display Adv. E-mail: gazadv@montrealgazette.com
Classified Adv. e-mail: classifieds@montrealgazette.com
Primary Website: www.montrealgazette.com
Published: Mon`Tues`Wed`Thur`Fri`Sat
Avg Paid Circ: 56064
Audit By: AAM
Audit Date: 31.03.2018
Personnel: Mario Belluscio (Dir., Finance, Postmedia); Donna Dudka (Mgr, Admin,Äì Eastern Region); Giancarlo Lanzetta (Dir., Integrated Adv.); David Klimek (Research Manager); St√©phane Le Gal (Regional Vice-President, Advertising - Eastern Canada); Charlene Assels (Director, Integrated Adv. & Strategy, 3i); Lucinda Chodan (Editor, Montreal Gazette & Vice-President, Editorial, Eastern Region, Postmedia); Sean Duckett (Manager, Advertising Sales); Jeff Blond (Executive Producer, Print); Edie Austin (Editorial Page Editor); June Thompson (Newsroom Administrator); Yves Levasseur

LE SOLEIL

Street address 1: 410 Blvd. Charest East
Street address city: Quebec
Street address province or territory: QC
Postal code: G1K 7J6
Country: Canada
Mailing address: PO Box 1547, Succ. Terminus
Mailing city: Quebec
Mailing province or territory: QC
Mailing code: G1K 7J6
General Phone: (418) 686-3233
General Fax: (418) 686-3225
Advertising Phone: (418) 686-3435
Advertising Fax: (418) 686-3260
Editorial Phone: (418) 686-3209
Editorial Fax: (418) 686-3374
Display Adv. E-mail: marketing@lesoleil.com
Editorial e-mail: redaction@lesoleil.com
Primary Website: www.lesoleil.ca
Published: Mon`Tues`Wed`Thur`Fri`Sat`Sun
Avg Paid Circ: 66826
Avg Free Circ: 10993
Audit By: AAM
Audit Date: 31.03.2016
Personnel: Claude Daniel (Pres.); Gilles Ouellet (Bus. Mgr.); Therese Cote (Supvr.); Louis Gendron (VP, Adv.); Andre-Philippe Cote (Cartoonist); Pierre-Paul Noreau (Editorial Page Ed.); Yves Bellefleur (Librarian); Daphne Bedard (Music Ed.); Michel Samson (Online Ed.); Gilles Angers (Real Estate); Maurice Dumas (Sports Dir.); Raymond Tardif (Travel Ed.); Gilles Garneau (Prodn. Dir.); Line Baillargeon (Prodn. Mgr., Graphic Arts); Claude Gagnon (Pub./Pres. & Ed.); Benoit Jobin (VP, Circ.); Patrick Paluck (Prod. Mgr.)

LE QUOTIDIEN

Street address 1: 1051, Boul. Talbot
Street address city: Saguenay
Street address province or territory: QC
Postal code: G7H 5C1
Country: Canada
Mailing address: 1051, Boul. Talbot
Mailing city: Saguenay
Mailing province or territory: QC
Mailing code: G7H 5C1
General Phone: (418) 545-4474
General Fax: (418) 690-8805
Advertising Phone: (418) 549-4444
Advertising Fax: (418) 690-8824
Editorial Phone: (418) 545-4474
Editorial Fax: (418) 690-8805
General/National Adv. E-mail: annonces@lequotidien.com
Display Adv. E-mail: annonces@lequotidien.com
Classified Adv. e-mail: classees@lequotidien.com
Editorial e-mail: redaction@lequotidien.com
Primary Website: www.lapresse.ca/le-quotidien/
Published: Mon`Tues`Wed`Thur`Fri`Sat`Sun
Avg Paid Circ: 22816
Avg Free Circ: 2735
Audit By: AAM
Audit Date: 31.03.2016
Personnel: Michel Simard (Pub.); Linda Cantin (Dir. Sales & Mktg.); Denis Bouchard (Ed. in Chief); Francois St-Gelais (Info. Mgr.); Bernard Bellei (Prodn. Mgr., Distr.); Jean Simard (Prod./Circ. Mgr.); Sylvaine Tremblay (Prod. Dir.)

LA TRIBUNE

Street address 1: 1950 Rue Roy
Street address city: Sherbrooke
Street address province or territory: QC
Postal code: J1K 2X8
Country: Canada
Mailing address: 1950 Rue Roy
Mailing city: Sherbrooke
Mailing province or territory: QC
Mailing code: J1K 2X8
General Phone: (819) 564-5450
General Fax: (819) 564-5480
Advertising Phone: (819) 564-5450
Advertising Fax: (819) 564-5482
Editorial Phone: (819) 564-5454
Editorial Fax: (819) 564-8098
General/National Adv. E-mail: latribune@latribune.qc.ca
Display Adv. E-mail: latribune@latribune.qc.ca
Classified Adv. e-mail: latribune@latribune.qc.ca
Editorial e-mail: latribune@latribune.qc.ca
Primary Website: www.cyberpresse.ca
Published: Mon`Tues`Wed`Thur`Fri`Sat`Sun
Avg Paid Circ: 23507
Audit By: AAM
Audit Date: 31.03.2017
Personnel: Louis Boisvert (Pres./Ed.); Alain LeClerc (Adv. Asst. Mgr.); Andre Custeau (Circ. Mgr.); Louis Eric Allard (Newsroom Dir.); Renee Marquis (Photo Dept. Mgr.); Andre Laroche (Radio/Television Ed.); Sonia Bolduc (Sports Ed.); Andre Roberge (Prodn. Mgr.); Steve Rancourt (Asst. Prod. Mgr.); Rene Beliveau (Prod. Mgr.); Louise Boisvert (Pub & Pres.); Maurice Cloutier (Ed.-in-Chief); Sylvain Denault (Adv. Dir.)

THE RECORD

Street address 1: 1195 Galt East
Street address city: Sherbrooke
Street address province or territory: QC
Postal code: J1H 1Y7
Country: Canada
Mailing address: 1195 Galt East
Mailing city: Sherbrooke
Mailing province or territory: QC
Mailing code: J1H 1Y7
General Phone: (819) 569-9525
General Fax: (819) 821-3179
Advertising Phone: (819) 569-9511
Advertising Fax: (819) 821-3179
Editorial Phone: (819) 569-6345
Editorial Fax: (819) 821-3179
Display Adv. E-mail:»Classified Adv. e-mail: classad@sherbrookerecord.com
Editorial e-mail: newsroom@sherbrookerecord.com
Primary Website: www.sherbrookerecord.com
Published: Mon`Tues`Wed`Thur`Fri
Avg Paid Circ: 4392
Audit By: AAM
Audit Date: 30.09.2011

LE NOUVELLISTE

Street address 1: 1920 rue Bellefeuille
Street address city: Trois-Rivieres
Street address province or territory: QC
Postal code: G9A 3Y2
Country: Canada
Mailing address: PO Box 668
Mailing city: Trois-Rivieres
Mailing province or territory: QC
Mailing code: G9A 3Y2
General Phone: (819) 376-2501
General Fax: (819) 376-0946
Advertising Fax:»Editorial Phone:»Editorial Fax:»General/National Adv. E-mail:»Display Adv. E-mail: pub@lenouvelliste.qc.ca
Editorial e-mail: information@lenouvelliste.qc.ca
Primary Website: www.lapresse.ca/le-nouvelliste
Published: Mon`Tues`Wed`Thur`Fri`Sat
Avg Paid Circ: 31123
Avg Free Circ: 4755
Audit By: AAM
Audit Date: 31.03.2016
Personnel: Marc Auger (Mgr., Personnel); Yves Neault (Adv. Dir.); Ginette Panneton (Mktg./Promo. Dir.); Patrick Glassom (Circ. Mgr.); Marc Rochette (Ed.); Stephen Frappier (Ed.-in-Chief); Raymond Pitre (Prodn. Mgr.); Pierre Cote (Prodn. Mgr., Printing); Raymond Tardif (Pres./Ed.); Alain Turcotte (Pres./Ed.)

LE JOURNAL DE QUEBEC

Street address 1: 450 Bechard Ave.
Street address city: Vanier
Street address province or territory: QC
Postal code: G1M 2E9
Country: Canada
Mailing address: 450 Bechard Ave.
Mailing city: Vanier
Mailing province or territory: QC
Mailing code: G1M 2E9
General Phone: (418) 683-1573
General Fax: (418) 683-8886
Advertising Fax: (418) 683-1027
Editorial Fax: (418) 688-8181
Display Adv. E-mail:»Classified Adv. e-mail:»Editorial e-mail:»Primary Website: www.journaldequebec.com
Published: Mon`Tues`Wed`Thur`Fri`Sat`Sun
Avg Paid Circ: 76585
Avg Free Circ: 44206
Audit By: CCAB
Audit Date: 20.11.2017
Personnel: Andre Berube (Vice Pres., Finance); Louis Ouellet (Controller); Daniel Houde (Adv. Vice Pres., Sales); Pierre Villeneuve (Mgr., Promo.); Marc Couture (Circ. Mgr.); Karen Vezilleneube (Entertainment Ed.); Donald Charette (Gen. Ed.); Louis Chretien (Data Processing Mgr.); Jean Pierre Robitaille (VP, Adv.); Maurice Vezina (Prodn. Mgr., Pre Press); Ulric Kusik (Prodn. Mgr., Pressroom); Louise Cordeau (Pub.); Georges Leveille (Circ. Mgr.); Sebastian Menard (Ed.-in-chief)

SASKATCHEWAN

PRINCE ALBERT DAILY HERALD

Street address 1: 30 10th St E
Street address city: Prince Albert
Street address province or territory: SK
Postal code: S6V 0Y5
Country: Canada
Mailing address: 30-10th St E
Mailing city: Prince Albert
Mailing province or territory: SK
Mailing code: S6V 0Y5
General Phone: (306) 764-4276
General Fax: (306) 922-4237

Advertising Phone: (306) 764-4276
Editorial Phone: (306) 764-4276
General/National Adv. E-mail: accounting@paherald.sk.ca
Display Adv. E-mail: ebergen@paherald.sk.ca
Classified Adv. e-mail: classifieds@paherald.sk.ca
Editorial e-mail: edotorial@paherald.sk.ca
Primary Website: www.paherald.sk.ca
Published: Tues`Wed`Thur`Fri`Sat`Mthly
Avg Paid Circ: 2500
Avg Free Circ: 27525
Audit By: Sworn/Estimate/Non-Audited
Audit Date: 01.10.2011
Personnel: Donna Pfeil (Pub.); Peter Lozinski (Managing Ed.); Jason Kerr (Editor); Lucas Punkari (Sports Ed.); Erin Bergen (Marketing Mgr.)

REGINA LEADERPOST

Street address 1: 1964 Park St.
Street address city: Regina
Street address province or territory: SK
Postal code: S4P 3G4
Country: Canada
Mailing address: PO Box 2020
Mailing city: Regina
Mailing province or territory: SK
Mailing code: S4P 3G4
General Phone: (306) 781-5211
General Fax: (306) 565-2588
Advertising Phone: (306) 781-5251
Advertising Fax: (306) 781-5350
Editorial Phone: (306) 781-5300
Editorial Fax: (306) 565-2588
General/National Adv. E-mail: advertising@leaderpost.com
Display Adv. E-mail: advertising@leaderpost.com
Classified Adv. e-mail: classifieds@leaderpost.com
Editorial e-mail: letters@leaderpost.com
Primary Website: www.leaderpost.com
Published: Mon`Tues`Wed`Thur`Fri`Sat
Avg Paid Circ: 15027
Avg Free Circ: 7429
Audit By: AAM
Audit Date: 31.03.2019
Personnel: Heather Persson (Ed.); Tim Switzer (Managing Ed.); Barb Pacholik; Austin Davis (Digital Co-ordinator)

SASKATOON STARPHOENIX

Street address 1: 204 5th Ave. N.
Street address city: Saskatoon
Street address province or territory: SK
Postal code: S7K 2P1
Country: Canada
Mailing address: 204 5th Ave. N.
Mailing city: Saskatoon
Mailing province or territory: SK
Mailing code: S7K 2P1
General Phone: (306) 657-6397
General Fax: (306) 657-6437
Advertising Phone: (306) 657-6340
Advertising Fax: (306) 657-6208
Editorial Phone: (306) 657-6231
Editorial Fax: (306) 657-6437
General/National Adv. E-mail: mluczka@postmedia.com
Display Adv. E-mail: mluczka@thestarphoenix.com
Classified Adv. e-mail: sdyck@thestarphoenix.com
Editorial e-mail: letters@thestarphoenix.com
Primary Website: www.thestarphoenix.com
Published: Mon`Tues`Wed`Thur`Fri`Sat
Avg Paid Circ: 17635
Avg Free Circ: 9867
Audit By: AAM
Audit Date: 31.03.2019
Personnel: Rob McLaughlin (Pub./Ed. in Chief); Rick Fraser (VP., Adv. Sales); Jeff Golding (Prod. Mgr.); Mark Kotellnikof (Circ. Dir.); Sharon Wacker (Mgr., HR); Heather Persson (Ed)

YUKON

WHITEHORSE STAR

Street address 1: 2149 2nd Ave.
Street address city: Whitehorse
Street address province or territory: YT
Postal code: Y1A 1C5
Country: Canada
Mailing address: 2149 2nd Ave.
Mailing city: Whitehorse
Mailing province or territory: YT
Mailing code: Y1A 1C5
General Phone: (867) 668-2002
General Fax: (867) 668-7130
Advertising Phone: (867) 668-2060
Advertising Fax: (867) 668-7130
Editorial Phone: (867) 667-4481
Editorial Fax: (867) 668-7130
General/National Adv. E-mail: advertising@whitehorsestar.com
Display Adv. E-mail: advertising@whitehorsestar.com
Classified Adv. e-mail: classifieds@whitehorsestar.com
Editorial e-mail: editor@whitehorsestar.com
Primary Website: www.whitehorsestar.com
Published: Mon`Tues`Wed`Thur`Fri
Avg Paid Circ: 912
Avg Free Circ: 123
Audit By: AAM
Audit Date: 31.03.2019
Personnel: Jackie Pierce (Pub.); Michele Pierce (Adv./Sales Mgr.); John Stuckey (Circ. Mgr.); Jim Butler (Editor); Vince Fedoroff (Photo Ed.); Eric Murphy (Wire Ed); Don Campbell (Head Pressman); Joni Pierce (Circulation Assistant); Chuck Tobin (Reporter); Stephanie Waddle (Reporter); Emily Blake (Reporter); Taylor Blewett (Reporter); McKayla Morgan (Advertising Rep.); Pat Wilson (Accounts)
Parent company (for newspapers): Whitehorse Star (77) Ltd.

Section II

Community & Niche Newspapers in the U.S. and Canada

COMMUNITY UNITED STATES NEWSPAPER

ALABAMA

ABBEVILLE HERALD

Street address 1: 135 Kirkland St
Street address city: Abbeville
Street address state: AL
Zip/Postal code: 36310-2113
General Phone: (334) 585-2331
General Fax: (334) 585-6835
General/National Adv. E-mail: heraldadv@centurytel.net
Editorial e-mail: heraldnews@centurytel.net
Primary Website: No Website
Year Established: 1912
Avg Paid Circ: 2350
Audit By: Sworn/Estimate/Non-Audited
Audit Date: 10.06.2019
Personnel: J. Edward Dodd (Ed.)

ALABAMA MESSENGER

Street address 1: 2100 1st Avenue North
Street address 2: Ste 240
Street address city: Birmingham
Street address state: AL
Zip/Postal code: 35203-3673
General Phone: (205) 252-3672
General Fax: (205) 252-3679
General/National Adv. E-mail: alamsgr@bellsouth.net
Editorial e-mail: alamsgr@bellsouth.net
Primary Website: alabamamessenger.com
Year Established: 1918
Avg Paid Circ: 1500
Avg Free Circ: 75
Audit By: Sworn/Estimate/Non-Audited
Audit Date: 10.06.2019
Personnel: Karen W. Abercrombie (Pub. / Gen. Mgr.); Traci Smeraglia (Mng. Ed.)

ALABASTER REPORTER

Street address 1: 115 N Main St
Street address city: Columbiana
Street address state: AL
Zip/Postal code: 35051-5359
General Phone: (205) 669-3131
General Fax: (205) 669-4217
General/National Adv. E-mail: news@shelbycountyreporter.com
Primary Website: alabasterreporter.com
Year Established: 1843
Avg Paid Circ: 7997
Avg Free Circ: 24500
Audit By: Sworn/Estimate/Non-Audited
Audit Date: 10.06.2019
Personnel: Matthew Allen (Adv. Mgr.); Tim Prince (Ed.); Jan Grissey (News Ed.)
Parent company (for newspapers): Boone Newspapers, Inc.; Shelby County Newspapers, Inc

ALASKA STAR

Street address 1: 11401 Old Glenn Hwy
Street address 2: Ste 105
Street address city: Eagle River
Street address state: AK
Zip/Postal code: 99577-7747
General Phone: (907) 694-2727
General Fax: (907) 694-1545
General/National Adv. E-mail: jada.nowling@morris.com
Editorial e-mail: cinthia.ritchie@alaskastar.com
Primary Website: alaskastar.com
Avg Paid Circ: 4800
Audit By: Sworn/Estimate/Non-Audited
Audit Date: 10.06.2019
Personnel: Cinthia Ritchie (Ed.); Jada Nowling (Adv. Media Consultant)

ATMORE ADVANCE

Street address 1: 301 S Main St
Street address city: Atmore
Street address state: AL
Zip/Postal code: 36502-2436
General Phone: (251) 368-2123
General Fax: (251) 368-2124
General/National Adv. E-mail: newsroom@atmoreadvance.com
Display Adv. E-mail: advertising@atmoreadvance.com
Primary Website: atmoreadvance.com
Avg Paid Circ: 3100
Avg Free Circ: 6000
Audit By: Sworn/Estimate/Non-Audited
Audit Date: 10.06.2019
Personnel: Allison Knowles (Circ. Mgr.); Andrew Garner (Editor); Blake Bell (Pres./Pub.)
Parent company (for newspapers): Boone Newspapers, Inc.

ATMORE NEWS

Street address 1: 128 S Main St
Street address city: Atmore
Street address state: AL
Zip/Postal code: 36502-2446
General Phone: (251) 368-6397
General Fax: (251) 368-3397
General/National Adv. E-mail: myrna@atmorenews.com
Display Adv. E-mail: myrna@atmorenews.com
Classified Adv. e-mail: myrna@atmorenews.com
Editorial e-mail: sherry@atmorenews.com
Primary Website: atmorenews.com
Year Established: 2005
Avg Paid Circ: 1300
Avg Free Circ: 50
Audit By: Sworn/Estimate/Non-Audited
Audit Date: 10.06.2019
Personnel: Myrna Monroe (Co-owner.); Sherry Digmon (Co-Pub.); Don Fletcher (Staff Writer); Ditto Gorme (Composing)

AUBURN VILLAGER

Street address 1: 687 N Dean Rd
Street address city: Auburn
Street address state: AL
Zip/Postal code: 36830-4044
General Phone: (334) 501-0600
General Fax: (334) 826-7700
Advertising Phone: (334) 501-0600
Advertising Fax: (334) 826-7700
General/National Adv. E-mail: dawn@auburnvillager.com
Editorial e-mail: editorial@auburnvillager.com
Primary Website: auburnvillager.com
Year Established: 2006
Avg Paid Circ: 3000
Avg Free Circ: 1000
Audit By: Sworn/Estimate/Non-Audited
Audit Date: 10.06.2019
Personnel: Allison Blankenship (Assoc. Ed); Brian Woodham (Assoc Ed); Rhonda Fields (Accts. Mgr.); Lance Radermacher (Advert. Mgr)

BIRMINGHAM BUSINESS JOURNAL

Street address 1: 2140 11th Ave S
Street address 2: Ste. 205
Street address city: Birmingham
Street address state: AL
Zip/Postal code: 35205-2840
General Phone: (205) 443-5600
General Fax: (205) 322-0040
Advertising Phone: (205) 443-5617
General/National Adv. E-mail: jwelker@bizjournals.com
Editorial e-mail: ccrawford@bizjournals.com
Primary Website: bizjournals.com/birmingham
Audit By: Sworn/Estimate/Non-Audited
Audit Date: 10.06.2019
Personnel: Joel Welker (Pres./Pub.); Cindy Crawford (Editor); Ty West (Ed.-in-chief); Ryan Phillips (Digital Prod.); Dan Bagwell (Research Dir); Derek Morrow (Prod. Dir); Ginger Gardner Aarons (Audience Dev Dir); Courtney Sanak (Events Mgr); Jana Branch (Business Mgr); Beth Hoff (Credit Mgr); Stephanie Rebman (Mng. Ed.)
Parent company (for newspapers): American City Business Journals

BLACKBELT GAZETTE

Street address 1: 115 E Washington St
Street address city: Demopolis
Street address state: AL
Zip/Postal code: 36732-2101
General Phone: (334) 289-2013
General Fax: (334) 289-4019
General/National Adv. E-mail: jeanne.glass@demopolistimes.com
Display Adv. E-mail: clara.gary@demopolistimes.com
Primary Website: demopolistimes.com/category/blackbelt-gazette
Audit By: Sworn/Estimate/Non-Audited
Audit Date: 10.06.2019
Personnel: Robert Bankenship (Pub. Ed.); Jeanne Glass (Adv. and Mktg. Rep.); Nicholas Finch (Sports Ed. & Staff Writer)
Parent company (for newspapers): Boone Newspapers, Inc.

CALL NEWS

Street address 1: 7870 State St
Street address city: Citronelle
Street address state: AL
Zip/Postal code: 36522-2486
General Phone: (251) 866-5998
General Fax: (251) 866-5981
Advertising Phone: (251) 866-5998
Advertising Fax: (251) 866-5981
General/National Adv. E-mail: callnews@bellsouth.net
Primary Website: thecallnews.com
Avg Paid Circ: 4550
Audit By: Sworn/Estimate/Non-Audited
Audit Date: 10.06.2019
Personnel: Willie Gray (Pub.); Rhonda Gray (Office Mgr.); William Gray (Adv. Mgr.)

CHEROKEE COUNTY HERALD

Street address 1: 100 E Main St
Street address city: Centre
Street address state: AL
Zip/Postal code: 35960-1517
General Phone: (256) 927-5037
General Fax: (256) 927-4853
General/National Adv. E-mail: vrobinson@cherokeeherald.com
Display Adv. E-mail: vrobinson@cherokeeherald.com
Editorial e-mail: tdean@cherokeeherald.com
Primary Website: cherokeeherald.com
Year Established: 1938
Avg Paid Circ: 2594
Avg Free Circ: 5872
Audit By: Sworn/Estimate/Non-Audited
Audit Date: 10.06.2019
Personnel: Terry Dean (Pub./Ed.); Buddie Norton (Layout Ed); Shannon Fagan (Sports Ed); Brenda Burger (Classified/Legal); Vickie Robinson (Adv. Mgr.)
Parent company (for newspapers): Rome News-Tribune

CHILKAT VALLEY NEWS

Street address 1: PO Box 630
Street address city: Haines
Street address state: AK
Zip/Postal code: 99827-0630
General Phone: (907) 766-2688
Advertising Phone: (907) 766-2688
General/National Adv. E-mail: cvn@chilkatvalleynews.com
Display Adv. E-mail: cvn@chilkatvalleynews.com
Editorial e-mail: cvn@chilkatvalleynews.com
Primary Website: chilkatvalleynews.com
Year Established: 1966
Avg Paid Circ: 1200
Avg Free Circ: 11
Audit By: Sworn/Estimate/Non-Audited
Audit Date: 10.06.2019
Personnel: Bonnie Hedrick (Pub.)

CHILTON COUNTY NEWS

Street address 1: 1203 7th St S
Street address city: Clanton
Street address state: AL
Zip/Postal code: 35045-3723
General Phone: (205) 755-0110
General/National Adv. E-mail: newscc@bellsouth.net; oltuck@bellsouth.net
Primary Website: beachbecky.com
Avg Paid Circ: 3000
Audit By: Sworn/Estimate/Non-Audited
Audit Date: 10.06.2019
Personnel: Robert M. Tucker (Ed.); Ben Tucker (Adv. Mgr.)

CHOCTAW SUN-ADVOCATE

Street address 1: PO Box 269
Street address 2: 13440 Choctaw Ave
Street address city: Gilbertown
Street address state: AL
Zip/Postal code: 36908-0269
General Phone: (251) 843-6397
General Fax: (251) 843-3233
General/National Adv. E-mail: choctawsun@millry.net
Primary Website: choctawsun.com
Mthly Avg Views: 55000
Mthly Avg Unique Visitors: 18500
Year Established: 1890
Avg Paid Circ: 4800
Audit By: Sworn/Estimate/Non-Audited
Audit Date: 10.06.2019
Personnel: Tommy Campbell (Publisher/Advertising Manager); Dee Ann Campbell (Editor)

CLARKE COUNTY DEMOCRAT

Street address 1: 261 N Jackson St
Street address city: Grove Hill
Street address state: AL
Zip/Postal code: 36451-3073
General Phone: (251) 275-3375
General Fax: (251) 275-3060
General/National Adv. E-mail: jimcox@tds.net
Editorial e-mail: jimcox@tds.net
Primary Website: clarkecountydemocrat.com
Year Established: 1856
Avg Paid Circ: 3700
Audit By: Sworn/Estimate/Non-Audited
Audit Date: 10.06.2019
Personnel: James A. Cox (Ed.); Jim Cox (Pub.)

CLAY TIMES-JOURNAL

Street address 1: 60132 Hwy 49
Street address city: Lineville
Street address state: AL
Zip/Postal code: 36266
General Phone: (256) 396-5760
General/National Adv. E-mail: claytimes97@gmail.com
Editorial e-mail: timesjournal97@gmail.com
Primary Website: claytimesjournal.com
Avg Paid Circ: 3800
Avg Free Circ: 99
Audit By: Sworn/Estimate/Non-Audited
Audit Date: 10.06.2019
Personnel: David Proctor (Ed.); Justin McCullers (Adv. Mgr.)

CLAYTON RECORD

Street address 1: 12 Eufaula Avenue
Street address city: Clayton
Street address state: AL

Zip/Postal code: 36016
General Phone: (334) 775-3254
General Fax: (334) 775-8554
General/National Adv. E-mail: advertising@claytonrecord.com
Primary Website: theclaytonrecordonline.com
Year Established: 1870
Avg Paid Circ: 2500
Audit By: Sworn/Estimate/Non-Audited
Audit Date: 10.06.2019
Personnel: Blake Gumprecht (Ed./Pub.)

COLBERT COUNTY REPORTER

Street address 1: 106 W 5th St
Street address city: Tuscumbia
Street address state: AL
Zip/Postal code: 35674-2412
General Phone: (256) 383-8471
General Fax: (256) 383-8476
General/National Adv. E-mail: colbertcountyreporter@earthlink.net
Primary Website: facebook.com/thecolbertcountyreporter
Avg Paid Circ: 4500
Audit By: Sworn/Estimate/Non-Audited
Audit Date: 10.06.2019
Personnel: Charlie Crawford (Adv. Mgr.); Jim Crawford (Ed.); Estelle Crawford-Whitehead (Mng. Ed.)

COOSA COUNTY NEWS

Street address 1: 10 Main St
Street address city: Rockford
Street address state: AL
Zip/Postal code: 35136
General Phone: (256) 377-2525
General Fax: (256) 377-2422
Editorial e-mail: editor@coosanews.com
Primary Website: facebook.com/coosacountynews
Avg Paid Circ: 1400
Avg Free Circ: 300
Audit By: Sworn/Estimate/Non-Audited
Audit Date: 10.06.2019
Personnel: Lewis Scarbrough (Owner); Carlton Jones (Pub. / Mgn. Ed. / Adv. mgr.)

COURIER JOURNAL

Street address 1: 219 W Tennessee St
Street address city: Florence
Street address state: AL
Zip/Postal code: 35630-5440
General Phone: (256) 764-4268
General Fax: (256) 760-9618
Advertising Phone: (256) 740-4701
Advertising Fax: (256) 760-9618
Editorial Phone: (256) 740-4701
Editorial Fax: (256) 760-9618
General/National Adv. E-mail: sadonna@courierjournal.net
Display Adv. E-mail: sadonna@courierjournal.net
Editorial e-mail: editor@courierjournal.net
Primary Website: courierjournal.net
Year Established: 1884
Avg Paid Circ: 19
Avg Free Circ: 73211
Audit By: CVC
Audit Date: 31.12.2018
Personnel: Thomas V. Magazzu (Pub./Ed.); Sadonna B. Magazzu (Adv. Mgr.); Jane Brasfield (Circ. Mgr.)
Parent company (for newspapers): Tennessee Valley Media Co., Inc.

DADEVILLE RECORD

Street address 1: 548 Cherokee Rd
Street address city: Alexander City
Street address state: AL
Zip/Postal code: 35010-2503
General Phone: (256) 234-4281
General Fax: (256) 234-6550
Advertising Phone: (256) 234-4281 x15
Editorial Phone: (256) 234-4281 x22
General/National Adv. E-mail: tippy.hunter@alexcityoutlook.com
Display Adv. E-mail: linda.ewing@alexcityoutlook.com
Editorial e-mail: virginia.spears@alexcityoutlook.com
Primary Website: alexcityoutlook.com
Avg Paid Circ: 1600
Audit By: Sworn/Estimate/Non-Audited
Audit Date: 10.06.2019
Personnel: Kenneth Boone (Pub.); Mary Lyman (Bookkeeper); Tippy Hunter (Adv. Rep.); David Kendrick; Cathy Higgins (Sports Ed.)
Parent company (for newspapers): Boone Newspapers, Inc.

DEMOPOLIS TIMES

Street address 1: 315 E Jefferson St
Street address city: Demopolis
Street address state: AL
Zip/Postal code: 36732-2255
General Phone: (334) 289-4017
General Fax: (334) 289-4019
Advertising Phone: (334) 289-4017
Advertising Fax: (334) 289-4019
Editorial Phone: (334) 289-4017
Editorial Fax: (334) 289-4019
General/National Adv. E-mail: hannah.riley@demopolistimes.com
Display Adv. E-mail: hannah.riley@demopolistimes.com
Classified Adv. e-mail: bernice.smith@demopolistimes.com
Editorial e-mail: news@demopolistimes.com
Primary Website: demopolistimes.com
Year Established: 1887
Avg Paid Circ: 2850
Sat. Circulation Paid: 2850
Sun. Circulation Paid: 2850
Audit By: Sworn/Estimate/Non-Audited
Audit Date: 10.06.2019
Personnel: Jason Cannon (Pub.); Bernice Smith (Gen. Mgr.); Jeremy Smith (Sports Ed.)
Parent company (for newspapers): Boone Newspapers, Inc.

DOTHAN PROGRESS

Street address 1: 227 N Oates St
Street address city: Dothan
Street address state: AL
Zip/Postal code: 36303-4555
General Phone: (334) 792-3141
General Fax: (334) 702-6043
General/National Adv. E-mail: advertising@dothaneagle.com
Display Adv. E-mail: classifieds@dothaneagle.com
Editorial e-mail: lgriffin@dothaneagle.com
Primary Website: dothaneagle.com
Avg Paid Circ: 25000
Audit By: Sworn/Estimate/Non-Audited
Audit Date: 10.06.2019
Personnel: Steve Smith (Pub.); Jerry Morgan (Regl. Sales Dir.); Elaine Brackin (Ed.); Kelly Bexley (Prodn. Mgr.); Lance Griffin (Mng. Ed.)
Parent company (for newspapers): BH Media Group

EAST LAUDERDALE NEWS

Street address 1: 1617 Lee St
Street address city: Rogersville
Street address state: AL
Zip/Postal code: 35652-7606
General Phone: (256) 247-5565
General Fax: (256) 247-1902
General/National Adv. E-mail: elnewsrog@aol.com
Primary Website: https://facebook.com/eastlauderdalenews
Avg Paid Circ: 4500
Audit By: Sworn/Estimate/Non-Audited
Audit Date: 10.06.2019
Personnel: Phyllis D. Cox (Co-Pub.); James B. Cox (Ed.)

ECLECTIC OBSERVER

Street address 1: 300 Green St
Street address city: Wetumpka
Street address state: AL
Zip/Postal code: 36092-2507
General Phone: (334) 567-7811
General Fax: (334) 567-3284
General/National Adv. E-mail: advertising@thewetumpkaherald.com
Display Adv. E-mail: shannon.elliott@wetumpkaherald.com
Editorial e-mail: kim.price@thewetumpkaherald.com
Primary Website: thewetumpkaherald.com/theeclecticobserver
Avg Paid Circ: 1200
Avg Free Circ: 100
Audit By: Sworn/Estimate/Non-Audited
Audit Date: 10.06.2019
Personnel: Kim Price (Pub.); Peggy Blackburn (Mng. Ed.); David Goodwin (Ed.); Shannon Elliott (Classified Adv. Mgr.)
Parent company (for newspapers): Boone Newspapers, Inc.

EUFAULA TRIBUNE

Street address 1: 514 E Barbour St
Street address city: Eufaula
Street address state: AL
Zip/Postal code: 36027-1704
General Phone: (334) 687-3506
General Fax: (334) 687-3229
General/National Adv. E-mail: dshelley@alsmg.com
Display Adv. E-mail: dshelley@alsmg.com
Editorial e-mail: editor@eufaulatribune.com
Primary Website: eufaulatribune.com
Year Established: 1929
Avg Paid Circ: 3500
Audit By: Sworn/Estimate/Non-Audited
Audit Date: 10.06.2019
Personnel: Dennis Shelley (Adv. Sales Rep.); Kyle Mooty (Gen. Mgr.)
Parent company (for newspapers): BH Media Group; World Media Enterprises Inc.

FRANKLIN COUNTY TIMES

Street address 1: 14131 Highway 43
Street address city: Russellville
Street address state: AL
Zip/Postal code: 35653-2847
General Phone: (256) 332-1881
General Fax: (256) 332-1883
Advertising Phone: (256) 332-1881 ext. 19
Editorial Phone: (256) 332-1881 ext. 16
General/National Adv. E-mail: nicole.pell@franklincountytimes.com
Display Adv. E-mail: nicole.pell@franklincountytimes.com
Editorial e-mail: kellie.singleton@franklincountytimes.com
Primary Website: franklincountytimes.com
Year Established: 1879
Avg Paid Circ: 3800
Audit By: Sworn/Estimate/Non-Audited
Audit Date: 10.06.2019
Personnel: Kellie Singleton (Ed.); Peggy Hyde (Adv. Mgr.); Nicole Pell (General Manager)
Parent company (for newspapers): Boone Newspapers, Inc.

FRONTIERSMAN

Street address 1: 5751 E Mayflower Ct
Street address city: Wasilla
Street address state: AK
Zip/Postal code: 99654-7880
General Phone: (907) 352-2250
General Fax: (907) 352-2277
Advertising Phone: (907) 352-2291
Editorial Phone: (907) 352-2268
General/National Adv. E-mail: tawni.davis@frontiersman.com
Display Adv. E-mail: classads@frontiersman.com
Editorial e-mail: sports@frontiersman.com
Primary Website: frontiersman.com
Mthly Avg Views: 400000
Mthly Avg Unique Visitors: 125000
Year Established: 1947
Avg Paid Circ: 1925
Avg Free Circ: 2352
Sun. Circulation Paid: 2689
Audit By: AAM
Audit Date: 30.06.2017
Personnel: Mike Jensen (Pub.); Jeremiah Bartz (Sports Ed.); Tawni Davis; Christy Pinkerton (Circ. Mgr.)
Parent company (for newspapers): Wick Communications

GADSDEN MESSENGER

Street address 1: 408 Broad St
Street address city: Gadsden
Street address state: AL
Zip/Postal code: 35901-3718
General Phone: (256) 547-1049
General Fax: (256) 547-1011
General/National Adv. E-mail: cmccarthy@gadsdenmessenger.com
Editorial e-mail: info@gadsdenmessenger.com
Primary Website: gadsdenmessenger.com
Avg Paid Circ: 8000
Audit By: Sworn/Estimate/Non-Audited
Audit Date: 10.06.2019
Personnel: Art Segers (Adv. Dir.); Keith Reason (Ed.)

GENEVA COUNTY REAPER

Street address 1: 506 S Commerce St
Street address city: Geneva
Street address state: AL
Zip/Postal code: 36340-2421
General Phone: (334) 684-2280
General Fax: (334) 684-3099
General/National Adv. E-mail: ads@genevareaper.com
Editorial e-mail: news@genevareaper.com
Primary Website: oppnewsonline.com
Year Established: 1899
Avg Paid Circ: 2500
Audit By: Sworn/Estimate/Non-Audited
Audit Date: 10.06.2019
Personnel: Brenda Pujol (Pub.); Jay Felsberg (Ed.)

GREENE COUNTY INDEPENDENT

Street address 1: 106 Main St
Street address city: Eutaw
Street address state: AL
Zip/Postal code: 35462-1104
General Phone: (205) 372-2232
General Fax: (205) 372-2232
General/National Adv. E-mail: greenecoind@aol.com
Primary Website: facebook.com/Greene-County-Independent-Inc-233365326677345
Year Established: 1986
Avg Paid Circ: 1500
Avg Free Circ: 19
Audit By: Sworn/Estimate/Non-Audited
Audit Date: 10.06.2019
Personnel: Betty C. Banks (Ed.); J. William McFarland (Special Reporter)

GREENSBORO WATCHMAN

Street address 1: 505 College St
Street address city: Greensboro
Street address state: AL
Zip/Postal code: 36744
General Phone: (334) 624-8323
General Fax: (334) 624-8327
Advertising Phone: 205-602-2627
Editorial Phone: 205-602-2627
General/National Adv. E-mail: greensborowatchman@gmail.com
Display Adv. E-mail: greensborowatchman@gmail.com
Classified Adv. e-mail: greensborowatchman@gmail.com
Editorial e-mail: greensborowatchman@gmail.com
Primary Website: greensborowatchman.com
Year Established: 1876
Avg Paid Circ: 3000
Audit By: Sworn/Estimate/Non-Audited
Audit Date: 10.06.2024
Personnel: Willie Jean Lowry Arrington (Ed.); John Clark (Publisher and Editor); Becky Johnson (Pub.); Waymon Johnson (Adv. Dir.)

HARTFORD NEWS-HERALD

Street address 1: 506 S Commerce St
Street address city: Geneva
Street address state: AL
Zip/Postal code: 36340-2421
General Phone: (334) 684-2280
General Fax: (334) 684-3099
General/National Adv. E-mail: ads@genevareaper.com
Editorial e-mail: news@genevareaper.com
Primary Website: oppnewsonline.com
Avg Paid Circ: 2500
Audit By: Sworn/Estimate/Non-Audited
Audit Date: 10.06.2019
Personnel: Brenda Pujol (Pub.); Jay Felsberg (Ed.)

HARTSELLE ENQUIRER

Street address 1: 407 Chestnut St NW
Street address city: Hartselle
Street address state: AL
Zip/Postal code: 35640-2407
General Phone: (256) 773-6566
General Fax: (256) 773-1953
General/National Adv. E-mail: randy.garrison@hartselleenquirer.com

Display Adv. E-mail: classifieds@hartselleenquirer.com
Editorial e-mail: news@hartselleenquirer.com
Primary Website: hartselleenquirer.com
Mthly Avg Views: 83949
Mthly Avg Unique Visitors: 19300
Year Established: 1933
Avg Paid Circ: 3100
Avg Free Circ: 3500
Audit By: Sworn/Estimate/Non-Audited
Audit Date: 10.06.2019
Personnel: Randy Cox (Pub.)
Parent company (for newspapers): Boone Newspapers, Inc.

HOMER NEWS

Street address 1: 3482 Landings St
Street address city: Homer
Street address state: AK
Zip/Postal code: 99603-7948
General Phone: (907) 235-7767
General Fax: (907) 235-4199
Editorial e-mail: news@homernews.com
Primary Website: homernews.com
Year Established: 1964
Audit By: Sworn/Estimate/Non-Audited
Audit Date: 10.06.2019
Personnel: Michael Armstrong (Ed.); Megan Pacer (Reporter)
Parent company (for newspapers): CherryRoad Media

JOURNAL RECORD

Street address 1: 401 State Highway 17
Street address city: Hamilton
Street address state: AL
Zip/Postal code: 35570-1477
General Phone: (205) 921-3104
General Fax: (205) 921-3105
General/National Adv. E-mail: jrads@centurytel.net
Editorial e-mail: jrpaper@centurytel.net
Primary Website: myjrpaper.com
Year Established: 1970
Avg Paid Circ: 5841
Avg Free Circ: 126
Audit By: Sworn/Estimate/Non-Audited
Audit Date: 10.06.2019
Personnel: Horace Moore (Pub.); Kristi White (Adv. Mgr.); Les Walters (Mgn. Ed.); Matthew Puckett (Managing Editor); Scott Johnson (News Editor); Michael Palmer (Staff Writer); Logan Meador (Ad Composition); Mandye Green (Staff Writer); Teresa Gray (Office Manager/Classifieds); Whitley Burroughs (Advertisement)
Parent company (for newspapers): Mid South Newspaper, Inc.

JUNEAU EMPIRE

Street address 1: 3100 Channel Drive
Street address city: Juneau
Street address state: AK
Zip/Postal code: 99801-7837
General Phone: (907) 586-3740
General Fax: (907) 586-9097
Editorial Phone: (907) 523-2263
General/National Adv. E-mail: editor@capweek.com
Editorial e-mail: editor@capweek.com
Primary Website: juneauempire.com
Year Established: 1980
Avg Free Circ: 30000
Audit By: Sworn/Estimate/Non-Audited
Audit Date: 10.06.2019
Personnel: Terry Ward (Pub.); Emily Russo Miller (Ed.); Greg McEwen (Circ. Mgr.)
Parent company (for newspapers): Sound Publishing, Inc.

LAFAYETTE SUN

Street address 1: 116 S Lafayette St
Street address city: Lafayette
Street address state: AL
Zip/Postal code: 36862-2044
General Phone: (334) 864-8885
General Fax: (334) 864-8310
General/National Adv. E-mail: advertising@thelafayettesun.com
Display Adv. E-mail: ledge@thelafayettesun.com
Editorial e-mail: mhand@thelafayettesun.com
Primary Website: thelafayettesun.com
Year Established: 1880
Avg Paid Circ: 2605
Avg Free Circ: 33
Audit By: Sworn/Estimate/Non-Audited
Audit Date: 10.06.2019
Personnel: Michael D. Hand (Ed. / Pub.); Lisa Edge (Gen. Mgr.); Kendra Gilmore (Adv. Mgr.)

LAMAR LEADER

Street address 1: 55071 Highway 17
Street address city: Sulligent
Street address state: AL
Zip/Postal code: 35586-3800
General Phone: (205) 698-8148
General Fax: (205) 698-8146
General/National Adv. E-mail: news@lamarleader.com
Display Adv. E-mail: news@lamarleader.com
Editorial e-mail: news@lamarleader.com
Primary Website: facebook.com/lamar.leader
Year Established: 1973
Avg Paid Circ: 3000
Audit By: Sworn/Estimate/Non-Audited
Audit Date: 10.06.2019
Personnel: Stephanie Minor (Ed.); Keith Bryson (Publisher, News Editor)
Parent company (for newspapers): Lamar Publishing, Inc.

LOWNDES SIGNAL

Street address 1: 118 Ellis Street
Street address city: Fort Deposit
Street address state: AL
Zip/Postal code: 36032
General Phone: (334) 382-3111
General Fax: (334) 382-7104
General/National Adv. E-mail: tracy.salter@greenvilleadvocate.com/
Display Adv. E-mail: tracy.branum@greenvilleadvocate.com
Editorial e-mail: andy.brown@greenvilleadvocate.com
Primary Website: lowndessignal.com
Avg Paid Circ: 1900
Audit By: Sworn/Estimate/Non-Audited
Audit Date: 10.06.2019
Personnel: Lea Fennell (Office Mgr.); Tracy Salter (Adv. Mgr.); Andy Brown (Managing Ed.)
Parent company (for newspapers): Boone Newspapers, Inc.

MARION TIMES-STANDARD

Street address 1: 424 Washington St
Street address city: Marion
Street address state: AL
Zip/Postal code: 36756-2334
General Phone: (334) 683-6318
General Fax: (334) 683-4616
Advertising Phone: (334) 683-6318
Editorial e-mail: mariontimesnews@qwestoffice.net
Primary Website: facebook.com/MarionTimesStandard
Year Established: 1839
Avg Paid Circ: 2000
Avg Free Circ: 25
Audit By: Sworn/Estimate/Non-Audited
Audit Date: 10.06.2019
Personnel: Robert E. Tribble (Pres.); Lorrie Rinehart (Pub.); Kimberly Clements (Adv. Mgr.)
Parent company (for newspapers): Trib Publications

MOUNDVILLE TIMES

Street address 1: 46 2ND AVE
Street address city: Moundville
Street address state: AL
Zip/Postal code: 35474
General Phone: (205) 371-2488
General Fax: (205) 371-2788
Editorial Fax: (205) 371-9010
General/National Adv. E-mail: times@mound.net
Primary Website: moundvilletimes.net
Avg Paid Circ: 1300
Audit By: Sworn/Estimate/Non-Audited
Audit Date: 10.06.2019
Personnel: Larry Taylor (Pub.); Cindy Bolling (Ed.)

NORTH JACKSON PROGRESS

Street address 1: 128 Oak Hill Cir
Street address city: Stevenson
Street address state: AL
Zip/Postal code: 35772-5411
General Phone: (256) 437-2395
General Fax: (256) 437-2592
General/National Adv. E-mail: njprogresslog@aol.com
Primary Website: No Website
Avg Paid Circ: 6000
Audit By: Sworn/Estimate/Non-Audited
Audit Date: 10.06.2019
Personnel: Larry O. Glass (Ed. / Pub.); Faye Glass (News Ed.)

NORTH JEFFERSON NEWS

Street address 1: 1110 Main St.
Street address city: Gardendale
Street address state: AL
Zip/Postal code: 35071
General Phone: (205) 631-8716
General Fax: (205) 631-9902
Advertising Phone: (205) 631-8716
Editorial Phone: (205) 631-8716
General/National Adv. E-mail: sadams@njeffersonnews.com
Editorial e-mail: editor@njeffersonnews.com
Primary Website: njeffersonnews.com
Year Established: 1970
Avg Paid Circ: 2310
Audit By: Sworn/Estimate/Non-Audited
Audit Date: 10.06.2019
Personnel: Bill Morgan (Pub.); Sam Mazzara (Circ. Mgr.); Danielle Cater (Gen. Mgr.); Melanie Patterson (Ed.); Stephen Adams (Sales); Rachel Davis (Ed.)
Parent company (for newspapers): CNHI, LLC

NORTHWEST ALABAMIAN

Street address 1: 1530 21st St
Street address city: Haleyville
Street address state: AL
Zip/Postal code: 35565-2099
General Phone: (205) 486-9461
General Fax: (205) 486-4849
General/National Adv. E-mail: news@mynwapaper.com
Display Adv. E-mail: ads@mynwapaper.com
Classified Adv. e-mail: mike@mynwapaper.com
Editorial e-mail: news@mynwapaper.com
Primary Website: mynwapaper.com
Year Established: 1915
Avg Paid Circ: 7500
Audit By: Sworn/Estimate/Non-Audited
Audit Date: 10.06.2019
Personnel: Mike Moore (Gen. Mgr.); Horace Moore (Editor/Publisher); Roger Carden (Adv. Mgr.); Shelly Hess (Mng. Ed.); Phillip Brooks (Prodn. Mgr.); Melica Allen (Advertising Director)
Parent company (for newspapers): Mid-South Newspapers, Inc.

PELHAM REPORTER

Street address 1: 115 N Main St
Street address city: Columbiana
Street address state: AL
Zip/Postal code: 35051-5359
General Phone: (205) 669-3131
General Fax: (205) 669-4217
Advertising Phone: (205) 280-5667
General/National Adv. E-mail: news@shelbycountyreporter.com
Primary Website: pelhamreporter.com
Year Established: 1843
Avg Paid Circ: 7997
Avg Free Circ: 24500
Audit By: Sworn/Estimate/Non-Audited
Audit Date: 10.06.2019
Personnel: Matthew Allen (Adv. Mgr.); Tim Prince (Ed.); Jan Grissey (News Ed.)
Parent company (for newspapers): Boone Newspapers, Inc.; Shelby County Newspapers, Inc

PETERSBURG PILOT

Street address 1: 207 N Nordic Dr
Street address city: Petersburg
Street address state: AK
Zip/Postal code: 99833
General Phone: (907) 772-9393
General Fax: (907) 772-4871
General/National Adv. E-mail: pilotpub@gmail.com
Display Adv. E-mail: pilotpub@gmail.com
Primary Website: petersburgpilot.com
Year Established: 1974
Avg Paid Circ: 1250
Avg Free Circ: 30
Audit By: Sworn/Estimate/Non-Audited
Audit Date: 10.06.2019
Personnel: Anne Loesch (Co-Owner/Pub.); Orin Pierson (Editor/Publisher); Ronald J. Loesch (Co-Owner/Pub./Ed.)

PICKENS COUNTY HERALD

Street address 1: 215 REFORM ST
Street address city: Carrollton
Street address state: AL
Zip/Postal code: 35447
General Phone: (205) 367-2217
General Fax: (205) 367-2217
General/National Adv. E-mail: pickenscnty@centurytel.net
Primary Website: pcherald.com
Year Established: 1848
Avg Paid Circ: 4000
Avg Free Circ: 27
Audit By: Sworn/Estimate/Non-Audited
Audit Date: 10.06.2019
Personnel: Douglas Sanders (Pub. / Ed.)

PIEDMONT JOURNAL

Street address 1: 4305 McClellan Blvd
Street address city: Anniston
Street address state: AL
Zip/Postal code: 36206-2812
General Phone: (256) 235-3563
General Fax: (256) 241-1990
Advertising Phone: (256) 235-9238
General/National Adv. E-mail: smartin@annistonstar.com
Primary Website: annistonstar.com/piedmont_journal
Year Established: 1907
Avg Paid Circ: 3300
Audit By: Sworn/Estimate/Non-Audited
Audit Date: 10.06.2019
Personnel: John Alred (Pub.); Shannon Martin (Adv. Dir.); Laura Johnson (News Ed.)
Parent company (for newspapers): Consolidated Publishing Co.

PRATTVILLE PROGRESS

Street address 1: 425 Molton St.
Street address city: Montgomery
Street address state: AL
Zip/Postal code: 36104
General Phone: (334) 262-1611
General/National Adv. E-mail: info@prattvilleprogress.com
Primary Website: montgomeryadvertiser.com/news/prattville
Avg Paid Circ: 8500
Avg Free Circ: 88
Audit By: Sworn/Estimate/Non-Audited
Audit Date: 10.06.2019
Personnel: Bob Krift (Exec. Ed.); Steve Arnold (Sr. Content Strategist/ Dig. News Dir.); Brad Zimanek (Consumer Experience Dir./ Sports Ed.)
Parent company (for newspapers): Gannett

REDSTON ROCKET

Street address 1: 201 1st Ave SE
Street address city: Decatur
Street address state: AL
Zip/Postal code: 35601-2333
General Phone: (256) 340-2463
General Fax: (256) 260-2211
Advertising Phone: (256) 260-2218
Primary Website: theredstonerocket.com
Audit By: Sworn/Estimate/Non-Audited
Audit Date: 10.06.2019
Personnel: Skip Vaughn (Ed.); French Salter (Gen. Mgr.); Donna Counts (Adv. Rep.); Kelly Lane (Copy Ed.); Bill Marks (Ed.-in-Chief)
Parent company (for newspapers): Tennessee Valley Media Co., Inc.

SAMSON LEDGER

Street address 1: 506 S Commerce St
Street address city: Geneva
Street address state: AL
Zip/Postal code: 36340-2421
General Phone: (334) 684-2280
General Fax: (334) 684-3099
General/National Adv. E-mail: ads@genevareaper.com
Editorial e-mail: news@genevareaper.com

Primary Website: oppnewsonline.com
Audit By: Sworn/Estimate/Non-Audited
Audit Date: 10.06.2019
Personnel: Brenda Pujol (Pub.); Jay Felsberg (Ed.)

SAND MOUNTAIN REPORTER

Street address 1: 1603 Progress Dr
Street address city: Albertville
Street address state: AL
Zip/Postal code: 35950-8547
General Phone: (256) 840-3000
General Fax: (256) 840-2987
Advertising Phone: (256) 840-3000 x120
Advertising Fax: (256) 840-2987
Editorial Phone: (256) 840-3000 x115
Editorial Fax: 256-840-2987
General/National Adv. E-mail: sherrie.hall@sandmountainreporter.com
Display Adv. E-mail: linda.allen@sandmountainreporter.com
Editorial e-mail: taylor.beck@sandmountainreporter.com
Primary Website: sandmountainreporter.com
Year Established: 1955
Avg Paid Circ: 4280
Avg Free Circ: 261
Sat. Circulation Paid: 7235
Audit By: AAM
Audit Date: 31.03.2019
Personnel: Kimberly Patterson (Pub.); Sherrie Hall (Adv. Mgr.); Michelle Rowell (Business Manager); Taylor Beck (Mng. Ed.); Tammy Walker (Cir. Mgr)
Parent company (for newspapers): Southern Newspapers Inc.

SHELBY COUNTY REPORTER

Street address 1: 115 N Main St
Street address city: Columbiana
Street address state: AL
Zip/Postal code: 35051-5359
General Phone: (205) 669-3131
General Fax: (205) 669-4217
Advertising Phone: (205) 669-3131 ext. 11
Editorial Phone: (205) 669-3131 ext. 19
General/National Adv. E-mail: alan.brown@shelbycountyreporter.com
Editorial e-mail: katie.mcdowell@shelbycountyreporter.com
Primary Website: shelbycountyreporter.com
Year Established: 1843
Avg Paid Circ: 7997
Avg Free Circ: 24500
Audit By: Sworn/Estimate/Non-Audited
Audit Date: 10.06.2019
Personnel: Matthew Allen (Adv. Mgr.); Tim Prince (Ed.); Jan Grissey (News Ed.)
Parent company (for newspapers): Boone Newspapers, Inc.; Shelby County Newspapers, Inc

ST. CLAIR NEWS-AEGIS

Street address 1: 1820 2nd Ave N
Street address city: Pell City
Street address state: AL
Zip/Postal code: 35125-1616
General Phone: (205) 884-2310
General Fax: (205) 884-2312
Advertising Phone: (205) 884-2310
Editorial Phone: (205) 884-2310
General/National Adv. E-mail: ads@newsaegis.com
Editorial e-mail: editor@newsaegis.com
Primary Website: newsaegis.com
Avg Paid Circ: 5500
Audit By: Sworn/Estimate/Non-Audited
Audit Date: 10.06.2019
Personnel: Gordon Roberts (Ed.); Katerine Miller (Pub.// Adv Director); Sam Mazarra (Circ. Mgr.)
Parent company (for newspapers): CNHI, LLC

STANDARD & TIMES

Street address 1: 106 W 5th St
Street address city: Tuscumbia
Street address state: AL
Zip/Postal code: 35674-2412
General Phone: (256) 383-8471
General Fax: (256) 383-8476
General/National Adv. E-mail: estelle0601@yahoo.com
Primary Website: No website
Avg Paid Circ: 1000
Audit By: Sworn/Estimate/Non-Audited
Audit Date: 10.06.2019
Personnel: Jim Crawford (Pub.); Charlie Crawford (Adv. Mgr.); Estelle Crawford-Whitehead (Mng. Ed.)

SUMTER COUNTY RECORD-JOURNAL

Street address 1: 210 S Washington St
Street address city: Livingston
Street address state: AL
Zip/Postal code: 35470
General Phone: (205) 652-6100
General Fax: (205) 652-4466
General/National Adv. E-mail: scrjmedia@yahoo.com
Primary Website: recordjournal.net
Avg Paid Circ: 5200
Avg Free Circ: 200
Audit By: Sworn/Estimate/Non-Audited
Audit Date: 10.06.2019
Personnel: Gena Doggett Robbins (Ed.); Tommy McGraw (Mng. Ed.); Herman B. Ward (Assoc. Ed.)

THE ADVERTISER-GLEAM

Street address 1: 2218 Taylor St
Street address city: Guntersville
Street address state: AL
Zip/Postal code: 35976-1126
General Phone: (256) 582-3232
General Fax: (256) 582-3231
General/National Adv. E-mail: ads@advertisergleam.com
Display Adv. E-mail: ads@advertisergleam.com
Editorial e-mail: news@advertisergleam.com
Primary Website: advertisergleam.com
Avg Paid Circ: 8140
Audit By: Sworn/Estimate/Non-Audited
Audit Date: 10.06.2019
Personnel: Taunya Buchanan (Circ. Mgr.); Anthony Campbell (Editor); Joe Cagle (Reporter); Cindy McGregor (Reporter); Kim Fitch (Gen. Mgr); Christy Graves (Advert. Sales); Stephanie Lemke (Advert. Sales)
Parent company (for newspapers): Tennessee Valley Printing

THE ARAB TRIBUNE

Street address 1: 619 S Brindlee Mountain Pkwy
Street address city: Arab
Street address state: AL
Zip/Postal code: 35016-1502
General Phone: (256) 586-3188
General Fax: (256) 586-3190
General/National Adv. E-mail: tribads@otelco.net
Editorial e-mail: tribnews@otelco.net
Primary Website: thearabtribune.com
Year Established: 1958
Avg Paid Circ: 6500
Audit By: Sworn/Estimate/Non-Audited
Audit Date: 10.06.2019
Personnel: Edwin H. Reed (Pub.); Charles Whisenant (Ed.); Marcus Johnson (VP/OPs); RayeLynne Wingrove (Class. Ads Mgr); Donna Matuszak (Sports Ed)

THE ARCTIC SOUNDER

Street address 1: 500 W Intl Airport Rd
Street address 2: Ste F
Street address city: Anchorage
Street address state: AK
Zip/Postal code: 99518-1175
General Phone: (907) 770-0820
General Fax: (907) 770-0822
Advertising Phone: (907) 770-0820
Editorial Phone: (907) 770-0820
General/National Adv. E-mail: ads@reportalaska.com
Display Adv. E-mail: ads@reportalaska.com
Editorial e-mail: crestino@reportalaska.com
Primary Website: thearcticsounder.com
Avg Paid Circ: 2000
Audit By: Sworn/Estimate/Non-Audited
Audit Date: 10.06.2019
Personnel: Jason Evans (Pub.); Carey Restino (News Ed.)
Parent company (for newspapers): Alaska Media LLC

THE BALDWIN TIMES INDEPENDENT

Street address 1: 901 N McKenzie St
Street address city: Foley
Street address state: AL
Zip/Postal code: 36535-3546
General Phone: (251) 928-2321
General Fax: (251) 928-9963
Advertising Phone: (251) 928-2321
Advertising Fax: (251) 928-9963
General/National Adv. E-mail: bcuddy@gulfcoastnewspapers.com
Editorial e-mail: timeseditor@gulfcoastnewspapers.com
Primary Website: gulfcoastnewstoday.com/baldwin-times
Year Established: 1890
Avg Paid Circ: 3200
Avg Free Circ: 4500
Audit By: Sworn/Estimate/Non-Audited
Audit Date: 10.06.2019
Personnel: Sudie Gambrell (Pub.); Ken Hilton (Prod. Dir.); Cathy Higgins (News Ed.); Bruce Cuddy (Adv. Mgr.)
Parent company (for newspapers): Gulf Coast Newspapers

THE BIRMINGHAM NEWS

Street address 1: 1731 1st Ave N
Street address city: Birmingham
Street address state: AL
Zip/Postal code: 35203-2055
General Phone: (205) 325.4444
General Fax: (205) 325-2283
Advertising Phone: (205) 325-2261
Advertising Fax: (205) 325-3217
Editorial Fax: (205) 325-2283
General/National Adv. E-mail: advertise@al.com
Classified Adv. e-mail: advertise@al.com
Primary Website: al.com/birmingham
Mthly Avg Views: 64000000
Mthly Avg Unique Visitors: 4200000
Avg Paid Circ: 30136
Sat. Circulation Paid: 4663
Sun. Circulation Paid: 106819
Audit By: Sworn/Estimate/Non-Audited
Audit Date: 10.06.2019
Personnel: Carl Bates (Adv. Dir., Bus. Devel.); Troy Niday (Circ./Vice Pres.); Pam Siddall (President); Dee Dee Mathis (VP, Digital Solutions); Michelle Holmes (VP, Content); Kurt Vantosky (VP, Sales/Mktg); Elaine Jackson (Nat'l Coord.); Kelley Kilgore (Nat'l Classifieds Adv. Rep.)
Parent company (for newspapers): Advance Publications, Inc.

THE BLOUNT COUNTIAN

Street address 1: 217 3rd St S
Street address city: Oneonta
Street address state: AL
Zip/Postal code: 35121-2189
General Phone: (205) 625-3231
General Fax: (205) 625-3239
General/National Adv. E-mail: countian@otelco.net
Primary Website: blountcountian.com
Avg Paid Circ: 6900
Avg Free Circ: 13000
Audit By: Sworn/Estimate/Non-Audited
Audit Date: 10.06.2019
Personnel: Molly Howard Ryan (Pub.); Rob Rice (Owner/Ed); Jenna Wood (Circ. Mgr.); Kim Hipp (Advert. Dir)

THE BREWTON STANDARD

Street address 1: 407 Saint Nicholas Ave
Street address city: Brewton
Street address state: AL
Zip/Postal code: 36426-1847
General Phone: (251) 867-4876
General Fax: (251) 867-4877
General/National Adv. E-mail: newsroom@brewtonstandard.com
Primary Website: brewtonstandard.com
Year Established: 1906
Avg Paid Circ: 3180
Avg Free Circ: 150
Audit By: Sworn/Estimate/Non-Audited
Audit Date: 10.06.2019
Personnel: Stephanie Nelson (Publisher); Corey Williams (Sports Ed); Jennifer Howard (Circ Mgr); Amy Booker (Advert. Rep); Lydia Grimes (Features Report.)
Parent company (for newspapers): Boone Newspapers, Inc.

THE BRISTOL BAY TIMES

Street address 1: 500 W Intl Airport Rd
Street address 2: Ste F
Street address city: Anchorage
Street address state: AK
Zip/Postal code: 99518-1175
General Phone: (907) 770-0820
General Fax: (907) 770-0822
Advertising Phone: (907) 770-0820
Editorial Phone: (907) 770-0820
General/National Adv. E-mail: ads@reportalaska.com
Display Adv. E-mail: ads@reportalaska.com
Editorial e-mail: crestino@reportalaska.com
Primary Website: thebristolbaytimes.com
Avg Paid Circ: 2000
Avg Free Circ: 552
Audit By: Sworn/Estimate/Non-Audited
Audit Date: 10.06.2019
Personnel: Jason Evans (Pub.); Carey Restino (News Ed.)
Parent company (for newspapers): Alaska Media LLC

THE CENTREVILLE PRESS

Street address 1: 32 Court Sq W
Street address city: Centreville
Street address state: AL
Zip/Postal code: 35042-2232
General Phone: (205) 926-9769
General Fax: (205) 926-9760
Advertising Phone: (205) 926-9769
General/National Adv. E-mail: billy@centrevillepress.com
Primary Website: centrevillepress.com/Community.html
Year Established: 1880
Avg Paid Circ: 4200
Avg Free Circ: 157
Audit By: Sworn/Estimate/Non-Audited
Audit Date: 10.06.2019
Personnel: Robert E. Tribble (Pres.); Lorrie Rinehart (Pub.); Billy Colley (Adv. Mgr.); Carol Belcher (Bookkeeper); Deborah Martin (Reporter); Essie Sanders (Typist); Ann Riley (Typist, Proofer); Jimmy Huett (Pressman)
Parent company (for newspapers): Trib Publications

THE CITIZEN OF EAST ALABAMA

Street address 1: 2401 Sportsman Dr
Street address city: Phenix City
Street address state: AL
Zip/Postal code: 36867-5402
General Phone: (334) 664-0145
General Fax: (334) 664-0154
Editorial e-mail: ddubois@citizenea.com
Primary Website: citizenofeastalabama.com
Year Established: 1954
Avg Paid Circ: 13500
Audit By: Sworn/Estimate/Non-Audited
Audit Date: 10.06.2019
Personnel: Denise DuBois (Executive Editor)

THE CLEBURNE NEWS

Street address 1: 926 Ross St
Street address city: Heflin
Street address state: AL
Zip/Postal code: 36264-1134
General Phone: (256) 463-2872
General Fax: (256) 463-7127
General/National Adv. E-mail: mpointer@cleburnenews.com
Editorial e-mail: news@cleburnenews.com
Primary Website: annistonstar.com/cleburne_news
Year Established: 1906
Avg Paid Circ: 3000
Audit By: Sworn/Estimate/Non-Audited
Audit Date: 10.06.2019
Personnel: John Alred (Pub.); Laura Camper (Ed.); Misty Pointer (Adv. Mgr.)
Parent company (for newspapers): Consolidated Publishing Co.

THE CORDOVA TIMES

Street address 1: 110 Nicholoff Way
Street address city: Cordova
Street address state: AK

Zip/Postal code: 99574
General Phone: (907) 424-7181
General Fax: (907) 424-5799
Advertising Phone: (907) 350-3993
Advertising Fax: (907) 222-7706
Editorial Phone: (907) 424-7181
General/National Adv. E-mail: lnewton@thecordovatimes.com
Display Adv. E-mail: lnewton@thecordovatimes.com
Editorial e-mail: editor@thecordovatimes.com
Primary Website: thecordovatimes.com
Year Established: 1906
Avg Paid Circ: 919
Avg Free Circ: 50
Audit By: Sworn/Estimate/Non-Audited
Audit Date: 10.06.2019
Personnel: Margaret Nelson (Pub./Pres.); Mary Beth Carr (Adv. Rep.); Tony Hall (Mng. Ed.); Joy Landaluce (News Ed.); Linda Newton (Adv. Mgr.)
Parent company (for newspapers): Alaska Newspapers, Inc. (OOB)

THE CORRIDOR MESSENGER

Street address 1: 1903 3rd Ave S
Street address city: Jasper
Street address state: AL
Zip/Postal code: 35501-5315
General Phone: (205) 282-4569
General Fax: (205) 572-4621
Advertising Phone: (2
General/National Adv. E-mail: ken@corridormessenger.com
Display Adv. E-mail: nicole@corridormessenger.com
Editorial e-mail: tanya@corridormessenger.com
Primary Website: corridormessenger.com
Avg Paid Circ: 2546
Audit By: Sworn/Estimate/Non-Audited
Audit Date: 10.06.2019
Personnel: David Lazenby (Pub./Ed.); Tanya Guin (Mng. Ed.)

THE CULLMAN TRIBUNE

Street address 1: 219 2nd Ave SE
Street address city: Cullman
Street address state: AL
Zip/Postal code: 35055-3513
General Phone: (256) 739-1351
General Fax: (256) 739-4422
General/National Adv. E-mail: news@culltrib.com
Display Adv. E-mail: news@culltrib.com
Editorial e-mail: news@culltrib.com
Primary Website: cullmansense.com
Avg Paid Circ: 13400
Audit By: Sworn/Estimate/Non-Audited
Audit Date: 10.06.2019
Personnel: Delton Blalock (Ed.)

THE DUTCH HARBOR FISHERMAN

Street address 1: 500 W Intl Airport Rd
Street address 2: Ste F
Street address city: Anchorage
Street address state: AK
Zip/Postal code: 99518-1175
General Phone: (907) 770-0820
General Fax: (907) 770-0822
Advertising Phone: (907) 770-0820
Editorial Phone: (907) 770-0820
General/National Adv. E-mail: ads@reportalaska.com
Display Adv. E-mail: ads@reportalaska.com
Editorial e-mail: crestino@reportalaska.com
Primary Website: thedutchharborfisherman.com
Avg Paid Circ: 2000
Avg Free Circ: 74
Audit By: Sworn/Estimate/Non-Audited
Audit Date: 10.06.2019
Personnel: Jason Evans (Pub.); Carey Restino (News Ed.)
Parent company (for newspapers): Alaska Media LLC

THE ELBA CLIPPER

Street address 1: 417 Buford St
Street address city: Elba
Street address state: AL
Zip/Postal code: 36323-1753
General Phone: (334) 897-2823
General Fax: (334) 897-3434
General/National Adv. E-mail: clipper@alaweb.com
Editorial e-mail: clipperace@alaweb.com
Primary Website: elba-clipper.com
Year Established: 1897
Avg Paid Circ: 2650
Audit By: Sworn/Estimate/Non-Audited
Audit Date: 10.06.2019
Personnel: John Ferrin Cox (Pub.); Linda Hodge (Ed.)
Parent company (for newspapers): HF Enterprises, Inc.

THE FAIRHOPE COURIER

Street address 1: 420 Fairhope Ave
Street address city: Fairhope
Street address state: AL
Zip/Postal code: 36532-2110
General Phone: (251) 928-2321
General Fax: (251) 928-9963
Advertising Phone: (251) 928-2321
Advertising Fax: (251) 928-9963
Editorial Phone: (251) 928-2321
Editorial Fax: (251) 928-9963
General/National Adv. E-mail: pjohnson@gulfcoastnewspapers.com
Editorial e-mail: courier@gulfcoastnewspapers.com
Primary Website: thefairhopecourier.com
Year Established: 1894
Avg Paid Circ: 1752
Audit By: Sworn/Estimate/Non-Audited
Audit Date: 10.06.2019
Personnel: Pat Johnson (Adv. Mgr.); Mike Odom (Ed.); Jessie Patterson (Pub.)
Parent company (for newspapers): Gulf Coast Newspapers

THE FLORALA NEWS

Street address 1: 1155 5th St
Street address city: Florala
Street address state: AL
Zip/Postal code: 36442-3243
General Phone: (334) 858-3342
General Fax: (334) 858-3786
General/National Adv. E-mail: floralanews@fairpoint.net
Display Adv. E-mail: windham@gtcom.net
Primary Website: No Website
Year Established: 1900
Avg Paid Circ: 1700
Audit By: Sworn/Estimate/Non-Audited
Audit Date: 10.06.2019
Personnel: Lisa Windham (Adv. Mgr.); Gary Woodham (Pub.)

THE GREENVILLE ADVOCATE

Street address 1: 103 Hickory St
Street address city: Greenville
Street address state: AL
Zip/Postal code: 36037-2609
General Phone: (334) 382-3111
General Fax: (334) 382-7104
General/National Adv. E-mail: news@theclintonjournal.com
Primary Website: greenvilleadvocate.com
Year Established: 1865
Avg Paid Circ: 3000
Avg Free Circ: 9700
Audit By: Sworn/Estimate/Non-Audited
Audit Date: 10.06.2019
Personnel: Adam Prestridge (Pub.); Mark Rogers (Mng. Ed.); Chloe Langston (Adv.)
Parent company (for newspapers): Boone Newspapers, Inc.

THE HUNTSVILLE TIMES

Street address 1: 200 Westside Sq
Street address 2: Ste 100
Street address city: Huntsville
Street address state: AL
Zip/Postal code: 35801-4894
General Phone: (256) 532-4000
General Fax: (256) 532-4420
Advertising Phone: (256) 532-4250
Advertising Fax: (256) 532-4183
Editorial Phone: (256) 532-4400
Editorial Fax: (256) 532-4420
General/National Adv. E-mail: sheila.runnels@htimes.com
Display Adv. E-mail: bill.joyner@htimes.com
Editorial e-mail: htimes@htimes.com
Primary Website: al.com/huntsville
Avg Paid Circ: 34196
Sat. Circulation Paid: 2147
Sun. Circulation Paid: 45532
Audit By: AAM
Audit Date: 30.06.2018
Personnel: Carol Casey (Mktg. Mgr.); Shelly Haskins (City Desk Ed.); Tom Bates (Pub); Robert D. Ludwig (Pres./Pub.); Steve Wilson (Adv. Mgr., Retail); Anita McCain (Asst. Controller); Robert Carothers (Controller); Sheila Runnels (Adv. Mgr., Classified); Joe Bagwell (Adv. Mgr., Major Accts.); Frank Maier (Circ. Dir.); Doug Mendenhall (Design Ed.); John Ehinger (Editorial Page Ed.); Deborah Storey (Entertainment/Leisure Ed.); Kenneth Kesner (Health Ed.); Stephen Lomax (Asst. News Ed.); Alan Clemons (Outdoors Ed.); Mike Mercier (Chief Photographer); Mike Hollis (Regl. Ed.); Yvonne Betowt (Religion Ed.); Joe Duncan (News Ed.)
Parent company (for newspapers): Advance Publications, Inc.

THE ISLANDER

Street address 1: 901 N McKenzie St
Street address city: Foley
Street address state: AL
Zip/Postal code: 36535-3546
General Phone: (251) 968-6414
General Fax: (251) 943-3441
Advertising Phone: (251) 943-2151
Advertising Fax: (251) 943-3441
Editorial Phone: (251) 968-6414
Editorial Fax: (251) 943-3441
General/National Adv. E-mail: hclarke@gulfcoastnewspapers.com
Editorial e-mail: theislander@gulfcoastnewspapers.com
Primary Website: gulfcoastnewstoday.com/the-islander
Year Established: 1977
Avg Paid Circ: 1737
Audit By: Sworn/Estimate/Non-Audited
Audit Date: 10.06.2019
Personnel: Sudie Gambrell (Pub.); John Mullen (Ed.); Harry Clarke (Adv. Mgr.)
Parent company (for newspapers): Gulf Coast Newspapers

THE JACKSONVILLE NEWS

Street address 1: 4305 McClellan Blvd
Street address city: Anniston
Street address state: AL
Zip/Postal code: 36206-2812
General Phone: (256) 435-5021
General Fax: (256) 435-1028
General/National Adv. E-mail: news@jaxnews.com
Primary Website: jaxnews.com
Year Established: 1936
Avg Paid Circ: 3300
Audit By: Sworn/Estimate/Non-Audited
Audit Date: 10.06.2019
Personnel: Phillip A. Sanguinetti (Pub.); Shannon Martin (Adv. Mgr.); John Alred (Ed.)
Parent company (for newspapers): Consolidated Publishing Co.

THE LUVERNE JOURNAL

Street address 1: 506 S Forest Ave
Street address city: Luverne
Street address state: AL
Zip/Postal code: 36049-1902
General Phone: (334) 335-3541
General Fax: (334) 335-4299
Advertising Phone: (334) 382-3111
Editorial Phone: (334) 335-3541
General/National Adv. E-mail: tracy.salter@greenvilleadvocate.com
Display Adv. E-mail: tracy.hadley@greenvilleadvocate.com
Editorial e-mail: kendra.bolling@luvernejournal.com
Primary Website: luvernejournal.com
Year Established: 1890
Avg Paid Circ: 2400
Audit By: Sworn/Estimate/Non-Audited
Audit Date: 10.06.2019
Personnel: Tracy Salter (Pub.); Regina Grayson; Beth Hyatt (Ed.)
Parent company (for newspapers): Boone Newspapers, Inc.

THE MADISON RECORD

Street address 1: 14 Main St
Street address 2: Ste C
Street address city: Madison
Street address state: AL
Zip/Postal code: 35758-2084
General Phone: (256) 772-6677
General Fax: (256) 772-6655
Display Adv. E-mail: classifieds@themadisonrecord.com
Primary Website: themadisonrecord.com
Audit By: Sworn/Estimate/Non-Audited
Audit Date: 10.06.2019
Personnel: Tammy Overman (Customer Service Rep.); Randy Cox (Pub.); Ashley Davis (Mktg. Consult.); Kari George (Class. Consult.)
Parent company (for newspapers): Boone Newspapers, Inc.

THE MONROE JOURNAL

Street address 1: 49 Hines St
Street address city: Monroeville
Street address state: AL
Zip/Postal code: 36460-1833
General Phone: (251) 575-3282
General Fax: (251) 575-3284
General/National Adv. E-mail: advertising@monroejournal.com
Editorial e-mail: news@monroejournal.com
Primary Website: monroejournal.com
Avg Paid Circ: 7800
Avg Free Circ: 11900
Audit By: Sworn/Estimate/Non-Audited
Audit Date: 10.06.2019
Personnel: Bo Bolton (Pub.); Mike Qualls (Ed.); Jodie Bolton (Art Dir.); Michael Lambeth (Adv. Mgr.)

THE MOULTON ADVERTISER

Street address 1: 659 Main St
Street address city: Moulton
Street address state: AL
Zip/Postal code: 35650-1512
General Phone: (256) 974-1114
General Fax: (256) 974-3097
General/National Adv. E-mail: teresa@moultonadvertiser.com
Display Adv. E-mail: classified@moultonadvertiser.com
Editorial e-mail: editor@moultonadvertiser.com
Primary Website: moultonadvertiser.com
Year Established: 1828
Avg Paid Circ: 4123
Avg Free Circ: 9550
Audit By: Sworn/Estimate/Non-Audited
Audit Date: 10.06.2019
Personnel: Teresa Woodruff (Adv. Mgr.); Misty Alexander (Ad Rep.); Jeff Edwards (Staff Writer); J.R. Tidewell (Staff Writer)
Parent company (for newspapers): Tennessee Valley Media Co., Inc.

THE NOME NUGGET

Street address 1: P.O. Box 610
Street address city: Nome
Street address state: AK
Zip/Postal code: 99672-0610
General Phone: (907) 443-5235
General Fax: (907) 443-5112
General/National Adv. E-mail: ads@nomenugget.com
Display Adv. E-mail: ads@nomenugget.com
Editorial e-mail: diana@nomenugget.com
Primary Website: nomenugget.net
Year Established: 1897
Avg Paid Circ: 6000
Audit By: Sworn/Estimate/Non-Audited
Audit Date: 10.06.2019
Personnel: Diana Haecker (News Ed./Reporter); Nils Hahn (Adv. Mgr.)

THE NORTHPORT GAZETTE

Street address 1: 401 20th Ave
Street address 2: Ste 2
Street address city: Northport
Street address state: AL
Zip/Postal code: 35476-5045
General Phone: (205) 759-3091

General Fax: (205) 759-5449
General/National Adv. E-mail: northportgazette@northportgazette.com
Primary Website: northportgazette.com
Year Established: 1998
Avg Paid Circ: 4500
Audit By: Sworn/Estimate/Non-Audited
Audit Date: 10.06.2019
Personnel: Paula Bryant (Gen. Mgr.)

THE ONLOOKER

Street address 1: 901 N McKenzie St
Street address city: Foley
Street address state: AL
Zip/Postal code: 36535-3546
General Phone: (251) 943-2151
General Fax: (251) 943-3441
General/National Adv. E-mail: frank@gulfcoastmedia.com
Display Adv. E-mail: classifieds@gulfcoastmedia.com
Editorial e-mail: john@gulfcoastmedia.com
Primary Website: gulfcoastnewstoday.com/the-onlooker
Year Established: 1907
Avg Paid Circ: 4600
Audit By: Sworn/Estimate/Non-Audited
Audit Date: 10.06.2019
Personnel: Parks Rogers (Pub.); John Underwood (Co-Ed); Jessica Vaughn (Co-Ed.)
Parent company (for newspapers): Gulf Coast Newspapers

THE OPP NEWS

Street address 1: 200 W Covington Ave
Street address city: Opp
Street address state: AL
Zip/Postal code: 36467-2046
General Phone: (334) 493-3595
General Fax: (334) 493-4901
General/National Adv. E-mail: opppublisher@centurytel.net
Editorial e-mail: oppnews@centurytel.net
Primary Website: oppnewsonline.com
Avg Paid Circ: 5300
Audit By: Sworn/Estimate/Non-Audited
Audit Date: 10.06.2019
Personnel: Moe Pujol (Pub.); Wanda Sasser (Adv. Mgr.); Jay Thomas (Ed.); Josh Richards (Ed.)

THE OZARK SOUTHERN STAR

Street address 1: 373 Ed Lisenby Dr
Street address city: Ozark
Street address state: AL
Zip/Postal code: 36360-1473
General Phone: (334) 774-2715
General Fax: (334) 774-9619
General/National Adv. E-mail: southstar@centurytel.net
Primary Website: thesouthernstaronline.com
Avg Paid Circ: 4900
Audit By: Sworn/Estimate/Non-Audited
Audit Date: 10.06.2019
Personnel: Charlie Dawkins (Adv. Mgr.); Joseph H. Adams (Ed.)

THE RANDOLPH LEADER

Street address 1: 524 Main St
Street address city: Roanoke
Street address state: AL
Zip/Postal code: 36274-1440
General Phone: (334) 863-2819
General Fax: (334) 863-4006
General/National Adv. E-mail: peggy@therandolphleader.com
Editorial e-mail: vanessa@therandolphleader.com
Primary Website: therandolphleader.com
Year Established: 1892
Avg Paid Circ: 7000
Audit By: Sworn/Estimate/Non-Audited
Audit Date: 10.06.2019
Personnel: John W. Stevenson (Ed. / Pub.); Peggy Seabolt (Adv. Mgr.); Vanessa Sorrell Burnside (News Ed.)

THE RED BAY NEWS

Street address 1: 120 4th Ave SE
Street address city: Red Bay
Street address state: AL
Zip/Postal code: 35582-4191
General Phone: (256) 356-2148
General Fax: (256) 356-2787
General/National Adv. E-mail: rbaynews@gmail.com
Display Adv. E-mail: rbaynews@gmail.com
Editorial e-mail: rbaynews@gmail.com
Primary Website: trbnews.net
Year Established: 1963
Avg Paid Circ: 2600
Avg Free Circ: 0
Audit By: Sworn/Estimate/Non-Audited
Audit Date: 10.06.2019
Personnel: LaVale Mills (Publisher Emeritus); Angel Gasaway (Advertising Manager); Bridget Berry (Managing Ed.)

THE SAINT CLAIR TIMES

Street address 1: 1911 Martin St S
Street address 2: Ste 7
Street address city: Pell City
Street address state: AL
Zip/Postal code: 35128-2372
General Phone: (205) 884-3400
General Fax: (205) 814-9194
Advertising Phone: (205) 884-3400
Editorial Phone: (205) 884-3400
General/National Adv. E-mail: dhalpin@dailyhome.com
Editorial e-mail: wheath@thestclairtimes.com
Primary Website: annistonstar.com/the_st_clair_times
Year Established: 2000
Avg Paid Circ: 34000
Avg Free Circ: 34000
Audit By: Sworn/Estimate/Non-Audited
Audit Date: 10.06.2019
Personnel: Ed Fowler (Pub.); Will Heath (Ed.); Gary Hanner (Assoc. Ed.); Dale Halpin (Adv. Sales); Polly T. Ramsey (Classifed Adv. Sales)
Parent company (for newspapers): Consolidated Publishing Co.

THE SEWARD PHOENIX LOG

Street address 1: 301 Calista Court
Street address 2: Suite B
Street address city: Seward
Street address state: AK
Zip/Postal code: 99518
General Phone: (907) 272-9830
Advertising Phone: (907) 348-2417
Editorial Phone: (907) 348-2428
General/National Adv. E-mail: banderson@alaskanewspapers.com
Display Adv. E-mail: classifiedlegal@alaskanewspapers.com
Editorial e-mail: ahall@alaskanewspapers.com
Primary Website: TheSewardPhoenixLOG.com
Year Established: 1966
Avg Paid Circ: 700
Avg Free Circ: 50
Audit By: Sworn/Estimate/Non-Audited
Audit Date: 10.06.2019
Personnel: Margaret Nelson (Pres./Pub.); Tony Hall (Mng. Ed.); Cinthia Ritchie; Mary Beth Carr (Adv. Mgr.)
Parent company (for newspapers): All Alaska News Unlimited

THE SOUTH ALABAMIAN

Street address 1: 1525 College Ave
Street address city: Jackson
Street address state: AL
Zip/Postal code: 36545-2418
General Phone: (251) 246-4494
General Fax: (251) 246-7486
General/National Adv. E-mail: Ads@thesouthalabamian.com
Editorial e-mail: News@thesouthalabamian.com
Primary Website: southalabamian.com
Avg Paid Circ: 4200
Avg Free Circ: 58
Audit By: Sworn/Estimate/Non-Audited
Audit Date: 10.06.2019
Personnel: Evan Carden (Ed.); Jerry Turner (Pub.); Travis Matthews (Adv. Mgr.)

THE TALLASSEE TRIBUNE

Street address 1: 548 Cherokee Road
Street address city: Alexander City
Street address state: AL
Zip/Postal code: 35010
General Phone: 2562344281
General Fax: (334) 283-6569
Advertising Phone: 3343503917
General/National Adv. E-mail: jayne.carr@alexcityoutlook.com
Display Adv. E-mail: heather.glenn@alexcityoutlook.com
Editorial e-mail: editor@tallasseetribune.com
Primary Website: tallasseetribune.com
Year Established: 1899
Avg Paid Circ: 4200
Audit By: Sworn/Estimate/Non-Audited
Audit Date: 10.06.2019
Personnel: Tippy Hunter (Advertising Director); Marilyn Hawkins (Regional Ad Manager); Carmen Rodgers (Reporter); David Granger (Managing Editor)
Parent company (for newspapers): Boone Newspapers, Inc.

THE THOMASVILLE TIMES

Street address 1: 24 W. Front St.
Street address city: Thomasville
Street address state: AL
Zip/Postal code: 36784
General Phone: (334) 636-2214
General Fax: (334) 636-9822
General/National Adv. E-mail: aloflin@hpe.com
Display Adv. E-mail: terri@thethomasvilletimes.net
Editorial e-mail: editor@tvilletimes.com
Primary Website: thethomasvilletimes.com
Year Established: 1921
Avg Paid Circ: 3700
Audit By: Sworn/Estimate/Non-Audited
Audit Date: 10.06.2019
Personnel: Renee Campbell (Sales, Book Keeping)

THE TIMES-RECORD

Street address 1: 106 1st St SE
Street address city: Fayette
Street address state: AL
Zip/Postal code: 35555-2702
General Phone: (205) 932-6271
General Fax: (205) 932-6998
General/National Adv. E-mail: tradvertising@centurytel.net
Editorial e-mail: trnews@centurytel.net
Primary Website: mytrpaper.com
Year Established: 1977
Avg Paid Circ: 5000
Audit By: Sworn/Estimate/Non-Audited
Audit Date: 10.06.2019
Personnel: Horace Moore (Pub.); Gina Lynn (Adv. Mgr.); Jerrie Elliott (Gen. Mgr.); Crystal Foster (Ed.); Michael Palmer (Mng. Ed.)

THE TRI-CITY LEDGER

Street address 1: 20766 Hwy 31
Street address city: Flomaton
Street address state: AL
Zip/Postal code: 36441
General Phone: (251) 296-3491
General Fax: (251) 296-0010
General/National Adv. E-mail: newsroom@tricityledger.com
Primary Website: No Website
Avg Paid Circ: 5300
Audit By: Sworn/Estimate/Non-Audited
Audit Date: 10.06.2019
Personnel: Joe Thomas (Ed.)

THE TUNDRA DRUMS

Street address 1: 232 4th Ave
Street address city: Seward
Street address state: AK
Zip/Postal code: 99664
General Phone: (907) 224-4888
General Fax: (907) 224-4888
Advertising Phone: (907) 224-4888
Editorial Phone: (907) 224-4888
Primary Website: TheTundraDrums.com
Year Established: 1974
Avg Paid Circ: 700
Avg Free Circ: 1000
Audit By: Sworn/Estimate/Non-Audited
Audit Date: 10.06.2019
Personnel: Annette Shacklett (Pub.)
Parent company (for newspapers): All Alaska News Unlimited

THE TUSKEGEE NEWS

Street address 1: 103 S Main St
Street address city: Tuskegee
Street address state: AL
Zip/Postal code: 36083-1801
General Phone: (334) 727-3020
Advertising Phone: (334) 727-3020
Editorial Phone: (334) 727-3020
General/National Adv. E-mail: tuskegeenews@bellsouth.net
Display Adv. E-mail: tuskegeenews@bellsouth.net
Editorial e-mail: tuskegeenews@bellsouth.net
Primary Website: thetuskegeenews.com
Year Established: 1865
Avg Paid Circ: 2500
Audit By: Sworn/Estimate/Non-Audited
Audit Date: 10.06.2019
Personnel: Scott Richardson (Pub. Asst.); Guy Rhodes (Ed./Pub.)

THE WESTERN STAR

Street address 1: 1709 3rd Ave N
Street address city: Bessemer
Street address state: AL
Zip/Postal code: 35020-0900
General Phone: (205) 424-7827
General Fax: (205) 424-8118
General/National Adv. E-mail: bessemercutoff@gmail.com
Editorial e-mail: editor@thewesternstarnews.com
Avg Paid Circ: 4200
Audit By: Sworn/Estimate/Non-Audited
Audit Date: 10.06.2019
Personnel: Matt Bryant (Pub.); Matthew McCrary (Ed.); Michelle Lambert (Office Mgr.)

THE WETUMPKA HERALD

Street address 1: 548 CHEROKEE RD
Street address city: Alexander City
Street address state: AL
Zip/Postal code: 35010-2503
General Phone: (334) 567-7811
General Fax: (334) 567-3284
General/National Adv. E-mail: tippy.hunter@alexcityoutlook.com
Display Adv. E-mail: tippy.hunter@alexcityoutlook.com
Editorial e-mail: david.granger@alexcityoutlook.com
Primary Website: thewetumpkaherald.com
Year Established: 1898
Avg Paid Circ: 5700
Avg Free Circ: 100
Audit By: Sworn/Estimate/Non-Audited
Audit Date: 10.06.2019
Personnel: Steve Baker (President/Publisher); David Granger (Managing Editor); Tippy Hunter (Advertising Director)
Parent company (for newspapers): Boone Newspapers, Inc.

VALDEZ STAR

Street address 1: 310 Pioneer St
Street address city: Valdez
Street address state: AK
Zip/Postal code: 99686
General Phone: (907) 835-2405
General/National Adv. E-mail: editor@valdezstar.net
Editorial e-mail: editor@valdezstar.net
Primary Website: valdezstar.net
Avg Paid Circ: 2020
Audit By: Sworn/Estimate/Non-Audited
Audit Date: 10.06.2019
Personnel: Lee Revis (Ed.); Marilyn Braighboy (Office/Business Mgr.); Mark Dickman (Graphics)

WASHINGTON COUNTY NEWS

Street address 1: 8350 North St
Street address city: Citronelle
Street address state: AL
Zip/Postal code: 36522-4008
General Phone: (251) 847-2599
General Fax: (251) 847-3847
General/National Adv. E-mail: williegray@thecallnews.com
Primary Website: washcountynews.com

Avg Paid Circ: 4000
Avg Free Circ: 75
Audit By: Sworn/Estimate/Non-Audited
Audit Date: 10.06.2019
Personnel: Willie Gray (Pub.); Jason Boothe
Parent company (for newspapers): Call News

WEST ALABAMA GAZETTE

Street address 1: PO Box 249
Street address city: Millport
Street address state: AL
Zip/Postal code: 35576-0249
General Phone: (205) 759-3091
General Fax: (205) 759-5449
General/National Adv. E-mail: gazettenews@frontiernet.net
Primary Website: facebook.com/pg/The-West-Alabama-Gazette-110067155713008
Year Established: 1967
Avg Paid Circ: 3000
Avg Free Circ: 500
Audit By: Sworn/Estimate/Non-Audited
Audit Date: 10.06.2019

WILCOX PROGRESSIVE ERA

Street address 1: 16 Water St
Street address city: Camden
Street address state: AL
Zip/Postal code: 36726-2111
General Phone: (334) 682-4422
General Fax: (334) 682-5163
General/National Adv. E-mail: progressiveera@mchsi.com
Display Adv. E-mail: progressiveera@mchsi.com
Editorial e-mail: progressiveera@mchsi.com
Primary Website: thewilcoxprogressiveera.com
Year Established: 2016
Avg Paid Circ: 1000
Audit By: Sworn/Estimate/Non-Audited
Audit Date: //0
Personnel: Glenda Curl (Editor/Publisher); Ethan Van Sice (Editor in Chief)

WRANGELL SENTINEL

Street address 1: 205 Front St
Street address city: Wrangell
Street address state: AK
Zip/Postal code: 99929
General Phone: (907) 874-2301
General Fax: (907) 874-2303
General/National Adv. E-mail: wrgsent@gmail.com
Display Adv. E-mail: wrgsent@gmail.com
Editorial e-mail: wrgsent@gmail.com
Primary Website: wrangellsentinel.com
Year Established: 1902
Avg Paid Circ: 1500
Avg Free Circ: 20
Audit By: Sworn/Estimate/Non-Audited
Audit Date: 10.06.2019
Personnel: Anne Loesch (Co-Owner/Pub.); Ron Loesch (Co-Owner/Pub./Ed.); Chris Reed (Adv. Mgr.)
Parent company (for newspapers): Jade River Publishing

ARIZONA

AHWATUKEE FOOTHILLS NEWS

Street address 1: 1620 West Fountainhead Parkway, Suite 219
Street address 2: Ste 219
Street address city: Tempe
Street address state: AZ
Zip/Postal code: 85282-1848
General Phone: (480) 898-5940
General Fax: (480) 898-6329
Advertising Phone: (480) 898-7900
Editorial Phone: (480) 898-7913
General/National Adv. E-mail: kmays@ahwatukee.com
Display Adv. E-mail: ecota@ahwatukee.com
Editorial e-mail: Pmaryniak@ahwatukee.com
Primary Website: ahwatukee.com
Year Established: 1978
Avg Free Circ: 27750
Audit By: Sworn/Estimate/Non-Audited
Audit Date: 10.06.2019
Personnel: Steve Strickbine (Pub.); Chuck Morales (Ops. Mgr.); Aaron Kolodny (Circ. Dir.); Lori Dionisio (Adv. Admin.); Elaine Cota (Class Mgr.)
Parent company (for newspapers): Times Media Group

AJO COPPER NEWS

Street address 1: 10 W Pajaro St
Street address city: Ajo
Street address state: AZ
Zip/Postal code: 85321-2435
General Phone: (520) 387-7688
General Fax: (520) 387-7505
Advertising Phone: (520) 387-7688
General/National Adv. E-mail: cunews@cunews.info
Display Adv. E-mail: advertising@cunews.info
Editorial e-mail: editor@cunews.info
Primary Website: cunews.info
Year Established: 1916
Avg Paid Circ: 1000
Avg Free Circ: 45
Audit By: Sworn/Estimate/Non-Audited
Audit Date: 10.06.2019
Personnel: H.J. David (Pub.); Michelle Pacheco (Off. Mgr.); Gabrielle David (Ed.)
Parent company (for newspapers): ANA Advertising Services, Inc. (Arizona Newspaper Association)

APACHE JUNCTION/GOLD CANYON INDEPENDENT

Street address 1: 23043 N 16th Ln
Street address city: Phoenix
Street address state: AZ
Zip/Postal code: 85027-1331
General Phone: (480) 982-7799
General Fax: (480) 671-0016
General/National Adv. E-mail: evads@newszap.com
Display Adv. E-mail: iniclassads@newszap.com
Editorial e-mail: ajeditor@newszap.com
Primary Website: apachejunctionindependent.com
Year Established: 1959
Avg Paid Circ: 0
Avg Free Circ: 20000
Audit By: Sworn/Estimate/Non-Audited
Audit Date: 10.06.2019
Personnel: Bret McKeand (Pub.); Richard Dyer (Mng. Ed.); Deb Richardson (General Manager)
Parent company (for newspapers): Independent Newsmedia Inc. USA

ARCADIA NEWS

Street address 1: 3850 E Indian School Rd
Street address 2: Ste 1
Street address city: Phoenix
Street address state: AZ
Zip/Postal code: 85018
General Phone: 602-840-6379
General Fax: 602-840-6592
Advertising Phone: 602-840-6379
Advertising Fax: 602-840-6592
Editorial Phone: 602-840-6379
Editorial Fax: 602-840-6592
General/National Adv. E-mail: business@arcadianews.com
Display Adv. E-mail: ads@arcadianews.com
Classified Adv. e-mail: ads@arcadianews.com
Editorial e-mail: editor@arcadianews.com
Primary Website: www.arcadianews.com
Mthly Avg Views: 13151
Mthly Avg Unique Visitors: 8700
Year Established: 1993
Avg Free Circ: 17768
Audit By: CVC
Audit Date: 30.06.2021
Personnel: Greg Bruns (Publisher); Roni Mier (Advertising & Marketing Manager); Mallory Gleich (Editor)

ARIZONA BUSINESS GAZETTE

Street address 1: 200 E Van Buren St
Street address city: Phoenix
Street address state: AZ
Zip/Postal code: 85004-2238
General Phone: (602) 444-8838
General Fax: (602) 444-7312
Primary Website: abgnews.com
Audit By: Sworn/Estimate/Non-Audited
Audit Date: 10.06.2019
Parent company (for newspapers): Gannett

ARIZONA CAPITOL TIMES

Street address 1: 1835 W Adams St
Street address city: Phoenix
Street address state: AZ
Zip/Postal code: 85007-2603
General Phone: (602) 258-7026
General Fax: (602) 258-2504
General/National Adv. E-mail: jschanfeldt@azcapitoltimes.com
Editorial e-mail: tom.spratt@azcapitoltimes.com
Primary Website: azcapitoltimes.com
Year Established: 1906
Avg Paid Circ: 1675
Avg Free Circ: 26
Audit By: Sworn/Estimate/Non-Audited
Audit Date: 10.06.2019
Personnel: Luige Del Puerto (Ed. / Pub.); Gary Grado (Mng. Ed.); Lisa Simpson (Adv.)
Parent company (for newspapers): BridgeTower Media

ARIZONA INFORMANT

Street address 1: 1301 E Washington St
Street address 2: Ste 101
Street address city: Phoenix
Street address state: AZ
Zip/Postal code: 85034-1173
General Phone: (602) 257-9300
General Fax: (602) 257-0547
General/National Adv. E-mail: aznewspaper@questoffice.net
Primary Website: azinformant.com
Year Established: 1971
Avg Paid Circ: 15000
Audit By: Sworn/Estimate/Non-Audited
Audit Date: 10.06.2019
Personnel: Roland Campbell (Pub.); Clovis C. Campbell (Ed.)

ARIZONA RANGE NEWS

Street address 1: 333 W Wilcox Dr
Street address 2: Ste 302
Street address city: Sierra Vista
Street address state: AZ
Zip/Postal code: 85635-1791
General Phone: (520) 384-3571
General Fax: (520) 384-3572
General/National Adv. E-mail: steve.reno@willcoxrangenews.com
Display Adv. E-mail: deedee.hicks@willcoxrangenews.com
Editorial e-mail: ainslee.wittig@willcoxrangenews.com
Primary Website: willcoxrangenews.com
Year Established: 1884
Avg Paid Circ: 1514
Audit By: Sworn/Estimate/Non-Audited
Audit Date: 10.06.2019
Personnel: Ainslee Wittig (Mng. Ed.); Steve Reno (Adv. Rep.); Rebecca Bradner (Pub.)
Parent company (for newspapers): Wick Communications

ARIZONA SILVER BELT

Street address 1: 298 N Pine St
Street address city: Globe
Street address state: AZ
Zip/Postal code: 85501-2516
General Phone: (928) 425-7121
General Fax: (928) 425-7001
Advertising Phone: (928) 425-7121
Editorial Phone: (928) 425-7121
General/National Adv. E-mail: sherri@silverbelt.com
Display Adv. E-mail: sherri@silverbelt.com
Editorial e-mail: news@silverbelt.com
Primary Website: silverbelt.com
Year Established: 1878
Avg Paid Circ: 1800
Audit By: Sworn/Estimate/Non-Audited
Audit Date: 10.06.2019
Personnel: Holly Sow (Ed.); Sherri Davis (Gen. Mgr.)
Parent company (for newspapers): San Luis Valley Publishing

AU-AUTHM ACTION NEWS

Street address 1: 10005 E Osborn Rd
Street address city: Scottsdale
Street address state: AZ
Zip/Postal code: 85256-4019
General Phone: (480) 362-7750
General Fax: (480) 362-5592
Advertising Phone: (480) 362-6699
General/National Adv. E-mail: dustin.hughes@srpmic-nsn.gov
Editorial e-mail: Dodie.Manuel@srpmic-nsn.gov
Primary Website: srpmic-nsn.gov
Audit By: Sworn/Estimate/Non-Audited
Audit Date: 10.06.2019
Personnel: Dodie Manuel (Mng. Ed.); Jessica Joaquin (Ad Sales)

BUCKEYE VALLEY NEWS

Street address 1: 122 S 4th St
Street address city: Buckeye
Street address state: AZ
Zip/Postal code: 85326
General Phone: (623) 386-4426
General Fax: (623) 386-4199
General/National Adv. E-mail: bvalnews@qwestoffice.net
Display Adv. E-mail: bvalnews@qwestoffice.net
Editorial e-mail: bvalnews@qwestoffice.net
Primary Website: buckeyevalleynews.net
Avg Paid Circ: 3000
Avg Free Circ: 8000
Audit By: Sworn/Estimate/Non-Audited
Audit Date: 10.06.2019
Personnel: Marlene Turner (Owner,Publisher); Sharon Torres (Editor, CFO)

BULLHEAD CITY BOOSTER

Street address 1: 2435 Miracle Mile
Street address city: Bullhead City
Street address state: AZ
Zip/Postal code: 86442-7311
General Phone: (928) 763-2505
General Fax: (928) 763-6752
Editorial Phone: (928) 763-2505 x 5144
General/National Adv. E-mail: mvdnews@mohavedailynews.com
Editorial e-mail: bmcmillen@mohavedailynews.com
Primary Website: mohavedailynews.com
Avg Free Circ: 12500
Audit By: Sworn/Estimate/Non-Audited
Audit Date: 10.06.2019
Personnel: Gary Milks (Pub.); Bill McMillen (News Ed.)
Parent company (for newspapers): Brehm Communications, Inc.; News West Publishing Company Inc. (OOB)

CAMP VERDE BUGLE

Street address 1: 283 3rd St
Street address city: Camp Verde
Street address state: AZ
Zip/Postal code: 86322
General Phone: (928) 634-2241
General Fax: (928) 634-2312
Advertising Phone: (928) 634-2241
Advertising Fax: (928) 634-2312
Editorial Phone: (928) 634-2241
Editorial Fax: (928) 634-2312
General/National Adv. E-mail: advertising@verdenews.com
Display Adv. E-mail: classified@verdenews.com
Editorial e-mail: dengler@verdenews.com
Primary Website: cvbugle.com
Year Established: 1947
Avg Paid Circ: 824
Audit By: Sworn/Estimate/Non-Audited
Audit Date: 10.06.2019
Personnel: Pam Miller (Pub.); Dan Engler (Ed.)
Parent company (for newspapers): Western News&Info, Inc.

CHINO VALLEY REVIEW

Street address 1: 110 W Center St
Street address 2: Ste A2
Street address city: Chino Valley
Street address state: AZ
Zip/Postal code: 86323-5961
General Phone: (928) 636-2653
General Fax: (928) 636-1334
Advertising Phone: (928) 636-2653
Editorial Phone: (928) 636-2653

General/National Adv. E-mail: theitzman@prescottaz.com
Editorial e-mail: hdfoster@prescottaz.com
Primary Website: cvrnews.com
Avg Paid Circ: 51
Avg Free Circ: 6691
Audit By: Sworn/Estimate/Non-Audited
Audit Date: 10.06.2019
Personnel: Heidi Dahms Foster (Ed.); Babette Cubitt (Adv. Dir.); Fred Ellison (Adv. Mgr.); Teri Bryant (Classified Adv. Mgr.); David Russell (Circ. Mgr.); Kit Atwell (Co-Pub.)
Parent company (for newspapers): Western News&Info, Inc.

COMBINED WITH CASA GRANDE DISPATCH

Street address 1: 190 N Main St
Street address city: Florence
Street address state: AZ
Zip/Postal code: 85132
General Phone: (520) 868-5897
General Fax: (520) 868-5898
General/National Adv. E-mail: info@florencereminder.com
Display Adv. E-mail: ads@florencereminder.com
Editorial e-mail: news@florencereminder.com
Primary Website: pinalcentral.com/florence_reminder_blade_tribune
Avg Paid Circ: 1623
Avg Free Circ: 8
Audit By: Sworn/Estimate/Non-Audited
Audit Date: 10.06.2019
Personnel: Joey Chenoweth (Editor)
Parent company (for newspapers): Casa Grande Valley Newspapers Inc.

COOLIDGE EXAMINER

Street address 1: 353 W Central Ave
Street address city: Coolidge
Street address state: AZ
Zip/Postal code: 85128-4706
General Phone: (520) 723-5441
General Fax: (520) 723-7899
General/National Adv. E-mail: coolidgeexaminer@yahoo.com
Primary Website: pinalcentral.com/coolidge_examiner
Avg Paid Circ: 1943
Audit By: Sworn/Estimate/Non-Audited
Audit Date: 10.06.2019
Personnel: Adam Gaub (County Team Ed.); Kelli Kent (Adv. Mgr.)
Parent company (for newspapers): Casa Grande Valley Newspapers Inc.

COPPER BASIN NEWS

Street address 1: 366 W Alden Rd
Street address city: Kearny
Street address state: AZ
Zip/Postal code: 85137-1208
General Phone: (520) 363-5554
General Fax: (520) 363-9663
General/National Adv. E-mail: michaelc@minersunbasin.com
Primary Website: copperarea.com
Year Established: 1958
Avg Paid Circ: 2403
Avg Free Circ: 23
Audit By: Sworn/Estimate/Non-Audited
Audit Date: 10.06.2019
Personnel: James Carnes (Adv. Mgr.); Jennifer Carnes (Mng. Ed.); Michael Carnes (Adv. Prodn.)

COPPER COUNTRY NEWS

Street address 1: 298 N Pine St
Street address city: Globe
Street address state: AZ
Zip/Postal code: 85501-2516
General Phone: (928) 425-0355
General Fax: (928) 425-6535
Editorial Phone: (928) 425-0355
General/National Adv. E-mail: globeccn@yahoo.com
Editorial e-mail: ed@coppercountrynews.com
Primary Website: coppercountrynews.com
Year Established: 1984
Avg Free Circ: 19000
Audit By: Sworn/Estimate/Non-Audited
Audit Date: 10.06.2019
Personnel: Marc Martin (Pub.); Ed Kuehneman (Ed.); Vicki Ross (Adv. Sales)
Parent company (for newspapers): San Luis Valley Publishing

COTTONWOOD JOURNAL EXTRA

Street address 1: 830 S Main St
Street address 2: Ste 1E
Street address city: Cottonwood
Street address state: AZ
Zip/Postal code: 86326-4621
General Phone: (928) 634-8551
General Fax: (928) 634-0823
General/National Adv. E-mail: bob@redrocknews.com
Primary Website: journalaz.com
Avg Paid Circ: 548
Avg Free Circ: 8500
Audit By: Sworn/Estimate/Non-Audited
Audit Date: 10.06.2019
Personnel: Robert Larson (Pub.); David Zarin (Adv. Mgr.); Greg Ruland (Ed.)
Parent company (for newspapers): Larson Newspapers

EAST VALLEY TRIBUNE

Street address 1: 1900 W. Broadway Roadad Parkway, Suite 219
Street address city: Tempe
Street address state: AZ
Zip/Postal code: 85282
General Phone: (480) 898-6500
General Fax: (480) 898-6463
Advertising Phone: (480) 898-6415
Editorial Phone: (480) 898-6512
Editorial Fax: (480) 898-6362
General/National Adv. E-mail: national@evtrib.com
Display Adv. E-mail: golocal@evtrib.com
Classified Adv. e-mail: classads@evtrib.com
Editorial e-mail: newstips@evtrib.com; newstips@evtrib.com
Primary Website: eastvalleytribune.com
Year Established: 1891
Avg Paid Circ: 0
Avg Free Circ: 139800
Sun. Circulation Free: 122000
Audit By: AAM
Audit Date: 30.06.2018
Personnel: Aaron Kolodny (Circ. Dir.); Zac Reynolds (Nat'l Adv. Dir.); Paul Maryniak (Exec. Ed.); Ruth Carlton (Graphic Des.)
Parent company (for newspapers): Times Media Group

EASTERN ARIZONA COURIER

Street address 1: 301 E Hwy 70
Street address 2: Ste A
Street address city: Safford
Street address state: AZ
Zip/Postal code: 85546
General Phone: (928) 428-2560
General Fax: (928) 428-5396
General/National Adv. E-mail: mwatson@eacourier.com
Display Adv. E-mail: classi@eacourier.com
Editorial e-mail: editor@eacourier.com
Primary Website: eacourier.com
Year Established: 1889
Avg Paid Circ: 4094
Avg Free Circ: 25
Audit By: VAC
Audit Date: 31.05.2017
Personnel: David Bell (Mng. Ed.); James Copeland (Circulation Manager); Monica Watson (Pub.)
Parent company (for newspapers): Wick Communications

ELOY ENTERPRISE

Street address 1: 190 N Main St
Street address city: Florence
Street address state: AZ
Zip/Postal code: 85132
General Phone: (520) 868-5897
General Fax: (520) 868-5898
General/National Adv. E-mail: ahowell@pinalcentral.com
Editorial e-mail: news@florencereminder.com
Primary Website: pinalcentral.com/florence_reminder_blade_tribune
Year Established: 1947
Avg Paid Circ: 1623
Avg Free Circ: 8
Audit By: Sworn/Estimate/Non-Audited
Audit Date: 10.06.2019
Personnel: Andy Howell (Editor)
Parent company (for newspapers): ANA Advertising Services, Inc. (Arizona Newspaper Association); Casa Grande Valley Newspapers Inc.

EXPLORER

Street address 1: 7225 N Mona Lisa Rd
Street address 2: Ste 125
Street address city: Tucson
Street address state: AZ
Zip/Postal code: 85741-2581
General Phone: (520) 797-4384
General Fax: (520) 575-8891
Advertising Phone: (520) 797-4384
Advertising Fax: (520) 575-8891
Editorial Phone: (520) 797-4384
Editorial Fax: (520) 575-8891
General/National Adv. E-mail: casey@TucsonLocalMedia.com
Display Adv. E-mail: casey@TucsonLocalMedia.com
Editorial e-mail: editor@explorernews.com
Primary Website: explorernews.com
Year Established: 1993
Avg Paid Circ: 14
Avg Free Circ: 43114
Audit By: CVC
Audit Date: 30.06.2018
Personnel: Jamie Hood (Gen. Mgr); Mari Herreras (Ed.); Jim Nintzel (News Ed.); Chelo Grubb (Web Ed.); Laura Horvath (Circulation Manager); Jason Joseph (Pres./Pub.); Casey Anderson (Adv. Mgr.)

FLAGSTAFF LIVE!

Street address 1: 1751 S Thompson St
Street address city: Flagstaff
Street address state: AZ
Zip/Postal code: 86001-8716
General Phone: (928) 774-4545
General Fax: (928) 773-1934
Advertising Phone: (928) 556-2287
Editorial Phone: (928) 556-2262
General/National Adv. E-mail: cbrady@azdailysun.com
Display Adv. E-mail: cbrady@azdailysun.com
Editorial e-mail: mchase@flaglive.com
Primary Website: flaglive.com
Year Established: 1995
Avg Free Circ: 8300
Audit By: Sworn/Estimate/Non-Audited
Audit Date: 10.06.2019
Personnel: Nancy Wiechec (Man. Ed.); MacKenzie Chase (Staff Writer); Gabriel Granillo (Staff Writer)
Parent company (for newspapers): Flagstaff Publishing; Dispatch-Argus

FLORENCE REMINDER & BLADE-TRIBUNE

Street address 1: 190 N Main St
Street address city: Florence
Street address state: AZ
Zip/Postal code: 85132
General Phone: (520) 868-5897
General Fax: (520) 868-5898
General/National Adv. E-mail: info@florencereminder.com
Display Adv. E-mail: ads@florencereminder.com
Editorial e-mail: news@florencereminder.com
Primary Website: pinalcentral.com/florence_reminder_blade_tribune
Avg Paid Circ: 1623
Avg Free Circ: 8
Audit By: Sworn/Estimate/Non-Audited
Audit Date: 10.06.2019
Personnel: Joey Chenoweth (Editor)
Parent company (for newspapers): Casa Grande Valley Newspapers Inc.

FOOTHILLS FOCUS

Street address 1: 46641 N Black Canyon Hwy
Street address 2: Ste 1
Street address city: New River
Street address state: AZ
Zip/Postal code: 85087-6941
General Phone: (623) 465-5808
General Fax: (623) 465-1363
General/National Adv. E-mail: foothillsfocus@qwestoffice.net
Editorial e-mail: ffeditorial@hotmail.com
Primary Website: thefoothillsfocus.com
Year Established: 2002
Audit By: Sworn/Estimate/Non-Audited
Audit Date: 10.06.2019
Personnel: John Alexander (Publisher & Editor)

FOOTHILLS NEWS

Street address 1: 7225 N Mona Lisa Rd
Street address 2: Ste 125
Street address city: Tucson
Street address state: AZ
Zip/Postal code: 85741-2581
General Phone: (520) 797-4384
General Fax: (520) 575-8891
General/National Adv. E-mail: Kristin@tucsonlocalmedia.com
Primary Website: tucsonlocalmedia.com/foothillsnews
Audit By: Sworn/Estimate/Non-Audited
Audit Date: 10.06.2019
Personnel: Jason Joseph (Pres.?Pub.); Jaime Hood (Gen. Mgr.); Casey Anderson (Adv. Dir.); Jim Nintzel (Circ. Mgr.)
Parent company (for newspapers): Times Media Group

GLENDALE TODAY

Street address 1: 17220 N Boswell Blvd
Street address 2: Ste 101
Street address city: Sun City
Street address state: AZ
Zip/Postal code: 85373-2065
General Phone: (623) 977-8351
General Fax: (623) 876-2589
Advertising Phone: (623) 876-2566
Editorial Phone: (623) 876-2534
General/National Adv. E-mail: paslandes@yourwestvalley.com
Display Adv. E-mail: sunclassads@yourwestvalley.com
Editorial e-mail: dmccarthy@yourwestvalley.com
Primary Website: yourwestvalley.com
Mthly Avg Views: 130000
Mthly Avg Unique Visitors: 60000
Year Established: 1995
Avg Paid Circ: 1
Avg Free Circ: 22384
Audit By: Sworn/Estimate/Non-Audited
Audit Date: 10.06.2019
Personnel: Marji Ranes (Pub.); Dan McCarthy (Exec. Ed.)
Parent company (for newspapers): Independent Newsmedia Inc. USA

GREEN VALLEY NEWS

Street address 1: 18705 S I 19 Frontage Rd
Street address 2: Ste 125
Street address city: Green Valley
Street address state: AZ
Zip/Postal code: 85614-5014
General Phone: (520) 625-5511
General/National Adv. E-mail: skeith@gvnews.com
Display Adv. E-mail: cnixon@gvnews.com
Editorial e-mail: dshearer@gvnews.com
Primary Website: gvnews.com
Avg Paid Circ: 7126
Avg Free Circ: 162
Audit By: Sworn/Estimate/Non-Audited
Audit Date: 10.06.2019
Personnel: Dru Sanchez (Pub.); Dan Shearer (Ed.); Sarah Keith (Adv. Mgr.); Graham Harrington (Production Mgr.); Bonnie Olsen (Circ. Mgr)
Parent company (for newspapers): Wick Communications

INSIDE TUCSON BUSINESS

Street address 1: 7225 N Mona Lisa Rd
Street address 2: Ste. 125
Street address city: Tucson
Street address state: AZ
Zip/Postal code: 85741-2581
General Phone: (520) 294-1200
General Fax: (520) 294-4040
General/National Adv. E-mail: jahearn@azbiz.com
Editorial e-mail: mevans@azbiz.com
Primary Website: insidetucsonbusiness.com
Avg Paid Circ: 1845
Avg Free Circ: 3047

Audit By: Sworn/Estimate/Non-Audited
Audit Date: 10.06.2019
Personnel: Mark Evans (Ed.); Jason Joseph (Pres./Pub.); Jim Nintzel (Circ.); Grace Heike (Sales Admin); Mari Herreras (Ed.)
Parent company (for newspapers): ANA Advertising Services, Inc. (Arizona Newspaper Association); Times Media Group

LAKE POWELL CHRONICLE

Street address 1: PO Box 1716
Street address city: Page
Street address state: AZ
Zip/Postal code: 86040-1716
General Phone: (928) 645-8888
General Fax: (928) 645-2209
General/National Adv. E-mail: ed@lakepowellchronicle.com
Editorial e-mail: editor@lakepowellchronicle.reporter@lakepowellchronicle.com
Primary Website: lakepowellchronicle.com
Year Established: 1965
Audit By: Sworn/Estimate/Non-Audited
Audit Date: 10.06.2019
Personnel: David Rupkalvis (Ed./Pub.); Kim Clark (Office Mgr.); Mary Chilton (Sales Rep.)
Parent company (for newspapers): San Luis Valley Publishing

LAUGHLIN ENTERTAINER

Street address 1: 2435 Miracle Mile
Street address city: Bullhead City
Street address state: AZ
Zip/Postal code: 86442-7311
General Phone: (928) 763-2505
General Fax: (928) 763-2232
Advertising Phone: (928) 763-2505 x7238
Editorial Phone: (928) 763-2505 x7232
General/National Adv. E-mail: laughlin.entertainer@gmail.com
Editorial e-mail: entertainereditor@gmail.com
Primary Website: laughlinentertainer.com
Year Established: 1985
Avg Free Circ: 55000
Audit By: Sworn/Estimate/Non-Audited
Audit Date: 10.06.2019
Personnel: Alan Marciocchi (Ed.)
Parent company (for newspapers): Brehm Communications, Inc.

LAUGHLIN NEVADA TIMES

Street address 1: 2435 Miracle Mile
Street address city: Bullhead City
Street address state: AZ
Zip/Postal code: 86442-7311
General Phone: (928) 763-2505
General Fax: (928) 763-6752
General/National Adv. E-mail: nwpad@nwppub.com
Display Adv. E-mail: classifieds@nwppub.com
Editorial e-mail: LaughlinTimes @gmail.com
Primary Website: laughlintimes.com
Year Established: 1990
Avg Paid Circ: 4300
Audit By: Sworn/Estimate/Non-Audited
Audit Date: 10.06.2019
Personnel: Gary Milks (Pub.); Julie Fariman (Ed.)
Parent company (for newspapers): Brehm Communications, Inc.; News West Publishing Company Inc. (OOB)

LET'S GO

Street address 1: 16508 E Laser Dr
Street address 2: Ste 101
Street address city: Fountain Hills
Street address state: AZ
Zip/Postal code: 85268-6512
General Phone: (480) 837-1925
General Fax: (480) 837-1951
General/National Adv. E-mail: brent@fhtimes.com
Editorial e-mail: mike@fhtimes.com
Primary Website: fhtimes.com/lets_go
Year Established: 1999
Avg Free Circ: 17000
Audit By: Sworn/Estimate/Non-Audited
Audit Date: 10.06.2019
Personnel: L. Alan Cruikshank (Pub.); Michael Scharnow (Ed.)
Parent company (for newspapers): Western States Publishers, Inc.

MARANA NEWS

Street address 1: 7225 N Mona Lisa Rd
Street address 2: Ste 125
Street address city: Tucson
Street address state: AZ
Zip/Postal code: 85741-2581
General Phone: (520) 797-4384
General Fax: (520) 908-0455
Advertising Phone: (520) 578-1505 ext.19
General/National Adv. E-mail: carolyn@newsmediacorp.com
Editorial e-mail: news@maranaweeklynews.com
Primary Website: themarananews.com
Year Established: 2007
Audit By: Sworn/Estimate/Non-Audited
Audit Date: 10.06.2019
Personnel: Tonja Greenfield (General Manager/Editor); Tom Legg (Dir., Nat'l Sales); Patricia Dixie (Nat'l Acct. Coord.); Jason Joseph (Pres./Pub.)
Parent company (for newspapers): Times Media Group

MARICOPA MONITOR

Street address 1: 21300 N John Wayne Pkwy
Street address 2: Ste 103
Street address city: Maricopa
Street address state: AZ
Zip/Postal code: 85139-8964
General Phone: (520) 568-4198
General Fax: (520) 560-2831
Advertising Phone: (520) 568-4198
Editorial Phone: (520) 568-4198
General/National Adv. E-mail: kdodge@trivalleycentral.com
Display Adv. E-mail: dcortez@trivalleycentral.com
Editorial e-mail: agaub@trivalleycentral.com
Primary Website: pinalcentral.com/maricopa_monitor
Year Established: 2003
Audit By: Sworn/Estimate/Non-Audited
Audit Date: 10.06.2019
Personnel: Adam Guab (Mng. Ed.); Brian Wright (News Ed.)
Parent company (for newspapers): Casa Grande Valley Newspapers Inc.

NOGALES INTERNATIONAL

Street address 1: 268 W View Point Dr
Street address city: Nogales
Street address state: AZ
Zip/Postal code: 85621-4114
General Phone: (337)365-6773
General Fax: (520) 761-3115
Advertising Phone: (520) 375-5764
Editorial Phone: (520) 375-5767
General/National Adv. E-mail: graphics@nogalesinternational.com
Display Adv. E-mail: classifieds@nogalesinternational.com
Editorial e-mail: editorial@nogalesinternational.com
Primary Website: nogalesinternational.com
Year Established: 1925
Avg Paid Circ: 1736
Avg Free Circ: 68
Audit By: CVC
Audit Date: 31.05.2017
Personnel: Manuel Coppola (Pub.); Jonathan Clark (Mng. Ed.); Ricardo Villarreal (Circ. Mgr.); Debbie Keller (Adv. Mgr.); Andrew Saenz (Int. Gen. Mgr.)
Parent company (for newspapers): Wick Communications

PEORIA INDEPENDENT

Street address 1: 17220 N Boswell Blvd
Street address 2: Ste 101
Street address city: Sun City
Street address state: AZ
Zip/Postal code: 85373-2065
General Phone: (623) 972-6101
General Fax: (623) 445-2720
Advertising Phone: (623) 445-2807
General/National Adv. E-mail: azmajoraccounts@newszap.com
Editorial e-mail: aznews@newszap.com
Primary Website: yourwestvalley.com
Year Established: 1999
Avg Paid Circ: 6
Avg Free Circ: 16340
Audit By: Sworn/Estimate/Non-Audited
Audit Date: 10.06.2019
Personnel: Rusty Bradshaw (News Ed.)
Parent company (for newspapers): Independent Newspapers, Inc. (Arizona)

PEORIA TIMES

Street address 1: 7122 N 59th Ave
Street address city: Glendale
Street address state: AZ
Zip/Postal code: 85301-2436
General Phone: (623) 842-6000
General Fax: (623) 842-6013
Advertising Phone: (623) 847-4601
Editorial Phone: (623) 847-4604
General/National Adv. E-mail: sales@star-times.com
Display Adv. E-mail: notices@star-times.com
Editorial e-mail: cdryer@star-times.com
Primary Website: peoriatimes.com
Year Established: 1952
Avg Paid Circ: 4200
Avg Free Circ: 800
Audit By: Sworn/Estimate/Non-Audited
Audit Date: 10.06.2019
Personnel: William E. Toops (Pub./Gen. Mng.); Roger W. Toops (Bus. Mgr.); Connie Williams (Adv. Mgr.); Carolyn Dryer (Ed.)
Parent company (for newspapers): Pueblo Publishers, Inc.

PRESCOTT VALLEY TRIBUNE

Street address 1: PO Box 370
Street address city: Chino Valley
Street address state: AZ
Zip/Postal code: 86323-0370
General Phone: (928) 445-3333
General Fax: (928) 772-3393
Advertising Phone: (928) 776-8122
Editorial Phone: (928) 445-3333 x 1020
General/National Adv. E-mail: bcubitt@prescottaz.com
Display Adv. E-mail: classifieds@prescottaz.com
Editorial e-mail: hdfoster@prescottaz.com
Primary Website: prescottvalleytribune.com
Avg Paid Circ: 131
Avg Free Circ: 15389
Audit By: Sworn/Estimate/Non-Audited
Audit Date: 10.06.2019
Personnel: Kelly Soldwedel (Pub.); Heidi Dahms Foster (Ed. Mgr.); Will Campbell (Adv. Mgr.); Babette Cubitt (Adv. Dir.); Teri Bryant (Classified Coord.)
Parent company (for newspapers): ANA Advertising Services, Inc. (Arizona Newspaper Association); Western News&Info, Inc.

QUEEN CREEK INDEPENDENT

Street address 1: 2066 W Apache Trl
Street address 2: Ste 110
Street address city: Apache Junction
Street address state: AZ
Zip/Postal code: 85120-3733
General Phone: (480) 982-7799
General Fax: (480) 671-0016
General/National Adv. E-mail: qcnews@newszap.com
Display Adv. E-mail: evads@newszap.com
Editorial e-mail: qcnews@newszap.com
Primary Website: queencreekindependent.com
Year Established: 2004
Avg Paid Circ: 0
Avg Free Circ: 10000
Audit By: Sworn/Estimate/Non-Audited
Audit Date: 10.06.2019
Personnel: Wendy Miller (Ed.); Bret McKeand (Pub.); Richard Dyer (Mng. Ed.); Deb Richardson (Adv. Consultant)
Parent company (for newspapers): Independent Newsmedia Inc. USA

SAHUARITA SUN

Street address 1: 18705 S I 19 Frontage Rd
Street address 2: Ste 125
Street address city: Green Valley
Street address state: AZ
Zip/Postal code: 85614-5014
General Phone: (520) 625-5511
General Fax: (520) 625-8046
General/National Adv. E-mail: skeith@sahuaritasun.com
Display Adv. E-mail: cnixon@sahuaritasun.com
Editorial e-mail: dshearer@sahuaritasun.com
Primary Website: sahuaritasun.com
Year Established: 2005
Avg Paid Circ: 813
Avg Free Circ: 8141
Audit By: Sworn/Estimate/Non-Audited
Audit Date: 10.06.2019
Personnel: Dru Sanchez (Pub.); Anne Maner (Bus. Mgr.); Dan Shearer (Ed.); Andrew Paxton (Asst. Ed.); Sarah Keith (Adv. Mgr.); Bonnie Olsen
Parent company (for newspapers): Wick Communications

SAN CARLOS APACHE MOCCASIN

Street address 1: 298 N Pine St
Street address city: Globe
Street address state: AZ
Zip/Postal code: 85501-2516
General Phone: (928) 425-7121
General Fax: (928) 425-7001
General/National Adv. E-mail: publisher@silverbelt.com
Primary Website: silverbelt.com
Avg Paid Circ: 1973
Audit By: Sworn/Estimate/Non-Audited
Audit Date: 10.06.2019
Personnel: Marc Marin (Pub.); Andrea Marcandi (Ed.)

SAN MANUEL MINER

Street address 1: 366 W Alden Rd
Street address city: Kearny
Street address state: AZ
Zip/Postal code: 85137-1208
General Phone: (520) 385-2266
General Fax: (520) 385-4666
Primary Website: copperarea.com
Avg Paid Circ: 3310
Avg Free Circ: 36
Audit By: Sworn/Estimate/Non-Audited
Audit Date: 10.06.2019
Personnel: James Carnes (Pub.); Pat Hernandez (Adv. Mgr.); Jan Carlson (Circ. Mgr.); Gayle Carnes (Mng. Ed.)
Parent company (for newspapers): ANA Advertising Services, Inc. (Arizona Newspaper Association)

SAN PEDRO VALLEY NEWS-SUN

Street address 1: 200 S Ocotillo Ave
Street address city: Benson
Street address state: AZ
Zip/Postal code: 85602-6407
General Phone: (520) 586-3382
General Fax: (520) 586-2382
Advertising Phone: (520) 586-3382
Advertising Fax: (520) 586-2382
General/National Adv. E-mail: newssun@bensonnews-sun.com
Display Adv. E-mail: sara.brown@bensonnews-sun.com
Editorial e-mail: chris.dabovich@bensonnews-sun.com
Primary Website: bensonnews-sun.com
Year Established: 1900
Avg Paid Circ: 1466
Audit By: VAC
Audit Date: 31.05.2017
Personnel: Chris Dabovich (Mng. Ed.); Joan Hancock (Bus. Mgr.); Adam Tanner (Adv. Rep.); Kendra Tanner (Classifieds Adv. Mgr.); Donna Fenn (Circ. Dir.); Francis Wick (Publisher)
Parent company (for newspapers): Wick Communications

SANTA CRUZ VALLEY SUN

Street address 1: 268 W View Point Dr
Street address city: Nogales
Street address state: AZ
Zip/Postal code: 85621-4114
General Phone: (520) 375-5760
General Fax: (520) 761-3115
Advertising Phone: (520) 625-5511
General/National Adv. E-mail: webmaster@nogalesinternational.com
Primary Website: nogalesinternational.com/santa_cruz_valley_sun
Avg Paid Circ: 0
Avg Free Circ: 18079
Audit By: Sworn/Estimate/Non-Audited
Audit Date: 10.06.2019

Personnel: Manuel Coppola (Pub.); Jonathan Clark (Mng. Ed.); Ricardo Villarreal (Circ. Mgr.); Debbie Keller (Adv. Mgr.)

SCOTTSDALE INDEPENDENT

Street address 1: 23043 N 16th Ln
Street address city: Phoenix
Street address state: AZ
Zip/Postal code: 85027-1331
General Phone: (623) 445-2777
General Fax: (623) 445-2740
General/National Adv. E-mail: neads@newszap.com
Display Adv. E-mail: iniclassads@newszap.com
Editorial e-mail: scottsdalenews@newszap.com
Primary Website: scottsdaleindependent.com
Year Established: 1984
Avg Paid Circ: 0
Avg Free Circ: 10000
Audit By: Sworn/Estimate/Non-Audited
Audit Date: 10.06.2019
Personnel: Bret McKeand (Publisher/President); Terrance Thornton (Ed.); Jan McKinney (Adv. Mgr.); Charlene Bisson (Pub.); Edward Dulin (Pres.)
Parent company (for newspapers): Independent Newsmedia Inc. USA

SEDONA RED ROCK NEWS

Street address 1: 298 Van Deren Rd
Street address city: Sedona
Street address state: AZ
Zip/Postal code: 86336-4826
General Phone: (928) 282-5580
General Fax: (928) 282-6011
Advertising Phone: (928) 282-5580
Editorial Phone: (928) 282-7795 x129
General/National Adv. E-mail: klarson@larsonnewspapers.com
Display Adv. E-mail: klarson@larsonnewspapers.com
Classified Adv. e-mail: classifieds@larsonnewspapers.com
Editorial e-mail: Editor@LarsonNewspapers.com
Primary Website: redrocknews.com
Year Established: 1963
Avg Paid Circ: 5600
Avg Free Circ: 8400
Audit By: Sworn/Estimate/Non-Audited
Audit Date: 10.06.2019
Personnel: Robert Larson (Pub.); George Werner (Copy Ed.); Kyle Larson (Adv. Dir.); Christopher Fox Graham (Managing Editor); Tim Perry; Trista Steers (Ed.); Robert Sterry; Austin Turner
Parent company (for newspapers): Larson Publishing, Inc.

SILVER CREEK HERALD

Street address 1: 200 E Hopi Dr
Street address city: Holbrook
Street address state: AZ
Zip/Postal code: 86025-2628
General Phone: (928) 524-6203
General Fax: (928) 524-3541
General/National Adv. E-mail: mbarger@cableone.net
Display Adv. E-mail: rbarger@cableone.net
Editorial e-mail: franciepayne@cableone.net
Primary Website: tribunenewsnow.com
Year Established: 1909
Avg Free Circ: 3200
Audit By: Sworn/Estimate/Non-Audited
Audit Date: 10.06.2019
Personnel: Matthew Barger (Pub.); Linda Kor (Ed./Gen. Mgr.); Debbie Barger (Off. Mgr.)

SONORAN NEWS

Street address 1: 6702 E Cave Creek Rd
Street address 2: Ste 3
Street address city: Cave Creek
Street address state: AZ
Zip/Postal code: 85331-8659
General Phone: (480) 488-2021
General Fax: (480) 488-6216
General/National Adv. E-mail: sales@sonorannews.com
Editorial e-mail: editorial@sonorannews.com
Primary Website: sonorannews.com/new
Avg Paid Circ: 62
Avg Free Circ: 43000
Audit By: Sworn/Estimate/Non-Audited
Audit Date: 10.06.2019
Personnel: Don Sorchych (Ed.)

SUN CITY INDEPENDENT

Street address 1: 17220 N Boswell Blvd
Street address 2: Ste 230
Street address city: Sun City
Street address state: AZ
Zip/Postal code: 85373-2065
General Phone: (623) 972-6101
General Fax: (623) 974-6004
Editorial Phone: 623-445-2725
General/National Adv. E-mail: rbradshaw@iniusa.org
Display Adv. E-mail: bwandling@iniusa.org
Editorial e-mail: wvnews@newszap.com
Primary Website: aznews@iniusa.org
Mthly Avg Views: 22000
Year Established: 1960
Avg Paid Circ: 9
Avg Free Circ: 20108
Audit By: AAM
Audit Date: 31.03.2019
Personnel: Charlene Bisson (CEO/president); Edward Dulin (Pres.); Bret McKeand (VP)
Parent company (for newspapers): Independent Newsmedia Inc. USA

SUN CITY WEST INDEPENDENT

Street address 1: 17220 N Boswell Blvd
Street address 2: Ste 101
Street address city: Sun City
Street address state: AZ
Zip/Postal code: 85373-2065
General Phone: (623) 972-6101
General Fax: (623) 974-6004
Advertising Phone: (623) 876-2569
General/National Adv. E-mail: kmahoney@newszap.com
Editorial e-mail: aznews@newszap.com
Primary Website: yourwestvalley.com
Year Established: 1978
Avg Paid Circ: 9
Avg Free Circ: 12767
Audit By: CAC
Audit Date: 31.03.2019
Personnel: Rusty Bradshaw (News Ed)
Parent company (for newspapers): Independent Newspapers, Inc. (Arizona)

SURPRISE INDEPENDENT

Street address 1: 17220 N Boswell Blvd
Street address 2: Ste 101
Street address city: Sun City
Street address state: AZ
Zip/Postal code: 85373-2065
General Phone: (623) 972-6101
General Fax: (623) 974-6004
General/National Adv. E-mail: wvads@newszap.com
Display Adv. E-mail: iniclassads@newszap.com
Editorial e-mail: wvnews@newszap.com
Primary Website: YourValley.nete
Year Established: 1997
Avg Free Circ: 32000
Audit By: CAC
Audit Date: 01.07.2017
Personnel: Charlene Patti-Bisson (Publisher); Bret McKeand (VP., Opns.); Edward Dulin (Pres.)
Parent company (for newspapers): Independent Newspapers, Inc. (Arizona); ANA Advertising Services, Inc. (Arizona Newspaper Association); Independent Newsmedia Inc. USA

THE APACHE JUNCTION/GOLD CANYON NEWS

Street address 1: 1075 S Idaho Rd
Street address 2: Ste 102
Street address city: Apache Junction
Street address state: AZ
Zip/Postal code: 85119-6497
General Phone: (480) 982-6397
General Fax: (480) 982-3707
General/National Adv. E-mail: ajnews@ajnews.com
Display Adv. E-mail: ajnews@ajnews.com
Editorial e-mail: ajnews@ajnews.com
Primary Website: ajnews.com
Year Established: 1997
Audit By: Sworn/Estimate/Non-Audited
Audit Date: 10.06.2019
Personnel: Chuck Baker (Co-Publisher)
Parent company (for newspapers): Foothills Publishing, Inc.

THE BISBEE OBSERVER

Street address 1: 7 Bisbee Rd Ste L
Street address 2: Ste. L
Street address city: Bisbee
Street address state: AZ
Zip/Postal code: 85603-1140
General Phone: (520) 432-7254
General Fax: (520) 432-4192
General/National Adv. E-mail: bisbeeobserver@cableone.net
Primary Website: thebisbeeobserver.com
Year Established: 1985
Avg Paid Circ: 2100
Avg Free Circ: 45
Audit By: Sworn/Estimate/Non-Audited
Audit Date: 10.06.2019
Personnel: Paul Lewis (Circ. Mgr.); Laura Swan (Prodn. Mgr.)
Parent company (for newspapers): ANA Advertising Services, Inc. (Arizona Newspaper Association)

THE BUCKEYE STAR

Street address 1: 108 N 4th St
Street address city: Buckeye
Street address state: AZ
Zip/Postal code: 85326-2402
General Phone: (623) 374-4303
General Fax: (623) 322-9686
General/National Adv. E-mail: publisher@thebuckeyestar.net
Primary Website: thebuckeyestar.net
Year Established: 2010
Audit By: Sworn/Estimate/Non-Audited
Audit Date: 10.06.2019
Personnel: Jonathan Stein (Pub.)

THE BUSINESS JOURNAL

Street address 1: 101 N 1st Ave Ste 2300
Street address 2: Suite 2300
Street address city: Phoenix
Street address state: AZ
Zip/Postal code: 85003-1903
General Phone: (602) 230-8400
General Fax: (602) 230-0955
Advertising Phone: (602) 308-6525
Editorial Phone: (602) 308-6513
General/National Adv. E-mail: sdenison@bizjournals.com
Editorial e-mail: ilowery@bizjournals.com
Primary Website: bizjournals.com/phoenix
Audit By: Sworn/Estimate/Non-Audited
Audit Date: 10.06.2019
Personnel: Ray Schey (Pub.); Llana Lwery (Ed.-in-Chief); Patrick O'Grady (Mng. Ed.); David Hostetler (Prod. Dir.); Rhonda Pringle (Adv. Dir.)

THE CAMP VERDE JOURNAL

Street address 1: 406 S. First St.
Street address city: Camp Verde
Street address state: AZ
Zip/Postal code: 86322
General Phone: (928) 567-3341
General Fax: (928) 567-2373
General/National Adv. E-mail: bob@redrocknews.com
Editorial e-mail: editor@larsonnewspapers.com
Primary Website: journalaz.com
Year Established: 1980
Avg Paid Circ: 2000
Avg Free Circ: 125
Audit By: Sworn/Estimate/Non-Audited
Audit Date: 10.06.2019
Personnel: David Zarn (Adv. Mgr.); Robert B. Larson (Pub.); Kyle Larson (Adv. Dir); Trista Steers (Ed.)
Parent company (for newspapers): Larson Newspapers

THE CATHOLIC SUN

Street address 1: 400 E Monroe St
Street address city: Phoenix
Street address state: AZ
Zip/Postal code: 85004-2336
General Phone: (602) 354-2139
General Fax: (602) 354-2429
Advertising Phone: (602) 354-2136
Editorial Phone: (602) 354-2131
General/National Adv. E-mail: advertising@catholicsun.org
Display Adv. E-mail: akearns@catholicsun.org
Editorial e-mail: jdlgarcia@catholicsun.org
Primary Website: catholicsun.org
Year Established: 1985
Audit By: Sworn/Estimate/Non-Audited
Audit Date: 10.06.2019
Personnel: Tony GutiÃ©rrez (Ed.); Jennifer Ellis (Adv. Rep.); Alana Kearns (Adv. Sales)

THE COPPER ERA

Street address 1: 301 E Hwy 70
Street address 2: Ste A
Street address city: Safford
Street address state: AZ
Zip/Postal code: 85546
General Phone: (928) 428-2560
General Fax: (928) 428-5396
General/National Adv. E-mail: mwatson@eacourier.com
Display Adv. E-mail: classi@eacourier.com
Editorial e-mail: business@eacourier.com
Primary Website: eacourier.com/copper_era
Year Established: 1899
Avg Paid Circ: 871
Audit By: VAC
Audit Date: 31.05.2017
Personnel: Monica Watson (Pub.); David Bell (Mng. Ed.)
Parent company (for newspapers): Wick Communications

THE DOUGLAS DISPATCH

Street address 1: 530 E 11th St
Street address city: Douglas
Street address state: AZ
Zip/Postal code: 85607-2014
General Phone: (337)365-6773
General Fax: (520) 364-6750
Advertising Phone: (520) 220-8775
Advertising Fax: (520) 364-6750
Editorial Phone: (520) 234-0145
Editorial Fax: (520) 364-6750
General/National Adv. E-mail: newsroom@douglasdispatch.com
Display Adv. E-mail: advertising@douglasdispatch.com
Editorial e-mail: editor@douglasdispatch.com
Primary Website: douglasdispatch.com
Year Established: 1902
Avg Paid Circ: 1435
Audit By: Sworn/Estimate/Non-Audited
Audit Date: 10.06.2019
Personnel: Kimberly Hicks (Bookkeeper); David Dominguez (Adv. Mgr.); Francisco Barrios (Circ. Mgr.); Bruce Whetten (Managing Ed.); Nancy Wykle (Pub.)
Parent company (for newspapers): Wick Communications

THE FOUNTAIN HILL TIMES

Street address 1: 16508 E Laser Dr
Street address 2: Ste 101
Street address city: Fountain Hills
Street address state: AZ
Zip/Postal code: 85268-6512
General Phone: (480) 837-1925
General Fax: (480) 837-1951
Advertising Phone: (480) 837-1925
Advertising Fax: (480) 837-1951
General/National Adv. E-mail: brent@fhtimes.com
Display Adv. E-mail: Tammie@fhtimes.com
Editorial e-mail: mike@fhtimes.com
Primary Website: fhtimes.com
Year Established: 1974
Avg Paid Circ: 5300
Audit By: Sworn/Estimate/Non-Audited
Audit Date: 10.06.2019
Personnel: L. Alan Cruikshank (Pub.); Michael G. Scharnow (Ed.); Kip Kirkendoll (Bus. Mgr.); Jennifer Gentry (Circ. Mgr.)
Parent company (for newspapers): Western States Publishers, Inc.

THE GLENDALE STAR

Street address 1: 7122 N 59th Ave
Street address city: Glendale
Street address state: AZ
Zip/Postal code: 85301-2436

General Phone: (623) 842-6000
General Fax: (623) 842-6013
Advertising Phone: (623) 847-4601
Editorial Phone: (623) 847-4604
General/National Adv. E-mail: wtoops@star-times.com
Display Adv. E-mail: sales@star-times.com
Editorial e-mail: cdryer@star-times.com
Primary Website: glendalestar.com
Year Established: 1978
Avg Paid Circ: 6000
Avg Free Circ: 1000
Audit By: Sworn/Estimate/Non-Audited
Audit Date: 10.06.2019
Personnel: William E. Toops (Pub./Gen.Mng.); Carolyn Dryer (Mng. Ed.); Roger W. Toops (Bus. Mgr.)
Parent company (for newspapers): Pueblo Publishers, Inc.

THE PARKER PIONEER

Street address 1: 1317 S Joshua Ave
Street address 2: Ste L
Street address city: Parker
Street address state: AZ
Zip/Postal code: 85344-5768
General Phone: (928) 669-2275
General Fax: (928) 669-9624
General/National Adv. E-mail: sales@havasunews.com
Editorial e-mail: bbowers@havasunews.com
Primary Website: parkerpioneer.net
Avg Paid Circ: 2075
Avg Free Circ: 32
Audit By: Sworn/Estimate/Non-Audited
Audit Date: 10.06.2019
Personnel: Michael E. Quinn (Pub.); Christine Hammers (Adv. Mgr.); Alexis Christensen (Circ. Mgr.); Cindy Taylor (Prod. Mgr.)
Parent company (for newspapers): Wick Communications; Western News&Info, Inc.

THE PAYSON ROUNDUP

Street address 1: 708 N Beeline Hwy
Street address city: Payson
Street address state: AZ
Zip/Postal code: 85541-3770
General Phone: (928) 474-5251
General Fax: (928) 474-1893
Advertising Phone: (928) 474-5251 x 104
Advertising Fax: (928) 474-1893
Editorial Phone: (928) 474-5251 x 115
Editorial Fax: (928) 474-1893
General/National Adv. E-mail: gtackett@payson.com
Display Adv. E-mail: classads@payson.com
Editorial e-mail: paleshire@payson.com
Primary Website: payson.com
Year Established: 1937
Avg Paid Circ: 5166
Avg Free Circ: 169
Audit By: Sworn/Estimate/Non-Audited
Audit Date: 10.06.2019
Personnel: Peter Aleshire (Ed.); Patty Behm (Circ. Mgr.); Julie Williams (Opns. Mgr.); Gary Tackett (Director of Sales)
Parent company (for newspapers): White Mountain Publishing

THE PINAL NUGGET

Street address 1: 366 W Alden Rd
Street address city: Kearny
Street address state: AZ
Zip/Postal code: 85137-1208
General Phone: (520) 385-2266
General Fax: (520) 385-4666
General/National Adv. E-mail: michaelc@minersunbasin.com
Primary Website: copperarea.com
Year Established: 2007
Audit By: Sworn/Estimate/Non-Audited
Audit Date: 10.06.2019

THE RECORD REPORTER

Street address 1: 2025 N 3rd St
Street address 2: Ste 155
Street address city: Phoenix
Street address state: AZ
Zip/Postal code: 85004-1425
General Phone: (602) 417-9900
General Fax: (602) 417-9910
General/National Adv. E-mail: Diane_Heuel@dailyjournal.com
Display Adv. E-mail: record_reporter@dailyjournal.com
Editorial e-mail: diane_heuel@dailyjournal.com
Primary Website: www.recordreporter.com
Year Established: 1914
Personnel: Diane Heuel (Pub.); Heather Gibson (Production Editor); Christopher Gilfillan (Ed.)
Parent company (for newspapers): DAILY JOURNAL CORPORATION

THE STANDARD

Street address 1: 221 E Beale St
Street address city: Kingman
Street address state: AZ
Zip/Postal code: 86401-5829
General Phone: (928) 753-1143
General Fax: (928) 753-1312
General/National Adv. E-mail: ads@thestandardnewspaper.net
Display Adv. E-mail: classifiedads@thestandardnewspaper.net
Primary Website: thestandardnewspaper.net
Year Established: 1990
Audit By: Sworn/Estimate/Non-Audited
Audit Date: 10.06.2019
Personnel: Erin Clark (Ed.)

THE TOMBSTONE NEWS

Street address 1: 525 E Allen St.
Street address 2: Ste. 4
Street address city: Tombstone
Street address state: AZ
Zip/Postal code: 85638
General Phone: (520) 457-3086
General Fax: (520) 457-3126
Editorial e-mail: editor@thetombstonenews.com
Primary Website: thetombstonenews.com
Year Established: 2005
Audit By: Sworn/Estimate/Non-Audited
Audit Date: 10.06.2019

THE TRIBUNE-NEWS

Street address 1: 200 E Hopi Dr
Street address city: Holbrook
Street address state: AZ
Zip/Postal code: 86025-2628
General Phone: (928) 524-6203
General Fax: (928) 524-3541
General/National Adv. E-mail: mikenilsson.adv@gmail.com
Display Adv. E-mail: mbarger@cableone.net
Editorial e-mail: franciepayne@cableone.net
Primary Website: tribunenewsnow.com
Avg Paid Circ: 2490
Avg Free Circ: 1538
Audit By: Sworn/Estimate/Non-Audited
Audit Date: 10.06.2019
Personnel: Matthew Barger (Pub./Adv. Dir.); Linda Kor (Mng. Ed.)
Parent company (for newspapers): Navajo County Publishers, Inc.

THE VERDE INDEPENDENT

Street address 1: 116 S Main St
Street address city: Cottonwood
Street address state: AZ
Zip/Postal code: 86326-3998
General Phone: (928) 634-2241
General Fax: (928) 634-2312
Advertising Phone: (928) 634-2241 ext. 6024
Advertising Fax: (928) 634-2312
Editorial Phone: (928) 634-2241 ext. 6032
Editorial Fax: (928) 634-2312
General/National Adv. E-mail: advertising@verdenews.com
Display Adv. E-mail: classified@verdenews.com
Editorial e-mail: dengler@verdenews.com
Primary Website: verdenews.com
Year Established: 1947
Avg Paid Circ: 2522
Audit By: Sworn/Estimate/Non-Audited
Audit Date: 10.06.2019
Personnel: Dan Engler (Ed.); Edward Dulin (Pres.); Bret McKeand (VP)
Parent company (for newspapers): Western News&Info, Inc.

THE WEEKLY BULLETIN

Street address 1: 268 W View Point Dr
Street address city: Nogales
Street address state: AZ
Zip/Postal code: 85621-4114
General Phone: (520) 375-5760
General Fax: (520) 761-3115
Advertising Phone: (520) 375-5764
Editorial Phone: (520) 375-5767
General/National Adv. E-mail: carmen.torres@nogalesinternational.com
Display Adv. E-mail: classifieds@nogalesinternational.com
Editorial e-mail: editorial@nogalesinternational.com
Primary Website: nogalesinternational.com/the_bulletin
Year Established: 1991
Avg Paid Circ: 515
Audit By: Sworn/Estimate/Non-Audited
Audit Date: 10.06.2019
Personnel: Manuel Coppola (Pub.); Jonathan Clark (Ed.)

TOWN OF PARADISE VALLEY INDEPENDENT

Street address 1: 23043 N 16th Ln
Street address city: Phoenix
Street address state: AZ
Zip/Postal code: 85027-1331
General Phone: (623) 445-2777
General Fax: (623) 445-2740
General/National Adv. E-mail: neads@newszap.com
Display Adv. E-mail: iniclassads@newszap.com
Editorial e-mail: pvalleynews@newszap.com
Primary Website: paradisevalleyindependent.com
Year Established: 1984
Avg Paid Circ: 0
Avg Free Circ: 8500
Audit By: Sworn/Estimate/Non-Audited
Audit Date: 10.06.2019
Personnel: Bret McKeand (VP); Terrance Thornton (Ed.); Jan McKinney (Adv. Mgr.); Edward Dulin (Pres.); Charlene Bisson (Pub.)
Parent company (for newspapers): Independent Newsmedia Inc. USA

WEST VALLEY VIEW

Street address 1: 250 N Litchfield Rd
Street address 2: Ste. 130
Street address city: Goodyear
Street address state: AZ
Zip/Postal code: 85338-1380
General Phone: (623) 535-8439
General Fax: (623) 935-2103
General/National Adv. E-mail: christina@timeslocalmedia.com
Display Adv. E-mail: lmeehan@timeslocalmedia.com
Editorial e-mail: christina@timeslocalmedia.com
Primary Website: westvalleyview.com
Mthly Avg Views: 149122
Mthly Avg Unique Visitors: 59092
Year Established: 1986
Avg Paid Circ: 0
Avg Free Circ: 72800
Audit By: Sworn/Estimate/Non-Audited
Audit Date: 10.06.2019
Personnel: Steve Strickbine (Pub.); Christina Fuoco-Karasinski (Ed.); Connor Dziawura (Asst. Ed.); Laura Meehan (Adv.); Aaron Kolodny (Circ.)

WHITE MOUNTAIN INDEPENDENT

Street address 1: 3191 S White Mountain Rd
Street address 2: Ste 3
Street address city: Show Low
Street address state: AZ
Zip/Postal code: 85901-7409
General Phone: (928) 537-5721
General Fax: (928) 537-1780
Advertising Phone: (928) 537-5721 x 234
Editorial Phone: (928) 537-5721 x 228
General/National Adv. E-mail: krippy@wmicentral.com
Display Adv. E-mail: classifieds@wmicentral.com
Editorial e-mail: sdieterich@wmicentral.com
Primary Website: wmicentral.com
Year Established: 1888
Avg Paid Circ: 11494
Avg Free Circ: 17
Audit By: Sworn/Estimate/Non-Audited
Audit Date: 10.06.2019
Personnel: Sean Dieterich (Ed.); Charlene Bisson (Pub.); Bret McKeand (VP); Edward Dulin (Pres.)

WICKENBURG SUN

Street address 1: 180 N Washington St
Street address city: Wickenburg
Street address state: AZ
Zip/Postal code: 85390-2263
General Phone: (928) 684-5454
Advertising Phone: (928) 684-5454
Editorial Phone: (928) 684-5454
General/National Adv. E-mail: publisher@wickenburgsun.com
Display Adv. E-mail: advertisingworks@wickenburgsun.com
Classified Adv. e-mail: classifieds@wickenburgsun.com
Editorial e-mail: editor@wickenburgsun.com
Primary Website: wickenburgsun.com
Year Established: 1934
Avg Paid Circ: 3000
Avg Free Circ: 3200
Audit By: Sworn/Estimate/Non-Audited
Audit Date: 10.06.2019
Personnel: Jeanie Hankins (Publisher)
Parent company (for newspapers): Brehm Communications, Inc.

WILLIAMS-GRAND CANYON NEWS

Street address 1: 118 S 3rd St
Street address city: Williams
Street address state: AZ
Zip/Postal code: 86046-2404
General Phone: (928) 635-4426
General Fax: (928) 635-4887
Editorial Phone: (928) 635-4426
General/National Adv. E-mail: advertising@williamsnews.com
Display Adv. E-mail: advertising@williamsnews.com
Editorial e-mail: editorial@williamsnews.com
Primary Website: williamsnews.com
Year Established: 1889
Avg Paid Circ: 3000
Audit By: Sworn/Estimate/Non-Audited
Audit Date: 10.06.2019
Personnel: Connie Hiemenz (Adv. Mgr.); Madeline Keith (Pub.); Yerian Loretta (Ed.)
Parent company (for newspapers): ANA Advertising Services, Inc. (Arizona Newspaper Association); Western News&Info, Inc.

WRANGLER NEWS

Street address 1: 2145 E Warner Rd
Street address 2: Ste 102
Street address city: Tempe
Street address state: AZ
Zip/Postal code: 85284-3497
General Phone: (480) 966-0845
General Fax: NA
Advertising Phone: (480) 966-0837
General/National Adv. E-mail: DON.KIRKLAND@WRANGLERNEWS.COM
Display Adv. E-mail: ANDREW.LWOWSKI@WRANGLERNEWS.COM
Editorial e-mail: editor@wranglernews.com
Primary Website: wranglernews.com
Year Established: 1991
Avg Free Circ: 20000
Audit By: Sworn/Estimate/Non-Audited
Audit Date: 10.06.2019
Personnel: ANDREW Tabat (Associate publisher); Don Kirkland; ANDREW LWOWSKI
Parent company (for newspapers): Newslink LLC

ARKANSAS

ADVANCE-MONTICELLONIAN

Street address 1: 314 N Main St
Street address city: Monticello
Street address state: AR
Zip/Postal code: 71655-4359
General Phone: (870) 367-5325

General/National Adv. E-mail: publisher@monticellonews.net
Display Adv. E-mail: advertising@monticellonews.net
Classified Adv. e-mail: classified@monticellonews.net
Editorial e-mail: editor@monticellonews.net
Primary Website: mymonticellonews.net
Year Established: 1870
Avg Paid Circ: 2519
Audit By: USPS
Audit Date: 10.10.2021
Personnel: Tom White (Publisher Editor); Harold Coggins (Ed.); Vicki Kelly (Ad Manager)
Parent company (for newspapers): Smith Newspapers

ARKANSAS FREE PRESS

Street address 1: 324 Carpenter Dr
Street address city: Little Rock
Street address state: AR
Zip/Postal code: 72205-4727
General Phone: (501) 224-4256
General/National Adv. E-mail: arkansasfreepress@gmail.com
Display Adv. E-mail: arkansasfreepress@gmail.com
Editorial e-mail: arkansasfreepress@gmail.com
Primary Website: arkansasfreepress.net
Year Established: 2011
Avg Free Circ: 25000
Audit By: Sworn/Estimate/Non-Audited
Audit Date: 30.09.2017
Personnel: Glen Schwarz (Circ. Mgr.); Dotty Oliver (Prodn. Mgr.); Tracy Crain (Publisher, Editor)

ARKANSAS TIMES

Street address 1: 201 E Markham St
Street address 2: Suite 200
Street address city: Little Rock
Street address state: AR
Zip/Postal code: 72201-1696
General Phone: (501) 375-2985
General Fax: (501) 375-3623
Advertising Phone: (501) 3752985
Editorial Phone: (501) 3752985
General/National Adv. E-mail: phyllis@arktimes.com
Display Adv. E-mail: luis@arktimes.com
Editorial e-mail: lindseymillar@arktimes.com
Primary Website: arktimes.com
Year Established: 1974
Avg Paid Circ: 616
Avg Free Circ: 19796
Audit By: Sworn/Estimate/Non-Audited
Audit Date: 10.06.2019
Personnel: Alan Leveritt (Pub.); Phyllis Britton (Adv. Mgr.); Anitra Hickman (Circ. Mgr.); Max Brantley (Ed.); Lindsey Millar (Editor)
Parent company (for newspapers): Arkansas Times Limited Partnership

ARKANSAS WEEKLY

Street address 1: 920 Harrison St
Street address 2: # C
Street address city: Batesville
Street address state: AR
Zip/Postal code: 72501-6949
General Phone: (870) 793-4196
General Fax: (870) 793-5222
Advertising Phone: (870) 793-4196 ext.21
Editorial Phone: (870) 793-4196 ext.13
General/National Adv. E-mail: mattjohnson21@swbell.net
Editorial e-mail: rgmax99@yahoo.com
Primary Website: arkansasweekly.com
Avg Free Circ: 21012
Audit By: Sworn/Estimate/Non-Audited
Audit Date: 10.06.2019
Personnel: Matt Johnson (Sales Mgr.); Rob Grace (Pres./Ed.); Gary Bridgman (Gen Mgr.)

ASHLEY COUNTY LEDGER

Street address 1: PO Box 471
Street address city: Hamburg
Street address state: AR
Zip/Postal code: 71646-0471
General Phone: (870) 853-2424
General Fax: (870) 853-8203
Advertising Phone: (870) 853-2424
General/National Adv. E-mail: ledgerads@att.net
Display Adv. E-mail: acledger@att.net
Editorial e-mail: editor@ashleycountyledger.com
Primary Website: ashleycountyledger.com
Avg Paid Circ: 3072
Audit By: Sworn/Estimate/Non-Audited
Audit Date: 10.06.2019
Personnel: Whitney White (Ed.)
Parent company (for newspapers): Ashley Publishing Inc.

ASHLEY NEWS OBSERVER

Street address 1: 102 Pine St
Street address city: Crossett
Street address state: AR
Zip/Postal code: 71635-2906
General Phone: (870) 364-5186
General Fax: (870) 364-2116
General/National Adv. E-mail: kcaldwell@ashleynewsobserver.com
Display Adv. E-mail: ads@ashleynewsobserver.com
Editorial e-mail: news@ashleynewsobserver.com
Primary Website: ashleynewsobserver.com
Avg Paid Circ: 4300
Avg Free Circ: 151
Audit By: Sworn/Estimate/Non-Audited
Audit Date: 10.06.2019
Personnel: Barney W. White (Pub.); Pat Tullos (Adv. Mgr.); Vershal Hogan (Mng. Ed.); Whitney White (Gen. Mgr.); Kelly White (Mktg./Adv. Dir.)
Parent company (for newspapers): Lancaster Management, Inc.

BOONEVILLE DEMOCRAT

Street address 1: 72 W 2nd St
Street address city: Booneville
Street address state: AR
Zip/Postal code: 72927-4043
General Phone: (479) 675-4455
General Fax: (479) 675-5457
Advertising Phone: (479) 675-4455
Advertising Fax: (479) 675-5457
Editorial Phone: (479) 675-4455
Editorial Fax: (479) 675-5457
General/National Adv. E-mail: ccoffee@boonevilledemocrat.com
Editorial e-mail: news@boonevilledemocrat.com
Primary Website: boonevilledemocrat.com
Year Established: 1899
Avg Paid Circ: 2900
Avg Free Circ: 12
Audit By: Sworn/Estimate/Non-Audited
Audit Date: 10.06.2019
Personnel: Glenn M. Parrish (Ed.); Christina Coffee (Circ. Mgr.); Christina Holmes (Office Mgr.); Kristyn Sims (Pub.)

CABOT STAR-HERALD

Street address 1: 206 Plaza Blvd
Street address 2: Ste G
Street address city: Cabot
Street address state: AR
Zip/Postal code: 72023-3748
General Phone: (501) 843-3534
General Fax: (501) 843-6447
Advertising Phone: (501) 843-3534
Advertising Fax: (501) 370-8391
Editorial Phone: (501) 843-3534
Editorial Fax: (501) 370-8391
General/National Adv. E-mail: tmason@cabotstarherald.com
Display Adv. E-mail: classifieds@cabotstarherald.com
Editorial e-mail: jpappas@nlr.com
Primary Website: lonokenews.net/cabot-star-herald
Year Established: 1955
Avg Paid Circ: 5461
Audit By: Sworn/Estimate/Non-Audited
Audit Date: 10.06.2019
Personnel: Theresa Hicks (Pub.); Teresa Mason (Retail Adv. Mgr.)

CARROLL COUNTY NEWS

Street address 1: 1105 S Main St
Street address city: Berryville
Street address state: AR
Zip/Postal code: 72616-4332
General Phone: (870) 423-6636
General Fax: (870) 423-6640
Advertising Phone: (870) 423-6636
Editorial Phone: (870) 423-6636
General/National Adv. E-mail: rhonda.w@cox-internet.com
Display Adv. E-mail: ccnlegals@cox-internet.com
Classified Adv. e-mail: ccnlegals@cox-internet
Editorial e-mail: carrollcountynews@cox-internet.com
Primary Website: carrollconews.com
Mthly Avg Views: 220000
Mthly Avg Unique Visitors: 29000
Year Established: 1871
Avg Paid Circ: 2797
Avg Free Circ: 215
Audit By: Sworn/Estimate/Non-Audited
Audit Date: 10.06.2019
Personnel: Bob Moore (Pub.); Samantha Jones (Associate Ed.); Kelby Newcomb (Reporter); Scott Loftis (Mng Ed); Tavi Ellis (Photograher); Ty Loftis (Sports)
Parent company (for newspapers): Rust Communications

CHARLESTON EXPRESS

Street address 1: 38 TOWN SQ
Street address city: Greenwood
Street address state: AR
Zip/Postal code: 72936
General Phone: (479) 965-7368
General Fax: (479) 965-7206
General/National Adv. E-mail: ksims@charlestonexpress.com
Editorial e-mail: pgramlich@charlestonexpress.com
Primary Website: charlestonexpress.com
Avg Paid Circ: 2050
Audit By: Sworn/Estimate/Non-Audited
Audit Date: 10.06.2019
Personnel: Kristyn Sims (Pub.); Rachel Henley (Inside Sales); Lindsey Neel (Multi-Media Sales Exec.); Paul Gramlich (Ed.)

CHICOT SPECTATOR

Street address 1: 105 N Court St
Street address city: Lake Village
Street address state: AR
Zip/Postal code: 71653-1917
General Phone: (870) 265-2071
General Fax: (870) 265-2807
General/National Adv. E-mail: ads@chicotnewspaper.com
Display Adv. E-mail: ads@chicotnewspaper.com
Editorial e-mail: news@chicotnewspapers.com
Primary Website: chicotnewspapers.com
Avg Paid Circ: 1250
Audit By: Sworn/Estimate/Non-Audited
Audit Date: 10.06.2019
Personnel: Gloria Emerson (Circ. Mgr.)
Parent company (for newspapers): Lancaster Management, Inc.

CLAY COUNTY COURIER

Street address 1: 810 N Missouri Ave
Street address city: Corning
Street address state: AR
Zip/Postal code: 72422-7187
General Phone: (870) 857-3531
General Fax: (870) 857-5204
Editorial e-mail: pam@claycountyliving.com
Primary Website: claycountyliving.com
Avg Paid Circ: 4000
Avg Free Circ: 60
Audit By: Sworn/Estimate/Non-Audited
Audit Date: 10.06.2019
Personnel: Fred Martin (Adv. Mgr.); J.V. Rockwell (Ed./Pub.); Bill Cobb (Prodn. Mgr.)
Parent company (for newspapers): CherryRoad Media

CLAY COUNTY TIMES-DEMOCRAT

Street address 1: 270 W Court St
Street address city: Piggott
Street address state: AR
Zip/Postal code: 72454-2640
General Phone: (870) 598-2201
General Fax: (870) 598-5189
Advertising Phone: (870) 598-2201
Editorial Phone: (870) 598-2201
General/National Adv. E-mail: ronkemp@centurytel.net
Editorial e-mail: ronkemp@centurytel.net
Primary Website: cctimesdemocrat.com
Year Established: 2011
Avg Paid Circ: 1900
Avg Free Circ: 86
Audit By: Sworn/Estimate/Non-Audited
Audit Date: 10.06.2019
Personnel: Nancy Kemp (Co-Pub., Co-Ed.); Ron Kemp (Co-Pub., Co-Ed.); Dianna Risinger (Office Mgr.)
Parent company (for newspapers): Rust Communications

CLAY-COUNTY TIMES DEMOCRAT

Street address 1: 270 W Court St
Street address city: Piggott
Street address state: AR
Zip/Postal code: 72454-2640
General Phone: (870) 598-2201
General Fax: (870) 598-5189
General/National Adv. E-mail: piggotttimes@centurytel.net
Primary Website: cctimesdemocrat.com
Avg Paid Circ: 3186
Avg Free Circ: 130
Audit By: Sworn/Estimate/Non-Audited
Audit Date: 10.06.2019
Personnel: Sheila Rouse (Pub.); Diana Risinger (Gen. Mgr.); Tim Blair (Reporter); Jordan Ralph (Sales); Terri Coleman (Reg. Sales Mgr.)

CLEVELAND COUNTY HERALD

Street address 1: 215 N MAIN ST
Street address city: Rison
Street address state: AR
Zip/Postal code: 71665
General Phone: (870) 325-6412
General Fax: (870) 325-6127
Advertising Phone: (870) 325-6412
Advertising Fax: (870) 325-6127
Editorial Phone: (870) 325-6412
Editorial Fax: (870) 325-6127
General/National Adv. E-mail: ccherald@tds.net
Display Adv. E-mail: ccherald@tds.net
Editorial e-mail: ccherald@tds.net
Primary Website: clevelandcountyherald.com
Year Established: 1888
Avg Paid Circ: 2200
Avg Free Circ: 30
Audit By: Sworn/Estimate/Non-Audited
Audit Date: 10.06.2019
Personnel: Britt Talent (Ed.); Douglas Boultinghouse (Circulation Manager/Graphic Arts)
Parent company (for newspapers): Talent Publishing LLC

CONWAY COUNTY PETIT JEAN COUNTRY HEADLIGHT

Street address 1: 908 W Broadway St
Street address city: Morrilton
Street address state: AR
Zip/Postal code: 72110-3329
General Phone: (501) 354-2451
General Fax: (501) 354-4225
General/National Adv. E-mail: pjch@fuddenlinkmail.com
Primary Website: headlightnews.com
Year Established: 1876
Avg Paid Circ: 6200
Audit By: Sworn/Estimate/Non-Audited
Audit Date: 10.06.2019
Personnel: David Fisher (Pub.); Sharon Judkins (Adv. Mgr.); Donna Ferren (Circ. Mgr.); Larry Miller (Ed.)

COURIER INDEX

Street address 1: 31 S Poplar St
Street address city: Marianna
Street address state: AR
Zip/Postal code: 72360-2319
General Phone: (870) 295-2521
General Fax: (870) 295-9662
General/National Adv. E-mail: cinews@sbcglobal.net
Primary Website: No Website
Year Established: 1872
Avg Paid Circ: 2500
Avg Free Circ: 13
Audit By: Sworn/Estimate/Non-Audited
Audit Date: 10.06.2019
Personnel: Weston M. Lewey (Pub.); Amanda Vondran (Ed.)

Parent company (for newspapers): Argent Arkansas News Media

DARDANELLE POST-DISPATCH

Street address 1: 218 N Front St
Street address city: Dardanelle
Street address state: AR
Zip/Postal code: 72834-3824
General Phone: (479) 229-2250
General Fax: (479) 229-1159
General/National Adv. E-mail: postdispatch@centurytel.net
Primary Website: dardanellepostdispatch.com
Avg Paid Circ: 2000
Avg Free Circ: 44
Audit By: Sworn/Estimate/Non-Audited
Audit Date: 10.06.2019
Personnel: David Meadows (Pub.); David Weber (Gen. Mgr.); Michelle Harris (Adv. Mgr.)

DE WITT ERA-ENTERPRISE

Street address 1: 140 Court Sq
Street address city: De Witt
Street address state: AR
Zip/Postal code: 72042-2049
General Phone: (870) 946-3933
General Fax: (870) 946-3934
General/National Adv. E-mail: manager@dewitt-ee.com
Display Adv. E-mail: graphics@dewitt-ee.com
Editorial e-mail: editor@dewitt-ee.com
Primary Website: dewitt-ee.com
Year Established: 1882
Avg Paid Circ: 2700
Avg Free Circ: 16
Audit By: Sworn/Estimate/Non-Audited
Audit Date: 10.06.2019
Personnel: Haley Watkins (Graphic Designer); Dawn Deane (Manager/Ad Sales); Kaley Webb (Ed.)
Parent company (for newspapers): Kingsett, LLC

DEQUEEN BEE

Street address 1: 404 W Dequeen Ave
Street address city: De Queen
Street address state: AR
Zip/Postal code: 71832-2834
General Phone: (870) 642-2111
General Fax: (870) 642-3138
Advertising Phone: (870) 642-2111
General/National Adv. E-mail: ads@dequeenbee.com
Editorial e-mail: editor@dequeenbee.com
Primary Website: dequeenbee.com
Year Established: 1897
Avg Paid Circ: 3600
Audit By: Sworn/Estimate/Non-Audited
Audit Date: 10.06.2019
Personnel: Clark Smith (Pub./Ed.); Doug Dunson (Sports Ed.); Linda Russell (Office Manager); Cindy Evans (Advertising); Linda Dollar (Advertising Director); Marty Bachman
Parent company (for newspapers): Lancaster Management, Inc.

DUMAS CLARION

Street address 1: 136 E Waterman St
Street address city: Dumas
Street address state: AR
Zip/Postal code: 71639-2227
General Phone: (870) 382-4925
General Fax: (870) 382-6421
Advertising Phone: (870) 382-4925
Advertising Fax: (870) 382-6421
Editorial Phone: (870) 382-4925
Editorial Fax: (870) 382-6421
General/National Adv. E-mail: ads@dumas-clarion.com
Display Adv. E-mail: ads@dumas-clarion.com
Editorial e-mail: editorial@dumas-clarion.com
Primary Website: facebook.com/dumas.clarion.5
Year Established: 1930
Avg Paid Circ: 2600
Audit By: Sworn/Estimate/Non-Audited
Audit Date: 10.06.2019
Personnel: Terry G. Hawkins (Pub.); Heather Lawrence (Office Mgr. / Circ.); Debra Conard (Prod. Mgr.); Linda Lambert (Ed.)
Parent company (for newspapers): 1976

EAST ARKANSAS ADVERTISER

Street address 1: 222 N Izard St
Street address city: Forrest City
Street address state: AR
Zip/Postal code: 72335-3324
General Phone: (870) 633-3131
General Fax: (870) 633-0599
General/National Adv. E-mail: publisher@thnews.com
Display Adv. E-mail: thnewsads@gmail.com
Classified Adv. e-mail: publisher@thnews.com
Editorial e-mail: publisher@thnews.com
Primary Website: thnews.com
Year Established: 1871
Avg Paid Circ: 500
Avg Free Circ: 4075
Audit By: Sworn/Estimate/Non-Audited
Audit Date: 15.09.2023
Personnel: Weston McCollum Lewey (Pub.); Tamara Johnson (Publisher); Bonner McCollum (Pub.); Bill McLoud (Advertising Manager); Ronnie Barnett (Circ. Mgr.); Tammy Long (ad sales)
Parent company (for newspapers): Argent Arkansas News Media

ENGLAND DEMOCRAT

Street address 1: 121 E Haywood St
Street address city: England
Street address state: AR
Zip/Postal code: 72046-1841
General Phone: (501) 842-3111
General Fax: (501) 842-3081
General/National Adv. E-mail: englanddemo@centurytel.net
Primary Website: No Website
Year Established: 1989
Avg Paid Circ: 1800
Audit By: Sworn/Estimate/Non-Audited
Audit Date: 10.06.2019
Personnel: Jerry M. Jackson (Ed.)

EUDORA ENTERPRISE

Street address 1: 105 N Court St
Street address city: Lake Village
Street address state: AR
Zip/Postal code: 71653-1917
General Phone: (870) 265-2071
General Fax: (870) 265-2807
General/National Adv. E-mail: news@chicotnewspapers.com
Display Adv. E-mail: ads@chicotnewspapers.com
Primary Website: No Website
Avg Paid Circ: 1250
Audit By: Sworn/Estimate/Non-Audited
Audit Date: 10.06.2019
Personnel: Barney White (Pub.); Gloria Emerson (Circ. Mgr.); Whitney White (Ed.); Justin Mazzanti (Reporter)
Parent company (for newspapers): Lancaster Management, Inc.

FORDYCE NEWS-ADVOCATE

Street address 1: 304 N Spring St
Street address city: Fordyce
Street address state: AR
Zip/Postal code: 71742-3318
General Phone: (870) 352-3144
General Fax: (870) 352-8091
Advertising Phone: (870) 352-3144
General/National Adv. E-mail: newsadvo@windstream.net
Primary Website: No Website
Avg Paid Circ: 2993
Avg Free Circ: 98
Audit By: Sworn/Estimate/Non-Audited
Audit Date: 10.06.2019
Personnel: Ann Mathews (Adv. Mgr.); W.R. Whitehead (Ed.)

GLENWOOD HERALD

Street address 1: 209 E Broadway
Street address city: Glenwood
Street address state: AR
Zip/Postal code: 71943-9200
General Phone: (870) 356-2111
General Fax: (870) 356-4400
General/National Adv. E-mail: gwherald@alltel.windstream.net
Primary Website: swarkansasnews.com/glenwood_herald
Year Established: 1926
Avg Paid Circ: 2439
Audit By: Sworn/Estimate/Non-Audited
Audit Date: 10.06.2019
Personnel: Mike Graves (Pub.); Kareth Baber (Adv. Mgr.); P.J. Tracey IV (Ed.); Donna Harwell (Comptroller); Kenny Jackson (Production); Natasha Worley (Advert./Web Mgr); Nikkole Vines (Office Mgr)
Parent company (for newspapers): Nashville Leader Publishing Company

GREENWOOD DEMOCRAT

Street address 1: 38 TOWN SQ
Street address city: Greenwood
Street address state: AR
Zip/Postal code: 72936
General Phone: (479) 996-4494
General Fax: (479) 996-4122
Advertising Phone: (479) 996-4494
Advertising Fax: (479) 996-4122
Editorial Phone: (479) 996-4494
Editorial Fax: (479) 996-4122
General/National Adv. E-mail: info@greenwooddemocrat.com
Display Adv. E-mail: info@greenwooddemocrat.com
Editorial e-mail: info@greenwooddemocrat.com
Primary Website: greenwooddemocrat.com
Year Established: 1881
Avg Paid Circ: 2280
Audit By: Sworn/Estimate/Non-Audited
Audit Date: 10.06.2019
Personnel: Summer Aina (Pub.); Pam Nutter (Adv. Mgr.); Michael Stromley (News Desk)

HERALD PUBLISHING CO.

Street address 1: PO Box 370
Street address 2: 111 Hwy. 70 East
Street address city: Hazen
Street address state: AR
Zip/Postal code: 72064-0370
General Phone: (870) 255-4538
General Fax: (870) 255-4538
Advertising Phone: (870) 255-4538
Advertising Fax: (870) 255-4538
Editorial Phone: (870) 255-4538
Editorial Fax: (870) 255-4538
General/National Adv. E-mail: heraldpublishing@gmail.com
Display Adv. E-mail: heraldpublishing@gmail.com
Classified Adv. e-mail: heraldpublishing@gmail.com
Editorial e-mail: heraldpublishing@gmail.com
Primary Website: herald-publishing.com
Year Established: 1900
Avg Paid Circ: 1000
Avg Free Circ: 50
Audit By: Sworn/Estimate/Non-Audited
Audit Date: 10.06.2019
Personnel: Roxanne Bradow (Owner/Pub.); Trudy Johnson (Circulation)
Parent company (for newspapers): Herald Publishing Co.

HOT SPRINGS VILLAGE VOICE

Street address 1: 3576 N Highway 7
Street address city: Hot Springs Village
Street address state: AR
Zip/Postal code: 71909-9608
General Phone: (501) 623-6397
General Fax: (501) 623-3131
Advertising Phone: (501) 623-6397
Editorial Phone: (501) 623-6397
General/National Adv. E-mail: jallen@hsvvoice.com
Display Adv. E-mail: jkegley@hsvvoice.com
Editorial e-mail: hdaste@hsvvoice.com
Primary Website: hsvvoice.com
Year Established: 1990
Avg Paid Circ: 7600
Avg Free Circ: 132
Audit By: Sworn/Estimate/Non-Audited
Audit Date: 10.06.2019
Personnel: Theresa Hicks (Pub.); Summer Benedict (Adv. Sales); Mae Washington (Circ. Dir.); Jeff Meek (Mng. Ed.); Jeff Meek (Managing Ed.)

JACKSONVILLE PATRIOT

Street address 1: 1 Riverfront Pl
Street address 2: Ste 615
Street address city: North Little Rock
Street address state: AR
Zip/Postal code: 72114-5650
General Phone: (501) 370-8300
General Fax: (501) 370-8391
Advertising Phone: (501) 843-3534
Editorial Phone: (501) 370-8318
General/National Adv. E-mail: advertising@jacksonvillepatriot.com
Display Adv. E-mail: ksatterfield@arkansasnews.com
Editorial e-mail: news@jacksonvillepatriot.com
Primary Website: pulaskinews.net/jacksonville-patriot
Year Established: 1958
Avg Paid Circ: 911
Avg Free Circ: 10
Audit By: Sworn/Estimate/Non-Audited
Audit Date: 10.06.2019
Personnel: Theresa Hicks (Gen. Mgr.); Theresa Hicks (Pub.); Mae Washington (Circ. Dir.); Lakita Cato (Adv. Mgr.); John Worthen (Ed.)

JOHNSON COUNTY GRAPHIC

Street address 1: 203 E Cherry St
Street address city: Clarksville
Street address state: AR
Zip/Postal code: 72830-3101
General Phone: (479) 754-2005
General Fax: (479) 754-2098
General/National Adv. E-mail: ads@thegraphic.org
Display Adv. E-mail: ads@thegraphic.org
Editorial e-mail: news@thegraphic.org
Primary Website: thegraphic.org
Mthly Avg Views: 8221
Mthly Avg Unique Visitors: 1687
Year Established: 1877
Avg Paid Circ: 5500
Audit By: Sworn/Estimate/Non-Audited
Audit Date: 10.06.2019
Personnel: Ron Wylie (Pub./Mng. Ed.); Gerald Sanders (Adv. Mgr.); Janice Penix (News/ Sports Ed.)

LAFAYETTE COUNTY PRESS

Street address 1: 221 Main St
Street address city: Stamps
Street address state: AR
Zip/Postal code: 71860-2827
General Phone: (870) 533-4708
General Fax: (870) 533-1368
Advertising Phone: (870) 533-4708
Editorial Phone: (870) 533-4708
General/National Adv. E-mail: lcpress@sbcglobal.net
Primary Website: lafayettecountypress.com
Avg Paid Circ: 1550
Audit By: Sworn/Estimate/Non-Audited
Audit Date: 10.06.2019
Personnel: Lucy Goodwin (Pub.); Tommy Goodwin (Ed.)

LAKE AREA WEEKLY

Street address 1: PO Box 1370
Street address city: Fairfield Bay
Street address state: AR
Zip/Postal code: 72088-1370
General Phone: (501) 884-6012
General Fax: (501) 884-6019
General/National Adv. E-mail: editor@lakeareaweekly.com
Display Adv. E-mail: volunteers@lakeareaweekly.com
Editorial e-mail: editor@lakeareaweekly.com
Primary Website: lakeareaweekly.com
Year Established: 1967
Avg Paid Circ: 1200
Avg Free Circ: 0
Audit By: Sworn/Estimate/Non-Audited
Audit Date: 10.06.2019
Personnel: Dan Feuer (Mng. Ed.)
Parent company (for newspapers): Fairfield Bay Community Club

LINCOLN LEDGER

Street address 1: 216 W Bradley St

Street address city: Star City
Street address state: AR
Zip/Postal code: 71667-5116
General Phone: (870) 628-4161
General Fax: (870) 628-3802
Advertising Phone: (870) 628-4161
Editorial Phone: (870) 628-4161
General/National Adv. E-mail: lincolnledger@centurytel.net
Primary Website: lincolnledger.weebly.com
Year Established: 1876
Avg Paid Circ: 3500
Audit By: Sworn/Estimate/Non-Audited
Audit Date: 10.06.2019
Personnel: Peggy Mason (Adv. Mgr.); Joe V. Mason (Ed.)

LITTLE RIVER NEWS

Street address 1: 614 E Wood St
Street address city: Ashdown
Street address state: AR
Zip/Postal code: 71822-3648
General Phone: (870) 898-3462
General Fax: (870) 898-6213
General/National Adv. E-mail: jamie.lrnews@gmail.com
Editorial e-mail: editor.lrnews@gmail.com
Primary Website: thelrnews.com
Year Established: 1898
Avg Paid Circ: 3000
Audit By: Sworn/Estimate/Non-Audited
Audit Date: 10.06.2019
Personnel: Quinton Bagley (Gen. Mgr.); Melanie Rhyne (Composing/Layout); Jamie Bagley
Parent company (for newspapers): Red River Media

LOG CABIN DEMOCRAT

Street address 1: 1025 Front St.
Street address city: Conway
Street address state: AR
Zip/Postal code: 72034
General Phone: (501) 327-6621
General Fax: n/a
Advertising Phone: (501) 327-6621
Editorial Phone: (501) 327-6621
General/National Adv. E-mail: editorial@thecabin.net
Display Adv. E-mail: amartin@thecabin.net
Editorial e-mail: editorial@thecabin.net
Primary Website: thecabin.net
Year Established: 1879
Audit By: Sworn/Estimate/Non-Audited
Personnel: Jeanette Stewart (Editor); Lisa Martin (Ad rep); Carrie Ramsey (Office Mgr.); Kolton Rutherford (News editor); Megan Bailey (Adv. Dir.); Mark Buffalo (Sports editor); Alex Kienlen (Ed.); Jordan Woodson (Reporter); Tina DeMuri (News clerk)
Parent company (for newspapers): Paxton Media Group

LONOKE DEMOCRAT

Street address 1: 402 N Center St
Street address city: Lonoke
Street address state: AR
Zip/Postal code: 72086-2851
General Phone: (501) 676-2463
General Fax: (501) 676-6231
Advertising Phone: (501) 843-3534
Advertising Fax: (501) 370-8391
Editorial Phone: (501) 843-3534
Editorial Fax: (501) 370-8391
General/National Adv. E-mail: ascott@arkansasnews.com
Display Adv. E-mail: classifieds@lonokedemocrat.com
Editorial e-mail: mdougherty@arkansasnews.com
Primary Website: lonokenews.net/lonoke-democrat
Year Established: 1872
Avg Paid Circ: 1929
Avg Free Circ: 100
Audit By: Sworn/Estimate/Non-Audited
Audit Date: 10.06.2019
Personnel: Theresa Hicks (Pub.); Jeff Meek (Exec. Ed.); Lakita Cato (Adv. Mgr.); Theresa Hicks (Gen. Mgr.); John Worthen

LOVELY COUNTY CITIZEN

Street address 1: 3022 E Van Buren
Street address 2: Ste H
Street address city: Eureka Springs
Street address state: AR
Zip/Postal code: 72632-9800
General Phone: (479) 253-0070
General Fax: (479) 253-0080
Advertising Phone: (479) 253-0070
Editorial Phone: (479) 981-9419
General/National Adv. E-mail: b.moore@cox-internet.com
Display Adv. E-mail: citizendesk@cox-internet.com
Classified Adv. e-mail: citizendesk@cox-internet.com
Editorial e-mail: citizen.editor.eureka@gmail.com
Primary Website: lovelycitizen.com
Mthly Avg Views: 64000
Mthly Avg Unique Visitors: 21000
Year Established: 1999
Avg Paid Circ: 5200
Audit By: CAC
Audit Date: 16.09.2017
Personnel: Bob Moore (Pub./Adv. Dir.); Scott Loftis (Mng Ed); Karen Horst (Adv. Mgr.); Melody Rust (Design Dir.); Samantha Jones (Associate Ed)
Parent company (for newspapers): Rust Communications

MARSHALL MOUNTAIN WAVE

Street address 1: 215 Highway 27 S
Street address city: Marshall
Street address state: AR
Zip/Postal code: 72650-7781
General Phone: (870) 448-3321
General Fax: (870) 448-5659
General/National Adv. E-mail: mmw@windstream.net
Primary Website: emountainwave.com
Year Established: 1891
Avg Paid Circ: 3200
Audit By: Sworn/Estimate/Non-Audited
Audit Date: 10.06.2019
Personnel: Leisa Younger (Adv. Mgr.); Jane Estes (Publisher/Editor)
Parent company (for newspapers): CherryRoad Media

MAUMELLE MONITOR

Street address 1: 1 Riverfront Pl
Street address 2: Ste 615
Street address city: North Little Rock
Street address state: AR
Zip/Postal code: 72114-5650
General Phone: (501) 370-8300
General Fax: (501) 370-8391
Advertising Phone: (501) 370-8317
Editorial Phone: (501) 370-8356
General/National Adv. E-mail: advertising@maumellemonitor.com
Display Adv. E-mail: ksatterfield@arkansasnews.com
Editorial e-mail: editor@maumellemonitor.com
Primary Website: pulaskinews.net/maumelle-monitor
Avg Paid Circ: 2906
Avg Free Circ: 15
Audit By: Sworn/Estimate/Non-Audited
Audit Date: 10.06.2019
Personnel: Theresa Hicks (Pub.); Theresa Hicks (Gen. Mgr.); Bill Lawson (managing Ed.); Mae Washington (Circ. Dir.); Lakita Cato (Adv. Mgr.)

MCGEHEE DERMOTT TIMES/NEWS

Street address 1: 211 N 2nd St
Street address city: Mc Gehee
Street address state: AR
Zip/Postal code: 71654-2201
General Phone: (870) 222-3922
General Fax: (870) 222-3726
Advertising Phone: (870) 222-3922
Advertising Fax: (870) 222-3726
Editorial Phone: (870) 222-3922
Editorial Fax: (870) 222-3726
General/National Adv. E-mail: advertising@themcgeheetimes.com
Display Adv. E-mail: advertising@themcgeheetimes.com
Editorial e-mail: editor@themcgeheetimes.com
Primary Website: themcgeheetimes.com
Avg Paid Circ: 3400
Audit By: Sworn/Estimate/Non-Audited
Audit Date: 10.06.2019
Personnel: Brenda Denton (Circ. Mgr.); Rachel Freeze (Pub./Ed.)
Parent company (for newspapers): McGehee Publishing Company Inc.

MONROE COUNTY HERALD

Street address 1: 322 W Cypress St
Street address city: Brinkley
Street address state: AR
Zip/Postal code: 72021-2733
General Phone: (870) 734-1056
General Fax: (870) 734-1494
General/National Adv. E-mail: brinkleyargus@sbcglobal.net
Editorial e-mail: argussubmissions@yahoo.com
Primary Website: facebook.com/Monroe-County-Herald-Shopper-108283809210276
Year Established: 1877
Avg Paid Circ: 2300
Avg Free Circ: 138
Audit By: Sworn/Estimate/Non-Audited
Audit Date: 10.06.2019
Personnel: Tricia Rogers (Ed.); Glenda Arnett (Assoc. Ed.); Doug Holloway (Prodn. Mgr.); Hayden Taylor (Owner)

MONTGOMERY COUNTY NEWS

Street address 1: 133 S. West Street
Street address city: Mount Ida
Street address state: AR
Zip/Postal code: 71957
General Phone: 8708673832
General/National Adv. E-mail: montcnews2@windstream.net
Primary Website: mcnews.online
Year Established: 1951
Avg Paid Circ: 875
Avg Free Circ: 0
Audit By: Sworn/Estimate/Non-Audited
Personnel: Lawrence Graves (Pub.); Dewayne Holloway (Publisher); Barbara Ingami (Adv. Mgr.); Danielle Cummings (Ed.)
Parent company (for newspapers): Nashville Leader Publishing Company

MURFREESBORO DIAMOND

Street address 1: 119 N Main St.
Street address city: Nashville
Street address state: AR
Zip/Postal code: 71852
General Phone: (870) 845-0600
General/National Adv. E-mail: contact@swarkansasnews.com
Primary Website: swarkansasnews.com
Avg Paid Circ: 1700
Audit By: Sworn/Estimate/Non-Audited
Audit Date: 10.06.2019
Personnel: Mike Graves (Pub.); Heather Grabin (Adv. Mgr.)

NEA TOWN CRIER

Street address 1: 100 W LAKE ST
Street address city: Manila
Street address state: AR
Zip/Postal code: 72442
General Phone: (870) 763-4461
General Fax: (870) 763-6874
General/National Adv. E-mail: tcoleman@neatowncourier.com
Display Adv. E-mail: classifieds@neatowncourier.com
Editorial e-mail: gwilliams@neatowncourier.com
Primary Website: neatowncourier.com
Avg Paid Circ: 2900
Avg Free Circ: 59
Audit By: Sworn/Estimate/Non-Audited
Audit Date: 10.06.2019
Personnel: Mark Brasfield (Gen. Mgr./ Ed.); Terri Coleman (Reg. Adv. Mgr.); Greydon Williams (News Reporter); Joseph Fondren (Sports Reporter); Sheila Gale (Classifieds and Circulation)
Parent company (for newspapers): Rust Communications

NEVADA COUNTY PICAYUNE

Street address 1: 522 W 3rd St
Street address city: Hope
Street address state: AR
Zip/Postal code: 71801-5001
General Phone: (870) 777-1501
General Fax: (870) 777-3311
Advertising Phone: (870) 777-1501
Advertising Fax: (870) 777-3311
Editorial Phone: (870) 777-1501
Editorial Fax: (870) 777-3311
General/National Adv. E-mail: lmartin@picayune-times.com
Editorial e-mail: ccobbs@thegurdontimes.com
Primary Website: picayune-times.com
Year Established: 1899
Avg Paid Circ: 2200
Audit By: Sworn/Estimate/Non-Audited
Audit Date: 10.06.2019
Personnel: Cherith Cobbs (Reporter); Marcia Hunt (Bus. Mgr.); Lisa Martin (Class. Mgr.); Ed Graves (Sr. Group Publisher)
Parent company (for newspapers): CherryRoad Media

NEWPORT INDEPENDENT

Street address 1: 2408 Highway 367 N
Street address city: Newport
Street address state: AR
Zip/Postal code: 72112-2324
General Phone: (870) 523-5855
General Fax: (870) 523-6540
General/National Adv. E-mail: ads@newportindependent.com
Display Adv. E-mail: ads@newportindependent.com
Editorial e-mail: gslagley@newportindependent.com
Primary Website: newportindependent.com
Year Established: 1907
Avg Paid Circ: 2300
Audit By: Sworn/Estimate/Non-Audited
Audit Date: 10.06.2019
Personnel: Ed Graves (Sr. Group Pub.); Gina Slagley (GM/ Adv); Stephanie Tiner (Bus. Mgr.); Jodi Arnold (Office Mgr./Classifieds/Circ. Mgr.); Tristan Mount (Reporter)
Parent company (for newspapers): CherryRoad Media

PACESETTING TIMES

Street address 1: 703 S Bend Dr
Street address city: Horseshoe Bend
Street address state: AR
Zip/Postal code: 72512-3740
General Phone: (870) 670-6397
General Fax: (870) 670-7223
Advertising Phone: (870) 670-6397
Advertising Fax: (870) 670-7223
Editorial Phone: (870) 670-6397
Editorial Fax: (870) 670-7223
General/National Adv. E-mail: pacesetting@centurytel.net
Display Adv. E-mail: pacesetting@centurytel.net
Editorial e-mail: pacesetting@centurytel.net
Primary Website: pacesettingtimesonline.com
Avg Paid Circ: 2400
Audit By: Sworn/Estimate/Non-Audited
Audit Date: 10.06.2019
Personnel: Karen Johnson (Pub./Ed.)

PARIS EXPRESS

Street address 1: 22 S Express St
Street address city: Paris
Street address state: AR
Zip/Postal code: 72855-3816
General Phone: (479) 963-2901
General Fax: (479) 963-3062
Advertising Phone: (479) 963-2901
Editorial Phone: (479) 963-2901
General/National Adv. E-mail: ads@paris-express.com
Display Adv. E-mail: ads@paris-express.com
Editorial e-mail: news@paris-express.com
Primary Website: paris-express.com
Year Established: 1980
Avg Paid Circ: 3600
Audit By: Sworn/Estimate/Non-Audited
Audit Date: 10.06.2019
Personnel: Vickey Wiggins (Pub.); Pat McHughes (Ed.)

PERRY COUNTY PETIT JEAN COUNTRY HEADLIGHT

Street address 1: 908 W Broadway St
Street address city: Morrilton
Street address state: AR
Zip/Postal code: 72110-3329
General Phone: (501) 354-2451
General Fax: (501) 354-4225
Advertising Phone: (501) 889-2331

Advertising Fax: (501) 889-2331
Editorial Phone: (501) 889-2331
Editorial Fax: (501) 889-2331
General/National Adv. E-mail: pjch@suddenlinkmail.com
Display Adv. E-mail: pjch@suddenlinkmail.com
Editorial e-mail: pjch@suddenlinkmail.com
Primary Website: headlightnews.com
Year Established: 1874
Avg Paid Circ: 1900
Audit By: Sworn/Estimate/Non-Audited
Audit Date: 10.06.2019
Personnel: Lary Miller (Ed.)
Parent company (for newspapers): Yell County Publishing, Inc.

PINE BLUFF COMMERCIAL

Street address 1: 1 Riverfront Pl
Street address 2: Ste 615
Street address city: North Little Rock
Street address state: AR
Zip/Postal code: 72114-5650
General Phone: (501) 370-8300
General Fax: (501) 370-8391
Advertising Phone: (501) 370-8309
Editorial Phone: (501) 370-8318
General/National Adv. E-mail: advertising@sherwoodvoice.com
Display Adv. E-mail: ksatterfield@arkansasnews.com
Editorial e-mail: news@sherwoodvoice.com
Primary Website: pbcommercial.com
Avg Paid Circ: 1964
Avg Free Circ: 15
Audit By: Sworn/Estimate/Non-Audited
Audit Date: 10.06.2019
Personnel: Theresa Hicks (Pub.); Theresa Hicks (Retail Adv.); Mae Washington (Circ. Dir.); Lakita Cato (Retail Adv.); John Worthen (Mng. Ed.); Ray King (Reporter)

POCAHONTAS STAR HERALD

Street address 1: 109 N Van Bibber St
Street address city: Pocahontas
Street address state: AR
Zip/Postal code: 72455-3319
General Phone: (870) 892-4451
General Fax: (870) 892-4453
Advertising Phone: (870) 892-4451
General/National Adv. E-mail: starheraldads@yahoo.com
Editorial e-mail: anita@starheraldnews.com
Primary Website: starheraldnews.com
Avg Paid Circ: 4500
Audit By: Sworn/Estimate/Non-Audited
Audit Date: 10.06.2019
Personnel: Jan V. Rockwell (Pub.); Anita Murphy (Editor); Tonya Long (Adv. Mgr.)
Parent company (for newspapers): CherryRoad Media

POINSETT COUNTY DEMOCRATE TRIBUNE

Street address 1: 201 Highway 463 N
Street address city: Trumann
Street address state: AR
Zip/Postal code: 72472-3503
General Phone: (870) 483-6317
General Fax: (870) 483-6031
General/National Adv. E-mail: poinsettdteditor@centurytel.net
Primary Website: democratetribune.com
Avg Paid Circ: 2500
Audit By: Sworn/Estimate/Non-Audited
Audit Date: 10.06.2019
Personnel: Ron Kemp (Pub.)

PRESS ARGUS-COURIER

Street address 1: 5111 Rogers Avenue
Street address 2: Suite 471
Street address city: Fort Smith
Street address state: AR
Zip/Postal code: 72903
General Phone: (479) 474-5215
General Fax: (479) 471-5607
Advertising Phone: (479) 474-5215
Editorial Phone: (479) 474-5215
General/National Adv. E-mail: lnietert@pressargus.com
Display Adv. E-mail: lnietert@pressargus.com
Editorial e-mail: bhorne@pressargus.com
Primary Website: pressargus.com
Year Established: 1858
Avg Paid Circ: 1900
Avg Free Circ: 50
Audit By: Sworn/Estimate/Non-Audited
Audit Date: 10.07.2019
Personnel: Kim Hattaway (Publisher); Bennett Horne (Editor)
Parent company (for newspapers): CherryRoad Media

SHERIDAN HEADLIGHT

Street address 1: 101 N Rose St
Street address city: Sheridan
Street address state: AR
Zip/Postal code: 72150-2137
General Phone: (870) 942-2142
General Fax: (870) 942-8823
Advertising Phone: (870) 942-2142
Editorial Phone: (870) 942-2142
General/National Adv. E-mail: ads@thesheridanheadlight.com
Editorial e-mail: kristin@thesheridanheadlight.com
Primary Website: thesheridanheadlight.com
Year Established: 1881
Avg Paid Circ: 4050
Audit By: Sworn/Estimate/Non-Audited
Audit Date: 10.06.2019
Personnel: LeAnn McTigrit (Prodn. Mgr.); Byron Tate (Pub.); Millie McClain (Mng. Ed.); LeAnn Brown (Adv. Dir./Graphic Dsgn.); Kathi Webb (Bus. Mgr.)

STONE COUNTY LEADER

Street address 1: 104 W Main St
Street address city: Mountain View
Street address state: AR
Zip/Postal code: 72560-6388
General Phone: (870) 269-3841
General Fax: (870) 269-2171
General/National Adv. E-mail: leaderads@mvtel.net
Display Adv. E-mail: pam@stonecountyleader.com
Editorial e-mail: lori@stonecountyleader.com
Primary Website: stonecountyleader.com
Year Established: 1952
Avg Paid Circ: 3554
Avg Free Circ: 60
Audit By: Sworn/Estimate/Non-Audited
Audit Date: 10.06.2019
Personnel: James R. Fraser (Pub., Owner); Karen Younger (Circ. Mgr.); Lori Freeze (Mng. Ed.)

THE BEEBE NEWS

Street address 1: 107 E Center St
Street address city: Beebe
Street address state: AR
Zip/Postal code: 72012-3011
General Phone: (501) 882-5414
General Fax: (501) 882-3576
General/National Adv. E-mail: tbn@beebenews.com
Editorial e-mail: tbn@beebenews.com
Primary Website: beebenews.com
Year Established: 1935
Avg Paid Circ: 2500
Audit By: Sworn/Estimate/Non-Audited
Audit Date: 10.06.2019
Personnel: Lee McLane (Ed. / Pub.)

THE CITIZEN

Street address 1: 200 S MAIN ST
Street address city: Waldron
Street address state: AR
Zip/Postal code: 72958
General Phone: (479) 637-4161
General Fax: (479) 637-4162
General/National Adv. E-mail: carla@waldronnews.com
Primary Website: waldronnews.com
Avg Paid Circ: 1875
Audit By: Sworn/Estimate/Non-Audited
Audit Date: 10.06.2019
Personnel: Don Jones (Adv. Dir.); Joe Ben Oiler (Ed.); Carla Harrison (Prodn. Dir.)

THE DOVER TIMES

Street address 1: 204 Avenue 1 NE
Street address city: Atkins
Street address state: AR
Zip/Postal code: 72823-4233
General Phone: (479) 331-3875
General Fax: (479) 331-4728
General/National Adv. E-mail: dovertimes@hotmail.com
Editorial e-mail: dovertimes@hotmail.com
Primary Website: atkinschronicle.com
Year Established: 1926
Avg Paid Circ: 1600
Audit By: Sworn/Estimate/Non-Audited
Audit Date: 10.06.2019
Personnel: Van A. Tyson (Pub.); Ginnie Tyson (Bus. Mgr.); Gail Tyson Murdoch (Gen. Mgr.); Beverly Davis (Circ. Mgr.); Elizabeth Brown (Ed.)

THE EAGLE DEMOCRAT

Street address 1: 200 W Cypress St
Street address city: Warren
Street address state: AR
Zip/Postal code: 71671-2743
General Phone: (870) 226-5831
General Fax: (870) 226-6601
Advertising Phone: (870) 226-5831
Editorial Phone: (870) 226-5831
General/National Adv. E-mail: eagledemocrat@hotmail.com
Primary Website: facebook.com/timkesslerEditor
Year Established: 1885
Avg Paid Circ: 3600
Audit By: Sworn/Estimate/Non-Audited
Audit Date: 10.06.2019
Personnel: Danny Cook (Adv. Mgr.); Deborah Rawls (Circ. Mgr.); Zack Plair (Ed.)

THE GURDON TIMES

Street address 1: 205 S 26th St
Street address city: Arkadelphia
Street address state: AR
Zip/Postal code: 71923-5423
General Phone: (870) 353-4482
General Fax: (870)887-2949
Advertising Phone: (870) 353-4482
Advertising Fax: (870)887-2949
Editorial Phone: (870) 353-4482
Editorial Fax: (870)887-2949
General/National Adv. E-mail: lmartin@picayune-times.com
Editorial e-mail: wiedbetter@siftingsherald.com
Primary Website: thegurdontimes.com
Avg Paid Circ: 1200
Audit By: Sworn/Estimate/Non-Audited
Audit Date: 10.06.2019
Personnel: John Tucker (Pub.); Wendy Ledbetter (Ed.); Donnie Hollis (Circ. Mgr.); Sherry Kelley (Reporter)
Parent company (for newspapers): CherryRoad Media

THE HELENA ARKANSAS DAILY WORLD

Street address 1: 417 YORK ST
Street address city: HELENA
Street address state: AR
Zip/Postal code: 72342-3232
General Phone: (870) 338-9181
General Fax: (870) 338-9184
General/National Adv. E-mail: advertising1@helena-arkansas.com
Display Adv. E-mail: advertising1@helena-arkansas.com
Classified Adv. e-mail: classified@helena-arkansas.com
Editorial e-mail: editorial@helena-arkansas.com
Primary Website: helena-arkansas.com
Avg Paid Circ: 2157
Audit By: Sworn/Estimate/Non-Audited
Audit Date: 10.06.2019
Personnel: Renee Durham (Gen. Mgr.); Philly Rains (Adv. Exec.)
Parent company (for newspapers): CherryRoad Media

THE LEADER

Street address 1: 404 Graham Rd
Street address city: Jacksonville
Street address state: AR
Zip/Postal code: 72076
General Phone: (501) 982-9421
General Fax: (501) 982-9421
Advertising Phone: (501) 982-9421
Advertising Fax: (501) 982-9421
Editorial Phone: (501) 982-9421
Editorial Fax: (501) 982-9421
General/National Adv. E-mail: johnhenderson@leaderpublishing.com
Display Adv. E-mail: johnhenderson@leaderpublishing.com
Editorial e-mail: johnhenderson@leaderpublishing.com
Primary Website: arkansasleader.com
Year Established: 1987
Avg Paid Circ: 16251
Audit By: Sworn/Estimate/Non-Audited
Audit Date: 10.06.2019
Personnel: Garrick Feldman (Ed. / Pub.); Eileen Feldman (Exec. Ed.); Aliya Feldman (Ed.); John Henderson (Gen. Mgr.); Susan Swift (Adv. Rep.)

THE MADISON COUNTY RECORD

Street address 1: 201 Church St
Street address city: Huntsville
Street address state: AR
Zip/Postal code: 72740
General Phone: (479) 738-2141
General Fax: (479) 738-1250
General/National Adv. E-mail: loripollock@mcrecordonline.com
Primary Website: mcrecordonline.com
Year Established: 1879
Avg Paid Circ: 3000
Avg Free Circ: 4600
Audit By: Sworn/Estimate/Non-Audited
Audit Date: 10.06.2019
Personnel: Preston Tolliver (Mng. Ed.); Shannon Hahn (Office Mgr.); Debbie Diver (Ed. Asst.); Johnna Cornett (Adv. Mgr.)
Parent company (for newspapers): Boone Newspapers, Inc.; The Madison County Record, Inc.

THE MENA STAR

Street address 1: 501 Mena St
Street address city: Mena
Street address state: AR
Zip/Postal code: 71953-3337
General Phone: (479) 394-1900
General Fax: (479) 394-1908
General/National Adv. E-mail: clark@menastar.com
Display Adv. E-mail: sales@menastar.com
Classified Adv. e-mail: classifieds@menastar.com
Editorial e-mail: editor@menastar.com
Primary Website: menastar.com
Year Established: 1898
Avg Paid Circ: 4700
Avg Free Circ: 26000
Audit By: Sworn/Estimate/Non-Audited
Audit Date: 10.06.2019
Personnel: Clark Smith (Pub.); Jessica Laws (Business Mgr.); Vicki Agee (Account Rep.); Linda Dollar (Advertising Director); Cheyenne Blake (Composing Manager); Jeri Pearson (Editor); Carlos Duck (Press Foreman)
Parent company (for newspapers): Lancaster Management, Inc.

THE MOUNTAINEER ECHO

Street address 1: 1277 Highway 178 N
Street address city: Flippin
Street address state: AR
Zip/Postal code: 72634-9653
General Phone: (870) 453-3731
General Fax: (870) 453-3071
General/National Adv. E-mail: estesd@suddenlinkmail.com
Primary Website: flippinonline.com
Avg Paid Circ: 2100
Audit By: Sworn/Estimate/Non-Audited
Audit Date: 10.06.2019
Personnel: Dale Estes (Adv. Mgr.); Jane Estes (Ed.)
Parent company (for newspapers): Jade Media, Inc.

THE NASHVILLE NEWS-LEADER

Street address 1: 119 N Main St
Street address city: Nashville
Street address state: AR
Zip/Postal code: 71852-2002
General Phone: (870) 845-0600
General Fax: (870) 845-5091
General/National Adv. E-mail: tracy@nashvilleleader.com
Editorial e-mail: jrs@nashvilleleader.com
Primary Website: swarkansasnews.com
Audit By: Sworn/Estimate/Non-Audited

Audit Date: 10.06.2019
Personnel: John Schirmer (Ed.); Tracy Denny-Bailey; Pam McAnelly (Office Mgr.); John Balch (Assoc. Ed.); Louie Graves (Co-Pub.); Jane Graves (Co-Pub)
Parent company (for newspapers): Nashville Leader Publishing Company

THE NEWS

Street address 1: 388 Highway 62 E
Street address city: Salem
Street address state: AR
Zip/Postal code: 72576-8074
General Phone: (870) 895-3207
General Fax: (870) 895-4277
Advertising Phone: (417) 264-3085
General/National Adv. E-mail: news@areawidenews.com
Primary Website: areawidenews.com
Audit By: Sworn/Estimate/Non-Audited
Audit Date: 10.06.2019
Personnel: Debra Perryman (Circ. Mgr.); Patti Sanders (Prodn. Mgr.); Ron Kemp (Pub.); Kacey Hollins (Adv. Exec.)
Parent company (for newspapers): Rust Communications

THE NORTH LITTLE ROCK TIMES

Street address 1: 1 Riverfront Pl
Street address 2: Ste 615
Street address city: North Little Rock
Street address state: AR
Zip/Postal code: 72114-5650
General Phone: (501) 370-8300
General Fax: (501) 370-8391
Advertising Phone: (501) 370-8309
Editorial Phone: (501) 370-8318
General/National Adv. E-mail: advertising@nlrtimes.com
Display Adv. E-mail: ksatterfield@arkansasnews.com
Editorial e-mail: editor@nlrtimes.com
Primary Website: pulaskinews.net/north-little-rock-times
Year Established: 1898
Avg Paid Circ: 4081
Avg Free Circ: 20
Audit By: Sworn/Estimate/Non-Audited
Audit Date: 10.06.2019
Personnel: Theresa Hicks (Pub.); Theresa Hicks (Gen. Mgr.); Mae Washington (Circ. Dir.); Lakita Cato (Adv. Mgr.); John Worthen (Ed.)

THE OSCEOLA TIMES

Street address 1: 112 N Poplar St
Street address city: Osceola
Street address state: AR
Zip/Postal code: 72370-2637
General Phone: (870) 563-2615
General Fax: (870) 563-2616
Advertising Phone: (870) 563-2615
Advertising Fax: (870) 563-2616
Editorial Phone: (870) 563-2615
Editorial Fax: (870) 563-2616
General/National Adv. E-mail: timesads@osceolatimes.com
Display Adv. E-mail: timesads@osceolatimes.com
Editorial e-mail: brand@osceolatimes.com
Primary Website: osceolatimes.com
Avg Paid Circ: 3000
Avg Free Circ: 9000
Audit By: Sworn/Estimate/Non-Audited
Audit Date: 10.06.2019
Personnel: David Tennyson (Pub.); Steve Knox (Adv. Mgr.); Sandra Brand (Ed.)
Parent company (for newspapers): Rust Communications; Tennyson Publishing Co.

THE SPECTATOR

Street address 1: 207 W Main St
Street address city: Ozark
Street address state: AR
Zip/Postal code: 72949-3231
General Phone: (479) 667-2136
General Fax: N/A
General/National Adv. E-mail: spectator@centurytel.net
Primary Website: ozarkspectator.net
Year Established: 1911
Avg Paid Circ: 3200
Audit By: Sworn/Estimate/Non-Audited
Audit Date: 10.06.2019
Personnel: Bob Bevil (Pub.); Tracey Kendrick (Adv. Mgr.); Pat Bevil (Circ. Mgr.); Jo Eveld (Ed.)

THE STANDARD

Street address 1: 132 W Thompson St
Street address city: Amity
Street address state: AR
Zip/Postal code: 71921-9135
General Phone: (870) 342-5007
General/National Adv. E-mail: southernstandard@yahoo.com
Primary Website: thesouthernstandard.com
Year Established: 1996
Audit By: Sworn/Estimate/Non-Audited
Audit Date: 10.06.2019

THE SUN-TIMES

Street address 1: 107 N 4th St
Street address city: Heber Springs
Street address state: AR
Zip/Postal code: 72543-3061
General Phone: (501) 362-2425
General Fax: (501) 362 5877
Advertising Phone: (501) 362-2425
Editorial Phone: (501) 362-2425
General/National Adv. E-mail: advertising@thesuntimes.com
Display Adv. E-mail: advertising@thesuntimes.com
Editorial e-mail: publisher@thesuntimes.com
Primary Website: thesuntimes.com
Avg Paid Circ: 5827
Audit By: Sworn/Estimate/Non-Audited
Audit Date: 10.06.2019
Personnel: Ed Graves (Sr. Grp. Pub.); James Jackson (Ed.); Regina Cantrell (Adv. Mgr.)
Parent company (for newspapers): CherryRoad Media

THE TIMES DISPATCH

Street address 1: 225 W Main St
Street address city: Walnut Ridge
Street address state: AR
Zip/Postal code: 72476-1934
General Phone: (870) 886-2464
General Fax: (870) 886-9369
Advertising Phone: (870) 886-2464
Editorial Phone: (870) 886-2464
General/National Adv. E-mail: advertising@thetd.com
Display Adv. E-mail: advertising@thetd.com
Editorial e-mail: editor@thetd.com
Primary Website: thetd.com
Avg Paid Circ: 4800
Audit By: Sworn/Estimate/Non-Audited
Audit Date: 10.06.2019
Personnel: Janice Hibbard (Adv. Mgr.); John A. Bland (Ed.); Gretchen Hunt (Mng. Ed.)

THE TIMES OF NORTHEAST BENTON COUNTY

Street address 1: 981 N Curtis Ave
Street address city: Pea Ridge
Street address state: AR
Zip/Postal code: 72751-2907
General Phone: (479) 451-1196
General Fax: (479) 451-9456
Editorial Phone: (479) 445-4081
General/National Adv. E-mail: prtnews@nwaonline.com
Primary Website: tnebc.nwaonline.com
Year Established: 1966
Avg Paid Circ: 1500
Audit By: Sworn/Estimate/Non-Audited
Audit Date: 10.06.2019
Personnel: Kent Marts (Weeklies Ed. & Gen. Mgr.); Annette Beard (Mng. Ed.)
Parent company (for newspapers): WEHCO Media, Inc.

THE WALDRON NEWS

Street address 1: 200 S MAIN ST
Street address city: Waldron
Street address state: AR
Zip/Postal code: 72958
General Phone: (479) 637-4161
General Fax: (479) 637-4162
General/National Adv. E-mail: ads@waldronnews.com
Display Adv. E-mail: office@waldronnews.com
Editorial e-mail: editor@waldronnews.com
Primary Website: waldronnews.com
Year Established: 1964
Avg Paid Circ: 2670
Avg Free Circ: 6000
Audit By: Sworn/Estimate/Non-Audited
Audit Date: 10.06.2019
Parent company (for newspapers): Lancaster Management, Inc.

THE WEEKLY VISTA

Street address 1: 313 Town Ctr W
Street address city: Bella Vista
Street address state: AR
Zip/Postal code: 72714-2442
General Phone: (479) 855-3724
General Fax: (479) 855-6992
General/National Adv. E-mail: bpaulos@nwaonline.com
Editorial e-mail: tthrone@nwaonline.com
Primary Website: bvwv.nwaonline.com
Avg Paid Circ: 5000
Audit By: Sworn/Estimate/Non-Audited
Audit Date: 10.06.2019
Personnel: Dani Beeman (Adv. Mgr.)
Parent company (for newspapers): Northwest Arkansas Newspapers LLC; WEHCO Media, Inc.; NAN LLC

WASHINGTON COUNTY ENTERPRISE-LEADER

Street address 1: 128 Southwinds Rd
Street address 2: Ste 1
Street address city: Farmington
Street address state: AR
Zip/Postal code: 72730-8652
General Phone: (479) 571-6418
General Fax: (501) 399-3681
Advertising Phone: (479) 841-6541
General/National Adv. E-mail: rturner@nwaonline.net
Display Adv. E-mail: wcel@nwaonline.com
Editorial e-mail: wcel@nwaonline.com
Primary Website: wcel.nwaonline.com
Audit By: Sworn/Estimate/Non-Audited
Audit Date: 10.06.2019
Personnel: Rusty Turner (Pub.)
Parent company (for newspapers): Northwest Arkansas Newspapers LLC; WEHCO Media, Inc.

WESTSIDE EAGLE OBSERVER

Street address 1: 101 N Mount Olive St
Street address city: Siloam Springs
Street address state: AR
Zip/Postal code: 72761-3156
General Phone: (479) 524-5144
Advertising Phone: (479) 549-8148
General/National Adv. E-mail: rturner@nwaonline.net
Display Adv. E-mail: rturner@nwaonline.net
Editorial e-mail: rturner@nwaonline.net
Primary Website: eagleobserver.com
Year Established: 2010
Audit By: Sworn/Estimate/Non-Audited
Audit Date: 10.06.2019
Personnel: Rusty Turner (Pub.); Randy Moll (Mng. Ed.)
Parent company (for newspapers): WEHCO Media, Inc.

WHITE HALL JOURNAL

Street address 1: 7400 Dollarway Rd
Street address 2: Ste E
Street address city: White Hall
Street address state: AR
Zip/Postal code: 71602-3067
General Phone: (870) 247-4700
General Fax: (870) 247-4755
Advertising Phone: (870) 247-4700
Advertising Fax: (870) 247-4755
Editorial Phone: (870) 247-4700
Editorial Fax: (870) 247-4755
General/National Adv. E-mail: vkelly@whitehalljournal.com
Editorial e-mail: tbennett@whitehalljournal.com
Primary Website: whitehalljournal.com
Year Established: 1983
Avg Paid Circ: 1800
Audit By: Sworn/Estimate/Non-Audited
Audit Date: 10.06.2019
Personnel: Ed Graves (Sr. Grp. Pub.); John Worthen (Mng. Ed.); Keanon Reep (Adv. Sales); Stephanie Tiner; Dawn Teer (Reporter and Columnist)
Parent company (for newspapers): CherryRoad Media

WHITE RIVER CURRENT

Street address 1: 15 W 1st St
Street address city: Calico Rock
Street address state: AR
Zip/Postal code: 72519-9099
General Phone: (870) 297-3010
General/National Adv. E-mail: wrcnews@centurytel.net
Display Adv. E-mail: wrcnews@centurytel.net
Editorial e-mail: news@whiterivercurrent.com
Primary Website: whiterivercurrent.com
Year Established: 1974
Avg Paid Circ: 1500
Avg Free Circ: 75
Audit By: Sworn/Estimate/Non-Audited
Audit Date: 10.06.2019
Personnel: Charles Francis (Pub.); Cindy Stewart (Ed.)

WOODRUFF COUNTY MONITOR-LEADER-ADVOCATE

Street address 1: 112 W 2nd St
Street address city: Mc Crory
Street address state: AR
Zip/Postal code: 72101-8062
General Phone: (870) 731-2263
General Fax: (870) 731-5899
Advertising Phone: (870) 731-2263
Editorial Phone: (870) 731-2263
General/National Adv. E-mail: wcm@centurytel.net
Primary Website: wcmla.net
Year Established: 1923
Avg Paid Circ: 2000
Avg Free Circ: 156
Audit By: Sworn/Estimate/Non-Audited
Audit Date: 10.06.2019
Personnel: Maryln Moody (Adv. Mgr.); Paula Barnett (Ed.)

WYNNE PROGRESS

Street address 1: 702 Falls Blvd N
Street address city: Wynne
Street address state: AR
Zip/Postal code: 72396-2209
General Phone: (870) 238-2375
General Fax: (870) 238-4655
Advertising Phone: (870) 238-2375
Editorial Phone: (870) 238-2375
General/National Adv. E-mail: ads@wynneprogressinc.com
Editorial e-mail: news@wynneprogressinc.com
Primary Website: facebook.com/WynneProgress
Avg Paid Circ: 2775
Avg Free Circ: 250
Audit By: Sworn/Estimate/Non-Audited
Audit Date: 10.06.2019
Personnel: David M. Boger (Pub.); Brandon Boger (Adv. Mgr.); James Jennings (Ed.); Sandra Boger (Prodn. Mgr.); David Owens
Parent company (for newspapers): Wynne Progress

CALIFORNIA

ACI, LAST MILE CALIFORNIA

Street address 1: 330 Golden Shore
Street address 2: Suite 410
Street address city: Long Beach
Street address state: CA
Zip/Postal code: 90802
General Phone: (562) 277-9320
General Fax: (5620 277-9320
General/National Adv. E-mail: jklunder@acicalifornialic.com
Primary Website: acilastmile.com
Avg Free Circ: 292851
Audit By: Sworn/Estimate/Non-Audited
Audit Date: 10.06.2019
Personnel: Jack Klunder (COO)

Parent company (for newspapers): ACI Media Group, Inc.

ADELANTE VALLE

Street address 1: 205 N. 8th Street
Street address city: El Centro
Street address state: CA
Zip/Postal code: 92243
General Phone: (760) 335-4646
General Fax: (760) 353-3003
Advertising Phone: (760) 337-3443
Editorial Phone: (760) 337-3446
General/National Adv. E-mail: advertising@ivpressonline.com
Display Adv. E-mail: classified@ivpressonline.com
Editorial e-mail: pdale@ivpressonline.com
Primary Website: ivpressonline.com
Avg Paid Circ: 4
Avg Free Circ: 10721
Audit By: Sworn/Estimate/Non-Audited
Audit Date: 10.06.2019
Personnel: Belinda Mills (Pub.); Alexis Singh (Adv. Dir.); Julio Navarro (Dist. Mgr.)
Parent company (for newspapers): Imperial Valley Press

ADOBE PRESS

Street address 1: 3200 Skyway Dr
Street address city: Santa Maria
Street address state: CA
Zip/Postal code: 93455-1824
General Phone: (805) 925-2691
General Fax: (805) 473-0571
General/National Adv. E-mail: dchavez@leecentralcoastnews.com
Primary Website: theadobepress.com
Avg Paid Circ: 7500
Audit By: Sworn/Estimate/Non-Audited
Audit Date: 10.06.2019
Personnel: Cynthia Schur (Pub.); Emily Slater (Mng. Ed.)

ALAMEDA JOURNAL

Street address 1: 1516 Oak St
Street address 2: Ste 105
Street address city: Alameda
Street address state: CA
Zip/Postal code: 94501-2953
General Phone: (510) 748-1658
General Fax: (510) 748-1680
General/National Adv. E-mail: jkohler@bayareanewsgroup.com
Display Adv. E-mail: classads@bayareanewsgroup.com
Editorial e-mail: dhatfield@bayareanewsgroup.com
Primary Website: eastbaytimes.com
Avg Paid Circ: 3356
Audit By: Sworn/Estimate/Non-Audited
Audit Date: 10.06.2019
Personnel: Bert Robinson (Mng. Ed.); Sharon Ryan (Pres./Pub.); Lisa Buckingham (Sr. VP/ COO)
Parent company (for newspapers): Digital First Media

ALISO VIEJO NEWS

Street address 1: 625 N Grand Ave
Street address city: Santa Ana
Street address state: CA
Zip/Postal code: 92701-4347
General Phone: (949) 454-7300
General Fax: (949) 454-7354
General/National Adv. E-mail: alisoviejonews@ocregister.com
Display Adv. E-mail: nationalads@ocregister.com
Editorial e-mail: letters@ocregister.com
Primary Website: ocregister.com/alisoviejo
Avg Paid Circ: 1611
Audit By: Sworn/Estimate/Non-Audited
Audit Date: 10.06.2019
Personnel: Aaron Kushner (Pub.); Ken Brusic (Ed.); Susan Verdon (Ed.)
Parent company (for newspapers): Times Media Group

ALMADEN RESIDENT

Street address 1: 4 North 2nd Street
Street address city: San Jose
Street address state: CA
Zip/Postal code: 95113
General Phone: (408) 200-1000
General Fax: (408) 200-1011
Editorial e-mail: mdianda@bayareanewsgroup.com
Primary Website: mercurynews.com
Year Established: 2003
Avg Paid Circ: 964
Audit By: Sworn/Estimate/Non-Audited
Audit Date: 10.06.2019
Personnel: Mario Dianda; David DeBolt (Reporter); Harry Harris (Reporter)
Parent company (for newspapers): Media News Group; Digital First Media

ALPINE SUN

Street address 1: 2144 Alpine Blvd
Street address city: Alpine
Street address state: CA
Zip/Postal code: 91901-2113
General Phone: (619) 445-3288
General Fax: (619) 445-6776
General/National Adv. E-mail: editor@thealpinesun.com
Primary Website: thealpinesun.com
Avg Paid Circ: 4400
Avg Free Circ: 2800
Audit By: Sworn/Estimate/Non-Audited
Audit Date: 10.06.2019
Personnel: Vonne Sanchez (Pub.); Lori Bledsoe (Ed.); Jennifer Tshida (Adv. Mgr.)

AMADOR LEDGER-DISPATCH

Street address 1: PO Box 1240
Street address city: Jackson
Street address state: CA
Zip/Postal code: 95642
General Phone: (209) 223-8761
General Fax: (209) 223-1264
General/National Adv. E-mail: jmitchell@ledger-dispatch.com
Primary Website: ledger.news
Year Established: 1855
Avg Paid Circ: 6000
Avg Free Circ: 193
Audit By: Sworn/Estimate/Non-Audited
Audit Date: 10.06.2019
Personnel: Jack Mitchell (Pub.); Beth Bernard (Adv. Dir.); Caitlyn Schaap (Ed.); Joe Svec (Circ. Coord.)
Parent company (for newspapers): Amador Hometown Media, LLC; Mainstreet Media Group, LLC

AMERICAN CANYON EAGLE

Street address 1: 1615 Soscol Ave
Street address city: Napa
Street address state: CA
Zip/Postal code: 94559-1901
General Phone: (707) 256-2269
General Fax: (707) 224-3963
Editorial e-mail: editor@americancanyoneagle.com
Primary Website: http://napavalleyregister.com/eagle/
Avg Paid Circ: 200
Avg Free Circ: 6000
Audit By: Sworn/Estimate/Non-Audited
Audit Date: 10.06.2019
Personnel: Davis Taylor (Pub.); Norma Kostecka (Disp. Dir.); Noel Brinkerhoff (Ed.); Sean Scully (Dir of News Content)

ANAHEIM BULLETIN

Street address 1: 625 N Grand Ave
Street address city: Santa Ana
Street address state: CA
Zip/Postal code: 92701-4347
General Phone: (714) 634-1567
General Fax: (714) 704-3714
General/National Adv. E-mail: anaheimhillsnews@ocregister.com
Display Adv. E-mail: nationalads@ocregister.com; retailads@ocregister.com; classifiedads@ocregister.com
Editorial e-mail: letters@ocregister.com
Primary Website: ocregister.com
Avg Paid Circ: 12749
Avg Free Circ: 14143
Audit By: Sworn/Estimate/Non-Audited
Audit Date: 10.06.2019
Personnel: Aaron Kushner; Heather McRea (City Ed.); Ken Brusic (Ed.); Frank Pine (Exec. Ed.); Todd Harmonson (Sr. Ed.)
Parent company (for newspapers): Times Media Group

ANDERSON VALLEY ADVERTISER

Street address 1: PO Box 459
Street address city: Boonville
Street address state: CA
Zip/Postal code: 95415-0459
General Phone: (707) 895-3016
General Fax: (707) 895-3355
General/National Adv. E-mail: ava@pacific.net
Primary Website: theava.com
Avg Paid Circ: 3000
Audit By: Sworn/Estimate/Non-Audited
Audit Date: 10.06.2019
Personnel: Bruce Anderson (Ed.)

APPLE VALLEY NEWS

Street address 1: 16925 Main St
Street address city: Hesperia
Street address state: CA
Zip/Postal code: 92345-6097
General Phone: (760) 242-1930
General Fax: (760) 244-6609
General/National Adv. E-mail: valleywide@valleywidenews.com
Primary Website: valleywidenews.com
Avg Free Circ: 24000
Audit By: Sworn/Estimate/Non-Audited
Audit Date: 10.06.2019
Personnel: Raymond Pryke (Ed.)
Parent company (for newspapers): Valley Wide Newspapers

ATASCADERO NEWS

Street address 1: PO Box 6068
Street address city: Atascadero
Street address state: CA
Zip/Postal code: 93423-6068
General Phone: (805) 466-2585
General Fax: (805) 466-2714
Advertising Phone: (805) 466-2585 x 116
Editorial Phone: (805) 466-2585 x 203
General/National Adv. E-mail: publisher@atascaderonews.com
Editorial e-mail: editor@atascaderonews.com
Primary Website: atascaderonews.com
Year Established: 1916
Avg Paid Circ: 12500
Avg Free Circ: 5800
Audit By: Sworn/Estimate/Non-Audited
Audit Date: 10.06.2019
Personnel: Ryan Cronk (Ed.); Adriana Novack (Ad. Mgr.); John Bartlett (Pub.); Michael bartlett (Gen. Mgr.); Autumn Thayer (Office Mgr.)
Parent company (for newspapers): San Luis Valley Publishing

AUBURN JOURNAL

Street address 1: 1030 High Street
Street address city: Auburn
Street address state: CA
Zip/Postal code: 95603
General Phone: (530) 885-5656
General/National Adv. E-mail: aj@goldcountrymedia.com
Display Adv. E-mail: advertising@goldcountrymedia.com
Classified Adv. e-mail: classifieds@goldcountrymedia.com
Editorial e-mail: billp@goldcountrymedia.com
Primary Website: auburnjournal.com
Avg Paid Circ: 2500
Avg Free Circ: 4000
Audit By: Sworn/Estimate/Non-Audited
Audit Date: 10.06.2019
Personnel: John Love (Publisher); Bill Sullivan (Associate Publisher); Carol Feineman (Managing Editor)
Parent company (for newspapers): Gold Country Media, Inc.; Gold Mountain California News Media, Inc.; Brehm Communications, Inc.

AZUSA HERALD HIGHLANDER

Street address 1: 605 E Huntington Dr
Street address 2: Suite 100
Street address city: Monrovia
Street address state: CA
Zip/Postal code: 91016-6353
General Phone: (626) 962-8811
General Fax: (626) 854-8719
Advertising Phone: (626) 544-0888
Editorial Phone: (626) 422-4305
General/National Adv. E-mail: mark.welches@sgvn.com
Primary Website: sgvtribune.com/highlanders
Avg Free Circ: 3490
Audit By: Sworn/Estimate/Non-Audited
Audit Date: 10.06.2019
Personnel: Ron Hasse (Pres./Pub.); Michael Anastasi (Exec. Ed./VP)

BEACH & BAY PRESS

Street address 1: 1621 Grand Ave
Street address 2: Ste C
Street address city: San Diego
Street address state: CA
Zip/Postal code: 92109-4458
General Phone: (858) 270-3103
General Fax: (858) 270-9325
Advertising Phone: (858) 270-3103 x 106
Advertising Fax: (858) 713-0095
Editorial Phone: (858) 270-3103 x133
General/National Adv. E-mail: julie@sdnews.com
Display Adv. E-mail: julie@sdnews.com
Editorial e-mail: bbp@sdnews.com
Primary Website: sdnews.com
Year Established: 1988
Avg Paid Circ: 29
Avg Free Circ: 18549
Audit By: Sworn/Estimate/Non-Audited
Audit Date: 10.06.2019
Personnel: Julie Main (Pub.); Tom Melville (Ed.)
Parent company (for newspapers): San Diego Community Newspaper Group, publishers of La Jolla Today, Peninsula Beacon and Beach & Bay Press

BEVERLY HILLS COURIER

Street address 1: 499 Canon Drive
Street address 2: Suite 100
Street address city: Beverly Hills
Street address state: CA
Zip/Postal code: 90210
General Phone: (310) 278-1322
General Fax: (310) 271-5118
Advertising Phone: (310) 278-1322 x 116
General/National Adv. E-mail: eportugal@bhcourier.com
Display Adv. E-mail: advertising@bhcourier.com
Editorial e-mail: editorial@bhcourier.com
Primary Website: bhcourier.com
Year Established: 1965
Avg Free Circ: 39975
Audit By: CVC
Audit Date: 31.03.2018
Personnel: Clifton S. Smith (Pub.); Marcia Wilson Hobbs (Associate Pub./Circ. Mgr); Ron Pingul (Sr. Sales Exec.); Ferry Simanjuntak (Prod. Mgr.)

BEVERLY HILLS WEEKLY

Street address 1: 140 S Beverly Dr
Street address 2: Ste 201
Street address city: Beverly Hills
Street address state: CA
Zip/Postal code: 90212-3050
General Phone: (310) 887-0788
General Fax: (310) 887-0789
General/National Adv. E-mail: josh@bhweekly.com
Display Adv. E-mail: josh@bhweekly.com
Editorial e-mail: josh@bhweekly.com
Primary Website: bhweekly.com
Year Established: 1999
Avg Paid Circ: 30
Avg Free Circ: 14890
Audit By: CVC
Audit Date: 21.12.2018
Personnel: Josh Gross (CEO/ Pub.); Steven Herbert (Sports Ed.); Katie Trojano (Reporter)

BIG BEAR GRIZZLY

Street address 1: 42007 Fox Farm Rd
Street address 2: Ste 3
Street address city: Big Bear Lake
Street address state: CA
Zip/Postal code: 92315
General Phone: (909) 866-3456

General Fax: (909) 866-2302
Advertising Phone: (909) 866-3456
Editorial Phone: (909) 866-3003 x 137
General/National Adv. E-mail: mweaver@bigbeargrizzly.net
Display Adv. E-mail: classified@bigbeargrizzly.net
Editorial e-mail: jbowers.grizzly@gmail.com
Primary Website: bigbeargrizzly.net
Mthly Avg Views: 129975
Mthly Avg Unique Visitors: 16200
Year Established: 1941
Avg Paid Circ: 4500
Avg Free Circ: 0
Audit By: Sworn/Estimate/Non-Audited
Audit Date: 10.06.2019
Personnel: Judi Bowers (Pub.); Kathy Portie (Sports Ed.); Karen Osuna-Sharamitaro (Business Manager)
Parent company (for newspapers): Brehm Communications, Inc.

BREA-LA HABRA STAR-PROGRESS

Street address 1: 625 N Grand Ave
Street address city: Santa Ana
Street address state: CA
Zip/Postal code: 92701-4347
General Phone: (877) 469-7344
General Fax: (949) 454-7354
Advertising Phone: (714) 796-3844
General/National Adv. E-mail: customerservice@ocregister.com
Display Adv. E-mail: ebrunelli@ocregister.com
Editorial e-mail: kbrusic@ocregister.com
Primary Website: ocregister.com
Avg Paid Circ: 4652
Avg Free Circ: 16000
Audit By: Sworn/Estimate/Non-Audited
Audit Date: 10.06.2019
Personnel: Chris Anderson (Pub.); Aaron Kushner (Pub.); Ken Brusic (Ed.); Nick Lapaceia (Adv. Mgr.); Tom Graves (Ed.)
Parent company (for newspapers): Times Media Group

BRENTWOOD NEWS

Street address 1: 2116 Wilshire Blvd
Street address 2: Ste 260
Street address city: Santa Monica
Street address state: CA
Zip/Postal code: 90403-5750
General Phone: (310) 310-2637
General Fax: (424) 744-8821
General/National Adv. E-mail: advertising@smmirror.com
Display Adv. E-mail: advertising@smmirror.com
Editorial e-mail: editor@smmirror.com
Primary Website: westsidetoday.com
Year Established: 1990
Avg Paid Circ: 0
Avg Free Circ: 1740
Audit By: AAM
Audit Date: 30.09.2018
Personnel: TJ Montemer (President/Publisher); Judy Swartz (Sales Mgr.)
Parent company (for newspapers): Digital First Media

BURBANK LEADER

Street address 1: 202 W 1st St
Street address 2: 2nd Floor
Street address city: Los Angeles
Street address state: CA
Zip/Postal code: 90012-4299
General Phone: (818) 637-3200
General Fax: (818) 241-1975
Advertising Phone: (818) 637-3200
General/National Adv. E-mail: jeffrey.young@latimes.com
Display Adv. E-mail: tcnclassifieds@latimes.com
Primary Website: burbankleader.com
Year Established: 1901
Avg Paid Circ: 15020
Avg Free Circ: 10387
Audit By: Sworn/Estimate/Non-Audited
Audit Date: 10.06.2019
Personnel: Dan Evans (Ed.); Scott Pompe (Pub.); Hector Cabral (Sales Dir.); Carlin Chesney (Classified Supervisor)
Parent company (for newspapers): Times Community News (TCN)

CALAVERAS CALIFORNIAN

Street address 1: 15 MAIN ST
Street address city: San Andreas
Street address state: CA
Zip/Postal code: 95249
General Phone: (209) 754-3861
General Fax: (209) 754-1805
Advertising Phone: (209) 754-3863
Editorial Phone: (209) 498-2078
Editorial Fax: (209) 754-4396
General/National Adv. E-mail: jmetzger@calaverasenterprise.com
Display Adv. E-mail: advertising@calacerasenterprise.com
Primary Website: calaverasenterprise.com
Year Established: 1923
Avg Free Circ: 12973
Audit By: Sworn/Estimate/Non-Audited
Audit Date: 10.06.2019
Personnel: Ralph Alldredge (Pub.); Joel Metzger (Ed./Pres.)

CALAVERAS ENTERPRISE

Street address 1: 15 Main St
Street address 2: 15 N. Main St.
Street address city: San Andreas
Street address state: CA
Zip/Postal code: 95249-9548
General Phone: (209) 754-3861
General Fax: (209) 754-1805
Advertising Phone: (209) 754-3863
Editorial Phone: (209) 498-2078
Editorial Fax: (209) 754-4396
General/National Adv. E-mail: advertising@calaverasenterprise.com
Display Adv. E-mail: class@calaverasenterprise.com
Editorial e-mail: editor@calaverasenterprise.com
Primary Website: calaverasenterprise.com
Year Established: 1960
Avg Paid Circ: 4500
Audit By: Sworn/Estimate/Non-Audited
Audit Date: 10.06.2019
Personnel: Talibah Al-Rafiq (Gen. Mgr.); Monty Wright (Circ. Sup.); Jock Piel (Adv. Mgr.); Sean Thomas (Ed)
Parent company (for newspapers): Calaveras First Co.

CALEXICO CHRONICLE

Street address 1: 128 W 5th St
Street address city: Holtville
Street address state: CA
Zip/Postal code: 92250-1214
General Phone: (760) 356-2995
General Fax: (760) 356-4915
General/National Adv. E-mail: holtvillenews@aol.com
Primary Website: tribwekchron.com
Year Established: 1904
Avg Paid Circ: 1500
Avg Free Circ: 11000
Audit By: Sworn/Estimate/Non-Audited
Audit Date: 10.06.2019
Personnel: Brenda Torres (Pub./Bus. Mgr./Adv. Mgr.); Rosa Nogueda (Office Mgr.)

CAMARILLO ACORN

Street address 1: 1203 Flynn Rd
Street address 2: Unit 140
Street address city: Camarillo
Street address state: CA
Zip/Postal code: 93012-6202
General Phone: (818)706-0266
General Fax: (805) 484-2313
General/National Adv. E-mail: camarillo@theacorn.com
Editorial e-mail: newstip@theacorn.com
Primary Website: thecamarilloacorn.com
Avg Free Circ: 26628
Audit By: Sworn/Estimate/Non-Audited
Audit Date: 10.06.2019
Personnel: Daniel Wolowicz (Ed.)
Parent company (for newspapers): J. Bee NP Publishing, Ltd.

CAMPBELL EXPRESS

Street address 1: 334 E Campbell Ave
Street address 2: Frnt
Street address city: Campbell
Street address state: CA
Zip/Postal code: 95008-2094
General Phone: (408) 374-9700
General Fax: (408) 374-0813
Advertising Phone: (408) 206-4720
General/National Adv. E-mail: info@campbellexpress.com; news@campbellexpress.com
Primary Website: campbellexpress.com
Avg Paid Circ: 2200
Audit By: Sworn/Estimate/Non-Audited
Audit Date: 10.06.2019
Personnel: Roberta Howe (Co Ed.); Matthew Howe (Co-Ed)

CAMPBELL REPORTER

Street address 1: 1095 the Alameda
Street address city: San Jose
Street address state: CA
Zip/Postal code: 95126-3142
General Phone: (408) 200-1000
General Fax: (408) 200-1011
Advertising Phone: (408) 200-1003
General/National Adv. E-mail: jclose@community-newspapers.com
Editorial e-mail: bbabcock@community-newspapers.com
Primary Website: mercurynews.com/campbell
Avg Paid Circ: 8250
Audit By: AAM
Audit Date: 30.09.2018
Personnel: Sharon Ryan (Pres./Pub.)
Parent company (for newspapers): Digital First Media

CAPISTRANO VALLEY NEWS

Street address 1: 625 N Grand Ave
Street address city: Santa Ana
Street address state: CA
Zip/Postal code: 92701-4347
General Phone: (877) 469-7344
General Fax: (949) 454-7354
Advertising Phone: (714) 796-3844
General/National Adv. E-mail: customerservice@ocregister.com
Display Adv. E-mail: ebrunelli@ocregister.com
Editorial e-mail: kbrusic@ocregister.com
Primary Website: ocregister.com/sections/city-pages/sanjuancapistrano
Avg Paid Circ: 2726
Audit By: Sworn/Estimate/Non-Audited
Audit Date: 10.06.2019
Personnel: Aaron Kushner (Pub.); Ken Brusic (Ed.)
Parent company (for newspapers): Times Media Group

CARMEL VALLEY NEWS

Street address 1: 380 Stevens Ave
Street address 2: Suite 316
Street address city: Solana Beach
Street address state: CA
Zip/Postal code: 92075-2069
General Phone: (858) 756-1403
General Fax: (858) 756-9912
Advertising Phone: (858) 459-4201
Editorial Phone: (858) 756-1451
General/National Adv. E-mail: donp@rsfreview.com
Editorial e-mail: editor@delmartimes.net
Primary Website: delmartimes.net/carmel-valley
Avg Paid Circ: 17226
Audit By: AAM
Audit Date: 31.12.2017
Personnel: Phyllis Pfeiffer (Pub.); Lorine Wright (Exec. Ed.); Don Parks (Adv. VP); Dara Elstein (Circ. Mgr.)
Parent company (for newspapers): NantMedia Holdings, LLC

CARMICHAEL TIMES

Street address 1: 7144 Fair Oaks Blvd
Street address 2: Ste 5
Street address city: Carmichael
Street address state: CA
Zip/Postal code: 95608-6464
General Phone: (916) 773-1111
General Fax: (916) 773-2999
General/National Adv. E-mail: publisher@mpg8.com
Display Adv. E-mail: publisher@mpg8.com
Editorial e-mail: Editor@MPG8.com
Primary Website: CarmichaelTimes.com
Mthly Avg Views: 5903
Mthly Avg Unique Visitors: 3177
Year Established: 1981
Avg Paid Circ: 103
Avg Free Circ: 8381
Audit By: CVC
Audit Date: 05.06.2018
Personnel: Paul Scholl (Pub.)
Parent company (for newspapers): Messenger Publishing Group

CENTURY CITY NEWS

Street address 1: 2116 Wilshire Blvd
Street address 2: Ste 260
Street address city: Santa Monica
Street address state: CA
Zip/Postal code: 90403-5750
General Phone: (310) 310-2637
General Fax: (424) 744-8821
General/National Adv. E-mail: advertising@smmirror.com
Display Adv. E-mail: advertising@smmirror.com
Editorial e-mail: editor@smmirror.com
Primary Website: westsidetoday.com
Year Established: 1990
Avg Paid Circ: 0
Avg Free Circ: 100000
Audit By: Sworn/Estimate/Non-Audited
Audit Date: 10.06.2019
Personnel: TJ Montemer (President/Publisher); Judy Swartz (Sales Mgr.)
Parent company (for newspapers): Mirror Media Group

CHESTER PROGRESSIVE

Street address 1: 135 MAIN ST
Street address city: Chester
Street address state: CA
Zip/Postal code: 96020
General Phone: (530) 283-0800
General Fax: (530) 283-3952
General/National Adv. E-mail: jtaborski@plumasnews.com
Display Adv. E-mail: mnewhouse@plumasnews.com
Editorial e-mail: dmoore@plumasnews.com
Primary Website: plumasnews.com
Year Established: 1946
Avg Paid Circ: 2150
Avg Free Circ: 2150
Audit By: Sworn/Estimate/Non-Audited
Audit Date: 10.06.2019
Personnel: Michael C. Taborski (Pub); Debra Moore (Ed)
Parent company (for newspapers): Feather Publishing Co., Inc.

CHINO CHAMPION

Street address 1: 13179 9th St
Street address city: Chino
Street address state: CA
Zip/Postal code: 91710-4216
General Phone: (909) 628-5501
General Fax: (909) 590-1217
Advertising Phone: (909) 628-5501 x22
Advertising Fax: (909) 591-6296
Editorial Phone: (909) 628-5501 x31
Editorial Fax: (909) 590-1217
General/National Adv. E-mail: ads@ChampionNewspapers.com
Display Adv. E-mail: Classified@ChampionNewspapers.com
Editorial e-mail: News@ChampionNewspapers.com
Primary Website: ChampionNewspapers.com
Mthly Avg Views: 39090
Mthly Avg Unique Visitors: 16991
Year Established: 1887
Avg Paid Circ: 1876
Avg Free Circ: 39745
Audit By: AAM
Audit Date: 31.03.2019
Personnel: Bruce M. Wood (Pub./Adv. Dir.); Mel Ewald (Mng. Ed.); Lynn Haws (Prodn. Mgr.); Tom Hebert (IT/Business Manager); Allen McCombs (Pub. Emeritus); William Fleet (Pres./CEO)
Parent company (for newspapers): Champion Newspapers

CLAREMONT COURIER

Street address 1: 114 Olive St

Street address 2: Ste 205B
Street address city: Claremont
Street address state: CA
Zip/Postal code: 91711-4924
General Phone: (909) 621-4761
General Fax: (909) 621-4072
General/National Adv. E-mail: maryrose@claremont-courier.com
Display Adv. E-mail: classified@claremont-courier.com
Editorial e-mail: editor@claremont-courier.com
Primary Website: claremont-courier.com
Year Established: 1908
Avg Paid Circ: 5600
Audit By: Sworn/Estimate/Non-Audited
Audit Date: 10.06.2019
Personnel: Peter Weinberger (Pub.); Kathryn Dunn (Ed.)

CLEAR LAKE OBSERVER-AMERICAN

Street address 1: 415 Talmage Rd Suite A
Street address city: Ukiah
Street address state: CA
Zip/Postal code: 95482
General Phone: (707) 263-5636
Advertising Phone: (707) 263-5636
Editorial Phone: (707) 263-5636
General/National Adv. E-mail: ahansmith@record-bee.com
Display Adv. E-mail: advertising@record-bee.com
Primary Website: record-bee.com
Year Established: 1961
Avg Paid Circ: 6000
Audit By: Sworn/Estimate/Non-Audited
Audit Date: 10.06.2019
Personnel: Kevin McConnell (Pub.)
Parent company (for newspapers): Digital First Media

COASTAL VIEW NEWS

Street address 1: 4856 Carpinteria Ave
Street address city: Carpinteria
Street address state: CA
Zip/Postal code: 93013-1935
General Phone: (805) 684-4428
General Fax: (805) 684-4655
General/National Adv. E-mail: dan@coastalview.com
Editorial e-mail: news@coastalview.com
Primary Website: coastalview.com
Year Established: 1994
Avg Paid Circ: 7000
Avg Free Circ: 7000
Audit By: CVC
Audit Date: 01.01.2017
Personnel: Michael Van Stry (Pub.); Lea Boyd (Ed.); Dan Terry (Advertising Manager)
Parent company (for newspapers): RMG VENTURES, LLC

COLFAX RECORD

Street address 1: 233 S Auburn St
Street address 2: Ste 205
Street address city: Colfax
Street address state: CA
Zip/Postal code: 95713-9753
General Phone: (916)774-7910
General Fax: (530) 346-2700
Advertising Phone: (530) 852-0225
Editorial Phone: (530) 346-2232
Editorial Fax: (530) 346-2700
General/National Adv. E-mail: mjh@goldcountrymedia.com
Display Adv. E-mail: classifieds@goldcountrymedia.com
Editorial e-mail: marthag@goldcountrymedia.com
Primary Website: colfaxrecord.com
Year Established: 1937
Avg Paid Circ: 736
Avg Free Circ: 0
Audit By: VAC
Audit Date: 31.12.2016
Personnel: Carol Feineman (Pub.); Martha Garcia (Ed.); Linda Shuman-Prins (Business Develop.)
Parent company (for newspapers): Brehm Communications, Inc.; Gold Country Media

COLUSA COUNTY SUN-HERALD

Street address 1: 1530 Ellis Lake Dr
Street address city: Marysville
Street address state: CA
Zip/Postal code: 95901-4258
General Phone: (530) 458-2121
General Fax: (530) 458-5711
Advertising Phone: (530) 934-6800
Editorial Phone: (530) 749-4767
General/National Adv. E-mail: dbaggett@appealdemocrat.com
Display Adv. E-mail: nbrown@appealdemocrat.com
Primary Website: colusa-sun-herald.com
Avg Paid Circ: 5000
Avg Free Circ: 3151
Audit By: Sworn/Estimate/Non-Audited
Audit Date: 10.06.2019
Personnel: Paula Patton (Pub.); Steve Miller (Ed.); Jamie Keith (nat'l Adv. Mgr.); Debbie Baggett (Adv./Retail/Mktg Mgr.); Nancy Brown (Classified Adv. Mgr.)
Parent company (for newspapers): Times Media Group

CORNING OBSERVER

Street address 1: 1530 Ellis Lake Dr
Street address city: Marysville
Street address state: CA
Zip/Postal code: 95901-4258
General Phone: (530) 824-5464
General Fax: (530) 824-4804
Advertising Phone: (530) 934-6800
Editorial Phone: (530) 749-4767
General/National Adv. E-mail: dbaggett@appealdemocrat.com
Display Adv. E-mail: smiller@appealdemocrat.com
Primary Website: corning-observer.com
Avg Paid Circ: 1500
Audit By: Sworn/Estimate/Non-Audited
Audit Date: 10.06.2019
Personnel: Paula Patton (Pub.); Steve Miller (Ed.); Jamie Keith (Nat'l Adv. Mgr.); Debbie Baggett (Adv./Retail/Mktg Dir.)
Parent company (for newspapers): Times Media Group

CORONADO EAGLE & JOURNAL

Street address 1: 122410th St Ste 103
Street address city: Coronado
Street address state: CA
Zip/Postal code: 92118-3402
General Phone: (619) 437-8800
General Fax: (619) 437-8635
General/National Adv. E-mail: editor.eaglenews@gmail.com
Display Adv. E-mail: patricia.eaglenews@gmail.com
Classified Adv. e-mail: classifieds.eaglenews@gmail.com
Editorial e-mail: editor.eaglenews@gmail.com
Primary Website: coronadonewsca.com
Mthly Avg Views: 50000
Year Established: 1912
Avg Free Circ: 12500
Audit By: Sworn/Estimate/Non-Audited
Audit Date: 10.06.2019
Personnel: Dean Eckenroth (Pub.); Dean Eckenroth, Jr. (Assoc. Pub. & Editor); Patricia Ross (Advertising Director); Daniel Teonnies (Adv. Dir.)
Parent company (for newspapers): Eagle Newspapers

COVINA PRESS COURIER HIGHLANDER

Street address 1: 605 E Huntington Dr
Street address 2: Suite 101
Street address city: Monrovia
Street address state: CA
Zip/Postal code: 91016-6353
General Phone: (626) 962-8811
General Fax: (626) 854-8719
Advertising Phone: (626) 962-8811
Editorial Phone: (626) 544-0811
General/National Adv. E-mail: jim.maurer@sgvn.com
Editorial e-mail: steve.hunt@sgvn.com
Primary Website: sgvtribune.com/highlanders
Avg Free Circ: 13075
Audit By: Sworn/Estimate/Non-Audited
Audit Date: 10.06.2019
Personnel: Steve Hunt (Sen. Ed.)

CURRENT

Street address 1: 625 N Grand Ave
Street address city: Santa Ana
Street address state: CA
Zip/Postal code: 92701-4347
General Phone: (877) 469-7344
General Fax: (949) 454-7354
Advertising Phone: (714) 796-3844
General/National Adv. E-mail: customerservice@ocregister.com
Display Adv. E-mail: ebrunelli@ocregister.com
Editorial e-mail: kbrusic@ocregister.com
Primary Website: ocregister.com
Avg Paid Circ: 9014
Audit By: Sworn/Estimate/Non-Audited
Audit Date: 10.06.2019
Personnel: Aaron Kushner (Pub.); Ken Brusic (Ed.)

DAILY MIDWAY DRILLER

Street address 1: 800 Center St
Street address city: Taft
Street address state: CA
Zip/Postal code: 93268-3129
General Phone: (661) 763-3171
General Fax: (661) 763-5638
General/National Adv. E-mail: cthompson@taftmidwaydriller.com
Editorial e-mail: editor@bay.rr.com
Primary Website: taftmidwaydriller.com
Year Established: 1916
Avg Paid Circ: 4900
Audit By: Sworn/Estimate/Non-Audited
Audit Date: 10.06.2019
Personnel: Deanna Long (Office Mgr.); Melissa Robertson (Circ. Mgr.); John Watkins (Pub.); Doug Keeler (Ed.); Sara Mitchell (Sports Ed.); Christine Thompson (Adv. Rep.); Kim Coker (Classified Adv. Mgr.); Roseanne Noble (Production Mgr.)
Parent company (for newspapers): CherryRoad Media

DANA POINT NEWS

Street address 1: 625 N Grand Ave
Street address city: Santa Ana
Street address state: CA
Zip/Postal code: 92701-4347
General Phone: (877) 469-7344
General Fax: (949) 454-7354
Advertising Phone: (714) 796-3844
General/National Adv. E-mail: customerservice@ocregister.com
Display Adv. E-mail: ebrunelli@ocregister.com
Editorial e-mail: kbrusic@ocregister.com
Primary Website: ocregister.com/sections/city-pages/danapoint
Avg Paid Circ: 3138
Audit By: Sworn/Estimate/Non-Audited
Audit Date: 10.06.2019
Personnel: Aaron Kushner (Pub.); Ken Brusic (Ed.)
Parent company (for newspapers): Times Media Group

DANA POINT TIMES

Street address 1: 34932 Calle Del Sol
Street address 2: Ste B
Street address city: Capistrano Beach
Street address state: CA
Zip/Postal code: 92624-1664
General Phone: (949) 388-7700
General Fax: (949) 388-9977
General/National Adv. E-mail: lloynes.picketfencemedia.com
Primary Website: danapointtimes.com
Audit By: Sworn/Estimate/Non-Audited
Audit Date: 10.06.2019
Personnel: Matt Cortina; Norb Garrett; Lauralyn Loynes; Tricia Zines (Prod. and Circ. Mgr.); Alyssa Garrett (Bus. Ops. Mgr.)
Parent company (for newspapers): Picket Fence Media

DEL MAR TIMES

Street address 1: 380 Stevens Ave
Street address 2: Suite 316
Street address city: Solana Beach
Street address state: CA
Zip/Postal code: 92075-2069
General Phone: (858) 756-1403
General Fax: (858) 756-9912
Advertising Phone: (858) 459-4201
Editorial Phone: (858) 756-1451
General/National Adv. E-mail: ashleyo@lajollalight.com
Display Adv. E-mail: donp@rsfreview.com
Editorial e-mail: editor@delmartimes.net
Primary Website: delmartimes.net
Year Established: 1995
Avg Paid Circ: 7051
Audit By: AAM
Audit Date: 31.12.2017
Personnel: Phyllis Pfeiffer (Pub.); Lorine Wright (Exec. Ed.); Don Parks (VP, Adv.); Dara Elstein (Circ. Mgr.)
Parent company (for newspapers): NantMedia Holdings, LLC

DESERT ENTERTAINER

Street address 1: 41995 Boardwalk
Street address 2: Ste L2
Street address city: Palm Desert
Street address state: CA
Zip/Postal code: 92211-9065
General Phone: (760) 776-5181
General Fax: (760) 776-5733
General/National Adv. E-mail: ads@desertentertainer.com
Display Adv. E-mail: ads@desertentertainer.com
Editorial e-mail: news@desertentertainer.com
Primary Website: http://desertentertainer.com
Year Established: 2003
Audit By: Sworn/Estimate/Non-Audited
Audit Date: 10.06.2019
Personnel: Jose De La Cruz (Ed)
Parent company (for newspapers): Brehm Communications, Inc.; Hi-Desert Publishing Co., Inc.

DESERT TRAIL

Street address 1: 6396 Adobe Rd
Street address city: Twentynine Palms
Street address state: CA
Zip/Postal code: 92277-2648
General Phone: (760) 367-3577
General Fax: (760) 367-1798
General/National Adv. E-mail: advertising@hidesertstar.com
Display Adv. E-mail: advertising@hidesertstar.com
Editorial e-mail: news@deserttrail.com
Primary Website: hidesertstar.com/the_desert_trail
Year Established: 1935
Avg Paid Circ: 3500
Audit By: Sworn/Estimate/Non-Audited
Audit Date: 10.06.2019
Personnel: Cindy Melland (Pub.); Kurt Schauppner (Ed./Gen. Mgr.)
Parent company (for newspapers): Brehm Communications, Inc.; Hi-Desert Publishing Co., Inc.

DIAMOND BAR HIGHLANDER

Street address 1: 605 E Huntington Dr Ste 100
Street address 2: Suite 100
Street address city: Monrovia
Street address state: CA
Zip/Postal code: 91016-6353
General Phone: (626) 962-8811
General Fax: (626) 854-8719
Advertising Phone: (626) 962-8811
Editorial Phone: (626) 544-0811
General/National Adv. E-mail: malfonso@scng.com
Editorial e-mail: fpine@scng.com
Primary Website: sgvtribune.com
Avg Free Circ: 1183
Audit By: Sworn/Estimate/Non-Audited
Audit Date: 10.06.2019
Personnel: Melene Alfonso (Advertising Vice President); Carla Asmundson (Classified Advertising Manager)
Parent company (for newspapers): Southern California News Group

DIXON TRIBUNE

Street address 1: 145 E A St
Street address city: Dixon
Street address state: CA
Zip/Postal code: 95620-3599
General Phone: (707) 678-5594
General Fax: (707) 678-5404
Editorial e-mail: editor@dixontribune.com
Primary Website: facebook.com/dixontribunesocialmedia
Avg Paid Circ: 5500
Avg Free Circ: 2000
Audit By: Sworn/Estimate/Non-Audited
Audit Date: 10.06.2019

Personnel: David L. Payne (Pub.); Sarah Villec (Adv. Mgr.); Brianna Boyd (Ed.)

DIXON'S INDEPENDENT VOICE

Street address 1: 1275 W H St
Street address city: Dixon
Street address state: CA
Zip/Postal code: 95620-2621
General Phone: (707) 678-8917
General/National Adv. E-mail: staff@independentvoice.com
Display Adv. E-mail: staff@independentvoice.com
Editorial e-mail: staff@independentvoice.com
Primary Website: independentvoice.com
Year Established: 1992
Avg Paid Circ: 280
Avg Free Circ: 4200
Audit By: Sworn/Estimate/Non-Audited
Audit Date: 10.06.2019
Personnel: David J. Scholl (Pub/Ed)

DOWNTOWN GAZETTE

Street address 1: 5225 E 2nd St
Street address city: Long Beach
Street address state: CA
Zip/Postal code: 90803-5326
General Phone: (562) 433-2000
General Fax: (562) 434-8826
General/National Adv. E-mail: advertising@gazettes.com
Display Adv. E-mail: classifieds@gazettes.com
Editorial e-mail: editor@gazettes.com
Primary Website: gazettes.com
Year Established: 1978
Avg Paid Circ: 0
Avg Free Circ: 17975
Audit By: CVC
Audit Date: 30.06.2016
Personnel: Simon Grieve (Pub./Adv. Mgr.); Henry Saltzgaver (Exec. Ed.); Michelle Shearer (Circ. Mgr.); Julie Mckibben (Circ. Mgr)
Parent company (for newspapers): MediaNews Group

DUNSMUIR NEWS

Street address 1: 924B N MOUNT SHASTA BLVD
Street address city: Mount Shasta
Street address state: CA
Zip/Postal code: 96067-8700
General Phone: (530) 926-5214
General Fax: (530) 926-4166
General/National Adv. E-mail: news@mtshastanews.com
Display Adv. E-mail: legals@mtshastanews.com
Primary Website: mtshastanews.com
Year Established: 1887
Avg Paid Circ: 1000
Avg Free Circ: 800
Audit By: Sworn/Estimate/Non-Audited
Audit Date: 10.06.2019
Personnel: Matt Guthrie (Pub.); Steve Gerace (Ed.)
Parent company (for newspapers): CherryRoad Media

EAST BAY BUSINESS TIMES

Street address 1: 275 Battery St
Street address 2: Ste 940
Street address city: San Francisco
Street address state: CA
Zip/Postal code: 94111-3332
General Phone: (415) 989-2522
General Fax: (415) 398-2494
Primary Website: bizjournals.com/eastbay
Audit By: Sworn/Estimate/Non-Audited
Audit Date: 10.06.2019
Personnel: Mary Huss (Pub.); Jim Gardner (Mng. Ed.)

EASTVALE COMMUNITY NEWS

Street address 1: 14144 Central Ave
Street address 2: Ste H
Street address city: Chino
Street address state: CA
Zip/Postal code: 91710-5763
General Phone: (909) 464-1200
General Fax: (909) 464-1257
General/National Adv. E-mail: diane@anapr.com
Editorial e-mail: editor@anapr.com
Primary Website: anapr.com
Audit By: Sworn/Estimate/Non-Audited
Audit Date: 10.06.2019
Personnel: Michael Armijo (Ed.); Sarah Armijo (Asst. Ed.); Joe A. Merica (Adv. Sales)
Parent company (for newspapers): Armijo News

EL SEGUNDO HERALD

Street address 1: 500 Center St
Street address city: El Segundo
Street address state: CA
Zip/Postal code: 90245-3201
General Phone: (310) 322-1830
General Fax: (310) 322-2787
General/National Adv. E-mail: classifieds@heraldpublishers.com
Display Adv. E-mail: classifieds@heraldpublications.com
Primary Website: heraldpublications.com
Avg Free Circ: 16000
Audit By: Sworn/Estimate/Non-Audited
Audit Date: 10.06.2019
Personnel: Heidi Maerker (CEO/Pub.); Martha Prieto (Classified Adv. Mgr.)

ELK GROVE CITIZEN

Street address 1: 8970 Elk Grove Blvd
Street address city: Elk Grove
Street address state: CA
Zip/Postal code: 95624-1971
General Phone: (209) 685-3945
General Fax: (916) 686-6675
General/National Adv. E-mail: DJacobson@herburger.net
Display Adv. E-mail: Classified@herburger.net
Editorial e-mail: cameronjmacdonald@gmail.com
Primary Website: egcitizen.com
Year Established: 1903
Avg Paid Circ: 5434
Audit By: Sworn/Estimate/Non-Audited
Audit Date: 10.06.2019
Personnel: David Herburger (Owner/Pub.); Cameron Macdonald (News Ed.); Kerensa Uyeta-Buckley (Sports Ed.); Lance Armstrong; Jim O'Donell (Adv. Mgr.); Diana Jacobson (Adv. Sales)
Parent company (for newspapers): Herburger Publications, Inc.

ENCINITAS ADVOCATE

Street address 1: 380 Stevens Ave
Street address 2: Suite 316
Street address city: Solana Beach
Street address state: CA
Zip/Postal code: 92075-2069
General Phone: (858) 876-7997
General Fax: (858) 756-9912
Advertising Phone: (858) 876-8853
Editorial e-mail: editor@rsfreview.com
Primary Website: delmartimes.net/encinitas-advocate
Avg Paid Circ: 23859
Audit By: AAM
Audit Date: 31.12.2017
Personnel: Phyllis Pfeiffer (President and General Manager); Lorine Wright (Executive Editor); Jeff Light (Publisher and Editor)
Parent company (for newspapers): NantMedia Holdings, LLC

ESCALON TIMES

Street address 1: 122 S 3rd Ave
Street address city: Oakdale
Street address state: CA
Zip/Postal code: 95361-3935
General Phone: (209) 847-3021
General Fax: (209) 847-9750
Advertising Phone: (209) 847-3021
Advertising Fax: (209) 847-9750
General/National Adv. E-mail: ads@oakdaleleader.com
Display Adv. E-mail: mkendig@oakdaleleader.com
Editorial e-mail: mjackson@escalontimes.com
Primary Website: escalontimes.com
Year Established: 1926
Avg Paid Circ: 11000
Avg Free Circ: 2800
Audit By: Sworn/Estimate/Non-Audited
Audit Date: 10.06.2019
Personnel: Hank Veen (Pub.); Marg Jackson (Ed.); Teresa Hammond (Circ. Mgr.)
Parent company (for newspapers): Morris Multimedia, Inc.

FEATHER RIVER BULLETIN

Street address 1: 287 Lawrence St
Street address city: Quincy
Street address state: CA
Zip/Postal code: 95971-9477
General Phone: (530) 283-0800
General Fax: (530) 283-3952
Advertising Phone: (530) 283-0800
Editorial Phone: (530) 283-0800
General/National Adv. E-mail: ccurran@plumasnews.com
Display Adv. E-mail: mnewhouse@plumasnews.com
Editorial e-mail: dmoore@plumasnews.com
Primary Website: plumasnews.com
Year Established: 1866
Avg Paid Circ: 2505
Audit By: Sworn/Estimate/Non-Audited
Audit Date: 10.06.2019
Personnel: Michael C. Taborski (Pub.); Debra Moore (Mng Ed)
Parent company (for newspapers): Feather Publishing Co., Inc.

FOLSOM TELEGRAPH

Street address 1: 101 Parkshore Drive
Street address city: Folsom
Street address state: CA
Zip/Postal code: 95603
General Phone: (916) 985-2581
General Fax:
Advertising Phone:
Editorial Phone:
Display Adv. E-mail: advertising@goldcountrymedia.com
Classified Adv. e-mail: classifieds@goldcountrymedia.com
Editorial e-mail: billp@goldcountrymedia.com
Primary Website: folsomtelegraph.com
Year Established: 1856
Avg Paid Circ: 800
Avg Free Circ: 3000
Audit By: Sworn/Estimate/Non-Audited
Audit Date: 10.06.2019
Personnel: Matt Long (Sports Ed.); Ken Larson (Pub.); Linda Shuman-Prins (Business Develop.); Lydia McNabb (Ed.)
Parent company (for newspapers): Brehm Communications, Inc.; Gold Mountain California News Media, Inc.; Gold Country Media

FOLSOM TELEGRAPH

Street address 1: 188 Cirby Way
Street address city: Roseville
Street address state: CA
Zip/Postal code: 95678-6481
General Phone: (916)774-7910
General Fax: (916) 985-0720
Advertising Phone: (916) 351-3750
Editorial Phone: (916) 351-3753
General/National Adv. E-mail: ryans@goldcountrymedia.com
Display Adv. E-mail: classifieds@goldcountrymedia.com
Editorial e-mail: donc@goldcountrymedia.com
Primary Website: folsomtelegraph.com
Year Established: 1856
Avg Paid Circ: 2275
Avg Free Circ: 11593
Audit By: Sworn/Estimate/Non-Audited
Audit Date: 10.06.2019
Personnel: Ryan Schuyler (Pub.); Lydia McNabb (Ed.); Sandy Stockton (National Advert); Bill Sullivan (Advert.)
Parent company (for newspapers): Brehm Communications, Inc.; Gold Country Media

FONTANA HERALD NEWS

Street address 1: 16981 Foothill Blvd
Street address 2: Suite F
Street address city: Fontana
Street address state: CA
Zip/Postal code: 92335-3566
General Phone: (909) 822-2231
General Fax: (909) 355-9358
Advertising Phone: (909) 797-9101
Advertising Fax: (909) 355-9358
General/National Adv. E-mail: advertising@fontanaheraldnews.com
Display Adv. E-mail: classifieds@fontanaheraldnews.com
Editorial e-mail: ringold@fontanaheraldnews.com
Primary Website: fontanaheraldnews.com
Avg Paid Circ: 266
Avg Free Circ: 181
Audit By: VAC
Audit Date: 30.09.2016
Personnel: Grace Barnett (Pub.); Russell Ingold (Ed.)
Parent company (for newspapers): Century Group Newspapers

FORT BRAGG ADVOCATE-NEWS

Street address 1: 690 S Main St
Street address city: Fort Bragg
Street address state: CA
Zip/Postal code: 95437-5108
General Phone: (707) 964-5642
General Fax: (707) 964-0424
Editorial Phone: (707) 964-5642 x96094
General/National Adv. E-mail: mrham@advocate-news.com
Display Adv. E-mail: classads@advocate-news.com
Editorial e-mail: editor@advocate-news.com
Primary Website: advocate-news.com
Year Established: 1889
Avg Paid Circ: 3800
Audit By: Sworn/Estimate/Non-Audited
Audit Date: 30.09.2017
Personnel: Sharon DiMauro (Pub.); Chris Calder (Editor); Kate Lee (Circulation Manager)
Parent company (for newspapers): Digital First Media

FOUNTAIN VALLEY VIEW

Street address 1: 625 N Grand Ave
Street address city: Santa Ana
Street address state: CA
Zip/Postal code: 92701-4347
General Phone: (877) 469-7344
General Fax: (949) 454-7354
Advertising Phone: (714) 796-3844
General/National Adv. E-mail: customerservice@ocregister.com
Display Adv. E-mail: ebrunelli@ocregister.com
Editorial e-mail: letters@ocregister.com
Primary Website: ocregister.com/sections/city-pages/fountainvalley
Avg Paid Circ: 3522
Audit By: Sworn/Estimate/Non-Audited
Audit Date: 10.06.2019
Personnel: Aaron Kushner (Pub.); Ken Brusic (Ed.)
Parent company (for newspapers): Times Media Group

FREMONT BULLETIN

Street address 1: 59 Marylinn Dr
Street address city: Milpitas
Street address state: CA
Zip/Postal code: 95035-4311
General Phone: (408) 262-2454
General Fax: (408) 263-9710
General/National Adv. E-mail: news@themilpitaspost.com
Primary Website: mercurynews.com/fremont
Avg Paid Circ: 500
Avg Free Circ: 29400
Audit By: Sworn/Estimate/Non-Audited
Audit Date: 10.06.2019
Personnel: Gloria Guillen (Bus. Mgr.); Liz Pollock (Sales Rep.); Robert J. Devincenzi (Ed.)
Parent company (for newspapers): Digital First Media

FULLERTON NEWS-TRIBUNE

Street address 1: 625 N Grand Ave
Street address city: Santa Ana
Street address state: CA
Zip/Postal code: 92701-4347
General Phone: (877) 469-7344
General Fax: (949) 454-7354
Advertising Phone: (714) 796-3844
General/National Adv. E-mail: fullertonnewstribune@ocregister.com
Display Adv. E-mail: ebrunelli@ocregister.com
Primary Website: ocregister.com
Avg Paid Circ: 9056
Avg Free Circ: 22000

Audit By: Sworn/Estimate/Non-Audited
Audit Date: 10.06.2019
Personnel: Terry Horne (Pub.); Aaron Kushner (Pub.); Ken Brusic (Ed.); Bob Ziebell (City Ed.)
Parent company (for newspapers): Times Media Group

GAN GABRIEL VALLEY TRIBUNE

Street address 1: 605 E Huntington Dr
Street address 2: Suite 102
Street address city: Monrovia
Street address state: CA
Zip/Postal code: 91016-6353
General Phone: (626) 962-8811
General Fax: (666) 338-9157
General/National Adv. E-mail: malfonso@scng.com
Display Adv. E-mail: casmundson@scng.com
Editorial e-mail: editor@scng.com
Primary Website: sgvtribune.com
Avg Paid Circ: 500
Avg Free Circ: 12450
Audit By: Sworn/Estimate/Non-Audited
Audit Date: 10.06.2019
Personnel: Ron Hasse (Pres./Pub.); Kyla Rodriguez (Sr. VP, Adv.); Frank Pine (Exec. Ed.); Dan Scofield (COO); Kat Wang (Circ. Dir.); Melaine Alfonso (Dir. Adv.)

GARDENA VALLEY NEWS

Street address 1: 15005 S Vermont Ave
Street address city: Gardena
Street address state: CA
Zip/Postal code: 90247-3004
General Phone: (310) 329-6351
General Fax: (310) 329-7501
Editorial Phone: (310) 329-6351 x 121
General/National Adv. E-mail: gvneditorial@gardenavalleynews.org
Primary Website: gardenavalleynews.org
Year Established: 1895
Avg Paid Circ: 10000
Audit By: Sworn/Estimate/Non-Audited
Audit Date: 10.06.2019
Personnel: Alan Moskal (Pub.); Gary Kohatsu (Ed.)

GEORGETOWN GAZETTE

Street address 1: 2775 Miners Flat Rd
Street address city: Georgetown
Street address state: CA
Zip/Postal code: 95634-9345
General Phone: (530) 333-4481
General Fax: (530) 333-0152
General/National Adv. E-mail: editor@gtgazette.com
Display Adv. E-mail: kay@gtgazette.com
Editorial e-mail: editor@gtgazette.com
Primary Website: gtgazette.com
Year Established: 1880
Avg Paid Circ: 1600
Avg Free Circ: 6700
Audit By: Sworn/Estimate/Non-Audited
Audit Date: 10.06.2019
Personnel: Wendy Thompson (Ed.)
Parent company (for newspapers): McNaughton Media

GONZALES TRIBUNE

Street address 1: 522 Broadway St
Street address 2: Ste B
Street address city: King City
Street address state: CA
Zip/Postal code: 93930-3243
General Phone: (831) 385-4880
General Fax: (831) 385-4799
General/National Adv. E-mail: soledadb@redshift.com
Primary Website: gonzalestribune.com
Avg Paid Circ: 650
Audit By: Sworn/Estimate/Non-Audited
Audit Date: 10.06.2019
Personnel: Sheryl Bailey (Adv. Mgr.); Tricia Bergeron (Ed./Gen. Mgr.)
Parent company (for newspapers): San Luis Valley Publishing

GREENFIELD NEWS

Street address 1: 522 Broadway St
Street address 2: Ste A
Street address city: King City
Street address state: CA
Zip/Postal code: 93930-3243
General Phone: (831) 385-4880
General Fax: (831) 385 4799
Editorial e-mail: editor@southcountynewspapers.com
Primary Website: greenfieldnews.com
Avg Paid Circ: 1400
Audit By: Sworn/Estimate/Non-Audited
Audit Date: 10.06.2019
Personnel: Sheryl Bailey (Adv. Mgr.); Tricia Bergeron (Ed./Gen Mgr.)
Parent company (for newspapers): San Luis Valley Publishing

GRIZZLY WEEKENDER

Street address 1: 42007 Fox Farm Road
Street address 2: Suite 3B, PO Box 1789
Street address city: Big Bear Lake
Street address state: CA
Zip/Postal code: 92315-1789
General Phone: (909) 866-3456
General Fax: (909) 866-2302
General/National Adv. E-mail: mweaver@bigbeargrizzly.net
Display Adv. E-mail: classified@bigbeargrizzly.net
Editorial e-mail: jbowers.grizzly@gmail.com
Primary Website: bigbeargrizzly.net
Year Established: 1993
Avg Free Circ: 6500
Audit By: Sworn/Estimate/Non-Audited
Audit Date: 10.06.2019
Personnel: Judi Bowers (Pub.); Karen Osuna-Sharamitaro (Bus. Mgr.); Kathy Portie (Sr. Ed.); Kelsey Bowers (Acct. Ex.)
Parent company (for newspapers): Brehm Communications, Inc.

GRUNION GAZETTE

Street address 1: 5225 E 2nd St
Street address city: Long Beach
Street address state: CA
Zip/Postal code: 90803-5326
General Phone: (562) 433-2000
General Fax: (562) 434-8826
General/National Adv. E-mail: sgrieve@gazettes.com
Display Adv. E-mail: sgrieve@gazettes.com
Editorial e-mail: sgrieve@gazettes.com
Primary Website: gazettes.com
Year Established: 1977
Avg Free Circ: 51476
Audit By: CVC
Audit Date: 30.06.2018
Personnel: Simon Grieve (Pub./Adv. Mgr.); Henry Saltzgaver (Exec. Ed.); Michelle Shearer (Circ. Mgr.); Julie Mckibben (Circ. Mgr)
Parent company (for newspapers): Digital First Media

HALF MOON BAY REVIEW

Street address 1: 714 Kelly St
Street address city: Half Moon Bay
Street address state: CA
Zip/Postal code: 94019-1919
General Phone: (650) 726-4424
General Fax: (650) 726-7054
General/National Adv. E-mail: karin@hmbreview.com
Display Adv. E-mail: karin@hmbreview.com
Editorial e-mail: clay@hmbreview.com
Primary Website: hmbreview.com
Mthly Avg Views: 350000
Year Established: 1898
Avg Paid Circ: 5600
Audit By: Sworn/Estimate/Non-Audited
Audit Date: 10.06.2019
Personnel: Barbara Anderson (Pub.); Clay Lambert (Ed.); Karin Litcher (Adv. Mgr.)
Parent company (for newspapers): Wick Communications

HESPERIA RESORTER

Street address 1: 16925 Main St
Street address 2: Ste A
Street address city: Hesperia
Street address state: CA
Zip/Postal code: 92345-6038
General Phone: (760) 244-0021
General Fax: (760) 244-6609
General/National Adv. E-mail: valleywide@valleywidenews.com
Primary Website: valleywidenewspaper.com
Year Established: 1959
Avg Free Circ: 20000
Audit By: Sworn/Estimate/Non-Audited
Audit Date: 10.06.2019
Personnel: Raymond Pryke (Pub.)
Parent company (for newspapers): Valley Wide Newspapers

HESPERIA STAR

Street address 1: 13891 Park Ave
Street address city: Victorville
Street address state: CA
Zip/Postal code: 92392-2435
General Phone: (760) 956-7827
General Fax: (760) 956-6803
Advertising Phone: (760) 956-7827
Editorial Phone: (760) 956-7827 x 224
Editorial e-mail: editor@hesperiastar.com
Primary Website: hesperiastar.com
Avg Free Circ: 20000
Audit By: Sworn/Estimate/Non-Audited
Audit Date: 10.06.2019
Personnel: Peter Day (Ed.)
Parent company (for newspapers): Times Media Group

HI-DESERT STAR

Street address 1: 56445 29 Palms Hwy
Street address city: Yucca Valley
Street address state: CA
Zip/Postal code: 92284-2861
General Phone: (760) 365-3315
General Fax: (760) 365-8686
General/National Adv. E-mail: advertising@hidesertstar.com
Display Adv. E-mail: advertising@hidesertstar.com
Editorial e-mail: editor@hidesertstar.com
Primary Website: hidesertstar.com
Avg Paid Circ: 7361
Avg Free Circ: 75
Audit By: Sworn/Estimate/Non-Audited
Audit Date: 10.06.2019
Personnel: Cindy Melland (Mktg. Dir.); Stacy Moore (Mng. Ed.)
Parent company (for newspapers): Brehm Communications, Inc.; Hi-Desert Publishing Co., Inc.

HIGHLAND COMMUNITY NEWS

Street address 1: 27000 Baseline St
Street address 2: Suite G
Street address city: Highland
Street address state: CA
Zip/Postal code: 92346-3169
General Phone: (909) 862-1771
General Fax: (909) 862-1787
Advertising Phone: (909) 797-9101
General/National Adv. E-mail: advertising@highlandnews.net
Display Adv. E-mail: classifieds@highlandnews.net
Editorial e-mail: editor@highlandnews.net
Primary Website: highlandnews.net
Year Established: 1994
Avg Paid Circ: 496
Avg Free Circ: 14248
Audit By: VAC
Audit Date: 30.09.2016
Personnel: Toebe Bush (Pub); James Folmer (Ed.); Hector Hernandez Jr. (News Dept.)
Parent company (for newspapers): Century Group Newspapers

HILMAR TIMES

Street address 1: 19920 1st St
Street address city: Hilmar
Street address state: CA
Zip/Postal code: 95324-9096
General Phone: (209) 669-0109
General/National Adv. E-mail: midvalleypub@aol.com
Primary Website: hilmartimes.weebly.com
Year Established: 1962
Avg Paid Circ: 4000
Audit By: Sworn/Estimate/Non-Audited
Audit Date: 10.06.2019
Personnel: Wendy Krier (Ed.)
Parent company (for newspapers): Mid Valley Publishing

HOLLISTER FREE LANCE

Street address 1: 350 6th St
Street address 2: Suite 102
Street address city: Hollister
Street address state: CA
Zip/Postal code: 95023-3882
General Phone: (831) 637-5566
General Fax: (831) 637-4104
Advertising Phone: (831) 637-5566
Advertising Fax: (831) 637-4104
General/National Adv. E-mail: info@freelancenews.com
Display Adv. E-mail: classified@freelancenews.com
Editorial e-mail: editor@freelancenews.com
Primary Website: sanbenitocountytoday.com
Year Established: 1873
Avg Paid Circ: 3221
Avg Free Circ: 9000
Audit By: Sworn/Estimate/Non-Audited
Audit Date: 10.06.2019
Personnel: Robert Rodriguez (Circ. Mgr.); Kollin Kosmicki (Ed.); Jeff Mitchell (Publisher)
Parent company (for newspapers): New SV Media, Inc

HOLTVILLE TRIBUNE

Street address 1: 128 W 5th St
Street address city: Holtville
Street address state: CA
Zip/Postal code: 92250-1214
General Phone: (760) 356-2995
General Fax: (760) 356-4915
General/National Adv. E-mail: holtvillenews@aol.com
Display Adv. E-mail: holtvillenews@aol.com
Primary Website: tribwekchron.com
Year Established: 1904
Avg Paid Circ: 2013
Audit By: Sworn/Estimate/Non-Audited
Audit Date: 10.06.2019
Personnel: Brenda Torres (Pub.)

HUGHSON CHRONICLE-DENAIR DISPATCH

Street address 1: 7012 Pine St.
Street address 2: STE 1
Street address city: Hughson
Street address state: CA
Zip/Postal code: 95326
General Phone: (209) 883-9215
General Fax: (209) 358-7108
General/National Adv. E-mail: info@midvalleypub.com
Primary Website: hughsonchronicle-denairdispatch.weebly.com
Avg Paid Circ: 7500
Audit By: Sworn/Estimate/Non-Audited
Audit Date: 10.06.2019
Personnel: Kelly Thomas (Office Mgr.); Wendy Krier (Chief Ed./Sales/Mktg.)
Parent company (for newspapers): Mid Valley Publishing

HUNTINGTON BEACH WAVE

Street address 1: 625 N Grand Ave
Street address city: Santa Ana
Street address state: CA
Zip/Postal code: 92701-4347
General Phone: (877) 469-7344
General Fax: (949) 454-7354
Advertising Phone: (714) 796-3844
General/National Adv. E-mail: customerservice@ocregister.com
Display Adv. E-mail: ebrunelli@ocregister.com
Editorial e-mail: letters@ocregister.com
Primary Website: ocregister.com/sections/city-pages/huntingtonbeach
Avg Paid Circ: 14073
Audit By: Sworn/Estimate/Non-Audited
Audit Date: 10.06.2019
Personnel: Aaron Kushner (Pub.); Ken Brusic (Ed.)
Parent company (for newspapers): Times Media Group

IDYLLWILD TOWN CRIER

Street address 1: 54405 North Circle Dr
Street address city: Idyllwild

Street address state: CA
Zip/Postal code: 92549
General Phone: (951) 659-2145
General Fax: (951) 659-2071
General/National Adv. E-mail: lisa@towncrier.com
Display Adv. E-mail: mandy@towncrier.com
Editorial e-mail: becky@towncrier.com
Primary Website: towncrier.com
Year Established: 1946
Avg Paid Circ: 2100
Avg Free Circ: 200
Audit By: Sworn/Estimate/Non-Audited
Audit Date: 10.06.2019
Personnel: J.P. Crumrine (News Ed.); Becky Clark (Ed./Pub.)
Parent company (for newspapers): Idyllwild House Publishing Co., Ltd.

IMPERIAL BEACH EAGLE & TIMES

Street address 1: 1116 Teneth Street
Street address city: Coronado
Street address state: CA
Zip/Postal code: 92118
General Phone: (619) 437-8800
General Fax: (619) 437-8635
General/National Adv. E-mail: sarah@eaglenewsca.com
Editorial e-mail: editorial@eaglenewsca.com
Primary Website: imperialbeachnewsca.com
Avg Free Circ: 7500
Audit By: Sworn/Estimate/Non-Audited
Audit Date: 10.06.2019
Personnel: Dean Eckenroth (Pub./Ed.)

INDEPENDENT COAST OBSERVER

Street address 1: PO Box 1200
Street address city: Gualala
Street address state: CA
Zip/Postal code: 95445-1200
General Phone: (707) 884-3501
General Fax: (707) 884-1710
Advertising Phone: (707) 884-3501
Advertising Fax: (707) 884-1710
General/National Adv. E-mail: display@mendonoma.com
Display Adv. E-mail: classads@mendonoma.com
Editorial e-mail: editor@mendonoma.com
Primary Website: mendonoma.com
Year Established: 1969
Avg Paid Circ: 3500
Avg Free Circ: 10
Audit By: Sworn/Estimate/Non-Audited
Audit Date: 10.06.2019
Personnel: Greg Oliver (Adv. Mgr.); J. Stephen McLaughlin (Pub./Ed.)

INDIAN VALLEY RECORD

Street address 1: PO Box 469
Street address city: Greenville
Street address state: CA
Zip/Postal code: 95947-0469
General Phone: (530) 283-0800
General Fax: (530) 283-3952
General/National Adv. E-mail: jtaborski@plumasnews.com
Display Adv. E-mail: mnewhouse@plumasnews.com
Editorial e-mail: dmoore@plumasnews.com
Primary Website: plumasnews.com
Year Established: 1930
Avg Paid Circ: 1175
Audit By: Sworn/Estimate/Non-Audited
Audit Date: 10.06.2019
Personnel: Michael C. Taborski (Pub.); Mary Newhouse (Classified and Circ. Mgr.); Debra Moore (Mng. Ed.)
Parent company (for newspapers): Feather Publishing Co., Inc.

INSIDE SACRAMENTO: ARDEN/ CARMICHAEL

Street address 1: 3104 O St
Street address 2: # 120
Street address city: Sacramento
Street address state: CA
Zip/Postal code: 95816-6519
General Phone: (916) 443-5087
Advertising Phone: (916) 443-5087
Editorial Phone: (916) 443-5087
General/National Adv. E-mail: Daniel@insidepublications.com
Editorial e-mail: Editor@insidepublications.com
Primary Website: Insidesacramento.com
Mthly Avg Views: 17500
Year Established: 1996
Avg Paid Circ: 900
Avg Free Circ: 20000
Audit By: Sworn/Estimate/Non-Audited
Audit Date: 10.06.2023
Personnel: Cecily Hastings (Publisher); Duffy Kelly (Acc. Rep.)
Parent company (for newspapers): Inside Publications

INSIDE SACRAMENTO: EAST SACRAMENTO

Street address 1: 3104 O St
Street address 2: # 120
Street address city: Sacramento
Street address state: CA
Zip/Postal code: 95816-6519
General Phone: (916) 443-5087
General/National Adv. E-mail: Daniel@insidepublications.com
Editorial e-mail: Editor@insidepublications.com
Primary Website: Insidesacramento.com
Year Established: 1996
Avg Paid Circ: 500
Avg Free Circ: 20000
Audit By: Sworn/Estimate/Non-Audited
Audit Date: 10.06.2023
Personnel: Cecily Hastings (Pub.); Ann Tracy (Acc. Rep.)
Parent company (for newspapers): Inside Publications

INSIDE SACRAMENTO: LAND PARK

Street address 1: 3104 O St
Street address 2: # 120
Street address city: Sacramento
Street address state: CA
Zip/Postal code: 95816-6519
General Phone: (916) 443-5087
General/National Adv. E-mail: Daniel@insidepublications.com
Editorial e-mail: Editor@insidepublications.com
Primary Website: Insidesacramento.com
Mthly Avg Views: 20000
Year Established: 1998
Avg Paid Circ: 250
Avg Free Circ: 20000
Audit By: Sworn/Estimate/Non-Audited
Audit Date: 10.06.2023
Personnel: Cecily Hastings (Pub.); A J Holm (Acc. Rep.)
Parent company (for newspapers): Inside Publications

INSIDE SACRAMENTO: POCKET

Street address 1: 3104 O St
Street address 2: # 120
Street address city: Sacramento
Street address state: CA
Zip/Postal code: 95816-6519
General Phone: (916) 443-5087
General/National Adv. E-mail: Daniel@insidepublications.com
Editorial e-mail: mbbizjak@aol,com
Primary Website: Insidesacramento.com
Mthly Avg Views: 17500
Year Established: 1996
Avg Paid Circ: 250
Avg Free Circ: 20000
Audit By: Sworn/Estimate/Non-Audited
Audit Date: 10.06.2023
Personnel: Cecily Hastings (Pub.)
Parent company (for newspapers): Inside Publications

INYO REGISTER

Street address 1: 407 W Line St
Street address 2: Ste 8
Street address city: Bishop
Street address state: CA
Zip/Postal code: 93514-3321
General Phone: (760) 873-3535
General Fax: (760) 873-3591
Advertising Phone: (760) 873-3535 x 207
Editorial Phone: (760) 873-3535 x 211
General/National Adv. E-mail: terry@inyoregister.com
Display Adv. E-mail: classy@inyoregister.com
Editorial e-mail: tvestal@inyoregister.com
Primary Website: inyoregister.com
Year Established: 1870
Avg Paid Circ: 3688
Avg Free Circ: 2400
Audit By: Sworn/Estimate/Non-Audited
Audit Date: 10.06.2019
Personnel: Rena Mlodecki (Publisher); Terrance Vestal (Managing Editor); Rena Mlodecki (Publisher); Michael Chacanaca (Associate Editor)
Parent company (for newspapers): Horizon Publications Inc.

IRVINE WORLD NEWS

Street address 1: 625 N Grand Ave
Street address city: Santa Ana
Street address state: CA
Zip/Postal code: 92701-4347
General Phone: (877) 469-7344
General Fax: (949) 454-7354
Advertising Phone: (714) 796-3844
General/National Adv. E-mail: customerservice@ocregister.com
Display Adv. E-mail: ebrunelli@ocregister.com
Editorial e-mail: letters@ocregister.com
Primary Website: ocregister.com/sections/city-pages/irvine
Avg Paid Circ: 8026
Audit By: Sworn/Estimate/Non-Audited
Audit Date: 10.06.2019
Personnel: Aaron Kushner (Pub.); Ken Brusic (Ed.)
Parent company (for newspapers): Times Media Group

JOINT FORCES JOURNAL

Street address 1: PO Box 13283
Street address city: Oakland
Street address state: CA
Zip/Postal code: 94661-0283
General Phone: (510) 428-2000
General Fax: (510) 595-7777
General/National Adv. E-mail: info@jointforcesjournal.com
Display Adv. E-mail: jointforcesjournal@aol.com
Primary Website: jointforcesjournal.com
Year Established: 1995
Avg Free Circ: 42000
Audit By: Sworn/Estimate/Non-Audited
Audit Date: 10.06.2019
Personnel: Ken Krause (Pub.); Jan Miller (Ed.)

JULIAN NEWS

Street address 1: 1453 Hollow Glen Rd
Street address city: Julian
Street address state: CA
Zip/Postal code: 92036
General Phone: (760) 765-2231
General Fax: (760) 765-2231
Advertising Phone: (760) 765-2231
Advertising Fax: (760) 765-2231
General/National Adv. E-mail: publisher@juliannews.com
Editorial e-mail: editor@juliannews.com
Primary Website: juliannews.com
Year Established: 1984
Avg Paid Circ: 1200
Avg Free Circ: 400
Audit By: Sworn/Estimate/Non-Audited
Audit Date: 10.06.2019
Personnel: Michele Harvey (Ed/Columnist); Michael Hart (Pub/ Produc Mgr.)

KERN VALLEY SUN

Street address 1: 6416 LAKE ISABELLA BLVD
Street address city: Lake Isabella
Street address state: CA
Zip/Postal code: 93240
General Phone: (760) 379-3667
General Fax: (760) 379-4343
Editorial Phone: (760) 379-3667 x 14
General/National Adv. E-mail: michelel@kvsun.com
Editorial e-mail: editor@kvsun.com
Primary Website: kvsun.com
Year Established: 1959
Avg Paid Circ: 6500
Avg Free Circ: 10500
Audit By: Sworn/Estimate/Non-Audited
Audit Date: 10.06.2019
Personnel: Marsha Smith (Pub.); Susan Barr (Ed.)

LA CANADA VALLEY SUN

Street address 1: 202 W 1st St
Street address 2: 2nd Floor
Street address city: Los Angeles
Street address state: CA
Zip/Postal code: 90012-4299
General Phone: (818) 495-4440
General Fax: (818) 790-5690
Advertising Phone: (818) 637-3200
Advertising Fax: (213) 237-6065
Editorial Phone: (818) 495-4161
General/National Adv. E-mail: marissa.contreras@latimes.com
Display Adv. E-mail: gil.cormaci@latimes.com
Editorial e-mail: lcnews@valleysun.net
Primary Website: lacanadaonline.com
Year Established: 1946
Audit By: Sworn/Estimate/Non-Audited
Audit Date: 10.06.2019
Parent company (for newspapers): Times Community News (TCN)

LA JOLLA LIGHT

Street address 1: 565 Pearl St
Street address 2: Ste 300
Street address city: La Jolla
Street address state: CA
Zip/Postal code: 92037-5051
General Phone: (858) 459-4201
General Fax: (858) 459-5250
Advertising Phone: (858) 875-5954
Advertising Fax: (858) 459-0977
Editorial Phone: (858) 875-5950
Editorial Fax: (858) 459-5250
General/National Adv. E-mail: donp@lajollalight.com
Display Adv. E-mail: mwilliams@mainstreetsd.com
Editorial e-mail: editor@lajollalight.com
Primary Website: lajollalight.com
Mthly Avg Views: 83195
Mthly Avg Unique Visitors: 42676
Year Established: 1913
Avg Paid Circ: 17806
Audit By: AAM
Audit Date: 31.12.2017
Personnel: Phyllis Pfeiffer (President/Gen Mgr); John Feagans (Graphics Mgr.); Susan DeMaggio (Exec. Ed.); Don Parks (Adv. Mgr.); Dara Elstein (Circ. Mgr.); Sandra Hood (Classified Adv. Mgr.)
Parent company (for newspapers): NantMedia Holdings, LLC

LA JOLLA VILLAGE NEWS

Street address 1: 1621 Grand Ave
Street address 2: Ste C
Street address city: San Diego
Street address state: CA
Zip/Postal code: 92109-4458
General Phone: (858) 270-3103
General Fax: (858) 713-0095
Advertising Phone: (858) 270-3103 x 115
Advertising Fax: (858) 713-0095
Editorial Phone: (858) 270-3103 x 131
General/National Adv. E-mail: julie@sdnews.com
Display Adv. E-mail: heather@sdnews.com
Classified Adv. e-mail: heather@sdnews.com
Editorial e-mail: Tom@sdnews.com
Primary Website: sdnews.com
Year Established: 1988
Avg Paid Circ: 25
Avg Free Circ: 160000
Audit By: CVC
Audit Date: 11.08.2023
Personnel: Julie Main (Publisher); Tom Melville (Editor in Chief)
Parent company (for newspapers): San Diego Community Newspaper Group, publishers of La Jolla Today, Peninsula Beacon and Beach & Bay Press

LA PRIDE

Street address 1: 2116 Wilshire Blvd
Street address 2: Ste 260
Street address city: Santa Monica
Street address state: CA
Zip/Postal code: 90403-5750
General Phone: (310) 310-2637
General Fax: (424) 744-8821

General/National Adv. E-mail: advertising@smmirror.com
Display Adv. E-mail: advertising@smmirror.com
Editorial e-mail: editor@smmirror.com
Primary Website: westsidetoday.com
Year Established: 1990
Avg Paid Circ: 0
Avg Free Circ: 100000
Audit By: Sworn/Estimate/Non-Audited
Audit Date: 10.06.2019
Personnel: TJ Montemer (President/Publisher); Judy Swartz (Sales Mgr.)
Parent company (for newspapers): Mirror Media Group

LA PUENTE HIGHLANDER

Street address 1: 181 W. Huntington Driver
Street address 2: Ste 209
Street address city: Monrovia
Street address state: CA
Zip/Postal code: 91016
General Phone: (626) 544-0777
General Fax: (626) 856-2758
Advertising Phone: (626) 544-0777
Editorial Phone: (626) 422-4305
General/National Adv. E-mail: advertising@scng.com
Display Adv. E-mail: advertising@scng.com
Classified Adv. e-mail: advertising@scng.com
Editorial e-mail: news.tribune@sgvn.com
Avg Free Circ: 987
Audit By: Sworn/Estimate/Non-Audited
Audit Date: 16.10.2023
Personnel: Melene Alfonso (VP Advertising); Carla Asmundson (Classified Advertising Manager); Ron Hasse (Publisher); Tom Bray (Senior Editor); Tom Bray
Parent company (for newspapers): Southern California News Group

LAGUNA BEACH NEWS POST

Street address 1: 625 N Grand Ave
Street address city: Santa Ana
Street address state: CA
Zip/Postal code: 92701-4347
General Phone: (877) 469-7344
General Fax: (949) 454-7354
Advertising Phone: (714) 796-3844
General/National Adv. E-mail: customerservice@ocregister.com
Display Adv. E-mail: ebrunelli@ocregister.com
Editorial e-mail: letters@ocregister.com
Primary Website: ocregister.com/sections/city-pages/lagunabeach
Avg Free Circ: 9643
Audit By: Sworn/Estimate/Non-Audited
Audit Date: 10.06.2019
Personnel: Aaron Kushner (Pub.); Ken Brusic (Ed.)

LAGUNA CITIZEN

Street address 1: 604 N Lincoln Way
Street address city: Galt
Street address state: CA
Zip/Postal code: 95632-8601
General Phone: (209) 745-1551
General Fax: (209) 745-4492
General/National Adv. E-mail: news@herburger.com
Primary Website: herburger.net
Avg Free Circ: 12593
Audit By: Sworn/Estimate/Non-Audited
Audit Date: 10.06.2019
Personnel: David Herburger (Pub.)
Parent company (for newspapers): Herburger Publications, Inc.

LAGUNA NEWS-POST

Street address 1: 625 N Grand Ave
Street address city: Santa Ana
Street address state: CA
Zip/Postal code: 92701-4347
General Phone: (714) 796-7954
General Fax: (949) 454-7354
General/National Adv. E-mail: lagunanewspost@ocregister.com
Primary Website: ocregister.com
Avg Paid Circ: 2170
Audit By: Sworn/Estimate/Non-Audited
Audit Date: 10.06.2019
Personnel: Rob Vardon (Ed.); Chris Boucly (Events Ed.)
Parent company (for newspapers): Times Media Group

LAGUNA NIGUEL NEWS

Street address 1: 2190 S. Towne Centre Place
Street address city: Anaheim
Street address state: CA
Zip/Postal code: 92806
General Phone: (714) 796-7000
Primary Website: ocregister.com/sections/city-pages/alisoviejo-lagunaniguel
Avg Paid Circ: 3768
Audit By: Sworn/Estimate/Non-Audited
Audit Date: 10.06.2019
Personnel: Ron Hasse (Pres./Pub.); Kyla Rodriguez (Sr. VP Adv.); Frank Pine (Ed.); Kat Wang (Circ. Dir.); Dan Scofield (COO)
Parent company (for newspapers): Times Media Group

LAGUNA WOODS GLOBE

Street address 1: 2190 S. Towne Centre Place
Street address city: Anaheim
Street address state: CA
Zip/Postal code: 92806
General Phone: (714) 796-7000
General/National Adv. E-mail: service@scng.com
Primary Website: ocregister.com/lagunawoods
Avg Paid Circ: 6747
Avg Free Circ: 619
Audit By: AAM
Audit Date: 31.03.2016
Personnel: Ron Hasse (Pres./ Pub.); Kyla Rodriguez (Sr. VP Adv.); Frank Pine (Ex. Ed.); Bill Van Laningham (VP Mktg); Dan Scofield (CFO); Kat Wang (Circ. Dir.); Erika Ritchie (Local Reporter)
Parent company (for newspapers): Times Media Group

LAMORINDA SUN

Street address 1: 2640 Shadelands Dr
Street address city: Walnut Creek
Street address state: CA
Zip/Postal code: 94598-2513
General Phone: (925) 935-2525
General Fax: (925) 933-0239
Advertising Phone: (925) 943-8119
Advertising Fax: (925) 933-0239
Editorial Phone: (925) 943-8241
Editorial Fax: (925) 933-0239
General/National Adv. E-mail: ccretailads@cctimes.com
Display Adv. E-mail: dsmith@bayareanewsgroup.com
Editorial e-mail: dbutler@bayareanewsgroup.com
Primary Website: contracostatimes.com/lafayette
Year Established: 1857
Avg Paid Circ: 2772
Audit By: AAM
Audit Date: 30.09.2018
Personnel: Dave Butler (Exec. Ed.); Samuel Richards (Ed.); Lisa Herendeen (Editorial Asst.)
Parent company (for newspapers): Digital First Media

LASSEN COUNTY TIMES

Street address 1: 100 Grand Ave
Street address city: Susanville
Street address state: CA
Zip/Postal code: 96130-4451
General Phone: (530) 257-5321
General Fax: (530) 257-0408
Advertising Phone: (530) 257-5321
Editorial Phone: (530) 257-5321
General/National Adv. E-mail: cwilliams@lassennews.com
Display Adv. E-mail: rmeadows@lassennews.com
Editorial e-mail: swilliams@lassennews.com
Primary Website: lassennews.com
Year Established: 1976
Avg Paid Circ: 6128
Avg Free Circ: 3598
Audit By: Sworn/Estimate/Non-Audited
Audit Date: 10.06.2019
Personnel: Michael C. Taborski (Pub); Sam Williams (Mgr. Ed); Rashelle Meadows (Class)
Parent company (for newspapers): Feather Publishing Co., Inc.

LEISURE WORLD GOLDEN RAIN NEWS

Street address 1: 13533 Seal Beach Blvd.
Street address 2: Amphitheater Bldg.
Street address city: Seal Beach
Street address state: CA
Zip/Postal code: 90740
General Phone: (562) 430-0534
General Fax: (562) 598-1617
Advertising Phone: (562) 472-1275
Editorial Phone: (562) 472-1278
General/National Adv. E-mail: davesaunders@lwsbnews.com
Display Adv. E-mail: davesaunders@lwsbnews.com
Editorial e-mail: davesaunders@lwsbnews.com
Primary Website: lwsb.com/newspaper
Year Established: 1963
Avg Paid Circ: 7000
Avg Free Circ: 2000
Audit By: Sworn/Estimate/Non-Audited
Audit Date: 10.06.2019
Personnel: Dave Saunders (Mng. Ed.); Karen McElwain (Adv. Sales)

LINCOLN NEWS MESSENGER

Street address 1: 1030 High Street
Street address city: Auburn
Street address state: CA
Zip/Postal code: 95603
General Phone: (916) 645-7733
Advertising Phone: (916) 774-7939
Editorial Phone: (916) 774-7972
Editorial Fax: (530) 887-1231
Display Adv. E-mail: advertising@goldcountrymedia.com
Classified Adv. e-mail: classifieds@goldcountrymedia.com
Editorial e-mail: billp@goldcountrymedia.com
Primary Website: www.lincolnnewsmessenger.com
Year Established: 1891
Avg Paid Circ: 2700
Avg Free Circ: 0
Audit By: Sworn/Estimate/Non-Audited
Audit Date: 31.12.2016
Personnel: Bill Sullivan (Associate Publisher); John Love (Publisher); Carol Feineman (Managing Editor)
Parent company (for newspapers): Brehm Communications, Inc.; Gold Mountain California News Media, Inc.; Gold Country Media

LOOMIS NEWS

Street address 1: 1030 High Street
Street address city: Auburn
Street address state: CA
Zip/Postal code: 95603
General Phone: 5308855656
General Fax:
Advertising Phone: 91677479393
Editorial Phone:
Display Adv. E-mail: advertising@goldcountrymedia.com
Classified Adv. e-mail: classified@goldcountrymedia.com
Editorial e-mail: billp@goldcountrymedia.com
Primary Website: theloomisnews.com
Year Established: 1940
Avg Paid Circ: 771
Avg Free Circ: 195
Audit By: Sworn/Estimate/Non-Audited
Audit Date: 30.08.2017
Personnel: Kelly Leibold (Circulation Mgr)
Parent company (for newspapers): Brehm Communications, Inc.; Gold Mountain California News Media, Inc.

LOS ALTOS TOWN CRIER

Street address 1: 138 Main St
Street address city: Los Altos
Street address state: CA
Zip/Postal code: 94022-2905
General Phone: (650) 948-9000
General Fax: (650) 948-9213
Advertising Phone: (650) 948-9000 x 307
General/National Adv. E-mail: info@latc.com
Display Adv. E-mail: jt@latc.com
Primary Website: latc.com
Year Established: 1947
Avg Paid Circ: 8598
Avg Free Circ: 7355
Audit By: Sworn/Estimate/Non-Audited
Audit Date: 10.06.2019
Personnel: Paul Nyberg (Pub.); Howard Bischoff (Circ. Mgr.); Bruce Barton (Ed.); Liz Nyberg (HR Dir); Howard Bischoff (Circulation Mgr)

LOS ANGELES DOWNTOWN NEWS

Street address 1: 1264 W 1st St
Street address city: Los Angeles
Street address state: CA
Zip/Postal code: 90026-5831
General Phone: (213) 481-1448
General Fax: (213) 250-4617
Advertising Phone: (213) 481-1448
Advertising Fax: (213) 250-4617
Editorial Phone: (213) 481-1448
Editorial Fax: (213) 250-4617
General/National Adv. E-mail: realpeople@downtownnews.com
Display Adv. E-mail: catherine@downtownnews.com
Editorial e-mail: regardie@downtownnews.com
Primary Website: downtownnews.com
Year Established: 1972
Avg Paid Circ: 31
Avg Free Circ: 37670
Audit By: VAC
Audit Date: 30.06.2017
Personnel: Dawn Eastin (Gen. Mgr.)

LOS ANGELES WAVE

Street address 1: 3731 Wilshire Blvd
Street address 2: Suite 840
Street address city: Los Angeles
Street address state: CA
Zip/Postal code: 90010-2851
General Phone: (323) 556-5720
General Fax: (213) 835-0584
Advertising Phone: (323) 556-5720 x 245
General/National Adv. E-mail: llodder@wavepublication.com
Display Adv. E-mail: llodder@wavepublication.com
Editorial e-mail: newsroom@wavepublication.com
Primary Website: wavenewspapers.com
Avg Free Circ: 49900
Audit By: Sworn/Estimate/Non-Audited
Audit Date: 10.06.2019
Personnel: Linda Lodder (Adv.)

LOS BANOS ENTERPRISE

Street address 1: 848 6th Street
Street address 2: Suite 7
Street address city: Los Banos
Street address state: CA
Zip/Postal code: 93635
General Phone: (209) 519-0230
General/National Adv. E-mail: editor@losbanosenterprise.com
Display Adv. E-mail: sales@losbanosenterprise.com
Classified Adv. e-mail: sales@losbanosenterprise.com
Editorial e-mail: sales@losbanosenterprise.com
Primary Website: losbanosenterprise.com
Mthly Avg Views: 70000
Year Established: 1891
Avg Paid Circ: 0
Avg Free Circ: 17000
Audit By: USPS
Audit Date: 09.09.2022
Personnel: Tisha Blackwood-Freitas (Editor); Gene Lieb (Outside Adv. Sales); Allen Payton (Interim Publisher); David Witte (Sports Reporter); Sydney Benton (Advertising Sales Representative); Corey Pride (Reporter); AJ Griem (Webmaster); Thaddeus Miller (Reporter); Beth Smith (Admin./Sales Asst.); Victor Patton (Managing. Ed.); Ken Riddick (Pres./Pub.); Deanna Whitmore (Adv. Dir.)
Parent company (for newspapers): Los Banos Enterprise, LLC; The McClatchy Company

MAMMOTH TIMES

Street address 1: 501 Old Mammoth Rd
Street address 2: Unit 9
Street address city: Mammoth Lakes
Street address state: CA
Zip/Postal code: 93546
General Phone: (760) 934-3929

General Fax: (760) 934-3951
Advertising Phone: (760) 934-3929 x 107
Editorial Phone: (760) 934-3929 x 116
General/National Adv. E-mail: ads@mammothtimes.com
Display Adv. E-mail: classifieds@mammothtimes.com
Editorial e-mail: editor@mammothtimes.com
Primary Website: mammothtimes.com
Year Established: 1987
Avg Paid Circ: 4200
Audit By: Sworn/Estimate/Non-Audited
Audit Date: 10.06.2019
Personnel: Mike Gervais (Managing Ed.); Wendi Grasseschi (Staff Writer); Blake Martines (Sales Rep); Josh Haywood (Classifieds/Circ)
Parent company (for newspapers): Horizon Publications Inc.

MARIN COUNTY POST

Street address 1: 405 14th St
Street address 2: Ste 1215
Street address city: Oakland
Street address state: CA
Zip/Postal code: 94612-2707
General Phone: (510) 287-8200
General Fax: (510) 287-8247
Advertising Phone: (510) 287-8220
Editorial e-mail: themarinpost@gmail.com
Primary Website: https://marinpost.org/
Year Established: 1963
Avg Paid Circ: 0
Avg Free Circ: 417
Audit By: VAC
Audit Date: 30.06.2017
Personnel: Paul Cobbs (Pub.)
Parent company (for newspapers): Post News Group

MARIPOSA GAZETTE

Street address 1: 5108 State Highway 140
Street address 2: Ste B
Street address city: Mariposa
Street address state: CA
Zip/Postal code: 95338-9249
General Phone: (209) 966-2500
General Fax: (209) 966-3384
General/National Adv. E-mail: nicole@mariposagazette.com
Display Adv. E-mail: nicole@mariposagazette.com
Editorial e-mail: greg@mariposagazette.com
Primary Website: mariposagazette.com
Year Established: 1854
Avg Paid Circ: 4200
Avg Free Circ: 100
Audit By: Sworn/Estimate/Non-Audited
Audit Date: 28.09.2023
Personnel: Greg Little (Editor); Nicole Little (Publisher); Matt Johnson (Assistant editor); Shantel Wight (Advertising director)

MARTINEZ NEWS-GAZETTE

Street address 1: 802 Alhambra Ave
Street address city: Martinez
Street address state: CA
Zip/Postal code: 94553-1604
General Phone: (925) 228-6400
General Fax: (925) 228-1536
General/National Adv. E-mail: gazette_ads@yahoo.com
Primary Website: martinezgazette.com
Avg Paid Circ: 2550
Avg Free Circ: 8399
Audit By: Sworn/Estimate/Non-Audited
Audit Date: 10.06.2019
Personnel: David L. Payne (Ed. in Chief); Samuel Li-Ron (Gen. Mgr.); Yael Li-Ron (Ed.); Erin Clark

MATTOS NEWSPAPERS, INC.

Street address 1: PO Box 878
Street address city: Newman
Street address state: CA
Zip/Postal code: 95360-0878
General Phone: (209) 604-8105
General Fax: (209) 862-4133
Advertising Phone: (209) 243-8170
Editorial Phone: (209) 243-8104
General/National Adv. E-mail: smattos@mattosnews.com
Primary Website: Website
Avg Paid Circ: 7500
Audit By: Sworn/Estimate/Non-Audited
Audit Date: 10.06.2019
Personnel: Susan Mattos (Pub.); Dean Harris (Ed.)

MENDOCINO COUNTY OBSERVER

Street address 1: 50 Ramsey Rd
Street address city: Laytonville
Street address state: CA
Zip/Postal code: 95454-9900
General Phone: (707) 984-6223
General Fax: (707) 984-8118
General/National Adv. E-mail: observer@pacific.net
Primary Website: No Website
Year Established: 1978
Avg Paid Circ: 3000
Audit By: Sworn/Estimate/Non-Audited
Audit Date: 10.06.2019
Personnel: Susan Shields (Adv. Mgr.); Jim Shields (Ed.)

MERCED COUNTY TIMES

Street address 1: 2221 K St
Street address city: Merced
Street address state: CA
Zip/Postal code: 95340-3868
General Phone: (209) 383-0433
General Fax: (209) 383-0344
Primary Website: mercedcountytimes.net
Year Established: 1962
Avg Paid Circ: 10000
Avg Free Circ: 25000
Audit By: Sworn/Estimate/Non-Audited
Audit Date: 10.06.2019
Personnel: John Whitaker (Chief Ed.); Mallori Resendez (Adv); Sergio Servin (Adv)
Parent company (for newspapers): Mid Valley Publishing

MERCED SUN-STAR

Street address 1: 1190 W. Olive Avenue
Street address 2: Suite F
Street address city: Merced
Street address state: CA
Zip/Postal code: 95348
General Phone: (209) 722-1511
General Fax: (209) 385-2460
Advertising Fax: (209) 384-2226
Editorial Fax: (209) 385-2460
General/National Adv. E-mail: rperes@mercedsunstar.com
Primary Website: mercedsunstar.com
Year Established: 1869
Avg Paid Circ: 14944
Avg Free Circ: 15000
Audit By: Sworn/Estimate/Non-Audited
Audit Date: 10.06.2019
Personnel: Tim Ritchie (Pres./Pub.); Rob Parsons (Ed.)
Parent company (for newspapers): The McClatchy Company

MILL VALLEY HERALD

Street address 1: 1301B Grant Ave
Street address city: Novato
Street address state: CA
Zip/Postal code: 94945-3143
General Phone: (415) 892-1516
General Fax: (415) 897-0940
Advertising Phone: (415) 892-1516 x 15
Editorial Phone: (415) 892-1516 x 31
General/National Adv. E-mail: mmckellips@marinscope.com
Display Adv. E-mail: mmckellips@marinscope.com
Editorial e-mail: shemmila@marinscope.com
Primary Website: marinscope.com/mill_valley_herald/news
Year Established: 1994
Avg Paid Circ: 121
Avg Free Circ: 4977
Audit By: Sworn/Estimate/Non-Audited
Audit Date: 10.06.2019
Personnel: Soren Hemmila (Ed.)
Parent company (for newspapers): Marinscope Community Newspapers

MOJAVE DESERT NEWS

Street address 1: 8016 California City Blvd St #7
Street address city: California City
Street address state: CA
Zip/Postal code: 93505-2662
General Phone: (760) 373-4812
General Fax: (760) 373-2941
General/National Adv. E-mail: admin@desertnews.com
Display Adv. E-mail: classified@desertnews.com
Editorial e-mail: sales@desertnews.com
Primary Website: desertnews.com
Year Established: 1938
Avg Paid Circ: 5500
Avg Free Circ: 500
Audit By: Sworn/Estimate/Non-Audited
Audit Date: 10.06.2019
Personnel: James Quiggle (Co-Pub./Ed.); Linda Love (Co-Pub.); Jerri Elford (Adv.); Misty Hickok (Adv. Sales)
Parent company (for newspapers): Times Media Group

MONTEREY COUNTY WEEKLY

Street address 1: 668 Williams Ave
Street address city: Seaside
Street address state: CA
Zip/Postal code: 93955-5736
General Phone: (831) 394-5656
General Fax: (831) 394-2909
General/National Adv. E-mail: erik@mcweekly.com
Display Adv. E-mail: erik@mcweekly.com
Editorial e-mail: erik@mcweekly.com
Primary Website: montereycountyweekly.com
Year Established: 1988
Avg Paid Circ: 0
Avg Free Circ: 36014
Audit By: CVC
Audit Date: 30.09.2018
Personnel: Erik Cushman (Publisher); Bradley Zeve (Exec. Ed. & CEO); Kevin Jones (Circ.)
Parent company (for newspapers): Milestones, Inc.

MOORPARK ACORN

Street address 1: 1203 Flynn Rd
Street address 2: Unit 140
Street address city: Camarillo
Street address state: CA
Zip/Postal code: 93012-6202
General Phone: (818) 706-0266
General Fax: (818) 706-8468
Editorial Fax: (818) 671-1873
General/National Adv. E-mail: AdRep@theacorn.com
Display Adv. E-mail: classads@theacorn.com
Editorial e-mail: newstip@theacorn.com
Primary Website: mpacorn.com
Avg Free Circ: 11530
Audit By: VAC
Audit Date: 30.09.2017
Personnel: Daniel Wolowicz (ed.)
Parent company (for newspapers): J. Bee NP Publishing, Ltd.

MORGAN HILL TIMES

Street address 1: 17500 Depot St
Street address 2: Ste 140
Street address city: Morgan Hill
Street address state: CA
Zip/Postal code: 95037-3886
General Phone: (408) 779-4106
General Fax: (408) 779-3886
Advertising Phone: (408) 842-2206
Advertising Fax: (408) 779-3886
Editorial Phone: (408) 847-7010
General/National Adv. E-mail: editor@morganhilltimes.com
Editorial e-mail: editor@morganhilltimes.com
Primary Website: morganhilltimes.com
Avg Paid Circ: 1375
Avg Free Circ: 9000
Audit By: Sworn/Estimate/Non-Audited
Audit Date: 10.06.2019
Personnel: Jeff Mitchell (Publisher); Michael Moore (Editor); Deborah Garcia (Ad Director)
Parent company (for newspapers): New SV Media, Inc

MOUNTAIN DEMOCRAT, INC.

Street address 1: 2889 Ray Lawyer Drive
Street address city: Placerville
Street address state: CA
Zip/Postal code: 95667
General Phone: (530) 622-1255
General Fax: (530) 622-7894
General/National Adv. E-mail: ibalentine@mtdemocrat.com
Display Adv. E-mail: ibalentine@mtdemocrat.com
Primary Website: mtdemocrat.com
Year Established: 1851
Avg Paid Circ: 6889
Avg Free Circ: 750
Audit By: AAM
Audit Date: 31.12.2018
Personnel: Richard B. Esposito (Pub.); Ian Balentine (Adv. Dir.); Gerry Ulm (Circ. Mgr.); Noel Stack (Editor); Mimi Escabar (Lifestyle Ed.); Jerry Heinzer (Sports Ed.); Letty Baumgardner (Graphics Manager)
Parent company (for newspapers): Mountain Democrat, Inc.

MOUNTAIN NEWS

Street address 1: P.O. Box 2410
Street address 2: PO Box 2410
Street address city: Lake Arrowhead
Street address state: CA
Zip/Postal code: 92352
General Phone: 9093376145
General Fax: 9093376145
Advertising Phone: 9093376145
Advertising Fax: 9093376145
Editorial Phone: 9093376145
Editorial Fax: 9093376145
General/National Adv. E-mail: hbradley@mountain-news.com
Display Adv. E-mail: hbradley@mountain-news.com
Classified Adv. e-mail: hbradley@mountain-news.com
Editorial e-mail: hbradley@mountain-news.com
Primary Website: mountain-news.com
Mthly Avg Views: 90000
Mthly Avg Unique Visitors: 30000
Year Established: 1924
Avg Paid Circ: 2000
Avg Free Circ: 500
Audit By: Sworn/Estimate/Non-Audited
Audit Date: 10.06.2022
Personnel: Harry Bradley (Publisher)
Parent company (for newspapers): Brehm Communications, Inc.; Horizon - Gold Mountain CA

MOUNTAIN VIEW VOICE

Street address 1: 450 Cambridge Ave
Street address city: Palo Alto
Street address state: CA
Zip/Postal code: 94306-1507
General Phone: (650) 964-6300
General Fax: (650) 223-7507
Advertising Phone: (650) 223-6570
Editorial Phone: (650) 223-6537
General/National Adv. E-mail: ads@mv-voice.com
Display Adv. E-mail: ads@mv-voice.com
Editorial e-mail: editor@mv-voice.com
Primary Website: mv-voice.com
Year Established: 1992
Avg Free Circ: 15000
Audit By: Sworn/Estimate/Non-Audited
Audit Date: 10.06.2019
Personnel: Andrea Gemmet (Ed.); Connie Jo Cotton (VP, Sales/Mktg)
Parent company (for newspapers): Embarcadero Media

MOUNTAINEER PROGRESS

Street address 1: 3407 State Highway 2
Street address city: Wrightwood
Street address state: CA
Zip/Postal code: 92397-9687
General Phone: (760) 249-3245
General Fax: (760) 249-4021
General/National Adv. E-mail: editorial@mtprogress.net
Display Adv. E-mail: displayads@mtprogress.net
Editorial e-mail: newsroom@mtprogress.net
Primary Website: mtprogress.net
Year Established: 1961
Avg Paid Circ: 3500
Avg Free Circ: 1200
Audit By: Sworn/Estimate/Non-Audited
Audit Date: 10.06.2019
Personnel: Steve Rinek (Pub.); Vicky Rinek (Ed.)

MT. SHASTA HERALD

Street address 1: 924 N Mount Shasta Blvd

Street address city: Mount Shasta
Street address state: CA
Zip/Postal code: 96067-8700
General Phone: (530) 926-5214
General Fax: (530) 926-4166
Advertising Phone: (530) 926-5214
General/National Adv. E-mail: mguthrie@siskiyoudaily.com
Display Adv. E-mail: classifieds@mtshastanews.com
Editorial e-mail: sgerace@mtshastanews.com
Primary Website: mtshastanews.com
Year Established: 1934
Avg Paid Circ: 6000
Audit By: Sworn/Estimate/Non-Audited
Audit Date: 10.06.2019
Personnel: Matt Guthrie (Pub.); Steve Gerace (Ed.)
Parent company (for newspapers): CherryRoad Media

MTSHASTA NEWS

Street address 1: 924 N Mount Shasta Blvd
Street address city: Mount Shasta
Street address state: CA
Zip/Postal code: 96067-8700
General Phone: (530) 926-5214
General Fax: (530) 926-4166
General/National Adv. E-mail: bbrown@mtshastanews.com
Display Adv. E-mail: classifieds@mtshastanews.com
Editorial e-mail: news@mtshastanews.com
Primary Website: mtshastanews.com
Avg Paid Circ: 1600
Avg Free Circ: 900
Audit By: Sworn/Estimate/Non-Audited
Audit Date: 10.06.2019
Personnel: Amy Lanier (Reg. Pub.); Skye Kinkade (Reg. Ed.); Cathy Athens (Classified Adv.); Haley Brown (Display Adv.)
Parent company (for newspapers): CherryRoad Media

NEEDLES DESERT STAR

Street address 1: 800 W Broadway St
Street address 2: Ste E
Street address city: Needles
Street address state: CA
Zip/Postal code: 92363-2755
General Phone: (760) 326-2222
General Fax: (760) 326-3480
Advertising Phone: (928) 763-2505
Editorial Phone: (760) 326-2222
General/National Adv. E-mail: needlesdesertstar@citlink.net
Primary Website: thedesertstar.com
Year Established: 1888
Avg Paid Circ: 1800
Avg Free Circ: 500
Audit By: Sworn/Estimate/Non-Audited
Audit Date: 10.06.2019
Personnel: Robin Richards (Ed); Don Orth (Circulation Mgr)
Parent company (for newspapers): Brehm Communications, Inc.; News West Publishing Company Inc. (OOB)

NEWS ENTERPRISE

Street address 1: 216 Main St
Street address city: Seal Beach
Street address state: CA
Zip/Postal code: 90740-6318
General Phone: (562) 431-1397
General Fax: (562) 493-2310
Advertising Phone: (562) 431-1397
Editorial Phone: (562) 431-1397 x 220
General/National Adv. E-mail: info@newsenterprise.net
Display Adv. E-mail: publisher@newsenterprise.net
Editorial e-mail: editor@newsenterprise.net
Primary Website: newsenterprise.net
Year Established: 1923
Avg Paid Circ: 1400
Avg Free Circ: 30000
Audit By: Sworn/Estimate/Non-Audited
Audit Date: 10.06.2019
Personnel: Vince Bodiford (Pub.); Ted Apodaca (Ed.); Alice Melamed (Advert. Acct Mgr); Jesus Ruiz (Sports Ed)

Parent company (for newspapers): CommunityMedia Co.

NORTH COAST JOURNAL

Street address 1: 310 F St
Street address city: Eureka
Street address state: CA
Zip/Postal code: 95501-1006
General Phone: (707) 442-1400
General Fax: (707) 442-1401
General/National Adv. E-mail: ncjournal@northcoastjournal.com
Display Adv. E-mail: classified@northcoastjournal.com
Editorial e-mail: thad@northcoastjournal.com
Primary Website: northcoastjournal.com
Year Established: 1990
Avg Paid Circ: 81
Avg Free Circ: 19559
Audit By: CVC
Audit Date: 31.03.2020
Personnel: Melissa Sanderson; Chuck Leishman (Adv. Mgr); Kimberley Wear (Reporter); Judy Hodgson (Pub. Mgr); Thad Greenson (Editor); Kyle Windham (Sales Manager); Henk Sims (Ed.); Linda Schwend (Prodn. Mgr.); Carolyn Fernandez (Circ. Mgr)
Parent company (for newspapers): C-VILLE Holdings LLC; Melissa Sanderson

NOVATO ADVANCE

Street address 1: 1301B Grant Ave
Street address 2: # B
Street address city: Novato
Street address state: CA
Zip/Postal code: 94945-3143
General Phone: (415) 892-1516
General Fax: (415) 897-0940
Advertising Phone: (415) 892-1516 x15
Editorial Phone: (415) 892-1516 x 13
General/National Adv. E-mail: scope@marinscope.com
Display Adv. E-mail: mmckellips@marinscope.com
Editorial e-mail: nbaptista@marinscope.com
Primary Website: marinscope.com/novato_advance
Year Established: 1922
Avg Paid Circ: 3725
Avg Free Circ: 3848
Audit By: Sworn/Estimate/Non-Audited
Audit Date: 10.06.2019
Personnel: Sherman Frederick (Pub.); Nicole Baptista (Ed.); Joe Wolfcale (Managing Ed); Soren Hemmila (Southern Marin Editor); Derek Wilson (Central Marin Ed)
Parent company (for newspapers): Marinscope Community Newspapers

OAKDALE LEADER

Street address 1: 122 S 3rd Ave
Street address city: Oakdale
Street address state: CA
Zip/Postal code: 95361-3993
General Phone: (209) 847-3021
General Fax: (209) 847-9750
Advertising Phone: (209) 847-3021
Advertising Fax: (209) 847-9750
Editorial Phone: (209) 847-3021
Editorial Fax: (209) 847-9750
General/National Adv. E-mail: mjackson@oakdaleleader.com
Display Adv. E-mail: ads@oakdaleleader.com
Editorial e-mail: mjackson@oakdaleleader.com
Primary Website: oakdaleleader.com
Avg Paid Circ: 6000
Avg Free Circ: 5000
Audit By: Sworn/Estimate/Non-Audited
Audit Date: 10.06.2019
Personnel: Hank Veen (Pub.); Marg Jackson (Ed.); Teresa Hammond (Circ. Mgr.); Corey Rogers (Asst. Adv. Dir.)
Parent company (for newspapers): Morris Multimedia, Inc.

OJAI VALLEY NEWS

Street address 1: 101 Vallerio Ave
Street address city: Ojai
Street address state: CA
Zip/Postal code: 93023-3631
General Phone: (805) 646-1476
General Fax: (805) 646-4281
Advertising Phone: (805) 646-1476
Editorial Phone: (805) 646-1476
General/National Adv. E-mail: editor@ojaivalleynews.com
Display Adv. E-mail: classified@ojaivalleynews.com
Editorial e-mail: editor@ojaivalleynews.com
Primary Website: ojaivalleynews.com
Year Established: 1891
Avg Paid Circ: 3800
Audit By: Sworn/Estimate/Non-Audited
Audit Date: 10.06.2019
Personnel: Tim Dewar (Pub.)
Parent company (for newspapers): Downhome Publishing LLC

ORANGE CITY NEWS

Street address 1: 625 N Grand Ave
Street address city: Santa Ana
Street address state: CA
Zip/Postal code: 92701-4347
General Phone: (714) 796-7954
General Fax: (714) 704-3714
General/National Adv. E-mail: orangecitynews@ocregister.com
Primary Website: ocregister.com/sections/city-pages/orange-villapark
Avg Paid Circ: 6959
Audit By: Sworn/Estimate/Non-Audited
Audit Date: 10.06.2019
Personnel: Aaron Kushner (Pub.); Ken Brusic (Ed.)
Parent company (for newspapers): Times Media Group

PACIFICA TRIBUNE

Street address 1: 1301B Grant Ave
Street address city: Novato
Street address state: CA
Zip/Postal code: 94945-3143
General Phone: (650) 359-6666
General Fax: (650) 359-3821
Editorial e-mail: jnorthrop@bayareanewsgroup.com
Primary Website: pacificatribune.com
Year Established: 1959
Avg Paid Circ: 3697
Avg Free Circ: 160
Audit By: Sworn/Estimate/Non-Audited
Audit Date: 10.06.2019
Personnel: J Northrop; Randall Keith (Mng. Dig. Ed.); Bert Robinson; Sharon Bryant (Pres./Pub.); Lisa Buckingham (Sr. VP/ COO)
Parent company (for newspapers): MediaNews Group

PALISADIAN-POST

Street address 1: 881 Alma Real Dr
Street address 2: Ste 213
Street address city: Pacific Palisades
Street address state: CA
Zip/Postal code: 90272-3737
General Phone: (310) 454-1321
General Fax: (310) 454-1078
General/National Adv. E-mail: info@palipost.com
Display Adv. E-mail: kendy@palipost.com
Editorial e-mail: editor@palipost.com
Primary Website: palipost.com
Year Established: 1928
Avg Paid Circ: 4950
Avg Free Circ: 24
Audit By: Sworn/Estimate/Non-Audited
Audit Date: 10.06.2019
Personnel: Roberta Donohue (Pub.)

PALO ALTO DAILY NEWS

Street address 1: 255 Constitution Dr
Street address city: Menlo Park
Street address state: CA
Zip/Postal code: 94025-1108
General Phone: (650) 391-1000
General Fax: (650) 391-1001
Advertising Phone: (650) 391-1028
Advertising Fax: (650) 391-1011
Editorial Phone: (650) 391-1337
General/National Adv. E-mail: letters@bayareanewsgroup.com
Display Adv. E-mail: adsales@dailynewsgroup.com
Editorial e-mail: news@paloaltodailynews.com
Primary Website: paloaltodailynews.com
Avg Paid Circ: 47585
Sat. Circulation Paid: 49282
Sun. Circulation Paid: 49464
Audit By: Sworn/Estimate/Non-Audited
Audit Date: 10.06.2019
Personnel: Mario Dianda (Exec. Ed.); Jason Green (City Ed.); Kevin Kelly (Copydesk Chief); Bud Geracie (Sports Editor); Paulo Pereira (Opns. Mgr.); Christine Eng (Prodn./Creative Servs. Mgr); Jennifer Belton (Adv. Sales Mgr.)
Parent company (for newspapers): Digital First Media

PALO VERDE VALLEY TIMES

Street address 1: 400 W Hobsonway
Street address city: Blythe
Street address state: CA
Zip/Postal code: 92225-1509
General Phone: (760) 922-3181
General Fax: (760) 922-3184
General/National Adv. E-mail: advertising@pvvt.com
Display Adv. E-mail: classifieds@pvvt.com
Editorial e-mail: editor@pvvt.com
Primary Website: paloverdevalleytimes.com
Year Established: 1925
Avg Paid Circ: 1770
Avg Free Circ: 55
Audit By: Sworn/Estimate/Non-Audited
Audit Date: 10.06.2019
Personnel: Debbie Hoel (Pub.); Jill Madsen (Adv. Rep.); Jaclyn Randall (Assoc. Ed.); Sylvia Rubalcaba (Classified Adv. Mgr.); Robin Echardt (Circ. Mgr.)
Parent company (for newspapers): Western News&Info, Inc.

PALOS VERDES PENINSULA NEWS

Street address 1: 609 Deep Valley Dr
Street address 2: Ste 200
Street address city: Rolling Hills Estates
Street address state: CA
Zip/Postal code: 90274-3614
General Phone: (310) 377-6877
General Fax: (310) 372-6113
General/National Adv. E-mail: jenifer.lemon@tbrnews.com
Display Adv. E-mail: jenifer.lemon@tbrnews.com
Editorial e-mail: lisa.jacobs@tbrnews.com
Primary Website: pvnews.com
Avg Paid Circ: 13444
Audit By: Sworn/Estimate/Non-Audited
Audit Date: 10.06.2019
Personnel: Lisa Jacobs (Ed.); Jennifer Lemon (Adv./Sales); Molly Moreno (Adv./Sales)
Parent company (for newspapers): Digital First Media

PARADISE POST

Street address 1: PO Box 70
Street address city: Paradise
Street address state: CA
Zip/Postal code: 95967-0070
General Phone: (530) 879-7888
Editorial e-mail: newsroom@paradisepost.com
Primary Website: paradisepost.com
Year Established: 1945
Avg Paid Circ: 2902
Audit By: Sworn/Estimate/Non-Audited
Audit Date: 10.06.2019
Personnel: Jean Chirsty (Circ. Mgr.); Rick Silva (Mng. Ed.); Jeri Luce (Prodn. Mgr.); Rowland Rebele; Gregg McConnell (Pub.); Jerry Urban (Adv. Dir.); Darren Holden (Advertising)

PARK LABREA NEWS & BEVERLY PRESS

Street address 1: 5150 Wilshire Blvd
Street address 2: Suite 330
Street address city: Los Angeles
Street address state: CA
Zip/Postal code: 90036-4480
General Phone: (323) 933-5518
Primary Website: beverlypress.com
Audit By: Sworn/Estimate/Non-Audited
Audit Date: 10.06.2019
Parent company (for newspapers): Times Community News (TCN)

PASADENA WEEKLY

Street address 1: 50 S De Lacey Ave
Street address 2: Ste 200
Street address city: Pasadena
Street address state: CA
Zip/Postal code: 91105-3806

General Phone: (626) 584-1500
General Fax: (626) 795-0149
General/National Adv. E-mail: jon@pasadenaweekly.com
Editorial e-mail: kevinu@pasadenaweekly.com
Primary Website: pasadenaweekly.com
Year Established: 1985
Avg Free Circ: 26691
Audit By: VAC
Audit Date: 30.09.2017
Personnel: Jon Guynn (Pub.); Kevin Uhrich (Ed.)
Parent company (for newspapers): Times Media Group

PASO ROBLES PRESS

Street address 1: 935 Riverside Ave.
Street address 2: Ste. 8A
Street address city: Paso Robles
Street address state: CA
Zip/Postal code: 93446
General Phone: (805) 237-6060
General Fax: (805) 237-6066
General/National Adv. E-mail: spotruch@pasoroblespress.com
Display Adv. E-mail: spotruch@pasoroblespress.com
Editorial e-mail: cfrank@pasoroblespress.com
Primary Website: pasoroblespress.com
Avg Paid Circ: 2821
Avg Free Circ: 12379
Audit By: Sworn/Estimate/Non-Audited
Audit Date: 10.06.2019
Personnel: Brian Williams (Ed.); Sheri Potruch (Mktg.)
Parent company (for newspapers): San Luis Valley Publishing

PATTERSON IRRIGATOR

Street address 1: 26 N 3rd St
Street address city: Patterson
Street address state: CA
Zip/Postal code: 95363-2507
General Phone: (209) 892-6187
General Fax: (209) 892-3761
Advertising Phone: (209) 892-6187
Advertising Fax: (209) 892-3761
General/National Adv. E-mail: news@pattersonirrigator.com
Display Adv. E-mail: marybeth@pattersonirrigator.com
Editorial e-mail: jenifer@pattersonirrigator.com
Primary Website: pattersonirrigator.com
Year Established: 1911
Avg Paid Circ: 8700
Avg Free Circ: 7000
Audit By: Sworn/Estimate/Non-Audited
Audit Date: 10.06.2019
Personnel: Robert Matthews (Pub.)

PAUL V SCHOLL

Street address 1: 7144 Fair Oaks Blvd
Street address 2: Ste 5
Street address city: Carmichael
Street address state: CA
Zip/Postal code: 95608-6464
General Phone: (916)773-1111
General Fax: (916) 773-2999
Advertising Phone: (916) 773-1111
Advertising Fax: (916) 773-2999
Editorial Phone: (916) 773-1111
General/National Adv. E-mail: Publisher@MPG8.com
Display Adv. E-mail: Publisher@MPG8.com
Editorial e-mail: Publisher@MPG8.com
Primary Website: placersentinel.com
Year Established: 1987
Avg Free Circ: 8000
Audit By: Sworn/Estimate/Non-Audited
Audit Date: 10.06.2019
Personnel: Paul Scholl (Owner/Pub.)
Parent company (for newspapers): Messenger Publishing Group

PENINSULA BEACON

Street address 1: 1621 Grand Ave
Street address 2: Ste C
Street address city: San Diego
Street address state: CA
Zip/Postal code: 92109-4458
General Phone: (858) 270-3103
General Fax: (858) 713-0095
Advertising Phone: (858) 270-3103 x 106
Advertising Fax: (858) 713-0095
Editorial Phone: (858) 270-3103 x 131
General/National Adv. E-mail: heather@sdnews.com
Display Adv. E-mail: kim@sdnews.com
Editorial e-mail: mail@sdnews.com
Primary Website: sdnews.com
Year Established: 1989
Avg Paid Circ: 21
Avg Free Circ: 20000
Audit By: Sworn/Estimate/Non-Audited
Audit Date: 10.06.2019
Personnel: Julie Main (Pub.); Heather Long (Ad Manager); Tom Melville (Editor)
Parent company (for newspapers): San Diego Community Newspaper Group, publishers of La Jolla Today, Peninsula Beacon and Beach & Bay Press

PERRIS PROGRESS

Street address 1: 277 E 4th St
Street address 2: Ste F
Street address city: Perris
Street address state: CA
Zip/Postal code: 92570-2256
General Phone: (951) 737-9784
General Fax: (951) 737-9785
General/National Adv. E-mail: SentinelWeekly@aol.com
Display Adv. E-mail: PerrisCityNews@aol.com
Primary Website: theperrisprogress.com
Year Established: 1900
Avg Free Circ: 5000
Audit By: Sworn/Estimate/Non-Audited
Audit Date: 10.06.2019
Personnel: Gary Lendennie (Ed.)

PETALUMA ARGUS-COURIER

Street address 1: 719 Southpoint Blvd
Street address 2: Ste C
Street address city: Petaluma
Street address state: CA
Zip/Postal code: 94954-8004
General Phone: (707) 762-4541
Advertising Phone: (707) 526-8551
Editorial Phone: (707) 776-8458
General/National Adv. E-mail: john.burns@arguscourier.com
Display Adv. E-mail: john.burns@arguscourier.com
Editorial e-mail: matt.brown@arguscourier.com
Primary Website: petaluma360.com
Year Established: 1855
Avg Paid Circ: 4314
Avg Free Circ: 244
Audit By: CVC
Audit Date: 30.03.2018
Personnel: kathi Schneider; Emily Charrier (Pub.); Joanne Herrfeldt (Adv.); Kris Patalano (Circ.)
Parent company (for newspapers): Sonoma Media Investments LLC

PHILIPPINES TODAY

Street address 1: 6454 Mission St
Street address 2: Suite 227
Street address city: Daly City
Street address state: CA
Zip/Postal code: 94014-2013
General Phone: (650) 872-3200
General Fax: (650) 8723208
Advertising Phone: (650) 8723200
Advertising Fax: (650) 8723208
Editorial Phone: same
Editorial Fax: same
General/National Adv. E-mail: advertising@philippinestodayus.com
Display Adv. E-mail: advertising@philippinestodayus.com
Editorial e-mail: editor@philippinestodayus.com
Primary Website: philippinestodayus.com
Year Established: 2008
Avg Paid Circ: 29855
Audit By: Sworn/Estimate/Non-Audited
Audit Date: 10.06.2019
Personnel: Marilyn King (VP, Sales)

PIEDMONTER

Street address 1: 1516 Oak St
Street address city: Alameda
Street address state: CA
Zip/Postal code: 94501-2947
General Phone: (510) 748-1666
General Fax: (510) 748-1680
Editorial Phone: (510) 748-1658
Primary Website: www.insidebayarea.com/piedmont
Avg Paid Circ: 3851
Audit By: AAM
Audit Date: 30.09.2018
Personnel: Ken McLaughlin (Reg. news editor); Frankel Mike (Asst. Mng. Ed. â€" Reg.); Chris Walker (News Ed.)
Parent company (for newspapers): Digital First Media

PLACENTIA NEWS TIMES

Street address 1: 625 N Grand Ave
Street address city: Santa Ana
Street address state: CA
Zip/Postal code: 92701-4347
General Phone: (877) 469-7344
General Fax: (949) 454-7354
Advertising Phone: (714) 796-3844
General/National Adv. E-mail: customerservice@ocregister.com
Display Adv. E-mail: ebrunelli@ocregister.com
Editorial e-mail: letters@ocregister.com
Primary Website: ocregister.com/sections/city-pages/placentia-yorbalinda
Avg Paid Circ: 3092
Audit By: AAM
Audit Date: 31.03.2016
Personnel: Aaron Kushner (Pub.); Ken Brusic (Ed.)
Parent company (for newspapers): Times Media Group

PLACER HERALD

Street address 1: 1030 High Street
Street address city: Auburn
Street address state: CA
Zip/Postal code: 95603
General Phone: 5308855656
Advertising Phone: 9167747939
General/National Adv. E-mail: johnl@goldcountrymedia.com
Display Adv. E-mail: classifieds@goldcountrymedia.com
Editorial e-mail: placerherald@goldcountrymedia.com
Primary Website: placerherald.com
Avg Paid Circ: 800
Avg Free Circ: 3800
Audit By: Sworn/Estimate/Non-Audited
Audit Date: 31.12.2016
Personnel: Krissi Khokhobashvili (Ed.); Linda Shuman-Prins (Business Develop.)
Parent company (for newspapers): Brehm Communications, Inc.; Gold Mountain California News Media, Inc.

PLEASANTON WEEKLY

Street address 1: 5506 Sunol Blvd
Street address 2: Ste 100
Street address city: Pleasanton
Street address state: CA
Zip/Postal code: 94566-7779
General Phone: (925) 600-0840
General Fax: (925) 600-9559
General/National Adv. E-mail: ads@pleasantonweekly.com
Display Adv. E-mail: ads@pleasantonweekly.com
Editorial e-mail: editor@pleasantonweekly.com
Primary Website: pleasantonweekly.com
Mthly Avg Views: 200000
Mthly Avg Unique Visitors: 60000
Year Established: 2000
Avg Free Circ: 14000
Audit By: Sworn/Estimate/Non-Audited
Audit Date: 10.06.2019
Personnel: Gina Channell (Pres.); Jeremy Walsh (Ed.); Carol Cano (Adv. Acct. Exec.); Karen Klein (Adv. Acct. Exec.)
Parent company (for newspapers): Embarcadero Media

POINT REYES LIGHT

Street address 1: 12781 Sir Francis Drake Blvd
Street address city: Inverness
Street address state: CA
Zip/Postal code: 94937-9736
General Phone: (415) 669-1200
General Fax: (415) 669-1216
Advertising Phone: (415) 669-1200
Advertising Fax: (415) 669-1216
Editorial Phone: (415) 669-1200
Editorial Fax: (415) 669-1216
General/National Adv. E-mail: editor@ptreyeslight.com
Display Adv. E-mail: renee@ptreyeslight.com
Editorial e-mail: editor@ptreyeslight.com
Primary Website: ptreyeslight.com
Year Established: 1948
Avg Paid Circ: 4256
Avg Free Circ: 26
Audit By: Sworn/Estimate/Non-Audited
Audit Date: 10.06.2019
Personnel: Donna Blum (Accounting); Renee Shannon (Adv. Mgr.); Tess Elliott (Ed.); Lys Plotkin (Pub.); Missy Patterson (Circ. Mgr.)

PORTOLA REPORTER

Street address 1: 96 E Sierra St
Street address city: Portola
Street address state: CA
Zip/Postal code: 96122-8436
General Phone: (530) 832-4646
General Fax: (530) 832-5319
General/National Adv. E-mail: ccurran@plumasnews.com
Display Adv. E-mail: mnewhouse@plumasnews.com
Editorial e-mail: dmoore@plumasnews.com
Primary Website: plumasnews.com
Year Established: 1927
Avg Paid Circ: 2270
Audit By: Sworn/Estimate/Non-Audited
Audit Date: 10.06.2019
Personnel: Michael Taborski (Pub); Debra Moore (Mng Ed)
Parent company (for newspapers): Feather Publishing Co., Inc.

POWAY NEWS CHIEFTAIN

Street address 1: 14023 Midland Rd
Street address city: Poway
Street address state: CA
Zip/Postal code: 92064-3959
General Phone: (858) 748-2311
General Fax: (858) 748-7695
General/National Adv. E-mail: ppfeiffer@lajollalight.com
Editorial e-mail: editor@pomeradonews.com
Primary Website: sandiegouniontribune.com/pomerado-news
Year Established: 2004
Avg Paid Circ: 14722
Audit By: AAM
Audit Date: 31.12.2017
Personnel: Steve Dreyer (Ed.); Douglas F. Manchester (Pub.); Phyllis Pfeiffer (VP, Adv.); Don Parks (Adv. Dir.)
Parent company (for newspapers): NantMedia Holdings, LLC

PRESS BANNER

Street address 1: 5215 Scotts Valley Dr
Street address 2: Ste F
Street address city: Scotts Valley
Street address state: CA
Zip/Postal code: 95066-3522
General Phone: (831) 438-2500
General Fax: (831) 438-4114
Advertising Phone: (831) 438-2500
Advertising Fax: (831) 438-4114
Editorial Phone: (831) 438-2500
Editorial Fax: (831) 438-4114
General/National Adv. E-mail: pbads@pressbanner.com
Display Adv. E-mail: pbads@pressbanner.com
Editorial e-mail: pbeditor@pressbanner.com
Primary Website: pressbanner.com
Year Established: 1960
Avg Paid Circ: 70
Avg Free Circ: 12780
Audit By: Sworn/Estimate/Non-Audited
Audit Date: 10.06.2019
Personnel: Barry Holtzclaw (Editor); Cherie Anderson (Advertising Director)
Parent company (for newspapers): TankTown Media

PRESS TRIBUNE

Street address 1: 188 Cirby Way
Street address city: Roseville
Street address state: CA

Zip/Postal code: 95678-6481
General Phone: (916) 786-8746
General Fax: (916) 783-1183
Advertising Phone: (916) 774-7910
Editorial Phone: (916) 774-7955
General/National Adv. E-mail: suzannes@goldcountrymedia.com
Display Adv. E-mail: classifieds@goldcountrymedia.com
Editorial e-mail: pteditor@goldcountrymedia.com
Primary Website: thepresstribune.com
Avg Paid Circ: 1418
Avg Free Circ: 11280
Audit By: CVC
Audit Date: 31.12.2016
Personnel: Krissi Khokhobashvili (Ed.)

QUARTZSITE TIMES

Street address 1: 400 W. Hobsonway
Street address city: Blythe
Street address state: CA
Zip/Postal code: 92225-2501
General Phone: (760) 922-3181
Advertising Phone: (760) 922-3181
Editorial Phone: (760) 922-3181
General/National Adv. E-mail: advertising@pvvt.com
Display Adv. E-mail: advertising@pvvt.com
Editorial e-mail: mbachman@pvvt.com
Primary Website: paloverdevalleytimes.com
Year Established: 1925
Avg Paid Circ: 78
Audit By: Sworn/Estimate/Non-Audited
Audit Date: 10.06.2019
Personnel: Debbie Hoel (Publisher); Jill Madsen (Adv. Rep.); Jaclyn Randall (Mng. Ed.)
Parent company (for newspapers): Western News&Info, Inc.

RANCHO BERNARDO NEWS-JOURNAL

Street address 1: 14023 Midland Rd
Street address city: Poway
Street address state: CA
Zip/Postal code: 92064-3959
General Phone: (858) 748-2311
General Fax: (858) 513-7203
Advertising Phone: (858) 218-7205
Editorial Phone: (858) 218-7207
General/National Adv. E-mail: donp@rsfreview.com
Display Adv. E-mail: mwilliams@mainstreetsd.com
Editorial e-mail: editor@pomeradonews.com
Primary Website: sandiegouniontribune.com/pomerado-news
Year Established: 2004
Avg Paid Circ: 16551
Audit By: AAM
Audit Date: 31.12.2017
Personnel: Steve Dreyer (Exec. Ed.); Phyllis Pfeiffer (VP, Adv.); Don Parks (Adv. Dir.); Douglas F. Manchester (Pub.)
Parent company (for newspapers): NantMedia Holdings, LLC

RANCHO SANTA FE NEWS

Street address 1: 315 S Coast Highway 101
Street address 2: Ste W
Street address city: Encinitas
Street address state: CA
Zip/Postal code: 92024-3555
General Phone: (760) 436-9737
General Fax: (760) 943-0850
General/National Adv. E-mail: advertising@coastnewsgroup.com
Display Adv. E-mail: classifieds@coastnewsgroup.com
Editorial e-mail: jgillette@coastnewsgroup.com
Primary Website: coastnewsgroup.com
Year Established: 2004
Avg Free Circ: 9935
Audit By: CVC
Audit Date: 30.06.2017
Personnel: Jim Kydd (Pub.); Anthony Cagala (Managing Ed.); Chris Kydd (Adv. Mgr./Assc. Pub.); Becky Roland (Circ. Mgr); Charles Steinman (Prod. Mgr); Phillys Mitchell (Prod.)
Parent company (for newspapers): Coast News Group, Inc.

RANCHO SANTA FE REVIEW

Street address 1: 380 Stevens Ave Ste 316
Street address 2: Suite 316
Street address city: Solana Beach
Street address state: CA
Zip/Postal code: 92075-2069
General Phone: (858) 876-7997
General Fax: (858) 756-9912
Advertising Phone: (858) 459-4201
Editorial Phone: (858) 756-1451
General/National Adv. E-mail: donp@rsfreview.com
Editorial e-mail: editor@rsfreview.com
Primary Website: www.ranchosantafereview.com
Mthly Avg Views: 24966
Mthly Avg Unique Visitors: 9411
Year Established: 1983
Avg Paid Circ: 6859
Audit By: AAM
Audit Date: 31.12.2017
Personnel: Phyllis Pfeiffer (VP/Gen. Mgr.); Lorine Wright (Exec. Ed.); Don Parks (VP, Adv.); Dara Elstein (Circ. Mgr.)
Parent company (for newspapers): NantMedia Holdings, LLC

RECORD GAZETTE

Street address 1: 218 N Murray St
Street address city: Banning
Street address state: CA
Zip/Postal code: 92220-5512
General Phone: (951) 849-4586
General Fax: (951) 849-2437
Advertising Phone: (951) 849-4586
Advertising Fax: (951) 849-2437
General/National Adv. E-mail: advertising@recordgazette.net
Display Adv. E-mail: advertising@recordgazette.net
Primary Website: recordgazette.net
Avg Paid Circ: 1537
Avg Free Circ: 18178
Audit By: VAC
Audit Date: 30.09.2016
Personnel: Art Reyes (Gen. Mgr.); Ron Smith (Ed.)
Parent company (for newspapers): Century Group Newspapers

RIVER VALLEY TIMES

Street address 1: 604 N Lincoln Way
Street address city: Galt
Street address state: CA
Zip/Postal code: 95632-8601
General Phone: (209) 745-1551
General Fax: (209) 745-4492
Advertising Phone: (209) 745-1551 x 112
General/National Adv. E-mail: advertising@herburger.net
Primary Website: herburger.net
Avg Paid Circ: 256
Avg Free Circ: 5600
Audit By: Sworn/Estimate/Non-Audited
Audit Date: 10.06.2019
Personnel: David Herburger (Pub.); Jim O'Donnell (Adv. Mgr.)
Parent company (for newspapers): Herburger Publications, Inc.

ROSE GARDEN RESIDENT

Street address 1: 4 North 2nd Street
Street address city: San Jose
Street address state: CA
Zip/Postal code: 95113
General Phone: (408) 200-1000
General Fax: (408) 200-1101
General/National Adv. E-mail: rgr@svcn.com
Primary Website: community-newspapers.com
Year Established: 2003
Avg Paid Circ: 4268
Audit By: AAM
Audit Date: 30.09.2018
Personnel: Mario Dianda (Ed. Local News); Sharon Ryan (Pres./Pub.)
Parent company (for newspapers): Media News Group; Digital First Media

ROSS VALLEY REPORTER

Street address 1: 1301B Grant Ave
Street address city: Novato
Street address state: CA
Zip/Postal code: 94945-3143
General Phone: (415) 892-1516
General Fax: (415) 897-0940
Advertising Phone: (415) 892-1516 x 15
Editorial Phone: (415) 892-1516 x 38
General/National Adv. E-mail: mmckellips@marinscope.com
Display Adv. E-mail: mmckellips@marinscope.com
Editorial e-mail: jwolfcale@marinscope.com
Primary Website: marinscope.com
Year Established: 1922
Avg Paid Circ: 54
Avg Free Circ: 5421
Audit By: Sworn/Estimate/Non-Audited
Audit Date: 10.06.2019
Personnel: Paul Hutcheson (Pub.); Joe Wolfcale (Ed.)

SACRAMENTO BUSINESS JOURNAL

Street address 1: 555 Capitol Mall
Street address 2: Ste 200
Street address city: Sacramento
Street address state: CA
Zip/Postal code: 95814-4557
General Phone: (916) 447-7661
General Fax: (916) 558-7898
General/National Adv. E-mail: sacramento@bizjournals.com
Primary Website: bizjournals.com/sacramento
Year Established: 1984
Audit By: Sworn/Estimate/Non-Audited
Audit Date: 10.06.2019
Personnel: David Lichtman (Pub.); Adam Steinhauer (Ed. in Chief)

SACRAMENTO GAZETTE

Street address 1: 428 J St.
Street address 2: Ste. 400
Street address city: Sacramento
Street address state: CA
Zip/Postal code: 95814-3361
General Phone: (916) 567-9654
General Fax: (888) 567-1193
Advertising Phone: (916) 567-9654
General/National Adv. E-mail: sacgazette@aol.com
Primary Website: Sacramento Gazette
Year Established: 1996
Avg Paid Circ: 1000
Audit By: Sworn/Estimate/Non-Audited
Audit Date: 10.06.2019
Personnel: David A. Fong (Ed.)

SADDLEBACK VALLEY NEWS

Street address 1: 627 N Grand Ave
Street address city: Santa Ana
Street address state: CA
Zip/Postal code: 92701-4347
General Phone: (714) 796-7955
General Fax: (949) 454-7355
Advertising Phone: (714) 796-2205
General/National Adv. E-mail: customerservice@ocregister.com
Display Adv. E-mail: ebrunelli@ocregister.com
Editorial e-mail: letters@ocregister.com
Primary Website: ocregister.com/sections/city-pages/lakeforest-lagunahills
Avg Paid Circ: 5276
Audit By: Sworn/Estimate/Non-Audited
Audit Date: 10.06.2019
Personnel: Alicia Robinson; Leo Smith (Ed.)
Parent company (for newspapers): Times Media Group

SADDLEBACK VALLEY NEWS - MISSION VIEJO

Street address 1: 625 N Grand Ave
Street address city: Santa Ana
Street address state: CA
Zip/Postal code: 92701-4347
General Phone: (877) 469-7344
General Fax: (949) 454-7354
Advertising Phone: (714) 796-2205
General/National Adv. E-mail: customerservice@ocregister.com
Display Adv. E-mail: ebrunelli@ocregister.com
Editorial e-mail: letters@ocregister.com
Primary Website: ocregister.com/sections/city-pages/missionviejo
Avg Paid Circ: 6291
Audit By: Sworn/Estimate/Non-Audited
Audit Date: 10.06.2019
Personnel: Aaron Kushner (Pub.); Ken Brusic (Ed.)
Parent company (for newspapers): Times Media Group

SALINAS VALLEY WEEKLY

Street address 1: 8 Upper Ragsdale Dr
Street address city: Monterey
Street address state: CA
Zip/Postal code: 93940-5730
General Phone: (831) 646-4301
General Fax: (831) 372-8401
Advertising Phone: (831) 646-4395
Editorial Phone: (831) 646-4381
General/National Adv. E-mail: rpowell@montereyherald.com
Editorial e-mail: rcalkins@montereyherald.com
Primary Website: montereyherald.com
Avg Free Circ: 35000
Audit By: Sworn/Estimate/Non-Audited
Audit Date: 10.06.2019
Personnel: Gary Omnerick (Pub.); Royal Calkins (Ed.); Lucia Fernandez (Prod. Coord.)
Parent company (for newspapers): The McClatchy Company

SAN CLEMENTE SUN POST

Street address 1: 625 N Grand Ave
Street address city: Santa Ana
Street address state: CA
Zip/Postal code: 92701-4347
General Phone: (877) 469-7344
General Fax: (949) 454-7354
Advertising Phone: (714) 796-2205
General/National Adv. E-mail: customerservice@ocregister.com
Display Adv. E-mail: ebrunelli@ocregister.com
Editorial e-mail: letters@ocregister.com
Primary Website: ocregister.com/sections/city-pages/sanclemente
Avg Paid Circ: 6133
Audit By: Sworn/Estimate/Non-Audited
Audit Date: 10.06.2019
Personnel: Aaron Kushner (Pub.); Ken Brusic (Ed.)
Parent company (for newspapers): Times Media Group

SAN CLEMENTE TIMES

Street address 1: 34932 Calle Del Sol
Street address 2: Ste B
Street address city: Capistrano Beach
Street address state: CA
Zip/Postal code: 92624-1664
General Phone: (949) 388-7700
General Fax: (949) 388-9977
General/National Adv. E-mail: slantz@picketfencemedia.com
Editorial e-mail: kpritchett@picketfencemedia.com
Primary Website: sanclementetimes.com
Audit By: Sworn/Estimate/Non-Audited
Audit Date: 10.06.2019
Personnel: Matt Cortina (Grp. Mng. Ed.); Norb Garrett (CEO/pUB.); Susie Lantz (Sales Associate); Rachel Mattice (M.E.)
Parent company (for newspapers): Picket Fence Media

SAN DIEGO UPTOWN NEWS

Street address 1: 123 Camino De La Reina
Street address 2: Ste 202
Street address city: San Diego
Street address state: CA
Zip/Postal code: 92108-3002
General Phone: (619) 519-7775
Advertising Phone: (619) 961-1951
General/National Adv. E-mail: david@sdcnn.com
Editorial e-mail: john@sdcnn.com
Primary Website: sdcnn.com
Year Established: 2009
Avg Free Circ: 23011

Audit By: CVC
Audit Date: 30.12.2016
Personnel: David Mannis (Pub./Circ. Mgr.); Mike Rosensteel (Adv. Mgr.)
Parent company (for newspapers): San Diego Community News Netwrok

SAN FRANCISCO EXAMINER

Street address 1: 835 Market St.
Street address 2: Suite 550
Street address city: San Francisco
Street address state: CA
Zip/Postal code: 94103
Avg Paid Circ: 0
Avg Free Circ: 108753
Sun. Circulation Paid: 0
Sun. Circulation Free: 254219
Audit By: CVC
Audit Date: 31.12.2016
Parent company (for newspapers): Black Press Group Ltd.; Clint Reilly Communications

SAN JOSE BUSINESS JOURNAL

Street address 1: 125 S Market St
Street address 2: Fl 11th
Street address city: San Jose
Street address state: CA
Zip/Postal code: 95113-2292
General Phone: (408) 295-5028
Advertising Phone: (408) 299-1814
Editorial Phone: (408) 299-1828
General/National Adv. E-mail: wkupiec@bizjournals.com
Display Adv. E-mail: wkupiec@bizjournals.com
Editorial e-mail: gbaumann@bizjournals.com
Primary Website: bizjournals.com/sanjose
Year Established: 1983
Audit By: Sworn/Estimate/Non-Audited
Audit Date: 10.06.2019
Personnel: James MacGregor (Pub.); Scott Ard (Ed.)

SAN RAFAEL NEWS POINTER

Street address 1: 1301B Grant Ave
Street address city: Novato
Street address state: CA
Zip/Postal code: 94945-3143
General Phone: (415) 892-1516
General Fax: (415) 897-0940
Advertising Phone: (415) 892-1516 x 15
Editorial Phone: (415) 892-1516 x 19
General/National Adv. E-mail: mmckellips@marinscope.com
Display Adv. E-mail: mmckellips@marinscope.com
Editorial e-mail: gandersen@marinscope.com
Primary Website: marinscope.com
Year Established: 1922
Avg Paid Circ: 65
Avg Free Circ: 4661
Audit By: Sworn/Estimate/Non-Audited
Audit Date: 10.06.2019
Personnel: Paul Hutcheson (Pub.); Greg Andersen (Ed.)
Parent company (for newspapers): Marinscope Community Newspapers

SANGER HERALD

Street address 1: 740 N St
Street address city: Sanger
Street address state: CA
Zip/Postal code: 93657-3114
General Phone: (559) 875-2511
General Fax: (559) 875-2521
General/National Adv. E-mail: mvpsanger@yahoo.com
Display Adv. E-mail: mvpsanger@yahoo.com
Editorial e-mail: sangerherald@yahoo.com
Primary Website: thesangerherald.com
Avg Paid Circ: 3100
Avg Free Circ: 14300
Audit By: Sworn/Estimate/Non-Audited
Audit Date: 10.06.2019
Personnel: Fred Hall (Pub.); Dick Sheppard (Editor)
Parent company (for newspapers): Mid Valley Publishing

SANTA CLARITA VALLEY SIGNAL

Street address 1: 24000 Creekside Rd
Street address city: Santa Clarita
Street address state: CA
Zip/Postal code: 91355-1726
General Phone: (661) 259-1234
General Fax: (661) 254-8068
Advertising Fax: (661) 259-2081
Editorial Fax: (661) 255-9689
General/National Adv. E-mail: ypreviture@signalscv.com
Display Adv. E-mail: yprevitire@signalscv.com
Editorial e-mail: psmith@signalscv.com
Primary Website: signalscv.com
Year Established: 1919
Avg Paid Circ: 8824
Avg Free Circ: 159
Sat. Circulation Paid: 8770
Sat. Circulation Free: 168
Sun. Circulation Paid: 12421
Sun. Circulation Free: 2079
Audit By: Sworn/Estimate/Non-Audited
Audit Date: 10.06.2019
Personnel: Richard Budman (Owner/ Pub.); Chris Budman (VP, Operations); Tim Whyte (Ed. in Cheif); Perry Smith (Mng. Ed.); Brad Lanfranco (Adv. Dir.); Maureen Daniels (Multi-media Acct. Mgr.)

SANTA MONICA MIRROR

Street address 1: 2116 Wilshire Blvd
Street address 2: Ste 260
Street address city: Santa Monica
Street address state: CA
Zip/Postal code: 90403-5750
General Phone: (310) 310-2637
General Fax: (424) 744-8821
General/National Adv. E-mail: advertising@smmirror.com
Display Adv. E-mail: advertising@smmirror.com
Editorial e-mail: editor@smmirror.com
Primary Website: westsidetoday.com
Year Established: 1990
Avg Paid Circ: 0
Avg Free Circ: 100000
Audit By: Sworn/Estimate/Non-Audited
Audit Date: 10.06.2019
Personnel: TJ Montemer (President/Publisher); Judy Swartz (Sales Mgr.)
Parent company (for newspapers): Mirror Media Group

SANTA YNEZ VALLEY NEWS/EXTRA

Street address 1: 423 2nd St
Street address city: Solvang
Street address state: CA
Zip/Postal code: 93463-3711
General Phone: (805) 688-5522
General Fax: (805) 688-7685
Advertising Phone: (805) 688-5522 x 6003
Editorial Phone: (805) 739-2143
General/National Adv. E-mail: cdelgado@syvnews.com
Display Adv. E-mail: sedwards@syvnews.com
Editorial e-mail: mcooley@syvnews.com
Primary Website: syvnews.com
Year Established: 1925
Avg Free Circ: 13500
Audit By: Sworn/Estimate/Non-Audited
Audit Date: 10.06.2019
Personnel: Cynthia Schur (Pub.); Marga Cooley (Mng. Ed.)

SARATOGA NEWS

Street address 1: 4 North 2nd Street
Street address 2: Suite 800
Street address city: San Jose
Street address state: CA
Zip/Postal code: 95113
General Phone: (408) 920-5000
General Fax: (408) 288-8060
General/National Adv. E-mail: sn@svcn.com
Primary Website: mercurynews.com/saratoga
Avg Paid Circ: 10227
Audit By: AAM
Audit Date: 30.09.2018
Personnel: Sharon Ryan (Pres./Pub.); Lisa Buckingham (Sr. VP/CFO); Bert Robinson (Mng. Ed.); Randall Keith (Mng. Ed. Dig.)
Parent company (for newspapers): Media News Group; Digital First Media

SAUSALITO MARINSCOPE

Street address 1: 1301B Grant Ave
Street address city: Novato
Street address state: CA
Zip/Postal code: 94945-3143
General Phone: (415) 892-1516
General Fax: (415) 897-0940
Advertising Phone: (415) 892-1516 x 15
Editorial Phone: (415) 892-1516 x 31
General/National Adv. E-mail: phutcheson@marinscope.com
Display Adv. E-mail: phutcheson@marinscope.com
Editorial e-mail: shemmila@marinscope.com
Primary Website: marinscope.com
Year Established: 1922
Avg Paid Circ: 867
Avg Free Circ: 311
Audit By: Sworn/Estimate/Non-Audited
Audit Date: 10.06.2019
Personnel: Paul Hutcheson (Pub./Adv. Mgr.); Soren Hemmila (Ed.); Linda Mallin (Circ. Mgr.)
Parent company (for newspapers): Marinscope Community Newspapers

SHAFTER PRESS

Street address 1: 1508 Corte Perito
Street address city: Bakersfield
Street address state: CA
Zip/Postal code: 93309-7155
General Phone: (661) 746-4942
General Fax: (661) 746-5571
Advertising Phone: (661) 303-7465
Editorial Phone: (661) 746-4942
General/National Adv. E-mail: shafterpress@earthlink.net
Editorial e-mail: shafterpress@earthlink.net
Primary Website: shafterpress.net
Year Established: 1927
Avg Paid Circ: 2300
Avg Free Circ: 4000
Audit By: Sworn/Estimate/Non-Audited
Audit Date: 10.06.2019
Personnel: Donald L. Reed (Pub.); Frank W. Reed (Pub.); Diane Givens (Circ. Mgr.); Jamie Stewart (Ed.)

SIERRA STAR

Street address 1: PO BOX 305
Street address city: Oakhurst
Street address state: CA
Zip/Postal code: 93644-0305
General Phone: (559) 683-4464
General Fax: (559) 683-8102
General/National Adv. E-mail: editorial@sierrastar.com
Display Adv. E-mail: editorial@sierrastar.com
Editorial e-mail: editorial@sierrastar.com
Primary Website: sierrastar.com
Year Established: 1957
Avg Paid Circ: 1504
Avg Free Circ: 19
Audit By: AAM
Audit Date: 31.03.2019
Personnel: Cherie Arambel (Pub.); Brian Wilkinson (Ed.)
Parent company (for newspapers): The McClatchy Company

SIERRA SUN

Street address 1: 10775 Pioneer Trl
Street address 2: Ste 101
Street address city: Truckee
Street address state: CA
Zip/Postal code: 96161-0233
General Phone: (530) 587-6061
General Fax: (530) 587-3763
General/National Adv. E-mail: drogers@theunion.com
Display Adv. E-mail: drogers@theunion.com
Editorial e-mail: editor@sierrasun.com
Primary Website: sierrasun.com
Year Established: 1869
Avg Paid Circ: 0
Avg Free Circ: 5852
Audit By: Sworn/Estimate/Non-Audited
Audit Date: 10.06.2019
Personnel: Don Rodgers (Pub.); Brian Hamilton; Ross Maak (City Ed.); Susan Kokenge (Adv.)
Parent company (for newspapers): Swift Communications, Inc.; Ogden Newspapers Inc.

SIMI VALLEY ACORN

Street address 1: 30423 Canwood St
Street address 2: Ste 108
Street address city: Agoura Hills
Street address state: CA
Zip/Postal code: 91301-4313
General Phone: (805) 367-8232
General Fax: (805) 367-8237
Advertising Phone: (818) 706-0266
Editorial Fax: (805) 367-8237
General/National Adv. E-mail: AdRep@theacorn.com
Display Adv. E-mail: classads@theacorn.com
Editorial e-mail: newstip@theacorn.com
Primary Website: theacorn.com
Avg Free Circ: 34041
Audit By: VAC
Audit Date: 30.09.2017
Personnel: Darleen Principe (Ed.)
Parent company (for newspapers): J. Bee NP Publishing, Ltd.

SOLANA BEACH SUN

Street address 1: 380 Stevens Ave
Street address 2: Suite 316
Street address city: Solana Beach
Street address state: CA
Zip/Postal code: 92075-2069
General Phone: (858) 756-1403
General Fax: (858) 756-9912
Advertising Phone: (858) 459-4201
Editorial Phone: (858) 756-1451
General/National Adv. E-mail: donp@rsfreview.com
Editorial e-mail: editor@delmartimes.net
Primary Website: delmartimes.net/solana-beach-sun
Year Established: 2004
Avg Paid Circ: 4312
Audit By: AAM
Audit Date: 31.12.2017
Personnel: Phyllis Pfeiffer (Pub.); Lorine Wright (Exec. Ed.); Don Parks (VP, Adv.); Dara Elstein (Circ. Mgr.)
Parent company (for newspapers): NantMedia Holdings, LLC

SOLEDAD BEE

Street address 1: 522 Broadway St
Street address 2: Ste B
Street address city: King City
Street address state: CA
Zip/Postal code: 93930-3243
General Phone: (831) 385-4880
General Fax: (831) 385-4799
General/National Adv. E-mail: sheryl@southcountynewspapers.com
Display Adv. E-mail: sheryl@southcountynewspapers.com
Editorial e-mail: editor@southcountynewspapers.com
Primary Website: soledadbee.com
Avg Paid Circ: 1500
Audit By: Sworn/Estimate/Non-Audited
Audit Date: 10.06.2019
Personnel: Aaron Crutchfield (Ed.)
Parent company (for newspapers): San Luis Valley Publishing

SONOMA WEST TIMES AND NEWS

Street address 1: 230 Center St
Street address city: Healdsburg
Street address state: CA
Zip/Postal code: 95448-4402
General Phone: (707) 823-7845
Primary Website: sonomawest.com
Avg Paid Circ: 3800
Audit By: Sworn/Estimate/Non-Audited
Audit Date: 10.06.2019
Personnel: Sarah Bradbury (Assoc. Pub); Greg Clementi (Sports Ed); Laura Hager-Rush; Bleys Rose; Elizabeth Hillin (Reporter); Eay Holley (Mgr. Editor)
Parent company (for newspapers): Sonoma West Publishers

SOUTH COUNTY NEWS

Street address 1: 415 Talmage Rd Suite A
Street address city: Ukiah
Street address state: CA
Zip/Postal code: 95482
General Phone: (707) 263-5636
Display Adv. E-mail: advertising@record-bee.com
Primary Website: record-bee.com
Avg Free Circ: 5700
Audit By: Sworn/Estimate/Non-Audited
Audit Date: 10.06.2019

Parent company (for newspapers): Digital First Media

SOUTH PASADENA REVIEW

Street address 1: 1020 Mission St
Street address 2: Unit C
Street address city: South Pasadena
Street address state: CA
Zip/Postal code: 91030-3172
General Phone: (626) 799-1161
General Fax: (626) 799-2404
General/National Adv. E-mail: advertising@southpasadenareview.com
Display Adv. E-mail: advertising@southpasadenareview.com
Editorial e-mail: bglazier@southpasadenareview.com
Primary Website: south.pasadenanow.com
Year Established: 1888
Avg Paid Circ: 4000
Audit By: Sworn/Estimate/Non-Audited
Audit Date: 10.06.2019
Personnel: William Ericson (Pub.); Nancy Lem (Adv. Mgr.); Bill Glazier (Ed.)

ST HELENA STAR

Street address 1: 1200 Main St
Street address 2: Ste C
Street address city: Saint Helena
Street address state: CA
Zip/Postal code: 94574-1901
General Phone: (707) 963-2731
General Fax: (707) 963-8957
Advertising Phone: (707) 256-2228
Editorial Phone: (707) 967-6800
General/National Adv. E-mail: nkostecka@napanews.com
Display Adv. E-mail: nkostecka@napanews.com
Editorial e-mail: editor@sthelenastar.com
Primary Website: StHelenaStar.com
Year Established: 1874
Avg Paid Circ: 2400
Audit By: Sworn/Estimate/Non-Audited
Audit Date: 10.06.2019
Personnel: David Stoneberg (Editor); Jesse Duarte (Staff writer)
Parent company (for newspapers): Napa Valley Publishing

SUN-POST NEWS

Street address 1: 625 N Grand Ave
Street address city: Santa Ana
Street address state: CA
Zip/Postal code: 92701-4347
General Phone: (949) 492-4316
General Fax: (714) 796-7000
Advertising Phone: (714) 796-3844
Editorial Phone: (949) 492-4316
General/National Adv. E-mail: sunpostnews@ocregister.com
Editorial e-mail: nteubner@ocregister.com
Primary Website: ocregister.com/sanclemente
Avg Paid Circ: 9296
Audit By: Sworn/Estimate/Non-Audited
Audit Date: 10.06.2019
Personnel: Nellene Teubner (Ed.)
Parent company (for newspapers): Times Media Group

TAHOE DAILY TRIBUNE

Street address 1: 3079 Harrison Ave
Street address city: South Lake Tahoe
Street address state: CA
Zip/Postal code: 96150-7976
General Phone: (530) 541-3880
Display Adv. E-mail: classifieds@sierranevadamedia.com
Editorial e-mail: editor@tahoedailytribune.com
Primary Website: tahoedailytribune.com
Year Established: 1952
Avg Paid Circ: 7078
Sat. Circulation Paid: 469
Sat. Circulation Free: 7943
Audit By: Sworn/Estimate/Non-Audited
Audit Date: 10.06.2019
Personnel: Rob Galloway (Pub.); Carolan LaCroix (Sr. Bus. Dvp. Mgr.); Annemarie Prudente (Adv. Acct. Exec.); Justine Dhollande (Acct. Mgr.); Ryan Hoffman (Ed.); Bill Rozak (Sports Ed.)
Parent company (for newspapers): Swift Communications, Inc.; Ogden Newspapers Inc.; Ogden Newspapers

THE ACORN

Street address 1: 30423 Canwood St
Street address 2: Ste 108
Street address city: Agoura Hills
Street address state: CA
Zip/Postal code: 91301-4313
General Phone: (818) 706-0266
General Fax: (818) 706-8468
Editorial Fax: (818) 671-1873
General/National Adv. E-mail: info@theacorn.com
Primary Website: theacorn.com
Avg Free Circ: 26650
Audit By: VAC
Audit Date: 30.09.2017
Personnel: Lisa Rule (Gen. Mgr.); John Loesing (Ed.)
Parent company (for newspapers): J. Bee NP Publishing, Ltd.

THE ALMANAC

Street address 1: 3525 Alameda De Las Pulgas
Street address city: Menlo Park
Street address state: CA
Zip/Postal code: 94025-6544
General Phone: (650) 854-2626
General Fax: (650) 854-0677
Advertising Phone: (650) 223-6570
Editorial Phone: (650) 223-6507
General/National Adv. E-mail: ads@almanacnews.com
Editorial e-mail: editor@almanacnews.com
Primary Website: almanacnews.com
Year Established: 1965
Avg Free Circ: 17000
Audit By: Sworn/Estimate/Non-Audited
Audit Date: 10.06.2019
Personnel: Neal Fine (Real Estate Sales Manager); Richard Hine (Editor); Connie Jo Cotton (Major Accounts Sales Mgr.)
Parent company (for newspapers): Embarcadero Media

THE ARGONAUT

Street address 1: 5355 McConnell Ave
Street address city: Los Angeles
Street address state: CA
Zip/Postal code: 90066-7025
General Phone: (310) 822-1629
General Fax: (310) 822-2089
General/National Adv. E-mail: Renee@Argonautnews.com
Display Adv. E-mail: Chantal@Argonautnews.com
Editorial e-mail: Vince@ArgonautNews.com
Primary Website: argonautnews.com
Mthly Avg Views: 32904
Mthly Avg Unique Visitors: 10764
Year Established: 1971
Avg Paid Circ: 13
Avg Free Circ: 29962
Audit By: Sworn/Estimate/Non-Audited
Audit Date: 10.06.2019
Personnel: David Comden (Pub.); David Maury; Tom Ponton (Circ. Mgr.)
Parent company (for newspapers): Times Media Group

THE ARK

Street address 1: 1550 Tiburon Blvd
Street address 2: Ste D
Street address city: Tiburon
Street address state: CA
Zip/Postal code: 94920-2537
General Phone: (415) 435-2652
General Fax: (415) 435-0849
Advertising Phone: (415) 435-1190
Advertising Fax: (415) 435-0849
Editorial Phone: (415) 435-2652
Editorial Fax: (415) 435-0849
General/National Adv. E-mail: ads@thearknewspaper.com
Display Adv. E-mail: ark.manager@thearknewspaper.com
Editorial e-mail: editor@thearknewspaper.com
Primary Website: thearknewspaper.com
Year Established: 1973
Avg Paid Circ: 2750
Avg Free Circ: 50
Audit By: Sworn/Estimate/Non-Audited
Audit Date: 10.06.2019
Personnel: Alison Gray (Owner-publisher); Kevin Hessel (Executive editor); Arthur Kern (Owner/pub.); Henriette Corn (Dir. of Bus & Adv.); Emily Lavin (Assist ed & Strawberry reporter); Matthew Hose (Belvedere & public safety reporter); Jeff Dempsey (Prod ed & youth reporter); Deirdre McCrohan (Tiburon reporter); Leigh Pagan (Accounts mgr); Diana Goodman (Copy ed. & calendar ed.)
Parent company (for newspapers): AMMI Publishing Co Inc

THE BERKELEY VOICE

Street address 1: 1050 Marina Way S
Street address city: Richmond
Street address state: CA
Zip/Postal code: 94804-3741
General Phone: (510) 262-2784
General Fax: (510) 748-1680
Primary Website: insidebayarea.com/berkeley
Avg Paid Circ: 6668
Audit By: AAM
Audit Date: 30.09.2018
Personnel: Mike Frankel (Asst. Mng. Ed. â€" Reg.); Ken McLaughlin (Reg. News Ed.); Chris Walker (Reg. News Ed.)
Parent company (for newspapers): Digital First Media

THE BUSINESS JOURNAL

Street address 1: 1315 Van Ness Ave
Street address 2: Ste 200
Street address city: Fresno
Street address state: CA
Zip/Postal code: 93721-1729
General Phone: (559) 490-3400
General Fax: (559) 490-3526
Advertising Phone: (559) 490-3422
Advertising Fax: (559) 490-3526
Editorial Phone: (559) 490-3467
Editorial Fax: (559) 490-3526
General/National Adv. E-mail: ashley@thebusinessjournal.com
Display Adv. E-mail: abner@thebusinessjournal.com
Editorial e-mail: gabriel@thebusinessjournal.com
Primary Website: thebusinessjournal.com
Year Established: 1886
Avg Paid Circ: 4500
Avg Free Circ: 3000
Audit By: CVC
Audit Date: 30.09.2022
Personnel: Gordon Webster (Pub.); Gabriel Dillard (Mng. Ed.); Kaysi Coelho (Adv. Mgr.); Ashley Webster (Associate Publisher)
Parent company (for newspapers): Pacific Publishing Group, Inc.

THE CAPISTRANO DISPATCH

Street address 1: 34932 Calle Del Sol
Street address 2: Ste B
Street address city: Capistrano Beach
Street address state: CA
Zip/Postal code: 92624-1664
General Phone: (949) 388-7700
General Fax: (949) 388-9977
General/National Adv. E-mail: kpritchett@picketfencemedia.com
Display Adv. E-mail: dwells@picketfencemedia.com
Primary Website: thecapistranodispatch.com
Audit By: Sworn/Estimate/Non-Audited
Audit Date: 10.06.2019
Personnel: Norb Garrett (Pub./CEO); Matt Cortina; Lauralyn Loynes; Tricia Zines; Alyssa Garrett; Shawn Raymundo (City Ed.)
Parent company (for newspapers): Picket Fence Media

THE CATALINA ISLANDER

Street address 1: 635 Crescent Ave
Street address 2: Ste A
Street address city: Avalon
Street address state: CA
Zip/Postal code: 90704
General Phone: (310) 510-0500
General Fax: (310) 510-2882
Advertising Phone: (310) 510-0500 x 250
Editorial Phone: (310) 510-0500
General/National Adv. E-mail: advertising@thecatalinaislander.com
Display Adv. E-mail: advertising@thecatalinaislander.com
Editorial e-mail: editor@thecatalinaislander.com
Primary Website: thecatalinaislander.com
Year Established: 1914
Avg Paid Circ: 3015
Avg Free Circ: 2000
Audit By: Sworn/Estimate/Non-Audited
Audit Date: 10.06.2019
Personnel: Vince Bodiford (Exec. Pub.); Dixie Redfearn (Editor); Jon Remy (General Manager)
Parent company (for newspapers): CommunityMedia Co.

THE CERES COURIER

Street address 1: 138 S Center St
Street address city: Turlock
Street address state: CA
Zip/Postal code: 95380-4508
General Phone: (209) 537-5032
General Fax: (209) 632-8813
Advertising Phone: (209) 537-5032
Advertising Fax: (209) 847-9750
Editorial Phone: (209) 537-5032
Editorial Fax: (209) 632-8813
General/National Adv. E-mail: tphillips@turlockjournal.com
Display Adv. E-mail: tphillips@turlockjournal.com
Editorial e-mail: jbenziger@cerescourier.com
Primary Website: cerescourier.com
Year Established: 1910
Avg Paid Circ: 4062
Avg Free Circ: 19500
Audit By: Sworn/Estimate/Non-Audited
Audit Date: 10.06.2019
Personnel: Jeff Benziger (Ed.); Hank Veen (Pub.); Kelli Wilson (Circ. Mgr.)
Parent company (for newspapers): Morris Multimedia, Inc.

THE CHOWCHILLA NEWS

Street address 1: 3033 G St
Street address city: Merced
Street address state: CA
Zip/Postal code: 95340-2108
General Phone: (559) 665-5751
General Fax: (559) 665-5462
Advertising Phone: (209) 385-2463
Editorial Phone: (559) 665-5751 x 101
General/National Adv. E-mail: lswanson@mercedsun-star.com
Display Adv. E-mail: lswanson@mercedsun-star.com
Editorial e-mail: pmandrell@mercedsun-star.com
Primary Website: thechowchillanews.com
Avg Paid Circ: 760
Avg Free Circ: 4
Audit By: AAM
Audit Date: 30.09.2017
Personnel: Patty Mandrell (Mng. Ed.); Deanna Whitmore (Adv. Dir.)
Parent company (for newspapers): The McClatchy Company

THE COAST NEWS

Street address 1: 315 S Coast Highway 101
Street address 2: Ste W
Street address city: Encinitas
Street address state: CA
Zip/Postal code: 92024-3555
General Phone: (760) 436-9737
General Fax: (760) 943-0850
General/National Adv. E-mail: advertising@coastnewsgroup.com
Display Adv. E-mail: advertising@coastnewsgroup.com
Editorial e-mail: jkydd@coastnewsgroup.com
Primary Website: coastnewsgroup.com
Year Established: 1987
Avg Paid Circ: 206
Avg Free Circ: 23356
Audit By: CVC
Audit Date: 30.06.2017
Personnel: James Kydd (Pub./Own.); Chris Kydd (Adv. Mgr./Assoc. Pub.); Becky Roland (Circ. Mgr); Phillys Mitchell (Prod.); Tony Cagala (Mng. Ed.)

Parent company (for newspapers): Coast News Group, Inc.

THE COMMUNITY VOICE

Street address 1: 100 Professional Center Dr
Street address 2: Ste 110
Street address city: Rohnert Park
Street address state: CA
Zip/Postal code: 94928-2137
General Phone: (707) 584-2222
General Fax: (707) 584-2233
Advertising Phone: (707) 584-2222 x10
Advertising Fax: (707) 584-2233
Editorial Phone: (707) 584-2222
Editorial Fax: (707) 584-2233
General/National Adv. E-mail: publisher@thecommunityvoice.com
Display Adv. E-mail: ads@thecommunityvoice.com
Classified Adv. e-mail: ads@thecommunityvoice.com
Editorial e-mail: news@thecommunityvoice.com
Primary Website: thecommunityvoice.com
Year Established: 1993
Avg Paid Circ: 2400
Avg Free Circ: 5600
Audit By: Sworn/Estimate/Non-Audited
Audit Date: 10.06.2019
Personnel: Yatin Shah (Pub.)

THE CORCORAN JOURNAL

Street address 1: 1012 Hale Ave
Street address city: Corcoran
Street address state: CA
Zip/Postal code: 93212-2309
General Phone: (559) 992-3115
General Fax: (559) 992-5543
General/National Adv. E-mail: tbotill@hotmail.com
Primary Website: thecorcoranjournal.net
Year Established: 1908
Avg Paid Circ: 2450
Audit By: Sworn/Estimate/Non-Audited
Audit Date: 10.06.2019
Personnel: Rob Atilano (Adv. Mgr.); Jeanette Todd (Ed.)

THE CUPERTINO COURIER

Street address 1: 1095 the Alameda
Street address city: San Jose
Street address state: CA
Zip/Postal code: 95126-3142
General Phone: (408) 200-1000
General Fax: (408) 200-1011
General/National Adv. E-mail: jkohler@bayareanewsgroup.com
Primary Website: mercurynews.com/cupertino
Year Established: 1947
Avg Paid Circ: 12312
Audit By: AAM
Audit Date: 30.09.2018
Personnel: Sharon Ryan (Pres./Pub.); David Butler (Ed./VP); Jeannette Close (Adv. Mgr.)
Parent company (for newspapers): Digital First Media

THE DAVIS ENTERPRISE

Street address 1: 315 G ST
Street address city: DAVIS
Street address state: CA
Zip/Postal code: 95616-4119
General Phone: (530) 756-0800
General Fax: (530) 756-7504
Advertising Phone: (530) 756-0800
Advertising Fax: (530) 756-7504
Editorial Phone: (530) 756-0800
Editorial Fax: (530) 756-1668
General/National Adv. E-mail: nhannell@davisenterprise.net
Display Adv. E-mail: classads@davisenterprise.net
Editorial e-mail: newsroom@davisenterprise.net
Primary Website: davisenterprise.com
Year Established: 1897
Avg Paid Circ: 5007
Avg Free Circ: 674
Sun. Circulation Paid: 5564
Sun. Circulation Free: 1186
Audit By: AAM
Audit Date: 31.03.2019
Personnel: Burt McNaughton (Pub./Vice Pres./Sec.); Nancy Hannell (Adv. Dir.); Jeff Hudson (Educ./Schools Ed.); Sebastion Onate (Editor)
Parent company (for newspapers): McNaughton Newspapers; McNaughton Newspapers

THE DEL NORTE TRIPLICATE

Street address 1: 312 H St
Street address city: Crescent City
Street address state: CA
Zip/Postal code: 95531-4018
General Phone: (707) 464-2141
General Fax: (707) 464-5102
General/National Adv. E-mail: tripads@triplicate.com
Editorial e-mail: mdurkee@triplicate.com
Primary Website: triplicate.com
Mthly Avg Views: 233973
Mthly Avg Unique Visitors: 24540
Year Established: 1879
Avg Paid Circ: 3905
Avg Free Circ: 114
Sat. Circulation Paid: 5850
Audit By: CVC
Audit Date: 30.09.2016
Personnel: Kyle Curtis (Operations Manager); Cindy Vosburg (Regional Pub.); Matt Durkee (Ed.); David Jeffcoat (Circ. Dir.); David DeLonge (Production Mgr.); Elizabeth Carter (Circ District Mgr); Kyle Curtis (Ops. Mgr.); Michael Zogg (Sports Ed); Emily Reed (Adv Acct Mgr)
Parent company (for newspapers): Country Media, Inc.

THE DINUBA SENTINEL

Street address 1: 145 S L St
Street address city: Dinuba
Street address state: CA
Zip/Postal code: 93618-2324
General Phone: (559) 591-4632
General Fax: (559) 591-1322
General/National Adv. E-mail: vanessa@midvalleypublishing.com
Display Adv. E-mail: classifieddinubasentinel@yahoo.com
Editorial e-mail: editor@thedinubasentinel.com
Primary Website: thedinubasentinel.com
Year Established: 1909
Avg Paid Circ: 3000
Audit By: Sworn/Estimate/Non-Audited
Audit Date: 10.06.2019
Personnel: Linda Renn (Ed.); Keven Geaney (Sports Writer); Jackson Moore (Reporter)
Parent company (for newspapers): Mid Valley Publishing

THE EAST COUNTY CALIFORNIAN

Street address 1: 119 N Magnolia Ave
Street address city: El Cajon
Street address state: CA
Zip/Postal code: 92020-3903
General Phone: (619) 441-0400
General Fax: (619) 441-0020
General/National Adv. E-mail: info@eccalifornian.com
Editorial e-mail: editor@eccalifornian.com
Primary Website: eccalifornian.com
Year Established: 1887
Avg Paid Circ: 1450
Avg Free Circ: 32500
Audit By: Sworn/Estimate/Non-Audited
Audit Date: 10.06.2019
Personnel: Albert Fulcher (Ed.)

THE FERNDALE ENTERPRISE

Street address 1: 207 Francis St
Street address city: Ferndale
Street address state: CA
Zip/Postal code: 95536
General Phone: (707) 786-3068
General Fax: (707) 786-4311
Advertising Phone: (707) 786-3068
Advertising Fax: (707) 786-4311
General/National Adv. E-mail: editor@ferndaleenterprise.us
Editorial e-mail: editor@ferndaleenterprise.us
Primary Website: ferndaleenterprise.us
Year Established: 1878
Avg Paid Circ: 1500
Audit By: Sworn/Estimate/Non-Audited
Audit Date: 10.06.2019
Personnel: Caroline Titus (Ed./Pub.); Donna Mays (Circ. Dir.)
Parent company (for newspapers): Cages Publishing, Inc.

THE FOOTHILLS SUN-GAZETTE

Street address 1: PO Box 7
Street address city: Exeter
Street address state: CA
Zip/Postal code: 93221-0007
General Phone: (559) 592-3171
General Fax: (559) 592-4308
General/National Adv. E-mail: ads@thesungazette.com
Display Adv. E-mail: ads@thesungazette.com
Primary Website: fsgnews.com
Year Established: 1901
Avg Paid Circ: 3000
Avg Free Circ: 20000
Audit By: Sworn/Estimate/Non-Audited
Audit Date: 10.06.2019
Personnel: Reggie Ellis (Pub.)
Parent company (for newspapers): Mineral King Publishing, Inc.

THE FRIDAY FLYER

Street address 1: 31558 Railroad Canyon Rd
Street address city: Canyon Lake
Street address state: CA
Zip/Postal code: 92587-9427
General Phone: (951)244-1966
General Fax: (951) 244-2748
Advertising Phone: (951) 244-1966
Advertising Fax: (951) 244-2748
Editorial Phone: (951) 244-1966
Editorial Fax: (951) 244-2748
General/National Adv. E-mail: greg@goldingpublications.com
Display Adv. E-mail: greg@goldingpublications.com
Classified Adv. e-mail: gina@goldingpublications.com
Editorial e-mail: news@goldingpublications.com
Primary Website: fridayflyer.com
Mthly Avg Views: 45417
Mthly Avg Unique Visitors: 8888
Year Established: 1990
Avg Paid Circ: 4041
Avg Free Circ: 1116
Audit By: Sworn/Estimate/Non-Audited
Audit Date: 10.06.2019
Personnel: Chuck Golding (Pub.); Greg Golding (Adv. Mgr.); Gina Wells (Classified Mgr.); Donna Ritchie (Editor)
Parent company (for newspapers): Golding Publications

THE GALT HERALD

Street address 1: 604 N Lincoln Way
Street address city: Galt
Street address state: CA
Zip/Postal code: 95632-8601
General Phone: (209) 745-1551
General Fax: (209) 745-4492
General/National Adv. E-mail: advertising@herburger.net
Display Adv. E-mail: classified@herburger.net
Editorial e-mail: editor_galtherald@herburger.net
Primary Website: galtheraldonline.com
Avg Paid Circ: 2453
Audit By: Sworn/Estimate/Non-Audited
Audit Date: 10.06.2019
Personnel: David Herburger (Pub.); Jim O'Donnell (Adv. Mgr.); Bonnie Rodriguez (Mng. Ed.)
Parent company (for newspapers): Herburger Publications, Inc.

THE GILROY DISPATCH

Street address 1: 64 W 6th St
Street address city: Gilroy
Street address state: CA
Zip/Postal code: 95020-6102
General Phone: (408) 842-6400
General Fax: (408) 842-2206
Advertising Fax: (408) 842-7105
Editorial Phone: (408) 847-7010
General/National Adv. E-mail: sstaloch@mainstreetmg.com
Display Adv. E-mail: cgault@svnewspapers.com
Editorial e-mail: mderry@gilroydispatch.com
Primary Website: gilroydispatch.com
Year Established: 1868
Avg Paid Circ: 4800
Avg Free Circ: 15600
Audit By: Sworn/Estimate/Non-Audited
Audit Date: 10.06.2019
Personnel: Chuck Gibbs (Prodn./IT Mgr.); Steve Staloch (Pub.); Deborah Garcia (Adv. Dir.); Jack Foley (Editor); Erin Redmond (Sports Ed)
Parent company (for newspapers): Mainstreet Media Group, LLC

THE GRIDLEY HERALD

Street address 1: 650 Kentucky St
Street address city: Gridley
Street address state: CA
Zip/Postal code: 95948-2118
General Phone: (530) 846-3661
General Fax: (530) 846-4519
General/National Adv. E-mail: jcalcagno@gridleyherald.com
Display Adv. E-mail: ajohnson-cooper@gridleyherald.com
Editorial e-mail: lvandehey@gridleyherald.com
Primary Website: gridleyherald.com
Avg Paid Circ: 2900
Avg Free Circ: 95
Audit By: Sworn/Estimate/Non-Audited
Audit Date: 10.06.2019
Personnel: Lisa Hey (Pub./Ed.)
Parent company (for newspapers): CherryRoad Media

THE HIGHLANDER - DIAMBOND BAR/WALNUT

Street address 1: 181 W. Huntington Drive
Street address 2: Ste 209
Street address city: Monrovia
Street address state: CA
Zip/Postal code: 91016
General Phone: (626) 544-0777
Advertising Phone: (626) 962-8811
Editorial Phone: (626) 544-0890
General/National Adv. E-mail: advertising@scng.com
Display Adv. E-mail: advertising@scng.com
Classified Adv. e-mail: advetising@scng.com
Editorial e-mail: news.tribune@sgvn.com
Avg Free Circ: 508
Audit By: Sworn/Estimate/Non-Audited
Audit Date: 13.10.2023
Personnel: Ron Hasse (Pres./Pub.); ron hasse (Senior Editor); Carla Asmundson (Regional Classified Manager); Frank Pine
Parent company (for newspapers): San Gabriel Valley News Group (Digital First Media)

THE HIGHLANDER - GLENDORA EDITION

Street address 1: 181 W. Huntington Drive
Street address 2: Suite 209
Street address city: Monrovia
Street address state: CA
Zip/Postal code: 91016-6353
General Phone: (626) 962-8811
Advertising Phone: (626) 962-8811
Editorial Phone: (626) 544-0811
General/National Adv. E-mail: advertising@scng.com
Display Adv. E-mail: advertising@scng.com
Classified Adv. e-mail: advertising@scng.com
Editorial e-mail: news.star-news@sgvn.com
Primary Website: sgvtribune.com/highlanders
Avg Free Circ: 1064
Audit By: Sworn/Estimate/Non-Audited
Audit Date: 16.10.2023
Personnel: Carla Asmundson (Regional Classified Manager); Melene Alfonso (VP, Advertising)
Parent company (for newspapers): San Gabriel Valley News Group (Digital First Media)

THE HIGHLANDER - LA PUENTE EDITION

Street address 1: 605 E Huntington Dr
Street address 2: Suite 100
Street address city: Monrovia
Street address state: CA
Zip/Postal code: 91016-6353
General Phone: (626) 544-0777
Advertising Phone: (626) 962-8811
Editorial Phone: (626) 544-0811
General/National Adv. E-mail: advertising@scng.com
Display Adv. E-mail: advertising@scng.com
Classified Adv. e-mail: advertising@scng.com

Editorial e-mail: news.tribune@sgvn.com
Primary Website: sgvtribune.com/highlander
Avg Free Circ: 987
Audit By: Sworn/Estimate/Non-Audited
Audit Date: 16.10.2023
Personnel: Ron Hasse (Publisher); Carla Asmundson (Regional Classified Manager); Tom Bray (Senior Editor); Melene Alfonso (VP, Advertising)
Parent company (for newspapers): San Gabriel Valley News Group (Digital First Media)

THE HUMBOLDT BEACON

Street address 1: 930 6th St
Street address city: Eureka
Street address state: CA
Zip/Postal code: 95501-1112
General Phone: (707) 441-0563
Advertising Phone: (707) 441-0599
Editorial Fax: (707) 441-0501
General/National Adv. E-mail: kmaynard@times-standard.com
Display Adv. E-mail: class@times-standard.com
Editorial e-mail: news@humboldtbeacon.com
Primary Website: humboldtbeacon.com
Year Established: 1903
Avg Paid Circ: 2500
Audit By: Sworn/Estimate/Non-Audited
Audit Date: 10.06.2019
Personnel: Franklin Stover (Ed.)
Parent company (for newspapers): Media news

THE INDEPENDENT

Street address 1: 2250 1st St
Street address city: Livermore
Street address state: CA
Zip/Postal code: 94550-3143
General Phone: (925) 447-8700
General Fax: (925) 447-0212
Advertising Phone: (925) 243-8010
Editorial Phone: (925) 243-8013
General/National Adv. E-mail: editmail@compuserve.com
Display Adv. E-mail: ramona@independentnews.com
Editorial e-mail: editmail@compuserve.com
Primary Website: independentnews.com
Year Established: 1963
Avg Free Circ: 48000
Audit By: Sworn/Estimate/Non-Audited
Audit Date: 10.06.2019
Personnel: Joan Kinney Seppala (Pub.); David T. Lowell (Assoc. Pub.); Tina Rose (Adv. Mgr.); Janet Armantrout (Ed./Prod. Mgr.)

THE INTERMOUNTAIN NEWS

Street address 1: PO Box 1030
Street address city: Burney
Street address state: CA
Zip/Postal code: 96013-1030
General Phone: (530) 725-0925
General Fax: (530) 303-1528
General/National Adv. E-mail: news@northstate.news
Display Adv. E-mail: katie@northstate.news
Editorial e-mail: news@northstate.news
Primary Website: northstate.news
Year Established: 1957
Avg Paid Circ: 2300
Audit By: Sworn/Estimate/Non-Audited
Audit Date: 10.06.2019
Personnel: Craig Harrington (Pres./Pub.); Katie Harrington (Mgr.)
Parent company (for newspapers): Cright, Inc.

THE JOURNAL - ALBANY

Street address 1: 2850 Shadelands Dr
Street address 2: Ste 101
Street address city: Walnut Creek
Street address state: CA
Zip/Postal code: 94598
General Phone: (925) 935-2525
Editorial e-mail: jhrobinson@bayareanewsgroup.com
Primary Website: eastbaytimes.com
Avg Paid Circ: 369
Avg Free Circ: 3982
Audit By: Sworn/Estimate/Non-Audited
Audit Date: 10.06.2019
Personnel: Sharon Ryan (Pub.); Lisa Buckingham (CFO/Sr. VP); Bert Robinson (Mng. Ed. Content); Randall Keith (Mng. Ed. Dig.)
Parent company (for newspapers): Digital First Media

THE KERMAN NEWS

Street address 1: 652 S Madera Ave
Street address city: Kerman
Street address state: CA
Zip/Postal code: 93630-1737
General Phone: (559) 846-6689
General Fax: (559) 846-8045
General/National Adv. E-mail: kerwest@msn.com
Primary Website: kerwestnewspapers.com
Year Established: 1906
Avg Paid Circ: 2000
Avg Free Circ: 6050
Audit By: Sworn/Estimate/Non-Audited
Audit Date: 10.06.2019
Personnel: Mark Kilen (Ed.)

THE KING CITY RUSTLER

Street address 1: 522 Broadway St
Street address 2: Ste B
Street address city: King City
Street address state: CA
Zip/Postal code: 93930-3243
General Phone: (831) 385-4880
Advertising Phone: (831) 225-0994
Editorial Phone: (831) 225-0995
General/National Adv. E-mail: jjohnson@weeklys.com
Display Adv. E-mail: jallred@weeklys.com
Classified Adv. e-mail: jallred@weeklys.com
Editorial e-mail: rcronk@weeklys.com
Primary Website: kingcityrustler.com
Avg Paid Circ: 1393
Audit By: USPS
Audit Date: 20.09.2023
Personnel: Jeanie Johnson (Pub.); Ryan Cronk (Ed.); Sheryl Bailey (Adv.); Jon Allred (Advertising Rep); Gail Esteban (Circ)
Parent company (for newspapers): San Luis Valley Publishing; NewSVMedia

THE KINGSBURG RECORDER

Street address 1: 300 W 6th St
Street address city: Hanford
Street address state: CA
Zip/Postal code: 93230-4518
General Phone: (559) 582-0471
General Fax: (559) 582-2341
Advertising Phone: (559) 583-2420
Editorial Phone: (559) 583-2421
General/National Adv. E-mail: jvikjord@HanfordSentinel.com
Display Adv. E-mail: jvikjord@HanfordSentinel.com
Editorial e-mail: jmcgill@kingsburgrecorder.com
Primary Website: hanfordsentinel.com/kingsburg_recorder
Avg Paid Circ: 1289
Audit By: AAM
Audit Date: 31.03.2016
Personnel: Davis Taylor (Pub.); Jenny Mcgill (Ed.); Gordon Weaver (Circulation Manager)
Parent company (for newspapers): Dispatch-Argus

THE LOG NEWSPAPER

Street address 1: 18475 Bandilier Cir
Street address city: Fountain Valley
Street address state: CA
Zip/Postal code: 92708-7000
General Phone: (949) 660-6150
General Fax: (949) 660-6172
Advertising Phone: (949) 660-6150 ext. 230
Editorial Phone: (949) 660-6150 ext. 226
General/National Adv. E-mail: susanne@thelog.com
Display Adv. E-mail: classifieds@thelog.com
Editorial e-mail: parimal@thelog.com
Primary Website: thelog.com
Year Established: 1971
Avg Paid Circ: 265
Avg Free Circ: 40000
Audit By: Sworn/Estimate/Non-Audited
Audit Date: 10.06.2019
Personnel: Duncan McIntosh (Pub.); Jeff Fleming (Associate Ed./Associate Pub.); Annabelle Zabala (National Adv. Mgr.); Susanne Diaz (Sales Manager)
Parent company (for newspapers): Duncan McIntosh Co., Inc.

THE LOMPOC RECORD

Street address 1: 3200 Skyway Dr
Street address city: Santa Maria
Street address state: CA
Zip/Postal code: 93455-1824
General Phone: (805) 736-2313
General Fax: (805) 736-5654
Advertising Phone: (805) 739-2150
Advertising Fax: (805) 736-5654
Editorial Phone: (805) 739-2143
Editorial Fax: (805) 736-5654
General/National Adv. E-mail: zchavez@lompocrecord.com
Display Adv. E-mail: sedwards@lompocrecord.com
Classified Adv. e-mail: bcunningham@lompocrecord.com
Editorial e-mail: mcooley@lompocrecord.com
Primary Website: lompocrecord.com
Year Established: 1979
Avg Paid Circ: 2688
Sun. Circulation Paid: 2805
Audit By: Sworn/Estimate/Non-Audited
Audit Date: 10.06.2019
Personnel: Cynthia Schur (Pub.); Tom Bolton (Exec. Ed.); Bo Poertner (City Ed.); Elliott Stern (Sports Ed.); Braxton Carroll (IT/Web Admin.); George Fischer (Prodn. Mgr.); Donna Dimock (Bus. Mgr.); Rich Macke (Circ. Dir.)
Parent company (for newspapers): Dispatch-Argus

THE MADERA TRIBUNE

Street address 1: 2591 Mitchell Ct
Street address 2: Ste 107
Street address city: Madera
Street address state: CA
Zip/Postal code: 93637-3807
General Phone: (559) 674-2424
General Fax: (559) 673-0944
Advertising Fax: (559) 673-6526
Editorial Phone: (559) 674-8134
General/National Adv. E-mail: maderatribune@maderatribunet.net
Editorial e-mail: cdoud@maderatribune.net
Primary Website: maderatribune.com
Year Established: 1892
Avg Paid Circ: 4213
Sat. Circulation Paid: 4485
Audit By: Sworn/Estimate/Non-Audited
Audit Date: 10.06.2019
Personnel: Nancy Simpson (CFO); Charles P. Doud (Ed.); Leonard Soliz (Dir., Opns.); Doug Caldwell (Pres./Pub.)

THE MALIBU SURFSIDE NEWS

Street address 1: PO Box 6854
Street address city: Malibu
Street address state: CA
Zip/Postal code: 90264-6854
General Phone: (708) 326-9170
General Fax: (708) 326-9179
General/National Adv. E-mail: mary@malibusurfsidenews.com
Display Adv. E-mail: mary@malibusurfsidenews.com
Editorial e-mail: lauren@malibusurfsidenews.com
Primary Website: malibusurfsidenews.com
Avg Free Circ: 6306
Audit By: AAM
Audit Date: 30.06.2018
Personnel: Andrew Nicks (Pres.); Joe Coughlin (Pub.); Lauren Coughlin (Ed.); Michael Ksycki (Circ. Dir.); Mary Hogan (Adv./Sales)
Parent company (for newspapers): 22nd Century Media

THE MALIBU TIMES

Street address 1: 3864 Las Flores Canyon Rd
Street address city: Malibu
Street address state: CA
Zip/Postal code: 90265-5239
General Phone: (310) 456-5507
General Fax: (310) 456-8986
Advertising Phone: (310) 456-5507
Advertising Fax: (310) 456-8986
Editorial Phone: (310) 456-5507
General/National Adv. E-mail: barbara@malibutimes.com
Display Adv. E-mail: classads@malibutimes.com
Editorial e-mail: editoral@malibutimes.com
Primary Website: malibutimes.com
Year Established: 1946
Avg Paid Circ: 500
Avg Free Circ: 11500
Audit By: Sworn/Estimate/Non-Audited
Audit Date: 10.06.2019
Personnel: Arnold G. York (Pub./Gen. Mgr.)

THE MENDOCINO BEACON

Street address 1: 690 S Main St
Street address city: Fort Bragg
Street address state: CA
Zip/Postal code: 95437-5108
General Phone: (707) 964-5642
General Fax: (707) 964-0424
Advertising Phone: (707) 964-5642
Editorial Phone: (707) 964-5642
General/National Adv. E-mail: mrharm@advocate-news.com
Display Adv. E-mail: classads@advocate-news.com
Editorial e-mail: editor@advocate-news.com
Primary Website: mendocinobeacon.com
Year Established: 1877
Avg Paid Circ: 1600
Avg Free Circ: 3
Audit By: Sworn/Estimate/Non-Audited
Audit Date: 10.06.2019
Personnel: Sharon DiMauro (Adv. Mgr.); Chris Calder (Ed); Kate Lee (Circulation Mgr); Cathy Stanley (Office Mgr)
Parent company (for newspapers): Digital First Media

THE MODOC COUNTY RECORD

Street address 1: 201 W Carlos St
Street address city: Alturas
Street address state: CA
Zip/Postal code: 96101-3919
General Phone: (530) 233-2632
General Fax: (530) 233-5113
General/National Adv. E-mail: record1@modocrecord.com
Display Adv. E-mail: classifieds@modocrecord.com
Editorial e-mail: rick@modocrecord.com
Primary Website: modocrecord.com
Year Established: 1892
Avg Paid Circ: 4500
Audit By: Sworn/Estimate/Non-Audited
Audit Date: 10.06.2019
Personnel: Jane Holloway (Ed.); Rick Holloway (Ed.)

THE MONTCLARION

Street address 1: 1516 Oak St
Street address city: Alameda
Street address state: CA
Zip/Postal code: 94501-2947
General Phone: (510) 748-1666
General Fax: (510) 748-1680
General/National Adv. E-mail: drounds@bayareanewsgroup.com
Primary Website: insidebayarea.com/montclair
Avg Paid Circ: 24209
Audit By: AAM
Audit Date: 30.09.2018
Personnel: Jon Kawamoto (Hills Ed.); David Rounds (Pub.); Chris Walker (Reg. News Ed.); Ken McLaughlin
Parent company (for newspapers): Digital First Media

THE MOUNTAIN ECHO

Street address 1: 43152 State Highway 299 E
Street address city: Fall River Mills
Street address state: CA
Zip/Postal code: 96028-9811
General Phone: (530) 336-6262
General Fax: (530) 336-6262
General/National Adv. E-mail: mtecho@shasta.com
Primary Website: mountainecho.com
Year Established: 1977
Avg Paid Circ: 3000
Avg Free Circ: 500
Audit By: Sworn/Estimate/Non-Audited
Audit Date: 10.06.2019
Personnel: Donna Caldwell (Pub.); Walt Caldwell (Ed.); Katie Clift (Adv. Mgr.)

THE NEWS REVIEW

Street address 1: 109 N Sanders St

Street address city: Ridgecrest
Street address state: CA
Zip/Postal code: 93555-3848
General Phone: (760) 371-4301
General Fax: (760) 371-4304
General/National Adv. E-mail: newsreview@iwvisp.com
Primary Website: news-ridgecrest.com
Avg Paid Circ: 7500
Avg Free Circ: 10728
Audit By: Sworn/Estimate/Non-Audited
Audit Date: 10.06.2019
Personnel: Patricia Farris (Pub.); Christine Scrivner (Adv. Mgr.); Patti Farris Cosner (Mng. Ed.); Rebecca Neipp (Prodn. Mgr.); Laura Auspin (Graphics)

THE NEWS-LEDGER

Street address 1: 1040 W Capitol Ave
Street address 2: Ste B
Street address city: West Sacramento
Street address state: CA
Zip/Postal code: 95691-2701
General Phone: (916) 371-8030
General Fax: (916) 371-8055
Advertising Phone: (916) 371-8030
Primary Website: news-ledger.com
Year Established: 1964
Avg Paid Circ: 2100
Audit By: Sworn/Estimate/Non-Audited
Audit Date: 10.06.2019
Personnel: Monica Stark (Editor)

THE PARAMOUNT JOURNAL

Street address 1: 8007 Somerset Blvd
Street address city: Paramount
Street address state: CA
Zip/Postal code: 90723-4334
General Phone: (800) 540-1870
General Fax: (562) 630-8141
Advertising Phone: (562) 833-1234 x 310
General/National Adv. E-mail: info@paramountjournal.org
Editorial e-mail: ckelly@paramountjournal.org
Primary Website: paramountjournal.org
Year Established: 2003
Avg Paid Circ: 4500
Audit By: Sworn/Estimate/Non-Audited
Audit Date: 10.06.2019
Personnel: Vince Bodiford (Pub.); Charles Kelly (Ed.)

THE PRESS

Street address 1: 248 Oak St
Street address city: Brentwood
Street address state: CA
Zip/Postal code: 94513-1337
General Phone: (925) 634-1441
Audit By: Sworn/Estimate/Non-Audited
Audit Date: 10.06.2019

THE REEDLEY EXPONENT

Street address 1: PO Box 432
Street address 2: 1130 G Street
Street address city: Reedley
Street address state: CA
Zip/Postal code: 93654-0432
General Phone: (559) 638-2244
General Fax: (559) 638-5021
General/National Adv. E-mail: janie@midvalleypublishing.com
Display Adv. E-mail: janie@midvalleypublishing.com
Editorial e-mail: jon@midvalleypublishing.com
Primary Website: reedleyexponent.com
Year Established: 1891
Audit By: Sworn/Estimate/Non-Audited
Audit Date: 10.06.2019
Personnel: Fred Hall (Publisher); Jon Earnest (Editor); Janie Lucio (Adv.)

THE RIVER NEWS-HERALD & ISLETON JOURNAL

Street address 1: 21 S Front St
Street address city: Rio Vista
Street address state: CA
Zip/Postal code: 94571-1822
General Phone: (707) 374-6431
General Fax: (707) 374-6322
Advertising Phone: (707) 374-6431
Advertising Fax: (707) 374-6322
General/National Adv. E-mail: rvads@citlink.net
Display Adv. E-mail: rvads@citlink.net
Editorial e-mail: rveditor@citlink.net
Primary Website: rivernewsherald.org
Year Established: 1890
Avg Paid Circ: 3900
Avg Free Circ: 1008
Audit By: Sworn/Estimate/Non-Audited
Audit Date: 10.06.2019
Personnel: David L. Payne (Pub.); Galen Kusic (Ed.)

THE RIVERBANK NEWS

Street address 1: 122 S 3rd Ave
Street address city: Oakdale
Street address state: CA
Zip/Postal code: 95361-3935
General Phone: (209) 847-3021
General Fax: (209) 847-9750
Advertising Phone: (209) 847-3021
Advertising Fax: (209) 847-9750
Editorial Phone: (209) 847-3021
Editorial Fax: (209) 847-9750
General/National Adv. E-mail: ads@oakdaleleader.com
Display Adv. E-mail: mkendig@oakdaleleader.com
Editorial e-mail: mjackson@oakdaleleader.com
Primary Website: theriverbanknews.com
Avg Paid Circ: 1100
Avg Free Circ: 6800
Audit By: Sworn/Estimate/Non-Audited
Audit Date: 10.06.2019
Personnel: Hank Veen (Pub.); Teresa Hammond (Circ. Mgr.); Marg Jackson (Ed.)
Parent company (for newspapers): Morris Multimedia, Inc.

THE SALINAS CALIFORNIAN

Street address 1: 123 W. Alisal Street
Street address city: Salinas
Street address state: CA
Zip/Postal code: 93901
General Phone: (831) 424-2221
General Fax: (831) 754-4104
Advertising Phone: (831) 754-4133
Advertising Fax: (831) 754-4104
Editorial Phone: (831) 754-4260
Editorial Fax: (831) 754-4104
General/National Adv. E-mail: chymovitz@thecalifornian.com
Display Adv. E-mail: chymovitz@thecalifornian.com
Classified Adv. e-mail: chymovitz@thecalifornian.com
Editorial e-mail: newsroom@thecalifornian.com
Primary Website: thecalifornian.com
Year Established: 1871
Avg Paid Circ: 5095
Avg Free Circ: 161
Sat. Circulation Paid: 9661
Sun. Circulation Paid: 70
Audit By: AAM
Audit Date: 31.03.2019
Personnel: Paula Goudreau (Publisher & President); Craig Hymovitz (Adv. Sales Mgr.); Katharine Ball (Digital Ed.); Paul Young (Major/Nat'l Sales); Karen Ferguson (Regional Publisher); Silas Lyons (Exec. Ed.)
Parent company (for newspapers): Gannett

THE SELMA ENTERPRISE

Street address 1: 300 W 6th St
Street address city: Hanford
Street address state: CA
Zip/Postal code: 93230-4518
General Phone: (559) 896-1976
General Fax: (559) 896-9160
Advertising Phone: (559) 583-2402
Editorial Phone: (559) 896-1976 x 1013
General/National Adv. E-mail: mdaniel@HanfordSentinel.com
Display Adv. E-mail: mdaniel@HanfordSentinel.com
Editorial e-mail: jmcgill@selmaenterprise.com
Primary Website: selmaenterprise.com
Year Established: 1851
Avg Paid Circ: 5000
Avg Free Circ: 1650
Audit By: Sworn/Estimate/Non-Audited
Audit Date: 10.06.2019
Personnel: Davis Taylor (Pub.); Jenny Mcgill (Ed.)

THE SONOMA INDEX-TRIBUNE

Street address 1: 17 W Napa St
Street address 2: Ste C
Street address city: Sonoma
Street address state: CA
Zip/Postal code: 95476
General Phone: (707) 933-2771
General/National Adv. E-mail: robert.lee@sonomanews.com
Display Adv. E-mail: robert.lee@sonomanews.com
Editorial e-mail: jason.walsh@sonomanews.com
Primary Website: sonomanews.com
Year Established: 1879
Avg Paid Circ: 3819
Avg Free Circ: 258
Audit By: CVC
Audit Date: 30.03.2018
Personnel: Emily Charrier (Pub.); Jason Walsh (Editor-in-chief); Katni Schneider; Robert Lee (Adv.); Kris Patalano (Circ.)
Parent company (for newspapers): Sonoma Media Investments

THE STAR-NEWS

Street address 1: 296 3rd Ave
Street address city: Chula Vista
Street address state: CA
Zip/Postal code: 91910-2701
General Phone: (619) 427-3000
General Fax: (619) 426-6346
Advertising Phone: (619) 427-3000 x 270
Editorial Phone: (619) 427-3000 x 220
General/National Adv. E-mail: legals@thestarnews.com
Display Adv. E-mail: classified@thestarnews.com
Editorial e-mail: carlos@thestarnews.com
Primary Website: thestarnews.com
Year Established: 1954
Avg Paid Circ: 270
Avg Free Circ: 35000
Audit By: Sworn/Estimate/Non-Audited
Audit Date: 10.06.2019
Personnel: Carlo Davalos (Ed.); John Moreno (Pub.); Jo Delgadillo (Circ. Mgr.); Jutta Vanderhayden (Business Mgr.)
Parent company (for newspapers): Community Media Group

THE SUNNYVALE SUN

Street address 1: 4 North 2nd Street
Street address city: San Jose
Street address state: CA
Zip/Postal code: 95113
General Phone: (408) 200-1000
General Fax: (408) 200-1011
Advertising Phone: (408) 200-1009
Editorial Phone: (408) 200-1039
Primary Website: mercurynews.com/location/sunnyvale
Year Established: 1993
Avg Paid Circ: 12015
Audit By: Sworn/Estimate/Non-Audited
Audit Date: 10.06.2019
Personnel: Bert Robinson (Mng. Ed); Sharon Ryan (Pres./Pub.); Lisa Buckingham (CFO/ Sr. VP)
Parent company (for newspapers): MediaNews Group; The McClatchy Company

THE TRINITY JOURNAL

Street address 1: 500 Main St.
Street address city: Weaverville
Street address state: CA
Zip/Postal code: 96093
General Phone: 530-623-2055
General Fax: 530-623-5382
General/National Adv. E-mail: editor@trinityjournal.com
Display Adv. E-mail: joelp@trinityjournal.com
Classified Adv. e-mail: tjoffice@trinityjournal.com
Editorial e-mail: editor@trinityjournal.com
Primary Website: www.trinityjournal.com
Mthly Avg Views: 50000
Year Established: 1856
Avg Paid Circ: 3050
Audit By: Sworn/Estimate/Non-Audited
Personnel: Wayne Agner (Editor & Publisher)
Parent company (for newspapers): WRA Enterprises, Inc.

THE UKIAH DAILY JOURNAL

Street address 1: 415 Talmage Rd Suite A
Street address city: Ukiah
Street address state: CA
Zip/Postal code: 95482-4912
General Phone: (707) 468-3500
Advertising Phone: (707) 468-3500
Editorial Phone: (707) 468-3500
General/National Adv. E-mail: udjemily@ukiahdj.com
Display Adv. E-mail: udjemily@ukiahdj.com
Classified Adv. e-mail: advertising@record-bee.com
Editorial e-mail: udj@ukiahdj.com
Primary Website: www.ukiahdailyjournal.com
Mthly Avg Views: 600000
Mthly Avg Unique Visitors: 90000
Year Established: 1860
Avg Paid Circ: 5070
Sat. Circulation Paid: 5070
Sun. Circulation Paid: 5344
Audit By: AAM
Audit Date: 30.09.2014
Personnel: Kevin McConnell (Pub.); Jody Martinez (Asst. Ed.); K.C. Meadows (Online Ed.); Sarah McGrath (General Manager/Advertising Manager); Brittany Dashiell (Webpage Ed.); Gail McAlister (Lake Mendo Group Dig. Dir.)
Parent company (for newspapers): Digital First Media; MediaNews Group

THE VALLEY CHRONICLE

Street address 1: 227 E Florida Ave
Street address city: Hemet
Street address state: CA
Zip/Postal code: 92543-4205
General Phone: (951) 652-6529
General Fax: (951) 652-4009
Advertising Phone: (951) 318-2908
General/National Adv. E-mail: knichols@thevalleychronicle.com
Editorial e-mail: jself@thevalleychronicle.com
Primary Website: thevalleychronicle.com
Avg Paid Circ: 2029
Avg Free Circ: 23152
Audit By: Sworn/Estimate/Non-Audited
Audit Date: 10.06.2019
Personnel: Eric Buskirk (Pub.); Mary Ann Morris (Ed.); Kathy McNeeley (Sales & Adv); David Burlison (Sales & Adv); Leo Monreal (Sales & Adv.); Rocky Zharp (Sales & Adv.); Rusty Strait (Journalist); Corey Evan; Jessica Self (Mng. Ed.); Debbie Mulvena (Journalist); Halima Haider (Journalist); Kyle Selby (Journalist); R.A. Calderon (Operations Dir.)
Parent company (for newspapers): Verican, Inc.

THE WEEKLY CALISTOGAN

Street address 1: PO Box 385
Street address city: Calistoga
Street address state: CA
Zip/Postal code: 94515-0385
General Phone: (707) 942-4035
Advertising Phone: (707) 967-6815
Editorial Phone: (707) 942-4035
General/National Adv. E-mail: editor@weeklycalistogan.com
Display Adv. E-mail: classified@napanews.com
Editorial e-mail: editor@weeklycalistogan.com
Primary Website: napavalleyregister.com/calistogan
Year Established: 1877
Avg Paid Circ: 300
Audit By: Sworn/Estimate/Non-Audited
Audit Date: 10.06.2019
Personnel: Cynthia Sweeney (Editor)
Parent company (for newspapers): Dispatch-Argus; Lee Enterprises

THE WILLITS NEWS

Street address 1: PO Box 628
Street address city: Willits
Street address state: CA
Zip/Postal code: 95490-0628
General Phone: (707) 459-4643
General Fax: (707) 459-1664
Advertising Phone: (707) 456-9520
Editorial Phone: (707) 456-9520
General/National Adv. E-mail: advertising@willitsnews.com

Display Adv. E-mail: classifieds@willitsnews.com
Editorial e-mail: editorial@willitsnews.com
Primary Website: willitsnews.com
Year Established: 1903
Avg Paid Circ: 2000
Audit By: Sworn/Estimate/Non-Audited
Audit Date: 10.06.2019
Personnel: Debbie Clark (Pub Emeritus); KC Meadows (Ed.); Kevin McConnell
Parent company (for newspapers): Digital First Media

THE WINDSOR TIMES

Street address 1: 230 Center St
Street address city: Healdsburg
Street address state: CA
Zip/Postal code: 95448-4402
General Phone: (707) 838-9211
General Fax: (707) 838-7791
General/National Adv. E-mail: sales@hbgtrib.com
Display Adv. E-mail: sales@hbgtrib.com
Editorial e-mail: editor@wdsrtimes.com
Primary Website: sonomawest.com/the_windsor_times
Avg Free Circ: 3600
Audit By: Sworn/Estimate/Non-Audited
Audit Date: 10.06.2019
Personnel: Rollie Atkinson (Pub.); Sarah Bradbury (Assoc. Pub.); Ray Holley (Mgr. editor)
Parent company (for newspapers): Sonoma West Publishers

THOUSAND OAKS ACORN

Street address 1: 30423 Canwood St
Street address 2: Ste 108
Street address city: Agoura Hills
Street address state: CA
Zip/Postal code: 91301-4313
General Phone: (805) 367-8232
General Fax: (805) 764-4432
Advertising Phone: (818) 706-0266
Editorial Fax: (805) 367-8237
General/National Adv. E-mail: AdRep@theacorn.com
Display Adv. E-mail: classads@theacorn.com
Editorial e-mail: newstip@theacorn.com
Primary Website: toacorn.com
Avg Free Circ: 40072
Audit By: VAC
Audit Date: 30.09.2017
Personnel: Kyle Jorrey (Ed.)
Parent company (for newspapers): J. Bee NP Publishing, Ltd.

TIMES-ADVOCATE

Street address 1: 720 N Broadway
Street address 2: Ste 108
Street address city: Escondido
Street address state: CA
Zip/Postal code: 92025-1870
General Phone: (760) 546-4000
Advertising Phone: (760) 546-4000
Editorial Phone: (760) 546-4000
Primary Website: times-advocate.com
Audit By: Sworn/Estimate/Non-Audited
Audit Date: 10.06.2019
Personnel: David Ross (Editor In Chief); Doug Green (Editor); Justin Salter (Publisher); Andrew Leyva (Advertising Account Manager)
Parent company (for newspapers): Roadrunner Publications, Inc.

TRACY PRESS

Street address 1: 145 W 10th St
Street address city: Tracy
Street address state: CA
Zip/Postal code: 95376-3903
General Phone: (209) 835-3030
General Fax: (209) 835-0655
Advertising Phone: (209) 830-4260
Advertising Fax: (209) 832-5383
General/National Adv. E-mail: tpads@tracypress.com
Display Adv. E-mail: tpads@tracypress.com
Editorial e-mail: mlangley@tracypress.com
Primary Website: tracypress.com
Year Established: 1898
Avg Paid Circ: 19000
Audit By: Sworn/Estimate/Non-Audited
Audit Date: 10.06.2019
Personnel: Ralph Alldredge (Co-Pub.); Michael Langley (Ed.); Vanessa Alfaro (Adv. Sales); Lisa Carcraft (Mktg. Mgr.); Diane Lopez (Adv. Rep.)

TRI-CITY VOICE

Street address 1: 39737 Paseo Padre Pkwy
Street address 2: Ste. B
Street address city: Fremont
Street address state: CA
Zip/Postal code: 94538-2997
General Phone: (510) 494-1999
General Fax: (510) 796-2462
Advertising Phone: (510) 494-1999
Editorial Phone: (510) 494-1999
General/National Adv. E-mail: tricityvoice@aol.com
Display Adv. E-mail: tricityvoice@aol.com
Editorial e-mail: tricityvoice@aol.com
Primary Website: tricityvoice.com
Year Established: 2002
Audit By: Sworn/Estimate/Non-Audited
Audit Date: 10.06.2019
Personnel: William Marshak (Pub.)

TRI-CITY WEEKLY

Street address 1: 930 6th St
Street address city: Eureka
Street address state: CA
Zip/Postal code: 95501-1112
General Phone: (707) 441-0500
General Fax: (707) 441-0565
Advertising Phone: (707) 441-0556
Advertising Fax: (707) 441-0565
Editorial Phone: (707) 441-0520
Editorial Fax: (707) 441-0501
General/National Adv. E-mail: ads@times-standard.com
Display Adv. E-mail: class@times-standard.com
Editorial e-mail: mvalles@times-standard.com
Primary Website: tricityweekly.com
Year Established: 1970
Avg Paid Circ: 0
Avg Free Circ: 32050
Audit By: Sworn/Estimate/Non-Audited
Audit Date: 10.06.2019
Personnel: Paula Patton (Pub.); Carmel Bonitatibus (Prod. Mgr.)
Parent company (for newspapers): Digital First Media

TUESDAY REVIEW

Street address 1: 1021 Fresno St
Street address city: Newman
Street address state: CA
Zip/Postal code: 95360-1303
General Phone: (209) 862-2222
General Fax: (209) 862-4133
Advertising Phone: (209) 862-2222
General/National Adv. E-mail: advertising@mattosnews.com
Display Adv. E-mail: advertising@mattosnews.com
Editorial e-mail: dharris@mattosnews.com
Primary Website: mattosnews.com
Avg Free Circ: 6500
Audit By: Sworn/Estimate/Non-Audited
Audit Date: 10.06.2019
Personnel: Susan Mattos (Pub.); Mary Beth Merin (Adv. Mgr.); Dean Harris (Ed.)

TURLOCK JOURNAL

Street address 1: 138 S Center St
Street address city: Turlock
Street address state: CA
Zip/Postal code: 95380-4508
General Phone: (209) 634-9141
General Fax: (209) 632-8813
Advertising Phone: (209) 634-9141
Advertising Fax: (209) 632-8813
Editorial Phone: (209) 634-9141
Editorial Fax: (209) 632-8813
General/National Adv. E-mail: adinfo@turlockjournal.com
Display Adv. E-mail: classifieds@turlockjournal.com
Editorial e-mail: news@turlockjournal.com
Primary Website: turlockjournal.com
Year Established: 1904
Avg Paid Circ: 6030
Avg Free Circ: 14500
Audit By: Sworn/Estimate/Non-Audited
Audit Date: 10.06.2019
Personnel: Hank Veen (Pub.); Kristina Hacker (Ed.); Victoria Batesole (Adv. Sales); Taylor Phillips (Adv. Mgr.)
Parent company (for newspapers): Morris Multimedia, Inc.

TWIN CITIES TIMES

Street address 1: 1301B Grant Ave
Street address city: Novato
Street address state: CA
Zip/Postal code: 94945-3143
General Phone: (415) 892-1516
General Fax: (415) 897-0940
Advertising Phone: (415) 892-1516 x 15
Editorial Phone: (415) 892-1516 x 19
General/National Adv. E-mail: mmckellips@marinscope.com
Display Adv. E-mail: mmckellips@marinscope.com
Editorial e-mail: gandersen@marinscope.com
Primary Website: marinscope.com
Year Established: 1922
Avg Paid Circ: 71
Avg Free Circ: 7351
Audit By: Sworn/Estimate/Non-Audited
Audit Date: 10.06.2019
Personnel: Paul Hutcheson (Pub.); Greg Andersen (Ed.); Linda Mallin (Circ. Mgr.)
Parent company (for newspapers): Marinscope Community Newspapers

UPTOWN GAZETTE

Street address 1: 5225 E 2nd St
Street address city: Long Beach
Street address state: CA
Zip/Postal code: 90803-5326
General Phone: (562) 433-2000
General Fax: (562) 434-8826
General/National Adv. E-mail: advertising@gazettes.com
Display Adv. E-mail: classifieds@gazettes.com
Editorial e-mail: editor@gazettes.com
Primary Website: gazettes.com
Year Established: 2008
Avg Free Circ: 17975
Audit By: CVC
Audit Date: 30.06.2016
Personnel: Simon Grieve (Pub.); Harry Saltzgaver (Exec. Ed.)

UPTOWN SAN DIEGO EXAMINER

Street address 1: 3601 30th St
Street address city: San Diego
Street address state: CA
Zip/Postal code: 92104-3508
General Phone: (619) 955-8960
General Fax: (619) 955-8962
Advertising Phone: (619) 955-8960
Advertising Fax: (619) 955-8962
General/National Adv. E-mail: kevin@uptownexaminer.com
Primary Website: uptownexaminer.com
Year Established: 1937
Avg Paid Circ: 50
Avg Free Circ: 15000
Audit By: Sworn/Estimate/Non-Audited
Audit Date: 10.06.2019
Personnel: Gary Shaw (Pub.); Kevin Specht (Legal Notice Rep.); Manny Cruz (Mng. Ed.)

VALLEY ROADRUNNER

Street address 1: 29115 Valley Center Rd
Street address city: Valley Center
Street address state: CA
Zip/Postal code: 92082-6553
General Phone: (760) 749-1112
General Fax: (760) 749-1688
General/National Adv. E-mail: advertising@valleycenter.com
Display Adv. E-mail: advertising@valleycenter.com
Editorial e-mail: News@ValleyCenter.com
Primary Website: valleycenter.com
Year Established: 1974
Avg Paid Circ: 3600
Avg Free Circ: 42
Audit By: Sworn/Estimate/Non-Audited
Audit Date: 10.06.2019
Personnel: David Ross (Ed); Kimberly Nichols (Acct. Exec.); Justin Salter (Publisher)
Parent company (for newspapers): Verican, Inc.

VENTURA COUNTY REPORTER

Street address 1: 700 E Main St
Street address city: Ventura
Street address state: CA
Zip/Postal code: 93001-2906
General Phone: (805) 648-2244
General Fax: (805) 648-2245
Advertising Phone: (805) 648-2244 x 237
General/National Adv. E-mail: diane@vcreporter.com
Display Adv. E-mail: tori@vcreporter.com
Editorial e-mail: editor@vcreporter.com
Primary Website: vcreporter.com
Year Established: 1976
Avg Paid Circ: 33000
Audit By: Sworn/Estimate/Non-Audited
Audit Date: 10.06.2019
Personnel: David Comden (Pub.); Michael Sullivan (Ed.)
Parent company (for newspapers): Times Media Group

VICTORVILLE DAILY PRESS

Street address 1: 13891 Park Ave
Street address city: Victorville
Street address state: CA
Zip/Postal code: 92392-2435
General Phone: (760) 248-7878
General Fax: (760) 248-2042
General/National Adv. E-mail: snakutin@vvdailypress.com
Display Adv. E-mail: snakutin@vvdailypress.com
Editorial e-mail: shunt@vvdailypress.com
Primary Website: lucernevalleyleader.com
Year Established: 1956
Avg Paid Circ: 4400
Audit By: Sworn/Estimate/Non-Audited
Audit Date: 10.06.2019
Personnel: Steve Hunt (Ed./Pub.); Mario Mejia (Circ. Dir.); Jason Vrtis (News Ed.); Steve Nakutin (Adv.)
Parent company (for newspapers): CherryRoad Media

VILLAGE LIFE

Street address 1: 2889 Ray Lawyer Dr
Street address city: Placerville
Street address state: CA
Zip/Postal code: 95667-3914
General Phone: (530) 622-1255
General Fax: (530) 622-7894
Advertising Phone: (530) 344-5048
Editorial Phone: (530) 344-5073
General/National Adv. E-mail: ibalentine@mtdemocrat.net
Display Adv. E-mail: ibalentine@mtdemocrat.net
Editorial e-mail: editor@villagelife.com
Primary Website: villagelife.com
Avg Paid Circ: 12000
Audit By: Sworn/Estimate/Non-Audited
Audit Date: 10.06.2019
Personnel: Noel Stack (Mng. Ed.); Richard Esposito (Pub.)
Parent company (for newspapers): McNaughton Newspapers

WATERFORD NEWS

Street address 1: 12717 Bentley St
Street address city: Waterford
Street address state: CA
Zip/Postal code: 95386-9012
General Phone: (209) 874-1927
General/National Adv. E-mail: midvalleypub@aol.com; info@yahoo.com
Primary Website: waterfordnews.weebly.com
Avg Free Circ: 7000
Audit By: Sworn/Estimate/Non-Audited
Audit Date: 10.06.2019
Personnel: Wendy Krier (Ed./ Sales and Mktg.)
Parent company (for newspapers): Mid Valley Publishing

WEST COVINA HIGHLANDER

Street address 1: 181 W. Huntington Drive
Street address 2: Suite 209
Street address city: Monrovia
Street address state: CA
Zip/Postal code: 91016
General Phone: (626) 544-0777

Advertising Phone: (626) 544-0890
Editorial Phone: (626) 544-0990
General/National Adv. E-mail: advertising@scng.com
Display Adv. E-mail: advertising@scng.com
Classified Adv. e-mail: advertising@scng.com
Editorial e-mail: news.tribune@sgvn.com
Avg Free Circ: 571
Audit By: Sworn/Estimate/Non-Audited
Audit Date: 16.10.2023
Personnel: Ron Hasse (Publisher); Melene Alfonso (VP Advertising); Carla Asmundson (Classified Advertising Manager)
Parent company (for newspapers): Southern California News Group

WEST COVINA HIGHLANDER

Street address 1: 1210 N Azusa Canyon Rd
Street address city: West Covina
Street address state: CA
Zip/Postal code: 91790-1003
General Phone: (626) 854-8700
General Fax: (626) 854-8719
Advertising Phone: (626) 962-8811
Editorial Phone: (626) 544-0990
General/National Adv. E-mail: lauree.sierra@sgvn.com
Display Adv. E-mail: Carla.asmundson@sgvn.com
Editorial e-mail: michael.anastasi@langnews.com
Primary Website: sgvtribune.com/highlanders
Avg Free Circ: 18450
Audit By: Sworn/Estimate/Non-Audited
Audit Date: 10.06.2019
Personnel: Ron Hasse (Pres./Pub.); Michael Anastasi (Exec. Ed./VP)

WESTMINSTER HERALD

Street address 1: 7441 Garden Grove Blvd
Street address 2: Ste G
Street address city: Garden Grove
Street address state: CA
Zip/Postal code: 92841-4209
General Phone: (714) 893-4501
General Fax: (714) 893-4502
General/National Adv. E-mail: westmherald@aol.com
Editorial e-mail: editor@westminsterheraldnews.com
Primary Website: westminsterheraldnews.com
Year Established: 1946
Avg Paid Circ: 5000
Audit By: Sworn/Estimate/Non-Audited
Audit Date: 10.06.2019
Personnel: Lloyd W. Thomas (Ed.)

WESTSIDE TODAY

Street address 1: 2116 Wilshire Blvd
Street address 2: Ste 260
Street address city: Santa Monica
Street address state: CA
Zip/Postal code: 90403-5750
General Phone: (310) 310-2637
General Fax: (424) 744-8821
General/National Adv. E-mail: advertising@smmirror.com
Display Adv. E-mail: advertising@smmirror.com
Editorial e-mail: editor@smmirror.com
Primary Website: westsidetoday.com
Year Established: 1990
Avg Paid Circ: 0
Avg Free Circ: 100000
Audit By: Sworn/Estimate/Non-Audited
Audit Date: 10.06.2019
Personnel: TJ Montemer (President/Publisher); Judy Swartz (Sales Mgr.)
Parent company (for newspapers): Mirror Media Group

WESTWOOD PINEPRESS

Street address 1: 100 Grand Ave
Street address city: Susanville
Street address state: CA
Zip/Postal code: 96130-4451
General Phone: (530) 257-5321
General Fax: (530) 257-0408
Advertising Phone: (530) 257-5321
Advertising Fax: (530) 257-0408
Editorial Phone: (530) 257-5321
Editorial Fax: (530) 257-0408
General/National Adv. E-mail: cmcintire@plumasnews.com
Display Adv. E-mail: rmeadows@lassennews.com
Editorial e-mail: swilliams@lassennews.com
Primary Website: lassennews.com
Year Established: 1977
Avg Free Circ: 750
Audit By: Sworn/Estimate/Non-Audited
Audit Date: 10.06.2019
Personnel: Michael Taborski (Pub.); Sam Williams (Mgr. Ed)
Parent company (for newspapers): Feather Publishing Co., Inc.

WINE COUNTRY THIS WEEK

Street address 1: 669 Broadway
Street address 2: Ste B
Street address city: Sonoma
Street address state: CA
Zip/Postal code: 95476-7085
General Phone: (707) 938-3494
General Fax: (707) 938-3674
Primary Website: winecountrythisweek.com
Audit By: Sworn/Estimate/Non-Audited
Audit Date: 10.06.2019
Personnel: Chandra Grant (Ed.)
Parent company (for newspapers): Brehm Communications, Inc.

WINTERS EXPRESS

Street address 1: 13 Russell St
Street address city: Winters
Street address state: CA
Zip/Postal code: 95694-1730
General Phone: (530) 795-4551
General/National Adv. E-mail: ads@wintersexpress.com
Display Adv. E-mail: ads@wintersexpress.com
Editorial e-mail: news@wintersexpress.com
Primary Website: wintersexpress.com
Year Established: 1884
Avg Paid Circ: 2000
Avg Free Circ: 100
Audit By: Sworn/Estimate/Non-Audited
Audit Date: 10.06.2019
Personnel: Charles R. Wallace (Pub.); Debra DeAngelo (Ed.)
Parent company (for newspapers): McNaughton Newspapers

WINTON TIMES

Street address 1: 6950 Gerard Ave
Street address city: Winton
Street address state: CA
Zip/Postal code: 95388
General Phone: (209) 358-5311
General Fax: (209) 358-7108
General/National Adv. E-mail: info@midvalleypub.com
Avg Paid Circ: 2500
Avg Free Circ: 50
Audit By: Sworn/Estimate/Non-Audited
Audit Date: 10.06.2019
Personnel: John M. Derby (Pub.); Kelly Thomas (Bookkeeper)
Parent company (for newspapers): Mid Valley Publishing

YO VENICE

Street address 1: 2116 Wilshire Blvd
Street address 2: Ste 260
Street address city: Santa Monica
Street address state: CA
Zip/Postal code: 90403-5750
General Phone: (310) 310-2637
General Fax: (424) 744-8821
General/National Adv. E-mail: advertising@smmirror.com
Display Adv. E-mail: advertising@smmirror.com
Editorial e-mail: editor@smmirror.com
Primary Website: westsidetoday.com
Year Established: 1990
Avg Paid Circ: 0
Avg Free Circ: 100000
Audit By: Sworn/Estimate/Non-Audited
Audit Date: 10.06.2019
Personnel: TJ Montemer (President/Publisher); Judy Swartz (Sales Mgr.)
Parent company (for newspapers): Mirror Media Group

YORBA LINDA STAR

Street address 1: 625 N Grand Ave
Street address city: Santa Ana
Street address state: CA
Zip/Postal code: 92701-4347
General Phone: (714) 634-1567
General Fax: (714) 704-3714
Editorial Phone: (714) 796-2226
General/National Adv. E-mail: yorbalindastar@ocregister.com
Primary Website: ocregister.com/sections/city-pages/placentia-yorbalinda
Avg Paid Circ: 5047
Audit By: Sworn/Estimate/Non-Audited
Audit Date: 10.06.2019
Personnel: Aaron Kushner (Ed.); Ken Brusic (Ed.); Heather McRea (Ed.)
Parent company (for newspapers): Times Media Group

YUCAIPA & CALIMESA NEWS-MIRROR

Street address 1: 35154 Yucaipa Blvd
Street address city: Yucaipa
Street address state: CA
Zip/Postal code: 92399-4339
General Phone: (909) 797-9101
General Fax: (909) 797-0502
General/National Adv. E-mail: ads@centurygroup.com
Display Adv. E-mail: ads@centurygroup.com
Editorial e-mail: tbush@centurygroup.com
Primary Website: newsmirror.net
Year Established: 1987
Avg Paid Circ: 2893
Avg Free Circ: 18819
Audit By: CVC
Audit Date: 30.06.2018
Personnel: Toebe Bush (Pub./VP); Pamela Eldridge (Adv.); Cheri Mitchell (Adv.)
Parent company (for newspapers): Century Group Newspapers

COLORADO

AG JOURNAL

Street address 1: 422 Colorado Ave
Street address city: La Junta
Street address state: CO
Zip/Postal code: 81050-2336
General Phone: (719) 384-8121
General Fax: (719) 384-8157
Advertising Phone: (719) 384-1430
Editorial Phone: (719) 384-1453
General/National Adv. E-mail: jason@ljtdmail.com
Display Adv. E-mail: classifieds@ljtdmail.com
Editorial e-mail: publisher@ljtdmail.com
Primary Website: agjournalonline.com
Avg Paid Circ: 10159
Avg Free Circ: 452
Audit By: Sworn/Estimate/Non-Audited
Audit Date: 10.06.2019
Personnel: Candy Hill (Pub./Ed.); Ken Hamrick (Sports Ed.); Jason Gallegos (Multimedia Sales Exec.); Rita Ojeda (Class. Adv. Mgr.)
Parent company (for newspapers): CherryRoad Media

AKRON NEWS-REPORTER

Street address 1: 69 Main Ave
Street address city: Akron
Street address state: CO
Zip/Postal code: 80720-1439
General Phone: (970) 345-2296
General Fax: (970) 345-6638
General/National Adv. E-mail: mmcmahill@akronnewsreporter.com
Display Adv. E-mail: mmcmahill@akronnewsreporter.com
Editorial e-mail: jbusing@akronnewsreporter.com
Primary Website: akronnewsreporter.com
Avg Paid Circ: 2000
Audit By: Sworn/Estimate/Non-Audited
Audit Date: 10.06.2019
Personnel: Iva Horner (Pub.); JoAnne Busing (Ed.)
Parent company (for newspapers): Digital First Media; Prairie Mountain Publishing

ARVADA PRESS

Street address 1: 722 Washington Ave Unit 210
Street address 2: Suite 210
Street address city: Golden
Street address state: CO
Zip/Postal code: 80401-5876
General Phone: (303) 566-4100
General Fax: (303) 468-2592
Advertising Phone: (303) 566-4074
Editorial Phone: (303) 566-4127
General/National Adv. E-mail: sales@milehighnews.com
Display Adv. E-mail: audreyb@milehighnews.com
Editorial e-mail: mkelly@ourcoloradonews.com
Primary Website: arvadapress.com
Avg Paid Circ: 37200
Avg Free Circ: 34603
Audit By: Sworn/Estimate/Non-Audited
Audit Date: 10.06.2019
Personnel: Jerry Healey (Pres. / Pub.); Robin Sant (Circ. Mgr.); Cari Witzel (Dir, Sales/Mktg.); Barb Stolte (Adv. Mgr.); Glenn Wallace (Mng. Ed.); Karen Earhart (Class. Sales)
Parent company (for newspapers): Colorado Community Media

AURORA SENTINEL

Street address 1: 12100 E Iliff Ave Ste 102
Street address 2: Suite 102
Street address city: Aurora
Street address state: CO
Zip/Postal code: 80014-1277
General Phone: (303) 750-7555
General Fax: (303) 750-7699
Advertising Phone: (303) 750-7555
Advertising Fax: (303) 750-7699
Editorial Phone: (303) 750-7555
Editorial Fax: (720) 449-9033
General/National Adv. E-mail: advertising@aurorasentinel.com
Display Adv. E-mail: advertise@aurorasentinel.com
Primary Website: aurorasentinel.com
Year Established: 1908
Avg Paid Circ: 7055
Audit By: Sworn/Estimate/Non-Audited
Audit Date: 10.06.2019
Personnel: James Gold (Pub.); Dave Perry (Ed.); Melanie Coker (Mktg. Dir.); Lindsay Nicoletti (Mktg. Mgr.)

BENT COUNTY DEMOCRAT

Street address 1: 510 Carson Ave
Street address city: Las Animas
Street address state: CO
Zip/Postal code: 81054-1732
General Phone: (719) 456-1333
Advertising Phone: (719) 384-4475
Editorial Phone: (719) 456-1333
General/National Adv. E-mail: tara@ljtdmail.com
Editorial e-mail: bcd@ljtdmail.com
Primary Website: bcdemocratonline.com
Avg Paid Circ: 1200
Audit By: Sworn/Estimate/Non-Audited
Audit Date: 10.06.2019
Personnel: Loreta Moss (Office Mgr.); Adrian Hart (Circ. Mgr.); Candi Hill (Pub.); Ken Hamrick (Sports Ed.); Jason Gallegos (Multimedia Sales Exec.); Tara Castaneda (Multimedia Sales Exec.)
Parent company (for newspapers): CherryRoad Media; CherryRoad Media

BIZWEST

Street address 1: 1550 E. Harmony Road
Street address 2: 2nd floor
Street address city: Fort Collins
Street address state: CO
Zip/Postal code: 80525
General Phone: (970) 221-5400
General Fax: (970) 221-5432
General/National Adv. E-mail: nmorse@bizwestmedia.com
Display Adv. E-mail: nmorse@bizwestmedia.com
Editorial e-mail: cwood@bizwest.com
Primary Website: bizwest.com
Year Established: 1995
Avg Paid Circ: 1640

Avg Free Circ: 2640
Audit By: CVC
Audit Date: 30.12.2017
Personnel: Chris Wood (Co-Owner/Ed./Pub.); Jeff Nuttall (Co-Owner/Pub.); Ken Amundson (Mng. Ed.); Bruce Dennis (Audience Development); Sandy Powell (Sales Manager); Bernie Simon (Prod.)
Parent company (for newspapers): BizWest Media LLC

BLACK FOREST NEWS & PALMER DIVIDE PIONEER

Street address 1: 6520 Shoup Rd
Street address city: Colorado Springs
Street address state: CO
Zip/Postal code: 80908-3865
General Phone: (719) 495-5924
General Fax: (719) 495-4367
General/National Adv. E-mail: blackforestnews@yahoo.com
Editorial e-mail: editor@blackforestnews-co.com
Primary Website: blackforestnews-co.com
Year Established: 1960
Avg Paid Circ: 928
Avg Free Circ: 77
Audit By: Sworn/Estimate/Non-Audited
Audit Date: 10.06.2019
Parent company (for newspapers): Poor & Piglets Newspaper

BRIGHTON STANDARD BLADE

Street address 1: 143 S. 2nd Place
Street address city: Brighton
Street address state: CO
Zip/Postal code: 80601-1626
General Phone: (303) 659-2522
General Fax: (303) 659-2901
Editorial e-mail: news@metrowestnewspapers.com
Primary Website: thebrightonblade.com
Avg Paid Circ: 3718
Avg Free Circ: 9109
Audit By: Sworn/Estimate/Non-Audited
Audit Date: 10.06.2019
Personnel: Steve Smith (Managing Editor); Sean Kennedy (Reporter/Designer); Belen Ward (Reporter); Teresa Alexis (Account Executive)
Parent company (for newspapers): Landmark Community Newspapers, LLC

BROOMFIELD ENTERPRISE

Street address 1: 2500 55th St
Street address 2: Ste 210
Street address city: Boulder
Street address state: CO
Zip/Postal code: 80301-5740
General Phone: (970) 215-4943
General Fax: (303) 466-8168
Advertising Phone: (720) 494-5445
Advertising Fax: (303) 466-8168
Editorial Phone: (303) 473-1362
Editorial Fax: (303) 466-8168
General/National Adv. E-mail: clabozan@prairiemountainmedia.com
Display Adv. E-mail: classifieds@prairiemountainmedia.com
Editorial e-mail: cwood@prairiemountainmedia.com
Primary Website: broomfieldenterprise.com
Year Established: 1975
Avg Free Circ: 20000
Audit By: Sworn/Estimate/Non-Audited
Audit Date: 10.06.2019
Personnel: Albert Manzi (Pub.); Carol Wood (Ed.)
Parent company (for newspapers): Prairie Mountain Publishing

BURLINGTON RECORD

Street address 1: 202 S 14th St
Street address city: Burlington
Street address state: CO
Zip/Postal code: 80807-2322
General Phone: (719) 346-5381
General Fax: (719) 346-5514
General/National Adv. E-mail: brecordadvertising@plainstel.com
Display Adv. E-mail: brecordadvertising@plainstel.com
Primary Website: burlington-record.com
Avg Paid Circ: 3350
Avg Free Circ: 15
Audit By: Sworn/Estimate/Non-Audited
Audit Date: 10.06.2019
Personnel: Rol Hudler (Pub.); Lucky Gipe (Ed.); Shannon Floyd (Adv. Mgr.)
Parent company (for newspapers): Digital First Media; Prairie Mountain Publishing

CASTLE ROCK NEWS PRESS

Street address 1: 9137 RIDGELINE BLVD
Street address 2: Suite 210
Street address city: HIGHLANDS RANCH
Street address state: CO
Zip/Postal code: 80129-2394
General Phone: (303) 566-4100
General Fax: (303) 566-4098
Advertising Phone: (303) 566-4092
General/National Adv. E-mail: jherbert@ourcoloradonews.com
Display Adv. E-mail: kearhart@ourcoloradonews.com
Primary Website: castlerocknewspress.net
Avg Free Circ: 15654
Audit By: CVC
Audit Date: 30.03.2016
Personnel: Jerry Healey (Pres/ Pub.); Chris Rotar (Mng. Ed.); Karen Earhart (Class. Sales); Maureen Shively (Adv. Mgr.)
Parent company (for newspapers): Colorado Community Media; Milehigh Newspapers

CENTENNIAL CITIZEN

Street address 1: 9137 Ridgeline Blvd
Street address 2: Suite 210
Street address city: Highlands Ranch
Street address state: CO
Zip/Postal code: 80129-2752
General Phone: (303) 566-4100
General Fax: (303) 566-4098
Advertising Phone: (303) 566-4074
Editorial Phone: (303) 566-4102
General/National Adv. E-mail: eaddenbrooke@ourcoloradonews.com
Display Adv. E-mail: kearhart@ourcoloradonews.com
Editorial e-mail: crotar@ourcoloradonews.com
Primary Website: centennialcitizen.net
Avg Paid Circ: 19
Avg Free Circ: 12441
Audit By: CVC
Audit Date: 30.03.2016
Personnel: Chris Rotar (Mng. Ed.); Jerry Healey (Pub.); Karen Earhart (Class. Sales); Dawn Brandt (Adv. Mgr.)
Parent company (for newspapers): Colorado Community Media

CENTER POST-DISPATCH

Street address 1: 835 1st Ave
Street address city: Monte Vista
Street address state: CO
Zip/Postal code: 81144-1474
General Phone: (719) 852-3531
General Fax: (719) 852-3387
General/National Adv. E-mail: bwilliams@valleypublishinginc.com
Display Adv. E-mail: bwilliams@valleypublishinginc.com
Classified Adv. e-mail: rbeutler@valleypublishinginc.com
Editorial e-mail: bwilliams@valleypublishinginc.com
Primary Website: centerpostdispatch.com
Avg Paid Circ: 315
Audit By: Sworn/Estimate/Non-Audited
Audit Date: 10.06.2019
Parent company (for newspapers): San Luis Valley Publishing

CLEAR CREEK COURANT

Street address 1: 1639 Miner St.
Street address city: Idaho Springs
Street address state: CO
Zip/Postal code: 80452
General Phone: (303) 567-4491
General Fax: (303) 567-0520
Advertising Phone: (303) 567-4491 x 14
Editorial Phone: (303) 567-4491
General/National Adv. E-mail: advertising@evergreenco.com
Display Adv. E-mail: tracy@evergreenco.com
Editorial e-mail: couranteditor@evergreenco.com
Primary Website: clearcreekcourant.com
Avg Paid Circ: 2000
Audit By: Sworn/Estimate/Non-Audited
Audit Date: 10.06.2019
Personnel: Ian Neligh (Ed.); Doug Bell (Ed.)
Parent company (for newspapers): Landmark Community Newspapers, LLC

COLORADO HOMETOWN WEEKLY

Street address 1: 2500 55th St
Street address 2: Ste 210
Street address city: Boulder
Street address state: CO
Zip/Postal code: 80301-5740
General Phone: (303) 684-5218
General Fax: (303) 442-1508
Advertising Phone: (720) 494-5445
Advertising Fax: (303) 442-1508
Editorial Phone: (303) 473-1362
Editorial Fax: (303) 442-1508
General/National Adv. E-mail: clabozan@prairiemountainmedia.com
Display Adv. E-mail: classifieds@prairiemountainmedia.com
Editorial e-mail: cwood@prairiemountainmedia.com
Primary Website: coloradohometownweekly.com
Avg Paid Circ: 6000
Audit By: Sworn/Estimate/Non-Audited
Audit Date: 10.06.2019
Personnel: Carol Wood (Editor)
Parent company (for newspapers): Prairie Mountain Media

COLORADO SPRINGS BUSINESS JOURNAL

Street address 1: 235 S Nevada Ave
Street address city: Colorado Springs
Street address state: CO
Zip/Postal code: 80903-1906
General Phone: (719) 634-5905
General Fax: (719) 577-4107
Editorial e-mail: amy.sweet@csbj.com
Primary Website: csbj.com
Year Established: 1989
Avg Paid Circ: 1130
Avg Free Circ: 1204
Audit By: CVC
Audit Date: 29.12.2017
Personnel: Amy Sweet (Exec. Ed./Pub.); Bryan Grossman (Ed.); Jeff Moore (Adv. Dir.)
Parent company (for newspapers): Colorado Publishing House

COLORADO STATESMAN

Street address 1: 1001 16th St
Street address 2: B-180 Pmb 113,
Street address city: Denver
Street address state: CO
Zip/Postal code: 80265-0005
General Phone: (303) 837-8600
General Fax: (303) 837-9015
General/National Adv. E-mail: info@coloradostatesman.com
Primary Website: coloradostatesman.com
Year Established: 1898
Avg Paid Circ: 2139
Avg Free Circ: 5000
Audit By: Sworn/Estimate/Non-Audited
Audit Date: 10.06.2019
Personnel: Jody Hope Strogoff (Ed.)

COLUMBINE COURIER

Street address 1: 27902 Meadow Dr
Street address 2: Unit 200
Street address city: Evergreen
Street address state: CO
Zip/Postal code: 80439-2106
General Phone: (303) 933-2233
General Fax: (303) 674-5534
Advertising Phone: (303) 933-2233 x 13
General/National Adv. E-mail: columbinesales@evergreenco.com
Display Adv. E-mail: columbinesales@evergreenco.com
Primary Website: columbinecourier.com
Year Established: 1989
Avg Free Circ: 30000
Audit By: Sworn/Estimate/Non-Audited
Audit Date: 10.06.2019
Personnel: Teresa Willmann (Pub.); John Libby (Adv. Dir.); Doug Bell (Ed.); Tom Fidley (Prodn. Mgr.)
Parent company (for newspapers): Landmark Communications, Inc.

COMMERCE CITY SENTINEL EXPRESS

Street address 1: 143 S. 2nd Place
Street address city: Brighton
Street address state: CO
Zip/Postal code: 80601-1626
General Phone: (303)Â 659-2522
General Fax: (303) 659-2901
General/National Adv. E-mail: talexis@metrowestnewspapers.com
Primary Website: commercecitysentinel.com
Avg Paid Circ: 745
Avg Free Circ: 56
Audit By: Sworn/Estimate/Non-Audited
Audit Date: 10.06.2019
Personnel: Steve Smith (Managing Editor); Sean Kennedy (Reporter/ Designer); Belen Ward (Reporter); Teresa Alexis (Account Executive)
Parent company (for newspapers): Landmark Community Newspapers, LLC

CORTEZ JOURNAL

Street address 1: 8 W Main St
Street address city: Cortez
Street address state: CO
Zip/Postal code: 81321-3141
General Phone: (970) 565-8527
General Fax: (970) 565-8532
Advertising Phone: (970) 565-8527
General/National Adv. E-mail: mdrudge@cortezjournal.com
Display Adv. E-mail: advertising@cortezjournal.com
Primary Website: cortezjournal.com
Avg Paid Circ: 7003
Audit By: Sworn/Estimate/Non-Audited
Audit Date: 10.06.2019
Personnel: Suzy Meyer (Pub./Ed.); Mark Drudge (Adv. Mgr.)

CRAIG DAILY PRESS

Street address 1: 466 Yampa Ave
Street address city: Craig
Street address state: CO
Zip/Postal code: 81625-2610
General Phone: (970) 824-7031
General Fax: (970) 824-6810
Advertising Phone: (970) 824-7031
Advertising Fax: (970) 824-6810
Editorial Phone: (970) 824-7031
Editorial Fax: (970) 824-6810
General/National Adv. E-mail: kbalfour@craigdailypress.com
Display Adv. E-mail: kbalfour@craigdailypress.com
Classified Adv. e-mail: veverard@SteamboatToday.com
Editorial e-mail: lschlichtman@SteamboatToday.com
Primary Website: www.craigdailypress.com
Year Established: 1891
Avg Paid Circ: 3400
Sat. Circulation Paid: 9600
Audit By: Sworn/Estimate/Non-Audited
Audit Date: 12.07.2019
Personnel: Renee Campbell (Pub.); Amy Fontenot (Circ. Mgr.); Day Kelsey (Designer); Thomas Martinez (Ed.)
Parent company (for newspapers): Swift Communications, Inc.; Ogden Newspapers Inc.

CRESTED BUTTE NEWS

Street address 1: 301 Belleview
Street address 2: Unit 6A
Street address city: Crested Butte
Street address state: CO
Zip/Postal code: 81224-8706
General Phone: (970) 349-0500
General Fax: (970) 349-9876
Advertising Phone: (970) 349-0500 x 111
General/National Adv. E-mail: nolan@crestedbuttenews.com
Display Adv. E-mail: classifieds@crestedbuttenews.com
Editorial e-mail: editorial@crestedbuttenews.com
Primary Website: crestedbuttenews.com
Avg Paid Circ: 5000
Audit By: Sworn/Estimate/Non-Audited
Audit Date: 10.06.2019

Personnel: Melissa Ruch (Circ. Mgr.); Mark Reaman (Ed.); Tyler Hansen (Prodn. Mgr.); Jeff Nolan (Adv. Rep.); Ashley Cahir (Adv. Rep.)

DENVER BUSINESS JOURNAL

Street address 1: 1700 Broadway
Street address 2: Ste 515
Street address city: Denver
Street address state: CO
Zip/Postal code: 80290-1700
General Phone: (303) 803-9200
General Fax: (303) 803-9203
Advertising Phone: (303) 803-9250
Editorial Phone: (303) 803-9220
General/National Adv. E-mail: djendrusch@bizjournals.com
Display Adv. E-mail: rhesterman@bizjournals.com
Editorial e-mail: nwestergaard@bizjournals.com
Primary Website: denver.bizjournals.com
Audit By: Sworn/Estimate/Non-Audited
Audit Date: 10.06.2019
Personnel: Scott Bemis (Pub.); Neil Westergaard (Ed.)

DOLORES STAR

Street address 1: 8 W Main St
Street address city: Cortez
Street address state: CO
Zip/Postal code: 81321-3141
General Phone: (970) 565-8527
General Fax: (970) 565-8532
Advertising Phone: (970) 565-8527
General/National Adv. E-mail: mdrudge@cortezjournal.com
Display Adv. E-mail: jjones@cortezjournal.com
Editorial e-mail: editor@cortezjournal.com
Primary Website: doloresstar.com
Year Established: 1897
Avg Paid Circ: 1400
Audit By: Sworn/Estimate/Non-Audited
Audit Date: 10.06.2019
Personnel: Suzy Meyer (Pub./Ed.); Mark Drudge (Adv. Dir.)

DOUGLAS COUNTY NEWS PRESS

Street address 1: 9137 Ridgeline Blvd
Street address 2: Suite 210
Street address city: Highlands Ranch
Street address state: CO
Zip/Postal code: 80129-2752
General Phone: (303) 566-4100
General Fax: (303) 660-4826
Advertising Phone: (303) 566-4074
Editorial Phone: (303) 566-4102
General/National Adv. E-mail: eaddenbrooke@ourcoloradonews.com
Display Adv. E-mail: kearhart@ourcoloradonews.com
Editorial e-mail: crotar@ourcoloradonews.com
Primary Website: douglascountynewspress.net
Avg Paid Circ: 554
Avg Free Circ: 376
Audit By: CVC
Audit Date: 30.03.2016
Personnel: Chris Rotar (Ed.); Erin Addenbrooke (Adv. Dir.); Sandra Arellano (Circ. Mgr.); Jerry Healey (Pub.); Karen Earhart (Class. Sales)
Parent company (for newspapers): Colorado Community Media

EASTERN COLORADO NEWS

Street address 1: 1522 Main St
Street address city: Strasburg
Street address state: CO
Zip/Postal code: 80136-7507
General Phone: (303) 622-9796
General Fax: (303) 622-9794
Advertising Phone: (303) 622-9796
General/National Adv. E-mail: dclaussen@i-70scout.com
Display Adv. E-mail: lstegner@i-70scout.com
Classified Adv. e-mail: lstegner@i-70scout.com
Editorial e-mail: dclaussen@i-70scout.com
Primary Website: i-70scout.com
Year Established: 1916
Avg Paid Circ: 1012
Avg Free Circ: 40
Audit By: Sworn/Estimate/Non-Audited
Audit Date: 10.06.2019
Personnel: Douglas Claussen (Ed.); Steven Vetter (Mng. Ed.); LuAnne Stegner (Off. Mng.)

EL PASO COUNTY ADVERTISER & NEWS

Street address 1: 120 E Ohio Ave
Street address city: Fountain
Street address state: CO
Zip/Postal code: 80817-2230
General Phone: (719) 382-5611
General Fax: (719) 382-5614
General/National Adv. E-mail: news@epcan.com
Display Adv. E-mail: ads@epcan.com
Editorial e-mail: news@epcan.com
Primary Website: epcan.com
Year Established: 1958
Avg Paid Circ: 4500
Avg Free Circ: 22
Audit By: Sworn/Estimate/Non-Audited
Audit Date: 10.06.2019
Personnel: Patricia St. Louis (Mng. Ed.); Karen Johnson (General Manager)
Parent company (for newspapers): Shopper Press, Inc.

ELBERT COUNTY NEWS

Street address 1: 9137 Ridgeline Blvd Ste 210
Street address 2: Suite 210
Street address city: Highlands Ranch
Street address state: CO
Zip/Postal code: 80129-2752
General Phone: (303) 566-4100
General Fax: (303) 566-4098
Advertising Phone: (303) 566-4074
Advertising Fax: (303) 566-4098
Editorial Phone: (303) 566-4102
General/National Adv. E-mail: eaddenbrooke@coloradocommunitymedia.com
Display Adv. E-mail: kearhart@coloradocommunitymedia.com
Editorial e-mail: crotar@coloradocommunitymedia.com
Primary Website: www.elbertcountynews.net
Avg Paid Circ: 376
Avg Free Circ: 26
Audit By: CVC
Audit Date: 30.03.2016
Personnel: Chris Rotar (Mng. Ed.); Erin Addenbrooke (Adv. Dir.); Jerry Healey (Pub.); Karen Earhart (Class. Sales)
Parent company (for newspapers): Colorado Community Media

ESTES PARK TRAIL-GAZETTE

Street address 1: 251 Moraine Ave
Street address city: Estes Park
Street address state: CO
Zip/Postal code: 80517
General Phone: (970) 586-3356
General Fax: (970) 586-9532
General/National Adv. E-mail: sales@eptrail.com
Editorial e-mail: tgeditor@eptrail.com
Primary Website: eptrail.com
Year Established: 1922
Avg Paid Circ: 2660
Avg Free Circ: 296
Audit By: Sworn/Estimate/Non-Audited
Audit Date: 10.06.2019
Personnel: Mike Romero (Pub.); Keith Kratochvil (Adv. Mgr.); Tony Wedick (Prodn. Mgr.); Scott Rowen (Mng. Ed.); David Persons (News Ed.); Mike O'Flaherty (Adv. Sales Rep.)
Parent company (for newspapers): Digital First Media

FORT LUPTON PRESS

Street address 1: 143 S 2nd Place
Street address city: Brighton
Street address state: CO
Zip/Postal code: 80601
General Phone: (303) 659-2522
General Fax: (303) 637-7955
Primary Website: ftluptonpress.com
Avg Paid Circ: 4500
Avg Free Circ: 35
Audit By: Sworn/Estimate/Non-Audited
Audit Date: 10.06.2019
Personnel: Taylor White (Ed.)
Parent company (for newspapers): Landmark Communications, Inc.; Landmark Community Newspapers, LLC

GOLDEN TRANSCRIPT

Street address 1: 722 Washington Ave Unit 210
Street address 2: Suite 225
Street address city: Golden
Street address state: CO
Zip/Postal code: 80401-5876
General Phone: (303) 566-4100
General Fax: (303) 566-4098
Advertising Phone: (303) 566-4074
General/National Adv. E-mail: eaddenbrooke@coloradocommunitymedia.com
Display Adv. E-mail: eaddenbrooke@coloradocommunitymedia.com
Primary Website: goldentranscript.net
Year Established: 1866
Avg Paid Circ: 2084
Avg Free Circ: 1936
Audit By: Sworn/Estimate/Non-Audited
Audit Date: 10.06.2019
Personnel: Erin Addenbrooke (VP Slaes & Advertising); Karen Earhart; Mindy Nelon (Adv. Mgr.); Jerry Healey (Pres./Pub.); Glenn Wallace (Mng. Ed.)
Parent company (for newspapers): Colorado Community Media; Milehigh Newspapers

GUNNISON COUNTRY TIMES

Street address 1: 218 N Wisconsin St
Street address city: Gunnison
Street address state: CO
Zip/Postal code: 81230-2626
General Phone: (970) 641-1414
General Fax: N//A
Advertising Phone: (970) 641-1414
Advertising Fax: N/A
Editorial Phone: (970) 641-1414
Editorial Fax: N/A
General/National Adv. E-mail: bobbie@gunnisontimes.com
Display Adv. E-mail: classifieds@gunnisontimes.com
Editorial e-mail: editor@gunnisontimes.com
Primary Website: gunnisontimes.com
Year Established: 1865
Avg Paid Circ: 4000
Audit By: Sworn/Estimate/Non-Audited
Audit Date: 10.06.2019
Personnel: Chris Dickey (Pub./Own.); Will Shoemaker (Ed.)

HAXTUN-FLEMING HERALD

Street address 1: 217 S COLORADO AVE
Street address city: Haxtun
Street address state: CO
Zip/Postal code: 80731
General Phone: (970) 774-6118
General Fax: (970) 774-7690
General/National Adv. E-mail: ads@hfherald.com
Primary Website: hfherald.com
Avg Paid Circ: 1000
Avg Free Circ: 50
Audit By: Sworn/Estimate/Non-Audited
Audit Date: 10.06.2019
Personnel: Candie Salyards (Co-Pub./Own./Mng. Ed./Adv. Rep.); Spring Atchison (Co-Pub./Own./Office Mgr./Adv. Mgr.)

HERALD DEMOCRAT

Street address 1: 717 Harrison Ave
Street address city: Leadville
Street address state: CO
Zip/Postal code: 80461-3561
General Phone: (719) 486-0641
General Fax: (719) 486-0611
Advertising Phone: (719) 486-0641 x 11
Editorial Phone: (719) 486-0641 x 10
General/National Adv. E-mail: advertise@leadvilleherald.com
Display Adv. E-mail: classifieds@leadvilleherald.com
Editorial e-mail: editor@leadvilleherald.com
Primary Website: leadvilleherald.com
Year Established: 1879
Avg Paid Circ: 2400
Audit By: Sworn/Estimate/Non-Audited
Audit Date: 10.06.2019
Personnel: Marcia Martinek (Ed.)
Parent company (for newspapers): Arkansas Valley Publishing

HIGHLANDS RANCH HERALD

Street address 1: 9137 Ridgeline Blvd
Street address 2: Suite 210
Street address city: Highlands Ranch
Street address state: CO
Zip/Postal code: 80129-2752
General Phone: (303) 566-4100
General Fax: (303) 794-1909
Advertising Phone: (303) 566-4078
Editorial Phone: (303) 566-4102
General/National Adv. E-mail: eaddenbrooke@ourcoloradonews.com
Display Adv. E-mail: kearhart@ourcoloradonews.com
Editorial e-mail: crotar@ourcoloradonews.com
Primary Website: highlandsranchherald.net
Avg Paid Circ: 9
Avg Free Circ: 27493
Audit By: CVC
Audit Date: 30.03.2016
Personnel: Chris Rotar (Mng. Ed.); Erin Addenbrooke (Adv. Dir.); Karen Earhart (Class. Sales); Maureen Shively (Adv. Mgr.); Jerry Healey (Pub.)
Parent company (for newspapers): Colorado Community Media

HOLYOKE ENTERPRISE

Street address 1: 130 N Interocean Ave
Street address city: Holyoke
Street address state: CO
Zip/Postal code: 80734-1013
General Phone: (970) 854-2811
General Fax: (970) 854-2232
General/National Adv. E-mail: bbholent@chase3000.com
Primary Website: holyokeenterprise.com
Year Established: 1900
Avg Paid Circ: 1470
Avg Free Circ: 40
Audit By: Sworn/Estimate/Non-Audited
Audit Date: 10.06.2019
Personnel: Brenda Brandt (Pub./Adv. Mgr.); Ashley Sullivan (Circ. Mgr.); Lori Pankonin (Accounting)
Parent company (for newspapers): Johnson Publications

JACKSON COUNTY STAR

Street address 1: PO Box 397
Street address city: Walden
Street address state: CO
Zip/Postal code: 80480-0397
General Phone: (970) 723-4404
General/National Adv. E-mail: jcstarmail@yahoo.com
Primary Website: jacksoncountystar.com
Year Established: 1913
Avg Paid Circ: 1250
Avg Free Circ: 30
Audit By: Sworn/Estimate/Non-Audited
Audit Date: 10.06.2019
Personnel: Matt Shuler (Ed./Pub.); Jim Dustin (Contrib. Ed.); Michelle Shuler (THE BOSS)

JULESBURG ADVOCATE

Street address 1: 114 W 1st St
Street address city: Julesburg
Street address state: CO
Zip/Postal code: 80737-1502
General Phone: (970) 474-3388
General/National Adv. E-mail: advertising@julesburgadvocate.com
Display Adv. E-mail: advertising@julesburgadvocate.com
Editorial e-mail: publisher@julesburgadvocate.com
Primary Website: julesburgadvocate.com
Year Established: 1899
Avg Paid Circ: 600
Audit By: Sworn/Estimate/Non-Audited
Audit Date: 10.06.2019
Parent company (for newspapers): Digital First Media; Prairie Mountain Publishing

KIOWA COUNTY PRESS

Street address 1: 1208 Maine St
Street address city: Eads
Street address state: CO

Zip/Postal code: 81036-9900
General Phone: (719) 438-5800
General/National Adv. E-mail: press@kiowacountypress.com
Primary Website: kiowacountypress.com
Avg Paid Circ: 800
Audit By: Sworn/Estimate/Non-Audited
Audit Date: 10.06.2019
Personnel: Chris Sorensen (Pub.); Connie McPherson (Ed.)

LAKEWOOD SENTINEL

Street address 1: 722 Washington Ave Unit 210
Street address 2: Suite 225
Street address city: Golden
Street address state: CO
Zip/Postal code: 80401-5876
General Phone: (303) 566-4100
General Fax: (303) 468-2592
Advertising Phone: (303) 566-4074
Editorial Phone: (303) 566-4127
General/National Adv. E-mail: eaddenbrooke@coloradocommunitymedia.com
Display Adv. E-mail: audreyb@milehighnews.com
Primary Website: www.coloradocommunitymedia.com
Avg Paid Circ: 437
Avg Free Circ: 14474
Audit By: Sworn/Estimate/Non-Audited
Audit Date: 10.06.2019
Personnel: Erin Addenbrooke; Glenn Wallace (Mng. Ed.); Jerry Healey (Pres./Pub.); Mindy Nelon (Adv. Mgr.); Karen Earhart (Class. Sales Mgr.)
Parent company (for newspapers): Colorado Community Media; Milehigh Newspapers

LONE TREE VOICE

Street address 1: 9137 Ridgeline Blvd
Street address 2: Suite 210
Street address city: Highlands Ranch
Street address state: CO
Zip/Postal code: 80129-2752
General Phone: (303) 566-4100
General Fax: (303) 566-4089
Advertising Phone: (303) 566-4074
Editorial Phone: (303) 566-4102
General/National Adv. E-mail: eaddenbrooke@ourcoloradonews.com
Display Adv. E-mail: vortega@ourcoloradonews.com
Editorial e-mail: crotar@ourcoloradonews.com
Primary Website: ourlonetreenews.com
Avg Paid Circ: 7
Avg Free Circ: 5469
Audit By: CVC
Audit Date: 30.03.2016
Personnel: Chris Rotar (Mng. Ed.); Erin Addenbrooke (Adv. Mgr.); Jerry Healey (Owner); Roy Schuster (Adv. Mgr.); Karen Earhart (Class. Sales)
Parent company (for newspapers): Colorado Community Media

MANCOS TIMES

Street address 1: 8 W Main St
Street address city: Cortez
Street address state: CO
Zip/Postal code: 81321-3141
General Phone: (970) 565-8527
General Fax: (970) 565-8532
Advertising Phone: (970) 565-8527
Editorial Phone: (970) 564-6040
Editorial e-mail: news@the-journal.com
Primary Website: mancostimes.com
Avg Paid Circ: 753
Avg Free Circ: 11
Audit By: Sworn/Estimate/Non-Audited
Audit Date: 10.06.2019
Personnel: Trent Stephens (Sr. Ed.); Patrick Armijo (City Ed./Staff Writer)

MORGAN TIMES REVIEW

Street address 1: 230 A Main St
Street address city: Fort Morgan
Street address state: CO
Zip/Postal code: 80701-2107
General Phone: (970) 867-5651
General Fax: (970) 867-7448
General/National Adv. E-mail: troberts@fortmorgantimes.com
Display Adv. E-mail: ecpcadvertising@dailycamera.com
Editorial e-mail: gbaumgartner@fortmorgantimes.com
Primary Website: fortmorgantimes.com
Year Established: 1884
Avg Free Circ: 6400
Audit By: Sworn/Estimate/Non-Audited
Audit Date: 10.06.2019
Personnel: Brian Porter (Pub.); Geoff Baumgartner (Ed.); Andrew Ohlson (Adv.); Teresa Roberts (Adv.); Sherrie Hunter (Circ. Mgr.)

MOUNTAIN GUIDE

Street address 1: 125 E 2nd St
Street address city: Salida
Street address state: CO
Zip/Postal code: 81201-2114
General Phone: (719) 539-6691
General Fax: (719) 539-6630
General/National Adv. E-mail: vickiesue@avpsalida.com
Display Adv. E-mail: classifieds@themountainmail.com
Primary Website: themountainmail.com
Year Established: 1977
Avg Free Circ: 7500
Audit By: Sworn/Estimate/Non-Audited
Audit Date: 10.06.2019
Personnel: Merle Baranczyk (Pub.); Vickie Vigil (Adv. Dir.); Sandra Christensen (Circ. Direc.); Morris Christensen (Prodn. Direc.); Paul Goetz (Managing Editor)
Parent company (for newspapers): Arkansas Valley Pubishing Co.

NORTH WELD HERALD

Street address 1: 216 1st St
Street address 2: Suite H
Street address city: Eaton
Street address state: CO
Zip/Postal code: 80615-3598
General Phone: (970) 454-5551
General/National Adv. E-mail: nwh@ltbroadband.net
Primary Website: nwherald.qwestoffice.net
Avg Paid Circ: 1950
Audit By: Sworn/Estimate/Non-Audited
Audit Date: 10.06.2019
Personnel: Brenda L. Bormann (Gen. Mgr.); Bruce J. Bormann (Ed.)

NORTHGLENN-THORNTON SENTINEL

Street address 1: 8753 Yates Dr
Street address 2: Suite 225
Street address city: Westminster
Street address state: CO
Zip/Postal code: 80031-6946
General Phone: (303) 566-4100
General Fax: (303) 426-4209
General/National Adv. E-mail: eaddenbrooke@coloradocommunitymedia.com
Display Adv. E-mail: eaddenbrooke@coloradocommunitymedia.com
Primary Website: northglenn-thorntonsentinel.com
Avg Paid Circ: 3124
Avg Free Circ: 1735
Audit By: Sworn/Estimate/Non-Audited
Audit Date: 10.06.2019
Personnel: Erin Addenbrooke (Major Accts. Mgr.); Barb Stolte (Opns. Mgr.); Jerry Healey (Pres./Pub.); Karen Earhart; Josh Sumner (Mng. Ed.)
Parent company (for newspapers): Colorado Community Media

PARKER CHRONICLE

Street address 1: 9137 Ridgeline Blvd
Street address 2: Suite 210
Street address city: Highlands Ranch
Street address state: CO
Zip/Postal code: 80129-2752
General Phone: (303) 566-4100
General Fax: (303) 566-4098
Advertising Phone: (303) 566-4075
Editorial Phone: (303) 566-4102
General/National Adv. E-mail: rmitchell@ourcoloradonews.com
Display Adv. E-mail: vortega@ourcoloradonews.com
Editorial e-mail: crotar@ourcoloradonews.com
Primary Website: parkerchronicle.net
Year Established: 2001
Avg Paid Circ: 12
Avg Free Circ: 20129
Audit By: CVC
Audit Date: 30.03.2016
Personnel: Chris Rotar (Mng. Ed.); Erin Addenbrooke (Adv. Dir.); Sandra Arellano (Circ. Mgr.); Jerry Healey (Pub.); Roy Schuster (Adv. Rep.); Karen Earhart (Class. Sales)
Parent company (for newspapers): Colorado Community Media

PINE RIVER TIMES

Street address 1: 110 Mill St
Street address city: Bayfield
Street address state: CO
Zip/Postal code: 81122
General Phone: (970) 884-2331
General Fax: (970) 884-4385
General/National Adv. E-mail: prt@pinerivertimes.com
Primary Website: pinerivertimes.com
Year Established: 1985
Avg Paid Circ: 1800
Avg Free Circ: 122
Audit By: Sworn/Estimate/Non-Audited
Audit Date: 10.06.2019
Personnel: Robert Mazur (Adv. Dir.); Melanie Brubaker Mazur (Ed.)

POST INDEPENDENT

Street address 1: 823 Blake Ave. STE 101
Street address city: Glenwood Springs
Street address state: CO
Zip/Postal code: 81601-3557
General Phone: (970) 945-8515
Editorial Phone: (970) 384-9114
General/National Adv. E-mail: lmassender@postindependent.com
Display Adv. E-mail: ahewitt@aspentimes.com
Classified Adv. e-mail: classifieds@postindependent.com
Editorial e-mail: editorial@postindependent.com
Primary Website: postindependent.com
Mthly Avg Views: 805889
Mthly Avg Unique Visitors: 187764
Year Established: 1891
Audit By: Sworn/Estimate/Non-Audited
Audit Date: 18.10.2021
Personnel: John Stroud (Ed.); Jerry Raehal (Pub/Ad. Dir.); Jake Marine (Circ. Dir.); Bryce Jacobson (Publisher); Peter Baumann (Editor); ???? ????; Joshua Carney (Sports Ed.); Lisa Curley (Adv. Mgr.)
Parent company (for newspapers): Swift Communications, Inc.; Ogden Newspapers Inc.

RANCHLAND NEWS

Street address 1: 115 Sioux Ave
Street address city: Simla
Street address state: CO
Zip/Postal code: 80835
General Phone: (719) 541-2288
General Fax: (719) 541-2289
Advertising Phone: (719) 541-2288
Advertising Fax: (719) 541-2289
General/National Adv. E-mail: ranchland@bigsandytelco.com
Primary Website: ranchland-news.com
Avg Paid Circ: 4000
Audit By: Sworn/Estimate/Non-Audited
Audit Date: 10.06.2019
Personnel: Mykayla Householder (Co-Pub.); Susan Lister (Co-Pub.); Nikki Lister (Adv. Mgr.); John Hill (Ed.)

RIO BLANCO HERALD TIMES

Street address 1: 304 4th St
Street address 2: PO Box 720
Street address city: Meeker
Street address state: CO
Zip/Postal code: 81641
General Phone: (970) 878-4017
General Fax: (970) 878-4016
Advertising Phone: (970) 878-4017
Editorial Phone: (970) 878-4017
General/National Adv. E-mail: ads@theheraldtimes.com
Display Adv. E-mail: ads@theheraldtimes.com
Classified Adv. e-mail: accounts@theheraldtimes.com
Editorial e-mail: editor@theheraldtimes.com
Primary Website: theheraldtimes.com
Mthly Avg Views: 40000
Mthly Avg Unique Visitors: 10000
Year Established: 1885
Avg Paid Circ: 850
Avg Free Circ: 50
Audit By: Sworn/Estimate/Non-Audited
Audit Date: 10.06.2019
Personnel: Debbie Watson (Front Office Mgr.); Niki Turner (Ed./Pub.); Caitlin Walker (Display Adv.); Lucas Turner; Patti Hoke (Front Office); Selena Steele; Pat Turner (Adv. Acct. Exec.); Jen Hill (Range Corresp.); Reed Kelley (Meeker Corresp.)
Parent company (for newspapers): Golden Lasso Media Inc; Solas Publications, Inc.

SAN MIGUEL BASIN FORUM

Street address 1: PO Box 9
Street address city: Nucla
Street address state: CO
Zip/Postal code: 81424-0009
General Phone: (970) 864-7425
General Fax: (970) 864-2298
General/National Adv. E-mail: ads@nntcwireless.com
Avg Paid Circ: 1397
Avg Free Circ: 15
Audit By: Sworn/Estimate/Non-Audited
Audit Date: 10.06.2019
Personnel: Roger Culver (Ed.); Tanner Nelson (Advertising Assistant)

SILVERTON STANDARD AND THE MINER

Street address 1: 1316 Snowden St.
Street address 2: Ste 308
Street address city: Silverton
Street address state: CO
Zip/Postal code: 81433
General Phone: (970) 387-5477
General Fax: (970) 387-5795
Editorial Phone: (970) 387-5477
General/National Adv. E-mail: silvertonads@gmail.com
Editorial e-mail: editor@silverrtonstandard.com
Primary Website: silvertonstandard.com
Year Established: 1875
Avg Paid Circ: 1050
Audit By: Sworn/Estimate/Non-Audited
Audit Date: 10.06.2019
Personnel: Mark Esper (Ed.)

SKY-HI NEWS

Street address 1: 424 E Agate Ave
Street address city: Granby
Street address state: CO
Zip/Postal code: 80446
General Phone: (970) 887-3334
General Fax: (970) 887-3204
Advertising Phone: (970) 887-3334
Editorial Phone: (970) 887-3334
General/National Adv. E-mail: etrainor@skyhinews.com
Display Adv. E-mail: classifieds@skyhinews.com
Editorial e-mail: bmartin@skyhinews.com
Primary Website: skyhinews.com
Year Established: 1881
Avg Free Circ: 5500
Audit By: Sworn/Estimate/Non-Audited
Audit Date: 10.06.2019
Personnel: Emma Trainor (Publisher); Bryce Martin (Editor)
Parent company (for newspapers): Swift Communications, Inc.; Ogden Newspapers Inc.; Ogden Newspapers

SNOWMASS SUN

Street address 1: 314 E Hyman Ave
Street address city: Aspen
Street address state: CO
Zip/Postal code: 81611-1918
General Phone: (970) 923-5829
General Fax: (970) 923-2571
General/National Adv. E-mail: afreitas@aspentimes.com
Display Adv. E-mail: classifieds@cmnm.org
Editorial e-mail: news@snowmasssun.com
Primary Website: aspentimes.com/news/snowmass
Avg Paid Circ: 2000
Avg Free Circ: 2000
Audit By: Sworn/Estimate/Non-Audited
Audit Date: 10.06.2019

Personnel: Louise Walker (Adv. Acct. Mgr.); Laura Glendenning (Ed.); Rick Carroll (Mng. Ed.); Maria Wimmer (Distrib. Mgr.)
Parent company (for newspapers): Swift Communications, Inc.; Ogden Newspapers Inc.; Ogden Newspapers

STEAMBOAT PILOT

Street address 1: 32 10th St.
Street address 2: Suite C1-C
Street address city: Steamboat Springs
Street address state: CO
Zip/Postal code: 80487
General Phone: (970) 879-1502
General Fax: (970) 879-2888
Advertising Phone: (970) 871-4213
Advertising Fax: (970) 879-7541
Editorial Phone: (970) 879-1502
Editorial Fax: (970) 879-2888
General/National Adv. E-mail: kgilchrist@SteamboatPilot.com
Display Adv. E-mail: Classifieds@SteamboatPilot.com
Editorial e-mail: news@SteamboatPilot.com
Primary Website: steamboatpilot.com
Year Established: 1884
Avg Paid Circ: 9830
Avg Free Circ: 10500
Audit By: Sworn/Estimate/Non-Audited
Audit Date: 10.06.2019
Personnel: Amanda Sundberg (Circ.); Julia Hebard (Adv. Dir.); Logan Molen (Pub.); Lisa Schlichtman (Ed.)
Parent company (for newspapers): Swift Communications, Inc.; Ogden Newspapers Inc.

STRATTON SPOTLIGHT

Street address 1: 210 Colorado Ave.
Street address city: Stratton
Street address state: CO
Zip/Postal code: 80836
General Phone: (719) 348-5913
General Fax: (719) 348-5913
General/National Adv. E-mail: strattonspotlight@yahoo.com
Primary Website: No Website
Avg Paid Circ: 650
Avg Free Circ: 24
Audit By: Sworn/Estimate/Non-Audited
Audit Date: 10.06.2019
Personnel: Nicki Lueck (Owner/Ed.)

THE BRUSH NEWS-TRIBUNE

Street address 1: 216 Clayton St
Street address 2: # 12
Street address city: Brush
Street address state: CO
Zip/Postal code: 80723-2104
General Phone: (970) 842-5516
General Fax: (970) 842-5519
General/National Adv. E-mail: horner@brushnewstribune.com
Display Adv. E-mail: horner@brushnewstribune.com
Editorial e-mail: horner@brushnewstribune.com
Primary Website: brushnewstribune.com
Year Established: 1896
Avg Paid Circ: 1000
Audit By: Sworn/Estimate/Non-Audited
Audit Date: 10.06.2019
Personnel: Iva Kay Horner (Pub./Ed.)
Parent company (for newspapers): Digital First Media; Prairie Mountain Publishing

THE CANYON COURIER

Street address 1: 27902 Meadow Dr
Street address 2: Unit 200
Street address city: Evergreen
Street address state: CO
Zip/Postal code: 80439-2106
General Phone: (303) 350-1039
General Fax: (303) 674-4104
Advertising Phone: (303) 350-1045
Advertising Fax: (303) 674-4104
Editorial Phone: (303) 350-1045
Editorial Fax: (303) 674-4104
General/National Adv. E-mail: sales@evergreenco.com
Display Adv. E-mail: sales@evergreenco.com
Editorial e-mail: circulation@canyoncourier.com
Primary Website: canyoncourier.com
Year Established: 1958
Avg Paid Circ: 9500
Audit By: Sworn/Estimate/Non-Audited
Audit Date: 10.06.2019
Personnel: Vern Manning (Pub./Ed.)
Parent company (for newspapers): Landmark Community Newspapers, LLC

THE CHAFFEE COUNTY TIMES

Street address 1: 209 W Main St
Street address city: Buena Vista
Street address state: CO
Zip/Postal code: 81211-9169
General Phone: (719) 395-8621
General Fax: (719) 395-8623
Advertising Phone: (719) 395-8621 x11
Editorial Phone: (719) 395-8621 x14
General/National Adv. E-mail: ckennedy@chaffeecountytimes.com
Display Adv. E-mail: judie@chaffeecountytimes.com
Editorial e-mail: editor@chaffeecountytimes.com
Primary Website: chaffeecountytimes.com
Year Established: 1879
Avg Paid Circ: 3000
Audit By: Sworn/Estimate/Non-Audited
Audit Date: 10.06.2019
Personnel: Dave Schiefelbein (Ed.); Cristie Kennedy (Advertising director)
Parent company (for newspapers): Arkansas Valley Publishing

THE CONEJOS COUNTY CITIZEN

Street address 1: 835 1st Ave
Street address city: Monte Vista
Street address state: CO
Zip/Postal code: 81144-1474
General Phone: (719) 852-3531
General Fax: (719) 852-3387
General/National Adv. E-mail: bwilliams@valleypublishinginc.com
Display Adv. E-mail: bwilliams@valleypublishinginc.com
Classified Adv. e-mail: rbeutler@valleypublishinginc.com
Editorial e-mail: bwilliams@valleypublishinginc.com
Primary Website: conejoscountycitizen.com
Avg Paid Circ: 250
Avg Free Circ: 30
Audit By: Sworn/Estimate/Non-Audited
Audit Date: 10.06.2019
Personnel: Brian Williams (General Manager/Editor); Shasta Hunter (Circ. Mgr.); Sylvia Lobato (Ed.); Beth Tooker (Class. Mgr.)
Parent company (for newspapers): San Luis Valley Publishing

THE DEL NORTE PROSPECTOR

Street address 1: 835 1st Ave
Street address city: Monte Vista
Street address state: CO
Zip/Postal code: 81144-1474
General Phone: (719) 852-3531
General Fax: (719) 852-3387
Editorial Phone: (719) 852-3531
General/National Adv. E-mail: bwilliams@valleypublishinginc.com
Display Adv. E-mail: bwilliams@valleypublishinginc.com
Classified Adv. e-mail: rbeutler@valleypublishinginc.com
Editorial e-mail: bwilliams@valleypublishinginc.com
Primary Website: delnorteprospector.com
Avg Paid Circ: 650
Audit By: Sworn/Estimate/Non-Audited
Audit Date: 10.06.2019
Personnel: Brian Williams (General Manager/Editor); Shasta Hunter (Circ. Mgr.); Sylvia Lobato (Ed.); Ellie Bone (Prodn. Mgr.); Beth Tooker (Office Mgr.)
Parent company (for newspapers): San Luis Valley Publishing

THE EAGLE VALLEY ENTERPRISE

Street address 1: 200 Lindbergh Drive
Street address city: Gypsum
Street address state: CO
Zip/Postal code: 81637
General Phone: (970) 328-6656
General Fax: (970) 328-6393
Advertising Phone: (970) 328-6656
Editorial Phone: (970) 328-6656
General/National Adv. E-mail: cbukovich@vaildaily.com
Display Adv. E-mail: pschultz@eaglevalleyenterprise.com
Editorial e-mail: pboyd@eaglevalleyenterprise.com
Primary Website: eaglevalleyenterprise.com
Avg Paid Circ: 3400
Avg Free Circ: 300
Audit By: Sworn/Estimate/Non-Audited
Audit Date: 10.06.2019
Personnel: Mark Wurzer (Pub.); Patrick Connolly (Adv. Dir.); David Hakes (Circ. Mgr.); Pam Boyd (Ed.); Carole Bukovich (Display Adv. Rep.)
Parent company (for newspapers): Swift Communications, Inc.; Ogden Newspapers Inc.; Ogden Newspapers

THE ENGLEWOOD HERALD

Street address 1: 9137 Ridgeline Blvd
Street address 2: Suite 210
Street address city: Highlands Ranch
Street address state: CO
Zip/Postal code: 80129-2752
General Phone: (303) 566-4100
General Fax: (303) 566-4099
Advertising Phone: (303) 566-4074
Editorial Phone: (303) 566-4102
General/National Adv. E-mail: eaddenbrooke@coloradocommunitymedia.com
Display Adv. E-mail: kearhart@ourcoloradonews.com
Editorial e-mail: crotar@ourcoloradonews.com
Primary Website: englewoodherald.net
Avg Paid Circ: 296
Avg Free Circ: 178
Audit By: CVC
Audit Date: 30.03.2016
Personnel: Erin Addenbrooke (Adv. Dir.); Karen Earhart; Dawn Brandt (Adv. Rep.); Chris Rotar (Mng. Ed.)
Parent company (for newspapers): Colorado Community Media; Milehigh Newspapers

THE FLORENCE CITIZEN

Street address 1: 201 E 2nd St
Street address city: Florence
Street address state: CO
Zip/Postal code: 81226-1518
General Phone: (719) 784-6383
General/National Adv. E-mail: florencecitizen@aol.com
Primary Website: facebook.com/The-Florence-Citizen-157955437616961
Year Established: 1898
Avg Paid Circ: 900
Avg Free Circ: 35
Audit By: Sworn/Estimate/Non-Audited
Audit Date: 10.06.2019
Personnel: Robert Wood (Ed.)

THE FOWLER TRIBUNE

Street address 1: 112 E Cranston Ave
Street address city: Fowler
Street address state: CO
Zip/Postal code: 81039-1119
General Phone: (719) 263-5311
General Fax: (719) 263-5900
Advertising Phone: (719) 384-1430
Editorial Phone: (719) 263-5311
General/National Adv. E-mail: jason@ljtdmail.com
Editorial e-mail: fowlereditor@ljtdmail.com
Primary Website: fowlertribune.com
Avg Paid Circ: 1475
Audit By: Sworn/Estimate/Non-Audited
Audit Date: 10.06.2019
Personnel: Candi Hill (Pub.); Jason Gallegos (Multimedia Sales Exec.); Ken Hamrick (Sports Ed.); Pam Spitzer (Fowler Tribune Office Mgr.); Rita Ojeda (Class. Adv.)
Parent company (for newspapers): CherryRoad Media; CherryRoad Media

THE JOHNSTOWN BREEZE

Street address 1: 7 S Parish Ave
Street address city: Johnstown
Street address state: CO
Zip/Postal code: 80534-9099
General Phone: (970) 587-4525
General Fax: (970) 587-5882
Advertising Phone: (970) 587-4525
General/National Adv. E-mail: ads@johnstownbreeze.com
Display Adv. E-mail: ads@johnstownbreeze.com
Editorial e-mail: editor@johnstownbreeze.com
Primary Website: johnstownbreeze.com
Mthly Avg Unique Visitors: 10000
Year Established: 1904
Avg Paid Circ: 1500
Avg Free Circ: 50
Audit By: Sworn/Estimate/Non-Audited
Audit Date: 10.06.2019
Personnel: Lesli Bangert (Pub.); Martin B. Hamilton (Ed.)

THE LAMAR LEDGER

Street address 1: 222 S Main St
Street address city: Lamar
Street address state: CO
Zip/Postal code: 81052-2833
General Phone: (719) 336-2266
General Fax: (719) 336-2526
General/National Adv. E-mail: rstagner@lamarledger.com, blasley@lamarledger.com
Display Adv. E-mail: tgodinez@lamarledger.com, ecpcadvertising@dailycamera.com
Editorial e-mail: editor@lamarledger.com
Primary Website: lamarledger.com
Year Established: 1907
Avg Paid Circ: 2000
Avg Free Circ: 3000
Audit By: Sworn/Estimate/Non-Audited
Audit Date: 10.06.2019
Personnel: Chris Frost (Gen. Mgr./Ed.); John Contreras (Sports Ed.); Rick Stagner (Advertising Consultant); Brenda Lasley (Advertising Consultant)
Parent company (for newspapers): Digital First Media

THE LIMON LEADER

Street address 1: 1062 Main St
Street address city: Limon
Street address state: CO
Zip/Postal code: 80828
General Phone: (719) 775-2064
General/National Adv. E-mail: Publisher@thelimonleader.com
Display Adv. E-mail: Publisher@thelimonleader.com
Editorial e-mail: Publisher@thelimonleader.com
Primary Website: thelimonleader.com
Year Established: 1911
Avg Paid Circ: 1000
Audit By: Sworn/Estimate/Non-Audited
Audit Date: 03.06.2024
Personnel: Mykayla Householder (Publisher); Will Bublitz (Ed.)
Parent company (for newspapers): SMH Publications LLC

THE LITTLETON INDEPENDENT

Street address 1: 9137 Ridgeline Blvd
Street address 2: Suite 210
Street address city: Highlands Ranch
Street address state: CO
Zip/Postal code: 80129-2752
General Phone: (303) 566-4100
General Fax: (303) 566-4099
Advertising Phone: (303) 566-4073
Editorial Phone: (303) 566-4102
General/National Adv. E-mail: cwoodman@ourcoloradonews.com
Display Adv. E-mail: vortega@ourcoloradonews.com
Editorial e-mail: crotar@ourcoloradonews.com
Primary Website: littletonindependent.net
Avg Paid Circ: 1407
Avg Free Circ: 236
Audit By: CVC
Audit Date: 30.03.2016
Personnel: Chris Rotar (Mng. Ed.); Sandra Arellano (Circ. Mgr.); Erin Addenbrooke (Adv. Dir.); Jerry Healey; Dawn Brandt (Adv. Rep.); Karen Earhart (Class. Sales)
Parent company (for newspapers): Colorado Community Media

THE LYONS RECORDER

Street address 1: 415 Main St
Street address 2: Ste C
Street address city: Lyons
Street address state: CO
Zip/Postal code: 80540
General Phone: (303) 823-6625
General Fax: n/a
Advertising Phone: (303) 823-6625
Advertising Fax: n/a

Editorial Phone: (303) 823-6625
Editorial Fax: n/a
General/National Adv. E-mail: ads@lyonsrecorder.com
Display Adv. E-mail: ads@lyonsrecorder.com
Classified Adv. e-mail: ads@lyonsrecorder.com
Editorial e-mail: editor@lyonsrecorder.com
Primary Website: lyonsrecorder.com
Year Established: 1900
Avg Paid Circ: 400
Avg Free Circ: 10
Sat. Circulation Paid: 0
Sat. Circulation Free: 0
Sun. Circulation Paid: 0
Sun. Circulation Free: 0
Audit By: Sworn/Estimate/Non-Audited
Audit Date: 10.06.2019
Personnel: Lora Gilson (Pub.); Joseph Lekarczyk (Ed.)

THE MINERAL COUNTY MINER

Street address 1: 835 1st Ave
Street address city: Monte Vista
Street address state: CO
Zip/Postal code: 81144-1474
General Phone: (719) 852-3531
General Fax: (719) 852-3387
Editorial Phone: (719) 852-3531
Display Adv. E-mail: montevistaads@gmail.com
Classified Adv. e-mail: montevistaclass@gmail.com
Editorial e-mail: montevistanews@gmail.com
Primary Website: mineralcountyminer.com
Avg Paid Circ: 650
Avg Free Circ: 30
Audit By: Sworn/Estimate/Non-Audited
Audit Date: 10.06.2019
Personnel: Jennifer Alonzo (Ed.); Beth Tooker (Office Mgr.)
Parent company (for newspapers): San Luis Valley Publishing

THE MONTE VISTA JOURNAL

Street address 1: 835 1st Ave
Street address city: Monte Vista
Street address state: CO
Zip/Postal code: 81144-1474
General Phone: (719) 852-3531
General Fax: (719) 852-3387
Editorial Phone: (719) 852-3531
Display Adv. E-mail: montevistaads@gmail.com
Classified Adv. e-mail: montevistaclass@gmail.com
Editorial e-mail: montevistanews@gmail.com
Primary Website: montevistajournal.com
Avg Paid Circ: 1200
Avg Free Circ: 30
Audit By: Sworn/Estimate/Non-Audited
Audit Date: 10.06.2019
Personnel: Jennifer Alonzo (Publisher); Beth Tooker
Parent company (for newspapers): San Luis Valley Publishing

THE NORWOOD POST

Street address 1: 307 E Colorado Ave
Street address city: Telluride
Street address state: CO
Zip/Postal code: 81435
General Phone: (970) 728-9788
General Fax: (970) 728-8061
Advertising Phone: (503) 477-2923 x 24
Editorial Phone: (503) 477-2923
General/National Adv. E-mail: dusty@telluridedailyplanet.com
Display Adv. E-mail: dusty@telluridedailyplanet.com
Editorial e-mail: norwoodpost@yahoo.com
Primary Website: telluridenews.com/norwood_post/front
Avg Paid Circ: 1000
Audit By: Sworn/Estimate/Non-Audited
Audit Date: 10.06.2019
Personnel: Andrew Mirrington (Pub.); Dusty Atheron (Assoc. Pub.); Lea St. Amand (Mktg./Sales Coord.); Shelly Bolus (Office Mgr.); Regan Tuttle (Ed.)

THE PAGOSA SPRINGS SUN

Street address 1: 466 Pagosa St
Street address city: Pagosa Springs
Street address state: CO
Zip/Postal code: 81147-9955
General Phone: (970) 264-2100
General Fax: (970) 264-2103
General/National Adv. E-mail: tjay@pagosasun.com
Display Adv. E-mail: classads@pagosasun.com
Editorial e-mail: editor@pagosasun.com
Primary Website: pagosasun.com
Year Established: 1909
Avg Paid Circ: 4645
Audit By: Sworn/Estimate/Non-Audited
Audit Date: 10.06.2019
Personnel: Terri House (Owner/Pub./Ed.); Shari Pierce (Adv. Mgr.); Randi Pierce (Asst. Ed.); Missy Phelan (Class. Adv.)

THE PIKES PEAK COURIER

Street address 1: 1200 E. Hwy. 24
Street address 2: Suite B
Street address city: Woodland Park
Street address state: CO
Zip/Postal code: 80863
General Phone: (719) 687-3006
General Fax: (719) 687-3009
Advertising Phone: (719) 686-6457
Editorial Phone: (719) 963-8831 x111
General/National Adv. E-mail: eaddenbrooke@ourcoloradonews.com
Display Adv. E-mail: eaddenbrooke@ourcoloradonews.com
Editorial e-mail: rcarrigan@ourcoloradonews.com
Primary Website: pikespeakcourier.net
Avg Paid Circ: 2500
Avg Free Circ: 250
Audit By: Sworn/Estimate/Non-Audited
Audit Date: 10.06.2019
Personnel: Rob Carrigan (Pub.); Danny Summers (Sports/News Reporter); David Lowe (Adv. Rep.)
Parent company (for newspapers): Pikes Peak Newspapers, Inc.

THE SIGNATURE

Street address 1: 124 N Main St
Street address city: La Veta
Street address state: CO
Zip/Postal code: 81055
General Phone: (719) 742-5591
General Fax: (719) 742-3183
Advertising Phone: (719) 742-5591
Advertising Fax: (719) 742-3183
Editorial e-mail: editor@signaturenewspaper.com
Primary Website: signaturenewspaper.com
Avg Paid Circ: 2500
Avg Free Circ: 100
Audit By: Sworn/Estimate/Non-Audited
Audit Date: 10.06.2019
Personnel: Renee Rinehart (Ed.)

THE SOPRIS SUN

Street address 1: 520 S 3rd St
Street address city: Carbondale
Street address state: CO
Zip/Postal code: 81623-2059
General Phone: (970) 510-3003
Advertising Phone: (970) 510-0246
General/National Adv. E-mail: news@soprissun.com
Editorial e-mail: news@soprissun.com
Primary Website: soprissun.com
Mthly Avg Views: 8900
Mthly Avg Unique Visitors: 2600
Year Established: 2009
Avg Free Circ: 4200
Audit By: Sworn/Estimate/Non-Audited
Audit Date: 10.06.2019

THE SOUTH FORK TINES

Street address 1: 835 1st Ave
Street address city: Monte Vista
Street address state: CO
Zip/Postal code: 81144-1474
General Phone: (719) 852-3531
General Fax: (719) 852-3387
Editorial Phone: (719) 852-3531
General/National Adv. E-mail: bwilliams@valleypublishinginc.com
Display Adv. E-mail: bwilliams@valleypublishinginc.com
Classified Adv. e-mail: rbeutler@valleypublishinginc.com
Editorial e-mail: bwilliams@valleypublishinginc.com
Primary Website: southforktines.com
Avg Paid Circ: 650
Avg Free Circ: 30
Audit By: Sworn/Estimate/Non-Audited
Audit Date: 10.06.2019
Personnel: Brian Williams (General Manager/Editor); Beth Tooker (Office Mgr.)
Parent company (for newspapers): San Luis Valley Publishing

THE TRIBUNE

Street address 1: 153 Washington St
Street address city: Monument
Street address state: CO
Zip/Postal code: 80132-9181
General Phone: (719) 686-6447
General Fax: (719) 687-3009
Advertising Phone: (719) 687-306 x 111
Editorial Phone: (719) 687-306 x 111
General/National Adv. E-mail: rcarrigan@ourcoloradonews.com
Display Adv. E-mail: vortega@ourcoloradonews.com
Editorial e-mail: rcarrigan@ourcoloradonews.com
Primary Website: pikespeaknewspapers.com
Year Established: 1964
Avg Paid Circ: 12000
Avg Free Circ: 107
Audit By: Sworn/Estimate/Non-Audited
Audit Date: 10.06.2019
Personnel: Rob Carrigan (pub.); Danny Summers (News/Sports Reporter); David Lowe (Advertising Rep.)
Parent company (for newspapers): Pikes Peak Newspapers, Inc.

TRI-COUNTY TRIBUNE

Street address 1: 625 2nd Ave
Street address city: Deer Trail
Street address state: CO
Zip/Postal code: 80105-8078
General Phone: (303) 769-4646
General Fax: (303) 769-4650
General/National Adv. E-mail: rbell357@aol.com
Avg Paid Circ: 450
Audit By: Sworn/Estimate/Non-Audited
Audit Date: 10.06.2019
Personnel: Harry L. Venter (Ed.)

VERISON

Street address 1: 321 Main Ave
Street address city: Flagler
Street address state: CO
Zip/Postal code: 80815-9237
General Phone: (719) 349-4448
General Fax: (719) 349-4448
Advertising Phone: (719) 349-4448
Advertising Fax: (719) 349-4448
Editorial Phone: (719) 349-4448
Editorial Fax: (719) 349-4448
General/National Adv. E-mail: advertise@milesaver.com
Year Established: 1911
Avg Paid Circ: 1400
Avg Free Circ: 60
Audit By: Sworn/Estimate/Non-Audited
Audit Date: 10.06.2019
Personnel: Thomas E. Bredehoft (Ed.)
Parent company (for newspapers): TBP Publishing, Inc.

WESTMINSTER WINDOW

Street address 1: 8753 Yates Dr
Street address 2: Suite 200
Street address city: Westminster
Street address state: CO
Zip/Postal code: 80031-6946
General Phone: (303) 566-4100
General Fax: (303) 566-4098
General/National Adv. E-mail: eaddenbrooke@coloradocommunitymedia.com
Display Adv. E-mail: kearhart@coloradocommunitymedia.com
Editorial e-mail: gwallace@coloradocommunitymedia.com
Primary Website: westminsterwindow.com
Avg Paid Circ: 2200
Avg Free Circ: 1150
Audit By: Sworn/Estimate/Non-Audited
Audit Date: 10.06.2019
Personnel: Erin Addenbrooke (Adv. Dir.); Barbara Stolte (Gen. Mgr./Mktg. Mgr.); Josh Sumner (Mng. Ed.)
Parent company (for newspapers): Colorado Community Media

WET MOUNTAIN TRIBUNE

Street address 1: 404 E Main St
Street address city: Westcliffe
Street address state: CO
Zip/Postal code: 81252-8307
General Phone: (719) 783-2361
General Fax: (719) 783-3725
General/National Adv. E-mail: ads@wetmountaintribune.com
Display Adv. E-mail: frontdesk@wetmountaintribune.com
Editorial e-mail: editor@wetmountaintribune.com
Primary Website: wetmountaintribune.com
Year Established: 1883
Avg Paid Circ: 3000
Avg Free Circ: 0
Audit By: Sworn/Estimate/Non-Audited
Audit Date: 10.06.2019
Personnel: James A. Little (Ed./Pub.); Charlotte Curtis (Graphic Dsgnr.); Lynne Tabb (Adv. Dir.); Blair Little (Admin. Asst.)
Parent company (for newspapers): Little Publishing Company, Inc.

WHEAT RIDGE TRANSCRIPT

Street address 1: 722 Washington Ave Unit 210
Street address 2: Suite 225
Street address city: Golden
Street address state: CO
Zip/Postal code: 80401-5876
General Phone: (303) 566-4100
General Fax: (303) 566-4098
Advertising Phone: (303) 566-4074
General/National Adv. E-mail: eaddenbrooke@coloradocommunitymedia.com
Display Adv. E-mail: eaddenbrooke@coloradocommunitymedia.com
Primary Website: goldentranscript.net
Year Established: 1866
Avg Paid Circ: 2084
Avg Free Circ: 1936
Audit By: Sworn/Estimate/Non-Audited
Audit Date: 10.06.2019
Personnel: Erin Addenbrooke (VP Slaes & Advertising); Karen Earhart; Mindy Nelon (Adv. Mgr.); Jerry Healey (Pres./Pub.); Glenn Wallace (Mng. Ed.)
Parent company (for newspapers): Colorado Community Media; Milehigh Newspapers

WINDSOR BEACON

Street address 1: 1300 Riverside Ave
Street address city: Fort Collins
Street address state: CO
Zip/Postal code: 80524-4353
General Phone: (970) 686-9646
General Fax: (970) 686-9647
Advertising Phone: (970) 416-3989
Editorial Phone: (970) 224-7755
General/National Adv. E-mail: jkurtyak@coloradoan.com
Display Adv. E-mail: jkurtyak@coloradoan.com
Editorial e-mail: editor@windsorbeacon.com
Primary Website: coloradoan.com/windsor-beacon
Year Established: 1806
Avg Paid Circ: 0
Avg Free Circ: 5914
Audit By: Sworn/Estimate/Non-Audited
Audit Date: 10.06.2019
Personnel: David Persons (Pub./Ed.); Mary Bline (Adv. Rep.); Jack Bline (Adv. Rep.)
Parent company (for newspapers): Gannett

WINDSOR NOW

Street address 1: 423 Main St
Street address city: Windsor
Street address state: CO
Zip/Postal code: 80550-5129
General Phone: (970) 674-1431
Advertising Phone: (970) 392-4406
General/National Adv. E-mail: advertising@greeleytribune.com
Display Adv. E-mail: advertising@greeleytribune.com
Editorial e-mail: editorial@greeleytribune.com
Primary Website: mywindsornow.com
Year Established: 2007
Avg Paid Circ: 8065

Audit By: Sworn/Estimate/Non-Audited
Audit Date: 10.06.2019
Personnel: Bart Smith (Pub.); Randy Bangert (Ed.); Bruce Dennis (Sales Mgr.); Becky Colvin (Acct. Mgr.)
Parent company (for newspapers): Swift Communications, Inc.; Greeley Publishing Company

CONNECTICUT

ANTIQUES & THE ARTS WEEKLY

Street address 1: 5 Church Hill Rd
Street address city: Newtown
Street address state: CT
Zip/Postal code: 06470-1605
General Phone: (203) 426-3141
General Fax: (203) 426-1394
Advertising Phone: (203) 426-8036
Advertising Fax: (203) 426-1394
General/National Adv. E-mail: sue@thebee.com
Editorial e-mail: antiques@thebee.com
Primary Website: antiquesandthearts.com
Year Established: 1963
Audit By: Sworn/Estimate/Non-Audited
Audit Date: 10.06.2019
Personnel: R. Scudder Smith (Pub & Ed)
Parent company (for newspapers): Bee Publishing Co., Inc.

BERLIN CITIZEN

Street address 1: 500 S Broad St
Street address 2: Ste 2
Street address city: Meriden
Street address state: CT
Zip/Postal code: 06450-6643
General Phone: (203) 235-1661
General Fax: (203) 639-0210
Advertising Phone: (203) 317-2312
Advertising Fax: (203) 235-4048
Editorial Phone: (203) 317-2447
General/National Adv. E-mail: advertising@record-journal.com
Editorial e-mail: newsroom@record-journal.com
Primary Website: berlincitizen.com
Year Established: 1997
Avg Free Circ: 9200
Audit By: Sworn/Estimate/Non-Audited
Audit Date: 10.06.2019
Personnel: Eliot C. White (Pub.); Kimberley Boath (Adv. Dir.); Robert Mayer (Mng. Ed.); Nick Carroll (Ed)
Parent company (for newspapers): The Record-Journal Publishing Co.

BRIDGEPORT NEWS

Street address 1: 1000 Bridgeport Ave
Street address city: Shelton
Street address state: CT
Zip/Postal code: 06484-4660
General Phone: (203) 926-2080
General Fax: (203) 926-2091
Advertising Phone: (203) 402-2329
Editorial Phone: (203) 402-2355
General/National Adv. E-mail: dpross@hersamacorn.com
Display Adv. E-mail: class@hersamacorn.com
Editorial e-mail: bridgeportnews@hersamacorn.com
Primary Website: thebridgeportnews.com
Year Established: 1985
Avg Paid Circ: 9797
Audit By: Sworn/Estimate/Non-Audited
Audit Date: 10.06.2019
Personnel: Susan Chaves (Ed.); Tom Nash (Pub.); Nancy Doniger (Mng. Ed.)

CITIZEN'S NEWS

Street address 1: 389 Meadow Street, P.O. Box 2090
Street address city: Waterbury
Street address state: CT
Zip/Postal code: 6722
General Phone: (203) 729-2228
General Fax: (203) 729-9099
Advertising Phone: (203) 729-2228 ext. 11
Editorial Phone: (203) 729-2228 ext. 20
Primary Website: mycitizensnews.com
Avg Free Circ: 15000
Audit By: Sworn/Estimate/Non-Audited
Audit Date: 10.06.2019
Parent company (for newspapers): American-Republican, Incorporated

COURANT COMMUNITY - COLCHESTER

Street address 1: 285 Broad St
Street address city: Hartford
Street address state: CT
Zip/Postal code: 06105-3785
General Phone: (860) 241-6200
General Fax: (860) 520-6941
Editorial Fax: (860) 520-69411
General/National Adv. E-mail: lckelleher@courant.com
Display Adv. E-mail: classifieds@courant.com
Editorial e-mail: agriffin@courant.com
Primary Website: courant.com/community/colchester-edition
Avg Free Circ: 13620
Audit By: Sworn/Estimate/Non-Audited
Audit Date: 10.06.2019
Personnel: Christine Neves (Community Sales Mgr.); Mary Lou Stoneburner (Adv. Sales); Brian McEnery (Circ.); Mary Lou Stoneburner (VP of Adv.); Andrew S. Julien (Pub.)

COURANT COMMUNITY - EAST HARTFORD

Street address 1: 285 Broad St
Street address city: Hartford
Street address state: CT
Zip/Postal code: 06105-3785
General Phone: (860) 241-6200
General Fax: (860) 520-6941
General/National Adv. E-mail: lckelleher@courant.com
Display Adv. E-mail: classifieds@courant.com
Editorial e-mail: agriffin@courant.com
Primary Website: courant.com/community/east-hartford
Mthly Avg Views: 85738
Mthly Avg Unique Visitors: 18205
Avg Free Circ: 13289
Audit By: Sworn/Estimate/Non-Audited
Audit Date: 10.06.2019
Personnel: Mary Lou Stoneburner (Adv. Sales); Christine Neves (Community Sales Mgr.); Brian McEnery (Circ. Mgr); Andrew S. Julien (Pub.); Mary Lou Stoneburner (VP of Adv.)

COURANT COMMUNITY - ENFIELD

Street address 1: 285 Broad St
Street address city: Hartford
Street address state: CT
Zip/Postal code: 06105-3785
General Phone: (860) 241-6200
General Fax: (860) 520-6941
General/National Adv. E-mail: lckelleher@courant.com
Display Adv. E-mail: classifieds@courant.com
Editorial e-mail: agriffin@courant.com
Primary Website: courant.com/community/enfield
Avg Free Circ: 18829
Audit By: Sworn/Estimate/Non-Audited
Audit Date: 10.06.2019
Personnel: Mary Lou Stoneburner (Adv. Sales); Brian McEnery (Circ.); Christine Neves (Community Sales Mgr.); Andrew S. Julien (Pub.Pub./Ed.-in-Chief); Mary Lou Stoneburner (VP of Adv.)

COURANT COMMUNITY - GLASTONBURY

Street address 1: 285 Broad St
Street address city: Hartford
Street address state: CT
Zip/Postal code: 06105-3785
General Phone: (860) 241-6200
General Fax: (860) 520-6941
General/National Adv. E-mail: lckelleher@courant.com
Display Adv. E-mail: classifieds@courant.com
Editorial e-mail: agriffin@courant.com
Primary Website: courant.com/community/glastonbury
Avg Free Circ: 9856
Audit By: Sworn/Estimate/Non-Audited
Audit Date: 10.06.2019
Personnel: Mary Lou Stoneburner (Adv. Sales); Brian McEnery (Circ.); Mary Lou Stoneburner (VP of Adv.); Christine Neves (Community Sales Mgr.); Andrew S. Julien (Pub./Ed.-in-Chief)

COURANT COMMUNITY - HEBRON

Street address 1: 285 Broad St
Street address city: Hartford
Street address state: CT
Zip/Postal code: 06105-3785
General Phone: (860) 241-6200
General Fax: (860) 520-6941
General/National Adv. E-mail: lckelleher@courant.com
Display Adv. E-mail: classifieds@courant.com
Editorial e-mail: agriffin@courant.com
Primary Website: courant.com/community/hebron-edition
Avg Free Circ: 7867
Audit By: Sworn/Estimate/Non-Audited
Audit Date: 10.06.2019
Personnel: Mary Lou Stoneburner (Adv. Sales); Brian McEnery (Circ.); Christine Neves (Community Sales Mgr.); Mary Lou Stoneburner (VP of Adv.); Andrew S. Julien (Pub./Ed.-in-Chief)

COURANT COMMUNITY - KILLINGLY

Street address 1: 285 Broad St
Street address city: Hartford
Street address state: CT
Zip/Postal code: 06105-3785
General Phone: (860) 241-6200
General Fax: (860) 520-6941
General/National Adv. E-mail: lckelleher@courant.com
Display Adv. E-mail: classifieds@courant.com
Editorial e-mail: agriffin@courant.com
Primary Website: courant.com/community
Avg Free Circ: 16076
Audit By: Sworn/Estimate/Non-Audited
Audit Date: 10.06.2019
Personnel: Mary Lou Stoneburner (Adv. Sales); Brian McEnery (Circ.); Christine Neves (Community Sales Mgr.); Mary Lou Stoneburner (VP of Adv.); Andrew S. Julien (Pub./Ed.-in-Chief)

COURANT COMMUNITY - MANCHESTER

Street address 1: 285 Broad St
Street address city: Hartford
Street address state: CT
Zip/Postal code: 06105-3785
General Phone: (860) 241-6200
General Fax: (860) 520-6941
General/National Adv. E-mail: lckelleher@courant.com
Display Adv. E-mail: classifieds@courant.com
Editorial e-mail: agriffin@courant.com
Primary Website: courant.com/community
Avg Free Circ: 15633
Audit By: Sworn/Estimate/Non-Audited
Audit Date: 10.06.2019
Personnel: Mary Lou Stoneburner (Adv. Sales); Brian McEnery (Circ.); Mary Lou Stoneburner (VP of Adv.); Christine Neves (Community Sales Mgr.); Andrew S. Julien (Pub./Ed.-in-Chief)

COURANT COMMUNITY - PUTNAM

Street address 1: 285 Broad St
Street address city: Hartford
Street address state: CT
Zip/Postal code: 06105-3785
General Phone: (860) 241-6200
General Fax: (860) 520-6941
General/National Adv. E-mail: lckelleher@courant.com
Display Adv. E-mail: classifieds@courant.com
Editorial e-mail: agriffin@courant.com
Primary Website: courant.com/community
Avg Free Circ: 9598
Audit By: Sworn/Estimate/Non-Audited
Audit Date: 10.06.2019
Personnel: Mary Lou Stoneburner (Adv. Sales); Brian McEnery (Circ.); Christine Neves (Community Sales Mgr.); Mary Lou Stoneburner (VP of Adv.); Andrew S. Julien (Pub./Ed.-in-Chief)

COURANT COMMUNITY - SOUTH WINDSOR

Street address 1: 285 Broad St
Street address city: Hartford
Street address state: CT
Zip/Postal code: 06105-3785
General Phone: (860) 241-6200
General Fax: (860) 520-6941
General/National Adv. E-mail: lckelleher@courant.com
Display Adv. E-mail: classifieds@courant.com
Editorial e-mail: agriffin@courant.com
Primary Website: courant.com/community
Avg Free Circ: 7604
Audit By: Sworn/Estimate/Non-Audited
Audit Date: 10.06.2019
Personnel: Mary Lou Stoneburner (Adv. Sales); Brian McEnery (Circ.); Andrew S. Julien (Pub./Ed.-in-Chief); Christine Neves (Community Sales Mgr.); Mary Lou Stoneburner (VP of Adv.)

COURANT COMMUNITY - STAFFORD

Street address 1: 285 Broad St
Street address city: Hartford
Street address state: CT
Zip/Postal code: 06105-3785
General Phone: (860) 241-6200
General Fax: (860) 520-6941
General/National Adv. E-mail: lckelleher@courant.com
Display Adv. E-mail: classifieds@courant.com
Editorial e-mail: agriffin@courant.com
Primary Website: courant.com/community
Avg Free Circ: 7607
Audit By: Sworn/Estimate/Non-Audited
Audit Date: 10.06.2019
Personnel: Mary Lou Stoneburner (Adv. Sales); Brian McEnery (Circ.); Andrew S. Julien (Pub./Ed.-in-Chief); Christine Neves (Community Sales Mgr.); Mary Lou Stoneburner (VP of Adv.)

COURANT COMMUNITY - VALLEY

Street address 1: 285 Broad St
Street address city: Hartford
Street address state: CT
Zip/Postal code: 06105-3785
General Phone: (860) 241-6200
General Fax: (860) 520-6941
General/National Adv. E-mail: lckelleher@courant.com
Display Adv. E-mail: classifieds@courant.com
Editorial e-mail: agriffin@courant.com
Primary Website: courant.com/community
Avg Free Circ: 7962
Audit By: Sworn/Estimate/Non-Audited
Audit Date: 10.06.2019
Personnel: Mary Lou Stoneburner (Adv. Sales); Brian McEnery (Circ.); Andrew S. Julien (Pub./Ed.-in-Chief); Christine Neves (Community Sales Mgr.); Mary Lou Stoneburner (VP of Adv.)

COURANT COMMUNITY - VERNON

Street address 1: 285 Broad St
Street address city: Hartford
Street address state: CT
Zip/Postal code: 06105-3785
General Phone: (860) 241-6200
General Fax: (860) 520-6941
General/National Adv. E-mail: lckelleher@courant.com
Display Adv. E-mail: classifieds@courant.com
Editorial e-mail: agriffin@courant.com
Primary Website: courant.com/community
Avg Free Circ: 15816
Audit By: Sworn/Estimate/Non-Audited
Audit Date: 10.06.2019
Personnel: Mary Lou Stoneburner (Adv. Sales); Brian McEnery (Circ.); Andrew S. Julien (Pub./Ed.-in-Chief); Christine Neves (Community Sales Mgr.); Mary Lou Stoneburner (VP of Adv.)

COURANT COMMUNITY - WEST HARTFORD

Street address 1: 285 Broad St
Street address city: Hartford
Street address state: CT
Zip/Postal code: 06105-3719
General Phone: (860) 241-6200
Editorial Fax: (860) 520-6941
General/National Adv. E-mail: lckelleher@courant.com
Display Adv. E-mail: classifieds@courant.com
Editorial e-mail: agriffin@courant.com
Audit By: Sworn/Estimate/Non-Audited
Audit Date: 10.06.2019

Personnel: Christine Neves (Community Sales Mgr.); Andrew S. Julien (Pub./Ed.-in-Chief); Alaine Griffin (Towns Ed.); Jeff Otterbein (Sports Ed.); Mary Lou Stoneburner (VP of Adv.); Mary Lou Stoneburner (VP of Adv.)

COURANT COMMUNITY - WETHERSFIELD

Street address 1: 285 Broad St
Street address city: Hartford
Street address state: CT
Zip/Postal code: 06105-3785
General Phone: (860) 241-6200
General Fax: (860) 520-6941
General/National Adv. E-mail: lckelleher@courant.com
Display Adv. E-mail: classifieds@courant.com
Editorial e-mail: agriffin@courant.com
Primary Website: courant.com/community
Audit By: Sworn/Estimate/Non-Audited
Audit Date: 10.06.2019
Personnel: Christine Neves (Community Sales Mgr.); Andrew S. Julien (Pub.); Alaine Griffin (Towns Ed.); Jeff Otterbein (Sports Ed.); Mary Lou Stoneburner (VP of Adv.)

COURANT COMMUNITY - WINDHAM

Street address 1: 285 Broad St
Street address city: Hartford
Street address state: CT
Zip/Postal code: 06105-3785
General Phone: (860) 241-6200
General Fax: (860) 520-6941
General/National Adv. E-mail: lckelleher@courant.com
Display Adv. E-mail: classifieds@courant.com
Editorial e-mail: agriffin@courant.com
Primary Website: courant.com/community
Avg Free Circ: 12734
Audit By: Sworn/Estimate/Non-Audited
Audit Date: 10.06.2019
Personnel: Mary Lou Stoneburner (Adv. Sales); Brian McEnery (Circ.); Andrew S. Julien (Pub./Ed.-in-Chief); Christine Neves (Community Sales Mgr.); Mary Lou Stoneburner (VP of Adv.)

COURANT COMMUNITY - WINDSOR

Street address 1: 285 Broad St
Street address city: Hartford
Street address state: CT
Zip/Postal code: 06105-3785
General Phone: (860) 241-6200
General Fax: (860) 520-6941
General/National Adv. E-mail: lckelleher@courant.com
Display Adv. E-mail: classifieds@courant.com
Editorial e-mail: agriffin@courant.com
Primary Website: courant.com/community
Avg Free Circ: 9689
Audit By: Sworn/Estimate/Non-Audited
Audit Date: 10.06.2019
Personnel: Mary Lou Stoneburner (Adv. Sales); Andrew S. Julien (Pub./Ed.-in-Chief); Brian McEnery (Circ.); Christine Neves (Community Sales Mgr.); Mary Lou Stoneburner (VP of Adv.)

COURANT COMMUNITY - WINDSOR LOCKS

Street address 1: 285 Broad St
Street address city: Hartford
Street address state: CT
Zip/Postal code: 06105-3785
General Phone: (860) 241-6200
General Fax: (860) 520-6941
General/National Adv. E-mail: lckelleher@courant.com
Display Adv. E-mail: classifieds@courant.com
Editorial e-mail: agriffin@courant.com
Primary Website: courant.com/community
Avg Free Circ: 9887
Audit By: Sworn/Estimate/Non-Audited
Audit Date: 10.06.2019
Personnel: Andrew S. Julien (Pub./Ed.-in-Chief); Mary Lou Stoneburner (Adv. Sales); Brian McEnery (Circ.); Christine Neves (Community Sales Mgr.); Mary Lou Stoneburner (VP of Adv.)

DARIEN NEWS

Street address 1: 410 State St
Street address city: Bridgeport
Street address state: CT
Zip/Postal code: 06604-4501
General Phone: (203) 333-161
General Fax: (203) 972-4404
Editorial Phone: (203) 330-6581
General/National Adv. E-mail: mmcabee@scni.com
Editorial e-mail: avarese@bcnnew.com
Primary Website: dariennewsonline.com
Avg Paid Circ: 784
Avg Free Circ: 12
Audit By: Sworn/Estimate/Non-Audited
Audit Date: 10.06.2019
Personnel: Jerrod Ferrari (Ed.); Doreen Madden; Paul Barbetta (Grp. Pub./Pres.); Bill Mason (Circ. Dir.); Anthony Parelli (Sports Ed.)
Parent company (for newspapers): Hearst Communications, Inc.

DARIEN TIMES

Street address 1: 10 Corbin Dr
Street address 2: Fl 3rd
Street address city: Darien
Street address state: CT
Zip/Postal code: 06820-5403
General Phone: (203) 656-4230
General Fax: (203) 656-4240
Advertising Phone: (203) 966-9541
Editorial Phone: (203) 656-4230
General/National Adv. E-mail: lspicehandler@hersamacorn.com
Display Adv. E-mail: class@hersamacorn.com
Editorial e-mail: editor@darientimes.com
Primary Website: darientimes.com
Year Established: 1993
Avg Paid Circ: 6015
Audit By: Sworn/Estimate/Non-Audited
Audit Date: 10.06.2019
Personnel: Susan Shultz (Ed.); Lauren Spicehandler (Acct. Exec.); Shelagh Barrett (Adv. Sales); Bruce McDougall (Circ. Mgr.); Stephen Spinosa (Adv. Dir.)
Parent company (for newspapers): HAN Network

EAST HAVEN COURIER

Street address 1: 724 Boston Post Rd
Street address 2: Ste 202
Street address city: Madison
Street address state: CT
Zip/Postal code: 06443-3039
General Phone: (203) 245-1877
General Fax: (203) 245-9773
General/National Adv. E-mail: advertising@shorepublishing.com
Editorial e-mail: b.boyd@shorepublishing.com
Primary Website: zip06.com
Year Established: 1996
Avg Free Circ: 9347
Audit By: CVC
Audit Date: 30.06.2018
Personnel: Robyn Wolcott (Pub.); Brian Boyd (Ed.); Julie Johnson (Prod. Mgr); Ed Majersky (Adv. Dir.)
Parent company (for newspapers): The Day Publishing Co.

EASTON COURIER

Street address 1: 16 Bailey Ave
Street address city: Ridgefield
Street address state: CT
Zip/Postal code: 06877-4512
General Phone: (203) 438-1183
General Fax: (203) 926-2091
Advertising Phone: (203) 402-2327
Editorial Phone: (203) 894-3343
General/National Adv. E-mail: dcosenza@hersamacorn.com
Editorial e-mail: ndoniger@hersamacorn.com
Primary Website: eastoncourier.com
Year Established: 1973
Avg Paid Circ: 1156
Avg Free Circ: 99
Audit By: Sworn/Estimate/Non-Audited
Audit Date: 10.06.2019
Personnel: Thomas Nash (Pub. Mgr); Mary Anne Hersam (Adv. Mgr); Nancy Doniger (Ed.); Donna Cosenza (Account Exec.); Bruce McDougall (Circ. Mgr.); Shelagh Barrett (Adv. Sales); Rose Sayers (Classifieds Adv. Mgr.); Greg Moy (Prod. Mgr)
Parent company (for newspapers): HAN Network

FAIRFIELD CITIZEN

Street address 1: 410 State St
Street address 2: 220 Carter Henry Dr
Street address city: Bridgeport
Street address state: CT
Zip/Postal code: 06604-4501
General Phone: (203) 337-4877
General Fax: (203) 367-8158
Advertising Phone: (203) 330-6409
Editorial Phone: (203) 255-4561 ext. 111
General/National Adv. E-mail: gdoucette@hearstmediact.com
Display Adv. E-mail: classified@ctpost.com
Editorial e-mail: jdoody@bcnnew.com
Primary Website: fairfieldcitizenonline.com
Avg Paid Circ: 1823
Audit By: Sworn/Estimate/Non-Audited
Audit Date: 10.06.2019
Personnel: Jerrod Ferrari (Ed.); Chris Elsberry (Sports Ed.); Paul Barbetta (Grp. Pub.); Doreen Madden (Exec Asst to Pub.); Bill Mason (Circ. Dir.)
Parent company (for newspapers): Hearst Communications, Inc.

FAIRFIELD MINUTEMAN

Street address 1: 100 Gando Dr
Street address city: New Haven
Street address state: CT
Zip/Postal code: 06513-1049
General Phone: (203) 752-2711
General Fax: (203) 789-5309
Advertising Phone: (203) 789-5484
Editorial Phone: (203) 789-5726
General/National Adv. E-mail: news@fairfieldminuteman.com
Display Adv. E-mail: pwalsh@journalregister.com
Editorial e-mail: editor@fairfieldminuteman.com
Primary Website: minutemannewscenter.com
Avg Paid Circ: 0
Avg Free Circ: 20524
Audit By: Sworn/Estimate/Non-Audited
Audit Date: 10.06.2019
Personnel: John Slater (Gen. Mgr.); Donna Saracco (Ed.); Ken Kopas (Adv. Dir.)
Parent company (for newspapers): Digital First Media

FAIRFIELD SUN

Street address 1: 1000 Bridgeport Ave
Street address city: Shelton
Street address state: CT
Zip/Postal code: 06484-4660
General Phone: (203) 438-1183
General Fax: (203) 926-2091
Advertising Phone: (203) 402-2327
Editorial Phone: (203)894-3343
General/National Adv. E-mail: dcosenza@hersamacorn.com
Editorial e-mail: ndoniger@hersamacorn.com
Primary Website: eastoncourier.com
Year Established: 1973
Avg Free Circ: 6548
Audit By: Sworn/Estimate/Non-Audited
Audit Date: 10.06.2019
Personnel: Thomas Nash (Pub. Mgr); Mary Anne Hersam (Adv. Sales); Nancy Doniger (Ed.); Donna Cosenza (Account Exec.); Rose Sayers (Classified Adv. Mgr.); Donald Hersam (Circ. Mgr.); Greg Moy (Prod. Mgr); John Kovach (Ed)

GLASTONBURY CITIZEN

Street address 1: 87 Nutmeg Ln
Street address city: Glastonbury
Street address state: CT
Zip/Postal code: 06033-2314
General Phone: (860) 633-4691
General Fax: (860) 657-3258
Advertising Phone: (860) 633-4691 ext. 237
Editorial Phone: (860) 633-4691 ext. 226
General/National Adv. E-mail: rivereast@snet.net
Editorial e-mail: citizen@snet.net
Primary Website: glcitizen.com
Avg Paid Circ: 7792
Audit By: Sworn/Estimate/Non-Audited
Audit Date: 10.06.2019
Personnel: Carole Saucier (Adv. Mgr.); Janki Buch (Circ. Mgr.); James Hallas (Ed. & Pub.); Chris Seymour (Sports Ed.)
Parent company (for newspapers): The Glastonbury Citizen, Inc.

GUILFORD COURIER

Street address 1: 724 Boston Post Rd
Street address 2: Ste 202
Street address city: Madison
Street address state: CT
Zip/Postal code: 06443-3039
General Phone: (203) 245-1877
General Fax: (203) 245-9773
Advertising Phone: (203) 245-1877, ext. 6142
Editorial Phone: (203) 245-1877 ext 6500
General/National Adv. E-mail: r.collins@shorepublishing.com
Display Adv. E-mail: classifieds@shorepublishing.com
Editorial e-mail: b.boyd@shorepublishing.com
Primary Website: zip06.com
Avg Free Circ: 7777
Audit By: CVC
Audit Date: 30.06.2018
Personnel: Robyn Collins (Pub.); Brian Boyd (Ed.); Alan Ellis (Prodn. Mgr.); Julie Johnson (Prod. Mgr.); Dave Ellis (Classified Adv. Mgr.); Ed Majersky
Parent company (for newspapers): The Day Publishing Co.

HARBOR NEWS

Street address 1: 724 Boston Post Rd
Street address 2: Ste 202
Street address city: Madison
Street address state: CT
Zip/Postal code: 06443-3039
General Phone: (203) 245-1877
General Fax: (203) 245-9773
Advertising Phone: (203) 245-1877 ext 6142
Editorial Phone: (203) 245-1877 ext 6500
General/National Adv. E-mail: e.majersky@shorepublishing.com
Display Adv. E-mail: e.majersky@shorepublishing.com
Editorial e-mail: r.collins@shorepublishing.com
Primary Website: zip06.com
Avg Free Circ: 10467
Audit By: CVC
Audit Date: 30.06.2018
Personnel: Robyn Collins (Pub.); Brian Boyd (Managing Editor); Alan Ellis (Prodn. Mgr.); Shannon Timme (Acct. Manager); Julie Johnson (Prod. Mgr); Ed Majersky
Parent company (for newspapers): Shore Publishing LLC

HARTFORD BUSINESS JOURNAL

Street address 1: 15 Lewis St
Street address 2: Ste 200
Street address city: Hartford
Street address state: CT
Zip/Postal code: 06103-2503
General Phone: (860) 236-9998
General Fax: (860) 570-2493
Advertising Phone: (860) 236-9998 ext. 139
Editorial Phone: (860) 236-9998 ext. 130
General/National Adv. E-mail: jrudy@hartfordbusiness.com
Display Adv. E-mail: jrudy@hartfordbusiness.com
Editorial e-mail: jzwiebel@hartfordbusiness.com
Primary Website: hartfordbusiness.com
Year Established: 1992
Avg Paid Circ: 608
Avg Free Circ: 8662
Audit By: CVC
Audit Date: 30.06.2017
Personnel: Joe Zwiebel (Pres./Pub.); Jamie Rudy (Adv.); Kelly Ansley (Circ.); Liz Saltzman (Prod.)
Parent company (for newspapers): New England Business Media

KILLINGLY VILLAGER

Street address 1: 283 Route 169
Street address city: Woodstock
Street address state: CT
Zip/Postal code: 06281-3332
General Phone: (860) 928-1818
General Fax: (860) 928-5940
Advertising Phone: (877) 888-2711
General/National Adv. E-mail: ads@villagernewspapers.com
Editorial e-mail: aminor@villagernewspapers.com
Primary Website: southbridgeeveningnews.com
Avg Free Circ: 9418

Audit By: Sworn/Estimate/Non-Audited
Audit Date: 10.06.2019
Personnel: Adam Minor (Ed.); Sarah Mortensen (Ad. Director)

MILFORD MIRROR

Street address 1: 1000 Bridgeport Ave
Street address city: Shelton
Street address state: CT
Zip/Postal code: 06484-4660
General Phone: (203) 926-2080
General Fax: (203) 926-2091
Advertising Phone: (203) 402-2335
Editorial Phone: (203) 402-2315
General/National Adv. E-mail: ads@hersamacorn.com
Primary Website: milfordmirror.com
Year Established: 1985
Avg Paid Circ: 2932
Avg Free Circ: 591
Audit By: Sworn/Estimate/Non-Audited
Audit Date: 10.06.2019
Personnel: Bill Bloxsom (Sports Ed.); Jill Dion (Ed.); Jim Chiappa (Account Exec.); Mary Anne Hersam (VP, Sales); Rose Sayers (Classified Adv. Mgr.); Donald Hersam (Circ. Mgr.); Greg Moy (Prod. Mgr)
Parent company (for newspapers): HAN Network

MONROE COURIER

Street address 1: 1000 Bridgeport Ave
Street address city: Shelton
Street address state: CT
Zip/Postal code: 06484-4660
General Phone: (203) 926-2080
General Fax: (203) 926-2091
Advertising Phone: (203) 402-2327
Editorial Phone: (203) 402-2313
Editorial Fax: (203) 926-2091
General/National Adv. E-mail: mahersam@ncadvertiser.com
Editorial e-mail: monroecourier@hersamacorn.com
Primary Website: monroecourier.com
Year Established: 1962
Avg Paid Circ: 2372
Avg Free Circ: 129
Audit By: Sworn/Estimate/Non-Audited
Audit Date: 10.06.2019
Personnel: Thomas Nash (Pub.); Bill Bloxsom (Sports Ed.); Mary Anne Hersam (VP of Sales); Donna Cosenza (Account Exec.); Donald Hersam (Circ. Mgr.); Greg Moy (Prod. Mgr); Brad Durrell (Ed)
Parent company (for newspapers): HAN Network

MYSTIC RIVER PRESS

Street address 1: 99 Mechanic St
Street address city: Pawcatuck
Street address state: CT
Zip/Postal code: 06379-2187
General Phone: (860) 495-8200
General Fax: (401) 348-5080
Editorial e-mail: news@thewesterlysun.com
Primary Website: mysticriverpress.com
Audit By: Sworn/Estimate/Non-Audited
Audit Date: 10.06.2019
Personnel: John Layton (Adv); Karen Davis (Classified Advertising)
Parent company (for newspapers): Sun Publishing Company

NEW CANAAN ADVERTISER

Street address 1: 42 Vitti St
Street address city: New Canaan
Street address state: CT
Zip/Postal code: 06840-4823
General Phone: (203) 966-9541
General Fax: (203) 966-8006
Advertising Phone: (203) 966-9541 ext 106
Editorial Phone: (203) 966-9541 ext 112
General/National Adv. E-mail: ads@hersamacorn.com
Editorial e-mail: editor@ncadvertiser.com
Primary Website: ncadvertiser.com
Year Established: 1908
Avg Paid Circ: 4236
Audit By: Sworn/Estimate/Non-Audited
Audit Date: 10.06.2019
Personnel: Paul Barbetta (Pub.); Matt DeRienzo (VP of News and Dig. Content); John Kovach (Ed.); Grace Duffield (Reporter); Justin Stock (Content Mgr.); Dave Stewart (Sports Ed.); Donald Hersam (Pub. Emeritus)
Parent company (for newspapers): HAN Network

NEW CANAAN NEWS

Street address 1: 410 State St
Street address city: Bridgeport
Street address state: CT
Zip/Postal code: 06604-4501
General Phone: (203) 333-0161
General Fax: (203) 972-4404
Advertising Phone: (203) 964-2357
Advertising Fax: (203) 972-4404
Editorial Phone: (203) 330-6581
Editorial Fax: (203) 972-4404
General/National Adv. E-mail: agonzalez@scni.com
Display Adv. E-mail: classifieds@ctpost.com
Editorial e-mail: avarese@bcnnew.com
Primary Website: newcanaannewsonline.com
Avg Paid Circ: 2710
Audit By: Sworn/Estimate/Non-Audited
Audit Date: 10.06.2019
Personnel: Claire Racine (Ed.); Anthony Parelli (Sports Ed.); Jerrod Ferrari (Ed.); Paul Barbetta (Group Pres./ Pub.); Doreen Madden (Exec. Asst. to Pub.)
Parent company (for newspapers): Hearst Communications, Inc.

NEW LONDON TIMES

Street address 1: 47 Eugene Oneill Dr
Street address city: New London
Street address state: CT
Zip/Postal code: 06320-6351
General Phone: (860) 442-2200
General Fax: (860) 437-1176
Advertising Phone: (860) 701-4203
Editorial Phone: (860) 701-4379
General/National Adv. E-mail: B.Briere@theday.com
Editorial e-mail: t.dwyer@theday.com
Primary Website: zip06.com
Avg Free Circ: 11261
Audit By: Sworn/Estimate/Non-Audited
Audit Date: 10.06.2019
Personnel: Timothy Dwyer (Exec. Ed.); Lisa Miksis (Pub.); Marisa Nadolny (Ed.); Bob Briere (Adv. Dir.); Gary Farrugia (Pub)
Parent company (for newspapers): The Day Publishing Co.

NEW MILFORD SPECTRUM

Street address 1: 43E Main Street
Street address city: New Milford
Street address state: CT
Zip/Postal code: 06776
General Phone: (203) 333-6688
General/National Adv. E-mail: jubicr@timesunion.com
Display Adv. E-mail: jubicr@timesunion.com
Editorial e-mail: ktorres@ctpost.com
Primary Website: newmilfordspectrum.com
Avg Paid Circ: 19771
Avg Free Circ: 20598
Audit By: Sworn/Estimate/Non-Audited
Audit Date: 10.06.2019
Personnel: Deborah Rose (Ed.); Keila Torres (Asst. Ed.); Stephen Spinosa (Ad. Dir.)
Parent company (for newspapers): Hearst Communications, Inc.

NEWINGTON TOWN CRIER

Street address 1: 1 Herald Sq
Street address city: New Britain
Street address state: CT
Zip/Postal code: 06051-5009
General Phone: (860) 225-4601
General Fax: (860) 223-8171
Advertising Phone: (860) 225-4601 ext 281
Editorial Phone: (860) 225-4601 ext 359
General/National Adv. E-mail: gcurran@centralctcommunications.com
Editorial e-mail: mbatterson@centralctcommunications.com
Primary Website: newingtontowncrier.com
Audit By: Sworn/Estimate/Non-Audited
Audit Date: 10.06.2019
Personnel: Gary Curran (Ad. Manger); Daniel Kline (Managing Editor); Michael Schroeder (Owner and Publisher)
Parent company (for newspapers): Central Connecticut Communications LLC

NORTH HAVEN COURIER

Street address 1: 724 Boston Post Rd
Street address 2: Ste 202
Street address city: Madison
Street address state: CT
Zip/Postal code: 06443-3039
General Phone: (203) 245-1877
General Fax: (203) 245-9773
Advertising Phone: (203) 245-1877 ext 6142
Editorial Phone: (203) 245-1877 ext 6500
General/National Adv. E-mail: r.collins@shorepublishing.com
Editorial e-mail: r.collins@shorepublishing.com
Primary Website: zip06.com/section
Avg Free Circ: 8518
Audit By: CVC
Audit Date: 30.06.2018
Personnel: Brian Boyd (Ed.); Robyn Collins (Pub.); John McKenna (Acct. Manager); Julie Johnson (Prod. Mgr); Ed Majersky
Parent company (for newspapers): The Day Publishing Co.

REDDING PILOT

Street address 1: 16 Bailey Ave
Street address city: Ridgefield
Street address state: CT
Zip/Postal code: 06877-4512
General Phone: (203) 894-3331
General Fax: (203) 438-3395
Advertising Phone: (203) 894-3324
Editorial Phone: (203) 894-3337
General/National Adv. E-mail: kforrest@hersamacorn.com
Editorial e-mail: pilot@thereddingpilot.com
Primary Website: thereddingpilot.com
Year Established: 1966
Avg Paid Circ: 1859
Audit By: Sworn/Estimate/Non-Audited
Audit Date: 10.06.2019
Personnel: Thomas B. Nash (Pub.); Martin V. Hersam (Gen. Mgr.); Mary Anne Hersam (VP of Sales); Susan Wolf (Ed.); Rocco Valluzzo (Sports Ed.); Donald Hersam (Circ. Mgr.)
Parent company (for newspapers): HAN Network

RIDGEFIELD PRESS

Street address 1: 16 Bailey Ave
Street address city: Ridgefield
Street address state: CT
Zip/Postal code: 06877-4512
General Phone: (203) 438-6544
General Fax: (203) 438-4269
Advertising Phone: (203) 894-3322
Editorial Phone: (203) 894-3350
General/National Adv. E-mail: lcampbell@hersamacorn.com
Primary Website: theridgefieldpress.com
Year Established: 1875
Avg Paid Circ: 5528
Audit By: Sworn/Estimate/Non-Audited
Audit Date: 10.06.2019
Personnel: Thomas B. Nash (Pub.); Martin V. Hersam (COO); Mary Anne Hersam (VP of Sales); Jack Sanders (Exec. Ed.); Macklin K. Reid (News Ed.); Tim Murphy (Sports Ed.); Laurie Campbell (Account Executive); Rose Sayers (Classifieds Adv. Mgr.)
Parent company (for newspapers): HAN Network

RIVEREAST NEWS BULLETIN

Street address 1: 87 Nutmeg Ln
Street address city: Glastonbury
Street address state: CT
Zip/Postal code: 06033-2314
General Phone: (860) 633-4691
General Fax: (860) 657-3258
Advertising Phone: (860) 633-4691 ext. 237
Editorial Phone: (860) 633-4691 ext. 225
General/National Adv. E-mail: bulletin@glcitizen.com
Editorial e-mail: bulletin@glcitizen.com
Primary Website: glcitizen.com
Avg Free Circ: 27050
Audit By: Sworn/Estimate/Non-Audited
Audit Date: 10.06.2019
Personnel: James Hallas (Pub.); Carole Saucier (Adv. Mgr.); Mike Thompson (Ed.)
Parent company (for newspapers): The Glastonbury Citizen, Inc.

SHELTON HERALD

Street address 1: 1000 Bridgeport Ave
Street address city: Shelton
Street address state: CT
Zip/Postal code: 06484-4660
General Phone: (203) 926-2080
General Fax: (203) 926-2091
Advertising Phone: (203) 402-2327
Editorial Phone: (203) 402-2332
General/National Adv. E-mail: ads@hersamacorn.com
Primary Website: sheltonherald.com
Year Established: 1981
Avg Paid Circ: 3306
Avg Free Circ: 125
Audit By: Sworn/Estimate/Non-Audited
Audit Date: 10.06.2019
Personnel: Thomas B. Nash (Pub.); Mary Anne Hersam (VP of Sales); Brad Durrell (Ed.); Donna Cosenza (Account Exec.); Donald Hersam (Circ. Mgr.); Greg Moy (Prod. Mgr); Kate Czaplinski (Ed)
Parent company (for newspapers): HAN Network

SHORE PUBLISHING

Street address 1: 724 Boston Post Road
Street address 2: Suite 202
Street address city: Madison
Street address state: CT
Zip/Postal code: 06443
General Phone: (203) 245-1877
General Fax: (203) 245-9773
General/National Adv. E-mail: e.majersky@shorepublishing.com
Display Adv. E-mail: e.majersky@shorepublishing.com
Editorial e-mail: news@shorepublishing.com
Primary Website: zip06.com
Avg Free Circ: 8546
Audit By: Sworn/Estimate/Non-Audited
Audit Date: 10.06.2019
Personnel: Robyn Wolcott (Pub.); Brian Boyd (Managing Ed.); Margaret McNellis (Asst. Ed.); Ed Majersky (Adv. Dir.)
Parent company (for newspapers): The Day Publishing Co.

SHORELINE TIMES

Street address 1: 100 Gando Drive
Street address city: New Haven
Street address state: CT
Zip/Postal code: 6513
General Phone: (203) 789-5200
General Fax: (203) 789-5309
Advertising Phone: (203) 789-5484
General/National Adv. E-mail: kkopas@westportminuteman.com
Primary Website: shorelinetimes.com
Avg Paid Circ: 42709
Audit By: AAM
Audit Date: 30.09.2017
Personnel: John Slater (Gen. Mgr.); Susan Braden (Editor); Ken Kopas (Ad. Dir.)
Parent company (for newspapers): Hearst Communications, Inc.

SOURCE

Street address 1: 724 Boston Post Rd
Street address 2: Ste 202
Street address city: Madison
Street address state: CT
Zip/Postal code: 06443-3039
General Phone: (203) 245-1877
General Fax: (203) 245-9773
Advertising Phone: (203) 245-1877 ext 6142
Editorial Phone: (203) 245-1877 ext 6500
General/National Adv. E-mail: advertising@shorepublishing.com
Display Adv. E-mail: r.collins@shorepublishing.com
Editorial e-mail: r.collins@shorepublishing.com
Primary Website: zip06.com
Year Established: 1996
Avg Free Circ: 8483
Audit By: CVC
Audit Date: 30.06.2018
Personnel: Denise Forrest (Acct. Manager); Robyn Collins (Pub.); Brian Boyd (Mng. Ed.); Julie Johnson (Prod. Mgr); Ed Majersky

Parent company (for newspapers): The Day Publishing Co.

STRATFORD STAR

Street address 1: 1000 Bridgeport Ave
Street address city: Shelton
Street address state: CT
Zip/Postal code: 06484-4660
General Phone: (203) 926-2080
General Fax: (203) 926-2091
Advertising Phone: (203) 402-2335
Editorial Phone: (203) 402-2319
General/National Adv. E-mail: jchiappa@hersamacorn.com
Editorial e-mail: stratfordstar@hersamacorn.com
Primary Website: stratfordstar.com
Year Established: 1985
Avg Paid Circ: 3146
Avg Free Circ: 607
Audit By: Sworn/Estimate/Non-Audited
Audit Date: 10.06.2019
Personnel: Thomas B. Nash (Pub.); Mary Anne Hersam (VP of Sales); Jim Chiappa (Account Exec.); Donald Hersam (Circ. Mgr.); Greg Moy (Prod. Mgr); Joseph Cole (Ed)
Parent company (for newspapers): HAN Network

THE CHESHIRE HERALD

Street address 1: 1079 S Main St
Street address city: Cheshire
Street address state: CT
Zip/Postal code: 06410-3414
General Phone: (203) 272-5316
General Fax: (203) 250-7145
General/National Adv. E-mail: ffonteyn@cheshireherald.com
Editorial e-mail: news@cheshireherald.com
Primary Website: cheshireherald.com
Year Established: 1953
Avg Paid Circ: 7200
Avg Free Circ: 197
Audit By: Sworn/Estimate/Non-Audited
Audit Date: 10.06.2019
Personnel: Joseph J. Jakubisyn (Pres./Pub.); Maureen Jakubisyn (Treasurer); Frank Fonteyn (Adv. Dir.); Debi Reeve (Circ. Mgr.); John Rook (Ed.)

THE EXPRESS

Street address 1: 99 Mechanic St
Street address city: Pawcatuck
Street address state: CT
Zip/Postal code: 06379-2187
General Phone: (401) 348-1000
General Fax: (401) 348-5080
Advertising Phone: (860) 495-8277
Advertising Fax: (401) 348-3080
Editorial Phone: (860) 495-8224
Editorial Fax: (401) 348-3080
General/National Adv. E-mail: news@thewesterlysun.com
Display Adv. E-mail: classified@thewesterlysun.com
Classified Adv. e-mail: classified@ thewesterlysun.com
Editorial e-mail: news@thewesterlysun.com
Primary Website: thewesterlysun.com
Avg Free Circ: 23680
Audit By: Sworn/Estimate/Non-Audited
Audit Date: 10.06.2019
Personnel: Jody Boucher; Corey Fyke (Ed.); Keith Kimberlin (Sports); Ken Sorenson (Sports); Dale Faulkner (Reporter); Kathy Enders
Parent company (for newspapers): Sun Publishing Company

THE FOOTHILLS TRADER

Street address 1: 59 Field St
Street address city: Torrington
Street address state: CT
Zip/Postal code: 06790-4942
General Phone: (860) 489-3121
General/National Adv. E-mail: dnaparstek@adtaxi.com
Primary Website: foothillstrader.com
Audit By: Sworn/Estimate/Non-Audited
Audit Date: 10.06.2019
Parent company (for newspapers): Digital First Media

THE GROTON TIMES

Street address 1: 47 Eugene Oneill Dr
Street address city: New London
Street address state: CT
Zip/Postal code: 06320-6306
General Phone: (860) 442-2200
General Fax: (860) 437-1176
Advertising Phone: (860) 701-4203
Editorial Phone: (860) 701-4379
General/National Adv. E-mail: B.Briere@theday.com
Editorial e-mail: t.dwyer@theday.com
Primary Website: zip06.com
Year Established: 1995
Avg Free Circ: 11687
Audit By: Sworn/Estimate/Non-Audited
Audit Date: 10.06.2019
Personnel: Gary Farrugia (Pub.); Timothy Dwyer (Exec. Ed.); Bob Briere (Ad. Dir.); Lisa Miksis (Pub./Circ. Mgr.); Tim Cotter (ed)
Parent company (for newspapers): The Day Publishing Co.

THE HAMDEN JOURNAL

Street address 1: 17 Hesse Rd
Street address city: Hamden
Street address state: CT
Zip/Postal code: 06517-2620
General Phone: (203) 687-3075
Advertising Phone: (203) 687-3075
Editorial Phone: (203) 687-3075
General/National Adv. E-mail: sales@thehamdenjournal.com
Display Adv. E-mail: sales@thehamdenjournal.com
Editorial e-mail: info@thehamdenjournal.com
Primary Website: goodnewspublishing.solutions
Year Established: 2010
Avg Free Circ: 7500
Audit By: Sworn/Estimate/Non-Audited
Audit Date: 10.06.2019
Personnel: Shala LaTorraca (Pub / EIC); Chris LaTorraca (Publisher / Director of Sales)
Parent company (for newspapers): Good News Publishing LLC

THE HOUR

Street address 1: 301 Merritt 7
Street address city: Norwalk
Street address state: CT
Zip/Postal code: 06851
General Phone: (203) 842-2500
General/National Adv. E-mail: dhanson@thehour.com
Display Adv. E-mail: classified@thehour.com
Editorial e-mail: cwright@thehour.com
Primary Website: thehour.com
Year Established: 1995
Avg Paid Circ: 800
Avg Free Circ: 5000
Audit By: Sworn/Estimate/Non-Audited
Audit Date: 10.06.2019
Personnel: Thane Grauel (Mng. Ed.); Jacky Smith (Ed. Pg. Ed.); Sean Barker; Lee Steele (Features Ed.)

THE LAKEVILLE JOURNAL

Street address 1: 64 Route 7 North
Street address city: Falls Village
Street address state: CT
Zip/Postal code: 6031
General Phone: (860) 435-9873
Advertising Phone: (860) 435-9873 x501
Advertising Fax: (860) 271-8282
Editorial Phone: (860) 435-9873 x601
Editorial Fax: (860) 271-8282
General/National Adv. E-mail: libbyh@lakevillejournal.com
Display Adv. E-mail: libbyh@lakevillejournal.com
Editorial e-mail: editor@lakevillejournal.com
Primary Website: tricornernews.com
Mthly Avg Views: 40000
Mthly Avg Unique Visitors: 8000
Year Established: 1897
Avg Paid Circ: 2824
Avg Free Circ: 98
Audit By: AAM
Audit Date: 31.12.2018
Personnel: Libby Hall Abeel
Parent company (for newspapers): The Lakeville Journal

THE LITCHFIELD COUNTY TIMES

Street address 1: 59 Field St
Street address city: Torrington
Street address state: CT
Zip/Postal code: 06790-4942
General Phone: (860) 489-3121
General Fax: (860) 489-6790
General/National Adv. E-mail: advertise@hearstmediact.com
Display Adv. E-mail: advertise@hearstmediact.com
Editorial e-mail: news@countytimes.com
Primary Website: countytimes.com
Year Established: 1981
Avg Paid Circ: 3335
Avg Free Circ: 25
Audit By: Sworn/Estimate/Non-Audited
Audit Date: 10.06.2019
Personnel: Catherine Guarnieri (Ed.); Helen Bennett Harvey (Exec. Ed.)
Parent company (for newspapers): Digital First Media

THE LYME TIMES

Street address 1: 47 Eugene Oneill Dr
Street address city: New London
Street address state: CT
Zip/Postal code: 06320-6306
General Phone: (860) 442-2200
General Fax: (860) 437-1176
Advertising Phone: (860) 701-4203
Editorial Phone: (860) 701-4379
General/National Adv. E-mail: B.Briere@theday.com
Editorial e-mail: t.dwyer@theday.com
Primary Website: zip06.com
Avg Free Circ: 14591
Audit By: Sworn/Estimate/Non-Audited
Audit Date: 10.06.2019
Personnel: Bob Briere (Adv. Dir.); Timothy Dwyer (Exec. Ed.); Lisa Miksis (Pub.); Dave Ellis (Classifieds Adv. Mgr.); Tim Cotter (Ed)
Parent company (for newspapers): The Day Publishing Co.

THE MILLERTON NEWS

Street address 1: 64 Route 7 North
Street address city: Falls Village
Street address state: CT
Zip/Postal code: 6031
General Phone: (860) 435-9873
General/National Adv. E-mail: libbyh@lakevillejournal.com
Display Adv. E-mail: libbyh@lakevillejournal.com
Editorial e-mail: editor@lakevillejournal.com
Primary Website: tricornernews.com
Avg Paid Circ: 1014
Avg Free Circ: 39
Audit By: AAM
Audit Date: 31.12.2018
Personnel: Libby Hall Abeel (Adv. Mgr.)
Parent company (for newspapers): The Lakeville Journal Company, LLC

THE MONTVILLE TIMES

Street address 1: 47 Eugene Oneill Dr
Street address city: New London
Street address state: CT
Zip/Postal code: 06320-6306
General Phone: (860) 442-2200
General Fax: (860) 437-1176
Advertising Phone: (860) 701-4203
Editorial Phone: (860) 701-4379
General/National Adv. E-mail: B.Briere@theday.com
Editorial e-mail: t.dwyer@theday.com
Primary Website: zip06.com
Avg Free Circ: 6980
Audit By: Sworn/Estimate/Non-Audited
Audit Date: 10.06.2019
Personnel: Timothy Dwyer (Exec. Ed.); Bob Briere (Adv. Dir.); Lisa Miksis (Pub.); Dave Ellis (Classified Adv. Mgr.)
Parent company (for newspapers): The Day

THE MYSTIC TIMES

Street address 1: 47 Eugene Oneill Dr
Street address city: New London
Street address state: CT
Zip/Postal code: 06320-6306
General Phone: (860) 442-2200
General Fax: (860) 437-1176
Advertising Phone: (860) 701-4203
Editorial Phone: (860) 701-4379
General/National Adv. E-mail: B.Briere@theday.com
Editorial e-mail: t.dwyer@theday.com
Primary Website: zip06.com
Avg Free Circ: 7465
Audit By: Sworn/Estimate/Non-Audited
Audit Date: 10.06.2019
Personnel: Gary Farrugia (Pub.); Timothy Dwyer (Exec. Ed.); Bob Briere (Ad. Dir.); Dave Ellis (Classified Adv. Mgr.); Tim Cotter (Ed)
Parent company (for newspapers): The Day Publishing Co.

THE NEWTOWN BEE

Street address 1: 5 Church Hill Rd
Street address city: Newtown
Street address state: CT
Zip/Postal code: 06470-1605
General Phone: (203) 426-3141
General Fax: (203) 426-5169
General/National Adv. E-mail: editor@thebee.com
Display Adv. E-mail: ellen@thebee.com
Classified Adv. e-mail: sandyt@thebee.com
Editorial e-mail: editor@thebee.com
Primary Website: newtownbee.com
Mthly Avg Views: 35000
Mthly Avg Unique Visitors: 25000
Year Established: 1877
Avg Paid Circ: 8000
Avg Free Circ: 6300
Audit By: Sworn/Estimate/Non-Audited
Audit Date: 10.06.2019
Personnel: R. Scudder Smith (Publisher); Ellen Therrien (Adv. Manager); John Voket (Editor);; Nancy Crevier (Ed.); Scott Baggett (Production & Circulation Manager); Sherri Baggett (Business Manager)
Parent company (for newspapers): Bee Publishing Co., Inc.

THE OBSERVER

Street address 1: 213 Spring St
Street address city: Southington
Street address state: CT
Zip/Postal code: 06489-1542
General Phone: (860) 621-6751
General/National Adv. E-mail: sales@StepSaver.com
Display Adv. E-mail: sales@StepSaver.com
Editorial e-mail: JGoralski@SouthingtonObserver.com
Primary Website: southingtonobserver.com
Avg Paid Circ: 5394
Avg Free Circ: 46
Audit By: Sworn/Estimate/Non-Audited
Audit Date: 10.06.2019
Personnel: John Goralski (Ed)

THE PLAINVILLE CITIZEN

Street address 1: 500 S Broad St
Street address 2: Ste 2
Street address city: Meriden
Street address state: CT
Zip/Postal code: 06450-6643
General Phone: (203) 235-1661
General Fax: (203) 639-0210
Advertising Phone: (203) 317-2312
Advertising Fax: (203) 235-4048
Editorial Phone: (203) 317-2449
General/National Adv. E-mail: kboath@record-journal.com
Display Adv. E-mail: advertising@plainvillecitizen.com
Editorial e-mail: news@theplainvillecitizen.com
Primary Website: plainvillecitizen.com
Year Established: 2002
Avg Free Circ: 9200
Audit By: Sworn/Estimate/Non-Audited
Audit Date: 10.06.2019
Personnel: Eliot C. White (Pub.); Crystal Maldonaldo (Mng. Ed.); Kimberley Booth (Ad. Dir.)
Parent company (for newspapers): The Record-Journal Publishing Co.

THE RESIDENT

Street address 1: 252 S Broad St
Street address city: Pawcatuck
Street address state: CT
Zip/Postal code: 06379-7924
General Phone: (860) 599-1221
General Fax: (860) 599-1400
Advertising Phone: (860) 608-0467
General/National Adv. E-mail: alexisinmystic@aol.com
Display Adv. E-mail: classifieds@theresident.com

Editorial e-mail: editor@theresident.com
Primary Website: theresident.com
Year Established: 1990
Avg Free Circ: 29251
Audit By: CVC
Audit Date: 05.02.2018
Personnel: Alexis Ann (Pub./Adv. Sales)

THE SOUND

Street address 1: 724 Boston Post Rd
Street address 2: Ste 202
Street address city: Madison
Street address state: CT
Zip/Postal code: 06443-3039
General Phone: (203) 245-1877
General Fax: (203) 245-9773
General/National Adv. E-mail: e.majersky@shorepublishing.com
Display Adv. E-mail: e.majersky@shorepublishing.com
Editorial e-mail: r.collins@shorepublishing.com
Primary Website: zip06.com
Year Established: 1994
Avg Free Circ: 12657
Audit By: CVC
Audit Date: 30.06.2018
Personnel: Robyn Collins (Pub.); Brian Boyd (Managing Ed.); Nikki Brinn (Acct. Manager); Julie Johnson (Prod. Mgr); Ed Majersky
Parent company (for newspapers): The Day Publishing Co.

THE SOUTHINGTON CITIZEN

Street address 1: 500 S Broad St
Street address 2: Ste 2
Street address city: Meriden
Street address state: CT
Zip/Postal code: 06450-6643
General Phone: (203) 235-1661
General Fax: (203) 639-0210
Advertising Phone: (203) 317-2312
Advertising Fax: (203) 235-4048
Editorial Phone: (860) 620-5960
General/National Adv. E-mail: kboath@record-journal.com
Display Adv. E-mail: advertising@thesouthingtoncitizen.com
Editorial e-mail: news@thesouthingtoncitizen.com
Primary Website: southingtoncitizen.com
Avg Free Circ: 9800
Audit By: Sworn/Estimate/Non-Audited
Audit Date: 10.06.2019
Personnel: Nick Carroll (News Editor); Carolyn Wallach (Managing Ed.); Kimberley Boath (Ad. Dir.); Eliot White (Pres./Pub.)
Parent company (for newspapers): The Record-Journal Publishing Co.

THE STONINGTON TIMES

Street address 1: 47 Eugene Oneill Dr
Street address city: New London
Street address state: CT
Zip/Postal code: 06320-6306
General Phone: (860) 442-2200
General Fax: (860) 437-1176
Advertising Phone: (860) 701-4203
Editorial Phone: (860) 701-4379
General/National Adv. E-mail: B.Briere@theday.com
Editorial e-mail: t.dwyer@theday.com
Primary Website: zip06.com
Avg Free Circ: 8791
Audit By: Sworn/Estimate/Non-Audited
Audit Date: 10.06.2019
Personnel: Lisa Miksis (Pub.); Bob Briere (Adv. Dir.); Timothy Dwyer (Exec. Ed.); Brian Boyd (Managing Ed.); Tim Cotter (Ed)
Parent company (for newspapers): The Day Publishing Co.

THE THAMES RIVER TIMES

Street address 1: 47 Eugene Oneill Dr
Street address city: New London
Street address state: CT
Zip/Postal code: 06320-6306
General Phone: (860) 442-2200
General Fax: (860) 437-1176
Advertising Phone: (860) 701-4203
Editorial Phone: (860) 701-4379
General/National Adv. E-mail: r.collins@shorepublishing.com
Editorial e-mail: t.dwyer@theday.com
Primary Website: zip06.com
Year Established: 1986
Avg Free Circ: 7626
Audit By: Sworn/Estimate/Non-Audited
Audit Date: 10.06.2019
Personnel: Timothy Dwyer (Executive Ed.); Bob Briere (Ad. Director); Lisa Miksis (Pub.); Tim Cotter (Ed)
Parent company (for newspapers): The Day

THE VALLEY PRESS

Street address 1: 540 Hopmeadow St
Street address 2: Ste 106
Street address city: Simsbury
Street address state: CT
Zip/Postal code: 06070-3197
General Phone: (860) 651-4700
General Fax: (860) 606-9599
Advertising Phone: (860) 978-1345
General/National Adv. E-mail: Melissa@TheValleyPress.net
Display Adv. E-mail: classifieds@thevalleypress.net
Editorial e-mail: AAlbair@TheValleyPress.net
Primary Website: turleyct.com/valley-press
Avg Free Circ: 39500
Audit By: Sworn/Estimate/Non-Audited
Audit Date: 10.06.2019
Personnel: Abigail Albair (Ed.-in-Chief); Melissa Friedman (Ad. Director); Keith Turley (Pub.)
Parent company (for newspapers): Valley Press Publishing, Inc.

THE WEST HARTFORD PRESS

Street address 1: 540 Hopmeadow St
Street address city: Simsbury
Street address state: CT
Zip/Postal code: 06070-2496
General Phone: (800) 651-4700
General Fax: (800) 606-9599
Advertising Phone: (800) 978-1345
General/National Adv. E-mail: Melissa@TheValleyPress.net
Display Adv. E-mail: classifieds@thevalleypress.net
Editorial e-mail: AAlbair@TheValleyPress.net
Primary Website: turleyct.com/west-hartford-press
Avg Free Circ: 12000
Audit By: Sworn/Estimate/Non-Audited
Audit Date: 10.06.2019
Personnel: Abigail Albair (Ed.); Melissa Friedman (Ad. Director); Keith Turley (Pub.); Ed Gunderson (Pub)
Parent company (for newspapers): Valley Press Publishing, Inc.

THE WINSTED JOURNAL

Street address 1: 452 Main St
Street address city: Winsted
Street address state: CT
Zip/Postal code: 06098-1537
General Phone: (860) 738-4418
General Fax: (860) 738-3709
General/National Adv. E-mail: advertising@lakevillejournal.com
Display Adv. E-mail: advertising@lakevillejournal.com
Editorial e-mail: winstedjournal@sbcglobal.net
Primary Website: winstedjournal.com
Year Established: 1996
Avg Paid Circ: 592
Audit By: Sworn/Estimate/Non-Audited
Audit Date: 10.06.2019
Personnel: Lauren Dimauro (Office Mgr.); Anna Mae Kupferer (Adv. Dir.); Helen Testa (Circ. Mgr.); Janet Manko (Pub. & Ed. in Chief); Michael Marciano (Ed.); James Clark (Prodn. Coord.)
Parent company (for newspapers): The Lakeville Journal

TOWN TIMES

Street address 1: 449 Main Street
Street address city: Watertown
Street address state: CT
Zip/Postal code: 06795
General Phone: (860) 274-6721
General Fax: (860) 945-3116
General/National Adv. E-mail: rdobos@towntimesnews.com
Display Adv. E-mail: rdobos@towntimesnews.com
Editorial e-mail: newsdept@towntimesnews.com
Primary Website: towntimesnews.com
Year Established: 2002
Avg Paid Circ: 96
Avg Free Circ: 12859
Audit By: AAM
Audit Date: 30.09.2018
Personnel: Rudy Mazurosky (Pres.); Eliot C. White (Pub.); Kimberley Boath (Adv. Dir.); Carolyn Wallach (Managing Ed.); Joy Boone (Adv. Sales); Stephanie Wilcox (Ed.)
Parent company (for newspapers): The Record-Journal Publishing Co.

TRUMBULL TIMES

Street address 1: 1000 Bridgeport Ave
Street address city: Shelton
Street address state: CT
Zip/Postal code: 06484-4660
General Phone: (203) 926-2080
General Fax: (203) 926-2091
Advertising Phone: (203) 402-2327
Editorial Phone: (203) 402-2311
General/National Adv. E-mail: mahersam@ncadvertiser.com
Editorial e-mail: trumbulltimes@hersamacorn.com
Primary Website: trumbulltimes.com
Year Established: 1959
Avg Paid Circ: 3760
Avg Free Circ: 136
Audit By: Sworn/Estimate/Non-Audited
Audit Date: 10.06.2019
Personnel: Thomas Nash (Pub.); Mary Anne Hersam (VP of Sales); Bill Bloxsom (Sports Ed.); Donna Cosenza (Account Executive); Donald Hersam (Circ. Mgr.); Greg Moy (Prod. Mgr); Don Eng (Ed)
Parent company (for newspapers): HAN Network

VALLEY COURIER

Street address 1: 724 Boston Post Rd
Street address 2: Ste 202
Street address city: Madison
Street address state: CT
Zip/Postal code: 06443-3039
General Phone: (203) 245-1877
General Fax: (203) 245-9773
Advertising Phone: (203) 245-1877 ext 6142
Editorial Phone: (203) 245-1877 ext 6500
General/National Adv. E-mail: r.collins@shorepublishing.com
Editorial e-mail: r.collins@shorepublishing.com
Primary Website: zip06.com
Avg Free Circ: 6043
Audit By: CVC
Audit Date: 30.06.2018
Personnel: Hollis Romanelli (Acct. Manager); Brian Boyd (Ed.); Robyn Collins (Pub.); Allan Ellis (Prodn. Mgr.); Ed Majersky
Parent company (for newspapers): The Day Publishing Co.

VOICES

Street address 1: P.O. Box 383
Street address city: Southbury
Street address state: CT
Zip/Postal code: 6488
General Phone: (203) 262-6631
General Fax: (203) 262-6691
Editorial e-mail: newsdesk@ctvoices.com
Primary Website: primepublishers.com/voicesnews
Avg Paid Circ: 352
Avg Free Circ: 27650
Audit By: AAM
Audit Date: 30.09.2018
Personnel: Rudy Mazurosky (Pres. & Pub.); James Scully (Advertising Mgr.)
Parent company (for newspapers): Prime Publisher's Inc.

WEST HARTFORD NEWS

Street address 1: 100 Gando Dr
Street address city: New Haven
Street address state: CT
Zip/Postal code: 06513-1049
General Phone: (860) 294-0157
General Fax: (860) 347-4425
Advertising Phone: (800) 922-7066
Editorial Phone: (860) 294-0157
General/National Adv. E-mail: jgallacher@registercitizen.com
Display Adv. E-mail: sam@middletownpress.com
Editorial e-mail: jberry@21st-centurymedia.com
Primary Website: westhartfordnews.com
Year Established: 1931
Avg Free Circ: 10000
Audit By: Sworn/Estimate/Non-Audited
Audit Date: 10.06.2019
Personnel: Douglas Clement (Exec. Ed.); John Berry (Ed.); Matt DeRienzo; Bob Reneson (Adv. Dir.)
Parent company (for newspapers): Digital First Media

WESTON FORUM

Street address 1: 16 Bailey Ave
Street address city: Ridgefield
Street address state: CT
Zip/Postal code: 06877-4512
General Phone: (203) 894-3332
General Fax: (203) 762-3120
Advertising Phone: (203) 402-2329
Editorial Phone: (203) 894-3328
General/National Adv. E-mail: dpross@hersamacorn.com
Editorial e-mail: editor@thewestonforum.com
Primary Website: thewestonforum.com
Year Established: 1970
Avg Paid Circ: 1859
Audit By: Sworn/Estimate/Non-Audited
Audit Date: 10.06.2019
Personnel: Thomas B. Nash (Pub.); Martin V. Hersam (Gen. Mgr.); Mary Anne Hersam (VP of Sales); Kimberly Donnelly (Ed.); Rocco Valluzzo (Sports Ed.); Dave Pross (Account Exec.); Donald Hersam (Circ. Mgr.)
Parent company (for newspapers): HAN Network

WESTPORT MINUTEMAN

Street address 1: 100 Gando Dr
Street address city: New Haven
Street address state: CT
Zip/Postal code: 06513-1049
General Phone: (203) 752-2711
General Fax: (203) 789-5309
Advertising Phone: (203) 789-5484
Editorial Phone: (203) 789-5750
General/National Adv. E-mail: kkopas@westportminuteman.com
Editorial e-mail: editor@westportminuteman.com
Primary Website: minutemannewscenter.com
Mthly Avg Views: 110000
Year Established: 1992
Avg Paid Circ: 0
Avg Free Circ: 11215
Audit By: Sworn/Estimate/Non-Audited
Audit Date: 10.06.2019
Personnel: John Slater (Gen. Mgr.); Ken Kopas (Ad. Director); Tom Henry (Ed.)
Parent company (for newspapers): 21st Century Media

WESTPORT NEWS

Street address 1: 410 State St
Street address city: Bridgeport
Street address state: CT
Zip/Postal code: 06604-4501
General Phone: (203) 255-4561
General Fax: (203) 255-0456
Advertising Phone: (203) 964-2357
Editorial Phone: (203) 255-4561 ext. 111
General/National Adv. E-mail: agonzalez@scni.com
Editorial e-mail: jdoody@bcnnew.com
Primary Website: westport-news.com
Avg Paid Circ: 2505
Audit By: Sworn/Estimate/Non-Audited
Audit Date: 10.06.2019
Personnel: Ryan Lacey (Sports Ed.); Jerrod Ferrari (Ed.); Bill Mason (Circ. Dir.); Paul Barbetta (Grp. Pub./Pres.); Doreen Madden (Exec. Asst. to Pub.)
Parent company (for newspapers): Hearst Communications, Inc.

WILTON BULLETIN

Street address 1: 16 Bailey Ave
Street address city: Ridgefield
Street address state: CT
Zip/Postal code: 06877-4512
General Phone: (203) 894-3330
General Fax: (203) 762-3120
Advertising Phone: (203) 894-3323
Editorial Phone: (203) 894-3333
General/National Adv. E-mail: tjackse@hersamacorn.com
Editorial e-mail: editor@wiltonbulletin.com

Primary Website: wiltonbulletin.com
Year Established: 1937
Avg Paid Circ: 2527
Audit By: Sworn/Estimate/Non-Audited
Audit Date: 10.06.2019
Personnel: Thomas B. Nash (Pub.); Martin V. Hersam (COO); Mary Anne Hersam (VP of Sales); Jeannette Ross (Ed.); Tim Murphy (Sports Ed.); Thomas Jackse (Account Exec.); Donald Hersam (Circ. Mgr.)
Parent company (for newspapers): HAN Network

DELAWARE

BEACHCOMBER

Street address 1: 33000 Coastal Hwy
Street address 2: Beachcomber
Street address city: Bethany Beach
Street address state: DE
Zip/Postal code: 19930-3712
General Phone: (302) 537-1881
General Fax: (302) 537-9630
General/National Adv. E-mail: wave@dmg.gannett.com
Primary Website: delmarvanow.com/news/delaware
Avg Free Circ: 25000
Audit By: Sworn/Estimate/Non-Audited
Audit Date: 10.06.2019
Personnel: Pat Purdum (Gen. Mgr.); Alyson Cunningham (Beachcomber Ed.); Michael Kilian (Exec.Ed.)
Parent company (for newspapers): Gannett

CAPE GAZETTE

Street address 1: 17585 Nassau Commons Blvd.
Street address city: Lewes
Street address state: DE
Zip/Postal code: 19958
General Phone: 302-645-7700
General Fax: 302-644-1664
Advertising Phone: 302-645-7700
Advertising Fax: 302-644-1664
Editorial Phone: 302-645-7700
Editorial Fax: 302-644-1664
General/National Adv. E-mail: info@capegazette.com
Display Adv. E-mail: adsales@capegazette.com
Classified Adv. e-mail: adsales@capegazette.com
Editorial e-mail: newsroom@capegazette.com
Primary Website: Capegazette.com
Mthly Avg Views: 2100000
Mthly Avg Unique Visitors: 425000
Year Established: 1993
Avg Paid Circ: 13000
Audit By: USPS
Audit Date: 30.09.2021
Personnel: Charity Vernon (HR/Office Manager); Dennis Fourney (Pub./Adv. Dir.); Trish Vernon (Ed.); Laura Ritter (Ed.); Teresa Rodriguez (Prod.); Cindy Bowlin (Adv. Mgr.); Chris Rausch (Sales Manager)
Parent company (for newspapers): Cape Gazette LLC

COASTAL POINT

Street address 1: 111 Atlantic Ave
Street address 2: Ste 2
Street address city: Ocean View
Street address state: DE
Zip/Postal code: 19970-9166
General Phone: (302) 539-1788
General Fax: (302) 539-3777
Advertising Phone: (302) 539-1788
Advertising Fax: (302) 539-3777
Editorial Phone: (302) 539-1788
Editorial Fax: (302) 539-3777
General/National Adv. E-mail: susan.lyons@coastalpoint.com
Display Adv. E-mail: susan.mutz@coastalpoint.com
Classified Adv. e-mail: jane.johnson@coastalpoint.com
Editorial e-mail: darin.mccann@coastalpoint.com
Primary Website: coastalpoint.com
Year Established: 2004
Avg Paid Circ: 40
Avg Free Circ: 18000
Audit By: Sworn/Estimate/Non-Audited
Audit Date: 10.06.2019
Personnel: Susan Lyons (Pub.); Darin McCann (Editor); Jane Johnson (Classified Manager); Susan Mutz (Advertising Manager)

DORCHESTER BANNER

Street address 1: 110 Galaxy Drive
Street address city: Dover
Street address state: DE
Zip/Postal code: 19901
General Phone: (410) 228-3131
General Fax: (410) 228-6547
Advertising Phone: (410) 228-3131
Editorial Phone: (410) 228-3131
General/National Adv. E-mail: banner@newszap.com
Display Adv. E-mail: classads@newszap.com
Editorial e-mail: dryan@newszap.com
Primary Website: baytobaynews.com
Year Established: 1897
Avg Paid Circ: 1886
Avg Free Circ: 121
Audit By: USPS
Audit Date: 30.09.2022
Personnel: Darel La Prade (Pub.); Konrad La Prade (Promotions Manager); Tim Gary (Major Accts. Adv. Mgr.); Dave Cannon (Advertising Manager)
Parent company (for newspapers): Independent Newsmedia Inc. USA

DOVER POST

Street address 1: 1196 S Little Creek Rd
Street address city: Dover
Street address state: DE
Zip/Postal code: 19901-4727
General Phone: (302) 678-3616
General Fax: (302) 678-8291
Advertising Phone: (302) 346-5434
Editorial Phone: (302) 346-5418
General/National Adv. E-mail: brigitte.mckinney@doverpost.com
Display Adv. E-mail: brandi.ford@doverpost.com
Editorial e-mail: jesse.chadderdon@doverpost.com
Primary Website: doverpost.com
Mthly Avg Views: 263461
Mthly Avg Unique Visitors: 66255
Year Established: 1975
Avg Paid Circ: 660
Avg Free Circ: 21088
Audit By: CVC
Audit Date: 30.06.2016
Personnel: Jesse Chadderdon (Exec. Ed.); Jennifer Hayes (News Ed.); Brigitte McKinney (Adv. Sales Mgr.); Jay Parsons (Prod. Dir.); Amanda Johnston (Adv. Sales Mgr); Stacey Poore (Circ. Mgr); Amy Dotson-Newton (Pub. & Adv. Dir.)
Parent company (for newspapers): CherryRoad Media

HOCKESSIN COMMUNITY NEWS

Street address 1: 24 W Main St
Street address city: Middletown
Street address state: DE
Zip/Postal code: 19709-1039
General Phone: (302) 378-9531
General Fax: (302) 378-0647
Advertising Phone: (302) 378-9531 ext. 13
Editorial Phone: (302) 346-5418
General/National Adv. E-mail: amanda.johnston@doverpost.com
Display Adv. E-mail: brandi.ford@doverpost.com
Editorial e-mail: jesse.chadderdon@doverpost.com
Primary Website: hockessincommunitynews.com
Year Established: 1983
Avg Paid Circ: 6
Avg Free Circ: 13626
Audit By: CVC
Audit Date: 30.06.2016
Personnel: Jay Parsons (Prod. Dir.); Amanda Johnston (Sales Mgr.); Jesse Chadderdon (Exec. Ed.); Keven Todd (Pres./Pub.); Clarissa Williams (Pub.); Brigitte McKinney; Stacey Poore (Circ. Mgr)
Parent company (for newspapers): CherryRoad Media

MILFORD BEACON

Street address 1: 1196 S Little Creek Rd
Street address city: Dover
Street address state: DE
Zip/Postal code: 19901-4727
General Phone: (302) 678-3616
General Fax: (302) 856-0925
Editorial Phone: (302) 346-5418
General/National Adv. E-mail: kathy.mcginty@doverpost.com
Display Adv. E-mail: brandi.ford@doverpost.com
Editorial e-mail: jesse.chadderdon@doverpost.com
Primary Website: milfordbeacon.com
Mthly Avg Views: 43823
Mthly Avg Unique Visitors: 19890
Year Established: 2004
Avg Paid Circ: 235
Avg Free Circ: 6149
Audit By: CVC
Audit Date: 30.06.2016
Personnel: Jay Parsons (Prod. Mgr.); Jesse Chadderdon (Exec. Ed.); Jennifer Hayes (News Ed.); Kathy McGinty (Sales Mgr.); Keven Todd (Pres./Pub.); Clarissa Williams (Pub.); Amanda Johnston (Adv. Mgr); Brigitte McKinney (Adv. Mgr); Stacey Poore (Circ. Mgr)
Parent company (for newspapers): CherryRoad Media

MILFORD CHRONICLE

Street address 1: 37A N WALNUT ST
Street address city: Milford
Street address state: DE
Zip/Postal code: 19963-1445
General Phone: (302) 422-1200
General Fax: (302) 422-1208
Advertising Phone: (302) 422-1200
Advertising Fax: (302) 422-1208
Editorial Phone: (302) 422-1200
Editorial Fax: (302) 422-1208
General/National Adv. E-mail: adsupport@newszap.com
Display Adv. E-mail: classads@newszap.com
Editorial e-mail: mc@newszap.com
Primary Website: milfordchronicle.net
Year Established: 1878
Avg Paid Circ: 235
Avg Free Circ: 161
Audit By: Sworn/Estimate/Non-Audited
Audit Date: 10.06.2019
Personnel: Darel La Prade (Publisher); Konrad La Prade (Promotions Manager); Tim Gary (Major Accts. Adv. Mgr.)
Parent company (for newspapers): Independent Newsmedia Inc. USA

SMYRNA/CLAYTON SUN-TIMES

Street address 1: 24 W Main St
Street address city: Middletown
Street address state: DE
Zip/Postal code: 19709-1039
General Phone: (302) 653-2083
General Fax: (302) 653-8821
Advertising Phone: (302) 346-5434
Editorial Phone: (302) 346-5418
General/National Adv. E-mail: brigitte.mckinney@doverpost.com
Display Adv. E-mail: brandi.ford@doverpost.com
Editorial e-mail: jesse.chadderdon@doverpost.com
Primary Website: scsuntimes.com
Mthly Avg Views: 81641
Mthly Avg Unique Visitors: 27690
Year Established: 1854
Avg Paid Circ: 1768
Avg Free Circ: 955
Audit By: CVC
Audit Date: 30.06.2016
Personnel: Brigitte McKinney (Adv. Mgr.); Ben Mace (Ed.); Keven Todd (Pres./Pub.); Clarissa Williams (Pub. Mgr); Amanda Johnston (Adv. Mgr); Stacey Poore (Circ. Mgr)
Parent company (for newspapers): CherryRoad Media

SUSSEX POST

Street address 1: 110 Galaxy Drive
Street address city: Dover
Street address state: DE
Zip/Postal code: 19901
General Phone: (302) 629-5505
General Fax: (302) 422-1208
Advertising Phone: (302) 629-5505
Advertising Fax: (302) 422-1208
Editorial Phone: (302) 629-5505
Editorial Fax: (302) 422-1208
General/National Adv. E-mail: sussexpost@iniusa.org
Display Adv. E-mail: classads@newszap.com
Editorial e-mail: sussexpost@newszap.com
Primary Website: BaytoBayNews.com
Mthly Avg Views: 200000
Mthly Avg Unique Visitors: 70000
Year Established: 1972
Avg Free Circ: 11837
Audit By: USPS
Audit Date: 10.[illegible]
Personnel: Darel LaPrade (Publisher); Ashley Dawson (Managing editor); Konrad La Prade (VP Advertising)
Parent company (for newspapers): Independent Newsmedia Inc. USA

THE DELAWARE WAVE

Street address 1: Route 1 Lem Hickman Plaza
Street address city: Bethany Beach
Street address state: DE
Zip/Postal code: 19973
General Phone: (302) 537-1881
General Fax: (302) 537-9630
Advertising Phone: (302) 537-1881 ext.125
Editorial Phone: (302) 537-1881 ext.200
General/National Adv. E-mail: rpousson@gannett.com
Display Adv. E-mail: rpousson@gannett.com
Editorial e-mail: acunningh@dmg.gannett.com
Primary Website: delmarvanow.com/news/delaware
Avg Free Circ: 20328
Audit By: AAM
Audit Date: 31.03.2018
Personnel: Mike Kilian (Exec. Ed.); Alyson Cunningham (Ed.); Ron Smith (Op. Dir.); Robb Scott (Dir. Sales); Pat Purdum (Sales Mgr.); Tom Claybaugh (Gen Mgr.); Ron Pousson (Adv. Dir.)
Parent company (for newspapers): Gannett

THE MIDDLETOWN TRANSCRIPT

Street address 1: 24 W Main St
Street address city: Middletown
Street address state: DE
Zip/Postal code: 19709-1039
General Phone: (302) 378-9531
General Fax: (302) 378-0114
Advertising Phone: (302) 378-9531 ext. 13
Editorial Phone: (302) 346-5418
General/National Adv. E-mail: amanda.johnston@doverpost.com
Display Adv. E-mail: brandi.ford@doverpost.com
Editorial e-mail: jesse.chadderdon@doverpost.com
Primary Website: middletowntranscript.com
Mthly Avg Views: 93391
Mthly Avg Unique Visitors: 29835
Year Established: 1868
Avg Paid Circ: 498
Avg Free Circ: 13206
Audit By: CVC
Audit Date: 30.06.2016
Personnel: Jay Parsons (Prod. Dir.); Jesse Chadderdon (Exec. Ed.); Ben Mace (Ed.); Amanda Johnston (Adv. Sales Mgr.); Keven Todd (Pres./Pub.); Clarissa Williams (Pub.); Brigitte McKinney (Adv. Sales Mgr); Stacey Poore (Circ. Mgr)
Parent company (for newspapers): CherryRoad Media

THE SUSSEX COUNTIAN

Street address 1: 1196 S Little Creek Rd
Street address city: Dover
Street address state: DE
Zip/Postal code: 19901-4727
General Phone: (302) 678-3616
General Fax: (302) 856-0925
Editorial Phone: (302) 346-5418
General/National Adv. E-mail: kathy.mcginty@doverpost.com
Display Adv. E-mail: brandi.ford@doverpost.com
Editorial e-mail: jesse.chadderdon@doverpost.com
Primary Website: sussexcountian.com
Mthly Avg Views: 42711
Mthly Avg Unique Visitors: 23318
Year Established: 1886
Avg Paid Circ: 202
Avg Free Circ: 1637
Audit By: CVC
Audit Date: 30.06.2016
Personnel: Jay Parsons (Prod. Dir.); Jesse Chadderdon (Exec. Ed.); Jennifer Hayes (Ed.); Kathy McGinty (Sales Mgr.); Keven Todd (Pres./Pub.); Clarissa Williams (Pub.); Amanda Johnston (Adv. Mgr); Brigitte McKinney (Adv. Mgr); Stacey Poore (Circ. Mgr)
Parent company (for newspapers): CherryRoad Media

DISTRICT OF

COLUMBIA

ALBERNI VALLEY NEWS

Street address 1: 4918 Napier Street,
Street address city: Port Alberni
Street address state: BC
Zip/Postal code: V9Y 6H2

DUPONT CURRENT

Street address 1: 5185 MacArthur Blvd NW
Street address 2: Ste 102
Street address city: Washington
Street address state: DC
Zip/Postal code: 20016-3349
General Phone: (202) 244-7223
General Fax: (202) 363-9850
Advertising Phone: (202) 244-7223
General/National Adv. E-mail: garysocha@currentnewspapers.com
Display Adv. E-mail: garysocha@currentnewspapers.com
Editorial e-mail: newsdesk@currentnewspapers.com
Primary Website: currentnewspapers.com
Avg Paid Circ: 3
Avg Free Circ: 12098
Audit By: Sworn/Estimate/Non-Audited
Audit Date: 10.06.2019
Personnel: Davis Kennedy (Pub./Ed.); Gary Socha (Adv. Dir.); Chris Kain (Mgn. Ed.); Chip Py (Acct. Exec.); Shani Madden (Acct. Exec.); George Steinbrauer (Service Dir./Classified Adv. Mgr.)

FOGGY BOTTOM CURRENT

Street address 1: 5185 MacArthur Blvd NW
Street address 2: Ste 102
Street address city: Washington
Street address state: DC
Zip/Postal code: 20016-3349
General Phone: (202) 244-7223
General Fax: (202) 363-9850
Advertising Phone: (202) 244-7223
General/National Adv. E-mail: garysocha@currentnewspapers.com
Display Adv. E-mail: garysocha@currentnewspapers.com
Editorial e-mail: newsdesk@currentnewspapers.com
Primary Website: currentnewspapers.com
Avg Paid Circ: 2
Avg Free Circ: 2132
Audit By: Sworn/Estimate/Non-Audited
Audit Date: 10.06.2019
Personnel: Davis Kennedy (Pub./Ed.); Gary Socha (Adv. Dir.); Chris Kain (Mgn. Ed.); George Steinbrauer (Service Dir./Classified Adv. Mgr.); Chip Py (Acct. Exec.); Shani Madden (Acct. Exec.)

GEORGETOWN CURRENT

Street address 1: 5185 MacArthur Blvd NW
Street address 2: Ste 102
Street address city: Washington
Street address state: DC
Zip/Postal code: 20016-3349
General Phone: (202) 244-7223
General Fax: (202) 363-9850
Advertising Phone: (202) 244-7223
General/National Adv. E-mail: garysocha@currentnewspapers.com
Display Adv. E-mail: garysocha@currentnewspapers.com
Editorial e-mail: newsdesk@currentnewspapers.com
Primary Website: currentnewspapers.com
Avg Paid Circ: 5
Avg Free Circ: 7789
Audit By: Sworn/Estimate/Non-Audited
Audit Date: 10.06.2019
Personnel: Davis Kennedy (Pub./Ed.); Gary Socha (Adv. Mgr.); Chris Kain; Shani Madden (Acct. Exec.); Chip Py (Acct. Exec.); George Steinbrauer (Service Dir./Classified Adv. Mgr.)

NORTHWEST CURRENT

Street address 1: 5185 MacArthur Blvd NW
Street address 2: Ste 102
Street address city: Washington
Street address state: DC
Zip/Postal code: 20016-3349
General Phone: (202) 244-7223
General Fax: (202) 363-9850
Advertising Phone: (202) 244-7223
General/National Adv. E-mail: garysocha@currentnewspapers.com
Display Adv. E-mail: garysocha@currentnewspapers.com
Editorial e-mail: newsdesk@currentnewspapers.com
Primary Website: currentnewspapers.com
Year Established: 1976
Avg Paid Circ: 31
Avg Free Circ: 23591
Audit By: Sworn/Estimate/Non-Audited
Audit Date: 10.06.2019
Personnel: Davis Kennedy (Pub./Ed.); Gary Socha (Adv. Dir.); Chris Kain (Mgn. Ed.); George Steinbrauer (Service Dir./Classified Adv. Mgr.); Chip Py (Acct. Exec.); Shani Madden (Acct. Exec.)

THE INTOWNER

Street address 1: 1730B Corcoran St NW
Street address city: Washington
Street address state: DC
Zip/Postal code: 20009-2406
General Phone: (202) 234-1717
Advertising Phone: (202) 234-1717
Editorial Phone: (202) 234-1717
General/National Adv. E-mail: advertising@intowner.com
Display Adv. E-mail: advertising@intowner.com
Editorial e-mail: newsroom@intowner.com
Primary Website: intowner.com
Year Established: 1968
Avg Free Circ: 20000
Audit By: Sworn/Estimate/Non-Audited
Audit Date: 10.06.2019
Personnel: P.L. Wolff (Mng Ed)
Parent company (for newspapers): InTowner Publishing Corp.

FLORIDA

ALACHUA COUNTY TODAY

Street address 1: 14804 Main St
Street address city: Alachua
Street address state: FL
Zip/Postal code: 32615-8590
General Phone: (386) 462-3355
General Fax: (386) 462-4569
General/National Adv. E-mail: ads@alachuatoday.com
Editorial e-mail: editor@alachuatoday.com
Primary Website: alachuatoday.com
Year Established: 2000
Avg Paid Circ: 5000
Audit By: Sworn/Estimate/Non-Audited
Audit Date: 10.06.2019
Personnel: Robert Boukari (Advertisement); Bryan Boukari (Publisher); Ellen Boukari (Executive Editor); Gail Luparello (Associate Publisher)

ANNA MARIA ISLAND SUN

Street address 1: 9801 Gulf Drive
Street address city: Anna Maria
Street address state: FL
Zip/Postal code: 34216
General Phone: (941) 778-3986
General Fax: (941) 778-6988
General/National Adv. E-mail: ads@amisun.com
Display Adv. E-mail: classifieds@amisun.com
Primary Website: amisun.com
Year Established: 2000
Avg Free Circ: 16000
Audit By: Sworn/Estimate/Non-Audited
Audit Date: 10.06.2019
Personnel: Mike Field (Publisher, Editor); Maggie Field (Co-Publisher); Chantelle Lewin (Advertisement)

APOPKA CHIEF (THE)

Street address 1: 400 N Park Ave
Street address city: Apopka
Street address state: FL
Zip/Postal code: 32712-4152
General Phone: (407) 886-2777
General Fax: (407) 889-4121
General/National Adv. E-mail: news@theapopkachief.com
Display Adv. E-mail: ads@theapopkachief..com
Editorial e-mail: news@theapopkachief..com
Primary Website: theapopkachief.com
Year Established: 1923
Avg Paid Circ: 5000
Avg Free Circ: 100
Audit By: Sworn/Estimate/Non-Audited
Audit Date: 10.06.2021
Personnel: John E. Ricketson (Pub.); Jackie Trefcer (Mktg. & Ad. Dir.); Neoma DeGard Knox (Gen. Mgr.); John Peery (Ed.); Elain Gibbons (Adv. Mgr.); Kathleen Jackson (Adv. Rep.); Kayla Leon (Adv. Rep.)

ARCADIAN

Street address 1: 108 S Polk Ave
Street address city: Arcadia
Street address state: FL
Zip/Postal code: 34266-3952
General Phone: (863) 494-7600
General Fax: (863) 494-3533
General/National Adv. E-mail: majoraccts@sun-herald.com
Display Adv. E-mail: gkotz@sun-herald.com
Editorial e-mail: feedback@sun-herald.com
Primary Website: yoursun.net
Audit By: Sworn/Estimate/Non-Audited
Audit Date: 10.06.2019
Personnel: Joe Gallimore (Pub.); Steve Bauer (Ed.); Mark Yero (Cird. Dir.); David Dunn-Rankin (Pres.); Jim Gouvellis (Exec. Ed.)
Parent company (for newspapers): Sun Coast Media Group - APG

BAY COUNTY BULLET

Street address 1: 1714 W 23rd St
Street address 2: Suite G
Street address city: Panama City
Street address state: FL
Zip/Postal code: 32405-2924
General Phone: (850) 640-0855
General Fax: (850) 391-6648
General/National Adv. E-mail: ads@baybullet.com
Display Adv. E-mail: classifieds@baybullet.com
Editorial e-mail: news@baybullet.com
Primary Website: baybullet.com
Year Established: 2009
Avg Paid Circ: 3300
Avg Free Circ: 2700
Audit By: Sworn/Estimate/Non-Audited
Audit Date: 10.06.2019
Personnel: Phil Lucas (Editor); Linda Lucas (Pub.)

BEACH BEACON

Street address 1: 9911 Seminole Blvd
Street address city: Seminole
Street address state: FL
Zip/Postal code: 33772-2536
General Phone: (727) 397-5563
General Fax: (727) 397-5902
General/National Adv. E-mail: jrey@tbnweekly.com
Display Adv. E-mail: wedwards@tbnweekly.com
Classified Adv. e-mail: wedwards@tbnweekly.com
Editorial e-mail: editorial@tbnweekly.com
Primary Website: tbnweekly.com
Mthly Avg Unique Visitors: 45
Year Established: 1980
Avg Free Circ: 14334
Audit By: Sworn/Estimate/Non-Audited
Audit Date: 10.06.2019
Personnel: Dan Autrey (Pub./Pres.); Jay Rey (Adv. Mgr.); Dave Brown (Prod. Mgr.); Don Henry (Dist. Mgr.)
Parent company (for newspapers): Tampa Bay Newspapers

BELLEAIR BEE

Street address 1: 9911 Seminole Blvd
Street address city: Seminole
Street address state: FL
Zip/Postal code: 33772-2536
General Phone: (727) 397-5563
General Fax: (727) 397-5902
General/National Adv. E-mail: jrey@tbnweekly.com
Display Adv. E-mail: wedwards@tbnweekly.com
Classified Adv. e-mail: wedwards@tbnweekly.com
Editorial e-mail: dautrey@tbnweekly.com
Primary Website: tbnweekly.com
Year Established: 1975
Avg Free Circ: 12100
Audit By: Sworn/Estimate/Non-Audited
Audit Date: 10.06.2019
Personnel: Dan Autrey (Pub./Pres.); Jay Rey (Adv. Mgr); Dave Brown (Prod. Mgr); Don Henry (Dist. Mgr.)
Parent company (for newspapers): Tampa Bay Newspapers, Inc.

BEST - CENTRAL

Street address 1: 1 Gannett Plaza
Street address city: Melbourne
Street address state: FL
Zip/Postal code: 32940
General Phone: (321) 242-3500
General Fax: (321) 242-6620
Advertising Phone: (321) 242-3765
Advertising Fax: (321) 610-5152
Editorial Phone: (321) 242-3774
Editorial Fax: (321) 242-6620
General/National Adv. E-mail: advertising@floridatoday.com
Editorial e-mail: sprice@floridatoday.com
Primary Website: floridatoday.com
Avg Paid Circ: 45000
Audit By: Sworn/Estimate/Non-Audited
Audit Date: 10.06.2019
Personnel: Jeff Kiel (President & Publisher); Bob Stover (Exec. Editor); Shona Price (Editor); Stephanie McLoughlin (Ad. Dir.)
Parent company (for newspapers): Gannett

BEST - NORTH

Street address 1: 1 Gannett Plaza
Street address city: Melbourne
Street address state: FL
Zip/Postal code: 32940
General Phone: (321) 242-3500
General Fax: (321) 242-6620
Advertising Phone: (321) 242-3765
Advertising Fax: (321) 610-5152
Editorial Phone: (321) 242-3774
Editorial Fax: (321) 242-6620
General/National Adv. E-mail: advertising@floridatoday.com
Editorial e-mail: sprice@floridatoday.com
Primary Website: floridatoday.com
Avg Paid Circ: 55000
Audit By: Sworn/Estimate/Non-Audited
Audit Date: 10.06.2019
Personnel: Jeff Kiel (President & Publisher); Bob Stover (Exec. Editor); Shona Price (Editor); Stephanie McLoughlin (Ad. Director)
Parent company (for newspapers): Gannett

BEST - SOUTH

Street address 1: 1 Gannett Plaza
Street address city: Melbourne
Street address state: FL
Zip/Postal code: 32940
General Phone: (321) 242-3500
General Fax: (321) 242-6620
Advertising Phone: (321) 242-3765
Advertising Fax: (321) 610-5152
Editorial Phone: (321) 242-3774
Editorial Fax: (321) 242-6620
General/National Adv. E-mail: advertising@floridatoday.com
Editorial e-mail: sprice@floridatoday.com
Primary Website: floridatoday.com
Avg Paid Circ: 55000
Audit By: Sworn/Estimate/Non-Audited
Audit Date: 10.06.2019
Personnel: Stephanie McLoughlin (Ad. Dir.); Shona Price (Editor); Bob Stover (Exec. Editor); Jeff Kiel (President & Publisher)
Parent company (for newspapers): Gannett

BOCA BEACON

Street address 1: 431 Park Ave
Street address city: Boca Grande
Street address state: FL
Zip/Postal code: 33921
General Phone: (941) 964-2995
General Fax: (941) 964-0372
General/National Adv. E-mail: info@bocabeacon.com
Primary Website: bocabeacon.com
Year Established: 1980

Avg Paid Circ: 3000
Avg Free Circ: 4000
Audit By: Sworn/Estimate/Non-Audited
Audit Date: 10.06.2019
Personnel: Dusty Hopkins (Publisher & General Manager); Karen Clark (Office Mgr.); Julianne Greenberg (Ad. Rep.); Dizey Lindquist (Adv. Rep.); Marcy Shortuse (Ed.)

BOCA RATON FORUM

Street address 1: 500 E Broward Blvd
Street address city: Fort Lauderdale
Street address state: FL
Zip/Postal code: 33394-3000
General Phone: (954) 698-6397
General Fax: (954) 429-1207
Editorial e-mail: PDoto@tribune.com
Primary Website: forumpubs.com
Year Established: 1973
Avg Paid Circ: 0
Avg Free Circ: 26960
Audit By: CVC
Audit Date: 6/31/2018
Personnel: Mark Ward (Circ.); Pam Doto; Ed Wilder
Parent company (for newspapers): Sun-Sentinel Co.

BONITA SPRINGS FLORIDA WEEKLY

Street address 1: 9051 Tamiami Trl N
Street address 2: Ste 202
Street address city: Naples
Street address state: FL
Zip/Postal code: 34108-2520
General Phone: (239) 325-1960
General/National Adv. E-mail: advertise@floridaweekly.com
Display Adv. E-mail: advertise@floridaweekly.com
Editorial e-mail: news@floridaweekly.com
Primary Website: floridaweekly.com
Avg Paid Circ: 35646
Audit By: Sworn/Estimate/Non-Audited
Audit Date: 10.06.2019
Personnel: J. Pason Gaddis (Pres./Pub.); Jeffrey Cull (VP and Exec. Ed.); Jim Dickerson (VP and Creative Dir.); Shelley Hobbs (Nat'l Adv. Mgr.)
Parent company (for newspapers): Florida Media Group LLC

BOYNTON FORUM

Street address 1: 500 E Broward Blvd
Street address city: Fort Lauderdale
Street address state: FL
Zip/Postal code: 33394-3000
General Phone: (954) 698-6397
General Fax: (954) 698-6719
General/National Adv. E-mail: gbehar@tribune.com
Primary Website: sun-sentinel.com/local/palm-beach/boynton-beach
Avg Paid Circ: 0
Avg Free Circ: 77744
Audit By: Sworn/Estimate/Non-Audited
Audit Date: 10.06.2019
Personnel: Lisa Goodlin; Mark Ward (Circ. Mgr.); Tom Adams (Pub./Pres.)
Parent company (for newspapers): Forum Publishing Group

BRADFORD COUNTY TELEGRAPH

Street address 1: 135 W Call St
Street address city: Starke
Street address state: FL
Zip/Postal code: 32091-3210
General Phone: (904) 964-6305
General Fax: (904) 964-8628
Advertising Phone: (904) 964-6305
General/National Adv. E-mail: darlene@bctelegraph.com
Display Adv. E-mail: classads@bctelegraph.com
Editorial e-mail: editor@bctelegraph.com
Primary Website: bctelegraph.com
Year Established: 1879
Avg Paid Circ: 5825
Avg Free Circ: 1000
Audit By: Sworn/Estimate/Non-Audited
Audit Date: 10.06.2019
Personnel: John Miller (Pub.); Mark Crawford (Ed.)

BRANDON NEWS & TRIBUNE

Street address 1: 202 S Parker St
Street address city: Tampa
Street address state: FL
Zip/Postal code: 33606-2379
General Phone: (813) 259-7711
Advertising Phone: (813) 259-7455
Advertising Fax: (813) 259-7903
General/National Adv. E-mail: adsolutions@tampatrib.com
Primary Website: tbo.com/brandon
Year Established: 1956
Avg Paid Circ: 16682
Avg Free Circ: 41318
Audit By: Sworn/Estimate/Non-Audited
Audit Date: 10.06.2019
Personnel: Carla Floyd (Pub.); Annette Demask (Adv. Mgr.); Susan Anastasia (Ed.); Russell Holecek (Mng. Ed.)
Parent company (for newspapers): Tampa Media Group

BUSINESS OBSERVER

Street address 1: 1970 Main St
Street address 2: Fl 3
Street address city: Sarasota
Street address state: FL
Zip/Postal code: 34236-5923
General Phone: (941)362-4848
General Fax: (941) 9362-4808
Advertising Phone: (941) 726-6145
Editorial Phone: (941) 362-4848 x303
General/National Adv. E-mail: dschaefer@BusinessObserverFL.com
Editorial e-mail: mgordon@BusinessObserverFL.com
Primary Website: businessobserverfl.com
Year Established: 1997
Avg Paid Circ: 1515
Avg Free Circ: 5139
Audit By: VAC
Audit Date: 30.09.2016
Personnel: Matthew G. Walsh (CEO/Pub./Ed.); Diane Schaefer (Assoc. Pub., Adv.); Mark Gordon (Ed.); Anne Shumate (Dir. Sales/Mktg.); Kat Hughes (Exec. Ed.)
Parent company (for newspapers): Observer Media Group Inc.

BUSINESS OBSERVER-COLLIER

Street address 1: 501 Goodlette Rd N
Street address 2: Ste D100
Street address city: Naples
Street address state: FL
Zip/Postal code: 34102-5666
General Phone: (239) 263-0122
General Fax: (239) 263-0112
Advertising Phone: (941) 726-6145
Advertising Fax: (239) 263-0112
Editorial Phone: (239) 275-2230
Editorial Fax: (239) 263-0112
General/National Adv. E-mail: dschaefer@BusinessObserverFL.com
Display Adv. E-mail: kboothroyd@BusinessObserverFL.com
Editorial e-mail: gruss@BusinessObserverFL.com
Primary Website: businessobserverfl.com
Year Established: 1997
Avg Paid Circ: 145
Avg Free Circ: 446
Audit By: Sworn/Estimate/Non-Audited
Audit Date: 10.06.2019
Personnel: Matthew G. Walsh (Publisher); Diane Schaefer (Assoc. Pub./Adv. Dir.); Jean Gruss (Ed.)
Parent company (for newspapers): Observer Media Group Inc.

BUSINESS OBSERVER-HILLSBOROUGH-PASCO

Street address 1: 1970 Main St
Street address 2: Ste 400
Street address city: Sarasota
Street address state: FL
Zip/Postal code: 34236-5921
General Phone: (941) 362-4848
General Fax: (941) 362-4808
Advertising Phone: (941) 726-6145
Advertising Fax: (941) 362-4808
Editorial Phone: (941) 362-4848
Editorial Fax: (941) 362-4808
General/National Adv. E-mail: dschaefer@BusinessObserverFL.com
Display Adv. E-mail: kboothroyd@BusinessObserverFL.com
Editorial e-mail: mwalsh@BusinessObserverFL.com
Primary Website: businessobserverfl.com
Year Established: 1997
Avg Paid Circ: 403
Avg Free Circ: 1112
Audit By: Sworn/Estimate/Non-Audited
Audit Date: 10.06.2019
Personnel: Matthew G. Walsh (Publisher); Diane Schaefer (Assoc. Pub./Adv. Dir.); Kat Hughes (Mng. Ed.)
Parent company (for newspapers): Observer Media Group Inc.

BUSINESS OBSERVER-LEE

Street address 1: 1970 Main St
Street address 2: Fl 3
Street address city: Sarasota
Street address state: FL
Zip/Postal code: 34236-5923
General Phone: (941) 906-9386
General Fax: (239) 936-1001
Advertising Phone: (941) 726-6145
Advertising Fax: (239) 936-1001
Editorial Phone: (239) 275-2230
Editorial Fax: (239) 936-1001
General/National Adv. E-mail: dschaefer@BusinessObserverFL.com
Display Adv. E-mail: kboothroyd@BusinessObserverFL.com
Editorial e-mail: gruss@BusinessObserverFL.com
Primary Website: businessobserverfl.com
Year Established: 1997
Avg Paid Circ: 202
Avg Free Circ: 590
Audit By: Sworn/Estimate/Non-Audited
Audit Date: 10.06.2019
Personnel: Matthew G. Walsh (Publisher); Diane Schaefer (Assoc. Pub./Adv. Dir.); Jean Gruss (Ed.)
Parent company (for newspapers): Observer Media Group Inc.

BUSINESS OBSERVER-PINELLAS

Street address 1: 14004 Roosevelt Blvd
Street address 2: Ste 604
Street address city: Clearwater
Street address state: FL
Zip/Postal code: 33762-3850
General Phone: (727) 447-7784
General Fax: (727) 447-3944
Advertising Phone: (941) 726-6145
Advertising Fax: (727) 447-3944
Editorial Phone: (727) 254-0976
Editorial Fax: (727) 447-3944
General/National Adv. E-mail: dschaefer@BusinessObserverFL.com
Display Adv. E-mail: kboothroyd@BusinessObserverFL.com
Editorial e-mail: khughes@BusinessObserverFL.com
Primary Website: businessobserverfl.com
Year Established: 1997
Avg Paid Circ: 185
Avg Free Circ: 696
Audit By: Sworn/Estimate/Non-Audited
Audit Date: 10.06.2019
Personnel: Matthew G. Walsh (Publisher); Diane Schaefer (Assoc. Pub./Adv. Dir.)
Parent company (for newspapers): Observer Media Group Inc.

CALOOSA BELLE

Street address 1: PO Box 518
Street address city: Labelle
Street address state: FL
Zip/Postal code: 33975-0518
General Phone: (863) 675-2541
Primary Website: http://caloosabelle.com
Audit By: Sworn/Estimate/Non-Audited
Audit Date: 10.06.2019
Personnel: Katrina Elsken (Exec. Ed.)
Parent company (for newspapers): Independent Newsmedia Inc. USA; Independent Newspapers, Inc. (Florida)

CAPE CORAL BREEZE

Street address 1: 2510 Del Prado Blvd S
Street address city: Cape Coral
Street address state: FL
Zip/Postal code: 33904-5750
General Phone: (239) 574-1110
General Fax: (239) 573-2318
Advertising Phone: (239) 574-1110
Advertising Fax: (239) 574-3403
Editorial Phone: (239) 574-1110
Editorial Fax: (239) 574-5693
Display Adv. E-mail: jkonig@breezenewspapers.com
Classified Adv. e-mail: jkonig@breezenewspapers.com
Editorial e-mail: sblonde@breezenewspapers.com
Primary Website: breezenewspapers.com
Year Established: 1951
Avg Paid Circ: 1742
Avg Free Circ: 71872
Audit By: CVC
Audit Date: 30.09.2017
Personnel: Scott Blonde (Pub.); Renee Brown (Adv. Dir.); Chris Strine (Mng. Ed.); Valarie Harring (Executive ed.); Michael Pistella (Photo Dept. Mgr.); Jim Linette (Sports Ed.); Henry Keim (Prodn. Mgr., Press); Smith Barbara (Circulation Director); Jim Konig (Advertisng Director); Tiffany Repecki (Assoc. ed.); Stephanie Struense (National & Major Account Sales Manager)
Parent company (for newspapers): Ogden Newspapers Inc.

CAPTIVA CURRENT

Street address 1: 695 Tarpon Bay Rd Unit 13
Street address 2: #13
Street address city: Sanibel
Street address state: FL
Zip/Postal code: 33957-3135
General Phone: (239) 472-1587
General Fax: (239) 472-8398
General/National Adv. E-mail: dpapoi@breezenewspapers.com
Editorial e-mail: mcassidy@breezenewspapers.com
Primary Website: captivasanibel.com
Year Established: 1990
Avg Paid Circ: 142
Avg Free Circ: 466
Audit By: Sworn/Estimate/Non-Audited
Audit Date: 10.06.2019
Personnel: Danielle Papoi (Ad. Sales); Scott Blonde (Pub.); Mckenzie Cassidy (Editor)
Parent company (for newspapers): Ogden Newspapers Inc.

CARROLLWOOD NEWS & TRIBUNE

Street address 1: 202 S Parker St
Street address city: Tampa
Street address state: FL
Zip/Postal code: 33606-2379
General Phone: (813) 259-7711
Advertising Phone: (813) 259-7455
Advertising Fax: (813) 259-7903
General/National Adv. E-mail: adsolutions@tampatrib.com
Primary Website: tbo.com/carrollwood
Avg Paid Circ: 12851
Avg Free Circ: 35800
Audit By: Sworn/Estimate/Non-Audited
Audit Date: 10.06.2019
Personnel: Denise Palmer (Pub.); Russell Holecek (Ed.)
Parent company (for newspapers): Tampa Media Group

CHIEFLAND CITIZEN

Street address 1: 624 W Park Ave
Street address city: Chiefland
Street address state: FL
Zip/Postal code: 32626-0430
General Phone: (352) 493-4796
General Fax: (352) 493-9336
Advertising Phone: (352) 493-4796
Advertising Fax: (352) 493-9336
Editorial Phone: (352) 493-4796
Editorial Fax: (352) 493-9336
General/National Adv. E-mail: circulation@chieflandcitizen.com
Display Adv. E-mail: circulation@chieflandcitizen.com

Editorial e-mail: circulation@chieflandcitizen.com
Primary Website: chieflandcitizen.com
Year Established: 1950
Avg Paid Circ: 6000
Audit By: Sworn/Estimate/Non-Audited
Audit Date: 10.06.2019
Personnel: Lou Elliott Jones (Ed.); Tom Broeck (Gen. Mgr.); Marcia Vaughn (Circ. Mgr.); Cheri Clark (Creative)
Parent company (for newspapers): Paxton Media Group; Landmark Community Newspapers, LLC

CLAY COUNTY LEADER

Street address 1: 3513 US Highway 17
Street address city: Fleming Island
Street address state: FL
Zip/Postal code: 32003-7122
General Phone: (904) 264-3200
General Fax: (904) 264-3285
Advertising Phone: (904) 579-2148
Editorial Phone: (904) 579-2151
General/National Adv. E-mail: jon@opcfla.com
Display Adv. E-mail: martha@opcfla.com
Editorial e-mail: eric@opcfla.com
Primary Website: claytodayonline.com
Mthly Avg Views: 19000
Mthly Avg Unique Visitors: 12000
Year Established: 1987
Avg Free Circ: 6975
Audit By: Sworn/Estimate/Non-Audited
Audit Date: 10.06.2019
Personnel: Jon Cantrell (Publisher); Peg Oddy; Rob Conwell (Circ. Mgr)
Parent company (for newspapers): Osteen Publishing Company

CLAY TODAY

Street address 1: 3513 US Highway 17
Street address city: Fleming Island
Street address state: FL
Zip/Postal code: 32003-7122
General Phone: (904) 264-3200
General Fax: (904) 264-3285
General/National Adv. E-mail: jon@opcfla.com
Display Adv. E-mail: martha@opcfla.com
Editorial e-mail: eric@opcfla.com
Primary Website: claytodayonline.com
Mthly Avg Views: 19000
Mthly Avg Unique Visitors: 12000
Year Established: 1950
Avg Paid Circ: 3637
Avg Free Circ: 838
Audit By: VAC
Audit Date: 16.12.2016
Personnel: Jon Cantrell (Pub.); Rob Conwell (Circ. Mgr.); Peg Oddy (Adv. Mgr.); Eric Cravey (Editor); Michele McNeil (Production); Justin Freeman (Prod. Mgr)
Parent company (for newspapers): Osteen Publishing Company

CLEARWATER BEACON

Street address 1: 9911 Seminole Blvd
Street address city: Seminole
Street address state: FL
Zip/Postal code: 33772-2536
General Phone: (727) 397-5563
General Fax: (727) 397-5902
General/National Adv. E-mail: dautrey@tbnweekly.com
Display Adv. E-mail: jrey@tbnweekly.com
Classified Adv. e-mail: wedwards@tbnweekly.com
Editorial e-mail: lmosby@tbnweekly.com
Primary Website: tbnweekly.com/pubs/clearwater_beacon
Mthly Avg Unique Visitors: 45000
Year Established: 1950
Avg Free Circ: 25241
Audit By: CVC
Audit Date: 30.09.2017
Personnel: Dan Autrey (Pub./Pres.); Jay Rey (Adv. Mgr); Dave Brown (Prod. Mgr); Logan Mosby (Ed.); Don Henry (Dist. Mgr.)
Parent company (for newspapers): Tampa Bay Newspapers, Inc.

COASTAL BREEZE NEWS

Street address 1: 1857 San Marco Rd
Street address 2: Ste C-216
Street address city: Marco Island
Street address state: FL
Zip/Postal code: 34145-6742
General Phone: (239) 393-4991
General Fax: (239) 393-4992
General/National Adv. E-mail: val@coastalbreezenews.com
Display Adv. E-mail: cherie@coastalbreezenews.com
Editorial e-mail: jessica@coastalbreezenews.com
Primary Website: coastalbreezenews.com
Mthly Avg Views: 43632
Mthly Avg Unique Visitors: 13393
Year Established: 2010
Avg Paid Circ: 0
Avg Free Circ: 17500
Audit By: CVC
Audit Date: 01.10.2017
Personnel: Val Simon (Pub)

COASTAL/GREENACRES OBSERVER

Street address 1: 1313 Central Ter
Street address city: Lake Worth
Street address state: FL
Zip/Postal code: 33460-1835
General Phone: (561) 585-9387
General Fax: (561) 585-5434
General/National Adv. E-mail: Adsales@lwherald.com
Display Adv. E-mail: Classifieds@lwherald.com
Editorial e-mail: Editor@lwherald.com
Primary Website: lwherald.com
Year Established: 1912
Avg Paid Circ: 1200
Avg Free Circ: 28000
Audit By: Sworn/Estimate/Non-Audited
Audit Date: 10.06.2019
Personnel: Mark J. Easton (Editor/Publisher)
Parent company (for newspapers): Lake Worth Herald Press, Inc.

CREATIVE LOAFING TAMPA BAY

Street address 1: 1911 N 13th St
Street address 2: Ste W200
Street address city: Tampa
Street address state: FL
Zip/Postal code: 33605-3652
General Phone: (813) 739-4800
General Fax: (813) 739-4801
Advertising Phone: (813) 739-4843
General/National Adv. E-mail: kelly.moroni@creativeloafing.com
Editorial e-mail: joe.bardi@creativeloafing.com
Primary Website: cltampa.com
Year Established: 1988
Avg Paid Circ: 0
Avg Free Circ: 33976
Audit By: VAC
Audit Date: 31.03.2016
Personnel: James Howard (Pub.); David Warner (Editor-in-Chief); Joe Bardi (Managing Ed.); Chris Madalena (Adv. Dir.); Kelly Moroni (Ad. Sales)
Parent company (for newspapers): Womack Newspapers, inc

CRESTVIEW NEWS BULLETIN

Street address 1: 638 N Ferdon Blvd
Street address city: Crestview
Street address state: FL
Zip/Postal code: 32536-2170
General Phone: (850) 682-6524
Classified Adv. e-mail: dawnb@crestviewbulletin.com
Primary Website: crestviewbulletin.com
Mthly Avg Views: 700000
Mthly Avg Unique Visitors: 70000
Year Established: 1975
Avg Paid Circ: 4000
Avg Free Circ: 13000
Audit By: Sworn/Estimate/Non-Audited
Audit Date: 10.06.2019
Personnel: Aaron Little (Ed.); Renee Bell (Ed. Asst.); Aaron Jacobs (Reporter); Jim Fletcher (Pub.); Jason Blakeney (Exec. Ed.); Sherrie Stanley (Adv.); Dale Robinson (Circ.)
Parent company (for newspapers): CherryRoad Media

DEERFIELD AND POMPANO FORUM

Street address 1: 500 E Broward Blvd
Street address city: Fort Lauderdale
Street address state: FL
Zip/Postal code: 33394-3000
General Phone: (954) 698-6397
General Fax: (954) 429-1207
Advertising Phone: (800) 974-7521
Advertising Fax: (954) 698-6719
Editorial Phone: (954) 596-5632
General/National Adv. E-mail: Kenwilliams@tribpub.com
Display Adv. E-mail: jshalek@tribune.com
Editorial e-mail: JZizzo@tribpub.com
Primary Website: forumpubs.com
Avg Paid Circ: 0
Avg Free Circ: 85704
Audit By: Sworn/Estimate/Non-Audited
Audit Date: 10.06.2019
Personnel: Gregg Behar (Senior Sales Manager); Mickie Carusos (Adv. Mgr.); Tom Adams (President); Pam Doto (Exec. Ed.); Pam Doto (VP/Exec. Ed.); Stewart Cady (Prodn. Mgr.); Judith Zizzo (Managing Editor); Mark Ward (Circ. Mgr.)
Parent company (for newspapers): Sun-Sentinel Co.

DELRAY TIMES

Street address 1: 1701 Green Rd
Street address 2: Ste B
Street address city: Deerfield Beach
Street address state: FL
Zip/Postal code: 33064
General Phone: (954) 356-4000
General Fax: (954) 698-6719
General/National Adv. E-mail: gbehar@tribune.com
Primary Website: sun-sentinel.com/local/palm-beach/delray-beach/
Avg Paid Circ: 0
Avg Free Circ: 27869
Audit By: CVC
Audit Date: 6/31/2018
Personnel: Mark Ward (Circ. Mgr.); Tom Adams (Pres./Pub.); Pam Doto
Parent company (for newspapers): Forum Publishing Group

DIXIE COUNTY ADVOCATE

Street address 1: 174 NE Highway 351
Street address city: Cross City
Street address state: FL
Zip/Postal code: 32628-3120
General Phone: (352) 498-3312
General Fax: (352) 507-4585
Advertising Phone: (352) 542-0131
General/National Adv. E-mail: adsdcadvocate@gmail.com
Display Adv. E-mail: news@dcadvocate.net
Editorial e-mail: editor@dcadvocate.net
Primary Website: dcadvocate.net
Year Established: 1921
Avg Paid Circ: 4200
Avg Free Circ: 10
Audit By: Sworn/Estimate/Non-Audited
Audit Date: 10.06.2019
Personnel: Katherine McKinney (Ed.); Becky Williams (Ad. Rep.)

DUNEDIN BEACON

Street address 1: 9911 Seminole Blvd
Street address city: Seminole
Street address state: FL
Zip/Postal code: 33772-2536
General Phone: (727) 397-5563
General Fax: (727) 397-5902
General/National Adv. E-mail: jrey@tbnweekly.com
Display Adv. E-mail: wedwards@tbnweekly.com
Classified Adv. e-mail: wedwards@tbnweekly.com
Editorial e-mail: tgermond@tbnweekly.com
Primary Website: tbnweekly.com
Mthly Avg Unique Visitors: 45000
Year Established: 2009
Avg Free Circ: 19421
Audit By: CVC
Audit Date: 30.09.2017
Personnel: Dan Autrey (Pres./Pub.); Jay Rey (Adv. Mgr.); Dave Brown (Prod. Mgr.); Don Henry (Dist. Mgr.)
Parent company (for newspapers): Tampa Bay Newspapers, Inc.

EAST COUNTY OBSERVER

Street address 1: 1970 Main St
Street address 2: Ste 300
Street address city: Sarasota
Street address state: FL
Zip/Postal code: 34236-5921
General Phone: (941) 366-3468
General Fax: (394) 362-4808
Advertising Phone: (941) 366-3468
Editorial Phone: (941) 366-3468
General/National Adv. E-mail: mwalsh@yourobserver.com
Display Adv. E-mail: mwalsh@yourobserver.com
Editorial e-mail: khughes@yourobserver.com
Primary Website: yourobserver.com
Year Established: 1998
Avg Paid Circ: 3
Avg Free Circ: 22250
Audit By: VAC
Audit Date: 31.05.2017
Personnel: Jill Raleigh (Adv. Dir.); Emily Walsh (Publisher)
Parent company (for newspapers): Observer Media Group Inc.

EAST SIDE FORUM

Street address 1: 500 E Broward Blvd
Street address city: Fort Lauderdale
Street address state: FL
Zip/Postal code: 33394-3000
General Phone: (954) 356-4000
General Fax: (954) 698-6719
General/National Adv. E-mail: gbehar@tribune.com
Primary Website: sun-sentinel.com
Avg Free Circ: 26805
Audit By: Sworn/Estimate/Non-Audited
Audit Date: 10.06.2019
Personnel: Lisa Goodlin; Tom Adams (Pres./Pub.); Mark Ward (Circ. Mgr.)
Parent company (for newspapers): Forum Publishing Group

EL OSCEOLA STAR

Street address 1: 220 E Monument Ave
Street address 2: Ste C
Street address city: Kissimmee
Street address state: FL
Zip/Postal code: 34741-5752
General Phone: (407) 933-0174
General Fax: (407) 933-0190
General/National Adv. E-mail: ad@elosceolastar.com
Primary Website: elosceolastar.com
Avg Free Circ: 15000
Audit By: Sworn/Estimate/Non-Audited
Audit Date: 10.06.2019
Personnel: Yolanda Lopez (Gen. Mgr.); Bill Hansen (Ed.)

ESCAMBIA SUN PRESS

Street address 1: 605 S Old Corry Field Rd
Street address city: Pensacola
Street address state: FL
Zip/Postal code: 32507-2129
General Phone: (850) 456-3121
General Fax: (850) 456-0103
Advertising Phone: (850) 456-3121
Advertising Fax: (850) 456-0103
Editorial Phone: Same
Editorial Fax: Same
General/National Adv. E-mail: stories@escambiasunpress.com
Display Adv. E-mail: stories@escambiasunpress.com
Editorial e-mail: stories@escambiasunpress.com
Primary Website: escambiasunpress.com
Year Established: 1948
Avg Paid Circ: 1600
Audit By: Sworn/Estimate/Non-Audited
Audit Date: 10.06.2019
Personnel: Michael J. Driver (Owner/Publisher); Denise Turner (Mng. Ed.); Phil Driver (Prodn. Mgr.)

FLORIDA KEYS FREE PRESS

Street address 1: 91731 Overseas Hwy
Street address city: Tavernier
Street address state: FL
Zip/Postal code: 33070-2649
General Phone: (305) 853-7277
General Fax: (305) 853-0556
General/National Adv. E-mail: sales@keysnews.com
Display Adv. E-mail: marnold@keysnews.com
Classified Adv. e-mail: marnold@keysnews.com
Editorial e-mail: freepress@keysnews.com
Primary Website: keysnews.com
Avg Paid Circ: 210
Avg Free Circ: 14000

Audit By: Sworn/Estimate/Non-Audited
Audit Date: 10.06.2019
Personnel: Paul Clarin (Pub.); Dan Campbell (Managing Ed.); Melanie Arnold (Dir, Adv.); Tammy Collins (Sales Consultant)
Parent company (for newspapers): Cooke Communications Florida, LLC

FOLIO WEEKLY

Street address 1: 45 W Bay St
Street address 2: Ste 103
Street address city: Jacksonville
Street address state: FL
Zip/Postal code: 32202-3632
General Phone: (904) 860-2465
General Fax: (904) 260-9773
Advertising Phone: (904) 860-2465
Editorial Phone: (904) 260-9770
General/National Adv. E-mail: sam@folioweekly.com
Display Adv. E-mail: fpiadmin@folioweekly.com
Editorial e-mail: mail@folioweekly.com
Primary Website: folioweekly.com
Year Established: 1987
Avg Paid Circ: 0
Avg Free Circ: 25349
Audit By: Sworn/Estimate/Non-Audited
Audit Date: 10.06.2019
Personnel: Sam Taylor (Adv. Mgr.); Georgio Valentino (Ed.); Lorraine Cover (Bus. Mgr.); Madison Gross (Art Dir.); Anne Schindler (Ed.); Kelly Lucas (Prodn. Mgr.)

FORT MEYERS BEACH BULLETIN

Street address 1: 2510 Del Prado Blvd
Street address city: Cape Coral
Street address state: FL
Zip/Postal code: 33904
General Phone: (239) 463-4421
General Fax: (239) 765-0846
Advertising Phone: (239) 765-0400 x107
Editorial Phone: (239) 765-0400
General/National Adv. E-mail: observer@breezenewspapers.com
Display Adv. E-mail: classifieds@breezenewspapers.com
Editorial e-mail: sblonde@breezenewspapers.com
Primary Website: fortmyersbeachtalk.com
Mthly Avg Views: 17320
Mthly Avg Unique Visitors: 6410
Year Established: 1978
Avg Paid Circ: 143
Avg Free Circ: 7353
Audit By: CVC
Audit Date: 30.12.2017
Personnel: Scott Blonde (Pub.); Natalie Zabala (Nat'l Sales Mgr.); Jim Konig (Adv. Dir.); Rhonda Marble (Prod. Mgr.); Cindy Gallagher (Adv. Mgr); Barbara Smith (Circ. Mgr); Cecilia Yndart (Prod. Mgr)
Parent company (for newspapers): Ogden Newspapers Inc.

FORT MYERS BEACH BULLETIN

Street address 1: 19260 San Carlos Blvd
Street address 2: Bldg C
Street address city: Fort Myers Beach
Street address state: FL
Zip/Postal code: 33931-2266
General Phone: (239) 463-4421
General Fax: (239) 765-0846
Editorial Phone: (239) 765-0400
General/National Adv. E-mail: beachbulletin@breezenewspapers.com
Display Adv. E-mail: classifieds@breezenewspapers.com
Editorial e-mail: rpetcher@breezenewspapers.com
Primary Website: fortmyersbeachtalk.com
Year Established: 1951
Avg Paid Circ: 35
Avg Free Circ: 6923
Audit By: Sworn/Estimate/Non-Audited
Audit Date: 10.06.2019
Personnel: Robert Petcher (Ed.); Melissa Schneider (Ed.)
Parent company (for newspapers): Ogden Newspapers Inc.

FORT MYERS FLORIDA WEEKLY

Street address 1: 4300 Ford St
Street address 2: Ste 105
Street address city: Fort Myers
Street address state: FL
Zip/Postal code: 33916-9318
General Phone: (239) 333-2135
General Fax: (239) 333-2140
General/National Adv. E-mail: advertise@floridaweekly.com
Display Adv. E-mail: advertise@floridaweekly.com
Editorial e-mail: news@floridaweekly.com
Primary Website: floridaweekly.com
Year Established: 2007
Avg Paid Circ: 35646
Audit By: Sworn/Estimate/Non-Audited
Audit Date: 10.06.2019
Personnel: J. Pason Gaddis (Pres./Pub.); Jeffrey Cull (Ed.); Jim Dickerson (VP and Creative Dir.); Cameo Hinman (Circ. Dir.)

GADSDEN COUNTY TIMES

Street address 1: 112 E Washington St
Street address city: Quincy
Street address state: FL
Zip/Postal code: 32351-2415
General Phone: (904) 627-7649
General Fax: (850) 627-7191
General/National Adv. E-mail: poconnell@gadcotimes.com
Display Adv. E-mail: classifieds@chronicle.com
Editorial e-mail: editor@gadcotimes.com
Primary Website: gadcotimes.com
Year Established: 1901
Avg Paid Circ: 3500
Avg Free Circ: 50
Audit By: Sworn/Estimate/Non-Audited
Audit Date: 10.06.2019
Personnel: Cheri Harris (Mng. Ed.); Mary Williams (Office Manager); Penny O'Connell (Ad sales rep); Erin Hill (Reporter)
Parent company (for newspapers): Landmark Community Newspapers, LLC; Priority News, Inc.

GILCHRIST COUNTY JOURNAL

Street address 1: 207 N Main St
Street address city: Trenton
Street address state: FL
Zip/Postal code: 32693-3439
General Phone: (352) 463-7135
General Fax: (352) 463-7393
General/National Adv. E-mail: gcjads@bellsouth.net
Editorial e-mail: gilchristjournal@bellsouth.net
Primary Website: gilchristcountyjournal.net
Avg Paid Circ: 4000
Audit By: Sworn/Estimate/Non-Audited
Audit Date: 10.06.2019
Personnel: John Ayers (Ed.); Chris Rogers (Adv.)

GLADES COUNTY DEMOCRAT

Street address 1: 107 SW 17th St
Street address city: Okeechobee
Street address state: FL
Zip/Postal code: 34974-6110
General Phone: (863) 763-3134
General Fax: (863) 763-5901
General/National Adv. E-mail: adsales@newszap.com
Display Adv. E-mail: classads@newszap.com
Primary Website: gladescountydemocrat.com
Year Established: 1915
Avg Paid Circ: 1300
Audit By: Sworn/Estimate/Non-Audited
Audit Date: 10.06.2019
Personnel: Suzanne Antonich (Adv. Consultant)
Parent company (for newspapers): Independent Newsmedia Inc. USA; Independent Newspapers, Inc. (Florida)

GULF BREEZE NEWS

Street address 1: 913 Gulf Breeze Pkwy
Street address 2: Harbourtown Suite 35
Street address city: Gulf Breeze
Street address state: FL
Zip/Postal code: 32561-4754
General Phone: (850) 932-8986
General Fax: (850) 932-8794
Advertising Phone: (850) 932-8986 ext. 104
Advertising Fax: (850) 932-8794
Editorial Phone: (850) 932-8986 ext. 111
Editorial Fax: 850-932-8794
General/National Adv. E-mail: news@gulfbreezenews.com
Display Adv. E-mail: class@gulfbreezenews.com
Editorial e-mail: news@gulfbreezenews.com
Primary Website: gulfbreezenews.com
Year Established: 2001
Avg Paid Circ: 2000
Avg Free Circ: 1000
Audit By: Sworn/Estimate/Non-Audited
Audit Date: 10.06.2019
Personnel: Lisa Newell (Publisher); Bob Newell (Ad Sales)
Parent company (for newspapers): Gulf Breeze News, Inc.

HERNANDO SUN

Street address 1: 13491 Simmons Lake Road
Street address city: Brooksville
Street address state: FL
Zip/Postal code: 34601
General Phone: (352) 675-6397
Advertising Phone: (352) 675-6397
General/National Adv. E-mail: editor@hernandosun.com
Display Adv. E-mail: sales@hernandosun.com
Classified Adv. e-mail: sales@hernandosun.com
Editorial e-mail: editor@hernandosun.com
Primary Website: hernandosun.com
Mthly Avg Views: 750000
Mthly Avg Unique Visitors: 150000
Year Established: 2015
Avg Paid Circ: 2325
Avg Free Circ: 1347
Audit By: USPS
Audit Date: 9/31/2023
Personnel: Julie Maglio (Pub.)
Parent company (for newspapers): Hernando Sun Publications LLC

HI-RISER - BROWARD

Street address 1: 1701 Green Rd
Street address city: Pompano Beach
Street address state: FL
Zip/Postal code: 33064-1074
General Phone: (954) 356-4000
General Fax: (954) 429-1207
Advertising Phone: (954) 574-5373
Editorial Phone: (954) 563-3311
General/National Adv. E-mail: tadams@tribune.com
Editorial e-mail: jzizzo@tribune.com
Primary Website: forumpubs.comm
Avg Free Circ: 16000
Audit By: Sworn/Estimate/Non-Audited
Audit Date: 10.06.2019
Personnel: Tom Adams (Pres./Pub.); Pam Doto (VP/Exec. Ed.); Judith Zizzo (Managing Ed.); Mark Ward (Circ. Mgr.)
Parent company (for newspapers): Sun-Sentinel Co.

HOLMES COUNTY TIMES-ADVERTISER

Street address 1: 1364 N Railroad Ave
Street address city: Chipley
Street address state: FL
Zip/Postal code: 32428-1456
General Phone: (850) 638-0212
General Fax: (850) 547-9414
General/National Adv. E-mail: ssmith@chipleypaper.com
Primary Website: chipleypaper.com
Avg Paid Circ: 4200
Audit By: Sworn/Estimate/Non-Audited
Audit Date: 10.06.2019
Personnel: Nicole Barefield (Pub.); Jay Selsberg (Ed.); Mickayla Boname (Adv.)
Parent company (for newspapers): Halifax Media; Neves Media Publishing

IMMOKALEE BULLETIN

Street address 1: 22 Fort Thompson Ave.
Street address city: Labelle
Street address state: FL
Zip/Postal code: 33975
General Phone: (863) 675-2541
Primary Website: http://immokaleebulletin.com
Audit By: Sworn/Estimate/Non-Audited
Audit Date: 10.06.2019
Personnel: Patty Brant (Editor/Publisher)
Parent company (for newspapers): Independent Newsmedia Inc. USA

ISLAND REPORTER

Street address 1: 2340 Periwinkle Way
Street address 2: Ste K1
Street address city: Sanibel
Street address state: FL
Zip/Postal code: 33957-3220
General Phone: (239) 472-1587
General Fax: (239) 472-8398
Advertising Phone: (239) 472-1587
Advertising Fax: (239) 472-8398
Editorial Phone: (239) 472-1587
Editorial Fax: (239) 472-8398
General/National Adv. E-mail: dpapoi@breezenewspapers.com
Display Adv. E-mail: dpapoi@breezenewspapers.com
Editorial e-mail: jlinette@breezenewspapers.com
Primary Website: captivasanibel.com
Year Established: 1973
Avg Paid Circ: 789
Avg Free Circ: 4752
Audit By: Sworn/Estimate/Non-Audited
Audit Date: 10.06.2019
Personnel: Scott Blonde (Pub.); Jim Linette (Ed.); Danielle Papoi (Adv. Sales); Betsy Judge
Parent company (for newspapers): Ogden Newspapers Inc.

ISLANDER NEWS

Street address 1: 104 Crandon Blvd
Street address 2: Ste 301
Street address city: Key Biscayne
Street address state: FL
Zip/Postal code: 33149-1556
General Phone: (305) 361-3333
General Fax: (305) 361-5051
General/National Adv. E-mail: lia@islandernews.com
Editorial e-mail: editor@islandernews.com
Primary Website: islandernews.com
Year Established: 1966
Avg Paid Circ: 3900
Avg Free Circ: 690
Audit By: Sworn/Estimate/Non-Audited
Audit Date: 10.06.2019
Personnel: Lia Esteban (Ad. Dir.); Nancye Ray (Ed. & Pub.); Jamie Millan (Art Dir.)

JACKSON COUNTY TIMES

Street address 1: 2866 Madison St
Street address city: Marianna
Street address state: FL
Zip/Postal code: 32448-4610
General Phone: (850) 526-1501
General Fax: (850) 526-1505
Advertising Phone: (850) 526-1501
Advertising Fax: (850-526-1505
Editorial Phone: (850) 526-1501
Editorial Fax: (850-526-1505
General/National Adv. E-mail: bo.jctimes@gmail.com
Display Adv. E-mail: liz@jacksoncountytimes.net
Editorial e-mail: editor@jacksoncountytimes.net
Primary Website: jacksoncountytimes.net
Year Established: 2006
Avg Paid Circ: 2500
Audit By: Sworn/Estimate/Non-Audited
Audit Date: 10.06.2019
Personnel: Stephanie Parker (Pub./Adv. Mgr.); Sid Riley (Managing Editor); Bo McMullian (Advertising)
Parent company (for newspapers): Hatcher Publications

JACKSONVILLE BUSINESS JOURNAL

Street address 1: 200 W Forsyth St
Street address 2: Ste 1350
Street address city: Jacksonville
Street address state: FL
Zip/Postal code: 32202-4349
General Phone: (904) 396-3502
General Fax: (904) 396-5706
Primary Website: bizjournals.com/jacksonville
Audit By: Sworn/Estimate/Non-Audited
Audit Date: 10.06.2019

Personnel: Sara Leutzinger (Pres./Pub.); Timothy Gibbons (Ed. in Cheif); James Cannon (Mng. Ed.); Scott Warofka (Adv. Mgr.); Deborah Green (Bus. Mgr.)

JASPER NEWS

Street address 1: 521 Demorest St SE
Street address city: Live Oak
Street address state: FL
Zip/Postal code: 32064-3320
General Phone: (386) 792-2487
General Fax: (386) 792-2934
General/National Adv. E-mail: jaspernews1@windstream.net
Primary Website: nflaonline.com
Year Established: 1870
Avg Paid Circ: 1450
Avg Free Circ: 30
Audit By: Sworn/Estimate/Non-Audited
Audit Date: 10.06.2019
Personnel: Myra Regan (Pub.); Monja Robinson (Ad. Dir.); Angie Sparks (Circ. Mgr.); Jeff Waters (Ed.); Dee Freeman (Prodn. Mgr.); Laura Rogers (Nat'l Adv. Mgr.)
Parent company (for newspapers): CNHI, LLC

JUPITER COURIER

Street address 1: 1939 SE Federal Hwy
Street address city: Stuart
Street address state: FL
Zip/Postal code: 34994-3915
General Phone: (772) 287-1550
Advertising Phone: (772) 221-4255
Editorial Phone: (561) 745-3311
General/National Adv. E-mail: jess.mcallister@scripps.com
Display Adv. E-mail: classified@stuartnews.com
Editorial e-mail: feedback@tcpalm.com
Primary Website: tcpalm.com
Year Established: 1957
Avg Paid Circ: 8500
Avg Free Circ: 8500
Audit By: Sworn/Estimate/Non-Audited
Audit Date: 10.06.2019
Personnel: Mark Tomasik (Ed.); Bob Brunjes (Pres./Pub.); Christine Stonecipher; Suzanne Antonich (Gen. Mgr.); Adam Neal (Managing Ed.)
Parent company (for newspapers): E. W. Scripps Co.

KENDALL GAZETTE

Street address 1: 6796 SW 62nd Ave
Street address city: South Miami
Street address state: FL
Zip/Postal code: 33143-3306
General Phone: (305) 669-7355
General Fax: (305) 662-6980
General/National Adv. E-mail: sales@communitynewspapers.com
Primary Website: communitynewspapers.com/kendall-gazett
Avg Free Circ: 10000
Audit By: Sworn/Estimate/Non-Audited
Audit Date: 10.06.2019
Personnel: Grant Miller (Co-Pub.); Michael Miller (Co-Pub.); Dan Palmer (Editor); Susan Miller (Sales)
Parent company (for newspapers): Miller Publishing

KEY WEST WEEKLY

Street address 1: 5450 MacDonald Avenue, Suite 5
Street address 2: No. 5
Street address city: Key West
Street address state: FL
Zip/Postal code: 33040
General Phone: (305) 453-6928
General Fax: (305) 509-7347
Primary Website: keysweekly.com
Avg Free Circ: 6977
Audit By: AAM
Audit Date: 30.09.2018
Personnel: Britt Myers (Pub.)
Parent company (for newspapers): Keys Weekly Newspapers

LAKE WORTH FORUM

Street address 1: 500 E Broward Blvd
Street address city: Fort Lauderdale
Street address state: FL
Zip/Postal code: 33394-3000
General Phone: (954) 698-6397
General Fax: (954) 429-1207
Advertising Phone: (800) 974-7521
Advertising Fax: (954) 698-6719
Editorial Phone: (954) 596-5632
General/National Adv. E-mail: Kenwilliams@tribpub.com
Display Adv. E-mail: jshalek@tribune.com
Editorial e-mail: JZizzo@tribpub.com
Primary Website: forumpubs.com
Avg Free Circ: 12775
Audit By: Sworn/Estimate/Non-Audited
Audit Date: 10.06.2019
Personnel: Pam Doto (VP/ Exec. Ed.); Tom Adams (President); Gregg Behar (Senior Sales Manager); Kari Barnett (Editor)
Parent company (for newspapers): Forum Publishing Group; Sun-Sentinel Co.

LAND O LAKES LAKER

Street address 1: 3632 Land O Lakes Blvd
Street address 2: Ste 102
Street address city: Land O Lakes
Street address state: FL
Zip/Postal code: 34639-4407
General Phone: (813) 909-2800
General Fax: (813) 909-2802
General/National Adv. E-mail: cbennett@lakerlutznews.com
Display Adv. E-mail: cbennett@lakerlutznews.com
Classified Adv. e-mail: cbennett@lakerlutznews.com
Editorial e-mail: bcmanion@lakerlutznews.com
Primary Website: lakerlutznews.com
Year Established: 1981
Avg Free Circ: 14560
Audit By: CVC
Audit Date: 30.12.2021
Personnel: Brian Calle (Publisher / owner.); B.C. Manion (Editor); Ken Rogers (Circulation Manager.)
Parent company (for newspapers): Street Media, LLC

LARGO LEADER

Street address 1: 9911 Seminole Blvd
Street address city: Seminole
Street address state: FL
Zip/Postal code: 33772-2536
General Phone: (727) 397-5563
General Fax: (727) 397-5900
General/National Adv. E-mail: jrey@tbnweekly.com
Display Adv. E-mail: wedwards@tbnweekly.com
Classified Adv. e-mail: wedwards@tbnweekly.com
Editorial e-mail: cgeorge@tbnweekly.com
Primary Website: tbnweekly.com
Mthly Avg Unique Visitors: 45000
Year Established: 1977
Avg Free Circ: 24316
Audit By: CVC
Audit Date: 30.09.2017
Personnel: Dan Autrey (Pub./Pres.); Jay Rey (Adv. Mgr); Dave Brown (Prod. Mgr); Don Henry (Distribution Manager)
Parent company (for newspapers): Tampa Bay Newspapers, Inc.

LEHIGH ACRES NEWS-STAR

Street address 1: 2510 Del Prado Blvd
Street address city: Cape Coral
Street address state: FL
Zip/Postal code: 33904
General Phone: (239) 574-1110
General Fax: (239) 574-3403
General/National Adv. E-mail: jkonig@breezenewspapers.com
Display Adv. E-mail: jkonig@breezenewspapers.com
Editorial e-mail: sblonde@breezenewspapers.com
Primary Website: lehighacrescitizen.com
Year Established: 1978
Avg Paid Circ: 11
Avg Free Circ: 5393
Audit By: CVC
Audit Date: 30.12.2017
Personnel: Scott Blonde (Pres./Pub.); Jim Konig (Adv.); Terry Reid (Circ.); Cecilia Yndart (Prod.)
Parent company (for newspapers): Gannett

LIVE WELLINGTON

Street address 1: 500 E Broward Blvd
Street address city: Fort Lauderdale
Street address state: FL
Zip/Postal code: 33394-3000
General Phone: (954) 356-4000
General Fax: (954) 429-1207
Advertising Phone: (954) 574-5373
Advertising Fax: (954) 698-6719
Editorial Phone: (954) 596-5632
General/National Adv. E-mail: TAdams@tribune.com
Editorial e-mail: KABarnett@tribune.com
Primary Website: sun-sentinel.com/local/palm-beach/wellington
Avg Free Circ: 16712
Audit By: Sworn/Estimate/Non-Audited
Audit Date: 10.06.2019
Personnel: Pam Doto (VP/Exec. Ed.); Tom Adams (President); Gregg Behar (Sr. Sales Mgr.); Kari Barnett (Editor)
Parent company (for newspapers): Forum Publishing Group; The Charleston Sun-Sentinel

LONGBOAT OBSERVER

Street address 1: 1970 Main St
Street address 2: Ste 300
Street address city: Sarasota
Street address state: FL
Zip/Postal code: 34236-5921
General Phone: (941) 366-3468
Advertising Phone: (941) 366-3468
Editorial Phone: (941) 366-3468
General/National Adv. E-mail: jraleigh@yourobserver.com
Display Adv. E-mail: mwalsh@yourobserver.com
Editorial e-mail: khughes@yourobserver.com
Primary Website: yourobserver.com
Year Established: 1978
Avg Paid Circ: 271
Avg Free Circ: 10409
Audit By: VAC
Audit Date: 31.05.2017
Personnel: Jill Raleigh (Ad. Dir.); Emily Walsh (Publisher)
Parent company (for newspapers): Observer Media Group Inc.

MADISON COUNTY CARRIER

Street address 1: 1695 S State Road 53
Street address city: Madison
Street address state: FL
Zip/Postal code: 32340-3331
General Phone: (850) 973-4141
General Fax: (850) 973-4121
General/National Adv. E-mail: greenepub@greenepublishing.com
Editorial e-mail: news@greenepublishing.com
Primary Website: greenepublishing.com
Year Established: 1964
Avg Paid Circ: 3700
Audit By: Sworn/Estimate/Non-Audited
Audit Date: 10.06.2019
Personnel: Emerald Greene (Pub.); Jeanette Dunn (Ad.); Jacob Bernbry (Editor)

MADISON ENTERPRISE-RECORDER

Street address 1: 1695 S State Road 53
Street address city: Madison
Street address state: FL
Zip/Postal code: 32340-3331
General Phone: (850) 973-4141
General Fax: (850) 973-4121
General/National Adv. E-mail: greenepub@greenepublishing.com
Editorial e-mail: news@greenepublishing.com
Primary Website: greenepublishing.com
Avg Paid Circ: 3700
Audit By: Sworn/Estimate/Non-Audited
Audit Date: 10.06.2019
Personnel: Emerald Greene (Publisher); Jacob Bernbry (Editor); Jeanette Dunn (Ad.)

MANDARIN NEWSLINE

Street address 1: 12443 San Jose Blvd
Street address 2: Ste 403
Street address city: Jacksonville
Street address state: FL
Zip/Postal code: 32223-8650
General Phone: (904) 886-4919
General Fax: (904) 379-5250
General/National Adv. E-mail: Linda@floridanewsline.com
Display Adv. E-mail: Linda@floridanewsline.com
Editorial e-mail: editor@floridanewsline.com
Primary Website: mandarinnewsline.com
Year Established: 2007
Avg Free Circ: 27178
Audit By: CVC
Audit Date: 31.12.2017
Personnel: Martie Thompson (Ed.); Linda Gay (Adv.)
Parent company (for newspapers): RT Publishing, Inc.

MARCO EAGLE

Street address 1: 1100 Immokalee Rd
Street address city: Naples
Street address state: FL
Zip/Postal code: 34110-4810
General Phone: (239) 213-6000
General Fax: (239) 213-5390
Advertising Phone: (239) 213-5301
Editorial Phone: (239) 263-4863
General/National Adv. E-mail: JLFuenmayor@Naplesnews.com
Display Adv. E-mail: classad@naplesnews.com
Editorial e-mail: manny.garcia@naplesnews.com
Primary Website: naplesnews.com/community/marco-eagle
Avg Free Circ: 15900
Audit By: Sworn/Estimate/Non-Audited
Audit Date: 10.06.2019
Personnel: Vince Modarelli (Ad. Dir.); Bill Barker (President/Publisher); Jay Schlichter (Editor)

MARGATE / COCONUT CREEK FORUM

Street address 1: 500 E Broward Blvd
Street address city: Fort Lauderdale
Street address state: FL
Zip/Postal code: 33394-3000
General Phone: (954) 574-5341
General Fax: (954) 698-6719
General/National Adv. E-mail: gbehar@tribune.com
Primary Website: forumpubs.com
Avg Free Circ: 20700
Audit By: Sworn/Estimate/Non-Audited
Audit Date: 10.06.2019
Personnel: Mark Ward (Circ. Mgr.); Tom Adams (Pres./Pub.)
Parent company (for newspapers): Forum Publishing Group

MAYO FREE PRESS

Street address 1: PO Box 370
Street address city: Live Oak
Street address state: FL
Zip/Postal code: 32064-0370
General Phone: (386) 362-1734
General Fax: (386) 364-5578
General/National Adv. E-mail: mayofreepress@windstream.net
Editorial e-mail: mayofreepress@windstream.net
Primary Website: suwanneedemocrat.com/mayo
Year Established: 1888
Avg Paid Circ: 900
Avg Free Circ: 50
Audit By: Sworn/Estimate/Non-Audited
Audit Date: 10.06.2019
Personnel: Jeff Waters (Editor); Myra Regan (Publisher)
Parent company (for newspapers): CNHI, LLC

MIAMI TODAY

Street address 1: 2000 S Dixie Hwy
Street address 2: Suite 100
Street address city: Miami
Street address state: FL
Zip/Postal code: 33133-2451
General Phone: (305) 358-2663
General Fax: (305) 358-4811
Advertising Phone: (305) 358-1008
Advertising Fax: (305) 358-4811
Editorial Phone: (305) 358-2663
Editorial Fax: (305) 358-4811
General/National Adv. E-mail: cblewis@miamitodaynews.com
Display Adv. E-mail: fgrande@miamitodaynews.com
Editorial e-mail: editor@miamitodaynews.com
Primary Website: miamitodaynews.com
Year Established: 1983
Avg Paid Circ: 172
Avg Free Circ: 27229
Audit By: BPA
Audit Date: 30.06.2017

Personnel: Carmen Betancourt-Lewis (VP)
Parent company (for newspapers): Today Enterprises Inc.

MONTICELLO NEWS

Street address 1: 180 W Washington St
Street address city: Monticello
Street address state: FL
Zip/Postal code: 32344-1954
General Phone: (850) 997-3568
General Fax: (850) 997-3774
General/National Adv. E-mail: glendaslater@embarqmail.com
Editorial e-mail: monticellonews@embarqmail.com
Primary Website: ecbpublishing.com
Avg Paid Circ: 3000
Avg Free Circ: 30
Audit By: Sworn/Estimate/Non-Audited
Audit Date: 10.06.2019
Personnel: Emerald Greene (Pub.); Glenda Slater (Adv. Exec.)

NAPLES FLORIDA WEEKLY

Street address 1: 9051 Tamiami Trl N
Street address 2: Ste 202
Street address city: Naples
Street address state: FL
Zip/Postal code: 34108-2520
General Phone: (239) 325-1960
General Fax: (239) 325-1964
General/National Adv. E-mail: advertise@floridaweekly.com
Display Adv. E-mail: advertise@floridaweekly.com
Editorial e-mail: news@floridaweekly.com
Primary Website: www.floridaweekly.com
Avg Paid Circ: 35646
Audit By: Sworn/Estimate/Non-Audited
Audit Date: 10.06.2019
Personnel: Jim Dickerson (VP and Creative Dir.); Jeffrey Cull (VP and Exec. Ed.); J. Pason Gaddis (Pres./Grp. Pub.); Angela Schivinski (Pub.); Shelley Hobbs (Nat'l Adv. Mgr.); Eric Strachan (Pub.)
Parent company (for newspapers): Florida Media Group LLC.

NASSAU COUNTY RECORD

Street address 1: 617317 Brandies Ave
Street address city: Callahan
Street address state: FL
Zip/Postal code: 32011-3704
General Phone: (904) 879-2727
General Fax: (904) 879-5155
General/National Adv. E-mail: advertising@nassaucountyrecord.com
Display Adv. E-mail: advertising@nassaucountyrecord.com
Classified Adv. e-mail: advertising@nassaucountyrecord.com
Editorial e-mail: editor@nassaucountyrecord.com
Primary Website: nassaucountyrecord.com
Year Established: 1930
Avg Paid Circ: 3000
Audit By: Sworn/Estimate/Non-Audited
Audit Date: 01.10.2021
Personnel: Foy Maloy (Pub.); Angeline Mudd (Bus. Office Mgr.); Robert Fiege (Prodn. Dir.); Amanda Ream (Editor); Kathie Sciullo (Reporter); Mariah Arnold (Advertising Specialist); Brad Spalding (National Sales); Joel Jenkins (Corp. Mktg. Dir.); John Gaddy (Circulation Manager); Samantha Coxwell (Marketing Associate)
Parent company (for newspapers): Community Newspapers, Inc.

NAVARRE PRESS

Street address 1: 7502 Harvest Village Ct
Street address city: Navarre
Street address state: FL
Zip/Postal code: 32566-7319
General Phone: (850) 939-8040
General Fax: (850) 939-4575
General/National Adv. E-mail: ads@navarrepress.com
Editorial e-mail: news@navarrepress.com
Primary Website: navarrepress.com
Avg Paid Circ: 4000
Audit By: Sworn/Estimate/Non-Audited
Audit Date: 10.06.2019
Personnel: Sandi Kemp (Pub.); Gail Acosta (Ad.)

NEWS-LEADER

Street address 1: 1235 S 10th St
Street address city: Fernandina Beach
Street address state: FL
Zip/Postal code: 32034
General Phone: (904) 261-3696
General Fax: (904) 261-3698
General/National Adv. E-mail: ads@fbnewsleader.com
Display Adv. E-mail: abutler@fbnewsleader.com
Editorial e-mail: tdishman@fbnewsleader.com
Primary Website: fbnewsleader.com
Mthly Avg Views: 87900
Mthly Avg Unique Visitors: 29000
Year Established: 1854
Avg Paid Circ: 8500
Audit By: Sworn/Estimate/Non-Audited
Audit Date: 10.06.2021
Personnel: Foy R. Maloy (Publisher); Robert Fiege (Prodn. Dir.); Angeline Mudd (Regional Business Office Manager); Beth Jones (Sports Ed.); Scott Bryan (Editor); Joel Jenkins (Corp. Mktg. Dir.); Peg Davis (Editor); John Gaddy (Circulation/Distribution Manager)
Parent company (for newspapers): Community Newspapers, Inc.

NORDSTJERNAN

Street address 1: 131 W Washington St
Street address 2: Suite 680
Street address city: Minneola
Street address state: FL
Zip/Postal code: 34755
General Phone: (203) 299-0380
Advertising Phone: (800) 827-9333
General/National Adv. E-mail: info@nordstjernan.com
Primary Website: www.nordstjernan.com
Year Established: 1872
Avg Paid Circ: 27000
Avg Free Circ: 300
Audit By: Sworn/Estimate/Non-Audited
Audit Date: 12.07.2021
Personnel: Mette Barslund (Circ. Mgr.); Ulf E. Barslund Martensson (Ed.); Amanda Olson Robison (Copy proof)

NORTH FORT MYERS NEIGHBOR

Street address 1: 2510 Del Prado Blvd S
Street address city: Cape Coral
Street address state: FL
Zip/Postal code: 33904-5750
General Phone: (239) 574-1110
General Fax: (239) 574-5693
Advertising Phone: (239) 220-2754
Editorial Phone: (239) 574-1110 x119
General/National Adv. E-mail: mjohnson@breezenewspapers.com
Editorial e-mail: vharring@breezenewspapers.com
Primary Website: northfortmyersneighbor.com
Year Established: 1999
Avg Paid Circ: 8
Avg Free Circ: 5626
Audit By: CVC
Audit Date: 31.12.2017
Personnel: Scott Blonde (Pub.); Valarie Harring (Ed.); Malcolm Johnson (Ad. Sales); Cindy Gallagher (Adv. Mgr); Barbara Smith (Circ. Mgr); Cecilia Yndart (Prod. Mgr)

NORTH LAKE OUTPOST

Street address 1: PO Box 1099
Street address city: Umatilla
Street address state: FL
Zip/Postal code: 32784-1099
General Phone: (352) 669-2430
General Fax: (352) 669-4644
General/National Adv. E-mail: northlakeoutpost@aol.com
Primary Website: thenorthlakeoutpost.com
Year Established: 1979
Avg Paid Circ: 3000
Audit By: Sworn/Estimate/Non-Audited
Audit Date: 10.06.2019
Personnel: Holly Newby (Publisher)

OBSERVER NEWS

Street address 1: 210 Woodland Estates Ave
Street address city: Ruskin
Street address state: FL
Zip/Postal code: 33570-4591
General Phone: (813) 645-3111
General Fax: (813) 645-4118
Advertising Phone: (813) 645-3111 ext 213
Advertising Fax: (813) 645-4118
Editorial Phone: (813) 645-3111 ext 210
Editorial Fax: (813) 645-4118
General/National Adv. E-mail: desi@observernews.net
Display Adv. E-mail: desi@observernews.net
Editorial e-mail: editor@observernews.net
Primary Website: observernews.net
Year Established: 1958
Avg Paid Circ: 0
Avg Free Circ: 51260
Audit By: CVC
Audit Date: 31.03.2018
Personnel: Brenda Knowles (Pub./Ed.); Vilma Stillwell (Sales Mgr.); Nan Kirk (Adv. Mgr.); Wes Mullins (Pub. Mgr); Chere Simmons (Prod. Mgr); Alexandria Reid (Circ.)
Parent company (for newspapers): M&M Printing Co. Inc.

OBSERVER NEWSPAPER

Street address 1: 201 N Federal Hwy
Street address 2: Suite 103
Street address city: Deerfield Beach
Street address state: FL
Zip/Postal code: 33441-3621
General Phone: (954) 428-9045
General Fax: (954) 428-9096
General/National Adv. E-mail: observerart@comcast.net
Display Adv. E-mail: observerfrontdesk@comcast.net
Primary Website: observernewspaperonline.com
Year Established: 1962
Avg Free Circ: 15000
Audit By: Sworn/Estimate/Non-Audited
Audit Date: 10.06.2019
Personnel: James Lust (Vice President); Jim Canavian (Adv. Mgr.); David Eller (Publisher); Diane Emeott (Editor); Rachel Galvin (Assistant Editor)

OCEAN BREEZE

Street address 1: 12443 San Jose Blvd
Street address 2: Ste 403
Street address city: Jacksonville
Street address state: FL
Zip/Postal code: 32223-8650
General Phone: (904) 886-4919
General Fax: (904) 379-5250
General/National Adv. E-mail: publisher@rtpublishinginc.com
Editorial e-mail: editor@rtpublishinginc.com
Primary Website: floridanewsline.com
Year Established: 2001
Avg Free Circ: 1800
Audit By: Sworn/Estimate/Non-Audited
Audit Date: 10.06.2019
Personnel: Rebecca Taus (Pub.); Wiliam Guthrie (Ed.); Heather Seay (Adv. Mgr.)
Parent company (for newspapers): RT Publishing, Inc.

OKEECHOBEE NEWS

Street address 1: 107 SW 17th St
Street address 2: Ste D
Street address city: Okeechobee
Street address state: FL
Zip/Postal code: 34974-6110
General Phone: (863) 763-3134
General Fax: (863) 763-5901
Advertising Fax: (863) 763-7949
General/National Adv. E-mail: adsales@newszap.com
Display Adv. E-mail: classads@newszap.com
Editorial e-mail: okeditor@newszap.com
Primary Website: okeechobeenews.net
Year Established: 1915
Avg Paid Circ: 2583
Avg Free Circ: 4000
Sat. Circulation Paid: 2583
Sun. Circulation Paid: 2583
Audit By: Sworn/Estimate/Non-Audited
Audit Date: 10.06.2019
Personnel: Judy Kasten (Adv. Dir.); Janet Madray (Circ. Mgr.); Katrina Elsken (Ed.); Charles Murphy (Sports Ed.); Ginny Guy (Prodn. Mgr., Pressroom)
Parent company (for newspapers): Independent Newsmedia Inc. USA; Independent Newspapers, Inc. (Florida)

ORLANDO BUSINESS JOURNAL

Street address 1: 255 S Orange Ave
Street address 2: Ste 700
Street address city: Orlando
Street address state: FL
Zip/Postal code: 32801-5007
General Phone: (407) 649-8470
General Fax: (407) 420-1625
Advertising Phone: (407) 241-2897
Advertising Fax: (407) 420-1625
Editorial Phone: (407) 241-2889
Editorial Fax: (407) 420-1625
General/National Adv. E-mail: rbobroff@bizjournals.com
Display Adv. E-mail: ekoshel@bizjournals.com
Editorial e-mail: cbarth@bizjournals.com
Primary Website: bizjournals.com/orlando
Mthly Avg Unique Visitors: 150490
Year Established: 1984
Avg Paid Circ: 9496
Audit By: Sworn/Estimate/Non-Audited
Audit Date: 10.06.2019
Personnel: Cindy Barth (Ed.); Robert Bobroff (Publisher)

OSCEOLA NEWS-GAZETTE

Street address 1: 108 Church St
Street address city: Kissimmee
Street address state: FL
Zip/Postal code: 34741-5055
General Phone: (407) 846-7600
General Fax: (407) 846-8516
Advertising Phone: (454) 654-4345
General/National Adv. E-mail: bberry@osceolanewsgazette.com
Display Adv. E-mail: bberry@osceolanewsgazette.com
Editorial e-mail: mplocha@osceolanewsgazette.com
Primary Website: aroundosceola.com
Mthly Avg Views: 92184
Mthly Avg Unique Visitors: 19663
Year Established: 1897
Avg Paid Circ: 582
Avg Free Circ: 39371
Audit By: CVC
Audit Date: 30.12.2017
Personnel: Matt Plocha (Pub. Mgr); Tom Overton (Pub.); Kathy Beckham (Circ. Mgr.); Bob Berry (Adv.); Kathy Beckham (Circ.); Steve Krause (Prod.); Kenny Jackson (Editor)
Parent company (for newspapers): Lakeway Publishers, Inc.

PALM BEACH GARDENS FLORIDA WEEKLY

Street address 1: 11380 Prosperity Farms Rd
Street address 2: Ste 103
Street address city: Palm Beach Gardens
Street address state: FL
Zip/Postal code: 33410-3450
General Phone: (561) 904-6470
General Fax: (561) 904-6456
General/National Adv. E-mail: advertise@floridaweekly.com
Display Adv. E-mail: advertise@floridaweekly.com
Editorial e-mail: news@floridaweekly.com
Primary Website: floridaweekly.com
Avg Paid Circ: 35646
Audit By: Sworn/Estimate/Non-Audited
Audit Date: 10.06.2019
Personnel: J. Pason Gaddis (President and Group Publisher); Jeffrey Cull (VP and Exec. Ed.); Jim Dickerson (VP and Creative Dir.)

PALM COAST OBSERVER

Street address 1: 1 Florida Park Dr N
Street address 2: Ste 103
Street address city: Palm Coast
Street address state: FL
Zip/Postal code: 32137-3843
General Phone: (386) 447-9723
General Fax: (386) 447-9963
General/National Adv. E-mail: jaclyn@palmcoastobserver.com
Display Adv. E-mail: randi@palmcoastobserver.com
Editorial e-mail: bmcmillan@palmcoastobserver.com

Primary Website: palmcoastobserver.com
Mthly Avg Views: 150000
Mthly Avg Unique Visitors: 75000
Year Established: 2010
Avg Paid Circ: 11
Avg Free Circ: 26787
Audit By: VAC
Audit Date: 31.03.2016
Personnel: John Walsh (Pub.); Brian McMillan (Managing Ed.); Jaci Beckett (Ad. Manager)
Parent company (for newspapers): Palm Coast Observer, LLC

PALM HARBOR BEACON

Street address 1: 9911 Seminole Blvd
Street address city: Seminole
Street address state: FL
Zip/Postal code: 33772-2536
General Phone: (727) 397-5563
General Fax: (727) 397-5900
General/National Adv. E-mail: jrey@tbnweekly.com
Display Adv. E-mail: wedwards@tbnweekly.com
Classified Adv. e-mail: wedwards@tbnweekly.com
Editorial e-mail: editorial@tbnweekly.com
Primary Website: tbnweekly.com
Mthly Avg Unique Visitors: 45000
Year Established: 2011
Avg Free Circ: 24563
Audit By: CVC
Audit Date: 17.12.2017
Personnel: Dan Autrey (President/Pub); Jay Rey (Adv. Mgr); Dave Brown (Prod. Mgr); Don Henry (Dist. Mgr.)
Parent company (for newspapers): Tampa Bay Newspapers, Inc.

PALMETTO BAY NEWS

Street address 1: 6796 SW 62nd Ave
Street address city: South Miami
Street address state: FL
Zip/Postal code: 33143-3306
General Phone: (305) 669-7355
General Fax: (305) 662-6980
General/National Adv. E-mail: sales@communitynewspapers.com
Primary Website: communitynewspapers.com
Year Established: 1958
Avg Free Circ: 5000
Audit By: Sworn/Estimate/Non-Audited
Audit Date: 10.06.2019
Personnel: Grant Miller (Co-Pub); Michael Miller (Co-Pub.); Susan Miller (Sales); Dan Palmer (Editor)
Parent company (for newspapers): Miller Publishing

PLANT CITY COURIER & TRIBUNE

Street address 1: 202 S Parker St
Street address city: Tampa
Street address state: FL
Zip/Postal code: 33606-2379
General Phone: (813) 259-7711
General Fax: (813) 259-7903
Advertising Phone: (813) 259-7455
Advertising Fax: (813) 259-7903
Editorial Phone: (813) 259-7711
Editorial Fax: (813) 259-7903
General/National Adv. E-mail: adsolutions@tampatrib.com
Display Adv. E-mail: adsolutions@tampatrib.com
Editorial e-mail: dnicholson@tampatrib.com
Primary Website: tbo.com/plant-city
Avg Paid Circ: 6621
Avg Free Circ: 2336
Audit By: Sworn/Estimate/Non-Audited
Audit Date: 10.06.2019
Personnel: David Nicholson (Mng. Ed.); Brian Burns (Pub.); Joe Gess (Dir, Nat'l Sales)
Parent company (for newspapers): Tampa Media Group

PLANT CITY OBSERVER

Street address 1: 1507 S Alexander St
Street address 2: #103
Street address city: Plant City
Street address state: FL
Zip/Postal code: 33563-8413
General Phone: (813) 704-6850
General Fax: (941) 362-4808
Advertising Phone: (813) 704-6850
Editorial Phone: (813) 704-6850
General/National Adv. E-mail: vprostko@PlantCityObserver.com
Display Adv. E-mail: llancaster@PlantCityObserver.com
Editorial e-mail: meng@PlantCityObserver.com
Primary Website: PlantCityObserver.com
Avg Paid Circ: 0
Avg Free Circ: 13246
Audit By: VAC
Audit Date: 31.05.2017
Personnel: Karen Berry (Pub.); Sarah Holt (Mng. Ed.); Robert Verner (Adv. Exec.); Justine Kline (Assoc. Ed./Sports Ed.); Breanne Williams (Staff Writer); Linda Lancaster (Circ./ Office Mgr.)
Parent company (for newspapers): Plant City Media LLC

PLANTATION/DAVIE FORUM

Street address 1: 333 S.W. 12th Ave.
Street address city: Deerfield Beach
Street address state: FL
Zip/Postal code: 33394-3000
General Phone: (954) 698-6397
General Fax: (954) 429-1207
General/National Adv. E-mail: placeanad.sun-sentinel.com
Display Adv. E-mail: ewilder@tribune.com
Editorial e-mail: JZizzo@tribpub.com
Primary Website: forumpubs.com
Year Established: 1973
Avg Paid Circ: 0
Avg Free Circ: 58872
Audit By: Sworn/Estimate/Non-Audited
Audit Date: 10.06.2019
Personnel: Tom Adams (Pres./Pub.); Ray Daley (Adv. Mgr.); Stewart Cady (Prodn. Mgr.)
Parent company (for newspapers): Sun-Sentinel Co.

PLAYERS JOURNAL

Street address 1: 12443 San Jose Blvd
Street address 2: Ste 403
Street address city: Jacksonville
Street address state: FL
Zip/Postal code: 32223-8650
General Phone: (904) 886-4919
General Fax: (904) 379-5250
General/National Adv. E-mail: publisher@rtpublishinginc.com
Editorial e-mail: editor@rtpublishinginc.com
Primary Website: floridanewsline.com
Year Established: 2001
Avg Free Circ: 1850
Audit By: Sworn/Estimate/Non-Audited
Audit Date: 10.06.2019
Personnel: Wiliam Guthrie (Ed.); Heather Seay (Adv. Mgr.)
Parent company (for newspapers): RT Publishing, Inc.

POLK COUNTY PRESS

Street address 1: 1020 N Church Ave
Street address city: Mulberry
Street address state: FL
Zip/Postal code: 33860-2040
General Phone: (863) 425-3411
Advertising Phone: same
General/National Adv. E-mail: polkcounrypress@yahoo.com
Editorial e-mail: editor@themulberrypress.com
Primary Website: none
Year Established: 1909
Avg Paid Circ: 3000
Avg Free Circ: 3000
Audit By: Sworn/Estimate/Non-Audited
Audit Date: 10.06.2019
Personnel: William M. Histed (Owner, Pub. & Ed.); Carole M. Histed (Circ. Mgr.); Robert B. Histed (Prodn. Mgr.)

PONTE VEDRA NEWSLINE

Street address 1: 12443 San Jose Blvd
Street address 2: Ste 403
Street address city: Jacksonville
Street address state: FL
Zip/Postal code: 32223-8650
General Phone: (904) 886-4919
General Fax: (904) 379-5250
General/National Adv. E-mail: Linda@floridanewsline.com
Display Adv. E-mail: Linda@floridanewsline.com
Editorial e-mail: editor@floridanewsline.com
Primary Website: floridanewsline.com
Year Established: 2014
Avg Free Circ: 22321
Audit By: CVC
Audit Date: 31.12.2017
Personnel: Martie Thompson (Ed.); Linda Gay (Adv.)
Parent company (for newspapers): Local Community News

PONTE VEDRA RECORDER

Street address 1: 1102 A1A N
Street address 2: Ste 108
Street address city: Ponte Vedra Beach
Street address state: FL
Zip/Postal code: 32082-4098
General Phone: (904) 285-8831
Advertising Phone: (904) 686-3938
Editorial Phone: (904) 285-8831
General/National Adv. E-mail: susan@opcfla.com
Editorial e-mail: Susan@opcfla.com
Primary Website: pontevedrarecorder.com
Year Established: 1969
Avg Paid Circ: 1814
Avg Free Circ: 8000
Audit By: CVC
Audit Date: 30.12.2017
Personnel: Ed Johnson (Sr. Acct. Exec.); Susan Griffin (Publisher); Rob Conwell (Circ. Mgr.); Kelly Hould (Ed.)

PUNTA GORDA/PORT CHARLOTTE FLORIDA WEEKLY

Street address 1: 1205 Elizabeth St
Street address 2: Ste G
Street address city: Punta Gorda
Street address state: FL
Zip/Postal code: 33950-6054
General Phone: (941) 621-3422
General Fax: (941) 621-3423
General/National Adv. E-mail: advertise@floridaweekly.com
Display Adv. E-mail: advertise@floridaweekly.com
Editorial e-mail: news@floridaweekly.com
Primary Website: floridaweekly.com
Avg Paid Circ: 35646
Audit By: Sworn/Estimate/Non-Audited
Audit Date: 10.06.2019
Personnel: Jeffrey Cull (VP and Exec. Ed.); J. Pason Gaddis (Pres./Grp. Pub.); Angela Schivinski (Pub.); Shelley Hobbs (Nat'l Adv. Mgr.); Kelli Carico (Classifieds Mgr.); Jim Dickerson (Creative Dir.)
Parent company (for newspapers): Florida Media Group LLC

PUTNAM COUNTY COURIER JOURNAL

Street address 1: 320 N Summit St
Street address city: Crescent City
Street address state: FL
Zip/Postal code: 32112-2300
General Phone: (386) 698-1644
General Fax: (386) 698-1994
General/National Adv. E-mail: ads@cjnewsfl.com
Display Adv. E-mail: classifieds@cjnewsfl.com
Editorial e-mail: news@cjnewsfl.com
Primary Website: cjnewsfl.com
Year Established: 1898
Avg Paid Circ: 3000
Audit By: Sworn/Estimate/Non-Audited
Audit Date: 10.06.2019
Personnel: Juliette Laurie (Ed./Pub.)
Parent company (for newspapers): Lakestreet Publishing Company

RIVERLAND NEWS

Street address 1: 20441 E Pennsylvania Ave
Street address city: Dunnellon
Street address state: FL
Zip/Postal code: 34432-6035
General Phone: (352) 489-2731
General Fax: (352) 489-6593
General/National Adv. E-mail: editor@riverlandnews.com
Primary Website: riverlandnews.com
Year Established: 1982
Avg Paid Circ: 3000
Audit By: Sworn/Estimate/Non-Audited
Audit Date: 10.06.2019
Personnel: John Murphy (Gen Mgr); Michele Northsea (Advertising sales); Jeff Bryan (Ed.); Gerry Mulligan (Pub.); John Provost (Gen. Mgr.)
Parent company (for newspapers): Paxton Media Group; Landmark Communications, Inc.; Landmark Community Newspapers, LLC

SANFORD HERALD

Street address 1: 217 E 1st St
Street address city: Sanford
Street address state: FL
Zip/Postal code: 32771-1376
General Phone: (407) 322-2611
General Fax: (407) 323-9408
General/National Adv. E-mail: rlavender@mysanfordherald.com
Display Adv. E-mail: WKourpanidis@MySanfordHerald.com
Editorial e-mail: rdelinski@mysanfordherald.com
Primary Website: mysanfordherald.com
Year Established: 1908
Avg Paid Circ: 6500
Audit By: Sworn/Estimate/Non-Audited
Audit Date: 10.06.2019
Personnel: Roxzie Lavender (Pub./Adv. Dir.); Rachel Delinski (Ed.); Wanda Kourpanidis (Circ. Mgr.)
Parent company (for newspapers): North Carolina Press Service, Inc.

SANIBEL-CAPTIVA ISLANDER

Street address 1: 2510 Del Prado Blvd S
Street address city: Cape Coral
Street address state: FL
Zip/Postal code: 33904-5750
General Phone: (239)-574-1110
General Fax: (239) 472-8398
Advertising Phone: (239) 472-1587
General/National Adv. E-mail: dpapoi@breezenewspapers.com
Editorial e-mail: mcassidy@breezenewspapers.com
Primary Website: captivasanibel.com
Year Established: 1960
Avg Paid Circ: 424
Avg Free Circ: 6606
Audit By: CVC
Audit Date: 31.12.2017
Personnel: Scott Blonde (Pub); Valarie Harring (Executive Editor); Mckenzie Cassidy (Editor); Danielle Papoi (Ad. Sales); Cindy Gallagher (Adv. Mgr); Barbara Smith (Circ. Mgr); Cecilia Yndart (Prod. Mgr)
Parent company (for newspapers): Ogden Newspapers Inc.

SANTA ROSA PRESS GAZETTE

Street address 1: 6576 Caroline St
Street address city: Milton
Street address state: FL
Zip/Postal code: 32570-4759
General Phone: (850) 623-2120
General Fax: (850) 623-2007
Advertising Phone: (850) 910-5316
Editorial Fax: (850) 623-2007
General/National Adv. E-mail: dcoon@srpressgazette.com
Display Adv. E-mail: rpratt@srpressgazette.com
Editorial e-mail: lhough@srpressgazette.com
Primary Website: srpressgazette.com
Year Established: 1908
Avg Paid Circ: 5000
Audit By: Sworn/Estimate/Non-Audited
Audit Date: 10.06.2019
Personnel: Jim Fletcher (Pub.); Debbie Coon (Ad. Accounts Exec.); Pamela Holt (Editor)
Parent company (for newspapers): Halifax Media

SARASOTA OBSERVER

Street address 1: 1970 Main St
Street address 2: Ste 300
Street address city: Sarasota
Street address state: FL
Zip/Postal code: 34236-5921
General Phone: (941) 366-3468
General Fax: (941) 362-4808
Advertising Phone: (941) 366-3468
Editorial Phone: (941) 366-3468
General/National Adv. E-mail: mwalsh@yourobserver.com
Display Adv. E-mail: mwalsh@yourobserver.com
Editorial e-mail: khughes@yourobserver.com

Primary Website: yourobserver.com
Year Established: 2004
Avg Paid Circ: 26
Avg Free Circ: 16743
Audit By: VAC
Audit Date: 31.05.2017
Personnel: Emily Walsh (Publisher)
Parent company (for newspapers): Observer Media Group Inc.

SEMINOLE BEACON

Street address 1: 9911 Seminole Blvd
Street address city: Seminole
Street address state: FL
Zip/Postal code: 33772-2536
General Phone: (727) 397-5563
General Fax: (727) 397-5900
Advertising Phone: (727) 397-5563
Editorial Phone: (727) 397-5563
General/National Adv. E-mail: jrey@tbnweekly.com
Display Adv. E-mail: wedwards@tbnweekly.com
Classified Adv. e-mail: wedwards@tbnweekly.com
Editorial e-mail: tgermond@tbnweekly.com
Primary Website: tbnweekly.com
Mthly Avg Unique Visitors: 45000
Year Established: 1977
Avg Free Circ: 27708
Audit By: CVC
Audit Date: 30.09.2017
Personnel: Dan Autrey (Pres./Pub.); Jay Rey (Ad Sales Dir.); Tiffany Razzano (Ed.); Dave Brown (Prod. Mgr); Don Henry (Dist. Mgr.)
Parent company (for newspapers): Tampa Bay Newspapers, Inc.

SIESTA KEY OBSERVER

Street address 1: 1970 Main St
Street address 2: Ste 300
Street address city: Sarasota
Street address state: FL
Zip/Postal code: 34236-5921
General Phone: (941) 366-3468
General Fax: (941) 362-4808
General/National Adv. E-mail: advertise@yourobserver.com
Editorial e-mail: khughes@yourobserver.com
Primary Website: yourobserver.com
Year Established: 1972
Avg Free Circ: 5109
Audit By: VAC
Audit Date: 31.05.2017
Personnel: Jill Raleigh (Adv. Dir.); Emily Walsh (Publisher)
Parent company (for newspapers): Observer Media Group Inc.

SOUTH DADE NEWS LEADER

Street address 1: 125 NE 8th St.
Street address 2: Suite 2
Street address city: Homestead
Street address state: FL
Zip/Postal code: 33030
General Phone: (305) 245-2311
General/National Adv. E-mail: mdill@calkins-media.com
Display Adv. E-mail: sdnlads@calkins-media.com
Editorial e-mail: letters@southdadenewsleader.com
Primary Website: southdadenewsleader.com
Year Established: 1912
Avg Paid Circ: 24000
Audit By: Sworn/Estimate/Non-Audited
Audit Date: 10.06.2019
Personnel: Dale Machesic (Pub.); Ann Machesic (Ed.)
Parent company (for newspapers): Calkins Media

SOUTH FLORIDA BUSINESS JOURNAL

Street address 1: 80 SW 8th St
Street address 2: Ste 2710
Street address city: Miami
Street address state: FL
Zip/Postal code: 33130-3057
General Phone: (954) 949-7600
General Fax: (954) 949-7591
Advertising Phone: (954) 949-7558
Advertising Fax: (954) 949-7599
General/National Adv. E-mail: southflorida@bizjournals.com
Primary Website: bizjournals.com/southflorida
Avg Free Circ: 9000
Audit By: Sworn/Estimate/Non-Audited
Audit Date: 10.06.2019
Personnel: Mel Melendez (Ed. in Chief); Eileen Cukier (Assoc. Ed.); Brian Bandell (Sr. Reporter); Yasmine Gahed (Adv. Dir.); Melanie Dickinson (Pres./Pub.)

SOUTH LAKE PRESS

Street address 1: 212 E Main St
Street address city: Leesburg
Street address state: FL
Zip/Postal code: 34748-5227
General Phone: (352) 394-2183
General Fax: (352) 394-8001
General/National Adv. E-mail: slpress@dailycommercial.com
Primary Website: southlakepress.com
Year Established: 1913
Avg Paid Circ: 40000
Audit By: Sworn/Estimate/Non-Audited
Audit Date: 10.06.2019
Personnel: Vanessa Hovater (Adv. Sales Mgr.); Jay Gillespie (Circ. Mgr.); Dan Fields (Mng. Ed.); Wayne Wicker (Prodn. Mgr.); Melanie Randall (New Majors/Nat'l Acct. Rep.); Steve Skaggs
Parent company (for newspapers): HarborPoint Media Group (OOB); Halifax Media

SOUTH MIAMI NEWS

Street address 1: 6796 SW 62nd Ave
Street address city: South Miami
Street address state: FL
Zip/Postal code: 33143-3306
General Phone: (305) 667-7481
General Fax: (305) 662-6980
General/National Adv. E-mail: cneditor@gate.net
Editorial e-mail: sales@communitynewspapers.com
Primary Website: communitynewspapers.com
Avg Free Circ: 18000
Audit By: Sworn/Estimate/Non-Audited
Audit Date: 10.06.2019
Personnel: Grant Miller (Co-Pub.); Dan Palmer (Editor); Michael Miller (Co-Pub.); Susan Miller (Sales)
Parent company (for newspapers): Miller Publishing

SOUTH TAMPA NEWS & TRIBUNE

Street address 1: 490 First Avenue South
Street address city: Saint Petersburg
Street address state: FL
Zip/Postal code: 33701
General Phone: (800) 888-7012
General/National Adv. E-mail: rmcghan@tampabay.com
Display Adv. E-mail: rmcghan@tampabay.com
Editorial e-mail: ksimpkins@tampabay.com
Primary Website: tampabay.com
Avg Paid Circ: 18680
Avg Free Circ: 26334
Audit By: Sworn/Estimate/Non-Audited
Audit Date: 10.06.2019
Personnel: Mark Katches (Ed); Amy Holyfield (Sr. Deputy Ed.); Barry Klein (Tampa Ed.); John Martin (Tampa News Ed.)
Parent company (for newspapers): Tampa Media Group

SUMTER COUNTY TIMES

Street address 1: 204 E McCollum Ave
Street address city: Bushnell
Street address state: FL
Zip/Postal code: 33513-6145
General Phone: (352) 793-2161
General Fax: (352) 793-1486
General/National Adv. E-mail: mtaylor@sctnews.com
Display Adv. E-mail: mtaylor@sctnews.com
Editorial e-mail: news@sctnews.com
Primary Website: sumtercountytimes.com
Year Established: 1881
Avg Paid Circ: 2600
Audit By: Sworn/Estimate/Non-Audited
Audit Date: 10.06.2019
Personnel: Gerard Mulligan (Pub.); Brenda Locklear (Circ. Mgr.); Bob Reichman (Ed.); Mike Taylor (Sales Rep); John Murphy (Mgr)
Parent company (for newspapers): Paxton Media Group; Landmark Communications, Inc.; Landmark Community Newspapers, LLC

SUMTER EXPRESS

Street address 1: 3347 CR 431
Street address city: Lake Panasoffkee
Street address state: FL
Zip/Postal code: 33538
General Phone: (352) 793-1671
Primary Website: No Website
Year Established: 2006
Avg Free Circ: 7000
Audit By: Sworn/Estimate/Non-Audited
Audit Date: 10.06.2019
Personnel: Rose Davis (Pub./Ed.); Dee Dee McCaslin (Circ./Adv. Dir.)

SUWANNEE DEMOCRAT

Street address 1: 521 Demorest St SE
Street address city: Live Oak
Street address state: FL
Zip/Postal code: 32064-3320
General Phone: (386) 362-1734
General Fax: (386) 364-5578
Advertising Phone: (386) 362-1734 x105
Editorial Phone: (386) 362-1734 x131
General/National Adv. E-mail: monja.slater@gaflnews.com
Display Adv. E-mail: louise.sheddan@gaflnews.com
Editorial e-mail: nf.editorial@gaflnews.com
Primary Website: suwanneedemocrat.com
Year Established: 1884
Avg Paid Circ: 3215
Audit By: Sworn/Estimate/Non-Audited
Audit Date: 10.06.2019
Personnel: Myra Regan (Pub.); Jamie Wachter (Editor); Monja Slater (Advertising Director); Jennifer Newham (Circulation)
Parent company (for newspapers): CNHI, LLC

TACO TIMES

Street address 1: 123 S Jefferson St
Street address city: Perry
Street address state: FL
Zip/Postal code: 32347-3232
General Phone: (850) 584-5513
General Fax: (850) 838-1566
General/National Adv. E-mail: ads@perrynewspapers.com
Display Adv. E-mail: classifieds@perrynewspapers.com
Editorial e-mail: newsdesk@perrynewspapers.com
Primary Website: perrynewspapers.com
Year Established: 1961
Avg Paid Circ: 5346
Audit By: Sworn/Estimate/Non-Audited
Audit Date: 10.06.2019
Personnel: Donald D. Lincoln (Pub.); Carol Lynn Dubose (Adv. Mgr.); Debbie Carlton (Circ. Mgr.); Susan H. Lincoln (Mng. Ed.)

TARPON SPRINGS BEACON

Street address 1: 9911 Seminole Blvd
Street address city: Seminole
Street address state: FL
Zip/Postal code: 33772-2536
General Phone: (727) 397-5563
General Fax: (727) 397-5900
Advertising Phone: (727) 397-5563
Editorial Phone: (727) 397-5563
General/National Adv. E-mail: dautrey@tbnweekly.com
Display Adv. E-mail: jrey@tbnweekly.com
Classified Adv. e-mail: dnoheji@suncoastnews.ocm
Editorial e-mail: rhibbs@suncoastnews.con
Primary Website: tbnweekly.com
Avg Free Circ: 21,7
Audit By: Sworn/Estimate/Non-Audited
Audit Date: 10.06.2019
Personnel: Dan Autrey (Pub. Mgr); Jay Rey (Adv. Mgr); Dave Brown (Prod. Mgr); Don Henry (Dist. Mgr.); Bob Hibbs (Editor)
Parent company (for newspapers): Times Publishing Company

THE APALACHICOLA CARRABELLE TIMES

Street address 1: 129 Commerce St
Street address city: Apalachicola
Street address state: FL
Zip/Postal code: 32320-1717
General Phone: (850) 653-8868
General Fax: (850) 653-8036
Editorial Phone: (850) 227-7827
General/National Adv. E-mail: rhoxie@starfl.com
Primary Website: apalachtimes.com
Avg Paid Circ: 5100
Audit By: Sworn/Estimate/Non-Audited
Audit Date: 10.06.2019
Personnel: Tim Croft (Ed.)
Parent company (for newspapers): CherryRoad Media

THE BAKER COUNTY PRESS

Street address 1: 104 S 5th St
Street address city: Macclenny
Street address state: FL
Zip/Postal code: 32063-2304
General Phone: (904) 259-2400
General Fax: (904) 259-6502
General/National Adv. E-mail: advertising@bakercountypress.com
Display Adv. E-mail: classifieds@bakercountypress.com
Editorial e-mail: editor@bakercountypress.com
Primary Website: bakercountypress.com
Year Established: 1929
Avg Paid Circ: 5400
Audit By: Sworn/Estimate/Non-Audited
Audit Date: 10.06.2019
Personnel: Karin Thomas (Bus. Mgr.); James C. McGauley (Pub./Ed.); Jessica Prevatt (Ad. Dir.); Joel Addington (Mng Ed.)

THE BANNER

Street address 1: 1100 Immokalee Rd
Street address city: Naples
Street address state: FL
Zip/Postal code: 34110-4810
General Phone: (239) 213-6000
General Fax: (239) 213-6099
Advertising Phone: (239) 263-4730
General/National Adv. E-mail: salesassist@naplesnews.com
Display Adv. E-mail: classad@naplesnews.com
Editorial e-mail: news@naplesnews.com
Primary Website: bonitabanner.com
Avg Free Circ: 43000
Audit By: Sworn/Estimate/Non-Audited
Audit Date: 10.06.2019
Personnel: Elysa Delcorto (Editor); Bill Barker (President/Publisher); Vince Modarelli (Ad. Director)

THE BAY BEACON

Street address 1: 1181 John Sims Pkwy E
Street address city: Niceville
Street address state: FL
Zip/Postal code: 32578-2752
General Phone: (850) 678-1080
Advertising Phone: (850) 678-1080
Editorial Phone: (850) 678-1080
General/National Adv. E-mail: info@baybeacon.com
Display Adv. E-mail: info@baybeacon.com
Editorial e-mail: info@baybeacon.com
Primary Website: baybeacon.com
Year Established: 1992
Avg Free Circ: 15000
Audit By: Sworn/Estimate/Non-Audited
Audit Date: 10.06.2019
Personnel: Stephen Kent (Ed. & Pub.)

THE BEACHES LEADER

Street address 1: 1372 Beach Blvd
Street address city: Jacksonville Beach
Street address state: FL
Zip/Postal code: 32250-3447
General Phone: (904) 249-9033
General Fax: (904) 249-1501
Advertising Phone: (904) 249-9033
Editorial Phone: (904) 246-9033
General/National Adv. E-mail: Sales@beachesleader.com
Display Adv. E-mail: classified@beachesleader.com
Editorial e-mail: Editor@beachesleader.com
Primary Website: BeachesLeader.com
Year Established: 1963
Avg Paid Circ: 7500

Audit By: Sworn/Estimate/Non-Audited
Audit Date: 10.06.2019
Personnel: Kathleen Bailey (Ed./Pub.); Hal Newsome (Web Ed.); Chelsea Wiggs (News/Edit.); Linda Borgstede (News/Edit.); Laura Kurtz (Display Ad Sales); David Bailey (Display Ad Sales); Marie Adams (Classified Adv.)

THE CALHOUN LIBERTY JOURNAL

Street address 1: 11493 NW Summers Rd
Street address city: Bristol
Street address state: FL
Zip/Postal code: 32321-3364
General Phone: (850) 643-3333
General Fax: (850) 643-3334
General/National Adv. E-mail: thejournal@fairpoint.net
Primary Website: cljnews.com
Year Established: 1981
Avg Paid Circ: 5200
Avg Free Circ: 18
Audit By: Sworn/Estimate/Non-Audited
Audit Date: 10.06.2019
Personnel: Johnny Eubanks (Pub.); Teresa Eubanks (Ed.)

THE CLEWISTON NEWS

Street address 1: 107 SW 17th St
Street address 2: Ste D
Street address city: Okeechobee
Street address state: FL
Zip/Postal code: 34974-6110
General Phone: (863) 763-3134
General Fax: (863) 983-7537
General/National Adv. E-mail: adsales@newszap.com
Display Adv. E-mail: classads@newszap.com
Primary Website: theclewistonnews.com
Year Established: 1920
Avg Paid Circ: 3700
Audit By: Sworn/Estimate/Non-Audited
Audit Date: 10.06.2019
Parent company (for newspapers): Independent Newsmedia Inc. USA; Independent Newspapers, Inc. (Florida)

THE COASTAL STAR

Street address 1: 5114 N Ocean Blvd
Street address city: Ocean Ridge
Street address state: FL
Zip/Postal code: 33435-7031
General Phone: (561) 337-1553
General Fax: (561) 337-1553
Advertising Phone: (561) 337-1553
Editorial Phone: (561) 337-1553
General/National Adv. E-mail: sales@thecoastalstar.com
Editorial e-mail: editor@thecoastalstar.com
Primary Website: thecoastalstar.com
Mthly Avg Views: 16306
Mthly Avg Unique Visitors: 4941
Year Established: 2008
Avg Paid Circ: 400
Avg Free Circ: 17000
Audit By: Sworn/Estimate/Non-Audited
Audit Date: 10.06.2019
Personnel: Jerry Lower (Publlisher); Mary Kate Leming (Ed.); Chris Bellard (Adv. Dir.)

THE COLLIER CITIZEN

Street address 1: 1100 Immokalee Rd
Street address city: Naples
Street address state: FL
Zip/Postal code: 34110-4810
General Phone: (239) 213-6000
General Fax: (239) 213-6076
Advertising Phone: (239) 263-4730
Editorial e-mail: penny.fisher@naplesnews.com
Primary Website: colliercitizen.com
Year Established: 2005
Avg Free Circ: 52118
Audit By: Sworn/Estimate/Non-Audited
Audit Date: 10.06.2019
Personnel: Penny Fisher (News Dir.)

THE COUNTY RECORD

Street address 1: PO Box 366
Street address city: Blountstown
Street address state: FL
Zip/Postal code: 32424-0366
General Phone: (850) 674-5041
General Fax: (850) 674-5008
General/National Adv. E-mail: displayads@thecountyrecord.net
Display Adv. E-mail: classifieds@thecountyrecord.net
Editorial e-mail: editor@thecountyrecord.net
Primary Website: thecountyrecord.net
Year Established: 1907
Audit By: Sworn/Estimate/Non-Audited
Audit Date: 10.06.2019
Personnel: Robert Turner (Editor&Publisher)

THE CREEKLINE

Street address 1: 12443 San Jose Blvd
Street address 2: Ste 403A
Street address city: Jacksonville
Street address state: FL
Zip/Postal code: 32223-8650
General Phone: (904) 886-4919
General/National Adv. E-mail: linda@floridanewsline.com
Display Adv. E-mail: linda@floridanewsline.com
Editorial e-mail: editor@floridanewsline.com
Primary Website: floridanewsline.com
Year Established: 2000
Avg Free Circ: 27299
Audit By: CVC
Audit Date: 31.12.2017
Personnel: Martie Thompson (Pub.); Linda Gay (Sales Consultant)
Parent company (for newspapers): Local Community News

THE DESTIN LOG

Street address 1: 2 Eglin Parkway NE
Street address city: Fort Walton Beach
Street address state: FL
Zip/Postal code: 32548
General Phone: (850) 315-4306
General/National Adv. E-mail: jkirkland@pcnh.com
Display Adv. E-mail: jkirkland@pcnh.com
Editorial e-mail: dricketts@nwfdailynews.com
Primary Website: thedestinlog.com
Audit By: Sworn/Estimate/Non-Audited
Audit Date: 10.06.2019
Personnel: Dusty Ricketts (Ed.); Joan Kirkland (Bus. Mgr.)
Parent company (for newspapers): CherryRoad Media

THE FORUM - SUNRISE & TAMARAC

Street address 1: 6501 Nob Hill Road
Street address city: Davie
Street address state: FL
Zip/Postal code: 33328
General Phone: (954) 698-6397
General Fax: (954) 429-1207
General/National Adv. E-mail: placeanad.sun-sentinel.com
Display Adv. E-mail: jshalek@tribune.com
Primary Website: sun-sentinel.com/local
Avg Free Circ: 15013
Audit By: Sworn/Estimate/Non-Audited
Audit Date: 10.06.2019
Personnel: Ed Wilder (Circ. Mgr.); Ruben Cueto (Ed.); Joann Zollo (Adv. Mgr.); Tom Adams (Pres./Pub.); Ed Wilder (Circ. Mgr.); Gregg Behar (Sr. Sales Mgr.); Ruben Cueto (Mng. Ed.); Mark Ward (Circ. Mgr.)
Parent company (for newspapers): Sun-Sentinel Co.

THE FREE PRESS

Street address 1: 1010 W Cass St
Street address city: Tampa
Street address state: FL
Zip/Postal code: 33606-1307
General Phone: (813) 254-5888
General Fax: (813) 902-6599
General/National Adv. E-mail: contact@4freepress.com
Editorial e-mail: contact@4freepress.com
Primary Website: 4freepress.com
Year Established: 1911
Avg Paid Circ: 507
Audit By: Sworn/Estimate/Non-Audited
Audit Date: 30.09.2017
Personnel: Cheryl Marshalsea (Ed.); Paul Clarion (Pub.); Tommy Todd (Adv. Dir.); Tammy Collins (Sales Consultant)

THE GAZETTE - PEMBROKE PINES & MIRAMAR

Street address 1: 500 E Broward Blvd
Street address city: Fort Lauderdale
Street address state: FL
Zip/Postal code: 33394-3000
General Phone: (954) 698-6397
General Fax: (954) 429-1207
Advertising Phone: (800) 974-7521
Advertising Fax: (954) 698-6719
Editorial Phone: (954) 596-5632
General/National Adv. E-mail: Kenwilliams@tribpub.com
Display Adv. E-mail: jshalek@tribune.com
Editorial e-mail: JZizzo@tribpub.com
Primary Website: forumpubs.com
Audit By: Sworn/Estimate/Non-Audited
Audit Date: 10.06.2019
Personnel: Dana Banker (Mng. Ed.); Howard Saltz (Pub.)

THE GRACEVILLE NEWS

Street address 1: 1004 10th Ave
Street address city: Graceville
Street address state: FL
Zip/Postal code: 32440-1906
General Phone: (850) 263-6015
General Fax: (850) 263-1042
General/National Adv. E-mail: gvnews@wfeca.net
Primary Website: facebook.com/thegracevillenews
Avg Paid Circ: 1750
Audit By: Sworn/Estimate/Non-Audited
Audit Date: 10.06.2019
Personnel: John Ferrin Cox (Pub.); Sharon Taylor (Ed.)

THE HERALD

Street address 1: 103 W 7th Ave
Street address city: Havana
Street address state: FL
Zip/Postal code: 32333-1660
General Phone: (850) 539-6586
General Fax: (850) 539-0454
General/National Adv. E-mail: colleen@prioritynews.net
Editorial e-mail: mail@prioritynews.net
Primary Website: TheHerald.onlin
Year Established: 1947
Avg Paid Circ: 3500
Audit By: Sworn/Estimate/Non-Audited
Audit Date: 10.06.2019
Personnel: Mark Pettus (Pub.)

THE HERALD-ADVOCATE

Street address 1: 115 S 7th Ave
Street address city: Wauchula
Street address state: FL
Zip/Postal code: 33873-2801
General Phone: (863) 773-3255
General Fax: (863) 773-0657
General/National Adv. E-mail: publisher@theheraldadvocate.com
Primary Website: theheraldadvocate.com
Year Established: 1955
Avg Paid Circ: 4750
Avg Free Circ: 50
Audit By: Sworn/Estimate/Non-Audited
Audit Date: 10.06.2019
Personnel: Jeanne Kelly (Circ. Mgr.); Jim Kelly (Ed. & Pub.); Cynthia Krahl (Mng. Ed.); Joan Seaman (News/Sports Ed.)

THE ISLAND REPORTER

Street address 1: 1331 Sea Gull Dr S
Street address city: South Pasadena
Street address state: FL
Zip/Postal code: 33707-3833
General Phone: (727) 631-4730
General Fax: (727) 864-6434
Advertising Phone: (727) 631-4730
Advertising Fax: (727) 864-6434
Editorial Phone: (727) 631-4730
Editorial Fax: (727) 864-6434
General/National Adv. E-mail: info@theislandreporter.com
Display Adv. E-mail: info@theislandreporter.com
Editorial e-mail: sloane@theislandreporter.com
Primary Website: theislandreporter.com
Year Established: 2003
Avg Free Circ: 30175
Audit By: CVC
Audit Date: 31.03.2016
Personnel: Betsy Judge (Pub./Ed.); Sloane Golden (Ed.)

THE ISLANDER

Street address 1: 3218 E Bay Dr
Street address city: Holmes Beach
Street address state: FL
Zip/Postal code: 34217-2039
General Phone: (941) 778-7978
General Fax: (941) 778-9392
General/National Adv. E-mail: toni@islander.org
Editorial e-mail: news@islander.org
Primary Website: islander.org
Year Established: 1992
Avg Paid Circ: 2900
Avg Free Circ: 15000
Audit By: Sworn/Estimate/Non-Audited
Audit Date: 10.06.2019
Personnel: Bonner Joy (Ed./Pub.); Toni Lyon (Adv. Dir.)

THE LAKE WORTH HERALD

Street address 1: 1313 Central Ter
Street address city: Lake Worth
Street address state: FL
Zip/Postal code: 33460-1835
General Phone: (561) 585-9387
General Fax: (561) 585-5434
General/National Adv. E-mail: Adsales@lwherald.com
Display Adv. E-mail: Classifieds@lwherald.com
Editorial e-mail: Editor@lwherald.com
Primary Website: lwherald.com
Year Established: 1912
Avg Paid Circ: 918
Avg Free Circ: 16000
Audit By: Sworn/Estimate/Non-Audited
Audit Date: 10.06.2019
Personnel: Mark J. Easton (Editor/Publisher)
Parent company (for newspapers): Lake Worth Herald Press, Inc.

THE LUTZ NEWS

Street address 1: 3632 Land O Lakes Blvd
Street address 2: Ste 102
Street address city: Land O Lakes
Street address state: FL
Zip/Postal code: 34639-4407
General Phone: (813) 909-2800
General Fax: (813) 909-2802
General/National Adv. E-mail: cbennett@lakerlutznews.com
Display Adv. E-mail: classifieds@lakerlutznews.com
Classified Adv. e-mail: classifieds@lakerlutznews.com
Editorial e-mail: bcmanion@lakerlutznews.com
Primary Website: lakerlutznews.com
Year Established: 1965
Avg Free Circ: 8927
Audit By: CVC
Audit Date: 30.12.2021
Personnel: Brian Calle (Pres./Pub.); B.C. Manion (Ed)
Parent company (for newspapers): Street Media, LLC

THE NEWS LEADER

Street address 1: 637 8th St
Street address city: Clermont
Street address state: FL
Zip/Postal code: 34711-2159
General Phone: (352) 242-9818
General Fax: (352) 242-9820
General/National Adv. E-mail: jkemp@clermontnewsleader.com
Display Adv. E-mail: nlclassifieds@cfl.rr.com
Editorial e-mail: lbriody@cfl.rr.com
Primary Website: clermontnewsleader.com
Year Established: 1982
Avg Free Circ: 38394
Audit By: Sworn/Estimate/Non-Audited
Audit Date: 10.06.2019
Personnel: Linda Briody (Ed.); Jodi Marano (Adv. Dir.); Dawn Hendry (Creative Director)

Parent company (for newspapers): Independent Publications Inc; Lakeway Publishers, Inc.; Sun Publications of Fla.

THE PINE ISLAND EAGLE

Street address 1: 2510 Del Prado Blvd
Street address city: Cape Coral
Street address state: FL
Zip/Postal code: 33904
General Phone: (239) 283-2022
General Fax: (239) 283-0232
Advertising Phone: (239) 574-1110 x171
Editorial Phone: (239) 574-1110 x119
General/National Adv. E-mail: cgallagher@breezenewspapers.com
Editorial e-mail: vharring@breezenewspapers.com
Primary Website: pineisland-eagle.com
Year Established: 1976
Avg Paid Circ: 185
Avg Free Circ: 7967
Audit By: CVC
Audit Date: 30.12.2017
Personnel: Scott Blonde (Pub.); Valarie Harring (Exec. Ed.); Natalie Gerreira (Nat'l Acct. Mgr.); Cynthia Gallagher (Adv. Dir.); Barbara Smith (Circ. Mgr); Cecilia Yndart (Prod. Mgr)
Parent company (for newspapers): Ogden Newspapers Inc.

THE PLANTER

Street address 1: 400 N Park Ave
Street address city: Apopka
Street address state: FL
Zip/Postal code: 32712-4152
General Phone: (407) 886-2777
General Fax: (407) 889-4121
General/National Adv. E-mail: news@theapopkachief.com
Display Adv. E-mail: ads@theapopkachief..com
Editorial e-mail: news@theapopkachief..com
Primary Website: theapopkachief.com
Year Established: 1965
Avg Paid Circ: 0
Avg Free Circ: 4500
Audit By: Sworn/Estimate/Non-Audited
Audit Date: 10.06.2019
Personnel: John E. Ricketson (Pub.); John Peery (Ed.)

THE POLK COUNTY NEWS AND DEMOCRAT

Street address 1: 99 3rd St NW
Street address city: Winter Haven
Street address state: FL
Zip/Postal code: 33881-4609
General Phone: (863) 533-4183
General Fax: (863) 533-0402
General/National Adv. E-mail: kedwards@scmginc.com
Display Adv. E-mail: aswain@scmginc.com
Editorial e-mail: jroslow@scmginc.com
Primary Website: polkcountydemocrat.com
Year Established: 1931
Avg Paid Circ: 2500
Avg Free Circ: 18000
Audit By: Sworn/Estimate/Non-Audited
Audit Date: 10.06.2019
Personnel: Chris Sexson (Pub.); Jeff Roslow (Ed.); Kim Edwards (Adv. Dir.)
Parent company (for newspapers): Sun Coast Media Group - APG

THE REPORTER

Street address 1: 171 Hood Ave
Street address 2: Ste 22
Street address city: Tavernier
Street address state: FL
Zip/Postal code: 33070-2645
General Phone: (305) 852-3216
Editorial Phone: (305) 440-3204
General/National Adv. E-mail: jdarden@keysreporter.com
Display Adv. E-mail: jpulis@keynoter.com
Editorial e-mail: dgoodhue@keysreporter.com
Primary Website: flkeysnews.com
Year Established: 1973
Avg Paid Circ: 7094
Avg Free Circ: 500
Audit By: Sworn/Estimate/Non-Audited
Audit Date: 10.06.2019
Personnel: Carter Townshend (Circ. Mgr.); David Goodhue (Ed.); Richard Tamborrino (Pub.); Joanne Pulis (Class/Web Mgr.)
Parent company (for newspapers): The McClatchy Company

THE SENTRY

Street address 1: 2500 SE 5th Ct
Street address city: Pompano Beach
Street address state: FL
Zip/Postal code: 33062-6108
General Phone: (954) 532-2000
General Fax: (954) 532-2002
General/National Adv. E-mail: advertise@flsentry.com
Editorial e-mail: editor@flsentry.com
Primary Website: flsentry.com
Year Established: 1980
Avg Paid Circ: 5000
Audit By: Sworn/Estimate/Non-Audited
Audit Date: 10.06.2019
Personnel: Karen M. Foley (Pub.); Ross Shulmister (Ed.); J.P. Bender (Reporter); Chas Rogers (Prodn. Mgr.)

THE STAR

Street address 1: 135 W Highway 98
Street address city: Port Saint Joe
Street address state: FL
Zip/Postal code: 32456-1871
General Phone: (850) 227-1278
General Fax: (850) 227-7212
Advertising Phone: (850) 227-7847
Editorial Phone: (850) 227-7827
General/National Adv. E-mail: kfortune@starfl.com
Display Adv. E-mail: starads@starfl.com
Editorial e-mail: tcroft@starfl.com
Primary Website: starfl.com
Avg Free Circ: 2600
Audit By: Sworn/Estimate/Non-Audited
Audit Date: 10.06.2019
Personnel: Tim Croft (Ed.); Kari Fortune (Ad. Rep.)
Parent company (for newspapers): Halifax Media

THE SUNCOAST NEWS

Street address 1: 6214 US Highway 19
Street address city: New Port Richey
Street address state: FL
Zip/Postal code: 34652-2528
General Phone: (727) 815-1000
General Fax: (727) 815-1025
Advertising Phone: (727) 815-1032
Editorial Phone: (727) 815-1064
General/National Adv. E-mail: dpleus@suncoastnews.com
Display Adv. E-mail: tribisi@suncoastnews.com
Editorial e-mail: rhibbs@suncoastnews.com
Primary Website: suncoastnews.com
Avg Free Circ: 90433
Audit By: Sworn/Estimate/Non-Audited
Audit Date: 10.06.2019
Personnel: Duayne Chichester (Pub.); Doug Pleus (Ad. Sales Manager); Robert Hibbs (Ed.); Timothy Wahl (Adv. Sales Mgr.)
Parent company (for newspapers): BH Media Group; Media General, Inc. (OOB)

THE TOWN-CRIER

Street address 1: 12794 Forest Hill Blvd
Street address 2: Ste 33
Street address city: Wellington
Street address state: FL
Zip/Postal code: 33414-4758
General Phone: (561) 793-7606
General/National Adv. E-mail: news@gotowncrier.com
Display Adv. E-mail: towncrierads@aol.com
Classified Adv. e-mail: classifieds@gotowncrier.com
Editorial e-mail: news@gotowncrier.com
Primary Website: gotowncrier.com
Year Established: 1980
Avg Free Circ: 25000
Audit By: Sworn/Estimate/Non-Audited
Audit Date: 10.06.2019
Personnel: Barry S. Manning (Publisher); Jody Gorran (Assoc. Pub.); Dawn Rivera (General Manager); Joshua I. Manning (Executive Editor); Ron Bukley (Managing Editor); Mark Lioi (News Ed.); Stephanie Rodriguez (Arts/Prodn. Mgr.)
Parent company (for newspapers): Newspaper Publishers LLC

THE WAKULLA NEWS

Street address 1: 3119A Crawfordville Hwy
Street address city: Crawfordville
Street address state: FL
Zip/Postal code: 32327-3148
General Phone: (850) 926-7102
General Fax: (850) 926-3815
General/National Adv. E-mail: lkinsey@thewakullanews.net
Display Adv. E-mail: advertising@thewakullanews.net
Editorial e-mail: editor@thewakullanews.net
Primary Website: thewakullanews.com
Year Established: 1897
Avg Paid Circ: 4500
Audit By: Sworn/Estimate/Non-Audited
Audit Date: 10.06.2019
Personnel: William Snowden (Ed)
Parent company (for newspapers): Landmark Community Newspapers, LLC

THE WALTON SUN

Street address 1: 5597 US Highway 98 W
Street address 2: Ste 204
Street address city: Santa Rosa Beach
Street address state: FL
Zip/Postal code: 32459-3283
General Phone: (850) 267-4555
General Fax: (850) 267-0929
Advertising Phone: (850) 654-8448
Editorial Phone: (850) 654-8440
General/National Adv. E-mail: agaffka@nwfdailynews.com
Editorial e-mail: whatfield@waltonsun.com
Primary Website: waltonsun.com
Avg Free Circ: 12000
Audit By: Sworn/Estimate/Non-Audited
Audit Date: 10.06.2019
Personnel: Donna Talla (Adv. Dir.); Matt Algarin (Managing Ed.)
Parent company (for newspapers): Halifax Media

THE WEST ORANGE TIMES & OBSERVER

Street address 1: 720 S Dillard St
Street address city: Winter Garden
Street address state: FL
Zip/Postal code: 34787-3908
General Phone: (407) 656-2121
General Fax: (407) 656-6075
Advertising Phone: (407) 656-2121
Editorial Phone: (407) 656-2121
General/National Adv. E-mail: advertising@orangeobserver.com
Display Adv. E-mail: classifieds@orangeobserver.com
Editorial e-mail: news@orangeobserver.com
Primary Website: orangeobserver.com
Year Established: 1905
Avg Paid Circ: 22000
Audit By: Sworn/Estimate/Non-Audited
Audit Date: 10.06.2019
Personnel: Dawn Willis (Pub.); Andrew Bailey (Circ. Mgr.); Amy Rhode
Parent company (for newspapers): Observer Media Group

THE WEST VOLUSIA BEACON

Street address 1: 110 W New York Ave
Street address city: Deland
Street address state: FL
Zip/Postal code: 32720-5416
General Phone: (386) 734-4622
General Fax: (386) 734-4641
General/National Adv. E-mail: info@beacononlinenews.com
Display Adv. E-mail: adsales@beacononlinenews.com
Classified Adv. e-mail: classified@beacononlinenews.com
Editorial e-mail: info@beacononlinenews.com
Primary Website: beacononlinenews.com
Year Established: 1992
Avg Paid Circ: 5000
Avg Free Circ: 9050
Audit By: CVC
Audit Date: 10.06.2019
Personnel: Joann Kramer (Co-Owner/Co-Pub.); Sammie Wiggins (Co-Pub.); Michael Jaeckle (General Manager); Barb Shepherd (Co-Pub./Ed.); Sona O'Connell (Co-Editor); Eli Witek (Co-Editor)

TWIN CITY NEWS

Street address 1: 314 W Washington St
Street address city: Chattahoochee
Street address state: FL
Zip/Postal code: 32324-1434
General Phone: (850) 663-2255
General/National Adv. E-mail: tcnews@fairpoint.net
Avg Paid Circ: 2000
Audit By: Sworn/Estimate/Non-Audited
Audit Date: 10.06.2019
Personnel: Nick Bert (Pub.); Kathy Johnson (Mng. Ed.)

UNION COUNTY TIMES

Street address 1: 131 W Call St
Street address city: Starke
Street address state: FL
Zip/Postal code: 32091-3210
General Phone: (904) 964-6305
General Fax: (904) 964-8628
Advertising Phone: (904) 964-6305
General/National Adv. E-mail: kmiller@bctelegraph.com
Display Adv. E-mail: classads@bctelegraph.com
Editorial e-mail: editor@bctelegraph.com
Primary Website: starkejournal.com
Year Established: 1912
Avg Paid Circ: 1000
Avg Free Circ: 1750
Audit By: Sworn/Estimate/Non-Audited
Audit Date: 10.06.2019
Personnel: Mark Crawford (Ed.); John Miller (Mng. Ed.)

VENICE GONDOLIER SUN

Street address 1: 200 E Venice Ave
Street address 2: Fl 1
Street address city: Venice
Street address state: FL
Zip/Postal code: 34285-1998
General Phone: (941) 207-1000
General Fax: (941) 484-8460
Editorial Fax: (941) 484-8460
General/National Adv. E-mail: majoraccts@sun-herald.com
Display Adv. E-mail: classified@sun-herald.com
Editorial e-mail: feedback@sun-herald.com
Primary Website: venicegondolier.com
Year Established: 1946
Avg Paid Circ: 14000
Avg Free Circ: 13000
Audit By: Sworn/Estimate/Non-Audited
Audit Date: 10.06.2019
Personnel: Ron Dupont (Ed.); Greg Giles (News Ed.); Kim Cool
Parent company (for newspapers): Sun Coast Media Group - APG

VOICE OF SOUTH MARION

Street address 1: 5513 SE 113th St
Street address city: Belleview
Street address state: FL
Zip/Postal code: 34420-4039
General Phone: (352) 245-3161
General Fax: (352) 347-7444
General/National Adv. E-mail: vosm@aol.com
Display Adv. E-mail: vosminfo@aol.com
Primary Website: thevosm.net
Year Established: 1969
Avg Paid Circ: 2800
Audit By: Sworn/Estimate/Non-Audited
Audit Date: 10.06.2019
Personnel: Clay Waldron (Adv. Mgr.); Sandy Waldron (Ed.)

WESLEY CHAPEL LAKER

Street address 1: 3632 Land O Lakes Blvd
Street address 2: Ste 102
Street address city: Land O Lakes
Street address state: FL
Zip/Postal code: 34639-4407
General Phone: (813) 909-2800
General Fax: (813) 909-2802
Advertising Phone: (813) 909-2800

Advertising Fax: (813) 909-2802
Editorial Phone: (813) 909-2800
Editorial Fax: (813) 909-2802
General/National Adv. E-mail: cbennett@lakerlutznews.com
Display Adv. E-mail: classifieds@lakerlutznews.com
Classified Adv. e-mail: classifieds@lakerlutznews.com
Editorial e-mail: bcmanion@lakerlutznews.com
Primary Website: lakerlutznews.com
Year Established: 1981
Avg Free Circ: 14298
Audit By: CVC
Audit Date: 30.08.2021
Personnel: Brian Calle (Pres./Pub.); B.C. Manion (Ed)
Parent company (for newspapers): Street Media, LLC

WEST BOCA FORUM

Street address 1: 500 E Broward Blvd
Street address 2: Ste 1710
Street address city: Fort Lauderdale
Street address state: FL
Zip/Postal code: 33394-3012
General Phone: (954) 698-6397
General Fax: (954) 429-1207
Advertising Phone: (800) 974-7521
Advertising Fax: (954) 698-6719
Editorial Phone: (954) 596-5632
General/National Adv. E-mail: Kenwilliams@tribpub.com
Display Adv. E-mail: jshalek@tribune.com
Editorial e-mail: JZizzo@tribpub.com
Primary Website: forumpubs.com
Avg Paid Circ: 0
Avg Free Circ: 23814
Audit By: Sworn/Estimate/Non-Audited
Audit Date: 10.06.2019
Personnel: Kari Barnett (Editor); Gregg Behar (Sr. Sales Mgr.); Tom Adams (Pres./Pub.); Pam Doto (VP/Exec. Ed.); Mark Ward (Circ. Mgr.)
Parent company (for newspapers): Forum Publishing Group; Sun-Sentinel Co.

WESTON GAZETTE

Street address 1: 500 E Broward Blvd
Street address city: Fort Lauderdale
Street address state: FL
Zip/Postal code: 33394-3000
General Phone: (954) 356-4000
General Fax: (954) 429-1207
Advertising Phone: (954) 698-6397
Editorial Phone: (954) 698-6397
General/National Adv. E-mail: placeanad.sun-sentinel.com
Display Adv. E-mail: ewilder@tribune.com
Editorial e-mail: ctouey@tribune.com
Primary Website: forumpubs.com
Year Established: 1973
Audit By: Sworn/Estimate/Non-Audited
Audit Date: 10.06.2019
Personnel: Tom Adams (Pub./Gen. Mgr.); Tracy Kolody (Mng. Ed.); Ray Daley (Adv. Mgr.); Stewart Cady (Prodn. Mgr.); Mark Ward (Circ. Mgr.)
Parent company (for newspapers): Sun-Sentinel Co.

WILLISTON PIONEER SUN NEWS

Street address 1: 607 SW 1st Ave
Street address city: Williston
Street address state: FL
Zip/Postal code: 32696-2515
General Phone: (352) 528-3343
Editorial Phone: (352) 528-3343
General/National Adv. E-mail: Chad.Thompson@chieflandcitizen.com
Display Adv. E-mail: classified@chieflandcitizen.com
Editorial e-mail: editor@willistonpioneer.com
Primary Website: willistonpioneer.com
Year Established: 1879
Avg Paid Circ: 1500
Audit By: Sworn/Estimate/Non-Audited
Audit Date: 10.06.2019
Personnel: Carolyn Ten Broeck (Ed.); Chad Thompson (Sales Representative)

Parent company (for newspapers): Landmark Community Newspapers, LLC; Landmark Communications, Inc.

WINTER PARK-MAITLAND OBSERVER

Street address 1: 1500 Park Center Dr
Street address city: Orlando
Street address state: FL
Zip/Postal code: 32835-5705
General Phone: (407) 563-7000
General Fax: (407) 563-7099
Editorial e-mail: meng@OrangeObserver.com
Primary Website: wpmobserver.com
Mthly Avg Views: 15000
Year Established: 1989
Avg Paid Circ: 5300
Audit By: Sworn/Estimate/Non-Audited
Audit Date: 10.06.2019
Personnel: Michael Eng (Ed.); Jackie Fanara (Pub.); Steven Ryzewski (Sports Ed.); Michelle Gentry (Adv. Ex.)
Parent company (for newspapers): Turnstile Media Group

ZEPHYRHILLS LAKER

Street address 1: 3632 Land O Lakes Blvd
Street address 2: Ste 102
Street address city: Land O Lakes
Street address state: FL
Zip/Postal code: 34639-4407
General Phone: (813) 909-2800
General Fax: (813) 909-2802
Advertising Phone: (813) 909-2800
Advertising Fax: (813) 909-2802
Editorial Phone: (813) 909-2800
Editorial Fax: (813) 909-2802
General/National Adv. E-mail: cbennett@lakerlutznews.com
Display Adv. E-mail: classifieds@lakerlutznews.com
Classified Adv. e-mail: classifieds@lakerlutznews.com
Editorial e-mail: bcmanion@lakerlutznews.com
Primary Website: lakerlutznews.com
Year Established: 1965
Avg Free Circ: 9126
Audit By: CVC
Audit Date: 31.12.2021
Personnel: Brian Calle (Pres./Pub.); B.C. Manion (Ed)
Parent company (for newspapers): Street Media, LLC

ZEPHYRHILLS NEWS

Street address 1: 38440 5th Avenue
Street address city: Zephyrhills
Street address state: FL
Zip/Postal code: 33542
General Phone: (813) 783-1300
General Fax: (813) 788-7987
Editorial e-mail: cdrews@pasconewspubs.com
Primary Website: zephyrhillsnewsonline.com
Year Established: 1911
Avg Paid Circ: 3539
Avg Free Circ: 469
Audit By: Sworn/Estimate/Non-Audited
Audit Date: 10.06.2019
Personnel: Chris Drews (Pub.); Krista Black (Sales); Greg First (Pub. Rel.)

GEORGIA

ADVOCATE DEMOCRAT

Street address 1: 107 N Main St
Street address city: Greensboro
Street address state: GA
Zip/Postal code: 30642-1143
General Phone: (706) 453-7988
General Fax: (706) 453-2311
Editorial e-mail: editor@heraldjournal.net
Primary Website: No Website
Avg Paid Circ: 900
Audit By: Sworn/Estimate/Non-Audited
Audit Date: 10.06.2019

Personnel: Beth Lyons (Adv. Mgr.); Carey Williams (Ed.)

ALPHARETTA NEIGHBOR

Street address 1: 10930 Crabapple Rd
Street address 2: Ste 9
Street address city: Roswell
Street address state: GA
Zip/Postal code: 30075-5812
General Phone: (770) 993-7400
General Fax: (770) 518-6062
Advertising Phone: 7704289411x 501
Display Adv. E-mail: adavis@mdjonline.com
Editorial e-mail: nfulton@neighbornewspapers.com
Primary Website: neighbornewspapers.com
Year Established: 1968
Avg Paid Circ: 3
Avg Free Circ: 11800
Audit By: Sworn/Estimate/Non-Audited
Audit Date: 10.06.2019
Personnel: Rachel Kellogg (Ed); Brian Clark (Mng. Ed.); Lee Brumby Garrett (Gen. Mgr.); Wade Stephens (VP, Sales/Mktg.)
Parent company (for newspapers): Neighbor Newspapers; Neighbor Newspapers, Inc.

ATLANTA BUSINESS CHRONICLE

Street address 1: 3384 Peachtree Rd NE
Street address 2: Ste 900
Street address city: Atlanta
Street address state: GA
Zip/Postal code: 30326-2828
General Phone: (404) 249-1000
General Fax: (404) 249-1048
Advertising Phone: (404) 249-1069
Advertising Fax: (404) 249-1048
Editorial Phone: (404) 249-1039
Editorial Fax: (404) 249-1048
General/National Adv. E-mail: eboyle@bizjournals.com
Display Adv. E-mail: ebaker@bizjournals.com
Editorial e-mail: dallison@bizjournals.com
Primary Website: bizjournals.com/atlanta
Year Established: 1978
Audit By: Sworn/Estimate/Non-Audited
Audit Date: 10.06.2019
Personnel: Ed Baker (Pub.); David Allison (Ed.); Mark Meltzer (Exec. Ed.); Jessica Saunders (Mng. Ed.)
Parent company (for newspapers): American City Business Journals

BARROW NEWS-JOURNAL

Street address 1: 33 Lee Street
Street address city: Jefferson
Street address state: GA
Zip/Postal code: 30549
General Phone: 706-367-5233
Advertising Phone: (706) 367-5233
Editorial Phone: (706) 367-5233
General/National Adv. E-mail: ads@mainstreetnews.com
Display Adv. E-mail: scott@mainstreetnews.com
Classified Adv. e-mail: classifieds@mainstreetnews.com
Editorial e-mail: mike@mainstreetnews.com
Primary Website: www.barrownewsjournal.com
Year Established: 1893
Avg Paid Circ: 4500
Avg Free Circ: 0
Audit By: Sworn/Estimate/Non-Audited
Audit Date: 12.07.2021
Personnel: Scott Buffington (Co-Pub); Mike Buffington (Co-Publisher)
Parent company (for newspapers): MainStreet Newspapers, Inc.

BOWDON BULLETIN

Street address 1: 901 Hays Mill Rd
Street address city: Carrollton
Street address state: GA
Zip/Postal code: 30117-9576
General Phone: (770) 834-6631
General Fax: (770) 830-9425
General/National Adv. E-mail: melissa@times-georgian.com
Primary Website: times-georgian.com
Avg Paid Circ: 1800
Avg Free Circ: 1200
Audit By: Sworn/Estimate/Non-Audited
Audit Date: 10.06.2019

Personnel: Leonard Woolsey (Pub.)

BRYAN COUNTY NEWS

Street address 1: 9998 Ford Ave
Street address 2: Suite 6
Street address city: Richmond Hill
Street address state: GA
Zip/Postal code: 31324
General Phone: (912) 756-2668
General Fax: (912) 756-5907
General/National Adv. E-mail: swilliamson@bryancountynews.com
Display Adv. E-mail: emattingly@bryancountynews.com
Editorial e-mail: jwhitten@bryancountynews.com
Primary Website: bryancountynews.net
Avg Paid Circ: 3000
Avg Free Circ: 1000
Audit By: Sworn/Estimate/Non-Audited
Audit Date: 10.06.2019
Personnel: Jeff Whitten (Ed.); Patty Leon (GM); Stephanie Williamson (Adv.); Darlene Redmon (Circ.)
Parent company (for newspapers): Morris Multimedia, Inc.

CALHOUN TIMES AND GORDON COUNTY NEWS

Street address 1: 215 W Line St
Street address city: Calhoun
Street address state: GA
Zip/Postal code: 30701-1815
General Phone: (706) 629-2231
General Fax: (706) 625-0899
General/National Adv. E-mail: calhountimes@calhountimes.com
Primary Website: calhountimes.com
Year Established: 1870
Avg Paid Circ: 8500
Audit By: Sworn/Estimate/Non-Audited
Audit Date: 10.06.2019
Personnel: Brandi Owczarz (Editor); Billy Steele (Adv. Mgr.); Dianne Tippens (Adv. Rep.); Alex Farrer (Sports Ed.); Rob Broadway (Prodn. Mgr.); Danika Trice (Classified / Legal)

CAMILLA ENTERPRISE

Street address 1: 13 S Scott St
Street address city: Camilla
Street address state: GA
Zip/Postal code: 31730-1705
General Phone: (229) 336-5265
General Fax: (229) 336-8476
General/National Adv. E-mail: camillaenterprise@camillaga.net
Primary Website: No Website
Avg Paid Circ: 3300
Audit By: Sworn/Estimate/Non-Audited
Audit Date: 10.06.2019
Personnel: Darrin Wilson (Pub.); Sandra Williams (Circ. Dir.)
Parent company (for newspapers): Trib Publications

CATOOSA COUNTY NEWS

Street address 1: 7513 Nashville St
Street address city: Ringgold
Street address state: GA
Zip/Postal code: 30736-2357
General Phone: (706) 935-2621
General Fax: (706) 965-5934
General/National Adv. E-mail: catoosacountynews@catoosanews.com
Primary Website: catoosawalkernews.com
Avg Paid Circ: 4261
Audit By: Sworn/Estimate/Non-Audited
Audit Date: 10.06.2019
Personnel: Don Stillwell (Pub.); Karen Keys (Adv. Mgr.); Kathy Bruce (Adv. Rep.); Misty Martin (Sports Ed.); Brenda Burger (VP, Ops.); William Steele (Rgl. Adv. Mgr.)
Parent company (for newspapers): Rome News-Tribune

CHARLTON COUNTY HERALD

Street address 1: 3781 Main St
Street address 2: Ste A
Street address city: Folkston
Street address state: GA
Zip/Postal code: 31537-7572

General Phone: (912) 496-3585
General Fax: (912) 496-4585
General/National Adv. E-mail: ads@charltonherald.com
Display Adv. E-mail: mail@charltonherald.com
Editorial e-mail: editor@charltonherald.com
Primary Website: charltoncountyherald.com
Year Established: 1898
Avg Paid Circ: 3000
Avg Free Circ: 100
Audit By: Sworn/Estimate/Non-Audited
Audit Date: 10.06.2019
Personnel: Marla Ogletree (Advertising); Matt Gardner (Ed.)
Parent company (for newspapers): Gardner Newspapers

CHATSWORTH TIMES

Street address 1: 224 N 3rd Ave
Street address city: Chatsworth
Street address state: GA
Zip/Postal code: 30705-2536
General Phone: (706) 695-4646
General Fax: (706) 695-7181
General/National Adv. E-mail: news@chatsworthtimes.com
Primary Website: chatsworthtimes.com
Avg Paid Circ: 6000
Audit By: Sworn/Estimate/Non-Audited
Audit Date: 10.06.2019
Personnel: Lorri Harrison (Ed./ Gen. Mgr.); Pat Oxford (Adv. Director); Cari Sluder (Classifieds & Legals)
Parent company (for newspapers): Cleveland Newspapers, Inc.

CHEROKEE LEDGER-NEWS

Street address 1: 521 E Main St
Street address city: Canton
Street address state: GA
Zip/Postal code: 30114-2805
General Phone: (770) 479-1441
General Fax: (770) 422-9533
General/National Adv. E-mail: wstephens@mdjonline.com
Display Adv. E-mail: wstephens@mdjonline.com
Editorial e-mail: rjohnston@cherokeetribune.com
Primary Website: cherokeetribune.com
Avg Free Circ: 10000
Audit By: Sworn/Estimate/Non-Audited
Audit Date: 10.06.2019
Personnel: Otis Brumby (Pub.); Rebecca Johnston (Ed.); Lee Brumby Garrett (Gen. Mgr.); Wade Stephens (VP, Sales)
Parent company (for newspapers): Neighbor Newspapers, Inc.

CLAXTON ENTERPRISE

Street address 1: 24 S Newton St
Street address city: Claxton
Street address state: GA
Zip/Postal code: 30417-2044
General Phone: (912) 739-2132
General Fax: (912) 739-2140
General/National Adv. E-mail: news@claxtonenterprise.com
Display Adv. E-mail: advertising@claxtonenterprise.com
Editorial e-mail: editor@claxtonenterprise.com
Primary Website: claxtonenterprise.com
Avg Paid Circ: 4200
Avg Free Circ: 50
Audit By: Sworn/Estimate/Non-Audited
Audit Date: 10.06.2019
Personnel: Mitchell E. Peace (Pub.); Pamela A. Peace (Pub.); Paula McNeely (Vice Pres., Opns./Adv.); Sarah Tarr (Ed.)

CLINCH COUNTY NEWS

Street address 1: 113 E Dame Ave
Street address city: Homerville
Street address state: GA
Zip/Postal code: 31634-2456
General Phone: (912) 487-5337
General Fax: (912) 487-3227
Editorial e-mail: clinnews@windstream.net
Primary Website: theclinchcountynews.com
Avg Paid Circ: 1800
Avg Free Circ: 70
Audit By: Sworn/Estimate/Non-Audited
Audit Date: 10.06.2019
Personnel: Carolyn Burtchaell (Bus. Mgr.); Casey Gray (Adv. Rep.); Len Robbins (Ed./Pub.); Bonnie Whitley (Prodn. Mgr.); Cari Fortner (Advertising Sales Rep)

CORDELE DISPATCH

Street address 1: 401 E 16th Ave
Street address 2: Ste F
Street address city: Cordele
Street address state: GA
Zip/Postal code: 31015-1669
General Phone: (229) 273-2277
General Fax: (229) 273-7239
Advertising Phone: (229) 273-2277
General/National Adv. E-mail: chris.lewis@cordeledispatch.com
Primary Website: cordeledispatch.com
Year Established: 1908
Avg Paid Circ: 4590
Sun. Circulation Paid: 4590
Audit By: Sworn/Estimate/Non-Audited
Audit Date: 10.06.2019
Personnel: Chris Lewis (Gen. Mngr./Adv. Mngr.); Beth Alston (Exec. Ed.); Harvey Simpson (Sports Ed.); Betty Ruis (Prodn. Compositor); Cathy Strickland (Prodn. Compositor); Rachel Wainwright (Circ. Dir.); Peggy King (Copy Ed); Laura Rogers (Adv. Mngr.)
Parent company (for newspapers): Boone Newspapers, Inc.

CROSSROADSNEWS

Street address 1: 2346 Candler Rd
Street address city: Decatur
Street address state: GA
Zip/Postal code: 30032-6406
General Phone: (404) 284-1888
General Fax: (404) 284-5007
General/National Adv. E-mail: editor@crossroadsnews.com
Display Adv. E-mail: advertising@crossroadsnews.com
Editorial e-mail: editor@crossroadsnews.com
Primary Website: crossroadsnews.com
Year Established: 1995
Avg Paid Circ: 11
Avg Free Circ: 27908
Audit By: VAC
Audit Date: 31.12.2016
Personnel: Curtis Parker (Prod. Mgr); Jennifer Parker (Ed./Pub.); Kathy Warner (Adv. Mgr); Jami French-Parker (Circ. Mgr)

DALLAS NEW ERA

Street address 1: 121 W Spring St
Street address city: Dallas
Street address state: GA
Zip/Postal code: 30132-4138
General Phone: (770) 445-3379
General Fax: (770) 445-5726
General/National Adv. E-mail: newerapr@bellsouth.net
Editorial e-mail: newerapr@bellsouth.net
Primary Website: thedallasnewera.com
Avg Paid Circ: 6500
Audit By: Sworn/Estimate/Non-Audited
Audit Date: 10.06.2019
Personnel: W.T. Parker (Pub.); Joe Parker (Circ. Mgr.)

DAWSON COUNTY NEWS

Street address 1: 30 SHOAL CREEK RD
Street address city: Dawsonville
Street address state: GA
Zip/Postal code: 30534
General Phone: (706) 265-3384
General Fax: (706) 265-3276
General/National Adv. E-mail: JLyness@dawsonnews.com
Display Adv. E-mail: jlyness@dawsonnews.com
Editorial e-mail: editor@dawsonnews.com
Primary Website: dawsonnews.com
Avg Paid Circ: 4024
Avg Free Circ: 8
Audit By: Sworn/Estimate/Non-Audited
Audit Date: 10.06.2019
Personnel: John Hall (Pub./Mktg. Dir.); Jennifer Lyness (Adv. Dir.); Stephanie Griffin (Ed.); Lisa Salinas (Circ. Dir.); Stephanie Woody (Gen. Mgr.)
Parent company (for newspapers): Swartz Media, LLC

DEKALB NEIGHBOR

Street address 1: 10930 Crabapple Rd
Street address 2: Ste 9
Street address city: Roswell
Street address state: GA
Zip/Postal code: 30075-5812
General Phone: (770) 454-9388
General Fax: (770) 454-9131
General/National Adv. E-mail: dweaver@neighbornewspapers.com
Display Adv. E-mail: adavis@mdjonline.com
Editorial e-mail: otis@mdjonline.com
Primary Website: mdjonline.com/neighbor_newspapers/dekalb/
Avg Paid Circ: 7
Avg Free Circ: 15552
Audit By: Sworn/Estimate/Non-Audited
Audit Date: 10.06.2019
Personnel: Otis A. Brumby (Pub.); Mark Maguire (Mng. Ed.); Lee Brumby Garrett (Gen. Mgr.); Wade Stephens (VP, Sales/Mktg)
Parent company (for newspapers): Neighbor Newspapers; Times-Journal, Inc.

DONALSONVILLE NEWS

Street address 1: 216 Cherry St
Street address city: Donalsonville
Street address state: GA
Zip/Postal code: 39845-1616
General Phone: (229) 524-2343
General Fax: (229) 524-2343
General/National Adv. E-mail: scott@donalsonvillenews.com
Display Adv. E-mail: classifieds@donalsonvillenews.com
Primary Website: donalsonvillenews.com
Avg Paid Circ: 3500
Audit By: Sworn/Estimate/Non-Audited
Audit Date: 10.06.2019
Personnel: Janet Hill (Circ. Mgr.); Waldo L. McLeod (Ed.)

DOUGLAS COUNTY SENTINEL

Street address 1: 8501 Bowden St
Street address city: Douglasville
Street address state: GA
Zip/Postal code: 30134-1705
General Phone: (770) 942-6571
General Fax: (770) 949-7556
Advertising Phone: (770) 942-6571
Advertising Fax: (770) 949-7556
Editorial Phone: (770) 942-6571
Editorial Fax: (770) 949-7556
General/National Adv. E-mail: melissa@times-georgian.com
Display Adv. E-mail: classifieds@douglascountysentinel.com
Editorial e-mail: news@douglascountysentinel.com
Primary Website: douglascountysentinel.com
Mthly Avg Views: 133656
Mthly Avg Unique Visitors: 94075
Year Established: 1902
Avg Paid Circ: 1608
Avg Free Circ: 1013
Sun. Circulation Paid: 2068
Sun. Circulation Free: 1283
Audit By: Sworn/Estimate/Non-Audited
Audit Date: 10.06.2019
Personnel: Ron Daniel (Mng. Ed.); Ricky Stilley (Systems Mgr.); Melissa Wilson (Adv. Dir.); Marvin Enderle (Pub.); Mark Golding (Cir. Mgr.); Derrick Mahone (Sports Ed.)
Parent company (for newspapers): Paxton Media Group

DUNWOODY CRIER

Street address 1: 5064 Nandina Ln
Street address 2: Ste C
Street address city: Dunwoody
Street address state: GA
Zip/Postal code: 30338-4115
General Phone: (770) 451-4147
General Fax: (770) 451-4223
General/National Adv. E-mail: jhart@criernewspapers.com
Display Adv. E-mail: dstevens@criernewspapers.com
Editorial e-mail: thecrier@mindspring.com
Primary Website: thecrier.net
Year Established: 1976
Avg Free Circ: 15564
Audit By: Sworn/Estimate/Non-Audited
Audit Date: 10.06.2019
Personnel: Jim Hart (Nat'l/Retail Adv. Dir.); Dick Williams (Ed.); Donna Stevens (Classified Adv. Mgr.); Kenyatta Taliafero (Prod. Mgr.)
Parent company (for newspapers): Crier Newspapers LLC

EAST COBB NEIGHBOR

Street address 1: 580 S Fairground St SE
Street address city: Marietta
Street address state: GA
Zip/Postal code: 30060-2751
General Phone: (770) 428-9411
General Fax: (770) 422-9533
General/National Adv. E-mail: mdjnews@mdjonline.com
Editorial e-mail: jkirby@mdjonline.com
Primary Website: mdjonline.com/neighbor_newspapers
Avg Free Circ: 32464
Audit By: Sworn/Estimate/Non-Audited
Audit Date: 10.06.2019
Personnel: Otis A. Brumby (Pub.); Lee Garrett (Gen. Mgr.); Billy Mitchell (Mng. Ed.); Wade Stephens (VP of Sales & Marketing)
Parent company (for newspapers): Times-Journal, Inc.

EFFINGHAM HERALD

Street address 1: 586 S Columbia Ave
Street address 2: Ste 13
Street address city: Rincon
Street address state: GA
Zip/Postal code: 31326-4174
General Phone: (912) 826-5012
General Fax: (912) 826-0381
General/National Adv. E-mail: jwilliams@effinghamherald.net
Display Adv. E-mail: jwilliams@effinghamherald.net
Editorial e-mail: mlastinger@effinghamherald.net
Primary Website: effinghamherald.net
Year Established: 1908
Avg Paid Circ: 2129
Avg Free Circ: 76
Audit By: AAM
Audit Date: 31.03.2019
Personnel: Karen Tanksley (Pub.); Mark Lastinger (Ed.); Jacqueline Williams (Adv./Sales Ex.); Kim Dennis (GM)

FORSYTH COUNTY NEWS

Street address 1: 302 Veterans Memorial Blvd
Street address city: Cumming
Street address state: GA
Zip/Postal code: 30040-2644
General Phone: (770) 887-3126
General Fax: (770) 889-6017
Advertising Phone: (770) 887-3126
Advertising Fax: (770) 744 9779
Editorial Phone: (770) 887-3126
General/National Adv. E-mail: adv@forsythnews.com
Display Adv. E-mail: rgarmon@forsythnews.com
Classified Adv. e-mail: classified@forsythnews.com
Editorial e-mail: editor@forsythnews.com
Primary Website: forsythnews.com
Mthly Avg Views: 500000
Mthly Avg Unique Visitors: 90000
Year Established: 1908
Avg Paid Circ: 12500
Sun. Circulation Paid: 13500
Audit By: Sworn/Estimate/Non-Audited
Audit Date: 10.06.2019
Personnel: Vince Johnson (Pub.); Ryan Garmon (Adv. Dir.); Kayla Robins (Ed.); Lisa Salinas (Circ. Mgr.); Cheri Bullard (Adv, Account Exec.); Connor Kelly (Adv. Acct Exec.); Allison Althauser (Adv. Acct. Exec.); Jim Dean (Online Ed.); Shana Patterson (Classified Adv.); Tracie Pike (Production Mgr.)
Parent company (for newspapers): Swartz Media, LLC

FRANKLIN COUNTY CITIZEN LEADER

Street address 1: 12150 Augusta Rd
Street address city: Lavonia
Street address state: GA
Zip/Postal code: 30553-1208
General Phone: (706) 356-8557
General Fax: (706) 356-2008

Advertising Phone: (864) 457-3337
Advertising Fax: (864) 457-5231
Editorial Phone: (864) 457-3337
Editorial Fax: (864) 457-5231
General/National Adv. E-mail: jdean@franklincountycitizen.com
Display Adv. E-mail: jphillips@franklincountycitizen.com
Editorial e-mail: fcc@franklincountycitizen.com
Primary Website: franklincountycitizen.com
Year Established: 1955
Avg Paid Circ: 4000
Avg Free Circ: 150
Audit By: Sworn/Estimate/Non-Audited
Audit Date: 10.06.2019
Personnel: Shane Scoggins (Pub.); Jennifer Phillips (Office Mgr.); Jan Dean (Adv. Rep.)
Parent company (for newspapers): Community Newspapers Inc.

GWINNETT DAILY POST

Street address 1: 725 Old Norcross Rd
Street address city: Lawrenceville
Street address state: GA
Zip/Postal code: 30046-4317
General Phone: (770) 963-9205
General Fax: (770) 277-5271
Advertising Phone: (770) 963-9205
Advertising Fax: (770) 338-7350
Editorial Phone: (770) 339-5850
Editorial Fax: (770) 339-8081
General/National Adv. E-mail: news@gwinnettdailypost.com
Display Adv. E-mail: advertising@gwinnettdailypost.com
Editorial e-mail: letters@gwinnettdailypost.com
Primary Website: gwinnettdailypost.com
Year Established: 1970
Avg Paid Circ: 335
Avg Free Circ: 49
Sun. Circulation Paid: 5053
Sun. Circulation Free: 69
Audit By: CVC
Audit Date: 30.09.2016
Personnel: J.K. Murphy (Vice President/Content SCNI newspapers); Bob McCray (Adv. Mgr., Major Accts.); Thom Bell (Vice President/Circulation Southern Community Newspapers, Inc.); Todd Cline (Ed.); Nate McCullough (Copy Desk Chief); Nicole Puckett (Graphics Ed.); Will Hammock (Sports Ed.); Lynn Ridder (Production Director); Jo Pearse (General Sales Manger); Cindy Carter (Adv. Mgr., Legal Notices); Tina Pethel (Controller); Mike Gebhart (Publisher)
Parent company (for newspapers): Southern Community Newspapers, Inc.

HAWKINSVILLE DISPATCH AND NEWS

Street address 1: 122 Commerce St
Street address city: Hawkinsville
Street address state: GA
Zip/Postal code: 31036-8418
General Phone: (478) 783-1291
General Fax: (478) 783-1293
General/National Adv. E-mail: dn@comsouth.net
Primary Website: No Wesbsite
Avg Paid Circ: 3000
Audit By: Sworn/Estimate/Non-Audited
Audit Date: 10.06.2019
Personnel: Chuck C. Southerland (Ed.)

HENRY DAILY HERALD

Street address 1: 38 Sloan St
Street address city: McDonough
Street address state: GA
Zip/Postal code: 30253-3102
General Phone: (770) 957-9161
General Fax: (770) 954-0282
Advertising Phone: (770) 478-5753 ext. 277
Editorial Phone: (770) 957-9161 ext. 228
General/National Adv. E-mail: ladams@henryherald.com
Display Adv. E-mail: rshirey@news-daily.com
Primary Website: henryherald.com
Avg Paid Circ: 2493
Avg Free Circ: 11
Audit By: Sworn/Estimate/Non-Audited
Audit Date: 10.06.2019
Personnel: Kathy Jefcoats (Editor); Bonnie Pratt (Pub.); Rita Camp (Classifieds Adv. Mgr.)
Parent company (for newspapers): Southern Community Newspapers, Inc.

HENRY NEIGHBOR

Street address 1: 47 Waddell Street
Street address city: Marietta
Street address state: GA
Zip/Postal code: 30060
General Phone: (678) 938-2387
General/National Adv. E-mail: alarry@mdjonline.com
Display Adv. E-mail: classifieds@mdjonline.com
Editorial e-mail: smetro@mdjonline.com
Primary Website: mdjonline.com/neighbor_newspapers
Avg Paid Circ: 2
Avg Free Circ: 40000
Audit By: Sworn/Estimate/Non-Audited
Audit Date: 10.06.2019
Personnel: Otis A. Brumby (Pub.); Noreen Cochran (Ed.)
Parent company (for newspapers): Times-Journal, Inc.; Neighbor Newspapers

HOGANSVILLE HOME NEWS

Street address 1: PO Box 426
Street address city: Manchester
Street address state: GA
Zip/Postal code: 31816-0426
General Phone: (706) 846-3188
General Fax: (706) 846-2206
General/National Adv. E-mail: starmarcurynews@charterinternet.com
Primary Website: smalltownpapers.com/newspapers/newspaper.php?id=175
Avg Paid Circ: 4300
Audit By: Sworn/Estimate/Non-Audited
Audit Date: 10.06.2019
Personnel: John Kuykendall (Ed.)
Parent company (for newspapers): Star-Mercury Publishing Co.

JACKSON PROGRESS-ARGUS

Street address 1: 129 S Mulberry St
Street address city: Jackson
Street address state: GA
Zip/Postal code: 30233-2056
General Phone: (770) 775-3107
General Fax: (770) 775-3855
Advertising Phone: (770) 775-3107 x 105
General/National Adv. E-mail: hpope@myjpa.com
Primary Website: jacksonprogress-argus.com
Year Established: 1873
Avg Paid Circ: 4600
Audit By: Sworn/Estimate/Non-Audited
Audit Date: 10.06.2019
Personnel: Bonnie Pratt (Gen. Sales Mgr.); Michael Davis (Ed.)
Parent company (for newspapers): Triple Crown Media

JEFF DAVIS LEDGER

Street address 1: 12 Latimer St
Street address city: Hazlehurst
Street address state: GA
Zip/Postal code: 31539-6110
General Phone: (912) 375-4225
General Fax: (912) 375-3704
General/National Adv. E-mail: news@jdledger.com
Primary Website: jdledger.com
Avg Paid Circ: 3850
Audit By: Sworn/Estimate/Non-Audited
Audit Date: 10.06.2019
Personnel: Kay Purser (Adv. Mgr.); Kelli Craft (Circ. Mgr.); Thomas H. Purser (Ed.); Anna Purser (Prodn. Mgr.)

JOHN'S CREEK HERALD

Street address 1: 319 N Main St
Street address city: Alpharetta
Street address state: GA
Zip/Postal code: 30009-2321
General Phone: (770)442-3278
General Fax: (770)475-1216
Advertising Phone: (770) 442-3278
General/National Adv. E-mail: advertising@northfulton.com
Display Adv. E-mail: lynn@northfulton.com
Editorial e-mail: hhurd@northfulton.com
Primary Website: NorthFulton.com
Avg Free Circ: 19975
Audit By: Sworn/Estimate/Non-Audited
Audit Date: 10.06.2019
Personnel: Hans Appen (Pub.); Hatcher Hurd (Exec. Ed./Ed.); Aldo Nahed (Mng. Ed./ Bus. Ed.); Kelly Brooks (Associate Pub.); Hans Appen (Gen. Mgr.); Georgie Tiernan (Circ. Mgr.); A. J. McNaughton (Prod. Mgr)

LAKE OCONEE BREEZE

Street address 1: 165 Garrett Way NW
Street address city: Milledgeville
Street address state: GA
Zip/Postal code: 31061-2318
General Phone: (478) 453-1432
Advertising Phone: (478) 453-1436
General/National Adv. E-mail: kmertz@unionrecorder.com
Display Adv. E-mail: cgiles@unionrecorder.com
Primary Website: lakeoconeebreeze.net
Avg Paid Circ: 6200
Audit By: Sworn/Estimate/Non-Audited
Audit Date: 10.06.2019
Personnel: Keith Barlow (Pub.); Natalie Davis (Ed.); Erin Simmons (Adv. Director)

LANIER COUNTY NEWS

Street address 1: 335 W Church St
Street address city: Lakeland
Street address state: GA
Zip/Postal code: 31635-1115
General Phone: (229) 896-2233
General Fax: (229) 896-7237
Primary Website: laniercountynewsonline.com
Avg Paid Circ: 1100
Audit By: Sworn/Estimate/Non-Audited
Audit Date: 10.06.2019
Personnel: Diana Cooper (Circ. Mgr.); Ann Knight (Ed.)

LANIER LIFE

Street address 1: 345 Green St NW
Street address city: Gainesville
Street address state: GA
Zip/Postal code: 30501-3370
General Phone: (770) 532-1234
General Fax: (770) 535-2859
Primary Website: gainesvilletimes.com
Audit By: Sworn/Estimate/Non-Audited
Audit Date: 10.06.2019
Parent company (for newspapers): Morris Multimedia, Inc.

MERIWETHER VINDICATOR

Street address 1: 3051 Roosevelt Hwy
Street address city: Manchester
Street address state: GA
Zip/Postal code: 31816-6406
General Phone: (706) 846-3188
General Fax: (706) 846-2206
General/National Adv. E-mail: starmercurynews@charterinternet.com
Primary Website: No Website
Avg Paid Circ: 2700
Audit By: Sworn/Estimate/Non-Audited
Audit Date: 10.06.2019
Personnel: John Kuykendall (Pub.); Rob Richardson (Ed.)
Parent company (for newspapers): Star-Mercury Publishing Co.

MILLER COUNTY LIBERAL

Street address 1: PO Box 37
Street address 2: 157 E Main St
Street address city: Colquitt
Street address state: GA
Zip/Postal code: 39837-0037
General Phone: (229) 758-5549
General Fax: (229) 758-5540
General/National Adv. E-mail: millercountyliberal@gmail.com
Editorial e-mail: terrytoole@mac.com
Primary Website: millercountyliberal.com
Year Established: 1897
Avg Paid Circ: 3000
Audit By: Sworn/Estimate/Non-Audited
Audit Date: 10.06.2019
Personnel: Betty Jo Toole (Gen. Mgr.); Terry Toole (Ed./Pub.); Wanda Griffin (Adv./Circ. Mgr.)

MILTON HERALD

Street address 1: 319 N Main St
Street address city: Alpharetta
Street address state: GA
Zip/Postal code: 30009-2321
General Phone: (770)442-3278
General Fax: (770)475-1216
Advertising Phone: (770) 442-3278
General/National Adv. E-mail: advertising@northfulton.com
Display Adv. E-mail: lynn@northfulton.com
Editorial e-mail: jcopsey@northfulton.com
Primary Website: NorthFulton.com
Avg Free Circ: 9308
Audit By: Sworn/Estimate/Non-Audited
Audit Date: 10.06.2019
Personnel: Hans Appen (Pub.); Jonathan Copsey (Ed.); Hatcher Hurd (Exec. Ed.); Aldo Nahed (Mng. Ed./ Bus. Ed.); Kelly Brooks (Associate Pub.); Wendy Goddard (Sr. Acct. Exec.); Anne O'Shaughnessy (Circ. Mgr.); A. J. McNaughton (Prod. Mgr)

MILTON NEIGHBOR

Street address 1: 10930 Crabapple Rd
Street address 2: Ste 9
Street address city: Roswell
Street address state: GA
Zip/Postal code: 30075-5812
General Phone: (770) 993-7400
General Fax: (770) 518-6062
General/National Adv. E-mail: lgarrett@mdjonline
Display Adv. E-mail: adavis@mdjonline.com
Editorial e-mail: nfulton@neighbornewspapers.com
Primary Website: neighbornewspapers.com
Year Established: 1968
Avg Paid Circ: 44
Avg Free Circ: 11986
Audit By: Sworn/Estimate/Non-Audited
Audit Date: 10.06.2019
Personnel: Rachel Kellogg (Ed); Lee Brumby Garrett (Gen. Mgr.); Wade Stephens (VP, Sales/Mktg)
Parent company (for newspapers): Neighbor Newspapers; Neighbor Newspapers, Inc.

MORGAN COUNTY CITIZEN

Street address 1: 259 N Second St
Street address city: Madison
Street address state: GA
Zip/Postal code: 30650-1317
General Phone: (706) 342-7440
General Fax: (706) 342-2140
General/National Adv. E-mail: citizen@morgancountycitizen.com
Primary Website: morgancountycitizen.com
Avg Paid Circ: 5000
Audit By: Sworn/Estimate/Non-Audited
Audit Date: 10.06.2019
Personnel: Sherry Stevens (Bus. Mgr.); Artrose Cooper (Adv./Circ. Mgr.); Kathryn Purcell (Mng. Ed.); Chris Muthig (Sports Ed.)
Parent company (for newspapers): Times-Journal, Inc.

NORTH COBB NEIGHBOR

Street address 1: 580 S Fairground St SE
Street address city: Marietta
Street address state: GA
Zip/Postal code: 30060-2751
General Phone: (770) 428-9411
General/National Adv. E-mail: bopitz@neighbornewspapers.com
Display Adv. E-mail: adavis@mdjonline.com
Editorial e-mail: bclark@neighbornewspapers.com
Primary Website: neighbornewspapers.com
Year Established: 1968
Avg Paid Circ: 1
Avg Free Circ: 23201
Audit By: Sworn/Estimate/Non-Audited
Audit Date: 10.06.2019
Personnel: Brian Clark (Mng. Ed.); Wade Stephens (VP, Sales/Mktg); Lee Brumby Garrett (Gen. Mgr.); Becky Opitz (Adv. Mgr.); Otis A. Brumby (Pub./CEO)

Parent company (for newspapers): Neighbor Newspapers, Inc.

NORTH GEORGIA NEWS

Street address 1: 266 Cleveland St
Street address city: Blairsville
Street address state: GA
Zip/Postal code: 30512-8537
General Phone: (706) 745-6343
General Fax: (706) 745-1830
General/National Adv. E-mail: northgeorgianews@hotmail.com
Editorial e-mail: ngnews@windstream.net
Primary Website: nganews.com
Avg Paid Circ: 10400
Audit By: Sworn/Estimate/Non-Audited
Audit Date: 10.06.2019
Personnel: Kenneth West (Pub.); Charles Duncan (Ed.); Todd Forrest (Staff Writer)

NORTHSIDE NEIGHBOR

Street address 1: 5290 Roswell Rd
Street address 2: Ste M
Street address city: Atlanta
Street address state: GA
Zip/Postal code: 30342-1978
General Phone: (404) 256-3100
General Fax: (404) 256-3292
General/National Adv. E-mail: nside@neighbornewspapers.com
Primary Website: neighbornewspapers.com
Audit By: Sworn/Estimate/Non-Audited
Audit Date: 10.06.2019
Personnel: Otis A. Brumby (Pub.); Stephanie DeJarnette (Adv. Mgr.); Matt Heck (Circ. Mgr.); Everett Catts (Ed.); Robert Nesmith (Prodn. Mgr.); Wade Stephens (VP, Sales/Mktg); Lee Brumby Garrett (Gen. Mgr.); Alice Davis (Classified Adv. Supervisor)
Parent company (for newspapers): Times-Journal, Inc.; Neighbor Newspapers

NORTHSIDE/SANDY SPRINGS/ VININGS/BROOKHAVEN NEIGHBOR

Street address 1: 5290 Roswell Rd
Street address 2: Ste M
Street address city: Sandy Springs
Street address state: GA
Zip/Postal code: 30342-1978
General Phone: (404) 256-3100
General Fax: (404) 256-3292
General/National Adv. E-mail: sdjarnette@neighbornewspapers.com
Primary Website: northside-neighbor.com
Avg Paid Circ: 27
Avg Free Circ: 27440
Audit By: Sworn/Estimate/Non-Audited
Audit Date: 10.06.2019
Personnel: Otis A. Brumby III (Pub.); Lee Garrett (Gen. Mgr.)
Parent company (for newspapers): Times-Journal, Inc.

OCONEE ENTERPRISE

Street address 1: 26 S Barnett Shoals Rd
Street address city: Watkinsville
Street address state: GA
Zip/Postal code: 30677-2500
General Phone: (706) 769-5175
General Fax: (706) 769-8532
General/National Adv. E-mail: oconeeenterprise@mindspring.com
Primary Website: oconeeenterprise.com
Avg Paid Circ: 4000
Audit By: Sworn/Estimate/Non-Audited
Audit Date: 10.06.2019
Personnel: Vinnie Williams (Pub.); Tracy Harmon (Adv. Rep.); Blake Giles (Ed.); Derek Wiley (Sports Ed.); Maridee Williams (Gen. Mgr./Adv. Director)

PAULDING NEIGHBOR

Street address 1: 580 S Fairground St SE
Street address city: Marietta
Street address state: GA
Zip/Postal code: 30060-2751
General Phone: (678) 831-3566
General Fax: (770) 445-0565
Advertising Phone: (770) 428-9411
General/National Adv. E-mail: Neighbors@mdjonline.com
Primary Website: neighbornewspapers.com
Avg Paid Circ: 2
Avg Free Circ: 11979
Audit By: Sworn/Estimate/Non-Audited
Audit Date: 10.06.2019
Personnel: Otis A. Brumby (Pub.); Furman Gardner (Mktg. Dir.); Russell H. Powell (Circ. Mgr.); Jeff Buice (Prodn. Mgr.); Wade Stephens (VP, Sales/Mktg.); Lee Brumby Garrett (Gen. Mgr.)
Parent company (for newspapers): Times-Journal, Inc.; Neighbor Newspapers

PIKE COUNTY JOURNAL AND REPORTER

Street address 1: 1 Courthouse Square
Street address city: Zebulon
Street address state: GA
Zip/Postal code: 30295
General Phone: (770) 567-3446
General Fax: (770) 567-8814
General/National Adv. E-mail: designsteam@barnesville.com
Primary Website: pikecountygeorgia.com
Avg Paid Circ: 3000
Audit By: Sworn/Estimate/Non-Audited
Audit Date: 10.06.2019
Personnel: Walter Geiger (Pub.); Rachel McDaniel (Ed./Rep.); Jennifer Taylor (Office Mgr.); Cathy Siegl (Adv.)

QUITMAN FREE PRESS

Street address 1: 112 N Lee St
Street address city: Quitman
Street address state: GA
Zip/Postal code: 31643-2124
General Phone: (229) 263-4615
General Fax: (229) 263-5282
Editorial Phone: (229) 263-4615
General/National Adv. E-mail: quitmanpress@windstream.net
Display Adv. E-mail: adelnewstribune@windstream.com
Primary Website: thequitmanfreepress.com
Year Established: 1876
Avg Paid Circ: 3400
Avg Free Circ: 60
Audit By: Sworn/Estimate/Non-Audited
Audit Date: 10.06.2019
Personnel: Bonnell Holmes (Editor)
Parent company (for newspapers): Cook Publishing Co.

REPORTER NEWSPAPERS

Street address 1: 6065 Roswell Rd Ste 225
Street address 2: Suite 225
Street address city: Atlanta
Street address state: GA
Zip/Postal code: 30328-4012
General Phone: (404) 917-2200
General Fax: (404) 917-2201
General/National Adv. E-mail: publisher@reporternewspapers.net
Display Adv. E-mail: publisher@reporternewspapers.net
Editorial e-mail: editor@reporternewspapers.net
Primary Website: reporternewspapers.net
Mthly Avg Views: 75000
Mthly Avg Unique Visitors: 45000
Year Established: 2006
Avg Free Circ: 100000
Audit By: Sworn/Estimate/Non-Audited
Audit Date: 10.06.2019
Personnel: Steve Levene (Fouder & Publisher)
Parent company (for newspapers): Springs Publishing LLC

ROSWELL NEIGHBOR

Street address 1: 10930 Crabapple Rd
Street address 2: Ste 9
Street address city: Roswell
Street address state: GA
Zip/Postal code: 30075-5812
General Phone: (770) 993-7400
General Fax: (770) 518-6062
General/National Adv. E-mail: lgarrett@mdjonline
Display Adv. E-mail: adavis@mdjonline.com
Editorial e-mail: nfulton@neighbornewspapers.com
Primary Website: neighbornewspapers.com
Year Established: 1968
Avg Paid Circ: 19553
Audit By: Sworn/Estimate/Non-Audited
Audit Date: 10.06.2019
Personnel: Rachel Kellogg (Ed.); Wade Stephens (VP, Sales/Mktg.); Lee Brumby Garrett (Gen. Mgr.)
Parent company (for newspapers): Neighbor Newspapers; Neighbor Newspapers, Inc.

SOPERTON NEWS

Street address 1: 4075 W Main St
Street address city: Soperton
Street address state: GA
Zip/Postal code: 30457-2325
General Phone: (912) 529-6624
General Fax: (912) 529-5399
General/National Adv. E-mail: sopertonnews@nlamerica.com
Avg Paid Circ: 2050
Avg Free Circ: 44
Audit By: Sworn/Estimate/Non-Audited
Audit Date: 10.06.2019
Personnel: Griffin Lodett (Pub.); Marilyn Knapp (Adv. Mgr.); Barney Willamson (Circ. Mgr.); Dubose Porter (Exec. Ed.)

SOUTH COBB NEIGHBOR

Street address 1: 580 S Fairground St SE
Street address city: Marietta
Street address state: GA
Zip/Postal code: 30060-2751
General Phone: (770) 428-9411
General Fax: (770) 422-9533
General/National Adv. E-mail: lgarrett@mdjonline
Display Adv. E-mail: adavis@mdjonline.com
Editorial e-mail: jkirby@mdjonline.com
Primary Website: mdjonline.com
Avg Paid Circ: 18737
Audit By: Sworn/Estimate/Non-Audited
Audit Date: 10.06.2019
Personnel: Otis Brumby (Pub.); Lee Garrett (Gen. Mgr.); Billy Mitchell (Mng. Ed.); Wade Stephens (VP, Sales/Mktg)
Parent company (for newspapers): Times-Journal, Inc.

SOUTH FULTON NEIGHBOR

Street address 1: 5442 Frontage Rd
Street address 2: Ste 130
Street address city: Forest Park
Street address state: GA
Zip/Postal code: 30297-2538
General Phone: (404) 363-8484
General Fax: (404) 363-0212
General/National Adv. E-mail: nlong@neighbornewspapers.com
Display Adv. E-mail: adavis@mdjonline.com
Primary Website: mdjonline.com/neighbor_newspapers
Avg Paid Circ: 3
Avg Free Circ: 24200
Audit By: Sworn/Estimate/Non-Audited
Audit Date: 10.06.2019
Personnel: Otis A. Brumby (Gen. Mgr.); Mary Cosgrove (Ed.); Bill Baldowski (Ed.); Wade Stephens (VP, Sales/Mktg.)
Parent company (for newspapers): Times-Journal, Inc.

SPARTA ISHMAELITE

Street address 1: 12671 Broad St
Street address city: Sparta
Street address state: GA
Zip/Postal code: 31087-1732
General Phone: (706) 444-5330
General Fax: (706) 444-9063
General/National Adv. E-mail: spartish@bellsouth.net
Primary Website: No Website
Year Established: 1878
Avg Paid Circ: 2210
Avg Free Circ: 80
Audit By: Sworn/Estimate/Non-Audited
Audit Date: 10.06.2019
Personnel: Lynda Reynolds (Office Mgr.); Chuck Reynolds (Ed.)

STARNEWS

Street address 1: 318 Newnan Rd
Street address city: Carrollton
Street address state: GA
Zip/Postal code: 30117-3418
General Phone: (770) 214-9900
General Fax: (770) 214-9600
General/National Adv. E-mail: suehorn.starnews@gmail.com
Display Adv. E-mail: suehorn.starnews@gmail.com
Editorial e-mail: suehorn.starnews@gmail.com
Primary Website: starnewsga.com
Mthly Avg Views: 227000
Year Established: 1995
Avg Paid Circ: 5200
Avg Free Circ: 4800
Audit By: Sworn/Estimate/Non-Audited
Audit Date: 10.06.2019
Personnel: Sue M. Horn Chappell (Ed./Pub.)

STEWART-WEBSTER JOURNAL

Street address 1: 106 Broad St
Street address city: Richland
Street address state: GA
Zip/Postal code: 31825-6106
General Phone: (229) 887-3674
General Fax: (229) 887-2800
General/National Adv. E-mail: swjpc@bellsouth.net
Primary Website: swjpc.com
Avg Paid Circ: 4654
Avg Free Circ: 20
Audit By: Sworn/Estimate/Non-Audited
Audit Date: 10.06.2019
Personnel: Ron T. Provencher (Adv. Mgr.); Linda Provencher (Mng. Ed.); Ron Provencher (Mng. Ed.)

TALBOTTON NEW ERA

Street address 1: 3051 Roosevelt Hwy
Street address city: Manchester
Street address state: GA
Zip/Postal code: 31816-6406
General Phone: (706) 846-3188
General Fax: (706) 846-2206
General/National Adv. E-mail: starmercurynews@charterinternet.com
Primary Website: No Website
Avg Paid Circ: 1000
Audit By: Sworn/Estimate/Non-Audited
Audit Date: 10.06.2019
Personnel: John Kuykendall (Pub.); Vann Chapman (Ed)
Parent company (for newspapers): Trib Publications

TALLAPOOSA JOURNAL

Street address 1: 901 Hays Mill Rd
Street address city: Carrollton
Street address state: GA
Zip/Postal code: 30117-9576
General Phone: (770) 834-6631
General Fax: (770) 834-9991
Advertising Phone: (770) 834-6631 ext. 225
Advertising Fax: (770) 834-9991
Editorial Phone: (770) 834-6631
Editorial Fax: (770) 834-9991
General/National Adv. E-mail: melissa@times-georgian.com
Display Adv. E-mail: publisher@times-georgian.com
Editorial e-mail: bbrowning@times-georgian.com
Primary Website: times-georgian.com/tallapoosa-journal
Audit By: Sworn/Estimate/Non-Audited
Audit Date: 10.06.2019
Personnel: Leonard Woolsey (Pub.); Bruce Browning (Mng. Ed.); Melissa Wilson (Adv. Dir.)

THE ADVANCE

Street address 1: 205 E 1st St
Street address city: Vidalia
Street address state: GA
Zip/Postal code: 30474-4717
General Phone: (912) 537-3131
General Fax: (912) 537-4899
Advertising Phone: (912) 537-3131
Editorial Phone: (912) 537-3131
General/National Adv. E-mail: theadvancenews@gmail.com
Display Adv. E-mail: gailadvance@gmail.com
Editorial e-mail: hiltadvance@gmail.com
Year Established: 1901
Avg Paid Circ: 7250
Avg Free Circ: 23000
Audit By: Sworn/Estimate/Non-Audited
Audit Date: 10.06.2019

Personnel: William F. Ledford (Gen. Mgr.); Daniel Ford (Adv. Mgr.); Gail Cauley (Circ. Mgr.); Cindy Shatto (Financial Manager)
Parent company (for newspapers): Advance Publications, Inc.

THE BANKS COUNTY NEWS

Street address 1: 33 Lee St
Street address city: Jefferson
Street address state: GA
Zip/Postal code: 30549-1345
General Phone: (706) 367-5233
General Fax: (706) 367-8056
General/National Adv. E-mail: news@mainstreetnews.com
Primary Website: mainstreetnews.com
Year Established: 1968
Avg Paid Circ: 3400
Avg Free Circ: 90
Audit By: Sworn/Estimate/Non-Audited
Audit Date: 10.06.2019
Personnel: Scott Buffington (Co-Pub./Adv. Mgr.); Debbie Castellaw (Circ. Mgr.); Angela Gary (Ed.); Thomas Toles (Printing Mgr.); Mike Buffington (Co-Pub.)

THE BERRIEN PRESS

Street address 1: 200 E McPherson Ave
Street address city: Nashville
Street address state: GA
Zip/Postal code: 31639-2250
General Phone: (229) 686-3523
General Fax: (229) 686-7771
General/National Adv. E-mail: theberrienpress@windstream.net
Editorial e-mail: localnews@windstream.net
Primary Website: theberrienpress.com
Avg Paid Circ: 4200
Avg Free Circ: 50
Audit By: Sworn/Estimate/Non-Audited
Audit Date: 10.06.2019
Personnel: Jonna Exum (Gen. Mgr.); Donald F. Boyd (Ed.); Maria Hardman

THE BLACKSHEAR TIMES

Street address 1: 121 SW Central Ave
Street address city: Blackshear
Street address state: GA
Zip/Postal code: 31516-2259
General Phone: (912) 449-6693
General Fax: (912) 449-1719
General/National Adv. E-mail: pparker@theblacksheartimes.com
Display Adv. E-mail: pparker@theblacksheartimes.com
Primary Website: theblacksheartimes.com
Avg Paid Circ: 3650
Avg Free Circ: 0
Audit By: Sworn/Estimate/Non-Audited
Audit Date: 10.06.2019
Personnel: Cheryl S. Williams (Assoc. Pub.); Paige Parker (Adv./Sales Mgr.); Wayne Hardy (Mng. Ed./ Gen. Mgr.); Robert M. Williams (Ed.); Tammie Cason (Prodn. Mgr.); Julie Cunningham (Production Layout); Jason Deal (Staff Writer)
Parent company (for newspapers): SouthFire Newspapers

THE CAIRO MESSENGER

Street address 1: 31 1st Ave NE
Street address city: Cairo
Street address state: GA
Zip/Postal code: 39828-2102
General Phone: (229) 377-2032
General Fax: (229) 377-4640
General/National Adv. E-mail: advertising@cairomessenger.com
Display Adv. E-mail: classifieds@cairomessenger.com
Editorial e-mail: letters@cairomessenger.com
Primary Website: cairomessenger.com
Year Established: 1904
Avg Paid Circ: 500
Avg Free Circ: 2750
Audit By: Sworn/Estimate/Non-Audited
Audit Date: 10.06.2019
Personnel: The Editor (Ed.)

THE CHAMPION

Street address 1: 114 New St
Street address 2: Ste E
Street address city: Decatur
Street address state: GA
Zip/Postal code: 30030-5356
General Phone: (404) 373-7779
General Fax: (404) 373-7721
General/National Adv. E-mail: JohnH@dekalbchamp.com
Display Adv. E-mail: JohnH@dekalbchamp.com
Editorial e-mail: Kathy@dekalbchamp.com
Primary Website: championnewspaper.com
Avg Paid Circ: 443
Avg Free Circ: 97
Audit By: CVC
Audit Date: 30.09.2018
Personnel: Carolyn Glenn (Pub.); John Hewitt (COO/Gen. Mgr.); Kathy Mitchell (Ed.); Gale Horton Gay (Mng. Ed.); Kemesha Hunt (Prodn. Mgr.); Travis Hutchins (Classic/Web Designer)

THE CITIZEN

Street address 1: 310 B. North Glynn Street
Street address city: Fayetteville
Street address state: GA
Zip/Postal code: 30214-1105
General Phone: (770) 719-1880
Editorial e-mail: editor@thecitizen.com
Primary Website: thecitizen.com
Year Established: 1993
Avg Free Circ: 32992
Audit By: CAC
Audit Date: 31.03.2018
Personnel: Cal Beverly (Ed./Pub.); Joyce Beverly (Adv. Sales Dir.); Diann Cupertino (Major Accts. Mgr.)
Parent company (for newspapers): Fayette Publishing

THE CLAYTON TRIBUNE

Street address 1: 120 N Main St
Street address city: Clayton
Street address state: GA
Zip/Postal code: 30525-4266
General Phone: (706) 782-3312
General Fax: (706) 782-4230
Advertising Phone: (706) 782-3312
Advertising Fax: (706) 782-4230
Editorial Phone: (706) 782-3312
Editorial Fax: (706) 782-4230
General/National Adv. E-mail: thetribune@theclaytontribune.com
Display Adv. E-mail: circulation@TheClaytonTribune.com
Editorial e-mail: thetribune@theclaytontribune.com
Primary Website: theclaytontribune.com
Year Established: 1897
Avg Paid Circ: 8000
Audit By: Sworn/Estimate/Non-Audited
Audit Date: 10.06.2019
Personnel: Michael Leonard (Pub.); Blake Spurney (Ed.); Cyndy Brogdon (Adv. Sales)
Parent company (for newspapers): Community Newspapers, Inc.

THE COASTAL COURIER

Street address 1: 125 S Main St
Street address city: Hinesville
Street address state: GA
Zip/Postal code: 31313-3217
General Phone: (912) 876-0156
General Fax: (912) 368-6329
General/National Adv. E-mail: vphillips@coastalcourier.com
Editorial e-mail: editor@coastalcourier.com
Primary Website: coastalcourier.com
Avg Paid Circ: 5000
Avg Free Circ: 192
Audit By: Sworn/Estimate/Non-Audited
Audit Date: 10.06.2019
Personnel: Marshall Griffin (Pub.); Kathryn Fox (Gen. Mgr.); Johnny Brown (Circ. Mgr.); Leslie Miller (Prodn. Mgr.); Pat Watkins (Web Ed.); ???? ????; Susan Nelson (Digital Sales Manager)
Parent company (for newspapers): Morris Multimedia, Inc.

THE COLUMBIA COUNTY NEWS-TIMES

Street address 1: 604 Government Center Way
Street address 2: Ste A
Street address city: Evans
Street address state: GA
Zip/Postal code: 30809-7606
General Phone: (706) 868-1222
General Fax: (706) 823-6062
Advertising Phone: (706) 868-1222
General/National Adv. E-mail: cnt@newstimesonline.com
Primary Website: newstimes.augusta.com
Year Established: 1881
Avg Paid Circ: 18500
Audit By: Sworn/Estimate/Non-Audited
Audit Date: 10.06.2019
Personnel: Suzanne Liverett (Office Mgr.); Jim Blaylock (Visual Journalist); Valerie Rowell (Staff Writer); Scott Rouch (Sports Writer)

THE COMMERCE NEWS

Street address 1: 33 Lee St
Street address city: Jefferson
Street address state: GA
Zip/Postal code: 30549-1345
General Phone: (706) 367-5233
General Fax: (706) 367-8056
General/National Adv. E-mail: news@mainstreetnews.com
Primary Website: commercenewstoday.com
Year Established: 1875
Avg Paid Circ: 3100
Audit By: Sworn/Estimate/Non-Audited
Audit Date: 10.06.2019
Personnel: Mike N. Buffington (Co. Pub.); Scott Buffington (Co-Pub./Adv. Mgr.); Debbie Castellaw (Classified/Billing Mgr.); Mark Beardsley (Ed.)

THE COVINGTON NEWS

Street address 1: 1166 Usher St NW
Street address city: Covington
Street address state: GA
Zip/Postal code: 30014-2451
General Phone: (770) 787-6397
General Fax: (770) 786-6451
General/National Adv. E-mail: cbwarren@covnews.com
Display Adv. E-mail: cbwarren@covnews.com
Editorial e-mail: jgutknecht@covnews.com
Primary Website: covnews.com
Year Established: 1865
Avg Paid Circ: 5500
Avg Free Circ: 43500
Audit By: Sworn/Estimate/Non-Audited
Audit Date: 10.07.2019
Personnel: Patrick Graham (Owner); Jackie Gutknecht (Pub./Ed.); Amanda Ellington (Circ. Mgr.); Cynthia Warren (Adv. Mgr.); Jason Cosby (Digital Mgr.)

THE DAHLONEGA NUGGET

Street address 1: 1074 Morrison Moore Pkwy W
Street address city: Dahlonega
Street address state: GA
Zip/Postal code: 30533-1425
General Phone: (706) 864-3613
General Fax: (706) 864-4360
Advertising Phone: (706) 864-3613
General/National Adv. E-mail: nugclass@windstream.net
Editorial e-mail: tellerbee@dahloneganugget.com
Primary Website: thedahloneganugget.com
Avg Paid Circ: 5025
Avg Free Circ: 25
Audit By: Sworn/Estimate/Non-Audited
Audit Date: 10.06.2019
Personnel: Terrie Ellerbee (Ed.); Matt Aiken (Pub.); Joel Jenkins (Corp. Mktg. Dir.)
Parent company (for newspapers): Community Newspapers, Inc.

THE DAWSON NEWS

Street address 1: 139 W Lee St
Street address city: Dawson
Street address state: GA
Zip/Postal code: 39842-1624
General Phone: (229) 995-2175
General Fax: (229) 995-2176
Advertising Phone: (229) 995-2175
Editorial Phone: (229) 995-2175
General/National Adv. E-mail: news@thedawsonnews.com
Display Adv. E-mail: news@thedawsonnews.com
Editorial e-mail: news@thedawsonnews.com
Primary Website: N/A
Year Established: 1866
Avg Paid Circ: 1300
Audit By: Sworn/Estimate/Non-Audited
Audit Date: 10.06.2019
Personnel: Janice French (Secretary, Bookkeeper); Tommy Rountree (Editor, Publisher & Owner)

THE DOUGLAS ENTERPRISE

Street address 1: 1823 Peterson Ave S
Street address city: Douglas
Street address state: GA
Zip/Postal code: 31535-4013
General Phone: (912) 384-2323
General Fax: (912) 383-0218
General/National Adv. E-mail: adsales@douglasenterprise.net
Display Adv. E-mail: classifieds@douglasenterprise.net
Editorial e-mail: editor@douglasenterprise.net
Primary Website: douglasenterprise.net
Year Established: 1888
Avg Paid Circ: 8000
Avg Free Circ: 5
Audit By: Sworn/Estimate/Non-Audited
Audit Date: 10.06.2019
Personnel: Kristen Kitchens (Ed.); Tracy Mayo (Pub.); Sherri Smith (Adv. / Sales)

THE DOUGLAS NEIGHBOR

Street address 1: 4471 Jimmy Lee Smith Pkwy
Street address 2: Ste C
Street address city: Hiram
Street address state: GA
Zip/Postal code: 30141-2727
General Phone: (770) 445-9401
General Fax: (770) 942-4348
General/National Adv. E-mail: douglas@neighbornewspapers.com
Primary Website: mdjonline.com/neighbor_newspapers
Avg Paid Circ: 1
Avg Free Circ: 21825
Audit By: Sworn/Estimate/Non-Audited
Audit Date: 10.06.2019
Personnel: Otis A. Brumby (Pub.); Tom Spigolon (Ed.); Monica Burge (Ed.)
Parent company (for newspapers): Times-Journal, Inc.; Neighbor Newspapers

THE ELBERTON STAR

Street address 1: 25 N Public Sq
Street address city: Elberton
Street address state: GA
Zip/Postal code: 30635-2416
General Phone: (706) 283-8500
General Fax: (706) 283-9700
General/National Adv. E-mail: star@elberton.com
Display Adv. E-mail: vevans@elberton.net
Classified Adv. e-mail: bslay@elberton.com
Editorial e-mail: star@elberton.com
Primary Website: elberton.com
Year Established: 1887
Avg Paid Circ: 3200
Avg Free Circ: 159
Audit By: Sworn/Estimate/Non-Audited
Audit Date: 10.06.2019
Personnel: Joel Jenkins (Corp. Mktg. Dir.); Gary Jones (Pub.); Barbara Slay (Office Manager); Valerie Evans (Advertising Director); Kerri Pruitt (Office Mgr.); Mark Wells (Reporter); Julie Weeks (Editor/Publisher); Rose Scoggins (Editor/Publisher); Shana Toney (Staff writer)
Parent company (for newspapers): Community Newspapers, Inc.

THE FOREST-BLADE

Street address 1: 416 W Moring St
Street address city: Swainsboro
Street address state: GA
Zip/Postal code: 30401-3177
General Phone: (478) 237-9971
General Fax: (478) 237-9451
General/National Adv. E-mail: advertising@forest-blade.com
Display Adv. E-mail: classifieds@forest-blade.com
Editorial e-mail: news@foreset-blade.com
Primary Website: emanuelcountylive.com
Year Established: 1861
Avg Paid Circ: 4200
Audit By: Sworn/Estimate/Non-Audited
Audit Date: 10.06.2019

Personnel: Madelyne Meeks (Gen. Mgr.)
Parent company (for newspapers): Smith Newspapers

THE FORSYTH HERALD

Street address 1: 319 N Main St
Street address city: Alpharetta
Street address state: GA
Zip/Postal code: 30009-2321
General Phone: (770) 442-3278
General Fax: (770) 475-1216
General/National Adv. E-mail: advertising@appenmediagroup.com
Display Adv. E-mail: lynn@northfulton.com
Editorial e-mail: hans@appenmediagroup.com
Primary Website: appenmediagroup.com
Year Established: 1998
Avg Free Circ: 16975
Audit By: CVC
Audit Date: 30.12.2017
Personnel: Hans Appen (Pub.); Jonathan Copsey (Ed.); Hatcher Hurd (Exec. Ed.); Aldo Nahed (Mng. Ed./ Bus. Ed.); Kelly Brooks (Associate Pub.); Anne O'Shaughnessy (Circ. Mgr.); A. J. McNaughton (Prod. Mgr)

THE GEORGIA POST

Street address 1: 58 S Dugger Ave
Street address city: Roberta
Street address state: GA
Zip/Postal code: 31078-4807
General Phone: (478) 836-3195
General Fax: (478) 836-9634
General/National Adv. E-mail: gapost@pstel.net
Display Adv. E-mail: gapostbyronbuzz@gmail.com
Primary Website: www.gapostbyronbuzz.com
Mthly Avg Views: 2100
Year Established: 1921
Avg Paid Circ: 3000
Avg Free Circ: 25
Audit By: USPS
Audit Date: 10.10.2023
Personnel: Victoria Simmons (Publisher/General Manager); Kristi Watkins (Advertising/News editor); Casey Moore (Legal Notices); Linda Reynolds (Assistant to the Publisher/Legals)

THE HARALSON COUNTY GATEWAY BEACON

Street address 1: 901 Hays Mill Rd
Street address 2: Ste A
Street address city: Carrollton
Street address state: GA
Zip/Postal code: 30117-9576
General Phone: (770) 537-2434
General Fax: (770) 537-8816
Advertising Phone: (770) 834-6631 x 225
General/National Adv. E-mail: melissa@times-georgian.com
Primary Website: times-georgian.com
Avg Paid Circ: 770
Audit By: Sworn/Estimate/Non-Audited
Audit Date: 10.06.2019
Personnel: Francis Pollard (Office Mgr.); Amy Lavender (Ed.)

THE HARRIS COUNTY JOURNAL

Street address 1: 112 S College St
Street address city: Hamilton
Street address state: GA
Zip/Postal code: 31811-5330
General Phone: (706) 846-3188
General Fax: (706) 846-2206
General/National Adv. E-mail: harriscountyjournal@charterinternet.com; starmercurynews@charterinternet.com
Primary Website: No Website
Avg Paid Circ: 4400
Audit By: Sworn/Estimate/Non-Audited
Audit Date: 10.06.2019
Personnel: John Kuykendall (Pub.); Laurie Lewis (Adv. Mgr.); Michael C. Snider (Assoc. Ed.)
Parent company (for newspapers): Star-Mercury Publishing Co.

THE HARTWELL SUN

Street address 1: 8 Benson St
Street address city: Hartwell
Street address state: GA
Zip/Postal code: 30643-1990
General Phone: (706) 376-8025
General Fax: (706) 376-3016
General/National Adv. E-mail: hartwellson@hartcom.net
Primary Website: thehartwellsun.com
Year Established: 1874
Avg Paid Circ: 6771
Audit By: Sworn/Estimate/Non-Audited
Audit Date: 10.06.2019
Personnel: Michael Hall (Ed.); Alan NeSmith (Reg. Pub.); Carole Byrum (Adv. Sales); Kerri Pruitt (Class.)
Parent company (for newspapers): Community Newspapers, Inc.

THE HERALD-LEADER

Street address 1: 202 E Central Ave
Street address city: Fitzgerald
Street address state: GA
Zip/Postal code: 31750-2503
General Phone: (229) 423-9331
General Fax: (229) 423-6533
General/National Adv. E-mail: hlnews@alltell.net
Display Adv. E-mail: andersonherald@gmail.com
Primary Website: herald-leader.net
Year Established: 1916
Avg Paid Circ: 5300
Audit By: Sworn/Estimate/Non-Audited
Audit Date: 10.06.2019
Personnel: Becky Anderson (Adv. Mgr.); Tim Anderson (Ed.)

THE HOUSTON HOME JOURNAL

Street address 1: 1210 Washington St
Street address city: Perry
Street address state: GA
Zip/Postal code: 31069-2556
General Phone: (478) 987-1823
General Fax: (478) 988-9193
Advertising Phone: (478) 987-1823
Advertising Fax: (478) 988-9193
General/National Adv. E-mail: cadams@sunmulti.com
Display Adv. E-mail: diannee@sunmulti.com
Editorial e-mail: kriner@sunmulti.com
Primary Website: hhjonline.com
Year Established: 1870
Avg Paid Circ: 13000
Sat. Circulation Paid: 14000
Audit By: Sworn/Estimate/Non-Audited
Audit Date: 10.06.2019
Personnel: Daniel F. Evans (Pub.); Jimmy Townsend (Prodn. Mgr., Mailroom); Billy Townsend (Prodn. Mgr., Opns.); Krystal Riner (Managing Ed.); Cheri Adams (VP, Major Accts. Rep.); Betty Stubs (Classified Adv. Mgr.); Don Moncrief (d.)
Parent company (for newspapers): Sun Multimedia Inc.

THE ISLANDER

Street address 1: 1604B Newcastle St
Street address city: Brunswick
Street address state: GA
Zip/Postal code: 31520-6729
General Phone: (912) 265-9654
General/National Adv. E-mail: ssislander@bellsouth.net
Primary Website: theislanderonline.com
Year Established: 1972
Avg Paid Circ: 3500
Avg Free Circ: 500
Audit By: Sworn/Estimate/Non-Audited
Audit Date: 10.06.2019
Personnel: Matthew Permar (Pub.); Pam Shierling (Ed.)

THE JACKSON HERALD

Street address 1: 33 Lee St
Street address city: Jefferson
Street address state: GA
Zip/Postal code: 30549-1345
General Phone: (706) 367-5233
General Fax: (706) 367-8056
General/National Adv. E-mail: ads@mainstreetnews.com
Display Adv. E-mail: ads@mainstreetnews.com
Primary Website: jacksonheraldtoday.com
Avg Paid Circ: 9500
Avg Free Circ: 210
Audit By: Sworn/Estimate/Non-Audited
Audit Date: 10.06.2019
Personnel: Scott Buffington (Co-Pub.); Thomas Toles (Bus./Printing Mgr.); Debbie Castellaw (Circ. Mgr.); Mike Buffington (Co-Pub.); Vickie Thomas (Prodn. Mgr.)

THE JONES COUNTY NEWS

Street address 1: 102 Stewart Ave
Street address city: Gray
Street address state: GA
Zip/Postal code: 31032-5219
General Phone: (478) 986-3929
General Fax: (478) 986-1935
Advertising Phone: (478) 986-3929
General/National Adv. E-mail: articles@jcnews.com
Display Adv. E-mail: legals@jcnews.com
Editorial e-mail: mynews@jcnews.com
Primary Website: jcnews.com
Year Established: 1895
Avg Paid Circ: 4300
Audit By: Sworn/Estimate/Non-Audited
Audit Date: 10.06.2019
Personnel: Debbie Lurie-Smith (Ed.); Joshua Lurie (Pub.); Jennifer Gibson (Office Mgr.); Karen Hunsinger (Adv. Rep.); Kelli Martin (Adv. Rep.)

THE JOURNAL SENTINEL

Street address 1: 114B N Main St
Street address city: Reidsville
Street address state: GA
Zip/Postal code: 30453-4800
General Phone: (912) 557-6761
General Fax: (912) 557-4132
General/National Adv. E-mail: mail@tattnalljournal.com
Primary Website: tattnalljs.com
Year Established: 1879
Avg Paid Circ: 6000
Audit By: Sworn/Estimate/Non-Audited
Audit Date: 10.06.2019
Personnel: Russell J. Rhoden (Pub.); Lillian Durrence (Circ. Mgr.); Allison Cobb (Ed.)

THE LINCOLN JOURNAL

Street address 1: 157 N Peachtree St
Street address city: Lincolnton
Street address state: GA
Zip/Postal code: 30817-5884
General Phone: (706) 359-3229
General Fax: (706) 359-2884
General/National Adv. E-mail: journal@nu-z.net
Primary Website: lincolnjournalonline.com
Avg Paid Circ: 2850
Audit By: Sworn/Estimate/Non-Audited
Audit Date: 10.06.2019
Personnel: Teri Eno (Mng. Ed.); Anne Price (Office Mgr.); Sparky Newsome (Ed./Pub.); Jacquelyn Johnson (News Ed.)

THE MADISON COUNTY JOURNAL

Street address 1: 33 Lee St
Street address city: Jefferson
Street address state: GA
Zip/Postal code: 30549-1345
General Phone: (706) 367-5233
General Fax: (706) 367-8056
General/National Adv. E-mail: ads@mainstreetnews.com
Display Adv. E-mail: ads@mainstreetnews.com
Editorial e-mail: news@mainstreetnews.com
Primary Website: madisonjournaltoday.com
Year Established: 1997
Avg Paid Circ: 3900
Avg Free Circ: 210
Audit By: Sworn/Estimate/Non-Audited
Audit Date: 10.06.2019
Personnel: Thomas Toles (Bus./Printing Mgr.); Scott Buffington (Co-Pub./Adv. Mgr.); Debbie Castellaw (Circ. Mgr.); Zach Mitcham (Ed.); Ginger Chappell (Prodn. Mgr.); Frank Gillispie; Mike Buffington (Co-Pub.)

THE MCDUFFIE MIRROR

Street address 1: 108 Railroad St
Street address city: Thomson
Street address state: GA
Zip/Postal code: 30824-2733
General Phone: (706) 597-0335
General Fax: (706) 843-9295
General/National Adv. E-mail: news@mcduffiemirror.com
Primary Website: mcduffiemirror.com
Avg Paid Circ: 3700
Audit By: Sworn/Estimate/Non-Audited
Audit Date: 10.06.2019
Personnel: Todd Rainwater (Ed.)

THE MCDUFFIE PROGRESS

Street address 1: 101 Church St
Street address city: Thomson
Street address state: GA
Zip/Postal code: 30824-2613
General Phone: (706) 595-1601
General Fax: (706) 597-8974
General/National Adv. E-mail: dbond@mcduffieprogress.com
Display Adv. E-mail: karen@mcduffieprogress.com
Classified Adv. e-mail: dbond@mcduffieprogress.com
Editorial e-mail: karen@mcduffieprogress.com
Primary Website: mcduffieprogress.com
Avg Paid Circ: 2500
Avg Free Circ: 128
Audit By: Sworn/Estimate/Non-Audited
Audit Date: 10.06.2019
Personnel: Dianne Bond (Office Mgr./Circ. Mgr.); Wayne Parham (Pub./Ed.); Karen Fioretti (Publisher & Editor)
Parent company (for newspapers): Lancaster Management, Inc.

THE METTER ADVERTISER

Street address 1: 15 S Rountree St
Street address city: Metter
Street address state: GA
Zip/Postal code: 30439-4416
General Phone: (912) 685-6566
General Fax: (912) 685-4901
General/National Adv. E-mail: ads@metteradvertiser.com
Display Adv. E-mail: ads@metteradvertiser.com
Primary Website: metteradvertiser.com
Year Established: 1912
Avg Paid Circ: 3200
Audit By: Sworn/Estimate/Non-Audited
Audit Date: 10.06.2019
Personnel: Jerri Goodman (Ed.); Carvy Snell (Ed.)

THE MONTGOMERY MONITOR

Street address 1: Second & Main Sts.
Street address city: Soperton
Street address state: GA
Zip/Postal code: 30457
General Phone: (912) 529-6624
General Fax: (912) 529-5399
General/National Adv. E-mail: monitor@nlamerica.com
Avg Paid Circ: 1950
Audit By: Sworn/Estimate/Non-Audited
Audit Date: 10.06.2019
Personnel: Griffin Lovett (Pub.); DuBose Porter (Exec. Ed.); Jason Halcombe (Mng. Ed.)

THE MONTICELLO NEWS

Street address 1: 247 W Washington St
Street address city: Monticello
Street address state: GA
Zip/Postal code: 31064-1241
General Phone: (706) 468-6511
General Fax: (706) 468-6576
General/National Adv. E-mail: news@themonticellonews.com
Classified Adv. e-mail: advertising@themonticellonews.com
Editorial e-mail: editor@themonticellonews.com
Primary Website: themonticellonews.com
Year Established: 1881
Avg Paid Circ: 2100
Audit By: USPS
Audit Date: 15.10.2021
Personnel: Jenny Murphy (Adv. Mgr.); Kathy Mudd (Ed.); Victoria Lawrence (Legal, Class Mgr); Susan Jacobs (Sports Ed); Hannah Hinesley (Circu Mgr)

THE NEWS LEADER

Street address 1: 12150 Augusta Rd
Street address city: Lavonia

Street address state: GA
Zip/Postal code: 30553-1208
General Phone: (706) 356-8557
General Fax: (706) 356-2008
Editorial e-mail: fcc@franklincountycitizen.com
Primary Website: franklincountycitizen.com
Avg Paid Circ: 1950
Audit By: Sworn/Estimate/Non-Audited
Audit Date: 10.06.2019
Personnel: Shane Scoggins (Pub.); Denise Matthews (Ed.); Jan Dean (Adv.)
Parent company (for newspapers): Community Newspapers, Inc.

THE NEWS-OBSERVER

Street address 1: 5748 Appalachian Hwy
Street address city: Blue Ridge
Street address state: GA
Zip/Postal code: 30513-4240
General Phone: (706) 632-2019
General Fax: (706) 632-2577
General/National Adv. E-mail: ads@thenewsobserver.com
Primary Website: thenewsobserver.com
Avg Paid Circ: 2372
Audit By: Sworn/Estimate/Non-Audited
Audit Date: 10.06.2019
Personnel: Glenn Harbison (Pub.); Joel Jenkins (Corp. Mktg. Dir.)
Parent company (for newspapers): Community Newspapers, Inc.

THE NEWS-REPORTER

Street address 1: 116 W Robert Toombs Ave
Street address city: Washington
Street address state: GA
Zip/Postal code: 30673-1664
General Phone: (706) 678-2636
General Fax: (706) 678-3857
General/National Adv. E-mail: mary@wilkespublishing.com
Display Adv. E-mail: online@wilkespublishing.com
Editorial e-mail: editor@news-reporter.com
Primary Website: news-reporter.com
Year Established: 1967
Avg Paid Circ: 3200
Avg Free Circ: 175
Audit By: Sworn/Estimate/Non-Audited
Audit Date: 10.06.2019
Personnel: Teri Eno (Circ. Mgr.); Sparky Newsome (Ed./Pub.); Mary Newsome (Mng. Ed.)

THE NEWTON CITIZEN

Street address 1: 969 S Main St NE
Street address city: Conyers
Street address state: GA
Zip/Postal code: 30012-4501
General Phone: (770) 483-7108
Advertising Fax: (770) 761-4048
Editorial Fax: (770) 787-8603
General/National Adv. E-mail: Advertising@rockdalecitizen.com
Display Adv. E-mail: Advertising@rockdalecitizen.com
Classified Adv. e-mail: Advertising@rockdalecitizen.com
Editorial e-mail: news@newtoncitizen.com
Primary Website: newtoncitizen.com
Avg Paid Circ: 1863
Avg Free Circ: 246
Audit By: CVC
Audit Date: 31.12.2016
Personnel: Brenda Bennett (Adv. Dir.); Thom Bell (Circ. Dir.); Alice Queen (Ed.)
Parent company (for newspapers): Triple Crown Media

THE NORTH BARTOW NEWS

Street address 1: 5943 Joe Frank Harris Pkwy NW
Street address 2: Ste D
Street address city: Adairsville
Street address state: GA
Zip/Postal code: 30103-2451
General Phone: (770) 773-3754
General Fax: (770) 773-3757
General/National Adv. E-mail: northbartownews@yahoo.com
Display Adv. E-mail: northbartownews@yahoo.com
Primary Website: No Website
Avg Paid Circ: 293
Avg Free Circ: 7000
Audit By: Sworn/Estimate/Non-Audited
Audit Date: 10.06.2019
Personnel: Alan Davis (Pub.); Eric Pass (Adv. Sales); Janice Reed (Classifieds Adv. Mgr.)

THE NORTHEAST GEORGIAN

Street address 1: 2440 Old Athens Hwy
Street address city: Cornelia
Street address state: GA
Zip/Postal code: 30531-5364
General Phone: (706) 778-4215
General Fax: (706) 778-4114
General/National Adv. E-mail: news@thenortheastgeorgian.com
Display Adv. E-mail: advertising@thenortheastgeorgian.com
Primary Website: thenortheastgeorgian.com
Year Established: 1892
Avg Paid Circ: 9000
Avg Free Circ: 50
Audit By: Sworn/Estimate/Non-Audited
Audit Date: 10.06.2019
Personnel: Alan NeSmith (Reg. Pub.); Mark VanTassel (Regl. Bus. Mgr.); Lane Gresham (Ed.); April Compton (Prodn. Mgr.); Joel Jenkins (Corp. Mktg. Dir.)
Parent company (for newspapers): Community Newspapers, Inc.

THE OCILLA STAR

Street address 1: 102 E 4th St
Street address city: Ocilla
Street address state: GA
Zip/Postal code: 31774-1541
General Phone: (229) 468-5433
General Fax: (229) 468-5045
General/National Adv. E-mail: ocillastar@windstream.net
Primary Website: theocillastar.com
Avg Paid Circ: 2000
Audit By: Sworn/Estimate/Non-Audited
Audit Date: 10.06.2019
Personnel: Bob Tribble (Pres.); Ann Knight (Pub.); Beverly Bradford (Adv. Mgr.); Diane Pless (Ed.)

THE PELHAM JOURNAL

Street address 1: 13 S Scott St
Street address city: Camilla
Street address state: GA
Zip/Postal code: 31730-1705
General Phone: (229) 336-5265
General Fax: (229) 336-8476
General/National Adv. E-mail: camillaenterprise@camillaga.net
Primary Website: No Website
Avg Paid Circ: 1800
Avg Free Circ: 10
Audit By: Sworn/Estimate/Non-Audited
Audit Date: 10.06.2019
Personnel: Darrin Wilson (Pub.); Roger Davis (Nat'l Adv. Mgr./Adv. Dir.); Sandra Williams (Circ. Dir.)
Parent company (for newspapers): Trib Publications

THE POLK COUNTY STANDARD JOURNAL

Street address 1: 213 Main St
Street address city: Cedartown
Street address state: GA
Zip/Postal code: 30125-3048
General Phone: (770) 748-1520
General Fax: (770) 748-1524
General/National Adv. E-mail: tbritt@npco.com
Editorial e-mail: kmyrick@npco.com
Primary Website: polkstandardjournal.com
Year Established: 1869
Avg Paid Circ: 3679
Audit By: Sworn/Estimate/Non-Audited
Audit Date: 10.06.2019
Personnel: Kevin Myrick (Ed./Pub.)

THE POST-SEARCHLIGHT

Street address 1: 301 N Crawford St
Street address city: Bainbridge
Street address state: GA
Zip/Postal code: 39817-3612
General Phone: (229) 246-2827
General Fax: (229) 246-7665
General/National Adv. E-mail: postsearch@e-postprint.com
Primary Website: thepostsearchlight.com
Mthly Avg Views: 145000
Mthly Avg Unique Visitors: 30000
Avg Paid Circ: 7167
Avg Free Circ: 242
Audit By: Sworn/Estimate/Non-Audited
Audit Date: 10.06.2019
Personnel: Jeff Findley (Pub.); Mark Pope (Gen. Mgr.); Ashley Johnson (Mng. Ed.); Joe Crine (Sports Ed.); Sammy Griffin (Adv. Mgr.); Isaac Manuel (Circ. Mgr.)
Parent company (for newspapers): Boone Newspapers, Inc.

THE PRESS-SENTINEL

Street address 1: 252 W Walnut St
Street address city: Jesup
Street address state: GA
Zip/Postal code: 31545-1331
General Phone: (912) 427-3757
General Fax: (912) 427-4092
General/National Adv. E-mail: thepsadvertising@bellsouth.net
Display Adv. E-mail: thepresslegals@bellsouth.net
Editorial e-mail: drewd01@bellsouth.net
Primary Website: thepress-sentinel.com
Year Established: 1865
Avg Paid Circ: 7000
Audit By: Sworn/Estimate/Non-Audited
Audit Date: 10.06.2019
Personnel: Eric Denty (Pub.); Bob Whitley (Circ. Mgr.); Drew Davis (Ed.); Sheila Hires (Prodn. Mgr.); Danny Strickland (Press Mgr.); Lynn Rice (Bus. Mgr.); Mallard Melisa (Adv. Mgr.)
Parent company (for newspapers): Press-Sentinel Newspapers Inc.

THE REVUE & NEWS

Street address 1: 319 N Main St
Street address city: Alpharetta
Street address state: GA
Zip/Postal code: 30009-2321
General Phone: (770) 442-3278
General Fax: (770) 475-1216
Advertising Phone: (770) 442-3278
General/National Adv. E-mail: advertising@northfulton.com
Primary Website: northfulton.com
Avg Paid Circ: 350
Avg Free Circ: 27625
Audit By: Sworn/Estimate/Non-Audited
Audit Date: 10.06.2019
Personnel: Hans Appen (Pub.); Jonathan Copsey (Ed.); Hatcher Hurd (Exec. Ed.); Aldo Nahed (Mng. Ed./ Bus. Ed.); Kelly Brooks (Associate Pub.); Anne O'Shaughnessy (Circ. Mgr.); A. J. McNaughton (Gen. Mgr.)

THE ROCKDALE CITIZEN

Street address 1: 969 S Main St NE
Street address city: Conyers
Street address state: GA
Zip/Postal code: 30012-4501
General Phone: (770) 483-7108
Advertising Phone: (770) 483-7108
Advertising Fax: (770) 761-4048
Editorial Phone: (770) 483-7108
Editorial Fax: (770) 483-5797
General/National Adv. E-mail: alice.queen@rockdalecitizen.com
Display Adv. E-mail: brenda.bennett@rockdalecitizen.com
Editorial e-mail: news@rockdalecitizen.com
Primary Website: rockdalecitizen.com
Year Established: 1953
Avg Paid Circ: 4267
Avg Free Circ: 452
Sun. Circulation Paid: 5257
Sun. Circulation Free: 242
Audit By: CVC
Audit Date: 31.12.2016
Personnel: Alice Queen (Ed.); Brenda Bennett (Adv. Dir.); Rachel Hayes (Retail Adv. Rep.); Thom Bell (Circ. Dir.); Jay Jones (Mng. Ed.); Karen Rohr (Features Ed.); Manny Fils (Sports Ed.); J.K. Murphy (Pub.)
Parent company (for newspapers): Southern Community Newspapers, Inc.

THE SANDERSVILLE PROGRESS

Street address 1: 118 E Haynes St
Street address city: Sandersville
Street address state: GA
Zip/Postal code: 31082-2108
General Phone: (478) 552-3161
General/National Adv. E-mail: advertising@thesandersvilleprogress.com
Display Adv. E-mail: advertising@thesandersvilleprogress.com
Editorial e-mail: publisher@thesandersvilleprogress.com
Primary Website: No Website
Avg Paid Circ: 4900
Avg Free Circ: 6700
Audit By: Sworn/Estimate/Non-Audited
Audit Date: 10.06.2019
Personnel: Teresa Hines (Pub.); Jackie Little (Adv.)
Parent company (for newspapers): Trib Publications

THE SUMMERVILLE NEWS

Street address 1: 20 Wildlife Lake Rd
Street address city: Summerville
Street address state: GA
Zip/Postal code: 30747-5300
General Phone: (706) 857-2494
General Fax: (706) 857-2393
Advertising Phone: (706) 857-2494
Advertising Fax: (706) 857-2393
Editorial Phone: (706) 857-2494
Editorial Fax: (706) 857-2393
General/National Adv. E-mail: thesummervillenews@gmail.com
Display Adv. E-mail: sumnews@aol.com
Editorial e-mail: sumnews@aol.com
Primary Website: thesummervillenews.com
Year Established: 1886
Avg Paid Circ: 7000
Avg Free Circ: 75
Audit By: Sworn/Estimate/Non-Audited
Audit Date: 10.06.2019
Personnel: Winston Eugene Espy (Ed.)

THE SYLVESTER LOCAL NEWS

Street address 1: 103 E Kelly St
Street address city: Sylvester
Street address state: GA
Zip/Postal code: 31791-2159
General Phone: (229) 776-3991
General Fax: (229) 776-4607
General/National Adv. E-mail: info@thesylvesterlocal.com
Primary Website: thesylvesterlocal.com
Year Established: 1884
Avg Paid Circ: 3800
Avg Free Circ: 20
Audit By: Sworn/Estimate/Non-Audited
Audit Date: 10.06.2019
Personnel: Leigh Ford (Ed.)

THE TELFAIR ENTERPRISE

Street address 1: 31 W Oak St
Street address city: Mc Rae
Street address state: GA
Zip/Postal code: 31055-4333
General Phone: (229) 868-6015
General Fax: (229) 868-5486
General/National Adv. E-mail: telfairenterprise@windstream.net
Primary Website: thetelfairenterprise.com
Avg Paid Circ: 3200
Avg Free Circ: 55
Audit By: Sworn/Estimate/Non-Audited
Audit Date: 10.06.2019
Personnel: Eric Denty (Pub.); Robert M. Williams (Pres.); Donna J. Bell (Gen. Mgr.); W.H. NeSmith (Pub.); Don Richardson (Ed.); Joel Jenkins (Corp. Mktg. Dir.)
Parent company (for newspapers): Community Newspapers, Inc.

THE TOCCOA RECORD

Street address 1: 151 W Doyle St
Street address city: Toccoa
Street address state: GA

Zip/Postal code: 30577-1788
General Phone: (706) 886-9476
General Fax: (706) 886-2161
Advertising Fax: (706) 886-1166
General/National Adv. E-mail: toccoarecord@windstream.net
Primary Website: thetoccoarecord.com
Avg Paid Circ: 7200
Audit By: Sworn/Estimate/Non-Audited
Audit Date: 10.06.2019
Personnel: Tom Law (Pub.); Ty Dooley (Adv. Rep.); Sue Fletcher (Adv. Rep.); Jessica Waters (News Ed.); Joel Jenkins (Corp. Mktg. Dir.)
Parent company (for newspapers): Community Newspapers, Inc.

THE TRUE CITIZEN

Street address 1: 629 Shadrack St
Street address city: Waynesboro
Street address state: GA
Zip/Postal code: 30830-1451
General Phone: (706) 554-2111
General/National Adv. E-mail: rchalker@bellsouth.net
Display Adv. E-mail: tclegals@gmail.com
Editorial e-mail: rchalker@bellsouth.net
Primary Website: thetruecitizen.com
Year Established: 1882
Avg Paid Circ: 4200
Audit By: Sworn/Estimate/Non-Audited
Audit Date: 10.06.2019
Personnel: Roy F. Chalker (Ed./Pub.); Elizabeth Billips (Assoc. Ed.); Marianne Smith (Class. & Legals); Ann Marie Kyzer (Staff Reporter); Jill Dumars; Martha Chalker; Lisa Chance (Gen. Mgr.)

THE VILLA RICAN

Street address 1: 901 Hays Mill Rd
Street address city: Carrollton
Street address state: GA
Zip/Postal code: 30117-9576
General Phone: (770) 834-6631
General Fax: (770) 834-9991
General/National Adv. E-mail: melissa@times-georgian.com
Display Adv. E-mail: melissa@times-georgian.com
Editorial e-mail: ken@times-georgian.com
Primary Website: times-georgian.com/villa-rican
Mthly Avg Views: 239329
Mthly Avg Unique Visitors: 135195
Avg Free Circ: 8200
Audit By: Sworn/Estimate/Non-Audited
Audit Date: 10.06.2019
Personnel: Ken Denney (Ed.)
Parent company (for newspapers): Paxton Media Group

THE WALTON TRIBUNE

Street address 1: 121 South Broad Street
Street address city: Monroe
Street address state: GA
Zip/Postal code: 30655
General Phone: (770) 267-8371
General Fax: (770) 267-7780
Advertising Phone: (770) 267-4428
Editorial Phone: (770) 267-2492
General/National Adv. E-mail: madison.graham@waltontribune.com
Display Adv. E-mail: madison.graham@waltontribune.com
Editorial e-mail: news@waltontribune.com
Primary Website: waltontribune.com
Year Established: 1900
Avg Paid Circ: 4415
Avg Free Circ: 1013
Audit By: AAM
Audit Date: 31.03.2019
Personnel: Maddison Graham (Adv. Dir.); Sheila Tiller (Composing Mgr.); Cynethia Brown (Asst. Circ. Mgr.); Kim Powers (Business Office Mgr.); Patrick Graham (Pub./Ed.); David Clemons (Managing Ed.)
Parent company (for newspapers): Monroe Media Inc.

THE WHEELER COUNTY EAGLE

Street address 1: 115 S Jefferson St
Street address city: Dublin
Street address state: GA
Zip/Postal code: 31021-5146
General Phone: (478) 272-5522 ext. 223
General Fax: (912) 529-5399
General/National Adv. E-mail: wheelercountyeagle@gmail.com
Primary Website: wheelercountyeagle.com
Year Established: 1921
Avg Paid Circ: 1150
Audit By: Sworn/Estimate/Non-Audited
Audit Date: 10.06.2019
Personnel: Griffin Lovett (Pub.); Dubose Porter (CEO)

THE WRIGHTSVILLE HEADLIGHT

Street address 1: 2527 E Elm St
Street address city: Wrightsville
Street address state: GA
Zip/Postal code: 31096-2003
General Phone: (478) 864-3528
General Fax: (478) 864-2166
General/National Adv. E-mail: wheadlight@bellsouth.net
Year Established: 1880
Avg Paid Circ: 1000
Audit By: Sworn/Estimate/Non-Audited
Audit Date: 10.06.2019
Personnel: Robert E. Tribble (Pres.); Theresa Hines (Pub.); Sandra Saunders (Ed.)
Parent company (for newspapers): Trib Publications

TIMES-COURIER

Street address 1: 47 River St
Street address city: Ellijay
Street address state: GA
Zip/Postal code: 30540-3174
General Phone: (706) 635-4313
General Fax: (706) 635-7006
Advertising Phone: (706) 635-7002
Advertising Fax: (706) 635-7006
Editorial Phone: (706) 635-7002
Editorial Fax: (706) 635-7006
General/National Adv. E-mail: adsales@timescourier.com
Display Adv. E-mail: Fcclassifieds@timescourier.com
Editorial e-mail: editor@timescourier.com
Primary Website: timescourier.com
Mthly Avg Views: 39000
Mthly Avg Unique Visitors: 5780
Year Established: 1875
Avg Paid Circ: 6600
Avg Free Circ: 60
Audit By: Sworn/Estimate/Non-Audited
Audit Date: 10.06.2019
Personnel: Shana Parks (Adv. Mgr.); Rhesa Chastain (Circ./Office Mgr.); Mark Millican (News Ed.); Robbie Bills (Sports Ed.); Ryan Rees (Staff Writer); Keli Fredrickson (Prod. Mgr.); Kathy Aker (Adv. Sales); Andy Hurst (Publisher)

TOWNS COUNTY HERALD

Street address 1: 446 N MAIN ST
Street address city: Hiawassee
Street address state: GA
Zip/Postal code: 30546
General Phone: (706) 896-4454
General Fax: (706) 896-1745
General/National Adv. E-mail: tcherald@windstream.net
Primary Website: townscountyherald.net
Avg Paid Circ: 4200
Audit By: Sworn/Estimate/Non-Audited
Audit Date: 10.06.2019
Personnel: Kenneth West (Pub.); Tracie Woodstrom (Adv. Mgr.)

TRIBUNE & GEORGIAN

Street address 1: 206 Osborne St
Street address city: Saint Marys
Street address state: GA
Zip/Postal code: 31558-8400
General Phone: (912) 882-4927
General Fax: (912) 882-6519
General/National Adv. E-mail: marketing@tribune-georgian.com
Display Adv. E-mail: classifieds@tribune-georgian.com
Editorial e-mail: editor1@tds.net
Primary Website: tribune-georgian.com
Year Established: 1894
Avg Paid Circ: 6437
Avg Free Circ: 228
Audit By: Sworn/Estimate/Non-Audited
Audit Date: 10.06.2019
Personnel: Jill Helton (Pub.); Mega Sumner (Circ. / Admin); Denise Carver (Adv. / Mktg.)
Parent company (for newspapers): Community Newspapers, Inc.

WALKER COUNTY MESSENGER

Street address 1: 102 N Main St
Street address city: La Fayette
Street address state: GA
Zip/Postal code: 30728-2418
General Phone: (706) 638-1859
General Fax: (706) 638-7045
General/National Adv. E-mail: walkercountymessenger@walkermessenger.com
Primary Website: walkermessenger.com
Avg Paid Circ: 4700
Avg Free Circ: 50
Audit By: Sworn/Estimate/Non-Audited
Audit Date: 10.06.2019
Personnel: Don Stilwell (Pub.); Angie Clark (Adv. Mgr.); Becky McDaniel (Ed.); Brenda Burger (VP, Ops.); William Steele (Rgl. Adv. Mgr.); Donna Hixon (Adv. Mgr.)
Parent company (for newspapers): Rome News-Tribune

WEST GEORGIA WEEKLY

Street address 1: 901 Hays Mill Rd
Street address city: Carrollton
Street address state: GA
Zip/Postal code: 30117-9576
General Phone: (770) 834-6631
General Fax: (770) 834-9991
General/National Adv. E-mail: melissa@times-georgian.com
Display Adv. E-mail: melissa@times-georgian.com
Editorial e-mail: bbrowning@times-georgian.com
Primary Website: times-georgian.com
Mthly Avg Views: 239329
Mthly Avg Unique Visitors: 135195
Avg Free Circ: 16000
Audit By: Sworn/Estimate/Non-Audited
Audit Date: 10.06.2019
Personnel: Corey Cusick (Sports Editor)
Parent company (for newspapers): Paxton Media Group

WHITE COUNTY NEWS

Street address 1: 13 E Jarrard St
Street address city: Cleveland
Street address state: GA
Zip/Postal code: 30528-1228
General Phone: (706) 865-4718
General Fax: (706) 865-3048
Advertising Phone: (706) 865-4718
Advertising Fax: (706) 865-4718
Editorial Phone: (706) 865-4718
Editorial Fax: (706) 865-4718
General/National Adv. E-mail: publisher@whitecountynews.net
Display Adv. E-mail: sales@whitecountynews.net
Editorial e-mail: publisher@whitecountynews.net
Primary Website: whitecountynews.net
Year Established: 1968
Avg Paid Circ: 5000
Audit By: Sworn/Estimate/Non-Audited
Audit Date: 10.06.2019
Personnel: Samantha Sinclair (Editor)
Parent company (for newspapers): Community Newspapers, Inc.; White County News

WIREGRASS FARMER

Street address 1: 109 N Gordon St
Street address city: Ashburn
Street address state: GA
Zip/Postal code: 31714-5208
General Phone: (229) 567-3655
General Fax: (229) 567-4402
General/National Adv. E-mail: wiregrassfarmer@yahoo.com
Primary Website: thewiregrassfarmer.com
Year Established: 1902
Avg Paid Circ: 2000
Avg Free Circ: 100
Audit By: Sworn/Estimate/Non-Audited
Audit Date: 10.06.2019
Personnel: Ben Baker (Ed.)

HAWAII

KAUAI MIDWEEK

Street address 1: 500 Ala Moana Blvd
Street address 2: Ste 7-500
Street address city: Honolulu
Street address state: HI
Zip/Postal code: 96813-4930
General Phone: (808) 529-4700
General Fax: (808) 585-6324
Advertising Fax: (808) 529-4898
General/National Adv. E-mail: displayads@thegardenisland.com
Display Adv. E-mail: tgiclassifieds@thegardenisland.com
Editorial e-mail: rnagasawa@midweek.com
Primary Website: midweekkauai.com
Year Established: 2010
Avg Free Circ: 23294
Audit By: AAM
Audit Date: 31.12.2017
Personnel: Dennis Francis (Pres.); Dave Kennedy (CRO); Jay Higa (VP Reg Sales); Bill Mossman (Exec Ed)
Parent company (for newspapers): Oahu Publications Inc.

MAUI TIME

Street address 1: 16 S Market Street
Street address 2: Suite 2K
Street address city: Wailuku
Street address state: HI
Zip/Postal code: 96793
General Phone: (808) 244-0777
Primary Website: mauitime.com
Year Established: 1997
Audit By: Sworn/Estimate/Non-Audited
Audit Date: 10.06.2019
Personnel: Tommy Russo (Pub.); Axel Beers (Ed.)
Parent company (for newspapers): Ogden Newspapers Inc.

MIDWEEK OAHU

Street address 1: 500 Ala Moana Blvd
Street address 2: Ste 7-500
Street address city: Honolulu
Street address state: HI
Zip/Postal code: 96813-4930
General Phone: (808) 529-4700
General Fax: (808) 585-6324
Advertising Fax: (808) 529-4898
General/National Adv. E-mail: displayads@staradvertiser.com
Display Adv. E-mail: classifieds@staradvertiser.com
Editorial e-mail: rnagasawa@midweek.com
Primary Website: midweek.com
Year Established: 1984
Avg Free Circ: 269041
Audit By: AAM
Audit Date: 31.12.2017
Personnel: Dennis Francis (Pres.); Ron Nagasawa (Pub.); Dave Kennedy (CRO); Patrick Klein (VP/Adv); Jay Higa (VP/Bus. Devt & Reg Sales); Bill Mossman (Exec Ed)
Parent company (for newspapers): Oahu Publications Inc.

NORTH HAWAII NEWS

Street address 1: 65-1279 Kawaihae Rd
Street address 2: Ste 216
Street address city: Kamuela
Street address state: HI
Zip/Postal code: 96743-8444
General Phone: (808) 930-8675
General Fax: (808) 885-0601
Advertising Phone: (808) 329-9311
Advertising Fax: (808) 329-3659
Editorial Phone: (808) 930-8675
Editorial Fax: (808) 885-0601
Display Adv. E-mail: johnson@northhawaiinews.net
Editorial e-mail: editor@northhawaiinews.com
Primary Website: northhawaiinews.com
Mthly Avg Unique Visitors: 3500
Year Established: 2000
Avg Paid Circ: 1798
Audit By: Sworn/Estimate/Non-Audited
Audit Date: 10.06.2019

Personnel: Tracey Fosso (Adv. Mgr. / Pub.); John Shackelford (Circ. Mgr.); Lisa Dahm (Mgn. Ed.)
Parent company (for newspapers): Oahu Publications Inc.

PACIFIC BUSINESS NEWS

Street address 1: 737 Bishop St
Street address 2: Ste 1590
Street address city: Honolulu
Street address state: HI
Zip/Postal code: 96813-3205
General Phone: (808) 955-8100
General Fax: (808) 955-8078
Advertising Phone: (808) 955-8053
Advertising Fax: (808) 955-8051
Editorial Phone: (808) 955-8041
General/National Adv. E-mail: mstofle@bizjournals.com
Editorial e-mail: pacific@bizjournals.com
Primary Website: bizjournals.com/pacific
Mthly Avg Views: 510000
Mthly Avg Unique Visitors: 185000
Year Established: 1963
Avg Free Circ: 12290
Audit By: Sworn/Estimate/Non-Audited
Audit Date: 10.06.2019
Personnel: Bob Charlet (Pub.); Janis Magin (Mgn. Ed.); Michelle Stofle (Adv. Mgr.)

STREET PULSE

Street address 1: 500 Ala Moana Blvd
Street address 2: Ste 7-500
Street address city: Honolulu
Street address state: HI
Zip/Postal code: 96813-4930
General Phone: (808) 529-4700
General Fax: (808) 585-4898
General/National Adv. E-mail: displayads@staradvertiser.com
Display Adv. E-mail: classifieds@staradvertiser.com
Primary Website: honolulustreetpulse.com
Year Established: 2012
Avg Free Circ: 44843
Audit By: AAM
Audit Date: 31.12.2017
Personnel: Dennis Francis (Pres.); Ron Nagasawa (Pub.); Patrick Klein (VP/Adv); Darin Nakakura (Dir. of Adv); Troy Fujimoto (VP/Dig Media); Dave Kennedy (CRO)
Parent company (for newspapers): Oahu Publications Inc.

THE MOLOKAI DISPATCH

Street address 1: 2 Kamoi St.
Street address 2: Ste. 5
Street address city: Kaunakakai
Street address state: HI
Zip/Postal code: 96748
General Phone: (808) 552-2781
General Fax: (808) 552-2334
Advertising Phone: (808) 552-2781
Editorial Phone: (808) 552-2781
General/National Adv. E-mail: sales@themolokaidispatch.com
Editorial e-mail: editor@themolokaidispatch.com
Primary Website: themolokaidispatch.com
Mthly Avg Views: 16000
Year Established: 1985
Avg Paid Circ: 300
Avg Free Circ: 3500
Audit By: Sworn/Estimate/Non-Audited
Audit Date: 10.06.2019
Personnel: Catherine Cluett Pactol (Ed. in Chief)

IDAHO

ABERDEEN TIMES

Street address 1: PO Box 856
Street address 2: 31 S. Main
Street address city: Aberdeen
Street address state: ID
Zip/Postal code: 83210-0856
General Phone: (208) 397-4440
General Fax: (208) 397-4440
General/National Adv. E-mail: times1@dcdi.net
Display Adv. E-mail: times1@dcdi.net
Editorial e-mail: times1@dcdi.net
Primary Website: press-times.com
Year Established: 1912
Avg Paid Circ: 900
Avg Free Circ: 30
Audit By: Sworn/Estimate/Non-Audited
Audit Date: 10.06.2019
Personnel: Vicki Gamble (Editor)
Parent company (for newspapers): Crompton Publishing Inc.

ARCO ADVERTISER

Street address 1: 146 S Front St
Street address city: Arco
Street address state: ID
Zip/Postal code: 83213
General Phone: (208) 527-3038
General Fax: (208) 527-8210
General/National Adv. E-mail: arcoadv@aol.com
Display Adv. E-mail: arcoadv@aol.com
Classified Adv. e-mail: arcoadv@aol.com
Editorial e-mail: arcoadv@aol.com
Year Established: 1909
Avg Paid Circ: 1500
Avg Free Circ: 55
Audit By: Sworn/Estimate/Non-Audited
Audit Date: 10.06.2019
Personnel: Thomas D. Cammack (Adv. Mgr.); Dartell Beard; Hillary Hyde

BONNERS FERRY HERALD

Street address 1: 7183 Main St
Street address city: Bonners Ferry
Street address state: ID
Zip/Postal code: 83805-8729
General Phone: (208) 267-5521
General Fax: (208) 267-5523
General/National Adv. E-mail: ljohnson@bonnersferryherald.com
Primary Website: bonnersferryherald.com
Mthly Avg Views: 5000
Year Established: 1891
Avg Paid Circ: 3200
Avg Free Circ: 200
Audit By: Sworn/Estimate/Non-Audited
Audit Date: 10.06.2019
Personnel: Linda Johnson (Office Mgr.); Mandi Bateman (Editor); Tanna Larsen; Ida Trower
Parent company (for newspapers): Hagadone Corporation

BUHL HERALD

Street address 1: PO Box 312
Street address city: Buhl
Street address state: ID
Zip/Postal code: 83316-0312
General Phone: (208) 543-4335
General Fax: (208) 543-6834
General/National Adv. E-mail: buhlherald@cableone.net
Avg Paid Circ: 2200
Audit By: Sworn/Estimate/Non-Audited
Audit Date: 10.06.2019
Personnel: Sandra Wisecaver (Ed.)

CLEARWATER TRIBUNE

Street address 1: 161 Main St
Street address city: Orofino
Street address state: ID
Zip/Postal code: 83544
General Phone: (208) 476-4571
General Fax: (208) 476-0765
General/National Adv. E-mail: cleartrib@cbridge.net
Primary Website: clearwatertribune.com
Year Established: 1912
Avg Paid Circ: 14
Avg Free Circ: 5061
Audit By: Sworn/Estimate/Non-Audited
Audit Date: 10.06.2019
Personnel: Marcie Stanton (Pub.)

COTTONWOOD CHRONICLE

Street address 1: 503 King St
Street address city: Cottonwood
Street address state: ID
Zip/Postal code: 83522-5263
General Phone: (208) 962-3851
General Fax: (208) 962-7131
Editorial e-mail: editor@cottonwoodchronicle.com
Primary Website: cottonwoodchronicle.com
Year Established: 1893
Avg Paid Circ: 577
Avg Free Circ: 10
Audit By: Sworn/Estimate/Non-Audited
Audit Date: 10.06.2019
Personnel: Greg A. Wherry (Pub.)

IDAHO BUSINESS REVIEW

Street address 1: 855 W Broad St
Street address 2: Suite 103
Street address city: Boise
Street address state: ID
Zip/Postal code: 83702-7158
General Phone: (208) 336-3768
General Fax: (208) 336-5534
Advertising Phone: (208) 639-3512
General/National Adv. E-mail: advertising@idahobusinessreview.com
Editorial e-mail: news@idahobusinessreview.com
Primary Website: idahobusinessreview.com
Avg Paid Circ: 2600
Avg Free Circ: 75
Audit By: Sworn/Estimate/Non-Audited
Audit Date: 10.06.2019
Personnel: Cindy Safa (Assoc. Pub.); Anne Allen (Ed.); Laura Butler (Admin Asst.); Corey Wong (Acct. Exec.); Rocky Cook (Acct. Exec.)

IDAHO COUNTY FREE PRESS

Street address 1: 900 W Main St
Street address city: Grangeville
Street address state: ID
Zip/Postal code: 83530-5192
General Phone: (208) 983-1200
General Fax: (208) 983-1336
Advertising Phone: (208) 983-1200
Advertising Fax: (208) 983-1336
Editorial Phone: (208) 983-1200
Editorial Fax: (208) 983-1336
General/National Adv. E-mail: freepressads@idahocountyfreepress.com
Display Adv. E-mail: wkunkel@idahocountyfreepress.com
Editorial e-mail: freepressnews@idahocountyfreepress.com
Primary Website: idahocountyfreepress.com
Year Established: 1886
Avg Paid Circ: 3600
Avg Free Circ: 68
Audit By: Sworn/Estimate/Non-Audited
Audit Date: 10.06.2019
Personnel: Linda Mort (Circ. Mgr.); Sarah Clement (Pub.); Lisa Adkison (Adv. Rep.); David Rauzi (Ed.)
Parent company (for newspapers): Eagle Newspapers, Inc.

IDAHO ENTERPRISE

Street address 1: 100 E 90 S
Street address city: Malad City
Street address state: ID
Zip/Postal code: 83252-1314
General Phone: (208) 766-4773
General Fax: (208) 766-4774
General/National Adv. E-mail: newsdesk@atcnet.net
Primary Website: idahoenterprise.com
Year Established: 1879
Avg Paid Circ: 1300
Audit By: Sworn/Estimate/Non-Audited
Audit Date: 10.06.2019
Personnel: Kristine Smith (Ed./Pub.); Helen Ravsten (Office Mgr.); Sherrie Wise (Adv. Exec.)
Parent company (for newspapers): Loyal Perch Media

IDAHO MOUNTAIN EXPRESS

Street address 1: 591 N 1st Ave
Street address city: Ketchum
Street address state: ID
Zip/Postal code: 83340
General Phone: (208) 726-8060
General Fax: (208) 726-2329
General/National Adv. E-mail: advertising@mtexpress.com
Display Adv. E-mail: classifieds@mtexpress.com
Editorial e-mail: news@mtexpress.com
Primary Website: mtexpress.com
Avg Paid Circ: 11
Avg Free Circ: 28394
Audit By: Sworn/Estimate/Non-Audited
Audit Date: 10.06.2019
Personnel: Pam Morris (Pub.); Tony Barriatua (Production Mgr.); John Ferry (Adv. Dir.); Sara Adamiec (Adv. Rep.)
Parent company (for newspapers): Express Publishing, Inc.

IDAHO WORLD

Street address 1: PO Box 220
Street address city: Idaho City
Street address state: ID
Zip/Postal code: 83631-0220
General Phone: (208) 429-1606
General Fax: (208) 445-2110
General/National Adv. E-mail: editor@idahoworld.com
Primary Website: idahoworld.com
Avg Paid Circ: 1300
Audit By: Sworn/Estimate/Non-Audited
Audit Date: 10.06.2019
Personnel: Wayne Hart (Adv. Mgr.); Erin Sturbaum (Ed.)

INDEPENDENT-ENTERPRISE

Street address 1: 124 S Main St
Street address city: Payette
Street address state: ID
Zip/Postal code: 83661-2851
General Phone: (208) 642-3357
General Fax: (208) 642-3560
General/National Adv. E-mail: andys@argusobserver.com
Display Adv. E-mail: lisap@argusobserver.com
Classified Adv. e-mail: joo@argusobserver.com
Editorial e-mail: editor@argusobserver.com
Primary Website: argusobserver.com/independent
Mthly Avg Views: 260000
Mthly Avg Unique Visitors: 75000
Year Established: 1891
Avg Paid Circ: 1245
Avg Free Circ: 16
Sun. Circulation Paid: 6201
Sun. Circulation Free: 10
Audit By: Sworn/Estimate/Non-Audited
Audit Date: 10.06.2019
Personnel: Stephanie Spiess (Pub.); Dawnita Haueter (Bus. Mgr.); Leslie Thompson (Ed.); Kelly Jones (Adv. Mgr.)
Parent company (for newspapers): Wick Communications

KUNA MELBA NEWS

Street address 1: 326 Avenue D
Street address city: Kuna
Street address state: ID
Zip/Postal code: 83634
General Phone: (208) 922-3008
General Fax: (208) 922-3009
General/National Adv. E-mail: kunamelbanews@aol.com
Primary Website: kunamelba.com
Mthly Avg Views: 4000
Year Established: 1983
Avg Paid Circ: 408
Audit By: CAC
Audit Date: 30.06.2017
Personnel: Cliff Wright (Pub.); Mark Barnes (Ed.); Karri Keller (Gen Mgr.)
Parent company (for newspapers): Adams Publishing Group, LLC

MESSENGER-INDEX

Street address 1: 120 N Washington Ave
Street address city: Emmett
Street address state: ID
Zip/Postal code: 83617-2973
General Phone: (208) 365-6066
General Fax: (208) 365-6068
Advertising Phone: (208) 365-6066 ext. 11
Editorial Phone: (208) 365-6066 ext. 17
General/National Adv. E-mail: dgray@messenger-index.com
Editorial e-mail: newsroom@messenger-index.com
Primary Website: messenger-index.com
Year Established: 1893
Avg Paid Circ: 1660

Avg Free Circ: 50
Audit By: Sworn/Estimate/Non-Audited
Audit Date: 10.06.2019
Personnel: Diana Baird (Gen. Mgr.); Del Gray (Managing Editor); Renee McMahon (Adv. Assoc.)
Parent company (for newspapers): Adams Publishing Group

MOUNTAIN HOME NEWS

Street address 1: 195 S 3rd E
Street address city: Mountain Home
Street address state: ID
Zip/Postal code: 83647-3020
General Phone: (208) 587-3331
General Fax: (208) 587-9205
General/National Adv. E-mail: bfincher@mountaintainhomenews.com
Display Adv. E-mail: advertising@mountainhomenews.com
Editorial e-mail: borban@mountainhomenews.com
Primary Website: mountainhomenews.com
Year Established: 1888
Avg Paid Circ: 2800
Audit By: Sworn/Estimate/Non-Audited
Audit Date: 10.06.2019
Personnel: Brian Orban (Ed); Cristena Ford (Bus Mgr)

NORTHWEST MARKET

Street address 1: 220 E 5th St
Street address 2: Rm 205
Street address city: Moscow
Street address state: ID
Zip/Postal code: 83843-2981
General Phone: (208) 882-5561
General Fax: (208) 883-8205
Editorial e-mail: editor@dnews.com
Primary Website: dnews.com
Year Established: 1911
Avg Free Circ: 10500
Audit By: Sworn/Estimate/Non-Audited
Audit Date: 10.06.2019
Personnel: Nathan Alford (Pub.); Fred Board (Gen. Mgr.); Angela Kay (Adv. Dir.); Mark Bryan (Circ. Dir.)
Parent company (for newspapers): TPC Holdings Inc.

POWER COUNTY PRESS

Street address 1: 174 Idaho St
Street address city: American Falls
Street address state: ID
Zip/Postal code: 83211-1234
General Phone: (208) 226-5294
General Fax: (208) 226-5295
General/National Adv. E-mail: press5@press-times.com
Display Adv. E-mail: press5@press-times.com
Editorial e-mail: press1@press-times.com
Primary Website: press-times.com
Year Established: 1902
Avg Paid Circ: 1600
Audit By: Sworn/Estimate/Non-Audited
Audit Date: 10.06.2019
Personnel: Debbie Crompton (Adv. Mgr.); Brett Crompton (Pub.); Daniel Moore (Staff Writer)
Parent company (for newspapers): Crompton Publishing Inc.

PRESTON CITIZEN

Street address 1: 1250 Industrial Park Rd
Street address city: Preston
Street address state: ID
Zip/Postal code: 83263-5686
General Phone: (208) 852-0155
General Fax: (208) 852-0158
General/National Adv. E-mail: addesign@prestoncitizen.com
Display Adv. E-mail: jjanke@prestoncitizen.com
Editorial e-mail: editor@prestoncitizen.com
Primary Website: prestoncitizen.com
Year Established: 1890
Avg Paid Circ: 3000
Avg Free Circ: 130
Audit By: Sworn/Estimate/Non-Audited
Audit Date: 10.06.2019
Personnel: Necia Seamons (Ed.); Stacey Comeau (Adv. Mgr.); Rhonda Gregorson (Circ. Mgr.)
Parent company (for newspapers): Adams Publishing Group, LLC

PRIEST RIVER TIMES

Street address 1: 310 Church St
Street address city: Sandpoint
Street address state: ID
Zip/Postal code: 83864-1345
General Phone: (208) 448-2431
General Fax: (208) 448-2938
General/National Adv. E-mail: prtimesadvertising@priestrivertimes.com
Editorial e-mail: tivie@priestrivertimes.com
Primary Website: priestrivertimes.com
Mthly Avg Views: 4000
Mthly Avg Unique Visitors: 20000
Year Established: 1914
Avg Paid Circ: 1427
Avg Free Circ: 9000
Audit By: Sworn/Estimate/Non-Audited
Audit Date: 10.06.2019
Personnel: Robin Herrin (Adv. Specialist); Kieth Kinnaird (Ed.); Jim McKiernan (Pub.)
Parent company (for newspapers): Hagadone Corporation

SAINT MARIES GAZETTE-RECORD

Street address 1: 610 Main Ave
Street address city: Saint Maries
Street address state: ID
Zip/Postal code: 83861-1838
General Phone: (208) 245-4538
General Fax: (208) 245-4011
General/National Adv. E-mail: dan@smgazette.com
Primary Website: gazetterecord.com
Year Established: 1906
Avg Paid Circ: 3500
Audit By: Sworn/Estimate/Non-Audited
Audit Date: 10.06.2019
Personnel: Daniel H. Hammes (Pub.)

TETON VALLEY NEWS

Street address 1: 75 N Main St
Street address city: Driggs
Street address state: ID
Zip/Postal code: 83422-5141
General Phone: (208) 354-8101
General Fax: (208) 354-8621
General/National Adv. E-mail: publisher@tetonvalley.net
Editorial e-mail: editor@tetonvalleynews.net
Primary Website: tetonvalleynews.net
Year Established: 1909
Avg Paid Circ: 2300
Avg Free Circ: 50
Audit By: Sworn/Estimate/Non-Audited
Audit Date: 10.06.2019
Personnel: Meg Heinen (Adv. Mgr.); Andy Pennington (Pub.); Scott Stuntz (Mng. Ed.)
Parent company (for newspapers): Adams Publishing Group, LLC

THE ADAMS COUNTY RECORD

Street address 1: 108 ILLINOIS AVE
Street address 2:
Street address city: Council
Street address state: ID
Zip/Postal code: 83612
General Phone: (208) 253-6961
General Fax: (208) 253-6801
General/National Adv. E-mail: advertising@theadamscountyrecord.com
Display Adv. E-mail: advertising@theadamscountyrecord.com
Editorial e-mail: editor@theadamscountyrecord.com
Primary Website: theadamscountyrecord.com
Year Established: 1908
Avg Paid Circ: 1200
Avg Free Circ: 75
Audit By: Sworn/Estimate/Non-Audited
Audit Date: 10.06.2019
Personnel: Lyle Sall (Pub.); Darcy Panak (Ed.); Dara Victorino (Office Mgr.)

THE CHALLIS MESSENGER

Street address 1: 310 Main
Street address city: Challis
Street address state: ID
Zip/Postal code: 83226
General Phone: (208) 879-4445
General Fax: (208) 879-5276
General/National Adv. E-mail: info@challismessenger.com
Display Adv. E-mail: sridenour@challismessenger.com
Classified Adv. e-mail: sridenour@challismessenger.com
Editorial e-mail: sridenour@challismessenger.com
Primary Website: challismessenger.com
Year Established: 1881
Avg Paid Circ: 1000
Avg Free Circ: 50
Audit By: USPS
Audit Date: 10.10.2022
Personnel: Shelley Ridenour (General manager); Jim Smirch (Leg., class., disp. ads); Veronica Weisbeck (Off. Mgr., circ., billing, class ads)
Parent company (for newspapers): Adams Publishing Group, LLC

THE CLEARWATER PROGRESS

Street address 1: 417 Main St
Street address city: Kamiah
Street address state: ID
Zip/Postal code: 83536-9700
General Phone: (208) 935-0838
General Fax: (208) 935-0973
General/National Adv. E-mail: progress@clearwaterprogress.com
Display Adv. E-mail: sales.theprogress@gmail.com
Primary Website: clearwaterprogress.com
Year Established: 1905
Avg Paid Circ: 400
Avg Free Circ: 3700
Audit By: Sworn/Estimate/Non-Audited
Audit Date: 10.06.2019
Personnel: John Bennett (Pub./Owner); Susan Bennett (Pub./Owner); Ben Jorgensen (Ed.); Angela Berger (Adv. Mgr.)

THE NEWS-EXAMINER

Street address 1: 847 Washington St
Street address city: Montpelier
Street address state: ID
Zip/Postal code: 83254-1455
General Phone: (208) 847-0552
General Fax: (208) 847-0553
General/National Adv. E-mail: newseditor@news-examiner.net
Display Adv. E-mail: adsales@news-examiner.net
Editorial e-mail: newseditor@news-examiner.net
Primary Website: news-examiner.net
Year Established: 1895
Avg Paid Circ: 1400
Avg Free Circ: 30
Audit By: Sworn/Estimate/Non-Audited
Audit Date: 10.06.2019
Personnel: Michelle Higley (Ed./ Gen. Mgr.)
Parent company (for newspapers): Adams Publishing Group

THE OWYHEE AVALANCHE

Street address 1: 20 E IDAHO AVE
Street address city: Homedale
Street address state: ID
Zip/Postal code: 83628
General Phone: (208) 337-4681
General Fax: (208) 337-4867
Advertising Phone: (208) 337-4866
Advertising Fax: (208) 337-4866
Editorial Phone: (208) 337-4866
Editorial Fax: (208) 337-4866
General/National Adv. E-mail: rob@owyhee.com
Display Adv. E-mail: jennifer@owyheeavalanche.com
Editorial e-mail: jon@owyheeavalanche.com
Primary Website: owyheepublishing.com
Year Established: 1865
Avg Paid Circ: 1800
Avg Free Circ: 34
Audit By: Sworn/Estimate/Non-Audited
Audit Date: 10.06.2019
Personnel: Joe E. Aman (Owner); Jon P. Brown (Mng. Ed.); Robert Aman (Composition)

THE STAR-NEWS

Street address 1: 1000 N 1st St
Street address city: McCall
Street address state: ID
Zip/Postal code: 83638-3848
General Phone: (208) 634-2123
Advertising Phone: (208) 634-2123
Editorial Phone: (208) 634-2123
General/National Adv. E-mail: tomigrote@gmail.com
Display Adv. E-mail: starclass@frontier.com
Editorial e-mail: starnews@frontier.com
Primary Website: mccallstarnews.com
Year Established: 1915
Avg Paid Circ: 4000
Avg Free Circ: 20
Audit By: Sworn/Estimate/Non-Audited
Audit Date: 10.06.2019
Personnel: Tom Grote (Ed./Pub.)

THE UPPER COUNTRY NEWS-REPORTER

Street address 1: 155 N Superior St
Street address city: Cambridge
Street address state: ID
Zip/Postal code: 83610-2001
General Phone: (208) 257-3515
General Fax: (208) 257-3540
General/National Adv. E-mail: buhlherald@cableone.net
Primary Website: facebook.com/theucnr
Year Established: 1889
Avg Paid Circ: 900
Audit By: Sworn/Estimate/Non-Audited
Audit Date: 10.06.2019
Personnel: Norman Dopf (Ed.)

WEISER SIGNAL AMERICAN

Street address 1: 18 E Idaho St
Street address city: Weiser
Street address state: ID
Zip/Postal code: 83672-2530
General Phone: (208) 549-1717
General Fax: (208) 549-1718
General/National Adv. E-mail: ads@signalamerican.org
Display Adv. E-mail: ads@signalamerican.org
Editorial e-mail: news@signalamerican.org
Primary Website: signalamerican.org
Year Established: 1882
Avg Paid Circ: 2200
Audit By: Sworn/Estimate/Non-Audited
Audit Date: 10.06.2019
Personnel: Sarah Imada (Gen. Mgr.); Stephanie McDaniel (Adv. Dir.); Steve Lyon (Ed.)

ILLINOIS

ADDISON SUBURBAN LIFE

Street address 1: 2001 Butterfield Rd Suite 105
Street address 2: Ste 260
Street address city: Downers Grove
Street address state: IL
Zip/Postal code: 60515
General Phone: (630) 368-1100
General Fax: (630) 969-0228
Advertising Phone: (630) 427-6213
Editorial Phone: (630) 427-6250
General/National Adv. E-mail: nshannon@shawmedia.com
Display Adv. E-mail: sbissell@shawmedia.com
Editorial e-mail: dgood@shawmedia.com
Primary Website: mysuburbanlife.com
Avg Paid Circ: 3193
Avg Free Circ: 757
Audit By: Sworn/Estimate/Non-Audited
Audit Date: 10.06.2019
Personnel: Katie Sherman (Marketing Dir.); Maureen Ringness (Major/Nat'l Accts./Grp. Sales Dir.); Ryan Wells (Gen. Mgr.); Laura Burke (Adv. Dir.)
Parent company (for newspapers): Shaw Media

ADVANTAGE NEWS - EDWARDSVILLE

Street address 1: 235 - A E Alton Square Mall Dr
Street address city: Alton
Street address state: IL
Zip/Postal code: 62002

General Phone: (618) 463-0612
General Fax: (618) 463-0733
Editorial Fax: (888) 532-4111
General/National Adv. E-mail: contactus@todaysadvantage.com
Display Adv. E-mail: contactus@todaysadvantage.com
Editorial e-mail: news@todaysadvantage.com
Primary Website: advantagenews.com
Year Established: 1986
Avg Free Circ: 38098
Audit By: Sworn/Estimate/Non-Audited
Audit Date: 10.06.2019
Personnel: Eric McRoy (President)

ADVANTAGE NEWS - GRANITE CITY

Street address 1: 1000 E Homer Adams Pkwy
Street address city: Godfrey
Street address state: IL
Zip/Postal code: 62035
General Phone: (618) 462-0612
General Fax: (618) 463-0733
Editorial Fax: (800) 532-4441
General/National Adv. E-mail: ericmcroy@advantagenews.com
Display Adv. E-mail: erinspain@advantagenews.com
Editorial e-mail: fredpollard@advantagenews.com
Primary Website: advantagenews.com
Year Established: 2001
Avg Free Circ: 18560
Audit By: Sworn/Estimate/Non-Audited
Audit Date: 10.06.2019
Personnel: Eric McRoy (VP); Fred Pollard (Ed.); Leigh McRoy (Office Mgr.); Erin Spain (Adv.); Angie Fulgham (Prod. Mgr.); Missy Long (Creat. Dir.)
Parent company (for newspapers): Rex Encore

ADVANTAGE NEWS-RIVERBEND

Street address 1: 1000 W Homer Adams Pkwy
Street address city: Godfrey
Street address state: IL
Zip/Postal code: 62035
General Phone: (618) 463-0612
General Fax: (618) 463-0733
General/National Adv. E-mail: ericmcroy@advantagenews.com
Display Adv. E-mail: erinspain@advantagenews.com
Editorial e-mail: fredpollard@advantagenews.com
Primary Website: advantagenews.com
Mthly Avg Views: 124061
Mthly Avg Unique Visitors: 29605
Year Established: 1986
Avg Free Circ: 38905
Audit By: Sworn/Estimate/Non-Audited
Audit Date: 10.06.2019
Personnel: Eric McRoy (VP, Rex Encore); Fred Pollard (Mng. Ed.); Erin Spain (Adv. Sales)
Parent company (for newspapers): Rex Encore

ARCOLA RECORD-HERALD

Street address 1: 118 E Main St
Street address city: Arcola
Street address state: IL
Zip/Postal code: 61910-1435
General Phone: (217) 268-4950
General Fax: (217) 268-4938
General/National Adv. E-mail: slackpub@consolidated.net
Primary Website: arcolarecordherald.com
Avg Paid Circ: 2200
Audit By: Sworn/Estimate/Non-Audited
Audit Date: 30.09.2017
Personnel: Chris Slack (Pub., Ed.)

ARGUS-SENTINEL

Street address 1: 140 S Prairie St
Street address city: Galesburg
Street address state: IL
Zip/Postal code: 61401-4605
General Phone: (309) 462-5758
General Fax: (309) 462-3221
General/National Adv. E-mail: argus@abingdon.net
Primary Website: facebook.com/abingdonargussentinel
Year Established: 1867
Avg Paid Circ: 1134
Avg Free Circ: 7
Audit By: Sworn/Estimate/Non-Audited
Audit Date: 10.06.2019
Personnel: Lynne Campbell (Pub.); Jane Hasley (Adv. Mgr); Lisa Tast (Adv. Mgr.); Deb Fowlks (Ed.); Deb Robinson (Ed.)
Parent company (for newspapers): CherryRoad Media

ARLINGTON HEIGHTS POST

Street address 1: 160 N. Stetson Avenue
Street address city: Chicago
Street address state: IL
Zip/Postal code: 60601
General Phone: (866) 399-0537
General Fax: (312) 222-2598
Advertising Phone: (866) 399-0537
Editorial Phone: (312) 222-3429
Editorial Fax: (312) 222-2598
General/National Adv. E-mail: jmcdermott@tribpub.com
Display Adv. E-mail: jmcdermott@tribpub.com
Editorial e-mail: pjurik@chicagotribune.com
Primary Website: chicagotribune.com/suburbs/arlington-heights
Year Established: 1912
Avg Paid Circ: 883
Audit By: Sworn/Estimate/Non-Audited
Audit Date: 10.06.2019
Personnel: Ed Rooney (Display Adv. Mgr.); Steve Walzer (Regl./Nat'l Adv. Mgr.); David Perham (Circ. Dir.); Kathy Catrambone (Bureau Chief); Robert Loerzel (Ed.)
Parent company (for newspapers): Tribune Publishing, Inc.

ARLINGTON HEIGHTS/BUFFALO GROVE/ROLLING MEADOWS/ WHEELING JOURNAL

Street address 1: 622 Graceland Ave
Street address city: Des Plaines
Street address state: IL
Zip/Postal code: 60016-4519
General Phone: (847) 299-5511
General Fax: (847) 298-8549
General/National Adv. E-mail: journalads@journal-topics.info
Editorial e-mail: journalnews@journal-topics.info
Primary Website: journal-topics.com
Audit By: Sworn/Estimate/Non-Audited
Audit Date: 10.06.2019
Personnel: Rick Wessell (Managing Ed.); Robert Wessell (Mktg. Mgr.); Todd Wessell (Ed./Pub.)

ARTHUR GRAPHIC CLARION

Street address 1: 113 E Illinois St
Street address city: Arthur
Street address state: IL
Zip/Postal code: 61911-1331
General Phone: (217) 543-2151
General Fax: (217) 543-2152
General/National Adv. E-mail: info@thearthurgraphic.com
Primary Website: thearthurgraphic.com
Audit By: Sworn/Estimate/Non-Audited
Audit Date: 10.06.2019
Personnel: Roger Borham (Ed.)
Parent company (for newspapers): The Miami Herald Publishing Co.

ASHLEY NEWS

Street address 1: 9 N Division St
Street address city: Du Quoin
Street address state: IL
Zip/Postal code: 62832-1405
General Phone: (618) 542-2133
General Fax: (618) 542-2726
General/National Adv. E-mail: dqnews@verizon.net
Primary Website: duquoin.com
Year Established: 1895
Avg Paid Circ: 85
Avg Free Circ: 10
Audit By: Sworn/Estimate/Non-Audited
Audit Date: 10.06.2019
Personnel: Craig Smith (Adv. Mgr.); John Croessman (Mng. Ed.)
Parent company (for newspapers): CherryRoad Media

ASHTON GAZETTE

Street address 1: 813 Main St
Street address city: Ashton
Street address state: IL
Zip/Postal code: 61006-9258
General Phone: (815) 453-2551
General Fax: (815) 453-2422
Editorial e-mail: monetta@ashtongazette.com
Primary Website: ashtongazette.com
Audit By: Sworn/Estimate/Non-Audited
Audit Date: 10.06.2019
Personnel: Monetta Young (Ed.); Mike Feltes (Gen. Mgr.)
Parent company (for newspapers): San Luis Valley Publishing

AUSTIN WEEKLY NEWS

Street address 1: 141 S Oak Park Ave
Street address 2: Ste 1
Street address city: Oak Park
Street address state: IL
Zip/Postal code: 60302-2972
General Phone: (773) 626-6332
General Fax: (708) 524-0447
General/National Adv. E-mail: dawn@austinweeklynews.com
Display Adv. E-mail: classifieds@austinweeklynews.com
Editorial e-mail: circulation@wjinc.com
Primary Website: austinweeklynews.com
Avg Free Circ: 12000
Audit By: Sworn/Estimate/Non-Audited
Audit Date: 10.06.2019
Personnel: Dan Haley (Pub.); Terry Dean (Ed.)

BARRINGTON COURIER-REVIEW

Street address 1: 3701 W Lake Ave
Street address city: Glenview
Street address state: IL
Zip/Postal code: 60026-1216
General Phone: (847) 486-7300
General Fax: (312) 222-2598
Advertising Phone: (866) 399-0537
Editorial Phone: (312) 321-2307
Editorial Fax: (312) 222-2598
General/National Adv. E-mail: display@pioneerlocal.com
Display Adv. E-mail: classifieds@stmedianetwork.com
Editorial e-mail: pjurik@chicagotribune.com
Primary Website: pioneerlocal.com
Year Established: 1889
Avg Paid Circ: 242
Audit By: Sworn/Estimate/Non-Audited
Audit Date: 10.06.2019
Personnel: Phil Jurik (Ed.); R. Bruce Dold (Pub./Ed.-in-Chief); Peter Kendall (Mng. Ed.); Jill McDermott (VP of Adv.); Maggie Wartik (Gen. Mgr. of Suburban Weeklies)
Parent company (for newspapers): Tribune Publishing, Inc.

BATAVIA CHRONICLE

Street address 1: 333 N Randall Rd
Street address 2: Ste 1
Street address city: St Charles
Street address state: IL
Zip/Postal code: 60174-1500
General Phone: (630) 232-9222
Editorial e-mail: editorial@kcchronicle.com
Primary Website: kcchronicle.com
Avg Paid Circ: 1532
Avg Free Circ: 220
Audit By: Sworn/Estimate/Non-Audited
Audit Date: 10.06.2019
Personnel: Sherri Dauskurdas (Ed.); Ryan Wells (GM/ Adv. Mgr.)
Parent company (for newspapers): Shaw Media

BEECHER CITY JOURNAL

Street address 1: 104 S Charles St
Street address city: Beecher City
Street address state: IL
Zip/Postal code: 62414-1137
General Phone: (618) 487-5634
General Fax: (618) 487-5180
General/National Adv. E-mail: news@beechercityjournal.com
Display Adv. E-mail: news@beechercityjournal.com
Classified Adv. e-mail: news@beechercityjournal.com
Editorial e-mail: news@beechercityjournal.com
Year Established: 1915
Avg Paid Circ: 1200
Audit By: Sworn/Estimate/Non-Audited
Audit Date: 23.10.2019
Personnel: P.J. Ryan (Pub.); Cherie Ryan (Mng. Ed.)

BENSENVILLE PRESS

Street address 1: 1101 31st St
Street address 2: Ste 100
Street address city: Downers Grove
Street address state: IL
Zip/Postal code: 60515-5581
General Phone: (630) 368-1100
General Fax: (630) 969-0228
Editorial Phone: (630) 368-1144
General/National Adv. E-mail: celebrations@mysuburbanlife.com
Editorial e-mail: letters@mysuburbanlife.com
Primary Website: mysuburbanlife.com
Avg Paid Circ: 296
Avg Free Circ: 0
Audit By: Sworn/Estimate/Non-Audited
Audit Date: 10.06.2019
Personnel: Brad Hanahan (Class Advt Mgr); Dave Lemery (Ed)

BERWYN SUBURBAN LIFE

Street address 1: 2001 Butterfield Rd
Street address 2: Ste 105
Street address city: Downers Grove
Street address state: IL
Zip/Postal code: 60515
General Phone: (844) 368-1100
General/National Adv. E-mail: nfossmeyer@shawmedia.com
Display Adv. E-mail: nfossmeyer@shawmedia.com
Editorial e-mail: brakow@shawmedia.com
Primary Website: mysuburbanlife.com
Avg Paid Circ: 3193
Avg Free Circ: 757
Audit By: AAM
Audit Date: 31.03.2018
Personnel: J. Tom Shaw (Pub.); Ryan Wells (Bus. Mgr.); Bill Korbel; Bob Rakow (News Ed.)
Parent company (for newspapers): Shaw Media

BEVERLY NEWS

Street address 1: 3840 147th St
Street address city: Midlothian
Street address state: IL
Zip/Postal code: 60445-3452
General Phone: (708) 388-2425
General Fax: (708) 385-7811
General/National Adv. E-mail: spressnews@aol.com
Year Established: 1948
Avg Paid Circ: 4080
Audit By: Sworn/Estimate/Non-Audited
Audit Date: 10.06.2019
Personnel: Luicinda Lysen (Pub./Co-owners); Linnea Lysen-Gavin (Ed./Co-Owners)
Parent company (for newspapers): Southwest Messenger Press, Inc.

BLUE MOUND LEADER

Street address 1: 205 W Niles St
Street address city: Blue Mound
Street address state: IL
Zip/Postal code: 62513
General Phone: (217) 692-2323
General Fax: (217) 692-2323
General/National Adv. E-mail: bmleader1@yahoo.com
Primary Website: bluemoundleader.com
Year Established: 1886
Avg Paid Circ: 850
Avg Free Circ: 25
Audit By: Sworn/Estimate/Non-Audited
Audit Date: 10.06.2019
Personnel: Cynthia L. Ervin (Pub./Ed.)

BOLINGBROOK SUBURBAN LIFE

Street address 1: 1101 31st St
Street address 2: Ste 260
Street address city: Downers Grove
Street address state: IL
Zip/Postal code: 60515-5585
General Phone: (630) 368-1100
General Fax: (630) 969-0228
Advertising Phone: (630) 427-6213
Advertising Fax: (630) 969-0228
Editorial Phone: (630) 427-6252
Editorial Fax: (630) 969-0228

General/National Adv. E-mail: nshannon@shawmedia.com
Display Adv. E-mail: sbissell@shawmedia.com
Editorial e-mail: rterrell@shawmedia.com
Primary Website: mysuburbanlife.com
Avg Paid Circ: 5256
Audit By: Sworn/Estimate/Non-Audited
Audit Date: 10.06.2019
Personnel: J. Tom Shaw (Pub.); Katie Sherman (Marketing Dir.); Maureen Ringness (Major/Nat'l Accts./Grp. Sales Dir.); Ryan Wells

BOONE COUNTY JOURNAL

Street address 1: 419 S State St
Street address 2: Suite A
Street address city: Belvidere
Street address state: IL
Zip/Postal code: 61008-3750
General Phone: (815) 544-4430
General Fax: (815) 544-4330
General/National Adv. E-mail: info@boonecountyjournal.com
Primary Website: boonecountyjournal.com
Year Established: 1996
Avg Free Circ: 10000
Audit By: Sworn/Estimate/Non-Audited
Audit Date: 10.06.2019
Personnel: David Larson (Owner/Pub.); James Middleton (Ed.)

BRIDGEPORT NEWS

Street address 1: 3506 S Halsted St
Street address 2: Ste 1
Street address city: Chicago
Street address state: IL
Zip/Postal code: 60609-1605
General Phone: (773) 927-0025
General Fax: (773) 337-6995
General/National Adv. E-mail: jrbridgeportnews@aol.com
Primary Website: bridgeportnews.net
Year Established: 1939
Avg Free Circ: 25300
Audit By: Sworn/Estimate/Non-Audited
Audit Date: 10.06.2019
Personnel: Joseph Feldman (Pub.); Janice Racinowski (Ed/Mgr)

BRIDGEVIEW INDEPENDENT

Street address 1: 3840 147th St
Street address city: Midlothian
Street address state: IL
Zip/Postal code: 60445-3452
General Phone: (708) 388-2425
General Fax: (708) 385-7811
General/National Adv. E-mail: spressnews@aol.com
Display Adv. E-mail: spressnews@aol.com
Editorial e-mail: spressnews@aol.com
Primary Website: southwestmessengerpress.com
Avg Paid Circ: 4500
Avg Free Circ: 500
Audit By: Sworn/Estimate/Non-Audited
Audit Date: 10.06.2019
Personnel: Carol Beymer (Adv. Mgr.); Margaret D. Lysen (Ed.)
Parent company (for newspapers): Southwest Messenger Press, Inc.

BRIGHTON PARK - MCKINLEY PARK LIFE

Street address 1: 2949 W Pope John Paul II Dr
Street address city: Chicago
Street address state: IL
Zip/Postal code: 60632-2554
General Phone: (773) 523-3663
General Fax: (773) 523-3983
General/National Adv. E-mail: brightonparklife@aol.com
Primary Website: brightonparklife.com
Year Established: 1932
Avg Free Circ: 21000
Audit By: Sworn/Estimate/Non-Audited
Audit Date: 10.06.2019
Personnel: Albert H. Silinski (Circ. Mgr.); Donna Rooney (Ed.)

BROWN COUNTY DEMOCRAT MESSAGE

Street address 1: 123 W MAIN ST
Street address city: Mt Sterling
Street address state: IL
Zip/Postal code: 62353-1223
General Phone: (217) 773-3371
General Fax: (217) 773-3369
General/National Adv. E-mail: thedmads@yahoo.com
Display Adv. E-mail: thedmads@yahoo.com
Classified Adv. e-mail: thedmads@yahoo.com
Editorial e-mail: thedmnews@yahoo.com
Year Established: 1871
Avg Paid Circ: 2200
Audit By: Sworn/Estimate/Non-Audited
Audit Date: 10.06.2019
Personnel: Robin Oitker (Publisher); Dan Long (Ed.)
Parent company (for newspapers): Coulson Publications

BUFFALO GROVE COUNTRYSIDE

Street address 1: 160 N. Stetson Avenue
Street address city: Chicago
Street address state: IL
Zip/Postal code: 60601
General Phone: (847) 486-7462
General Fax: (847) 486-7434
Editorial Phone: (312) 321-2307
General/National Adv. E-mail: advertisinginfo@suntimes.com
Display Adv. E-mail: classifieds@stmedianetwork.com
Editorial e-mail: cberman@pioneerlocal.com
Primary Website: buffalogrove.chicagotribune.com
Year Established: 1912
Avg Paid Circ: 970
Audit By: AAM
Audit Date: 31.03.2017
Personnel: David Perham (Circ. Dir.); Kathy Catrambone (Bureau Chief); Mary Hendricks (Production Ed.); R. Bruce Dold (Pub./Ed.-in-Chief); Phil Jurik (Ed.); Jill McDermott (VP of Adv.); Maggie Wartik (Gen. Mgr. of Suburban Weeklies); Peter Kendall (Mng. Ed.)
Parent company (for newspapers): Tribune Publishing, Inc.

BUGLE NEWSPAPERS

Street address 1: 23856 W Andrew Rd
Street address city: Plainfield
Street address state: IL
Zip/Postal code: 60585-8770
General Phone: (815) 436-2431
General Fax: (815) 436-2592
General/National Adv. E-mail: sholmgren@buglenewspapers.com
Display Adv. E-mail: linda@enterprisepublications.com
Editorial e-mail: news@enterprisepublications.com
Primary Website: buglenewspapers.com
Year Established: 1887
Avg Paid Circ: 7100
Avg Free Circ: 32600
Audit By: Sworn/Estimate/Non-Audited
Audit Date: 10.06.2019
Personnel: Andrew Samaan (GM/ Vice Pres. Adv./Mktg.); Mark Gregory (News Dir.)
Parent company (for newspapers): Voyager Media Publications

BURBANK-STICKNEY INDEPENDENT

Street address 1: 3840 147th St
Street address city: Midlothian
Street address state: IL
Zip/Postal code: 60445-3452
General Phone: (708) 388-2425
General Fax: (708) 385-7811
Editorial e-mail: spressnews@aol.com
Primary Website: southwestmessengerpress.com
Avg Paid Circ: 6110
Audit By: Sworn/Estimate/Non-Audited
Audit Date: 10.06.2019
Personnel: Margaret Lysen (Pub.); Lucinda Lysen (Ed.)
Parent company (for newspapers): Southwest Messenger Press, Inc.

BURBANK-STICKNEY INDEPENDENT - SCOTTSDALE EDITION

Street address 1: 3840 147th St
Street address city: Midlothian
Street address state: IL
Zip/Postal code: 60445-3452
General Phone: (708) 388-2425
General Fax: (708) 385-7811
General/National Adv. E-mail: info@southwestmessengerpress.com
Display Adv. E-mail: info@southwestmessengerpress.com
Editorial e-mail: info@southwestmessengerpress.com
Primary Website: southwestmessengerpress.com
Avg Paid Circ: 5975
Audit By: Sworn/Estimate/Non-Audited
Audit Date: 10.06.2019
Personnel: Margaret Lysen (Pub.)
Parent company (for newspapers): Southwest Messenger Press, Inc.

BUREAU COUNTY REPUBLICAN

Street address 1: 800 Ace Rd
Street address city: Princeton
Street address state: IL
Zip/Postal code: 61356-2049
General Phone: (815) 875-4461
General Fax: (815) 875-1235
General/National Adv. E-mail: advertising@bcrnews.com
Display Adv. E-mail: classified@bcrnews.com
Editorial e-mail: news@bcrnews.com
Primary Website: bcrnews.com
Year Established: 1847
Audit By: Sworn/Estimate/Non-Audited
Audit Date: 10.06.2019
Personnel: Sam R. Fisher (Pub./Gen. Mgr.); Sandy Pistole (Adv. Mgr.); Terri Simon (Ed.); Abbie Clark (Circ. Mgr.)
Parent company (for newspapers): Shaw Media

BUREAU VALLEY CHIEF

Street address 1: 108 W Main St
Street address city: Tiskilwa
Street address state: IL
Zip/Postal code: 61368-9652
General Phone: (815) 646-4731
General Fax: (815) 646-4376
General/National Adv. E-mail: bvchief@comcast.net
Year Established: 1875
Avg Paid Circ: 1100
Avg Free Circ: 200
Audit By: Sworn/Estimate/Non-Audited
Audit Date: 10.06.2019
Personnel: John Murphy (Adv. Mgr.); Ginger Murphy (Ed.)

CALHOUN NEWS-HERALD

Street address 1: 310 S County Rd
Street address city: Hardin
Street address state: IL
Zip/Postal code: 62047-4414
General Phone: (618) 576-2345
General Fax: (630) 206-0320
Advertising Phone: (618) 498-1234
General/National Adv. E-mail: jkallal@campbellpublications.net
Display Adv. E-mail: jkallal@campbellpublications.net
Editorial e-mail: cnhnews@campbellpublications.net
Primary Website: calhounnewsherald.com
Year Established: 1872
Avg Paid Circ: 2000
Avg Free Circ: 50
Audit By: Sworn/Estimate/Non-Audited
Audit Date: 10.06.2019
Personnel: Julie Boren (Pub.); Robert Lyons (regional editori)
Parent company (for newspapers): Campbell Publishing Co., Inc.

CAMBRIDGE CHRONICLE IN ILLINOIS

Street address 1: 119 W Exchange St
Street address city: Cambridge
Street address state: IL
Zip/Postal code: 61238-1158
General Phone: (309) 944-2119
General Fax: (309) 944-5615
General/National Adv. E-mail: ewalker@geneseorepublic.com
Display Adv. E-mail: kclementz@geneseorepublic.com
Primary Website: cambridgechron.com
Year Established: 1858
Avg Paid Circ: 1050
Audit By: Sworn/Estimate/Non-Audited
Audit Date: 10.06.2019
Personnel: Dee Evans (Pub.); Marnie Eggan (Circ. Mgr.); Mindy Carls (Mng. Ed.)
Parent company (for newspapers): CherryRoad Media

CAMP POINT JOURNAL

Street address 1: 202 E State St
Street address city: Camp Point
Street address state: IL
Zip/Postal code: 62320-1114
General Phone: (217) 593-6515
General Fax: (217) 593-7720
General/National Adv. E-mail: lisa@elliott-publishing.com
Editorial e-mail: gina@elliott-publishing.com
Primary Website: elliott-publishing.com
Year Established: 1873
Avg Paid Circ: 970
Audit By: Sworn/Estimate/Non-Audited
Audit Date: 10.06.2019
Personnel: James W. Elliott (Pres.); Marcia Elliott (Gen. Mgr.); Gina Maddox (Bookkeeping); Newell Lisa (Advertising)
Parent company (for newspapers): Elliott Publishing, Inc.

CARBONDALE TIMES

Street address 1: 2015 W. Main St.
Street address city: Carbondale
Street address state: IL
Zip/Postal code: 62901
General Phone: (618) 549-2799
Advertising Phone: (618) 549-2799
Editorial Phone: (618) 549-2799
General/National Adv. E-mail: kgordon@carbondaletimes.com
Editorial e-mail: gritter@localsouthernnews.com
Primary Website: carbondaletimes.com
Year Established: 1997
Avg Free Circ: 9000
Audit By: Sworn/Estimate/Non-Audited
Audit Date: 10.06.2019
Personnel: Geoffrey Ritter (Ed.)
Parent company (for newspapers): Paddock Publications

CAROL STREAM SUBURBAN LIFE

Street address 1: 2001 Butterfield Rd Suite 105
Street address 2: Suite 100
Street address city: Downers Grove
Street address state: IL
Zip/Postal code: 60515
General Phone: (630) 368-1100
General Fax: (630) 969-0228
Advertising Phone: (630) 427-6213
Editorial Phone: (630) 427-6248
Editorial Fax: (630) 969-0228
General/National Adv. E-mail: bkorbel@shawmedia.com
Display Adv. E-mail: bhanahan@shawmedia.com
Editorial e-mail: aschier@shawmedia.com
Primary Website: mysuburbanlife.com
Avg Paid Circ: 121
Avg Free Circ: 24
Audit By: AAM
Audit Date: 31.03.2018
Personnel: J. Tom Shaw (Pub); Katie Sherman (Marketing Dir); Anna Schier (Ed.); Maureen Ringness (Major/Nat'l Accts./Grp. Sales Dir.); Ryan Wells
Parent company (for newspapers): Shaw Media

CARROLL COUNTY MIRROR-DEMOCRAT

Street address 1: 308 N Main St
Street address city: Mount Carroll
Street address state: IL
Zip/Postal code: 61053-1024

General Phone: (815) 244-2411
General Fax: (815) 244-2965
Advertising Phone: (815) 244-2411
Advertising Fax: (815) 244-2965
Editorial Phone: (815) 244-2411
Editorial Fax: (815) 244-2965
General/National Adv. E-mail: mirrordem@grics.net
Display Adv. E-mail: mirrordem@grics.net
Editorial e-mail: mirrordem@grics.net
Primary Website: mirrordemocrat.com
Year Established: 1860
Avg Paid Circ: 4000
Avg Free Circ: 8000
Audit By: Sworn/Estimate/Non-Audited
Audit Date: 10.06.2019
Personnel: Robert (Bob) Watson (Ed./Pub./Owner); Mary Maszk (Office/Circ. Mgr.); Pam Villalobos (Times-Journal Office Mgr./Adv. Rep.); Angie Field (Reporter/ Adv. Rep.); Janice Smith (Graphic Designer)
Parent company (for newspapers): Mirror-Democrat Co.; Northwestern Illinois Dispatch; Savanna Times-Journal

CARROLL COUNTY REVIEW

Street address 1: 809 W Main St
Street address city: Thomson
Street address state: IL
Zip/Postal code: 61285-7776
General Phone: (815) 259-2131
General Fax: (815) 259-3226
Primary Website: gocarrollcounty.com
Year Established: 1863
Avg Paid Circ: 2066
Avg Free Circ: 130
Audit By: Sworn/Estimate/Non-Audited
Audit Date: 10.06.2019
Personnel: Jonathan K. Whitney (Pub.)

CASEY WESTFIELD REPORTER

Street address 1: 610 Archer Ave
Street address city: Marshall
Street address state: IL
Zip/Postal code: 62441-1268
General Phone: (217) 826-3600
General Fax: (217) 826-3700
Advertising Phone: (217) 932-5211
Advertising Fax: (217) 826-3700
Editorial Phone: (217) 826-5487
Editorial Fax: (217) 826-3700
General/National Adv. E-mail: stromnewspapers@gmail.com
Display Adv. E-mail: strohmnews@joink.com
Editorial e-mail: stromnewspapers@gmail.com
Primary Website: strohmnews.com
Year Established: 1996
Avg Paid Circ: 1900
Avg Free Circ: 7416
Audit By: Sworn/Estimate/Non-Audited
Audit Date: 10.06.2019
Personnel: Gary Strohm (Pub.); Melody Strohm (Pub.)

CASS COUNTY STAR-GAZETTE

Street address 1: 1210 Wall St
Street address city: Beardstown
Street address state: IL
Zip/Postal code: 62618-2327
General Phone: (217) 323-1010
General Fax: (217) 323-1644
General/National Adv. E-mail: stargazette@casscomm.com
Primary Website: beardstownnewspapers.com
Year Established: 1844
Avg Paid Circ: 640
Audit By: Sworn/Estimate/Non-Audited
Audit Date: 10.06.2019
Personnel: Jamila Khalil (Pub.); Patricia Wellenkamp (Adv. Mgr.)

CHATHAM CLARION

Street address 1: 110 North Fifth Street
Street address city: Auburn
Street address state: IL
Zip/Postal code: 62615
General Phone: 217-438-6155
General Fax: (217) 438-6156
Advertising Phone: (217) 438-6155
Advertising Fax: (217) 438-6156
General/National Adv. E-mail: chathamclarion@royell.org
Display Adv. E-mail: southco@royell.org
Classified Adv. e-mail: southco@royell.org
Editorial e-mail: chathamclarion@royell.org
Primary Website: southcountypublications.net
Year Established: 1963
Avg Paid Circ: 1800
Audit By: Sworn/Estimate/Non-Audited
Audit Date: 10.06.2019
Personnel: Joe Michelich; Connie Michelich (Adv. Mgr.); Joe Pritchett (Ed.)
Parent company (for newspapers): South County Publications

CHICAGO RIDGE CITIZEN

Street address 1: 3840 147th St
Street address city: Midlothian
Street address state: IL
Zip/Postal code: 60445-3452
General Phone: (708) 388-2425
General Fax: (708) 385-7811
General/National Adv. E-mail: info@southwestmessengerpress.com
Display Adv. E-mail: info@southwestmessengerpress.com
Editorial e-mail: info@southwestmessengerpress.com
Primary Website: southwestmessengerpress.com
Avg Paid Circ: 2915
Avg Free Circ: 600
Audit By: Sworn/Estimate/Non-Audited
Audit Date: 10.06.2019
Personnel: Margaret Lysen (Pub.); Lori Taylor (Ed.)
Parent company (for newspapers): Southwest Messenger Press, Inc.

CHICAGO'S NORTHWEST SIDE PRESS

Street address 1: 4937 N Milwaukee Ave
Street address city: Chicago
Street address state: IL
Zip/Postal code: 60630-2114
General Phone: (773) 286-6100
General Fax: (773) 286-8151
General/National Adv. E-mail: nadignewspapers@aol.com
Display Adv. E-mail: nadignewspapers@aol.com
Editorial e-mail: nadignewspapers@aol.com
Primary Website: nadignewspapers.com
Year Established: 1940
Avg Free Circ: 30000
Audit By: Sworn/Estimate/Non-Audited
Audit Date: 10.06.2019
Personnel: Brian Nadig (Pub.); Glenn Nadig (Pub.); Randy Erickson (Ed.)

CHILLICOTHE TIMES-BULLETIN

Street address 1: PO Box 9426
Street address city: Peoria
Street address state: IL
Zip/Postal code: 61612-9426
General Phone: (309) 274-2185
General Fax: (309) 686-3101
Advertising Phone: (309) 274-2185
Advertising Fax: (309) 686-3122
Editorial Phone: (309) 686-3016
Editorial Fax: (309) 686-3101
General/National Adv. E-mail: mgillespie@timestoday.com
Display Adv. E-mail: lsmithbrown@timestoday.com
Editorial e-mail: ctb@timestoday.com
Primary Website: chillicothetimesbulletin.com
Year Established: 1883
Avg Free Circ: 3220
Audit By: Sworn/Estimate/Non-Audited
Audit Date: 10.06.2019
Personnel: Ken Mauser (Pres. / Pub.); David Adams (Pub.); Tom Kelling (Display Adv. Mgr.); Sandy Norbits (Adv. Rep.); Jeanette Brickner (Exec. Ed.); Tim Rosenberg (Mng. Ed.)
Parent company (for newspapers): CherryRoad Media

CHRISMAN LEADER

Street address 1: 118 E. Jefferson Ave.
Street address city: Chrisman
Street address state: IL
Zip/Postal code: 61924
General Phone: (217) 269-4166
General/National Adv. E-mail: chrismanleader@insightbb.com
Primary Website: facebook.com/thechrismanleader
Avg Paid Circ: 1000
Audit By: Sworn/Estimate/Non-Audited
Audit Date: 10.06.2019
Personnel: Alice Lientz (Owner/Manager)

CISSNA PARK NEWS

Street address 1: 119 W Garfield Ave
Street address city: Cissna Park
Street address state: IL
Zip/Postal code: 60924-6125
General Phone: (815) 457-2245
General Fax: (815) 457-3245
General/National Adv. E-mail: rickbaier@yahoo.com
Primary Website: No Website
Year Established: 1958
Audit By: Sworn/Estimate/Non-Audited
Audit Date: 10.06.2019
Personnel: Rick A. Baier (Pub.)

CLAY COUNTY REPUBLICAN

Street address 1: 126 Church St
Street address city: Louisville
Street address state: IL
Zip/Postal code: 62858
General Phone: (618) 665-3135
General Fax: (618) 665-3135
General/National Adv. E-mail: ccrnews@wabash.net
Display Adv. E-mail: ccrnews@wabash.net
Editorial e-mail: ccrnews@wabash.net
Primary Website: No Website
Avg Paid Circ: 2200
Avg Free Circ: 95
Audit By: Sworn/Estimate/Non-Audited
Audit Date: 10.06.2019
Personnel: Lindell Smith (Ed.)

CLINTON COUNTY NEWS

Street address 1: 314 E Church St
Street address 2: Ste 1
Street address city: Mascoutah
Street address state: IL
Zip/Postal code: 62258-2100
General Phone: (618) 566-8282
General Fax: (618) 566-8283
General/National Adv. E-mail: ccn@cbnstl.com
Primary Website: heraldpubs.com
Avg Paid Circ: 1131
Audit By: Sworn/Estimate/Non-Audited
Audit Date: 10.06.2019
Personnel: Greg Hoskins (Pub.); Tam Rensing (Ed.)

CLINTON JOURNAL

Street address 1: 111 S Monroe St
Street address city: Clinton
Street address state: IL
Zip/Postal code: 61727-2057
General Phone: (217) 935-3171
General Fax: (217) 935-6086
General/National Adv. E-mail: kpyne@theclintonjournal.com
Display Adv. E-mail: kpyne@theclintonjournal.com
Editorial e-mail: gwoods@theclintonjournal.com
Primary Website: theclintonjournal.com
Avg Paid Circ: 1800
Avg Free Circ: 6600
Sat. Circulation Paid: 6500
Sat. Circulation Free: 6500
Audit By: Sworn/Estimate/Non-Audited
Audit Date: 10.06.2019
Personnel: Diane Robertson (Classified Adv. Mgr.); Gordon Woods (Gen. Mgr./Ed.); Katy O'Grady-Pyne; Susan Munoz (Sales Rep.)
Parent company (for newspapers): San Luis Valley Publishing

COAL COUNTRY TIMES

Street address 1: 125 E Main St
Street address city: Carlinville
Street address state: IL
Zip/Postal code: 62626-1726
General Phone: (217) 854-2534
General Fax: (217) 854-2535
General/National Adv. E-mail: mcednews@campbellpublications.net
Primary Website: enquirerdemocrat.com
Avg Paid Circ: 4100
Audit By: Sworn/Estimate/Non-Audited
Audit Date: 10.06.2019
Personnel: Julie Boren (Pub.)

COUNTY JOURNAL

Street address 1: 1101 E Pine St
Street address city: Percy
Street address state: IL
Zip/Postal code: 62272-1333
General Phone: (618) 497-8272
General Fax: (618) 497-2607
Advertising Phone: (618) 497-8272
Advertising Fax: (618) 497-2607
Editorial Phone: (618) 497-8272
Editorial Fax: (618) 497-2607
General/National Adv. E-mail: cjournal@egyptian.net
Display Adv. E-mail: cjournal@egyptian.net
Editorial e-mail: cjournal@egyptian.net
Primary Website: countyjournal.org
Year Established: 1980
Avg Paid Circ: 7000
Avg Free Circ: 75
Audit By: Sworn/Estimate/Non-Audited
Audit Date: 21.09.2021
Personnel: John Falkenhein (Adv. Mgr.); Larry Willis (Co-Pub.); Sarah Gordon; Kristin Anderson (Co-Owner); Gerald Willis (Co-Pub./Adv. Mgr.)
Parent company (for newspapers): Willis Publishing

COURIER

Street address 1: 100 Ford Ln
Street address city: Washington
Street address state: IL
Zip/Postal code: 61571-2668
General Phone: (309) 444-3139
General Fax: (309) 444-8505
General/National Adv. E-mail: joi67@mtco.com
Primary Website: courierpaper.com
Year Established: 1973
Avg Free Circ: 20000
Audit By: Sworn/Estimate/Non-Audited
Audit Date: 10.06.2019
Personnel: James Strauss (Pub.); Joi DeArmond (Ed.)

CROWN POINT STAR

Street address 1: 435 N Michigan Ave
Street address city: Chicago
Street address state: IL
Zip/Postal code: 60611-4066
General Phone: (866) 399-0537
General Fax: (312) 222-2598
Advertising Phone: (866) 399-0537
Advertising Fax: (312) 222-3232
Editorial Phone: (312) 222-3429
Editorial Fax: (312) 222-2598
General/National Adv. E-mail: jmcdermott@tribpub.com
Display Adv. E-mail: jmcdermott@tribpub.com
Editorial e-mail: pjurik@chicagotribune.com
Primary Website: chicagotribune.com/suburbs/post-tribune/crown-point
Year Established: 1871
Avg Paid Circ: 290
Audit By: Sworn/Estimate/Non-Audited
Audit Date: 10.06.2019
Personnel: Sue Medved (Adv. Consultant); Maggie Wartik (Gen. Mgr. of Suburban Weeklies); R. Bruce Dold (Pub./Ed.-in-Chief); Peter Kendall (Mng. Ed.); Phil Jurik (Ed.); Jill McDermott (VP of Adv.)
Parent company (for newspapers): Tribune Publishing, Inc.

DAILY UNION

Street address 1: 100 W Main St
Street address city: Shelbyville
Street address state: IL
Zip/Postal code: 62565-1652
General Phone: (217) 774-2161
General Fax: (217) 774-5732
Advertising Phone: (217) 774-2161
Advertising Fax: (217) 774-5732
Editorial Phone: (217) 774-2161
Editorial Fax: (217) 774-5732
General/National Adv. E-mail: publisher@shelbyvilledailyunion.com

Display Adv. E-mail: deanna.sickles@shelbyvilledailyunion.com
Editorial e-mail: news@shelbyvilledailyunion.com
Primary Website: shelbyvilledailyunion.com
Year Established: 1863
Avg Paid Circ: 4156
Audit By: Sworn/Estimate/Non-Audited
Audit Date: 10.06.2019
Personnel: Ryan Beitz (Circ. Mgr./Off. Mgr.); John Curtis (Sports Ed.); Deanna Sickles (Adv. Mgr); Darrell Lewis (Pub.); Jeff Long (Ed.)
Parent company (for newspapers): CNHI, LLC

DECATUR TRIBUNE

Street address 1: 132 S Water St
Street address 2: Ste 424
Street address city: Decatur
Street address state: IL
Zip/Postal code: 62523-6043
General Phone: (217) 422-9702
General Fax: (217) 422-7320
General/National Adv. E-mail: decaturtribune@aol.com
Display Adv. E-mail: decaturtribune@aol.com
Editorial e-mail: decaturtribune@aol.com
Primary Website: decaturtribune.com
Year Established: 1968
Avg Paid Circ: 7000
Avg Free Circ: 0
Audit By: Sworn/Estimate/Non-Audited
Audit Date: 10.06.2019
Personnel: Paul Osborne (Ed./Pub.)

DEERFIELD REVIEW

Street address 1: 160 N. Stetson Avenue
Street address city: Chicago
Street address state: IL
Zip/Postal code: 60601
General Phone: (866) 399-0537
General Fax: (312) 222-2598
Advertising Phone: (866) 399-0537
Editorial Phone: (312) 222-3429
Editorial Fax: (312) 222-2598
General/National Adv. E-mail: jmcdermott@tribpub.com
Display Adv. E-mail: jmcdermott@tribpub.com
Editorial e-mail: pjurik@chicagotribune.com
Primary Website: chicagotribune.com/suburbs/deerfield
Year Established: 1912
Avg Paid Circ: 655
Audit By: AAM
Audit Date: 31.03.2017
Personnel: Maggie Wartik (Gen. Mgr. of Suburban Weeklies); R. Bruce Dold (Pub./Ed.-in-Chief); Peter Kendall (Mng. Ed.); Phil Jurik (Ed.)
Parent company (for newspapers): Tribune Publishing, Inc.

DES PLAINES JOURNAL

Street address 1: 622 Graceland Ave
Street address city: Des Plaines
Street address state: IL
Zip/Postal code: 60016-4519
General Phone: (847) 299-5511
General Fax: (847) 298-8549
General/National Adv. E-mail: journalnews@mail.com
Primary Website: journal-topics.com/news/des_plaines
Year Established: 1930
Audit By: Sworn/Estimate/Non-Audited
Audit Date: 10.06.2019
Personnel: Todd Wessell (Managing Ed.); Rick Wessell (Adv. Dir.); Robert Wessell (Classified Mgr.)

DOWNERS GROVE SUBURBAN LIFE

Street address 1: 2001 Butterfield Rd Suite 105
Street address 2: Ste 260
Street address city: Downers Grove
Street address state: IL
Zip/Postal code: 60515
General Phone: (630) 368-1100
General Fax: (630) 969-0228
Advertising Phone: (630) 427-6213
Editorial Phone: (630) 427-6252
Editorial Fax: (630) 969-0228
General/National Adv. E-mail: nshannon@shawmedia.com
Display Adv. E-mail: sbissell@shawmedia.com
Editorial e-mail: rterrell@shawmedia.com
Primary Website: mysuburbanlife.com
Year Established: 1883
Avg Paid Circ: 3193
Avg Free Circ: 7173
Audit By: AAM
Audit Date: 31.03.2018
Personnel: J. Tom Shaw (Pub.); Katie Sherman (Marketing Dir.); Ryan Terrell (Ed.); Maureen Ringness (Major/Nat'l Accts./Grp. Sales Dir.); Ryan Wells
Parent company (for newspapers): Shaw Media

EAST PEORIA TIMES-COURIER

Street address 1: 1 News Plz
Street address city: Peoria
Street address state: IL
Zip/Postal code: 61643-0001
General Phone: (309) 692-6600
Editorial Fax: (309) 691-7857
General/National Adv. E-mail: eptc@timestoday.com
Primary Website: eastpeoriatimescourier.com
Year Established: 1927
Avg Paid Circ: 1872
Audit By: Sworn/Estimate/Non-Audited
Audit Date: 10.06.2019
Personnel: Jeanette Kendall (Ed.)
Parent company (for newspapers): CherryRoad Media

ELK GROVE JOURNAL

Street address 1: 622 Graceland Ave
Street address city: Des Plaines
Street address state: IL
Zip/Postal code: 60016-4519
General Phone: (847) 299-5511
General Fax: (847) 298-8549
General/National Adv. E-mail: journalnews@mail.com
Primary Website: journal-topics.com/news/des_plaines
Audit By: Sworn/Estimate/Non-Audited
Audit Date: 10.06.2019
Personnel: Robert Wessell (Classified Mgr.); Todd Wessell (Managing Ed.); Rick Wessell (Adv. Dir.)

ELMHURST SUBURBAN LIFE

Street address 1: 2001 Butterfield Rd Suite 105
Street address 2: Ste 105
Street address city: Downers Grove
Street address state: IL
Zip/Postal code: 60515
General Phone: (630) 368-1100
General Fax: (630) 969-0228
Advertising Phone: (630) 427-6213
Editorial Phone: (630) 427-6270
Editorial Fax: (630) 969-0228
General/National Adv. E-mail: bkorbel@shawmedia.com
Display Adv. E-mail: bhanahan@shawmedia.com
Editorial e-mail: dgood@shawmedia.com
Primary Website: mysuburbanlife.com
Avg Paid Circ: 561
Avg Free Circ: 3927
Audit By: AAM
Audit Date: 31.03.2018
Personnel: J. Tom Shaw (Pub.); Katie Sherman (Marketing Dir.); David Good (Ed.); Maureen Ringness (Major/Nat'l Accts./Grp. Sales Dir.); Ryan Wells
Parent company (for newspapers): Shaw Media

ELMWOOD PARK LEAVES

Street address 1: 435 N Michigan Ave
Street address city: Chicago
Street address state: IL
Zip/Postal code: 60611-4066
General Phone: (312) 321-2028
General Fax: (847) 486-7454
Editorial Phone: (312) 321-2864
General/National Adv. E-mail: advertisinginfo@suntimes.com
Display Adv. E-mail: classifieds@stmedianetwork.com
Primary Website: chicagotribune.com/suburbs/elmwood-park
Year Established: 1912
Avg Paid Circ: 210
Audit By: AAM
Audit Date: 31.03.2017
Personnel: Jill McDemott (North); R. Bruce Dold (Pub./Ed.-in-Chief); Peter Kendall (Mng. Ed.); Jill McDermott (VP of Adv.); Phil Jurik (Ed.); Maggie Wartik (Gen. Mgr. of Suburban Weeklies)
Parent company (for newspapers): Tribune Publishing, Inc.

EVANSTON REVIEW

Street address 1: 160 N. Stetson Avenue
Street address city: Chicago
Street address state: IL
Zip/Postal code: 60601
General Phone: (847) 486-9200
Advertising Phone: (847) 486-7300
Editorial Phone: (312) 321-2678
Editorial Fax: (847) 486-7451
General/National Adv. E-mail: advertisinginfo@suntimes.com
Display Adv. E-mail: classifieds@stmedianetwork.com
Primary Website: chicagotribune.com/suburbs/evanston
Year Established: 1912
Avg Paid Circ: 306
Audit By: AAM
Audit Date: 31.03.2017
Personnel: Maggie Wartik (Gen. Mgr. of Suburban Weeklies); R. Bruce Dold (Pub./Ed.-in-Chief); Peter Kendall (Mng. Ed.); Phil Jurik (Ed.); Jill McDermott (VP of Adv.)
Parent company (for newspapers): Tribune Publishing, Inc.

EVERGREEN PARK COURIER

Street address 1: 3840 147th St
Street address city: Midlothian
Street address state: IL
Zip/Postal code: 60445-3452
General Phone: (708) 388-2425
General Fax: (708) 385-7811
General/National Adv. E-mail: info@southwestmessengerpress.com
Primary Website: southwestmessengerpress.com
Avg Paid Circ: 8729
Avg Free Circ: 800
Audit By: Sworn/Estimate/Non-Audited
Audit Date: 10.06.2019
Personnel: Margaret Lysen (Pub.)
Parent company (for newspapers): Southwest Messenger Press, Inc.

EXAMINER PUBLICATIONS, INC.

Street address 1: 4N781 Gerber Rd
Street address city: Bartlett
Street address state: IL
Zip/Postal code: 60103-2021
General Phone: (630) 830-4145
Advertising Phone: (630) 830-4145
Editorial Phone: (630) 830-4145
General/National Adv. E-mail: staff@examinerpublications.com
Display Adv. E-mail: classads@examinerpublications.com
Classified Adv. e-mail: classads@examinerpublications.com
Editorial e-mail: news@examinerpublications.com
Primary Website: examinerpublications.com
Year Established: 1976
Avg Paid Circ: 33447
Avg Free Circ: 4353
Audit By: Sworn/Estimate/Non-Audited
Audit Date: 10.06.2019
Personnel: Randall Petrik (Pres, Pub.)
Parent company (for newspapers): Examiner Publications, Inc.

FAIRVIEW HEIGHTS TRIBUNE

Street address 1: 314 E Church St
Street address city: Mascoutah
Street address state: IL
Zip/Postal code: 62258-2100
General Phone: (618) 566-8282
General Fax: (618) 566-8282
General/National Adv. E-mail: adv@heraldpubs.com
Editorial e-mail: tribune@heraldpubs.com
Primary Website: heraldpubs.com
Avg Paid Circ: 1250
Audit By: Sworn/Estimate/Non-Audited
Audit Date: 10.06.2019
Personnel: Greg Hoskins (Pub.)

FARINA NEWS

Street address 1: 109 N Walnut St
Street address city: Farina
Street address state: IL
Zip/Postal code: 62838-1326
General Phone: (618) 245-6216
General Fax: (618) 245-6216
General/National Adv. E-mail: farinanews@yahoo.com
Year Established: 1882
Avg Paid Circ: 850
Audit By: Sworn/Estimate/Non-Audited
Audit Date: 10.06.2019
Personnel: Sara Hunley (Ed./Pub.)

FARMER'S REPORT

Street address 1: 703 Illinois Ave
Street address city: Mendota
Street address state: IL
Zip/Postal code: 61342-1637
General Phone: (815) 39-9396
General Fax: (815) 539-7862
General/National Adv. E-mail: kmeaker@mendotareporter.com
Display Adv. E-mail: acaylor@mendotareporter.com
Editorial e-mail: bmorris@mendotareporter.com
Primary Website: mendotareporter.com
Avg Paid Circ: 2100
Avg Free Circ: 8000
Audit By: Sworn/Estimate/Non-Audited
Audit Date: 10.06.2019
Personnel: Jennifer Sommer (Ed.)
Parent company (for newspapers): News Media Corporation

FARMERS WEEKLY REVIEW

Street address 1: 100 Manhattan Rd
Street address 2: Suite 2
Street address city: Joliet
Street address state: IL
Zip/Postal code: 60433-2764
General Phone: (815) 727-4811
General Fax: (815) 727-5570
Advertising Phone: (815) 727-4811
Advertising Fax: (815) 727-5570
Editorial Phone: (815) 727-4811
Editorial Fax: (815) 727-5570
General/National Adv. E-mail: debbie@willcfb.com
Display Adv. E-mail: debbie@willcfb.com
Editorial e-mail: farmersweekly@sbcglobal.net
Primary Website: facebook.com/farmersweekly1921
Year Established: 1921
Avg Paid Circ: 12900
Avg Free Circ: 50
Audit By: Sworn/Estimate/Non-Audited
Audit Date: 10.06.2019
Personnel: Debbie Werner (Adv. Mgr.); Michael J. Cleary (Pub.); Nick Reiher (Ed.)

FORD COUNTY RECORD

Street address 1: 208 N Market St
Street address city: Paxton
Street address state: IL
Zip/Postal code: 60957-1124
General Phone: (217) 379-2356
General Fax: (217) 379-3104
Editorial Phone: (217) 722-1042 or (217) 379-2356
General/National Adv. E-mail: sschunke@news-gazette.com
Display Adv. E-mail: pkillion@news-gazette.com
Editorial e-mail: wbrumleve@fordcountyrecord.com
Primary Website: fordcountyrecord.com
Year Established: 1865
Avg Paid Circ: 452
Sat. Circulation Paid: 33291
Sun. Circulation Paid: 36877
Audit By: AAM
Audit Date: 30.09.2018
Personnel: William Brumleve (Editor); John Foreman (Pub.); Tom Zalabak (Adv. Dir.)
Parent company (for newspapers): The News-Gazette

FOREST LEAVES

Street address 1: 435 N Michigan Ave
Street address city: Chicago
Street address state: IL
Zip/Postal code: 60611-4066
General Phone: (312) 321-2034
General Fax: (312) 321-9310
General/National Adv. E-mail: display@pioneerlocal.com

Display Adv. E-mail: classifieds@pioneerlocal.com
Primary Website: chicagotribune.com/suburbs/river-forest
Avg Paid Circ: 384
Audit By: Sworn/Estimate/Non-Audited
Audit Date: 10.06.2019
Personnel: Maggie Wartik (Gen. Mgr. of Suburban Weeklies); Peter Kendall (Mng. Ed.); R. Bruce Dold (Pub.); Phil Jurik (Ed.); Jill McDermott (VP of Adv.)

FOREST PARK REVIEW

Street address 1: 141 S Oak Park Ave
Street address 2: Ste 3
Street address city: Oak Park
Street address state: IL
Zip/Postal code: 60302-2900
General Phone: (708) 366-0600
General Fax: (708) 524-0447
General/National Adv. E-mail: dawn@forestparkreview.com
Display Adv. E-mail: classifieds@forestparkreview.com
Editorial e-mail: circulation@wjinc.com
Primary Website: forestparkreview.com
Mthly Avg Views: 70734
Mthly Avg Unique Visitors: 18273
Year Established: 1886
Avg Paid Circ: 2400
Avg Free Circ: 400
Audit By: Sworn/Estimate/Non-Audited
Audit Date: 10.06.2019
Personnel: Dan Haley (Pub.)

FORRESTON JOURNAL

Street address 1: 113 S Peoria Ave
Street address city: Dixon
Street address state: IL
Zip/Postal code: 61021-2905
General Phone: (815) 732-6166
General Fax: (815) 732-4238
Advertising Phone: (815) 625-3600, Ext. 5613
Editorial Phone: (815) 732-6166
General/National Adv. E-mail: leisenberg@oglecountynews.com
Display Adv. E-mail: classifieds@svnmail.com; advertising@svnmail.com
Editorial e-mail: vwells@oglecountynews.com
Primary Website: oglecountynews.com
Avg Paid Circ: 967
Avg Free Circ: 24
Audit By: Sworn/Estimate/Non-Audited
Audit Date: 10.06.2019
Personnel: Earleen Hinton (Gen. Mgr.); Kris Boggs (HR); Trevis Mayfield (Pub.); Jennifer Baratta (Adv. Dir.); Vinde Wells (Ed.); Chris Johnson (Reporter)
Parent company (for newspapers): Shaw Media

FRANKLIN PARK HERALD-JOURNAL

Street address 1: 160 N. Stetson Avenue
Street address city: Chicago
Street address state: IL
Zip/Postal code: 60601
General Phone: (866) 399-0537
General Fax: (312) 222-2598
Advertising Phone: (866) 399-0537
Editorial Phone: (312) 222-3429
Editorial Fax: (312) 222-2598
General/National Adv. E-mail: jmcdermott@tribpub.com
Display Adv. E-mail: jmcdermott@tribpub.com
Editorial e-mail: pjurik@chicagotribune.com
Primary Website: chicagotribune.com/suburbs/franklin-park
Year Established: 1912
Avg Paid Circ: 127
Audit By: AAM
Audit Date: 31.03.2017
Personnel: Phil Jurik (Ed.); Peter Kendall (Mng. Ed.); R. Bruce Dold (Pub./Ed.-in-Chief); Maggie Wartik (Gen. Mgr. of Suburban Weeklies); Jill McDermott (VP of Adv.)
Parent company (for newspapers): Tribune Publishing, Inc.

FREE PRESS-PROGRESS

Street address 1: 112 W State St
Street address city: Nokomis
Street address state: IL
Zip/Postal code: 62075-1657
General Phone: (217) 563-2115
General Fax: (217) 563-7464
General/National Adv. E-mail: freepress@consolidated.net
Primary Website: nokomisonline.com
Avg Paid Circ: 2150
Avg Free Circ: 1900
Audit By: Sworn/Estimate/Non-Audited
Audit Date: 10.06.2019
Personnel: Thomas J. Phillips (Pub.); Tom Latonis (Ed.); John Broux (Editor)

FULTON DEMOCRAT

Street address 1: 31 S Main St
Street address city: Canton
Street address state: IL
Zip/Postal code: 61520-2605
General Phone: (309) 647-9501
General Fax: (309) 543-6844
General/National Adv. E-mail: fultondemocrat@att.net
Primary Website: fultondemocrat.com
Year Established: 1855
Avg Paid Circ: 3000
Avg Free Circ: 4000
Audit By: Sworn/Estimate/Non-Audited
Audit Date: 10.06.2019
Personnel: Robert L. Martin (Pub.)
Parent company (for newspapers): Martin Publishing Company

FULTON JOURNAL

Street address 1: 1009 4th St
Street address 2: Frnt Main
Street address city: Fulton
Street address state: IL
Zip/Postal code: 61252-1791
General Phone: (815) 589-2424
General Fax: (815) 589-2714
General/National Adv. E-mail: journal@whitesidesentinel.com
Year Established: 1854
Audit By: Sworn/Estimate/Non-Audited
Audit Date: 10.06.2019
Personnel: Sue Patten (Pub.)
Parent company (for newspapers): WNS Publications Inc.

GALLATIN DEMOCRAT

Street address 1: 288 N LINCOLN BLVD E
Street address city: Shawneetown
Street address state: IL
Zip/Postal code: 62984
General Phone: (618) 269-3147
General Fax: (618) 269-3147
General/National Adv. E-mail: gallatin@yourclearwave.com
Primary Website: facebook.com/pages/The-Gallatin-Democrat/152210741460695
Year Established: 1888
Avg Paid Circ: 1150
Audit By: Sworn/Estimate/Non-Audited
Audit Date: 10.06.2019
Personnel: George Wilson (Ed.); Brian DeNeal (Ed.); David Adams (Pub.)
Parent company (for newspapers): CherryRoad Media

GALVA NEWS

Street address 1: 348 Front St
Street address city: Galva
Street address state: IL
Zip/Postal code: 61434-1365
General Phone: (309) 932-2103
General Fax: (309) 932-3282
Editorial e-mail: dboock@galvanews.com
Primary Website: galvanews.com
Avg Paid Circ: 1200
Audit By: Sworn/Estimate/Non-Audited
Audit Date: 10.06.2019
Personnel: David Adams (Pub.); Mike Landis (Ed.); Lisa Leemans (Adv. Mgr.)

GAZETTE-NEWS

Street address 1: 150 S Washington St
Street address city: Bunker Hill
Street address state: IL
Zip/Postal code: 62014-1316
General Phone: (618) 585-4411
General Fax: (618) 585-3354
General/National Adv. E-mail: gazette8@frontiernet.net
Primary Website: bunkerhillpublications.com
Year Established: 1866
Avg Paid Circ: 1650
Audit By: Sworn/Estimate/Non-Audited
Audit Date: 10.06.2019
Personnel: John M. Galer (Pub.); Laura Dabbs (Prodn. Mgr.)

GENESEO REPUBLIC

Street address 1: 108 W 1st St
Street address city: Geneseo
Street address state: IL
Zip/Postal code: 61254-1342
General Phone: (309) 944-2119
General Fax: (309) 944-5615
Editorial e-mail: editor@geneseorepublic.com
Primary Website: geneseorepublic.com
Avg Paid Circ: 4800
Audit By: Sworn/Estimate/Non-Audited
Audit Date: 10.06.2019
Personnel: Dee Evans (Gen. Mgr.); Marnie Eggen (Circ. Mgr.); Lisa Depies (Ed.); David Adams (Pub.)
Parent company (for newspapers): CherryRoad Media

GENEVA CHRONICLE

Street address 1: 333 N Randall Rd
Street address 2: Ste 2
Street address city: St Charles
Street address state: IL
Zip/Postal code: 60174-1500
General Phone: (630)232-9222
General Fax: (630) 444-1641
General/National Adv. E-mail: lsiebolds@shawmedia.com
Display Adv. E-mail: lsiebolds@shawmedia.com
Editorial e-mail: kgresey@shawmedia.com
Primary Website: kcchronicle.com
Avg Paid Circ: 271
Avg Free Circ: 8465
Audit By: Sworn/Estimate/Non-Audited
Audit Date: 10.06.2019
Personnel: Kathy Gresey; Maureen Ringness (Group Sales Dir/Major Nat'l Accts); Jason Rossi (Sports Ed.)
Parent company (for newspapers): Shaw Media

GLEN ELLYN SUBURBAN LIFE

Street address 1: 2001 Butterfield Rd Suite 105
Street address 2: Ste 260
Street address city: Downers Grove
Street address state: IL
Zip/Postal code: 60515
General Phone: (630) 368-1100
General Fax: (630) 969-0228
Advertising Phone: (630) 427-6213
Editorial Phone: (630) 427-6248
General/National Adv. E-mail: nshannon@shawmedia.com
Display Adv. E-mail: sbissell@shawmedia.com
Editorial e-mail: aschier@shawmedia.com
Primary Website: mysuburbanlife.com
Avg Paid Circ: 327
Avg Free Circ: 2907
Audit By: AAM
Audit Date: 31.03.2018
Personnel: J. Tom Shaw (Pub.); Katie Sherman (Marketing Dir.); David Lemery (Ed.); Ryan Wells
Parent company (for newspapers): Shaw Media

GLENCOE NEWS

Street address 1: 160 N. Stetson Avenue
Street address city: Chicago
Street address state: IL
Zip/Postal code: 60601
General Phone: (866) 399-0537
General Fax: (312) 222-2598
Advertising Phone: (866) 399-0537
Editorial Phone: (312) 222-3429
Editorial Fax: (312) 222-2598
General/National Adv. E-mail: jmcdermott@tribpub.com
Display Adv. E-mail: jmcdermott@tribpub.com
Editorial e-mail: pjurik@chicagotribune.com
Primary Website: chicagotribune.com/suburbs/glencoe
Avg Paid Circ: 439
Audit By: Sworn/Estimate/Non-Audited
Audit Date: 10.06.2019
Personnel: Mike Bivona (Mng. Ed.); R. Bruce Dold (Pub./Ed.-in-Chief); Phil Jurik (Ed.); Maggie Wartik (Gen. Mgr. of Suburban Weeklies); Peter Kendall (Mng. Ed.); Jill McDermott (VP of Adv.)
Parent company (for newspapers): Tribune Publishing Company

GLENVIEW ANNOUNCEMENTS

Street address 1: 160 N. Stetson Avenue
Street address city: Chicago
Street address state: IL
Zip/Postal code: 60601
General Phone: (866) 399-0537
General Fax: (312) 222-2598
Advertising Phone: (866) 399-0537
Editorial Phone: (312) 222-3429
Editorial Fax: (312) 222-2598
General/National Adv. E-mail: jmcdermott@tribpub.com
Display Adv. E-mail: jmcdermott@tribpub.com
Editorial e-mail: pjurik@chicagotribune.com
Primary Website: chicagotribune.com/suburbs/glenview
Year Established: 1912
Avg Paid Circ: 1171
Audit By: Sworn/Estimate/Non-Audited
Audit Date: 10.06.2019
Personnel: Cathy Backer (Ed.); R. Bruce Dold (Pub./Ed.-in-Chief); Phil Jurik (Ed.); Maggie Wartik (Gen. Mgr. of Suburban Weeklies); Peter Kendall (Mng. Ed.); Jill McDermott (VP of Adv.)
Parent company (for newspapers): Tribune Publishing Company

GLENVIEW JOURNAL

Street address 1: 622 Graceland Ave
Street address city: Des Plaines
Street address state: IL
Zip/Postal code: 60016-4519
General Phone: (847) 299-5511
General Fax: (847) 298-8549
General/National Adv. E-mail: journalnews@mail.com
Primary Website: journal-topics.com/news/glenview
Audit By: Sworn/Estimate/Non-Audited
Audit Date: 10.06.2019
Personnel: Rick Wessell (Adv. Dir.); Robert Wessell (Classified Mgr.); Todd Wessell (Managing Ed.)

GOLDEN-CLAYTON NEW ERA

Street address 1: 202 E State St
Street address city: Camp Point
Street address state: IL
Zip/Postal code: 62320-1114
General Phone: (217) 593-6515
General Fax: (217) 593-7720
General/National Adv. E-mail: lisa@elliott-publishing.com
Editorial e-mail: gina@elliott-publishing.com
Primary Website: elliott-publishing.com
Year Established: 1876
Avg Paid Circ: 600
Audit By: Sworn/Estimate/Non-Audited
Audit Date: 10.06.2019
Personnel: James W. Elliott (Pub.); Marcia Elliott (Ed.); Gina Maddox (Receptionist); Lisa Newell (Graphics)
Parent company (for newspapers): Elliott Publishing, Inc.

GOREVILLE GAZETTE

Street address 1: 205 S BROADWAY
Street address city: Goreville
Street address state: IL
Zip/Postal code: 62939
General Phone: (618) 995-9445
General Fax: (618) 658-4322
General/National Adv. E-mail: gorevillegazette@frontier.com
Primary Website: gorevillegazette.com
Year Established: 1977
Avg Paid Circ: 800
Audit By: Sworn/Estimate/Non-Audited
Audit Date: 10.06.2019
Personnel: Lonnie Hinton (Pub.); Sandra Lively (Ed.)

GREENE PRAIRIE PRESS

Street address 1: 516 N Main St
Street address city: Carrollton
Street address state: IL

Zip/Postal code: 62016-1027
General Phone: (217) 942-9100
General Fax: (630) 206-0320
Advertising Phone: (618) 498-1234
General/National Adv. E-mail: jkallal@campbellpublications.net
Display Adv. E-mail: jkallal@campbellpublications.net
Editorial e-mail: gppnews@campbellpublications.net
Primary Website: greenprairiepress.com
Year Established: 1846
Avg Paid Circ: 2200
Avg Free Circ: 10
Audit By: Sworn/Estimate/Non-Audited
Audit Date: 10.06.2019
Personnel: Julie Boren (Pub.); Robert Lyons (regional editor)
Parent company (for newspapers): Campbell Publishing Co., Inc.

HANCOCK COUNTY JOURNAL-PILOT

Street address 1: 31 N Washington St
Street address city: Carthage
Street address state: IL
Zip/Postal code: 62321-1450
General Phone: (217) 357-2149
General Fax: (217) 357-2177
General/National Adv. E-mail: advertising@journalpilot.com
Display Adv. E-mail: classified@journalpilot.com
Editorial e-mail: editor@journalpilot.com
Primary Website: journalpilot.com
Audit By: Sworn/Estimate/Non-Audited
Audit Date: 10.06.2019
Personnel: Ethan Lillard (Sports Ed.); Emma VanArsdale (Ed.); Andria Miller (Adv. Dir.); Bobbi Cleesen (Clas. Adv./Circ.)
Parent company (for newspapers): Community Media Group

HENRY NEWS REPUBLICAN

Street address 1: 709 3rd St
Street address city: Henry
Street address state: IL
Zip/Postal code: 61537-1446
General Phone: (309) 364-3250
General Fax: (309) 364-3858
General/National Adv. E-mail: henrynews@frontier.com
Avg Paid Circ: 2000
Audit By: Sworn/Estimate/Non-Audited
Audit Date: 10.06.2019
Personnel: Amy Ziegler (Ed.)

HERALD LIFE

Street address 1: 909 Liberty St
Street address city: Morris
Street address state: IL
Zip/Postal code: 60450-1594
Advertising Phone: (815) 280-4100
Advertising Fax: (815) 729-2019
General/National Adv. E-mail: ads@morrisdailyherald.com
Avg Free Circ: 100
Audit By: Sworn/Estimate/Non-Audited
Audit Date: 10.06.2019
Personnel: Jon Styf (Ed.); Steve Vanisko (Gen. Mgr.); Denise Pankey (Adv. Mgr.)
Parent company (for newspapers): Shaw Media

HERALD-ENTERPRISE

Street address 1: 211 E Main St
Street address city: Golconda
Street address state: IL
Zip/Postal code: 62938
General Phone: (618) 683-3531
General Fax: (618) 683-3831
General/National Adv. E-mail: herald@shawneelink.net
Year Established: 1858
Avg Paid Circ: 1100
Avg Free Circ: 25
Audit By: Sworn/Estimate/Non-Audited
Audit Date: 28.09.2023
Personnel: Sandra Cowsert (Ed.)

HERSCHER PILOT

Street address 1: 100 S Main St
Street address city: Herscher
Street address state: IL
Zip/Postal code: 60941-9522
General Phone: (815) 426-2132
General Fax: (815) 426-2132
Advertising Phone: (815) 426-2132
Advertising Fax: (815) 426-2132
Editorial Phone: (815) 426-2132
Editorial Fax: (815) 426-2132
General/National Adv. E-mail: editor@herscherpilot.com
Display Adv. E-mail: editor@herscherpilot.com
Editorial e-mail: editor@herscherpilot.com
Primary Website: herscherpilot.com
Year Established: 1976
Avg Paid Circ: 1200
Audit By: Sworn/Estimate/Non-Audited
Audit Date: 10.06.2019

HICKORY HILLS CITIZEN

Street address 1: 3840 147th St
Street address city: Midlothian
Street address state: IL
Zip/Postal code: 60445-3452
General Phone: (708) 388-2425
General Fax: (708) 385-7811
General/National Adv. E-mail: spressnews@aol.com
Display Adv. E-mail: spressnews@aol.com
Editorial e-mail: spressnews@aol.com
Avg Paid Circ: 3530
Avg Free Circ: 400
Audit By: Sworn/Estimate/Non-Audited
Audit Date: 10.06.2019
Personnel: Margaret Lysen (Pub.); Carol Beymer (Adv. Mgr.); Lori Taylor (Ed.)
Parent company (for newspapers): Southwest Messenger Press, Inc.

HIGHLAND NEWS LEADER

Street address 1: 1 Woodcrest Professional Park
Street address city: Highland
Street address state: IL
Zip/Postal code: 62249-1254
General Phone: (618) 654-2366
General Fax: (618) 654-1181
General/National Adv. E-mail: gbentlage@bnd.com
Editorial e-mail: hnlnews@bnd.com
Primary Website: highlandnl.com
Year Established: 1861
Avg Paid Circ: 28334
Audit By: AAM
Audit Date: 31.12.2018
Personnel: Gay Bentlage (Adv. Mgr.); Curt Libbra (News Editor)

HIGHLAND PARK NEWS

Street address 1: 160 N. Stetson Avenue
Street address city: Chicago
Street address state: IL
Zip/Postal code: 60601
General Phone: (847) 486-9200
Editorial Phone: (312) 321-2328
General/National Adv. E-mail: advertisinginfo@suntimes.com
Display Adv. E-mail: classifieds@stmedianetwork.com
Primary Website: pioneerlocal.com
Year Established: 1912
Avg Paid Circ: 1213
Audit By: Sworn/Estimate/Non-Audited
Audit Date: 10.06.2019
Personnel: R. Bruce Dold (Pub./Ed.-in-Chief); Phil Jurik (Ed.); Maggie Wartik (Gen. Mgr. of Suburban Weeklies); Peter Kendall (Mng. Ed.); Jill McDermott (VP of Adv.)
Parent company (for newspapers): Tribune Publishing Company

HINSDALE SUBURBAN LIFE

Street address 1: 2001 Butterfield Road, Suite 105
Street address 2: Ste 260
Street address city: Downers Grove
Street address state: IL
Zip/Postal code: 60515-5585
General Phone: (630) 368-1100
General Fax: (630) 969-0228
Advertising Phone: (630) 427-6213
Editorial Phone: (630) 427-6270
Editorial Fax: (630) 969-0228
General/National Adv. E-mail: nshannon@shawmedia.com
Display Adv. E-mail: sbissell@shawmedia.com
Editorial e-mail: dgood@shawmedia.com
Primary Website: mysuburbanlife.com
Year Established: 1926
Avg Paid Circ: 6434
Avg Free Circ: 1132
Audit By: AAM
Audit Date: 31.03.2018
Personnel: J. Tom Shaw (Pub.); Katie Sherman (Marketing Dir.); David Good (Ed.); Maureen Ringness (Major/Nat'l Accts./Grp. Sales Dir.); Ryan Wells
Parent company (for newspapers): Shaw Media

HYDE PARK HERALD

Street address 1: 1525 E 53rd St
Street address 2: Ste 920
Street address city: Chicago
Street address state: IL
Zip/Postal code: 60615-4530
General Phone: (773) 643-8533
General Fax: (773) 643-8542
General/National Adv. E-mail: display@hpherald.com
Display Adv. E-mail: classifi@hpherald.com
Editorial e-mail: editor@hpherald.com
Primary Website: hpherald.com
Year Established: 1882
Avg Paid Circ: 5400
Avg Free Circ: 195
Audit By: Sworn/Estimate/Non-Audited
Audit Date: 10.06.2019
Personnel: Bruce Sagan (Pub.); Susan J. Walker (VP/Gen. Mgr.); Carol Cichocki (Adv. Mgr.); Gabriel Piemonte (Ed.); Mary Petrassi (Bus. Mgr.)
Parent company (for newspapers): Herald Newspapers, Inc.

ILLINOIS SUBURBAN JOURNALS

Street address 1: 2 Eastport Executive Dr
Street address city: Collinsville
Street address state: IL
Zip/Postal code: 62234
General Phone: (618) 344-0264
General Fax: (618) 344-3611
General/National Adv. E-mail: metroeastnews@yourjournal.com
Primary Website: stltoday.com/suburban-journals/illinois
Year Established: 1922
Avg Free Circ: 40335
Audit By: Sworn/Estimate/Non-Audited
Audit Date: 10.06.2019
Personnel: Greg Uptain (Ed.); Mary Ann Wagner (Promotions Dir./Niche Pub.)
Parent company (for newspapers): Dispatch-Argus

INDEPENDENT NEWS

Street address 1: 2202 Kickapoo Dr
Street address city: Danville
Street address state: IL
Zip/Postal code: 61832-5379
General Phone: (217) 443-8484
General Fax: (217) 443-8490
General/National Adv. E-mail: indnews@news-gazette.com
Display Adv. E-mail: indnews@news-gazette.com
Editorial e-mail: indnews@news-gazette.com
Primary Website: the-independent-news.com
Year Established: 1975
Avg Paid Circ: 330
Audit By: Sworn/Estimate/Non-Audited
Audit Date: 10.06.2019
Personnel: John Foreman (Pub.); Tim Evans (Gen. Mgr.); Vicki Delhaye (Editor/office manager)
Parent company (for newspapers): News Gazette Community News; The News-Gazette

JESEY COUNTY JOURNAL

Street address 1: 832 S State St
Street address city: Jerseyville
Street address state: IL
Zip/Postal code: 62052-2343
General Phone: (618) 498-1234
General Fax: (630) 206-0320
Advertising Phone: (618) 498-1234
Primary Website: jerseycountyjournal.com
Year Established: 2003
Avg Free Circ: 10600
Audit By: Sworn/Estimate/Non-Audited
Audit Date: 10.06.2019
Personnel: Julie Boren (Pub.); Robert Lyons (regional editor)
Parent company (for newspapers): Campbell Publishing Co., Inc.

KANE COUNTY CHRONICLE

Street address 1: 333 N Randall Rd
Street address 2: Ste 11
Street address city: Saint Charles
Street address state: IL
Zip/Postal code: 60174-1500
General Phone: (630) 232-9222
General Fax: (630) 444-1645
Advertising Phone: (630) 845-5228
Advertising Fax: (630) 444-1645
Editorial Phone: (630) 845-5355
Editorial Fax: (630) 444-1641
General/National Adv. E-mail: advertising@kcchronicle.com
Display Adv. E-mail: advertising@kcchronicle.com
Classified Adv. e-mail: classified@shawsuburban.com
Editorial e-mail: editorial@kcchronicle.com
Primary Website: kcchronicle.com
Year Established: 1881
Avg Paid Circ: 5090
Avg Free Circ: 260
Sat. Circulation Paid: 10254
Audit By: AAM
Audit Date: 30.06.2018
Personnel: Don Bricker (Pub.); Kathy Greser (Ed.); Shelly Bissell (Adv. Dir., Classified); Leslie Shambo (Mktg. Coord.); Kara Hansen (Circ. Mgr., Distr./Sales); Jay Schwab (Sports Ed.); Kevin Elder (Prodn. Dir.); Clem Garcia (Prodn. Mgr., Mailroom); Ted Robinson (Prodn. Mgr., Pressroom); Maureen Ringness (Group Sales Dir.); Rebecca Dienhart (Major Sales Coord.)
Parent company (for newspapers): Shaw Media

KENDALL COUNTY RECORD, OSWEGO LEDGER, SANDWICH RECORD, PLANO RECORD

Street address 1: 109 W Veterans Pkwy
Street address city: Yorkville
Street address state: IL
Zip/Postal code: 60560-1905
General Phone: (630) 553-7034
General Fax: (630) 553-7085
Display Adv. E-mail: ads@kendallcountynow.com
Editorial e-mail: news@kendallcountynow.com
Primary Website: kendallcountynow.com
Year Established: 1864
Avg Paid Circ: 5997
Avg Free Circ: 444
Audit By: Sworn/Estimate/Non-Audited
Audit Date: 10.06.2019
Personnel: Joshua Welge (Sports Ed.)

LACON HOME JOURNAL

Street address 1: 204 S Washington St
Street address city: Lacon
Street address state: IL
Zip/Postal code: 61540-1498
General Phone: (309) 246-2865
General Fax: (309) 246-3214
General/National Adv. E-mail: sonbtp@aol.com
Primary Website: laconhomejournal.com
Year Established: 1847
Avg Paid Circ: 1800
Audit By: Sworn/Estimate/Non-Audited
Audit Date: 10.06.2019
Personnel: William H. Sondag (Ed.)

LAGRANGE SUBURBAN LIFE

Street address 1: 2001 Butterfield Rd
Street address 2: Ste 105
Street address city: Downers Grove
Street address state: IL
Zip/Postal code: 60515-5479
General Phone: (630) 368-1100
General Fax: (630) 969-0228
Advertising Phone: (630) 427-6213
Editorial Phone: (630) 427-6254
Editorial Fax: (630) 969-0228
General/National Adv. E-mail: bkorbel@shawmedia.com
Display Adv. E-mail: bhanahan@shawmedia.com
Editorial e-mail: mhendrickson@shawmedia.com

Primary Website: mysuburbanlife.com
Avg Paid Circ: 1630
Avg Free Circ: 162
Audit By: AAM
Audit Date: 31.03.2018
Personnel: J. Tom Shaw (Pub.); Matthew Hendrickson (Ed.); Maureen Ringness (Major/Nat'l Accts./Grp. Sales Dir.); Ryan Wells
Parent company (for newspapers): Shaw Media

LAKE COUNTY JOURNAL

Street address 1: PO Box 343
Street address city: Grayslake
Street address state: IL
Zip/Postal code: 60030-0343
General Phone: (847) 223-8161
General Fax: (847) 543-1139
General/National Adv. E-mail: circulation@nwnewsgroup.com
Primary Website: lakecountyjournals.com
Year Established: 1956
Avg Free Circ: 8000
Audit By: Sworn/Estimate/Non-Audited
Audit Date: 10.06.2019
Personnel: John Rung (Exec. Vice Pres./Gen. Mgr.); Cassandra Dowell (Sr. Reporter); Yadira Sanchez Olson (Reporter)
Parent company (for newspapers): Shaw Media

LAKE FORESTER

Street address 1: 435 N Michigan Ave
Street address city: Chicago
Street address state: IL
Zip/Postal code: 60611-4066
General Phone: (847) 599-6900
General Fax: (847) 486-7454
Editorial Phone: (312) 321-2328
General/National Adv. E-mail: advertisinginfo@suntimes.com
Display Adv. E-mail: classifieds@stmedianetwork.com
Primary Website: pioneerlocal.com
Year Established: 1912
Avg Paid Circ: 1466
Audit By: Sworn/Estimate/Non-Audited
Audit Date: 10.06.2019
Personnel: R. Bruce Dold (Pub./Ed.-in-Chief); Phil Jurik (Ed.); Maggie Wartik (Gen. Mgr. of Suburban Weeklies); Peter Kendall (Mng. Ed.); Jill McDermott (VP of Adv.)

LAKE ZURICH COURIER

Street address 1: 160 N. Stetson Avenue
Street address city: Chicago
Street address state: IL
Zip/Postal code: 60601
General Phone: (866) 399-0537
General Fax: (312) 222-2598
Advertising Phone: (866) 399-0537
Editorial Phone: (312) 222-3429
Editorial Fax: (312) 222-2598
General/National Adv. E-mail: jmcdermott@tribpub.com
Display Adv. E-mail: jmcdermott@tribpub.com
Editorial e-mail: pjurik@chicagotribune.com
Primary Website: chicagotribune.com/suburbs/lake-zurich
Year Established: 1912
Avg Paid Circ: 644
Audit By: Sworn/Estimate/Non-Audited
Audit Date: 10.06.2019
Personnel: R. Bruce Dold (Pub./Ed.-in-Chief); Phil Jurik (Ed.); Maggie Wartik (Gen. Mgr. of Suburban Weeklies); Peter Kendall (Mng. Ed.); Jill McDermott (VP of Adv.)
Parent company (for newspapers): Tribune Publishing Company

LANDMARK

Street address 1: 141 S Oak Park Ave
Street address 2: Ste 1
Street address city: Oak Park
Street address state: IL
Zip/Postal code: 60302-2972
General Phone: (708) 524-8300
General Fax: (708) 524-0447
Primary Website: rblandmark.com
Avg Paid Circ: 2500
Avg Free Circ: 1100
Audit By: Sworn/Estimate/Non-Audited
Audit Date: 10.06.2019
Personnel: Dawn Ferencak (Advertising Manager); Bob Uphues (Ed.)
Parent company (for newspapers): Wednesday Journal, Inc.

LAWRENCE COUNTY NEWS

Street address 1: 1209 State St
Street address city: Lawrenceville
Street address state: IL
Zip/Postal code: 62439-2332
General Phone: (618) 943-2331
General Fax: (618) 943-3976
Advertising Phone: (618) 943-2331
Advertising Fax: (618) 943-3976
Editorial Phone: (618) 943-2331
Editorial Fax: (618) 943-3976
General/National Adv. E-mail: syoung@lawdailyrecord.com
Display Adv. E-mail: lkocher@lawdailyrecord.com
Editorial e-mail: mvandorn@lawdailyrecord.com
Primary Website: lawdailyrecord.com
Avg Paid Circ: 300
Audit By: Sworn/Estimate/Non-Audited
Audit Date: 10.06.2019
Personnel: Michael Van Dorn (Ed.); Beverly Johnson (Gen. Mgr.); Bev Johnson (Prodn. Mgr.)
Parent company (for newspapers): Lewis Newspapers

LEDGER-SENTINEL

Street address 1: 109 W Veterans Pkwy
Street address city: Yorkville
Street address state: IL
Zip/Postal code: 60560-1905
General Phone: (630) 553-7034
General Fax: (630) 553-7085
Editorial Phone: (630) 554-8573
General/National Adv. E-mail: adsales@kendallcountynow.com
Editorial e-mail: news@kendallcountynow.com
Primary Website: kendallcountynow.com
Avg Paid Circ: 7900
Avg Free Circ: 23
Audit By: Sworn/Estimate/Non-Audited
Audit Date: 10.06.2019
Personnel: Jeffrey A. Farren (Pub.); Kristin Hawkins (Adv. Mgr.); John Etheridge (Mng. Ed.)

LEMONT SUBURBAN LIFE

Street address 1: 1101 W. 31st Street
Street address 2: Ste 260
Street address city: Downers Grove
Street address state: IL
Zip/Postal code: 60515
General Phone: (630) 368-1100
General Fax: (630) 969-0228
Advertising Phone: (630) 427-6213
Editorial Phone: (630) 427-6248
General/National Adv. E-mail: nshannon@shawmedia.com
Display Adv. E-mail: sbissell@shawmedia.com
Editorial e-mail: aschier@shawmedia.com
Primary Website: mysuburbanlife.com
Avg Paid Circ: 654
Avg Free Circ: 80
Audit By: AAM
Audit Date: 31.03.2018
Personnel: J. Tom Shaw (Pub.); Katie Sherman (Marketing Dir.); Anna Schier; Maureen Ringness (Major/Nat'l Accts./Grp. Sales Dir.); Ryan Wells
Parent company (for newspapers): Shaw Media

LIBERTYVILLE REVIEW

Street address 1: 160 N. Stetson Avenue
Street address city: Chicago
Street address state: IL
Zip/Postal code: 60601
General Phone: (866) 399-0537
General Fax: (312) 222-2598
Advertising Phone: (866) 399-0537
Editorial Phone: (312) 222-3429
Editorial Fax: (312) 222-2598
General/National Adv. E-mail: jmcdermott@tribpub.com
Display Adv. E-mail: jmcdermott@tribpub.com
Editorial e-mail: pjurik@chicagotribune.com
Primary Website: chicagotribune.com/suburbs/libertyville
Year Established: 1912
Avg Paid Circ: 806
Audit By: Sworn/Estimate/Non-Audited
Audit Date: 10.06.2019
Personnel: R. Bruce Dold (Pub./Ed.-in-Chief); Phil Jurik (Ed.); Maggie Wartik (Gen. Mgr. of Suburban Weeklies); Peter Kendall (Mng. Ed.); Jill McDermott (VP of Adv.)
Parent company (for newspapers): Tribune Publishing Company

LIMESTONE INDEPENDENT NEWS

Street address 1: 114 Roosevelt St
Street address city: Bartonville
Street address state: IL
Zip/Postal code: 61607-1910
General Phone: (309) 697-1851
General Fax: (309) 697-1851
General/National Adv. E-mail: limestonenews@yahoo.com
Primary Website: facebook.com/LIN715
Year Established: 1967
Avg Paid Circ: 2300
Audit By: Sworn/Estimate/Non-Audited
Audit Date: 10.06.2019
Personnel: Barbara Widener (Ed.)

LINCOLNSHIRE REVIEW

Street address 1: 160 N. Stetson Avenue
Street address city: Chicago
Street address state: IL
Zip/Postal code: 60601
General Phone: (847) 329-2000
Editorial Phone: (312) 321-2324
General/National Adv. E-mail: advertisinginfo@suntimes.com
Display Adv. E-mail: classifieds@stmedianetwork.com
Primary Website: pioneerlocal.com
Year Established: 1912
Avg Paid Circ: 210
Audit By: Sworn/Estimate/Non-Audited
Audit Date: 10.06.2019
Personnel: Jill McDermott (VP of Adv.); R. Bruce Dold (Pub./Ed.-in-Chief); Phil Jurik (Ed.); Maggie Wartik (Gen. Mgr. of Suburban Weeklies); Peter Kendall (Mng. Ed.)
Parent company (for newspapers): Tribune Publishing Company

LINCOLNWOOD REVIEW

Street address 1: 160 N. Stetson Avenue
Street address city: Chicago
Street address state: IL
Zip/Postal code: 60601
General Phone: (847) 486-9200
General Fax: (847) 696-3229
Editorial Phone: (312) 321-3277
General/National Adv. E-mail: advertisinginfo@suntimes.com
Display Adv. E-mail: classifieds@stmedianetwork.com
Primary Website: pioneerlocal.com
Year Established: 1912
Avg Paid Circ: 290
Audit By: Sworn/Estimate/Non-Audited
Audit Date: 10.06.2019
Personnel: R. Bruce Dold (Pub./Ed.-in-Chief); Phil Jurik (Ed.); Maggie Wartik (Gen. Mgr. of Suburban Weeklies); Peter Kendall (Mng. Ed.); Jill McDermott (VP of Adv.)
Parent company (for newspapers): Tribune Publishing Company

LISLE SUBURBAN LIFE

Street address 1: 1101 31st St
Street address 2: Ste 260
Street address city: Downers Grove
Street address state: IL
Zip/Postal code: 60515-5585
General Phone: (630) 368-1100
General Fax: (630) 969-0228
Advertising Phone: (630) 427-6213
Editorial Phone: (630) 427-6252
General/National Adv. E-mail: nshannon@shawmedia.com
Display Adv. E-mail: sbissell@shawmedia.com
Editorial e-mail: rterrell@shawmedia.com
Primary Website: mysuburbanlife.com
Avg Paid Circ: 72
Avg Free Circ: 3411
Audit By: Sworn/Estimate/Non-Audited
Audit Date: 10.06.2019
Personnel: J. Tom Shaw (Pub.); Katie Sherman (Marketing Dir.); Ryan Terrell (Ed.); Maureen Ringness (Major/Nat'l Accts./Grp. Sales Dir.); Ryan Wells

LOMBARD SUBURBAN LIFE

Street address 1: 2001 Butterfield Rd Suite 105
Street address 2: Ste 260
Street address city: Downers Grove
Street address state: IL
Zip/Postal code: 60515
General Phone: (630) 368-1100
General Fax: (630) 969-0228
Advertising Phone: (630) 427-6213
Editorial Phone: (630) 427-6270
General/National Adv. E-mail: nshannon@shawmedia.com
Display Adv. E-mail: sbissell@shawmedia.com
Editorial e-mail: dgood@shawmedia.com
Primary Website: mysuburbanlife.com
Avg Paid Circ: 123
Avg Free Circ: 43
Audit By: AAM
Audit Date: 31.03.2018
Personnel: J. Tom Shaw (Pub.); Katie Sherman (Marketing Dir.); David Good (Ed.); Maureen Ringness (Major/Nat'l Accts./Grp. Sales Dir.); Ryan Wells (GM)
Parent company (for newspapers): Shaw Media

LOMBARDIAN

Street address 1: 929 S Main St
Street address 2: Ste 102
Street address city: Lombard
Street address state: IL
Zip/Postal code: 60148-3325
General Phone: (630) 627-7010
General Fax: (630) 627-7027
General/National Adv. E-mail: lombardian@sbcglobal.net
Primary Website: lombardian.info
Year Established: 1959
Avg Paid Circ: 11000
Audit By: Sworn/Estimate/Non-Audited
Audit Date: 10.06.2019
Personnel: Scott D. MacKay (Co-Pub.); Marguerite Micken (Adv. Mgr.); Bonnie MacKay (Ed./Pub.)

MACOUPIN COUNTY ENQUIRER DEMOCRAT

Street address 1: 125 E Main St
Street address city: Carlinville
Street address state: IL
Zip/Postal code: 62626-1726
General Phone: (217) 854-2534
General Fax: (217) 854-2535
General/National Adv. E-mail: mcednews@campbellpublications.net
Primary Website: enquirerdemocrat.com
Year Established: 1852
Avg Paid Circ: 4800
Avg Free Circ: 200
Audit By: Sworn/Estimate/Non-Audited
Audit Date: 10.06.2019
Personnel: Julie Boren (Pub.); Daniel Winningham; Eric Becker (Ed. Dept.)

MACOUPIN COUNTY JOURNAL

Street address 1: 431 S Main St
Street address city: Hillsboro
Street address state: IL
Zip/Postal code: 62049-1433
General Phone: (217) 532-3933
General Fax: (217) 532-3632
General/National Adv. E-mail: advertisejn@consolidated.net
Display Adv. E-mail: advertisejn@consolidated.net
Primary Website: thejournal-news.net
Year Established: 1852
Avg Free Circ: 13200
Audit By: Sworn/Estimate/Non-Audited
Audit Date: 10.06.2019
Personnel: John Galer (Ed./Gen. Mgr.); Cheri Ozee (Classifieds Mgr.)

MADISON COUNTY CHRONICLE

Street address 1: 125 E Wall St
Street address 2: Apt 9
Street address city: Worden

Street address state: IL
Zip/Postal code: 62097-1331
General Phone: (618) 459-3655
General Fax: (618) 459-3655
Advertising Phone: (618) 459-3655
Advertising Fax: (618) 459-3655
Editorial Phone: (618) 459-3655
Editorial Fax: (618) 459-3655
General/National Adv. E-mail: chronicl@madisontelco.com
Year Established: 1976
Avg Paid Circ: 650
Audit By: Sworn/Estimate/Non-Audited
Audit Date: 10.06.2019
Personnel: John M. Galer (Pub.); Vera Eckhardt (Prodn. Mgr.)

MAHOMET CITIZEN

Street address 1: 303 E Main St
Street address 2: Ste D
Street address city: Mahomet
Street address state: IL
Zip/Postal code: 61853-7448
General Phone: (217) 586-2512
General Fax: (217) 586-4821
Advertising Phone: (217) 586-2512
Editorial Phone: (217) 586-2512
General/National Adv. E-mail: mcitizen@news-gazette.com
Display Adv. E-mail: jneidel@news-gazette.com
Editorial e-mail: abenner@news-gazette.com
Primary Website: mcitizen.com
Year Established: 1853
Avg Paid Circ: 774
Sat. Circulation Paid: 33291
Sun. Circulation Paid: 36877
Audit By: AAM
Audit Date: 30.09.2018
Personnel: John Foreman (Pub.); Amelia Benner (Ed.); Tom Zalabak (Adv. Dir.)
Parent company (for newspapers): The News-Gazette

MARSHALL ADVOCATE

Street address 1: 610 Archer Ave
Street address city: Marshall
Street address state: IL
Zip/Postal code: 62441-1268
General Phone: (217) 826-3600
General Fax: (217) 826-3700
Advertising Phone: (217) 932-5211
Advertising Fax: (217) 826-3700
Editorial Phone: (217) 826-5487
Editorial Fax: (217) 826-3700
General/National Adv. E-mail: stromnewspapers@gmail.com
Display Adv. E-mail: strohmnews@joink.com
Editorial e-mail: stromnewspapers@gmail.com
Primary Website: strohmnews.com
Year Established: 1996
Avg Paid Circ: 1900
Avg Free Circ: 7416
Sat. Circulation Free: 7426
Audit By: Sworn/Estimate/Non-Audited
Audit Date: 10.06.2019
Personnel: Gary Strohm (Pub.); Melody Strohm (Pub.)

MASON CITY BANNER TIMES

Street address 1: 126 N Tonica St
Street address city: Mason City
Street address state: IL
Zip/Postal code: 62664-1115
General Phone: (217) 482-3276
General Fax: (217) 482-3277
General/National Adv. E-mail: btpublications@frontiernet.net
Display Adv. E-mail: btpublications@frontiernet.net
Editorial e-mail: btpublications@frontiernet.net
Year Established: 1867
Avg Paid Circ: 1000
Audit By: Sworn/Estimate/Non-Audited
Audit Date: 03.06.2024
Personnel: Mark Rickard (Pub.); Angela Harris (Owner / Publisher); Lois Rickard (Ed.)
Parent company (for newspapers): 1867 Publishing LLC

MASON COUNTY DEMOCRAT

Street address 1: 219 W Market St
Street address city: Havana
Street address state: IL
Zip/Postal code: 62644-1145
General Phone: (309) 543-3311
General Fax: (309) 543-6844
General/National Adv. E-mail: mcdemo@havanaprint.com
Primary Website: masoncountydemocrat.com
Year Established: 1849
Avg Paid Circ: 3900
Avg Free Circ: 2400
Audit By: Sworn/Estimate/Non-Audited
Audit Date: 10.06.2019
Personnel: Robert L. Martin (Pub.); Dan Pitcher (Circ. Mgr.); Wendy Martin (Vice-Chmn.)

MCDONOUGH COUNTY VOICE

Street address 1: 26 W Side Sq
Street address city: Macomb
Street address state: IL
Zip/Postal code: 61455-2219
General Phone: (309) 837-4428
General Fax: (309) 833-2346
General/National Adv. E-mail: eaglepub@macomb.com
Editorial e-mail: eaglepub@macomb.com
Primary Website: mcdonoughvoice.com
Year Established: 1999
Avg Paid Circ: 2047
Avg Free Circ: 26
Audit By: Sworn/Estimate/Non-Audited
Audit Date: 10.06.2019
Personnel: David Adams (Pub.); Interim Editor (Ed.); Michelle Ringenberger
Parent company (for newspapers): CherryRoad Media

MCDONOUGH-DEMOCRAT

Street address 1: 358 E Main St
Street address city: Bushnell
Street address state: IL
Zip/Postal code: 61422-1338
General Phone: (309) 772-2129
General Fax: (309) 772-3994
General/National Adv. E-mail: info@themcdonoughdemocrat.com
Primary Website: themcdonoughdemocrat.com
Year Established: 1884
Avg Paid Circ: 1400
Audit By: Sworn/Estimate/Non-Audited
Audit Date: 10.06.2019
Personnel: David S. Norton (Ed.)

MENARD COUNTY REVIEW

Street address 1: 235 E Sangamon Ave
Street address city: Petersburg
Street address state: IL
Zip/Postal code: 62675-1245
General Phone: (217) 632-2236
General Fax: (217) 632-2237
General/National Adv. E-mail: observer@casscomm.com
Display Adv. E-mail: observer@casscomm.com
Editorial e-mail: observer@casscomm.com
Year Established: 1971
Avg Paid Circ: 1500
Avg Free Circ: 12
Audit By: Sworn/Estimate/Non-Audited
Audit Date: 14.06.2023
Personnel: Jane Cutright (Pub.)

MENDON DISPATCH-TIMES

Street address 1: 202 E State St
Street address city: Camp Point
Street address state: IL
Zip/Postal code: 62320-1114
General Phone: (217) 593-6515
General Fax: (217) 593-7720
General/National Adv. E-mail: lisa@elliott-publishing.com
Editorial e-mail: gina@elliott-publishing.com
Primary Website: elliott-publishing.com
Year Established: 1871
Avg Paid Circ: 845
Audit By: Sworn/Estimate/Non-Audited
Audit Date: 10.06.2019
Personnel: Jim Elliott (Pub.); Marcia Elliott (Ed.); Gina Maddox (Receptionist); Lisa Newell (Graphics)
Parent company (for newspapers): Elliott Publishing, Inc.

MENDOTA REPORTER

Street address 1: 703 Illinois Ave
Street address city: Mendota
Street address state: IL
Zip/Postal code: 61342-1637
General Phone: (815) 539-9396
General Fax: (815) 539-7862
Advertising Phone: (815) 539-9396
Advertising Fax: (815) 539-7862
General/National Adv. E-mail: editor@mendotareporter.com
Display Adv. E-mail: mark@mendotareporter.com
Editorial e-mail: editor@mendotareporter.com
Primary Website: mendotareporter.com
Year Established: 1878
Avg Paid Circ: 4000
Avg Free Circ: 8000
Audit By: Sworn/Estimate/Non-Audited
Audit Date: 10.06.2019
Personnel: Kip Cheek (Pub.); Mark Elston (Gen. Mgr.); Bonnie Morris (Ed.)
Parent company (for newspapers): San Luis Valley Publishing

METROPOLIS PLANET

Street address 1: 111 E 5th St
Street address city: Metropolis
Street address state: IL
Zip/Postal code: 62960-2108
General Phone: (618) 524-2141
General Fax: (618) 524-4727
General/National Adv. E-mail: ads@metropolisplanet.com
Display Adv. E-mail: classifieds@metropolisplanet.com
Editorial e-mail: news@metropolisplanet.com
Primary Website: metropolisplanet.com
Year Established: 1865
Avg Paid Circ: 4100
Avg Free Circ: 11850
Audit By: Sworn/Estimate/Non-Audited
Audit Date: 10.06.2019
Personnel: Areia Hathcock (Gen. Mgr.); Linda Kennedy (News Ed.)
Parent company (for newspapers): Paxton Media Group

MIDLOTHIAN-BREMEN MESSENGER

Street address 1: 3840 147th St
Street address city: Midlothian
Street address state: IL
Zip/Postal code: 60445-3452
General Phone: (708) 388-2425
General Fax: (708) 385-7811
General/National Adv. E-mail: info@southwestmessengerpress.com
Display Adv. E-mail: info@southwestmessengerpress.com
Editorial e-mail: info@southwestmessengerpress.com
Primary Website: southwestmessengerpress.com
Year Established: 1930
Avg Paid Circ: 10200
Avg Free Circ: 1106
Audit By: Sworn/Estimate/Non-Audited
Audit Date: 10.06.2019
Personnel: Linnea Gavin (Pub.)
Parent company (for newspapers): Southwest Messenger Press, Inc.

MILFORD HERALD-NEWS

Street address 1: 18 S Axtel Ave
Street address city: Milford
Street address state: IL
Zip/Postal code: 60953-1271
General Phone: (815) 889-9930
General Fax: (815) 889-9930
General/National Adv. E-mail: milfordnews@netoptioninc.com
Primary Website: No Website
Year Established: 1928
Avg Paid Circ: 750
Audit By: Sworn/Estimate/Non-Audited
Audit Date: 10.06.2019
Personnel: Joy Claire (Adv. Mgr.)

MONDAY'S PUB

Street address 1: 112 Lafayette St
Street address city: Anna
Street address state: IL
Zip/Postal code: 62906-1544
General Phone: (618) 833-2158
General Fax: (618) 833-5813
General/National Adv. E-mail: news@annanews.com
Display Adv. E-mail: news@annanews.com
Editorial e-mail: news@annanews.com
Primary Website: annanews.com
Year Established: 1979
Avg Free Circ: 13000
Audit By: Sworn/Estimate/Non-Audited
Audit Date: 10.06.2019
Personnel: Jerry L. Reppert (Pub.); James West (Gen. Mgr.); Dianne Reppert (Circ. Mgr.); Geoffrey Skinner (Ed.); Barbara Wilson (Ed.)

MORRIS HERALD-NEWS

Street address 1: 909 Liberty St.
Street address city: MORRIS
Street address state: IL
Zip/Postal code: 60450
General Phone: (815) 280-4100
General Fax: (815) 729-2019
Advertising Phone: (815) 280-4101
Advertising Fax: (815) 729-2019
Editorial Phone: (815) 280-4100
General/National Adv. E-mail: dpankey@shawmedia.com
Editorial e-mail: news@morrisdailyherald.com
Primary Website: morrisherald-news.com
Year Established: 1880
Audit By: Sworn/Estimate/Non-Audited
Audit Date: 10.06.2019
Personnel: Steve Vanisko; Kevin Solari (Editor); Denise Pankey
Parent company (for newspapers): Shaw Media

MORTON GROVE CHAMPION

Street address 1: 160 N. Stetson Avenue
Street address city: Chicago
Street address state: IL
Zip/Postal code: 60601
General Phone: (866) 399-0537
General Fax: (312) 222-2598
Advertising Phone: (866) 399-0537
Editorial Phone: (312) 222-3429
Editorial Fax: (312) 222-2598
General/National Adv. E-mail: jmcdermott@tribpub.com
Display Adv. E-mail: jmcdermott@tribpub.com
Editorial e-mail: pjurik@chicagotribune.com
Primary Website: chicagotribune.com/suburbs/morton-grove
Year Established: 1912
Avg Paid Circ: 569
Audit By: Sworn/Estimate/Non-Audited
Audit Date: 10.06.2019
Personnel: Susan Karol (Vice Pres., Adv.); Steve Walzer (Regl./Nat'l Adv. Mgr.); Kyle Leonard (Mgr., Niche Publications); David Perham (Circ. Dir.); John Ambrosia (Exec. Ed.); Randy Blaser (Bureau Chief); Dan Obermaier (Ed.); Gary Taylor (Ed.); Mike Martinez (Mng. Ed.); R. Bruce Dold (Pub./Ed.-in-Chief); Phil Jurik (Ed.); Maggie Wartik (Gen. Mgr. of Suburban Weeklies); Peter Kendall (Mng. Ed.); Jill McDermott (VP of Adv.)
Parent company (for newspapers): Tribune Publishing Company

MORTON TIMES-NEWS

Street address 1: 306 Court St
Street address city: Pekin
Street address state: IL
Zip/Postal code: 61554-3104
General Phone: (309) 346-1111
Advertising Phone: (309) 346-1111
Advertising Fax: (309) 686-3122
Editorial Phone: (309) 346-1111
General/National Adv. E-mail: mmehl@timestoday.com
Display Adv. E-mail: mmehl@timestoday.com
Editorial e-mail: TCnews@timestoday.com
Primary Website: mortontimesnews.com
Avg Free Circ: 28210
Audit By: Sworn/Estimate/Non-Audited

Audit Date: 10.06.2019
Personnel: Mike Mehl (Sales Mgr); Jeanette Kendall (Executive Ed)
Parent company (for newspapers): CherryRoad Media

MOUNT GREENWOOD EXPRESS

Street address 1: 3840 147th St
Street address city: Midlothian
Street address state: IL
Zip/Postal code: 60445-3452
General Phone: (708) 388-2425
General Fax: (708) 385-7811
General/National Adv. E-mail: info@southwestmessengerpress.com
Display Adv. E-mail: info@southwestmessengerpress.com
Editorial e-mail: info@southwestmessengerpress.com
Primary Website: southwestmessengerpress.com
Avg Paid Circ: 8729
Avg Free Circ: 800
Audit By: Sworn/Estimate/Non-Audited
Audit Date: 10.06.2019
Personnel: Margaret Lysen (Pub.)
Parent company (for newspapers): Southwest Messenger Press, Inc.

MOUNT GREENWOOD EXPRESS - ALSIP EDITION

Street address 1: 3840 147th St
Street address city: Midlothian
Street address state: IL
Zip/Postal code: 60445-3452
General Phone: (708) 388-2425
General Fax: (708) 385-7811
General/National Adv. E-mail: info@southwestmessengerpress.com
Display Adv. E-mail: info@southwestmessengerpress.com
Editorial e-mail: info@southwestmessengerpress.com
Primary Website: southwestmessengerpress.com
Avg Paid Circ: 8729
Avg Free Circ: 800
Audit By: Sworn/Estimate/Non-Audited
Audit Date: 10.06.2019
Personnel: Margaret Lysen (Pub.)
Parent company (for newspapers): Southwest Messenger Press, Inc.

MOUNT OLIVE HERALD

Street address 1: 102 E Main St
Street address city: Mount Olive
Street address state: IL
Zip/Postal code: 62069-1702
General Phone: (217) 999-3941
General Fax: (217) 999-5105
General/National Adv. E-mail: moherald1880@yahoo.com
Primary Website: No Website
Avg Paid Circ: 1550
Audit By: Sworn/Estimate/Non-Audited
Audit Date: 10.06.2019
Personnel: John M. Galer (Pub.); Linda Hasquin (Ed.)

MOUNT PROSPECT JOURNAL

Street address 1: 622 Graceland Ave
Street address city: Des Plaines
Street address state: IL
Zip/Postal code: 60016-4519
General Phone: (847) 299-5511
General Fax: (847) 298-8549
General/National Adv. E-mail: journalnews@mail.com
Primary Website: journal-topics.com/news/mt_prospect
Avg Paid Circ: 22000
Avg Free Circ: 68996
Audit By: Sworn/Estimate/Non-Audited
Audit Date: 10.06.2019
Personnel: Robert Wessell (Classified Mgr.); Todd Wessell (Managing Ed.); Rick Wessell (Adv. Dir.)

MT. MORRIS TIMES

Street address 1: 113 S Peoria Ave
Street address city: Dixon
Street address state: IL
Zip/Postal code: 61021-2905
General Phone: (815) 732-6166
General Fax: (815) 732-4238
Advertising Phone: (815) 625-3600, Ext. 5614
General/National Adv. E-mail: leisenberg@oglecountynews.com
Primary Website: oglecountynews.com
Avg Paid Circ: 878
Audit By: Sworn/Estimate/Non-Audited
Audit Date: 10.06.2019
Personnel: Earleen Hinton (Gen. Mgr); Vinde Wells (Ed.)
Parent company (for newspapers): Shaw Media

MUNDELEIN REVIEW

Street address 1: 160 N. Stetson Avenue
Street address city: Chicago
Street address state: IL
Zip/Postal code: 60601
General Phone: (866) 399-0537
General Fax: (312) 222-2598
Advertising Phone: (866) 399-0537
Editorial Phone: (312) 222-3429
Editorial Fax: (312) 222-2598
General/National Adv. E-mail: jmcdermott@tribpub.com
Display Adv. E-mail: jmcdermott@tribpub.com
Editorial e-mail: pjurik@chicagotribune.com
Primary Website: chicagotribune.com/suburbs/mundelein
Year Established: 1912
Avg Paid Circ: 437
Audit By: Sworn/Estimate/Non-Audited
Audit Date: 10.06.2019
Personnel: R. Bruce Dold (Pub./Ed.-in-Chief); Phil Jurik (Ed.); Maggie Wartik (Gen. Mgr. of Suburban Weeklies); Peter Kendall (Mng. Ed.); Jill McDermott (VP of Adv.)
Parent company (for newspapers): Tribune Publishing Company

NEW BERLIN BEE

Street address 1: 110 N 5th St
Street address city: Auburn
Street address state: IL
Zip/Postal code: 62615-1449
General Phone: (217) 438-6155
General Fax: (217) 438-6156
General/National Adv. E-mail: southco@royell.org
Primary Website: No Website
Avg Paid Circ: 650
Audit By: Sworn/Estimate/Non-Audited
Audit Date: 10.06.2019
Personnel: Joseph Michelich (Pub.); Connie Michelich (Adv. Mgr.)
Parent company (for newspapers): South County Publications

NEWS-PROGRESS

Street address 1: 100 W Monroe St
Street address city: Sullivan
Street address state: IL
Zip/Postal code: 61951-1400
General Phone: (217) 728-7381
General Fax: (217) 728-2020
General/National Adv. E-mail: ads@newsprogress.com
Display Adv. E-mail: class@newsprogress.com
Editorial e-mail: newspro@newsprogress.com
Primary Website: newsprogress.com
Year Established: 1857
Avg Paid Circ: 3720
Avg Free Circ: 15
Audit By: Sworn/Estimate/Non-Audited
Audit Date: 10.06.2019
Personnel: Robert R. Best (Pub.); Barry Morgan (Adv. Mgr.); Carolyn Collier (Class. Mgr.); Keith Stewart (Ed.)

NEWS-STAR

Street address 1: 6221 N Clark St
Street address city: Chicago
Street address state: IL
Zip/Postal code: 60660-1207
General Phone: (773) 465-9700
General Fax: (773) 465-9800
General/National Adv. E-mail: insidepublicationschicago@gmail.com
Display Adv. E-mail: inside1958@gmail.com
Primary Website: insideonline.com
Year Established: 1906
Avg Paid Circ: 36
Avg Free Circ: 3701
Audit By: CVC
Audit Date: 30.08.2017
Personnel: Ron Roenigk (Pub.)

NEWTON PRESS-MENTOR

Street address 1: 700 W Washington St
Street address city: Newton
Street address state: IL
Zip/Postal code: 62448-1129
General Phone: (618) 783-2324
General Fax: (618) 783-2325
Advertising Phone: (618) 393-2931
Advertising Fax: (618) 392-2953
General/National Adv. E-mail: cslunaker@olneydailymail.com
Display Adv. E-mail: abrian@olneydailymail.coom
Editorial e-mail: vking@pressmentor.com
Primary Website: pressmentor.com
Year Established: 1860
Avg Paid Circ: 2500
Avg Free Circ: 6150
Audit By: Sworn/Estimate/Non-Audited
Audit Date: 10.06.2019
Personnel: Vanette King (Mng. Ed.); Kerry Kocher (Publisher)
Parent company (for newspapers): CherryRoad Media

NILES HERALD-SPECTATOR

Street address 1: 160 N. Stetson Avenue
Street address city: Chicago
Street address state: IL
Zip/Postal code: 60601
General Phone: (847) 696-3133
General Fax: (847) 696-3229
Advertising Phone: (847) 486-7300
Editorial Phone: (312) 321-2864
General/National Adv. E-mail: advertisinginfo@suntimes.com
Display Adv. E-mail: classifieds@stmedianetwork.com
Editorial e-mail: bmeyerson@pioneerlocal.com
Primary Website: pioneerlocal.com
Year Established: 1912
Avg Paid Circ: 393
Audit By: Sworn/Estimate/Non-Audited
Audit Date: 10.06.2019
Personnel: Steve Walzer (Regl./Nat'l Adv. Mgr.); John Ambrosia (Exec. Ed.); Tom Ganz (Bureau Chief); Rich Behren (Ed.); Anne Lunde (Ed.); Lloyd Weston (Ed.); R. Bruce Dold (Pub./Ed.-in-Chief); Phil Jurik (Ed.); Maggie Wartik (Gen. Mgr. of Suburban Weeklies); Peter Kendall (Mng. Ed.); Jill McDermott (VP of Adv.)
Parent company (for newspapers): Tribune Publishing Company

NILES JOURNAL

Street address 1: 622 Graceland Ave
Street address city: Des Plaines
Street address state: IL
Zip/Postal code: 60016-4519
General Phone: (847) 299-5511
General Fax: (847) 298-8549
General/National Adv. E-mail: journalads@journal-topics.info
Editorial e-mail: journalnews@journal-topics.info
Primary Website: journal-topics.com/news/niles
Audit By: Sworn/Estimate/Non-Audited
Audit Date: 10.06.2019
Personnel: Robert Wessell (Classified Mgr.); Rick Wessell (Adv. Dir.); Todd Wessell (Managing Ed.)

NORRIDGE-HARWOOD HEIGHTS NEWS

Street address 1: 160 N. Stetson Avenue
Street address city: Chicago
Street address state: IL
Zip/Postal code: 60601
General Phone: (866) 399-0537
General Fax: (312) 222-2598
Advertising Phone: (866) 399-0537
Editorial Phone: (312) 222-3429
Editorial Fax: (312) 222-2598
General/National Adv. E-mail: jmcdermott@tribpub.com
Display Adv. E-mail: jmcdermott@tribpub.com
Editorial e-mail: pjurik@chicagotribune.com
Primary Website: chicagotribune.com/suburbs/norridge
Year Established: 1984
Avg Paid Circ: 866
Audit By: Sworn/Estimate/Non-Audited
Audit Date: 10.06.2019
Personnel: R. Bruce Dold (Pub./Ed.-in-Chief); Phil Jurik (Ed.); Maggie Wartik (Gen. Mgr. of Suburban Weeklies); Peter Kendall (Mng. Ed.); Jill McDermott (VP of Adv.)
Parent company (for newspapers): Tribune Publishing Company

NORTH COUNTY NEWS

Street address 1: 124 S Main St
Street address city: Red Bud
Street address state: IL
Zip/Postal code: 62278-1103
General Phone: (618) 282-3803
General Fax: (618) 282-6134
General/National Adv. E-mail: ncnews@htc.net
Display Adv. E-mail: incnews@htc.net
Classified Adv. e-mail: nccomp@htc.net
Editorial e-mail: ncnews@htc.net
Primary Website: northcountynews.org
Year Established: 1959
Avg Paid Circ: 4000
Audit By: Sworn/Estimate/Non-Audited
Audit Date: 10.06.2019
Personnel: Victor L. Mohr (Publisher); Jesse Heidel (Advertising Manager); Jana Kueker (Circ. Mgr./Asst. Ed.); Mary Koester (Managing Ed.); Joel Heidel (Classifieds/Composition)

NORTHBROOK STAR

Street address 1: 160 N. Stetson Avenue
Street address city: Chicago
Street address state: IL
Zip/Postal code: 60601
General Phone: (866) 399-0537
General Fax: (312) 222-2598
Advertising Phone: (866) 399-0537
Editorial Phone: (312) 222-3429
Editorial Fax: (312) 222-2598
General/National Adv. E-mail: jmcdermott@tribpub.com
Display Adv. E-mail: jmcdermott@tribpub.com
Editorial e-mail: pjurik@chicagotribune.com
Primary Website: chicagotribune.com/suburbs/northbrook
Year Established: 1912
Avg Paid Circ: 1238
Audit By: Sworn/Estimate/Non-Audited
Audit Date: 10.06.2019
Personnel: Steve Walzer (Regl./Nat'l Adv. Mgr.); R. Bruce Dold (Pub./Ed.-in-Chief); Phil Jurik (Ed.); Maggie Wartik (Gen. Mgr. of Suburban Weeklies); Peter Kendall (Mng. Ed.); Jill McDermott (VP of Adv.)
Parent company (for newspapers): Tribune Publishing Company

NORTHWESTERN ILLINOIS FARMER

Street address 1: 119 W Railroad St
Street address city: Lena
Street address state: IL
Zip/Postal code: 61048-9038
General Phone: (815) 369-2811
General Fax: (815) 369-2816
General/National Adv. E-mail: news@nwilfarmer.com
Year Established: 1867
Avg Paid Circ: 2090
Audit By: Sworn/Estimate/Non-Audited
Audit Date: 10.06.2019
Personnel: Norman Templin (Ed.)

NORTHWESTERN NEWS

Street address 1: PO Box 157
Street address city: Palmyra
Street address state: IL
Zip/Postal code: 62674-0157
General Phone: (217) 436-2424
General Fax: (217) 965-4512
General/National Adv. E-mail: ads@gnnews.net
Editorial e-mail: editor@gnnews.net
Primary Website: gnnews.net
Year Established: 1969
Avg Paid Circ: 1100
Audit By: Sworn/Estimate/Non-Audited
Audit Date: 10.06.2019
Personnel: Nathan E. Jones (Adv. Mgr.); Julie Westerhausen (Circ. Mgr.)

Parent company (for newspapers): Paddock Publications

OAK LAWN INDEPENDENT

Street address 1: 3840 147th St
Street address city: Midlothian
Street address state: IL
Zip/Postal code: 60445-3452
General Phone: (708) 388-2425
General Fax: (708) 385-7811
General/National Adv. E-mail: spressnews@aol.com
Display Adv. E-mail: spressnews@aol.com
Editorial e-mail: spressnews@aol.com
Primary Website: southwestmessengerpress.com
Avg Paid Circ: 76000
Avg Free Circ: 700
Audit By: Sworn/Estimate/Non-Audited
Audit Date: 10.06.2019
Personnel: Margaret Lysen (Pub.)
Parent company (for newspapers): Southwest Messenger Press, Inc.

OAK LEAVES

Street address 1: 435 N Michigan Ave
Street address city: Chicago
Street address state: IL
Zip/Postal code: 60611-4066
General Phone: (866) 399-0537
General Fax: (312) 222-2598
Advertising Phone: (866) 399-0537
Editorial Phone: (312) 222-3429
Editorial Fax: (312) 222-2598
General/National Adv. E-mail: jmcdermott@tribpub.com
Display Adv. E-mail: jmcdermott@tribpub.com
Editorial e-mail: pjurik@chicagotribune.com
Primary Website: chicagotribune.com/suburbs/oak-park
Year Established: 1912
Avg Paid Circ: 893
Audit By: Sworn/Estimate/Non-Audited
Audit Date: 10.06.2019
Personnel: R. Bruce Dold (Pub./Ed.-in-Chief); Phil Jurik (Ed.); Maggie Wartik (Gen. Mgr. of Suburban Weeklies); Peter Kendall (Mng. Ed.); Jill McDermott (VP of Adv.)

O'FALLON PROGRESS

Street address 1: 120 S Illinois St
Street address city: Belleville
Street address state: IL
Zip/Postal code: 62220-2130
General Phone: (618) 239-2500
General/National Adv. E-mail: ofprogress@bnd.com
Primary Website: bnd.com/news/local/community/ofallon-progress
Year Established: 1858
Avg Paid Circ: 7000
Avg Free Circ: 12000
Audit By: Sworn/Estimate/Non-Audited
Audit Date: 10.06.2019
Personnel: Jeffry Couch (Ed.); Don Bradley (Prod. Dir.)
Parent company (for newspapers): The McClatchy Company

OGLE COUNTY LIFE

Street address 1: 311 E Washington St
Street address city: Oregon
Street address state: IL
Zip/Postal code: 61061-9564
General Phone: (815) 732-2156
General Fax: (815) 732-6154
General/National Adv. E-mail: leisenberg@oglecountynews.com
Primary Website: oglecountylife.com
Audit By: Sworn/Estimate/Non-Audited
Audit Date: 10.06.2019
Personnel: Vinde Wells (Ed.); Earleen Hinton (Gen. Mgr.); Luke Eisenberg (Adv. Mgr.)
Parent company (for newspapers): San Luis Valley Publishing

OLYMPIA REVIEW & MANITO REVIEW

Street address 1: 126 N. Tonica
Street address city: Mason City
Street address state: IL
Zip/Postal code: 62664
General Phone: (217) 482-3276
General Fax: (217) 482-3277
General/National Adv. E-mail: btpublications@frontiernet.net
Editorial e-mail: btpublications@frontiernet.net
Avg Paid Circ: 700
Audit By: Sworn/Estimate/Non-Audited
Audit Date: 03.06.2024
Personnel: Mark Rickard (Pub.); Angela Harris (Owner / Publisher)
Parent company (for newspapers): 1867 Publishing LLC

OREGON REPUBLICAN REPORTER

Street address 1: 113 S Peoria Ave
Street address city: Dixon
Street address state: IL
Zip/Postal code: 61021-2905
General Phone: (815) 732-6166
General Fax: (815) 732-4238
Advertising Phone: (815) 625-3600, Ext. 5615
General/National Adv. E-mail: leisenberg@oglecountynews.com
Primary Website: oglecountynews.com
Year Established: 1851
Avg Paid Circ: 1495
Audit By: Sworn/Estimate/Non-Audited
Audit Date: 10.06.2019
Personnel: Earleen Hinton (Gen. Mgr.); Vinde Wells (Ed.)
Parent company (for newspapers): Shaw Media

ORION GAZETTE

Street address 1: 1018 4th St
Street address city: Orion
Street address state: IL
Zip/Postal code: 61273-7731
General Phone: (309) 526-8085
Editorial e-mail: mcarls@oriongazette.com
Primary Website: oriongazette.com
Year Established: 1992
Audit By: Sworn/Estimate/Non-Audited
Audit Date: 10.06.2019
Personnel: Dee Evans (Pub.); Mindy Carls (Ed.)

ORLAND TOWNSHIP MESSENGER

Street address 1: 3840 147th St
Street address city: Midlothian
Street address state: IL
Zip/Postal code: 60445-3452
General Phone: (708) 388-2425
General Fax: (708) 385-7811
General/National Adv. E-mail: spressnews@aol.com
Display Adv. E-mail: spressnews@aol.com
Editorial e-mail: spressnews@aol.com
Primary Website: southwestmessengerpress.com
Avg Paid Circ: 3788
Audit By: Sworn/Estimate/Non-Audited
Audit Date: 10.06.2019
Personnel: Margaret D. Lysen (Pub.)
Parent company (for newspapers): Southwest Messenger Press, Inc.

PALATINE JOURNAL

Street address 1: 622 Graceland Ave
Street address city: Des Plaines
Street address state: IL
Zip/Postal code: 60016-4519
General Phone: (847) 299-5511
General Fax: (847) 298-8549
General/National Adv. E-mail: journalnews@mail.com
Primary Website: journal-topics.com/news/palatine
Audit By: Sworn/Estimate/Non-Audited
Audit Date: 10.06.2019
Personnel: Rick Wessell (Adv. Dir.); Todd Wessell (Managing Ed.); Robert Wessell (Classified Mgr.)

PALOS CITIZEN

Street address 1: 3840 147th St
Street address city: Midlothian
Street address state: IL
Zip/Postal code: 60445-3452
General Phone: (708) 388-2425
General Fax: (708) 385-7811
General/National Adv. E-mail: info@southwestmessengerpress.com
Display Adv. E-mail: info@southwestmessengerpress.com
Editorial e-mail: info@southwestmessengerpress.com
Primary Website: southwestmessengerpress.com
Avg Paid Circ: 4600
Avg Free Circ: 450
Audit By: Sworn/Estimate/Non-Audited
Audit Date: 10.06.2019
Personnel: Margaret Lysen (Pub.); Lori Taylor (Ed.)
Parent company (for newspapers): Southwest Messenger Press, Inc.

PANA NEWS-PALLADIUM

Street address 1: 205 S Locust St
Street address city: Pana
Street address state: IL
Zip/Postal code: 62557-1605
General Phone: (217) 562-2113
General Fax: (217) 562-3729
General/National Adv. E-mail: pananews@consolidated.net
Primary Website: pananewsonline.net
Year Established: 1864
Avg Paid Circ: 3500
Avg Free Circ: 152
Audit By: Sworn/Estimate/Non-Audited
Audit Date: 10.06.2019
Personnel: Thomas J. Phillips (Pub.); Thomas R. Latonis (Ed.)
Parent company (for newspapers): Nokomis Free Press-Progress; Morrisonville Times-OOB; Assumption Golden Prairie News

PARK RIDGE HERALD ADVOCATE

Street address 1: 160 N. Stetson Avenue
Street address city: Chicago
Street address state: IL
Zip/Postal code: 60601
General Phone: (866) 399-0537
General Fax: (312) 222-2598
Advertising Phone: (866) 399-0537
Editorial Phone: (312) 222-3429
Editorial Fax: (312) 222-2598
General/National Adv. E-mail: jmcdermott@tribpub.com
Display Adv. E-mail: jmcdermott@tribpub.com
Editorial e-mail: pjurik@chicagotribune.com
Primary Website: chicagotribune.com/suburbs/park-ridge
Year Established: 1912
Avg Paid Circ: 1909
Audit By: Sworn/Estimate/Non-Audited
Audit Date: 10.06.2019
Personnel: Maggie Wartik (Gen. Mgr. of Suburban Weeklies); R. Bruce Dold (Pub./Ed.-in-Chief); Jill McDermott (VP of Adv.); Phil Jurik (Ed.); Peter Kendall (Mng. Ed.)
Parent company (for newspapers): Tribune Publishing Company

PARK RIDGE JOURNAL

Street address 1: 622 Graceland Ave
Street address city: Des Plaines
Street address state: IL
Zip/Postal code: 60016-4519
General Phone: (847) 299-5511
General Fax: (847) 298-8549
General/National Adv. E-mail: journalnews@mail.com
Primary Website: journal-topics.com/news/park_ridge
Audit By: Sworn/Estimate/Non-Audited
Audit Date: 10.06.2019
Personnel: Rick Wessell (Adv. Dir.); Todd Wessell (Managing Ed.); Robert Wessell (Classified Mgr.)

PAWNEE POST

Street address 1: 110 N 5th St
Street address city: Auburn
Street address state: IL
Zip/Postal code: 62615-1449
General Phone: (217) 438-6155
General Fax: (217) 438-6156
General/National Adv. E-mail: southco@royell.org
Primary Website: southcountypublications.net
Avg Paid Circ: 600
Avg Free Circ: 10
Audit By: Sworn/Estimate/Non-Audited
Audit Date: 10.06.2019
Personnel: Connie Michelich (Adv. Mgr.); Joseph M. Michelich (Ed.)
Parent company (for newspapers): South County Publications

PIATT COUNTY JOURNAL-REPUBLICAN

Street address 1: 118 E Washington St
Street address city: Monticello
Street address state: IL
Zip/Postal code: 61856-1641
General Phone: (217) 762-2511
General Fax: (217) 762-8591
General/National Adv. E-mail: jrads@news-gazette.com
Display Adv. E-mail: journal@journal-republican.com
Editorial e-mail: journal@journal-republican.com
Primary Website: journal-republican.com
Year Established: 1874
Avg Paid Circ: 2672
Audit By: Sworn/Estimate/Non-Audited
Audit Date: 10.06.2019
Personnel: Tim Evans (Vice Pres./Gen. Mgr.); John Foreman (Pub.); Melinda Carpenter (Circ. Mgr.); Steve Hoffman (Editor); Tom Zalabak (Adv. Dir.)
Parent company (for newspapers): The News-Gazette; News Gazette Community News

PIKE COUNTY EXPRESS

Street address 1: 129 N Madison St
Street address city: Pittsfield
Street address state: IL
Zip/Postal code: 62363-1405
General Phone: (217) 285-5415
General Fax: (217) 285-9564
General/National Adv. E-mail: pikecountyexpressnews@yahoo.com
Avg Paid Circ: 4600
Audit By: Sworn/Estimate/Non-Audited
Audit Date: 10.06.2019
Personnel: Robin Oitker (Publisher/Owner)
Parent company (for newspapers): Coulson Publications

PLANO RECORD

Street address 1: 109 W Veterans Pkwy
Street address city: Yorkville
Street address state: IL
Zip/Postal code: 60560-1905
General Phone: (630) 553-7034
General Fax: (630) 553-7085
General/National Adv. E-mail: news@kendallcountyrecord.com
Display Adv. E-mail: ads@kendallcountyrecord.com
Year Established: 1974
Avg Paid Circ: 1395
Avg Free Circ: 298
Audit By: Sworn/Estimate/Non-Audited
Audit Date: 10.06.2019
Personnel: Jeffery A. Farren (Pub.)

PLEASANT PLAINS PRESS

Street address 1: 110 N 5th St
Street address city: Auburn
Street address state: IL
Zip/Postal code: 62615-1449
General Phone: (217) 438-6155
General Fax: (217) 438-6156
General/National Adv. E-mail: southco@royell.org
Avg Paid Circ: 475
Audit By: Sworn/Estimate/Non-Audited
Audit Date: 10.06.2019
Personnel: Connie Michelich (Adv. Mgr.); Joseph M. Michelich (Ed.)
Parent company (for newspapers): South County Publications

POST JOURNAL

Street address 1: 11512 N 2nd St
Street address city: Machesney Park
Street address state: IL
Zip/Postal code: 61115-1101
General Phone: (815) 877-4044
General Fax: (815) 654-4857
General/National Adv. E-mail: mbayer@rvpublishing.com
Display Adv. E-mail: mbayer@rvpublishing.com
Editorial e-mail: news@rvpublishing.com
Primary Website: rvpnews.com

Year Established: 1968
Avg Free Circ: 845
Audit By: Sworn/Estimate/Non-Audited
Audit Date: 10.06.2019
Personnel: Doug Schroder; Maxine Bayer (Adv. Mgr.); Linda Sweet (Circ. Mgr.); Linda Lano (Prodn. Mgr.)
Parent company (for newspapers): Rock Valley Publishing LLC

PROPHETSTOWN ECHO

Street address 1: 342 Washington St
Street address city: Prophetstown
Street address state: IL
Zip/Postal code: 61277-1115
General Phone: (815) 772-7244
General Fax: (815) 537-2658
General/National Adv. E-mail: echo@whitesidesentinel.com
Primary Website: facebook.com/TheProphetstownEcho
Avg Paid Circ: 1975
Avg Free Circ: 113
Audit By: Sworn/Estimate/Non-Audited
Audit Date: 10.06.2019
Personnel: Tony Komlanc (Owner/Ed.); Marilyn Vegter (Circ. Mgr.); Sue Patten
Parent company (for newspapers): WNS Publications Inc.

PROSPECT HEIGHTS JOURNAL

Street address 1: 622 Graceland Ave
Street address city: Des Plaines
Street address state: IL
Zip/Postal code: 60016-4519
General Phone: (847) 299-5511
General Fax: (847) 298-8549
General/National Adv. E-mail: journalnews@mail.com
Primary Website: journal-topics.com/news/prospect_hts
Audit By: Sworn/Estimate/Non-Audited
Audit Date: 10.06.2019
Personnel: Rick Wessell (Adv. Dir.); Todd Wessell (Managing Ed.); Robert Wessell (Classified Mgr.)

RAMSEY NEWS-JOURNAL

Street address 1: 223 S. Superior St
Street address 2: PO Box 218
Street address city: Ramsey
Street address state: IL
Zip/Postal code: 62080-2095
General Phone: (618) 423-4142
General Fax: (618) 423-4144
General/National Adv. E-mail: ramseynewsjournal@gmail.com
Display Adv. E-mail: ramseynewsjournal@gmail.com
Editorial e-mail: ramseynewsjournal@gmail.com
Primary Website: ramseynewsjournal.net
Year Established: 1886
Avg Paid Circ: 1770
Avg Free Circ: 74
Audit By: Sworn/Estimate/Non-Audited
Audit Date: 10.06.2019
Personnel: Robert (B.J.) Mueller (Ed.)

RANDOLPH COUNTY HERALD TRIBUNE

Street address 1: PO Box 184
Street address city: Du Quoin
Street address state: IL
Zip/Postal code: 62832-0184
General Phone: (616) 826-2385
General Fax: (618) 826-5181
General/National Adv. E-mail: eraby@randolphcountyheraldtribune.com
Display Adv. E-mail: srahn@randolphcountyheraldtribune.com
Editorial e-mail: editor@randolphcountyheraldtribune.com
Primary Website: randolphcountyheraldtribune.com
Year Established: 1862
Avg Paid Circ: 1100
Avg Free Circ: 0
Audit By: Sworn/Estimate/Non-Audited
Audit Date: 10.06.2019
Personnel: Sherri Rahn (Office Mgr.); Eric Raby (Multi-Media Sales); Pete Spitler (Ed.)
Parent company (for newspapers): Paddock Publications

RANKIN INDEPENDENT

Street address 1: 119 W Garfield Ave
Street address city: Cissna Park
Street address state: IL
Zip/Postal code: 60924-6125
General Phone: (815) 457-2245
General Fax: (815) 457-3245
General/National Adv. E-mail: rickbaier@yahoo.com
Year Established: 1958
Avg Paid Circ: 1858
Audit By: Sworn/Estimate/Non-Audited
Audit Date: 10.06.2019
Personnel: Rick A. Baier (Pub.); Steve Scott (Ed.)

RANTOUL PRESS

Street address 1: 216 E Sangamon Ave
Street address 2: Ste A
Street address city: Rantoul
Street address state: IL
Zip/Postal code: 61866-3300
General Phone: (217) 892-9613
General Fax: (217) 892-9451
Advertising Phone: (217) 892-9613
Editorial Phone: (217) 892-9613
General/National Adv. E-mail: tevans@news-gazette.com
Display Adv. E-mail: kturner@news-gazette.com
Editorial e-mail: news@rantoulpress.com
Primary Website: rantoulpress.com
Year Established: 1875
Avg Paid Circ: 475
Audit By: AAM
Audit Date: 30.09.2018
Personnel: John Foreman (Pub.); Tim Evans (Gen. Mgr.); Melinda Carpenter (Circ. Mgr.); Dave Hinton (Ed. in Chief); Bob Sheldon (Prod. Mgr.); Tom Zalabak (Adv. Dir.)
Parent company (for newspapers): The News-Gazette

REDEYE

Street address 1: 435 N Michigan Ave
Street address city: Chicago
Street address state: IL
Zip/Postal code: 60611-4066
General Phone: (312) 222-4970
General/National Adv. E-mail: advertisingredeye@tribpub.com
Editorial e-mail: redeye@tribune.com
Primary Website: redeyechicago.com
Audit By: Sworn/Estimate/Non-Audited
Audit Date: 10.06.2019
Personnel: Jenny McCabe (Adv.); Chris Sosa (Sports Ed.); Elise De Los Santos (Exec. Ed.); Michelle Lopes (Digital Ed.); Aly Morris (Dsgn. Dir.)

REGISTER-NEWS

Street address 1: PO Box 370
Street address city: Effingham
Street address state: IL
Zip/Postal code: 62401-0370
General Phone: (618) 242-0113
General Fax: (618) 242-8286
Editorial Fax: (618) 242-2797
General/National Adv. E-mail: sheonna.hill@register-news.com
Display Adv. E-mail: sheonna.hill@register-news.com
Classified Adv. e-mail: melissa.hungate@register-news.com
Editorial e-mail: rick.hayes@register-news.com
Primary Website: register-news.com
Year Established: 1871
Avg Paid Circ: 10260
Sat. Circulation Paid: 10260
Audit By: Sworn/Estimate/Non-Audited
Audit Date: 10.06.2019
Personnel: Alana Parker (Adv. Mgr.); Tesa Glass (Mng. Ed.); Darrell Lewis (Pub.)
Parent company (for newspapers): CNHI, LLC

REPORTER JOURNAL

Street address 1: 4937 N Milwaukee Ave
Street address city: Chicago
Street address state: IL
Zip/Postal code: 60630-2114
General Phone: (773) 286-6100
General Fax: (773) 286-8151
General/National Adv. E-mail: nadignewpapers@aol.com
Display Adv. E-mail: ads@nadignewspapers.com
Primary Website: nadignewspapers.com
Year Established: 1965
Avg Paid Circ: 3000
Avg Free Circ: 10000
Audit By: Sworn/Estimate/Non-Audited
Audit Date: 10.06.2019
Personnel: Brian Nadig (Pub.); Glenn Nadig (Pub.); Randy Erickson (Ed.); Joe Czech (Circ.)

RIVERSIDE & BROOKFIELD SUBURBAN LIFE

Street address 1: 2001 Butterfield Rd
Street address 2: Ste 105
Street address city: Downers Grove
Street address state: IL
Zip/Postal code: 60515-5479
General Phone: (630) 368-1100
General Fax: (630) 969-0228
Advertising Phone: (630) 427-6213
Editorial Phone: (630) 427-6254
Editorial Fax: (630) 969-0228
General/National Adv. E-mail: bkorbel@shawmedia.com
Display Adv. E-mail: bhanahan@shawmedia.com
Editorial e-mail: mhendrickson@shawmedia.com
Primary Website: mysuburbanlife.com
Avg Paid Circ: 1087
Avg Free Circ: 98
Audit By: AAM
Audit Date: 31.03.2018
Personnel: J. Tom Shaw (Pub.); Katie Sherman (Marketing Dir.); Matthew Hendrickson (Ed.); Maureen Ringness (Major/Nat'l Accts./Grp. Sales Dir.); Ryan Wells
Parent company (for newspapers): Shaw Media

RIVERTON/TRI-CITY REGISTER

Street address 1: 110 N 5th
Street address city: Auburn
Street address state: IL
Zip/Postal code: 62615
General Phone: (217) 629-9221
General Fax:
General/National Adv. E-mail: southcountypub@att.net
Primary Website: southcountypublications.net
Audit By: Sworn/Estimate/Non-Audited
Audit Date: 10.06.2019
Personnel: Byron Painter (Ed)
Parent company (for newspapers): South County Publications

ROCHESTER TIMES

Street address 1: 110 N 5th St
Street address city: Auburn
Street address state: IL
Zip/Postal code: 62615-1449
General Phone: (217) 438-6155
General Fax: (217) 438-6156
General/National Adv. E-mail: southco@royell.org
Primary Website: southcountypublications.net
Avg Paid Circ: 875
Avg Free Circ: 3
Audit By: Sworn/Estimate/Non-Audited
Audit Date: 10.06.2019
Personnel: Connie Michelich (Adv. Mgr.); Joseph M. Michelich (Ed.)
Parent company (for newspapers): South County Publications

ROSELLE ITASCA PRESS

Street address 1: 1101 31st St
Street address 2: Ste 100
Street address city: Downers Grove
Street address state: IL
Zip/Postal code: 60515-5581
General Phone: (630) 368-1100
General Fax: (630) 368-1188
Editorial e-mail: cbrokamp@mysuburbanlife.com
Primary Website: mysuburbanlife.com
Avg Paid Circ: 741
Avg Free Circ: 18
Audit By: Sworn/Estimate/Non-Audited
Audit Date: 10.06.2019
Personnel: Bill Korbel (Local Sales Mgr); Brad Hanahan (Class Advt Mgr); Dave Lemery (Ed)
Parent company (for newspapers): CherryRoad Media

ROSEMONT JOURNAL

Street address 1: 622 Graceland Ave
Street address city: Des Plaines
Street address state: IL
Zip/Postal code: 60016-4519
General Phone: (847) 299-5511
General Fax: (847) 298-8549
General/National Adv. E-mail: journalads@mail.com
Display Adv. E-mail: journalads@mail.com
Primary Website: journal-topics.com
Audit By: Sworn/Estimate/Non-Audited
Audit Date: 10.06.2019
Personnel: Robert Wessell (Classified Mgr.); Todd Wessell (Managing Ed.); Rick Wessell (Adv. Dir.)

ROSEVILLE INDEPENDENT

Street address 1: 140 S Prairie St
Street address city: Galesburg
Street address state: IL
Zip/Postal code: 61401-4605
General Phone: (309) 255-7581
General Fax: (309) 833-2346
General/National Adv. E-mail: abingdonargus@gmail.com
Editorial e-mail: eaglepub@macomb.com
Primary Website: eaglepublications.com
Avg Paid Circ: 605
Avg Free Circ: 3
Audit By: Sworn/Estimate/Non-Audited
Audit Date: 10.06.2019
Personnel: Phil Gerding (Ed.)
Parent company (for newspapers): CherryRoad Media

SANDWICH RECORD

Street address 1: 222 S Bridge St
Street address city: Yorkville
Street address state: IL
Zip/Postal code: 60560-1502
General Phone: (630) 553-7034
General Fax: (630) 553-7085
General/National Adv. E-mail: news@kendallcountyrecord.com
Display Adv. E-mail: ads@kendallcountyrecord.com
Year Established: 1985
Avg Free Circ: 5482
Audit By: Sworn/Estimate/Non-Audited
Audit Date: 10.06.2019
Personnel: Jeff Farren (Pub.); Kristen Hawkins (Adv. Mgr.)

SAVANNA TIMES-JOURNAL

Street address 1: 315 Main St
Street address city: Savanna
Street address state: IL
Zip/Postal code: 61074-1629
General Phone: (815) 273-2277
General Fax: (815) 273-2715
General/National Adv. E-mail: savtj@grics.net
Primary Website: savannatimes-journal.com
Avg Paid Circ: 2050
Avg Free Circ: 10
Audit By: Sworn/Estimate/Non-Audited
Audit Date: 10.06.2019
Personnel: Pam Villalobos (Adv. Mgr.); Robert W. Watson (Ed./Pub.)

SCOTT AFB FLIER

Street address 1: 314 E Church St
Street address city: Mascoutah
Street address state: IL
Zip/Postal code: 62258-2100
General Phone: (618)566-8282
General Fax: (618)566-8283
General/National Adv. E-mail: adv@heraldpubs.com
Editorial e-mail: mascherald@heraldpubs.com
Primary Website: heraldpubs.com
Audit By: Sworn/Estimate/Non-Audited
Audit Date: 10.06.2019
Personnel: Greg Hoskins

SCOTT COUNTY TIMES

Street address 1: 4 S Hill St

Street address city: Winchester
Street address state: IL
Zip/Postal code: 62694-1212
General Phone: (217) 742-3313
General Fax: (630) 206-0320
Advertising Phone: (217) 285-2345
Editorial Phone: (217) 285-2345
General/National Adv. E-mail: nllehr@campellpublications.net
Display Adv. E-mail: ppnews@campbellpublications.net
Editorial e-mail: ppnews@campbellpublications.net
Primary Website: scottcountytimes.com
Year Established: 1865
Avg Paid Circ: 800
Avg Free Circ: 20
Audit By: Sworn/Estimate/Non-Audited
Audit Date: 10.06.2019
Personnel: Julie Boren (Pub.)
Parent company (for newspapers): Campbell Publishing Co., Inc.

SKOKIE REVIEW

Street address 1: 160 N. Stetson Avenue
Street address city: Chicago
Street address state: IL
Zip/Postal code: 60601
General Phone: (866) 399-0537
General Fax: (312) 222-2598
Advertising Phone: (866) 399-0537
Editorial Phone: (312) 222-3429
Editorial Fax: (312) 222-2598
General/National Adv. E-mail: jmcdermott@tribpub.com
Display Adv. E-mail: jmcdermott@tribpub.com
Editorial e-mail: pjurik@chicagotribune.com
Primary Website: chicagotribune.com/suburbs/skokie
Year Established: 1912
Avg Paid Circ: 1167
Avg Free Circ: 5
Audit By: Sworn/Estimate/Non-Audited
Audit Date: 10.06.2019
Personnel: Phil Jurik (Ed.); Maggie Wartik (Gen. Mgr. of Suburban Weeklies); R. Bruce Dold (Pub./Ed.-in-Chief); Jill McDermott (VP of Adv.); Peter Kendall (Mng. Ed.)
Parent company (for newspapers): Tribune Publishing Company

SOUTHERN CHAMPAIGN CO. TODAY

Street address 1: 5-7 S. Main Street
Street address city: Villa Grove
Street address state: IL
Zip/Postal code: 61956-1522
General Phone: (217) 832-4201
General Fax: (217) 832-4001
General/National Adv. E-mail: vgnews@mchsi.com
Primary Website: facebook.com/pages/Southern-Champaign-County-Today/401543786583214?rf=162292340455904
Year Established: 1971
Avg Free Circ: 2685
Audit By: Sworn/Estimate/Non-Audited
Audit Date: 10.06.2019
Personnel: John Broux (Ed.); Jamie Morse

SOUTHERN PIATT RECORD HERALD

Street address 1: 113 E Illinois St
Street address city: Arthur
Street address state: IL
Zip/Postal code: 61911-1331
General Phone: (217) 543-2151
General Fax: (217) 543-2152
General/National Adv. E-mail: recordherald@consolidated.net
Primary Website: facebook.com/SouthernPiattRecordHerald
Avg Paid Circ: 1772
Avg Free Circ: 8
Audit By: Sworn/Estimate/Non-Audited
Audit Date: 10.06.2019
Personnel: Stephanie Wierman (Gen. Mgr./Adv. Mgr.); Roger Borham (Ed.)

SOUTHWEST MESSENGER PRESS, INC.

Street address 1: 3840 West 147th St
Street address city: Midlothian
Street address state: IL
Zip/Postal code: 60445-3452
General Phone: (708) 388-2425
General Fax: (708) 385-7811
General/National Adv. E-mail: linfo@southwestmessengerpress.com
Audit By: Sworn/Estimate/Non-Audited
Audit Date: 01.06.2024
Personnel: Margaret Lysen (Pub.)

SOUTHWEST NEWS-HERALD

Street address 1: 7676 W 63rd St
Street address city: Summit
Street address state: IL
Zip/Postal code: 60501-1812
General Phone: (708) 496-0265
General Fax: (708) 496-3019
General/National Adv. E-mail: vonpub@aol.com
Primary Website: swnewsherald.com
Year Established: 1924
Avg Paid Circ: 9300
Audit By: Sworn/Estimate/Non-Audited
Audit Date: 10.06.2019
Personnel: James Vondrak (Pub.); Bob Gusanders (Gen. Mgr.); Dave Anderson (Circ. Mgr.); Tim Hadac (Ed.); Renee Lawrence (Display Adv. Dir.)
Parent company (for newspapers): Southwest Communiy Newspapers

SOUTHWEST SUBURBAN NEWS-HERALD

Street address 1: 7676 W 63rd St
Street address city: Summit
Street address state: IL
Zip/Postal code: 60501-1812
General Phone: (708) 496-0265
General Fax: (708) 496-3019
General/National Adv. E-mail: vonpub@aol.com
Primary Website: swnewsherald.com
Year Established: 1924
Audit By: Sworn/Estimate/Non-Audited
Audit Date: 10.06.2019
Personnel: James Vondrak (Pub.); Bob Gusanders (Gen. Mgr.); John Briggs (Circ. Mgr.); Tim Hadac (Ed.)

SOUTHWESTERN JOURNAL

Street address 1: 150 N Washington
Street address city: Bunker Hill
Street address state: IL
Zip/Postal code: 62014
General Phone: 6185854411
General Fax: 6185853354
General/National Adv. E-mail: swjnews@sbcglobal.net
Primary Website: facebook.com/Southwestern-Journal-News-101665105809
Year Established: 1971
Avg Paid Circ: 1150
Audit By: Sworn/Estimate/Non-Audited
Audit Date: 10.06.2019
Personnel: John M. Galer (Pub.); LuAnne Woody (Editor); Cheri Petroline

ST. CHARLES CHRONICLE

Street address 1: 333 N Randall Rd
Street address 2: Ste 2
Street address city: St Charles
Street address state: IL
Zip/Postal code: 60174-1500
General Phone: (630) 232-9222
General Fax: (630) 444-1641
General/National Adv. E-mail: lsiebolds@shawmedia.com
Display Adv. E-mail: lsiebolds@shawmedia.com
Editorial e-mail: kgresey@shawmedia.com
Primary Website: kcchronicle.com
Avg Paid Circ: 311
Avg Free Circ: 11906
Audit By: Sworn/Estimate/Non-Audited
Audit Date: 10.06.2019
Personnel: Brad Hanahan (Group Classified Dir.); Kathy Balcazar (Ed.)
Parent company (for newspapers): Shaw Media

ST. CHARLES COUNTY SUBURBAN JOURNALS

Street address 1: 2 Eastport Executive Dr
Street address city: Collinsville
Street address state: IL
Zip/Postal code: 62234
General Phone: (618) 344-0264
General Fax: (618) 344-3831
General/National Adv. E-mail: goodnews@yourjournal.com
Primary Website: yourjournal.com
Avg Free Circ: 19800
Audit By: Sworn/Estimate/Non-Audited
Audit Date: 10.06.2019
Personnel: Mary Ann Wagner (Promotions Dir./Niche Pub.); Greg Uptain (Ed.)

ST. ELMO BANNER

Street address 1: 7 Do It Dr
Street address city: Altamont
Street address state: IL
Zip/Postal code: 62411-1135
General Phone: (618) 829-3246
General Fax: (618) 483-5177
General/National Adv. E-mail: altnewsban@frontiernet.net
Primary Website: altnewsban.com
Year Established: 1880
Avg Paid Circ: 1000
Avg Free Circ: 1000
Audit By: Sworn/Estimate/Non-Audited
Audit Date: 10.06.2019
Personnel: Clyde Barr (Ed.)

STAUNTON STAR-TIMES

Street address 1: 108 W Main St
Street address city: Staunton
Street address state: IL
Zip/Postal code: 62088-1453
General Phone: (618) 635-2000
General Fax: (618) 635-5281
General/National Adv. E-mail: startime@madisontelco.com
Display Adv. E-mail: startime@madisontelco.com
Editorial e-mail: startime@madisontelco.com
Primary Website: stauntonstartimes.com
Year Established: 1878
Avg Paid Circ: 3730
Avg Free Circ: 240
Audit By: Sworn/Estimate/Non-Audited
Audit Date: 10.06.2019
Personnel: Walter F. Haase (Pub.)

STEELEVILLE LEDGER

Street address 1: PO Box 184
Street address city: Du Quoin
Street address state: IL
Zip/Postal code: 62832-0184
General Phone: (618) 826-2385
General Fax: (618) 826-5181
General/National Adv. E-mail: eraby@randolphcountyheraldtribune.com
Display Adv. E-mail: srahn@randolphcountyheraldtribune.com
Editorial e-mail: editor@randolphcountyheraldtribune.com
Primary Website: facebook.com/SteelevilleLedger
Year Established: 1893
Avg Paid Circ: 85
Avg Free Circ: 0
Audit By: Sworn/Estimate/Non-Audited
Audit Date: 10.06.2019
Personnel: Sherri Rahn (Office Mgr.); Pete Spitler (Ed.)
Parent company (for newspapers): Paddock Publications

TEUTOPOLIS PRESS-DIETERICH SPECIAL GAZETTE

Street address 1: PO Box 151
Street address city: Newton
Street address state: IL
Zip/Postal code: 62448-0151
General Phone: (217) 857-3116
General Fax: (217) 857-3623
General/National Adv. E-mail: tpress@frontiernet.net
Editorial e-mail: rmcgrew@olneydailymail.com
Primary Website: teutopolispress.com
Year Established: 1898
Avg Paid Circ: 1100
Audit By: Sworn/Estimate/Non-Audited
Audit Date: 10.06.2019
Personnel: Ray McGrew (Pub.)

THE ADVOCATE

Street address 1: 330 N 4th St
Street address city: Clifton
Street address state: IL
Zip/Postal code: 60927-7232
General Phone: (815) 694-2122
General Fax: (815) 694-2649
General/National Adv. E-mail: advocate@dloque.net
Primary Website: cliftonadvocate.com
Year Established: 1893
Avg Paid Circ: 1441
Audit By: Sworn/Estimate/Non-Audited
Audit Date: 10.06.2019
Personnel: Therese Simoneau (Ed.)

THE ALTAMONT NEWS

Street address 1: 7 Do It Dr
Street address city: Altamont
Street address state: IL
Zip/Postal code: 62411-1135
General Phone: (618) 483-6176
General Fax: (618) 483-5177
General/National Adv. E-mail: altnewsban@frontiernet.net
Primary Website: altnewsban.com
Year Established: 1881
Avg Paid Circ: 900
Audit By: Sworn/Estimate/Non-Audited
Audit Date: 10.06.2019
Personnel: Greg Hoskins (Owner); Barbara Gathe-Barr (Pub.); Clyde Barr (Ed.)
Parent company (for newspapers): The Miami Herald Publishing Co.

THE AMBOY NEWS

Street address 1: 703 Illinois Ave
Street address city: Mendota
Street address state: IL
Zip/Postal code: 61342
General Phone: (815) 857-2311
General/National Adv. E-mail: amboyedit@amboynews.com
Primary Website: amboynews.com
Avg Paid Circ: 800
Avg Free Circ: 30
Audit By: Sworn/Estimate/Non-Audited
Personnel: Tonja Greenfield (Publisher); Jennifer Griffith (Office Manager/Circulation/Legals); Bonnie Morris (Ed.); Brandon LaChance (Editor); Brandon LaChance; Mary Mays (Circ. Mgr.)
Parent company (for newspapers): San Luis Valley Publishing

THE ASTORIA SOUTH FULTON ARGUS

Street address 1: 100 N Pearl St
Street address city: Astoria
Street address state: IL
Zip/Postal code: 61501-9545
General Phone: (309) 329-2151
General Fax: (309) 329-2344
General/National Adv. E-mail: argus@kkspc.com
Primary Website: kkspc.com/argus
Avg Paid Circ: 2000
Avg Free Circ: 62
Audit By: Sworn/Estimate/Non-Audited
Audit Date: 10.06.2022
Personnel: Jodie Ragle (circulation & editor); Judy Beaird (Ed.); Thomas Stevens (Pub.); Paul Sager (Adv. Sales Rep.); Ellen Stevens (Ad Design); Laura Hickle (Layout and Design)

THE BELVIDERE REPUBLICAN

Street address 1: 130 S State St
Street address 2: Ste 101
Street address city: Belvidere
Street address state: IL
Zip/Postal code: 61008-3772
General Phone: (815) 547-0084
General Fax: (815) 547-3045
Advertising Phone: (815) 547-0084
Editorial Phone: (815) 547-0084
General/National Adv. E-mail: vicki@southernlakesnewspapers.com

Display Adv. E-mail: vicki@southernlakesnewspapers.com
Classified Adv. e-mail: dwerner@rvpublishing.com
Editorial e-mail: bdrnews@rvpublishing.com
Primary Website: belvideredailyrepublican.net
Year Established: 1894
Avg Paid Circ: 3175
Avg Free Circ: 4275
Audit By: Sworn/Estimate/Non-Audited
Audit Date: 10.06.2019
Personnel: Pete Cruger (Pub.); Lindy Sweet (Circ. Mgr.); Sue Lange (General Manager); Vicki Vanderwerff (Advertising Director)
Parent company (for newspapers): Rock Valley Publishing LLC; Southern Lakes Newspapers

THE BREESE JOURNAL

Street address 1: 8060 Old US Highway 50
Street address city: Breese
Street address state: IL
Zip/Postal code: 62230-3924
General Phone: (618) 526-7211
General Fax: (618) 526-2590
General/National Adv. E-mail: sales@breesepub.com
Primary Website: breesepub.com
Year Established: 1921
Avg Paid Circ: 5058
Avg Free Circ: 85
Audit By: Sworn/Estimate/Non-Audited
Audit Date: 10.06.2019
Personnel: Dave Mahlandt (Pub.); Vickie Albers (Ed.); Kelly Ross

THE BUGLE

Street address 1: 23856 W Andrew Rd
Street address 2: Ste 104
Street address city: Plainfield
Street address state: IL
Zip/Postal code: 60585-8771
General Phone: (815) 436-2431
General Fax: (815) 436-2592
Advertising Phone: (815) 436-2431 ext. 103
Editorial Phone: (815) 436-2431 ext.118
General/National Adv. E-mail: advertising@verdenews.com
Display Adv. E-mail: advertising@verdenews.com
Editorial e-mail: nreiher@buglenewspapers.com
Primary Website: buglenewspapers.com
Year Established: 1957
Avg Paid Circ: 500
Avg Free Circ: 10000
Audit By: Sworn/Estimate/Non-Audited
Audit Date: 10.06.2019
Personnel: Michael James (Gen. Mgr./VP Adv./Mktg); Linda Martin (Classified Adv. Mgr.)
Parent company (for newspapers): Voyager Media Publications

THE CAIRO CITIZEN

Street address 1: 231 16th St
Street address city: Cairo
Street address state: IL
Zip/Postal code: 62914-1904
General Phone: (618) 734-4242
General Fax: (618) 734-4244
General/National Adv. E-mail: thecairocitizen@gmail.com
Primary Website: cairocitizen.com
Avg Paid Circ: 3500
Audit By: Sworn/Estimate/Non-Audited
Audit Date: 10.06.2019
Personnel: Jerry L. Reppert (Pub.); Scarlett Tarpley (Gen. Mgr.); Dianne Reppert (Circ. Mgr.); George Lamboley (Ed.)

THE CHRONICLE

Street address 1: 308 E Main St
Street address city: Hoopeston
Street address state: IL
Zip/Postal code: 60942-1505
General Phone: (217) 283-5111
General Fax: (217) 283-5846
General/National Adv. E-mail: chronoffice@verizon.net
Primary Website: thehoopestonchronicle.com
Avg Paid Circ: 1100
Audit By: Sworn/Estimate/Non-Audited
Audit Date: 10.06.2019
Personnel: Misty Courtney (Advertising Executive)
Parent company (for newspapers): Community Media Group

THE CLAY COUNTY ADVOCATE-PRESS

Street address 1: 105 W North Ave
Street address city: Flora
Street address state: IL
Zip/Postal code: 62839-1613
General Phone: (618) 662-2108
General Fax: (618) 662-2939
Advertising Phone: (618) 662-2108
Advertising Fax: (618) 662-2939
Editorial Phone: (618) 662-2108
Editorial Fax: (618) 662-2939
General/National Adv. E-mail: admanager@advocatepress.com
Display Adv. E-mail: classifieds@advocatepress.com
Editorial e-mail: rmcgrew@olneydailymail.com
Primary Website: advocatepress.com
Year Established: 1886
Avg Paid Circ: 3166
Audit By: Sworn/Estimate/Non-Audited
Audit Date: 10.06.2019
Personnel: Jennifer Lewis (Circ. Mgr.); Mary Ann Maxwell (News Ed.); Chip Barche (Sports Ed.); Bob Hiemenz (Pub./Adv. Mgr.)
Parent company (for newspapers): CherryRoad Media

THE COAL CITY COURANT

Street address 1: 271 S Broadway St
Street address city: Coal City
Street address state: IL
Zip/Postal code: 60416-1534
General Phone: (815) 634-0315
General Fax: (815) 634-0317
Advertising Phone: (815) 476-7966 ext. 209
Advertising Fax: (815) 476-7002
General/National Adv. E-mail: fpnads@cbcast.com
Display Adv. E-mail: fpnads@cbcast.com
Primary Website: freepressnewspapers.com
Year Established: 1976
Avg Paid Circ: 2125
Avg Free Circ: 30
Audit By: Sworn/Estimate/Non-Audited
Audit Date: 10.06.2019
Personnel: Eric Fisher (Pub.); Ann Gill (Ed.)
Parent company (for newspapers): Free Press Newspapers

THE DOINGS Â€" CLARENDON HILLS

Street address 1: 435 N Michigan Ave
Street address city: Chicago
Street address state: IL
Zip/Postal code: 60611-4066
General Phone: (866) 399-0537
General Fax: (312) 222-2598
Advertising Phone: (866) 399-0537
Editorial Phone: (312) 222-3429
Editorial Fax: (312) 222-2598
General/National Adv. E-mail: jmcdermott@tribpub.com
Primary Website: chicagotribune.com/suburbs/clarendon-hills
Year Established: 1912
Audit By: Sworn/Estimate/Non-Audited
Audit Date: 10.06.2019
Personnel: Phil Jurik (Ed.); Peter Kendall (Mng. Ed.); Maggie Wartik (Gen. Mgr. of Suburban Weeklies); R. Bruce Dold (Pub./Ed.-in-Chief); Jill McDermott (VP of Adv.)

THE DOINGS Â€" HINSDALE

Street address 1: 435 N Michigan Ave
Street address city: Chicago
Street address state: IL
Zip/Postal code: 60611-4066
General Phone: (866) 399-0537
General Fax: (312) 222-2598
Advertising Phone: (866) 399-0537
Editorial Phone: (312) 222-3429
Editorial Fax: (312) 222-2598
General/National Adv. E-mail: jmcdermott@tribpub.com
Primary Website: chicagotribune.com/suburbs/hinsdale
Year Established: 1912
Audit By: Sworn/Estimate/Non-Audited
Audit Date: 10.06.2019
Personnel: Phil Jurik (Ed.); Peter Kendall (Mng. Ed.); Maggie Wartik (Gen. Mgr. of Suburban Weeklies); R. Bruce Dold (Pub./Ed.-in-Chief); Jill McDermott (VP of Adv.)

THE DOINGS Â€" LA GRANGE

Street address 1: 435 N Michigan Ave
Street address city: Chicago
Street address state: IL
Zip/Postal code: 60611-4066
General Phone: (866) 399-0537
General Fax: (312) 222-2598
Advertising Phone: (866) 399-0537
Editorial Phone: (312) 222-3429
Editorial Fax: (312) 222-2598
General/National Adv. E-mail: jmcdermott@tribpub.com
Primary Website: chicagotribune.com/suburbs/la-grange
Year Established: 1912
Audit By: Sworn/Estimate/Non-Audited
Audit Date: 10.06.2019
Personnel: Phil Jurik (Ed.); Peter Kendall (Mng. Ed.); Maggie Wartik (Gen. Mgr. of Suburban Weeklies); R. Bruce Dold (Pub./Ed.-in-Chief); Jill McDermott (VP of Adv.)

THE DOINGS Â€" OAK BROOK AND ELMHURST

Street address 1: 435 N Michigan Ave
Street address city: Chicago
Street address state: IL
Zip/Postal code: 60611-4066
General Phone: (866) 399-0537
General Fax: (312) 222-2598
Advertising Phone: (866) 399-0537
Editorial Phone: (312) 222-3429
Editorial Fax: (312) 222-2598
General/National Adv. E-mail: jmcdermott@tribpub.com
Primary Website: chicagotribune.com/suburbs/oak-brook
Year Established: 1912
Audit By: Sworn/Estimate/Non-Audited
Audit Date: 10.06.2019
Personnel: Phil Jurik (Ed.); Peter Kendall (Mng. Ed.); Maggie Wartik (Gen. Mgr. of Suburban Weeklies); R. Bruce Dold (Pub./Ed.-in-Chief); Jill McDermott (VP of Adv.)

THE DOINGS Â€" WESTERN SPRINGS

Street address 1: 435 N Michigan Ave
Street address city: Chicago
Street address state: IL
Zip/Postal code: 60611-4066
General Phone: (866) 399-0537
General Fax: (312) 222-2598
Advertising Phone: (866) 399-0537
Editorial Phone: (312) 222-3429
Editorial Fax: (312) 222-2598
General/National Adv. E-mail: jmcdermott@tribpub.com
Primary Website: chicagotribune.com/suburbs/western-springs
Year Established: 1912
Audit By: Sworn/Estimate/Non-Audited
Audit Date: 10.06.2019
Personnel: Phil Jurik (Ed.); Peter Kendall (Mng. Ed.); Maggie Wartik (Gen. Mgr. of Suburban Weeklies); R. Bruce Dold (Pub./Ed.-in-Chief); Jill McDermott (VP of Adv.)

THE DOINGS WEEKLY Â€" BURR RIDGE

Street address 1: 435 N Michigan Ave
Street address city: Chicago
Street address state: IL
Zip/Postal code: 60611-4066
General Phone: (866) 399-0537
General Fax: (312) 222-2598
Advertising Phone: (866) 399-0537
Editorial Phone: (312) 222-3429
Editorial Fax: (312) 222-2598
General/National Adv. E-mail: jmcdermott@tribpub.com
Primary Website: chicagotribune.com/suburbs/burr-ridge
Year Established: 1912
Audit By: Sworn/Estimate/Non-Audited
Audit Date: 10.06.2019
Personnel: Phil Jurik (Ed.); Peter Kendall (Mng. Ed.); Maggie Wartik (Gen. Mgr. of Suburban Weeklies); R. Bruce Dold (Pub./Ed.-in-Chief); Jill McDermott (VP of Adv.)

THE ELBURN HERALD

Street address 1: 333 N Randall Rd
Street address 2: Ste 111
Street address city: St Charles
Street address state: IL
Zip/Postal code: 60174-1500
General Phone: (630) 365-6446
General Fax: (630) 365-2251
General/National Adv. E-mail: adgraphics@kcchronicle.com
Display Adv. E-mail: bhanahan@shawmedia.com
Editorial e-mail: sdauskurdas@shawmedia.com
Primary Website: elburnherald.com
Year Established: 1908
Avg Paid Circ: 1390
Avg Free Circ: 25
Audit By: AAM
Audit Date: 31.03.2017
Personnel: Leslie Flint (Adv. Mgr.); Ryan Wells (Ed.); Sandy Bressner (Ed.)
Parent company (for newspapers): Shaw Media

THE ELMHURST INDEPENDENT

Street address 1: 11512 N 2nd St
Street address city: Machesney Park
Street address state: IL
Zip/Postal code: 61115-1101
Primary Website: rvpublishing.com
Avg Paid Circ: 7
Avg Free Circ: 7138
Audit By: Sworn/Estimate/Non-Audited
Audit Date: 10.06.2019
Personnel: Randy Johnson

THE EXAMINER OF CAROL STREAM

Street address 1: 4N781 Gerber Rd
Street address city: Bartlett
Street address state: IL
Zip/Postal code: 60103-2021
General Phone: (630) 830-4145
Advertising Phone: (630) 830-4145
Editorial Phone: (630) 830-4145
General/National Adv. E-mail: staff@examinerpublications.com
Display Adv. E-mail: ads@examinerpublications.com
Classified Adv. e-mail: classads@examinerpublications.com
Editorial e-mail: news@examinerpublications.com
Primary Website: examinerpublications.com
Year Established: 1977
Avg Paid Circ: 1672
Avg Free Circ: 4892
Audit By: Sworn/Estimate/Non-Audited
Audit Date: 10.06.2019
Personnel: Randall Petrik (Pres./Pub.)
Parent company (for newspapers): Examiner Publications, Inc.

THE EXAMINER OF HANOVER PARK

Street address 1: 4N781 Gerber Rd
Street address city: Bartlett
Street address state: IL
Zip/Postal code: 60103-2021
General Phone: (630) 830-4145
Advertising Phone: (630) 830-4145
Editorial Phone: (630) 830-4145
General/National Adv. E-mail: staff@examinerpublications.com
Display Adv. E-mail: ads@examinerpublications.com
Classified Adv. e-mail: classads@examinerpublications.com
Editorial e-mail: news@examinerpublications.com
Primary Website: examinerpublications.com
Year Established: 1993
Avg Paid Circ: 5500
Audit By: Sworn/Estimate/Non-Audited
Audit Date: 10.06.2019

Personnel: Randall Petrik (Pres. Pub.)

THE EXAMINER OF SOUTH ELGIN

Street address 1: 4N781 Gerber Rd
Street address city: Bartlett
Street address state: IL
Zip/Postal code: 60103-2021
General Phone: (630) 830-4145
Advertising Phone: (630) 830-4145
Editorial Phone: (630) 830-4145
General/National Adv. E-mail: staff@examinerpublications.com
Display Adv. E-mail: ads@examinerpublications.com
Classified Adv. e-mail: classads@examinerpublications.com
Editorial e-mail: news@examinerpublications.com
Primary Website: examinerpublications.com
Year Established: 2005
Avg Paid Circ: 4950
Avg Free Circ: 2050
Audit By: Sworn/Estimate/Non-Audited
Audit Date: 10.06.2019
Personnel: Randall Petrik (Pres./Pub.)
Parent company (for newspapers): Examiner Publications, Inc.

THE EXAMINER OF STREAMWOOD

Street address 1: 4N781 Gerber Rd
Street address city: Bartlett
Street address state: IL
Zip/Postal code: 60103-2021
General Phone: (630) 830-4145
Advertising Phone: (630) 830-4145
Editorial Phone: (630) 830-4145
General/National Adv. E-mail: staff@examinerpublications.com
Display Adv. E-mail: ads@examinerpublications.com
Classified Adv. e-mail: classads@examinerpublications.com
Editorial e-mail: news@examinerpublications.com
Primary Website: examinerpublications.com
Year Established: 1997
Avg Paid Circ: 1030
Avg Free Circ: 5682
Audit By: Sworn/Estimate/Non-Audited
Audit Date: 10.06.2019
Personnel: Randall Petrik (Pres./Pub.)
Parent company (for newspapers): Examiner Publications, Inc.

THE EXAMINER OF WAYNE

Street address 1: 4N781 Gerber Rd
Street address city: Bartlett
Street address state: IL
Zip/Postal code: 60103-2021
General Phone: (630) 830-4145
Advertising Phone: (630) 830-4145
Editorial Phone: (630) 830-4145
General/National Adv. E-mail: staff@examinerpublications.com
Display Adv. E-mail: classads@examinerpublications.com
Classified Adv. e-mail: ads@examinerpublications.com
Editorial e-mail: news@examinerpublications.com
Primary Website: examinerpublications.com
Year Established: 1978
Avg Paid Circ: 1593
Avg Free Circ: 4864
Audit By: Sworn/Estimate/Non-Audited
Audit Date: 10.06.2019
Personnel: Randall Petrik (Pres./Pub.)
Parent company (for newspapers): Examiner Publications, Inc.

THE FRANKFORT STATION

Street address 1: 11516 183rd Pl
Street address 2: Unit Swofccondo # 3
Street address city: Orland Park
Street address state: IL
Zip/Postal code: 60467-9455
General Phone: (708) 326-9170
General Fax: (708) 326-9179
General/National Adv. E-mail: m.vinci@22ndcenturymedia.com
Display Adv. E-mail: m.vinci@22ndcenturymedia.com
Editorial e-mail: jon@frankfortstation.com
Primary Website: 22ndcenturymedia.com
Year Established: 2005
Avg Free Circ: 9673
Audit By: AAM
Audit Date: 30.06.2018
Personnel: Andrew Nicks (Pres.); Joe Coughlin (Pub.); Michael Ksycki (Circ. Dir.); Nuria Mathog (Ed.); Dana Anderson (Adv./Sales)
Parent company (for newspapers): 22nd Century Media

THE FREEBURG TRIBUNE

Street address 1: 820 S State St
Street address city: Freeburg
Street address state: IL
Zip/Postal code: 62243-1548
General Phone: (618) 539-3320
General Fax: (618) 539-3346
General/National Adv. E-mail: newsroom@freeburgtribune.com
Display Adv. E-mail: Tom@freeburgtribune.com
Editorial e-mail: newsroom@freeburgtribune.com
Primary Website: freeburgtribune.com
Year Established: 1897
Avg Paid Circ: 2600
Audit By: Sworn/Estimate/Non-Audited
Audit Date: 10.06.2019
Personnel: Harold G. Carpenter (Ed. Emertis); Thomas Carpenter (Gen. Mgr.); Judy Carpenter (News Ed.); Hal Carpenter (Vice Pres.)
Parent company (for newspapers): Freeburg Printing and Publishing, Inc.

THE GAZETTE

Street address 1: 111 W 4th St
Street address city: Pecatonica
Street address state: IL
Zip/Postal code: 61063-7712
General Phone: (815) 239-1028
General Fax: (815) 239-9198
General/National Adv. E-mail: rmarshall@rvpublishing.com
Primary Website: rvpublishing.com
Avg Paid Circ: 2341
Avg Free Circ: 5020
Audit By: Sworn/Estimate/Non-Audited
Audit Date: 10.06.2019
Personnel: Pete Crugar (Pub.); Randall Johnson (Gen. Mgr.); Rhonda Marshall (Adv. Mgr.); Lindy Sweet (Circ. Mgr.); Charlie Plumb (Mng. Ed.)

THE GAZETTE-DEMOCRAT

Street address 1: 112 Lafayette St
Street address city: Anna
Street address state: IL
Zip/Postal code: 62906-1544
General Phone: (618) 833-2158
General Fax: (618) 833-5813
General/National Adv. E-mail: news@annanews.com
Primary Website: annanews.com
Year Established: 1849
Avg Paid Circ: 2696
Audit By: Sworn/Estimate/Non-Audited
Audit Date: 10.06.2019
Personnel: Jerry L. Reppert (Pub.); James West (Adv. Mgr.); Dianne Reppert (Circ. Mgr.); Geoffrey Skinner (Ed.)

THE GILMAN STAR

Street address 1: 203 N Central St
Street address city: Gilman
Street address state: IL
Zip/Postal code: 60938-1218
General Phone: (815) 265-7332
General Fax: (815) 265-7880
General/National Adv. E-mail: gstar7332@yahoo.com
Primary Website: thegilmanstar.com
Avg Paid Circ: 2200
Audit By: Sworn/Estimate/Non-Audited
Audit Date: 10.06.2019
Personnel: John T. Elliott (Ed.); Kent Johnson (Prodn. Mgr.)

THE GIRARD GAZETTE

Street address 1: 174 W Center St
Street address city: Girard
Street address state: IL
Zip/Postal code: 62640-1222
General Phone: (217) 627-2115
General Fax: (217) 965-4512
General/National Adv. E-mail: nj331@royell.net
Year Established: 1879
Avg Paid Circ: 1290
Avg Free Circ: 1320
Audit By: Sworn/Estimate/Non-Audited
Audit Date: 10.06.2019
Personnel: Nathan Jones (Adv. Mgr.); Norris E. Jones (Ed.); Martin Jones (Prodn. Mgr.)
Parent company (for newspapers): Paddock Publications

THE GLENCOE ANCHOR

Street address 1: 60 Revere Dr
Street address 2: Suite 888
Street address city: Northbrook
Street address state: IL
Zip/Postal code: 60062-1580
General Phone: (847) 272-4565
General Fax: (847) 272-4648
General/National Adv. E-mail: a.nicks@22ndcenturymedia.com
Display Adv. E-mail: j.nemec@22ndcenturymedia.com
Editorial e-mail: jacqueline@winnetkacurrent.com
Primary Website: glencoeanchor.com
Avg Free Circ: 2743
Audit By: AAM
Audit Date: 30.06.2018
Personnel: Andrew Nicks (Adv. Dir.); Renee Burker (Nat. Sales Dir.); Michael Ksycki (Circ. Dir.); Eric DeGrechie (Mng. Ed.); Joe Caughlin (Pub.)
Parent company (for newspapers): 22nd Century Media

THE GLENVIEW LANTERN

Street address 1: 60 Revere Dr
Street address 2: Ste 888
Street address city: Northbrook
Street address state: IL
Zip/Postal code: 60062-1580
General Phone: (847) 272-4565
General Fax: (847) 272-4648
General/National Adv. E-mail: g.eisenberg@22ndcenturymedia.com
Display Adv. E-mail: g.eisenberg@22ndcenturymedia.com
Editorial e-mail: jason@glenviewlantern.com
Primary Website: 22ndcenturymedia.com
Year Established: 2011
Avg Free Circ: 15911
Audit By: AAM
Audit Date: 30.06.2018
Personnel: Andrew Nicks (Pres.); Joe Coughlin (Pub.); Jason Addy (Ed.); Michael Dwojak (Sports Ed.); Michael Ksycki (Circ. Dir.); Kate Lynch (Circ. Asst.); Collins Mony (CIO/ CTO); Heather Warthen (CMO); Gail Eisenberg (Adv. and Sales)
Parent company (for newspapers): 22nd Century Media

THE HANCOCK-HENDERSON QUILL

Street address 1: 102 N Broadway St
Street address city: Stronghurst
Street address state: IL
Zip/Postal code: 61480-5023
General Phone: (309) 924-1871
General Fax: (309) 924-1212
General/National Adv. E-mail: quill@hcil.net
Primary Website: quillnewspaper.com
Year Established: 1926
Avg Paid Circ: 1689
Avg Free Circ: 50
Audit By: Sworn/Estimate/Non-Audited
Audit Date: 10.06.2019
Personnel: Dessa L. Rodeffer (Adv. Mgr.); Shirley Linder (Ed.)

THE HERALD

Street address 1: 11512 N 2nd St
Street address city: Machesney Park
Street address state: IL
Zip/Postal code: 61115-1101
General Phone: (815) 654-4850
General Fax: (815) 654-4857
General/National Adv. E-mail: heraldads@rvpublishing.com
Display Adv. E-mail: heraldads@rvpublishing.com
Editorial e-mail: mbradley@rvpublishing.com
Primary Website: rvpublishing.com
Avg Paid Circ: 2942
Avg Free Circ: 6015
Audit By: Sworn/Estimate/Non-Audited
Audit Date: 10.06.2019
Personnel: Randall Johnson (Gen. Mgr.); Melanie Bradley (Ed.)
Parent company (for newspapers): Rock Valley Publishing LLC

THE HERALD/COUNTRY MARKET

Street address 1: 500 Brown Blvd
Street address city: Bourbonnais
Street address state: IL
Zip/Postal code: 60914-2328
General Phone: (815) 933-1131
General Fax: (815) 933-3785
General/National Adv. E-mail: sales@bbherald.com
Editorial e-mail: news@bbherald.com
Primary Website: bbherald.com
Year Established: 1975
Avg Paid Circ: 3000
Avg Free Circ: 39000
Audit By: Sworn/Estimate/Non-Audited
Audit Date: 10.06.2019
Personnel: Jon Olszewski (Gen. Mgr.); Toby Olszewski (Ed.); Nancy Cross (Adv. Sales)

THE HERALD-STAR

Street address 1: 103 S Eaton St
Street address city: Edinburg
Street address state: IL
Zip/Postal code: 62531-9700
General Phone: (217) 623-5523
General Fax: (217) 623-5523
General/National Adv. E-mail: heraldstar@consolidated.net
Editorial e-mail: heraldstar@consolidated.net
Primary Website: No Website
Year Established: 1882
Avg Paid Circ: 610
Avg Free Circ: 34
Audit By: Sworn/Estimate/Non-Audited
Audit Date: 10.06.2019
Personnel: Elizabeth Conoway (Pub.)

THE HIGHLAND PARK LANDMARK

Street address 1: 60 Revere Dr
Street address 2: Suite 888
Street address city: Northbrook
Street address state: IL
Zip/Postal code: 60062-1580
General Phone: (847) 272-4565
General Fax: (847) 272-4648
General/National Adv. E-mail: t.lippert@22ndcenturymedia.com
Display Adv. E-mail: t.lippert@22ndcenturymedia.com
Editorial e-mail: erin@hplandmark.com
Primary Website: hplandmark.com
Avg Free Circ: 9665
Audit By: AAM
Audit Date: 30.06.2018
Personnel: Andrew Nicks (Pres.); Joe Caughlin (Pub.); Erin Yarnall (Ed.); Teresa Lippert (Adv./Sales); Michael Ksycki (Circ. Dir.)
Parent company (for newspapers): 22nd Century Media

THE HOMER HORIZON

Street address 1: 11516 183rd Pl
Street address 2: Unit Swofccondo # 3
Street address city: Orland Park
Street address state: IL
Zip/Postal code: 60467-9455
General Phone: (708) 326-9170
General Fax: (708) 326-9179
General/National Adv. E-mail: j.mcdermed@22ndcenturymedia.com
Display Adv. E-mail: j.mcdermed@22ndcenturymedia.com
Editorial e-mail: a.datta@22ndcenturymedia.com
Primary Website: homerhorizon.com
Year Established: 2005
Avg Free Circ: 8064
Audit By: AAM
Audit Date: 30.06.2018
Personnel: Andrew Nicks (Pres.); Joe Coughlin (Pub.); Michael Ksycki (Circ. Dir.); Julie McDermed (Adv. Sales); Abhinanda Datta (Ed.)

Parent company (for newspapers): 22nd Century Media

THE HOOPESTON CHRONICLE

Street address 1: 308 E Main St
Street address city: Hoopeston
Street address state: IL
Zip/Postal code: 60942-1505
General Phone: (217) 283-5111
General Fax: (217) 283-5846
Display Adv. E-mail: chronoffice@frontier.com
Primary Website: newsbug.info/hoopeston_chronicle
Audit By: Sworn/Estimate/Non-Audited
Audit Date: 10.06.2019
Personnel: Cyndi Grace (Circ.)
Parent company (for newspapers): Community Media Group

THE JOURNAL-NEWS

Street address 1: 431 S Main St
Street address city: Hillsboro
Street address state: IL
Zip/Postal code: 62049-1433
General Phone: (217) 532-3933
General Fax: (217) 532-3632
General/National Adv. E-mail: thejournal-news@consolidated.net
Display Adv. E-mail: advertisejn@consolidated.net
Primary Website: thejournal-news.net
Year Established: 1852
Avg Paid Circ: 6450
Avg Free Circ: 129
Audit By: Sworn/Estimate/Non-Audited
Audit Date: 10.06.2019
Personnel: Mike Plunkett (Pub.)
Parent company (for newspapers): Hillsboro Journal, Inc.

THE LAKE FOREST LEADER

Street address 1: 60 Revere Dr
Street address 2: Suite 888
Street address city: Northbrook
Street address state: IL
Zip/Postal code: 60062-1580
General Phone: (847) 272-4565
General Fax: (847) 272-4648
General/National Adv. E-mail: t.lippert@22ndcenturymedia.com
Display Adv. E-mail: t.lippert@22ndcenturymedia.com
Editorial e-mail: alyssa@lakeforestleader.com
Primary Website: lakeforestleader.com
Avg Free Circ: 7764
Audit By: AAM
Audit Date: 30.06.2018
Personnel: Andrew Nicks (Pres.); Joe Caughlin (Pub.); Alyssa Groh (Ed.); Michael Ksycki (Circ. Dir.); Teresa Lippert (Adv./Sales)
Parent company (for newspapers): 22nd Century Media

THE LEADER

Street address 1: 429 W WARREN ST
Street address city: Saint Joseph
Street address state: IL
Zip/Postal code: 61873
General Phone: (217) 469-0045
General Fax: (217) 469-0089
Advertising Phone: (217) 351-5252
Editorial Phone: (217) 469-0045
General/National Adv. E-mail: nmaberry@news-gazette.com
Display Adv. E-mail: mstenzel@news-gazette.com
Editorial e-mail: nmaberry@news-gazette.com
Primary Website: leaderlandnews.com
Year Established: 1977
Avg Paid Circ: 942
Audit By: Sworn/Estimate/Non-Audited
Audit Date: 10.06.2019
Personnel: John Foreman (Pub.); Nora Maberry (Ed.)
Parent company (for newspapers): The News-Gazette; News Gazette Community News

THE LEADER-UNION

Street address 1: 229 S 5th St
Street address city: Vandalia
Street address state: IL
Zip/Postal code: 62471-2703
General Phone: (618) 283-3374
General Fax: (618) 283-0977
General/National Adv. E-mail: sales@leaderunion.com
Display Adv. E-mail: classifieds@leaderunion.com
Editorial e-mail: rbauer@leaderunion.com
Primary Website: leaderunion.com
Year Established: 1864
Avg Paid Circ: 4000
Audit By: Sworn/Estimate/Non-Audited
Audit Date: 10.06.2019
Personnel: Lovetta Lockart (Office Mgr.); Susie Pontious (Class Adv. mgr.)
Parent company (for newspapers): Landmark Community Newspapers, LLC

THE LIBERTY BEE-TIMES

Street address 1: 103 E Hannibal St
Street address city: Liberty
Street address state: IL
Zip/Postal code: 62347-1055
General Phone: (217) 645 -3033
General Fax: (217) 645 -3083
General/National Adv. E-mail: libertyb@adams.net
Primary Website: elliott-publishing.com
Avg Paid Circ: 3600
Audit By: Sworn/Estimate/Non-Audited
Audit Date: 10.06.2019
Personnel: James W. Elliott (Pub.); Marcia Elliott (Ed.)
Parent company (for newspapers): Elliott Publishing, Inc.

THE LOCKPORT LEGEND

Street address 1: 11516 183rd Pl
Street address 2: Unit Swofccondo # 3
Street address city: Orland Park
Street address state: IL
Zip/Postal code: 60467-9455
General Phone: (708) 326-9170
General Fax: (708) 326-9179
General/National Adv. E-mail: j.mcdermed@22ndcenturymedia.com
Display Adv. E-mail: j.mcdermed@22ndcenturymedia.com
Editorial e-mail: max@lockportlegend.com
Primary Website: 22ndcenturymedia.com
Year Established: 2010
Avg Free Circ: 10916
Audit By: AAM
Audit Date: 30.06.2018
Personnel: Andrew Nicks (Pres.); Joe Coughlin (Pub.); Max Lapthorne (Ed.); Julie McDermed (Adv. Sales); Michael Ksycki (Circ. Dir.)
Parent company (for newspapers): 22nd Century Media

THE MASCOUTAH HERALD

Street address 1: 314 E Church St
Street address 2: Ste 1
Street address city: Mascoutah
Street address state: IL
Zip/Postal code: 62258-2100
General Phone: (618) 566-8282
General Fax: (618) 566-8282
General/National Adv. E-mail: adv@heraldpubs.com
Editorial e-mail: mascherald@heraldpubs.com
Primary Website: heraldpubs.com
Avg Paid Circ: 2400
Audit By: Sworn/Estimate/Non-Audited
Audit Date: 10.06.2019
Personnel: Greg Hoskins (Pub.)

THE MIDWEEK

Street address 1: 1586 Barber Greene Rd
Street address city: Dekalb
Street address state: IL
Zip/Postal code: 60115-7900
General Phone: (815) 756-4841
General Fax: (815) 758-5059
General/National Adv. E-mail: jbabbitt@shawmedia.com
Display Adv. E-mail: jbabbitt@shawmedia.com
Editorial e-mail: ikoch@shawmedia.com
Primary Website: midweeknews.com
Audit By: Sworn/Estimate/Non-Audited
Audit Date: 10.06.2019
Personnel: Inger Koch (Ed.)
Parent company (for newspapers): Shaw Media

THE MOKENA MESSENGER

Street address 1: 11516 183rd Pl
Street address 2: Unit Swofccondo # 3
Street address city: Orland Park
Street address state: IL
Zip/Postal code: 60467-9455
General Phone: (708) 326-9170
General Fax: (708) 326-9179
General/National Adv. E-mail: l.healy@22ndcenturymedia.com
Display Adv. E-mail: l.healy@22ndcenturymedia.com
Editorial e-mail: tj@mokenamessenger.com
Primary Website: 22ndcenturymedia.com
Year Established: 2007
Avg Free Circ: 8502
Audit By: AAM
Audit Date: 30.06.2018
Personnel: Andrew Nicks (Pres.); Joe Coughlin (Pub.); T.J. Kremer (Ed.); Lora Healy (Adv./Sales); Michael Ksycki (Circ. Dir.)
Parent company (for newspapers): 22nd Century Media

THE MOMENCE PROGRESS REPORTER

Street address 1: 110 W River St
Street address city: Momence
Street address state: IL
Zip/Postal code: 60954-1516
General Phone: (815) 472-2000
General Fax: (815) 472-3877
General/National Adv. E-mail: m.reporter@mchsi.com
Primary Website: momenceprogressreporter.com
Year Established: 1903
Avg Paid Circ: 900
Audit By: Sworn/Estimate/Non-Audited
Audit Date: 10.06.2019
Personnel: H. Gene Lincoln (Pub.); Anita Allison (Display Adv.); Sue Lincoln (Ed.)

THE MT. ZION REGION NEWS

Street address 1: 433 N State Route 121
Street address city: Mount Zion
Street address state: IL
Zip/Postal code: 62549-1514
General Phone: (217) 864-4212
General Fax: (217) 864-4711
General/National Adv. E-mail: mtzionregionnews@comcast.net
Year Established: 1959
Avg Paid Circ: 1784
Avg Free Circ: 150
Audit By: Sworn/Estimate/Non-Audited
Audit Date: 10.06.2019
Personnel: Greg Hoskins (Pub.)
Parent company (for newspapers): The Miami Herald Publishing Co.

THE NAPERVILLE SUN

Street address 1: 435 N Michigan Ave
Street address 2: Fl 10
Street address city: Chicago
Street address state: IL
Zip/Postal code: 60611-7556
General Phone: (866) 399-0537
General Fax: (312) 222-2598
Advertising Phone: (866) 399-0537
Editorial Phone: (312) 222-3429
Editorial Fax: (312) 222-2598
General/National Adv. E-mail: jmcdermott@tribpub.com
Primary Website: chicagotribune.com/suburbs/naperville-sun
Year Established: 1935
Avg Paid Circ: 3886
Sun. Circulation Paid: 13399
Audit By: Sworn/Estimate/Non-Audited
Audit Date: 10.06.2019
Personnel: Jill McDermott (VP of Adv.); Phil Jurik (Ed.); R. Bruce Dold (Pub./Ed.-in-Chief); Maggie Wartik (Gen. Mgr. of Suburban Weeklies); Peter Kendall (Mng. Ed.)

THE NASHVILLE NEWS

Street address 1: 211 W Saint Louis St
Street address city: Nashville
Street address state: IL
Zip/Postal code: 62263-1161
General Phone: (618) 327-3411
General Fax: (618) 327-3299
General/National Adv. E-mail: news@nashnews.net
Editorial e-mail: news@nashnews.net
Primary Website: nash-news.com
Year Established: 1933
Avg Paid Circ: 5300
Audit By: Sworn/Estimate/Non-Audited
Audit Date: 10.06.2019
Personnel: Pam Smith (Pub.); Alex Haglund (Ed.)

THE NAVIGATOR

Street address 1: 19 W Main St
Street address city: Albion
Street address state: IL
Zip/Postal code: 62806-1006
General Phone: (618) 445-2355
General Fax: (618) 445-3459
General/National Adv. E-mail: stevesads@nwcable.net
Display Adv. E-mail: gatorbills@nwcable.net
Editorial e-mail: gatoreditor@nwcable.net
Primary Website: navigatorjournal.com
Year Established: 1995
Avg Paid Circ: 3400
Avg Free Circ: 12500
Audit By: Sworn/Estimate/Non-Audited
Audit Date: 10.06.2019
Personnel: Patrick Seil (Pub.); Steve Hartsock (Adv. Mgr.); T.J. Hug (Editor)
Parent company (for newspapers): S&R Media, LLC

THE NEW LENOX PATRIOT

Street address 1: 11516 183rd Pl
Street address 2: Unit Swofccondo # 3
Street address city: Orland Park
Street address state: IL
Zip/Postal code: 60467-9455
General Phone: (708) 326-9170
General Fax: (708) 326-9179
General/National Adv. E-mail: l.healy@22ndcenturymedia.com
Display Adv. E-mail: l.healy@22ndcenturymedia.com
Editorial e-mail: sean@newlenoxpatriot.com
Primary Website: newlenoxpatriot.com
Year Established: 2007
Avg Free Circ: 10560
Audit By: AAM
Audit Date: 30.06.2018
Personnel: Andrew Nicks (Pres.); Joe Coughlin (Pub.); Sean Hastings (Ed.); Lora Healy (Adv./Sales); Michael Ksycki (Circ. Dir.)
Parent company (for newspapers): 22nd Century Media

THE NEWMAN INDEPENDENT

Street address 1: 207 W Yates St
Street address city: Newman
Street address state: IL
Zip/Postal code: 61942-9444
General Phone: (217) 837-2414
General Fax: (217) 837-2071
General/National Adv. E-mail: news1@tni-news.com
Primary Website: newman.net
Year Established: 1874
Avg Paid Circ: 480
Avg Free Circ: 20
Audit By: Sworn/Estimate/Non-Audited
Audit Date: 10.06.2019
Personnel: Cathy Hales (Owner, publisher); Dana Hales (Adv. Mgr.)

THE NORTHBROOK TOWER

Street address 1: 60 Revere Dr
Street address 2: Ste 888
Street address city: Northbrook
Street address state: IL
Zip/Postal code: 60062-1580
General Phone: (847) 272-4565
General/National Adv. E-mail: g.eisenberg@22ndcenturymedia.com
Display Adv. E-mail: g.eisenberg@22ndcenturymedia.com
Editorial e-mail: martin@northbrooktower.com
Primary Website: 22ndcenturymedia.com
Year Established: 2011
Avg Free Circ: 14464

Audit By: AAM
Audit Date: 30.06.2018
Personnel: Andrew Nicks (Pres.); Joe Coughlin (Pub.); Heather Warthen (COO); Martin Carlino (Ed.); Gail Eisenberg (Sales); Eric DeGrechie (Mng. Ed.); Michael Ksycki (Circ. Dir.)
Parent company (for newspapers): 22nd Century Media

THE OKAWVILLE TIMES

Street address 1: 109 E Walnut St
Street address 2: P.O. Box 68
Street address city: Okawville
Street address state: IL
Zip/Postal code: 62271-1883
General Phone: (618) 243-5563
General Fax: (618) 243-5563
Advertising Phone: (618) 243-5563
Advertising Fax: (618) 243-5563
General/National Adv. E-mail: press1@okawvilletimes.com
Display Adv. E-mail: press1@okawvilletimes.com
Editorial e-mail: press1@okawvilletimes.com
Primary Website: okawvilletimes.com
Year Established: 1893
Avg Paid Circ: 2550
Audit By: Sworn/Estimate/Non-Audited
Audit Date: 10.06.2019
Personnel: Gary W. Stricker (Pub.); Travis Volz (Ed.)

THE ORLAND PARK PRAIRIE

Street address 1: 11516 183rd Pl
Street address 2: Unit Swofccondo # 3
Street address city: Orland Park
Street address state: IL
Zip/Postal code: 60467-9455
General Phone: (708) 326-9170
General Fax: (708) 326-9179
Editorial e-mail: bill@opprairie.com
Primary Website: 22ndcenturymedia.com
Year Established: 2006
Avg Free Circ: 21529
Audit By: AAM
Audit Date: 30.06.2018
Personnel: Andrew Nicks (Pres.); Joe Coughlin (Pub.); Michael Ksycki (Circ. Dir.); Bill Jones (Ed.); Dana Anderson (Adv./Sales)
Parent company (for newspapers): 22nd Century Media

THE PANHANDLE PRESS

Street address 1: 169 W. Jackson St
Street address city: Virden
Street address state: IL
Zip/Postal code: 62690
General Phone: (217) 227-4425
Editorial e-mail: editor@gnnews.com
Primary Website: gnnews.net/index.php
Year Established: 1964
Avg Paid Circ: 951
Avg Free Circ: 30
Audit By: Sworn/Estimate/Non-Audited
Audit Date: 10.06.2019
Personnel: Sandy Webb (Ed.)
Parent company (for newspapers): Gold Nugget Publications, Inc.

THE PETERSBURG OBSERVER

Street address 1: 235 E Sangamon Ave
Street address city: Petersburg
Street address state: IL
Zip/Postal code: 62675-1245
General Phone: (217) 632-2236
General Fax: (217) 632-2237
General/National Adv. E-mail: observer@casscomm.com
Year Established: 1874
Avg Paid Circ: 3000
Avg Free Circ: 39
Audit By: Sworn/Estimate/Non-Audited
Audit Date: 10.06.2019
Personnel: Jane Cutright (Ed.); Curtis Davis; Jason Cutright; Denise Boeker; Norman Wiseman

THE PRAIRIE POST

Street address 1: 19 W Main St
Street address city: Albion
Street address state: IL
Zip/Postal code: 62806-1006
General Phone: (618) 445-2355
General Fax: (618) 445-3459
General/National Adv. E-mail: gatoreditor@nwcable.net
Primary Website: navigatorjournal.com/prairie_post
Avg Free Circ: 13100
Audit By: Sworn/Estimate/Non-Audited
Audit Date: 10.06.2019
Personnel: Patrick Seil (Pub.); Steve Hartsock (Adv. Mgr.); Tj Hug (Ed.)
Parent company (for newspapers): S & R Media

THE PRAIRIE PRESS

Street address 1: 101 N Central Ave
Street address city: Paris
Street address state: IL
Zip/Postal code: 61944-1704
General Phone: (217) 921-3216
General Fax: (217) 921-3309
General/National Adv. E-mail: rtucker@prairiepress.net
Classified Adv. e-mail: becky@prairiepress.net
Editorial e-mail: ghenry@prairiepress.net
Primary Website: prairiepress.net
Year Established: 1848/2014
Avg Paid Circ: 2100
Avg Free Circ: 0
Audit By: Sworn/Estimate/Non-Audited
Audit Date: 26.09.2023
Personnel: Robby Tucker (Publisher); Gary Henry (Staff Writer)
Parent company (for newspapers): Prairie Beacon LLC

THE REGIONAL NEWS

Street address 1: 12243 S Harlem Ave
Street address city: Palos Heights
Street address state: IL
Zip/Postal code: 60463-1431
General Phone: (708) 448-4000
General Fax: (708) 448-4012
General/National Adv. E-mail: theregional@comcast.net
Primary Website: theregionalnews.com
Year Established: 1941
Avg Paid Circ: 4000
Avg Free Circ: 95
Audit By: Sworn/Estimate/Non-Audited
Audit Date: 10.06.2019
Personnel: Amy Richards (Pub.); Anthony Caciopo (Ed.)
Parent company (for newspapers): Regional Publishing

THE REPORTER

Street address 1: 12243 S Harlem Ave
Street address city: Palos Heights
Street address state: IL
Zip/Postal code: 60463-1431
General Phone: (708) 448-6161
General Fax: (708) 448-4012
General/National Adv. E-mail: thereporteronline@comcast.net
Primary Website: thereporteronline.net
Year Established: 1960
Avg Paid Circ: 4000
Audit By: Sworn/Estimate/Non-Audited
Audit Date: 10.06.2019
Personnel: Amy Richards (Pub.); Joe Boyle (Ed.)
Parent company (for newspapers): Regional Publishing

THE REVIEW

Street address 1: 1100 N High St
Street address city: Port Byron
Street address state: IL
Zip/Postal code: 61275-9031
General Phone: (815) 772-7244
General Fax: (309) 659-7751
General/National Adv. E-mail: review@whitesitesentinel.com
Year Established: 1857
Avg Paid Circ: 1803
Avg Free Circ: 14
Audit By: Sworn/Estimate/Non-Audited
Audit Date: 10.06.2019
Personnel: Anthony M. Komlanc (Pub. Owner); Beth Armstrong (Adv. Mgr.); Judy James (Ed.)
Parent company (for newspapers): Shaw Media

THE ROBINSON CONSTITUTION

Street address 1: 302 S Cross St
Street address city: Robinson
Street address state: IL
Zip/Postal code: 62454-2137
General Phone: (618) 544-2101
General Fax: (618) 544-9533
Advertising Phone: (618) 544-2101
Advertising Fax: (618) 544-9533
Editorial Phone: (618) 544-2101
Editorial Fax: (618) 544-9533
General/National Adv. E-mail: wpiper@robdailynews.com
Display Adv. E-mail: classifieds@robdailynews.com
Editorial e-mail: gbilbrey@robdailynews.com
Primary Website: robdailynews.com
Year Established: 1865
Avg Paid Circ: 176
Audit By: Sworn/Estimate/Non-Audited
Audit Date: 10.06.2019
Personnel: Winnie Piper (Nat'l Adv. Mgr.); Greg Bilbrey (Ed.)
Parent company (for newspapers): Lewis Newspapers

THE ROCHELLE NEWS LEADER

Street address 1: 211 E Il Route 38
Street address city: Rochelle
Street address state: IL
Zip/Postal code: 61068-2303
General Phone: (815) 562-4171
General Fax: (815) 562-2161
Editorial Phone: (815) 561-2151
General/National Adv. E-mail: kprice@rochellenews-leader.com
Editorial e-mail: jsimmons@rochellenews-leader.com
Primary Website: rochellenews-leader.com
Avg Paid Circ: 5500
Avg Free Circ: 585
Audit By: Sworn/Estimate/Non-Audited
Audit Date: 10.06.2019
Personnel: John Shank (Pub.); Kelly Price (Adv. Mgr); Wanda Brimhall (Circ.); Jennifer Simmons (Managing Ed.); Russell Hodges (Sports Editor)
Parent company (for newspapers): San Luis Valley Publishing

THE ROCK RIVER TIMES

Street address 1: 128 N Church St
Street address city: Rockford
Street address state: IL
Zip/Postal code: 61101-1002
General Phone: (815) 964-9767
General Fax: (815) 964-9825
Advertising Phone: (815) 964-9767
Advertising Fax: (815) 964-9825
Editorial Phone: (815) 964-9767
Editorial Fax: (815) 964-9825
General/National Adv. E-mail: contact@rockrivertimes.com
Display Adv. E-mail: contact@rockrivertimes.com
Editorial e-mail: contact@rockrivertimes.com
Primary Website: rockrivertimes.com
Year Established: 1987
Avg Paid Circ: 6
Avg Free Circ: 19504
Audit By: CVC
Audit Date: 31.12.2017
Personnel: Frank Schier (Pub./Ed./Adv.); Shane Nicholson (Managing Ed.); Josh Johnson

THE RUSHVILLE TIMES

Street address 1: 110 E Lafayette St
Street address city: Rushville
Street address state: IL
Zip/Postal code: 62681-1412
General Phone: (217) 322-3321
General Fax: (217) 322-2770
Editorial e-mail: editor@rushvilletimes.com
Year Established: 1848
Avg Paid Circ: 3612
Avg Free Circ: 88
Audit By: Sworn/Estimate/Non-Audited
Audit Date: 10.06.2019
Personnel: Teresa Haines (Adv. Mgr.); Alan Icenogle (Ed./Owner)

THE SENTINEL

Street address 1: 311 W Matilda St
Street address city: Illiopolis
Street address state: IL
Zip/Postal code: 62539-3605
General Phone: (217) 486-6496
General/National Adv. E-mail: thesentinel@comcast.net
Primary Website: illiopolis.com/pages/members/illiopolis_sentinel.htm
Avg Paid Circ: 1000
Audit By: Sworn/Estimate/Non-Audited
Audit Date: 10.06.2019
Personnel: Cindy Wilson (Ed./Pub.)

THE SUMNER PRESS

Street address 1: 216 S Christy Ave
Street address city: Sumner
Street address state: IL
Zip/Postal code: 62466-1142
General Phone: (618) 936-2212
General Fax: (618) 936-2858
General/National Adv. E-mail: sumpress@frontier.com
Editorial e-mail: sumpress@frontier.com
Primary Website: sumnerpress.com
Year Established: 1876
Avg Paid Circ: 850
Audit By: Sworn/Estimate/Non-Audited
Audit Date: 10.06.2019
Personnel: Tasha Legg (Office manager); Cristy Wilson (Advertising/Graphics Designer)

THE TEMPO

Street address 1: 418 W Blackhawk Dr
Street address 2: # LL3
Street address city: Byron
Street address state: IL
Zip/Postal code: 61010-8634
General Phone: (815) 234-4821
General Fax: (815) 234-4809
General/National Adv. E-mail: rmarshall@rvpublishing.com
Primary Website: rvpublishing.com
Audit By: Sworn/Estimate/Non-Audited
Audit Date: 10.06.2019
Personnel: Randy Johnson (Gen. Mgr.); Doug Schroder (Ed.); Rhonda Marshall (Adv. Mgr.)

THE TIMES RECORD

Street address 1: 219 S College Ave
Street address city: Aledo
Street address state: IL
Zip/Postal code: 61231-1734
General Phone: (309) 582-5112
General Fax: (309) 582-5319
Primary Website: aledotimesrecord.com
Avg Paid Circ: 3300
Avg Free Circ: 7387
Audit By: Sworn/Estimate/Non-Audited
Audit Date: 10.06.2019
Personnel: Teresa Welch (Adv. Dir.); Susie Swearingen (Multi-Media Sales Ex.); Penny Doyle (Admin. Asst.); John Pulliam (Ed.)
Parent company (for newspapers): CherryRoad Media

THE TIMES WEEKLY

Street address 1: 254 E Cass St
Street address city: Joliet
Street address state: IL
Zip/Postal code: 60432-2813
General Phone: (815) 723-0325
General Fax: (815) 723-0326
Advertising Phone: (815) 723-0325 ext. 303
General/National Adv. E-mail: ads@thetimesweekly.com
Display Adv. E-mail: ads@thetimesweekly.com
Editorial e-mail: editor@thetimesweekly.com
Primary Website: thetimesweekly.com
Year Established: 1986
Avg Free Circ: 25000
Audit By: Sworn/Estimate/Non-Audited
Audit Date: 10.06.2019
Personnel: Jayme Cain (Pres./Pub.)

Parent company (for newspapers): M.I.A. Media Group

THE TINLEY JUNCTION

Street address 1: 11516 183rd Pl
Street address 2: Unit Swofccondo # 3
Street address city: Orland Park
Street address state: IL
Zip/Postal code: 60467-9455
General Phone: (708) 326-9170
General Fax: (708) 326-9179
General/National Adv. E-mail: r.burke@22ndcenturymedia.com
Display Adv. E-mail: r.burke@22ndcenturymedia.com
Editorial e-mail: jacquelyn@tinleyjunction.com
Primary Website: 22ndcenturymedia.com
Year Established: 2008
Avg Free Circ: 18542
Audit By: AAM
Audit Date: 30.06.2018
Personnel: Andrew Nicks (Pres.); Joe Coughlin (Pub.); Jacquelyn Schlabach (Ed.); Michael Ksycki (Circ. Dir.); Renee Burker (Adv.)
Parent company (for newspapers): 22nd Century Media

THE TRENTON SUN

Street address 1: 15 W Broadway
Street address city: Trenton
Street address state: IL
Zip/Postal code: 62293-1303
General Phone: (618) 224-9422
General Fax: (618) 224-2646
General/National Adv. E-mail: mike@trentonsun.net
Primary Website: trentonsun.net
Year Established: 1880
Avg Paid Circ: 1700
Audit By: Sworn/Estimate/Non-Audited
Audit Date: 10.06.2019
Personnel: Michael Conley (Ed./Pub.)

THE VEDETTE

Street address 1: 120 W North St
Street address city: Peotone
Street address state: IL
Zip/Postal code: 60468-9226
General Phone: (708) 258-3473
General Fax: (708) 258-6295
General/National Adv. E-mail: newsdesk@cornerstone-media.net
Display Adv. E-mail: wendy.massat@clrdigitalsolutions.com
Editorial e-mail: info@russell-publications.com
Primary Website: russell-publications.com
Year Established: 1942
Avg Paid Circ: 2700
Avg Free Circ: 98
Audit By: Sworn/Estimate/Non-Audited
Audit Date: 10.06.2019
Personnel: Nancy Cross (Adv. Mgr.); Cindy O'Connell (Circ. Mgr.); Christopher Russell (Ed.)
Parent company (for newspapers): Cornerstone Media; Russell Publications, Inc.

THE VIENNA TIMES

Street address 1: 305 E Main St
Street address city: Vienna
Street address state: IL
Zip/Postal code: 62995-1823
General Phone: (618) 658-4321
General Fax: (618) 658-4322
General/National Adv. E-mail: viennatimes@frontier.com
Display Adv. E-mail: viennatimes@frontier.com
Editorial e-mail: viennatimes@frontier.com
Primary Website: theviennatimes.com
Year Established: 1879
Avg Paid Circ: 2424
Avg Free Circ: 57
Audit By: Sworn/Estimate/Non-Audited
Audit Date: 10.06.2019
Personnel: Lonnie Hinton (Ed.)

THE WEEKLY MESSENGER

Street address 1: 115 W Jefferson St
Street address city: Pittsfield
Street address state: IL
Zip/Postal code: 62363-1424
General Phone: (217) 285-2345
General Fax: (630) 206-0320
General/National Adv. E-mail: nliehr@campbellpublications.net
Display Adv. E-mail: ppnews@campbellpublications.net
Editorial e-mail: ppnews@campbellpublications.net
Year Established: 1912
Avg Paid Circ: 600
Audit By: Sworn/Estimate/Non-Audited
Audit Date: 10.06.2019
Personnel: Julie Boren (Pub./Ed.); Nichole Liehr (Gen. Mgr./Adv. Dir.)
Parent company (for newspapers): Campbell Publishing Co., Inc.

THE WILMETTE BEACON

Street address 1: 60 Revere Dr
Street address 2: Ste 888
Street address city: Northbrook
Street address state: IL
Zip/Postal code: 60062-1580
General Phone: (847) 272-4565
General Fax: (847) 272-4648
General/National Adv. E-mail: p.hansen@22ndcenturymedia.com
Display Adv. E-mail: p.hansen@22ndcenturymedia.com
Editorial e-mail: eric@wilmettebeacon.com
Primary Website: 22ndcenturymedia.com
Year Established: 2010
Avg Free Circ: 9191
Audit By: AAM
Audit Date: 30.06.2018
Personnel: Andrew Nicks (Pres.); Michael Ksycki (Circ. Dir.); Eric DeGrechie (Ed.); Peter Hansen (Adv. Sales)
Parent company (for newspapers): 22nd Century Media

THE WINNETKA CURRENT

Street address 1: 60 Revere Dr
Street address 2: Ste 888
Street address city: Northbrook
Street address state: IL
Zip/Postal code: 60062-1580
General Phone: (847) 272-4565
General Fax: (847) 272-4648
General/National Adv. E-mail: p.hansen@22ndcenturymedia.com
Display Adv. E-mail: p.hansen@22ndcenturymedia.com
Editorial e-mail: megan@glencoeanchor.com
Primary Website: winnetkacurrent.com
Year Established: 2010
Avg Free Circ: 5936
Audit By: AAM
Audit Date: 30.06.2018
Personnel: Andrew Nicks (Pres.); Joe Coughlin (Pub.); Megan Bernard (Ed.); Michael Ksycki (Circ. Dir.); Peter Hansen (Adv. Sales)
Parent company (for newspapers): 22nd Century Media

THE WOODFORD COUNTY JOURNAL

Street address 1: 1926 S Main St
Street address city: Eureka
Street address state: IL
Zip/Postal code: 61530-1666
General Phone: (309) 467-3314
General Fax: (309) 467-4563
Advertising Phone: (309) 467-3314 Ext. 203
Editorial Phone: (309) 467-3314 Ext. 211
General/National Adv. E-mail: hbowman@pantagraph.com
Display Adv. E-mail: hhowman@panteetpm
Editorial e-mail: cwolfe@pantagraph.com
Primary Website: woodcojo.com
Year Established: 1867
Avg Paid Circ: 1224
Audit By: AAM
Audit Date: 31.03.2016
Personnel: Barry Winterland (Pub.); Mark Barra (Gen. Mgr.); Cheryl Wolfe (Ed.)

TOLEDO DEMOCRAT

Street address 1: 116 Courthouse Sq
Street address city: Toledo
Street address state: IL
Zip/Postal code: 62468-1052
General Phone: (217) 849-2000
General Fax: (217) 849-3237
General/National Adv. E-mail: tdnews@cell1net.net
Primary Website: facebook.com/Toledo-Democrat-134064103434272
Year Established: 1857
Avg Paid Circ: 1900
Audit By: Sworn/Estimate/Non-Audited
Audit Date: 10.06.2019
Personnel: Billie Chambers (Ed.)

TONICA NEWS

Street address 1: 800 Ace Rd
Street address city: Princeton
Street address state: IL
Zip/Postal code: 61356-9201
General Phone: (815) 875-4461
General Fax: (815) 875-1235
General/National Adv. E-mail: advertising@tonicanews.com
Display Adv. E-mail: cwagner@bcrnews.com
Editorial e-mail: news@tonicanews.com
Primary Website: tonicanews.com
Avg Paid Circ: 585
Avg Free Circ: 50
Audit By: Sworn/Estimate/Non-Audited
Audit Date: 10.06.2019
Personnel: Sam R. Fisher (Pub.); Terri Simon (Ed.); Ashley Oliver (Adv. Sales)
Parent company (for newspapers): Shaw Media

TRI-COUNTY PRESS

Street address 1: 113 S Peoria Ave
Street address city: Dixon
Street address state: IL
Zip/Postal code: 61021-2905
General Phone: (815) 732-6166 ext. 5901
General Fax: (815) 732-4238
General/National Adv. E-mail: leisenberg@oglecountynews.com
Editorial e-mail: vwells@oglecountynews.com
Primary Website: oglecountynews.com
Avg Paid Circ: 1200
Audit By: Sworn/Estimate/Non-Audited
Audit Date: 10.06.2019
Personnel: Earleen Hinton (Gen. Mgr.); Vinde Wells (Ed.); Luke Eisenberg (Adv. Sales Mgr.)
Parent company (for newspapers): Shaw Media

TROY TIMES-TRIBUNE

Street address 1: 201 E Market St
Street address 2: Stop 6
Street address city: Troy
Street address state: IL
Zip/Postal code: 62294-1518
General Phone: (618) 667-3111
General Fax: (618) 667-3128
General/National Adv. E-mail: troy.il.news@gmail.com
Display Adv. E-mail: TroyNews@aol.com
Editorial e-mail: editor.times.tribune@gmail.com
Primary Website: troytimes-tribune.com
Avg Paid Circ: 3300
Audit By: Sworn/Estimate/Non-Audited
Audit Date: 10.06.2019
Personnel: Paul Ping (Adv. Mgr.); Steve Rensberry (Ed.); Jerry Campbell (Sports Reporter); Charles Feldman (Reporter); Angela Simmons (Reporter); Masja LaRue (Office Manager)

VALLEY LIFE

Street address 1: 1586 Barber Greene Rd
Street address city: Dekalb
Street address state: IL
Zip/Postal code: 60115-7900
General Phone: (815) 756-4841
General Fax: (815) 758-5059
General/National Adv. E-mail: vfpads@vfpnews.com
Display Adv. E-mail: vfpads@vfpnews.com
Editorial e-mail: vfpnews@vfpnews.com
Primary Website: valleylifepress.com
Avg Free Circ: 15000
Audit By: Sworn/Estimate/Non-Audited
Audit Date: 10.06.2019
Personnel: Rob Dancey (Adv. Sales); Debbie Behrends (Ed.)
Parent company (for newspapers): Shaw Media

VERNON HILLS REVIEW

Street address 1: 160 N. Stetson Avenue
Street address city: Chicago
Street address state: IL
Zip/Postal code: 60601
General Phone: (847) 317-0500
Editorial Phone: (312) 321-2328
General/National Adv. E-mail: advertisinginfo@suntimes.com
Display Adv. E-mail: classifieds@stmedianetwork.com
Primary Website: pioneerlocal.com
Year Established: 1912
Avg Paid Circ: 363
Audit By: Sworn/Estimate/Non-Audited
Audit Date: 10.06.2019
Personnel: Jill McDermott (VP of Adv.); Phil Jurik (Ed.); R. Bruce Dold (Pub./Ed.-in-Chief); Peter Kendall (Mng. Ed.); Maggie Wartik (Gen. Mgr. of Suburban Weeklies)
Parent company (for newspapers): Tribune Publishing Company

VILLA GROVE NEWS

Street address 1: 57 S Main St
Street address city: Villa Grove
Street address state: IL
Zip/Postal code: 61956-1522
General Phone: (217) 832-4201
General Fax: (217) 832-4001
General/National Adv. E-mail: vgads@mediacombb.net
Display Adv. E-mail: vgnews@mchsi.com
Editorial e-mail: vgnews@mchsi.com
Primary Website: facebook.com/TheVillaGroveNews/?ref=page_internal
Avg Paid Circ: 1200
Audit By: Sworn/Estimate/Non-Audited
Audit Date: 10.06.2019
Personnel: John Broux (Gen. Mgr./Ed.); Jamie Morse (Advertising Representative); Nathan Thompson (Editor)
Parent company (for newspapers): The Miami Herald Publishing Co.

VILLA PARK REVIEW

Street address 1: 929 S Main St
Street address 2: Ste 102
Street address city: Lombard
Street address state: IL
Zip/Postal code: 60148-3325
General Phone: (630) 627-7010
General Fax: (630) 627-7027
General/National Adv. E-mail: lombardian@sbcglobal.net
Primary Website: lombardian.info
Year Established: 1959
Avg Paid Circ: 9000
Audit By: Sworn/Estimate/Non-Audited
Audit Date: 10.06.2019
Personnel: Bonnie MacKay (Ed./Pub.)

VILLA PARK SUBURBAN LIFE

Street address 1: 1101 W. 31st Street
Street address 2: Ste 260
Street address city: Downers Grove
Street address state: IL
Zip/Postal code: 60515
General Phone: (630) 368-1100
General Fax: (630) 969-0228
Advertising Phone: (630) 427-6213
Editorial Phone: (630) 427-6270
Editorial Fax: (630) 969-0228
General/National Adv. E-mail: nshannon@shawmedia.com
Display Adv. E-mail: sbissell@shawmedia.com
Editorial e-mail: rwells@shawmedia.com
Primary Website: mysuburbanlife.com
Avg Paid Circ: 219
Avg Free Circ: 27
Audit By: AAM
Audit Date: 31.03.2018
Personnel: J. Tom Shaw (Pub.); Katie Sherman (Marketing Dir.); David Good (Ed.); Maureen Ringness (Major/Nat'l Accts./Grp. Sales Dir.); Ryan Wells
Parent company (for newspapers): Shaw Media

VIRDEN RECORDER

Street address 1: 169 E. Dean St.

Street address city: Virden
Street address state: IL
Zip/Postal code: 62690
General Phone: (217) 965-3355
General Fax: (217) 965-4512
General/National Adv. E-mail: ads@gnnews.net
Editorial e-mail: editor@gnnews.net
Primary Website: gnnews.net
Year Established: 1916
Avg Paid Circ: 6100
Avg Free Circ: 30
Audit By: Sworn/Estimate/Non-Audited
Audit Date: 10.06.2019
Personnel: Nathan Jones (Adv. Mgr.); Julie Westerhausen (Circ. Mgr.)
Parent company (for newspapers): Paddock Publications

WASHINGTON TIMES REPORTER

Street address 1: 306 Court St
Street address city: Pekin
Street address state: IL
Zip/Postal code: 61554-3104
General Phone: (309) 346-1111 ext. 660
General Fax: (309) 346-1446
Advertising Phone: (309) 686-3106
Advertising Fax: (309) 346-9815
Editorial Phone: (309) 686-3054
Editorial Fax: (309) 346-1446
General/National Adv. E-mail: mmehl@timestoday.com
Display Adv. E-mail: lscott@pekintimes.com
Editorial e-mail: wtr@timestoday.com
Primary Website: washingtontimesreporter.com
Year Established: 1840
Avg Paid Circ: 171
Avg Free Circ: 9488
Audit By: Sworn/Estimate/Non-Audited
Audit Date: 10.06.2019
Personnel: Jeanette Kendall (Exec. Ed.); Donna Reaska (Office Mgr.); Linda Smith Brown (Gen. Sales Mgr.); Ken Mauser (Pub.)
Parent company (for newspapers): CherryRoad Media

WAVERLY JOURNAL

Street address 1: 130 S Pearl St
Street address city: Waverly
Street address state: IL
Zip/Postal code: 62692-1166
General Phone: (217) 435-9221
General Fax: (217) 435-4511
General/National Adv. E-mail: journaltrib@mchsi.com
Editorial e-mail: journaltrib@mchsi.com
Primary Website: facebook.com/pages/Waverly-Journal/169529479729692
Avg Paid Circ: 1350
Avg Free Circ: 20
Audit By: Sworn/Estimate/Non-Audited
Audit Date: 10.06.2019
Personnel: Nancy P. Copelin (Pub.); Julie A. Springer (Ed.)

WAYNE COUNTY PRESS

Street address 1: 213 E Main St
Street address city: Fairfield
Street address state: IL
Zip/Postal code: 62837-2028
General Phone: (618) 842-2662
General Fax: (618) 842-7912
Advertising Phone: (618) 842-2662
Editorial Phone: (618) 842-2662
General/National Adv. E-mail: news@waycopress.com
Display Adv. E-mail: news@waycopress.com
Editorial e-mail: news@waycopress.com
Primary Website: waycopress.com
Year Established: 1866
Avg Paid Circ: 4925
Avg Free Circ: 50
Audit By: Sworn/Estimate/Non-Audited
Audit Date: 10.06.2019
Personnel: Thomas Mathews (Pub./Gen. Mgr.); Elizabeth Gonzalez (Advertising Manager); Elizabeth Gonzalez (Adv. Mgr.); Brian Turner (Editor)

WEDNESDAY JOURNAL OF OAK PARK & RIVER FOREST

Street address 1: 141 S Oak Park Ave
Street address 2: Ste 1
Street address city: Oak Park
Street address state: IL
Zip/Postal code: 60302-2972
General Phone: (708) 524-8300
General Fax: (708) 524-0447
General/National Adv. E-mail: dawn@oakpark.com
Display Adv. E-mail: maryellen@oakpark.com
Editorial e-mail: dhaley@wjinc.com
Primary Website: oakpark.com
Mthly Avg Views: 300000
Mthly Avg Unique Visitors: 18000
Year Established: 1980
Avg Paid Circ: 5450
Avg Free Circ: 1400
Audit By: Sworn/Estimate/Non-Audited
Audit Date: 10.06.2019
Personnel: Dan Haley (Pub.); Andy Mead (Prodn. Mgr.)

WENONA INDEX

Street address 1: 709 3rd St
Street address city: Henry
Street address state: IL
Zip/Postal code: 61537-1446
General Phone: (309) 364-3250
General Fax: (309) 364-3858
Avg Paid Circ: 711
Audit By: Sworn/Estimate/Non-Audited
Audit Date: 10.06.2019
Personnel: Sheila Healy

WEST CHICAGO SUBURBAN LIFE

Street address 1: 2001 Butterfield Rd Suite 105
Street address 2: Ste 105
Street address city: Downers Grove
Street address state: IL
Zip/Postal code: 60515
General Phone: (844) 368-1100
General/National Adv. E-mail: bkorbel@shawmedia.com
Display Adv. E-mail: nfossmeyer@shawmedia.com
Editorial e-mail: rwells@shawmedia.com
Primary Website: mysuburbanlife.com
Avg Paid Circ: 141
Avg Free Circ: 33
Audit By: AAM
Audit Date: 31.03.2018
Personnel: J. Tom Shaw (Pub.); Katie Sherman (Marketing Dir.); Maureen Ringness (Major/Nat'l Accts./Grp. Sales Dir.); Ryan Wells; Bob Rakow (Ed.)
Parent company (for newspapers): Shaw Media

WEST VIGO TIMES

Street address 1: 610 Archer Ave
Street address city: Marshall
Street address state: IL
Zip/Postal code: 62441-1268
General Phone: (217) 826-3600
General Fax: (217) 826-3700
Advertising Phone: (217) 932-5211
Advertising Fax: (217) 826-3700
Editorial Phone: (217) 826-5487
Editorial Fax: (217) 826-3700
General/National Adv. E-mail: stromnewspapers@gmail.com
Display Adv. E-mail: strohmnews@joink.com
Editorial e-mail: stromnewspapers@gmail.com
Primary Website: strohmnews.com
Year Established: 1996
Avg Paid Circ: 1900
Avg Free Circ: 7416
Audit By: Sworn/Estimate/Non-Audited
Audit Date: 10.06.2019
Personnel: Gary Strohm (Pub.); Melody Strohm (Pub.)

WESTMONT SUBURBAN LIFE

Street address 1: 2001 Butterfield Rd Suite 105
Street address 2: Ste 260
Street address city: Downers Grove
Street address state: IL
Zip/Postal code: 60515
General Phone: (630) 368-1100
General Fax: (630) 969-0228
Advertising Phone: (630) 427-6213
Editorial Phone: (630) 427-6252
General/National Adv. E-mail: nshannon@shawmedia.com
Display Adv. E-mail: sbissell@shawmedia.com
Editorial e-mail: rwells@shawmedia.com
Primary Website: mysuburbanlife.com
Avg Paid Circ: 506
Avg Free Circ: 46
Audit By: AAM
Audit Date: 31.03.2018
Personnel: J. Tom Shaw (Pub.); Katie Sherman (Marketing Dir.); Ryan Terrell (Ed.); Maureen Ringness (Major/Nat'l Accts./Grp. Sales Dir.); Ryan Wells
Parent company (for newspapers): Shaw Media

WHEATON SUBURBAN LIFE

Street address 1: 2001 Butterfield Rd Suite 105
Street address 2: Ste 260
Street address city: Downers Grove
Street address state: IL
Zip/Postal code: 60515
General Phone: (630) 368-1100
General Fax: (630) 969-0228
Advertising Phone: (630) 427-6213
Editorial Phone: (630) 427-6248
General/National Adv. E-mail: nshannon@shawmedia.com
Display Adv. E-mail: sbissell@shawmedia.com
Editorial e-mail: rwells@shawmedia.com
Primary Website: mysuburbanlife.com
Avg Paid Circ: 202
Avg Free Circ: 4926
Audit By: CAC
Audit Date: 31.03.2018
Personnel: J. Tom Shaw (Pub.); Katie Sherman (Marketing Dir.); Anna Schier (Ed.); Maureen Ringness (Major/Nat'l Accts./Grp. Sales Dir.); Ryan Wells
Parent company (for newspapers): Shaw Media

WHITESIDE NEWS SENTINEL

Street address 1: 100 E Main St
Street address city: Morrison
Street address state: IL
Zip/Postal code: 61270-2694
General Phone: (815) 772-7244
General Fax: (815) 772-4105
Advertising Phone: (815) 772-7244
Advertising Fax: (815) 772-4105
Editorial Phone: (815) 772-7244
Editorial Fax: (815) 772-7244
General/National Adv. E-mail: wnssentinel@gmail.com
Display Adv. E-mail: wnssentinel@gmail.com
Editorial e-mail: wnssentinel@gmail.com
Year Established: 1857
Avg Paid Circ: 2425
Avg Free Circ: 22
Audit By: Sworn/Estimate/Non-Audited
Audit Date: 10.06.2019
Personnel: Sue Patten (Pub./Adv. Mgr.); Jerry Lindsey (Editor); Anthony M. Komlanc (Owner/Mng. Ed.); Nancy Rutledge (Prodn. Mgr.)
Parent company (for newspapers): WNS Publications Inc.

WILLIAMSVILLE-SHERMAN SUN TIMES

Street address 1: 110 N 5th
Street address city: Auburn
Street address state: IL
Zip/Postal code: 62615
General Phone: (217) 629-9221
General/National Adv. E-mail: southcountypub@att.net
Primary Website: southcountypublications.net
Audit By: Sworn/Estimate/Non-Audited
Audit Date: 10.06.2019
Personnel: Byron Painter (Editor)
Parent company (for newspapers): South County Publications

WILMETTE LIFE

Street address 1: 160 N. Stetson Avenue
Street address city: Chicago
Street address state: IL
Zip/Postal code: 60601
General Phone: (866) 399-0537
General Fax: (312) 222-2598
Advertising Phone: (866) 399-0537
Editorial Phone: (312) 222-3429
Editorial Fax: (312) 222-2598
General/National Adv. E-mail: jmcdermott@tribpub.com
Display Adv. E-mail: jmcdermott@tribpub.com
Editorial e-mail: pjurik@chicagotribune.com
Primary Website: chicagotribune.com/suburbs/wilmette
Avg Paid Circ: 895
Audit By: Sworn/Estimate/Non-Audited
Audit Date: 10.06.2019
Personnel: Jeff Wisser (Ed. in Chief); Carol Goddard (Sr. Ed.); Randy Blaser (Sr. Ed.); Cathy Backer (Mng. Ed.); Phil Jurik (Ed.); R. Bruce Dold (Pub./Ed.-in-Chief); Peter Kendall (Mng. Ed.); Jill McDermott (VP of Adv.); Maggie Wartik (Gen. Mgr. of Suburban Weeklies)
Parent company (for newspapers): Tribune Publishing Company

WINNETKA TALK

Street address 1: 160 N. Stetson Avenue
Street address city: Chicago
Street address state: IL
Zip/Postal code: 60601
General Phone: (866) 399-0537
General Fax: (312) 222-2598
Advertising Phone: (866) 399-0537
Editorial Phone: (312) 222-3429
Editorial Fax: (312) 222-2598
General/National Adv. E-mail: jmcdermott@tribpub.com
Display Adv. E-mail: jmcdermott@tribpub.com
Editorial e-mail: pjurik@chicagotribune.com
Primary Website: chicagotribune.com/suburbs/winnetka
Year Established: 1912
Avg Paid Circ: 858
Audit By: Sworn/Estimate/Non-Audited
Audit Date: 10.06.2019
Personnel: Peggy Cunniff (Adv. Dir.); Paul Sassone (Exec. Ed.); Jeff Wisser (Ed. in Chief); Phil Jurik (Ed.); R. Bruce Dold (Pub./Ed.-in-Chief); Peter Kendall (Mng. Ed.); Jill McDermott (VP of Adv.); Maggie Wartik (Gen. Mgr. of Suburban Weeklies)
Parent company (for newspapers): Tribune Publishing Company

WOODFORD COUNTY JOURNAL ROANOKE-MINONK EDITION

Street address 1: 105 E Broad St
Street address city: Roanoke
Street address state: IL
Zip/Postal code: 61561-7547
General Phone: (309) 923-5841
General Fax: (309) 467-4563
Advertising Phone: (309) 467-3314 Ext 202
Editorial Phone: (309) 467-3314 Ext 211
General/National Adv. E-mail: mbarra@mtco.com
Display Adv. E-mail: wendiwcj@mtco.com
Editorial e-mail: cwolfe@mtco.com
Primary Website: pantagraph.com
Year Established: 1936
Avg Paid Circ: 893
Audit By: AAM
Audit Date: 31.03.2016
Personnel: Mark Pickering (Ed.)

WOODFORD COURIER

Street address 1: 100 Ford Ln
Street address city: Washington
Street address state: IL
Zip/Postal code: 61571-2668
General Phone: (309) 444-3139
General Fax: (309) 444-8505
Editorial Phone: (309)444-3139, x12
General/National Adv. E-mail: bookkper@courierpapers.com
Display Adv. E-mail: bookkper@courierpapers.com
Editorial e-mail: Joi67@courierpapers.com
Primary Website: courierpapers.com
Avg Free Circ: 4600
Audit By: Sworn/Estimate/Non-Audited
Audit Date: 10.06.2019
Personnel: James Strauss (Ed./News Dept.); Joi DeArmond (Pub.); Dawn Farrar (Office Mgr.)
Parent company (for newspapers): Courier Newspapers

WOODFORD TIMES

Street address 1: PO Box 430
Street address city: Pekin
Street address state: IL
Zip/Postal code: 61555-0430
General Phone: (309) 346-1111
General/National Adv. E-mail: sales@timestoday.com
Display Adv. E-mail: snorbits@timestoday.com
Editorial e-mail: jbrickner@timestoday.com

Primary Website: WoodfordTimes.com
Year Established: 2010
Avg Free Circ: 4819
Audit By: Sworn/Estimate/Non-Audited
Audit Date: 10.06.2019
Personnel: Jeanette Brickner (Ex. Ed.); Tom Kelling (Display Adv. Mgr.); Sandy Norbits (Adv.); Ken Mauser (Pub.); David Adams (Pub.)
Parent company (for newspapers): CherryRoad Media

WOODRIDGE SUBURBAN LIFE

Street address 1: 2001 Butterfield Rd Suite 105
Street address 2: Ste 260
Street address city: Downers Grove
Street address state: IL
Zip/Postal code: 60515
General Phone: (630) 368-1100
General Fax: (630) 969-0228
Advertising Phone: (630) 427-6213
Editorial Phone: (630) 427-6252
General/National Adv. E-mail: nshannon@shawmedia.com
Display Adv. E-mail: sbissell@shawmedia.com
Editorial e-mail: rwells@shawmedia.com
Primary Website: mysuburbanlife.com
Avg Paid Circ: 368
Avg Free Circ: 163
Audit By: AAM
Audit Date: 31.03.2018
Personnel: J. Tom Shaw (Pub.); Katie Sherman (Marketing Dir.); Ryan Terrell (Ed.); Maureen Ringness (Major/Nat'l Accts./Grp. Sales Dir.); Ryan Wells
Parent company (for newspapers): Shaw Media

WORTH CITIZEN

Street address 1: 3840 147th St
Street address city: Midlothian
Street address state: IL
Zip/Postal code: 60445-3452
General Phone: (708) 388-2425
General Fax: (708) 385-7811
General/National Adv. E-mail: info@southwestmessengerpress.com
Primary Website: southwestmessengerpress.com
Avg Paid Circ: 8729
Avg Free Circ: 800
Audit By: Sworn/Estimate/Non-Audited
Audit Date: 10.06.2019
Personnel: Margaret Lysen (Pub.)
Parent company (for newspapers): Southwest Messenger Press, Inc.

ZION BENTON NEWS

Street address 1: 2711 Sheridan Rd
Street address 2: Ste. 202
Street address city: Zion
Street address state: IL
Zip/Postal code: 60099-2650
General Phone: (847) 746-9000
General Fax: (847) 746-9150
General/National Adv. E-mail: mpobiecke@kenoshanews.com
Display Adv. E-mail: zion@kenoshanews.com
Editorial e-mail: mona@zion-bentonnews.com
Primary Website: zion-bentonnews.com
Avg Free Circ: 22000
Audit By: Sworn/Estimate/Non-Audited
Audit Date: 10.06.2019
Personnel: Frank M. Misureli (Pub.); Mona Shannon (Ed.)
Parent company (for newspapers): United Communications Corporation

INDIANA

ADVANCE NEWS

Street address 1: 126 E Plymouth St
Street address city: Bremen
Street address state: IN
Zip/Postal code: 46506-1236
General Phone: (574) 546-2941
Advertising Phone: (574) 936-3101
Advertising Fax: (574) 936-7491
Editorial Fax: (574) 546-5170
Display Adv. E-mail: class@thepilotnews.com
Editorial e-mail: AdvanceNews@yahoo.com
Year Established: 1879
Avg Paid Circ: 918
Audit By: Sworn/Estimate/Non-Audited
Audit Date: 10.06.2019
Personnel: Cindy Stockton (Ad. Dir.); Shawn McGrath (Editor)
Parent company (for newspapers): Heritage Publications (2003) Inc.

ALBION NEW ERA

Street address 1: 407 S Orange St
Street address city: Albion
Street address state: IN
Zip/Postal code: 46701-1132
General Phone: (260) 636-2727
General Fax: (260) 636-2042
Primary Website: kpcnews.com
Year Established: 1876
Avg Paid Circ: 6004
Audit By: Sworn/Estimate/Non-Audited
Audit Date: 10.06.2019
Personnel: Bob Allman (Pub and Sales); Matt Getts; David Rigas (Adv. Sales)
Parent company (for newspapers): KPC Media Group, Inc.

ALEXANDRIA TIMES-TRIBUNE

Street address 1: 317 S Anderson St
Street address city: Elwood
Street address state: IN
Zip/Postal code: 46036-2018
General Phone: (765) 724-4469
General Fax: (765) 552-3358
General/National Adv. E-mail: alextribune@elwoodpublishing.com
Display Adv. E-mail: alextribune@elwoodpublishing.com
Primary Website: elwoodpublishing.com
Year Established: 1885
Avg Paid Circ: 1200
Audit By: Sworn/Estimate/Non-Audited
Audit Date: 10.06.2019
Personnel: Robert Nash (Pub.); Cindy Tyner (Adv. Director); Jenny Corbett (Managing Ed.); Randy Bayne (Prodn. Mgr.)
Parent company (for newspapers): Elwood Publishing Co., Inc.

BERNE TRI WEEKLY NEWS

Street address 1: 153 S Jefferson St
Street address city: Berne
Street address state: IN
Zip/Postal code: 46711-2157
General Phone: (260) 589-2101
General Fax: (260) 589-8614
Advertising Fax: (260) 589-8614
General/National Adv. E-mail: news@bernetriweekly.com
Primary Website: bernetriweekly.com
Year Established: 1896
Avg Paid Circ: 2000
Audit By: Sworn/Estimate/Non-Audited
Audit Date: 10.06.2019
Personnel: Roger Muselman (Pub.); Jessica Elvey (Adv. Mgr.)
Parent company (for newspapers): Dynamic Resource Group

BOURBON NEWS-MIRROR

Street address 1: 214 N Michigan St
Street address city: Plymouth
Street address state: IN
Zip/Postal code: 46563-2135
General Phone: (574) 936-3101
Advertising Fax: (574) 936-7491
Editorial Fax: (574) 342-8002
General/National Adv. E-mail: ads@thepilotnews.com
Primary Website: thepilotnews.com
Year Established: 1870
Avg Paid Circ: 911
Audit By: Sworn/Estimate/Non-Audited
Audit Date: 10.06.2019
Personnel: Cindy Stockton (Adv. Mgr.)
Parent company (for newspapers): Heritage Publications (2003) Inc.

BROOK REPORTER

Street address 1: 305 E Graham St
Street address city: Kentland
Street address state: IN
Zip/Postal code: 47951-1235
General Phone: (219) 474-5532
Advertising Fax: (219) 866-3775
General/National Adv. E-mail: daily@renssrep.com
Primary Website: facebook.com/NewtonCountyNewspapers
Year Established: 1895
Audit By: Sworn/Estimate/Non-Audited
Audit Date: 10.06.2019
Personnel: Cindy Brandenburg (Mng. Ed); Connie Nimz (Adv); Betty Long (Office Admin)
Parent company (for newspapers): Kankakee Valley Publishing

BROWN COUNTY DEMOCRAT

Street address 1: 147 E Main St
Street address city: Nashville
Street address state: IN
Zip/Postal code: 47448-7008
General Phone: (812) 988-2221
Advertising Fax: (812) 988-6502
Editorial Fax: (812) 988-6502
General/National Adv. E-mail: ads@democrat.com
Display Adv. E-mail: ads@democrat.com
Editorial e-mail: newsroom@bcdemocrat.com
Primary Website: bcdemocrat.com
Year Established: 1870
Avg Paid Circ: 3800
Avg Free Circ: 42
Audit By: Sworn/Estimate/Non-Audited
Audit Date: 10.06.2019
Personnel: Steve Marshall (Gen. Mgr.); Keith L. Fleener (Adv. Mgr.); Sara Clifford (Ed.)
Parent company (for newspapers): AIM Media Indiana

CARROLL COUNTY COMET

Street address 1: 14 E Main St
Street address city: Flora
Street address state: IN
Zip/Postal code: 46929-1351
General Phone: (574) 967-4135
General Fax: (574) 967-3384
General/National Adv. E-mail: comet@carrollcountycomet.com
Display Adv. E-mail: comet@carrollcountycomet.com
Editorial e-mail: editor@carrollcountycomet.com
Primary Website: carrollcountycomet.com
Mthly Avg Views: 43431
Mthly Avg Unique Visitors: 17898
Year Established: 1974
Avg Paid Circ: 2912
Avg Free Circ: 67
Audit By: USPS
Audit Date: 01.10.2021
Personnel: Joe Moss (Adv. Mgr.); Susan Scholl (Co-Publisher)
Parent company (for newspapers): Carroll Papers, Inc.

CEDAR LAKE JOURNAL

Street address 1: 116 Clark St
Street address city: Lowell
Street address state: IN
Zip/Postal code: 46356-1702
General Phone: (219) 696-7711
General Fax: (219) 696-7713
General/National Adv. E-mail: pilcherpubco@comcast.net
Avg Paid Circ: 1500
Audit By: Sworn/Estimate/Non-Audited
Audit Date: 10.06.2019
Personnel: Mary Jeanette Pilcher (Pub.); Gary A. Pilcher (Adv. Mgr.); Connie Schrombeck (Ed.); Matt Pilcher (Prodn. Mgr.)

CHESTERTON TRIBUNE

Street address 1: 209 S Calumet Rd
Street address 2: Suite 3
Street address city: Chesterton
Street address state: IN
Zip/Postal code: 46304
General Phone: (219) 926-1131
Advertising Phone: (219) 926-1131
Editorial Phone: (219) 926-1131
General/National Adv. E-mail: ads@chestertontribune.com
Display Adv. E-mail: ads@chestertontribune.com
Classified Adv. e-mail: ads@chestertontribune.com
Editorial e-mail: news@chestertontribune.com
Primary Website: www.chestertontribune.com
Mthly Avg Views: 200000
Mthly Avg Unique Visitors: 40000
Year Established: 1884
Avg Paid Circ: 3200
Avg Free Circ: 300
Audit By: AAM
Audit Date: 12.07.2019
Personnel: David Canright (Managing Ed./Pub.); Amy Lavalley (Executive editor); TR Harlan (Sports Ed.); Margaret Willis (Co-Pub.)
Parent company (for newspapers): Chesterton Tribune, Inc.; Hoosier Media Group LLC; Hurd Media Group

CHURUBUSCO NEWS

Street address 1: 123 N Main St
Street address city: Churubusco
Street address state: IN
Zip/Postal code: 46723-1708
General Phone: (260) 693-3949
General Fax: (260) 693-6545
Advertising Fax: (260) 693-6545
General/National Adv. E-mail: chnews@app-printing.com
Display Adv. E-mail: classifieds@kpcmedia.com
Editorial e-mail: nminier@kpcmedia.com
Primary Website: app-printing.com
Year Established: 1872
Avg Paid Circ: 2000
Audit By: Sworn/Estimate/Non-Audited
Audit Date: 10.06.2019
Personnel: Lynche Donley (Adv. Dir.); Robert Allman (Pub.)
Parent company (for newspapers): KPC Media Group, Inc.

CLARION NEWS

Street address 1: 301 N Capitol Ave
Street address city: Corydon
Street address state: IN
Zip/Postal code: 47112-1140
General Phone: (812) 738-2211
General Fax: (812) 738-1909
General/National Adv. E-mail: ads@corydondemocrat.com
Display Adv. E-mail: classifiedad@corydondemocrat.com
Editorial e-mail: cadams@clarionnews.net
Primary Website: clarionnews.net
Avg Free Circ: 16600
Audit By: Sworn/Estimate/Non-Audited
Audit Date: 10.06.2019
Personnel: Jonathan O'Bannon (Pub.); Cathy Riddle (Circ. Mgr.); Chris Adams (Ed.)
Parent company (for newspapers): O'Bannon Publishing Co., Inc.

CROTHERSVILLE TIMES

Street address 1: 69 N Main St
Street address city: Scottsburg
Street address state: IN
Zip/Postal code: 47170
General Phone: (812) 793-2188
General Fax: (812) 793-2188
Advertising Phone: (812) 793-2188
Advertising Fax: (812) 793-2188
Editorial Phone: (812) 793-2188
Editorial Fax: (812) 793-2188
General/National Adv. E-mail: ctimes@frontier.com
Display Adv. E-mail: ctimes@frontier.com
Editorial e-mail: ctimes@frontier.com
Primary Website: crothersvilletimes.com
Year Established: 1980
Avg Paid Circ: 1800
Audit By: USPS
Audit Date: 01.10.2022

Personnel: Curt Kovener (Owner, Publisher, Editor, & Complaint Department)

DUNKIRK NEWS AND SUN

Street address 1: 209 S Main St
Street address city: Dunkirk
Street address state: IN
Zip/Postal code: 47336-1243
General Phone: (765) 768-6022
General Fax: (260) 726-8143
Advertising Fax: (260) 726-8143
General/National Adv. E-mail: cr.ads@comcast.net
Year Established: 1952
Avg Paid Circ: 1000
Avg Free Circ: 12
Audit By: Sworn/Estimate/Non-Audited
Audit Date: 10.06.2019
Personnel: John C. Ronald (Pub.)
Parent company (for newspapers): Graphic Printing Co., Inc.

FERDINAND NEWS

Street address 1: PO Box 38
Street address 2: 113 W 6th St
Street address city: Ferdinand
Street address state: IN
Zip/Postal code: 47532-0038
General Phone: (812) 367-2041
General Fax: (812) 367-2371
General/National Adv. E-mail: ferdnews@psci.net
Display Adv. E-mail: ads@psci.net
Editorial e-mail: ferdnews@psci.net
Primary Website: ferdinandnews.com/v2/content.aspx?IsHome=1&MemberID=1995&ID=24232
Year Established: 1906
Avg Paid Circ: 2700
Audit By: Sworn/Estimate/Non-Audited
Audit Date: 10.06.2019
Personnel: Kathy Tretter (Ed./publisher); Brian Bohne (Sports Ed.); Lisa Hoppenjans (writer); Casey Uebelhor (writer); Linda Simpson (Advertising manager); Stacy Brown (Office manager); Debbie Powell (graphics)
Parent company (for newspapers): Dubois Spencer Counties Pubishing Co., Inc.

FOUNTAIN COUNTY NEIGHBOR

Street address 1: 113 S Perry St
Street address city: Attica
Street address state: IN
Zip/Postal code: 47918-1349
General Phone: (765) 762-2411
General Fax: (765) 762-1547
General/National Adv. E-mail: atticasales@sbcglobal.net
Display Adv. E-mail: atticasales@sbcglobal.net
Classified Adv. e-mail: fcnhembree@sbcglobal.net
Editorial e-mail: atticaeditor@sbcglobal.net
Primary Website: fountaincountyneighbor.com
Avg Paid Circ: 1803
Audit By: Sworn/Estimate/Non-Audited
Audit Date: 10.06.2019
Personnel: Greg Willhite (Gen. Mgr.); Roberta Hembree (Office Mgr.); Gretchen Stone (Ed)
Parent company (for newspapers): Community Media Group

FRANKLIN TOWNSHIP INFORMER

Street address 1: 8822 Southeastern Ave
Street address city: Indianapolis
Street address state: IN
Zip/Postal code: 46239-1341
General Phone: (317) 862-1774
Advertising Fax: (317) 862-1775
General/National Adv. E-mail: ftinformer@sbcglobal.net
Display Adv. E-mail: ftinformer-adsales@sbcglobal.net
Primary Website: ftcivicleague.org/informer
Year Established: 1971
Avg Paid Circ: 1500
Avg Free Circ: 0
Audit By: Sworn/Estimate/Non-Audited
Audit Date: 10.06.2019
Personnel: Kasie Foster (Editor)
Parent company (for newspapers): Franklin Township Civic League, Inc.

GREATER FORT WAYNE BUSINESS WEEKLY

Street address 1: 3306 Independence Dr
Street address city: Fort Wayne
Street address state: IN
Zip/Postal code: 46808-4510
General Phone: (260) 426-2640
Editorial Phone: (260) 426-2640 Ext. 3311
Editorial e-mail: lcardenas@kpcmedia.com
Primary Website: fwbusiness.com
Year Established: 2005
Audit By: Sworn/Estimate/Non-Audited
Audit Date: 10.06.2019
Personnel: Terry Householder (Pres.); Lisa Long (Ed.); S. Rick Mitchell (CFO); Doug LeDuc (Reporter); Linda Lipp (Assoc. Ed.); Christy Day (Circ. Acct. Mgr.); Bobbi Jenks (Sales Mgr.)
Parent company (for newspapers): KPC Media Group, Inc.

GREENWOOD AND SOUTHSIDE CHALLENGER

Street address 1: 400 E Main St
Street address city: Greenwood
Street address state: IN
Zip/Postal code: 46143-1362
General Phone: (317) 888-3376
General Fax: (317) 888-3377
Advertising Phone: (317) 888-3376
Advertising Fax: (317) 888-3377
Editorial Phone: (317) 888-3376
Editorial Fax: (317) 888-3377
General/National Adv. E-mail: sgoldsby@hspa.com
Display Adv. E-mail: sgoldsby@hspa.com
Editorial e-mail: news@hspa.com
Primary Website: facebook.com/GreenwoodSouthsideChallengerNewspapers
Year Established: 1972
Avg Paid Circ: 5813
Avg Free Circ: 2000
Audit By: Sworn/Estimate/Non-Audited
Audit Date: 10.06.2019
Personnel: Doug L. Chambers (Pub./Ed.); Steve Key (Exec. Dir.); Shawn Goldsby (Nat'l Adv. Mgr./Classifieds Adv. Mgr.); Pamela Lego (Mktg. Mgr/Adv. Dir.)
Parent company (for newspapers): Greenwood Newspapers, Inc.

HARRISON PRESS

Street address 1: 126 W High St
Street address city: Lawrenceburg
Street address state: IN
Zip/Postal code: 47025-1908
General Phone: (812) 537-0063
General Fax: (812) 537-5576
Advertising Phone: (812) 537-0063
Advertising Fax: (812) 537-5576
Editorial Phone: (812) 537-0063
Editorial Fax: 812-537-5576
General/National Adv. E-mail: afritch@registerpublications.com
Display Adv. E-mail: customerservice@registerpublications.com
Editorial e-mail: jawad@registerpublications.com
Primary Website: theharrison-press.com
Year Established: 1928
Avg Paid Circ: 4000
Avg Free Circ: 110
Audit By: Sworn/Estimate/Non-Audited
Audit Date: 10.06.2019
Personnel: Joe Awad (Ed.); April Fritch (Gen. Mgr.)
Parent company (for newspapers): Delphos Herald Newspapers of Indiana, Inc.

HENDRICKS COUNTY FLYER

Street address 1: 8109 Kingston St
Street address 2: Ste 500
Street address city: Avon
Street address state: IN
Zip/Postal code: 46123-8211
General Phone: (317) 272-5800
General Fax: (317) 272-5887
Advertising Phone: (317) 272-5800 ext. 126
Advertising Fax: (317) 272-5887
Editorial Phone: (317) 272-5800 ext. 134
Editorial Fax: (317) 272-5887
General/National Adv. E-mail: david.johnson@flyergroup.com
Display Adv. E-mail: ashley.gauger@flyergroup.com
Editorial e-mail: kathy.linton@flyergroup.com
Primary Website: flyergroup.com
Year Established: 1994
Avg Paid Circ: 2750
Avg Free Circ: 28800
Audit By: Sworn/Estimate/Non-Audited
Audit Date: 10.06.2019
Personnel: Harold Allen (Pub.); Cathy Wilson (Bus. Mgr.); Kathy Linton (Ed.); Terry Ballard (Prodn. Dir.); Jared Selch (Adv. Mgr.)
Parent company (for newspapers): CNHI, LLC

INDIANAPOLIS BUSINESS JOURNAL

Street address 1: 41 E Washington St
Street address 2: Ste 200
Street address city: Indianapolis
Street address state: IN
Zip/Postal code: 46204-3517
General Phone: (317) 634-6200
General Fax: (317) 263-5400
Advertising Phone: (317) 472-5321
Advertising Fax: (317) 472-5321
Editorial Phone: (317) 472-5378
General/National Adv. E-mail: ibradley@ibj.com
Editorial e-mail: gandrews@ibj.com
Primary Website: ibj.com
Mthly Avg Views: 800000
Mthly Avg Unique Visitors: 215000
Year Established: 1980
Avg Paid Circ: 10637
Avg Free Circ: 494
Audit By: AAM
Audit Date: 17.09.2016
Personnel: Greg Morris (Pub.); Greg Andrews (Ed.); Lisa Bradley (Adv. Dir.); Patricia Keiffner (Prod. Dir.); Bill Wright (Circ. Mgr.); Lesley Weidenbener (Managing Ed.)
Parent company (for newspapers): IBJ Media Corporation

KANKAKEE VALLEY POST-NEWS

Street address 1: 827 S Halleck St
Street address city: Demotte
Street address state: IN
Zip/Postal code: 46310-8342
General Phone: (219) 987-5111
General Fax: (219) 987-5119
Editorial Fax: (219) 987-5119
General/National Adv. E-mail: adsales@kvpost.net
Display Adv. E-mail: Classifieds@kvpost.net
Editorial e-mail: editor@kvpost.net
Primary Website: kvonline.info
Year Established: 1932
Avg Paid Circ: 2800
Avg Free Circ: 19000
Audit By: Sworn/Estimate/Non-Audited
Audit Date: 10.06.2019
Personnel: Greg Perrotto (Gen. Mgr.); Cheri Shelhart (Ed.); Cyndi Grace (Circ.)
Parent company (for newspapers): Community Media Group; Kankakee Valley Publishing

KNIGHTSTOWN BANNER

Street address 1: 24 N Washington St
Street address city: Knightstown
Street address state: IN
Zip/Postal code: 46148-1275
General Phone: (765) 345-2292
General Fax: (765) 345-2113
General/National Adv. E-mail: thebanner@embarqmail.com
Display Adv. E-mail: thebanner@embarqmail.com
Editorial e-mail: thebanner@embarqmail.com
Primary Website: thebanneronline.com
Year Established: 1867
Avg Paid Circ: 1400
Avg Free Circ: 15
Audit By: Sworn/Estimate/Non-Audited
Audit Date: 10.06.2019
Personnel: Stacy Cox (General Manager); Eric M. Cox (Ed.)

KOKOMO HERALD

Street address 1: 207 N Buckeye St
Street address city: Kokomo
Street address state: IN
Zip/Postal code: 46901-4521
General Phone: (765) 452-5942
General Fax: (765) 452-3037
General/National Adv. E-mail: scrouch@kokomoherald.com
Primary Website: kokomoherald.com
Year Established: 1971
Audit By: Sworn/Estimate/Non-Audited
Audit Date: 10.06.2019

LAGRANGE NEWS

Street address 1: PO Box 148
Street address 2: 0410 East 100 South
Street address city: Lagrange
Street address state: IN
Zip/Postal code: 46761-0148
General Phone: (260) 463-2166
General Fax: (260) 463-2734
Advertising Fax: (260) 463-2734
Editorial Fax: (260) 463-2734
General/National Adv. E-mail: advertising@lagrangepublishing.com
Display Adv. E-mail: advertising@lagrangepublishing.com
Editorial e-mail: editor@lagrangepublishing.com
Primary Website: lagrangepublishing.com
Year Established: 1861
Avg Paid Circ: 5000
Audit By: Sworn/Estimate/Non-Audited
Audit Date: 10.06.2019
Personnel: William Connelly (Pub.); Scott Faust (Adv. Mgr.); Guy Thompson
Parent company (for newspapers): LaGrange Publishing, Co.

LAGRANGE STANDARD

Street address 1: PO Box 148
Street address city: Lagrange
Street address state: IN
Zip/Postal code: 46761-0148
General Phone: (260) 463-2166
General Fax: (260) 463-2734
Advertising Fax: (260) 463-2734
Editorial Fax: (260) 463-2734
General/National Adv. E-mail: advertising@lagrangepublishing.com
Display Adv. E-mail: advertising@lagrangepublishing.com
Editorial e-mail: editor@lagrangepublishing.com
Primary Website: lagrangepublishing.com
Year Established: 1856
Avg Paid Circ: 5200
Audit By: Sworn/Estimate/Non-Audited
Audit Date: 10.06.2019
Personnel: William Connelly (Pub.); Scott Faust (Adv. Mgr.); Guy Thompson (editor)
Parent company (for newspapers): LaGrange Publishing, Co.

LEADER-TRIBUNE REVIEW EAST

Street address 1: 116 S Main St
Street address 2: Ste A
Street address city: Tipton
Street address state: IN
Zip/Postal code: 46072-1864
General Phone: (765) 675-2115
General Fax: (765) 675-4147
Advertising Phone: (765) 675-2115
Advertising Fax: (765) 675-4147
Editorial Phone: (765) 675-2115
Editorial Fax: (765) 675-4147
General/National Adv. E-mail: tiptonads@elwoodpublishing.com
Display Adv. E-mail: tiptonads@elwoodpublishing.com
Classified Adv. e-mail: tiptonads@elwoodpublishing.com
Editorial e-mail: tiptoneditor@elwoodpublishing.com
Primary Website: elwoodpublishing.com
Avg Paid Circ: 5400
Avg Free Circ: 5298
Audit By: Sworn/Estimate/Non-Audited
Audit Date: 10.06.2019
Personnel: Jack Barnes (Pres.); Robert Nash (Pub.); Jackie Henry (Mng. Ed.); Scott Blaylock (Adv. Mgr.); Tammy Boyer (Circ. Mgr.)

Parent company (for newspapers): Elwood Publishing Co., Inc.; Ray Barnes Newspapers, Inc.

LEADER-TRIBUNE REVIEW WEST

Street address 1: 116 S Main St
Street address 2: Ste A
Street address city: Tipton
Street address state: IN
Zip/Postal code: 46072-1864
General Phone: (765) 675-2115
General Fax: (765) 675-4147
Advertising Phone: (765) 675-2115
Advertising Fax: (765) 675-4147
Editorial Phone: (765) 675-2115
Editorial Fax: (765) 675-4147
General/National Adv. E-mail: tiptonads@elwoodpublishing.com
Display Adv. E-mail: tiptonads@elwoodpublishing.com
Classified Adv. e-mail: tiptonads@elwoodpublishing.com
Editorial e-mail: tiptoneditor@elwoodpublishing.com
Primary Website: elwoodpublishing.com
Avg Paid Circ: 5400
Avg Free Circ: 5298
Audit By: Sworn/Estimate/Non-Audited
Audit Date: 10.06.2019
Personnel: Jack Barnes (Pres.); Robert Nash (Pub.); Jackie Henry (Mng. Ed.); Scott Blaylock (Adv. Mgr.); Tammy Boyer (Circ. Mgr.)
Parent company (for newspapers): Elwood Publishing Co., Inc.; Ray Barnes Newspapers, Inc.

LOWELL TRIBUNE

Street address 1: PO Box 191
Street address city: Lowell
Street address state: IN
Zip/Postal code: 46356-0191
General Phone: (219) 696-7711
General Fax: (219) 696-7713
General/National Adv. E-mail: pilcherpubco@comcast.net
Display Adv. E-mail: pilcherpubco@comcast.net
Editorial e-mail: tribune@pilcherpublishing.com
Primary Website: thelowelltribune.com
Avg Paid Circ: 4650
Audit By: Sworn/Estimate/Non-Audited
Audit Date: 10.06.2019
Personnel: Matt Pilcher (Pub.); Gary A. Pilcher (Adv. Mgr.); Connie Schrombeck (Ed.); Craig Pilcher (Prodn. Mgr.)

MOROCCO COURIER

Street address 1: 305 E Graham St
Street address city: Kentland
Street address state: IN
Zip/Postal code: 47951-1235
General Phone: (219) 474-5532
General Fax: (219) 866-3775
Advertising Fax: (219) 866-3775
General/National Adv. E-mail: daily@rensselaerrepublican.com
Display Adv. E-mail: daily@rensselaerrepublican.com
Editorial e-mail: daily@rensselaerrepublican.com
Primary Website: newsbug.info/rensselaer_republican
Year Established: 1877
Avg Paid Circ: 450
Avg Free Circ: 10
Audit By: Sworn/Estimate/Non-Audited
Audit Date: 10.06.2019
Personnel: Carla Waters (Pub); Cindy Brandenburg; Connie Nimz; Betty Long
Parent company (for newspapers): Kankakee Valley Publishing

MOUNT VERNON DEMOCRAT

Street address 1: 132 E 2nd St
Street address 2: Ste B
Street address city: Mount Vernon
Street address state: IN
Zip/Postal code: 47620-1805
General Phone: (812) 838-4811
Advertising Fax: (812) 838-3696
General/National Adv. E-mail: mvdemocrat_ads@insightbb.com
Display Adv. E-mail: advertising@mvdemocrat.com
Editorial e-mail: editor@mvdemocrat.com
Primary Website: mvdemocrat.com
Year Established: 1867
Avg Paid Circ: 1500
Avg Free Circ: 6100
Audit By: Sworn/Estimate/Non-Audited
Audit Date: 10.06.2019
Personnel: Sondra Reich (Sales Rep); Alicia Bell (Adv. Sales); Mike Webster (Ed.)
Parent company (for newspapers): Landmark Community Newspapers, LLC

NEW PALESTINE PRESS

Street address 1: 22 W New Rd
Street address city: Greenfield
Street address state: IN
Zip/Postal code: 46140-1090
General Phone: (317) 467-6000
General Fax: (317) 467-6017
Advertising Phone: (317) 467-6001
Advertising Fax: (317) 467-6009
Editorial Phone: (317) 467-6022
Editorial Fax: (317) 467-6017
General/National Adv. E-mail: advert@newpalestinepress.com
Display Adv. E-mail: class@newpalestinepress.com
Editorial e-mail: news@newpalestinepress.com
Primary Website: greenfieldreporter.com
Avg Paid Circ: 2500
Audit By: Sworn/Estimate/Non-Audited
Audit Date: 10.06.2019
Personnel: Chuck Wells (Pub.); Scott Slade (Community Ed.); John Senger (Adv. Dir.)

NEWS & REVIEW

Street address 1: 202 Rickey Rd
Street address city: Monticello
Street address state: IN
Zip/Postal code: 47960-1539
General Phone: (765) 884-1902
General Fax: (765) 813-0700
Advertising Phone: (765)884-1902
Advertising Fax: (765) 813-0700
Editorial Phone: (765)884-1902
Editorial Fax: (765) 813-0700
General/National Adv. E-mail: bentonreviewads@gmail.com
Display Adv. E-mail: bentonreviewads@gmail.com
Editorial e-mail: bentonreviewads@gmail.com
Primary Website: smalltownpapers.com
Year Established: 1887
Avg Paid Circ: 1300
Avg Free Circ: 200
Audit By: Sworn/Estimate/Non-Audited
Audit Date: 10.06.2019
Personnel: Don Hurd (Pub.)
Parent company (for newspapers): Hoosier Media Group LLC

NORTHWEST NEWS

Street address 1: 15605 Lima Rd
Street address city: Huntertown
Street address state: IN
Zip/Postal code: 46748-9372
General Phone: (260) 637-9003
Advertising Fax: (260) 637-8598
General/National Adv. E-mail: nweditor@app-printing.com
Primary Website: thenorthwestnews.com
Year Established: 1997
Avg Paid Circ: 1500
Audit By: Sworn/Estimate/Non-Audited
Audit Date: 10.06.2019
Personnel: Robert L. Allman (Pub.); Dave Kurtz (Exec. Ed.); Terry Householder (Pres./Pub.)
Parent company (for newspapers): All Printing & Publishing, Inc

OAK HILL TIMES

Street address 1: 407 E Main St
Street address city: Gas City
Street address state: IN
Zip/Postal code: 46933-1532
General Phone: (765) 674-0070
General Fax: (765) 674-3496
Advertising Phone: (270) 442-7389
Advertising Fax: (270) 442-5220
Editorial Phone: (765) 583-0368
Editorial Fax: (765) 674-3496
General/National Adv. E-mail: kpicphelps@gmail.com
Display Adv. E-mail: kpirebekah@gmail.com
Editorial e-mail: kpilayout@gmail.com
Year Established: 1902
Avg Paid Circ: 3130
Avg Free Circ: 5000
Audit By: Sworn/Estimate/Non-Audited
Audit Date: 10.06.2019
Parent company (for newspapers): Kentucky Publishing, Inc.

OAKLAND CITY JOURNAL

Street address 1: 100 N Gibson St
Street address city: Princeton
Street address state: IN
Zip/Postal code: 47670-1855
General Phone: (812) 385-2525
General Fax: (812) 386-6199
General/National Adv. E-mail: jeff@pdclarion.com
Display Adv. E-mail: classifieds@pdclarion.com
Editorial e-mail: news@pdclarion.com
Primary Website: tristate-media.com
Year Established: 1899
Avg Paid Circ: 400
Avg Free Circ: 0
Audit By: Sworn/Estimate/Non-Audited
Audit Date: 10.06.2019
Personnel: Andrea Howe (Editor); Jeff Schumacher (Pub./CEO)
Parent company (for newspapers): Brehm Communications, Inc.; Princeton Publishing Co., Inc.

OSGOOD JOURNAL

Street address 1: 115 S Washington St
Street address city: Versailles
Street address state: IN
Zip/Postal code: 47042-8016
General Phone: (812) 689-6364
Advertising Fax: (812) 689-6508
General/National Adv. E-mail: lchandler@ripleynews.com
Display Adv. E-mail: publication@ripleynews.com
Editorial e-mail: publication@ripleynews.com
Primary Website: ripleynews.com
Year Established: 1865
Avg Paid Circ: 5200
Avg Free Circ: 48
Audit By: Sworn/Estimate/Non-Audited
Audit Date: 10.06.2019
Personnel: Linda Chandler (Pub./Adv. Mgr.); Cindy Roberts (Officer Mgr.); Wanda Burnett (Ed.)
Parent company (for newspapers): Ripley Publishing

PAOLI NEWS-REPUBLICAN

Street address 1: 131 S Court St
Street address city: Paoli
Street address state: IN
Zip/Postal code: 47454-1323
General Phone: (812) 482-2626
General/National Adv. E-mail: news@ocpnews.com
Display Adv. E-mail: aabrams@suncommercial.com
Editorial e-mail: news@ocpnews.com
Primary Website: ocpnews.com
Year Established: 1875
Avg Paid Circ: 2800
Audit By: Sworn/Estimate/Non-Audited
Audit Date: 10.06.2019
Personnel: Arthur Hampton (Pub.); Michael Stanley (News Editor); Peggy Manship (Adv. Mgr.); Tim Young (Editor); Dennis Eller (Ed.); Dennis Ellis (Ed.)
Parent company (for newspapers): Paxton Media Group; Orange County Publishing, Inc.

PARKE COUNTY SENTINEL

Street address 1: 125 W High St
Street address city: Rockville
Street address state: IN
Zip/Postal code: 47872-1735
General Phone: (765) 569-2033
General Fax: (765) 569-1424
Advertising Fax: (765) 569-1424
General/National Adv. E-mail: knelson@parkecountysentinel.com
Editorial e-mail: Lbemis@parkecountysentinel.com
Primary Website: parkecountysentinel.com
Year Established: 1977
Avg Paid Circ: 3500
Avg Free Circ: 49
Audit By: Sworn/Estimate/Non-Audited
Audit Date: 10.06.2019
Personnel: Mary Harney (Pub.); Larry Bemis (Ed.); Christina Valdes (Circ. Mgr.); Lisa Wood (Business/News Coordinator)
Parent company (for newspapers): Torch Newspapers, Inc.

PENDLETON TIMES-POST

Street address 1: 126 W State St
Street address city: Pendleton
Street address state: IN
Zip/Postal code: 46064-1034
General Phone: (765) 778-2324
General Fax: (765) 778-7152
Advertising Phone: (765) 778-2324
Advertising Fax: (765) 778-7152
Editorial Phone: (765) 778-2324
Editorial Fax: (765) 778-7152
General/National Adv. E-mail: mjones@ptlpnews.com
Display Adv. E-mail: mjones@ptlpnews.com
Editorial e-mail: sslade@ptlpnews.com
Primary Website: pendletontimespost.com
Year Established: 1897
Avg Paid Circ: 2400
Audit By: Sworn/Estimate/Non-Audited
Audit Date: 10.06.2019
Personnel: Chuck Wells (Pub.); Scott Slade (Ed.); John Senger (Ad. Director)
Parent company (for newspapers): AIM Media Indiana

PERRY COUNTY NEWS

Street address 1: 9266 Hidden Acres Rd
Street address city: Tell City
Street address state: IN
Zip/Postal code: 47586-8879
General Phone: (812) 547-3424
Advertising Fax: (812) 547-2847
General/National Adv. E-mail: publisher@perrycountynews.com
Primary Website: perrycountynews.com
Year Established: 1891
Avg Paid Circ: 6792
Audit By: Sworn/Estimate/Non-Audited
Audit Date: 10.06.2019
Personnel: Dave Eldridge (Pub.); Cindy Dauby (Adv. Mgr.); Joyce Dauby (Circ. Mgr.); Vince Leucke (Ed.); Larry Goffinet (Sports Ed.); Gary Smith (Production Manager); Sara Sommer (Adv. Sales Rep.); Corliss Krueger (Classified Adv. Mgr.); Trina Severson (Editorial Department)
Parent company (for newspapers): Landmark Community Newspapers, LLC

ROYAL CENTER RECORD

Street address 1: 102 S Chicago St
Street address city: Royal Center
Street address state: IN
Zip/Postal code: 46978-9997
General Phone: (574) 643-3165
General Fax: (574) 643-9440
General/National Adv. E-mail: rcrecord@mac.com
Primary Website: rcr.stparchive.com
Year Established: 1890
Avg Paid Circ: 802
Avg Free Circ: 50
Audit By: Sworn/Estimate/Non-Audited
Audit Date: 10.06.2019
Personnel: Jeffrey C. Funk (Ed.)

RUSHVILLE REPUBLICAN

Street address 1: 315 N Main St
Street address city: Rushville
Street address state: IN
Zip/Postal code: 46173-1635
General Phone: (765) 932-2222
General Fax: (765) 932-4358
Advertising Phone: (765) 932-2222
Advertising Fax: (765) 932-4358
Editorial Phone: (765) 932-2222
Editorial Fax: (765) 932-4358
General/National Adv. E-mail: marilyn.land@rushvillerepublican.com
Display Adv. E-mail: marilyn.land@rushvillerepublican.com
Classified Adv. e-mail: marilyn.land@rushvillerepublican.com
Editorial e-mail: aaron.kirchoff@rushvillerepublican.com
Primary Website: rushvillerepublican.com
Mthly Avg Views: 548000

Mthly Avg Unique Visitors: 111700
Year Established: 1840
Avg Paid Circ: 3682
Sat. Circulation Paid: 3682
Audit By: Sworn/Estimate/Non-Audited
Audit Date: 10.06.2019
Personnel: Aaron Kirchoff (Managing Ed.); Shelley Barton; Lisa Spangler (Rgl. Controller); Laura Welborn (Rgl. Pub.); Denver E. Sullivan; Keith Wells (Rgl. Adv. Dir.); Lisa Huff (Regl. Circ. Mgr.); Susan Peters (Graphic Arts Dir.); Marilyn Land (Adv. Mgr.)
Parent company (for newspapers): McNaughton Newspapers; CNHI, LLC

SOUTH GIBSON STAR TIMES

Street address 1: 203 S McCreary St
Street address city: Fort Branch
Street address state: IN
Zip/Postal code: 47648-1317
General Phone: (812) 753-3553
General Fax: (812) 753-4251
Advertising Fax: (812) 753-4251
General/National Adv. E-mail: ads@sgstartimes.com
Display Adv. E-mail: classifieds@sgstartimes.com
Editorial e-mail: editor@sgstartimes.com
Primary Website: sgstartimes.com
Year Established: 1955
Avg Paid Circ: 4952
Avg Free Circ: 21
Audit By: Sworn/Estimate/Non-Audited
Audit Date: 10.06.2019
Personnel: Frank Heuring (Pres./Pub.); John Heuring (Adv. Mgr.); Rachael Heuring (Circ. Mgr.); Andrea Preston (Ed.)
Parent company (for newspapers): Pike Publishing

SOUTHSIDE TIMES

Street address 1: 7670 US 31 S
Street address city: Indianapolis
Street address state: IN
Zip/Postal code: 46227-8547
General Phone: (317) 300-8782
General Fax: (317) 300-8786
General/National Adv. E-mail: Rickm@ss-Times.com
Editorial e-mail: news@ss-times.com
Primary Website: ss-times.com
Year Established: 1928
Avg Free Circ: 17500
Audit By: Sworn/Estimate/Non-Audited
Audit Date: 10.06.2019
Personnel: Rick Myers (The Southside Times); Nicole Davis (Ed.); Steve Laughlin (Sales Rep.)
Parent company (for newspapers): Times-Leader Publications, LLC

SOUTHSIDER VOICE

Street address 1: 6025 Madison Ave
Street address 2: Ste B
Street address city: Indianapolis
Street address state: IN
Zip/Postal code: 46227-4722
General Phone: (317) 781-0023
General Fax: (317) 781-0253
General/National Adv. E-mail: kelly.sawyers@southsidervoice.com
Display Adv. E-mail: ads@southsidervoice.com
Editorial e-mail: news@southsidervoice.com
Primary Website: southsidervoice.com
Year Established: 1939
Avg Free Circ: 24811
Audit By: Sworn/Estimate/Non-Audited
Audit Date: 10.06.2019
Personnel: Kelly Sawyers (Pub./Owner); Denise Summers (Ed./Owner)

SPENCER COUNTY JOURNAL-DEMOCRAT

Street address 1: 541 Main St
Street address city: Rockport
Street address state: IN
Zip/Postal code: 47635-1429
General Phone: (812) 649-9196
General Fax: (812) 649-9197
Editorial e-mail: news@spencercountyjournal.com
Primary Website: spencercountyjournal.com
Year Established: 1855
Avg Paid Circ: 5700
Audit By: Sworn/Estimate/Non-Audited
Audit Date: 10.06.2019
Personnel: Dave Eldridge (Pub); Cindy Dauby (Rgl. Adv. Mgr.); Vince Leucke (Ed.); Melissa Strawn (Adv. Consultant); Jennifer Heady (Classified Adv. Mgr.)
Parent company (for newspapers): Paxton Media Group; Landmark Communications, Inc.; Landmark Community Newspapers, LLC

SPENCER COUNTY LEADER

Street address 1: 208 E Medcalf St
Street address city: Dale
Street address state: IN
Zip/Postal code: 47523-9040
General Phone: (812) 367-2041
Advertising Fax: (812) 367-2371
General/National Adv. E-mail: ferdnews@psci.net
Primary Website: ferdinandnews.com
Year Established: 1960
Avg Paid Circ: 2100
Audit By: Sworn/Estimate/Non-Audited
Audit Date: 10.06.2019
Personnel: Richard Tretter (Co-Pub.); Kathy Tretter (Ed.); Cheryl Hurst (Mng. Ed.); Brian Bohne (Sports Ed.)
Parent company (for newspapers): Dubois Spencer Counties Pubishing Co., Inc.

SPRINGS VALLEY HERALD

Street address 1: 8481 W College St
Street address city: French Lick
Street address state: IN
Zip/Postal code: 47432-1069
General Phone: (812) 723-2592
Advertising Fax: (812) 723-2592
General/National Adv. E-mail: peg@ocpnews.com
Display Adv. E-mail: peg@ocpnews.com
Editorial e-mail: art@ocpnews.com
Primary Website: springsvalleyherald.com
Year Established: 1903
Avg Paid Circ: 2200
Audit By: Sworn/Estimate/Non-Audited
Audit Date: 10.06.2019
Personnel: Peggy Manship (Adv. Mgr.); Arthur Hampton (Ed.)
Parent company (for newspapers): Orange County Publishing, Inc.

THE ADVANCE LEADER

Street address 1: 102 N Main St
Street address city: Kendallville
Street address state: IN
Zip/Postal code: 46755-1714
General Phone: (260) 302-1346
General Fax: (260) 347-2693
Advertising Phone: (260) 347-0400 Ext. 1002
Advertising Fax: (260) 347-7282
General/National Adv. E-mail: info@kpcmedia.com
Display Adv. E-mail: classified@kpcmedia.com
Editorial e-mail: leader@kpcmedia.com
Primary Website: kpcnews.com/latest/advanceleader
Year Established: 1880
Avg Paid Circ: 94
Audit By: AAM
Audit Date: 31.12.2018
Personnel: Terry Housholder (Pub.); Bob Buttgen (Ed.); Bruce Hakala (Circ. Dir.); Joy Newman (Adv. Dir.)
Parent company (for newspapers): KPC Media Group, Inc.

THE BANNER-GAZETTE

Street address 1: 490 E State Road 60
Street address city: Pekin
Street address state: IN
Zip/Postal code: 47165-7928
General Phone: (812) 967-3176
General Fax: (812) 967-3194
General/National Adv. E-mail: sales@gbpnews.com
Display Adv. E-mail: classifieds@gbpnews.com
Editorial e-mail: gbrowning@gbpnews.com
Primary Website: gbpnews.com
Avg Paid Circ: 0
Avg Free Circ: 18021
Audit By: Sworn/Estimate/Non-Audited
Audit Date: 10.06.2019
Personnel: Joe Green (Pub.); April Falk (Adv. Mgr.); Leslie Gertin (Circ. Mgr.); George Browning (Ed.); Heather Marlman (Prodn. Mgr.); Harry Sanford (Circ. Mgr)
Parent company (for newspapers): Green Banner Publications, Inc.

THE BENTON REVIEW

Street address 1: 205 E 5th St
Street address city: Fowler
Street address state: IN
Zip/Postal code: 47944-1445
General Phone: (765) 884-1902
General Fax: (765) 813-0700
Advertising Phone: (765) 884-1902
Advertising Fax: (765) 884-8110
Editorial Phone: (765) 884-1902
Editorial Fax: 765-813-0700
General/National Adv. E-mail: bentonreviewads@gmail.com
Display Adv. E-mail: bentonreviewads#gmail.com
Editorial e-mail: bentonreview@sbcglobal.net
Year Established: 1875
Avg Paid Circ: 3000
Avg Free Circ: 76
Audit By: Sworn/Estimate/Non-Audited
Audit Date: 10.06.2019
Personnel: Don Hurd (Pub.)
Parent company (for newspapers): Hoosier Media Group, LLC

THE BROOKVILLE AMERICAN

Street address 1: 531 Main St
Street address city: Brookville
Street address state: IN
Zip/Postal code: 47012-1407
General Phone: (765) 647-4221
General Fax: (765) 647-4811
General/National Adv. E-mail: info@whitewaterpub.com
Display Adv. E-mail: info@whitewaterpub.com
Editorial e-mail: info@whitewaterpub.com
Primary Website: whitewaterpub.com
Year Established: 1838
Avg Paid Circ: 5000
Avg Free Circ: 62
Audit By: Sworn/Estimate/Non-Audited
Audit Date: 10.06.2019
Personnel: Gary L. Wolf (Pub.); Mary Ross (Adv. Mgr.); Donna Schuler (Circ. Mgr.); John Estridge (Ed.)
Parent company (for newspapers): Whitewater Publications

THE BUTLER BULLETIN

Street address 1: 118 W 9th St
Street address city: Auburn
Street address state: IN
Zip/Postal code: 46706-2225
General Phone: (260) 868-5501
General Fax: (260) 925-2625
Advertising Phone: (260) 925-2611 x 2547
Advertising Fax: (260) 925-2625
Editorial Fax: (260) 925-2625
General/National Adv. E-mail: ldonley@kpcmedia.com
Display Adv. E-mail: ldonley@kpcmedia.com
Primary Website: kpcnews.com/butlerbulletin
Year Established: 1976
Avg Paid Circ: 52
Audit By: AAM
Audit Date: 31.12.2018
Personnel: Terry Housholder (Pres./CEO)
Parent company (for newspapers): KPC Media Group, Inc.

THE CLAY CITY NEWS

Street address 1: 717 Main St
Street address city: Clay City
Street address state: IN
Zip/Postal code: 47841-1331
General Phone: (812) 939-2163
Advertising Fax: (812) 939-2286
General/National Adv. E-mail: ccnews@claycitynews.com
Editorial e-mail: ccnews@claycitynews.com
Year Established: 1912
Avg Paid Circ: 1800
Audit By: Sworn/Estimate/Non-Audited
Audit Date: 10.06.2019
Personnel: Kim Howell (Adv. Mgr.); Travis Curoi (Mng. Ed.)
Parent company (for newspapers): Spencer Evening World

THE CORYDON DEMOCRAT

Street address 1: 301 N Capitol Ave
Street address city: Corydon
Street address state: IN
Zip/Postal code: 47112-1151
General Phone: (812) 738-2211
Advertising Fax: (812) 738-1909
General/National Adv. E-mail: ads@corydondemocrat.com
Display Adv. E-mail: ads@corydondemocrat.com
Editorial e-mail: ctimberlake@corydondemocrat.com
Primary Website: corydondemocrat.com
Year Established: 1856
Avg Paid Circ: 6800
Avg Free Circ: 17600
Audit By: Sworn/Estimate/Non-Audited
Audit Date: 10.06.2019
Personnel: Jonathan O'Bannon (Pres./Pub.); Jan Crosby (Adv. Mgr.); Jo Ann Saylor (Ed.); Soni O'Bannon
Parent company (for newspapers): O'Bannon Publishing Co., Inc.

THE CULVER CITIZEN

Street address 1: 214 N Michigan St
Street address city: Plymouth
Street address state: IN
Zip/Postal code: 46563-2135
General Phone: (574) 936-3101
General Fax: (574) 936-3844
Advertising Phone: (800) 933-0356
Advertising Fax: (574) 936-7491
Editorial Phone: (574) 216-0075
General/National Adv. E-mail: culvercitizen@gmail.com
Display Adv. E-mail: ads@thepilotnews.com
Classified Adv. e-mail: class@thepilotnews.com
Editorial e-mail: news@thepilotnews.com
Primary Website: thepilotnews.com
Year Established: 1894
Avg Paid Circ: 900
Audit By: Sworn/Estimate/Non-Audited
Audit Date: 10.06.2019
Personnel: Cindy Stockton (Adv. Mgr.); James Radican (Circ. Mgr.); Greg Hildebrand (Prodn. Mgr.); Lois Tomaszewski (Ed.); Jeff Kenney (Ed.)
Parent company (for newspapers): Heritage Publications (2003) Inc.

THE DEARBORN COUNTY REGISTER

Street address 1: 126 W High St
Street address city: Lawrenceburg
Street address state: IN
Zip/Postal code: 47025-1908
General Phone: (812) 537-0063
General Fax: (812) 537-5576
Advertising Fax: (812) 537-5576
Editorial Phone: (513) 537-0063
General/National Adv. E-mail: bthies@registerpublications.com
Display Adv. E-mail: afritch@registerpublications.com
Editorial e-mail: newsroom@registerpublications.com
Primary Website: thedcregister.com
Year Established: 1841
Avg Paid Circ: 6000
Audit By: Sworn/Estimate/Non-Audited
Audit Date: 10.06.2019
Personnel: Chip Munich (Adv. Rep.); Joe Awad (Managing Ed.); April Fitch (Gen. Mgr.)
Parent company (for newspapers): Delphos Herald, Inc.; Register Publications

THE ELLETTSVILLE JOURNAL

Street address 1: 211 N Sale St
Street address city: Ellettsville
Street address state: IN
Zip/Postal code: 47429-1423
General Phone: (812) 876-2254
Advertising Fax: (812) 876-2853
General/National Adv. E-mail: journal@bluemarble.net
Editorial e-mail: journal@bluemarble.net
Year Established: 1939
Avg Paid Circ: 1500
Audit By: Sworn/Estimate/Non-Audited
Audit Date: 10.06.2019
Personnel: Travis Curry (Editor)

Parent company (for newspapers): Spencer Evening World

THE FRANKLIN CHALLENGER

Street address 1: 400 E Main St
Street address city: Greenwood
Street address state: IN
Zip/Postal code: 46143-1362
General Phone: (317) 888-3376
General Fax: (317) 888-3377
Advertising Phone: (317) 888-3376
Advertising Fax: (317) 888-3377
Editorial Phone: (317) 888-3376
Editorial Fax: (317) 888-3377
General/National Adv. E-mail: sgoldsby@hspa.com
Display Adv. E-mail: sgoldsby@hspa.com
Editorial e-mail: news@hspa.com
Primary Website: challengernewspapers.com
Year Established: 1984
Avg Paid Circ: 3819
Avg Free Circ: 1500
Audit By: Sworn/Estimate/Non-Audited
Audit Date: 10.06.2019
Personnel: Doug L. Chambers (Ed./Pub.); Pamela Lego (Mktg. Mgr./Adv. Dir.); Shawn Goldsby (Nat'l Adv. Mgr./ Classifieds Adv. Mgr.); Steve Key (Exec. Dir.)
Parent company (for newspapers): Greenwood Newspapers, Inc.

THE GARRETT CLIPPER

Street address 1: 118 W 9th St
Street address city: Auburn
Street address state: IN
Zip/Postal code: 46706-2225
General Phone: (260) 925-2611 x 45
Advertising Phone: (260) 347-0400 Ext. 1002
Advertising Fax: (260) 925-2625
Editorial Phone: (260) 925-2611 Ext. 2545
General/National Adv. E-mail: garrettclipper@kpcnews.net
Display Adv. E-mail: garrettclipper@kpcnews.net
Editorial e-mail: garrettclipper@kpcnews.net
Primary Website: kpcnews.com
Year Established: 1885
Avg Paid Circ: 141
Audit By: AAM
Audit Date: 31.12.2018
Personnel: Terry Housholder (Pres./Pub.); Sue Carpenter (Ed.); Joy Newman (Adv. Dir.)
Parent company (for newspapers): KPC Media Group, Inc.

THE GIVEAWAY

Street address 1: PO Box 159
Street address city: Scottsburg
Street address state: IN
Zip/Postal code: 47170-0159
General Phone: (812) 752-3171
General Fax: (812) 967-3194
General/National Adv. E-mail: sales@gbpnews.com
Display Adv. E-mail: april@gbpnews.com
Editorial e-mail: mamos@gbpnews.com
Primary Website: gbpnews.com
Mthly Avg Views: 378669
Mthly Avg Unique Visitors: 137646
Year Established: 1933
Avg Free Circ: 17970
Audit By: Sworn/Estimate/Non-Audited
Audit Date: 10.06.2019
Personnel: Joe Green (Publisher); April Falk (Adv. Mgr); Leslie Gertin (Distribution Manager); Marcus Amos (Editor); Harry Sanford (Circ. Mgr.); Heather Marlman (Production Manager); Judy Lizenby (Acct. Exec.)
Parent company (for newspapers): Green Banner Publications, Inc.

THE GREENSBURG TIMES

Street address 1: 135 S Franklin St
Street address city: Greensburg
Street address state: IN
Zip/Postal code: 47240-2023
General Phone: (812) 663-3111
General Fax: (812) 663-2985
Advertising Phone: (812) 663-3111 x7034
Editorial Phone: (812) 663-3111 x7010
General/National Adv. E-mail: natalie.acra@greensburgdailynews.com
Editorial e-mail: news@greensburgdailynews.com
Primary Website: greensburgdailynews.com
Year Established: 1894
Avg Paid Circ: 692
Avg Free Circ: 3
Audit By: Sworn/Estimate/Non-Audited
Audit Date: 10.06.2019
Personnel: Kevin Green (Mng. Ed.); Laura Welborn (Reg. Pub.); James Howell (Sports Ed.); Natalie Arca (Adv. Ops. Mgr.); Jeanie York (Adv.)
Parent company (for newspapers): CNHI, LLC

THE HERALD-TRIBUNE

Street address 1: 475 N Huntersville Rd
Street address city: Batesville
Street address state: IN
Zip/Postal code: 47006-9205
General Phone: (812) 934-4343
General Fax: (812) 934-6406
General/National Adv. E-mail: bonnie.motz@batesvilleheraldtribune.com
Display Adv. E-mail: tawnya.birden@indianamediagroup.com
Editorial e-mail: TheHeraldTribune@batesvilleheraldtribune.com
Primary Website: batesvilleheraldtribune.com
Year Established: 1891
Avg Paid Circ: 2000
Audit By: Sworn/Estimate/Non-Audited
Audit Date: 10.06.2019
Personnel: Debbie Blank (Mng Ed.); Lisa Huff (Reg Dir of Audience Development); Laura Welborn (publisher); Sheridan Mark (sales director); Diane Raver (assistant editor); Will Fehlinger (sports writer); Bonnie Motz (advertising representative); Marilyn Schwegman (advertising representative)
Parent company (for newspapers): CNHI, LLC

THE HUNTINGBURG PRESS

Street address 1: 327 E 4th St
Street address 2: Fl 2
Street address city: Huntingburg
Street address state: IN
Zip/Postal code: 47542-1337
General Phone: (812) 683-5899
Advertising Fax: (812) 683-5897
General/National Adv. E-mail: kpirebekah@gmail.com
Display Adv. E-mail: kpirebekah@gmail.com
Editorial e-mail: kpiads@ky-news.com
Year Established: 1905
Avg Paid Circ: 1100
Avg Free Circ: 8900
Audit By: Sworn/Estimate/Non-Audited
Audit Date: 10.06.2019
Personnel: Greg LeNeave (Publisher); Rebekah Tatum (Advertising Account Executive)
Parent company (for newspapers): Kentucky Publishing, Inc.

THE INDIANAPOLIS RECORDER

Street address 1: 2901 N Tacoma Ave
Street address city: Indianapolis
Street address state: IN
Zip/Postal code: 46218-2737
General Phone: (317) 924-5143
General Fax: (317) 921-6653
Advertising Fax: (317) 921-6653
Editorial Fax: (317) 921-5148
General/National Adv. E-mail: michaelf@indyrecorder.com
Display Adv. E-mail: michaelf@indyrecorder.com
Editorial e-mail: newsroom@indyrecorder.com
Primary Website: indianapolisrecorder.com
Year Established: 1895
Avg Paid Circ: 4729
Avg Free Circ: 395
Audit By: CVC
Audit Date: 30.03.2016
Personnel: William Mays (Pub.); Shannon Williams (Gen. Mgr.); Victoria Davis (Newsroom Mgr.)
Parent company (for newspapers): Recorder Media Group

THE JACKSON COUNTY BANNER

Street address 1: 116 E Cross St
Street address city: Brownstown
Street address state: IN
Zip/Postal code: 47220-2011
General Phone: (812) 358-2111
Advertising Fax: (812) 358-5606
General/National Adv. E-mail: ads@thebanner.com
Display Adv. E-mail: ads@thebanner.com
Editorial e-mail: news@thebanner.com
Primary Website: thebanner.com
Year Established: 1869
Avg Paid Circ: 1730
Avg Free Circ: 4140
Audit By: Sworn/Estimate/Non-Audited
Audit Date: 10.06.2019
Personnel: Nick Hedrick (Ed); Aaron Wright (Office Mgr.)
Parent company (for newspapers): AIM Media Indiana

THE JOURNAL-PRESS

Street address 1: 126 W High St
Street address city: Lawrenceburg
Street address state: IN
Zip/Postal code: 47025-1908
General Phone: (812) 537-0063
Editorial Fax: (812) 537-5576
General/National Adv. E-mail: afritch@registerpublications.com
Display Adv. E-mail: afritch@registerpublications.com
Editorial e-mail: erussell@registerpublications.com
Primary Website: thejournal-press.com
Year Established: 1975
Avg Paid Circ: 6300
Audit By: Sworn/Estimate/Non-Audited
Audit Date: 10.06.2019
Personnel: Erika Schmidt Russell (News Ed.); Tom Brooker (Pub.); Loretta Day (Adv. Dir.)
Parent company (for newspapers): Register Publications

THE LEADER

Street address 1: 382 Main Cross St
Street address city: Charlestown
Street address state: IN
Zip/Postal code: 47111-1230
General Phone: (812) 256-3377
General Fax: (812) 256-3377
General/National Adv. E-mail: sales@gbpnews.com
Display Adv. E-mail: classifieds@gbpnews.com
Editorial e-mail: jross@gbpnews.com
Primary Website: gbpnews.com
Mthly Avg Views: 378669
Mthly Avg Unique Visitors: 137646
Year Established: 1933
Avg Free Circ: 14964
Audit By: Sworn/Estimate/Non-Audited
Audit Date: 10.06.2019
Personnel: Joe Green (Pub.); April Falk (Sales Mgr.); Janna Ross (Manager Ed.); Heather Marlman (Prodn. Mgr.); Harry Sanford (Circ. Mgr.); Leslie Gertin (Dist. Mgr.)
Parent company (for newspapers): Green Banner Publications, Inc.

THE LEADER

Street address 1: 214 N Michigan St
Street address city: Plymouth
Street address state: IN
Zip/Postal code: 46563-2135
General Phone: (574) 772-2101
General Fax: (574) 936-7491
Advertising Phone: (800) 933-0356
Advertising Fax: (574) 772-7041
General/National Adv. E-mail: theleader@nitline.net
Display Adv. E-mail: class@thepilotnews.com
Primary Website: thepilotnews.com
Mthly Avg Views: 378669
Mthly Avg Unique Visitors: 137646
Year Established: 1868
Avg Paid Circ: 3600
Audit By: Sworn/Estimate/Non-Audited
Audit Date: 10.06.2019
Personnel: Cindy Stockton (Adv. Mgr.)
Parent company (for newspapers): Heritage Publications (2003) Inc.

THE LOOGOOTEE TRIBUNE

Street address 1: 514 N John F Kennedy Ave
Street address city: Loogootee
Street address state: IN
Zip/Postal code: 47553-1102
General Phone: (812) 295-2500
General Fax: (812) 295-5221
Advertising Phone: (812) 295-2500
Advertising Fax: (812) 295-5221
Editorial Phone: (812) 295-2500
Editorial Fax: (812) 295-5221
General/National Adv. E-mail: advertising@loogooteetribune.com
Display Adv. E-mail: advertising@loogooteetribune.com
Editorial e-mail: news@loogooteetribune.com
Primary Website: loogooteetribune.com
Year Established: 1873
Audit By: Sworn/Estimate/Non-Audited
Audit Date: 10.06.2019
Personnel: Larry Hembree (Pub./Ed.)
Parent company (for newspapers): Hembree Communications

THE MAIL-JOURNAL

Street address 1: 206 S Main St
Street address 2: 206 S Main Street
Street address city: Milford
Street address state: IN
Zip/Postal code: 46542-3004
General Phone: (574) 658-4111
General Fax: (800) 886-3796
Advertising Fax: (800) 886-3796
General/National Adv. E-mail: smeadows@the-papers.com
Display Adv. E-mail: smeadows@the-papers.com
Editorial e-mail: dpatterson@the-papers.com
Primary Website: the-papers.com
Year Established: 1888
Avg Paid Circ: 3000
Audit By: Sworn/Estimate/Non-Audited
Audit Date: 16.09.2023
Personnel: Ron Baumgartner (Pub.); Steve Meadows (Advertising Director); Deb Patterson (Editor-in-chief); Kip Schumm (Dir., Mktg.); Jeri Seely (Ed.)
Parent company (for newspapers): The Papers Incorporated

THE MIDDLEBURY INDEPENDENT

Street address 1: PO Box 68
Street address 2: 201 South Main Street
Street address city: Middlebury
Street address state: IN
Zip/Postal code: 46540-0068
General Phone: (574) 825-9112
General Fax: (260) 463-2734
Advertising Fax: (260) 463-2734
Editorial Fax: (260) 463-2734
General/National Adv. E-mail: advertising@lagrangepublishing.com
Display Adv. E-mail: advertising@lagrangepublishing.com
Editorial e-mail: editor@lagrangepublishing.com
Primary Website: lagrangepublishing.com
Year Established: 1946
Avg Paid Circ: 890
Avg Free Circ: 44
Audit By: Sworn/Estimate/Non-Audited
Audit Date: 10.06.2019
Personnel: Bill Connelly (Pub.); Scott Faust (Adv. Mgr.); Guy Thompson
Parent company (for newspapers): LaGrange Publishing, Co.

THE MIDDLETOWN NEWS

Street address 1: 106 N 5th St
Street address city: Middletown
Street address state: IN
Zip/Postal code: 47356-1439
General Phone: (765) 354-2221
General Fax: (765) 354-2221
General/National Adv. E-mail: sue@themiddletownnews.com
Display Adv. E-mail: sue@themiddletownnews.com
Editorial e-mail: frontpage@themiddletownnews.com
Primary Website: themiddletownnews.com
Year Established: 1885
Avg Paid Circ: 2000
Audit By: Sworn/Estimate/Non-Audited
Audit Date: 10.06.2019
Personnel: Joey Cooper (Co-Pub.); Drew Cooper (Co-Pub.); Michael Cooper (Design Ed.); Sue Cooper (Office Mgr./Copy Ed.)

THE MOORESVILLE-DECATUR TIMES

Street address 1: 60 S Jefferson St
Street address city: Martinsville
Street address state: IN

Zip/Postal code: 46151-1968
General Phone: (317) 831-0280
General Fax: (317) 831-7068
Advertising Phone: (812) 331-4291
Advertising Fax: (317) 831-7068
Editorial Phone: (765) 342-3311 ext. 4412
General/National Adv. E-mail: cgiddens@heraldt.com
Display Adv. E-mail: cgiddens@heraldt.com
Editorial e-mail: bculp@reporter-times.com
Primary Website: reporter-times.com/mdt
Year Established: 1879
Avg Paid Circ: 5700
Audit By: Sworn/Estimate/Non-Audited
Audit Date: 10.06.2019
Personnel: Chad Giddens (Adv. Mgr.); Tim Smith (Circ. Mgr.); Laurie Ragle (Adv. Dir.); Cory Bollinger (Managing Ed.); Cory Bollinger (Pub.)
Parent company (for newspapers): Schurz Communications Inc

THE NEWS-JOURNAL

Street address 1: 606 N State Road 13
Street address city: Wabash
Street address state: IN
Zip/Postal code: 46992-7735
General Phone: (260) 982-6383
Advertising Fax: (260) 982-8233
General/National Adv. E-mail: mreese@thepaperofwabash.com
Primary Website: nmpaper.com
Year Established: 1865
Avg Paid Circ: 2000
Audit By: Sworn/Estimate/Non-Audited
Audit Date: 10.06.2019
Personnel: Mike Rees (Pub.); Mike McLaughlin (Office Mgr.); Carrie Vineyard (Adv. Mgr.); Eric Christiansen (Ed.)
Parent company (for newspapers): The Paper of Wabash Co. Inc.

THE NEWTON COUNTY ENTERPRISE

Street address 1: 305 E Graham St
Street address city: Kentland
Street address state: IN
Zip/Postal code: 47951-1235
General Phone: (219) 474-5532
General Fax: (219) 474-5354
General/National Adv. E-mail: nceeditor@centurylink.net
Display Adv. E-mail: ncesales@centurylink.net
Editorial e-mail: nceeditor@centurylink.net
Primary Website: newsbug.info; newtoncountyenterprise.com
Avg Paid Circ: 1600
Audit By: Sworn/Estimate/Non-Audited
Audit Date: 10.06.2019
Personnel: Connie Nimz (Adv. Mgr.); Betty Long (Classifieds/Legal Notice); Carla Waters (Mng. Ed.); Cindy Brandenburg (Staff Reporter); Bette Schmid (Pub.); Charlotte Sparks (Adv. Sales Rep.)
Parent company (for newspapers): Community Media Group

THE NORTH VERNON SUN

Street address 1: 528 E O and M Ave
Street address city: North Vernon
Street address state: IN
Zip/Postal code: 47265-1217
General Phone: (812) 346-3973
Advertising Fax: (812) 346-8368
General/National Adv. E-mail: advertising@northvernon.com
Display Adv. E-mail: classifiedspds@northvernon.com
Editorial e-mail: bmayer@northvernon.com
Primary Website: plaindealer-sun.com
Year Established: 1872
Avg Paid Circ: 5000
Avg Free Circ: 52
Audit By: Sworn/Estimate/Non-Audited
Audit Date: 10.06.2019
Personnel: Bryce Mayer (Ed.); Sharon Hamilton (Sports Ed.); Barbara King (Pub); Sue Ross (advertisingn rep); ???? ????; Billie Taylor (Adv)
Parent company (for newspapers): North Vernon Plain Dealer & Sun, Inc.

THE ODON JOURNAL

Street address 1: 102 W Main St
Street address city: Odon
Street address state: IN
Zip/Postal code: 47562-1306
General Phone: (812) 636-7350
Advertising Fax: (812) 636-7359
General/National Adv. E-mail: journal@rtccom.net
Editorial e-mail: journal@rtccom.net
Primary Website: facebook.com/The-Odon-Journal-110477855656975
Year Established: 1873
Avg Paid Circ: 2990
Audit By: Sworn/Estimate/Non-Audited
Audit Date: 10.06.2019
Personnel: Sue Myers (Adv. Mgr.); John L. Myers (Ed.)
Parent company (for newspapers): Myers Enterprises, Inc.

THE OHIO COUNTY NEWS/RISING SUN RECORDER

Street address 1: 235 Main St
Street address city: Rising Sun
Street address state: IN
Zip/Postal code: 47040-1224
General Phone: (812) 438-2011
General Fax: (812) 438-3228
Advertising Phone: (812) 537-0063
Advertising Fax: (812)537-5576
General/National Adv. E-mail: afritch@registerpublications.com
Editorial e-mail: risingsun@registerpublications.com
Primary Website: theohiocountynews.com
Year Established: 1833
Avg Paid Circ: 1700
Audit By: Sworn/Estimate/Non-Audited
Audit Date: 10.06.2019
Personnel: April Fritch (Gen. Mgr.); Joe Awad (Mng. Ed.); Chip Munich (Adv. Rep.)
Parent company (for newspapers): Delphos Herald, Inc.; Register Publications

THE OSSIAN JOURNAL

Street address 1: 1002 Dehner Dr
Street address city: Ossian
Street address state: IN
Zip/Postal code: 46777-9787
General Phone: (260) 622-4108
Advertising Fax: (260) 622-6439
General/National Adv. E-mail: ossianj@adamswells.com
Editorial e-mail: ossianj@adamswells.com
Primary Website: sunrisernews.com
Year Established: 1912
Avg Paid Circ: 500
Avg Free Circ: 10
Audit By: Sworn/Estimate/Non-Audited
Audit Date: 10.06.2019
Personnel: Jean Bordner (Adv. Dir); Mark Miller (Ed.)
Parent company (for newspapers): News-Banner Publications, Inc.

THE PAPER - KOSCIUSKO EDITION

Street address 1: PO Box 188
Street address 2: 206 S. Main Street
Street address city: Milford
Street address state: IN
Zip/Postal code: 46542-0188
General Phone: (574) 658-4111
General Fax: (800) 886-3796
Advertising Phone: (574) 658-4111
Advertising Fax: (800) 886-3796
Editorial Phone: (574) 658-4111
Editorial Fax: (800) 886-3796
General/National Adv. E-mail: kschumm@the-papers.com
Display Adv. E-mail: kschumm@the-papers.com
Classified Adv. e-mail: kschumm@the-papers.com
Editorial e-mail: jseely@the-papers.com
Primary Website: the-papers.com
Year Established: 1971
Avg Free Circ: 24198
Audit By: CVC
Audit Date: 30.06.2022
Personnel: Ron Baumgartner (Pub.); Elaine Pearson (Circ. Mgr.); Kip Schumm (Adv. Mgr.); Todd Clark (Prod. Mgr.); Carl Lauster (Advertising Representative); Susan Littlefield (Advertising Representative); Jeri Seely (Ed. in Chief); Jerry Straka (Circulation); Rebecca Whitesel (Ed.); Collette Knepp (Business Manager); Phoebe Muthart (Associate Editor); Tim Ashley (Associate Editor); Amil Bischof (Warsaw Office Manager); Kristine Marshall (Syracuse Office Manager); Cindy Hathaway (Advertising Representative); Toni Ryan (Advertising Representative); Barb Walter (Commercial Printing Sales Rep); Bruce Bultemeier (Commercial Printing Sales Rep)
Parent company (for newspapers): The Papers Incorporated

THE POSEY COUNTY NEWS

Street address 1: 641 3rd St
Street address city: New Harmony
Street address state: IN
Zip/Postal code: 47631-9800
General Phone: (812) 682-3950
General Fax: (812) 682-3944
Advertising Phone: (812) 459-4206
Advertising Fax: (812) 682-3944
General/National Adv. E-mail: ads@poseycountynews.com
Display Adv. E-mail: news1@poseycountynews.com
Editorial e-mail: news1@poseycountynews.com
Primary Website: poseycountynews.com
Year Established: 1955
Avg Paid Circ: 4500
Audit By: Sworn/Estimate/Non-Audited
Audit Date: 10.06.2019
Personnel: David Pearce (Owner/Pub.)

THE POST AND MAIL (TUESDAY)

Street address 1: 927 W Connexion Way
Street address city: Columbia City
Street address state: IN
Zip/Postal code: 46725-1031
General Phone: (260) 244-5153
General Fax: (260) 244-7598
General/National Adv. E-mail: publisher@thepostandmail.com
Display Adv. E-mail: postandmailclassifieds@earthlink.net
Primary Website: thepostandmail.com
Audit By: Sworn/Estimate/Non-Audited
Audit Date: 10.06.2019
Personnel: Cindy Stockton (Publisher/Advertising Mgr.); Rick Kreps (Pub.); Nicole Ott (Ed.); Sally Ballard (Circu.)
Parent company (for newspapers): Horizon Publications Inc.

THE PRESS-DISPATCH

Street address 1: 820 E Poplar St
Street address 2: PO Box 68
Street address city: Petersburg
Street address state: IN
Zip/Postal code: 47567-1258
General Phone: (574) 936-3101
General Fax: (574) 936-3844
Advertising Phone: (800) 933-0356
General/National Adv. E-mail: ads@pressdispatch.net
Display Adv. E-mail: classifieds@pressdispatch.net
Editorial e-mail: news@pressdispatch.net
Primary Website: pressdispatch.net
Year Established: 1898
Avg Paid Circ: 5000
Audit By: Sworn/Estimate/Non-Audited
Audit Date: 10.06.2019
Personnel: Frank Heuring (Pres./Pub.); John Heuring (Adv. Mgr.); Greg Hildebrand (Managing Ed.); Michele Louderback (Acct. Mgr.)
Parent company (for newspapers): Pike Publishing

THE PROGRESS EXAMINER

Street address 1: 233 S 2nd St
Street address city: Orleans
Street address state: IN
Zip/Postal code: 47452-1601
General Phone: (812) 865-3242
Advertising Fax: (812) 865-3242
General/National Adv. E-mail: penews@blueriver.net
Display Adv. E-mail: lmac1@blueriver.net
Primary Website: N/A
Year Established: 1879
Avg Paid Circ: 1684
Avg Free Circ: 44
Audit By: Sworn/Estimate/Non-Audited
Audit Date: 10.06.2019
Personnel: Neva Stroud (Adv. Mgr.); John F. Noblitt (Ed.); Gretchen Nelson (Pub./Asst. Ed.)

THE PULASKI COUNTY JOURNAL

Street address 1: 114 W Main St
Street address city: Winamac
Street address state: IN
Zip/Postal code: 46996-1208
General Phone: (574) 946-6628
General Fax: (574) 946-7471
Advertising Fax: (574) 946-7471
General/National Adv. E-mail: ads@pulaskijournal.com
Display Adv. E-mail: ads@pulaskijournal.com
Editorial e-mail: news@pulaskijournal.com
Primary Website: pulaskijournal.com
Year Established: 1859
Avg Paid Circ: 3000
Audit By: Sworn/Estimate/Non-Audited
Audit Date: 10.06.2019
Personnel: John Haley (Pub./Exec. Ed.); Chris Ford (Adv. Rep.); Kari Beth Stout (Creative Dir.)
Parent company (for newspapers): Winamac Publishers, LLC

THE PULASKI COUNTY JOURNAL

Street address 1: 114 W Main St
Street address city: Winamac
Street address state: IN
Zip/Postal code: 46996-1208
General Phone: (574) 946-6628
General/National Adv. E-mail: admin@pulaskijournal.com
Display Adv. E-mail: sales@pulaskijournal.com
Classified Adv. e-mail: sales@pulaskijournal.com
Editorial e-mail: news@pulaskijournal.com
Primary Website: www.pulaskijournal.com
Year Established: 1977
Avg Paid Circ: 1600
Audit By: USPS
Audit Date: 13.10.2023
Personnel: John Haley (Publisher/Owner); Kari Beth Stout (Mng. Ed.); Carrie Intravaia (Advertising Director); Andrew Van Auken (Advertising Sales Manager)

THE REGIONAL NEWS

Street address 1: PO Box 828
Street address city: Westville
Street address state: IN
Zip/Postal code: 46391-0828
General Phone: (219) 785-2234
Advertising Fax: (219) 785-2442
Primary Website: facebook.com/pg/TheRegionalNews46
Year Established: 1922
Avg Paid Circ: 525
Avg Free Circ: 50
Audit By: Sworn/Estimate/Non-Audited
Audit Date: 10.06.2019
Personnel: Galen Armstrong (Ed.)
Parent company (for newspapers): Paw Prints Publishing

THE REPUBLICAN

Street address 1: 6 E Main St
Street address city: Danville
Street address state: IN
Zip/Postal code: 46122-1818
General Phone: (317) 745-2777
Advertising Fax: (317) 745-2777
General/National Adv. E-mail: therepublican@sbcglobal.net
Display Adv. E-mail: therepublican@sbcglobal.net
Editorial e-mail: therepublican@sbcglobal.net
Year Established: 1847
Avg Paid Circ: 1600
Audit By: Sworn/Estimate/Non-Audited
Audit Date: 10.06.2019
Personnel: Betty Bartley (Editor)
Parent company (for newspapers): Hendricks County Republican, Inc.

THE REVIEW REPUBLICAN

Street address 1: 113 S Perry St
Street address city: Attica
Street address state: IN
Zip/Postal code: 47918-1349

General Phone: (765) 762-3322
General Fax: (765) 762-1547
Advertising Phone: (765) 762-3322
Advertising Fax: (765) 762-1547
Editorial Phone: (765) 762-3322
Editorial Fax: (765) 762-1547
General/National Adv. E-mail: atticasales@sbcglobal.net
Display Adv. E-mail: fcbhembree@sbcglobal.net
Editorial e-mail: revrep@sbcglobal.net
Primary Website: newsbug.info/williamsport_review_republican
Year Established: 1914
Audit By: Sworn/Estimate/Non-Audited
Audit Date: 10.06.2019
Personnel: Greg Willhite (Acct. Exec.); Gretchen Stone (Ed.); Cyndi Grace (Circ.)
Parent company (for newspapers): Kankakee Valley Publishing

THE SALEM DEMOCRAT

Street address 1: 117 E Walnut St
Street address city: Salem
Street address state: IN
Zip/Postal code: 47167-2044
General Phone: (812) 883-3281
General Fax: (812) 883-4446
Advertising Phone: (812) 883-3281
Advertising Fax: (812) 883-4446
Editorial Phone: (812) 883-3281
Editorial Fax: (812) 883-4446
General/National Adv. E-mail: am@salemleader.com
Display Adv. E-mail: am@salemleader.com
Editorial e-mail: stephanie@salemleader.com
Primary Website: salemleader.com
Year Established: 1827
Avg Paid Circ: 6000
Audit By: Sworn/Estimate/Non-Audited
Audit Date: 10.06.2019
Personnel: Stephanie Ferriell (Senior Editor); Debbi Hayes (Sales and Marketing Mgr.); Nancy Grossman (Publisher); Rhonda Smith (Gen. Mgr.); Dennis Miller (Production Manager)
Parent company (for newspapers): Leader Publishing Co.

THE SALEM LEADER

Street address 1: 117 E Walnut St
Street address city: Salem
Street address state: IN
Zip/Postal code: 47167-2044
General Phone: (812) 883-3281
General Fax: (812) 883-4446
General/National Adv. E-mail: am@salemleader.com
Display Adv. E-mail: am@salemleader.com
Editorial e-mail: stephanie@salemleader.com
Primary Website: salemleader.com
Year Established: 1878
Avg Paid Circ: 5800
Avg Free Circ: 324
Audit By: Sworn/Estimate/Non-Audited
Audit Date: 10.06.2019
Personnel: Nancy Grossman (Gen. Mgr.); Debbie Hayes (Adv. Mgr.); Stephanie Taylor (Ed.); Dennis Miller (Prodn. Mgr.)
Parent company (for newspapers): Leader Publishing Co.

THE SCOTT CO. JOURNAL & CHRONICLE

Street address 1: 183 E McClain Ave
Street address city: Scottsburg
Street address state: IN
Zip/Postal code: 47170-1845
General Phone: (812) 752-3171
Advertising Fax: (812) 752-6486
General/National Adv. E-mail: sales@gbpnews.com
Display Adv. E-mail: sales@gbpnews.com
Editorial e-mail: mamos@gbpnews.com
Primary Website: gbpnews.com
Year Established: 1899
Avg Paid Circ: 4794
Audit By: Sworn/Estimate/Non-Audited
Audit Date: 10.06.2019
Personnel: Marcus Amos (Ed.); April Falk (Adv. Mgr.)

THE SHOALS NEWS

Street address 1: 311 High St
Street address city: Shoals
Street address state: IN
Zip/Postal code: 47581-5502
General Phone: (812) 247-2828
Advertising Fax: (812) 247-2243
General/National Adv. E-mail: steve@theshoalsnews.com
Display Adv. E-mail: steve@theshoalsnews.com
Editorial e-mail: steve@theshoalsnews.com
Primary Website: theshoalsnews.com
Year Established: 1888
Avg Paid Circ: 2750
Avg Free Circ: 39
Audit By: Sworn/Estimate/Non-Audited
Audit Date: 10.06.2019
Personnel: Stephen A. Deckard (Editor and Publisher)

THE SWITZERLAND DEMOCRAT

Street address 1: 111 W Market St
Street address city: Vevay
Street address state: IN
Zip/Postal code: 47043-1159
General Phone: (812) 427-2311
Advertising Fax: (812) 427-2793
General/National Adv. E-mail: vevaynews@gmail.com
Display Adv. E-mail: vevaynews@gmail.com
Editorial e-mail: vevaynews@gmail.com
Primary Website: vevaynewspapers.com
Year Established: 1839
Avg Paid Circ: 600
Audit By: Sworn/Estimate/Non-Audited
Audit Date: 10.06.2019
Personnel: Eerin Williams (Adv. Mgr.); Ginny Leap (Circ. Mgr.); Patrick Lanman (Pub.)
Parent company (for newspapers): Vevay Newspapers, Inc.

THE WARWICK COUNTY STANDARD

Street address 1: 131 S. Warwick St.
Street address 2: P.O. Box 266
Street address city: Boonville
Street address state: IN
Zip/Postal code: 47601
General Phone: (812) 897-2330
Advertising Fax: (812) 897-3703
General/National Adv. E-mail: advertising@warricknews.com
Display Adv. E-mail: classifieds@warricknews.com
Editorial e-mail: newsroom@warricknews.com
Primary Website: warricknews.com
Year Established: 1874
Avg Paid Circ: 4000
Avg Free Circ: 2000
Audit By: Sworn/Estimate/Non-Audited
Audit Date: 10.06.2019
Personnel: Bob Rigg (Adv.); Marisa Patwa (Gen. Rep.); Don Wilkins (Grp. Ed.); Lisa Polk (Circ.)
Parent company (for newspapers): Paxton Media Group

THE WASHINGTON COUNTY EDITION

Street address 1: 105 E Walnut St
Street address city: Salem
Street address state: IN
Zip/Postal code: 47167-2044
General Phone: (812) 883-5555
General Fax: (812) 967-3194
General/National Adv. E-mail: sales@gbpnews.com
Display Adv. E-mail: april@gbpnews.com
Editorial e-mail: gbrowning@gbpnews.com
Primary Website: gbpnews.com
Mthly Avg Views: 378669
Mthly Avg Unique Visitors: 137646
Year Established: 1933
Avg Free Circ: 11338
Audit By: Sworn/Estimate/Non-Audited
Audit Date: 10.06.2019
Personnel: Joe Green (Pub.); April Falk (Adv. Mgr.); Leslie Gertin (Circ. Mgr.); Harry Sanford (Circ. Mgr.); Heather Marlman (Prodn. Mgr.)
Parent company (for newspapers): Green Banner Publications, Inc.

THE WEEKEND FLYER

Street address 1: 8109 Kingston St
Street address 2: Ste 500
Street address city: Avon
Street address state: IN
Zip/Postal code: 46123-8211
General Phone: (317) 272-5800
General Fax: (317) 272-5887
Advertising Phone: (317) 272-5800 ext. 126
Advertising Fax: (317) 272-5887
Editorial Phone: (317) 272-5800 ext. 134
Editorial Fax: (317) 272-5887
General/National Adv. E-mail: flyer@flyergroup.com
Editorial e-mail: Kathy.Linton@flyergroup.com
Primary Website: flyergroup.com
Avg Free Circ: 16000
Audit By: Sworn/Estimate/Non-Audited
Audit Date: 10.06.2019
Personnel: Harold Allen (Pub.); Cathy Wilson (Bus. Mgr.); Bill Jarchow (Adv. Dir.); Kathy Linton (Ed.); Terry Ballard (Prodn. Dir.); David Johnson (Adv. Dir.)
Parent company (for newspapers): CNHI, LLC

TRI-COUNTY NEWS

Street address 1: 748 S 28th St
Street address city: South Bend
Street address state: IN
Zip/Postal code: 46615-2222
General Phone: (574) 232-8590
General Fax: (574) 232-8592
General/National Adv. E-mail: admin@tricountynewsinc.com
Display Adv. E-mail: admin@tricountynewsinc.com
Editorial e-mail: admin@tricountynewsinc.com
Primary Website: tricountynewsinc.com
Avg Paid Circ: 1000
Audit By: Sworn/Estimate/Non-Audited
Audit Date: 10.06.2019
Personnel: Lisa J. Andrysiak (Gen. Mgr.); Cherie Jolly (Ed.)

VERSAILLES REPUBLICAN

Street address 1: 115 S Washington St
Street address city: Versailles
Street address state: IN
Zip/Postal code: 47042-8016
General Phone: (812) 689-6364
General Fax: (812) 689-6508
General/National Adv. E-mail: publication@ripleynews.com
Display Adv. E-mail: publication@ripleynews.com
Editorial e-mail: lchandler@ripleynews.com
Primary Website: ripleynews.com
Year Established: 1865
Avg Paid Circ: 5200
Avg Free Circ: 48
Audit By: Sworn/Estimate/Non-Audited
Audit Date: 10.06.2019
Personnel: Linda Chandler (Pub.); Cindy Roberts (Office Mgr.); Mary Mattingly (Ed.)
Parent company (for newspapers): Ripley Publishing

VEVAY REVEILLE-ENTERPRISE

Street address 1: 111 W Market St
Street address city: Vevay
Street address state: IN
Zip/Postal code: 47043-1159
General Phone: (812) 427-2311
Advertising Fax: (812) 427-2793
General/National Adv. E-mail: news@vevaynewspapers.com
Primary Website: vevaynewspapers.com
Year Established: 1816
Avg Paid Circ: 3000
Audit By: Sworn/Estimate/Non-Audited
Audit Date: 10.06.2019
Personnel: Erin Williams (Ad. Director); Ginny Leap (Circ. Mgr.); Patrick Lanman (Pub)
Parent company (for newspapers): Vevay Newspapers, Inc.

WARRICK COUNTY TODAY

Street address 1: 204 W Locust St
Street address city: Boonville
Street address state: IN
Zip/Postal code: 47601-1522
General Phone: (812) 897-2330
General Fax: (812) 897-3703
General/National Adv. E-mail: advertising@warricknews.com
Display Adv. E-mail: advertising@warricknews.com
Editorial e-mail: newsroom@warricknews.com
Primary Website: warricknews.com
Mthly Avg Views: 700000
Mthly Avg Unique Visitors: 157000
Year Established: 1875
Avg Paid Circ: 4000
Avg Free Circ: 12000
Audit By: Sworn/Estimate/Non-Audited
Audit Date: 10.06.2019
Personnel: Debi Neal (TSM Sales Coord.); Emily May (Managing Ed.); Karen Hullett (Adv.); Lavinia Brookshire (Publications Ad. Sales)
Parent company (for newspapers): Brehm Communications, Inc.

WEST SIDE COMMUNITY NEWS & WEST INDIANAPOLIS COMMUNITY NEWS

Street address 1: 608 S Vine St
Street address city: Indianapolis
Street address state: IN
Zip/Postal code: 46241-0800
General Phone: (317) 241-7363
General Fax: (317) 240-6397
General/National Adv. E-mail: commnews@communitypapers.net
Year Established: 1965
Avg Free Circ: 25000
Audit By: Sworn/Estimate/Non-Audited
Audit Date: 10.06.2019
Personnel: Jackie F. Deppe (Pub./Gen. Mgr./Adv. Mgr.)
Parent company (for newspapers): Community Papers, Inc.

YOUR ADVANTAGE

Street address 1: 117 E Walnut St
Street address city: Salem
Street address state: IN
Zip/Postal code: 47167-2044
General Phone: (812) 883-3281
General Fax: (812) 883-4446
Display Adv. E-mail: office@salemleader.com
Avg Free Circ: 12400
Audit By: Sworn/Estimate/Non-Audited
Audit Date: 10.06.2019
Personnel: Nancy Grossman (Pub.); Debbie Hayes (Adv. Mgr.); Stephanie Serriell (Ed.); Dennis Miller (Prodn. Mgr.)

ZIONSVILLE TIMES SENTINEL

Street address 1: 250 S Elm St
Street address city: Zionsville
Street address state: IN
Zip/Postal code: 46077-1601
General Phone: (317) 873-6397
Advertising Fax: (317) 873-6259
General/National Adv. E-mail: rick.whiteman@timessentinel.com
Display Adv. E-mail: rick.whiteman@timessentinel.com
Editorial e-mail: news@timessentinel.com
Primary Website: timessentinel.com
Year Established: 1860
Avg Paid Circ: 4300
Audit By: Sworn/Estimate/Non-Audited
Audit Date: 10.06.2019
Personnel: Rick Whiteman (Sales Mgr)
Parent company (for newspapers): CNHI, LLC

IOWA

ACKLEY WORLD JOURNAL

Street address 1: 701 Park Ave
Street address city: Ackley
Street address state: IA
Zip/Postal code: 50601-1538
General Phone: (641) 847-2592
General Fax: (641) 847-3010
Advertising Phone: (641) 847-2592
Advertising Fax: (641) 847-3010
Editorial Phone: (641) 847-2592
Editorial Fax: (641) 847-3010
General/National Adv. E-mail: ackleywj@iafalls.com
Display Adv. E-mail: circulation@iafalls.com
Editorial e-mail: news@iafalls.com
Primary Website: ackleyworldjournal.com
Audit By: Sworn/Estimate/Non-Audited

Audit Date: 10.06.2019
Personnel: Becky Schipper (Ed.); Joy Walker (Adv. Mgr.)
Parent company (for newspapers): United Daily News Group; Times Citizen Communications, Inc

ADAIR COUNTY FREE PRESS

Street address 1: 141 Public Sq
Street address city: Greenfield
Street address state: IA
Zip/Postal code: 50849-1266
General Phone: (641) 743-6121
General Fax: (641) 743-6378
General/National Adv. E-mail: ads@adairpress.com
Display Adv. E-mail: d.mitchell@adairpress.com
Editorial e-mail: editor@adairpress.com
Avg Paid Circ: 2000
Audit By: Sworn/Estimate/Non-Audited
Audit Date: 10.06.2019
Personnel: Denna Mitchell (Circ. Mgr.); Tammy Pearson (editor); Hesper Christensen; Steve Thompson (Sports E.); Melissa Brewer; Sandy McCurdy
Parent company (for newspapers): Herald Publishing Company

ADAIR NEWS

Street address 1: 403 Audubon St
Street address city: Adair
Street address state: IA
Zip/Postal code: 50002-7708
General Phone: (641) 742-3241
General Fax: (641) 742-3489
Advertising Phone: (641) 742-3241
Advertising Fax: (641) 742-3489
Editorial Phone: (641) 742-3241
Editorial Fax: (641) 742-3489
General/National Adv. E-mail: adairnews@iowatelecom.net
Display Adv. E-mail: adairnews@iowatelecom.net
Editorial e-mail: adairnews@iowatelecom.net
Year Established: 1881
Audit By: Sworn/Estimate/Non-Audited
Audit Date: 10.06.2019
Personnel: William Littler (Pub./Ed.)

ADAMS COUNTY FREE PRESS

Street address 1: 618 Davis Ave
Street address city: Corning
Street address state: IA
Zip/Postal code: 50841-1623
General Phone: (641)322-3161
General Fax: (641) 322-3461
Advertising Phone: (641) 322-4126
Editorial Phone: (641) 322-4126
General/National Adv. E-mail: advertising@acfreepress.com
Display Adv. E-mail: advertising@acfreepress.com
Editorial e-mail: editor@acfreepress.com
Primary Website: acfreepress.com
Year Established: 1882
Avg Paid Circ: 2000
Audit By: Sworn/Estimate/Non-Audited
Audit Date: 10.06.2019
Personnel: Don Groves (Publisher)

AFTON STAR-ENTERPRISE

Street address 1: 412 E Filmore
Street address city: Afton
Street address state: IA
Zip/Postal code: 50830
General Phone: (641) 347-8721
General Fax: (641) 347-8721
General/National Adv. E-mail: aftonstar@iowatelecom.net
Primary Website: No Website
Avg Paid Circ: 700
Avg Free Circ: 20
Audit By: Sworn/Estimate/Non-Audited
Audit Date: 10.06.2019
Personnel: Wayne Hill (Pub.); K'Lea Johnson (Publisher/Editor)

AKRON HOMETOWNER

Street address 1: 110 Reed St
Street address city: Akron
Street address state: IA
Zip/Postal code: 51001-7739
General Phone: (712) 568-2208
General Fax: (712) 568-2271
General/National Adv. E-mail: akronht@hickorytech.net
Primary Website: akronhometowner.com
Year Established: 2001
Avg Paid Circ: 1400
Audit By: Sworn/Estimate/Non-Audited
Audit Date: 10.06.2019
Personnel: Julie Ann Madden (Ed.); Joe Hook (Advertising)
Parent company (for newspapers): The Akron Hometowner, Inc.

ALBIA UNION-REPUBLICAN

Street address 1: 109 Benton Ave E
Street address city: Albia
Street address state: IA
Zip/Postal code: 52531-2034
General Phone: (641) 932-7121
General Fax: (641) 932-2822
General/National Adv. E-mail: dave@albianews.com
Primary Website: albianews.com
Year Established: 1862
Avg Paid Circ: 3500
Avg Free Circ: 3000
Audit By: Sworn/Estimate/Non-Audited
Audit Date: 10.06.2019
Personnel: Carol Ann Faber (Adv. Mgr.); David A. Paxton (Ed.)
Parent company (for newspapers): Lancaster Management, Inc.

ALTOONA HERALD-INDEX

Street address 1: 400 Locust St
Street address 2: Ste 500
Street address city: Des Moines
Street address state: IA
Zip/Postal code: 50309-2355
General Phone: (515) 699-7000
General Fax: (515) 699-7098
General/National Adv. E-mail: adwilson@dmreg.com
Primary Website: altoonaherald.com
Audit By: Sworn/Estimate/Non-Audited
Audit Date: 10.06.2019

ANAMOSA PUBLICATIONS

Street address 1: PO Box 108
Street address 2: P.O. Box 108
Street address city: Anamosa
Street address state: IA
Zip/Postal code: 52205-0108
General Phone: (319) 462-3511
General Fax: (319) 462-4540
Advertising Phone: (319) 462-3511
Advertising Fax: (319) 462-4540
Editorial Phone: (319) 462-3511
Editorial Fax: (319) 462-3511
General/National Adv. E-mail: admin@journal-eureka.com
Display Adv. E-mail: admin@journal-eureka.com
Editorial e-mail: News@journal-eureka.com
Primary Website: Journal-Eureka.com
Year Established: 1856
Avg Paid Circ: 2500
Avg Free Circ: 11223
Audit By: Sworn/Estimate/Non-Audited
Audit Date: 10.06.2019
Personnel: W. James Johnson (Pub)
Parent company (for newspapers): Anamosa Publications

ANITA TRIBUNE

Street address 1: 850 Main
Street address city: Anita
Street address state: IA
Zip/Postal code: 50020
General Phone: (712) 762-4188
General Fax: (712) 762-4189
General/National Adv. E-mail: gandrews@midlands.net
Primary Website: facebook.com/pages/The-Anita-Tribune/232703986773881
Year Established: 1883
Avg Paid Circ: 1100
Audit By: Sworn/Estimate/Non-Audited
Audit Date: 10.06.2019
Personnel: Gene Andrews (Pub./Gen. Mgr./Adv. Mgr.); Dana Larsen (Ed.); Deanna Andrews (Prod. Mgr.)

ANKENY REGISTER & PRESS CITIZEN

Street address 1: 400 Locust St
Street address 2: Ste 500
Street address city: Des Moines
Street address state: IA
Zip/Postal code: 50309-2355
General Phone: (515) 284-8000
General Fax: (515) 284-8420
Advertising Phone: (515) 238-2334
Advertising Fax: (515) 284-8420
Editorial Phone: (515) 284-8256
General/National Adv. E-mail: jhanson@dmreg.com
Display Adv. E-mail: sucruz@desmoine.gannett.com
Editorial e-mail: mlagesch@dmreg.com
Primary Website: desmoinesregister.com/communities/ankeny
Year Established: 1953
Avg Free Circ: 24000
Audit By: Sworn/Estimate/Non-Audited
Audit Date: 10.06.2019
Personnel: Jolene Hanson (Account Executive); Jody Savage (Account Executive)
Parent company (for newspapers): Gannett

ANTHON SIOUX VALLEY NEWS

Street address 1: PO Box 299
Street address city: Anthon
Street address state: IA
Zip/Postal code: 51004-0299
General Phone: (712) 373-5571
General Fax: (712) 373-5389
General/National Adv. E-mail: siouxvalleynews@ruralwaves.us
Audit By: Sworn/Estimate/Non-Audited
Audit Date: 10.06.2019

ARMSTRONG JOURNAL

Street address 1: 529 6th St
Street address city: Armstrong
Street address state: IA
Zip/Postal code: 50514-7711
General Phone: (712) 868-3460
General Fax: (712) 864-3028
Advertising Phone: (712) 868-3460
Advertising Fax: (712) 868-3460
Editorial Phone: (712) 868-3460
Editorial Fax: (712) 868-3460
General/National Adv. E-mail: ads@armstrongjournal.com
Display Adv. E-mail: clint@armstrongjournal.com
Editorial e-mail: clint@armstrongjournal.com
Primary Website: statelinepubs.com
Avg Paid Circ: 850
Audit By: Sworn/Estimate/Non-Audited
Audit Date: 10.06.2019
Personnel: Kristin Grabinoski (Publisher); Dorothy Cronk (Editor); Clinton Davis (Office Manager)
Parent company (for newspapers): Stateline Publications

AUDUBON COUNTY ADVOCATE JOURNAL

Street address 1: 517 Leroy St
Street address city: Audubon
Street address state: IA
Zip/Postal code: 50025-0268
General Phone: (712) 563-2741
General Fax: (712) 563-2740
Editorial Phone: (712) 563-2741
Editorial Fax: (712) 563-2740
General/National Adv. E-mail: jeannem@auduboncountynews.com
Display Adv. E-mail: dianab@auduboncountynews.com
Editorial e-mail: dianab@auduboncountynews.com
Primary Website: auduboncountynews.com
Year Established: 1879
Avg Paid Circ: 2100
Avg Free Circ: 8022
Audit By: Sworn/Estimate/Non-Audited
Audit Date: 10.06.2019
Personnel: Diana Ballou (Composition)
Parent company (for newspapers): Community Media Group

AURELIA STAR

Street address 1: PO Box 248
Street address city: Aurelia
Street address state: IA
Zip/Postal code: 51005-0248
General Phone: (712) 229-5492
General/National Adv. E-mail: aurstar@gmail.com
Primary Website: aureliastar.webs.com
Avg Paid Circ: 380
Avg Free Circ: 20
Audit By: Sworn/Estimate/Non-Audited
Audit Date: 10.06.2019
Personnel: Marci Brown (Owner/Ed.)

BARR'S POST CARD NEWS

Street address 1: 108 E 5th St
Street address city: Vinton
Street address state: IA
Zip/Postal code: 52349-1759
General Phone: (319) 472-4713
General Fax: (319) 472-3117
Primary Website: barrspcn.com
Audit By: Sworn/Estimate/Non-Audited
Audit Date: 10.06.2019
Personnel: Shelly Haefner (Circ. Mgr.)
Parent company (for newspapers): Community Media Group

BELLEVUE HERALD-LEADER

Street address 1: 118 S 2nd St
Street address city: Bellevue
Street address state: IA
Zip/Postal code: 52031-1318
General Phone: (563) 872-4159
General Fax: (563) 872-4298
General/National Adv. E-mail: bhleader@bellevueheraldleader.com
Primary Website: bellevueheraldleader.com
Year Established: 1871
Avg Paid Circ: 2770
Avg Free Circ: 12
Audit By: Sworn/Estimate/Non-Audited
Audit Date: 10.06.2019
Personnel: Judy Reed (Circ. Mgr.); David Namanny (Ed.)

BELLEVUE LEADER

Street address 1: 300 W Broadway
Street address 2: Ste 108
Street address city: Council Bluffs
Street address state: IA
Zip/Postal code: 51503
General Phone: (402) 733-7300
General Fax: 712-325-5717
Advertising Phone: 712-325-5798
Advertising Fax: 712-325-5717
Editorial Phone: (402) 733-7300
Editorial Fax: 712-325-5776
General/National Adv. E-mail: news@bellevueleader.com
Display Adv. E-mail: njohnson@owh.com
Classified Adv. e-mail: classifieds@bellevueleader.com
Editorial e-mail: news@bellevueleader.com
Primary Website: bellevueleader.com
Mthly Avg Views: 22
Mthly Avg Unique Visitors: 11
Year Established: 1971
Avg Paid Circ: 1000
Audit By: USPS
Audit Date: 01.10.2022
Personnel: Melissa Vanek (Circ. Mgr.); Amy Corrigan (Production Control Manager); Scott Stewart (Assistant Editor); Tony Digilio (Local Retail Sales Manager); Scott Stewart (Assistant Editor); Tony Digilio (Local Retail Sales Manager); Amy McKay (Gen Man); Paul Swanson (Adv. Mgr.); Ron Petak (Exec. Ed.)
Parent company (for newspapers): BH Media Group; Lee Enterprises; Lee Enterprises

BETTENDORF NEWS

Street address 1: 500 E 3rd St
Street address city: Davenport
Street address state: IA
Zip/Postal code: 52801-1708
General Phone: (563) 383-2200

General Fax: (563) 383-2370
Editorial Phone: (563) 383-2396
Editorial Fax: (563) 383-2370
General/National Adv. E-mail: bettnews@qctimes.com
Editorial e-mail: newsroom@qctimes.com
Primary Website: qctimes.com/bettnews
Year Established: 1927
Avg Paid Circ: 9700
Avg Free Circ: 2453
Audit By: Sworn/Estimate/Non-Audited
Audit Date: 10.06.2019
Personnel: Greg Veon (Pub.); Ann Boyd (Adv. Mgr.); Glenda Verdick (Event Mgr.); Janet Hill (Ed.); Brett Riley (Classified Adv. Dir.)
Parent company (for newspapers): Dispatch-Argus

BLOOMFIELD DEMOCRAT

Street address 1: 207 S Madison St
Street address city: Bloomfield
Street address state: IA
Zip/Postal code: 52537-1622
General Phone: (641) 664-2334
General Fax: (641) 664-2316
General/National Adv. E-mail: ads@bdemo.com
Display Adv. E-mail: ads@bdemo.com
Editorial e-mail: bdemo@netins.net
Primary Website: bdemo.com
Mthly Avg Views: 26000
Mthly Avg Unique Visitors: 19000
Year Established: 1869
Avg Paid Circ: 1661
Audit By: Sworn/Estimate/Non-Audited
Audit Date: 10.06.2019
Personnel: Karen Spurgeon (Pub)

BOONE NEWS-REPUBLICAN

Street address 1: 2136 Mamie Eisenhower Ave
Street address city: Boone
Street address state: IA
Zip/Postal code: 50036-4437
General Phone: (515) 432-6694
General Fax: (515) 432-7811
General/National Adv. E-mail: mscott@amestrib.com
Display Adv. E-mail: mscott@amestrib.com
Classified Adv. e-mail: gtaylor@newsrepublican.com
Editorial e-mail: lkahler@newsrepublican.com
Primary Website: newsrepublican.com
Mthly Avg Unique Visitors: 31173
Year Established: 1888
Avg Paid Circ: 1399
Avg Free Circ: 0
Sat. Circulation Paid: 1433
Sat. Circulation Free: 0
Audit By: Sworn/Estimate/Non-Audited
Audit Date: 10.06.2019
Personnel: Logan Kahler (News Ed.); Randy Terwilliger (Circ. Dir.); Sandi Hilsabeck (Circ. Mgr.); Mary Beth Scott (Sales Mgr.)

BREMER COUNTY INDEPENDENT

Street address 1: 311 W Bremer Ave
Street address city: Waverly
Street address state: IA
Zip/Postal code: 50677-3144
General Phone: (319) 352-3334
General Fax: (319) 352-5135
Advertising Phone: (319) 352-3334
Advertising Fax: (319) 352-5135
Editorial Phone: (319) 352-3334
Editorial Fax: (319) 352-5135
General/National Adv. E-mail: ads@oelweindailyregister.com
Display Adv. E-mail: classifieds@oelweindailyregister.com
Editorial e-mail: news@waverlynewspapers.com
Primary Website: waverlynewspapers.com
Year Established: 1858
Audit By: Sworn/Estimate/Non-Audited
Audit Date: 10.06.2019
Personnel: Deb Weigel (Pub.); Anelia Dimitrova
Parent company (for newspapers): Community Media Group

BRITT NEWS-TRIBUNE

Street address 1: 105 S Clark St
Street address city: Forest City
Street address state: IA
Zip/Postal code: 50436-1710
General Phone: (641) 585-2112
General Fax: (641) 585-4442
General/National Adv. E-mail: news@brittnewstribune.com
Primary Website: brittnewstribune.com
Audit By: Sworn/Estimate/Non-Audited
Audit Date: 10.06.2019

BUFFALO CENTER TRIBUNE

Street address 1: 124 N Main St
Street address city: Buffalo Center
Street address state: IA
Zip/Postal code: 50424-7752
General Phone: (641) 562-2606
General Fax: (641) 562-2636
General/National Adv. E-mail: bctrib@wctatel.net
Primary Website: buffalocentertribune.com
Mthly Avg Views: 2000
Mthly Avg Unique Visitors: 700
Avg Paid Circ: 1595
Audit By: Sworn/Estimate/Non-Audited
Audit Date: 10.06.2019
Personnel: Lanita Kardoes (Pub.)

BUTLER COUNTY TRIBUNE JOURNAL

Street address 1: 422 N Main St
Street address city: Allison
Street address state: IA
Zip/Postal code: 50602-7710
General Phone: (319) 267-2731
General Fax: (319) 267-2731
General/National Adv. E-mail: tribunejournal@netins.net
Primary Website: butlercountytribune.com
Avg Paid Circ: 1600
Audit By: Sworn/Estimate/Non-Audited
Audit Date: 10.06.2019
Personnel: Brad Hicks (Ed.)

CALMAR COURIER

Street address 1: PO Box 507
Street address city: Calmar
Street address state: IA
Zip/Postal code: 52132-0507
General Phone: (563) 562-3488
General Fax: (563) 562-3486
General/National Adv. E-mail: calmarcourier@hotmail.com
Primary Website: calmarcourier.com
Year Established: 2005
Avg Paid Circ: 1800
Audit By: Sworn/Estimate/Non-Audited
Audit Date: 10.06.2019
Personnel: Tina Hageman (Pub.)

CASCADE PIONEER

Street address 1: PO Box 9
Street address city: Cascade
Street address state: IA
Zip/Postal code: 52033-0009
General Phone: (563) 852-3217
General Fax: (563) 852-7188
Advertising Phone: (563) 852-3217
Editorial Phone: (563) 852-3217
General/National Adv. E-mail: cascadesales@wcinet.com
Display Adv. E-mail: cascadesales@wcinet.com
Editorial e-mail: cascadeeditor@wcinet.com
Primary Website: cpioneer.com
Year Established: 1876
Avg Paid Circ: 1875
Audit By: Sworn/Estimate/Non-Audited
Audit Date: 10.06.2019
Personnel: Mary Ungs-Sogaard (Publisher); Theresa Collins (Reporter/Photo.)
Parent company (for newspapers): Woodward Communications, Inc.

CHARITON HERALD-PATRIOT

Street address 1: 815 Braden Ave
Street address city: Chariton
Street address state: IA
Zip/Postal code: 50049-1742
General Phone: (641) 774-2137
General Fax: (641) 774-2139
General/National Adv. E-mail: charnews@charitonleader.com
Primary Website: charitonleader.com
Year Established: 1857
Avg Paid Circ: 3100
Avg Free Circ: 19
Audit By: Sworn/Estimate/Non-Audited
Audit Date: 10.06.2019
Personnel: David A. Paxton (Pub.); Susan Smith (Adv. Mgr.)
Parent company (for newspapers): Lancaster Management, Inc.

CHEROKEE CHRONICLE TIMES

Street address 1: 111 S 2nd St
Street address city: Cherokee
Street address state: IA
Zip/Postal code: 51012-1839
General Phone: (712) 225-5111
General Fax: (712) 225-2910
Advertising Phone: (712) 225-5111
Advertising Fax: (712) 225-2910
Editorial Phone: (712) 225-5111
Editorial Fax: (712) 225-2910
General/National Adv. E-mail: ads@ctimes.biz
Display Adv. E-mail: troyv@ctimes.biz
Classified Adv. e-mail: ads@ctimes.biz
Editorial e-mail: pauls@ctimes.biz
Primary Website: chronicletimes.com
Mthly Avg Views: 85000
Mthly Avg Unique Visitors: 15000
Year Established: 1870
Avg Paid Circ: 2389
Audit By: Sworn/Estimate/Non-Audited
Audit Date: 10.06.2019
Personnel: Paul Struck (Assc. Pub. & Ed. In Chief); Troy Valentine (Assc. Pub./Adv. Mgr.); Rhonda Fassler (Ad.); Chris Reed (Ad.); Diana Otto (Circ.); Ken Ross (Staff Writer); Dan Whitney (Staff Writer)
Parent company (for newspapers): Rust Communications

CLARION WRIGHT COUNTY MONITOR

Street address 1: 107 2nd Ave NE
Street address city: Clarion
Street address state: IA
Zip/Postal code: 50525-1430
General Phone: (515) 532-2871
General Fax: (515) 532-2872
General/National Adv. E-mail: cmonitor@mchsi.com
Primary Website: clarionnewsonline.com
Audit By: Sworn/Estimate/Non-Audited
Audit Date: 10.06.2019

CLEAR LAKE MIRROR REPORTER

Street address 1: 12 N 4th St
Street address city: Clear Lake
Street address state: IA
Zip/Postal code: 50428-1815
General Phone: (641) 357-2131
General Fax: (641) 357-2133
General/National Adv. E-mail: office@clreporter.com
Primary Website: clreporter.com
Year Established: 1869
Avg Paid Circ: 2500
Avg Free Circ: 45
Audit By: Sworn/Estimate/Non-Audited
Audit Date: 10.06.2019
Personnel: Michael J. Finnegan (Pub.); Marianne Morf (Ed.)

COLUMBUS GAZETTE

Street address 1: 209 Main St
Street address city: Columbus Junction
Street address state: IA
Zip/Postal code: 52738-1136
General Phone: (319) 728-2413
General Fax: (319) 728-3272
General/National Adv. E-mail: cjgaz@windstream.net
Primary Website: thecolumbusgazette.com
Year Established: 1886
Avg Paid Circ: 1370
Audit By: Sworn/Estimate/Non-Audited
Audit Date: 10.06.2019
Personnel: Donna Carpenter (Pub.); Carmen Lawrence (Circ. Mgr.); John M. Carpenter (Ed.); Tammy K. Virzi (Sports Ed.); Katie Martin (Prodn. Mgr.)

COON RAPIDS ENTERPRISE

Street address 1: 504 Main St
Street address city: Coon Rapids
Street address state: IA
Zip/Postal code: 50058-1612
General Phone: (712) 999-6397
General Fax: (712) 999-2821
Editorial e-mail: news@coonrapidsenterprise.com
Primary Website: coonrapidsenterprise.com
Year Established: 1881
Avg Paid Circ: 1700
Audit By: Sworn/Estimate/Non-Audited
Audit Date: 10.06.2019
Personnel: Charles Nixon (Pub.)

CORYDON TIMES REPUBLICAN

Street address 1: PO Box 258
Street address 2: 204 S. Franklin St.
Street address city: Corydon
Street address state: IA
Zip/Postal code: 50060-0258
General Phone: (641) 872-1234
General/National Adv. E-mail: rbennett@corydontimes.com
Display Adv. E-mail: rbennett@corydontimes.com
Editorial e-mail: rbennett@corydontimes.com
Primary Website: corydontimes.com
Year Established: 1865
Avg Paid Circ: 1000
Audit By: Sworn/Estimate/Non-Audited
Audit Date: 10.06.2021
Personnel: Rhonda Bennett (Publisher)

CRESCO TIMES-PLAIN DEALER

Street address 1: 214 N Elm St
Street address city: Cresco
Street address state: IA
Zip/Postal code: 52136-1522
General Phone: (563) 547-3601
General Fax: (553) 547-4602
General/National Adv. E-mail: ads1@crescotimes.com
Display Adv. E-mail: ads1@crescotimes.com
Editorial e-mail: tpdeditor@crescotimes.com
Primary Website: crescotimes.com
Year Established: 1855
Avg Paid Circ: 2500
Avg Free Circ: 6000
Audit By: Sworn/Estimate/Non-Audited
Audit Date: 10.06.2019
Personnel: Nate Troy (Sports Editor)
Parent company (for newspapers): Evans Printing & Publishing, Inc.

DAYTON REVIEW

Street address 1: 25 S Main St
Street address city: Dayton
Street address state: IA
Zip/Postal code: 50530-7698
General Phone: (515) 547-2811
General Fax: (515) 547-2337
General/National Adv. E-mail: daytonreview@lvcta.com
Year Established: 1877
Avg Paid Circ: 1100
Avg Free Circ: 20
Audit By: Sworn/Estimate/Non-Audited
Audit Date: 10.06.2019
Personnel: Glenn Schreiber (Pub.)

DECORAH PUBLIC OPINION

Street address 1: 107 E Water St
Street address city: Decorah
Street address state: IA
Zip/Postal code: 52101-1801
General Phone: (563) 382-4221
General Fax: (563) 382-5949
General/National Adv. E-mail: news@decorahnewspapers.com
Display Adv. E-mail: ude@decorahnewspapers.com
Editorial e-mail: fromm@decorahnewspapers.com
Primary Website: decorahnewspapers.com
Year Established: 1898
Avg Paid Circ: 5200

Avg Free Circ: 80
Audit By: Sworn/Estimate/Non-Audited
Audit Date: 10.06.2019
Personnel: Julie Ude (Adv. Mgr.); Richard M. Fromm (Ed.); Stephanie Langreck (Production manager); Amy Usgaard (Bookkeeper)

DELAWARE COUNTY LEADER

Street address 1: 101 1st St SE
Street address city: Hopkinton
Street address state: IA
Zip/Postal code: 52237-7765
General Phone: (563) 926-2626
General Fax: (563) 926-2045
General/National Adv. E-mail: hopleader@yahoo.com
Avg Paid Circ: 1420
Audit By: Sworn/Estimate/Non-Audited
Audit Date: 10.06.2019
Personnel: Mary Helle (Pub.); Cathy Smith (Adv. Mgr.); Cathy Harris (Ed.)

DENVER FORUM

Street address 1: PO Box 509
Street address city: Denver
Street address state: IA
Zip/Postal code: 50622-0509
General Phone: (319) 984-6179
General/National Adv. E-mail: ads@denveriaforum.com
Display Adv. E-mail: ads@denveriaforum.com
Editorial e-mail: news@denveriaforum.com
Primary Website: denveriaforum.com
Mthly Avg Views: 15917
Mthly Avg Unique Visitors: 1219
Year Established: 1976
Avg Paid Circ: 500
Audit By: Sworn/Estimate/Non-Audited
Audit Date: 10.06.2019
Personnel: Kim Adams (Publisher)
Parent company (for newspapers): Horizon Publishing Company

DES MOINES BUSINESS RECORD

Street address 1: 100 4th St
Street address city: Des Moines
Street address state: IA
Zip/Postal code: 50309-4742
General Phone: (515) 288-3336
General Fax: (515) 288-0309
General/National Adv. E-mail: advertising@bpcdm.com
Editorial e-mail: newsroom@bpcdm.com
Primary Website: businessrecord.com
Year Established: 1983
Avg Paid Circ: 2857
Avg Free Circ: 2765
Audit By: VAC
Audit Date: 30.09.2017
Personnel: Janette Larkin (Pub.)
Parent company (for newspapers): Business Publications Corporation Inc.

DES MOINES COUNTY NEWS

Street address 1: 301 Hwy t1
Street address city: Wapello
Street address state: IA
Zip/Postal code: 52653
General Phone: 319-523-4631
General Fax: 319-523-8167
General/National Adv. E-mail: lpc@louisacomm.net
Primary Website: No Website
Avg Paid Circ: 1250
Avg Free Circ: 15
Audit By: Sworn/Estimate/Non-Audited
Audit Date: 10.06.2019
Personnel: Michael A. Hodges (Pub.); Ernie Appleyard (Publisher)
Parent company (for newspapers): Sycamore Media; Sycamore Media

DICKINSON COUNTY NEWS

Street address 1: 3000 18th St
Street address 2: Ste 400
Street address city: Spirit Lake
Street address state: IA
Zip/Postal code: 51360-7471
General Phone: (712) 336-1211
General Fax: (712) 336-1219
General/National Adv. E-mail: dcn@dickinsoncountynews.com
Primary Website: dickinsoncountynews.com
Mthly Avg Views: 46000
Mthly Avg Unique Visitors: 15000
Avg Paid Circ: 3500
Audit By: Sworn/Estimate/Non-Audited
Audit Date: 10.06.2019
Personnel: Russ Mitchell (Editor)
Parent company (for newspapers): Rust Communications

DOON PRESS

Street address 1: 209 Hubbard Ave
Street address city: Doon
Street address state: IA
Zip/Postal code: 51235-7716
General Phone: (712) 726-3313
General Fax: (712) 726-3134
General/National Adv. E-mail: pressgal@hickorytech.net
Primary Website: No Website
Year Established: 1872
Avg Paid Circ: 2600
Audit By: Sworn/Estimate/Non-Audited
Audit Date: 10.06.2019
Personnel: Cheri Groeneweg (Circ. Mgr.); Bridget Vander Tuin (Co-Ed.)

DUNLAP REPORTER

Street address 1: 114 Iowa Ave
Street address city: Dunlap
Street address state: IA
Zip/Postal code: 51529-1047
General Phone: (712) 643-5380
General Fax: (712) 643-2173
General/National Adv. E-mail: reporter@iowatelecom.net
Display Adv. E-mail: dianne@iowatelecom.net
Primary Website: dunlapiowa.com
Year Established: 1870
Avg Paid Circ: 560
Avg Free Circ: 10
Audit By: Sworn/Estimate/Non-Audited
Audit Date: 10.06.2019
Personnel: Dianne Walker (Owner, Publisher/Editor); Mary Crilly (Office Mngr.); Bonnie McCullough (Page design, billing)

DYERSVILLE COMMERCIAL

Street address 1: 223 1st Ave E
Street address city: Dyersville
Street address state: IA
Zip/Postal code: 52040-1202
General Phone: (563) 875-7131
General Fax: (563) 875-2279
Advertising Phone: (563) 875-7131
Advertising Fax: (563) 875-2279
Editorial Phone: (563) 875-7131
Editorial Fax: (563) 875-2279
General/National Adv. E-mail: mungs-sogaard@wcinet.com
Display Adv. E-mail: mungs-sogaard@wcinet.com
Editorial e-mail: mungs-sogaard@wcinet.com
Primary Website: dyersvillecommercial.com
Year Established: 1873
Avg Paid Circ: 3950
Audit By: Sworn/Estimate/Non-Audited
Audit Date: 10.06.2019
Personnel: Mary Ungs-Sogaard (Publisher); Beth Lutgen (Managing Editor)
Parent company (for newspapers): Woodward Communications, Inc.

EAGLE GROVE EAGLE

Street address 1: 314 W Broadway St
Street address city: Eagle Grove
Street address state: IA
Zip/Postal code: 50533-1712
General Phone: (515) 448-4745
General Fax: (515) 448-3182
General/National Adv. E-mail: egeagle@goldfieldaccess.net
Primary Website: theeaglegroveeagle.com
Avg Paid Circ: 2317
Audit By: Sworn/Estimate/Non-Audited
Audit Date: 10.06.2019
Personnel: Leigh Banwell (Adv. Mgr.); Kim Demory (Ed.)

EASTERN IOWA BIZZZY BEE

Street address 1: 214 N Second St.
Street address city: Eldridge
Street address state: IA
Zip/Postal code: 52748-0200
General Phone: (563) 285-8111
General Fax: (563) 285-8114
General/National Adv. E-mail: btubbs@northscottpress.com
Display Adv. E-mail: jmartens@northscottpress.com
Classified Adv. e-mail: btubbs@northscottpress.com
Editorial e-mail: btubbs@northscottpress.com
Primary Website: www.northscottpress.com
Year Established: 1968
Avg Paid Circ: 19000
Audit By: Sworn/Estimate/Non-Audited
Audit Date: 25.09.2021
Personnel: William F. Tubbs (Pub); Scott Campbell (Mng. Ed.); Jeff Martens (Adv. Mgr.); Scott Campbell (Ed.); Jeff Martens (Advertising Mgr); Linda Tubbs (Co-Pub.); Mark Ridolfi (Assist. Ed.)
Parent company (for newspapers): North Scott Press, Inc.

EDGEWOOD REMINDER

Street address 1: PO Box 458
Street address 2: 109 North Washington St.
Street address city: Edgewood
Street address state: IA
Zip/Postal code: 52042-0458
General Phone: (563) 928-6876
General/National Adv. E-mail: edgewood.reminder@yahoo.com
Display Adv. E-mail: edgewood.reminder@yahoo.com
Editorial e-mail: edgewood.reminder@yahoo.com
Primary Website: No Website
Avg Paid Circ: 1100
Avg Free Circ: 17
Audit By: Sworn/Estimate/Non-Audited
Audit Date: 10.06.2019
Personnel: Julie Miller (Owner/Ed.)

ELDORA NEWSPAPERS

Street address 1: 1513 Edgington Ave
Street address city: Eldora
Street address state: IA
Zip/Postal code: 50627-1623
General Phone: (641) 939-5051
General Fax: (641) 939-5541
General/National Adv. E-mail: ads@eldoranewspaper.com
Editorial e-mail: news@eldoranewspaper.com
Primary Website: eldoranewspapers.com
Year Established: 1860
Avg Paid Circ: 1750
Audit By: Sworn/Estimate/Non-Audited
Audit Date: 10.06.2019
Personnel: Pam Warren (Adv. Mgr.); Rick Patrie (Ed.); Scott Bierle; Betty Gotto (Adv. Mgr.)

ESTHERVILLE NEWS

Street address 1: 10 N 7th St
Street address city: Estherville
Street address state: IA
Zip/Postal code: 51334-2232
General Phone: (712) 362-2622
General Fax: (712) 362-2624
Advertising Phone: (712) 362-2622
Advertising Fax: (712) 362-2624
Editorial Phone: (712) 362-2622
Editorial Fax: (712) 362-2624
General/National Adv. E-mail: disaackson@esthervillenews.net
Display Adv. E-mail: disaackson@esthervillenews.net
Classified Adv. e-mail: classifieds@esthervillenews.net
Editorial e-mail: dswartz@esthervillenews.net
Primary Website: esthervilledailynews.com
Mthly Avg Views: 22870
Mthly Avg Unique Visitors: 7623
Avg Paid Circ: 2282
Sat. Circulation Paid: 2282
Audit By: Sworn/Estimate/Non-Audited
Audit Date: 10.06.2019
Personnel: Glen Caron (Pub./Classified Adv. Mgr./Business Mgr.); David Swartz (Sports Ed.); Dar Isaackson (Adv. Dir.); Tessa Peterson (Bus. Mgr.)
Parent company (for newspapers): Ogden Newspapers Inc.

FAIRFIELD TOWN CRIER

Street address 1: 112 E Broadway Ave
Street address city: Fairfield
Street address state: IA
Zip/Postal code: 52556-3202
General Phone: (641) 472-4129
General Fax: (641) 472-1916
General/National Adv. E-mail: adv@ffledger.com
Display Adv. E-mail: classifieds@ffledger.com
Editorial e-mail: news@ffledger.com
Primary Website: goldentrianglenewspapers.com
Year Established: 1980
Avg Free Circ: 10499
Audit By: Sworn/Estimate/Non-Audited
Audit Date: 10.06.2019
Personnel: Kim Stout (Circ. Mgr.); Amy Sparby (Pub); Sherry Jipp (Advt Mgr)
Parent company (for newspapers): The Siebold Company, Inc. (TSC)

FAYETTE COUNTY UNION

Street address 1: 119 S Vine St
Street address city: West Union
Street address state: IA
Zip/Postal code: 52175-1354
General Phone: (563) 422-3888
General Fax: (563) 422-3488
General/National Adv. E-mail: lanews@thefayettecountyunion.com
Primary Website: westunionfayettecountyunion.com
Year Established: 1866
Avg Paid Circ: 2600
Avg Free Circ: 4400
Audit By: Sworn/Estimate/Non-Audited
Audit Date: 10.06.2019
Personnel: LeAnn Larson (Pub.); Jerry Blue (Vice President); Steve Murray (Graphic Design Supervisor)
Parent company (for newspapers): Community Media Group

FAYETTE LEADER

Street address 1: 119 S Vine St
Street address city: West Union
Street address state: IA
Zip/Postal code: 52175-1354
General Phone: (563) 422-5410
General Fax: (563) 422-3488
General/National Adv. E-mail: shermen@fayettepublishing.com
Display Adv. E-mail: shermen@fayettepublishing.com
Editorial e-mail: zkriener@fayettepublishing.com
Primary Website: fayettepublishing.com
Avg Paid Circ: 812
Audit By: Sworn/Estimate/Non-Audited
Audit Date: 10.06.2019
Personnel: LeAnn Larson (Pub.); Steph Hermen (Adv. Exec.); Zak Kriener (News Writer / Sports Writer)
Parent company (for newspapers): Community Media Group

FOREST CITY SUMMIT

Street address 1: 105 S Clark St
Street address city: Forest City
Street address state: IA
Zip/Postal code: 50436-1710
General Phone: (641) 585-2112
General Fax: (641) 585-4442
General/National Adv. E-mail: news@forestcitysummit.com
Primary Website: northiowanews.com
Audit By: Sworn/Estimate/Non-Audited
Audit Date: 10.06.2019
Parent company (for newspapers): Dispatch-Argus

FREMONT-MILLS BEACON-ENTERPRISE

Street address 1: PO Box 129
Street address city: Malvern
Street address state: IA
Zip/Postal code: 51551-0129
General Phone: (712) 624-8512
General Fax: (712) 624-9250
General/National Adv. E-mail: leaderbeacon@qwestoffice.net

Primary Website: No Website
Avg Paid Circ: 800
Audit By: Sworn/Estimate/Non-Audited
Audit Date: 10.06.2019
Personnel: Margaret Waugh (Adv. Mgr.); Karol Siekman (Ed.)

GOWRIE NEWS

Street address 1: 1108 Market St
Street address city: Gowrie
Street address state: IA
Zip/Postal code: 50543-7714
General Phone: (515) 352-3325
General Fax: (515) 352-3309
General/National Adv. E-mail: gnews@wccta.net
Primary Website: daytongowrienews.com
Audit By: Sworn/Estimate/Non-Audited
Audit Date: 10.06.2019

GREENE RECORDER

Street address 1: PO Box 370
Street address city: Greene
Street address state: IA
Zip/Postal code: 50636-0370
General Phone: (641) 816-4525
General Fax: (641) 816-4765
General/National Adv. E-mail: news@greenerecorder.com
Primary Website: greenerecorder.com
Year Established: 1901
Avg Paid Circ: 1250
Avg Free Circ: 20
Audit By: Sworn/Estimate/Non-Audited
Audit Date: 10.06.2019
Personnel: Ross Hawker (Pub.); Fred J. Hawker (Ed.); Sylvia J. Hawker (Ed.)

GRETNA BREEZE

Street address 1: 300 W Broadway
Street address 2: Ste 108
Street address city: Council Bluffs
Street address state: IA
Zip/Postal code: 51503
General Phone: (402) 733-7300
General Fax: 712-325-5717
Advertising Phone: 712-325-5798
Advertising Fax: 712-325-5717
Editorial Phone: 402-733-7300
Editorial Fax: 712-325-5776
General/National Adv. E-mail: news@bellevueleader.com
Display Adv. E-mail: njohnson@owh.com
Classified Adv. e-mail: classifieds@bellevueleader.com
Editorial e-mail: news@bellevueleader.com
Primary Website: gretnabreeze.com
Mthly Avg Views: 25
Mthly Avg Unique Visitors: 9
Year Established: 1971
Avg Paid Circ: 600
Audit By: USPS
Audit Date: 01.10.2022
Personnel: Melissa Vanek (Circ. Mgr.); Amy McKay (Gen Man); Paul Swanson (Adv. Mgr.); Amy Corrigan (Prod Control Mgr); Scott Stewart (Assistant Editor); Ron Petak (Exec. Ed.); Tony Digilio (Local Retail Sales Manager)
Parent company (for newspapers): BH Media Group; Lee Enterprises

GRINNELL HERALD-REGISTER

Street address 1: 813 5th Ave
Street address city: Grinnell
Street address state: IA
Zip/Postal code: 50112-1653
General Phone: (641) 236-3113
General Fax: (641) 236-5135
Advertising Phone: (641) 236-3113
Advertising Fax: (641) 236-5135
Editorial Phone: (641) 236-3113
Editorial Fax: (641) 236-5135
General/National Adv. E-mail: ghr@iowatelecom.net
Display Adv. E-mail: ghr@iowatelecom.net
Editorial e-mail: ghr@iowatelecom.net
Year Established: 1936
Audit By: Sworn/Estimate/Non-Audited
Audit Date: 10.06.2019
Personnel: Dorothy Pinder (Pub.); Martha Pinder (Ed.); Peggy Pinder-Elliot (News Ed.); John DeGrado (Adv. Mgr.); Betty Broders (Adv. Sales Rep.)

GRISWOLD AMERICAN

Street address 1: 519 MAIN ST
Street address city: Griswold
Street address state: IA
Zip/Postal code: 51535
General Phone: (712) 778-4337
General Fax: (712) 778-4350
General/National Adv. E-mail: grisamer@netins.net
Primary Website: griswoldamerican.com
Year Established: 1880
Avg Paid Circ: 800
Avg Free Circ: 30
Audit By: Sworn/Estimate/Non-Audited
Audit Date: 10.06.2019
Personnel: Donna Forsyth (Owner/Ed./Pub.)

GRUNDY CENTER REGISTER

Street address 1: 601 G Ave
Street address city: Grundy Center
Street address state: IA
Zip/Postal code: 50638-1549
General Phone: (319) 824-6958
General Fax: (319) 824-6288
General/National Adv. E-mail: registerads@gcmuni.net
Editorial e-mail: editor@gcmuni.net
Primary Website: thegrundyregister.com
Audit By: Sworn/Estimate/Non-Audited
Audit Date: 10.06.2019
Personnel: Mitchell Krmpotich (Sports Ed.)

GUTHRIE CENTER TIMES

Street address 1: 205 State St
Street address city: Guthrie Center
Street address state: IA
Zip/Postal code: 50115-1370
General Phone: (641) 332-2380
General Fax: (641) 332-2382
Editorial e-mail: gctimes@netins.net
Primary Website: guthriecountynewspapers.com
Avg Paid Circ: 1350
Avg Free Circ: 17
Audit By: Sworn/Estimate/Non-Audited
Audit Date: 10.06.2019
Personnel: Beth Stanley (Adv. Mgr.); Beth Rogers (Circ. Mgr.); Scott P. Gonzales (Ed.); Caitlin Ware (Reporter)

GUTHRIE COUNTY VEDETTE

Street address 1: 111 E Main St
Street address city: Panora
Street address state: IA
Zip/Postal code: 50216-1155
General Phone: (641) 755-2115
General Fax: (641) 755-2425
General/National Adv. E-mail: gctimes@netins.net
Avg Paid Circ: 1200
Audit By: Sworn/Estimate/Non-Audited
Audit Date: 10.06.2019
Personnel: Gordon Castile (Gen. Mgr.); Scott P. Gonzales (Ed.); Caitlin Ware (Rptr.)

GUTTENBERG PRESS

Street address 1: 10 Schiller St
Street address city: Guttenberg
Street address state: IA
Zip/Postal code: 52052-9057
General Phone: (563) 252-2421
General Fax: (563) 252-1275
General/National Adv. E-mail: gbpress@alpinecom.net
Primary Website: guttenbergpress.com
Year Established: 1896
Avg Paid Circ: 2600
Audit By: Sworn/Estimate/Non-Audited
Audit Date: 10.06.2019
Personnel: Gary Howe (Pub.); Jane Thein (Circ. Mgr.)
Parent company (for newspapers): Clayton County Register

HAMBURG REPORTER

Street address 1: 1009 Main St
Street address city: Hamburg
Street address state: IA
Zip/Postal code: 51640-1231
General Phone: (712) 382-1234
General Fax: (712) 382-1222
General/National Adv. E-mail: hamburgreporter@qwestoffice.net
Display Adv. E-mail: classad@ncnewspress.com
Primary Website: hamburgreporter.com
Avg Paid Circ: 1100
Audit By: Sworn/Estimate/Non-Audited
Audit Date: 10.06.2019
Personnel: Tammy Schumacher (Ed./Adv. Dir.); Roxanne Schutz (Classified Sales)
Parent company (for newspapers): CherryRoad Media; CherryRoad Media

HAMPTON CHRONICLE

Street address 1: 9 2nd St NW
Street address city: Hampton
Street address state: IA
Zip/Postal code: 50441-1903
General Phone: (641) 456-2585
General Fax: (641) 456-2587
General/National Adv. E-mail: chroniclenews@iowaconnect.com
Primary Website: hamptonchronicle.com
Audit By: Sworn/Estimate/Non-Audited
Audit Date: 10.06.2019

HARDIN COUNTY INDEX

Street address 1: 1513 Edgington Ave
Street address city: Eldora
Street address state: IA
Zip/Postal code: 50627-1623
General Phone: (641) 939-5051
General Fax: (641) 939-5541
General/National Adv. E-mail: ads@eldoranewspaper.com
Editorial e-mail: news@eldoranewspaper.com
Primary Website: eldoranewspapers.com
Year Established: 1865
Avg Paid Circ: 1500
Audit By: Sworn/Estimate/Non-Audited
Audit Date: 10.06.2019
Personnel: Clint Poock (Pub.); Scott Bierle (Gen Mgr.); Rick Patrie (Ed.); Betty Gotto (Adv. Mgr.)
Parent company (for newspapers): Washington Advertising Company,LLC

HARTLEY SENTINEL-NEWS

Street address 1: 71 1st St SE
Street address city: Hartley
Street address state: IA
Zip/Postal code: 51346-1403
General Phone: (712) 834-2388
General Fax: (712) 928-2223
General/National Adv. E-mail: sentinel@tcaexpress.net
Avg Paid Circ: 1800
Avg Free Circ: 32
Audit By: Sworn/Estimate/Non-Audited
Audit Date: 10.06.2019
Personnel: Nick Pedley (Ed.); Mike Peterson (Sports Ed.); Kaity Harms (Pub. Adv. Mgr.)

HAWARDEN INDEPENDENT/IRETON EXAMINER

Street address 1: 926 Avenue F
Street address city: Hawarden
Street address state: IA
Zip/Postal code: 51023-2275
General Phone: (712) 551-1051
General Fax: (712) 551-1057
General/National Adv. E-mail: independent@longlines.com
Primary Website: independentexaminer.net
Year Established: 1878
Avg Paid Circ: 1256
Avg Free Circ: 21
Audit By: Sworn/Estimate/Non-Audited
Audit Date: 10.06.2019
Personnel: Bruce Odson (Publisher); Mylan Schroeder (General Manager); Pam Banta (Office Manager); Kim Fickett (Reporter/Photographer); Nicole Hoogland (Reporter/Photographer)

HUDSON HERALD

Street address 1: 411 Jefferson St
Street address city: Hudson
Street address state: IA
Zip/Postal code: 50643-9719
General Phone: (319) 988-3855
General Fax: n/a
General/National Adv. E-mail: hudherald@gmail.com
Display Adv. E-mail: hudherald@gmail.com
Classified Adv. e-mail: hudherald@gmail.com
Editorial e-mail: hudherald@gmail.com
Primary Website: hudherald.com
Year Established: 1911
Avg Paid Circ: 700
Avg Free Circ: 25
Audit By: Sworn/Estimate/Non-Audited
Audit Date: 10.06.2019
Personnel: Bonniesue Joy (Ed, Pub)

HUMBOLDT INDEPENDENT

Street address 1: 512 Sumner Ave
Street address city: Humboldt
Street address state: IA
Zip/Postal code: 50548-1759
General Phone: (515) 332-2514
General Fax: (515) 332-1505
General/National Adv. E-mail: independent@humboldtnews.com
Primary Website: humboldtnews.com
Year Established: 1985
Avg Paid Circ: 3623
Avg Free Circ: 197
Audit By: Sworn/Estimate/Non-Audited
Audit Date: 10.06.2019
Personnel: James Gargano (Pub./Gen. Mgr); Jeffrey Gargano (Ed.)

IDA COUNTY COURIER

Street address 1: 214 Main St
Street address city: Ida Grove
Street address state: IA
Zip/Postal code: 51445-1311
General Phone: (712) 364-3131
General Fax: (712) 364-3010
General/National Adv. E-mail: idacourier@frontiernet.net
Display Adv. E-mail: idacourier@frontiernet.net
Editorial e-mail: editor@idacountycourier.com
Primary Website: idacountycourier.com
Year Established: 1975
Avg Paid Circ: 2099
Avg Free Circ: 120
Audit By: Sworn/Estimate/Non-Audited
Audit Date: 10.06.2019
Personnel: Roger D. Rector (Pub.); Peg Peters (Circ. Mgr.); Beth Wolterman (Ed.); Amy Forbes (Business Mgr.); Mike Thornhill (Sports Ed.); Deb Loger (Reporter)

INDEPENDENCE BULLETIN JOURNAL

Street address 1: 900 5th Ave NE
Street address 2: Ste A
Street address city: Independence
Street address state: IA
Zip/Postal code: 50644-1464
General Phone: (319) 334-2557
General Fax: (319) 334-6752
General/National Adv. E-mail: editor@bulletinjournal.com
Primary Website: bulletinjournal.com
Audit By: Sworn/Estimate/Non-Audited
Audit Date: 10.06.2019
Parent company (for newspapers): Community Media Group

IOWA FALLS IOWA FARM BUREAU SPOKESMAN

Street address 1: 406 Stevens St
Street address city: Iowa Falls
Street address state: IA
Zip/Postal code: 50126-2214
General Phone: (641) 648-2521
General Fax: (641) 648-4606
General/National Adv. E-mail: spokesman406@gmail.com
Primary Website: iowafarmbureau.com
Audit By: Sworn/Estimate/Non-Audited

Audit Date: 10.06.2019

JASPER COUNTY TRIBUNE

Street address 1: 1 W Howard St
Street address city: Colfax
Street address state: IA
Zip/Postal code: 50054-1213
General Phone: (515) 674-3591
General Fax: (515) 674-3591
Advertising Phone: (515) 674-3591
Advertising Fax: (515) 674-3591
Editorial Phone: (515) 674-3591
Editorial Fax: (515) 674-3591
General/National Adv. E-mail: ads@jaspercountytribune.com
Display Adv. E-mail: ads@jaspercountytribune.com
Editorial e-mail: news@jaspercountytribune.com
Primary Website: Jasper County Tribune
Year Established: 1895
Avg Paid Circ: 860
Avg Free Circ: 0
Audit By: Sworn/Estimate/Non-Audited
Audit Date: 10.06.2019
Personnel: Mike Mendenhall (Editor); Alex Olp (Reporter)
Parent company (for newspapers): Shaw Media

JESUP CITIZEN HERALD

Street address 1: 930 6th St
Street address city: Jesup
Street address state: IA
Zip/Postal code: 50648-1177
General Phone: (319) 827-1128
General Fax: (319) 827-1125
General/National Adv. E-mail: ads@jesupcitizenherald.com
Display Adv. E-mail: ads@jesupcitizenherald.com
Editorial e-mail: editor@jesupcitizenherald.com
Primary Website: jesupcitizenherald.com
Mthly Avg Views: 92500
Mthly Avg Unique Visitors: 2667
Year Established: 1899
Avg Paid Circ: 1020
Audit By: Sworn/Estimate/Non-Audited
Audit Date: 10.06.2019
Personnel: Kim Edward Adams (Pub.); Nancy Steinbron (Editor)
Parent company (for newspapers): Horizon Publishing Company

JOURNAL HERALD

Street address 1: 931 Main St
Street address city: Manson
Street address state: IA
Zip/Postal code: 50563-5135
General Phone: (712) 469-3381
General Fax: (712) 469-2648
General/National Adv. E-mail: journal@journalherald.com
Display Adv. E-mail: journal@journalherald.com
Editorial e-mail: journal@journalherald.com
Primary Website: journalherald.com
Year Established: 1910
Avg Paid Circ: 1300
Audit By: Sworn/Estimate/Non-Audited
Audit Date: 10.06.2019
Personnel: Gary D. Dudley (Pub.); Ron Sturgis (Ed.)

JOURNAL TRIBUNE

Street address 1: 208 W State St
Street address city: Williamsburg
Street address state: IA
Zip/Postal code: 52361-4708
General Phone: (319) 668-1240
General Fax: (319) 668-9112
General/National Adv. E-mail: cvonahse@dmreg.com
Primary Website: yourweeklypaper.com
Year Established: 1901
Avg Paid Circ: 2487
Avg Free Circ: 85
Audit By: AAM
Audit Date: 30.09.2018
Personnel: Diane Goodlow (Pub.)
Parent company (for newspapers): Gannett

KEOTA EAGLE

Street address 1: 310 E Broadway Ave
Street address city: Keota
Street address state: IA
Zip/Postal code: 52248-9402
General Phone: (641) 622-3110
General Fax: (641) 340-0805
General/National Adv. E-mail: keomahmanager@midamericapub.com
Display Adv. E-mail: keomahmanager@midamericapub.com
Editorial e-mail: keotanews@midamericapub.com
Primary Website: keotaeagle.com
Year Established: 1875
Audit By: Sworn/Estimate/Non-Audited
Audit Date: 10.06.2019
Personnel: Mike Burvee (Sports Ed.); Amy Stourac (Ed.); Amie Van Patten (Adv.)
Parent company (for newspapers): Mid-America Publishing

KINGSLEY NEWS-TIMES

Street address 1: 120 Main St
Street address city: Kingsley
Street address state: IA
Zip/Postal code: 51028-7725
General Phone: (712) 378-2770
General Fax: (712) 378-2274
General/National Adv. E-mail: knewest@evertek.net
Avg Paid Circ: 1000
Audit By: Sworn/Estimate/Non-Audited
Audit Date: 10.06.2019
Personnel: Randy List (Pub.); Earl Horlyk (Ed.)

KOSSUTH COUNTY ADVANCE

Street address 1: 14 E Nebraska St
Street address city: Algona
Street address state: IA
Zip/Postal code: 50511-2630
General Phone: (515) 295-3535
General Fax: (515) 295-7217
General/National Adv. E-mail: ads@algona.com
Display Adv. E-mail: ads@algona.com
Editorial e-mail: news@algona.com
Primary Website: algona.com
Mthly Avg Views: 30000
Year Established: 1866
Avg Paid Circ: 2550
Audit By: Sworn/Estimate/Non-Audited
Audit Date: 15.09.2021
Personnel: Brad Hicks (Publisher)

LAKE MILLS GRAPHIC

Street address 1: 204 N Mill St
Street address city: Lake Mills
Street address state: IA
Zip/Postal code: 50450-1316
General Phone: (641) 592-4222
General Fax: (641) 592-6397
General/National Adv. E-mail: graphic@wctatel.net
Primary Website: lmgraphic.com
Year Established: 1872
Avg Paid Circ: 1650
Avg Free Circ: 0
Audit By: Sworn/Estimate/Non-Audited
Audit Date: 10.06.2019
Personnel: Terry Gasper (Pub.); Sherylee Gasper (Editor/Owner/Publisher/Graphic Designer)

LAMONI CHRONICLE

Street address 1: 120 N Linden St
Street address city: Lamoni
Street address state: IA
Zip/Postal code: 50140-1046
General Phone: (641) 784-6397
General Fax: (641) 784-7669
General/National Adv. E-mail: newnews@grm.net
Year Established: 1891
Audit By: Sworn/Estimate/Non-Audited
Audit Date: 10.06.2019
Personnel: Michelle Morris (Business Manager)

LAMONT LEADER

Street address 1: 621 Bush St
Street address city: Lamont
Street address state: IA
Zip/Postal code: 50650-9041
General Phone: (563) 924-2361
General Fax: (563) 924-2159
General/National Adv. E-mail: lamontleader@iowatelecom.net
Avg Paid Circ: 700
Audit By: Sworn/Estimate/Non-Audited
Audit Date: 10.06.2019
Personnel: Steven C. Sanders (Ed.)

LAURENS SUN

Street address 1: 218 N Main St
Street address city: Pocahontas
Street address state: IA
Zip/Postal code: 50574-1605
General Phone: (712) 335-3553
General Fax: (712) 335-3856
Advertising Phone: (712) 335-3553
Advertising Fax: (712) 335-3856
Editorial Phone: (712) 335-3553
Editorial Fax: (712) 335-3856
General/National Adv. E-mail: ads@laurenssun.com
Display Adv. E-mail: ads@laurenssun.com
Editorial e-mail: publisher@laurenssun.com
Avg Paid Circ: 500
Audit By: Sworn/Estimate/Non-Audited
Audit Date: 10.06.2019
Personnel: Chris Vrba (Owner/Pub./Ed.)

LENOX TIME TABLE

Street address 1: 101 E Temple St
Street address 2: # 12
Street address city: Lenox
Street address state: IA
Zip/Postal code: 50851-1210
General Phone: (641) 333-2810
General/National Adv. E-mail: timetable@lenoxia.com
Primary Website: No Website
Year Established: 1874
Avg Paid Circ: 975
Audit By: Sworn/Estimate/Non-Audited
Audit Date: 10.06.2019
Personnel: Randy Larimer (Ed.)

LINN NEWS-LETTER

Street address 1: 38 4th St N
Street address city: Central City
Street address state: IA
Zip/Postal code: 52214-7700
General Phone: (319) 438-1313
General Fax: (319) 438-1838
Advertising Phone: (319) 438-1313
Advertising Fax: (319) 438-1838
Editorial Phone: (319) 438-1313
Editorial Fax: (319) 438-1838
General/National Adv. E-mail: linnnewsletter@iowatelecom.net
Display Adv. E-mail: linnnewsletter@iowatelecom.net
Editorial e-mail: linnnewsletter@iowatelecom.net
Primary Website: linncolettershoppr.com
Year Established: 1888
Audit By: Sworn/Estimate/Non-Audited
Audit Date: 10.06.2019
Personnel: Rae Ann Holub (Ed.)

LITTLE ROCK FREE LANCE

Street address 1: PO Box 185
Street address city: Little Rock
Street address state: IA
Zip/Postal code: 51243-0185
General Phone: (712) 479-2270
General/National Adv. E-mail: vksc@mtcnet.net
Year Established: 1978
Avg Paid Circ: 810
Audit By: Sworn/Estimate/Non-Audited
Audit Date: 10.06.2019
Personnel: Virginia Klaassen (Pub.)

LOWDEN SUN-NEWS AND ADVERTISER

Street address 1: 124 W 5th St
Street address city: Tipton
Street address state: IA
Zip/Postal code: 52772-1728
General Phone: (563) 886-2131
General Fax: (563) 886-6466
General/National Adv. E-mail: tcadvertising@yahoo.com
Audit By: Sworn/Estimate/Non-Audited
Audit Date: 10.06.2019

LYON COUNTY NEWS

Street address 1: 113 E Michigan Ave
Street address city: George
Street address state: IA
Zip/Postal code: 51237-7751
General Phone: (712) 475-3351
General Fax: (712) 475-3353
General/National Adv. E-mail: lyonconews@mtcnet.net
Display Adv. E-mail: lyonconewsck@mtcnet.net
Editorial e-mail: lyonconewsck@mtcnet.net
Year Established: 1906
Avg Paid Circ: 750
Avg Free Circ: 80
Audit By: Sworn/Estimate/Non-Audited
Audit Date: 10.06.2019
Personnel: Milli Krull (Circ. Mgr.); Cheryl Koerselman (Ed.); Brian Hulshof (Advertising); Leann Kruger (Ad Sales/Graphic Artist)

LYON COUNTY REPORTER

Street address 1: 310 1st Ave
Street address city: Rock Rapids
Street address state: IA
Zip/Postal code: 51246-1595
General Phone: (712) 472-2525
General Fax: (712) 472-3414
Advertising Phone: (712) 472-2525
Advertising Fax: (712) 472-3414
Editorial Phone: (712) 472-2525
Editorial Fax: (712) 472-3414
General/National Adv. E-mail: lmiller@ncppub.com
Display Adv. E-mail: lkuehl@ncppub.com
Editorial e-mail: jjensen@ncppub.com
Primary Website: lyoncountyreporter.com
Avg Paid Circ: 1200
Audit By: Sworn/Estimate/Non-Audited
Audit Date: 10.06.2019
Personnel: Jim Hensley (Pub./COO); Jessica Jensen (Ed.); Lisa Miller (Gen. Mgr.)
Parent company (for newspapers): New Century Press

MADRID REGISTER-NEWS

Street address 1: 102 S Main St
Street address city: Madrid
Street address state: IA
Zip/Postal code: 50156-1232
General Phone: (515) 795-2730
General Fax: (515) 795-2012
General/National Adv. E-mail: wilcoxprinting@mchsi.com
Year Established: 1881
Avg Paid Circ: 1250
Audit By: Sworn/Estimate/Non-Audited
Audit Date: 10.06.2019
Personnel: Jennifer Williams (Ed.); Ken Williams

MANILLA TIMES

Street address 1: 448 Main St
Street address city: Manilla
Street address state: IA
Zip/Postal code: 51454-7708
General Phone: (712) 654-2911
General Fax: (712) 654-2910
General/National Adv. E-mail: manillatimesads@fmctc.com
Editorial e-mail: manillatimes@fmctc.com
Year Established: 1899
Avg Paid Circ: 782
Avg Free Circ: 18
Audit By: Sworn/Estimate/Non-Audited
Audit Date: 10.06.2019
Personnel: Joleen Sievertsen (Office Mgr); Michele Ertz (Graphic Des, Tech Supp); Kay Rutherford (Adv Mgr)

MANLY JUNCTION SIGNAL

Street address 1: 801 Central Ave
Street address city: Northwood
Street address state: IA
Zip/Postal code: 50459-1519
General Phone: (641) 324-1051
General Fax: (641) 324-2432
General/National Adv. E-mail: jane@northwoodanchor.net
Audit By: Sworn/Estimate/Non-Audited
Audit Date: 10.06.2019

Personnel: Kris Kenison (Editor)

MANNING MONITOR

Street address 1: 411 Main St
Street address city: Manning
Street address state: IA
Zip/Postal code: 51455-1032
General Phone: (712) 653-3854
General Fax: (712) 653-9430
General/National Adv. E-mail: manningmonitor@iowatelecom.net
Primary Website: No Website
Year Established: 1893
Avg Paid Circ: 1550
Audit By: Sworn/Estimate/Non-Audited
Audit Date: 10.06.2019
Personnel: Ronald A. Colling (Ed.)

MAPLETON PRESS

Street address 1: 502 Main St
Street address city: Mapleton
Street address state: IA
Zip/Postal code: 51034-1215
General Phone: (712) 881-1101
General Fax: (712) 881-1330
General/National Adv. E-mail: ads@mapletonpress.com
Display Adv. E-mail: ads@mapletonpress.com
Editorial e-mail: news@mapletonpress.com
Primary Website: mapletonpress.com
Year Established: 1874
Avg Paid Circ: 1300
Audit By: Sworn/Estimate/Non-Audited
Audit Date: 10.06.2019
Personnel: Brad Swenson (Publisher)
Parent company (for newspapers): Enterprise Media Group

MAQUOKETA SENTINEL-PRESS

Street address 1: 108 W Quarry St
Street address city: Maquoketa
Street address state: IA
Zip/Postal code: 52060-2244
General Phone: (563) 652-2441
General Fax: (563) 652-6094
General/National Adv. E-mail: mspress@mspress.net
Primary Website: maqnews.com
Avg Paid Circ: 5050
Audit By: Sworn/Estimate/Non-Audited
Audit Date: 10.06.2019
Personnel: Rosie Morehead (Adv. Mgr.); Douglas D. Melvold (Ed.)

MARENGO PIONEER-REPUBLICAN

Street address 1: 1152 Marengo Ave
Street address city: Marengo
Street address state: IA
Zip/Postal code: 52301-1523
General Phone: (319) 642-5506
General Fax: (319) 642-5509
General/National Adv. E-mail: publish@netins.net
Primary Website: yourweeklypaper.com
Avg Paid Circ: 2542
Audit By: Sworn/Estimate/Non-Audited
Audit Date: 10.06.2019
Personnel: Martin Bunge (Pub.); Paul Thompson (Adv. Sales Mgr.)
Parent company (for newspapers): Gannett

MEDIAPOLIS NEWS

Street address 1: 616 Main St
Street address city: Mediapolis
Street address state: IA
Zip/Postal code: 52637-7731
General Phone: (319) 394-3174
General Fax: (319) 394-3134
General/National Adv. E-mail: meponews@mepotelco.net
Display Adv. E-mail: meponews@mepotelco.net
Primary Website: mediapolisnews.com
Year Established: 1874
Avg Paid Circ: 1000
Avg Free Circ: 600
Audit By: Sworn/Estimate/Non-Audited
Audit Date: 10.06.2019

MISSOURI VALLEY TIMES-NEWS

Street address 1: 501 E Erie St
Street address city: Missouri Valley
Street address state: IA
Zip/Postal code: 51555-1646
General Phone: (712) 642-2791
General Fax: (712) 642-2595
General/National Adv. E-mail: advertising@missourivalleytimes.com
Display Adv. E-mail: classifieds@missourivalleytimes.com
Editorial e-mail: news@missourivalleytimes.com
Primary Website: missourivalleytimes.com
Year Established: 1868
Avg Paid Circ: 1900
Audit By: Sworn/Estimate/Non-Audited
Audit Date: 10.06.2019
Personnel: Mark Rhoades (President); Brad Swenson (Publisher)
Parent company (for newspapers): Enterprise Media Group

MITCHELL COUNTY PRESS-NEWS

Street address 1: 112 N 6th St
Street address city: Osage
Street address state: IA
Zip/Postal code: 50461-1202
General Phone: (641) 732-3721
General Fax: (641) 732-5689
General/National Adv. E-mail: editor@mcpress.com
Display Adv. E-mail: ads@mcpress.com
Editorial e-mail: editor@mcpress.com
Primary Website: mcpress.com
Avg Paid Circ: 6900
Audit By: Sworn/Estimate/Non-Audited
Audit Date: 10.06.2019
Personnel: David Namanny (Mng. Ed.); Howard Query (Pub./Gen. Mgr.); Greg Wilderman (Adv. Mgr.)
Parent company (for newspapers): Dispatch-Argus

MONROE COUNTY NEWS

Street address 1: 109 Benton Ave E
Street address city: Albia
Street address state: IA
Zip/Postal code: 52531-2034
General Phone: (641) 932-7121
General Fax: (641) 932-2822
General/National Adv. E-mail: brian@albianews.com
Primary Website: albianews.com
Avg Paid Circ: 2850
Avg Free Circ: 900
Audit By: Sworn/Estimate/Non-Audited
Audit Date: 10.06.2019
Personnel: David A. Paxton (Ed.)
Parent company (for newspapers): Lancaster Management, Inc.

MONROE LEGACY

Street address 1: 213 W Mills St
Street address city: Monroe
Street address state: IA
Zip/Postal code: 50170-7920
General Phone: (641) 259-2708
General/National Adv. E-mail: mmml@iowatelecom.net
Primary Website: monroelegacy.com
Year Established: 1873
Audit By: Sworn/Estimate/Non-Audited
Audit Date: 10.06.2019

MORNING SUN NEWS-HERALD

Street address 1: 11 Division St
Street address 2: # 8
Street address city: Morning Sun
Street address state: IA
Zip/Postal code: 52640-7616
General Phone: (319) 868-7509
General Fax: (319) 868-7509
General/National Adv. E-mail: lpc@louisacomm.net
Year Established: 1881
Audit By: Sworn/Estimate/Non-Audited
Audit Date: 10.06.2019

MOUNT AYR RECORD-NEWS

Street address 1: 122 W Madison St
Street address city: Mount Ayr
Street address state: IA
Zip/Postal code: 50854-1630
General Phone: (641) 464-2440
General Fax: (641) 464-2229
General/National Adv. E-mail: staff@mtayrnews.com
Primary Website: mtayrnews.com
Year Established: 1864
Avg Paid Circ: 1550
Avg Free Circ: 485
Audit By: Sworn/Estimate/Non-Audited
Audit Date: 10.09.2023
Personnel: Tom Hawley (Ed & Pub); LuAnn Jackson (Prodn. Mgr.); Lora Stull (Office Mgr); Jennifer Kellner; Michael Edwards (Ad Designer); Darrell Dodge (News Ed); Sue Carson (Proofreader); Chanse Hall (Reporter)
Parent company (for newspapers): Paragon Publications

MOUNT VERNON-LISBON SUN

Street address 1: 108 1st St SW
Street address city: Mount Vernon
Street address state: IA
Zip/Postal code: 52314-4706
General Phone: (319) 895-6216
General Fax: (319) 895-6217
General/National Adv. E-mail: advertising@mtvernonlisbonsun.com
Editorial e-mail: news@mtvernonlisbonsun.com
Primary Website: mvlsun.com
Year Established: 1869
Avg Paid Circ: 2500
Avg Free Circ: 3000
Audit By: Sworn/Estimate/Non-Audited
Audit Date: 10.06.2019
Personnel: Richard Eskelsen (Adv. Mgr.); Jake Krob (Pub.); Margaret Stevens (Ed.); Nathan Countryman
Parent company (for newspapers): Woodward Communications Inc

NASHUA REPORTER

Street address 1: 10 N Chestnut Ave
Street address city: New Hampton
Street address state: IA
Zip/Postal code: 50659-1349
General Phone: (641) 394-2111
General Fax: (641) 394-2113
General/National Adv. E-mail: nashuareporter@gmail.com
Primary Website: nashuareporter.com
Audit By: Sworn/Estimate/Non-Audited
Audit Date: 10.06.2019
Parent company (for newspapers): Hallmark Integrated Media, Inc.

NEVADA JOURNAL

Street address 1: 317 5th St
Street address city: Ames
Street address state: IA
Zip/Postal code: 50010-6101
General Phone: (515) 382-2161
General Fax: (515) 382-4299
General/National Adv. E-mail: results@nevadaiowajournal.com
Primary Website: nevadaiowajournal.com
Audit By: Sworn/Estimate/Non-Audited
Audit Date: 10.06.2019
Personnel: Jayme Ollendieck (Multi. Sales exec.)

NEW HAMPTON TRIBUNE

Street address 1: 10 N Chestnut Ave
Street address city: New Hampton
Street address state: IA
Zip/Postal code: 50659-1349
General Phone: (641) 394-2111
General Fax: (641) 394-2113
General/National Adv. E-mail: tribune@nhtrib.com
Avg Paid Circ: 2600
Audit By: Sworn/Estimate/Non-Audited
Audit Date: 10.06.2019

Personnel: Dave Stanley (Pub)

NEW LONDON JOURNAL

Street address 1: 138 W Main St
Street address city: New London
Street address state: IA
Zip/Postal code: 52645-1334
General Phone: (319) 367-2366
General Fax: (319) 367-2366
Advertising Phone: 319-523-4631
General/National Adv. E-mail: lpc@louisacomm.net
Avg Paid Circ: 850
Audit By: Sworn/Estimate/Non-Audited
Audit Date: 10.06.2019
Personnel: Ernier Appleyard (publisher); Michael A. Hodges (Pub.); Evelyn Garmoe (Ed.)
Parent company (for newspapers): Sycamore Media; Sycamore Media

NEWS-ADVERTISER

Street address 1: 1114 7th St
Street address 2: P O Box 721
Street address city: Harlan
Street address state: IA
Zip/Postal code: 51537-1338
General Phone: (712) 755-3111
General Fax: (712) 755-3324
General/National Adv. E-mail: news2@harlanonline.com
Primary Website: harlanonline.com
Year Established: 1870
Avg Paid Circ: 4000
Avg Free Circ: 43000
Audit By: Sworn/Estimate/Non-Audited
Audit Date: 10.06.2019
Personnel: Alan Mores (Co-Pub.); Steven Mores (Co-Pub.); Mike Kolbe (Adv. Mgr./Mktg. Dir.); Bob Bjoin (Ed.)
Parent company (for newspapers): Tribune Newspapers Inc

NORA SPRINGS ROCKFORD REGISTER

Street address 1: PO Box 107
Street address city: Northwood
Street address state: IA
Zip/Postal code: 50459-0107
General Phone: (641) 324-1051
General Fax: (641) 324-2432
General/National Adv. E-mail: jane@northwoodanchor.net
Audit By: Sworn/Estimate/Non-Audited
Audit Date: 10.06.2019
Personnel: Jane Podgorniak (Publisher); Jennifer Moe (Sales); Julie Salisbury

NORTH IOWA TIMES

Street address 1: 220 Main St
Street address city: Mc Gregor
Street address state: IA
Zip/Postal code: 52157-8718
General Phone: (563) 873-2210
General Fax: (608) 326-2443
General/National Adv. E-mail: howeads@mhtc.net
Editorial e-mail: nitelitor@mhtc.net
Primary Website: northiowatimes.com
Year Established: 1856
Avg Paid Circ: 750
Avg Free Circ: 20000
Audit By: Sworn/Estimate/Non-Audited
Audit Date: 10.06.2019
Personnel: Gary Howe (Publisher); Audrey Posten (Editor)
Parent company (for newspapers): Courier Press

NORTH LIBERTY LEADER

Street address 1: 206 E. Main Street
Street address city: Solon
Street address state: IA
Zip/Postal code: 52333
General Phone: (319) 624-2233
General Fax: (319) 624-1356
General/National Adv. E-mail: advertising@economistleader.com
Editorial e-mail: economist@economistleader.com
Primary Website: northlibertyleader.com
Avg Paid Circ: 925

Audit By: Sworn/Estimate/Non-Audited
Audit Date: 10.06.2019
Personnel: Doug Lindner (Pub.)
Parent company (for newspapers): Woodward Communications

NORTH WARREN TOWN AND COUNTY NEWS

Street address 1: PO Box 325
Street address city: Norwalk
Street address state: IA
Zip/Postal code: 50211-0325
General Phone: (515) 989-3251
Avg Paid Circ: 1722
Audit By: Sworn/Estimate/Non-Audited
Audit Date: 10.06.2019
Personnel: Steven Klein (Pub.)

NORTHERN-SUN PRINT

Street address 1: 423 2nd St
Street address city: Gladbrook
Street address state: IA
Zip/Postal code: 50635-7720
General Phone: (641) 473-2102
General Fax: (641) 473-1004
General/National Adv. E-mail: editor@northernsunprint.com
Editorial e-mail: editor@northernsunprint.com
Primary Website: northernsunprint.com
Avg Paid Circ: 1100
Audit By: Sworn/Estimate/Non-Audited
Audit Date: 10.06.2019
Personnel: Betty Dahms (Ed.)
Parent company (for newspapers): Ogden Newspapers Inc.

NORTHWOOD ANCHOR

Street address 1: 801 Central Ave
Street address city: Northwood
Street address state: IA
Zip/Postal code: 50459-1519
General Phone: (641) 324-1051
General Fax: (641) 324-2432
General/National Adv. E-mail: anchor@northwoodanchor.net
Audit By: Sworn/Estimate/Non-Audited
Audit Date: 10.06.2019
Personnel: Kris Kenison (Editor); Jane Podgorniak

N'WEST IOWA REVIEW

Street address 1: 227 9th St
Street address city: Sheldon
Street address state: IA
Zip/Postal code: 51201-1419
General Phone: (712) 324-5347
General Fax: (712) 324-2345
General/National Adv. E-mail: editor@iowainformation.com
Display Adv. E-mail: ads@iowainformation.com
Editorial e-mail: editor@iowainformation.com
Primary Website: nwestiowa.com
Year Established: 1972
Avg Paid Circ: 6647
Audit By: Sworn/Estimate/Non-Audited
Audit Date: 10.06.2019
Personnel: Peter W. Wagner (Pub.); Jeff Wagner (Gen. Mgr.); Jeff Grant (Ed.); Connie Wagner (Prodn. Mgr.)
Parent company (for newspapers): Iowa Information, Inc.

OAKLAND HERALD

Street address 1: 146 MAIN ST
Street address city: Oakland
Street address state: IA
Zip/Postal code: 51560
General Phone: (888) 343-2154
General/National Adv. E-mail: avocajh@iowatelecom.net
Audit By: Sworn/Estimate/Non-Audited
Audit Date: 10.06.2019
Personnel: Rich Price (Editor)

OGDEN REPORTER

Street address 1: 222 W Walnut St
Street address 2: 222 West Walnut St.
Street address city: Ogden
Street address state: IA
Zip/Postal code: 50212-2004
General Phone: (515) 275-4101
General Fax: (515) 275-2678
Advertising Phone: (515) 275-2101
Advertising Fax: (515) 275-2678
General/National Adv. E-mail: alban@netins.net
Display Adv. E-mail: sharonalban@gmail.com
Editorial e-mail: alban@netins.net
Primary Website: ogdenreporter.com
Year Established: 1884
Avg Paid Circ: 1850
Audit By: Sworn/Estimate/Non-Audited
Audit Date: 10.06.2019
Personnel: Sharon Alban (Pub.)

ONAWA DEMOCRAT

Street address 1: 720 Iowa Ave
Street address city: Onawa
Street address state: IA
Zip/Postal code: 51040-1628
General Phone: (712) 423-2411
General Fax: (712) 423-2411
General/National Adv. E-mail: democrat@longlines.com
Audit By: Sworn/Estimate/Non-Audited
Audit Date: 10.06.2019

OPINION-TRIBUNE

Street address 1: 116 S Walnut St
Street address city: Glenwood
Street address state: IA
Zip/Postal code: 51534-1665
General Phone: (712) 527-3191
General Fax: (712) 527-3193
General/National Adv. E-mail: news@opinion-tribune.com
Primary Website: opinion-tribune.com
Year Established: 1864
Avg Paid Circ: 3900
Avg Free Circ: 6000
Audit By: Sworn/Estimate/Non-Audited
Audit Date: 10.06.2019
Personnel: Joe Foreman (Ed.); Greg Orear (Pub.); Melissa Lorang (Adv. Sales); Karen Herzberg (Circ. Mgr./Classifieds)
Parent company (for newspapers): Landmark Communications, Inc.; Landmark Community Newspapers, LLC

OSCEOLA COUNTY GAZETTE-TRIBUNE

Street address 1: 201 9th St
Street address 2: Ste 1
Street address city: Sibley
Street address state: IA
Zip/Postal code: 51249-1846
General Phone: (712) 754-2551
General Fax: (712) 754-2552
General/National Adv. E-mail: gtnews@nethtc.net
Primary Website: No Website
Year Established: 1872
Avg Paid Circ: 1500
Avg Free Circ: 4800
Audit By: Sworn/Estimate/Non-Audited
Audit Date: 10.06.2019
Personnel: Chris Godfredsen (Pub.)

OSCEOLA SENTINEL-TRIBUNE

Street address 1: 111 E Washington St
Street address city: Osceola
Street address state: IA
Zip/Postal code: 50213-1244
General Phone: (641) 342-2131
General Fax: (641) 342-2060
General/National Adv. E-mail: ccpnews@osceolaiowa.com
Editorial e-mail: ccpeditor@osceolaiowa.com
Primary Website: osceolaiowa.com
Avg Paid Circ: 3200
Avg Free Circ: 11000
Audit By: CVC
Audit Date: 17.06.2017
Personnel: Rich Paulsen (Pub.); Scott Vicker (Mng., Ed.)
Parent company (for newspapers): Shaw Media

OSSIAN BEE

Street address 1: 119 S Vine St
Street address city: West Union
Street address state: IA
Zip/Postal code: 52175-1354
General Phone: (563) 422-5410
General Fax: (563) 422-3488
General/National Adv. E-mail: thebee@alpinecom.net
Primary Website: newspapersoffayettecounty.com
Year Established: 1889
Avg Paid Circ: 400
Audit By: Sworn/Estimate/Non-Audited
Audit Date: 10.06.2019
Personnel: Zak Kriener (News Writer / Sports Writer); Amy Stracener (Executive Advertising Director); LeAnn Larson (Pub.); Steph Hermen (Adv. Dir.)
Parent company (for newspapers): Community Media Group

PAPILLION TIMES

Street address 1: 300 W Broadway
Street address 2: Ste 108
Street address city: Council Bluffs
Street address state: IA
Zip/Postal code: 51503
General Phone: (402) 733-7300
General Fax: 712-325-5717
Advertising Phone: 712-325-5798
Advertising Fax: 712-325-5717
Editorial Phone: (402) 733-7300
Editorial Fax: 712-325-5776
General/National Adv. E-mail: news@papilliontimes.com
Display Adv. E-mail: njohnson@owh.com
Classified Adv. e-mail: classifieds@bellevueleader.com
Editorial e-mail: news@papilliontimes.com
Primary Website: papilliontimes.com
Mthly Avg Views: 22
Mthly Avg Unique Visitors: 12
Year Established: 1874
Avg Paid Circ: 825
Audit By: USPS
Audit Date: 01.10.2022
Personnel: Melissa Vanek (Circ. Mgr.); Amy McKay (General Manager); Amy Corrigan (Creative Servs. Mgr.); Paul Swanson (Mktg. Dir.); Scott Stewart (Assistant Editor); Ron Petak (Exec. Ed.); Tony Digilio (Local Retail Sales Manager); Dan Matuella (Adv. Mgr.)
Parent company (for newspapers): Lee Enterprises; BH Media Group

PARKERSBURG ECLIPSE-NEWS-REVIEW

Street address 1: 503 Coates St
Street address city: Parkersburg
Street address state: IA
Zip/Postal code: 50665-7733
General Phone: (319) 346-1461
General Fax: (319) 346-1461
General/National Adv. E-mail: butlersales.map@gmail.com
Avg Paid Circ: 1500
Avg Free Circ: 16
Audit By: Sworn/Estimate/Non-Audited
Audit Date: 10.06.2019
Personnel: John Jensen (Mgr Ed); Danielle Potkonak (Office Mgr/Designer); Ian Murphy (Reg Sports Ed)
Parent company (for newspapers): Mid-America Publishing

PELLA CHRONICLE

Street address 1: 812 Main St
Street address city: Pella
Street address state: IA
Zip/Postal code: 50219-1522
General Phone: (641) 628-3882
General Fax: (641) 628-3905
General/National Adv. E-mail: thechronicle@iowatelecom.net; chroniclenews@iowatelecom.net
Display Adv. E-mail: chronicleads@iowatelecom.net
Editorial e-mail: chroniclenews@iowatelecom.net
Primary Website: pellachronicle.com
Mthly Avg Views: 15000
Mthly Avg Unique Visitors: 7000
Year Established: 1866
Avg Paid Circ: 2000
Audit By: Sworn/Estimate/Non-Audited
Audit Date: 10.06.2019
Personnel: Maureen Miller (Pub.); Clint Brown (Ed.)
Parent company (for newspapers): CNHI, LLC

PERRY CHIEF

Street address 1: 1316 2nd St
Street address 2: Ste B
Street address city: Perry
Street address state: IA
Zip/Postal code: 50220-1549
General Phone: (515) 465-4666
General Fax: (515) 465-3087
General/National Adv. E-mail: publisher@theperrychief.com
Display Adv. E-mail: ads@theperrychief.com
Editorial e-mail: news@theperrychief.com
Primary Website: theperrychief.com
Year Established: 1874
Avg Paid Circ: 1900
Avg Free Circ: 14500
Audit By: Sworn/Estimate/Non-Audited
Audit Date: 10.06.2019
Personnel: Patricia Snyder (Publisher); Linda Schumacher (Adv. Mgr.); Don Thomas (Prodn. Mgr.); Lori Lott (Gen. Mgr.); Dana Fink (Adv. Sales Rep.); Melissa Todelo (Columnist / Reporter)
Parent company (for newspapers): CherryRoad Media

PILOT TRIBUNE

Street address 1: 527 Cayuga St
Street address city: Storm Lake
Street address state: IA
Zip/Postal code: 50588-2319
General Phone: (712) 732-3130
General Fax: (712) 732-3152
General/National Adv. E-mail: sledt@ncn.net
Primary Website: stormlakepilottribune.com
Avg Paid Circ: 3085
Audit By: Sworn/Estimate/Non-Audited
Audit Date: 10.06.2019
Personnel: Dana Larsen (Mng. Ed.); Tim Marlow (Prodn. Mgr.); Paula Buerger (Pub.)
Parent company (for newspapers): Rust Communications

POCAHONTAS RECORD-DEMOCRAT

Street address 1: 218 N Main St
Street address 2: Ste 1
Street address city: Pocahontas
Street address state: IA
Zip/Postal code: 50574-1612
General Phone: (712) 335-3553
General Fax: (712) 335-3856
Advertising Phone: (712) 335-3553
Advertising Fax: (712) 335-3856
Editorial Phone: (712) 335-3553
Editorial Fax: (712) 335-3856
General/National Adv. E-mail: ads@pokyrd.com
Display Adv. E-mail: ads@pokyrd.com
Editorial e-mail: publisher@pokyrd.com
Avg Paid Circ: 1800
Avg Free Circ: 44
Audit By: Sworn/Estimate/Non-Audited
Audit Date: 10.06.2019
Personnel: Marcia Hamp (Adv. Mgr.); Mary Phillips (Classified Mgr.); Chris Vrba (Owner/Pub./Ed.); Jamie Whitney (Staff writer)

POSTVILLE HERALD

Street address 1: 101 N Lawler St
Street address city: Postville
Street address state: IA
Zip/Postal code: 52162-7799
General Phone: (563) 864-3333
General Fax: (563) 864-3400
General/National Adv. E-mail: ads@postvilleherald.com
Display Adv. E-mail: ads@postvilleherald.com
Editorial e-mail: news@postvilleherald.com
Year Established: 1892
Avg Paid Circ: 1107
Avg Free Circ: 0
Audit By: Sworn/Estimate/Non-Audited
Audit Date: 10.06.2019

Personnel: Jason Meyer (Pub.); Sharon Drahn (Ed.); Nadine Brock (Circ. Mgr.); R. Craig White (Adv. Mgr.)

POWESHIEK COUNTY CHRONICLE-REPUBLICAN

Street address 1: 925 Broad St
Street address city: Grinnell
Street address state: IA
Zip/Postal code: 50112-2047
General Phone: (641) 522-7155
General Fax: (641) 236-0625
General/National Adv. E-mail: powcr@dmreg.com
Audit By: Sworn/Estimate/Non-Audited
Audit Date: 10.06.2019
Parent company (for newspapers): Gannett

PRAIRIE CITY NEWS

Street address 1: 104 E 5th St
Street address city: Prairie City
Street address state: IA
Zip/Postal code: 50228-7765
General Phone: (515) 994-2349
General/National Adv. E-mail: prairiecitynews@aol.com
Year Established: 1874
Audit By: Sworn/Estimate/Non-Audited
Audit Date: 10.06.2019

PRESTON TIMES

Street address 1: 4 N Stephens St
Street address 2: PO Box 9
Street address city: Preston
Street address state: IA
Zip/Postal code: 52069-7742
General Phone: (563) 689-3841
General Fax: (563) 689-3842
General/National Adv. E-mail: prestontimes@netins.net
Display Adv. E-mail: prestontimes@netins.net
Editorial e-mail: prestontimes@netins.net
Primary Website: prestontimesonline.com
Year Established: 1847
Avg Paid Circ: 1000
Avg Free Circ: 25
Audit By: Sworn/Estimate/Non-Audited
Audit Date: 10.06.2019
Personnel: Krista Schap (Graphics/ Sales)
Parent company (for newspapers): The Richlen Group LLC

RED OAK EXPRESS

Street address 1: 2012 Commerce Drive
Street address 2: P.O. Box 377
Street address city: Red Oak
Street address state: IA
Zip/Postal code: 51566-0377
General Phone: (712) 623-2566
General Fax: (712) 623-2568
Primary Website: redoakexpress.com
Year Established: 1868
Avg Paid Circ: 3500
Audit By: Sworn/Estimate/Non-Audited
Audit Date: 10.06.2019
Personnel: Nick Johansen (Reporter); Tess Nelson (Ed./Pub.)
Parent company (for newspapers): Landmark Communications, Inc.; Red Oak Publications, LLC; Landmark Community Newspapers, LLC

REINBECK COURIER

Street address 1: 107 Broad St
Street address city: Reinbeck
Street address state: IA
Zip/Postal code: 50669-1013
General Phone: (319) 345-2031
General Fax: (319) 345-6767
Editorial e-mail: editor@reinbeckcourier.com
Primary Website: reinbeckcourier.com
Avg Paid Circ: 1112
Audit By: Sworn/Estimate/Non-Audited
Audit Date: 10.06.2019
Personnel: Mike Schlesinger (Pub.); Molly Dahms (Adv. Mgr.)
Parent company (for newspapers): Ogden Newspapers Inc.

REMSEN BELL-ENTERPRISE

Street address 1: 41 1st Ave NE
Street address city: Le Mars
Street address state: IA
Zip/Postal code: 51031-3535
General Phone: (712) 786-1196
General Fax: (712) 786-1257
General/National Adv. E-mail: remsenbell@midlands.net
Display Adv. E-mail: systems@semissourian.com
Editorial e-mail: systems@semissourian.com
Primary Website: No Website
Year Established: 1887
Avg Paid Circ: 1100
Avg Free Circ: 4
Audit By: Sworn/Estimate/Non-Audited
Audit Date: 10.06.2019
Personnel: Megan Sabin (Office Mgr.); Randy List (Pub.); Monte Jost (Sr Gen. Mgr.)
Parent company (for newspapers): Rust Communications

REPORTER

Street address 1: PO Box 13
Street address city: Lone Tree
Street address state: IA
Zip/Postal code: 52755-0013
General Phone: (319) 629-5207
General Fax: (319) 629-4203
General/National Adv. E-mail: ltnews@iowatelecom.net
Primary Website: thelonetreereporter.com
Year Established: 1897
Avg Paid Circ: 775
Audit By: Sworn/Estimate/Non-Audited
Audit Date: 10.06.2019
Personnel: Ronald C. Slechta (Pub.); Helen Slechta (Circ. Mgr.)

REPORTER-DEMOCRAT

Street address 1: 1901 Main St
Street address city: Emmetsburg
Street address state: IA
Zip/Postal code: 50536-2440
General Phone: (712) 852-2323
General Fax: (712) 852-3184
General/National Adv. E-mail: advertising@emmetsburgnews.com
Display Adv. E-mail: advertising@emmetsburgnews.com
Primary Website: emmetsburgnews.com
Avg Paid Circ: 2700
Audit By: Sworn/Estimate/Non-Audited
Audit Date: 10.06.2019
Personnel: Dan McCain (Pub./Adv. Mgr.); Jane Whitmore (Ed.); Linda Hill (Circ.)
Parent company (for newspapers): Ogden Newspapers Inc.

RICEVILLE RECORDER

Street address 1: 111 E 2nd St
Street address city: Riceville
Street address state: IA
Zip/Postal code: 50466-7717
General Phone: (641) 985-2142
General Fax: (641) 985-4185
General/National Adv. E-mail: recorder@myomnitel.com
Primary Website: facebook.com/RicevilleRecorder
Year Established: 1886
Avg Paid Circ: 1350
Audit By: Sworn/Estimate/Non-Audited
Audit Date: 10.06.2019
Personnel: Daniel Evans (Pub.); Casander Leff (Ed.)

RINGSTED DISPATCH

Street address 1: 520 6th St
Street address city: Armstrong
Street address state: IA
Zip/Postal code: 50514-7711
General Phone: (712) 868-3460
General Fax: (712) 868-3028
Advertising Phone: (712) 868-3460
Advertising Fax: (712) 868-3460
Editorial Phone: (712) 868-3460
Editorial Fax: (712) 868-3460
General/National Adv. E-mail: ads@armstrongjournal.com
Display Adv. E-mail: clint@armstrongjournal.com
Editorial e-mail: clint@armstrongjournal.com
Primary Website: statelinepubs.com
Avg Paid Circ: 400
Audit By: Sworn/Estimate/Non-Audited
Audit Date: 10.06.2019
Personnel: Kris Grabinoski (Publisher); Clinton Davis (Office Manager)
Parent company (for newspapers): Stateline Publications

ROCK VALLEY BEE

Street address 1: 1442 Main St
Street address city: Rock Valley
Street address state: IA
Zip/Postal code: 51247-1224
General Phone: (712) 476-2795
General Fax: (712) 476-2796
General/National Adv. E-mail: rvbee@mtcnet.net
Avg Paid Circ: 1400
Avg Free Circ: 4500
Audit By: Sworn/Estimate/Non-Audited
Audit Date: 10.06.2019
Personnel: Chris Godfredsen (Pub.)

ROCKWELL PIONEER ENTERPRISE

Street address 1: 304 Main St E
Street address city: Rockwell
Street address state: IA
Zip/Postal code: 50469-7755
General Phone: (641) 822-3193
General Fax: (641) 822-3193
General/National Adv. E-mail: pioneerenterprise@qwestoffice.net
Primary Website: pioneerenterprise.com
Audit By: Sworn/Estimate/Non-Audited
Audit Date: 10.06.2019

SANBORN PIONEER

Street address 1: 121 Main St
Street address city: Sanborn
Street address state: IA
Zip/Postal code: 51248-7727
General Phone: (712) 729-3201
General Fax: (712) 729-3202
General/National Adv. E-mail: spioneer@tcaexpress.net
Year Established: 1871
Audit By: Sworn/Estimate/Non-Audited
Audit Date: 10.06.2019
Personnel: scott Chrisman (Pub./Ed.)

SCRANTON JOURNAL

Street address 1: PO Box 187
Street address city: Scranton
Street address state: IA
Zip/Postal code: 51462-0187
General Phone: (712) 651-2321
General/National Adv. E-mail: ciapub@netins.net
Year Established: 1880
Avg Paid Circ: 832
Audit By: Sworn/Estimate/Non-Audited
Audit Date: 01.10.2023
Personnel: Luann Waldo (Ed.)

SHEFFIELD PRESS

Street address 1: 305 Gilman St
Street address city: Sheffield
Street address state: IA
Zip/Postal code: 50475-5007
General Phone: (641) 892-4636
General/National Adv. E-mail: jzpress@frontiernet.net
Primary Website: thesheffieldpress.com
Audit By: Sworn/Estimate/Non-Audited
Audit Date: 10.06.2019

SHELDON MAIL-SUN

Street address 1: 227 9th St
Street address city: Sheldon
Street address state: IA
Zip/Postal code: 51201-1419
General Phone: (712) 324-5347
General Fax: (712) 324-2345
General/National Adv. E-mail: drust@iowainformation.com
Primary Website: nwestiowa.com
Year Established: 1862
Avg Paid Circ: 2220
Avg Free Circ: 13
Audit By: Sworn/Estimate/Non-Audited
Audit Date: 10.06.2019
Personnel: Peter W. Wagner (Pub.); Jeff Wagner (Gen. Mgr.); Derrick Vander Waal (Ed.); Dawn Cermak (Prodn. Mgr.)

SIDNEY ARGUS-HERALD

Street address 1: 614 Main St
Street address 2: PO Box 190
Street address city: Sidney
Street address state: IA
Zip/Postal code: 51652-2053
General Phone: (712) 370-1275
General Fax: (712)374-2251
Advertising Phone: (712) 374-2241
Advertising Fax: (712) 374-2251
Editorial Phone: (712) 374-2251
Editorial Fax: (712) 374-2251
General/National Adv. E-mail: news@argusherald.com
Display Adv. E-mail: news@argusherald.com
Editorial e-mail: news@argusherald.com
Primary Website: N.A.
Year Established: 1927
Avg Paid Circ: 700
Audit By: Sworn/Estimate/Non-Audited
Audit Date: 10.06.2019
Personnel: Ellen West Longman (Owner); Tess Gruber Nelson (Managing Editor)
Parent company (for newspapers): ()

SIOUX COUNTY CAPITAL-DEMOCRAT

Street address 1: 113 Central Ave SE
Street address city: Orange City
Street address state: IA
Zip/Postal code: 51041-1738
General Phone: (712) 737-4266
General Fax: (712) 737-3896
General/National Adv. E-mail: pluimpub@orangecitycomm.net
Display Adv. E-mail: pluimpub@orangecitycomm.net
Editorial e-mail: pluimpub@orangecitycomm.net
Primary Website: siouxcountynews.com
Year Established: 1882
Avg Paid Circ: 1800
Avg Free Circ: 25
Audit By: Sworn/Estimate/Non-Audited
Audit Date: 10.06.2019
Personnel: Dale H. Pluim (Pub.); Bob Hulstein (Gen. Mgr.); Dennis Den Hartog (Adv. Mgr.); Doug Calsbeek (Ed.)

SIOUX COUNTY INDEX-REPORTER

Street address 1: 1013 1st St
Street address city: Hull
Street address state: IA
Zip/Postal code: 51239-7718
General Phone: (712) 439-1075
General Fax: (712) 439-2001
General/National Adv. E-mail: jvisser@ncppub.com
Primary Website: ncppub.com/pages/?cat=58
Avg Paid Circ: 1221
Avg Free Circ: 25
Audit By: Sworn/Estimate/Non-Audited
Audit Date: 10.06.2019
Personnel: Lois Keuhl (Adv. Mgr.); James Hensley (Gen. Mgr.); Robbie Kooistra (Circ. Mgr.); Joseph Stearns (Writer)

SIOUXLAND PRESS

Street address 1: 105 Ash St
Street address city: Hospers
Street address state: IA
Zip/Postal code: 51238
General Phone: (712) 752-8401
General Fax: (712) 752-8405
General/National Adv. E-mail: slpress@nethtc.net
Display Adv. E-mail: slpress@nethtc.net
Editorial e-mail: siouxlandpress@htc.net
Year Established: 1970
Avg Paid Circ: 1800

Avg Free Circ: 50
Audit By: Sworn/Estimate/Non-Audited
Audit Date: 10.06.2019
Personnel: Harlan Rouse (Ed.); Katie Rouse (Ed.)

SLECHTA COMMUNICATIONS, INC.

Street address 1: 419 B Ave
Street address city: Kalona
Street address state: IA
Zip/Postal code: 52247-7719
Audit By: Sworn/Estimate/Non-Audited
Audit Date: 10.06.2019
Parent company (for newspapers): Anamosa Publications

SOUTH HAMILTON RECORD-NEWS

Street address 1: 602 Main St
Street address city: Jewell
Street address state: IA
Zip/Postal code: 50130-2012
General Phone: (515) 827-5931
General Fax: (515) 827-5760
General/National Adv. E-mail: shrecnew@netins.net
Primary Website: iowanewspapersonline.com
Avg Paid Circ: 933
Avg Free Circ: 17
Audit By: Sworn/Estimate/Non-Audited
Audit Date: 10.06.2019
Personnel: Kenneth Scott Ervin (Ed.)

ST. ANSGAR ENTERPRISE JOURNAL

Street address 1: 204 E 4th St
Street address city: Saint Ansgar
Street address state: IA
Zip/Postal code: 50472-9606
General Phone: (641) 713-4541
General Fax: (641) 713-2399
General/National Adv. E-mail: staej@iowatelecom.net
Primary Website: staej.com
Avg Paid Circ: 1300
Audit By: Sworn/Estimate/Non-Audited
Audit Date: 10.06.2019
Personnel: Deb Stickney (Gen. Mgr.); Chuck Peterson (Ed.)

STAR PRESS UNION

Street address 1: 832 12th St
Street address city: Belle Plaine
Street address state: IA
Zip/Postal code: 52208-1761
General Phone: (319) 444-2520
General Fax: (319) 444-2522
General/National Adv. E-mail: bpunions@netins.net
Primary Website: yourweeklypaper.com
Avg Paid Circ: 1348
Audit By: Sworn/Estimate/Non-Audited
Audit Date: 10.06.2019
Personnel: Jim Magdefrau (Pub.)
Parent company (for newspapers): Gannett

STATE CENTER MID IOWA ENTERPRISE

Street address 1: 201 Main St W
Street address 2: # 634
Street address city: State Center
Street address state: IA
Zip/Postal code: 50247-7770
General Phone: (641) 483-2120
Editorial Phone: (641) 483-2120
General/National Adv. E-mail: midiaenterprise@partnercom.net
Primary Website: midiaenterprise.com
Avg Paid Circ: 1000
Audit By: Sworn/Estimate/Non-Audited
Audit Date: 10.06.2019
Personnel: Christine Davis (Pub.); Jamie Burdorf (Ed.)

STRATFORD COURIER

Street address 1: 820 Shakespeare Ave
Street address city: Stratford
Street address state: IA
Zip/Postal code: 50249-7771
General Phone: (515) 838-2494
General Fax: (515) 838-2958
General/National Adv. E-mail: shrecnew@netins.net
Primary Website: No Website
Avg Paid Circ: 700
Audit By: Sworn/Estimate/Non-Audited
Audit Date: 10.06.2019
Personnel: Scott Ervin (Ed.)

STRAWBERRY PT. PRESS JOURNAL

Street address 1: 107 W Mission St
Street address city: Strawberry Point
Street address state: IA
Zip/Postal code: 52076-4400
General Phone: (563) 933-4370
General Fax: (563) 933-4370
General/National Adv. E-mail: pressj@iowatelecom.net
Primary Website: No Website
Avg Paid Circ: 1600
Audit By: Sworn/Estimate/Non-Audited
Audit Date: 10.06.2019
Personnel: Harry L. Nolda (Pub.); Kay Behrens

STUART HERALD

Street address 1: 119 NW 2nd St
Street address city: Stuart
Street address state: IA
Zip/Postal code: 50250-7704
General Phone: (515) 523-1010
General Fax: (515) 523-2825
General/National Adv. E-mail: ads@thestuartherald.com
Display Adv. E-mail: ads@thestuartherlad.com
Classified Adv. e-mail: ads@thestuartherald.com
Editorial e-mail: news@thestuartherald.com
Primary Website: facebook.com/pages/The-Stuart-Herald-Newspaper-and-Four-County-Bulletin/182134119688
Year Established: 1871
Avg Paid Circ: 1100
Avg Free Circ: 200
Audit By: Sworn/Estimate/Non-Audited
Audit Date: 10.06.2019

SULLY HOMETOWN PRESS

Street address 1: 301 7th Ave
Street address 2: Ste 101
Street address city: Sully
Street address state: IA
Zip/Postal code: 50251-1098
General Phone: (641) 594-3200
General Fax: (641) 594-3243
Advertising Phone: (641) 594-3200
Advertising Fax: (641) 594-3243
Editorial Phone: (641) 594-3200
Editorial Fax: (641) 594-3243
General/National Adv. E-mail: press@netins.net
Display Adv. E-mail: press@netins.net
Classified Adv. e-mail: press@netins.net
Editorial e-mail: press@netins.net
Year Established: 2009
Avg Paid Circ: 1160
Audit By: Sworn/Estimate/Non-Audited
Audit Date: 10.06.2019
Personnel: Margaret VanderWeert (Editor)
Parent company (for newspapers): Co-Line

TABOR BEACON-ENTERPRISE

Street address 1: 704 Main St
Street address city: Tabor
Street address state: IA
Zip/Postal code: 51653-2067
General Phone: (712) 629-2255
General Fax: (712) 624-9250
General/National Adv. E-mail: leaderbeacon@qwestoffice.net
Avg Paid Circ: 1000
Audit By: Sworn/Estimate/Non-Audited
Audit Date: 10.06.2019
Personnel: Karol Siekman (Ed.)

THE AVOCA JOURNAL-HERALD

Street address 1: 164 S Elm St
Street address city: Avoca
Street address state: IA
Zip/Postal code: 51521-4003
General Phone: (712) 343-2154
General Fax: (712) 343-2262
General/National Adv. E-mail: avocajh@iowatelecom.net
Primary Website: No Website
Avg Paid Circ: 1600
Audit By: Sworn/Estimate/Non-Audited
Audit Date: 10.06.2019
Personnel: Donald L. Nielson (Pub.); Rich Price (Ed.)

THE BANCROFT REGISTER

Street address 1: 101 N Portland St
Street address city: Bancroft
Street address state: IA
Zip/Postal code: 50517-8012
General Phone: (515) 885-2531
General Fax: (515) 885-2771
Advertising Phone: (712) 868-3460
Advertising Fax: (712) 868-3460
Editorial Phone: (712) 868-3460
Editorial Fax: (712) 868-3460
General/National Adv. E-mail: krisg@armstrongjournal.com
Display Adv. E-mail: clint@armstrongjournal.com
Editorial e-mail: bancroftregister@yahoo.com
Primary Website: statelinepubs.com
Avg Paid Circ: 800
Audit By: Sworn/Estimate/Non-Audited
Audit Date: 10.06.2019
Personnel: Kristin Grabinoski (Publisher); Kim Meyer (Editor)
Parent company (for newspapers): Stateline Publications

THE BEDFORD TIMES-PRESS

Street address 1: 404 Main St
Street address city: Bedford
Street address state: IA
Zip/Postal code: 50833-1357
General Phone: (712) 523-2525
General/National Adv. E-mail: btimespress@gmail.com
Primary Website: bedfordtimespress.com
Avg Paid Circ: 1700
Audit By: Sworn/Estimate/Non-Audited
Audit Date: 10.06.2019
Personnel: Colleen Larimer (Pub.)

THE BEE

Street address 1: 200 N Wilson Ave
Street address city: Jefferson
Street address state: IA
Zip/Postal code: 50129-1923
General Phone: (515) 386-4161
General Fax: (515) 386-4162
General/National Adv. E-mail: news@beeherald.com
Primary Website: beeherald.com
Avg Free Circ: 7500
Audit By: Sworn/Estimate/Non-Audited
Audit Date: 10.06.2019
Personnel: Deb Geisler (Adv. Mgr.); Frederick G. Morain (Ed.)

THE BELMOND INDEPENDENT

Street address 1: 215 E Main St
Street address city: Belmond
Street address state: IA
Zip/Postal code: 50421-1122
General Phone: (641) 444-3333
General Fax: (641) 444-7777
General/National Adv. E-mail: belmondnews@frontiernet.net
Primary Website: belmondnews.com
Year Established: 1885
Avg Paid Circ: 1400
Avg Free Circ: 5
Audit By: Sworn/Estimate/Non-Audited
Audit Date: 10.06.2019
Personnel: Dirk J. Vanderlinden (Pub.); Lee H. Vanderlinden (Pub.)

THE CARLISLE CITIZEN

Street address 1: 210 S 1st St
Street address city: Carlisle
Street address state: IA
Zip/Postal code: 50047-7601
General Phone: (515) 989-0525
General Fax: (515) 989-0743
General/National Adv. E-mail: news@carlislecitizen.com
Display Adv. E-mail: news@carlislecitizen.com
Editorial e-mail: news@carlislecitizen.com
Primary Website: No Website
Year Established: 1926
Avg Paid Circ: 1600
Audit By: Sworn/Estimate/Non-Audited
Audit Date: 10.06.2019
Personnel: Steven Klein (Pub.); Sara Davis (Ed.)

THE CHARITON LEADER

Street address 1: 815 Braden Ave
Street address city: Chariton
Street address state: IA
Zip/Postal code: 50049-1742
General Phone: (641) 774-2137
General Fax: (641) 774-2139
General/National Adv. E-mail: charnews@charitonleader.com
Primary Website: charitonleader.com
Avg Paid Circ: 2500
Audit By: Sworn/Estimate/Non-Audited
Audit Date: 10.06.2019
Personnel: Susan Smith (Sales Rep.); David A. Paxton (Pub.)
Parent company (for newspapers): Lancaster Management, Inc.

THE CHRONICLE

Street address 1: 216 S Main St
Street address city: Odebolt
Street address state: IA
Zip/Postal code: 51458-7605
General Phone: (712) 668-2253
General Fax: (712) 668-4364
General/National Adv. E-mail: paper@netins.net
Primary Website: No Website
Avg Paid Circ: 1500
Audit By: Sworn/Estimate/Non-Audited
Audit Date: 10.06.2019
Personnel: Jerry Wiseman (Pub.); Mary Linda Mack (Ed.); Mary Linda Mack (Ed.)

THE CLARINDA HERALD-JOURNAL

Street address 1: 114 W Main St
Street address 2: Ste B
Street address city: Clarinda
Street address state: IA
Zip/Postal code: 51632-2127
General Phone: (712) 542-2181
General Fax: (712) 542-5424
General/National Adv. E-mail: news@clarindaherald.com
Display Adv. E-mail: ads@clarindaherald.com
Primary Website: clarindaherald.com
Year Established: 1859
Avg Paid Circ: 2250
Avg Free Circ: 75
Audit By: Sworn/Estimate/Non-Audited
Audit Date: 10.06.2019
Personnel: Marilyn Jones (Circ. Mgr.); Kent Dinnebier (Ed.); John Van Nostrand (publisher); Laurie Urich (graphic design)
Parent company (for newspapers): BH Media Group

THE CLARION-PLAINSMAN

Street address 1: 107 S Richland St
Street address city: Richland
Street address state: IA
Zip/Postal code: 52585-9226
General Phone: (319) 456-6641
General Fax: (319) 456-6641
General/National Adv. E-mail: lpc@louisacomm.net
Year Established: 1881
Audit By: Sworn/Estimate/Non-Audited
Audit Date: 10.06.2019

THE CLARKSVILLE STAR

Street address 1: 422 N Main St
Street address city: Clarksville
Street address state: IA
Zip/Postal code: 50619
General Phone: (319) 278-4641
General Fax: (319) 278-4641
General/National Adv. E-mail: clarksvillestar@butler-bremer.com
Primary Website: theclarksvillestar.com
Year Established: 1865
Avg Paid Circ: 1058
Avg Free Circ: 31
Audit By: Sworn/Estimate/Non-Audited

Audit Date: 10.06.2019
Personnel: Pat Racette (Ed.)

THE CLAYTON COUNTY REGISTER

Street address 1: 205 S Main St
Street address city: Elkader
Street address state: IA
Zip/Postal code: 52043-9078
General Phone: (563) 245-1311
General Fax: (563) 245-1312
General/National Adv. E-mail: ccrads@alpinecom.net
Display Adv. E-mail: ccrads@alpinecom.net
Editorial e-mail: ccrnews@alpinecom.net
Primary Website: claytoncountyregister.com
Year Established: 1878
Avg Paid Circ: 1200
Avg Free Circ: 21000
Audit By: Sworn/Estimate/Non-Audited
Audit Date: 10.06.2019
Personnel: Gary Howe (Pub.); Pam Reinig (Ed.); Dana Richard (Bus. Mgr.)
Parent company (for newspapers): Clayton County Register

THE DECORAH JOURNAL

Street address 1: 107 E Water St
Street address city: Decorah
Street address state: IA
Zip/Postal code: 52101-1801
General Phone: (563) 382-4221
General Fax: (563) 382-5949
General/National Adv. E-mail: fromm@decorahnewspapers.com
Primary Website: decorahnewspapers.com
Year Established: 1895
Avg Paid Circ: 5185
Avg Free Circ: 16000
Audit By: Sworn/Estimate/Non-Audited
Audit Date: 10.06.2019
Personnel: Joanne Stevenson (Circ. Mgr.); Richard M. Fromm (Mng. Ed.); Destiny Langreck (Prodn. Mgr.)

THE DEMOCRAT

Street address 1: 1122 Broadway St
Street address 2: Ste B
Street address city: Emmetsburg
Street address state: IA
Zip/Postal code: 50536-1767
General Phone: (712) 852-2323
General Fax: (712) 852-3184
General/National Adv. E-mail: advertising@emmetsburgnews.com
Display Adv. E-mail: advertising@emmetsburgnews.com
Editorial e-mail: jwhitmore@emmetsburgnews.com
Primary Website: emmetsburgnews.com
Year Established: 1882
Audit By: Sworn/Estimate/Non-Audited
Audit Date: 10.06.2019
Personnel: Dan McCain (Adv. Mgr.); Jane Whitmore (Pub.); Linda Hill (Circ. Mgr.)

THE DYSART REPORTER

Street address 1: 317 Main St
Street address city: Dysart
Street address state: IA
Zip/Postal code: 52224
General Phone: (319) 476-3550
General Fax: (319) 476-2813
Editorial e-mail: editor@dysartreporter.com
Primary Website: dysartreporter.com
Avg Paid Circ: 800
Avg Free Circ: 10
Audit By: Sworn/Estimate/Non-Audited
Audit Date: 10.06.2019
Personnel: Mike Schlesinger (Pub.); Kelly Jantzen (Adv. Mgr.)
Parent company (for newspapers): Ogden Newspapers Inc.

THE ELGIN ECHO

Street address 1: 119 S Vine St
Street address city: West Union
Street address state: IA
Zip/Postal code: 52175-1354
General Phone: (563) 422-5410
General Fax: (563) 422-3488
General/National Adv. E-mail: shermen@fayettepublishing.com
Display Adv. E-mail: areiling@fayettepublishing.com
Editorial e-mail: zkriener@fayettepublishing.com
Primary Website: fayettecountynewspapers.com
Year Established: 1886
Avg Paid Circ: 875
Audit By: Sworn/Estimate/Non-Audited
Audit Date: 10.06.2019
Personnel: LeAnn Larson (Pub.); Steph Hermen (Acc. Exec.); Amanda Reiling (Prodn. Sup.); Zak Kriener (News Writer / Sports Writer); Danielle Luchsinger (Graphic Designer)
Parent company (for newspapers): Community Media Group

THE EMMETSBURG REPORTER

Street address 1: 1122 Broadway St
Street address 2: Stuite B
Street address city: Emmetsburg
Street address state: IA
Zip/Postal code: 50536-1767
General Phone: (712) 852-2323
General Fax: (712) 852-3184
General/National Adv. E-mail: mdune@emmetsburgnews.com
Display Adv. E-mail: lhill@emmetsburgnews.com
Editorial e-mail: jwhitmore@emmetsburgnews.com
Primary Website: emmetsburgnews.com
Year Established: 1876
Avg Paid Circ: 2400
Audit By: Sworn/Estimate/Non-Audited
Audit Date: 10.06.2019
Personnel: Dan McCain (Pub./Gen. Mgr.); Jane Whitmore (Ed.); Linda Hill (Circ. Mgr.)
Parent company (for newspapers): Ogden Newspapers Inc.

THE ESSEX INDEPENDENT

Street address 1: 617 W. Sheridan Ave.
Street address city: Shenandoah
Street address state: IA
Zip/Postal code: 51601
General Phone: (712) 246-3097
General Fax: (712) 246-3099
General/National Adv. E-mail: ads@valleynewstoday.com
Display Adv. E-mail: ads@valleynewstoday.com
Editorial e-mail: editorial@valleynewstoday.com
Primary Website: valleynewstoday.com
Year Established: 1953
Avg Paid Circ: 300
Avg Free Circ: 7
Audit By: Sworn/Estimate/Non-Audited
Audit Date: 10.06.2019
Personnel: John VanNostrand; Kimberly Kellison (Circ.); Cybill Erickson (Ed.)

THE GLIDDEN GRAPHIC

Street address 1: 122 Idaho St.
Street address city: Glidden
Street address state: IA
Zip/Postal code: 51443
General Phone: (712) 790-6999
General/National Adv. E-mail: news@gliddengraphic.com
Primary Website: facebook.com/pages/Glidden-Graphic/155359484478487
Year Established: 1889
Avg Paid Circ: 600
Audit By: Sworn/Estimate/Non-Audited
Audit Date: 10.06.2019
Personnel: Bill Brown (Pub.)

THE GRAETTINGER TIMES

Street address 1: 104 W ROBINS ST
Street address city: Graettinger
Street address state: IA
Zip/Postal code: 51342
General Phone: (712) 859-3780
General Fax: (712) 859-3039
General/National Adv. E-mail: grtimes@netins.net
Primary Website: facebook.com/The-Graettinger-Times-183153428799597
Year Established: 1847
Avg Paid Circ: 1300
Audit By: Sworn/Estimate/Non-Audited
Audit Date: 10.06.2019
Personnel: Penny Tonderum (Pub.)

THE GRAPHIC ADVOCATE

Street address 1: 505 4th St
Street address city: Rockwell City
Street address state: IA
Zip/Postal code: 50579-1901
General Phone: (712) 297-7544
General Fax: (712) 297-7544
Advertising Phone: (712) 464-3188
General/National Adv. E-mail: lcgraphic@iowatelecom.net
Editorial e-mail: gaeditor@iowatelecom.net
Primary Website: thegraphic-advocate.com
Year Established: 1889
Avg Paid Circ: 700
Audit By: Sworn/Estimate/Non-Audited
Audit Date: 10.06.2019
Personnel: Teresa Snyder (Adv. Mgr.); Ken Ross (Ed.)

THE HUMESTON NEWS ERA

Street address 1: 204 S Franklin St
Street address city: Corydon
Street address state: IA
Zip/Postal code: 50060-1520
General Phone: (641) 872-1234
General/National Adv. E-mail: rbennett@corydontimes.com
Display Adv. E-mail: rbennett@corydontimes.com
Editorial e-mail: rbennett@corydontimes.com
Primary Website: corydontimes.com
Avg Paid Circ: 500
Audit By: Sworn/Estimate/Non-Audited
Audit Date: 10.06.2019
Personnel: Rhonda Bennett (Pub)
Parent company (for newspapers): Lancaster Management, Inc.

THE JEFFERSON HERALD

Street address 1: 200 N Wilson Ave
Street address city: Jefferson
Street address state: IA
Zip/Postal code: 50129-1923
General Phone: (515) 386-4161
General Fax: (515) 386-4162
General/National Adv. E-mail: news@beeherald.com
Primary Website: beeherald.com
Avg Paid Circ: 2294
Audit By: Sworn/Estimate/Non-Audited
Audit Date: 10.06.2019
Personnel: Deb Geisler (Adv. Mgr.)

THE KALONA NEWS

Street address 1: 419 B Ave
Street address city: Kalona
Street address state: IA
Zip/Postal code: 52247-7719
General Phone: (319) 656-2273
General Fax: (319) 656-2299
General/National Adv. E-mail: adsales@kalonanews.com
Display Adv. E-mail: classifieds@kctc.net
Editorial e-mail: news@kalonanews.com
Primary Website: kalonanews.com
Year Established: 1891
Avg Paid Circ: 2360
Audit By: Sworn/Estimate/Non-Audited
Audit Date: 10.06.2019
Personnel: Dan Ehl (News Editor)
Parent company (for newspapers): Anamosa Publications; Slechta Communications, Inc.

THE KNOXVILLE JOURNAL-EXPRESS

Street address 1: 122 E Robinson St
Street address city: Knoxville
Street address state: IA
Zip/Postal code: 50138-2329
General Phone: (641) 842-2155
General Fax: (641) 842-2929
Display Adv. E-mail: classified@journalexpress.net
Editorial e-mail: editor@journalexpress.net
Primary Website: journalexpress.net
Year Established: 1855
Avg Paid Circ: 1800
Audit By: Sworn/Estimate/Non-Audited
Audit Date: 10.06.2019
Personnel: Rebecca Maxwell (Publisher)
Parent company (for newspapers): Raycom Media

THE LAKE CITY GRAPHIC-ADVOCATE

Street address 1: 121 N Center St
Street address city: Lake City
Street address state: IA
Zip/Postal code: 51449-1701
General Phone: (712) 464-3188
General Fax: (712) 464-3380
General/National Adv. E-mail: lcgraphic@iowatelecom.net
Primary Website: thegraphic-advocate.com
Avg Paid Circ: 1150
Audit By: Sworn/Estimate/Non-Audited
Audit Date: 10.06.2019
Personnel: Ken Ross (Pub.)
Parent company (for newspapers): Mid-America Publishing

THE LEADER

Street address 1: 365 State St
Street address city: Garner
Street address state: IA
Zip/Postal code: 50438-1236
General Phone: (641) 923-2684
General Fax: (641) 923-2685
General/National Adv. E-mail: gleader@qwestoffice.net
Primary Website: theleaderonline.net
Avg Paid Circ: 2500
Avg Free Circ: 40
Audit By: Sworn/Estimate/Non-Audited
Audit Date: 10.06.2019
Personnel: Ryan Harvey (President/CEO/Publisher); Ana Olsthoorn (Office and Production Manager); Rebecca Peter (News Editor)
Parent company (for newspapers): Mid-America Publishing

THE LEON JOURNAL-REPORTER

Street address 1: 110 N Main St
Street address 2: Ste B
Street address city: Leon
Street address state: IA
Zip/Postal code: 50144-1890
General Phone: (641) 446-4151
General Fax: (641) 446-7645
General/National Adv. E-mail: jrnews@grm.net
Year Established: 1865
Avg Paid Circ: 2100
Avg Free Circ: 24
Audit By: Sworn/Estimate/Non-Audited
Audit Date: 10.06.2019
Personnel: Corey R. Lindsey (Pub.)

THE LOGAN HERALD-OBSERVER

Street address 1: 107 N 4th Ave
Street address 2: Ste 3
Street address city: Logan
Street address state: IA
Zip/Postal code: 51546-1365
General Phone: (712) 644-2705
General Fax: (712) 644-2788
General/National Adv. E-mail: news@loganwoodbine.com
Editorial e-mail: news@loganwoodbine.com
Primary Website: loganwoodbine.com
Avg Paid Circ: 1400
Audit By: Sworn/Estimate/Non-Audited
Audit Date: 10.06.2019
Personnel: Mary Darling (Ed.)

THE MALVERN LEADER

Street address 1: PO Box 129
Street address city: Malvern
Street address state: IA
Zip/Postal code: 51551-0129
General Phone: (712) 624-8512
General Fax: (712) 624-9250
General/National Adv. E-mail: leaderbeacon@qwestoffice.net
Primary Website: No Website
Avg Paid Circ: 800
Audit By: Sworn/Estimate/Non-Audited
Audit Date: 10.06.2019

Personnel: Margaret Waugh (Adv. Mgr.); Karol Siekman (Ed.)

THE MANCHESTER PRESS

Street address 1: 109 E Delaware St
Street address city: Manchester
Street address state: IA
Zip/Postal code: 52057-2208
General Phone: (563) 927-2020
General Fax: (563) 927-4945
General/National Adv. E-mail: manpress@mchsi.com
Primary Website: manchesterpress.com
Avg Paid Circ: 4800
Audit By: Sworn/Estimate/Non-Audited
Audit Date: 10.06.2019
Personnel: Mary Ungs-Sogaard (Pub.); Beth Lutgen

THE MONITOR REVIEW

Street address 1: 117 S Broad St
Street address city: Stacyville
Street address state: IA
Zip/Postal code: 50476-5041
General Phone: (641) 710-2119
General Fax: (641) 710-3119
General/National Adv. E-mail: themonitorreview@gmail.com
Primary Website: facebook.com/TheMonitorReviewNewspaper
Avg Paid Circ: 1400
Avg Free Circ: 19
Audit By: Sworn/Estimate/Non-Audited
Audit Date: 10.06.2019
Personnel: Robert Adams (Ed.)

THE MONTICELLO EXPRESS

Street address 1: 111 E Grand St
Street address city: Monticello
Street address state: IA
Zip/Postal code: 52310-1688
General Phone: (319) 465-3555
General Fax: (319) 465-4611
General/National Adv. E-mail: advertising@monicelloexpress.com
Primary Website: monticelloexpress.com
Year Established: 1865
Avg Paid Circ: 3450
Audit By: Sworn/Estimate/Non-Audited
Audit Date: 10.06.2019
Personnel: Dan Goodyear (Co-Pub.); Mark Spensley (Co-Pub.); Kim Brooks (Ed.); Abby Manternach (Graph. Dsgn.)

THE MUSCATINE POST

Street address 1: 301 E 3rd St
Street address city: Muscatine
Street address state: IA
Zip/Postal code: 52761-4116
General Phone: (563) 263-2331
General Fax: (563) 263-7240
Primary Website: muscatinejournal.com
Avg Paid Circ: 1
Avg Free Circ: 14913
Audit By: Sworn/Estimate/Non-Audited
Audit Date: 10.06.2019
Personnel: Debbie Anselm (Pub.); Ariel Olsen (Adv.)

THE NEWS-REVIEW

Street address 1: 120 East Washington
Street address city: Sigourney
Street address state: IA
Zip/Postal code: 52591
General Phone: (641) 622-3110
General/National Adv. E-mail: keomahmanager@midamericapub.com
Display Adv. E-mail: keomahmanager@midamericapub.com
Editorial e-mail: keokukconews@midamericapub.com
Primary Website: sigourneynewsreview.com
Year Established: 1860
Avg Paid Circ: 2500
Audit By: Sworn/Estimate/Non-Audited
Audit Date: 10.06.2019

Personnel: Charlie Comfort (Ed.); Amie Van Patten (Adv. Sales Mgr./ Reg. Mgr.); Mike Burvee

THE OBSERVER

Street address 1: 512 7th St
Street address city: De Witt
Street address state: IA
Zip/Postal code: 52742-1610
General Phone: (563) 659-3121
General Fax: (563) 659-3778
General/National Adv. E-mail: obsgm@iowatelecom.net
Display Adv. E-mail: obsgm@iowatelecom.net
Editorial e-mail: observer@iowatelecom.net
Primary Website: dewittobserver.com
Year Established: 1865
Avg Paid Circ: 4174
Audit By: Sworn/Estimate/Non-Audited
Audit Date: 10.06.2019
Personnel: Jean Bormann (Adv. Mgr.); Mary Rueter (Gen. Mgr.); Rhonda Richards (Prodn. Mgr.); Linda Watson (News editor)

THE OCHEYEDAN PRESS-MELVIN NEWS

Street address 1: 859 Main St
Street address city: Ocheyedan
Street address state: IA
Zip/Postal code: 51354-7726
General Phone: (712) 758-3140
General Fax: (712) 758-3186
General/National Adv. E-mail: pressinc@nethtc.net
Avg Paid Circ: 1000
Avg Free Circ: 17
Audit By: Sworn/Estimate/Non-Audited
Audit Date: 10.06.2019
Personnel: Arlyn Pedley (Gen. Mgr.); Jan Reiste Pedley (Ed.)

THE PROGRESS-REVIEW

Street address 1: 213 Main St
Street address city: La Porte City
Street address state: IA
Zip/Postal code: 50651-1235
General Phone: (319) 342-2429
General Fax: (319) 342-2433
General/National Adv. E-mail: news@theprogressreview.co
Primary Website: theprogressreview.com
Year Established: 1865
Avg Paid Circ: 1360
Audit By: Sworn/Estimate/Non-Audited
Audit Date: 10.06.2019
Personnel: Mike Whittlesey (Pub./Ed.)

THE RECORD

Street address 1: 238 Main St
Street address 2: Box 546
Street address city: Moville
Street address state: IA
Zip/Postal code: 51039
General Phone: (712) 873-3141
General Fax: (712) 873-3142
Advertising Phone: (712) 873-3141
Advertising Fax: (712) 873-3142
Editorial Phone: (712) 873-3141
Editorial Fax: (712) 873-3142
General/National Adv. E-mail: record@wiatel.net
Display Adv. E-mail: record@wiatel.net
Editorial e-mail: blake@wiatel.net
Primary Website: movillerecord.com
Mthly Avg Views: 4000
Mthly Avg Unique Visitors: 2400
Year Established: 1943
Avg Paid Circ: 2500
Avg Free Circ: 20
Audit By: Sworn/Estimate/Non-Audited
Audit Date: 10.06.2019
Personnel: Blake Stubbs (Editor/Publisher); Blake Stubbs (Pub & Ed); Lisa Fouts (Office/Circu/Bus Mgr); Brian Johnson (Composition Mgr); Pam Clark (Kingsley Office Mgr); Karen Newman (Sioux Valley News Mgr)
Parent company (for newspapers): Baker Newspapers, Inc.

THE SAC SUN

Street address 1: 406 Williams St
Street address city: Sac City
Street address state: IA
Zip/Postal code: 50583-1739
General Phone: (712) 662-7161
General Fax: (712) 662-4198
Advertising Phone: (712) 662-7161
Advertising Fax: (712) 662-4198
Editorial Phone: (712) 662-7161
Editorial Fax: (712) 662-4198
General/National Adv. E-mail: sacsuneditor@gmail.com
Display Adv. E-mail: sacsunads@gmail.com
Classified Adv. e-mail: sacsunads@gmail.com
Editorial e-mail: sacsuneditor@gmail.com
Year Established: 1871
Avg Paid Circ: 1400
Avg Free Circ: 85
Audit By: Sworn/Estimate/Non-Audited
Audit Date: 10.06.2024
Personnel: Dale P. Wegner (Ed./Gen. Mgr.); Trinity Carlson (Office Manager); Brenda Fiscus (Adv./Graphic Design); Bridget Harms (Office Mgr/Billing); Galen Grote (Advt Sales)
Parent company (for newspapers): Sac County Newspapers

THE SERGEANT BLUFF ADVOCATE

Street address 1: 204 1st St
Street address 2: Ste A2
Street address city: Sergeant Bluff
Street address state: IA
Zip/Postal code: 51054-8589
General Phone: (712) 943-2583
General Fax: (712) 943-4606
Advertising Phone: (712) 943-2583
Advertising Fax: (712) 943-4606
General/National Adv. E-mail: advocate@longlines.com
Display Adv. E-mail: advocate@longlines.com
Editorial e-mail: advocate@longlines.com
Primary Website: N/A
Year Established: 1970
Avg Paid Circ: 1200
Avg Free Circ: 50
Audit By: Sworn/Estimate/Non-Audited
Audit Date: 10.06.2022
Personnel: Wayne Dominowski (Pblr/Editor)
Parent company (for newspapers): Domino Publishers, Inc.

THE SEYMOUR HERALD

Street address 1: 206 N 4th St
Street address city: Seymour
Street address state: IA
Zip/Postal code: 52590-1310
General Phone: (641) 898-7554
General Fax: (641) 898-7554
General/National Adv. E-mail: seymourherald@iowatelecom.net
Primary Website: No Website
Year Established: 1884
Avg Paid Circ: 1500
Audit By: Sworn/Estimate/Non-Audited
Audit Date: 10.06.2019
Personnel: Karen Young (Ed.); Vicky Decker (Ed.)

THE SOLON ECONOMIST

Street address 1: 206 E. Main Street
Street address city: Solon
Street address state: IA
Zip/Postal code: 52333
General Phone: (319) 624-2233
General Fax: (319) 624-1356
General/National Adv. E-mail: advertising@economistleader.com
Editorial e-mail: economist@economistleader.com
Primary Website: soloneconomist.com
Year Established: 1896
Avg Paid Circ: 1270
Audit By: Sworn/Estimate/Non-Audited
Audit Date: 10.06.2019
Personnel: Doug Lindner (Pub.)

THE STANDARD

Street address 1: 15 1st St NW
Street address city: Waukon
Street address state: IA
Zip/Postal code: 52172-1659
General Phone: (563) 568-3431
General/National Adv. E-mail: ads@waukonstandard.com
Display Adv. E-mail: adsales@waukonstandard.com
Editorial e-mail: news@waukonstandard.com
Primary Website: waukonstandard.com
Mthly Avg Views: 41175
Mthly Avg Unique Visitors: 31603
Year Established: 1858
Avg Paid Circ: 2075
Audit By: Sworn/Estimate/Non-Audited
Audit Date: 10.06.2019
Personnel: Brianne Grimstad (Office Manager/Circulation Manager/Ad Sales); Robin Johnson (Bookkeeper)
Parent company (for newspapers): Finger Publishing, Inc.

THE STORM LAKE TIMES

Street address 1: 220 W Railroad St
Street address city: Storm Lake
Street address state: IA
Zip/Postal code: 50588-2464
General Phone: (712) 732-4991
General Fax: (712) 732-4331
General/National Adv. E-mail: sales@stormlake.com
Display Adv. E-mail: sales@stormlake.com
Editorial e-mail: times@stormlake.com
Primary Website: stormlake.com
Year Established: 1990
Avg Paid Circ: 2900
Audit By: Sworn/Estimate/Non-Audited
Audit Date: 10.06.2019
Personnel: John Cullen (Publisher); Art Cullen (Editor); Jeff DeHaan (Advertising Manager); Rob McCartney (Circulation Manager)

THE STORY CITY HERALD

Street address 1: PO Box 380
Street address city: Ames
Street address state: IA
Zip/Postal code: 50010-0380
General Phone: (515) 733-4318
General Fax: (515) 733-4319
Advertising Phone: (515) 663-6963
General/National Adv. E-mail: rrong@amestrib.com
Display Adv. E-mail: rrong@amestrib.com
Editorial e-mail: mcrumb@amestrib.com
Primary Website: storycityherald.com
Year Established: 1881
Avg Paid Circ: 1963
Audit By: Sworn/Estimate/Non-Audited
Audit Date: 10.06.2019
Personnel: Scott Anderson (Pub.); Michael Crumb (Ed.); Randy Terwilliger (Circ. Dir.)
Parent company (for newspapers): CherryRoad Media

THE TAMA NEWS-HERALD

Street address 1: 220 W 3rd St
Street address city: Tama
Street address state: IA
Zip/Postal code: 52339-2308
General Phone: (641) 484-2841
General Fax: (641) 484-5705
General/National Adv. E-mail: nsund@tamatoledonews.com
Display Adv. E-mail: nsund@tamatoledonews.com
Editorial e-mail: jspeer@tamatoledonews.com
Primary Website: tamatoledonews.com
Year Established: 1925
Avg Paid Circ: 1951
Audit By: Sworn/Estimate/Non-Audited
Audit Date: 10.06.2019
Personnel: Nancy Sund (Gen. Mgr.); John Speer (Ed.); Abigail Pelzer (Publisher)
Parent company (for newspapers): Ogden Newspapers Inc.

THE THOMPSON COURIER

Street address 1: PO Box 318
Street address city: Thompson
Street address state: IA
Zip/Postal code: 50478-0318
General Phone: (641) 584-2770
General/National Adv. E-mail: thompsoncourier.rakeregister@gmail.com
Primary Website: thompsoncourier.info
Avg Paid Circ: 600

Audit By: Sworn/Estimate/Non-Audited
Audit Date: 10.06.2019
Personnel: Gretchen Daniels (Editor)

THE TRAER STAR-CLIPPER

Street address 1: 625 2nd St
Street address city: Traer
Street address state: IA
Zip/Postal code: 50675-1230
General Phone: (319) 478-2323
General Fax: (319) 478-2818
General/National Adv. E-mail: editor@traerstarclipper.com
Display Adv. E-mail: legals@traerstarclipper.com
Editorial e-mail: editor@traerstarclipper.com
Primary Website: traerstarclipper.com
Avg Paid Circ: 2500
Audit By: Sworn/Estimate/Non-Audited
Audit Date: 10.06.2019
Personnel: CJ Eilers (Ed.)
Parent company (for newspapers): Ogden Newspapers Inc.

THE TRI-COUNTY TIMES

Street address 1: 317 5th St
Street address 2: Ste B
Street address city: Ames
Street address state: IA
Zip/Postal code: 50010-6101
General Phone: (515) 232-2160
General Fax: (515) 382-4299
General/National Adv. E-mail: results@tricountytimes.com
Primary Website: tricountytimes.com
Avg Paid Circ: 2500
Audit By: Sworn/Estimate/Non-Audited
Audit Date: 10.06.2019
Personnel: Marlys Barker (Gen. Mgr.); John Greving (Adv. Mgr.); Jayme Ollendieck (Multi. Sales Exec.)
Parent company (for newspapers): Iowa Newspapers, Inc.

THE WOODBINE TWINER

Street address 1: 503 Walker St.
Street address city: Woodbine
Street address state: IA
Zip/Postal code: 51579-1267
General Phone: (712) 647-2821
General Fax: (712) 647-3081
General/National Adv. E-mail: ads@loganwoodbine.com
Display Adv. E-mail: ads@loganwoodbine.com
Editorial e-mail: news@loganwoodbine.com
Primary Website: loganwoodbine.com
Year Established: 1878
Avg Paid Circ: 1200
Audit By: Sworn/Estimate/Non-Audited
Audit Date: 10.06.2019
Personnel: Jacob Snyder (Ed.)

TIPTON CONSERVATIVE AND ADVERTISER

Street address 1: 124 W 5th St
Street address city: Tipton
Street address state: IA
Zip/Postal code: 52772-1728
General Phone: (563) 886-2131
General Fax: (563) 886-6466
General/National Adv. E-mail: StuartC108@aol.com
Primary Website: tiptonconservative.com
Year Established: 1853
Avg Paid Circ: 4582
Avg Free Circ: 10
Audit By: Sworn/Estimate/Non-Audited
Audit Date: 10.06.2019
Personnel: Pat Kroemer (Adv. Mgr.); Darla Walling (Circ. Mgr.); Stuart Clark (Ed.)

TITONKA TOPIC

Street address 1: 162 Main St N
Street address city: Titonka
Street address state: IA
Zip/Postal code: 50480-7724
General Phone: (515) 928-2723
General Fax: (515) 928-2506
Advertising Fax: (515) 928-2506
General/National Adv. E-mail: titonkatopic@netins.net
Display Adv. E-mail: titonkatopic@netins.net
Year Established: 1898
Avg Paid Circ: 550
Avg Free Circ: 10
Audit By: Sworn/Estimate/Non-Audited
Audit Date: 10.06.2019
Personnel: Mary Ullmann (Ed.)

TOLEDO CHRONICLE

Street address 1: 220 W 3rd St
Street address city: Tama
Street address state: IA
Zip/Postal code: 52339-2308
General Phone: (641) 484-2841
General Fax: (641) 484-5705
General/National Adv. E-mail: nsund@tamatoledonews.com
Display Adv. E-mail: nsund@tamatoledonews.com
Editorial e-mail: jspeer@tamatoledonews.com
Primary Website: tamatoledonews.com
Year Established: 1853
Avg Paid Circ: 1950
Audit By: Sworn/Estimate/Non-Audited
Audit Date: 10.06.2019
Personnel: Nancy Sund (Adv. Mgr.); John Speer (Ed.); Abigail Pelzer (Publisher)
Parent company (for newspapers): Ogden Newspapers Inc.

VALLEY NEWS TODAY

Street address 1: 617 W Sheridan Ave
Street address city: Shenandoah
Street address state: IA
Zip/Postal code: 51601-1707
General Phone: (712) 246-3097
General Fax: (712) 246-3099
Advertising Phone: (712) 246-3097 ext. 111
Advertising Fax: (712) 246-3099
Editorial Phone: (712) 246-3097 ext. 105
Editorial Fax: (712) 246-3099
General/National Adv. E-mail: ads@valleynewstoday.com
Display Adv. E-mail: ads@valleynewstoday.com
Classified Adv. e-mail: ads@valleynewstoday.com
Editorial e-mail: editorial@valleynewstoday.com
Primary Website: valleynewstoday.com
Mthly Avg Views: 35000
Mthly Avg Unique Visitors: 5259
Year Established: 1882
Avg Paid Circ: 2300
Avg Free Circ: 23000
Sun. Circulation Paid: 2300
Audit By: Sworn/Estimate/Non-Audited
Audit Date: 10.06.2019
Personnel: Kate Thompson (Pub.); Tess Gruber Nelson (Ed.); Erica Matya (Acct. Exec.); Jason Glenn (Sports Ed.)
Parent company (for newspapers): BH Media Group

VAN BUREN COUNTY REGISTER

Street address 1: 102 Elm St
Street address city: Farmington
Street address state: IA
Zip/Postal code: 52626-9537
General Phone: (319) 878-4111
General Fax: (319) 293-3198
General/National Adv. E-mail: vbregister@netins.net
Avg Paid Circ: 1786
Audit By: Sworn/Estimate/Non-Audited
Audit Date: 10.06.2019
Personnel: Donna Muir (Gen. Mgr.); Russell Ebert (Ed.)
Parent company (for newspapers): Sycamore Media

VILLISCA REVIEW

Street address 1: 201 S 5th Ave
Street address city: Villisca
Street address state: IA
Zip/Postal code: 50864-1132
General Phone: (712) 826-2142
General Fax: (712) 826-8888
General/National Adv. E-mail: newspapr@netins.net; wordchick@villiscareview.com
Display Adv. E-mail: adchick@villiscareview.com
Primary Website: facebook.com/Villisca-Review-Stanton-Viking-1703231826555199
Year Established: 1871
Avg Paid Circ: 1300
Audit By: Sworn/Estimate/Non-Audited
Audit Date: 10.06.2019
Personnel: Peggy Vermillion (Pub./GM); Anne Harter (Ed.)

WAPELLO REPUBLICAN

Street address 1: 301 Highway 61 N
Street address city: Wapello
Street address state: IA
Zip/Postal code: 52653-1242
General Phone: (319) 523-4631
General Fax: (319) 523-8167
General/National Adv. E-mail: lpc@louisacomm.net
Primary Website: facebook.com/The-Wapello-Republican-378443352532
Year Established: 1851
Avg Paid Circ: 2300
Avg Free Circ: 6
Audit By: Sworn/Estimate/Non-Audited
Audit Date: 10.06.2019
Personnel: Ernie Appleyard (Publisher)
Parent company (for newspapers): Sycamore Media; ????

WELLMAN ADVANCE

Street address 1: 230 8th Ave
Street address city: Wellman
Street address state: IA
Zip/Postal code: 52356-4707
General Phone: (319) 646-2712
General Fax: (319) 646-5904
General/National Adv. E-mail: wellnews@netins.net
Primary Website: wellmanadvance.com
Year Established: 1898
Avg Paid Circ: 1227
Avg Free Circ: 16
Audit By: Sworn/Estimate/Non-Audited
Audit Date: 10.06.2019
Personnel: Ranee Fladung (Pub)
Parent company (for newspapers): Anamosa Publications

WEST BRANCH TIMES

Street address 1: 124 W Main St
Street address city: West Branch
Street address state: IA
Zip/Postal code: 52358-9636
General Phone: (319) 643-2131
General/National Adv. E-mail: wbtimes@lcom.net; info@westbranchtimes.com
Primary Website: westbranchtimes.com
Year Established: 1875
Avg Paid Circ: 673
Audit By: Sworn/Estimate/Non-Audited
Audit Date: 10.06.2019
Personnel: Jake Krob (Pub.); Stuart Clark (Pub.); Gregory Norfleet (Editor); Joanne Salemink (Production); Tom Burger (Adv. Mgr.)
Parent company (for newspapers): West Branch Communications; Conservative Publishing

WEST LIBERTY INDEX

Street address 1: 214 N 2nd St
Street address city: Eldridge
Street address state: IA
Zip/Postal code: 52748-1271
General Phone: (563) 285-8111
General Fax: (563) 285-8114
General/National Adv. E-mail: adsales@northscottpress.com
Display Adv. E-mail: adsales@northscottpress.com
Classified Adv. e-mail: Jeff Martens <adsales@northscottpress.com>
Primary Website: northscottpress.com
Year Established: 1968
Avg Paid Circ: 5000
Audit By: Sworn/Estimate/Non-Audited
Audit Date: 10.06.2019
Personnel: William F. Tubbs (Pub.); Jeff Martens (Adv. Mgr.); Scott Campbell (Ed.); Linda Tubbs (Co-Pub.); Mark Ridolfi (Assist. Ed.)

WEST LIBERTY INDEX

Street address 1: 219 N Calhoun St
Street address city: West Liberty
Street address state: IA
Zip/Postal code: 52776-1537
General Phone: (319) 627-2814
General Fax: (319) 627-2110
General/National Adv. E-mail: index@Lcom.net
Primary Website: westlibertyindex.com
Audit By: Sworn/Estimate/Non-Audited
Audit Date: 10.06.2019
Personnel: Tom Burger (GM/Adv. Mgr.); John Hawkins (Circ.); Jake Krob (Pub.); Stuart Clark (Pub.)

WEST LYON HERALD

Street address 1: 211 South Main
Street address 2: Box 340
Street address city: Inwood
Street address state: IA
Zip/Postal code: 51240-7807
General Phone: (712) 753-2258
General Fax: (712) 753-4864
General/National Adv. E-mail: ads@ncppub.com
Display Adv. E-mail: vschilling@ncppub.com
Editorial e-mail: jjensen@ncppub.com
Primary Website: ncppub.com
Year Established: 1890
Avg Paid Circ: 1400
Audit By: Sworn/Estimate/Non-Audited
Audit Date: 10.06.2019
Personnel: Jessica Jensen (Ed.); Nathan Broek (Sports Ed.); Kari Jurrens (Adv. Rep.); Jim Hensley (COO)
Parent company (for newspapers): New Century Press

WESTSIDE OBSERVER

Street address 1: 324 1st St
Street address city: Westside
Street address state: IA
Zip/Postal code: 51467
General Phone: (712) 663-4362
General Fax: (712) 663-4363
General/National Adv. E-mail: observer@win-4-u.net
Primary Website: westsideobserveronline.com
Avg Paid Circ: 1140
Avg Free Circ: 35
Audit By: Sworn/Estimate/Non-Audited
Audit Date: 10.06.2019
Personnel: Janine Kock (Ed./Pub.); Doreen Jons (Office Mgr.); Jessica Berger (Office Asst.)
Parent company (for newspapers): Kock Publishing Inc.

WHITTEMORE INDEPENDENT

Street address 1: 419 Broad St
Street address city: Whittemore
Street address state: IA
Zip/Postal code: 50598-8512
General Phone: (515)884-2648
General Fax: (515)884-2648
General/National Adv. E-mail: wjournal@ncn.net
Primary Website: No website
Year Established: 1988
Avg Paid Circ: 235
Audit By: Sworn/Estimate/Non-Audited
Audit Date: 10.06.2019
Personnel: Karen Schwartzkopf (Pub.)

WILTON-DURANT ADVOCATE NEWS

Street address 1: 410 Cedar St
Street address city: Wilton
Street address state: IA
Zip/Postal code: 52778-9495
General Phone: (563) 732-2029
General Fax: (563) 732-3144
Advertising Phone: (563) 732-2029
Advertising Fax: (563) 732-3144
Editorial Phone: (563) 732-2029
Editorial Fax: (563) 732-3144
General/National Adv. E-mail: anads@netwtc.net
Display Adv. E-mail: adnews@netwtc.net
Editorial e-mail: dsawvell@netwtc.net
Primary Website: Wilton-Durant Advocate News
Audit By: Sworn/Estimate/Non-Audited
Audit Date: 10.06.2019
Personnel: Derek Sawvell (Mng. Ed.); Bill Tubs (Adv. Mgr.)

WINFIELD BEACON / WAYLAND NEWS

Street address 1: 107 E Elm St
Street address city: Winfield
Street address state: IA
Zip/Postal code: 52659-9780
General Phone: (319) 257-6813

General Fax: (319) 257-6902
General/National Adv. E-mail: newspapers2@iowatelecom.net
Primary Website: No Website
Audit By: Sworn/Estimate/Non-Audited
Audit Date: 10.06.2019
Personnel: Cathy Lauderdale (Pub.)

WINTERSET MADISONIAN

Street address 1: 215 N 1st Ave
Street address city: Winterset
Street address state: IA
Zip/Postal code: 50273-1506
General Phone: (515) 462-2101
General Fax: (515) 462-2102
General/National Adv. E-mail: madisonianads@i-rule.net
Editorial e-mail: vpolk@i-rule.net
Primary Website: wintersetmadisonian.com
Year Established: 1856
Avg Paid Circ: 3580
Audit By: Sworn/Estimate/Non-Audited
Audit Date: 10.06.2019
Personnel: Dave Braga (Ed.); Ted C. Gorman (Pub.); Vickie Polk (Prodn. Mgr.)

WINTHROP NEWS

Street address 1: 225 W Madison St
Street address city: Winthrop
Street address state: IA
Zip/Postal code: 50682-7705
General Phone: (319) 935-3027
General Fax: (319) 935-3082
General/National Adv. E-mail: news@thewinthropnews.com
Primary Website: thewinthropnews.com
Year Established: 1892
Avg Paid Circ: 3800
Audit By: Sworn/Estimate/Non-Audited
Audit Date: 10.06.2019
Personnel: Steven Smith (Adv. Mgr.); Mary Beth Smith (Ed.)

KANSAS

ADVOCATE OF PHILLIPS COUNTY

Street address 1: 265 F St
Street address city: Phillipsburg
Street address state: KS
Zip/Postal code: 67661-1918
General Phone: (785) 543-2349
General Fax: (785) 543-2364
Editorial e-mail: theadvocate@ruraltel.net
Primary Website: facebook.com/pages/The-Advocate-of-Phillips-County/143662349001002
Audit By: Sworn/Estimate/Non-Audited
Audit Date: 10.06.2019
Personnel: Ron Lower (Pub); Lee Lower (Pub); Kathy Merklein (Ed)

ANDERSON COUNTY ADVOCATE

Street address 1: 117 E 4th Ave
Street address city: Garnett
Street address state: KS
Zip/Postal code: 66032-1502
General Phone: (785) 448-7000
General Fax: (785) 448-9800
General/National Adv. E-mail: garnettadvocate@yahoo.com
Editorial e-mail: news@andersoncountynewsline.com
Primary Website: http://andersoncountynewsline.com/
Audit By: Sworn/Estimate/Non-Audited
Audit Date: 10.06.2019
Personnel: Vern Brown

ANDERSON COUNTY REVIEW

Street address 1: 112 W 6th Ave
Street address city: Garnett
Street address state: KS
Zip/Postal code: 66032-1402
General Phone: (785) 448-3121
General Fax: (785) 448-6253
General/National Adv. E-mail: Review@garnett-ks.com
Editorial e-mail: Review@garnett-ks.com
Primary Website: garnett-ks.com
Year Established: 1865
Avg Paid Circ: 2318
Avg Free Circ: 44
Audit By: Sworn/Estimate/Non-Audited
Audit Date: 10.06.2019
Personnel: Dane Hicks (Publisher)

ANTHONY REPUBLICAN

Street address 1: 121 E Main St
Street address 2: PO Box 31
Street address city: Anthony
Street address state: KS
Zip/Postal code: 67003-2720
General Phone: (620) 842-5129
General Fax: (620) 842-5115
General/National Adv. E-mail: anthonyrepublican@att.net
Display Adv. E-mail: anthonyrepublican@att.net
Classified Adv. e-mail: anthonyrepublican@att.net
Editorial e-mail: anthonyrepublican@att.net
Primary Website: anthonyrepublicannews.com
Year Established: 1878
Avg Paid Circ: 1900
Audit By: Sworn/Estimate/Non-Audited
Audit Date: 10.06.2019
Personnel: Larry Dunn (Pub); Ross Downing (Editor)

ARK VALLEY NEWS

Street address 1: 210 W Main St
Street address city: Valley Center
Street address state: KS
Zip/Postal code: 67147-2216
General Phone: (316) 755-0821
General Fax: (316) 755-0644
General/National Adv. E-mail: ads@arkvalleynews.com
Editorial e-mail: news@arkvalleynews.com
Primary Website: arkvalleynews.com
Avg Paid Circ: 3000
Avg Free Circ: 93
Audit By: Sworn/Estimate/Non-Audited
Audit Date: 30.09.2017
Personnel: Chris Strunk (Pub.)

ATCHISON GLOBE

Street address 1: 308 Commercial St
Street address city: Atchison
Street address state: KS
Zip/Postal code: 66002-2519
General Phone: (913) 367-0583
General Fax: (913) 367-7531
Advertising Phone: (913) 367-0583 ext. 20406
Advertising Fax: (913) 367-7531
Editorial Phone: (913) 367-0583 ext. 20411
Editorial Fax: (913) 367-7531
General/National Adv. E-mail: christym@npgco.com
Display Adv. E-mail: christym@npgco.com
Classified Adv. e-mail: jim.ervin@npgco.com
Editorial e-mail: joewarren@npgco.com
Primary Website: atchisondailyglobenow.com
Year Established: 1877
Avg Paid Circ: 3293
Sat. Circulation Paid: 3293
Audit By: Sworn/Estimate/Non-Audited
Audit Date: 10.06.2019
Personnel: Joe Warren (Pub./Ed.); Marilyn Andre (Bus. Mgr./Circ.); Christy McKibben (Adv. Mgr.); Jim Ervin (Adv. Rep.); Logan Jackson (News Ed.); Adam Gardner (Sports Ed.); Joey May (Lady A Ed.)
Parent company (for newspapers): News-Press & Gazette Co.

ATTICA INDEPENDENT

Street address 1: 422 N Logan St
Street address city: Attica
Street address state: KS
Zip/Postal code: 67009-9224
General Phone: (620) 254-7660
Primary Website: facebook.com/pages/Attica-Independent/152138318133485
Audit By: Sworn/Estimate/Non-Audited
Audit Date: 10.06.2019
Personnel: Ray Howell (Ed./Pub.)

BELOIT CALL

Street address 1: 119 E Main St
Street address city: Beloit
Street address state: KS
Zip/Postal code: 67420-3234
General Phone: (785) 738-3537
General Fax: (785) 738-6442
General/National Adv. E-mail: beloitcall@nckcn.com
Display Adv. E-mail: beloitcall@nckcn.com
Editorial e-mail: beloitcall@nckcn.com
Primary Website: beloitcall.com
Audit By: Sworn/Estimate/Non-Audited
Audit Date: 10.06.2019
Personnel: Brad Lowell (Pub.); Sharon Hesket Sahlfeld (Ed.)

BIRD CITY TIMES

Street address 1: PO Box 1050
Street address city: Saint Francis
Street address state: KS
Zip/Postal code: 67756-1050
General Phone: (785) 332-3162
General Fax: (785) 332-3001
General/National Adv. E-mail: tburr@nwkansas.com
Editorial e-mail: normamartinez@wildblue.net
Primary Website: nwkansas.com
Avg Paid Circ: 565
Avg Free Circ: 3
Audit By: Sworn/Estimate/Non-Audited
Audit Date: 10.06.2019
Personnel: Norma Martinez (Ed.)
Parent company (for newspapers): Haynes Publishing Co.

BLUE RAPIDS FREE PRESS

Street address 1: 203 W 5th St
Street address city: Blue Rapids
Street address state: KS
Zip/Postal code: 66411-1201
General Phone: (785) 363-7779
General/National Adv. E-mail: brfreepress@kansas.net
Editorial e-mail: brfreepress@kansas.net
Primary Website: bluerapidsfreepress.com
Year Established: 2009
Audit By: Sworn/Estimate/Non-Audited
Audit Date: 10.06.2019
Personnel: Jon Brake (Editor/Publisher/Ad Director)

BUCKLIN BANNER

Street address 1: PO Box 528
Street address 2: 101 N Main
Street address city: Cimarron
Street address state: KS
Zip/Postal code: 67835-0528
General Phone: (620) 338-3071
General Fax: (620) 855-2489
General/National Adv. E-mail: bucklinbanner@ucom.net
Display Adv. E-mail: bucklinbanner@ucom.net
Classified Adv. e-mail: bucklinbanner@ucom.net
Editorial e-mail: bucklinbanner@ucom.net
Year Established: 1901
Avg Paid Circ: 200
Audit By: Sworn/Estimate/Non-Audited
Audit Date: 10.06.2020
Personnel: Kirk Anderson (Editor)
Parent company (for newspapers): Golden Plains Publishing

CALDWELL MESSENGER

Street address 1: 111 S Main St
Street address city: Caldwell
Street address state: KS
Zip/Postal code: 67022-1607
General Phone: (620) 845-2320
General Fax: (620) 845-6461
General/National Adv. E-mail: messenger@kanokla.net
Editorial e-mail: messenger@kanokla.net
Primary Website: facebook.com/pages/Caldwell-Messenger/152565398090263
Avg Paid Circ: 1350
Audit By: Sworn/Estimate/Non-Audited
Audit Date: 10.06.2019
Personnel: Pat Weber (Ed.)

CHAPMAN & ENTERPRISE NEWS-TIMES

Street address 1: 437 N Marshall St
Street address city: Chapman
Street address state: KS
Zip/Postal code: 67431
General Phone: (785) 922-6450
General Fax: (785) 922-6027
General/National Adv. E-mail: chapmannewstimes@gmail.com
Primary Website: chapmannewstimes.com
Audit By: Sworn/Estimate/Non-Audited
Audit Date: 10.06.2019
Personnel: John Baetz

CHASE COUNTY LEADER-NEWS

Street address 1: PO Box K
Street address 2: 306 Broadway St
Street address city: Cottonwood Falls
Street address state: KS
Zip/Postal code: 66845-0436
General Phone: (620) 273-6391
General Fax: (620) 273-8674
Advertising Phone: (620) 273-6391
Advertising Fax: (620) 273-8674
Editorial Phone: (620) 273-6391
Editorial Fax: (620) 273-8674
General/National Adv. E-mail: ccleadernews@gmail.com
Display Adv. E-mail: ccleadernews@gmail.com
Editorial e-mail: ccleadernews@gmail.com
Primary Website: facebook.com/chasecountyleadernews
Year Established: 1871
Avg Paid Circ: 1200
Avg Free Circ: 15
Audit By: Sworn/Estimate/Non-Audited
Audit Date: 10.06.2019
Personnel: Jerry Schwilling (Prodn. Mgr.); Cheri Hopson (advertising, business manager); Marion Weaver (Bus. Mgr.)

CHEROKEE COUNTY NEWS-ADVOCATE

Street address 1: 217 S Kansas Ave
Street address city: Columbus
Street address state: KS
Zip/Postal code: 66725-1718
General Phone: (620) 429-2773
General Fax: (620) 429-3223
Advertising Phone: (620) 429-2773
Advertising Fax: (620) 429-3223
Editorial Phone: (620) 429-2773
Editorial Fax: (620) 429-3223
General/National Adv. E-mail: advertising@sekvoice.com
Display Adv. E-mail: classifieds@sekvoice.com
Editorial e-mail: news@sekvoice.com
Primary Website: sekvoice.com
Year Established: 1882
Avg Paid Circ: 3300
Audit By: Sworn/Estimate/Non-Audited
Audit Date: 10.06.2019
Personnel: Chris Zimmerman (Pub.); Pat Richardson (Ed.); Cheryl Franklin (Pub.); Morgan Downs (Digital Dir.)
Parent company (for newspapers): Larry Hiatt; CherryRoad Media

CHERRYVALE CHRONICLE

Street address 1: 115 N Labette St
Street address city: Cherryvale
Street address state: KS
Zip/Postal code: 67335
General Phone: (620) 336-2100
General Fax: (620) 336-2101
General/National Adv. E-mail: chroniclenews@cox.net
Primary Website: taylornews.org
Avg Paid Circ: 3100
Audit By: Sworn/Estimate/Non-Audited
Audit Date: 10.06.2019
Personnel: Rudy M. Taylor (Pub.); Amy Taylor (Adv. Mgr.); Kathy Taylor (Mng. Ed.)

CLARK COUNTY GAZETTE

Street address 1: PO Box 463
Street address city: Minneola
Street address state: KS
Zip/Postal code: 67865-0463
General Phone: (620) 339-9217
General/National Adv. E-mail: gazette@clarkcountygazette.com
Editorial e-mail: gazette@clarkcountygazette.com

Primary Website: clarkcountygazette.com
Audit By: Sworn/Estimate/Non-Audited
Audit Date: 10.06.2019
Personnel: Denise Kuhns (Editor & Publisher)

CLYDE REPUBLICAN

Street address 1: 305 Washington St
Street address 2: PO Box 397
Street address city: Clyde
Street address state: KS
Zip/Postal code: 66938-9664
General Phone: (785) 446-2201
General Fax: (785) 446-2201
General/National Adv. E-mail: clyderepublican@hotmail.com
Primary Website: facebook.com/TheClydeRepublican
Year Established: 1900
Avg Paid Circ: 1000
Audit By: Sworn/Estimate/Non-Audited
Audit Date: 10.06.2019
Personnel: Margene Cash (Ed.); Matthew Jorgenson (Co-Owner/Pub.); Crystal Jorgenson (Co-Owner)

COFFEY COUNTY REPUBLICAN

Street address 1: 324 Hudson St
Street address city: Burlington
Street address state: KS
Zip/Postal code: 66839-1327
General Phone: (620) 364-5325
General Fax: (620) 364-2607
General/National Adv. E-mail: repubads1@gmail.com
Display Adv. E-mail: repubclass@gmail.com
Editorial e-mail: ccrepub@gmail.com
Primary Website: coffeycountyonline.com
Year Established: 1856
Avg Paid Circ: 3000
Audit By: Sworn/Estimate/Non-Audited
Audit Date: 10.06.2019
Personnel: Chris Faimon (Pub.); Jeff Birkatad (Adv. Mgr.); Kathy Payne (Circ. Mgr.); Mark Petterson (Ed.)

COFFEYVILLE JOURNAL

Street address 1: 302 W 8th St
Street address city: Coffeyville
Street address state: KS
Zip/Postal code: 67337-5829
General Phone: (620) 251-3300
General Fax: (620) 251-1905
Advertising Phone: (620) 251-3300
Advertising Fax: (620) 251-1905
General/National Adv. E-mail: advertising@cj.kscoxmail.com
Display Adv. E-mail: classifieds@cj.kscoxmail.com
Editorial e-mail: gcraven@cj.kscoxmail.com
Primary Website: facebook.com/TheCoffeyvilleJournal/?ref=page_internal
Year Established: 1875
Avg Paid Circ: 4103
Avg Free Circ: 10000
Sun. Circulation Paid: 4103
Audit By: Sworn/Estimate/Non-Audited
Audit Date: 10.06.2019
Personnel: Darrell Sumner (Owner/Pub.); Scott Wood; Bill Noel (Adv. Dir.); Hayley Henderson (Classified Adv.); Deanna Evans (Sr. Ed.)
Parent company (for newspapers): Kansas Press Association

COLUMBUS NEWS REPORT

Street address 1: 105 S Pennsylvania Ave
Street address city: Columbus
Street address state: KS
Zip/Postal code: 66725-1710
General Phone: (620) 429-4684
General Fax: (620) 429-4694
General/National Adv. E-mail: newsreport@columbus-ks.com
Editorial e-mail: newsreport@columbus-ks.com
Primary Website: columbusnews-report.com
Year Established: 2010
Avg Paid Circ: 1377
Audit By: Sworn/Estimate/Non-Audited
Audit Date: 10.06.2019
Personnel: Larry Hiatt (Editor & Publisher)

COURTLAND JOURNAL

Street address 1: 420 Main St
Street address city: Courtland
Street address state: KS
Zip/Postal code: 66939-9712
General Phone: (785) 374-4428
General Fax: (785) 374-4209
General/National Adv. E-mail: cjournal@courtland.net
Editorial e-mail: cjournal@courtland.net
Primary Website: facebook.com/CourtlandJournal
Year Established: 1903
Avg Paid Circ: 700
Avg Free Circ: 20
Audit By: Sworn/Estimate/Non-Audited
Audit Date: 10.06.2019
Personnel: Colleen Mainquist (Ed.)

COWLEY COURIER TRAVELER

Street address 1: PO Box 543
Street address city: Winfield
Street address state: KS
Zip/Postal code: 67156-0543
General Phone: (620) 221-1050
General Fax: (620) 221-1101
General/National Adv. E-mail: advertising1@ctnewsonline.com
Display Adv. E-mail: classified@ctnewsonline.com
Editorial e-mail: news1@ctnewsonline.com
Primary Website: ctnewsonline.com
Audit By: Sworn/Estimate/Non-Audited
Audit Date: 10.06.2019
Personnel: David A. Seaton (Pub.); Marsha Wesler (Dir. Sales/Mktg.); Arty Hicks
Parent company (for newspapers): Winfield Publishing Co., Inc.

CUNNINGHAM COURIER

Street address 1: 209 E 1st St
Street address city: Cunningham
Street address state: KS
Zip/Postal code: 67035-8824
General Phone: (620) 298-2659
General Fax: (620) 298-4047
General/National Adv. E-mail: ckclipper@juno.com
Editorial e-mail: cunninghamcourier@gmail.com
Primary Website: cunninghamks.com
Audit By: Sworn/Estimate/Non-Audited
Audit Date: 10.06.2019
Personnel: David Steffen (Pub.); Kerri Steffen (Ed.)

DERBY INFORMER

Street address 1: 219 E Madison Ave
Street address city: Derby
Street address state: KS
Zip/Postal code: 67037-1711
General Phone: (316) 788-4006
General Fax: (316) 788-4573
General/National Adv. E-mail: mail@derbyinformer.com
Primary Website: derbyinformer.com
Mthly Avg Views: 85000
Mthly Avg Unique Visitors: 11000
Year Established: 1998
Avg Paid Circ: 2789
Audit By: Sworn/Estimate/Non-Audited
Audit Date: 10.06.2019
Personnel: Jeff Cott (Publisher/Owner)

DOWNS NEWS AND TIMES

Street address 1: 717 Railroad St
Street address city: Downs
Street address state: KS
Zip/Postal code: 67437-1633
General Phone: (785) 454-3514
General Fax: (785) 454-3866
General/National Adv. E-mail: downsnews@ruraltel.net
Primary Website: mainstreetmedia.us
Avg Paid Circ: 1155
Audit By: Sworn/Estimate/Non-Audited
Audit Date: 10.06.2019
Personnel: Jack Krier (Pub.); Kathy Krier (Pub.); LaRhea Cole (Ed.)
Parent company (for newspapers): Main Street Media, Inc.

EDWARDS COUNTY SENTINEL

Street address 1: 221 E 6th St
Street address city: Kinsley
Street address state: KS
Zip/Postal code: 67547-1109
General Phone: (620) 659-2080
General Fax: (620) 855-2489
General/National Adv. E-mail: edcsentinel@hotmail.com
Avg Paid Circ: 1200
Audit By: Sworn/Estimate/Non-Audited
Audit Date: 10.06.2019
Personnel: Mark Anderson (Pub); Faith BroKar (Editor)
Parent company (for newspapers): Golden Plains Publishing

ELLINWOOD LEADER

Street address 1: 105 N Main St
Street address city: Ellinwood
Street address state: KS
Zip/Postal code: 67526-1639
General Phone: (620) 564-3116
General Fax: (620) 564-2550
General/National Adv. E-mail: dsettle@idn.kscoxmail.com
Editorial e-mail: theellinwoodleadernews@yahoo.com
Primary Website: midksnews.com
Year Established: 1894
Avg Paid Circ: 1053
Avg Free Circ: 613
Audit By: Sworn/Estimate/Non-Audited
Audit Date: 10.06.2019
Personnel: John M. Settle (Pub.); Dennis Martin (Circ. Mgr.)
Parent company (for newspapers): Hi Neighbor Newspapers

ERIE RECORD

Street address 1: 213 S Main St
Street address city: Erie
Street address state: KS
Zip/Postal code: 66733-1334
General Phone: (620) 244-3371
General Fax: (620) 244-3371
Editorial e-mail: news@erierecord.com
Primary Website: facebook.com/pages/The-Erie-Record/100524630008815
Audit By: Sworn/Estimate/Non-Audited
Audit Date: 10.06.2019
Personnel: Eddi Hibbs (Pub.)

FAIRVIEW ENTERPRISE

Street address 1: 715 New York
Street address city: Lawrence
Street address state: KS
Zip/Postal code: 66044
General Phone: (785) 217-7023
Advertising Phone: (785) 217-7023
Editorial Phone: (785) 217-7023
General/National Adv. E-mail: dflambertson@gmail.com
Display Adv. E-mail: thefairviewenterprise@gmail.com
Classified Adv. e-mail: dflambertson@gmail.com
Editorial e-mail: dflambertson@gmail.com
Year Established: 1888
Avg Paid Circ: 300
Avg Free Circ: 25
Audit By: Sworn/Estimate/Non-Audited
Audit Date: 10.06.2019
Personnel: David Lambertson (Pub.)

FARM TALK

Street address 1: 1801 S US Highway 59
Street address city: Parsons
Street address state: KS
Zip/Postal code: 67357-4958
General Phone: (800) 356-8255
General Fax: (620) 421-9473
General/National Adv. E-mail: farmtalk@terraworld.net
Display Adv. E-mail: farmtalk@terraworld.net
Editorial e-mail: farmtalk@terraworld.net
Primary Website: farmtalknewspaper.com
Year Established: 1974
Audit By: Sworn/Estimate/Non-Audited
Audit Date: 10.06.2019
Personnel: Lance Markley (Co-Pub./Adv. Mgr.)

FRANKFORT AREA NEWS

Street address 1: 116 E 2nd St
Street address city: Frankfort
Street address state: KS
Zip/Postal code: 66427-1403
General Phone: (785) 292-4726
General/National Adv. E-mail: fan@bluevalley.net
Display Adv. E-mail: fan@bluevalley.net
Editorial e-mail: fan@bluevalley.net
Primary Website: frankfortareanews.com
Year Established: 1991
Avg Paid Circ: 700
Audit By: Sworn/Estimate/Non-Audited
Audit Date: 10.06.2019
Personnel: Connie Musil (Ed.)

GALENA SENTINEL-TIMES

Street address 1: 511 S Main St
Street address city: Galena
Street address state: KS
Zip/Postal code: 66739-1292
General Phone: (620) 783-5034
General Fax: (620) 783-1388
Editorial e-mail: gstimes@kans.com
Primary Website: sentineltimes.com
Year Established: 1880
Audit By: Sworn/Estimate/Non-Audited
Audit Date: 10.06.2019
Personnel: David Nelson (Pub)

GOODLAND STAR-NEWS

Street address 1: 1205 Main Ave
Street address city: Goodland
Street address state: KS
Zip/Postal code: 67735-2946
General Phone: (785) 899-2338
General Fax: (785) 899-6186
General/National Adv. E-mail: kbentley@nwkansas.com
Editorial e-mail: star.news@nwkansas.com
Primary Website: nwkansas.com
Year Established: 1993
Avg Paid Circ: 2004
Audit By: Sworn/Estimate/Non-Audited
Audit Date: 10.06.2019
Personnel: Pat Schiefen (Society Ed./composition); Jessica Corbin (ad designer/traffic manager); Steve Haynes (president); Sheila Smith (Circ. Mgr./office manager); Kevin Bottrell (Ed)
Parent company (for newspapers): Haynes Publishing Co.

GOVE COUNTY ADVOCATE

Street address 1: 304 Main St
Street address city: Quinter
Street address state: KS
Zip/Postal code: 67752-9526
General Phone: (785) 754-3651
General Fax: (785) 754-3878
General/National Adv. E-mail: advocate@ruraltel.net
Primary Website: facebook.com/pages/Gove-County-Advocate/124124657634832
Avg Paid Circ: 1800
Avg Free Circ: 100
Audit By: Sworn/Estimate/Non-Audited
Audit Date: 10.06.2019
Personnel: Roxane K. Broeckelman (Pub.); Tom W. Broeckelman (Ed.)

GRASS & GRAIN

Street address 1: 1531 Yuma St
Street address city: Manhattan
Street address state: KS
Zip/Postal code: 66502-4228
General Phone: (785) 539-7558
General Fax: (785) 539-2679
General/National Adv. E-mail: agpress2@agpress.com
Editorial e-mail: gandgeditor@agpress.com
Primary Website: grassandgrain.com
Year Established: 1953
Avg Paid Circ: 14000
Audit By: Sworn/Estimate/Non-Audited
Audit Date: 10.06.2019
Personnel: Donna Sullivan (Ed.)

GREELEY COUNTY REPUBLICAN

Street address 1: 507 Broadway Ave
Street address city: Tribune
Street address state: KS
Zip/Postal code: 67879-7702

General Phone: (620) 376-4264
General Fax: (620) 376-2433
General/National Adv. E-mail: newspaper@sunflowertelco.com
Primary Website: gcrnews.com
Avg Paid Circ: 900
Avg Free Circ: 14
Audit By: Sworn/Estimate/Non-Audited
Audit Date: 10.06.2019
Personnel: Dan M. Epp (Ed.); Jan Epp (Ed.)

HARPER ADVOCATE

Street address 1: 907 Central St
Street address 2: # 36
Street address city: Harper
Street address state: KS
Zip/Postal code: 67058-1112
General Phone: (620) 896-7311
General/National Adv. E-mail: harperadvocate@sbcglobal.net
Display Adv. E-mail: same as above
Editorial e-mail: harperadvocate@sbcglobal.net
Primary Website: NA
Year Established: 1882
Avg Paid Circ: 1200
Audit By: Sworn/Estimate/Non-Audited
Audit Date: 10.06.2019
Personnel: Ken Leu (Pub.)

HARVEY COUNTY NOW

Street address 1: 706 N Main St
Street address city: Newton
Street address state: KS
Zip/Postal code: 67114
General Phone: 3162817899
Advertising Phone: 3166171095
Editorial Phone: 3167122125
General/National Adv. E-mail: subscriber@harveycountynow.com
Display Adv. E-mail: bruce@harveycountynow.com
Classified Adv. e-mail: shelley@harveycountynow.com
Editorial e-mail: joey@harveycountynow.com
Primary Website: https://harveycountynow.com
Mthly Avg Views: 40000
Year Established: 1881
Avg Paid Circ: 3950
Avg Free Circ: 50
Audit By: USPS
Audit Date: 10.10.2021
Personnel: Karen Jacobs (Ed)
Parent company (for newspapers): Kansas Publishing Ventures, LLC

HAYSVILLE SUN-TIMES

Street address 1: 325 N Main St
Street address city: Haysville
Street address state: KS
Zip/Postal code: 67060-1159
General Phone: (316) 524-6868
General Fax: (316) 522-8668
Advertising Phone: (316) 540-3111
Editorial Phone: (316) 540-0500
General/National Adv. E-mail: graphicsdept@tsnews.com
Display Adv. E-mail: classifieds@tsnews.com
Editorial e-mail: haysvillesuntimes@yahoo.com
Primary Website: tsnews.com
Avg Paid Circ: 1100
Audit By: Sworn/Estimate/Non-Audited
Audit Date: 10.06.2019
Personnel: Travis Mounts (Pub)
Parent company (for newspapers): Times-Sentinel Newspapers LLC

HESSTON RECORD

Street address 1: PO Box 340
Street address city: Hesston
Street address state: KS
Zip/Postal code: 67062-0340
General Phone: (620) 327-4831
General Fax: (620) 327-4830
General/National Adv. E-mail: ads@hesstonrecord.com
Editorial e-mail: jackie@hesstonrecord.com
Primary Website: hesstonrecord.com
Avg Paid Circ: 1074
Avg Free Circ: 130
Audit By: Sworn/Estimate/Non-Audited
Audit Date: 10.06.2019
Personnel: Robb Reeves (Pub.); Jackie Nelson (Ed.); Blake Spurney

HIAWATHA WORLD

Street address 1: 607 Utah St
Street address city: Hiawatha
Street address state: KS
Zip/Postal code: 66434-2319
General Phone: (785) 742-2111
General Fax: (785) 742-2276
General/National Adv. E-mail: christym@npgco.com
Display Adv. E-mail: world@npgco.com
Editorial e-mail: joewarren@npgco.com
Primary Website: hiawathaworldonline.com
Year Established: 1908
Avg Paid Circ: 2300
Audit By: Sworn/Estimate/Non-Audited
Audit Date: 10.06.2019
Personnel: Joe Warren (Pub/Ed); Sarah Davies (Adv. Mgr.); Joey May (Managing Ed.)
Parent company (for newspapers): News-Press & Gazette Co.

HIGH PLAINS JOURNAL

Street address 1: 1500 E Wyatt Earp Blvd
Street address city: Dodge City
Street address state: KS
Zip/Postal code: 67801-7001
General Phone: (620) 227-7171
General Fax: (620) 227-7173
Advertising Phone: (620) 227-1847
Editorial Phone: (620) 227-1806
General/National Adv. E-mail: art@hpj.com
Display Adv. E-mail: ads@hpj.com
Editorial e-mail: journal@hpj.com
Primary Website: hpj.com
Year Established: 1949
Avg Paid Circ: 44232
Avg Free Circ: 0
Audit By: Sworn/Estimate/Non-Audited
Audit Date: 10.06.2019
Personnel: Holly Martin (Ed)

HILLSBORO FREE PRESS

Street address 1: 116 S Main St
Street address city: Hillsboro
Street address state: KS
Zip/Postal code: 67063-1526
General Phone: (620) 947-5702
General Fax: (620) 947-5940
Advertising Phone: (620) 947-5702
Advertising Fax: (620) 947-5940
Editorial Phone: (620) 947-5702
Editorial Fax: (620) 947-5940
General/National Adv. E-mail: natalie@hillsborofreepress.com
Display Adv. E-mail: nicole@hillsborofreepress.com
Editorial e-mail: joey@hillsborofreepress.com
Primary Website: hillsborofreepress.com
Mthly Avg Views: 26544
Mthly Avg Unique Visitors: 5078
Year Established: 1998
Avg Paid Circ: 120
Avg Free Circ: 7140
Audit By: Sworn/Estimate/Non-Audited
Audit Date: 10.06.2019
Personnel: Joey Young (Pub.); Natalie Hoffman (Adv. Mgr.)
Parent company (for newspapers): Kansas Publishing Ventures

HILLSBORO STAR-JOURNAL

Street address 1: 110 N Main St
Street address city: Hillsboro
Street address state: KS
Zip/Postal code: 67063-1139
General Phone: (620) 947-3975
General Fax: (620) 382-2262
General/National Adv. E-mail: advertising@starj.com
Display Adv. E-mail: advertising@starj.com
Editorial e-mail: news@starj.com
Primary Website: http://starj.com/
Year Established: 1908
Avg Paid Circ: 1200
Avg Free Circ: 100
Audit By: Sworn/Estimate/Non-Audited
Audit Date: 10.06.2019
Personnel: Debra Steele (Advertising sales representative); Jean Stuchlik (Business and circulation manager); Eric Meyer (President and publisher); Melvin Honeyfield (Production director); Adam Stewart (News editor); Ben Kleine (Reporter); David Colburn (Reporter); Jennifer Stultz (Reporter); Rowena Plett (Reporter); Tena Lundgren (Accounting coordinator)
Parent company (for newspapers): Hoch Publishing Co. Inc.

HORTON HEADLIGHT

Street address 1: 133 W 8th St
Street address 2: PO Box 269
Street address city: Horton
Street address state: KS
Zip/Postal code: 66439-1601
General Phone: (785) 486-2512
General Fax: (785) 486-2512
General/National Adv. E-mail: headlight@carsoncomm.com
Editorial e-mail: headlight@carsoncomm.com
Primary Website: NA
Avg Paid Circ: 1300
Audit By: Sworn/Estimate/Non-Audited
Audit Date: 10.06.2019
Personnel: Dana Foley (Pub.); Linda Messer (Mng. Ed.); Susan Higley (Ed.); Dave Christensen (Prodn. Mgr.)

JACKSONIAN

Street address 1: 101 S Main St
Street address city: Cimarron
Street address state: KS
Zip/Postal code: 67835-8856
General Phone: (620) 855-3902
General Fax: (620) 855-2489
General/National Adv. E-mail: jacksoniannews@me.com
Editorial e-mail: jacksoniannews@me.com
Avg Paid Circ: 905
Audit By: Sworn/Estimate/Non-Audited
Audit Date: 10.06.2020
Personnel: Mark Anderson (Publisher); Kirk Anderson (Ed.)
Parent company (for newspapers): Golden Plains Publishing

JETMORE REPUBLICAN

Street address 1: 415 Main
Street address city: Jetmore
Street address state: KS
Zip/Postal code: 67854
General Phone: (620) 357-8316
General/National Adv. E-mail: jetrepub@fairpoint.net
Editorial e-mail: jetrepub@fairpoint.net
Primary Website: facebook.com/pages/Jetmore-Republican/128074637238247
Audit By: Sworn/Estimate/Non-Audited
Audit Date: 10.06.2019
Personnel: Mark Anderson (Pub.); Mike Thornburg (Ed.)

JEWELL COUNTY RECORD

Street address 1: 111 E Main St
Street address city: Mankato
Street address state: KS
Zip/Postal code: 66956-2214
General Phone: (785) 378-3191
General Fax: (785) 378-3782
General/National Adv. E-mail: bblauvelt@windstream.net
Editorial e-mail: jcr@nckcn.com
Primary Website: superiorne.com
Year Established: 1970
Avg Paid Circ: 700
Audit By: Sworn/Estimate/Non-Audited
Audit Date: 10.06.2019
Personnel: Bill Blauvelt (Pub.); Joanne Freeman (Office Manager)
Parent company (for newspapers): Superior Publishing Company

KANSAS CITY RECORD

Street address 1: 14690 Parallel Rd
Street address city: Basehor
Street address state: KS
Zip/Postal code: 66007-3007
General Phone: (913) 362-1988
General/National Adv. E-mail: jon@recordnews.com
Editorial e-mail: news@recordnews.com
Year Established: 1888
Audit By: Sworn/Estimate/Non-Audited
Audit Date: 10.06.2019
Personnel: Jon Males (Pub)

KINGMAN LEADER-COURIER

Street address 1: 140 N Main St
Street address city: Kingman
Street address state: KS
Zip/Postal code: 67068-1301
General Phone: (620) 532-3151
General Fax: (620) 532-3152
General/National Adv. E-mail: advertise@kcnonline.com
Display Adv. E-mail: iarensdorf@kcnonline.com
Editorial e-mail: jjump@kcnonline.com
Primary Website: kcnonline.com
Year Established: 1878
Avg Paid Circ: 2400
Avg Free Circ: 50
Audit By: Sworn/Estimate/Non-Audited
Audit Date: 10.06.2019
Personnel: Jason Jump (Pub.); Irene Arensdorf (Sub.); Stephanie Jump (Bus. Mgr.); Bob Morris (Education and Sports Ed.)

KIOWA COUNTY SIGNAL

Street address 1: 320 S Main St
Street address city: Pratt
Street address state: KS
Zip/Postal code: 67124-2706
General Phone: (620) 723-2115
General Fax: (620) 723-1031
Advertising Phone: (620) 672-5511
Editorial Phone: (620) 672-5511
General/National Adv. E-mail: cnemec@pratttribune.com
Editorial e-mail: jguy@kiowacountysignal.com
Primary Website: kiowacountysignal.com
Year Established: 1886
Avg Free Circ: 900
Audit By: Sworn/Estimate/Non-Audited
Audit Date: 10.06.2019
Personnel: Jennifer Stultz (Ed.); Dena Sattler (Pub.); Kim Smith (Adv.); Shannon Briles (Circ. Mgr.)
Parent company (for newspapers): CherryRoad Media; CherryRoad Media

LABETTE AVENUE

Street address 1: 711 4th St
Street address city: Oswego
Street address state: KS
Zip/Postal code: 67356-1601
General Phone: (620) 795-2550
General Fax: (620) 795-4712
Advertising Phone: (800) 592-7606
General/National Adv. E-mail: adv@taylornews.org
Display Adv. E-mail: adv@taylornews.org
Editorial e-mail: labetteavenue@taylornews.org
Primary Website: taylornews.org
Year Established: 1879
Avg Paid Circ: 1865
Avg Free Circ: 24
Audit By: Sworn/Estimate/Non-Audited
Audit Date: 10.06.2019
Personnel: Rudy Taylor (Co-Pub.); Kathy Taylor (Co-Pub.); Emalee Mikel (Adv. Dir.); Rena Russell (Ed.)
Parent company (for newspapers): Taylor Newspapers

LEDGER (MOUNDRIDGE)

Street address 1: 107 S Christian Ave
Street address city: Moundridge
Street address state: KS
Zip/Postal code: 67107-9000
General Phone: (620) 345-6353
General Fax: (620) 345-2170
General/National Adv. E-mail: ads@hesstonrecord.com
Editorial e-mail: ledge@mtelco.net
Primary Website: ledgernewspaper.net
Audit By: Sworn/Estimate/Non-Audited
Audit Date: 10.06.2019
Personnel: Randy Frogg (Ed)

LINCOLN SENTINEL-REPUBLICAN

Street address 1: 141 W Lincoln Ave
Street address city: Lincoln

Street address state: KS
Zip/Postal code: 67455-1917
General Phone: (785) 524-4200
General Fax: (785) 524-4242
General/National Adv. E-mail: lincolnksads@gmail.com
Editorial e-mail: johnbaetz@gmail.com
Primary Website: lincolnsentinel.com
Avg Paid Circ: 1750
Avg Free Circ: 1750
Audit By: Sworn/Estimate/Non-Audited
Audit Date: 10.06.2019
Personnel: Bree McReynolds Baetz (Co-Owner); John Baetz (Co-Pub.)

LINN-PALMER RECORD

Street address 1: 405 2nd St
Street address city: Linn
Street address state: KS
Zip/Postal code: 66953-9562
General Phone: (785) 348-5581
General Fax: (785) 348-5549
General/National Adv. E-mail: lpr@bluevalley.net
Editorial e-mail: editor@bluevalley.net
Year Established: 1891
Avg Paid Circ: 700
Avg Free Circ: 13
Audit By: Sworn/Estimate/Non-Audited
Audit Date: 10.06.2019
Personnel: Lorene Rieth (Linn Ed)

LOS TIEMPOS

Street address 1: 16 S Kansas Ave
Street address city: Liberal
Street address state: KS
Zip/Postal code: 67901-3732
General Phone: (620) 624-2541
General Fax: (620) 624-0735
General/National Adv. E-mail: ads@swdtimes.com
Primary Website: facebook.com/pages/Los-Tiempos/174782409548429
Avg Free Circ: 8500
Audit By: Sworn/Estimate/Non-Audited
Audit Date: 10.06.2019
Personnel: Larry Reynolds (Pub.); Tammy Garth (Bus. Mgr.); James Gutzmer (Mng. Ed.)

LUCAS-SYLVAN NEWS

Street address 1: 203 S Main St
Street address city: Lucas
Street address state: KS
Zip/Postal code: 67648-9718
General Phone: (785) 525-6355
General Fax: (785) 525-6356
General/National Adv. E-mail: lusynews@gmail.com
Primary Website: lucas-sylvan-news.com
Year Established: 1899
Avg Paid Circ: 675
Audit By: Sworn/Estimate/Non-Audited
Audit Date: 10.06.2019
Personnel: LaRee Bretz (Ed.); Rita Sharp (Owner/Publisher)

MANHATTAN FREE PRESS

Street address 1: 313 Spruce
Street address city: Wamego
Street address state: KS
Zip/Postal code: 66547
General Phone: (785) 556-1694
Advertising Phone: (785) 556-1694
General/National Adv. E-mail: freepress@kansas.net
Primary Website: manhattanfreepress.com
Year Established: 1991
Audit By: Sworn/Estimate/Non-Audited
Audit Date: 10.06.2019
Personnel: Jon Brake (Co-Pub); Linda Brake (Co-Pub)

MARION COUNTY RECORD

Street address 1: 117 S 3rd St
Street address city: Marion
Street address state: KS
Zip/Postal code: 66861-1621
General Phone: (620) 382-2165
General Fax: (620) 382-2262
General/National Adv. E-mail: record@MarionCountyRecord.com
Display Adv. E-mail: advertising@MarionCountyRecord.com
Classified Adv. e-mail: classified@MarionCountyRecord.com
Editorial e-mail: news@MarionCountyRecord.com
Primary Website: MarionCountyRecord.com
Mthly Avg Views: 15754656
Mthly Avg Unique Visitors: 73531
Year Established: 1869
Avg Paid Circ: 4721
Avg Free Circ: 212
Audit By: USPS
Audit Date: 25.09.2024
Personnel: Eric Meyer (Editor and publisher); Debra Steele (Sales Manager); Pat Wick (Columnist)
Parent company (for newspapers): Hoch Publishing Co. Inc.

MARYSVILLE ADVOCATE

Street address 1: 107 S 9th St
Street address city: Marysville
Street address state: KS
Zip/Postal code: 66508-1825
General Phone: (785) 562-2317
General Fax: (785) 562-5589
Advertising Phone: (785) 562-2317
Advertising Fax: (785) 562-5589
Editorial Phone: (785) 562-2317
Editorial Fax: (785) 562-5589
General/National Adv. E-mail: skessinger@marysvilleonline.net
Display Adv. E-mail: wkruse@marysvilleonline.net
Classified Adv. e-mail: mkeller@marysvilleonline.net
Editorial e-mail: skessinger@marysvilleonline.net
Primary Website: marysvilleonline.net
Year Established: 1885
Avg Paid Circ: 3000
Avg Free Circ: 100
Audit By: Sworn/Estimate/Non-Audited
Audit Date: 10.06.2022
Personnel: Sharon Kessinger (Editor emeritus); Sarah Kessinger (Editor, publisher, owner); Sally Gray (News editor); Julie Perry (Sports writer); Mandy Keller (Ad sales); Wayne Kruse (Advertising director); Kelsey Smith (Obituary writer, public notices); Paul Kessinger (Reporter); JoAnn Shum (reporter); Chris Pannbacker (Reporter); Audrey Plisl (Circulation manager); Angela Schmale (Circulation manager, business office)
Parent company (for newspapers): Advocate Publishing Co.

MEADE COUNTY NEWS

Street address 1: 105 S Fowler St
Street address city: Meade
Street address state: KS
Zip/Postal code: 67864-6404
General Phone: (620) 873-2118
General Fax: (620) 873-5456
General/National Adv. E-mail: mcnews@mcnewsonline.com
Editorial e-mail: mcnews@mcnewsonline.com
Primary Website: mcnewsonline.com
Year Established: 1885
Avg Paid Circ: 1300
Audit By: Sworn/Estimate/Non-Audited
Audit Date: 10.06.2019
Personnel: Denise Kuhns (Ed.)

MERCHANT'S DIRECTORY

Street address 1: 318 E. KINGMAN AVE
Street address city: Mullinville
Street address state: KS
Zip/Postal code: 67109-7116
General Phone: (620) 548-2678
General Fax: (620) 548-2638
General/National Adv. E-mail: merchantsdirectory@yahoo.com
Primary Website: facebook.com/merchantsdirectory
Year Established: 1969
Avg Paid Circ: 390
Avg Free Circ: 10
Audit By: Sworn/Estimate/Non-Audited
Audit Date: 10.06.2019
Personnel: Paul Kendall (Ed.)

MINNEAPOLIS MESSENGER

Street address 1: 108 N Concord St
Street address city: Minneapolis
Street address state: KS
Zip/Postal code: 67467-2320
General Phone: (785) 392-2129
General Fax: (785) 392-2026
General/National Adv. E-mail: submit@mymessengerks.com
Editorial e-mail: submit@mymessengerks.com
Primary Website: facebook.com/pg/MyMessengerKS
Avg Paid Circ: 2300
Avg Free Circ: 33
Audit By: Sworn/Estimate/Non-Audited
Audit Date: 10.06.2019
Personnel: Jason Parks (Pub/Ed); Erik Shupe (Pub/Ed)

MONITOR-JOURNAL

Street address 1: 270 Main St
Street address city: Little River
Street address state: KS
Zip/Postal code: 67457-9072
General Phone: (620) 897-6234
General Fax: (620) 897-6287
General/National Adv. E-mail: themonitor@lrmutual.com
Display Adv. E-mail: themonitor@lrmutual.com
Editorial e-mail: themonitor@lrmutual.com
Year Established: 1886
Avg Paid Circ: 400
Audit By: Sworn/Estimate/Non-Audited
Audit Date: 10.06.2019
Personnel: Denice Dater (Co-Pub); Greg Dater (Co-Pub)

MONTGOMERY COUNTY CHRONICLE

Street address 1: 202 W 4th Ave
Street address city: Caney
Street address state: KS
Zip/Postal code: 67333-1462
General Phone: (620) 879-2156
General Fax: (620) 879-2855
General/National Adv. E-mail: adv@taylornews.org
Display Adv. E-mail: adv@taylornews.org
Editorial e-mail: chronicle@taylornews.org
Primary Website: taylornews.org
Audit By: Sworn/Estimate/Non-Audited
Audit Date: 10.06.2019
Personnel: Rudy Taylor; Kathy Taylor; Andy Taylor (Ed)
Parent company (for newspapers): Taylor Newspapers

NATOMA LURAY INDEPENDENT

Street address 1: 120 N Main St
Street address city: Natoma
Street address state: KS
Zip/Postal code: 67651-9731
General Phone: (785) 885-4582
General Fax: (785) 885-4582
General/National Adv. E-mail: natomanews@ruraltel.net
Primary Website: mainstreetmedia.us
Avg Paid Circ: 6000
Avg Free Circ: 54
Audit By: Sworn/Estimate/Non-Audited
Audit Date: 10.06.2019
Personnel: Jack Krier (Pub.); Della Richmond (Ed.)
Parent company (for newspapers): Main Street Media, Inc.

NEODESHA DERRICK

Street address 1: 502 Main St
Street address city: Neodesha
Street address state: KS
Zip/Postal code: 66757-1739
General Phone: (620) 325-3000
General Fax: (620) 325-2880
General/National Adv. E-mail: thederrick@cableone.net
Primary Website: shopthederrick.com
Avg Paid Circ: 1800
Avg Free Circ: 99
Audit By: Sworn/Estimate/Non-Audited
Audit Date: 10.06.2019
Personnel: Dee Anne Tigner (Adv. Mgr.); Jo Anne Hartley Harper (Ed.)

NESS COUNTY NEWS

Street address 1: 110 S Kansas Ave
Street address city: Ness City
Street address state: KS
Zip/Postal code: 67560-1814
General Phone: (785) 798-2213
General Fax: (785) 798-2214
General/National Adv. E-mail: nessnews@gbta.net
Primary Website: facebook.com/pages/Ness-County-News/147247601986003
Avg Paid Circ: 2200
Avg Free Circ: 48
Audit By: Sworn/Estimate/Non-Audited
Audit Date: 10.06.2019
Personnel: Jerry Clarke (Ed.)

NEWSLEAF

Street address 1: 417 MAIN ST
Street address city: Effingham
Street address state: KS
Zip/Postal code: 66023
General Phone: (913) 833-4180
General Fax: (267) 295-8020
General/National Adv. E-mail: cap@thenewsleaf.com
Primary Website: thenewsleaf.com
Audit By: Sworn/Estimate/Non-Audited
Audit Date: 10.06.2019
Personnel: Steve Caplinger (Pub)

NINNESCAH VALLEY NEWS

Street address 1: 201 S Maple St
Street address city: Pretty Prairie
Street address state: KS
Zip/Postal code: 67570-8619
General Phone: (620) 459-6322
General Fax: (620) 459-6729
Advertising Phone: (620) 459-6322
Advertising Fax: (620) 459-6729
Editorial Phone: (620) 459-6322
Editorial Fax: (620) 459-6729
General/National Adv. E-mail: nvn@embarqmail.com
Display Adv. E-mail: nvn@embarqmail.com
Editorial e-mail: nvn@embarqmail.com
Primary Website: facebook.com/pages/Ninnescah-Valley-News/142191375827044
Audit By: Sworn/Estimate/Non-Audited
Audit Date: 10.06.2019
Personnel: Nancy Stucky (Pub.)

NORWICH NEWS

Street address 1: 215 S 8th St
Street address city: Conway Springs
Street address state: KS
Zip/Postal code: 67031-8817
General Phone: (620) 456-2232
General Fax: (620) 456-2432
General/National Adv. E-mail: ajprinting@havilandtelco.com
Editorial e-mail: ajprinting@havilandtelco.com
Audit By: Sworn/Estimate/Non-Audited
Audit Date: 10.06.2019
Personnel: A.J. Bozarth (Pub/Ed)

OBERLIN HERALD, THE

Street address 1: 170 S Penn Ave
Street address city: Oberlin
Street address state: KS
Zip/Postal code: 67749-2243
General Phone: (785) 475-2206
General Fax: (785) 475-2800
General/National Adv. E-mail: oberlin.ads@nwkansas.com
Display Adv. E-mail: oberlin.ads@nwkansas.com
Editorial e-mail: oberlin.editor@nwkansas.com
Primary Website: nwkansas.com
Year Established: 1879
Avg Paid Circ: 1724
Avg Free Circ: 91
Audit By: Sworn/Estimate/Non-Audited
Audit Date: 10.06.2019
Personnel: Steve Haynes (Ed.); Kimberly Davis (Gen. Mng)
Parent company (for newspapers): Haynes Publishing Co.

ONAGA HERALD

Street address 1: 302 Leonard St
Street address city: Onaga
Street address state: KS
Zip/Postal code: 66521-9484
General Phone: (785) 889-4681
General/National Adv. E-mail: oherald@bluevalley.net
Editorial e-mail: oherald@bluevalley.net

Primary Website: facebook.com/pages/The-Onaga-Herald/105298976204089
Audit By: Sworn/Estimate/Non-Audited
Audit Date: 10.06.2019
Personnel: Joe Harder (Pub.)

OSBORNE COUNTY FARMER

Street address 1: 210 W Main St
Street address city: Osborne
Street address state: KS
Zip/Postal code: 67473-2405
General Phone: (785) 346-5424
General Fax: (785) 346-5400
General/National Adv. E-mail: ospubco@ruraltel.net
Primary Website: mainstreetmedia.us
Year Established: 1872
Avg Paid Circ: 2500
Avg Free Circ: 100
Audit By: Sworn/Estimate/Non-Audited
Audit Date: 10.06.2019
Personnel: Jack Krier (Pub.); Stephanie Baxa (Ed.)
Parent company (for newspapers): Main Street Media, Inc.

OSKALOOSA INDEPENDENT

Street address 1: 607 Delaware St
Street address city: Oskaloosa
Street address state: KS
Zip/Postal code: 66066-5431
General Phone: (785) 863-2520
General Fax: (785) 863-2730
General/National Adv. E-mail: independent@centurylink.net
Display Adv. E-mail: independent@centurylink.net
Editorial e-mail: independent@centurylink.net
Primary Website: jeffcountynews.com
Year Established: 1860
Avg Paid Circ: 1530
Avg Free Circ: 29
Audit By: Sworn/Estimate/Non-Audited
Audit Date: 10.06.2019
Personnel: Clarke Davis (Pub.); Corey Davis (Prodn. Mgr.); Rick Nichols (Ed.)
Parent company (for newspapers): Davis Publications Inc.

PEABODY GAZETTE-BULLETIN

Street address 1: 113 N Walnut St
Street address city: Peabody
Street address state: KS
Zip/Postal code: 66866-1059
General Phone: (620) 382-2165
General Fax: (620) 983-2700
General/National Adv. E-mail: advertising@peabodykansas.com
Display Adv. E-mail: classified@peabodykansas.com
Editorial e-mail: news@peabodykansas.com
Primary Website: peabodykansas.com
Avg Paid Circ: 1400
Avg Free Circ: 9
Audit By: Sworn/Estimate/Non-Audited
Audit Date: 10.06.2019
Personnel: Debra Steele (Adv. Mgr.); Jean Stuchlik (Circ. Mgr.); Susan Marshall (Ed.)
Parent company (for newspapers): Hoch Publishing Co. Inc.

PHILLIPS COUNTY REVIEW

Street address 1: 683 3rd St
Street address city: Phillipsburg
Street address state: KS
Zip/Postal code: 67661-2138
General Phone: (785) 543-5242
General Fax: (785) 543-5243
General/National Adv. E-mail: pcreview@mainstreetmedia.us
Editorial e-mail: news@phillipscountyreview.com
Primary Website: phillipscountyreview.com
Year Established: 1889
Avg Paid Circ: 2000
Audit By: Sworn/Estimate/Non-Audited
Audit Date: 10.06.2019
Personnel: Kirby Ross (Ed.); Irene Allen (Page Design); Ronda Hueneke (Adv. Sales)
Parent company (for newspapers): Main Street Media, Inc.

PLAINVILLE TIMES

Street address 1: PO Box 40
Street address 2: 400 W Mill St
Street address city: Plainville
Street address state: KS
Zip/Postal code: 67663-0040
General Phone: (785) 434-4525
General Fax: (785) 434-2527
General/National Adv. E-mail: pvtimes@ruraltel.net
Primary Website: mainstreetmedia.us
Avg Paid Circ: 1200
Avg Free Circ: 40
Audit By: Sworn/Estimate/Non-Audited
Audit Date: 10.06.2019
Personnel: Frank Mercer (Pub.); Janice Bendick (Adv. Mgr. Office Mgr); Candace Rachel (Ed.)
Parent company (for newspapers): Main Street Media, Inc.

PRAIRIE STAR

Street address 1: 226 E Main St
Street address city: Sedan
Street address state: KS
Zip/Postal code: 67361-1629
General Phone: (620) 725-3176
General Fax: (620) 725-3272
General/National Adv. E-mail: adv@taylornews.org
Display Adv. E-mail: adv@taylornews.org
Editorial e-mail: taylornews@taylornews.org
Primary Website: taylornews.org
Year Established: 1870
Avg Paid Circ: 1325
Avg Free Circ: 25
Audit By: Sworn/Estimate/Non-Audited
Audit Date: 10.06.2019
Personnel: Rudy Taylor (Mng. Ed.); Kathy Taylor; Jenny Diveley (Ed); Julie Beckley

PROTECTION PRESS

Street address 1: 301 N Broadway Ave
Street address city: Protection
Street address state: KS
Zip/Postal code: 67127
General Phone: (620) 622-4288
General Fax: (620) 622-4370
General/National Adv. E-mail: propress@unitedwireless.com
Display Adv. E-mail: ProPress@unitedwireless.com
Editorial e-mail: propress@unitedwireless.com
Year Established: 1986
Avg Paid Circ: 770
Avg Free Circ: 14
Audit By: Sworn/Estimate/Non-Audited
Audit Date: 10.06.2019
Personnel: Susan Edmonston (Ed.)

RILEY COUNTIAN

Street address 1: 207 S Broadway St
Street address city: Riley
Street address state: KS
Zip/Postal code: 66531-9559
General Phone: (785) 485-2290
General Fax: (785) 485-2290
General/National Adv. E-mail: countian@twinvalley.net
Primary Website: facebook.com/pg/The-Riley-Countian-155651394453413
Avg Paid Circ: 1200
Audit By: Sworn/Estimate/Non-Audited
Audit Date: 10.06.2019
Personnel: Donna Sullivan (Editor/Publisher); June Campbell (Office Manager)

RURAL MESSENGER

Street address 1: 115 S Kansas St
Street address city: Haven
Street address state: KS
Zip/Postal code: 67543-9261
General Phone: (620) 465-4636
General Fax: (620) 465-2309
Advertising Phone: (620) 465-4636
Advertising Fax: (620) 465-2309
Editorial Phone: (620) 465-4636
Editorial Fax: (620) 465-2309
General/National Adv. E-mail: anita@ruralmessenger.com
Display Adv. E-mail: anita@ruralmessenger.com
Classified Adv. e-mail: anita@ruralmessenger.com
Editorial e-mail: tammie@ruralmessenger.com
Primary Website: RuralMessenger.com
Mthly Avg Views: 36000
Mthly Avg Unique Visitors: 18000
Year Established: 2004
Avg Free Circ: 11000
Audit By: Sworn/Estimate/Non-Audited
Audit Date: 10.06.2019
Personnel: Mike Alfers (Pub); Anita Stuckey (Marketing Manager)

RUSH COUNTY NEWS

Street address 1: 112 W 8th St
Street address city: La Crosse
Street address state: KS
Zip/Postal code: 67548-9603
General Phone: (785) 222-2555
General Fax: (785) 222-2557
General/National Adv. E-mail: rcn@gbta.net
Editorial e-mail: rcn@gbta.net
Primary Website: facebook.com/pages/Rush-County-News/153454468030266
Year Established: 1941
Audit By: Sworn/Estimate/Non-Audited
Audit Date: 10.06.2019
Personnel: Mary Engel (Pub); Tim Engel (Ed)

SHAWNEE DISPATCH

Street address 1: 6301 Pflumm Rd
Street address 2: Ste 102
Street address city: Shawnee
Street address state: KS
Zip/Postal code: 66216-2497
General Phone: (913) 962-3000
General Fax: (913) 962-3004
Advertising Phone: (913) 962-3000
General/National Adv. E-mail: scantrell@ljworld.com
Display Adv. E-mail: smilgram@ljworld.com
Editorial e-mail: jkendall@shawneedispatch.com
Primary Website: shawneedispatch.com
Year Established: 2003
Avg Free Circ: 20108
Audit By: VAC
Audit Date: 31.12.2016
Personnel: Jason Kendall (Ed); Scott Stanford (Pub.); Mike Countryman; Ed Ciambrone (Circulation Manager); Kathleen Johnson (Advertising Manager)
Parent company (for newspapers): Lawrence Journal-World

SPEARVILLE NEWS

Street address 1: 400 N Main St
Street address city: Spearville
Street address state: KS
Zip/Postal code: 67876-9501
General Phone: (620) 385-2200
General Fax: (620) 385-2610
General/National Adv. E-mail: spnews@ucom.net
Display Adv. E-mail: spnews@ucom.net
Editorial e-mail: spnews@ucom.net
Primary Website: facebook.com/pages/Spearville-News-Inc/161631100525188
Year Established: 1899
Avg Paid Circ: 575
Avg Free Circ: 20
Audit By: Sworn/Estimate/Non-Audited
Audit Date: 10.06.2019
Personnel: Bruce Vierthaler (Pub.); Cynthia Vierthaler (Ed.)

SPRING HILL NEW ERA

Street address 1: 936 E Santa Fe St
Street address city: Gardner
Street address state: KS
Zip/Postal code: 66030-1549
General Phone: (913) 856-7615
General Fax: (913) 856-6707
General/National Adv. E-mail: submissions@gardnernews.com
Primary Website: gardnernews.com
Avg Paid Circ: 2000
Avg Free Circ: 10
Audit By: Sworn/Estimate/Non-Audited
Audit Date: 10.06.2019
Personnel: Rhonda Humble (Pub.); David Highfill (Adv. Mgr.); Michelle Whitaker (Circ. Mgr.); Mark Taylor (Ed.)

ST. FRANCIS HERALD

Street address 1: 310 W Washington St
Street address city: Saint Francis
Street address state: KS
Zip/Postal code: 67756-9606
General Phone: (785) 332-3162
General Fax: (785) 332-3001
General/National Adv. E-mail: sf.herald@nwkansas.com
Primary Website: nwkansas.com
Year Established: 1912
Avg Paid Circ: 1288
Avg Free Circ: 4
Audit By: Sworn/Estimate/Non-Audited
Audit Date: 10.06.2019
Personnel: Karen Krien (Publisher); Leslie McCormick (Circ. Mgr.)
Parent company (for newspapers): Haynes Publishing Co.

ST. JOHN NEWS

Street address 1: 320 S. Main St.
Street address 2: P.O. Box 909
Street address city: Pratt
Street address state: KS
Zip/Postal code: 97124
General Phone: (620) 672-5511
Primary Website: sjnewsonline.com
Year Established: 1878
Avg Paid Circ: 700
Avg Free Circ: 14
Audit By: Sworn/Estimate/Non-Audited
Audit Date: 10.06.2019
Personnel: Dena Sattler (Pub.)
Parent company (for newspapers): CherryRoad Media; CherryRoad Media

ST. MARYS STAR

Street address 1: 117 S 6th St
Street address city: Saint Marys
Street address state: KS
Zip/Postal code: 66536-1606
General Phone: (785) 437-2935
General Fax: (785) 437-2935
General/National Adv. E-mail: star@oct.net
Editorial e-mail: star@oct.net
Primary Website: thesmstar.com
Year Established: 1884
Avg Paid Circ: 1850
Audit By: Sworn/Estimate/Non-Audited
Audit Date: 10.06.2019
Personnel: Lori Hickey (Adv. Mgr.); Steven Tetlow (Pub./Gen. Mgr.)
Parent company (for newspapers): The White Corporation

STERLING BULLETIN

Street address 1: 107 N Broadway Ave
Street address city: Sterling
Street address state: KS
Zip/Postal code: 67579-2130
General Phone: (620) 278-2114
General Fax: (620) 278-2330
General/National Adv. E-mail: ads@sterlingbulletin.com
Display Adv. E-mail: ads@sterlingbulletin.com
Editorial e-mail: news@sterlingbulletin.com
Primary Website: sterlingbulletin.com
Year Established: 1876
Avg Paid Circ: 90
Avg Free Circ: 47
Audit By: Sworn/Estimate/Non-Audited
Audit Date: 10.06.2019
Personnel: Rene Wilson (Editor); Koni Hendricks (Advertising Director)

STOCKTON SENTINEL

Street address 1: 414 Main St
Street address city: Stockton
Street address state: KS
Zip/Postal code: 67669-1930
General Phone: (785) 425-6354
General Fax: (785) 425-7292
General/National Adv. E-mail: stkpaper@ruraltel.net

Editorial e-mail: stkpaper@ruraltel.net
Primary Website: stocktonsentinel.com
Year Established: 1989
Avg Paid Circ: 1851
Audit By: Sworn/Estimate/Non-Audited
Audit Date: 10.06.2019
Personnel: Bob Hamilton (Pub); Deb Dix (News Ed); Virginia Laska (Editorial Writer)

TELEGRAPH

Street address 1: 113 Commercial St
Street address city: Waterville
Street address state: KS
Zip/Postal code: 66548
General Phone: (785) 363-2061
General Fax: (785) 363-2075
General/National Adv. E-mail: telegraph@bluevalley.net
Primary Website: facebook.com/pages/The-Telegraph/146721058690272
Avg Paid Circ: 750
Avg Free Circ: 5
Audit By: Sworn/Estimate/Non-Audited
Audit Date: 10.06.2019
Personnel: Donald H. King (Ed.)

THE BELLE PLAINE NEWS

Street address 1: 402 N. Merchant
Street address 2: P.O. Box 128
Street address city: Belle Plaine
Street address state: KS
Zip/Postal code: 67013-9117
General Phone: (620) 488-2234
General/National Adv. E-mail: newsbelleplaine@gmail.com
Display Adv. E-mail: newsbelleplaine@gmail.com
Editorial e-mail: newsbelleplaine@gmail.com
Primary Website: BellePlaineNews.com
Avg Paid Circ: 500
Avg Free Circ: 48
Audit By: Sworn/Estimate/Non-Audited
Audit Date: 10.06.2019
Personnel: Bill Rhiley (Publisher)
Parent company (for newspapers): Main Street Publishing LLC

THE BELLE PLAINE NEWS & THE OXFORD REGISTER

Street address 1: 217 W 5th Ave
Street address city: Belle Plaine
Street address state: KS
Zip/Postal code: 67013-9117
General Phone: (620) 488-2234
General/National Adv. E-mail: newsbelleplaine@gmail.com
Display Adv. E-mail: newsbelleplaine@gmail.com
Editorial e-mail: newsbelleplaine@gmail.com
Year Established: 1879
Avg Paid Circ: 500
Avg Free Circ: 24
Audit By: Sworn/Estimate/Non-Audited
Audit Date: 10.06.2019
Personnel: Bill Rhiley (Publisher)
Parent company (for newspapers): Main Street Publishing LLC

THE BELLEVILLE TELESCOPE

Street address 1: 1805 N St
Street address city: Belleville
Street address state: KS
Zip/Postal code: 66935-2247
General Phone: (785) 527-2244
General Fax: (785) 527-2225
General/National Adv. E-mail: susanism2@yahoo.com
Display Adv. E-mail: susanism2@yahoo.com
Editorial e-mail: dhadachek@gmail.com
Primary Website: thebellevilletelescope.com
Avg Paid Circ: 3500
Audit By: Sworn/Estimate/Non-Audited
Audit Date: 10.06.2019
Personnel: Fred Arnold (Pub.); Deb Hadachek (Ed.); Susan Bartels (Adv Dir)

THE BUTLER COUNTY TIMES-GAZETTE

Street address 1: 204 E 5th Ave
Street address city: Augusta
Street address state: KS
Zip/Postal code: 67010-1012
General Phone: (316) 321-1120
General Fax: (316) 775-3220
Advertising Phone: (316) 321-1120
Advertising Fax: (316) 775-3220
Editorial Phone: (316) 321-1120
Editorial Fax: (316) 321-7722
General/National Adv. E-mail: awickwire@butlercountytimesgazette.com
Display Adv. E-mail: awickwire@butlercountytimesgazette.com
Classified Adv. e-mail: kadams@butlercountytimesgazette.com
Editorial e-mail: jclements@butlercountytimesgazette.com
Primary Website: butlercountytimesgazette.com
Year Established: 1902
Avg Paid Circ: 2247
Audit By: Sworn/Estimate/Non-Audited
Audit Date: 10.06.2019
Personnel: Cristina Janney (Pub.); Michelle Griffith (Business Mgr.); Julie Clements (Managing Ed.); Belinda Larsen (Augusta City Ed.); Jeremy Costello (Sports Ed.); April Wickwire (Adv. Coord.); Amy Motter (Adv. Exec.); Jennifer Wilson (Adv. Exec.); Kim Lucas (Classifieds Adv.); Rhonda Zinn (Legal Adv.); Lori Sibley (Circ. Mgr.); Levi Yager (El Dorado City Ed.)
Parent company (for newspapers): CherryRoad Media

THE CLARION

Street address 1: 314 N Main St
Street address city: Andale
Street address state: KS
Zip/Postal code: 67001-9700
General Phone: (316) 445-2444
General Fax: (316) 445-2446
Advertising Phone: (316) 712-2125
Editorial Phone: (316) 712-2125
General/National Adv. E-mail: marketingdesk@clarionpaper.com
Display Adv. E-mail: joey@kspublishingventures.com
Editorial e-mail: editor@clarionpaper.com
Primary Website: clarionpaper.com
Avg Paid Circ: 1500
Audit By: Sworn/Estimate/Non-Audited
Audit Date: 10.06.2019
Personnel: Joey Young (Pub & Owner); Lindsey Young (Mng Ed)
Parent company (for newspapers): Kansas Publishing Ventures

THE COURIER-TRIBUNE

Street address 1: 512 Main St
Street address city: Seneca
Street address state: KS
Zip/Postal code: 66538-1928
General Phone: (785) 336-2175
General Fax: (785) 336-3475
General/National Adv. E-mail: ctseneca@nvcs.com
Editorial e-mail: ctseneca@nvcs.com
Primary Website: couriertribuneonline.com
Year Established: 1863
Avg Paid Circ: 3100
Avg Free Circ: 1800
Audit By: Sworn/Estimate/Non-Audited
Audit Date: 10.06.2019
Personnel: Dan Diehl (Pub.); Matt Diehl (Mng. Ed.); Kylee Luckeroth (Ad Director)

THE DIGHTON HERALD

Street address 1: 113 E Long St
Street address city: Dighton
Street address state: KS
Zip/Postal code: 67839
General Phone: (620) 397-5347
General/National Adv. E-mail: dherald@st-tel.net
Editorial e-mail: dherald@st-tel.net
Year Established: 1885
Avg Paid Circ: 1000
Audit By: Sworn/Estimate/Non-Audited
Audit Date: 10.06.2019
Personnel: Jerry Anderson (Pub.); Mary Hartman (Ed.)

THE ELLIS REVIEW

Street address 1: 1020 Washington St
Street address city: Ellis
Street address state: KS
Zip/Postal code: 67637-2221
General Phone: (785) 726-4583
General Fax: (785) 726-3821
General/National Adv. E-mail: review@gbta.net
Primary Website: mainstreetmedia.us
Year Established: 1880
Avg Paid Circ: 1130
Avg Free Circ: 32
Audit By: Sworn/Estimate/Non-Audited
Audit Date: 10.06.2019
Personnel: Nickole Byers (Ed.); Frank Mercer (Publisher); Jack Krier (Pub.)
Parent company (for newspapers): Main Street Media, Inc.

THE ELLSWORTH COUNTY INDEPENDENT-REPORTER

Street address 1: 304 N Douglas Ave
Street address city: Ellsworth
Street address state: KS
Zip/Postal code: 67439-3218
General Phone: (785) 472-5085
General Fax: (785) 472-5087
Advertising Phone: (785) 472-5085
General/National Adv. E-mail: eciads@eaglecom.net
Display Adv. E-mail: eciads@eaglecom.net
Editorial e-mail: indy@eaglecom.net
Primary Website: indyrepnews.com
Year Established: 1999
Avg Paid Circ: 2700
Avg Free Circ: 45
Audit By: Sworn/Estimate/Non-Audited
Audit Date: 10.06.2019
Personnel: Linda Mowery-Denning (Pub/Ed); Juanita Kepka (Bus. Mgr.)
Parent company (for newspapers): Morris Multimedia, Inc.

THE EUREKA HERALD

Street address 1: 822 E River St
Street address 2: Ste 100
Street address city: Eureka
Street address state: KS
Zip/Postal code: 67045-2132
General Phone: (620) 583-5721
General Fax: (620) 583-5922
General/National Adv. E-mail: news@eurekaherald.com
Editorial e-mail: news@eurekaherald.com
Primary Website: eurekaherald.com
Year Established: 1868
Avg Paid Circ: 2300
Avg Free Circ: 40
Audit By: Sworn/Estimate/Non-Audited
Audit Date: 10.06.2019
Personnel: Rachel Clasen (Pub); Robin Wunderlich (Ed)

THE GYP HILL PREMIERE

Street address 1: 108 N Main St
Street address city: Medicine Lodge
Street address state: KS
Zip/Postal code: 67104-1317
General Phone: (620) 886-5654
General Fax: (620) 886-5617
General/National Adv. E-mail: rnoland@cyberlodg.com
Display Adv. E-mail: rnoland@cyberlodg.com
Editorial e-mail: doris@medicinelodge.com
Primary Website: gyphillpremiere.com
Avg Paid Circ: 1200
Audit By: Sworn/Estimate/Non-Audited
Audit Date: 10.06.2019
Personnel: Kevin J. Noland (Pub.); Ronda D. Noland (Adv. Mgr.); Doris Sorg (Ed.)

THE HASKELL COUNTY MONITOR-CHIEF

Street address 1: 114 S. Inman St.
Street address city: Sublette
Street address state: KS
Zip/Postal code: 67877
General Phone: (620) 675-2204
General Fax: (620) 675-2204
General/National Adv. E-mail: monitorchief27@att.net
Editorial e-mail: monitorchief27@att.net
Year Established: 1891
Avg Paid Circ: 800
Audit By: Sworn/Estimate/Non-Audited
Audit Date: 10.06.2019
Personnel: Mark Anderson (Pub.)
Parent company (for newspapers): Golden Plains Publishing

THE HERINGTON TIMES

Street address 1: 106 N Broadway
Street address city: Herington
Street address state: KS
Zip/Postal code: 67449-2225
General Phone: (785) 366-6186
General Fax: (316) 445-2446
General/National Adv. E-mail: ads@heringtontimes.com
Display Adv. E-mail: ads@heringtontimes.com
Editorial e-mail: editor@heringtontimes.com
Primary Website: heringtontimes.com
Year Established: 1889
Avg Paid Circ: 800
Avg Free Circ: 50
Audit By: Sworn/Estimate/Non-Audited
Audit Date: 10.06.2019
Personnel: Kristi Lovett (Ed.)
Parent company (for newspapers): Kansas Publishing Ventures

THE HILL CITY TIMES

Street address 1: 110 N Pomeroy Ave
Street address city: Hill City
Street address state: KS
Zip/Postal code: 67642-1870
General Phone: (785) 421-5700
General Fax: (785) 421-5712
General/National Adv. E-mail: times@ruraltel.net
Editorial e-mail: times@ruraltel.net
Avg Paid Circ: 1400
Avg Free Circ: 10
Audit By: Sworn/Estimate/Non-Audited
Audit Date: 30.09.2021
Personnel: James Logback (Ed.); Diane Boyd (Associate Editor); SUZIE MCDOWELL (Associate Editor)

THE HOLTON RECORDER

Street address 1: 109 W 4th St
Street address city: Holton
Street address state: KS
Zip/Postal code: 66436-1701
General Phone: (785) 364-3141
General Fax: (785) 364-3422
General/National Adv. E-mail: holtonrecorder@embarqmail.com
Editorial e-mail: holtonrecorder@embarqmail.com
Primary Website: holtonrecorder.net
Year Established: 1867
Avg Paid Circ: 4200
Avg Free Circ: 2700
Audit By: Sworn/Estimate/Non-Audited
Audit Date: 10.06.2019
Personnel: Connie Powls (Co-Owner); David M. Powls (Ed.); Allen Bowser (Prodn. Mgr.)

THE HUGOTON HERMES

Street address 1: 522 S Main St
Street address city: Hugoton
Street address state: KS
Zip/Postal code: 67951-2428
General Phone: (620) 544-4321
General Fax: (620) 544-7321
General/National Adv. E-mail: hermes10@pld.com
Display Adv. E-mail: hermes10@pld.com
Editorial e-mail: hermesro@pld.com
Primary Website: hugotonhermes.com
Year Established: 1887
Avg Paid Circ: 1600
Audit By: Sworn/Estimate/Non-Audited
Audit Date: 10.06.2019
Personnel: RoGlenda Coulter (Co-Owner); Kay McDaniels (Co-Owner); Ruthie Winget (Co-Owner)

THE KANSAS CHIEF

Street address 1: 317 E Saint Joseph St
Street address city: Wathena
Street address state: KS
Zip/Postal code: 66090-1204
General Phone: (785) 989-4415
General Fax: (785) 989-4416
General/National Adv. E-mail: Kschief@carsoncomm.com

Primary Website: NA
Year Established: 1857
Avg Paid Circ: 2050
Avg Free Circ: 25
Audit By: Sworn/Estimate/Non-Audited
Audit Date: 10.06.2019
Personnel: Lori Vertin (Circ. Mgr.); Dana Foley (Ed.)

THE KIOWA NEWS

Street address 1: 614 Main St
Street address city: Kiowa
Street address state: KS
Zip/Postal code: 67070-1414
General Phone: (620) 825-4229
General Fax: (620) 825-4229
General/National Adv. E-mail: kionews@sctelcom.net
Editorial e-mail: kionews@sctelcom.net
Primary Website: kiowanews.com
Year Established: 1893
Avg Paid Circ: 1250
Avg Free Circ: 34
Audit By: Sworn/Estimate/Non-Audited
Audit Date: 10.06.2019
Personnel: Rex Zimmerman (Ed.)

THE LAKIN INDEPENDENT

Street address 1: 118 N Main St
Street address city: Lakin
Street address state: KS
Zip/Postal code: 67860-9474
General Phone: (620) 355-6162
General Fax: (620) 355-6300
Advertising Phone: (620) 355-6162
Advertising Fax: (620) 355-6162
Editorial Phone: (620) 355-6162
Editorial Fax: 620-355-6162
General/National Adv. E-mail: indpndt@pld.com
Display Adv. E-mail: indpndt@pld.com
Editorial e-mail: indpndt@pld.com
Year Established: 1885
Avg Paid Circ: 1450
Audit By: Sworn/Estimate/Non-Audited
Audit Date: 10.06.2019
Personnel: Kathy McVey (Ed.)

THE LEDGER

Street address 1: 105 N Main St
Street address city: Hesston
Street address state: KS
Zip/Postal code: 67062-9143
General Phone: (620) 327-4831
General Fax: (620) 345-2170
Advertising Phone: (863) 802-7400
Editorial Phone: (863) 802-7504
General/National Adv. E-mail: ledg@mtelco.net
Display Adv. E-mail: classifieds@theledger.com
Editorial e-mail: lenore.devore@theledger.com
Primary Website: ledgernewspaper.com
Avg Paid Circ: 1300
Audit By: Sworn/Estimate/Non-Audited
Audit Date: 10.06.2019
Personnel: Lenore Devore (Ed.)

THE LEGAL RECORD

Street address 1: 1701 E Cedar St
Street address 2: Ste 111
Street address city: Olathe
Street address state: KS
Zip/Postal code: 66062-1775
General Phone: (913) 780-5790
General Fax: (913) 780-5747
General/National Adv. E-mail: dvalenti@thelegalrecord.net
Display Adv. E-mail: dvalenti@thelegalrecord.net
Editorial e-mail: dvalenti@thelegalrecord.net
Primary Website: thelegalrecord.net
Audit By: Sworn/Estimate/Non-Audited
Personnel: John Lewis (Pub.); Emily Campbell (Ed.); Debra Valenti; Debra Valenti
Parent company (for newspapers): Lewis Legal News, Inc.; Lewis Legal News, Inc.

THE LEOTI STANDARD

Street address 1: 114 S 4th St
Street address city: Leoti
Street address state: KS
Zip/Postal code: 67861-7032
General Phone: (620) 375-2631
General/National Adv. E-mail: standard@fairpoint.net
Avg Paid Circ: 1000
Avg Free Circ: 30
Audit By: Sworn/Estimate/Non-Audited
Audit Date: 10.06.2019
Personnel: Mark Anderson (Pub.); Shonda Taylor (Editor)
Parent company (for newspapers): Golden Plains Publishing

THE LINDSBORG NEWS-RECORD

Street address 1: 114 S Main St
Street address city: Lindsborg
Street address state: KS
Zip/Postal code: 67456-2418
General Phone: (785) 227-3348
General Fax: (785) 227-3740
General/National Adv. E-mail: frontdesk@lindsborgnewsrecord.com
Display Adv. E-mail: kathy@lindsborgnewsrecord.com
Classified Adv. e-mail: frontdesk@lindsborgnewsrecord.com
Editorial e-mail: lnreditor@mainstreetmedia.us
Primary Website: mainstreetmedia.us
Year Established: 1881
Avg Paid Circ: 812
Audit By: USPS
Audit Date: 28.09.2022
Personnel: Kathy Lindsborg; Kathy George (Advertising Sales); Andrea Evans (Office Clerk); Angela Rider (Graphic Artist); Kelly Lindsborg; Allena McNichols (Editor/ Reporter)
Parent company (for newspapers): Main Street Media, Inc.

THE LINN COUNTY NEWS

Street address 1: 808 Main St
Street address city: Pleasanton
Street address state: KS
Zip/Postal code: 66075-4077
General Phone: (913) 352-6235
General Fax: (913) 352-6607
General/National Adv. E-mail: raquel@linncountynews.net
Display Adv. E-mail: lisa@linncountynews.net
Editorial e-mail: story@linncountynews.net
Primary Website: linncountynews.net
Avg Paid Circ: 2600
Audit By: Sworn/Estimate/Non-Audited
Audit Date: 10.06.2019
Personnel: Jacquelyn I. Taylor (Pub/Ed); Lisa Fort (Circ. Mgr.); Deb Cougill (Reporter)

THE LOGAN REPUBLICAN

Street address 1: 101 E Main St
Street address city: Logan
Street address state: KS
Zip/Postal code: 67646-5169
General Phone: (785) 689-4339
General Fax: (785) 689-4338
General/National Adv. E-mail: loganrep@ruraltel.net
Primary Website: facebook.com/pages/Logan-Republican/151744111503720
Avg Paid Circ: 1000
Audit By: Sworn/Estimate/Non-Audited
Audit Date: 10.06.2019
Personnel: John Sullivan (Ed.)

THE LYONS NEWS

Street address 1: 210 W Commercial St
Street address city: Lyons
Street address state: KS
Zip/Postal code: 67554-2716
General Phone: (620) 257-2368
General Fax: (620) 257-2369
General/National Adv. E-mail: advertising@ldn.kscoxmail.com
Display Adv. E-mail: advertising@ldn.kscoxmail.com
Editorial e-mail: admin@ldn.kscoxmail.com
Primary Website: midksnews.com
Year Established: 1906
Avg Paid Circ: 2321
Audit By: Sworn/Estimate/Non-Audited
Audit Date: 10.06.2019
Personnel: David Settle (Ed.); Anita Settle (Office Mgr./ Adv. Mgr.); John M. Settle (Pub.); Jennifer Renollet (Office Asst.); Debbie Peters (Distribution); Darla Graf (Office Asst,); Silver Ingram (Distribution); Ryan Carlson (Reporter); Mike Courson (Sports Reporter)
Parent company (for newspapers): Star Communications

THE MADISON NEWS

Street address 1: 225 W Main St
Street address 2: # 12
Street address city: Madison
Street address state: KS
Zip/Postal code: 66860-9569
General Phone: (620) 437-2433
General Fax: (620) 437-2433
General/National Adv. E-mail: madnews@madtel.net
Editorial e-mail: madnews@madtel.net
Primary Website: facebook.com/The-Madison-News-253840751628/
Avg Paid Circ: 850
Avg Free Circ: 15
Audit By: Sworn/Estimate/Non-Audited
Audit Date: 10.06.2019
Personnel: Tammy Seimears (Editor and Publisher); Patsy Murphy (Gen. Mgr.)

THE MARQUETTE TRIBUNE

Street address 1: 112 N Washington St
Street address city: Marquette
Street address state: KS
Zip/Postal code: 67464-4010
General Phone: (785) 546-2266
General Fax: (785) 546-2266
General/National Adv. E-mail: marquettetribune@eagalecom.net
Editorial e-mail: marquettetribune@eagalecom.net
Avg Paid Circ: 600
Audit By: Sworn/Estimate/Non-Audited
Audit Date: 10.06.2019
Personnel: Dori Weber (Ed.)
Parent company (for newspapers): Morris Multimedia, Inc.

THE MIAMI COUNTY REPUBLIC

Street address 1: 121 S Pearl St
Street address city: Paola
Street address state: KS
Zip/Postal code: 66071-1754
General Phone: (913) 294-2311
General Fax: (913) 294-5318
General/National Adv. E-mail: republic@miconew.com
Display Adv. E-mail: classifieds@miconews.com
Editorial e-mail: republic@miconew.com
Primary Website: republic-online.com
Year Established: 1866
Avg Paid Circ: 5140
Avg Free Circ: 10
Audit By: Sworn/Estimate/Non-Audited
Audit Date: 10.06.2019
Personnel: Sandy Nelson (Group Pub.); Brian McMauley (Ed.); Teresa Morrow (Adv. Mgr.)
Parent company (for newspapers): News-Press & Gazette Co.

THE MILTONVALE RECORD

Street address 1: 10 W Spruce Ave
Street address 2: PO Box 278
Street address city: Miltonvale
Street address state: KS
Zip/Postal code: 67466-5026
General Phone: (785) 427-2680
General Fax: none
General/National Adv. E-mail: miltonvalerecord@twinvalley.net
Display Adv. E-mail: same
Editorial e-mail: miltonvalerecord@twinvalley.net
Primary Website: none
Year Established: 1898
Avg Paid Circ: 411
Avg Free Circ: 0
Audit By: Sworn/Estimate/Non-Audited
Audit Date: 10.06.2019
Personnel: Sarah Lacy (Circ. Dir.); Jeannie Hauck (Advertising, Office Work)
Parent company (for newspapers): Concordia Blade-Empire

THE MIRROR

Street address 1: 520 E 4th St
Street address city: Tonganoxie
Street address state: KS
Zip/Postal code: 66086-8920
General Phone: (913) 845-2222
General Fax: (913) 845-9451
General/National Adv. E-mail: mgriffin@theworldco.info
Display Adv. E-mail: weeklyclassifieds@ljworld.com
Editorial e-mail: slinenberger@theworldco.info
Primary Website: tonganoxiemirror.com
Year Established: 1882
Avg Paid Circ: 2256
Avg Free Circ: 299
Audit By: Sworn/Estimate/Non-Audited
Audit Date: 10.06.2019
Personnel: Shawn Linenberger (News Ed)

THE NORTON TELEGRAM

Street address 1: 215 S Kansas Ave
Street address city: Norton
Street address state: KS
Zip/Postal code: 67654-2131
General Phone: (785) 877-3361
General Fax: (785) 877-3732
General/National Adv. E-mail: dpaxton@nwkansas.com
Editorial e-mail: nortontelegram@nwkansas.com
Primary Website: nwkansas.com
Avg Paid Circ: 2704
Audit By: Sworn/Estimate/Non-Audited
Audit Date: 10.06.2019
Personnel: Steven Haynes (Co-Owner); Cynthia Haynes (Co-Owner); Sherry Hickman (Circ. Mgr.); Harriett Gill (Society/Women's Ed.)
Parent company (for newspapers): Haynes Publishing Co.

THE OAKLEY GRAPHIC

Street address 1: 118 Center Ave
Street address city: Oakley
Street address state: KS
Zip/Postal code: 67748-1712
General Phone: (785) 672-3228
General/National Adv. E-mail: graphic@st-tel.net
Editorial e-mail: graphic@st-tel.net
Avg Paid Circ: 1200
Audit By: Sworn/Estimate/Non-Audited
Audit Date: 10.06.2019
Personnel: Anita Gabel (Ed.); Mark Anderson (Pub.)
Parent company (for newspapers): Kansas Press Association

THE OLATHE NEWS

Street address 1: 514 S Kansas Ave
Street address city: Olathe
Street address state: KS
Zip/Postal code: 66061
General Phone: (913) 764-2212
Classified Adv. e-mail: classfeedback@kcstar.com
Editorial e-mail: mfannin@kcstar.com
Primary Website: kansascity.com
Year Established: 1960
Avg Paid Circ: 25000
Sat. Circulation Paid: 17182
Audit By: Sworn/Estimate/Non-Audited
Audit Date: 10.06.2019
Personnel: Mike Fannin; Greg Farmer (Mng. Ed.)
Parent company (for newspapers): The McClatchy Company

THE OSAGE COUNTY HERALD-CHRONICLE

Street address 1: 527 Market St
Street address city: Osage City
Street address state: KS
Zip/Postal code: 66523-1157
General Phone: (785) 528-3511
General Fax: (785) 528-4811
General/National Adv. E-mail: ochcads@gmail.com
Display Adv. E-mail: ochcads@gmail.com
Editorial e-mail: ochcnews@gmail.com
Primary Website: ocherald-chronicle.com
Year Established: 1869
Avg Paid Circ: 4000
Audit By: Sworn/Estimate/Non-Audited
Audit Date: 10.06.2019

Personnel: Catherine Faimon (Pub.)

THE OTTAWA HERALD

Street address 1: 214 S Hickory St
Street address city: Ottawa
Street address state: KS
Zip/Postal code: 66067-2392
General Phone: (785) 242-4700
General Fax: (785) 242-9420
General/National Adv. E-mail: ads@ottawaherald.com
Display Adv. E-mail: legals@ottawaherald.com
Classified Adv. e-mail: classifieds@ottawaherald.com
Editorial e-mail: jgulley@ottawaherald.com
Primary Website: ottawaherald.com
Year Established: 1869
Avg Paid Circ: 4100
Avg Free Circ: 700
Sat. Circulation Paid: 4500
Audit By: Sworn/Estimate/Non-Audited
Audit Date: 10.06.2019
Personnel: Leon Toon (GM/Adv. Dir.); Jeff Gulley (Ed.); Clinton Dick
Parent company (for newspapers): CherryRoad Media

THE PRAIRIE POST

Street address 1: 108 E MacKenzie St
Street address city: White City
Street address state: KS
Zip/Postal code: 66872-0326
General Phone: (785) 349-5516
General Fax: (785) 349-5516
General/National Adv. E-mail: ppost@tctelco.net
Display Adv. E-mail: ppost@tctelco.net
Classified Adv. e-mail: ppost@tctelco.net
Editorial e-mail: ppost@tctelco.net
Primary Website: https://www.p-post.net
Year Established: 1993
Avg Paid Circ: 550
Avg Free Circ: 15
Audit By: USPS
Audit Date: 23.09.2023
Personnel: Gloria Smith (Adv. Mgr.); Joann Kahnt (Ed.)

THE PRATT TRIBUNE

Street address 1: 320 S Main St
Street address 2: P.O. Box 909
Street address city: Pratt
Street address state: KS
Zip/Postal code: 67124-2706
General Phone: (620) 672-5511
General Fax: (620) 672-5514
Advertising Phone: (620) 672-5511
Advertising Fax: (620) 672-5514
Editorial Phone: (620) 672-5511
Editorial Fax: (620) 672-5514
General/National Adv. E-mail: editor@pratttribune.com
Display Adv. E-mail: bcain@pratttribune.com
Classified Adv. e-mail: jlang@pratttribune.com
Editorial e-mail: editor@pratttribune.com
Primary Website: pratttribune.com
Year Established: 1917
Avg Paid Circ: 2000
Audit By: Sworn/Estimate/Non-Audited
Audit Date: 10.06.2019
Personnel: Dena Sattler (Pub.); Jennifer Stultz (Ed.); Kim Smith (Adv. Sales); Shannon Briles (Circ. Mgr.); Sheryl Kutz (Off. Mgr.)
Parent company (for newspapers): CherryRoad Media

THE RECORD

Street address 1: 107 S Burns St
Street address city: Turon
Street address state: KS
Zip/Postal code: 67583-9513
General Phone: (620) 497-6448
General/National Adv. E-mail: record@sctelcom.net
Editorial e-mail: record@sctelcom.net
Primary Website: facebook.com/pages/Record/133088910068883
Avg Paid Circ: 550
Avg Free Circ: 26
Audit By: Sworn/Estimate/Non-Audited
Audit Date: 10.06.2019
Personnel: Stephen Green (Pub)

THE RUSSELL COUNTY NEWS

Street address 1: 958 E WICHITA AVE
Street address city: Russell
Street address state: KS
Zip/Postal code: 67665
General Phone: (785) 483-2116
General Fax: (785) 483-4012
General/National Adv. E-mail: russell@mainstreetmedia.us
Primary Website: mainstreetmedia.us
Avg Paid Circ: 2300
Audit By: Sworn/Estimate/Non-Audited
Audit Date: 10.06.2019
Personnel: Chuck Krier (Pub.); Ruth Newman (Gen. Mgr.); Pam Soetaert (Adv. Mgr.); Richelle Twenter (Cir. Mgr.); Justin Ashlaw (Ed.)
Parent company (for newspapers): Main Street Media, Inc.

THE SABETHA HERALD

Street address 1: 1024 Main St
Street address city: Sabetha
Street address state: KS
Zip/Postal code: 66534-1831
General Phone: (785) 284-3300
General Fax: (785) 284-2320
General/National Adv. E-mail: advertising@sabethaherald.com.
Display Adv. E-mail: advertising@sabethaherald.com.
Editorial e-mail: sabethaherald@sabethaherald.com
Primary Website: sabethaherald.com
Year Established: 1884
Avg Paid Circ: 2542
Avg Free Circ: 50
Audit By: Sworn/Estimate/Non-Audited
Audit Date: 10.06.2019
Personnel: Tim Kellenburger (Pub.)

THE SHERIDAN SENTINEL

Street address 1: 716 Main St
Street address city: Hoxie
Street address state: KS
Zip/Postal code: 67740-8800
General Phone: (785) 675-3321
General/National Adv. E-mail: sentinel@sheridansentinel.com
Display Adv. E-mail: advertising@sheridansentinel.com
Editorial e-mail: editor@sheridansentinel.com
Primary Website: sheridansentinel.com
Mthly Avg Views: 500
Mthly Avg Unique Visitors: 300
Year Established: 29.[illegible].16
Avg Paid Circ: 800
Avg Free Circ: 50
Audit By: Sworn/Estimate/Non-Audited
Audit Date: 10.06.2019
Personnel: Viktorija Briggs (Owner/Ed/Pub)
Parent company (for newspapers): Sheridan Sentinel, LLC

THE SOUTH HAVEN NEW ERA

Street address 1: 215 S 8th St
Street address city: Conway Springs
Street address state: KS
Zip/Postal code: 67031-8817
General Phone: (620) 456-2232
General Fax: (620) 456-2432
General/National Adv. E-mail: ajprinting@havilandtelco.com
Primary Website: facebook.com/pages/South-Haven-New-Era/154024557969923
Avg Paid Circ: 330
Avg Free Circ: 35
Audit By: Sworn/Estimate/Non-Audited
Audit Date: 10.06.2019
Personnel: A.J. Bozarth (Ed.)

THE STAFFORD COURIER

Street address 1: 114 E Broadway St
Street address city: Stafford
Street address state: KS
Zip/Postal code: 67578-1803
General Phone: (620) 234-5241
General Fax: (620) 234-5242
General/National Adv. E-mail: staffordcourier@sbcglobal.net
Editorial e-mail: staffordcourier@sbcglobal.net
Primary Website: facebook.com/pages/Courier-Office/123680691012380
Year Established: 1903
Avg Paid Circ: 1000
Audit By: Sworn/Estimate/Non-Audited
Audit Date: 10.06.2019
Personnel: David Green (Pub.); Karen Kalmer (Ed.)

THE SYRACUSE JOURNAL

Street address 1: 123 N Main St
Street address city: Syracuse
Street address state: KS
Zip/Postal code: 67878-7881
General Phone: (620) 384-5640
General Fax: (620) 384-5228
General/National Adv. E-mail: editor@thesyracusejournal.com
Display Adv. E-mail: editor@thesyracusejournal.com
Editorial e-mail: editor@thesyracusejournal.com
Primary Website: thesyracusejournal.com
Year Established: 1885
Avg Paid Circ: 650
Avg Free Circ: 30
Audit By: USPS
Audit Date: 10.10.2021
Personnel: Marcus Ashlock (Owner/Ed.); Michele Boy (Owner/Editor)
Parent company (for newspapers): N Highway 27 Productions LLC

THE TILLER & TOILER

Street address 1: 115 W 5th St
Street address city: Larned
Street address state: KS
Zip/Postal code: 67550-9983
General Phone: (620) 285-3111
General Fax: (620) 285-6062
General/National Adv. E-mail: tiller@star.kscoxmail.com
Editorial e-mail: tiller@star.kscoxmail.com
Primary Website: midksnews.com
Avg Paid Circ: 1434
Audit By: Sworn/Estimate/Non-Audited
Audit Date: 10.06.2019
Personnel: Marshall Settle (Pres.); John M. Settle (Pub.); Bryan Martin (Adv. Rep.); Paula Settle (Adv. Rep.); Shirley Strassburg (Circ. Mgr.); Mark Zwink (Sports Ed.); Lisa Springer (Online Mgr.); Bob Crawford (Prodn. Mgr., Pressroom); David Settle (Adv. Mgr.); Mike Gilmore (Managing Ed.)
Parent company (for newspapers): Hi Neighbor Newspapers

THE ULYSSES NEWS

Street address 1: 218 N Main St
Street address city: Ulysses
Street address state: KS
Zip/Postal code: 67880-2129
General Phone: (620) 356-1201
General Fax: (620) 356-4610
General/National Adv. E-mail: ulynews3@pld.com
Editorial e-mail: ulynews@pld.com
Primary Website: ulyssesnewsonline.com
Avg Paid Circ: 2200
Avg Free Circ: 16
Audit By: Sworn/Estimate/Non-Audited
Audit Date: 10.06.2019
Personnel: Shayla Hernandez-Jaquez (Adv. Mgr.)
Parent company (for newspapers): Southwest Kansas Publications Inc.

THE WABAUNSEE COUNTY SIGNAL-ENTERPRISE

Street address 1: 323 Missouri Ave
Street address city: Alma
Street address state: KS
Zip/Postal code: 66401-9810
General Phone: (785) 765-3327
General/National Adv. E-mail: signal@embarqmail.com
Editorial e-mail: signal@embarqmail.com
Primary Website: signal-enterprise.com
Year Established: 1884
Avg Paid Circ: 1300
Avg Free Circ: 12
Audit By: Sworn/Estimate/Non-Audited
Audit Date: 10.06.2019
Personnel: Lori Daniel (Owner / Publisher / Editor)

THE WAMEGO TIMES

Street address 1: 407 Lincoln Ave
Street address city: Wamego
Street address state: KS
Zip/Postal code: 66547-1631
General Phone: (785) 456-2602
General Fax: (785) 456-8484
General/National Adv. E-mail: advertising@wamegonews.com
Display Adv. E-mail: advertising@wamegonews.com
Classified Adv. e-mail: office@wamegonews.com
Editorial e-mail: office@wamegonews.com
Primary Website: wamegotimes.com
Year Established: 1889
Avg Paid Circ: 950
Audit By: Sworn/Estimate/Non-Audited
Audit Date: 10.06.2019
Personnel: Shannon Fritz (Advertising Executive); Beth Day (Editor)
Parent company (for newspapers): Seaton Publications

THE WESTERN STAR

Street address 1: 113 S Central St
Street address city: Coldwater
Street address state: KS
Zip/Postal code: 67029-2943
General Phone: (620) 582-2101
Advertising Phone: (620) 582-2101
Editorial Phone: (620) 582-2101
General/National Adv. E-mail: weststar@gmaxx.us
Display Adv. E-mail: weststar@gmaxx.us
Classified Adv. e-mail: weststar@gmaxx.us
Editorial e-mail: weststar@gmaxx.us
Year Established: 1884
Avg Paid Circ: 750
Avg Free Circ: 30
Audit By: Sworn/Estimate/Non-Audited
Audit Date: 10.06.2019
Personnel: Dennies Andersen (Ed./Pub.)

TIMES SENTINEL

Street address 1: 125 N Main St
Street address city: Cheney
Street address state: KS
Zip/Postal code: 67025-8844
General Phone: (316) 540-0500
General/National Adv. E-mail: news@tsnews.com
Display Adv. E-mail: prhodes@tsnews.com
Editorial e-mail: news@tsnews.com
Primary Website: tsnews.com
Year Established: 1894
Avg Paid Circ: 3000
Audit By: USPS
Audit Date: 01.10.2021
Personnel: Paul Rhodes (Owner/Pub.); Travis Mounts (Mng. Ed/Co-Owner)

TOPEKA METRO NEWS

Street address 1: 800 SW Jackson St
Street address 2: Ste 1118
Street address city: Topeka
Street address state: KS
Zip/Postal code: 66612-1244
General Phone: (785) 232-8600
General/National Adv. E-mail: legal@topekametronews.com
Editorial e-mail: legal@topekametronews.com
Primary Website: topekametro.com
Audit By: Sworn/Estimate/Non-Audited
Audit Date: 10.06.2019

VALLEY FALLS VINDICATOR

Street address 1: 416 Broadway St
Street address city: Valley Falls
Street address state: KS
Zip/Postal code: 66088-1304
General Phone: (785) 945-3257
General Fax: (785) 945-3444
General/National Adv. E-mail: vindicator@embarqmail.com
Primary Website: jeffcountynews.com
Year Established: 1890
Avg Paid Circ: 1865
Avg Free Circ: 35

Audit By: Sworn/Estimate/Non-Audited
Audit Date: 10.06.2019
Personnel: Clarke Davis (Pub/Ed); Corey Davis (Mgr.); Marveta Davis (Society Ed)
Parent company (for newspapers): Davis Publications Inc.

WAMEGO SMOKE SIGNAL

Street address 1: 407 Lincoln Ave
Street address city: Wamego
Street address state: KS
Zip/Postal code: 66547-1631
General Phone: (785) 456-2602
General Fax: (785) 456-8484
General/National Adv. E-mail: advertising@wamegonews.com
Display Adv. E-mail: advertising@wamegonews.com
Editorial e-mail: office@wamegonews.com
Primary Website: thewamegosmokesignal.com
Avg Free Circ: 9823
Audit By: Sworn/Estimate/Non-Audited
Audit Date: 10.06.2019
Personnel: Michelle Wilken
Parent company (for newspapers): The White Corporation

WASHINGTON COUNTY NEWS

Street address 1: 323 C St
Street address city: Washington
Street address state: KS
Zip/Postal code: 66968-1908
General Phone: (785) 325-2219
General Fax: (785) 325-3255
General/National Adv. E-mail: editor@bluevalley.net
Display Adv. E-mail: jen@bluevalley.net
Classified Adv. e-mail: sales@bluevalley.net
Editorial e-mail: editor@bluevalley.net
Primary Website: backroadsnews.com
Year Established: 1869
Avg Paid Circ: 2000
Avg Free Circ: 10
Audit By: Sworn/Estimate/Non-Audited
Audit Date: 10.06.2019
Personnel: Judy Wiechman (Circ. Mgr.); Dan Thalmann (Ed.)

WELLINGTON DAILY NEWS

Street address 1: 113 W Harvey Ave
Street address city: Wellington
Street address state: KS
Zip/Postal code: 67152-3840
General Phone: (620) 326-3326
General/National Adv. E-mail: jwilson@butlercountytimesgazette.com
Display Adv. E-mail: jfullerton@wellingtondailynews.com
Classified Adv. e-mail: jfullerton@wellingtondailynews.com
Editorial e-mail: acatlin@wellingtondailynews.com
Primary Website: wellingtondailynews.com
Year Established: 1901
Avg Paid Circ: 2000
Audit By: Sworn/Estimate/Non-Audited
Audit Date: 10.06.2019
Personnel: Adam Catlin (Ed.); Jennifer Wilson (Adv. Sales)
Parent company (for newspapers): CherryRoad Media; CherryRoad Media

WESTERN KANSAS WORLD

Street address 1: 205 N Main St
Street address city: Wakeeney
Street address state: KS
Zip/Postal code: 67672-2104
General Phone: (785) 743-2155
General Fax: (785) 743-5340
General/National Adv. E-mail: westernkansasworld@yahoo.com
Editorial e-mail: westernkansasworld@yahoo.com
Primary Website: facebook.com/pages/Western-Kansas-World-World-Print/146562978706908
Avg Paid Circ: 1700
Avg Free Circ: 400
Audit By: Sworn/Estimate/Non-Audited
Audit Date: 10.06.2019
Personnel: Megan Mowery (Office Mgr.); Jerry Millard (Ed.); Cathy Millard (Mng. Ed.)

WICHITA BUSINESS JOURNAL

Street address 1: 121 N Mead St
Street address 2: Ste 100
Street address city: Wichita
Street address state: KS
Zip/Postal code: 67202-2784
General Phone: (316) 267-6406
General Fax: (316) 267-8570
General/National Adv. E-mail: arobuck@bizjournals.com
Display Adv. E-mail: arobuck@bizjournals.com
Editorial e-mail: broy@bizjournals.com
Primary Website: wichitabusinessjournal.com
Year Established: 1986
Audit By: Sworn/Estimate/Non-Audited
Audit Date: 10.06.2019
Personnel: John Ek (Pub); Bill Roy (Ed); Angela Robuck (Adv)

WILSON COUNTY CITIZEN

Street address 1: 406 N 7th St
Street address city: Fredonia
Street address state: KS
Zip/Postal code: 66736-1315
General Phone: (620) 378-4415
General Fax: (620) 378-4688
General/National Adv. E-mail: news@wilsoncountycitizen.com
Editorial e-mail: news@wilsoncountycitizen.com
Primary Website: wilsoncountycitizen.com
Year Established: 1870
Avg Paid Circ: 3000
Avg Free Circ: 69
Audit By: Sworn/Estimate/Non-Audited
Audit Date: 10.06.2019
Personnel: Meredith Odell (Adv. Mgr.); Joseph Relph (Ed.); Rita Relph (Ed.); Mina S. DeBerry (Mng. Ed.); Ross Relph (Photography/IT)

WYANDOTTE COUNTY BUSINESS NEWS

Street address 1: PO Box 13235
Street address city: Kansas City
Street address state: KS
Zip/Postal code: 66113-0235
General Phone: (913) 422-8232
General/National Adv. E-mail: notices@wyandottecountylegalnews.com
Display Adv. E-mail: notices@wyandottecountylegalnews.com
Editorial e-mail: notices@wyandottecountylegalnews.com
Primary Website: wybiznews.com
Audit By: Sworn/Estimate/Non-Audited
Audit Date: 10.06.2019
Personnel: Emily Campbell (Ed)

WYANDOTTE DAILY NEWS WEEKLY PRINT EDITION

Street address 1: 2 S 14th St
Street address 2: Ste 100
Street address city: Kansas City
Street address state: KS
Zip/Postal code: 66102-5041
General Phone: (913) 788-5565
General Fax: (816) 979-1122
General/National Adv. E-mail: ads@wyandottedailynews.com
Display Adv. E-mail: ads@WyandotteDaily.com
Editorial e-mail: maryr@WyandotteDaily.com
Primary Website: wyandottedaily.com
Year Established: 1968
Avg Paid Circ: 1500
Avg Free Circ: 10000
Audit By: Sworn/Estimate/Non-Audited
Audit Date: 10.06.2019
Personnel: Richard Ward (Pub.); Mary Rupert (Ed.); Lexie Cocker (Adv.)
Parent company (for newspapers): TrulyLocal Media

WYANDOTTE ECHO

Street address 1: 450 N 17th St
Street address city: Kansas City
Street address state: KS
Zip/Postal code: 66102-4202
General Phone: (913) 342-2444
General Fax: (913) 362-8406
Advertising Phone: (913) 342-2444
Advertising Fax: (913) 362-8406
Editorial Phone: (913) 342-2444
Editorial Fax: (913) 362-8406
General/National Adv. E-mail: mjpkck@aol.com
Display Adv. E-mail: mjpkck@aol.com
Editorial e-mail: mjpkck@aol.com
Primary Website: wyandotteecho.com
Audit By: Sworn/Estimate/Non-Audited
Audit Date: 10.06.2019
Personnel: Roberta Peterson (Pub.)

YATES CENTER NEWS

Street address 1: 113 S Main St
Street address 2: P.O. Box 285
Street address city: Yates Center
Street address state: KS
Zip/Postal code: 66783-1425
General Phone: (620) 625-2181
General Fax: (620) 625-2081
General/National Adv. E-mail: ycn@sekansas.com
Editorial e-mail: ycn@sekansas.com
Avg Paid Circ: 1500
Avg Free Circ: 40
Audit By: Sworn/Estimate/Non-Audited
Audit Date: 10.06.2019
Personnel: Stewart Braden (Ed.)

KENTUCKY

ADAIR COUNTY COMMUNITY VOICE

Street address 1: 316 Public Sq
Street address city: Columbia
Street address state: KY
Zip/Postal code: 42728-1456
General Phone: (270) 384-9454
Advertising Phone: 270-634-0350
General/National Adv. E-mail: snburton@duo-county.com
Display Adv. E-mail: sales@adairvoice.com
Editorial e-mail: newsroom@adairvoice.com
Primary Website: adairvoice.com
Year Established: 1989
Avg Paid Circ: 2400
Audit By: Sworn/Estimate/Non-Audited
Audit Date: 10.06.2019
Personnel: Mindy Yarberry (Gen. Mgr.); Sharon Burton (Pub./Ed.); Toni Humphress (General Manager); Hailey Stotts (Sales and marketing rep)

ADAIR PROGRESS

Street address 1: 98 Grant Ln
Street address city: Columbia
Street address state: KY
Zip/Postal code: 42728-2233
General Phone: (270) 384-6471
General Fax: (270) 384-6474
General/National Adv. E-mail: advertising@adairprogress.com
Display Adv. E-mail: advertising@adairprogress.com
Editorial e-mail: editorial@adairprogress.com
Primary Website: adairprogress.com
Year Established: 1987
Avg Paid Circ: 4900
Audit By: Sworn/Estimate/Non-Audited
Audit Date: 10.06.2019
Personnel: Donna Hancock (Pub.); Melanie Ollery (Circ. Mgr.); Zachery Oakes (Ed.); Ann Melton (Asst Ed); Jeremy Birdwell (Prodn. Mgr.); April Burton (Advt)

ADVOCATE

Street address 1: 214 Knox St
Street address city: Barbourville
Street address state: KY
Zip/Postal code: 40906-1428
General Phone: (606) 546-9225
General Fax: (606) 546-3175
Advertising Fax: 6066220078
Editorial Fax: (606) 546-2830
General/National Adv. E-mail: advertising@mountainadvocate.com
Display Adv. E-mail: advertising@mountainadvocate.com
Editorial e-mail: editor@mountainadvocate.com
Primary Website: mountainadvocate.com
Avg Paid Circ: 4200
Avg Free Circ: 25
Audit By: Sworn/Estimate/Non-Audited
Audit Date: 10.06.2019
Personnel: Charles Myrick (Publisher / General Manager); Jay Nolan (Pub); Tim Terrell (Advertising Manager)

BATH COUNTY BULLETIN

Street address 1: 28 N Court St
Street address city: Owingsville
Street address state: KY
Zip/Postal code: 40360
General Phone: (606) 674-2260
General Fax: (606) 674-2260
Advertising Phone: (606) 674-2260
Advertising Fax: (606) 674-2260
Editorial Phone: (606) 674-2260
Editorial Fax: (606) 674-2260
General/National Adv. E-mail: bathcountynews@gmail.com
Display Adv. E-mail: bathcountynews@gmail.com
Editorial e-mail: bathcountynews@gmail.com
Primary Website: facebook.com/Bath-County-Bulletin-208017657623
Year Established: 2009
Audit By: Sworn/Estimate/Non-Audited
Audit Date: 10.06.2019
Personnel: Chris Bailey (Pub./Ed.)

BEATTYVILLE ENTERPRISE

Street address 1: 149 Main Street
Street address city: Beattyville
Street address state: KY
Zip/Postal code: 41311-7491
General Phone: (606) 464-2444
General/National Adv. E-mail: thebeattyvilleenterprise@gmail.com
Editorial e-mail: thebeattyvilleenterprise@gmail.com
Primary Website: nolangroupmedia.com/beattyville_enterprise
Year Established: 1883
Avg Paid Circ: 4000
Audit By: Sworn/Estimate/Non-Audited
Audit Date: 10.06.2019
Personnel: Glenn Gray (Pub.); Cheryle Walton (Adv. Dir.); Edmund Shelby (Ed.)

BOONE COMMUNITY RECORDER

Street address 1: 226 Grandview Dr
Street address city: Fort Mitchell
Street address state: KY
Zip/Postal code: 41017-2702
General Phone: (859) 578-5501
General Fax: (859) 578-5515
General/National Adv. E-mail: ndaly@communitypress.com
Display Adv. E-mail: llawrence@enquirer.com
Editorial e-mail: kynews@communitypress.com
Primary Website: communitypress.com
Year Established: 2001
Avg Paid Circ: 15
Avg Free Circ: 5907
Audit By: Sworn/Estimate/Non-Audited
Audit Date: 10.06.2019
Personnel: Sharon Schachleiter (Circ. Mgr.); Nancy Daly (Sr. Ed.)
Parent company (for newspapers): Gannett

BOURBON COUNTY CITIZEN

Street address 1: 123 W 8th St
Street address city: Paris
Street address state: KY
Zip/Postal code: 40361-1343
General Phone: (859) 987-1870
General Fax: (859) 987-3729
General/National Adv. E-mail: citadinc@bellsouth.net
Editorial e-mail: citadinc@bellsouth.net
Primary Website: facebook.com/thebourboncountycitizenadvertiser
Year Established: 1984
Avg Paid Circ: 3000
Audit By: Sworn/Estimate/Non-Audited
Audit Date: 10.06.2019

Personnel: Beverly Brannon (Adv. Mgr.); Jimmy Brannon (Ed.); Genevieve Brannon (Mng. Ed.); Rebecca Brannon Lawyer (Prodn. Mgr.)

CAMPBELL COUNTY RECORDER

Street address 1: 226 Grandview Dr
Street address city: Fort Mitchell
Street address state: KY
Zip/Postal code: 41017-2702
General Phone: (859) 283-0404
General Fax: (859) 283-7285
General/National Adv. E-mail: kynews@communitypress.com
Primary Website: communitypress.com
Year Established: 2001
Avg Paid Circ: 1747
Avg Free Circ: 7898
Audit By: Sworn/Estimate/Non-Audited
Audit Date: 10.06.2019
Personnel: Debbie Maggard (Adv. Mgr); Sharon Schachleiter (Circ. Mgr.); Nancy Daly (Sr. Ed.)
Parent company (for newspapers): Gannett

CARROLLTON NEWS-DEMOCRAT

Street address 1: 122 6th St
Street address city: Carrollton
Street address state: KY
Zip/Postal code: 41008-1009
General Phone: (502) 732-4261
General Fax: (502) 732-0453
General/National Adv. E-mail: dgarrett@mycarrollnews.com
Editorial e-mail: jwright@mycarrollnews.com
Primary Website: mycarrollnews.com
Year Established: 1868
Avg Paid Circ: 2841
Avg Free Circ: 17
Audit By: Sworn/Estimate/Non-Audited
Audit Date: 10.06.2019
Personnel: Carla Kidwell (Circ. Mgr.); Jeff Moore (Pub./Ed.); Kristin Sherrard (News Ed.); Deborah Garrett (Adv. Consultant); Phyllis McLaughlin
Parent company (for newspapers): Landmark Community Newspapers, LLC; Main Street Media, Inc.; Landmark Communications, Inc.

CASEY COUNTY NEWS

Street address 1: 720 Campbellsville St
Street address city: Liberty
Street address state: KY
Zip/Postal code: 42539-3106
General Phone: (606) 787-7171
General Fax: (606) 787-8306
General/National Adv. E-mail: bemerson@caseynews.net
Display Adv. E-mail: bemerson@caseynews.net
Editorial e-mail: lrowell@caseynews.net
Primary Website: caseynews.net
Avg Paid Circ: 6000
Avg Free Circ: 14
Audit By: Sworn/Estimate/Non-Audited
Audit Date: 10.06.2019
Personnel: Charlie VanLeuven (Ed.); Joy Coppage (Adv. Mgr.); Zach Johnson (Reporter); Amanda Richards (Circ. Mgr.)
Parent company (for newspapers): Paxton Media Group; Landmark Community Newspapers, LLC

CENTRAL CITY LEADER NEWS

Street address 1: 1730 W EVERLY BROTHERS BLVD
Street address city: Central City
Street address state: KY
Zip/Postal code: 42330
General Phone: (270) 754-3000
General Fax: (270) 754-9484
General/National Adv. E-mail: advp@ky-leadernews.com
Display Adv. E-mail: typist@ky-leadernews.com
Editorial e-mail: editor@ky-leadernews.com
Primary Website: ky-leadernews.com
Audit By: Sworn/Estimate/Non-Audited
Audit Date: 10.06.2019
Personnel: Jenny Earle (Sales); Jowanna Bandy (Gen Mgr)

CENTRAL KENTUCKY NEWS-JOURNAL

Street address 1: 200 Albion Way
Street address city: Campbellsville
Street address state: KY
Zip/Postal code: 42718-1565
General Phone: (270) 465-8111
General Fax: (270) 465-2500
General/National Adv. E-mail: cmagers@cknj.com
Display Adv. E-mail: cmagers@cknj.com
Editorial e-mail: publisher@cknj.com
Primary Website: cknj.com
Year Established: 1910
Avg Paid Circ: 7600
Avg Free Circ: 12000
Audit By: Sworn/Estimate/Non-Audited
Audit Date: 10.06.2019
Personnel: Rebecca Cassell (Ed.); Jeff Moreland (Pub/Ed); Suzanne Houk (Prodn. Mgr.); Cheryl Magers (Adv. Mgr.); Andrea Yates (Circulation Sales Representative); Richard Robards (Pub.); Melissa Netherland (Ad. Sales Rep.)
Parent company (for newspapers): Paxton Media Group; Landmark Communications, Inc.; Landmark Community Newspapers, LLC

CITIZEN VOICE & TIMES

Street address 1: 108 S Court St
Street address 2: PO Box 660
Street address city: Irvine
Street address state: KY
Zip/Postal code: 40336-1079
General Phone: (606) 723-5161
General Fax: (606) 723-5509
General/National Adv. E-mail: cvtnews@windstream.net
Display Adv. E-mail: cvtads@windstream.net
Editorial e-mail: lisa@hatfieldnewspapers.com
Primary Website: cvt-news.com
Year Established: 1973
Avg Paid Circ: 3600
Audit By: Sworn/Estimate/Non-Audited
Audit Date: 10.06.2019
Personnel: Teresa Hatfield-Barger (Adv. Mgr.); Megan Parker (Ad Composition Classified); Lisa Bicknell (Editor)

CLINTON COUNTY NEWS

Street address 1: 116 N Washington St
Street address city: Albany
Street address state: KY
Zip/Postal code: 42602-1302
General Phone: (606) 387-5144
General Fax: (606) 387-7949
General/National Adv. E-mail: gpcompany@kih.net
Primary Website: clintonnews.net
Year Established: 1949
Avg Paid Circ: 3100
Audit By: Sworn/Estimate/Non-Audited
Audit Date: 10.10.2023
Personnel: Al Gibson (Publisher); Janie Gibson (Office Mng); Brett Gibson (News, Advt); Amanda Sharpe (Advt)

CUMBERLAND COUNTY NEWS

Street address 1: 412 Courthouse Sq.
Street address 2: PO Box 307
Street address city: Burkesville
Street address state: KY
Zip/Postal code: 42717
General Phone: 2708643891
General Fax: 2708643891
Advertising Phone: 2708643891
General/National Adv. E-mail: ccn@burkesville.com
Display Adv. E-mail: ccn@burkesville.com
Classified Adv. e-mail: ccn@burkesville.com
Editorial e-mail: ccn@burkesville.com
Primary Website: cumberlandcountynewspaper.com
Year Established: 1923
Avg Paid Circ: 2900
Audit By: USPS
Audit Date: 10.06.2020
Personnel: Jeff Jobe (Publisher); Billy Guffey (Design and Layout); Greg Wells (Editor); Jessica Pitcock (Sports Typesetting); JR Jessie (Sales Director); Cyndi Pritchett (Ed.); Paula Gunderman (Typesetter); Kimberly Johnson (Advertising Manager)
Parent company (for newspapers): Jobe Publications

CYNTHIANA DEMOCRAT

Street address 1: 302 Webster Ave
Street address city: Cynthiana
Street address state: KY
Zip/Postal code: 41031-1647
General Phone: (859) 234-1035
General Fax: (859) 234-8096
General/National Adv. E-mail: ads@cynthianademocrat.com
Editorial e-mail: bbarnes@cynthianademocrat.com
Primary Website: cynthianademocrat.com
Avg Paid Circ: 5500
Audit By: Sworn/Estimate/Non-Audited
Audit Date: 10.06.2019
Personnel: Patricia Jenkins (Gen. Mgr.); Becky Barnes (Ed.); Josh Guthrie
Parent company (for newspapers): Paxton Media Group; Landmark Communications, Inc.; Landmark Community Newspapers, LLC

EAGLE POST

Street address 1: 1618 E 9th St
Street address city: Hopkinsville
Street address state: KY
Zip/Postal code: 42240-4430
General Phone: (270) 887-3241
General Fax: (270) 439-5142
Advertising Phone: (270) 887-3274
Editorial Phone: (270) 887-3295
General/National Adv. E-mail: trodgers@kentuckynewera.com
Display Adv. E-mail: sellis@kentuckynewera.com
Editorial e-mail: dsnow@theeaglepost.us
Primary Website: theeaglepost.us
Year Established: 2008
Avg Paid Circ: 5490
Avg Free Circ: 12000
Audit By: Sworn/Estimate/Non-Audited
Audit Date: 10.06.2019
Personnel: David Snow (Ed.)
Parent company (for newspapers): Kentucky New Era

EDMONSON NEWS

Street address 1: 101 S Main St
Street address city: Brownsville
Street address state: KY
Zip/Postal code: 42210-7233
General Phone: (270) 597-3115
General Fax: (270) 597-3115
General/National Adv. E-mail: ednews@winstream.net
Display Adv. E-mail: ednews@winstream.net
Editorial e-mail: ednews@winstream.net
Primary Website: edmonsonvoice.com/-news
Avg Paid Circ: 4200
Audit By: Sworn/Estimate/Non-Audited
Audit Date: 10.06.2019
Parent company (for newspapers): Jobe Publishing

ELLIOTT COUNTY NEWS

Street address 1: 142 Prestonsburg St
Street address city: West Liberty
Street address state: KY
Zip/Postal code: 41472-1028
General Phone: (606) 743-3551
General Fax: (606) 743-3565
General/National Adv. E-mail: courier@mrtc.com
Display Adv. E-mail: courier@mrtc.com
Classified Adv. e-mail: courier@mrtc.com
Avg Paid Circ: 1800
Audit By: Sworn/Estimate/Non-Audited
Audit Date: 10.06.2019
Personnel: Flora Whitley (Ed.)

FALMOUTH OUTLOOK

Street address 1: 210 Main St
Street address city: Falmouth
Street address state: KY
Zip/Postal code: 41040-1265
General Phone: (859) 654-3332
General Fax: (859) 654-4365
General/National Adv. E-mail: ads@falmouthoutlook.com
Display Adv. E-mail: classifieds@falmouthoutlook.com
Editorial e-mail: news@falmouthoutlook.com
Primary Website: falmouthoutlook.com
Year Established: 1907
Avg Paid Circ: 2199
Audit By: Sworn/Estimate/Non-Audited
Audit Date: 22.09.2019
Personnel: Jackie Vaughn (News Ed); Neil Belcher (Pub); Jessie Beckett (Graphics Coord); Carolyn Reid (Editor)
Parent company (for newspapers): Delphos Herald, Inc.; Independent....Newmar Media LLC

FLORENCE RECORDER

Street address 1: 226 Grandview Dr
Street address city: Fort Mitchell
Street address state: KY
Zip/Postal code: 41017-2702
General Phone: (859) 578-5501
General Fax: (859) 578-5515
General/National Adv. E-mail: kynews@communitypress.com
Primary Website: communitypress.com
Year Established: 2001
Avg Paid Circ: 1398
Avg Free Circ: 13304
Audit By: Sworn/Estimate/Non-Audited
Audit Date: 10.06.2019
Personnel: Sharon Schachleiter (Circ. Mgr.); Nancy Daly (Sr. Ed.)
Parent company (for newspapers): Gannett

FLOYD COUNTY TIMES

Street address 1: 263 S Central Ave
Street address city: Prestonsburg
Street address state: KY
Zip/Postal code: 41653-1958
General Phone: (606) 886-8506
General Fax: (606) 886-3603
General/National Adv. E-mail: fctadvertising@floydcountytimes.com
Display Adv. E-mail: fctclassifieds@floydcountytimes.com
Editorial e-mail: web@floydcountytimes.com
Primary Website: floydcountytimes.com
Year Established: 1927
Avg Paid Circ: 8200
Avg Free Circ: 110
Audit By: Sworn/Estimate/Non-Audited
Audit Date: 10.06.2019
Personnel: Joshua Byers (Pub.); Jamie Vaenhoose (Adv Mgr); Ralph B. Davis (Mng. Ed.); Steve LeMaster (Sports Ed.)
Parent company (for newspapers): Lancaster Management, Inc.

FORT THOMAS RECORDER

Street address 1: 226 Grandview Dr
Street address city: Fort Mitchell
Street address state: KY
Zip/Postal code: 41017-2702
General Phone: (859) 283-0404
General Fax: (859) 283-7285
General/National Adv. E-mail: kynews@communitypress.com
Primary Website: communitypress.com
Year Established: 2001
Avg Paid Circ: 1024
Avg Free Circ: 4294
Audit By: Sworn/Estimate/Non-Audited
Audit Date: 10.06.2019
Personnel: Debbie Maggard (Adv. Mgr); Sharon Schachleiter (Circ. Mgr.); Nancy Daly (Sr. Ed.)
Parent company (for newspapers): Gannett

FRANKLIN FAVORITE

Street address 1: 103 N High St
Street address city: Franklin
Street address state: KY
Zip/Postal code: 42134-1801
General Phone: (270) 586-4481
General Fax: (270) 586-6031
Primary Website: franklinfavorite.com
Year Established: 1859
Avg Paid Circ: 4000
Audit By: Sworn/Estimate/Non-Audited
Audit Date: 10.06.2019
Personnel: Megan Purazrang (Ed.); Jennifer Sturm (Adv. Ex.); Jodi Camp (Staff Writer); Keith Pyles (Reporter)

GARRARD CENTRAL RECORD

Street address 1: 106 Richmond St
Street address city: Lancaster
Street address state: KY
Zip/Postal code: 40444-1158
General Phone: (859) 792-2831
General Fax: (859) 792-3448

General/National Adv. E-mail: ads@garrardcentralrecord.com
Display Adv. E-mail: ads@garrardcentralrecord.com
Editorial e-mail: news@garrardcentralrecord.com
Primary Website: garrardcentralrecord.com
Year Established: 1889
Avg Paid Circ: 3993
Avg Free Circ: 95
Audit By: Sworn/Estimate/Non-Audited
Audit Date: 10.06.2019
Personnel: Jim Cox (Pub.); Oneida Black (Exec. Sec./Adv. Mgr.); Pattie Cox (Mng. Ed.); Danny Elam (Sports Ed.); Melanie Arnold; Ted Cox; Pam Fathergill (Graphic artist)

GEORGETOWN NEWS-GRAPHIC

Street address 1: 1481 Cherry Blossom Way
Street address city: Georgetown
Street address state: KY
Zip/Postal code: 40324-8953
General Phone: (502) 863-1111
General Fax: (502) 863-6296
General/National Adv. E-mail: mscogin@news-graphic.com
Display Adv. E-mail: classifieds@news-graphic.com
Editorial e-mail: news@news-graphic.com
Primary Website: news-graphic.com
Year Established: 1867
Avg Paid Circ: 5780
Avg Free Circ: 622
Audit By: Sworn/Estimate/Non-Audited
Audit Date: 10.06.2019
Personnel: Mike Scogin (Pres./Pub.); Jerry Boggs (Ed.)
Parent company (for newspapers): Lancaster Management, Inc.

GRANT COUNTY NEWS AND EXPRESS

Street address 1: 1406 N Main St
Street address 2: Ste 2
Street address city: Williamstown
Street address state: KY
Zip/Postal code: 41097-8500
General Phone: (859) 824-3343
General Fax: (859) 824-5888
General/National Adv. E-mail: grantads@grantky.com
Display Adv. E-mail: kstone@grantky.com
Editorial e-mail: gceditorial@grantky.com
Primary Website: grantky.com
Year Established: 1906
Avg Paid Circ: 5000
Avg Free Circ: 12900
Audit By: Sworn/Estimate/Non-Audited
Audit Date: 10.06.2019
Personnel: Ken Stone (Pub.); Jamie Baker-Nantz (Ed.); Janet McKee (Adv. Asst.); Ken Stone (Publisher); Anita Appler (Classified, Circulation Manager); May Evans (Assistant Sales to Mr. Stone)
Parent company (for newspapers): Landmark Communications, Inc.; Landmark Community Newspapers, LLC

GRAYSON COUNTY NEWS-GAZETTE

Street address 1: 52 Public Square
Street address city: Leitchfield
Street address state: KY
Zip/Postal code: 42754
General Phone: (270) 259-9622
General Fax: (270) 259-5537
Advertising Phone: (270) 259-9622, ext. 2012
Primary Website: gcnewsgazette.com
Mthly Avg Views: 79000
Mthly Avg Unique Visitors: 15000
Year Established: 1890
Avg Paid Circ: 3000
Audit By: Sworn/Estimate/Non-Audited
Audit Date: 10.06.2019
Personnel: Matt Lasley (Ed.); Amy Lindsey (Reporter); Tracey Collins
Parent company (for newspapers): Paxton Media Group

GRAYSON JOURNAL-ENQUIRER

Street address 1: 211 S Carol Malone Blvd
Street address city: Grayson
Street address state: KY
Zip/Postal code: 41143-1355
General Phone: (606) 474-5101
General Fax: (606) 474-0013
General/National Adv. E-mail: dduncan@journal-times.com
Display Adv. E-mail: dduncan@journal-times.com
Editorial e-mail: tpreston@journal-times.com
Primary Website: journal-times.com
Year Established: 1916
Avg Paid Circ: 2700
Avg Free Circ: 100
Audit By: Sworn/Estimate/Non-Audited
Audit Date: 10.06.2019
Personnel: Dan Duncan (Adv. Dir.); Keith Kappes (Publisher and Editor)
Parent company (for newspapers): CNHI, LLC

GREENSBURG RECORD-HERALD

Street address 1: 102 W Court St
Street address city: Greensburg
Street address state: KY
Zip/Postal code: 42743-1564
General Phone: (270) 932-4381
General Fax: (270) 932-4441
General/National Adv. E-mail: advertising@record-herald.com
Display Adv. E-mail: advertising@record-herald.com
Editorial e-mail: news2@record-herald.com
Primary Website: record-herald.com
Year Established: 1895
Avg Paid Circ: 3500
Avg Free Circ: 3300
Audit By: Sworn/Estimate/Non-Audited
Audit Date: 10.06.2019
Personnel: Anne Gorin (Office Mgr.); Walter C. Gorin (Adv. Mgr.); Barbara Harris (Circ. Mgr.); Tom Mills (Ed.)

GREENUP COUNTY NEWS-TIMES

Street address 1: 1407 Beth Ann Dr
Street address city: Flatwoods
Street address state: KY
Zip/Postal code: 41139
General Phone: (606) 356-7509
Primary Website: greenupbeacon.com
Avg Paid Circ: 3600
Audit By: Sworn/Estimate/Non-Audited
Audit Date: 10.06.2019
Personnel: Hank Bond (Ed./Pub.)
Parent company (for newspapers): CNHI, LLC

HART COUNTY NEWS HERALD

Street address 1: 570 S Dixie St
Street address city: Horse Cave
Street address state: KY
Zip/Postal code: 42749-1253
General Phone: (270) 786-2676
General Fax: (270) 786-4470
General/National Adv. E-mail: print@jpinews.com
Display Adv. E-mail: print@jpinews.com
Editorial e-mail: print@jpinews.com
Primary Website: jpinews.com
Avg Paid Circ: 8000
Avg Free Circ: 4000
Audit By: Sworn/Estimate/Non-Audited
Audit Date: 10.06.2019
Personnel: Jeff S. Jobe (CEO); Jerry Matera (Ed.)

HENRY COUNTY LOCAL

Street address 1: 18 S Penn Ave
Street address city: Eminence
Street address state: KY
Zip/Postal code: 40019-1036
General Phone: (502) 845-2858
General Fax: (502) 845-2921
General/National Adv. E-mail: advertising@hclocal.com
Display Adv. E-mail: advertising@hclocal.com
Editorial e-mail: news@hclocal.com
Primary Website: hclocal.com
Avg Paid Circ: 4500
Audit By: Sworn/Estimate/Non-Audited
Audit Date: 10.06.2019
Personnel: Jonna Spelbring Priester (Pub.); Brad Bowman (Reporter); Barbara Didier (Adv Sales); Phyllis Banta (Office Mgr); Tawnja Morris (Circ Mgr)
Parent company (for newspapers): Landmark Community Newspapers, LLC

JACKSON COUNTY SUN

Street address 1: 101 Main St
Street address city: Mc Kee
Street address state: KY
Zip/Postal code: 40447
General Phone: (606) 287-7197
General Fax: (606) 287-7196
General/National Adv. E-mail: jcsun@prtcnet.org
Editorial e-mail: tammy@thejacksoncountysun.com
Primary Website: thejacksoncountysun.com
Year Established: 1926
Avg Paid Circ: 4050
Audit By: Sworn/Estimate/Non-Audited
Audit Date: 10.06.2019
Personnel: Glenn Gray (Pub.); Tammy Spurlock (Adv. Mgr.)

JACKSON TIMES-VOICE

Street address 1: 22 Howell Lane
Street address city: Jackson
Street address state: KY
Zip/Postal code: 41339-1036
General Phone: (606) 666-2451
General Fax: (606) 666-5706
General/National Adv. E-mail: advertising@jacksontimesky.com
Display Adv. E-mail: advertising@jacksontimesky.com
Editorial e-mail: info@jacksontimesky.com
Primary Website: jacksontimesvoice.com
Year Established: 1893
Avg Paid Circ: 4000
Audit By: Sworn/Estimate/Non-Audited
Audit Date: 10.06.2019
Personnel: James David Fugate (Gen. Mgr.); Cheryl Campbell; Jeff Noble
Parent company (for newspapers): Nolan Media Group

KENTUCKY MONTHLY

Street address 1: 102 Consumer Ln
Street address city: Frankfort
Street address state: KY
Zip/Postal code: 40601-8489
General Phone: (502) 227-0053
General Fax: (502) 227-5009
General/National Adv. E-mail: ads@kentuckymonthly.com
Display Adv. E-mail: lindsey@kentuckymonthly.com
Editorial e-mail: patty@kentuckymonthly.com
Primary Website: kentuckymonthly.com
Mthly Avg Views: 35000
Year Established: 1998
Avg Paid Circ: 35000
Avg Free Circ: 5000
Audit By: Sworn/Estimate/Non-Audited
Audit Date: 13.10.2023
Personnel: Stephen Vest (Pub/Ed); Ranft Patty (Executive Editor); Lindsey Collins (Sales Director); Deborah Kohl Kremer
Parent company (for newspapers): Vested Interest Publication

KENTUCKY STANDARD

Street address 1: 110 W Stephen Foster Ave
Street address city: Bardstown
Street address state: KY
Zip/Postal code: 40004-1416
General Phone: (502) 348-9003
General Fax: (502) 348-1971
General/National Adv. E-mail: jsizemore@kystandard.com
Display Adv. E-mail: classifieds@kystandard.com
Editorial e-mail: news@kystandard.com
Primary Website: kystandard.com
Year Established: 1900
Avg Paid Circ: 7536
Audit By: Sworn/Estimate/Non-Audited
Audit Date: 10.06.2019
Personnel: Jamie Sizemore (Pub.); Forrest Berkshire (Ed); Alice Burgen (Class Advt Mgr); Toni Heady (Bus Office Mgr); Arlie Hash (Circulation Manager)
Parent company (for newspapers): Paxton Media Group; Landmark Community Newspapers, LLC

LARUE COUNTY HERALD NEWS

Street address 1: 40 Shawnee Dr
Street address city: Hodgenville
Street address state: KY
Zip/Postal code: 42748-1639
General Phone: (270) 358-3118
General Fax: (270) 358-4852
General/National Adv. E-mail: publisher@laruecountyherald.com
Display Adv. E-mail: publisher@laruecountyherald.com
Classified Adv. e-mail: publsiher@laruecountyherald.com
Editorial e-mail: editor@laruecountyherald.com
Primary Website: laruecountyherald.com
Year Established: 1885
Avg Paid Circ: 2842
Avg Free Circ: 3900
Audit By: Sworn/Estimate/Non-Audited
Audit Date: 10.06.2019
Personnel: Allison Shepherd (Pub); Doug Ponder (Ed)
Parent company (for newspapers): Paxton Media Group; Landmark Community Newspapers, LLC; Paxton Media Group; Landmark Communications, Inc.

LEBANON ENTERPRISE

Street address 1: 115 S Proctor Knott Ave
Street address city: Lebanon
Street address state: KY
Zip/Postal code: 40033-1259
General Phone: (270) 692-6026
General Fax: (270) 692-2118
Advertising Phone: (270) 692-6026
Editorial Phone: (270) 692-6027
General/National Adv. E-mail: editor@lebanonenterprise.com
Display Adv. E-mail: awalker@thespringfieldsun.com
Classified Adv. e-mail: awalker@thespringfieldsun.com
Editorial e-mail: editor@lebanonenterprise.com
Primary Website: www.lebanonenterprise.com
Year Established: n/a
Avg Paid Circ: 3181
Audit By: Sworn/Estimate/Non-Audited
Audit Date: 29.09.2023
Personnel: Stevie Lowery (Gen. Mgr.); Denis House (General Manager, Editor); Steve Lowery (Ed.); Alice Walker (Advertising Manager); Stephen Lega (Other)
Parent company (for newspapers): Paxton Media Group; Landmark Communications, Inc.; Paxton Media Group; Landmark Community Newspapers, LLC

LEWIS COUNTY HERALD

Street address 1: 187 Main St
Street address city: Vanceburg
Street address state: KY
Zip/Postal code: 41179-1031
General Phone: (606) 796-6182
General Fax: (606) 796-3110
General/National Adv. E-mail: heraldadvertising@yahoo.com
Display Adv. E-mail: heraldadvertising@yahoo.com
Editorial e-mail: dkb.lch@gmail.com
Primary Website: lewiscountyherald.com
Avg Paid Circ: 4400
Audit By: Sworn/Estimate/Non-Audited
Audit Date: 10.06.2019
Personnel: Patricia Bloomfield (Mng. Ed.); Gary Kidwell (Sports Ed.)

LIVINGSTON LEDGER

Street address 1: 130 E Adair St
Street address city: Smithland
Street address state: KY
Zip/Postal code: 42081-9998
General Phone: (270) 442-7389
General/National Adv. E-mail: kpiads@ky-news.com
Primary Website: ky-news.com
Avg Paid Circ: 3400
Avg Free Circ: 30
Audit By: Sworn/Estimate/Non-Audited
Audit Date: 10.06.2019
Personnel: Pat Thomann (Pub.); Pat Thomann (Ed.)
Parent company (for newspapers): Kentucky Publishing, Inc.

LOUISVILLE BUSINESS FIRST

Street address 1: 462 S 4th St
Street address 2: Ste 450
Street address city: Louisville
Street address state: KY
Zip/Postal code: 40202-4403
General Phone: (502) 583-1731

Advertising Phone: (502) 498-1946
Editorial Phone: (502) 498-1958
General/National Adv. E-mail: gtyler@bizjournals.com
Display Adv. E-mail: gtyler@bizjournals.com
Editorial e-mail: Lisa.benson@bizjournals.com
Primary Website: www.bizjournals.com/louisville
Year Established: 1984
Avg Paid Circ: 9749
Audit By: AAM
Audit Date: 30.01.2018
Personnel: Gary Tyler (Adv. Dir.); Lisa Benson (Ed.); Krysteen Cissell (Ad. Dir.)
Parent company (for newspapers): American City Business Journals

MARSHALL COUNTY TRIBUNE COURIER

Street address 1: 86 Commerce Blvd
Street address city: Benton
Street address state: KY
Zip/Postal code: 42025-1110
General Phone: (270) 527-3162
General Fax: (270) 527-4567
General/National Adv. E-mail: ads@tribunecourier.com
Display Adv. E-mail: sales@tribunecourier.com
Editorial e-mail: editor@tribunecourier.com
Primary Website: kentuckybarkleynews.com/benton_tribune_courier
Year Established: 1972
Avg Paid Circ: 5000
Audit By: Sworn/Estimate/Non-Audited
Audit Date: 10.06.2019
Personnel: Selena Ward (Adv. Mgr.); Venita Fritz (Gen. Mgr.)

MCLEAN COUNTY NEWS

Street address 1: 165 E 2nd St
Street address city: Calhoun
Street address state: KY
Zip/Postal code: 42327-2205
General Phone: (270) 273-3287
General Fax: (270) 273-3544
Advertising Phone: (270) 691-7285
Editorial Phone: (270) 691-7296
General/National Adv. E-mail: news@mcleannews.com
Editorial e-mail: news@mcleannews.com
Primary Website: messenger-inquirer.com
Year Established: 1884
Avg Paid Circ: 3000
Avg Free Circ: 350
Audit By: Sworn/Estimate/Non-Audited
Audit Date: 10.06.2019
Personnel: Bob Morris (Pub.); Faye Murry (Adv. Mgr.); Austin Ramsey (Editor)

MENIFEE COUNTY NEWS

Street address 1: 722 W 1st St
Street address city: Morehead
Street address state: KY
Zip/Postal code: 40351-1404
General Phone: (606) 784-4116
General Fax: (606) 784-7337
Primary Website: facebook.com/Menifee-County-News-Outlook-190065967691341
Avg Paid Circ: 500
Audit By: Sworn/Estimate/Non-Audited
Audit Date: 10.06.2019
Personnel: Brad Toy (Adv. Mgr.); Stephanie Ockerman (Mng. Ed.)

MT. STERLING ADVOCATE

Street address 1: 219 Midland Trl
Street address city: Mount Sterling
Street address state: KY
Zip/Postal code: 40353-9070
General Phone: (859) 498-2222
General Fax: (859) 498-2228
General/National Adv. E-mail: advertising@msadvocate.com
Display Adv. E-mail: classified@msadvocate.com
Editorial e-mail: news@msadvocate.com
Primary Website: msadvocate.com
Year Established: 1890
Avg Paid Circ: 7500
Avg Free Circ: 38
Audit By: Sworn/Estimate/Non-Audited
Audit Date: 10.06.2019
Personnel: Matt Hall (Pub.); Sharon Manning (Adv. Mgr.); Jamie Vinson (Ed.); Tom Marshall (Staff Writer)

NEWS JOURNAL

Street address 1: 215 N Main St
Street address city: Corbin
Street address state: KY
Zip/Postal code: 40701-1451
General Phone: (606) 528-9767
General Fax: (606) 528-9779
General/National Adv. E-mail: advertising@corbinnewsjournal.com
Display Adv. E-mail: advertising@corbinnewsjournal.com
Editorial e-mail: destep@corbinnewsjournal.com
Primary Website: thenewsjournal.net
Year Established: 1908
Avg Paid Circ: 7774
Audit By: Sworn/Estimate/Non-Audited
Audit Date: 10.06.2019
Personnel: Linda Carpenter (Production Mgr.); Melissa Hudsonc (Adv. Mgr.); Jennifer Benfield (Circ. Mgr.); Don Estep (Publisher); Trent Knuckles (Managing Ed.); Jim McAlister (Sports Ed.); Mark White (Ed.); Melissa Netherland (Adv. Sales Rep.)
Parent company (for newspapers): Forcht Group

OLDHAM ERA

Street address 1: 202 S 1st Ave
Street address 2: Ste 1
Street address city: La Grange
Street address state: KY
Zip/Postal code: 40031-2208
General Phone: (502) 222-7183
General Fax: (502) 222-7194
General/National Adv. E-mail: barbara@oldhamera.com
Display Adv. E-mail: barbara@oldhamera.com
Editorial e-mail: editor@oldhamera.com
Primary Website: oldhamera.com
Year Established: 1876
Avg Paid Circ: 3134
Audit By: Sworn/Estimate/Non-Audited
Audit Date: 10.06.2019
Personnel: Talon Hampton (Graphic Designer); Barbara Duncan (Advertising Representative); Tawnja Morris (Circulation manager); Sam Draut (Sports Ed.); Amanda Manning; Glenn Jennings (Reporter); Jane Ashley Pace (Pub.)
Parent company (for newspapers): Paxton Media Group; Landmark Community Newspapers, LLC

OLIVE HILL TIMES

Street address 1: 187 RAILROAD ST
Street address city: Olive Hill
Street address state: KY
Zip/Postal code: 41164
General Phone: (606) 286-4201
General Fax: (606) 286-0120
General/National Adv. E-mail: dduncan@journal-times.com
Display Adv. E-mail: dduncan@journal-times.com
Editorial e-mail: tpreston@themoreheadnews.com
Primary Website: journal-times.com
Year Established: 1935
Avg Paid Circ: 1800
Avg Free Circ: 100
Audit By: Sworn/Estimate/Non-Audited
Audit Date: 10.06.2019
Personnel: Dan Duncan (Adv. Mgr.); Keith Kappes (Publisher and Editor)
Parent company (for newspapers): CNHI, LLC

OWENTON NEWS-HERALD

Street address 1: 154 W. Bryan St.
Street address 2: Ste 1
Street address city: Owenton
Street address state: KY
Zip/Postal code: 40359-1440
General Phone: (502) 484-3431
General Fax: (502) 484-3221
Primary Website: owentonnewsherald.com
Year Established: 1868
Avg Paid Circ: 4129
Audit By: Sworn/Estimate/Non-Audited
Audit Date: 10.06.2019
Personnel: Sherry Lyons (Circ. Mgr.); John Whitlock (News Ed.); Patti Clark (Pub./Ed./Gen. Mgr.); Scott Hubbard (Adv. Sales Rep.)
Parent company (for newspapers): Landmark Communications, Inc.; Landmark Community Newspapers, LLC

PINEVILLE SUN

Street address 1: PO Box 250
Street address city: Pineville
Street address state: KY
Zip/Postal code: 40977-0250
General Phone: (606) 337-2333
General Fax: (606) 337-2360
General/National Adv. E-mail: news@pinevillesun.net
Primary Website: facebook.com/pages/The-Pineville-Sun-Cumberland-Courier/129776610402283
Avg Paid Circ: 3500
Avg Free Circ: 41
Audit By: Sworn/Estimate/Non-Audited
Audit Date: 10.06.2019
Personnel: Rhonda Droughton (Adv. Dir.); Gary Ferguson (Ed.); Sam Gambrell (Ed.)

PIONEER NEWS

Street address 1: 455 N Buckman St
Street address city: Shepherdsville
Street address state: KY
Zip/Postal code: 40165-5902
General Phone: (502) 543-2288
General Fax: (502) 955-9704
General/National Adv. E-mail: editor@pioneernews.net
Display Adv. E-mail: editor@pioneernews.net
Editorial e-mail: editor@pioneernews.net
Primary Website: pioneernews.net
Year Established: 1882
Avg Paid Circ: 5300
Audit By: Sworn/Estimate/Non-Audited
Audit Date: 10.06.2019
Personnel: Mike Farner (Sports Ed.); Thomas J. Barr (Pub.); Laura Felts
Parent company (for newspapers): Landmark Communications, Inc.; Landmark Community Newspapers, LLC

SALYERSVILLE INDEPENDENT

Street address 1: 900 Parkway Dr
Street address city: Salyersville
Street address state: KY
Zip/Postal code: 41465-9251
General Phone: (606) 349-2915
General Fax: (888) 704-6789
General/National Adv. E-mail: vanessa@salyersvilleindependent.com
Display Adv. E-mail: jo@salyersvilleindependent.com
Primary Website: salyersvilleindependent.com
Year Established: 1821
Audit By: Sworn/Estimate/Non-Audited
Audit Date: 10.06.2019
Personnel: David Prater (Pub.)

SOUTH KENTON RECORDER

Street address 1: 226 Grandview Dr
Street address city: Fort Mitchell
Street address state: KY
Zip/Postal code: 41017-2702
General Phone: (859) 283-0404
General Fax: (859) 283-7285
Advertising Phone: (513) 768-8338
Editorial Phone: (859) 283-0404
General/National Adv. E-mail: kynews@communitypress.com
Display Adv. E-mail: llawrence@enquirer.com
Editorial e-mail: kynews@communitypress.com
Primary Website: communitypress.com
Year Established: 2011
Avg Paid Circ: 911
Avg Free Circ: 13423
Audit By: Sworn/Estimate/Non-Audited
Audit Date: 10.06.2019
Personnel: Sharon Schachleiter (Circ. Mgr.); Nancy Daly (Sr. Ed.)
Parent company (for newspapers): Gannett

SPENCER MAGNET

Street address 1: 100 W Main St
Street address city: Taylorsville
Street address state: KY
Zip/Postal code: 40071-8624
General Phone: (502) 477-2239
General Fax: (502) 477-2110
Advertising Phone: (502) 477-2239 ext 25
Editorial Phone: (502) 477-2239 ext 24
General/National Adv. E-mail: lmason@spencermagnet.com
Display Adv. E-mail: lmason@spencermagnet.com
Editorial e-mail: lmason@spencermagnet.com
Primary Website: spencermagnet.com
Year Established: 1867
Avg Paid Circ: 3600
Audit By: Sworn/Estimate/Non-Audited
Audit Date: 10.06.2019
Personnel: Jeff Sopland (graphics designer); Lynette Mason (Publisher); Susan Collins (Circulation Manager); John Shindlebower (Editor)
Parent company (for newspapers): Paxton Media Group; Landmark Community Newspapers, LLC; Landmark Communications, Inc.

SPRINGFIELD SUN

Street address 1: 108 Progress Ave
Street address city: Springfield
Street address state: KY
Zip/Postal code: 40069-1400
General Phone: (859) 336-3716
General Fax: (859) 336-7718
General/National Adv. E-mail: shorty@thespringfieldsun.com
Display Adv. E-mail: shorty@thespringfieldsun.com
Editorial e-mail: bmattingly@thespringfieldsun.com
Primary Website: thespringfieldsun.com
Avg Paid Circ: 3500
Audit By: Sworn/Estimate/Non-Audited
Audit Date: 10.06.2019
Personnel: Renee Webb (Circ. Mgr./Bookkeeper); Shorty Lassitter (Gen. Mgr./Adv. Mgr.); Geoff Hamill (Ed.); Brandon Mattingly (Sports and news reporter); Lula Mae Adams (News clerk)
Parent company (for newspapers): Paxton Media Group; Landmark Community Newspapers, LLC

THE ADVANCE YEOMAN

Street address 1: 1540 McCracken Blvd
Street address city: Paducah
Street address state: KY
Zip/Postal code: 42001-9192
General Phone: (270) 519-3395
General Fax: (270) 442-5220
General/National Adv. E-mail: larrah@ky-news.com
Display Adv. E-mail: larrah@ky-news.com
Editorial e-mail: advanceyeoman@gmail.com
Primary Website: ky-news.com
Year Established: 1889
Avg Paid Circ: 4300
Avg Free Circ: 45
Audit By: Sworn/Estimate/Non-Audited
Audit Date: 10.06.2019
Personnel: Greg Leneave (Pub.); Larrah Workman (Adv. Mgr.); Bobby Mayberry (Ed.); Gregory Vaught (Prodn. Mgr.)

THE ANDERSON NEWS

Street address 1: PO Box 410
Street address city: Lawrenceburg
Street address state: KY
Zip/Postal code: 40342-0410
General Phone: (502) 839-6906
General Fax: (502) 839-3118
General/National Adv. E-mail: advertising@theandersonnews.com
Display Adv. E-mail: classifieds@theandersonnews.com
Editorial e-mail: news@theandersonnews.com
Primary Website: theandersonnews.com
Mthly Avg Views: 50000
Year Established: 1877
Avg Paid Circ: 5200
Audit By: Sworn/Estimate/Non-Audited
Audit Date: 10.06.2019
Personnel: Ben Carlson (Ed./Pub.); Bud Garrison (Adv. Mgr.); Claudia Kuhn (Adv. Sales Rep.); Shirley Morgan (Classified Adv. Mgr.)
Parent company (for newspapers): Landmark Communications, Inc.; Landmark Community Newspapers, LLC

THE APPALACHIAN NEWS-EXPRESS

Street address 1: 129 Caroline Ave
Street address city: Pikeville

Street address state: KY
Zip/Postal code: 41501-1101
General Phone: (606) 437-4054
General Fax: (606) 437-4246
General/National Adv. E-mail: mkeller@news-expressky.com
Display Adv. E-mail: mkeller@news-expressky.com
Editorial e-mail: editor@news-expressky.com
Primary Website: news-expressky.com
Avg Paid Circ: 11000
Audit By: Sworn/Estimate/Non-Audited
Audit Date: 10.06.2019
Personnel: Jeff Vanderbeck (Pub.); Lisa Moore (Circ. Mgr); Russ Cassady (Ed.); Melissa Keller (Adv. Dir)
Parent company (for newspapers): Lancaster Management, Inc.

THE BEREA CITIZEN

Street address 1: 711 Chestnut St
Street address 2: Ste 2
Street address city: Berea
Street address state: KY
Zip/Postal code: 40403-1916
General Phone: (859) 986-0959
General Fax: (859) 986-0960
General/National Adv. E-mail: bereacitizen@windstream.net
Editorial e-mail: www.bereacitizen@windstream.net
Primary Website: citizen.nolangroupmedia.com
Avg Paid Circ: 4000
Audit By: Sworn/Estimate/Non-Audited
Audit Date: 10.06.2019
Personnel: Teresa Scenters (Pub.); Beth Myers (Ed.)

THE BIG SANDY NEWS

Street address 1: PO Box 766
Street address city: Louisa
Street address state: KY
Zip/Postal code: 41230-0766
General Phone: (606) 638-4581
General Fax: (606) 638-9949
General/National Adv. E-mail: bcrum@bigsandynews.com
Display Adv. E-mail: classifieds@bigsandynews.com
Editorial e-mail: info@bigsandynews.com
Primary Website: bigsandynews.com
Year Established: 1885
Avg Paid Circ: 12000
Audit By: Sworn/Estimate/Non-Audited
Audit Date: 10.06.2019
Personnel: Becky Crum (Adv. Mgr.); Doug McDavid (Circ. Mgr.); Tony Fyffe (Mng. Ed.)

THE BRACKEN COUNTY NEWS

Street address 1: 216 Frankfort St
Street address city: Brooksville
Street address state: KY
Zip/Postal code: 41004-8306
General Phone: (606) 735-2198
General Fax: (606) 735-2199
Editorial e-mail: brackencountynews@gmail.com
Primary Website: thebrackencountynews.com
Year Established: 1927
Avg Paid Circ: 3000
Avg Free Circ: 114
Audit By: Sworn/Estimate/Non-Audited
Audit Date: 10.06.2019
Personnel: Kathy Bay (Pub.); Amy Meyer (Circ. Mgr.); Lynn Darnell (Ed.)

THE CADIZ RECORD

Street address 1: 58 Nunn Blvd
Street address city: Cadiz
Street address state: KY
Zip/Postal code: 42211-7968
General Phone: (270) 522-6605
General Fax: (270) 522-3001
General/National Adv. E-mail: ads@cadizrecord.com
Display Adv. E-mail: chazelmyer@cadizrecord.com
Editorial e-mail: news@cadizrecord.com
Primary Website: cadizrecord.com
Avg Paid Circ: 4800
Avg Free Circ: 97
Audit By: Sworn/Estimate/Non-Audited
Audit Date: 10.06.2019
Personnel: Mary Beth Carlock (Gen. Mgr.); Connie Puglisi (Adv. Exec.); Cynthia Mitchell (Adv. Mgr.); Justin McGill (Exec. Ed.); Jennifer Wallace (Prodn. Mgr.)

THE CARLISLE COUNTY NEWS

Street address 1: 1540 McCracken Blvd
Street address city: Paducah
Street address state: KY
Zip/Postal code: 42001-9192
General Phone: (270) 628-5490
General Fax: (270) 442-5220
General/National Adv. E-mail: ccn1@galaxycable.net
Primary Website: ky-news.com
Year Established: 1894
Avg Paid Circ: 1625
Avg Free Circ: 77
Audit By: Sworn/Estimate/Non-Audited
Audit Date: 10.06.2019
Personnel: Greg Leneave (Pub.); Lilly Morefield (Ed.); Kate Prince (Staff Writer); STEPHANIE DAWSON (AD SALES)

THE CITIZEN-TIMES

Street address 1: 611 E Main St
Street address city: Scottsville
Street address state: KY
Zip/Postal code: 42164-1628
General Phone: (270) 237-3441
General Fax: (270) 237-4943
General/National Adv. E-mail: ctines@nctc.com
Editorial e-mail: ctimes@nctc.com
Primary Website: thecitizen-times.com
Year Established: 1918
Avg Paid Circ: 6000
Avg Free Circ: 212
Audit By: Sworn/Estimate/Non-Audited
Audit Date: 10.06.2019
Personnel: Robert Burns Pitchford (Pub.); Jeannetta Stinson (Adv. Mgr.); Matthew James Pedigo (Ed.)

THE CLAY CITY TIMES

Street address 1: 4477 Main St
Street address city: Clay City
Street address state: KY
Zip/Postal code: 40380
General Phone: (606) 663-5540
General Fax: (606) 663-6397
General/National Adv. E-mail: cctimesnews@bellsouth.net
Display Adv. E-mail: cctads@windstream.net
Primary Website: claycity-times.com
Year Established: 1899
Avg Paid Circ: 3200
Audit By: Sworn/Estimate/Non-Audited
Audit Date: 10.06.2019
Personnel: Teresa Hatfield-Barger (Publisher)

THE CRITTENDEN PRESS

Street address 1: 125 E Bellville St
Street address city: Marion
Street address state: KY
Zip/Postal code: 42064-1409
General Phone: (270) 965-3191
General Fax: (270) 965-2516
General/National Adv. E-mail: advertising@the-press.com
Display Adv. E-mail: information@the-press.com
Editorial e-mail: thepress@the-press.com
Primary Website: the-press.com
Avg Paid Circ: 3800
Avg Free Circ: 64
Audit By: Sworn/Estimate/Non-Audited
Audit Date: 10.06.2019
Personnel: Chris Evans (Pub.); Allison Mick-Evans (Adv. Mgr.); Daryl Tabor (Mng. Ed)

THE DAWSON SPRINGS PROGRESS

Street address 1: 131 S Main St
Street address city: Dawson Springs
Street address state: KY
Zip/Postal code: 42408-1745
General Phone: (270) 797-3271
General Fax: (270) 797-3273
General/National Adv. E-mail: progress@vci.net
Editorial e-mail: progress@vci.net
Primary Website: dawsonspringsprogress.com
Year Established: 1919
Avg Paid Circ: 1800
Avg Free Circ: 35
Audit By: Sworn/Estimate/Non-Audited
Audit Date: 10.06.2019
Personnel: Melissa Larimore (Managing editor); Lucas Johnson (editorial assistant)

THE EDMONTON HERALD-NEWS

Street address 1: 116 S MAIN ST
Street address city: Edmonton
Street address state: KY
Zip/Postal code: 42129
General Phone: (270) 432-3291
General Fax: (270) 432-4414
Advertising Phone: (270) 590-6625
General/National Adv. E-mail: heraldnews@jpinews.com
Classified Adv. e-mail: heraldnews@jpinews.com
Editorial e-mail: heraldnews@jpinews.com
Primary Website: jpinews.com
Year Established: 1894
Avg Paid Circ: 2500
Audit By: Sworn/Estimate/Non-Audited
Audit Date: 10.06.2019
Personnel: Jeffrey Jobe (Pub./Owner)
Parent company (for newspapers): Jobe Publishing Inc.

THE ERLANGER RECORDER

Street address 1: 226 Grandview Dr
Street address city: Fort Mitchell
Street address state: KY
Zip/Postal code: 41017-2702
General Phone: (859) 283-0404
General Fax: (859) 283-7285
General/National Adv. E-mail: kynews@communitypress.com
Primary Website: communitypress.com
Year Established: 2001
Avg Paid Circ: 130
Avg Free Circ: 7201
Audit By: Sworn/Estimate/Non-Audited
Audit Date: 10.06.2019
Personnel: Debbie Maggard (Adv. Mgr); Sharon Schachleiter (Circ. Mgr.); Nancy Daly (Sr. Ed.)
Parent company (for newspapers): Gannett

THE FULTON LEADER

Street address 1: 214 Main St
Street address city: Fulton
Street address state: KY
Zip/Postal code: 42041
General Phone: (270) 472-1121
General/National Adv. E-mail: fultonleader@bellsouth.net
Primary Website: thecurrent.press
Year Established: 1898
Avg Paid Circ: 2261
Avg Free Circ: 31
Audit By: Sworn/Estimate/Non-Audited
Audit Date: 10.06.2019
Personnel: Benita Fuzzell (Pub.); Barbara Atwill (Billing/Subs.); Bonnie Collier; Clay McWherther (Sales); Rebecca Meadows (Reporter)
Parent company (for newspapers): Magic Valley Publishing Co., Inc

THE GALLATIN COUNTY NEWS

Street address 1: 211 3rd St
Street address city: Warsaw
Street address state: KY
Zip/Postal code: 41095-2002
General Phone: (859) 567-5051
General Fax: (859) 567-6397
General/National Adv. E-mail: galnews@zoomtown.com
Editorial e-mail: galnews@zoomtown.com
Primary Website: thegallatincountynews.com
Year Established: 1880
Avg Paid Circ: 2400
Avg Free Circ: 37
Audit By: Sworn/Estimate/Non-Audited
Audit Date: 10.06.2019
Personnel: Denny K. Warnick (Pub.); Clay Warnick (Adv. Mgr.); Kelly Warnick (Mng. Ed.); Terry Combs-Caldwell (Prodn. Mgr.)

THE GOLD STANDARD

Street address 1: PO Box 1000
Street address 2: 125 Sixth Ave. Bldg 1110, 2nd Floor, Wing B
Street address city: Fort Knox
Street address state: KY
Zip/Postal code: 40121-1000
General Phone: (502) 624-1095
General Fax: (502) 624-2096
Editorial Phone: (502) 624-1095
General/National Adv. E-mail: melissalove@thenewsenterprise.com
Editorial e-mail: bsheroan@thenewsenterprise.com
Primary Website: fkgoldstandard.com
Audit By: Sworn/Estimate/Non-Audited
Audit Date: 10.06.2019
Personnel: Chris Ordway (Pub.); Ben Sheroan (Ed.); Larry Jobe

THE HANCOCK CLARION

Street address 1: 230 Main St
Street address city: Hawesville
Street address state: KY
Zip/Postal code: 42348-2626
General Phone: (270) 927-6945
General Fax: (270) 927-6947
Advertising Phone: (270) 927-6945
General/National Adv. E-mail: hancockclarion@bellsouth.net
Display Adv. E-mail: hancockclarion@bellsouth.net
Editorial e-mail: hancockclarion@bellsouth.net
Primary Website: hancockclarion.com
Year Established: 1893
Avg Paid Circ: 3683
Audit By: Sworn/Estimate/Non-Audited
Audit Date: 10.06.2019
Personnel: Donn K. Wimmer (Ed.); Steve Wimmer (Mng. Ed.); Ralph Dickerson (News Ed.); Dave Taylor (Adv Mgr)

THE HARRODSBURG HERALD

Street address 1: 101 W Broadway St
Street address city: Harrodsburg
Street address state: KY
Zip/Postal code: 40330-1527
General Phone: (859) 734-2726
General Fax: (859) 734-0737
General/National Adv. E-mail: advertising@harrodsburgherald.com
Display Adv. E-mail: classifieds@harrodsburgherald.com
Editorial e-mail: newssroom@harrodsburgherald.com
Primary Website: harrodsburgherald.com
Year Established: 1884
Avg Paid Circ: 3326
Audit By: Sworn/Estimate/Non-Audited
Audit Date: 10.06.2019
Personnel: Cathy Caton (Adv. Mgr.); Barbara Yeast (Circ. Mgr.); April Ellis (Owner/Gen. Mgr)

THE HAZARD HERALD

Street address 1: 439 High St
Street address city: Hazard
Street address state: KY
Zip/Postal code: 41701-1701
General Phone: (606) 436-5771
General Fax: (606) 436-3140
Advertising Phone: (606) 436-5771
General/National Adv. E-mail: bskeens@hazard-herald.com
Display Adv. E-mail: jjones@hazard-herald.com
Editorial e-mail: hazardherald1@gmail.com
Primary Website: hazard-herald.com
Year Established: 1911
Avg Paid Circ: 4000
Audit By: Sworn/Estimate/Non-Audited
Audit Date: 10.06.2019
Personnel: Jenny Jones (Off Mgr.); Barb Skeens (Sr. Sales Rep.); Jeff Vanderbeck (Pub.); Danny Coleman (Adv. Rep.); Russ Cassidy (Ed.)

Parent company (for newspapers): Lancaster Management, Inc.

THE HERALD-LEDGER

Street address 1: 143 W Main St
Street address city: Eddyville
Street address state: KY
Zip/Postal code: 42038-7762
General Phone: (270) 388-2269
General Fax: (270) 388-5540
General/National Adv. E-mail: sales@heraldledger.com
Display Adv. E-mail: sales@heraldledger.com
Editorial e-mail: news@heraldledger.com
Primary Website: heraldledger.com
Year Established: 1901
Avg Paid Circ: 2000
Audit By: Sworn/Estimate/Non-Audited
Audit Date: 10.06.2019
Personnel: Rae Wagoner (Pub.); Becky Fields (Office Mgr.); Jody Norwood (Ed.)

THE HICKMAN COUNTY GAZETTE

Street address 1: 308 S Washington St
Street address 2: Ste 101
Street address city: Clinton
Street address state: KY
Zip/Postal code: 42031-1340
General Phone: (270) 653-3381
General Fax: (270) 653-3322
General/National Adv. E-mail: gazette3322@bellsouth.net
Primary Website: magicvalleypublishing.com
Year Established: 1843
Avg Paid Circ: 2000
Avg Free Circ: 25
Audit By: Sworn/Estimate/Non-Audited
Audit Date: 10.06.2019
Personnel: Dennis Richardson (Pub.); Nancy Evans (Adv. Mgr.); Gaye Bencini (Ed.)

THE HICKMAN COUNTY TIMES

Street address 1: 104 S Jefferson St
Street address city: Clinton
Street address state: KY
Zip/Postal code: 42031-1318
General Phone: (270) 653-4040
General/National Adv. E-mail: tommy@thehctimes.com
Editorial e-mail: tommy@thehctimes.com
Primary Website: risnerweb.com
Year Established: 2011
Audit By: Sworn/Estimate/Non-Audited
Audit Date: 10.06.2019
Personnel: Gaye Bencini (Co-Owner); Tommy Kimbro (Co-Owner)

THE INTERIOR JOURNAL

Street address 1: 301 W Main St
Street address city: Stanford
Street address state: KY
Zip/Postal code: 40484-1215
General Phone: (606) 365-2104
General Fax: (606) 365-2105
Advertising Phone: (859) 469-6429
General/National Adv. E-mail: Larry.hensley@theinteriorjournal.com
Display Adv. E-mail: Carrie.shields@theinteriorjournal.com
Classified Adv. e-mail: Bonnie.kolasa@theinteriorjournal.com
Editorial e-mail: Abigail.whitehouse@theinteriorjournal.com
Primary Website: theinteriorjournal.com
Year Established: 1860
Avg Paid Circ: 2400
Audit By: Sworn/Estimate/Non-Audited
Audit Date: 10.06.2019
Personnel: Bonnie Kolasa; Larry Hensley (Pub.); Abigail Whitehouse (Editor); Nancy Leedy (Sports Editor)
Parent company (for newspapers): Boone Newspapers, Inc.

THE JESSAMINE JOURNAL

Street address 1: 507 N Main St
Street address city: Nicholasville
Street address state: KY
Zip/Postal code: 40356-1156
General Phone: (859) 885-5381
General Fax: (859) 887-2966
General/National Adv. E-mail: joe.hall@jessaminejournal.com
Display Adv. E-mail: finditky@jessaminejournal.com
Editorial e-mail: brittany.fuller@jessaminejournal.com
Primary Website: jessamineonline.com
Year Established: 1873
Avg Paid Circ: 3500
Audit By: Sworn/Estimate/Non-Audited
Audit Date: 10.06.2019
Personnel: Brittany Fuller (Ed.); Michael Caldwell (Pres./Pub.)
Parent company (for newspapers): Boone Newspapers, Inc.

THE JOURNAL ENTERPRISE

Street address 1: 114 N Broadway St
Street address city: Providence
Street address state: KY
Zip/Postal code: 42450-1220
General Phone: (270) 667-2068
General Fax: (270) 667-9160
General/National Adv. E-mail: chust@journalenterprise.com
Editorial e-mail: matt@journalenterprise.com
Primary Website: journalenterprise.com
Year Established: 1905
Avg Paid Circ: 4500
Audit By: Sworn/Estimate/Non-Audited
Audit Date: 10.06.2019
Personnel: Matt Hughes (News Ed.); Charles Hust (Ed)

THE LAKE NEWS

Street address 1: 153 E 5th Ave
Street address city: Calvert City
Street address state: KY
Zip/Postal code: 42029-9998
General Phone: (270) 395-5858
General Fax: (270) 395-5858
General/National Adv. E-mail: news@thelakenews.com
Display Adv. E-mail: news@thelakenews.com
Editorial e-mail: news@thelakenews.com
Primary Website: thelakenews.com
Year Established: 1984
Avg Paid Circ: 1900
Audit By: USPS
Audit Date: 01.10.2022
Personnel: Loyd Ford (Ed./Pub.)

THE LESLIE COUNTY NEWS

Street address 1: 22009 Main St
Street address city: Hyden
Street address state: KY
Zip/Postal code: 41749-8568
General Phone: (606) 672-2841
General Fax: (606) 672-7409
General/National Adv. E-mail: rebab@tds.net
Primary Website: facebook.com/pages/Leslie-County-News/141938412518523
Avg Paid Circ: 3500
Avg Free Circ: 25
Audit By: Sworn/Estimate/Non-Audited
Audit Date: 10.06.2019
Personnel: Vernon Baker (Pub.); Jan Estep (Circ. Mgr.)

THE LETCHER COUNTY COMMUNITY PRESS

Street address 1: 73 Community Dr
Street address city: Cromona
Street address state: KY
Zip/Postal code: 41810-9000
General Phone: (606) 855-4541
General Fax: (606) 855-9290
Advertising Phone: (606) 855-4541
Editorial Phone: (606) 855-4542
General/National Adv. E-mail: Paul@superiorprinting.org
Display Adv. E-mail: Tina@superiorprinting.org
Editorial e-mail: Paul@superiorprinting.org
Primary Website: http://lch.stparchive.com
Year Established: 1959
Avg Paid Circ: 2000
Avg Free Circ: 20
Audit By: Sworn/Estimate/Non-Audited
Audit Date: 10.06.2019
Personnel: Bobbie Whitaker (Adv. Mgr.); Charles W. Whitaker (Ed.); William M. Whitaker (Mng. Ed.)

THE MADISON COUNTY ADVERTISER

Street address 1: 380 Big Hill Ave
Street address city: Richmond
Street address state: KY
Zip/Postal code: 40475-2012
General Phone: (859) 623-1669
General Fax: (859) 623-2337
Advertising Phone: (859) 624-6685
Editorial Phone: (859) 624-6690
General/National Adv. E-mail: tmerlon@richmondregister.com
Display Adv. E-mail: pbowlin@richmondregister.com
Editorial e-mail: editor@richmondregister.com
Primary Website: richmondregister.com
Avg Free Circ: 28000
Audit By: Sworn/Estimate/Non-Audited
Audit Date: 10.06.2019
Personnel: Jonathan Greene; Dave Eldridge; Tim Merlin
Parent company (for newspapers): CNHI, LLC

THE MANCHESTER ENTERPRISE

Street address 1: 103 3rd St
Street address city: Manchester
Street address state: KY
Zip/Postal code: 40962-1119
General Phone: (606) 598-2319
General Fax: (606) 598-2330
Display Adv. E-mail: cblair@themanchesterenterprise.com
Primary Website: themanchesterenterprise.com
Avg Paid Circ: 6500
Audit By: Sworn/Estimate/Non-Audited
Audit Date: 10.06.2019
Personnel: Glenn Gray (Pub.); Rodney Miller (Adv Mgr)

THE MAYFIELD MESSENGER

Street address 1: 111 S 7th St
Street address city: Mayfield
Street address state: KY
Zip/Postal code: 42066-2341
General Phone: (270) 247-5223
General Fax: (270) 247-6336
Advertising Phone: (270) 247-5223
Advertising Fax: (270) 247-6336
Editorial Phone: (270) 247-1516
Editorial Fax: (270) 247-6336
General/National Adv. E-mail: sbseay@mayfield-messenger.com
Display Adv. E-mail: mellen@mayfield-messenger.com
Classified Adv. e-mail: sbseay@mayfield-messenger.com
Editorial e-mail: news@mayfield-messenger.com
Primary Website: mayfield-messenger.com
Year Established: 1900
Avg Paid Circ: 2000
Audit By: Sworn/Estimate/Non-Audited
Audit Date: 10.06.2019
Personnel: Tom Berry (Ed.)
Parent company (for newspapers): Paxton Media Group

THE MCCREARY COUNTY VOICE

Street address 1: 57 Oaks Ln
Street address city: Whitley City
Street address state: KY
Zip/Postal code: 42653-6173
General Phone: (606) 376-5500
General Fax: (606) 376-8609
General/National Adv. E-mail: susie@tmcvoice.com
Display Adv. E-mail: susie@tmcvoice.com
Editorial e-mail: editor@tmcvoice.com
Primary Website: themccrearyvoice.com
Year Established: 2000
Audit By: Sworn/Estimate/Non-Audited
Audit Date: 10.06.2019
Personnel: Greg Bird (Ed.)

THE MEADE COUNTY MESSENGER

Street address 1: 138 Broadway St
Street address 2: Ste A
Street address city: Brandenburg
Street address state: KY
Zip/Postal code: 40108-1272
General Phone: (270) 422-2155
General Fax: (270) 422-2110
General/National Adv. E-mail: mcmsales@bbtel.com
Display Adv. E-mail: typesetter@bbtel.com
Editorial e-mail: messenger@bbtel.com
Primary Website: meadecountymessenger.com
Year Established: 1882
Avg Paid Circ: 5460
Avg Free Circ: 142
Audit By: Sworn/Estimate/Non-Audited
Audit Date: 10.06.2019
Personnel: Rena Singleton (Pub.); Jim Mansfield (Ed)

THE MONROE COUNTY CITIZEN

Street address 1: 201 N Main St
Street address 2: Ste A
Street address city: Tompkinsville
Street address state: KY
Zip/Postal code: 42167-1685
General Phone: (270) 487-8666
General Fax: (270) 786-4470
Advertising Phone: (270) 590-6625
General/National Adv. E-mail: citizen@jpinews.com
Display Adv. E-mail: citizen@jpinews.com
Editorial e-mail: jobe@jobeinc.com
Primary Website: jobeforkentucky.com
Avg Paid Circ: 1026
Avg Free Circ: 4874
Audit By: Sworn/Estimate/Non-Audited
Audit Date: 10.06.2019
Personnel: Jeff Jobe (Pub.)
Parent company (for newspapers): Jobe Publishing Inc.

THE MOREHEAD NEWS

Street address 1: 710 W 1st St
Street address city: Morehead
Street address state: KY
Zip/Postal code: 40351-1436
General Phone: (606) 784-4116
General Fax: (606) 784-7337
General/National Adv. E-mail: dduncan@themoreheadnews.com
Display Adv. E-mail: dduncan@themoreheadnews.com
Editorial e-mail: sockerman@themoreheadnews.com
Primary Website: themoreheadnews.com
Year Established: 1883
Avg Paid Circ: 4200
Avg Free Circ: 100
Audit By: Sworn/Estimate/Non-Audited
Audit Date: 10.06.2019
Personnel: Dan Duncan (Adv. Dir.); Stephanie Ockermann (Ed.); Eddie Blakeley (Pub.)
Parent company (for newspapers): CNHI, LLC

THE MOUNTAIN CITIZEN

Street address 1: 20 W MAIN ST
Street address city: Inez
Street address state: KY
Zip/Postal code: 41224
General Phone: (606) 298-7570
General Fax: (606) 298-3711
General/National Adv. E-mail: mountaincitizen@bellsouth.net
Editorial e-mail: mountaincitizen@bellsouth.net
Year Established: 1975
Avg Paid Circ: 6000
Avg Free Circ: 100
Audit By: Sworn/Estimate/Non-Audited
Audit Date: 10.06.2019
Personnel: Roger Smith (Pub.); Diane Smith (Adv. Mgr.); Becky Smith (Circ. Mgr.); Gary Ball (Ed.)

THE MOUNTAIN EAGLE

Street address 1: 41 N Webb St
Street address city: Whitesburg
Street address state: KY
Zip/Postal code: 41858-7324
General Phone: (606) 633-2252
General Fax: (606) 633-2843
General/National Adv. E-mail: mtneagle@bellsouth.net
Editorial e-mail: mtneagle@bellsouth.net
Primary Website: themountaineagle.com
Year Established: 1907
Avg Paid Circ: 4748
Avg Free Circ: 92
Audit By: AAM
Audit Date: 31.03.2017

Personnel: Thomas Gish (Pub.); Freddy Oakes (Adv. Mgr.); Benjamin T. Gish (Ed.)

THE NEWS DEMOCRAT & LEADER

Street address 1: 250 N Main St
Street address city: Russellville
Street address state: KY
Zip/Postal code: 42276-1841
General Phone: (270) 726-8394
General Fax: (270) 726-8396
Editorial e-mail: edit-ndl@bellsouth.net
Primary Website: newsdemocratleader.com
Avg Paid Circ: 6000
Audit By: Sworn/Estimate/Non-Audited
Audit Date: 10.06.2019
Personnel: Lola Nash (Adv. Mgr.); Heather Justice (Adv. Sales Rep.); O.J. Stapleton (Ed.); Chris Cooper (Mng. Ed.)

THE NEWS-ENTERPRISE

Street address 1: 200 Sycamore St.
Street address 2: Suite 134
Street address city: Elizabethtown
Street address state: KY
Zip/Postal code: 42701-2455
General Phone: (270) 769-1200
Advertising Phone: (270) 505-1411
Editorial Phone: (270) 505-1418
General/National Adv. E-mail: ne@thenewsenterprise.com
Display Adv. E-mail: vserra@thenewsenterprise.com
Classified Adv. e-mail: bchism@thenewsenterprise.com
Editorial e-mail: ne@thenewsenterprise.com
Primary Website: www.thenewsenterprise.com
Mthly Avg Views: 880000
Mthly Avg Unique Visitors: 120000
Year Established: 1974
Avg Paid Circ: 5680
Sun. Circulation Paid: 10590
Sun. Circulation Free: 432
Audit By: AAM
Audit Date: 9/31/2018
Personnel: Chris Ordway (Pub.); Lydia Leasor (Graphic Design Mgr); Ben Sheroan (Publisher); Chuck Jones (Sports Ed.); Valerie Serra (Advertising Director); David Dickens (Production Mgr.); Gina Clear (Editor); Jenny Simpson (Circulation Director); Charles Love (Prodn. Press Team Leader); Lisa D'Alessio (Business Mgr.); Erin Hahn (Adv. Dir.); Tom Siemers (Circ. Mgr.)
Parent company (for newspapers): Paxton Media Group; Landmark Communications, Inc.

THE OHIO COUNTY TIMES

Street address 1: 314 S Main St
Street address city: Hartford
Street address state: KY
Zip/Postal code: 42347-1129
General Phone: (270) 298-7100
General Fax: (270) 298-9572
General/National Adv. E-mail: ads@octimesnews.com
Primary Website: octimesnews.com
Avg Paid Circ: 6700
Avg Free Circ: 75
Audit By: Sworn/Estimate/Non-Audited
Audit Date: 10.06.2019
Personnel: Andy Anderson (Pub.); Seth Dukes (Ed.); Georgina Dockery (Community Ed.)
Parent company (for newspapers): Delphos Herald, Inc.

THE PAINTSVILLE HERALD

Street address 1: 978 Broadway St
Street address city: Paintsville
Street address state: KY
Zip/Postal code: 41240-1346
General Phone: (606) 789-5315
General Fax: (606) 789-9717
General/National Adv. E-mail: ads@paintsvilleherald.com
Display Adv. E-mail: classifieds@paintsvilleherald.com
Editorial e-mail: news@paintsvilleherald.com
Primary Website: paintsvilleherald.com
Year Established: 1901
Avg Paid Circ: 5200
Audit By: Sworn/Estimate/Non-Audited
Audit Date: 10.06.2019
Personnel: Paula Halm (Pub.)
Parent company (for newspapers): Lancaster Management, Inc.

THE RECORD

Street address 1: 209C W. White Oak Street
Street address city: Leitchfield
Street address state: KY
Zip/Postal code: 42754-5816
General Phone: (270) 259-6061
General Fax: (270) 230-8405
General/National Adv. E-mail: gm@graysonrecord.com
Display Adv. E-mail: circulation@graysonrecord.com
Editorial e-mail: news@graysonrecord.com
Primary Website: graysonrecord.com
Year Established: 1980
Avg Paid Circ: 3167
Avg Free Circ: 6
Audit By: Sworn/Estimate/Non-Audited
Audit Date: 10.06.2019
Personnel: Rebecca Morris (Ed./Gen. Mgr.); Nancy Farmer (Adv. Rep.); Alicia Carter (Circ./Off. Mgr.); Michaela Priddy (Adv. Rep.)
Parent company (for newspapers): Paxton Media Group; Landmark Community Newspapers Inc.

THE RUSSELL COUNTY NEWS-REGISTER

Street address 1: 120 Wilson St
Street address city: Russell Springs
Street address state: KY
Zip/Postal code: 42642-4315
General Phone: (270) 866-3191
General Fax: (270) 866-3198
General/National Adv. E-mail: advertising@russellcountynewspapers.com
Display Adv. E-mail: advertising@russellcountynewspapers.com
Editorial e-mail: news@russellcountynewspapers.com
Primary Website: russellcountynewspapers.com
Avg Free Circ: 10000
Audit By: Sworn/Estimate/Non-Audited
Audit Date: 10.06.2019
Personnel: Stephanie Smith (Adv. Mgr.); Derek Aaron (Ed); Michelle Maldonado (Office Mgr)

THE SENTINEL-ECHO

Street address 1: 115 C V B Drive
Street address city: London
Street address state: KY
Zip/Postal code: 40741-1837
General Phone: (606) 878-7400
General Fax: (606) 878-7404
General/National Adv. E-mail: advertising@sentinel-echo.com
Display Adv. E-mail: advertising@sentinel-echo.com
Classified Adv. e-mail: thumphrey@thetimetribune.com
Editorial e-mail: jslaven@sentinel-echo.com
Primary Website: sentinel-echo.com
Year Established: 1873
Avg Paid Circ: 9800
Avg Free Circ: 10000
Audit By: USPS
Audit Date: 10.06.2019
Personnel: Willie Sawyers (Pub.); Shari Serier (Prodn. Mgr.); Mark Walker (Publisher); Kathy Jones (Adv. Mgr.); Janie Slaven (Editor); Earletta Sparkman (Circ. Mgr.); Lisa Harrison (Advertising); Jessie Eldridge (Advertising); Denis House (Sports Ed.)
Parent company (for newspapers): CNHI, LLC

THE SENTINEL-NEWS

Street address 1: 703 Taylorsville Rd
Street address city: Shelbyville
Street address state: KY
Zip/Postal code: 40065-9125
General Phone: (502) 633-2526
General Fax: (502) 633-2618
Editorial e-mail: tmartin@sentinelnews.com
Primary Website: sentinelnews.com
Year Established: 1866
Avg Paid Circ: 7500
Avg Free Circ: 18000
Audit By: Sworn/Estimate/Non-Audited
Audit Date: 10.06.2019
Personnel: Todd Martin (Ed.); Kerry Jonson (Pub.); Dan Barry (Adv. Mgr.); Diana Olson (Bookkeeper)
Parent company (for newspapers): Paxton Media Group; Landmark Community Newspapers, LLC; Landmark Communications, Inc.

THE TIMES JOURNAL

Street address 1: 120 Wilson St
Street address city: Russell Springs
Street address state: KY
Zip/Postal code: 42642-4315
General Phone: (270) 866-3191
General Fax: (270) 866-3198
General/National Adv. E-mail: advertising@russellcountynewspapers.com
Display Adv. E-mail: advertising@russellcountynewspapers.com
Editorial e-mail: news@russellcountynewspapers.com
Primary Website: russellcounty.net
Year Established: 1949
Avg Paid Circ: 5000
Avg Free Circ: 235
Audit By: Sworn/Estimate/Non-Audited
Audit Date: 10.06.2019
Personnel: David Davenport (Pub.); Kim Haydon (Bus. Mgr.); Stephanie Smith (Adv. Mgr.); Greg Wells (Mng. Ed.); Derek Aaron (News/Sports Ed.); Renee Daffron (Prodn. Mgr.)

THE TIMES-ARGUS

Street address 1: 202 W Broad St
Street address city: Central City
Street address state: KY
Zip/Postal code: 42330-1540
General Phone: (270) 754-2331
General Fax: (270) 754-1805
General/National Adv. E-mail: timesargus@bellsouth.net
Primary Website: timesargus.com
Year Established: 1906
Avg Paid Circ: 2600
Audit By: Sworn/Estimate/Non-Audited
Audit Date: 10.06.2019
Personnel: Debbie Harris (Adv. Mgr.); Mark Stone (President); Richard Deavers (Mng. Ed.)

THE TRI-CITY NEWS

Street address 1: 805 E Main St
Street address city: Cumberland
Street address state: KY
Zip/Postal code: 40823-1711
General Phone: (606) 589-2588
General Fax: (606) 589-2589
General/National Adv. E-mail: tricitynewsky@gmail.com
Display Adv. E-mail: tricitynewsky@gmail.com
Editorial e-mail: tricitynews@yahoo.com
Primary Website: facebook.com/pg/tcnky
Year Established: 1929
Avg Paid Circ: 2500
Avg Free Circ: 39
Audit By: Sworn/Estimate/Non-Audited
Audit Date: 10.06.2019
Personnel: Lindsay Collier (Adv. Mgr.); Rachel Ison (Publishing Ed.); Paul J. Wilder (Ed.)

THE VOICE-TRIBUNE

Street address 1: 607 West Main Street
Street address city: Louisville
Street address state: KY
Zip/Postal code: 40202
General Phone: (502) 897-8900
General Fax: (502) 897-8915
General/National Adv. E-mail: smitchell@voice-tribune.com
Display Adv. E-mail: eclark@leoweekly.com
Editorial e-mail: circ@voice-tribune.com
Primary Website: voice-tribune.com
Year Established: 1987
Avg Paid Circ: 11587
Avg Free Circ: 1850
Audit By: Sworn/Estimate/Non-Audited
Audit Date: 10.06.2019
Personnel: Tracy Blue (Pub.); Angie Fenton (Ed.)

THE WAYNE COUNTY OUTLOOK

Street address 1: 45 E Columbia Ave
Street address city: Monticello
Street address state: KY
Zip/Postal code: 42633-1293
General Phone: (606) 348-3338
General Fax: (606) 348-8848
General/National Adv. E-mail: advertising@wcoutlook.com
Display Adv. E-mail: wcoclass@windstream.net
Editorial e-mail: news@wcoutlook.com
Primary Website: wcoutlook.com
Avg Paid Circ: 5800
Audit By: Sworn/Estimate/Non-Audited
Audit Date: 10.06.2019
Personnel: Melinda Jones (Adv. Mgr.); Melodie Phelps (News Ed.)
Parent company (for newspapers): CNHI, LLC

TIMES LEADER

Street address 1: 607 W Washington St
Street address city: Princeton
Street address state: KY
Zip/Postal code: 42445-1941
General Phone: (270) 365-5588
General Fax: (270) 365-7299
General/National Adv. E-mail: advertising@timesleader.net
Display Adv. E-mail: classifieds@timesleader.net
Editorial e-mail: newsroom@timesleader.net
Primary Website: timesleader.net
Year Established: 1871
Avg Paid Circ: 5490
Avg Free Circ: 45
Audit By: Sworn/Estimate/Non-Audited
Audit Date: 10.06.2019
Personnel: Willie McGregor (Prodn. Mgr.); Sherry McGregor (Ad Rep/Graphic Designer); Todd Griffin (Sports Ed); Jared Nelson (Editor & General Manager); Debbie Frisch (Business Manager); Stacey Menser (Lifestyles/Features); Kayla Stevenson (Circulation/Advertising); Roberta Thompson (Printing Rep); Shelia Brennan (Photo tech/Online content)
Parent company (for newspapers): Kentucky New Era

TODD COUNTY STANDARD

Street address 1: 41 Public Sq
Street address city: Elkton
Street address state: KY
Zip/Postal code: 42220-8822
General Phone: (270) 265-2439
General Fax: (270) 265-2571
General/National Adv. E-mail: tcstandard@kypress.com
Editorial e-mail: tcstandard@kypress.com
Primary Website: toddcountynews.blogspot.com
Year Established: 1893
Avg Paid Circ: 2500
Audit By: Sworn/Estimate/Non-Audited
Audit Date: 10.06.2019
Personnel: Ryan Craig (Ed.)

TOMPKINSVILLE NEWS

Street address 1: 105 N Main St
Street address city: Tompkinsville
Street address state: KY
Zip/Postal code: 42167-1507
General Phone: (270) 487-5576
General Fax: (270) 487-8839
Advertising Phone: (270) 487-5576
Advertising Fax: (270) 487-8839
Editorial Phone: (270) 487-5576
Editorial Fax: (270) 487-8839
General/National Adv. E-mail: admanager@tompkinsvillenews.com
Display Adv. E-mail: classifieds@tompkinsvillenews.com
Editorial e-mail: tvillenews@tompkinsvillenews.com
Primary Website: tompkinsvillenews.com
Year Established: 1903
Avg Paid Circ: 3594
Avg Free Circ: 488
Audit By: Sworn/Estimate/Non-Audited
Audit Date: 10.06.2019
Personnel: Blanche B. Trimble (Publisher); Mark Elam (Gen. Mgr.); Ronda Elam (Ed.); Ledeana Creech (Graphics); Kristin Turner (Advertising); Brenda Bradstreet (Circulation mgr); Carolyn Jordan (Office Mgr., Bookkeeping)

Parent company (for newspapers): Monroe County Press, Inc.

TRIMBLE BANNER

Street address 1: 127 Highway 42 E
Street address city: Bedford
Street address state: KY
Zip/Postal code: 40006-7621
General Phone: (502) 255-3205
General Fax: (502) 732-4261
General/National Adv. E-mail: dgarrett@mytrimblenews.com
Editorial e-mail: lgillock@mytrimblenews.com
Primary Website: mytrimblenews.com
Year Established: 1879
Avg Paid Circ: 1325
Avg Free Circ: 5
Audit By: Sworn/Estimate/Non-Audited
Audit Date: 10.06.2019
Personnel: Jeff Moore (Pub.); Carla Kidwell (Circ. Mgr.); Deborah Garrett (Adv. Sales Consult.); Lorrie Gillock (Ed.)
Parent company (for newspapers): Paxton Media Group; Landmark Community Newspapers, LLC; Landmark Communications, Inc.

TROUBLESOME CREEK TIMES

Street address 1: 27 Main St E
Street address 2: Ste 1
Street address city: Hindman
Street address state: KY
Zip/Postal code: 41822-9998
General Phone: (606) 785-5134
General Fax: (606) 785-5134
Advertising Phone: (606) 785-5134
Advertising Fax: (606) 785-5134
Editorial Phone: (606) 785-5134
Editorial Fax: (606) 785-5134
General/National Adv. E-mail: shall@troublesomecreektimes.com
Display Adv. E-mail: shall@troublesomecreektimes.com
Editorial e-mail: shall@troublesomecreektimes.com
Primary Website: troublesomecreektimes.com
Year Established: 1980
Avg Paid Circ: 4000
Avg Free Circ: 250
Audit By: Sworn/Estimate/Non-Audited
Audit Date: 10.06.2019
Personnel: Sharon Kay Hall (Co-Pub.); Karen Jones Cody (Co- Publisher/ Exec. Editor); Jordan Thomas Hall (Asst. Gen. Mgr./Photographer); Tommy Curtis Hall (Advertising Sales); Tim Cody (Classifieds/Production)
Parent company (for newspapers): Knott County Publishing Co., Inc.

UNION COUNTY ADVOCATE

Street address 1: 214 W Main St
Street address city: Morganfield
Street address state: KY
Zip/Postal code: 42437-1479
General Phone: (270) 389-1833
General/National Adv. E-mail: uca@ucadvocate.com
Display Adv. E-mail: uca@ucadvocate.com
Editorial e-mail: uca@ucadvocate.com
Primary Website: thegleaner.com
Year Established: 1885
Avg Paid Circ: 5000
Avg Free Circ: 11
Audit By: Sworn/Estimate/Non-Audited
Audit Date: 10.06.2019
Personnel: Jack Pate (Pub.); Colby Girten (GM); Jessica Paris (News/ Sports Ed.)

UNION RECORDER

Street address 1: 226 Grandview Dr
Street address city: Fort Mitchell
Street address state: KY
Zip/Postal code: 41017-2702
General Phone: (859) 578-5501
General Fax: (859) 578-5515
General/National Adv. E-mail: kynews@communitypress.com
Primary Website: communitypress.com
Year Established: 2001
Audit By: Sworn/Estimate/Non-Audited
Audit Date: 10.06.2019

Personnel: Sharon Schachleiter (Circ. Mgr); Nancy Daly (Sr. Ed)

WOODFORD SUN

Street address 1: PO Box 29
Street address city: Versailles
Street address state: KY
Zip/Postal code: 40383-0029
General Phone: (859) 873-4131
General Fax: (859) 873-0300
General/National Adv. E-mail: news@woodfordsun.com
Primary Website: woodfordsun.com
Year Established: 1869
Audit By: Sworn/Estimate/Non-Audited
Audit Date: 10.06.2019

LOUISIANA

AMITE TANGI-DIGEST

Street address 1: 120 NE Central Ave
Street address city: Amite
Street address state: LA
Zip/Postal code: 70422-2547
General Phone: (985) 748-7156
General Fax: (985) 748-7104
General/National Adv. E-mail: suzanne.lee@tangilena.com
Display Adv. E-mail: classifieds@tangilena.com
Editorial e-mail: carol.brooke@tangilena.com
Primary Website: tangilena.com
Year Established: 1868
Avg Paid Circ: 1500
Avg Free Circ: 19866
Audit By: Sworn/Estimate/Non-Audited
Audit Date: 10.06.2019
Personnel: Marcia Sims (Circ. Mgr.); Jennifer Decota (Business Mgr.)

AVOYELLES JOURNAL

Street address 1: 105 N Main St
Street address city: Marksville
Street address state: LA
Zip/Postal code: 71351-2405
General Phone: (318) 253-5413
General Fax: (318) 253-7223
General/National Adv. E-mail: ads@avoyelles.com
Display Adv. E-mail: ads@avoyelles.com
Primary Website: avoyelles.com
Year Established: 1978
Avg Free Circ: 16000
Audit By: Sworn/Estimate/Non-Audited
Audit Date: 10.06.2019
Personnel: Kathy Lipe (Circ. Mgr.); Randy DeCuir (Pub./Ed.); Amy Ducote (Adv. Mgr.)
Parent company (for newspapers): LSN Publishing Company LLC

BANNER-DEMOCRAT

Street address 1: 313 Lake St
Street address city: Lake Providence
Street address state: LA
Zip/Postal code: 71254-2629
General Phone: (318) 559-2750
General Fax: (318) 559-2750
General/National Adv. E-mail: bannerdemocrat@bellsouth.net
Editorial e-mail: bannerdemocrat@bellsouth.net
Primary Website: facebook.com/The-Banner-Democrat-127683417309400
Year Established: 1887
Avg Paid Circ: 1825
Avg Free Circ: 42
Audit By: Sworn/Estimate/Non-Audited
Audit Date: 10.06.2019
Personnel: Judy Whitaker (Adv. Mgr.); Billy Coleman (Reporter); Judy Whitaker (Adv, Mgr.); Jimmy Neighbours (Circ. Mgr.); Lynn Bearden (Managing Editor)

BEAUREGARD DAILY NEWS

Street address 1: 903 W 1st St
Street address city: Deridder
Street address state: LA
Zip/Postal code: 70634-3701
General Phone: (337) 462-0616
General Fax: (337) 463-5347
General/National Adv. E-mail: csherman@beauregarddailynews.net
Display Adv. E-mail: llaborde@beauregarddailynews.net
Classified Adv. e-mail: classifieds@beauregarddailynews.net
Editorial e-mail: lblankenship@beauregarddailynews.net
Primary Website: beauregarddailynews.net
Year Established: 1945
Avg Paid Circ: 2800
Avg Free Circ: 5500
Sun. Circulation Paid: 13500
Audit By: Sworn/Estimate/Non-Audited
Audit Date: 10.06.2019
Personnel: Clarice Touhey (Pub.); Lauren Blankenship (Ed.); Cindy Sherman (Multi Media Sales Executive); Kurt Oswald (GM); Larissa Williams (Office Manager)
Parent company (for newspapers): CherryRoad Media

BIENVILLE DEMOCRAT

Street address 1: 1952 N Railroad Ave
Street address city: Arcadia
Street address state: LA
Zip/Postal code: 71001-3422
General Phone: (318) 263-2922
General Fax: (318) 263-8897
General/National Adv. E-mail: news@bienvilledemocrat.com
Primary Website: facebook.com/pages/The-Bienville-Democrat/148805565147072
Avg Paid Circ: 1903
Audit By: Sworn/Estimate/Non-Audited
Audit Date: 10.06.2019
Personnel: Priscilla Smith (Ed./Adv. Mgr.); Wayne R. Dring (Pub.)
Parent company (for newspapers): Natchitoches Times Newspapers

BOGALUSA DAILY NEWS

Street address 1: 525 Avenue V
Street address city: Bogalusa
Street address state: LA
Zip/Postal code: 70427-4493
General Phone: (985) 732-2565
General Fax: (985) 732-4036
Primary Website: bogalusadailynews.com
Year Established: 1927
Avg Paid Circ: 3200
Sun. Circulation Paid: 5195
Audit By: Sworn/Estimate/Non-Audited
Audit Date: 10.06.2019
Personnel: Carol Case (Adv. Dir.); Mildred Newman (Business Office Mgr.); Justin Schuver (Publisher and Editor)
Parent company (for newspapers): Boone Newspapers, Inc.

BOSSIER PRESS-TRIBUNE

Street address 1: 6346 Venecia Dr
Street address city: Bossier City
Street address state: LA
Zip/Postal code: 71111-7454
General Phone: (318) 747-7900
General Fax: (318) 747-5298
General/National Adv. E-mail: ads@bossierpress.com
Display Adv. E-mail: ads@bossierpress.com
Editorial e-mail: newsroom@bossierpress.com
Primary Website: bossierpress.com
Year Established: 1927
Avg Paid Circ: 5000
Audit By: Sworn/Estimate/Non-Audited
Audit Date: 10.06.2019
Personnel: Randy Brown (Pub); David A. Specht (Vice President & Publisher); Sean Green (Mng. Ed.); Hedges Russell (Sports Ed.); Amanda Simmons (Managing Editor); Kathleen Weir (Composing Director); Jamie Green (Legals/Classifieds Manager); Dianna Smathers (Sales Manager)
Parent company (for newspapers): Specht Newspapers Inc

BUNKIE RECORD

Street address 1: 637 Evergreen St
Street address city: Bunkie
Street address state: LA
Zip/Postal code: 71322-3903
General Phone: (318) 346-7251
General Fax: (318) 346-7253
Advertising Phone: (318) 253-5413
General/National Adv. E-mail: bunkierecord@yahoo.com
Primary Website: avoyellestoday.com
Year Established: 1888
Avg Paid Circ: 1500
Avg Free Circ: 18000
Audit By: Sworn/Estimate/Non-Audited
Audit Date: 10.06.2019
Personnel: Penny St. Romain (Gen. Mgr.)
Parent company (for newspapers): LSN Publishing Company LLC

CADDO CITIZEN

Street address 1: 203 S Spruce St
Street address city: Vivian
Street address state: LA
Zip/Postal code: 71082-2841
General Phone: (318) 375-3294
General Fax: (318) 375-3380
General/National Adv. E-mail: caddocitizen@centurytel.net
Primary Website: facebook.com/The-Caddo-Citizen-425796657560617
Avg Paid Circ: 1350
Audit By: Sworn/Estimate/Non-Audited
Audit Date: 10.06.2019
Personnel: Mary Haddox (Pub.)

CATAHOULA NEWS BOOSTER

Street address 1: 103 Third St
Street address city: Jonesville
Street address state: LA
Zip/Postal code: 71343-2339
General Phone: (318) 339-7242
General Fax: (318) 339-7243
General/National Adv. E-mail: catahoulanewsmedia@gmail.com
Display Adv. E-mail: catahoulanewsmedia@gmail.com
Editorial e-mail: catahoulanewsmedia@gmail.com
Primary Website: catahoulanewsbooster.com
Year Established: 1853
Avg Paid Circ: 3200
Avg Free Circ: 10
Audit By: Sworn/Estimate/Non-Audited
Audit Date: 10.06.2019
Personnel: Kim Cloessner (Ed./Pub.)

CENLA FOCUS MAGAZINE

Street address 1: 3911 Parliament Dr
Street address city: Alexandria
Street address state: LA
Zip/Postal code: 71303-3016
General Phone: (318) 442-8277
General Fax: (318) 484-3745
General/National Adv. E-mail: contact@cenlafocus.com
Primary Website: cenlafocus.com
Year Established: 1997
Audit By: Sworn/Estimate/Non-Audited
Audit Date: 10.06.2019
Personnel: Willie Harp (Pub.)

CENTRAL CITY NEWS

Street address 1: PO Box 1
Street address city: Greenwell Springs
Street address state: LA
Zip/Postal code: 7073-90001
General Phone: (225) 261-5055
General Fax: (225) 261-5022
General/National Adv. E-mail: centralcitynews@hotmail.com
Primary Website: centralcitynews.us
Audit By: Sworn/Estimate/Non-Audited
Audit Date: 10.06.2019

CONCORDIA SENTINEL

Street address 1: 1308 1st St
Street address city: Ferriday
Street address state: LA
Zip/Postal code: 71334-2847
General Phone: (318) 757-3646
General Fax: (318) 757-3001

General/National Adv. E-mail: admanager@concordiasentinel.com
Display Adv. E-mail: admanager@concordiasentinel.com
Classified Adv. e-mail: legals@concordiasentinel.com
Editorial e-mail: news@concordiasentinel.com
Primary Website: concordiasentinel.com
Mthly Avg Views: 189432
Year Established: 1876
Avg Paid Circ: 4700
Audit By: Sworn/Estimate/Non-Audited
Audit Date: 10.10.2023
Personnel: Lesley H. Capdepon (Mng. Ed.); Sam Hanna Jr. (Ed); Cora Morace (Circ. Mgr.); Joey Martin (Sport Ed); Kay Killen (Office Manager, Public Notices, Classified, Circulation); Stanley Nelson (Ed.); Mary Sue Hanna (Pub.); Gerry Meraz (Advertising Director)
Parent company (for newspapers): Hanna Publishing Co.

COUNTRY ROADS MAGAZINE

Street address 1: 758 Saint Charles St
Street address city: Baton Rouge
Street address state: LA
Zip/Postal code: 70802-6446
General Phone: (225) 343-3714
General Fax: (815) 550-2272
General/National Adv. E-mail: sales@countryroadsmag.com
Display Adv. E-mail: ashley@countryroadsmag.com
Editorial e-mail: lucie@countryroadsmag.com
Primary Website: countryroadsmagazine.com
Year Established: 1983
Avg Free Circ: 27000
Audit By: Sworn/Estimate/Non-Audited
Audit Date: 10.06.2019
Personnel: Ashley Fox-Smith (Associate Pub.); Dorcas Brown (Pres.); James Fox-Smith (Pub.); Lucie Monk Carter (Mng. Ed.); Kourtney Zimmerman (Creative Dir.)

DAILY WORLD

Street address 1: 5367 I 49 S Service Rd
Street address city: Opelousas
Street address state: LA
Zip/Postal code: 70570-0743
General Phone: (337) 942-4971
General Fax: (337) 943-7067
Advertising Phone: (337) 942-4971
Advertising Fax: (337) 943-7067
Editorial Phone: (337) 942-4971
Editorial Fax: (337) 943-7067
General/National Adv. E-mail: cmcross@gannett.com
Display Adv. E-mail: scarr2@mediaacadien.com
Classified Adv. e-mail: scarr2@mediaacadien.com
Editorial e-mail: cmcross@gannett.com
Primary Website: dailyworld.com
Year Established: 1939
Avg Paid Circ: 2329
Sat. Circulation Paid: 57
Sun. Circulation Paid: 5119
Sun. Circulation Free: 11
Audit By: AAM
Audit Date: 31.03.2019
Personnel: Vera Bridges (Pres./Pub.); Scott Carr (Adv. Sales Dir.); Jim Keeble (Circ. Distribution Dir.); Dean Taylor (Home Delivery Mgr.); Cheryl Devall (City Ed.); Freddie Herpin (Photographer); Cindy McCurry-Ross (Exec. Ed.)
Parent company (for newspapers): Gannett

GONZALES WEEKLY CITIZEN

Street address 1: 231 W Cornerview St
Street address city: Gonzales
Street address state: LA
Zip/Postal code: 70737-2841
General Phone: (225) 644-6397
General Fax: (225) 644-2069
Advertising Phone: (225) 644-6397
Editorial Phone: (225) 644-6397
General/National Adv. E-mail: cbarrett@gatehousemedia.com
Display Adv. E-mail: bgautreau@weeklycitizen.com
Editorial e-mail: editor@weeklycitizen.com
Primary Website: weeklycitizen.com
Year Established: 1998
Avg Paid Circ: 2500
Avg Free Circ: 250
Audit By: Sworn/Estimate/Non-Audited
Audit Date: 10.06.2019
Personnel: Marie Schexnaydre (Circ. Mgr.); Brenda Gautreau (Classified Adv. Mgr.); Stephanie Schexnaydre (General Manager/Bookkeeper); Crystal Barrett (Advertising Manager)
Parent company (for newspapers): CherryRoad Media

GUEYDAN JOURNAL

Street address 1: 311 Main St
Street address city: Gueydan
Street address state: LA
Zip/Postal code: 70542-3631
General Phone: (337) 536-6016
General Fax: (337) 536-9997
General/National Adv. E-mail: angie.longon@vermiliontoday.com
Display Adv. E-mail: angie.longon@vermiliontoday.com
Editorial e-mail: judy.leblanc@vermiliontoday.com
Primary Website: gueydantoday.com
Avg Paid Circ: 1200
Avg Free Circ: 15
Audit By: Sworn/Estimate/Non-Audited
Audit Date: 10.06.2019
Personnel: Angie Longon (Adv. Mgr.)
Parent company (for newspapers): LSN Publishing Company LLC

HOMER GUARDIAN-JOURNAL

Street address 1: 620 N Main St
Street address city: Homer
Street address state: LA
Zip/Postal code: 71040-3847
General Phone: (318) 927-3541
General Fax: (318) 927-3542
General/National Adv. E-mail: Guardian-Journal@ClaiborneOne.com
Editorial e-mail: Guardian-Journal@ClaiborneOne.com
Primary Website: claiborneone.org
Avg Paid Circ: 3200
Audit By: Sworn/Estimate/Non-Audited
Audit Date: 10.06.2019
Personnel: Michelle Bates (Ed); Kathryn H. Hightower (Co-Owner); Geraldine Hightower (Pub.)

KINDER COURIER NEWS

Street address 1: 1024 3rd Ave
Street address city: Kinder
Street address state: LA
Zip/Postal code: 70648-3413
General Phone: (337) 738-5642
General Fax: (337) 738-5630
General/National Adv. E-mail: kindernews@yahoo.com
Display Adv. E-mail: kindernews@yahoo.com
Editorial e-mail: kindernews@centurytel.net
Primary Website: kindernow.com
Year Established: 1979
Avg Paid Circ: 880
Audit By: Sworn/Estimate/Non-Audited
Audit Date: 10.06.2019
Personnel: David Ortego (Pub.); Rebekah Ogea (Office Mgr.); Marcus Norris (Adv. Mgr.); Jennifer Alision (Circ. Mgr.); Mark Leibson (Mng. Ed.)
Parent company (for newspapers): LSN Publishing Company LLC

LAFOURCHE GAZETTE

Street address 1: 12958 E MAIN ST
Street address city: Larose
Street address state: LA
Zip/Postal code: 70373
General Phone: (985) 693-7229
General Fax: (985) 693-8282
General/National Adv. E-mail: ads@TLGnewspaper.com
Display Adv. E-mail: ads@TLGnewspaper.com
Editorial e-mail: editor@TLGnewspaper.com
Primary Website: TLGnewspaper.com
Mthly Avg Views: 33000
Mthly Avg Unique Visitors: 4800
Year Established: 1965
Avg Free Circ: 15675
Audit By: CVC
Audit Date: 01.09.2018
Personnel: Addy Legendre (Ed.); Brandi LeBlanc (Adv.); Vicki Chaisson (Circ.)

L'OBSERVATEUR

Street address 1: 116 Newspaper Dr
Street address city: La Place
Street address state: LA
Zip/Postal code: 70068-4509
General Phone: (985) 652-9545
General Fax: (985) 652-1633
General/National Adv. E-mail: lobpress@bellsouth.net
Display Adv. E-mail: lobpress@bellsouth.net
Editorial e-mail: lobnews@bellsouth.net
Primary Website: lobservateur.com
Avg Paid Circ: 5000
Audit By: Sworn/Estimate/Non-Audited
Audit Date: 10.06.2019
Personnel: David Vitrano (Gen. Mgr/Mng. Ed.); Rhett Triche (Circ. Mgr)
Parent company (for newspapers): Boone Newspapers, Inc.; Carpenter Newsmedia

LOUISIANA FOOTBALL MAGAZINE

Street address 1: PO Box 86638
Street address city: Baton Rouge
Street address state: LA
Zip/Postal code: 70879-6638
General Phone: (225) 262-7667
General/National Adv. E-mail: info@lafootballmagazine.com
Editorial e-mail: info@lafootballmagazine.com
Primary Website: lafootballmagazine.com
Year Established: 1996
Audit By: Sworn/Estimate/Non-Audited
Audit Date: 10.06.2019
Personnel: Lee Brecheen

MADISON JOURNAL

Street address 1: 300 S Chestnut St
Street address city: Tallulah
Street address state: LA
Zip/Postal code: 71282-4206
General Phone: (318) 574-1404
General Fax: (318) 574-4219
General/National Adv. E-mail: publisher@madisonjournal.com
Avg Paid Circ: 2000
Audit By: Sworn/Estimate/Non-Audited
Audit Date: 10.06.2019
Parent company (for newspapers): 1976

NATCHITOCHES TIMES

Street address 1: 904 South Dr
Street address city: Natchitoches
Street address state: LA
Zip/Postal code: 71457-3053
General Phone: (318) 352-3618
General Fax: (318) 352-7842
Advertising Phone: (318) 352-3618
Advertising Fax: (318) 352-7842
Editorial Phone: (318) 352-3618
Editorial Fax: (318) 352-7842
General/National Adv. E-mail: news@natchitochestimes.com
Display Adv. E-mail: advertising@natchitochestimes.com
Classified Adv. e-mail: classifieds@natchitochestimes.com
Editorial e-mail: reporter@natchitochestimes.com
Primary Website: natchitochestimes.com
Year Established: 1903
Avg Paid Circ: 4805
Sat. Circulation Paid: 4805
Audit By: Sworn/Estimate/Non-Audited
Audit Date: 10.06.2019
Personnel: Lovan Thomas (Pres./Pub.); Steve Clowell (Mgr., Mktg./Promo.); Jerry Hooper (Circ. Mgr.); Carolyn Roy (Ed.); Ernie Davis (Prodn. Mgr.); Dennis Doll (Systems Mgr.)

NEW ORLEANS CITY BUSINESS

Street address 1: 3350 Ridgelake Drive
Street address 2: Suite 281
Street address city: Metairie
Street address state: LA
Zip/Postal code: 70002-3768
General Phone: (504) 834-9292
General/National Adv. E-mail: lbaldini@nopg.com
Display Adv. E-mail: lbaldini@nopg.com
Editorial e-mail: nchandler@nopg.com
Primary Website: neworleanscitybusiness.com
Avg Paid Circ: 3311
Avg Free Circ: 2380
Audit By: Sworn/Estimate/Non-Audited
Audit Date: 10.06.2019
Personnel: Lisa Blossman (Pub.); Natalie Chandler (Ed.); Lance Traweek (Ed.); Liz Baldini (Adv. Exec.)

PLAQUEMINES GAZETTE

Street address 1: 7962 Highway 23
Street address city: Belle Chasse
Street address state: LA
Zip/Postal code: 70037-2432
General Phone: (504) 392-1619
General Fax: (504) 392-7526
General/National Adv. E-mail: ads@plaqueminesgazette.com
Display Adv. E-mail: ads@plaqueminesgazette.com
Editorial e-mail: copy@plaqueminesgazette.com
Primary Website: plaqueminesgazette.com
Year Established: 1928
Avg Paid Circ: 2846
Avg Free Circ: 26
Audit By: Sworn/Estimate/Non-Audited
Audit Date: 10.06.2019
Personnel: Norris Babin (Circ. Mgr.); Dale Benoit (Ed.); Brandi Rollo (Graphic Designer, Layout Artist)

POINT OF VUE

Street address 1: 6160 W Park Ave
Street address city: Houma
Street address state: LA
Zip/Postal code: 70364-1700
General Phone: (985) 868-7515
General Fax: (985) 873-9009
General/National Adv. E-mail: sales@rushing-media.com
Display Adv. E-mail: sales@rushing-media.com
Editorial e-mail: editor@rushing-media.com
Primary Website: povhouma.com
Year Established: 2007
Audit By: Sworn/Estimate/Non-Audited
Audit Date: 10.06.2019
Personnel: Brian Rushing (Pub.); Terry Trahan Jr. (Ed.); Gavin Stevens (Creative Dir.)

POST SOUTH

Street address 1: 23520 Eden St.
Street address 2: Suite E
Street address city: Plaquemine
Street address state: LA
Zip/Postal code: 70764
General Phone: (225) 687-3288
Advertising Phone:
General/National Adv. E-mail: cbarrett@gatehousemedia.com
Display Adv. E-mail: legals@postsouth.com
Editorial e-mail: gfischer@weeklycitizen.com
Primary Website: postsouth.com
Year Established: 1957
Avg Paid Circ: 5500
Avg Free Circ: 12
Audit By: Sworn/Estimate/Non-Audited
Audit Date: 10.06.2019
Personnel: Clarice Touhey (Pub.); Crystall Barrett (Adv. Mgr.); Greg Fischer (Ed.)
Parent company (for newspapers): CherryRoad Media

RICHLAND BEACON-NEWS

Street address 1: 603 Louisa St
Street address city: Rayville
Street address state: LA
Zip/Postal code: 71269-2112
General Phone: (318) 728-6467
General Fax: (318) 728-5991
General/National Adv. E-mail: maryterry@bellsouth.net
Primary Website: richlandtoday.com
Year Established: 1868
Avg Paid Circ: 3000
Avg Free Circ: 10000
Audit By: Sworn/Estimate/Non-Audited
Audit Date: 10.06.2019
Personnel: Mary Terry (Pub.); Darryl Riser (Mng. Ed.)
Parent company (for newspapers): LSN Publishing Company LLC

RIVERSIDE READER

Street address 1: 570 N Jefferson Ave
Street address 2: Ste A
Street address city: Port Allen
Street address state: LA

Zip/Postal code: 70767-2412
General Phone: (225) 336-0749
General Fax: (225) 336-4157
General/National Adv. E-mail: Advertising@riversidereader.com
Primary Website: riversidereader.com
Audit By: Sworn/Estimate/Non-Audited
Audit Date: 10.06.2019
Personnel: John Michael Lockhart (Pub.); Rachel Thornhill (Adv. Sales); Josh Ledet (Circ. Mgr.)

SOUTHWEST DAILY NEWS

Street address 1: 120 S Huntington St
Street address city: Sulphur
Street address state: LA
Zip/Postal code: 70663-3332
General Phone: (337) 527-7075
General Fax: (337) 528-9557
Advertising Phone: (337) 527-7075
Advertising Fax: (337) 528-9557
Editorial Phone: (337) 527-7075
Editorial Fax: (337) 528-9557
General/National Adv. E-mail: sdneditorial@yahoo.com
Display Adv. E-mail: swtdaily@yahoo.com
Classified Adv. e-mail: andyjacobson61@gmail.com
Editorial e-mail: sdneditorial@yahoo.com
Primary Website: sulphurdailynews.com
Year Established: 1930
Avg Paid Circ: 4631
Sun. Circulation Paid: 4631
Audit By: Sworn/Estimate/Non-Audited
Audit Date: 10.06.2019
Personnel: Brian Trahan (Rgl. Exec. Ed.); Suzanne Peveto-Nelson (Rgl. Pub.); Marilyn Monroe (Newsroom Mgr.); Rodrick Anderson (Sports Ed.); Joan Stevens (Multimedia Acct. Specialist); Bernadine Consundado (Multimedia Acct. Specialist); Tracy Bumgardner (Adv. Exec.)
Parent company (for newspapers): Shearman Corporation; Boone Newspapers, Inc.

SPRINGHILL PRESS & NEWS-JOURNAL

Street address 1: 403 Butler St
Street address city: Springhill
Street address state: LA
Zip/Postal code: 71075-2735
General Phone: (318) 539-3511
General Fax: (318) 539-3512
General/National Adv. E-mail: nittimes@wnonline.net
Primary Website: facebook.com/pages/Springhill-Press-News-Journal/115652755161535
Year Established: 1937
Avg Paid Circ: 4000
Avg Free Circ: 9100
Audit By: Sworn/Estimate/Non-Audited
Audit Date: 10.06.2019
Personnel: Vicky Darst (Ed.)
Parent company (for newspapers): Natchitoches Times Newspapers

ST. CHARLES HERALD-GUIDE

Street address 1: 14236 Highway 90
Street address city: Boutte
Street address state: LA
Zip/Postal code: 70039-3516
General Phone: (985) 758-2795
General Fax: (985) 758-7000
General/National Adv. E-mail: ads@heraldguide.com
Display Adv. E-mail: ads@heraldguide.com
Editorial e-mail: editorial@heraldguide.com
Primary Website: heraldguide.com
Year Established: 1993
Avg Paid Circ: 4600
Audit By: Sworn/Estimate/Non-Audited
Audit Date: 10.06.2019
Personnel: Jaunita Guidry (Office Mgr.); Brent Madere (Adv. Sales Mgr.); Ann Talyor (Circ. Mgr.); Joe Lopez

ST. FRANCISVILLE DEMOCRAT

Street address 1: 4749 Johnson St
Street address city: Saint Francisville
Street address state: LA
Zip/Postal code: 70775-4330
General Phone: (225) 635-3366
General Fax: (225) 635-3398
General/National Adv. E-mail: sfdemocrat@bellsouth.net
Primary Website: facebook.com/pg/SFDemocrat/about
Avg Paid Circ: 2000
Audit By: Sworn/Estimate/Non-Audited
Audit Date: 10.06.2019
Personnel: Randall Newsom (Pub.)

ST. HELENA ECHO

Street address 1: Corner of Main and Lafette
Street address city: Greensburg
Street address state: LA
Zip/Postal code: 70441
General Phone: (225) 222-4541
General Fax: (225) 222-4542
General/National Adv. E-mail: echo@tangilena.com
Display Adv. E-mail: echo@tangilena.com
Editorial e-mail: echo@tangilena.com
Primary Website: facebook.com/St-Helena-Echo-305375052815206
Year Established: 1857
Avg Paid Circ: 1150
Avg Free Circ: 4438
Audit By: Sworn/Estimate/Non-Audited
Audit Date: 10.06.2019
Personnel: Marcia Sims (Circ. Mgr.); Gary Miller (Pub); Stephanie Warren (Ed)

TECHE NEWS

Street address 1: 214 N Main St
Street address city: Saint Martinville
Street address state: LA
Zip/Postal code: 70582-4028
General Phone: (337) 394-6232
General Fax: (337) 394-7511
General/National Adv. E-mail: advertise@techetoday.com
Display Adv. E-mail: cynthia.dore@techetoday.com
Editorial e-mail: sally.angelle@techetoday.com
Primary Website: techetoday.com
Year Established: 1886
Audit By: Sworn/Estimate/Non-Audited
Audit Date: 10.06.2019
Personnel: Ken Grissom; Henri Bienvenu
Parent company (for newspapers): LSN Publishing Company LLC

THE BASILE WEEKLY

Street address 1: 3014 Stagg Ave
Street address city: Basile
Street address state: LA
Zip/Postal code: 70515-5578
General Phone: (337) 432-6807
General Fax: (337) 432-6822
General/National Adv. E-mail: thebasileweekly@hotmail.com
Display Adv. E-mail: thebasileweeklyads@yahoo.com
Editorial e-mail: thebasileweekly@hotmail.com
Primary Website: facebook.com/thebasileweekly
Year Established: 1964
Avg Paid Circ: 800
Audit By: Sworn/Estimate/Non-Audited
Audit Date: 10.06.2019
Personnel: Rachel Fontenot (Adv. Mgr.); Darrel B. LeJeune (Ed.)
Parent company (for newspapers): LSN Publishing Company LLC; La. State Newspapers

THE BERNICE BANNER

Street address 1: 227 Boyette Rd
Street address city: Bernice
Street address state: LA
Zip/Postal code: 71222-5327
General Phone: (318) 285-7424
General Fax: (318) 285-7420
Advertising Phone: (318) 285-7424
Advertising Fax: (318) 285-7420
Editorial Phone: (318) 285-7424
Editorial Fax: (318) 285-7420
General/National Adv. E-mail: bernicebanner@oeccwildblue.com
Display Adv. E-mail: bernicebanner@oeccwildblue.com
Editorial e-mail: bernicebanner@oeccwildblue.com
Primary Website: bernicebanner.weebly.com
Year Established: 1995
Audit By: Sworn/Estimate/Non-Audited
Audit Date: 10.06.2019
Personnel: Jessie Kelley Boyett (Pub./Ed.)

THE DELHI DISPATCH

Street address 1: 603 Louisa St
Street address city: Rayville
Street address state: LA
Zip/Postal code: 71269-2112
General Phone: (318) 878-2444
General Fax: (318) 728-5991
General/National Adv. E-mail: maryterry@bellsouth.net
Avg Paid Circ: 1000
Avg Free Circ: 39
Audit By: Sworn/Estimate/Non-Audited
Audit Date: 10.06.2019
Personnel: Mary Terry (Pub.); Darryl Riser (Ed.)
Parent company (for newspapers): LSN Publishing Company LLC

THE DEQUINCY NEWS

Street address 1: 203 E Harrison St
Street address city: Dequincy
Street address state: LA
Zip/Postal code: 70633-3545
General Phone: (337) 786-8004
General Fax: (337) 786-8131
General/National Adv. E-mail: dequincynews@centurytel.net
Display Adv. E-mail: classifieds@centurytel.net
Editorial e-mail: dequincynews@centurytel.net
Primary Website: dequincynews.com
Mthly Avg Views: 5000
Year Established: 1923
Avg Paid Circ: 3600
Audit By: Sworn/Estimate/Non-Audited
Audit Date: 10.06.2019
Personnel: Joy Wise (Pub.); Jeffrey DeViney (Adv. Mgr.); Jerry Wise (Ed.)

THE DONALDSONVILLE CHIEF

Street address 1: 120 Railroad Ave
Street address city: Donaldsonville
Street address state: LA
Zip/Postal code: 70346-2520
General Phone: (225) 473-3101
General Fax: (225) 473-4060
General/National Adv. E-mail: cbarrett@gatehousemedia.com
Display Adv. E-mail: jsagona@donaldsonvillechief.com
Editorial e-mail: news@donaldsonvillechief.com
Primary Website: donaldsonvillechief.com
Year Established: 1871
Avg Paid Circ: 1000
Avg Free Circ: 50
Audit By: Sworn/Estimate/Non-Audited
Audit Date: 10.06.2019
Personnel: Bob Prejean (Multi Media Sales Representative); Greg Fischer (Editor); Julie Sagona (Office manager)
Parent company (for newspapers): CherryRoad Media

THE DRUM

Street address 1: 17253 Lavigne Rd
Street address city: Ponchatoula
Street address state: LA
Zip/Postal code: 70454-2485
General Phone: (225) 927-3717
General/National Adv. E-mail: news@thedrumnews.com
Display Adv. E-mail: news@thedrumnews.com
Editorial e-mail: news@thedrumnews.com
Primary Website: thedrumnewspaper.info
Year Established: 1985
Avg Free Circ: 2000
Audit By: Sworn/Estimate/Non-Audited
Audit Date: 10.06.2019
Personnel: Eddie Ponds (Ed.)

THE ENTERPRISE

Street address 1: 2677 HIGHWAY 20
Street address city: Vacherie
Street address state: LA
Zip/Postal code: 70090
General Phone: (225) 265-2120
General Fax: (225) 265-2133
General/National Adv. E-mail: karenenterprise@bellsouth.net
Primary Website: vacherienews.com
Avg Paid Circ: 1800
Audit By: Sworn/Estimate/Non-Audited
Audit Date: 10.06.2019
Personnel: Wilbur Reynaud (Pub.); David Reynaud (Ed.)

THE ENTERPRISE & INTERSTATE PROGRESS

Street address 1: 202 Adams St
Street address city: Mansfield
Street address state: LA
Zip/Postal code: 71052-2430
General Phone: (318) 872-4120
General Fax: (318) 872-6038
General/National Adv. E-mail: enterprise@wnonline.net
Editorial e-mail: enterprise@wnonline.net
Primary Website: ent.stparchive.com
Year Established: 1889
Avg Paid Circ: 4000
Audit By: Sworn/Estimate/Non-Audited
Audit Date: 10.06.2019
Personnel: Lovan Thomas (Pub.); Bennie Hall (Gen. Mgr.); Cindy Williams (Ed.)
Parent company (for newspapers): Natchitoches Times Newspapers

THE ERA-LEADER

Street address 1: 1137 Main St
Street address city: Franklinton
Street address state: LA
Zip/Postal code: 70438-2083
General Phone: (985) 839-9077
General Fax: (985) 839-9096
General/National Adv. E-mail: info@era-leader.com
Display Adv. E-mail: sheila@era-leader.com
Editorial e-mail: info@era-leader.com
Primary Website: era-leader.com
Year Established: 1910
Avg Paid Circ: 4088
Audit By: Sworn/Estimate/Non-Audited
Audit Date: 10.06.2019
Personnel: Steve Kuperstock (Pub.)
Parent company (for newspapers): 1976

THE EUNICE NEWS

Street address 1: 456 Aymond St
Street address city: Eunice
Street address state: LA
Zip/Postal code: 70535-6601
General Phone: (337) 457-3061
General Fax: (337) 457-3122
Advertising Phone: (337) 457-3061
Advertising Fax: (337) 457-3122
Editorial Phone: (337) 457-3061
Editorial Fax: (337) 457-3122
General/National Adv. E-mail: misty.deaville@eunicetoday.com
Display Adv. E-mail: tiffany.joubert@eunicetoday.com
Editorial e-mail: harlan.kirgan@eunicetoday.com
Primary Website: eunicetoday.com
Year Established: 1903
Avg Paid Circ: 3000
Audit By: Sworn/Estimate/Non-Audited
Audit Date: 10.06.2019
Personnel: Darrell Guillory (COO/Pub.)
Parent company (for newspapers): LSN Publishing Company LLC

THE FORUM

Street address 1: 1158 Texas Ave
Street address city: Shreveport
Street address state: LA
Zip/Postal code: 71101-3343
General Phone: (318) 222-409
General/National Adv. E-mail: angela@theforumnews.com
Display Adv. E-mail: angela@theforumnews.com
Editorial e-mail: editor@theforumnews.com
Primary Website: theforumnews.com
Year Established: 1988
Avg Paid Circ: 43
Avg Free Circ: 22755
Audit By: Sworn/Estimate/Non-Audited
Audit Date: 10.06.2019
Personnel: Jay Covington (Pub.); Fayline Bass (Adv. Mgr/Gen. Mgr.); Chris Welch (Circ. Mgr); Jill French (Prod. Mgr); Angela Haacker (Sales Mgr.)

Parent company (for newspapers): Forum Communications Co.

THE FRANKLIN SUN

Street address 1: 514 Prairie St
Street address city: Winnsboro
Street address state: LA
Zip/Postal code: 71295-2737
General Phone: (318) 435-4521
General Fax: (318) 435-9220
General/National Adv. E-mail: joecurtis@franklinsun.com
Display Adv. E-mail: admanager@franklinsun.com
Classified Adv. e-mail: admanager@franklinsun.com
Editorial e-mail: Samhannajr@samhannajr.com
Primary Website: franklinsun.com
Mthly Avg Views: 135862
Year Established: 1856
Avg Paid Circ: 6200
Audit By: Sworn/Estimate/Non-Audited
Audit Date: 10.10.2023
Personnel: Monica Huff (Photographer Advertising); Nicki Vines (Circ. Mgr.); Lesley Capdepon (Gen Mgr); Sam Hanna Jr. (Ed); Joe Curtis (Editor); Wanda Berry (Public Notice/Class.); Marcy Thompson (Community Editor General Assignments); Rebecca Beach (Public Notices/Subscriptions/Classifieds); Amy Thomas (Advertising)
Parent company (for newspapers): Hanna Publishing Co.

THE GAZETTE

Street address 1: 104 N Washington St
Street address city: Farmerville
Street address state: LA
Zip/Postal code: 71241-2916
General Phone: (318) 368-9732
General Fax: (318) 368-7331
General/National Adv. E-mail: hillary@fgazette.com
Display Adv. E-mail: nicole@fgazette.com
Editorial e-mail: news@fgazette
Primary Website: fgazette.com
Year Established: 1886
Avg Paid Circ: 3300
Audit By: Sworn/Estimate/Non-Audited
Audit Date: 10.06.2019
Personnel: Mark Rainwater (Editor); Hillary Newcomb (Advertising sales); Nicole Morgan (Circulation manager)

THE HAYNESVILLE NEWS

Street address 1: 604 N Main St
Street address city: Homer
Street address state: LA
Zip/Postal code: 71040-3806
General Phone: (318) 927-3721
General/National Adv. E-mail: THN@ClaiborneOne.org
Display Adv. E-mail: THN@ClaiborneOne.org
Editorial e-mail: THN@ClaiborneOne.org
Primary Website: claiborneone.org/thn
Year Established: 1924
Avg Paid Circ: 1200
Avg Free Circ: 8233
Audit By: Sworn/Estimate/Non-Audited
Audit Date: 10.06.2019
Personnel: Jackie Roberts (Ed.)

THE JACKSON INDEPENDENT

Street address 1: 624 Hudson Ave
Street address city: Jonesboro
Street address state: LA
Zip/Postal code: 71251-3851
General Phone: (318) 259-2551
General Fax: (318) 259-8537
General/National Adv. E-mail: graphics@thejacksonindependent.com
Display Adv. E-mail: accounting@thejacksonindependent.com
Editorial e-mail: news@thejacksonindependent.com
Avg Paid Circ: 3400
Avg Free Circ: 3000
Audit By: Sworn/Estimate/Non-Audited
Audit Date: 10.06.2019
Personnel: Chris Smith (Ed.)

THE JENA-TIMES/OLLA-TULLOS-URANIA SIGNAL

Street address 1: 1509 N 3RD ST
Street address city: Jena
Street address state: LA
Zip/Postal code: 71342
General Phone: (318) 992-4121
General Fax: (318) 992-2287
General/National Adv. E-mail: sales@thejenatimes.net
Display Adv. E-mail: classifieds@thejenatimes.net
Editorial e-mail: editor@thejenatimes.net
Primary Website: thejenatimes.net
Year Established: 1905
Avg Paid Circ: 4000
Audit By: Sworn/Estimate/Non-Audited
Audit Date: 17.09.2021
Personnel: Sammy Franklin (Pub., Ed.); Ashley Keene (Business Mgr.); Kristie Taylor (Classifieds/subscriptions); Sherry Steele (Shop Foreman); Libby Warwick (Advertising Sales); Morgan Smith (Reporter/Photographer); Craig Franklin (Writer/photographer)

THE KAPLAN HERALD

Street address 1: 219 N Cushing Ave
Street address city: Kaplan
Street address state: LA
Zip/Postal code: 70548-4119
General Phone: (337) 643-8002
General Fax: (337) 643-1382
General/National Adv. E-mail: ejbheart@hotmail.com
Display Adv. E-mail: ejbheart@hotmail.com
Editorial e-mail: judy.mire@vermiliontoday.com
Primary Website: kaplantoday.com
Avg Paid Circ: 2000
Audit By: Sworn/Estimate/Non-Audited
Audit Date: 10.06.2019
Personnel: Kathy Cormier (Pub.); June Breaux (Adv. Mgr.); Judy Mire (Ed.)
Parent company (for newspapers): LSN Publishing Company LLC

THE KENTWOOD NEWS-LEDGER

Street address 1: 234 Avenue F
Street address city: Kentwood
Street address state: LA
Zip/Postal code: 70444-2522
General Phone: (985) 229-8607
General Fax: (985) 229-8698
General/National Adv. E-mail: editor.newsledger@tangilena.com
Editorial e-mail: editor.newsledger@tangilena.com
Primary Website: tangilena.com
Year Established: 1934
Avg Paid Circ: 1525
Audit By: Sworn/Estimate/Non-Audited
Audit Date: 10.06.2019
Personnel: Joy Lofton (Ed.); Karen Walker (Acct. Exec.); Cathy Chapman (Ed.)

THE LEESVILLE DAILY LEADER

Street address 1: 206 E Texas St
Street address city: Leesville
Street address state: LA
Zip/Postal code: 71446-4056
General Phone: (337) 239-3444
General Fax: (337) 238-1152
Advertising Phone: (337) 239-3444
Advertising Fax: (337) 238-1152
Editorial Phone: (337) 239-3444
Editorial Fax: (337) 238-1152
General/National Adv. E-mail: advertising@leesvilledailyleader.com
Display Adv. E-mail: advertising@leesvilledailyleader.com
Classified Adv. e-mail: classified@leesvilledailyleader.com
Editorial e-mail: news@leesvilledailyleader.com
Primary Website: leesvilledailyleader.com
Year Established: 1898
Avg Paid Circ: 2800
Avg Free Circ: 5000
Sun. Circulation Paid: 3794
Audit By: Sworn/Estimate/Non-Audited
Audit Date: 10.06.2019
Personnel: Larissa Williams (Office Manager); Rachel Steffan (Editor)
Parent company (for newspapers): CherryRoad Media

THE LIVINGSTON PARISH NEWS

Street address 1: 688 Hatchell Ln
Street address city: Denham Springs
Street address state: LA
Zip/Postal code: 70726-3015
General Phone: (225) 665-5176
General Fax: (225) 667-0167
General/National Adv. E-mail: advertising@livingstonparishnews.com
Display Adv. E-mail: classifieds@livingstonparishnews.com
Editorial e-mail: editor@livingstonparishnews.com
Primary Website: livingstonparishnews.com
Mthly Avg Views: 185000
Mthly Avg Unique Visitors: 125000
Year Established: 1898
Avg Paid Circ: 30000
Audit By: Sworn/Estimate/Non-Audited
Audit Date: 10.06.2019
Personnel: McHugh David (Pub.)

THE MAMOU ACADIAN PRESS

Street address 1: PO Box 220
Street address city: Ville Platte
Street address state: LA
Zip/Postal code: 70586-0220
General Phone: (337) 363-2103
General Fax: (337) 363-2841
Advertising Phone: (337) 363-2103
Advertising Fax: (337) 363-2841
Editorial Phone: (337) 363-2103
Editorial Fax: (337) 363-2841
General/National Adv. E-mail: kathy.gazette@yahoo.com
Display Adv. E-mail: classifieds.vp@centurytel.net
Editorial e-mail: vpgaz@centurytel.net
Primary Website: evangelinetoday.com
Avg Free Circ: 3000
Audit By: Sworn/Estimate/Non-Audited
Audit Date: 10.06.2019
Personnel: David L. Ortego (Pub.); Kathy Longino (Adv. Mgr.); Jennifer Allison (Circ. Mgr.); Mike Bordelon (Ed.)
Parent company (for newspapers): LSN Publishing Company LLC

THE MARKSVILLE WEEKLY NEWS

Street address 1: PO Box 36
Street address city: Marksville
Street address state: LA
Zip/Postal code: 71351-0036
General Phone: (318) 253-5413
General Fax: (318) 253-7223
General/National Adv. E-mail: ads@avoyelles.com
Editorial e-mail: avoyellesjournal@yahoo.com
Primary Website: avoyelles.com
Avg Paid Circ: 3500
Audit By: Sworn/Estimate/Non-Audited
Audit Date: 10.06.2019
Personnel: Randy DeCuir (Pub.)
Parent company (for newspapers): LSN Publishing Company LLC

THE OAKDALE JOURNAL

Street address 1: 231 E 6th Ave
Street address city: Oakdale
Street address state: LA
Zip/Postal code: 71463-2617
General Phone: (318) 335-0635
General Fax: (318) 335-0431
General/National Adv. E-mail: oakdalejournal@bellsouth.net
Display Adv. E-mail: oakdalejournal@bellsouth.net
Editorial e-mail: oakdalejournal@bellsouth.net
Primary Website: facebook.com/pages/Oakdale-Journal/143123332400740
Year Established: 1913
Avg Paid Circ: 1700
Avg Free Circ: 12939
Audit By: Sworn/Estimate/Non-Audited
Audit Date: 10.06.2019
Personnel: David Ortego (Pub.); Peggy Byrd (Adv. Mgr.); Jennifer Allison (Circ. Mgr.); Barbara Doyle (Ed.)
Parent company (for newspapers): LSN Publishing Company LLC

THE OUACHITA CITIZEN

Street address 1: 4423 Cypress St
Street address city: West Monroe
Street address state: LA
Zip/Postal code: 71291-7405
General Phone: (318) 322-3161
General Fax: (318) 325-2285
General/National Adv. E-mail: news@ouachitacitizen.com
Editorial e-mail: News@ouachitacitizen.com
Primary Website: hannapub.com/ouachitacitizen
Year Established: 1924
Avg Paid Circ: 5200
Audit By: Sworn/Estimate/Non-Audited
Audit Date: 10.06.2019
Personnel: Sam Hanna (Publisher); Scott Rogers (Ed.)

THE POINTE COUPEE BANNER

Street address 1: 123 Saint Mary St
Street address city: New Roads
Street address state: LA
Zip/Postal code: 70760-3529
General Phone: (225) 638-7155
General Fax: (225) 638-8442
General/National Adv. E-mail: ThePCBanner@yahoo.com
Display Adv. E-mail: ThePCBanner@yahoo.com
Editorial e-mail: ThePCBanner@yahoo.com
Primary Website: pointecoupeereporter.com
Year Established: 1880
Avg Paid Circ: 5000
Audit By: Sworn/Estimate/Non-Audited
Audit Date: 10.06.2019
Personnel: Mary LaCour (Pub.); Brent Roy (Pub.); Tommy Comeaux (Ed.)

THE PONCHATOULA TIMES

Street address 1: PO Box 743
Street address 2: 170 N 7th Street
Street address city: Ponchatoula
Street address state: LA
Zip/Postal code: 70454-0743
General Phone: (985) 386-2877
General Fax: (985) 386-0458
General/National Adv. E-mail: ads@ponchatoula.com; ptimes@ponchatoula.com
Display Adv. E-mail: ads@ponchatoula.com
Editorial e-mail: editor@ponchatoula.com
Primary Website: ponchatoula.com/ptimes
Year Established: 1981
Avg Paid Circ: 9047
Avg Free Circ: 3500
Audit By: Sworn/Estimate/Non-Audited
Audit Date: 10.06.2019
Personnel: Bryan T. McMahon (Pub./Ed.)

THE RAYNE-ACADIAN TRIBUNE

Street address 1: 108 N Adams Ave
Street address city: Rayne
Street address state: LA
Zip/Postal code: 70578-5918
General Phone: (337) 334-3186
General Fax: (337) 334-8474
General/National Adv. E-mail: admin@raynetoday.com
Display Adv. E-mail: admin@raynetoday.com
Editorial e-mail: admin@raynetoday.com
Primary Website: raynetoday.com
Year Established: 1904
Avg Paid Circ: 4105
Avg Free Circ: 8400
Audit By: Sworn/Estimate/Non-Audited
Audit Date: 10.06.2019
Personnel: Josie Henry (Adv. Rep.)
Parent company (for newspapers): LSN Publishing Company LLC

THE SABINE INDEX

Street address 1: 875 San Antonio Ave
Street address city: Many
Street address state: LA
Zip/Postal code: 71449-3140
General Phone: (318) 256-3495
General Fax: (318) 256-9151
General/National Adv. E-mail: sales@sabineindex.net

Display Adv. E-mail: classifieds@sabineindex.net
Editorial e-mail: news@sabineindex.net
Primary Website: thesabineindex.com
Year Established: 1879
Avg Paid Circ: 6130
Avg Free Circ: 25
Audit By: Sworn/Estimate/Non-Audited
Audit Date: 10.06.2019
Personnel: Robert Gentry (Pub.); Daniel Jones

THE ST. BERNARD VOICE

Street address 1: 234 Mehle St
Street address city: Arabi
Street address state: LA
Zip/Postal code: 70032-1054
General Phone: (504) 279-7488
General Fax: (504) 309-5532
General/National Adv. E-mail: ads@thestbernardvoice.com
Display Adv. E-mail: ads@thestbernardvoice.com
Editorial e-mail: copy@thestbernardvoice.com
Primary Website: thestbernardvoice.com
Year Established: 1890
Avg Paid Circ: 3150
Audit By: Sworn/Estimate/Non-Audited
Audit Date: 10.06.2019
Personnel: Brandi Rollo (Graphic Designer); Norris Babin (Publisher); Amber Prattini (Reporter)

THE TIMES-PICAYUNE

Street address 1: 365 Canal St
Street address 2: Ste 3100
Street address city: New Orleans
Street address state: LA
Zip/Postal code: 70130-6509
General Phone: (800) 925-0000
General Fax: (504) 826-3636
Advertising Phone: (504) 826-3075
Advertising Fax: (504) 826-3800
Editorial Phone: (504) 826-3300
Editorial Fax: (504) 826-3007
General/National Adv. E-mail: ads@timespicayune.com
Display Adv. E-mail: ads@timespicayune.com
Editorial e-mail: editor@timespicayune.com
Primary Website: nola.com
Year Established: 1837
Avg Paid Circ: 99851
Sat. Circulation Paid: 17249
Sun. Circulation Paid: 118475
Audit By: AAM
Audit Date: 30.09.2018
Personnel: Kelly Rose (Vice Pres., Adv); Jim Amoss (Ed.); Ricky Mathews (Pub.); David Francis (Vice Pres./Bus. Mgr.); Mark Rose (VP Digital Solutions); Brad Breuhl (Asst. Adv. Dir.)
Parent company (for newspapers): Advance Publications, Inc.

THE TOWN TALK

Street address 1: 1201 3rd St
Street address city: Alexandria
Street address state: LA
Zip/Postal code: 71301-8246
General Phone: (318) 487-6397
General Fax: (318) 487-2950
Advertising Phone: (318) 487-6388
Advertising Fax: (318) 487-2950
Editorial Phone: (318) 487-6409
Editorial Fax: (318) 487-2950
General/National Adv. E-mail: christina.pierce@thetowntalk.com
Display Adv. E-mail: christina.pierce@thetowntalk.com
Classified Adv. e-mail: legals@thetowntalk.com
Editorial e-mail: news@thetowntalk.com
Primary Website: thetowntalk.com
Year Established: 1883
Avg Paid Circ: 10888
Avg Free Circ: 22
Sat. Circulation Paid: 15983
Sun. Circulation Paid: 21384
Audit By: AAM
Audit Date: 31.12.2018
Personnel: Jim Smilie (Engagement & Community Content Editor); Christina Pierce (Gen. Mgr./Adv. Dir.); Deborah Schulte (Distribution Mgr.)
Parent company (for newspapers): Gannett

THE WATCHMAN

Street address 1: 11317B CHURCH ST
Street address city: Clinton
Street address state: LA
Zip/Postal code: 70722
General Phone: (225) 683-5196
General Fax: (225) 683-4276
General/National Adv. E-mail: tabatha.alcina@felicianatoday.com
Display Adv. E-mail: tabatha.alcina@felicianatoday.com
Editorial e-mail: tabatha.alcina@felicianatoday.com
Primary Website: felicianatoday.com
Year Established: 1878
Avg Paid Circ: 18900
Audit By: Sworn/Estimate/Non-Audited
Audit Date: 10.06.2019
Personnel: Tabatha Alcina (Ed)

THE WELSH CITIZEN

Street address 1: 119 S Elms St
Street address city: Welsh
Street address state: LA
Zip/Postal code: 70591-4211
General Phone: (337) 734-2891
General Fax: (337) 734-4457
General/National Adv. E-mail: welshcitizen@centurytel.net
Primary Website: jeffdavistoday.com
Year Established: 1958
Avg Paid Circ: 1000
Audit By: Sworn/Estimate/Non-Audited
Audit Date: 10.06.2019
Personnel: Bengt Lindell (Ed.)

THE WEST CARROLL GAZETTE

Street address 1: 512 S Constitution Ave
Street address city: Oak Grove
Street address state: LA
Zip/Postal code: 71263-2514
General Phone: (318) 428-3207
General Fax: (318) 428-2747
General/National Adv. E-mail: wcarrollgazette@bellsouth.net
Display Adv. E-mail: wcarrollgazette@bellsouth.net
Editorial e-mail: wcarrollgazette@bellsouth.net
Primary Website: westcarrollgazette.com
Year Established: 1910
Avg Paid Circ: 2000
Avg Free Circ: 100
Audit By: Sworn/Estimate/Non-Audited
Audit Date: 10.06.2019
Personnel: Mary Terry (Pub./Gen. Mgr.); Melba West (Office Mgr.); Renee Graham (Adv. Mgr.); Johney S. Turner (Ed.); Jessica Townsend (Lifestyle Ed.)
Parent company (for newspapers): LSN Publishing Company LLC

THE ZACHARY PLAINSMAN-NEWS

Street address 1: PO Box 588
Street address city: Baton Rouge
Street address state: LA
Zip/Postal code: 70821-0588
General Phone: (225) 654-6841
General Fax: (225) 654-8271
General/National Adv. E-mail: wendy.pate@zacharytoday.com
Display Adv. E-mail: cindy.munn@zacharytoday.com
Editorial e-mail: stacy.gill@zacharytoday.com
Primary Website: zacharytoday.com
Year Established: 1953
Avg Paid Circ: 2000
Audit By: Sworn/Estimate/Non-Audited
Audit Date: 10.06.2019
Personnel: Stacy Gill (Ed.); Gary Miller (Pub); Wendy Pate (Sales Mgr); Cindy Munn (Classified Mgr)

TRI-PARISH TIMES & BUSINESS NEWS

Street address 1: 4924 Highway 311
Street address city: Houma
Street address state: LA
Zip/Postal code: 70360-2873
General Phone: (985) 876-3008
General Fax: (985) 876-0950
Advertising Phone: (985) 876-3008
Advertising Fax: (985) 876-0950
Editorial Phone: (985) 876-3008
Editorial Fax: (985) 876-0950
General/National Adv. E-mail: sales@tri-parishtimes.com
Display Adv. E-mail: sales@tri-parishtimes.com
Editorial e-mail: editor@tri-parishtimes.com
Primary Website: tri-parishtimes.com
Year Established: 1997
Avg Paid Circ: 5076
Avg Free Circ: 943
Audit By: Sworn/Estimate/Non-Audited
Audit Date: 10.06.2019
Personnel: Shell Armstrong (Exec. Ed.); Brad Thibodaux (Adv. Dir); Darrin Guidry (Pub)

VINTON NEWS

Street address 1: 716 E Napoleon St
Street address city: Sulphur
Street address state: LA
Zip/Postal code: 70663-3402
General Phone: (337) 527-7075
General Fax: (337) 528-3044
General/National Adv. E-mail: sdneditorial@yahoo.com
Primary Website: sulphurdailynews.com
Avg Paid Circ: 4200
Avg Free Circ: 11800
Audit By: Sworn/Estimate/Non-Audited
Audit Date: 10.06.2019
Personnel: Suzanne Peveto-Nelson (Pub.)
Parent company (for newspapers): Shearman Corporation

WEST SIDE JOURNAL

Street address 1: 668 N Jefferson Ave
Street address city: Port Allen
Street address state: LA
Zip/Postal code: 70767-2414
General Phone: (225) 343-2540
General Fax: (225) 344-0923
General/National Adv. E-mail: advertising@thewestsidejournal.com
Display Adv. E-mail: advertising@thewestsidejournal.com
Editorial e-mail: editor@thewestsidejournal.com
Primary Website: thewestsidejournal.com
Year Established: 1937
Avg Paid Circ: 2473
Audit By: Sworn/Estimate/Non-Audited
Audit Date: 10.06.2019
Personnel: Darrell Guilbeau (Pub.); Aaron Williams (Ed.); Cole Williams (Graphic Artist)

WINN PARISH ENTERPRISE-NEWS AMERICAN

Street address 1: 500 E Main St
Street address city: Winnfield
Street address state: LA
Zip/Postal code: 71483-4301
General Phone: (318) 628-2712
General Fax: (318) 628-6196
General/National Adv. E-mail: adsales@winnparishenterprise.com
Display Adv. E-mail: advertising@winnparishenterprise.com
Editorial e-mail: news@winnparishenterprise.com
Primary Website: winnparishenterprise.com
Year Established: 1924
Avg Paid Circ: 3995
Avg Free Circ: 75
Audit By: Sworn/Estimate/Non-Audited
Audit Date: 10.06.2019
Personnel: Nanie Young (Adv. Mgr.); Verlene Henderson (Circ. Mgr.); Crystal Evans (Ed.)
Parent company (for newspapers): Natchitoches Times Newspapers

MAINE

ADVERTISER DEMOCRAT

Street address 1: 1 Pikes Hl
Street address city: Norway
Street address state: ME
Zip/Postal code: 04268-4350
General Phone: (207) 743-7011
General Fax: (207) 743-2256
Advertising Phone: (207) 743-7011
Advertising Fax: (207) 743-2256
Editorial Phone: (207) 743-7011
Editorial Fax: (207) 743-2256
General/National Adv. E-mail: ads@advertiserdemocrat.com
Display Adv. E-mail: ads@advertiserdemocrat.com
Editorial e-mail: newsteam@advertiserdemocrat.com
Primary Website: advertiserdemocrat.com
Year Established: 1826
Avg Paid Circ: 4000
Avg Free Circ: 100
Audit By: Sworn/Estimate/Non-Audited
Audit Date: 10.06.2019
Personnel: A.M. Sheehan (Ed); Lisa DeSisto (Pub.)
Parent company (for newspapers): Sun Media Group

AMERICAN JOURNAL

Street address 1: 5 Fundy Rd
Street address 2: Ste 1
Street address city: Falmouth
Street address state: ME
Zip/Postal code: 04105-1771
General Phone: (207) 854-2577
General Fax: (207) 854-0018
Advertising Phone: (207) 854-2577
Advertising Fax: (207) 854-0018
Editorial Phone: (207) 854-2577
Editorial Fax: (207) 854-0018
General/National Adv. E-mail: sales@keepmecurrent.com
Display Adv. E-mail: sales@keepmecurrent.com
Editorial e-mail: jlord@keepmecurrent.com
Primary Website: keepmecurrent.com
Year Established: 1950
Avg Paid Circ: 7600
Avg Free Circ: 556
Audit By: Sworn/Estimate/Non-Audited
Audit Date: 10.06.2019
Personnel: Mark Hews (Circ. Mgr.)
Parent company (for newspapers): Current Publishing

AROOSTOOK REPUBLICAN AND NEWS

Street address 1: PO Box 510
Street address city: Presque Isle
Street address state: ME
Zip/Postal code: 04769-0510
General Phone: (207) 496-3251
General Fax: (207) 492-4351
General/National Adv. E-mail: republicansales@bangordailynews.com
Display Adv. E-mail: republican@bangordailynews.com
Editorial e-mail: republican@bangordailynews.com
Primary Website: thecounty.me
Year Established: 1880
Avg Paid Circ: 2643
Avg Free Circ: 32
Audit By: Sworn/Estimate/Non-Audited
Audit Date: 10.06.2019
Personnel: Rick Levasseur (Editor); Danielle Camping (Sales Manager)
Parent company (for newspapers): Bangor Publishing Company

BIDDEFORD COURIER

Street address 1: 6 Digital Drive
Street address city: Biddeford
Street address state: ME
Zip/Postal code: 04005
General Phone: (207) 282-4337
General Fax: (207) 282-4339
Advertising Phone: (207) 282-4337
Advertising Fax: (207) 282-4339
General/National Adv. E-mail: ads@mainelymediallc.com
Display Adv. E-mail: sacoads@inthecourier.com
Editorial e-mail: editor@inthecourier.com
Primary Website: mainelymediallc.com
Avg Free Circ: 22500
Audit By: Sworn/Estimate/Non-Audited
Audit Date: 10.06.2019
Personnel: David Clark (Adv. Mgr./Gen. Mgr.); Molly Lovell (Mng. Ed.); Dina Mendros (Executive Editor); Sandy Porrazo (Bus. Mgr.); Steve Betts (Ed.)

Parent company (for newspapers): Mainely Media, LLC

BOOTHBAY REGISTER

Street address 1: 97 Townsend Ave
Street address city: Boothbay Harbor
Street address state: ME
Zip/Postal code: 04538-1843
General Phone: (207) 633-4620
General Fax: (207) 633-7123
Display Adv. E-mail: classifieds@boothbayregister.com
Editorial e-mail: kevinburnham@boothbayregister.com
Primary Website: boothbayregister.com
Year Established: 1876
Avg Paid Circ: 3555
Avg Free Circ: 300
Audit By: Sworn/Estimate/Non-Audited
Audit Date: 10.06.2019
Personnel: Kathy Frizzell (Adv. Mgr.); Kevin G. Burnham (Editor); A.R. Tandy (Pub.)
Parent company (for newspapers): Maine-OK Enterprises, Inc.

CASTINE PATRIOT

Street address 1: 13 Main St
Street address city: Blue Hill
Street address state: ME
Zip/Postal code: 04614-5985
General Phone: (207) 374-2341
General Fax: (207) 374-2343
Advertising Phone: (207) 367-2200
Advertising Fax: (207) 367-6397
Editorial Phone: (207) 374-2341
Editorial Fax: (207) 374-2343
General/National Adv. E-mail: info@pbp.me
Display Adv. E-mail: ads@pbp.me
Classified Adv. e-mail: classifieds@pbp.me
Editorial e-mail: news@pbp.me
Primary Website: penobscotbaypress.com
Year Established: 1980
Avg Paid Circ: 400
Avg Free Circ: 40
Audit By: Sworn/Estimate/Non-Audited
Audit Date: 23.09.2021
Personnel: R. Nathaniel W. Barrows (Owner/Pub.); Cathy Marshall (Circulation Mgr); Debra Larrabee (Financial Manager); Jean Lamontanaro (Director of Sales); Faith DeAmbrose (Mng. Ed.); Tegan McGuire (Classifieds & Coming Events Manager); Heather Oliver (Sales Rep.)
Parent company (for newspapers): Penobscot Bay Press, Inc.

CENTRAL MAINE SUNDAY

Street address 1: 295 Gannett Drive
Street address city: South Portland
Street address state: ME
Zip/Postal code: 4106
General Phone: (207) 791-6204
General/National Adv. E-mail: vciampi@mainetoday.com
Display Adv. E-mail: vciampi@mainetoday.com
Avg Paid Circ: 13886
Avg Free Circ: 86
Audit By: AAM
Audit Date: 31.03.2019
Personnel: Vince Ciampi (VP Advertising)
Parent company (for newspapers): MaineToday Media Inc.

COASTAL JOURNAL

Street address 1: 3 Business Parkway
Street address city: Brunswick
Street address state: ME
Zip/Postal code: 04011
General Phone: (207) 386-5230
General Fax: (207) 443-5605
Advertising Phone: (207) 443-6241
Advertising Fax: (207) 443-5605
General/National Adv. E-mail: ads@coastaljournal.com
Display Adv. E-mail: ads@coastaljournal.com
Editorial e-mail: editor@coastaljournal.com
Primary Website: timesrecord.com/coastal-journal
Year Established: 1966
Avg Free Circ: 19200
Audit By: Sworn/Estimate/Non-Audited
Audit Date: 10.06.2019
Personnel: Jason Pafundi (Assoc. Ed.); John Swinconeck (Exec. Ed.); Dennis Gears (Sales Dir.)

COMMUNITY ADVERTISER

Street address 1: 20 Peter Path
Street address city: Farmingdale
Street address state: ME
Zip/Postal code: 04344-2930
General Phone: (207) 582-8486
General Fax: (207) 512-5388
Advertising Phone: (207) 582-8486
Advertising Fax: (207) 512-5388
Editorial Phone: (207) 582-8486
Editorial Fax: (207) 512-5388
General/National Adv. E-mail: ads@comadvertiser.com
Display Adv. E-mail: ads@comadvertiser.com
Editorial e-mail: ads@comadvertiser.com
Primary Website: facebook.com/Community-Advertiser-138769906840
Year Established: 1938
Avg Free Circ: 15000
Audit By: Sworn/Estimate/Non-Audited
Audit Date: 10.06.2019
Personnel: Keith E. Peters (Ed.)

EASTERN GAZETTE

Street address 1: 97 Church St
Street address city: Dexter
Street address state: ME
Zip/Postal code: 04930-1332
General Phone: (207) 924-7402
General/National Adv. E-mail: ads@easterngazette.com
Display Adv. E-mail: ads@easterngazette.com
Editorial e-mail: news@easterngazette.com
Primary Website: easterngazette.com
Year Established: 1853
Avg Free Circ: 17000
Audit By: Sworn/Estimate/Non-Audited
Audit Date: 10.06.2019
Personnel: Robert H. Shank (Ed./Pub.); Janice Shank (Co-Pub.); Michele Lancaster (Gen. Mgr.); Joanne Henderson (Sales/Mktg.); Kelsee Bowman (Opns. Mgr.)
Parent company (for newspapers): The Gazette Inc.

FRANKLIN JOURNAL

Street address 1: 187 Wilton Rd
Street address city: Farmington
Street address state: ME
Zip/Postal code: 04938-6120
General Phone: (207) 778-2075
General Fax: (207) 778-6970
General/National Adv. E-mail: mblanchet@sunjournal.com
Display Adv. E-mail: mblanchet@sunjournal.com
Editorial e-mail: editor@thefranklinjournal.com
Primary Website: thefranklinjournal.com
Year Established: 1840
Avg Paid Circ: 2500
Audit By: Sworn/Estimate/Non-Audited
Audit Date: 10.06.2019
Personnel: Mike Blanchet (Adv. Acct. Exec.); Barry Matulaitis (Editor)
Parent company (for newspapers): Sun Media Group

FREE PRESS

Street address 1: 8 N Main St
Street address 2: Ste 101
Street address city: Rockland
Street address state: ME
Zip/Postal code: 04841-3154
General Phone: (207) 596-0055
General Fax: (207) 596-6698
Advertising Phone: (207) 596-0055
Advertising Fax: (207) 596-6698
Editorial Phone: (207) 596-0055
Editorial Fax: (207) 596-6698
General/National Adv. E-mail: admanager@freepressonline.com
Display Adv. E-mail: admanager@freepressonline.com
Editorial e-mail: editor@freepressonline.com
Primary Website: freepressonline.com
Year Established: 1985
Avg Free Circ: 12500
Audit By: Sworn/Estimate/Non-Audited
Audit Date: 10.06.2019
Personnel: Steve Davis (Adv. Mgr.); Glenn Billington (Sr. Sales Rep.); Alice McFadden (Pub.); Patty Poe (Ed.); Wendell Greer (Prodn. Mgr.)

HOULTON PIONEER TIMES

Street address 1: 23 Court St
Street address 2: Unit 1
Street address city: Houlton
Street address state: ME
Zip/Postal code: 04730-1747
General Phone: (207) 532-2281
General Fax: (207) 532-2403
General/National Adv. E-mail: hptsales@bangordailynews.com
Display Adv. E-mail: pioneertimes@bangordailynews.com
Editorial e-mail: pioneertimes@bangordailynews.com
Primary Website: thecounty.me
Year Established: 1857
Avg Paid Circ: 4188
Avg Free Circ: 12
Audit By: Sworn/Estimate/Non-Audited
Audit Date: 10.06.2019
Personnel: David Bates (Sales Rep.); Rick Levasseur (Editor)
Parent company (for newspapers): Bangor Publishing Company

ISLAND AD-VANTAGES

Street address 1: 69 Main St
Street address city: Stonington
Street address state: ME
Zip/Postal code: 4681
General Phone: (207) 367-2200
General Fax: (207) 367-6397
Advertising Phone: (207) 367-2200
Advertising Fax: (207) 367-6397
Editorial Phone: (207) 367-2200
Editorial Fax: (207) 367-6397
General/National Adv. E-mail: ads@pbp.me
Display Adv. E-mail: classifieds@pbp.me
Editorial e-mail: news@pbp.me
Primary Website: islandadvantages.com
Year Established: 1882
Avg Paid Circ: 1684
Avg Free Circ: 29
Audit By: Sworn/Estimate/Non-Audited
Audit Date: 10.06.2019
Personnel: R. Nathaniel W. Barrows (Ed.); Faith DeAmbrose (Managing Ed.); Cathy Marshall (Circ. Mgr.)

KENNEBUNK POST

Street address 1: 180 Main St
Street address city: Biddeford
Street address state: ME
Zip/Postal code: 04005-2410
General Phone: (207) 282-4337
General Fax: (207) 282-4339
Advertising Phone: (207) 282-4337
Advertising Fax: (207) 282-4339
Editorial Phone: (207) 282-4337
Editorial Fax: (207) 282-4339
General/National Adv. E-mail: ads@kennebunkpost.com
Display Adv. E-mail: ads@kennebunkpost.com
Editorial e-mail: editor@kennebunkpost.com
Primary Website: mainelymediallc.com
Audit By: Sworn/Estimate/Non-Audited
Audit Date: 10.06.2019
Personnel: David Clark (Gen. Mgr./Adv. Mgr.); Dan King (Ed.)
Parent company (for newspapers): Mainely Media, LLC

LINCOLN NEWS

Street address 1: PO Box 35
Street address 2: 78 W Broadway
Street address city: Lincoln
Street address state: ME
Zip/Postal code: 04457-0035
General Phone: (207) 794-6532
General Fax: (207) 794-2004
General/National Adv. E-mail: news@lincnews.com
Display Adv. E-mail: news@lincnews.com
Editorial e-mail: editor@lincnews.com
Primary Website: lincnews.com
Year Established: 1959
Avg Paid Circ: 6450
Avg Free Circ: 19
Audit By: Sworn/Estimate/Non-Audited
Audit Date: 10.06.2019
Personnel: Laverne Carll (Office Mgr.); David Whalen (Gen. Mgr.)

LIVERMORE FALLS ADVERTISER

Street address 1: 59 Main St
Street address city: Livermore Falls
Street address state: ME
Zip/Postal code: 04254-1528
General Phone: (207) 897-4321
General Fax: (207) 897-4322
Advertising Phone: (207) 897-4321
Advertising Fax: (207) 897-4322
Editorial Phone: (207) 897-4321
Editorial Fax: (207) 897-4322
General/National Adv. E-mail: Lfanews@myfairpoint.net
Display Adv. E-mail: Lfanews@myfairpoint.net
Editorial e-mail: Lfanews@myfairpoint.net
Primary Website: lfadvertiser.com
Avg Paid Circ: 3000
Audit By: Sworn/Estimate/Non-Audited
Audit Date: 10.06.2019
Personnel: James R. Costello (Pres.); Barry Matulaitis (Ed.)
Parent company (for newspapers): Sun Media Group

MACHIAS VALLEY NEWS OBSERVER

Street address 1: 41 Broadway
Street address city: Machias
Street address state: ME
Zip/Postal code: 04654-1105
General Phone: (207) 255-6561
General Fax: (207) 255-4058
Advertising Phone: (207) 255-6561
Advertising Fax: (207) 255-4058
Editorial Phone: (207) 255-6561
Editorial Fax: (207) 255-4058
General/National Adv. E-mail: sales@machiasnews.com
Display Adv. E-mail: sales@machiasnews.com
Editorial e-mail: editor@machiasnews.com
Primary Website: machiasnews.com
Year Established: 1852
Avg Paid Circ: 2971
Avg Free Circ: 70
Audit By: Sworn/Estimate/Non-Audited
Audit Date: 10.06.2019
Personnel: Jay B. Hinson (Pub. Emiritus); Patricia Townsend (Pub.); Karen Hinson (Ed./Pub.); Wendy Dyer (Reporter); Mary Bury (Bus. Mgr.)

MAINEBIZ

Street address 1: 48 Free St
Street address 2: Ste 109
Street address city: Portland
Street address state: ME
Zip/Postal code: 04101-3874
General Phone: (207) 761-8379
General Fax: (207) 761-0732
Advertising Phone: (207) 761-8379
Advertising Fax: (207) 761-0732
Editorial Phone: (207) 761-8379
Editorial Fax: (207) 761-0732
General/National Adv. E-mail: leila@mainebiz.biz
Display Adv. E-mail: leila@mainebiz.biz
Editorial e-mail: dbrassard@mainebiz.biz
Primary Website: mainebiz.biz
Mthly Avg Unique Visitors: 20000
Year Established: 1994
Avg Paid Circ: 875
Avg Free Circ: 8731
Audit By: CVC
Audit Date: 30.09.2017
Personnel: Donna Brassard (Pub.); Rebekah Roy (Mktg. Mgr.); Leila Musacchio (Adv. Dir.)
Parent company (for newspapers): New England Business Media

MAKING IT AT HOME

Street address 1: 180 Main St
Street address city: Biddeford
Street address state: ME
Zip/Postal code: 04005-2410
General Phone: (207) 282-4337

General Fax: (207) 282-4339
Advertising Phone: (207) 282-4337 ext. 214
Advertising Fax: (207) 282-4339
Editorial Phone: (207) 282-4337
Editorial Fax: (207) 282-4339
General/National Adv. E-mail: ads@mainelymediallc.com
Display Adv. E-mail: ads@mainelymediallc.com
Editorial e-mail: editor@scarboroughleader.com
Primary Website: mainelymediallc.com
Audit By: Sworn/Estimate/Non-Audited
Audit Date: 10.06.2019
Personnel: David Clark (Gen. Mgr./Adv. Mgr.); Sandy Porrazzo (Bus. Mgr.); Molly Lovell (Mng. Ed.); Dan King (Ed.)
Parent company (for newspapers): Mainely Media, LLC

MOUNT DESERT ISLANDER

Street address 1: 310 Main St
Street address city: Bar Harbor
Street address state: ME
Zip/Postal code: 04609-1638
General Phone: (207) 288-0556
General Fax: (207) 288-0559
Advertising Phone: (207) 288-0556
Advertising Fax: (207) 288-0559
Editorial Phone: (207) 288-0556
Editorial Fax: (207) 288-0559
General/National Adv. E-mail: jclark@ellsworthamerican.com
Display Adv. E-mail: jclark@ellsworthamerican.com
Editorial e-mail: news@mdislander.com
Primary Website: mdislander.com
Year Established: 1851
Avg Paid Circ: 4369
Avg Free Circ: 65
Audit By: Sworn/Estimate/Non-Audited
Audit Date: 10.06.2019
Personnel: Alan L. Baker (Pub.)

PENOBSCOT TIMES

Street address 1: 282 Main St
Street address city: Old Town
Street address state: ME
Zip/Postal code: 04468-1529
General Phone: (207) 827-4451
General Fax: (207) 827-2280
General/National Adv. E-mail: news@thepenobscottimes.com
Display Adv. E-mail: news@thepenobscottimes.com
Editorial e-mail: news@thepenobscottimes.com
Primary Website: thepenobscottimes.com
Year Established: 1888
Avg Paid Circ: 4500
Audit By: Sworn/Estimate/Non-Audited
Audit Date: 10.06.2019
Personnel: Lynn Higgins (Pub.); Greg Fish (Ed.)
Parent company (for newspapers): Sun Media Group

PRESQUE ISLE STAR-HERALD

Street address 1: 40 North St
Street address 2: 40 North St
Street address city: Presque Isle
Street address state: ME
Zip/Postal code: 04769-2287
General Phone: (207) 768-5431
General Fax: (207) 764-7585
Advertising Phone: (207) 768-5431
Advertising Fax: (207) 764-7585
Editorial Phone: (207) 768-5431
Editorial Fax: (207) 764-7585
General/National Adv. E-mail: starheraldsales@nepublish.com
Display Adv. E-mail: starheraldsales@nepublish.com
Editorial e-mail: starherald@nepublish.com
Primary Website: starherald-me.com
Year Established: 1871
Avg Paid Circ: 7500
Avg Free Circ: 52
Audit By: Sworn/Estimate/Non-Audited
Audit Date: 10.06.2019
Personnel: Mark Putnam (Managing Ed.)

REGISTER GAZETTE

Street address 1: 180 Main St
Street address city: Biddeford
Street address state: ME
Zip/Postal code: 04005-2410
General Phone: (207) 282-4337
General Fax: (207) 282-4339
Advertising Phone: (207) 282-4337 ext. 214
Advertising Fax: (207) 282-4339
Editorial Phone: (207) 282-4337
Editorial Fax: (207) 282-4339
General/National Adv. E-mail: ads@intheregister.com
Display Adv. E-mail: ads@mainelymediallc.com
Editorial e-mail: editor@scarboroughleader.com
Primary Website: mainelymediallc.com
Audit By: Sworn/Estimate/Non-Audited
Audit Date: 10.06.2019
Personnel: David Clark (Gen. Mgr./Adv. Mgr.); Sandy Porrazzo (Bus. Mgr.); Molly Lovell (Mng. Ed.); Dan King (Ed.)
Parent company (for newspapers): Mainely Media, LLC

REPORTER

Street address 1: 1 City Center
Street address city: Portland
Street address state: ME
Zip/Postal code: 04101
General Phone: (207) 780-9086
General/National Adv. E-mail: cbell@keepmecurrent.com
Display Adv. E-mail: nladd@keepmecurrent.com
Editorial e-mail: acanfield@keepmecurrent.com
Primary Website: keepmecurrent.com
Year Established: 2001
Audit By: Sworn/Estimate/Non-Audited
Audit Date: 10.06.2019
Personnel: Mo Mehlsak (Exec. Ed.); Amy Canfield (Mng. Ed.); Cyndy Bell (Adv.)
Parent company (for newspapers): Current Publishing

ROLLING THUNDER EXPRESS

Street address 1: 134A Main St
Street address city: Newport
Street address state: ME
Zip/Postal code: 04953-3105
General Phone: (207) 876-4957
General Fax: (207) 368-5513
Advertising Phone: (207) 368-2028
Advertising Fax: (207) 368-5513
Editorial Phone: (207) 368-2028
Editorial Fax: (207) 368-5513
General/National Adv. E-mail: info@rollingthunderexpress.com
Display Adv. E-mail: info@rollingthunderexpress.com
Editorial e-mail: info@rollingthunderexpress.com
Primary Website: rollingthunderexpress.com
Year Established: 1985
Avg Free Circ: 16200
Audit By: Sworn/Estimate/Non-Audited
Audit Date: 10.06.2019
Personnel: Sylvia Angel-Currier (Pub.); Dawn Angel (Office Mgr.); David Dube (Circ. Mgr.); Colleen Theriault (Mng. Ed.)

RUMFORD FALLS TIMES

Street address 1: 69 Congress St
Street address city: Rumford
Street address state: ME
Zip/Postal code: 04276-2015
General Phone: (207) 364-7893
General Fax: (207) 369-0170
Advertising Phone: (207) 364-7893
Advertising Fax: (207) 369-0170
Editorial Phone: (207) 364-7893
Editorial Fax: (207) 369-0170
General/National Adv. E-mail: spenney@sunjournal.com
Display Adv. E-mail: spenney@sunjournal.com
Editorial e-mail: editor@rumfordfallstimes.com
Primary Website: rumfordfallstimes.com
Year Established: 1883
Avg Paid Circ: 4000
Avg Free Circ: 26
Audit By: Sworn/Estimate/Non-Audited
Audit Date: 10.06.2019
Personnel: Bruce Farrin (Mng. Ed.)
Parent company (for newspapers): MaineToday Media Inc.

SOUTH PORTLAND-CAPE/ ELIZABETH SENTRY

Street address 1: 180 Main St
Street address city: Biddeford
Street address state: ME
Zip/Postal code: 04005-2410
General Phone: (207) 282-4337
General Fax: (207) 282-4339
Advertising Phone: (207) 282-4337
Advertising Fax: (207) 282-4339
Editorial Phone: (207) 282-4337
Editorial Fax: (207) 282-4339
General/National Adv. E-mail: ads@mainelymediallc.com
Display Adv. E-mail: ads@mainelymediallc.com
Editorial e-mail: editor@scarboroughleader.com
Primary Website: mainelymediallc.com
Audit By: Sworn/Estimate/Non-Audited
Audit Date: 10.06.2019
Personnel: David Clark (Adv. Mgr./Gen. Mgr); Molly Lovell (Mng. Ed.)
Parent company (for newspapers): Mainely Media, LLC

ST. JOHN VALLEY TIMES

Street address 1: 328 Main St
Street address 2: # 102
Street address city: Madawaska
Street address state: ME
Zip/Postal code: 04756-1166
General Phone: (207) 728-3336
General Fax: (207) 728-3825
General/National Adv. E-mail: advertising@sjvalley-times.com
Display Adv. E-mail: linda.pelletier@sjvalley-times.com
Editorial e-mail: don.eno@sjvalley-times.com
Primary Website: sjvalley-times.com
Year Established: 1957
Avg Paid Circ: 4415
Audit By: Sworn/Estimate/Non-Audited
Audit Date: 10.06.2019
Personnel: Tessie Dubois (Pub./Ed.); Dan Doyon (Press Mgr.); Alison Voisine (Print Shop Customer Service Director); Jessica Blalock (General Manager); Crystal Berube (Bookkeeper); Don Eno (News Director); Monique Labbe (Reporter); Linda Pelletier (Circulation Director); Sharon Williams (Print Shop Assistant)
Parent company (for newspapers): Cleveland Newspapers, Inc.

SUN CHRONICLE

Street address 1: 840 Main St
Street address city: Westbrook
Street address state: ME
Zip/Postal code: 04092-2847
General Phone: (207) 854-2577
General Fax: (207) 854-0018
Advertising Phone: (207) 854-2577
Advertising Fax: (207) 854-0018
Editorial Phone: (207) 854-2577
Editorial Fax: (207) 854-0018
General/National Adv. E-mail: sales@keepmecurrent.com
Display Adv. E-mail: sales@keepmecurrent.com
Editorial e-mail: info@keepmecurrent.com
Primary Website: keepmecurrent.com
Year Established: 2001
Audit By: Sworn/Estimate/Non-Audited
Audit Date: 10.06.2019
Personnel: Jane P. Lord (Ed.); Mark Hews; Ben Bragdon
Parent company (for newspapers): Current Publishing

THE BETHEL CITIZEN

Street address 1: 19 Main St
Street address city: Bethel
Street address state: ME
Zip/Postal code: 04217-4014
General Phone: (207) 824-2444
General Fax: (207) 824-2426
Advertising Phone: (207) 824-2444
Advertising Fax: (207) 824-2426
General/National Adv. E-mail: ads@bethelcitizen.com
Display Adv. E-mail: ads@bethelcitizen.com
Editorial e-mail: news@bethelcitizen.com
Primary Website: bethelcitizen.com
Year Established: 1895
Avg Paid Circ: 3600
Audit By: Sworn/Estimate/Non-Audited
Audit Date: 10.06.2019
Personnel: Edward M. Snook (Pub.); Allison Aloisio (Ed.); Nancy Forest (Prodn. Mgr.)
Parent company (for newspapers): Sun Media Group

THE BRIDGTON NEWS

Street address 1: 118 Main St
Street address city: Bridgton
Street address state: ME
Zip/Postal code: 04009-1127
General Phone: (207) 647-2851
General Fax: (207) 647-5001
Advertising Phone: (207) 647-2851
Advertising Fax: (207) 647-5001
General/National Adv. E-mail: bnewsads@roadrunner.com
Display Adv. E-mail: bnewsads@roadrunner.com
Classified Adv. e-mail: bnews@roadrunner.com
Editorial e-mail: bnews@roadrunner.com
Primary Website: bridgton.com
Year Established: 1870
Avg Paid Circ: 5500
Audit By: Sworn/Estimate/Non-Audited
Audit Date: 10.06.2019
Personnel: Eric Gulbrandsen (Adv.)

THE BUCKSPORT ENTERPRISE

Street address 1: 105 Main St
Street address city: Bucksport
Street address state: ME
Zip/Postal code: 04416-4028
General Phone: (207) 469-6722
General/National Adv. E-mail: theenterpr@aol.com
Display Adv. E-mail: theenterpr@aol.com
Editorial e-mail: theenterpr@aol.com
Primary Website: bucksportenterprise.com
Year Established: 1991
Avg Paid Circ: 2300
Audit By: Sworn/Estimate/Non-Audited
Audit Date: 10.06.2019
Personnel: Donald M. Houghton (Ed.)

THE CALAIS ADVERTISER

Street address 1: 23 Church St
Street address city: Calais
Street address state: ME
Zip/Postal code: 04619-1639
General Phone: (207) 454-3561
General Fax: (207) 454-3458
General/National Adv. E-mail: advertising@thecalaisadvertiser.com
Display Adv. E-mail: advertising@thecalaisadvertiser.com
Editorial e-mail: editorcalais@gmail.com
Primary Website: thecalaisadvertiser.com
Year Established: 1836
Avg Paid Circ: 3200
Avg Free Circ: 15
Audit By: Sworn/Estimate/Non-Audited
Audit Date: 10.06.2019
Personnel: John Rogers (Sports Ed.); Cheryl Stabinski (Graphic Designer); Lura Jackson (Managing editor); Beth McCray (advertising manager); Nada Williams-White (proof reader)

THE CAMDEN HERALD

Street address 1: 91 Camden St
Street address 2: Ste 403
Street address city: Rockland
Street address state: ME
Zip/Postal code: 04841-2421
General Phone: (207) 236-8511
General Fax: (207) 236-2816
General/National Adv. E-mail: sales@courierpublicationsllc.com
Display Adv. E-mail: sales@courierpublicationsllc.com
Editorial e-mail: news@courierpublicationsllc.com
Primary Website: knox.villagesoup.com
Year Established: 1869
Avg Paid Circ: 8438
Avg Free Circ: 1407
Audit By: Sworn/Estimate/Non-Audited
Audit Date: 10.06.2019

Personnel: Reade Brower (Owner); Bryan Gess (Operations Dir.); Stephanie Grinnell (Ed.); Christine Dunkle (Prodn. Mgr.)
Parent company (for newspapers): Courier Publications, LLC

THE CURRENT

Street address 1: 840 Main St
Street address city: Westbrook
Street address state: ME
Zip/Postal code: 04092-2847
General Phone: (207) 854-2577
General Fax: (207) 854-0018
Advertising Phone: (207) 854-2577
Advertising Fax: (207) 854-0018
Editorial Phone: (207) 854-2577
Editorial Fax: (207) 854-0018
General/National Adv. E-mail: sales@keepmecurrent.com
Display Adv. E-mail: sales@keepmecurrent.com
Editorial e-mail: info@keepmecurrent.com
Primary Website: keepmecurrent.com
Year Established: 2001
Audit By: Sworn/Estimate/Non-Audited
Audit Date: 10.06.2019
Personnel: Jane P. Lord (Ed.); Mark Hews (Ad. Director)
Parent company (for newspapers): Current Publishing

THE ELLSWORTH AMERICAN

Street address 1: 30 Water St
Street address city: Ellsworth
Street address state: ME
Zip/Postal code: 04605-2033
General Phone: (207)667-2576
General Fax: (207) 667-7656
Advertising Phone: (207) 667-2576
Advertising Fax: (207) 667-3431
Editorial Phone: (207) 667-2576
Editorial Fax: (207) 667-7656
General/National Adv. E-mail: skimball@ellsworthamerican.com
Display Adv. E-mail: skimball@ellsworthamerican.com
Editorial e-mail: sfay@ellsworthamerican.com
Primary Website: ellsworthamerican.com
Year Established: 1851
Avg Paid Circ: 8477
Audit By: Sworn/Estimate/Non-Audited
Audit Date: 10.06.2019
Personnel: Alan L. Baker (Pub.); Terry Carlisle (Gen. Mgr.); Sally Hutchins (Acct Mgr); Scott Kimball (Adv Dir); Matt Martin (Production Manager)
Parent company (for newspapers): Ellsworth American, Inc.

THE FORECASTER

Street address 1: 5 Fundy Rd
Street address 2: Ste 1
Street address city: Falmouth
Street address state: ME
Zip/Postal code: 04105-1771
General Phone: (207) 781-3661
General Fax: (207) 781-2060
Advertising Phone: (207) 781-3661
Advertising Fax: (207) 781-2060
Editorial Phone: (207) 781-3661
Editorial Fax: (207) 781-2060
General/National Adv. E-mail: cgardner@theforecaster.net
Display Adv. E-mail: jallen@theforecaster.net
Editorial e-mail: editor@theforecaster.net
Primary Website: theforecaster.net
Year Established: 1986
Avg Free Circ: 60000
Audit By: Sworn/Estimate/Non-Audited
Audit Date: 10.06.2019
Personnel: Mo Mehlsak (Ed.); Michael Hoffer (Sports Ed.); Suzanne Piecuch (Production Mgr.); David W. Costello (Pres.); Karen Wood (Publisher)
Parent company (for newspapers): Sun Media Group

THE LAKES REGION WEEKLY

Street address 1: 840 Main St
Street address city: Westbrook
Street address state: ME
Zip/Postal code: 04092-2847
General Phone: (207) 854-2577
General Fax: (207) 854-0018
Advertising Phone: (207) 854-2577
Advertising Fax: (207) 854-0018
Editorial Phone: (207) 854-2577
Editorial Fax: (207) 854-0018
General/National Adv. E-mail: sales@keepmecurrent.com
Display Adv. E-mail: sales@keepmecurrent.com
Editorial e-mail: info@keepmecurrent.com
Primary Website: keepmecurrent.com
Year Established: 2001
Avg Paid Circ: 5800
Audit By: Sworn/Estimate/Non-Audited
Audit Date: 10.06.2019
Personnel: Lee Hewes-Casler (Pub.); Mark Hews (Circ. Mgr.); Brendan Moran (Ed.); Jane P. Lord (Exec. Ed.)
Parent company (for newspapers): Current Publishing

THE LINCOLN COUNTY NEWS

Street address 1: 116 Mills Rd
Street address city: Newcastle
Street address state: ME
Zip/Postal code: 04553-3408
General Phone: (207) 563-3171
General Fax: (207) 563-3127
Advertising Phone: (207) 563-3171
Advertising Fax: (207) 563-3127
Editorial Phone: (207) 563-3171
Editorial Fax: (207) 563-3127
General/National Adv. E-mail: info@lcnme.com
Editorial e-mail: info@lcnme.com
Primary Website: lcnme.com
Year Established: 1875
Audit By: Sworn/Estimate/Non-Audited
Audit Date: 10.06.2019
Personnel: Christopher Roberts (Publisher); John Roberts (Associate Publisher); J.W. Oliver; Maia Zewert (Acting Editor)

THE PISCATAQUIS OBSERVER

Street address 1: 12 E Main St
Street address 2: Ste A
Street address city: Dover Foxcroft
Street address state: ME
Zip/Postal code: 04426-1414
General Phone: (207) 564-8355
General Fax: (207) 564-7056
General/National Adv. E-mail: observersales@bangordailynews.com
Display Adv. E-mail: observersales@bangordailynews.com
Editorial e-mail: observer@bangordailynews.com
Primary Website: observer-me.com
Year Established: 1838
Avg Paid Circ: 2000
Avg Free Circ: 10
Audit By: Sworn/Estimate/Non-Audited
Audit Date: 10.06.2019
Personnel: Mike Dowd (Manager); Keri Foster (Sales)
Parent company (for newspapers): Bangor Publishing Company

THE REPUBLICAN JOURNAL

Street address 1: 161 High St
Street address city: Belfast
Street address state: ME
Zip/Postal code: 04915-6548
General Phone: (207) 338-3333
General Fax: (207) 338-5498
Advertising Phone: (207) 338-3333
Advertising Fax: (207) 338-5498
General/National Adv. E-mail: sales@courierpublicationsllc.com
Display Adv. E-mail: sales@courierpublicationsllc.com
Editorial e-mail: news@villagesoup.com
Primary Website: villagesoup.com
Year Established: 1829
Avg Paid Circ: 8000
Avg Free Circ: 162
Audit By: Sworn/Estimate/Non-Audited
Audit Date: 10.06.2019
Personnel: Reade Brower (Pres./Pub.); Dave Libby (Sales Dir.); Bryan Gess (Oper. Mgr.); Daniel Dunkle (Ed.)
Parent company (for newspapers): Courier Publications, LLC; Crescent Publishing Company LLC; Village Netmedia, Inc.

THE WEEKLY

Street address 1: 491 Main St
Street address city: Bangor
Street address state: ME
Zip/Postal code: 04401-6296
General Phone: (207) 990-8000
General Fax: (207) 990-8041
Advertising Phone: (207) 990-8000
Advertising Fax: (207) 990-8041
Editorial Phone: (207) 990-8175
Editorial Fax: (207) 990-8041
General/National Adv. E-mail: advertising@bangordailynews.net
Display Adv. E-mail: tmcleod@bangordailynews.com
Editorial e-mail: syoung@bangordailynews.com
Primary Website: bangordailynews.com/weekly
Avg Paid Circ: 24775
Audit By: Sworn/Estimate/Non-Audited
Audit Date: 10.06.2019
Personnel: Richard J. Warren (Pub.); Robert W. Stairs (Vice Pres.); Timothy Reynolds (Controller); Mike Kearney (Adv. Dir.); Jim Hayes (Circ. Dir.); A. Mark Woodward (Exec. Ed.); Michael J. Dowd (Mng. Ed.); Joseph McLaughlin (Sports Ed.); Charles Villard (Prodn. Mgr.)

THE WEEKLY PACKET

Street address 1: 13 Main St
Street address city: Blue Hill
Street address state: ME
Zip/Postal code: 04614-5985
General Phone: (207) 374-2341
General Fax: (207) 374-2343
Advertising Phone: (207) 374-2341
Advertising Fax: (207) 374-2343
Editorial Phone: (207) 374-2341
Editorial Fax: (207) 374-2343
General/National Adv. E-mail: ads@pbp.me
Display Adv. E-mail: classifieds@pbp.me
Editorial e-mail: news@pbp.me
Primary Website: weeklypacket.com
Year Established: 1960
Avg Paid Circ: 1610
Avg Free Circ: 22
Audit By: Sworn/Estimate/Non-Audited
Audit Date: 10.06.2019
Personnel: R. Nathaniel W. Barrows (Ed.); Cathy Marshall (Circ. Mgr.); Faith DeAmbrose (Managing Editor)

TOWN LINE

Street address 1: PO Box 89
Street address city: South China
Street address state: ME
Zip/Postal code: 04358-0089
General Phone: (207) 445-2234
General Fax: (207) 445-2265
Advertising Phone: (207) 445-2234
Advertising Fax: (207) 445-2265
Editorial Phone: (207) 445-2234
Editorial Fax: (207) 445-2265
General/National Adv. E-mail: townline@fairpoint.net
Display Adv. E-mail: townline@fairpoint.net
Editorial e-mail: townline@fairpoint.net
Primary Website: townline.org
Year Established: 1989
Audit By: Sworn/Estimate/Non-Audited
Audit Date: 10.06.2019
Personnel: Roland Hallee (Mng. Ed.); Claire Breton (Circulation Director)

TRI-TOWN WEEKLY

Street address 1: 840 Main St
Street address city: Westbrook
Street address state: ME
Zip/Postal code: 04092-2847
General Phone: (207) 854-2577
General Fax: (207) 854-0018
Advertising Phone: (207) 854-2577
Advertising Fax: (207) 854-0018
Editorial Phone: (207) 854-2577
Editorial Fax: (207) 854-0018
General/National Adv. E-mail: sales@keepmecurrent.com
Display Adv. E-mail: sales@keepmecurrent.com
Editorial e-mail: info@keepmecurrent.com
Primary Website: keepmecurrent.com
Year Established: 2001
Audit By: Sworn/Estimate/Non-Audited
Audit Date: 10.06.2019
Personnel: Jane P. Lord (Ed.); Mark Hews (Ad. Dir.)
Parent company (for newspapers): Current Publishing

WEEKLY OBSERVER

Street address 1: 840 Main St
Street address city: Westbrook
Street address state: ME
Zip/Postal code: 04092-2847
General Phone: (207) 854-2577
General Fax: (207) 854-0018
Advertising Phone: (207) 854-2577
Advertising Fax: (207) 854-0018
Editorial Phone: (207) 854-2577
Editorial Fax: (207) 854-0018
General/National Adv. E-mail: sales@keepmecurrent.com
Display Adv. E-mail: sales@keepmecurrent.com
Editorial e-mail: info@keepmecurrent.com
Primary Website: keepmecurrent.com
Year Established: 2001
Audit By: Sworn/Estimate/Non-Audited
Audit Date: 10.06.2019
Personnel: Jane P. Lord (Ed.); Mark Hews (Ad. Dir.)
Parent company (for newspapers): Current Publishing

WEEKLY SENTINEL

Street address 1: 952 Post Rd
Street address 2: Unit 10
Street address city: Wells
Street address state: ME
Zip/Postal code: 04090-4142
General Phone: (207) 646-8448
General Fax: (207) 646-8477
General/National Adv. E-mail: ads@theweeklysentinel.com
Editorial e-mail: editor@theweeklysentinel.com
Primary Website: theweeklysentinel.com
Year Established: 2005
Avg Free Circ: 39592
Audit By: Sworn/Estimate/Non-Audited
Audit Date: 10.06.2019
Personnel: Dan Brennan (Operations Mgr.); David Kennedy (Acct. Mgr.)

WISCASSET NEWSPAPER

Street address 1: 97 Townsend Ave
Street address city: Boothbay Harbor
Street address state: ME
Zip/Postal code: 04538-1843
General Phone: (207) 633-4620
General Fax: (207) 633-7123
General/National Adv. E-mail: newsdesk@wiscassetnewspaper.com
Display Adv. E-mail: classifieds@boothbayregister.com
Editorial e-mail: newsdesk@wiscassetnewspaper.com
Primary Website: wiscassetnewspaper.com
Year Established: 1970
Avg Paid Circ: 690
Avg Free Circ: 23
Audit By: Sworn/Estimate/Non-Audited
Audit Date: 10.06.2019
Personnel: A.R. Tandy (Pub.); Pat Schmid (Bus. Mgr.); Kathy Frizzell (Adv. Mgr.); Kevin Burnham (Ed.)
Parent company (for newspapers): Maine-OK Enterprises, Inc.

YORK COUNTY COAST STAR

Street address 1: 85 Main Street
Street address city: Kennebunk
Street address state: ME
Zip/Postal code: 04043
General Phone: (207) 985-5901
Primary Website: seacoastonline.com
Audit By: Sworn/Estimate/Non-Audited
Audit Date: 10.06.2019
Personnel: Howard Altschiller (Ed.); Vince Ciampi (Adv. Dir.); John Tabor (Pub.); Dennis Thompson
Parent company (for newspapers): Dow Jones Local Media Group-OOB; Seacoast Media Group

MARYLAND

ARBUTUS TIMES

Street address 1: 501 N Calvert St
Street address city: Baltimore

Street address state: MD
Zip/Postal code: 21278-1000
General Phone: (410) 332-6000
General Fax: (410) 332-6977
Advertising Phone: (410) 332-6300
Advertising Fax: (410) 332-6977
Editorial Phone: (410) 332-6000
Editorial Fax: (410) 332-6977
General/National Adv. E-mail: advertise@baltsun.com
Display Adv. E-mail: advertise@baltsun.com
Editorial e-mail: talkback@baltimoresun.com
Primary Website: arbutustimes.com
Avg Paid Circ: 415
Avg Free Circ: 204
Audit By: Sworn/Estimate/Non-Audited
Audit Date: 10.06.2019
Personnel: Jim Quimby (Pub.); Keith Meisel (Mng. Ed.); Judith Berman (Sr. VP, Sales/Mktg); Matt Cimino (Nat'l Adv. Majors/Sales Mgr.); Susan Duchin (Dir, Nat'l Adv.); Jim Alvey (Dir., Direct Mktg.); Wayne Lowman (Dir, Classified Adv.)
Parent company (for newspapers): Tribune Publishing, Inc.

BALTIMORE BUSINESS JOURNAL

Street address 1: 36 S Charles St
Street address 2: Ste 2500
Street address city: Baltimore
Street address state: MD
Zip/Postal code: 21201-3107
General Phone: (410) 576-1161
General Fax: (410) 752-3112
General/National Adv. E-mail: baltimore@bizjournals.com
Display Adv. E-mail: baltimore@bizjournals.com
Editorial e-mail: baltimore@bizjournals.com
Primary Website: baltimorebusinessjournal.com
Year Established: 1983
Avg Paid Circ: 9206
Audit By: Sworn/Estimate/Non-Audited
Audit Date: 10.06.2019
Personnel: John Dinkel (President & Publisher); Joanna Sullivan (Ed.); Eileen Silberfeld (Aud. Dev. Dir.); Mike Gillispie (Prod. Dir.); Linda Schummers (Bus. Mgr.)

BALTIMORE GUIDE SOUTH

Street address 1: 2935 Odonnell St
Street address city: Baltimore
Street address state: MD
Zip/Postal code: 21224-4823
General Phone: (410) 732-6600
General Fax: (410) 732-6336
Advertising Phone: (410) 732-6600
Advertising Fax: (410) 732-6336
Editorial Phone: (410) 732-6600
Editorial Fax: (410) 732-6336
General/National Adv. E-mail: lnemec@baltimoreguide.com
Display Adv. E-mail: jchaney@baltimoreguide.com
Editorial e-mail: ezygmont@baltimoreguide.com
Primary Website: baltimoreguide.com
Year Established: 1927
Avg Free Circ: 25000
Audit By: Sworn/Estimate/Non-Audited
Audit Date: 10.06.2019
Personnel: Perry Corsetti (Pub.); Erik Zygmont (Ed.); Jackie Miller (Office Mgr.); Lisa Nemec (Acct. Exec); Jessica Chaney (Acct. Exec.)

BAY WEEKLY

Street address 1: 1160 Spa Rd
Street address 2: Ste 1A
Street address city: Annapolis
Street address state: MD
Zip/Postal code: 21403-1097
General Phone: (410) 626-9888
General Fax: (410) 626-0008
General/National Adv. E-mail: ads@bayweekly.com
Display Adv. E-mail: ads@bayweekly.com
Editorial e-mail: editor@bayweekly.com
Primary Website: bayweekly.com
Year Established: 1993
Avg Free Circ: 17000
Audit By: Sworn/Estimate/Non-Audited
Audit Date: 10.06.2019
Personnel: Sandra Martin (Ed./Pub.); J. Alex Knoll (Gen. Mgr.); Lisa Edler Knoll (Mktg. Dir.); Betsy Kehne (Prod. Mgr.); Kathy Knotts (Editorial assistant)
Parent company (for newspapers): New Bay Enterprises

BAYSIDE GAZETTE

Street address 1: 8200 Coastal Hwy
Street address city: Ocean City
Street address state: MD
Zip/Postal code: 21842
General Phone: (410) 723-6397
General Fax: (410) 723-6511
Advertising Phone: (410) 723-6397 x107
Editorial Phone: (410) 723-6397 x110
Editorial Fax: (410) 641-0085
General/National Adv. E-mail: ebrady@baysidegazette.com
Display Adv. E-mail: classifieds@oceancitytoday.net
Editorial e-mail: editor@baysidegazette.com
Primary Website: baysideoc.com
Year Established: 2004
Avg Free Circ: 7500
Audit By: Sworn/Estimate/Non-Audited
Audit Date: 10.06.2019
Personnel: Elaine Brady (Associate Publisher)
Parent company (for newspapers): Ocean City Today

BOWIE BLADE-NEWS

Street address 1: 2000 Capital Dr
Street address city: Annapolis
Street address state: MD
Zip/Postal code: 21401-3155
General Phone: (410) 268-5000
General Fax: (410) 268-4643
Advertising Phone: (410) 268-5000
Advertising Fax: (410) 280-5974
General/National Adv. E-mail: localads@capgaznews.com
Display Adv. E-mail: classifieds@capgaznews.com
Editorial e-mail: tips@capgaznews.com
Primary Website: capitalgazette.com/bowie_bladenews
Year Established: 1900
Avg Free Circ: 35000
Audit By: Sworn/Estimate/Non-Audited
Audit Date: 10.06.2019
Personnel: Pat Richardson (Pub.); Rob Pryor (Circ. Dir.)
Parent company (for newspapers): Landmark Media Enterprises, LLC

BOWIE STAR

Street address 1: 13501 Konterra Dr
Street address city: Laurel
Street address state: MD
Zip/Postal code: 20707-6505
General Phone: (240) 473-7500
General Fax: (240) 473-7501
General/National Adv. E-mail: editor@gazette.net
Primary Website: gazette.net
Avg Free Circ: 22769
Audit By: Sworn/Estimate/Non-Audited
Audit Date: 10.06.2019
Personnel: David Simon

CATONSVILLE TIMES

Street address 1: 300 E. Cromwell Street
Street address city: Baltimore
Street address state: MD
Zip/Postal code: 21230
General Phone: (410) 788-4500
Editorial Fax: (410) 997-4564
General/National Adv. E-mail: catonsvilletimes@patuxent.com
Primary Website: patuxent.com
Avg Paid Circ: 1243
Avg Free Circ: 111
Audit By: AAM
Audit Date: 30.09.2018
Personnel: Judith Berman (Sr. VP Sales & Mkting.); Matt Cimino (Nat'l Adv & Majors Sales Mgr); Susan Duchin (Dir Nat'l Adv & Majors)
Parent company (for newspapers): Baltimore Sun Media Group; Tribune Publishing, Inc.

CECIL WHIG

Street address 1: 601 N Bridge St
Street address city: Elkton
Street address state: MD
Zip/Postal code: 21921-5307
General Phone: (410) 398-3311
General Fax: (410) 398-4044
Advertising Phone: (443) 245-5045
Advertising Fax: (410) 398-4044
Editorial Phone: (410) 398-3311
Editorial Fax: (443) 245-5043
General/National Adv. E-mail: mfoglio@chespub.com
Display Adv. E-mail: mfoglio@chespub.com
Classified Adv. e-mail: mfoglio@chespub.com
Editorial e-mail: jowens@cecilwhig.com
Primary Website: cecildaily.com
Year Established: 1841
Avg Paid Circ: 12163
Audit By: Sworn/Estimate/Non-Audited
Audit Date: 10.06.2019
Personnel: David Fike (Pub.); Jake Owens (News Ed.); Dara McBride (Features Ed.); Chuck Ristano (Sports Ed.); Maria Foglio (Adv. Dir.)
Parent company (for newspapers): Adams Publishing Group, LLC

COLUMBIA FLIER

Street address 1: 10750 Little Patuxent Pkwy
Street address city: Columbia
Street address state: MD
Zip/Postal code: 21044-3106
General Phone: (443) 692-9011
Editorial Fax: (410) 997-4564
General/National Adv. E-mail: wartuscooper@baltsun.com
Display Adv. E-mail: wartuscooper@baltsun.com
Editorial e-mail: sam.davis@baltsun.com
Primary Website: baltimoresun.com
Avg Paid Circ: 1079
Avg Free Circ: 42304
Audit By: CAC
Audit Date: 30.09.2018
Personnel: Triffon Alatzas (Pub./Ed.-in-Chief); Samuel Davis (Mng. Ed.); Wanda Artus-Cooper (Adv. Mgr.); Sharon Nevins (VP, Adv.)
Parent company (for newspapers): Baltimore Sun Media Group

COMMUNITY TIMES

Street address 1: 201 Railroad Ave
Street address city: Westminster
Street address state: MD
Zip/Postal code: 21157-4823
General Phone: (410) 875-5400
General Fax: (410) 857-8749
Primary Website: carrollcountytimes.com
Avg Paid Circ: 500
Avg Free Circ: 11500
Audit By: Sworn/Estimate/Non-Audited
Audit Date: 10.06.2019
Personnel: Erin Hahn (Adv. Dir.); Jim Lee (Ed.)

CRISFIELD-SOMERSET COUNTY TIMES

Street address 1: 914 W Main St
Street address city: Crisfield
Street address state: MD
Zip/Postal code: 21817-1016
General Phone: (410) 968-1188
General Fax: (410) 968-1197
Advertising Phone: (410) 968-1189
Advertising Fax: (410) 968-1197
Editorial Phone: (410) 968-1188
Editorial Fax: (410) 968-1197
General/National Adv. E-mail: adsales@newszap.com
Display Adv. E-mail: classads@newszap.com
Editorial e-mail: crisfieldnews@newszap.com
Primary Website: csctimes.com
Year Established: 1889
Avg Paid Circ: 1047
Avg Free Circ: 53
Audit By: AAM
Audit Date: 31.12.2016
Personnel: Darel LaPrade (Pub.); Richard Crumbaker (Ed./Gen Mgr.); Karen Riggin (Adv. Consultant)
Parent company (for newspapers): Independent Newsmedia Inc. USA

CROFTON-WEST COUNTY GAZETTE

Street address 1: 2000 Capital Dr
Street address city: Annapolis
Street address state: MD
Zip/Postal code: 21401-3155
General Phone: (410) 268-5000
General Fax: (410) 268-4643
Advertising Phone: (410) 268-5000
Advertising Fax: (410) 280-5974
Editorial Phone: (410) 280-5959
Editorial Fax: (410) 280-5953
General/National Adv. E-mail: localads@capgaznews.com
Display Adv. E-mail: classifieds@capgaznews.com
Editorial e-mail: cwcgazette@capgaznews.com
Primary Website: capitalgazette.com/crofton_westcounty
Year Established: 1995
Audit By: Sworn/Estimate/Non-Audited
Audit Date: 10.06.2019
Personnel: Pat Richardson (Pub.); Steve Gunn (Ed.); Marty Padden (Adv. Dir.)
Parent company (for newspapers): Landmark Media Enterprises, LLC

DELAWARE COAST PRESS

Street address 1: 115 S. Division St.
Street address city: Salisbury
Street address state: MD
Zip/Postal code: 21801
General Phone: (410) 749-7171
General/National Adv. E-mail: rpousson@localiq.com
Display Adv. E-mail: sbyclass@gannett.com
Editorial e-mail: lbenedic@dmg.gannett.com
Primary Website: delmarvanow.com/news/delaware
Year Established: 1897
Avg Free Circ: 16628
Audit By: AAM
Audit Date: 31.12.2018
Personnel: Mike Kilian (Exec. Ed.); Alyson Cunningham (Ed.); Ron Smith (Operations Dir.); Robb Scott (Dir. of Sales); Pat Purdum (Sales Mgr.); Lou Haut (Circ. Mgr.); Laurie Benedict (News Dir.)
Parent company (for newspapers): Gannett

EAST COUNTY TIMES

Street address 1: 513 Eastern Blvd
Street address city: Baltimore
Street address state: MD
Zip/Postal code: 21221-6702
General Phone: (410) 780-3303
General Fax: (410) 780-2616
Advertising Phone: (410) 780-3303
Advertising Fax: (410) 780-2616
Editorial Phone: (410) 780-3303
Editorial Fax: (410) 780-2616
General/National Adv. E-mail: ectsales@comcast.net
Display Adv. E-mail: classified@eastcountytimesonline.com
Editorial e-mail: ecteditorial@comcast.net
Primary Website: eastcountytimesonline.com
Year Established: 1995
Avg Free Circ: 31325
Audit By: VAC
Audit Date: 31.03.2017
Personnel: George Wilbanks (Pub./Gen. Mgr.); Linda K. Mrok (Adv. Mgr.); Mike Wilbanks (Opns. Mgr.); Allison McAlister (Ed.); Angie Hess (Art. Dir.)
Parent company (for newspapers): Chatsworth Enterprises, Inc.

EASTERN SHORE BARGAINEER

Street address 1: 29088 Airpark Dr
Street address city: Easton
Street address state: MD
Zip/Postal code: 21601-7000
General Phone: (410) 822-1500
General Fax: (410) 770-4019
Primary Website: stardem.com
Audit By: Sworn/Estimate/Non-Audited
Audit Date: 10.06.2019
Personnel: Josh Griep (Ed.)
Parent company (for newspapers): Adams Publishing Group, LLC

GREENBELT NEWS REVIEW

Street address 1: 15 Crescent Rd
Street address 2: Ste 100
Street address city: Greenbelt
Street address state: MD
Zip/Postal code: 20770-0807
General Phone: (301) 474-4131
General Fax: (301) 474-5880
Advertising Phone: (301) 474-4131
Advertising Fax: (301) 474-5880

Editorial Phone: (301) 474-4131
Editorial Fax: (301) 474-5880
General/National Adv. E-mail: newsreview@verizon.net
Display Adv. E-mail: newsreview@verizon.net
Editorial e-mail: newsreview@verizon.net
Primary Website: greenbeltnewsreview.com
Year Established: 1937
Avg Paid Circ: 80
Avg Free Circ: 9400
Audit By: Sworn/Estimate/Non-Audited
Audit Date: 10.06.2019
Personnel: Eileen Farnham (Pres.); Thomas X. White (Vice Pres.); Judy Bell (Treasurer); Diane Oberg (Bus. Mgr.); Carol Griffith (Sec.); Ian Tuckman (Circ. Mgr.); Mary Lou Williamson (Ed.); Barbara Likowski (Asst. Ed.); Elaine Skolnik (News Ed.)

HOWARD COUNTY TIMES

Street address 1: 10750 Little Patuxent Pkwy
Street address city: Columbia
Street address state: MD
Zip/Postal code: 21044-3106
General Phone: (410) 730-3620
Advertising Phone: (410) 730-3620
Editorial Fax: (410) 997-4564
General/National Adv. E-mail: mcimino@baltsun.com
Display Adv. E-mail: wayne.lowman@baltsun.com
Primary Website: howardcountytimes.com
Avg Paid Circ: 4105
Avg Free Circ: 6108
Audit By: AAM
Audit Date: 30.09.2018
Personnel: Paul Milton (Exec. Dir.); Allison Thompson (Adv.); Judith Berman (Sr VP Sales & Mkting); Susan Duchin (Dir, Nat'l Adv & Majors); Matt Cimino (Nat'l Adv & Majors Sales Mgr)
Parent company (for newspapers): Tribune Publishing, Inc.

JEFFERSONIAN

Street address 1: 409 Washington Ave
Street address city: Towson
Street address state: MD
Zip/Postal code: 21204-4920
General Phone: (410) 337-2400
General Fax: (410) 337-2490
General/National Adv. E-mail: jtynes@patuxent.com
Primary Website: thejeffersonian.com
Avg Paid Circ: 292
Avg Free Circ: 187
Audit By: CAC
Audit Date: 30.09.2017
Personnel: Trish Carroll (Pub.); David Piel (Circ. Mgr.); Michael Aaron (Ed.); Matt Cimino (Nat'l Adv & Majors, Sales Mgr); Judith Berman (Sr VP Sales & Mkting); Susan Duchin (Dir, Nat'l Adv & Majors)
Parent company (for newspapers): Tribune Publishing, Inc.

KENT COUNTY NEWS

Street address 1: 217 High St
Street address city: Chestertown
Street address state: MD
Zip/Postal code: 21620-1517
General Phone: (410) 778-2011
General Fax: (410) 778-6522
Advertising Phone: (410) 778-2011
Editorial Phone: (410) 778-2011
General/National Adv. E-mail: eastonad@chespub.com
Display Adv. E-mail: eastonad@chespub.com
Editorial e-mail: editor@thekentcountynews.com
Primary Website: thekentcountynews.com
Avg Paid Circ: 7506
Avg Free Circ: 12
Audit By: Sworn/Estimate/Non-Audited
Audit Date: 10.06.2019
Personnel: Mary Burton (Pub./Gen. Mgr./Adv. Mgr.); David Fike (VP/Pub.); Betty Jean Bryden (Classified Adv. Mgr.); Trish McGee (Ed.); Kathleen McLaughlin (Circ. Exec.)
Parent company (for newspapers): Adams Publishing Group, LLC

LAUREL LEADER

Street address 1: 300 E. Cromwell Street
Street address city: Baltimore
Street address state: MD
Zip/Postal code: 21230
General Phone: (410) 332-6594
General Fax: (410) 332-6594
Editorial Phone: (410) 332-6594
Editorial Fax: (410) 332-6594
General/National Adv. E-mail: jduchman@baltsun.com
Display Adv. E-mail: classifieds@baltsun.com
Editorial e-mail: Laurelleadernews@tronc.com
Primary Website: laurelleader.com
Year Established: 1897
Avg Paid Circ: 12057
Avg Free Circ: 18067
Audit By: AAM
Audit Date: 30.09.2018
Personnel: Melanie Dzwonchyk (Ed.); Triffon Alatzas
Parent company (for newspapers): Baltimore Sun Media Group; Tribune Publishing, Inc.

MARYLAND BEACHCOMBER

Street address 1: 12417 Ocean Gtwy
Street address 2: Ste 7
Street address city: Ocean City
Street address state: MD
Zip/Postal code: 21842-9522
General Phone: (410) 213-9442
General Fax: (410) 213-9459
Primary Website: marylandbeachcomber.com
Year Established: 1965
Avg Free Circ: 22000
Audit By: Sworn/Estimate/Non-Audited
Audit Date: 10.06.2019
Personnel: Greg Desset (Pub.); Kelsey Collins (Ed.)
Parent company (for newspapers): Gannett

MARYLAND COAST DISPATCH

Street address 1: 10012 Old Ocean City Blvd
Street address city: Berlin
Street address state: MD
Zip/Postal code: 21811-1145
General Phone: (410) 641-4561
General Fax: (410) 641-0966
General/National Adv. E-mail: editor@mdcoastdispatch.com
Display Adv. E-mail: classifieds@mdcoastdispatch.com
Editorial e-mail: editor@mdcoastdispatch.com
Primary Website: mdcoastdispatch.com
Year Established: 1984
Avg Paid Circ: 500
Avg Free Circ: 25000
Audit By: Sworn/Estimate/Non-Audited
Audit Date: 10.06.2019
Personnel: Steven Green (Pub.); Terry French (VP, Sales); Patricia Lohmeyer (Office Mgr.); J. Steven Green (Ed.); Shawn Soper (News Ed.)

MONTGOMERY COUNTY SENTINEL

Street address 1: 22 W Jefferson St
Street address 2: Ste 309
Street address city: Rockville
Street address state: MD
Zip/Postal code: 20850-4259
General Phone: (301) 838-0788
General Fax: (301) 838-3458
Advertising Phone: (301) 306-9500
Advertising Fax: (301) 306-0134
Editorial Phone: (301) 838-0788
Editorial Fax: (301) 838-3458
General/National Adv. E-mail: lonnie@thesentinel.com
Display Adv. E-mail: lonnie@thesentinel.com
Editorial e-mail: editor-mc@thesentinel.com
Primary Website: thesentinel.com
Year Established: 1855
Avg Paid Circ: 10000
Audit By: Sworn/Estimate/Non-Audited
Audit Date: 10.06.2019
Personnel: Lynn Kapiloff (CEO); Brian Karen (Ed.); Lonnie Johnson (Adv. Mgr.); Mark Kapiloff; Sharmia Bush; Pete Hajiantoni (Strategic Information Mgr.)

NEWARK POST

Street address 1: 601 N Bridge St
Street address city: Elkton
Street address state: MD
Zip/Postal code: 21921-5307
General Phone: (302) 737-0724
General Fax: (302) 737-9019
Primary Website: newarkpostonline.com
Avg Paid Circ: 12500
Audit By: Sworn/Estimate/Non-Audited
Audit Date: 10.06.2019
Personnel: Marty Valania (Gen. Mgr.); Ed Hoffman (Adv. Mgr.); Bill Sims (Circ. Dir.); Scott Goss (Ed.)

OCEAN CITY TODAY

Street address 1: 8200 Coastal Hwy
Street address city: Ocean City
Street address state: MD
Zip/Postal code: 21842-2834
General Phone: (410) 723-6397
General Fax: (410) 723-6511
General/National Adv. E-mail: ebrady@oceancitytoday.net
Display Adv. E-mail: sales@oceancitytoday.net
Editorial e-mail: editor@oceancitytoday.net
Primary Website: oceancitytoday.net
Year Established: 1993
Avg Free Circ: 16500
Audit By: Sworn/Estimate/Non-Audited
Audit Date: 10.06.2019
Personnel: Stewart Dobson (Ed./Pub.); Elaine Brady (Sales Manager); Lisa Capitelli (Managing Editor); Phil Jacobs

OCEAN PINES INDEPENDENT

Street address 1: 11021 Nicholas Ln
Street address 2: Ste 10
Street address city: Berlin
Street address state: MD
Zip/Postal code: 21811-3244
General Phone: (410) 213-9442
General Fax: (410) 213-9458
Editorial e-mail: Newshub@DelmarvaNow.com
Primary Website: oceanpinesindependent.com
Avg Free Circ: 8600
Audit By: Sworn/Estimate/Non-Audited
Audit Date: 10.06.2019
Personnel: Michael Kilian (Exec. Ed.)
Parent company (for newspapers): Gannett

OWINGS MILLS TIMES

Street address 1: 501 N Calvert St
Street address city: Baltimore
Street address state: MD
Zip/Postal code: 21278-1000
General Phone: (410) 337-2400
General Fax: (410) 997-0885
General/National Adv. E-mail: owingsmillstimes@patuxent.com
Primary Website: owingsmillstimes.com
Avg Paid Circ: 92
Avg Free Circ: 33794
Audit By: CAC
Audit Date: 30.09.2017
Personnel: Pat Sweeney (Adv. Mgr.); Janice Jewell (Ed.); Matt Cimino (Nat'l Adv. & Majors Sales Mgr.); Susan Duchin (Dir, Nat'l Adv & Majors); Judith Berman (Sr VP Sales & Mkting)
Parent company (for newspapers): Baltimore Sun Media Group

PRINCE GEORGE'S POST

Street address 1: 15207 Marlboro Pike
Street address 2: Ste B
Street address city: Upper Marlboro
Street address state: MD
Zip/Postal code: 20772-3112
General Phone: (301) 627-0900
General Fax: (301) 627-8147
Advertising Phone: (301) 627-0900
Advertising Fax: (301) 627-6260
Editorial Phone: (301) 627-0900
Editorial Fax: (301) 627-6260
General/National Adv. E-mail: pgpost@gmail.com
Display Adv. E-mail: pgpost@gmail.com
Editorial e-mail: pgpost@gmail.com
Primary Website: pgpost.com
Year Established: 1932
Avg Paid Circ: 15000
Audit By: Sworn/Estimate/Non-Audited
Audit Date: 10.06.2019
Personnel: Michal Frangia (Ed.); Brenda Boice (Gen. Mgr./Adv. Mgr.); Lea Greve (Managing Ed.)

QUEEN ANNE'S RECORD OBSERVER

Street address 1: 114 Broadway
Street address city: Centreville
Street address state: MD
Zip/Postal code: 21617-1006
General Phone: (410) 758-1400
General Fax: (410) 758-1701
Advertising Phone: (410) 758-1400
Editorial Phone: (410) 758-1400
General/National Adv. E-mail: recordobserver@chespub.com
Editorial e-mail: newsroom@recordobserver.com
Primary Website: myeasternshoremd.com
Avg Paid Circ: 5000
Audit By: Sworn/Estimate/Non-Audited
Audit Date: 10.06.2019
Personnel: David Fike (Pub.); Tiffany Hardey (Adv. Exec.); Janice Colvin (Ed.)
Parent company (for newspapers): Adams Publishing Group, LLC

SALISBURY INDEPENDENT

Street address 1: PO Box 1385
Street address city: Salisbury
Street address state: MD
Zip/Postal code: 21802-1385
General Phone: (410) 543-4500
Advertising Phone: (410) 543-4500
Editorial Phone: (410) 543-4500
General/National Adv. E-mail: salisburysales@newszap.com
Display Adv. E-mail: classads@newszap.com
Editorial e-mail: SalisburyIndependent@newszap.com
Primary Website: salisburyindependent.net
Year Established: 2014
Avg Free Circ: 14060
Audit By: CAC
Audit Date: 31.03.2019
Personnel: Greg Bassett (Ed./Gen. Mgr.); Darel La Prade (Publisher)
Parent company (for newspapers): Independent Newsmedia Inc. USA

SOMERSET HERALD

Street address 1: 618 Beam St
Street address city: Salisbury
Street address state: MD
Zip/Postal code: 21801-7803
General Phone: (410) 651-1600
Advertising Phone: (410) 749-7171
General/National Adv. E-mail: cstubbs@dmg.gannett.com
Display Adv. E-mail: pmaher@gannett.com
Editorial e-mail: somersetherald@gannett.com
Primary Website: delmarvanow.com
Year Established: 1828
Avg Paid Circ: 4000
Audit By: Sworn/Estimate/Non-Audited
Audit Date: 10.06.2019
Personnel: Robb Scott (Sales Dir.); Liz Holland (Ed.); Michael Kilian (Executive Editor)
Parent company (for newspapers): Gannett

THE ADVOCATE OF ELDERSBURG AND SYKESVILLE

Street address 1: 201 Railroad Ave
Street address city: Westminster
Street address state: MD
Zip/Postal code: 21157-4823
General Phone: (410) 857-4400
General Fax: (410) 857-8749
Advertising Phone: (410) 857-7888
General/National Adv. E-mail: erin.hahn@carrollcountytimes.com
Display Adv. E-mail: erin.hahn@carrollcountytimes.com
Primary Website: eldersburgadvocate.com
Year Established: 2004
Avg Paid Circ: 4160
Avg Free Circ: 9740
Audit By: Sworn/Estimate/Non-Audited
Audit Date: 10.06.2019
Personnel: Pat Richardson (Pub.)

THE AEGIS

Street address 1: 501 North Calvert Street
Street address city: Baltimore
Street address state: MD
Zip/Postal code: 21278
General Phone: (410) 838-4400
General Fax: (410) 638-0357
General/National Adv. E-mail: news@theaegis.com

Primary Website: theaegis.com
Avg Paid Circ: 13938
Avg Free Circ: 82
Audit By: AAM
Audit Date: 30.09.2017
Personnel: John D. Worthington (Pub.); Mary Anne Pfeiffer (Mktg. Dir.); Ted Hendricks (Exec. Ed.); Judith Berman (Sr VP Sales & Mkting); Susan Duchin (Dir, Nat'l Adv & Majors); Wayne Carter (Ed.)
Parent company (for newspapers): Tribune Publishing, Inc.

THE AVENUE NEWS

Street address 1: 4 N Center Pl
Street address city: Dundalk
Street address state: MD
Zip/Postal code: 21222-4300
General Phone: (410) 687-7775
General Fax: (410) 687-7881
Editorial e-mail: aveeditorial@chespub.com
Primary Website: avenuenews.com
Avg Free Circ: 55423
Audit By: Sworn/Estimate/Non-Audited
Audit Date: 10.06.2019
Personnel: David Fike (Vice. Pres./Pub.); Claudio Nimmo (Gen, Mgr.); Shiela Malatesta (Adv. Mgr.); Konrad LaPrade (Reg. Dir., Adv.); Harry Porter (Dir., Adv.); Bill Sims (Reg, Dir., Circ.); Mary Ferguson (Circ. Mgr.); Amy Graziano (Ed.); Brian Doane (Adv. Dir.)
Parent company (for newspapers): Adams Publishing Group, LLC

THE BALTIMORE GUIDE

Street address 1: 2935 Odonnell St
Street address city: Baltimore
Street address state: MD
Zip/Postal code: 21224-4823
General Phone: (410) 732-6600
General Fax: (410) 732-6336
Advertising Phone: (410) 732-6616
Advertising Fax: (410) 732-6336
General/National Adv. E-mail: lnemec@baltimoreguide.com
Display Adv. E-mail: ehoffman@baltimoreguide.com
Editorial e-mail: editor@baltimoreguide.com
Primary Website: baltimoreguide.com
Year Established: 1927
Avg Free Circ: 35000
Audit By: Sworn/Estimate/Non-Audited
Audit Date: 10.06.2019
Personnel: Perry Corsetti (Pub.); Erik Zygmont (Editor); Ed Hoffman (Pub.)
Parent company (for newspapers): Ascend Publishing

THE BAY TIMES

Street address 1: 300 Abruzzi Dr
Street address 2: Ste C
Street address city: Chester
Street address state: MD
Zip/Postal code: 21619-2395
General Phone: (410) 643-7770
General Fax: (410) 643-8374
General/National Adv. E-mail: baytimes@kibaytimes.com
Display Adv. E-mail: classads@chespub.com
Editorial e-mail: baytimes@kibaytimes.com
Primary Website: kibaytimes.com
Year Established: 1963
Avg Paid Circ: 6000
Avg Free Circ: 106
Audit By: Sworn/Estimate/Non-Audited
Audit Date: 10.06.2019
Personnel: David Fike (VP/Pub); Angela Price (Ed.); Gail Ruppe (Advertising Manager)
Parent company (for newspapers): Adams Publishing Group, LLC

THE CALVERT RECORDER

Street address 1: 134 Main St
Street address 2: Ste 102
Street address city: Prince Frederick
Street address state: MD
Zip/Postal code: 20678-6150
General Phone: (410) 535-1234
General Fax: (443) 378-3498
Advertising Phone: (410) 535-1234
Advertising Fax: (443) 378-3498
Editorial Phone: (410) 535-1234
Editorial Fax: (443) 378-3498
General/National Adv. E-mail: bash@chespub.com
Display Adv. E-mail: chesAds@chespub.com
Editorial e-mail: mcady@somdnews.com
Primary Website: somdnews.com/recorder
Year Established: 1971
Avg Paid Circ: 10500
Audit By: Sworn/Estimate/Non-Audited
Audit Date: 10.06.2019
Personnel: Art Crofoot (Pub)
Parent company (for newspapers): Adams Publishing Group, LLC

THE CARROLL EAGLE

Street address 1: 501 N Calvert St Fl 3
Street address 2: Third Floor
Street address city: Baltimore
Street address state: MD
Zip/Postal code: 21278-1000
General Phone: (410) 386-334
General Fax: (410) 386-0340
Primary Website: explorecarroll.com
Year Established: 2009
Audit By: Sworn/Estimate/Non-Audited
Audit Date: 10.06.2019
Personnel: Paul Milton

THE DORCHESTER STAR

Street address 1: 29088 Airpark Dr.
Street address city: Easton
Street address state: MD
Zip/Postal code: 21601
General Phone: (410) 228-0222
General Fax: (410) 228-0685
Advertising Phone: (410) 228-0222
Editorial Phone: (410) 228-0222
General/National Adv. E-mail: news@dorchesterstar.com
Primary Website: dorchesterstar.com
Avg Free Circ: 10000
Audit By: Sworn/Estimate/Non-Audited
Audit Date: 10.06.2019
Personnel: Jim Normandin (Publisher); David Fike (VP/Pub.); Angela Price (Editor); Mike Detmer (Reporter); Paul Myers (Adv. Mgr.); Gail Dean (Ed.); Anthony David (Advertising)
Parent company (for newspapers): Adams Publishing Group, LLC

THE DUNDALK EAGLE

Street address 1: 4 N Center Pl
Street address city: Dundalk
Street address state: MD
Zip/Postal code: 21222-4300
General Phone: (410) 288-6060
General Fax: (410) 288-6963
Advertising Phone: (410) 288-6060
Advertising Fax: (410) 288-2712
Editorial Phone: (410) 288-6060
Editorial Fax: (410) 288-6963
General/National Adv. E-mail: ads@dundalkeagle.net
Display Adv. E-mail: classifieds@dundalkeagle.net
Editorial e-mail: editor@dundalkeagle.net
Primary Website: dundalkeagle.com
Year Established: 1969
Avg Paid Circ: 18000
Audit By: Sworn/Estimate/Non-Audited
Audit Date: 10.06.2019
Personnel: Deborah Cornely (Pub.); Steve Matrazzo (Editor); Jason O'Neill (Advertising Director); Paul Rosenberger (Gen. Mgr.); Jonathan O'Neill (Editor)

THE ENQUIRER-GAZETTE

Street address 1: 7 Industrial Park Dr
Street address city: Waldorf
Street address state: MD
Zip/Postal code: 20602-2753
General Phone: (301) 627-2833
General Fax: (301) 627-2795
General/National Adv. E-mail: princegeorges@gazette.net
Primary Website: somdnews.com
Avg Paid Circ: 2475
Audit By: Sworn/Estimate/Non-Audited
Audit Date: 10.06.2019
Personnel: Karen Acton (Pub.); Vanessa Harrton (Ed.); Christy Bailey (Adv. Mgr.); Ron Notter (Circ. Dir.); Kim Minopoli (Adv. Mgr.)
Parent company (for newspapers): Southern Maryland Newspapers

THE ENTERPRISE

Street address 1: 22685 Three Notch Road
Street address 2: Suite D
Street address city: California
Street address state: MD
Zip/Postal code: 20619
General Phone: (301) 862-2111
General Fax: (301) 737-2896
General/National Adv. E-mail: adaily@somdnews.com
Primary Website: somdnews.com
Avg Paid Circ: 11260
Audit By: Sworn/Estimate/Non-Audited
Audit Date: 10.06.2019
Personnel: Donnie Morgan (Exec. Ed.); Jessie Yeatmen (Dep. Ed.); Paul Watson (Sports Ed.); Brook Ash (Adv. Mgr.); Jim Normandin (Reg. Pres.); David Fike (CRO); Mark Elliott (Pub.); Doug Mcavoy (Reg. Circ. Dir.)
Parent company (for newspapers): Adams Publishing Group, LLC

THE GARRETT COUNTY WEEKENDER

Street address 1: 19 Baltimore St
Street address city: Cumberland
Street address state: MD
Zip/Postal code: 21502-3023
General Phone: (301) 722-4600
General Fax: (301) 722-2021
Advertising Phone: (301) 722-4600
Advertising Fax: (301) 722-4870
Editorial Phone: (301) 722-4600
Editorial Fax: (301) 722-5270
General/National Adv. E-mail: advertising@times-news.com
Display Adv. E-mail: classified@times-news.com
Editorial e-mail: weeklies@times-news.com
Primary Website: times-news.com
Avg Free Circ: 18000
Audit By: Sworn/Estimate/Non-Audited
Audit Date: 10.06.2019
Personnel: Robin Quillion (Pub.); Craig Springer (Advertising Director); John Smith (Managing Editor); Jeff Clark (Circulation Manager)
Parent company (for newspapers): Community Newspaper Holdings Inc.

THE GAZETTE - DAMASCUS / CLARKSBURG

Street address 1: 9030 Comprint Ct
Street address city: Gaithersburg
Street address state: MD
Zip/Postal code: 20877-1307
General Phone: (301) 948-3120
General Fax: (301) 670-7183
Advertising Phone: (301) 670-2500
General/National Adv. E-mail: editor@gazette.net
Display Adv. E-mail: circulation@gazette.net; classifieds@gazette.net
Editorial e-mail: sports@gazette.net
Primary Website: gazette.net
Year Established: 1988
Avg Free Circ: 7486
Audit By: Sworn/Estimate/Non-Audited
Audit Date: 10.06.2019
Personnel: James Mannarino (Pub.); Cliff Chiet (Vice Pres., Sales); Maria Lampos (Adv. Coord.); Jean Casey (Circ. Dir.); Lisa Merhi (Prodn. Mgr.); Melissa A. Chadwick (Ed.); John Wehmueller (Sports Ed.); Mona Bass (Corp. Classified Dir.); Dennis Wilston (Corp. Adv. Dir.)
Parent company (for newspapers): Post Newsweek Media, LLC

THE GAZETTE - POTOMAC / NORTH POTOMAC

Street address 1: 9030 Comprint Ct
Street address city: Gaithersburg
Street address state: MD
Zip/Postal code: 20877-1307
General Phone: (301) 948-3120
General Fax: (301) 670-7183
Advertising Phone: (301) 670-2500
General/National Adv. E-mail: editor@gazette.net
Display Adv. E-mail: classifieds@gazette.net
Editorial e-mail: editor@gazette.net
Primary Website: gazette.net
Year Established: 1988
Avg Free Circ: 16463
Audit By: Sworn/Estimate/Non-Audited
Audit Date: 10.06.2019
Personnel: James Mannarino (Pub.); Cliff Chiet (Vice Pres., Sales); Maria Lampos (Adv. Coord.); Jean Casey (Circ. Dir.); Lisa Merhi (Prodn. Mgr.); Melissa A. Chadwick (Ed.); John Wehmueller (Sports Ed.); Mona Bass (Corp. Classified Dir.); Dennis Wilston (Corp. Adv. Dir.)
Parent company (for newspapers): Post Newsweek Media, LLC

THE HANCOCK NEWS

Street address 1: 105 West Main Street
Street address city: Hancock
Street address state: MD
Zip/Postal code: 21750-1098
General Phone: (301) 678-6255
General Fax: 304-258-8441
General/National Adv. E-mail: ads@morganmessenger.com
Display Adv. E-mail: ads@morganmessenger.com
Editorial e-mail: news@hancocknews.us
Primary Website: www,thehancocknews.com
Year Established: 1914
Avg Paid Circ: 1800
Audit By: Sworn/Estimate/Non-Audited
Audit Date: 10.06.2019
Personnel: Sandra Buzzerd (Mgr Ed.); Jody Crouse (Managing Editor); Kate Shunney (Editor); Kate Shunney (Ed)
Parent company (for newspapers): The Morgan Messenger

THE MARYLAND GAZETTE

Street address 1: 501 N. Calvert St
Street address city: Baltimore
Street address state: MD
Zip/Postal code: 21278
General Phone: (443) 482-3154
General/National Adv. E-mail: mpadden@capgaznews.com
Display Adv. E-mail: mpadden@capgaznews.com
Editorial e-mail: gazstaff@capgaznews.com
Primary Website: capitalgazette.com
Year Established: 1727
Avg Paid Circ: 8703
Avg Free Circ: 2527
Audit By: AAM
Audit Date: 30.09.2018
Personnel: Marty Padden (Adv. Dir.); Rob Pryor (Circ. Dir.); Rick Hutzell (Ed.); Carolyn Gooden (Classified Adv. Mgr.)
Parent company (for newspapers): Tribune Publishing, Inc.

THE MARYLAND INDEPENDENT

Street address 1: 4475 Regency Pl
Street address 2: Ste 301
Street address city: White Plains
Street address state: MD
Zip/Postal code: 20695-3077
General Phone: (301) 645-9480
General Fax: (301) 884-9403
Advertising Phone: (301) 645-9480
Advertising Fax: (301) 884-9403
Editorial Phone: (301) 645-9480
Editorial Fax: (301) 884-9403
General/National Adv. E-mail: kminopoli@somdnews.com
Display Adv. E-mail: sheadley@somdnews.com
Editorial e-mail: abreck@somdnews.com
Primary Website: somdnews.com
Year Established: 1872
Avg Paid Circ: 15140
Audit By: Sworn/Estimate/Non-Audited
Audit Date: 10.06.2019
Personnel: Karen Acton (Pub.); Kim Minopoli (Adv. Dir.); Ron Notter (Circ. Mgr.); Angela Breck (Ed.); Joel Davis (Mng. Ed.); Ellen Pankake (Prodn. Mgr.); Phyllis Dietz (Circ. Mgr.)
Parent company (for newspapers): Adams Publishing Group, LLC

THE PRINCE GEORGE'S SENTINEL

Street address 1: 9458 Lanham Severn Rd
Street address 2: Ste 200
Street address city: Seabrook

Street address state: MD
Zip/Postal code: 20706-2661
General Phone: (301) 306-9500
General Fax: (301) 306-0134
Advertising Phone: (301) 306-9500
Advertising Fax: (301) 306-0134
Editorial Phone: (301) 306-9500
Editorial Fax: (301) 306-0134
General/National Adv. E-mail: lonnie@thesentinel.com
Display Adv. E-mail: lonnie@thesentinel.com
Editorial e-mail: editor-pg@thesentinel.com
Primary Website: thesentinel.com
Year Established: 1932
Avg Paid Circ: 4000
Avg Free Circ: 20000
Audit By: Sworn/Estimate/Non-Audited
Audit Date: 10.06.2019
Personnel: Lynn Kapiloff (CEO); Lonnie Johnson (Adv. Dir.); Donna Lechly (Mng. Ed.); Pete Hajiantoni (Strategic Information Mgr.)

THE RECORD

Street address 1: 10 N Hays St
Street address city: Bel Air
Street address state: MD
Zip/Postal code: 21014-3643
General Phone: (410) 838-4451
General Fax: (410) 838-7867
General/National Adv. E-mail: apowers@baltsun.com
Display Adv. E-mail: apowers@baltsun.com
Primary Website: hdgrecordonline.com
Avg Paid Circ: 919
Avg Free Circ: 55
Audit By: AAM
Audit Date: 31.03.2019
Personnel: John D. Worthington (Pub.); Ted Hendricks (Exec. Ed.); Judith Berman (Sr VP Sales & Mkting); Susan Duchin (Dir, Nat'l Adv & Majors); Matt Cimino (Nat'l Adv & Majors, Sales Mgr.); Jim Alvey (Dir, Direct Mktg.); Amy Powers (Adv. Dir.)
Parent company (for newspapers): Tribune Publishing, Inc.

THE TIMES RECORD

Street address 1: 212 Market St
Street address city: Denton
Street address state: MD
Zip/Postal code: 21629-1037
General Phone: (410) 479-1800
General Fax: (410) 479-3174
Advertising Phone: (410) 479-1800
Editorial Phone: (410) 479-1800
Primary Website: myeasternshoremd.com
Avg Paid Circ: 4200
Audit By: Sworn/Estimate/Non-Audited
Audit Date: 10.06.2019
Personnel: Larry Effingham (Pub.); Margaret Iovino (Adv. Mgr.); John Evans (Ed.)
Parent company (for newspapers): Adams Publishing Group, LLC

THE VALLEY CITIZEN

Street address 1: 101 W Potomac St
Street address city: Brunswick
Street address state: MD
Zip/Postal code: 21716-1114
General Phone: (301) 834-7722
General/National Adv. E-mail: citizen@mip.net
Primary Website: citizennewspapers.com
Year Established: 1990
Avg Paid Circ: 2200
Audit By: Sworn/Estimate/Non-Audited
Audit Date: 10.06.2019
Personnel: Julie Maynard (Ed.)

THE WEEKENDER

Street address 1: 10 N Hays St
Street address city: Bel Air
Street address state: MD
Zip/Postal code: 21014-3643
General Phone: (410) 838-4400
General Fax: (410) 638-0357
General/National Adv. E-mail: news@theaegis.com
Primary Website: theaegis.com
Avg Free Circ: 87000
Audit By: Sworn/Estimate/Non-Audited
Audit Date: 10.06.2019
Personnel: Jim Quimby (Pres.); John D. Worthington (Pub.); Mary Anne Pfeffer (Adv. Dir.); Ted Hendricks (Exec. Ed.); Judith Berman (Sr. VP. Sales/Mktg.); Susan Duchin (Dir. Nat'l Adv.); Matt Cimino (Nat'l Adv./Sales Mgr.); Jim Alvey (Dir. Direct Mktg.); Wayne Lowman (Classified Adv. Dir.)
Parent company (for newspapers): Tribune Publishing, Inc.

TOWSON TIMES

Street address 1: 300 E. Cromwell Street
Street address 2: Fl 3
Street address city: Baltimore
Street address state: MD
Zip/Postal code: 21230
General Phone: (410) 332-6100
Advertising Phone: (410) 332-6300
Primary Website: baltimoresun.com/towson
Year Established: 1958
Avg Paid Circ: 1015
Avg Free Circ: 25096
Audit By: AAM
Audit Date: 30.09.2018
Personnel: Elizabeth Eck (AME, Community News, Baltimore Sun Media Group)
Parent company (for newspapers): Tribune Publishing, Inc.

MASSACHUSETTS

ABINGTON MARINER

Street address 1: 165 Enterprise Dr
Street address city: Marshfield
Street address state: MA
Zip/Postal code: 02050-2132
General Phone: (781) 837-4500
General Fax: (781) 837-4540
Advertising Phone: (781) 837-4500
Advertising Fax: (781) 837-4540
Editorial Phone: (781) 837-4500
Editorial Fax: (781) 837-4540
General/National Adv. E-mail: salesteam@wickedlocal.com
Display Adv. E-mail: salesteam@wickedlocal.com
Editorial e-mail: sjacobson@wickedlocal.com
Primary Website: wickedlocal.com/abington
Avg Paid Circ: 609
Audit By: Sworn/Estimate/Non-Audited
Audit Date: 10.06.2019
Personnel: Mark Olivieri (Pub.); Paul Harber (Sports Ed.); Seth Jacobson (Ed.); Gregory Mathis (Ed. in Chief)
Parent company (for newspapers): CherryRoad Media

AGAWAM ADVERTISER NEWS

Street address 1: 23 Southwick St
Street address city: Feeding Hills
Street address state: MA
Zip/Postal code: 01030
General Phone: (413) 786-7747
General Fax: (413) 786-8457
Advertising Phone: (413) 786-7747
Advertising Fax: (413) 786-8457
Editorial Phone: (413) 786-7747
Editorial Fax: (413) 786-8457
General/National Adv. E-mail: jbaskin@turley.com
Display Adv. E-mail: classifieds@turley.com
Editorial e-mail: aan@turley.com
Primary Website: agawamnewsonline.com
Year Established: 1965
Avg Paid Circ: 6500
Audit By: Sworn/Estimate/Non-Audited
Audit Date: 10.06.2019
Personnel: Patrick H. Turley (Pub.); Beth Baker (Adv. Mgr.); Jennifer Wroblewski (Ed.)
Parent company (for newspapers): Turley Publications, Inc.

ALLSTON-BRIGHTON TAB

Street address 1: 254 2nd Ave
Street address city: Needham
Street address state: MA
Zip/Postal code: 02494-2829
General Phone: (781) 433-8365
General Fax: (781) 433-8202
Advertising Phone: (781) 433-8204
Advertising Fax: (781) 433-8202
Editorial Phone: (781) 433-8384
Editorial Fax: (781) 433-8202
General/National Adv. E-mail: landler@wickedlocal.com
Display Adv. E-mail: landler@wickedlocal.com
Editorial e-mail: jcohen@wickedlocal.com
Primary Website: wickedlocal.com/allston
Year Established: 1996
Avg Paid Circ: 146
Audit By: Sworn/Estimate/Non-Audited
Audit Date: 10.06.2019
Personnel: Chuck Goodrich (Pub.); Jesse Floyd (Ed. in Chief); Julie Cohen (Ed.); Kathleen Cordeiro (Adv. Dir.)
Parent company (for newspapers): Community Newspaper Co.-Metro; CherryRoad Media

AMESBURY NEWS

Street address 1: 75 Sylvan St
Street address 2: Ste C105
Street address city: Danvers
Street address state: MA
Zip/Postal code: 01923-2765
General Phone: (978) 739-1347
General Fax: (978) 739-8501
Advertising Phone: (978) 739-1350
Advertising Fax: (978) 739-8501
Editorial Phone: (978) 739-8506
Editorial Fax: (978) 739-8501
General/National Adv. E-mail: ameltzer@wickedlocal.com
Display Adv. E-mail: pfraney@wickedlocal.com
Editorial e-mail: amesbury@wickedlocal.com
Primary Website: wickedlocal.com/amesbury
Avg Paid Circ: 7767
Avg Free Circ: 295
Audit By: Sworn/Estimate/Non-Audited
Audit Date: 10.06.2019
Personnel: Chuck Goodrich (Pub.); Pete Chianca (Ed.-in-Chief); Rosemary Herbert (Ed.); Mark Cohen (Vice Pres., Adv.); James McEvoy (Nat'l Adv. Mgr.); John Lockwood (Ed.); Janet Mackay Smith (News Ed.); Dom NiCastro (Sports Ed.); Pat Coen (Prodn. Mgr.); Kathleen Cordeiro (Adv. Dir.)
Parent company (for newspapers): Community Newspaper Co.-North-OOB; CherryRoad Media

AMHERST BULLETIN

Street address 1: 115 Conz St
Street address city: Northampton
Street address state: MA
Zip/Postal code: 01060-4444
General Phone: (413) 584-5000
General Fax: (413) 585-5299
Advertising Phone: (413) 585-5357
Advertising Fax: (413) 549-8181
Editorial Phone: (413) 584-5000
Editorial Fax: (413) 549-8181
General/National Adv. E-mail: sales@gazettenet.com
Display Adv. E-mail: sales@gazettenet.com
Editorial e-mail: editor@gazettenet.com
Primary Website: amherstbulletin.com
Mthly Avg Views: 1000699
Mthly Avg Unique Visitors: 191262
Year Established: 1786
Avg Paid Circ: 108
Avg Free Circ: 12750
Audit By: Sworn/Estimate/Non-Audited
Audit Date: 10.06.2019
Personnel: Jeff Good (Exec Editor); Michael Rifanburg (Pub.)
Parent company (for newspapers): Newspapers of New England

ANDOVER TOWNSMAN

Street address 1: 33 Chestnut St
Street address city: Andover
Street address state: MA
Zip/Postal code: 01810-3623
General Phone: (978) 475-7000
General Fax: (978) 470-2819
Advertising Phone: (978) 475-7000
Advertising Fax: (978) 470-2819
Editorial Phone: (978) 475-7000
Editorial Fax: (978) 470-2819
General/National Adv. E-mail: Adsales@andovertownsman.com
Display Adv. E-mail: Adsales@andovertownsman.com
Editorial e-mail: bkirk@andovertownsman.com
Primary Website: andovertownsman.com
Mthly Avg Views: 64000
Mthly Avg Unique Visitors: 24000
Year Established: 1887
Avg Paid Circ: 5000
Avg Free Circ: 500
Audit By: Sworn/Estimate/Non-Audited
Audit Date: 10.06.2019
Personnel: Karen Andreas (Reg. Pub.); Cathy Goss (Adv. Dir.); James Falzone (Ops. Dir.); Steve Baskin (Circ. Dir.); Bill Kirk (Ed.)
Parent company (for newspapers): CNHI, LLC

ARLINGTON ADVOCATE

Street address 1: 9 Meriam St
Street address city: Lexington
Street address state: MA
Zip/Postal code: 02420-5300
General Phone: (781) 674-7726
General Fax: (781) 674-7735
Advertising Phone: (978) 371-5717
Advertising Fax: (978) 371-5712
Editorial Phone: (781) 674-7726
Editorial Fax: (781) 674-7735
General/National Adv. E-mail: pgaudette@wickedlocal.com
Display Adv. E-mail: classifieds@wickedlocal.com
Editorial e-mail: arlington@wickedlocal.com
Primary Website: arlington.wickedlocal.com
Avg Paid Circ: 6624
Avg Free Circ: 2830
Audit By: Sworn/Estimate/Non-Audited
Audit Date: 10.06.2019
Personnel: Chuck Goodrich (Pub.); Mark Cohen (Vice Pres., Adv.); Anne Marie Magerman (Adv. Mgr.); Mike Murphy (Adv. Mgr., Display); Eileen Kennedy (Ed.); Kathleen Cordiero (Ed. in Chief); Mike Bentle (Sales Mgr.); Ron Bright (Classified Adv. Mgr.)
Parent company (for newspapers): CherryRoad Media

ASHLAND TAB

Street address 1: 33 New York Ave
Street address city: Framingham
Street address state: MA
Zip/Postal code: 01701-8857
General Phone: (508) 626-3957
General Fax: (508) 626-4400
Advertising Phone: (508) 626-3984
Advertising Fax: (508) 626-4400
Editorial Phone: (508) 626-3957
Editorial Fax: (508) 626-4400
General/National Adv. E-mail: crobinso@wickedlocal.com
Display Adv. E-mail: crobinso@wickedlocal.com
Editorial e-mail: ashland@wickedlocal.com
Primary Website: wickedlocal.com/ashland
Avg Paid Circ: 987
Audit By: Sworn/Estimate/Non-Audited
Audit Date: 10.06.2019
Personnel: Anne Brennan (Ed. in Chief); Alison Bosma (News Coverage); Kathleen Cordeiro (Dig. Dir.)
Parent company (for newspapers): Community Newspaper Co.-West-OOB; CherryRoad Media

AUBURN NEWS

Street address 1: 25 Elm St
Street address city: Southbridge
Street address state: MA
Zip/Postal code: 01550-2605
General Phone: (508) 764-4325
General Fax: (508) 764-8102
Advertising Phone: (508) 909-4104
Advertising Fax: (508) 764-8102
Editorial Phone: (508) 909-4130
Editorial Fax: (508) 764-8102
General/National Adv. E-mail: jashton@stonebridgepress.com
Display Adv. E-mail: classifieds@stonebridgepress.com
Editorial e-mail: aminor@stonebridgepress.com
Primary Website: theheartofmassachusetts.com
Avg Paid Circ: 1600
Avg Free Circ: 8
Audit By: Sworn/Estimate/Non-Audited
Audit Date: 10.06.2019
Personnel: Frank Chilinski (Pub.); Ron Tremblay (CFO); Jean Ashton (Adv. Mgr.); Adam Minor (Ed.)

Parent company (for newspapers): Stonebridge Press, Inc.

AVON MESSENGER

Street address 1: 1324 Belmont St
Street address 2: Unit 102
Street address city: Brockton
Street address state: MA
Zip/Postal code: 02301-4435
General Phone: (508) 967-3523
General Fax: (508) 967-3501
Advertising Phone: (781) 837-4591
Advertising Fax: (508) 967-3501
Editorial Phone: (508) 427-4038
Editorial Fax: (508) 967-3501
General/National Adv. E-mail: wmurphy@wickedlocal.com
Display Adv. E-mail: rbright@wickedlocal.com
Editorial e-mail: newsroom@enterprisenews.com
Primary Website: wickedlocal.com/avon
Avg Paid Circ: 1022
Audit By: Sworn/Estimate/Non-Audited
Audit Date: 10.06.2019
Personnel: Ron Bright (Class. Adv. Mgr.); Kathleen Cordeiro (Adv. Dir.)

BARNSTABLE PATRIOT

Street address 1: 4 Ocean Ave
Street address city: Hyannis
Street address state: MA
Zip/Postal code: 02601-4419
General Phone: (508) 771-1427
General Fax: (508) 790-3997
General/National Adv. E-mail: advertising@barnstablepatriot.com
Display Adv. E-mail: classified@capecodonline.com
Editorial e-mail: news@barnstablepatriot.com
Primary Website: barnstablepatriot.com
Mthly Avg Views: 59000
Mthly Avg Unique Visitors: 29837
Year Established: 1830
Avg Paid Circ: 4905
Avg Free Circ: 350
Audit By: Sworn/Estimate/Non-Audited
Audit Date: 10.06.2019
Personnel: April Miller (Adv. Mgr.); Craig Salters (Ed.); Bronwen Howells Walsh (Asst. Ed.)
Parent company (for newspapers): Dow Jones Local Media Group-OOB

BARRE GAZETTE

Street address 1: 5 Exchange St
Street address city: Barre
Street address state: MA
Zip/Postal code: 01005-8702
General Phone: (978) 355-4000
General Fax: (978) 355-6274
Advertising Phone: (978) 355-4000
Advertising Fax: (978) 355-6274
Editorial Phone: (978) 355-4000
Editorial Fax: (978) 355-6274
General/National Adv. E-mail: bbaker@turley.com
Display Adv. E-mail: classifieds@turley.com
Editorial e-mail: edowner@turley.com
Primary Website: barregazette.turley.com
Year Established: 1834
Avg Paid Circ: 2666
Audit By: Sworn/Estimate/Non-Audited
Audit Date: 10.06.2019
Personnel: Patrick H. Turley (Owner); Ellie Downer (Ed.); Beth Baker (Adv. Mgr.); Charlann Griswold (Circ. Mgr.); Tim Kane (Exec. Ed.); David Forbes (Sports Ed.)
Parent company (for newspapers): Turley Publications, Inc.

BEDFORD MINUTEMAN

Street address 1: 150 Baker Avenue Ext
Street address 2: Ste 101
Street address city: Concord
Street address state: MA
Zip/Postal code: 01742-2199
General Phone: (978) 371-5796
General Fax: (978) 371-5711
Advertising Phone: (978) 371-5723
Advertising Fax: (978) 371-5712
Editorial Phone: (978) 371-5796
Editorial Fax: (978) 371-5711
General/National Adv. E-mail: pcalder@wickedlocal.com
Display Adv. E-mail: classifieds@wickedlocal.com
Primary Website: bedford.wickedlocal.com
Year Established: 1956
Avg Paid Circ: 7996
Avg Free Circ: 5815
Audit By: Sworn/Estimate/Non-Audited
Audit Date: 10.06.2019
Personnel: Rob Fucci; Pamela Calder; Debra Ryan; Kathleen Cordeiro; Nicole Simmons (Dir. of Dig.)
Parent company (for newspapers): CherryRoad Media

BELLINGHAM BULLETIN

Street address 1: 36 Rakeville Cir
Street address city: Bellingham
Street address state: MA
Zip/Postal code: 02019-2132
General Phone: (508) 883-3252
General Fax: (508) 883-3252
Advertising Phone: (508) 883-3252
Advertising Fax: (508) 883-3252
Editorial Phone: (508) 883-3252
Editorial Fax: (508) 883-3252
General/National Adv. E-mail: cyndyrogers@charter.net
Display Adv. E-mail: cyndyrogers@charter.net
Editorial e-mail: email@BellinghamBulletin.com
Primary Website: bellinghambulletin.com
Year Established: 1994
Audit By: Sworn/Estimate/Non-Audited
Audit Date: 10.06.2019
Personnel: Cyndy Rogers (Adv. Dir.)

BELMONT CITIZEN HERALD

Street address 1: 9 Meriam St.
Street address city: Lexington
Street address state: MA
Zip/Postal code: 02420
General Phone: (781) 674-7723
Avg Free Circ: 2305
Audit By: Sworn/Estimate/Non-Audited
Audit Date: 10.06.2019
Personnel: Kathleen Cordeiro (Regional Director of News & Operations)
Parent company (for newspapers): CherryRoad Media

BERKSHIRE BEACON

Street address 1: PO Box 312
Street address city: Lenox Dale
Street address state: MA
Zip/Postal code: 01242-0312
General Phone: (413) 637-2250
General Fax: (413) 637-2250
Advertising Phone: (413) 637-2250
Advertising Fax: (413) 637-2250
Editorial Phone: (413) 637-2250
Editorial Fax: (413) 637-2250
General/National Adv. E-mail: ads@berkshirebeacon.comÃ‚
Display Adv. E-mail: ads@berkshirebeacon.com
Editorial e-mail: news@berkshirebeacon.com
Primary Website: berkshirebeacon.com
Mthly Avg Unique Visitors: 26000
Year Established: 2011
Audit By: Sworn/Estimate/Non-Audited
Audit Date: 10.06.2019
Personnel: George Jordan III (Ed./Pub.); Kameron Spaulding (Editorial Assistant); Catherine Krummy (Copy Ed.); Susan Robinson (Graphic Designer)

BERKSHIRE JEWISH VOICE

Street address 1: 196 South Street
Street address 2: Jewish Federation of the Berkshires
Street address city: Pittsfield
Street address state: MA
Zip/Postal code: 01201
General Phone: 413-442-4360
Advertising Phone: 413-442-4360
Editorial Phone: 413-442-4360
General/National Adv. E-mail: astern@jewishberkshires.org
Editorial e-mail: astern@jewishberkshires.org
Primary Website: https://jewishberkshires.org/community-events/berkshire-jewish-voice/berkshire-jewish-voice-highlights
Year Established: 1989
Avg Free Circ: 5000
Personnel: Dara Kaufman (Exec. Dir.); Albert Stern (Editor); Jenny Greenfield (Office Mgr.)
Parent company (for newspapers): Jewish Federation of the Berkshires; Joseph Jacobs Organization

BEVERLY CITIZEN

Street address 1: 75 Sylvan St
Street address 2: Ste C105
Street address city: Danvers
Street address state: MA
Zip/Postal code: 01923-2765
General Phone: (978) 927-2777
General Fax: (978) 739-8501
Advertising Phone: (978) 739-1320
Advertising Fax: (978) 739-1391
Editorial Phone: (978) 927-2777
Editorial Fax: (978) 739-8501
General/National Adv. E-mail: mkasper@wickedlocal.com
Display Adv. E-mail: classifieds@wickedlocal.com
Editorial e-mail: beverly@wickedlocal.com
Primary Website: beverly.wickedlocal.com
Year Established: 1851
Avg Paid Circ: 6284
Avg Free Circ: 470
Audit By: AAM
Audit Date: 31.03.2018
Personnel: Chuck Goodrich (Pub.); Kathleen Cordeiro (Adv. Dir.)
Parent company (for newspapers): CherryRoad Media

BILLERICA MINUTEMAN

Street address 1: 150 Baker Avenue Ext
Street address city: Concord
Street address state: MA
Zip/Postal code: 01742-2126
General Phone: (978) 667-2156
General Fax: (978) 371-5212
Advertising Phone: (978) 667-2156
Advertising Fax: (978) 371-5212
Editorial Phone: (978) 667-2156
Editorial Fax: (978) 371-5212
General/National Adv. E-mail: speters@wickedlocal.com
Display Adv. E-mail: rbright@wickedlocal.com
Editorial e-mail: kcordeiro@wickedlocal.com
Primary Website: billerica.wickedlocal.com
Avg Paid Circ: 7996
Avg Free Circ: 3360
Audit By: AAM
Audit Date: 31.03.2018
Personnel: Chuck Goodrich (Pub.); Kathleen Cordeiro (Ed. in Chief); Doug Hastings (Sports Ed.)
Parent company (for newspapers): CherryRoad Media

BLACKSTONE VALLEY TRIBUNE

Street address 1: 25 Elm St
Street address city: Southbridge
Street address state: MA
Zip/Postal code: 01550-2605
General Phone: (508) 764-4325
General Fax: (508) 764-8102
Advertising Phone: (508) 909-4111
Editorial Phone: (508) 909-4111
General/National Adv. E-mail: jsima@stonebridgepress.news
Display Adv. E-mail: classifieds@stonebridgepress.news
Editorial e-mail: news@stonebridgepress.news
Primary Website: blackstonevalleytribune.com
Year Established: 1949
Avg Paid Circ: 15000
Audit By: Sworn/Estimate/Non-Audited
Audit Date: 10.06.2019
Personnel: Brendan Berube (Ed.); Nick Ethier (Sports Ed.); Kerri Peterson (Circulation Director)
Parent company (for newspapers): Stonebridge Press, Inc.

BOSTON BUSINESS JOURNAL

Street address 1: 160 Federal St
Street address 2: Fl 12th
Street address city: Boston
Street address state: MA
Zip/Postal code: 02110-1700
General Phone: (617) 330-1000
General Fax: (617) 330-1015
Advertising Phone: (617) 330-1000
Advertising Fax: (617) 330-1015
Editorial Phone: (617) 330-1000
Editorial Fax: (617) 330-1015
General/National Adv. E-mail: boston@bizjournals.com
Display Adv. E-mail: boston@bizjournals.com
Editorial e-mail: newsroom@masshightech.com
Primary Website: amcity.com/boston
Year Established: 1981
Audit By: Sworn/Estimate/Non-Audited
Audit Date: 10.06.2019
Personnel: Heather Lacey (Controller)

BOSTON HAITIAN REPORTER

Street address 1: 150 Mount Vernon St
Street address 2: Ste 120
Street address city: Dorchester
Street address state: MA
Zip/Postal code: 02125-3135
General Phone: (617) 436-1222
General Fax: (617) 825-5516
Advertising Phone: (617) 436-1222
Advertising Fax: (617) 825-5516
Editorial Phone: (617) 436-1222
Editorial Fax: (617) 825-5516
General/National Adv. E-mail: addesk@dotnews.com
Display Adv. E-mail: addesk@dotnews.com
Editorial e-mail: newseditor@dotnews.com
Primary Website: bostonhaitian.com
Year Established: 1983
Audit By: Sworn/Estimate/Non-Audited
Audit Date: 10.06.2019
Personnel: Edward Forrey (Pub.); William Forry (Ed.); Jack Conboy (Ad. Director); Barbara Langis (Prod. Mgr.)
Parent company (for newspapers): Boston Neighborhood News, Inc.

BOSTON IRISH REPORTER

Street address 1: 150 Mount Vernon St
Street address 2: Ste 120
Street address city: Dorchester
Street address state: MA
Zip/Postal code: 02125-3135
General Phone: (617) 436-1222
General Fax: (617) 825-5516
Advertising Phone: (617) 436-1222
Advertising Fax: (617) 825-5516
Editorial Phone: (617) 436-1222
Editorial Fax: (617) 825-5516
General/National Adv. E-mail: addesk@dotnews.com
Display Adv. E-mail: addesk@dotnews.com
Editorial e-mail: newseditor@dotnews.com
Primary Website: bostonirish.com
Year Established: 1983
Audit By: Sworn/Estimate/Non-Audited
Audit Date: 10.06.2019
Personnel: Edward Forrey (Pub.); William Forry (Ed.); Jack Conboy (Ad. Director); Barbara Langis (Prod. Mgr.)
Parent company (for newspapers): Boston Neighborhood News, Inc.

BOURNE COURIER

Street address 1: 319 Main St
Street address city: Hyannis
Street address state: MA
Zip/Postal code: 02601-4037
General Phone: (508) 888-0000
General Fax: (508) 375-4903
Advertising Phone: (781) 433-6934
Advertising Fax: (508) 375-4903
Editorial Phone: (508) 375-4945
Editorial Fax: (508) 375-4903
General/National Adv. E-mail: salesteam@wickedlocal.com
Display Adv. E-mail: salesteam@wickedlocal.com
Editorial e-mail: jbasile@wickedlocal.com
Primary Website: wickedlocal.com/bourne
Audit By: Sworn/Estimate/Non-Audited
Audit Date: 10.06.2019
Personnel: Mark Olivieri (Pub.); John Basile (Mng. Ed.); Kathleen Cordeiro (Adv. Dir.)
Parent company (for newspapers): Community Newspaper Co. - South

BRAINTREE FORUM

Street address 1: 15 Pacella Park Dr
Street address 2: Ste 120

Street address city: Randolph
Street address state: MA
Zip/Postal code: 02368-1700
General Phone: (781) 682-4850
General Fax: (781) 682-4851
Advertising Phone: (781) 682-4850
Advertising Fax: (781) 682-4851
Editorial Phone: (781) 682-4850
Editorial Fax: (781) 682-4851
General/National Adv. E-mail: sgenerous@wickedlocal.com
Display Adv. E-mail: toliver@wickedlocal.com
Editorial e-mail: Bfonda@wickedlocal.com
Primary Website: wickedlocal.com/braintree
Avg Paid Circ: 1471
Audit By: AAM
Audit Date: 31.03.2018
Personnel: Mark Olivieri (Pub.); Bill Fonda (Ed.); Gregory Mathis (Ed. in Chief); Kathleen Cordeiro (Adv. Dir.)
Parent company (for newspapers): CherryRoad Media

BRIDGEWATER INDEPENDENT

Street address 1: 370 Paramount Dr
Street address 2: Ste 3
Street address city: Raynham
Street address state: MA
Zip/Postal code: 02767-5419
General Phone: (508) 967-3520
General Fax: (508) 967-3501
Advertising Phone: (781) 837-4598
Advertising Fax: (508) 967-3501
Editorial Phone: (508) 967-3505
Editorial Fax: (508) 967-3501
General/National Adv. E-mail: dteehan@wickedlocal.com
Display Adv. E-mail: rbright@wickedlocal.com
Editorial e-mail: acoyle@wickedlocal.com
Primary Website: wickedlocal.com/bridgewater
Year Established: 1875
Avg Paid Circ: 310
Avg Free Circ: 1530
Audit By: AAM
Audit Date: 31.03.2018
Personnel: Alice Coyle (Managing Ed.); Kathleen Cordeiro (Adv. Dir.)
Parent company (for newspapers): CherryRoad Media

BROOKLINE TAB

Street address 1: 254 2nd Ave
Street address city: Needham
Street address state: MA
Zip/Postal code: 02494-2829
General Phone: (781) 433-8334
General Fax: (781) 433-8202
Advertising Phone: (781) 433-6925
Advertising Fax: (781) 433-8202
Editorial Phone: (781) 433-8334
Editorial Fax: (781) 433-8202
General/National Adv. E-mail: cwarren@wickedlocal.com
Display Adv. E-mail: landler@wickedlocal.com
Editorial e-mail: eclossey@wickedlocal.com
Primary Website: wickedlocal.com/brookline
Avg Free Circ: 14302
Audit By: AAM
Audit Date: 31.03.2018
Personnel: Charles Goodrich (Pub.); Erin Clossey (News Ed.); Kathleen Cordeiro (Adv. Dir.)
Parent company (for newspapers): CherryRoad Media

BURLINGTON UNION

Street address 1: 150 Baker Avenue Ext
Street address city: Concord
Street address state: MA
Zip/Postal code: 01742-2126
General Phone: (781) 371-5742
Advertising Phone: (978) 739-1364
Editorial Phone: (978) 371-5742
General/National Adv. E-mail: aninos@wickedlocal.com
Display Adv. E-mail: cncclassads@wickedlocal.com
Editorial e-mail: Burlington@wickedlocal.com
Primary Website: burlington.wickedlocal.com
Year Established: 1963
Avg Paid Circ: 1319
Audit By: AAM
Audit Date: 31.03.2018
Personnel: Chuck Goodrich (Pub.); Linda Vahey (Circ. Mgr.); Christine Herter Warren (Ed.); Doug Hastings (Sports Ed.); Kathleen Cordeiro (Adv. Dir.)
Parent company (for newspapers): CherryRoad Media

CAMBRIDGE CHRONICLE & TAB

Street address 1: 80 Central St
Street address city: Somerville
Street address state: MA
Zip/Postal code: 02143-1612
General Phone: (617) 629-3387
General Fax: (617) 629-3381
Advertising Phone: (781) 433-8253
Advertising Fax: (617) 629-3381
Editorial Phone: (617) 629-3382
Editorial Fax: (617) 629-3381
General/National Adv. E-mail: cwarren@wickedlocal.com
Display Adv. E-mail: esiegal@wickedlocal.com
Editorial e-mail: cambridge@wickedlocal.com
Primary Website: wickedlocal.com/cambridge
Year Established: 1846
Avg Paid Circ: 659
Avg Free Circ: 4500
Audit By: AAM
Audit Date: 31.03.2018
Personnel: Amy Saltzman (Ed.); Erin Baldassari (Assist. Ed.); Cris Warren (Reg. Adv. Dir.); Kathleen Cordeiro (Adv. Dir.)
Parent company (for newspapers): CherryRoad Media

CANTON CITIZEN

Street address 1: 866 Washington St
Street address city: Canton
Street address state: MA
Zip/Postal code: 02021-2514
General Phone: (781) 821-4418
General Fax: (781) 821-4419
Advertising Phone: (781) 821-4418
Advertising Fax: (781) 821-4419
Editorial Phone: (781) 821-4418
Editorial Fax: (781) 821-4419
General/National Adv. E-mail: ads@thecantoncitizen.com
Display Adv. E-mail: ads@thecantoncitizen.com
Editorial e-mail: submissions@thecantoncitizen.com
Primary Website: thecantoncitizen.com
Year Established: 1987
Avg Paid Circ: 3600
Avg Free Circ: 20
Audit By: Sworn/Estimate/Non-Audited
Audit Date: 10.06.2019
Personnel: Beth Erickson (Ed./Pub.); Connor Erickson (Adv. Mgr.); Jay Turner (Assistant Editor)

CANTON JOURNAL

Street address 1: 370 Paramount Dr
Street address 2: Ste 3
Street address city: Raynham
Street address state: MA
Zip/Postal code: 02767-5419
General Phone: (508) 967-3515
General Fax: (508) 967-3501
Advertising Phone: (508) 967-3515
Advertising Fax: (508) 967-3501
Editorial Phone: (508) 967-3515
Editorial Fax: (508) 967-3501
General/National Adv. E-mail: canton@cnc.com
Display Adv. E-mail: rbright@wickedlocal.com
Editorial e-mail: acoyle@wickedlocal.com
Primary Website: wickedlocal.com/canton
Year Established: 1876
Avg Free Circ: 169
Audit By: AAM
Audit Date: 31.12.2017
Personnel: Alice Coyle (Managing Ed.); Stuart Green (News Ed.); Kathleen Cordeiro (Adv. Dir.)
Parent company (for newspapers): CherryRoad Media

CAPE ANN BEACON

Street address 1: 75 Sylvan St
Street address 2: Ste C105
Street address city: Danvers
Street address state: MA
Zip/Postal code: 01923-2765
General Phone: (978) 739-1300
General Fax: (978) 739-8501
Advertising Phone: (978) 739-1320
Advertising Fax: (978) 739-1391
Editorial Phone: (978) 739-1300
Editorial Fax: (978) 739-8501
General/National Adv. E-mail: mkasper@wickedlocal.com
Display Adv. E-mail: classifieds@wickedlocal.com
Editorial e-mail: capeann@wickedlocal.com
Primary Website: gloucester.wickedlocal.com
Avg Free Circ: 5500
Audit By: AAM
Audit Date: 31.03.2016
Personnel: Peter Chianca (Ed.-in-Chief); Janet Mackay-Smith (Managing Ed.); Kathleen Cordeiro (Adv. Dir.)
Parent company (for newspapers): Community Newspaper Co.-North-OOB

CARLISLE MOSQUITO

Street address 1: 662A Bedford Rd
Street address city: Carlisle
Street address state: MA
Zip/Postal code: 01741-1859
General Phone: (978) 369-8313
General Fax: (978) 369-3569
Advertising Phone: (978) 369-8313
Advertising Fax: (978) 369-3569
Editorial Phone: (978) 369-8313
Editorial Fax: (978) 369-3569
General/National Adv. E-mail: ads@carlislemosquito.org
Display Adv. E-mail: ads@carlislemosquito.org
Editorial e-mail: mail@carlislemosquito.org
Primary Website: carlislemosquito.org
Year Established: 1972
Avg Free Circ: 2100
Audit By: Sworn/Estimate/Non-Audited
Audit Date: 10.06.2019
Personnel: Susan Emmons (Gen. Mgr.); Susan Mills (Adv. Mgr.); Ann Quenin (Features Ed.); Betsy Fell (News Ed.); Penny Zezima (Asst. Ed.)

CARVER REPORTER

Street address 1: 182 Standish Ave
Street address city: Plymouth
Street address state: MA
Zip/Postal code: 02360-4162
General Phone: (508) 591-6605
General Fax: (508) 591-6601
Advertising Phone: (508) 591-6605
Advertising Fax: (508) 591-6601
Editorial Phone: (508) 591-6605
Editorial Fax: (508) 591-6601
General/National Adv. E-mail: salesteam@wickedlocal.com
Display Adv. E-mail: salesteam@wickedlocal.com
Editorial e-mail: dsmith@wickedlocal.com
Primary Website: wickedlocal.com/carver
Year Established: 1980
Avg Paid Circ: 651
Audit By: AAM
Audit Date: 9/31/2018
Personnel: Mark Olivieri (Pub.); Tim Oliver (Sales Mgr.); Bobbi Sistrunk (Reporter); Adam Ellis (Sports Ed.); Kathleen Cordeiro (Adv. Dir.)
Parent company (for newspapers): CherryRoad Media

CHARLTON VILLAGER

Street address 1: 25 Elm St
Street address city: Southbridge
Street address state: MA
Zip/Postal code: 01550-2605
General Phone: (508) 764-4325
General Fax: (508) 764-8102
Advertising Phone: (508) 909-4104
Advertising Fax: (508) 764-8102
Editorial Phone: (508) 909-4130
Editorial Fax: (508) 764-8102
General/National Adv. E-mail: jashton@stonebridgepress.com
Display Adv. E-mail: classifieds@stonebridgepress.com
Editorial e-mail: aminor@stonebridgepress.com
Primary Website: theheartofmassachusetts.com
Audit By: Sworn/Estimate/Non-Audited
Audit Date: 10.06.2019
Personnel: Adam Minor (Ed.); Jean Ashton (Ad. Director)

CHELMSFORD INDEPENDENT

Street address 1: 150 Baker Avenue Ext
Street address city: Concord
Street address state: MA
Zip/Postal code: 01742-2126
General Phone: (978) 256-7196
General Fax: (978) 371-5212
Advertising Phone: (978) 256-7196
Advertising Fax: (978) 371-5212
Editorial Phone: (978) 256-7196
Editorial Fax: (978) 371-5212
General/National Adv. E-mail: speters@wickedlocal.com
Display Adv. E-mail: rbright@wickedlocal.com
Editorial e-mail: chelmsford@wickedlocal.com
Primary Website: wickedlocal.com/chelmsford
Avg Paid Circ: 1336
Audit By: AAM
Audit Date: 31.03.2018
Personnel: Chuck Goodrich (Pub.); Kathleen Cordeiro; Kathleen Cordeiro (Adv. Dir.); Margaret Smith (Ed.)
Parent company (for newspapers): CherryRoad Media

CHELSEA RECORD

Street address 1: 385 Broadway
Street address 2: Ste 105
Street address city: Revere
Street address state: MA
Zip/Postal code: 02151-3049
General Phone: (781) 284-2400
General Fax: (781) 485-1403
Advertising Phone: (781) 284-2400
Advertising Fax: (781) 485-1403
Editorial Phone: (781) 284-2400
Editorial Fax: (781) 485-1403
General/National Adv. E-mail: ads.journal@verizon.net
Display Adv. E-mail: ads.journal@verizon.net
Editorial e-mail: editor@chelsearecord.com
Primary Website: chelsearecord.com
Year Established: 1890
Avg Paid Circ: 4500
Audit By: Sworn/Estimate/Non-Audited
Audit Date: 10.06.2019
Personnel: Joshua Resnek (Vice Pres./executive editor); Debra DiGregorio (Adv. Mgr.); Cary Shuman (Ed. in Chief); Stephen Quigley (Prodn. Mgr.)
Parent company (for newspapers): Independent Newspaper Group

COHASSET MARINER

Street address 1: 73 South St
Street address city: Hingham
Street address state: MA
Zip/Postal code: 02043-2421
General Phone: (781) 749-0031
General Fax: (781) 741-2931
Advertising Phone: (781) 749-0031
Advertising Fax: (781) 741-2931
Editorial Phone: (781) 749-0031
Editorial Fax: (781) 741-2931
General/National Adv. E-mail: coliver@wickedlocal.com
Display Adv. E-mail: toliver@wickedlocal.com
Editorial e-mail: cohasset@wickedlocal.com
Primary Website: wickedlocal.com/cohasset
Avg Paid Circ: 1449
Avg Free Circ: 36
Audit By: AAM
Audit Date: 31.03.2018
Personnel: Mark Olivieri (Pub.); Gregory Mathis (Ed. in Chief); Mary Ford (Ed.); Claudia Oliver (Act. Exec.); Kathleen Cordeiro (Adv. Dir.)
Parent company (for newspapers): CherryRoad Media

COMMUNITY ADVOCATE

Street address 1: 32 South St
Street address city: Westborough
Street address state: MA
Zip/Postal code: 01581-1619
General Phone: (508) 366-5500
General Fax: (508) 366-2812
Advertising Phone: (508) 366-5500
Advertising Fax: (508) 366-2812
General/National Adv. E-mail: adguy@communityadvocate.com
Display Adv. E-mail: adguy@communityadvocate.com
Editorial e-mail: news@communityadvocate.com
Primary Website: communityadvocate.com
Year Established: 1974
Avg Paid Circ: 16000
Avg Free Circ: 5194
Audit By: Sworn/Estimate/Non-Audited

Audit Date: 10.06.2019
Personnel: Tracy Nickerson (Office Mgr.); David Bagdon (Ed.); Barbara Polan (Mng. Ed.)

COUNTRY JOURNAL

Street address 1: 5 Main St
Street address city: Huntington
Street address state: MA
Zip/Postal code: 01050-9678
General Phone: (413) 667-3211
General Fax: (413) 667-3011
General/National Adv. E-mail: bbaker@turley.com
Display Adv. E-mail: classifieds@turley.com
Editorial e-mail: countryjournal@turley.com
Primary Website: turley.com/countryjournal.html
Year Established: 1979
Avg Free Circ: 3317
Audit By: Sworn/Estimate/Non-Audited
Audit Date: 10.06.2019
Personnel: Christine Charnosky (Ed.); Patrick H. Turley (Pub.); Beth Baker (Ad. Director)
Parent company (for newspapers): Turley Publications, Inc.

DANVERS HERALD

Street address 1: 75 Sylvan St
Street address 2: Ste C105
Street address city: Danvers
Street address state: MA
Zip/Postal code: 01923-2765
General Phone: (978) 774-0505
General Fax: (978) 739-8501
Advertising Phone: (978) 774-0505
Advertising Fax: (978) 739-8501
Editorial Phone: (978) 774-0505
Editorial Fax: (978) 739-8501
General/National Adv. E-mail: danvers@cnc.com; obits@cnc.com; photoreprints@cnc.com; mypaper@cnc.com
Display Adv. E-mail: salesteam@wickedlocal.com
Editorial e-mail: legals@cnc.com
Primary Website: wickedlocal.com/danvers
Avg Paid Circ: 1465
Avg Free Circ: 192
Audit By: AAM
Audit Date: 31.03.2018
Personnel: Charles Goodrich (Pub.); Jeffrey Pope (Ed.); Pete Chianca (Ed. in Chief); Kathleen Cordeiro (Adv. Dir.)
Parent company (for newspapers): CherryRoad Media

DOVER-SHERBORN PRESS

Street address 1: 254 2nd Ave
Street address city: Needham
Street address state: MA
Zip/Postal code: 02494-2829
General Phone: (781) 433-8226
General Fax: (781) 433-8202
Advertising Phone: (781) 433-8313
Advertising Fax: (781) 433-8202
Editorial Phone: (781) 433-6925
Editorial Fax: (781) 433-8202
General/National Adv. E-mail: cwarren@wickedlocal.com
Display Adv. E-mail: dmaher@wickedlocal.com
Editorial e-mail: wbraverman@wickedlocal.com
Primary Website: wickedlocal.com/dover
Avg Paid Circ: 400
Audit By: AAM
Audit Date: 31.03.2018
Personnel: Chuck Goodrich (Pub.); Cris Warren (Reg. Adv. Dir.); Wayne Braverman (Mng. Ed.); Jesse Floyd (Ed. in Chief); Kathleen Cordeiro (Adv. Dir.)
Parent company (for newspapers): CherryRoad Media

DUXBURY CLIPPER

Street address 1: 11 S Station St
Street address city: Duxbury
Street address state: MA
Zip/Postal code: 02332-4534
General Phone: (781) 934-2811
General Fax: (781) 934-5917
General/National Adv. E-mail: newsroom@duxburyclipper.com
Display Adv. E-mail: ads@duxburyclipper.com
Editorial e-mail: editor@duxburyclipper.com
Primary Website: duxburyclipper.com
Year Established: 1950
Avg Paid Circ: 4500
Audit By: Sworn/Estimate/Non-Audited
Audit Date: 10.06.2019
Personnel: Deborah Anderson (Pub.); Gillian Smith (Ed.); Amy McWilliams (Office Mgr.); Robin Nudd (Adv. Asst.); Mike Halloran (Sports Ed.); Lindsey Gardner (Prodn. Mgr.)
Parent company (for newspapers): Duxbury Clipper

DUXBURY REPORTER

Street address 1: 165 Enterprise Dr
Street address city: Marshfield
Street address state: MA
Zip/Postal code: 02050-2132
General Phone: (781) 837-4545
General Fax: (781) 837-4543
Advertising Phone: (781) 837-4545
Advertising Fax: (781) 837-4543
Editorial Phone: (781) 837-4545
Editorial Fax: (781) 837-4543
Primary Website: wickedlocal.com/duxbury
Year Established: 1987
Avg Paid Circ: 0
Avg Free Circ: 2725
Audit By: Sworn/Estimate/Non-Audited
Audit Date: 10.06.2019
Personnel: Mark Olivieri (Pub.); David Smith (Ed.)
Parent company (for newspapers): Community Newspaper Co. - South; CherryRoad Media

EAST BOSTON TIMES

Street address 1: 385 Broadway
Street address 2: Ste 105
Street address city: Revere
Street address state: MA
Zip/Postal code: 02151-3049
General Phone: (781) 485-0588
General Fax: (781) 485-1403
Advertising Phone: (781) 485-0588
Advertising Fax: (781) 485-1403
Editorial Phone: (781) 485-0588
Editorial Fax: (781) 485-1403
General/National Adv. E-mail: ads.journal@verizon.net
Display Adv. E-mail: ADS.JOURNAL@VERIZON.NET
Primary Website: eastietimes.com
Avg Free Circ: 8000
Audit By: Sworn/Estimate/Non-Audited
Audit Date: 10.06.2019
Personnel: Joshua Resnek (Vice Pres.); Stephen Quigley (Prodn. Mgr.)
Parent company (for newspapers): Independent Newspaper Group

EASTON JOURNAL

Street address 1: 370 Paramount Dr
Street address 2: Ste 3
Street address city: Raynham
Street address state: MA
Zip/Postal code: 02767-5419
General Phone: (508) 967-3510
General Fax: (508) 967-3501
Advertising Phone: (508) 967-3510
Advertising Fax: (508) 967-3501
Editorial Phone: (508) 967-3510
Editorial Fax: (508) 967-3501
General/National Adv. E-mail: msutherland@wickedlocal.com
Display Adv. E-mail: rbright@wickedlocal.com
Editorial e-mail: acoyle@wickedlocal.com
Primary Website: wickedlocal.com/easton
Avg Paid Circ: 301
Audit By: AAM
Audit Date: 31.12.2018
Personnel: Mark Olivieri (Pub.); Alice Coyla (Mng. Ed.); John Quattrucci (Sports Ed.); Kathleen Cordeiro (Adv. Dir.)
Parent company (for newspapers): CherryRoad Media

EVERETT INDEPENDENT

Street address 1: 385 Broadway
Street address 2: Ste 105
Street address city: Revere
Street address state: MA
Zip/Postal code: 02151-3049
General Phone: (781) -485-0588
General Fax: (781) 485-1403
Editorial Phone: (781) 284-2400
Editorial Fax: (781) 485-1403
General/National Adv. E-mail: ads.journal@verizon.net
Display Adv. E-mail: ads.journal@verizon.net
Editorial e-mail: editor@everettindependent.com
Primary Website: everettindependent.com
Avg Free Circ: 12500
Audit By: Sworn/Estimate/Non-Audited
Audit Date: 10.06.2019
Personnel: Kane Di-Masso Scott (Ed.); Deb Gregorio (Adv., Dir. of Mktg.)
Parent company (for newspapers): Independent Newspaper Group

EVERETT LEADER HERALD NEWS GAZETTE

Street address 1: 28 Church St
Street address city: Everett
Street address state: MA
Zip/Postal code: 02149-2719
General Phone: (617) 387-4570
General Fax: (617) 387-0409
Advertising Phone: (617) 387-4570
Advertising Fax: (617) 387-0409
Editorial Phone: (617) 387-4570
Editorial Fax: (617) 387-0409
General/National Adv. E-mail: everettleader@comcast.net
Display Adv. E-mail: everettleader@comcast.net
Editorial e-mail: everettleader@comcast.net
Primary Website: facebook.com/pages/Everett-Leader-Herald-News-Gazette/155161251187065
Year Established: 1885
Avg Free Circ: 15000
Audit By: Sworn/Estimate/Non-Audited
Audit Date: 10.06.2019
Personnel: Joseph A. Curnane (Pub.)

FRAMINGHAM TAB

Street address 1: 33 New York Ave
Street address city: Framingham
Street address state: MA
Zip/Postal code: 01701-8857
General Phone: (508) 626-3800
General Fax: (508) 626-4400
Advertising Phone: (508) 626-3800
Advertising Fax: (508) 626-4400
Editorial Phone: (508) 626-3800
Editorial Fax: (508) 626-4400
General/National Adv. E-mail: salesteam@wickedlocal.com
Display Adv. E-mail: salesteam@wickedlocal.com
Editorial e-mail: framingham@wickedlocal.com
Primary Website: wickedlocal.com/framingham
Avg Free Circ: 4536
Audit By: AAM
Audit Date: 31.03.2018
Personnel: Richard Lodge (Ed. in Chief); Phil Maddocks (Ed.); Paul Farrell (Dir. Corp. Sales)
Parent company (for newspapers): CherryRoad Media

GEORGETOWN RECORD

Street address 1: 75 Sylvan St
Street address 2: Ste C105
Street address city: Danvers
Street address state: MA
Zip/Postal code: 01923-2765
General Phone: (978) 739-8506
General Fax: (978) 739-8501
Advertising Phone: (781) 433-6925
Advertising Fax: (781) 433-7951
Editorial Phone: (978) 739-8506
Editorial Fax: (781) 433-6965
General/National Adv. E-mail: salesteam@wickedlocal.com
Display Adv. E-mail: salesteam@wickedlocal.com
Editorial e-mail: georgetown@wickedlocal.com
Primary Website: wickedlocal.com/georgetown
Avg Paid Circ: 592
Avg Free Circ: 0
Audit By: AAM
Audit Date: 31.03.2018
Personnel: Charles Goodrich (Pub.); Linda Vahey (Cir. Mgr.); Pete Chianca (Ed. in Chief); Tim McCarthy (Ed.); Kathleen Cordeiro (Adv. Dir.)
Parent company (for newspapers): Community Newspaper Co.-North-OOB; CherryRoad Media

GROTON LANDMARK

Street address 1: 78 Barnum Rd
Street address city: Devens
Street address state: MA
Zip/Postal code: 01434-3508
General Phone: (978) 772-0777
General Fax: (978) 772-4012
Advertising Phone: (978) 772-0777
Advertising Fax: (978) 772-4012
Editorial Phone: (978) 772-0777
Editorial Fax: (978) 772-4012
General/National Adv. E-mail: Advertising@MediaOneMarketPlace.com
Display Adv. E-mail: Advertising@MediaOneMarketPlace.com
Editorial e-mail: editor@nashobapub.com
Primary Website: grotonlandmark.com
Year Established: 1869
Avg Paid Circ: 695
Audit By: Sworn/Estimate/Non-Audited
Audit Date: 10.06.2019
Personnel: Mark O'Neil (Pub.); Kate King (Mng. Ed.)

HALIFAX-PLYMPTON REPORTER

Street address 1: 165 Enterprise Dr
Street address city: Marshfield
Street address state: MA
Zip/Postal code: 02050-2132
General Phone: (508) 746-5555
General Fax: (508) 747-2148
Advertising Phone: (508) 746-5555
Advertising Fax: (508) 747-2148
Editorial Phone: (508) 746-5555
Editorial Fax: (508) 747-2148
General/National Adv. E-mail: newsroom@mpgnews.com
Primary Website: plymptonhalifaxexpress.com
Year Established: 1983
Avg Paid Circ: 750
Avg Free Circ: 1
Audit By: Sworn/Estimate/Non-Audited
Audit Date: 10.06.2019
Personnel: Gregory Mathis (Ed.-in-Chief); Mark Olivieri (Publisher)
Parent company (for newspapers): Community Newspaper Co. - South; CherryRoad Media

HAMILTON-WENHAM CHRONICLE

Street address 1: 75 Sylvan St
Street address 2: Ste C105
Street address city: Danvers
Street address state: MA
Zip/Postal code: 01923-2765
General Phone: (978) 468-1911
General Fax: (978) 739-8501
Advertising Phone: (978) 468-1911
Advertising Fax: (978) 739-8501
Editorial Phone: (978) 468-1911
Editorial Fax: (978) 739-8501
General/National Adv. E-mail: salesteam@wickedlocal.com
Display Adv. E-mail: salesteam@wickedlocal.com
Editorial e-mail: hamilton-wenham@wickedlocal.com
Primary Website: wickedlocal.com/hamilton
Avg Paid Circ: 942
Audit By: AAM
Audit Date: 31.03.2018
Personnel: Charles Goodrich (Pub.); Pete Chianca (Ed. in Chief); Janet Mackay-Smith (Managing Ed.); Jennie Omeig (News Ed.); Kathleen Cordeiro (Adv. Dir.)
Parent company (for newspapers): CherryRoad Media

HANOVER MARINER

Street address 1: 165 Enterprise Dr
Street address city: Marshfield
Street address state: MA
Zip/Postal code: 02050-2132
General Phone: (781) 837-4560
General Fax: (781) 837-4540
Advertising Phone: (781) 837-4560
Advertising Fax: (781) 837-4540
Editorial Phone: (781) 837-4560
Editorial Fax: (781) 837-4540
General/National Adv. E-mail: hanover@cnc.com
Display Adv. E-mail: hanover@cnc.com
Editorial e-mail: hanover@cnc.com
Primary Website: wickedlocal.com/hanover
Year Established: 1980
Avg Paid Circ: 939
Audit By: AAM
Audit Date: 31.03.2018

Personnel: Mark Olivieri (Pub.); Gregory Mathis (Sr. Mng. Ed.); Kathleen Cordeiro (Adv. Dir.)
Parent company (for newspapers): CherryRoad Media

HARWICH ORACLE

Street address 1: 5 Namskaket Rd
Street address city: Orleans
Street address state: MA
Zip/Postal code: 02653-3202
General Phone: (508) 247-3255
General Fax: (508) 247-3203
Advertising Phone: (508) 247-3255
Advertising Fax: (508) 247-3203
Editorial Phone: (508) 247-3255
Editorial Fax: (508) 247-3203
General/National Adv. E-mail: harwich@cnc.com; obits@cnc.com
Display Adv. E-mail: salesteam@wickedlocal.com
Editorial e-mail: harwich@cnc.com
Primary Website: wickedlocal.com
Year Established: 1986
Avg Paid Circ: 1304
Audit By: Sworn/Estimate/Non-Audited
Audit Date: 10.06.2019
Personnel: Douglas Karlson (Ed.); Kathleen Cordeiro (Adv. Dir.)
Parent company (for newspapers): Community Newspaper Co. - South; CherryRoad Media

HINGHAM JOURNAL

Street address 1: 73 South St
Street address city: Hingham
Street address state: MA
Zip/Postal code: 02043-2421
General Phone: (781) 749-0031
General Fax: (781) 741-2931
Advertising Phone: (781) 749-0031
Advertising Fax: (781) 741-2931
Editorial Phone: (781) 749-0031
Editorial Fax: (781) 741-2931
General/National Adv. E-mail: srussell@wickedlocal.com
Display Adv. E-mail: salesteam@wickedlocal.com
Editorial e-mail: mford@wickedlocal.com
Primary Website: wickedlocal.com/hingham
Avg Paid Circ: 3414
Avg Free Circ: 235
Audit By: AAM
Audit Date: 31.03.2018
Personnel: Mark Olivieri (Pub.); Jeff McEvoy (Natl. Adv. Dir.); Mary Ford (News Ed.); William Wassersug (Sports Ed.); Kathleen Cordeiro (Adv. Dir.)
Parent company (for newspapers): CherryRoad Media

HOLBROOK SUN

Street address 1: 15 Pacella Park Dr
Street address 2: Ste 200
Street address city: Randolph
Street address state: MA
Zip/Postal code: 02368-1700
General Phone: (781) 682-4850
General Fax: (781) 682-4851
Advertising Phone: (781) 837-4547
Advertising Fax: (781) 682-4851
Editorial Phone: (781) 837-4560
Editorial Fax: (781) 682-4851
General/National Adv. E-mail: salesteam@wickedlocal.com
Display Adv. E-mail: toliver@wickedlocal.com
Classified Adv. e-mail: kwillette@wickedlocal.com
Editorial e-mail: bfonda@wickedlocal.com
Primary Website: wickedlocal.com/holbrook
Mthly Avg Views: 1154957
Mthly Avg Unique Visitors: 244866
Year Established: 1958
Avg Paid Circ: 330
Audit By: AAM
Audit Date: 31.03.2018
Personnel: Mark Olivieri (Pub.); Paul Harber (Sports Ed.); Kathleen Cordeiro (Adv. Dir.)
Parent company (for newspapers): CherryRoad Media

HOLLISTON TAB

Street address 1: 33 New York Ave
Street address city: Framingham
Street address state: MA
Zip/Postal code: 01701-8857
General Phone: (508) 323-3957
General Fax: (508) 626-4400
Advertising Phone: (508) 323-3957
Advertising Fax: (508) 626-4400
Editorial Phone: (508) 323-3957
Editorial Fax: (508) 626-4400
General/National Adv. E-mail: crobinso@wickedlocal.com
Display Adv. E-mail: salesteam@wickedlocal.com
Editorial e-mail: joconnell@wickedlocal.com
Primary Website: wickedlocal.com/holliston
Avg Paid Circ: 1343
Audit By: Sworn/Estimate/Non-Audited
Audit Date: 10.06.2019
Personnel: Joe O'Connell (Tab Ed.); Kathleen Cordeiro (Adv. Dir.)
Parent company (for newspapers): Community Newspaper Co.-West-OOB; CherryRoad Media

HOPKINTON CRIER

Street address 1: 33 New York Ave
Street address city: Framingham
Street address state: MA
Zip/Postal code: 01701-8857
General Phone: (508) 626-4412
General Fax: (508) 626-4400
Advertising Phone: (508) 626-4412
Advertising Fax: (508) 626-4400
Editorial Phone: (508) 626-4332
Editorial Fax: (508) 626-4400
General/National Adv. E-mail: salesteam@wickedlocal.com
Display Adv. E-mail: salesteam@wickedlocal.com
Editorial e-mail: hopkinton@wickedlocal.com
Primary Website: wickedlocal.com/hopkinton
Year Established: 1987
Avg Paid Circ: 195
Audit By: AAM
Audit Date: 31.03.2018
Personnel: Alison McCall (Ed.); Richard Lodge (Ed. in Chief); Elizabeth Banks; Kathleen Cordeiro (Adv. Dir.)
Parent company (for newspapers): CherryRoad Media

HUDSON SUN

Street address 1: 33 New York Ave
Street address city: Framingham
Street address state: MA
Zip/Postal code: 01701-8857
General Phone: (508) 490-7455
General Fax: (508) 626-4400
Advertising Phone: (508) 626-3833
Advertising Fax: (508) 626-4400
Editorial Phone: (508) 626-3926
Editorial Fax: (508) 626-4400
General/National Adv. E-mail: lgreen@wickedlocal.com
Editorial e-mail: hudson@wickedlocal.com
Primary Website: wickedlocal.com/hudson
Avg Paid Circ: 726
Audit By: AAM
Audit Date: 31.03.2018
Personnel: Richard Lodge (Ed. in Chief); Cathy Buday (Ed.); Chuck Goodrich (Pub.); Kathleen Cordeiro (Adv. Dir.)
Parent company (for newspapers): CherryRoad Media

HYDE PARK BULLETIN

Street address 1: 661 Washington St
Street address 2: Ste 202
Street address city: Norwood
Street address state: MA
Zip/Postal code: 02062-3529
General Phone: (617) 361-8400
General Fax: (617) 361-1933
Advertising Phone: (617) 361-8400
Advertising Fax: (617) 361-1933
Editorial Phone: (617) 361-8400
Editorial Fax: (617) 361-1933
General/National Adv. E-mail: news@hydeparkbulletin.com
Display Adv. E-mail: bulletingraphics@aol.com
Editorial e-mail: news@hydeparkbulletin.com
Primary Website: bulletinnewspapers.com
Year Established: 1992
Avg Free Circ: 5500
Audit By: Sworn/Estimate/Non-Audited
Audit Date: 10.06.2019
Personnel: Paul DiModica (Pub.); Susan Yandell (Adv.)

IPSWICH CHRONICLE

Street address 1: 75 Sylvan St
Street address 2: # 105
Street address city: Danvers
Street address state: MA
Zip/Postal code: 01923-2763
General Phone: (978) 739-1303
General Fax: (978) 739-8501
Advertising Phone: (978) 739-1303
Advertising Fax: (978) 739-8501
Editorial Phone: (978) 739-1303
Editorial Fax: (978) 739-8501
General/National Adv. E-mail: salesteam@wickedlocal.com
Display Adv. E-mail: salesteam@wickedlocal.com
Editorial e-mail: ipswich@wickedlocal.com
Primary Website: wickedlocal.com/ipswich
Avg Paid Circ: 2233
Avg Free Circ: 2
Audit By: Sworn/Estimate/Non-Audited
Audit Date: 10.06.2019
Personnel: Charles Goodrich (Pub.); Wendall Waters (Ed.); Dan Mac Alpine (Ed.); Janet Mackay Smith (Mng. Ed.); Kathleen Cordeiro (Adv. Dir.)
Parent company (for newspapers): Community Newspaper Co.-North-OOB; CherryRoad Media

ITEM LIVE

Street address 1: 110 Munroe St.
Street address city: Lynn
Street address state: MA
Zip/Postal code: 01901
General Phone: (781) 593-7700
Advertising Phone: (781) 593-7700 ext. 2
Editorial Phone: (781) 593-7700 ext. 3
General/National Adv. E-mail: advertising@itemlive.com
Display Adv. E-mail: advertising@itemlive.com
Editorial e-mail: news@itemlive.com
Primary Website: weeklynews.net
Avg Free Circ: 19263
Audit By: Sworn/Estimate/Non-Audited
Audit Date: 10.06.2019
Personnel: Stephen Krause; E Carpenter (Adv.); T Jourgensen (Ed.)

KINGSTON REPORTER

Street address 1: 182 Standish Ave
Street address city: Plymouth
Street address state: MA
Zip/Postal code: 02360-4162
General Phone: (781) 837-4504
General Fax: (508) 591-6601
Advertising Phone: (781) 433-6934
Advertising Fax: (508) 591-6601
Editorial Phone: (508) 591-6605
Editorial Fax: (508) 591-6601
General/National Adv. E-mail: salesteam@wickedlocal.com
Display Adv. E-mail: salesteam@wickedlocal.com
Editorial e-mail: scsmith@wickedlocal.com
Primary Website: wickedlocal.com/kingston
Avg Paid Circ: 195
Avg Free Circ: 0
Audit By: AAM
Audit Date: 31.03.2017
Personnel: Mark Olivieri (Pub.); Gregory Mathis (Ed. in Chief); Scott Smith (Mng. Ed.); Kathleen Cordeiro (Adv. Dir.)
Parent company (for newspapers): CherryRoad Media

LEOMINSTER CHAMPION

Street address 1: 285 Central St
Street address 2: Ste 202
Street address city: Leominster
Street address state: MA
Zip/Postal code: 01453-6144
General Phone: (978) 534-6006
General Fax: (978) 534-6004
Advertising Phone: (978) 534-6006
Advertising Fax: (978) 534-6004
General/National Adv. E-mail: sales@leominsterchamp.com
Display Adv. E-mail: sales@centralmassclass.com
Editorial e-mail: editor@leominsterchamp.com
Primary Website: leominsterchamp.com
Mthly Avg Views: 28136
Mthly Avg Unique Visitors: 7518
Year Established: 2006
Avg Free Circ: 5984
Audit By: Sworn/Estimate/Non-Audited
Audit Date: 10.06.2019
Personnel: David Dore (Ed.); Barbara Brown (Pub.); Tom Signa (Adv. Mgr); Don Cloutier (Prod. Mgr)
Parent company (for newspapers): Holden Landmark Corp

LEXINGTON MINUTEMAN

Street address 1: 9 Meriam St
Street address city: Lexington
Street address state: MA
Zip/Postal code: 02420-5300
General Phone: (781) 674-7725
Advertising Phone: (978) 371-5717
Editorial Phone: (781) 674-7725
General/National Adv. E-mail: pgaudette@wickedlocal.com
Editorial e-mail: lexington@wickedlocal.com
Primary Website: lexington.wickedlocal.com
Year Established: 1870
Avg Paid Circ: 2840
Avg Free Circ: 1454
Audit By: AAM
Audit Date: 31.03.2018
Personnel: Chuck Goodrich (Pub.); Jim O'Rourke (Circ. Mgr.); Bryan Mahoney (Ed.); Kathleen Cordeiro (Adv. Dir.)
Parent company (for newspapers): CherryRoad Media

LINCOLN JOURNAL

Street address 1: 50 Baker Ave. Ext.
Street address 2: Ste 101
Street address city: Concord
Street address state: MA
Zip/Postal code: 01742-2199
General Phone: (978) 371-5759
General/National Adv. E-mail: dryan@wickedlocal.com
Display Adv. E-mail: dryan@wickedlocal.com
Editorial e-mail: kcordeiro@wickedlocal.com
Primary Website: wickedlocal.com/lincoln
Avg Paid Circ: 439
Avg Free Circ: 37
Audit By: AAM
Audit Date: 31.03.2018
Personnel: Chuck Goodrich (Pub.); Kathy Cordeiro (Ed. in Chief); Kathie Ragsdale (Ed.); Kathleen Cordeiro (Adv. Dir.)
Parent company (for newspapers): CherryRoad Media

LITTLETON INDEPENDENT

Street address 1: 150 Baker Avenue Ext
Street address 2: Ste 101
Street address city: Concord
Street address state: MA
Zip/Postal code: 01742-2199
General Phone: (978) 371-5713
General/National Adv. E-mail: pcalder@wickedlocal.com
Display Adv. E-mail: classifieds@wickedlocal.com
Editorial e-mail: kcordeiro@wickedlocal.com
Primary Website: wickedlocal.com/littleton
Avg Paid Circ: 779
Avg Free Circ: 225
Audit By: AAM
Audit Date: 31.03.2018
Personnel: Chuck Goodrich (Pub.); Kathy Cordeiro (Ed. in Chief); Pamela Calder (Adv. Mgr., Display)
Parent company (for newspapers): CherryRoad Media

MALDEN OBSERVER

Street address 1: 48 Dunham Road
Street address 2: Suite 3100
Street address city: Beverly
Street address state: MA
Zip/Postal code: 01915
General Phone: (781) 393-1827
General Fax: (617) 629-3381
General/National Adv. E-mail: nprag@wickedlocal.com
Display Adv. E-mail: classifieds@wickedlocal.com
Editorial e-mail: pchianca@wickedlocal.com
Primary Website: wickedlocal.com/malden
Avg Paid Circ: 809
Avg Free Circ: 0
Audit By: AAM

Audit Date: 31.03.2018
Personnel: Charles Goodrich (Pub.); Pete Chianca (Ed. in Chief); Nell Escobar Coakley (Ed.); Chris Hurley (Sports Ed.); Kathleen Cordeiro (Adv. Dir.)
Parent company (for newspapers): CherryRoad Media

MANSFIELD NEWS

Street address 1: 165 Enterprise Dr
Street address city: Marshfield
Street address state: MA
Zip/Postal code: 02050-2132
General Phone: (508) 967-3500
General Fax: (508) 967-3501
Advertising Phone: (508) 967-3500
Advertising Fax: (508) 967-3501
Editorial Phone: (508) 967-3500
Editorial Fax: (508) 967-3501
General/National Adv. E-mail: mansfield@cnc.com
Display Adv. E-mail: salesteam@wickedlocal.com
Editorial e-mail: mansfield@cnc.com
Primary Website: wickedlocal.com
Year Established: 1872
Avg Paid Circ: 236
Audit By: AAM
Audit Date: 31.12.2018
Personnel: Mark Olivieri (Pub.); Kathleen Cordeiro (Adv. Dir.)
Parent company (for newspapers): CherryRoad Media

MARBLEHEAD REPORTER

Street address 1: 48 Dunham Road
Street address 2: Suite 3100
Street address city: Beverly
Street address state: MA
Zip/Postal code: 01915
General Phone: (781) 639-4800
Display Adv. E-mail: classifieds@wickedlocal.com
Editorial e-mail: pchianca@wickedlocal.com
Primary Website: marblehead.wickedlocal.com
Avg Paid Circ: 3239
Avg Free Circ: 68
Audit By: AAM
Audit Date: 31.03.2018
Personnel: Charles Goodrich (Pub.); Peter Chianca (Ed. in Chief); Kathleen Cordeiro (Adv. Dir.); Mary Reines (Arts and More Section Ed.)
Parent company (for newspapers): CherryRoad Media

MARLBOROUGH ENTERPRISE

Street address 1: 33 New York Ave
Street address city: Framingham
Street address state: MA
Zip/Postal code: 01701-8857
General Phone: (508) 490-7455
General Fax: (508) 490-7471
Advertising Phone: (508) 490-7455
Editorial Phone: (508) 490-7455
General/National Adv. E-mail: crobinson@wickedlocal.com
Display Adv. E-mail: salesteam@wickedlocal.com
Editorial e-mail: marlborough@wickedlocal.com
Primary Website: wickedlocal.com/marlborough
Avg Paid Circ: 1746
Audit By: Sworn/Estimate/Non-Audited
Audit Date: 10.06.2019
Personnel: Richard Lodge (Ed. in Chief); Meghan Kelly (Digital Ed.); Art Davidson (Sports Ed.); Kathleen Cordeiro (Adv. Dir.)
Parent company (for newspapers): Community Newspaper Co.-West-OOB; CherryRoad Media

MARSHFIELD MARINER

Street address 1: 600 Cordwainer Drive
Street address city: Norwell
Street address state: MA
Zip/Postal code: 02061
General Phone: (781) 837-4500
General Fax: (781) 837-4540
General/National Adv. E-mail: ccrimmins@wickedlocal.com
Display Adv. E-mail: classifieds@wickedlocal.com
Editorial e-mail: mburridge@wickedlocal.com
Primary Website: wickedlocal.com/marshfield
Avg Paid Circ: 2409
Avg Free Circ: 142
Audit By: AAM
Audit Date: 31.03.2018
Personnel: Mark Olivieri (Pub.); Mark Burridge (Print Ed.); Gregory Mathis (Regional Director of News & Operations); Michael Kane (Dep. Dir. Multimedia); Crissy Crimmins (Adv. Sales); Chris Avis (Adv. Mgr.)
Parent company (for newspapers): CherryRoad Media

MASSACHUSETTS LAWYERS WEEKLY

Street address 1: 40 Court Street
Street address 2: 5th Floor
Street address city: Boston
Street address state: MA
Zip/Postal code: 02108
General Phone: (617) 451-7300
Advertising Phone: (617) 451-7300
Editorial Phone: (617) 451-7300
Display Adv. E-mail: sziegler@lawyersweekly.com
Editorial e-mail: hcampagne@lawyersweekly.com.
Primary Website: masslawyersweekly.com
Year Established: 1972
Audit By: Sworn/Estimate/Non-Audited
Audit Date: 10.06.2019
Personnel: Susan Bocamazo (Pub.); Henriette Campagne (Ed.); Charlene Smith (Ad. Dir)

MATTAPAN REPORTER

Street address 1: 150 Mount Vernon St
Street address 2: Ste 120
Street address city: Dorchester
Street address state: MA
Zip/Postal code: 02125-3135
General Phone: (617) 436-1222
General Fax: (617) 825-5516
Advertising Phone: (617) 436-1222
Advertising Fax: (617) 825-5516
Editorial Phone: (617) 436-1222
Editorial Fax: (617) 825-5516
General/National Adv. E-mail: addesk@dotnews.com
Display Adv. E-mail: addesk@dotnews.com
Editorial e-mail: newseditor@dotnews.com
Primary Website: dotnews.com/mattapan
Year Established: 1983
Audit By: Sworn/Estimate/Non-Audited
Audit Date: 10.06.2019
Personnel: Edward Forrey (Pub.); William Forry (Ed.); Jack Conboy (Ad. Director); Barbara Langis (Prod. Mgr.)
Parent company (for newspapers): Boston Neighborhood News, Inc.

MEDFIELD PRESS

Street address 1: 1 Speen St.
Street address 2: Ste 200
Street address city: Framingham
Street address state: MA
Zip/Postal code: 01701
General Phone: (781) 433-6700
General/National Adv. E-mail: medfield@wickedlocal.com
Display Adv. E-mail: classifieds@wickedlocal.com
Editorial e-mail: medfield@wickedlocal.com
Primary Website: wickedlocal.com/medfield
Avg Paid Circ: 491
Avg Free Circ: 0
Audit By: AAM
Audit Date: 31.03.2018
Personnel: Chuck Goodrich (Pub.); Max Bowen (Ed.); Kathleen Cordeiro (Adv. Dir.)
Parent company (for newspapers): CherryRoad Media

MEDFORD TRANSCRIPT

Street address 1: 75 Sylvan St
Street address 2: Ste C105
Street address city: Danvers
Street address state: MA
Zip/Postal code: 01923-2765
General Phone: (781) 396-1982
General Fax: (781) 393-1821
Advertising Phone: (978) 739-1350
Advertising Fax: (781) 393-1821
Editorial Phone: (781) 396-1982
Editorial Fax: (781) 393-1821
General/National Adv. E-mail: ameltzer@wickedlocal.com
Display Adv. E-mail: salesteam@wickedlocal.com
Editorial e-mail: medford@wickedlocal.com
Primary Website: wickedlocal.com/medford
Avg Paid Circ: 2036
Avg Free Circ: 0
Audit By: AAM
Audit Date: 31.03.2018
Personnel: Charles Goodrich (Pub.); Pete Chianca (Ed. in Chief); Nell Escobar-Coakley (Ed.); Chris Hurley (Sports Ed.); Kathleen Cordeiro (Adv. Dir.)
Parent company (for newspapers): CherryRoad Media

MELROSE FREE PRESS

Street address 1: 75 Sylvan St
Street address 2: Ste C105
Street address city: Danvers
Street address state: MA
Zip/Postal code: 01923-2765
General Phone: (978) 739-1314
General Fax: (978) 739-8501
Advertising Phone: (978) 739-1350
Advertising Fax: (978) 739-1391
Editorial Phone: (978) 739-1314
Editorial Fax: (978) 739-8501
General/National Adv. E-mail: thosker@wickedlocal.com
Display Adv. E-mail: classifieds@wickedlocal.com
Editorial e-mail: pchianca@wickedlocal.com
Primary Website: melrose.wickedlocal.com
Year Established: 1901
Avg Paid Circ: 1372
Audit By: AAM
Audit Date: 31.03.2018
Personnel: Chuck Goodrich (Pub.); Pete Chianca (Ed.-in-Chief); Nell Escobar Coakley (Mng. Ed.); Kathleen Cordeiro (Adv. Dir.)
Parent company (for newspapers): CherryRoad Media

MIDDLEBORO GAZETTE

Street address 1: 148 W Grove St
Street address city: Middleboro
Street address state: MA
Zip/Postal code: 02346-1457
General Phone: (508) 947-1760
General Fax: (508) 947-9426
General/National Adv. E-mail: news@gazettenewsonline.com
Editorial e-mail: editor@gazattenewsonline.com
Primary Website: southcoasttoday.com
Year Established: 1852
Avg Paid Circ: 4802
Avg Free Circ: 184
Audit By: Sworn/Estimate/Non-Audited
Audit Date: 10.06.2019
Personnel: Mary-Ann Cole (Adv. Rep.); Jane Lopes (Ed.); April Belanger (Office manager); Susan Duff (Circ. Mgr.)
Parent company (for newspapers): Dow Jones Local Media Group-OOB

MILLBURY-SUTTON CHRONICLE

Street address 1: 101 Water St
Street address city: Worcester
Street address state: MA
Zip/Postal code: 01604-5033
General Phone: (508) 749-3164
General Fax: (508) 865-7979
Advertising Phone: (508) 749-3164
Advertising Fax: (508) 865-7979
Editorial Phone: (508) 749-3164
Editorial Fax: (508) 865-7979
General/National Adv. E-mail: sales@millburysutton.com
Display Adv. E-mail: sales@centralmassclass.com
Editorial e-mail: editor@millburysutton.com
Primary Website: millburysutton.com
Audit By: Sworn/Estimate/Non-Audited
Audit Date: 10.06.2019
Personnel: Joshua Farnsworth (Ed.); Rebecca White (Ad. Exec.)

MILTON TIMES

Street address 1: 372 Granite Ave
Street address 2: Ste 6
Street address city: Milton
Street address state: MA
Zip/Postal code: 02186
General Phone: (617) 696-7758
Advertising Phone: (617) 696-7758
Advertising Fax: (617) 696-3681
Editorial Phone: (617) 696-7758
General/National Adv. E-mail: Ads@miltontimes.com
Display Adv. E-mail: ads@miltontimes.com
Editorial e-mail: editor@miltontimes.com
Primary Website: miltontimes.com
Mthly Avg Views: 25000
Mthly Avg Unique Visitors: 9000
Year Established: 1995
Avg Paid Circ: 4600
Audit By: USPS
Audit Date: 10.10.2023
Personnel: Nadine Leary (Ad. Director); Genevieve Santilli (Editor); Pat Desmond (Publisher); Karen Wilkinson (circulation manager); Douglas Scibeck (Editor)

NANTUCKET TODAY

Street address 1: 1 Old South Rd
Street address city: Nantucket
Street address state: MA
Zip/Postal code: 02554-2836
General Phone: (508) 228-0001
General Fax: (508) 325-5089
Primary Website: nantuckettodayonline.com
Audit By: Sworn/Estimate/Non-Audited
Audit Date: 10.06.2019
Personnel: Kevin Stanton (Circ.)
Parent company (for newspapers): Dow Jones Local Media Group-OOB

NASHOBA VALLEY VOICE

Street address 1: 491 Dutton St
Street address city: Lowell
Street address state: MA
Zip/Postal code: 01854-4290
General Phone: (978) 459-1300
General Fax: (978) 970-4891
General/National Adv. E-mail: enajeeullah@mediaonene.com
Editorial e-mail: jpaluzzi@nashobavalleyvoice.com
Primary Website: nashobavalleyvoice.com
Year Established: 2015
Avg Paid Circ: 3500
Avg Free Circ: 15000
Audit By: Sworn/Estimate/Non-Audited
Audit Date: 10.06.2019
Personnel: Mike Sheehan (Vice Pres. Circ.); Kevin Corrado (Pub.); Eddie Najeeullah (Reg. Dir. of Adv.)
Parent company (for newspapers): MediaNews Group

NATICK BULLETIN & TAB

Street address 1: 33 New York Ave
Street address city: Framingham
Street address state: MA
Zip/Postal code: 01701-8857
General Phone: (508) 626-4437
General Fax: (508) 626-4400
Advertising Phone: (781) 433-6930
Advertising Fax: (781) 433-7951
Editorial Phone: (866) 746-8603
Editorial Fax: (508) 626-4400
General/National Adv. E-mail: crobinso@wickedlocal.com
Display Adv. E-mail: salesteam@wickedlocal.com
Editorial e-mail: natick@wickedlocal.com
Primary Website: wickedlocal.com/natick
Year Established: 1986
Avg Paid Circ: 4696
Audit By: Sworn/Estimate/Non-Audited
Audit Date: 10.06.2019
Personnel: Richard Lodge (Ed. in Chief); Kathleen Cordeiro (Adv. Dir.)
Parent company (for newspapers): CherryRoad Media

NEEDHAM TIMES

Street address 1: 254 2nd Ave
Street address 2: Ste 1
Street address city: Needham
Street address state: MA
Zip/Postal code: 02494-2829
General Phone: (781) 433-6905
General Fax: (781) 433-8202
Advertising Phone: (781) 433-8313
Advertising Fax: (781) 433-8202
Editorial Phone: (781) 433-8366
Editorial Fax: (781) 433-8202
General/National Adv. E-mail: cwarren@wickedlocal.com
Display Adv. E-mail: salesteam@wickedlocal.com
Editorial e-mail: vzic@wickedlocal.com

Primary Website: wickedlocal.com/needham
Year Established: 1874
Avg Free Circ: 9687
Audit By: AAM
Audit Date: 31.03.2018
Personnel: Chuck Goodrich (Pub.); Valentina Zic (Ed.); Wei-Huan Chen (Reporter); Kathleen Cordeiro (Adv. Dir.)
Parent company (for newspapers): CherryRoad Media

NEWBURYPORT CURRENT

Street address 1: 75 Sylvan St
Street address 2: Ste C105
Street address city: Danvers
Street address state: MA
Zip/Postal code: 01923-2765
General Phone: (978) 739-1331
General Fax: (978) 739-8501
Advertising Phone: (978) 739-1350
Advertising Fax: (978) 739-8501
Editorial Phone: (978) 739-1331
Editorial Fax: (978) 739-8501
General/National Adv. E-mail: ameltzer@wickedlocal.com
Display Adv. E-mail: salesteam@wickedlocal.com
Editorial e-mail: newburyport@wickedlocal.com
Primary Website: wickedlocal.com/newburyport
Avg Free Circ: 7428
Audit By: Sworn/Estimate/Non-Audited
Audit Date: 10.06.2019
Personnel: Chuck Goodrich (Pub.); Pete Chianca (Ed. in Chief); John Lockwood (Ed.); Janet Mackay-Smith (ed.); Kathleen Cordeiro (Adv. Dir.)
Parent company (for newspapers): Community Newspaper Co.-North-OOB; CherryRoad Media

NEWTON TAB

Street address 1: 1 Speen St.
Street address city: Framingham
Street address state: MA
Zip/Postal code: 01701
General Phone: (781) 433-6700
General/National Adv. E-mail: jmann@wickedlocal.com
Display Adv. E-mail: classifieds@wickedlocal.com
Editorial e-mail: kcordeiro@wickedlocal.com
Primary Website: wickedlocal.com/newton
Avg Free Circ: 27884
Audit By: AAM
Audit Date: 31.03.2018
Personnel: Chuck Goodrich (Pub.); Kathleen Cordeiro (News Dir.); Jenn Mann (Adv.)
Parent company (for newspapers): CherryRoad Media

NORTH ANDOVER CITIZEN

Street address 1: 75 Sylvan St
Street address 2: Ste C105
Street address city: Danvers
Street address state: MA
Zip/Postal code: 01923-2765
General Phone: (978) 739-1300
General Fax: (978) 739-8501
Advertising Phone: (978) 739-1350
Advertising Fax: (978) 739-8501
Editorial Phone: (978) 739-1320
Editorial Fax: (978) 739-8501
General/National Adv. E-mail: ameltzer@wickedlocal.com
Display Adv. E-mail: salesteam@wickedlocal.com
Editorial e-mail: northandover@wickedlocal.com
Primary Website: wickedlocal.com/northandover
Avg Paid Circ: 513
Avg Free Circ: 0
Audit By: AAM
Audit Date: 31.03.2018
Personnel: Chuck Goodrich (Pub.); Pete Chianca (Ed. in Chief); Tim McCarthy (Ed.); Joe McConnel (Sports Ed.); Kathleen Cordeiro (Adv. Dir.)
Parent company (for newspapers): CherryRoad Media

NORTH ATTLEBORO FREE PRESS

Street address 1: 31 N Washington St
Street address 2: Unit 7
Street address city: North Attleboro
Street address state: MA
Zip/Postal code: 02760-1650
General Phone: (508) 699-6755
General Fax: (508) 699-8545
Advertising Phone: (508) 699-6755
Advertising Fax: (508) 699-8545
Editorial Phone: (508) 699-6755
Editorial Fax: (508) 699-8545
General/National Adv. E-mail: ads@nafreepress.com
Display Adv. E-mail: ads@nafreepress.com
Editorial e-mail: news@nafreepress.com
Primary Website: wickedlocal.com/northattleborough
Year Established: 1987
Avg Free Circ: 16993
Audit By: Sworn/Estimate/Non-Audited
Audit Date: 10.06.2019
Personnel: Peter Cox (Ed.); Jim Orourke (Pub.); John Andre (Ed.); Kathleen Cordeiro (Adv. Dir.)

NORTH READING TRANSCRIPT

Street address 1: 26 Albion St
Street address city: Wakefield
Street address state: MA
Zip/Postal code: 01880-2803
General Phone: (781)245-0080
General Fax: (781) 246-0061
Advertising Phone: (781)245-0080
Advertising Fax: (781) 246-0061
Editorial Phone: (781)245-0080
Editorial Fax: (781) 246-0061
General/National Adv. E-mail: ads@wakefielditem.com
Display Adv. E-mail: ads@wakefielditem.com
Editorial e-mail: nrtranscript@rcn.com
Year Established: 1956
Avg Paid Circ: 4000
Avg Free Circ: 290
Audit By: Sworn/Estimate/Non-Audited
Audit Date: 10.06.2019
Personnel: Robert Turosz (Ed.); Phil Solmonson (Adv. Dir.); Bob Burgess
Parent company (for newspapers): Wakefield Item

NORTH SHORE SUNDAY

Street address 1: 75 Sylvan St
Street address 2: Ste C105
Street address city: Danvers
Street address state: MA
Zip/Postal code: 01923-2765
General Phone: (978) 739-1347
General Fax: (978) 739-8501
Advertising Phone: (978) 739-1350
Advertising Fax: (978) 739-8501
Editorial Phone: (978) 739-1347
Editorial Fax: (978) 739-8501
General/National Adv. E-mail: ameltzer@wickedlocal.com
Display Adv. E-mail: dwinder@wickedlocal.com
Editorial e-mail: northshore@wickedlocal.com
Primary Website: wickedlocal.com/northofboston
Avg Free Circ: 18168
Audit By: Sworn/Estimate/Non-Audited
Audit Date: 10.06.2019
Personnel: Chuck Goodrich (Pub.); Pete Chianca (Ed. in Chief); Janet Mackay-Smith (Mng. Ed.); Kathleen Cordeiro (Adv. Dir.)
Parent company (for newspapers): Community Newspaper Co.-North-OOB; CherryRoad Media

NORTON MIRROR

Street address 1: 370 Paramount Dr
Street address 2: Ste 3
Street address city: Raynham
Street address state: MA
Zip/Postal code: 02767-5419
General Phone: (508) 967-3510
General Fax: (508) 967-3501
Advertising Phone: (508) 967-3510
Advertising Fax: (508) 967-3501
Editorial Phone: (508) 967-4593
Editorial Fax: (508) 967-3501
General/National Adv. E-mail: msutherland@wickedlocal.com
Display Adv. E-mail: rbright@wickedllocal.com
Editorial e-mail: acoyle@wickedlocal.com
Primary Website: wickedlocal.com/norton
Year Established: 1987
Avg Paid Circ: 721
Audit By: Sworn/Estimate/Non-Audited
Audit Date: 10.06.2019
Personnel: Mark Olivieri (Pub.); Alice Coyle (Ed.); Kathleen Cordeiro (Adv. Dir.)
Parent company (for newspapers): Community Newspaper Co.-West-OOB; CherryRoad Media

NORWELL MARINER

Street address 1: 165 Enterprise Dr
Street address city: Marshfield
Street address state: MA
Zip/Postal code: 02050-2132
General Phone: (781) 837-3500
General Fax: (781) 837-4543
Advertising Phone: (781) 837-3500
Advertising Fax: (781) 837-4543
Editorial Phone: (781) 837-3500
Editorial Fax: (781) 837-4543
General/National Adv. E-mail: srussell@wickedlocal.com
Display Adv. E-mail: salesteam@wickedlocal.com
Editorial e-mail: molivieri@wickedlocal.com
Primary Website: wickedlocal.com/norwell
Year Established: 1974
Avg Paid Circ: 962
Avg Free Circ: 0
Audit By: AAM
Audit Date: 31.03.2018
Personnel: Gregory Mathis (Ed. in Chief); Erin Tiernan (Editor); Kathleen Cordeiro (Adv. Dir.)
Parent company (for newspapers): CherryRoad Media

NORWOOD TRANSCRIPT & BULLETIN

Street address 1: 254 2nd Ave
Street address city: Needham
Street address state: MA
Zip/Postal code: 02494-2829
General Phone: (781) 433-8322
General Fax: (781) 433-8375
Advertising Phone: (781) 433-8313
Advertising Fax: (781) 433-8375
Editorial Phone: (781) 433-8322
Editorial Fax: (781) 433-8375
General/National Adv. E-mail: ageisinger@wickedlocal.com
Display Adv. E-mail: salesteam@wickedlocal.com
Editorial e-mail: psalisbury@wickedlocal.com
Primary Website: wickedlocal.com/norwood
Avg Paid Circ: 628
Avg Free Circ: 0
Audit By: AAM
Audit Date: 31.03.2018
Personnel: Chuck Goodrich (Pub.); Phil Salisbury (Ed.); Kathleen Cordeiro (Adv. Dir.)
Parent company (for newspapers): CherryRoad Media

OLD COLONY MEMORIAL

Street address 1: 182 Standish Ave
Street address city: Plymouth
Street address state: MA
Zip/Postal code: 02360-4162
General Phone: (508) 591-6623
General/National Adv. E-mail: salesteam@wickedlocal.com
Display Adv. E-mail: salesteam@wickedlocal.com
Editorial e-mail: scsmith@wickedlocal.com
Primary Website: wickedlocal.com/plymouth
Avg Paid Circ: 4572
Avg Free Circ: 22
Audit By: Sworn/Estimate/Non-Audited
Audit Date: 10.06.2019
Personnel: Sarah Carr (News Sub.); Emily Clark (News Coverage); Gregory Mathis (Reg. Dir. News and Ops.); Mark Olivieri (Group Pub.); Michael Spellman (Adv. Dir.); Chris Avis (Adv. Mgr.)
Parent company (for newspapers): CherryRoad Media

PEMBROKE MARINER & EXPRESS

Street address 1: 165 Enterprise Dr
Street address city: Marshfield
Street address state: MA
Zip/Postal code: 02050-2132
General Phone: (781) 837-4500
General Fax: (781) 837-4540
General/National Adv. E-mail: pembroke@cnc.com
Editorial e-mail: gmathis@wickedlocal.com
Primary Website: wickedlocal.com/pembroke
Year Established: 1983
Avg Paid Circ: 1275
Audit By: Sworn/Estimate/Non-Audited
Audit Date: 10.06.2019
Personnel: Mark Olivieri (Pub.); Kathleen Cordeiro (Adv. Dir.)
Parent company (for newspapers): Community Newspaper Co. - South; CherryRoad Media

PEPPERELL FREE PRESS

Street address 1: 78 Barnum Rd
Street address city: Devens
Street address state: MA
Zip/Postal code: 01434-3508
General Phone: (978) 772-0777
General Fax: (978) 772-4012
Advertising Phone: (978) 772-0777
Advertising Fax: (978) 772-4012
Editorial Phone: (978) 772-0777
Editorial Fax: (978) 772-4012
General/National Adv. E-mail: hconry@mediaonene.com
Display Adv. E-mail: Advertising@MediaOneMarketPlace.com
Editorial e-mail: editor@nashobapub.com
Primary Website: pepperellfreepress.com
Year Established: 1869
Avg Paid Circ: 1023
Audit By: Sworn/Estimate/Non-Audited
Audit Date: 10.06.2019
Personnel: Rebecca Pellerin (Office Coord.); Mike Sheehan (Circ. Mgr.); Kate King (Mng. Ed.); Ed Niser (Sports Ed.); Bill Walker (Opns. Dir.); Larry Hubner (Pub.)

PLYMPTON-HALIFAX EXPRESS

Street address 1: PO Box 60
Street address 2: 1000 Main Street
Street address city: Hanson
Street address state: MA
Zip/Postal code: 02341-0060
General Phone: (781) 293-0420
General Fax: (781) 293-0421
General/National Adv. E-mail: ads@whphexpress.com
Display Adv. E-mail: ads@whphexpress.com
Editorial e-mail: editor@whphexpress.com
Primary Website: plymptonhalifaxexpress.com
Year Established: 2014
Avg Paid Circ: 528
Avg Free Circ: 23
Audit By: Sworn/Estimate/Non-Audited
Audit Date: 10.06.2019
Personnel: Deborah Anderson (Pub); Tracey Seelye (Ed.)
Parent company (for newspapers): Anderson Newspapers, Inc., d/b/a Express Newspapers

PROVINCETOWN BANNER

Street address 1: P.O. Box 977
Street address city: Provincetown
Street address state: MA
Zip/Postal code: 02657
General Phone: (508) 487-7400
General Fax: (508) 487-7144
General/National Adv. E-mail: sales@provincetownbanner.com
Display Adv. E-mail: classsub@provincetownbanner.com
Editorial e-mail: ppronovost@capecodonline.com
Primary Website: wickedlocal.com/provincetown
Year Established: 1995
Avg Paid Circ: 3199
Avg Free Circ: 316
Audit By: AAM
Audit Date: 31.03.2018
Personnel: Peter Meyer (Pub.); Paul Pronovost (Ed.-in-Chief); K.C. Meyers (Ed.); Molly Evans (Adv./Sales)
Parent company (for newspapers): CherryRoad Media

QUABOAG CURRENT

Street address 1: 80 Main St
Street address city: Ware
Street address state: MA
Zip/Postal code: 01082-1318
General Phone: (413) 967-3505
General Fax: (413) 967-6009
Advertising Phone: (413) 967-3505
Advertising Fax: (413) 967-6009
Editorial Phone: (413) 967-3505
Editorial Fax: (413) 967-6009
General/National Adv. E-mail: bbaker@turley.com
Display Adv. E-mail: classifieds@turley.com
Editorial e-mail: tkane@turley.com

Primary Website: quaboagcurrent.com
Audit By: Sworn/Estimate/Non-Audited
Audit Date: 10.06.2019
Personnel: Tim Kane (Ed.); Beth Baker (Ad. Director)

RANDOLPH HERALD

Street address 1: 15 Pacella Park Dr
Street address city: Randolph
Street address state: MA
Zip/Postal code: 02368-1772
General Phone: (508) 967-3515
General Fax: (508) 967-3501
Advertising Phone: (781) 837-4591
Advertising Fax: (508) 967-3501
Editorial Phone: (508) 967-3505
Editorial Fax: (508) 967-3501
General/National Adv. E-mail: ccrimmins@wickedlocal.com
Display Adv. E-mail: ccrimmins@wickedlocal.com
Editorial e-mail: gmathis@wickedlocal.com
Primary Website: wickedlocal.com/randolph
Year Established: 1924
Avg Paid Circ: 107
Avg Free Circ: 2513
Audit By: AAM
Audit Date: 31.03.2018
Personnel: Mark Olivieri (Pub.); Beth Doyle (Ed.); Gregory Mathis (News Dir.); Crissy Crimmons (Adv.)
Parent company (for newspapers): CherryRoad Media

READING ADVOCATE

Street address 1: 48 Dunham Road
Street address 2: Suite 3100
Street address city: Danvers
Street address state: MA
Zip/Postal code: 01915
General Phone: (781) 942-2252
General Fax: (978) 371-5214
Advertising Phone: (978) 739-1320
Advertising Fax: (978) 739-1391
General/National Adv. E-mail: rmurphy@wickedlocal.com
Display Adv. E-mail: classifieds@wickedlocal.com
Editorial e-mail: pchianca@wickedlocal.com
Primary Website: reading.wickedlocal.com
Avg Paid Circ: 520
Audit By: AAM
Audit Date: 31.03.2018
Personnel: Chuck Goodrich (Pub.); Pete Chianca (Ed. in Chief); Steve Ryan (Ed.); Kathleen Cordeiro (Adv. Dir.)
Parent company (for newspapers): CherryRoad Media

REMINDER METROWEST / CHICOPEE HERALD

Street address 1: 280 N Main St
Street address city: East Longmeadow
Street address state: MA
Zip/Postal code: 01028-1868
General Phone: (413) 525-3247
General Fax: (413) 525-5882
Advertising Phone: (413) 525-3247
Advertising Fax: (413) 525-5882
Editorial Phone: (413) 525-3247
Editorial Fax: (413) 525-5882
General/National Adv. E-mail: marketing@reminderpublications.com
Display Adv. E-mail: marketing@reminderpublications.com
Editorial e-mail: news@reminderpublications.com
Primary Website: thereminder.com
Year Established: 1962
Avg Paid Circ: 2
Avg Free Circ: 8926
Audit By: Sworn/Estimate/Non-Audited
Audit Date: 10.06.2019
Personnel: Christopher Buendo (Pub.); Daniel Buendo (Co-Pub.); Barbara Perry (Adv. Mgr.); Holly Mulligan (Circ. Mgr.); Michael Dobbs (Editorial Mgr.); Beth Thurber (Prodn. Mgr.)
Parent company (for newspapers): Reminder Publications

RHODE ISLAND LAWYERS WEEKLY

Street address 1: 10 Milk St
Street address 2: Ste 1000
Street address city: Boston
Street address state: MA
Zip/Postal code: 02108-4620
General Phone: (617) 451-7300
General Fax: (617) 451-7324
Advertising Phone: (617) 451-7300
Advertising Fax: (617) 451-7324
Editorial Phone: (617) 451-7300
Editorial Fax: (617) 451-7324
General/National Adv. E-mail: charlene.smith@lawyersweekly.com
Display Adv. E-mail: charlene.smith@lawyersweekly.com
Editorial e-mail: henriette.campagne@lawyersweekly.com
Primary Website: rilawyersweekly.com
Audit By: Sworn/Estimate/Non-Audited
Audit Date: 10.06.2019
Personnel: Henriette Campagne (Ed.); Charlene Smith (Ad. Director); Susan Bocamazo (Pub)

ROCKLAND STANDARD

Street address 1: 165 Enterprise Dr
Street address city: Marshfield
Street address state: MA
Zip/Postal code: 02050-2132
General Phone: (781) 837-3500
General Fax: (781) 837-4543
Advertising Phone: (781) 837-4519
Advertising Fax: (781) 837-4543
Editorial Phone: (781) 837-4560
Editorial Fax: (781) 837-4543
General/National Adv. E-mail: coliver@wickedlocal.com
Display Adv. E-mail: salesteam@wickedlocal.com
Editorial e-mail: gmathis@wickedlocal.com
Primary Website: wickedlocal.com/rockland
Avg Free Circ: 1064
Audit By: Sworn/Estimate/Non-Audited
Audit Date: 10.06.2019
Personnel: Mark Olivieri (Pub.); Seth Jacobson (Ed.); Gregory Mathis (Ed. in Chief); Kathleen Cordeiro (Adv. Dir.)
Parent company (for newspapers): Community Newspaper Co. - South; CherryRoad Media

ROSLINDALE TRANSCRIPT

Street address 1: 1 Speen St.
Street address city: Framingham
Street address state: MA
Zip/Postal code: 01701
General Phone: (781) 433-6700
General/National Adv. E-mail: jmann@wickedlocal.com
Display Adv. E-mail: classifieds@wickedlocal.com
Editorial e-mail: kcordeiro@wickedlocal.com
Primary Website: wickedlocal.com/roslindale
Avg Paid Circ: 191
Audit By: AAM
Audit Date: 31.03.2018
Personnel: Kathleen Cordeiro (News Dir.); Jenn Mann (Adv.)
Parent company (for newspapers): CherryRoad Media

SALEM GAZETTE

Street address 1: 75 Sylvan St
Street address 2: Ste C105
Street address city: Danvers
Street address state: MA
Zip/Postal code: 01923-2765
General Phone: (978) 739-1312
General Fax: (978) 739-8501
Advertising Phone: (978) 739-1350
Advertising Fax: (978) 739-8501
Editorial Phone: (978) 739-1312
Editorial Fax: (978) 739-8501
General/National Adv. E-mail: ameltzer@wickedlocal.com
Display Adv. E-mail: salesteam@wickedlocal.com
Editorial e-mail: salem@wickedlocal.com
Primary Website: wickedlocal.com/salem
Audit By: Sworn/Estimate/Non-Audited
Audit Date: 10.06.2019
Personnel: Pete Chianca (Ed.-in-Chief); Janet Mackay-Smith (Managing Ed.); Kathleen Cordeiro (Adv. Dir.)
Parent company (for newspapers): Community Newspaper Co.-North-OOB; CherryRoad Media

SANDWICH BROADSIDER

Street address 1: 923 Route 6A
Street address 2: Unit G
Street address city: Yarmouth Port
Street address state: MA
Zip/Postal code: 02675-2159
General Phone: (508) 375-4947
General Fax: (508) 375-4903
Advertising Phone: (508) 375-4928
Advertising Fax: (508) 375-4903
Editorial Phone: (508) 375-4945
Editorial Fax: (508) 375-4903
Display Adv. E-mail: salesteam@wickedlocal.com
Editorial e-mail: jbasile@wickedlocal.com
Primary Website: wickedlocal.com/sandwich
Year Established: 2007
Avg Paid Circ: 2332
Audit By: Sworn/Estimate/Non-Audited
Audit Date: 10.06.2019
Personnel: Carol Dumas (Senior Managing Ed.); Kathleen Cordeiro (Adv. Dir.)
Parent company (for newspapers): Community Newspaper Co. - South; CherryRoad Media

SAUGUS ADVERTISER

Street address 1: 75 Sylvan St
Street address 2: Ste C
Street address city: Danvers
Street address state: MA
Zip/Postal code: 01923-2763
General Phone: (978) 739-1395
General Fax: (978) 739-8501
Display Adv. E-mail: classifieds@wickedlocal.com
Editorial e-mail: pchianca@wickedlocal.com
Primary Website: saugus.wickedlocal.com
Avg Paid Circ: 1362
Audit By: AAM
Audit Date: 31.03.2018
Personnel: Chuck Goodrich (Pub.); Pete Chianca (Ed. in Chief); Michael Gaffney (Ed.); Joe McConnell (Sports Ed.); Nell Escobar Coakley (Mng. Ed.)
Parent company (for newspapers): CherryRoad Media

SCITUATE MARINER

Street address 1: 165 Enterprise Dr
Street address city: Marshfield
Street address state: MA
Zip/Postal code: 02050-2132
General Phone: (781) 837-3500
General Fax: (781) 837-4543
Advertising Phone: (781) 837-4519
Advertising Fax: (781) 837-4543
Editorial Phone: (781) 837-4560
Editorial Fax: (781) 837-4543
General/National Adv. E-mail: coliver@wickedlocal.com
Display Adv. E-mail: salesteam@wickedlocal.com
Editorial e-mail: gmathis@wickedlocal.com
Primary Website: wickedlocal.com/scituate
Avg Paid Circ: 2088
Avg Free Circ: 211
Audit By: AAM
Audit Date: 31.03.2018
Personnel: Gregory Mathis (Ed. in Chief); Kathleen Cordeiro (Adv. Dir.)
Parent company (for newspapers): CherryRoad Media

SHARON ADVOCATE

Street address 1: 254 2nd Ave
Street address city: Needham
Street address state: MA
Zip/Postal code: 02494-2829
General Phone: (781) 784-1487
General Fax: (781) 433-8375
Advertising Phone: (781) 433-8313
Advertising Fax: (781) 433-8375
Editorial Phone: (781) 433-8325
Editorial Fax: (781) 433-8375
General/National Adv. E-mail: cwarren@wickedlocal.com
Display Adv. E-mail: salesteam@wickedlocal.com
Editorial e-mail: wbraverman@wickedlocal.com
Primary Website: wickedlocal.com/sharon
Avg Paid Circ: 215
Audit By: AAM
Audit Date: 31.12.2017
Personnel: Chuck Goodrich (Pub.); Jesse Floyd (Ed. in Chief); Wayne Braverman (Mng. Ed.); Kathleen Cordeiro (Adv. Dir.)
Parent company (for newspapers): CherryRoad Media

SHIRLEY ORACLE

Street address 1: 78 Barnum Rd
Street address city: Devens
Street address state: MA
Zip/Postal code: 01434-3508
General Phone: (978) 772-0777
General Fax: (978) 772-4012
Advertising Phone: (978) 772-0777
Advertising Fax: (978) 772-4012
Editorial Phone: (978) 772-0777
Editorial Fax: (978) 772-4012
General/National Adv. E-mail: advertising@mediaonemarketplace.com
Display Adv. E-mail: advertising@mediaonemarketplace.com
Editorial e-mail: editor@nashobapub.com
Primary Website: shirleyoracle.com
Avg Paid Circ: 278
Audit By: Sworn/Estimate/Non-Audited
Audit Date: 10.06.2019
Personnel: Mark O'Neil (Pub.); Rebecca Pellerin (Office Coord.); Mike Sheehan (Circ. Mgr.); Kate King (Mng. Ed.); Ed Niser (Sports Ed.); Bill Walker (Opns. Dir.)

SHREWSBURY CHRONICLE

Street address 1: 1 Speen St.
Street address city: Framingham
Street address state: MA
Zip/Postal code: 01701
General Phone: (508) 626-3800
General/National Adv. E-mail: ccrimmins@wickedlocal.com
Display Adv. E-mail: classifieds@wickedlocal.com
Editorial e-mail: abrennan@wickedlocal.com
Primary Website: wickedlocal.com/shrewsbury
Avg Paid Circ: 1904
Avg Free Circ: 2146
Audit By: AAM
Audit Date: 31.03.2018
Personnel: Anne Brennan (Ed-In-Chief); Sandy Meindersma (News Dir.); Crissy Crimmons (Adv.)
Parent company (for newspapers): CherryRoad Media

SOMERVILLE JOURNAL

Street address 1: 48 Dunham Road
Street address 2: Suite 3100
Street address city: Beverly
Street address state: MA
Zip/Postal code: 01915
General Phone: (617) 433-6700
General/National Adv. E-mail: jmann@wickedlocal.com
Display Adv. E-mail: classifieds@wickedlocal.com
Editorial e-mail: pchianca@wickedlocal.com
Primary Website: wickedlocal.com/somerville
Year Established: 1870
Avg Paid Circ: 1085
Audit By: AAM
Audit Date: 31.03.2018
Personnel: Chuck Goodrich (Pub.); Peter Chianca (News Dir.); Jenn Mann (Adv.)
Parent company (for newspapers): CherryRoad Media

SOUTHWICK SUFFIELD NEWS

Street address 1: 23 Southwick St
Street address city: Feeding Hills
Street address state: MA
Zip/Postal code: 01030-2023
General Phone: (413) 786-7747
General Fax: (413) 786-8457
Advertising Phone: (413) 786-7747
Advertising Fax: (413) 786-8457
Editorial Phone: (413) 786-7747
Editorial Fax: (413) 786-8457
General/National Adv. E-mail: bbaker@turley.com
Display Adv. E-mail: classifieds@turley.com
Editorial e-mail: tkane@turley.com
Primary Website: southwicknewsonline.com
Year Established: 1967
Avg Free Circ: 9000
Audit By: Sworn/Estimate/Non-Audited
Audit Date: 10.06.2019
Personnel: Tim Kane (Ed.); Patrick H. Turley (Pub.); Kathleen Cordeiro (Adv. Dir.)

Parent company (for newspapers): Turley Publications, Inc.

SPENCER NEW LEADER

Street address 1: 25 Elm St
Street address city: Southbridge
Street address state: MA
Zip/Postal code: 01550-2605
General Phone: (508) 764-4325
General Fax: (508) 764-8015
Advertising Phone: (508) 764-4325
Advertising Fax: (508) 764-8015
Editorial Phone: (508) 764-4325
Editorial Fax: (508) 764-8015
General/National Adv. E-mail: frank@stonebridgepress.com
Display Adv. E-mail: classifieds@stonebridgepress.com
Editorial e-mail: aminor@stonebridgepress.com
Primary Website: spencernewleader.com
Avg Free Circ: 17200
Audit By: Sworn/Estimate/Non-Audited
Audit Date: 10.06.2019
Personnel: Frank Chilinski (President & Publisher); Jean Ashton (Adv. Dir.)
Parent company (for newspapers): Stonebridge Press, Inc.

SPRINGFIELD REMINDER

Street address 1: 280 N Main St
Street address city: East Longmeadow
Street address state: MA
Zip/Postal code: 01028-1868
General Phone: (413) 525-3247
General Fax: (413) 525-5882
Advertising Phone: (413) 525-3247
Advertising Fax: (413) 525-5882
Editorial Phone: (413) 525-3247
Editorial Fax: (413) 525-5882
General/National Adv. E-mail: marketing@reminderpublications.com
Display Adv. E-mail: marketing@reminderpublications.com
Editorial e-mail: news@reminderpublications.com
Primary Website: thereminder.com
Year Established: 1962
Avg Paid Circ: 2
Avg Free Circ: 5931
Audit By: Sworn/Estimate/Non-Audited
Audit Date: 10.06.2019
Personnel: Christopher Buendo (Pub.); Daniel Buendo (Co-Pub.); Michael Dobbs (Editorial Mgr.); Beth Thurber (Prodn. Mgr.); Doug Fabian (Adv. Dir.); Gail Breton (Circ. Mgr.); Barbara Perry (Adv. Mgr.); Holly Mulligan (Circ. Mgr.)
Parent company (for newspapers): Reminder Publications

STONEHAM SUN

Street address 1: 20 Holland St
Street address 2: Ste 40
Street address city: Somerville
Street address state: MA
Zip/Postal code: 02144-2749
General Phone: (978) 739-8509
General Fax: (781) 393-1821
Advertising Phone: (978) 739-1344
Advertising Fax: (781) 393-1821
Editorial Phone: (978) 739-8509
Editorial Fax: (781) 393-1821
General/National Adv. E-mail: ameltzer@wickedlocal.com
Display Adv. E-mail: salesteam@wickedlocal.com
Editorial e-mail: stoneham@wickedlocal.com
Primary Website: wickedlocal.com/stoneham
Avg Free Circ: 3821
Audit By: Sworn/Estimate/Non-Audited
Audit Date: 10.06.2019
Personnel: Chuck Goodrich (Pub.); Pete Chianca (Ed. in Chief); Matt Reid (Ed.); Kathleen Cordeiro (Adv. Dir.)
Parent company (for newspapers): Community Newspaper Co.-North-OOB; CherryRoad Media

STOUGHTON JOURNAL

Street address 1: 370 Paramount Dr
Street address 2: Ste 3
Street address city: Raynham
Street address state: MA
Zip/Postal code: 02767-5419
General Phone: (508) 967-3515
General Fax: (508) 967-3501
Display Adv. E-mail: salesteam@wickedlocal.com
Editorial e-mail: acoyle@wickedlocal.com
Primary Website: wickedlocal.com/stoughton
Year Established: 1989
Avg Paid Circ: 156
Audit By: AAM
Audit Date: 31.12.2018
Personnel: Alice Coyle (Managing Ed.); Stuart Green (Ed.); Kathleen Cordeiro (Adv. Dir.)
Parent company (for newspapers): CherryRoad Media

STURBRIDGE VILLAGER

Street address 1: 25 Elm St
Street address city: Southbridge
Street address state: MA
Zip/Postal code: 01550-2605
General Phone: (508) 764-4325
General Fax: (508) 764-8102
Advertising Phone: (508) 909-4104
Advertising Fax: (508) 764-8102
Editorial Phone: (508) 909-4130
Editorial Fax: (508) 764-8102
General/National Adv. E-mail: jashton@stonebridgepress.com
Display Adv. E-mail: classifieds@stonebridgepress.com
Editorial e-mail: aminor@stonebridgepress.com
Primary Website: theheartofmassachusetts.com
Audit By: Sworn/Estimate/Non-Audited
Audit Date: 10.06.2019
Personnel: Adam Minor (Ed.); Sarah Mortensen (Adv. Dir.); Jean Ashton (Dir. Sales/Mktg.)

SUDBURY TOWN CRIER

Street address 1: 33 New York Ave
Street address city: Framingham
Street address state: MA
Zip/Postal code: 01701-8857
General Phone: (508) 626-3926
General Fax: (508) 626-4400
Advertising Phone: (508) 626-3913
Editorial Phone: (508) 626-3926
General/National Adv. E-mail: subury@wickedlocal.com
Editorial e-mail: sudbury@wickedlocal.com
Primary Website: wickedlocal.com/sudbury
Avg Paid Circ: 3969
Audit By: Sworn/Estimate/Non-Audited
Audit Date: 10.06.2019
Personnel: Sean Burke (President, Group Publisher); Richard Lodge (Ed. in Chief)
Parent company (for newspapers): CherryRoad Media

SWAMPSCOTT REPORTER

Street address 1: 48 Dunham Road
Street address 2: Suite 3100
Street address city: Beverly
Street address state: MA
Zip/Postal code: 01915
General Phone: (781) 639-4800
General/National Adv. E-mail: nprag@wickedlocal.com
Display Adv. E-mail: classifieds@wickedlocal.com
Editorial e-mail: pchianca@wickedlocal.com
Primary Website: wickedlocal.com/swampscott
Mthly Avg Views: 1154957
Mthly Avg Unique Visitors: 244866
Year Established: 1850
Avg Paid Circ: 94
Avg Free Circ: 1228
Audit By: AAM
Audit Date: 31.03.2018
Personnel: Charles Goodrich (Pub.); Janet Mackay-Smith (Senior Ed.); Pete Chianca (Ed. in Chief); Mary Reines (Arts and More Section Ed.)
Parent company (for newspapers): CherryRoad Media

TEWKSBURY ADVOCATE

Street address 1: 150 Baker Ave. Ext.
Street address 2: Suite 101
Street address city: Concord
Street address state: MA
Zip/Postal code: 01742
General Phone: (978) 371-5744
General/National Adv. E-mail: speters@wickedlocal.com
Display Adv. E-mail: classifieds@wickedlocal.com
Editorial e-mail: kcordeiro@wickedlocal.com
Primary Website: wickedlocal.com/tewksbury
Avg Paid Circ: 247
Audit By: AAM
Audit Date: 31.03.2018
Personnel: Chuck Goodrich (Pub.); Kathy Cordeiro (Ed. in Chief); Mac McEntire (Ed.); Kathleen Cordeiro (Adv. Dir.)
Parent company (for newspapers): CherryRoad Media

THE ADVOCATE

Street address 1: PO Box 711
Street address city: Fairhaven
Street address state: MA
Zip/Postal code: 02719-0700
General Phone: (508) 992-1522
General Fax: (508) 961-2245
General/National Adv. E-mail: theadvocatenewspaper@yahoo.com; editor@advocatenewsonline.com
Avg Paid Circ: 1518
Avg Free Circ: 141
Audit By: Sworn/Estimate/Non-Audited
Audit Date: 10.06.2019
Personnel: Warren A. Hathaway (Pub.); Barry Harrington (Gen. Mgr.); Michael Medeiros (Ed.)
Parent company (for newspapers): Dow Jones Local Media Group-OOB

THE BACK BAY SUN

Street address 1: 385 Broadway
Street address 2: Ste 105
Street address city: Revere
Street address state: MA
Zip/Postal code: 02151-3049
General Phone: (617) 523-9490
General Fax: (617) 523-8668
Advertising Phone: (617) 523-9490
Advertising Fax: (617) 523-8668
Editorial Phone: (617) 523-9490
Editorial Fax: (617) 523-8668
General/National Adv. E-mail: tverhoogen@backbaysun.com
Display Adv. E-mail: tverhoogen@backbaysun.com
Editorial e-mail: editor@backbaysun.com
Primary Website: backbaysun.com
Audit By: Sworn/Estimate/Non-Audited
Audit Date: 10.06.2019
Personnel: Karen Cord Taylor (Exec. Ed. & Pub.); Jacqueline Harris (Mng. Dir.); Therese Verhoogen (Ad. Director)
Parent company (for newspapers): Independent Newspaper Group

THE BANNER

Street address 1: 156 Church St
Street address city: Clinton
Street address state: MA
Zip/Postal code: 01510-2563
General Phone: (508) 835-4865
General Fax: (978) 368-1151
Advertising Phone: (508) 835-4865
Advertising Fax: (978) 368-1151
Editorial Phone: (508) 835-4865
Editorial Fax: (978) 368-1151
General/National Adv. E-mail: itemads@telegram.com
Display Adv. E-mail: itemads@telegram.com
Editorial e-mail: bannews@yahoo.com
Primary Website: weeklybanner.com
Year Established: 1978
Avg Paid Circ: 1800
Audit By: Sworn/Estimate/Non-Audited
Audit Date: 10.06.2019
Personnel: Gary Hutner (Pub.); Michael Kane (Ed.); Jan Gottesman (Mng. Ed.); Patricia Houck (Prodn. Mgr.)
Parent company (for newspapers): Coulter Press

THE BEACON HILL TIMES

Street address 1: 25 Myrtle St
Street address city: Boston
Street address state: MA
Zip/Postal code: 02114-4509
General Phone: (617) 523-9490
General Fax: (617) 523-8668
Advertising Phone: (617) 523-9490
Advertising Fax: (617) 523-8668
Editorial Phone: (617) 523-9490
Editorial Fax: (617) 523-8668
General/National Adv. E-mail: tverhoogen@beaconhilltimes.com
Display Adv. E-mail: tverhoogen@beaconhilltimes.com
Editorial e-mail: editor@beaconhilltimes.com
Primary Website: beaconhilltimes.com
Year Established: 1995
Avg Free Circ: 10500
Audit By: Sworn/Estimate/Non-Audited
Audit Date: 10.06.2019
Personnel: Karen Cord Taylor (Ed. & Pub.); Suzanne Besser (Mng. Ed.)
Parent company (for newspapers): Independent Newspaper Group

THE BEACON-VILLAGER

Street address 1: 150 Baker Avenue Ext
Street address 2: Ste 105
Street address city: Concord
Street address state: MA
Zip/Postal code: 01742-2198
General Phone: (978) 371-5714
General/National Adv. E-mail: pcalder@wickedlocal.com
Display Adv. E-mail: classifieds@wickedlocal.com
Primary Website: acton.wickedlocal.com
Avg Paid Circ: 1939
Avg Free Circ: 971
Audit By: AAM
Audit Date: 31.03.2018
Personnel: Chuck Goodrich (Pub.); Kathleen Cordeiro (Adv. Dir.); Steve Tobey (Sports Ed.)
Parent company (for newspapers): CherryRoad Media

THE BERKSHIRE RECORD

Street address 1: 21 Elm St
Street address city: Great Barrington
Street address state: MA
Zip/Postal code: 01230-1516
General Phone: (413) 528-5380
General Fax: (413) 528-9449
Advertising Phone: (413) 528-5380
Advertising Fax: (413) 528-9449
Editorial Phone: (413) 528-5380
Editorial Fax: (413) 528-9449
General/National Adv. E-mail: berkads@bcn.net
Display Adv. E-mail: berkads@bcn.net
Editorial e-mail: berkrec@bcn.net
Primary Website: berkshirerecord.net
Avg Paid Circ: 14000
Audit By: Sworn/Estimate/Non-Audited
Audit Date: 10.06.2019
Personnel: Anthony Prisendorf (Pub.); Donna Prisendorf (Ed.)
Parent company (for newspapers): Limestone Communications Inc

THE BOLTON COMMON

Street address 1: 150 Baker Avenue Ext
Street address 2: Ste 101
Street address city: Concord
Street address state: MA
Zip/Postal code: 01742-2199
General Phone: (781) 433-6905
General Fax: (781) 433-6965
Advertising Phone: (978) 371-5737
Editorial Phone: (978) 371-5759
General/National Adv. E-mail: mmanuppelli@wickedlocal.com
Display Adv. E-mail: mmanuppelli@wickedlocal.com
Editorial e-mail: hcamero@wickedlocal.com
Primary Website: wickedlocal.com/bolton
Year Established: 1988
Avg Paid Circ: 1141
Audit By: Sworn/Estimate/Non-Audited
Audit Date: 10.06.2019
Personnel: Chuck Goodrich (Pub.); Holly Camero (Ed.); Kathleen Cordeiro (Ed. in Chief); Kathleen Cordeiro (Adv. Dir.)
Parent company (for newspapers): CherryRoad Media

THE BOSTON BULLETIN

Street address 1: 661 Washington Street
Street address 2: Ste. 202
Street address city: Norwood
Street address state: MA
Zip/Postal code: 02062
General Phone: (617) 361-8400
General Fax: (617) 361-1933
Advertising Phone: (617) 361-8400
Advertising Fax: (617) 361-1933
Editorial Phone: (617) 361-8400

Editorial Fax: (617) 361-1933
General/National Adv. E-mail: info@bulletinnewspapers.com
Display Adv. E-mail: info@bulletinnewspapers.com
Editorial e-mail: news@bulletinnewspapers.com
Primary Website: bulletinnewspapers.com
Avg Free Circ: 3000
Audit By: Sworn/Estimate/Non-Audited
Audit Date: 10.06.2019
Personnel: Paul DiModica (Pub.); Dennis Cawley (Ed./Co-Pub.); Susan Yandell (Adv. Mgr.)

THE BOURNE ENTERPRISE

Street address 1: 50 Depot Ave
Street address city: Falmouth
Street address state: MA
Zip/Postal code: 02540-2302
General Phone: (508) 548-4700
General Fax: (508) 540-8407
Advertising Phone: (508) 548-4700
Advertising Fax: (508) 540-8407
Editorial Phone: (508) 548-4700
Editorial Fax: (508) 540-8407
General/National Adv. E-mail: ads@capenews.net
Display Adv. E-mail: ads@capenews.net
Editorial e-mail: paradise@capenews.net
Primary Website: capenews.net
Year Established: 1895
Audit By: Sworn/Estimate/Non-Audited
Audit Date: 10.06.2019
Personnel: Bill Hough (Ed./Pub.); John Paradise (Managing Ed.); Sean Randall (Ad. Director)
Parent company (for newspapers): Enterprise

THE BULLETIN

Street address 1: 923 Route 6A
Street address 2: Unit G
Street address city: Yarmouth Port
Street address state: MA
Zip/Postal code: 02675-2159
General Phone: (508) 888-0000
General Fax: (508) 375-4903
Advertising Phone: (508) 888-0000
Advertising Fax: (508) 375-4903
Editorial Phone: (508) 888-0000
Editorial Fax: (508) 375-4903
General/National Adv. E-mail: salesteam@wickedlocal.com
Display Adv. E-mail: salesteam@wickedlocal.com
Editorial e-mail: jbasile@wickedlocal.com
Primary Website: wickedlocal.com/falmouth
Year Established: 2007
Avg Paid Circ: 6525
Audit By: Sworn/Estimate/Non-Audited
Audit Date: 10.06.2019
Personnel: Mark Olivieri (Pub.); John Basile (Ed.); Kathleen Cordeiro (Adv. Dir.)
Parent company (for newspapers): CherryRoad Media

THE CAPE COD CHRONICLE

Street address 1: 60 Munson Meeting Way
Street address 2: Ste C
Street address city: Chatham
Street address state: MA
Zip/Postal code: 02633-1992
General Phone: (508) 945-2220
General Fax: (508) 945-2579
Advertising Phone: (508) 945-2229
Advertising Fax: (508) 945-2579
Editorial Phone: (508) 945-2220
Editorial Fax: (508) 945-2579
General/National Adv. E-mail: debbie@capecodchronicle.com
Display Adv. E-mail: debbie@capecodchronicle.com
Editorial e-mail: twood@capecodchronicle.com
Primary Website: capecodchronicle.com
Avg Paid Circ: 27404
Avg Free Circ: 721
Audit By: Sworn/Estimate/Non-Audited
Audit Date: 10.06.2019
Personnel: Tim Wood (Ed.); Deb DeCosta (Adv. Mgr.)

THE CAPE CODDER

Street address 1: 5 Namskaket Rd
Street address city: Orleans
Street address state: MA
Zip/Postal code: 02653-3202
General Phone: (508) 247-3255
General Fax: (508) 247-3203
Advertising Phone: (508) 247-3255
Advertising Fax: (508) 247-3203
Editorial Phone: (508) 247-3255
Editorial Fax: (508) 247-3203
General/National Adv. E-mail: codder@cnc.com
Display Adv. E-mail: codder@cnc.com
Editorial e-mail: cdumas@cnc.com
Primary Website: wickedlocal.com
Year Established: 1946
Avg Paid Circ: 10653
Avg Free Circ: 10587
Audit By: AAM
Audit Date: 31.03.2018
Personnel: Carol Dumas (Editor)
Parent company (for newspapers): CherryRoad Media

THE CHARLESTOWN PATRIOT-BRIDGE

Street address 1: 385 Broadway
Street address 2: Ste 105
Street address city: Revere
Street address state: MA
Zip/Postal code: 02151
General Phone: (781) 485-0588
General Fax: (781) 485-1403
General/National Adv. E-mail: tverhoogen@charlestownbridge.com
Display Adv. E-mail: tverhoogen@charlestownbridge.com
Editorial e-mail: editor@charlestownbridge.com
Primary Website: charlestownbridge.com
Avg Paid Circ: 4500
Audit By: Sworn/Estimate/Non-Audited
Audit Date: 10.06.2019
Personnel: Karen Cord Taylor (Ed./Pub.); Therese Herhoogen (Adv. Mgr.); Alexandra Bowers (Mng. Ed.)
Parent company (for newspapers): Independent Newspaper Group

THE CHICOPEE REGISTER

Street address 1: 333 Front St
Street address 2: Ste 5
Street address city: Chicopee
Street address state: MA
Zip/Postal code: 01013-2798
General Phone: (413) 592-3599
General Fax: (413) 592-3568
Advertising Phone: (413) 592-3599
Advertising Fax: (413) 592-3568
Editorial Phone: (413) 592-3599
Editorial Fax: (413) 592-3568
General/National Adv. E-mail: bbaker@turley.com
Display Adv. E-mail: classifieds@turley.com
Editorial e-mail: kmitchell@turley.com
Primary Website: chicopeeregister.turley.com
Year Established: 1970
Avg Free Circ: 17000
Audit By: Sworn/Estimate/Non-Audited
Audit Date: 10.06.2019
Personnel: Kathy Mitchell (Ed.); Patrick H. Turley (Pub.); Beth Baker (Ad. Director)
Parent company (for newspapers): Turley Publications, Inc.

THE CHRONICLE

Street address 1: 25 Elm St
Street address city: New Bedford
Street address state: MA
Zip/Postal code: 02740-6228
General Phone: (508) 979-4431
General Fax: (508) 997-7491
General/National Adv. E-mail: chronnews@aol.com
Avg Paid Circ: 3995
Avg Free Circ: 196
Audit By: Sworn/Estimate/Non-Audited
Audit Date: 10.06.2019
Personnel: Phil Devitt (Gen. Mgr.); Robert Barboza (Ed.)
Parent company (for newspapers): Dow Jones Local Media Group-OOB

THE CONCORD JOURNAL

Street address 1: 150 Baker Avenue Ext
Street address 2: Ste 101
Street address city: Concord
Street address state: MA
Zip/Postal code: 01742-2199
General Phone: (978) 369-2800
General Fax: (978) 371-5220
Advertising Phone: (978) 371-5723
Advertising Fax: (978) 371-5220
Editorial Phone: (978) 371-5742
Editorial Fax: (978) 371-5220
General/National Adv. E-mail: pcalder@wickedlocal.com
Display Adv. E-mail: rbright@wickedlocal.com
Editorial e-mail: kragsdale@wickedlocal.com
Primary Website: wickedlocal.com/concord
Avg Paid Circ: 3002
Avg Free Circ: 714
Audit By: AAM
Audit Date: 31.03.2018
Personnel: Chuck Goodrich (Pub.); Kathy Cordeiro (Ed. in Chief); Kathie Ragsdale (Ed.); Kathleen Cordeiro (Adv. Dir.)
Parent company (for newspapers): CherryRoad Media

THE COUNTRY GAZETTE

Street address 1: 197 Main St
Street address city: Milford
Street address state: MA
Zip/Postal code: 01757-2635
General Phone: (508) 634-7500
General Fax: (508) 634-7568
Advertising Phone: (508) 626-3984
Advertising Fax: (508) 634-7568
Editorial Phone: (508) 634-7584
Editorial Fax: (508) 634-7568
General/National Adv. E-mail: crobinson@wickedlocal.com
Display Adv. E-mail: salesteam@wickedlocal.com
Editorial e-mail: gazette@wickedlocal.com
Primary Website: wickedlocal.com/franklin
Year Established: 1985
Avg Free Circ: 20114
Audit By: AAM
Audit Date: 31.03.2018
Personnel: Richard Lodge (Ed. in Chief); Heather McCarron (Ed.); Kathleen Cordeiro (Adv. Dir.)
Parent company (for newspapers): CherryRoad Media

THE DEDHAM TRANSCRIPT

Street address 1: 1 Speen St.
Street address 2: Ste 200
Street address city: Framingham
Street address state: MA
Zip/Postal code: 01701
General Phone: (781) 433-6700
General/National Adv. E-mail: dedham@wickedlocal.com
Display Adv. E-mail: classifieds@wickedlocal.com
Editorial e-mail: msullivan@wickedlocal.com
Primary Website: dedham.wickedlocal.com
Year Established: 1873
Avg Paid Circ: 453
Audit By: AAM
Audit Date: 31.03.2018
Personnel: Maureen Sullivan (News Dir.)
Parent company (for newspapers): CherryRoad Media

THE DISPATCH NEWS

Street address 1: 491 Dutton St
Street address city: Lowell
Street address state: MA
Zip/Postal code: 01854-4289
General Phone: (978) 458-7100
General Fax: (978) 970-4723
Advertising Phone: (978) 458-3311
Advertising Fax: (978) 970-4723
Editorial Phone: (978) 970-4623
Editorial Fax: (978) 970-4723
General/National Adv. E-mail: fsplaine@mediaonene.com
Display Adv. E-mail: fsplaine@mediaonene.com
Editorial e-mail: backtalk@lowellsun.com
Primary Website: thevalleydispatch.com
Avg Free Circ: 18000
Audit By: Sworn/Estimate/Non-Audited
Audit Date: 10.06.2019
Personnel: Mark O'Neil (Pres./Pub.); Kendall Wallace (CEO); Mike Sheehan (Dir., Circ.); Gary Wright (Circ. Opns. Mgr.); James Campanini (Ed.); Kris Pisarik (Mng. Ed.); Tom Zuppa (Mng. Ed.)

THE DORCHESTER REPORTER

Street address 1: 150 Mount Vernon St
Street address 2: Ste 120
Street address city: Dorchester
Street address state: MA
Zip/Postal code: 02125-3135
General Phone: (617) 436-1222
General Fax: (617) 825-5516
Advertising Phone: (617) 436-1222
Advertising Fax: (617) 825-5516
Editorial Phone: (617) 436-1222
Editorial Fax: (617) 825-5516
General/National Adv. E-mail: addesk@dotnews.com
Display Adv. E-mail: addesk@dotnews.com
Editorial e-mail: newseditor@dotnews.com
Primary Website: dotnews.com
Year Established: 1983
Avg Paid Circ: 22000
Audit By: Sworn/Estimate/Non-Audited
Audit Date: 10.06.2019
Personnel: Edward W. Forry (Pub.); Jack Conboy (Adv. Mgr.); William Forry (Mng. Ed.); Barbara Langis (Prodn. Mgr.)

THE FALMOUTH ENTERPRISE

Street address 1: 50 Depot Ave
Street address city: Falmouth
Street address state: MA
Zip/Postal code: 02540-2302
General Phone: (508) 548-4700
General Fax: (508) 540-8407
Advertising Phone: (508) 548-4700
Advertising Fax: (508) 540-8407
Editorial Phone: (508) 548-4700
Editorial Fax: (508) 540-8407
General/National Adv. E-mail: ptheall@capenews.net
Display Adv. E-mail: ads@capenews.net
Editorial e-mail: bennett@capenews.net
Primary Website: capenews.net
Year Established: 1895
Avg Paid Circ: 7759
Avg Free Circ: 66
Audit By: AAM
Audit Date: 30.09.2016
Personnel: Bill Hough (Pub./Ed.); Patti Theall (Sales Director)
Parent company (for newspapers): Enterprise

THE FOXBORO REPORTER

Street address 1: 36 Mechanic St
Street address 2: Ste 107
Street address city: Foxboro
Street address state: MA
Zip/Postal code: 02035-2073
General Phone: (508) 543-4851
General Fax: (508) 543-4888
Advertising Phone: (508) 543-4851
Advertising Fax: (508) 543-4888
Editorial Phone: (508) 543-4851
Editorial Fax: (508) 543-4888
General/National Adv. E-mail: msutherland@thesunchronicle.com
Display Adv. E-mail: msutherland@thesunchronicle.com
Editorial e-mail: foxboronews@yahoo.com
Primary Website: foxbororeporter.com
Avg Paid Circ: 2500
Audit By: Sworn/Estimate/Non-Audited
Audit Date: 10.06.2019
Personnel: Bill Stedman (Managing Ed.); Ruth Jackson (Office manager); Bera Dunau (Reporter)
Parent company (for newspapers): United Communications Corp

THE GRAFTON VILLAGER

Street address 1: 90 Milford Rd
Street address city: South Grafton
Street address state: MA
Zip/Postal code: 01560-1214
General Phone: (508) 736-5893
General Fax: (508) 839-5235
Advertising Phone: (508) 839-2838
Advertising Fax: (508) 839-5235
Editorial Phone: (508) 839-2259
Editorial Fax: (508) 839-5235
General/National Adv. E-mail: graftonvillager@gmail.com
Display Adv. E-mail: graftonvillager@gmail.com
Editorial e-mail: editor@thegraftonnews.com
Primary Website: thegraftonvillager.com
Year Established: 1958

Avg Paid Circ: 4024
Avg Free Circ: 60
Audit By: Sworn/Estimate/Non-Audited
Audit Date: 10.06.2019
Personnel: Wendy Watkins (Graphic Designer); Richard Price (Editor)

THE HARVARD POST

Street address 1: 150 Baker Avenue Ext
Street address 2: Ste 101
Street address city: Concord
Street address state: MA
Zip/Postal code: 01742-2198
General Phone: (978) 371-5759
Display Adv. E-mail: classifieds@wickedlocal.com
Primary Website: harvard.wickedlocal.com
Year Established: 1973
Avg Free Circ: 83
Audit By: Sworn/Estimate/Non-Audited
Audit Date: 10.06.2019
Personnel: Chuck Goodrich (Pub.); Kathy Cordeiro (Ed. in Chief); Mike Bentle (Multi-Media Sales); Debra Ryan (Adv.)
Parent company (for newspapers): CherryRoad Media

THE HARVARD PRESS

Street address 1: 1 Still River Rd
Street address 2: Fl 3rd
Street address city: Harvard
Street address state: MA
Zip/Postal code: 01451-1330
General Phone: (978) 456-3700
General Fax: (978) 456-0330
Advertising Phone: (978) 456-3700
Advertising Fax: (978) 456-0330
Editorial Phone: (978) 456-3700
Editorial Fax: (978) 456-0330
General/National Adv. E-mail: classifieds@harvardpress.com
Display Adv. E-mail: classifieds@harvardpress.com
Editorial e-mail: editor@harvardpress.com
Primary Website: harvardpress.com
Mthly Avg Views: 20000
Mthly Avg Unique Visitors: 5000
Audit By: Sworn/Estimate/Non-Audited
Audit Date: 10.06.2019
Personnel: Matthew Cook (Ed.)

THE HAVERHILL GAZETTE

Street address 1: 100 Turnpike St
Street address city: North Andover
Street address state: MA
Zip/Postal code: 01845-5033
General Phone: (978) 946-2000
General Fax: (978) 521-6790
Advertising Phone: (978) 946-2152
Advertising Fax: (978) 521-6790
Editorial Phone: (978) 946-2215
Editorial Fax: (978) 521-6790
General/National Adv. E-mail: ewholley@eagletribune.com
Display Adv. E-mail: ewholley@eagletribune.com
Editorial e-mail: editor@hgazette.com
Primary Website: hgazette.com
Year Established: 1821
Avg Paid Circ: 3590
Avg Free Circ: 292
Audit By: Sworn/Estimate/Non-Audited
Audit Date: 10.06.2019
Personnel: Al Getler (Pub.); Tim Brady (Adv. Dir.); Steve Milone (Circ. Dir.)
Parent company (for newspapers): CNHI, LLC

THE HERALD

Street address 1: 280 N Main St
Street address city: East Longmeadow
Street address state: MA
Zip/Postal code: 01028-1868
General Phone: (413) 525-6661
General Fax: (413) 525-5882
Advertising Phone: (413) 525-6661
Advertising Fax: (413) 525-5882
Editorial Phone: (413) 525-6661
Editorial Fax: (413) 525-5882
General/National Adv. E-mail: bperry@reminderpublications.com
Display Adv. E-mail: KBarba@ReminderPublications.com
Editorial e-mail: mdobbs@ReminderPublications.com
Primary Website: thereminder.com
Avg Free Circ: 10000
Audit By: Sworn/Estimate/Non-Audited
Audit Date: 10.06.2019
Personnel: Christopher M. Buendo (Pub.); Barbara Perry (Adv. Mgr.); Diane Damarjian (Circ. Mgr.); Holly Mulligan (Circ. Mgr.); G. Michael Dobbs (Ed.); Beth Thurber (Prodn. Mgr.)

THE HOLYOKE SUN

Street address 1: 333 Front St
Street address city: Chicopee
Street address state: MA
Zip/Postal code: 01013-3194
General Phone: (413) 612-2310
General Fax: (413) 592-3568
Advertising Phone: (413) 612-2310
Advertising Fax: (413) 592-3568
Editorial Phone: (413) 612-2310
Editorial Fax: (413) 592-3568
General/National Adv. E-mail: bbaker@turley.com
Display Adv. E-mail: classifieds@turley.com
Editorial e-mail: kwill@turley.com
Primary Website: sun.turley.com
Year Established: 1995
Avg Free Circ: 10000
Audit By: Sworn/Estimate/Non-Audited
Audit Date: 10.06.2019
Personnel: Patrick H. Turley (Pub.); Kristin Will (Ed.); Beth Baker (Ad. Director)
Parent company (for newspapers): Turley Publications, Inc.

THE HULL TIMES

Street address 1: 412 Nantasket Ave
Street address city: Hull
Street address state: MA
Zip/Postal code: 02045-2712
General Phone: (781) 925-9266
General Fax: (781) 925-0336
General/National Adv. E-mail: hulltimes@aol.com
Display Adv. E-mail: hulltimes@aol.com
Editorial e-mail: hulltimes@aol.com
Primary Website: hulltimes.com
Year Established: 1930
Avg Paid Circ: 3000
Audit By: Sworn/Estimate/Non-Audited
Audit Date: 10.06.2019
Personnel: Susan Ovans (Ed.); Roger Jackson (Prodn. Mgr.)

THE INQUIRER AND MIRROR

Street address 1: 1 Old South Rd
Street address city: Nantucket
Street address state: MA
Zip/Postal code: 02554-2836
General Phone: (508) 228-0001
General Fax: (508) 325-5089
Advertising Phone: (508) 228-0001
Advertising Fax: (508) 325-5089
Editorial Phone: (508) 228-0001
Editorial Fax: (508) 325-5089
General/National Adv. E-mail: advertising@inkym.com
Display Adv. E-mail: classified@inkym.com
Editorial e-mail: newsroom@inkym.com
Primary Website: ack.net
Year Established: 1865
Avg Paid Circ: 8903
Avg Free Circ: 162
Audit By: Sworn/Estimate/Non-Audited
Audit Date: 10.06.2019
Personnel: Lynda St. Peter (Office Mgr.); Lora Kebbati (Adv. Mgr.); Marianne Stanton (Ed.); Joshua H. Balling (Mng. Ed.); Greg Derr (Prodn. Dir.); Kevin Stanton (Circulation/Classified Manager); Joshua Balling (Assistant Editor); Denese B. Allen (Circ. Dir.); Sean Kalman (Prodn. Dir.); Jason Graziadei
Parent company (for newspapers): Dow Jones Local Media Group-OOB

THE ITEM

Street address 1: 156 Church St
Street address 2: Ste 1
Street address city: Clinton
Street address state: MA
Zip/Postal code: 01510-2563
General Phone: (978) 368-0176
General Fax: (978) 368-1151
Advertising Phone: (978) 368-0176
Advertising Fax: (978) 368-1151
Editorial Phone: (978) 368-0176
Editorial Fax: (978) 368-1151
General/National Adv. E-mail: itemads@telegram.com
Display Adv. E-mail: itemads@telegram.com
Editorial e-mail: clintonitem@yahoo.com
Primary Website: clintonitem.com
Year Established: 1893
Avg Paid Circ: 5100
Avg Free Circ: 100
Audit By: Sworn/Estimate/Non-Audited
Audit Date: 10.06.2019
Personnel: Gary Hutner (Pub.); Ed Grant (Circ. Mgr.); Jan Gottesman (Ed.); Graham Entwistle (Sports Ed.)
Parent company (for newspapers): Coulter Press

THE JOURNAL REGISTER

Street address 1: 24 Water St
Street address city: Palmer
Street address state: MA
Zip/Postal code: 01069-1885
General Phone: (413) 283-8393
General Fax: (413) 289-1977
Advertising Phone: (413) 283-8393
Advertising Fax: (413) 289-1977
Editorial Phone: (413) 283-8393
Editorial Fax: (413) 289-1977
General/National Adv. E-mail: bbaker@turley.com
Display Adv. E-mail: classifieds@turley.com
Editorial e-mail: journalregister@turley.com
Primary Website: palmerjr.com
Year Established: 1850
Avg Paid Circ: 5200
Audit By: Sworn/Estimate/Non-Audited
Audit Date: 10.06.2019
Personnel: Doug Farmer (Ed.); Patrick H. Turley (Pub.); Beth Baker (Ad. Director)
Parent company (for newspapers): McNaughton Newspapers; Turley Publications, Inc.

THE LAKEVILLE CALL

Street address 1: 1324 Belmont St
Street address 2: Ste 102
Street address city: Brockton
Street address state: MA
Zip/Postal code: 02301-4435
General Phone: (508) 967-3520
General Fax: (508) 967-3501
Advertising Phone: (781) 837-4598
Advertising Fax: (508) 967-3501
Editorial Phone: (508) 967-3520
Editorial Fax: (508) 967-3501
General/National Adv. E-mail: dteehan@wickedlocal.com
Display Adv. E-mail: rbright@wickedlocal.com
Editorial e-mail: molivieri@wickedlocal.com
Primary Website: lakeville.wickedlocal.com
Audit By: Sworn/Estimate/Non-Audited
Audit Date: 10.06.2019
Personnel: Alice Coyle (Ed.); Kathleen Cordeiro (Adv. Dir.)
Parent company (for newspapers): Community Newspaper Co. - South

THE LANDMARK

Street address 1: 1105A Main St
Street address city: Holden
Street address state: MA
Zip/Postal code: 01520-1219
General Phone: (508) 829-5981
General Fax: (508) 749-3165
Advertising Phone: (508) 829-5981
Advertising Fax: (508) 749-3165
Editorial Phone: (508) 829-5981
Editorial Fax: (508) 749-3165
General/National Adv. E-mail: sales@holdenlandmark.com
Display Adv. E-mail: sales@centralmassclass.com
Editorial e-mail: editor@thelandmark.com
Primary Website: thelandmark.com
Year Established: 1976
Avg Paid Circ: 8909
Avg Free Circ: 350
Audit By: Sworn/Estimate/Non-Audited
Audit Date: 10.06.2019
Personnel: Kirk A. Davis (Pres.); Barbara Brown (Sales/Gen. Mgr.); Tom Sidna (Circ. Mgr.); Don Cloutier (Prodn. Mgr.)

THE LYNN JOURNAL

Street address 1: 385 Broadway
Street address 2: Ste 105
Street address city: Revere
Street address state: MA
Zip/Postal code: 02151-3049
General Phone: (781) 485-0588
General Fax: (781) 485-1403
General/National Adv. E-mail: deb@reverejournal.com
Display Adv. E-mail: deb@reverejournal.com
Editorial e-mail: Editor@lynnjournal.com
Primary Website: lynnjournal.com
Year Established: 1998
Avg Free Circ: 10000
Audit By: Sworn/Estimate/Non-Audited
Audit Date: 10.06.2019
Personnel: Cary Shuman (Ed.); Debra DiGregerio (Dir. Mktg.); Stephen Quigley (Pres.)
Parent company (for newspapers): Independent Newspaper Group

THE LYNNFIELD VILLAGER

Street address 1: 26 Albion St
Street address city: Wakefield
Street address state: MA
Zip/Postal code: 01880-2803
General Phone: (781) 334-6319
General Fax: (781) 246-0061
Advertising Phone: (781) 334-6319
Advertising Fax: (781) 246-0061
Editorial Phone: (781) 334-6319
Editorial Fax: (781) 246-0061
General/National Adv. E-mail: ads@wakefielditem.com
Display Adv. E-mail: ads@wakefielditem.com
Editorial e-mail: greatoakadguy@aol.com
Primary Website: wp.localheadlinenews.com/?cat=4
Year Established: 1973
Avg Paid Circ: 1615
Avg Free Circ: 207
Audit By: Sworn/Estimate/Non-Audited
Audit Date: 10.06.2019
Personnel: Glenn Golbeare (Pub./Ed.); Phil Solmonson (Adv. Dir.); Robert Burgess (Ed.)
Parent company (for newspapers): Great Oak Publications

THE MANCHESTER CRICKET

Street address 1: 11 Beach St
Street address city: Manchester
Street address state: MA
Zip/Postal code: 01944
General Phone: (978) 526-7171
Advertising Phone: (978) 526-7171
Editorial Phone: (978) 526-7171
General/National Adv. E-mail: news@cricketpress.com
Display Adv. E-mail: info@cricketpress.com
Editorial e-mail: news@cricketpress.com
Primary Website: thecricket.com
Year Established: 1888
Avg Paid Circ: 3400
Audit By: Sworn/Estimate/Non-Audited
Audit Date: 10.06.2021
Personnel: Erika Brown (Publisher); Patricia C. Slade (Ed.)
Parent company (for newspapers): The Manchester Cricket, LLC

THE MARTHA'S VINEYARD TIMES

Street address 1: 30 Beach Rd
Street address city: Vineyard Haven
Street address state: MA
Zip/Postal code: 02568-5582
General Phone: (508) 693-6100
General Fax: (508) 693-6000
Advertising Phone: (508) 693-6100
Advertising Fax: (508) 693-6000
Editorial Phone: (508) 693-6100
Editorial Fax: (508) 693-6000
General/National Adv. E-mail: carrie@mvtimes.com
Display Adv. E-mail: class@mvtimes.com
Editorial e-mail: mvt@mvtimes.com
Primary Website: mvtimes.com
Mthly Avg Views: 2700000
Mthly Avg Unique Visitors: 860000

Year Established: 1984
Avg Paid Circ: 250
Avg Free Circ: 16000
Audit By: Sworn/Estimate/Non-Audited
Audit Date: 10.06.2019
Personnel: Barbara Oberfest (Pub.); Peter Oberfest (Pub.); Doug Cabral (Ed.); Carrie Waltersdorf (Adv. Dir.); Jim Osborn (Circ. Mgr.); Susan Safford (Production mgr.); Linda Wood (Classified Adv. Mgr.)

THE MASHPEE ENTERPRISE

Street address 1: 50 Depot Ave
Street address city: Falmouth
Street address state: MA
Zip/Postal code: 02540-2302
General Phone: (508) 548-4700
General Fax: (508) 540-8407
Advertising Phone: (508) 548-4700
Advertising Fax: (508) 540-8407
Editorial Phone: (508) 548-4700
Editorial Fax: (508) 540-8407
General/National Adv. E-mail: ads@capenews.net
Display Adv. E-mail: ads@capenews.net
Editorial e-mail: kehrl@capenews.net
Primary Website: capenews.net
Year Established: 1895
Audit By: Sworn/Estimate/Non-Audited
Audit Date: 10.06.2019
Personnel: Sean Randall (Ad. Director); Brian Kehrl (Mng. Ed.); Jim Kinsella (Ed.)
Parent company (for newspapers): Enterprise

THE PITTSFIELD GAZETTE

Street address 1: 10 Wendell Avenue Ext
Street address 2: Ste 101
Street address city: Pittsfield
Street address state: MA
Zip/Postal code: 01201-6284
General Phone: (413) 443-2010
General Fax: (413) 443-2445
General/National Adv. E-mail: info@pittsfieldgazette.com
Display Adv. E-mail: info@pittsfieldgazette.com
Editorial e-mail: info@pittsfieldgazette.com
Primary Website: pittsfieldgazette.com
Year Established: 1991
Avg Paid Circ: 1500
Avg Free Circ: 0
Audit By: Sworn/Estimate/Non-Audited
Audit Date: 10.06.2019
Personnel: Jonathan Levine (Ed.)

THE QUINCY SUN

Street address 1: 1372 Hancock St
Street address 2: Ste 102
Street address city: Quincy
Street address state: MA
Zip/Postal code: 02169-5107
General Phone: (617) 471-3100
General Fax: (617) 472- 3963
Advertising Phone: (617) 471-3100
Advertising Fax: (617) 472- 3963
Editorial Phone: (617) 471-3100
Editorial Fax: (617) 472- 3963
General/National Adv. E-mail: quincysunads@verizon.net
Display Adv. E-mail: quincysunads@verizon.net
Editorial e-mail: rbosworth@thequincysun.com
Primary Website: thequincysun.com
Year Established: 1968
Avg Paid Circ: 7000
Audit By: Sworn/Estimate/Non-Audited
Audit Date: 10.06.2019
Personnel: Robert H. Bosworth (Ed. & Pub.); Michelle Collins (Adv. Dir.); Donna Gray (Circ. Mgr.); Dolly Newman (Asst. Mgr.)

THE RAYNHAM CALL

Street address 1: 5 Cohannet St
Street address city: Taunton
Street address state: MA
Zip/Postal code: 02780-3903
General Phone: (508) 967-3518
General Fax: (508) 967-3501
General/National Adv. E-mail: ccrimmins@wickedlocal.com
Display Adv. E-mail: classifieds@wickedlocal.com
Editorial e-mail: bdoyle@wickedlocal.com
Primary Website: wickedlocal.com/raynham
Avg Paid Circ: 136
Avg Free Circ: 1700
Audit By: AAM
Audit Date: 31.03.2018
Personnel: Mark Olivieri (Pub.); Beth Doyle (Ed.); Crissy Crimmons (Adv.)
Parent company (for newspapers): CherryRoad Media

THE REGISTER

Street address 1: 319 Main St
Street address city: Hyannis
Street address state: MA
Zip/Postal code: 02601-4037
General Phone: (508) 375-4945
General Fax: (508) 375-4903
Advertising Phone: (508) 375-4917
Advertising Fax: (508) 375-4901
Editorial Phone: (508) 375-4945
Editorial Fax: (508) 375-4903
General/National Adv. E-mail: lporter@wickedlocal.com
Display Adv. E-mail: lporter@wickedlocal.com
Editorial e-mail: jbasile@wickedlocal.com
Primary Website: wickedlocal.com/capecod
Year Established: 1836
Avg Paid Circ: 4000
Audit By: Sworn/Estimate/Non-Audited
Audit Date: 10.06.2019
Personnel: John Basile (Managing Ed.)
Parent company (for newspapers): CherryRoad Media

THE REGISTER

Street address 1: 2341 Boston Rd
Street address 2: Ste B200
Street address city: Wilbraham
Street address state: MA
Zip/Postal code: 01095-1244
General Phone: (413) 682-0007
General/National Adv. E-mail: lmarulli@turley.com
Display Adv. E-mail: classifieds@turley.com
Editorial e-mail: ludlowregister@turley.com
Primary Website: register.turley.com
Year Established: 1946
Avg Free Circ: 12500
Audit By: Sworn/Estimate/Non-Audited
Audit Date: 10.06.2019
Personnel: Richard Wirth (Ed.); Luis Fieldman (Writer); Lisa Marulli (Adv. Sales)
Parent company (for newspapers): Turley Publications, Inc.

THE REMINDER

Street address 1: 280 N Main St
Street address 2: Ste 1
Street address city: East Longmeadow
Street address state: MA
Zip/Postal code: 01028-1814
General Phone: (413) 525-3247
General Fax: (413) 525-5882
Advertising Phone: (413) 525-3247
Advertising Fax: (413) 525-5882
Editorial Phone: (413) 525-3247
Editorial Fax: (413) 525-5882
General/National Adv. E-mail: marketing@reminderpublications.com
Display Adv. E-mail: marketing@reminderpublications.com
Editorial e-mail: news@reminderpublications.com
Primary Website: thereminder.com
Year Established: 1962
Avg Paid Circ: 8
Avg Free Circ: 94904
Audit By: CVC
Audit Date: 12.12.2017
Personnel: Barbara Perry (Pub.); Daniel Buendo (Co-Pub.); Holly Mulligan (Circ. Mgr.); Michael Dobbs (Editorial Mgr.); Beth Thurber (Prodn. Mgr.)
Parent company (for newspapers): Reminder Publications

THE REVERE JOURNAL

Street address 1: 385 Broadway
Street address 2: Ste 105
Street address city: Revere
Street address state: MA
Zip/Postal code: 02151-3049
General Phone: (781) 485-0588
General Fax: (781) 485-1403
Advertising Phone: (781) 485-0588
Advertising Fax: (781) 485-1403
Editorial Phone: (781) 485-0588
Editorial Fax: (781) 485-1403
General/National Adv. E-mail: tverhoogen@charlestownbridge.com
Display Adv. E-mail: tverhoogen@charlestownbridge.com
Editorial e-mail: editor@reverejournal.com
Primary Website: reverejournal.com
Avg Paid Circ: 7500
Audit By: Sworn/Estimate/Non-Audited
Audit Date: 10.06.2019
Personnel: Karen Cord Taylor (Pub.); Glenda Harris (Circ. Mgr.); David O'Connor (Ed.); Debra DiGregorio (Adv. Dir.)
Parent company (for newspapers): Independent Newspaper Group

THE SANDWICH ENTERPRISE

Street address 1: 50 Depot Ave
Street address city: Falmouth
Street address state: MA
Zip/Postal code: 02540-2302
General Phone: (508) 548-4700
General Fax: (508) 540-8407
Advertising Phone: (508) 548-4700
Advertising Fax: (508) 540-8407
Editorial Phone: (508) 548-4700
Editorial Fax: (508) 540-8407
General/National Adv. E-mail: ads@capenews.net
Display Adv. E-mail: ads@capenews.net
Editorial e-mail: paradise@capenews.net
Primary Website: capenews.net
Year Established: 1895
Audit By: Sworn/Estimate/Non-Audited
Audit Date: 10.06.2019
Personnel: Bill Hough (Ed./Pub.); John Paradise (Ed.); Sean Randall (Ad. Director)
Parent company (for newspapers): Enterprise

THE SENTINEL

Street address 1: 10 S Main St
Street address city: Belchertown
Street address state: MA
Zip/Postal code: 01007-8829
General Phone: (413) 323-5999
General Fax: (413) 323-9424
Advertising Phone: (413) 323-5999
Advertising Fax: (413) 323-9424
Editorial Phone: (413) 323-5999
Editorial Fax: (413) 323-9424
General/National Adv. E-mail: mmcgarrett@turley.com
Display Adv. E-mail: classifieds@turley.com
Editorial e-mail: ahenderson@turley.com
Primary Website: belchertownsentinelonline.com
Year Established: 1915
Avg Free Circ: 10054
Audit By: Sworn/Estimate/Non-Audited
Audit Date: 10.06.2019
Personnel: Patrick Turley (Pub.); Aimee Henderson (Ed.); David Anderson (Gen. Mgr.); Beth Baker (Ad. Director); Charlann Griswold (Circulation Director)
Parent company (for newspapers): Turley Publications, Inc.

THE SENTINEL

Street address 1: 182 Standish Ave
Street address city: Plymouth
Street address state: MA
Zip/Postal code: 02360-4162
General Phone: (508) 591-6628
General/National Adv. E-mail: cavis@wickedlocal.com
Display Adv. E-mail: classifieds@wickedlocal.com
Editorial e-mail: fmulligan@wickedlocal.com
Primary Website: wickedlocal.com/marion
Year Established: 1822
Avg Paid Circ: 0
Avg Free Circ: 461
Audit By: AAM
Audit Date: 31.03.2018
Personnel: Michael Olivieri (Pub.); Frank Mulligan (News Dir.); Chris Avis (Adv. Mgr.)
Parent company (for newspapers): CherryRoad Media

THE SOMERVILLE TIMES

Street address 1: 699 Broadway
Street address city: Somerville
Street address state: MA
Zip/Postal code: 02144-2223
General Phone: (617) 666-4010
General Fax: (617) 628-0422
Advertising Phone: (617) 666-4010
Advertising Fax: (617) 628-0422
Editorial Phone: (617) 666-4010
Editorial Fax: (617) 628-0422
General/National Adv. E-mail: ads@thesomervilletimes.com
Display Adv. E-mail: ads@thesomervilletimes.com
Editorial e-mail: jimclark@thesomervilletimes.com
Primary Website: thesomervillenews.com
Year Established: 1969
Audit By: Sworn/Estimate/Non-Audited
Audit Date: 10.06.2019
Personnel: Jim Clark (Ed.); Bobbie Toner (Adv. Dir.)

THE SPECTATOR

Street address 1: 25 Elm St
Street address city: New Bedford
Street address state: MA
Zip/Postal code: 02740-6228
General Phone: (508) 674-4656
General Fax: (508) 677-1210
General/National Adv. E-mail: crohland@s-t.com
Display Adv. E-mail: ksilvia@s-t.com
Editorial e-mail: jdriscoll@s-t.com
Primary Website: southcoasttoday.com
Year Established: 1932
Avg Paid Circ: 4338
Avg Free Circ: 105
Audit By: Sworn/Estimate/Non-Audited
Audit Date: 10.06.2019
Personnel: Peter Meyer (Pub./Pres.); Chris Rohland (Adv. Mgr.); Jennifer Driscoll (Ed.)
Parent company (for newspapers): CherryRoad Media

THE STONEHAM INDEPENDENT

Street address 1: 200F Main St
Street address 2: Ste 343
Street address city: Stoneham
Street address state: MA
Zip/Postal code: 02180-1619
General Phone: (781) 438-1660
General Fax: (781) 438-6762
Advertising Phone: (781) 438-1660
Advertising Fax: (781) 438-6762
Editorial Phone: (781) 438-1660
Editorial Fax: (781) 438-6762
General/National Adv. E-mail: news@stonehamindependent.com
Display Adv. E-mail: news@stonehamindependent.com
Editorial e-mail: news@stonehamindependent.com
Primary Website: homenewshere.com
Year Established: 1870
Avg Paid Circ: 3000
Audit By: Sworn/Estimate/Non-Audited
Audit Date: 10.06.2019
Personnel: Peter M. Haggerty (Pub.); Mark J. Haggerty (Business Manager); Paul Whalen (Adv. Mgr.); Jay M. Haggerty (Prodn. Mgr.); Patrick Blais (Reporter)
Parent company (for newspapers): Woburn Daily Times, Inc.

THE TANTASQUA TOWN COMMON

Street address 1: 24 Water St
Street address city: Palmer
Street address state: MA
Zip/Postal code: 01069-1885
General Phone: (413) 283-8393
General Fax: (413) 289-1977
Advertising Phone: (413) 283-8393
Advertising Fax: (413) 289-1977
Editorial Phone: (413) 283-8393
Editorial Fax: (413) 289-1977
General/National Adv. E-mail: jbonsall@turley.com
Display Adv. E-mail: classifieds@turley.com
Editorial e-mail: towncommon@turley.com
Primary Website: thetantasquatowncommon.com
Audit By: Sworn/Estimate/Non-Audited
Audit Date: 10.06.2019
Personnel: Tim Kane (Ed.); Jeanna Bonsall (Adv. Rep.); Jacqueline Haesaert-Perrot (Adv. Rep.)

THE TOWN COMMON

Street address 1: 77 Wethersfield St

Street address city: Rowley
Street address state: MA
Zip/Postal code: 01969-1713
General Phone: (978) 948-8696
General Fax: (978) 948-2564
Advertising Phone: (978) 948-8696
Advertising Fax: (978) 948-2564
Editorial Phone: (978) 948-8696
Editorial Fax: (978) 948-2564
General/National Adv. E-mail: advertise@thetowncommon.com
Display Adv. E-mail: advertise@thetowncommon.com
Editorial e-mail: editor@thetowncommon.com
Primary Website: thetowncommon.com
Year Established: 2004
Audit By: Sworn/Estimate/Non-Audited
Audit Date: 10.06.2019
Personnel: Marc Maravalli (Pub./Ed.)

THE VILLAGER

Street address 1: 33 New York Ave
Street address city: Framingham
Street address state: MA
Zip/Postal code: 01701-8857
General Phone: (508) 490-7454
General Fax: (508) 490-7471
Advertising Phone: (508) 626-3984
Advertising Fax: (508) 490-7471
Editorial Phone: (508) 490-7454
Editorial Fax: (508) 490-7471
General/National Adv. E-mail: crobinso@wickedlocal.com
Display Adv. E-mail: salesteam@wickedlocal.com
Editorial e-mail: northboro-southboro@wickedlocal.com
Primary Website: wickedlocal.com/northborough
Avg Paid Circ: 429
Avg Free Circ: 4
Audit By: Sworn/Estimate/Non-Audited
Audit Date: 10.06.2019
Personnel: Glenda Hazard (Ed.); Richard Lodge (Ed. in Chief); Kathleen Cordeiro (Adv. Dir.)
Parent company (for newspapers): CherryRoad Media

THE WALPOLE TIMES

Street address 1: 1 Speen St.
Street address 2: Ste 200
Street address city: Framingham
Street address state: MA
Zip/Postal code: 01701
General Phone: (781) 433-6700
General Fax: (508) 668-5174
General/National Adv. E-mail: walpole@wickedlocal.com
Display Adv. E-mail: classifieds@wickedlocal.com
Editorial e-mail: rtremblay@wickedlocal.com
Primary Website: wickedlocal.com/walpole
Avg Paid Circ: 460
Audit By: AAM
Audit Date: 31.12.2017
Personnel: Bob Tremblay
Parent company (for newspapers): CherryRoad Media

THE WANDERER

Street address 1: 55 County Rd
Street address city: Mattapoisett
Street address state: MA
Zip/Postal code: 02739-1652
General Phone: (508) 758-9055
Advertising Phone: (508) 758-9055
Editorial Phone: (508) 758-9055
General/National Adv. E-mail: office@wanderer.com
Display Adv. E-mail: office@wanderer.com
Editorial e-mail: news@wanderer.com
Primary Website: wanderer.com
Year Established: 1992
Avg Free Circ: 4700
Audit By: Sworn/Estimate/Non-Audited
Audit Date: 10.06.2019
Personnel: Paul R. Lopes (Pub.)

THE WEBSTER TIMES

Street address 1: 25 Elm St
Street address city: Southbridge
Street address state: MA
Zip/Postal code: 01550-2605
General Phone: (508) 764-4325
General Fax: (508) 764-8102
Advertising Phone: (508) 909-4104
Advertising Fax: (508) 764-8102
Editorial Phone: (508) 909-4130
Editorial Fax: (508) 764-8102
General/National Adv. E-mail: jashton@stonebridgepress.com
Display Adv. E-mail: classifieds@stonebridgepress.com
Editorial e-mail: aminor@stonebridgepress.com
Primary Website: webstertimes.net
Avg Paid Circ: 15200
Avg Free Circ: 17000
Audit By: Sworn/Estimate/Non-Audited
Audit Date: 10.06.2019
Personnel: Frank Chilinski (President & Publisher); Jean Ashton (Adv. Mgr.); Walter Bird (Exec. Ed.); Adam Minor (Ed.)
Parent company (for newspapers): Stonebridge Press, Inc.

THE WESTBOROUGH NEWS

Street address 1: 33 New York Ave
Street address city: Framingham
Street address state: MA
Zip/Postal code: 01701-8857
General Phone: (508) 836-3700
General Fax: (508) 490-7471
Advertising Phone: (508) 626-3984
Advertising Fax: (508) 490-7471
Editorial Phone: (508) 626-3871
Editorial Fax: (508) 490-7471
General/National Adv. E-mail: crobinson@wickedlocal.com
Display Adv. E-mail: salesteam@wickedlocal.com
Editorial e-mail: smeindersma@wickedlocal.com
Primary Website: wickedlocal.com/westborough
Avg Paid Circ: 986
Audit By: AAM
Audit Date: 31.03.2018
Personnel: Richard Lodge (Ed. in Chief); Kathleen Cordeiro (Adv. Dir.); Sandy Meindersma (News Dir.)
Parent company (for newspapers): CherryRoad Media

THE WINCHENDON COURIER

Street address 1: 44 Central St
Street address city: Winchendon
Street address state: MA
Zip/Postal code: 01475-1608
General Phone: (978) 297-0050
General Fax: (978) 297-2177
General/National Adv. E-mail: ruth@stonebridgepress.news
Primary Website: winchendoncourier.com
Year Established: 1878
Avg Paid Circ: 1500
Avg Free Circ: 120
Audit By: Sworn/Estimate/Non-Audited
Audit Date: 10.06.2019
Personnel: Frank Chilinski (Pub.); Ruth DeAmicis (Ed./Adv Mgr.); Kerri Peterson (Circ. Mgr.)
Parent company (for newspapers): Stonebridge Press, Inc.

TIMES & COURIER

Street address 1: 150 Baker Avenue Ext
Street address 2: Ste 101
Street address city: Concord
Street address state: MA
Zip/Postal code: 01742-2199
General Phone: (978) 371-5759
General Fax: (978) 371-5711
Advertising Phone: (978) 371-5737
Editorial Phone: (978) 371-5740
General/National Adv. E-mail: times-courier@wickedlocal.com
Display Adv. E-mail: rbright@wickedlocal.com
Editorial e-mail: times-courier.sports@wickedlocal.com
Primary Website: wickedlocal.com/clinton
Avg Paid Circ: 2809
Audit By: Sworn/Estimate/Non-Audited
Audit Date: 10.06.2019
Personnel: Chuck Goodrich (Pub.); Christine Herter Warren (Ed.); Mark Cohen (Vice Pres., Adv.); Kathleen Cordeiro (Ed.-in-Chief); Ron Bright (Classified Adv. Mgr.); Jeff McEvoy (National Adv. Mgr.); Chris Eck (Online Adv. Mgr.); Kathleen Cordeiro (Adv. Dir.)
Parent company (for newspapers): CherryRoad Media

TOWN CRIER

Street address 1: 1 Arrow Dr
Street address city: Woburn
Street address state: MA
Zip/Postal code: 01801-2039
General Phone: (978) 658-2346 x100
General Fax: (978) 658-2266
Advertising Phone: (978) 658-2346 x100
Advertising Fax: (978) 658-2266
Editorial Phone: (978) 658-2346 x100
Editorial Fax: (978) 658-2266
General/National Adv. E-mail: office@yourtowncrier.com
Display Adv. E-mail: bruce@yourtowncrier.com
Editorial e-mail: jayne@yourtowncrier.com
Primary Website: HomeNewsHere.com
Year Established: 1955
Avg Paid Circ: 6000
Avg Free Circ: 500
Audit By: Sworn/Estimate/Non-Audited
Audit Date: 10.06.2019
Personnel: Peter Haggarty (Pub.); Joel Haggerty (Office Mgr.); Stu Neilson (Mng. Ed.); Jayne Miller (News Editor); Bruce Hilliard (Advertising Rep)
Parent company (for newspapers): Daily Times Chronicle

TOWN REMINDER

Street address 1: 136 College St
Street address 2: Ste 2
Street address city: South Hadley
Street address state: MA
Zip/Postal code: 01075-1402
General Phone: (413) 536-5333
General Fax: (413) 536-5334
Advertising Phone: (413) 536-5333
Advertising Fax: (413) 536-5334
Editorial Phone: (413) 536-5333
Editorial Fax: (413) 536-5334
General/National Adv. E-mail: bbaker@turley.com
Display Adv. E-mail: classifieds@turley.com
Editorial e-mail: kwill@turley.com
Primary Website: townreminderonline.com
Year Established: 1968
Avg Free Circ: 12000
Audit By: Sworn/Estimate/Non-Audited
Audit Date: 10.06.2019
Personnel: Patrick H. Turley (Pub.); Kristin Will (Ed.); Beth Baker (Ad. Director)
Parent company (for newspapers): Turley Publications, Inc.

TOWNSEND TIMES

Street address 1: 78 Barnum Rd
Street address city: Devens
Street address state: MA
Zip/Postal code: 01434-3508
General Phone: (978) 772-0777
General Fax: (978) 772-4012
Advertising Phone: (978) 772-0777
Advertising Fax: (978) 772-4012
Editorial Phone: (978) 772-0777
Editorial Fax: (978) 772-4012
General/National Adv. E-mail: hconry@MediaOneNE.com
Display Adv. E-mail: hconry@MediaOneNE.com
Editorial e-mail: editor@nashobapub.com
Primary Website: nashobapublishing.com/townsend_times
Avg Paid Circ: 643
Audit By: Sworn/Estimate/Non-Audited
Audit Date: 10.06.2019
Personnel: Mark O'Neil (Pub.); Rebecca Pellerin (Office Coord.); Mike Sheehan (Circ. Mgr.); Kathleen Walsh (Mng. Ed.); Ken Blanchette (Sports Ed.); Bill Walker (Opns. Dir.)

TRI-TOWN TRANSCRIPT

Street address 1: 75 Sylvan St
Street address 2: Ste C
Street address city: Danvers
Street address state: MA
Zip/Postal code: 01923-2763
General Phone: (978) 739-1300
General Fax: (978) 739-8501
Advertising Phone: (978) 739-1350
Advertising Fax: (978) 739-8501
Editorial Phone: (978) 739-1393
Editorial Fax: (978) 739-8501
General/National Adv. E-mail: ameltzer@wickedlocal.com
Display Adv. E-mail: salesteam@wickedlocal.com
Editorial e-mail: tritown@wickedlocal.com
Primary Website: wickedlocal.com/boxford
Avg Paid Circ: 2604
Audit By: Sworn/Estimate/Non-Audited
Audit Date: 10.06.2019
Personnel: Chuck Goodrich (Pub.); Pete Chianca (Ed. in Chief); Kathryn O'Brien (Ed.); Joshua Boyd (Sports Ed.); Kathleen Cordeiro (Adv. Dir.)
Parent company (for newspapers): Community Newspaper Co.-North-OOB; CherryRoad Media

VINEYARD GAZETTE

Street address 1: 34 S Summer St
Street address city: Edgartown
Street address state: MA
Zip/Postal code: 02539-8104
General Phone: (508) 627-4311
General Fax: (508) 627-7444
Advertising Phone: (508) 627-4311
Advertising Fax: (508) 627-7444
Editorial Phone: (508) 627-4311
Editorial Fax: (508) 627-7444
General/National Adv. E-mail: ads@mvgazette.com
Display Adv. E-mail: classifieds@mvgazette.com
Editorial e-mail: news@mvgazette.com
Primary Website: vineyardgazette.com
Year Established: 1846
Avg Paid Circ: 9000
Avg Free Circ: 150
Audit By: Sworn/Estimate/Non-Audited
Audit Date: 10.06.2019
Personnel: Sarah Gifford (Business Mgr.); Julia Wells (Ed.); Bill Eville (Mng. Ed.); Steve Durkee (Prodn. Mgr.); Jane Seagrave (Pub.); Skip Finley (Director of Sales and Marketing)
Parent company (for newspapers): Vineyard Gazette LLC

WAKEFIELD OBSERVER

Street address 1: 48 Dunham Road
Street address 2: Suite 3100
Street address city: Beverly
Street address state: MA
Zip/Postal code: 01915
General Phone: (978) 739-8504
General/National Adv. E-mail: rmurphy@wickedlocal.com
Display Adv. E-mail: classifieds@wickedlocal.com
Editorial e-mail: pchianca@wickedlocal.com
Primary Website: wickedlocal.com/wakefield
Avg Paid Circ: 200
Audit By: AAM
Audit Date: 31.03.2018
Personnel: Joe McConnell (Sports); Peter Chianca (Reg. Dir. News & Ops); Nancy Prag (News Cov. Real Estate); Michael Gaffney (IT); Rich Tenorio (News Sub.); Linc Murphy (Retail Adv.)
Parent company (for newspapers): CherryRoad Media

WALTHAM NEWS TRIBUNE

Street address 1: 9 Meriam St.
Street address city: Lexington
Street address state: MA
Zip/Postal code: 02420
General Phone: (781) 433-6700
General/National Adv. E-mail: jmann@wickedlocal.com
Display Adv. E-mail: classifieds@wickedlocal.com
Editorial e-mail: kcordeiro@wickedlocal.com
Primary Website: waltham.wickedlocal.com
Avg Paid Circ: 2005
Audit By: AAM
Audit Date: 31.03.2018
Personnel: Kathleen Cordeiro (Reg. Dir. of News & Ops); Kerry Feltner (News Cov.); Melissa Russell (Prod.)
Parent company (for newspapers): CherryRoad Media

WARE RIVER NEWS

Street address 1: 80 Main St
Street address city: Ware
Street address state: MA
Zip/Postal code: 01082-1318
General Phone: (413) 967-3505
General Fax: (413) 967-6009
Advertising Phone: (413) 967-3505
Advertising Fax: (413) 967-6009
Editorial Phone: (413) 967-3505
Editorial Fax: (413) 967-6009
General/National Adv. E-mail: jhaesaert@turley.com

Display Adv. E-mail: classifieds@turley.com
Editorial e-mail: tkane@turley.com
Primary Website: warenewsonline.com
Year Established: 1887
Avg Paid Circ: 4429
Audit By: Sworn/Estimate/Non-Audited
Audit Date: 10.06.2019
Personnel: Patrick H. Turley (Pub.); Tim Kane (Ed.); Beth Baker (Dir., Adv.)
Parent company (for newspapers): Turley Publications, Inc.

WAREHAM COURIER

Street address 1: 182 Standish Ave
Street address city: Plymouth
Street address state: MA
Zip/Postal code: 02360-4162
General Phone: (508) 591-6628
General/National Adv. E-mail: cavis@wickedlocal.com
Display Adv. E-mail: classifieds@wickedlocal.com
Editorial e-mail: gmathis@wickedlocal.com
Primary Website: wickedlocal.com/wareham
Year Established: 1964
Avg Paid Circ: 925
Audit By: AAM
Audit Date: 31.03.2018
Personnel: Mark Olivieri (Pub.); Chris Avis (Adv. Mgr.); Gregory Mathis (Reg. Dir. News & Ops.); Frank Mulligan (News Dir.)
Parent company (for newspapers): CherryRoad Media

WATERTOWN TAB

Street address 1: 9 Meriam Street
Street address city: Lexington
Street address state: MA
Zip/Postal code: 02420
General Phone: (781)433-6700
General/National Adv. E-mail: jmann@wickedlocal.com
Display Adv. E-mail: classifieds@wickedlocal.com
Editorial e-mail: watertown@wickedlocal.com
Primary Website: watertown.wickedlocal.com
Avg Paid Circ: 1386
Audit By: AAM
Audit Date: 31.03.2018
Personnel: Kathleen Cordeiro (News Dir.); Bob Tremblay; Jenn Mann (Adv. Sales)
Parent company (for newspapers): CherryRoad Media

WAYLAND TOWN CRIER

Street address 1: 33 New York Ave
Street address city: Framingham
Street address state: MA
Zip/Postal code: 01701-8857
General Phone: (508) 626-4441
General Fax: (508) 626-4400
Advertising Phone: (508) 626-3984
Advertising Fax: (508) 626-4400
Editorial Phone: (508) 626-4441
Editorial Fax: (508) 626-4400
General/National Adv. E-mail: crobinso@wickedlocal.com
Display Adv. E-mail: salesteam@wickedlocal.com
Editorial e-mail: wayland@wickedlocal.com
Primary Website: wickedlocal.com/wayland
Avg Paid Circ: 2362
Audit By: Sworn/Estimate/Non-Audited
Audit Date: 10.06.2019
Personnel: Mark Olivieri (Pub.); Richard Lodge (Ed. in Chief); Michael Wyner (Ed.); Kathleen Cordeiro (Adv. Dir.)
Parent company (for newspapers): CherryRoad Media

WELLESLEY TOWNSMAN

Street address 1: 254 2nd Ave
Street address 2: Ste 1
Street address city: Needham
Street address state: MA
Zip/Postal code: 02494-2829
General Phone: (781) 431-2000
General Fax: (781) 431-2001
Advertising Phone: (781) 433-8276
Advertising Fax: (781) 431-2001
Editorial Phone: (781) 431-2003
Editorial Fax: (781) 431-2001
General/National Adv. E-mail: cwarren@wickedlocal.com
Display Adv. E-mail: salesteam@wickedlocal.com
Editorial e-mail: wellesley@wickedlocal.com
Primary Website: wickedlocal.com/wellesley
Avg Paid Circ: 2948
Avg Free Circ: 129
Audit By: AAM
Audit Date: 31.03.2018
Personnel: Chuck Goodrich (Pub.); Jesse Floyd (Ed.-in-Chief); Cathy Brauner (Ed.); Tom Wilcox (Sports Ed.); Kathleen Cordeiro (Adv. Dir.)
Parent company (for newspapers): CherryRoad Media

WEST COUNTY NEWS

Street address 1: 87 Bridge St
Street address city: Shelburne Falls
Street address state: MA
Zip/Postal code: 01370-1102
General Phone: (413) 625-4660
General Fax: (413) 625-4661
General/National Adv. E-mail: wcnews@turley.com
Primary Website: turley.com
Year Established: 1979
Avg Free Circ: 21629
Audit By: Sworn/Estimate/Non-Audited
Audit Date: 10.06.2019
Personnel: Patrick H. Turley (Pub.); Beth Baker (Adv. Mgr.); Patrick O'Connor (Ed.)

WEST ROXBURY TRANSCRIPT

Street address 1: 1 Spleen St.
Street address city: Framingham
Street address state: MA
Zip/Postal code: 01701
General Phone: (781) 433-6700
General Fax: (781) 433-8202
General/National Adv. E-mail: jmann@wickedlocal.com
Display Adv. E-mail: classifieds@wickedlocal.com
Editorial e-mail: west-roxbury@wickedlocal.com
Primary Website: wickedlocal.com/west-roxbury
Avg Paid Circ: 508
Audit By: AAM
Audit Date: 31.03.2018
Personnel: Kathleen Cordeiro (Ed.); Jenn Mann (News Dir.); Jesse Floyd (Adv. Sales)
Parent company (for newspapers): CherryRoad Media

WEST ROXBURY/ROSINDALE BULLETIN

Street address 1: 1 Westinghouse Plz
Street address city: Hyde Park
Street address state: MA
Zip/Postal code: 02136-2075
General Phone: (617) 361-8400
General Fax: (617) 361-1933
Advertising Phone: (617) 361-8400
Advertising Fax: (617) 361-1933
Editorial Phone: (617) 361-8400
Editorial Fax: (617) 361-1933
General/National Adv. E-mail: news@westroxburybulletin.com; news@bulletinnewspapers.com
Editorial e-mail: news@bulletinnewspapers.com
Primary Website: bulletinnewspapers.com
Year Established: 1992
Avg Free Circ: 11500
Audit By: Sworn/Estimate/Non-Audited
Audit Date: 10.06.2019
Personnel: Paul DiModica (Pub.); Dennis Cawley (Pub.); Susan Yandell (Adv. Mgr.); Joe Mont (Ed.)

WEST SPRINGFIELD RECORD

Street address 1: 516 Main St
Street address city: West Springfield
Street address state: MA
Zip/Postal code: 01089-3973
General Phone: (413) 736-1587
General Fax: (413) 739-2477
Advertising Phone: (413) 736-1587
Advertising Fax: (413) 739-2477
General/National Adv. E-mail: wsrecord@comcast.net
Display Adv. E-mail: wsrecord@comcast.net
Editorial e-mail: wsrecord@comcast.net
Primary Website: facebook.com/westspringfield.record
Year Established: 1953
Avg Paid Circ: 5600
Audit By: Sworn/Estimate/Non-Audited
Audit Date: 10.06.2019
Personnel: Marie Coburn (Gen. Mgr.); Tom Coburn (Ed.)

WESTFORD EAGLE

Street address 1: 150 Baker Avenue Ext
Street address 2: Ste 101
Street address city: Concord
Street address state: MA
Zip/Postal code: 01742-2199
General Phone: (978) 371-5729
General Fax: (978) 371-5711
General/National Adv. E-mail: speters@wickedlocal.com
Display Adv. E-mail: classifieds@wickedlocal.com
Editorial e-mail: westford@wickedlocal.com
Primary Website: westford.wickedlocal.com
Avg Paid Circ: 1477
Avg Free Circ: 536
Audit By: AAM
Audit Date: 31.03.2018
Personnel: Chuck Goodrich (Pub.); Mark Cohen (Vice Pres., Adv.); Kathy Cordeiro (Ed. in Chief); Joyce Crane (Ed.); Kathleen Cordeiro (Adv. Dir.)
Parent company (for newspapers): CherryRoad Media

WESTON TOWN CRIER

Street address 1: 1 Speen St.
Street address city: Framingham
Street address state: MA
Zip/Postal code: 01701
General Phone: (508) 626-3800
General/National Adv. E-mail: mwyner@wickedlocal.com
Display Adv. E-mail: classifieds@wickedlocal.com
Editorial e-mail: weston@wickedlocal.com
Primary Website: wickedlocal.com/weston
Avg Free Circ: 1131
Audit By: AAM
Audit Date: 31.03.2018
Personnel: Anne Brennan (Exec. Ed.); Michael Wyner (News Dir.); Mark Cohen (VP., Adv.); Kathleen Cordeiro (Adv. Dir.)
Parent company (for newspapers): CherryRoad Media

WESTWOOD PRESS

Street address 1: 1 Speen St.
Street address 2: Ste 200
Street address city: Framingham
Street address state: MA
Zip/Postal code: 01701
General Phone: (781) 433-6700
General/National Adv. E-mail: westwood@wickedlocal.com
Display Adv. E-mail: classifieds@wickedlocal.com
Editorial e-mail: msullivan@wickedlocal.com
Primary Website: westwood.wickedlocal.com
Avg Paid Circ: 440
Audit By: AAM
Audit Date: 31.03.2018
Personnel: Chuck Goodrich (Pub.); Maureen Sullivan (News. Dir.); Max Bowen (Ed.); Jesse Floyd (Ed. in Chief); Kathleen Cordeiro (Adv. Dir.)
Parent company (for newspapers): CherryRoad Media

WEYMOUTH NEWS

Street address 1: 15 Pacella Park Dr
Street address 2: Ste 120
Street address city: Randolph
Street address state: MA
Zip/Postal code: 02368-1700
General Phone: (781) 682-4850
General Fax: (781) 682-4851
Advertising Phone: (617) 786-7190
Advertising Fax: (781) 682-4851
Editorial Phone: (781) 837-4560
Editorial Fax: (781) 682-4851
General/National Adv. E-mail: sswindell@wickedlocal.com
Display Adv. E-mail: classifieds@wickedlocal.com
Editorial e-mail: gmathis@wickedlocal.com
Primary Website: wickedlocal.com/weymouth
Avg Paid Circ: 1740
Audit By: AAM
Audit Date: 31.03.2018
Personnel: Mark Olivieri (Pub.); Timothy Oliver (Adv. Mgr., Retail); Bill Fonda (Ed.); Gregory Mathis (Ed. in Chief); Kathleen Cordeiro (Adv. Dir.); Beth Doyle (Ed.)
Parent company (for newspapers): CherryRoad Media

WHITMAN-HANSON EXPRESS

Street address 1: 1000 Main St
Street address city: Hanson
Street address state: MA
Zip/Postal code: 02341-1560
General Phone: (781) 293-0420
General Fax: (781) 293-0421
General/National Adv. E-mail: ads@whphexpress.com
Display Adv. E-mail: ads@whphexpress.com
Editorial e-mail: editor@whphexpress.com
Primary Website: whitmanhansonexpress.com
Year Established: 2002
Avg Paid Circ: 2022
Avg Free Circ: 58
Audit By: Sworn/Estimate/Non-Audited
Audit Date: 10.06.2019
Personnel: Deborah Anderson (Pub); Tracey Seelye (Ed.)
Parent company (for newspapers): Anderson Newspapers, Inc., d/b/a Express Newspapers

WILBRAHAM-HAMPDEN TIMES

Street address 1: 2341 Boston Rd
Street address 2: Wilbraham Shops, Ste B200
Street address city: Wilbraham
Street address state: MA
Zip/Postal code: 01095-1244
General Phone: (413) 682-0007
Advertising Phone: (413) 682-0007
Editorial Phone: (413) 682-0007
General/National Adv. E-mail: jwalker@turley.com
Display Adv. E-mail: classifieds@turley.com
Editorial e-mail: twitkop@turley.com
Primary Website: wilbrahamhampdentimes.turley.com
Year Established: 2002
Avg Free Circ: 9300
Audit By: Sworn/Estimate/Non-Audited
Audit Date: 10.06.2019
Personnel: Tyler Witkop (Ed.); Dave Forbes (Sports); Jocelyn Walker (Display Adv.); Deana Sloat (Graphics Dept.)
Parent company (for newspapers): Turley Publications, Inc.

WILMINGTON ADVOCATE

Street address 1: 150 Baker Avenue Ext
Street address 2: Ste 101
Street address city: Concord
Street address state: MA
Zip/Postal code: 01742-2199
General Phone: (978) 371-5744
General Fax: (978) 371-5214
Advertising Phone: (978) 371-5707
Advertising Fax: (978) 371-5214
Editorial Phone: (978) 371-5744
Editorial Fax: (978) 371-5214
General/National Adv. E-mail: speters@wickedlocal.com
Display Adv. E-mail: speters@wickedlocal.com
Editorial e-mail: kcordeiro@wickedlocal.com
Primary Website: wickedlocal.com/wilmington
Avg Free Circ: 685
Audit By: AAM
Audit Date: 31.03.2018
Personnel: Chuck Goodrich (Pub.); Mac McEntire (Ed.); Kathleen Cordeiro (Ed. in Chief); Sandy Peters (Adv.); Rob Fucci (News. Mgr.)
Parent company (for newspapers): CherryRoad Media

WINCHESTER STAR

Street address 1: 9 Meriam St
Street address city: Lexington
Street address state: MA
Zip/Postal code: 02420-5300
General Phone: (781) 674-7740
General Fax: (781) 674-7735
Advertising Phone: (978) 371-5717
Advertising Fax: (781) 674-7735
Editorial Phone: (781) 674-7740
Editorial Fax: (781) 674-7735
General/National Adv. E-mail: kcordeiro@wickedlocal.com
Display Adv. E-mail: rbright@wickedlocal.com
Editorial e-mail: kcordeiro@wickedlocal.com
Primary Website: wickedlocal.com/winchester
Avg Paid Circ: 2032
Avg Free Circ: 489

Audit By: AAM
Audit Date: 31.03.2018
Personnel: Chuck Goodrich (Pub.); Kathy Cordeiro (Ed. in Chief); Stephen Toby (Sports Ed.); Kathleen Cordeiro (Adv. Dir.)
Parent company (for newspapers): CherryRoad Media

WINTHROP SUN-TRANSCRIPT

Street address 1: 385 Broadway
Street address 2: Ste 105
Street address city: Revere
Street address state: MA
Zip/Postal code: 02151-3049
General Phone: (781) 284-2400
General Fax: (781) 485-1403
General/National Adv. E-mail: ads.journal@verizon.net
Primary Website: reverejournal.com
Avg Paid Circ: 4300
Audit By: Sworn/Estimate/Non-Audited
Audit Date: 10.06.2019
Personnel: Stephen Quigley (Pres.); Joshua Resnek (Mng. Ed.)
Parent company (for newspapers): Independent Newspaper Group

WOBURN ADVOCATE

Street address 1: 150 Baker Ave
Street address 2: Ste 101
Street address city: Concord
Street address state: MA
Zip/Postal code: 01742-2117
General Phone: (978) 371-5744
General Fax: (978) 371-5711
Advertising Phone: (978) 739-1320
Advertising Fax: (978) 371-5711
Editorial Phone: (978) 371-5744
Editorial Fax: (978) 371-5711
General/National Adv. E-mail: woburn@wickedlocal.com
Display Adv. E-mail: woburn@wickedlocal.com
Editorial e-mail: kcordeiro@wickedlocal.com
Primary Website: woburn.wickedlocal.com
Avg Free Circ: 3627
Audit By: AAM
Audit Date: 31.03.2018
Personnel: Chuck Goodrich (Pub.); Kathleen Cordeiro (Ed.); Kathleen Cordeiro (Adv. Dir.)
Parent company (for newspapers): CherryRoad Media

WORCESTER BUSINESS JOURNAL

Street address 1: 172 Shrewsbury St
Street address 2: Ste 2
Street address city: Worcester
Street address state: MA
Zip/Postal code: 01604-4636
General Phone: (508) 755-8004
General Fax: (508) 755-8860
General/National Adv. E-mail: bleroux@wbjournal.com
Editorial e-mail: Rsaia@wbjournal.com
Primary Website: wbjournal.com
Year Established: 1990
Avg Paid Circ: 453
Avg Free Circ: 8465
Audit By: CVC
Audit Date: 12.12.2017
Personnel: Rick Saia (Ed.); Peter Stanton (Pub.); Mark Murray; Kelly Ansley; Kira Beaudoin (Prod.)
Parent company (for newspapers): New England Business Media

MICHIGAN

ADVERTISER TIMES

Street address 1: 13650 11 Mile Road
Street address city: Warren
Street address state: MI
Zip/Postal code: 48089
General Phone: (586) 498-8000
General Fax: (586) 498-9631
Advertising Phone: (586) 498-1032
Editorial Phone: (586) 498-1053
General/National Adv. E-mail: emyers@candgnews.com
Display Adv. E-mail: emyers@candgnews.com
Editorial e-mail: jdemers@candgnews.com
Primary Website: candgnews.com
Year Established: 1981
Avg Free Circ: 24288
Audit By: Sworn/Estimate/Non-Audited
Audit Date: 10.06.2019
Personnel: Gregg Demers (Owner); Jeff Demers (Adv. Mgr.); Gilbert Demers (Mng. Ed.); Keith Demers (Prodn. Mgr.); Elaine Myers (Adv. Mgr); David Demers (Circ. Mgr); Barry Bernard (Prod. Mgr)
Parent company (for newspapers): C & G Newspapers; C&G Publishing

ALBION RECORDER

Street address 1: 125 E Cass St
Street address city: Albion
Street address state: MI
Zip/Postal code: 49224-1726
General Phone: (517) 629-0041
General Fax: (517) 629-5210
General/National Adv. E-mail: therecorder@frontiernet.net
Avg Paid Circ: 1100
Audit By: Sworn/Estimate/Non-Audited
Audit Date: 10.06.2019
Personnel: Kathy Palon (Adv. Mgr., Ed.); Kara DeChalk (Mgr., Adv. Consultant)

ALCONA COUNTY REVIEW

Street address 1: 111 N Lake St
Street address city: Harrisville
Street address state: MI
Zip/Postal code: 48740-9696
General Phone: (989) 724-6384
General Fax: (989) 724-6655
Advertising Phone: (989) 724-6384
Advertising Fax: (989)724-6655
Editorial Phone: (989) 724-6384
Editorial Fax: (989) 724-6655
General/National Adv. E-mail: comp@alconareview.com
Display Adv. E-mail: subscribe@alconareview.com
Editorial e-mail: editor@alconareview.com
Primary Website: alconareview.com
Year Established: 1877
Avg Paid Circ: 3200
Audit By: Sworn/Estimate/Non-Audited
Audit Date: 10.06.2019
Personnel: Cheryl L. Peterson (Pub./Ed.); John Boufford (Prodn. Mgr.); Eileen Roe (Office/Circ. Mgr.)

ALLEGAN COUNTY NEWS

Street address 1: 241 Hubbard St
Street address city: Allegan
Street address state: MI
Zip/Postal code: 49010-1320
General Phone: (269) 673-5534
General Fax: (269) 673-5535
Advertising Phone: (269) 673-5534
Advertising Fax: (269) 673-5535
Editorial Phone: (269) 673-5534
Editorial Fax: (269) 673-5535
General/National Adv. E-mail: accountsrec@allegannews.com
Display Adv. E-mail: accountsrec@allegannews.com
Editorial e-mail: editor@allegannews.com
Primary Website: allegannews.com
Year Established: 1858
Avg Paid Circ: 3361
Avg Free Circ: 83
Audit By: Sworn/Estimate/Non-Audited
Audit Date: 10.06.2019
Personnel: Ryan Lewis (Ed.); Mike Wilcox (Publisher, owner)
Parent company (for newspapers): Kaechele Publications, Inc.

ANN ARBOR OBSERVER

Street address 1: 2390 Winewood Ave
Street address city: Ann Arbor
Street address state: MI
Zip/Postal code: 48103-3841
General Phone: (734) 769-3175
General Fax: (734) 769-3375
General/National Adv. E-mail: ads@aaobserver.com
Display Adv. E-mail: adsales@aaobserver.com
Editorial e-mail: editor@aaobserver.com
Primary Website: aaobserver.com
Mthly Avg Views: 500000
Year Established: 1976
Avg Paid Circ: 2125
Avg Free Circ: 28534
Audit By: Sworn/Estimate/Non-Audited
Audit Date: 10.06.2019
Personnel: Caron Valentine-Marsh (Creative Director)

ARENAC COUNTY INDEPENDENT

Street address 1: 1010 W Cedar St
Street address city: Standish
Street address state: MI
Zip/Postal code: 48658-9421
General Phone: (989) 846-4531
General Fax: (989) 846-9868
General/National Adv. E-mail: sales@arenacindependent.com
Display Adv. E-mail: classifieds@arenacindependent.com
Editorial e-mail: news@arenacindependent.com
Primary Website: arenacindependent.com
Year Established: 1883
Avg Paid Circ: 6000
Audit By: Sworn/Estimate/Non-Audited
Audit Date: 30.09.2017
Personnel: Elizabeth Gorske (Pub.); Eric Young (Mng. Ed.); Carla Reeves (Sales)

BANNER

Street address 1: 4241 Main St
Street address city: Brown City
Street address state: MI
Zip/Postal code: 48416-7715
General Phone: (810) 346-2753
General Fax: (810) 346-2579
General/National Adv. E-mail: bcbanner@lapeergroup.com
Display Adv. E-mail: ads@mihomepaper.com
Editorial e-mail: lettersbcb@mihomepaper.com
Primary Website: browncitybanner.mihomepaper.com
Avg Paid Circ: 1814
Audit By: Sworn/Estimate/Non-Audited
Audit Date: 10.06.2019
Personnel: Peter Neil (Pub.); Wes Smith

BEDFORD NOW

Street address 1: 20 W 1st St
Street address city: Monroe
Street address state: MI
Zip/Postal code: 48161-2333
General Phone: (734) 242-1100
General Fax: (734) 242-0937
Advertising Phone: (734) 240-5712
Editorial Phone: (734) 240-5776
General/National Adv. E-mail: trent@monroenews.com
Display Adv. E-mail: ebaldock@monroenews.com
Classified Adv. e-mail: dzewicky@monroenews.com
Primary Website: bedfordnow.com
Audit By: Sworn/Estimate/Non-Audited
Audit Date: 10.06.2019
Personnel: Paula Wethington (Reporter); Vince Bodiford (Pub.); Jeff Stahl (Circ. Mgr.); Ray Kisonas (Exec. Ed.); Colleen Morden (Adv. Sales)
Parent company (for newspapers): CherryRoad Media

BELLEVILLE-AREA INDEPENDENT

Street address 1: 152 Main St
Street address 2: Ste 9
Street address city: Belleville
Street address state: MI
Zip/Postal code: 48111-3911
General Phone: (734) 699-9020
General Fax: (734) 699-8962
General/National Adv. E-mail: mail@bellevilleareaindependent.com
Primary Website: bellevilleareaindependent.com
Year Established: 1995
Avg Paid Circ: 342
Avg Free Circ: 6600
Audit By: Sworn/Estimate/Non-Audited
Audit Date: 10.06.2019
Personnel: Robert Mytych (Adv. Mgr.); Rosemary K. Otzman (PUB.); James Otzman (Prodn. Mgr.); Janet Millard

BERRIEN COUNTY RECORD

Street address 1: 206 Main St
Street address city: Buchanan
Street address state: MI
Zip/Postal code: 49107-1376
General Phone: (269) 695-3878
General Fax: (269) 695-3880
Editorial e-mail: bcrnews@bcrnews.net
Primary Website: bcrnews.net
Year Established: 1865
Avg Paid Circ: 2600
Avg Free Circ: 176
Audit By: Sworn/Estimate/Non-Audited
Audit Date: 10.06.2019
Personnel: Survey Contact

BIRMINGHAM ECCENTRIC

Street address 1: 615 W Lafayette Blvd
Street address 2: # 2
Street address city: Detroit
Street address state: MI
Zip/Postal code: 48226-3124
General Phone: (866) 887-2737
Advertising Phone: (800) 579-7355
Editorial Phone: (313) 222-5397
General/National Adv. E-mail: fcibor@hometownlife.com
Display Adv. E-mail: cewilson@hometownlife.com
Editorial e-mail: srosiek@hometownlife.com
Primary Website: hometownlife.com
Year Established: 1869
Avg Paid Circ: 1748
Avg Free Circ: 4705
Audit By: Sworn/Estimate/Non-Audited
Audit Date: 10.06.2019
Personnel: Phillip Allmen (Consumer Exp. Dir.)
Parent company (for newspapers): Gannett

BIRMINGHAM-BLOOMFIELD EAGLE

Street address 1: 13650 11 Mile Road
Street address city: Warren
Street address state: MI
Zip/Postal code: 48089
General Phone: (586) 498-8000
General Fax: (586) 498-9631
Advertising Phone: (586) 498-1051
Editorial Phone: (586) 498-1071
General/National Adv. E-mail: emyers@candgnews.com
Display Adv. E-mail: emyers@candgnews.com
Editorial e-mail: jdemers@candgnews.com
Primary Website: candgnews.com
Year Established: 2003
Avg Free Circ: 33334
Audit By: AAM
Audit Date: 31.03.2018
Personnel: Jeff Demers (Adv. Sales Mgr.); Gregg Demers (Ed.); Elaine Myers (Adv. Mgr); David Demers (Circ. Mgr); Barry Bernard (Prod. Mgr)
Parent company (for newspapers): C & G Newspapers; C&G Publishing

BLUE WATER VOICE

Street address 1: 19176 Hall Rd
Street address 2: Ste 200
Street address city: Clinton Township
Street address state: MI
Zip/Postal code: 48038-6914
General Phone: (586) 716-8100
General Fax: (586) 719-8918
General/National Adv. E-mail: dawn.emke@voicenews.com
Display Adv. E-mail: classified.voice@voicenews.com
Editorial e-mail: editor@voicenews.com
Primary Website: voicenews.com
Year Established: 1983
Avg Paid Circ: 40
Avg Free Circ: 9697
Audit By: Sworn/Estimate/Non-Audited
Audit Date: 10.06.2019
Personnel: Debbie Loggins (Gen. Mgr.); Jeff Payne (Ed.); Don Wyatt (VP)
Parent company (for newspapers): Digital First Media

CANTON EAGLE

Street address 1: 502 Forest Ave
Street address city: Plymouth
Street address state: MI
Zip/Postal code: 48170-1752
General Phone: (734) 467-1900

General Fax: (734) 729-1840
General/National Adv. E-mail: ads@journalgroup.com
Editorial e-mail: editor@journalgroup.com
Primary Website: journalgroup.com
Year Established: 2002
Avg Paid Circ: 15000
Audit By: Sworn/Estimate/Non-Audited
Audit Date: 10.06.2019
Personnel: Susan Willett (Pub.)
Parent company (for newspapers): Associated Newspapers of Michigan

CANTON OBSERVER

Street address 1: 615 W Lafayette Blvd
Street address 2: # 2
Street address city: Detroit
Street address state: MI
Zip/Postal code: 48226-3124
General Phone: (866) 887-2737
Advertising Phone: (800) 579-7355
Editorial Phone: (313) 222-5397
General/National Adv. E-mail: fcibor@hometownlife.com
Display Adv. E-mail: cewilson@hometownlife.com
Editorial e-mail: srosiek@hometownlife.com
Primary Website: hometownlife.com
Year Established: 1869
Avg Paid Circ: 2232
Avg Free Circ: 4350
Audit By: Sworn/Estimate/Non-Audited
Audit Date: 10.06.2019
Personnel: Darrell Clem (Reporter)
Parent company (for newspapers): Gannett

CASS CITY CHRONICLE

Street address 1: 6550 Main St
Street address city: Cass City
Street address state: MI
Zip/Postal code: 48726-1561
General Phone: (989) 872-2010
General Fax: (989) 872-3810
General/National Adv. E-mail: sales@ccchronicle.net
Display Adv. E-mail: sales@ccchronicle.net
Editorial e-mail: tom@ccchronicle.net
Primary Website: ccchronicle.net
Year Established: 1899
Avg Paid Circ: 2400
Audit By: Sworn/Estimate/Non-Audited
Audit Date: 10.06.2019
Personnel: Tom Montgomery (Ed.); Clarke Blank (Sports)

CASSOPOLIS VIGILANT

Street address 1: 217 N 4th St
Street address city: Niles
Street address state: MI
Zip/Postal code: 49120-2301
General Phone: (269) 683-2101
General Fax: (269) 683-2175
General/National Adv. E-mail: phil.langer@leaderpub.com
Display Adv. E-mail: donna.knight@leaderpub.com
Editorial e-mail: ambrosia.neldon@leaderpub.com
Primary Website: cassopolisvigilant.com
Avg Paid Circ: 800
Audit By: Sworn/Estimate/Non-Audited
Audit Date: 10.06.2019
Personnel: Scott Novak (Community ed.)
Parent company (for newspapers): Boone Newspapers, Inc.

CHARLEVOIX COURIER

Street address 1: 411 Bridge St
Street address city: Charlevoix
Street address state: MI
Zip/Postal code: 49720-1416
General Phone: (231) 547-6558
General Fax: (231) 547-4992
General/National Adv. E-mail: jfoley@charlevoixcourier.com
Display Adv. E-mail: haugust@petoskeynews.com
Editorial e-mail: news@charlevoixcourier.com
Primary Website: petoskeynews.com/charlevoix
Year Established: 1883
Avg Paid Circ: 3500
Audit By: Sworn/Estimate/Non-Audited
Audit Date: 10.06.2019
Personnel: Doug Caldwell (Pub.); Lisa Sladek (Gen. Mgr.); Christy Lyons (Adv. Dir.)
Parent company (for newspapers): Schurz Communications Inc

CITIZEN

Street address 1: 12 South St
Street address city: Ortonville
Street address state: MI
Zip/Postal code: 48462-7717
General Phone: (248) 627-4332
General Fax: (248) 627-4408
Advertising Phone: (248) 627-4332
Advertising Fax: (248) 627-4408
Editorial Phone: (248) 627-4332
General/National Adv. E-mail: citads@citnewspaper.com
Display Adv. E-mail: citads@citnewspaper.com
Editorial e-mail: citnews@citnewspaper.com
Primary Website: thecitizenonline.com
Year Established: 1995
Avg Free Circ: 11800
Audit By: Sworn/Estimate/Non-Audited
Audit Date: 10.06.2019
Personnel: Jim Sherman (Pub); Jackie Nowiki (Adv. Mgr.)
Parent company (for newspapers): Waxa

CLARKSTON NEWS

Street address 1: 5 S Main St
Street address 2: Ste 1
Street address city: Clarkston
Street address state: MI
Zip/Postal code: 48346-1597
General Phone: (248) 625-3370
General Fax: (248) 625-0706
Advertising Phone: (248) 625-3370
Editorial Phone: (248) 625-3370
General/National Adv. E-mail: don@shermanpublications.org
Display Adv. E-mail: don@shermanpublications.org
Editorial e-mail: shermanpub@aol.com
Primary Website: clarkstonnews.com
Year Established: 1929
Avg Paid Circ: 2419
Avg Free Circ: 0
Audit By: CVC
Audit Date: 30.06.2018
Personnel: James A. Sherman (Pub.); Don Rush (Gen. Mgr.); Phil Custodio (Ed.)
Parent company (for newspapers): Waxa

COLON EXPRESS

Street address 1: PO Box 483
Street address 2: 212 East State Street
Street address city: Colon
Street address state: MI
Zip/Postal code: 49040-0483
General Phone: (269) 432-3488
General/National Adv. E-mail: sales@fabmagic.com
Display Adv. E-mail: sales@fabmagic.com
Editorial e-mail: sales@fabmagic.com
Primary Website: thecolonexpress.com
Year Established: 2015
Avg Paid Circ: 1111
Avg Free Circ: 27
Audit By: Sworn/Estimate/Non-Audited
Audit Date: 10.06.2019
Personnel: Rick Fisher (Publisher,editor)
Parent company (for newspapers): FAB Magic Mfg Company

COUNTY PRESS

Street address 1: PO Box 279
Street address 2: 11501 Mackie Rd
Street address city: Parma
Street address state: MI
Zip/Postal code: 49269-0279
General Phone: (517) 531-4542
General Fax: (517) 531-3576
General/National Adv. E-mail: advertising@jxncopress.com
Editorial e-mail: editor@jxncopress.com
Primary Website: jxncopress.com
Year Established: 1868
Avg Paid Circ: 1500
Avg Free Circ: 0
Audit By: Sworn/Estimate/Non-Audited
Audit Date: 10.06.2019
Personnel: Erika Sponsler (Publ./Bus Mgr.); Lucas Sponsler (Ed./Pub.)

COURIER-LEADER

Street address 1: 32280 E Red Arrow Hwy
Street address city: Paw Paw
Street address state: MI
Zip/Postal code: 49079-8764
General Phone: (269) 657-3072
General Fax: (269) 657-5723
General/National Adv. E-mail: ads@vineyardpress.biz
Display Adv. E-mail: sales@vineyardpress.biz
Editorial e-mail: couriereditorial@vineyardpress.biz
Primary Website: pawpawcourierleader.com
Year Established: 1844
Avg Paid Circ: 2987
Avg Free Circ: 16300
Audit By: Sworn/Estimate/Non-Audited
Audit Date: 10.06.2019
Personnel: Steven A. Racette (Gen. Mgr.); Robin Griffin (Mng. Ed.); Ashley Moore (Adv.)

CRAWFORD COUNTY AVALANCHE

Street address 1: 102 E Michigan Ave
Street address city: Grayling
Street address state: MI
Zip/Postal code: 49738-1741
General Phone: (989) 348-6811
General Fax: (989) 348-6806
General/National Adv. E-mail: avalanche@i2k.net
Primary Website: crawfordcountyavalanche.com
Year Established: 1879
Avg Paid Circ: 5000
Audit By: Sworn/Estimate/Non-Audited
Audit Date: 10.06.2019
Personnel: Linda Golnick (Gen. Mgr.); Caleb Casey (Managing Ed.)

DEARBORN TIMES-HERALD

Street address 1: 13730 Michigan Ave
Street address city: Dearborn
Street address state: MI
Zip/Postal code: 48126-3520
General Phone: (313) 584-4000
General Fax: (313) 584-1357
General/National Adv. E-mail: timesheraldads@yahoo.com
Display Adv. E-mail: timesheraldclassifieds@yahoo.com
Editorial e-mail: DbnTHerald@aol.com
Primary Website: downriversundaytimes.com
Year Established: 1963
Avg Paid Circ: 5639
Avg Free Circ: 847
Audit By: Sworn/Estimate/Non-Audited
Audit Date: 10.06.2019
Personnel: Michael Bewick (Pub.); Jonh Manzi (Adv. Mgr.); Jon Walton (Circ. Mgr.)

DECATUR REPUBLICAN

Street address 1: 121 S Phelps St
Street address city: Decatur
Street address state: MI
Zip/Postal code: 49045-1117
General Phone: (269) 423-2411
Primary Website: facebook.com/pages/Decatur-Republican/144973075525863
Avg Paid Circ: 1960
Avg Free Circ: 49
Audit By: Sworn/Estimate/Non-Audited
Audit Date: 10.06.2019
Personnel: David D. Moormann (Ed.)

DELTA WAVERLY COMMUNITY NEWS

Street address 1: 120 E Lenawee St
Street address city: Lansing
Street address state: MI
Zip/Postal code: 48919-1000
General Phone: (517) 377-1000
Advertising Phone: (517) 377-1082
General/National Adv. E-mail: sking@lsj.com
Display Adv. E-mail: classifieds@lsj.com
Editorial e-mail: sangel@lsj.com
Primary Website: lsj.com
Year Established: 1856
Avg Free Circ: 4344
Audit By: Sworn/Estimate/Non-Audited
Audit Date: 10.06.2019
Personnel: Brian Priester (Pub.); Stacia King (Adv. Mgr); Mark Conover (Circ. Mgr); Jack Conaboy (Prod. Mgr)

DEWITT BATH REVIEW

Street address 1: 120 E Lenawee St
Street address city: Lansing
Street address state: MI
Zip/Postal code: 48919-1000
General Phone: (517) 377-1000
Advertising Phone: (517) 377-1082
General/National Adv. E-mail: sking@lsj.com
Display Adv. E-mail: classifieds@lsj.com
Editorial e-mail: sangel@lsj.com
Primary Website: lsj.com
Year Established: 1856
Avg Paid Circ: 5
Avg Free Circ: 6261
Audit By: Sworn/Estimate/Non-Audited
Audit Date: 10.06.2019
Personnel: Brian Priester (Pub.); Stacia King (Adv. Mgr); Mark Conover (Circ. Mgr); Jack Conaboy (Prod. Mgr)

DOWNRIVER VOICE

Street address 1: 19176 Hall Rd
Street address 2: Ste 200
Street address city: Clinton Township
Street address state: MI
Zip/Postal code: 48038-6914
General Phone: (586) 716-8100
General Fax: (586) 716-8918
General/National Adv. E-mail: debbie.loggins@voicenews.com
Display Adv. E-mail: classified.voice@voicenews.com
Editorial e-mail: editor@voicenews.com
Primary Website: voicenews.com
Year Established: 1983
Avg Free Circ: 9234
Audit By: Sworn/Estimate/Non-Audited
Audit Date: 10.06.2019
Personnel: Debra Loggins (Gen. Mgr.); Jeff Payne (Ed.); Rene Allard (Circ. Mgr.)

EATON RAPIDS COMMUNITY NEWS

Street address 1: 120 E Lenawee St
Street address city: Lansing
Street address state: MI
Zip/Postal code: 48919-1000
General Phone: (517) 377-1000
Advertising Phone: (517) 377-1082
General/National Adv. E-mail: sking@lsj.com
Display Adv. E-mail: classifieds@lsj.com
Editorial e-mail: sangel@lsj.com
Primary Website: lsj.com
Year Established: 1856
Avg Paid Circ: 3
Avg Free Circ: 4321
Audit By: Sworn/Estimate/Non-Audited
Audit Date: 10.06.2019
Personnel: Brian Priester (Pub.); Stacia King (Adv. Mgr); Mark Conover (Circ. Mgr); Jack Conaboy (Prod. Mgr)

EDWARDSBURG ARGUS

Street address 1: 217 N 4th St
Street address city: Niles
Street address state: MI
Zip/Postal code: 49120-2301
General Phone: (269) 683-2100
General Fax: (269) 683-2175
Editorial Phone: (269) 687-7713
General/National Adv. E-mail: phil.langer@leaderpub.com
Editorial e-mail: ambrosia.neldon@leaderpub.com
Primary Website: edwardsburgargus.com
Avg Paid Circ: 800
Avg Free Circ: 21
Audit By: Sworn/Estimate/Non-Audited
Audit Date: 10.06.2019
Personnel: Scott Novak (Community Ed.)
Parent company (for newspapers): Boone Newspapers, Inc.

FARMERS ADVANCE

Street address 1: 331 E Bell St
Street address city: Camden
Street address state: MI

Zip/Postal code: 49232-9613
General Phone: (517) 368-0365
General Fax: (517) 368-5131
General/National Adv. E-mail: jhite@gannett.com
Primary Website: farmersadvance.com
Avg Paid Circ: 12000
Audit By: Sworn/Estimate/Non-Audited
Audit Date: 10.06.2019
Personnel: Cindy George-Bealer (Pub.)

FARMINGTON OBSERVER

Street address 1: 615 W Lafayette Blvd
Street address 2: # 2
Street address city: Detroit
Street address state: MI
Zip/Postal code: 48226-3124
General Phone: (866) 887-2737
General Fax: (313) 223-3318
Advertising Phone: (800) 579-7355
Primary Website: www.hometownlife.com
Avg Paid Circ: 895
Avg Free Circ: 7190
Audit By: AAM
Audit Date: 31.12.2018
Personnel: Jani Hayden (Dir. Adv.)
Parent company (for newspapers): Gannett

FARMINGTON PRESS

Street address 1: 13650 11 Mile Road
Street address city: Warren
Street address state: MI
Zip/Postal code: 48089
General Phone: (586) 498-8000
General Fax: (586) 498-9631
Advertising Phone: (586) 498-1032
Editorial Phone: (586) 498-1071
General/National Adv. E-mail: emyers@candgnews.com
Display Adv. E-mail: emyers@candgnews.com
Editorial e-mail: jdemers@candgnews.com
Primary Website: candgnews.com
Year Established: 2008
Avg Free Circ: 37805
Audit By: AAM
Audit Date: 31.03.2018
Personnel: Jeff Demers (Dir of Sales); Elaine Myers (Adv. Mgr); David Demers (Circ. Mgr); Barry Bernard (Prod. Mgr)
Parent company (for newspapers): C & G Newspapers; C&G Publishing

FLASHES ADVERTISING & NEWS

Street address 1: 241 S Cochran Ave
Street address city: Charlotte
Street address state: MI
Zip/Postal code: 48813-1584
General Phone: (517) 543-1099
General Fax: (517) 543-1993
Advertising Phone: (517) 543-1099 ext 225
Advertising Fax: (517) 543-1993
Editorial Phone: (517) 543-1099 ext 227
Editorial Fax: (517) 543-1993
General/National Adv. E-mail: cgwing@county-journal.com
Display Adv. E-mail: cgwing@county-journal.com
Classified Adv. e-mail: sales@county-journal.com
Editorial e-mail: news@county-journal.com
Primary Website: www.county-journal.com
Year Established: 1945
Avg Paid Circ: 15
Avg Free Circ: 5000
Audit By: CVC
Audit Date: 12.07.2020
Personnel: Cindy Gaedert (Publisher/Sales/Owner); Travis Silvas (Circ. Mgr)
Parent company (for newspapers): The County Journal

FLINT TOWNSHIP VIEW

Street address 1: 1521 Imlay City Rd
Street address city: Lapeer
Street address state: MI
Zip/Postal code: 48446
General Phone: (810) 664-0811
General Fax: (810) 687-8308
General/National Adv. E-mail: pclinton@mihomepaper.comc
Display Adv. E-mail: pclinton@mihomepaper.com
Editorial e-mail: wsmith@mihomepaper.com
Primary Website: mihomepaper.com
Year Established: 2010
Avg Free Circ: 8078
Audit By: CVC
Audit Date: 30.06.2018
Personnel: Wes Smith (Pub./Ed.); Pete Clinton (Adv. Mgr); Sharon DeFrain (Circ.); Liz LaFave (Prod.)
Parent company (for newspapers): View Newspaepr Group

FRANKENMUTH NEWS

Street address 1: 527 N Franklin St
Street address 2: Ste A
Street address city: Frankenmuth
Street address state: MI
Zip/Postal code: 48734-2011
General Phone: (989) 652-3246
General Fax: (989) 652-2417
General/National Adv. E-mail: frankenmuthnews@airadvantage.net
Display Adv. E-mail: frankenmuthnews@airadv.net
Editorial e-mail: swenzel@airadv.net
Primary Website: frankenmuthnews.com
Year Established: 1906
Avg Paid Circ: 5000
Audit By: Sworn/Estimate/Non-Audited
Audit Date: 10.06.2019
Personnel: Steven Grainger (Pub.); Vicky Hayden (Adv. Mgr.); Scott Wenzel (Ed.)

FRASER-CLINTON CHRONICLE

Street address 1: 13650 11 Mile Road
Street address city: Warren
Street address state: MI
Zip/Postal code: 48089
General Phone: (586) 498-8000
General Fax: (586) 498-9631
Advertising Phone: (586) 498-1032
Editorial Phone: (586) 498-1059
General/National Adv. E-mail: emyers@candgnews.com
Display Adv. E-mail: emyers@candgnews.com
Editorial e-mail: nmordowanec@candgnews.com
Primary Website: candgnews.com
Year Established: 1989
Avg Free Circ: 32409
Audit By: CVC
Audit Date: 30.03.2018
Personnel: Nick Mordowanec; Jeff Demers (Adv. Mgr.); Keith Demers (Circ. Mgr.); Barry Bernard (Prodn. Mgr.); Elaine Myers (Adv. Mgr); David Demers (Circ. Mgr); Barry Bernard (Prod. Mgr)
Parent company (for newspapers): C & G Newspapers; C&G Publishing

FREMONT TIMES-INDICATOR

Street address 1: 44 W Main St
Street address city: Fremont
Street address state: MI
Zip/Postal code: 49412-1176
General Phone: (231) 924-4400
General Fax: (231) 924-4066
General/National Adv. E-mail: tinews@comcast.net
Primary Website: timesindicator.com
Year Established: 1878
Avg Paid Circ: 7500
Audit By: Sworn/Estimate/Non-Audited
Audit Date: 10.06.2019
Personnel: Richard C. Wheater (Ed.)

GARDEN CITY OBSERVER

Street address 1: 615 W Lafayette Blvd
Street address 2: # 2
Street address city: Detroit
Street address state: MI
Zip/Postal code: 48226-3124
General Phone: (866) 887-2737
Advertising Phone: (800) 579-7355
Editorial Phone: (313) 222-5397
Editorial Fax: (313) 223-3318
General/National Adv. E-mail: fcibor@hometownlife.com
Display Adv. E-mail: cewilson@hometownlife.com
Editorial e-mail: srosiek@hometownlife.com
Primary Website: hometownlife.com
Year Established: 1869
Avg Paid Circ: 4262
Avg Free Circ: 5680
Audit By: AAM
Audit Date: 30.09.2016
Personnel: Jani Hayden (Dir. Adv.); Philip Allmen
Parent company (for newspapers): Gannett

GAYLORD HERALD TIMES

Street address 1: 2058 S Otsego Ave
Street address city: Gaylord
Street address state: MI
Zip/Postal code: 49735-9422
General Phone: (989) 732-1111
General Fax: (989) 732-3490
General/National Adv. E-mail: editor@gaylordheraldtimes.com
Primary Website: gaylordheraldtimes.com
Year Established: 1875
Avg Paid Circ: 7000
Avg Free Circ: 13000
Audit By: Sworn/Estimate/Non-Audited
Audit Date: 10.06.2019
Personnel: Jeremy Speer (Ed.)
Parent company (for newspapers): Schurz Communications Inc

GENESEE COUNTY HERALD, INC.

Street address 1: G 10098 N Dort Hwy
Street address city: Clio
Street address state: MI
Zip/Postal code: 48420
General Phone: (810) 686-3840
General Fax: (810) 686-9181
Primary Website: myherald.net
Avg Free Circ: 22153
Audit By: Sworn/Estimate/Non-Audited
Audit Date: 10.06.2019
Personnel: Mike Harrington (Pub.)

GLADWIN COUNTY RECORD

Street address 1: 700 E Cedar Ave
Street address city: Gladwin
Street address state: MI
Zip/Postal code: 48624-2218
General Phone: (989) 426-9411
General Fax: (989) 426-2023
General/National Adv. E-mail: sdoane@thegladwincountyrecord.com
Display Adv. E-mail: dlaidlaw@thegladwincountyrecord.com
Editorial e-mail: npaisley@thegladwincountyrecord.com
Primary Website: gladwinmi.com
Year Established: 1877
Avg Paid Circ: 4200
Avg Free Circ: 120
Audit By: Sworn/Estimate/Non-Audited
Audit Date: 10.06.2019
Personnel: Dawn Laidlaw (Office Mgr.)
Parent company (for newspapers): Adams Publishing Group, LLC

GRAND BLANC NEWS

Street address 1: 200 E 1st St
Street address city: Flint
Street address state: MI
Zip/Postal code: 48502-1911
General Phone: (810) 766-6323
General Fax: (810) 766-6393
Primary Website: thecommunitynewspapers.com
Avg Paid Circ: 14951
Audit By: Sworn/Estimate/Non-Audited
Audit Date: 10.06.2019
Personnel: Dave Sharp (Pub.); Mary Alexander (Adv. Mgr.); Katie Bach (Ed.)
Parent company (for newspapers): Advance Publications, Inc.

GRAND BLANC VIEW

Street address 1: 220 N Main St
Street address city: Davison
Street address state: MI
Zip/Postal code: 48423-1432
General Phone: (810) 653-3511
General Fax: (810) 667-6309
Editorial Phone: (810) 653-3511 ext. 211
General/National Adv. E-mail: pclinton@mihomepaper.com
Display Adv. E-mail: pclinton@mihomepaper.com
Editorial e-mail: ggould@mihomepaper.com
Primary Website: http://grandblancview.mihomepaper.com/
Year Established: 2005
Avg Free Circ: 27641
Audit By: CVC
Audit Date: 30.06.2017
Personnel: Wes Smith (Pub./Ed.); Pete Clinton (Adv. Mgr); Dale Phillips (Circ. Mgr); Rick Burrough (Owner)
Parent company (for newspapers): View Newspaper Group

GRAND LEDGE INDEPENDENT

Street address 1: 120 E. Lenawee Street
Street address 2: Ste 300
Street address city: Lansing
Street address state: MI
Zip/Postal code: 48919
General Phone: (517) 377-1000
General Fax: (517) 627-3497
Advertising Phone: (517) 377-1082
General/National Adv. E-mail: sking@lsj.com
Display Adv. E-mail: classifieds@lsj.com
Editorial e-mail: sangel@lsj.com
Primary Website: lsj.com
Year Established: 1856
Avg Paid Circ: 6
Avg Free Circ: 7643
Audit By: Sworn/Estimate/Non-Audited
Audit Date: 10.06.2019
Personnel: Brian Priester (Pub.); Stacia King (Adv. Mgr); Mark Conover (Circ. Mgr); Jack Conaboy (Prod. Mgr)
Parent company (for newspapers): Gannett Company Inc.

GRATIOT COUNTY HERALD

Street address 1: 123 N Main St
Street address city: Ithaca
Street address state: MI
Zip/Postal code: 48847-1131
General Phone: (989) 875-4151
General Fax: (989) 875-3159
General/National Adv. E-mail: gcherald@gcherald.com
Editorial e-mail: greg@gcherald.com
Primary Website: gcherald.com
Avg Paid Circ: 6727
Audit By: Sworn/Estimate/Non-Audited
Audit Date: 10.06.2019
Personnel: Greg Nelson (Ed.); Tom MacDonald (Pub.)

GREEN SHEET CLASSIFIEDS

Street address 1: 323 E. Grand River Avenue
Street address city: Howell
Street address state: MI
Zip/Postal code: 48843
General Phone: (517) 377-1001
Primary Website: michigan.com
Avg Free Circ: 41967
Audit By: AAM
Audit Date: 30.09.2018
Personnel: Rebecca Poynter (Pres.)
Parent company (for newspapers): Gannett - USA Today Network

GROSSE POINTE NEWS

Street address 1: 21316 Mack Ave
Street address city: Grosse Pointe Woods
Street address state: MI
Zip/Postal code: 48236-1047
General Phone: (313) 882-6900
General Fax: (313) 343-5569
Advertising Phone: (313) 882-3500
Advertising Fax: (313) 882-1585
Editorial Phone: (313) 882-0294
Editorial Fax: (313) 882-1585
General/National Adv. E-mail: schambers@grossepointenews.com
Display Adv. E-mail: apanski@grossepointenews.com
Editorial e-mail: editor@grossepointenews.com
Primary Website: grossepointenews.com
Year Established: 1940
Avg Paid Circ: 12014
Audit By: Sworn/Estimate/Non-Audited
Audit Date: 10.06.2019

Personnel: Scott Chambers (Pub.)

GROSSE POINTE TIMES

Street address 1: 13650 11 Mile Road
Street address city: Warren
Street address state: MI
Zip/Postal code: 48089
General Phone: (586) 498-8000
General Fax: (586) 498-9631
Advertising Phone: (586) 279-1113
Editorial Phone: (586) 498-1053
General/National Adv. E-mail: emyers@candgnews.com
Display Adv. E-mail: emyers@candgnews.com
Editorial e-mail: jdemers@candgnews.com
Primary Website: candgnews.com
Year Established: 1982
Avg Free Circ: 18810
Audit By: AAM
Audit Date: 30.09.2018
Personnel: Jeff Demers (Adv. Mgr.); Elaine Myers (Adv. Mgr); David Demers (Circ. Mgr); Barry Bernard (Prod. Mgr)
Parent company (for newspapers): C & G Newspapers; C&G Publishing

HARBOR COUNTRY NEWS

Street address 1: 122 N Whittaker St
Street address city: New Buffalo
Street address state: MI
Zip/Postal code: 49117-1169
General Phone: (800) 726-5735
Advertising Phone: (219) 874-7211
General/National Adv. E-mail: news@harborcountry-news.com
Display Adv. E-mail: lsherman@harborcountry-news.com
Editorial e-mail: news@harborcountry-news.com
Primary Website: harborcountry-news.com
Year Established: 1984
Avg Free Circ: 9200
Audit By: Sworn/Estimate/Non-Audited
Audit Date: 10.06.2019
Personnel: Isis Cains (Adv. Dir.); Dave Johnson (Ed.)
Parent company (for newspapers): Paxton Media Group

HARBOR LIGHT

Street address 1: 211 E 3rd St
Street address city: Harbor Springs
Street address state: MI
Zip/Postal code: 49740-1534
General Phone: (231) 526-2191
General Fax: (231) 526-7634
General/National Adv. E-mail: michelle@ncpublish.com
Display Adv. E-mail: michelle@ncpublish.com
Editorial e-mail: news@ncpublish.com
Primary Website: harborlightnews.com
Year Established: 1970
Avg Paid Circ: 2000
Avg Free Circ: 69
Audit By: Sworn/Estimate/Non-Audited
Audit Date: 10.06.2019
Personnel: Michelle Ketterer (Adv. Mgr.); Charles O'Neill (Ed.); Kate Bassett (News Editor)

HERALD REVIEW

Street address 1: 115 N Michigan Ave
Street address city: Big Rapids
Street address state: MI
Zip/Postal code: 49307-1401
General Phone: (231) 832-5566
General Fax: (231) 796-1152
General/National Adv. E-mail: bbriscoe@pioneergroup.com
Display Adv. E-mail: classified@pioneergroup.com
Editorial e-mail: heraldreview@pioneergroup.com
Primary Website: theheraldreview.com
Year Established: 1862
Avg Paid Circ: 3500
Avg Free Circ: 15
Audit By: Sworn/Estimate/Non-Audited
Audit Date: 10.06.2019
Personnel: John Norton (Pub.); Jim Crees (Ed.)
Parent company (for newspapers): Pioneer Group

HURON COUNTY VIEW

Street address 1: 592 N Port Crescent St
Street address city: Bad Axe
Street address state: MI
Zip/Postal code: 48413-1209
General Phone: (989) 269-9918
General Fax: (989) 269-7730
General/National Adv. E-mail: sales@mihomepaper.com
Display Adv. E-mail: sales@mihomepaper.com
Editorial e-mail: bmuir@mihomepaper.com
Primary Website: huroncountyview.com
Year Established: 1980
Avg Free Circ: 18457
Audit By: CVC
Audit Date: 30.11.2018
Personnel: Jane Vanderpoel (Pub.)
Parent company (for newspapers): JAMS Media

INGHAM COUNTY COMMUNITY NEWS

Street address 1: 120 E Lenawee St
Street address city: Lansing
Street address state: MI
Zip/Postal code: 48919-1000
General Phone: (517) 377-1000
Advertising Phone: (517) 377-1082
General/National Adv. E-mail: slucius@gannett.com
Display Adv. E-mail: classifieds@lsj.com
Editorial e-mail: sangel@lsj.com
Primary Website: lsj.com
Year Established: 1856
Avg Free Circ: 6993
Audit By: Sworn/Estimate/Non-Audited
Audit Date: 10.06.2019
Personnel: Brian Priester (Pub.); Stacia King (Adv. Mgr); Mark Conover (Circ. Mgr); Jack Conaboy (Prod. Mgr)

IOSCO COUNTY NEWS HERALD

Street address 1: 110 W State St
Street address city: East Tawas
Street address state: MI
Zip/Postal code: 48730-1229
General Phone: (989) 362-3456
General Fax: (989) 362-6601
General/National Adv. E-mail: advertising@iosconews.com
Editorial e-mail: editor@iosconews.com
Primary Website: iosconews.com
Avg Paid Circ: 3400
Audit By: Sworn/Estimate/Non-Audited
Audit Date: 10.11.2021
Personnel: Julie Carroll (General Manager)
Parent company (for newspapers): Community Media Group

JOURNAL

Street address 1: 13650 E 11 Mile Rd
Street address city: Warren
Street address state: MI
Zip/Postal code: 48089-1422
General Phone: (586) 498-8000
General Fax: (586) 498-9631
Advertising Phone: (586) 498-1032
Editorial Phone: (586) 498-1059
General/National Adv. E-mail: emyers@candgnews.com
Display Adv. E-mail: emyers@candgnews.com
Editorial e-mail: jdemers@candgnews.com
Primary Website: candgnews.com
Year Established: 1988
Avg Free Circ: 32888
Audit By: AAM
Audit Date: 31.03.2018
Personnel: Keith Demers (Prodn. Mgr.); Jeff Demers (Pub.); Elaine Myers (Adv. Mgr); David Demers (Circ. Mgr); Barry Bernard (Prod. Mgr); Gregg Demers
Parent company (for newspapers): C & G Newspapers

LA VIEW

Street address 1: 1521 Imlay City Rd
Street address city: Lapeer
Street address state: MI
Zip/Postal code: 48446-3175
General Phone: (810) 664-0811
General Fax: (810) 667-6309
General/National Adv. E-mail: pclinton@mihomepaper.com
Display Adv. E-mail: pclinton@mihomepaper.com
Editorial e-mail: jhogan@mihomepaper.com
Primary Website: http://lapeerareaview.mihomepaper.com/
Year Established: 2003
Avg Free Circ: 34904
Audit By: CVC
Audit Date: 30.06.2016
Personnel: Wes Smith (Pub./Ed.); Pete Clinton (Adv. Mgr); Dale Phillips (Circ. Mgr); Donna Ashby (Prod. Mgr)
Parent company (for newspapers): View Newspaper Group

LAKE COUNTY STAR

Street address 1: 851 Michigan Ave
Street address city: Baldwin
Street address state: MI
Zip/Postal code: 49304-8140
General Phone: (231) 745-4635
General Fax: (231) 745-7733
General/National Adv. E-mail: lcstar@pioneergroup.com
Display Adv. E-mail: starclass@pioneergroup.com
Editorial e-mail: lcstar@pioneergroup.com
Primary Website: lakecountystar.com
Year Established: 1873
Avg Paid Circ: 2976
Audit By: Sworn/Estimate/Non-Audited
Audit Date: 10.06.2019
Personnel: John S. Norton (Pub.); Kym Roldan (Prod. Mgr.)
Parent company (for newspapers): Pioneer Group

LAKE ORION ECCENTRIC

Street address 1: 615 W Lafayette Blvd
Street address 2: # 2
Street address city: Detroit
Street address state: MI
Zip/Postal code: 48226-3124
General Phone: (866) 887-2737
General Fax: (313) 223-3318
General/National Adv. E-mail: fcibor@hometownlife.com
Primary Website: hometownlife.com
Avg Paid Circ: 382
Avg Free Circ: 86005
Audit By: Sworn/Estimate/Non-Audited
Audit Date: 10.06.2019
Personnel: Carol McCloud (Mktg./Research Mgr.); Mark Warren (Circ. Dir.); Susan Rosiek (Exec. Ed.); Darren Jasey (IT Mgr.); Mark Vines (Prodn. Mgr.)
Parent company (for newspapers): Gannett

L'ANSE SENTINEL

Street address 1: 202 N Main St
Street address city: Lanse
Street address state: MI
Zip/Postal code: 49946-1118
General Phone: (906) 524-6194
General Fax: (906) 524-6197
General/National Adv. E-mail: sentinel1886@gmail.com
Primary Website: lansesentinel.net
Year Established: 1880
Avg Paid Circ: 2200
Audit By: Sworn/Estimate/Non-Audited
Audit Date: 10.06.2019
Personnel: Ed Danner (Pub.); Barry Drue (Ed.); Gale Eilola (Production. Mgr.); Nancy Besonen (Reporter); Melissa Newland (Reporter); Tammy Golde (Composition/Photo Editor); Mary Rogala (Ad Design/Graphic Artist)

LANSING CITY COMMUNITY NEWS

Street address 1: 300 S Washington Sq
Street address 2: Ste 300
Street address city: Lansing
Street address state: MI
Zip/Postal code: 48933-2102
General Phone: (517) 377-1000
Advertising Phone: (517) 377-1082
General/National Adv. E-mail: sholmes@gannett.com
Display Adv. E-mail: classifieds@lsj.com
Editorial e-mail: sangel@lsj.com
Primary Website: lsj.com
Year Established: 1856
Avg Paid Circ: 3
Avg Free Circ: 27120
Audit By: Sworn/Estimate/Non-Audited
Audit Date: 10.06.2019
Personnel: Brian Priester (Pub.); Stacia King (Adv. Mgr); Mark Conover (Circ. Mgr); Jack Conaboy (Prod. Mgr)

LANSING STATE JOURNAL

Street address 1: 300 S. Washington Square
Street address 2: Ste 300
Street address city: Lansing
Street address state: MI
Zip/Postal code: 48933-2102
General Phone: (517) 377-1000
Advertising Phone: (517) 377-1082
General/National Adv. E-mail: sholmes@gannett.com
Display Adv. E-mail: classifieds@lsj.com
Editorial e-mail: sangel@lsj.com
Primary Website: lansingstatejournal.com
Year Established: 1856
Avg Paid Circ: 2
Avg Free Circ: 6259
Audit By: Sworn/Estimate/Non-Audited
Audit Date: 10.06.2019
Personnel: Stephanie Angel (Ex. Ed.); Staci Holmes (Adv. Sales Mgr.); Matt Hund (Engagement Ed.)

LEELANAU ENTERPRISE

Street address 1: 7200 E Duck Lake Rd
Street address city: Lake Leelanau
Street address state: MI
Zip/Postal code: 49653
General Phone: 2312569827
Display Adv. E-mail: Kelli@leelanaunews.com
Classified Adv. e-mail: classifieds@leelanaunews.com
Editorial e-mail: editor@leelanaunews.com
Primary Website: leelanaunews.com
Mthly Avg Views: 56200
Mthly Avg Unique Visitors: 12400
Year Established: 1876
Avg Paid Circ: 8500
Audit By: USPS
Audit Date: 01.10.2021
Personnel: Debra Campbell (Adv. Mgr.); John Eichert (Publisher); Amy Hubbell (Editor); Alan C. Campbell (Ed.); Amy Hubbell (Mng. Ed.); Kelli Ameling (Sales Manager); Ken Lorincz (Print Manager); Mike Anderson (Creative Director)

LIVONIA OBSERVER

Street address 1: 615 W Lafayette Blvd
Street address 2: # 2
Street address city: Detroit
Street address state: MI
Zip/Postal code: 48226-3124
General Phone: (866) 887-2737
Advertising Phone: (800) 579-7355
Editorial Phone: (313) 222-5397
General/National Adv. E-mail: fcibor@hometownlife.com
Display Adv. E-mail: cewilson@hometownlife.com
Editorial e-mail: srosiek@hometownlife.com
Primary Website: hometownlife.com
Year Established: 1869
Avg Paid Circ: 2892
Avg Free Circ: 6805
Audit By: AAM
Audit Date: 30.06.2018
Personnel: Mark Warren (Circ. Dir.); Susan Rosiek (Executive Editor/Publisher)
Parent company (for newspapers): Gannett

LOWELL LEDGER

Street address 1: 105 N Broadway St
Street address city: Lowell
Street address state: MI
Zip/Postal code: 49331-1085
General Phone: (616) 897-9261
General Fax: (616) 897-4809
General/National Adv. E-mail: displayads@lowellbuyersguide.com
Display Adv. E-mail: classifieds@lowellbuyersguide.com
Editorial e-mail: ledger@lowerssbuyersguide.com
Primary Website: lowellbuyersguide.com
Year Established: 1893
Avg Paid Circ: 4000

Avg Free Circ: 200
Audit By: Sworn/Estimate/Non-Audited
Audit Date: 10.06.2019
Personnel: Tammy Janowich (Circ. Mgr.); Jon Jacobs (Ed.)

MACKINAW JOURNAL

Street address 1: 308 N Main St
Street address city: Cheboygan
Street address state: MI
Zip/Postal code: 49721-1545
General Phone: (231) 627-7144
General/National Adv. E-mail: nkidder@cheboygantribune.com
Display Adv. E-mail: classifieds@cheboygantribune.com
Editorial e-mail: gary@cheboygantribune.com
Primary Website: cheboygannews.com
Audit By: Sworn/Estimate/Non-Audited
Audit Date: 10.06.2019
Personnel: Matt Friday (Ed.); Mary Whaley (Circ. Mgr.); Kortney Hahn (Reporter); Jared Greenleaf (Sports Ed.)
Parent company (for newspapers): CherryRoad Media

MACOMB CHRONICLE

Street address 1: 13650 E 11 Mile Rd
Street address city: Warren
Street address state: MI
Zip/Postal code: 48089-1422
General Phone: (586) 498-8000
General Fax: (586) 498-9631
Advertising Phone: (586) 498-1072
Editorial Phone: (586) 498-1059
General/National Adv. E-mail: emyers@candgnews.com
Display Adv. E-mail: emyers@candgnews.com
Editorial e-mail: jdemers@candgnews.com
Primary Website: candgnews.com
Year Established: 1989
Avg Free Circ: 29747
Audit By: AAM
Audit Date: 31.03.2018
Personnel: Jeff Demers (Adv. Sales Mgr.); Gregg Demers (Ed.); Elaine Myers (Adv. Mgr); David Demers (Circ. Mgr); Barry Bernard (Prod. Mgr)
Parent company (for newspapers): C & G Newspapers

MADISON-PARK NEWS

Street address 1: 13650 11 Mile Road
Street address city: Warren
Street address state: MI
Zip/Postal code: 48089
General Phone: (586) 498-8000
General Fax: (586) 498-9631
Advertising Phone: (586) 498-1083
Editorial Phone: (586) 498-1059
General/National Adv. E-mail: emyers@candgnews.com
Display Adv. E-mail: emyers@candgnews.com
Editorial e-mail: jdemers@candgnews.com
Primary Website: candgnews.com
Year Established: 1982
Avg Free Circ: 19292
Audit By: AAM
Audit Date: 30.09.2018
Personnel: Jeff Demers (Adv. Mgr.); David Demers (Circ. Mgr); Elaine Myers (Adv. Mgr); Barry Bernard (Prod. Mgr)
Parent company (for newspapers): C & G Newspapers; C&G Publishing

MAYVILLE MONITOR

Street address 1: 6037 Fox St
Street address city: Mayville
Street address state: MI
Zip/Postal code: 48744-9004
General Phone: (989) 843-6242
General Fax: (989) 843-6242
Advertising Phone: (989) 843-6242
Editorial Phone: (989) 843-6242
General/National Adv. E-mail: mayvillemonitor@hotmail.com
Display Adv. E-mail: mayvillemonitor@hotmail.com
Classified Adv. e-mail: mayvillemonitor@hotmail.com
Editorial e-mail: mayvillemonitor@hotmail.com
Year Established: 1884
Avg Paid Circ: 600
Audit By: Sworn/Estimate/Non-Audited
Audit Date: 10.06.2019
Personnel: Gale Langford (Editor & Publisher)

MIBIZ

Street address 1: 65 Monroe Center St NW
Street address 2: Suite 500
Street address city: Grand Rapids
Street address state: MI
Zip/Postal code: 49503-2936
General Phone: (616) 608-6170
General Fax: (616) 608-6182
Advertising Phone: (616) 608-6170
Advertising Fax: (616) 608-6182
General/National Adv. E-mail: sales@mibiz.com
Display Adv. E-mail: sales@mibiz.com
Editorial e-mail: editor@mibiz.com
Primary Website: mibiz.com
Mthly Avg Views: 200000
Mthly Avg Unique Visitors: 35000
Year Established: 1988
Avg Free Circ: 11345
Audit By: Sworn/Estimate/Non-Audited
Audit Date: 10.06.2019
Personnel: Brian Edwards (Pub)
Parent company (for newspapers): REVUE Holding Company, Inc.

MILFORD TIMES

Street address 1: 615 W Lafayette Blvd
Street address 2: # 2
Street address city: Detroit
Street address state: MI
Zip/Postal code: 48226-3124
General Phone: (866) 887-2737
General Fax: (313) 223-3318
General/National Adv. E-mail: news@milfordtimes.com
Primary Website: hometownlife.com
Avg Paid Circ: 1720
Avg Free Circ: 210
Audit By: AAM
Audit Date: 30.06.2018
Personnel: Susan Rosiek (Exec. Ed./Pub.); Jani Hayden (Dir. Adv.)
Parent company (for newspapers): Gannett

NEW BUFFALO TIMES

Street address 1: 430 S Whittaker St
Street address city: New Buffalo
Street address state: MI
Zip/Postal code: 49117-1764
General Phone: (269) 469-1100
General Fax: (269) 469-1754
General/National Adv. E-mail: info@newbuffalotimes.com
Display Adv. E-mail: advertising@newbuffalotimes.com
Editorial e-mail: editorial@newbuffalotimes.com
Primary Website: newbuffalotimes.com
Year Established: 1943
Avg Paid Circ: 5000
Audit By: Sworn/Estimate/Non-Audited
Audit Date: 10.06.2019
Personnel: Mary Beth Moriarty (Ed.)

NEWS-HERALD

Street address 1: 1 Heritage Dr
Street address 2: Ste 100
Street address city: Southgate
Street address state: MI
Zip/Postal code: 48195-3047
General Phone: (734) 246-0800
General Fax: (734) 284-2117
General/National Adv. E-mail: westadvertising@heritage.com
Display Adv. E-mail: classifieds@heritage.com
Editorial e-mail: editor@thenewsherald.com
Primary Website: thenewsherald.com
Year Established: 1986
Avg Paid Circ: 17219
Avg Free Circ: 33120
Audit By: Sworn/Estimate/Non-Audited
Audit Date: 10.06.2019
Personnel: Rick Kessler (Mng. Ed.); Jeannie Parent (Pub.); Jason Alley (Editor)
Parent company (for newspapers): Digital First Media

NORTHEASTERN SHOPPER SOUTH

Street address 1: 711 W Pickard St
Street address 2: Ste P
Street address city: Mount Pleasant
Street address state: MI
Zip/Postal code: 48858-1587
General Phone: (989) 362-6111
General Fax: (989) 362-7080
Editorial e-mail: afrattura@journalregister.com
Primary Website: morningstarnewspapers.com
Year Established: 1954
Audit By: Sworn/Estimate/Non-Audited
Audit Date: 10.06.2019
Personnel: Al Frattura

NORTHERN EXPRESS

Street address 1: 129 1/2 E Front St
Street address 2: Ste 305
Street address city: Traverse City
Street address state: MI
Zip/Postal code: 49684-2508
General Phone: (231) 947-8787
General Fax: (231) 947-2425
General/National Adv. E-mail: ads@northernexpress.com
Editorial e-mail: info@northernexpress.com
Primary Website: northernexpress.com
Year Established: 1992
Avg Free Circ: 34000
Audit By: Sworn/Estimate/Non-Audited
Audit Date: 10.06.2019
Personnel: Robert Downes (Ed.)
Parent company (for newspapers): Express Publications, Inc.

NORTHERN MICHIGAN NEWS

Street address 1: 130 N Mitchell St
Street address city: Cadillac
Street address state: MI
Zip/Postal code: 49601-1856
General Phone: (231) 775-6565
General Fax: (231) 775-8790
General/National Adv. E-mail: customerservice@cadillacnews.com
Display Adv. E-mail: jbailey@cadillacnews.com
Primary Website: cadillacnews.com
Year Established: 1872
Avg Free Circ: 28500
Audit By: Sworn/Estimate/Non-Audited
Audit Date: 10.06.2019
Personnel: Christopher Huckle (Pub./Gen. Mgr.); Matthew Seward (Mng. Ed.); Ken Koch (Prodn. Mgr.); Josh Bailey (Sales and Marketing Leader)

NORTHVILLE EAGLE

Street address 1: 502 Forest Ave
Street address city: Plymouth
Street address state: MI
Zip/Postal code: 48170-1752
General Phone: (734) 467-1900
General Fax: (734) 729-1840
General/National Adv. E-mail: ads@journalgroup.com
Editorial e-mail: editor@journalgroup.com
Primary Website: journalgroup.com
Year Established: 2002
Avg Paid Circ: 4662
Audit By: Sworn/Estimate/Non-Audited
Audit Date: 10.06.2019
Personnel: Susan Willett (Pub.)
Parent company (for newspapers): Associated Newspapers of Michigan

NORTHVILLE RECORD

Street address 1: 615 W Lafayette Blvd
Street address 2: # 2
Street address city: Detroit
Street address state: MI
Zip/Postal code: 48226-3124
General Phone: (866) 887-2737
General Fax: (313) 223-3318
Advertising Phone: (800) 579-7355
Primary Website: hometownlife.com
Avg Paid Circ: 1905
Avg Free Circ: 210
Audit By: AAM
Audit Date: 30.06.2018
Personnel: Susan Rosiek (Exec. Ed./Pub.); Jani Hayden (Dir. Adv.)
Parent company (for newspapers): Gannett

NOVI NEWS

Street address 1: 615 W Lafayette Blvd
Street address 2: # 2
Street address city: Detroit
Street address state: MI
Zip/Postal code: 48226-3124
General Phone: (866) 887-2737
General Fax: (313) 223-3318
General/National Adv. E-mail: sunnewslink@freedom.com
Primary Website: hometownlife.com
Avg Paid Circ: 1155
Avg Free Circ: 255
Audit By: AAM
Audit Date: 30.06.2018
Personnel: Grace Perry (Gen. Mgr.); Jani Hayden (Dir. Adv.)
Parent company (for newspapers): Gannett

OBSERVER & ECCENTRIC MEDIA

Street address 1: 615 W Lafayette Blvd
Street address 2: # 2
Street address city: Detroit
Street address state: MI
Zip/Postal code: 48226-3124
General Phone: (866) 887-2737
Editorial e-mail: pallmen@hometownlife.com
Primary Website: hometownlife.com
Avg Paid Circ: 13871
Avg Free Circ: 39261
Audit By: AAM
Audit Date: 30.06.2018
Personnel: Jani Hayden (Dir. Adv.); Philip Allmen (News Dir.)
Parent company (for newspapers): Gannett

OCEANA'S HERALD-JOURNAL

Street address 1: 123 S State St
Street address city: Hart
Street address state: MI
Zip/Postal code: 49420-1124
General Phone: (231) 873-5602
General Fax: (231) 873-4775
General/National Adv. E-mail: clerk@oceanaheraldjournal.com
Classified Adv. e-mail: clerk@oceanaheraldjournal.com
Editorial e-mail: editor@oceanaheraldjournal.com
Primary Website: oceanaheraldjournal.com
Avg Paid Circ: 3085
Avg Free Circ: 15
Audit By: Sworn/Estimate/Non-Audited
Audit Date: 30.09.2021
Personnel: Ray McGrew (Publisher); Andy Skinner (Ed.); Amanda Dodge
Parent company (for newspapers): Community Media Group

OGEMAW COUNTY HERALD

Street address 1: 215 W Houghton Ave
Street address city: West Branch
Street address state: MI
Zip/Postal code: 48661-1219
General Phone: (989) 345-0044
General Fax: (989) 345-5609
General/National Adv. E-mail: sales2@ogemawherald.com
Display Adv. E-mail: classifieds@ogemawherald.com
Editorial e-mail: editor@ogemawherald.com
Primary Website: ogemawherald.com
Year Established: 1878
Avg Paid Circ: 6700
Avg Free Circ: 76
Audit By: Sworn/Estimate/Non-Audited
Audit Date: 10.06.2019
Personnel: Liz Gorske (Pub.); Eric Young (Ed.)

OGEMAW/OSCODA COUNTY STAR

Street address 1: 420 W Houghton Ave
Street address city: West Branch
Street address state: MI
Zip/Postal code: 48661-1224
General Phone: (989) 345-0510
General Fax: (989) 345-3750
General/National Adv. E-mail: cturner@michigannewspapers.com

Display Adv. E-mail: classifieds@michigannewspapers.com
Editorial e-mail: rmills@michigannewspapers.com
Primary Website: themorningsun.com/about_us/ogemawoscoda
Year Established: 1976
Avg Free Circ: 14654
Audit By: Sworn/Estimate/Non-Audited
Audit Date: 10.06.2019
Personnel: Jeannie Parent (Pub.); Tammy Fisher (Adv. Mgr.); Christine Fox (Circ. Mgr.); Ron Martin (Prod. Mgr.)
Parent company (for newspapers): Morning Star Publishing Company

OSCODA PRESS

Street address 1: 311 S State St
Street address city: Oscoda
Street address state: MI
Zip/Postal code: 48750-1636
General Phone: (989) 739-2054
General Fax: (989) 739-3201
Advertising Phone: advertising@iosconews.com
General/National Adv. E-mail: comp@iosconews.com
Display Adv. E-mail: comp@iosconews.com
Editorial e-mail: editor1@oscodapress.com
Primary Website: iosconews.com/oscoda_press
Year Established: 1879
Avg Paid Circ: 2550
Avg Free Circ: 5500
Audit By: Sworn/Estimate/Non-Audited
Audit Date: 01.11.2021
Personnel: Julie Carroll (Ed.); Jim Young (Gen. Mgr.)
Parent company (for newspapers): Community Media Group

OXFORD LEADER

Street address 1: 666 S Lapeer Rd
Street address city: Oxford
Street address state: MI
Zip/Postal code: 48371-5034
General Phone: (248) 628-4801
General Fax: (248) 628-9750
Advertising Phone: (248) 628-4801 ext.20
Editorial Phone: (248) 628-4801
General/National Adv. E-mail: shermanpub@aol.com
Primary Website: oxfordleader.com
Year Established: 1889
Avg Paid Circ: 2300
Avg Free Circ: 97
Audit By: Sworn/Estimate/Non-Audited
Audit Date: 10.06.2019
Personnel: James A. Sherman (Pub.); Don Rush (Asst. Pub); Eric Lewis (Adv. Mgr.); C.J. Carnacchis (Ed.)
Parent company (for newspapers): Waxa

PIONEER EAST

Street address 1: 115 N Michigan Ave
Street address city: Big Rapids
Street address state: MI
Zip/Postal code: 49307-1401
General Phone: (231) 796-4831
General Fax: (231) 796-1152
General/National Adv. E-mail: advertising@pioneergroup.com
Display Adv. E-mail: classified@pioneergroup.com
Primary Website: pioneereastshopper.com
Avg Free Circ: 8000
Audit By: Sworn/Estimate/Non-Audited
Audit Date: 10.06.2019
Personnel: Danette Doyle (Adv. Mgr.)

PIONEER TRIBUNE

Street address 1: 212 Walnut St
Street address city: Manistique
Street address state: MI
Zip/Postal code: 49854-1445
General Phone: (906) 341-5200
General Fax: (906) 341-5914
General/National Adv. E-mail: ads@pioneertribune.com
Display Adv. E-mail: ads@pioneertribune.com
Editorial e-mail: editor@pioneertribune.com
Primary Website: pioneertribune.com
Year Established: 1876
Avg Paid Circ: 3500
Audit By: Sworn/Estimate/Non-Audited
Audit Date: 10.06.2019
Personnel: Lisa A. Demers (Pub.)

PLYMOUTH EAGLE

Street address 1: 502 Forest Ave
Street address city: Plymouth
Street address state: MI
Zip/Postal code: 48170-1752
General Phone: (734) 467-1900
General Fax: (734) 729-1840
General/National Adv. E-mail: ads@journalgroup.com
Editorial e-mail: swillett@journalgroup.com
Primary Website: journalgroup.com
Year Established: 2000
Avg Paid Circ: 6000
Audit By: Sworn/Estimate/Non-Audited
Audit Date: 10.06.2019
Personnel: Susan Willett (Pub.)
Parent company (for newspapers): Associated Newspapers of Michigan

PLYMOUTH OBSERVER

Street address 1: 615 W Lafayette Blvd
Street address 2: # 2
Street address city: Detroit
Street address state: MI
Zip/Postal code: 48226-3124
General Phone: (866) 887-2737
General Fax: (313) 223-3318
Advertising Phone: (800) 579-7355
General/National Adv. E-mail: fcibor@hometownlife.com
Display Adv. E-mail: cewilson@hometownlife.com
Editorial e-mail: srosiek@hometownlife.com
Primary Website: hometownlife.com
Year Established: 1869
Avg Paid Circ: 1187
Avg Free Circ: 210
Audit By: AAM
Audit Date: 30.06.2018
Personnel: Mark Warren (Circ. Dir.); Choya Jordan (Mktg. Mgr.); Marty Carry (Adv. Dir.)
Parent company (for newspapers): Gannett

PORTLAND REVIEW & OBSERVER

Street address 1: 300 S Washington Sq
Street address city: Lansing
Street address state: MI
Zip/Postal code: 48933-2100
General Phone: (517) 377-1000
Advertising Phone: (517) 377-1082
General/National Adv. E-mail: sholmes@gannett.com
Display Adv. E-mail: classifieds@lsj.com
Editorial e-mail: sangel@lsj.com
Primary Website: lsj.com
Year Established: 1856
Avg Paid Circ: 4
Avg Free Circ: 5168
Audit By: Sworn/Estimate/Non-Audited
Audit Date: 10.06.2019
Personnel: Brian Priester (Pub); Stacia King (Adv. Mgr); Mark Conover (Circ. Mgr); Jack Conaboy (Prod. Mgr)
Parent company (for newspapers): Gannett

PRESQUE ISLE COUNTY ADVANCE

Street address 1: 104 S Third St
Street address city: Rogers City
Street address state: MI
Zip/Postal code: 49779-1710
General Phone: (989) 734-2105
General Fax: (989) 734-3053
Editorial e-mail: editor@piadvance.com
Primary Website: piadvance.com
Year Established: 1878
Avg Paid Circ: 3800
Avg Free Circ: 50
Audit By: Sworn/Estimate/Non-Audited
Audit Date: 10.06.2019
Personnel: Richard W. Lamb (Pub)

PRESS & GUIDE

Street address 1: 1 Heritage Dr
Street address 2: Ste 100
Street address city: Southgate
Street address state: MI
Zip/Postal code: 48195-3047
General Phone: (734) 246-0800
General Fax: (734) 246-2727
General/National Adv. E-mail: Subscribe@pressandguide.com
Display Adv. E-mail: Subscribe@pressandguide.com
Editorial e-mail: jalley@thenewsherald.com
Primary Website: pressandguide.com
Year Established: 1918
Avg Paid Circ: 1256
Avg Free Circ: 7384
Audit By: AAM
Audit Date: 31.03.2019
Personnel: Jason Alley (Ed.); Don Wyatt; Greg Mazanec (Pub.); Dave Swantek (GM)
Parent company (for newspapers): Digital First Media; MediaNews Group

REDFORD OBSERVER

Street address 1: 615 W Lafayette Blvd
Street address 2: # 2
Street address city: Detroit
Street address state: MI
Zip/Postal code: 48226-3124
General Phone: (866) 887-2737
Advertising Phone: (800) 579-7355
Editorial Phone: (313) 222-5397
General/National Adv. E-mail: fcibor@hometownlife.com
Display Adv. E-mail: cewilson@hometownlife.com
Editorial e-mail: srosiek@hometownlife.com
Primary Website: hometownlife.com
Year Established: 1869
Avg Paid Circ: 1220
Avg Free Circ: 6
Audit By: AAM
Audit Date: 30.06.2018
Personnel: Susan Rosiek (Executive Editor/Publisher); Mark Warren (Circ. Dir.); Jani Hayden (Dir. Adv.)
Parent company (for newspapers): Gannett

REGISTER-TRIBUNE

Street address 1: 15 W Pearl St
Street address city: Coldwater
Street address state: MI
Zip/Postal code: 49036-1912
General Phone: (517) 278-2318
General Fax: (517) 278-6041
General/National Adv. E-mail: editor@thedailyreporter.com
Avg Paid Circ: 1150
Avg Free Circ: 125
Audit By: Sworn/Estimate/Non-Audited
Audit Date: 10.06.2019
Personnel: Candice Phelps (Mng. Ed.); Troy Tennyson (Sports Ed.); Karen Allard

REPORTER

Street address 1: 801 W Adams St
Street address city: Iron River
Street address state: MI
Zip/Postal code: 49935-1218
General Phone: (906) 265-9927
General Fax: (906) 265-5755
General/National Adv. E-mail: sales@ironcountyreporter.com
Display Adv. E-mail: sales@ironcountyreporter.com
Editorial e-mail: news@ironcountyreporter.com
Primary Website: ironcountyreporter.com
Year Established: 1885
Avg Paid Circ: 5000
Audit By: Sworn/Estimate/Non-Audited
Audit Date: 10.06.2019
Personnel: Jerry DeRoche (Ed.)

ROCHESTER POST

Street address 1: 13650 11 Mile Road
Street address city: Warren
Street address state: MI
Zip/Postal code: 48089
General Phone: (586) 498-8000
General Fax: (586) 498-9631
Advertising Phone: (586) 498-1032
Editorial Phone: (586) 498-1071
General/National Adv. E-mail: emyers@candgnews.com
Display Adv. E-mail: emyers@candgnews.com
Editorial e-mail: jdemers@candgnews.com
Primary Website: candgnews.com
Year Established: 2005
Avg Free Circ: 39362
Audit By: AAM
Audit Date: 30.09.2018
Personnel: Jeff Demers (Dir of Sales); Elaine Myers (Ad. Mgr); David Demers (Circ. Mgr); Barry Bernard (Prod. Mgr)
Parent company (for newspapers): C & G Newspapers; C&G Publishing

ROCKFORD SQUIRE

Street address 1: 331 Northland Dr NE
Street address city: Rockford
Street address state: MI
Zip/Postal code: 49341-1025
General Phone: (616) 866-4465
General Fax: (616) 866-3810
General/National Adv. E-mail: squiresalesteam@gmail.com
Display Adv. E-mail: squiresales@gmail.com
Editorial e-mail: squiremail@aol.com
Primary Website: rockfordsquire.com
Year Established: 1871
Avg Free Circ: 11300
Audit By: Sworn/Estimate/Non-Audited
Audit Date: 10.06.2019
Personnel: Beth Altena (Owner/Ed.); Kym Steffes (Adv. Sales Rep.)

ROYAL OAK REVIEW

Street address 1: 13650 11 Mile Road
Street address city: Warren
Street address state: MI
Zip/Postal code: 48089
General Phone: (586) 498-8000
General Fax: (586) 498-9631
Advertising Phone: (586) 498-1031
Editorial Phone: (586) 498-1053
General/National Adv. E-mail: emyers@candgnews.com
Display Adv. E-mail: emyers@candgnews.com
Editorial e-mail: Royal Oak Review
Primary Website: candgnews.com
Year Established: 2003
Avg Free Circ: 32006
Audit By: AAM
Audit Date: 31.03.2018
Personnel: Jeff Demers (Dir of Sales); Elaine Myers (Adv. Mgr); David Demers (Circ. Mgr); Barry Bernard (Prod. Mgr)
Parent company (for newspapers): C & G Newspapers; C&G Publishing

SAGINAW PRESS

Street address 1: 100 S Michigan Ave
Street address city: Saginaw
Street address state: MI
Zip/Postal code: 48602-2054
General Phone: (989) 793-8070
General Fax: (989) 921-7225
Editorial e-mail: editor@thesaginawnews.com
Avg Paid Circ: 448
Avg Free Circ: 6
Audit By: Sworn/Estimate/Non-Audited
Audit Date: 10.06.2019
Personnel: George W. Baxter (Circ. Dir.); Jodi Mcfarland (Ed)

SANILAC COUNTY NEWS

Street address 1: 65 S Elk St
Street address city: Sandusky
Street address state: MI
Zip/Postal code: 48471-1337
General Phone: (810) 648-4000
General Fax: (810) 648-4526
Advertising Phone: (810) 648-4000
Advertising Fax: (810) 648-4526
Editorial Phone: (810) 648-4000
Editorial Fax: (810) 648-4526
General/National Adv. E-mail: sales@mihomepaper.com
Display Adv. E-mail: sales@mihomepaper.com
Editorial e-mail: jvanderpoel@mihomepaper.com
Primary Website: mihomepaper.com
Year Established: 1971
Avg Paid Circ: 4818
Avg Free Circ: 30
Audit By: Sworn/Estimate/Non-Audited
Audit Date: 10.06.2019
Personnel: Jane Vanderpoel (Pub.); Eric Levine (Ed.)

Parent company (for newspapers): JAMS Media

SHELBY-UTICA NEWS

Street address 1: 13650 11 Mile Road
Street address city: Warren
Street address state: MI
Zip/Postal code: 48089
General Phone: (586) 498-8000
General Fax: (586) 498-9631
Advertising Phone: (586) 498-1091
Editorial Phone: (586) 498-1053
General/National Adv. E-mail: emyers@candgnews.com
Display Adv. E-mail: emyers@candgnews.com
Editorial e-mail: jdemers@candgnews.com
Primary Website: candgnews.com
Year Established: 1992
Avg Free Circ: 31103
Audit By: AAM
Audit Date: 31.03.2018
Personnel: Elaine Myers (Adv. Mgr); David Demers (Circ. Mgr); Barry Bernard (Prod. Mgr); Jeff Demers (Pub.)
Parent company (for newspapers): C & G Newspapers; C&G Publishing

SOUTH ADVANCE

Street address 1: 2141 Port Sheldon St
Street address city: Jenison
Street address state: MI
Zip/Postal code: 49428-9315
General Phone: (616) 669-2700
General Fax: (616) 669-1162
General/National Adv. E-mail: retailsales@advancenewspapers.com
Primary Website: advancenewspapers.com
Year Established: 1965
Avg Paid Circ: 256
Avg Free Circ: 14860
Audit By: Sworn/Estimate/Non-Audited
Audit Date: 10.06.2019
Personnel: Joel Holland (Pub./Mktg. Dir./Adv. Mgr.); Terry Alvesteffer (Circ. Mgr.); Marilyn Dreisenga (Prodn. Mgr.)
Parent company (for newspapers): Advance Publications, Inc.

SOUTH HAVEN TRIBUNE

Street address 1: 3450 Hollywood Rd.
Street address city: St. Joseph
Street address state: MI
Zip/Postal code: 49085
General Phone: (269) 637-1104
General Fax: (269) 637-8415
Advertising Phone: (269) 429-2400 ext.405
Editorial Phone: (269) 637-1104 ext.14
General/National Adv. E-mail: news@southhaventribune.com
Display Adv. E-mail: shorton@TheHP.com
Classified Adv. e-mail: shorton@TheHP.com
Editorial e-mail: news@southhaventribune.com
Primary Website: https://www.heraldpalladium.com/southhaventribune/
Year Established: 1899
Avg Free Circ: 13665
Sun. Circulation Free: 13500
Audit By: Sworn/Estimate/Non-Audited
Audit Date: 10.06.2019
Personnel: David Holgate (Pub.); Becky Burkert (Ed./Gen. Mgr.); Stacey Ramsey (Adv. Dir.); Sara Horton (Advertising Director); Barry Whitman (Circ. Dir.); Julie Simpleman (Circulation Director)
Parent company (for newspapers): Paxton Media Group

SOUTH LYON HERALD

Street address 1: 615 W Lafayette Blvd
Street address 2: # 2
Street address city: Detroit
Street address state: MI
Zip/Postal code: 48226-3124
General Phone: (866) 887-2737
General Fax: (313) 223-3318
General/National Adv. E-mail: news@southlyonherald.com
Primary Website: hometownlife.com
Avg Paid Circ: 1790
Avg Free Circ: 210
Audit By: AAM
Audit Date: 30.06.2018
Personnel: Lisa Dranginis (Adv. Mgr.); Jani Hayden (Adv. Dir.)
Parent company (for newspapers): Gannett

SOUTH OAKLAND ECCENTRIC

Street address 1: 615 W Lafayette Blvd
Street address 2: # 2
Street address city: Detroit
Street address state: MI
Zip/Postal code: 48226-3124
General Phone: (866) 887-2737
General Fax: (313) 223-3318
Advertising Phone: (800) 579-7355
General/National Adv. E-mail: sdobkin@hometownlife.com
Display Adv. E-mail: cewilson@hometownlife.com
Editorial e-mail: sarmbruster@hometownlife.com
Primary Website: hometownlife.com
Avg Paid Circ: 450
Avg Free Circ: 8658
Audit By: CAC
Audit Date: 9/31/2015
Personnel: Mark Warren (Circ. Dir.); Peter Neill (Gen. Mgr.); Marty Carry (Adv. Dir.); Jani Hayden (Adv. Dir.)
Parent company (for newspapers): Gannett

SOUTHFIELD SUN

Street address 1: 13650 11 Mile Road
Street address city: Warren
Street address state: MI
Zip/Postal code: 48089
General Phone: (586) 498-8000
General Fax: (586) 498-9631
Advertising Phone: (586) 498-1032
Editorial Phone: (586) 498-1071
General/National Adv. E-mail: emyers@candgnews.com
Display Adv. E-mail: emyers@candgnews.com
Editorial e-mail: jdemers@candgnews.com
Primary Website: candgnews.com
Year Established: 2004
Avg Free Circ: 32135
Audit By: AAM
Audit Date: 31.03.2018
Personnel: Jeff Demers (Dir of Sales); Elaine Myers (Ad. Mgr); David Demers (Circ. Mgr); Barry Bernard (Prod. Mgr)
Parent company (for newspapers): C & G Newspapers; C&G Publishing

SPINAL COLUMN NEWSWEEKLY

Street address 1: 1103 South Milford Road
Street address city: Highland
Street address state: MI
Zip/Postal code: 48357-1426
General Phone: (248) 360-7355
General Fax: (248) 360-5308
Advertising Phone: (248) 360-7355 x21
Advertising Fax: (248) 360-5308
Editorial Phone: (248) 360-7355 x12
General/National Adv. E-mail: jimstevenson@scnmail.com
Display Adv. E-mail: lynndonohue@scnmail.com
Editorial e-mail: anne@scnmail.com
Primary Website: spinalcolumnonline.com
Mthly Avg Views: 17700
Mthly Avg Unique Visitors: 360700
Year Established: 1961
Avg Free Circ: 13300
Audit By: Sworn/Estimate/Non-Audited
Audit Date: 01.10.2021
Personnel: Jim Stevenson (Publisher/Owner); Phil Catlain (Partner); Bob Ely (Partner); Cindie Audia (Sales Leader/Asst. pub.)
Parent company (for newspapers): Kingsett, LLC

SPRINGPORT SIGNAL

Street address 1: 123 W Main St
Street address city: Springport
Street address state: MI
Zip/Postal code: 49284-9501
General Phone: (517) 857-2500
General Fax: (517) 857-2887
Editorial e-mail: springportsignal@springcom.com
Primary Website: springportmi.com/newspaper.htm
Avg Paid Circ: 1100
Avg Free Circ: 10
Audit By: Sworn/Estimate/Non-Audited
Audit Date: 10.06.2019
Personnel: Dawn Doner (Ed.)

ST. CLAIR SHORES SENTINEL

Street address 1: 13650 11 Mile Road
Street address city: Warren
Street address state: MI
Zip/Postal code: 48089
General Phone: (586) 498-8000
General Fax: (586) 498-9631
Advertising Phone: (586) 498-8117
Editorial Phone: (586) 498-1059
General/National Adv. E-mail: emyers@candgnews.com
Display Adv. E-mail: emyers@candgnews.com
Editorial e-mail: jdemers@candgnews.com
Primary Website: candgnews.com
Year Established: 1981
Avg Free Circ: 27151
Audit By: AAM
Audit Date: 31.03.2018
Personnel: Jeff Demers (Pub.); Elaine Myers (Adv. Mgr); David Demers (Circ. Mgr); Barry Bernard (Prod. Mgr)
Parent company (for newspapers): C & G Newspapers; C&G Publishing

STATE LINE OBSERVER

Street address 1: 120 North St
Street address city: Morenci
Street address state: MI
Zip/Postal code: 49256-1446
General Phone: (517) 458-6811
General Fax: (517) 458-6811
Editorial e-mail: editor@statelineobserver.com
Primary Website: statelineobserver.com
Year Established: 1872
Avg Paid Circ: 2321
Audit By: Sworn/Estimate/Non-Audited
Audit Date: 10.06.2019
Personnel: David G. Green (Ed.)

STERLING HEIGHTS SENTRY

Street address 1: 13650 11 Mile Road
Street address city: Warren
Street address state: MI
Zip/Postal code: 48089
General Phone: (586) 498-8000
General Fax: (586) 498-9631
Advertising Phone: (586) 498-1032
Editorial Phone: (586) 498-1071
General/National Adv. E-mail: emyers@candgnews.com
Display Adv. E-mail: emyers@candgnews.com
Editorial e-mail: jdemers@candgnews.com
Primary Website: candgnews.com
Year Established: 1990
Avg Free Circ: 48431
Audit By: AAM
Audit Date: 31.03.2018
Personnel: Jeff Demers (Pub.); Keith Demers (Circ. Mgr.); Barry Bernard (Prodn. Mgr.); Elaine Myers (Adv. Mgr); David Demers (Circ. Mgr)
Parent company (for newspapers): C & G Newspapers; C&G Publishing

STRAITSLAND RESORTER

Street address 1: 3636 S Straits Hwy
Street address city: Indian River
Street address state: MI
Zip/Postal code: 49749-5136
General Phone: (231) 238-7362
General Fax: (231) 238-1290
General/National Adv. E-mail: ads@resorter.com
Display Adv. E-mail: ads@resorter.com
Editorial e-mail: editor@resorter.com
Primary Website: resorter.com
Year Established: 1963
Avg Paid Circ: 3200
Avg Free Circ: 65
Audit By: Sworn/Estimate/Non-Audited
Audit Date: 10.06.2019
Personnel: Kathy Swanson (Pub.); Scott Swanson (Ed.)

SUN & NEWS

Street address 1: 1351 N M43 Hwy
Street address city: Hastings
Street address state: MI
Zip/Postal code: 49058
General Phone: (269) 945-9554
General Fax: (269) 945-5192
Display Adv. E-mail: ads@j-adgraphics.com
Year Established: 1949
Avg Paid Circ: 170
Avg Free Circ: 13025
Audit By: Sworn/Estimate/Non-Audited
Audit Date: 10.06.2019
Personnel: Fred Jacobs (Pub.)
Parent company (for newspapers): J-Ad Graphics

SUNDAY INDEPENDENT

Street address 1: 1907 W. M-21
Street address city: Owosso
Street address state: MI
Zip/Postal code: 48867
General Phone: (989) 723-1118
General Fax: (989) 725-1834
Editorial e-mail: indysales@chartermi.net
Primary Website: owossoindependent.com
Year Established: 1968
Avg Free Circ: 32035
Audit By: Sworn/Estimate/Non-Audited
Audit Date: 10.06.2019
Personnel: Michael Flores (Pub.); William Constine (Ed.); Kim Lazar (Adv. Mgr.`)

SWARTZ CREEK VIEW

Street address 1: 220 N Main St
Street address city: Davison
Street address state: MI
Zip/Postal code: 48423-1432
General Phone: (810) 653-3511
General Fax: (810) 667-6309
Advertising Phone: (810) 664-0811
General/National Adv. E-mail: pclinton@mihomepaper.comc
Display Adv. E-mail: pclinton@mihomepaper.com
Editorial e-mail: ggould@mihomepaper.com
Primary Website: http://swartzcreekview.mihomepaper.com/
Year Established: 2010
Avg Free Circ: 9418
Audit By: CVC
Audit Date: 30.06.2016
Personnel: Wes Smith (Pub./Ed.); Pete Clinton (Adv. Mgr)
Parent company (for newspapers): View Newspaper Group

THE ADVANCE

Street address 1: 121 Newspaper St
Street address city: Blissfield
Street address state: MI
Zip/Postal code: 49228-1248
General Phone: (517) 486-2400
General Fax: (517) 486-4675
General/National Adv. E-mail: joel_holland@mlive.com
Display Adv. E-mail: advancenewsclassified@mlive.com
Editorial e-mail: news@blissfieldadvance.com
Primary Website: blissfieldadvance.com
Year Established: 1874
Avg Paid Circ: 2700
Audit By: Sworn/Estimate/Non-Audited
Audit Date: 10.06.2019
Personnel: Marcia Loader (Ed.); Liz Gaynor (Business Mgr.)
Parent company (for newspapers): River Raisin Publications, Inc.

THE ADVISOR & SOURCE

Street address 1: 19176 Hall Rd
Street address 2: Ste 200
Street address city: Clinton Township
Street address state: MI
Zip/Postal code: 48038-6914
General Phone: (586) 716-8100
General Fax: (586) 716-8533
General/National Adv. E-mail: noelle.klomp@oakpress.com
Display Adv. E-mail: noelle.klomp@oakpress.com
Editorial e-mail: jhoard@digitalfirstmedia.com
Primary Website: sourcenewspapers.com
Avg Free Circ: 115389
Audit By: Sworn/Estimate/Non-Audited
Audit Date: 10.06.2019

Personnel: Jeff Hoard (Ed.); Greg Mazanec (Pub.); Noelle Klomp (Adv. Mgr.)
Parent company (for newspapers): Media News Group

THE ANN ARBOR NEWS

Street address 1: 111 N Ashley St
Street address 2: Ste 100
Street address city: Ann Arbor
Street address state: MI
Zip/Postal code: 48104-1307
General Phone: (734) 623-2500
Advertising Phone: (900) 878-1400
Editorial Phone: (734) 623-2500
General/National Adv. E-mail: aanews@mlive.com
Display Adv. E-mail: aanews@mlive.com
Editorial e-mail: aanews@mlive.com
Primary Website: mlive.com/ann-arbor
Year Established: 2009
Avg Paid Circ: 12950
Avg Free Circ: 2481
Sat. Circulation Paid: 299
Sat. Circulation Free: 685
Sun. Circulation Paid: 14624
Sun. Circulation Free: 4681
Audit By: AAM
Audit Date: 31.03.2019
Personnel: Meyer Erin (Mktg. Analyst)
Parent company (for newspapers): Advance Publications, Inc.

THE ARMADA TIMES

Street address 1: 19176 Hall Rd
Street address 2: Ste 200
Street address city: Clinton Township
Street address state: MI
Zip/Postal code: 48038-6914
General Phone: (586) 716-8100
General Fax: (586) 716-8918
Advertising Phone: (800) 561-2248
Advertising Fax: (586) 716-8533
General/National Adv. E-mail: debbie.loggins@voicenews.com
Display Adv. E-mail: classified.voice@voicenews.com
Editorial e-mail: editor@voicenews.com
Primary Website: voicenews.com
Year Established: 1887
Avg Free Circ: 59500
Audit By: Sworn/Estimate/Non-Audited
Audit Date: 10.06.2019
Personnel: Debra Loggins (Gen. Mgr.); Anna Eerola (Adv. Asst.); Rene Allard (Circ. Mgr.); Jeff Payne (Ed.)

THE BAY VOICE

Street address 1: 19176 Hall Rd
Street address 2: Ste 200
Street address city: Clinton Township
Street address state: MI
Zip/Postal code: 48038-6914
General Phone: (586) 716-8100
General Fax: (586) 719-8918
General/National Adv. E-mail: debbie.loggins@voicenews.com
Display Adv. E-mail: classified.voice@voicenews.com
Editorial e-mail: editor@voicenews.com
Primary Website: voicenews.com
Year Established: 1983
Avg Paid Circ: 40
Avg Free Circ: 9697
Audit By: Sworn/Estimate/Non-Audited
Audit Date: 10.06.2019
Personnel: Debbie Loggins (Gen. Mgr.); Jeff Payne (Ed.); Rene Allard (Circ. Mgr.)
Parent company (for newspapers): Digital First Media

THE BELLEVILLE ENTERPRISE

Street address 1: 152 Main St
Street address 2: Suite 9
Street address city: Belleville
Street address state: MI
Zip/Postal code: 48111-3911
General Phone: (734) 699-9020
General Fax: (734) 699-8962
General/National Adv. E-mail: mail@bellevilleareaindependent.com
Editorial e-mail: rotzman@ameritech.net
Primary Website: http://bellevilleareaindependent.com/
Avg Paid Circ: 1900
Audit By: Sworn/Estimate/Non-Audited
Audit Date: 10.06.2019
Personnel: Rosemary Otzman (Ed.)
Parent company (for newspapers): Associated Newspapers of Michigan

THE BENZIE COUNTY RECORD-PATRIOT

Street address 1: 5885 Frankfort Hwy
Street address city: Benzonia
Street address state: MI
Zip/Postal code: 49616
General Phone: (231) 408-3531
General Fax: (231) 352-7874
General/National Adv. E-mail: recpat@pioneergroup.com
Display Adv. E-mail: classrecpat@pioneergroup.com
Classified Adv. e-mail: classrecpat@pioneergroup.com
Editorial e-mail: recpat@pioneergroup.com
Primary Website: recordpatriot.com
Mthly Avg Views: 425
Mthly Avg Unique Visitors: 35000
Year Established: 1888
Avg Paid Circ: 1275
Audit By: Sworn/Estimate/Non-Audited
Audit Date: 10.06.2019
Personnel: Jeff Bergin (President, Community Newspapers at Hearst Newspapers); John Norton (Pub.)
Parent company (for newspapers): Pioneer Group; Hearst Newspapers

THE BROWN CITY BANNER

Street address 1: 65 S Elk St
Street address city: Sandusky
Street address state: MI
Zip/Postal code: 48471-1337
Primary Website: mihomepaper.com
Avg Paid Circ: 676
Avg Free Circ: 95
Audit By: CVC
Audit Date: 30.06.2016
Personnel: Pete Clinton (Adv. Mgr); Dale Phillips (Circ. Mgr); Donna Ashby (Prod. Mgr)

THE BURTON NEWS

Street address 1: 200 E 1st St
Street address city: Flint
Street address state: MI
Zip/Postal code: 48502-1911
General Phone: (810) 766-6100
General Fax: (810) 766-7518
General/National Adv. E-mail: theburtonnews@communitynewspapers.com
Primary Website: burtonsuburbannews.com
Year Established: 2002
Avg Paid Circ: 15000
Audit By: Sworn/Estimate/Non-Audited
Audit Date: 10.06.2019
Personnel: Katie Bach (Ed.)
Parent company (for newspapers): Advance Publications, Inc.

THE CHELSEA STANDARD

Street address 1: 1 Heritage Dr
Street address 2: Suite 100
Street address city: Southgate
Street address state: MI
Zip/Postal code: 48195-3047
General Phone: (734) 475-1371
General Fax: (734) 429-3621
General/National Adv. E-mail: westadvertising@heritage.com
Display Adv. E-mail: classifieds@heritage.com
Editorial e-mail: editor@chelseastandard.com
Primary Website: chelseastandard.com
Year Established: 1873
Avg Paid Circ: 1811
Avg Free Circ: 16
Audit By: Sworn/Estimate/Non-Audited
Audit Date: 10.06.2019
Personnel: Jason Alley (Ed); Teresa Goodrich (VP); Jeannie Parent (Pub.)
Parent company (for newspapers): Digital First Media; Heritage Newspapers, Inc.-OOB

THE CLARE COUNTY REVIEW

Street address 1: 2141 E Ludington Dr
Street address city: Clare
Street address state: MI
Zip/Postal code: 48617-8801
General Phone: (989) 386-4414
General Fax: (989) 386-2412
General/National Adv. E-mail: info@clarecountyreview.com
Display Adv. E-mail: info@clarecountyreview.com
Editorial e-mail: info@clarecountyreview.com
Primary Website: clarecountyreview.com
Year Established: 1947
Avg Paid Circ: 473
Avg Free Circ: 9557
Audit By: Sworn/Estimate/Non-Audited
Audit Date: 10.06.2019
Personnel: Patricia Maurer (Owner/Pub.)

THE CLIMAX CRESCENT

Street address 1: 150 N Main St
Street address city: Climax
Street address state: MI
Zip/Postal code: 49034-9637
General Phone: (269) 746-4331
General/National Adv. E-mail: scribe@ctsmail.net
Primary Website: theclimaxcrescent.com
Year Established: 1912
Avg Paid Circ: 1050
Audit By: Sworn/Estimate/Non-Audited
Audit Date: 10.06.2019
Personnel: Bruce Rolfe (Ed.)

THE CLINTON LOCAL

Street address 1: 108 Tecumseh Rd
Street address city: Clinton
Street address state: MI
Zip/Postal code: 49236-9507
General Phone: (517) 456-4100
General Fax: (517) 456-4100
Advertising Phone: (517) 456-4100
Advertising Fax: (517) 456-4100
Editorial Phone: (517) 442-8616
Display Adv. E-mail: localcokelady@comcast.net
Primary Website: theclintonlocal.com
Year Established: 1884
Avg Paid Circ: 1500
Audit By: Sworn/Estimate/Non-Audited
Audit Date: 10.06.2019
Personnel: Maryann Habrick (Ed.)
Parent company (for newspapers): The Clinton Local

THE COMMERCIAL RECORD

Street address 1: 3217 Blue Star Hwy
Street address city: Saugatuck
Street address state: MI
Zip/Postal code: 49453-9723
General Phone: (269) 857-2570
General Fax: (269) 857-4637
General/National Adv. E-mail: commrec@allegannews.com
Editorial e-mail: editorcommrec@allegannews.com
Primary Website: thecommercialrecord.com
Year Established: 1869
Avg Paid Circ: 1020
Avg Free Circ: 21
Audit By: Sworn/Estimate/Non-Audited
Audit Date: 10.06.2019
Personnel: Cheryl Kaechele (Pub); Connie Ellis (Office Mgr.)
Parent company (for newspapers): Kaechele Publications, Inc.

THE CONNECTION

Street address 1: 21316 Mack Ave
Street address city: Grosse Pointe Woods
Street address state: MI
Zip/Postal code: 48236-1047
General Phone: (313) 882-6900
General Fax: (313) 882-1585
General/National Adv. E-mail: jminnis@grossepointenews.com
Primary Website: grossepointenews.com
Avg Free Circ: 30000
Audit By: Sworn/Estimate/Non-Audited
Audit Date: 10.06.2019
Personnel: Peter Birkner (Adv. Mgr.); Jill Carlsen (Circ. Mgr.)

THE COUNTY JOURNAL

Street address 1: 241 S. Cochran Ave.
Street address city: Charlotte
Street address state: MI
Zip/Postal code: 48813
General Phone: (517) 543-1099
General Fax: (517) 543-1993
Advertising Phone: (517) 543-1099 ext 225
Advertising Fax: (517) 543-1993
Editorial Phone: (517) 543-1099 ext 227
Editorial Fax: (517) 543-1993
General/National Adv. E-mail: cgwing@county-journal.com
Display Adv. E-mail: cgwing@county-journal.com
Classified Adv. e-mail: sales@county-journal.com
Editorial e-mail: news@county-journal.com
Primary Website: county-journal.com
Year Established: 2006
Avg Paid Circ: 28
Avg Free Circ: 15000
Audit By: CVC
Audit Date: 30.06.2020
Personnel: Cindy Gaedert (Owner, Pub. & Sales); Cindy Gaedert (Publisher/Owner); Travis Silvas (Circ. Mgr.); Denise Ensley
Parent company (for newspapers): Flashes Advertising & News

THE COUNTY PRESS

Street address 1: 1521 Imlay City Rd
Street address city: Lapeer
Street address state: MI
Zip/Postal code: 48446-3195
General Phone: (810) 664-0811
General Fax: (810) 667-6309
General/National Adv. E-mail: info@mihomepaper.com
Display Adv. E-mail: sales@mihomepaper.com
Editorial e-mail: editor@mihomepaper.com
Primary Website: http://thecountypress.mihomepaper.com/
Year Established: 1839
Avg Paid Circ: 7941
Avg Free Circ: 233
Audit By: AAM
Audit Date: 31.12.2017
Personnel: Theresa Richey (Circ. Mgr.); Jeff Hogan (Ed.); Wes Smith (Adv. Dir.)

THE CURRENT

Street address 1: 3003 Washtenaw Ave
Street address 2: Ste 3
Street address city: Ann Arbor
Street address state: MI
Zip/Postal code: 48104-5107
General Phone: (734) 668-4044
General Fax: (734) 668-0555
General/National Adv. E-mail: a2sales@adamsstreetpublishing.com
Display Adv. E-mail: sales@adamsstreetpublishing.com
Editorial e-mail: cjacobs@toledocitypaper.com
Primary Website: ecurrent.com/contact
Avg Paid Circ: 1500
Avg Free Circ: 150
Audit By: Sworn/Estimate/Non-Audited
Audit Date: 10.06.2019
Personnel: Bob Wurzer (Pub.); Patricia Pollard (Ed.); Vicki Underhill (Adv. Mgr.); Elaine Thom (Comp. Mgr.)

THE DAVISON INDEX

Street address 1: 220 N Main St
Street address city: Davison
Street address state: MI
Zip/Postal code: 48423-1432
General Phone: (810) 653-3511
General Fax: (810) 653-6309
Advertising Phone: (810) 653-3511
Editorial Phone: (810) 452-2650
General/National Adv. E-mail: pclinton@mihomepaper.com
Display Adv. E-mail: pclinton@mihomepaper.com
Editorial e-mail: ggould@mihomepaper.com
Primary Website: http://davisonindex.mihomepaper.com/
Year Established: 1889
Avg Free Circ: 14593

Audit By: VAC
Audit Date: 30.06.2017
Personnel: Wes Smith (Pub.); Gary Gould (Ed); Pete Clinton (Adv. Mgr); Dale Phillips (Circ. Mgr); Donna Ashby (Prod. Mgr)
Parent company (for newspapers): View Newspaper Group

THE EASTSIDER

Street address 1: 13650 E 11 Mile Rd
Street address city: Warren
Street address state: MI
Zip/Postal code: 48089-1422
General Phone: (586) 498-8000
General Fax: (586) 498-9631
Advertising Phone: (586) 498-1088
Editorial Phone: (586) 498-1053
General/National Adv. E-mail: emyers@candgnews.com
Display Adv. E-mail: emyers@candgnews.com
Editorial e-mail: jdemers@candgnews.com
Primary Website: candgnews.com
Year Established: 1982
Avg Free Circ: 31035
Audit By: AAM
Audit Date: 30.09.2018
Personnel: Jeff Demers (Pub.); Elaine Myers (Adv. Mgr); David Demers (Circ. Mgr); Barry Bernard (Prod. Mgr)
Parent company (for newspapers): C & G Newspapers

THE EXPONENT

Street address 1: 160 S Main St
Street address city: Brooklyn
Street address state: MI
Zip/Postal code: 49230-8588
General Phone: (517) 592-2122
General Fax: (517) 592-3241
General/National Adv. E-mail: dorothy@theexponent.com
Display Adv. E-mail: sell@theexponent.com
Editorial e-mail: news@theexponent.com
Primary Website: theexponent.com
Year Established: 1881
Avg Paid Circ: 5000
Audit By: Sworn/Estimate/Non-Audited
Audit Date: 10.06.2019
Personnel: Matt Schepeler (Pub.); Dorothy Booth (Adv. Mgr.)

THE FENTON PRESS

Street address 1: 200 E 1st St
Street address city: Flint
Street address state: MI
Zip/Postal code: 48502-1911
General Phone: (810) 766-6100
General Fax: (810) 767-7518
General/National Adv. E-mail: weeklyjournal@fledjournal.com
Primary Website: mlive.com
Avg Free Circ: 16486
Audit By: Sworn/Estimate/Non-Audited
Audit Date: 10.06.2019
Personnel: Barb Modrack (Ed.); Brooke Rausch (Mng. Ed.)
Parent company (for newspapers): Advance Publications, Inc.

THE HASTINGS BANNER

Street address 1: 1351 N M-43 Hwy
Street address city: Hastings
Street address state: MI
Zip/Postal code: 49058
General Phone: (269) 945-9554
General Fax: (269) 945-5192
Advertising Phone: (269) 945-9554
Advertising Fax: (269) 945-5522
General/National Adv. E-mail: news@j-adgraphics.com
Display Adv. E-mail: news@j-adgraphics.com
Editorial e-mail: news@j-adgraphics.com
Primary Website: hastingsbanner.com
Year Established: 1856
Avg Paid Circ: 4998
Avg Free Circ: 30000
Audit By: Sworn/Estimate/Non-Audited
Audit Date: 10.06.2019
Personnel: John Jacobs (Pres./Pub.); Dennis Rasey (Circ. Mgr.)
Parent company (for newspapers): J-Ad Graphics

THE HOMER INDEX

Street address 1: 119 W Main St
Street address city: Homer
Street address state: MI
Zip/Postal code: 49245-1023
General Phone: (517) 568-4646
General Fax: (517) 568-4346
General/National Adv. E-mail: ads@homerindex.com
Display Adv. E-mail: ads@homerindex.com
Editorial e-mail: news@homerindex.com
Primary Website: homerindex.com
Year Established: 1872
Avg Paid Circ: 1150
Avg Free Circ: 20
Audit By: Sworn/Estimate/Non-Audited
Audit Date: 10.06.2019
Personnel: Sharon Warner (Gen. Mgr.); Mike Warner (Ed.)

THE HOUGHTON LAKE RESORTER

Street address 1: 4049 W Houghton Lake Dr
Street address city: Houghton Lake
Street address state: MI
Zip/Postal code: 48629-9208
General Phone: (989) 366-5341
General Fax: (989) 366-4472
General/National Adv. E-mail: news@houghtonlakeresorter.com
Display Adv. E-mail: ads@houghtonlakeresorter.com
Editorial e-mail: news@houghtonlakeresorter.com
Primary Website: houghtonlakeresorter.com
Year Established: 1939
Avg Paid Circ: 7800
Avg Free Circ: 58
Audit By: Sworn/Estimate/Non-Audited
Audit Date: 10.06.2019
Personnel: Jo Ann Juruzel (Office Mgr.); Thomas W. Hamp (Pub./Ed.); Eric M. Hamp (Mng. Ed.); Bryan Hamp (Prodn. Mgr.)

THE INKSTER LEDGER STAR

Street address 1: 502 Forest Ave
Street address city: Plymouth
Street address state: MI
Zip/Postal code: 48170-1752
General Phone: (734) 467-1900
General Fax: (734) 729-1840
General/National Adv. E-mail: ads@journalgroup.com
Editorial e-mail: swillett@journalgroup.com
Primary Website: journalgroup.com
Year Established: 1947
Avg Paid Circ: 1940
Avg Free Circ: 1263
Audit By: Sworn/Estimate/Non-Audited
Audit Date: 10.06.2019
Personnel: Susan Willett (Pub.)
Parent company (for newspapers): Associated Newspapers of Michigan

THE JEFFERSONIAN

Street address 1: 65 S Elk St
Street address city: Sandusky
Street address state: MI
Zip/Postal code: 48471-1337
General Phone: (810) 648-4000
General Fax: (810) 648-4526
Advertising Phone: (810) 648-4000
Advertising Fax: (810) 648-4526
Editorial Phone: (810) 648-4000
Editorial Fax: (810) 648-4526
General/National Adv. E-mail: jvanderpoel@mihomepaper.com
Display Adv. E-mail: jvanderpoel@mihomepaper.com
Editorial e-mail: jvanderpoel@mihomepaper.com
Primary Website: mihomepaper.com
Year Established: 1971
Avg Paid Circ: 262
Avg Free Circ: 151
Audit By: AAM
Audit Date: 30.09.2018
Personnel: Eric Levine (Ed.); Jane Vanderpoel (Pub.)
Parent company (for newspapers): Tribune Publishing, Inc.

THE JOURNAL ERA

Street address 1: 101 W Ferry St
Street address city: Berrien Springs
Street address state: MI
Zip/Postal code: 49103-1154
General Phone: (269) 473-5421
General Fax: (269) 471-1362
Advertising Phone: (269) 473-1533
General/National Adv. E-mail: thejournalera@yahoo.com
Primary Website: thejournalera.com
Year Established: 1874
Avg Paid Circ: 2000
Audit By: Sworn/Estimate/Non-Audited
Audit Date: 10.06.2019
Personnel: Kathy Pullano (Ed.)

THE LAKE ORION REVIEW

Street address 1: 30 N Broadway St
Street address city: Lake Orion
Street address state: MI
Zip/Postal code: 48362-3100
General Phone: (248) 693-8331
General Fax: (248) 693-5712
Advertising Phone: (248) 628-4801 ext20
Editorial Phone: (248) 693-8331
General/National Adv. E-mail: lakeorionreview@gmail.com
Primary Website: lakeorionreview.com
Year Established: 1881
Avg Paid Circ: 2500
Avg Free Circ: 66
Audit By: Sworn/Estimate/Non-Audited
Audit Date: 10.06.2019
Personnel: Jim Sherman (Pub.); Don Rush (Asst. Pub.); Eric Lewis (Adv. Mgr.); jim newell
Parent company (for newspapers): Waxa

THE LEADER AND THE KALKASKIAN

Street address 1: 415 Cass St
Street address 2: Ste 2D
Street address city: Traverse City
Street address state: MI
Zip/Postal code: 49684-2589
General Phone: (231) 486-0072
General Fax: (231) 486-2203
Advertising Phone: (231) 620-5707
Editorial Phone: (231) 620-5707
General/National Adv. E-mail: plein@michigannewspapers.com
Display Adv. E-mail: dlein@michigannewspapers.com
Editorial e-mail: news@grandtraverseinsider.com
Primary Website: themorningsun.com
Avg Paid Circ: 3517
Avg Free Circ: 25
Audit By: Sworn/Estimate/Non-Audited
Audit Date: 10.06.2019
Personnel: Dave Lein (Ed.); Pam Lein (Adv. Mgr.)
Parent company (for newspapers): Morning Star

THE MACOMB VOICE

Street address 1: 19176 Hall Rd
Street address 2: Ste 200
Street address city: Clinton Township
Street address state: MI
Zip/Postal code: 48038-6914
General Phone: (586) 716-8100
General Fax: (586) 716-8918
Advertising Fax: (586) 716-8533
General/National Adv. E-mail: debbie.loggins@voicenews.com
Display Adv. E-mail: classified.voice@voicenews.com
Editorial e-mail: editor@voicenews.com
Primary Website: voicenews.com
Year Established: 1983
Avg Paid Circ: 4000
Audit By: Sworn/Estimate/Non-Audited
Audit Date: 10.06.2019
Personnel: Debra Loggins (Gen. Mgr.); Jeff Payne (Ed.); Rene Allard (Circ. Mgr.)
Parent company (for newspapers): Digital First Media

THE MARCELLUS NEWS

Street address 1: PO Box 277
Street address city: Marcellus
Street address state: MI
Zip/Postal code: 49067-5102
General Phone: (269) 646-2101
General/National Adv. E-mail: editor@marcellusnews.com
Editorial e-mail: editor@marcellusnews.com
Primary Website: marcellusnews.com
Year Established: 1876
Avg Paid Circ: 1600
Audit By: Sworn/Estimate/Non-Audited
Audit Date: 10.06.2019
Personnel: ???? ????; Ramona Moormann (Ed.)

THE MARION PRESS

Street address 1: 301 E. Mill St.
Street address city: Marion
Street address state: MI
Zip/Postal code: 49665
General Phone: (231) 743-2481
General Fax: (989) 386-2412
Editorial e-mail: yourmarionpress@gmail.com
Primary Website: marion-press.com
Avg Paid Circ: 1941
Avg Free Circ: 10
Audit By: Sworn/Estimate/Non-Audited
Audit Date: 10.06.2019
Personnel: Mike Wilcox (Publ)

THE MINDEN CITY HERALD

Street address 1: 1524 Main St
Street address city: Minden City
Street address state: MI
Zip/Postal code: 48456-9404
General Phone: (989) 864-3630
General Fax: (989) 864-5363
Editorial e-mail: mcherald@hbch.com
Avg Paid Circ: 1500
Audit By: Sworn/Estimate/Non-Audited
Audit Date: 10.06.2019
Personnel: Paul Engel (Ed.)

THE MONTMORENCY COUNTY TRIBUNE

Street address 1: 12625 State St.
Street address city: Atlanta
Street address state: MI
Zip/Postal code: 49709
General Phone: (989) 785-4214
General Fax: (989) 785-3118
General/National Adv. E-mail: office@montmorencytribune.com
Display Adv. E-mail: office@montmorencytribune.com
Editorial e-mail: editor@montmorencytribune.com
Primary Website: montmorencytribune.com
Year Established: 1886
Avg Paid Circ: 5200
Audit By: Sworn/Estimate/Non-Audited
Audit Date: 10.06.2019
Personnel: James Young (Ed.)

THE MUNISING NEWS

Street address 1: 132 E Superior St
Street address city: Munising
Street address state: MI
Zip/Postal code: 49862-1122
General Phone: (906) 387-3282
General Fax: (906) 387-4054
Advertising Phone: (906) 387-3282
Editorial Phone: (906) 387-3282
General/National Adv. E-mail: munisingnews@jamadots.com
Display Adv. E-mail: munisingnews@jamadots.com
Editorial e-mail: munisingnews@jamadots.com
Primary Website: themunisingnews.com
Year Established: 1896
Avg Paid Circ: 2250
Avg Free Circ: 5000
Audit By: Sworn/Estimate/Non-Audited
Audit Date: 10.06.2019
Personnel: Willie J. Peterson (Pub.)
Parent company (for newspapers): Peterson Publishing, Inc

THE NEWBERRY NEWS

Street address 1: 316 Newberry Ave
Street address city: Newberry

Street address state: MI
Zip/Postal code: 49868-1105
General Phone: (906) 293-8401
General Fax: (906) 293-8815
General/National Adv. E-mail: nbyads@jamadots.com
Display Adv. E-mail: nbynews@jamadots.com
Editorial e-mail: nbynews@att.net
Primary Website: newberry-news.com
Year Established: 1886
Avg Paid Circ: 3600
Audit By: Sworn/Estimate/Non-Audited
Audit Date: 10.06.2019
Personnel: James Diem (Ed.); Caroline Diem (Bus. Mgr.); Teri Petrie (Adv. Mgr.)

THE NEWS HERALD

Street address 1: 2125 Butterfield Road
Street address 2: Suite 102N
Street address city: Troy
Street address state: MI
Zip/Postal code: 48084
General Phone: (248) 322-2186
General/National Adv. E-mail: ckruemmer@digitalfirstmedia.com
Display Adv. E-mail: classifiedads@newspaperclassifieds.com
Editorial e-mail: jalley@thenewsherald.com
Primary Website: thenewsherald.com
Avg Paid Circ: 6364
Avg Free Circ: 22741
Audit By: AAM
Audit Date: 31.03.2019
Personnel: Jason Alley (Ed.); Greg Mazanec (Pub. MI Press); Carol Kruemer (Adv.); Dave Swantek (GM)
Parent company (for newspapers): MediaNews Group

THE NORTH MACOMB VOICE

Street address 1: 19176 Hall Rd
Street address 2: Ste 200
Street address city: Clinton Township
Street address state: MI
Zip/Postal code: 48038-6914
General Phone: (586) 716-8100
General Fax: (586) 716-8918
Advertising Fax: (586) 716-8533
General/National Adv. E-mail: debbie.loggins@voicenews.com
Display Adv. E-mail: classified.voice@voicenews.com
Editorial e-mail: editor@voicenews.com
Primary Website: voicenews.com
Year Established: 1983
Avg Free Circ: 9636
Audit By: Sworn/Estimate/Non-Audited
Audit Date: 10.06.2019
Personnel: Jeff Payne (Ed.); Debbie Loggins (Adv.); Rene Allard (Circ. Mgr.)
Parent company (for newspapers): Digital First Media

THE ONTONAGON HERALD

Street address 1: 326 River Street
Street address city: Ontonagon
Street address state: MI
Zip/Postal code: 49953-1612
General Phone: (906) 884-2826
General Fax: (906) 884-2939
General/National Adv. E-mail: herald@ontonagonherald.com
Primary Website: ontonagonherald.com
Year Established: 1881
Avg Paid Circ: 1350
Avg Free Circ: 20
Audit By: Sworn/Estimate/Non-Audited
Audit Date: 29.06.2022
Personnel: Barbara Kilmer (Ed.)

THE ROMULUS ROMAN

Street address 1: 502 Forest Ave
Street address city: Plymouth
Street address state: MI
Zip/Postal code: 48170-1752
General Phone: (734) 467-1900
General Fax: (734) 729-1840
General/National Adv. E-mail: ads@journalgroup.com
Editorial e-mail: swillett@journalgroup.com
Primary Website: journalgroup.com
Year Established: 1885
Avg Paid Circ: 1163
Avg Free Circ: 307
Audit By: Sworn/Estimate/Non-Audited
Audit Date: 10.06.2019
Personnel: Susan Willett (Ed./Pub.)
Parent company (for newspapers): Associated Newspapers of Michigan

THE SALINE REPORTER

Street address 1: 1 Heritage Dr
Street address 2: Suite 100
Street address city: Southgate
Street address state: MI
Zip/Postal code: 48195-3047
General Phone: (734) 246-0800
Editorial e-mail: jalley@thenewsherald.com
Primary Website: salinereporter.com
Year Established: 1883
Avg Paid Circ: 1835
Avg Free Circ: 42
Audit By: Sworn/Estimate/Non-Audited
Audit Date: 10.06.2019
Personnel: Jason Alley (Ed.)

THE ST. IGNACE NEWS

Street address 1: 359 Reagon St
Street address city: Saint Ignace
Street address state: MI
Zip/Postal code: 49781-1134
General Phone: (906) 643-9150
General Fax: (906) 643-9122
General/National Adv. E-mail: ads@SaintIgnaceNews.com
Editorial e-mail: news@SaintIgnaceNews.com
Primary Website: saintignacenews.com
Year Established: 1878
Avg Paid Circ: 4985
Audit By: Sworn/Estimate/Non-Audited
Audit Date: 10.06.2019
Personnel: Mary Maurer (Bus. Mgr.); Wendy Colegrove (Circ. Mgr.); Wesley H. Jr. Maurer (Pub); Ellen Paquin (Ed.)

THE SUN TIMES NEWS

Street address 1: 9573 Dexter Pinckney Rd
Street address city: Pinckney
Street address state: MI
Zip/Postal code: 48169-9667
General Phone: (734) 562-2325
General Fax: (734) 562-2398
General/National Adv. E-mail: info@thesuntimesnews.com
Display Adv. E-mail: Advertising@thesuntimesnews.com
Editorial e-mail: Wendy@thesuntimesnews.com
Primary Website: https://thesuntimesnews.com
Year Established: 1878
Avg Paid Circ: 358
Avg Free Circ: 16561
Audit By: Sworn/Estimate/Non-Audited
Audit Date: 10.06.2019
Personnel: Robert Nester (Owner/Pub.)

THE SWARTZ CREEK NEWS

Street address 1: 200 E 1st St
Street address city: Flint
Street address state: MI
Zip/Postal code: 48502-1911
General Phone: (810) 766-6100
General Fax: (810) 767-7518
General/National Adv. E-mail: tcn@thecommunitynewspapers.com
Primary Website: theswartznews.com
Avg Free Circ: 7455
Audit By: Sworn/Estimate/Non-Audited
Audit Date: 10.06.2019
Personnel: Brooke Rausch (Mng. Ed.)
Parent company (for newspapers): Advance Publications, Inc.

THE TECUMSEH HERALD

Street address 1: 110 E Logan St
Street address city: Tecumseh
Street address state: MI
Zip/Postal code: 49286-1559
General Phone: (517) 423-2174
General Fax: (517) 423-6258
General/National Adv. E-mail: brian@tecumsehherald.com
Display Adv. E-mail: sharonm@tecumsehherald.com
Editorial e-mail: managingeditor@tecumsehherald.com
Primary Website: tecumsehherald.com
Year Established: 1850
Avg Paid Circ: 4000
Audit By: Sworn/Estimate/Non-Audited
Audit Date: 10.06.2019
Personnel: James C. Lincoln (Pub.); Mickey Alvarado (Ed.); Patti Brugger (Circ. Mgr.); Brian Callaghan (Adv. Mgr.)

THE TOWNSHIP TIMES

Street address 1: PO Box 396
Street address city: Breckenridge
Street address state: MI
Zip/Postal code: 48615-0396
General Phone: (989) 799-3200
General Fax: (989) 799-7085
Advertising Phone: (989) 842-3164
General/National Adv. E-mail: tari@twptimes.com
Editorial e-mail: nicole@twptimes.com
Primary Website: twptimes.com
Year Established: 1964
Avg Paid Circ: 4360
Avg Free Circ: 293
Audit By: Sworn/Estimate/Non-Audited
Audit Date: 10.06.2019
Personnel: Ed Belles (Pub.); Lisa Guthrie (Gen. Mgr.); Tari Newvine (Sales Assoc.); Nicole Wagner (Mng. Ed.)

THE VALLEY FARMER

Street address 1: 410 Raymond St
Street address city: Bay City
Street address state: MI
Zip/Postal code: 48706-4377
General Phone: (989) 893-6507
General Fax: (989) 893-6507
General/National Adv. E-mail: dbhebert1@charter.net
Year Established: 1929
Avg Paid Circ: 600
Avg Free Circ: 20
Audit By: Sworn/Estimate/Non-Audited
Audit Date: 10.06.2019
Personnel: David Hebert (Pub.)

THE VASSAR PIONEER TIMES

Street address 1: 344 N State St
Street address city: Caro
Street address state: MI
Zip/Postal code: 48723-1538
General Phone: (989) 678-3181
General Fax: (989) 673-5662
General/National Adv. E-mail: ads@tcadvertiser.com
Primary Website: facebook.com/pg/Vassar-Pioneer-Times-106721472696367
Year Established: 1856
Avg Paid Circ: 1500
Avg Free Circ: 9
Audit By: Sworn/Estimate/Non-Audited
Audit Date: 10.06.2019
Personnel: Tim Murphy (Adv.)
Parent company (for newspapers): Hearst Communications, Inc.

THE VOICE

Street address 1: 19176 Hall Rd
Street address 2: Ste 200
Street address city: Clinton Township
Street address state: MI
Zip/Postal code: 48038-6914
General Phone: (586) 716-8100
General Fax: (586) 716-8533
General/National Adv. E-mail: dawn.emke@voicenews.com
Display Adv. E-mail: classified.voice@voicenews.com
Editorial e-mail: editor@voicenews.com
Primary Website: voicenews.com
Audit By: Sworn/Estimate/Non-Audited
Audit Date: 10.06.2019
Personnel: Jeannie Parent (Pub.); Teresa Goodrich (VP); Jeff Payne (Ed.)

THE WAYNE EAGLE

Street address 1: 502 Forest Ave
Street address city: Plymouth
Street address state: MI
Zip/Postal code: 48170-1752
General Phone: (734) 467-1900
General Fax: (734) 729-1840
General/National Adv. E-mail: ads@journalgroup.com
Editorial e-mail: swillett@journalgroup.com
Primary Website: journalgroup.com
Avg Paid Circ: 1253
Avg Free Circ: 998
Audit By: Sworn/Estimate/Non-Audited
Audit Date: 10.06.2019
Personnel: Susan Willett (Pub.)
Parent company (for newspapers): Associated Newspapers of Michigan

THE WESTLAND EAGLE

Street address 1: 502 Forest Ave
Street address city: Plymouth
Street address state: MI
Zip/Postal code: 48170-1752
General Phone: (734) 467-1900
General Fax: (734) 729-1840
General/National Adv. E-mail: ads@journalgroup.com
Editorial e-mail: swillett@journalgroup.com
Primary Website: associatednewspapers.net
Year Established: 1885
Avg Paid Circ: 100
Avg Free Circ: 1300
Audit By: Sworn/Estimate/Non-Audited
Audit Date: 10.06.2019
Personnel: Susan Willett (Pub.)
Parent company (for newspapers): Associated Newspapers of Michigan

THE YALE EXPOSITOR

Street address 1: 21 S Main St
Street address city: Yale
Street address state: MI
Zip/Postal code: 48097-3317
General Phone: (810) 387-2300
General Fax: (810) 387-9490
Advertising Phone: (810) 387-2300
Editorial Phone: (810) 387-2300
General/National Adv. E-mail: YaleExpositor@gmail.com
Display Adv. E-mail: YaleExpositor@gmail.com
Editorial e-mail: YaleExpositor@gmail.com
Primary Website: YaleExpositor.com
Year Established: 1882
Avg Paid Circ: 2500
Avg Free Circ: 0
Audit By: Sworn/Estimate/Non-Audited
Audit Date: 10.06.2019
Personnel: Barbara Stasik (Ed); James Brown (Pub); Caitlin Chandler (Office Manager); Melissa Hughes (Advertising/Sales)

THE ZONE

Street address 1: 214 S Jackson St
Street address city: Jackson
Street address state: MI
Zip/Postal code: 49201-2267
General Phone: (517) 787-2300
General Fax: (517) 789-1249
Primary Website: mlive.com/citpat
Avg Free Circ: 30000
Audit By: Sworn/Estimate/Non-Audited
Audit Date: 10.06.2019
Personnel: Sandra Petykiewicz (Pub.); Margaret Parshall (Adv. Mgr.)

TOWNSHIP VIEW

Street address 1: 110 S Chapman St
Street address city: Chesaning
Street address state: MI
Zip/Postal code: 48616-1221
General Phone: (989) 393-4100
General Fax: (989) 845-4397
Advertising Fax:
General/National Adv. E-mail: jvanderpoel@mihomepaper.com
Display Adv. E-mail: jvanderpoel@mihomepaper.com
Editorial e-mail: jvanderpoel@mihomepaper.com
Primary Website: http://townshipview.mihomepaper.com/
Year Established: 2010
Avg Free Circ: 20268
Audit By: CVC
Audit Date: 30.06.2017

Personnel: Wes Smith (Pub./Ed.); Jane Vanderpoel (General Manager)
Parent company (for newspapers): View Newspaper Group

TRIBUNE RECORDER LEADER

Street address 1: 43 S Elk St
Street address city: Sandusky
Street address state: MI
Zip/Postal code: 48471-1353
General Phone: (810) 648-5282
General Fax: (810) 376-4058
Editorial e-mail: sandusky.tribune@gmail.com
Primary Website: tribunerecorderleader.com
Year Established: 1893
Avg Paid Circ: 1500
Avg Free Circ: 10
Audit By: Sworn/Estimate/Non-Audited
Audit Date: 10.06.2019
Personnel: Douglas Regentin (Ed.)
Parent company (for newspapers): Hearst Communications, Inc.

TRI-CITY TIMES

Street address 1: 594 N Almont Ave
Street address city: Imlay City
Street address state: MI
Zip/Postal code: 48444-1000
General Phone: (810) 724-2615
General Fax: (810) 724-8552
General/National Adv. E-mail: rjorgensen@pageone-inc.com
Display Adv. E-mail: rjorgensen@pageone-inc.com
Editorial e-mail: cminolli@pageone-inc.com
Primary Website: tricitytimes-online.com
Avg Paid Circ: 5771
Avg Free Circ: 1229
Audit By: Sworn/Estimate/Non-Audited
Audit Date: 10.06.2019
Personnel: Delores Heim (Pub.)

TRI-COUNTY CITIZEN

Street address 1: 110 S. Chapman St.
Street address city: Chesaning
Street address state: MI
Zip/Postal code: 48616
General Phone: (989) 341-4806
General Fax: (989) 845-4397
General/National Adv. E-mail: tccsales@mihomepaper.com
Display Adv. E-mail: tccsales@mihomepaper.com
Editorial e-mail: tccnews@mihomepaper.com
Primary Website: tricountycitizen.mihomepaper.com
Year Established: 1983
Avg Free Circ: 17844
Audit By: Sworn/Estimate/Non-Audited
Audit Date: 10.06.2019
Personnel: Keith Salisbury (Ed.); Mark Hayden (Adv.)

TRI-COUNTY TIMES

Street address 1: 256 N Fenway Dr
Street address city: Fenton
Street address state: MI
Zip/Postal code: 48430-2699
General Phone: (810) 629-8282
General Fax: (810) 629-9227
Advertising Phone: (810) 433-6778
General/National Adv. E-mail: tallen@tctimes.com
Display Adv. E-mail: hpoyner@tctimes.com
Editorial e-mail: sstone@tctimes.com
Primary Website: tctimes.com
Year Established: 1955
Avg Paid Circ: 9881
Avg Free Circ: 19800
Audit By: Sworn/Estimate/Non-Audited
Audit Date: 10.06.2019
Personnel: John Evans (Bus Mgr); Terese Allen (Marketing Director); Jennifer Ward (General Manager); Craig Rockman (Publisher); Sharon Stone (Editor)
Parent company (for newspapers): Rockman Communications, Inc

TROY TIMES

Street address 1: 13650 11 Mile Road
Street address city: Warren
Street address state: MI
Zip/Postal code: 48089
General Phone: (586) 498-8000
General Fax: (586) 498-9631
Advertising Phone: (586) 498-1087
Editorial Phone: (586) 498-1071
General/National Adv. E-mail: emyers@candgnews.com
Display Adv. E-mail: emyers@candgnews.com
Editorial e-mail: jdemers@candgnews.com
Primary Website: candgnews.com
Year Established: 1985
Avg Free Circ: 31455
Audit By: CVC
Audit Date: 31.03.2018
Personnel: Jeff Demers (Circ. Mgr.); Elaine Myers (Adv. Mgr); Barry Bernard (Prod. Mgr); David Demers (Circ. Mgr)
Parent company (for newspapers): C & G Newspapers; C&G Publishing

TUSCOLA COUNTY ADVERTISER

Street address 1: 344 N State St
Street address city: Caro
Street address state: MI
Zip/Postal code: 48723-1538
General Phone: (989) 673-3181
General Fax: (989) 673-5662
General/National Adv. E-mail: ads@tcadvertiser.com
Primary Website: tuscolatoday.com
Year Established: 1868
Avg Paid Circ: 8220
Audit By: Sworn/Estimate/Non-Audited
Audit Date: 10.06.2019
Personnel: Tim Murphy (Pub.); Deborah Stahl (Adv Mgr.); Ven Stark (Circ. Mgr.)

UNION ENTERPRISE

Street address 1: 231 Trowbridge St
Street address 2: Ste 17
Street address city: Allegan
Street address state: MI
Zip/Postal code: 49010-1330
General Phone: (269) 673-5534
General Fax: (269) 673-5535
Advertising Phone: (269) 673-5534
Advertising Fax: (269) 673-5535
Editorial Phone: (269) 673-5534
Editorial Fax: (269) 673-5535
General/National Adv. E-mail: publisher@allegannews.com
Display Adv. E-mail: advertising@allegannews.com
Editorial e-mail: editor@allegannews.com
Primary Website: allegannews.com
Year Established: 1871
Avg Paid Circ: 519
Avg Free Circ: 35
Audit By: Sworn/Estimate/Non-Audited
Audit Date: 10.06.2019
Personnel: Cheryl A. Kaechele (Pub.); Ryan Lewis (Ed.)
Parent company (for newspapers): Kaechele Publications, Inc.

WAKEFIELD NEWS/ BESSEMER PICK & AXE

Street address 1: 405 Sunday Lake St
Street address city: Wakefield
Street address state: MI
Zip/Postal code: 49968-1337
General Phone: (906) 224-9561
General Fax: (906) 224-9921
Editorial e-mail: news@wnbpa.net
Year Established: 1925
Avg Paid Circ: 1700
Avg Free Circ: 48
Audit By: Sworn/Estimate/Non-Audited
Audit Date: 10.06.2019
Personnel: Andrew Hill (Ed.)

WARREN WEEKLY

Street address 1: 13650 11 Mile Road
Street address city: Warren
Street address state: MI
Zip/Postal code: 48089
General Phone: (586) 498-8000
General Fax: (586) 498-9631
Advertising Phone: (586) 498-1078
Editorial Phone: (586) 498-1059
General/National Adv. E-mail: emyers@candgnews.com
Display Adv. E-mail: emyers@candgnews.com
Editorial e-mail: jdemers@candgnews.com
Primary Website: candgnews.com
Year Established: 1981
Avg Free Circ: 55976
Audit By: AAM
Audit Date: 31.03.2018
Personnel: Jeff Demers (Pub.); Barry Bernard (Prod. Mgr.); Elaine Myers (Adv. Mgr); David Demers (Circ. Mgr)
Parent company (for newspapers): C & G Newspapers; C&G Publishing

WEST BLOOMFIELD BEACON

Street address 1: 13650 E 11 Mile Rd
Street address city: Warren
Street address state: MI
Zip/Postal code: 48089-1422
General Phone: (586) 498-1071
Editorial e-mail: abates@candgnews.com
Primary Website: candgnews.com
Year Established: 2004
Avg Free Circ: 27536
Audit By: AAM
Audit Date: 30.09.2018
Personnel: Jeff Demers (Pub.); Annie Bates (Ed.); Elaine Myers (Adv. Mgr); David Demers (Circ. Mgr); Barry Bernard (Prod. Mgr)
Parent company (for newspapers): C & G Newspapers

WESTLAND OBSERVER

Street address 1: 615 W Lafayette Blvd
Street address 2: # 2
Street address city: Detroit
Street address state: MI
Zip/Postal code: 48226-3124
General Phone: (866) 887-2737
General Fax: (313) 223-3318
Advertising Phone: (800) 579-7355
Primary Website: hometownlife.com
Avg Paid Circ: 950
Avg Free Circ: 5400
Audit By: AAM
Audit Date: 31.12.2018
Personnel: Philip Allmen (Cons. Exp. Dir.)
Parent company (for newspapers): Gannett

WHITE LAKE BEACON

Street address 1: 123 S State St
Street address city: Hart
Street address state: MI
Zip/Postal code: 49420
General Phone: (231) 873-5602
General/National Adv. E-mail: editor@whitelakebeacon.com
Display Adv. E-mail: monica@whitelakebeacon.com
Editorial e-mail: editor@whitelakebeacon.com
Primary Website: whitelakebeacon.com
Year Established: 1983
Avg Paid Circ: 1760
Avg Free Circ: 3170
Audit By: Sworn/Estimate/Non-Audited
Audit Date: 01.11.2021
Personnel: Andy Roberts (Editor)
Parent company (for newspapers): Community Media Group

WOODWARD TALK

Street address 1: 13650 11 Mile Road
Street address city: Warren
Street address state: MI
Zip/Postal code: 48089
General Phone: (586) 498-8000
General Fax: (586) 498-9631
Advertising Phone: (586) 498-1032
Editorial Phone: (586) 498-1053
General/National Adv. E-mail: emyers@candgnews.com
Display Adv. E-mail: emyers@candgnews.com
Editorial e-mail: dwallace@candgnews.com
Primary Website: candgnews.com
Year Established: 2004
Avg Free Circ: 20028
Audit By: CVC
Audit Date: 31.03.2018
Personnel: Gregg Demers (Ed. Dir.); David Wallace (Ed.); Jeff Demers (Dir of Sales); Elaine Myers (Adv. Mgr); David Demers (Circ. Mgr); Barry Bernard (Prod. Mgr)
Parent company (for newspapers): C & G Newspapers; C&G Publishing

ZEELAND RECORD

Street address 1: 16 S Elm St
Street address city: Zeeland
Street address state: MI
Zip/Postal code: 49464-1751
General Phone: (616) 772-2131
General Fax: (616) 772-9771
General/National Adv. E-mail: advertising@zeelandrecord.net
Display Adv. E-mail: advertising@zeelandrecord.net
Editorial e-mail: newsrelease@zeelandrecord.net
Year Established: 1893
Avg Paid Circ: 1100
Audit By: Sworn/Estimate/Non-Audited
Audit Date: 10.06.2019
Personnel: Kraig Van Koevering (Adv. Mgr.); Kurt Van Koevering (Ed.)

MINNESOTA

ACCESS PRESS

Street address 1: 161 Saint Anthony Ave
Street address 2: Ste 910
Street address city: Saint Paul
Street address state: MN
Zip/Postal code: 55103-2454
General Phone: (651) 644-2133
General Fax: (651) 644-2136
Advertising Phone: (651) 807-1078
General/National Adv. E-mail: access@accesspress.org
Display Adv. E-mail: Michelle@accesspress.org
Editorial e-mail: tim@accesspress.org
Primary Website: accesspress.org
Year Established: 1990
Avg Paid Circ: 550
Avg Free Circ: 12000
Audit By: Sworn/Estimate/Non-Audited
Audit Date: 10.06.2019
Personnel: Tim Benjamin (Publisher/Editor)

AGRI NEWS

Street address 1: 18 1st Ave SE
Street address city: Rochester
Street address state: MN
Zip/Postal code: 55904-3722
General Phone: (507) 285-7600
General Fax: (507) 281-7436
Advertising Phone: (507) 285-7607
General/National Adv. E-mail: lschell@postbulletin.com
Display Adv. E-mail: classifieds@agrinews.com
Editorial e-mail: wilmes@agrinews.com
Primary Website: agrinews.com
Year Established: 1975
Avg Paid Circ: 7772
Avg Free Circ: 419
Audit By: Sworn/Estimate/Non-Audited
Audit Date: 10.06.2019
Personnel: Todd Heroff (Circ. Mgr.); Mychal Wilmes (Mng. Ed.); Lisa Schell (Adv Mgr.)

AITKIN INDEPENDENT AGE

Street address 1: 213 Minnesota Ave N
Street address city: Aitkin
Street address state: MN
Zip/Postal code: 56431-1411
General Phone: (218) 927-3761
General Fax: (218) 927-3763
Advertising Phone: (218) 927-3761
Advertising Fax: (218) 927-3763
Editorial Phone: (218) 927-3761
Editorial Fax: 218-927-3763
General/National Adv. E-mail: rbouley@aitkinage.com
Display Adv. E-mail: subscriptions@aitkinage.com
Editorial e-mail: news@aitkinage.com
Primary Website: aitkinage.com
Year Established: 1883
Avg Paid Circ: 3800

Audit By: Sworn/Estimate/Non-Audited
Audit Date: 10.06.2019
Personnel: Roxanne Bouley (Operations Mgr.); Brielle Bredsten (Ed.)
Parent company (for newspapers): Adams Publishing Group, LLC

ANNANDALE ADVOCATE

Street address 1: 73 Oak Ave S
Street address city: Annandale
Street address state: MN
Zip/Postal code: 55302-1205
General Phone: (320) 274-3052
General Fax: (320) 274-2301
General/National Adv. E-mail: ads@annandaleadvocate.com
Editorial e-mail: news@annandaleadvocate.com
Primary Website: annandaleadvocate.com
Avg Paid Circ: 2515
Audit By: Sworn/Estimate/Non-Audited
Audit Date: 10.06.2019
Personnel: Steven Prinsen (Pub.); Sharon Schumacher (Co-Pub.); Paul Downer (Ed.)

ANOKA COUNTY UNION HERALD

Street address 1: 4095 Coon Rapids Blvd.
Street address city: Coon Rapids
Street address state: MN
Zip/Postal code: 55433-2525
General Phone: (763) 421-4444
General Fax: (763) 421-4315
Advertising Phone: (763) 712-3520
Editorial Phone: (763) 712-3514
Editorial Fax: (763) 712-3519
General/National Adv. E-mail: steve.gall@ecm-inc.com
Display Adv. E-mail: steve.gall@ecm-inc.com
Editorial e-mail: matthew.hankey@ecm-inc.com
Primary Website: hometownsource.com
Mthly Avg Views: 204663
Mthly Avg Unique Visitors: 55607
Year Established: 1865
Avg Paid Circ: 3563
Avg Free Circ: 173
Audit By: Sworn/Estimate/Non-Audited
Audit Date: 10.06.2019
Personnel: Matthew Hankey (Mng Ed.); Steve Gall (Adv. Dir.)
Parent company (for newspapers): Adams Publishing Group, LLC

ARLINGTON ENTERPRISE

Street address 1: 402 W Alden St
Street address city: Arlington
Street address state: MN
Zip/Postal code: 55307-2214
General Phone: (507) 964-5547
General Fax: (507) 964-2423
General/National Adv. E-mail: info@arlingtonMNnews.com
Display Adv. E-mail: info@arlingtonmnnews.com
Editorial e-mail: KurtM@arlingtonmnnews.com
Primary Website: arlingtonMNnews.com
Year Established: 1884
Avg Paid Circ: 1040
Avg Free Circ: 400
Audit By: Sworn/Estimate/Non-Audited
Audit Date: 10.06.2019
Personnel: Kurt Menk (Ed)
Parent company (for newspapers): McLeod Publishing, Inc.

ASKOV AMERICAN

Street address 1: 6351 Kobmagergade
Street address city: Askov
Street address state: MN
Zip/Postal code: 55704-4280
General Phone: (320) 838-3151
General Fax: (320) 838-3152
General/National Adv. E-mail: askovamerican@scicable.net
Display Adv. E-mail: askovamerican@scicable.net
Classified Adv. e-mail: askovamerican@scicable.net
Editorial e-mail: askovamerican@scicable.com
Primary Website: askovamerican.com
Year Established: 1914
Avg Paid Circ: 1786
Audit By: Sworn/Estimate/Non-Audited
Audit Date: 10.06.2019
Personnel: Shawn Jansen (Editor)

BALATON PRESS TRIBUNE

Street address 1: 220 Central Ave S
Street address city: Balaton
Street address state: MN
Zip/Postal code: 56115-1032
General Phone: (507) 734-5421
General Fax: (507) 734-5457
General/National Adv. E-mail: balatonpublishing@yahoo.com
Year Established: 1910
Avg Paid Circ: 415
Audit By: Sworn/Estimate/Non-Audited
Audit Date: 10.06.2019
Personnel: Connie Skaug (Office Manager); Mckenzie Swanson (Editor); Donna Miller (Accounting)
Parent company (for newspapers): Balaton Press Tribune

BARNESVILLE RECORD REVIEW

Street address 1: 424 Front St S
Street address city: Barnesville
Street address state: MN
Zip/Postal code: 56514-3825
General Phone: (218) 354-2606
General Fax: (218) 354-2246
General/National Adv. E-mail: adsrecordreview@bvillemn.net
Editorial e-mail: newsrecordreview@bvillemn.net
Primary Website: barnesvillerecordreview.net
Year Established: 1903
Avg Paid Circ: 1725
Audit By: Sworn/Estimate/Non-Audited
Audit Date: 10.06.2019
Personnel: Eugene A. Prim (Ed.)
Parent company (for newspapers): Prim Group

BATTLE LAKE REVIEW

Street address 1: 114 N Lake Ave
Street address city: Battle Lake
Street address state: MN
Zip/Postal code: 56515-4049
General Phone: (218) 864-5952
General Fax: (218) 864-5212
Editorial e-mail: blreview@arvig.net
Primary Website: battlelakereview.com
Year Established: 1884
Avg Paid Circ: 2026
Audit By: Sworn/Estimate/Non-Audited
Audit Date: 10.06.2019
Personnel: Jon Tamke (Ed.)

BELLE PLAINE HERALD

Street address 1: 113 E Main St
Street address city: Belle Plaine
Street address state: MN
Zip/Postal code: 56011-1821
General Phone: (952) 873-2261
General Fax: (952) 873-2262
Editorial e-mail: bpherald@frontiernet.net
Primary Website: belleplaineherald.com
Year Established: 1882
Avg Paid Circ: 3834
Audit By: Sworn/Estimate/Non-Audited
Audit Date: 10.06.2019
Personnel: C. Edward Townsend (Pub.)

BENTON COUNTY NEWS

Street address 1: 1061 Hwy 23
Street address 2: Suite 2A
Street address city: Foley
Street address state: MN
Zip/Postal code: 56329-8802
General Phone: (320) 968-7220
General Fax: (320) 968-8821
Advertising Phone: (320) 352-6577
Advertising Fax: (320) 352-5647
Editorial Phone: same
Editorial Fax: same
General/National Adv. E-mail: missy@saukherald.com
Display Adv. E-mail: missy@saukherald.com
Classified Adv. e-mail: missy@saukherald.com
Editorial e-mail: natasha@saukherald.com
Primary Website: bentonconews.com
Year Established: 1932
Avg Paid Circ: 1300
Audit By: Sworn/Estimate/Non-Audited
Audit Date: 10.06.2019
Personnel: Missy Traeger (Sales Mgr.); Natasha Barber (Ed.); Elizabeth Haug
Parent company (for newspapers): Star Publications

BIRD DOG & RETRIEVER NEWS

Street address 1: 563 17th Ave NW
Street address city: Saint Paul
Street address state: MN
Zip/Postal code: 55112-6514
General Phone: (612) 868-9169
Advertising Phone: (612) 868-9169
General/National Adv. E-mail: publisher@Bird-dog-news.com
Display Adv. E-mail: publisher@Bird-dog-news.com
Editorial e-mail: publisher@Bird-dog-news.com
Primary Website: Bdarn.com
Year Established: 1992
Avg Paid Circ: 10000
Avg Free Circ: 17000
Audit By: Sworn/Estimate/Non-Audited
Audit Date: 10.06.2019
Personnel: Dennis Guldan (Pub.)

BIRD ISLAND UNION

Street address 1: 750 ASH AVE
Street address city: Bird Island
Street address state: MN
Zip/Postal code: 55310
General Phone: (320) 365-3266
General Fax: (320) 365-4506
General/National Adv. E-mail: union@willmar.com
Editorial e-mail: newsmir@hcctel.net
Year Established: 1936
Avg Paid Circ: 325
Audit By: Sworn/Estimate/Non-Audited
Audit Date: 10.06.2019
Personnel: John N. Hubin (Pub.); Aaron Hubin (Adv. Mgr.)

BLAINE-SPRING LAKE PARK LIFE

Street address 1: 4101 Coon Rapids Blvd NW
Street address city: Coon Rapids
Street address state: MN
Zip/Postal code: 55433-2525
General Phone: (763) 421-4444
General Fax: (763) 421-4315
Display Adv. E-mail: class@ecm-inc.com
Editorial e-mail: jonathan.young@ecm-inc.com
Primary Website: abcnewspapers.com
Mthly Avg Views: 204000
Mthly Avg Unique Visitors: 61122
Year Established: 1969
Avg Paid Circ: 145
Avg Free Circ: 15756
Audit By: Sworn/Estimate/Non-Audited
Audit Date: 10.06.2019
Personnel: Jonathon Young (Mng. Ed.); Jeremy Bradfield (Adv. Dir.)
Parent company (for newspapers): Adams Publishing Group, LLC

BLOOMINGTON SUN-CURRENT

Street address 1: 10917 Valley View Rd
Street address city: Eden Prairie
Street address state: MN
Zip/Postal code: 55344-3730
General Phone: (952) 392-6800
General Fax: (952) 392-6802
Advertising Phone: (952) 392-6888
Editorial Phone: (763) 424-7352
General/National Adv. E-mail: jeremy.bradfield@ecm-inc.com
Display Adv. E-mail: krista.jech@ecm-inc.com
Editorial e-mail: matthew.hankey@ecm-inc.com
Primary Website: http://current.mnsun.com/
Year Established: 1954
Avg Paid Circ: 391
Avg Free Circ: 24491
Audit By: Sworn/Estimate/Non-Audited
Audit Date: 10.06.2019
Personnel: Nancy Etzel (Adv. Sales); Joseph Palmersheim (Mng. Ed.)
Parent company (for newspapers): Adams Publishing Group, LLC; Sun Newspapers

BONANZA VALLEY VOICE

Street address 1: 131 Central Ave N
Street address city: Brooten
Street address state: MN
Zip/Postal code: 56316-4665
General Phone: (320) 346-2400
General Fax: (320) 346-2379
General/National Adv. E-mail: bonanzavalvoice@tds.net
Display Adv. E-mail: bonanzavalvoice@tds.net
Editorial e-mail: bonanzavalvoice@tds.net
Primary Website: bonanzavalleyvoice.com
Year Established: 1969
Avg Paid Circ: 1450
Audit By: Sworn/Estimate/Non-Audited
Audit Date: 10.06.2019
Personnel: Jennifer Murphey (Ad Design/Layout)

BROOKLYN CENTER/BROOKLYN PARK SUN-POST

Street address 1: 33 2nd St NE
Street address city: Osseo
Street address state: MN
Zip/Postal code: 55369-1252
General Phone: (952) 392-6800
General Fax: (763) 424-7388
Advertising Phone: (952) 392-6888
Editorial Phone: (763) 425-3323
General/National Adv. E-mail: cheri.obannon@ecm-inc.com
Display Adv. E-mail: tena.wensman@ecm-inc.com
Editorial e-mail: peggy.bakken@ecm-inc.com
Primary Website: http://post.mnsun.com/
Year Established: 1938
Avg Paid Circ: 62
Avg Free Circ: 6969
Audit By: Sworn/Estimate/Non-Audited
Audit Date: 10.06.2019
Personnel: Peggy Bakken (Ed.); Cheri Oâ€™Bannon (Adv. Dir.); Mark Weber (Gen. Mgr.)
Parent company (for newspapers): Adams Publishing Group, LLC; Sun Newspapers

BROWERVILLE BLADE

Street address 1: 609 Main St N
Street address city: Browerville
Street address state: MN
Zip/Postal code: 56438-5186
General Phone: (320) 594-2911
General Fax: (218) 756-2126
General/National Adv. E-mail: cindy@inhnews.com
Editorial e-mail: blade@inhnews.com
Primary Website: inhnews.com
Year Established: 1906
Avg Paid Circ: 1382
Avg Free Circ: 6500
Audit By: Sworn/Estimate/Non-Audited
Audit Date: 10.06.2019
Personnel: Ray Benning (Pub.); Marlo Benning (Pub.); Kathy Maquardt (Mng. Ed.)

BUFFALO RIDGE NEWSPAPERS

Street address 1: 320 Aetna St
Street address city: Ruthton
Street address state: MN
Zip/Postal code: 56170-5005
General Phone: (507) 658-3919
General Fax: (507) 658-3404
Editorial e-mail: brgazette@woodstocktel.net
Primary Website: http://photos.buffaloridgenews.com/
Year Established: 1873
Avg Paid Circ: 740
Audit By: Sworn/Estimate/Non-Audited
Audit Date: 10.06.2019
Personnel: Chuck Hunt (Pub.)

BYRON REVIEW

Street address 1: 1011 Tompkins Dr NE
Street address city: Byron
Street address state: MN
Zip/Postal code: 55920-3001
General Phone: (507) 775-6180
General Fax: (507) 374-9327

General/National Adv. E-mail: communitynewscorp@kmtel.com
Display Adv. E-mail: communitynewscorp@kmtel.com
Editorial e-mail: communitynewscorp@kmtel.com
Primary Website: communitynewscorp.com
Year Established: 1958
Avg Paid Circ: 1200
Audit By: Sworn/Estimate/Non-Audited
Audit Date: 10.06.2019
Personnel: Larry Dobson (Adv. Mgr.); Melanie Dobson (Ed.)
Parent company (for newspapers): Community News Corporation

CANBY NEWS

Street address 1: 123 1st St E
Street address city: Canby
Street address state: MN
Zip/Postal code: 56220-1342
General Phone: (507) 223-5303
General Fax: (507) 223-5404
General/National Adv. E-mail: cnews@frontiernet.net
Display Adv. E-mail: ads.cnews@gmail.com
Editorial e-mail: thecanbynews@thecanbynews.com
Primary Website: frontiernet.net/~cnews
Year Established: 1878
Avg Paid Circ: 1799
Audit By: Sworn/Estimate/Non-Audited
Audit Date: 10.06.2019
Personnel: Richard Gail (Pub); Sara Stokes (Adv. Mgr.)

CANNON FALLS BEACON

Street address 1: 120 4th St S
Street address city: Cannon Falls
Street address state: MN
Zip/Postal code: 55009-2433
General Phone: (507) 263-3991
General Fax: (507) 263-2300
Advertising Fax: (507) 263-2319
General/National Adv. E-mail: beacon@cannonfalls.com
Display Adv. E-mail: dave@cannonfalls.com
Editorial e-mail: dick@cannonfalls.com
Primary Website: cannonfalls.com
Year Established: 1876
Avg Paid Circ: 3900
Audit By: Sworn/Estimate/Non-Audited
Audit Date: 10.06.2019
Personnel: G. Richard Dalton (Pub.); Dick Dalton (Ed.)

CARVER COUNTY NEWS

Street address 1: 8 S Elm St
Street address city: Waconia
Street address state: MN
Zip/Postal code: 55387-1412
General Phone: (952) 442-4414
General Fax: (952) 442-1272
General/National Adv. E-mail: rick.brauer@ecm-inc.com
Display Adv. E-mail: norma.carstensen@ecm-inc.com
Editorial e-mail: jason.schmucker@ecm-inc.com
Primary Website: http://sunpatriot.com/tag/ccn/
Year Established: 1976
Avg Free Circ: 44
Audit By: Sworn/Estimate/Non-Audited
Audit Date: 10.06.2019
Personnel: Rick Brauer (Adv.); Melissa Priebe (Comm. Ed.); Jason Schmucker (Ed.)
Parent company (for newspapers): Adams Publishing Group, LLC

CHAMPLIN-DAYTON PRESS

Street address 1: 33 2nd St NE
Street address city: Osseo
Street address state: MN
Zip/Postal code: 55369-1252
General Phone: (763) 425-3323
General Fax: (763) 425-2945
General/National Adv. E-mail: jeremy.bradfield@ecm-inc.com
Display Adv. E-mail: mike.specht@ecm-inc.com
Editorial e-mail: peggy.bakken@ecm-inc.com
Primary Website: pressnews.com
Avg Paid Circ: 47
Avg Free Circ: 6214
Audit By: Sworn/Estimate/Non-Audited
Audit Date: 10.06.2019
Personnel: Peggy Bakken (Ed.); Mark Weber (Gen. Mgr.); Jeremy Bradfield (Adv. Dir.)
Parent company (for newspapers): Adams Publishing Group, LLC; American Community Newspapers LLC

CHANHASSEN VILLAGER

Street address 1: 123 W 2nd St
Street address city: Chaska
Street address state: MN
Zip/Postal code: 55318-1907
General Phone: (952) 934-5045
General Fax: (952) 448-3146
Advertising Phone: (952) 345-6477
General/National Adv. E-mail: jhiltunen@swpub.com
Display Adv. E-mail: classified@swpub.com
Editorial e-mail: editor@chanvillager.com
Primary Website: swnewsmedia.com/chanhassen_villager
Avg Free Circ: 4532
Audit By: Sworn/Estimate/Non-Audited
Audit Date: 10.06.2019
Personnel: Richard Crawford (Ed); Bill Davis (Pub./Gen. Mgr.); Jen Hiltunen (Adv. Dir)
Parent company (for newspapers): Red Wing Publishing Co.

CHASKA HERALD

Street address 1: 123 W 2nd St
Street address city: Chaska
Street address state: MN
Zip/Postal code: 55318-1907
General Phone: (952) 448-2650
General Fax: (952) 448-3146
Advertising Phone: (952) 345-6477
Editorial Phone: (952) 345-6574
General/National Adv. E-mail: jhiltunen@swpub.com
Display Adv. E-mail: classified@swpub.com
Editorial e-mail: editor@chaskaherald.com
Primary Website: swnewsmedia.com/chaska_herald
Year Established: 1862
Avg Paid Circ: 4532
Avg Free Circ: 290
Audit By: Sworn/Estimate/Non-Audited
Audit Date: 10.06.2019
Personnel: Bob Suel (Adv); Mark Olson (Ed.)
Parent company (for newspapers): Red Wing Publishing Co.

CHISAGO COUNTY PRESS

Street address 1: 12631 Lake Blvd
Street address city: Lindstrom
Street address state: MN
Zip/Postal code: 55045-9344
General Phone: (651) 257-5115
General Fax: (651) 257-5500
Editorial e-mail: chisago@citlink.net
Primary Website: chisagocountypress.com
Year Established: 1898
Avg Paid Circ: 3413
Avg Free Circ: 115
Audit By: Sworn/Estimate/Non-Audited
Audit Date: 10.06.2019
Personnel: Matt Silver (Pub.); Denise Martin (Mng. Ed.); Laure Peterson (Prod. Mgr.)

CHOKIO REVIEW

Street address 1: 121 Main St
Street address city: Chokio
Street address state: MN
Zip/Postal code: 56221
General Phone: (320) 324-2405
General Fax: (320) 324-2449
Editorial e-mail: chreview@fedtel.net
Primary Website: chokioreview.com
Year Established: 1897
Avg Paid Circ: 744
Avg Free Circ: 35
Audit By: Sworn/Estimate/Non-Audited
Audit Date: 10.06.2019
Personnel: Kay Grossman (Pub.); Nick Ripperger (Ed.)
Parent company (for newspapers): Free Scout Press, Inc

CITIZEN'S ADVOCATE

Street address 1: 412 Douglas Ave
Street address city: Henning
Street address state: MN
Zip/Postal code: 56551-4001
General Phone: (218) 548-5585
General Fax: (218) 548-5582
General/National Adv. E-mail: news@henningadvocate.com
Primary Website: henningadvocate.com
Year Established: 1891
Avg Paid Circ: 910
Avg Free Circ: 27
Audit By: Sworn/Estimate/Non-Audited
Audit Date: 10.06.2019
Personnel: Chad Koenen; Danielle Koenen
Parent company (for newspapers): Henning Publications, LLC

CLAY COUNTY UNION

Street address 1: 112 2nd St NE
Street address city: Ulen
Street address state: MN
Zip/Postal code: 56585-4200
General Phone: (218) 596-8813
General Fax: (218) 483-4457
General/National Adv. E-mail: news@claycountyunion.net
Editorial e-mail: marc@hawleyherald.net
Primary Website: claycountyunion.net
Avg Paid Circ: 1226
Audit By: Sworn/Estimate/Non-Audited
Audit Date: 10.06.2019
Personnel: John Kolness (Ed.); Renne Nyestvold (Adv)

CLEARWATER TRIBUNE

Street address 1: 29 Lake St S
Street address city: Big Lake
Street address state: MN
Zip/Postal code: 55309-4588
General Phone: (763) 263-3602
Advertising Phone: (763) 263-3602
Editorial Phone: (763) 263-3602
General/National Adv. E-mail: sales.westrib@izoom.net
Editorial e-mail: editor@westsherburnetribune.net
Primary Website: westsherburnetribune.com
Mthly Avg Views: 38768
Mthly Avg Unique Visitors: 17463
Year Established: 1984
Avg Paid Circ: 24
Avg Free Circ: 4942
Audit By: Sworn/Estimate/Non-Audited
Audit Date: 10.06.2019
Personnel: Gary W. Meyer (Ed. / Pub); Gail Evans (Circ. Mgr.)
Parent company (for newspapers): West Sherburne Tribune

COLD SPRING RECORD

Street address 1: 403 Westwind Ct
Street address 2: PO Box 456
Street address city: Cold Spring
Street address state: MN
Zip/Postal code: 56320-4560
General Phone: (320) 685-8621
General Fax: (320) 685-8885
General/National Adv. E-mail: ads-csrecord@midconetwork.com
Editorial e-mail: csrecord@midconetwork.com
Primary Website: csrecord.net
Year Established: 1899
Avg Paid Circ: 3400
Avg Free Circ: 12
Audit By: Sworn/Estimate/Non-Audited
Audit Date: 10.06.2019
Personnel: Mike Austreng (Ed.); Jeanie Austreng (Adv. Mgr.)

COLUMBIA HEIGHTS/FRIDLEY SUN FOCUS

Street address 1: 10917 Valley View Rd
Street address city: Eden Prairie
Street address state: MN
Zip/Postal code: 55344-3730
General Phone: (952) 392-6800
General Fax: (763) 424-7388
Advertising Phone: (952) 392-6888
General/National Adv. E-mail: cheri.obannon@ecm-inc.com
Display Adv. E-mail: krista.jech@ecm-inc.com
Editorial e-mail: matthew.hankey@ecm-inc.com
Primary Website: http://focus.mnsun.com
Year Established: 1968
Avg Paid Circ: 36
Avg Free Circ: 14254
Audit By: Sworn/Estimate/Non-Audited
Audit Date: 10.06.2019
Personnel: Kassie Petermann (Ed.); Mark Weber (Gen. Mgr.); Krista Jech (Mktg. Mgr.)
Parent company (for newspapers): Adams Publishing Group, LLC; American Community Newspapers LLC

COMFREY TIMES

Street address 1: 112 Brown St W
Street address city: Comfrey
Street address state: MN
Zip/Postal code: 56019-7701
General Phone: (507) 877-2281
General Fax: (507) 877-2251
Editorial e-mail: comfreytimes@frontiernet.net
Avg Paid Circ: 650
Audit By: Sworn/Estimate/Non-Audited
Audit Date: 10.06.2019
Personnel: Steve Christiansen (Ed.)

COOK COUNTY NEWS-HERALD

Street address 1: 15 1st Ave W
Street address city: Grand Marais
Street address state: MN
Zip/Postal code: 55604-3131
General Phone: (218) 387-1025
General Fax: (218) 387-9500
General/National Adv. E-mail: heraldads@boreal.org
Editorial e-mail: starnews@boreal.org
Primary Website: cookcountynews-herald.com
Year Established: 1881
Avg Paid Circ: 4010
Avg Free Circ: 66
Audit By: Sworn/Estimate/Non-Audited
Audit Date: 10.06.2019
Personnel: Deidre Kettunen (Pub.); Hal Kettunen (Pub.); Rhonda Silence (Ed.); Mary Fleace (Adv. Mgr.)
Parent company (for newspapers): CherryRoad Media

COON RAPIDS HERALD

Street address 1: 4101 Coon Rapids Blvd NW
Street address city: Coon Rapids
Street address state: MN
Zip/Postal code: 55433-2525
General Phone: (763) 421-4444
General Fax: (763) 421-4315
General/National Adv. E-mail: steve.rajtar@ecm-inc.com
Display Adv. E-mail: kjel.nordstrom@ecm-inc.com
Editorial e-mail: mandy.froemming@ecm-inc.com
Primary Website: abcnewspapers.com
Mthly Avg Views: 205457
Mthly Avg Unique Visitors: 44852
Year Established: 1875
Avg Paid Circ: 2650
Avg Free Circ: 76
Audit By: Sworn/Estimate/Non-Audited
Audit Date: 10.06.2019
Personnel: Julian Andersen (Pub.); Peter Bodley (Mng. Ed.); Tom Murray (Gen. Mgr.)

COTTONWOOD COUNTY CITIZEN

Street address 1: 260 10th St
Street address city: Windom
Street address state: MN
Zip/Postal code: 56101-1411
General Phone: (507) 831-3455
General Fax: (507) 831-3740
General/National Adv. E-mail: jenw@windomnews.com
Display Adv. E-mail: terriw@windomnews.com
Editorial e-mail: rahnl@windomnews.com
Primary Website: windomnews.com
Year Established: 1883
Avg Paid Circ: 2579
Avg Free Circ: 188
Audit By: Sworn/Estimate/Non-Audited
Audit Date: 10.06.2019
Personnel: Trevor Slette (Pub.); Rahn Larson (Ed.); Michelle Riihl (Office Mgr.); Teri Scott (Circ. Mgr.)

CROSBY-IRONTON COURIER

Street address 1: 12 E Main St

Street address city: Crosby
Street address state: MN
Zip/Postal code: 56441-1614
General Phone: (218) 546-5029
General Fax: (218) 546-8352
Editorial e-mail: courier@crosbyironton.net
Primary Website: cicourierinc.com
Year Established: 1911
Avg Paid Circ: 3341
Audit By: Sworn/Estimate/Non-Audited
Audit Date: 10.06.2019
Personnel: T.M. Swensen (Pub.); Lori LaBorde (Gen. Mgr.)

DAKOTA COUNTY TRIBUNE

Street address 1: 15322 Galaxie Ave
Street address 2: Suite 219
Street address city: Apple Valley
Street address state: MN
Zip/Postal code: 55124-3150
General Phone: (952) 894-1111
General Fax: (952) 846-2010
General/National Adv. E-mail: ads.thisweek@ecm-inc.com
Display Adv. E-mail: class.thisweek@ecm-inc.com
Editorial e-mail: tad.johnson@ecm-inc.com
Primary Website: http://sunthisweek.com/dakota-county-tribune/
Year Established: 1887
Avg Paid Circ: 19
Avg Free Circ: 12687
Audit By: Sworn/Estimate/Non-Audited
Audit Date: 10.06.2019
Personnel: Mike Jetchick (Gen Mgr.); Tad Johnson (Ed.); Julian Andersen (Pub.)
Parent company (for newspapers): Adams Publishing Group, LLC

DASSEL-COKATO ENTERPRISE DISPATCH

Street address 1: 185 3rd St SW
Street address city: Cokato
Street address state: MN
Zip/Postal code: 55321-4595
General Phone: (320) 286-2118
General/National Adv. E-mail: hj@heraldjournal.com
Display Adv. E-mail: ads@heraldjournal.com
Editorial e-mail: news@dasselcokato.com
Primary Website: dasselcokato.com
Year Established: 1885
Avg Paid Circ: 1550
Audit By: USPS
Audit Date: 30.09.2021
Personnel: Chris Schultz
Parent company (for newspapers): Herald Journal Publishing, Inc.

DAWSON SENTINEL

Street address 1: 674 CHESTNUT ST
Street address city: Dawson
Street address state: MN
Zip/Postal code: 56232
General Phone: (320) 769-2497
General Fax: (320) 769-2459
Editorial e-mail: dawsonsentinel@frontiernet.net
Primary Website: dawsonmn.com
Year Established: 1884
Avg Paid Circ: 1662
Avg Free Circ: 15
Audit By: Sworn/Estimate/Non-Audited
Audit Date: 10.06.2019
Personnel: Bill Klaimon (Pub.); Dave Hickey (Ed.)

DELANO HERALD JOURNAL

Street address 1: 127 Bridge Ave E
Street address 2: Suite 216
Street address city: Delano
Street address state: MN
Zip/Postal code: 55328-4643
General Phone: (763) 972-1028
General/National Adv. E-mail: delano@heraldjournal.com
Display Adv. E-mail: ads@heraldjournal.com
Editorial e-mail: delano@heraldjournal.com
Primary Website: delanoheraldjournal.com
Year Established: 2006
Avg Paid Circ: 1650
Audit By: USPS
Audit Date: 30.09.2021
Personnel: Chris Schultz; Dale Kovar (Gen. Mgr.); Gabe Licht (Ed.)
Parent company (for newspapers): Herald Journal Publishing, Inc.

DETROIT LAKES TRIBUNE

Street address 1: 511 Washington Ave
Street address city: Detroit Lakes
Street address state: MN
Zip/Postal code: 56501-3007
General Phone: (218) 847-3151
General Fax: (218) 847-9409
Editorial e-mail: recordtribune@dlnewspapers.com
Primary Website: dl-online.com
Year Established: 1872
Avg Paid Circ: 3400
Avg Free Circ: 59
Audit By: VAC
Audit Date: 30.03.2017
Personnel: Viola Anderson (Circ. Mgr.); Melissa Swenson (Publisher); Paula Quam (Editor)
Parent company (for newspapers): Forum Communications Co.

DODGE CENTER STAR-HERALD

Street address 1: 40 W Main St
Street address city: Dodge Center
Street address state: MN
Zip/Postal code: 55927-9117
General Phone: (507) 374-6531
Advertising Phone: (507) 633-9327
General/National Adv. E-mail: dcstar@kmtel.com
Display Adv. E-mail: cncads@kmtel.com
Editorial e-mail: cnceditor@kmtel.com
Primary Website: communitynewscorp.com
Year Established: 1869
Avg Paid Circ: 1774
Avg Free Circ: 50
Audit By: Sworn/Estimate/Non-Audited
Audit Date: 10.06.2019
Personnel: Larry Dobson (Pub.); Melanie Dobson (Ed.)

DODGE COUNTY INDEPENDENT

Street address 1: 301 S. Mantorville Av/
Street address 2: Suite 200
Street address city: Kasson
Street address state: MN
Zip/Postal code: 55944-1456
General Phone: (507) 634-7503
General Fax: N/A
General/National Adv. E-mail: dci@kmtel.com
Editorial e-mail: editordci@kmtel.com
Primary Website: dodgecountyindependent.com
Avg Paid Circ: 1849
Audit By: Sworn/Estimate/Non-Audited
Audit Date: 10.06.2019
Personnel: June Howard (Adv. Mgr.); Keith Hansen (Publisher); Randy Carlsen (Ed.)

DULUTH BUDGETEER NEWS

Street address 1: 424 W 1st St
Street address city: Duluth
Street address state: MN
Zip/Postal code: 55802-1596
General Phone: (218) 723-5281
General Fax: (218) 723-5295
Advertising Phone: (218) 590-7592
Editorial Phone: (218) 723-5235
General/National Adv. E-mail: web@duluthnews.com
Display Adv. E-mail: dwruck@duluthnews.com
Editorial e-mail: budgeteer@duluthbudgeteer.com
Primary Website: duluthnewstribune.com
Year Established: 1931
Avg Free Circ: 21606
Audit By: Sworn/Estimate/Non-Audited
Audit Date: 10.06.2019
Personnel: Peter Baumann (Ed.); Rick Lubbers (Exec. Ed.); Katie Rohman (Reg. Ed.); Megan Keller (Adv.); Neal Ronquist (Pub.)
Parent company (for newspapers): Forum Communications Co.

DULUTH-ZENITH NEWS

Street address 1: PO Box 3280
Street address city: Duluth
Street address state: MN
Zip/Postal code: 55803-3280
General Phone: (218) 940-3132
General/National Adv. E-mail: zenithcityweekly@yahoo.com
Primary Website: zenithcitynews.com
Year Established: 2007
Avg Free Circ: 11000
Audit By: Sworn/Estimate/Non-Audited
Audit Date: 10.06.2019
Personnel: Taylor Martin-Romme (Pub.)

EAST SIDE REVIEW

Street address 1: 2515 7th Ave E
Street address city: North St Paul
Street address state: MN
Zip/Postal code: 55109-3004
General Phone: (651) 777-8800
General Fax: (651) 777-8288
Advertising Phone: (651) 748-7860
Editorial Phone: (651) 748-7820
General/National Adv. E-mail: tfragnito@lillienews.com
Display Adv. E-mail: rnisswandt@lillienews.com
Editorial e-mail: mlhagert@lillienews.com
Primary Website: lillienews.com/east-side-review
Year Established: 1938
Avg Paid Circ: 20
Avg Free Circ: 9277
Audit By: VAC
Audit Date: 31.05.2017
Personnel: Jeffery R. Enright (Co-Pub.); Ted H. Lillie (Co-Pub.); Tony Fragnito (Adv. Dir.); Laura Young (Circ. Mgr.); Mary Lee Hagert (Mng. Ed.)
Parent company (for newspapers): Lillie Suburban Newspapers

ECHO JOURNAL

Street address 1: 4285 W Lake St
Street address city: Pequot Lakes
Street address state: MN
Zip/Postal code: 56472-3014
General Phone: (218) 829-4705
Advertising Phone: (218) 855-5836
Editorial Phone: (218) 855-5877
Primary Website: pineandlakes.com
Audit By: Sworn/Estimate/Non-Audited
Audit Date: 10.06.2019
Personnel: Susie Alters (Adv. Mgr.); Nancy Vogt (Ed.); Pete Mohs (Pub.)
Parent company (for newspapers): Forum Communications Co.

ECHO-PRESS

Street address 1: 225 7th Ave E
Street address city: Alexandria
Street address state: MN
Zip/Postal code: 56308-1831
General Phone: (320) 763-3133
General Fax: (320) 763-3258
Advertising Phone: (320) 763-3133
Advertising Fax: (320) 763-3258
Editorial Phone: (320) 763-3133
Editorial Fax: (320) 763-3258
General/National Adv. E-mail: jhanson@echopress.com
Display Adv. E-mail: mweller@echopress.com
Classified Adv. e-mail: echo@echopress.com
Editorial e-mail: revavold@echopress.com
Primary Website: echopress.com
Year Established: 1891
Avg Paid Circ: 6920
Audit By: Sworn/Estimate/Non-Audited
Audit Date: 10.06.2019
Personnel: Jody Hanson (Pub.); Lynn Mounsdon (Circ. Mgr.); Diann Drew (Bus. Mgr.); Al Edenloff (News Ed./ Opinion Page Ed.); Jeff Beach (Ed.)
Parent company (for newspapers): Forum Communications Co.

EDEN PRAIRIE NEWS

Street address 1: 250 Prairie Center Dr Ste 211
Street address 2: Suite 211
Street address city: Eden Prairie
Street address state: MN
Zip/Postal code: 55344-7911
General Phone: (952) 942-7885
General Fax: (952) 942-7975
Advertising Phone: (952) 345-6477
General/National Adv. E-mail: netzel@swpub.com
Display Adv. E-mail: classified@swpub.com
Editorial e-mail: editor@edenprairienews.com
Primary Website: edenprairienews.com
Year Established: 1976
Avg Free Circ: 11632
Audit By: Sworn/Estimate/Non-Audited
Audit Date: 10.06.2019
Personnel: Mark Weber (Pub.); Ruby Mohlin (Circ. Mgr.); Karla Wennerstrom (Ed.)
Parent company (for newspapers): Red Wing Publishing Co.

EDEN PRAIRIE SUN-CURRENT

Street address 1: 10917 Valley View Rd
Street address city: Eden Prairie
Street address state: MN
Zip/Postal code: 55344-3730
General Phone: (952) 392-6800
General Fax: (763) 424-7388
Advertising Phone: (952) 392-6888
General/National Adv. E-mail: nancy.etzel@ecm-inc.com
Display Adv. E-mail: pam.miller@ecm-inc.com
Editorial e-mail: matthew.hankey@ecm-inc.com
Primary Website: current.mnsun.com
Year Established: 1954
Avg Paid Circ: 86
Avg Free Circ: 14760
Audit By: Sworn/Estimate/Non-Audited
Audit Date: 10.06.2019
Personnel: Mark Webber (Gen. Mgr.); Matthew Hankey (Ed.); Krista Jech (Mktg. Mgr.)
Parent company (for newspapers): Adams Publishing Group, LLC; American Community Newspapers LLC

EDGERTON ENTERPRISE

Street address 1: 831 MAIN ST
Street address city: Edgerton
Street address state: MN
Zip/Postal code: 56128-1151
General Phone: (507) 442-6161
General Fax: (507) 631-7542
Editorial e-mail: edgent@iw.net
Primary Website: edgertonenterprise.com
Year Established: 1883
Avg Paid Circ: 1679
Audit By: Sworn/Estimate/Non-Audited
Audit Date: 10.06.2019
Personnel: Jill Fennema (Pub.); Irene Gunnink (Pub.); Ashley Stoel (Asst. Ed)

EDINA SUN-CURRENT

Street address 1: 10917 Valley View Rd
Street address city: Eden Prairie
Street address state: MN
Zip/Postal code: 55344-3730
General Phone: (952) 392-6800
General Fax: (952) 392-6802
Advertising Phone: (952) 392-6888
General/National Adv. E-mail: lisa.kaczke@ecm-inc.com
Display Adv. E-mail: nicole.jorgenson@ecm-inc.com
Editorial e-mail: lisa.kaczke@ecm-inc.com
Primary Website: http://current.mnsun.com/
Year Established: 1954
Avg Paid Circ: 219
Avg Free Circ: 15755
Audit By: Sworn/Estimate/Non-Audited
Audit Date: 10.06.2019
Personnel: Gene Carr (CEO); Bernie Kelcher (Gen. Mgr.); Pam Miller (Adv. Mgr.); Craig Anderson (Dist. Mgr.); Peggy Bakken (Mng. Ed.)
Parent company (for newspapers): Adams Publishing Group, LLC; American Community Newspapers LLC

ELY TIMBERJAY

Street address 1: 414 Main St
Street address city: Tower
Street address state: MN
Zip/Postal code: 55790-5105
General Phone: (218) 365-3114
General Fax: (218) 753-2916
Advertising Phone: (218) 753-2950
Editorial Phone: (218) 365-3114
General/National Adv. E-mail: editor@timberjay.com
Editorial e-mail: editor@timberjay.com
Primary Website: timberjay.com
Avg Paid Circ: 1208

Audit By: Sworn/Estimate/Non-Audited
Audit Date: 10.06.2019
Personnel: Marshall Helmberger (Pub.)

ELYSIAN ENTERPRISE

Street address 1: 200 Main St E
Street address city: New Prague
Street address state: MN
Zip/Postal code: 56071-2438
General Phone: (507) 267-4323
General Fax: (507) 362-4458
General/National Adv. E-mail: ads@newpraguetimes.com
Display Adv. E-mail: classifieds@newpraguetimes.com
Editorial e-mail: news@newpraguetimes.com
Primary Website: newpraguetimes.com/category/publication/elysian-enterprise
Avg Paid Circ: 422
Audit By: Sworn/Estimate/Non-Audited
Audit Date: 10.06.2019
Personnel: E. Charles Wann (Pub.); Jay Schneider (Ed.); Mark Slavik (Adv. Dir.)

ENTERPRISE BULLETIN

Street address 1: 222 2nd Ave SE
Street address 2: Frnt
Street address city: Perham
Street address state: MN
Zip/Postal code: 56573-1706
General Phone: (218) 346-5900
General Fax: (218) 346-5901
General/National Adv. E-mail: perhameb@eot.com
Editorial e-mail: louish@eot.com
Primary Website: eotfocus.com
Year Established: 1882
Avg Paid Circ: 3200
Avg Free Circ: 50
Audit By: Sworn/Estimate/Non-Audited
Audit Date: 10.06.2019
Personnel: Kathy Bope (Bus. Mgr.); Melissa Swenson (Adv. Mgr.); Louis Hoglund (Ed.)
Parent company (for newspapers): Forum Communications Co.

EXCELSIOR/SHOREWOOD/ CHANHASSEN SUN SAILOR

Street address 1: 10917 Valley View Rd
Street address city: Eden Prairie
Street address state: MN
Zip/Postal code: 55344-3730
General Phone: (952) 392-6800
General Fax: (952) 392-6802
Advertising Phone: (952) 392-6888
General/National Adv. E-mail: chris.dillmann@ecm-inc.com
Display Adv. E-mail: cheri.obannon@ecm-inc.com
Editorial e-mail: chris.dillmann@ecm-inc.com
Primary Website: http://sailor.mnsun.com/
Year Established: 1970
Avg Paid Circ: 60
Avg Free Circ: 5963
Audit By: Sworn/Estimate/Non-Audited
Audit Date: 10.06.2019
Personnel: Gene Carr (CEO); Bob Cole (Pub.); Jeremy Bradford (Adv. Mgr.); Pam Miller (Class. Adv. Mgr.); Krista Jech (Mktg. Mgr.); Mark Weber (Gen Mgr); Paul Groessel (Mng. Ed.)
Parent company (for newspapers): Adams Publishing Group, LLC; American Community Newspapers LLC

FAIRFAX STANDARD GAZETTE

Street address 1: 102 SE First St.
Street address city: Fairfax
Street address state: MN
Zip/Postal code: 55332
General Phone: (507) 426-7235
General Fax: (507) 426-7264
General/National Adv. E-mail: fxstandardcomp@gmail.com
Editorial e-mail: fxstandardnews@gmail.com
Primary Website: standard-gazette.com
Year Established: 2000
Avg Paid Circ: 1423
Audit By: Sworn/Estimate/Non-Audited
Audit Date: 10.06.2019
Personnel: Daniel McGonigle (Ed.)

Parent company (for newspapers): D&D Publications LLC

FARIBAULT COUNTY REGISTER

Street address 1: 125 N Main St
Street address city: Blue Earth
Street address state: MN
Zip/Postal code: 56013-1960
General Phone: (507) 526-7324
General Fax: (507) 526-4080
General/National Adv. E-mail: lnauman@faribaultcountyregister.com
Display Adv. E-mail: lnauman@faribaultcountyregister.com
Classified Adv. e-mail: lnauman@faribaultcountyregister.com
Editorial e-mail: chunt@faribaultcountyregister.com
Primary Website: faribaultcountyregister.com
Mthly Avg Views: 45000
Year Established: 1868
Avg Paid Circ: 3000
Audit By: Sworn/Estimate/Non-Audited
Audit Date: 10.06.2019
Personnel: Lori Nauman (Publisher/GM/Ad Director); Chuck Hunt (Editor); Hanna Ann (Circ. Mng.)
Parent company (for newspapers): Ogden Newspapers Inc.

FARMERS INDEPENDENT

Street address 1: 102 N Main Ave
Street address city: Bagley
Street address state: MN
Zip/Postal code: 56621-8317
General Phone: (218) 694-6265
General Fax: (218) 694-6015
General/National Adv. E-mail: farmpubads@gvtel.com
Editorial e-mail: farmpub@gvtel.com
Year Established: 1918
Avg Paid Circ: 2350
Audit By: Sworn/Estimate/Non-Audited
Audit Date: 10.06.2019
Personnel: Tom Burford (Ed.)

FILLMORE COUNTY JOURNAL

Street address 1: 136 Saint Anthony St S
Street address 2: P.O. Box 496
Street address city: Preston
Street address state: MN
Zip/Postal code: 55965-1151
General Phone: (507) 765-2151
General Fax: (507) 765-2468
General/National Adv. E-mail: jason@fillmorecountyjournal.com
Display Adv. E-mail: ads@fillmorecountyjournal.com
Classified Adv. e-mail: news@fillmorecountyjournal.com
Editorial e-mail: news@fillmorecountyjournal.com
Primary Website: fillmorecountyjournal.com
Mthly Avg Views: 24158
Mthly Avg Unique Visitors: 10663
Year Established: 1985
Avg Paid Circ: 200
Avg Free Circ: 13026
Audit By: CVC
Audit Date: 30.09.2018
Personnel: Jason Sethre (Pres & Pub); Ellen Whalen (Asst. Ed.); Amanda Sethre (Assoc. Pub); Jana Boyum (Creative Dir.)
Parent company (for newspapers): Sethre Media Group, Inc.

FILLMORE COUNTY NEWS LEADER

Street address 1: 124 Main St SE
Street address 2: Ste 200
Street address city: Preston
Street address state: MN
Zip/Postal code: 55965-1202
General Phone: (507) 765-2752
General Fax: (507) 765-2752
General/National Adv. E-mail: ads@bluffcountrynews.com
Display Adv. E-mail: classifieds@bluffcountrynews.com
Editorial e-mail: mvanderplas@bluffcountrynews.com
Primary Website: fillmorecountynewsleader.com
Avg Paid Circ: 1412
Audit By: Sworn/Estimate/Non-Audited
Audit Date: 10.06.2019
Personnel: David Phillips (Pub.)

Parent company (for newspapers): Bluffs Country Newspaper Group

FOREST LAKE LOWDOWN

Street address 1: 4779 Bloom Ave
Street address city: White Bear Lake
Street address state: MN
Zip/Postal code: 55110-2764
General Phone: (651) 407-1200
General Fax: (651) 429-1242
Advertising Phone: (651) 407-1208
General/National Adv. E-mail: lowdown3@presspubs.com
Display Adv. E-mail: classified@presspubs.com
Editorial e-mail: lowdownnews@presspubs.com
Primary Website: presspubs.com/forest_lake
Year Established: 1903
Avg Paid Circ: 58
Avg Free Circ: 11584
Audit By: VAC
Audit Date: 28.09.2017
Personnel: Carter Johnson (Pub.); Greg Workman (Circ. Mgr.)
Parent company (for newspapers): Press Publications, Inc.

FOREST LAKE TIMES

Street address 1: 146 Lake St N
Street address 2: Ste 125
Street address city: Forest Lake
Street address state: MN
Zip/Postal code: 55025-2109
General Phone: (651) 464-4601
General Fax: (651) 464-4605
General/National Adv. E-mail: clint.riese@ecm-inc.com
Display Adv. E-mail: nicholas.hall@ecm-inc.com
Editorial e-mail: ryan.howard@ecm-inc.com
Primary Website: forestlaketimes.com
Mthly Avg Views: 71380
Mthly Avg Unique Visitors: 13746
Year Established: 1903
Avg Paid Circ: 175
Avg Free Circ: 12901
Audit By: Sworn/Estimate/Non-Audited
Audit Date: 10.06.2019
Personnel: Jeff Andres (Gen. Mgr.); Cliff Buchan (Ed.); Jerry Gloe (Adv. Dir.)
Parent company (for newspapers): Adams Publishing Group, LLC

FRAZEE-VERGAS FORUM

Street address 1: 112 W Main Ave
Street address city: Frazee
Street address state: MN
Zip/Postal code: 56544
General Phone: (218) 334-3566
General Fax: (218) 334-3567
General/National Adv. E-mail: fforum@loretel.net
Primary Website: frazeeforum.com
Year Established: 1960
Avg Paid Circ: 1750
Avg Free Circ: 25
Audit By: Sworn/Estimate/Non-Audited
Audit Date: 10.06.2019
Personnel: Delair Kaas (Gen. Mgr.); Gale Kaas (Ed.)

FULDA FREE PRESS

Street address 1: 118 N St Paul Ave
Street address city: Fulda
Street address state: MN
Zip/Postal code: 56131-4463
General Phone: (507) 425-2303
General Fax: (507) 425-2501
General/National Adv. E-mail: text@fuldafreepress.net
Editorial e-mail: photo@fuldafreepress.net
Primary Website: fuldafreepress.net
Year Established: 1879
Avg Paid Circ: 1148
Audit By: Sworn/Estimate/Non-Audited
Audit Date: 10.06.2019
Personnel: Gerald D. Johnson (Ed.)

GRAND RAPIDS HERALD-REVIEW

Street address 1: 301 NW 1st Ave
Street address city: Grand Rapids
Street address state: MN

Zip/Postal code: 55744-2704
General Phone: (218) 326-6623
General Fax: (218) 326-6627
General/National Adv. E-mail: grads@grandrapidsheraldreview.net
Display Adv. E-mail: beiesland@grandrapidsheraldreview.net
Editorial e-mail: barendt@grandrapidsheraldreview.net
Primary Website: grandrapidsmn.com
Year Established: 1894
Avg Paid Circ: 7883
Audit By: Sworn/Estimate/Non-Audited
Audit Date: 10.06.2019
Personnel: Britta Arendt (Ed.); Mark Roy (Pub)
Parent company (for newspapers): APG Media

GRANITE FALLS-CLARKFIELD ADVOCATE-TRIBUNE

Street address 1: 713 Prentice St
Street address city: Granite Falls
Street address state: MN
Zip/Postal code: 56241-1519
General Phone: (320) 564-2126
General Fax: (320) 564-4293
General/National Adv. E-mail: bsommervold@granitefallsnews.com
Editorial e-mail: stedrick@granitefallsnews.com
Primary Website: granitefallsnews.com
Avg Paid Circ: 2108
Audit By: Sworn/Estimate/Non-Audited
Audit Date: 10.06.2019
Personnel: David Smiglewski (Pub.); Mike Dupere (Gen. Mgr); Scott Tedrick (Ed.); Bev Sommervold (Adv. Mgr.)
Parent company (for newspapers): CherryRoad Media

GRANT COUNTY HERALD

Street address 1: 35 Central Ave N
Street address city: Elbow Lake
Street address state: MN
Zip/Postal code: 56531-4123
General Phone: (218) 685-5326
General Fax: (218) 685-5327
Advertising Phone: (218) 685-5326
Advertising Fax: (218) 685-5327
Editorial Phone: (218) 685-5326
Editorial Fax: (218) 685-5327
General/National Adv. E-mail: gcanne@runestone.net
Display Adv. E-mail: gcanne@runestone.net
Classified Adv. e-mail: gcanne@runestone.net
Editorial e-mail: gcnews@runestone.net
Primary Website: www.grantherald.com
Year Established: 1879
Avg Paid Circ: 1900
Avg Free Circ: 35
Audit By: Sworn/Estimate/Non-Audited
Audit Date: 08.08.2021
Personnel: Nikki Eystad; Penny Pederson (Circ. Mgr.); Reed/Shelly Anfinson (Publishers); Christopher A. Ray (Ed.); Anne O'Flynn (General Manager); Pauline Martinson (Prodn. Mgr.); chris Ray (Editor); Kimber Wolfe (Accounts Rec./Circulation); Darla Johnson; Christine Jacobson (Graphic Design); April Franken (Advertising Coordinator); Kara Engquist (Designer)
Parent company (for newspapers): Whitney Rae Publishing

HASTINGS STAR GAZETTE

Street address 1: 120 W. Fourth St.
Street address city: Cannon Falls
Street address state: MN
Zip/Postal code: 55009
General Phone: 507-263-3991
General/National Adv. E-mail: OMGmnNews@orourkemediagroup.com
Primary Website: hastingsstargazette.com
Mthly Avg Views: 69000
Mthly Avg Unique Visitors: 23000
Audit By: Sworn/Estimate/Non-Audited
Audit Date: 10.06.2019
Personnel: Steven R. Messick (Pub.); Jim Johnson (Managing editor); Chad Richardson (Ed.); Jim Johnson (Managing editor); Steve Engelhart (Adv. Dir.)
Parent company (for newspapers): Forum Communications Co.; O'Rourke Media Group; O'Rourke Media Group

HENDERSON INDEPENDENT

Street address 1: 407 Main St
Street address city: Henderson

Street address state: MN
Zip/Postal code: 56044-7742
General Phone: (507) 248-3223
General Fax: (507) 248-3611
General/National Adv. E-mail: hendersonmnnews@gmail.com
Display Adv. E-mail: hendersonmnnews@gmail.com
Editorial e-mail: hendersonind@frontiernet.net
Primary Website: facebook.com/HendersonIndependent
Year Established: 1874
Avg Paid Circ: 785
Avg Free Circ: 85
Audit By: Sworn/Estimate/Non-Audited
Audit Date: 10.06.2019
Personnel: C. Edward Townsend (Pub.)

HERALD JOURNAL

Street address 1: 120 6th St N
Street address city: Winsted
Street address state: MN
Zip/Postal code: 55395-1024
General Phone: (320) 485-2535
General Fax: (320) 485-2878
General/National Adv. E-mail: hj@heraldjournal.com
Display Adv. E-mail: ads@heraldjournal.com
Editorial e-mail: news@heraldjournal.com
Primary Website: herald-journal.com
Avg Paid Circ: 2500
Audit By: Sworn/Estimate/Non-Audited
Audit Date: 10.06.2019
Personnel: Dale Kovar (Gen. Mgr.); Chris Schultz (Adv. Mgr.)
Parent company (for newspapers): Herald Journal Publishing, Inc.

HERALD JOURNAL

Street address 1: PO Box 129
Street address city: Winsted
Street address state: MN
Zip/Postal code: 55395-0129
General Phone: (320) 485-2535
General Fax: (320) 485-2878
General/National Adv. E-mail: hj@heraldjournal.com
Display Adv. E-mail: ads@heraldjournal.com
Primary Website: www.herald-journal.com
Year Established: 1885
Avg Paid Circ: 2000
Audit By: USPS
Audit Date: 30.09.2021
Personnel: Dale Kovar (Gen. Mgr.)
Parent company (for newspapers): Herald Journal Publishing, Inc.

HERMAN-HOFFMAN TRIBUNE

Street address 1: 408 Berlin Ave S
Street address city: Herman
Street address state: MN
Zip/Postal code: 56248-1044
General Phone: (320)677-2229
General Fax: (320) 677-2229
Editorial e-mail: hcreview@frontiernet.net
Primary Website: hermanhoffmantribune.com
Year Established: 1900
Avg Paid Circ: 1250
Audit By: Sworn/Estimate/Non-Audited
Audit Date: 10.06.2019
Personnel: Nick Ripperger (Pub.)
Parent company (for newspapers): Grant County Herald

HERMANTOWN STAR

Street address 1: 4940 Lightning Dr
Street address city: Hermantown
Street address state: MN
Zip/Postal code: 55811-1355
General Phone: (218) 727-0419
General Fax: (218) 722-5821
Editorial e-mail: wpetrich@hermantownstar.com
Primary Website: hermantownstar.com
Avg Paid Circ: 1752
Audit By: Sworn/Estimate/Non-Audited
Audit Date: 10.06.2019
Personnel: Wade Petrich (Pub.)

HILLS CRESCENT

Street address 1: 117 W Main St
Street address city: Luverne
Street address state: MN
Zip/Postal code: 56156-1843
General Phone: (507) 283-2333
General Fax: (507) 283-2335
General/National Adv. E-mail: sales@star-herald.com
Editorial e-mail: hceditor@star-herald.com
Primary Website: star-herald.com/crescent
Avg Paid Circ: 394
Audit By: Sworn/Estimate/Non-Audited
Audit Date: 10.06.2019
Personnel: Rick Peterson (General manager); Lori Ehde (Ed.); Rick Peterson (Gen. Mgr.)

HINCKLEY NEWS

Street address 1: 115 Main St E
Street address city: Hinckley
Street address state: MN
Zip/Postal code: 55037-8763
General Phone: (320) 384-6188
General Fax: (320) 384-7844
General/National Adv. E-mail: hinckleynews@scicable.com
Primary Website: hinckleynews.com
Year Established: 1891
Avg Paid Circ: 1600
Audit By: Sworn/Estimate/Non-Audited
Audit Date: 10.06.2019
Personnel: Tim Franklin (Pub.); Mary Franklin (Adv. Mgr.); Steve Klumb

HUDSON STAR-OBSERVER

Street address 1: 120 W. Fourth St.
Street address city: Cannon Falls
Street address state: MN
Zip/Postal code: 55009
General Phone: 507-263-0478
General/National Adv. E-mail: OMGmnNews@orourkemediagroup.com
Primary Website: hudsonstarobserver.com
Mthly Avg Views: 387000
Mthly Avg Unique Visitors: 81000
Year Established: 1854
Avg Paid Circ: 7275
Avg Free Circ: 50
Audit By: Sworn/Estimate/Non-Audited
Audit Date: 10.06.2019
Personnel: Neal Ronquist (Pub.); Jim Johnson (Managing Editor); Doug Stohlberg (Ed.); Steve Engelhart (Adv. Dir.)
Parent company (for newspapers): Forum Communications Co.; O'Rourke Media Group

HUTCHINSON LEADER

Street address 1: 170 Shady Ridge Rd NW
Street address 2: Ste 100
Street address city: Hutchinson
Street address state: MN
Zip/Postal code: 55350-2490
General Phone: (320) 587-5000
General Fax: (320) 587-6104
Advertising Phone: (320) 234-4141
Editorial Phone: (320) 234-4156
General/National Adv. E-mail: addirector@hutchinsonleader.com
Display Adv. E-mail: warden@hutchinsonleader.com
Editorial e-mail: hanneman@hutchinsonleader.com
Primary Website: crowrivermedia.com/hutchinsonleader
Year Established: 1880
Avg Paid Circ: 3986
Avg Free Circ: 379
Audit By: Sworn/Estimate/Non-Audited
Audit Date: 10.06.2019
Personnel: Matt McMillan (Pub.); Tina McMillan (Adv. Mgr.); Doug Hanneman (Ed.); Kevin True (Adv. Dir.)
Parent company (for newspapers): Red Wing Publishing Co.

INDEPENDENT NEWS HERALD

Street address 1: 310 Main St W
Street address city: Clarissa
Street address state: MN
Zip/Postal code: 56440-2200
General Phone: (218) 756-2131
General Fax: (218) 756-2126
General/National Adv. E-mail: cindy@inhnews.com
Editorial e-mail: kathy@inhnews.com
Primary Website: inhnews.com
Avg Paid Circ: 2375
Avg Free Circ: 92
Audit By: Sworn/Estimate/Non-Audited
Audit Date: 10.06.2019
Personnel: Marlo Benning (Pub.); Ray Benning (Pub.); Katrina Nauber (Adv. Mgr.); Danielle Hanson (Circ. Mgr.)

INDEPENDENT REVIEW

Street address 1: 217 N Sibley Ave
Street address city: Litchfield
Street address state: MN
Zip/Postal code: 55355-2140
General Phone: (320) 693-3266
General Fax: (320) 693-9177
General/National Adv. E-mail: esser@independentreview.net
Display Adv. E-mail: esser@independentreview.net
Editorial e-mail: bonelli@independentreview.net
Primary Website: crowrivermedia.com/independentreview
Avg Paid Circ: 2659
Avg Free Circ: 11
Audit By: Sworn/Estimate/Non-Audited
Audit Date: 10.06.2019
Personnel: Brent Schacherer (Pub.); Kevin True (Ad. Dir.); Cam Bonelli (Ed.)

INTERCOM

Street address 1: 314 Jefferson St S
Street address city: Wadena
Street address state: MN
Zip/Postal code: 56482-1534
General Phone: (218) 631-2561
General Fax: (218) 631-1621
General/National Adv. E-mail: editorial@wadenapj.com
Primary Website: wadenapj.com
Avg Paid Circ: 0
Avg Free Circ: 9325
Audit By: VAC
Audit Date: 30.09.2017
Personnel: Steve Schultz (Ed.)
Parent company (for newspapers): Forum Communications Co.

ISANTI COUNTY NEWS

Street address 1: 234 Main St S
Street address city: Cambridge
Street address state: MN
Zip/Postal code: 55008-1611
General Phone: (763) 689-1981
General Fax: (763) 689-4372
General/National Adv. E-mail: neil.anderson@ecm-inc.com
Editorial e-mail: editor.countynews@ecm-inc.com
Primary Website: isanticountynews.com
Year Established: 1900
Avg Paid Circ: 125
Avg Free Circ: 12948
Audit By: Sworn/Estimate/Non-Audited
Audit Date: 10.06.2019
Personnel: Jeff Andres (Rgl Gen. Mgr.); Rachel Kytonen (Ed.)
Parent company (for newspapers): Adams Publishing Group, LLC

ISANTI-CHISAGO COUNTY STAR

Street address 1: 930 Cleveland St S
Street address city: Cambridge
Street address state: MN
Zip/Postal code: 55008-1785
General Phone: (763) 698-1181
General Fax: (763) 698-1185
General/National Adv. E-mail: akrist@moraminn.com
Display Adv. E-mail: starclass@countystar.com
Editorial e-mail: editor@countystar.com
Primary Website: http://isanti-chisagocountystar.com
Year Established: 1905
Avg Free Circ: 8263
Audit By: VAC
Audit Date: 30.06.2017
Personnel: Keith Hansen (Pub.); Eric Champion (Adv. Mgr.); Scott Kittelson (Circ. Mgr.); Becky Glander (Ed.); Matt Mcolly (Prod. Mgr.)
Parent company (for newspapers): Northstar Media, Inc.

JACKSON COUNTY PILOT

Street address 1: 310 2nd St
Street address city: Jackson
Street address state: MN
Zip/Postal code: 56143-1640
General Phone: (507) 847-3771
General Fax: (507) 847-5822
General/National Adv. E-mail: info@livewireprinting.com
Display Adv. E-mail: eileenc@livewireprinting.com
Editorial e-mail: editor@livewireprinting.com
Primary Website: jacksoncountypilot.com
Avg Paid Circ: 1700
Audit By: Sworn/Estimate/Non-Audited
Audit Date: 10.06.2019
Personnel: Justin Lessman (Pub.); Ryan Brinks (Ed.); Dallas Luhmann (Adv. Sales Rep.); Marilyn Knutson (Circ. Mgr.)

JANESVILLE ARGUS

Street address 1: 107 N Main St
Street address city: Janesville
Street address state: MN
Zip/Postal code: 56048-9538
General Phone: (507) 835-3380
General Fax: (507) 835-3435
General/National Adv. E-mail: kbiehn@wasecacountynews.com
Display Adv. E-mail: classifieds@wasecacountynews.com
Editorial e-mail: srook@wasecacountynews.com
Primary Website: southernminn.com/janesville_argus/
Avg Paid Circ: 764
Avg Free Circ: 2
Audit By: Sworn/Estimate/Non-Audited
Audit Date: 10.06.2019
Personnel: Julie Frazier (Pub.); Suzanne Rook (Ed.)

JORDAN INDEPENDENT

Street address 1: 109 Rice St S
Street address city: Jordan
Street address state: MN
Zip/Postal code: 55352-1513
General Phone: (952) 492-2224
General Fax: (952) 492-2231
Advertising Phone: (952) 345-6477
General/National Adv. E-mail: jhiltunen@swpub.com
Display Adv. E-mail: classified@swpub.com
Editorial e-mail: editor@jordannews.com
Primary Website: swnewsmedia.com/jordan_independent
Avg Paid Circ: 1709
Audit By: Sworn/Estimate/Non-Audited
Audit Date: 10.06.2019
Personnel: Laurie Hartmann (Pub.); Ruby Winings (Circ. Mgr.); Mathias Baden (Ed.); Jen Hiltunen (Adv. Mgr.)
Parent company (for newspapers): Red Wing Publishing Co.

KANABEC COUNTY TIMES

Street address 1: 107 Park St S
Street address city: Mora
Street address state: MN
Zip/Postal code: 55051-1459
General Phone: (320) 679-2661
General Fax: (320) 679-2663
Advertising Phone: (320) 225-5124
Advertising Fax: (320) 679-2661
Editorial Phone: (320) 225-5128
Editorial Fax: (320) 679-2661
General/National Adv. E-mail: akrist@moraminn.com
Display Adv. E-mail: frontdesk@moraminn.com
Editorial e-mail: editor@moraminn.com
Primary Website: moraminn.com
Avg Paid Circ: 3000
Audit By: Sworn/Estimate/Non-Audited
Audit Date: 10.06.2019
Personnel: Wade Weber (Pub.); Annette Krist (Adv. Mgr.); Kristen Faurie (Ed.)

KENYON LEADER

Street address 1: 638 2nd St
Street address city: Kenyon
Street address state: MN

Zip/Postal code: 55946-1334
General Phone: (507) 789-6161
Advertising Phone: (507) 333-3148
General/National Adv. E-mail: nbrandon@faribault.com
Display Adv. E-mail: echristensen@southernminndigital.com
Editorial e-mail: editor@thekenyonleader.com
Primary Website: southernminn.com/the_kenyon_leader
Year Established: 1885
Avg Paid Circ: 636
Avg Free Circ: 2334
Audit By: Sworn/Estimate/Non-Audited
Audit Date: 10.06.2019
Personnel: Terri Lenz (Ed./Pub.); Kris Johnson (Circ. Mgr.)
Parent company (for newspapers): Adams Publishing Group, LLC

KERKHOVEN BANNER

Street address 1: 1001 Atlantic Ave.
Street address city: Kerkhoven
Street address state: MN
Zip/Postal code: 56252
General Phone: (320) 264-3071
General Fax: (320) 264-3070
General/National Adv. E-mail: kbanner@midstate.tds.net
Editorial e-mail: kbanner@tds.net
Avg Paid Circ: 1000
Audit By: Sworn/Estimate/Non-Audited
Audit Date: 10.10.2021
Personnel: Theodore J. Almen (Ed.)

KITTSON COUNTY ENTERPRISE

Street address 1: 118 2nd St S
Street address city: Hallock
Street address state: MN
Zip/Postal code: 56728-4320
General Phone: (218) 843-2868
General/National Adv. E-mail: kce@wiktel.com
Display Adv. E-mail: kce@wiktel.com
Editorial e-mail: kce@wiktel.com
Primary Website: kittsonarea.com
Year Established: 1881
Avg Paid Circ: 1000
Audit By: Sworn/Estimate/Non-Audited
Audit Date: 27.09.2023
Personnel: Michael Moore (Pub.)

LAFAYETTE NICOLLET LEDGER

Street address 1: 750 Main Ave
Street address city: Lafayette
Street address state: MN
Zip/Postal code: 56054-4401
General Phone: (507) 228-8985
General Fax: (507) 228-8779
Editorial e-mail: ledger@prairiepublishingmn.com
Primary Website: prairiepublishingmn.com
Year Established: 1904
Avg Paid Circ: 1263
Avg Free Circ: 11
Audit By: Sworn/Estimate/Non-Audited
Audit Date: 10.06.2019
Personnel: Michael Koob (Pub)
Parent company (for newspapers): Prairie Publishing, Inc

LAKE AREA PRESS

Street address 1: 511 Washington Ave
Street address city: Detroit Lakes
Street address state: MN
Zip/Postal code: 56501-3007
General Phone: (218) 847-3151
General Fax: (218) 847-9409
Advertising Phone: (218) 844-1451
Editorial Phone: (218) 844-1466
General/National Adv. E-mail: MSWENSON@DLNEWSPAPERS.COM
Display Adv. E-mail: lholmer@dlnewspapers.com
Editorial e-mail: pquam@dlnewspapers.com
Primary Website: dl-online.com
Avg Free Circ: 9958
Audit By: VAC
Audit Date: 30.03.2017
Personnel: Melissa Swenson (Publisher)
Parent company (for newspapers): Forum Communications Co.

LAKE COUNTRY ECHO

Street address 1: 4285 W Lake St
Street address city: Pequot Lakes
Street address state: MN
Zip/Postal code: 56472-3014
General Phone: (218) 568-8521
General Fax: (218) 568-5407
General/National Adv. E-mail: news@pequotlakesecho.com
Display Adv. E-mail: kathy.bittnerlee@pequotlakesecho.com
Editorial e-mail: nancy.vogt@pequotlakesecho.com
Primary Website: pineandlakes.com
Mthly Avg Views: 106516
Mthly Avg Unique Visitors: 20572
Year Established: 1972
Avg Paid Circ: 2820
Avg Free Circ: 59
Audit By: CVC
Audit Date: 3//2013
Personnel: Pete Mohs (Pub.); Nancy Vogt (Ed.)

LAKE COUNTY NEWS-CHRONICLE

Street address 1: 109 Waterfront Dr
Street address city: Two Harbors
Street address state: MN
Zip/Postal code: 55616-1525
General Phone: (218) 834-2141
General Fax: (218) 834-2144
General/National Adv. E-mail: chronicle@lcnewschronicle.com
Display Adv. E-mail: class@lcnewschronicle.com
Editorial e-mail: rlubbers@duluthnews.com
Primary Website: twoharborsmn.com
Year Established: 1890
Avg Paid Circ: 2031
Audit By: Sworn/Estimate/Non-Audited
Audit Date: 10.06.2019
Personnel: Adelle Whitefoot (Com. Ed); Neal Ronquist (Pub.); Rick Lubbers (Ed.)
Parent company (for newspapers): Forum Communications Co.

LAKE CRYSTAL TRIBUNE

Street address 1: 101 W Humphrey St
Street address city: Lake Crystal
Street address state: MN
Zip/Postal code: 56055-2035
General Phone: (507) 726-2133
General Fax: (507) 726-2265
General/National Adv. E-mail: tribune@hickorytech.net
Year Established: 1882
Avg Paid Circ: 1150
Avg Free Circ: 33
Audit By: Sworn/Estimate/Non-Audited
Audit Date: 10.06.2019
Personnel: Don R. Marben (Ed.); Mindy Kranz (Office Manager/Subscription/Accouonts Payable)

LAKE PARK JOURNAL

Street address 1: PO Box 709
Street address city: Hawley
Street address state: MN
Zip/Postal code: 56549-0709
General Phone: (218) 238-6872
General Fax: (218) 483-4457
General/National Adv. E-mail: ads@hawleyherald.net
Display Adv. E-mail: frontdesk@hawleyherald.net
Editorial e-mail: marc@hawleyherald.net
Year Established: 1922
Avg Paid Circ: 1712
Audit By: Sworn/Estimate/Non-Audited
Audit Date: 10.06.2019
Personnel: Eugene Prim (Pub.); Marc Ness (Ed.)

LAKE REGION LIFE

Street address 1: 200 Main St E
Street address city: New Prague
Street address state: MN
Zip/Postal code: 56071-2438
General Phone: (952) 758-4435
General Fax: (952) 758-4135
General/National Adv. E-mail: ads@newpraguetimes.com
Display Adv. E-mail: classifieds@newpraguetimes.com
Editorial e-mail: news@newpraguetimes.com
Primary Website: newpraguetimes.com
Year Established: 1970
Avg Paid Circ: 1425
Avg Free Circ: 65
Audit By: Sworn/Estimate/Non-Audited
Audit Date: 10.06.2019
Personnel: Chuck Wann (Pub.); Lisa Ingebrand (Adv. Mgr.); Debbie Atherton (Circ. Mgr.); Jay Schneider (Ed.)

LAKEFIELD STANDARD

Street address 1: 403 Main St
Street address city: Lakefield
Street address state: MN
Zip/Postal code: 56150-1201
General Phone: (507) 662-5555
General Fax: (507) 662-6770
General/National Adv. E-mail: info@livewireprinting.com
Editorial e-mail: editor@livewireprinting.com
Primary Website: lakefieldstandard.com
Avg Paid Circ: 1055
Avg Free Circ: 41
Audit By: Sworn/Estimate/Non-Audited
Audit Date: 10.06.2019
Personnel: Justin Lessman (Ed.)

LAKES AREA REVIEW

Street address 1: 106 Norwood St SW
Street address city: New London
Street address state: MN
Zip/Postal code: 56273-8520
General Phone: (320) 354-2945
General Fax: (320) 354-6300
General/National Adv. E-mail: brettb@nlslakesareareview.com
Display Adv. E-mail: sales@nlslakesareareview.com
Classified Adv. e-mail: sales@nlslakesareareview.com
Editorial e-mail: brettb@nlslakesareareview.com
Year Established: 1899
Avg Paid Circ: 145
Avg Free Circ: 6500
Audit By: Sworn/Estimate/Non-Audited
Audit Date: 04.06.2024
Personnel: Theodore ALMEN (PUBLISHER)
Parent company (for newspapers): Village Ink Ltd.

LAKESHORE WEEKLY NEWS

Street address 1: 12925 Eagle Creek Parkway
Street address city: Savage
Street address state: MN
Zip/Postal code: 55378
General Phone: (952) 445-3333
Editorial e-mail: editor@chanvillager.com
Primary Website: swnewsmedia.com/lakeshore_weekly
Avg Paid Circ: 11
Avg Free Circ: 14280
Audit By: CAC
Audit Date: 30.04.2019
Personnel: Laurie Hartmann (Pub.); Todd Molldrem (CRO); Ruby Winings (Circ. Dir.); Mark Olson (Reg. Ed.); Melissa Turtinen (Comm. Ed.)

LAMBERTON NEWS

Street address 1: 218 S Main St
Street address city: Lamberton
Street address state: MN
Zip/Postal code: 56152-1389
General Phone: (507) 752-7181
General Fax: (507) 752-7181
Editorial e-mail: lambnews@centurylink.net
Year Established: 1923
Avg Paid Circ: 1700
Avg Free Circ: 4
Audit By: Sworn/Estimate/Non-Audited
Audit Date: 10.06.2019
Personnel: J.G. Dietl (Ed.)

LE SUEUR NEWS-HERALD

Street address 1: 62 E Minnesota St
Street address city: Le Center
Street address state: MN
Zip/Postal code: 56057-1502
General Phone: (507) 665-3332
General Fax: (507) 665-3334
Advertising Phone: (507) 931-8574
Editorial Phone: (507) 931-8571
General/National Adv. E-mail: news@lesueurnews-herald.com
Editorial e-mail: editor@lesueurnews-herald.com
Primary Website: lesueurnews-herald.com
Avg Paid Circ: 864
Avg Free Circ: 45
Audit By: Sworn/Estimate/Non-Audited
Audit Date: 10.06.2019
Personnel: Suzanne Rook (Reg Mgr Ed); Chad Hjellming (Reg Gen Mgr)
Parent company (for newspapers): Adams Publishing Group, LLC

LEADER RECORD

Street address 1: 239 2ND AVE
Street address city: Gonvick
Street address state: MN
Zip/Postal code: 56644
General Phone: (218) 487-5225
General Fax: (218) 487-5251
Editorial e-mail: richards@gvtel.com
Primary Website: tricocanary.com/leader-record
Avg Paid Circ: 1535
Audit By: Sworn/Estimate/Non-Audited
Audit Date: 10.06.2019
Personnel: Richard D. Richards (Pub.); Corrine J. Richards (Ed.)

LEWISTON JOURNAL

Street address 1: 924 Whitewater Ave
Street address city: Saint Charles
Street address state: MN
Zip/Postal code: 55972-1131
General Phone: (507) 523-2119
General Fax: (507) 932-5537
Primary Website: lewistonjournal.net
Avg Paid Circ: 974
Audit By: Sworn/Estimate/Non-Audited
Audit Date: 10.06.2019
Personnel: Daniel Y. Stumpf (Pub.); Carol A. Boynton (Ed.)
Parent company (for newspapers): Stumpf Publishing Co., Inc.

LONSDALE AREA NEWS-REVIEW

Street address 1: PO Box 352
Street address city: Lonsdale
Street address state: MN
Zip/Postal code: 55046-0352
General Phone: (507) 744-2551
Advertising Phone: (507) 645-1120
Editorial Phone: (507) 744-2551
General/National Adv. E-mail: jpetsche@northfieldnews.com
Display Adv. E-mail: njohnson@faribault.com
Editorial e-mail: editor@northfieldnews.com
Primary Website: southernminn.com/lonsdale_area_news_review
Avg Paid Circ: 17
Avg Free Circ: 2445
Audit By: Sworn/Estimate/Non-Audited
Audit Date: 10.06.2019
Personnel: Suzanne Rook; Misty Schwab (Reporter)
Parent company (for newspapers): Adams Publishing Group, LLC

LONSDALE NEWS - REVIEW

Street address 1: PO Box 352
Street address 2: 102 5th Ave. NW
Street address city: Lonsdale
Street address state: MN
Zip/Postal code: 55046-0352
General Phone: (507) 744-2551
General Fax: (507) 645-6005
Advertising Phone: (507) 645-1120
General/National Adv. E-mail: jpetsche@northfieldnews.com
Display Adv. E-mail: njohnson@faribault.com
Editorial e-mail: mschwab@lonsdalenewsreview.com
Primary Website: lonsdalenewsreview.com
Year Established: 2006
Avg Paid Circ: 0
Avg Free Circ: 2555
Audit By: Sworn/Estimate/Non-Audited
Audit Date: 10.06.2019

Personnel: Misty Schwab (Reporter); Suzanne Rook (Reg. Mng. Ed.); Anne Kopas (Reporter/ Edit. Asst.)
Parent company (for newspapers): Adams Publishing Group, LLC

MADELIA TIMES-MESSENGER

Street address 1: 112 W Main St
Street address city: Madelia
Street address state: MN
Zip/Postal code: 56062-1440
General Phone: (507) 642-3636
General Fax: (507) 642-3535
Editorial e-mail: tm@prairiepublishingmn.com
Primary Website: prairiepublishingmn.com
Year Established: 1871
Avg Paid Circ: 875
Avg Free Circ: 16
Audit By: Sworn/Estimate/Non-Audited
Audit Date: 10.06.2019
Personnel: Michael Koob (Pub.); Shari Kilmer (Adv.)
Parent company (for newspapers): Prairie Publishing, Inc

MAPLE LAKE MESSENGER

Street address 1: 218 Division St W
Street address city: Maple Lake
Street address state: MN
Zip/Postal code: 55358-4576
General Phone: (320) 963-3813
General Fax: (320) 963-6114
General/National Adv. E-mail: ads@maplelakemessenger.com
Display Adv. E-mail: vicki@maplelakemessenger.com
Editorial e-mail: news@maplelakemessenger.com
Primary Website: maplelakemessenger.com
Avg Paid Circ: 1113
Audit By: Sworn/Estimate/Non-Audited
Audit Date: 10.06.2019
Personnel: Kayla Erickson (Adv. Mgr.); Michele Pawlenty (Pub.)

MAPLE RIVER MESSENGER

Street address 1: 309 Main St W
Street address city: Mapleton
Street address state: MN
Zip/Postal code: 56065-2062
General Phone: (507) 524-3212
General Fax: (507) 524-4249
General/National Adv. E-mail: mrm@prairiepublishingmn.com
Editorial e-mail: editor@maplerivermessenger.com
Primary Website: maplerivermessenger.com
Avg Paid Circ: 1113
Avg Free Circ: 8
Audit By: Sworn/Estimate/Non-Audited
Audit Date: 10.06.2019
Personnel: Michael Koob (Pub.); Kelly Spillman (Ed.)

MAPLEWOOD REVIEW

Street address 1: 2515 7th Ave E
Street address city: North Saint Paul
Street address state: MN
Zip/Postal code: 55109-3098
General Phone: (651) 777-8800
General Fax: (651) 777-8288
Advertising Phone: (651) 748-7862
Editorial Phone: (651) 748-7820
General/National Adv. E-mail: tfragnito@lillienews.com
Display Adv. E-mail: rnisswandt@lillienews.com
Editorial e-mail: mlhagert@lillienews.com
Primary Website: lillienews.com/ramsey-co-maplewood-review
Avg Paid Circ: 36
Avg Free Circ: 4554
Audit By: VAC
Audit Date: 30.09.2017
Personnel: Jeffery R. Enright (Co-Pub.); Ted H. Lillie (Co-Pub.); Tony Fragnito (Adv. Mgr.); Laura Young (Circ. Mgr.); Mary Lee Hagert (Mng. Ed.); Holly Wenzel (Ed.)
Parent company (for newspapers): Lillie Suburban Newspapers

MCINTOSH TIMES

Street address 1: 115 Broadway NW
Street address city: Mcintosh
Street address state: MN
Zip/Postal code: 56556-5777
General Phone: (218) 563-3585
General Fax: (218) 487-5251
General/National Adv. E-mail: richards@gvtel.com
Editorial e-mail: mcintoshtimes@gmail.com
Primary Website: tricocanary.com/contact
Year Established: 1888
Avg Paid Circ: 939
Audit By: Sworn/Estimate/Non-Audited
Audit Date: 10.06.2019
Personnel: Richard D. Richards (Pub.); Kim Hedlund (Ed.)

MELROSE BEACON

Street address 1: 408 E Main St
Street address city: Melrose
Street address state: MN
Zip/Postal code: 56352-1186
General Phone: (320) 256-3240
General Fax: (320) 256-3363
General/National Adv. E-mail: missy@saukherald.com
Display Adv. E-mail: kayla@saukherald.com
Editorial e-mail: carol@melrosebeacon.com
Primary Website: melrosebeacon.com
Avg Paid Circ: 1900
Avg Free Circ: 2300
Audit By: Sworn/Estimate/Non-Audited
Audit Date: 10.06.2019
Personnel: Carol Moorman (Ed.); Joyce Frericks (Bus. Mgr.); Pat Turner (Prod. Mgr.)

MESSENGER

Street address 1: PO Box 96
Street address city: Scandia
Street address state: MN
Zip/Postal code: 55073-0096
General Phone: (651) 433-3845
General Fax: (651) 433-3158
General/National Adv. E-mail: sales@osceolasun.com
Editorial e-mail: editor@countrymessenger.com
Primary Website: countrymessenger.com
Year Established: 1986
Avg Paid Circ: 1600
Audit By: Sworn/Estimate/Non-Audited
Audit Date: 10.06.2019
Personnel: Teresa Holmdahl (Ad. Sales); Carrie Larson (Circ. Mgr.); Tom Stangl

MESSENGER BANNER

Street address 1: 586 Pacific Ave
Street address city: Stephen
Street address state: MN
Zip/Postal code: 56757
General Phone: (218) 478-2210
General Fax: (218) 478-2210
Editorial e-mail: messenger@wiktel.com
Year Established: 1882
Avg Paid Circ: 1499
Audit By: Sworn/Estimate/Non-Audited
Audit Date: 10.06.2019
Personnel: Keith Sustad (Ed.)

MIDDLE RIVER HONKER

Street address 1: 655 2nd St N
Street address city: Middle River
Street address state: MN
Zip/Postal code: 56737-4136
General Phone: (218) 222-3501
General/National Adv. E-mail: honkernews@wiktel.com
Display Adv. E-mail: honkernews@wiktel.com
Editorial e-mail: honkernews@wiktel.com
Primary Website: thehonker.com
Year Established: 2006
Avg Paid Circ: 1100
Avg Free Circ: 15
Audit By: Sworn/Estimate/Non-Audited
Audit Date: 10.06.2019
Personnel: Babara Geer (Pub.); Brianna Geer (Publisher)

MILLE LACS COUNTY TIMES

Street address 1: 208 N Rum River Dr
Street address 2: Ste 1
Street address city: Princeton
Street address state: MN
Zip/Postal code: 55371-1632
General Phone: (763) 389-1222
General Fax: (763) 389-1728
General/National Adv. E-mail: brigitte.larson@ecm-inc.com
Display Adv. E-mail: becky.southard@ecm-inc.com
Editorial e-mail: jeff.hage@ecm-inc.com
Primary Website: millelacscountytimes.com
Avg Paid Circ: 1559
Audit By: Sworn/Estimate/Non-Audited
Audit Date: 10.06.2019
Personnel: Jeff Andres (Gen. Mgr.); Jeff Hage (Ed); Jerry Gloe (Adv. Dir.)
Parent company (for newspapers): Adams Publishing Group, LLC

MILLE LACS MESSENGER

Street address 1: PO Box 26
Street address 2: 280 W. Main St.
Street address city: Isle
Street address state: MN
Zip/Postal code: 56342-0026
General Phone: (320) 676-3123
General Fax: (320) 676-8450
General/National Adv. E-mail: phototech@millelacsmessenger.com
Display Adv. E-mail: phototech@millelacsmessenger.com
Editorial e-mail: vlamoore@millelacsmessenger.com
Primary Website: millelacsmessenger.com
Year Established: 1913
Avg Paid Circ: 3800
Audit By: Sworn/Estimate/Non-Audited
Audit Date: 10.06.2019
Personnel: Monica Weets (Adv.); Shauna Tetrault (Ed.); RoxAnne Bouley (Operations Mgr.)
Parent company (for newspapers): Adams Publishing Group, LLC

MINNEOTA MASCOT

Street address 1: 201 N JEFFERSON ST
Street address city: Minneota
Street address state: MN
Zip/Postal code: 56264
General Phone: (507) 872-6492
General Fax: (507) 872-6840
General/National Adv. E-mail: byron@minneotamascot.com
Display Adv. E-mail: same
Editorial e-mail: same
Primary Website: theminneotamascot.com
Year Established: 1891
Avg Paid Circ: 1200
Audit By: Sworn/Estimate/Non-Audited
Audit Date: 10.06.2019
Personnel: Byron Higgin (Pub.)

MINNESOTA LAKE TRIBUNE

Street address 1: PO Box 214
Street address city: Minnesota Lake
Street address state: MN
Zip/Postal code: 56068-0214
General Phone: (507) 462-3321
General Fax: (507) 462-3321
General/National Adv. E-mail: mltrib@bevcomm.net
Editorial e-mail: mltrib@bevcomm.net
Year Established: 1985
Avg Paid Circ: 896
Avg Free Circ: 25
Audit By: Sworn/Estimate/Non-Audited
Audit Date: 10.06.2019
Personnel: Donald Kain (Pub.)

MINNETONKA/DEEPHAVEN/ HOPKINS SUN SAILOR

Street address 1: 33 Second St. N.E.
Street address city: Osseo
Street address state: MN
Zip/Postal code: 55369
General Phone: (763) 425-3323
General Fax: (763) 425-2945
General/National Adv. E-mail: advertise@ecm-inc.com
Display Adv. E-mail: advertise@ecm-inc.com
Editorial e-mail: sabina.badola@ecm-inc.com
Primary Website: hometownsource.com
Year Established: 1970
Avg Paid Circ: 88
Avg Free Circ: 18076
Audit By: Sworn/Estimate/Non-Audited
Audit Date: 10.06.2019
Personnel: Gretchen Schlosser (Mng. Ed.); Steve Gall (Adv. Dir.); Mandy Froemming (Exec. Ed.); Craig Anderson (Dist. Mgr.); Keith Anderson (Dir. of News)
Parent company (for newspapers): Adams Publishing Group, LLC; Sun Newspapers

MONITOR REVIEW

Street address 1: 318 W Main St
Street address city: Adams
Street address state: MN
Zip/Postal code: 55909-9771
General Phone: (507) 582-3542
General Fax: (507) 582-3542
General/National Adv. E-mail: monitor@omnitelcom.com
Editorial e-mail: themonitorreview@gmail.com
Avg Paid Circ: 1127
Avg Free Circ: 19
Audit By: Sworn/Estimate/Non-Audited
Audit Date: 10.06.2019
Personnel: Robert Adams (Ed.)

MONTEVIDEO AMERICAN-NEWS

Street address 1: 223 S 1st St
Street address city: Montevideo
Street address state: MN
Zip/Postal code: 56265-1412
General Phone: (320) 269-2156
General Fax: (320) 269-2159
General/National Adv. E-mail: mbutzin@montenews.com
Display Adv. E-mail: kchristians@montenews.com
Editorial e-mail: bolson@montenews.com
Primary Website: montenews.com
Avg Paid Circ: 3257
Avg Free Circ: 41
Audit By: Sworn/Estimate/Non-Audited
Audit Date: 10.06.2019
Personnel: Donna Moe (Circ. Mgr.); Bruce Olson (Ed.); Janell Sjurseth (Prod. Mgr.)
Parent company (for newspapers): CherryRoad Media

MONTGOMERY MESSENGER

Street address 1: 310 1st St S
Street address city: Montgomery
Street address state: MN
Zip/Postal code: 56069-1604
General Phone: (507) 364-8601
General Fax: (507) 364-8602
Advertising Phone: (507) 364-8601
Editorial Phone: (507) 364-8601
General/National Adv. E-mail: wade@montgomerymnnews.com
Display Adv. E-mail: wade@montgomerymnnews.com
Editorial e-mail: wade@montgomerymnnews.com
Avg Paid Circ: 1777
Avg Free Circ: 15
Audit By: Sworn/Estimate/Non-Audited
Audit Date: 10.06.2019
Personnel: E. Charles Wann (Pub.); Wade Young (Ed.)
Parent company (for newspapers): Suel Printing Co.

MONTICELLO TIMES

Street address 1: 540 Walnut St
Street address 2: PO Box 420
Street address city: Monticello
Street address state: MN
Zip/Postal code: 55362-8663
General Phone: (763) 295-3131
General Fax: (763) 295-3080
Primary Website: monticellotimes.com
Avg Paid Circ: 1312
Avg Free Circ: 18
Audit By: Sworn/Estimate/Non-Audited
Audit Date: 10.06.2019
Personnel: Jeff Hage (Ed.); Josh Dungan (Sports); Jeremy Bradfield (Adv. Dir.); Craig Dahlberg (Sales)
Parent company (for newspapers): Adams Publishing Group, LLC; American Community Newspapers LLC

MOOSE LAKE STAR GAZETTE

Street address 1: 308 Elm Ave
Street address city: Moose Lake
Street address state: MN
Zip/Postal code: 55767-7706
General Phone: (218) 485-4406
General Fax: (218) 485-0237

Editorial e-mail: evergreen@mooselakestargazette.com
Primary Website: mooselakestargazette.com
Avg Paid Circ: 3865
Audit By: Sworn/Estimate/Non-Audited
Audit Date: 10.06.2019
Personnel: Connie Berruungf (Pub.)

MORGAN MESSENGER

Street address 1: 510 2ND ST W
Street address city: Morgan
Street address state: MN
Zip/Postal code: 56266
General Phone: (507) 249-3130
General Fax: (507) 249-3131
General/National Adv. E-mail: fxstandardnews@gmail.com
Display Adv. E-mail: fxstandardnews@gmail.com
Editorial e-mail: morganmess@yahoo.com
Primary Website: standard-gazette.com/aboutus.html
Avg Paid Circ: 968
Avg Free Circ: 50
Audit By: Sworn/Estimate/Non-Audited
Audit Date: 10.06.2019
Personnel: Daniel McGonigle (Ed.); Denise Bonsack (Pub.); Marilyn Brandel (Gen. Mgr.)

MORRISON COUNTY RECORD

Street address 1: 216 1st St SE
Street address city: Little Falls
Street address state: MN
Zip/Postal code: 56345-3004
General Phone: (320) 632-2345
General Fax: (320) 632-2348
General/National Adv. E-mail: mcr@mcrecord.com
Display Adv. E-mail: mcr@mcrecord.com
Classified Adv. e-mail: mcr@mcrecord.com
Editorial e-mail: terry.lehrke@mcrecord.com
Primary Website: mcrecord.com
Mthly Avg Views: 238641
Mthly Avg Unique Visitors: 21751
Year Established: 1969
Avg Paid Circ: 350
Avg Free Circ: 18114
Audit By: CAC
Audit Date: 6/31/2017
Personnel: Judy Espino (Bus. Mgr.); Karen Grittner (Circ. Mgr.); Terry Lehrke (News Ed.); Carmen Meyer (General Manager); Tena Wensman (Sales Manager)
Parent company (for newspapers): Adams Publishing Group, LLC

MOUNDS VIEW/NEW BRIGHTON SUN FOCUS

Street address 1: 10917 Valley View Rd
Street address city: Eden Prairie
Street address state: MN
Zip/Postal code: 55344-3730
General Phone: (952) 392-6800
General Fax: (952) 392-6802
Advertising Phone: (952) 392-6888
General/National Adv. E-mail: kassie.petermann@ecm-inc.com
Display Adv. E-mail: krista.jech@ecm-inc.com
Editorial e-mail: kassie.petermann@ecm-inc.com
Primary Website: http://focus.mnsun.com
Year Established: 1968
Avg Paid Circ: 12
Avg Free Circ: 9309
Audit By: Sworn/Estimate/Non-Audited
Audit Date: 10.06.2019
Personnel: Peggy Bakken (Ed.); Mike Erickson (Prod. Mgr.); Jeff Coolman (Gen. Mgr.)
Parent company (for newspapers): Adams Publishing Group, LLC

MOUNTAIN LAKE/BUTTERFIELD OBSERVER-ADVOCATE

Street address 1: 1025 2nd Ave
Street address 2: Ste 2
Street address city: Mountain Lake
Street address state: MN
Zip/Postal code: 56159-1456
General Phone: (507) 427-2725
General Fax: (507) 427-2724
General/National Adv. E-mail: suef@mtlakenews.com
Editorial e-mail: rahnl@windomnews.com
Primary Website: mtlakenews.com
Avg Paid Circ: 1141
Audit By: Sworn/Estimate/Non-Audited
Audit Date: 10.06.2019
Personnel: Trevor Slette (Gen. Mgr.); Sue Frederickson (Sales Mgr.); Kris Langland (Ed.)

MOWER COUNTY INDEPENDENT

Street address 1: 135 East Main Street
Street address city: LeRoy
Street address state: MN
Zip/Postal code: 55951
General Phone: 507-324-5325
General Fax: 507-324-5267
Advertising Phone: (507) 324-5325
Advertising Fax: (507) 324-5267
Editorial Phone: (507) 324-5325
Editorial Fax: (507) 324-5267
General/National Adv. E-mail: evansppc@mediacombb.net
Display Adv. E-mail: evansppc@mediacombb.net
Classified Adv. e-mail: evansppc@mediacombb.net
Editorial e-mail: evansppc@mediacombb.net
Primary Website: NONE
Year Established: 1876
Avg Paid Circ: 1500
Audit By: USPS
Audit Date: 9/31/2023
Personnel: Dan Evans (Pub.); Sarah Mensink (Ad Layout/Graphics/Coordinator); Marciel Skifter (Ed)
Parent company (for newspapers): Evans Printing & Publishing, Inc.; Evans Publishing & Printing, Inc.

MURRAY COUNTY NEWS

Street address 1: 2627 Broadway Ave
Street address city: Slayton
Street address state: MN
Zip/Postal code: 56172-1311
General Phone: (507) 836-8929
General Fax: (507) 836-6162
Primary Website: murraycountynews.net
Avg Paid Circ: 950
Audit By: Sworn/Estimate/Non-Audited
Audit Date: 10.06.2019
Personnel: Gerald D. Johnson (Pub.)

NEW BRIGHTON BULLETIN

Street address 1: 2515 7th Ave E
Street address city: North St Paul
Street address state: MN
Zip/Postal code: 55109-3004
General Phone: (651) 777-8800
General Fax: (651) 777-8288
Advertising Phone: (651) 777-7860
Editorial Phone: (651) 748-7820
General/National Adv. E-mail: tfragnito@lillienews.com
Display Adv. E-mail: sanderson@lillienews.com
Editorial e-mail: mlhagert@lillienews.com
Primary Website: lillienews.com/articles/new-brighton-mounds-view-bulletin-news
Avg Paid Circ: 12
Avg Free Circ: 5245
Audit By: VAC
Audit Date: 30.09.2016
Personnel: Ted H. Lillie (Co-Pub); Jeff R. Enright (Co-Pub.); Tony Fragnito (Adv. Dir.); Laura Young (Circ. Mgr.); Mary Hagert (Ed.)
Parent company (for newspapers): Lillie Suburban Newspapers

NEW BRIGHTON-MOUNDS VIEW BULLETIN

Street address 1: 2515 7th Ave E
Street address city: North Saint Paul
Street address state: MN
Zip/Postal code: 55109-3004
General Phone: (651) 777-8800
General Fax: (651) 777-8288
Advertising Phone: (651) 748-7860
Editorial Phone: (651) 748-7800
General/National Adv. E-mail: tfragnito@lillienews.com
Display Adv. E-mail: sanderson@lillienews.com
Editorial e-mail: mlhagert@lillienews.com
Primary Website: lillienews.com/articles/new-brighton-mounds-view-bulletin-news
Avg Paid Circ: 230
Avg Free Circ: 26000
Audit By: Sworn/Estimate/Non-Audited
Audit Date: 10.06.2019
Personnel: Laura Young (Circ. Mgr.); Mary Lee Hagert (Exec. Ed.); Tony Fragnito (Adv. Mgr.)
Parent company (for newspapers): Lillie Suburban Newspapers

NEW YORK MILLS HERALD

Street address 1: 106 S Boardman Ave
Street address city: New York Mills
Street address state: MN
Zip/Postal code: 56567-4101
General Phone: (218) 385-7720
General Fax: (218) 548-5582
General/National Adv. E-mail: nymdispatch@arvig.net
Editorial e-mail: news@nymdispatch.com
Primary Website: http://nymdispatch.com
Avg Paid Circ: 1835
Audit By: Sworn/Estimate/Non-Audited
Audit Date: 10.06.2019
Personnel: Chad Koenen (Co-Pub.); Dani Koenen (Co-Pub.); Connie Vandermay (Ed.)
Parent company (for newspapers): Forum Communications Co.

NEWS HOPPER

Street address 1: 21 Washington St
Street address city: Brainerd
Street address state: MN
Zip/Postal code: 56401-3334
General Phone: (218) 772-0300
General Fax: (218) 772-0301
Editorial e-mail: hopper@crosbyironton.net
Primary Website: newshopper.net
Year Established: 2000
Avg Free Circ: 17141
Audit By: CVC
Audit Date: 30.09.2018
Personnel: Laura Heglund (Owner); Eric Heglund (Adv. Mgr)
Parent company (for newspapers): NewsHopper Publications Inc.

NEWS-RECORD

Street address 1: 225 S Main St
Street address city: Zumbrota
Street address state: MN
Zip/Postal code: 55992-1698
General Phone: (507) 732-7617
General Fax: (507) 732-7619
General/National Adv. E-mail: same
Display Adv. E-mail: same
Editorial e-mail: news@zumbrota.com
Primary Website: zumbrota.com
Avg Paid Circ: 2246
Avg Free Circ: 9411
Audit By: USPS
Audit Date: 05.06.2024
Personnel: Peter K. Grimsrud (Adv. Mgr.); Matthew Grimsrud (Ed.)

NOBLES COUNTY REVIEW

Street address 1: 108 Maine Ave
Street address city: Adrian
Street address state: MN
Zip/Postal code: 56110-1192
General Phone: (507) 483-2213
General Fax: (507) 483-2219
Editorial e-mail: ncreview@frontier.com
Primary Website: noblescountyreview.net
Avg Paid Circ: 1067
Avg Free Circ: 1300
Audit By: Sworn/Estimate/Non-Audited
Audit Date: 10.06.2019
Personnel: Gerald Johnson (Pub.); Kathryn A. Burzlaff (Ed.)
Parent company (for newspapers): Johnson Publishing Company

NORMAN COUNTY INDEX

Street address 1: 307 W Main St
Street address city: Ada
Street address state: MN
Zip/Postal code: 56510-1251
General Phone: (218) 784-2541
General Fax: (218) 784-2551
General/National Adv. E-mail: nci@loretel.net
Editorial e-mail: nci@loretel.net
Year Established: 1880
Avg Paid Circ: 1200
Audit By: Sworn/Estimate/Non-Audited
Audit Date: 27.09.2023
Personnel: Ross Pfund (Pub.)
Parent company (for newspapers): Index Printing, Inc.

NORTH CROW RIVER NEWS

Street address 1: 33 2nd St NE
Street address city: Osseo
Street address state: MN
Zip/Postal code: 55369-1252
General Phone: (763) 425-3323
General Fax: (763) 425-2945
General/National Adv. E-mail: jeremy.bradfield@ecm-inc.com
Display Adv. E-mail: mike.specht@ecm-inc.com
Editorial e-mail: peggy.bakken@ecm-inc.com
Primary Website: pressnews.com
Year Established: 1963
Avg Paid Circ: 3280
Avg Free Circ: 6214
Audit By: Sworn/Estimate/Non-Audited
Audit Date: 10.06.2019
Personnel: Peggy Bakken (Ed.); Jeremy Bradfield (Adv. Dir.); Mark Weber (Gen. Mgr.)
Parent company (for newspapers): Adams Publishing Group, LLC; American Community Newspapers LLC

NORTH NEWS

Street address 1: 125 W Broadway Ave
Street address 2: Ste 130
Street address city: Minneapolis
Street address state: MN
Zip/Postal code: 55411-2245
General Phone: (651) 245-2647
Advertising Phone: (651) 245-2647
Editorial Phone: (651) 245-2647
General/National Adv. E-mail: okeefek@puc-mn.org
Display Adv. E-mail: okeefek@puc-mn.org
Editorial e-mail: okeefek@puc-mn.org
Primary Website: facebook.com/mynorthnews
Year Established: 1991
Avg Free Circ: 10000
Audit By: Sworn/Estimate/Non-Audited
Audit Date: 10.06.2019
Parent company (for newspapers): Pillsbury United Communities

NORTH STAR NEWS

Street address 1: 204 Main St S
Street address city: Karlstad
Street address state: MN
Zip/Postal code: 56732-4002
General Phone: (218) 436-2157
General Fax: (218) 436-3271
General/National Adv. E-mail: norstar@wiktel.com
Display Adv. E-mail: nsads@wiktel.com
Editorial e-mail: dan@wiktel.com
Primary Website: page1publications.com
Year Established: 1904
Avg Paid Circ: 1490
Audit By: Sworn/Estimate/Non-Audited
Audit Date: 10.06.2019
Personnel: Rollin Bergman (Pub.); Larina Berggren (Adv. Mgr.); Julie M. Nordine (Ed.)
Parent company (for newspapers): Page One Publications

NORTHEASTER

Street address 1: 2844 Johnson St NE
Street address city: Minneapolis
Street address state: MN
Zip/Postal code: 55418-3056
General Phone: (612) 788-9003
General Fax: (612) 788-3299
General/National Adv. E-mail: contact@mynortheaster.com
Display Adv. E-mail: contact@MyNortheaster.com
Classified Adv. e-mail: contact@mynortheaster.com
Editorial e-mail: contact@mynortheaster.com
Primary Website: MyNortheaster.com
Mthly Avg Views: 7000
Mthly Avg Unique Visitors: 5000
Year Established: 1978
Avg Paid Circ: 31
Avg Free Circ: 31000
Audit By: CVC
Audit Date: 31.03.2022

Personnel: Margo Ashmore (Pub.); Vince Brown (Circ./Prod.)
Parent company (for newspapers): Pro Media, Inc

NORTHERN STAR

Street address 1: 128 Main St
Street address city: Clinton
Street address state: MN
Zip/Postal code: 56225-5174
General Phone: (320) 325-5152
General Fax: (320) 325-5280
Editorial e-mail: northernstar@mchsi.com
Year Established: 1965
Avg Paid Circ: 1802
Avg Free Circ: 20
Audit By: Sworn/Estimate/Non-Audited
Audit Date: 10.06.2019
Personnel: Sue Kaercher (Pub.); Denese Gustafson (Adv. Mgr.); Lois Torgerson (Mng. Ed.)
Parent company (for newspapers): Kaercher Publications

NORTHERN WATCH

Street address 1: 324 Main Ave N
Street address city: Thief River Falls
Street address state: MN
Zip/Postal code: 56701-1906
General Phone: (218) 681-4450
General Fax: (218) 681-4455
General/National Adv. E-mail: sales@trftimes.com
Display Adv. E-mail: classified@trftimes.com
Editorial e-mail: dhill@trftimes.com
Primary Website: trftimes.com/northernwatch
Year Established: 1910
Avg Free Circ: 22000
Audit By: Sworn/Estimate/Non-Audited
Audit Date: 10.06.2019
Personnel: Dede Coltam (Adv. Mgr.); Sue Philip (Circ. Mgr.); Dave Hill (Ed.)

NORTHFIELD NEWS

Street address 1: 115 5th St W
Street address city: Northfield
Street address state: MN
Zip/Postal code: 55057-2017
General Phone: (507) 645-5615
General Fax: (507) 645-6005
Advertising Phone: (507) 645-1110
Editorial Phone: (507) 645-1136
General/National Adv. E-mail: jpetsche@northfieldnews.com
Display Adv. E-mail: chjellming@northfieldnews.com
Editorial e-mail: ngerhardt@northfieldnews.com
Primary Website: northfieldnews.com
Year Established: 1876
Avg Paid Circ: 2850
Avg Free Circ: 0
Audit By: Sworn/Estimate/Non-Audited
Audit Date: 10.06.2019
Personnel: Sam Gett (Pub.); Roger Stolley (Prodn. Mgr.); Chad Hjellming (Pub.)
Parent company (for newspapers): Adams Publishing Group, LLC

NORTHLAND PRESS

Street address 1: 13833 Riverwood Ln
Street address 2: Ste 2
Street address city: Crosslake
Street address state: MN
Zip/Postal code: 56442-2823
General Phone: (218) 692-5842
General Fax: (218) 792-5844
Advertising Phone: (218) 692-5842
Advertising Fax: (218) 792-5844
Editorial Phone: (218) 692-5842
Editorial Fax: (218) 792-5844
General/National Adv. E-mail: news@northlandpress.com
Display Adv. E-mail: news@northlandpress.com
Editorial e-mail: news@northlandpress.com
Primary Website: northlandpress.com
Year Established: 2005
Avg Free Circ: 5331
Audit By: CVC
Audit Date: 30.09.2018

Personnel: Joanne Boblett (Publisher); Paul Boblett (Editor and Advertising Manager)

NORWOOD YOUNG AMERICA TIMES

Street address 1: PO Box 5
Street address city: Waconia
Street address state: MN
Zip/Postal code: 55387-0005
General Phone: (952) 442-4414
General Fax: (952) 442-6815
Editorial e-mail: jason.schmucker@ecm-inc.com
Primary Website: hometownsource.com/sun_patriot/
Avg Paid Circ: 2550
Avg Free Circ: 41
Audit By: Sworn/Estimate/Non-Audited
Audit Date: 10.06.2019
Personnel: Jason Schmucker (Ed.); Al Lohman (Comm. Ed.); Keith Anderson (News Dir.); Mark Webber (Reg. Pres.)
Parent company (for newspapers): Adams Publishing Group, LLC

OAKDALE LAKE ELMO REVIEW

Street address 1: 2515 7th Ave E
Street address city: North Saint Paul
Street address state: MN
Zip/Postal code: 55109-3098
General Phone: (651) 777-8800
General Fax: (651) 777-8288
Advertising Phone: (651) 748-7863
Editorial Phone: (651) 748-7820
General/National Adv. E-mail: tfragnito@lillienews.com
Display Adv. E-mail: rnisswandt@lillienews.com
Editorial e-mail: mlhagert@lillienews.com
Primary Website: lillienews.com/oakdale-lake-elmo-review
Year Established: 1986
Avg Paid Circ: 37
Avg Free Circ: 6710
Audit By: VAC
Audit Date: 30.09.2017
Personnel: Jeffery R. Enright (Co-Pub.); Ted H. Lillie (Co-Pub.); Tony Fragnito (Adv. Dir.); Laura Young (Circ. Mgr.); Mary Lee Hagert (Mng. Ed.)
Parent company (for newspapers): Lillie Suburban Newspapers

OLMSTED COUNTY JOURNAL

Street address 1: 136 Saint Anthony St S
Street address city: Preston
Street address state: MN
Zip/Postal code: 55965-1151
General Phone: (507) 288-5201
General Fax: (507) 288-9560
General/National Adv. E-mail: news@olmstedcountyjournal.com
Display Adv. E-mail: bob@olmstedcountyjournal.com
Editorial e-mail: jade@olmstedcountyjournal.com
Year Established: 2011
Avg Free Circ: 36986
Audit By: Sworn/Estimate/Non-Audited
Audit Date: 10.06.2019
Personnel: Jason Sethre (Pub.)

OSAKIS REVIEW

Street address 1: PO Box 5
Street address city: Alexandria
Street address state: MN
Zip/Postal code: 56308-0005
General Phone: (320) 859-2143
General Fax: (320) 763-3258
Advertising Phone: (320) 763-1225
General/National Adv. E-mail: achaffins@osakisreview.com
Editorial e-mail: news@theosakisreview.com
Primary Website: theosakisreview.com
Year Established: 1890
Avg Paid Circ: 1147
Avg Free Circ: 28
Audit By: Sworn/Estimate/Non-Audited
Audit Date: 10.06.2019
Personnel: Jody Hanson (Pub.); Greta Petrich (Mng. Ed.); Lynn Mounsdon (Circ. Mgr.)
Parent company (for newspapers): Forum Communications Co.

OSSEO-MAPLE GROVE PRESS

Street address 1: 33 2nd St NE
Street address city: Osseo
Street address state: MN
Zip/Postal code: 55369-1252
General Phone: (763) 425-3323
General Fax: (763) 425-2945
Advertising Phone: (763) 424-7355
General/National Adv. E-mail: jeremy.bradfield@ecm-inc.com
Display Adv. E-mail: mike.specht@ecm-inc.com
Editorial e-mail: peggy.bakken@ecm-inc.com
Primary Website: pressnews.com
Year Established: 1924
Avg Paid Circ: 3280
Avg Free Circ: 6214
Audit By: Sworn/Estimate/Non-Audited
Audit Date: 10.06.2019
Personnel: Peggy Bakken (Ed.); Mark Weber (Gen. Mgr.); Jeremy Bradfield (Adv. Dir.)
Parent company (for newspapers): Adams Publishing Group, LLC; American Community Newspapers LLC

PARK RAPIDS ENTERPRISE

Street address 1: 203 Henrietta Ave N
Street address city: Park Rapids
Street address state: MN
Zip/Postal code: 56470-2617
General Phone: (218) 732-3364
General Fax: (218) 732-8757
Advertising Phone: (218) 237-1816
Editorial Phone: (218) 237-1815
General/National Adv. E-mail: cparks@parkrapidsenterprise.com
Display Adv. E-mail: mharmon@parkrapidsenterprise.com
Editorial e-mail: kcederstrom@parkrapidsenterprise.com
Primary Website: parkrapidsenterprise.com
Avg Paid Circ: 3341
Avg Free Circ: 73
Audit By: VAC
Audit Date: 30.09.2017
Personnel: Rory Palm (Pub.); Candy Parks (Adv. Mgr.); Kathy Dennis (Circ. Mgr)
Parent company (for newspapers): Forum Communications Co.

PAYNESVILLE PRESS

Street address 1: 211 Washburne Ave
Street address city: Paynesville
Street address state: MN
Zip/Postal code: 56362-1642
General Phone: (320) 243-3772
General Fax: (320) 243-4492
General/National Adv. E-mail: adsales@paynesvillepress.com
Display Adv. E-mail: classifieds@paynesvillepress.com
Editorial e-mail: editor@paynesvillepress.com
Primary Website: paynesvillearea.com
Year Established: 1887
Avg Paid Circ: 2142
Avg Free Circ: 177
Audit By: Sworn/Estimate/Non-Audited
Audit Date: 10.06.2019
Personnel: Michael Jacobson (Ed.)

PELICAN RAPIDS PRESS

Street address 1: 29 W Mill Ave
Street address city: Pelican Rapids
Street address state: MN
Zip/Postal code: 56572-4228
General Phone: (218) 863-1421
General Fax: (218) 863-1423
General/National Adv. E-mail: adsprpress@loretel.net
Display Adv. E-mail: joprpress@loretel.net
Editorial e-mail: jeffprpress@loretel.net
Primary Website: pelicanrapidspress.com
Year Established: 1897
Avg Paid Circ: 2470
Audit By: Sworn/Estimate/Non-Audited
Audit Date: 10.06.2019
Personnel: Julie Meyer (Pub.); Jeff Meyer (Adv. Mgr.)

PERHAM FOCUS

Street address 1: 222 2nd Ave SE
Street address city: Perham
Street address state: MN
Zip/Postal code: 56573-1707
General Phone: (218) 346-5900
General Fax: (218) 346-5901
General/National Adv. E-mail: kdobberstein@perhamfocus.com
Display Adv. E-mail: jbrown@perhamfocus.com
Editorial e-mail: pquam@perhamfocus.com
Primary Website: perhamfocus.com
Avg Paid Circ: 2100
Audit By: Sworn/Estimate/Non-Audited
Audit Date: 10.06.2019
Personnel: Kim Dobberstein (Adv. Mgr.); Jason Miller (Publisher)
Parent company (for newspapers): Forum Communications Co.

PIERCE COUNTY HERALD

Street address 1: 2760 N Service Drive
Street address city: Red Wing
Street address state: MN
Zip/Postal code: 55066
General Phone: (800) 535-1660
Primary Website: piercecountyherald.com
Avg Paid Circ: 3000
Avg Free Circ: 28
Audit By: Sworn/Estimate/Non-Audited
Audit Date: 10.06.2019
Personnel: Steve Dzubay (Pub.); Anne Jacobson (News Dir.); Michael Brun (MultiMed. Ed.); Sarah Nigbor (Reg Ed.)
Parent company (for newspapers): Forum Communications Co.

PINE CITY PIONEER

Street address 1: 405 2nd Ave SE
Street address city: Pine City
Street address state: MN
Zip/Postal code: 55063-1504
General Phone: (320) 629-6771
General Fax: (320) 629-6772
Advertising Phone: (320) 225-5124
General/National Adv. E-mail: ads@pinecitymn.com
Editorial e-mail: editor@pinecitymn.com
Primary Website: pinecitymn.com
Year Established: 1895
Avg Paid Circ: 2588
Avg Free Circ: 104
Audit By: Sworn/Estimate/Non-Audited
Audit Date: 10.06.2019
Personnel: Annette Krist (Pub.); Mike Gainor (Ed.)

PINE CONE PRESS CITIZEN

Street address 1: 166 Hardy Ln.
Street address 2: STE 100
Street address city: Longville
Street address state: MN
Zip/Postal code: 56655
General Phone: (218) 363-2002
General Fax: (218) 363-3043
Editorial e-mail: presscit@arvig.net
Primary Website: pineconepresscitizen.com
Year Established: 1984
Avg Paid Circ: 250
Avg Free Circ: 6986
Audit By: Sworn/Estimate/Non-Audited
Audit Date: 10.06.2019
Personnel: Marilyn Ford (Ed/Office Mgr.); Dave DeLost (Sales Mgr.); Bill DeLost (Ed.)

PINE COUNTY COURIER

Street address 1: 405 2nd Ave SE
Street address city: Pine City
Street address state: MN
Zip/Postal code: 55063-1504
General Phone: (320) 245-2368
General Fax: (320) 245-2438
General/National Adv. E-mail: ads@pinecitymn.com
Editorial e-mail: editor@pinecitymn.com
Primary Website: pinecitymn.com
Year Established: 1894
Avg Paid Circ: 1744
Avg Free Circ: 90
Audit By: Sworn/Estimate/Non-Audited
Audit Date: 10.06.2019
Personnel: Annette Krist (Pub.); Mike Gainor (Ed.)

PINEANDLAKES ECHO JOURNAL

Street address 1: 506 James St
Street address city: Brainerd

Street address state: MN
Zip/Postal code: 56401-2942
General Phone: (218) 829-4705
General Fax:
General/National Adv. E-mail:
Display Adv. E-mail:
Editorial e-mail: nancy.vogt@pequotlakesecho.com
Primary Website: pineandlakes.com
Mthly Avg Views: 108003
Mthly Avg Unique Visitors: 20428
Year Established: 1935
Avg Paid Circ: 3400
Avg Free Circ: 52
Audit By: Sworn/Estimate/Non-Audited
Audit Date: 10.06.2019
Personnel: Pete Mohs (Pub.)

PIPESTONE COUNTY STAR

Street address 1: 115 2nd St NE
Street address 2: Ste 100
Street address city: Pipestone
Street address state: MN
Zip/Postal code: 56164-1957
General Phone: (507) 825-3333
General Fax: (507) 825-2168
General/National Adv. E-mail: pipepub@pipestonestar.com
Display Adv. E-mail: plorang@pipestonestar.com
Classified Adv. e-mail: news@pipestonestar.com
Editorial e-mail: editor@pipestonestar.com
Primary Website: pipestonestar.com
Year Established: 1879
Avg Paid Circ: 1850
Avg Free Circ: 15
Audit By: Sworn/Estimate/Non-Audited
Audit Date: 27.09.2023
Personnel: John C. Draper (Publisher); Paul Lorang (Adv. Mgr.); Kyle Kuphal (Ed.)

POPE COUNTY TRIBUNE

Street address 1: 14 1st Ave SE
Street address city: Glenwood
Street address state: MN
Zip/Postal code: 56334-0157
General Phone: (320) 634-4571
General Fax: (320) 634-5522
General/National Adv. E-mail: design@pctribune.com
Display Adv. E-mail: design@pctribune.com
Editorial e-mail: tdouglass@pctribune.com
Primary Website: pctribune.com
Mthly Avg Views: 800000
Mthly Avg Unique Visitors: 40000
Year Established: 1920
Avg Paid Circ: 3200
Audit By: USPS
Audit Date: 10.06.2019
Personnel: Tim Douglass (Pub./Ed.)

PORTAGE NEWS

Street address 1: 121 W 7th Ave
Street address city: Floodwood
Street address state: MN
Zip/Postal code: 55736-1200
General Phone: (218) 476-3210
General Fax: (218) 476-3211
General/National Adv. E-mail: portage.ads@frontier.com
Editorial e-mail: vpofmg.sec@frontiernet.net
Primary Website: thevoyageurpress.com/portagenews.html
Audit By: Sworn/Estimate/Non-Audited
Audit Date: 10.06.2019
Personnel: John Grones (Pub); Pat Murphy (Gen. Mgr./Adv.)

PRAIRIE TIMES

Street address 1: 411 E Main St
Street address city: Blooming Prairie
Street address state: MN
Zip/Postal code: 55917-1439
General Phone: (507) 583-4431
General Fax: (507) 583-4445
Editorial e-mail: dcieditorial@gmail.com
Primary Website: bloomingprairieonline.com
Avg Paid Circ: 1073
Audit By: Sworn/Estimate/Non-Audited
Audit Date: 10.06.2019
Personnel: Rick Bussler (Pub.); Alex Malm (News Ed.)

PRINCETON UNION-EAGLE

Street address 1: 208 N Rum River Dr
Street address 2: Ste 1
Street address city: Princeton
Street address state: MN
Zip/Postal code: 55371-1632
General Phone: (763) 389-1222
General Fax: (763) 389-1728
General/National Adv. E-mail: becky.southard@ecm-inc.com
Display Adv. E-mail: brigitte.alday@ecm-inc.com
Editorial e-mail: jeff.hage@ecm-inc.com
Primary Website: princetonunioneagle.com
Mthly Avg Views: 74319
Mthly Avg Unique Visitors: 13433
Year Established: 1876
Avg Paid Circ: 1806
Audit By: Sworn/Estimate/Non-Audited
Audit Date: 10.06.2019
Personnel: Jeff Andres (Gen. Mgr.); Jeff Hage (Ed.); Jerry Gloe (Adv. Dir.)
Parent company (for newspapers): Adams Publishing Group, LLC

PRIOR LAKE AMERICAN

Street address 1: 12925 Eagle Creek Pkwy
Street address city: Savage
Street address state: MN
Zip/Postal code: 55378-1271
General Phone: (952) 447-6669
General Fax: (952) 447-6671
Advertising Phone: (952) 345-6477
Editorial Phone: (952) 345-6378
General/National Adv. E-mail: jhiltunen@swpub.com
Display Adv. E-mail: classified@swpub.com
Editorial e-mail: editor@plamerican.com
Primary Website: swnewsmedia.com/prior_lake_american
Year Established: 1960
Avg Paid Circ: 740
Avg Free Circ: 8340
Audit By: Sworn/Estimate/Non-Audited
Audit Date: 10.06.2019
Personnel: Laurie Hartmann (Op. Dir.); Lorie Carlson (Ed.); Bill Davis (Gen. Mgr.)
Parent company (for newspapers): Red Wing Publishing Co.

PROCTOR JOURNAL

Street address 1: 215 5th St
Street address city: Proctor
Street address state: MN
Zip/Postal code: 55810-1628
General Phone: (218) 624-3344
General Fax: (218) 624-7037
Advertising Phone: (218) 624-3344
Advertising Fax: (218) 624-7037
Editorial Phone: (218) 624-3344
Editorial Fax: (218) 624-7037
General/National Adv. E-mail: journal@proctormn.com
Display Adv. E-mail: journal@proctormn.com
Classified Adv. e-mail: journal@proctormn.com
Editorial e-mail: journal@proctormn.com
Primary Website: proctorjournal.com
Mthly Avg Views: 12100
Mthly Avg Unique Visitors: 1392
Year Established: 1906
Avg Paid Circ: 1800
Audit By: USPS
Audit Date: 10.06.2019
Personnel: Diane Giuliani (Gen. Mgr.); Jake Benson (Ed.); Lauren Anderson (Associate Editor)

QUAD COMMUNITY PRESS

Street address 1: 4779 Bloom Ave
Street address city: White Bear Lake
Street address state: MN
Zip/Postal code: 55110-2764
General Phone: (365) 407-1200
General Fax: (651) 429-1242
General/National Adv. E-mail: quadpressrep@presspubs.com
Display Adv. E-mail: classified@presspubs.com
Editorial e-mail: quadnews@presspubs.com
Primary Website: presspubs.com
Year Established: 1981
Avg Paid Circ: 708
Avg Free Circ: 5987
Audit By: VAC
Audit Date: 30.09.2017
Personnel: Eugene D. Johnson (Pub.); Patti Carlson (Adv.); Amy Johnson (Circ. Mgr.)
Parent company (for newspapers): Press Publications, Inc.

RAMSEY COUNTY REVIEW

Street address 1: 2515 7th Ave E
Street address city: North Saint Paul
Street address state: MN
Zip/Postal code: 55109-3098
General Phone: (651) 777-8800
General Fax: (651) 777-8288
Advertising Phone: (651) 748-7862
Editorial Phone: (651) 748-7820
General/National Adv. E-mail: tfragnito@lillienews.com
Display Adv. E-mail: rnisswandt@lillienews.com
Editorial e-mail: mlhagert@lillienews.com
Primary Website: lillienews.com/ramsey-co-maplewood-review
Year Established: 1938
Avg Paid Circ: 39
Avg Free Circ: 2503
Audit By: VAC
Audit Date: 30.09.2017
Personnel: Laura Young (Circ. Mgr.); Mary Lee Hagert (Exec. Ed.); Tony Fragnito (Adv. Dir.)
Parent company (for newspapers): Lillie Suburban Newspapers

RENVILLE COUNTY REGISTER

Street address 1: 110 NW Dupont Ave
Street address city: Renville
Street address state: MN
Zip/Postal code: 56284
General Phone: (320) 329-3324
General Fax: (320) 329-3432
Advertising Phone: (320) 329-3324
Advertising Fax: (320) 329-3432
Editorial Phone: (320) 523-2032
Editorial Fax: (320) 523-2033
General/National Adv. E-mail: oproduction@rencopub.com
Display Adv. E-mail: oclassifieds@rencopub.com
Editorial e-mail: editor@rencopub.com
Year Established: 1872
Avg Paid Circ: 1800
Audit By: Sworn/Estimate/Non-Audited
Audit Date: 10.06.2019
Personnel: Rose Hettig (Publisher); Karen Harrier (Circ. Mgr.); Luke Stadther (Editor)

REPUBLICAN EAGLE

Street address 1: 2760 N Service Dr
Street address city: Red Wing
Street address state: MN
Zip/Postal code: 55066-1985
General Phone: (651) 388-8235
General Fax: (651) 388-3404
Advertising Phone: (651) 301-7855
Editorial Phone: (651) 301-7870
General/National Adv. E-mail: pfrebault@rivertowns.net
Display Adv. E-mail: chjelming@rivertowns.net
Classified Adv. e-mail: classifieds@rivertowns.net
Editorial e-mail: letters@republican-eagle.com
Primary Website: republican-eagle.com
Mthly Avg Views: 433764
Mthly Avg Unique Visitors: 48782
Year Established: 1857
Avg Paid Circ: 5414
Sat. Circulation Paid: 5824
Audit By: Sworn/Estimate/Non-Audited
Audit Date: 10.06.2019
Personnel: Steve Messick (Pub.); Michael Keuhn (Gen. Mgr.); Anne Jacobson (News Ed.); Steve Gall (Adv. Dir.); Neal Ronquist; Neal Ronquist
Parent company (for newspapers): Forum Communications Co.

REVIEW PERSPECTIVES

Street address 1: 2515 7th Ave E
Street address city: North Saint Paul
Street address state: MN
Zip/Postal code: 55109-3004
General Phone: (651) 777-8800
General Fax: (651) 777-8288
Editorial Phone: (651) 748-7820
General/National Adv. E-mail: tfragnito@lillienews.com
Display Adv. E-mail: rnisswandt@lillienews.com
Editorial e-mail: mlhagert@lillienews.com
Primary Website: lillienews.com/perspectives
Avg Free Circ: 6613
Audit By: Sworn/Estimate/Non-Audited
Audit Date: 10.06.2019
Personnel: Jeffery R. Enright (Co-Pub.); Ted H. Lillie (Co-Pub.); Tony Fragnito (Adv. Dir.); Laura Young (Circ. Mgr.); Mary Lee Hagert (Ed.)
Parent company (for newspapers): Lillie Suburban Newspapers

RICHFIELD SUN-CURRENT

Street address 1: 10917 Valley View Rd
Street address city: Eden Prairie
Street address state: MN
Zip/Postal code: 55344-3730
General Phone: (952) 392-6800
General Fax: (952) 392-6802
Advertising Phone: (952) 392-6888
General/National Adv. E-mail: jorgensonnicole@hotmail.com
Display Adv. E-mail: krista.jech@ecm-inc.com
Editorial e-mail: andrew.wig@ecm-inc.com
Primary Website: current.mnsun.com
Year Established: 1954
Avg Paid Circ: 163
Avg Free Circ: 9831
Audit By: Sworn/Estimate/Non-Audited
Audit Date: 10.06.2019
Personnel: Mike Erickson (Prod. Mgr.); Peggy Baken (Mng. Ed.); Krista Jech (Mktg. Mgr.)
Parent company (for newspapers): Adams Publishing Group, LLC

ROCKFORD AREA NEWS LEADER

Street address 1: 33 2nd St NE
Street address city: Osseo
Street address state: MN
Zip/Postal code: 55369-1252
General Phone: (763) 425-3323
General Fax: (763) 425-2945
General/National Adv. E-mail: jeremy.bradfield@ecm-inc.com
Display Adv. E-mail: mike.specht@ecm-inc.com
Editorial e-mail: peggy.bakken@ecm-inc.com
Primary Website: pressnews.com
Year Established: 1963
Avg Paid Circ: 780
Avg Free Circ: 3149
Audit By: Sworn/Estimate/Non-Audited
Audit Date: 10.06.2019
Personnel: Peggy Bakken (Ed.); Jeremy Bradfield (Adv Dir); Mark Weber (Gen. Mgr.)
Parent company (for newspapers): Press and News Publications

ROSEAU TIMES-REGION

Street address 1: 1307 3rd St NE
Street address 2: Suite 109
Street address city: Roseau
Street address state: MN
Zip/Postal code: 56751-2105
General Phone: (218) 463-1521
General Fax: (218) 463-1530
Editorial e-mail: rtr@mncable.net
Primary Website: roseautimes.com
Year Established: 1892
Avg Paid Circ: 3191
Audit By: Sworn/Estimate/Non-Audited
Audit Date: 10.06.2019
Personnel: Jodi Driscoll (Pub.)

ROSEVILLE REVIEW

Street address 1: 2515 7th Ave E
Street address city: North Saint Paul
Street address state: MN
Zip/Postal code: 55109-3098
General Phone: (651) 777-8800
General Fax: (651) 777-8288
Advertising Phone: (651) 748-7864
Editorial Phone: (651) 748-7820
General/National Adv. E-mail: tfragnito@lillienews.com
Display Adv. E-mail: rnisswandt@lillienews.com

Editorial e-mail: mlhagert@lillienews.com
Primary Website: lillienews.com/roseville-little-canada-review
Year Established: 1938
Avg Paid Circ: 18
Avg Free Circ: 12276
Audit By: VAC
Audit Date: 30.09.2017
Personnel: Jeffery R. Enright (Co-Pub.); Ted H. Lillie (Co-Pub.); Tony Fragnito (Adv. Dir); George Fairbank (Ed.); Mary Lee Hagert (Mng. Ed.)
Parent company (for newspapers): Lillie Suburban Newspapers

SARTELL-ST. STEPHEN NEWSLEADER

Street address 1: 1622 11th Ave. SE
Street address city: St. Cloud
Street address state: MN
Zip/Postal code: 56304
General Phone: (320) 363-7741
Advertising Phone: Option 1
Editorial Phone: Option 2
General/National Adv. E-mail: news@thenewsleaders.com
Display Adv. E-mail: janellev@thenewsleaders.com
Editorial e-mail: editor@thenewsleaders.com
Primary Website: thenewsleaders.com
Mthly Avg Views: 20000
Mthly Avg Unique Visitors: 12000
Year Established: 1995
Avg Free Circ: 9724
Audit By: CVC
Audit Date: 30.09.2021
Personnel: Janelle Von Pinnon (CEO/Owner/Publisher); Tara Wiese (Production Manager/Designer); Carolyn Bertsch (Assignment Editor); Dennis Dalman (Editor); Leanne Loyu (Editor); Rajahna Wanick (General manager); Marg Crumley (Graphics designer)
Parent company (for newspapers): Von Meyer Publishing Inc.

SAUK CENTRE HERALD

Street address 1: 522 Sinclair Lewis Ave
Street address city: Sauk Centre
Street address state: MN
Zip/Postal code: 56378-1246
General Phone: (320) 352-6577
General Fax: (320) 352-5647
General/National Adv. E-mail: missy@saukherald.com
Display Adv. E-mail: office@saukherald.com
Editorial e-mail: diane@saukherald.com
Primary Website: saukherald.com
Year Established: 1868
Avg Paid Circ: 3276
Audit By: Sworn/Estimate/Non-Audited
Audit Date: 10.06.2019
Personnel: Joyce Frierick (Bus. Mgr.); Missy Traeger (Sales Mgr.); Diane Leukam (Ed.)

SAVAGE PACER

Street address 1: 12925 Eagle Creek Pkwy
Street address city: Savage
Street address state: MN
Zip/Postal code: 55378-1271
General Phone: (952) 440-1234
General Fax: (952) 445-3335
Advertising Phone: (952) 345-6477
General/National Adv. E-mail: jhiltunen@swpub.com
Display Adv. E-mail: classified@swpub.com
Editorial e-mail: editor@savagepacer.com
Primary Website: swnewsmedia.com/savage_pacer
Avg Free Circ: 5614
Audit By: Sworn/Estimate/Non-Audited
Audit Date: 10.06.2019
Personnel: Laurie Hartmann (Op. Dir.); Ruby Winings (Circ. Mgr.); Richard Crawford (Ed.)
Parent company (for newspapers): Red Wing Publishing Co.

SHAKOPEE VALLEY NEWS

Street address 1: 12925 Eagle Creek Pkwy
Street address city: Savage
Street address state: MN
Zip/Postal code: 55378-1271
General Phone: (952) 445-3333
General Fax: (952) 445-3335
Advertising Phone: (952) 345-6470
General/National Adv. E-mail: editor@shakopeenews.com
Display Adv. E-mail: classified@swpub.comÃ‚Â Ã‚Â
Editorial e-mail: editor@shakopeenews.com
Primary Website: shakopeenews.com
Avg Paid Circ: 4602
Audit By: Sworn/Estimate/Non-Audited
Audit Date: 10.06.2019
Personnel: Laurie Hartman (Pub.); Tess Lee (Adv. Rep.); Pat Minelli (Ed.); Ruby Winings (Circulation)
Parent company (for newspapers): Red Wing Publishing Co.

SHERBURNE COUNTY CITIZEN

Street address 1: 14054 Bank St
Street address city: Becker
Street address state: MN
Zip/Postal code: 55308-8865
General Phone: (763) 261-5880
General Fax: (763) 261-5884
General/National Adv. E-mail: citizensads@midconetwork.com
Display Adv. E-mail: citizensads@midconetwork.com
Editorial e-mail: citizennewspaper@midconetwork.com
Primary Website: citizennewspaper.com
Mthly Avg Views: 58182
Mthly Avg Unique Visitors: 20818
Year Established: 1994
Avg Paid Circ: 30
Avg Free Circ: 10995
Audit By: CVC
Audit Date: 30.09.2018
Personnel: Gary W. Meyer (Pub.); Mary Nehring (Adv.); Roberta Hibbison (Circ. Mgr); Melissa Werner (Prod.)
Parent company (for newspapers): Meyer Publications

SHOREVIEW ARDEN HILLS BULLETIN

Street address 1: 2515 7th Ave E
Street address city: North Saint Paul
Street address state: MN
Zip/Postal code: 55109-3004
General Phone: (651) 777-8800
General Fax: (651) 777-8288
Advertising Phone: (651) 748-7860
Editorial Phone: (651) 748-7820
General/National Adv. E-mail: tfragnito@lillienews.com
Display Adv. E-mail: sanderson@lillienews.com
Editorial e-mail: mlhagert@lillienews.com
Primary Website: lillienews.com/articles/shoreview-arden-hills-bulletin-news
Avg Paid Circ: 38
Avg Free Circ: 19683
Audit By: Sworn/Estimate/Non-Audited
Audit Date: 10.06.2019
Personnel: Jeffery J. Enright (Co-Pub.); Ted H. Lillie (Co-Pub.); Tony Fragnito (Adv. Dir.); Mary Lee Hagert (Exec. Ed.)
Parent company (for newspapers): Lillie Suburban Newspapers

SHOREVIEW BULLETIN

Street address 1: 2515 7th Ave E
Street address city: North Saint Paul
Street address state: MN
Zip/Postal code: 55109-3004
General Phone: (651) 777-8800
General Fax: (651) 777-8288
Advertising Phone: (651) 748-7860
Editorial Phone: (651) 748-7820
General/National Adv. E-mail: tfragnito@lillienews.com
Display Adv. E-mail: sanderson@lillienews.com
Editorial e-mail: mlhagert@lillienews.com
Primary Website: lillienews.com/articles/shoreview-arden-hills-bulletin-news
Avg Paid Circ: 10
Avg Free Circ: 6333
Audit By: VAC
Audit Date: 30.09.2017
Personnel: Jeffery R. Enright (Co-Pub.); Ted H. Lillie (Co-Pub.); Tony Fragnito (Adv. Dir.); Laura Young (Circ. Mgr.); Mary Lee Hagert (Mng. Ed.)
Parent company (for newspapers): Lillie Suburban Newspapers

SLEEPY EYE HERALD-DISPATCH

Street address 1: 119 Main St E
Street address city: Sleepy Eye
Street address state: MN
Zip/Postal code: 56085-1352
General Phone: (507) 794-3511
General Fax: (507) 794-5031
General/National Adv. E-mail: aberg@sleepyeyenews.com
Editorial e-mail: dmoldaschel@sleepyeyenews.com
Primary Website: sleepyeyenews.com
Year Established: 1880
Avg Paid Circ: 1515
Audit By: Sworn/Estimate/Non-Audited
Audit Date: 10.06.2019
Personnel: Deb Moldaschel (Ed.); Jenna Friton (Circ.); Robin Havemeier (Prod. Mgr); Lisa Drafall (Pub.)
Parent company (for newspapers): CherryRoad Media

SOUTH CROW RIVER NEWS

Street address 1: 33 2nd St NE
Street address city: Osseo
Street address state: MN
Zip/Postal code: 55369-1252
General Phone: (763) 425-3323
General Fax: (763) 425-2945
General/National Adv. E-mail: jeremy.bradfield@ecm-inc.com
Display Adv. E-mail: mike.specht@ecm-inc.com
Editorial e-mail: peggy.bakken@ecm-inc.com
Primary Website: pressnews.com
Year Established: 1963
Avg Paid Circ: 715
Avg Free Circ: 420
Audit By: Sworn/Estimate/Non-Audited
Audit Date: 10.06.2019
Personnel: Peggy Bakken (Ed.); Mark Weber (Gen. Mgr.); Jeremy Bradfield (Adv. Mgr)
Parent company (for newspapers): Adams Publishing Group, LLC; Press and News Publications

SOUTH ST. PAUL - SOUTH WEST REVIEW

Street address 1: 2515 7th Ave E
Street address city: North St Paul
Street address state: MN
Zip/Postal code: 55109-3004
General Phone: (651) 777-8800
General Fax: (651) 777-8288
Advertising Phone: (651) 748-7860
Editorial Phone: (651) 748-7820
General/National Adv. E-mail: tfragnito@lillienews.com
Display Adv. E-mail: rnisswandt@lillienews.com
Editorial e-mail: mlhagert@lillienews.com
Primary Website: lillienews.com/articles/south-st-paul
Year Established: 1938
Avg Paid Circ: 21
Avg Free Circ: 4696
Audit By: VAC
Audit Date: 30.09.2017
Personnel: Tony Fragnito (Adv. Dir.); Mary Hagert (Ed.); Laura Young (Circ. Mgr.)
Parent company (for newspapers): Lillie Suburban Newspapers

SOUTH WASHINGTON COUNTY BULLETIN

Street address 1: 217 Ramsey St
Street address city: Hastings
Street address state: MN
Zip/Postal code: 55033-1220
General Phone: (651) 319-4280
General Fax: (651) 459-9491
Advertising Phone: (651) 319-4515
Editorial Phone: (651) 459-7600
Editorial e-mail: editor@swcbulletin.com
Primary Website: swcbulletin.com
Avg Paid Circ: 4529
Audit By: Sworn/Estimate/Non-Audited
Audit Date: 10.06.2019
Personnel: Steven R. Messick (Pub.); Jeffrey Patterson (Gen. Mgr.); Patricia Drey (Mng. Ed.); Thomas Bonneville (Prodn. Mgr.)
Parent company (for newspapers): Forum Communications Co.

SOUTHWEST JOURNAL

Street address 1: 1115 Hennepin Ave
Street address city: Minneapolis
Street address state: MN
Zip/Postal code: 55403-1705
General Phone: (612) 825-9205
General Fax: (612) 825-0929
Advertising Phone: (612) 825-9205
Advertising Fax: (612) 825-0929
Editorial Phone: (612) 825-9205
Editorial Fax: (612) 825-0929
General/National Adv. E-mail: sales@mnpubs.com
Display Adv. E-mail: tgahan@swjournal.com
Editorial e-mail: dthomas@swjournal.com
Primary Website: swjournal.com
Audit By: Sworn/Estimate/Non-Audited
Audit Date: 10.06.2019
Personnel: Sarah McKenzie (Ed.); Chris Damio (Gen. Mgr.); Janis Hall (Pub.)
Parent company (for newspapers): Minnesota Premier Publications

SOUTH-WEST REVIEW

Street address 1: 2515 7th Ave E
Street address city: North Saint Paul
Street address state: MN
Zip/Postal code: 55109-3004
General Phone: (651) 777-8800
General Fax: (651) 777-8288
Advertising Phone: (651) 748-7860
Editorial Phone: (651) 748-7820
General/National Adv. E-mail: tfragnito@lillienews.com
Display Adv. E-mail: rnisswandt@lillienews.com
Editorial e-mail: mlhagert@lillienews.com
Primary Website: bulletin-news.com/south-west-review
Year Established: 1938
Avg Paid Circ: 46
Avg Free Circ: 10975
Audit By: Sworn/Estimate/Non-Audited
Audit Date: 10.06.2019
Personnel: Tony Fragnito (Adv. Dir.); Laura Young (Circ. Mgr.); Mary Lee Hagert (Mng. Ed.)
Parent company (for newspapers): Lillie Suburban Newspapers

SPRING GROVE HERALD

Street address 1: 115 W Main St
Street address city: Spring Grove
Street address state: MN
Zip/Postal code: 55974-1276
General Phone: (507) 498-3868
General Fax: (507) 498-6397
General/National Adv. E-mail: sgherald@bluffcountrynews.com
Editorial e-mail: hgray@bluffcountrynews.com
Primary Website: springgroveherald.com
Year Established: 1892
Avg Paid Circ: 1099
Avg Free Circ: 15
Audit By: Sworn/Estimate/Non-Audited
Audit Date: 10.06.2019
Personnel: Dave Phillips (Pub.); Heather Gray (Ed.)
Parent company (for newspapers): Bluff Country Newspaper Group; Bluffs Country Newspaper Group

SPRING VALLEY TRIBUNE

Street address 1: 112 N Broadway St
Street address city: Spring Valley
Street address state: MN
Zip/Postal code: 55975-1224
General Phone: (507) 346-7365
General Fax: (507) 346-7366
General/National Adv. E-mail: svtribune@bluffcountrynews.com
Display Adv. E-mail: classifieds@bluffcountrynews.com
Editorial e-mail: svtribune@bluffcountrynews.com
Primary Website: svtribune.com
Year Established: 1880
Avg Paid Circ: 1219
Audit By: Sworn/Estimate/Non-Audited
Audit Date: 10.06.2019
Personnel: Dave Phillips (Pub.); Debbie Groth (Circ. Mgr.); Sue Bly (Adv.)
Parent company (for newspapers): Bluff Country Newspaper Group; Bluffs Country Newspaper Group

SPRINGFIELD ADVANCE-PRESS

Street address 1: 13 S Marshall Ave
Street address city: Springfield
Street address state: MN
Zip/Postal code: 56087-1612
General Phone: (507) 723-4225

General Fax: (507) 723-4400
Editorial e-mail: comp.aps@newulmtel.net
Primary Website: springfieldap.com
Year Established: 1888
Avg Paid Circ: 1813
Avg Free Circ: 39
Audit By: Sworn/Estimate/Non-Audited
Audit Date: 10.06.2019
Personnel: P.C. Hedstrom (Pub.); Doris M. Weber (Ed.)

ST JAMES PLAINDEALER

Street address 1: 604 1st Ave S
Street address city: Saint James
Street address state: MN
Zip/Postal code: 56081-1729
General Phone: (507) 375-3161
General Fax: (507) 375-3221
General/National Adv. E-mail: ddurheim@stjamesnews.com
Primary Website: stjamesnews.com
Avg Paid Circ: 1145
Avg Free Circ: 40
Audit By: Sworn/Estimate/Non-Audited
Audit Date: 10.06.2019
Personnel: Lisa Drafall (Pub.); Kyle Nordhausen (Adv. Mgr.); Sean Ellertson (Ed.)
Parent company (for newspapers): CherryRoad Media

ST. ANTHONY BULLETIN

Street address 1: 2515 7th Ave E
Street address city: North Saint Paul
Street address state: MN
Zip/Postal code: 55109-3004
General Phone: (651) 777-8800
General Fax: (651) 633-3846
Advertising Phone: (651) 748-7866
Editorial Phone: (651) 748-7820
General/National Adv. E-mail: tfragnito@lillienews.com
Display Adv. E-mail: sanderson@lillienews.com
Editorial e-mail: mlhagert@lillienews.com
Primary Website: bulletin-news.com/articles/st-anthony-bulletin-news
Avg Paid Circ: 1
Avg Free Circ: 2046
Audit By: VAC
Audit Date: 30.09.2017
Personnel: Jeffery R. Enright (Co-Pub.); Ted H. Lillie (Co-Pub.); Tony Fragnito (Adv. Dir.); George Fairbank (Ed.); Mary Lee Hagert (Mng. Ed.)
Parent company (for newspapers): Lillie Suburban Newspapers

ST. CHARLES PRESS

Street address 1: 924 Whitewater Ave
Street address city: Saint Charles
Street address state: MN
Zip/Postal code: 55972-1131
General Phone: (507) 932-3663
General Fax: (507) 932-5537
General/National Adv. E-mail: scpress@hbcsc.com
Editorial e-mail: dan@rochesterbg.com
Primary Website: gmdmedia.net/st-charles-press
Avg Paid Circ: 1475
Audit By: Sworn/Estimate/Non-Audited
Audit Date: 10.06.2019
Personnel: Daniel Stumpf (Pub.); Nathan Cambell (Ed.)
Parent company (for newspapers): Stumpf Publishing Co., Inc.

ST. JOSEPH NEWSLEADER

Street address 1: 1622 11th Ave. SE
Street address city: St. Cloud
Street address state: MN
Zip/Postal code: 56304
General Phone: (320) 363-7741
Advertising Phone: Option 1
Editorial Phone: Option 2
General/National Adv. E-mail: news@thenewsleaders.com
Display Adv. E-mail: janellev@thenewsleaders.com
Editorial e-mail: editor@thenewsleaders.com
Primary Website: thenewsleaders.com
Mthly Avg Views: 20000
Mthly Avg Unique Visitors: 12000
Year Established: 1989
Avg Free Circ: 4042
Audit By: CVC
Audit Date: 30.09.2021
Personnel: Janelle Von Pinnon (Publisher); Tara Wiese (Production Manager/Designer); Carolyn Bertsch (Assignment Editor); Dennis Dalman (Editor); Leanne Loy (Editor); Rajahna Wanick (General manager); Marg Crumley (Graphics designer)
Parent company (for newspapers): Von Meyer Publishing Inc.

ST. LOUIS PARK SUN SAILOR

Street address 1: 33 2nd St NE
Street address city: Osseo
Street address state: MN
Zip/Postal code: 55369-1252
General Phone: (763) 425-3323
General Fax: (763) 425-2945
General/National Adv. E-mail: cheri.obannon@ecm-inc.com
Display Adv. E-mail: robbie.shoemaker@ecm-inc.com
Editorial e-mail: peggy.bakken@ecm-inc.com
Primary Website: sailor.mnsun.com
Year Established: 1970
Avg Paid Circ: 148
Avg Free Circ: 10821
Audit By: Sworn/Estimate/Non-Audited
Audit Date: 10.06.2019
Personnel: Cheri Oâ€™Bannon (Adv. Dir.); Mark Weber (Gen. Mgr.); Peggy Bakken (Ed.)
Parent company (for newspapers): Adams Publishing Group, LLC

ST. PETER HERALD

Street address 1: 311 S Minnesota Ave
Street address city: Saint Peter
Street address state: MN
Zip/Postal code: 56082-2523
General Phone: (507) 931-4520
General/National Adv. E-mail: kdavies@stpeterherald.com
Display Adv. E-mail: njohnson@faribault.com
Editorial e-mail: editor@stpeterherald.com
Primary Website: southernminn.com
Avg Paid Circ: 1191
Avg Free Circ: 200
Audit By: Sworn/Estimate/Non-Audited
Audit Date: 10.06.2019
Personnel: Chad Hjellming (Reg. Pub.); Kathleen Davies (Adv. Mgr.); Suzanne Rook (Mng. Ed.); Phillip Weyhe (Ed.); Nancy Madsen (Asst. Ed.)
Parent company (for newspapers): Adams Publishing Group, LLC

STAPLES WORLD

Street address 1: 224 4th St NE
Street address city: Staples
Street address state: MN
Zip/Postal code: 56479-2428
General Phone: (218) 894-1112
General Fax: (218) 894-3570
General/National Adv. E-mail: info@staplesworld.com
Display Adv. E-mail: office@staplesworld.com
Editorial e-mail: editor@staplesworld.com
Primary Website: staplesworld.com
Year Established: 1890
Avg Paid Circ: 1800
Audit By: Sworn/Estimate/Non-Audited
Audit Date: 10.06.2019
Personnel: Brenda Halvorson (Gen. Mgr.); Kathy Odden (Circ. Mgr.); Gary Mueller (Adv. Mgr.); Mark Anderson (Ed.); Dawn Timbs; Janice Winter (graphic designer/photo tech)
Parent company (for newspapers): Devlin Newspapers, Inc.; RMM Publications

STAR EAGLE

Street address 1: 128 Broadway Ave N
Street address city: New Richland
Street address state: MN
Zip/Postal code: 56072-2020
General Phone: (507) 463-8112
General Fax: (507) 463-0504
Editorial e-mail: steagle@hickorytech.net
Primary Website: newrichlandstar.com
Year Established: 1887
Avg Paid Circ: 2000
Audit By: Sworn/Estimate/Non-Audited
Audit Date: 10.06.2019
Personnel: Jim Lutgens (Ed.)

STEARNS-MORRISON ENTERPRISE

Street address 1: 561 Railroad Ave
Street address city: Albany
Street address state: MN
Zip/Postal code: 56307-9804
General Phone: (320) 845-2700
General Fax: (320) 845-4805
General/National Adv. E-mail: missy@saukherald.com
Display Adv. E-mail: kayla@saukherald.com
Editorial e-mail: liz@albanyenterprise.com
Primary Website: albanyenterprise.com
Avg Paid Circ: 1870
Avg Free Circ: 3150
Audit By: Sworn/Estimate/Non-Audited
Audit Date: 10.06.2019
Personnel: Peggy Bakken (Co-Pub.); Bruce Treichler (Co-Pub.); Michael Kosik (Ed.)
Parent company (for newspapers): Star Publications/Upper Michigan LLC

STEVENS COUNTY TIMES

Street address 1: 607 Pacific Avenue
Street address 2: P.O. Box 470
Street address city: Morris
Street address state: MN
Zip/Postal code: 56267-1942
General Phone: (320) 589-2525
General Fax: (320) 589-4357
General/National Adv. E-mail: sales@stevenscountytimes.com
Display Adv. E-mail: classifieds@stevenscountytimes.com
Editorial e-mail: news@stevenscountytimes.com
Primary Website: stevenscountytimes.com
Mthly Avg Views: 29000
Mthly Avg Unique Visitors: 4500
Year Established: 1899
Avg Paid Circ: 2400
Audit By: Sworn/Estimate/Non-Audited
Audit Date: 10.06.2019
Personnel: Sue Dieter (Pub.); Heidi Rolland (Bus. Mgr.); Rae Yost (Editor)
Parent company (for newspapers): Forum Communications Co.

STEWARTVILLE STAR

Street address 1: 101 4th Street NE
Street address 2: #2
Street address city: Stewartville
Street address state: MN
Zip/Postal code: 55976
General Phone: (507) 533-4271
General/National Adv. E-mail: starads@stewiestar.com
Editorial e-mail: editor@stewiestar.com
Primary Website: thinkstewartville.com
Year Established: 1891
Avg Paid Circ: 1575
Avg Free Circ: 4800
Audit By: Sworn/Estimate/Non-Audited
Audit Date: 10.06.2019
Personnel: Sharon Moehnke (Circ. Mgr.); Mark Peterson (Ed.); Bill Schroeder (Owner/Pub.); Judy Schroeder (Owner/Pub.); Bill Schroeder (Owner/Pub.); Judy Schroeder (Owner/Pub.)
Parent company (for newspapers): Galaxy Publications LLC

STILLWATER GAZETTE

Street address 1: 1931 Curve Crest Blvd W
Street address city: Stillwater
Street address state: MN
Zip/Postal code: 55082-6063
General Phone: (651) 439-3130
General Fax: (651) 439-4713
Advertising Phone: (651) 796-1116
Advertising Fax: (651) 439-4713
Editorial Phone: (651) 796-1112
Editorial Fax: (651) 439-4713
General/National Adv. E-mail: doug.lacher@ecm-inc.com
Display Adv. E-mail: brad.solem@ecm-inc.com
Classified Adv. e-mail: michelle.ahrens@ecm-inc.com
Primary Website: stillwatergazette.com
Year Established: 1870
Avg Paid Circ: 1591
Avg Free Circ: 24
Audit By: Sworn/Estimate/Non-Audited
Audit Date: 10.06.2019
Personnel: Doug Lacher (Adv. Acct. Exec.); Brad Solem (Adv. Acct. Exec.); Stuart Groskreutz (Sports Ed.); Jonathan Young (Mng Ed)
Parent company (for newspapers): Adams Publishing Group, LLC

SUN CURRENT- BLOOMINGTON

Street address 1: 4095 Coon Rapids Blvd.
Street address city: Coon Rapids
Street address state: MN
Zip/Postal code: 55433
General Phone: (763) 712-3544
General/National Adv. E-mail: advertise@ecm-inc.com
Display Adv. E-mail: advertise@ecm-inc.com
Editorial e-mail: matthew.hankey@ecm-inc.com
Primary Website: hometownsource.com
Year Established: 1938
Avg Paid Circ: 19
Avg Free Circ: 12099
Audit By: CVC
Audit Date: 31.03.2018
Personnel: Mark Webber (Reg. Pres.); Mathew Hankey (Mng. Ed.); Sean Miner (Community Ed.); Jason Olsen (Sports Ed.); Sharon Brauer (Adv.); Steve Gall (Adv. Dir.); Mandy Froemming (Exec. Ed.); Craig Anderson (Dist. Dir.)
Parent company (for newspapers): Adams Publishing Group, LLC; American Community Newspapers LLC

SUN THISWEEK APPLE VALLEY

Street address 1: 15322 Galaxie Ave
Street address 2: Suite 219
Street address city: Apple Valley
Street address state: MN
Zip/Postal code: 55124-3150
General Phone: (952) 894-1111
General Fax: (952) 846-2010
Advertising Phone: (952) 846-2019
General/National Adv. E-mail: ads.thisweek@ecm-inc.com
Editorial e-mail: andrew.miller@ecm-inc.com
Primary Website: sunthisweek.com
Mthly Avg Views: 100000
Mthly Avg Unique Visitors: 27000
Year Established: 1979
Avg Paid Circ: 25
Avg Free Circ: 11248
Audit By: Sworn/Estimate/Non-Audited
Audit Date: 10.06.2019
Personnel: Tad Johnson (Mng. Ed.); Mike Jetchick (Sales Mgr.)
Parent company (for newspapers): Adams Publishing Group, LLC

SUN THISWEEK LAKEVILLE

Street address 1: 15322 Galaxie Ave
Street address 2: Suite 219
Street address city: Apple Valley
Street address state: MN
Zip/Postal code: 55124-3150
General Phone: (952) 894-1111
General Fax: (952) 846-2010
General/National Adv. E-mail: sharon.buechner@ecm-inc.com
Editorial e-mail: tad.johnson@ecm-inc.com
Primary Website: sunthisweek.com
Year Established: 1979
Avg Paid Circ: 22
Avg Free Circ: 16807
Audit By: Sworn/Estimate/Non-Audited
Audit Date: 10.06.2019
Personnel: Tad Johnson (Mng. Ed.); John Gessner (Ed.)
Parent company (for newspapers): Adams Publishing Group, LLC

SWIFT COUNTY MONITOR & NEWS

Street address 1: 101 12th St S
Street address city: Benson
Street address state: MN
Zip/Postal code: 56215-1844
General Phone: (320) 843-4111
General Fax: (320) 843-3246
General/National Adv. E-mail: reed@swiftcountymonitor.com
Display Adv. E-mail: ads@monitor-news.com
Classified Adv. e-mail: ads@monitor-news.com
Editorial e-mail: reed@swiftcountymonitor-com

Primary Website: swiftcountymonitor.com
Year Established: 1886
Avg Paid Circ: 2299
Audit By: Sworn/Estimate/Non-Audited
Audit Date: 10.06.2019
Personnel: Reed W. Anfinson (Publisher); Nancy Ridler (Advertising)
Parent company (for newspapers): Swift County Monitor-News

THE AMERICAN

Street address 1: 1320 Neilson Ave SE
Street address city: Bemidji
Street address state: MN
Zip/Postal code: 56601-5406
General Phone: (218) 333-9200
General Fax: (218) 333-9819
General/National Adv. E-mail: advertising@bemidjipioneer.com
Display Adv. E-mail: advertising@bemidjipioneer.com
Classified Adv. e-mail: classifieds@bemidjipioneer.com
Editorial e-mail: bldknews@blackduckamerican.com
Primary Website: bemidjipioneer.com
Year Established: 1901
Avg Paid Circ: 525
Audit By: Sworn/Estimate/Non-Audited
Audit Date: 10.06.2019
Personnel: Dennis Doeden (Pub.)
Parent company (for newspapers): Forum Communications Co.

THE APPLETON PRESS

Street address 1: 241 W Snelling Ave
Street address city: Appleton
Street address state: MN
Zip/Postal code: 56208-1396
General Phone: (320) 289-1323
General Fax: (320) 289-2702
General/National Adv. E-mail: ads@appletonpress.com
Editorial e-mail: editor@appletonpress.com
Primary Website: appletonpress.com
Avg Paid Circ: 2110
Audit By: Sworn/Estimate/Non-Audited
Audit Date: 10.06.2019
Personnel: April Coots (Adv. Mgr.); Leslie Ehrenberg (Ed.)

THE BELGRADE OBSERVER

Street address 1: 303 Washburn Ave
Street address city: Belgrade
Street address state: MN
Zip/Postal code: 56312-4626
General Phone: (320) 254-8250
General Fax: (320) 254-3215
Editorial e-mail: observer@belgradearea.com
Primary Website: belgradearea.com
Avg Paid Circ: 1075
Audit By: Sworn/Estimate/Non-Audited
Audit Date: 10.06.2019
Personnel: James Lemmer (Pub./Ed./Adv. Mgr.)

THE BUSINESS JOURNAL

Street address 1: 333 S 7th St
Street address 2: Suite 350
Street address city: Minneapolis
Street address state: MN
Zip/Postal code: 55402-2466
General Phone: (612) 288-2100
General Fax: (612) 288-2121
Advertising Phone: (612) 288-2134
General/National Adv. E-mail: gsundeen@bizjournals.com
Display Adv. E-mail: asullivan@bizjournals.com
Editorial e-mail: ddeyoung@bizjournals.com
Primary Website: bizjournals.com/twincities
Year Established: 1983
Audit By: Sworn/Estimate/Non-Audited
Audit Date: 10.06.2019
Personnel: Tammy Mencel (Pub.); Kathy Robideau (Adv. Dir.); Dirk DeYoung (Ed.)

THE CALEDONIA ARGUS

Street address 1: 225 S. Kingston
Street address 2: PO Box 227
Street address city: Caledonia
Street address state: MN
Zip/Postal code: 55921-1040
General Phone: (507) 724-3475
General Fax: (507) 725-8610
General/National Adv. E-mail: amanda.ninneman@ecm-inc.com
Editorial e-mail: dan.mcgonigle@ecm-inc.com
Primary Website: hometownsource.com/caledonia
Year Established: 1875
Avg Paid Circ: 2094
Avg Free Circ: 3748
Audit By: Sworn/Estimate/Non-Audited
Audit Date: 10.06.2019
Personnel: Daniel McGonigle (Ed.); Stuart Sherry (Sales Mgr.); Jenna Nelson (Circulation)
Parent company (for newspapers): Adams Publishing Group, LLC

THE CASS LAKE TIMES

Street address 1: 128 2nd St NW
Street address city: Cass Lake
Street address state: MN
Zip/Postal code: 56633-3623
General Phone: (218) 335-2290
General Fax: (218) 335-2290
Advertising Phone: (218) 689-7290
Editorial e-mail: cltimes1@arvig.net
Primary Website: lakeandpine.com/46691/2205/the-cass-lake-timespdf
Avg Paid Circ: 1077
Avg Free Circ: 11
Audit By: Sworn/Estimate/Non-Audited
Audit Date: 10.06.2019
Personnel: Allan Olson (Adv. Mgr.); Tim Bloomquist (Ed.)

THE CHATFIELD NEWS

Street address 1: 220 Main St S
Street address city: Chatfield
Street address state: MN
Zip/Postal code: 55923-1225
General Phone: (507) 867-3870
General Fax: (507) 867-3870
General/National Adv. E-mail: info@bluffcountrynews.com
Display Adv. E-mail: classifieds@bluffcountrynews.com
Editorial e-mail: chatfieldnews@bluffcountrynews.com
Primary Website: http://bluffcountrynews.com/Content/The-Chatfield-News/44
Avg Paid Circ: 1413
Audit By: Sworn/Estimate/Non-Audited
Audit Date: 10.06.2019
Personnel: Dave Phillips (Ed.); Pan Bluhm (Ed.)
Parent company (for newspapers): Bluff Country Reader; Bluff Country Newspaper Group

THE CHISHOLM TRIBUNE PRESS

Street address 1: 131 W Lake St
Street address 2: Ste 2
Street address city: Chisholm
Street address state: MN
Zip/Postal code: 55719-3748
General Phone: (218) 254-4432
Editorial e-mail: tribune@chisholmtribunepress.com
Avg Paid Circ: 900
Avg Free Circ: 143
Audit By: Sworn/Estimate/Non-Audited
Audit Date: 10.06.2019
Personnel: Deb Baker
Parent company (for newspapers): Adams Publishing Group, LLC

THE CLARA CITY HERALD

Street address 1: 14 NW 4th Street
Street address city: Clara City
Street address state: MN
Zip/Postal code: 56222-1182
General Phone: (320) 847-3130
General Fax: (320) 847-2630
Editorial e-mail: ccherald@hcinet.net
Primary Website: claracityherald.com
Year Established: 1895
Avg Paid Circ: 1275
Avg Free Circ: 40
Audit By: Sworn/Estimate/Non-Audited
Audit Date: 10.06.2019
Personnel: T.J. Almen (Pub.); Josie Oliver (Ed); Billie Jo Rassat (Editor); Laura Prosser (Co-Ed.)

THE COURIER-SENTINEL

Street address 1: 405 W Center St
Street address city: Kiester
Street address state: MN
Zip/Postal code: 56051
General Phone: (507) 294-3400
General Fax: (507) 294-3400
Editorial e-mail: coursent@smig.net
Year Established: 1900
Avg Paid Circ: 1393
Audit By: Sworn/Estimate/Non-Audited
Audit Date: 10.06.2019
Personnel: Tamra Aadsen (Adv. Mgr.); Nicole Swanson (Pub./Ed.)

THE DETROIT LAKES TRIBUNE

Street address 1: 511 Washington Ave
Street address city: Detroit Lakes
Street address state: MN
Zip/Postal code: 56501-3007
General Phone: (218) 847-3151
General Fax: (218) 847-9409
Editorial e-mail: recordtribune@dlnewspapers.com
Primary Website: dl-online.com
Avg Paid Circ: 3584
Avg Free Circ: 94
Audit By: Sworn/Estimate/Non-Audited
Audit Date: 10.06.2019
Personnel: Dennis Winskowski (Pub.); Mary Brenk (Adv. Mgr.); Viola Anderson (Circ. Mgr.); Nathan Bowe (Ed.)
Parent company (for newspapers): Forum Communications Co.

THE DOWNTOWN JOURNAL

Street address 1: 1115 Hennepin Ave
Street address city: Minneapolis
Street address state: MN
Zip/Postal code: 55403-1705
General Phone: (612) 825-9205
General Fax: (612)825-0929
General/National Adv. E-mail: sales@mnpubs.com
Display Adv. E-mail: tgahan@journalmpls.com
Editorial e-mail: dthomas@journalmpls.com
Primary Website: journalmpls.com
Avg Paid Circ: 220
Avg Free Circ: 30000
Audit By: Sworn/Estimate/Non-Audited
Audit Date: 10.06.2019
Personnel: Janis Hall (Pub.); Terry Gahan (Adv. Mgr.); Sarah McKenzie (Ed.)

THE ELY ECHO

Street address 1: 15 E Chapman St
Street address city: Ely
Street address state: MN
Zip/Postal code: 55731-1227
General Phone: (218) 365-3141
General Fax: (218) 365-3142
General/National Adv. E-mail: elyecho@aol.com
Display Adv. E-mail: ads@elyecho.com
Classified Adv. e-mail: elyecho@aol.com
Editorial e-mail: elyecho@aol.com
Primary Website: elyecho.com
Year Established: 1972
Avg Paid Circ: 3329
Avg Free Circ: 32
Audit By: Sworn/Estimate/Non-Audited
Audit Date: 30.09.2023
Personnel: Anne Swenson (Pub.); Nick Wognum (Publisher); Tom Coombe (Mng. Ed.); Lisa Vidal-Sainio (Advt Dir)
Parent company (for newspapers): Milestones, Inc.

THE ERSKINE ECHO

Street address 1: 309 1st St S
Street address city: Erskine
Street address state: MN
Zip/Postal code: 56535-4142
General Phone: (218) 687-3775
General Fax: (218) 687-3744
General/National Adv. E-mail: echonews@gvtel.com
Year Established: 1899
Avg Paid Circ: 969
Avg Free Circ: 23
Audit By: Sworn/Estimate/Non-Audited
Audit Date: 10.06.2019
Personnel: Robert Hole (Ed.)

THE EXPONENT

Street address 1: 207 2nd Ave NE
Street address city: East Grand Forks
Street address state: MN
Zip/Postal code: 56721-2405
General Phone: (218) 773-2808
General Fax: (218) 773-9212
General/National Adv. E-mail: ads@page1publications.com
Editorial e-mail: exponent@rrv.net
Primary Website: page1publications.com
Avg Paid Circ: 1343
Audit By: Sworn/Estimate/Non-Audited
Audit Date: 10.06.2019
Personnel: Bruce Brierley (Bus. Mgr.); Linda Forseide (Creative Dir.); Jaclyn Hicks (Reporter); Kim Mathiason (Adv. Consult.)
Parent company (for newspapers): Page One Publications

THE FARMINGTON INDEPENDENT

Street address 1: 2760 N Service Drive
Street address city: Red Wing
Street address state: MN
Zip/Postal code: 55066
General Phone: (800) 535-1660
General Fax: (651) 463-7730
Advertising Phone: (888) 567-9694
General/National Adv. E-mail: editor@farmingtonindependent.com
Editorial e-mail: editor@farmingtonindependent.com
Primary Website: farmingtonindependent.com
Avg Paid Circ: 2500
Audit By: Sworn/Estimate/Non-Audited
Audit Date: 10.06.2019
Personnel: Michael Brun (Multimedia Ed.); Anne Jacobson (News Dir.); Sarah Nigbor (Reg. Ed.); Neal Ronquist
Parent company (for newspapers): Forum Communications Co.

THE FERTILE JOURNAL

Street address 1: 214 N MILL ST
Street address city: Fertile
Street address state: MN
Zip/Postal code: 56540
General Phone: (218) 945-6120
General Fax: (218) 945-6125
Editorial e-mail: fertjou@gvtel.com
Primary Website: fertilejournal.com/mobile
Year Established: 1882
Avg Paid Circ: 1348
Audit By: Sworn/Estimate/Non-Audited
Audit Date: 10.06.2019
Personnel: Rod Thoreson (Ed.); Karie Kirschbaum (Pub.)

THE FM EXTRA

Street address 1: 810 4th Ave S
Street address 2: Suite 120
Street address city: Moorhead
Street address state: MN
Zip/Postal code: 56560-2800
General Phone: (218) 284-1288
General Fax: (218) 284-1289
General/National Adv. E-mail: extra@ncppub.com
Display Adv. E-mail: Extramediasales@aol.com
Classified Adv. e-mail: Extramediasales@aol.com
Editorial e-mail: Tfinney@ncppub.com
Primary Website: thefmextra.com
Mthly Avg Views: 8507
Mthly Avg Unique Visitors: 3472
Year Established: 2001
Avg Free Circ: 5335
Audit By: CVC
Audit Date: 01.07.2021
Personnel: Tammy Finney (Editor); Lisa Miller (Pub.); Tasha Lange (Circ. Mgr); Diane Strom (Adv. Sales)

THE GAZETTE

Street address 1: 105 Main Ave S
Street address city: Red Lake Falls
Street address state: MN
Zip/Postal code: 56750-4701
General Phone: (218) 253-2594
General Fax: (218) 253-4114

Editorial e-mail: rlfgaz@gvtel.com
Primary Website: redlakefallsgazette.com
Avg Paid Circ: 1171
Audit By: Sworn/Estimate/Non-Audited
Audit Date: 10.06.2019
Personnel: Rod Thoreson (Circ. Mgr.); Don Johanneck (Prod. Mgr.); Karie Kirschbaum (Pub.)

THE GRYGLA EAGLE

Street address 1: 127 S MAIN AVE
Street address city: Grygla
Street address state: MN
Zip/Postal code: 56727
General Phone: (218) 294-6220
General Fax: (218) 487-5251
General/National Adv. E-mail: richards@gvtel.com
Avg Paid Circ: 700
Audit By: Sworn/Estimate/Non-Audited
Audit Date: 10.06.2019
Personnel: Richard D. Richards (Pub.); Kari Sundberg (Ed.)

THE HANCOCK RECORD

Street address 1: 607 Pacific Ave
Street address city: Morris
Street address state: MN
Zip/Postal code: 56267-1942
General Phone: (320) 392-5527
General Fax: (320) 589-4357
General/National Adv. E-mail: ads@morrissuntribune.com
Display Adv. E-mail: classifieds@morrissuntribune.com
Editorial e-mail: news@hancockrecord.com
Primary Website: hancockrecord.com
Year Established: 1899
Avg Paid Circ: 759
Avg Free Circ: 15
Audit By: Sworn/Estimate/Non-Audited
Audit Date: 10.06.2019
Personnel: Sue Dieter (Pub.); Katie Erdman (Ed.); Christine McKenzie (Circ. Dir.)
Parent company (for newspapers): Forum Communications Co.

THE HANSKA HERALD

Street address 1: 112 W Main St
Street address city: Madelia
Street address state: MN
Zip/Postal code: 56062-1440
General Phone: (507) 642-3636
General Fax: (507) 642-3535
Editorial e-mail: hh@prairiepublishingmn.com
Primary Website: hanskaherald.com
Avg Paid Circ: 349
Audit By: Sworn/Estimate/Non-Audited
Audit Date: 10.06.2019
Personnel: David Parker (Pub.); N. Ross Becken (Ed.)

THE HAWLEY HERALD

Street address 1: 119 6th St
Street address city: Hawley
Street address state: MN
Zip/Postal code: 56549-4121
General Phone: (218) 483-3306
General Fax: (218) 483-4457
General/National Adv. E-mail: ads@hawleyherald.net
Editorial e-mail: marc@hawleyherald.net
Primary Website: hawleyherald.net
Year Established: 1927
Avg Paid Circ: 1712
Audit By: Sworn/Estimate/Non-Audited
Audit Date: 10.06.2019
Personnel: Marc Ness (Ed.)

THE HENDRICKS PIONEER

Street address 1: 202 S Main St
Street address city: Hendricks
Street address state: MN
Zip/Postal code: 56136-1244
General Phone: (507) 275-3197
General Fax: (507) 275-3108
Editorial e-mail: hendrickspioneer@gmail.com
Primary Website: thehendrickspioneer.com
Year Established: 1900
Avg Paid Circ: 748
Audit By: Sworn/Estimate/Non-Audited
Audit Date: 10.06.2019
Personnel: Diane Clark (Co-Pub.); William Clark (Co-Pub.); Robert Wolsington (Ed.)

THE HOUSTON BANNER

Street address 1: 205 S Ellsworth St
Street address city: Houston
Street address state: MN
Zip/Postal code: 55943-8627
General Phone: (507) 896-2107
General Fax: (507) 896-2107
General/National Adv. E-mail: banner@acegroup.cc
Year Established: 1999
Avg Paid Circ: 578
Avg Free Circ: 15
Audit By: Sworn/Estimate/Non-Audited
Audit Date: 10.06.2019
Personnel: Ellyn Baumann (Ed.)

THE HUGO CITIZEN

Street address 1: 4779 Bloom Ave
Street address city: White Bear Lake
Street address state: MN
Zip/Postal code: 55110-2764
General Phone: (651) 407-1200
General Fax: (651) 407-1242
General/National Adv. E-mail: wbpressad3@presspubs.com
Display Adv. E-mail: classified@presspubs.com
Editorial e-mail: citizen@presspubs.com
Primary Website: readthecitizen.com
Year Established: 1998
Avg Free Circ: 8262
Audit By: Sworn/Estimate/Non-Audited
Audit Date: 10.06.2019
Personnel: Carter Johnson (Pub)
Parent company (for newspapers): Press Publications, Inc.

THE IVANHOE TIMES

Street address 1: 315 N Norman St
Street address city: Ivanhoe
Street address state: MN
Zip/Postal code: 56142-9580
General Phone: (507) 694-1246
General Fax: (507) 694-1246
Editorial e-mail: luminamin@yahoo.com
Primary Website: http://ivanhoetimes-com.webs.com
Avg Paid Circ: 847
Audit By: Sworn/Estimate/Non-Audited
Audit Date: 10.06.2019
Personnel: Brent Breck (Adv./Prod. Mgr.); Ellen Beck (Mng. Ed.)

THE JOURNAL

Street address 1: 1602 Highway 71
Street address city: International Falls
Street address state: MN
Zip/Postal code: 56649-2161
General Phone: (218) 285-7411
General Fax: (218) 285-7206
Advertising Phone: (218) 283-3377 ext 225
Advertising Fax: (218) 285-7206
Editorial Phone: (218) 283-3377 ext. 230
Editorial Fax: (218) 285-7206
General/National Adv. E-mail: karley@ifallsjournal.com
Display Adv. E-mail: wendy@ifallsjournal.com
Classified Adv. e-mail: classifieds@ifallsjournal.com
Editorial e-mail: laurel@ifallsdailyjournal.com
Primary Website: ifallsjournal.com
Year Established: 1911
Avg Paid Circ: 3109
Audit By: Sworn/Estimate/Non-Audited
Audit Date: 10.06.2019
Personnel: Rob Davenport (Pub.); Laurel Beager (Ed.); Emily Gedde (Reporter); Tammie Calder (Lifestyle Editor)
Parent company (for newspapers): Red Wing Publishing Co.

THE LAKE CITY GRAPHIC

Street address 1: 111 S 8th St
Street address city: Lake City
Street address state: MN
Zip/Postal code: 55041-1666
General Phone: (651) 345-3316
General Fax: (651) 345-4200
General/National Adv. E-mail: graphic@lakecitygraphic.com
Display Adv. E-mail: ads@lakecitygraphic.com
Classified Adv. e-mail: ads@lakecitygraphic.com
Editorial e-mail: andrew@lakecitygraphic.com
Primary Website: lakecitygraphic.com
Mthly Avg Views: 15000
Mthly Avg Unique Visitors: 5500
Year Established: 1861
Avg Paid Circ: 2250
Audit By: Sworn/Estimate/Non-Audited
Audit Date: 23.10.2019
Personnel: Terry Schumacher (Pub.); Dean Schumacher (Adv. Mgr.); Andrew Eggenberger (Editor)
Parent company (for newspapers): Lake City Printing Company

THE LAKER

Street address 1: 8 S Elm St
Street address city: Waconia
Street address state: MN
Zip/Postal code: 55387-1412
General Phone: (952) 442-4414
General Fax: (952) 442-6815
General/National Adv. E-mail: kristi.pexa@ecm-inc.com
Display Adv. E-mail: norma.carstensen@ecm-inc.com
Editorial e-mail: jason.schmucker@ecm-inc.com
Primary Website: lakerpioneer.com
Avg Paid Circ: 10
Avg Free Circ: 6499
Audit By: Sworn/Estimate/Non-Audited
Audit Date: 10.06.2019
Personnel: Kristi Pexa (Adv. Mgr.); Jason Schmucker (Ed.); Norma Carstensen (Class. Adv.)
Parent company (for newspapers): Adams Publishing Group, LLC

THE LITTLEFORK TIMES

Street address 1: 720 3rd Ave
Street address city: Littlefork
Street address state: MN
Zip/Postal code: 56653-2001
General Phone: (218) 278-4143
General Fax: (218) 278-4147
General/National Adv. E-mail: msfair@northwinds.net
Editorial e-mail: littleforktimes@frontiernet.net
Audit By: Sworn/Estimate/Non-Audited
Audit Date: 10.06.2019
Personnel: Stephanie Fairchild (Pub)

THE LONG PRAIRIE LEADER

Street address 1: 21 3rd St S
Street address city: Long Prairie
Street address state: MN
Zip/Postal code: 56347-1195
General Phone: (320) 732-2151
General Fax: (320) 732-2152
General/National Adv. E-mail: advertising@lpleader.com
Display Adv. E-mail: info@lpleader.com
Editorial e-mail: news@lpleader.com
Primary Website: lpleader.com
Year Established: 1883
Avg Paid Circ: 2392
Audit By: Sworn/Estimate/Non-Audited
Audit Date: 10.06.2019
Personnel: Jason Brown (Ed./Pub); Gary Brown (Bus. Mgr.); Susan Lubbers (Adv.)

THE LOWDOWN - FOREST LAKE AREA

Street address 1: 4779 Bloom Ave
Street address city: White Bear Lake
Street address state: MN
Zip/Postal code: 55110-2764
General Phone: (651) 407-1200
General Fax: (651) 429-1242
Advertising Phone: (651) 407-1213
Advertising Fax: (651) 429-1242
Editorial Phone: (651) 407-1200
Editorial Fax: (651) 429-1242
General/National Adv. E-mail: lowdown@presspubs.com
Display Adv. E-mail: classified@presspubs.com
Editorial e-mail: lowdownnews@presspubs.com
Primary Website: presspubs.com
Year Established: 1996
Avg Paid Circ: 62
Avg Free Circ: 2923
Audit By: Sworn/Estimate/Non-Audited
Audit Date: 10.10.2022
Personnel: Carter Johnson (Pub.)
Parent company (for newspapers): Press Publications, Inc.

THE LOWDOWN - ST. CROIX VALLEY AREA

Street address 1: 4779 Bloom Ave
Street address city: White Bear Lake
Street address state: MN
Zip/Postal code: 55110-2764
General Phone: (365) 407-1200
General Fax: (651) 429-1242
Advertising Phone: (651) 407-1213
Advertising Fax: (651) 429-1242
Editorial Phone: (651) 407-1200
Editorial Fax: (651) 407-1242
General/National Adv. E-mail: wbpressad3@presspubs.com
Display Adv. E-mail: classified@presspubs.com
Editorial e-mail: whitebearnews@presspubs.com
Primary Website: presspubs.com
Year Established: 1903
Avg Paid Circ: 125
Avg Free Circ: 2850
Audit By: VAC
Audit Date: 30.09.2017
Personnel: Carter Johnson (Pub)
Parent company (for newspapers): Press Publications, Inc.

THE MAHNOMEN PIONEER

Street address 1: 207 North Main Street
Street address city: Mahnomen
Street address state: MN
Zip/Postal code: 56557
General Phone: (218) 935-5296
General Fax: (218) 935-2555
General/National Adv. E-mail: mahpioneer@arvig.net
Editorial e-mail: mahedit@arvig.net
Primary Website: mahnomenpioneer.com
Year Established: 1905
Avg Paid Circ: 1600
Avg Free Circ: 100
Audit By: Sworn/Estimate/Non-Audited
Audit Date: 10.06.2019
Personnel: Sue Gruman Kraft (Ed.)

THE MARTIN COUNTY STAR

Street address 1: 30 N MAIN ST
Street address city: Sherburn
Street address state: MN
Zip/Postal code: 56171
General Phone: (507) 764-6681
General Fax: (507) 764-2756
Editorial e-mail: mcstar@frontiernet.net
Avg Paid Circ: 775
Audit By: Sworn/Estimate/Non-Audited
Audit Date: 10.06.2019
Personnel: Sheila Yurcek (Office Mgr.); Al Klein (Ed.)

THE MCLEOD COUNTY CHRONICLE

Street address 1: 716 E. 10th St.
Street address 2: PO Box 188
Street address city: Glencoe
Street address state: MN
Zip/Postal code: 55336-2212
General Phone: (320) 864-5518
General Fax: (320) 864-5510
General/National Adv. E-mail: brendaf@glencoenews.com
Display Adv. E-mail: suek@glencoenews.com
Editorial e-mail: bulletinnews@embarqmail.com
Primary Website: glencoenews.com
Avg Paid Circ: 3367
Avg Free Circ: 50
Audit By: Sworn/Estimate/Non-Audited
Audit Date: 10.06.2019
Personnel: Karin Ramige (Pub.); John Mueller (Ed.); Brenda Fogarty (Adv. Mgr.); Tom Carothers (Sports Ed.)

THE NEW PRAGUE TIMES

Street address 1: 200 Main St E
Street address city: New Prague

Street address state: MN
Zip/Postal code: 56071-2438
General Phone: (952) 758-4435
General Fax: (952) 758-4135
General/National Adv. E-mail: ads@newpraguetimes.com
Display Adv. E-mail: classifieds@newpraguetimes.com
Editorial e-mail: news@newpraguetimes.com
Primary Website: newpraguetimes.com
Year Established: 1889
Avg Paid Circ: 3700
Audit By: Sworn/Estimate/Non-Audited
Audit Date: 10.06.2019
Personnel: E. Charles Wann (Pub.); Mark Slavik (Adv. Mgr.); Chuck Kajer (Mng. Ed.)

THE NEWS MIRROR

Street address 1: 201 S. Main
Street address city: Hector
Street address state: MN
Zip/Postal code: 55342
General Phone: (320) 848-2248
General Fax: (320) 848-2249
General/National Adv. E-mail: newsmir@hcctel.net
Year Established: 1977
Avg Paid Circ: 1495
Audit By: Sworn/Estimate/Non-Audited
Audit Date: 10.06.2019
Personnel: Aaron Hubin (Adv. Mgr.); John Hubin (Ed.)

THE NORTHERN LIGHT REGION

Street address 1: 212 Main Ave. N
Street address 2: Suite A
Street address city: Baudette
Street address state: MN
Zip/Postal code: 56623
General Phone: (218) 634-2700
General Fax: (218) 634-2777
General/National Adv. E-mail: mikeh@wiktel.com
Editorial e-mail: norlight@wiktel.com
Primary Website: page1publications.com
Avg Paid Circ: 1415
Avg Free Circ: 38
Audit By: Sworn/Estimate/Non-Audited
Audit Date: 10.06.2019
Personnel: Julie M. Bergman (Pub.); Doris Knutson (Ed.)
Parent company (for newspapers): Page One Publications

THE OKLEE HERALD

Street address 1: 301 Main St
Street address city: Oklee
Street address state: MN
Zip/Postal code: 56742
General Phone: (218) 796-5181
General Fax: (218) 487-5251
General/National Adv. E-mail: richards@gvtel.com
Avg Paid Circ: 895
Audit By: Sworn/Estimate/Non-Audited
Audit Date: 10.06.2019
Personnel: Richard D. Richards (Pub.); Bonita Cote (Ed.)

THE ORTONVILLE INDEPENDENT

Street address 1: 789 US Highway 75
Street address city: Ortonville
Street address state: MN
Zip/Postal code: 56278-4084
General Phone: (320) 839-6163
General/National Adv. E-mail: mail@ortonvilleindependent.com
Display Adv. E-mail: ads@ortonvilleindependent.com
Classified Adv. e-mail: mail@ortonvilleindependent.com
Editorial e-mail: mail@ortonvilleindependent.com
Primary Website: ortonvilleindependent.com
Year Established: 1920
Avg Paid Circ: 2619
Avg Free Circ: 100
Audit By: Sworn/Estimate/Non-Audited
Audit Date: 10.06.2019
Personnel: Philip Blake (Pub.)
Parent company (for newspapers): Kaercher Publications, Inc.

THE PARK BUGLE

Street address 1: 2190 Como Ave
Street address city: Saint Paul
Street address state: MN
Zip/Postal code: 55108-1850
General Phone: (651) 646-5369
General/National Adv. E-mail: bradley.wolfe@parkbugle.org
Display Adv. E-mail: classifieds@parkbugle.org
Editorial e-mail: editor@parkbugle.org
Primary Website: parkbugle.com
Year Established: 1974
Audit By: Sworn/Estimate/Non-Audited
Audit Date: 10.06.2019
Personnel: Kristal Leebrick (Ed); Steve Parker (Prod. Mgr.); Bradley Wolfe (Adv. Mgr.)

THE PARKERS PRAIRIE INDEPENDENT, LLC

Street address 1: 117 N Otter Ave
Street address city: Parkers Prairie
Street address state: MN
Zip/Postal code: 56361-4996
General Phone: (218) 338-2741
General Fax: (218) 338-2745
Advertising Phone: (218) 338-2741
Advertising Fax: (218) 338-2745
Editorial Phone: (218) 338-2741
Editorial Fax: (218) 338-2745
General/National Adv. E-mail: ppinews@me.com
Display Adv. E-mail: ppinews@me.com
Editorial e-mail: ppinews@me.com
Primary Website: ppindependent.net
Year Established: 1902
Avg Paid Circ: 950
Audit By: Sworn/Estimate/Non-Audited
Audit Date: 10.06.2019
Personnel: Jakki Wehking (Co-Pub/Ed.); Jennifer Marquard (Pub.)

THE PILOT-INDEPENDENT

Street address 1: 408 MINNESOTA AVE
Street address city: Walker
Street address state: MN
Zip/Postal code: 56484
General Phone: (218) 547-1000
General Fax: (218) 547-3000
General/National Adv. E-mail: pilotads@pilotindependent.com
Display Adv. E-mail: pilotclassifieds@pilotindependent.com
Editorial e-mail: dmorrill@pilotindependent.com
Primary Website: walkermn.com
Year Established: 1900
Avg Paid Circ: 2200
Audit By: Sworn/Estimate/Non-Audited
Audit Date: 10.06.2019
Personnel: Dean Morrill (Ed.); Terri Fierstine (Gen. Mgr.); Deb Bitker (Circ. Mgr)

THE PINE JOURNAL

Street address 1: 424 W 1st St
Street address city: Duluth
Street address state: MN
Zip/Postal code: 55802-1516
General Phone: (218) 879-1950
General Fax: (218) 879-2078
Advertising Phone: (218) 590-8392
Editorial Phone: (218) 879-1950
General/National Adv. E-mail: news@pinejournal.com
Display Adv. E-mail: ads@pinejournal.com
Editorial e-mail: jpeterson@pinejournal.com
Primary Website: pinejournal.com
Year Established: 1884
Avg Paid Circ: 4471
Audit By: Sworn/Estimate/Non-Audited
Audit Date: 10.06.2019
Personnel: Neal Ronquist (Pub.); Jana Peterson (Ed); Mike Mazzio (Adv. Dir); Julie Fchulz (Bus. Mgr.)
Parent company (for newspapers): Forum Communications Co.

THE PIONEER

Street address 1: 8 S Elm St
Street address city: Waconia
Street address state: MN
Zip/Postal code: 55387-1412
General Phone: (952) 442-4414
General Fax: (952) 442-6815
General/National Adv. E-mail: kristi.pexa@ecm-inc.com
Display Adv. E-mail: norma.carstensen@ecm-inc.com
Editorial e-mail: jason.schmucker@ecm-inc.com
Primary Website: lakerpioneer.com
Avg Paid Circ: 15
Avg Free Circ: 11459
Audit By: Sworn/Estimate/Non-Audited
Audit Date: 10.06.2019
Personnel: Kristi Pexa (Adv. Mgr.); Norma Carstensen (Class. Adv.); Jason Schmucker (Ed.)
Parent company (for newspapers): Adams Publishing Group, LLC

THE POST REVIEW

Street address 1: 234 Main St S
Street address city: Cambridge
Street address state: MN
Zip/Postal code: 55008-1611
General Phone: (763) 691-6000
General Fax: (763) 689-4372
General/National Adv. E-mail: helen.rosing@ecm-inc.com
Editorial e-mail: derrick.knutson@ecm-inc.com
Primary Website: ecmpostreview.com
Year Established: 1875
Avg Paid Circ: 1259
Avg Free Circ: 0
Audit By: Sworn/Estimate/Non-Audited
Audit Date: 10.06.2019
Personnel: Julian Anderson (Pub.); Mary Eslinger (Adv. Mgr.); Mary Helen Swanson (Ed.)
Parent company (for newspapers): Adams Publishing Group, LLC

THE REDWOOD FALLS GAZETTE

Street address 1: 219 S Washington St
Street address city: Redwood Falls
Street address state: MN
Zip/Postal code: 56283-1700
General Phone: (507) 637-2929
General Fax: (507) 637-3175
General/National Adv. E-mail: sdahmes@redwoodfallsgazette.com
Display Adv. E-mail: sdahmes@redwoodfallsgazette.com
Editorial e-mail: t.krause@redwoodfallsgazette.com
Primary Website: redwoodfallsgazette.com
Avg Paid Circ: 1401
Audit By: Sworn/Estimate/Non-Audited
Audit Date: 10.06.2019
Personnel: Troy Krause (Ed.); Lisa Drafall (Gen Mgr)
Parent company (for newspapers): CherryRoad Media

THE REVIEW MESSENGER

Street address 1: 112 Minnesota Ave W
Street address city: Sebeka
Street address state: MN
Zip/Postal code: 56477-6004
General Phone: (218) 837-5558
General Fax: (218) 837-5560
General/National Adv. E-mail: remess@wcta.net
Display Adv. E-mail: remess@wcta.net
Classified Adv. e-mail: remess@wcta.net
Editorial e-mail: remess@wcta.net
Primary Website: lakeandpine.com
Year Established: 1898
Avg Paid Circ: 2958
Audit By: Sworn/Estimate/Non-Audited
Audit Date: 10.06.2019
Personnel: Timothy M. Bloomquist (Ed./Pub.); Bernice Eckenrode (Adv. Mgr.)

THE ROCK COUNTY STAR HERALD

Street address 1: 117 W Main St
Street address city: Luverne
Street address state: MN
Zip/Postal code: 56156-1843
General Phone: (507) 283-2333
General Fax: (507) 283-2335
General/National Adv. E-mail: sales@star-herald.com
Editorial e-mail: editor@star-herald.com
Primary Website: star-herald.com
Year Established: 1940
Avg Paid Circ: 2300
Audit By: Sworn/Estimate/Non-Audited
Audit Date: 10.06.2019
Personnel: Rick Peterson (Gen. Mgr.); Lori Ehde (Ed.); Glenda McGaffee (Ed.)

THE ROSEMOUNT TOWN PAGES

Street address 1: 312 Oak St
Street address city: Farmington
Street address state: MN
Zip/Postal code: 55024-1359
General Phone: (651) 460-6606
General Fax: (651) 463-7730
General/National Adv. E-mail: info@rosemounttownpages.com
Editorial e-mail: editor@rosemounttownpages.com
Primary Website: rosemounttownpages.com
Avg Paid Circ: 1594
Audit By: Sworn/Estimate/Non-Audited
Audit Date: 10.06.2019
Personnel: Chad Haelming (Gen. Mgr.); Nathan Hansen (Ed.); Jeff Mores (Mng. Ed.)
Parent company (for newspapers): Forum Communications Co.

THE ST. PAUL VOICE, DOWNTOWN ST. PAUL VOICE, SOUTH ST. PAUL VOICE AND LA VOZ LATINA

Street address 1: 1643 Robert St S
Street address 2: Suite 60B
Street address city: West St Paul
Street address state: MN
Zip/Postal code: 55118-4582
General Phone: (651) 457-1177
General/National Adv. E-mail: info@stpaulpublishing.com
Editorial e-mail: tim@stpaulpublishing.com
Primary Website: stpaulpublishing.com
Year Established: 1966
Avg Free Circ: 37500
Audit By: Sworn/Estimate/Non-Audited
Personnel: Tim Spitzack (Pub./Ed.); John Ahlstrom (Adv. Mgr.); Jake Spitzack (reporter); Caitlyn Fekete (Marketing Manager); John Ahlstrom (Sports writer); Leslie Martin (Copy editor)
Parent company (for newspapers): St. Paul Publishing Co.

THE STARBUCK TIMES

Street address 1: 14 1st Ave SE
Street address city: Glenwood
Street address state: MN
Zip/Postal code: 56334-1621
General Phone: (320) 239-2244
General Fax: (320) 239-2254
General/National Adv. E-mail: ads@pctribune.com
Display Adv. E-mail: locals@pctribune.com
Editorial e-mail: news.times@hcinet.net
Primary Website: pctribune.com/starbuck.php
Avg Paid Circ: 1320
Audit By: Sworn/Estimate/Non-Audited
Audit Date: 10.06.2019
Personnel: Tim Douglas (Pub); Zach Anderson (Ed); Erika Andreas (Gen. Mgr)

THE THIRTEEN TOWNS

Street address 1: 118 Johnson Ave N
Street address city: Fosston
Street address state: MN
Zip/Postal code: 56542-1328
General Phone: (218) 435-1313
General Fax: (218) 435-1309
General/National Adv. E-mail: ads13towns@gvtel.com
Editorial e-mail: 13towns@gvtel.com
Primary Website: 13Towns.com
Year Established: 1884
Avg Paid Circ: 1600
Audit By: Sworn/Estimate/Non-Audited
Audit Date: 10.06.2019
Personnel: Michael Moore (Pub.); Ed Lavelle (Ed.)
Parent company (for newspapers): Thirteen Towns of Fosston

THE VERNDALE SUN

Street address 1: 121 W Farewell St
Street address city: Verndale
Street address state: MN
Zip/Postal code: 56481
General Phone: (218) 445-6397
General Fax: (218) 756-2126

General/National Adv. E-mail: cindy@inhnews.com
Display Adv. E-mail: verndalesun@inhnews.com
Editorial e-mail: kathy@inhnews.com
Primary Website: inhnews.com
Avg Paid Circ: 870
Audit By: Sworn/Estimate/Non-Audited
Audit Date: 10.06.2019
Personnel: Marlo Benning (Co-Pub.); Ray Benning (Co-Pub.); Kathy Marquardt (Ed.)

THE VOYAGEUR PRESS OF MCGREGOR

Street address 1: 15 Country House Ln
Street address city: McGregor
Street address state: MN
Zip/Postal code: 55760-1417
General Phone: (218) 768-3405
General Fax: (218) 768-7046
General/National Adv. E-mail: vpofmg@frontiernet.net
Editorial e-mail: port
Primary Website: thevoyageurpress.com
Year Established: 2000
Avg Paid Circ: 1162
Audit By: Sworn/Estimate/Non-Audited
Audit Date: 10.06.2019
Personnel: John Grones (Pub.); Dora Potts (Ed/Office Mgr.); Lucia Grones (Circ. Mgr.)

THE WACONIA PATRIOT

Street address 1: 8 S Elm St
Street address city: Waconia
Street address state: MN
Zip/Postal code: 55387-1412
General Phone: (952) 442-4414
General Fax: (952) 442-6815
General/National Adv. E-mail: kristi.pexa@ecm-inc.com
Display Adv. E-mail: norma.carstensen@ecm-inc.com
Editorial e-mail: jason.schmucker@ecm-inc.com
Primary Website: waconiapatriot.com
Year Established: 1976
Avg Paid Circ: 4640
Avg Free Circ: 6528
Audit By: Sworn/Estimate/Non-Audited
Audit Date: 10.06.2019
Personnel: Marge Winkelman (Pres./COO); Kristi Pexa (Adv. Mgr.); Jason Schmucker (Ed.)
Parent company (for newspapers): Adams Publishing Group, LLC

THE WESTERN GUARD

Street address 1: 216 6th Ave
Street address city: Madison
Street address state: MN
Zip/Postal code: 56256-1309
General Phone: (320) 598-7521
General Fax: (320) 598-7523
General/National Adv. E-mail: ads.thewesternguard@gmail.com
Display Adv. E-mail: ads.thewesternguard@gmail.com
Editorial e-mail: news.thewesternguard@gmail.com
Year Established: 1891
Avg Paid Circ: 1691
Avg Free Circ: 15
Audit By: Sworn/Estimate/Non-Audited
Audit Date: 10.06.2019
Personnel: Adam Conroy (Pub.)
Parent company (for newspapers): RBM News

THE WINTHROP NEWS

Street address 1: 110 N Carver St
Street address city: Winthrop
Street address state: MN
Zip/Postal code: 55396-2800
General Phone: (507) 647-5357
General Fax: (507) 647-5358
Editorial e-mail: winthropnews@gmail.com
Avg Paid Circ: 1148
Audit By: Sworn/Estimate/Non-Audited
Audit Date: 10.06.2019
Personnel: Doug Hanson (Pub.); Michael Mattison (Ed.)

THIEF RIVER FALLS TIMES

Street address 1: 324 Main Ave N
Street address city: Thief River Falls
Street address state: MN
Zip/Postal code: 56701-1906
General Phone: (218) 681-4450
General Fax: (218) 681-4455
General/National Adv. E-mail: sales@trftimes.com
Display Adv. E-mail: classified@trftimes.com
Editorial e-mail: dhill@trftimes.com
Primary Website: trftimes.com
Year Established: 1910
Avg Paid Circ: 4997
Avg Free Circ: 71
Audit By: Sworn/Estimate/Non-Audited
Audit Date: 10.06.2019
Personnel: Dave Hill (Ed.); Sue Philipp (Circ. Mgr.); Kathy Svidal
Parent company (for newspapers): MCM Ohio LLC

THISWEEK BURNSVILLE-EAGAN SUN

Street address 1: 15322 Galaxie Ave
Street address 2: Suite 219
Street address city: Apple Valley
Street address state: MN
Zip/Postal code: 55124-3150
General Phone: (952) 894-1111
General Fax: (952) 846-2010
Advertising Phone: (952) 846-2000
General/National Adv. E-mail: gina.lee@ecm-inc.com
Display Adv. E-mail: judy.johnson@ecm-inc.com
Editorial e-mail: john.gessner@ecm-inc.com
Primary Website: sunthisweek.com
Year Established: 1979
Avg Paid Circ: 77
Avg Free Circ: 25733
Audit By: Sworn/Estimate/Non-Audited
Audit Date: 10.06.2019
Personnel: John Gessner (Ed.); Gina Lee (Adv.); Tad Johnson (Ed.)
Parent company (for newspapers): Adams Publishing Group, LLC

THISWEEK NEWSPAPERS

Street address 1: 15322 Galaxie Ave
Street address 2: Suite 219
Street address city: Apple Valley
Street address state: MN
Zip/Postal code: 55124-3150
General Phone: (952) 469-2181
General Fax: (952) 846-2010
General/National Adv. E-mail: mike.jetchick@ecm-inc.com
Editorial e-mail: tad.johnson@ecm-inc.com
Primary Website: http://sunthisweek.com/
Year Established: 1884
Avg Free Circ: 62000
Audit By: Sworn/Estimate/Non-Audited
Audit Date: 10.06.2019
Personnel: Julian Andereson (Pub.); Tad Johnson (Ed.); John Gessner (Ed.)
Parent company (for newspapers): CherryRoad Media

TIMBERJAY

Street address 1: 414 Main St
Street address city: Tower
Street address state: MN
Zip/Postal code: 55790-5105
General Phone: (218) 753-2950
General Fax: (218) 753-2916
General/National Adv. E-mail: editor@timberjay.com
Editorial e-mail: editor@timberjay.com
Primary Website: timberjay.com
Year Established: 1989
Avg Paid Circ: 3430
Avg Free Circ: 80
Audit By: Sworn/Estimate/Non-Audited
Audit Date: 10.06.2019
Personnel: Marshall Helmberger (Pub.); Jodi Summit (Adv. Mgr./Ed.); Mickey White (Circ. Mgr.); Keith Vandervort

TOWN & COUNTRY SHOPPER

Street address 1: 604 1st Ave S
Street address city: Saint James
Street address state: MN
Zip/Postal code: 56081-1729
General Phone: (507) 375-3161
General Fax: (507) 375-3221
General/National Adv. E-mail: ddurheim@stjamesnews.com
Avg Free Circ: 9648
Audit By: CVC
Audit Date: 03.09.2017
Personnel: Duane (Doc) Durheim (Gen. Mgr.)
Parent company (for newspapers): CherryRoad Media

TRACY HEADLIGHT-HERALD

Street address 1: 207 4th St
Street address city: Tracy
Street address state: MN
Zip/Postal code: 56175-1221
General Phone: (507) 629-4300
General Fax: (507) 629-4301
General/National Adv. E-mail: admanager@headlightherald.com
Display Adv. E-mail: kris@headlightherald.com
Editorial e-mail: per@headlightherald.com
Primary Website: headlightherald.com
Year Established: 1879
Avg Paid Circ: 1685
Avg Free Circ: 4600
Audit By: Sworn/Estimate/Non-Audited
Audit Date: 10.06.2019
Personnel: Lisa Sell (Adv. Mgr.); Seth Schmidt (Pub./Gen. Mgr.); Per Peterson (Ed.)
Parent company (for newspapers): Tracy Publishing Company, Inc

TRI COUNTY NEWS

Street address 1: 1 Barstad Rd N
Street address city: Cottonwood
Street address state: MN
Zip/Postal code: 56229-2269
General Phone: (507) 423-6239
General Fax: (507) 423-6230
Editorial e-mail: tcedit@mvtvwireless.com
Year Established: 1989
Avg Paid Circ: 842
Audit By: Sworn/Estimate/Non-Audited
Audit Date: 10.06.2019
Personnel: David Smigelski (Pub.)

TRI COUNTY NEWS

Street address 1: PO Box 227
Street address 2: 931 2nd Ave
Street address city: Heron Lake
Street address state: MN
Zip/Postal code: 56137-0227
General Phone: (507) 793-2327
General Fax: (507) 793-2327
Advertising Phone: (507) 793-2327
Advertising Fax: (507) 793-2327
Editorial Phone: (507) 793-2327
Editorial Fax: (507) 793-2327
General/National Adv. E-mail: tcnews@mysmbs.com
Display Adv. E-mail: tcnews@mysmbs.com
Editorial e-mail: tcnews@mysmbs.com
Primary Website: tricountynewsmn.net
Year Established: 1885
Avg Paid Circ: 797
Audit By: Sworn/Estimate/Non-Audited
Audit Date: 10.06.2019
Personnel: Gerald D. Johnson (Pub.); Carol Schreiber (Ed.)

TRIBUNE

Street address 1: 192 Hill St.
Street address city: Greenbush
Street address state: MN
Zip/Postal code: 56726
General Phone: (218) 782-2275
General/National Adv. E-mail: tribune@wiktel.com
Editorial e-mail: mavis@wiktel.com
Primary Website: page1publications.com
Avg Paid Circ: 986
Audit By: Sworn/Estimate/Non-Audited
Audit Date: 10.06.2019
Personnel: Rollin Bergman (Pub.); Julie Nordine (Ed.)
Parent company (for newspapers): Page 1 Publications. Inc/; Page One Publications

TRI-COUNTY NEWS

Street address 1: 70 S Main St
Street address city: Kimball
Street address state: MN
Zip/Postal code: 55353-1205
General Phone: (320) 398-5000
General Fax: (320) 398-5000
General/National Adv. E-mail: news@tricountynews.com
Display Adv. E-mail: ads@tricountynews.com
Editorial e-mail: editor@tricountynews.com
Primary Website: tricountynews.com
Mthly Avg Unique Visitors: 60000
Year Established: 1948
Avg Paid Circ: 1000
Avg Free Circ: 5500
Audit By: Sworn/Estimate/Non-Audited
Audit Date: 10.06.2019
Personnel: Jean Matua (Owner/Pub./Ed.); Maxine Doran (Office Asst); Barb Rose

TRI-COUNTY RECORD

Street address 1: 300 S Mill St
Street address 2: Ste 1
Street address city: Rushford
Street address state: MN
Zip/Postal code: 55971-8824
General Phone: (507) 864-7700
General Fax: (507) 864-2356
Advertising Phone: (507) 864-7700
Editorial Phone: (507) 864-7700
General/National Adv. E-mail: info@bluffcountrynews.com
Display Adv. E-mail: classifieds@bluffcountrynews.com
Editorial e-mail: sbestul@bluffcountrynews.com
Primary Website: rushford.net
Year Established: 1915
Avg Paid Circ: 1063
Avg Free Circ: 53
Audit By: Sworn/Estimate/Non-Audited
Audit Date: 10.06.2019
Personnel: David Phillips (Publisher)
Parent company (for newspapers): Bluff Country Newspaper Group; Phillips Publishing, Inc. - Bluff Country Newspaper Group

TRUMAN TRIBUNE

Street address 1: 118 E Ciro St
Street address city: Truman
Street address state: MN
Zip/Postal code: 56088-2017
General Phone: (507) 776-2751
General Fax: (507) 776-2751
General/National Adv. E-mail: neal@thetrumantribune.com
Editorial e-mail: thetrumantribune@gmail.com
Primary Website: thetrumantribune.com
Year Established: 1899
Avg Paid Circ: 821
Avg Free Circ: 250
Audit By: Sworn/Estimate/Non-Audited
Audit Date: 10.06.2019
Personnel: Nicole Meyer (Pub); Neal Meyer (Adv. Mgr.)

TYLER TRIBUTE

Street address 1: 124 N Tyler St
Street address city: Tyler
Street address state: MN
Zip/Postal code: 56178-1160
General Phone: (507) 247-5502
General Fax: (507) 247-5502
General/National Adv. E-mail: tributeadvertising@gmail.com
Editorial e-mail: tributeeditor@gmail.com
Primary Website: tylertribute.com
Avg Paid Circ: 1081
Avg Free Circ: 134
Audit By: Sworn/Estimate/Non-Audited
Audit Date: 10.06.2019
Personnel: Diane Clark (Co-Pub.); Robert Wolfington (Ed.); Mark Whimes (Co-Pub./Ed)

VADNAIS HEIGHTS PRESS

Street address 1: 4779 Bloom Ave
Street address city: White Bear Lake
Street address state: MN
Zip/Postal code: 55110-2764
General Phone: (365) 407-1200
General Fax: (651) 429-1242
Advertising Phone: (651) 407-1200
Advertising Fax: (651) 429-1242
Editorial Fax: (651) 429-1242
General/National Adv. E-mail: wbpressad1@presspubs.com
Display Adv. E-mail: classified@presspubs.com

Editorial e-mail: vadnaisheightsnews@presspubs.com
Primary Website: www.presspubs.com
Year Established: 1975
Avg Paid Circ: 226
Avg Free Circ: 3312
Audit By: VAC
Audit Date: 10.10.2022
Personnel: Carter Johnson (Pub.); Jill Twedt (Classified Adv. Mgr.); Patty Steele (Multi Marketing Director); Amy Johnson (Circulation Manager)
Parent company (for newspapers): Press Publications, Inc.

VILLAGER

Street address 1: 757 Snelling Ave S
Street address city: Saint Paul
Street address state: MN
Zip/Postal code: 55116-2296
General Phone: (651) 699-1462
General Fax: (651) 699-6501
General/National Adv. E-mail: vci@myvillager.com
Display Adv. E-mail: vci@myvillager.com
Editorial e-mail: vci@myvillager.com
Primary Website: myvillager.com
Year Established: 1953
Avg Paid Circ: 59
Avg Free Circ: 59830
Audit By: CVC
Audit Date: 18.03.2018
Personnel: Michael Mischke (Pub)

WABASSO STANDARD

Street address 1: 1034 Cedar St
Street address city: Wabasso
Street address state: MN
Zip/Postal code: 56293-1408
General Phone: (507) 342-5143
General Fax: (507) 342-5144
General/National Adv. E-mail: manderson@wabasso-standard.com
Editorial e-mail: manderson@wabasso-standard.com
Avg Paid Circ: 1200
Audit By: Sworn/Estimate/Non-Audited
Audit Date: 10.06.2019
Personnel: Pat Schmidt (Pub.)

WADENA PIONEER JOURNAL

Street address 1: 314 Jefferson St S
Street address city: Wadena
Street address state: MN
Zip/Postal code: 56482-1534
General Phone: (218) 631-2561
General Fax: (218) 631-1621
Editorial Phone: (218) 346-5900 x226
Editorial e-mail: editorial@wadenapj.com
Primary Website: wadenapj.com
Avg Paid Circ: 1860
Avg Free Circ: 38
Audit By: VAC
Audit Date: 30.09.2017
Personnel: Paula Quam (Ed.)
Parent company (for newspapers): Forum Communications Co.

WARREN SHEAF

Street address 1: 127 W Johnson Ave
Street address city: Warren
Street address state: MN
Zip/Postal code: 56762-1102
General Phone: (218) 745-5174
General Fax: (218) 745-5175
Editorial e-mail: warrensheaf@mncable.net
Primary Website: warrensheaf.net
Year Established: 1880
Avg Paid Circ: 1929
Audit By: Sworn/Estimate/Non-Audited
Audit Date: 10.06.2019
Personnel: Eric N. Mattson (Ed.)

WASECA COUNTY NEWS

Street address 1: 213 2nd St NW
Street address city: Waseca
Street address state: MN
Zip/Postal code: 56093-2401
General Phone: (507) 835-3380
General Fax: (507) 835-3435
General/National Adv. E-mail: kbiehn@wasecacountynews.com
Display Adv. E-mail: classifieds@wasecacountynews.com
Editorial e-mail: jfrazier@wasecacountynews.com
Primary Website: southernminn.com/waseca_county_news
Year Established: srook@wasecacountynews.com
Avg Paid Circ: 1907
Avg Free Circ: 100
Audit By: Sworn/Estimate/Non-Audited
Audit Date: 10.06.2019
Personnel: Suzanne Rook (Ed); Kristie Biehn (Adv.); Chad Hjellming (Gen. Mgr)
Parent company (for newspapers): Adams Publishing Group, LLC

WAYZATA/ORONO/PLYMOUTH/LONG LAKE SUN SAILOR

Street address 1: 10917 Valley View Rd
Street address city: Eden Prairie
Street address state: MN
Zip/Postal code: 55344-3730
General Phone: (952) 392-6800
General Fax: (952) 392-6802
Advertising Phone: (952) 392-6888
General/National Adv. E-mail: robbie.shoemaker@ecm-inc.com
Display Adv. E-mail: linda.bank@ecm-inc.com
Editorial e-mail: jared.huizenga@ecm-inc.com
Primary Website: http://sailor.mnsun.com/
Year Established: 1970
Avg Paid Circ: 146
Avg Free Circ: 18039
Audit By: Sworn/Estimate/Non-Audited
Audit Date: 10.06.2019
Personnel: Bob Cole (Pub.); Nathen Bliss (Adv. Dir.); Yvonne Klinnert (Mng. Ed.); Herb Hesse (Circ. Mgr.)
Parent company (for newspapers): Adams Publishing Group, LLC; American Community Newspapers LLC

WELLS MIRROR

Street address 1: 40 W Franklin St
Street address city: Wells
Street address state: MN
Zip/Postal code: 56097-1927
General Phone: (507) 553-3131
General Fax: (507) 553-3132
General/National Adv. E-mail: mirror.shopper@gmail.com
Editorial e-mail: mirror.shopper@gmail.com
Primary Website: https://facebook.com/Wells-Mirror-Shopper-461335810602923/about/?ref=page_internal
Avg Paid Circ: 1396
Avg Free Circ: 71
Audit By: Sworn/Estimate/Non-Audited
Audit Date: 10.06.2019
Personnel: Diana Brooks (Sales and Customer Service Representative); Jacob Winter (Staff Writer)

WEST DOUGLAS COUNTY RECORD

Street address 1: 510 Central Ave N
Street address city: Brandon
Street address state: MN
Zip/Postal code: 56315-4626
General Phone: (320) 834-4924
Editorial e-mail: wdrecord@gctel.com
Primary Website: westdouglascountyrecord.com
Year Established: 1979
Avg Paid Circ: 32
Avg Free Circ: 1530
Audit By: CVC
Audit Date: 30.09.2018
Personnel: Dave Bedore (Pub.)

WEST SHERBURNE TRIBUNE

Street address 1: 29 Lake St S
Street address city: Big Lake
Street address state: MN
Zip/Postal code: 55309-4588
General Phone: (763) 263-3602
General Fax: (763) 263-8458
General/National Adv. E-mail: westrib@sherbtel.net
Editorial e-mail: editor@westsherburnetribune.net
Primary Website: westsherburnetribune.com
Mthly Avg Views: 43376
Mthly Avg Unique Visitors: 17422
Year Established: 1979
Avg Paid Circ: 33
Avg Free Circ: 10920
Audit By: CVC
Audit Date: 30.09.2016
Personnel: Gary W. Meyer (Ed./Pub.); Shelley Berthiaume (Prod. Mgr.); Kathy LaClaire (Designer)

WESTBROOK SENTINEL TRIBUNE

Street address 1: 611 1st Ave
Street address city: Westbrook
Street address state: MN
Zip/Postal code: 56183-9500
General Phone: (507) 274-6136
General Fax: (507) 274-6137
General/National Adv. E-mail: pharms@ncppub.com
Editorial e-mail: sebeling@ncppub.com
Primary Website: ncppub.com
Avg Paid Circ: 997
Audit By: Sworn/Estimate/Non-Audited
Audit Date: 10.06.2019
Personnel: Jessica Jensen (Ed)
Parent company (for newspapers): New Century Press

WESTERN ITASCA REVIEW

Street address 1: 15 1st St NE
Street address city: Deer River
Street address state: MN
Zip/Postal code: 56636-8769
General Phone: (218) 246-8533
General Fax: (218) 246-8540
Editorial e-mail: drpub@paulbunyan.net
Primary Website: deerriverreviewmn.com
Year Established: 1896
Avg Paid Circ: 1618
Avg Free Circ: 22
Audit By: Sworn/Estimate/Non-Audited
Audit Date: 10.06.2019
Personnel: Rebecca Passeri (Pub.)

WHEATON GAZETTE

Street address 1: 1114 Broadway
Street address city: Wheaton
Street address state: MN
Zip/Postal code: 56296-1308
General Phone: (320) 563-8146
General Fax: (320) 563-8147
Editorial e-mail: wgazette@frontiernet.net
Year Established: 1885
Avg Paid Circ: 1750
Avg Free Circ: 26643
Audit By: Sworn/Estimate/Non-Audited
Audit Date: 10.06.2019
Personnel: Michael P. Kremer (Mng. Ed.)

WHITE BEAR PRESS

Street address 1: 4779 Bloom Ave
Street address city: White Bear Lake
Street address state: MN
Zip/Postal code: 55110-2764
General Phone: 651) 407-1200
General Fax: (651) 429-1242
General/National Adv. E-mail: ppinfo@presspubs.com
Display Adv. E-mail: marketing@presspubs.com
Editorial e-mail: news@presspubs.com
Primary Website: presspubs.com
Year Established: 1903
Audit By: VAC
Audit Date: 22.10.2021
Personnel: Carter Johnson (Pub.); Eugene Johnson (Pub Emeritus); Patty Steele; Greg Workman
Parent company (for newspapers): Press Publications, Inc.

WINONA POST

Street address 1: 64 E 2nd St
Street address city: Winona
Street address state: MN
Zip/Postal code: 55987-3409
General Phone: (507) 452-1262
General Fax: (507) 454-6409
General/National Adv. E-mail: farkas@winonapost.com
Display Adv. E-mail: class@winonapost.com
Editorial e-mail: winpost@winonapost.com
Primary Website: winonapost.com
Mthly Avg Views: 162885
Mthly Avg Unique Visitors: 12780
Year Established: 1971
Avg Paid Circ: 75
Avg Free Circ: 21973
Audit By: CVC
Audit Date: 30.09.2018
Personnel: Patrick Marek (VP/Pub.); Sarah Squires (Ed); Kim Farkas (Adv. Mgr); Twila Lorenz (Class. Adv); Mary Veraguth (Circ. Dir)

WOODBURY BULLETIN

Street address 1: PO Box 277
Street address city: Hastings
Street address state: MN
Zip/Postal code: 55033-0277
General Phone: (651) 319-4270
General Fax: (651) 702-0977
General/National Adv. E-mail: sengelhart@woodburybulletin.com
Editorial e-mail: editor@woodburybulletin.com
Primary Website: woodburybulletin.com
Avg Free Circ: 4892
Audit By: Sworn/Estimate/Non-Audited
Audit Date: 10.06.2019
Personnel: Hank Long (Ed.); Steve Engelhart (Adv. Dir); Jean Marie Brown
Parent company (for newspapers): Forum Communications Co.

WRIGHT COUNTY JOURNAL-PRESS

Street address 1: 108 Central Ave
Street address city: Buffalo
Street address state: MN
Zip/Postal code: 55313-1521
General Phone: (763) 682-1221
General Fax: (763) 682-5458
General/National Adv. E-mail: ads@thedummer.com
Editorial e-mail: edd@thedrummer.com
Primary Website: thedrummer.com
Year Established: 1887
Avg Paid Circ: 5230
Audit By: Sworn/Estimate/Non-Audited
Audit Date: 10.06.2019
Personnel: James P. McDonnell (Ed.)

MISSISSIPPI

BALDWYN NEWS

Street address 1: 102 W Main St
Street address city: Baldwyn
Street address state: MS
Zip/Postal code: 38824-1814
General Phone: (662) 365-3232
General Fax: (662) 365-7989
General/National Adv. E-mail: thebaldwynnews@dixie-net.com
Editorial e-mail: thebaldwynnews@dixie-net.com
Primary Website: facebook.com/The-Baldwyn-News-101395283376480
Avg Paid Circ: 2500
Avg Free Circ: 20
Audit By: Sworn/Estimate/Non-Audited
Audit Date: 10.06.2019
Personnel: Tammy Bullock (Mng. Ed.)

BANNER INDEPENDENT

Street address 1: 208 N Main St
Street address city: Booneville
Street address state: MS
Zip/Postal code: 38829-3317
General Phone: (662) 728-6214
General Fax: (662) 728-1636
Advertising Phone: (662) 287-6111 x339
Editorial Phone: (662) 287-6111 340
General/National Adv. E-mail: rterry@paxtonmedia.com
Display Adv. E-mail: classad@dailycorinthian.com
Classified Adv. e-mail: classad@dailycorinthian.com
Editorial e-mail: editor@boonevillebanner.com
Year Established: 1898
Avg Paid Circ: 3000
Avg Free Circ: 35
Audit By: Sworn/Estimate/Non-Audited
Audit Date: 10.06.2023

Personnel: Reese Terry (Publisher); Renee Johnson (Adv. Mgr.); Brant Sappington (Editor); Tom Tiernan (Sales Manager); Chris Enderle (Circ. Mgr.); Kenny Goode (Ed.)

BILOXI-D'IBERVILLE PRESS

Street address 1: 819 Jackson St
Street address city: Biloxi
Street address state: MS
Zip/Postal code: 39530-4235
General Phone: (228) 435-0720
General Fax: (228) 436-7737
General/National Adv. E-mail: ads@biloxi-diberville-press.com
Display Adv. E-mail: legal@biloxi-diberville-press.com
Editorial e-mail: news@biloxi-diberville-press.com
Primary Website: biloxi-diberville-press.com
Year Established: 1973
Avg Paid Circ: 4000
Avg Free Circ: 1000
Audit By: Sworn/Estimate/Non-Audited
Audit Date: 10.06.2019
Personnel: Vicki Fox (Production Mgr.); Cindy Picard (Pub.)
Parent company (for newspapers): Bay Corporation, Inc.

CHICKASAW JOURNAL

Street address 1: 225 E Madison St
Street address city: Houston
Street address state: MS
Zip/Postal code: 38851-2320
General Phone: (662) 456-3771
General Fax: (662) 456-5202
General/National Adv. E-mail: web@chickasawjournal.com
Display Adv. E-mail: advertising@chickasawjournal.com
Editorial e-mail: news@chickasawjournal.com
Primary Website: chickasawjournal.com
Avg Paid Circ: 2000
Avg Free Circ: 10500
Audit By: Sworn/Estimate/Non-Audited
Audit Date: 10.06.2019
Personnel: Lisa Boyles (Pub.)
Parent company (for newspapers): Journal Publishing Company

CLARKE COUNTY TRIBUNE

Street address 1: 101 Main St
Street address city: Quitman
Street address state: MS
Zip/Postal code: 39355-2119
General Phone: (601) 776-3726
General Fax: (601) 776-5793
General/National Adv. E-mail: mcranford@clarkecountytrib.com
Editorial e-mail: cbaxley@clarkecountytrib.com
Primary Website: http://clarkecountytrib.com/
Avg Paid Circ: 3735
Avg Free Circ: 50
Audit By: Sworn/Estimate/Non-Audited
Audit Date: 10.06.2019
Personnel: Wyatt Emmerich (Owner); Wade Bolen (Adv. Mgr.); Cindy Baxley (Ed.)
Parent company (for newspapers): 1976

COPIAH COUNTY COURIER

Street address 1: 103 S Ragsdale Ave
Street address city: Hazlehurst
Street address state: MS
Zip/Postal code: 39083-3037
General Phone: (601) 894-3141
General Fax: (601) 894-3144
General/National Adv. E-mail: Publisher@copiahcountycourier.com
Display Adv. E-mail: Office@copiahcountycourier.com
Editorial e-mail: Publisher@copiahcountycourier.com
Primary Website: copiahcountycourier.com
Year Established: 1874
Avg Paid Circ: 4400
Avg Free Circ: 1600
Audit By: Sworn/Estimate/Non-Audited
Audit Date: 10.06.2019
Personnel: John Carney (Publisher, Marketing Director, Account Rep Editor, Sports Director)

DEER CREEK PILOT

Street address 1: 145 N First St
Street address city: Rolling Fork
Street address state: MS
Zip/Postal code: 39159-2749
General Phone: (662) 873-4354
General Fax: (662) 873-4355
General/National Adv. E-mail: deercreekpilot@bellsouth.net
Editorial e-mail: deercreekpilot@bellsouth.net
Avg Paid Circ: 1500
Avg Free Circ: 50
Audit By: Sworn/Estimate/Non-Audited
Audit Date: 10.06.2019
Personnel: Ray Mosby (Ed.)

DESOTO TIMES-TRIBUNE

Street address 1: 2445 Highway 51 S
Street address city: Hernando
Street address state: MS
Zip/Postal code: 38632-1734
General Phone: (662) 429-6397
General Fax: (662) 429-5229
Advertising Phone: (662) 429-6397 ext. 227
Advertising Fax: (662) 429-5229
Editorial Phone: (662) 429-6397 ext. 247
Editorial Fax: (662) 429-5229
General/National Adv. E-mail: lyla@dttclick.com
Display Adv. E-mail: classifieds@desototimestribune.com
Classified Adv. e-mail: classifieds@desototimestribune.com
Editorial e-mail: editor@desototimestribune.com
Primary Website: desototimes.com
Year Established: 1839
Avg Paid Circ: 7810
Sat. Circulation Paid: 7810
Audit By: Sworn/Estimate/Non-Audited
Audit Date: 10.06.2019
Personnel: Terri Smith (News Ed.); Angie Pittman (Dir. of Marketing & Adv.)

FAYETTE CHRONICLE

Street address 1: 501 Main St
Street address city: Fayette
Street address state: MS
Zip/Postal code: 39069
General Phone: (601) 786-3661
General Fax: (601) 786-3661
General/National Adv. E-mail: fayettenews@hotmail.com
Display Adv. E-mail: fayette1866@aol.com
Editorial e-mail: fayettenews@hotmail.com
Primary Website: http://fayettenews.tripod.com/
Avg Paid Circ: 2500
Avg Free Circ: 35
Audit By: Sworn/Estimate/Non-Audited
Audit Date: 10.06.2019
Personnel: Tenodra M. Shepphard (Adv. Mgr.); Ashanta A. Shepphard (Circ. Mgr.); Charles K. Shepphard (Ed.); Joe Turner (Office Manager)

FRANKLIN ADVOCATE

Street address 1: 111 MAIN ST E
Street address city: Meadville
Street address state: MS
Zip/Postal code: 39653
General Phone: (601) 384-2484
General Fax: (601) 384-2276
General/National Adv. E-mail: advocate@telepak.net
Primary Website: http://franklinadvocate.com/
Year Established: 1890
Avg Paid Circ: 3200
Avg Free Circ: 12
Audit By: Sworn/Estimate/Non-Audited
Audit Date: 10.06.2019
Personnel: Mary Lou Webb (Pub. Emeritus); Heather Jacobs (Pub./Ed.); Marsha Webb (Ed./Pub.)

GEORGE COUNTY TIMES

Street address 1: 5133 Main St
Street address city: Lucedale
Street address state: MS
Zip/Postal code: 39452-6523
General Phone: (601) 947-2967
General Fax: (601) 947-6828
General/National Adv. E-mail: gctimes@bellsouth.net
Avg Paid Circ: 6300
Audit By: Sworn/Estimate/Non-Audited
Audit Date: 10.06.2019
Personnel: O.G. Sellers (Ed.)

GREENE COUNTY HERALD

Street address 1: 431 MAIN STREET
Street address 2: P.O. BOX 220
Street address city: Leakesville
Street address state: MS
Zip/Postal code: 39451-6502
General Phone: (601) 394-5070
General Fax: (601)394-4389
General/National Adv. E-mail: herald@tds.net
Display Adv. E-mail: advertising_gcherald@tds.net
Editorial e-mail: herald@tds.net
Primary Website: greenecountyheraldonline.com
Year Established: 1898
Avg Paid Circ: 2200
Avg Free Circ: 52
Audit By: Sworn/Estimate/Non-Audited
Audit Date: 12.10.2023
Personnel: Russell Turner (Ed.); Leola Turner (Pub.); Joni Cooley McMillon (Adv. Dir.)
Parent company (for newspapers): THE TURNER GROUP LLC

HATTIESBURG AMERICAN

Street address 1: 4200 Mamie St
Street address 2: Ste 200
Street address city: Hattiesburg
Street address state: MS
Zip/Postal code: 39402-1729
General Phone: (601) 582-4321
General Fax: (601) 584-3075
Advertising Phone: (601) 582-4321
Advertising Fax: (601)584-3074
Editorial Phone: (601)584-3070
Editorial Fax: (601) 584-3130
General/National Adv. E-mail: tfowler@hattiesburgamerican.com
Display Adv. E-mail: tfowler@hattiesburgamerican.com
Classified Adv. e-mail: tfowler@hattiesburgamerican.com
Editorial e-mail: tfowler@hattiesburgamerican.com
Primary Website: hattiesburgamerican.com
Mthly Avg Unique Visitors: 248190
Year Established: 1897
Avg Paid Circ: 6722
Avg Free Circ: 61
Sat. Circulation Paid: 6886
Sat. Circulation Free: 106
Sun. Circulation Paid: 9461
Audit By: AAM
Audit Date: 31.12.2018
Personnel: Sam Hall (Exec. Ed.); Adrianne Dunn (Dir. of Sales); Elizabeth Morgan (Reg Acct Exec)
Parent company (for newspapers): Gannett

HOLMES COUNTY HERALD

Street address 1: 308 Court Sq
Street address city: Lexington
Street address state: MS
Zip/Postal code: 39095-3636
General Phone: (662) 834-1151
General Fax: (662) 834-1074
General/National Adv. E-mail: hcherald@gmail.com
Primary Website: holmescountyherald.com
Year Established: 1959
Avg Paid Circ: 2000
Audit By: Sworn/Estimate/Non-Audited
Audit Date: 10.06.2019
Personnel: Julie Ellison (General Manager); Matthew Breazeale (Editor)

KEMPER COUNTY MESSENGER

Street address 1: 102 Main Ave
Street address city: De Kalb
Street address state: MS
Zip/Postal code: 39328-6381
General Phone: (601) 743-5760
General Fax: (601) 743-4430
Editorial Phone: (601) 938-2471
Primary Website: http://kempercountymessenger.com/
Avg Paid Circ: 2100
Avg Free Circ: 85
Audit By: Sworn/Estimate/Non-Audited
Audit Date: 10.06.2019
Personnel: Jim Prince (Pub.); Carver Rayburen (Ed.)

LAUREL LEADER-CALL

Street address 1: 318 N Magnolia St
Street address city: Laurel
Street address state: MS
Zip/Postal code: 39440-3932
General Phone: (601) 649-9388
General Fax: (601) 649-9390
General/National Adv. E-mail: reporter@leader-call.com
Display Adv. E-mail: legals@leader-call.com
Classified Adv. e-mail: classifieds@leader-call.net
Editorial e-mail: murph@leader-call.com
Primary Website: leader-call.com
Year Established: 1911
Avg Paid Circ: 7500
Sat. Circulation Paid: 7100
Audit By: Sworn/Estimate/Non-Audited
Audit Date: 10.06.2019
Personnel: Mark Thornton (Editor); Robin Bice (Gen. Mgr.); Sean Murphy (Managing editor); Jim Cegielski (Publisher)
Parent company (for newspapers): CNHI, LLC

LAWRENCE COUNTY PRESS

Street address 1: 296 F E Sellers Hwy
Street address city: Monticello
Street address state: MS
Zip/Postal code: 39654-9555
General Phone: (601) 587-2781
General/National Adv. E-mail: info@lawrencecountypress.com
Display Adv. E-mail: info@lawrencecountypress.com
Editorial e-mail: info@lawrencecountypress.com
Primary Website: lawrencecountypress.com
Year Established: 1888
Avg Paid Circ: 1600
Audit By: Sworn/Estimate/Non-Audited
Audit Date: 10.06.2019
Personnel: J.J. Carney (Assoc. Ed.); John H. Carney (Pub./Ed./News Ed./Adv. Mgr.); Kelsey Wells Lambert (Mng Ed.)

LELAND PROGRESS

Street address 1: 119 E 3rd St
Street address city: Leland
Street address state: MS
Zip/Postal code: 38756-2705
General Phone: (662) 771-4012
General Fax: (662) 580-4068
General/National Adv. E-mail: editor@thelelandprogress.com
Display Adv. E-mail: editor@thelelandprogress.com
Editorial e-mail: editor@thelelandprogress.com
Primary Website: thelelandprogress.com
Year Established: 1897
Avg Paid Circ: 1000
Avg Free Circ: 50
Audit By: Sworn/Estimate/Non-Audited
Audit Date: 10.06.2019
Personnel: Stephanie Patton (Publisher/Editor)

MACON BEACON

Street address 1: 2904 Jefferson St
Street address city: Macon
Street address state: MS
Zip/Postal code: 39341-2273
General Phone: (662) 726-4747
General Fax: (662) 726-4742
General/National Adv. E-mail: maconbeacon@aol.com
Display Adv. E-mail: maconbeacon@aol.com
Editorial e-mail: maconbeacon@aol.com
Primary Website: facebook.com/MaconBeacon
Year Established: 1849
Avg Paid Circ: 3100
Avg Free Circ: 40
Audit By: Sworn/Estimate/Non-Audited
Audit Date: 10.06.2019
Personnel: R. Scott Boyd (Ed.)

MADISON COUNTY JOURNAL

Street address 1: 293 Commerce Park Dr
Street address city: Ridgeland

Street address state: MS
Zip/Postal code: 39157-2233
General Phone: (601) 853-4222
General Fax: (601) 856-9419
General/National Adv. E-mail: msimmons@onlinemadison.com
Display Adv. E-mail: msimmons@onlinemadison.com
Editorial e-mail: msimmons@onlinemadison.com
Primary Website: onlinemadison.com
Year Established: 1982
Avg Paid Circ: 3600
Audit By: Sworn/Estimate/Non-Audited
Audit Date: 10.06.2019
Personnel: Jim Prince (Ed.); Michael Simmons (Associate Ed/Pub)
Parent company (for newspapers): Prince Newspaper Holdings

MISSISSIPPI BUSINESS JOURNAL

Street address 1: 200 N Congress St
Street address 2: Suite 400
Street address city: Jackson
Street address state: MS
Zip/Postal code: 39201-1902
General Phone: (601) 364-1011
General Fax: (601) 364-1007
Advertising Phone: (601) 364-1011
Editorial Phone: (601) 364-1018
Editorial Fax: (601) 364-1035
General/National Adv. E-mail: tami.jones@msbusiness.com
Display Adv. E-mail: tami.jones@msbusiness.com
Editorial e-mail: ross.reily@msbusiness.com
Primary Website: msbusiness.com
Year Established: 1978
Avg Paid Circ: 3941
Avg Free Circ: 174
Audit By: Sworn/Estimate/Non-Audited
Audit Date: 10.06.2019
Personnel: Alan Turner; Ross Reily (Editor); Tami Jones (Associate Publisher); Tacy Rayburn (Prod Mgr); Charins Rhodes (Circ. Mng.)
Parent company (for newspapers): Journal Inc.

MONROE COUNTY JOURNAL

Street address 1: 115 Main St S
Street address city: Amory
Street address state: MS
Zip/Postal code: 38821-3407
General Phone: (662) 256-5647
General Fax: (662) 256-5701
General/National Adv. E-mail: advertisingmonroe@journalinc.com
Display Adv. E-mail: advertisingmonroe@journalinc.com
Editorial e-mail: news1monroe@journalinc.com
Primary Website: djournal.com/monroe
Avg Paid Circ: 7300
Avg Free Circ: 132
Audit By: Sworn/Estimate/Non-Audited
Audit Date: 10.06.2019
Personnel: Chris Wilson (Ed.)
Parent company (for newspapers): Journal Publishing Company

NEW ALBANY GAZETTE

Street address 1: PO Box 300
Street address city: New Albany
Street address state: MS
Zip/Postal code: 38652-0300
General Phone: (662) 534-6321
General Fax: (662) 534-6355
General/National Adv. E-mail: advertising@newalbanygazette.com
Display Adv. E-mail: classifieds@newalbanygazette.com
Editorial e-mail: news@newalbanygazette.com
Primary Website: djournal.com/new-albany
Year Established: 1889
Avg Paid Circ: 4200
Avg Free Circ: 12000
Audit By: Sworn/Estimate/Non-Audited
Audit Date: 10.06.2019
Personnel: T. Wayne Mitchell (Pub.); David Johnson (Managing Ed.); J. Lynn West (Editor)
Parent company (for newspapers): Journal Inc.

NORTH MISSISSIPPI HERALD

Street address 1: 416 N Main St
Street address city: Water Valley
Street address state: MS
Zip/Postal code: 38965-2506
General Phone: (662) 473-1473
General Fax: (662) 473-9133
Editorial Phone: (662) 473-8444
General/National Adv. E-mail: heraldads@bellsouth.net
Editorial e-mail: dhowl@bellsouth.net
Primary Website: yalnews.com
Avg Paid Circ: 2900
Avg Free Circ: 102
Audit By: Sworn/Estimate/Non-Audited
Audit Date: 10.06.2019
Personnel: Betty Shearer (Gen. Mgr.); David Howell (Ed.)

NORTHSIDE SUN

Street address 1: 246 Briarwood Dr
Street address city: Jackson
Street address state: MS
Zip/Postal code: 39206-3027
General Phone: (601) 957-1122
General Fax: (601) 957-1533
Advertising Phone: (601) 977-8181
Editorial Phone: (601) 957-1123
General/National Adv. E-mail: jennifer@northsidesun.com
Display Adv. E-mail: lauren@northsidesun.com
Editorial e-mail: jimmye@northsidesun.com
Primary Website: northsidesun.com
Avg Paid Circ: 11144
Avg Free Circ: 548
Audit By: Sworn/Estimate/Non-Audited
Audit Date: 10.06.2019
Personnel: J. Wyatt Emmerich (Pub./Adv. Mgr.); Jimmye Sweat (Ed.); Dani Poe (Circ. Mgr.)
Parent company (for newspapers): 1976

OCEAN SPRINGS RECORD

Street address 1: 807 Holcomb Blvd
Street address city: Ocean Springs
Street address state: MS
Zip/Postal code: 39564-3943
General Phone: (228)207-4709
General Fax: (228)207-4678
General/National Adv. E-mail: adv@osrecord.com
Display Adv. E-mail: adv@osrecord.com
Editorial e-mail: editor@osrecord.com
Primary Website: osrecord.com
Year Established: 1965
Avg Paid Circ: 3500
Avg Free Circ: 500
Audit By: Sworn/Estimate/Non-Audited
Audit Date: 10.06.2019
Personnel: Gene Coleman (Editor); Leigh Colman (Pub.)

OKOLONA MESSENGER

Street address 1: 249 W Main St
Street address city: Okolona
Street address state: MS
Zip/Postal code: 38860-1498
General Phone: (662) 447-5501
General/National Adv. E-mail: okmessenger@bellsouth.net
Primary Website: facebook.com/pages/Okolona-Messenger
Avg Paid Circ: 1300
Avg Free Circ: 19
Audit By: Sworn/Estimate/Non-Audited
Audit Date: 10.06.2019
Personnel: Murry Blankenship (Ed.)

PONTOTOC PROGRESS

Street address 1: 13 E Jefferson St
Street address city: Pontotoc
Street address state: MS
Zip/Postal code: 38863-2807
General Phone: (662) 489-3511
General Fax: (662) 489-6714
General/National Adv. E-mail: pontotoc.advertising@journainc.com
Display Adv. E-mail: pontotoc.advertising@journainc.com
Editorial e-mail: pontotoc.news@journalinc.com
Primary Website: http://pontotoc-progress.com/
Year Established: 1929
Avg Paid Circ: 7800
Avg Free Circ: 221
Audit By: Sworn/Estimate/Non-Audited
Audit Date: 10.06.2019
Personnel: Brenda Owen (Mng. Ed.)
Parent company (for newspapers): Journal Publishing Company

PRENTISS HEADLIGHT

Street address 1: 1020 Third St
Street address city: Prentiss
Street address state: MS
Zip/Postal code: 39474-6002
General Phone: (601) 792-4221
General Fax: (601) 792-4222
General/National Adv. E-mail: editor@prentissheadlight.com
Display Adv. E-mail: business@prentissheadlight.com
Editorial e-mail: holley.cochran@prentissheadlight.com
Primary Website: dailyleader.com/prentiss
Year Established: 1906
Avg Paid Circ: 1568
Avg Free Circ: 25
Audit By: Sworn/Estimate/Non-Audited
Audit Date: 10.06.2019
Personnel: Karen Sanford (Ed./Gen. Mgr.); Rick Reynolds (Pres./Pub.)
Parent company (for newspapers): Prentiss Publishers, Inc

RANKIN COUNTY NEWS

Street address 1: 207 E Government St
Street address city: Brandon
Street address state: MS
Zip/Postal code: 39042-3151
General Phone: (601) 825-8333
General Fax: (601) 825-8334
General/National Adv. E-mail: rankincn@bellsouth.net
Display Adv. E-mail: rankincn@bellsouth.net
Editorial e-mail: rankincn@aol.com
Primary Website: rankincn.com
Year Established: 1852
Avg Paid Circ: 8000
Audit By: Sworn/Estimate/Non-Audited
Audit Date: 10.06.2019
Personnel: Marcus R. Bowers (Ed.)

SCOTT COUNTY TIMES

Street address 1: 311 Smith Ave
Street address city: Forest
Street address state: MS
Zip/Postal code: 39074-4159
General Phone: (601) 469-2561
General Fax: (601) 469-2004
General/National Adv. E-mail: blatham@sctonline.net
Display Adv. E-mail: charrell@sctonline.net
Editorial e-mail: cbaker@sctonline.net
Primary Website: sctonline.net
Avg Paid Circ: 5500
Avg Free Circ: 4000
Audit By: Sworn/Estimate/Non-Audited
Audit Date: 10.06.2019
Personnel: Tim Beeland (Pub.); Courtney Robinson (Features Ed.); Chris Allen Baker (Sports Ed.)
Parent company (for newspapers): 1976

SEA COAST ECHO

Street address 1: 124 Court St
Street address city: Bay Saint Louis
Street address state: MS
Zip/Postal code: 39520-4516
General Phone: (228) 467-5473
General Fax: (228) 467-0333
Advertising Phone: (228) 467-5474
Advertising Fax: (228) 467-0333
General/National Adv. E-mail: gbelcher@seacoastecho.com
Display Adv. E-mail: classifieds@seacoastecho.com
Editorial e-mail: rponder@seacoastecho.com
Primary Website: seacoastecho.com
Mthly Avg Views: 350000
Mthly Avg Unique Visitors: 80000
Year Established: 1892
Avg Paid Circ: 6100
Audit By: Sworn/Estimate/Non-Audited
Audit Date: 10.06.2019
Personnel: James Randy Ponder (Pub./Ed.); Geoff Belcher (News Ed)
Parent company (for newspapers): Lancaster Management, Inc.

SIMPSON COUNTY NEWS

Street address 1: 206 Main Ave N
Street address city: Magee
Street address state: MS
Zip/Postal code: 39111-3536
General Phone: (601) 847-2525
General Fax: (601) 847-2571
Advertising Phone: (601) 849-3434
Editorial Phone: (601) 849-3434
General/National Adv. E-mail: nbrown@mageecourier.ms
Display Adv. E-mail: mbratcher@countynews.ms
Editorial e-mail: pbrown@mageecourier.ms
Primary Website: simpsoncounty.ms
Avg Paid Circ: 3750
Avg Free Circ: 40
Audit By: Sworn/Estimate/Non-Audited
Audit Date: 10.06.2019
Personnel: Marsha Bratcher (Circ. Mgr.); Pat Brown (Ed.)
Parent company (for newspapers): 1976

SMITH COUNTY REFORMER

Street address 1: 153 MAIN ST
Street address city: Raleigh
Street address state: MS
Zip/Postal code: 39153
General Phone: (601) 782-4358
General Fax: (601) 782-9081
General/National Adv. E-mail: ads@smithcountyreformer.net
Display Adv. E-mail: legals@smithcountyreformer.net
Editorial e-mail: ads@smithcountyreformer.net
Year Established: 1889
Avg Paid Circ: 2965
Avg Free Circ: 720
Audit By: Sworn/Estimate/Non-Audited
Audit Date: 10.06.2019
Personnel: Brenda Ingram (Gen. Mgr./Marketing)
Parent company (for newspapers): Buckley Newspapers

SOUTH REPORTER

Street address 1: 157 S Center St
Street address city: Holly Springs
Street address state: MS
Zip/Postal code: 38635-3040
General Phone: (662) 252-4261
General Fax: (662) 252-3388
General/National Adv. E-mail: southreporter@dixie-net.com
Display Adv. E-mail: southreporter@dixie-net.com
Editorial e-mail: southreporter@dixie-net.com
Primary Website: southreporter.com
Year Established: 1865
Avg Paid Circ: 5200
Avg Free Circ: 52
Audit By: Sworn/Estimate/Non-Audited
Audit Date: 10.06.2019
Personnel: Barry Burleson (Ed.); Barbara Taylor (Prodn. Mgr.)

SOUTHERN ADVOCATE

Street address 1: 1701 City Ave N
Street address city: Ripley
Street address state: MS
Zip/Postal code: 38663-1124
General Phone: (662) 837-8111
General Fax: (662) 837-4504
General/National Adv. E-mail: advertising@tippah360.com
Display Adv. E-mail: advertising@tippah360.com
Editorial e-mail: news@tippah360.com
Primary Website: http://southern-advocate.com
Avg Paid Circ: 1600
Audit By: Sworn/Estimate/Non-Audited
Audit Date: 10.06.2019
Personnel: Tim Watson (Pub.); Gene Ladnier (Mng. Ed.)
Parent company (for newspapers): Journal Publishing Company

SOUTHERN SENTINEL

Street address 1: 1701 City Ave N
Street address city: Ripley
Street address state: MS

Zip/Postal code: 38663-1124
General Phone: (662) 837-8111
General Fax: (662) 837-4504
General/National Adv. E-mail: advertising@tippah360.com
Display Adv. E-mail: advertising@tippah360.com
Editorial e-mail: news@tippah360.com
Primary Website: http://southern-advocate.com
Year Established: 1879
Avg Paid Circ: 6800
Audit By: Sworn/Estimate/Non-Audited
Audit Date: 10.06.2019
Personnel: Tina Campbell (Asst. Pub.); Jessica Davis (Office Mgr.); Joyce Brock (News Ed.); Tim Watson (Pub.)
Parent company (for newspapers): Journal Publishing Company

SOUTHWEST SUN

Street address 1: 113 OLIVER EMMERICH DR
Street address city: McComb
Street address state: MS
Zip/Postal code: 39648
General Phone: (601) 684-2421
General Fax: (601) 684-0836
General/National Adv. E-mail: advertising@enterprise-journal.com
Display Adv. E-mail: classifieds@enterprise-journal.com
Editorial e-mail: publisher@enterprise-journal.com
Primary Website: enterprise-journal.com
Avg Free Circ: 8500
Audit By: Sworn/Estimate/Non-Audited
Audit Date: 10.06.2019
Personnel: Lauren Devereaux (Adv. Mgr.); Tammy Britt (Circ. Mgr.); Jack Ryan (Ed.); Matt Williamson (Mng. Ed.); Keith Hux (Prodn. Mgr.)
Parent company (for newspapers): 1976

STONE COUNTY ENTERPRISE

Street address 1: 143 First St S
Street address city: Wiggins
Street address state: MS
Zip/Postal code: 39577-2733
General Phone: (601) 928-4802
General Fax: (601) 928-2191
General/National Adv. E-mail: sales@stonecountyenterprise.com
Display Adv. E-mail: classifieds@stonecountyenterprise.com
Editorial e-mail: editor@stonecountyenterprise.com
Primary Website: stonecountyenterprise.com
Year Established: 1916
Avg Paid Circ: 3000
Avg Free Circ: 25
Audit By: Sworn/Estimate/Non-Audited
Audit Date: 10.06.2019
Personnel: Heather Anderson (Ed./Pub.); Jody O'Hara (Staff Writer); Alexis Nichols (Classified Clerk); Abigail Voda (Marketing Specialist)
Parent company (for newspapers): Lancaster Management, Inc.

THE BELZONI BANNER

Street address 1: 115 E Jackson St
Street address city: Belzoni
Street address state: MS
Zip/Postal code: 39038-3641
General Phone: (662) 247-3373
General Fax: (662) 247-3372
General/National Adv. E-mail: editor@thebelzonibanner.com
Display Adv. E-mail: editor@thebelzonibanner.com
Editorial e-mail: editor@thebelzonibanner.com
Primary Website: thebelzonibanner.com
Year Established: 1914
Avg Paid Circ: 950
Avg Free Circ: 25
Audit By: Sworn/Estimate/Non-Audited
Audit Date: 10.06.2019
Personnel: Julian Toney (Ed.)

THE CALHOUN COUNTY JOURNAL

Street address 1: PO Box 278
Street address city: Bruce
Street address state: MS
Zip/Postal code: 38915-0278
General Phone: (662) 983-2570
General Fax: (662) 983-7667
Advertising Phone: (662) 983-2570
Advertising Fax: (662) 983-7667
Editorial Phone: (662) 983-2570
Editorial Fax: (662) 983-7667
General/National Adv. E-mail: joelmcneece@gmail.com
Display Adv. E-mail: lisamcneece@gmail.com
Editorial e-mail: calhouncountyjournal@gmail.com
Primary Website: calhouncountyjournal.com
Year Established: [illegible].53
Avg Paid Circ: 4700
Audit By: Sworn/Estimate/Non-Audited
Audit Date: 10.06.2019
Personnel: Joel McNeece (Pub.); Lisa McNeece (Adv. Mgr.)

THE CARTHAGINIAN

Street address 1: 123 E Main St
Street address city: Carthage
Street address state: MS
Zip/Postal code: 39051-4102
General Phone: (601) 267-4501
General Fax: (601) 267-5290
General/National Adv. E-mail: ads@thecarthaginian.com
Display Adv. E-mail: ads@thecarthaginian.com
Editorial e-mail: brendah@thecarthaginian.com
Primary Website: thecarthaginian.com
Year Established: 1872
Avg Paid Circ: 5700
Avg Free Circ: 59
Audit By: Sworn/Estimate/Non-Audited
Audit Date: 10.06.2019
Personnel: Waid Prather (Ed./Pub.); Jacob Grimes (News-sports); Moore Jimmy (Circulation Director); Bobby Latham (Ad director); Brenda Howell (Office manager)
Parent company (for newspapers): The 'Ginian, LLC

THE CHARLESTON SUN-SENTINEL

Street address 1: 16 S Square St
Street address city: Charleston
Street address state: MS
Zip/Postal code: 38921-2335
General Phone: (662) 647-8462
General Fax: (662) 647-3830
General/National Adv. E-mail: krista@charlestonsun.net
Display Adv. E-mail: krista@charlestonsun.net
Editorial e-mail: clay@charlestonsun.net
Primary Website: tallahatchienews.ms
Year Established: 1856
Avg Paid Circ: 1526
Avg Free Circ: 123
Audit By: Sworn/Estimate/Non-Audited
Audit Date: 10.06.2019
Personnel: Clay McFerrin (Ed./Pub.); Krista McFerrin (Adv. Mgr.)
Parent company (for newspapers): 1976

THE CHOCTAW PLAINDEALER

Street address 1: 48 N LOUISVILLE ST
Street address city: Ackerman
Street address state: MS
Zip/Postal code: 39735
General Phone: (662) 285-6248
General Fax: (662) 285-6695
General/National Adv. E-mail: ads@websterprogresstimes.com
Editorial e-mail: newsroom@winstoncountyjournal.com
Primary Website: choctawplaindealer.com
Avg Paid Circ: 1200
Avg Free Circ: 100
Audit By: Sworn/Estimate/Non-Audited
Audit Date: 10.06.2019
Personnel: Chasatie Fisher (Circ.); Brenda Perry (Circ. Mgr.); Joseph McCain (Ed.)
Parent company (for newspapers): 1976

THE CLARKSDALE PRESS REGISTER

Street address 1: 128 E 2nd St
Street address city: Clarksdale
Street address state: MS
Zip/Postal code: 38614-4206
General Phone: (662) 627-2201
General Fax: (662) 624-5125
General/National Adv. E-mail: bkeller@pressregister.com
Display Adv. E-mail: sandyhite@pressregister.com
Classified Adv. e-mail: bkeller@pressregister.com
Editorial e-mail: publisher@pressregister.com
Primary Website: pressregister.com
Year Established: 1826
Avg Paid Circ: 3175
Sun. Circulation Paid: 5200
Audit By: Sworn/Estimate/Non-Audited
Audit Date: 10.06.2019
Personnel: Sandy Hite (Office Mgr.); Troy Catchings (Photography Ed.)
Parent company (for newspapers): 1976

THE CLEVELAND CURRENT

Street address 1: 125 S Court St
Street address 2: Ste 1
Street address city: Cleveland
Street address state: MS
Zip/Postal code: 38732-2635
General Phone: (662) 843-2700
General/National Adv. E-mail: kristy@theclevelandcurrent.com
Editorial e-mail: pam@theclevelandcurrent.com
Primary Website: theclevelandcurrent.com
Audit By: Sworn/Estimate/Non-Audited
Audit Date: 10.06.2019
Personnel: Scott Coopwood (Pub.); Kristy Kitchings (Ads.); Pam Parker (Managing Ed.)
Parent company (for newspapers): Coopwood Newspapers, Inc

THE COFFEEVILLE COURIER

Street address 1: 14259 Main St
Street address city: Coffeeville
Street address state: MS
Zip/Postal code: 38922-2596
General Phone: (662) 675-2446
General Fax: (662) 675-2416
General/National Adv. E-mail: coffeevillecourier@bellsouth.net
Editorial e-mail: coffeevillecourier@bellsouth.net
Avg Paid Circ: 2100
Avg Free Circ: 50
Audit By: Sworn/Estimate/Non-Audited
Audit Date: 10.06.2019
Personnel: Sarah H. Williams (Mng. Ed.)

THE COLUMBIAN-PROGRESS

Street address 1: 318 Second St
Street address city: Columbia
Street address state: MS
Zip/Postal code: 39429-2954
General Phone: (601) 736-2611
General Fax: (601) 736-4507
General/National Adv. E-mail: kimgingell@columbianprogress.com
Display Adv. E-mail: lmizell@columbianprogress.com
Editorial e-mail: csmith@columbianprogress.com
Primary Website: columbianprogress.com
Year Established: 1882
Avg Paid Circ: 5700
Audit By: Sworn/Estimate/Non-Audited
Audit Date: 10.06.2019
Personnel: Bonnie Hudson (Office Mgr.); Kim Gingell (Adv. Mgr.); Mark Rogers (Managing Ed.)
Parent company (for newspapers): 1976

THE CONSERVATIVE

Street address 1: 401 Summit St
Street address 2: Rm 108
Street address city: Winona
Street address state: MS
Zip/Postal code: 38967-2240
General Phone: (662) 283-1131
General Fax: (662) 283-5374
General/National Adv. E-mail: wandaroche@winonatimes.com
Display Adv. E-mail: bookkeeping@winonatimes.com
Editorial e-mail: publisher@winonatimes.com
Primary Website: winonatimes.com
Year Established: 1865
Avg Paid Circ: 1350
Avg Free Circ: 14
Audit By: Sworn/Estimate/Non-Audited
Audit Date: 10.06.2019
Personnel: Amanda Sexton (Ed.)
Parent company (for newspapers): 1976

THE DEMOCRAT

Street address 1: 219 E Main St
Street address city: Senatobia
Street address state: MS
Zip/Postal code: 38668-2123
General Phone: (662) 562-4414
General Fax: (662) 562-8866
General/National Adv. E-mail: strimm@taterecord.com
Display Adv. E-mail: classifieds@taterecord.com
Editorial e-mail: pageeditor@taterecord.com
Primary Website: taterecord.com
Avg Paid Circ: 5200
Audit By: Sworn/Estimate/Non-Audited
Audit Date: 10.06.2019
Personnel: Joseph B. Lee (Pub.); Shirley Trimm (Adv. Mgr.); Melissa Turner (Ed.)

THE ENTERPRISE-TOCSIN

Street address 1: 114 Main St
Street address city: Indianola
Street address state: MS
Zip/Postal code: 38751-2844
General Phone: (662) 887-2222
General Fax: (662) 887-2999
General/National Adv. E-mail: advertising@enterprise-tocsin.com
Editorial e-mail: news@enterprise-tocsin.com
Primary Website: enterprise-tocsin.com
Year Established: 1888
Avg Paid Circ: 4000
Avg Free Circ: 50
Audit By: Sworn/Estimate/Non-Audited
Audit Date: 10.06.2019
Personnel: Charlie Smith (Editor/Publisher); Mary Gray (Adv. Mgr.)
Parent company (for newspapers): 1976

THE GRENADA STAR

Street address 1: 355 W. Monroe St.
Street address city: Grenada
Street address state: MS
Zip/Postal code: 38901-2823
General Phone: (662) 226-4321
General Fax: (662) 226-8310
Advertising Phone: (662) 226-4321
Advertising Fax: (662) 226-8310
Editorial Phone: (662) 226-4321
Editorial Fax: (662) 226-8310
General/National Adv. E-mail: bookkeeping@grenadastar.com
Display Adv. E-mail: aprestridge@grenadastar.com
Classified Adv. e-mail: mengle@grenadastar.com
Editorial e-mail: editor@grenadastar.com
Primary Website: www.grenadastar.com
Mthly Avg Views: 63487
Mthly Avg Unique Visitors: 11346
Year Established: 1854
Avg Paid Circ: 4200
Audit By: USPS
Audit Date: 31.10.2023
Personnel: Fred Adams (Gen. Mgr.); Adam Prestridge (Publisher/Editor); Joseph B. Lee (Pub./Ed.); Stephanie Dees (Bookkeeper/Circulation Clerk); Marsha Engle (Creative Director/Classifieds Clerk); Brenda R. Lee (Sec./Treasurer); Anita Turner (Adv. Sales); Chuck Hathcock (Sports Editor/News Reporter); Stephanie Dees (Circ. Dir.); Marie Harrison (Marketing Consultant); Nannette Lascer (Managing Ed.); Tami Mitchell (Marketing Consultant); Chuck Hathcock (Sports Ed.); Duke Bullin (Mailroom Clerk/Delivery Driver); Musset McPhail (Creative Servs. Mgr.); Kathy Blair (Inserter)
Parent company (for newspapers): Emmerich Newspapers, Inc.

THE HATTIESBURG POST

Street address 1: 103 N 40th Ave
Street address city: Hattiesburg
Street address state: MS
Zip/Postal code: 39401-6606
General Phone: (601) 268-2331
General Fax: (601) 268-2965
General/National Adv. E-mail: kristen@hubcityspokes.com
Primary Website: hubcityspokes.com
Year Established: 2013
Avg Paid Circ: 9000

Audit By: Sworn/Estimate/Non-Audited
Audit Date: 10.06.2019
Personnel: David Gustafson (Ed./Pub.); Beth Bunch (Mng Ed.); Kristen Brock (Adv. Mgr.)
Parent company (for newspapers): 1976

THE ITAWAMBA COUNTY TIMES

Street address 1: 106 W Main St
Street address city: Fulton
Street address state: MS
Zip/Postal code: 38843-1146
General Phone: (662) 655-2141
General/National Adv. E-mail: itawamba.advertising@journalinc.com
Display Adv. E-mail: itawamba.classifieds@journalinc.com
Editorial e-mail: itawamba.times@journalinc.com
Primary Website: djournal.com/itawamba
Year Established: 1945
Avg Paid Circ: 1290
Avg Free Circ: 45
Audit By: Sworn/Estimate/Non-Audited
Audit Date: 13.10.2023
Personnel: Harvey Parson (General Manager); Charlotte Wolfe; Adam Armour
Parent company (for newspapers): Journal Publishing Company

THE JASPER COUNTY NEWS

Street address 1: 3362 HIGHWAY 15
Street address city: Bay Springs
Street address state: MS
Zip/Postal code: 39422-5181
General Phone: (601) 764-3104
General Fax: (601) 764-3106
Editorial Phone: (601) 764-9776
General/National Adv. E-mail: bni@teleclipse.net
Editorial e-mail: news@jaspercountynews.net
Avg Paid Circ: 2772
Avg Free Circ: 110
Audit By: Sworn/Estimate/Non-Audited
Audit Date: 10.06.2019
Personnel: Ronnie L. Buckley (Pub.); Kristie Scott (Sales Rep.); Ellen Paul (Circ. Mgr.); Anna King (Ed.); Missy Clark (Prodn. Mgr.)

THE LAMAR TIMES

Street address 1: 103 N 40th Ave
Street address city: Hattiesburg
Street address state: MS
Zip/Postal code: 39401-6606
General Phone: (601) 268-2331
General Fax: (601) 268-2965
General/National Adv. E-mail: kristen@hubcityspokes.com
Display Adv. E-mail: missy@hubcityspokes.com
Editorial e-mail: beth@hubcityspokes.com
Primary Website: hubcityspokes.com/lamar-times
Avg Paid Circ: 5000
Audit By: Sworn/Estimate/Non-Audited
Audit Date: 10.06.2019
Personnel: Beth Bunch (Mng. Ed.); Samantha Mlot (Adv. Mgr.); David Gustafson (Ed./Pub.); Emily Hall (Art Dir.)
Parent company (for newspapers): Hattiesburg Publishing, Inc.

THE LAUREL CHRONICLE

Street address 1: 130 Leontyne Price Blvd
Street address city: Laurel
Street address state: MS
Zip/Postal code: 39440-4428
General Phone: (601) 651-2000
General Fax: (601) 651-2020
Advertising Phone: (601) 651-2006
Editorial Phone: (601) 651-2010
General/National Adv. E-mail: mrobinson@thechronicle.ms
Editorial e-mail: jniblett@thechronicle.ms
Year Established: 2012
Audit By: Sworn/Estimate/Non-Audited
Audit Date: 10.06.2019
Personnel: Jason Niblett (Ed./Pub.); Dale McKee (Sports Ed.); Marquita Robinson (Ad Sales); Julie Whatley (Ad Sales); Sonya James (Office Mgr.); Lisa Miller (Circ. Mgr.)
Parent company (for newspapers): 1976

THE MAGEE COURIER

Street address 1: PO Box 338
Street address city: Magee
Street address state: MS
Zip/Postal code: 39111-0338
General Phone: (601) 849-3434
General Fax: (601) 849-6828
General/National Adv. E-mail: nbrown@mageecourier.ms
Editorial e-mail: dminsky@mageecourier.ms
Primary Website: simpsoncounty.ms
Year Established: 1899
Avg Paid Circ: 3750
Avg Free Circ: 125
Audit By: Sworn/Estimate/Non-Audited
Audit Date: 10.06.2019
Personnel: Marsha Bratcher (Circ. Mgr.); John Pat Brown (Ed.)
Parent company (for newspapers): 1976

THE MAGNOLIA GAZETTE

Street address 1: 280 Magnolia St
Street address city: Magnolia
Street address state: MS
Zip/Postal code: 39652-2828
General Phone: (601) 783-2441
General Fax: (601) 783-2091
General/National Adv. E-mail: magnoliagazette@bellsouth.net
Primary Website: magnoliagazette.com
Avg Paid Circ: 1400
Audit By: Sworn/Estimate/Non-Audited
Audit Date: 10.06.2019
Personnel: Joy Reeves (Adv. Mgr.); Luke Lampton (Ed.); Donna DeLee (Mng. Ed.)

THE METEOR INC.

Street address 1: 201 E Georgetown St
Street address city: Crystal Springs
Street address state: MS
Zip/Postal code: 39059-2516
General Phone: (601) 892-2581
General Fax: (601) 892-2249
General/National Adv. E-mail: info@themeteor.com
Editorial e-mail: info@themeteor.com
Primary Website: http://themeteor.com/index.html
Year Established: 1881
Avg Paid Circ: 3615
Avg Free Circ: 1385
Audit By: Sworn/Estimate/Non-Audited
Audit Date: 10.06.2019
Personnel: Henry Carney (Ed.)

THE MISSISSIPPI PRESS

Street address 1: 909 CONVENT AVE
Street address city: Pascagoula
Street address state: MS
Zip/Postal code: 39567
General Phone: (228) 762-1111
General Fax: (228) 934-1454
Advertising Phone: (228) 762-1111
Advertising Fax: (228) 934-1454
Editorial Phone: (228) 934-1424
Editorial Fax: (228) 934-1474
General/National Adv. E-mail: msnews@themississippipress.com
Display Adv. E-mail: pressads@themississippipress.com
Classified Adv. e-mail: pressads@themississippipress.com
Editorial e-mail: msnews@themississippipress.com
Primary Website: gulflive.com/mississippipress
Year Established: 1964
Avg Paid Circ: 5749
Sun. Circulation Paid: 7208
Audit By: Sworn/Estimate/Non-Audited
Audit Date: 10.06.2019
Personnel: Wanda Heary Jacobs (Pub.); Gareth Clary (Pub.); Roy May (Adv. Mgr.); Susan Ruddiman (Features Ed.)
Parent company (for newspapers): Advance Publications, Inc.

THE NESHOBA DEMOCRAT

Street address 1: 439 E Beacon St
Street address city: Philadelphia
Street address state: MS
Zip/Postal code: 39350-2950
General Phone: (601) 656-4000
General Fax: (601) 656-6379
General/National Adv. E-mail: samantha@neshobademocrat.com
Display Adv. E-mail: advertising@neshobademocrat.com
Classified Adv. e-mail: advertising@neshobademocrat.com
Editorial e-mail: jprince@neshobademocrat.com
Primary Website: neshobademocrat.com
Mthly Avg Views: 52000
Mthly Avg Unique Visitors: 2496
Year Established: 1881
Avg Paid Circ: 7500
Avg Free Circ: 70
Audit By: Sworn/Estimate/Non-Audited
Audit Date: 01.10.2023
Personnel: Jim Prince (Editors and Publisher); Wayne Ceacey (Adv. Dir.); Irda Wards (Circ. Mgr.); Carver Rayburn (Assoc. Ed.); Debbie Myers (Mng. Ed.)
Parent company (for newspapers): Prince Media Group

THE NEWS-COMMERCIAL

Street address 1: 104 1st St
Street address city: Collins
Street address state: MS
Zip/Postal code: 39428-4140
General Phone: (601) 765-8275
General Fax: (601) 765-6952
General/National Adv. E-mail: thenewscommercial@att.net
Display Adv. E-mail: thenewscommercial@att.net
Editorial e-mail: thenewscommercial@att.net
Primary Website: facebook.com/thenewscommercial
Avg Paid Circ: 4200
Avg Free Circ: 35
Audit By: Sworn/Estimate/Non-Audited
Audit Date: 10.06.2019
Personnel: Analyn Arrington-Goff (Ed.); Jimmy Goff (Ed.)

THE NEWTON COUNTY APPEAL

Street address 1: 105 Main St
Street address city: Union
Street address state: MS
Zip/Postal code: 39365-2519
General Phone: (601) 774-9433
General Fax: (601) 774-8301
Advertising Phone: (601) 683-7810
Editorial Phone: (601) 774-9433
General/National Adv. E-mail: askinner@newtoncountyappeal.com
Display Adv. E-mail: mfarrow@newtoncountyappeal.com
Editorial e-mail: dthompson@newtoncountyappeal.com
Primary Website: thenewtoncountyappeal.com
Year Established: 1910
Avg Paid Circ: 3200
Audit By: Sworn/Estimate/Non-Audited
Audit Date: 10.06.2019
Personnel: Demetrius Thompson (Managing Editor); Luke Horton (Publisher); Michael Miller (Adv Director); Austin Bishop (Sports)
Parent company (for newspapers): 1976

THE PANOLIAN

Street address 1: 363 Highway 51 N
Street address city: Batesville
Street address state: MS
Zip/Postal code: 38606-2311
General Phone: (662) 563-4591
General Fax: (662) 563-5610
General/National Adv. E-mail: publisher@panolian.com
Display Adv. E-mail: classifieds@panolian.com
Editorial e-mail: news@panolian.com
Primary Website: panolian.com
Mthly Avg Views: 45000
Mthly Avg Unique Visitors: 6200
Year Established: 1882
Avg Paid Circ: 2419
Avg Free Circ: 1200
Audit By: Sworn/Estimate/Non-Audited
Audit Date: 10.06.2019
Personnel: Rebecca Alexander (Publisher); Rupert Howell (Mng. Ed.); Rita W. Howell (News Ed.); Myra Bean (Sports Ed.); Margaret Buntin (Advt Mgr, Graphic Designer)
Parent company (for newspapers): Boone Newsmedia

THE PETAL NEWS

Street address 1: 103 N 40th Ave
Street address city: Hattiesburg
Street address state: MS
Zip/Postal code: 39401-6606
General Phone: (601) 268-2331
General Fax: (601) 268-2965
General/National Adv. E-mail: kristen@HubCitySPOKES.com
Display Adv. E-mail: missyHubCitySPOKES.com
Editorial e-mail: beth@hubcityspokes.com
Primary Website: hubcityspokes.com
Avg Paid Circ: 3000
Audit By: Sworn/Estimate/Non-Audited
Audit Date: 10.06.2019
Personnel: David Gustafson (Editor/Publisher); Kristen Brock (Adv. Mgr.); Beth Bunch (Mng. Ed.)
Parent company (for newspapers): 1976

THE POPLARVILLE DEMOCRAT

Street address 1: 418 S Main St
Street address city: Poplarville
Street address state: MS
Zip/Postal code: 39470-2826
General Phone: (601) 795-2247
General Fax: (601) 795-2232
General/National Adv. E-mail: laci.lee@picayuneitem.com
Display Adv. E-mail: laura.henley@picayuneitem.com
Editorial e-mail: jeremy.pittari@picayuneitem.com
Primary Website: picayuneitem.com
Year Established: 1976
Avg Paid Circ: 2222
Avg Free Circ: 14
Audit By: Sworn/Estimate/Non-Audited
Audit Date: 10.06.2019
Personnel: Butch Weir (Ed.); Kevin Warren (Publisher); Julie Bounds (Adv. Mgr.); Mary Jim Weems (Adv. Dir.)
Parent company (for newspapers): CNHI, LLC

THE PORT GIBSON REVEILLE

Street address 1: 708 Market St
Street address city: Port Gibson
Street address state: MS
Zip/Postal code: 39150-2332
General Phone: (601) 437-5103
General Fax: (601) 437-4410
General/National Adv. E-mail: reveille@bellsouth.net
Display Adv. E-mail: reveille@bellsouth.net
Avg Paid Circ: 1600
Avg Free Circ: 51
Audit By: Sworn/Estimate/Non-Audited
Audit Date: 10.06.2019
Personnel: Janice G. Bufkin (Adv./Circ. Mgr.); Emma F. Crisler (Pub./Ed.); Marjorie Bufkin (Adv. Manager)

THE RICHTON DISPATCH

Street address 1: 110 Walnut St
Street address city: Richton
Street address state: MS
Zip/Postal code: 39476
General Phone: (601) 788-6031
General Fax: (601) 788-6031
General/National Adv. E-mail: news@therichtondispatch.com
Display Adv. E-mail: news@therichtondispatch.com
Editorial e-mail: news@therichtondispatch.com
Primary Website: therichtondispatch.com
Year Established: 1905
Avg Paid Circ: 1825
Avg Free Circ: 8
Audit By: Sworn/Estimate/Non-Audited
Audit Date: 10.06.2019
Personnel: Dean Wilson (Gen. Mgr.); Larry A. Wilson (Ed.)

THE SOUTHERN HERALD

Street address 1: 260 Main St
Street address city: Liberty
Street address state: MS
Zip/Postal code: 39645
General Phone: (601) 657-4818
General Fax: (601) 657-4818
General/National Adv. E-mail: southernherald@bellsouth.net
Display Adv. E-mail: southernherald@bellsouth.net

Editorial e-mail: southernherald@bellsouth.net
Primary Website: facebook.com/The-Southern-Herald-215266298536196
Year Established: 1825
Avg Paid Circ: 900
Avg Free Circ: 25
Audit By: Sworn/Estimate/Non-Audited
Audit Date: 10.06.2019
Personnel: Richard H. Stratton (Ed./owner)

THE SOUTHERN REPORTER

Street address 1: 211 S Pocahontas St
Street address city: Sardis
Street address state: MS
Zip/Postal code: 38666-1625
General Phone: (662) 487-1551
General Fax: (662) 487-1552
General/National Adv. E-mail: southernreporter@bellsouth.net
Avg Paid Circ: 2250
Avg Free Circ: 343
Audit By: Sworn/Estimate/Non-Audited
Audit Date: 10.06.2019
Personnel: David Howell (Ed.)

THE STAR-HERALD

Street address 1: 104 N. Jackson St.
Street address city: Kosciusko
Street address state: MS
Zip/Postal code: 39090-3626
General Phone: (662) 289-2251
General Fax: (662) 289-2254
Advertising Phone: (662) 289-2251
Editorial Phone: (662) 289-2251
General/National Adv. E-mail: news@starherald.net
Display Adv. E-mail: kfioretti@starherald.net
Classified Adv. e-mail: jmccaskill@starherald.net
Editorial e-mail: news@starherald.net
Primary Website: starherald.net
Year Established: 1866
Avg Paid Circ: 4200
Avg Free Circ: 100
Audit By: Sworn/Estimate/Non-Audited
Audit Date: 10.06.2019
Personnel: Karen Fioretti (Publisher)
Parent company (for newspapers): 1976; Emmerich Newspapers

THE TUNICA TIMES

Street address 1: 986 Magnolia St
Street address city: Tunica
Street address state: MS
Zip/Postal code: 38676-9742
General Phone: (662) 363-1511
General Fax: (662) 363-9969
General/National Adv. E-mail: ads@tunicatimes.com
Display Adv. E-mail: ads@tunicatimes.com
Editorial e-mail: news@tunicatimes.com
Primary Website: tunicatimes.com
Year Established: 1904
Avg Paid Circ: 2400
Audit By: Sworn/Estimate/Non-Audited
Audit Date: 10.06.2019
Personnel: Brooks N. Taylor (Publisher); Meg Coker (Managing Editor)

THE TYLERTOWN TIMES

Street address 1: 727 Beulah Ave
Street address city: Tylertown
Street address state: MS
Zip/Postal code: 39667-2709
General Phone: (601) 876-5111
General Fax: (601) 876-5280
General/National Adv. E-mail: tylertowntimes@bellsouth.net
Display Adv. E-mail: tylertowntimes@bellsouth.net
Editorial e-mail: tylertowntimes@bellsouth.net
Primary Website: thetylertowntimes.org
Year Established: 1907
Avg Paid Circ: 3248
Avg Free Circ: 6729
Audit By: Sworn/Estimate/Non-Audited
Audit Date: 10.06.2019
Personnel: Carolyn Dillon (Owner/Ed./Pub.)

THE WAYNE COUNTY NEWS

Street address 1: 716 South Street
Street address city: Waynesboro
Street address state: MS
Zip/Postal code: 39367
General Phone: 601-735-4341
General Fax: 601-735-1111
Advertising Phone: 601-735-4341
Advertising Fax: 601-735-1111
Editorial Phone: 601-735-4341
Editorial Fax: 601-735-1111
General/National Adv. E-mail: publisher@thewaynecountynews.com
Display Adv. E-mail: advertising@thewaynecountynews.com
Classified Adv. e-mail: legals@thewaynecountynews.com
Editorial e-mail: news@thewaynecountynews.com
Primary Website: thewaynecountynews.com
Mthly Avg Views: 45000
Mthly Avg Unique Visitors: 12000
Year Established: 1873
Avg Paid Circ: 3000
Avg Free Circ: 0
Audit By: Sworn/Estimate/Non-Audited
Personnel: Paul Keane (Publisher/Editor); Doris Keane (Advertising Director); Anna Dearmon (Legals, Circulation, Office Manager)
Parent company (for newspapers): Keane Media, Inc.

THE WINONA TIMES

Street address 1: 401 Summit St
Street address 2: Rm 108
Street address city: Winona
Street address state: MS
Zip/Postal code: 38967-2240
General Phone: (662) 283-1131
General Fax: (662) 283-5374
General/National Adv. E-mail: wandaroche@winonatimes.com
Display Adv. E-mail: bookkeeping@winonatimes.com
Editorial e-mail: publisher@winonatimes.com
Primary Website: winonatimes.com
Year Established: 1881
Avg Paid Circ: 3650
Avg Free Circ: 61
Audit By: Sworn/Estimate/Non-Audited
Audit Date: 10.06.2019
Personnel: Amanda Sexton (Pub.)
Parent company (for newspapers): 1976

THE WOODVILLE REPUBLICAN

Street address 1: 425 Depot St
Street address city: Woodville
Street address state: MS
Zip/Postal code: 39669-3597
General Phone: (601) 888-4293
General Fax: (601) 888-6156
General/National Adv. E-mail: wrepublican@bellsouth.net
Display Adv. E-mail: wrepublican@bellsouth.net
Editorial e-mail: wrepublican@bellsouth.net
Primary Website: smalltownpapers.com/newspapers
Year Established: 1824
Avg Paid Circ: 1950
Avg Free Circ: 50
Audit By: Sworn/Estimate/Non-Audited
Audit Date: 10.06.2019
Personnel: Elise R. Lewis (Adv. Mgr.); Andrew J. Lewis (Ed.)

THE YAZOO HERALD

Street address 1: 1025 GRAND AVE
Street address city: Yazoo City
Street address state: MS
Zip/Postal code: 39194-2946
General Phone: (662) 746-4911
General Fax: (662) 746-4915
General/National Adv. E-mail: sharon@yazooherald.net
Display Adv. E-mail: sheila@yazooherald.net
Classified Adv. e-mail: sheila@yazooherald.net
Editorial e-mail: jason@yazooherald.net
Primary Website: yazooherald.net
Year Established: 1871
Avg Paid Circ: 3200
Avg Free Circ: 25
Audit By: Sworn/Estimate/Non-Audited
Audit Date: 10.06.2019
Personnel: Jason Patterson (Ed & Pub); Jamie Patterson (Mng Ed); Cathryn Cartwright (Staff Writer)
Parent company (for newspapers): 1976

TISHOMINGO COUNTY NEWS

Street address 1: PO Box 70
Street address city: Iuka
Street address state: MS
Zip/Postal code: 38852-0070
General Phone: (662) 423-2211
General Fax: (662) 423-2214
General/National Adv. E-mail: tcnews@bellsouth.net
Display Adv. E-mail: tcnews@bellsouth.net
Editorial e-mail: tcnews@bellsouth.net
Primary Website: facebook.com/pages/The-Tishomingo-County-NewsThe-Vidette
Year Established: 1877
Avg Paid Circ: 6000
Avg Free Circ: 100
Audit By: Sworn/Estimate/Non-Audited
Audit Date: 10.06.2019
Personnel: John H. Biggs (Pub.); Charlotte McVay (Ed.)

WEBSTER PROGRESS-TIMES

Street address 1: 58 N Dunn St
Street address city: Eupora
Street address state: MS
Zip/Postal code: 39744-2631
General Phone: (662) 773-6241
General Fax: (662) 258-6474
Advertising Phone: (662) 258-7532
Editorial Phone: (662) 258-3109
General/National Adv. E-mail: ads@websterprogresstimes.com
Display Adv. E-mail: ads@websterprogresstimes.com
Editorial e-mail: news@websterprogresstimes.com
Primary Website: websterprogresstimes.com
Year Established: 1968
Avg Paid Circ: 2500
Avg Free Circ: 6500
Audit By: Sworn/Estimate/Non-Audited
Audit Date: 10.06.2019
Personnel: Joseph McCain (Pub.); Russell Hood (News Ed.)

WILK-AMITE RECORD

Street address 1: 243 E Main St
Street address city: Gloster
Street address state: MS
Zip/Postal code: 39638-9009
General Phone: (601) 225-9200
General Fax: (601) 225-4531
General/National Adv. E-mail: wilkamiterecord@yahoo.com
Display Adv. E-mail: wilkamiterecord@yahoo.com
Editorial e-mail: info@wilkamiterecord.com
Primary Website: wilkamiterecord.com
Year Established: 1892
Avg Paid Circ: 2400
Avg Free Circ: 10
Audit By: Sworn/Estimate/Non-Audited
Audit Date: 10.06.2019
Personnel: Bettty N. Stevens (Ed.)

WINSTON COUNTY JOURNAL

Street address 1: 233 N Court Ave
Street address city: Louisville
Street address state: MS
Zip/Postal code: 39339-2648
General Phone: (662) 773-6241
General Fax: (662) 773-6242
Advertising Phone: (662) 773-6241 x25
Editorial Phone: (662) 773-6241 x12
General/National Adv. E-mail: lwhite@winstoncountyjournals.com
Display Adv. E-mail: sales@winstoncountyjournal.com
Editorial e-mail: newsroom@winstoncountyjournal.com
Primary Website: winstoncountyjournal.com
Avg Paid Circ: 2703
Avg Free Circ: 20
Audit By: Sworn/Estimate/Non-Audited
Audit Date: 10.06.2019
Personnel: Brenda Perry (Circ. Mgr.); Joseph McCain (Ed.)
Parent company (for newspapers): 1976

MISSOURI

APPLETON CITY JOURNAL

Street address 1: 104 E 4th St
Street address city: Appleton City
Street address state: MO
Zip/Postal code: 64724-1122
General Phone: (660) 476-5566
General Fax: (660) 646-8015
General/National Adv. E-mail: sacosagenews@centurytel.net
Editorial e-mail: sacosagenews@centurytel.net
Avg Paid Circ: 1200
Avg Free Circ: 64
Audit By: Sworn/Estimate/Non-Audited
Audit Date: 10.06.2019
Personnel: Mike Crawford (Ed.)
Parent company (for newspapers): Main Street Media, Inc.

ASH GROVE COMMONWEALTH

Street address 1: 100 E Main St
Street address city: Ash Grove
Street address state: MO
Zip/Postal code: 65604-9096
General Phone: (417) 363-7025
General Fax: (417) 751-3499
Editorial e-mail: agcommonwealth@sbcglobal.net
Primary Website: greenecountycommonwealth.com
Avg Paid Circ: 2000
Avg Free Circ: 3725
Audit By: Sworn/Estimate/Non-Audited
Audit Date: 10.06.2019
Personnel: Laura Scott (Pub.)

ATCHISON COUNTY MAIL

Street address 1: 300 S Main St
Street address city: Rock Port
Street address state: MO
Zip/Postal code: 64482-1534
General Phone: (660) 744-6245
General Fax: (660) 744-2645
Editorial e-mail: amail@rpt.coop
Primary Website: http://farmerpublishing.com/weekly-editions/atchison-county-mail/
Avg Paid Circ: 2200
Avg Free Circ: 30
Audit By: Sworn/Estimate/Non-Audited
Audit Date: 10.06.2019
Personnel: William C. Farmer (Ed.); Mike Farmer (Mng. Ed.)

AURORA ADVERTISER

Street address 1: 33 W Olive St
Street address city: Aurora
Street address state: MO
Zip/Postal code: 65605-1430
General Phone: (417) 678-2115
General Fax: (417) 678-2117
General/National Adv. E-mail: pward@auroraadvertiser.net
Display Adv. E-mail: classifieds@auroraadvertiser.net
Editorial e-mail: news@auroraadvertiser.net
Primary Website: auroraadvertiser.net
Year Established: 1886
Avg Paid Circ: 1100
Avg Free Circ: 7000
Audit By: Sworn/Estimate/Non-Audited
Audit Date: 10.06.2019
Personnel: Judy Dingman (Gen. Mgr.); Paul Ward (Adv. Mgr.); Krissy Garoutte (Circ. Mgr.)
Parent company (for newspapers): CherryRoad Media; Sexton Media Group

BARRY COUNTY ADVERTISER

Street address 1: 904 West St
Street address city: Cassville
Street address state: MO
Zip/Postal code: 65625-1356
General Phone: (417) 847-4475
General Fax: (417) 847-4523
General/National Adv. E-mail: ads@4bca.com
Display Adv. E-mail: class@4bca.com
Classified Adv. e-mail: class@4bca.com
Editorial e-mail: editor@4bca.com

Primary Website: 4bcaonline.com
Mthly Avg Views: 70000
Mthly Avg Unique Visitors: 20000
Year Established: 1966
Avg Paid Circ: 200
Avg Free Circ: 13200
Audit By: Sworn/Estimate/Non-Audited
Audit Date: 10.06.2019
Personnel: Marty Jenkins (Prodn. Mgr.); Charlea Estes (Editor); Shana Harter (Bookkeeping)
Parent company (for newspapers): Melton Publications

BENTON COUNTY ENTERPRISE

Street address 1: 107 Main St
Street address city: Warsaw
Street address state: MO
Zip/Postal code: 65355
General Phone: (660) 438-6312
General Fax: (660) 438-3464
General/National Adv. E-mail: carrierieman@bentoncountyenterprise.com
Editorial e-mail: jameswhite@bentoncountyenterprise.com
Primary Website: bentoncountyenterprise.com
Avg Paid Circ: 5700
Avg Free Circ: 30
Audit By: Sworn/Estimate/Non-Audited
Audit Date: 10.06.2019
Personnel: James Mahlon White (Pub.); Jane Salley (Asst. Pub.); Lisa Firsick (Prod. Dir.)

BETHANY REPUBLICAN-CLIPPER

Street address 1: 202 N 16th St
Street address city: Bethany
Street address state: MO
Zip/Postal code: 64424-1204
General Phone: (660) 425-6325
General Fax: (660) 425-3441
General/National Adv. E-mail: ad1@grm.net
Display Adv. E-mail: ad2@grm.net
Editorial e-mail: news@grm.net
Primary Website: bethanyclipper.com
Avg Paid Circ: 3550
Avg Free Circ: 10000
Audit By: Sworn/Estimate/Non-Audited
Audit Date: 10.06.2019
Personnel: Kathy Conger (Circ. Mgr.); Philip G. Conger (Ed.)

BOLIVAR HERALD-FREE PRESS

Street address 1: 335 S Springfield Ave
Street address city: Bolivar
Street address state: MO
Zip/Postal code: 65613-2040
General Phone: (417) 326-7636
General Fax: (417) 326-8701
Advertising Phone: (417) 777-9731
General/National Adv. E-mail: deannam@bolivarmonews.com
Display Adv. E-mail: amandao@bolivarmonews.com
Editorial e-mail: jessicam@bolivarmonews.com
Primary Website: bolivarmonews.com
Mthly Avg Views: 93705
Mthly Avg Unique Visitors: 21847
Year Established: 1868
Avg Paid Circ: 5061
Avg Free Circ: 77
Audit By: Sworn/Estimate/Non-Audited
Audit Date: 10.06.2019
Personnel: Dave Berry (Pub.); Deanna Moore (Adv. Mgr.); Charlotte Marsch (Ed.); Ted Lawrence (Adv. Sales)
Parent company (for newspapers): Community Publishers, Inc.

BOONE COUNTY JOURNAL

Street address 1: 201 S Henry Clay Blvd
Street address city: Ashland
Street address state: MO
Zip/Postal code: 65010-9437
General Phone: (573) 657-2334
General Fax: (573) 657-2002
General/National Adv. E-mail: reporter@bocojo.com
Primary Website: bocojo.com
Year Established: 1969
Avg Paid Circ: 2000
Avg Free Circ: 150
Audit By: Sworn/Estimate/Non-Audited
Audit Date: 10.06.2019
Personnel: Bruce Wallace (Pub.)

BOONVILLE DAILY NEWS

Street address 1: 412 High St
Street address city: Boonville
Street address state: MO
Zip/Postal code: 65233-1242
General Phone: (660) 882-5335
General Fax: (660) 882-2256
General/National Adv. E-mail: jreynolds@gatehousemedia.com
Display Adv. E-mail: classifieds@boonvilledailynews.com
Classified Adv. e-mail: classifieds@boonvilledailynews.com
Editorial e-mail: afennewald@gatehousemedia.com
Primary Website: boonvilledailynews.com
Year Established: 1919
Avg Paid Circ: 2484
Audit By: Sworn/Estimate/Non-Audited
Audit Date: 10.06.2019
Personnel: James Bright (Pub.); Allen Fennewald (Reg. News Ed.); Jamie Reynolds (Reg. Adv. Dir.)
Parent company (for newspapers): CherryRoad Media; CherryRoad Media

BOWLING GREEN TIMES

Street address 1: PO Box 110
Street address 2: 106 W Main St
Street address city: Bowling Green
Street address state: MO
Zip/Postal code: 63334-0110
General Phone: (573) 324-2222
General Fax: (573) 324-3991
General/National Adv. E-mail: bgtads@lcs.net
Display Adv. E-mail: bgtads@lcs.net
Editorial e-mail: bgted@lcs.net
Primary Website: bowlinggreentimes.com
Mthly Avg Views: 401000
Mthly Avg Unique Visitors: 8825
Year Established: 1874
Avg Paid Circ: 3125
Audit By: Sworn/Estimate/Non-Audited
Audit Date: 10.06.2019
Personnel: Linda Luebrecht (Pub.); Amy Patterson (Advertising); Amanda Chamberlain (Circulation); Ethan Colbert (Editor)
Parent company (for newspapers): Lakeway Publishers, Inc.

BRANSON TRI-LAKES NEWS

Street address 1: 200 Industrial Park Dr
Street address city: Hollister
Street address state: MO
Zip/Postal code: 65672-5327
General Phone: (417) 334-3161
General Fax: (417) 334-1460
General/National Adv. E-mail: shane@bransontrilakesnews.com
Display Adv. E-mail: classifieds@bransontrilakesnews.com
Editorial e-mail: csain@bransontrilakesnews.com
Primary Website: bransontrilakesnews.com
Year Established: 1895
Avg Paid Circ: 9300
Avg Free Circ: 19000
Sat. Circulation Paid: 11170
Audit By: Sworn/Estimate/Non-Audited
Audit Date: 10.06.2019
Personnel: Robert Erickson (Bus. Office); Cliff Sain (Ed.); Shane Walton (Advertising Manager)
Parent company (for newspapers): Lancaster Management, Inc.

BUFFALO REFLEX

Street address 1: 114 E LINCOLN ST
Street address city: Buffalo
Street address state: MO
Zip/Postal code: 65622
General Phone: (417) 345-2224
General Fax: (417) 345-2235
General/National Adv. E-mail: sherryb@buffaloreflex.com
Display Adv. E-mail: joyb@buffaloreflex.com
Primary Website: buffaloreflex.com
Mthly Avg Views: 35818
Mthly Avg Unique Visitors: 8709
Year Established: 1869
Avg Paid Circ: 4000
Avg Free Circ: 380
Audit By: Sworn/Estimate/Non-Audited
Audit Date: 10.06.2019
Personnel: Paul Campbell (Ed./Gen. Mngr.)
Parent company (for newspapers): Phillips Media Group LLC

CABOOL ENTERPRISE

Street address 1: 525 Main St
Street address city: Cabool
Street address state: MO
Zip/Postal code: 65689-8104
General Phone: (417) 962-4411
General Fax: (417) 962-4455
General/National Adv. E-mail: cabent@centurytel.net
Display Adv. E-mail: ads@thecaboolenterprise.com
Editorial e-mail: news@thecaboolenterprise.com
Primary Website: thecaboolenterprise.com
Year Established: 1884
Avg Paid Circ: 1369
Avg Free Circ: 41
Audit By: Sworn/Estimate/Non-Audited
Audit Date: 10.06.2019
Personnel: Dala Whittaker (Pub.)

CALIFORNIA DEMOCRAT

Street address 1: 319 S High St
Street address city: California
Street address state: MO
Zip/Postal code: 65018-1807
General Phone: (573) 796-2135
General Fax: (573) 796-4220
Advertising Phone: ext. 22
Editorial Phone: ext. 27
General/National Adv. E-mail: denise@californiademocrat.com
Display Adv. E-mail: denise@californiademocrat.com
Editorial e-mail: editor@californiandemocrat.com
Primary Website: californiademocrat.com
Year Established: 1858
Avg Paid Circ: 2750
Audit By: Sworn/Estimate/Non-Audited
Audit Date: 10.06.2019
Personnel: Elizabeth Morales (Reporter); Kevin Labotka (Sports Reporter); Danisha Hogue (Reporter)
Parent company (for newspapers): Central Missouri Newspapers Inc.

CAMERON CITIZEN-OBSERVER

Street address 1: 403 E Evergreen St
Street address city: Cameron
Street address state: MO
Zip/Postal code: 64429-2096
General Phone: (816) 632-6543
Display Adv. E-mail: composing@mycameronnews.com
Classified Adv. e-mail: classifieds@mycameronnews.com
Editorial e-mail: editor@mycameronnews.com
Primary Website: mycameronnews.com
Avg Paid Circ: 2000
Audit By: Sworn/Estimate/Non-Audited
Audit Date: 30.04.2019
Personnel: Jeff King (Production Director); Debbie Wiedmier (CFO); Kristin Ryan (Classified/Receptionist); Amy Keeney (Publisher); Abby Lewey (Editor); Helen Guffey (Head Composer); Tina Svoboda (Publisher); Chris Johnson (Editor)

CASH-BOOK JOURNAL/THE WEEKENDER

Street address 1: 210 W Main St
Street address city: Jackson
Street address state: MO
Zip/Postal code: 63755-1822
General Phone: (573) 243-3515
General Fax: (573) 243-3517
General/National Adv. E-mail: stephanie.watkins@thecash-book.com
Display Adv. E-mail: cbjadvleg@socket.net
Editorial e-mail: denise.kinder@thecash-book.com
Primary Website: thecash-book.com
Year Established: 1870
Avg Paid Circ: 6000
Avg Free Circ: 4000
Audit By: Sworn/Estimate/Non-Audited
Audit Date: 10.06.2019
Personnel: Gina Raffety (Pub.); Jim Salzman (Adv. Mgr.); Elaine Hale (Circ. Mgr.); David Bloom (Asst. Pub.); Greg Dullum (Prodn. Mgr.)

CASSVILLE DEMOCRAT

Street address 1: 600 Main St
Street address city: Cassville
Street address state: MO
Zip/Postal code: 65625-1420
General Phone: (417) 847-2610
General Fax: (417) 847-3092
General/National Adv. E-mail: community@monett-times.com
Display Adv. E-mail: darlene@caseville-democrat.com
Editorial e-mail: editor@cassville-democrat.com
Primary Website: cassville-democrat.com
Year Established: 1871
Avg Paid Circ: 3000
Audit By: Sworn/Estimate/Non-Audited
Audit Date: 10.06.2019
Personnel: Jacob Brower (Pub.); Kyle Troutman (Ed.); Lisa Craft (Mktg. Dir.)
Parent company (for newspapers): Rust Communications

CEDAR COUNTY REPUBLICAN/ STOCKTON JOURNAL

Street address 1: 26 Public Sq
Street address city: Stockton
Street address state: MO
Zip/Postal code: 65785-7617
General Phone: (417) 276-4211
General Fax: (417) 276-5760
General/National Adv. E-mail: marilyne@cedarrepublican.com
Editorial e-mail: robertj@cedarrepublican.com
Primary Website: cedarrepublican.com
Mthly Avg Views: 28186
Mthly Avg Unique Visitors: 5489
Year Established: 1885
Avg Paid Circ: 2714
Avg Free Circ: 267
Audit By: Sworn/Estimate/Non-Audited
Audit Date: 10.06.2019
Personnel: Dave Berry (Pub.); Marilyn Ellis (Adv. Mgr.); Robert Jackson (Ed.)
Parent company (for newspapers): Community Publishers, Inc.

CHESTERFIELD JOURNAL

Street address 1: 900 N Tucker Blvd
Street address city: Saint Louis
Street address state: MO
Zip/Postal code: 63101-1069
General Phone: (314) 821-1110
General Fax: (314) 821-3408
Editorial e-mail: mshatiro@yourjournal.com
Primary Website: stltoday.com/suburban-journals
Avg Free Circ: 17000
Audit By: Sworn/Estimate/Non-Audited
Audit Date: 10.06.2019
Personnel: Bob Williams (Pub.); Dan Crockwell (Circ. Mgr.); Mary Ann Wagner (Promo. Dir)

CHRISTIAN COUNTY HEADLINER NEWS

Street address 1: 114 N 2nd Ave
Street address city: Ozark
Street address state: MO
Zip/Postal code: 65721-8453
General Phone: (417) 581-3541
General Fax: (417) 581-3577
General/National Adv. E-mail: triciac@ccheadliner.com
Display Adv. E-mail: ashleys@ccheadliner.com
Editorial e-mail: ameliaw@ccheadliner.com
Primary Website: ccheadliner.com
Mthly Avg Views: 47039
Mthly Avg Unique Visitors: 13480
Year Established: 1961
Avg Paid Circ: 3412
Avg Free Circ: 377
Audit By: Sworn/Estimate/Non-Audited
Audit Date: 10.06.2019

Personnel: Amelia Wigton (Ed.); Dave Berry (Pub.); Tricia Chapman (Gen. Mgr.)

CITIZEN JOURNAL

Street address 1: 14522 S Outer 40 Rd
Street address city: Town And Country
Street address state: MO
Zip/Postal code: 63017-5737
General Phone: (314) 821-1110
General Fax: (314) 821-3408
General/National Adv. E-mail: service@stltoday.com
Editorial e-mail: gbailon@post-dispatch.com
Primary Website: suburbanjournals.stltoday.com
Year Established: 1940
Avg Free Circ: 15500
Audit By: Sworn/Estimate/Non-Audited
Audit Date: 10.06.2019
Personnel: Bob Williams (Adv. Mgr.); Dan Crockwell (Circ. Mgr.); Monika Kleban (Mng. Ed.)

CLARENCE COURIER

Street address 1: 106 E Maple St
Street address city: Clarence
Street address state: MO
Zip/Postal code: 63437-1723
General Phone: (660) 699-2344
General Fax: (660) 699-2194
General/National Adv. E-mail: advertising@clarencecourier.com
Editorial e-mail: editor@clarencecourier.com
Avg Paid Circ: 1600
Avg Free Circ: 118
Audit By: Sworn/Estimate/Non-Audited
Audit Date: 10.06.2019
Personnel: Dennis Williams (Pub., Ed.)

COURIER TRIBUNE

Street address 1: 104 N. Main St.
Street address city: Kearney
Street address state: MO
Zip/Postal code: 64068
General Phone: (816) 628-6010
General Fax: (816) 628-4422
Advertising Phone: (816) 454-9660
Editorial Phone: (816) 454-9660
General/National Adv. E-mail: advertise@mycouriertribune.com
Display Adv. E-mail: classifieds@mycouriertribune.com
Editorial e-mail: news@mycouriertribune.com
Primary Website: mycouriertribune.com
Avg Paid Circ: 4000
Audit By: Sworn/Estimate/Non-Audited
Audit Date: 10.06.2019
Personnel: Sandy Nelson (Pub.); Ryan Johnson (Adv. Mgr.); Amanda Lubinski (Ed.)

CRANE CHRONICLE/STONE COUNTY REPUBLICAN

Street address 1: 114 Main St
Street address city: Crane
Street address state: MO
Zip/Postal code: 65633-7359
General Phone: (417) 723-5248
General Fax: (417) 723-8490
General/National Adv. E-mail: screditor@centurylink.net
Display Adv. E-mail: scrclassified@centurylink.net
Editorial e-mail: screditor@centurylink.net
Primary Website: ccscrnews.com
Year Established: 1876
Avg Paid Circ: 1104
Avg Free Circ: 45
Audit By: Sworn/Estimate/Non-Audited
Audit Date: 10.06.2019
Personnel: Isaac Estes-Jones (Editor); Shana Harter (Legals); Judy Waisner (Reception/Classifieds)
Parent company (for newspapers): Stone County Publishing, Inc.

CROSS COUNTRY TIMES

Street address 1: 100 E JACKSON ST
Street address city: Willard
Street address state: MO
Zip/Postal code: 65781
General Phone: (417) 685-4328
General Fax: (417) 751-3499
Editorial e-mail: editor@crosscountrytimes.com
Year Established: 1979
Avg Paid Circ: 1500
Audit By: Sworn/Estimate/Non-Audited
Audit Date: 10.06.2019
Personnel: Cimmy Abbott (Mgr.); Laura Scott (Ed.)
Parent company (for newspapers): Greene County Commonwealth and continuing the Republic Monitor

CURRENT WAVE LLC

Street address 1: 102 PLUM ST
Street address city: Eminence
Street address state: MO
Zip/Postal code: 65466
General Phone: (573) 226-5229
General Fax: (573) 226-3335
General/National Adv. E-mail: cwave128@gmail.com
Editorial e-mail: cwave128@gmail.com
Primary Website: shannoncountycurrentwave.com
Year Established: 1874
Avg Paid Circ: 1600
Avg Free Circ: 24
Audit By: Sworn/Estimate/Non-Audited
Audit Date: 10.06.2019
Personnel: Susie Gates (Office Mgr.); Roger Dillon (Ed.); julie Anderson (Bookkeeper, Ad design)

DEKALB COUNTY RECORD-HERALD

Street address 1: 201 N Polk St
Street address city: Maysville
Street address state: MO
Zip/Postal code: 64469-9089
General Phone: (816) 449-2121
General Fax: (816) 449-2808
Primary Website: http://maysville.k12.mo.us/
Avg Paid Circ: 1900
Avg Free Circ: 73
Audit By: Sworn/Estimate/Non-Audited
Audit Date: 10.06.2019
Personnel: Terry Pearl (Pub.); Chrissy Jestes (Ed.)

DELTA NEWS CITIZEN

Street address 1: PO Box 669
Street address city: Kennett
Street address state: MO
Zip/Postal code: 63857-0669
General Phone: (573) 276-5148
General Fax: (573) 276-3687
General/National Adv. E-mail: csummers@dddnews.com
Editorial e-mail: srouse@stategazette.com
Primary Website: deltanewscitizen.com
Year Established: 1997
Avg Paid Circ: 2500
Audit By: Sworn/Estimate/Non-Audited
Audit Date: 10.06.2019
Personnel: Shelia Rose (Pub.); Trina Bell (Ed.); Mike Smith (Gen. Mgr.)
Parent company (for newspapers): Rust Communications

DEMOCRAT NEWS

Street address 1: 131 S Main St
Street address city: Fredericktown
Street address state: MO
Zip/Postal code: 63645-1451
General Phone: (573) 783-3366
General Fax: (573) 783-6890
General/National Adv. E-mail: mboren@dailyjournalonline.com
Display Adv. E-mail: 33.tripp.33@gmail.com
Editorial e-mail: dsmith@dailyjournalonline.com
Primary Website: dailyjournalonline.com/dn
Year Established: 1870
Avg Paid Circ: 2300
Avg Free Circ: 300
Audit By: Sworn/Estimate/Non-Audited
Audit Date: 10.06.2019
Personnel: Doug Smith (Ed.); Kevin Saylor (Circ. Dir.); Lawana Starkey (Adv.); Donny Cheatham (Adv.); Matt Kingman (Sports Ed.)
Parent company (for newspapers): Dispatch-Argus

DIXON PILOT NEWSPAPER AND PRINT SHOP

Street address 1: 302 N Locust St
Street address city: Dixon
Street address state: MO
Zip/Postal code: 65459-6055
General Phone: (573) 759-2127
General Fax: (573) 759-6226
General/National Adv. E-mail: dixonpilotnews@yahoo.com; news@dixonpilot.com
Primary Website: dixonpilot.com
Year Established: 1915
Avg Paid Circ: 2200
Audit By: Sworn/Estimate/Non-Audited
Audit Date: 10.06.2019
Personnel: Rick Blackburn (Co Publishers); Connie Erisman

DOUGLAS COUNTY HERALD

Street address 1: 302 E Washington Ave
Street address city: Ava
Street address state: MO
Zip/Postal code: 65608-5547
General Phone: (417) 683-4181
General Fax: (417) 683-4102
Primary Website: douglascountyherald.com
Year Established: 1887
Avg Paid Circ: 3150
Avg Free Circ: 15
Audit By: Sworn/Estimate/Non-Audited
Audit Date: 10.06.2019
Personnel: Keith Moore (Ed.); Sue Jones

EAST PRAIRIE EAGLE & ENTERPRISE-COURIER

Street address 1: 101 E Main St
Street address city: East Prairie
Street address state: MO
Zip/Postal code: 63845-1136
General Phone: (573) 683-3351
General Fax: (573) 649-9530
General/National Adv. E-mail: advertising@enterprisecourier.com
Editorial e-mail: news@enterprisecourier.com
Primary Website: enterprisecourier.com
Avg Paid Circ: 2500
Audit By: Sworn/Estimate/Non-Audited
Audit Date: 10.06.2019
Personnel: Carlin Bennett (Publisher); Adam Rhodes (Editor)

EL DORADO SPRINGS SUN

Street address 1: 125 N Main St
Street address city: El Dorado Springs
Street address state: MO
Zip/Postal code: 64744-1141
General Phone: (417) 876-3841
General Fax: (417) 876-3848
Editorial e-mail: sunnews@socket.net
Primary Website: eldoradospringsmo.com
Year Established: 1890
Avg Paid Circ: 3800
Avg Free Circ: 3580
Audit By: Sworn/Estimate/Non-Audited
Audit Date: 10.06.2019
Personnel: Kimball S. Long (Pub.); Kenneth W. Long (Ed.)

ELDON ADVERTISER

Street address 1: 415 S Maple St
Street address city: Eldon
Street address state: MO
Zip/Postal code: 65026-1856
General Phone: (573) 392-5658
General Fax: (573) 392-7755
General/National Adv. E-mail: advertiser@vernonpublishing.com
Editorial e-mail: tvernon@vernonpublishing.com
Primary Website: vernonpublishing.com
Avg Paid Circ: 3550
Avg Free Circ: 52
Audit By: Sworn/Estimate/Non-Audited
Audit Date: 10.06.2019
Personnel: Trevor Vernon (Publisher); Tim Flora (Editor); Trevor Vernon (Pub.)
Parent company (for newspapers): Vernon Publishing, Inc

FARMINGTON PRESS

Street address 1: 1513 S Saint Joe Dr
Street address city: Park Hills
Street address state: MO
Zip/Postal code: 63601-2402
General Phone: (573) 431-2010
General Fax: (573) 431-7640
Advertising Fax: (573) 518-0765
Editorial e-mail: dsmith@dailyjournalonline.com
Primary Website: pressleader.com
Audit By: Sworn/Estimate/Non-Audited
Audit Date: 10.06.2019
Personnel: Doug Smith (Ed.); Eugene Jackson (Pub.); George Easley (Circ. Dir.)

FAYETTE ADVERTISER

Street address 1: 203 N Main St
Street address city: Fayette
Street address state: MO
Zip/Postal code: 65248-1421
General Phone: (660) 248-2235
General Fax: (660) 248-1200
General/National Adv. E-mail: advertising@fayettenews.com
Display Adv. E-mail: advertising@fayettenews.com
Editorial e-mail: proll@fayettenews.com
Primary Website: fayettenewspapers.com
Year Established: 1840
Avg Paid Circ: 1800
Audit By: Sworn/Estimate/Non-Audited
Audit Date: 10.06.2019
Personnel: Patrick Roll (Publisher); Linda Vroman (Office Mgr); Mike Ursery (Sports Editor)

FLORISSANT/BLACK JACK-NORTH COUNTY JOURNAL

Street address 1: 7751 N Lindbergh Blvd
Street address city: Hazelwood
Street address state: MO
Zip/Postal code: 63042-2135
General Phone: (314) 972-1111
General Fax: (314) 831-7643
Editorial e-mail: cmarty@yourjournal.com
Primary Website: suburbanjournals.stltoday.com
Avg Free Circ: 35000
Audit By: Sworn/Estimate/Non-Audited
Audit Date: 10.06.2019
Personnel: Mary Ann Wagner (Promotions Dir); Tammie Sprinkle (Adv. Mgr.)

FORT LEONARD WOOD GUIDON

Street address 1: 4079 Illinois Ave
Street address city: Fort Leonard Wood
Street address state: MO
Zip/Postal code: 65473-9105
General Phone: (573) 563-5014
General Fax: (573) 336-5487
Advertising Phone: (417) 837-1904
General/National Adv. E-mail: dgunter@gannett.com
Editorial e-mail: guidoneditor@myguidon.com
Primary Website: myguidon.com
Audit By: Sworn/Estimate/Non-Audited
Audit Date: 10.06.2019
Personnel: Mike Bowers (Ed.); Marti Yoshida (Asst. Ed.); Amanda Thompson (Adv.)

GALLATIN NORTH MISSOURIAN

Street address 1: 609B S Main St
Street address city: Gallatin
Street address state: MO
Zip/Postal code: 64640-1447
General Phone: (660) 663-2154
General Fax: (660) 663-2498
Advertising Phone: (660) 663-2154
Advertising Fax: (660) 663-2498
Editorial Phone: (660) 663-2154
Editorial Fax: (660) 663-2498
General/National Adv. E-mail: GPC@GPCink.com
Display Adv. E-mail: ads@GPCink.com
Classified Adv. e-mail: ads@GPCink.com
Editorial e-mail: news@GPCink.com
Primary Website: NorthMissourian.com
Mthly Avg Views: 2561
Mthly Avg Unique Visitors: 1888
Year Established: 1864
Avg Paid Circ: 1700
Audit By: Sworn/Estimate/Non-Audited
Audit Date: 10.06.2019

Personnel: Liz Wilkinson (Owner/Pub.); Darryl Wilkinson (Owner/Pub.)

GASCONADE COUNTY REPUBLICAN

Street address 1: 106 E Washington Ave
Street address city: Owensville
Street address state: MO
Zip/Postal code: 65066-1316
General Phone: (573) 437-2323
General/National Adv. E-mail: dwarden@wardpub.com
Display Adv. E-mail: dwarden@wardpub.com
Editorial e-mail: news@wardpub.com
Primary Website: gasconadecountyrepublican.com
Year Established: 1905
Avg Paid Circ: 2800
Audit By: Sworn/Estimate/Non-Audited
Audit Date: 10.06.2019
Personnel: Don Warden (Assoc.); Dennis Warden (Publisher); Dave Marner (Ed.)

GLADSTONE DISPATCH

Street address 1: 104 N Main St
Street address city: Liberty
Street address state: MO
Zip/Postal code: 64068-1640
General Phone: (816) 454-9660
General Fax: (816) 781-0909
General/National Adv. E-mail: quinn.gregg@npgco.com
Display Adv. E-mail: rachel.chrisman@npgco.com
Editorial e-mail: amy.neal@npgco.com
Primary Website: gladstonedispatch.com
Audit By: Sworn/Estimate/Non-Audited
Audit Date: 10.06.2019
Personnel: Amy Neal (Ed.); Sandy Nelson (Pub.)

HALE HORIZONS

Street address 1: 29236 Highway J
Street address city: Hale
Street address state: MO
Zip/Postal code: 64643
General Phone: (660) 565-2555
General Fax: (660) 565-2556
Editorial e-mail: halehorizons@cvalley.net
Primary Website: facebook.com/pages/Hale-Horizons/133432296718836
Year Established: 1996
Avg Paid Circ: 750
Audit By: Sworn/Estimate/Non-Audited
Audit Date: 10.06.2019
Personnel: Cynthia Corf (Publisher)

HIGGINSVILLE ADVANCE

Street address 1: 3002 Highway 13 Blvd
Street address city: Higginsville
Street address state: MO
Zip/Postal code: 64037-1870
General Phone: (660) 584-3611
General Fax: (660) 584-7966
General/National Adv. E-mail: bmackie@ctcis.net
Display Adv. E-mail: bmackie@ctcis.net
Editorial e-mail: higvladv@ctcis.net
Primary Website: mainstreetmedia.us
Year Established: 1876
Avg Paid Circ: 1700
Avg Free Circ: 15
Audit By: Sworn/Estimate/Non-Audited
Audit Date: 10.06.2019
Personnel: Frank Mercer (Pub)
Parent company (for newspapers): Main Street Media, Inc

HOUSTON HERALD

Street address 1: 113 N Grand Ave
Street address city: Houston
Street address state: MO
Zip/Postal code: 65483-1223
General Phone: (417) 967-2000
General Fax: (417) 967-2096
General/National Adv. E-mail: ads@houstonherald.com
Display Adv. E-mail: ads@houstonherald.com
Classified Adv. e-mail: ads@houstonherald.com
Editorial e-mail: news@houstonherald.com
Primary Website: houstonherald.com
Mthly Avg Views: 2000000
Mthly Avg Unique Visitors: 100000
Year Established: 1878
Avg Paid Circ: 4075
Avg Free Circ: 6100
Audit By: Sworn/Estimate/Non-Audited
Audit Date: 10.06.2019
Personnel: Bradley G. Gentry (Publisher); Jeff McNiell (Ed.)

HUMANSVILLE STAR-LEADER

Street address 1: 117 N Ohio St
Street address city: Humansville
Street address state: MO
Zip/Postal code: 65674-8734
General Phone: (417) 754-2228
General Fax: (417) 646-8015
General/National Adv. E-mail: humansvillestarleader@gmail.com
Display Adv. E-mail: sacosageads@centurytel.net
Editorial e-mail: sacosagenews@centurytel.net
Primary Website: mainstreetmedia.us
Year Established: 1887
Avg Paid Circ: 1715
Avg Free Circ: 10
Audit By: Sworn/Estimate/Non-Audited
Audit Date: 10.06.2019
Personnel: Donna White (Adv. Mgr.); Michael Crawford (Ed.)
Parent company (for newspapers): Main Street Media, Inc.

INDEPENDENT NEWS

Street address 1: 25 Saint Anthony Ln
Street address city: Florissant
Street address state: MO
Zip/Postal code: 63031-6720
General Phone: (314) 831-4645
General Fax: (314) 831-4566
Advertising Phone: (314) 831-4645
Advertising Fax: (314) 831-4566
Editorial Phone: (314) 831-4645
Editorial Fax: (314) 831-4566
General/National Adv. E-mail: independentnws@aol.com
Display Adv. E-mail: independentnws@aol.com
Editorial e-mail: independentnws@aol.com
Primary Website: flovalleynews.com
Mthly Avg Views: 50000
Mthly Avg Unique Visitors: 2500
Year Established: 1987
Avg Free Circ: 25506
Audit By: CVC
Audit Date: 12.12.2017
Personnel: Phil Tankersley (Circ. Mgr.); Robert Lindsey (Editor-Publisher); Carol Arnett (Reporter); Tom Anselm (Sales Mgr.); Patricia Lindsey (Assistant editor- Entertainment); Nichole Richardson (Copy& Associate Editor)
Parent company (for newspapers): Two Rivers Publishing o. Inc.

JACKSON COUNTY ADVOCATE

Street address 1: 1102 Main St
Street address 2: Suite A
Street address city: Grandview
Street address state: MO
Zip/Postal code: 64030-2480
General Phone: (816) 761-6200
General Fax: (816) 761-8215
General/National Adv. E-mail: mwilson@jcadvocate.com
Display Adv. E-mail: bdavis@jcadvocate.com
Editorial e-mail: mwilson@jcadvocate.com
Primary Website: http://jcadvocate.blogspot.com/
Year Established: 1953
Avg Paid Circ: 6000
Avg Free Circ: 175
Audit By: Sworn/Estimate/Non-Audited
Audit Date: 10.06.2019
Personnel: Mary Wilson (Editor)

KANSAS CITY BUSINESS JOURNAL

Street address 1: 1100 Main St
Street address 2: Ste 2450
Street address city: Kansas City
Street address state: MO
Zip/Postal code: 64105-5189
General Phone: (816) 421-5900
General Fax: (816) 472-4010
Primary Website: kansascity.bizjournals.com
Year Established: 1982
Avg Paid Circ: 10500
Audit By: Sworn/Estimate/Non-Audited
Audit Date: 10.06.2019
Personnel: Stacie Prosser (Pub.); Brian Kaberline (Ed.); Russel Gray (Mng. Ed.)

KNOB NOSTER ITEM

Street address 1: 111 N Jackson Ave
Street address city: Knob Noster
Street address state: MO
Zip/Postal code: 65336-1315
General Phone: (660) 563-3606
Editorial e-mail: knobnosteritem@sbcglobal.net
Year Established: 1958
Avg Paid Circ: 800
Avg Free Circ: 10
Audit By: Sworn/Estimate/Non-Audited
Audit Date: 10.06.2019
Personnel: Stan Hall (Ed.)

LAMAR DEMOCRAT

Street address 1: 100 E 11th St
Street address city: Lamar
Street address state: MO
Zip/Postal code: 64759-1943
General Phone: (417) 682-5529
General Fax: (417) 682-5595
Advertising Phone: (417) 682-5529 x11
Editorial Phone: (417) 682-5529 x16
General/National Adv. E-mail: melissa@lamardemocrat.com
Editorial e-mail: melodymetzger@lamardemocrat.com
Primary Website: lamardemocrat.com
Year Established: 1920
Avg Paid Circ: 3335
Audit By: Sworn/Estimate/Non-Audited
Audit Date: 10.06.2019
Personnel: Douglas D. Davis (Pub.); Melody Metzger (Circ. Mgr.); Rayma B. Davis (Ed.)

LAWRENCE COUNTY RECORD

Street address 1: 312 S Hickory St
Street address city: Mount Vernon
Street address state: MO
Zip/Postal code: 65712-1450
General Phone: (417) 466-2185
General Fax: (417) 466-7865
General/National Adv. E-mail: recordadvertising@centurytel.net
Display Adv. E-mail: recordadvertising@centurytel.net
Editorial e-mail: thepaper@lawrencecountyrecord.com
Primary Website: lawrencecountyrecord.com
Year Established: 1876
Avg Paid Circ: 4000
Avg Free Circ: 7600
Audit By: Sworn/Estimate/Non-Audited
Audit Date: 10.06.2019
Personnel: Ryan Squibb (Pub./Ed.); Cheryl Reynolds (Adv. Mgr.)

LEE'S SUMMIT JOURNAL

Street address 1: 1601 McGee St.
Street address city: Kansas City
Street address state: MO
Zip/Postal code: 64108
General Phone: (816) 234-4345
Editorial e-mail: gfarmer@kcstar.com
Primary Website: lsjournal.com
Year Established: 1881
Avg Paid Circ: 3369
Avg Free Circ: 2521
Audit By: Sworn/Estimate/Non-Audited
Audit Date: 10.06.2019
Personnel: Mike Fannin (VP./ Exec. Ed.); Maria Martin (Ed.); Dave McQueen (Sports Ed.)
Parent company (for newspapers): The McClatchy Company

LEE'S SUMMIT TRIBUNE

Street address 1: 219 SE Douglas St
Street address city: Lees Summit
Street address state: MO
Zip/Postal code: 64063-2328
General Phone: (816) 524-0061
Advertising Phone: (816) 524-0061
Editorial Phone: (816) 524-0061
Editorial Fax: (816) 600-6102
General/National Adv. E-mail: editor@lstribune.net
Display Adv. E-mail: editor@lstribune.net
Editorial e-mail: Linda@lstribune.net
Primary Website: lstribune.net
Mthly Avg Views: 100000
Mthly Avg Unique Visitors: 44000
Year Established: 2002
Avg Paid Circ: 3500
Audit By: Sworn/Estimate/Non-Audited
Audit Date: 10.06.2019
Personnel: Linda Ahern (Owner/Pub.)

LINN COUNTY LEADER

Street address 1: 314 N Main St
Street address 2: PO Box 40
Street address city: Brookfield
Street address state: MO
Zip/Postal code: 64628-1601
General Phone: (660) 258-7237
General Fax: (660) 258-7238
General/National Adv. E-mail: lmeissen@linncountyleader.com
Display Adv. E-mail: tniemeier@linncountyleader.com
Editorial e-mail: dwatson@linncountyleader.com
Primary Website: linncountyleader.com
Year Established: 2001
Avg Paid Circ: 3300
Audit By: Sworn/Estimate/Non-Audited
Audit Date: 10.06.2019
Personnel: Matt Ragsdale (News Ed.); Henry Janssen (Sports Ed.); Honi Brown (Reg. Ad. Dir.)
Parent company (for newspapers): CherryRoad Media; CherryRoad Media

LOUISIANA PRESS JOURNAL

Street address 1: 14522 S Outer 40 Rd
Street address city: Town And Country
Street address state: MO
Zip/Postal code: 63017-5737
General Phone: (314) 821-1110
General Fax: (314) 821-0745
General/National Adv. E-mail: service@stltoday.com
Editorial e-mail: gbailon@post-dispatch.com
Primary Website: suburbanjournals.stltoday.com
Year Established: 1922
Avg Paid Circ: 89722
Avg Free Circ: 226000
Audit By: Sworn/Estimate/Non-Audited
Audit Date: 10.06.2019
Personnel: Bob Williams (Pub.); Keith Carpenter (Adv. Dir.); Dan Crockwell (Circ. Dir.); Monika Kieban (Mng. Ed.)
Parent company (for newspapers): Lakeway Publishers, Inc.

MARIES COUNTY GAZETTE

Street address 1: 218 S MAIN ST
Street address city: Vienna
Street address state: MO
Zip/Postal code: 65582
General Phone: (573) 422-3441
General Fax: (573) 422-3441
Primary Website: facebook.com/pages/maries-county-gazette/163412607020457
Avg Paid Circ: 1500
Audit By: Sworn/Estimate/Non-Audited
Audit Date: 10.06.2019
Personnel: Kurt Lewis (Pub.); Nichoel Snodgrass (Ed.)

MCDONALD COUNTY NEWS-GAZETTE

Street address 1: 11248 US-71
Street address city: Pineville
Street address state: MO
Zip/Postal code: 64856
General Phone: (417) 223-4675
General Fax: (418) 223-4049
Editorial e-mail: thepress@olemac.net
Avg Paid Circ: 1431
Audit By: Sworn/Estimate/Non-Audited
Audit Date: 10.06.2019
Personnel: George Pogue (Pub.); Donnie Parlet; Rick Peck (Mng. Ed.)

MCDONALD COUNTY PRESS

Street address 1: 11248 US-71

Street address city: Pineville
Street address state: MO
Zip/Postal code: 64856
General Phone: (417) 223-4675
General Fax: (417) 223-4049
Editorial e-mail: thepress@olemac.net
Primary Website: stephensmedia.com/newspapers/missouri
Avg Paid Circ: 6127
Audit By: Sworn/Estimate/Non-Audited
Audit Date: 10.06.2019
Personnel: Rick Peck (Ed.); George Pogue (Pub.); Donnie Parlet
Parent company (for newspapers): WEHCO Media, Inc.

MEMPHIS DEMOCRAT

Street address 1: 121 S Main St
Street address city: Memphis
Street address state: MO
Zip/Postal code: 63555-1423
General Phone: (660) 465-7016
General Fax: (660) 465-2803
General/National Adv. E-mail: memdemoc@nemr.net
Display Adv. E-mail: chris@memphisdemocrat.com
Editorial e-mail: chris@memphisdemocrat.com
Primary Website: memphisdemocrat.com
Year Established: 1872
Avg Paid Circ: 2780
Audit By: Sworn/Estimate/Non-Audited
Audit Date: 10.06.2019
Personnel: Chris Feeney (Ed.)

MILLER COUNTY AUTOGRAM SENTINEL

Street address 1: 415 S Maple St
Street address city: Eldon
Street address state: MO
Zip/Postal code: 65026-1856
General Phone: (573) 392-5658
General Fax: (573) 392-7755
Advertising Phone: (573) 392-5658
General/National Adv. E-mail: autogram-sentinel@vernonpublishing.com
Display Adv. E-mail: dfair@vernonpublishing.com
Editorial e-mail: gduffield@vernonpublishing.com
Primary Website: vernonpublishing.com/Autogram-Sentine
Year Established: 1883
Avg Paid Circ: 1875
Avg Free Circ: 20
Audit By: Sworn/Estimate/Non-Audited
Audit Date: 10.06.2019
Personnel: Trevor Vernon (Pub.); Ginny Duffield (Ed.); Debbie Fair (Ad Sales)
Parent company (for newspapers): Vernon Publishing, Inc

MISSISSIPPI COUNTY TIMES

Street address 1: 207 S Main St
Street address city: Charleston
Street address state: MO
Zip/Postal code: 63834-1639
General Phone: (573) 683-6689
General Fax: (573) 683-4291
General/National Adv. E-mail: countytimes@sbcglobal.net
Editorial e-mail: countytimes@sbcglobal.net
Primary Website: misscotimes.com
Avg Free Circ: 40000
Audit By: Sworn/Estimate/Non-Audited
Audit Date: 10.06.2019
Personnel: Richard Scheffer (Ed.)

MISSOURIAN-NEWS

Street address 1: 413 E Main St
Street address city: Portageville
Street address state: MO
Zip/Postal code: 63873-1617
General Phone: (573) 379-5355
General Fax: (573) 379-5488
General/National Adv. E-mail: lcollins@dddnews.com
Editorial e-mail: sseal@dddnews.com
Primary Website: pvmonews.com
Avg Paid Circ: 1700
Audit By: Sworn/Estimate/Non-Audited
Audit Date: 10.06.2019
Personnel: Bud Hunt (Pub.); H. Scott Seal (Ed./Gen. Mgr.)

Parent company (for newspapers): Rust Communications

MONROE COUNTY APPEAL

Street address 1: 230 N Main St
Street address city: Paris
Street address state: MO
Zip/Postal code: 65275-1329
General Phone: (314) 574-4401
General Fax: (660) 327-4847
Advertising Phone: (314) 574-4401
Editorial Phone: (314) 574-4401
General/National Adv. E-mail: ads@monroecountyappeal.com
Display Adv. E-mail: ads@monroecountyappeal.com
Editorial e-mail: news@monroecountyappeal.com
Primary Website: monroecountyappeal.com
Year Established: 1868
Avg Paid Circ: 1000
Avg Free Circ: 0
Audit By: Sworn/Estimate/Non-Audited
Audit Date: 10.06.2019
Personnel: Dan Crockwell (Pub); Margie Crockwell (Ad Design)
Parent company (for newspapers): Lewis County Press

MONTGOMERY STANDARD

Street address 1: 115 W 2nd St
Street address city: Montgomery City
Street address state: MO
Zip/Postal code: 63361-1812
General Phone: (573) 564-2339
General Fax: (573) 564-2313
Editorial e-mail: standard@socket.net
Year Established: 1868
Avg Paid Circ: 3200
Avg Free Circ: 73
Audit By: Sworn/Estimate/Non-Audited
Audit Date: 10.06.2019
Personnel: John Fisher (Ed.)

MORGAN COUNTY PRESS

Street address 1: 104 W Jasper Street
Street address city: Versailles
Street address state: MO
Zip/Postal code: 65084
General Phone: (573) 378-5441
General Fax: 573-378-4292
General/National Adv. E-mail: news@morgancountypress.com
Display Adv. E-mail: ads@morgancountypress.com
Editorial e-mail: news@morgancountypress.com
Primary Website: morgancountypress.com
Year Established: 1911
Avg Paid Circ: 1100
Avg Free Circ: 279
Audit By: Sworn/Estimate/Non-Audited
Audit Date: 10.10.2021
Personnel: Bryan Jones (owner, publisher)
Parent company (for newspapers): Pipistrelle Press, LLC

MOUND CITY NEWS

Street address 1: 511 State St
Street address city: Mound City
Street address state: MO
Zip/Postal code: 64470-1144
General Phone: (660) 442-5423
General Fax: (660) 442-5423
Editorial e-mail: moundcitynews@socket.net
Primary Website: moundcitynews.com
Year Established: 1879
Avg Paid Circ: 2600
Audit By: Sworn/Estimate/Non-Audited
Audit Date: 10.06.2019
Personnel: Adam Johnson (Ed.)

MOUNTAIN GROVE NEWS-JOURNAL

Street address 1: 150 E 1st St
Street address city: Mountain Grove
Street address state: MO
Zip/Postal code: 65711-1742
General Phone: (417) 926-5148
General Fax: (417) 926-6648
General/National Adv. E-mail: classifieds@news-journal.net
Display Adv. E-mail: classifieds@news-journal.net
Editorial e-mail: doug@news-journal.net
Primary Website: news-journal.net
Year Established: 1882
Avg Paid Circ: 3200
Avg Free Circ: 9850
Audit By: Sworn/Estimate/Non-Audited
Audit Date: 10.06.2019
Personnel: Sandy Anderson (Pub.); Doug Berger (Ed.)
Parent company (for newspapers): Lebanon Publishing Co.

MOUNTAIN VIEW STANDARD

Street address 1: 1004 E US Highway 60
Street address city: Mountain View
Street address state: MO
Zip/Postal code: 65548-8070
General Phone: (417) 934-2025
General Fax: (417) 934-1591
General/National Adv. E-mail: standardnews@centurytel.net
Display Adv. E-mail: brian@mvstandard.com
Editorial e-mail: tianna@mvstandard.com
Primary Website: mountainviewstandard.com
Year Established: 1906
Avg Paid Circ: 7600
Avg Free Circ: 550
Audit By: Sworn/Estimate/Non-Audited
Audit Date: 10.06.2019
Personnel: Tianna Brook (Ed.)

NEVADA HERALD

Street address 1: 131 S Cedar St
Street address city: Nevada
Street address state: MO
Zip/Postal code: 64772-3309
General Phone: (417) 667-3344
General Fax: (417) 667-8384
General/National Adv. E-mail: ndmcomposing@gmail.com
Display Adv. E-mail: lmcvay@nevadadailymail.com
Editorial e-mail: ndmeditorial@gmail.com
Primary Website: nevadadailymail.com
Year Established: 1883
Avg Paid Circ: 5500
Avg Free Circ: 105
Audit By: Sworn/Estimate/Non-Audited
Audit Date: 10.06.2019
Personnel: Lorie Harter (Pub./Adv. Mgr.); Ralph Pokorny (Ed.); Chris Jones (Prod. Mgr.); Linda Shankel (Circ. Mgr.)

NEW HAVEN LEADER

Street address 1: 136 E 4th St
Street address city: Hermann
Street address state: MO
Zip/Postal code: 65041-1177
General Phone: (573) 237-3222
General Fax: (573) 237-7222
General/National Adv. E-mail: hacmgr@lcs.net
Editorial e-mail: nhleditor@lcs.net
Primary Website: newhavenleader.com
Year Established: 1895
Avg Paid Circ: 1700
Audit By: Sworn/Estimate/Non-Audited
Audit Date: 10.06.2019
Personnel: Buck Collier (Ed.)

NEWS-XPRESS

Street address 1: 5 N Main St
Street address city: Butler
Street address state: MO
Zip/Postal code: 64730-2135
General Phone: (660) 679-6126
General Fax: (660) 679-4905
General/National Adv. E-mail: butlerxchanger@gmail.com
Editorial e-mail: newsxpress@yourxgroup.com
Primary Website: yourxgroup.com
Year Established: 1984
Avg Paid Circ: 2570
Avg Free Circ: 65
Audit By: Sworn/Estimate/Non-Audited
Audit Date: 10.06.2019

Personnel: Paula Schowengerdt (Adv. Mgr.); C.A. Moore (Pub./Editor)

NEWTON COUNTY NEWS

Street address 1: 200 S Jefferson St
Street address city: Neosho
Street address state: MO
Zip/Postal code: 64850-1753
General Phone: (409) 379-2416
Editorial e-mail: newtonnews@valornet.com
Primary Website: newtoncountynews.net
Avg Paid Circ: 2500
Avg Free Circ: 10
Audit By: Sworn/Estimate/Non-Audited
Audit Date: 10.06.2019
Personnel: Sean Wilkerson (Ed.)

NIXA NEWS ENTERPRISE

Street address 1: 123 W Sherman Way
Street address 2: Ste 101
Street address city: Nixa
Street address state: MO
Zip/Postal code: 65714-7657
General Phone: (417) 725-3745
General Fax: (417) 725-3683
General/National Adv. E-mail: paulj@ccheadliner.com
Editorial e-mail: ameliaw@ccheadliner.com
Primary Website: http://ccheadliner.com/
Avg Paid Circ: 2463
Audit By: Sworn/Estimate/Non-Audited
Audit Date: 10.06.2019
Personnel: Chuck Branch (Gen. Mgr.); Matt Roberts (Ed.)

NODAWAY NEWS LEADER

Street address 1: 116 E 3rd St
Street address city: Maryville
Street address state: MO
Zip/Postal code: 64468-1640
General Phone: (660) 562-4747
General Fax: (660) 562-3607
General/National Adv. E-mail: ldalton@nodawaynews.com
Display Adv. E-mail: ldalton@nodawaynews.com
Editorial e-mail: kwilson@nodawaynews.com
Primary Website: nodawaynews.com
Year Established: 1996
Avg Paid Circ: 2649
Audit By: Sworn/Estimate/Non-Audited
Audit Date: 10.06.2019
Personnel: Kay Wilson (Pub./Owner); Lisa Dalton (Adv. Mgr.)

NORBORNE DEMOCRAT-LEADER

Street address 1: 106 S Pine St
Street address city: Norborne
Street address state: MO
Zip/Postal code: 64668-1238
General Phone: (660) 593-3712
General Fax: (660) 593-3712
General/National Adv. E-mail: leader@greenhills.net
Editorial e-mail: leader@greenhills.net
Avg Paid Circ: 1300
Audit By: Sworn/Estimate/Non-Audited
Audit Date: 10.06.2019
Personnel: Frank Mercer (Ed.)
Parent company (for newspapers): Main Street Media, Inc.; Main Street Media, Inc.-OOB

NORTH SIDE JOURNAL

Street address 1: 14522 S Outer 40 Rd
Street address 2: Ste 300
Street address city: Chesterfield
Street address state: MO
Zip/Postal code: 63017-5755
General Phone: (314) 340-8000
General Fax: (314) 831-4986
Advertising Phone: (314) 340-8500
Editorial Phone: (314) 340-3139
General/National Adv. E-mail: cmarty@yourjournal.com
Editorial e-mail: mkoenig@post-dispatch.com
Primary Website: yourjournal.com
Avg Free Circ: 31000
Audit By: Sworn/Estimate/Non-Audited
Audit Date: 10.06.2019

Personnel: Carolyn Marty (Pub.); Dan Crockwell (Circ Dir); Rich Sisak (Circ. Mgr.); Mary Ann Wagner (Promo. Dir)

OVERLAND/ST. ANN JOURNAL-NORTH COUNY JOURNAL

Street address 1: 7751 N Lindbergh Blvd
Street address city: Hazelwood
Street address state: MO
Zip/Postal code: 63042-2135
General Phone: (314) 972-1111
General Fax: (314) 831-7643
Editorial e-mail: cmarty@yourjournal.com
Primary Website: suburbanjournals.stltoday.com
Avg Free Circ: 22260
Audit By: Sworn/Estimate/Non-Audited
Audit Date: 10.06.2019
Personnel: Carolyn Marty (Pub.); Tammy Mortensen (Adv. Mgr.); Dan Crockwell (Circ. Mgr.)

OZARK COUNTY TIMES

Street address 1: 504 Third Street
Street address city: Gainesville
Street address state: MO
Zip/Postal code: 65655
General Phone: (417) 679-4641
General Fax: (417) 679-3423
General/National Adv. E-mail: jenny@ozarkcountytimes.com
Display Adv. E-mail: norene@ozarkcountytimes.com
Editorial e-mail: editor@ozarkcountytimes.com
Primary Website: ozarkcountytimes.com
Year Established: 1876
Avg Paid Circ: 3050
Audit By: Sworn/Estimate/Non-Audited
Audit Date: 10.06.2019
Personnel: Norene Prososki (Pub.); Jennifer Yarger (Adv. Mgr.); Sue Ann Jones (Ed.); Jessi Dreckman (Online manager/reporter)
Parent company (for newspapers): Ozark County Media LLC

PALMYRA SPECTATOR

Street address 1: 304 S Main St
Street address city: Palmyra
Street address state: MO
Zip/Postal code: 63461-1652
General Phone: (573) 769-3111
General Fax: (573) 769-3554
General/National Adv. E-mail: advertising@palmyra-spectator.com
Display Adv. E-mail: office@palmyra-spectator.com
Editorial e-mail: editorial@palmyra-spectator.com
Primary Website: palmyra-spectator.com
Year Established: 1839
Avg Paid Circ: 2628
Avg Free Circ: 75
Audit By: Sworn/Estimate/Non-Audited
Audit Date: 10.06.2019
Personnel: Mark Cheffey (Pub.)

PIERCE CITY LEADER-JOURNAL

Street address 1: PO Box 400
Street address city: Sarcoxie
Street address state: MO
Zip/Postal code: 64862-0400
General Phone: (417) 548-3311
General Fax: (417) 548-3312
General/National Adv. E-mail: fstop@centurytel.net
Year Established: 1903
Avg Paid Circ: 950
Avg Free Circ: 50
Audit By: Sworn/Estimate/Non-Audited
Audit Date: 10.06.2019
Personnel: Paul E. Donley (Ed.); Katrina Keys (Gen Mgr)

PLEASANT HILL TIMES

Street address 1: 126 S 1st St
Street address city: Pleasant Hill
Street address state: MO
Zip/Postal code: 64080-1604
General Phone: (816) 540-3500
General Fax: (816) 987-5699
General/National Adv. E-mail: cheryl.phtimes@comcast.net
Editorial e-mail: editor.phtimes@comcast.net
Primary Website: phtimes.net
Year Established: 1901
Audit By: Sworn/Estimate/Non-Audited
Audit Date: 10.06.2019
Personnel: F. Erik Powell (Pub./Ed.); Jan Powell (Pub.)

PRINCETON POST-TELEGRAPH

Street address 1: 704 W Main St
Street address city: Princeton
Street address state: MO
Zip/Postal code: 64673-1141
General Phone: (660) 748-3266
General Fax: (660) 748-3267
General/National Adv. E-mail: posttele@grm.net
Editorial e-mail: posttele@grm.net
Year Established: 1873
Avg Paid Circ: 1100
Avg Free Circ: 5200
Audit By: Sworn/Estimate/Non-Audited
Audit Date: 10.06.2019
Personnel: Ron Kinzler (Pub.); Preston J. Cole (Ed.)

PULASKI COUNTY MIRROR

Street address 1: 555 Marshall Dr
Street address city: Saint Robert
Street address state: MO
Zip/Postal code: 65584-5601
General Phone: (573) 336-5359
General Fax: (573) 336-7619
General/National Adv. E-mail: ldr-lrbarker@lebanondailyrecord.com
Display Adv. E-mail: anitav@lebanondailyrecord.com
Editorial e-mail: ssmith@pulaskicountymirror.com
Primary Website: pulaskicountymirror.com
Avg Paid Circ: 1200
Avg Free Circ: 10150
Audit By: Sworn/Estimate/Non-Audited
Audit Date: 10.06.2019
Personnel: Steve Smith (Ed.); Rene Barker (Adv. Sales Mgr.); Anita Hooser (Class. Adv. Mgr.)

PUXICO PRESS

Street address 1: 141 S E L HAWKS ST
Street address city: Puxico
Street address state: MO
Zip/Postal code: 63960
General Phone: (573) 222-3243
General Fax: (573) 222-6327
Editorial e-mail: puxpress@sbcglobal.net
Primary Website: darnews.com/Daily_American_Republic/Contact_Us.html
Year Established: 1884
Avg Paid Circ: 1285
Avg Free Circ: 3021
Audit By: Sworn/Estimate/Non-Audited
Audit Date: 10.06.2019
Personnel: Don Schrieber (Pub.); Sierra John (Ed.)
Parent company (for newspapers): Rust Communications

RALLS COUNTY HERALD-ENTERPRISE

Street address 1: 404 S Main St
Street address city: New London
Street address state: MO
Zip/Postal code: 63459-1326
General Phone: (573) 985-3420
General Fax: (573) 985-5531
Editorial e-mail: danielcrockwell@rallshe.com
Primary Website: rallscountypaper.com
Year Established: 1865
Avg Paid Circ: 1300
Avg Free Circ: 0
Audit By: Sworn/Estimate/Non-Audited
Audit Date: 10.06.2019
Personnel: Judith Statler (Pub.); Gene Statler (Ed.); Carolyn Trower (Ed.)

RICH HILL MINING REVIEW

Street address 1: 602 E Park Ave
Street address city: Rich Hill
Street address state: MO
Zip/Postal code: 64779-1224
General Phone: (417) 395-4131
General Fax: (417) 646-8015
Editorial e-mail: sacosagenews@centurytel.net
Avg Paid Circ: 1000
Avg Free Circ: 0
Audit By: Sworn/Estimate/Non-Audited
Audit Date: 10.06.2019
Personnel: Micheal Crawford (Pub.)
Parent company (for newspapers): Main Street Media, Inc.

RICHMOND NEWS

Street address 1: 204 W North Main St
Street address city: Richmond
Street address state: MO
Zip/Postal code: 64085-1610
General Phone: (816) 776-5454
General Fax: (816) 470-6397
Advertising Phone: (816) 776-5454
Advertising Fax: (816) 470-6397
General/National Adv. E-mail: marie@richmond-dailynews.com
Display Adv. E-mail: ads@richmond-dailynews.com
Classified Adv. e-mail: sales@richmond-dailynews.com
Editorial e-mail: editor@richmond-dailynews.com
Primary Website: richmond-dailynews.com
Year Established: 1914
Avg Paid Circ: 2050
Avg Free Circ: 8940
Audit By: Sworn/Estimate/Non-Audited
Audit Date: 10.06.2019
Personnel: JoEllen Black (Pub.); Marie King (Sales Mgr.); Tess Harris (Print/Dig Media Consultant); Joy Tipping (Mng. Ed.); Russ Green (Sports Ed.); Arron Sander (Pressman/Prod. Supervisor)
Parent company (for newspapers): Excelsior Springs Publishing

SALT RIVER JOURNAL

Street address 1: 200 N 3rd St
Street address city: Hannibal
Street address state: MO
Zip/Postal code: 63401-3504
General Phone: (573) 221-2800
General Fax: (573) 221-1568
Advertising Phone: (573) 248-2711
Editorial Phone: (573) 248-2750
General/National Adv. E-mail: jreynolds@gatehousemedia.com
Display Adv. E-mail: samara.campen@courierpost.com
Editorial e-mail: eric.dundon@courierpost.com
Primary Website: hannibal.net/saltriverjournal
Year Established: 1838
Avg Paid Circ: 5383
Avg Free Circ: 9230
Audit By: Sworn/Estimate/Non-Audited
Audit Date: 10.06.2019
Personnel: Jenetta Cranmer (Circ Mgr); Catherine Ripley (News Ed); Jessica Spurgron (Gen. Mgr.); Forest Gosset (Ed.)

SAVANNAH REPORTER AND ANDREW COUNTY DEMOCRAT

Street address 1: 107 W US Highway 71
Street address 2: Suite E
Street address city: Savannah
Street address state: MO
Zip/Postal code: 64485-2305
General Phone: (816) 324-3149
General Fax: (816) 324-3632
General/National Adv. E-mail: adsales@stjoelive.com
Editorial e-mail: editor@stjoelive.com
Primary Website: thesavannahreporter.com
Year Established: 1876
Avg Paid Circ: 2700
Audit By: Sworn/Estimate/Non-Audited
Audit Date: 10.06.2019
Personnel: Guy Speckman (Pub.); Leslie Speckman (Ed.); Brandi Abbott (Ad Sales)

SENECA NEWS-DISPATCH

Street address 1: 1108 Cherokee Ave
Street address city: Seneca
Street address state: MO
Zip/Postal code: 64865-9207
General Phone: (417) 776-2236
General Fax: (417) 776-2204
General/National Adv. E-mail: newsdis@netins.net
Editorial e-mail: jimmy@thenewsdispatch.net
Primary Website: senecanewsdispatch.com
Year Established: 1882
Avg Paid Circ: 1800
Avg Free Circ: 0
Audit By: Sworn/Estimate/Non-Audited
Audit Date: 10.06.2019
Personnel: Diane Friend (Ed.)

SHELBY COUNTY HERALD

Street address 1: 109 E Main St
Street address city: Shelbyville
Street address state: MO
Zip/Postal code: 63469-1433
General Phone: (573) 633-2261
General Fax: (573) 633-2133
General/National Adv. E-mail: news@shelbycountyherald.com
Primary Website: shelbycountyherald.com
Avg Paid Circ: 1500
Avg Free Circ: 40
Audit By: Sworn/Estimate/Non-Audited
Audit Date: 10.06.2019
Personnel: Martha Jane East (Ed.)
Parent company (for newspapers): NEMOnews Media Group, LLC

SLATER MAIN STREET NEWS

Street address 1: 222 Main St
Street address city: Slater
Street address state: MO
Zip/Postal code: 65349-1412
General Phone: (660) 529-2249
General Fax: (660) 529-2474
General/National Adv. E-mail: slaternews@socket.net
Year Established: 1886
Avg Paid Circ: 1200
Avg Free Circ: 13
Audit By: Sworn/Estimate/Non-Audited
Audit Date: 10.06.2019
Personnel: James Stanfield (Adv. Mgr.); Jean E. Black (Ed.); Suzette Large (Receptionist)

SOUTH COUNTY MAIL

Street address 1: 115 E Center St
Street address city: Rogersville
Street address state: MO
Zip/Postal code: 65742-9703
General Phone: (417) 753-2800
General Fax: (417) 753-2792
General/National Adv. E-mail: debbiec@marshfieldmail.com
Editorial e-mail: debbiec@marshfieldmail.com
Primary Website: http://marshfieldmail.com/rogersville/
Avg Paid Circ: 1200
Avg Free Circ: 10
Audit By: Sworn/Estimate/Non-Audited
Audit Date: 10.06.2019
Personnel: Dave Berry (Pub); Scott Kerber (Ed./GM)
Parent company (for newspapers): Community Publishers, Inc.

SOUTH COUNTY TIMES

Street address 1: 122 W Lockwood Ave
Street address 2: Fl 2
Street address city: Saint Louis
Street address state: MO
Zip/Postal code: 63119-2916
General Phone: (314) 968-2699
General Fax: (314) 968-2961
General/National Adv. E-mail: mchambers@timesnewspapers.com
Display Adv. E-mail: classifieds@timesnewspapers.com
Editorial e-mail: newsroom@timesnewspapers.com
Primary Website: timesnewspapers.com
Year Established: 1947
Avg Free Circ: 37489
Audit By: CVC
Audit Date: 31.12.2017
Personnel: Dwight Bitikofer (Pub.); Don Corrigan (Ed.); Mary Chambers (Adv. Mgr); Kevin Murphy (Mng. Ed.); Kim Besterfeldt (Circ. Mgr); Randy Drilingas (Prod. Mgr); Dustin Bitikofer (circulation manager)
Parent company (for newspapers): Webster-Kirkwood Times, Inc.

SOUTH MISSOURIAN-NEWS

Street address 1: 109 Chestnut St
Street address city: Thayer
Street address state: MO

Zip/Postal code: 65791-1201
General Phone: (417) 264-3085
General Fax: (417) 264-3814
Advertising Phone: (870) 895-3207
Editorial e-mail: news@areawidenews.com
Primary Website: areawidenews.com/
Avg Paid Circ: 1500
Avg Free Circ: 19600
Audit By: Sworn/Estimate/Non-Audited
Audit Date: 30.09.2017
Personnel: Janie Flynn (Pub.); Tammy Curtis (Mng. Ed.); Richard Irby (Ed.); Debra Perryman (Circ. Mgr.)
Parent company (for newspapers): Rust Communications

SOUTHWEST COUNTY JOURNAL

Street address 1: 14522 S Outer 40 Rd
Street address city: Town And Country
Street address state: MO
Zip/Postal code: 63017-5737
General Phone: (314) 821-1110
General Fax: (314) 821-0843
General/National Adv. E-mail: service@stltoday.com
Editorial e-mail: gballon@post-dispatch.com
Primary Website: suburbanjournals.stltoday.com
Avg Free Circ: 29000
Audit By: Sworn/Estimate/Non-Audited
Audit Date: 10.06.2019
Personnel: Dan Crockwell (Circ. Dir.)

SPRINGFIELD BUSINESS JOURNAL

Street address 1: 313 Park Central W
Street address city: Springfield
Street address state: MO
Zip/Postal code: 65806-1244
General Phone: (417) 831-3238
General Fax: (417) 831-5478
General/National Adv. E-mail: tbrierly@sbj.net
Editorial e-mail: eolson@sbj.net
Primary Website: sbj.net
Year Established: 1980
Avg Paid Circ: 3785
Avg Free Circ: 1039
Audit By: CVC
Audit Date: 30.09.2017
Personnel: Eric Olson (Ed.); Jennifer Jackson (Pub.); Dianne Elizabeth Weber (Circ.); Marty Goodnight (Adv.)

ST. CHARLES COUNTY JOURNAL

Street address 1: 330 N Main St
Street address 2: Ste 202
Street address city: Saint Charles
Street address state: MO
Zip/Postal code: 63301-2028
General Phone: (636)724-1080
General Fax: (636) 724-1080
Classified Adv. e-mail: journalpubs@stcharlescountyjournal.com
Editorial e-mail: shannon@pulselegal.com
Primary Website: pulselegal.com
Year Established: 2010
Avg Free Circ: 18600
Audit By: Sworn/Estimate/Non-Audited
Audit Date: 10.06.2019
Personnel: Shannon Grindinger (Pub.)

ST. CLAIR CO. COURIER

Street address 1: 285 Pine St
Street address city: Osceola
Street address state: MO
Zip/Postal code: 64776-7466
General Phone: (417) 646-2211
General Fax: (417) 646-8015
General/National Adv. E-mail: sacosageads@centurytel.net
Editorial e-mail: sacosagenews@centurytel.net
Primary Website: https://facebook.com/St-Clair-County-Courier-150568565081049/about/?ref=page_internal
Avg Paid Circ: 2165
Avg Free Circ: 24000
Audit By: Sworn/Estimate/Non-Audited
Audit Date: 10.06.2019
Personnel: John Farrell (Reporter); Michael Crawford (Pub.); Derek Wood (Ad. Sales)

Parent company (for newspapers): Main Street Media, Inc.

ST. LOUIS BUSINESS JOURNAL

Street address 1: 815 Olive St
Street address 2: Suite 100
Street address city: Saint Louis
Street address state: MO
Zip/Postal code: 63101-1509
General Phone: (314) 421-6200
General Fax: (314) 621-5031
Advertising Phone: (314) 421-8340
Editorial Phone: (314) 421-8324
General/National Adv. E-mail: gwells@bizjournals.com
Display Adv. E-mail: mceresia@bizjournals.com
Editorial e-mail: jdwyer@bizjournals.com
Primary Website: bizjournals.com/stlouis
Year Established: 1980
Audit By: Sworn/Estimate/Non-Audited
Audit Date: 10.06.2019
Personnel: Ellen Sherberg (Pub.); Patricia Miller (Ed.); Glynelle Wells (Adv. Dir.)

ST. LOUIS/SOUTHERN ILLINOIS LABOR TRIBUNE

Street address 1: 505 S Ewing Ave
Street address city: Saint Louis
Street address state: MO
Zip/Postal code: 63103-2901
General Phone: (314) 535-9660
General Fax: (314) 535-9013
Advertising Phone: (314) 256-4136
Advertising Fax: Same
Editorial Phone: (314) 535-9660
Editorial Fax: (314) 535-9013
General/National Adv. E-mail: advertising@labortribune.com
Display Adv. E-mail: advertising@labortribune.com
Editorial e-mail: news@labortribune.com
Primary Website: labortribune.com
Year Established: 1937
Avg Paid Circ: 31219
Avg Free Circ: 610
Audit By: Sworn/Estimate/Non-Audited
Audit Date: 10.06.2019
Personnel: Ed Finkelstein (Publisher); Tim Rowden (Associate Editor); Marvin Naftolin (Gen. Mgr.)
Parent company (for newspapers): Tribune Publishing, Inc.

STE. GENEVIEVE HERALD

Street address 1: 330 Market St
Street address city: Sainte Genevieve
Street address state: MO
Zip/Postal code: 63670-1638
General Phone: (573) 883-2222
General Fax: (573) 883-2833
General/National Adv. E-mail: jgettinger@stegenherald.com
Display Adv. E-mail: afox@stegenherald.com
Editorial e-mail: tcarrig@stegenherald.com
Primary Website: stegenherald.com
Mthly Avg Views: 50000
Mthly Avg Unique Visitors: 17000
Year Established: 1882
Avg Paid Circ: 3665
Avg Free Circ: 76
Audit By: Sworn/Estimate/Non-Audited
Audit Date: 10.06.2019
Personnel: Toby Carrig (Pub./Ed.); Jill Gettinger (Adv. Mgr.); Lindsay Resinger (Circ. Mgr.)
Parent company (for newspapers): Ste. Genevieve Media, LLC

STEELVILLE STAR-CRAWFORD MIRROR

Street address 1: 103 W MAIN ST
Street address city: Steelville
Street address state: MO
Zip/Postal code: 65565
General Phone: (573) 775-5454
General Fax: (573) 775-2668
General/National Adv. E-mail: matt@threeriverspublishing.com
Display Adv. E-mail: dforbes@steelvillestar.com
Editorial e-mail: ccase@cubafreepress.com
Primary Website: steelvillestar.com
Year Established: 1872
Avg Paid Circ: 3500
Avg Free Circ: 2250
Audit By: Sworn/Estimate/Non-Audited
Audit Date: 10.06.2019
Personnel: Rob Viehman (Pub.); Chris Case (Ed.); Janice McMillen (Circ. Mgr.)
Parent company (for newspapers): Three Rivers Publishing, Inc.

SULLIVAN INDEPENDENT NEWS

Street address 1: 411 Scottsdale Dr
Street address city: Sullivan
Street address state: MO
Zip/Postal code: 63080-1307
General Phone: (573) 468-6511
General Fax: (573) 468-4046
Advertising Phone: (573) 468-6511
Advertising Fax: (573) 468-4046
Editorial Phone: (573) 468-6511
General/National Adv. E-mail: nuz4u@fidnet.com
Display Adv. E-mail: nuz4u@fidnet.com
Editorial e-mail: nuz4u@fidnet.com
Primary Website: mysullivannews.com
Mthly Avg Views: 1200
Year Established: 1964
Avg Paid Circ: 5960
Avg Free Circ: 240
Audit By: Sworn/Estimate/Non-Audited
Audit Date: 10.06.2019
Personnel: James Bartle (Owner Mng. Ed.); Mark Hilse (Adv. Mgr.); Jennifer Manion (Owner); Carmin Ball (Office/Bus Mgr); Chris Hopwood (Mngr.)
Parent company (for newspapers): New Haven Independent Newspaper - Parent Company is Sullivan Independent Newspaper

THE ALBANY LEDGER

Street address 1: 213 W Clay St
Street address city: Albany
Street address state: MO
Zip/Postal code: 64402-1603
General Phone: (660) 726-3998
General Fax: (660) 726-3997
General/National Adv. E-mail: taradodge@aledger.net
Display Adv. E-mail: christy@aledger.net
Editorial e-mail: news@aledger.net
Primary Website: aledger.net
Year Established: 1868
Avg Paid Circ: 1500
Avg Free Circ: 45
Audit By: Sworn/Estimate/Non-Audited
Audit Date: 10.06.2019
Personnel: Don Groves (Ed.); Tara Dodge (Ad); Christy Groves (Pub./Graphic Artist)

THE ANDERSON GRAPHIC

Street address 1: 11248 US-71
Street address city: Pineville
Street address state: MO
Zip/Postal code: 64856
General Phone: (417) 223-4675
General Fax: (417) 223-4049
Editorial e-mail: thepress@olemac.net
Primary Website: stephensmedia.com/newspapers/missouri
Avg Paid Circ: 683
Audit By: Sworn/Estimate/Non-Audited
Audit Date: 10.06.2019
Personnel: Donnie Parlet (Adv. Mgr.); Rick Peck (Sports Ed.); George Pogue (Pub.)

THE BANNER-PRESS

Street address 1: 103 WALNUT ST
Street address city: Marble Hill
Street address state: MO
Zip/Postal code: 63764
General Phone: (573) 238-2821
General Fax: (573) 238-0020
Editorial e-mail: banpress@hotmail.com
Primary Website: thebannerpress.com
Year Established: 1881
Avg Paid Circ: 4200
Audit By: Sworn/Estimate/Non-Audited
Audit Date: 10.06.2019

Personnel: Gera LeGrand (Pub.); Linda Redeffer (Gen. Mgr.)
Parent company (for newspapers): Rust Communications

THE BELLE BANNER

Street address 1: 217 S. Alvarado Ave.
Street address city: Belle
Street address state: MO
Zip/Postal code: 65013
General Phone: (573) 859-3328
General Fax: (573) 859-6274
General/National Adv. E-mail: kjl@socket.net
Year Established: 1906
Avg Paid Circ: 2000
Avg Free Circ: 200
Audit By: Sworn/Estimate/Non-Audited
Audit Date: 10.06.2019
Personnel: Kurt J. Lewis (Pub.); Ron J. Lewis (Ed.)

THE BLAND COURIER

Street address 1: 217 S. Alvarado Ave.
Street address city: Belle
Street address state: MO
Zip/Postal code: 65013
General Phone: (573) 859-3328
General Fax: (573) 859-6274
General/National Adv. E-mail: kjl@sockets.net
Avg Paid Circ: 728
Avg Free Circ: 30
Audit By: Sworn/Estimate/Non-Audited
Audit Date: 10.06.2019
Personnel: Kurt J. Lewis (Pub.); Ron J. Lewis (Ed.)

THE BRUNSWICKER

Street address 1: 118 E Broadway St
Street address city: Brunswick
Street address state: MO
Zip/Postal code: 65236-1232
General Phone: (660) 548-3171
General Fax: (660) 388-6688
General/National Adv. E-mail: ps@cvalley.net
Year Established: 1847
Avg Paid Circ: 1630
Avg Free Circ: 50
Audit By: Sworn/Estimate/Non-Audited
Audit Date: 10.06.2019
Personnel: Susan K. Baxley (Pub.); Colleen Johnson (Office Mgr.); Larry M. Baxley (Ed.)

THE CALDWELL COUNTY NEWS

Street address 1: 101 S Davis St
Street address city: Hamilton
Street address state: MO
Zip/Postal code: 64644-1405
General Phone: (816) 583-2116
General Fax: (816) 583-2118
General/National Adv. E-mail: ads@mycaldwellcounty.com
Display Adv. E-mail: ads@mycaldwellcounty.com
Editorial e-mail: news@mycaldwellcounty.com
Primary Website: mycaldwellcounty.com
Year Established: 1869
Avg Paid Circ: 1140
Avg Free Circ: 72
Audit By: Sworn/Estimate/Non-Audited
Audit Date: 10.06.2019
Personnel: Anne L. Tezon (Publisher and editor); Debbie Rankin (Ed.); Stephanie Hunry (Owner/Marketing Consultant)

THE CANTON PRESS-NEWS JOURNAL

Street address 1: 109 N 4th St
Street address city: La Grange
Street address state: MO
Zip/Postal code: 63448-1342
General Phone: (573) 288-5668
General Fax: (573) 288-0000
General/National Adv. E-mail: ads@lewispnj.com
Editorial e-mail: rita1@lewispnj.com
Primary Website: lewispnj.com
Avg Paid Circ: 3000
Audit By: Sworn/Estimate/Non-Audited
Audit Date: 10.06.2019

Personnel: Jennifer Pegler (Adv. Mgr.); Daniel Steinbeck (Ed.)

THE CENTRALIA FIRESIDE GUARD

Street address 1: 123 N Allen St
Street address city: Centralia
Street address state: MO
Zip/Postal code: 65240-1301
General Phone: (573) 682-2133
General Fax: (573) 682-3361
General/National Adv. E-mail: cfgcomp@lcs.net
Display Adv. E-mail: cfgads@lcs.net
Editorial e-mail: cfged@lcs.net
Primary Website: firesideguard.com
Year Established: 1868
Avg Paid Circ: 3700
Audit By: Sworn/Estimate/Non-Audited
Audit Date: 10.06.2019
Personnel: Walt Gilbert (Pub.); Jeff Grimes (General manager)
Parent company (for newspapers): Lakeway Publishers, Inc.

THE CITIZEN OBSERVER

Street address 1: 403 E Evergreen St
Street address city: Cameron
Street address state: MO
Zip/Postal code: 64429-2096
General Phone: (816) 632-6543
General Fax: (816) 632-4508
General/National Adv. E-mail: sales@mycameronnews.com
Display Adv. E-mail: classifieds@mycameronnews.com
Editorial e-mail: editor@mycameronnews.com
Primary Website: mycameronnews.com
Avg Paid Circ: 2000
Avg Free Circ: 14000
Audit By: Sworn/Estimate/Non-Audited
Audit Date: 10.06.2019
Personnel: Jeff King (Prodn. Dir.); Tina Svoboda (Pub.); Debbie Wiedmaier (Office Mgr.); Helen Guffey (Lead Composer); Tara Wallace (Editor); Heidi Bench (Classifieds)
Parent company (for newspapers): Smith Newspapers

THE CLINTON COUNTY LEADER

Street address 1: 102 E Maple St
Street address city: Plattsburg
Street address state: MO
Zip/Postal code: 64477-1246
General Phone: (816) 539-2111
General Fax: (816) 539-3530
General/National Adv. E-mail: nikki@clintoncountyleader.com
Display Adv. E-mail: ads@clintoncountyleader.com
Editorial e-mail: leader@clintoncountyleader.com
Primary Website: ClintonCountyLeader.com
Year Established: 1895
Avg Paid Circ: 2400
Audit By: Sworn/Estimate/Non-Audited
Audit Date: 10.06.2019
Personnel: Steven Tinnen (Pub); Betty Dickinson (Gen. Mgr)

THE CONCORDIAN

Street address 1: 714 S Main St
Street address city: Concordia
Street address state: MO
Zip/Postal code: 64020-9602
General Phone: (660) 463-7522
General Fax: (660) 463-7942
General/National Adv. E-mail: amilligan@marshallnews.com
Display Adv. E-mail: concordianclass@centurytel.net
Editorial e-mail: sreed@marshallnews.com
Primary Website: theconcordianonline.com
Year Established: 1893
Avg Paid Circ: 2635
Audit By: Sworn/Estimate/Non-Audited
Audit Date: 10.06.2019
Personnel: Bob Stewart (Ed.); Abbey Milligan (Adv.); Alyssa Pfannkuch (Off. Rec.)
Parent company (for newspapers): Rust Communications

THE COURIER TRIBUNE

Street address 1: 104 N. Main St.
Street address city: Liberty
Street address state: MO
Zip/Postal code: 64068
General Phone: (816) 781-4941
General Fax: (816) 414-3340
Advertising Phone: (816) 454-9660
Editorial Phone: (816) 454-9660
General/National Adv. E-mail: advertise@mycouriertribune.com
Display Adv. E-mail: classifieds@mycouriertribune.com
Editorial e-mail: news@mycouriertribune.com
Primary Website: MyCourierTribune.com
Year Established: 1888
Avg Paid Circ: 2000
Audit By: Sworn/Estimate/Non-Audited
Audit Date: 10.06.2019
Personnel: Sandy Nelson (Pub.); Amy Neal (Mng. Ed.); Quinn Gregg (Adv. Acct. Mgr.)

THE CUBA FREE PRESS

Street address 1: 501 E Washington St
Street address city: Cuba
Street address state: MO
Zip/Postal code: 65453-1834
General Phone: (573) 885-7460
General Fax: (573) 885-3803
General/National Adv. E-mail: advertising@threeriverspublishing.com
Display Adv. E-mail: smorice@cubafreepress.com
Editorial e-mail: news@cubafreepress.com
Primary Website: threeriverspublishing.com
Year Established: 1960
Avg Paid Circ: 3450
Audit By: Sworn/Estimate/Non-Audited
Audit Date: 10.06.2019
Personnel: Rob Viehman (Pub.); Chris Case (Ed.); Sandy Morice (Advertising)
Parent company (for newspapers): Three Rivers Publishing, Inc.

THE CURRENT LOCAL

Street address 1: 504 Ash St
Street address city: Van Buren
Street address state: MO
Zip/Postal code: 63965
General Phone: (573) 323-4515
General Fax: (573) 323-4515
General/National Adv. E-mail: currentlocal@centurytel.net
Display Adv. E-mail: currentlocal@centurytel.net
Editorial e-mail: currentlocal@centurytel.net
Primary Website: currentlocal@centurytel.net
Year Established: 1884
Avg Paid Circ: 1700
Avg Free Circ: 0
Audit By: Sworn/Estimate/Non-Audited
Audit Date: 10.06.2019
Personnel: Ryan VanWinkle (Pub./Ed.)

THE DEMOCRAT ARGUS

Street address 1: 1011 Truman Blvd
Street address city: Caruthersville
Street address state: MO
Zip/Postal code: 63830-1745
General Phone: (573) 333-4336
General Fax: (573) 333-2307
General/National Adv. E-mail: news@democratargus.com
Editorial e-mail: news@democratargus.com
Primary Website: democratargus.com
Year Established: 1868
Avg Paid Circ: 2417
Avg Free Circ: 30
Audit By: Sworn/Estimate/Non-Audited
Audit Date: 10.06.2019
Personnel: David Tennyson (Pub.); Lisa Helfer (Gen. Mgr.); Lisa Bryant (Adv. Mgr.); Ashley Sides (Circ. Mgr.); Herbie Smith (Ed.)
Parent company (for newspapers): Rust Communications

THE EDINA SENTINEL

Street address 1: 207 N Main St
Street address city: Edina
Street address state: MO
Zip/Postal code: 63537-1350
General Phone: (660) 397-2226
General Fax: (660) 397-3558
General/National Adv. E-mail: edinasentinel@att.net
Editorial e-mail: themedia@centurytel.net
Primary Website: nemonews.net
Year Established: 1868
Avg Paid Circ: 1600
Audit By: Sworn/Estimate/Non-Audited
Audit Date: 10.06.2019
Personnel: Donna Otte (Circ. Mgr.); Mike Scott (Ed.)

THE ELSBERRY DEMOCRAT

Street address 1: 106 N 3rd St
Street address 2: Ste A
Street address city: Elsberry
Street address state: MO
Zip/Postal code: 63343-1344
General Phone: (573) 898-2318
General Fax: (573) 898-2173
General/National Adv. E-mail: edgenmgr@lcs.net
Display Adv. E-mail: edgenmgr@lcs.net
Editorial e-mail: edgenmgr@lcs.net
Primary Website: elsberrydemocrat.com
Year Established: 1901
Avg Paid Circ: 1350
Avg Free Circ: 5
Audit By: Sworn/Estimate/Non-Audited
Audit Date: 10.06.2019
Personnel: Walter Gilbert (Pub.); Michael Short (Ed.); Jordan Lanham (Reporter)
Parent company (for newspapers): Lakeway Publishers, Inc.

THE FAIRFAX FORUM

Street address 1: 119 E Main St
Street address city: Fairfax
Street address state: MO
Zip/Postal code: 64446-9305
General Phone: (660) 686-2741
General Fax: (660) 686-3442
Advertising Phone: (660) 736-4111
General/National Adv. E-mail: amail.rpt.coop
Editorial e-mail: forum@fairfaxmo.net
Primary Website: http://farmerpublishing.com/
Year Established: 1892
Avg Paid Circ: 800
Avg Free Circ: 14
Audit By: Sworn/Estimate/Non-Audited
Audit Date: 10.06.2019
Personnel: Lori Shaw

THE FARMINGTON PRESS

Street address 1: 227 E Columbia St
Street address city: Farmington
Street address state: MO
Zip/Postal code: 63640-3106
General Phone: (573) 756-8927
General Fax: (573) 756-9160
General/National Adv. E-mail: mnicholson@farmingtonpressonline.com
Display Adv. E-mail: mnicholson@farmingtonpressonline.com
Editorial e-mail: srobinson@farmingtonpressonline.com
Primary Website: http://dailyjournalonline.com/farmington-press/
Year Established: 1928
Audit By: Sworn/Estimate/Non-Audited
Audit Date: 10.06.2019
Personnel: Shawnna Robinson (Mng. Ed)

THE FAYETTE ADVERTISER

Street address 1: 203 N Main St
Street address city: Fayette
Street address state: MO
Zip/Postal code: 65248-1421
General Phone: (660) 248-2235
General Fax: (660) 248-1200
General/National Adv. E-mail: advertising@fayettenews.com
Display Adv. E-mail: advertising@fayettenews.com
Editorial e-mail: gjackson@fayettenews.com
Primary Website: fayettenewspapers.com
Year Established: 1840
Avg Paid Circ: 2300
Audit By: Sworn/Estimate/Non-Audited
Audit Date: 10.06.2019
Personnel: James H. Steele (Ed.); Patrick Roll; Greg Jackson; Linda Vroman; Carol Leech

THE HAMILTON ADVOCATE

Street address 1: 412 S Davis St
Street address city: Hamilton
Street address state: MO
Zip/Postal code: 64644-1432
General Phone: (816) 583-2116
General Fax: (816) 583-2118
General/National Adv. E-mail: news@lipublications.com
Primary Website: caldwell-countynews.com
Year Established: 1869
Avg Paid Circ: 1450
Avg Free Circ: 77
Audit By: Sworn/Estimate/Non-Audited
Audit Date: 10.06.2019
Personnel: Marshall Tezon (Pub.); Ann Childs (Circ. Mgr.); Anne L. Tezon (Ed.)

THE HERMANN ADVERTISER-COURIER

Street address 1: 136 E 4th St
Street address city: Hermann
Street address state: MO
Zip/Postal code: 65041-1177
General Phone: (573) 486-5418
General Fax: (573) 486-5524
General/National Adv. E-mail: hacmgr@lcs.net
Editorial e-mail: monews@lcs.net
Primary Website: hermannadvertisercourier.com
Mthly Avg Views: 110000
Year Established: 1837
Avg Paid Circ: 3900
Audit By: Sworn/Estimate/Non-Audited
Audit Date: 10.06.2019
Personnel: Cathi Utley (Publisher)
Parent company (for newspapers): Lakeway Publishers, Inc.

THE HOME PRESS

Street address 1: 115 N. Rubey
Street address city: Macon
Street address state: MO
Zip/Postal code: 63552
General Phone: (660) 395-4663
General/National Adv. E-mail: sharon@maconhomepress.com
Display Adv. E-mail: leeann@maconhomepress.com
Editorial e-mail: shon@maconhomepress.com
Primary Website: maconhomepress.com
Year Established: 1876
Audit By: Sworn/Estimate/Non-Audited
Audit Date: 10.06.2019
Personnel: Shon Coram (Pub.)

THE HOPKINS JOURNAL

Street address 1: 411 E Barnard St
Street address city: Hopkins
Street address state: MO
Zip/Postal code: 64461
General Phone: (660) 778-3205
General Fax: (660) 778-3205
Editorial e-mail: hopkinsjournal@embarqmail.com
Year Established: 1875
Avg Paid Circ: 750
Avg Free Circ: 100
Audit By: Sworn/Estimate/Non-Audited
Audit Date: 10.06.2019
Personnel: Steve Thompson (Adv. Mgr.); Darla Thompson (Ed.)

THE INDEPENDENT-JOURNAL

Street address 1: 119 E High St
Street address city: Potosi
Street address state: MO
Zip/Postal code: 63664-1906
General Phone: (573) 438-5141
General Fax: (573) 438-4472
Editorial e-mail: ijnews@centurytel.net
Year Established: 1872
Avg Paid Circ: 4485
Avg Free Circ: 425
Audit By: Sworn/Estimate/Non-Audited
Audit Date: 10.06.2019

Personnel: Kris Richards (Adv. Mgr.); Neil Richards (Ed.)

THE INDEX

Street address 1: 109 W. Polk St.
Street address city: Hermitage
Street address state: MO
Zip/Postal code: 65668
General Phone: (417) 745-6404
General Fax: (417) 745-2222
General/National Adv. E-mail: jfoltz@vernonpublishing.com
Editorial e-mail: tvernon@vernonpublishing.com
Primary Website: https://vernonpublishing.com/index
Year Established: 1903
Avg Paid Circ: 2300
Audit By: Sworn/Estimate/Non-Audited
Audit Date: 10.06.2019
Personnel: Trevor Vernon (Publisher); Charles Dryer (Advertising Specialist); Aliea Ream (Editor)
Parent company (for newspapers): Vernon Publishing, Inc

THE LANDMARK

Street address 1: 252 Main St
Street address city: Platte City
Street address state: MO
Zip/Postal code: 64079-8461
General Phone: (816) 858-0363
General Fax: (816) 858-2313
General/National Adv. E-mail: news@plattecountylandmark.com
Display Adv. E-mail: advertising@plattecountylandmark.com
Editorial e-mail: ivan@plattecountylandmark.com
Primary Website: plattecountylandmark.com
Year Established: 1865
Avg Paid Circ: 3600
Avg Free Circ: 100
Audit By: Sworn/Estimate/Non-Audited
Audit Date: 10.06.2019
Personnel: Ivan Foley (Ed.)

THE LAWSON REVIEW

Street address 1: 405 N Pennsylvania Ave
Street address city: Lawson
Street address state: MO
Zip/Postal code: 64062-9402
General Phone: (816) 296-3412
General Fax: (816) 296-3412
Editorial e-mail: lawsonreview@juno.com
Primary Website: https://facebook.com/thelawsonreview
Year Established: 1881
Avg Paid Circ: 2200
Audit By: Sworn/Estimate/Non-Audited
Audit Date: 10.06.2019
Personnel: R. Cress Hewitt (Pub.); David Blyth (Ed.)

THE LEXINGTON NEWS

Street address 1: 1009 Franklin Ave
Street address city: Lexington
Street address state: MO
Zip/Postal code: 64067-1333
General Phone: (660) 259-2266
General Fax: (660) 259-4870
Editorial e-mail: lexingtonnews@mbarkmail.com
Primary Website: mainstreetmedia.us
Year Established: 1868
Avg Paid Circ: 4000
Avg Free Circ: 30
Audit By: Sworn/Estimate/Non-Audited
Audit Date: 10.06.2019
Personnel: Frank W. Mercer (Pub.); Devon Ellis-Miranda (Bus Mgr.); Marian Couch (Adv. Mgr.); Nancy Oles (Circ. Mgr.); Joe Parmon (Ed.)
Parent company (for newspapers): Main Street Media, Inc.; Main Street Media

THE LICKING NEWS

Street address 1: 115 S Main St
Street address city: Licking
Street address state: MO
Zip/Postal code: 65542
General Phone: (573) 674-2412
General Fax: (573) 674-4892
General/National Adv. E-mail: news_ads@thelickingnews.com
Editorial e-mail: news_ads@thelickingnews.com
Primary Website: thelickingnews.com
Year Established: 1893
Avg Paid Circ: 2421
Audit By: Sworn/Estimate/Non-Audited
Audit Date: 10.06.2019
Personnel: Donald Dodd (Pub.); Angela Barnes (Mng. Ed.)

THE LINCOLN COUNTY JOURNAL

Street address 1: 20 Business Park Dr
Street address city: Troy
Street address state: MO
Zip/Postal code: 63379-2819
General Phone: (636) 528-9550
General Fax: (636) 528-6694
Advertising Phone: (636) 528-9550
Advertising Fax: (636) 528-6694
Editorial Phone: (636) 528-9550
Editorial Fax: (636) 528-6694
General/National Adv. E-mail: lcjpub@lcs.net
Display Adv. E-mail: lcjpub@lcs.net
Editorial e-mail: lcjpub@lcs.net
Primary Website: lincolncountyjournal.com
Year Established: 1986
Avg Paid Circ: 18900
Avg Free Circ: 18800
Audit By: Sworn/Estimate/Non-Audited
Audit Date: 10.06.2019
Personnel: Bob Simmons (Editor)
Parent company (for newspapers): Lakeway Publishers, Inc.

THE LOUISIANA PRESS-JOURNAL

Street address 1: PO Box 110
Street address city: Bowling Green
Street address state: MO
Zip/Postal code: 63334-0110
General Phone: (573) 754-5566
General Fax: (573) 754-4749
General/National Adv. E-mail: lpjads@lcs.net
Editorial e-mail: lpjed@lcs.net
Primary Website: louisianapressjournal.com
Year Established: 1855
Avg Paid Circ: 3175
Avg Free Circ: 21
Audit By: Sworn/Estimate/Non-Audited
Audit Date: 10.06.2019
Personnel: Valerie Gilbert (Pub.); Dave Moller (Ed.); Neil Darnell (Adv. Mgr.)
Parent company (for newspapers): Lakeway Publishers of Missouri

THE MANSFIELD MIRROR/WRIGHT CO. REPUBLICAN

Street address 1: 300 E Commercial St
Street address city: Mansfield
Street address state: MO
Zip/Postal code: 65704-2502
General Phone: (417) 924-3226
General Fax: (417) 924-3227
General/National Adv. E-mail: susie@mansfieldmirror.com
Editorial e-mail: larry@mansfieldmirror.com
Primary Website: mansfieldmirror.com
Year Established: 1908
Avg Paid Circ: 2158
Avg Free Circ: 17
Audit By: Sworn/Estimate/Non-Audited
Audit Date: 10.06.2019
Personnel: Larry Dennis (Ed./Pub.); Suzann Choate (Assist. Pub.)

THE MARSHFIELD MAIL

Street address 1: 225 N Clay St
Street address city: Marshfield
Street address state: MO
Zip/Postal code: 65706-1652
General Phone: (417) 468-2013
General Fax: (417) 859-7930
General/National Adv. E-mail: debbiec@marshfieldmail.com
Display Adv. E-mail: janc@marshfieldmail.com
Editorial e-mail: scottk@marshfieldmail.com
Primary Website: marshfieldmail.com
Mthly Avg Views: 38832
Mthly Avg Unique Visitors: 8992
Year Established: 1891
Avg Paid Circ: 4814
Avg Free Circ: 99
Audit By: Sworn/Estimate/Non-Audited
Audit Date: 10.06.2019
Personnel: Debbie Chapman (Adv. Mgr.); Dave Berry (Pub); Scott Kerber (Gen. Mgr/Ed.); Jim Kennedy (Circ.)
Parent company (for newspapers): Phillips Media Group LLC

THE MEDIA

Street address 1: 178 W Main St
Street address city: Kahoka
Street address state: MO
Zip/Postal code: 63445-1637
General Phone: (660) 727-3395
General Fax: (660) 727-2475
Editorial e-mail: themedia@thecenturytel.net
Primary Website: http://nemonews.net/category/kahoka-news/
Year Established: 1977
Avg Paid Circ: 2650
Audit By: Sworn/Estimate/Non-Audited
Audit Date: 10.06.2019
Personnel: Mike Scott (Pub.); Sue Scott (Ed.); Vicki Gutting (Office Manager)

THE MOUNTAIN ECHO

Street address 1: 110 N Main St
Street address city: Ironton
Street address state: MO
Zip/Postal code: 63650-1108
General Phone: (573) 546-3917
Advertising Phone: (573) 546-3917
Editorial Phone: (573) 546-3917
General/National Adv. E-mail: sue@myironcountynews.com
Display Adv. E-mail: sue@myironcountynews.com
Classified Adv. e-mail: sue@myironcountynews.com
Editorial e-mail: randy@myironcountynews.com
Primary Website: myironcountynews.com
Year Established: 1937
Avg Paid Circ: 1407
Avg Free Circ: 4976
Audit By: Sworn/Estimate/Non-Audited
Audit Date: 10.06.2019
Personnel: Susan Pribble (Off. Mgr/Owner); Randall Pribble (Ed/Pub/owner)

THE NEWS-DISPATCH

Street address 1: 212 E. Main St.
Street address city: Neosho
Street address state: MO
Zip/Postal code: 64850
General Phone: (417) 451-3798
Primary Website: thenewsdispatch.net
Year Established: 1882
Avg Paid Circ: 200
Audit By: Sworn/Estimate/Non-Audited
Audit Date: 10.06.2019
Personnel: Jim Cummins (Ed.)

THE NORTHEAST NEWS

Street address 1: 5715 Saint John Ave
Street address city: Kansas City
Street address state: MO
Zip/Postal code: 64123-1819
General Phone: (816) 241-0765
General Fax: (816) 241-3255
General/National Adv. E-mail: northeastnews@socket.net
Display Adv. E-mail: dorri@northeastnews.net
Editorial e-mail: mbushnell@northeastnews.net
Primary Website: northeastnews.net
Year Established: 1932
Avg Paid Circ: 28
Avg Free Circ: 10000
Audit By: CVC
Audit Date: 12.12.2017
Personnel: Michael Bushnell (Pub./Adv.); Paul Thompson (Managing Editor); Bryan Stalder (Creative Director); Dorri Partain (Account Executive)

THE NORTH-STODDARD COUNTIAN

Street address 1: 133 S Walnut St
Street address city: Dexter
Street address state: MO
Zip/Postal code: 63841-2141
General Phone: (573) 624-4545
General Fax: (573) 624-7449
General/National Adv. E-mail: cnoles@dailystatesman.com
Primary Website: dailystatesman.com/nsc
Year Established: 1877
Avg Paid Circ: 2000
Audit By: Sworn/Estimate/Non-Audited
Audit Date: 10.06.2019
Personnel: Bud Hunt (Pub.); Betty Watkins (Adv. Mgr.); Corey Noles (Ed.)

THE ODESSAN

Street address 1: 212 W Mason St
Street address city: Odessa
Street address state: MO
Zip/Postal code: 64076-1263
General Phone: (816) 230-5311
General Fax: None
Advertising Phone: (816) 230-5311
Advertising Fax: (816) 633-8430
Editorial Phone: (816) 230-5311
Editorial Fax: None
General/National Adv. E-mail: spaar@iland.net
Display Adv. E-mail: spaar@iland.net
Editorial e-mail: spaar@iland.net
Primary Website: theodessan.net
Year Established: 1880
Avg Paid Circ: 4200
Audit By: Sworn/Estimate/Non-Audited
Audit Date: 10.06.2019
Personnel: Betty S. Spaar (Owner); Renee Spaar (Gen. Mgr.); John Spaar (Adv. Mgr.); Joe Spaar (Prod. Mgr.); Hannah Spaar (news editor)

THE PEOPLE'S TRIBUNE

Street address 1: 17 N Main Cross St
Street address city: Bowling Green
Street address state: MO
Zip/Postal code: 63334-1643
General Phone: (573) 324-6111
General Fax: (573) 324-2551
General/National Adv. E-mail: peoplestribune@sbcglobal.net
Editorial e-mail: april@thepeoplestribune.com
Primary Website: thepeoplestribune.com
Year Established: 1996
Avg Free Circ: 8500
Audit By: Sworn/Estimate/Non-Audited
Audit Date: 10.06.2019
Personnel: Nancy Case (Gen. Mgr.); Jerry L. Hickerson (Pub.); April M. Fronick. (Ed.)

THE PERRY COUNTY REPUBLIC-MONITOR

Street address 1: 10 W Sainte Marie St
Street address city: Perryville
Street address state: MO
Zip/Postal code: 63775-1347
General Phone: (573) 547-4567
General Fax: (573) 547-1643
Advertising Phone: (573) 547-4567
Editorial Phone: (573) 547-4567
General/National Adv. E-mail: sales@perryvillenews.com
Display Adv. E-mail: republic-monitor@perryvillenews.com
Editorial e-mail: editor@perryvillenenws.com
Primary Website: perryvillenews.com
Mthly Avg Views: 50000
Year Established: 1889
Avg Paid Circ: 3800
Audit By: Sworn/Estimate/Non-Audited
Audit Date: 10.06.2019
Personnel: Beth Durreman (Pub.)
Parent company (for newspapers): PTS, Inc.

THE PLATTE COUNTY CITIZEN

Street address 1: PO Box 888
Street address 2: 812 Third Street
Street address city: Platte City
Street address state: MO
Zip/Postal code: 64079-0888
General Phone: (816) 858-5154
General Fax: (816) 858-2154
General/National Adv. E-mail: advertising@plattecountycitizen.com

Display Adv. E-mail: advertising@plattecountycitizen.com
Editorial e-mail: editor@plattecountycitizen.com
Primary Website: plattecountycitizen.com
Mthly Avg Views: 16800
Mthly Avg Unique Visitors: 4800
Year Established: 1962
Avg Paid Circ: 3560
Avg Free Circ: 7300
Audit By: Sworn/Estimate/Non-Audited
Audit Date: 10.06.2019
Personnel: Will Johnson (Adv)

THE PROSPECT-NEWS

Street address 1: 110 Washington St
Street address city: Doniphan
Street address state: MO
Zip/Postal code: 63935-1761
General Phone: (573) 996-2103
General Fax: (573) 996-2217
General/National Adv. E-mail: pnpaper@windstream.net
Year Established: 1874
Avg Paid Circ: 3000
Audit By: Sworn/Estimate/Non-Audited
Audit Date: 10.06.2019
Personnel: Don Schrieber (Pub.); Barbie Rogers (Ed.)
Parent company (for newspapers): Butler County Publishing

THE SALEM NEWS

Street address 1: P.O. Box 798
Street address 2: 500 North Washington Street
Street address city: Salem
Street address state: MO
Zip/Postal code: 65560
General Phone: (573) 729-4126
General Fax: (573) 729-4920
Advertising Phone: (573) 729-4126
Advertising Fax: (573) 729-4920
Editorial Phone: (573) 729-4126
Editorial Fax: (573) 729-4920
General/National Adv. E-mail: salemnews@thesalemnewsonline.com
Display Adv. E-mail: salemnews@thesalemnewsonline.com
Classified Adv. e-mail: salemnews@thesalemnewsonline.com
Editorial e-mail: salemnews@thesalemnewsonline.com
Primary Website: thesalemnewsonline.com
Mthly Avg Views: 100000
Year Established: 1918
Avg Paid Circ: 2100
Avg Free Circ: 4200
Audit By: Sworn/Estimate/Non-Audited
Audit Date: 10.10.2023
Personnel: Donald Dodd (Pub.); Karen Barred (Adv. Mgr.); Catherine Wynn (Managing Editor)
Parent company (for newspapers): Salem Publishing Company

THE SANTA FE TIMES

Street address 1: 106 3rd St.
Street address 2: Ste 1
Street address city: Alma
Street address state: MO
Zip/Postal code: 64001
General Phone: (660) 674-2250
General Fax: (660) 674-2250
General/National Adv. E-mail: safetnews@yahoo.com
Primary Website: mainstreetnewsgroup.com
Avg Paid Circ: 800
Avg Free Circ: 20
Audit By: Sworn/Estimate/Non-Audited
Audit Date: 10.06.2019
Personnel: Frank Mercer (Pub.); Klarissa Olvera (Mng. Ed)
Parent company (for newspapers): Main Street Media, Inc.; Main Street Media, Inc.-OOB

THE SARCOXIE RECORD

Street address 1: 101 N 6th St
Street address city: Sarcoxie
Street address state: MO
Zip/Postal code: 64862-9453
General Phone: (417) 548-3311
General Fax: (417) 548-3312
Advertising Fax: (417) 548-3312
General/National Adv. E-mail: fstop@centurytel.net
Year Established: 1901
Avg Paid Circ: 1150
Audit By: Sworn/Estimate/Non-Audited
Audit Date: 10.06.2019
Personnel: Paul E. Donley (Pub.); Katrina Keys (Gen Mgr)

THE SOUTHWEST CITY REPUBLIC

Street address 1: 11248 US-71
Street address city: Pineville
Street address state: MO
Zip/Postal code: 64856
General Phone: (417) 223-4675
General Fax: (417) 223-4049
Editorial e-mail: thepress@olemac.net
Primary Website: stephensmedia.com/newspapers/missouri
Avg Paid Circ: 5500
Audit By: Sworn/Estimate/Non-Audited
Audit Date: 10.06.2019
Personnel: George Pogue (Pub.); Donnie Parlet (Adv. Mgr.); Rick Peck (Ed.)

THE STAR

Street address 1: 105 S Main St
Street address city: El Dorado Springs
Street address state: MO
Zip/Postal code: 64744-1123
General Phone: (417) 876-2500
General Fax: (417) 876-5986
Editorial e-mail: thestar@socket.net
Year Established: 1987
Avg Paid Circ: 550
Avg Free Circ: 5
Audit By: Sworn/Estimate/Non-Audited
Audit Date: 10.06.2019
Personnel: Mae McNeece (Gen. Mgr.); Patsy Brownlee (Ed.)

THE STEELE ENTERPRISE

Street address 1: 227 W Main St
Street address city: Steele
Street address state: MO
Zip/Postal code: 63877-1435
General Phone: (573) 695-3415
General Fax: (573) 695-2114
General/National Adv. E-mail: steeleenterprise63877@yahoo.com
Editorial e-mail: steelenews@steelemoenterprise.com
Primary Website: http://couriernews.net/
Year Established: 1922
Avg Paid Circ: 2250
Audit By: Sworn/Estimate/Non-Audited
Audit Date: 10.06.2019
Personnel: David Tennyson (Pub.); Lisa Rhoades (Ed.)
Parent company (for newspapers): Rust Communications

THE TARKIO AVALANCHE

Street address 1: 521 Main St
Street address city: Tarkio
Street address state: MO
Zip/Postal code: 64491-1546
General Phone: (660) 736-4111
General Fax: (660) 736-5700
General/National Adv. E-mail: avalanche@rpt.com
Editorial e-mail: amail@rpt.coop
Primary Website: http://farmerpublishing.com
Year Established: 1884
Avg Paid Circ: 2000
Avg Free Circ: 230
Audit By: Sworn/Estimate/Non-Audited
Audit Date: 10.06.2019
Personnel: Joy L. Johnson (Pub.); William W. Johnson (Ed.)

THE TIPTON TIMES

Street address 1: 113 E Morgan St
Street address city: Tipton
Street address state: MO
Zip/Postal code: 65081-8322
General Phone: (660) 433-5721
General Fax: (660) 433-2222
General/National Adv. E-mail: times@vernonpublishing.com
Display Adv. E-mail: times@vernonpublishing.com
Classified Adv. e-mail: times@vernonpublishing.com
Editorial e-mail: times@vernonpublishing.com
Primary Website: tiptontimes.com
Year Established: 1875
Avg Paid Circ: 1465
Audit By: Sworn/Estimate/Non-Audited
Audit Date: 28.09.2028
Personnel: Dane Vernon (Pub.); Becky Holloway (Ed.); Trevor Vernon (Publisher)
Parent company (for newspapers): Vernon Publishing, Inc

THE VANDALIA LEADER

Street address 1: 108 W State St
Street address city: Vandalia
Street address state: MO
Zip/Postal code: 63382-1737
General Phone: (573) 594-2222
General Fax: (573) 594-6741
General/National Adv. E-mail: tvlads@lcs.net
Editorial e-mail: tvlgenmgr@lcs.net
Primary Website: vandalialeader.com
Year Established: 1874
Avg Paid Circ: 2217
Avg Free Circ: 9
Audit By: Sworn/Estimate/Non-Audited
Audit Date: 10.06.2019
Personnel: Ron Schott (Gen. Mgr./Ed.)
Parent company (for newspapers): Lakeway Publishers, Inc.

THE VEDETTE

Street address 1: 7 N Main St Suite 2
Street address city: Greenfield
Street address state: MO
Zip/Postal code: 65661-1128
General Phone: (417) 637-2712
General/National Adv. E-mail: krista@greenfieldvedette.com
Classified Adv. e-mail: krista@greenfieldvedette.com
Editorial e-mail: krista@greenfieldvedette.com
Primary Website: greenfieldvedette.com
Year Established: 1866
Avg Paid Circ: 1145
Audit Date: 01.[illegible]
Personnel: Krista Guy (Owner/GM); Gina Langston (Ed./Pub.)
Parent company (for newspapers): The Vedette & Lake Stockton Shopper LLC; Lewis Co.Press

THE VERSAILLES LEADER-STATESMAN

Street address 1: 104 W Jasper St
Street address city: Versailles
Street address state: MO
Zip/Postal code: 65084-1020
General Phone: (573) 378-5441
General Fax: (573) 378-4292
General/National Adv. E-mail: leader-statesman@vernonpublishing.com
Display Adv. E-mail: dbatson@vernonpublishing.com
Editorial e-mail: bjones@vernonpublishing.com
Primary Website: http://leader-statesman.com/
Year Established: 1878
Avg Paid Circ: 4100
Avg Free Circ: 100
Audit By: Sworn/Estimate/Non-Audited
Audit Date: 10.06.2019
Personnel: Dane Vernon (Pub); Bryan Jones (Ed)
Parent company (for newspapers): Vernon Publishing, Inc

THE WEEKLY

Street address 1: 412 High St
Street address city: Boonville
Street address state: MO
Zip/Postal code: 65233-1242
General Phone: (660) 882-5335
General Fax: (660) 882-2256
General/National Adv. E-mail: jsmith@boonvilledailynews.com
Display Adv. E-mail: classifieds@boonvilledailynews.com
Classified Adv. e-mail: classifieds@boonvilledailynews.com
Editorial e-mail: news@boonvilledailynews.com
Primary Website: boonvilledailynews.com
Year Established: 1911
Avg Paid Circ: 2144
Avg Free Circ: 11000
Audit By: Sworn/Estimate/Non-Audited
Audit Date: 10.06.2019
Personnel: Deborah Marshall (Adv. Mgr.); Paul Zacharias (Gen. Mgr.); Marlene Ridgeway (Pub.); Nate Birt (Ed.); Lisa Glasscock (Circ. Mgr.)
Parent company (for newspapers): CherryRoad Media

THE WEEKLY RECORD

Street address 1: 218 Main St
Street address city: New Madrid
Street address state: MO
Zip/Postal code: 63869-1911
General Phone: (573) 748-2120
General Fax: (573) 748-5435
General/National Adv. E-mail: ed@weeklyrecord.net
Editorial e-mail: ed@weeklyrecord.net
Primary Website: weeklyrecord.net
Year Established: 1866
Avg Paid Circ: 1000
Avg Free Circ: 60
Audit By: Sworn/Estimate/Non-Audited
Audit Date: 10.06.2019
Personnel: Ed Thomason (Pub.)

THE WINDSOR REVIEW

Street address 1: 205 S Main St
Street address city: Windsor
Street address state: MO
Zip/Postal code: 65360-1869
General Phone: (660) 647-2121
General Fax: (660) 647-2122
Editorial e-mail: news@windsornews.net
Year Established: 1876
Avg Paid Circ: 1850
Audit By: Sworn/Estimate/Non-Audited
Audit Date: 10.06.2019
Personnel: Frank Mercer (Pub.); Colby Gordon (Gen. Mgr.)
Parent company (for newspapers): Main Street Media, Inc.

TIMES OBSERVER

Street address 1: 119 W Nodaway St
Street address city: Oregon
Street address state: MO
Zip/Postal code: 64473
General Phone: (660) 446-3331
General Fax: (660) 446-3077
Editorial e-mail: drlogo5@ofmlive.net
Avg Paid Circ: 2000
Avg Free Circ: 10
Audit By: Sworn/Estimate/Non-Audited
Audit Date: 10.06.2019
Personnel: Robert E. Ripley (Ed.)

TRI-COUNTY WEEKLY

Street address 1: 103 S Broadway
Street address city: Jamesport
Street address state: MO
Zip/Postal code: 64648
General Phone: (660) 684-6515
General Fax: (660) 684-6515
Editorial e-mail: nert@grm.net
Primary Website: jamesporttricountyweekly.com
Avg Paid Circ: 1500
Audit By: Sworn/Estimate/Non-Audited
Audit Date: 10.06.2019
Personnel: Natha McAllister (Ed.)

TROY FREE PRESS

Street address 1: 20 Business Park Dr
Street address city: Troy
Street address state: MO
Zip/Postal code: 63379-2819
General Phone: (636) 528-9550
General Fax: (636) 528-6694
General/National Adv. E-mail: lcjpub@lcs.net
Display Adv. E-mail: lcjpub@lcs.net
Editorial e-mail: lcjeditor@lcs.net
Primary Website: lincolncountyjournal.com
Avg Paid Circ: 1000
Audit By: Sworn/Estimate/Non-Audited
Audit Date: 10.06.2019
Personnel: Bob Simmons (Ed)

Parent company (for newspapers): Lakeway Publishers

UNIONVILLE REPUBLICAN

Street address 1: 111 S 16th St
Street address city: Unionville
Street address state: MO
Zip/Postal code: 63565-1624
General Phone: (660) 947-2222
General Fax: (660) 947-2223
General/National Adv. E-mail: unionvillerepublican@mac.com
Editorial e-mail: urep@nemr.net
Primary Website: unionvillerepublicanonline.com
Year Established: 1865
Avg Paid Circ: 1700
Avg Free Circ: 5000
Audit By: Sworn/Estimate/Non-Audited
Audit Date: 10.06.2019
Personnel: Ron Kinzler (Ed./Pub)

UNTERRIFIED DEMOCRAT

Street address 1: 300 E Main St
Street address city: Linn
Street address state: MO
Zip/Postal code: 65051-9000
General Phone: (573) 897-3150
Editorial e-mail: DWarden@wardpub.com
Year Established: 1866
Avg Paid Circ: 7100
Audit By: Sworn/Estimate/Non-Audited
Audit Date: 10.06.2019
Personnel: Dennis Warden (Pub.)

WARREN COUNTY RECORD

Street address 1: 103 E Booneslick Rd
Street address city: Warrenton
Street address state: MO
Zip/Postal code: 63383-2003
General Phone: (636) 456-6397
General Fax: (636) 456-6150
General/National Adv. E-mail: jtodd@warrencountyrecord.com
Display Adv. E-mail: recordclass@warrencountyrecord.com
Editorial e-mail: recordnews@warrencountyrecord.com
Primary Website: warrencountyrecord.com
Year Established: 1896
Avg Paid Circ: 3555
Audit By: Sworn/Estimate/Non-Audited
Audit Date: 10.06.2019
Personnel: William L. Miller (Pub.); Jana Todd (Adv. Dir.); Kate Miller (Ed.)
Parent company (for newspapers): Missourian Publishing Co.

WASHINGTON MISSOURIAN

Street address 1: 6321 Bluff Rd
Street address city: Washington
Street address state: MO
Zip/Postal code: 63090
General Phone: (636) 239-7701
General Fax: (636) 239-0915
Advertising Phone: (636) 390-3013
General/National Adv. E-mail: Yorkj@emissourian.com
Display Adv. E-mail: yorkj@emissourian.com
Editorial e-mail: bmillerjr@emissourian.com
Primary Website: emissourian.com
Year Established: 1937
Avg Paid Circ: 8713
Avg Free Circ: 0
Audit By: Sworn/Estimate/Non-Audited
Audit Date: 29.11.2018
Personnel: Bill Miller (ed./Pub.); Jeanine York (Adv. Dir.); Susan Miller Warden (Mng. Ed.); Gregg Jones (Asst. Mgr. Ed.)
Parent company (for newspapers): The Missourian Publshing Co.

WAYNE COUNTY JOURNAL-BANNER

Street address 1: 101 West Elm
Street address 2: P.O. Box 97
Street address city: Piedmont
Street address state: MO
Zip/Postal code: 63957-1417
General Phone: (573) 223-7122
General Fax: (573) 223-7871
General/National Adv. E-mail: susane@waynecojournalbanner.com
Display Adv. E-mail: jhaggett@waynecojournalbanner.com
Editorial e-mail: harold@waynecojounalbanner.com
Primary Website: waynecojournalbanner.com
Year Established: 1876
Avg Paid Circ: 3200
Avg Free Circ: 70
Audit By: Sworn/Estimate/Non-Audited
Audit Date: 10.06.2019
Personnel: Kimberly Combs (Gen. Mgr.); Josh Crum (Adv. Sales Rep.); Stacy Gillette (Graphic Artist)
Parent company (for newspapers): Ellinghouse Publishing Co., Inc.

WEBB CITY SENTINEL

Street address 1: 8 S Main St
Street address city: Webb City
Street address state: MO
Zip/Postal code: 64870-2326
General Phone: (417) 673-2421
General Fax: (417) 673-5308
General/National Adv. E-mail: sales@webbcity.net
Display Adv. E-mail: sales@webbcity.net
Classified Adv. e-mail: sales@webbcity.net
Editorial e-mail: news@webbcity.net
Primary Website: webbcity.net
Year Established: 1879
Avg Paid Circ: 2000
Avg Free Circ: 50
Audit By: Sworn/Estimate/Non-Audited
Audit Date: 10.06.2019
Personnel: Bob Foos (Ed.)

WEBSTER COUNTY CITIZEN

Street address 1: 221 S Commercial St
Street address city: Seymour
Street address state: MO
Zip/Postal code: 65746-8743
General Phone: (417) 935-2257
General Fax: (417) 935-2487
General/National Adv. E-mail: anna@webstercountycitizen.com
Display Adv. E-mail: citizen190@gmail.com
Editorial e-mail: citizen@webstercountycitizen.com
Primary Website: webstercountycitizen.com
Year Established: 1907
Avg Paid Circ: 2005
Avg Free Circ: 7
Audit By: Sworn/Estimate/Non-Audited
Audit Date: 10.06.2019
Personnel: Dan Wehmer (Ed.); Beverly Hannum (Prod. Mgr.); Anna Sturdefant (Gen. Mgr.)

WEBSTER-KIRKWOOD TIMES, INC.

Street address 1: 122 W Lockwood Ave
Street address 2: Fl 2
Street address city: Saint Louis
Street address state: MO
Zip/Postal code: 63119-2916
General Phone: (314) 968-2699
General Fax: (314) 968-2961
General/National Adv. E-mail: mchambers@timesnewspapers.com
Display Adv. E-mail: classified@timesnewspapers.com
Editorial e-mail: newsroom@timesnewspapers.com
Primary Website: timesnewspapers.com
Year Established: 1978
Avg Free Circ: 40277
Audit By: CVC
Audit Date: 31.12.2017
Personnel: Dwight Bitikofer (Pub.); Don Corrigan (Ed.); Kevin Murphy (Mng. Ed.); Mary Chambers (Adv. Mgr); Kim Besterfeldt (Circ. Mgr); Randy Drilingas (Prod. Mgr); Dustin Bitikofer (circulation manager)
Parent company (for newspapers): Webster-Kirkwood Times, Inc.

WEST END WORD

Street address 1: 122 W Lockwood Ave
Street address city: Saint Louis
Street address state: MO
Zip/Postal code: 63119-2916
General Phone: (314) 968-2699
General Fax: (314) 968-2961
General/National Adv. E-mail: advertising@timesnewspapers.com
Display Adv. E-mail: classified@timesnewspapers.com
Editorial e-mail: corrigan@timesnewspapers.com
Primary Website: westendword.com
Mthly Avg Views: 106485
Mthly Avg Unique Visitors: 5099
Year Established: 1972
Avg Free Circ: 17117
Audit By: CVC
Audit Date: 30.06.2018
Personnel: Don Corrigan (Ed.); Kevin Murphy (Mng. Ed.); Mary Chambers (Adv. Mgr); Kim Besterfeldt (Circ. Mgr); Randy Drilingas (Prod. Mgr); Dwight Bitikofer (publisher); Dustin Bitikofer (circulation manager); Fran Mannino (Managing Editor)
Parent company (for newspapers): Webster-Kirkwood Times, Inc.

WESTON CHRONICLE

Street address 1: 18275 Hwy. 45 N.
Street address city: Weston
Street address state: MO
Zip/Postal code: 64098
General Phone: (816) 640-2251
Advertising Phone: (816) 640-2251
Editorial Phone: (816) 640-2251
General/National Adv. E-mail: wcnews@embarqmail.com
Display Adv. E-mail: wcads@embarqmail.com
Editorial e-mail: wcnews@embarqmail.com
Primary Website: plattechronicle.com
Year Established: 1872
Avg Paid Circ: 1600
Audit By: Sworn/Estimate/Non-Audited
Audit Date: 10.06.2019
Personnel: Jim McPherson (Adv. & Sports); Beth McPherson (Ed. & Pub.); Bev Knoll (Ad Designer)

MONTANA

ANACONDA LEADER

Street address 1: 121 Main St
Street address city: 121 Main St
Street address state: MT
Zip/Postal code: 59711-2251
General Phone: (406) 563-5283
General Fax: (406) 563-5284
General/National Adv. E-mail: leadernews@anacondaleader.com
Display Adv. E-mail: advertising@anacondaleader.com
Editorial e-mail: leadernews@anacondaleader.com
Primary Website: facebook.com/pages/Anaconda-Leader/153849391344489
Year Established: 1972
Avg Paid Circ: 3816
Avg Free Circ: 59
Audit By: Sworn/Estimate/Non-Audited
Audit Date: 10.06.2019
Personnel: Van Neitz (Owner); Kathie Miller (Ed.); Debbie Johns (Prodn. Mgr.)

BELGRADE NEWS

Street address 1: 29 W Main St
Street address city: Belgrade
Street address state: MT
Zip/Postal code: 59714-3716
General Phone: (406) 388-5101
General Fax: (406) 388-5103
Advertising Phone: (406) 388-5101 x10
Editorial Phone: (406) 388-5101 x12
General/National Adv. E-mail: ghoffman@belgrade-news.com
Display Adv. E-mail: ghoffman@belgrade-news.com
Editorial e-mail: editor@belgrade-news.com
Primary Website: belgrade-news.com
Mthly Avg Views: 55000
Mthly Avg Unique Visitors: 16000
Year Established: 2004
Avg Paid Circ: 300
Avg Free Circ: 4500
Audit By: Sworn/Estimate/Non-Audited
Audit Date: 10.06.2019
Personnel: Stephanie Pressly (Pub.); Michael Tucker (Ed.); George Hoffman (Adv. Dir.)
Parent company (for newspapers): Adams Publishing Group, LLC

BIG HORN COUNTY NEWS

Street address 1: 204 N Center Ave
Street address city: Hardin
Street address state: MT
Zip/Postal code: 59034-1908
General Phone: (406) 665-1008
General Fax: (406) 665-1012
General/National Adv. E-mail: news@bighorncountynews.com
Display Adv. E-mail: classifieds@bighorncountynews.com
Editorial e-mail: news@bighorncountynews.com
Primary Website: bighorncountynews.com
Mthly Avg Views: 24000
Year Established: 1908
Avg Paid Circ: 2200
Avg Free Circ: 50
Audit By: Sworn/Estimate/Non-Audited
Audit Date: 10.06.2019
Personnel: Andrew Turck (Ed.); Frank Perea (Pub.); Jim Eshleman (Gen. Mngr.); Barb Eben (Sub/Classifieds); Janene McKenney (Finance)
Parent company (for newspapers): Yellowstone Communications

BILLINGS TIMES

Street address 1: 2919 Montana Ave
Street address city: Billings
Street address state: MT
Zip/Postal code: 59101-2143
General Phone: (406) 245-4994
General Fax: (406) 245-5115
General/National Adv. E-mail: mail@billingstimes.net
Editorial e-mail: mail@billingstimes.net
Primary Website: billingstimes.net
Year Established: 1891
Audit By: Sworn/Estimate/Non-Audited
Audit Date: 10.06.2019
Personnel: Scott Turner (Editor & Publisher)

BITTERROOT STAR

Street address 1: 215 Main St
Street address city: Stevensville
Street address state: MT
Zip/Postal code: 59870-2112
General Phone: (406) 777-3928
General Fax: (406) 777-4265
General/National Adv. E-mail: editor@bitterrootstar.com
Display Adv. E-mail: editor@bitterrootstar.com
Editorial e-mail: editor@bitterrootstar.com
Primary Website: bitterrootstar.com
Mthly Avg Views: 400000
Mthly Avg Unique Visitors: 150000
Year Established: 1985
Avg Paid Circ: 400
Avg Free Circ: 6800
Audit By: Sworn/Estimate/Non-Audited
Audit Date: 10.06.2019
Personnel: Jean Schurman (Adv. Sales Consultant); Michael Howell (Ed.); Victoria Howell (Prodn. Mgr.)
Parent company (for newspapers): Jesse and Sasha Mullen

CARBON COUNTY NEWS

Street address 1: 202 S Hauser Ave
Street address city: Red Lodge
Street address state: MT
Zip/Postal code: 59068-9128
General Phone: (406) 446-2222
General Fax: (406) 446-2225
General/National Adv. E-mail: ads@carboncountynews.com
Display Adv. E-mail: ccnsales@carboncountynews.com
Editorial e-mail: news@carboncountynews.com
Primary Website: carboncountynews.com
Year Established: 1909
Avg Paid Circ: 3100
Avg Free Circ: 500
Audit By: Sworn/Estimate/Non-Audited
Audit Date: 10.06.2019
Personnel: Alastair Baker (Ed.); Frank Perea (Publisher); Tim Craig (Pub.); Edith Achermann (Circ. Mgr.); Terri Newby (Adv)

Parent company (for newspapers): Yellowstone Communications

CASCADE COURIER

Street address 1: 17 FRONT ST N
Street address city: Cascade
Street address state: MT
Zip/Postal code: 59421-4801
General Phone: (406) 468-9231
General/National Adv. E-mail: cascadecourier@mcn.net
Editorial e-mail: cascadecourier@mcn.net
Primary Website: WWW.CASCADENEWSPAPER.COM
Year Established: 1910
Avg Paid Circ: 560
Avg Free Circ: 400
Audit By: Sworn/Estimate/Non-Audited
Audit Date: 10.06.2019
Personnel: Marie Castellanos (Publisher); Judith Dotson (Ed.); Felicia O'Brien (Pub./Ed.)
Parent company (for newspapers): Montana Newspaper Advertising Service, Inc.

CHOTEAU ACANTHA

Street address 1: 216 1st Ave NW
Street address city: Choteau
Street address state: MT
Zip/Postal code: 59422
General Phone: (406) 466-2403
General Fax: (406) 466-2403
Advertising Phone: (406) 466-2403
Editorial Phone: (406) 466-2403
General/National Adv. E-mail: tetonads@3rivers.net
Display Adv. E-mail: tetonads@3rivers.net
Classified Adv. e-mail: tetonads@3rivers.net
Editorial e-mail: acantha@3rivers.net
Primary Website: choteauacantha.com
Year Established: 1893
Avg Paid Circ: 1500
Avg Free Circ: 31
Audit By: Sworn/Estimate/Non-Audited
Audit Date: 28.09.2023
Personnel: Jeffrey O. Martinsen (Publisher/co-owner); Melody Martinsen (Editor)

CLARK FORK VALLEY PRESS

Street address 1: 105 Lynch St
Street address city: Plains
Street address state: MT
Zip/Postal code: 59859
General Phone: (406) 826-3402
General Fax: (406) 826-5577
Advertising Phone: (406) 826-3403
Editorial Phone: (406) 826-5599
General/National Adv. E-mail: llarson@vp-mi.com
Display Adv. E-mail: cminemyer@vp-mi.com
Editorial e-mail: editor@vp-mi.com
Primary Website: vp-mi.com
Mthly Avg Views: 2500
Mthly Avg Unique Visitors: 2000
Avg Paid Circ: 586
Audit By: CAC
Audit Date: 31.03.2018
Personnel: Dan Drewry (Pub.); Laurie Ramos (Adv. Mgr.); Matt Unrau (Ed.)
Parent company (for newspapers): Hagadone Corporation

CUT BANK PIONEER PRESS

Street address 1: 19 S Central Ave
Street address city: Cut Bank
Street address state: MT
Zip/Postal code: 59427-2914
General Phone: (406) 873-2201
General Fax: (406) 873-2443
General/National Adv. E-mail: pressads@bresnan.net
Primary Website: cutbankpioneerpress.com
Avg Paid Circ: 1600
Audit By: Sworn/Estimate/Non-Audited
Audit Date: 10.06.2019
Personnel: Brian Kavanagh (Pub.); Jonna Tafelmeyer (Adv. Mgr.); LeAnne Kavanagh (Ed.); Steven Gall; Samantha Radtke

DANIELS COUNTY LEADER

Street address 1: 214 Main St
Street address city: Scobey
Street address state: MT
Zip/Postal code: 59263
General Phone: (406) 487-5303
General Fax: (406) 487-5304
General/National Adv. E-mail: 2leader@nemont.net
Editorial e-mail: 2leader@nemont.net
Primary Website: danielscountyleader.com
Year Established: 1922
Avg Paid Circ: 1100
Audit By: Sworn/Estimate/Non-Audited
Audit Date: 10.06.2023
Personnel: Burl Bowler (Owner/Publisher); Milton Gunderson (Ed.)

DILLON TRIBUNE

Street address 1: 31 S Idaho St
Street address city: Dillon
Street address state: MT
Zip/Postal code: 59725-2509
General Phone: (406) 683-2331
General Fax: (406) 683-2332
Advertising Phone: (406) 988-7983
Editorial Phone: (406) 988-7986
General/National Adv. E-mail: ads@dillontribune.com
Display Adv. E-mail: accounts@dillontribune.com
Editorial e-mail: editor@dillontribune.com
Primary Website: dillontribune.com
Year Established: 1881
Avg Paid Circ: 2700
Avg Free Circ: 0
Audit By: Sworn/Estimate/Non-Audited
Audit Date: 10.06.2019
Personnel: Dick Crockford (pUB.); Jennifer Engstrom (Office Mgr.); Kayla Parker (Advertising Mgr.); J.P. Plutt (Managing Ed.); Debbie Melle (Dist. Mgr.); Jesse Alberi (Sports Reporter); Cassie Scheidecker (Graphics Artist)
Parent company (for newspapers): Yellowstone Communications

FAIRFIELD TIMES & GREAT FALLS LEADER

Street address 1: PO Box 578
Street address 2: 409 Central Ave.
Street address city: Fairfield
Street address state: MT
Zip/Postal code: 59436-0578
General Phone: (406) 467-2334
Advertising Phone: (406) 467-2334
Editorial Phone: (406) 467-2334
General/National Adv. E-mail: suntimes@3rivers.net
Display Adv. E-mail: suntimes@3rivers.net
Classified Adv. e-mail: suntimes@3rivers.net
Editorial e-mail: suntimes@3rivers.net
Primary Website: fairfieldsuntimes.com
Mthly Avg Views: 200000
Mthly Avg Unique Visitors: 15000
Year Established: 1916
Avg Paid Circ: 544
Avg Free Circ: 10
Audit By: Sworn/Estimate/Non-Audited
Audit Date: 10//2023
Personnel: Darryl Flowers (Ed., Pub., Propr.); Samantha Carlsson (Reporter; Office Clerk); Herbet Carlsson
Parent company (for newspapers): Sun Times Printing & Publishing, LLC

FALLON COUNTY TIMES

Street address 1: 115 S Main St
Street address city: Baker
Street address state: MT
Zip/Postal code: 59313-9013
General Phone: (406) 778-3344
General Fax: (406) 778-3347
General/National Adv. E-mail: fctimes@midrivers.com
Editorial e-mail: fctimes@midrivers.com
Primary Website: falloncountytimes.com
Year Established: 1916
Avg Paid Circ: 1200
Avg Free Circ: 49
Audit By: Sworn/Estimate/Non-Audited
Audit Date: 10.06.2019
Personnel: Darlene Hornung (Ed.); Tammy O'Donnell (Mktg.); Tina Rost (General Manager); Megan Slagter (Graphic Artist)
Parent company (for newspapers): Country Media Inc.; Badlands Patriot LLC; Country Media, Inc

FLATHEAD BEACON

Street address 1: 17 Main St
Street address city: Kalispell
Street address state: MT
Zip/Postal code: 59901-4449
General Phone: (406) 257-9220
General Fax: (406) 257-9231
Advertising Phone: (406) 407-9547
General/National Adv. E-mail: hunt@flatheadbeacon.com
Display Adv. E-mail: hunt@flatheadbeacon.com
Editorial e-mail: hunt@flatheadbeacon.com
Primary Website: flatheadbeacon.com
Mthly Avg Views: 700000
Mthly Avg Unique Visitors: 250000
Year Established: 2007
Avg Free Circ: 25000
Audit By: Sworn/Estimate/Non-Audited
Audit Date: 10.06.2019
Personnel: Kellyn Brown (Ed); Bob Hunt (Adv. Dir.)

GLACIER REPORTER

Street address 1: 208 N PIEGAN ST
Street address city: Browning
Street address state: MT
Zip/Postal code: 59417
General Phone: (406) 338-2090
General Fax: (406) 338-2410
General/National Adv. E-mail: pressads@bresnan.net
Editorial e-mail: cbpress@bresnan.net
Primary Website: http://cutbankpioneerpress.com/glacier_reporter/
Avg Paid Circ: 2362
Audit By: Sworn/Estimate/Non-Audited
Audit Date: 10.06.2019
Personnel: Brian Kavanagh (Pub.); Marlene Augare (Adv. Sales); John McGill (Editor)

GLENDIVE RANGER-REVIEW

Street address 1: 119 W Bell St
Street address city: Glendive
Street address state: MT
Zip/Postal code: 59330-1614
General Phone: (406) 377-3303
General Fax: (406) 377-5435
General/National Adv. E-mail: rrads@rangerreview.com
Display Adv. E-mail: rrads@rangerreview.com
Editorial e-mail: rrnews@rangerreview.com
Primary Website: rangerreview.com
Year Established: 1881
Avg Paid Circ: 3200
Avg Free Circ: 20
Audit By: Sworn/Estimate/Non-Audited
Audit Date: 10.06.2019
Personnel: Jamie Crisafulli (Pub.); Pamela Ruth (Adv. Sales)
Parent company (for newspapers): Montana Newspaper Advertising Service, Inc.; Yellowstone Communications

HUNGRY HORSE NEWS

Street address 1: 926 Nucleus Avenue
Street address 2: PO BOX 189
Street address city: Columbia Falls
Street address state: MT
Zip/Postal code: 59912-0189
General Phone: (406) 892-2151
General Fax: (406) 892-5600
Advertising Phone: (406) 892-2151
Editorial Phone: (406) 892-2151
General/National Adv. E-mail: abrowning@hungryhorsenews.com
Display Adv. E-mail: classifieds@dailyinterlake.com
Editorial e-mail: editor@hungryhorsenews.com
Primary Website: hungryhorsenews.com
Year Established: 1947
Avg Paid Circ: 1880
Avg Free Circ: 0
Audit By: CAC
Audit Date: 31.03.2018
Personnel: Rick Weaver (Pub); Chris Peterson (Ed.); Andrea Browning (Adv. Director)
Parent company (for newspapers): Hagadone Corporation

INDEPENDENT OBSERVER

Street address 1: 7 3rd Ave SE
Street address city: Conrad
Street address state: MT
Zip/Postal code: 59425-2039
General Phone: (406) 271-5561
General/National Adv. E-mail: indobserv@3rivers.net
Display Adv. E-mail: indobserv@3rivers.net
Editorial e-mail: indobserv@3rivers.net
Primary Website: theindependentobserver.com
Year Established: 1906
Avg Paid Circ: 1900
Avg Free Circ: 60
Audit By: Sworn/Estimate/Non-Audited
Audit Date: 10.06.2019
Personnel: Patricia Lee (Pub.); Julie Anderson (Office Mgr.); Barb Stratman (Production-Adv. Mgr.); Donna Arvidson (Adv. Asst.); McKenzie Graye (Reporter)

JOURNAL NEWS OPINION

Street address 1: 217 Indiana St
Street address city: Chinook
Street address state: MT
Zip/Postal code: 59523-9716
General Phone: (406) 357-2680
General Fax: (406) 357-3736
Advertising Phone: (406) 357-3573
General/National Adv. E-mail: bcjnews@ttc-cmc.net
Editorial e-mail: bcjnews@itstriangle.com
Primary Website: blainecountyjournal.com
Year Established: 1890
Avg Paid Circ: 2150
Avg Free Circ: 48
Audit By: Sworn/Estimate/Non-Audited
Audit Date: 10.06.2019
Personnel: Keith A. Hanson (Prodn. Mngr.); Keri Hanson (Ed.)

JUDITH BASIN PRESS

Street address 1: PO Box 900
Street address city: Lewistown
Street address state: MT
Zip/Postal code: 59457-0900
General Phone: (406) 566-2471
General Fax: (406) 566-2312
General/National Adv. E-mail: advertising1@lewistownnews.com
Editorial e-mail: pressoffice@itstriangle.com
Year Established: 1909
Avg Paid Circ: 500
Audit By: Sworn/Estimate/Non-Audited
Audit Date: 10.06.2019
Personnel: Jacques Rutten (Pub.); Vicky McCray (Editor); Kimberlee Smith (Adv.)
Parent company (for newspapers): Yellowstone Communications

KOOTENAI VALLEY RECORD

Street address 1: 507 Mineral Ave
Street address city: Libby
Street address state: MT
Zip/Postal code: 59923-1957
General Phone: (406) 293-2424
General Fax: (406) 293-5263
General/National Adv. E-mail: kvrecord@gmail.com
Editorial e-mail: kvrecord@gmail.com
Primary Website: facebook.com/pages/Kootenai-Valley-Record/387373364659815
Year Established: 2007
Audit By: Sworn/Estimate/Non-Audited
Audit Date: 10.06.2019
Personnel: Lee Bothman (Publisher/Ad Mgr./Ed.); Chris Nelson (Reporter)

LAKE COUNTY LEADER

Street address 1: 108 1st St E
Street address city: Polson
Street address state: MT
Zip/Postal code: 59860-2310
General Phone: (406) 883-4343
General Fax: (406) 883-4349
General/National Adv. E-mail: lramos@leaderadvertiser.com
Display Adv. E-mail: elonnivik@leaderadvertiser.com

Editorial e-mail: editor@leaderadvertiser.com
Primary Website: leaderadvertiser.com
Year Established: 1910
Avg Paid Circ: 1486
Audit By: CAC
Audit Date: 31.03.2018
Personnel: Laurie Ramos (Adv. Dir./Gen. Mgr.)
Parent company (for newspapers): Hagadone Corporation

LAUREL OUTLOOK

Street address 1: 415 E Main St
Street address city: Laurel
Street address state: MT
Zip/Postal code: 59044-3120
General Phone: (406) 628-4412
General Fax: (406) 628-8260
Advertising Phone: (406) 628-4412 x102
Editorial Phone: (406) 628-4412 x103
General/National Adv. E-mail: ads@laureloutlook.com
Display Adv. E-mail: classifieds@laureloutlook.com
Editorial e-mail: publisher@laureloutlook.com
Primary Website: laureloutlook.com
Year Established: 1906
Avg Paid Circ: 2500
Avg Free Circ: 100
Audit By: Sworn/Estimate/Non-Audited
Audit Date: 10.06.2019
Personnel: Stacey Osborne (Designer); Evan Bruce (Designer); Chris McConnell (Writer); Crystal Nagel (Bookeeper); Scott Toombs (Ad sales); Linda Swaggerty (Specialty ad sales)
Parent company (for newspapers): Yellowstone Communications

LEWISTOWN NEWS-ARGUS

Street address 1: 521 W Main St
Street address city: Lewistown
Street address state: MT
Zip/Postal code: 59457-2603
General Phone: (406) 535-3401
General Fax: (406) 535-3405
General/National Adv. E-mail: advertising@lewistownnews.com
Display Adv. E-mail: classified@lewistownnews.com
Editorial e-mail: editor@lewistownnews.com
Primary Website: lewistownnews.com
Year Established: 1883
Avg Paid Circ: 4551
Avg Free Circ: 108
Audit By: Sworn/Estimate/Non-Audited
Audit Date: 10.06.2019
Personnel: Darlene Hodik (Adv. Mgr.); Jacques Rutten (Pub.); Tim Hartford (Prodn. Mgr.)
Parent company (for newspapers): Montana Newspaper Advertising Service, Inc.; Yellowstone Communications

LIBERTY COUNTY TIMES

Street address 1: 46 1st St E
Street address city: Chester
Street address state: MT
Zip/Postal code: 59522
General Phone: (406) 759-5355
General Fax: (406) 759-5261
General/National Adv. E-mail: lctimes@itstriangle.com
Editorial e-mail: lctimes@itstriangle.com
Primary Website: libertycountytimes.net
Year Established: 1905
Avg Paid Circ: 1202
Avg Free Circ: 17
Audit By: Sworn/Estimate/Non-Audited
Audit Date: 10.06.2019
Personnel: Paul Overlie (Pub.)

MINERAL INDEPENDENT

Street address 1: 105 Lynch St
Street address city: Plains
Street address state: MT
Zip/Postal code: 59859
General Phone: (406) 826-3402
General Fax: (406) 826-5577
General/National Adv. E-mail: llarson@vp-mi.com
Display Adv. E-mail: cminemyer@vp-mi.com
Editorial e-mail: editor@vp-mi.com
Primary Website: vp-mi.com
Mthly Avg Views: 2500
Mthly Avg Unique Visitors: 2000
Year Established: 1910
Avg Paid Circ: 483
Audit By: CAC
Audit Date: 31.03.2018
Personnel: Dan Drewry (Pub.); Laurie Ramos (Adv. Mgr.); Matt Unrau (Ed.)
Parent company (for newspapers): Hagadone Corporation

SANDERS COUNTY LEDGER

Street address 1: 603 W Main St
Street address city: Thompson Falls
Street address state: MT
Zip/Postal code: 59873
General Phone: (406) 827-3421
General Fax: (406) 827-4375
Advertising Phone: 4068273421
Editorial Phone: 4068273421
General/National Adv. E-mail: info@scledger.net
Display Adv. E-mail: advertising@scledger.net
Classified Adv. e-mail: advertising@scledger.net
Editorial e-mail: editor@scledger.net
Primary Website: scledger.net
Year Established: 1983
Avg Paid Circ: 2300
Audit By: Sworn/Estimate/Non-Audited
Audit Date: 01.10.2024
Personnel: Annie Wooden (Ed./Pub.); Sherry Hagerman Benton (Adv. Mgr.); Tom Eggensperger (Off. Mgr./Classifieds)

SEELEY SWAN PATHFINDER

Street address 1: 3166 Highway 83 N
Street address city: Seeley Lake
Street address state: MT
Zip/Postal code: 59868
General Phone: (406) 677-2022
Advertising Phone: (406) 677-2155
General/National Adv. E-mail: pathfinder@seeleylake.com
Primary Website: seeleylake.com
Year Established: 1984
Avg Paid Circ: 1250
Avg Free Circ: 50
Audit By: Sworn/Estimate/Non-Audited
Audit Date: 10.06.2019
Personnel: Andi Bourne (Editor & Publisher); Nathan Bourne (Mailing & Advertising)
Parent company (for newspapers): Montana Newspaper Advertising Service, Inc.

SHERIDAN COUNTY NEWS

Street address 1: 115 N Main St
Street address city: Plentywood
Street address state: MT
Zip/Postal code: 59254-1817
General Phone: (406) 765-2190
General Fax: (406) 765-3333
General/National Adv. E-mail: scnews@nemont.net
Editorial e-mail: scnews@nemont.net
Year Established: 1995
Avg Paid Circ: 2418
Avg Free Circ: 25
Audit By: Sworn/Estimate/Non-Audited
Audit Date: 10.06.2019
Personnel: Tim Polk (Adv. Mgr.); Angie Tommerup (Circ. Mgr.); Joe Nistler (Ed.); Deanna Hellegaard (Business Manager)

SIDNEY HERALD

Street address 1: 310 2nd Ave NE
Street address city: Sidney
Street address state: MT
Zip/Postal code: 59270-4404
General Phone: (406) 433-2403
General Fax: (406) 433-7802
General/National Adv. E-mail: adrep@sidneyherald.com
Display Adv. E-mail: classifieds@sidneyherald.com
Editorial e-mail: editor@sidneyherald.com
Primary Website: sidneyherald.com
Year Established: 1907
Avg Paid Circ: 2192
Audit By: VAC
Audit Date: 30.09.2016
Personnel: Kelly Miller (Pub.); Bill Vander Weele (Ed.); Keri Brown (Circ.)
Parent company (for newspapers): Wick Communications

SILVER STATE POST

Street address 1: 312 Missouri Ave
Street address city: Deer Lodge
Street address state: MT
Zip/Postal code: 59722-1077
General Phone: (406) 846-2424
General Fax: (406) 846-2453
General/National Adv. E-mail: mgr@sspmt.com
Display Adv. E-mail: design@sspmt.com
Editorial e-mail: news@sspmt.com
Primary Website: sspmt.com
Year Established: 1887
Avg Paid Circ: 1900
Avg Free Circ: 2200
Audit By: Sworn/Estimate/Non-Audited
Audit Date: 10.06.2019
Personnel: Myra Hopkins (Office Mgr.); Jared Cooksey (Ed.); Christina Bledsoe (Ad. Design); Brendan Goble (Accounting); Grace Silverstein (Ad. Sales); Melissa Jenkins (Advertising Manager)

THE BIG TIMBER PIONEER

Street address 1: 105 E 2nd Ave
Street address city: Big Timber
Street address state: MT
Zip/Postal code: 59011-8800
General Phone: (406) 932-5298
General Fax: (406) 932-4931
Advertising Phone: (406) 932-5298
General/National Adv. E-mail: ads@bigtimberpioneer.net
Editorial e-mail: editor@bigtimberpioneer.net
Primary Website: http://bigtimberpioneer.net/
Year Established: 1890
Avg Paid Circ: 1768
Audit By: Sworn/Estimate/Non-Audited
Audit Date: 10.06.2019
Personnel: Laura Nelson (Editor / General Manager); Lois Huffman
Parent company (for newspapers): Yellowstone Communications

THE BIGFORK EAGLE

Street address 1: 8299 Mt Highway 35
Street address 2: Ste 4
Street address city: Bigfork
Street address state: MT
Zip/Postal code: 59911-3574
General Phone: (406) 837-5131
General Fax: (406) 837-1132
Advertising Phone: (406) 758-4410
Editorial Phone: (406) 837-5131
General/National Adv. E-mail: kfritz@dailyinterlake.com
Display Adv. E-mail: classifieds@dailyinterlake.com
Editorial e-mail: editor@bigforkeagle.com
Primary Website: bigforkeagle.com
Avg Paid Circ: 14954
Avg Free Circ: 403
Audit By: Sworn/Estimate/Non-Audited
Audit Date: 10.06.2019
Personnel: Ken Varga (Prodn. Mgr. & Circulation Director); Rick Weaver (Publisher); Dave Reese (Editor); Laurie Ramos (General Manager)

THE BOULDER MONITOR

Street address 1: 104 W Centennial Ave
Street address city: Boulder
Street address state: MT
Zip/Postal code: 59632
General Phone: (406) 225-3822
General Fax: (406) 225-3821
General/National Adv. E-mail: ads1@jeffersoncountycourier.com
Primary Website: boulder-monitor.com, jeffersoncountycourier.com
Audit By: Sworn/Estimate/Non-Audited
Audit Date: 10.06.2019
Personnel: David Anderson (Pub.); Jan Anderson (Ed.)

THE BUTTE WEEKLY

Street address 1: PO Box 4898
Street address city: Butte
Street address state: MT
Zip/Postal code: 59702-4898
General Phone: (406) 782-3820
Advertising Phone: (406) 782-3820
Editorial Phone: (406) 782-3820
General/National Adv. E-mail: butte.news@butteweekly.com
Display Adv. E-mail: butte.news@butteweekly.com
Editorial e-mail: editor@butteweekly.com
Primary Website: butteweekly.com
Year Established: 1992
Avg Free Circ: 5500
Audit By: Sworn/Estimate/Non-Audited
Audit Date: 10.06.2019
Personnel: Linda Anderson (Publisher/owner)
Parent company (for newspapers): Butte Weekly

THE CIRCLE BANNER

Street address 1: 219 Main St,
Street address city: Circle
Street address state: MT
Zip/Postal code: 59215
General Phone: (406) 974-3409
General Fax: (406) 485-2330
General/National Adv. E-mail: banner@midrivers.com
Primary Website: circlebanner.com
Year Established: 1914
Avg Paid Circ: 1150
Audit By: Sworn/Estimate/Non-Audited
Audit Date: 10.06.2019
Personnel: Kathy Boshart (Pub.); Ryan Grigg (Mng. Ed.); Marcie Brost (Owner/Editor); Marcie Brost
Parent company (for newspapers): Montana Newspaper Advertising Service, Inc.

THE EKALAKA EAGLE

Street address 1: 307 N Main St
Street address city: Ekalaka
Street address state: MT
Zip/Postal code: 59324
General Phone: (406) 775-6245
General Fax: (719) 623-0209
General/National Adv. E-mail: ekeagle@midrivers.com
Editorial e-mail: ekeagle@midrivers.com
Year Established: 1909
Avg Paid Circ: 1100
Audit By: Sworn/Estimate/Non-Audited
Audit Date: 10.06.2019
Personnel: Jeanette Adams (Adv. Mgr.); M. Brice Lambert (Ed.)
Parent company (for newspapers): Montana Newspaper Advertising Service, Inc.

THE GLASGOW COURIER

Street address 1: 341 3rd Ave S
Street address city: Glasgow
Street address state: MT
Zip/Postal code: 59230-2401
General Phone: (406) 228-9301
General Fax: (406) 228-2665
General/National Adv. E-mail: sales@glasgowcourier.com
Editorial e-mail: courier@glasgowcourier.com
Primary Website: glasgowcourier.com
Year Established: 1913
Avg Paid Circ: 2707
Avg Free Circ: 95
Audit By: Sworn/Estimate/Non-Audited
Audit Date: 10.06.2019
Personnel: Jim Orr (Publisher); Samar Fay (Editor); Terry Trang (Office manager); Stan Sonsteng (Production manager)
Parent company (for newspapers): Stevenson/Hicks Newspapers

THE HERALD-NEWS

Street address 1: 408 Main St
Street address city: Wolf Point
Street address state: MT
Zip/Postal code: 59201-1534
General Phone: (406) 653-2222
General Fax: (406) 653-2221
General/National Adv. E-mail: herald@nemont.net
Editorial e-mail: herald@nemont.net
Primary Website: wolfpointherald.com
Avg Paid Circ: 2000
Avg Free Circ: 30
Audit By: Sworn/Estimate/Non-Audited
Audit Date: 10.06.2019

Personnel: Darla Shumway (Publisher); Bill Weele (Ed.)

THE INDEPENDENT PRESS

Street address 1: 192 N 10th Ave
Street address city: Forsyth
Street address state: MT
Zip/Postal code: 59327
General Phone: (406) 346-2149
General Fax: (406) 346-2140
General/National Adv. E-mail: ip-ads@rangeweb.net
Display Adv. E-mail: classified@rangeweb.net
Editorial e-mail: ip-news@rangeweb.net
Primary Website: yellowstonecommunications.com
Avg Paid Circ: 1375
Avg Free Circ: 23
Audit By: Sworn/Estimate/Non-Audited
Audit Date: 10.06.2019
Personnel: Connie Brown (Adv. Mgr.); Christy Suits (Managing Editor); Krista Bartz (Admin. Assistant/ Bookkeeper)
Parent company (for newspapers): Yellowstone Communications

THE MADISONIAN

Street address 1: 65 Mt Highway 287
Street address city: Ennis
Street address state: MT
Zip/Postal code: 59729-9117
General Phone: (406) 682-7755
General Fax: (406) 682-5013
General/National Adv. E-mail: ads@madisoniannews.com
Editorial e-mail: editor@madisoniannews.com
Primary Website: madisoniannews.com
Mthly Avg Views: 16000
Year Established: 1873
Avg Paid Circ: 2300
Audit By: Sworn/Estimate/Non-Audited
Audit Date: 10.06.2019
Personnel: Erin Leonard (Owner/Adv. Dir.); Susanne Hill (Owner/Dir., Sales/Mktg); Abigail Dennis (News Ed.)

THE MEAGHER COUNTY NEWS

Street address 1: 13 E Main St
Street address city: White Sulphur Springs
Street address state: MT
Zip/Postal code: 59645-9000
General Phone: (406) 547-3831
General Fax: (406) 547-3832
General/National Adv. E-mail: mcnews@mtintouch.net
Editorial e-mail: mcnews@mtintouch.net
Primary Website: meagher-county-news.com
Year Established: 1889
Avg Paid Circ: 1200
Audit By: Sworn/Estimate/Non-Audited
Audit Date: 10.06.2019
Personnel: Jason Phillips (Ed.)

THE MONTANIAN

Street address 1: 317 California Ave
Street address city: Libby
Street address state: MT
Zip/Postal code: 59923-1937
General Phone: (406) 293-8202
General/National Adv. E-mail: news@montanian.com
Display Adv. E-mail: news@montanian.com
Editorial e-mail: news@montanian.com
Primary Website: facebook.com/The.Montanian
Year Established: 1989
Avg Free Circ: 3400
Audit By: Sworn/Estimate/Non-Audited
Audit Date: 10.06.2019
Personnel: Carol J. Latham (Owner/Publisher); David F. Latham (Ed.)

THE MOUNTAINEER

Street address 1: 122 Johannas Ave
Street address city: Big Sandy
Street address state: MT
Zip/Postal code: 59520
General Phone: (406) 378-2176
General Fax: (406) 378-2176
Advertising Phone: (406)378-2176
General/National Adv. E-mail: bsmnews@mtintouch.net
Editorial e-mail: bcjnews@itstriangle.com
Primary Website: bigsandymountaineer.com
Year Established: 1911
Avg Paid Circ: 926
Avg Free Circ: 99
Audit By: Sworn/Estimate/Non-Audited
Audit Date: 10.06.2019
Personnel: Keith Hanson (Mng. Ed.); Lorrie Merrill (Editor/Owner)

THE PHILIPSBURG MAIL

Street address 1: 410 W Broadway St
Street address city: Philipsburg
Street address state: MT
Zip/Postal code: 59858
General Phone: (406) 859-3223
General/National Adv. E-mail: ads@pburgmail.com
Display Adv. E-mail: ads@pburgmail.com
Editorial e-mail: news@pburgmail.com
Primary Website: pburgmail.com
Year Established: 1887
Avg Paid Circ: 1400
Avg Free Circ: 13
Audit By: Sworn/Estimate/Non-Audited
Audit Date: 10.06.2019
Personnel: Ann Mullen (Pub./Owner); Emily Petrovski (Ed.)
Parent company (for newspapers): Montana Newspaper Advertising Service, Inc.

THE PHILLIPS COUNTY NEWS

Street address 1: 220 N CENTRAL AVE
Street address city: Malta
Street address state: MT
Zip/Postal code: 59538
General Phone: (406) 654-2020
General Fax: (406) 654-1410
Advertising Phone: (406) 654-2020
General/National Adv. E-mail: sarahpcnews@gmail.com
Editorial e-mail: markpcnews@gmail.com
Year Established: 1896
Avg Paid Circ: 2324
Avg Free Circ: 52
Audit By: Sworn/Estimate/Non-Audited
Audit Date: 10.06.2019
Personnel: Bonnie Starr (Pub.); Curtis H. Starr (Ed.)
Parent company (for newspapers): Main Street Media, Inc.

THE RIVER PRESS

Street address 1: 114 Front St.
Street address city: Fort Benton
Street address state: MT
Zip/Postal code: 59442
General Phone: (406) 622-3311
General Fax: (406) 622-5446
General/National Adv. E-mail: riverpress@live.com
Editorial e-mail: riverpress@live.com
Primary Website: riverpressnews.com
Year Established: 1880
Avg Paid Circ: 2000
Avg Free Circ: 50
Audit By: Sworn/Estimate/Non-Audited
Audit Date: 10.06.2019
Personnel: Lindsey Kraus (Adv. Mgr.); Tim Burmeister (Ed.)

THE ROUNDUP

Street address 1: 111 E Main St
Street address city: Sidney
Street address state: MT
Zip/Postal code: 59270-4107
General Phone: (406) 433-3306
General Fax: (406) 433-4114
Advertising Phone: (406) 433-3306
General/National Adv. E-mail: adsales@esidney.com
Display Adv. E-mail: classads@esidney.com
Editorial e-mail: publisher@esidney.com
Primary Website: roundupweb.com
Year Established: 1994
Avg Free Circ: 9500
Audit By: Sworn/Estimate/Non-Audited
Audit Date: 10.06.2019
Personnel: Jody Wells (Pub.); Dianne Swanson (Adv. Mgr.)

THE ROUNDUP RECORD-TRIBUNE/ WINNETT TIMES

Street address 1: 24 Main St
Street address city: Roundup
Street address state: MT
Zip/Postal code: 59072-2828
General Phone: (406) 323-1105
General Fax: (406) 323-1761
General/National Adv. E-mail: rrtnews@midrivers.com
Editorial e-mail: rrtnews@midrivers.com
Year Established: 1908
Avg Paid Circ: 2600
Avg Free Circ: 88
Audit By: Sworn/Estimate/Non-Audited
Audit Date: 10.06.2019
Personnel: Eric N. Rasmussen (Prodn. Mgr.)

THE SEARCHLIGHT

Street address 1: 11 Broadway
Street address city: Culbertson
Street address state: MT
Zip/Postal code: 59218
General Phone: (406) 787-5821
General Fax: (406) 787-5271
Advertising Phone: (406) 787-5821
Editorial Phone: (406) 653-2222
General/National Adv. E-mail: searchlight@nemont.net
Primary Website: northeastmontananews.com
Year Established: 1902
Avg Paid Circ: 850
Audit By: Sworn/Estimate/Non-Audited
Audit Date: 10.06.2019
Personnel: Darla Shumway (Pub.)

THE SHELBY PROMOTER

Street address 1: 119 2nd Ave S
Street address city: Shelby
Street address state: MT
Zip/Postal code: 59474-1962
General Phone: (406) 434-5171
General Fax: (406) 434-5955
General/National Adv. E-mail: promoadmgr@3rivers.net
Display Adv. E-mail: pressads2@bresnan.net
Editorial e-mail: cbpress@bresnan.net
Primary Website: http://cutbankpioneerpress.com/shelby_promoter/
Avg Paid Circ: 2125
Avg Free Circ: 0
Audit By: Sworn/Estimate/Non-Audited
Audit Date: 10.06.2019
Personnel: Brian Kavanagh (Pub.); Leanne Kavanagh (Pub.)
Parent company (for newspapers): Montana Newspaper Advertising Service, Inc.

THE STILLWATER COUNTY NEWS

Street address 1: 38 N 4th St
Street address city: Columbus
Street address state: MT
Zip/Postal code: 59019-7364
General Phone: (406) 322-5212
General Fax: (406) 322-5391
General/National Adv. E-mail: ads@stillwatercountynews.com
Display Adv. E-mail: classifieds@stillwatercountynews.com
Editorial e-mail: editor@stillwatercountynews.com
Primary Website: stillwatercountynews.com
Avg Paid Circ: 2100
Avg Free Circ: 5
Audit By: Sworn/Estimate/Non-Audited
Audit Date: 10.06.2019
Personnel: Frank Perea II (Pub.); Melany Preece (Adv); Jillian Shoemaker (Ed.); Amy Spaulding (Prodn. Mgr.)
Parent company (for newspapers): Yellowstone Communications

THE TERRY TRIBUNE

Street address 1: 204 S Logan Ave
Street address city: Terry
Street address state: MT
Zip/Postal code: 59349
General Phone: (406) 635-5513
General Fax: (406) 635-2149
General/National Adv. E-mail: tribune@midriver.com
Year Established: 1907
Avg Paid Circ: 856
Avg Free Circ: 17
Audit By: Sworn/Estimate/Non-Audited
Audit Date: 10.06.2019
Personnel: Dan Killoy (Pub.); Dawn Olson (Adv. Mgr.); Kay Johnson (Ed.)
Parent company (for newspapers): Montana Newspaper Advertising Service, Inc.; Yellowstone Communications

THE TIMES CLARION

Street address 1: 111 Central Ave S
Street address city: Harlowton
Street address state: MT
Zip/Postal code: 59036-5034
General Phone: (406) 632-5633
General Fax: (406) 632-5644
General/National Adv. E-mail: harlotms@mtintouch.net
Year Established: 1917
Avg Paid Circ: 1325
Avg Free Circ: 5
Audit By: Sworn/Estimate/Non-Audited
Audit Date: 10.06.2019
Personnel: Shelli Randles (Adv. Mgr.); Shirley Wagner (Ed.)

THE VALIERIAN

Street address 1: 19 S Central Ave
Street address city: Cut Bank
Street address state: MT
Zip/Postal code: 59427-2914
General Phone: (406) 279-3440
General Fax: (406) 873-2443
General/National Adv. E-mail: valierian@bresnan.net
Primary Website: thevalierian.com
Audit By: Sworn/Estimate/Non-Audited
Audit Date: 10.06.2019

THE WESTERN NEWS

Street address 1: 311 California Ave
Street address city: Libby
Street address state: MT
Zip/Postal code: 59923-1937
General Phone: (406) 293-4124
General Fax: (406) 293-7187
Display Adv. E-mail: classads@thewesternnews.com
Primary Website: thewesternnews.com
Mthly Avg Views: 60000
Year Established: 1902
Avg Paid Circ: 1804
Audit By: CAC
Audit Date: 31.03.2018
Personnel: Suzanne Resch (Adv. Dir.); Teresa Johnston (Adv. Sales); Paul Sievers (Photo Journalist)
Parent company (for newspapers): Hagadone Corporation

THE WHITEFISH PILOT

Street address 1: 312 2nd St E
Street address city: Whitefish
Street address state: MT
Zip/Postal code: 59937-2414
General Phone: (406) 862-3505
General Fax: (406) 862-3636
Advertising Phone: (406) 862-3505
Editorial Phone: (406) 862-3505
General/National Adv. E-mail: kfritz@dailyinterlake.com
Display Adv. E-mail: classifieds@dailyinterlake.com
Editorial e-mail: editor@whitefishpilot.com
Primary Website: whitefishpilot.com
Mthly Avg Views: 20000
Year Established: 1904
Avg Paid Circ: 1930
Audit By: CAC
Audit Date: 31.03.2018
Personnel: Heidi Desch (Reporter)
Parent company (for newspapers): Hagadone Corporation; Montana Newspaper Advertising Service, Inc.

THE WIBAUX PIONEER-GAZETTE

Street address 1: 106 1st Ave SE
Street address city: Wibaux

Street address state: MT
Zip/Postal code: 59353-8004
General Phone: (406) 796-2218
General/National Adv. E-mail: wibaux@midrivers.com
Avg Paid Circ: 880
Audit By: Sworn/Estimate/Non-Audited
Audit Date: 10.06.2019
Personnel: Frank Datta (Ed.); Carmen Hahn (Editor/Publisher)

THE YELLOWSTONE COUNTY NEWS

Street address 1: 113 Northern Ave
Street address city: Huntley
Street address state: MT
Zip/Postal code: 59037-9101
General Phone: (406) 348-2649
General Fax: (406) 348-2302
Advertising Phone: (406) 348-2650
General/National Adv. E-mail: ads@yellowstonecountynews.com
Editorial e-mail: info@yellowstonecountynews.com
Primary Website: facebook.com/pages/Yellowstone-County-News/337310421752
Year Established: 1976
Avg Paid Circ: 1900
Audit By: Sworn/Estimate/Non-Audited
Audit Date: 10.06.2019
Personnel: Jeanne Travisono (Adv. Mgr.); Rebecca Tescher Robison (Ed.)

TOBACCO VALLEY NEWS

Street address 1: 200 Cliff Ave.
Street address city: Eureka
Street address state: MT
Zip/Postal code: 59917
General Phone: (406) 297-2514
General Fax: (406) 297-7807
General/National Adv. E-mail: robnewman22@gmail.com
Display Adv. E-mail: robnewman22@gmail.com
Editorial e-mail: eurekaeditor@tobaccovalleynews.com
Primary Website: tobaccovalleynews.com
Year Established: 1960
Avg Paid Circ: 2101
Avg Free Circ: 13
Audit By: Sworn/Estimate/Non-Audited
Audit Date: 10.06.2019
Personnel: Steve Newman (Ed.); Robin Newman (Mng. Ed.)

VALLEY JOURNAL

Street address 1: 331 Main St SW
Street address 2: Ste A
Street address city: Ronan
Street address state: MT
Zip/Postal code: 59864-2708
General Phone: (406) 676-8989
General Fax: (406) 676-8990
General/National Adv. E-mail: boone@valleyjournal.net
Editorial e-mail: vjeditor@valleyjournal.net
Primary Website: valleyjournal.net
Year Established: 2004
Avg Free Circ: 8400
Audit By: Sworn/Estimate/Non-Audited
Audit Date: 10.06.2019

WHITEHALL LEDGER

Street address 1: 15 W Legion St
Street address city: Whitehall
Street address state: MT
Zip/Postal code: 59759-9784
General Phone: (406) 287-5301
General Fax: (406) 287-5352
General/National Adv. E-mail: advertising@whitehallledger.com
Editorial e-mail: info@whitehallledger.com
Primary Website: whitehallledger.com
Year Established: 1984
Avg Paid Circ: 1400
Avg Free Circ: 16
Audit By: Sworn/Estimate/Non-Audited
Audit Date: 10.06.2019
Personnel: Greg Corr (Prodn. Mgr.)
Parent company (for newspapers): Montana Newspaper Advertising Service, Inc.

NEBRASKA

AINSWORTH STAR-JOURNAL

Street address 1: 921 E 4th St
Street address city: Ainsworth
Street address state: NE
Zip/Postal code: 69210-1218
General Phone: (402) 387-2844
General Fax: (402) 387-1234
General/National Adv. E-mail: ainsworthnews@ainsworthnews.com
Primary Website: ainsworthnews.com
Avg Paid Circ: 1375
Audit By: Sworn/Estimate/Non-Audited
Audit Date: 10.06.2019
Personnel: Rodney Worrell (Pub.); Kathy S. Worrell (Ed.)
Parent company (for newspapers): Great Plains Publishing Co., Inc.

ALBION NEWS

Street address 1: 328 W Church St
Street address city: Albion
Street address state: NE
Zip/Postal code: 68620-1260
General Phone: (402) 395-2115
General Fax: (402) 395-2772
General/National Adv. E-mail: brachow@frontier.com
Display Adv. E-mail: julied@frontiernet.net
Editorial e-mail: albnnuz@frontiernet.net
Primary Website: albionnewsonline.com
Year Established: 1879
Avg Paid Circ: 1850
Audit By: Sworn/Estimate/Non-Audited
Audit Date: 10.06.2019
Personnel: Jim Dickerson (Ed and co-pub)
Parent company (for newspapers): Dickerson Newspapers, Inc.

ARAPAHOE PUBLIC MIRROR

Street address 1: 420 Nebraska Ave
Street address city: Arapahoe
Street address state: NE
Zip/Postal code: 68922-2762
General Phone: (308) 962-7261
General Fax: (308) 962-7865
General/National Adv. E-mail: arapmir@atcjet.net
Primary Website: arapahoemirror.org
Year Established: 18
Avg Paid Circ: 950
Audit By: Sworn/Estimate/Non-Audited
Audit Date: 10.06.2019
Personnel: T.M. (Ted) Gill (Pub.); Gayle L. Schutz (Pub); Cheri Gill (Circ. Mgr.)

ARLINGTON CITIZEN

Street address 1: 138 N 16th St
Street address city: Blair
Street address state: NE
Zip/Postal code: 68008-1633
General Phone: (402) 426-2121
General Fax: (402) 426-2227
Advertising Phone: (402) 426-2121
Advertising Fax: (402) 426-2227
Editorial Phone: (402) 426-2121
Editorial Fax: (402) 426-2227
General/National Adv. E-mail: mrhoades@enterprisepub.com
Display Adv. E-mail: lhansen@enterprisepub.com
Classified Adv. e-mail: classifieds@enterprisepub.com
Editorial e-mail: editor@enterprisepub.com
Primary Website: enterprisepub.com
Year Established: 1954
Avg Paid Circ: 457
Audit By: USPS
Audit Date: 01.10.2021
Personnel: Mark Rhoades (Publisher/Owner); Lynette Hansen (Sales Manager); Leanna Ellis (Editor); Greg Forbes (Managing Editor); Jen Stolz (Art Director); Tracy Prettyman (Business Manager)
Parent company (for newspapers): Enterprise Media Group

ARNOLD SENTINEL

Street address 1: 113 S Walnut
Street address city: Arnold
Street address state: NE
Zip/Postal code: 69120-6872
General Phone: (308) 848-2511
General/National Adv. E-mail: arnoldsentinel@gpcom.net
Primary Website: None
Avg Paid Circ: 800
Audit By: Sworn/Estimate/Non-Audited
Audit Date: 10.06.2019
Personnel: Fallon Gibson (Circulation); Janet Larreau (Man.Ed.); Lacy McCarthy (Pub.)
Parent company (for newspapers): The Arnold Sentinel LLC

AURORA NEWS-REGISTER

Street address 1: 1320 K St
Street address city: Aurora
Street address state: NE
Zip/Postal code: 68818-2119
General Phone: (402) 694-2131
General Fax: (402) 694-2133
General/National Adv. E-mail: advertising@hamilton.net
Editorial e-mail: newsregister@hamilton.net
Primary Website: auroranewsregister.com
Year Established: 1929
Avg Paid Circ: 3000
Audit By: Sworn/Estimate/Non-Audited
Audit Date: 10.06.2019
Personnel: Kurt Johnson (Pub.); Paula Johnson (Pub.); Dave Bradley (Adv. Mgr.); Laurie Pfeifer (Mng. Ed.); Marc Russell (Prodn. Mgr.)
Parent company (for newspapers): Porchlight Publishing Inc

BLUE HILL LEADER

Street address 1: 565 W Gage St
Street address city: Blue Hill
Street address state: NE
Zip/Postal code: 68930-8000
General Phone: (402) 756-2077
General Fax: (402) 756-2583
General/National Adv. E-mail: bluehillleader@gtmc.net
Display Adv. E-mail: bluehillleader@gtmc.net
Editorial e-mail: bluehillleader@gtmc.net
Primary Website: mainstreetmedia.us
Year Established: 1887
Avg Paid Circ: 950
Audit By: Sworn/Estimate/Non-Audited
Audit Date: 10.06.2019
Personnel: Frank Mercer (Publisher); Rick Houchin (Editor); Melissa Lounsbury (Office Manager/Billing/Advertising)
Parent company (for newspapers): Main Street Media, Inc.

BRIDGEPORT NEWS-BLADE

Street address 1: 801 Main St
Street address city: Bridgeport
Street address state: NE
Zip/Postal code: 69336-4046
General Phone: (308) 262-0675
General Fax: (308) 262-0675
General/National Adv. E-mail: ads@newsblade.net
Display Adv. E-mail: ads@newsblade.net
Editorial e-mail: editor@newsblade.net
Primary Website: NewsBlade.com
Year Established: 1900
Avg Paid Circ: 1200
Avg Free Circ: 50
Audit By: Sworn/Estimate/Non-Audited
Audit Date: 10.06.2019
Personnel: John Erickson (Pub)
Parent company (for newspapers): MOCO RENOVO LLC

BURT COUNTY PLAINDEALER

Street address 1: 707 S 13th St
Street address city: Tekamah
Street address state: NE
Zip/Postal code: 68061-1326
General Phone: (402) 374-2226
General Fax: (402) 374-2739
General/National Adv. E-mail: renee.lombardo@lee.net
Editorial e-mail: katie.novak@lee.net
Primary Website: burtcountyplaindealer.com
Year Established: 1934
Avg Paid Circ: 1057
Avg Free Circ: 121
Audit By: Sworn/Estimate/Non-Audited
Audit Date: 10.06.2019
Personnel: Joe Zink (Gen. Mgr.); Jodie Jordan (Circ. Mgr.)
Parent company (for newspapers): Dispatch-Argus

CAMBRIDGE CLARION

Street address 1: 706 Patterson St
Street address city: Cambridge
Street address state: NE
Zip/Postal code: 69022-6598
General Phone: (308) 697-3326
General Fax: (308) 697-3326
General/National Adv. E-mail: clarion@cambridgeclarion.com
Primary Website: cambridgeclarion.com
Year Established: 1920
Avg Paid Circ: 1100
Avg Free Circ: 70
Audit By: Sworn/Estimate/Non-Audited
Audit Date: 10.06.2019
Personnel: Jolene Miller (Ed.)

CEDAR COUNTY NEWS

Street address 1: 102 W Main St
Street address city: Hartington
Street address state: NE
Zip/Postal code: 68739-3005
General Phone: (402) 254-3997
General Fax: (402) 254-3999
General/National Adv. E-mail: advertising@hartel.net
Editorial e-mail: ccnews@hartel.net
Primary Website: hartington.net
Year Established: 1898
Avg Paid Circ: 1640
Audit By: Sworn/Estimate/Non-Audited
Audit Date: 10.06.2019
Personnel: Peggy Year (Pub.); Rob Dump (Ed.)
Parent company (for newspapers): Northeast Nebraska News Co.

CEDAR RAPIDS PRESS

Street address 1: 206 W Main St
Street address city: Cedar Rapids
Street address state: NE
Zip/Postal code: 68627-5600
General Phone: (308) 358-0440
General Fax: (308) 358-0440
General/National Adv. E-mail: crpress@hotmail.com
Display Adv. E-mail: crpress@hotmail.com
Editorial e-mail: crpress@hotmail.com
Year Established: 1947
Avg Paid Circ: 350
Avg Free Circ: 10
Audit By: Sworn/Estimate/Non-Audited
Audit Date: 10.06.2019
Personnel: David Bopp (Ed.); Kim Schilousky (Location News Reporter)

CHAPPELL REGISTER

Street address 1: 273 Vincent Ave
Street address city: Chappell
Street address state: NE
Zip/Postal code: 69129-9701
General Phone: (308) 874-2207
General Fax: (308) 874-2207
General/National Adv. E-mail: chapregister@embarqmail.com
Avg Paid Circ: 1000
Audit By: Sworn/Estimate/Non-Audited
Audit Date: 10.06.2019
Personnel: Michael Talbott (Ed.)

CLAY COUNTY NEWS

Street address 1: 207 N Saunders Ave
Street address city: Sutton
Street address state: NE
Zip/Postal code: 68979-2511
General Phone: (402) 773-5576
General Fax: (402) 773-5577
General/National Adv. E-mail: ccntory@gmail.com
Editorial e-mail: claycountynews@gmail.com
Primary Website: theclaycountynews.com
Year Established: 1875
Avg Paid Circ: 2805
Avg Free Circ: 50

Audit By: Sworn/Estimate/Non-Audited
Audit Date: 10.06.2019
Personnel: Tory Duncan (Ed.)

CLEARWATER RECORD-EWING NEWS

Street address 1: 419 M St
Street address city: Neligh
Street address state: NE
Zip/Postal code: 68756-1422
General Phone: (402) 887-4840
General Fax: (402) 887-4711
General/National Adv. E-mail: jwright@nelighnews.com
Editorial e-mail: lschindler@nelighnews.com
Primary Website: nelighnews.com/clearwater_ewing
Avg Paid Circ: 600
Audit By: Sworn/Estimate/Non-Audited
Audit Date: 10.06.2019
Personnel: Joan Wright (Pub.)
Parent company (for newspapers): JD Printing & Publishing Co

COLERIDGE BLADE THIS NEWSPAPER HAS CEASED PUBLICATION

Street address 1: 102 W Main St
Street address city: Hartington
Street address state: NE
Zip/Postal code: 68739
General Phone: (402) 283-4267
General Fax: (402) 254-3999
General/National Adv. E-mail: advertising@hartel.net
Primary Website: northeastnebraskanews.us/category/cedar-county/coleridge
Avg Paid Circ: 445
Avg Free Circ: 35
Audit By: Sworn/Estimate/Non-Audited
Audit Date: 10.06.2019
Personnel: Rob Dump (Ed.)
Parent company (for newspapers): Northeast Nebraska News Co.

COLFAX COUNTY PRESS

Street address 1: 242 Pine St
Street address city: Clarkson
Street address state: NE
Zip/Postal code: 68629-4093
General Phone: (402) 892-3544
General Fax: (402) 892-3544
General/National Adv. E-mail: ccpress@megavision.com
Avg Paid Circ: 1397
Audit By: Sworn/Estimate/Non-Audited
Audit Date: 10.06.2019
Personnel: Helen Evans (Gen. Mgr.); T.A. Evans (Ed.)

CRAWFORD CLIPPER/HARRISON SUN LLC

Street address 1: 427 2nd St
Street address city: Crawford
Street address state: NE
Zip/Postal code: 69339-1053
General Phone: (308) 665-2310
General Fax: (308) 665-1146
General/National Adv. E-mail: crawfordclipper@gmail.com
Year Established: 1979
Avg Paid Circ: 1050
Avg Free Circ: 50
Audit By: Sworn/Estimate/Non-Audited
Audit Date: 10.06.2019
Personnel: Jessica Espinoza (Owner/Editor Prodn. Mgr.); Diane Clark (Reporter/Photographer)

CREIGHTON NEWS

Street address 1: 816 Main St
Street address city: Creighton
Street address state: NE
Zip/Postal code: 68729-4003
General Phone: (402) 358-5220
General Fax: (402) 358-5132
General/National Adv. E-mail: jforbes@creightonnews.com
Primary Website: creightonnews.com
Avg Paid Circ: 1400
Audit By: Sworn/Estimate/Non-Audited
Audit Date: 10.06.2019
Personnel: Dave Wright (Pub.); Rhea Landholm (Ed.)
Parent company (for newspapers): JD Printing & Publishing Co

CRETE NEWS

Street address 1: 129 S. 6th Street
Street address city: Seward
Street address state: NE
Zip/Postal code: 68434
General Phone: (402) 643-3676
General/National Adv. E-mail: nichole@sewardindependent.com
Display Adv. E-mail: office@sewardindependent.com
Editorial e-mail: emily@sewardindependent.com
Primary Website: sewardindependent.com/crete
Year Established: 1871
Avg Paid Circ: 3500
Audit By: Sworn/Estimate/Non-Audited
Audit Date: 10.06.2019
Personnel: Emily Hemphill (Mng. Ed.); Kevin Zadina (Pub.); Stephanie Croston (Sports Ed./Asst. Ed.); Nichole Javorsky (Ad consultant)

CUSTER COUNTY CHIEF

Street address 1: 305 S 10th Ave
Street address city: Broken Bow
Street address state: NE
Zip/Postal code: 68822-2019
General Phone: (308) 872-2471
General Fax: (308) 872-2415
General/National Adv. E-mail: chiefads@custercountychief.com
Primary Website: custercountychief.com
Year Established: 1892
Avg Paid Circ: 3900
Audit By: Sworn/Estimate/Non-Audited
Audit Date: 10.06.2019
Personnel: Mona Weatherly (Mng. Ed.); Donnis Hueftle-Bullock (Gen. Mgr.)
Parent company (for newspapers): Horizon Publications Inc.

DAKOTA COUNTY STAR

Street address 1: 7990 County Road P35
Street address city: Blair
Street address state: NE
Zip/Postal code: 68008-6562
General Phone: (402) 426-9860
General Fax: (402) 426-9860
Advertising Phone: (402) 426-9860
Advertising Fax: (402) 426-9860
Editorial Phone: (402) 426-9860
Editorial Fax: (402) 426-9860
General/National Adv. E-mail: mrhoades@enterprisepub.com
Display Adv. E-mail: mrhoades@enterprisepub.com
Editorial e-mail: mrhoades@enterprisepub.com
Primary Website: dakotacountystar.net
Avg Paid Circ: 2200
Avg Free Circ: 78
Audit By: Sworn/Estimate/Non-Audited
Audit Date: 10.06.2019
Personnel: Mark Rhoades (Owner/Pub.); Blake Branch (Ed.); Chris Rhoades (Associate Publisher)

DESHLER RUSTLER

Street address 1: 706 4th St
Street address city: Deshler
Street address state: NE
Zip/Postal code: 68340-1801
General Phone: (402) 365-7221
General Fax: (402) 365-4439
General/National Adv. E-mail: deshlerrustler@gpcom.net
Avg Paid Circ: 1300
Audit By: Sworn/Estimate/Non-Audited
Audit Date: 10.06.2019
Personnel: Jennifer Czeki (Assistant Editor); Dawn Schleif (Circ. Mgr., Ad Mgr., Billing); Lois Struve (Ed.); Paulette Hynek (Assistant)

DODGE CRITERION

Street address 1: 140 N Oak St
Street address city: Dodge
Street address state: NE
Zip/Postal code: 68633-3094
General Phone: (402) 693-2415
General Fax: (402) 693-2415
General/National Adv. E-mail: dodgecriterion@gpcom.net
Year Established: 1888
Avg Paid Circ: 650
Avg Free Circ: 9
Audit By: Sworn/Estimate/Non-Audited
Audit Date: 26.09.2022
Personnel: Kathleen Kauffold (Editor); Ken H. Kauffold (Ed.)

FAIRBURY JOURNAL-NEWS

Street address 1: 510 C St.
Street address city: Fairbury
Street address state: NE
Zip/Postal code: 68352
General Phone: (402) 729-6141
General Fax: (402) 729-5652
General/National Adv. E-mail: info@fairburyjournalnews.com
Display Adv. E-mail: info@fairburyjournalnews.com
Editorial e-mail: Trevor.gill@fairburyjournalnews.com
Primary Website: fairburyjournalnews.com
Year Established: 1892
Avg Paid Circ: 4500
Audit By: Sworn/Estimate/Non-Audited
Audit Date: 10.06.2019
Personnel: Trevor Gill (Ed./CFO); Timothy Linscott (Owner/Pub.)
Parent company (for newspapers): Linscott Media, LLC

FALLS CITY JOURNAL

Street address 1: 1709 Stone St
Street address city: Falls City
Street address state: NE
Zip/Postal code: 68355-2026
General Phone: (402) 245-2431
General Fax: (402) 245-4404
General/National Adv. E-mail: fcjournalads@sentco.net
Editorial e-mail: sschock@sentco.net
Primary Website: fcjournal.net
Avg Paid Circ: 4100
Audit By: Sworn/Estimate/Non-Audited
Audit Date: 10.06.2019
Personnel: George W. Schock (Pub.); Chelsie Alexander (Book Keeper); Nikki McKim (Adv. Mgr.); Scott Schock (Ed.)

FRIEND SENTINEL

Street address 1: 129 S. 6th Street
Street address city: Seward
Street address state: NE
Zip/Postal code: 68434
General Phone: (402) 643-3676
General/National Adv. E-mail: nichole@sewardindependent.com
Display Adv. E-mail: office@sewardindependent.com
Editorial e-mail: emily@sewardindependent.com
Primary Website: sewardindependent.com/friend
Audit By: Sworn/Estimate/Non-Audited
Audit Date: 10.06.2019
Personnel: Emily Hemphill (Mng. Ed.); Kevin Zadina (Pub.); Stephanie Croston (Sports Ed./Asst Ed.); Brenda Clark (Adv.)

GARDEN COUNTY NEWS

Street address 1: 204 Main St
Street address city: Oshkosh
Street address state: NE
Zip/Postal code: 69154-6130
General Phone: (308) 772-3555
General Fax: (308) 772-4475
General/National Adv. E-mail: gardencountynews@gmail.com
Display Adv. E-mail: gardencountynews@gmail.com
Editorial e-mail: gardencountynews@gmail.com
Primary Website: gardencountynews.com
Year Established: 1905
Avg Paid Circ: 1300
Audit By: Sworn/Estimate/Non-Audited
Audit Date: 10.06.2019
Personnel: Kelly Reece (Pub.)

GERING COURIER

Street address 1: 1405 Broadway
Street address city: Scottsbluff
Street address state: NE
Zip/Postal code: 69361-3151
General Phone: (308) 436-2222
General Fax: (308) 436-7127
General/National Adv. E-mail: doug.southard@starherald.com
Display Adv. E-mail: class@starherald.com
Editorial e-mail: brad.staman@geringcourier.com
Primary Website: geringcourier.com
Year Established: 1887
Avg Paid Circ: 2118
Audit By: Sworn/Estimate/Non-Audited
Audit Date: 10.06.2019
Personnel: Brad Staman (Pub.); Jeff Fielder (Ed.)
Parent company (for newspapers): BH Media Group

GOTHENBURG TIMES

Street address 1: 406 10th St
Street address city: Gothenburg
Street address state: NE
Zip/Postal code: 69138-1922
General Phone: (308) 537-3636
General Fax: (308) 537-7554
General/National Adv. E-mail: ads@gothenburgtimes.com
Display Adv. E-mail: ads@gothenburgtimes.com
Editorial e-mail: news@gothenburgtimes.com
Primary Website: gothenburgtimes.com
Year Established: 1908
Avg Paid Circ: 1800
Avg Free Circ: 0
Audit By: Sworn/Estimate/Non-Audited
Audit Date: 10.06.2019
Personnel: Ellen Morternsen (GM)
Parent company (for newspapers): Platte Valley Media LLC

GRANT COUNTY NEWS

Street address 1: 206 S Grant Ave
Street address city: Hyannis
Street address state: NE
Zip/Postal code: 69350
General Phone: (308) 458-2425
General Fax: (308) 458-2425
General/National Adv. E-mail: gcn@neb-sandhills.net
Year Established: 1896
Avg Paid Circ: 550
Avg Free Circ: 35
Audit By: Sworn/Estimate/Non-Audited
Audit Date: 10.06.2019
Personnel: Sharon M. Wheelock (Ed)

HARLAN COUNTY JOURNAL

Street address 1: 711 Main St
Street address city: Alma
Street address state: NE
Zip/Postal code: 68920-2164
General Phone: (308) 928-2143
General Fax: (308) 928-9914
General/National Adv. E-mail: journal@frontiernet.net
Primary Website: mainstreetmedia.us
Avg Paid Circ: 1600
Avg Free Circ: 67
Audit By: Sworn/Estimate/Non-Audited
Audit Date: 10.06.2019
Personnel: Jack Krier (Ed.)
Parent company (for newspapers): Main Street Media, Inc.

HAYES CENTER TIMES REPUBLICAN

Street address 1: 311 Tate St
Street address city: Hayes Center
Street address state: NE
Zip/Postal code: 69032-9747
General Phone: (308) 286-3325
Editorial Phone: (308) 222-0380
General/National Adv. E-mail: times@gpcom.net
Avg Paid Circ: 867
Audit By: Sworn/Estimate/Non-Audited
Audit Date: 10.06.2019
Personnel: Alysia MESSERSMITH
Parent company (for newspapers): Southwest Nebraska News, LLC

HEBRON JOURNAL-REGISTER

Street address 1: 318 Lincoln Ave

Street address city: Hebron
Street address state: NE
Zip/Postal code: 68370-1524
General Phone: (402) 768-6602
General Fax: (402) 768-7354
General/National Adv. E-mail: hebronjr@windstream.net
Primary Website: hebronjournalregister.com
Avg Paid Circ: 2500
Audit By: Sworn/Estimate/Non-Audited
Audit Date: 10.06.2019
Personnel: Mike Edgecombe (Ed.)

HI-LINE ENTERPRISE

Street address 1: 208 Center Ave
Street address city: Curtis
Street address state: NE
Zip/Postal code: 69025-3024
General Phone: (308) 367-4144
General Fax: (308) 367-8616
General/National Adv. E-mail: advertising@blairnebraska.com
Display Adv. E-mail: advertising@blairnebraska.com
Editorial e-mail: editor@hilineenterprise.com
Primary Website: hilineenterprise.com
Avg Paid Circ: 1500
Audit By: Sworn/Estimate/Non-Audited
Audit Date: 10.06.2019
Personnel: Mark Rhoades (Pub.); Lynette Hansen (Adv. Mgr.)

HITCHOCK COUNTY NEWS

Street address 1: 346 Main St
Street address city: Trenton
Street address state: NE
Zip/Postal code: 69044-1809
General Phone: (308) 334-5226
General Fax: (308) 334-5225
Avg Paid Circ: 1142
Avg Free Circ: 21
Audit By: Sworn/Estimate/Non-Audited
Audit Date: 10.06.2019
Personnel: Amy Frederick (Gen. Mgr.); Kathy Broz (Circ. Mgr.); Jason Frederick (Prodn. Mgr.)

HOLT COUNTY INDEPENDENT

Street address 1: 114 N 4th St
Street address city: O' Neill
Street address state: NE
Zip/Postal code: 68763-1503
General Phone: (402) 336-1220
General Fax: (402) 336-1222
General/National Adv. E-mail: ads@holtindependent.com
Editorial e-mail: editor@holtindependent.com
Primary Website: holtindependent.com
Year Established: 1880
Avg Paid Circ: 2500
Avg Free Circ: 20
Audit By: Sworn/Estimate/Non-Audited
Audit Date: 03.06.2024
Personnel: James T. Miles (Publisher); Joni Isom; Levi Stewart; Amanda Sindelar (Editor)

HOOKER COUNTY TRIBUNE

Street address 1: 306 NW 1st St
Street address city: Mullen
Street address state: NE
Zip/Postal code: 69152
General Phone: (308) 546-2242
General/National Adv. E-mail: tribune@nebnet.net
Primary Website: www.hookercountytribune.com
Year Established: 1887
Avg Paid Circ: 750
Audit By: Sworn/Estimate/Non-Audited
Audit Date: 10.06.2019
Personnel: Gerri Peterson (Ed.)

HOWELLS JOURNAL

Street address 1: 122 N 3rd St
Street address city: Howells
Street address state: NE
Zip/Postal code: 68641-3087
General Phone: (402) 986-1777
General/National Adv. E-mail: howellsjournal@msn.com
Editorial e-mail: howellsjournal@msn.com
Primary Website: ci.howells.ne.us/commclub.asp
Avg Paid Circ: 915
Audit By: Sworn/Estimate/Non-Audited
Audit Date: 10.06.2019
Personnel: Cheryl Sudbeck (Pub., Ed.)

HUMBOLDT STANDARD

Street address 1: 317 W Square St
Street address city: Humboldt
Street address state: NE
Zip/Postal code: 68376-6043
General Phone: (402) 862-2200
General Fax: (402) 862-2209
General/National Adv. E-mail: hs40231@windstream.net
Display Adv. E-mail: hs40231@windstream.net
Editorial e-mail: hs40231@windstream.net
Year Established: 1882
Avg Paid Circ: 750
Audit By: Sworn/Estimate/Non-Audited
Audit Date: 10.06.2019
Personnel: Roxanne Sailors (Editor)

IMPERIAL REPUBLICAN

Street address 1: 622 Broadway
Street address city: Imperial
Street address state: NE
Zip/Postal code: 69033-3136
General Phone: (308) 882-4453
General Fax: (308) 882-5167
General/National Adv. E-mail: imperialads@jpipapers.com
Display Adv. E-mail: frontdesk@jpipapers.com
Editorial e-mail: schultzjan@jpipapers.com
Primary Website: imperialrepublican.com
Year Established: 1885
Avg Paid Circ: 1614
Avg Free Circ: 36
Audit By: Sworn/Estimate/Non-Audited
Audit Date: 10.06.2019
Personnel: Jan Schultz (Managing editor); Lori Pankonin (Co-Publisher); Jana Pribbeno (Ad Rep); Vivian Berry (Accounts Payable manager); Russ Pankonin (Co-Publisher); Alan Carman (Pressman); Amanda Courter (Office/Circ Mgr.); Hayes Karen (Production Mgr.); Jenn Huff (Production Asst); Becky Kuntzelman (Reporter); Frank Perea

KEITH COUNTY NEWS

Street address 1: 116 W A St
Street address city: Ogallala
Street address state: NE
Zip/Postal code: 69153-2543
General Phone: (308) 284-4046
General Fax: (308) 284-4048
General/National Adv. E-mail: newsboy@ogallalakcnews.com
Editorial e-mail: newsboy@ogallalakcnews.com
Primary Website: ogallalakcnews.com
Year Established: 1885
Avg Paid Circ: 2200
Avg Free Circ: 400
Audit By: Sworn/Estimate/Non-Audited
Audit Date: 10.06.2019
Personnel: Marilee Perlinger (Adv. Mgr.); Jeff Headley (Publisher); Judy Curtis (Bookkepper)

LAUREL ADVOCATE

Street address 1: 106 E 2nd St
Street address city: Laurel
Street address state: NE
Zip/Postal code: 68745-1990
General Phone: (402) 256-3200
General Fax: (402) 254-3999
General/National Adv. E-mail: banners@hartington.net
Primary Website: hartington.net/category/laurel-advocate
Avg Paid Circ: 950
Audit By: Sworn/Estimate/Non-Audited
Audit Date: 10.06.2019
Personnel: Rob Dump (Ed.)
Parent company (for newspapers): Northeast Nebraska News Co.

LEXINGTON CLIPPER-HERALD

Street address 1: 114 W 5th St
Street address city: Lexington
Street address state: NE
Zip/Postal code: 68850-1903
General Phone: (308) 324-5511
General Fax: (308) 324-5240
General/National Adv. E-mail: ads@lexch.com
Display Adv. E-mail: carol.meyer@lexch.com
Editorial e-mail: malena.ward@lexch.com
Primary Website: lexch.com
Avg Paid Circ: 3000
Avg Free Circ: 5200
Audit By: Sworn/Estimate/Non-Audited
Audit Date: 10.06.2019
Personnel: Chrissy Wagener (Circ. Mgr.)
Parent company (for newspapers): BH Media Group

LINCOLN JOURNAL STAR

Street address 1: 926 P St
Street address city: Lincoln
Street address state: NE
Zip/Postal code: 68508-3615
General Phone: (402) 475-4200
General Fax: (402) 473-7159
Advertising Phone: (402) 473-7450
Editorial Phone: (402) 473-7306
General/National Adv. E-mail: advertising@journalstar.com
Editorial e-mail: dbundy@journalstar.com
Primary Website: neighborhoodextra.com
Year Established: 1990
Avg Paid Circ: 33000
Audit By: Sworn/Estimate/Non-Audited
Audit Date: 10.06.2019
Personnel: Ava Thomas (Publisher); Dennis Buckley (Ed.)
Parent company (for newspapers): Dispatch-Argus

LYONS MIRROR-SUN

Street address 1: 217 N Oakland Ave
Street address city: Oakland
Street address state: NE
Zip/Postal code: 68045-1338
General Phone: (402) 685-5624
General Fax: (402) 685-5625
General/National Adv. E-mail: oindependent@abbnebraska.com
Editorial e-mail: oindependent@abbnebraska.com
Primary Website: burtcountynews.net
Avg Paid Circ: 900
Avg Free Circ: 30
Audit By: Sworn/Estimate/Non-Audited
Audit Date: 10.06.2019
Personnel: Mark Rhodes (Pres./Pub.)
Parent company (for newspapers): Enterprise Media Group

MIDWEST MESSENGER

Street address 1: 707 S 13th St
Street address city: Tekamah
Street address state: NE
Zip/Postal code: 68061-1326
General Phone: (402) 374-2226
General Fax: (402) 374-2739
Advertising Phone: (402) 374-2226
Advertising Fax: (402) 374-2739
Editorial Phone: (402) 374-2226
Editorial Fax: (402) 374-2739
General/National Adv. E-mail: deanna.ray@midwestmessenger.com
Display Adv. E-mail: renee.lombardo@midwestmessenger.com
Editorial e-mail: terry.anderson@lee.net
Primary Website: midwestmessenger.com
Year Established: 1968
Avg Paid Circ: 0
Avg Free Circ: 100000
Audit By: Sworn/Estimate/Non-Audited
Audit Date: 10.06.2019
Personnel: Terry Anderson (News Ed.); Joe Zink (Gen. Mgr.); Deanna Ray (Adv. Mgr.); Mike Wood (Pub.)
Parent company (for newspapers): Dispatch-Argus

MILFORD TIMES

Street address 1: 129 S. 6th Street
Street address city: Seward
Street address state: NE
Zip/Postal code: 68434
General Phone: (402) 643-3676
General/National Adv. E-mail: nichole@sewardindependent.com
Display Adv. E-mail: office@sewardindependent.com
Editorial e-mail: emily@sewardindependent.com
Primary Website: milfordtimes.net
Avg Paid Circ: 1100
Avg Free Circ: 10
Audit By: Sworn/Estimate/Non-Audited
Audit Date: 10.06.2019
Personnel: Kevin Zadina (Pub.); Emily Hemphill (Mng. Ed.); Stephanie Croston (Sports Ed./Asst. Ed.); Jenny Brinkmeyer (Office Mgr.); Nichole Javorsky (Advertising consultant)

NEBRASKA CITY NEWS-PRESS

Street address 1: 823 Central Ave
Street address city: Nebraska City
Street address state: NE
Zip/Postal code: 68410-2408
General Phone: (402) 873-3334
General Fax: (402) 873-5436
Advertising Phone: (402) 209-8020
Advertising Fax: (402) 873-5436
Editorial Phone: (402) 873-3334
Editorial Fax: (402) 873-5436
General/National Adv. E-mail: ldavis@ncnewspress.com
Display Adv. E-mail: classad@ncnewspress.com
Classified Adv. e-mail: classad@ncnewspress.com
Editorial e-mail: kmanion@ncnewspress.com
Primary Website: ncnewspress.com
Mthly Avg Unique Visitors: 20000
Year Established: 1858
Avg Paid Circ: 2110
Audit By: Sworn/Estimate/Non-Audited
Audit Date: 10.06.2019
Personnel: Tammy Schumacher (Gen. Mgr.); Kirt Manion (Sports Ed.); Roxanne Schutz (Classified Adv. Mgr.)
Parent company (for newspapers): CherryRoad Media

NEBRASKA SIGNAL

Street address 1: 131 N 9th St
Street address city: Geneva
Street address state: NE
Zip/Postal code: 68361-2017
General Phone: (402) 759-3117
General Fax: (402) 759-4214
General/National Adv. E-mail: signal@thenebraskasignal.com
Editorial e-mail: signal@thenebraskasignal.com
Primary Website: thenebraskasignal.com
Year Established: 1881
Avg Paid Circ: 2500
Audit By: Sworn/Estimate/Non-Audited
Audit Date: 10.06.2019
Personnel: John Edgecombe (Pub., Circ. Mgr., Ed.)

NEMAHA COUNTY HERALD

Street address 1: 830 Central Ave
Street address city: Auburn
Street address state: NE
Zip/Postal code: 68305-1614
General Phone: (402) 274-3185
General Fax: (402) 274-3273
General/National Adv. E-mail: kendall@anewspaper.net
Primary Website: anewspaper.net
Year Established: 1888
Avg Paid Circ: 3245
Audit By: Sworn/Estimate/Non-Audited
Audit Date: 30.09.2017
Personnel: Kendall Neiman (Pub.); Darrell Wellman (Ed.); Will McQue (Prodn. Mgr.)

NEWMAN GROVE REPORTER

Street address 1: 509 Hale Ave
Street address city: Newman Grove
Street address state: NE
Zip/Postal code: 68758-6033
General Phone: (402) 447-6012
General/National Adv. E-mail: editor@ngreporter.com
Primary Website: ngreporter.com
Year Established: 1882
Avg Paid Circ: 625
Avg Free Circ: 12
Audit By: Sworn/Estimate/Non-Audited
Audit Date: 10.06.2019

Personnel: Steve & Gail Johnson (Owners/Publishers)

NIOBRARA TRIBUNE

Street address 1: 2544 Park Ave
Street address city: Niobrara
Street address state: NE
Zip/Postal code: 68760-7073
General Phone: (402) 857-3737
General Fax: (402) 388-4336
Advertising Phone: (402) 857-3737
General/National Adv. E-mail: niobraratribune@yahoo.com
Editorial e-mail: Editor@atkinsongraphic.com
Avg Paid Circ: 520
Audit By: Sworn/Estimate/Non-Audited
Audit Date: 10.06.2019
Personnel: Kevin Henseler (Pub.); Valerie Zach (Ed.)

NORTH BEND EAGLE

Street address 1: 730 Main St
Street address city: North Bend
Street address state: NE
Zip/Postal code: 68649-5003
General Phone: (402) 652-8312
General Fax: (402) 652-8312
General/National Adv. E-mail: eagleads@gmail.com
Display Adv. E-mail: eagleads@gmail.com
Editorial e-mail: nbeagle@gmail.com
Primary Website: northbendeagle.com
Year Established: 1897
Avg Paid Circ: 1100
Avg Free Circ: 10
Audit By: Sworn/Estimate/Non-Audited
Audit Date: 10.06.2019
Personnel: Nathan Arneal (Ed & Pub)

NUCKOLLS COUNTY LOCOMOTIVE-GAZETTE

Street address 1: 63 E 4th
Street address city: Nelson
Street address state: NE
Zip/Postal code: 68961
General Phone: (402) 225-2301
General Fax: (402) 225-2301
General/National Adv. E-mail: ncignews@gmail.com
Year Established: 1884
Avg Paid Circ: 700
Audit By: Sworn/Estimate/Non-Audited
Audit Date: 10.06.2019
Personnel: Mary Statz (Ed.)
Parent company (for newspapers): Superior Publishing Co; Superior Publishing Company

OAKLAND INDEPENDENT

Street address 1: 217 N Oakland Ave
Street address city: Oakland
Street address state: NE
Zip/Postal code: 68045-1338
General Phone: (402) 685-5624
General Fax: (402) 685-5625
General/National Adv. E-mail: ali@enterprisepub.com
Editorial e-mail: oindependent@abbnebraska.com
Primary Website: burtcountynews.net
Audit By: Sworn/Estimate/Non-Audited
Audit Date: 10.06.2019
Personnel: Mark Rhodes (Pres./Pub.)
Parent company (for newspapers): Enterprise Media Group

OXFORD STANDARD

Street address 1: 104 W South Railway St
Street address city: Oxford
Street address state: NE
Zip/Postal code: 68967
General Phone: (308) 824-3582
General Fax: (308) 824-3582
General/National Adv. E-mail: oxstandard@gmail.com
Year Established: 1896
Avg Paid Circ: 800
Audit By: Sworn/Estimate/Non-Audited
Audit Date: 10.06.2019
Personnel: Jolene Miller

PETERSBURG PRESS

Street address 1: 328 W Church St
Street address city: Albion
Street address state: NE
Zip/Postal code: 68620-1225
General Phone: (402) 395-2115
General Fax: (402) 395-2772
General/National Adv. E-mail: albnnuz@frontiernet.net
Primary Website: albionnewsonline.com/category/petersburg-press
Year Established: 1888
Avg Paid Circ: 380
Audit By: Sworn/Estimate/Non-Audited
Audit Date: 10.06.2019
Personnel: Jim Dickerson (co-publisher)
Parent company (for newspapers): Dickerson Newspapers, Inc.

POLK COUNTY NEWS

Street address 1: PO Box 365
Street address city: Stromsburg
Street address state: NE
Zip/Postal code: 68666-0365
General Phone: (402) 764-5341
General Fax: (402) 764-5341
General/National Adv. E-mail: polkcountynews@yahoo.com
Primary Website: polkcountynewspaper.com
Avg Paid Circ: 1800
Avg Free Circ: 20
Audit By: Sworn/Estimate/Non-Audited
Audit Date: 10.06.2019
Personnel: Dave Thompson (Pub.); Sandy Thompson (Pub.)

REPUBLICAN-NONPAREIL

Street address 1: 802 C Ave
Street address city: Central City
Street address state: NE
Zip/Postal code: 68826-1738
General Phone: (308) 946-3081
General Fax: (308) 946-3614
General/National Adv. E-mail: republicannonpareil@gmail.com
Primary Website: republicannonpareil.com
Avg Paid Circ: 1995
Audit By: Sworn/Estimate/Non-Audited
Audit Date: 10.06.2019
Personnel: Penni Jensen (Adv. Mgr.); Robert M. Jensen (Ed.)

ROCK COUNTY LEADER

Street address 1: 118 Clark St
Street address city: Bassett
Street address state: NE
Zip/Postal code: 68714-6012
General Phone: (402) 684-3771
General/National Adv. E-mail: news@rcleader.com
Avg Paid Circ: 1500
Audit By: Sworn/Estimate/Non-Audited
Audit Date: 10.06.2019
Personnel: Mariel Fegley (Ed.)

RUSTLER SENTINEL

Street address 1: 310 Main Street Suite C
Street address 2: PO Box 370
Street address city: Scribner
Street address state: NE
Zip/Postal code: 68057-0370
General Phone: (402) 664-3198
General Fax: (402) 664-3141
Advertising Phone: (402) 664-3198
Advertising Fax: 402 664 3141
Editorial Phone: (402) 664-3198
Editorial Fax: 402 664 3141
General/National Adv. E-mail: rustlersentinel@gpcom.net
Display Adv. E-mail: rustlersentinel@gpcom.net
Classified Adv. e-mail: rustlersentinel@gpcom.net
Editorial e-mail: rustlersentinel@gpcom.net
Year Established: 1884
Avg Paid Circ: 700
Avg Free Circ: 100
Audit By: USPS
Audit Date: 27.09.2023
Personnel: Kathy Lodl (Pub); Chris Heitshusen (Managing Editor); Kathy Buhrman (Reporter)

SARGENT LEADER

Street address 1: 757 H St
Street address city: Burwell
Street address state: NE
Zip/Postal code: 68823-4110
General Phone: (308) 346-4504
General/National Adv. E-mail: bwtrib@tribune2000.com
Primary Website: tribune2000.com
Avg Paid Circ: 500
Audit By: Sworn/Estimate/Non-Audited
Audit Date: 10.06.2019
Personnel: Lawrence Johnson (Pub.)

SEWARD COUNTY INDEPENDENT

Street address 1: 129 S 6th St
Street address city: Seward
Street address state: NE
Zip/Postal code: 68434-2078
General Phone: (402) 643-3676
General Fax: (402) 643-6774
General/National Adv. E-mail: nichole@sewardindependent.com
Display Adv. E-mail: office@sewardindependent.com
Editorial e-mail: emily@sewardindependent.com
Primary Website: sewardindependent.com
Year Established: 1893
Avg Paid Circ: 3200
Avg Free Circ: 25
Audit By: Sworn/Estimate/Non-Audited
Audit Date: 10.06.2019
Personnel: Mark Rhoades (Owner); Kevin L. Zadina (Pub.); Emily Hemphill (Mng. Ed.); Nichole Javorsky (Adv. Consult)

SHELTON CLIPPER

Street address 1: 113 C St
Street address city: Shelton
Street address state: NE
Zip/Postal code: 68876-9688
General Phone: (308) 647-5158
General Fax: (308) 647-6953
General/National Adv. E-mail: info@clipperpubco.com
Primary Website: clipperpubco.com
Avg Paid Circ: 1001
Audit By: Sworn/Estimate/Non-Audited
Audit Date: 10.06.2019
Personnel: Barb Berglund (Gen. Mgr.); Steven L. Glenn (Ed.)
Parent company (for newspapers): Clipper Publishing, Inc

SHERIDAN COUNTY JOURNAL STAR

Street address 1: 400 N Main St
Street address city: Gordon
Street address state: NE
Zip/Postal code: 69343-1264
General Phone: (308) 282-0118
General Fax: (866) 309-1774
General/National Adv. E-mail: scjsads@gmail.com
Display Adv. E-mail: scjsads@gmail.com
Editorial e-mail: scjsnews@gmail.com
Primary Website: sheridancountyjournalstar.net
Year Established: 1891
Avg Paid Circ: 1700
Audit By: Sworn/Estimate/Non-Audited
Audit Date: 10.06.2019
Personnel: Jordan Huether (Managing Editor)

SIDNEY SUN-TELEGRAPH

Street address 1: 817 12th Ave
Street address city: Sidney
Street address state: NE
Zip/Postal code: 69162-1625
General Phone: (308) 254-2818
General Fax: (308) 254-3925
General/National Adv. E-mail: ads@suntelegraph.com
Display Adv. E-mail: legals@suntelegraph.com
Classified Adv. e-mail: adrep@suntelegraph.com
Editorial e-mail: editor@suntelegraph.com
Primary Website: suntelegraph.com
Year Established: 1873
Avg Paid Circ: 1476
Audit By: Sworn/Estimate/Non-Audited
Audit Date: 10.06.2019
Personnel: Keith Hansen (Pub.)
Parent company (for newspapers): Stevenson Newspapers

SPALDING ENTERPRISE

Street address 1: 140 S Cedar St
Street address city: Spalding
Street address state: NE
Zip/Postal code: 68665
General Phone: (308) 497-2153
General Fax: (308) 497-2153
General/National Adv. E-mail: spalding2002@hotmail.com
Year Established: 1900
Avg Paid Circ: 730
Avg Free Circ: 15
Audit By: Sworn/Estimate/Non-Audited
Audit Date: 10.06.2019
Personnel: David Bopp (Ed.)

SPRINGVIEW HERALD

Street address 1: 102 S Main St
Street address city: Springview
Street address state: NE
Zip/Postal code: 68778-9603
General Phone: (402) 497-3651
General Fax: (402) 497-2651
Editorial e-mail: editor@springviewherald.com
Primary Website: facebook.com/SpringviewHerald
Year Established: 1886
Avg Paid Circ: 750
Avg Free Circ: 25
Audit By: Sworn/Estimate/Non-Audited
Audit Date: 10.06.2019
Personnel: Amy Johnson (Editor); Kelsi McGee (Assistant Editor)

STANTON REGISTER

Street address 1: 907 Ivy St
Street address city: Stanton
Street address state: NE
Zip/Postal code: 68779-2348
General Phone: (402) 439-2173
General Fax: (402) 439-2273
General/National Adv. E-mail: assistregister@stanton.net
Editorial e-mail: register@stanton.net
Year Established: 1878
Avg Paid Circ: 1514
Avg Free Circ: 20
Audit By: Sworn/Estimate/Non-Audited
Audit Date: 10.06.2019
Personnel: Laura M. Forker (Pub.)
Parent company (for newspapers): Pitzer Digital

STAPLETON ENTERPRISE

Street address 1: 238 Main St
Street address city: Stapleton
Street address state: NE
Zip/Postal code: 69163-9701
General Phone: (308) 636-2444
General Fax: (308) 636-2445
General/National Adv. E-mail: creativeprinters@gpcom.net
Year Established: 1912
Avg Paid Circ: 650
Audit By: Sworn/Estimate/Non-Audited
Audit Date: 10.06.2019
Personnel: Audrey M. French (Pub.); Marcia R. Hora (Gen. Mgr.); Traci Frey (Circ. Mgr.)
Parent company (for newspapers): The Arnold Sentinel LLC

SYRACUSE JOURNAL-DEMOCRAT

Street address 1: 123 W 17th St
Street address city: Syracuse
Street address state: NE
Zip/Postal code: 68446
General Phone: (402) 269-2135
General Fax: (402) 269-2392
General/National Adv. E-mail: tschumacher@ncnewspress.com
Editorial e-mail: tpearson@ncnewspress.com
Primary Website: journaldemocrat.com
Year Established: 1876
Avg Paid Circ: 1550
Avg Free Circ: 74
Audit By: Sworn/Estimate/Non-Audited

Audit Date: 10.06.2019
Personnel: Tammy Schumacher (Gen. Mgr.); Tammy Pearson (Exec. Ed.)
Parent company (for newspapers): CherryRoad Media; CherryRoad Media

THE ARTHUR ENTERPRISE

Street address 1: PO Box 165
Street address city: Arthur
Street address state: NE
Zip/Postal code: 69121-0165
General Phone: (308) 764-2402
General/National Adv. E-mail: artent@neb-sandhills.net
Year Established: 1911
Avg Paid Circ: 320
Avg Free Circ: 30
Audit By: Sworn/Estimate/Non-Audited
Audit Date: 10.06.2019
Personnel: Karen A. Sizer (Ed.)

THE ASHLAND GAZETTE

Street address 1: 1432 Silver St
Street address city: Ashland
Street address state: NE
Zip/Postal code: 68003-1846
General Phone: (402) 944-3397
General Fax: (402) 944-3398
General/National Adv. E-mail: advertising@wahoonewspaper.com
Editorial e-mail: news@ashland-gazette.com
Primary Website: ashland-gazette.com
Year Established: 1879
Avg Paid Circ: 1800
Audit By: Sworn/Estimate/Non-Audited
Audit Date: 10.06.2019
Personnel: Suzi Nelson (Ed.); Lisa Brichacek (Exec. Ed.)
Parent company (for newspapers): BH Media Group

THE ATKINSON GRAPHIC

Street address 1: 207 E Main St
Street address city: Atkinson
Street address state: NE
Zip/Postal code: 68713
General Phone: (402) 925-5411
General Fax: (402) 925-5411
General/National Adv. E-mail: advertising@atkinsongraphic.com
Editorial e-mail: editor@atkinsongraphic.com
Primary Website: atkinsongraphic.com
Avg Paid Circ: 2300
Audit By: Sworn/Estimate/Non-Audited
Audit Date: 10.06.2019
Personnel: Roxanne Hollingsworth (Pub./Gen. Mgr.); Jerry Hollingsworth (Ed.)

THE BEACON-OBSERVER

Street address 1: 215 N Tyler St
Street address city: Elm Creek
Street address state: NE
Zip/Postal code: 68836-1536
General Phone: (308) 856-4770
General Fax: (308) 856-0055
Editorial e-mail: happ.michael@gmail.com
Primary Website: beaconobserver.com
Year Established: 1898
Avg Paid Circ: 1380
Avg Free Circ: 60
Audit By: Sworn/Estimate/Non-Audited
Audit Date: 10.06.2019
Personnel: Michael Happ (Ed.)

THE BENKELMAN POST AND NEWS-CHRONICLE

Street address 1: 513 Chief St
Street address city: Benkelman
Street address state: NE
Zip/Postal code: 69021-3065
General Phone: (308) 423-2337
General Fax: (308) 423-5555
General/National Adv. E-mail: bpost@bwtelcom.net
Year Established: 1993
Avg Paid Circ: 1245
Avg Free Circ: 35
Audit By: Sworn/Estimate/Non-Audited
Audit Date: 10.06.2019
Personnel: Amy Fredrick (Pub.); Trenton Frederick (Manager)

THE BLOOMFIELD MONITOR

Street address 1: 110 N Broadway St
Street address city: Bloomfield
Street address state: NE
Zip/Postal code: 68718-4406
General Phone: (402) 373-2332
General Fax: (402) 373-2887
General/National Adv. E-mail: bmonitor@yahoo.com
Year Established: 1890
Avg Paid Circ: 1300
Audit By: Sworn/Estimate/Non-Audited
Audit Date: 10.06.2019
Personnel: Mary Ellen Skrivan (Gen. Mgr.); Joseph M. Skrivan (Ed.)

THE BURWELL TRIBUNE

Street address 1: 757 H St
Street address city: Burwell
Street address state: NE
Zip/Postal code: 68823-4110
General Phone: (308) 346-4504
General/National Adv. E-mail: bwtrib@tribune2000.com
Primary Website: tribune2000.com
Year Established: 1891
Avg Paid Circ: 1000
Avg Free Circ: 50
Audit By: Sworn/Estimate/Non-Audited
Audit Date: 10.06.2019
Personnel: Lawrence Johnson (Ed.)

THE BUSINESS FARMER

Street address 1: 22 W 17th St
Street address city: Scottsbluff
Street address state: NE
Zip/Postal code: 69361-3156
General Phone: (308) 635-3110
General Fax: (308) 635-7435
General/National Adv. E-mail: farmads@thebusinessfarmer.com
Editorial e-mail: farmnews@thebusinessfarmer.com
Primary Website: thebusinessfarmer.com
Avg Paid Circ: 2300
Audit By: Sworn/Estimate/Non-Audited
Audit Date: 10.06.2019
Personnel: Rob Mortimore (Pub.); Danielle Maychrzak (Adv. Dir./ GM); Andrew Brosig (Ed.)
Parent company (for newspapers): San Luis Valley Publishing

THE BUTTE GAZETTE

Street address 1: PO Box 6
Street address city: Butte
Street address state: NE
Zip/Postal code: 6872-20006
General Phone: (402) 775-2431
General Fax: (402) 775-2431
General/National Adv. E-mail: advocate@nntc.net
Avg Paid Circ: 400
Audit By: Sworn/Estimate/Non-Audited
Audit Date: 10.06.2019
Personnel: Sadie Wells (Ed.)

THE CALLAWAY COURIER

Street address 1: 206 E Morse St
Street address city: Callaway
Street address state: NE
Zip/Postal code: 68825-2611
General Phone: (308) 836-2200
General/National Adv. E-mail: ccourier@gpcom.net
Year Established: 1968
Avg Paid Circ: 680
Audit By: Sworn/Estimate/Non-Audited
Audit Date: 10.06.2019
Personnel: Michael Wendorff (Editor/Publisher); Suzanne Wendorff (Ed.)

THE CHADRON RECORD

Street address 1: 248 W 2nd St
Street address city: Chadron
Street address state: NE
Zip/Postal code: 69337-2337
General Phone: (308) 432-5511
General Fax: (308) 432-2385
General/National Adv. E-mail: julie.pfister@lee.net
Display Adv. E-mail: raelynn.nuno@lee.net
Editorial e-mail: chadron.record@lee.net
Primary Website: thechadronnews.com
Year Established: 1884
Avg Paid Circ: 2100
Avg Free Circ: 4700
Audit By: Sworn/Estimate/Non-Audited
Audit Date: 10.06.2019
Personnel: Kerri Rempp (Ed.); Julie Pfister (Adv. Mgr.)
Parent company (for newspapers): Dispatch-Argus

THE COLUMBUS TELEGRAM

Street address 1: 1254 27th Ave
Street address city: Columbus
Street address state: NE
Zip/Postal code: 68601
General Phone: (402) 564-2741
Editorial e-mail: mlindberg@columbustelegram.com
Primary Website: columbustelegram.com
Year Established: 1875
Avg Paid Circ: 2800
Audit By: Sworn/Estimate/Non-Audited
Audit Date: 10.06.2019
Personnel: Vincent Laboy (Reg. Pub.); Matt Lindberg (Mng. Ed.); Sam Pimper (News Ed.); Kelly Muchmore (Adv. Mgr.)
Parent company (for newspapers): Dispatch-Argus

THE COURIER-TIMES

Street address 1: 824 1st St
Street address city: Sutherland
Street address state: NE
Zip/Postal code: 69165-2155
General Phone: (308) 386-4617
General/National Adv. E-mail: suthcourier@gpcom.net
Year Established: 1895
Avg Paid Circ: 1200
Audit By: Sworn/Estimate/Non-Audited
Audit Date: 10.06.2019
Personnel: Trenda Seifer (Ed.)

THE CROFTON JOURNAL

Street address 1: 108 W Main St
Street address city: Crofton
Street address state: NE
Zip/Postal code: 68730-3310
General Phone: (402) 388-4355
General Fax: (402) 388-4336
General/National Adv. E-mail: journal@gpcom.net
Editorial e-mail: plainviewnews@nyecom.net
Primary Website: croftonjournal.com
Avg Paid Circ: 1000
Audit By: Sworn/Estimate/Non-Audited
Audit Date: 10.06.2019
Personnel: Kevin Henseler (Pub.)

THE DONIPHAN HERALD

Street address 1: 206 W Walnut St
Street address city: Doniphan
Street address state: NE
Zip/Postal code: 68832-8903
General Phone: (402) 845-2937
Editorial e-mail: rsadd@hamilton.net
Primary Website: doniphanherald.com
Year Established: 1972
Avg Paid Circ: 712
Avg Free Circ: 23
Audit By: Sworn/Estimate/Non-Audited
Audit Date: 10.06.2019
Personnel: Randy Sadd (Ed.)

THE DOUGLAS COUNTY POST GAZETTE

Street address 1: 2929 N 204th St
Street address 2: Ste 117
Street address city: Elkhorn
Street address state: NE
Zip/Postal code: 68022-1230
General Phone: (402) 289-2329
General Fax: (402) 289-0861
General/National Adv. E-mail: mike@dcpostgazette.com
Display Adv. E-mail: info@dcpostgazette.com
Editorial e-mail: dcpostgazette@dcpostgazette.com
Primary Website: dcpostgazette.com
Year Established: 1984
Avg Paid Circ: 3400
Avg Free Circ: 12200
Audit By: Sworn/Estimate/Non-Audited
Audit Date: 10.06.2019
Personnel: Mike Overmann (Pub.); Penny Overmann (Co-Pub.); Andrea Whery (Circ. Mgr.); Mary Lou Rodgers (Ed.)

THE ELGIN REVIEW

Street address 1: 116 S 2nd St
Street address city: Elgin
Street address state: NE
Zip/Postal code: 68636-4409
General Phone: (402) 843-5500
General Fax: (402) 843-5422
General/National Adv. E-mail: elgnrev@gpcom.net
Primary Website: elginreview.com
Year Established: 1897
Avg Paid Circ: 1043
Audit By: Sworn/Estimate/Non-Audited
Audit Date: 10.06.2019
Personnel: Lynell Morgan (Ed.); Dennis Morgan (Ed.)

THE GENOA LEADER-TIMES

Street address 1: 524 Willard Ave
Street address city: Genoa
Street address state: NE
Zip/Postal code: 68640-3039
General Phone: (402) 993-2205
General/National Adv. E-mail: gltimes@cablene.com
Avg Paid Circ: 600
Audit By: Sworn/Estimate/Non-Audited
Audit Date: 10.06.2019
Personnel: Mary K. Johnson (Pub.); Cindy Mohr (Gen. Mgr.)

THE GIBBON REPORTER

Street address 1: 113 C St
Street address city: Shelton
Street address state: NE
Zip/Postal code: 68876-9688
General Phone: (308) 647-5158
General Fax: (308) 647-6953
General/National Adv. E-mail: info@clipperpubco.com
Primary Website: clipperpubco.com
Avg Paid Circ: 1097
Avg Free Circ: 36
Audit By: Sworn/Estimate/Non-Audited
Audit Date: 10.06.2019
Personnel: Steven L. Glenn (Pub.); Barb Berglund (Ed.)
Parent company (for newspapers): Clipper Publishing, Inc

THE GRANT TRIBUNE SENTINEL

Street address 1: PO Box 67
Street address 2: 327 Central Ave.
Street address city: Grant
Street address state: NE
Zip/Postal code: 69140-0067
General Phone: (308) 352-4311
General Fax: (308) 352-4101
General/National Adv. E-mail: tribads@gpcom.net
Display Adv. E-mail: tribads@gpcom.net
Editorial e-mail: granttribune@gpcom.net
Primary Website: granttribune.com
Year Established: 1897
Avg Paid Circ: 1200
Audit By: Sworn/Estimate/Non-Audited
Audit Date: 10.06.2019
Personnel: Brooke Robertson (Editor); Samantha Goff (Publication Manager)
Parent company (for newspapers): Johnson Publications

THE GRETNA GUIDE & NEWS

Street address 1: 620 N Highway 6
Street address city: Gretna
Street address state: NE
Zip/Postal code: 68028-8090
General Phone: (402) 332-3232
General Fax: (402) 332-4733
General/National Adv. E-mail: mike@gretnaguide.com
Editorial e-mail: gretnaguide@gretnaguide.com
Primary Website: gretnaguide.com
Year Established: 1963
Avg Paid Circ: 1170

Avg Free Circ: 3380
Audit By: Sworn/Estimate/Non-Audited
Audit Date: 10.06.2019
Personnel: Mike Overmann (Adv. Mgr.); Andrea Bartman (Ed.)

THE HEMINGFORD LEDGER

Street address 1: 714 Box Butte Ave
Street address city: Hemingford
Street address state: NE
Zip/Postal code: 69348-9706
General Phone: (308) 487-3334
General/National Adv. E-mail: tammy.berry@ledgeronline.com
Display Adv. E-mail: tammy.berry@ledgeronline.com
Editorial e-mail: kay.bakkehaug@ledgeronline.com
Primary Website: starherald.com
Year Established: 1907
Avg Paid Circ: 1400
Audit By: Sworn/Estimate/Non-Audited
Audit Date: 10.06.2019
Personnel: Roger Tollefson (Pub.); Kay Bakkehaug (Ed.); Tammy Berry (Adv. Sales)
Parent company (for newspapers): Midland Newspapers Inc

THE HENDERSON NEWS

Street address 1: PO Box 606
Street address 2: 1021 N Main
Street address city: Henderson
Street address state: NE
Zip/Postal code: 68371-0606
General Phone: (402) 723-5861
General Fax: (402) 723-5863
General/National Adv. E-mail: servpress@mainstaycomm.net
Year Established: 1977
Avg Paid Circ: 350
Avg Free Circ: 20
Audit By: Sworn/Estimate/Non-Audited
Audit Date: 10.06.2019
Personnel: Jan Edgecombe (Pub.)

THE MADISON STAR-MAIL

Street address 1: 211 S Main St
Street address city: Madison
Street address state: NE
Zip/Postal code: 68748-6485
General Phone: (402) 454-3818
General Fax: (402) 454-3893
Editorial Phone: (402) 640-1268
General/National Adv. E-mail: starmail@telebeep.com
Display Adv. E-mail: starmail@telebeep.com
Editorial e-mail: starmail@telebeep.com
Primary Website: madisonstar-mail.com
Year Established: 1878
Avg Paid Circ: 700
Avg Free Circ: 50
Audit By: Sworn/Estimate/Non-Audited
Audit Date: 10.06.2019
Personnel: Niko Gronenthal (Pub., Adv. Mgr., Ed.); Greig Gronenthal (Owners)

THE MINDEN COURIER

Street address 1: 429 N Colorado Ave
Street address city: Minden
Street address state: NE
Zip/Postal code: 68959-1654
General Phone: (308) 832-2220
General Fax: (308) 832-2221
General/National Adv. E-mail: mindencourier@gtmc.net
Primary Website: themindencourier.com
Year Established: mindencourier@gtmc.net
Avg Paid Circ: 2300
Audit By: Sworn/Estimate/Non-Audited
Audit Date: 10.06.2019
Personnel: Michele Edgecombe (Pub.); Jim Edgecombe (Adv. Mgr.)

THE NELIGH NEWS AND LEADER

Street address 1: 419 M St
Street address city: Neligh
Street address state: NE
Zip/Postal code: 68756-1422
General Phone: (402) 887-4840
General Fax: (402) 887-4711
General/National Adv. E-mail: jpellatz@nelighnews.com
Primary Website: nelighnews.com
Avg Paid Circ: 1500
Audit By: Sworn/Estimate/Non-Audited
Audit Date: 10.06.2019
Personnel: Joan Wright (Pub.); David Wright (Ed.)
Parent company (for newspapers): JD Printing & Publishing Co

THE NEWS

Street address 1: 14541 Castlewood St
Street address 2: Ste 300
Street address city: Waverly
Street address state: NE
Zip/Postal code: 68462-1526
General Phone: (402) 786-2344
General Fax: (402) 786-2343
General/National Adv. E-mail: news@newswaverly.com
Primary Website: newswaverly.com
Avg Paid Circ: 1810
Avg Free Circ: 73
Audit By: Sworn/Estimate/Non-Audited
Audit Date: 10.06.2019
Personnel: Michael Wunder (News Ed.); Lisa Brichacek (Exec. Ed.)

THE ORCHARD NEWS

Street address 1: 230 Windom St
Street address city: Orchard
Street address state: NE
Zip/Postal code: 68764-5077
General Phone: (402) 893-2535
General Fax: (402) 893-2535
General/National Adv. E-mail: orchardnews@juno.com
Editorial e-mail: orchardnews@juno.com
Avg Paid Circ: 600
Audit By: Sworn/Estimate/Non-Audited
Audit Date: 10.06.2019
Personnel: Lucy Ferguson (Prodn. Mgr.); Logan Lawson (Reporter/Videographer); Natalie Bruzon (Ed.)

THE ORD QUIZ

Street address 1: 305 S 16th St
Street address city: Ord
Street address state: NE
Zip/Postal code: 68862-1752
General Phone: (308) 728-3262
General Fax: (308) 728-5715
General/National Adv. E-mail: quizadv@frontier.com
Editorial e-mail: quizeditor@frontier.com
Primary Website: ordquiz.com
Year Established: 1882
Avg Paid Circ: 2050
Avg Free Circ: 40
Audit By: Sworn/Estimate/Non-Audited
Audit Date: 10.06.2019
Personnel: Lynn Griffith (Pub./Adv. Mgr.); Cori Nickels (Office Mgr.); Bonnie Griffith (Society Ed.); Larry Kearns (Prodn. Mgr.); Nick Hon (Ed.)

THE OSMOND REPUBLICAN

Street address 1: 340 N State St
Street address city: Osmond
Street address state: NE
Zip/Postal code: 68765-5723
General Phone: (402) 748-3666
General Fax: (402) 748-3666
General/National Adv. E-mail: osmondnews@abbnebraska.com
Primary Website: northeastnebraskanews.us/category/cedar-county/osmond
Year Established: 1890
Avg Paid Circ: 510
Audit By: Sworn/Estimate/Non-Audited
Audit Date: 10.06.2019
Personnel: Rob Dump (Pub.); Regina Lorenz (Office Mgr); Bernice Blecha
Parent company (for newspapers): Northeast Nebraska News Co.

THE PAWNEE REPUBLICAN

Street address 1: 600 G St
Street address city: Pawnee City
Street address state: NE
Zip/Postal code: 68420
General Phone: (402) 852-2575
General/National Adv. E-mail: ads@pawneenews.com
Editorial e-mail: ronald@pawneenews.com
Primary Website: pawneenews.com
Year Established: 1867
Avg Paid Circ: 1500
Avg Free Circ: 52
Audit By: Sworn/Estimate/Non-Audited
Audit Date: 10.06.2019
Personnel: Beverly J. Puhalla (Pub.); Ronald J. Puhalla (Pub.); Ray Cappel (Ed.)
Parent company (for newspapers): Sunrise Publications, Inc

THE PENDER TIMES

Street address 1: 313 Main St
Street address city: Pender
Street address state: NE
Zip/Postal code: 68047
General Phone: (402) 385-3013
Editorial e-mail: ptimes@abbnebraska.com
Primary Website: penderthurston.com
Avg Paid Circ: 1450
Avg Free Circ: 75
Audit By: Sworn/Estimate/Non-Audited
Audit Date: 10.06.2019
Personnel: Jason Struek (Owner/Pub.)

THE PHONOGRAPH-HERALD

Street address 1: 406 Howard Ave
Street address city: Saint Paul
Street address state: NE
Zip/Postal code: 68873-2141
General Phone: (308) 754-4401
General Fax: (308) 754-4498
General/National Adv. E-mail: maryjo@phonographherald.com
Editorial e-mail: connie@phonographherald.com
Year Established: 1873
Avg Paid Circ: 2452
Audit By: Sworn/Estimate/Non-Audited
Audit Date: 10.06.2019
Personnel: Connie M. Thompson (Pub.)

THE PILOT TRIBUNE / ENTERPRISE

Street address 1: 138 N 16th St
Street address city: Blair
Street address state: NE
Zip/Postal code: 68008-1633
General Phone: (402) 426-2121
General Fax: (402) 426-2227
Advertising Phone: (402) 426-2121
Advertising Fax: (402) 426-2227
Editorial Phone: (402) 426-2121
Editorial Fax: (402) 426-2227
General/National Adv. E-mail: mrhoades@enterprisepub.com
Display Adv. E-mail: subscribe@enterprisepub.com
Editorial e-mail: editor@enterprisepub.com
Primary Website: enterprisepub.com
Mthly Avg Views: 112000
Mthly Avg Unique Visitors: 72000
Year Established: 1869
Avg Paid Circ: 14900
Avg Free Circ: 11700
Audit By: Sworn/Estimate/Non-Audited
Audit Date: 10.06.2019
Personnel: Mark Rhoades (Pub.); Lynette Hansen (Adv. Mgr.); Rich Hain (Circ. Mgr.); Jen Stolz (Prodn. Mgr.); Katie Rohman (managing editor)
Parent company (for newspapers): Enterprise Media Group

THE PLAINVIEW NEWS

Street address 1: 508 W Locust Ave
Street address city: Plainview
Street address state: NE
Zip/Postal code: 68769-4119
General Phone: (402) 582-4921
General Fax: (402) 582-4922
General/National Adv. E-mail: plainviewnews@nyecom.net
Editorial e-mail: plainviewnews@nyecom.net
Primary Website: theplainviewnews.com
Year Established: 1892
Avg Paid Circ: 1900
Audit By: Sworn/Estimate/Non-Audited
Audit Date: 10.06.2019
Personnel: Brook Curtiss (Pub.)

THE PLATTSMOUTH JOURNAL

Street address 1: 410 Main St
Street address city: Plattsmouth
Street address state: NE
Zip/Postal code: 68048-1960
General Phone: (402) 296-2141
General Fax: (402) 296-3401
General/National Adv. E-mail: PLAClassifieds@lee.net
Display Adv. E-mail: PLAClassifieds@lee.net
Editorial e-mail: PLANews@lee.net
Primary Website: fremonttribune.com/cass-news
Year Established: 1881
Avg Paid Circ: 5200
Avg Free Circ: 16250
Audit By: Sworn/Estimate/Non-Audited
Audit Date: 10.06.2019
Personnel: Patti Jo Peterson (Ed.); Caroline Dall (Adv. Rep.)
Parent company (for newspapers): Dispatch-Argus

THE RANDOLPH TIMES

Street address 1: 121 W Broadway St
Street address city: Randolph
Street address state: NE
Zip/Postal code: 68771-2516
General Phone: (402) 337-0488
General Fax: (402) 337-0488
General/National Adv. E-mail: randolph@cedarcountynews.net
Primary Website: northeastnebraskanews.us/category/cedar-county/randolph
Audit By: Sworn/Estimate/Non-Audited
Audit Date: 10.06.2019
Personnel: Rob Dump
Parent company (for newspapers): Northeast Nebraska News Co.

THE RAVENNA NEWS

Street address 1: 322 Grand Ave
Street address city: Ravenna
Street address state: NE
Zip/Postal code: 68869-1398
General Phone: (308) 452-3411
General Fax: (308) 452-3511
General/National Adv. E-mail: ranews@cornhusker.net
Year Established: 1886
Avg Paid Circ: 1152
Avg Free Circ: 3
Audit By: Sworn/Estimate/Non-Audited
Audit Date: 10.06.2019
Personnel: T.M. (Ted) Gill (Pub./Adv. Mgr.); Nancy Jackson (co-publisher)

THE RED CLOUD CHIEF

Street address 1: 484 N. Webster
Street address city: Red Cloud
Street address state: NE
Zip/Postal code: 68970
General Phone: (402) 746-3700
General Fax: (402) 746-2368
General/National Adv. E-mail: chief@gpcom.net
Editorial e-mail: chief@gpcom.net
Primary Website: mainstreetmedia.us
Avg Paid Circ: 1682
Audit By: Sworn/Estimate/Non-Audited
Audit Date: 10.06.2019
Personnel: Mary Ann Linda
Parent company (for newspapers): Main Street Media, Inc.

THE SCHUYLER SUN

Street address 1: 1112 C St
Street address city: Schuyler
Street address state: NE
Zip/Postal code: 68661-1914
General Phone: (402) 352-2424
General Fax: (402) 352-3332
General/National Adv. E-mail: thesunads@qwestoffice.net
Editorial e-mail: thesun@qwestoffice.net
Primary Website: schuyler-sun.com
Mthly Avg Views: 3840
Year Established: 1871
Avg Paid Circ: 3200
Audit By: Sworn/Estimate/Non-Audited

Audit Date: 10.06.2019
Personnel: Tyler Ellyson (Interim Ed.)
Parent company (for newspapers): Dispatch-Argus

THE SPENCER ADVOCATE

Street address 1: 100 S Thayer St
Street address city: Spencer
Street address state: NE
Zip/Postal code: 68777-9784
General Phone: (402) 589-1010
General Fax: (402) 589-1010
General/National Adv. E-mail: advocate@nntc.net
Avg Paid Circ: 1056
Avg Free Circ: 21
Audit By: Sworn/Estimate/Non-Audited
Audit Date: 10.06.2019
Personnel: Sadie Wells (Ed.)

THE ST. EDWARD ADVANCE

Street address 1: 105 N 3rd St
Street address city: Saint Edward
Street address state: NE
Zip/Postal code: 68660-4559
General Phone: (402) 678-2771
General Fax: (402) 678-2556
General/National Adv. E-mail: advance@gpcom.net
Display Adv. E-mail: advance@gpcom.net
Editorial e-mail: advance@gpcom.net
Year Established: 1900
Avg Paid Circ: 582
Avg Free Circ: 8
Audit By: Sworn/Estimate/Non-Audited
Audit Date: 10.06.2019
Personnel: Stephanie A. Dawson (Ed.)

THE SUPERIOR EXPRESS

Street address 1: 148 E 3rd St
Street address city: Superior
Street address state: NE
Zip/Postal code: 68978-1705
General Phone: (402) 879-3291
General Fax: (402) 879-3463
General/National Adv. E-mail: tse@superiorne.com
Primary Website: superiorne.com
Year Established: 1900
Avg Paid Circ: 2900
Avg Free Circ: 116
Audit By: Sworn/Estimate/Non-Audited
Audit Date: 10.06.2019
Personnel: Bill Blauvelt (Ed.)
Parent company (for newspapers): Superior Publishing Co; Superior Publishing Company

THE TECUMSEH CHIEFTAIN

Street address 1: 241 Clay St
Street address city: Tecumseh
Street address state: NE
Zip/Postal code: 68450-2317
General Phone: (402) 335-3394
General Fax: (402) 335-3496
General/National Adv. E-mail: ads@tecumsehchieftain.com
Editorial e-mail: news@tecumsehchieftain.com
Primary Website: tecumsehchieftain.com
Avg Paid Circ: 1630
Audit By: Sworn/Estimate/Non-Audited
Audit Date: 10.06.2019
Personnel: Bev Puhalla (Owner, Pub); Ann Wickett (Ed.)
Parent company (for newspapers): Sunrise Publications, Inc

THE TRI-CITY TRIBUNE

Street address 1: 320 W 8th St
Street address city: Cozad
Street address state: NE
Zip/Postal code: 69130-1772
General Phone: (308) 784-3644
General Fax: (308) 784-3647
General/National Adv. E-mail: ads@tricitytrib.com
Editorial e-mail: news@tricitytrib.com
Primary Website: tricitytrib.com
Year Established: 1965
Avg Paid Circ: 3450
Audit By: Sworn/Estimate/Non-Audited
Audit Date: 10.06.2019
Personnel: Nancy Dorsey (Pub.)

THE WAKEFIELD REPUBLICAN

Street address 1: 201 Main St
Street address city: Wakefield
Street address state: NE
Zip/Postal code: 68784
General Phone: (402) 287-2323
General/National Adv. E-mail: wakenews@huntel.net
Primary Website: wakefieldrepublican.com
Year Established: 1882
Avg Paid Circ: 1050
Avg Free Circ: 50
Audit By: Sworn/Estimate/Non-Audited
Audit Date: 10.06.2019
Personnel: Brook Curtiss (Pub.)

THE WAUNETA BREEZE

Street address 1: 324 N Tecumseh
Street address city: Wauneta
Street address state: NE
Zip/Postal code: 69045-9509
General Phone: (308) 394-5389
General Fax: (308) 394-5931
General/National Adv. E-mail: breeze.office@jpipapers.com
Display Adv. E-mail: breeze.office@jpipapers.com
Editorial e-mail: breeze.editor@jpipapers.com
Primary Website: waunetanebraska.com
Year Established: 1887
Avg Paid Circ: 817
Audit By: Sworn/Estimate/Non-Audited
Audit Date: 10.06.2019
Personnel: Lori Pankonin (Co-Publisher); Russ Pankonin (Co-Publisher); Christi Christner (News Editor)
Parent company (for newspapers): Johnson Publications

THE WAUSA GAZETTE

Street address 1: 510 E Broadway St
Street address city: Wausa
Street address state: NE
Zip/Postal code: 68786-1558
General Phone: (402) 586-2661
General Fax: (402) 586-2661
General/National Adv. E-mail: wausagazette@gpcom.net
Primary Website: northeastnebraskanews.us/category/wausa-county
Avg Paid Circ: 963
Avg Free Circ: 2
Audit By: Sworn/Estimate/Non-Audited
Audit Date: 10.06.2019
Personnel: Rob Dump (Ed.)
Parent company (for newspapers): Northeast Nebraska News Co.

THE WAVERLY NEWS

Street address 1: 14541 Castlewood St
Street address 2: Ste 300
Street address city: Waverly
Street address state: NE
Zip/Postal code: 68462-1526
General Phone: (402) 786-2344
General Fax: (402) 786-2343
General/National Adv. E-mail: advertising@newswaverly.com
Display Adv. E-mail: advertising@newswaverly.com
Primary Website: wahoo-ashland-waverly.com
Avg Paid Circ: 925
Audit By: Sworn/Estimate/Non-Audited
Audit Date: 10.06.2019
Personnel: Lisa Brichacek (Exec. Ed.)
Parent company (for newspapers): BH Media Group

THE WAYNE HERALD

Street address 1: 114 Main St
Street address city: Wayne
Street address state: NE
Zip/Postal code: 68787-1940
General Phone: (402) 375-2600
General Fax: (402) 375-1888
General/National Adv. E-mail: melissa@wayneherald.com
Display Adv. E-mail: whclass@inebraska.com
Editorial e-mail: sports@wayneherald.com
Primary Website: mywaynenews.com
Avg Paid Circ: 2100
Audit By: Sworn/Estimate/Non-Audited
Audit Date: 10.06.2019
Personnel: Kevin Peterson (Pub.); Melissa Urbanec (Gen. Mgr.); Michael Carnes (Ed.); Linda Granfield (Circ. Mgr.)
Parent company (for newspapers): Smith Newspapers

THE WOLBACH MESSENGER

Street address 1: PO Box 38
Street address city: Wolbach
Street address state: NE
Zip/Postal code: 68882-0038
General Phone: (308) 754-4401
General Fax: (308) 754-4498
General/National Adv. E-mail: maryjo@phonographherald.com
Editorial e-mail: connie@phonographherald.com
Year Established: 1900
Avg Paid Circ: 447
Audit By: Sworn/Estimate/Non-Audited
Audit Date: 10.06.2019
Personnel: Connie M. Thompson (Pub.)

THE WOOD RIVER SUNBEAM

Street address 1: 113 C St
Street address city: Shelton
Street address state: NE
Zip/Postal code: 68876-9688
General Phone: (308) 647-5158
General Fax: (308) 647-6953
General/National Adv. E-mail: info@clipperpubco.com
Primary Website: clipperpubco.com
Avg Paid Circ: 1083
Avg Free Circ: 9
Audit By: Sworn/Estimate/Non-Audited
Audit Date: 10.06.2019
Personnel: Steven L. Glenn (Pub.); Barb Berglund (Ed.)
Parent company (for newspapers): Clipper Publishing, Inc

THOMAS COUNTY HERALD

Street address 1: 238 Main St
Street address city: Stapleton
Street address state: NE
Zip/Postal code: 69163-9701
General Phone: (308) 636-2444
General Fax: (308) 636-2445
General/National Adv. E-mail: creativeprinters@gpcom.net
Avg Paid Circ: 600
Audit By: Sworn/Estimate/Non-Audited
Audit Date: 10.06.2019
Personnel: Marcia Hora (Adv. Mgr.); Traci Frey (Ed.)
Parent company (for newspapers): The Arnold Sentinel LLC

TWIN CITY WEEKLY

Street address 1: 1405 Broadway
Street address city: Scottsbluff
Street address state: NE
Zip/Postal code: 69361-3151
General Phone: (308) 632-9000
General Fax: (308) 632-9001
General/National Adv. E-mail: doug.southard@starherald.com
Editorial e-mail: bart.schaneman@starherald.com
Primary Website: starherald.com
Avg Paid Circ: 5869
Avg Free Circ: 6528
Audit By: Sworn/Estimate/Non-Audited
Audit Date: 10.06.2019
Personnel: Jim Holland (Pub.); Roger Tollefson (Gen. Mgr.); Doug Southard (Adv. Mgr.); Steve Frederick (Ed.)

VALENTINE MIDLAND NEWS

Street address 1: 146 W 2nd St
Street address city: Valentine
Street address state: NE
Zip/Postal code: 69201-1822
General Phone: (402) 376-2833
General Fax: (402) 376-1946
General/National Adv. E-mail: valentinenews@valentinenews.com
Primary Website: valentinenews.com
Year Established: 1989
Avg Paid Circ: 2050
Audit By: Sworn/Estimate/Non-Audited
Audit Date: 10.06.2019
Personnel: Dana Anderson (Office Mgr.); Laura Vorman (Ed.)
Parent company (for newspapers): Great Plains Publishing Co., Inc.

VOICE NEWS

Street address 1: 114 Locust St
Street address 2: Ste B
Street address city: Hickman
Street address state: NE
Zip/Postal code: 68372-9525
General Phone: (402) 792-2255
General Fax: (402) 792-2256
General/National Adv. E-mail: voicenews@inebraska.com
Primary Website: voicenewsnebraska.com
Year Established: 1978
Avg Paid Circ: 3304
Avg Free Circ: 260
Audit By: Sworn/Estimate/Non-Audited
Audit Date: 10.06.2019
Personnel: Wendy Doyle (Adv. Dir.); Sevoey Anderson (Mktg. Coor.); katherine Crawford (Creative Dir.); Darren Ivy (Co Pub.); Cassandra Ivy (Co Pub.)

WAHOO NEWSPAPER

Street address 1: 564 N Broadway St
Street address city: Wahoo
Street address state: NE
Zip/Postal code: 68066-1653
General Phone: (402) 443-4162
General Fax: (402) 443-4459
General/National Adv. E-mail: advertising@wahoonewspaper.com
Display Adv. E-mail: classifieds@wahoonewspaper.com
Editorial e-mail: news@wahoonewspaper.com
Primary Website: wahoo-ashland-waverly.com
Mthly Avg Views: 40000
Mthly Avg Unique Visitors: 13000
Year Established: 1886
Avg Paid Circ: 2850
Audit By: Sworn/Estimate/Non-Audited
Audit Date: 10.06.2019
Personnel: Candi Puren (Advertising Manager); Amy McKay (General Manager)
Parent company (for newspapers): BH Media Group

WASHINGTON COUNTY ENTERPRISE

Street address 1: 138 N 16th St
Street address city: Blair
Street address state: NE
Zip/Postal code: 68008-1633
General Phone: (402) 426-2121
General Fax: (402) 426-2227
Advertising Phone: (402) 426-2121
Advertising Fax: (402) 426-2227
Editorial Phone: (402) 426-2121
Editorial Fax: (402) 426-2227
General/National Adv. E-mail: lhansen@enterprisepub.com
Display Adv. E-mail: lhansen@enterprisepub.com
Classified Adv. e-mail: classifieds@enterprisepub.com
Editorial e-mail: editor@enterprisepub.com
Primary Website: enterprisepub.com
Year Established: 1869
Avg Paid Circ: 2900
Avg Free Circ: 8200
Audit By: USPS
Audit Date: 01.10.2021
Personnel: Mark Rhoades (Publisher); Lynette Hansen (Sales Manager); Rich Hain (Distribution Manager); Jen Stolz (Art Director); Greg Forbes (Managing Editor); Katie Rohman (Mng. Ed.); Tracy Prettyman (Business Manager); Chris Rhoades (Associate Publisher)
Parent company (for newspapers): Enterprise Media Group

WEST POINT NEWS

Street address 1: 134 E Grove St
Street address city: West Point
Street address state: NE
Zip/Postal code: 68788-1823
General Phone: (402) 372-2461
General Fax: (402) 372-3530
General/National Adv. E-mail: admanager@wpnews.com

Display Adv. E-mail: adrep7@wpnews.com
Editorial e-mail: editor@wpnews.com
Primary Website: wpnews.com
Year Established: 1869
Avg Paid Circ: 2500
Avg Free Circ: 165
Audit By: Sworn/Estimate/Non-Audited
Audit Date: 10.06.2019
Personnel: Tom Kelly (Pub./Gen. Mgr.); Colleen Ernesti (Circ. Mgr.); Willis Mahannah (Ed.); Warren Wesche (Prodn. Mgr.); Karey Rahn (Adv. Mgr.)

WESTERN NEBRASKA OBSERVER

Street address 1: 118 E 2nd St
Street address city: Kimball
Street address state: NE
Zip/Postal code: 69145-1209
General Phone: (308) 235-3631
General Fax: (308) 235-3632
Advertising Phone: (308) 235-3631
General/National Adv. E-mail: ads@westernnebraskaobserver.net
Editorial e-mail: editor@westernnebraskaobserver.net
Primary Website: westernnebraskaobserver.net
Year Established: 1885
Avg Paid Circ: 1910
Audit By: Sworn/Estimate/Non-Audited
Audit Date: 10.06.2019
Personnel: Jacob Misener (Editor & Publisher)

WILBER REPUBLICAN

Street address 1: 129 S. 6th Street
Street address city: Seward
Street address state: NE
Zip/Postal code: 68434
General Phone: (402) 643-3676
General/National Adv. E-mail: nichole@sewardindependent.com
Display Adv. E-mail: office@sewardindependent.com
Editorial e-mail: emily@sewardindependent.com
Primary Website: sewardindependent.com/wilber
Avg Paid Circ: 2000
Avg Free Circ: 37
Audit By: Sworn/Estimate/Non-Audited
Audit Date: 10.06.2019
Personnel: Kevin Zadina (Pub.); Emily Hemphill (Mng. Ed.); Stephanie Croston (Sports Ed./Asst. Ed.); Doris Jiskra (Office Mgr.)

WISNER NEWS-CHRONICLE

Street address 1: 1014 Avenue E
Street address city: Wisner
Street address state: NE
Zip/Postal code: 68791-2248
General Phone: (402) 529-3228
General Fax: (402) 529-3279
General/National Adv. E-mail: wisnewsad@gpcom.net
Editorial e-mail: wisnews@gpcom.net
Primary Website: wpnews.com
Avg Paid Circ: 1991
Avg Free Circ: 30
Audit By: Sworn/Estimate/Non-Audited
Audit Date: 10.06.2019
Personnel: Tom Kelly (Pub.); Kristy Dunbar (Copy Ed.)

WYMORE ARBOR STATE

Street address 1: 204 S 7th St
Street address city: Wymore
Street address state: NE
Zip/Postal code: 68466-2102
General Phone: (402) 645-3344
General Fax: (402) 645-3345
General/National Adv. E-mail: wymorearborstate@windstream.net
Primary Website: wymorearborstate.com
Year Established: 1882
Avg Paid Circ: 1000
Avg Free Circ: 78
Audit By: Sworn/Estimate/Non-Audited
Audit Date: 10.06.2019
Personnel: Dale Crawford (Ed.)

NEVADA

BATTLE MOUNTAIN BUGLE

Street address 1: 1022 Grass Valley Rd
Street address city: Winnemucca
Street address state: NV
Zip/Postal code: 89445-4045
General Phone: (775) 635-2230
General Fax: (775) 635-2644
General/National Adv. E-mail: k.koseck@winnemuccapublishing.net
Display Adv. E-mail: bmb.office@winnemuccapublishing.net
Editorial e-mail: editorial@winnemuccapublishing.net
Primary Website: insidenorthernnevada.com
Year Established: 1978
Audit By: Sworn/Estimate/Non-Audited
Audit Date: 10.06.2019
Personnel: Michelle Cook (Ed.)

BOULDER CITY REVIEW

Street address 1: 508 Nevada Way
Street address 2: Ste 1
Street address city: Boulder City
Street address state: NV
Zip/Postal code: 89005-2400
General Fax: (702) 586-9565
Advertising Phone: (702) 823-1457
Editorial Phone: (702) 586-9523
Editorial Fax: (702) 586-9565
General/National Adv. E-mail: news@bouldercityreview.com
Display Adv. E-mail: volsen@bouldercityreview.com
Editorial e-mail: hsaylor@bouldercityreview.com
Primary Website: bouldercityreview.com
Year Established: 2009
Avg Paid Circ: 1600
Audit By: AAM
Audit Date: 30.06.2018
Personnel: Hali Bernstein Saylor (Ed); Val Olsen (Display Advertising Sales Executive); Noah Cusick (Publisher); Celia Shortt Goodyear (Reporter); Angela Metcalf (Office coordinator)
Parent company (for newspapers): Las Vegas Review-Journal Inc.

COMSTOCK CHRONICLE

Street address 1: 66 N B St
Street address city: Virginia City
Street address state: NV
Zip/Postal code: 89440
General Phone: (775) 847-0765
General Fax:
General/National Adv. E-mail: storeystories@gmail.com
Year Established: 1988
Avg Paid Circ: 1000
Audit By: Sworn/Estimate/Non-Audited
Audit Date: 10.06.2019
Personnel: Richard Mann (Pub.); Angela Mann (Ed.)

DESERT VALLEY TIMES

Street address 1: 355 W Mesquite Blvd
Street address 2: Ste. C10
Street address city: Mesquite
Street address state: NV
Zip/Postal code: 89027-8128
General Phone: (702) 323-7922
General Fax: (702) 346-7494
Editorial e-mail: news@dvtnv.com
Primary Website: dvtonline.com
Year Established: 1986
Avg Free Circ: 8000
Audit By: Sworn/Estimate/Non-Audited
Audit Date: 10.06.2019
Personnel: Lucas Thomas (Reporter); Sarah Gambles (Reporter); Steve Kiggins (Exec Ed); Jolene Schwartz Classified Sales
Parent company (for newspapers): Gannett

ELY TIMES

Street address 1: 515 Murry St
Street address city: Ely
Street address state: NV
Zip/Postal code: 89301-1950
General Phone: (775) 289-4491
General Fax: (775) 289-4566
General/National Adv. E-mail: elytimes.teresa@gmail.com
Display Adv. E-mail: elytimes.linda@gmail.com
Editorial e-mail: elytimes.marty@gmail.com
Primary Website: elynews.com
Year Established: 1920
Avg Paid Circ: 2700
Audit By: Sworn/Estimate/Non-Audited
Audit Date: 10.06.2019
Personnel: Marty Bachman (Ed.); Sherman Frederick (Pub.)
Parent company (for newspapers): Battle Born Media LLC

HIGH DESERT ADVOCATE

Street address 1: 2028 Elko Ave
Street address 2: PO Box 2028
Street address city: Wendover
Street address state: NV
Zip/Postal code: 89883-3237
General Phone: (775) 664-3415
General Fax: (775) 664-3415
General/National Adv. E-mail: advocate@cut.net
Display Adv. E-mail: ccopelan@cut.net
Editorial e-mail: advocate@cut.net
Primary Website: coyote-tv.com
Year Established: 1984
Avg Paid Circ: 5500
Audit By: Sworn/Estimate/Non-Audited
Audit Date: 10.06.2019
Personnel: Howard Copelan (Ed.); Corinne Copelan (Prodn. Mgr.)

LAHONTAN VALLEY NEWS & FALLON EAGLE STANDARD

Street address 1: 37 S Maine St
Street address city: Fallon
Street address state: NV
Zip/Postal code: 89406-3301
General Phone: (775) 423-6041
General Fax: (775) 423-0474
General/National Adv. E-mail: ahorn@lahontanvalleynews.com
Display Adv. E-mail: classifieds@sierranevadamedia.com
Editorial e-mail: rgalloway@sierranevadamedia.com
Primary Website: nevadaappeal.com
Avg Paid Circ: 1371
Avg Free Circ: 106
Audit By: AAM
Audit Date: 31.03.2019
Personnel: AJ Horn (Adv. Mgr.); Rob Galloway (Pub.)
Parent company (for newspapers): Swift Communications, Inc.

LAS VEGAS BUSINESS PRESS

Street address 1: 1111 W Bonanza Rd
Street address city: Las Vegas
Street address state: NV
Zip/Postal code: 89106-3545
General Phone: (702) 383-4617
Advertising Phone: (702) 383-0383
Editorial Phone: (702) 3830299
General/National Adv. E-mail: adhelp@reviewjournal.com
Display Adv. E-mail: ddyer@reviewjournal.com
Editorial e-mail: news@businesspress.vegas
Primary Website: businesspress.vegas
Year Established: 1983
Avg Paid Circ: 365
Avg Free Circ: 9874
Audit By: AAM
Audit Date: 30.07.2016
Personnel: Lyn Collier (Ed.)
Parent company (for newspapers): Las Vegas Review-Journal, Inc.

LINCOLN COUNTY RECORD

Street address 1: 407 Highway 93
Street address city: Alamo
Street address state: NV
Zip/Postal code: 89001
General Phone: (775) 725-3232
General/National Adv. E-mail: contact.lcrecord@gmail.com
Display Adv. E-mail: contact.lcrecord@gmail.com
Editorial e-mail: contact.lcrecord@gmail.com
Primary Website: lccentral.com
Mthly Avg Views: 4000
Year Established: 1870
Avg Paid Circ: 1700
Avg Free Circ: 40
Audit By: Sworn/Estimate/Non-Audited
Audit Date: 10.06.2019
Personnel: Ben Rowley (Ed.)
Parent company (for newspapers): Battle Born Media LLC

LOVELOCK REVIEW-MINER

Street address 1: 1022 Grass Valley Rd
Street address city: Winnemucca
Street address state: NV
Zip/Postal code: 89445-4045
General Phone: (775) 623-5011
General/National Adv. E-mail: l.enget@winnemuccapublishing.net
Display Adv. E-mail: lrm.office@winnemuccapublishing.net
Editorial e-mail: editorial@winnemuccapublishing.net
Primary Website: http://insidenorthernnevada.com
Year Established: 1904
Avg Paid Circ: 1350
Avg Free Circ: 26
Audit By: Sworn/Estimate/Non-Audited
Audit Date: 10.06.2019
Personnel: Michelle Cook (Ed.)

MESQUITE LOCAL NEWS

Street address 1: 12 W Mesquite Blvd
Street address 2: Ste 109
Street address city: Mesquite
Street address state: NV
Zip/Postal code: 89027-4774
General Phone: (702) 346-6397
Advertising Phone: (702) 346-6397
Editorial Phone: (702) 346-6397
General/National Adv. E-mail: steph.bbm@gmail.com
Display Adv. E-mail: steph.bbm@gmail.com
Editorial e-mail: barb@bjellestad.com
Primary Website: mesquitelocalnews.com
Year Established: 2004
Avg Paid Circ: 4
Avg Free Circ: 7500
Audit By: Sworn/Estimate/Non-Audited
Audit Date: 10.06.2019
Personnel: Stephanie Frehner (Class Sales Exec); Barbara Ellestad (Ed); Teri Nehrenz (Office/Writer/Calendar)
Parent company (for newspapers): Battle Born Media LLC

MINERAL COUNTY INDEPENDENT NEWS

Street address 1: 420 3rd St
Street address city: Hawthorne
Street address state: NV
Zip/Postal code: 89415
General Phone: (775) 945-2414
General Fax: (775) 945-1270
General/National Adv. E-mail: hbunchmcin@gmail.com
Editorial e-mail: mcin.cw@gmail.com
Primary Website: http://mcindependentnews.com/
Year Established: 1933
Avg Paid Circ: 4500
Avg Free Circ: 80
Audit By: Sworn/Estimate/Non-Audited
Audit Date: 10.06.2019
Personnel: Ben Rowley (Web. Ed.); Kirk Kern (COO)
Parent company (for newspapers): Battle Born Media LLC

MOAPA VALLEY PROGRESS

Street address 1: 2885 N Moapa Valley Blvd
Street address city: Logandale
Street address state: NV
Zip/Postal code: 89021
General Phone: (702) 397-6246
General Fax: (702) 397-6247
General/National Adv. E-mail: progress@mvdsl.com
Primary Website: mvprogress.com
Year Established: 1987
Avg Paid Circ: 80
Avg Free Circ: 5600
Audit By: Sworn/Estimate/Non-Audited

Audit Date: 10.06.2019
Personnel: Vernon Robison (Ed.)

NIFTY NICKEL

Street address 1: 1111 W Bonanza Rd
Street address city: Las Vegas
Street address state: NV
Zip/Postal code: 89106-3545
General Phone: (702) 383-0383
General Fax: (702) 380-4561
Advertising Phone: 702-383-0383
Advertising Fax: (702) 383-0389
General/National Adv. E-mail: jlevin@reviewjournal.com
Display Adv. E-mail: ddyer@reviewjournal.com
Editorial e-mail: ddyer@reviewjournal.com
Primary Website: niftynickel.vegas
Year Established: 1967
Avg Paid Circ: 0
Avg Free Circ: 72000
Audit By: Sworn/Estimate/Non-Audited
Audit Date: 10.06.2019
Personnel: Deidre Dyer (Sales Mgr)
Parent company (for newspapers): 1971

PAHRUMP VALLEY TIMES

Street address 1: 1570 E HIGHWAY 372
Street address city: Pahrump
Street address state: NV
Zip/Postal code: 89048-4638
General Phone: (775) 727-5102
General Fax: (775) 727-5692
Advertising Phone: (702) 383-0388
Advertising Fax: (702) 383-0389
Primary Website: pvtimes.com
Year Established: 1971
Avg Paid Circ: 4683
Audit By: Sworn/Estimate/Non-Audited
Audit Date: 10.06.2019
Personnel: Noah Cusick (Publisher); David Jacobs (Ed.); Tom Rysinski (Sports Ed.)

RENO NEWS & REVIEW

Street address 1: 760 Margrave Drive
Street address 2: Ste 100
Street address city: Reno
Street address state: NV
Zip/Postal code: 89502
General Phone: (775) 324-4440
General Fax: (775) 324-2515
General/National Adv. E-mail: bizmgr@newsreview.com
Editorial e-mail: editor@newsreview.com
Primary Website: newsreview.com/reno/home
Year Established: 1995
Avg Paid Circ: 4
Avg Free Circ: 19062
Audit By: Sworn/Estimate/Non-Audited
Audit Date: 10.06.2019
Personnel: Brad Bynum (Ass. Ed.)
Parent company (for newspapers): Chico Community Publishing Inc.

SPARKS TRIBUNE

Street address 1: 155 Glendale Ave
Street address 2: Ste 10
Street address city: Sparks
Street address state: NV
Zip/Postal code: 89431-5751
General Phone: (775) 358-8062
General Fax: (775) 359-3837
Advertising Phone: (775) 358-8062 ext 238
General/National Adv. E-mail: advertising@dailysparkstribune.com
Display Adv. E-mail: carolyn@dailysparkstribune.com
Classified Adv. e-mail: classifieds@dailysparkstribune.com
Editorial e-mail: deckles@dailysparkstribune.com
Year Established: 1910
Audit By: Sworn/Estimate/Non-Audited
Audit Date: 10.06.2019
Personnel: Sherman Frederick (Pub.); Eric Dahlberg (Ed.)

THE EUREKA SENTINEL

Street address 1: 515 Murry St
Street address city: Ely
Street address state: NV
Zip/Postal code: 89301-1950
General Phone: (775) 289-4491
General Fax: (775) 289-4566
General/National Adv. E-mail: elytimes.teresa@gmail.com
Display Adv. E-mail: elytimes.linda@gmail.com
Editorial e-mail: elytimes.lukas@gmail.com
Primary Website: http://eurekasentinel.com/
Year Established: 1870
Avg Paid Circ: 500
Avg Free Circ: 50
Audit By: Sworn/Estimate/Non-Audited
Audit Date: 10.06.2019
Personnel: Gary Cook (Ed.)
Parent company (for newspapers): Battle Born Media LLC

THE HUMBOLDT SUN

Street address 1: 1022 Grass Valley Rd
Street address city: Winnemucca
Street address state: NV
Zip/Postal code: 89445-4045
General Phone: (775) 623-5011
General Fax: (775) 623-5243
General/National Adv. E-mail: r.coleman@winnemuccapublishing.net
Primary Website: news4nevada.com
Year Established: 1960
Avg Paid Circ: 3650
Audit By: Sworn/Estimate/Non-Audited
Audit Date: 10.06.2019
Personnel: Holly Rudy-James (Gen. Mgr.)

THE RECORD-COURIER

Street address 1: 1503 US Highway 395 N
Street address 2: Ste G
Street address city: Gardnerville
Street address state: NV
Zip/Postal code: 89410-5227
General Phone: (775) 782-5121
General Fax: (775) 782-6132
General/National Adv. E-mail: pbridges@nevadaappeal.com
Display Adv. E-mail: classifieds@sierranevadamedia.com
Editorial e-mail: rgalloway@sierranevadamedia.com
Primary Website: recordcourier.com
Avg Paid Circ: 3458
Avg Free Circ: 260
Audit By: AAM
Audit Date: 26.03.2019
Personnel: Rob Galloway (Pub.)
Parent company (for newspapers): Swift Communications, Inc.

THE SUNDAY

Street address 1: 2275 Corporate Cir
Street address city: Henderson
Street address state: NV
Zip/Postal code: 89074-7719
Primary Website: thesunday.com
Avg Free Circ: 54438
Audit By: VAC
Audit Date: 31.12.2016

TONOPAH TIMES-BONANZA AND GOLDFIELD NEWS

Street address 1: 150 Main St
Street address city: Tonopah
Street address state: NV
Zip/Postal code: 89049
General Phone: (775) 482-3365
General Fax: (775) 482-5042
General/National Adv. E-mail: broberts@tonopahtimes.com
Year Established: 1903
Avg Paid Circ: 1800
Audit By: Sworn/Estimate/Non-Audited
Audit Date: 10.06.2019
Personnel: Nancy Ann Whipperman (Pub.); Bobby Jean Roberts (Adv. Mgr.)
Parent company (for newspapers): CherryRoad Media

VIEW NEIGHBORHOOD NEWSPAPERS

Street address 1: 1111 W Bonanza Rd
Street address city: Las Vegas
Street address state: NV
Zip/Postal code: 89106-3545
General Phone: (702) 380-4589
General Fax: (702) 477-3852
Advertising Phone: (702) 383-0388
Advertising Fax: (702) 383-0389
Editorial Phone: (702) 380-4553
General/National Adv. E-mail: ctrares@reviewjournal.com
Display Adv. E-mail: bnelson@reviewjournal.com
Editorial e-mail: jmosier@viewnews.com
Primary Website: viewnews.com
Year Established: 1993
Avg Paid Circ: 97924
Avg Free Circ: 502633
Audit By: Sworn/Estimate/Non-Audited
Audit Date: 10.06.2019
Personnel: Jeff Mosier (Ed.)

NEW HAMPSHIRE

AMHERST CITIZEN

Street address 1: 16 Pine Acres Rd
Street address city: Amherst
Street address state: NH
Zip/Postal code: 03031-2710
General Phone: 6036205835
General Fax: 6036205835
Advertising Phone: 6036205835
Advertising Fax: None
Editorial Phone: 6036205835
Editorial Fax: None
General/National Adv. E-mail: jaswales@mac.com
Display Adv. E-mail: jaswales@mac.com
Classified Adv. e-mail: None
Editorial e-mail: jaswales@mac.com
Primary Website: amherstcitizen.net
Year Established: 1992
Audit Date: 10.06.2019
Personnel: Cliff Ann Wales (Pub./Ed.); James Wales (Adv. Dir.)
Parent company (for newspapers): None

BEDFORD BULLETIN

Street address 1: 100 William Loeb Dr
Street address city: Manchester
Street address state: NH
Zip/Postal code: 03109-5309
General Phone: (603) 314-0447
General Fax: (603) 206-7801
Advertising Phone: (603) 668-4321 x241
Editorial Phone: (603) 668-4321 x757
General/National Adv. E-mail: ul@unionleader.com
Display Adv. E-mail: classified@unionleader.com
Editorial e-mail: editor@yourneighborhoodnews.com
Primary Website: yourneighborhoodnews.com
Year Established: 1970
Avg Paid Circ: 56
Avg Free Circ: 10000
Audit By: Sworn/Estimate/Non-Audited
Audit Date: 10.06.2019
Personnel: Christine Heiser (Exec. Ed.); Robert Bennett (Circ. Mgr.); Holly Davis (Ed.); Pam Young (Prodn. Mgr.); Debra Dooley (Circ. Dir.)
Parent company (for newspapers): Neighborhood News (OOB)

BEDFORD JOURNAL

Street address 1: 54 School St
Street address city: Milford
Street address state: NH
Zip/Postal code: 03055-4543
General Phone: (603) 673-3100
General Fax: (603) 673-8250
Advertising Phone: (603) 594-1219
General/National Adv. E-mail: cabnews@cabinet.com
Editorial e-mail: cabnews@cabinet.com
Primary Website: cabinet.com
Year Established: 1802
Avg Free Circ: 9100
Audit By: Sworn/Estimate/Non-Audited
Audit Date: 10.06.2019
Personnel: Sandy Bucknam (Managing Ed.)
Parent company (for newspapers): Ogden Newspapers Inc.

CARRIAGE TOWNE NEWS

Street address 1: 14 Church St
Street address city: Kingston
Street address state: NH
Zip/Postal code: 03848-3062
General Phone: (603) 642-4499
General Fax: (603) 642-7750
Advertising Phone: (603) 734-9048
Editorial Phone: (603) 734-9050
General/National Adv. E-mail: advertise@carriagetownenews.com
Editorial e-mail: elisha@carriagetownenews.com
Primary Website: carriagetownenews.com
Year Established: 1983
Avg Free Circ: 25776
Audit By: Sworn/Estimate/Non-Audited
Audit Date: 10.06.2019
Personnel: Elisha Blaisdell (Ed.); Corinne Lester (Prod. Mgr.)
Parent company (for newspapers): CNHI, LLC

CARROLL COUNTY INDEPENDENT

Street address 1: 35 Center St
Street address 2: Clarke Plaza
Street address city: Wolfeboro
Street address state: NH
Zip/Postal code: 03894-4324
General Phone: (603) 569-3126
General Fax: (603) 569-4743
General/National Adv. E-mail: maureen@salmonpress.com
Display Adv. E-mail: jumbo@salmonpress.com
Editorial e-mail: tbeeler@salmonpress.news
Primary Website: carrollcountyindependent.com
Year Established: 1881
Avg Paid Circ: 4500
Audit By: Sworn/Estimate/Non-Audited
Audit Date: 10.06.2019
Personnel: Thomas Beeler (Ed.); Frank Chilinski
Parent company (for newspapers): Salmon Press

DERRY NEWS

Street address 1: 46 W Broadway
Street address city: Derry
Street address state: NH
Zip/Postal code: 03038-2329
General Phone: (603) 437-7000
General Fax: (603) 432-4510
General/National Adv. E-mail: advertising@derrynews.com
Display Adv. E-mail: classifieds@derrynews.com
Editorial e-mail: rford@derrynews.com
Primary Website: derrynews.com
Year Established: 1880
Avg Paid Circ: 7000
Avg Free Circ: 26000
Audit By: Sworn/Estimate/Non-Audited
Audit Date: 10.06.2019
Personnel: Karen Andreas (Pub.); Cathy Goss (Adv. Dir.); Steve Milone (Circ. Mgr.)
Parent company (for newspapers): CNHI, LLC

EXETER NEWS-LETTER

Street address 1: 111 NH Ave
Street address 2: Rockingham
Street address city: Portsmouth
Street address state: NH
Zip/Postal code: 03801-2864
General Phone: (800) 439-0303
General Fax: (603) 433-5760
Advertising Fax: (603) 427-0550
General/National Adv. E-mail: advertising@seacoastonline.com
Display Adv. E-mail: advertising@seacoastonline.com
Editorial e-mail: news@seacoastonline.com
Primary Website: seacoastonline.com
Avg Paid Circ: 294
Audit By: AAM
Audit Date: 31.12.2018
Personnel: Howard Altschiller (Ed.); Vince Ciampi (Adv. Dir.); John Tabor (Pub.); Dennis Thompson

Parent company (for newspapers): CherryRoad Media

GOFFSTOWN NEWS

Street address 1: 100 William Loeb Dr
Street address city: Manchester
Street address state: NH
Zip/Postal code: 03109-5309
General Phone: (603) 206-7800
General Fax: (603) 206-7801
Advertising Phone: (603) 668-4321 x241
Editorial Phone: (603) 668-4321 x757
General/National Adv. E-mail: ul@unionleader.com
Display Adv. E-mail: classified@unionleader.com
Editorial e-mail: editor@yourneighborhoodnews.com
Primary Website: yourneighborhoodnews.com
Year Established: 1957
Avg Free Circ: 9000
Audit By: Sworn/Estimate/Non-Audited
Audit Date: 10.06.2019
Personnel: Rob Bennett (Circ. Mgr.); Christine Heiser (Exec. Ed.); Pam Fahey (Prodn. Mgr.)
Parent company (for newspapers): Neighborhood News (OOB)

GRANITE STATE NEWS

Street address 1: 35 Center St
Street address 2: Clarke Plaza
Street address city: Wolfeboro
Street address state: NH
Zip/Postal code: 03894-4324
General Phone: (603) 569-3126
General Fax: (603) 569-3126
General/National Adv. E-mail: maureen@salmonpress.com
Display Adv. E-mail: jumbo@salmonpress.com
Editorial e-mail: tbeeler@salmonpress.news
Primary Website: granitestatenews.com
Year Established: 1859
Avg Paid Circ: 5800
Audit By: Sworn/Estimate/Non-Audited
Audit Date: 10.06.2019
Personnel: Frank Chilinski (Pub.); Thomas Beeler (Ed.)
Parent company (for newspapers): Salmon Press

HOLLIS BROOKLINE JOURNAL

Street address 1: 54 School St
Street address city: Milford
Street address state: NH
Zip/Postal code: 03055-4543
General Phone: (603) 673-3100
General Fax: (603) 673-8250
Advertising Phone: (603) 594-6460
Advertising Fax: (603) 594-6569
Editorial Phone: (603) 673-3100
Editorial Fax: (603) 673-8250
General/National Adv. E-mail: sbucknam@cabinet.com
Editorial e-mail: sbucknam@cabinet.com
Primary Website: cabinet.com
Year Established: 1802
Avg Free Circ: 4700
Audit By: Sworn/Estimate/Non-Audited
Audit Date: 10.06.2019
Personnel: Sandy Bucknam (Managing Ed.)
Parent company (for newspapers): Independent Publications Inc

HOOKSETT BANNER

Street address 1: 100 William Loeb Dr
Street address city: Manchester
Street address state: NH
Zip/Postal code: 03109-5309
General Phone: (603) 314-0447
General Fax: (603) 206-7801
Advertising Phone: (603) 668-4321 x241
Editorial Phone: (603) 668-4321 x757
General/National Adv. E-mail: ul@unionleader.com
Display Adv. E-mail: classified@unionleader.com
Editorial e-mail: editor@yourneighborhoodnews.com
Primary Website: yourneighborhoodnews.com
Year Established: 1961
Avg Paid Circ: 50
Avg Free Circ: 11050
Audit By: Sworn/Estimate/Non-Audited
Audit Date: 10.06.2019
Personnel: Henry Metz (Ed.); Pam Fahey (Prodn. Mgr.); Amy Vellucci (Pub./Sales Dir.)
Parent company (for newspapers): Neighborhood News (OOB)

HUDSON-LITCHFIELD NEWS

Street address 1: 1 Campbell Ave
Street address city: Hudson
Street address state: NH
Zip/Postal code: 03051-4202
General Phone: (603) 880-1516
General Fax: (603) 879-9707
General/National Adv. E-mail: sales@areanewsgroup.com
Editorial e-mail: len@areanewsgroup.com
Primary Website: areanewsgroup.com
Avg Paid Circ: 20
Avg Free Circ: 13900
Audit By: Sworn/Estimate/Non-Audited
Audit Date: 10.06.2019
Personnel: Len Lathrop (Pub.); Mike Falzone (Sales Rep.); Robin Rodgers (Ed.)
Parent company (for newspapers): Area News Group

INTERTOWN RECORD

Street address 1: PO Box 162
Street address city: North Sutton
Street address state: NH
Zip/Postal code: 03260-0162
General Phone: 6039274028
General Fax: 6039274028
General/National Adv. E-mail: info@intertownrecord.com
Display Adv. E-mail: info@intertownrecord.com
Classified Adv. e-mail: info@intertownrecord.com
Editorial e-mail: info@intertownrecord.com
Primary Website: intertownrecord.com
Mthly Avg Views: 1600
Mthly Avg Unique Visitors: 843
Year Established: 1993
Avg Paid Circ: 1475
Avg Free Circ: 35
Audit By: Sworn/Estimate/Non-Audited
Audit Date: 12.10.2023
Personnel: Annette Vogel (Pub./Gen. Mgr.)

LITTLETON COURIER

Street address 1: 5 Water St.
Street address city: Meredith
Street address state: NH
Zip/Postal code: 03253
General Phone: (603) 279-4516
General Fax: (603) 279-3331
General/National Adv. E-mail: courierreporter@salmonpress.com
Editorial e-mail: courierreporter@salmonpress.com
Primary Website: newhampshirelakesandmountains.com
Year Established: 1889
Avg Paid Circ: 6500
Audit By: Sworn/Estimate/Non-Audited
Audit Date: 10.06.2019
Personnel: Tara Giles (Ed.); Tracy Lewis (Sales Rep.)
Parent company (for newspapers): Salmon Press

LONDONDERRY TIMES

Street address 1: 118 Hardy Rd
Street address city: Londonderry
Street address state: NH
Zip/Postal code: 03053-2625
General Phone: (603) 537-2760
General/National Adv. E-mail: dpaul@nutpub.com
Editorial e-mail: dpaul@nutpub.net
Primary Website: londonderrytimes.net
Year Established: 2000
Avg Paid Circ: 0
Avg Free Circ: 11000
Audit By: Sworn/Estimate/Non-Audited
Audit Date: 10.06.2019
Personnel: Debra Paul (Publisher); Chris Paul (Art Dir.); Leslie O'Donnell (Ed.)
Parent company (for newspapers): Nutfield Publishing, LLC

MEREDITH NEWS

Street address 1: 5 Water St
Street address city: Meredith
Street address state: NH
Zip/Postal code: 03253-6233
General Phone: (603) 279-4516
General Fax: (603) 279-3331
Advertising Phone: (603) 279-4516 x 120
General/National Adv. E-mail: jeffd@salmonpress.com
Display Adv. E-mail: jumbo@salmonpress.com
Editorial e-mail: mnews@salmonpress.com
Primary Website: newhampshirelakesandmountains.com
Year Established: 1880
Avg Paid Circ: 5300
Audit By: Sworn/Estimate/Non-Audited
Audit Date: 10.06.2019
Personnel: Erin Plummer (Ed.); Tracy Lewis (Pub.)
Parent company (for newspapers): Salmon Press

MERRIMACK JOURNAL

Street address 1: 54 School St
Street address city: Milford
Street address state: NH
Zip/Postal code: 03055-4543
General Phone: (603) 673-3100
General Fax: (603) 673-8250
General/National Adv. E-mail: sbucknam@cabinet.com
Editorial e-mail: sbucknam@cabinet.com
Primary Website: cabinet.com
Year Established: 1826
Avg Free Circ: 10400
Audit By: Sworn/Estimate/Non-Audited
Audit Date: 10.06.2019
Personnel: Sandy Bucknam
Parent company (for newspapers): Ogden Newspapers Inc.

MESSENGER

Street address 1: 246 W Main St
Street address city: Hillsborough
Street address state: NH
Zip/Postal code: 03244-5251
General Phone: (603) 464-3388
General Fax: (603) 464-4106
General/National Adv. E-mail: granitequill@mcttelecom.com
Primary Website: granitequill.com
Avg Free Circ: 25000
Audit By: Sworn/Estimate/Non-Audited
Audit Date: 10.06.2019
Personnel: Leigh Bosse (Pub.); Joyce Bosse (Ed.)

MONADNOCK LEDGER-TRANSCRIPT

Street address 1: 20 Grove St
Street address 2: Ste 120
Street address city: Peterborough
Street address state: NH
Zip/Postal code: 03458-1466
General Phone: (603) 924-7172
General Fax: (603) 924-3681
General/National Adv. E-mail: ads@ledgertranscript.com
Display Adv. E-mail: ads@ledgertranscript.com
Classified Adv. e-mail: classifieds@ledgertranscript.com
Editorial e-mail: news@ledgertranscript.com
Primary Website: ledgertranscript.com
Mthly Avg Views: 132382
Mthly Avg Unique Visitors: 51959
Year Established: 1849
Avg Paid Circ: 4059
Avg Free Circ: 220
Audit By: Sworn/Estimate/Non-Audited
Audit Date: 16.10.2023
Personnel: Heather McKernan (Pub.); Bill Fonda (Ed.); Kimberly Poorte (Circ. Mgr.)
Parent company (for newspapers): Newspapers of New England

MONADNOCK SHOPPER NEWS

Street address 1: 445 West St
Street address city: Keene
Street address state: NH
Zip/Postal code: 03431-2448
General Phone: (603) 352-5250
General Fax: (603) 357-9351
General/National Adv. E-mail: sales@shoppernews.com
Display Adv. E-mail: classified@shoppernews.com
Editorial e-mail: editorial@shoppernews.com
Primary Website: shoppernews.com
Year Established: 1958
Audit By: Sworn/Estimate/Non-Audited
Audit Date: 10.06.2019
Personnel: Michelle Green (Asst. Pub./Ed.); Mitchell G. Shakour (Pres./Pub.)

NUTFIELD NEWS

Street address 1: 2 Litchfield Rd
Street address city: Londonderry
Street address state: NH
Zip/Postal code: 03053-2625
General Phone: (603) 537-2760
General Fax: (603) 537-2765
General/National Adv. E-mail: dpaul@nutpub.com
Editorial e-mail: lodonnell@nutpub.com
Primary Website: nutpub.net
Year Established: 2000
Avg Free Circ: 9996
Audit By: Sworn/Estimate/Non-Audited
Audit Date: 10.06.2019
Personnel: Debra Paul (Publisher); Leslie O'Donnell (Ed.); Chris Paul (Art Dir.)
Parent company (for newspapers): Nutfield Publishing, LLC

PELHAM/WINDHAM NEWS

Street address 1: 1 Campbell Ave
Street address city: Hudson
Street address state: NH
Zip/Postal code: 03051-4202
General Phone: (603) 880-1516
General Fax: (603) 879-9707
General/National Adv. E-mail: sales@areanewsgroup.com
Editorial e-mail: len@areanewsgroup.com
Primary Website: areanewsgroup.com
Year Established: 2001
Avg Free Circ: 10058
Audit By: Sworn/Estimate/Non-Audited
Audit Date: 10.06.2019
Personnel: Sandy Russo (Sales Rep); Mike Fizone (Sales)
Parent company (for newspapers): Area News Group

PLYMOUTH RECORD ENTERPRISE

Street address 1: 5 Water St
Street address city: Meredith
Street address state: NH
Zip/Postal code: 03253-6233
General Phone: (603) 279-4516
General Fax: (603) 279-3331
Advertising Phone: (603) 279-4516 ext. 132
Advertising Fax: (603) 279-3331
Editorial Phone: (603) 279-4516 ext. 111
Editorial Fax: (603) 279-3331
General/National Adv. E-mail: courierstj@salmonpress.com
Display Adv. E-mail: courierstj@salmonpress.com
Editorial e-mail: record@salmonpress.com
Primary Website: salmonpress.com
Audit By: Sworn/Estimate/Non-Audited
Audit Date: 10.06.2019
Personnel: Brendan Berube (Ed.); Tracy Lewis (Adv. Mgr.); Tracy Lewis (Pub.)

ROCHESTER TIMES

Street address 1: 18 Main St
Street address 2: Unit 2D
Street address city: Dover
Street address state: NH
Zip/Postal code: 03820-3812
General Phone: (603) 332-2300
General Fax: (603) 330-3162
General/National Adv. E-mail: thetimes@fosters.com
Primary Website: fosters.com
Year Established: 1993
Avg Free Circ: 15000
Audit By: Sworn/Estimate/Non-Audited
Audit Date: 10.06.2019
Parent company (for newspapers): George J. Foster Co., Inc.

SALEM COMMUNITY PATRIOT

Street address 1: 1 Campbell Ave
Street address city: Hudson
Street address state: NH
Zip/Postal code: 03051-4202
General Phone: (603) 880-1516

General Fax: (603) 879-9707
General/National Adv. E-mail: news@areanewsgroup.com
Primary Website: areanewsgroup.com
Year Established: 2007
Avg Free Circ: 14763
Audit By: Sworn/Estimate/Non-Audited
Audit Date: 10.06.2019
Personnel: Mike Falzone (customer service)
Parent company (for newspapers): Area News Group

THE BAYSIDER

Street address 1: Clark Plaza
Street address city: Wolfeboro Falls
Street address state: NH
Zip/Postal code: 3896
General Phone: (603) 569-3126
General Fax: (603) 569-4743
General/National Adv. E-mail: maureen@salmonpress.com
Display Adv. E-mail: jumbo@salmonpress.com
Editorial e-mail: baysider@salmonpress.com
Primary Website: salmonpress.com
Year Established: 2005
Audit By: Sworn/Estimate/Non-Audited
Audit Date: 10.06.2019
Personnel: Frank Chilinski (Pub.); Brendan Berube (Ed.); Tara Giles; Cathy Cardinal-Grondin (Adv. Sales); Lori Lynch (Adv. Sales); Samantha Lovett (Circ. Mgr.)
Parent company (for newspapers): Salmon Press

THE BERLIN DAILY SUN

Street address 1: 164 MAIN ST
Street address 2: STE 1
Street address city: BERLIN
Street address state: NH
Zip/Postal code: 03570-2477
General Phone: (603) 752-5858
General Fax: (866) 475-4429
Advertising Phone: (603) 733-5808
Advertising Fax: (603) 356-0435
Editorial Phone: (603) 326-6100
Editorial Fax: (866) 475-4429
General/National Adv. E-mail: joyce@conwaydailysun.com
Display Adv. E-mail: ads@conwaydailysun.com
Classified Adv. e-mail: louise@conwaydailysun.com
Editorial e-mail: barbara@berlindailysun.com
Primary Website: berlindailysun.com
Year Established: 1989
Avg Paid Circ: 8925
Audit By: Sworn/Estimate/Non-Audited
Audit Date: 10.06.2019
Personnel: Mark Guerringue (Pub.); Joyce Brothers (Ass. Pub.); Adam Hirshan (Ed.); Frank Haddy (Prodn. Mgr.); Barbara Tetreault (Managing Ed.); Tee Johnson (Adv. Rep.)

THE BERLIN REPORTER

Street address 1: 79 Main St
Street address city: Lancaster
Street address state: NH
Zip/Postal code: 03584-3027
General Phone: (603) 788-4939
General Fax: (603) 788-3022
General/National Adv. E-mail: courierreporter@salmonpress.com
Editorial e-mail: courierreporter@salmonpress.com
Primary Website: breporter.com
Year Established: 1838
Avg Paid Circ: 4250
Audit By: Sworn/Estimate/Non-Audited
Audit Date: 10.06.2019
Personnel: Darin Wipperman (Ed.); Tracy Lewis (Pub.)
Parent company (for newspapers): Salmon Press

THE COCHECO TIMES

Street address 1: 515 Endicott St N
Street address city: Laconia
Street address state: NH
Zip/Postal code: 03246-1725
General Phone: (888) 308-8463
General Fax: (603) 366-7301
Advertising Phone: (888) 308-8463
Advertising Fax: (603) 366-7301
Editorial Phone: (603) 366-8463 x 317
General/National Adv. E-mail: sales@weirs.com
Display Adv. E-mail: sales@weirs.com
Editorial e-mail: dlawton@weirs.com
Primary Website: weirs.com
Mthly Avg Views: 7950
Mthly Avg Unique Visitors: 3524
Year Established: 1992
Avg Free Circ: 27789
Audit By: Sworn/Estimate/Non-Audited
Audit Date: 10.06.2019
Personnel: David M. Lawton (Pub.); Starr Lawton (Off. Mgr.); Bredan Smith (Ed.)
Parent company (for newspapers): Weirs Publishing Co Inc.

THE COOS COUNTY DEMOCRAT

Street address 1: 79 Main St
Street address city: Lancaster
Street address state: NH
Zip/Postal code: 03584-3027
General Phone: (603) 788-4939
General Fax: (603) 788-3022
General/National Adv. E-mail: courierreporter@salmonpress.com
Editorial e-mail: courierreporter@salmonpress.com
Primary Website: cooscountydemocrat.com
Year Established: 1838
Avg Paid Circ: 5520
Audit By: Sworn/Estimate/Non-Audited
Audit Date: 10.06.2019
Personnel: Darin Wipperman; Tracy Lewis (Pub.)
Parent company (for newspapers): Salmon Press

THE GILFORD STEAMER

Street address 1: 5 Water St
Street address city: Meredith
Street address state: NH
Zip/Postal code: 03253-6233
General Phone: (603) 279-4516
General Fax: (603) 279-3331
Advertising Phone: (603) 279-4516 x 120
General/National Adv. E-mail: jeffd@salmonpress.com
Display Adv. E-mail: jumbo@salmonpress.com
Editorial e-mail: record@salmonpress.com
Primary Website: salmonpress.com
Mthly Avg Views: 100000
Mthly Avg Unique Visitors: 50000
Year Established: 2004
Avg Free Circ: 6800
Audit By: Sworn/Estimate/Non-Audited
Audit Date: 10.06.2019
Personnel: Frank Chilnski (Pub.); Breandan Berube (Ed.); Jefferey DeFrancesco
Parent company (for newspapers): Salmon Press

THE HAMPTON UNION

Street address 1: 111 NH Ave
Street address city: Portsmouth
Street address state: NH
Zip/Postal code: 03801-2864
General Phone: (800) 439-0303
General Fax: (603) 433-5760
Advertising Fax: (603) 427-0550
General/National Adv. E-mail: adreps@seacoastonline.com
Editorial e-mail: news@seacoastonline.com
Primary Website: seacoastonline.com
Avg Paid Circ: 1553
Audit By: AAM
Audit Date: 31.12.2018
Personnel: John Tabor (Pub.); Dennis Thompson (Circ. Dir.); Howard Altschiller (Exec. Ed.); Andrew Chernoff (Ad Director)
Parent company (for newspapers): CherryRoad Media

THE MILFORD CABINET

Street address 1: 54 School St
Street address city: Milford
Street address state: NH
Zip/Postal code: 03055-4543
General Phone: (603) 673-3100
General Fax: (603) 673-8250
General/National Adv. E-mail: sbucknam@cabinet.com
Editorial e-mail: sbucknam@cabinet.com
Primary Website: cabinet.com
Year Established: 1802
Avg Paid Circ: 6700
Avg Free Circ: 78
Audit By: Sworn/Estimate/Non-Audited
Audit Date: 10.06.2019
Personnel: Sandy Bucknam
Parent company (for newspapers): Ogden Newspapers Inc.

THE NEWS AND SENTINEL

Street address 1: 6 Bridge St
Street address city: Colebrook
Street address state: NH
Zip/Postal code: 03576-3033
General Phone: (603) 237-5501
General/National Adv. E-mail: butchladd@colebrooknewsandsentinel.com
Editorial e-mail: editor@colebrooknewsandsentinel.com
Primary Website: colbsent.com
Mthly Avg Views: 1500
Year Established: 1870
Avg Paid Circ: 3466
Avg Free Circ: 197
Audit By: Sworn/Estimate/Non-Audited
Audit Date: 10.06.2021
Personnel: Karen Harrigan (Ed./Pub.); Jake Mardin (News Rep./Sports); Linda Young (Sales Staff); Tracey Bagley (Ad Designer); Butch Ladd (Sales Staff); Eric Raymond (Sales Staff)

THE WEIRS TIMES

Street address 1: 515 Endicott St N
Street address city: Laconia
Street address state: NH
Zip/Postal code: 03246-1725
General Phone: (603) 366-8463
General Fax: (603) 366-7301
Advertising Phone: (603) 366-8463
Advertising Fax: (603) 366-7301
Editorial Phone: (603) 366-8463
Editorial Fax: (603) 366-7301
General/National Adv. E-mail: advertise@weirs.com
Display Adv. E-mail: advertise@weirs.com
Editorial e-mail: dlawton@weirs.com
Primary Website: theweirstimes.com
Mthly Avg Views: 7950
Mthly Avg Unique Visitors: 3524
Year Established: 1992
Avg Free Circ: 27789
Audit By: Sworn/Estimate/Non-Audited
Audit Date: 10.06.2019
Personnel: David M. Lawton (Managing Ed.); Brendan Smith (Ed.); Craig Richardson (Circ, Mgr.)
Parent company (for newspapers): Weirs Publishing Co Inc.

THE YORK WEEKLY

Street address 1: 111 NH Ave
Street address city: Portsmouth
Street address state: NH
Zip/Postal code: 03801-2864
General Phone: (800) 439-0303
General Fax: (603) 433-5760
Advertising Fax: (603) 427-0550
General/National Adv. E-mail: adreps@seacoastonline.com
Editorial e-mail: news@seacoastonline.com
Primary Website: seacoastonline.com
Avg Paid Circ: 3900
Audit By: Sworn/Estimate/Non-Audited
Audit Date: 10.06.2019
Personnel: John Tabor (Pub.); Dennis Thompson (Circ. Mgr.); Vince Ciampi; Howard Altschiller
Parent company (for newspapers): Dow Jones Local Media Group-OOB; Seacoast Media Group

TRI-TOWN TIMES

Street address 1: 2 Litchfield Rd
Street address city: Londonderry
Street address state: NH
Zip/Postal code: 03053-2625
General Phone: (603) 537-2760
General Fax: (603) 537-2765
General/National Adv. E-mail: dpaul@nutpub.com
Editorial e-mail: lodonnell@nutpub.com
Primary Website: nutpub.net
Year Established: 2006
Avg Free Circ: 8699
Audit By: Sworn/Estimate/Non-Audited
Audit Date: 10.06.2019
Personnel: Debra Paul (Pub.); Chris Paul (Art Dir.); Leslie O'Donnell (Ed.)
Parent company (for newspapers): Nutfield Publishing, LLC

WINNISQUAM ECHO

Street address 1: 5 Water St
Street address city: Meredith
Street address state: NH
Zip/Postal code: 03253-6233
General Phone: (603) 279-4516
General Fax: (603) 279-3331
Advertising Phone: (603) 279-4516 x 120
General/National Adv. E-mail: maureen@salmonpress.com
Display Adv. E-mail: jumbo@salmonpress.com
Editorial e-mail: record@salmonpress.com
Primary Website: salmonpress.com
Year Established: 2004
Avg Free Circ: 9200
Audit By: Sworn/Estimate/Non-Audited
Audit Date: 10.06.2019
Personnel: Frank Chilinski (Pub.); Breandan Berube (Ed.)
Parent company (for newspapers): Salmon Press

NEW JERSEY

ADVERTISER NEWS (NORTH EDITION)

Street address 1: 31 Newton Sparta Rd
Street address city: Andover
Street address state: NJ
Zip/Postal code: 07860
General Phone: (973) 300-0890
Advertising Phone: (973) 300-0890
Editorial Phone: (973) 300-0890
General/National Adv. E-mail: njoffice@strausnews.com
Display Adv. E-mail: sales@strausnews.com
Editorial e-mail: njoffice@strausnews.com
Primary Website: advertisernewsnorth.com
Avg Paid Circ: 0
Avg Free Circ: 10147
Audit By: USPS
Personnel: Jeanne Straus (Pres.); Mike Zummo (Mng. Ed.)

ADVERTISER NEWS (SOUTH EDITION)

Street address 1: 31 Newton Sparta Rd
Street address 2: Ste 9
Street address city: Newton
Street address state: NJ
Zip/Postal code: 07860
General Phone: (973) 300-0890
Advertising Phone: (973) 300-0890
Editorial Phone: (973) 300-0890
General/National Adv. E-mail: njoffice@strausnews.com
Display Adv. E-mail: sales@strausnews.com
Editorial e-mail: njoffice@strausnews.com
Primary Website: advertisernewssouth.com
Avg Paid Circ: 0
Avg Free Circ: 10000
Audit By: USPS
Personnel: Jeanne Straus (Pres.); Mike Zummo (Mng. Ed.)

AIM JEFFERSON

Street address 1: 100 Commons Way
Street address city: Rockaway
Street address state: NJ
Zip/Postal code: 07866-2038
General Phone: (973) 586-8195
Advertising Phone: (973) 283-5608
Editorial Phone: (973) 283-5611
General/National Adv. E-mail: adhelp@northjersey.com
Primary Website: northjersey.com
Avg Paid Circ: 0
Avg Free Circ: 8196
Audit By: Sworn/Estimate/Non-Audited
Audit Date: 10.06.2019
Personnel: Rick Green (Ed.)

Parent company (for newspapers): North Jersey Media Group Inc.

AIM VERNON

Street address 1: 505 Main St
Street address city: Butler
Street address state: NJ
Zip/Postal code: 07405-1095
General Phone: (973) 569-7000
General Fax: (973) 569-7268
Advertising Phone: (973) 569-7269
Editorial Phone: (973) 569-7100
General/National Adv. E-mail: aim@northjersey.com
Primary Website: northjersey.com/vernon
Year Established: 2009
Avg Paid Circ: 0
Avg Free Circ: 8840
Audit By: Sworn/Estimate/Non-Audited
Audit Date: 10.06.2019
Personnel: Rick Green (Ed.)
Parent company (for newspapers): North Jersey Media Group Inc.

AIM WEST MILFORD

Street address 1: 505 Main St
Street address city: Butler
Street address state: NJ
Zip/Postal code: 07405-1095
General Phone: (973) 283-5600
Advertising Phone: (973) 569-7269
Editorial Phone: (973) 569-7100
General/National Adv. E-mail: adhelp@northjersey.com
Display Adv. E-mail: marketplace@northjersey.com
Editorial e-mail: newsroom@northjersey.com
Primary Website: northjersey.com
Avg Paid Circ: 0
Avg Free Circ: 10051
Audit By: Sworn/Estimate/Non-Audited
Audit Date: 10.06.2019
Personnel: Rick Green (Ed.)
Parent company (for newspapers): North Jersey Media Group Inc.

ARGUS

Street address 1: 505 Main St
Street address city: Butler
Street address state: NJ
Zip/Postal code: 07405-1095
General Phone: (973) 283-5618
Advertising Phone: (973) 569-7269
Editorial Phone: (973) 569-7100
General/National Adv. E-mail: adhelp@northjersey.com
Display Adv. E-mail: marketplace@northjersey.com
Editorial e-mail: newsroom@northjersey.com
Primary Website: northjersey.com
Avg Paid Circ: 0
Avg Free Circ: 9847
Audit By: Sworn/Estimate/Non-Audited
Audit Date: 10.06.2019
Personnel: Rick Green (Ed.)
Parent company (for newspapers): North Jersey Media Group Inc.

ATLANTICVILLE

Street address 1: 198 US Highway 9
Street address 2: Ste 100
Street address city: Manalapan
Street address state: NJ
Zip/Postal code: 07726-3073
General Phone: (732) 358-5200
General Fax: (732) 780-4678
General/National Adv. E-mail: gmsales@gmnews.com
Editorial e-mail: aville@gmnews.com
Primary Website: gmnews.com
Avg Paid Circ: 5
Avg Free Circ: 17595
Audit By: Sworn/Estimate/Non-Audited
Audit Date: 10.06.2019
Personnel: Gloria Stravelli (Mng. Ed.)
Parent company (for newspapers): Newspaper Media Group-OOB

BAYONNE COMMUNITY NEWS

Street address 1: 447 Broadway
Street address city: Bayonne
Street address state: NJ
Zip/Postal code: 07002-3623
General Phone: (201) 798-7800
General Fax: (201) 798-0018
Advertising Phone: (201) 798-7800
Advertising Fax: (201) 798-0018
Editorial Phone: (201) 798-7800
Editorial Fax: (201) 798-0018
General/National Adv. E-mail: dunger@hudsonreporter.com
Display Adv. E-mail: classified@hudsonreporter.com
Editorial e-mail: editorial@hudsonreporter.com
Primary Website: hudsonreporter.com
Year Established: 1978
Avg Paid Circ: 0
Avg Free Circ: 45808
Audit By: Sworn/Estimate/Non-Audited
Audit Date: 10.06.2019
Personnel: Lucha Malato (Co-Pub.); David S. Unger (Co-Pub.); Cecilia Martinez (Ed.); Tish Kraszyk; Roberto Lopez (Circ. Dir.)
Parent company (for newspapers): Hudson Reporter Associates, Lp

BEACH HAVEN TIMES

Street address 1: 3600 Highway 66
Street address city: Neptune
Street address state: NJ
Zip/Postal code: 7754
General Phone: (732) 922-6000
General/National Adv. E-mail: HTowns@njpressmedia.com
Display Adv. E-mail: appclass@gannett.com
Editorial e-mail: lreddington@njpressmedia.com
Primary Website: app.com
Avg Paid Circ: 49198
Audit By: AAM
Audit Date: 30.09.2018
Personnel: Tom Donovan (Pres./Pub.); Hollis Towns (Exec. Ed./VP)
Parent company (for newspapers): Gannett

BELLEVILLE POST

Street address 1: 1291 Stuyvesant Ave
Street address city: Union
Street address state: NJ
Zip/Postal code: 07083-3854
General Phone: (908) 686-7700
General Fax: (908) 686-4169
General/National Adv. E-mail: ads@thelocalsource.com
Display Adv. E-mail: class@thelocalsource.com
Editorial e-mail: editorial@thelocalsource.com
Primary Website: essexnewsdaily.com
Year Established: 1982
Avg Paid Circ: 231
Audit By: Sworn/Estimate/Non-Audited
Audit Date: 10.06.2019
Personnel: David Worrall (Pub.); Raymond Worrall (Gen. Mgr.); Peter Worrall (IT / Production Manager Circulation Manager); Nancy Worrall
Parent company (for newspapers): Worrall Community Newspapers, Inc.

BELLEVILLE TIMES

Street address 1: 90 Centre St
Street address city: Nutley
Street address state: NJ
Zip/Postal code: 07110-3720
General Phone: (973) 667-2100
General Fax: (973) 667-3904
Advertising Phone: (973) 233-5007
General/National Adv. E-mail: bellevilletimes@northjersey.com
Primary Website: northjersey.com/towns/belleville
Year Established: 1909
Avg Paid Circ: 1201
Audit By: Sworn/Estimate/Non-Audited
Audit Date: 10.06.2019
Personnel: Rick Green (Ed.)
Parent company (for newspapers): Gannett - USA Today Network

BERNARDSVILLE NEWS

Street address 1: 17-19 Morristown Rd
Street address city: Bernardsville
Street address state: NJ
Zip/Postal code: 07924-2372
General Phone: (908) 766-3900
General Fax: (908) 766-5375
General/National Adv. E-mail: advertising@newjerseyhills.com
Display Adv. E-mail: nicoleb@Newjerseyhills.com
Editorial e-mail: czavalick@Newjerseyhills.com
Primary Website: recordernewspapers.com
Year Established: 1897
Avg Paid Circ: 6488
Avg Free Circ: 101
Audit By: Sworn/Estimate/Non-Audited
Audit Date: 10.06.2019
Personnel: Elizabeth K. Parker (Co-Pub.); Stephen W. Parker (Co-Pub.); Jerry O'Donnell (Adv. Dir.); Linda Campbell (Prodn. Mgr.); Diane Howard (Gen. Off. Mgr); Philip Nardone (Ass. Exec. Ed.); Charles Zavalick (Ed.)
Parent company (for newspapers): New Jersey Hills Media Group

BLACK RIVER NEWS

Street address 1: 5 Vista Dr
Street address city: Flanders
Street address state: NJ
Zip/Postal code: 07836
General Phone: (973) 252-9889
General Fax: (240) 332-7489
General/National Adv. E-mail: joe@newviewmg.com
Display Adv. E-mail: joe@newviewmg.com
Primary Website: newviewmediagroup.com
Year Established: 2003
Avg Free Circ: 8853
Audit By: CVC
Audit Date: 6/31/2018
Personnel: Joe Nicastro (Pub./Adv. Mgr./Circ, Mgr.)
Parent company (for newspapers): New View Media Group LLC

BLOOMFIELD LIFE

Street address 1: 1 Garret Mountain Plaza
Street address city: Woodland Park
Street address state: NJ
Zip/Postal code: 7424
General Phone: (973) 569-7000
General Fax: (973) 569-7268
Advertising Phone: (973) 233-5007
General/National Adv. E-mail: bloomfieldlife@northjersey.com
Primary Website: northjersey.com/towns/bloomfield
Year Established: 1981
Avg Paid Circ: 1149
Audit By: CAC
Audit Date: 31.12.2017
Personnel: Rick Green (Ed.)
Parent company (for newspapers): Gannett - USA Today Network

BOGOTA BULLETIN

Street address 1: 210 Knickerbocker Rd
Street address city: Cresskill
Street address state: NJ
Zip/Postal code: 07626-1801
General Phone: (201) 894-6700
Advertising Phone: (973) 569-7269
Editorial Phone: (973) 569-7100
General/National Adv. E-mail: adhelp@northjersey.com
Display Adv. E-mail: marketplace@northjersey.com
Editorial e-mail: newsroom@northjersey.com
Primary Website: northjersey.com/bogota
Year Established: 2007
Avg Free Circ: 638
Audit By: Sworn/Estimate/Non-Audited
Audit Date: 10.06.2019
Personnel: Rick Green (Ed.)
Parent company (for newspapers): North Jersey Community Newspapers

BORDENTOWN CURRENT

Street address 1: 15 Princess Rd
Street address 2: Ste K
Street address city: Lawrence
Street address state: NJ
Zip/Postal code: 08648-2301
General Phone: (609)396-1511
Advertising Phone: (609)396-1511 x110
Editorial Phone: (609)396-1511 x121
General/National Adv. E-mail: tfritts@mercerspace.com
Editorial e-mail: ssciarrotta@mercerspace.com
Primary Website: bordentowncurrent.com
Avg Free Circ: 8508
Audit By: Sworn/Estimate/Non-Audited
Audit Date: 10.06.2019
Personnel: Samantha Sciarrotta (Ed.)

BRIGANTINE BEACHCOMBER

Street address 1: 206 W Parkway Dr
Street address city: Egg Harbor Township
Street address state: NJ
Zip/Postal code: 08234-5106
General Phone: (609) 383-8994
General/National Adv. E-mail: adpro@thebeachcombernews.com
Display Adv. E-mail: adpro@thebeachcombernews.com
Primary Website: thebeachcombernews.com
Avg Free Circ: 3450
Audit By: Sworn/Estimate/Non-Audited
Audit Date: 10.06.2019
Personnel: Marc Blum (Pub.); Steve Mehl (Adv. Dir.); Bill Barlow (Ed.)
Parent company (for newspapers): Catamaran Media

BURLINGTON TOWNSHIP SUN

Street address 1: 108 Kings Hwy E
Street address city: Haddonfield
Street address state: NJ
Zip/Postal code: 08033-2099
General Phone: (856) 779-3800
Advertising Phone: (856) 528-4844
General/National Adv. E-mail: jgallo@newspapermediagroup.com
Primary Website: burlingtontownshipsun.com
Audit By: Sworn/Estimate/Non-Audited
Audit Date: 10.06.2019
Personnel: Arlene Reyes (Adv. Dir.); Angela Smith (Mktg. Dir.)
Parent company (for newspapers): Newspaper Media Group-OOB

CAPE MAY COUNTY HERALD

Street address 1: 1508 Route 47
Street address city: Rio Grande
Street address state: NJ
Zip/Postal code: 08242
General Phone: 609-886-8600
General Fax: 609-886-1879
Advertising Phone: 609-886-8600 x122
Advertising Fax: 609-886-1879
Editorial Phone: 609-886-8600 x130
Editorial Fax: 609-886-1879
General/National Adv. E-mail: Admin@cmcHerald.com
Display Adv. E-mail: Advertise@cmcHerald.com
Classified Adv. e-mail: Classified@cmcHerald.com
Editorial e-mail: Editor@cmcHerald.com
Primary Website: CapeMayCountyHerald.com
Mthly Avg Views: 1000000
Mthly Avg Unique Visitors: 100000
Year Established: 1967
Avg Paid Circ: 1000
Avg Free Circ: 16000
Audit By: CVC
Audit Date: 31.12.2020
Personnel: Arthur R. Hall (Pub.); Arthur Hall (Publisher); Benjamin Hall (Associate Publisher); Al Camtbell (Ed.); Karen Dickinson (Adv. Sales); Preston Gibson (CEO); Karen Dickinson (Advertising Manager); Janet Seitz (Classified Advertising Manager); Robert Kosinski (Circ. Dir.); Steven Dunwoody (Prod.); Jodee Clifford (Media & Marketing Manager); Kim Enteado (Finance, HR, Office Manager)
Parent company (for newspapers): The Seawave Corporation

CAPE MAY STAR AND WAVE

Street address 1: PO Box 2427
Street address city: West Cape May
Street address state: NJ
Zip/Postal code: 08204-7427
General Phone: (609) 884-3466
General Fax: (609) 884-2893
General/National Adv. E-mail: cmstarwaveadvertise@comcast.net
Editorial e-mail: cmstarwave@comcast.net
Primary Website: starandwave.com
Year Established: 1854
Avg Paid Circ: 3395
Avg Free Circ: 386
Audit By: Sworn/Estimate/Non-Audited
Audit Date: 10.06.2019

Personnel: David Nahan (Pub.); Rob Elder (Adv. Mgr.); Jack Fichter (Ed.)
Parent company (for newspapers): Sample Media Inc

CHATHAM COURIER

Street address 1: 100 S. Jefferson Road
Street address 2: Suite 104
Street address city: Whippany
Street address state: NJ
Zip/Postal code: 07981
General Phone: (908) 766-3900, 240
Advertising Phone: (973) 766-3900 ext. 230
Advertising Fax: (908) 766-2773
Editorial Phone: (908) 766-3900, ext. 240
Editorial Fax: (908) 766-2773
General/National Adv. E-mail: advertising@Newjerseyhills.com
Display Adv. E-mail: theag@newjerseyhills.com
Editorial e-mail: eparker@newjerseyhills.com
Primary Website: recordernewspapers.com
Year Established: 1945
Avg Paid Circ: 1856
Avg Free Circ: 12
Audit By: CAC
Audit Date: 30.09.2018
Personnel: Elizabeth Parker (Pub.); Stephen W. Parker (Pub.); Jeerry O'Donnell (VP Sales/ Mkt); Garry Herzog (Mng. Ed.)
Parent company (for newspapers): New Jersey Hills Media Group

CHERRY HILL SUN

Street address 1: 108 Kings Hwy E
Street address city: Haddonfield
Street address state: NJ
Zip/Postal code: 08033-2099
General Phone: (856) 779-3800
Advertising Phone: (856) 528-4844
General/National Adv. E-mail: jgallo@newspapermediagroup.com
Primary Website: cherryhillsun.com
Audit By: Sworn/Estimate/Non-Audited
Audit Date: 10.06.2019
Personnel: Arlene Reyes (Adv. Dir.); Angela Smith (Mktg. Dir.)
Parent company (for newspapers): Newspaper Media Group-OOB

CINNAMINSON SUN

Street address 1: 108 Kings Hwy E
Street address city: Haddonfield
Street address state: NJ
Zip/Postal code: 08033-2099
General Phone: (856) 779-3800
Advertising Phone: (856) 528-4844
General/National Adv. E-mail: jgallo@newspapermediagroup.com
Primary Website: cinnaminsonsun.com
Audit By: Sworn/Estimate/Non-Audited
Audit Date: 10.06.2019
Personnel: Arlene Reyes (Adv. Dir.); Angela Smith (Mktg. Dir.)
Parent company (for newspapers): Newspaper Media Group-OOB

CLIFFSIDE PARK CITIZEN

Street address 1: 210 Knickerbocker Rd
Street address city: Cresskill
Street address state: NJ
Zip/Postal code: 07626-1801
General Phone: (201) 894-6700
Advertising Phone: (973) 569-7269
Editorial Phone: (973) 569-7100
General/National Adv. E-mail: adhelp@northjersey.com
Display Adv. E-mail: marketplace@northjersey.com
Editorial e-mail: newsroom@northjersey.com
Primary Website: northjersey.com
Year Established: 2006
Avg Free Circ: 10618
Audit By: Sworn/Estimate/Non-Audited
Audit Date: 10.06.2019
Personnel: Rick Green (Ed.)
Parent company (for newspapers): North Jersey Media Group

CLIFTON JOURNAL

Street address 1: 777 Passaic Ave
Street address 2: Ste 575
Street address city: Clifton
Street address state: NJ
Zip/Postal code: 07012-1873
General Phone: (973) 778-2500
Advertising Phone: (973) 569-7269
Editorial Phone: (973) 569-7100
General/National Adv. E-mail: adhelp@northjersey.com
Display Adv. E-mail: marketplace@northjersey.com
Editorial e-mail: newsroom@northjersey.com
Primary Website: northjersey.com
Year Established: 1917
Avg Paid Circ: 0
Avg Free Circ: 31542
Audit By: Sworn/Estimate/Non-Audited
Audit Date: 10.06.2019
Personnel: Rick Green (Ed.)
Parent company (for newspapers): North Jersey Media Group Inc.

COASTER

Street address 1: 1011 Main St
Street address 2: Ste B
Street address city: Asbury Park
Street address state: NJ
Zip/Postal code: 07712-5963
General Phone: (732) 775-3010
General Fax: (732) 775-8345
Display Adv. E-mail: advertising@thecoaster.net
Editorial e-mail: editor@thecoaster.net
Primary Website: thecoaster.net
Year Established: 1983
Avg Paid Circ: 5100
Audit By: Sworn/Estimate/Non-Audited
Audit Date: 10.06.2019
Personnel: Michael Booth (Adv. Mgr.); Ellen Carroll (Ed.)

COMMUNITY NEWS

Street address 1: 12-38 River Rd
Street address city: Fair Lawn
Street address state: NJ
Zip/Postal code: 07410-1802
General Phone: (201) 791-8994
General Fax: (201) 794-3259
Editorial e-mail: dsforza@gannett.com
Primary Website: northjersey.com
Year Established: 1948
Avg Paid Circ: 0
Avg Free Circ: 66888
Audit By: Sworn/Estimate/Non-Audited
Audit Date: 10.06.2019
Personnel: Daniel Sforza (Ed.)

COMMUNITY NEWS SERVICE - HAMILTON POST

Street address 1: 15 Princess Rd
Street address 2: Ste K
Street address city: Lawrence
Street address state: NJ
Zip/Postal code: 08648-2301
General Phone: (609)396-1511
General Fax: (609)844-0180
General/National Adv. E-mail: advertise@communitynews.org
Editorial e-mail: news@communitynews.org
Primary Website: communitynews.org
Year Established: 1982
Avg Free Circ: 42101
Audit By: Sworn/Estimate/Non-Audited
Audit Date: 10.06.2019
Personnel: Rob Anthes (Ed.)

CRANBURY PRESS

Street address 1: 300 Witherspoon St
Street address city: Princeton
Street address state: NJ
Zip/Postal code: 08542-3401
General Phone: (609) 924-3244
General Fax: (609) 921-2714
Advertising Fax: (609) 921-2714
Editorial Fax: (609) 924-3842
General/National Adv. E-mail: feedback@centraljersey.com
Display Adv. E-mail: advertising@centraljersey.com
Editorial e-mail: ckim@centraljersey.com
Primary Website: centraljersey.com/news/the_cranbury_press
Year Established: 1885
Avg Paid Circ: 77
Avg Free Circ: 1614
Audit By: Sworn/Estimate/Non-Audited
Audit Date: 10.06.2019
Personnel: Joe Eisele (Pub.); Aubrey Huston (Ed.)

CRANFORD CHRONICLE

Street address 1: 309 South St
Street address city: New Providence
Street address state: NJ
Zip/Postal code: 07974-2110
General Phone: (908) 464-1025
General Fax: (908) 464-9085
General/National Adv. E-mail: union@njnpublishing.com
Primary Website: nj.com
Year Established: 1893
Avg Paid Circ: 3300
Audit By: Sworn/Estimate/Non-Audited
Audit Date: 10.06.2019
Personnel: Eileen Bickel (Pub.); Mary Krovacin (Circ. Mgr.); Jon Babicz (Adv. Dir.)
Parent company (for newspapers): Advance Publications, Inc.

CUMBERLAND REMINDER

Street address 1: 2 W Vine St
Street address city: Millville
Street address state: NJ
Zip/Postal code: 08332-3823
General Phone: (856) 825-8811
General Fax: (856) 825-0011
General/National Adv. E-mail: thereminderbeth@comcast.net
Display Adv. E-mail: thereminderbeth@comcast.net
Editorial e-mail: keirs1@comcast.net
Primary Website: reminderusa.net
Year Established: 1992
Avg Paid Circ: 11
Avg Free Circ: 14864
Audit By: CVC
Audit Date: 30.06.2017
Personnel: Karen Keirsey (Pub.); Patricia Haserick (Adv. Mgr); David Mitchell (Prod.); Patricia Catalano (Circ.)

EAST BRUNSWICK SENTINEL

Street address 1: 198 US Highway 9
Street address 2: Ste 100
Street address city: Manalapan
Street address state: NJ
Zip/Postal code: 07726-3073
General Phone: (732) 358-5200
General Fax: (732) 780-4678
General/National Adv. E-mail: gmsales@gmnews.com
Editorial e-mail: ebsent@newspapermediagroup.com
Primary Website: gmnews.com
Avg Paid Circ: 12
Avg Free Circ: 32428
Audit By: Sworn/Estimate/Non-Audited
Audit Date: 10.06.2019
Personnel: Ben Bannizzaro (Pub.); Robert Waitt (Adv. Dir.); Debra Parana (Circ. Mgr.); Gene Lennon (Prodn. Mgr.); Jennifer Amato (Mng. Ed.)

ECHOES-SENTINEL

Street address 1: 17-19 Morristown Rd
Street address city: Bernardsville
Street address state: NJ
Zip/Postal code: 07924-2372
General Phone: (908) 766-3900
General Fax: (908) 766-2773
Advertising Phone: 9087663900 ext 230
Editorial Phone: 9087663900 ext 241
General/National Adv. E-mail: advertising@Newjerseyhills.com
Display Adv. E-mail: lindap@newjerseyhills.com
Editorial e-mail: eparker@newjerseyhills.com
Primary Website: echoes-sentinel.com
Year Established: 1959
Avg Paid Circ: 1251
Avg Free Circ: 11
Audit By: Sworn/Estimate/Non-Audited
Audit Date: 10.06.2019
Personnel: Elizabeth K. Parker (Pub./Ed.); Stephen W. Parker (Pub.)
Parent company (for newspapers): New Jersey Hills Media Group

EDGEWATER VIEW

Street address 1: 210 Knickerbocker Rd
Street address city: Cresskill
Street address state: NJ
Zip/Postal code: 07626-1801
General Phone: (201) 894-6700
Advertising Phone: (973) 569-7269
Editorial Phone: (973) 569-7100
General/National Adv. E-mail: adhelp@northjersey.com
Display Adv. E-mail: marketplace@northjersey.com
Editorial e-mail: newsroom@northjersey.com
Primary Website: northjersey.com/edgewater
Year Established: 2004
Avg Free Circ: 6279
Audit By: Sworn/Estimate/Non-Audited
Audit Date: 10.06.2019
Personnel: Rick Green (Ed.)
Parent company (for newspapers): North Jersey Media Group Inc.

EDISON/NETUCHEN SENTINEL

Street address 1: 198 US Highway 9
Street address 2: Ste 100
Street address city: Manalapan
Street address state: NJ
Zip/Postal code: 07726-3073
General Phone: (732) 358-5200
General Fax: (732) 780-4678
General/National Adv. E-mail: gmsales@gmnews.com
Editorial e-mail: sentnorth@gmnews.com
Primary Website: gmnews.com
Avg Paid Circ: 7
Avg Free Circ: 24239
Audit By: Sworn/Estimate/Non-Audited
Audit Date: 10.06.2019
Personnel: Josef Ornegri (Adv. Mgr.); Kathy Herban (Circ. Mgr.); Gregory Bean (Ed.); Melissa Kress (Mng. Ed.); Gene Lennon (Prodn. Mgr.)

ELMER TIMES

Street address 1: 21 State St
Street address city: Elmer
Street address state: NJ
Zip/Postal code: 08318-2145
General Phone: (856) 358-6171
General/National Adv. E-mail: elmertimes@hotmail.com
Year Established: 1885
Avg Paid Circ: 1900
Audit By: Sworn/Estimate/Non-Audited
Audit Date: 10.06.2019
Personnel: Mark Foster (Pub.); Prestons Foster (Ed.)

ENGLEWOOD SUBURBANITE

Street address 1: 210 Knickerbocker Rd
Street address city: Cresskill
Street address state: NJ
Zip/Postal code: 07626-1801
General Phone: (201) 894-6700
Advertising Phone: (973) 569-7269
Editorial Phone: (973) 569-7100
General/National Adv. E-mail: adhelp@northjersey.com
Display Adv. E-mail: marketplace@northjersey.com
Editorial e-mail: newsroom@northjersey.com
Primary Website: northjersey.com
Avg Free Circ: 6435
Audit By: Sworn/Estimate/Non-Audited
Audit Date: 10.06.2019
Personnel: Rick Green (Ed.)
Parent company (for newspapers): North Jersey Media Group Inc.

EXAMINER

Street address 1: 198 US Highway 9
Street address 2: Ste 100
Street address city: Manalapan
Street address state: NJ
Zip/Postal code: 07726-3073
General Phone: (732) 358-5200
General Fax: (732) 780-4678
General/National Adv. E-mail: gmsales@gmnews.com
Editorial e-mail: examiner@gmnews.com
Primary Website: centraljersey.com
Avg Paid Circ: 4

Avg Free Circ: 7263
Audit By: Sworn/Estimate/Non-Audited
Audit Date: 10.06.2019
Personnel: Joe Eisele (Pub.)
Parent company (for newspapers): Newspaper Media Group-OOB

FLORHAM PARK EAGLE

Street address 1: 17-19 Morristown Rd
Street address city: Bernardsville
Street address state: NJ
Zip/Postal code: 07924-2372
General Phone: (908) 766-3900
Editorial Phone: (908) 766-3900 ext 246
General/National Adv. E-mail: advertising@Newjerseyhills.com
Display Adv. E-mail: lindap@newjerseyhills.com
Editorial e-mail: eparker@newjerseyhills.com
Primary Website: florhamparkeagle.com
Year Established: 1979
Avg Paid Circ: 1210
Avg Free Circ: 5
Audit By: Sworn/Estimate/Non-Audited
Audit Date: 10.06.2019
Personnel: Elizabeth K. Parker (Pub.); Stephen W. Parker (Pub.); Douglas McBride (Adv. Mgr.); Dave Nelson (Circ. Mgr.); Linda Campbell (Prodn. Mgr.); Christine Lee (Ed.)
Parent company (for newspapers): New Jersey Hills Media Group

FORT LEE SUBURBANITE

Street address 1: 210 Knickerbocker Rd
Street address city: Cresskill
Street address state: NJ
Zip/Postal code: 07626-1801
General Phone: (201) 894-6700
Advertising Phone: (973) 569-7269
Editorial Phone: (973) 569-7100
General/National Adv. E-mail: adhelp@northjersey.com
Display Adv. E-mail: marketplace@northjersey.com
Editorial e-mail: newsroom@northjersey.com
Primary Website: northjersey.com/fortlee
Year Established: 2003
Avg Free Circ: 17288
Audit By: Sworn/Estimate/Non-Audited
Audit Date: 10.06.2019
Personnel: Rick Green (Ed.)
Parent company (for newspapers): North Jersey Media Group Inc.

FRANKLIN LAKES/OAKLAND SUBURBAN NEWS

Street address 1: 41 Oak St
Street address city: Ridgewood
Street address state: NJ
Zip/Postal code: 07450-3805
General Phone: (201) 612-5415
General Fax: (201) 612-5421
General/National Adv. E-mail: suburbannews@northjersey.com
Editorial e-mail: green@northjersey.com
Primary Website: http://archive.northjersey.com/towns/franklin-lakes
Avg Free Circ: 7915
Audit By: Sworn/Estimate/Non-Audited
Audit Date: 10.06.2019
Personnel: Rick Green (Ed.)
Parent company (for newspapers): North Jersey Media Group Inc.

GLEN RIDGE VOICE

Street address 1: 1 Garret Mountain Plaza
Street address city: Woodland Park
Street address state: NJ
Zip/Postal code: 7424
General Phone: (973) 569-7000
General Fax: (973) 569-7268
Advertising Phone: (973) 233-5007
General/National Adv. E-mail: glenridgevoice@northjersey.com
Primary Website: northjersey.com/towns/glen-ridge
Year Established: 1995
Avg Paid Circ: 522
Audit By: AAM
Audit Date: 31.12.2017
Personnel: Rick Green (Ed.)
Parent company (for newspapers): Gannett - USA Today Network

GLEN ROCK GAZETTE

Street address 1: 41 Oak St
Street address city: Ridgewood
Street address state: NJ
Zip/Postal code: 07450-3805
General Phone: (201) 612-5432
General Fax: (201) 612-5436
General/National Adv. E-mail: glenrock@northjersey.com
Primary Website: northjersey.com
Avg Paid Circ: 0
Avg Free Circ: 3904
Audit By: Sworn/Estimate/Non-Audited
Audit Date: 10.06.2019
Personnel: Cindy Probert (Mng. Ed.); Janice Friedman (Pub.); Glenn Garvie (Vice Pres., Prodn.); Ellen Zitis (Adv. Mgr.); Rick Green (Ed.)
Parent company (for newspapers): North Jersey Media Group Inc.

GLOUCESTER CITY NEWS

Street address 1: 34 S Broadway
Street address city: Gloucester City
Street address state: NJ
Zip/Postal code: 08030-1710
General Phone: (856) 456-1199
General Fax: (856) 456-1330
General/National Adv. E-mail: gcneditor@verizon.net
Display Adv. E-mail: gcnads@verizon.net
Primary Website: gloucitynews.com
Year Established: 1927
Avg Paid Circ: 2900
Avg Free Circ: 200
Audit By: Sworn/Estimate/Non-Audited
Audit Date: 10.06.2019
Personnel: Albert J. Countryman (Pub./Ed.)

HACKENSACK CHRONICLE

Street address 1: 210 Knickerbocker Rd
Street address city: Cresskill
Street address state: NJ
Zip/Postal code: 07626-1801
General Phone: (201) 894-6700
Advertising Phone: (201) 894-6722
Editorial Phone: (973) 569-7100
General/National Adv. E-mail: adhelp@northjersey.com
Display Adv. E-mail: marketplace@northjersey.com
Editorial e-mail: newsroom@northjersey.com
Primary Website: northjersey.com/hackensack
Year Established: 2005
Avg Free Circ: 20139
Audit By: Sworn/Estimate/Non-Audited
Audit Date: 10.06.2019
Personnel: Rick Green (Ed.)
Parent company (for newspapers): North Jersey Media Group Inc.

HADDONFIELD SUN

Street address 1: 108 Kings Hwy E
Street address 2: Ste 300
Street address city: Haddonfield
Street address state: NJ
Zip/Postal code: 08033-2099
General Phone: (856) 779-3800
Advertising Phone: (856) 528-4844
General/National Adv. E-mail: jgallo@newspapermediagroup.com
Primary Website: haddonfieldsun.com
Audit By: Sworn/Estimate/Non-Audited
Audit Date: 10.06.2019
Personnel: Arlene Reyes (Adv. Dir.); Angela Smith (Mktg. Dir.)
Parent company (for newspapers): Newspaper Media Group-OOB

HAMILTON POST

Street address 1: 15 Princess Road
Street address 2: Suite K
Street address city: Lawrence
Street address state: NJ
Zip/Postal code: 08648
General Phone: (609) 396-1511
General Fax: (609) 844-0180
General/National Adv. E-mail: advertise@communitynews.org
Display Adv. E-mail: advertise@communitynews.org
Editorial e-mail: news@communitynews.org
Primary Website: centraljersey.com
Avg Paid Circ: 3725
Avg Free Circ: 6107
Audit By: Sworn/Estimate/Non-Audited
Audit Date: 10.06.2019
Personnel: Ed Gen (Ed.)

HAMMONTON NEWS

Street address 1: 891 E Oak Rd
Street address 2: Unit A
Street address city: Vineland
Street address state: NJ
Zip/Postal code: 08360-2311
General Phone: (609) 561-2300
General Fax: (609) 567-2249
Advertising Phone: (609) 561-2300
General/National Adv. E-mail: djclass@gannett.com
Primary Website: thehammontonnews.com
Avg Paid Circ: 5037
Audit By: Sworn/Estimate/Non-Audited
Audit Date: 10.06.2019
Personnel: Joe Calchi (Pub./Pres.); John Garrahan (Ed.)
Parent company (for newspapers): Gannett

HANOVER EAGLE

Street address 1: 17-19 Morristown Rd
Street address city: Bernardsville
Street address state: NJ
Zip/Postal code: 07924-2372
General Phone: (908) 766-3900
General Fax: (908) 766-2773
General/National Adv. E-mail: advertising@Newjerseyhills.com
Display Adv. E-mail: classified@recordernewspapers.com
Editorial e-mail: jlent@Newjerseyhills.com
Primary Website: recordernewspapers.com
Avg Paid Circ: 1645
Avg Free Circ: 18
Audit By: Sworn/Estimate/Non-Audited
Audit Date: 10.06.2019
Personnel: Elizabeth K. Parker (Pub.); Stephen W. Parker (Pub.); Dave Nelson (Circ. Mgr.); Jim Lent (Ed.)
Parent company (for newspapers): New Jersey Hills Media Group

HILLSBOROUGH BEACON

Street address 1: 421 US Highway 206
Street address city: Hillsborough
Street address state: NJ
Zip/Postal code: 08844-5097
General Phone: (609) 924-3244
General Fax: (609) 921-2714
Advertising Fax: (609) 921-2714
Editorial Phone: (609) 874-2163
Editorial Fax: (609) 924-3842
General/National Adv. E-mail: SBriggin@centraljersey.com
Editorial e-mail: amartins@centraljersey.com
Primary Website: hillsboroughbeacon.com
Year Established: 1955
Avg Paid Circ: 1298
Avg Free Circ: 2038
Audit By: Sworn/Estimate/Non-Audited
Audit Date: 10.06.2019
Personnel: James B. Kilgore (Pub); Andrew Martins (Mgr Ed)
Parent company (for newspapers): Newspaper Media Group-OOB

HOPEWELL VALLEY NEWS

Street address 1: 300 Witherspoon St
Street address city: Princeton
Street address state: NJ
Zip/Postal code: 08542-3401
General Phone: (609) 924-3244
General Fax: (609) 921-2714
Advertising Fax: (609) 921-2714
Editorial Fax: (609) 924-3842
General/National Adv. E-mail: scampo@centraljersey.com
Editorial e-mail: ahuston@centraljersey.com
Primary Website: hopewellvalleynews.com
Year Established: 1956
Avg Paid Circ: 167
Avg Free Circ: 3241
Audit By: Sworn/Estimate/Non-Audited
Audit Date: 10.06.2019
Personnel: Joe Eisele (Pub.); Aubrey Huston (Ed.)
Parent company (for newspapers): Newspaper Media Group-OOB

HUNTERDON COUNTY DEMOCRAT

Street address 1: 200 Route 31 North, Suite 200
Street address 2: Ste 200
Street address city: Flemington
Street address state: NJ
Zip/Postal code: 08822-5819
General Phone: (908) 782-4747
General Fax: (908) 782-6572
General/National Adv. E-mail: Akratzer@express-times.com
Display Adv. E-mail: Akratzer@express-times.com
Primary Website: njnpublishing.info
Year Established: 1847
Avg Paid Circ: 8786
Avg Free Circ: 8634
Audit By: AAM
Audit Date: 30.06.2017
Personnel: Judith A. Morgan (Circ. Mgr.); Rick Epstein (Mng. Ed.); Jay Langley (Ed.); Al Kratzer (Adv. Dir.); Dennis Carletta (VP, Circ.); Joseph Gioioso (Pres./Pub.)
Parent company (for newspapers): Advance Publications, Inc.

HUNTERDON OBSERVER

Street address 1: 8 Minneakoning Rd
Street address city: Flemington
Street address state: NJ
Zip/Postal code: 08822-5725
General Phone: (908) 782-4747
General Fax: (908) 782-6572
General/National Adv. E-mail: news@hcdemocrat.com
Primary Website: nj.com
Year Established: 1987
Avg Free Circ: 48256
Audit By: Sworn/Estimate/Non-Audited
Audit Date: 10.06.2019
Personnel: Judy Morgan (Circ. Mgr.); Jay Langley (Ed.); Rick Epstein (Mng. Ed.); Eileen Bickel (Pub./Adv. Mgr.)
Parent company (for newspapers): NJN Publishing

HUNTERDON REVIEW

Street address 1: 100 S Jefferson Rd
Street address 2: Ste 104
Street address city: Whippany
Street address state: NJ
Zip/Postal code: 07981-1009
General Phone: (908) 766-3900
General Fax: (908) 766-6365
Advertising Phone: (908) 766-3900 ext 234
Editorial Phone: (908) 7663-900 ext 255
General/National Adv. E-mail: info@newjerseyhills.com
Display Adv. E-mail: heatherh@newjerseyhills.com
Classified Adv. e-mail: theag@newjerseyhills.com
Editorial e-mail: wobrien@newjerseyhills.com
Primary Website: hunterdonreview.com
Year Established: 1868
Avg Paid Circ: 813
Avg Free Circ: 35
Audit By: Sworn/Estimate/Non-Audited
Audit Date: 10.06.2019
Personnel: Elizabeth K. Parker (Pub.); Stephen Parker (Pub.); Linda Campbell (Prod. Mgr.); Diane Howard; Philip Nardone (Ass. Exec. Ed.); Walter O'Brien (Editor, Hunterdon Review and Today in Hunterdon)
Parent company (for newspapers): New Jersey Hills Media Group

INDEPENDENT PRESS

Street address 1: 309 South St
Street address 2: Ste 1
Street address city: New Providence
Street address state: NJ
Zip/Postal code: 07974-2110
General Phone: (908) 464-1025
General Fax: (908) 464-9085
General/National Adv. E-mail: ipeditors@njnpublishing.com
Primary Website: nj.com/independentpress
Year Established: 1964
Avg Paid Circ: 496

Avg Free Circ: 34581
Audit By: Sworn/Estimate/Non-Audited
Audit Date: 10.06.2019
Personnel: Michael J. Kelly (Pub.); Lewis King (Circ. Mgr.); Patricia E. Meola (Ed.); Eileen Bickle (Adv. Sales)
Parent company (for newspapers): Advance Publications, Inc.

IRVINGTON HERALD

Street address 1: 1291 Stuyvesant Ave
Street address city: Union
Street address state: NJ
Zip/Postal code: 07083-3854
General Phone: (908) 686-7700
General Fax: (908) 686-4169
General/National Adv. E-mail: ads@thelocalsource.com
Display Adv. E-mail: class@thelocalsource.com
Editorial e-mail: editorial@thelocalsource.com
Primary Website: essexnewsdaily.com
Year Established: 1911
Avg Paid Circ: 455
Avg Free Circ: 46
Audit By: Sworn/Estimate/Non-Audited
Audit Date: 10.06.2019
Personnel: David Worrall (Pub.); Raymond Worrall (Gen. Mgr.); Nancy Worrall (Bus. Mgr.); Peter Worrall (Adv. Mgr.)
Parent company (for newspapers): Worrall Community Newspapers, Inc.

JEWISH VOICE

Street address 1: 1301 Springdale Rd
Street address 2: Ste 250
Street address city: Cherry Hill
Street address state: NJ
Zip/Postal code: 08003-2763
General Phone: (856) 751-9500 x1217
General Fax: (856) 489-8253
Editorial Phone: (856) 751-9500 x1237
General/National Adv. E-mail: jvoice@jfedsnj.org
Editorial e-mail: dportnoe@jfedsnj.org
Primary Website: jewishvoicesnj.org
Audit By: Sworn/Estimate/Non-Audited
Audit Date: 10.06.2019
Personnel: Stuart Abraham (Pub.); Howard Gases (Pub.); Judy Robinowitz (Adv. Mgr.); Lauren Silver (Ed.); Oscar Trugler (Prodn. Mgr.)
Parent company (for newspapers): Joseph Jacobs Organization

LAWRENCE GAZETTE - COMMUNITY NEWS SERVICE

Street address 1: 15 Princess Rd
Street address 2: Ste K
Street address city: Lawrence
Street address state: NJ
Zip/Postal code: 08648-2301
General Phone: (609)396-1511
General Fax: (609)844-0180
Editorial e-mail: news@mercerspace.com
Primary Website: mercerspace.com
Avg Free Circ: 16856
Audit By: Sworn/Estimate/Non-Audited
Audit Date: 10.06.2019
Personnel: Samantha Sciarrotta (Ed.)

LEDGER SOMERSET OBSERVER

Street address 1: 309 South St
Street address city: New Providence
Street address state: NJ
Zip/Postal code: 07974-2110
General Phone: (908) 575-6660
General Fax: (908) 575-6726
Primary Website: nj.com
Avg Paid Circ: 5797
Audit By: Sworn/Estimate/Non-Audited
Audit Date: 10.06.2019
Personnel: David Tomasini (Pub.); Craig Turpin (Mng. Ed.)
Parent company (for newspapers): Advance Publications, Inc.

LEONIA LIFE

Street address 1: 210 Knickerbocker Rd
Street address city: Cresskill
Street address state: NJ
Zip/Postal code: 07626-1801
General Phone: (201) 894-6700
Advertising Phone: (973) 569-7269
Editorial Phone: (973) 569-7100
General/National Adv. E-mail: adhelp@northjersey.com
Display Adv. E-mail: marketplace@northjersey.com
Editorial e-mail: newsroom@northjersey.com
Primary Website: northjersey.com/leonia
Year Established: 2005
Avg Free Circ: 3354
Audit By: Sworn/Estimate/Non-Audited
Audit Date: 10.06.2019
Personnel: Rick Green (Ed.)
Parent company (for newspapers): North Jersey Community Newspapers

LITTLE FERRY LOCAL

Street address 1: 210 Knickerbocker Rd
Street address city: Cresskill
Street address state: NJ
Zip/Postal code: 07626-1801
General Phone: (201) 894-6700
Advertising Phone: (973) 569-7269
Editorial Phone: (973) 569-7100
General/National Adv. E-mail: adhelp@northjersey.com
Display Adv. E-mail: marketplace@northjersey.com
Editorial e-mail: newsroom@northjersey.com
Primary Website: northjersey.com
Year Established: 2007
Avg Free Circ: 879
Audit By: Sworn/Estimate/Non-Audited
Audit Date: 10.06.2019
Personnel: Rick Green (Ed.)
Parent company (for newspapers): North Jersey Community Newspapers

MADISON EAGLE

Street address 1: 17-19 Morristown Rd
Street address city: Bernardsville
Street address state: NJ
Zip/Postal code: 07924-2372
General Phone: (908) 766-3900
General Fax: (908) 766-2773
Editorial Phone: (908) 766-3900 ext 240
General/National Adv. E-mail: advertising@Newjerseyhills.com
Display Adv. E-mail: lindap@newjerseyhills.com
Editorial e-mail: gherzog@Newjerseyhills.com
Primary Website: madisoneagle.com
Year Established: 1880
Avg Paid Circ: 2235
Avg Free Circ: 60
Audit By: Sworn/Estimate/Non-Audited
Audit Date: 10.06.2019
Personnel: Elizabeth K. Parker (Pub.); Stephen W. Parker (Pub.); Douglas McBride (Adv. Mgr.); Garry Herzog (Ed.)
Parent company (for newspapers): BH Media Group; New Jersey Hills Media Group

MAHWAH SUBURBAN NEWS

Street address 1: 41 Oak St
Street address city: Ridgewood
Street address state: NJ
Zip/Postal code: 07450-3805
General Phone: (201) 612-5400
General Fax: (201) 612-5421
General/National Adv. E-mail: suburbannews@northjersey.com
Primary Website: northjersey.com
Avg Free Circ: 7442
Audit By: Sworn/Estimate/Non-Audited
Audit Date: 10.06.2019
Personnel: Stephen Borg (Pres.); Ellen Zitis (Adv. Mgr.); Rick Green (Ed.)
Parent company (for newspapers): North Jersey Media Group Inc.

MARLTON SUN

Street address 1: 108 Kings Hwy E
Street address city: Haddonfield
Street address state: NJ
Zip/Postal code: 08033-2099
General Phone: (856) 779-3800
Advertising Phone: (856) 528-4844
General/National Adv. E-mail: jgallo@newspapermediagroup.com
Primary Website: marltonsun.com
Audit By: Sworn/Estimate/Non-Audited
Audit Date: 10.06.2019
Personnel: Arlene Reyes (Adv. Dir.); Angela Smith (Mktg. Dir.)
Parent company (for newspapers): Newspaper Media Group-OOB

MEDFORD SUN

Street address 1: 108 Kings Hwy E
Street address city: Haddonfield
Street address state: NJ
Zip/Postal code: 08033-2099
General Phone: (856) 779-3800
Advertising Phone: (856) 528-4844
General/National Adv. E-mail: jgallo@newspapermediagroup.com
Primary Website: medfordsun.com
Audit By: Sworn/Estimate/Non-Audited
Audit Date: 10.06.2019
Personnel: Arlene Reyes (Adv. Dir.); Angela Smith (Mktg. Dir.)
Parent company (for newspapers): Newspaper Media Group-OOB

MIDLAND PARK SUBURBAN NEWS

Street address 1: 41 Oak St
Street address city: Ridgewood
Street address state: NJ
Zip/Postal code: 07450-3805
General Phone: (201) 612-5415
General Fax: (201) 612-5421
General/National Adv. E-mail: suburbannews@northjersey.com
Editorial e-mail: green@northjersey.com
Primary Website: http://archive.northjersey.com/towns/midland-park
Avg Free Circ: 2400
Audit By: Sworn/Estimate/Non-Audited
Audit Date: 10.06.2019
Personnel: Rick Green (Ed.); Janice Friedman (Vice Pres./Pub.); Ellen Zitis (Adv. Mgr.)
Parent company (for newspapers): North Jersey Media Group Inc.

MOORESTOWN SUN

Street address 1: 108 Kings Hwy E
Street address city: Haddonfield
Street address state: NJ
Zip/Postal code: 08033-2099
General Phone: (856) 779-3800
Advertising Phone: (856) 528-4844
General/National Adv. E-mail: jgallo@newspapermediagroup.com
Primary Website: moorestownsun.com
Audit By: Sworn/Estimate/Non-Audited
Audit Date: 10.06.2019
Personnel: Arlene Reyes (Adv. Dir.); Angela Smith (Mktg. Dir.)
Parent company (for newspapers): Newspaper Media Group-OOB

MORRIS NEWS-BEE

Street address 1: 17-19 Morristown Rd
Street address city: Bernardsville
Street address state: NJ
Zip/Postal code: 07924-2372
General Phone: (908) 766-3900
General Fax: (908) 766-2773
General/National Adv. E-mail: advertising@Newjerseyhills.com
Display Adv. E-mail: classified@recordernewspapers.com
Editorial e-mail: jlent@Newjerseyhills.com
Primary Website: morrisnewsbee.com
Avg Paid Circ: 714
Avg Free Circ: 23
Audit By: Sworn/Estimate/Non-Audited
Audit Date: 10.06.2019
Personnel: Elizebeth Parker (Pub.); Douglas McBride (Adv. Mgr.); Jim Lent (Ed.)
Parent company (for newspapers): New Jersey Hills Media Group

MOUNT OLIVE CHRONICLE

Street address 1: 17-19 Morristown Rd
Street address city: Bernardsville
Street address state: NJ
Zip/Postal code: 07924-2372
General Phone: (908) 879-4100
General Fax: (908) 879-0799
Editorial Phone: (908) 766-3900 ext 251
General/National Adv. E-mail: advertising@Newjerseyhills.com
Display Adv. E-mail: classified@recordernewspapers.com
Editorial e-mail: pgarber@Newjerseyhills.com
Primary Website: recordernewspapers.com
Year Established: 1979
Avg Paid Circ: 2000
Avg Free Circ: 13
Audit By: Sworn/Estimate/Non-Audited
Audit Date: 10.06.2019
Personnel: Allison Spinella (Adv. Mgr.); David Nelson (Circ. Mgr.); Phil Garber (Ed.); Stephen Parker (Co-Pub.); Elizabeth Parker (Co-Pub.)
Parent company (for newspapers): New Jersey Hills Media Group

MR.

Street address 1: 447 Broadway
Street address city: Bayonne
Street address state: NJ
Zip/Postal code: 07002-3623
General Phone: (201) 798-7800
General Fax: (201) 798-0018
General/National Adv. E-mail: dunger@hudsonreporter.com
Display Adv. E-mail: dunger@hudsonreporter.com
Editorial e-mail: editorial@hudsonreporter.com
Primary Website: hudsonreporter.com
Year Established: 1983
Avg Paid Circ: 0
Avg Free Circ: 9823
Audit By: Sworn/Estimate/Non-Audited
Audit Date: 10.06.2019
Personnel: Lucha M. Malato (Pub.); David S. Unger (Adv. Dir.); Roberto Lopez (Circ. Mgr.); Caren Matzner (Ed.); Tish Kraszyk (Advt Mgr)

MT. LAUREL SUN

Street address 1: 108 Kings Hwy E
Street address city: Haddonfield
Street address state: NJ
Zip/Postal code: 08033-2099
General Phone: (856) 779-3800
Advertising Phone: (856) 528-4844
General/National Adv. E-mail: jgallo@newspapermediagroup.com
Primary Website: mtlaurelsun.com
Audit By: Sworn/Estimate/Non-Audited
Audit Date: 10.06.2019
Personnel: Arlene Reyes (Adv. Dir.); Angela Smith (Mktg. Dir.)
Parent company (for newspapers): Newspaper Media Group-OOB

NEIGHBOR NEWS

Street address 1: 100 Commons Way
Street address city: Rockaway
Street address state: NJ
Zip/Postal code: 07866-2038
General Phone: (973) 586-8190
Advertising Phone: (973) 586-8195
General/National Adv. E-mail: adhelp@northjersey.com
Primary Website: northjersey.com
Year Established: 1987
Avg Paid Circ: 0
Avg Free Circ: 35796
Audit By: Sworn/Estimate/Non-Audited
Audit Date: 10.06.2019
Personnel: Rick Green (Ed.)
Parent company (for newspapers): North Jersey Media Group Inc.

NEW JERSEY LAW JOURNAL

Street address 1: 24 Commerce St
Street address 2: Ste 425
Street address city: Newark
Street address state: NJ
Zip/Postal code: 07102-4005
General Phone: (973) 642-0075
General Fax: (973) 642-0920
Editorial Phone: (973) 854-2950
General/National Adv. E-mail: njladvertising@alm.com
Editorial e-mail: rfleury@alm.com
Primary Website: law.com/njlawjournal
Year Established: 1878

Audit By: Sworn/Estimate/Non-Audited
Audit Date: 10.06.2019
Personnel: Adam Sklanka (Dir. of Sales)
Parent company (for newspapers): ALM

NEWS TRANSCRIPT

Street address 1: 198 US Highway 9
Street address 2: Ste 100
Street address city: Manalapan
Street address state: NJ
Zip/Postal code: 07726-3073
General Phone: (732) 358-5210
General Fax: (732) 780-4678
General/National Adv. E-mail: gmsales@gmnews.com
Editorial e-mail: gmntnews@gmnews.com
Primary Website: gmnews.com
Avg Paid Circ: 13
Avg Free Circ: 38917
Audit By: Sworn/Estimate/Non-Audited
Audit Date: 10.06.2019
Personnel: Rick Feinblatt (Pub.); Debra Parana (Circ. Mgr.); Mark R. Rosman (Mng. Ed.); Gene Lennon (Dir., Prodn.)
Parent company (for newspapers): Newspaper Media Group-OOB

NEWS-RECORD OF MAPLEWOOD & SOUTH ORANGE

Street address 1: 1291 Stuyvesant Ave
Street address city: Union
Street address state: NJ
Zip/Postal code: 07083-3854
General Phone: (908) 686-7700
General Fax: (908) 686-4169
General/National Adv. E-mail: ads@thelocalsource.com
Display Adv. E-mail: class@thelocalsource.com
Editorial e-mail: editorial@thelocalsource.com
Primary Website: essexnewsdaily.com
Year Established: 1889
Avg Paid Circ: 6168
Avg Free Circ: 148
Audit By: Sworn/Estimate/Non-Audited
Audit Date: 10.06.2019
Personnel: David Worrall (Pub.); Nancy Worrall (Bus. Mgr.); Raymond Worrall (Gen. Mgr.); Peter Worrall (Adv. Mgr.)
Parent company (for newspapers): Worrall Community Newspapers, Inc.

NJTODAY.NET

Street address 1: PO Box 1061
Street address 2: Suite 503
Street address city: Rahway
Street address state: NJ
Zip/Postal code: 07065-1061
General Phone: (908) 352-3100
Advertising Phone: (732) 574-1200
Editorial Phone: (908) 352-3100
General/National Adv. E-mail: ads@njtoday.net
Display Adv. E-mail: sales@njtoday.net
Editorial e-mail: news@njtoday.net
Primary Website: njtoday.net
Year Established: 1822
Avg Paid Circ: 136656
Avg Free Circ: 3344
Audit By: Sworn/Estimate/Non-Audited
Audit Date: 10.06.2019
Personnel: Lisa McCormick (Pub.); Paul Hadsall (Ed.); Bob Milici (Assc. Pub./Dir. Sales Ops.)
Parent company (for newspapers): CMD Media LLC

NORTH/SOUTH BRUNSWICK SENTINEL

Street address 1: 198 Route 9 North
Street address 2: Suite 100
Street address city: Manalapan
Street address state: NJ
Zip/Postal code: 07726-3073
General Phone: (732) 358-5200
General Fax: (732) 780-4678
Advertising Phone: (732) 358-5200 x8282
General/National Adv. E-mail: jeisele@centraljersey.com
Display Adv. E-mail: gmclassified@newspapermediagroup.com
Editorial e-mail: nssent@newspapermediagroup.com
Primary Website: centraljersey.com/news/sentinel_north_south_brunswick
Avg Paid Circ: 8
Avg Free Circ: 15884
Audit By: Sworn/Estimate/Non-Audited
Audit Date: 10.06.2019
Personnel: Jennifer Amato (Mng. Ed.); Tony Naturale (Adv. Sales); Joe Eisele (Pub.)
Parent company (for newspapers): Newspaper Media Group-OOB

NORTHEAST TIMES

Street address 1: 1810 Underwood Blvd
Street address city: Delran
Street address state: NJ
Zip/Postal code: 08075
General Phone: (215) 354â€"3000
General/National Adv. E-mail: info@northeasttimes.com
Display Adv. E-mail: info@northeasttimes.com
Editorial e-mail: TWaring@bsmphilly.com
Primary Website: northeasttimes.com
Year Established: 1934
Avg Free Circ: 135286
Audit By: CVC
Audit Date: 30.03.2017
Personnel: Tom Waring (Ed.); ???? ????; Perry Corsetti (COO); Kevin Stuski (Sales); Joe Eisele; Melissa Mitman (Mng. Ed.)
Parent company (for newspapers): Review Publishing; Newspaper Media Group; ????

NORTHERN VALLEY SUBURBANITE

Street address 1: 210 Knickerbocker Rd
Street address city: Cresskill
Street address state: NJ
Zip/Postal code: 07626-1801
General Phone: (201) 894-6700
Advertising Phone: (973) 569-7269
Editorial Phone: (973) 569-7100
General/National Adv. E-mail: adhelp@northjersey.com
Display Adv. E-mail: marketplace@northjersey.com
Editorial e-mail: newsroom@northjersey.com
Primary Website: northjersey.com
Avg Paid Circ: 0
Avg Free Circ: 13116
Audit By: Sworn/Estimate/Non-Audited
Audit Date: 10.06.2019
Personnel: Rick Green (Ed.)
Parent company (for newspapers): North Jersey Media Group Inc.

NUTLEY JOURNAL

Street address 1: 1291 Stuyvesant Ave
Street address city: Union
Street address state: NJ
Zip/Postal code: 07083-3854
General Phone: (908) 686-7700
General Fax: (908) 686-4169
General/National Adv. E-mail: ads@thelocalsource.com
Display Adv. E-mail: class@thelocalsource.com
Editorial e-mail: essexcty@thelocalsource.com
Primary Website: essexnewsdaily.com
Year Established: 1982
Avg Paid Circ: 270
Avg Free Circ: 5122
Audit By: Sworn/Estimate/Non-Audited
Audit Date: 10.06.2019
Personnel: David Worrall (Pub.); Raymond Worrall (Gen. Mgr.); Peter Worrall (Adv. Mgr.); Nancy Worrall (Controller)
Parent company (for newspapers): Worrall Community Newspapers, Inc.

NUTLEY SUN

Street address 1: 1 Garret Mountain Plaza
Street address city: Woodland Park
Street address state: NJ
Zip/Postal code: 7424
General Phone: (973) 569-7000
General Fax: (973) 569-7268
Advertising Phone: (973) 233-5007
General/National Adv. E-mail: nutleysun@northjersey.com
Primary Website: northjersey.com/towns/nutley
Year Established: 1902
Avg Paid Circ: 2174
Audit By: AAM
Audit Date: 31.12.2017
Personnel: Rick Green (Ed.)
Parent company (for newspapers): Gannett - USA Today Network

OBSERVER TRIBUNE

Street address 1: 17-19 Morristown Rd
Street address city: Bernardsville
Street address state: NJ
Zip/Postal code: 07924-2372
General Phone: (908) 879-4100
General Fax: (908) 879-0799
Editorial Phone: (908) 766-3900 ext 251
General/National Adv. E-mail: advertising@Newjerseyhills.com
Display Adv. E-mail: classified@recordernewspapers.com
Editorial e-mail: pgarber@Newjerseyhills.com
Primary Website: recordernewspapers.com
Year Established: 1936
Avg Paid Circ: 4501
Avg Free Circ: 53
Audit By: Sworn/Estimate/Non-Audited
Audit Date: 10.06.2019
Personnel: Dave Nelson (Circ. Mgr.); Phil Garber (Ed.); Elizabeth Parker (Co-Pub.); Stephen Parker (Co-Pub.)
Parent company (for newspapers): New Jersey Hills Media Group

OCEAN CITY SENTINEL

Street address 1: 801 Asbury Ave
Street address 2: Ste 310
Street address city: Ocean City
Street address state: NJ
Zip/Postal code: 08226-3641
General Phone: (609) 399-5411
Advertising Phone: (609) 399-1220
Advertising Fax: (609) 399-9304
Editorial Phone: (609) 399-5411
Editorial Fax: (609) 399-0416
Primary Website: ocsentinel.com
Year Established: 1880
Avg Paid Circ: 10000
Avg Free Circ: 15000
Audit By: Sworn/Estimate/Non-Audited
Audit Date: 10.06.2019
Personnel: David Nahan (Editor and Publisher)
Parent company (for newspapers): Sample Media, Inc.

OUR TOWN

Street address 1: 19 W Pleasant Ave
Street address city: Maywood
Street address state: NJ
Zip/Postal code: 07607-1320
General Phone: (201) 843-5700
General Fax: (201) 843-5781
General/National Adv. E-mail: rtownmaywoodrp@aol.com
Display Adv. E-mail: rtownmaywoodrp@aol.com
Editorial e-mail: news@ourtownnews.com
Primary Website: ourtownnewsonline.com
Year Established: 1948
Avg Paid Circ: 3800
Avg Free Circ: 90
Audit By: Sworn/Estimate/Non-Audited
Audit Date: 10.06.2019
Personnel: Camille Hornes (Ed.); James Hornes (Ed.)

PALMYRA SUN

Street address 1: 108 Kings Hwy E
Street address city: Haddonfield
Street address state: NJ
Zip/Postal code: 08033-2099
General Phone: (856) 779-3800
Advertising Phone: (856) 528-4844
General/National Adv. E-mail: jgallo@newspapermediagroup.com
Primary Website: palmyrasun.com
Audit By: Sworn/Estimate/Non-Audited
Audit Date: 10.06.2019
Personnel: Arlene Reyes (Adv. Dir.); Angela Smith (Mktg. Dir.)
Parent company (for newspapers): Newspaper Media Group-OOB

PARSIPPANY LIFE

Street address 1: 100 Commons Way
Street address city: Rockaway
Street address state: NJ
Zip/Postal code: 07866-2038
General Phone: (973) 586-8190
General Fax: (973) 586-8199
General/National Adv. E-mail: parsippany@northjersey.com
Primary Website: parsippanylife.com
Avg Paid Circ: 0
Avg Free Circ: 12060
Audit By: Sworn/Estimate/Non-Audited
Audit Date: 10.06.2019
Personnel: Rick Green (Ed.)
Parent company (for newspapers): North Jersey Media Group Inc.

PASCACK VALLEY COMMUNITY LIFE

Street address 1: 372 Kinderkamack Rd
Street address 2: Ste 5
Street address city: Westwood
Street address state: NJ
Zip/Postal code: 07675-1657
General Phone: (201) 664-2501
General Fax: (201) 664-1332
General/National Adv. E-mail: pvcommunitylife@northjersey.com
Avg Paid Circ: 0
Avg Free Circ: 11024
Audit By: Sworn/Estimate/Non-Audited
Audit Date: 10.06.2019
Personnel: Rick Green (Ed.)
Parent company (for newspapers): North Jersey Media Group Inc.

PASSAIC VALLEY TODAY

Street address 1: 1 Garret Mountain Plz
Street address city: Woodland Park
Street address state: NJ
Zip/Postal code: 07424-3320
General Phone: (973) 569-7377
Advertising Phone: (973) 569-7201
Editorial Phone: (973) 569-7393
General/National Adv. E-mail: adhelp@northjersey.com
Primary Website: northjersey.com
Avg Paid Circ: 0
Avg Free Circ: 11187
Audit By: Sworn/Estimate/Non-Audited
Audit Date: 10.06.2019
Personnel: Rick Green (Ed.)
Parent company (for newspapers): North Jersey Media Group Inc.

RAMSEY SUBURBAN NEWS

Street address 1: 41 Oak St
Street address city: Ridgewood
Street address state: NJ
Zip/Postal code: 07450-3805
General Phone: (201) 612-5416
General Fax: (201) 612-5421
Advertising Phone: (973) 569-7269
Editorial Phone: (973) 569-7100
General/National Adv. E-mail: adhelp@northjersey.com
Display Adv. E-mail: marketplace@northjersey.com
Editorial e-mail: green@northjersey.com
Primary Website: northjersey.com/ramsey
Avg Free Circ: 3615
Audit By: Sworn/Estimate/Non-Audited
Audit Date: 10.06.2019
Personnel: Rick Green (Ed.)
Parent company (for newspapers): North Jersey Media Group Inc.

RECORD-TRANSCRIPT OF EAST ORANGE AND ORANGE

Street address 1: 1291 Stuyvesant Ave
Street address city: Union
Street address state: NJ
Zip/Postal code: 07083-3854
General Phone: (908) 686-7700
General Fax: (908) 686-4169
General/National Adv. E-mail: ads@thelocalsource.com
Display Adv. E-mail: class@thelocalsource.com
Editorial e-mail: editorial@thelocalsource.com
Primary Website: essexnewsdaily.com
Year Established: 1899
Avg Paid Circ: 2967
Avg Free Circ: 86

Audit By: Sworn/Estimate/Non-Audited
Audit Date: 10.06.2019
Personnel: David Worrall (Pub.); Raymond Worrall (Gen. Mgr.); Peter Worrall (Adv. Mgr.); Nancy Worrall (Controller)
Parent company (for newspapers): Worrall Community Newspapers, Inc.

REGISTER-NEWS

Street address 1: 300 Witherspoon St
Street address city: Princeton
Street address state: NJ
Zip/Postal code: 08542-3401
General Phone: (609) 924-3244
General Fax: (609) 924-3842
Advertising Fax: (609) 921-2714
Editorial e-mail: ahuston@centraljersey.com
Primary Website: registernews.com
Avg Paid Circ: 4662
Avg Free Circ: 54
Audit By: Sworn/Estimate/Non-Audited
Audit Date: 10.06.2019
Personnel: Aubrey Huston (Ed.); Joe Eisele (Pub.)

REPORTE HISPANO

Street address 1: 42 Dorann Ave
Street address city: New Jersey
Street address state: NJ
Zip/Postal code: 08540-3906
General Phone: (609) 933-1400
General Fax: (609) 924-5392
Advertising Phone: 6099331400
Advertising Fax: (609) 924-5392
Editorial Phone: (609) 933-7367
Editorial Fax: (609) 924-5392
General/National Adv. E-mail: caramarcano@reportehispano.com
Display Adv. E-mail: Publisher@ReporteHispano.com
Editorial e-mail: Kleibeel@ReporteHispano.com
Primary Website: reportehispano.com
Mthly Avg Views: 250000
Mthly Avg Unique Visitors: 250000
Year Established: 2006
Avg Paid Circ: 0
Avg Free Circ: 54900
Audit By: CAC
Audit Date: 15.10.2017
Personnel: Cara Marcano (Pub.); Kleibeel Marcano (Ed.)

RIDGEFIELD PARK PATRIOT

Street address 1: 210 Knickerbocker Rd
Street address city: Cresskill
Street address state: NJ
Zip/Postal code: 07626-1801
General Phone: (201) 894-6700
Advertising Phone: (973) 569-7269
Editorial Phone: (973) 569-7100
General/National Adv. E-mail: adhelp@northjersey.com
Display Adv. E-mail: marketplace@northjersey.com
Editorial e-mail: newsroom@northjersey.com
Primary Website: northjersey.com
Year Established: 2006
Avg Free Circ: 978
Audit By: Sworn/Estimate/Non-Audited
Audit Date: 10.06.2019
Personnel: Rick Green (Ed.)
Parent company (for newspapers): North Jersey Community Newspapers

ROXBURY REGISTER

Street address 1: 17-19 Morristown Rd
Street address city: Bernardsville
Street address state: NJ
Zip/Postal code: 07924-2372
General Phone: (908) 766-3900
General Fax: (908) 766-1083
Editorial Phone: (908) 766-3900 ext 223
General/National Adv. E-mail: advertising@Newjerseyhills.com
Display Adv. E-mail: lindap@newjerseyhills.com
Editorial e-mail: mcondon@Newjerseyhills.com
Primary Website: recordernewspapers.com
Year Established: 1988
Avg Paid Circ: 1213
Avg Free Circ: 12
Audit By: Sworn/Estimate/Non-Audited
Audit Date: 10.06.2019
Personnel: Elizabeth K. Parker (Pub.); Stephen W. Parker (Pub.); Michael Condon (Ed.)
Parent company (for newspapers): New Jersey Hills Media Group

SECAUCUS REPORTER

Street address 1: 447 Broadway
Street address city: Bayonne
Street address state: NJ
Zip/Postal code: 07002-3623
General Phone: (201) 798-7800
General Fax: (201) 798-0018
General/National Adv. E-mail: dunger@hudsonreporter.com
Display Adv. E-mail: classified@hudsonreporter.com
Editorial e-mail: editorial@hudsonreporter.com
Primary Website: hudsonreporter.com
Year Established: 1983
Avg Paid Circ: 0
Avg Free Circ: 33028
Audit By: Sworn/Estimate/Non-Audited
Audit Date: 10.06.2019
Personnel: Lucha Malato (Co-Pub.); David S. Unger (Co-Pub); Roberto Lopez (Circ. Mgr.); Caren Matzner (Ed.)
Parent company (for newspapers): Hudson Reporter Associates, Lp

SHAMONG SUN

Street address 1: 108 Kings Hwy E
Street address city: Haddonfield
Street address state: NJ
Zip/Postal code: 08033-2099
General Phone: (856) 779-3800
Advertising Phone: (856) 528-4844
General/National Adv. E-mail: jgallo@newspapermediagroup.com
Primary Website: shamongsun.com
Audit By: Sworn/Estimate/Non-Audited
Audit Date: 10.06.2019
Personnel: Arlene Reyes (Adv. Dir.); Angela Smith (Mktg. Dir.)
Parent company (for newspapers): Newspaper Media Group-OOB

SHORE NEWS TODAY

Street address 1: 507 Route US 9 S
Street address city: Marmora
Street address state: NJ
Zip/Postal code: 08223-1258
General Phone: (609) 624-8900
Primary Website: shorenewstoday.com
Audit By: Sworn/Estimate/Non-Audited
Audit Date: 10.06.2019
Personnel: Anthony Falduto (Gen. Mgr.)
Parent company (for newspapers): BH Media Group

SICKLERVILLE SUN

Street address 1: 108 Kings Hwy E
Street address city: Haddonfield
Street address state: NJ
Zip/Postal code: 08033-2099
General Phone: (856) 779-3800
Advertising Phone: (856) 528-4844
General/National Adv. E-mail: jgallo@newspapermediagroup.com
Primary Website: sicklervillesun.com
Audit By: Sworn/Estimate/Non-Audited
Audit Date: 10.06.2019
Personnel: Arlene Reyes (Adv. Dir.); Angela Smith (Mktg. Dir.)
Parent company (for newspapers): Newspaper Media Group-OOB

SNJ TODAY NEWSPAPER

Street address 1: 600 G St
Street address city: Millville
Street address state: NJ
Zip/Postal code: 08332-2111
General Phone: (856) 327-8800
General Fax: (856) 457-7816
General/National Adv. E-mail: dcongdon@snjtoday.com
Display Adv. E-mail: dfrie@snjtoday.com
Editorial e-mail: news@snjtoday.com
Primary Website: snjtoday.com
Year Established: 2008
Avg Free Circ: 23000
Audit By: Sworn/Estimate/Non-Audited
Audit Date: 10.06.2019
Personnel: Jeffrey Schwachter (Ed.)
Parent company (for newspapers): SNJ Today

SOUTH BERGENITE

Street address 1: PO Box 471
Street address city: Little Falls
Street address state: NJ
Zip/Postal code: 07424-0471
General Phone: (201) 933-1166
General Fax: (201) 933-5496
Advertising Phone: (800) 472-0158
Advertising Fax: (973) 569-7440
General/National Adv. E-mail: adhelp@northjersey.com
Primary Website: northjersey.com/southbergen
Year Established: 1970
Avg Paid Circ: 0
Avg Free Circ: 30071
Audit By: Sworn/Estimate/Non-Audited
Audit Date: 10.06.2019
Personnel: Rick Green (Ed.)
Parent company (for newspapers): North Jersey Media Group Inc.

SOUTH PHILLY REVIEW

Street address 1: 2 Executive Campus
Street address 2: Ste 400
Street address city: Cherry Hill
Street address state: NJ
Zip/Postal code: 08002-4102
General Phone: (215) 336-2500
General Fax: (215) 336-1112
General/National Adv. E-mail: bchamberlain@bsmphilly.com
Display Adv. E-mail: bchamberlain@bsmphilly.com
Editorial e-mail: news@southphillyreview.com
Primary Website: southphillyreview.com
Year Established: 1947
Avg Paid Circ: 30
Avg Free Circ: 56555
Audit By: Sworn/Estimate/Non-Audited
Audit Date: 10.06.2019
Personnel: John C. Gallo (Pub./COO); Perry Corsetti; Brandon Chamberlain (GM); Tom Beck (Ed.)
Parent company (for newspapers): Review Publishing

SOUTH PLAINFIELD OBSERVER

Street address 1: 1110 Hamilton Blvd
Street address 2: Ste 1B
Street address city: South Plainfield
Street address state: NJ
Zip/Postal code: 07080-2031
General Phone: (908) 668-0010
General Fax: (908) 669-8819
Advertising Phone: (908) 668-0010
Advertising Fax: (908) 668-8819
Editorial Phone: (908) 668-0010
General/National Adv. E-mail: spobserver@comcast.net
Display Adv. E-mail: spobserver@comcast.net
Editorial e-mail: spobserver@comcast.net
Year Established: 1997
Avg Paid Circ: 2500
Audit By: Sworn/Estimate/Non-Audited
Audit Date: 24.11.2021
Personnel: Nancy Grennier (Pub.)
Parent company (for newspapers): G&G Graphics Inc.; G&G Graphics Inc.

SPARTA INDEPENDENT

Street address 1: 1A Main St
Street address city: Sparta
Street address state: NJ
Zip/Postal code: 07871-1909
General Phone: (973) 300-0890
General Fax: (973) 726-0018
Editorial e-mail: njoffice@strausnews.com
Primary Website: strausnews.com
Year Established: 1986
Avg Free Circ: 7000
Audit By: USPS
Audit Date: //2024
Personnel: Jeanne Straus (Pres.); Voelker Sheila (Strategic Marketing Executive); Mike Zummo (Mng. Ed.)
Parent company (for newspapers): Straus News

STAR-GAZETTE

Street address 1: 8 Minneakoning Rd
Street address city: Flemington
Street address state: NJ
Zip/Postal code: 08822-5725
General Phone: (908) 782-6572
General Fax: (908) 782-6572
General/National Adv. E-mail: news@hcdemocrat.com
Primary Website: nj.com
Avg Paid Circ: 336
Avg Free Circ: 4
Audit By: Sworn/Estimate/Non-Audited
Audit Date: 10.06.2019
Personnel: Craig Turpin (Exec. Ed.)
Parent company (for newspapers): Advance Publications, Inc.

SUBURBAN

Street address 1: 198 US Highway 9
Street address 2: Ste 100
Street address city: Manalapan
Street address state: NJ
Zip/Postal code: 07726-3073
General Phone: (732) 358-5200
General Fax: (732) 780-4678
General/National Adv. E-mail: gmsales@gmnews.com
Editorial e-mail: ebsent@gmnews.com
Primary Website: gmnews.com
Avg Paid Circ: 9
Avg Free Circ: 29685
Audit By: Sworn/Estimate/Non-Audited
Audit Date: 10.06.2019
Personnel: Ben Cannizzaro (Pub.); Kate Rochelle (Promo. Coord.); Rich Klypka (Circ. Mgr.); Brian Donohue (Mng. Ed.); Gene Lennon (Prodn. Mgr.)
Parent company (for newspapers): Newspaper Media Group-OOB

SUBURBAN NEWS

Street address 1: 309 South St
Street address 2: Ste 1
Street address city: New Providence
Street address state: NJ
Zip/Postal code: 07974-2110
General Phone: (908) 464-1025
General Fax: (908) 464-9085
General/National Adv. E-mail: suburbannews@northjersey.com
Year Established: 1948
Avg Paid Circ: 14
Avg Free Circ: 63972
Audit By: Sworn/Estimate/Non-Audited
Audit Date: 10.06.2019
Personnel: Eileen Bickel (Vice Pres., Adv.); Carol Hladun (Adv. Dir.); Ted Meadowcroft (Circ. Mgr.); Ellen Dooley (Ed.); Russ Crespolini (Sports Ed.)
Parent company (for newspapers): Advance Publications, Inc.

SUBURBAN NEWS

Street address 1: 41 Oak St
Street address city: Ridgewood
Street address state: NJ
Zip/Postal code: 07450-3805
Advertising Phone: (973) 569-7269
Editorial Phone: (973) 569-7100
General/National Adv. E-mail: adhelp@northjersey.com
Display Adv. E-mail: marketplace@northjersey.com
Editorial e-mail: green@northjersey.com
Primary Website: northjersey.com/ridgewood
Avg Paid Circ: 0
Avg Free Circ: 33730
Audit By: Sworn/Estimate/Non-Audited
Audit Date: 10.06.2019
Personnel: Rick Green (Ed.)
Parent company (for newspapers): North Jersey Media Group Inc.

SUBURBAN TRENDS

Street address 1: 505 Main St
Street address city: Butler
Street address state: NJ
Zip/Postal code: 07405-1095
General Phone: (973) 283-5600
Advertising Phone: (973) 569-7269

Editorial Phone: (973) 569-7100
General/National Adv. E-mail: adhelp@northjersey.com
Display Adv. E-mail: marketplace@northjersey.com
Editorial e-mail: newsroom@northjersey.com
Primary Website: northjersey.com
Avg Paid Circ: 4201
Audit By: AAM
Audit Date: 31.12.2017
Personnel: Rick Green (Ed.)
Parent company (for newspapers): Gannett - USA Today Network

TABERNACLE SUN

Street address 1: 108 Kings Hwy E
Street address city: Haddonfield
Street address state: NJ
Zip/Postal code: 08033-2099
General Phone: (856) 779-3800
Advertising Phone: (856) 528-4844
General/National Adv. E-mail: jgallo@newspapermediagroup.com
Primary Website: tabernaclesun.com
Audit By: Sworn/Estimate/Non-Audited
Audit Date: 10.06.2019
Personnel: Arlene Reyes (Adv. Dir.); Angela Smith (Mktg. Dir.)
Parent company (for newspapers): Newspaper Media Group-OOB

TEANECK SUBURBANITE

Street address 1: 210 Knickerbocker Rd
Street address city: Cresskill
Street address state: NJ
Zip/Postal code: 07626-1801
General Phone: (201) 894-6700
Advertising Phone: (973) 569-7269
Editorial Phone: (973) 569-7100
General/National Adv. E-mail: adhelp@northjersey.com
Display Adv. E-mail: marketplace@northjersey.com
Editorial e-mail: newsroom@northjersey.com
Primary Website: northjersey.com/teaneck
Avg Paid Circ: 0
Avg Free Circ: 13651
Audit By: Sworn/Estimate/Non-Audited
Audit Date: 10.06.2019
Personnel: Rick Green (Ed.)
Parent company (for newspapers): North Jersey Media Group Inc.

TENAFLY SUBURBANITE

Street address 1: 210 Knickerbocker Rd
Street address city: Cresskill
Street address state: NJ
Zip/Postal code: 07626-1801
General Phone: (201) 894-6700
Advertising Phone: (973) 569-7269
Editorial Phone: (973) 569-7100
General/National Adv. E-mail: adhelp@northjersey.com
Display Adv. E-mail: marketplace@northjersey.com
Editorial e-mail: newsroom@northjersey.com
Primary Website: northjersey.com
Avg Free Circ: 4267
Audit By: Sworn/Estimate/Non-Audited
Audit Date: 10.06.2019
Personnel: Rick Green (Ed.)
Parent company (for newspapers): North Jersey Media Group Inc.

THE BEACON

Street address 1: 300 Witherspoon St
Street address city: Princeton
Street address state: NJ
Zip/Postal code: 08542-3401
General Phone: (609) 924-3244
General Fax: (609) 921-2714
Advertising Fax: (609) 921-2714
Editorial Fax: (609) 924-3842
General/National Adv. E-mail: msamano@centraljersey.com
Display Adv. E-mail: dscarpati@centraljersey.com
Editorial e-mail: ahuston@centraljersey.com
Primary Website: beaconnews.com
Year Established: 1845
Avg Paid Circ: 768
Audit By: Sworn/Estimate/Non-Audited
Audit Date: 10.06.2019
Personnel: Aubrey Huston (Ed.); Joe Eisele (Pub.)
Parent company (for newspapers): Newspaper Media Group-OOB

THE BERLIN SUN

Street address 1: 108 Kings Hwy E
Street address 2: Ste 300
Street address city: Haddonfield
Street address state: NJ
Zip/Postal code: 08033-2099
General Phone: (856) 779-3800
Advertising Phone: (856) 528-4844
General/National Adv. E-mail: jgallo@newspapermediagroup.com
Primary Website: theberlinsun.com
Audit By: Sworn/Estimate/Non-Audited
Audit Date: 10.06.2019
Personnel: Arlene Reyes (Adv. Dir.); Angela Smith (Mktg. Dir.)
Parent company (for newspapers): Newspaper Media Group-OOB

THE CENTRAL RECORD

Street address 1: 32 S Main St
Street address 2: Ste A
Street address city: Medford
Street address state: NJ
Zip/Postal code: 08055-2455
General Phone: (609) 654-5000
General Fax: (609) 654-0391
Editorial Phone: (609) 654-5000 ext 18
Editorial e-mail: news@medfordcentralrecord.com
Primary Website: southjerseylocalnews.com
Year Established: 1896
Avg Paid Circ: 1174
Audit By: Sworn/Estimate/Non-Audited
Audit Date: 10.06.2019
Personnel: John Berry (Mng. Ed.)
Parent company (for newspapers): Digital First Media

THE CITIZEN

Street address 1: 17-19 Morristown Rd
Street address city: Bernardsville
Street address state: NJ
Zip/Postal code: 07924-2372
General Phone: (908) 766-3900
General Fax: (908) 766-1083
Advertising Phone: (908) 766-3900
Advertising Fax: (908) 766-6365
Editorial Phone: (908) 766-3900 ext 241
General/National Adv. E-mail: advertising@newjerseyhills.com
Display Adv. E-mail: nicoleb@Newjerseyhills.com
Editorial e-mail: mcondon@newjerseyhills.com
Primary Website: recordernewspapers.com
Year Established: 1946
Avg Paid Circ: 2345
Avg Free Circ: 107
Audit By: Sworn/Estimate/Non-Audited
Audit Date: 10.06.2019
Personnel: Elizabeth K. Parker; Stephen Parker (Pub.); Jerry O'Donnell; Linda Campbell; Philip Nardone; Diane Howard; Mike Condon (Ed.)
Parent company (for newspapers): New Jersey Hills Media Group

THE COAST STAR

Street address 1: 13 Broad St
Street address city: Manasquan
Street address state: NJ
Zip/Postal code: 08736-2906
General Phone: (732) 223-0076
General Fax: (732) 223-8212
General/National Adv. E-mail: publisher@starnewsgroup.com
Primary Website: starnewsgroup.com
Year Established: 1877
Avg Paid Circ: 12500
Audit By: Sworn/Estimate/Non-Audited
Audit Date: 10.06.2019
Personnel: James M. Manser (Pub.); Frederick Tuccillo (Ed.); Alison Manser Ertl (General Manager)

THE CURRENT

Street address 1: 206 W Parkway Dr
Street address city: Egg Harbor Township
Street address state: NJ
Zip/Postal code: 08234-5106
General Phone: (609) 383-8994
General Fax: (609) 383-0056
General/National Adv. E-mail: current@shorenewstoday.com
Primary Website: shorenewstoday.com
Avg Free Circ: 13957
Audit By: Sworn/Estimate/Non-Audited
Audit Date: 10.06.2019
Personnel: Bill Barlow (Ed.)
Parent company (for newspapers): Catamaran Media

THE GAZETTE

Street address 1: 12-38 River Rd
Street address city: Fair Lawn
Street address state: NJ
Zip/Postal code: 07410-1802
General Phone: (201) 791-8994
General Fax: (201) 794-3259
Advertising Phone: (973) 569-7263
Advertising Fax: (973) 569-7259
General/National Adv. E-mail: thegazette@northjersey.com
Year Established: 1948
Avg Paid Circ: 0
Avg Free Circ: 15918
Audit By: Sworn/Estimate/Non-Audited
Audit Date: 10.06.2019
Personnel: Richard Mardekian (Ed.); Ellen Zitis (Ad. Director); Janice Friedman (Pub.)
Parent company (for newspapers): North Jersey Media Group

THE GAZETTE

Street address 1: 1000 W Washington Ave
Street address city: Pleasantville
Street address state: NJ
Zip/Postal code: 08232-3861
General Phone: (609) 624-8900
General Fax: (609) 624-3470
General/National Adv. E-mail: info@shorenewstoday.com
Primary Website: archive.northjersey.com/towns/the-gazette
Avg Paid Circ: 5
Avg Free Circ: 6968
Audit By: Sworn/Estimate/Non-Audited
Audit Date: 10.06.2019
Personnel: Bill Barlow (Ed.)
Parent company (for newspapers): Catamaran Media

THE GLEN RIDGE PAPER

Street address 1: 1291 Stuyvesant Ave
Street address city: Union
Street address state: NJ
Zip/Postal code: 07083-3854
General Phone: (908) 686-7700
General Fax: (908) 686-4169
General/National Adv. E-mail: ads@thelocalsource.com
Display Adv. E-mail: class@thelocalsource.com
Editorial e-mail: editorial@thelocalsource.com
Primary Website: essexnewsdaily.com
Year Established: 1935
Avg Paid Circ: 679
Audit By: Sworn/Estimate/Non-Audited
Audit Date: 10.06.2019
Personnel: David Worrall (Pub.); Raymond Worrall (Gen. Mgr.); Peter Worrall (Adv. Mgr.); Nancy Worrall (Controller)
Parent company (for newspapers): Worrall Community Newspapers, Inc.

THE HOBOKEN REPORTER

Street address 1: 447 Broadway
Street address city: Bayonne
Street address state: NJ
Zip/Postal code: 07002-3623
General Phone: (201) 798-7800
General Fax: (201) 798-7800
Advertising Phone: (201) 798-0018
Advertising Fax: (201) 798-0018
General/National Adv. E-mail: dunger@hudsonreporter.com
Display Adv. E-mail: tishk@hudsonreporter.com
Classified Adv. e-mail: tishk@hudsonreporter.com
Editorial e-mail: editorial@hudsonreporter.com
Primary Website: hudsonreporter.com
Year Established: 1983
Avg Paid Circ: 0
Avg Free Circ: 11925
Audit By: Sworn/Estimate/Non-Audited
Audit Date: 10.06.2019
Personnel: Lucha M. Malato (Pub.); David S. Unger (Pub.); Tish Kraszyk (Adv. Mgr.); Roberto Lopez (Circ. Mgr.); Caren Lissner (Ed.)
Parent company (for newspapers): Hudson Reporter Associates, Lp

THE HUB

Street address 1: 198 US Highway 9
Street address 2: Ste 100
Street address city: Manalapan
Street address state: NJ
Zip/Postal code: 07726-3073
General Phone: (732) 358-5200
General Fax: (732) 780-4678
General/National Adv. E-mail: gmsales@gmnews.com
Editorial e-mail: hubeditor@gmnews.com
Primary Website: gmnews.com
Avg Paid Circ: 6
Avg Free Circ: 17427
Audit By: Sworn/Estimate/Non-Audited
Audit Date: 10.06.2019
Personnel: Robert Waitt (Adv. Dir.); Gloria Stravelli (Mng. Ed.)
Parent company (for newspapers): Newspaper Media Group-OOB

THE INDEPENDENT

Street address 1: 198 Route 9 North
Street address 2: Suite 100
Street address city: Manalapan
Street address state: NJ
Zip/Postal code: 07726-3073
General Phone: (732) 358-5200
General Fax: (732) 780-4678
Advertising Phone: (732) 358-5200 x8282
General/National Adv. E-mail: jeisele@centraljersey.com
Display Adv. E-mail: gmclassified@newspapermediagroup.com
Primary Website: centraljersey.com/news/independent
Avg Paid Circ: 7
Avg Free Circ: 32799
Audit By: Sworn/Estimate/Non-Audited
Audit Date: 10.06.2019
Personnel: Joe Eisele; Bruce Moran (Ed.); Denise Binn (Adv. Sales); Ken Downey (Ed. Lifestyle Special Sections)
Parent company (for newspapers): Newspaper Media Group-OOB

THE INDEPENDENT PRESS OF BLOOMFIELD

Street address 1: 1291 Stuyvesant Ave
Street address city: Union
Street address state: NJ
Zip/Postal code: 07083-3854
General Phone: (908) 686-7700
General Fax: (908) 686-4169
General/National Adv. E-mail: ads@thelocalsource.com
Display Adv. E-mail: class@thelocalsource.com
Editorial e-mail: editorial@thelocalsource.com
Primary Website: essexnewsdaily.com
Year Established: 1883
Avg Paid Circ: 2378
Avg Free Circ: 418
Audit By: Sworn/Estimate/Non-Audited
Audit Date: 10.06.2019
Personnel: David Worrall (Pub./Pres.); Nancy Worrall (Bus. Mgr.); Raymond Worrall (Vice Pres., Editorial)
Parent company (for newspapers): Worrall Community Newspapers, Inc.

THE ITEM OF MILLBURN AND SHORT HILLS

Street address 1: 181 Millburn Ave
Street address 2: Ste 201
Street address city: Millburn
Street address state: NJ
Zip/Postal code: 07041-1811
General Phone: (973) 921-6451
General Fax: (973) 921-6458
Advertising Phone: (973) 569-7269
Editorial Phone: (973) 569-7100

General/National Adv. E-mail: adhelp@northjersey.com
Display Adv. E-mail: marketplace@northjersey.com
Editorial e-mail: newsroom@northjersey.com
Primary Website: theitemonline.com
Year Established: 1888
Avg Paid Circ: 3120
Avg Free Circ: 696
Audit By: Sworn/Estimate/Non-Audited
Audit Date: 10.06.2019
Personnel: Rick Green (Ed.)
Parent company (for newspapers): North Jersey Media Group Inc.

THE LACEY BEACON

Street address 1: 3600 State Route 66
Street address city: Neptune
Street address state: NJ
Zip/Postal code: 07753-2605
General Phone: (732) 922-6000
General Fax: (732) 643-4014
Editorial Phone: (800) 822-9770 ext 4110
Editorial e-mail: htowns@gannettnj.com
Primary Website: app.com
Avg Paid Circ: 1486
Avg Free Circ: 4
Audit By: Sworn/Estimate/Non-Audited
Audit Date: 10.06.2019
Personnel: Tom Donovan (Pub.); Hollis Towns (Exec. Ed./ VP); Karen Guarasi (Vice Pres., Adv.)
Parent company (for newspapers): Gannett

THE LAWRENCE LEDGER

Street address 1: 300 Witherspoon St
Street address city: Princeton
Street address state: NJ
Zip/Postal code: 08542-3401
General Phone: (609) 924-3244
General Fax: (609-921-2714
Advertising Fax: (609) 921-2714
Editorial Fax: (609) 924-3842
General/National Adv. E-mail: mnebbia@centraljersey.com
Editorial e-mail: ahuston@centraljersey.com
Primary Website: lawrenceledger.com
Year Established: 1968
Avg Paid Circ: 1560
Avg Free Circ: 452
Audit By: Sworn/Estimate/Non-Audited
Audit Date: 10.06.2019
Personnel: Aubrey Huston (Ed.)
Parent company (for newspapers): Newspaper Media Group-OOB

THE MONTCLAIR TIMES

Street address 1: 130 Valley Rd
Street address city: Montclair
Street address state: NJ
Zip/Postal code: 07042-2369
General Phone: (973) 233-5000
Advertising Phone: (973) 569-7269
Editorial Phone: (973) 569-7100
General/National Adv. E-mail: adhelp@northjersey.com
Display Adv. E-mail: marketplace@northjersey.com
Editorial e-mail: newsroom@northjersey.com
Primary Website: montclairtimes.com
Year Established: 1877
Avg Paid Circ: 4615
Audit By: AAM
Audit Date: 31.12.2017
Personnel: Rick Green (Ed.)
Parent company (for newspapers): Gannett - USA Today Network

THE NORTH BERGEN REPORTER

Street address 1: 447 Broadway
Street address city: Bayonne
Street address state: NJ
Zip/Postal code: 07002-3623
General Phone: (201) 798-7800
General Fax: (201) 798-0018
General/National Adv. E-mail: dunger@hudsonreporter.com
Display Adv. E-mail: tishk@hudsonreporter.com
Classified Adv. e-mail: tishk@hudsonreporter.com
Editorial e-mail: editorial@hudsonreporter.com
Primary Website: hudsonreporter.com
Year Established: 1983
Avg Paid Circ: 0
Avg Free Circ: 12112
Audit By: Sworn/Estimate/Non-Audited
Audit Date: 10.06.2019
Personnel: Lucha M. Malato (Pub.); David S. Unger (Pub.); Tish Kraszyk (Adv. Mgr.); Roberto Lopez (Circ. Mgr.); Caren matzner (Ed.)
Parent company (for newspapers): Hudson Reporter Associates, Lp

THE OBSERVER

Street address 1: PO Box 445
Street address city: Hasbrouck Heights
Street address state: NJ
Zip/Postal code: 07604-0445
General Phone: (201) 288-0333
General/National Adv. E-mail: theobsads@verizon.net
Display Adv. E-mail: theobsads@verizon.net
Editorial e-mail: theobsnews@verizon.net
Year Established: 1925
Avg Paid Circ: 2300
Audit By: Sworn/Estimate/Non-Audited
Audit Date: 10.06.2019
Personnel: Connie Doheny (Ed.)

THE PRINCETON PACKET

Street address 1: PO Box 350
Street address city: Princeton
Street address state: NJ
Zip/Postal code: 08542-0350
General Phone: (609) 924-3244
General Fax: (609) 921-2714
Advertising Fax: (609) 921-2714
Editorial Fax: (609) 924-3842
General/National Adv. E-mail: feedback@centraljerseycom
Editorial e-mail: ahuston@centraljersey.com
Primary Website: centraljersey.com
Year Established: 1786
Avg Paid Circ: 423
Avg Free Circ: 15151
Audit By: Sworn/Estimate/Non-Audited
Audit Date: 10.06.2019
Personnel: Aubrey Huston (Ed.)

THE PROGRESS

Street address 1: 6 Brookside Ave
Street address city: Caldwell
Street address state: NJ
Zip/Postal code: 07006-5604
General Phone: (973) 978-4809
General Fax: (973) 933-2247
General/National Adv. E-mail: advertising@Newjerseyhills.com
Display Adv. E-mail: classified@recordernewspapers.com
Editorial e-mail: lgreenspan@Newjerseyhills.com
Primary Website: theprogressnj.com
Year Established: 1911
Avg Paid Circ: 5900
Audit By: Sworn/Estimate/Non-Audited
Audit Date: 10.06.2019
Personnel: Steven Parker (Pub.); Mary Carroll (Circ. Mgr.); Rita Annan-Brady (Lifestyles Ed.); Elizabeth Parker; Megan Crouse (Reporter); Robert Corio (Advertising representative); Theresa Caporizzo (Advertising representative); Russ Crespolini (Ed.)
Parent company (for newspapers): New Jersey Hills Media Group

THE RANDOLPH REPORTER

Street address 1: 100 South Jefferson Road
Street address 2: Suite 104
Street address city: Whippany
Street address state: NJ
Zip/Postal code: 07981
General Phone: (908) 766-3900
General Fax: (908) 766-6365
Editorial Phone: (908) 766-3900 ext 244
General/National Adv. E-mail: mliloia@newjerseyhills.com
Display Adv. E-mail: TheaG@newjerseyhills.com
Editorial e-mail: pnardone@newjerseyhills.com
Primary Website: recordernewspapers.com
Year Established: 1978
Avg Paid Circ: 1973
Avg Free Circ: 22
Audit By: Sworn/Estimate/Non-Audited
Audit Date: 10.06.2019
Personnel: Stephen Parker (Co. Pub./ Bus. Mgr.); Elizabeth K. Parker (Co. Pub./ Exec. Ed.); Jerry O'Donnel (Adv. Dir.); Philip Nardone; Jake Yaniak (Prod. Mgr.); Pat Robinson (Editor); Loretta Kieffer (Sales Rep.)
Parent company (for newspapers): New Jersey Hills Media Group

THE RETROSPECT

Street address 1: 732 Haddon Ave
Street address city: Collingswood
Street address state: NJ
Zip/Postal code: 08108-3712
General Phone: (856) 854-1400
General/National Adv. E-mail: publisher@theretrospect.com
Display Adv. E-mail: retrospectsteve@gmail.com
Classified Adv. e-mail: graphics@theretrospect.com
Editorial e-mail: editor@theretrospect.com
Primary Website: theretrospect.com
Year Established: 1902
Avg Paid Circ: 5500
Avg Free Circ: 384
Audit By: Sworn/Estimate/Non-Audited
Audit Date: 10.10.2021
Personnel: Brett Ainsworth (Pub.); Susan Ainsworth (Bus)

THE RIDGEWOOD NEWS

Street address 1: 1 Garret Mountain Plaza
Street address city: Woodland Park
Street address state: NJ
Zip/Postal code: 7424
General Phone: (201) 612-5400
General Fax: (201) 612-5410
General/National Adv. E-mail: ridgewoodnews@northjersey.com
Primary Website: http://archive.northjersey.com/towns/ridgewood
Year Established: 1889
Avg Paid Circ: 1795
Audit By: AAM
Audit Date: 31.03.2019
Personnel: Rick Green (Ed.)
Parent company (for newspapers): Gannett - USA Today Network

THE SENTINEL OF GLOUCESTER COUNTY

Street address 1: 330 Oak Avenue
Street address city: Malaga
Street address state: NJ
Zip/Postal code: 08328-0903
General Phone: (856) 694-1600
General Fax: (856) 694-0469
General/National Adv. E-mail: ftsentinel@comcast.net
Primary Website: thenjsentinel.com
Year Established: 1942
Avg Paid Circ: 1200
Avg Free Circ: 200
Audit By: Sworn/Estimate/Non-Audited
Audit Date: 10.06.2021
Personnel: Cindy Merckx (Owner/Ed.)

THE TIMES OF SCOTCH PLAINS-FANWOOD

Street address 1: 425 North Ave E
Street address city: Westfield
Street address state: NJ
Zip/Postal code: 07090-1499
General Phone: (908) 232-4407
General/National Adv. E-mail: sales@goleader.com
Editorial e-mail: press@goleader.com
Primary Website: goleader.com
Year Established: 1890
Avg Paid Circ: 6000
Avg Free Circ: 100
Audit By: Sworn/Estimate/Non-Audited
Audit Date: 10.06.2023
Personnel: David Corbin (Asst. Pub.); Lauren Barr (Publisher); Horace R. Corbin (Pub.); Paul Peyton (Ed.)

THE TWO RIVER TIMES

Street address 1: 75 W Front St
Street address 2: Ste 2
Street address city: Red Bank
Street address state: NJ
Zip/Postal code: 07701-1660
General Phone: (732) 219-5788
General Fax: (732) 747-7213
General/National Adv. E-mail: ads@tworivertimes.com
Editorial e-mail: editor@tworivertimes.com
Primary Website: http://trtnj.com/
Year Established: 1990
Avg Paid Circ: 20000
Avg Free Circ: 12000
Audit By: Sworn/Estimate/Non-Audited
Audit Date: 10.06.2019
Personnel: Donna Rovere (Gen. Mgr.); Melissa McGuire (Circ. Mgr.); Eileen Moon (Ed.); Chris Draper (Prodn. Mgr.); Ellen McCarthy (Publisher)

THE UKRAINIAN WEEKLY

Street address 1: 2200 State Rt 10
Street address city: Parsippany
Street address state: NJ
Zip/Postal code: 07054-5304
General Phone: (973) 292-9800
General Fax: (973) 644-9510
General/National Adv. E-mail: staff@ukrweekly.com
Editorial e-mail: staff@ukrweekly.com
Primary Website: www.ukrweekly.com
Year Established: 1933
Avg Paid Circ: 5000
Audit By: Sworn/Estimate/Non-Audited
Audit Date: 12.07.2019
Personnel: Walter Honcharyk (Adv./Circ. Mgr.); Romana Hadzewycz (Ed. in Chief); Andrew Nynka (Editor-in-chief)
Parent company (for newspapers): Ukrainian National Association

THE WARREN REPORTER

Street address 1: 8 Minneakoning Rd
Street address city: Flemington
Street address state: NJ
Zip/Postal code: 08822-5725
General Phone: (908) 782-4747
General Fax: (908) 782-6572
General/National Adv. E-mail: ourtown@lehighvalleylive.com
Primary Website: nj.com/warrenreporter
Year Established: 1968
Avg Free Circ: 52934
Audit By: Sworn/Estimate/Non-Audited
Audit Date: 10.06.2019
Personnel: Robin Von Ohlsen (Adv. Dir.); Craig Turpin (Exec. Ed.); Kevin Lechiski (Ed.); Jessica King (News Ed,); Linda Zetterberg (Prodn. Mgr.)
Parent company (for newspapers): Advance Publications, Inc.

THE WEEHAWKEN REPORTER

Street address 1: 447 Broadway
Street address city: Bayonne
Street address state: NJ
Zip/Postal code: 07002-3623
General Phone: (201) 798-7800
General Fax: (201) 798-0018
General/National Adv. E-mail: dunger@hudsonreporter.com
Display Adv. E-mail: classified@hudsonreporter.com
Editorial e-mail: editorial@hudsonreporter.com
Primary Website: hudsonreporter.com
Year Established: 1983
Avg Paid Circ: 0
Avg Free Circ: 2986
Audit By: Sworn/Estimate/Non-Audited
Audit Date: 10.06.2019
Personnel: Lucha M. Malato (Co-Pub.); David S. Unger (Co-Pub.); Roberto Lopez (Circ. Mgr.); Caren Lissner (Ed.); Tish Kraszyk (Adv. Mgr.)
Parent company (for newspapers): Hudson Reporter Associates, Lp

THE WEST MILFORD MESSENGER

Street address 1: 1499 Union Valley Rd
Street address city: West Milford
Street address state: NJ
Zip/Postal code: 07480-1361
General Phone: (973)728-2200
Editorial e-mail: njoffice@strausnews.com
Primary Website: westmilfordmessenger.com
Avg Paid Circ: 313
Avg Free Circ: 10156
Audit By: USPS

Personnel: Sheila Voelker (Strategic Marketing Exectuive); Mike Zummo (Mng. Ed.)
Parent company (for newspapers): Straus News

THE WESTFIELD LEADER

Street address 1: 425 North Ave E
Street address city: Westfield
Street address state: NJ
Zip/Postal code: 07090-1499
General Phone: (908) 232-4407
General/National Adv. E-mail: editor@goleader.com
Display Adv. E-mail: sales@goleader.com
Classified Adv. e-mail: classifieds@goleader.com
Editorial e-mail: editor@goleader.com
Primary Website: goleader.com
Mthly Avg Views: 3752779
Mthly Avg Unique Visitors: 1364475
Year Established: 1890
Avg Paid Circ: 8000
Avg Free Circ: 59
Audit By: USPS
Audit Date: 10.06.2023
Personnel: Horace R. Corbin (Pub.); Lauren Barr (Publisher); David Corbin (Asst. Pub.); Fred Lecomte (Adv. Dir.)

THEMONMOUTHJOURNAL.COM

Street address 1: 421 Higgins Avenue
Street address 2: No. 300
Street address city: Brielle
Street address state: NJ
Zip/Postal code: 08730
General Phone: (732) 747-7007
Advertising Phone: 7327477007
Editorial Phone: 7327477007
General/National Adv. E-mail: info@themonmouthjournal.com
Display Adv. E-mail: sales@themonmouthjournal.com
Editorial e-mail: news@themonmouthjournal.com
Primary Website: themonmouthjournal.com
Mthly Avg Views: 200000
Mthly Avg Unique Visitors: 75000
Year Established: 2004
Audit By: Sworn/Estimate/Non-Audited
Audit Date: 10.10.2023
Personnel: Susan Paviluk (Gen. Mgr.); Ryan Walker (Sales Associate); Douglas Paviluk (Editor & Publisher); Lori Schwartz (Sales Associate); Paul Gundlach (Photographer); Ryan Walker (Sales Associate); Douglas Paviluk (Publisher); Lori Schwartz (Sales Associate); Paul Gundlach (Photographer); Gary Chapman (Ed.)
Parent company (for newspapers): Monmouth News Media, LLC; Monmouth News Media, LLC

TOMS RIVER OBSERVER-REPORTER

Street address 1: 3600 State Route 66
Street address city: Neptune
Street address state: NJ
Zip/Postal code: 07753-2605
General Phone: (800) 822-9770
Editorial Phone: (800) 822-9770 ext 4110
General/National Adv. E-mail: observer@app.com
Editorial e-mail: htowns@gannettnj.com
Primary Website: app.com
Avg Free Circ: 115000
Audit By: Sworn/Estimate/Non-Audited
Audit Date: 10.06.2019
Personnel: Thomas M. Donovan (Pub.)
Parent company (for newspapers): Gannett

TOWN JOURNAL

Street address 1: 41 Oak St
Street address city: Ridgewood
Street address state: NJ
Zip/Postal code: 07450-3805
General Phone: (201) 612-5434
General Fax: (201) 612-5436
Advertising Phone: (973) 569-7269
Editorial Phone: (973) 569-7100
General/National Adv. E-mail: adhelp@northjersey.com
Display Adv. E-mail: marketplace@northjersey.com
Editorial e-mail: green@northjersey.com
Avg Paid Circ: 0
Avg Free Circ: 6775
Audit By: Sworn/Estimate/Non-Audited
Audit Date: 10.06.2019
Personnel: Rick Green (Ed.)
Parent company (for newspapers): North Jersey Media Group Inc.

TOWN NEWS

Street address 1: 41 Oak St
Street address city: Ridgewood
Street address state: NJ
Zip/Postal code: 07450-3805
General Phone: (201) 612-5426
General Fax: (201) 612-5421
Advertising Phone: (973) 569-7269
Editorial Phone: (973) 569-7100
General/National Adv. E-mail: adhelp@northjersey.com
Display Adv. E-mail: marketplace@northjersey.com
Editorial e-mail: green@northjersey.com
Primary Website: northjersey.com/townnews
Avg Paid Circ: 0
Avg Free Circ: 9069
Audit By: Sworn/Estimate/Non-Audited
Audit Date: 10.06.2019
Personnel: Rick Green
Parent company (for newspapers): North Jersey Media Group Inc.

TOWN TOPICS

Street address 1: 4438 Route 27
Street address city: Kingston
Street address state: NJ
Zip/Postal code: 08528-9613
General Phone: (609) 924-2200
General Fax: (609) 924-8818
General/National Adv. E-mail: robin.broomer@towntopics.com
Display Adv. E-mail: classifieds@towntopics.com
Editorial e-mail: editor@towntopics.com
Primary Website: towntopics.com
Mthly Avg Views: 1946
Year Established: 1946
Avg Free Circ: 15000
Audit By: Sworn/Estimate/Non-Audited
Audit Date: 10.06.2019
Personnel: Lynn A. Smith (Ed.)

TOWNSHIP JOURNAL

Street address 1: 1A Main St
Street address 2: Ste 9
Street address city: Sparta
Street address state: NJ
Zip/Postal code: 07871-1909
General Phone: (973) 300-0890
General Fax: (973) 726-0018
Editorial e-mail: njoffice@strausnews.com
Primary Website: strausnews.com
Year Established: 1995
Avg Paid Circ: 0
Avg Free Circ: 17037
Audit By: Sworn/Estimate/Non-Audited
Audit Date: 10.06.2019
Personnel: Jeanne Straus (Pub.)
Parent company (for newspapers): Straus News

TRI-TOWN NEWS

Street address 1: 198 US Highway 9
Street address 2: Ste 100
Street address city: Manalapan
Street address state: NJ
Zip/Postal code: 07726-3073
General Phone: (732) 780-4192
General Fax: (732) 780-4678
General/National Adv. E-mail: gmsales@gmnews.com
Editorial e-mail: gmntnews@gmnews.com
Primary Website: gmnews.com
Avg Paid Circ: 7
Avg Free Circ: 27600
Audit By: Sworn/Estimate/Non-Audited
Audit Date: 10.06.2019
Personnel: Ben Cannizzaro (Pub.); Robert D. Waitt (Adv. Dir.); Greg Bean (Exec. Ed.); Mark Rosman (Mng. Ed.); Gene Lennon (Prodn./System Mgr.)
Parent company (for newspapers): Newspaper Media Group-OOB

TUCKERTON BEACON

Street address 1: 3600 State Route 66
Street address city: Neptune
Street address state: NJ
Zip/Postal code: 07753-2605
General Phone: (732) 922-6000
General Fax: (732) 557-5658
General/National Adv. E-mail: tbletter@app.com
Editorial e-mail: htowns@gannettnj.com
Primary Website: app.com
Year Established: 1889
Avg Paid Circ: 2184
Avg Free Circ: 2184
Audit By: Sworn/Estimate/Non-Audited
Audit Date: 10.06.2019
Personnel: Thomas Donovan (Pub.); Hollis Towns (Ed.)
Parent company (for newspapers): Gannett

TWIN-BORO NEWS

Street address 1: 210 Knickerbocker Rd
Street address 2: Ste 5
Street address city: Cresskill
Street address state: NJ
Zip/Postal code: 07626-1801
General Phone: (201) 894-6700
Advertising Phone: (973) 569-7269
Editorial Phone: (973) 569-7100
General/National Adv. E-mail: adhelp@northjersey.com
Display Adv. E-mail: marketplace@northjersey.com
Editorial e-mail: newsroom@northjersey.com
Primary Website: northjersey.com
Avg Paid Circ: 0
Avg Free Circ: 15427
Audit By: Sworn/Estimate/Non-Audited
Audit Date: 10.06.2019
Personnel: Janice Friedman (Pub.); William Slossar (Ed.); Glenn Garvie (Vice Pres., Prodn.); Ellen Zitis (Adv. Mgr.)
Parent company (for newspapers): North Jersey Media Group Inc.

UNION COUNTY LOCAL SOURCE

Street address 1: 1291 Stuyvesant Ave
Street address city: Union
Street address state: NJ
Zip/Postal code: 07083-3854
General Phone: (908) 686-7700
General Fax: (908) 686-4169
General/National Adv. E-mail: ads@thelocalsource.com
Display Adv. E-mail: class@thelocalsource.com
Editorial e-mail: editorial@thelocalsource.com
Primary Website: unionnewsdaily.com
Year Established: 1917
Avg Paid Circ: 4156
Avg Free Circ: 217
Audit By: Sworn/Estimate/Non-Audited
Audit Date: 10.06.2019
Personnel: David Worrall (Pub.); Peter Worrall (Adv. Mgr.); Raymond Worrall (General Manager); Nancy Worrall (Controller)
Parent company (for newspapers): Worrall Community Newspapers, Inc.

VERONA-CEDAR GROVE TIMES

Street address 1: 130 Valley Rd
Street address 2: Rear
Street address city: Montclair
Street address state: NJ
Zip/Postal code: 07042-2369
General Phone: (973) 233-5048
Advertising Phone: (973) 569-7269
Editorial Phone: (973) 569-7100
General/National Adv. E-mail: adhelp@northjersey.com
Display Adv. E-mail: marketplace@northjersey.com
Editorial e-mail: newsroom@northjersey.com
Primary Website: http://archive.northjersey.com/towns/verona-cedar-grove
Year Established: 1948
Avg Paid Circ: 2290
Audit By: AAM
Audit Date: 31.12.2017
Personnel: Rick Green (Ed.)
Parent company (for newspapers): Gannett - USA Today Network

VOORHEES SUN

Street address 1: 108 Kings Hwy E
Street address city: Haddonfield
Street address state: NJ
Zip/Postal code: 08033-2099
General Phone: (856) 779-3800
Advertising Phone: (856) 528-4844
General/National Adv. E-mail: jgallo@newspapermediagroup.com
Primary Website: voorheessun.com
Audit By: Sworn/Estimate/Non-Audited
Audit Date: 10.06.2019
Personnel: Arlene Reyes (Adv. Dir.); Angela Smith (Mktg. Dir.)
Parent company (for newspapers): Newspaper Media Group-OOB

WALDWICK SUBURBAN NEWS

Street address 1: 41 Oak St
Street address city: Ridgewood
Street address state: NJ
Zip/Postal code: 07450-3805
General Phone: (201) 612-5415
Advertising Phone: (973) 569-7269
Editorial Phone: (973) 569-7100
General/National Adv. E-mail: adhelp@northjersey.com
Display Adv. E-mail: marketplace@northjersey.com
Editorial e-mail: green@northjersey.com
Avg Free Circ: 2801
Audit By: Sworn/Estimate/Non-Audited
Audit Date: 10.06.2019
Personnel: Rick Green (Ed.)
Parent company (for newspapers): North Jersey Media Group Inc.

WAYNE TODAY

Street address 1: 1 Garret Mountain Plz
Street address city: Woodland Park
Street address state: NJ
Zip/Postal code: 07424-3320
General Phone: (973) 569-7393
General Fax: (973) 569-7377
General/National Adv. E-mail: today@northjersey.com
Display Adv. E-mail: deyoung@northjersey.com
Editorial e-mail: today@northjersey.com
Primary Website: northjersey.com/wayne
Avg Paid Circ: 0
Avg Free Circ: 18206
Audit By: Sworn/Estimate/Non-Audited
Audit Date: 10.06.2019
Personnel: Rick Green (Ed.)
Parent company (for newspapers): North Jersey Media Group Inc.

WEST ESSEX TRIBUNE

Street address 1: 495 S Livingston Ave
Street address city: Livingston
Street address state: NJ
Zip/Postal code: 07039-4327
General Phone: (973) 992-1771
General Fax: (973) 992-7015
General/National Adv. E-mail: tribune.jenny@gmail.com
Display Adv. E-mail: WETribune@gmail.com
Classified Adv. e-mail: tribuneclassifieds@gmail.com
Editorial e-mail: WestEssexTribune@gmail.com
Primary Website: westessextribune.net
Year Established: 1929
Avg Paid Circ: 5213
Avg Free Circ: 197
Audit By: Sworn/Estimate/Non-Audited
Audit Date: 01.10.2023
Personnel: Jennifer Cone Chciuk (Pub.); Christine Sablynski (Mng. Ed.); Karen Trachtenberg (Prodn. Mgr.); Michelle Bent (Editor)

WEST NEW YORK/UNION CITY REPORTER

Street address 1: 1400 Washington St
Street address city: Hoboken
Street address state: NJ
Zip/Postal code: 07030-9402
General Phone: (201) 798-7800
General Fax: (201) 798-0018
General/National Adv. E-mail: dunger@hudsonreporter.com
Display Adv. E-mail: classified@hudsonreporter.com
Editorial e-mail: editorial@hudsonreporter.com
Primary Website: hudsonreporter.com
Year Established: 1983
Avg Paid Circ: 0
Avg Free Circ: 2285
Audit By: Sworn/Estimate/Non-Audited
Audit Date: 10.06.2019

Personnel: Lucha M. Malato (Pub.); David S. Unger (Co-Pub.); Roberto Lopez (Circ. Mgr.); Tish Kraszyk (Advertising Manager)
Parent company (for newspapers): Hudson Reporter Associates, Lp

WEST ORANGE CHRONICLE

Street address 1: 1291 Stuyvesant Ave
Street address city: Union
Street address state: NJ
Zip/Postal code: 07083-3854
General Phone: (908) 686-7700
General Fax: (908) 686-4169
General/National Adv. E-mail: ads@thelocalsource.com
Display Adv. E-mail: class@thelocalsource.com
Editorial e-mail: editorial@thelocalsource.com
Primary Website: essexnewsdaily.com
Year Established: 1930
Avg Paid Circ: 2968
Avg Free Circ: 1272
Audit By: Sworn/Estimate/Non-Audited
Audit Date: 10.06.2019
Personnel: David Worrall (Pub.); Raymond Worrall (Vice Pres.); Peter Worrall (Prodn. Dir.); Nancy Worrall (Controller)
Parent company (for newspapers): Worrall Community Newspapers, Inc.

WILDWOOD LEADER

Street address 1: 1000 W. Washington Ave.
Street address city: Pleasantville
Street address state: NJ
Zip/Postal code: 08232-3806
General Phone: (609) 272-7231
General Fax: (609) 272-7224
General/National Adv. E-mail: RBuffone@pressofac.com
Display Adv. E-mail: RBuffone@pressofac.com
Editorial e-mail: letters@pressofac.com
Primary Website: pressofatlanticcity.com
Avg Free Circ: 3339
Audit By: Sworn/Estimate/Non-Audited
Audit Date: 10.06.2019
Personnel: Kevin Post; Michelle Rice (VP Adv.); Carol Steiger (Circ.); Mark Blum (Pub.); Kris Worrell (VP of News)
Parent company (for newspapers): Shore News Today

WINDSOR-HIGHTS HERALD

Street address 1: 300 Witherspoon St
Street address city: Princeton
Street address state: NJ
Zip/Postal code: 08542-3401
General Phone: (609) 924-3244
General Fax: (609) 921-2714
Advertising Fax: (609) 921-2714
Editorial Fax: (609) 924-3842
General/National Adv. E-mail: Jclerico@centraljersey.com
Display Adv. E-mail: classified@centraljersey.com
Editorial e-mail: green@northjersey.com
Primary Website: windsorhightsherald.com
Year Established: 1965
Avg Paid Circ: 170
Avg Free Circ: 2302
Audit By: Sworn/Estimate/Non-Audited
Audit Date: 10.06.2019
Personnel: Rick Green (Ed.)
Parent company (for newspapers): Newspaper Media Group-OOB

WYCKOFF SUBURBAN NEWS

Street address 1: 41 Oak St
Street address city: Ridgewood
Street address state: NJ
Zip/Postal code: 07450-3805
General Phone: (201) 612-5415
General Fax: (201) 612-5421
Advertising Phone: (973) 569-7269
Editorial Phone: (973) 569-7100
General/National Adv. E-mail: adhelp@northjersey.com
Display Adv. E-mail: marketplace@northjersey.com
Editorial e-mail: green@northjersey.com
Avg Free Circ: 5569
Audit By: Sworn/Estimate/Non-Audited
Audit Date: 10.06.2019
Personnel: Rick Green (Ed.)
Parent company (for newspapers): North Jersey Media Group Inc.

NEW MEXICO

ALBUQUERQUE BUSINESS FIRST

Street address 1: 6565 Americas Pkwy NE
Street address 2: Suite 202
Street address city: Albuquerque
Street address state: NM
Zip/Postal code: 87110-8177
General Phone: (505) 768-7008
General Fax: (505) 768-0890
Advertising Phone: (505) 348-8326
Editorial Phone: (505) 768-7008
General/National Adv. E-mail: dschrimsher@bizjournals.com
Editorial e-mail: cortiz@bizjournals.com
Primary Website: bizjournals.com/albuquerque
Year Established: 1993
Avg Paid Circ: 5400
Audit By: Sworn/Estimate/Non-Audited
Audit Date: 10.06.2019
Personnel: Candace Beeke (Pub.)
Parent company (for newspapers): ACBJ

CIBOLA BEACON

Street address 1: PO Box 579
Street address city: Grants
Street address state: NM
Zip/Postal code: 87020-0579
General Phone: (505) 287-4411
General Fax: (505) 287-7822
General/National Adv. E-mail: advertising@cibolabeacon.com
Display Adv. E-mail: classifieds@cibolabeacon.com
Editorial e-mail: editor@cibolabeacon.com
Primary Website: cibolabeacon.com
Year Established: 1945
Avg Paid Circ: 3400
Avg Free Circ: 5300
Audit By: Sworn/Estimate/Non-Audited
Audit Date: 10.06.2019
Personnel: Donald Jaramillo (Gen. Mgr.); Sylvia Gonzales (Adv. Mgr.); Alaina Jaramillo (Adv. Acct. Mgr.); Vanessa Garcia (Adv. Acct. Mgr.); Ramona MontaÃ±o (Composing Supervisor); Aaryn Tribbey (Circulation Dept. Manager); Rosanne Boyett (Senior Staff Writer); Ham Lujan (Ed.)
Parent company (for newspapers): New Mexico Press Association; Orion El Faro Publishing

CLOVIS LIVESTOCK MARKET NEWS

Street address 1: 181 East Sumner Ave
Street address city: Fort Sumner
Street address state: NM
Zip/Postal code: 88119
General Phone: (575) 355-2462
General Fax: (575) 355-7253
General/National Adv. E-mail: pecospub@plateautel.net
Year Established: 1993
Avg Paid Circ: 1350
Audit By: Sworn/Estimate/Non-Audited
Audit Date: 10.06.2019
Personnel: Scot Stinnett (Pub./Ed.); Lisa Stinnett (Bus. Mgr.)

DE BACA COUNTY NEWS

Street address 1: 181 E Sumner Ave
Street address city: Fort Sumner
Street address state: NM
Zip/Postal code: 88119
General Phone: (575) 355-2462
General Fax: (575) 355-7253
General/National Adv. E-mail: pecospub@plateautel.net
Year Established: 1900
Avg Paid Circ: 1000
Avg Free Circ: 15
Audit By: Sworn/Estimate/Non-Audited
Audit Date: 10.06.2019
Personnel: Scot Stinnett (Pub.); Lisa Stinnett (Bus. Mgr.)
Parent company (for newspapers): Pecos Publishing

EASTERN NEW MEXICO NEWS

Street address 1: 521 Pile St
Street address city: Clovis
Street address state: NM
Zip/Postal code: 88101-6637
General Phone: (575) 763-3431
General Fax: (575) 762-3879
Advertising Phone: (575) 763-3431
Advertising Fax: (575) 762-3879
Editorial Phone: (575) 763-3431
Editorial Fax: (575) 742-1349
General/National Adv. E-mail: cnjadvertising@thenews.email
Display Adv. E-mail: cnjadvertising@thenews.email
Classified Adv. e-mail: classified@thenews.email
Editorial e-mail: dstevens@thenews.email
Primary Website: easternnewmexiconews.com
Mthly Avg Views: 565596
Mthly Avg Unique Visitors: 84751
Year Established: 1929
Avg Paid Circ: 5235
Sun. Circulation Paid: 6125
Audit By: Sworn/Estimate/Non-Audited
Audit Date: 10.06.2019
Personnel: ROB LANGRELL (PUB); David Stevens (Ed.); Cindy Cole (Circ. Dir.); Joyce Cruce (Hum. Res. Dir.); Shawn Luscombe (Creative Services Director); Kevin Wilson (Managing Editor); Annie Stout (Business Manager)
Parent company (for newspapers): Stevenson Newspapers

EL DEFENSOR CHIEFTAIN

Street address 1: 200 Winkler St
Street address city: Socorro
Street address state: NM
Zip/Postal code: 87801-4200
General Phone: (575) 835-0520
General Fax: (575) 835-1837
General/National Adv. E-mail: advertising@dchieftain.com
Display Adv. E-mail: classifieds@dchieftain.com
Editorial e-mail: editorial@dchieftain.com
Primary Website: dchieftain.com
Year Established: 1860
Avg Paid Circ: 72020
Audit By: Sworn/Estimate/Non-Audited
Audit Date: 10.06.2019
Personnel: Scott Turner (Pub./Ed.)

HEALTH CITY SUN

Street address 1: 6300 Montano Rd NW
Street address 2: Ste G3
Street address city: Albuquerque
Street address state: NM
Zip/Postal code: 87120-1826
General Phone: (505) 242-3010
General Fax: (505) 842-5464
General/National Adv. E-mail: legal@healthcitysun.com
Primary Website: healthcitysun.com
Year Established: 1929
Avg Paid Circ: 2000
Avg Free Circ: 250
Audit By: Sworn/Estimate/Non-Audited
Audit Date: 10.06.2019
Personnel: Jill Stone (Pub.)

HIDALGO COUNTY HERALD

Street address 1: 212 E Motel Dr
Street address 2: Ste B
Street address city: Lordsburg
Street address state: NM
Zip/Postal code: 88045-1906
General Phone: (575) 542-8705
General Fax: (575) 542-8837
General/National Adv. E-mail: hcherald@hotmail.com
Avg Paid Circ: 1500
Avg Free Circ: 300
Audit By: Sworn/Estimate/Non-Audited
Audit Date: 10.06.2019
Personnel: Brenda Hood (Pub. Ed.); Glenda Greene (Adv. Mgr.)

LAS VEGAS OPTIC

Street address 1: 720 University Ave
Street address 2: Ste B
Street address city: LAS VEGAS
Street address state: NM
Zip/Postal code: 87701
General Phone: (505) 425-6796
General Fax: (505) 425-1005
Advertising Phone: (505) 425-6796
Advertising Fax: (505) 425-1005
Editorial Phone: (505) 425-6796
Editorial Fax: (505) 425-1005
General/National Adv. E-mail: optic@lasvegasoptic.com
Primary Website: lasvegasoptic.com
Year Established: 1879
Avg Paid Circ: 3850
Sun. Circulation Paid: 3850
Audit By: Sworn/Estimate/Non-Audited
Audit Date: 10.06.2019
Personnel: Cynthia Fitch (Advertising Manager); Jason Brooks (Editor); Ashley Ortega (Circulation Coordinator)
Parent company (for newspapers): New Mexico Press Association; O'Rourke Media Group

LINCOLN COUNTY NEWS

Street address 1: 309 Central Ave
Street address city: Carrizozo
Street address state: NM
Zip/Postal code: 88301
General Phone: (575) 648-2333
General Fax: (575) 648-2333
General/National Adv. E-mail: j.p.aguilar44@hotmail.com
Year Established: 1905
Avg Paid Circ: 1858
Avg Free Circ: 60
Audit By: Sworn/Estimate/Non-Audited
Audit Date: 10.06.2019
Personnel: Peter Aguilar (Prodn. Mgr.); Steve Mathis (Pub./Ed.); P. Dawn Mathis (office Mgr./Adv. Mgr.)

LOVINGTON LEADER

Street address 1: 14 W Avenue B
Street address city: Lovington
Street address state: NM
Zip/Postal code: 88260-4404
General Phone: (505) 396-2844
General Fax: (505) 396-5775
General/National Adv. E-mail: lovingtonleader@yahoo.com
Display Adv. E-mail: leader@leaco.net
Classified Adv. e-mail: lovingtonleader@yahoo.com
Editorial e-mail: leader@leaco.net
Primary Website: lovingtonleaderonline.com
Avg Paid Circ: 1495
Sun. Circulation Paid: 1495
Audit By: Sworn/Estimate/Non-Audited
Audit Date: 10.06.2019
Personnel: Joyce Clemens (Adv. Mgr.); John Graham (Ed./Pub.); Jeanine Graham (Society Ed.); Neil Granath (Sports Ed.); Hop Graham (Prodn. Pressman); Gina Ford (Classified Adv. Mgr.)

MOUNTAIN VIEW TELEGRAPH

Street address 1: 215 Old Route 66
Street address 2: Building 1 Suite 4
Street address city: Moriarty
Street address state: NM
Zip/Postal code: 87035
General Phone: (505) 823-7101
General Fax: (505) 823-7107
Advertising Phone: (505) 823-7108
Editorial Phone: (505) 823-7102
General/National Adv. E-mail: btrujillo@mvtelegraph.com
Display Adv. E-mail: class@mvtelegraph.com
Editorial e-mail: editor@mvtelegraph.com
Primary Website: mvtelegraph.com
Avg Paid Circ: 7000
Audit By: Sworn/Estimate/Non-Audited
Audit Date: 10.06.2019

Personnel: Tod Dickson (Ed.)

QUAY COUNTY SUN

Street address 1: 902 S 1st St
Street address city: Tucumcari
Street address state: NM
Zip/Postal code: 88401-3217
General Phone: (575) 461-1952
General Fax: (575) 461-1965
Editorial Phone: (800) 819-9925
General/National Adv. E-mail: cnjadvertising@cnjonline.com
Display Adv. E-mail: rsullivan@cnjonline.com
Primary Website: qcsunonline.com
Avg Paid Circ: 4200
Avg Free Circ: 30
Audit By: Sworn/Estimate/Non-Audited
Audit Date: 10.06.2019
Personnel: Viola Gonzales (Ad. Director); Lorinda Martinez (Classifieds Mgr.); David Gragg (Ed.); Marilyn Parker (Bookkeeper); ROB LANGRELL (PUBLISHER)
Parent company (for newspapers): Clovis Media Inc.

RIO GRANDE SUN

Street address 1: 123 N Railroad Ave
Street address city: Espanola
Street address state: NM
Zip/Postal code: 87532-2627
General Phone: (505) 753-2126
General Fax: (505) 753-2140
General/National Adv. E-mail: rgsunads@riograndesun.com
Display Adv. E-mail: classifieds@riograndesun.com
Editorial e-mail: rgsunedit@riograndesun.com
Primary Website: riograndesun.com
Year Established: 1956
Avg Paid Circ: 11500
Audit By: Sworn/Estimate/Non-Audited
Audit Date: 10.06.2019
Personnel: Robert Trapp (Pub./Co-owner); Maria Lopez Garcia (Adv./Mktg.); Jennifer Garcia (News Ed.)

SANTA FE REPORTER

Street address 1: 132 E Marcy St
Street address city: Santa Fe
Street address state: NM
Zip/Postal code: 87501-2054
General Phone: (505) 988-5541
General Fax: (505) 988-5348
Advertising Phone: (505) 988-5541 x205
General/National Adv. E-mail: advertising@sfreporter.com
Editorial e-mail: editor@sfreporter.com
Primary Website: sfreporter.com
Year Established: 1974
Avg Free Circ: 15000
Audit By: Sworn/Estimate/Non-Audited
Audit Date: 10.06.2019
Personnel: Julie Ann Grimm (Pub./Ed.); Anna Maggiore (Advertising director and associate publisher)
Parent company (for newspapers): City of Roses Newspaper Company

SIERRA COUNTY SENTINEL

Street address 1: 1747 E 3rd Ave
Street address city: Truth Or Consequences
Street address state: NM
Zip/Postal code: 87901-2042
General Phone: (575) 894-3088
General Fax: (575) 894-3998
Advertising Phone: (575) 894-3088
Advertising Fax: (575) 894-3998
General/National Adv. E-mail: sentinel@gpkmedia.com
Primary Website: gpkmedia.com
Year Established: 1967
Avg Paid Circ: 4580
Avg Free Circ: 30
Audit By: Sworn/Estimate/Non-Audited
Audit Date: 10.06.2019
Personnel: Frances Luna (Pub.)
Parent company (for newspapers): New Mexico Press Association

THE GUADALUPE COUNTY COMMUNICATOR

Street address 1: 241 S. 4th St.
Street address city: Santa Rosa
Street address state: NM
Zip/Postal code: 88435-2322
General Phone: (575) 472-3555
General Fax: (575) 472-5555
General/National Adv. E-mail: comsilvercom@plateautel.net
Display Adv. E-mail: comsilvercom@plateautel.net
Editorial e-mail: tmcdonald.srnm@gmail.com
Year Established: 1983
Avg Paid Circ: 1547
Avg Free Circ: 314
Audit By: Sworn/Estimate/Non-Audited
Audit Date: 10.06.2019
Personnel: Tom McDonald (Editor and Publisher)
Parent company (for newspapers): Gazette Media Services LLC

THE HERALD

Street address 1: 1204 N Date St
Street address city: Truth Or Consequences
Street address state: NM
Zip/Postal code: 87901-1754
General Phone: (575) 894-2143
General Fax: (575) 894-7824
General/National Adv. E-mail: herald@torcherald.com
Primary Website: theheraldtorc.com
Year Established: 1928
Avg Paid Circ: 4000
Audit By: Sworn/Estimate/Non-Audited
Audit Date: 10.06.2019
Personnel: Mike Tooley (Pub.); Carlos Padilla (Ed.); Cindy Tooley-Harrison (Associate Publisher)
Parent company (for newspapers): Herald Newspapers, Inc.

THE INDEPENDENT

Street address 1: 95 N.M. 344
Street address city: Edgewood
Street address state: NM
Zip/Postal code: 87015
General Phone: (505) 286-1212
General/National Adv. E-mail: independent@lobo.net
Display Adv. E-mail: independent@lobo.net
Editorial e-mail: leota@lobo.net
Primary Website: edgewood.news
Year Established: 1999
Avg Paid Circ: 3000
Avg Free Circ: 500
Audit By: Sworn/Estimate/Non-Audited
Audit Date: 10.06.2019
Personnel: Debbie Ohler (Business Manager); Leota Harriman (Editor & Publisher)

THE JAL RECORD

Street address 1: 101 E Panther
Street address city: Jal
Street address state: NM
Zip/Postal code: 88252
General Phone: (575) 395-9970
General Fax: (575) 395-9971
Advertising Phone: (575) 395-9970
General/National Adv. E-mail: Contact-us@jalrecord.net
Editorial e-mail: Contact_us@jalrecord.net
Primary Website: jalrecordonline.com
Year Established: 1939
Avg Paid Circ: 1475
Avg Free Circ: 26
Audit By: Sworn/Estimate/Non-Audited
Audit Date: 10.06.2019
Personnel: John Chance (Publisher/ Owner)

THE LAS CRUCES BULLETIN

Street address 1: 1740 Calle De Mercado
Street address 2: Ste A
Street address city: Las Cruces
Street address state: NM
Zip/Postal code: 88005-8254
General Phone: (575) 524-8061
General Fax: (575) 526-4621
General/National Adv. E-mail: shellie@lascrucesbulletin.com
Display Adv. E-mail: jamie@lascrucesbulletin.com
Editorial e-mail: brook@lascrucesbulletin.com
Primary Website: lascrucesbulletin.com
Year Established: 1969
Avg Paid Circ: 1000
Avg Free Circ: 20000
Audit By: Sworn/Estimate/Non-Audited
Audit Date: 10.06.2019
Personnel: Richard Coltharp (Pub.); Susie Ouderkirk (News Ed.); Brook Stockberger (Managing Editor)
Parent company (for newspapers): OPC News, LLC

THE NUCLEUS

Street address 1: 409 NM Hwy 528
Street address 2: Ste 101
Street address city: Rio Rancho
Street address state: NM
Zip/Postal code: 87124
General Phone: (505) 892-8080
General Fax: (505) 892-5719
General/National Adv. E-mail: lross@rrobserver.com
Primary Website: kafbnucleus.com
Audit By: Sworn/Estimate/Non-Audited
Audit Date: 10.06.2019
Parent company (for newspapers): RR Community Publishing LLC

THE RIO RANCHO OBSERVER

Street address 1: 409 NM 528 NE
Street address 2: Ste 101
Street address city: Rio Rancho
Street address state: NM
Zip/Postal code: 87124
General Phone: (505) 892-8080
General Fax: (505) 892-5719
General/National Adv. E-mail: mhartranft @rrobserver.com
Display Adv. E-mail: observerclass@rrobserver.com
Editorial e-mail: mhartranft @rrobserver.com
Primary Website: rrobserver.com
Year Established: 1973
Avg Free Circ: 23500
Audit By: Sworn/Estimate/Non-Audited
Audit Date: 10.06.2019
Personnel: Argen Duncan (Ed.); Gary Herron (Sports Ed.)
Parent company (for newspapers): New Mexico Press Association

THE RUIDOSO NEWS

Street address 1: 104 Park Ave
Street address city: Ruidoso
Street address state: NM
Zip/Postal code: 88345-6154
General Phone: (575) 257-4001
General Fax: (575) 257-7053
Editorial e-mail: jonsurez@gannett.com
Primary Website: ruidosonews.com
Year Established: 1946
Avg Paid Circ: 2214
Avg Free Circ: 45
Audit By: AAM
Audit Date: 30.06.2018
Personnel: Carol BUrgess (Gen. Mgr.); Kelly Brooks Vestal (Mng. Ed.); Frank Leto (Adv. Dir.); Chris Gonzales (Circ. Mgr.); Jessica Onsuarez (News Dir.); Rynni Henderson (Reg. Sales Dir.); Duane Barbati (News Ed.)
Parent company (for newspapers): New Mexico Press Association

THE TAOS NEWS

Street address 1: 226 Albright St
Street address city: Taos
Street address state: NM
Zip/Postal code: 87571-6312
General Phone: (575) 758-2241
General Fax: (575) 758-9647
General/National Adv. E-mail: admanager@taosnews.com
Display Adv. E-mail: admanager@taosnews.com
Editorial e-mail: editor@taosnews.com
Primary Website: taosnews.com
Year Established: 1959
Avg Paid Circ: 6871
Avg Free Circ: 14
Audit By: VAC
Audit Date: 30.09.2017
Personnel: Staci Matlock (Editor)

UNION COUNTY LEADER

Street address 1: 15 N 1st St
Street address city: Clayton
Street address state: NM
Zip/Postal code: 88415-3501
General Phone: (575) 374-2587
General Fax: (575) 374-8117
General/National Adv. E-mail: ucleader@plateautel.net
Year Established: 1928
Avg Paid Circ: 2300
Avg Free Circ: 95
Audit By: Sworn/Estimate/Non-Audited
Audit Date: 10.06.2019
Personnel: Brandy Payton (Ed.); Terry Martin (Ed./Pub.); Susan Richardson (Expeditor); Patricia Herrera (Adv. Mgr./Office Mgr.); Deborah Snider (Adv. Sales Rep.)
Parent company (for newspapers): New Mexico Press Association

VALENCIA COUNTY NEWS-BULLETIN

Street address 1: 1837 Camino Del Llano
Street address city: Belen
Street address state: NM
Zip/Postal code: 87002-2619
General Phone: (505) 864-4472
General Fax: (505) 864-3549
General/National Adv. E-mail: bchandler@news-bulletin.com
Display Adv. E-mail: classifieds@news-bulletin.com
Editorial e-mail: cgarcia@news-bulletin.com
Primary Website: news-bulletin.com
Year Established: 1910
Avg Paid Circ: 2855
Avg Free Circ: 12174
Audit By: Sworn/Estimate/Non-Audited
Audit Date: 10.06.2019
Personnel: Clara Garcia (Ed.)
Parent company (for newspapers): Albuquerque Publishing Co.

NEW YORK

ADVANCE NEWS

Street address 1: 308 Isabella St
Street address city: Ogdensburg
Street address state: NY
Zip/Postal code: 13669-1409
General Phone: (315) 393-1003
General Fax: (315) 393-5108
General/National Adv. E-mail: journal@ogd.com
Display Adv. E-mail: class@ogd.com
Primary Website: ogd.com
Avg Paid Circ: 10700
Audit By: Sworn/Estimate/Non-Audited
Audit Date: 10.06.2019
Personnel: Barb Ward (Adv. Mgr.); Charles W. Kelly (Ed.)

AKRON BUGLE

Street address 1: 7263 Downey Rd
Street address city: Akron
Street address state: NY
Zip/Postal code: 14001-9714
General Phone: (716) 542-9615
General Fax: (716) 210-8947
General/National Adv. E-mail: akronbugle@gmail.com
Display Adv. E-mail: classifieds@akronbugle.com
Editorial e-mail: editor@akronbugle.com
Primary Website: akronbugle.com
Year Established: 1981
Avg Paid Circ: 1895
Avg Free Circ: 15
Audit By: Sworn/Estimate/Non-Audited
Audit Date: 10.06.2019
Personnel: Marilyn J. Kasperek (Pub.); Kenneth B. Kasperek (Adv. Mgr.)

ALBANY BUSINESS REVIEW

Street address 1: 40 British American Blvd
Street address 2: Ste 9
Street address city: Latham
Street address state: NY
Zip/Postal code: 12110-1424
General Phone: (518) 640-6800
General Fax: (518) 640-6801
Advertising Phone: (518) 640-6820
Editorial Phone: (518) 640-6808
General/National Adv. E-mail: tgiroux@bizjournals.com

Editorial e-mail: mhendricks@bizjournals.com
Primary Website: albany.bizjournals.com
Audit By: Sworn/Estimate/Non-Audited
Audit Date: 10.06.2019
Personnel: Mike Hendricks (Editor-in-Chief); Melissa Mangini (Mgn. Editor)

ALDEN ADVERTISER

Street address 1: 13200 Broadway St
Street address city: Alden
Street address state: NY
Zip/Postal code: 14004-1313
General Phone: (716) 937-9226
General/National Adv. E-mail: aldenadvertiser@rochester.rr.com
Editorial e-mail: aldenadvertiser@rochester.rr.com
Primary Website: aldenadvertisernews.com
Year Established: 1914
Avg Paid Circ: 3550
Avg Free Circ: 108
Audit By: Sworn/Estimate/Non-Audited
Audit Date: 10.06.2019
Personnel: Leonard A. Weisbeck (Gen. Mgr. & Ed.)

AMHERST BEE

Street address 1: 5564 Main St
Street address city: Williamsville
Street address state: NY
Zip/Postal code: 14221-5473
General Phone: (716) 632-4700
General Fax: (716) 633-8601
Advertising Phone: (716) 204-4934
General/National Adv. E-mail: salesdept@beenews.com
Display Adv. E-mail: classified@beenews.com
Editorial e-mail: kdepriest@beenews.com
Primary Website: beenews.com
Year Established: 1879
Avg Paid Circ: 5000
Avg Free Circ: 25000
Audit By: Sworn/Estimate/Non-Audited
Audit Date: 10.06.2019
Personnel: Trey Measer (Pub.); Michael Measer (Exec. Vice Pres); Keaton DePriest (Ed.); Mary Anne Cappon (Adv. Dir.); David Passalugo (Sales Mgr.); Holly Schiferle (Classifieds Mgr.)
Parent company (for newspapers): Bee Group Newspapers

ARCADE HERALD

Street address 1: 223 Main St
Street address city: Arcade
Street address state: NY
Zip/Postal code: 14009-1209
General Phone: (585) 492-2525
General Fax: (585) 492-2667
General/National Adv. E-mail: heraldads@roadrunner.com
Editorial e-mail: heraldnews@roadrunner.com
Primary Website: mywnynews.com/arcade_warsaw
Year Established: 1891
Avg Paid Circ: 5000
Audit By: Sworn/Estimate/Non-Audited
Audit Date: 10.06.2019
Personnel: Grant M. Hamilton (Pub.); Cyndi Gradi (Ad. Mgr.)
Parent company (for newspapers): Neighbor to Neighbor News, Inc.

ASTORIA TIMES

Street address 1: 4102 Bell Blvd
Street address city: Bayside
Street address state: NY
Zip/Postal code: 11361-2792
General Phone: (718) 229-0300
General Fax: (718) 225-7117
Advertising Phone: (718) 229-0300
Advertising Fax: (718) 225-7117
Editorial Phone: (718) 229-0300
Editorial Fax: (718) 225-7117
General/National Adv. E-mail: brice@cnglocal.com
Display Adv. E-mail: classified@cnglocal.com
Editorial e-mail: timesledgernews@cnglocal.com
Primary Website: astoriatimes.com
Avg Paid Circ: 1983
Audit By: Sworn/Estimate/Non-Audited
Audit Date: 10.06.2019
Personnel: Roz Liston (Ed.)
Parent company (for newspapers): Queens Village Times (OOB)

BALDWIN HERALD

Street address 1: 2 Endo Blvd
Street address city: Garden City
Street address state: NY
Zip/Postal code: 11530-6707
General Phone: (516) 569-4000
General Fax: (516) 569-4942
Advertising Phone: (516) 569-400 x250
General/National Adv. E-mail: baldwineditor@liherald.com
Display Adv. E-mail: sales@liherald.com
Primary Website: liherald.com
Avg Paid Circ: 5291
Audit By: Sworn/Estimate/Non-Audited
Audit Date: 10.06.2019
Personnel: Clifford Richner (Pub.); Michael Bologna (VP, Ops./Gen. Mgr.); Rhonda Glickman (Adv. Mgr.)
Parent company (for newspapers): Richner Communications, Inc.

BALDWINSVILLE MESSENGER

Street address 1: 2501 James St
Street address 2: Ste 100
Street address city: Syracuse
Street address state: NY
Zip/Postal code: 13206-2996
General Phone: (315) 434-8889
General Fax: (315) 434-8883
General/National Adv. E-mail: messenger@cnylink.com
Primary Website: baldwinsvillemessenger.com
Avg Paid Circ: 6100
Audit By: Sworn/Estimate/Non-Audited
Audit Date: 10.06.2019
Personnel: Dave Tyler (Pub.); Jack Gardner (Adv. Dir.); Lori Newcomb (Prodn. Mgr.); Mac Green (Circ. Mgr.)

BALLSTON JOURNAL

Street address 1: PO Box 319
Street address city: Ballston Spa
Street address state: NY
Zip/Postal code: 12020-0319
General Phone: (518) 885-5238
General Fax: (518) 885-3752
General/National Adv. E-mail: jpublisher@theballstonjournal.com
Editorial e-mail: jpublisher@theballstonjournal.com
Primary Website: theballstonjournal.com
Year Established: 1798
Avg Free Circ: 151000
Audit By: Sworn/Estimate/Non-Audited
Audit Date: 10.06.2019
Personnel: Angela Miller McFarland (Owner/Pub.)

BAY NEWS

Street address 1: 1 Metrotech Ctr N
Street address 2: Fl 10
Street address city: Brooklyn
Street address state: NY
Zip/Postal code: 11201-3875
General Phone: (718) 260-2500
Advertising Phone: (718) 260-2510
Advertising Fax: (718) 260-2549
General/National Adv. E-mail: JStern@CNGLocal.com
Display Adv. E-mail: Classified@CNGLocal.com
Editorial e-mail: editorial@cnglocal.com
Primary Website: brooklyndaily.com
Avg Free Circ: 32000
Audit By: Sworn/Estimate/Non-Audited
Audit Date: 12.07.2019
Personnel: Vince DiMiceli (EIC)
Parent company (for newspapers): Community News Group; Courier Life Publications, Inc.

BAYSIDE TIMES

Street address 1: 4102 Bell Blvd
Street address 2: Ste 1
Street address city: Bayside
Street address state: NY
Zip/Postal code: 11361-2794
General Phone: (718) 229-0300
General Fax: (718) 224-2934
General/National Adv. E-mail: brice@cnglocal.com
Display Adv. E-mail: classified@cnglocal.com
Editorial e-mail: timesledgernews@cnglocal.com
Primary Website: timesledger.com
Year Established: 1935
Avg Paid Circ: 11042
Audit By: Sworn/Estimate/Non-Audited
Audit Date: 10.06.2019
Personnel: Roz Liston (Ed.)
Parent company (for newspapers): Community News Group

BEACON FREE PRESS

Street address 1: 84 E Main St
Street address city: Wappingers Falls
Street address state: NY
Zip/Postal code: 12590-2504
General Phone: (845) 297-3723
General Fax: (845) 297-6810
General/National Adv. E-mail: sdnadvertising@aol.com
Editorial e-mail: newsplace@aol.com
Primary Website: sdutchessnews.com
Avg Free Circ: 8002
Audit By: Sworn/Estimate/Non-Audited
Audit Date: 10.06.2019
Personnel: Albert M. Osten (Pub.); Ray Fashona (Ed.); Janet Way (Ad.); Roxane Hoffman (Ad.)
Parent company (for newspapers): Southern Dutchess News

BELLMORE HERALD

Street address 1: 2 Endo Blvd
Street address city: Garden City
Street address state: NY
Zip/Postal code: 11530-6707
General Phone: (516) 569-4000
General Fax: (516) 569-4942
General/National Adv. E-mail: sales@liherald.com
Editorial e-mail: AOReilly@liherald.com
Primary Website: liherald.com
Avg Paid Circ: 5251
Audit By: Sworn/Estimate/Non-Audited
Audit Date: 10.06.2019
Personnel: Clifford Richner (Pub.); Stuart Richner (Pub.); Anthony O'Reily (Ed.); Dianne Ramdass (Circ. Dir.)
Parent company (for newspapers): Richner Communications, Inc.

BOONVILLE HERALD & ADIRONDACK TOURIST

Street address 1: 105 E Schuyler St
Street address city: Boonville
Street address state: NY
Zip/Postal code: 13309-1103
General Phone: (315) 942-4449
General Fax: (315) 942-4440
General/National Adv. E-mail: boonherald@aol.com
Primary Website: boonvilleherald.com
Year Established: 1852
Avg Paid Circ: 4200
Avg Free Circ: 217
Audit By: Sworn/Estimate/Non-Audited
Audit Date: 10.06.2019
Personnel: Joe Kelly (Pub. & Sr. Ed.); Sandra Hrim (Ed.); Hal Muthig (Sales Mgr.)

BRIGHTON-PITTSFORD POST

Street address 1: 73 Buffalo St
Street address city: Canandaigua
Street address state: NY
Zip/Postal code: 14424-1001
General Phone: (585) 394-0770
General Fax: (585) 394-4160
Editorial Phone: (585) 337-4276
General/National Adv. E-mail: bkesel@messengerpostmedia.com
Display Adv. E-mail: classifieds@messengerpostmedia.com
Editorial e-mail: bdoane@messengerpostmedia.com
Primary Website: mpnnow.com
Mthly Avg Views: 700000
Mthly Avg Unique Visitors: 200000
Avg Paid Circ: 147
Avg Free Circ: 8305
Audit By: Sworn/Estimate/Non-Audited
Audit Date: 10.06.2019
Personnel: Beth Kesel (Pres./Pub.)
Parent company (for newspapers): Messenger Post Media

BRONX PRESS-REVIEW

Street address 1: PO Box 1252
Street address city: Bronx
Street address state: NY
Zip/Postal code: 10471-0620
General Phone: (718) 543-5200
General Fax: (718) 543-4206
General/National Adv. E-mail: rnilva@aol.com
Editorial e-mail: bxny@aol.com
Primary Website: bronxpresspolitics.blogspot.com
Year Established: 1942
Avg Free Circ: 20000
Audit By: Sworn/Estimate/Non-Audited
Audit Date: 10.06.2019
Personnel: Andrew Wolf (Pub.); Joel Pal (Prodn. Mgr.)

BRONX TIMES REPORTER

Street address 1: 3604 E Tremont Ave
Street address 2: Ste B
Street address city: Bronx
Street address state: NY
Zip/Postal code: 10465-2050
General Phone: (718) 260-4597
Advertising Phone: (718) 260-4593
Advertising Fax: (718) 518-0038
Editorial Phone: (718) 742-3396
General/National Adv. E-mail: LGuerriero@cnglocal.com
Display Adv. E-mail: classified@cnglocal.com
Editorial e-mail: BronxTimes@cnglocal.com
Primary Website: bxtimes.com
Avg Free Circ: 26000
Audit By: Sworn/Estimate/Non-Audited
Audit Date: 10.06.2019
Personnel: Laura Guerriero (Pub.); John Collazzi (Ed.)
Parent company (for newspapers): Community Newspaper Group

BROOKHAVEN REVIEW

Street address 1: 27 W Main St
Street address city: Smithtown
Street address state: NY
Zip/Postal code: 11787-2602
General Phone: (631) 265-3500
General Fax: (631) 265-3504
General/National Adv. E-mail: messenger127e@aol.com
Avg Paid Circ: 2415
Avg Free Circ: 835
Audit By: Sworn/Estimate/Non-Audited
Audit Date: 10.06.2019
Personnel: Phillip Sciarillo (Pub.)
Parent company (for newspapers): P & S News Group

BROOKLYN COURIER

Street address 1: 1 Metrotech Ctr N
Street address 2: Fl 10
Street address city: Brooklyn
Street address state: NY
Zip/Postal code: 11201-3875
General Phone: (718) 260-2500
General/National Adv. E-mail: jstern@cnglocal.com
Display Adv. E-mail: classified@cnglocal.com
Editorial e-mail: editorial@cnglocal.com
Primary Website: brooklypaper.com
Audit By: Sworn/Estimate/Non-Audited
Audit Date: 10.06.2019
Personnel: Amanda Tarley (Classified Adv. Mgr.); Clifford Luster (Pub.)
Parent company (for newspapers): Community Newspaper Group; Courier Life Publications, Inc.

BROOKLYN DOWNTOWN STAR

Street address 1: 4523 47th St
Street address city: Woodside
Street address state: NY
Zip/Postal code: 11377-5225
General Phone: (718) 639-7000
General/National Adv. E-mail: ads@queensledger.com
Editorial e-mail: news@queensledger.com
Primary Website: BrooklynDowntownstar.com
Year Established: 2004
Avg Paid Circ: 500
Avg Free Circ: 14500

Audit By: Sworn/Estimate/Non-Audited
Audit Date: 10.06.2019
Personnel: Tammy Sanchez (Gen. Mgr.); Walter H. Sanchez (Ed.); John Sanchez (director of marketing)
Parent company (for newspapers): BQE Publishing Inc.

BROOKLYN HEIGHTS PRESS & COBBLE HILL NEWS

Street address 1: 16 Court St
Street address 2: Ste 3000
Street address city: Brooklyn
Street address state: NY
Zip/Postal code: 11241-1013
General Phone: (718) 858-2300
General Fax: (718) 858-4483
General/National Adv. E-mail: kat@brooklyneagle.com
Display Adv. E-mail: kat@brooklyneagle.com
Editorial e-mail: jdh@brooklyneagle.com
Primary Website: brooklyneagle.com
Year Established: 1937
Avg Paid Circ: 12500
Audit By: Sworn/Estimate/Non-Audited
Audit Date: 10.06.2019
Personnel: Dozier Hasty (Pub.); Pat Higgins (Adv. Mgr.); Henrick Kroquis (Ed.)
Parent company (for newspapers): Everything Brooklyn Media

BUFFALO BUSINESS FIRST

Street address 1: 465 Main St
Street address 2: Ste 100
Street address city: Buffalo
Street address state: NY
Zip/Postal code: 14203-1717
General Phone: (716) 854-5822
General Fax: (716) 854-3394
General/National Adv. E-mail: buffalo@bizjournals.com
Primary Website: buffalo.bizjournals.com
Audit By: Sworn/Estimate/Non-Audited
Audit Date: 10.06.2019
Personnel: Jack Connors (Pub.)

BUFFALO LAW JOURNAL

Street address 1: 465 Main St
Street address 2: Ste 100
Street address city: Buffalo
Street address state: NY
Zip/Postal code: 14203-1717
General Phone: (716) 541-1650
General Fax: (716) 854-3826
Editorial e-mail: jconnors@bizjournals.com
Primary Website: lawjournalbuffalo.com
Audit By: Sworn/Estimate/Non-Audited
Audit Date: 10.06.2019
Personnel: Kim Schaus (General Mgr.); Jack Connors (Pub.)

BUFFALO ROCKET

Street address 1: 9195 Main St
Street address city: Clarence
Street address state: NY
Zip/Postal code: 14031-1931
General Phone: (716) 861-3304
General Fax: (716) 873-8586
Advertising Phone: (716) 861-3304
Editorial Phone: (716) 861-3304
General/National Adv. E-mail: barbarag.gallagherprinting@gmail.com
Display Adv. E-mail: barbarag.gallagherprinting@gmail.com
Classified Adv. e-mail: barbarag.gallagherprinting@gmail.com
Editorial e-mail: barbarag.gallagherprinting@gmail.com
Primary Website: buffalorocket.com
Year Established: 1969
Avg Free Circ: 14100
Audit By: Sworn/Estimate/Non-Audited
Audit Date: 10.06.2019
Personnel: Barbara Gilboy (Ed.)
Parent company (for newspapers): Gallagher Printing

BUSINESS FIRST OF BUFFALO

Street address 1: 465 Main St
Street address 2: Ste 100
Street address city: Buffalo
Street address state: NY
Zip/Postal code: 14203-1717
General Phone: (716) 541-1600
General Fax: (716) 854-3394
General/National Adv. E-mail: buffalo@bizjournals.com
Primary Website: buffalo.bizjournals.com
Year Established: 1984
Audit By: Sworn/Estimate/Non-Audited
Audit Date: 10.06.2019
Personnel: Jack Connors (Pub.)

CANARSIE COURIER

Street address 1: 1142 E 92nd St
Street address city: Brooklyn
Street address state: NY
Zip/Postal code: 11236-3624
General Phone: (718) 257-0600
General Fax: (718) 272-0870
General/National Adv. E-mail: canarsiec@aol.com
Display Adv. E-mail: canarsiec@aol.com
Editorial e-mail: canarsiec@aol.com
Primary Website: canarsiecourier.com
Year Established: 1921
Avg Paid Circ: 10000
Audit By: Sworn/Estimate/Non-Audited
Audit Date: 10.06.2019
Personnel: Donna M. Marra (Pub.); Linda Steinmuller

CARTHAGE REPUBLICAN TRIBUNE

Street address 1: 7567 S STATE ST
Street address city: LOWVILLE
Street address state: NY
Zip/Postal code: 13367-1512
General Phone: (315) 493-1270
General Fax: (315) 376-4136
Advertising Phone: (315) 376-4997
Editorial Phone: (315) 493-1270
General/National Adv. E-mail: tribunenews@lowville.com
Display Adv. E-mail: caucter@lowville.com
Classified Adv. e-mail: dfinster@lowville.com
Editorial e-mail: jpapineau@lowville.com
Primary Website: carthagerepublicantribune.com
Year Established: 1860
Avg Paid Circ: 104
Audit By: AAM
Audit Date: 31.12.2017
Personnel: Jeremiah Papineau (Managing Editor)
Parent company (for newspapers): Johnson Newspaper Corp.

CATSKILL MOUNTAIN NEWS

Street address 1: 43414 State Hwy. 28
Street address city: Arkville
Street address state: NY
Zip/Postal code: 12406
General Phone: (845) 586-2601
General Fax: (845) 586-2366
General/National Adv. E-mail: news@catskillmountainnews.com
Primary Website: catskillmountainnews.com
Year Established: 1863
Avg Paid Circ: 4100
Avg Free Circ: 6
Audit By: Sworn/Estimate/Non-Audited
Audit Date: 10.06.2019
Personnel: Linda Schebesta (Circ. Mgr.); Doris Warner (Adv. Mgr.); Richard D. Sanford (Ed.)

CAZENOVIA REPUBLICAN

Street address 1: 2501 James St
Street address 2: Ste 100
Street address city: Syracuse
Street address state: NY
Zip/Postal code: 13206-2996
General Phone: (315) 434-8889
General Fax: (315) 434-8883
General/National Adv. E-mail: llewis@eaglenewsonline.com
Editorial e-mail: editor@cazenoviarepublican.com
Primary Website: cazenoviarepublican.com
Year Established: 1854
Avg Paid Circ: 103
Avg Free Circ: 3294
Audit By: CVC
Audit Date: 30.09.2017
Personnel: Jason Emerson (Ed.); Lori Lewis (Adv. Mgr.); David Tyler (Pub.); Lori Newcomb (Circ. Mgr)

CHAIN DRUG REVIEW

Street address 1: 126 Fifth Avenue
Street address city: New York
Street address state: NY
Zip/Postal code: 10011
General Phone: (212) 213-6000
General Fax: (212) 725-4594
General/National Adv. E-mail: pnavarre@racherpress.com
Display Adv. E-mail: pnavarre@racherpress.com
Editorial e-mail: dpinto@racherpress.com
Primary Website: chaindrugreview.com
Year Established: 1978
Avg Paid Circ: 87
Avg Free Circ: 42977
Audit By: CVC
Audit Date: 18.12.2018
Personnel: Susan Schinitsky (Pub.); David Pinto (Ed.); Peggy Navvare (Adv.); Andrea Fallin (Adv.)
Parent company (for newspapers): Racher Press

CHATHAM COURIER

Street address 1: 1 Hudson City Ctr
Street address 2: Ste 202
Street address city: Hudson
Street address state: NY
Zip/Postal code: 12534-2355
General Phone: (518) 828-1616
General Fax: (518) 671-6043
Advertising Phone: (518) 828-1616
Advertising Fax: (518) 671-6043
Editorial Phone: (518) 828-1616
Editorial Fax: (518) 671-6043
General/National Adv. E-mail: advertising@registerstar.com
Display Adv. E-mail: classifieds@registerstar.com
Editorial e-mail: chathamcourier@registerstar.com
Primary Website: chathamcourier.net
Year Established: 1862
Avg Paid Circ: 1200
Audit By: Sworn/Estimate/Non-Audited
Audit Date: 10.06.2019
Personnel: Mark Vinciguerra (Pub.); Karrie Allen (Ed.); Lori Anander (Managing editor)
Parent company (for newspapers): Johnson Newspaper Corp.

CHEEKTOWAGA BEE

Street address 1: 5564 Main St
Street address city: Williamsville
Street address state: NY
Zip/Postal code: 14221-5410
General Phone: (716) 632-4700
General Fax: (716) 633-8601
Advertising Phone: (716) 204-4934
General/National Adv. E-mail: Salesdept@BeeNews.com
Display Adv. E-mail: classified@beenews.com
Editorial e-mail: bjackson@beenews.com
Primary Website: beenews.com
Year Established: 1977
Avg Paid Circ: 1800
Audit By: Sworn/Estimate/Non-Audited
Audit Date: 10.06.2019
Personnel: Bryan Jackson (Ed.); Trey Measer (Pub.); Michael Measer (Exec. Vice Pres.); Mary Ann Cappon (Adv. Sales Dir.)
Parent company (for newspapers): Bee Group Newspapers

CHELSEA CLINTON NEWS

Street address 1: 242 W 30th St
Street address city: New York
Street address state: NY
Zip/Postal code: 10001-4903
General Phone: (212) 868-0190
General Fax: (212) 268-2935
General/National Adv. E-mail: sales@strausnews.com
Editorial e-mail: nyoffice@strausnews.com
Primary Website: nypress.com
Year Established: 1939
Avg Paid Circ: 138
Audit By: Sworn/Estimate/Non-Audited
Audit Date: 10.06.2019
Personnel: Jeanne Straus (Pres.); Alexis Gelber (Ed-in-Chief)

CLARENCE BEE

Street address 1: 5564 Main St
Street address city: Williamsville
Street address state: NY
Zip/Postal code: 14221-5410
General Phone: (716) 632-4700
General Fax: (716) 633-8601
Advertising Phone: (716) 204-4934
General/National Adv. E-mail: Salesdept@BeeNews.com
Display Adv. E-mail: classified@beenews.com
Editorial e-mail: epowers@beenews.com
Primary Website: beenews.com
Year Established: 1937
Avg Paid Circ: 3700
Avg Free Circ: 16
Audit By: Sworn/Estimate/Non-Audited
Audit Date: 10.06.2019
Personnel: Trey Measer (Pub.); Michael Measer (Exec. Vice Pres.); Ethan Powers (Ed.)
Parent company (for newspapers): Bee Group Newspapers

COLONIE/LOUDONVILLE SPOTLIGHT

Street address 1: 341 Delaware Ave
Street address city: Delmar
Street address state: NY
Zip/Postal code: 12054-1920
General Phone: (518) 439-4949
General Fax: (518) 439-5198
General/National Adv. E-mail: Advertise@spotlightnews.com
Display Adv. E-mail: classified@spotlightnews.com
Editorial e-mail: news@spotlightnews.com
Primary Website: spotlightnews.com
Year Established: 1955
Avg Paid Circ: 10000
Audit By: Sworn/Estimate/Non-Audited
Audit Date: 10.06.2019
Personnel: John McIntyre (Pub.); Bo Berezansky (VP of Sales); Michael Hallisey (Mng. Ed.)
Parent company (for newspapers): Community Media Group

COMMUNITY JOURNAL

Street address 1: 2042 N Country Rd
Street address 2: Ste 204
Street address city: Wading River
Street address state: NY
Zip/Postal code: 11792-1639
General Phone: (631) 929-8882
General Fax: (631) 929-4560
Editorial e-mail: LettersCJ25A@aol.com
Avg Paid Circ: 7500
Audit By: Sworn/Estimate/Non-Audited
Audit Date: 10.06.2019
Personnel: Bernadette S. Budd (Ed.)

COMMUNITY NEWS

Street address 1: 20 Lake Ave
Street address city: Saratoga Springs
Street address state: NY
Zip/Postal code: 12866-2314
General Phone: (518) 583-8729 ext 224
General Fax: (518) 371-0933
Advertising Phone: (518) 583-8716
General/National Adv. E-mail: cnews@saratogian.com; cnews@nycap.rr.com
Editorial e-mail: cnews@saratogian.com
Primary Website: cnweekly.com
Avg Free Circ: 26000
Audit By: Sworn/Estimate/Non-Audited
Audit Date: 10.06.2019
Personnel: Charlie Kraebel (Mng. Ed.); Michael O'Sullivan (Pub.)
Parent company (for newspapers): Digital First Media

CO-OP CITY NEWS

Street address 1: 135 Dreiser Loop
Street address city: Bronx
Street address state: NY
Zip/Postal code: 10475-2704
General Phone: (718) 320-3071
General Fax: (718) 320-7059

General/National Adv. E-mail: bronxnews@gmail.com
Editorial e-mail: bronxnews@gmail.com
Primary Website: https://sites.google.com/site/citynewsbx/
Avg Free Circ: 16000
Audit By: Sworn/Estimate/Non-Audited
Audit Date: 10.06.2019
Personnel: Christopher G. Hagedorn (Pub.); Mike Horowitz (Ed.)

CO-OP CITY TIMES

Street address 1: 2049 Bartow Ave
Street address 2: Rm 21
Street address city: Bronx
Street address state: NY
Zip/Postal code: 10475-4613
General Phone: (718) 320-3300
General Fax: (718) 320-2595
Advertising Phone: (718) 320-3300 Ext.3379/84
Editorial Phone: (718) 320-3300 Ext. 3375/77/6
General/National Adv. E-mail: cctimes@riverbaycorp.com
Display Adv. E-mail: sgreen@riverbaycorp.com
Classified Adv. e-mail: jflynn@riverbaycorp.com
Editorial e-mail: rboone@riverbaycorp.com
Primary Website: coopcity.com
Year Established: 1966
Avg Paid Circ: 0
Avg Free Circ: 18000
Audit By: Sworn/Estimate/Non-Audited
Audit Date: 10.06.2019
Personnel: Rozaan Boone (Ed.)
Parent company (for newspapers): Riverbay Corporation

COOPERSTOWN CRIER

Street address 1: 21 Railroad Ave
Street address 2: Ste 25
Street address city: Cooperstown
Street address state: NY
Zip/Postal code: 13326-1169
General Phone: (607) 547-9493
Primary Website: coopercrier.com
Audit By: Sworn/Estimate/Non-Audited
Audit Date: 10.06.2019
Parent company (for newspapers): CNHI, LLC

COUNTRY FOLKS - EAST ZONE

Street address 1: 6113 State Highway 5
Street address city: Palatine Bridge
Street address state: NY
Zip/Postal code: 13428-2809
General Phone: (518) 673-3763
General Fax: (518) 673-2381
Advertising Phone: (518) 673-0104
Editorial Phone: (518) 673-0143
General/National Adv. E-mail: info@leepub.com
Display Adv. E-mail: classifieds@leepub.com
Editorial e-mail: cfeditor@leepub.com
Primary Website: countryfolks.com
Year Established: 1970
Avg Paid Circ: 8900
Avg Free Circ: 1100
Audit By: Sworn/Estimate/Non-Audited
Audit Date: 10.06.2019
Personnel: Joan Kark-Wren (Ed.); Gary Elliott (Ed.); Bruce Button (Ad. Sales)
Parent company (for newspapers): Dispatch-Argus

COURIER STANDARD ENTERPRISE

Street address 1: 1 Venner Rd
Street address city: Amsterdam
Street address state: NY
Zip/Postal code: 12010-5617
General Phone: (518) 843-1100x103
General Fax: (518) 843-1100x103
General/National Adv. E-mail: sales@recordernews.com
Editorial e-mail: news@recordernews.com
Primary Website: courierstandardenterprise.com
Year Established: 1876
Avg Paid Circ: 2000
Avg Free Circ: 100
Audit By: Sworn/Estimate/Non-Audited
Audit Date: 10.06.2019
Personnel: Geoff Dylong (Assoc. Pub.); Kevin McClary (Pub.); Brian Krohn (Ad. Director); Joshua Thomas (Ed.)
Parent company (for newspapers): McClary Media, Inc.

CUBA PATRIOT & FREE PRESS

Street address 1: 25 W Main St
Street address city: Cuba
Street address state: NY
Zip/Postal code: 14727-1403
General Phone: (585) 968-2580
General Fax: (585) 968-2622
General/National Adv. E-mail: sales@cubapatriot.com
Editorial e-mail: mail@cubapatriot.com
Primary Website: cubapatriot.com
Year Established: 1862
Avg Paid Circ: 3870
Audit By: Sworn/Estimate/Non-Audited
Audit Date: 10.06.2019
Personnel: Melodie Farwell (Managing Ed.); Christina Arden-Hopkins (Pub.); Donna Falandys (Ad. Sales)

DAN'S PAPERS LLC

Street address 1: 158 County Road 39
Street address 2: Ste 2
Street address city: Southampton
Street address state: NY
Zip/Postal code: 11968-5252
General Phone: (631) 537-0500
General Fax: (631) 537-6374
General/National Adv. E-mail: mcable@danshamptons.com
Display Adv. E-mail: mcable@danshamptons.com
Editorial e-mail: editor@danspapers.com
Primary Website: danspapers.com
Mthly Avg Views: 1000000
Mthly Avg Unique Visitors: 200000
Year Established: 1960
Avg Free Circ: 32940
Audit By: Sworn/Estimate/Non-Audited
Audit Date: 10.06.2019
Personnel: Stacy Dermont (Sr. Ed.); Dan Rattiner (Pres./ Ed.)
Parent company (for newspapers): Manhattan Media LLC

DEPEW BEE

Street address 1: 5564 Main St
Street address city: Williamsville
Street address state: NY
Zip/Postal code: 14221-5410
General Phone: (716) 632-4700
General Fax: (716) 633-8601
Advertising Phone: (716) 204-4934
General/National Adv. E-mail: Salesdept@BeeNews.com
Display Adv. E-mail: classified@beenews.com
Editorial e-mail: julieh@beenews.com
Primary Website: beenews.com
Year Established: 1893
Avg Paid Circ: 3700
Avg Free Circ: 0
Audit By: Sworn/Estimate/Non-Audited
Audit Date: 10.06.2019
Personnel: Trey Measer (Pub.); Michael Measer (Vice Pres.)
Parent company (for newspapers): Bee Group Newspapers

DIRT MAGAZINE

Street address 1: 20 West Ave
Street address city: Chester
Street address state: NY
Zip/Postal code: 10918-1032
General Phone: (845) 469-9000
General/National Adv. E-mail: artdept@strausnews.com
Display Adv. E-mail: artdept@strausnews.com
Editorial e-mail: editor.dirt@strausnews.com
Primary Website: dirt-mag.com
Year Established: 2011
Avg Free Circ: 20233
Audit By: Sworn/Estimate/Non-Audited
Audit Date: 10.06.2019
Personnel: Mike Zummo (Mng. Ed); Jeanne Straus (Pub.)
Parent company (for newspapers): Straus News

EAGLE BULLETIN

Street address 1: 2501 James St
Street address 2: Ste 100
Street address city: Syracuse
Street address state: NY
Zip/Postal code: 13206-2996
General Phone: (315) 434-8889
General Fax: (315) 434-8883
General/National Adv. E-mail: llewis@eaglenewsonline.com
Editorial e-mail: editor@eaglebulletin.com
Primary Website: eaglebulletin.com
Avg Paid Circ: 56
Avg Free Circ: 5902
Audit By: CVC
Audit Date: 30.09.2017
Personnel: Lori Newcomb (Gen. Mgr); David Tyler (Pub.); Jason Emerson (Ed); Lori Lewis (Advt rep)

EAGLE OBSERVER

Street address 1: 2501 James St
Street address 2: Ste 100
Street address city: Syracuse
Street address state: NY
Zip/Postal code: 13206-2996
Editorial e-mail: dtyler@eaglenewsonline.com
Primary Website: eagle-observer.com
Audit By: Sworn/Estimate/Non-Audited
Audit Date: 10.06.2019
Personnel: David Tyler (Pub.)

EAGLE STAR REVIEW

Street address 1: 2501 James St
Street address 2: Ste 100
Street address city: Syracuse
Street address state: NY
Zip/Postal code: 13206-2996
General Phone: (315) 434-8889
General Fax: (315) 434-8883
General/National Adv. E-mail: newsroom@eaglenewsonline.com
Editorial e-mail: editor@eaglestarreview.com
Primary Website: eaglenewsonline.com
Avg Paid Circ: 21
Avg Free Circ: 5542
Audit By: CVC
Audit Date: 30.09.2017
Personnel: David Tyler (Pub.)

EAST AURORA ADVERTISER

Street address 1: 710 Main St
Street address city: East Aurora
Street address state: NY
Zip/Postal code: 14052-2406
General Phone: (716) 652-0320
General Fax: (716) 652-8383
General/National Adv. E-mail: ads@eastaurorany.com
Editorial e-mail: eanews@eastaurorany.com
Primary Website: mywnynews.com/east_aurora_advertiser
Year Established: 1872
Avg Paid Circ: 4440
Avg Free Circ: 340
Audit By: Sworn/Estimate/Non-Audited
Audit Date: 10.06.2019
Personnel: Adam Zeremski (Mng. Ed.)
Parent company (for newspapers): Neighbor to Neighbor News, Inc.

EAST AURORA BEE

Street address 1: 5564 Main St
Street address city: Williamsville
Street address state: NY
Zip/Postal code: 14221-5410
General Phone: (716) 632-4700
General Fax: (716) 633-8601
Advertising Phone: (716) 204-4934
General/National Adv. E-mail: Salesdept@BeeNews.com
Display Adv. E-mail: classified@beenews.com
Editorial e-mail: katep@beenews.com
Primary Website: beenews.com
Year Established: 1987
Avg Paid Circ: 2100
Audit By: Sworn/Estimate/Non-Audited
Audit Date: 10.06.2019
Personnel: Trey Measer (Pub./Pres.); Mary Anne Cappon (Adv. Sales Dir.); Scott Patterson (Adv. Sales); David Passalugo (Sales Mgr.); Michael Measer (Exec. Vice Pres.); Kate Pelczynski (Ed.); David Sherman (Mng. Ed.); Beth Hutchinson (Copy Ed.); Karl Scheitheir (Prodn. Mgr.)
Parent company (for newspapers): Bee Group Newspapers

EAST MEADOW BEACON

Street address 1: 5 Centre St
Street address city: Hempstead
Street address state: NY
Zip/Postal code: 11550-2422
General Phone: (516) 481-5400
General Fax: (516) 481-8773
General/National Adv. E-mail: thebeaconnews5@aol.com
Avg Paid Circ: 5600
Audit By: Sworn/Estimate/Non-Audited
Audit Date: 10.06.2019
Personnel: Kathleen Hoegl (Pub.); Barbara Yohe (Ed.)
Parent company (for newspapers): Nassau County Publications

EAST MEADOW HERALD

Street address 1: 2 Endo Blvd
Street address city: Garden City
Street address state: NY
Zip/Postal code: 11530-6707
General Phone: (516) 569-4000
General Fax: (516) 569-4942
General/National Adv. E-mail: sales@liherald.com
Editorial e-mail: bStieglitz@liherald.com
Primary Website: liherald.com
Avg Paid Circ: 4068
Avg Free Circ: 225
Audit By: Sworn/Estimate/Non-Audited
Audit Date: 10.06.2019
Personnel: Clifford Richner (Pub.); Stuart Richner (Pub.); Michael Bologna (Gen. Mgr.); Rhonda Glickman (Adv. Mgr.); Brian Stieglitz (Ed.)
Parent company (for newspapers): Richner Communications, Inc.

EAST ROCHESTER-FAIRPORT POST

Street address 1: 73 Buffalo St
Street address city: Canandaigua
Street address state: NY
Zip/Postal code: 14424-1001
General Phone: (585) 394-0770
General Fax: (585) 394-4160
General/National Adv. E-mail: bkesel@messengerpostmedia.com
Display Adv. E-mail: classifieds@messengerpostmedia.com
Editorial e-mail: byoung@messengerpostmedia.com
Primary Website: mpnnow.com
Mthly Avg Views: 700000
Mthly Avg Unique Visitors: 200000
Avg Paid Circ: 108
Avg Free Circ: 5179
Audit By: Sworn/Estimate/Non-Audited
Audit Date: 10.06.2019
Personnel: Beth Kesel (Pres./Pub.)
Parent company (for newspapers): Messenger Post Media

ECUADOR NEWS

Street address 1: 6403 Roosevelt Ave
Street address 2: Fl 2
Street address city: Woodside
Street address state: NY
Zip/Postal code: 11377-3643
General Phone: (718) 205-7014
General Fax: (718) 205-6580
Editorial e-mail: ecuanews@inch.com
Primary Website: ecuadornews.com.ec
Year Established: 1996
Audit By: Sworn/Estimate/Non-Audited
Audit Date: 10.06.2019
Personnel: Marcelo Segovia (CEO & Editor-in-Chief); Leonardo Ottati (Business Rep.); Carmen Arboleda (Adv. Mgr.)

ELMA REVIEW

Street address 1: 710 Main St

Street address city: East Aurora
Street address state: NY
Zip/Postal code: 14052-2406
General Phone: (716) 652-0320
General Fax: (716) 652-8383
General/National Adv. E-mail: ads@eastaurorany.com
Editorial e-mail: eanews@eastaurorany.com
Primary Website: mywnynews.com/east_aurora_advertiser
Year Established: 1979
Avg Paid Circ: 1030
Audit By: Sworn/Estimate/Non-Audited
Audit Date: 10.06.2019
Personnel: Grant M. Hamilton; Adam Zeremski (Ed.)
Parent company (for newspapers): Neighbor to Neighbor News, Inc.

FAIRFIELD COUNTY BUSINESS JOURNAL

Street address 1: 3 Gannett Dr
Street address 2: Ste G7
Street address city: White Plains
Street address state: NY
Zip/Postal code: 10604-3402
General Phone: (914) 694-3600
General Fax: (914) 694-3699
Advertising Phone: (914) 694-3600
Advertising Fax: (914) 694-3699
Editorial Phone: (914) 358-0745
Editorial Fax: (914) 694-3680
General/National Adv. E-mail: dee@westfairinc.com
Display Adv. E-mail: mrose@westfairinc.com
Editorial e-mail: bobr@westfairinc.com
Primary Website: westfaironline.com
Avg Paid Circ: 1453
Avg Free Circ: 3757
Audit By: Sworn/Estimate/Non-Audited
Audit Date: 10.06.2019
Personnel: Dee DelBello (Pub.); Bob Rozycki (Mng. Ed.); Sylvia Sikoutris (Circ. Mgr.)
Parent company (for newspapers): Westfair Communications Inc.

FARMINGDALE OBSERVER

Street address 1: 132 E 2nd St
Street address city: Mineola
Street address state: NY
Zip/Postal code: 11501-3522
General Phone: (516) 747-8282
General Fax: (516) 742-5867
General/National Adv. E-mail: advertising@antonnews.com
Display Adv. E-mail: classified@antonnews.com
Editorial e-mail: frizzo@antonmediagroup.com
Primary Website: http://farmingdale-observer.com/
Year Established: 1960
Avg Paid Circ: 5130
Audit By: Sworn/Estimate/Non-Audited
Audit Date: 10.06.2019
Personnel: Angela Susan Anton (Pub.); Iris Picone (Adv. Mgr.); Joy DiDonato (Circ. Mgr.); Frank Rizzo (Ed.); Carrie Seaman (Mng. Ed.)
Parent company (for newspapers): Anton Community Newspapers

FLUSHING TIMES

Street address 1: 4102 Bell Blvd
Street address city: Bayside
Street address state: NY
Zip/Postal code: 11361-2792
General Phone: (718) 229-0300
General Fax: (718) 229-7117
Advertising Phone: (718) 229-0300
Advertising Fax: (718) 229-7117
Editorial Phone: (718) 229-0300
Editorial Fax: (718) 229-7117
General/National Adv. E-mail: brice@cnglocal.com
Display Adv. E-mail: classified@cnglocal.com
Editorial e-mail: timesledgernews@cnglocal.com
Primary Website: timesledger.com
Year Established: 1992
Avg Paid Circ: 5015
Audit By: Sworn/Estimate/Non-Audited
Audit Date: 10.06.2019
Personnel: Roz Liston (Mng. Ed.); Brian Rice (Display/Online Adv.)
Parent company (for newspapers): Queens Village Times (OOB)

FOREST HILLS LEDGER

Street address 1: 4102 Bell Blvd
Street address city: Bayside
Street address state: NY
Zip/Postal code: 11361-2792
General Phone: (718) 229-0300
General Fax: (718) 224-2934
General/National Adv. E-mail: brice@cnglocal.com
Display Adv. E-mail: classified@cnglocal.com
Editorial e-mail: timesledgernews@cnglocal.com
Primary Website: timesledger.com
Avg Paid Circ: 2503
Audit By: Sworn/Estimate/Non-Audited
Audit Date: 10.06.2019
Personnel: Roz Liston (Ed.)
Parent company (for newspapers): Queens Village Times (OOB)

FOREST HILLS/REGO PARK TIMES

Street address 1: 6960 Grand Ave
Street address city: Maspeth
Street address state: NY
Zip/Postal code: 11378-1828
General Phone: (718) 639-7000
General Fax: (718) 429-1234
General/National Adv. E-mail: ads@queensledger.com
Editorial e-mail: news@queensledger.com
Primary Website: foresthillstimes.com
Year Established: 1995
Avg Paid Circ: 18000
Avg Free Circ: 165
Audit By: Sworn/Estimate/Non-Audited
Audit Date: 10.06.2019
Personnel: Walter H. Sanchez (Pub.); Tammy Sanchez (Gen. Mgr.)
Parent company (for newspapers): BQE Publishing Inc.

FORWARD NEWSPAPER

Street address 1: 125 Maiden Ln
Street address 2: Fl 8
Street address city: New York
Street address state: NY
Zip/Postal code: 10038-5015
General Phone: (212) 889-8200
Advertising Phone: (212) 453-9420
Advertising Fax: (212) 689-4255
Editorial Fax: (212) 447-6406
General/National Adv. E-mail: advertising@forward.com
Display Adv. E-mail: classified@forward.com
Editorial e-mail: newsdesk@forward.com
Primary Website: forward.com
Year Established: 1897
Avg Paid Circ: 29479
Audit By: Sworn/Estimate/Non-Audited
Audit Date: 10.06.2019
Personnel: Samuel Norich (CEO/Pub.); Jane Eisner (Ed.); Dan Friedman (Managing Ed.); Kim Rosenberg Amzallag (Adv. Dir.); Bob Goldfarb (Mktg. Dir.)

FRANKLIN SQUARE/ELMONT HERALD

Street address 1: 2 Endo Blvd
Street address city: Garden City
Street address state: NY
Zip/Postal code: 11530-6707
General Phone: (516) 569-4000
General Fax: (516) 569-4942
General/National Adv. E-mail: sales@liherald.com
Display Adv. E-mail: sales@liherald.com
Primary Website: liherald.com
Avg Paid Circ: 6096
Audit By: Sworn/Estimate/Non-Audited
Audit Date: 10.06.2019
Personnel: Jeff Bessen (Executive Ed.); Rhonda Glickman (Adv. Mgr.)
Parent company (for newspapers): Richner Communications, Inc.

FRESH MEADOWS TIMES

Street address 1: 4102 Bell Blvd
Street address city: Bayside
Street address state: NY
Zip/Postal code: 11361-2792
General Phone: (718) 260-2500
General Fax: (718) 260-2549
Advertising Phone: (718) 260-2500
Advertising Fax: (718) 260-2549
Editorial Phone: (718) 260-2500
Editorial Fax: (718) 260-2549
General/National Adv. E-mail: brice@cnglocal.com
Display Adv. E-mail: classified@cnglocal.com
Editorial e-mail: timesledgernews@cnglocal.com
Primary Website: timesledger.com
Avg Paid Circ: 21000
Audit By: Sworn/Estimate/Non-Audited
Audit Date: 10.06.2019
Personnel: Roz Liston (Ed.); Amanda Tarley (Classified Advertising Director); Brian Rice (Display & Online Advertising)
Parent company (for newspapers): Community Newspaper Group; Queens Village Times (OOB)

GARDEN CITY LIFE

Street address 1: 132 E 2nd St
Street address city: Mineola
Street address state: NY
Zip/Postal code: 11501-3522
General Phone: (516) 747-8282
General Fax: (641) 742-5867
General/National Adv. E-mail: advertising@antonnews.com
Display Adv. E-mail: classified@antonnews.com
Editorial e-mail: gardencitylife@antonnews.com
Primary Website: http://gardencity-life.com/
Year Established: 1985
Avg Paid Circ: 6010
Audit By: Sworn/Estimate/Non-Audited
Audit Date: 10.06.2019
Personnel: Angela Susan Anton (Pub.); Iris Picone (Adv. Mgr.); Joy DiDonato (Circ. Mgr.); Dave Gil de Rubio (Ed.); Cary Sieman (Mng. Ed.)
Parent company (for newspapers): Anton Community Newspapers

GARDEN CITY NEWS

Street address 1: 821 Franklin Ave
Street address 2: Ste 208
Street address city: Garden City
Street address state: NY
Zip/Postal code: 11530-4519
General Phone: (516) 294-8900
General Fax: (516) 294-8924
Advertising Phone: (516) 294-8900
Advertising Fax: (516) 294-8924
Editorial Phone: (516) 294-8900
Editorial Fax: (516) 294-8924
General/National Adv. E-mail: kpiltz@gcnews.com
Display Adv. E-mail: sdaly@gcnews.com
Editorial e-mail: editor@gcnews.com
Primary Website: gcnews.com
Avg Paid Circ: 8481
Audit By: Sworn/Estimate/Non-Audited
Audit Date: 10.06.2019
Personnel: Meg Morgan Norris (Ed./Pub.); Ken Piltz (Adv. Sales)
Parent company (for newspapers): Litmor Publishing

GATES-CHILI POST

Street address 1: 73 Buffalo St
Street address city: Canandaigua
Street address state: NY
Zip/Postal code: 14424-1001
General Phone: (585) 394-0770
General Fax: (585) 394-4160
General/National Adv. E-mail: bkesel@messengerpostmedia.com
Display Adv. E-mail: classifieds@messengerpostmedia.com
Editorial e-mail: jbattaglia@messengerpostmedia.com
Primary Website: mpnnow.com
Mthly Avg Views: 700000
Mthly Avg Unique Visitors: 200000
Avg Paid Circ: 52
Avg Free Circ: 4973
Audit By: Sworn/Estimate/Non-Audited
Audit Date: 10.06.2019
Personnel: Beth Kesel (Pres./Pub.)
Parent company (for newspapers): Messenger Post Media

GENESEE COUNTRY EXPRESS

Street address 1: 113 Main St
Street address 2: Ste 2
Street address city: Dansville
Street address state: NY
Zip/Postal code: 14437-1611
General Phone: (585) 335-2271
General Fax: (585) 335-6957
General/National Adv. E-mail: lesbowen@dansvilleonline.com
Display Adv. E-mail: kellyschecter@dansvilleonline.com
Editorial e-mail: lesbowen@dansvilleonline.com
Primary Website: dansvilleonline.com
Year Established: 1851
Avg Paid Circ: 2500
Avg Free Circ: 6
Audit By: Sworn/Estimate/Non-Audited
Audit Date: 10.06.2019
Personnel: Melissa VanSkiver (Advertising Director); Rick Emanuel (Regional Publisher); John Anderson (Editor); Judy Smith-Cronk (Multi-Media Sales Executive)
Parent company (for newspapers): CherryRoad Media

GLEN COVE RECORD-PILOT

Street address 1: 132 E 2nd St
Street address city: Mineola
Street address state: NY
Zip/Postal code: 11501-3522
General Phone: (516) 747-8282
General Fax: (516) 742-5867
General/National Adv. E-mail: advertising@antonnews.com
Display Adv. E-mail: classified@antonnews.com
Editorial e-mail: jnossa@antonmediagroup.com
Primary Website: antonnews.com
Year Established: 1953
Avg Paid Circ: 5344
Avg Free Circ: 1128
Audit By: Sworn/Estimate/Non-Audited
Audit Date: 10.06.2019
Personnel: Angela Susan Anton (Pub.); Iris Picone (Adv. Mgr.); Joy DiDonato (Circ. Mgr.); Jill Nossa (Ed.); Cary Seaman (Mng. Ed.)
Parent company (for newspapers): Anton Community Newspapers

GLENDALE REGISTER

Street address 1: 6960 Grand Ave
Street address city: Maspeth
Street address state: NY
Zip/Postal code: 11378-1828
General Phone: (718) 639-7000
General Fax: (718) 429-1234
General/National Adv. E-mail: ads@queensledger.com
Editorial e-mail: news@queensledger.com
Primary Website: queensledger.com
Year Established: 1935
Avg Paid Circ: 1320
Avg Free Circ: 165
Audit By: Sworn/Estimate/Non-Audited
Audit Date: 10.06.2019
Personnel: Tammy Sanchez (Gen. Mgr.); Walter H. Sanchez (Ed.)
Parent company (for newspapers): BQE Publishing Inc.

GOLD COAST GAZETTE

Street address 1: 57 Glen St
Street address city: Glen Cove
Street address state: NY
Zip/Postal code: 11542-2755
General Phone: (516) 671-2360
General Fax: (516) 569-4942
General/National Adv. E-mail: mail@goldcoastgazette.net
Primary Website: goldcoastherald.com
Audit By: Sworn/Estimate/Non-Audited
Audit Date: 10.06.2019
Personnel: Kevin Horton (Ed./Pub.)

Parent company (for newspapers): Richner Communications, Inc.

GOWANDA NEWS

Street address 1: 75 Boxwood Ln
Street address city: Buffalo
Street address state: NY
Zip/Postal code: 14227-2707
General Phone: (716) 532-2288
General Fax: (716) 532-3056
Editorial Phone: (716) 532-2288 ext 104
General/National Adv. E-mail: mstockdale@metrowny.com
Editorial e-mail: mpankow@metrowny.com
Primary Website: metrowny.com
Mthly Avg Views: 1640
Mthly Avg Unique Visitors: 1032
Year Established: 1827
Avg Free Circ: 9059
Audit By: Sworn/Estimate/Non-Audited
Audit Date: 10.06.2019
Personnel: Mary Pankow (Ed.); Maureen Stockdale (Ad. Sales); Judy Covert (Off. Mgr.); Gary Durawa (Pub.); Bill Marshall (Circ. Mgr)
Parent company (for newspapers): Metro Group, Inc.

GREAT NECK NEWS

Street address 1: 105 Hillside Ave
Street address 2: Ste I
Street address city: Williston Park
Street address state: NY
Zip/Postal code: 11596-2311
General Phone: (516) 307-1045
General Fax: (516) 307-1046
Advertising Phone: (516) 307-1045 Ext. 212
Editorial Phone: (516) 307-1045 Ext. 201
General/National Adv. E-mail: mspitalnick@theislandnow.com
Display Adv. E-mail: lmatinale@theislandnow.com
Editorial e-mail: sblank@theislandnow.com
Primary Website: theislandnow.com
Mthly Avg Views: 116000
Mthly Avg Unique Visitors: 38000
Year Established: 1926
Avg Paid Circ: 4033
Audit By: Sworn/Estimate/Non-Audited
Audit Date: 10.06.2019
Personnel: Steven Blank (Ed & Pub); Holly Blank (Circulation Mgr); Joe Nikic (Reporter); Melissa Spitalnick (ACCT EXECUTIVE)
Parent company (for newspapers): Blank Slate Media LLC

GREAT NECK RECORD

Street address 1: 132 E 2nd St
Street address city: Mineola
Street address state: NY
Zip/Postal code: 11501-3522
General Phone: (516) 747-8282
General Fax: (516) 482-4491
General/National Adv. E-mail: advertising@antonnews.com
Display Adv. E-mail: classified@antonnews.com
Editorial e-mail: sarbitaljacoby@antonmediagroup.com
Primary Website: http://greatneckrecord.com/
Year Established: 1933
Avg Paid Circ: 6998
Avg Free Circ: 988
Audit By: Sworn/Estimate/Non-Audited
Audit Date: 10.06.2019
Personnel: Angela S. Anton (Pub.); Joy DiDonato (Circ. Mgr.); Sheri ArbitalJacoby (Mng. Ed.); Karen Mengel (Prod. Dir.)
Parent company (for newspapers): Anton Community Newspapers

GREECE POST

Street address 1: 73 Buffalo St
Street address city: Canandaigua
Street address state: NY
Zip/Postal code: 14424-1001
General Phone: (585) 394-0770
General Fax: (585) 394-4160
General/National Adv. E-mail: bkesel@messengerpostmedia.com
Display Adv. E-mail: classifieds@messengerpostmedia.com
Editorial e-mail: bdoane@messengerpostmedia.com
Primary Website: mpnnow.com
Mthly Avg Views: 700000
Mthly Avg Unique Visitors: 200000
Avg Paid Circ: 88
Avg Free Circ: 14569
Audit By: Sworn/Estimate/Non-Audited
Audit Date: 10.06.2019
Personnel: Beth Kesel (Gen. Mgr./Adv. Dir.); Brian Doane (Pres./Pub.)
Parent company (for newspapers): Messenger Post Media

GREENBUSH LIFE

Street address 1: 270 River Triangle
Street address 2: Suite 202B
Street address city: Troy
Street address state: NY
Zip/Postal code: 12180
General Phone: (518) 270-1200
General Fax: (518) 270-1251
Advertising Phone: (518) 290-3896
Advertising Fax: (518) 583-8014
Editorial Phone: (518) 290-3909
General/National Adv. E-mail: ttergeoglou@freemanonline.com
Display Adv. E-mail: aschaal@digitalfirstmedia.com
Editorial e-mail: ckraebel@digitalfirstmedia.com
Primary Website: troyrecord.com/greenbush
Audit By: Sworn/Estimate/Non-Audited
Audit Date: 10.06.2019
Personnel: Timothy Tergeoglou (Regional Advertising Director); Charlie Krabel (Ed.); Michael O'Sullivan

GREENE COUNTY NEWS

Street address 1: 1 Hudson City Ctr
Street address 2: Ste 202
Street address city: Hudson
Street address state: NY
Zip/Postal code: 12534-2355
General Phone: (518) 828-1616
General Fax: (518) 671-6043
Editorial Phone: (518) 828-1616
Editorial Fax: (518) 828-3870
General/National Adv. E-mail: advertising@registerstar.com
Display Adv. E-mail: Classifieds@registerstar.com
Editorial e-mail: lanander.windhamjournal@registerstar.com
Primary Website: registerstar.com/greene_county_news
Year Established: 1907
Avg Paid Circ: 668
Audit By: Sworn/Estimate/Non-Audited
Audit Date: 10.06.2019
Personnel: Mark Vinciguerra (Pub.)

GREENPOINT STAR & NORTHSIDE WEEKLY NEWS

Street address 1: 4523 47th St
Street address city: Woodside
Street address state: NY
Zip/Postal code: 11377-5225
General Phone: (718) 639-7000
General/National Adv. E-mail: ads@queensledger.com
Editorial e-mail: news@queensledger.com
Primary Website: greenpointstar.com
Year Established: 1898
Avg Paid Circ: 2000
Avg Free Circ: 13000
Audit By: Sworn/Estimate/Non-Audited
Audit Date: 10.06.2019
Personnel: Tammy Sanchez (Gen. Mgr.); Walter H. Sanchez (Ed.)
Parent company (for newspapers): BQE Publishing Inc.

HAMILTON COUNTY EXPRESS

Street address 1: 2892 State Route 30
Street address city: Speculator
Street address state: NY
Zip/Postal code: 12164
General Phone: (518) 843-1100
General Fax: (518) 843-6580
Editorial Phone: (518) 843-1100 x312
Editorial Fax: (518) 843-6580
General/National Adv. E-mail: briankrohn@recordernews.com
Display Adv. E-mail: advertising@recordernews.com
Editorial e-mail: editor@hamiltoncountyexpress.com
Primary Website: hamiltoncountyexpress.com
Year Established: 1949
Avg Paid Circ: 2681
Avg Free Circ: 81
Audit By: Sworn/Estimate/Non-Audited
Audit Date: 10.06.2019
Personnel: Kevin McClary (Pub.); Brian Krohn (Mktg. Dir); Gwendolyn Girsdansky (Ed.)
Parent company (for newspapers): Port Jackson Media LLC

HAMLIN CLARKSON HERALD

Street address 1: 1776 Hilton Parma Corners Rd
Street address city: Spencerport
Street address state: NY
Zip/Postal code: 14559-9501
General Phone: (585) 352-3411
General Fax: (585) 352-4811
Advertising Phone: (585) 352-3411 ext. 128
Editorial Phone: (585) 352-3411 ext. 127
General/National Adv. E-mail: production@westsidenewsny.com
Display Adv. E-mail: classified.advertising@westsidenewsny.com
Editorial e-mail: editor@westsidenewsny.com
Primary Website: westsidenewsonline.com
Year Established: 1988
Avg Paid Circ: 10
Avg Free Circ: 5915
Audit By: CVC
Audit Date: 30.09.2017
Personnel: Keith Ryan (Pub.); Evelyn Dow (Editor); Karen Fien (Ad. & Production Manager)
Parent company (for newspapers): Westside News

HICKSVILLE ILLUSTRATED NEWS

Street address 1: 132 E 2nd St
Street address city: Mineola
Street address state: NY
Zip/Postal code: 11501-3522
General Phone: (516) 747-8282
General Fax: (516) 742-5867
Editorial e-mail: aeichler@antonmediagroup.com
Primary Website: hicksvillenews.com
Year Established: 1986
Avg Paid Circ: 5000
Audit By: Sworn/Estimate/Non-Audited
Audit Date: 10.06.2019
Personnel: Allison Eichler (Ed.); Angela Susan Anton (Pub.); Frank Virga (Pres./COO)
Parent company (for newspapers): Anton Community Newspapers

HICKSVILLE MID-ISLAND TIMES

Street address 1: 821 Franklin Ave
Street address 2: Ste 206
Street address city: Garden City
Street address state: NY
Zip/Postal code: 11530-4519
General Phone: (516) 294-8900
General Fax: (516) 294-8924
Advertising Phone: (516) 294-8900
Advertising Fax: (516) 294-8924
Editorial Phone: (516) 294-8900
Editorial Fax: (516) 294-8924
General/National Adv. E-mail: kpiltz@gcnews.com
Display Adv. E-mail: sdaly@gcnews.com
Editorial e-mail: editor@gcnews.com
Primary Website: gcnews.com
Avg Paid Circ: 2765
Audit By: Sworn/Estimate/Non-Audited
Audit Date: 10.06.2019
Personnel: Meg Morgan Norris (Pub.); Ken Piltz (Adv. Mgr.)
Parent company (for newspapers): Litmor Publishing

HOME REPORTER AND SUNSET NEWS

Street address 1: 8723 3rd Ave
Street address city: Brooklyn
Street address state: NY
Zip/Postal code: 11209-5103
General Phone: (718) 238-6600
General Fax: (718) 238-6630
General/National Adv. E-mail: ads@homereporternews.com
Editorial e-mail: editorial@homereporternews.com
Primary Website: homereporter.com
Avg Paid Circ: 9696
Audit By: Sworn/Estimate/Non-Audited
Audit Date: 10.06.2019
Personnel: J. Frank Griffin (Pub.); Rick Buttacavoli (Ed.)

HUDSON VALLEY NEWS

Street address 1: PO Box 268
Street address city: Hyde Park
Street address state: NY
Zip/Postal code: 12538-0268
General Phone: (845) 233-4651
General/National Adv. E-mail: advertising@thehudsonvalleynews.com
Editorial e-mail: editorial@thehudsonvalleynews.com
Primary Website: thehudsonvalleynews.com
Audit By: Sworn/Estimate/Non-Audited
Audit Date: 10.06.2019
Personnel: Jim Langan (Exec. Ed.); Mahlon Goer (Adv. Dir.); Caroline Carey (Pub.)

HUDSON VALLEY PRESS

Street address 1: PO Box 2160
Street address city: Newburgh
Street address state: NY
Zip/Postal code: 12550-0332
General Phone: (845) 562-1313
General Fax: (845) 562-1348
General/National Adv. E-mail: sales@hvpress.net
Display Adv. E-mail: ads@hvpress.net
Editorial e-mail: editor@hypress.net
Primary Website: hvpress.net
Year Established: 1983
Audit By: Sworn/Estimate/Non-Audited
Audit Date: 10.06.2019
Personnel: Chuck Stewart (Exec. Ed & Pub.)

INDEPENDENT MIRROR

Street address 1: 80 N Jefferson St
Street address city: Mexico
Street address state: NY
Zip/Postal code: 13114-3001
General Phone: (315) 963-7813
General Fax: (315) 963-4087
General/National Adv. E-mail: ocwadvertising@cnymail.com
Display Adv. E-mail: ocwadvertising@cnymail.com
Editorial e-mail: ocweeklies@cnymail.com
Primary Website: oswegocountyweeklies.com
Year Established: 1861
Avg Paid Circ: 3260
Audit By: Sworn/Estimate/Non-Audited
Audit Date: 10.06.2019
Personnel: Rose Ann Parsons (Mng. Ed.)

IRONDEQUOIT POST

Street address 1: 73 Buffalo St
Street address city: Canandaigua
Street address state: NY
Zip/Postal code: 14424-1001
General Phone: (585) 394-0770
General Fax: (585) 394-4160
General/National Adv. E-mail: bkesel@messengerpostmedia.com
Display Adv. E-mail: classifieds@messengerpostmedia.com
Editorial e-mail: lquinlan@messengerpostmedia.com
Primary Website: mpnnow.com
Mthly Avg Views: 700000
Mthly Avg Unique Visitors: 200000
Avg Paid Circ: 83
Avg Free Circ: 7104
Audit By: Sworn/Estimate/Non-Audited
Audit Date: 10.06.2019
Personnel: Beth Kesel; Brian Doane
Parent company (for newspapers): Messenger Post Media

ISLAND DISPATCH

Street address 1: 1859 Whitehaven Rd
Street address city: Grand Island
Street address state: NY
Zip/Postal code: 14072-1803
General Phone: (716) 773-7676
General Fax: (716) 773-7190
General/National Adv. E-mail: majoraccounts@wnypapers.com

Display Adv. E-mail: Grandislandsales@wnypapers.com
Classified Adv. e-mail: nfpclassified@wnypapers.com
Editorial e-mail: dispatch@wnypapers.com
Primary Website: wnypapers.com
Year Established: 1944
Avg Paid Circ: 1550
Avg Free Circ: 0
Audit By: Sworn/Estimate/Non-Audited
Audit Date: 10.06.2019
Personnel: A. Skip Mazenauer (Pub.); Larry Austin (Ed.); Terry Duffy (Mng. Ed.); Josh Maloney (editor)
Parent company (for newspapers): Niagara Frontier Publications

ISLIP BULLETIN

Street address 1: 20 Medford Ave
Street address 2: Ste 112
Street address city: Patchogue
Street address state: NY
Zip/Postal code: 11772-1220
General Phone: (631) 475-1000
General Fax: (631) 475-1565
Advertising Phone: (631) 475-1000 x17
Editorial Phone: (631) 475-1000 x13
General/National Adv. E-mail: ttlia@optonline.net
Editorial e-mail: scnibletter@optonline.net
Primary Website: islipbulletin.net
Year Established: 1948
Avg Paid Circ: 1500
Audit By: Sworn/Estimate/Non-Audited
Audit Date: 10.06.2019
Personnel: John T. Tuthill (Pub.); Joanne LaBarca (Gen. Mgr.); Liz Finnigan (Editor); Terry Tuthill (Asst. Pub.); Monica Musetti-Carlin (Ad.)

ITHACA TIMES

Street address 1: 109 N Cayuga St
Street address 2: Ste A
Street address city: Ithaca
Street address state: NY
Zip/Postal code: 14850-4340
General Phone: (607) 277-7000
General Fax: (607) 277-1012
General/National Adv. E-mail: jbilinski@ithacatimes.com
Primary Website: ithaca.com
Avg Free Circ: 22936
Audit By: Sworn/Estimate/Non-Audited
Audit Date: 10.06.2019

JACKSON HEIGHTS TIMES

Street address 1: 4102 Bell Blvd
Street address city: Bayside
Street address state: NY
Zip/Postal code: 11361-2792
General Phone: (718) 260-2500
General Fax: (718) 260-2549
Advertising Phone: (718) 260-2500
Advertising Fax: (718) 260-2549
Editorial Phone: (718) 260-2500
Editorial Fax: (718) 260-2549
General/National Adv. E-mail: brice@cnglocal.com
Display Adv. E-mail: classified@cnglocal.com
Editorial e-mail: timesledgernews@cnglocal.com
Primary Website: timesledger.com
Avg Paid Circ: 21000
Audit By: Sworn/Estimate/Non-Audited
Audit Date: 10.06.2019
Personnel: Roz Liston (Ed.); Amanda Tarley (Classified Advertising Director); Brian Rice (Display & Online Advertising)
Parent company (for newspapers): Community Newspaper Group; Queens Village Times (OOB)

JAMAICA TIMES

Street address 1: 4102 Bell Blvd
Street address city: Bayside
Street address state: NY
Zip/Postal code: 11361-2792
General Phone: (718) 260-2500
General Fax: (718) 260-2549
Advertising Phone: (718) 260-2500
Advertising Fax: (718) 260-2549
Editorial Phone: (718) 260-2500
Editorial Fax: (718) 260-2549
General/National Adv. E-mail: brice@cnglocal.com
Display Adv. E-mail: classified@cnglocal.com
Editorial e-mail: timesledgernews@cnglocal.com
Primary Website: timesledger.com
Avg Paid Circ: 21000
Audit By: Sworn/Estimate/Non-Audited
Audit Date: 10.06.2019
Personnel: Roz Liston (Mng. Ed.); Amanda Tarley (Classified Advertising Director); Brian Rice (Display & Online Advertising)
Parent company (for newspapers): Community Newspaper Group; Queens Village Times (OOB)

JEFFERSON COUNTY JOURNAL

Street address 1: 7 Main St
Street address city: Adams
Street address state: NY
Zip/Postal code: 13605-1228
General Phone: (315) 232-2141
General Fax: (315) 232-4586
General/National Adv. E-mail: jcjesfucn@citlink.net
Year Established: 1844
Avg Paid Circ: 3500
Audit By: Sworn/Estimate/Non-Audited
Audit Date: 10.06.2019
Personnel: Karl A. Fowler (Ed.)

JERICHO NEWS JOURNAL

Street address 1: 821 Franklin Ave
Street address 2: Ste 206
Street address city: Garden City
Street address state: NY
Zip/Postal code: 11530-4519
General Phone: (516) 294-8900
General Fax: (516) 294-8924
Advertising Phone: (516) 294-8900
Advertising Fax: (516) 294-8924
Editorial Phone: (516) 294-8900
Editorial Fax: (516) 294-8924
General/National Adv. E-mail: kpiltz@gcnews.com
Display Adv. E-mail: sdaly@gcnews.com
Editorial e-mail: editor@gcnews.com
Primary Website: gcnews.com
Avg Paid Circ: 2727
Audit By: Sworn/Estimate/Non-Audited
Audit Date: 10.06.2019
Personnel: Meg Morgan Norris (Ed.); Ken Piltz (Adv. Dir.)
Parent company (for newspapers): Litmor Publishing

JOURNAL AND REPUBLICAN

Street address 1: 7567 S State St
Street address city: Lowville
Street address state: NY
Zip/Postal code: 13367-1512
General Phone: (315) 376-3525
General Fax: (315) 376-4136
Advertising Phone: (315) 376-4997
Advertising Fax: (315) 376-4136
Editorial Phone: (315) 376-6851
General/National Adv. E-mail: caucter@lowville.com
Display Adv. E-mail: dfinster@lowville.com
Editorial e-mail: jpapineau@lowville.com
Primary Website: journalandrepublican.com
Year Established: 1830
Avg Paid Circ: 4106
Avg Free Circ: 22
Audit By: Sworn/Estimate/Non-Audited
Audit Date: 10.06.2019
Personnel: Jeremiah Papineau (Managing Editor)
Parent company (for newspapers): Johnson Newspaper Corp.

KEN-TON BEE

Street address 1: 5564 Main St
Street address city: Williamsville
Street address state: NY
Zip/Postal code: 14221-5410
General Phone: (716) 632-4700
General Fax: (716) 633-8601
Advertising Phone: (716) 204-4934
General/National Adv. E-mail: Salesdept@BeeNews.com
Display Adv. E-mail: classified@beenews.com
Editorial e-mail: awalters@beenews.com
Primary Website: beenews.com
Year Established: 1982
Avg Paid Circ: 1800
Avg Free Circ: 10
Audit By: Sworn/Estimate/Non-Audited
Audit Date: 10.06.2019
Personnel: Michael Measer (Exec. Vice Pres.); Trey Measer (Pub.); David Passalugo (Adv. Mgr.); Mike Measer (Circ. Mgr.); Anna Walters (Ed.)
Parent company (for newspapers): Bee Group Newspapers

KINGSTON TIMES

Street address 1: 322 Wall St
Street address city: Kingston
Street address state: NY
Zip/Postal code: 12401-3820
General Phone: (845) 334-8200
General Fax: (845) 334-8202
General/National Adv. E-mail: info@ulsterpublishing.com
Display Adv. E-mail: classifieds@ulsterpublishing.com
Editorial e-mail: kingstontimes@ulsterpublishing.com
Primary Website: kingstonx.com
Avg Paid Circ: 1550
Audit By: Sworn/Estimate/Non-Audited
Audit Date: 10.06.2019
Personnel: Dan Barton (Ed.); Genia Wickwire (Adv. Dir./Circ Mgr./Classified Adv.); Brian Hollander (Pub.)
Parent company (for newspapers): Ulster Publishing

LANCASTER BEE

Street address 1: 5564 Main St
Street address city: Williamsville
Street address state: NY
Zip/Postal code: 14221-5410
General Phone: (716) 632-4700
General Fax: (716) 633-8601
Advertising Phone: (716) 204-4934
General/National Adv. E-mail: Salesdept@BeeNews.com
Display Adv. E-mail: classified@beenews.com
Editorial e-mail: arobb@beenews.com
Primary Website: beenews.com
Year Established: 1877
Audit By: Sworn/Estimate/Non-Audited
Audit Date: 10.06.2019
Personnel: Trey Measer (Pub); Michael Measer (Exec. Vice Pres.)
Parent company (for newspapers): Bee Group Newspapers

LATHAM LIFE

Street address 1: 270 River Triangle
Street address 2: Suite 202B
Street address city: Troy
Street address state: NY
Zip/Postal code: 12180
General Phone: (518) 270-1200
Advertising Phone: (518) 270-1204
Advertising Fax: (518) 583-8014
Editorial Phone: (518) 290-3909
General/National Adv. E-mail: letters@troyrecord.com
Editorial e-mail: llewis@troyrecord.com
Primary Website: troyrecord.com/
Audit By: Sworn/Estimate/Non-Audited
Audit Date: 10.06.2019
Personnel: Timothy Tergeoglou (Ad. Sales Mgr.); Charlie Krabel (Ed.); Michael O'Sullivan (Pub.)

LAURELTON TIMES

Street address 1: 4102 Bell Blvd
Street address city: Bayside
Street address state: NY
Zip/Postal code: 11361-2792
General Phone: (718) 260-2500
General Fax: (718) 260-2549
Advertising Phone: (718) 260-2500
Advertising Fax: (718) 260-2549
Editorial Phone: (718) 260-2500
Editorial Fax: (718) 260-2549
General/National Adv. E-mail: brice@cnglocal.com
Display Adv. E-mail: classified@cnglocal.com
Editorial e-mail: timesledgernews@cnglocal.com
Primary Website: timesledger.com
Avg Paid Circ: 21000
Audit By: Sworn/Estimate/Non-Audited
Audit Date: 10.06.2019
Personnel: Roz Liston (Ed.); Amanda Tarley (Classified Advertising Director); Brian Rice (Display & Online Advertising)
Parent company (for newspapers): Community Newspaper Group; Queens Village Times (OOB)

LE ROY PENNYSAVER & NEWS

Street address 1: 1 Church St
Street address city: Le Roy
Street address state: NY
Zip/Postal code: 14482-1017
General Phone: (585) 768-2201
General Fax: (585) 768-6334
General/National Adv. E-mail: pennysaver@leroyny.com
Display Adv. E-mail: office@leroyny.com
Editorial e-mail: editor@leroyny.com
Primary Website: leroyny.com
Mthly Avg Views: 2783
Mthly Avg Unique Visitors: 938
Year Established: 1935
Avg Free Circ: 6733
Audit By: CVC
Audit Date: 30.09.2017
Personnel: David Grayson (Pub./Ed.); Terry Guilford (Prod. Mgr); Tom Cuskey (Sales Dir.)
Parent company (for newspapers): Dray Enterprises Inc.

LEVITTOWN TRIBUNE

Street address 1: 132 E 2nd St
Street address city: Mineola
Street address state: NY
Zip/Postal code: 11501-3522
General Phone: (516) 747-8282
General Fax: (516) 742-5867
General/National Adv. E-mail: advertising@antonnews.com
Display Adv. E-mail: classified@antonnews.com
Editorial e-mail: jfauci@antonmediagroup.com
Primary Website: http://levittown-tribune.com/
Year Established: 1948
Avg Paid Circ: 3290
Avg Free Circ: 764
Audit By: Sworn/Estimate/Non-Audited
Audit Date: 10.06.2019
Personnel: Angela Anton (Pub.); Jennifer Fauci (Ed.); Joy DiDonato (Circ. Mgr.)
Parent company (for newspapers): Anton Community Newspapers

LEWISTON-PORTER SENTINEL

Street address 1: 1859 Whitehaven Rd
Street address city: Grand Island
Street address state: NY
Zip/Postal code: 14072-1803
General Phone: (716) 773-7676
General Fax: (716) 773-7190
General/National Adv. E-mail: majoraccounts@wnypapers.com
Display Adv. E-mail: Sentinelsales@wnypapers.com
Classified Adv. e-mail: nfpclassified@wnypapers.com
Editorial e-mail: sentinel@wnypapers.com
Primary Website: wnypapers.com
Year Established: 1987
Avg Paid Circ: 0
Avg Free Circ: 10800
Sat. Circulation Paid: 0
Sat. Circulation Free: 10800
Audit By: Sworn/Estimate/Non-Audited
Audit Date: 10.06.2019
Personnel: A. Skip Mazenauer (Pub/ CEO); Terry Duffy (Mng. Ed.); Josh Malone
Parent company (for newspapers): Niagara Frontier Publications

LONG BEACH HERALD

Street address 1: 2 Endo Blvd
Street address city: Garden City
Street address state: NY
Zip/Postal code: 11530-6707
General Phone: (516) 569-4000
General Fax: (516) 569-4942
General/National Adv. E-mail: sales@liherald.com
Editorial e-mail: lbeditor@liherald.com
Primary Website: liherald.com
Avg Paid Circ: 6544
Avg Free Circ: 1356
Audit By: Sworn/Estimate/Non-Audited
Audit Date: 10.06.2019

Personnel: Clifford Richner (Pub.); Stuart Richner (Pub.); Michael Bologna (Gen. Mgr.); Rhonda Glickman (Adv. Mgr.)
Parent company (for newspapers): Richner Communications, Inc.

LONG ISLAND ADVANCE

Street address 1: 20 Medford Ave
Street address 2: Ste 112
Street address city: Patchogue
Street address state: NY
Zip/Postal code: 11772-1220
General Phone: (631) 475-1000
General Fax: (631) 475-1565
Advertising Phone: (631) 475-1000 x28
Editorial Phone: (631) 475-1000 x21
General/National Adv. E-mail: ttlia@optonline.net
Display Adv. E-mail: ttlia@optonline.net
Classified Adv. e-mail: classifieds@longislandadvance.net
Editorial e-mail: advletters@optonline.net
Primary Website: longislandadvance.net
Mthly Avg Views: 80000
Mthly Avg Unique Visitors: 12000
Year Established: 1871
Avg Paid Circ: 5000
Audit By: Sworn/Estimate/Non-Audited
Audit Date: 19.09.2022
Personnel: Terry Tuthill (Publisher); Nicole Fuentes (Editor); Joanne Solowey-LaBarca (Gen. Mgr.); Doug Marino (Controller/Office Manager); Nicole Allegrezza (Editor)

LONG ISLAND BUSINESS NEWS

Street address 1: 2150 Smithtown Ave
Street address 2: Ste 7
Street address city: Ronkonkoma
Street address state: NY
Zip/Postal code: 11779-7348
General Phone: (631) 737-1700
Advertising Phone: (631) 913-4233
Editorial Phone: (631) 913-4257
General/National Adv. E-mail: jgiametta@libn.com
Editorial e-mail: editor@libn.com
Primary Website: libn.com
Year Established: 1953
Avg Paid Circ: 4000
Avg Free Circ: 1000
Audit By: VAC
Audit Date: 30.09.2016
Personnel: Joe Giametta (Pub.); Joe Parrino (Adv. Acct. Mgr.); Joe Dowd (Bus. Mgr.); Bernadette Starzee (Special Sections Ed.)
Parent company (for newspapers): BridgeTower Media

LONG ISLAND CITY/ASTORIA/ JACKSON HEIGHTS JOURNAL

Street address 1: 4523 47th St
Street address city: Woodside
Street address state: NY
Zip/Postal code: 11377-5225
General Phone: (718) 639-7000
General/National Adv. E-mail: ads@queensledger.com
Editorial e-mail: news@queensledger.com
Primary Website: LICJournal.com
Year Established: 1986
Avg Paid Circ: 1100
Avg Free Circ: 17000
Audit By: Sworn/Estimate/Non-Audited
Audit Date: 10.06.2019
Personnel: Tammy Sanchez (Gen. Mgr.); Walter H. Sanchez (Ed.); John Sanchez (director of marketing)
Parent company (for newspapers): BQE Publishing Inc.

LONG ISLAND PRESS

Street address 1: 6901 Jericho Tpke
Street address 2: Ste 215
Street address city: Syosset
Street address state: NY
Zip/Postal code: 11791-4447
General Phone: (516) 284-3300
General Fax: (516) 284-3310
General/National Adv. E-mail: felice@longislandpress.com
Primary Website: longislandpress.com
Avg Free Circ: 40000
Audit By: Sworn/Estimate/Non-Audited
Audit Date: 10.06.2019
Personnel: John Kominicki (Pub)
Parent company (for newspapers): Schneps Communications

LYNBROOK/EAST ROCKAWAY HERALD

Street address 1: 2 Endo Blvd
Street address city: Garden City
Street address state: NY
Zip/Postal code: 11530-6707
General Phone: (516) 569-4000
General Fax: (516) 569-4942
Advertising Phone: (516) 569-4000 x250
Editorial Phone: (516) 5694000 x202
General/National Adv. E-mail: sales@liherald.com
Primary Website: liherald.com
Avg Paid Circ: 5272
Avg Free Circ: 1293
Audit By: Sworn/Estimate/Non-Audited
Audit Date: 10.06.2019
Personnel: Clifford Richner (Pub.); Stuart Richner (Pub.); Michael Bologna (Gen. Mgr.); Rhonda Glickman (Adv. Mgr.)
Parent company (for newspapers): Richner Communications, Inc.

MAHOPAC NEWS

Street address 1: 334 Route 202
Street address 2: # 1
Street address city: Somers
Street address state: NY
Zip/Postal code: 10589-3207
General Phone: (845) 208-0774
Advertising Phone: (845) 621-1116
Editorial Phone: (845) 208-0774
General/National Adv. E-mail: forhan@halstonmedia.com
Display Adv. E-mail: forhan@halstonmedia.com
Editorial e-mail: marschhauser@halstonmedia.com
Primary Website: mahopacnews.com
Audit By: Sworn/Estimate/Non-Audited
Audit Date: 10.06.2019
Personnel: Brett Freeman (Pub.); Marc Weinreich (Ed.); Shelley Kilcoyne (Adv. Mgr.)

MALVERNE/WEST HEMPSTEAD HERALD

Street address 1: 2 Endo Blvd
Street address city: Garden City
Street address state: NY
Zip/Postal code: 11530-6707
General Phone: (516) 569-4000
General Fax: (516) 569-4942
Advertising Phone: (516) 569-4000 x250
General/National Adv. E-mail: sales@liherald.com
Editorial e-mail: ahackmack@liherald.com
Primary Website: liherald.com
Avg Paid Circ: 3286
Audit By: Sworn/Estimate/Non-Audited
Audit Date: 10.06.2019
Personnel: Clifford Richner (Pub.); Stuart Richner (Pub.); Rhonda Glickman (Adv. Mgr.); Michael Bologna (Gen. Mgr.)
Parent company (for newspapers): Richner Communications, Inc.

MANHASSET PRESS

Street address 1: 132 E 2nd St
Street address city: Mineola
Street address state: NY
Zip/Postal code: 11501-3522
General Phone: (516) 747-8282
General Fax: (516) 742-5867
General/National Adv. E-mail: advertising@antonnews.com
Display Adv. E-mail: classified@antonnews.com
Editorial e-mail: ejohnson@antonmediagroup.com
Primary Website: antonnews.com
Year Established: 1934
Avg Paid Circ: 3801
Avg Free Circ: 304
Audit By: Sworn/Estimate/Non-Audited
Audit Date: 10.06.2019
Personnel: Angela Anton (Pub.); Elizabeth Johnson (Ed.)
Parent company (for newspapers): Anton Community Newspapers

MANHASSET TIMES

Street address 1: 22 Planting Field Road
Street address city: Roslyn Heights
Street address state: NY
Zip/Postal code: 11577
General Phone: 516.307.1045
General Fax: 516.307.1046
Advertising Phone: (516) 307-1045
Editorial Phone: (516) 307-1045
General/National Adv. E-mail: sblank@theislandnow.com
Display Adv. E-mail: sblank@theislandnow.com
Classified Adv. e-mail: dflynn@theislandnow.com
Editorial e-mail: sblank@theislandnow.com
Primary Website: theislandnow.com
Mthly Avg Views: 400000
Mthly Avg Unique Visitors: 900000
Year Established: 2014
Avg Paid Circ: 2563
Audit By: Sworn/Estimate/Non-Audited
Audit Date: 10.10.2021
Personnel: Steven Blank (Editor and publisher)
Parent company (for newspapers): Blank Slate Media

MASS MARKET RETAILERS

Street address 1: 126 Fifth Avenue
Street address 2: 12th Floor
Street address city: New York
Street address state: NY
Zip/Postal code: 10011
General Phone: (212) 213-6000
General Fax: (212) 213-6106
General/National Adv. E-mail: pnavarre@racherpress.com
Display Adv. E-mail: pnavarre@racherpress.com
Editorial e-mail: dpinto@racherpress.com
Primary Website: massmarketretailers.com
Year Established: 1983
Avg Paid Circ: 91
Avg Free Circ: 23276
Audit By: CVC
Audit Date: 19.12.2018
Personnel: Susan Schinitsky (Pub.); David Pinto (Ed.); John Dioguardi (Dir., Sales & Mktg.); Peggy Navvare (Adv.)
Parent company (for newspapers): Racher Press

MASSAPEQUA POST

Street address 1: 85 Broadway
Street address 2: Ste A
Street address city: Amityville
Street address state: NY
Zip/Postal code: 11701-2778
General Phone: (516) 798-5100
General Fax: (631) 264-5310
Advertising Phone: (631) 608-4495
Advertising Fax: (631) 264-5310
General/National Adv. E-mail: acjads@optonline.net
Display Adv. E-mail: acjads@optonline.net
Editorial e-mail: acjnews@rcn.com
Primary Website: massapequapost.com
Year Established: 1954
Avg Paid Circ: 2800
Avg Free Circ: 400
Audit By: Sworn/Estimate/Non-Audited
Audit Date: 10.06.2019
Personnel: Alfred James (Pub.); Carolyn James (Exec. Ed.)
Parent company (for newspapers): CJ Publishers Inc.

MASSAPEQUAN OBSERVER

Street address 1: 132 E 2nd St
Street address city: Mineola
Street address state: NY
Zip/Postal code: 11501-3522
General Phone: (516) 747-8282
General Fax: (516) 742-5867
General/National Adv. E-mail: advertising@antonnews.com
Display Adv. E-mail: classified@antonnews.com
Editorial e-mail: smosco@antonmediagroup.com
Primary Website: massapequaobserver.com
Year Established: 1959
Avg Paid Circ: 4920
Avg Free Circ: 631
Audit By: Sworn/Estimate/Non-Audited
Audit Date: 10.06.2019
Personnel: Angela Anton (Pub.); Jennifer Fauci (Ed.)
Parent company (for newspapers): Anton Community Newspapers

MERRICK HERALD

Street address 1: 2 Endo Blvd
Street address city: Garden City
Street address state: NY
Zip/Postal code: 11530-6707
General Phone: (516) 569-4000
General Fax: (516) 569-4942
General/National Adv. E-mail: sales@liherald.com
Primary Website: liherald.com
Avg Paid Circ: 3846
Audit By: Sworn/Estimate/Non-Audited
Audit Date: 10.06.2019
Personnel: Clifford Richner (Pub.); Stuart Richner (Pub.); Michael Bologna (Gen. Mgr.); Rhonda Glickman (Adv. Mgr.); Scott Brinton (Ed.)
Parent company (for newspapers): Richner Communications, Inc.

MESSENGER POST MEDIA

Street address 1: 73 Buffalo St
Street address city: Canandaigua
Street address state: NY
Zip/Postal code: 14424-1001
General Phone: (585) 394-0770
General Fax: (585) 394-1675
General/National Adv. E-mail: bkesel@messengerpostmedia.com
Display Adv. E-mail: classifieds@messengerpostmedia.com
Classified Adv. e-mail: classifieds@messengerpostmedia.com
Editorial e-mail: jreed@messengerpostmedia.com
Primary Website: mpnnow.com
Year Established: 1970
Avg Paid Circ: 0
Avg Free Circ: 8975
Audit By: Sworn/Estimate/Non-Audited
Audit Date: 10.06.2019
Personnel: Beth Kesel (GM/ Adv.); Jennifer Reed (Ed.); Mike Murphy
Parent company (for newspapers): CherryRoad Media

MID YORK WEEKLY

Street address 1: 221 Oriskany St E
Street address city: Utica
Street address state: NY
Zip/Postal code: 13501-1201
General Phone: (315)792-5000
General Fax: (315)792-5017
Advertising Phone: (315)792-5107
Editorial Phone: (315)792-5008
General/National Adv. E-mail: srosenburgh@uticaod.com
Display Adv. E-mail: srosenburgh@uticaod.com
Editorial e-mail: tcascioli@uticaod.com
Primary Website: uticaod.com
Year Established: 2004
Avg Paid Circ: 1984
Avg Free Circ: 0
Audit By: CVC
Audit Date: 30.09.2017
Personnel: Terry Cascioli (Pub.); Scott Rosenburgh (Adv.); Robert Gall (Circ.); Eric West (Prod.)

MID-HUDSON TIMES

Street address 1: 300 Stony Brook Ct
Street address 2: Ste B
Street address city: Newburgh
Street address state: NY
Zip/Postal code: 12550-6535
General Phone: (845) 561-0170
General Fax: (845) 561-3967
Advertising Phone: (845) 561-0170
Display Adv. E-mail: advertising@tcnewspapers.com
Editorial e-mail: editor@tcnewspapers.com
Primary Website: timescommunitypapers.com
Year Established: 1989
Avg Paid Circ: 2700
Avg Free Circ: 100
Audit By: Sworn/Estimate/Non-Audited
Audit Date: 10.06.2019
Personnel: Carl J. Aiello (Ed. & Pub.)

Parent company (for newspapers): Times Community Newspapers

MILL-MARINE COURIER & CANARSIE DIGEST

Street address 1: 1 Metrotech Ctr
Street address 2: Suite 1001
Street address city: Brooklyn
Street address state: NY
Zip/Postal code: 11201-3949
General Phone: (718) 260-2500
General Fax: (718) 615-3828
Editorial Phone: (718) 260-8303
General/National Adv. E-mail: JStern@CNGLocal.com
Display Adv. E-mail: Classified@CNGLocal.com
Editorial e-mail: Editorial@CNGLocal.com
Primary Website: brooklyndaily.com
Year Established: 1959
Avg Paid Circ: 8645
Avg Free Circ: 1490
Audit By: Sworn/Estimate/Non-Audited
Audit Date: 10.06.2019
Personnel: Clifford Luster (Pub.); Dan Holt (Gen. Mgr.); Jennifer Stern (Circ. Mgr.); Ken Brown (Ed.)
Parent company (for newspapers): Courier Life Publications, Inc.

MINEOLA AMERICAN

Street address 1: 132 E 2nd St
Street address city: Mineola
Street address state: NY
Zip/Postal code: 11501-3522
General Phone: (516) 747-8282
General Fax: (516) 742-5867
General/National Adv. E-mail: advertising@antonnews.com
Display Adv. E-mail: classified@antonnews.com
Editorial e-mail: mineola@antonnews.com
Primary Website: http://mineolaamerican.com/
Year Established: 1952
Avg Paid Circ: 4873
Audit By: Sworn/Estimate/Non-Audited
Audit Date: 10.06.2019
Personnel: Angela Anton (Pub.)
Parent company (for newspapers): Anton Community Newspapers

MOUNTAIN EAGLE

Street address 1: 9 Railroad Ave
Street address city: Stamford
Street address state: NY
Zip/Postal code: 12167-1229
General Phone: (607) 652-5252
General Fax: (607) 652-5253
Advertising Phone: (518) 763-6854
Advertising Fax: (607) 652-5253
Editorial Phone: (518) 763-6854
Editorial Fax: 607-652-5253
General/National Adv. E-mail: mountaineaglenews@gmail.com
Display Adv. E-mail: mountaineaglenews@gmail.com
Classified Adv. e-mail: mountaineaglenews@gmail.com
Editorial e-mail: mountaineaglenews@gmail.com
Primary Website: the-mountaineagle.com
Mthly Avg Views: 80000
Mthly Avg Unique Visitors: 50000
Year Established: 1982
Avg Paid Circ: 3200
Avg Free Circ: 150
Audit By: Sworn/Estimate/Non-Audited
Audit Date: 25.08.2023
Personnel: Matthew Avitabile (Ed.)
Parent company (for newspapers): Schoharie News LLC

MY SHOPPER - MOHAWK VALLEY EDITION

Street address 1: 2403 State Route 7
Street address 2: Ste 4
Street address city: Cobleskill
Street address state: NY
Zip/Postal code: 12043-5740
General Phone: (518) 234-8215
General Fax: (518) 234-8520
General/National Adv. E-mail: production@pennysaveronline.com
Primary Website: www.myshopperonline.com
Year Established: 1987
Avg Free Circ: 11499
Audit By: CVC
Audit Date: 12.[illegible]
Personnel: Russ Foote (Corporate Sales Manager)
Parent company (for newspapers): Snyder Communication Corp.

NASSAU HERALD

Street address 1: 2 Endo Blvd
Street address city: Garden City
Street address state: NY
Zip/Postal code: 11530-6707
General Phone: (516) 569-4000
General Fax: (516) 569-4942
Advertising Phone: (516) 569-4000 x250
Editorial Phone: (516) 5694000 x201
General/National Adv. E-mail: sales@liherald.com
Primary Website: liherald.com
Avg Paid Circ: 8771
Audit By: Sworn/Estimate/Non-Audited
Audit Date: 10.06.2019
Personnel: Clifford Richner (Pub.); Stuart Richner (Pub.); Michael Bologna (Gen. Mgr.); Rhonda Glickman (Adv. Mgr.); Jeff Bessen (Ed.)
Parent company (for newspapers): Richner Communications, Inc.

NEW HYDE PARK HERALD COURIER

Street address 1: 22 Planting Field Road
Street address city: Roslyn Heights
Street address state: NY
Zip/Postal code: 11577
General Phone: (516) 307-1045
General Fax: (516) 307-1046
Advertising Phone: (516) 307-1045 Ext. 201
Advertising Fax: (516) 307-1046
Editorial Phone: (516) 307-1045 Ext. 201
Editorial Fax: (516) 307-1046
General/National Adv. E-mail: sblank@theislandnow.com
Display Adv. E-mail: dflynn@theislandnow.com
Editorial e-mail: sblank@theislandnow.com
Primary Website: theislandnow.com
Year Established: 1936
Avg Paid Circ: 3643
Audit By: Sworn/Estimate/Non-Audited
Audit Date: 10.10.2021
Personnel: Steven Blank (Pub); Holly Blank (Circ. Mgr.); Stacy Shaughnessy (Adv. Dir.)
Parent company (for newspapers): Blank Slate Media LLC

NEW HYDE PARK ILLUSTRATED

Street address 1: 132 E 2nd St
Street address city: Mineola
Street address state: NY
Zip/Postal code: 11501-3522
General Phone: (516) 747-8282
General Fax: (516) 742-5867
General/National Adv. E-mail: advertising@antonnews.com
Display Adv. E-mail: classified@antonnews.com
Editorial e-mail: jscotchie@antonmediagroup.com
Primary Website: http://newhydeparkillustrated.com/
Year Established: 1930
Avg Paid Circ: 4200
Avg Free Circ: 847
Audit By: Sworn/Estimate/Non-Audited
Audit Date: 10.06.2019
Personnel: Angela Anton (Pub.); Joy DiDonato (Circ. Mgr.); Joe Scotchie (Ed.)
Parent company (for newspapers): Anton Community Newspapers

NEW PALTZ TIMES

Street address 1: 29 S Chestnut St
Street address city: New Paltz
Street address state: NY
Zip/Postal code: 12561-1948
General Phone: (845) 255-7000
General Fax: (845) 255-7005
General/National Adv. E-mail: ads@ulsterpublishing.com
Display Adv. E-mail: classifieds@ulsterpublishing.com
Editorial e-mail: newpaltztimes@ulsterpublishing.com
Primary Website: newpaltzx.com
Avg Paid Circ: 4850
Audit By: Sworn/Estimate/Non-Audited
Audit Date: 10.06.2019
Personnel: Geddy Sveikauskas (Owner/Pub.); Genia Wickwire (Ad. Dir.); Debbie Alexsa (Ed.)
Parent company (for newspapers): Ulster Publishing

NEWFIELD NEWS

Street address 1: 1009 N Cayuage St
Street address city: Ithaca
Street address state: NY
Zip/Postal code: 14850
General Phone: (607) 277-7000
General Fax: (607) 277-1012
General/National Adv. E-mail: tolson@ithacatimes.com
Editorial e-mail: editor@flcn.org
Primary Website: ithaca.com
Avg Paid Circ: 475
Avg Free Circ: 30
Audit By: Sworn/Estimate/Non-Audited
Audit Date: 10.06.2019
Personnel: James Bilinski (Pub.); Nick Reynolds (Ed.)
Parent company (for newspapers): Finger Lakes Community Newspapers

NIAGARA-WHEATFIELD TRIBUNE

Street address 1: 1859 Whitehaven Rd
Street address city: Grand Island
Street address state: NY
Zip/Postal code: 14072-1803
General Phone: (716) 773-7676
General Fax: (716) 773-7190
General/National Adv. E-mail: majoraccounts@wnypapers.com
Display Adv. E-mail: tribunesales@wnypapers.com
Classified Adv. e-mail: nfpclassified@wnypapers.com
Editorial e-mail: tribune@wnypapers.com
Primary Website: wnypapers.com
Year Established: 1944
Avg Paid Circ: 0
Avg Free Circ: 11500
Audit By: Sworn/Estimate/Non-Audited
Audit Date: 10.06.2019
Personnel: A. Skip Mazenauer (Pub/ CEO); Terry Duffy (Mng. Ed.); David Yarger (editor)
Parent company (for newspapers): Niagara Frontier Publications

NORTH COUNTRY CATHOLIC

Street address 1: 622 Washington St
Street address city: Ogdensburg
Street address state: NY
Zip/Postal code: 13669-1724
General Phone: (315) 608-7556
Editorial e-mail: mkilian@dioogdensburg.org
Primary Website: northcountrycatholic.org
Year Established: 1946
Audit By: Sworn/Estimate/Non-Audited
Audit Date: 10.06.2019
Personnel: Bishop Robert J. Cunningham (Pub.); Darcy Fargo (Ed.)
Parent company (for newspapers): Diocese of Ogdensburg

NORTH COUNTRY FREE PRESS

Street address 1: 14 E Main St
Street address city: Granville
Street address state: NY
Zip/Postal code: 12832-1334
General Phone: (518) 642-1234
General Fax: (518) 642-1344
Advertising Phone: (518) 642-1234
Advertising Fax: (518) 642-1344
Editorial Phone: (518) 642-1234
Editorial Fax: (518) 642-1344
General/National Adv. E-mail: advertising@manchesternewspapers.com
Display Adv. E-mail: classifieds@manchesternewspapers.com
Editorial e-mail: publisher@manchesternewspapers.com
Primary Website: manchesternewspapers.com
Year Established: 1995
Avg Paid Circ: 0
Avg Free Circ: 17172
Audit By: CVC
Audit Date: 30.09.2017
Personnel: Lisa Manchester (Exec. VP); John MacArthur Manchester (Pub./ Nat'l Adv. Mgr.); Bill Toscano (Ed.); Ann Hilder (Circ. Mgr); Jane Cosey (Prodn. Mgr./ Adv. Mgr.)
Parent company (for newspapers): Manchester Newspapers, Inc.

NORTH COUNTRY THIS WEEK

Street address 1: 4 Clarkson Ave.
Street address city: Potsdam
Street address state: NY
Zip/Postal code: 13676-0975
General Phone: (315) 265-1000
General Fax: (315) 268-8701
Advertising Phone: (315) 265-1000
Advertising Fax: (315) 268-8701
Editorial Phone: (315) 265-1000
Editorial Fax: (315) 268-8701
General/National Adv. E-mail: thisweek@northcountrynow.com
Display Adv. E-mail: Classifieds@northcountrynow.com
Classified Adv. e-mail: classifieds@northcountrynow.com
Editorial e-mail: news@northcountrynow.com
Primary Website: northcountrynow.com
Mthly Avg Views: 2619555
Mthly Avg Unique Visitors: 184518
Year Established: 1984
Avg Paid Circ: 4
Avg Free Circ: 16460
Sat. Circulation Free: 7740
Audit By: CVC
Audit Date: 01.12.2021
Personnel: Bill Shumway (Pub.); John Basham (Adv. Mgr.)

NORTHERN DUTCHESS NEWS

Street address 1: 84 E Main St
Street address city: Wappingers Falls
Street address state: NY
Zip/Postal code: 12590-2599
General Phone: (845) 297-3723
General Fax: (845) 297-6810
General/National Adv. E-mail: sdnadvertising@aol.com
Editorial e-mail: northerndutchess@sdutchessnews.com
Primary Website: sdutchessnews.com
Audit By: Sworn/Estimate/Non-Audited
Audit Date: 10.06.2019
Personnel: Ray Fashona (Ed.); Albert M. Osten (Pub.)
Parent company (for newspapers): Southern Dutchess News

NORTHERN WESTCHESTER EXPRESS

Street address 1: 1 Gannett Dr
Street address city: White Plains
Street address state: NY
Zip/Postal code: 10604-3402
General Phone: (914) 694-9300
Advertising Phone: (914) 694-5158
Editorial Phone: (914) 694-9300
General/National Adv. E-mail: gpaganodec@lohud.com
Display Adv. E-mail: gtroyano@lohud.com
Editorial e-mail: jhasson@lohud.com
Primary Website: lohud.com/Westchester
Avg Free Circ: 86008
Audit By: Sworn/Estimate/Non-Audited
Audit Date: 10.06.2019
Personnel: George Troyano (Vice Pres.); Kathleen Ryan O'Conner (Ed.); Ed Forbes (Consumer Exper. Dir)

OCEANSIDE-ISLAND PARK HERALD

Street address 1: 2 Endo Blvd
Street address city: Garden City
Street address state: NY
Zip/Postal code: 11530-6707
General Phone: (516) 569-4000
General Fax: (516) 569-4942
General/National Adv. E-mail: sales@liherald.com
Editorial e-mail: MSmollins@liherald.com
Primary Website: liherald.com
Avg Paid Circ: 5015
Avg Free Circ: 1281
Audit By: Sworn/Estimate/Non-Audited
Audit Date: 10.06.2019
Personnel: Clifford Richner (Pub.); Michael Smollins (Ed.)

Parent company (for newspapers): Richner Communications, Inc.

ONONDAGA VALLEY NEWS

Street address 1: 750 W Genesee St
Street address city: Syracuse
Street address state: NY
Zip/Postal code: 13204-2306
General Phone: (315) 472-7825
General Fax: (315) 478-1434
Editorial e-mail: editorial@scotsmanpress.com
Primary Website: scotsmanonline.com
Year Established: 1990
Avg Paid Circ: 22
Avg Free Circ: 7903
Audit By: Sworn/Estimate/Non-Audited
Audit Date: 10.06.2019
Personnel: A. Loren Colburn (Pub.); Thomas C. Cuskey (Adv. Mgr.); Deb Lum (Ed.)
Parent company (for newspapers): Scotsman Press

ORANGE COUNTY POST

Street address 1: PO Box 406
Street address city: Vails Gate
Street address state: NY
Zip/Postal code: 12584-0406
General Phone: (845) 496-9997
General Fax: (845) 496-9949
Display Adv. E-mail: ocpads@frontiernet.net
Editorial e-mail: ocpnews@frontiernet.net
Primary Website: ocpostsentinel.com
Year Established: 1936
Avg Paid Circ: 2400
Avg Free Circ: 150
Audit By: Sworn/Estimate/Non-Audited
Audit Date: 10.06.2019
Personnel: Howard JP Spear (Editor)
Parent company (for newspapers): EWSmith Publishing

ORCHARD PARK BEE

Street address 1: 5564 Main St
Street address city: Williamsville
Street address state: NY
Zip/Postal code: 14221-5410
General Phone: (716) 632-4700
General Fax: (716) 633-8601
Advertising Phone: (716) 204-4934
General/National Adv. E-mail: Salesdept@BeeNews.com
Display Adv. E-mail: classified@beenews.com
Editorial e-mail: cgraham@beenews.com
Primary Website: orchardparkbee.com
Year Established: 1986
Avg Paid Circ: 2140
Audit By: Sworn/Estimate/Non-Audited
Audit Date: 10.06.2019
Personnel: Chris Graham (Ed.); Brenda Denk (Sales Mgr.); David Sherman; Patrick Nagy (Reporter); Nicholas Konotopskyi (Reporter)
Parent company (for newspapers): Bee Group Newspapers

OUR TOWN EASTSIDE

Street address 1: 110 W Crooked Hill Rd
Street address city: Pearl River
Street address state: NY
Zip/Postal code: 10965-1012
General Phone: (845) 735-1342
General Fax: (845) 620-9533
General/National Adv. E-mail: ads@ourtownnews.com
Editorial e-mail: news@ourtownnews.com
Primary Website: ourtownnews.com
Year Established: 1970
Avg Paid Circ: 0
Avg Free Circ: 19999
Audit By: Sworn/Estimate/Non-Audited
Audit Date: 10.06.2019
Personnel: Jeanne Straus (Pres.); Kate Raffa (Mng. Ed.)
Parent company (for newspapers): Straus News

OVID GAZETTE

Street address 1: 109 N Cayuga St
Street address city: Ithaca
Street address state: NY
Zip/Postal code: 14850-4341
General Phone: (607) 277-7000
General Fax: (607) 277 1012
General/National Adv. E-mail: jbilinski@ithacatimes.com
Editorial e-mail: editor@flcn.org
Primary Website: ithaca.com
Year Established: 1801
Avg Paid Circ: 575
Avg Free Circ: 63
Audit By: Sworn/Estimate/Non-Audited
Audit Date: 10.06.2019
Personnel: James Bilinski (Pub.)
Parent company (for newspapers): Finger Lakes Community Newspapers

OYSTER BAY ENTERPRISE PILOT

Street address 1: 132 E 2nd St
Street address city: Mineola
Street address state: NY
Zip/Postal code: 11501-3522
General Phone: (516) 747-8282
General Fax: (516) 742-5867
General/National Adv. E-mail: advertising@antonnews.com
Display Adv. E-mail: classified@antonnews.com
Editorial e-mail: smosco@antonmediagroup.com
Primary Website: http://oysterbayenterprisepilot.com/
Year Established: 1882
Avg Paid Circ: 1892
Avg Free Circ: 492
Audit By: Sworn/Estimate/Non-Audited
Audit Date: 10.06.2019
Personnel: Angela Anton (Pub.); Steve Mosco (Ed.)
Parent company (for newspapers): Anton Community Newspapers

OYSTER BAY GUARDIAN

Street address 1: 2 Endo Blvd
Street address city: Garden City
Street address state: NY
Zip/Postal code: 11530-6707
General Phone: (516) 922-4215 X327
General Fax: (516) 922-4227
Advertising Phone: (516) 569-4000 x272
General/National Adv. E-mail: llane@oysterbayguardian.com
Editorial e-mail: llane@liherald.com
Primary Website: oysterbayguardian.com
Year Established: 1899
Avg Paid Circ: 3500
Avg Free Circ: 50
Audit By: Sworn/Estimate/Non-Audited
Audit Date: 10.06.2019
Personnel: Laura Lane (Ed.); Clifford Richner (Pub.); Rhonda Glickman (Ad. Mgr.)
Parent company (for newspapers): Richner Communications, Inc.

PARKCHESTER NEWS

Street address 1: 135 Dreiser Loop
Street address city: Bronx
Street address state: NY
Zip/Postal code: 10475-2704
General Phone: (718) 320-3071
General Fax: (718) 320-7059
General/National Adv. E-mail: bronxnews@gmail.com
Editorial e-mail: bronxnews@gmail.com
Primary Website: https://sites.google.com/site/parkchesternewsbx/Ã‚Â
Avg Free Circ: 12200
Audit By: Sworn/Estimate/Non-Audited
Audit Date: 10.06.2019
Personnel: Christopher G. Hagedorn (Pub.); Daniel Gesslein (Ed.); Al Zezula (Mktg. Dir.)
Parent company (for newspapers): Hagedorn Communications

PENFIELD POST

Street address 1: 73 Buffalo St
Street address city: Canandaigua
Street address state: NY
Zip/Postal code: 14424-1001
General Phone: (585) 394-0770
General Fax: (585) 394-4160
General/National Adv. E-mail: bkesel@messengerpostmedia.com
Display Adv. E-mail: classifieds@mpnewspapers.com
Editorial e-mail: byoung@messengerpostmedia.com
Primary Website: mpnnow.com
Mthly Avg Views: 700000
Mthly Avg Unique Visitors: 200000
Year Established: 1971
Avg Paid Circ: 94
Avg Free Circ: 3241
Audit By: Sworn/Estimate/Non-Audited
Audit Date: 10.06.2019
Personnel: Alison Cooper (Ed.); Brian Doane; Beth Kesel
Parent company (for newspapers): Messenger Post Media

PERRY HERALD

Street address 1: 75 South Main Street
Street address city: Perry
Street address state: NY
Zip/Postal code: 14530
General Phone: (585) 237-2212
General Fax: (585) 237-2211
General/National Adv. E-mail: ads@perryshopper.com
Primary Website: perryshopper.com
Year Established: 1878
Avg Paid Circ: 772
Avg Free Circ: 7
Audit By: Sworn/Estimate/Non-Audited
Audit Date: 10.06.2019
Personnel: Lorraine Sturm (Ed.)

PHOENIX REGISTER

Street address 1: 80 N Jefferson St
Street address city: Mexico
Street address state: NY
Zip/Postal code: 13114-3001
General Phone: (315) 963-7813
General Fax: (315) 963-4087
General/National Adv. E-mail: ocwadvertising@cnymail.com
Display Adv. E-mail: ocwadvertising@cnymail.com
Editorial e-mail: ocweeklies@cnymail.com
Primary Website: oswegocountyweeklies.com
Year Established: 1858
Avg Paid Circ: 2272
Audit By: Sworn/Estimate/Non-Audited
Audit Date: 10.06.2019
Personnel: Rose Ann Parsons (Mng. Ed.)

PHOTO NEWS

Street address 1: 20 West Ave
Street address 2: Ste 201
Street address city: Chester
Street address state: NY
Zip/Postal code: 10918-1053
General Phone: (845) 469-9000
General Fax: (845) 469-9001
General/National Adv. E-mail: sales@strausnews.com
Editorial e-mail: nyoffice@strausnews.com
Primary Website: thephoto-news.com
Year Established: 1986
Avg Free Circ: 6701
Audit By: Sworn/Estimate/Non-Audited
Audit Date: 10.06.2019
Personnel: Jeanne Straus (Pres.); Mike Zummo (Mng. Ed.)
Parent company (for newspapers): Straus News

PLAINVIEW/OLD BETHPAGE HERALD

Street address 1: 132 E 2nd St
Street address city: Mineola
Street address state: NY
Zip/Postal code: 11501-3522
General Phone: (516) 747-8282
General Fax: (516) 742-5867
General/National Adv. E-mail: advertising@antonnews.com
Display Adv. E-mail: classified@antonnews.com
Editorial e-mail: plainview@antonnews.com
Primary Website: antonnews.com
Year Established: 1956
Avg Paid Circ: 3225
Avg Free Circ: 447
Audit By: Sworn/Estimate/Non-Audited
Audit Date: 10.06.2019
Personnel: Angela Anton (Pub.); Cary Seaman (Mng. Ed.)
Parent company (for newspapers): Anton Community Newspapers

PORT WASHINGTON NEWS

Street address 1: 270 Main St
Street address city: Port Washington
Street address state: NY
Zip/Postal code: 11050-2753
General Phone: (516) 747-8282
General Fax: (516) 767-0036
General/National Adv. E-mail: advertising@antonnews.com
Display Adv. E-mail: classified@antonnews.com
Editorial e-mail: portwashington@antonnews.com
Primary Website: antonnews.com
Year Established: 1903
Avg Paid Circ: 6501
Avg Free Circ: 329
Audit By: Sworn/Estimate/Non-Audited
Audit Date: 30.09.2017
Personnel: Angela Anton (Pub.); Joy DiDonato (Circ. Mgr.); Elizabeth Johnson (Ed.)
Parent company (for newspapers): Anton Community Newspapers

PORT WASHINGTON TIMES

Street address 1: 22 Planting Field Road
Street address city: Roslyn Heights
Street address state: NY
Zip/Postal code: 11577
General Phone: 516.307.1045
Advertising Phone: (516) 307-1045
Editorial Phone: (516) 307-1045
General/National Adv. E-mail: sblank@theislandnow.com
Display Adv. E-mail: sblank@theislandnow.com
Classified Adv. e-mail: dflynn@theislandnow.com
Editorial e-mail: sblank@theislandnow.com
Primary Website: theislandnow.com
Mthly Avg Views: 400000
Mthly Avg Unique Visitors: 900000
Year Established: 2014
Avg Paid Circ: 2731
Audit By: Sworn/Estimate/Non-Audited
Audit Date: 10.10.2021
Personnel: Steven Blank
Parent company (for newspapers): Blank Slate Media

POST-HERALD

Street address 1: 6784 Main St.
Street address city: Red Creek
Street address state: NY
Zip/Postal code: 13143
General Phone: (315) 754-6229
General Fax: (315) 754-6431
General/National Adv. E-mail: advertising@wayuga.com
Editorial e-mail: editor@wayuga.com
Primary Website: wayuga.com
Avg Paid Circ: 1884
Avg Free Circ: 23
Audit By: Sworn/Estimate/Non-Audited
Audit Date: 10.06.2019
Personnel: Charles Palermo (Pub. & Adv. Mgr.); Tammy Whitacre (Ed.)

PUTNAM COUNTY NEWS & RECORDER

Street address 1: 3 Stone St
Street address city: Cold Spring
Street address state: NY
Zip/Postal code: 10516-3020
General Phone: (845) 265-2468
General Fax: (845) 809-5572
Advertising Phone: (845) 265-2468
Advertising Fax: (845) 809-5572
Editorial Phone: (845) 265-2468
General/National Adv. E-mail: ads@pcnr.com
Display Adv. E-mail: ads@pcnr.com
Editorial e-mail: editor@pcnr.com
Primary Website: pcnr.com
Year Established: 1866
Avg Paid Circ: 2000
Audit By: Sworn/Estimate/Non-Audited
Audit Date: 17.09.2022

Personnel: Douglas Cunningham (Pub)

PUTNAM COUNTY PRESS

Street address 1: PO Box 608
Street address city: Mahopac
Street address state: NY
Zip/Postal code: 10541-0608
General Phone: (845) 628-8400
General Fax: (845) 628-8400
Advertising Phone: (845) 628-8400
Advertising Fax: (845) 628-8400
Editorial Phone: (845) 628-8401
Editorial Fax: (845) 628-8400
General/National Adv. E-mail: advertising@putnampresstimes.com
Display Adv. E-mail: advertising@putnampresstimes.com
Editorial e-mail: putnampress@aol.com
Primary Website: putnampresstimes.com
Avg Paid Circ: 3200
Audit By: Sworn/Estimate/Non-Audited
Audit Date: 10.06.2019
Personnel: Don Hall (Pub.); Holly Toal (Ed-in-Chief); Christine Groppe (Adv. Mgr.)

PUTNAM COUNTY TIMES

Street address 1: PO Box 608
Street address city: Mahopac
Street address state: NY
Zip/Postal code: 10541-0608
General Phone: (845) 628-8400
General Fax: (845) 628-8400
Advertising Phone: (845) 628-8400
Advertising Fax: (845) 628-8400
Editorial Phone: (845) 628-8400
Editorial Fax: (845) 628-8400
General/National Adv. E-mail: advertising@putnampresstimes.com
Display Adv. E-mail: advertising@putnampresstimes.com
Editorial e-mail: putnampress@aol.com
Primary Website: putnampresstimes.com
Audit By: Sworn/Estimate/Non-Audited
Audit Date: 10.06.2019
Personnel: Don Hall (Pub.); Holly Toal (Ed-in-Chief); Christine Groppe (Adv. Mgr./Graphic Designer)

PUTNAM EXPRESS

Street address 1: 1 GANNETT DR
Street address city: White Plains
Street address state: NY
Zip/Postal code: 10604
General Phone: (914) 694-9300
Advertising Phone: (914) 694-5158
Editorial Phone: (914) 694-9300
General/National Adv. E-mail: gtroyano@lohud.com
Display Adv. E-mail: gtroyano@lohud.com
Editorial e-mail: jhasson@lohud.com
Primary Website: lohud.com/Putnam
Audit By: Sworn/Estimate/Non-Audited
Audit Date: 10.06.2019
Personnel: George Troyano (Vice Pres.); Ed Forbes (Adv. Dir.); Kathleen Ryan O'Conner (Ed.)

QUEEN CENTRAL NEWS

Street address 1: 39 Main St
Street address city: Camden
Street address state: NY
Zip/Postal code: 13316-1301
General Phone: (315)245-1849
General Fax: (315)245-1880
General/National Adv. E-mail: theqcn@gmail.com
Editorial e-mail: theqcn@gmail.com
Primary Website: queencentralnews.com
Year Established: 1974
Audit By: Sworn/Estimate/Non-Audited
Audit Date: 10.06.2019
Personnel: Jim Van Winkle (Ed & Owner); Dori Monteith (Ad. Mgr.)

QUEENS LEDGER / BROOKLYN STAR

Street address 1: 45-23 47 Street
Street address city: Woodside
Street address state: NY
Zip/Postal code: 11377
General Phone: 718-639-7000
Advertising Phone: 718-426-7200
Editorial Phone: 718-639-7000
General/National Adv. E-mail: news@queensledger.com
Display Adv. E-mail: ads@queensledger.com
Classified Adv. e-mail: ads@queensledger.com
Editorial e-mail: news@queensledger.com
Primary Website: www.queensledger.com
Mthly Avg Views: 200000
Mthly Avg Unique Visitors: 30000
Year Established: 1873
Avg Paid Circ: 21500
Avg Free Circ: 53000
Audit By: USPS
Audit Date: 27.09.2021
Personnel: Walter H. Sanchez (Pub.); Tammy Sanchez (Office Mgr.); Shane Miller (Ed.)
Parent company (for newspapers): BQE Publishing Inc.

RECORD-REVIEW

Street address 1: PO Box 455
Street address city: Bedford Hills
Street address state: NY
Zip/Postal code: 10507-0455
General Phone: (914) 244-0533
General Fax: (914) 244-0537
General/National Adv. E-mail: flynch@scarsdalenews.com
Display Adv. E-mail: gryan@scarsdalenews.com
Editorial e-mail: recordreview@optonline.net
Primary Website: record-review.com
Year Established: 1995
Avg Paid Circ: 3300
Avg Free Circ: 100
Audit By: Sworn/Estimate/Non-Audited
Audit Date: 10.06.2019
Personnel: Deborah White (Pub.); Ed Baum (Ed.)

RIDGEWOOD LEDGER

Street address 1: 4102 Bell Blvd
Street address city: Bayside
Street address state: NY
Zip/Postal code: 11361-2792
General Phone: (718) 260-2500
General Fax: (718) 260-2549
Advertising Phone: (718) 260-2500
Advertising Fax: (718) 260-2549
Editorial Phone: (718) 260-2500
Editorial Fax: (718) 260-2549
General/National Adv. E-mail: brice@cnglocal.com
Display Adv. E-mail: classified@cnglocal.com
Editorial e-mail: timesledgernews@cnglocal.com
Primary Website: timesledger.com
Avg Paid Circ: 21000
Audit By: Sworn/Estimate/Non-Audited
Audit Date: 10.06.2019
Personnel: Roz Liston (Mng. Ed.); Amanda Tarley (Classified Advertising Director); Brian Rice (Display & Online Advertising)
Parent company (for newspapers): Community Newspaper Group; Queens Village Times (OOB)

RIVERDALE REVIEW

Street address 1: PO Box 1252
Street address city: Bronx
Street address state: NY
Zip/Postal code: 10471-0620
General Phone: (718) 543-5200
General Fax: (718) 543-4206
General/National Adv. E-mail: Bxny@aol.com
Editorial e-mail: bxny@aol.com
Primary Website: bronxpresspolitics.blogspot.com
Year Established: 1993
Avg Free Circ: 20000
Audit By: Sworn/Estimate/Non-Audited
Audit Date: 10.06.2019
Personnel: Robert Nilva (Adv. Mgr.); Andrew Wolf (Ed.); Joel Pal (Prodn. Mgr.)

RIVERHEAD NEWS-REVIEW

Street address 1: 7785 Main Rd
Street address city: Mattituck
Street address state: NY
Zip/Postal code: 11952-1518
General Phone: (631) 298-3200
General Fax: (631) 298-3287
Advertising Phone: (631) 354-8043
Editorial Phone: (631) 354-8045
General/National Adv. E-mail: jtumminello@timesreview.com
Display Adv. E-mail: classifieds@timesreview.com
Editorial e-mail: mwhite@timesreview.com
Primary Website: http://riverheadnewsreview.timesreview.com/
Mthly Avg Views: 215000
Mthly Avg Unique Visitors: 22000
Year Established: 1868
Avg Paid Circ: 5255
Avg Free Circ: 61
Audit By: Sworn/Estimate/Non-Audited
Audit Date: 10.06.2019
Personnel: Andrew Olsen (Pub.); Grant Parpan (Exec. Ed.); Sonja Reinholt Derr (Sales & Marketing Dir.)
Parent company (for newspapers): Time Review Newsgroup

ROCHESTER BUSINESS JOURNAL

Street address 1: 16 W. Main St.
Street address 2: Suite 341
Street address city: Rochester
Street address state: NY
Zip/Postal code: 14614
General Phone: (866) 941-4130
General/National Adv. E-mail: lgallemore@bridgetowermedia.com
Display Adv. E-mail: lgallemore@bridgetowermedia.com
Editorial e-mail: bjacobs@bridgetowermedia.com
Primary Website: rbj.net
Year Established: 1985
Avg Paid Circ: 4827
Avg Free Circ: 2526
Audit By: CVC
Audit Date: 31.12.2017
Personnel: Ben Jacobs (Ed.); Susanne Fischer-Huettner (Grp Pub.); Lyanne Gallemore (Adv. Mgr.); Jean Moorhouse (Acct. Mgr.)
Parent company (for newspapers): CherryRoad Media

ROCKLAND COUNTY EXPRESS

Street address 1: 1 Gannett Dr
Street address city: White Plains
Street address state: NY
Zip/Postal code: 10604-3402
General Phone: (914) 694-9300
Advertising Phone: (914) 694-5158
Editorial Phone: (914) 694-9300
Editorial e-mail: mdolan@lohud.com
Primary Website: lohud.com
Avg Free Circ: 77646
Audit By: AAM
Audit Date: 31.03.2018
Personnel: Mary Dolan
Parent company (for newspapers): Gannett

ROCKLAND COUNTY TIMES

Street address 1: 119 Main St
Street address city: Nanuet
Street address state: NY
Zip/Postal code: 10954-2882
General Phone: (845) 627-1414
General Fax: (845) 627-1411
General/National Adv. E-mail: editor@rocklandcountytimes.com
Editorial e-mail: editor@rocklandcountytimes.com
Primary Website: rocklandtimes.com
Year Established: 1888
Avg Paid Circ: 3100
Avg Free Circ: 4400
Audit By: Sworn/Estimate/Non-Audited
Audit Date: 10.06.2019
Personnel: Dylan Skriloff (Ed. in Chief/Pub.)
Parent company (for newspapers): Citizens Publishing Corporation of Rockland

ROCKVILLE CENTRE HERALD

Street address 1: 2 Endo Blvd
Street address city: Garden City
Street address state: NY
Zip/Postal code: 11530-6707
General Phone: (516) 569-4000
General Fax: (516) 569-4942
General/National Adv. E-mail: sales@liherald.com
Editorial e-mail: bstrack@liherald.com
Primary Website: liherald.com
Avg Paid Circ: 6367
Avg Free Circ: 1646
Audit By: Sworn/Estimate/Non-Audited
Audit Date: 10.06.2019
Personnel: Clifford Richner (Pub.); Stuart Richner (Pub.); Michael Bologna (Gen. Mgr.); Rhonda Glickman (Adv. Mgr.); Brian Kacharaba (Ed.); Ben Strack (Ed.)
Parent company (for newspapers): Richner Communications, Inc.

ROSLYN NEWS

Street address 1: 132 E 2nd St
Street address city: Mineola
Street address state: NY
Zip/Postal code: 11501-3522
General Phone: (516) 747-8282
General Fax: (516) 742-5867
General/National Adv. E-mail: advertising@antonnews.com
Display Adv. E-mail: classified@antonnews.com
Editorial e-mail: jscotchie@antonmediagroup.com
Primary Website: http://roslyn-news.com/
Year Established: 1877
Avg Paid Circ: 4800
Avg Free Circ: 821
Audit By: Sworn/Estimate/Non-Audited
Audit Date: 10.06.2019
Personnel: Angela Anton (Pub.); Joe Scotchie (Ed.)
Parent company (for newspapers): Anton Community Newspapers

ROSLYN TIMES

Street address 1: 22 Planting Field Road
Street address city: Roslyn Heights
Street address state: NY
Zip/Postal code: 11577
General Phone: (516) 307-1045
General Fax: (516) 307-1046
Advertising Phone: (516) 307-1045
Editorial Phone: (516) 307-1045
General/National Adv. E-mail: sblank@theislandnow.com
Display Adv. E-mail: sblank@theislandnow.com
Classified Adv. e-mail: dflynn@theislandnow.com
Editorial e-mail: sblank@theislandnow.com
Primary Website: https://theislandnow.com
Mthly Avg Views: 400000
Mthly Avg Unique Visitors: 900000
Year Established: 2014
Avg Paid Circ: 2955
Audit By: Sworn/Estimate/Non-Audited
Audit Date: 10.06.2019
Personnel: steven blank (Ed/Pub.); Steven Blank (Publisher)
Parent company (for newspapers): Blank Slate Media

RUSH-HENRIETTA POST

Street address 1: 73 Buffalo St
Street address city: Canandaigua
Street address state: NY
Zip/Postal code: 14424-1001
General Phone: (585) 394-0770
General Fax: (585) 394-4160
General/National Adv. E-mail: bkesel@messengerpostmedia.com
Display Adv. E-mail: classifieds@messengerpostmedia.com
Editorial e-mail: mshippers@messengerpostmedia.com
Primary Website: mpnnow.com
Mthly Avg Views: 700000
Mthly Avg Unique Visitors: 200000
Avg Paid Circ: 68
Avg Free Circ: 2924
Audit By: Sworn/Estimate/Non-Audited
Audit Date: 10.06.2019
Personnel: Allison Cooper (Mng. Ed.); Brian Doane (Pub.); Beth Kesel
Parent company (for newspapers): Messenger Post Media

SACANDAGA EXPRESS

Street address 1: 1 Venner Rd
Street address city: Amsterdam
Street address state: NY
Zip/Postal code: 12010-5617
General Phone: (518) 843-1100
General Fax: (518) 843-1338
Primary Website: sacandagaexpress.com
Avg Free Circ: 4500

Audit By: Sworn/Estimate/Non-Audited
Audit Date: 10.06.2019
Personnel: Geoff Dylong (Associate Pub.); Carla Kolbe (Ed.); Brian Krohn (Ad. Director)
Parent company (for newspapers): Port Jackson Media LLC

SALMON RIVER NEWS

Street address 1: 80 N Jefferson St
Street address city: Mexico
Street address state: NY
Zip/Postal code: 13114-3001
General Phone: (315) 963-7813
General Fax: (315) 963-4087
General/National Adv. E-mail: ocwadvertising@cnymail.com
Display Adv. E-mail: ocwadvertising@cnymail.com
Editorial e-mail: ocweeklies@cnymail.com
Primary Website: oswegocountyweeklies.com
Year Established: 1973
Avg Paid Circ: 5145
Audit By: Sworn/Estimate/Non-Audited
Audit Date: 10.06.2019
Personnel: Rose Ann Parsons (Mgn. Ed.)

SARATOGA TODAY

Street address 1: 2254 Route 50 South
Street address city: Saratoga Springs
Street address state: NY
Zip/Postal code: 12866
General Phone: (518) 581-2480
General Fax: (518) 581-2487
Advertising Phone: (518) 581-2480 x 209
Editorial Phone: (518) 581-2480 x 212
General/National Adv. E-mail: jdaley@saratogapublishing.com
Editorial e-mail: cbeatty@saratogapublishing.com
Primary Website: saratogatodaynewspaper.com
Mthly Avg Views: 500000
Year Established: 2006
Avg Free Circ: 10000
Audit By: Sworn/Estimate/Non-Audited
Audit Date: 10.06.2019
Personnel: Chad Beatty (Pub & Ed.); Jim Daley (Ad.)
Parent company (for newspapers): Saratoga Publishing

SAUGERTIES TIMES

Street address 1: 322 Wall St
Street address city: Kingston
Street address state: NY
Zip/Postal code: 12401-3820
General Phone: (845) 334-8200
General Fax: (845) 334-8202
General/National Adv. E-mail: info@ulsterpublishing.com
Display Adv. E-mail: classifieds@ulsterpublishing.com
Editorial e-mail: saugertiestimes@ulsterpublishing.com
Primary Website: saugertiesx.com
Avg Paid Circ: 1700
Audit By: Sworn/Estimate/Non-Audited
Audit Date: 10.06.2019
Personnel: Brian Hollander (Ed.); Dan Barton (Ed.); Genia Wickwire (Ad. Dir.)
Parent company (for newspapers): Ulster Publishing

SHAWANGUNK JOURNAL

Street address 1: PO Box 669
Street address city: Ellenville
Street address state: NY
Zip/Postal code: 12428-0669
General Phone: (845) 647-9190
General Fax: (845) 647-8713
General/National Adv. E-mail: ads@gunkjournal.com
Editorial e-mail: info@gunkjournal.com
Primary Website: shawangunkjournal.com
Year Established: 1849
Audit By: Sworn/Estimate/Non-Audited
Audit Date: 10.06.2019
Personnel: Alex Shiffer (Exec. Ed.); Paul Smart (Mgn. Ed.); Tara Dalton (Sales & Marketing)

SHELTER ISLAND REPORTER

Street address 1: 50 N Ferry Rd
Street address city: Shelter Island
Street address state: NY
Zip/Postal code: 11964
General Phone: (631) 749-1000
General Fax: (631) 749-0144
Advertising Phone: (631) 749-1000 x14
Editorial Phone: (631) 749-1000 x18
General/National Adv. E-mail: sales@sireporter.com
Display Adv. E-mail: classifieds@timesreview.com
Editorial e-mail: a.clancy@sireporter.com
Primary Website: http://shelterislandreporter.timesreview.com/
Mthly Avg Views: 50000
Mthly Avg Unique Visitors: 7000
Avg Paid Circ: 2191
Audit By: Sworn/Estimate/Non-Audited
Audit Date: 10.06.2019
Personnel: Andrew Olsen (Pub.); Grant Parpan (Exec. Ed.)
Parent company (for newspapers): Times Review Newsgroup

SHERBURNE NEWS

Street address 1: 17 E State St
Street address city: Sherburne
Street address state: NY
Zip/Postal code: 13460-9751
General Phone: (607) 674-6071
General Fax: (607) 264-2436
Advertising Phone: (607) 674-6071
Advertising Fax: (607) 674-6071
Editorial Phone: (607) 674-6071
Editorial Fax: 607 674-6071
General/National Adv. E-mail: thesherburnenews@gmail.com
Display Adv. E-mail: shernews@frontiernet.net
Editorial e-mail: info@sherburnenews.net
Primary Website: sherburnenews.net
Year Established: 1864
Avg Paid Circ: 2000
Audit By: Sworn/Estimate/Non-Audited
Audit Date: 10.06.2019
Personnel: James McDaniel (Adv. Mgr.)

SKANEATELES PRESS

Street address 1: 2501 James St
Street address 2: Ste 100
Street address city: Syracuse
Street address state: NY
Zip/Postal code: 13206-2996
General Phone: (315) 685-8338
General Fax: (315) 685-8338
General/National Adv. E-mail: press_observer@cnylink.com
Editorial e-mail: dtyler@eaglenewsonline.com
Primary Website: eaglenewsonline.com
Year Established: 1808
Avg Paid Circ: 146
Avg Free Circ: 2973
Audit By: CVC
Audit Date: 30.09.2017
Personnel: Richard K. Keene (Pres.); Matt Green (Adv. Mgr.); Lori Newcomb (Prodn. Mgr.); David Tyler (Pub.)

SMITHTOWN MESSENGER

Street address 1: 27 W Main St
Street address city: Smithtown
Street address state: NY
Zip/Postal code: 11787-2602
General Phone: (631) 265-3500
General Fax: (631) 265-3504
General/National Adv. E-mail: messenger127e@aol.com
Year Established: 1887
Avg Paid Circ: 8500
Audit By: Sworn/Estimate/Non-Audited
Audit Date: 10.06.2019
Personnel: Phillip L. Sciarillo (Pub.)
Parent company (for newspapers): P & S News Group

SOUTH BUFFALO NEWS

Street address 1: 2703 S Park Ave
Street address city: Lackawanna
Street address state: NY
Zip/Postal code: 14218-1511
General Phone: (716) 823-8222
General/National Adv. E-mail: frontpagegroupinc@gmail.com
Editorial e-mail: newsroomfpg@wny.twcbc.com
Avg Paid Circ: 3000
Audit By: Sworn/Estimate/Non-Audited
Audit Date: 10.06.2019
Personnel: Darryl McPherson (Ex Ed)
Parent company (for newspapers): Front Page Group Inc

SOUTHERN DUTCHESS NEWS

Street address 1: 84 E Main St
Street address city: Wappingers Falls
Street address state: NY
Zip/Postal code: 12590-2599
General Phone: (845) 297-3723
General Fax: (845) 297-6810
General/National Adv. E-mail: sdnadvertising@aol.com
Editorial e-mail: newsplace@aol.com
Primary Website: sdutchessnews.com
Year Established: 1952
Avg Paid Circ: 7947
Audit By: Sworn/Estimate/Non-Audited
Audit Date: 10.06.2019
Personnel: Albert M. Osten (Pub.); Janet Way (Ad.); Ray Fashona (Ed.); Roxane Hoffman (Ad.)
Parent company (for newspapers): Southern Dutchess News

SPENCER RANDOM HARVEST WEEKELY

Street address 1: 109 N Cayuga St
Street address city: Ithaca
Street address state: NY
Zip/Postal code: 14850-4341
General Phone: (607) 277-7000
General Fax: (607) 277-1012
General/National Adv. E-mail: jbilinski@ithacatimes.com
Editorial e-mail: editor@flcn.org
Primary Website: ithaca.com
Year Established: 1980
Avg Paid Circ: 826
Audit By: Sworn/Estimate/Non-Audited
Audit Date: 10.06.2019
Personnel: James Bilinski (Pub.)
Parent company (for newspapers): Finger Lakes Community Newspapers

SPOTLIGHT NEWSPAPERS

Street address 1: 341 Delaware Ave
Street address city: Delmar
Street address state: NY
Zip/Postal code: 12054-1920
General Phone: (518) 439-4949
General Fax: (518) 439-5198
General/National Adv. E-mail: news@spotlightnews.com
Primary Website: spotlightnews.com
Avg Paid Circ: 5389
Avg Free Circ: 16371
Audit By: CVC
Audit Date: 30.12.2017
Personnel: John McIntyre (Pub.); Bo Berezansky (VP of Advertising); Hallisey Michael (Mng. Ed.)

SPRING CREEK SUN

Street address 1: 1540 Van Siclen Ave
Street address 2: Ste. 4
Street address city: Brooklyn
Street address state: NY
Zip/Postal code: 11239-2429
General Phone: (718) 240-4554
Advertising Phone: (718) 240-4554
Editorial Phone: (718) 240-4554
Editorial Fax: (718) 240-4599
General/National Adv. E-mail: pstern@springcreektowers.com
Display Adv. E-mail: pstern@springcreektowers.com
Classified Adv. e-mail: pstern@springcreektowers.com
Editorial e-mail: pstern@springcreektowers.com
Primary Website: springcreeksunonline.com
Year Established: 1974
Avg Free Circ: 8500
Audit By: Sworn/Estimate/Non-Audited
Audit Date: 10.06.2019
Personnel: Amanda Moses (Reporter); Pamela Stern
Parent company (for newspapers): Starrett City Inc.

SPRINGVILLE JOURNAL

Street address 1: 75 Boxwood Ln
Street address city: Buffalo
Street address state: NY
Zip/Postal code: 14227-2707
General Phone: (716) 592-4550
General Fax: (716) 592-4663
Editorial Phone: (716) 592-4550 ext. 24
General/National Adv. E-mail: info@springvillejournal.com
Editorial e-mail: lschumer@springvillejournal.com
Primary Website: metrowny.com
Mthly Avg Views: 7293
Mthly Avg Unique Visitors: 5071
Year Established: 1939
Avg Paid Circ: 0
Avg Free Circ: 7420
Audit By: Sworn/Estimate/Non-Audited
Audit Date: 10.06.2019
Personnel: Denny Guastaferro (Pub.); Lizz Schumer (Ed.); Sandy Dashnaw (Circ. Mgr.); Gary Durawa (Pub.); Judy Beckwith (Adv. Mgr); Bill Marshall (Circ. Mgr)
Parent company (for newspapers): Metro Group, Inc.

ST. LAWRENCE PLAINDEALER

Street address 1: 1 Main St
Street address 2: Ste 103
Street address city: Canton
Street address state: NY
Zip/Postal code: 13617-1279
General Phone: (315) 386-8521
General Fax: (315) 393-5108
General/National Adv. E-mail: pdealer@ogd.com
Primary Website: watertowndailytimes.com/section/news05
Avg Paid Circ: 156
Avg Free Circ: 1
Audit By: Sworn/Estimate/Non-Audited
Audit Date: 10.06.2019
Personnel: Pery White (Mng. Ed.)

STEUBEN COURIER-ADVOCATE

Street address 1: 10 W Steuben St
Street address city: Bath
Street address state: NY
Zip/Postal code: 14810-1512
General Phone: (607) 776-2121
General/National Adv. E-mail: trounsville@steubencourier.com
Display Adv. E-mail: trounsville@steubencourier.com
Primary Website: steubencourier.com
Year Established: 1968
Avg Free Circ: 11113
Audit By: Sworn/Estimate/Non-Audited
Audit Date: 10.06.2019
Personnel: Sean Vargo (Ed.); Jamie Stopka (Circ. Mgr.); Teresa Rounsville (Sales Mgr.); Anna Devaul (Graphics)
Parent company (for newspapers): CherryRoad Media

SUBURBAN NEWS NORTH

Street address 1: 1776 Hilton Parma Corners Rd
Street address city: Spencerport
Street address state: NY
Zip/Postal code: 14559-9501
General Phone: (585) 352-3411
General Fax: (585) 352-4811
Advertising Phone: (585) 352-3411 ext 128
Editorial Phone: (585) 3523411 ext 127
General/National Adv. E-mail: info@westsidenewsny.com
Display Adv. E-mail: classified.advertising@westsidenewsny.com
Editorial e-mail: editor@westsidenewsny.com
Primary Website: westsidenewsonline.com
Year Established: 1953
Avg Paid Circ: 6
Avg Free Circ: 7094
Audit By: CVC
Audit Date: 30.09.2017
Personnel: Keith Ryan (Publisher); Evelyn Dow (Editor); Karen Fien (Production manager)
Parent company (for newspapers): Westside News

SUBURBAN NEWS SOUTH

Street address 1: 1776 Hilton Parma Corners Rd
Street address city: Spencerport
Street address state: NY
Zip/Postal code: 14559-9501
General Phone: (585) 352-3411
General Fax: (585) 352-4811

General/National Adv. E-mail: production@westsidenewsny.com
Display Adv. E-mail: classified.advertising@westsidenewsny.com
Editorial e-mail: editor@westsidenewsny.com
Primary Website: westsidenewsonline.com
Year Established: 1988
Avg Paid Circ: 38
Avg Free Circ: 11887
Audit By: CVC
Audit Date: 30.09.2017
Personnel: Keith Ryan (Publisher); Evelyn Dow (Editor); Karen Fien (Production manager)
Parent company (for newspapers): Westside News

SUBURBAN NEWS WEST

Street address 1: 1776 Hilton Parma Corners Rd
Street address city: Spencerport
Street address state: NY
Zip/Postal code: 14559-9501
General Phone: (585) 352-3411
General Fax: (585) 352-4811
General/National Adv. E-mail: production@westsidenewsny.com
Display Adv. E-mail: classified.advertising@westsidenewsny.com
Editorial e-mail: editor@westsidenewsny.com
Primary Website: westsidenewsonline.com
Year Established: 1989
Avg Paid Circ: 8
Avg Free Circ: 8817
Audit By: CVC
Audit Date: 30.09.2017
Personnel: Keith Ryan (Publisher); Evelyn Dow (Editor); Karen Fien (Production manager)
Parent company (for newspapers): Westside News

SUFFOLK COUNTY NEWS

Street address 1: 20 Medford Ave
Street address 2: Ste 112
Street address city: Patchogue
Street address state: NY
Zip/Postal code: 11772-1220
General Phone: (631) 475-1000
General Fax: (631) 475-1565
Advertising Phone: (631) 475-1000 x17
Editorial Phone: (631) 475-1000 x13
General/National Adv. E-mail: ibscnsales@suffolkcountynews.net
Editorial e-mail: scnibletter@optonline.net
Primary Website: suffolkcountynews.net
Year Established: 1884
Avg Paid Circ: 53000
Audit By: Sworn/Estimate/Non-Audited
Audit Date: 10.06.2019
Personnel: John T. Tuthill (Pub.); Joanne LaBarca (Gen. Mgr.); Liz Finnigan (Ed.); Monica Musetti-Carlin

SULLIVAN COUNTY DEMOCRAT

Street address 1: 5 Lower Main St
Street address city: Callicoon
Street address state: NY
Zip/Postal code: 12723-5000
General Phone: (845) 887-5200
General Fax: (845) 887-5386
General/National Adv. E-mail: lizt@sc-democrat.com
Display Adv. E-mail: class@sc-democrat.com
Editorial e-mail: editor@sc-democrat.com
Primary Website: scdemocratonline.com
Year Established: 1891
Avg Paid Circ: 9000
Audit By: Sworn/Estimate/Non-Audited
Audit Date: 10.06.2019
Personnel: Joseph Abraham (Co-Editor); Matt Shortall (Co-Editor); Liz Tucker (Advertising Director); Fred Stabbert III (Publisher); Sue Owens (Business Manager)
Parent company (for newspapers): Catskill-Delaware Publications

SYOSSET/JERICHO TRIBUNE

Street address 1: 132 E 2nd St
Street address city: Mineola
Street address state: NY
Zip/Postal code: 11501-3522
General Phone: (516) 747-8282
General Fax: (516) 742-5867
General/National Adv. E-mail: advertising@antonnews.com
Display Adv. E-mail: classified@antonnews.com
Editorial e-mail: nlockwood@AntonMediaGroup.com
Primary Website: http://syossetjerichotribune.com/
Year Established: 1958
Avg Paid Circ: 4220
Avg Free Circ: 753
Audit By: Sworn/Estimate/Non-Audited
Audit Date: 10.06.2019
Personnel: Angela Anton (Pub.); Joy DiDonato (Circ. Mgr.); Nicole Lockwood (Ed.)
Parent company (for newspapers): Anton Community Newspapers

THE ADIRONDACK EXPRESS

Street address 1: 2955 St. RT. 28
Street address city: Old Forge
Street address state: NY
Zip/Postal code: 13420
General Phone: (315) 369-2237
General Fax: (315) 369-3378
General/National Adv. E-mail: dgraydon@adirondackexpress.com
Display Adv. E-mail: office@adirondackexpress.com
Editorial e-mail: editor@adirondackexpress.com
Primary Website: adirondackexpress.com
Avg Paid Circ: 2000
Avg Free Circ: 12500
Audit By: Sworn/Estimate/Non-Audited
Audit Date: 10.06.2019
Personnel: Kevin McClary (Pub.); Brian Krohn (Dir., Adv./Mktg.); Debbie Graydon (Adv. Sales Mgr.); M. Lisa Monroe (Ed)
Parent company (for newspapers): McClary Media

THE ADIRONDACK JOURNAL SUN

Street address 1: 14 Hand Ave
Street address city: Elizabethtown
Street address state: NY
Zip/Postal code: 12932
General Phone: (518) 873-6368
General Fax: (518) 873-6360
Advertising Phone: (518) 585-9173
Advertising Fax: (518) 585-9175
General/National Adv. E-mail: ads@suncommunitynews.com
Display Adv. E-mail: susan@suncommunitynews.com
Editorial e-mail: dan@suncommunitynews.com
Primary Website: suncommmunitynews.com
Mthly Avg Views: 9508
Mthly Avg Unique Visitors: 1882
Year Established: 1948
Avg Paid Circ: 94
Avg Free Circ: 8087
Audit By: CVC
Audit Date: 30.09.2017
Personnel: Daniel E. Alexander (Pres./Pub.); Edward Coats (Pres./Pub.); Thom Randall (Ed.); John Gereau (Ed.); Bill Coats (Prodn. Mgr.); Scarlette Merfeld (Adv. Mgr); Jennifer Tower (Circ. Mgr); Susan Zackarenko (Office Mgr)
Parent company (for newspapers): Sun Community News, Published by:Denton Publications, Inc.

THE ADVERTISER-NEWS (NORTH)

Street address 1: 20 West Ave
Street address 2: Ste 101
Street address city: Chester
Street address state: NY
Zip/Postal code: 10918-1053
General Phone: (845) 469-9000
General Fax: (845) 469-9001
General/National Adv. E-mail: njoffice@strausnews.com
Primary Website: strausnews.com
Avg Free Circ: 20619
Audit By: Sworn/Estimate/Non-Audited
Audit Date: 10.06.2019
Personnel: Jeanne Straus (Pres.); Mike Zummo (Mng. Ed.)
Parent company (for newspapers): Straus News

THE ALFRED SUN

Street address 1: 764 State Rt 244
Street address city: Alfred
Street address state: NY
Zip/Postal code: 14802
General Phone: (607) 587-8110
Advertising Phone: 607-382-5308
General/National Adv. E-mail: alfredsun.news@gmail.com
Primary Website: n/a
Year Established: 1883
Avg Paid Circ: 959
Avg Free Circ: 50
Audit By: Sworn/Estimate/Non-Audited
Audit Date: 10.06.2019
Personnel: David L. Snyder (Ed. and Pub.)

THE ALTAMONT ENTERPRISE & ALBANY COUNTY POST

Street address 1: 120 Maple Ave
Street address city: Altamont
Street address state: NY
Zip/Postal code: 12009-7718
General Phone: (518) 861-4026
General Fax: (518) 595-8211
Editorial Phone: (518) 861-5005
General/National Adv. E-mail: ads@altamontenterprise.com
Display Adv. E-mail: classifieds@altamontenterprise.com
Editorial e-mail: MHale-Spencer@AltamontEnterprise.com
Primary Website: altamontenterprise.com
Year Established: 1884
Avg Paid Circ: 4757
Avg Free Circ: 111
Audit By: Sworn/Estimate/Non-Audited
Audit Date: 10.06.2019
Personnel: Melissa Hale-Spencer (Ed co-pub); Marcello Iaia (digital ed, co-pub); Gary Spencer (Co-pub)

THE AMITYVILLE RECORD

Street address 1: 85 Broadway
Street address 2: Ste A
Street address city: Amityville
Street address state: NY
Zip/Postal code: 11701-2778
General Phone: (631) 264-0077
General Fax: (631) 264-5310
Advertising Phone: (631) 608-4495
Advertising Fax: (631) 264-5310
General/National Adv. E-mail: acjads@optonline.net
Display Adv. E-mail: acjads@optonline.net
Editorial e-mail: acjnews@rcn.com
Primary Website: amityvillerecord.com
Year Established: 1904
Avg Paid Circ: 2800
Avg Free Circ: 300
Audit By: Sworn/Estimate/Non-Audited
Audit Date: 10.06.2019
Personnel: Alfred James (Pres./Pub.); Carolyn James (Exec. Ed.)
Parent company (for newspapers): CJ Publishers Inc.

THE BEACON

Street address 1: 65 Deer Park Ave
Street address 2: Ste 2
Street address city: Babylon
Street address state: NY
Zip/Postal code: 11702-2820
General Phone: (631) 587-5612
General Fax: (631) 587-0198
Editorial Phone: same
General/National Adv. E-mail: acjads@optonline.net
Display Adv. E-mail: acjads@optonline.net
Editorial e-mail: acjnews@rcn.com
Primary Website: babylonbeacon.com
Year Established: 1966
Avg Paid Circ: 2800
Avg Free Circ: 400
Audit By: Sworn/Estimate/Non-Audited
Audit Date: 10.06.2019
Personnel: Alfred James (Pub.); Carolyn James (Pub.); Helene Pagano (Circ. Mgr.); Maryann Heins (Adv. Mgr.)
Parent company (for newspapers): CJ Publishers Inc.

THE BRONX FREE PRESS

Street address 1: 5030 Broadway
Street address 2: Ste 801
Street address city: New York
Street address state: NY
Zip/Postal code: 10034-1666
General Phone: (212) 569-5800
General Fax: (212) 544-9545
Editorial e-mail: editor@manhattantimesnews.com
Primary Website: thebronxfreepress.com
Audit By: Sworn/Estimate/Non-Audited
Audit Date: 10.06.2019
Personnel: Debralee Santos (Ed.); Roberto Ramirez, Sr. (Pub.); Luis A. Miranda, Jr. (Pub.)

THE BRONX NEWS

Street address 1: 135 Dreiser Loop
Street address city: Bronx
Street address state: NY
Zip/Postal code: 10475-2704
General Phone: (718) 320-3071
General Fax: (718) 320-7059
General/National Adv. E-mail: bronxnews@gmail.com
Editorial e-mail: bronxnews@gmail.com
Primary Website: https://sites.google.com/site/bronxnews/Ã‚Â
Year Established: 1976
Avg Paid Circ: 6000
Avg Free Circ: 4000
Audit By: Sworn/Estimate/Non-Audited
Audit Date: 10.06.2019
Personnel: Christopher G. Hagedorn (Pub.); Daniel Gesslein (Ed.); Al Zezula (Mktg. Dir.)
Parent company (for newspapers): Hagedorn Communications

THE BROOKLYN PAPERS

Street address 1: 1 Metrotech Ctr N
Street address 2: Ste 1001
Street address city: Brooklyn
Street address state: NY
Zip/Postal code: 11201-3832
General Phone: (718) 260-2500
Advertising Phone: (718) 260-2510
Advertising Fax: (718) 260-2579
General/National Adv. E-mail: RDonofrio@cnglocal.com
Display Adv. E-mail: classified@cnglocal.com
Editorial e-mail: editorial@cnglocal.com
Primary Website: brooklynpaper.com
Avg Free Circ: 25600
Audit By: Sworn/Estimate/Non-Audited
Audit Date: 10.06.2019
Personnel: Vince DiMirceli (Ed.-in-Chief); Clifford Luster; Nathan Tempey (Deputy Ed.)
Parent company (for newspapers): Community Newspaper Group

THE BROOKLYN SPECTATOR

Street address 1: 9733 4th Ave
Street address city: Brooklyn
Street address state: NY
Zip/Postal code: 11209-8104
General Phone: (718) 238-6600
General Fax: (718) 238-6630
General/National Adv. E-mail: clatorre@brooklynreporter.com
Display Adv. E-mail: clatorre@brooklynreporter.com
Editorial e-mail: editorial@brooklynreporter.com
Primary Website: http://brooklynspectator.com/
Avg Paid Circ: 800
Avg Free Circ: 10000
Audit By: Sworn/Estimate/Non-Audited
Audit Date: 10.06.2019
Personnel: Joshua Schneps (Pub); Christine LaTorre (VP, S&O); Helen Klein (EiC)
Parent company (for newspapers): Schneps Communications

THE CANDOR CHRONICLE

Street address 1: 109 N Cayuga St
Street address city: Ithaca
Street address state: NY
Zip/Postal code: 14850-4341
General Phone: (607) 277-7700
General Fax: (607) 277-1012
Primary Website: ithaca.com/news/candor
Audit By: Sworn/Estimate/Non-Audited
Audit Date: 10.06.2019
Personnel: Nick Reynolds (Ed.)
Parent company (for newspapers): Finger Lakes Community Newspapers

THE CENTRAL NEW YORK BUSINESS JOURNAL

Street address 1: 269 W Jefferson St

Street address city: Syracuse
Street address state: NY
Zip/Postal code: 13202-2334
General Phone: (315) 579-3900
Advertising Phone: (315) 579-3907
Editorial Phone: (315) 579-3902
General/National Adv. E-mail: mlamacchia@cnybj.com
Editorial e-mail: arombel@cnybj.com
Primary Website: cnybj.com
Mthly Avg Views: 39000
Mthly Avg Unique Visitors: 8700
Audit By: Sworn/Estimate/Non-Audited
Audit Date: 10.06.2019
Personnel: Adam Rombel (Ed.-in-Chief); Norman Poltenson (Pub.)

THE CHENANGO AMERICAN/ WHITNEY POINT REPORTER/ OXFORD REVIEW-TIMES

Street address 1: 9 1/2 S Chenango St
Street address city: Greene
Street address state: NY
Zip/Postal code: 13778-1212
General Phone: (607) 656-4511
General Fax: (607) 656-8544
General/National Adv. E-mail: hometownnews@frontiernet.net
Editorial e-mail: hometownnews@frontiernet.net
Primary Website: tritownnews.com
Avg Paid Circ: 2100
Avg Free Circ: 131
Audit By: Sworn/Estimate/Non-Audited
Audit Date: 10.06.2019
Personnel: Allison Collins (Ed.); Ken Paden (Pub.)

THE CHRONICLE

Street address 1: 15 Ridge St
Street address city: Glens Falls
Street address state: NY
Zip/Postal code: 12801-3608
General Phone: (518) 792-1126
General Fax: (518) 793-1587
Advertising Phone: (518) 792-1126
Editorial Phone: (518) 792-1126
General/National Adv. E-mail: ads@loneoak.com
Display Adv. E-mail: ads@loneoak.com
Editorial e-mail: chronicle@loneoak.com
Primary Website: readthechronicle.com
Year Established: 1980
Avg Paid Circ: 500
Avg Free Circ: 28000
Audit By: Sworn/Estimate/Non-Audited
Audit Date: 10.06.2019
Personnel: Mark Frost (Owner/Pub.); Gordon Woodworth (News Ed.); Cathy DeDe (Mng. Ed.); Sandra Hutchinson (Chief Operating Officer); Valerie Erceg (Advertising Sales Guru)

THE CHRONICLE-EXPRESS

Street address 1: 138 Main St
Street address city: Penn Yan
Street address state: NY
Zip/Postal code: 14527-1299
General Phone: (315) 536-4422
General Fax: (315) 536-0682
General/National Adv. E-mail: CandyScutt@chronicle-express.com
Display Adv. E-mail: CandyScutt@chronicle-express.com
Editorial e-mail: News@chronicle-express.com
Primary Website: chronicle-express.com
Year Established: 1824
Avg Paid Circ: 3200
Avg Free Circ: 11245
Audit By: Sworn/Estimate/Non-Audited
Audit Date: 10.06.2019
Personnel: Karen Morris (Pub.); Candy Scutt (Ad. Mgr); Gwen Chamberlain (Ed.)
Parent company (for newspapers): CherryRoad Media

THE CITIZEN OUTLET

Street address 1: 80 N Jefferson St
Street address city: Mexico
Street address state: NY
Zip/Postal code: 13114-3001
General Phone: (315) 963-7813
General Fax: (315) 963-4087
General/National Adv. E-mail: ocwadvertising@cnymail.com
Display Adv. E-mail: ocwadvertising@cnymail.com
Editorial e-mail: rparsons@oswegonews.com
Primary Website: oswegocountyweeklies.com
Year Established: 1950
Avg Paid Circ: 4889
Audit By: Sworn/Estimate/Non-Audited
Audit Date: 10.06.2019
Personnel: Rose Ann Parsons (Mng. Ed.)

THE COLUMBIA PAPER

Street address 1: PO Box 482
Street address city: Ghent
Street address state: NY
Zip/Postal code: 12075-0482
General Phone: (518) 392-1122
General/National Adv. E-mail: ads@columbiapaper.com
Display Adv. E-mail: ads@columbiapaper.com
Editorial e-mail: letters@columbiapaper.com
Primary Website: columbiapaper.com
Mthly Avg Views: 25400
Mthly Avg Unique Visitors: 6400
Year Established: 2009
Avg Paid Circ: 2200
Audit By: Sworn/Estimate/Non-Audited
Audit Date: 10.06.2019
Personnel: Diane Valden (Associate Ed.); Parry Teasdale (Ed. & Pub.); Emilia Teasdale (Deputy Pub.)

THE CORNWALL LOCAL

Street address 1: 55 Quaker Ave
Street address 2: Suite 204
Street address city: Cornwall
Street address state: NY
Zip/Postal code: 12518-2026
General Phone: (845) 534-7771
General/National Adv. E-mail: joegill@thecornwalllocal.com
Editorial e-mail: kencashman@thecornwalllocal.com
Primary Website: thecornwalllocal.com
Year Established: 1888
Avg Paid Circ: 1676
Avg Free Circ: 67
Audit By: Sworn/Estimate/Non-Audited
Audit Date: 10.06.2019
Personnel: Joseph V. Gill (VP & Pub.); Ken Cashman (Ed.)
Parent company (for newspapers): News of the Highlands Inc.

THE COUNTRY COURIER

Street address 1: 1035 Conklin Rd
Street address city: Conklin
Street address state: NY
Zip/Postal code: 13748-1102
General Phone: (607) 775-0472
General Fax: (607) 775-5863
General/National Adv. E-mail: Deinstein@stny.rr.com
Primary Website: wecoverthetowns.com
Year Established: 1981
Avg Paid Circ: 1300
Audit By: Sworn/Estimate/Non-Audited
Audit Date: 10.06.2019
Personnel: Donald Einstein (Pub. & Ad.); Elizabeth Einstein (Ed.)
Parent company (for newspapers): Newspaper Publishers LLC

THE DEPOSIT COURIER

Street address 1: 24 Laurel Bank Ave
Street address 2: Ste 2
Street address city: Deposit
Street address state: NY
Zip/Postal code: 13754-1251
General Phone: (607) 467-3600
General Fax: (607) 467-5330
General/National Adv. E-mail: couriernews@tds.net
Display Adv. E-mail: couriernews@tds.net
Year Established: 1848
Avg Paid Circ: 2050
Avg Free Circ: 32
Audit By: Sworn/Estimate/Non-Audited
Audit Date: 10.06.2019
Personnel: Ann Schmitz (Adv. Mgr.); Hilton A. Evans (Ed.)

THE DOWNTOWN EXPRESS

Street address 1: One Metrotech Center North
Street address 2: 10th Floor
Street address city: Brooklyn
Street address state: NY
Zip/Postal code: 11201
General Phone: (212) 229-1890
General Fax: (212) 229-2790
Advertising Phone: (212) 229-1890 x2496
General/National Adv. E-mail: ads@thevillager.com
Editorial e-mail: lincoln@thevillager.com
Primary Website: thevillager.com
Avg Free Circ: 40000
Audit By: Sworn/Estimate/Non-Audited
Audit Date: 10.06.2019
Personnel: Victoria Schneps-Yunis (Pres./Pub.); Joshua Schneps (CEO/Co-Pub.); Lincoln Anderson (Ed.)
Parent company (for newspapers): NYC Community Media, LLC

THE DRUMMER PENNYSAVER

Street address 1: 2 Apollo Dr
Street address city: Batavia
Street address state: NY
Zip/Postal code: 14020-3002
General Phone: (585) 343-2055
General Fax: (585) 344-2050
Display Adv. E-mail: batads@batavianews.com
Primary Website: drummerpennysaver.com
Year Established: 1979
Avg Free Circ: 15200
Audit By: Sworn/Estimate/Non-Audited
Audit Date: 10.06.2019
Personnel: Michael Messerly (Pub.); Kim Pasierb (Ad. Dir.)
Parent company (for newspapers): Johnson Newspaper Corp.

THE DRYDEN COURIER

Street address 1: 109 N Cayuga St
Street address city: Ithaca
Street address state: NY
Zip/Postal code: 14850-4341
General Phone: (607) 277-7700
General Fax: (607) 277-1012
Primary Website: ithaca.com/news/candor
Audit By: Sworn/Estimate/Non-Audited
Audit Date: 10.06.2019
Personnel: Nick Reynolds (Ed.)
Parent company (for newspapers): Finger Lakes Community Newspapers

THE EAGLE

Street address 1: 2501 James St
Street address 2: Ste 100
Street address city: Syracuse
Street address state: NY
Zip/Postal code: 13206-2996
General Phone: (315) 434-8889
General Fax: (315) 434-8883
Advertising Phone: (315) 434-8889 x312
Editorial Phone: (315) 434-8889 x320
General/National Adv. E-mail: news@theeaglenewspaper.com
Display Adv. E-mail: EagleNews@gmail.com
Primary Website: theeaglecny.com
Avg Paid Circ: 1
Avg Free Circ: 4850
Audit By: Sworn/Estimate/Non-Audited
Audit Date: 10.06.2019
Personnel: David Tyler; Jennifer Wing (Ed.); James Robison (Ad.)

THE EAST HAMPTON STAR

Street address 1: 153 Main St
Street address city: East Hampton
Street address state: NY
Zip/Postal code: 11937-2716
General Phone: (631) 324-0002
General Fax: (631) 324-7943
General/National Adv. E-mail: ads@ehstar.com
Display Adv. E-mail: classy@easthamptonstar.com
Editorial e-mail: editor@easthamptonstar.com
Primary Website: easthamptonstar.com
Mthly Avg Views: 530000
Mthly Avg Unique Visitors: 53000
Year Established: 1885
Avg Paid Circ: 11000
Avg Free Circ: 612
Audit By: Sworn/Estimate/Non-Audited
Audit Date: 10.06.2019
Personnel: Helen S. Rattray (Pub.); Isabel Hefner (Adv. Mgr.); David E. Rattray (Ed.); Kathy Kovach (Prodn. Mgr.)

THE EASTWICK PRESS

Street address 1: 13 Babcock Lake Rd
Street address city: Cropseyville
Street address state: NY
Zip/Postal code: 12052-2200
General Phone: (518) 203-7574
General Fax: none
Advertising Phone: (518) 491-1613
Advertising Fax: none
Editorial Phone: (518) 491-1613
Editorial Fax: none
General/National Adv. E-mail: news@eastwickpress.cpm
Display Adv. E-mail: ads@eastwickpress.com
Classified Adv. e-mail: ads@eastwickpress.com
Editorial e-mail: news@eastwickpress.com
Primary Website: eastwickpress.com
Mthly Avg Views: 5000
Mthly Avg Unique Visitors: 200
Year Established: 2017
Avg Paid Circ: 1800
Avg Free Circ: 50
Audit By: Sworn/Estimate/Non-Audited
Audit Date: 10.10.2021
Personnel: Alex Brooks (Graphic Design, Reporter); Doug La Rocque (Publisher, editor); Bea Peterson (Copy Editor); Tom Withcuskey (Publisher, Advertising); Steve Bradley (Photo Journalist); Amy Modesti (Photo Journalist); Miranda Sehl; Heidi Woofenden; Thaddeus Flint (Photo Journalist); Chris Tergliafera; Ed Palitsch; Denise Wright
Parent company (for newspapers): Eastwick Press LLC

THE EXAMINER

Street address 1: PO Box 611
Street address city: Mount Kisco
Street address state: NY
Zip/Postal code: 10549-0611
General Phone: (914) 864-0878
Advertising Phone: (914) 864-0878
Editorial Phone: (914) 419-0390
General/National Adv. E-mail: advertising@theexaminernews.com
Display Adv. E-mail: astone@theexaminernews.com
Editorial e-mail: mwilbur@theexaminernews.com
Primary Website: theexaminernews.com
Year Established: 2007
Avg Paid Circ: 0
Avg Free Circ: 6475
Audit By: Sworn/Estimate/Non-Audited
Audit Date: 10.06.2019
Personnel: Adam Stone (Pub.); Martin Wilbur (Ed.)
Parent company (for newspapers): Examiner Media

THE EXPRESS

Street address 1: 30 Walnut St
Street address 2: Fl 1
Street address city: Mechanicville
Street address state: NY
Zip/Postal code: 12118-1040
General Phone: (518) 664-3335
Advertising Phone: (518) 664-3335
Editorial Phone: (518) 664-3335
General/National Adv. E-mail: info.expresspaper@gmail.com
Display Adv. E-mail: info.expresspaper@gmail.com
Editorial e-mail: info.expresspaper@gmail.com
Primary Website: theexpressweeklynews.com
Mthly Avg Views: 4000
Mthly Avg Unique Visitors: 3500
Year Established: 1981
Avg Paid Circ: 2700
Avg Free Circ: 0
Audit By: Sworn/Estimate/Non-Audited
Audit Date: 10.06.2019

Personnel: Cindy Mahoney (Owner/Ed.); Tom Mahoney (Owner & Pub.); Melissa LeMay (V.P. Sales and Marketing)

THE EXPRESS

Street address 1: 22 Division Street
Street address city: Sag Harbor
Street address state: NY
Zip/Postal code: 11963
General Phone: (631) 725-1700
General Fax: (631) 725-1584
General/National Adv. E-mail: gmenu@sagharborexpress.com
Display Adv. E-mail: classifieds@sagharborexpress.com
Editorial e-mail: editor@sagharborexpress.com
Primary Website: sagharborexpress.com
Year Established: 1859
Avg Paid Circ: 3000
Avg Free Circ: 1000
Audit By: Sworn/Estimate/Non-Audited
Audit Date: 10.06.2019
Personnel: Gavin Menu (Ad. Dir.); Kathryn Menu (Ed)

THE FORUM

Street address 1: 15519 Lahn St
Street address city: Howard Beach
Street address state: NY
Zip/Postal code: 11414-2858
General Phone: (718) 845-3221
General Fax: (718) 738-7645
General/National Adv. E-mail: forumsouth@gmail.com
Editorial e-mail: michael@theforumnewsgroup.com
Primary Website: theforumnewsgroup.com
Avg Free Circ: 25000
Audit By: Sworn/Estimate/Non-Audited
Audit Date: 10.06.2019
Personnel: Michael Cusenza (Editor-in-Chief)
Parent company (for newspapers): The Forum Newspaper, Inc.

THE GOUVERNEUR TRIBUNE-PRESS

Street address 1: 74 Trinity Ave
Street address city: Gouverneur
Street address state: NY
Zip/Postal code: 13642-1126
General Phone: (315) 287-2100
General Fax: (315) 287-2397
General/National Adv. E-mail: tribunepress@verizon.net
Primary Website: gouverneurtribunepress.com
Avg Paid Circ: 3724
Avg Free Circ: 301
Audit By: Sworn/Estimate/Non-Audited
Audit Date: 10.06.2019
Personnel: M. Dan McClelland (Pub.); Rachel Hunter (Ed.); Curran Wade (Ad.)

THE GRANVILLE SENTINEL

Street address 1: 14 E Main St
Street address city: Granville
Street address state: NY
Zip/Postal code: 12832-1334
General Phone: (518) 642-1234
General Fax: (518) 642-1344
Advertising Phone: (518) 642-1234
Advertising Fax: (518) 642-1344
Editorial Phone: (518) 642-1234
Editorial Fax: (518) 642-1344
General/National Adv. E-mail: advertising@manchesternewspapers.com
Display Adv. E-mail: classifieds@manchesternewspapers.com
Editorial e-mail: publisher@manchesternewspapers.com
Primary Website: manchesternewspapers.com
Year Established: 1875
Avg Paid Circ: 2800
Audit By: Sworn/Estimate/Non-Audited
Audit Date: 10.06.2019
Personnel: John MacArthur Manchester (Pub.); Lisa Manchester (Exec. VP); Jane Casey (Prodc. Mgr & Ad.)
Parent company (for newspapers): Manchester Newspapers, Inc.

THE GREENPOINT GAZETTE

Street address 1: 597 Manhattan Ave
Street address 2: Apt 1
Street address city: Brooklyn
Street address state: NY
Zip/Postal code: 11222-3924
General Phone: (718) 389-6067
General Fax: (718) 349-3471
General/National Adv. E-mail: jeff@greenpointnews.com
Editorial e-mail: jeff@greenpointnews.com
Primary Website: greenpointnews.com
Year Established: 1973
Avg Paid Circ: 9000
Audit By: Sworn/Estimate/Non-Audited
Audit Date: 10.06.2019
Personnel: Jeff Mann (Ed. & Pub.)

THE GREENWICH JOURNAL & SALEM PRESS

Street address 1: 171 Windy Hill Road
Street address city: GREENWICH
Street address state: NY
Zip/Postal code: 12834
General Phone: (518) 692-2266
General Fax: (518) 338-9908
General/National Adv. E-mail: gjpreporter@aol.com
Display Adv. E-mail: news@greenwichjournalsalempress.com
Editorial e-mail: gjpreporter@aol.com
Primary Website: greenwichjournalsalempress.com
Year Established: 1842
Avg Paid Circ: 900
Audit By: Sworn/Estimate/Non-Audited
Audit Date: 10.06.2019
Personnel: Meghan Phalen (Mng. Ed.)

THE HANCOCK HERALD

Street address 1: 102 E Front St
Street address city: Hancock
Street address state: NY
Zip/Postal code: 13783-1200
General Phone: (607) 637-3591
General Fax: (607) 637-4383
General/National Adv. E-mail: jill@hancockherald.com
Display Adv. E-mail: Mary@hancockherald.com
Editorial e-mail: hancockherald@hancock.net
Primary Website: hancockherald.com
Year Established: 1873
Avg Paid Circ: 2000
Audit By: Sworn/Estimate/Non-Audited
Audit Date: 10.06.2019
Personnel: Sally Zegers (Pub./Ed.)

THE HEMPSTEAD BEACON

Street address 1: 5 Centre St
Street address 2: Ste 3
Street address city: Hempstead
Street address state: NY
Zip/Postal code: 11550-2422
General Phone: (516) 481-5400
General Fax: (516) 481-8773
General/National Adv. E-mail: thebeaconnews5@aol.com
Avg Paid Circ: 4800
Audit By: Sworn/Estimate/Non-Audited
Audit Date: 10.06.2019
Personnel: Kathleen Hoegl (Pub.); Barbara Yohe (Ed.)
Parent company (for newspapers): Nassau County Publications

THE INDEPENDENT

Street address 1: 74 Montauk Hwy
Street address 2: Unit 16
Street address city: East Hampton
Street address state: NY
Zip/Postal code: 11937-3268
General Phone: (631) 324-2500
General Fax: (631) 324-2544
General/National Adv. E-mail: ads@indyeastend.com
Display Adv. E-mail: classifieds@indyeastend.com
Editorial e-mail: news@indyeastend.com
Primary Website: indyeastend.com
Year Established: 1993
Avg Paid Circ: 12
Avg Free Circ: 14000
Audit By: Sworn/Estimate/Non-Audited
Audit Date: 10.06.2019
Personnel: Rick Murphy (Ed.); James Mackin (Pub.); Joanna Froschl (Adv. Sales)
Parent company (for newspapers): East Hampton Media Holdings llc

THE INTERLAKEN REVIEW

Street address 1: 1009 N Cayuage St
Street address city: Ithaca
Street address state: NY
Zip/Postal code: 14850
General Phone: (607) 277-7000
General Fax: (607) 277-1012
General/National Adv. E-mail: tolson@ithacatimes.com
Editorial e-mail: editor@flcn.org
Primary Website: ithaca.com
Avg Paid Circ: 351
Avg Free Circ: 42
Audit By: Sworn/Estimate/Non-Audited
Audit Date: 10.06.2019
Personnel: James Bilinski (Pub.); Nick Reynolds (Mng. Ed.)
Parent company (for newspapers): Finger Lakes Community Newspapers

THE JEWISH PRESS

Street address 1: 3692 Bedford Avenue
Street address city: Brooklyn
Street address state: NY
Zip/Postal code: 11229
General Phone: 718-330-1100
General Fax: 718/624-4106
Advertising Phone: 718-645-7297
Editorial Phone: 718-330-1100
General/National Adv. E-mail: editor@jewishpress.com
Display Adv. E-mail: arthurklass@jewishpress.com
Classified Adv. e-mail: arthurklass@jewishpress.com
Editorial e-mail: editor@jewishpress.com
Primary Website: www.jewishpress.com
Mthly Avg Views: 300000
Year Established: 1959
Avg Paid Circ: 96000
Audit By: Sworn/Estimate/Non-Audited
Audit Date: 15.10.2020
Personnel: Irene Klass (Pub.); Arthur Klass (Director of Business Development); Heshy Kornblit (Display Dept. Mgr.); Joseph Hochberg (Circ. Mgr.); Jason Maoz (Sr. Ed.); Jerry Greenwald (Mng. Ed.)

THE LAKE PLACID NEWS

Street address 1: 6179 Sentinel Rd
Street address city: Lake Placid
Street address state: NY
Zip/Postal code: 12946-3509
General Phone: (518) 523-4401
Advertising Phone: (518) 891-2600
Editorial Phone: (518) 523-4401
General/National Adv. E-mail: advertising@lakeplacidnews.com
Display Adv. E-mail: classifieds@adirondackdailyenterprise.com
Editorial e-mail: news@lakeplacidnews.com
Primary Website: lakeplacidnews.com
Year Established: 1905
Avg Paid Circ: 2500
Audit By: Sworn/Estimate/Non-Audited
Audit Date: 10.06.2019
Personnel: Catherine Moore (Pub.)
Parent company (for newspapers): Ogden Newspapers Inc.

THE LAKES REGION FREE PRESS

Street address 1: 14 E Main St
Street address city: Granville
Street address state: NY
Zip/Postal code: 12832-1334
General Phone: (518) 642-1234
General Fax: (518) 642-1344
Advertising Phone: (518) 642-1234
Advertising Fax: (518) 642-1344
Editorial Phone: (518) 642-1234
Editorial Fax: (518) 642-1344
General/National Adv. E-mail: advertising@manchesternewspapers.com
Display Adv. E-mail: classifieds@manchesternewspapers.com
Editorial e-mail: publisher@manchesternewspapers.com
Primary Website: manchesternewspapers.com
Year Established: 1995
Avg Free Circ: 8039
Audit By: CVC
Audit Date: 30.09.2017
Personnel: John Manchester (Pub./Nat'l Adv. Mgr.); Lisa Manchester (Vice Pres.); Jane Cosey (Prodn. Mgr.); Bill Toscano (Ed.); Ann Hilder (Circ. Mgr)
Parent company (for newspapers): Manchester Newspapers, Inc.

THE LANSING LEDGER

Street address 1: 109 N Cayuga St
Street address city: Ithaca
Street address state: NY
Zip/Postal code: 14850-4341
General Phone: (607) 277-7700
General Fax: (607) 277-1012
Primary Website: ithaca.com/news/lansing
Audit By: Sworn/Estimate/Non-Audited
Audit Date: 10.06.2019
Parent company (for newspapers): Finger Lakes Community Newspapers

THE LEADER

Street address 1: 336 Forest Ave
Street address city: Locust Valley
Street address state: NY
Zip/Postal code: 11560-2122
General Phone: (516) 676-1434
General Fax: (516) 676-1414
General/National Adv. E-mail: advertising@theleaderonline.com
Display Adv. E-mail: classifieds@theleaderonline.com
Editorial e-mail: news@theleaderonline.com
Primary Website: theleaderonline.com
Avg Paid Circ: 3200
Avg Free Circ: 80
Audit By: Sworn/Estimate/Non-Audited
Audit Date: 10.06.2019
Personnel: Lawrence Laily (Pub.); LC Colgate (Mng. Ed.)

THE LEADER-OBSERVER OF WOODHAVEN

Street address 1: 6960 Grand Ave
Street address city: Maspeth
Street address state: NY
Zip/Postal code: 11378-1828
General Phone: (718) 639-7000
General Fax: (718) 429-1234
General/National Adv. E-mail: ads@queensledger.com
Editorial e-mail: news@queensledger.com
Primary Website: leaderobserver.com
Year Established: 1909
Avg Paid Circ: 25000
Audit By: Sworn/Estimate/Non-Audited
Audit Date: 10.06.2019
Personnel: Tammy Sanchez (Gen. Mgr.); Walter H. Sanchez (Ed.)
Parent company (for newspapers): BQE Publishing Inc.

THE LEGISLATIVE GAZETTE

Street address 1: PO Box 7329
Street address city: Albany
Street address state: NY
Zip/Postal code: 12224-0329
General Phone: (518) 486-6513
Advertising Phone: (518) 473-9739
General/National Adv. E-mail: gvadney@legislativegazette.com
Primary Website: legislativegazette.com
Year Established: 1978
Audit By: Sworn/Estimate/Non-Audited
Audit Date: 10.06.2019
Personnel: James Gormley (Editor); Alan Chartock (Pub.)

THE LITTLE NECK LEDGER

Street address 1: 4102 Bell Blvd
Street address city: Bayside
Street address state: NY
Zip/Postal code: 11361-2792
General Phone: (718) 229-0300
General Fax: (718) 225-7117
General/National Adv. E-mail: news@timesledger.com
Display Adv. E-mail: classified@cnglocal.com
Editorial e-mail: timesledgernews@cnglocal.com
Primary Website: timesledger.com
Avg Paid Circ: 1686

Audit By: Sworn/Estimate/Non-Audited
Audit Date: 10.06.2019
Personnel: Roz Liston (Ed.); Brian Rice (Display & Online Advertising); Amanda Tarley (Classified Advertising)
Parent company (for newspapers): Queens Village Times (OOB)

THE LIVINGSTON COUNTY NEWS

Street address 1: 122 Main St
Street address city: Geneseo
Street address state: NY
Zip/Postal code: 14454-1230
General Phone: (585) 243-0296
General Fax: (585) 243-0348
Advertising Phone: (585) 243-0296
Advertising Fax: (585) 243-0348
Editorial Phone: (585) 243-0296
Editorial Fax: (585) 243-0348
General/National Adv. E-mail: jzambito@batavianews.com
Display Adv. E-mail: jzambito@batavianews.com
Editorial e-mail: ben@livingstonnews.com
Primary Website: thelcn.com
Avg Paid Circ: 5789
Audit By: Sworn/Estimate/Non-Audited
Audit Date: 10.06.2019
Personnel: Ben Beagle (Gen Mgr/Mng. Ed.); Kim Roberts (Sales Rep.); Chris Metcalf (Sports Ed); Matt Leader (Reporter); Gary Durawa (Advt Dir)
Parent company (for newspapers): Johnson Newspaper Corporation

THE LONG-ISLANDER NEWS

Street address 1: 44 Broadway
Street address 2: Ste 1
Street address city: Greenlawn
Street address state: NY
Zip/Postal code: 11740
General Phone: (631) 427-7000
General Fax: (631) 427-5820
Advertising Phone: (631) 427-7000 x10
Advertising Fax: (631) 427-5820
Editorial Phone: (631) 427-7000
Editorial Fax: (631) 427-5820
General/National Adv. E-mail: info@longislandernews.com
Display Adv. E-mail: info@longislandernews.com
Classified Adv. e-mail: jvk@longislandernews.com
Editorial e-mail: info@longislandernews.com
Primary Website: longislandernews.com
Mthly Avg Views: 15000
Mthly Avg Unique Visitors: 11000
Year Established: 1838
Avg Paid Circ: 24000
Audit By: Sworn/Estimate/Non-Audited
Audit Date: 10.06.2019
Personnel: Peter Sloggatt (Pub./Mng.Ed.); James Kelly (Owner/General Manager); Andrew Wroblewski (Ed.)
Parent company (for newspapers): Tribco LLC-OOB; Spend Navigator, LLC

THE MERRICK BEACON

Street address 1: 5 Centre St
Street address 2: Ste 3
Street address city: Hempstead
Street address state: NY
Zip/Postal code: 11550-2422
General Phone: (516) 481-5400
General Fax: (516) 481-8773
General/National Adv. E-mail: thebeaconnews5@aol.com
Year Established: 1950
Avg Paid Circ: 3700
Audit By: Sworn/Estimate/Non-Audited
Audit Date: 10.06.2019
Personnel: Kathleen Hoegl (Pub.); Barbara Yohe (Ed.)
Parent company (for newspapers): Nassau County Publications

THE NEW YORK OBSERVER

Street address 1: 1 WHITEHALL STREET
Street address 2: Fl 7
Street address city: New York
Street address state: NY
Zip/Postal code: 10004
General Phone: (212) 755-2400
General Fax: (212) 668-4889
Advertising Phone: (212) 407-9389
General/National Adv. E-mail: sales@observer.com
Display Adv. E-mail: sales@observer.com
Editorial e-mail: editorial@observer.com
Primary Website: observermedia.com
Year Established: 1987
Avg Paid Circ: 52000
Audit By: Sworn/Estimate/Non-Audited
Audit Date: 10.06.2019
Personnel: james Karklins (Pres.); Max Gross (Ed. In Chief); Lauren Bell (Adv.)

THE NEWS ENTERPRISE SUN

Street address 1: 14 Hand Ave
Street address city: Elizabethtown
Street address state: NY
Zip/Postal code: 12932
General Phone: (518) 873-6368
General Fax: (518) 873-6360
Advertising Phone: (518) 585-9173
General/National Adv. E-mail: ads@suncommunitynews.com
Display Adv. E-mail: susan@suncommunitynews.com
Editorial e-mail: johng@suncommunitynews.com
Primary Website: suncommunitynews.com
Mthly Avg Views: 18747
Mthly Avg Unique Visitors: 2534
Year Established: 1948
Avg Paid Circ: 39
Avg Free Circ: 3414
Audit By: VAC
Audit Date: 30.09.2016
Personnel: Daniel E. Alexander (Pub.); Edward Coats (Assoc. Pub.); Ashley Alexander (Adv. Dir.); Dan Alexander (Gen. Mgr.); John Gereau (Mng. Ed.); William Coats (Plant Operations Mgr.); Scarlette Merfeld (Southern Adirondacks Publishing Group Manager); Jennifer Tower (Circ. Mgr)
Parent company (for newspapers): Sun Community News, Published by:Denton Publications, Inc.

THE NEWS OF THE HIGHLANDS

Street address 1: C/O 55 Quaker Ave.
Street address 2: Ste 204
Street address city: Cornwall
Street address state: NY
Zip/Postal code: 12518
General Phone: (845) 534-7771
General Fax: (845) 534-3855
General/National Adv. E-mail: joegill@thecornwalllocal.com
Editorial e-mail: newsofthehighlands@gmail.com
Primary Website: thenewsofthehighlands.com
Year Established: 1891
Avg Paid Circ: 919
Avg Free Circ: 730
Audit By: Sworn/Estimate/Non-Audited
Audit Date: 10.06.2019
Personnel: Joseph V. Gill (VP & Gen. Mgr.); Mary Jane Pitt (Ed.)
Parent company (for newspapers): News of the Highlands Inc.

THE NORTH COUNTRY FREE PRESS

Street address 1: 14 E Main St
Street address city: Granville
Street address state: NY
Zip/Postal code: 12832-1334
General Phone: (518) 642-1234
General Fax: (518) 642-1344
Advertising Phone: (518) 642-1234
Advertising Fax: (518) 642-1344
Editorial Phone: (518) 642-1234
Editorial Fax: (518) 642-1344
General/National Adv. E-mail: advertising@manchesternewspapers.com
Display Adv. E-mail: classifieds@manchesternewspapers.com
Editorial e-mail: publisher@manchesternewspapers.com
Primary Website: manchesternewspapers.com
Year Established: 1995
Avg Free Circ: 17172
Audit By: VAC
Audit Date: 30.09.2016
Personnel: Lisa Manchester (Exec. VP); John MacArthur Manchester (Pub.); Jane Cosey (Prodn. Mgr./Adv. Mgr.); Ann Hilder (Circ. Mgr)
Parent company (for newspapers): Manchester Newspapers, Inc.

THE NORTH COUNTRYMAN SUN

Street address 1: 14 Hand Ave
Street address city: Elizabethtown
Street address state: NY
Zip/Postal code: 12932
General Phone: (518) 873-6368
General Fax: (518) 873-6360
General/National Adv. E-mail: ashley@suncommunitynews.com
Display Adv. E-mail: ashley@suncommunitynews.com
Classified Adv. e-mail: shannonc@suncommunitynews.com
Editorial e-mail: pete@suncommunitynews.com
Primary Website: suncommunitynews.com
Mthly Avg Views: 25249
Mthly Avg Unique Visitors: 9893
Year Established: 1927
Avg Paid Circ: 37
Avg Free Circ: 8281
Sat. Circulation Paid: 197
Sat. Circulation Free: 63484
Audit By: VAC
Audit Date: 30.09.2016
Personnel: Daniel E. Alexander (Pub.); Bill Coats (Prodn. Mgr.); Pete DeMola (Mgr Ed); Ashley Alexander (Advt Dir); Edward Coats (Associate Pub); Scarlette Merfeld (Adv. Mgr); Jennifer Tower (Circ. Mgr)
Parent company (for newspapers): Sun Community News, Published by:Denton Publications, Inc.

THE NORTHERN WESTCHESTER EXAMINER

Street address 1: PO Box 611
Street address city: Mount Kisco
Street address state: NY
Zip/Postal code: 10549-0611
General Phone: (914) 864-0878
Advertising Phone: (914) 864-0878
Editorial Phone: (914) 729-4242
General/National Adv. E-mail: advertising@theexaminernews.com
Display Adv. E-mail: astone@theexaminernews.com
Editorial e-mail: rpezzullo@theexaminernews.com
Primary Website: theexaminernews.com
Year Established: 2007
Avg Paid Circ: 0
Avg Free Circ: 7360
Audit By: Sworn/Estimate/Non-Audited
Audit Date: 10.06.2019
Personnel: Adam Stone (Pub.); Rick Pezzullo (Ed.)
Parent company (for newspapers): Examiner Media

THE NORTHPORT JOURNAL

Street address 1: 44 Broadway
Street address 2: Suite 1
Street address city: greenlawn
Street address state: NY
Zip/Postal code: 11740
General Phone: (631) 427-7000
General Fax: (631) 427-5820
Advertising Phone: (631) 427-7000 x10
General/National Adv. E-mail: info@longislandernews.com
Display Adv. E-mail: info@longislandernews.com
Classified Adv. e-mail: info@longislandernews.com
Editorial e-mail: info@longislandernews.com
Primary Website: longislandernews.com
Mthly Avg Views: 15000
Mthly Avg Unique Visitors: 11000
Year Established: 1838
Avg Paid Circ: 4000
Avg Free Circ: 200
Audit By: Sworn/Estimate/Non-Audited
Audit Date: 10.06.2019
Personnel: Andrew Wroblewski (Pres./Pub.); Peter Sloggatt (Mng. Ed.); James Kelly (Owner / General Manager)
Parent company (for newspapers): Tribco LLC-OOB; Spend Navigator LLC

THE OBSERVER

Street address 1: 270 Lake St
Street address 2: Ste 11
Street address city: Penn Yan
Street address state: NY
Zip/Postal code: 14527-1832
General Phone: (607) 243-7600
General Fax: (607) 243-5833
General/National Adv. E-mail: obsrev@gmail.com
Editorial e-mail: obsrev@gmail.com
Primary Website: observer-review.com
Year Established: 1878
Avg Paid Circ: 1400
Avg Free Circ: 300
Audit By: Sworn/Estimate/Non-Audited
Audit Date: 10.06.2019
Personnel: George Lawson (Pres. and Pub.); Debbie Lawson (Bus. Mgr.)
Parent company (for newspapers): Finger Lakes Media, Inc.

THE ONEIDA DAILY DISPATCH

Street address 1: 130 Broad Street
Street address city: Oneida
Street address state: NY
Zip/Postal code: 13421
General Phone: (315) 363-5100
General Fax: (315) 363-9832
General/National Adv. E-mail: advertising@oneidadispatch.com
Display Adv. E-mail: classifieds@oneidadispatch.com
Classified Adv. e-mail: classifieds@oneidadispatch.com
Editorial e-mail: newsroom@oneidadispatch.com
Primary Website: oneidadispatch.com
Year Established: 1873
Avg Paid Circ: 5396
Avg Free Circ: 1751
Sun. Circulation Paid: 6209
Audit By: Sworn/Estimate/Non-Audited
Audit Date: 10.06.2019
Personnel: Kevin Corrado (Pub.); Karen Alvord (GM/ Adv. Dir.); Joe Sciacca (Reg. Ed.); Leah McDonald (Online Ed.)
Parent company (for newspapers): MediaNews Group

THE PALLADIUM-TIMES

Street address 1: 67 S 2nd St
Street address city: Fulton
Street address state: NY
Zip/Postal code: 13069-1725
General Phone: (315) 592-2459
General Fax: (315) 598-6618
General/National Adv. E-mail: tbarnes@palltimes.com
Display Adv. E-mail: adesantis@palltimes.com
Editorial e-mail: apoole@palltimes.com
Primary Website: valleynewsonline.com
Avg Paid Circ: 8230
Avg Free Circ: 5000
Audit By: Sworn/Estimate/Non-Audited
Audit Date: 10.06.2019
Personnel: Jon Spaulding (Pub.); Andrew Poole (Ad. Mgr.)

THE PHOENIX

Street address 1: 16 Court St
Street address 2: Ste 1208
Street address city: Brooklyn
Street address state: NY
Zip/Postal code: 11241-1012
General Phone: (718) 858-2300
General Fax: (718) 858-4483
General/National Adv. E-mail: edit@brooklyneagle.net
Editorial e-mail: publisher@BrooklynEagle.com
Primary Website: brooklyneagle.com
Year Established: 1972
Avg Paid Circ: 13000
Audit By: Sworn/Estimate/Non-Audited
Audit Date: 10.06.2019
Personnel: J.D. Hasty (Pub.); Samanhta Samel (Mng. Ed.)
Parent company (for newspapers): Everything Brooklyn Media

THE PORT TIMES-RECORD

Street address 1: 185 Main St
Street address 2: Ste 4
Street address city: Setauket
Street address state: NY
Zip/Postal code: 11733-2870
General Phone: (631) 751-7744
General Fax: (631) 751-4165
Advertising Phone: ext 118

Editorial Phone: ext 130
General/National Adv. E-mail: kjm@tbrnewspapers.com
Display Adv. E-mail: class@tbrnewspapers.com
Editorial e-mail: news@tbrnewspapers.com
Primary Website: tbrnewsmedia.com
Year Established: 1989
Avg Paid Circ: 8814
Audit By: Sworn/Estimate/Non-Audited
Audit Date: 10.06.2019
Personnel: Leah S. Dunaief (Pub.); Johness Watts Kuisel (Gen. Mgr.); Kathryn Mandracchia (Adv. Mgr.)
Parent company (for newspapers): Times Beacon Record News Media

THE PRESS OF SOUTHEAST QUEENS

Street address 1: 15050 14th Rd
Street address city: Whitestone
Street address state: NY
Zip/Postal code: 11357-2609
General Phone: (718) 357-7400
General Fax: (718) 357-9417
General/National Adv. E-mail: sales@queenstribune.com
Display Adv. E-mail: sales@queenstribune.com
Editorial e-mail: editor@queenstribune.com
Primary Website: queenstribune.com
Avg Free Circ: 25000
Audit By: Sworn/Estimate/Non-Audited
Audit Date: 10.06.2019
Personnel: Michael Nussbaum (Pub.); Steven Ferrari (Ed.); Maureen Coppola (Adv. Admin.)
Parent company (for newspapers): Tribco LLC-OOB

THE PUTNAM COUNTY COURIER

Street address 1: 144 Main St
Street address 2: Ste 1
Street address city: Cold Spring
Street address state: NY
Zip/Postal code: 10516-2854
General Phone: (845) 265-2468
General Fax: (845) 225-1914
Advertising Phone: (845) 265-2468
Advertising Fax: (845) 265-2144
Editorial Phone: (845) 265-2468
Editorial Fax: 845-265-2144
General/National Adv. E-mail: ads@pcnr.com
Display Adv. E-mail: ads@pcnr.com
Editorial e-mail: editor@pcnr.com
Primary Website: putnamcountycourier.com
Year Established: 1841
Avg Paid Circ: 2100
Audit By: Sworn/Estimate/Non-Audited
Audit Date: 10.06.2019
Personnel: Douglas Cunningham (Pub. & Editor-in-Chief)

THE PUTNAM EXAMINER

Street address 1: PO Box 611
Street address city: Mount Kisco
Street address state: NY
Zip/Postal code: 10549-0611
General Phone: (914) 864-0878
Advertising Phone: (914) 864-0878
Editorial Phone: (914) 671-5595
General/National Adv. E-mail: advertising@theexaminernews.com
Display Adv. E-mail: astone@theexaminernews.com
Editorial e-mail: dpropper@theexaminernews.com
Primary Website: theexaminernews.com
Year Established: 2007
Avg Paid Circ: 0
Avg Free Circ: 5841
Audit By: Sworn/Estimate/Non-Audited
Audit Date: 10.06.2019
Personnel: Adam Stone (Pub.); David Propper (Ed.)
Parent company (for newspapers): Examiner Media

THE QUEENS COURIER

Street address 1: 3815 Bell Blvd
Street address city: Bayside
Street address state: NY
Zip/Postal code: 11361-2058
General Phone: (718) 224-5863
General Fax: (718) 224-5441
Advertising Phone: (718) 224-5863 ext 231
General/National Adv. E-mail: bbrennan@queenscourier.com
Editorial e-mail: editorial@queenscourier.com
Primary Website: queenscourier.com
Year Established: 1985
Avg Paid Circ: 6000
Avg Free Circ: 70000
Audit By: Sworn/Estimate/Non-Audited
Audit Date: 10.06.2019
Personnel: Victoria Schneps-Yunis (Pub.); Robert Pozarycki (Editor-in-chief)

THE QUEENS EXAMINER

Street address 1: 454-23 47 Street
Street address city: Woodside
Street address state: NY
Zip/Postal code: 11377
General Phone: (718) 639-7000
General/National Adv. E-mail: ads@queensledger.com
Editorial e-mail: news@queensledger.com
Primary Website: queensexaminer.com
Year Established: 1999
Avg Paid Circ: 5000
Avg Free Circ: 12000
Audit By: Sworn/Estimate/Non-Audited
Audit Date: 10.06.2019
Personnel: Tammy Sanchez (Gen. Mgr.); Walter H. Sanchez (Ed.); John Sanchez (Director of marketing)
Parent company (for newspapers): BQE Publishing Inc.

THE RAVENA NEWS-HERALD

Street address 1: PO Box 178
Street address city: Ravena
Street address state: NY
Zip/Postal code: 12143-0178
General Phone: (518) 828-1616
General Fax: (518)671-6043
Advertising Phone: (518) 828-1616
Advertising Fax: (518) 671-6043
Editorial Phone: (518) 828-1616
General/National Adv. E-mail: advertisingregisterstar.com
Display Adv. E-mail: classifieds@wdt.net
Classified Adv. e-mail: tullrich@registerstar.com
Editorial e-mail: editorial@registerstar.com
Primary Website: hudsonvalley360.com
Mthly Avg Views: 1048368
Mthly Avg Unique Visitors: 162011
Year Established: 2010
Avg Paid Circ: 514
Audit By: Sworn/Estimate/Non-Audited
Audit Date: 10.06.2019
Personnel: Mark Vinciguerra (Pub.); Melanie Lekocevic (Ed.); Marlene McTigue (Multi-Media Consultant); Tammi Ullrich (Personnel Administrator)
Parent company (for newspapers): Johnson Newspaper Corp.

THE RECORD

Street address 1: 44 Broadway
Street address 2: Suite 1
Street address city: Greenlawn
Street address state: NY
Zip/Postal code: 11740
General Phone: (631) 427-7000
General Fax: (631) 427-5820
Advertising Phone: (631) 427-7000 x10
Advertising Fax: (631) 427-5820
Editorial Phone: (631) 427-7000
Editorial Fax: (631) 427-5820
General/National Adv. E-mail: info@longislandernews.com
Display Adv. E-mail: info@longislandernews.com
Classified Adv. e-mail: jvk@longislandernews.com
Editorial e-mail: info@longislandernews.com
Primary Website: longislandernews.com
Mthly Avg Views: 15000
Mthly Avg Unique Visitors: 11000
Year Established: 1838
Avg Paid Circ: 5000
Avg Free Circ: 200
Audit By: Sworn/Estimate/Non-Audited
Audit Date: 10.06.2019
Personnel: Peter Sloggatt (Mng. Ed.); James Kelly (Owner / General Manager); Andrew Wroblewski (Ed.); David Viejo (Adv. Mgr.); George Wallace (Circ. Mgr.); Rob Nieter (Prodn. Mgr.)

Parent company (for newspapers): Tribco LLC-OOB; Spend Navigator LLC

THE REPORTER

Street address 1: 97 Main St
Street address 2: Ste 5
Street address city: Delhi
Street address state: NY
Zip/Postal code: 13753-1231
General Phone: (607) 865-4131
General Fax: (607) 865-8689
General/National Adv. E-mail: sales@waltonreporter.com
Editorial e-mail: news@waltonreporter.com
Primary Website: the-reporter.net
Year Established: 1881
Avg Paid Circ: 6800
Avg Free Circ: 50
Audit By: Sworn/Estimate/Non-Audited
Audit Date: 10.06.2019
Personnel: Randy Shepard (Pub./Ed.); Bernice Bates (Adv. Sales)

THE REVEILLE/BETWEEN THE LAKES

Street address 1: 5 Walnut St S
Street address city: Waterloo
Street address state: NY
Zip/Postal code: 13165-1337
General Phone: (315) 651-4372
General Fax: (315) 873-3540
Advertising Phone: (315) 224-2768
Editorial Phone: (315) 224-2768
General/National Adv. E-mail: revbetweenthelakes@gmail.com
Display Adv. E-mail: revbetweenthelakes@gmail.com
Editorial e-mail: revbetweenthelakes@gmail.com
Year Established: 1855
Avg Paid Circ: 1100
Avg Free Circ: 400
Audit By: Sworn/Estimate/Non-Audited
Audit Date: 10.06.2019
Personnel: John Stoughtenger (Pub); Constance Stoughtenger (CFO)
Parent company (for newspapers): Fingerlakes Marketing & Print Services Inc

THE RIVER REPORTER

Street address 1: 93 Erie Ave
Street address city: Narrowsburg
Street address state: NY
Zip/Postal code: 12764-6423
General Phone: (845) 252-7414
General Fax: (845) 252-3298
Advertising Phone: (845) 25207414 ext. 34
Editorial Phone: (845) 252-7414, ext. 28
General/National Adv. E-mail: sales@riverreporter.com
Display Adv. E-mail: eileen@riverreporter.com
Editorial e-mail: editor@riverreporter.com
Primary Website: riverreporter.com
Year Established: 1975
Avg Paid Circ: 3000
Avg Free Circ: 265
Audit By: Sworn/Estimate/Non-Audited
Audit Date: 10.06.2019
Personnel: Laurie Stuart (Pub.); Fritz Mayer (Ed.); Amanda Reed (Prod. Mgr.)
Parent company (for newspapers): Stuart Communications Inc.

THE RIVERDALE PRESS

Street address 1: 5676 Riverdale Ave
Street address 2: Ste 311
Street address city: Bronx
Street address state: NY
Zip/Postal code: 10471-2100
General Phone: (718) 543-6065
General Fax: (718) 548-4038
General/National Adv. E-mail: newsroom@riverdalepress.com
Display Adv. E-mail: classified@riverdalepress.com
Classified Adv. e-mail: classified@riverdalepress.com
Editorial e-mail: newsroom@riverdalepress.com
Primary Website: riverdalepress.com
Year Established: 1950
Avg Paid Circ: 8140
Avg Free Circ: 2500
Audit By: Sworn/Estimate/Non-Audited
Audit Date: 10.06.2019
Personnel: Stuart Richner (Publisher); Jim Rotche (General Manager); Michael Hinman (Executive Editor); Jason Chirevas (Editor); Cheryl Ortiz (Sales Manager)
Parent company (for newspapers): Richner Communications, Inc.

THE RIVERTOWNS ENTERPRISE

Street address 1: 95 Main St
Street address city: Dobbs Ferry
Street address state: NY
Zip/Postal code: 10522-1673
General Phone: (914) 478-2787
General Fax: (914) 478-2863
Advertising Phone: (914) 478-2787 x12
Editorial Phone: (914) 478-2787 x11
General/National Adv. E-mail: displayads@rivertownsenterprise.net
Display Adv. E-mail: classifiedads@rivertownsenterprise.net
Editorial e-mail: tlamorte@rivertownsenterprise.net
Primary Website: rivertownsenterprise.net
Year Established: 1975
Avg Paid Circ: 6000
Avg Free Circ: 200
Audit By: Sworn/Estimate/Non-Audited
Audit Date: 10.06.2019
Personnel: Deborah G. White (Pub.); Timothy LaMorte (Ed.)

THE SALAMANCA PRESS

Street address 1: 36 River St
Street address city: Salamanca
Street address state: NY
Zip/Postal code: 14779-1474
General Phone: (716) 945-1644
General Fax: (716) 945-4285
Advertising Phone: (716) 945-1644
Advertising Fax: (716) 945-4285
Editorial Phone: (716) 945-1644
Editorial Fax: (716) 945-4285
General/National Adv. E-mail: salpressads@gmail.com
Display Adv. E-mail: salpressclass@gmail.com
Editorial e-mail: salamanacapress@gmail.com
Primary Website: salamancapress.com
Year Established: 1867
Avg Paid Circ: 1200
Avg Free Circ: 0
Audit By: Sworn/Estimate/Non-Audited
Audit Date: 10.06.2019
Personnel: Rich Place (Gen Mgr./Mng. Ed.); Sam Wilson (Sports Ed.); Kellen Quigley (Reporter); Preston Cochran (Adv); Jamie Ervay (Webmaster)
Parent company (for newspapers): Bradford Publishing

THE SENTINEL

Street address 1: PO Box 406
Street address city: Vails Gate
Street address state: NY
Zip/Postal code: 12584-0406
General Phone: (845) 562-1218
General Fax: (845) 562-0488
General/National Adv. E-mail: sentinelnews@hvcbiz.rr.com
Primary Website: thesentinel-online.com
Year Established: 1979
Avg Paid Circ: 7000
Audit By: Sworn/Estimate/Non-Audited
Audit Date: 10.06.2019
Personnel: Everett W. Smith (Ed.)

THE SMITHTOWN NEWS

Street address 1: 1 Brooksite Dr
Street address city: Smithtown
Street address state: NY
Zip/Postal code: 11787-3454
General Phone: (631) 265-2100
General Fax: (631) 265-6237
General/National Adv. E-mail: ads@smithtownnews.com
Display Adv. E-mail: ads@smithtownnews.com
Editorial e-mail: info@smithtownnews.com
Primary Website: thesmithtownnews.northshorenewsgroup.com
Avg Paid Circ: 10647
Audit By: Sworn/Estimate/Non-Audited
Audit Date: 10.06.2019

Personnel: Jennifer Paley (Pres.); Bernard Paley (Ed.)

THE SOUTHAMPTON PRESS

Street address 1: 135 Windmill Ln
Street address city: Southampton
Street address state: NY
Zip/Postal code: 11968-4840
General Phone: (631) 283-4100
General Fax: (631) 283-4927
General/National Adv. E-mail: ads@pressnewsgroup.com
Editorial e-mail: joeshaw@pressnewsgroup.com
Primary Website: southamptonpress.com
Year Established: 1897
Avg Paid Circ: 8382
Avg Free Circ: 209
Audit By: Sworn/Estimate/Non-Audited
Audit Date: 10.06.2019
Personnel: Joseph P. Louchheim (Pub.); Joseph P. Shaw (Ed.); Paul Conroy (Sales Mgr.)

THE SPOTLIGHT

Street address 1: 341 Delaware Ave
Street address city: Delmar
Street address state: NY
Zip/Postal code: 12054-1920
General Phone: (518) 439-4949
General Fax: (518) 439-5198
General/National Adv. E-mail: advertise@spotlightnews.com
Display Adv. E-mail: classified@spotlightnews.com
Editorial e-mail: news@spotlightnews.com
Primary Website: spotlightnews.com
Year Established: 1955
Avg Paid Circ: 7270
Avg Free Circ: 18983
Audit By: Sworn/Estimate/Non-Audited
Audit Date: 10.06.2019
Personnel: John McIntyre (Pub.); Bo Berezansky (Ad.); Michael Hallisey (Ed.)
Parent company (for newspapers): Community Media Group

THE SUFFOLK TIMES

Street address 1: 7785 Main Rd
Street address city: Mattituck
Street address state: NY
Zip/Postal code: 11952-1518
General Phone: (631) 298-3200
General Fax: (631) 298-3287
Advertising Phone: (631) 354-8053
Editorial Phone: (631) 354-8045
General/National Adv. E-mail: tvolinski@timesreview.com
Display Adv. E-mail: classifieds@timesreview.com
Editorial e-mail: mwhite@timesreview.com
Primary Website: suffolktimes.com
Mthly Avg Views: 230000
Mthly Avg Unique Visitors: 23000
Year Established: 1857
Avg Paid Circ: 8723
Avg Free Circ: 200
Audit By: Sworn/Estimate/Non-Audited
Audit Date: 10.06.2019
Personnel: Andrew Olsen (Pub.); Sonja Reinholt Derr (Sales & Marketing Dir.); Grant Parpan (Exec. Ed.)
Parent company (for newspapers): Times Review Newsgroup

THE SUN AND ERIE COUNTY INDEPENDENT

Street address 1: 141 Buffalo St
Street address 2: Hamburg Village Plaza
Street address city: Hamburg
Street address state: NY
Zip/Postal code: 14075-5010
General Phone: (716) 649-4040
General Fax: (716) 649-3231
Editorial Phone: (716) 649-4040 ext 255
General/National Adv. E-mail: news@thesunnews.net
Editorial e-mail: jowen@thesunnews.net
Primary Website: thesunnews.net
Mthly Avg Views: 11799
Mthly Avg Unique Visitors: 8535
Year Established: 1875
Avg Paid Circ: 10000
Audit By: Sworn/Estimate/Non-Audited
Audit Date: 10.06.2019
Personnel: Teri Scott (Dist. Mgr); Lizz Schumer (Editor); Denny Guastaferro (Pub); Felice Krycia (Assoc. Ed.); Michael Petro (Sports Ed); Michael Canfield (Community Reporter)
Parent company (for newspapers): Metro Group, Inc.

THE TIMES OF TI SUN

Street address 1: 14 Hand Ave
Street address city: Elizabethtown
Street address state: NY
Zip/Postal code: 12932
General Phone: (518) 873-6368
General Fax: (518) 873-6360
Advertising Phone: (518) 585-9173
Advertising Fax: (518) 585-9175
General/National Adv. E-mail: ads@suncommunitynews.com
Display Adv. E-mail: ads@suncommunitynews.com
Editorial e-mail: dan@suncommunitynews.com
Primary Website: suncommunitynews.com
Mthly Avg Views: 18747
Mthly Avg Unique Visitors: 2534
Year Established: 1948
Avg Paid Circ: 77
Avg Free Circ: 7214
Audit By: CVC
Audit Date: 30.09.2017
Personnel: Daniel E. Alexander (Pub.); Edward Coats (Assoc. Pub.); Ashley Alexander (Adv. Dir.); Dan Alexander (Prod. Mgr.); John Gereau (Mng. Ed.); William Coats (Plant Operations Mgr.); Scarlette Merfeld (Southern Adirondacks Publishing Group Mgr/ Ad. Mgr); Jennifer Tower (Circ. Mgr)
Parent company (for newspapers): Sun Community News, Published by:Denton Publications, Inc.

THE TRUMANSBURG FREE PRESS

Street address 1: 109 N Cayuga St
Street address city: Ithaca
Street address state: NY
Zip/Postal code: 14850-4341
General Phone: (607) 277-7000
General Fax: (607) 387-9421
General/National Adv. E-mail: tolson@ithacatimes.com
Editorial e-mail: editor@flcn.org
Primary Website: ithaca.com
Year Established: 1865
Avg Paid Circ: 1100
Avg Free Circ: 85
Audit By: Sworn/Estimate/Non-Audited
Audit Date: 10.06.2019
Personnel: James Bilinski (Pub.); Bill Chaisson (Mng. Ed.); Glynis Hart (Mng. Ed.)
Parent company (for newspapers): Finger Lakes Community Newspapers

THE UNIONDALE BEACON

Street address 1: 5 Centre St
Street address 2: Ste 3
Street address city: Hempstead
Street address state: NY
Zip/Postal code: 11550-2422
General Phone: (516) 481-5400
General Fax: (516) 481-8773
General/National Adv. E-mail: thebeaconnews5@aol.com
Avg Paid Circ: 5000
Audit By: Sworn/Estimate/Non-Audited
Audit Date: 10.06.2019
Personnel: Kathleen Hoegl (Pub.); Barbara Yohe (Ed.)
Parent company (for newspapers): Nassau County Publications

THE VALLEY NEWS

Street address 1: 67 S 2nd St
Street address city: Fulton
Street address state: NY
Zip/Postal code: 13069-1259
General Phone: (315) 598-6397
General Fax: (315) 598-6618
Display Adv. E-mail: classifieds@valleynewsonline.com
Editorial e-mail: colin@fultonvalleynews.com
Primary Website: valleynewsonline.com
Year Established: 1947
Avg Paid Circ: 8105
Avg Free Circ: 5000
Audit By: Sworn/Estimate/Non-Audited
Audit Date: 10.06.2019
Personnel: Colin Hogan (Ed.)

THE VALLEY NEWS SUN

Street address 1: 14 Hand Ave
Street address city: Elizabethtown
Street address state: NY
Zip/Postal code: 12932
General Phone: (518) 873-6368
General Fax: (518) 873-6360
General/National Adv. E-mail: ashley@suncommunitynews.com
Display Adv. E-mail: ashley@suncommunitynews.com
Editorial e-mail: dan@suncommunitynews.com
Primary Website: suncommunitynews.com
Mthly Avg Views: 10315
Mthly Avg Unique Visitors: 1745
Year Established: 1948
Avg Paid Circ: 67
Avg Free Circ: 15249
Audit By: CVC
Audit Date: 30.09.2017
Personnel: John Gereau (Mng. Ed.); Bill Coats (Plant Operations Mgr); Ashley Alexander (Adv. Dir.); Daniel E. Alexander (Pub.); Scarlette Merfeld (Ad. Mgr); Jennifer Tower (Circ. Mgr); Pete Demola (Asst Mgr Ed)
Parent company (for newspapers): Sun Community News, Published by:Denton Publications, Inc.

THE VILLAGE TIMES HERALD

Street address 1: 185 Main St
Street address 2: Ste 4
Street address city: Setauket
Street address state: NY
Zip/Postal code: 11733-2870
General Phone: (631) 751-7744
General Fax: (631) 751-4165
Advertising Phone: ext 118
Editorial Phone: ext 130
General/National Adv. E-mail: kjm@tbrnewspapers.com
Display Adv. E-mail: class@tbrnewspapers.com
Editorial e-mail: news@tbrnewspapers.com
Primary Website: tbrnewsmedia.com
Year Established: 1976
Avg Paid Circ: 10060
Audit By: Sworn/Estimate/Non-Audited
Audit Date: 10.06.2019
Personnel: Leah S. Dunaief (Pub.); Johness Watts Kuisel (Gen. Mgr.); Kathryn Mandracchia (Adv. Dir.)

THE VILLAGER

Street address 1: 1 Metrotech Ctr N
Street address 2: 10th Floor
Street address city: Brooklyn
Street address state: NY
Zip/Postal code: 11201-3832
General Phone: (212) 229-1890
General Fax: (212) 229-2790
General/National Adv. E-mail: ads@downtownexpress.com
Display Adv. E-mail: ads@downtownexpress.com
Editorial e-mail: lincoln@thevillager.com
Primary Website: thevillager.com
Audit By: Sworn/Estimate/Non-Audited
Audit Date: 10.06.2019
Personnel: Lincoln Anderson (Ed. in Chief); Joshua Schneps (CEO/Co-Pub.); Victoria Schneps-Yunis (Pres./Pub.); Amanda Tarley (Adv.)
Parent company (for newspapers): Schneps Communications

THE VILLAGER

Street address 1: 1 Metrotech Ctr
Street address 2: 10th Floor
Street address city: Brooklyn
Street address state: NY
Zip/Postal code: 11201-3948
General Phone: (646) 452-2464
Advertising Phone: (718) 260-8340
General/National Adv. E-mail: ads@downtownexpress.com
Display Adv. E-mail: ads@downtownexpress.com
Editorial e-mail: news@thevillager.com
Primary Website: thevillager.com
Year Established: 1933
Avg Paid Circ: 20000
Audit By: Sworn/Estimate/Non-Audited
Audit Date: 10.06.2019
Personnel: John W. Sutter (Pub.)
Parent company (for newspapers): NYC Community Media, LLC

THE WATERVILLE TIMES

Street address 1: 129 W Main St
Street address city: Waterville
Street address state: NY
Zip/Postal code: 13480-1165
General Phone: (315) 841-4105
General Fax: (315) 841-4104
General/National Adv. E-mail: advertising@cnymail.com
Editorial e-mail: watervilletimes@cnymail.com
Primary Website: watervilleny.com/timesindex.htm
Year Established: 1856
Avg Paid Circ: 2516
Avg Free Circ: 73
Audit By: Sworn/Estimate/Non-Audited
Audit Date: 10.06.2019
Personnel: Patricia Louise (Pub.); Kristi Kosmoski (Adv. Mgr.); Kim Kupris (Office Mgr.)

THE WATKINS REVIEW & EXPRESS

Street address 1: PO Box 207
Street address city: Watkins Glen
Street address state: NY
Zip/Postal code: 14891-0207
General Phone: (607) 535-1500
General Fax: (607) 243-5833
General/National Adv. E-mail: obsrev@gmail.com
Primary Website: observer-review.com
Year Established: 1854
Avg Paid Circ: 1350
Avg Free Circ: 300
Audit By: Sworn/Estimate/Non-Audited
Audit Date: 10.06.2019
Personnel: George Lawson (Pres. and Pub.)
Parent company (for newspapers): Finger Lakes Media. Inc.

THE WAVE

Street address 1: 8808 Rockaway Beach Blvd
Street address city: Rockaway Beach
Street address state: NY
Zip/Postal code: 11693-1608
General Phone: (718) 634-4000
General Fax: (718) 945-0913
General/National Adv. E-mail: ads@rockawave.com
Display Adv. E-mail: classifieds@rockawave.com
Editorial e-mail: editor@rockawave.com
Primary Website: rockawave.com
Year Established: 1893
Avg Paid Circ: 9000
Avg Free Circ: 100
Audit By: Sworn/Estimate/Non-Audited
Audit Date: 10.06.2019
Personnel: Susan B. Locke (Pub.); Sanford Bernstein (Gen. Mgr.); Felicia Scarola-Edwards (Adv. Mgr.); Mark Healey (Managing Editor.)

THE WEEKENDER

Street address 1: 14 E Main St
Street address city: Granville
Street address state: NY
Zip/Postal code: 12832-1334
General Phone: (518) 642-1234
General Fax: (518) 642-1344
General/National Adv. E-mail: advertising@manchesternewspapers.com
Display Adv. E-mail: classifieds@manchesternewspapers.com
Editorial e-mail: publisher@manchesternewspapers.com
Primary Website: manchesternewspapers.com
Year Established: 1995
Avg Free Circ: 5517
Audit By: CVC
Audit Date: 30.09.2017
Personnel: Lisa Manchester (Exec. VP); John MacArthur Manchester (Pub.); Jane Cosey (Prodn. Mgr./Adv. Mgr.); Ann Hilder (Circ. Mgr)
Parent company (for newspapers): Manchester Newspapers, Inc.

THE WEEKLY ADIRONDACK

Street address 1: Route 28
Street address city: Old Forge
Street address state: NY

Zip/Postal code: 13420
General Phone: (315) 369-9982
General Fax: (315) 369-9983
Advertising Phone: (315) 369-9982
Advertising Fax: (315) 369-9983
Editorial Phone: (315) 369-9982
Editorial Fax: (315) 369-9983
General/National Adv. E-mail: weeklyadk@yahoo.com
Display Adv. E-mail: weeklyadk@yahoo.com
Editorial e-mail: weeklyadk@yahoo.com
Primary Website: weeklyadk.com
Audit By: Sworn/Estimate/Non-Audited
Audit Date: 10.06.2019
Personnel: Jay Lawson (Pub./Ed./Adv. Mgr.); Marianne Christy (Adv. Sales Rep.)

THE WESTFIELD REPUBLICAN

Street address 1: 41 E Main St
Street address city: Westfield
Street address state: NY
Zip/Postal code: 14787-1303
General Phone: (716) 326-3163
General Fax: (716) 326-3165
General/National Adv. E-mail: jsaxton@westfieldrepublican.com
Display Adv. E-mail: ads@westfieldrepublican.com
Editorial e-mail: editorial@westfieldrepublican.com
Primary Website: westfieldrepublican.com
Avg Paid Circ: 2100
Avg Free Circ: 5256
Audit By: Sworn/Estimate/Non-Audited
Audit Date: 10.06.2019
Personnel: Mike Bird (Publisher); Jim Saxton (General Manager & Ad. Dir.)
Parent company (for newspapers): Ogden Newspapers Inc.

THE WESTSIDER

Street address 1: 63 W 38th St
Street address city: New York
Street address state: NY
Zip/Postal code: 10018-3818
General Phone: (212) 868-0190
General Fax: (212) 268-2935
General/National Adv. E-mail: sales@strausnews.com
Editorial e-mail: nyoffice@strausnews.com
Primary Website: nypress.com
Year Established: 1972
Avg Paid Circ: 326
Audit By: Sworn/Estimate/Non-Audited
Audit Date: 10.06.2019
Personnel: Jeanne Straus (Pres.); Alex Gelber (Ed.-in-Chief)

THE WHITE PLAINS EXAMINER

Street address 1: PO Box 611
Street address city: Mount Kisco
Street address state: NY
Zip/Postal code: 10549-0611
General Phone: (914) 864-0878
Advertising Phone: (914) 864-0878
Editorial Phone: (914) 588-5583
General/National Adv. E-mail: advertising@theexaminernews.com
Display Adv. E-mail: astone@theexaminernews.com
Editorial e-mail: pcasey@theexaminernews.com
Primary Website: theexaminernews.com
Year Established: 2007
Avg Paid Circ: 0
Avg Free Circ: 5226
Audit By: Sworn/Estimate/Non-Audited
Audit Date: 10.06.2019
Personnel: Adam Stone (Pub.); Pat Casey (Ed.)
Parent company (for newspapers): Examiner Media

THE WHITEHALL TIMES

Street address 1: 14 E Main St
Street address city: Granville
Street address state: NY
Zip/Postal code: 12832-1334
General Phone: (518) 642-1234
General Fax: (518) 642-1344
General/National Adv. E-mail: advertising@manchesternewspapers.com
Display Adv. E-mail: classifieds@manchesternewspapers.com
Editorial e-mail: publisher@manchesternewspapers.com
Primary Website: manchesternewspapers.com
Year Established: 1815
Avg Paid Circ: 1400
Audit By: Sworn/Estimate/Non-Audited
Audit Date: 10.06.2019
Personnel: John MacArthur Manchester (Ed.); Lisa Manchester (Exec. VP); Jane Casey (Prodc. Mgr. & Ad.)
Parent company (for newspapers): Manchester Newspapers, Inc.

THE WHITESTONE TIMES

Street address 1: 4102 Bell Blvd
Street address city: Bayside
Street address state: NY
Zip/Postal code: 11361-2792
General Phone: (718) 229-0300
General Fax: (718) 225-7117
Advertising Phone: (718) 229-0300
Advertising Fax: (718) 225-7117
Editorial Phone: (718) 229-0300
Editorial Fax: (718) 225-7117
General/National Adv. E-mail: brice@cnglocal.com
Display Adv. E-mail: classified@cnglocal.com
Editorial e-mail: timesledgernews@cnglocal.com
Primary Website: timesledger.com
Avg Paid Circ: 5015
Audit By: Sworn/Estimate/Non-Audited
Audit Date: 10.06.2019
Personnel: Roz Liston (Mng. Ed.); Brian Rice (Display & Online Advertising); Amanda Tarley (Classified Advertising)
Parent company (for newspapers): Queens Village Times (OOB)

THE WINDSOR STANDARD

Street address 1: 1035 Conklin Rd
Street address city: Conklin
Street address state: NY
Zip/Postal code: 13748-1102
General Phone: (607) 775-0472
General Fax: (607) 775-5863
General/National Adv. E-mail: deinstein@stny.rr.com
Primary Website: wecoverthetowns.com
Year Established: 1878
Avg Paid Circ: 1300
Avg Free Circ: 70
Audit By: Sworn/Estimate/Non-Audited
Audit Date: 12.10.2202
Personnel: Donald Einstein (Pub and Adv. Mgr.); Elizabeth Einstein (Ed.)
Parent company (for newspapers): Newspaper Publishers LLC

THIS WEEK

Street address 1: 25 Dill St
Street address city: Auburn
Street address state: NY
Zip/Postal code: 13021-3605
General Phone: (315) 282-2200
General Fax: (315) 253-6031
Advertising Phone: (315) 282-2213
Editorial Phone: (315) 282-2231
General/National Adv. E-mail: Jeffrey.Weigand@lee.net
Display Adv. E-mail: Jeffrey.Weigand@lee.net
Editorial e-mail: news@auburnpub.com
Primary Website: skaneatelesjournal.com
Avg Free Circ: 7500
Audit By: Sworn/Estimate/Non-Audited
Audit Date: 10.06.2019
Personnel: Rob Forcey (Pub.); Daniel Pelletier (Adv. Dir.)
Parent company (for newspapers): Cayuga Media

THOUSAND ISLAND SUN

Street address 1: Route 12
Street address city: Alexandria Bay
Street address state: NY
Zip/Postal code: 13607
General Phone: (315) 482-2581
General Fax: (315) 482-6315
General/National Adv. E-mail: tisun@gisco.net
Primary Website: thousandislandssun.net
Year Established: 1901
Avg Paid Circ: 6397
Avg Free Circ: 25
Audit By: Sworn/Estimate/Non-Audited
Audit Date: 10.06.2019
Personnel: Craig Snow (Gen. Mgr.); David Swartzentruber (Ed.)

TIMES COMMUNITY NEWSPAPERS

Street address 1: 500 Stony Brook Ct
Street address 2: Suite 2
Street address city: Newburgh
Street address state: NY
Zip/Postal code: 12550
General Phone: 8455610170
General Fax: 8455613967
General/National Adv. E-mail: editor@tcnewspapers.com
Display Adv. E-mail: advertising@tcnewspapers.com
Classified Adv. e-mail: classifieds@tcnewspapers.com
Editorial e-mail: editor@tcnewspapers.com
Primary Website: www.timeshudsonvalley.com

TIMES NEWSWEEKLY

Street address 1: 3815 Bell Blvd
Street address city: Bayside
Street address state: NY
Zip/Postal code: 11361-2058
General Phone: (718) 821-7503
General Fax: (718) 456-0120
Advertising Phone: (718) 821-7500
Advertising Fax: (718) 456-0120
General/National Adv. E-mail: info@timesnewsweekly.com
Display Adv. E-mail: d.cusick@timesnewsweekly.com
Editorial e-mail: info@timesnewsweekly.com
Primary Website: timesnewsweekly.com; ridgewoodtimes.net
Year Established: 1908
Avg Paid Circ: 20000
Avg Free Circ: 0
Audit By: Sworn/Estimate/Non-Audited
Audit Date: 10.06.2019
Personnel: Victoria Schneps-Yunis (Pub.)

TIMES-JOURNAL

Street address 1: 108 Division St
Street address 2: Ste A
Street address city: Cobleskill
Street address state: NY
Zip/Postal code: 12043-4699
General Phone: (518) 234-2515
General Fax: (518) 234-7898
General/National Adv. E-mail: tjournalads@yahoo.com
Display Adv. E-mail: tjournalclassified@yahoo.com
Editorial e-mail: tjournalnews@yahoo.com
Primary Website: timesjournalonline.com
Year Established: 1877
Avg Paid Circ: 6800
Avg Free Circ: 76
Audit By: Sworn/Estimate/Non-Audited
Audit Date: 10.06.2019
Personnel: James Poole (Pub.); Patsy Nicosia (Ed.); Bruce Tryon (Sales manager)

TOMPKINS WEEKLY

Street address 1: 3100 N. Triphammer Road
Street address 2: Suite 100
Street address city: Lansing
Street address state: NY
Zip/Postal code: 14882
General Phone: 607-533-0057
Advertising Phone: 607-591-0682
Editorial Phone: 607-533-0057 x203
General/National Adv. E-mail: info@VizellaMedia.com
Display Adv. E-mail: ToddM@VizellaMedia.com
Classified Adv. e-mail: TinaM@VizellaMedia.com
Editorial e-mail: editorial@VizellaMedia.com
Primary Website: www.TompkinsWeekly.com
Mthly Avg Views: 26324
Mthly Avg Unique Visitors: 23052
Year Established: 2006
Avg Paid Circ: 10
Avg Free Circ: 5300
Audit By: CVC
Audit Date: 30.09.2022
Personnel: Todd Mallinson (Publisher / Advertising Manager); Tina Mallinson (VP/Business Manager); Jaime Hughes (Managing Editor)
Parent company (for newspapers): Vizella Media

TRI-TOWN NEWS

Street address 1: 5 Winkler Rd
Street address city: Sidney
Street address state: NY
Zip/Postal code: 13838-1057
General Phone: (607) 561-3526
General Fax: (607) 563-8999
General/National Adv. E-mail: ttnews@tritownnews.com
Display Adv. E-mail: advertising@tritownnews.com
Primary Website: tritownnews.com
Year Established: 1856
Avg Paid Circ: 3400
Audit By: Sworn/Estimate/Non-Audited
Audit Date: 10.06.2019
Personnel: Allison Collins (Ed.); Ryan Dalpiaz (Sales and Office Manager); Anna Ritchey (Ad. Director)

TUPPER LAKE FREE PRESS

Street address 1: 136 Park St
Street address city: Tupper Lake
Street address state: NY
Zip/Postal code: 12986-1818
General Phone: (518) 359-2166
General Fax: (518) 359-2295
General/National Adv. E-mail: tlfreepress@yahoo.com
Primary Website: tupperlakepress.com
Year Established: 1931
Avg Paid Circ: 3800
Avg Free Circ: 89
Audit By: Sworn/Estimate/Non-Audited
Audit Date: 10.06.2019
Personnel: Judy McClelland (Gen. Mgr./Adv. Mgr.); M. Dan McClelland (Pub.); Sue Mitchell (Ed.)

UTICA PHOENIX

Street address 1: 1113 Linwood Pl
Street address city: Utica
Street address state: NY
Zip/Postal code: 13501-3911
General Phone: (315) 797-2417
General Fax: (315) 797-7025
General/National Adv. E-mail: uticaphoenix@gmail.com
Primary Website: uticaphoenix.net
Year Established: 2002
Avg Free Circ: 365
Audit By: Sworn/Estimate/Non-Audited
Audit Date: 10.06.2019
Personnel: Theresa Mancuso (Office and Distribution Manager, Online Editor); Cassandra Harris-Lockwood (Pub.)

VESTAL TOWN CRIER

Street address 1: 1035 Conklin Rd
Street address city: Conklin
Street address state: NY
Zip/Postal code: 13748-1102
General Phone: (607) 775-0472
General Fax: (607) 775-5863
General/National Adv. E-mail: eeinstein7@gmail.com
Primary Website: wecoverthetowns.com
Year Established: 1979
Avg Paid Circ: 1200
Audit By: Sworn/Estimate/Non-Audited
Audit Date: 10.06.2019
Personnel: Donald Einstein (Pub.); Elizabeth Einstein (Ed.)
Parent company (for newspapers): Newspaper Publishers LLC

VICTOR POST

Street address 1: 73 Buffalo St
Street address city: Canandaigua
Street address state: NY
Zip/Postal code: 14424-1001
General Phone: (585) 394-0770
General Fax: (585) 394-4160
General/National Adv. E-mail: bkesel@messengerpostmedia.com
Display Adv. E-mail: classifieds@messengerpostmedia.com
Editorial e-mail: bdoane@messengerpostmedia.com
Primary Website: mpnnow.com
Mthly Avg Views: 700000

Mthly Avg Unique Visitors: 200000
Avg Paid Circ: 16
Avg Free Circ: 3674
Audit By: Sworn/Estimate/Non-Audited
Audit Date: 10.06.2019
Personnel: Brian Doane (Pres./Pub.); Beth Kesel (General Mgr./Adv. Director)
Parent company (for newspapers): CherryRoad Media

WALLKILL VALLEY TIMES

Street address 1: 300 Stony Brook Ct
Street address city: Newburgh
Street address state: NY
Zip/Postal code: 12550-6534
General Phone: (845) 561-0170
General Fax: (845) 561-3967
General/National Adv. E-mail: advertising@tcnewspapers.com
Display Adv. E-mail: classifieds@tcnewspapers.com
Editorial e-mail: editor@tcnewspapers.com
Primary Website: timescommunitypapers.com
Year Established: 1983
Avg Paid Circ: 5000
Avg Free Circ: 53
Audit By: Sworn/Estimate/Non-Audited
Audit Date: 10.06.2019
Personnel: Carl J. Aiello (Editor & Publisher)
Parent company (for newspapers): Times Community Newspapers

WARSAW PENNYSAVER

Street address 1: 72 N Main St
Street address city: Warsaw
Street address state: NY
Zip/Postal code: 14569-1329
General Phone: (585) 786-8161
General Fax: (585) 786-5159
General/National Adv. E-mail: ads@warsawpennysaver.com
Display Adv. E-mail: ads@warsawpennysaver.com
Primary Website: warsawpennysaver.com
Year Established: 1943
Avg Paid Circ: 9280
Audit By: Sworn/Estimate/Non-Audited
Audit Date: 10.06.2019
Personnel: Colleen Kennedy (Treasurer Co-owner); Christine Kennedy-Till (President Co-owner)

WARSAW'S COUNTRY COURIER

Street address 1: 11 S Main St
Street address city: Warsaw
Street address state: NY
Zip/Postal code: 14569-1501
General Phone: (585) 786-3080
General Fax: (585) 786-3083
General/National Adv. E-mail: tammy-courierads@roadrunner.com
Editorial e-mail: news@couriercountry.com
Primary Website: www.couriercountry.com
Year Established: 1997
Audit By: USPS
Audit Date: 10.09.2019
Personnel: Tammy Hobson (Ad. Director); Grant M. Hamilton (Pub.); Julia Merulla (Mng. Ed.); Natalie Spink (Editor)
Parent company (for newspapers): Neighbor to Neighbor News, Inc.

WARWICK ADVERTISER

Street address 1: 20 West Ave
Street address 2: Ste 201
Street address city: Chester
Street address state: NY
Zip/Postal code: 10918-1053
General Phone: (845) 469-9000
General Fax: (845) 469-9001
General/National Adv. E-mail: sales@strausnews.com
Editorial e-mail: nyoffice@strausnews.com
Primary Website: warwickadvertiser.com
Year Established: 1866
Avg Free Circ: 6617
Audit By: Sworn/Estimate/Non-Audited
Audit Date: 10.06.2019
Personnel: Jeanne Straus (Pres.); Mike Zummo (Mng. Ed.)
Parent company (for newspapers): Straus News

WARWICK VALLEY DISPATCH

Street address 1: 2 Oakland Ave
Street address city: Warwick
Street address state: NY
Zip/Postal code: 10990-1530
General Phone: (845) 986-2216
General Fax: (845) 987-1180
General/National Adv. E-mail: ads@wvdispatch.com
Display Adv. E-mail: ads@wvdispatch.com
Classified Adv. e-mail: ads@wvdispatch.com
Editorial e-mail: editor@wvdispatch.com
Primary Website: wvdispatch.com
Year Established: 1885
Avg Paid Circ: 2500
Avg Free Circ: 50
Audit By: Sworn/Estimate/Non-Audited
Audit Date: 10.06.2019
Personnel: F. Eugene Wright (Publisher/Owner); Lon Tytell (Adv. Mgr.); Marion Maroski (Mng. Ed.); David DeWitt (Prodn. Mgr.); Eleanor Horoshun; Evelyn Card; Eric Meyer; Margaret Bezares; Myrek Zastavnyi; Mary Klym; Sue Mykytsei; Jennifer O'Connor (Ed.)

WAYNE COUNTY MAIL

Street address 1: 46 North Ave
Street address city: Webster
Street address state: NY
Zip/Postal code: 14580-3008
General Phone: (585) 671-1533
General Fax: (585) 671-7067
General/National Adv. E-mail: wcmail@empirestateweeklies.com
Year Established: 1901
Avg Paid Circ: 2500
Avg Free Circ: 200
Audit By: Sworn/Estimate/Non-Audited
Audit Date: 10.06.2019
Personnel: W. David Young (Pub.); Mike Sorenson (Ed.)
Parent company (for newspapers): Empire State Weeklies

WAYNE POST

Street address 1: 73 Buffalo St
Street address city: Canandaigua
Street address state: NY
Zip/Postal code: 14424-1001
General Phone: (585) 394-0770
General Fax: (585) 394-4160
General/National Adv. E-mail: bkesel@messengerpostmedia.com
Display Adv. E-mail: classifieds@messengerpostmedia.com
Editorial e-mail: bdoane@messengerpostmedia.com
Primary Website: mpnnow.com
Mthly Avg Views: 700000
Mthly Avg Unique Visitors: 200000
Year Established: 1876
Avg Paid Circ: 1317
Avg Free Circ: 170
Audit By: Sworn/Estimate/Non-Audited
Audit Date: 10.06.2019
Personnel: Beth Kesel (Gen. Mgr./Adv. Dir.); Brian Doane (Pres./Pub.)
Parent company (for newspapers): CherryRoad Media

WEBSTER HERALD

Street address 1: 46 North Ave
Street address city: Webster
Street address state: NY
Zip/Postal code: 14580-3008
General Phone: (585) 671-1533
General Fax: (585) 671-7067
General/National Adv. E-mail: websterherald@empirestateweeklies.com
Avg Paid Circ: 4000
Avg Free Circ: 800
Audit By: Sworn/Estimate/Non-Audited
Audit Date: 10.06.2019
Personnel: W. David Young (Pub.); Mike Sorenson (Mng. Ed.)
Parent company (for newspapers): Empire State Weeklies

WEBSTER POST

Street address 1: 73 Buffalo St
Street address city: Canandaigua
Street address state: NY
Zip/Postal code: 14424-1001
General Phone: (585) 394-0770
General Fax: (585) 394-4160
General/National Adv. E-mail: bkesel@messengerpostmedia.com
Display Adv. E-mail: classifieds@messengerpostmedia.com
Editorial e-mail: bdoane@messengerpostmedia.com
Primary Website: mpnnow.com
Mthly Avg Views: 700000
Mthly Avg Unique Visitors: 200000
Avg Paid Circ: 71
Avg Free Circ: 4750
Audit By: Sworn/Estimate/Non-Audited
Audit Date: 10.06.2019
Personnel: Beth Kesel (Gen. Mgr./Adv. Dir.); Brian Doane (Pres./Pub.)
Parent company (for newspapers): Messenger Post Media

WEST HEMPSTEAD BEACON

Street address 1: 5 Centre St
Street address 2: Ste 3
Street address city: Hempstead
Street address state: NY
Zip/Postal code: 11550-2422
General Phone: (516) 481-5400
General Fax: (516) 481-8773
General/National Adv. E-mail: thebeaconnews5@aol.com
Avg Paid Circ: 5200
Audit By: Sworn/Estimate/Non-Audited
Audit Date: 10.06.2019
Personnel: Katherine Hoegl (Pub.); Barbara Yohr (Ed.)
Parent company (for newspapers): Nassau County Publications

WEST SENECA BEE

Street address 1: 5564 Main St
Street address city: Williamsville
Street address state: NY
Zip/Postal code: 14221-5410
General Phone: (716) 632-4700
General Fax: (716) 633-8601
Advertising Phone: (716) 204-4934
General/National Adv. E-mail: Salesdept@BeeNews.com
Display Adv. E-mail: classified@beenews.com
Editorial e-mail: jwaters@beenews.com
Primary Website: beenews.com
Year Established: 1980
Avg Paid Circ: 5200
Avg Free Circ: 14
Audit By: Sworn/Estimate/Non-Audited
Audit Date: 10.06.2019
Personnel: Michael Measer (Exec. Vice Pres.); Trey Measer (Pub.); Jenee Waters (Ed.)
Parent company (for newspapers): Bee Group Newspapers

WEST SIDE SPIRIT

Street address 1: 28th St and 7th Ave
Street address city: New York
Street address state: NY
Zip/Postal code: 10001
General Phone: (212) 868-190
General Fax: (212) 268-0503
General/National Adv. E-mail: sales@strausnews.com
Editorial e-mail: nyoffice@strausnews.com
Primary Website: westsidespirit.com
Year Established: 1985
Audit By: Sworn/Estimate/Non-Audited
Audit Date: 10.06.2019
Personnel: Jeanne Straus (Pres); Alexis Gelber (Ed-in-chief)
Parent company (for newspapers): Straus News

WESTBURY TIMES

Street address 1: 132 E 2nd St
Street address city: Mineola
Street address state: NY
Zip/Postal code: 11501-3522
General Phone: (516) 747-8282
General Fax: (516) 742-5867
General/National Adv. E-mail: advertising@antonnews.com
Display Adv. E-mail: classified@antonnews.com
Editorial e-mail: babraham@antonmediagroup.com
Primary Website: http://thewestburytimes.com/
Year Established: 1933
Avg Paid Circ: 3445
Audit By: Sworn/Estimate/Non-Audited
Audit Date: 10.06.2019
Personnel: Angela Anton (Pub.); Betsy Abraham (Ed.)
Parent company (for newspapers): Anton Community Newspapers

WESTCHESTER COUNTY BUSINESS JOURNAL

Street address 1: 3 Gannett Dr
Street address 2: Ste G7
Street address city: White Plains
Street address state: NY
Zip/Postal code: 10604-3402
General Phone: (914) 694-3600
General Fax: (914) 694-3699
Advertising Phone: (914) 694-3600
Advertising Fax: (914) 694-3699
Editorial Phone: (914) 358-0745
Editorial Fax: (914) 694-3680
General/National Adv. E-mail: dee@westfairinc.com
Display Adv. E-mail: mrose@westfairinc.com
Editorial e-mail: bobr@westfairinc.com
Primary Website: westfaironline.com
Avg Paid Circ: 1697
Avg Free Circ: 4496
Audit By: Sworn/Estimate/Non-Audited
Audit Date: 10.06.2019
Personnel: Dee DelBello (Pub.); Bob Rozycki (Mng. Ed.); Sylvia Sikoutris (Circ. Mgr.)
Parent company (for newspapers): Westfair Communications Inc.

WESTCHESTER MAGAZINE

Street address 1: 2 Clinton Avenue
Street address city: Rye
Street address state: NY
Zip/Postal code: 10580
General Phone: (914) 345-0601
General/National Adv. E-mail: jdambrosio@westchestermagazine.com
Display Adv. E-mail: jdambrosio@westchestermagazine.com
Editorial e-mail: jturiano@westchestermagazine.com
Primary Website: westchestermagazine.com
Avg Paid Circ: 698
Avg Free Circ: 17750
Audit By: CVC
Audit Date: 19.12.2018
Personnel: John Bruno Turiano (Ed.); Amy Partridge (Mng. Ed.); Ralph Martinelli (Grp. Pub.); Samuel Wender (Pub.); Matthew Bonnani (Adv. Mgr.); Jennifer Dambrosio (Adv. Dir.); Paul Greicius (Dist. Mgr.); Gregory Wolfe (Ed.); Russel Marth (Circ. Mgr.)

WESTFIELD REPUBLICAN

Street address 1: 41 E Main St
Street address city: Westfield
Street address state: NY
Zip/Postal code: 14787-1303
General Phone: (716) 326-3163
General Fax: (716) 326-3165
General/National Adv. E-mail: jsaxton@westfieldrepublican.com
Display Adv. E-mail: ads@westfieldrepublican.com
Editorial e-mail: editorial@westfieldrepublican.com
Primary Website: westfieldrepublican.com
Avg Paid Circ: 900
Avg Free Circ: 25
Audit By: Sworn/Estimate/Non-Audited
Audit Date: 10.06.2019
Personnel: Jim Saxton (BM & Ad. Dir.); Mike Bird (Pub.)
Parent company (for newspapers): Ogden Newspapers Inc.

WESTMORE NEWS

Street address 1: 327 Irving Avenue
Street address city: Port Chester
Street address state: NY
Zip/Postal code: 10573
General Phone: (914) 939-6864
Advertising Phone: (914) 939-6864
Advertising Fax: (914) 939-6877
Editorial Phone: (914) 939-6864

General/National Adv. E-mail: publisher@westmorenews.com
Display Adv. E-mail: publisher@westmorenews.com
Editorial e-mail: editor@westmorenews.com
Primary Website: westmorenews.com
Year Established: 1964
Avg Paid Circ: 2254
Avg Free Circ: 774
Audit By: USPS
Audit Date: 30.09.2022
Personnel: Richard Abel (Publisher); Jananne Abel (Editor)

WILLISTON TIMES

Street address 1: 22 Planting Field Road
Street address 2:
Street address city: Roslyn Heights
Street address state: NY
Zip/Postal code: 11577
General Phone: (516) 307-1045
General Fax: (516) 307-1046
Advertising Phone: (516) 307-1045 Ext. 201
Advertising Fax: (516) 307-1046
Editorial Phone: (516) 307-1045 Ext. 201
Editorial Fax: (516) 307-1046
General/National Adv. E-mail: sblank@theislandnow.com
Display Adv. E-mail: bflynn@theislandnow.com
Editorial e-mail: sblank@theislandnow.com
Primary Website: theislandnow.com
Mthly Avg Views: 400000
Mthly Avg Unique Visitors: 900000
Year Established: 1940
Avg Paid Circ: 3470
Audit By: Sworn/Estimate/Non-Audited
Audit Date: 06.10.2021
Personnel: Steven Blank (Ed.); Holly Blank (Cir. Mgr.); Gail Hicka (Acct Exc)
Parent company (for newspapers): Blank Slate Media LLC

WINDHAM JOURNAL

Street address 1: 414 Main St
Street address city: Catskill
Street address state: NY
Zip/Postal code: 12414-1303
General Phone: (518) 943-2100
General Fax: (518) 943-2063
General/National Adv. E-mail: advertising@thedailymail.net
Editorial e-mail: lanander.windhamjournal@registerstar.com
Primary Website: columbiagreenemedia.com/windham_journal
Year Established: 1857
Avg Paid Circ: 2400
Audit By: Sworn/Estimate/Non-Audited
Audit Date: 10.06.2019
Personnel: Mark Vinciguerra (Pub.); Pam Geskie (Adv. Mgr.); Lori Anander (Ed.)

WOODSIDE HERALD

Street address 1: 4311 Greenpoint Ave
Street address city: Sunnyside
Street address state: NY
Zip/Postal code: 11104-2605
General Phone: (718) 729-3772
General/National Adv. E-mail: SherilynSabba@WoodsideHerald.com
Editorial e-mail: Rob@WoodsideHerald.com
Primary Website: woodsideherald.com
Avg Paid Circ: 14000
Avg Free Circ: 5000
Audit By: Sworn/Estimate/Non-Audited
Audit Date: 10.06.2019
Personnel: Sharilyn Sabba (Prodn. Mgr.)

WOODSTOCK TIMES

Street address 1: 322 Wall St
Street address city: Kingston
Street address state: NY
Zip/Postal code: 12401-3820
General Phone: (845) 334-8200
General Fax: (845) 334-8202
General/National Adv. E-mail: info@ulsterpublishing.com
Display Adv. E-mail: classifieds@ulsterpublishing.com
Editorial e-mail: wtedit@gmail.com
Primary Website: woodstockx.com
Avg Paid Circ: 4400
Audit By: Sworn/Estimate/Non-Audited
Audit Date: 10.06.2019
Personnel: Brian Hollander (Ed.); Genia Wickwire (Ad. Director)
Parent company (for newspapers): Ulster Publishing

YONKERS RISING

Street address 1: 25 Warburton Ave
Street address city: Yonkers
Street address state: NY
Zip/Postal code: 10701-7079
General Phone: (914) 965-4000
General Fax: (914) 965-2892
General/National Adv. E-mail: pgerken@risingmediagroup.com
Editorial e-mail: dmurphy@risingmediagroup.com
Primary Website: yonkersrising.com
Avg Free Circ: 16476
Audit By: Sworn/Estimate/Non-Audited
Audit Date: 10.06.2019
Personnel: Nick Sprayregen (Pub.); Daniel Murphy (Ed. in Chief); Paul Gerken (Ad. Sales)

YORKTOWN NEWS, MAHOPAC NEWS, THE SOMERS RECORD, NORTH SALEM NEWS

Street address 1: 334 Route 202
Street address 2: Bailey Court
Street address city: Somers
Street address state: NY
Zip/Postal code: 10589-3207
General Phone: (845)621-1116
Advertising Phone: (845)621-1116
Editorial Phone: (845)208-8151
General/National Adv. E-mail: ads@halstonmedia.com
Display Adv. E-mail: kilcoyne@halstonmedia.com
Classified Adv. e-mail: classifieds@halstonmedia.com
Editorial e-mail: freeman@halstonmedia.com
Primary Website: tapintoyorktown.net
Mthly Avg Views: 35000
Year Established: 2015
Avg Free Circ: 25500
Audit By: Sworn/Estimate/Non-Audited
Audit Date: 10.06.2019
Personnel: Brett Freeman (Pub.)
Parent company (for newspapers): Halston Media LLC

YOUR VALLEY

Street address 1: 221 Oriskany St E
Street address city: Utica
Street address state: NY
Zip/Postal code: 13501-1201
General Phone: (315) 792-5000
Advertising Phone: (315) 792-5103
Advertising Fax: (315) 792-5085
Editorial Phone: (315) 792-5004
Editorial Fax: (315) 792-5033
General/National Adv. E-mail: epittman@uticaod.com
Editorial e-mail: kworrell@uticaod.com
Primary Website: uticaod.com/pennysaver
Year Established: 2006
Avg Paid Circ: 0
Avg Free Circ: 9895
Audit By: CVC
Audit Date: 30.09.2017
Personnel: Kris Worrell (Ed.); Erin Pittman (Ad. Dir); Robert Gall (Circ. Mgr); Zoran Music (Prod. Mgr); Terry Cascioli (Pub.)
Parent company (for newspapers): CherryRoad Media

NORTH CAROLINA

ADVANTAGE NEWSPAPER CONSULTANTS

Street address 1: 2850 Village Dr
Street address 2: Ste 102
Street address city: Fayetteville
Street address state: NC
Zip/Postal code: 28304-3864
General Phone: (910) 323-0349
General Fax: (910) 323-9280
General/National Adv. E-mail: info@newspaperconsultants.com
Primary Website: newspaperconsultants.com
Year Established: 1996
Audit By: Sworn/Estimate/Non-Audited
Audit Date: 10.06.2019
Personnel: Timothy O. Dellinger (President); Susan M. Jolley (General Mgr.); Marie Smith (Exec. Dir. of Sales)

ARCHDALE TRINITY NEWS

Street address 1: 213 Woodbine St
Street address city: High Point
Street address state: NC
Zip/Postal code: 27260-8339
General Phone: (336) 434-2716
Advertising Phone: (336) 888-3625
Editorial Phone: (336) 434-2716
General/National Adv. E-mail: csaunders@hpenews.com
Display Adv. E-mail: classified@hpenews.com
Editorial e-mail: jseaboltt@atnonline.net
Primary Website: atnonline.net
Year Established: 1978
Avg Paid Circ: 3500
Avg Free Circ: 15
Audit By: Sworn/Estimate/Non-Audited
Audit Date: 10.06.2019
Personnel: John McClure (Adv. Dir.); Rick Bean (Pub.)

BANNER NEWS

Street address 1: 128-C N Main St
Street address city: Belmont
Street address state: NC
Zip/Postal code: 28012-3166
General Phone: (704) 484-1047
General Fax: (704) 484-1067
General/National Adv. E-mail: mike@cfmedia.info
Display Adv. E-mail: mike@cfmedia.info
Editorial e-mail: greg@cfmedia.info
Primary Website: banner-news.com
Year Established: 1935
Avg Paid Circ: 0
Avg Free Circ: 4000
Audit By: Sworn/Estimate/Non-Audited
Audit Date: 10.06.2019
Personnel: Greg Ledford (Pub.); Mike Marlow (Adv./Circ.)
Parent company (for newspapers): Gemini Newspapers

BERTIE LEDGER-ADVANCE

Street address 1: 105 E Granville St
Street address city: Windsor
Street address state: NC
Zip/Postal code: 27983-6753
General Phone: (252) 794-3185
General Fax: (252) 794-2835
General/National Adv. E-mail: jmobley@ncweeklies.com
Editorial e-mail: twhite@ncweeklies.com
Primary Website: facebook.com/Bertie-Ledger-Advance-540014596016586
Year Established: 1930
Avg Paid Circ: 4200
Audit By: Sworn/Estimate/Non-Audited
Audit Date: 10.06.2019
Personnel: Jay Jenkins (Pub.); Thadd White (Ed)
Parent company (for newspapers): Cooke Communications North Carolina, LLC

BLACK MOUNTAIN NEWS

Street address 1: 111 Richardson Blvd
Street address city: Black Mountain
Street address state: NC
Zip/Postal code: 28711-3526
General Phone: (828) 669-8727
General Fax: (828) 669-8619
General/National Adv. E-mail: lfprince@gannett.com
Display Adv. E-mail: lfprince@gannett.com
Editorial e-mail: news@blackmountainnews.com
Primary Website: blackmountainnews.com
Year Established: 1945
Avg Paid Circ: 3000
Avg Free Circ: 135
Audit By: Sworn/Estimate/Non-Audited
Audit Date: 10.06.2019
Personnel: Lyn Prince (Adv. Mgr.); Fred McCormick (Staff Writer); Christi Penland (Office Mgr.)
Parent company (for newspapers): Gannett

BLADEN JOURNAL

Street address 1: 138 W BROAD ST
Street address city: Elizabethtown
Street address state: NC
Zip/Postal code: 28337
General Phone: (910) 862-4163
General Fax: (910) 862-6602
General/National Adv. E-mail: ads@bladenjournal.com
Display Adv. E-mail: cjudson@civitasmedia.com
Editorial e-mail: cvincent@civitasmedia.com
Primary Website: bladenjournal.com
Year Established: 1978
Avg Paid Circ: 4400
Avg Free Circ: 3800
Audit By: Sworn/Estimate/Non-Audited
Audit Date: 10.06.2019
Personnel: Curt Vincent (Ed./Gen. Mgr.); Charlotte Smith (Adv. Sales Rep.); David Perkins (Adv. Dir.)
Parent company (for newspapers): Champion Media

CARTERET COUNTY NEWS-TIMES

Street address 1: 5039 Executive Drive
Street address 2: Suite 300
Street address city: Morehead City
Street address state: NC
Zip/Postal code: 28557-2942
General Phone: (252) 726-7081
General Fax: (252) 726-6016
Advertising Phone: (252) 726-7081 x263
General/National Adv. E-mail: lockwood@thenewstimes.com
Display Adv. E-mail: kim@thenewstimes.com
Classified Adv. e-mail: classifieds@thenewstimes.com
Editorial e-mail: richard@thenewstimes.com
Primary Website: carolinacoastonline.com
Mthly Avg Views: 443282
Mthly Avg Unique Visitors: 190065
Year Established: 1942
Avg Paid Circ: 6800
Audit By: Sworn/Estimate/Non-Audited
Audit Date: 01.09.2021
Personnel: Lockwood Phillips (Pub.); Kim Moseley (Adv. Dir.); Rachael Phillips (Assoc. Editor/Publisher); Walter D. Phillips (Ed.); Beth Blake (Mng. Ed.)
Parent company (for newspapers): Carteret Publishing Co.

CASWELL MESSENGER

Street address 1: 137 MAIN ST
Street address city: Yanceyville
Street address state: NC
Zip/Postal code: 27379
General Phone: (336) 694-4145
General Fax: (336) 694-5637
General/National Adv. E-mail: ads@caswellmessenger.com
Display Adv. E-mail: cmofficemanager@caswellmessenger.com
Editorial e-mail: editor@caswellmessenger.com
Primary Website: caswellmessenger.com
Year Established: 1926
Avg Paid Circ: 4000
Avg Free Circ: 142
Audit By: Sworn/Estimate/Non-Audited
Audit Date: 10.06.2019
Personnel: Patricia Cheek (Office Mgr.); Patti O'Keefe (Ed.); Jonathan Pettiford (Acc. Exec.)
Parent company (for newspapers): Womack Publishing Co.

CHAPEL HILL NEWS

Street address 1: 1530 N Gregson St
Street address 2: Ste 2A
Street address city: Durham
Street address state: NC
Zip/Postal code: 27701-1164
General Phone: (919) 932-2003
General Fax: (919) 932-8799
Advertising Phone: (919) 932-8776
General/National Adv. E-mail: chdisplay@newsobserver.com
Display Adv. E-mail: drogers@newsobserver.com
Editorial e-mail: editor@newsobserver.com
Primary Website: chapelhillnews.com
Year Established: 1932
Avg Paid Circ: 2

Avg Free Circ: 44233
Audit By: Sworn/Estimate/Non-Audited
Audit Date: 10.06.2019
Personnel: Mark Schultz (Pub.); Mark Alston (Adv. Dir.); Doug Rogers (Adv. Dir.)
Parent company (for newspapers): The News & Observer Publishing Co.

CHARLOTTE BUSINESS JOURNAL

Street address 1: 550 S Caldwell St
Street address 2: Suite 910
Street address city: Charlotte
Street address state: NC
Zip/Postal code: 28202-2881
General Phone: (704) 973-1100
General Fax: (704) 973-1102
Editorial e-mail: kpitts@bizjournals.com
Primary Website: charlottebusinessjournal.com
Audit By: Sworn/Estimate/Non-Audited
Audit Date: 10.06.2019
Personnel: Robert Morris (Ed); Kevin Pitts (Pres/Pub)

CHEROKEE SCOUT

Street address 1: 89 Sycamore St
Street address city: Murphy
Street address state: NC
Zip/Postal code: 28906-2954
General Phone: (828) 837-5122
General Fax: (828) 837-5832
General/National Adv. E-mail: news@cherokeescout.com
Display Adv. E-mail: advertising@cherokeescout.com
Classified Adv. e-mail: classifieds@cherokeescout.com
Editorial e-mail: news@cherokeescout.com
Primary Website: cherokeescout.com
Mthly Avg Views: 40000
Mthly Avg Unique Visitors: 12000
Year Established: 1889
Avg Paid Circ: 6000
Avg Free Circ: 100
Audit By: Sworn/Estimate/Non-Audited
Audit Date: 01.10.2023
Personnel: David Brown (Publisher); Donna Cook (Adv. Mgr.); Jared Putnam (Editor); Matthew Osborne (Ed.)
Parent company (for newspapers): Community Newspapers, Inc.

CLAY COUNTY PROGRESS

Street address 1: 43 Main St
Street address city: Hayesville
Street address state: NC
Zip/Postal code: 28904-5808
General Phone: (828) 389-8431
General Fax: (828) 389-9997
General/National Adv. E-mail: ads@claycountyprogress.com
Display Adv. E-mail: classifieds@claycountyprogress.com
Editorial e-mail: news@claycountyprogress.com
Primary Website: claycountyprogress.com
Year Established: 1980
Avg Paid Circ: 4400
Audit By: Sworn/Estimate/Non-Audited
Audit Date: 10.06.2019
Personnel: Tracy Smith (Adv. Mgr.); Danny Hughes (Circ. Mgr.); Becky Long (Pub.); Joel Jenkins (Corp. Mktg. Dir.)
Parent company (for newspapers): Community Newspapers, Inc.

CLAYTON NEWS-STAR

Street address 1: 421 Fayetteville Street
Street address 2: Suite 104
Street address city: Raleigh
Street address state: NC
Zip/Postal code: 27601
General Phone: (919) 829-4500
General Fax: (919) 553-5858
Editorial e-mail: rtomlin@newsobserver.com
Primary Website: newsobserver.com
Year Established: 1911
Avg Paid Circ: 19
Avg Free Circ: 18699
Audit By: Sworn/Estimate/Non-Audited
Audit Date: 10.06.2019
Personnel: Robyn Tomlin (Exec. Ed.); Jane Elizabeth; Susan Spring (Newsrm Dir. Ops.)
Parent company (for newspapers): The News & Observer Publishing Co.

CROSSROADS CHRONICLE

Street address 1: 196 Burns St.
Street address 2: Ste. 1
Street address city: Cashiers
Street address state: NC
Zip/Postal code: 28717
General Phone: (828) 743-5101
General Fax: (828) 743-4173
General/National Adv. E-mail: mhenry@CrossroadsChronicle.com
Display Adv. E-mail: Classifieds@CrossroadsChronicle.com
Editorial e-mail: Editor@CrossroadsChronicle.com
Primary Website: crossroadschronicle.com
Mthly Avg Views: 4038
Mthly Avg Unique Visitors: 2244
Year Established: 1983
Avg Paid Circ: 2200
Audit By: Sworn/Estimate/Non-Audited
Audit Date: 10.06.2019
Personnel: Mike Henry (Pub.); Don Richeson (Editor)
Parent company (for newspapers): Community Newspapers, Inc.

DAVIE COUNTY ENTERPRISE-RECORD

Street address 1: 171 S Main St
Street address city: Mocksville
Street address state: NC
Zip/Postal code: 27028-2424
General Phone: (336) 751-2120
General Fax: (336) 751-9760
General/National Adv. E-mail: erads2@davie-enterprise.com
Display Adv. E-mail: classifieds@salisburypost.com
Editorial e-mail: ernews@davie-enterprise.com
Primary Website: ourdavie.com
Year Established: 1899
Avg Paid Circ: 8500
Avg Free Circ: 32
Audit By: Sworn/Estimate/Non-Audited
Audit Date: 10.06.2019
Personnel: Mike Barnhardt (Mng Ed.); Ray Tutterow (Adv. Dir.); Dwight Sparks (Ed.)
Parent company (for newspapers): Salisbury Newsmedia

DUPLIN TIMES

Street address 1: 102 Front St
Street address city: Kenansville
Street address state: NC
Zip/Postal code: 28349
General Phone: (910) 296-0239
General Fax: (910) 296-9545
General/National Adv. E-mail: duplinads@ncweeklies.com
Editorial e-mail: tnormile@ncweeklies.com
Primary Website: http://theduplintimes.com
Year Established: 1935
Avg Paid Circ: 6100
Avg Free Circ: 11125
Audit By: Sworn/Estimate/Non-Audited
Audit Date: 10.06.2019
Personnel: Trevor Normile (Editor)
Parent company (for newspapers): Cooke Communications North Carolina, LLC

ENTERPRISE & WEEKLY HERALD

Street address 1: 106 W Main St
Street address city: Williamston
Street address state: NC
Zip/Postal code: 27892-2471
General Phone: (252) 792-1181
General Fax: (252) 792-1921
General/National Adv. E-mail: lavan@ncweeklies.com
Editorial e-mail: kstephens@ncweeklies.com
Primary Website: facebook.com/pages/The-Enterprise/171082442937848
Year Established: 1899
Avg Paid Circ: 5100
Avg Free Circ: 21
Audit By: Sworn/Estimate/Non-Audited
Audit Date: 10.06.2019
Personnel: Lou Ann VanLandingham (Adv.); Jay Jenkins (Gen. Mgr.)
Parent company (for newspapers): Cooke Communications North Carolina, LLC

FOUR OAKS-BENSON NEWS IN REVIEW

Street address 1: 110 E Main St
Street address city: Benson
Street address state: NC
Zip/Postal code: 27504
General Phone: (919) 894-3331
General Fax: (919) 894-1069 (Call ((919)) 894-3331 first)
General/National Adv. E-mail: fobnews@aol.com
Primary Website: www.bensonfouroaksnews.com
Avg Paid Circ: 2459
Avg Free Circ: 541
Audit By: Sworn/Estimate/Non-Audited
Audit Date: 09.10.2023
Personnel: Norman Delano (Pub.); Mike Dart (Owner)
Parent company (for newspapers): Dart Media Group

GARNER-CLEVELAND RECORD

Street address 1: 215 S McDowell St
Street address city: Raleigh
Street address state: NC
Zip/Postal code: 27601-1331
General Phone: (919) 829-4500
General/National Adv. E-mail: smcleod@newsobserver.com
Editorial e-mail: jwhitfield@newsobserver.com
Primary Website: garnercleveland.com
Avg Free Circ: 33870
Audit By: Sworn/Estimate/Non-Audited
Audit Date: 10.06.2019
Personnel: Kaki Berkeley (Adv. Dir.); Johnny Whitfield (Ed.)
Parent company (for newspapers): The News & Observer Publishing Co.

GATES COUNTY INDEX

Street address 1: 801 Parker Ave E
Street address city: Ahoskie
Street address state: NC
Zip/Postal code: 27910-3641
General Phone: (252) 332-2123
General Fax: (252) 332-3940
Advertising Phone: (252) 332-7217
Advertising Fax: (252) 332-3940
Editorial Phone: (252) 332-7207
Editorial Fax: (252) 332-3940
General/National Adv. E-mail: judy.farmer@r-cnews.com
Display Adv. E-mail: anna.phipps@r-cnews.com
Editorial e-mail: cal.bryant@r-cnews.com
Primary Website: roanoke-chowannewsherald.com
Avg Paid Circ: 1500
Audit By: Sworn/Estimate/Non-Audited
Audit Date: 10.06.2019
Personnel: Cal Bryant (Ed.); Tony Clark (Pub)
Parent company (for newspapers): Boone Newspapers, Inc.

HARNETT COUNTY NEWS

Street address 1: 407 MAIN ST
Street address city: Lillington
Street address state: NC
Zip/Postal code: 27546
General Phone: (910) 893-5121
General Fax: (910) 893-6128
Editorial e-mail: editor@harnettcountynews.com
Primary Website: harnettcountynews.com
Avg Paid Circ: 2118
Avg Free Circ: 11
Audit By: Sworn/Estimate/Non-Audited
Audit Date: 10.06.2019
Personnel: Bart S. Adams (Pub.); Tom Woerner (Ed.)

INDEPENDENT TRIBUNE

Street address 1: 363 Church Street
Street address city: Concord
Street address state: NC
Zip/Postal code: 28025
General Phone: (704) 782-3155
General Fax: (704) 786-0645
Advertising Phone: (704) 789-9125
Advertising Fax: (704) 789-9159
Editorial Phone: (704) 789-9103
Editorial Fax: (704) 786-0645
General/National Adv. E-mail: bbarker@independenttribune.com
Display Adv. E-mail: classifieds@independenttribune.com
Classified Adv. e-mail: jdunham@independenttribune.com
Editorial e-mail: mplemmons@independenttribune.com
Primary Website: independenttribune.com
Mthly Avg Views: 77684
Mthly Avg Unique Visitors: 4381
Year Established: 1996
Avg Paid Circ: 6208
Avg Free Circ: 99
Sun. Circulation Paid: 10513
Audit By: AAM
Audit Date: 18.03.2019
Personnel: Mark Plemmons (Ed.); Bruce Barker (Adv.); Rhonda Hargenrader (Bus Mgr)
Parent company (for newspapers): BH Media Group; Lee Enterprises, Incorporated

JAMESTOWN NEWS

Street address 1: 206 E Main St
Street address 2: Ste 1A
Street address city: Jamestown
Street address state: NC
Zip/Postal code: 27282-8005
General Phone: (336) 841-4933
General Fax: (336) 841-4953
General/National Adv. E-mail: publisher@yesweeekly.com
Display Adv. E-mail: jamestownnews@northstate.net
Editorial e-mail: jamestownnews@northstate.net
Primary Website: jamestownnews.com
Year Established: 1978
Avg Paid Circ: 4000
Avg Free Circ: 10
Audit By: Sworn/Estimate/Non-Audited
Audit Date: 10.06.2019
Personnel: Charles A. Womack (Pub.); Carol Brooks (Editor)
Parent company (for newspapers): Womack Newspapers

JEFFERSON POST

Street address 1: 203 S. 2nd Ave.
Street address city: West Jefferson
Street address state: NC
Zip/Postal code: 28694
General Phone: (336) 846-7164
General Fax: (336) 846-7165
General/National Adv. E-mail: tlaws@civitasmedia.com
Editorial e-mail: editorial@jeffersonpost.com
Primary Website: jeffersonpost.com
Year Established: 1931
Avg Paid Circ: 6500
Audit By: Sworn/Estimate/Non-Audited
Audit Date: 10.06.2019
Personnel: Cliff Clark (Ed.); Cabot Hamilton (Pub.); Teresa Laws (Gen. Mgr.); Ron Clausen (Pub.)
Parent company (for newspapers): Champion Media

KENLY NEWS

Street address 1: 201 W 2ND ST
Street address city: Kenly
Street address state: NC
Zip/Postal code: 27542
General Phone: (919) 284-2295
General Fax: (919) 284-6397
General/National Adv. E-mail: debra@kenlynews.com
Editorial e-mail: rstewart@kenlynews.com
Primary Website: kenlynews.com
Year Established: 1973
Avg Paid Circ: 3200
Avg Free Circ: 180
Audit By: Sworn/Estimate/Non-Audited
Audit Date: 10.06.2019
Personnel: Rick Stewart (Pub.); Keith Barnes (News Ed.); Debra Malarchik (Adv. Dir.)

KERNERSVILLE NEWS

Street address 1: 300 E Mountain St
Street address city: Kernersville
Street address state: NC
Zip/Postal code: 27284-2943
General Phone: (336) 993-2161

General Fax: (336) 993-0931
General/National Adv. E-mail: ad_director@kernersvillenews.com
Display Adv. E-mail: classifieds@kernersvillenews.com
Editorial e-mail: editor@kernersvillenews.com
Primary Website: kernersvillenews.com
Year Established: 1938
Avg Paid Circ: 6000
Avg Free Circ: 17850
Audit By: Sworn/Estimate/Non-Audited
Audit Date: 10.06.2019
Personnel: Meredith Harrell (Assist. Pub/Ed); Tracy Cardwell (Adv. Dir); John Owensby (Ed.); Connie Owensby (Vice Pres./Bus. Mgr)

KINGS MOUNTAIN HERALD

Street address 1: 219 S Battleground Ave
Street address 2: Suite 6, PO Box 769
Street address city: Kings Mountain
Street address state: NC
Zip/Postal code: 28086
General Phone: (704) 739-7496
Primary Website: kmherald.com
Year Established: 1886
Avg Paid Circ: 1200
Avg Free Circ: 1000
Audit By: Sworn/Estimate/Non-Audited
Audit Date: 10.06.2019
Personnel: Wendy Isbell (Pub.); Elizabeth Stewart (Ed); Gary Stewart (Sports)
Parent company (for newspapers): Community First Media

LAKE GASTON GAZETTE-OBSERVER

Street address 1: 378 Lizard Creek Rd
Street address city: Littleton
Street address state: NC
Zip/Postal code: 27850-8390
General Phone: (252) 586-2700
General Fax: (252) 586-3522
General/National Adv. E-mail: ads@lakegastongazette-observer.com
Editorial e-mail: news@lakegastongazette-observer.com
Primary Website: lakegastongazette-observer.com
Year Established: 1955
Audit By: Sworn/Estimate/Non-Audited
Audit Date: 10.06.2019
Personnel: Della Rose; Carol Griffin (Office Mgr.); Mary Lou Cheek (Adv. Mgr.)
Parent company (for newspapers): Womack Publishing Co.

LINCOLN TIMES-NEWS

Street address 1: 119 W Water St
Street address city: Lincolnton
Street address state: NC
Zip/Postal code: 28092-2623
General Phone: (704) 735-3031
General Fax: (704) 735-3037
Advertising Phone: (704) 735-3031
Advertising Fax: (704) 735-3996
Editorial Fax: (704) 735-1278
General/National Adv. E-mail: advertising@lincolntimesnews.com
Display Adv. E-mail: classifieds@lincolntimesnews.com
Editorial e-mail: editor@lincolntimesnews.com
Primary Website: lincolntimesnews.com
Year Established: 1873
Avg Paid Circ: 10500
Audit By: Sworn/Estimate/Non-Audited
Audit Date: 10.06.2019
Personnel: Jerry G. Leedy (Pub.); Lisa Matthews (Adv. Mgr.); Michael Gebelein (Mng. Ed.)
Parent company (for newspapers): Western Publishing Co

LUMINA NEWS

Street address 1: 7232 Wrightsville Ave
Street address city: Wilmington
Street address state: NC
Zip/Postal code: 28403-7223
General Phone: (910) 256-6569
General Fax: (910) 256-6512
Advertising Phone: (910) 256-6569
General/National Adv. E-mail: szmiller980@gmail.com
Editorial e-mail: pub@luminanews.com
Primary Website: luminanews.com
Audit By: Sworn/Estimate/Non-Audited
Audit Date: 10.06.2019
Personnel: Marimar McNaughton (Ed.); Jill Sabourin (Account Exec.); Pat Bradford (Pub./Circ. Mgr.)

MIDTOWN RALEIGH NEWS

Street address 1: 215 S McDowell St
Street address city: Raleigh
Street address state: NC
Zip/Postal code: 27601-1331
General Phone: (919) 829-4500
Advertising Phone: (919) 836-5909
General/National Adv. E-mail: ptompkins@newsobserver.com
Display Adv. E-mail: sbewley@newsobserver.com
Editorial e-mail: nrnews@newsobserver.com
Primary Website: midtownraleighnews.com
Avg Free Circ: 75189
Audit By: Sworn/Estimate/Non-Audited
Audit Date: 10.06.2019
Personnel: Shelley Bewley (Adv Sales Mgr)
Parent company (for newspapers): The News & Observer Publishing Co.

MITCHELL NEWS-JOURNAL

Street address 1: 261 Locust St
Street address city: Spruce Pine
Street address state: NC
Zip/Postal code: 28777-2713
General Phone: (828) 765-2071
General Fax: (828) 765-1616
General/National Adv. E-mail: adrep@mitchellnews.com
Editorial e-mail: editor@mitchellnews.com
Primary Website: mitchellnews.com
Year Established: 1927
Avg Paid Circ: 4922
Avg Free Circ: 135
Audit By: Sworn/Estimate/Non-Audited
Audit Date: 10.06.2019
Personnel: Brandon Roberts (Ed.); Cindy Lindsey (Adv. Mgr.); Joel Jenkins (Mktg. Dir.); Mariel Williams (Editor)
Parent company (for newspapers): Community Newspapers, Inc.

MONTGOMERY HERALD

Street address 1: 139 Bruton St
Street address city: Troy
Street address state: NC
Zip/Postal code: 27371-2815
General Phone: (910) 576-6051
General Fax: (910) 576-1050
General/National Adv. E-mail: advertise@montgomeryhrald.com
Display Adv. E-mail: advertise@montgomeryhrald.com
Editorial e-mail: sendnews@montgomeryherald.com
Primary Website: montgomeryherald.com
Year Established: 1880s
Avg Paid Circ: 4700
Avg Free Circ: 556
Audit By: Sworn/Estimate/Non-Audited
Audit Date: 10.06.2019
Personnel: Tammy Dunn (Publisher); Josh Bowles (Office Manager); Jon Galloway (Sports Editor)
Parent company (for newspapers): Womack Publishing Co.

MOORESVILLE TRIBUNE

Street address 1: 147 E. Center Avenue
Street address city: Mooresville
Street address state: NC
Zip/Postal code: 28115
General Phone: (704) 696-2950
General Fax: (704) 664-3614
Advertising Phone: (704) 562-9067
Editorial Phone: (704) 696-2941
General/National Adv. E-mail: advertising@mooresvilletribune.com
Display Adv. E-mail: classified@mooresvilletribune.com
Editorial e-mail: ldunlap@mooresvilletribune.com
Primary Website: mooresvilletribune.com
Year Established: 1937
Avg Paid Circ: 925
Avg Free Circ: 9500
Audit By: AAM
Audit Date: 31.03.2019
Personnel: LeAnna Dunlap (Adv. Mgr.); Bud Welch (Circ. Mgr.); Dale Gowing (Ed)
Parent company (for newspapers): BH Media Group; Lee Enterprises, Incorporated

MOUNT OLIVE TRIBUNE

Street address 1: 214 N Center St
Street address city: Mount Olive
Street address state: NC
Zip/Postal code: 28365-1702
General Phone: (919) 658-9456
General Fax: (919) 658-9559
General/National Adv. E-mail: ads@mountolivetribune.com
Editorial e-mail: editor@mountolivetribune.com
Primary Website: mountolivetribune.com
Year Established: 1904
Avg Paid Circ: 2000
Avg Free Circ: 49
Audit By: Sworn/Estimate/Non-Audited
Audit Date: 10.06.2019
Personnel: Barry Merrill (Pub)

MOUNTAIN XPRESS

Street address 1: 2 Wall St
Street address city: Asheville
Street address state: NC
Zip/Postal code: 28801-2721
General Phone: (828) 251-1333
General/National Adv. E-mail: xpress@mountainx.com
Display Adv. E-mail: advertise@mountainx.com
Editorial e-mail: news@mountainx.com
Primary Website: www.mountainx.com
Mthly Avg Views: 146000
Mthly Avg Unique Visitors: 70600
Year Established: 1994
Avg Paid Circ: 10
Avg Free Circ: 18035
Audit By: CVC
Audit Date: 30.06.2023
Personnel: Jeff Fobes (Pub.); Susan Hutchinson (Advertising Manager); Patty Levesque (Office Mgr.); Cindy Kunst (Circ Coordinator); Rebecca Sulock (Arts & Entertainment/Managing Editor); Thomas Calder (Editor); Stefan Colosimo (Techn. Mgr.); Carrie Lare (Art & Design Manager); Margaret Williams (News/ Managing Editor); Kyle Kirkpatrick (Webmaster)

NEWS-RECORD AND SENTINEL

Street address 1: 58 Back St.
Street address city: Marshall
Street address state: NC
Zip/Postal code: 28753
General Phone: (828) 649-1075
General Fax: (828) 649-9426
Editorial e-mail: info@newsrecordsentinel.com
Year Established: 1901
Avg Paid Circ: 6500
Avg Free Circ: 50
Audit By: Sworn/Estimate/Non-Audited
Audit Date: 10.06.2019
Personnel: Christina Rice (Gen. Mgr./Ed.)
Parent company (for newspapers): Gannett

NORTH CAROLINA LAWYERS WEEKLY

Street address 1: 130 N. McDowell St.
Street address 2: Ste. B
Street address city: Charlotte
Street address state: NC
Zip/Postal code: 28204
General Phone: (800) 876-5297
General/National Adv. E-mail: andrea.mounts@nclawyersweekly.com
Display Adv. E-mail: andrea.mounts@nclawyersweekly.com
Editorial e-mail: david.donovan@nclawyersweekly.com
Primary Website: nclawyersweekly.com
Year Established: 1987
Audit By: Sworn/Estimate/Non-Audited
Audit Date: 10.06.2019
Personnel: Grady Johnson (Pub.); David Donovan (Ed.); Andrea Mounts (Ad. Dir)
Parent company (for newspapers): The Dolan Company

NORTH RALEIGH NEWS

Street address 1: 215 S McDowell St
Street address city: Raleigh
Street address state: NC
Zip/Postal code: 27601-1331
General Phone: (919) 829-4500
Advertising Fax: (919) 829-4589
General/National Adv. E-mail: trevor.holland@newsobserver.com
Display Adv. E-mail: brookie.holloway@newsobserver.com
Editorial e-mail: nrnews@newsobserver.com
Primary Website: northraleighnews.com
Year Established: 2003
Avg Free Circ: 73782
Audit By: Sworn/Estimate/Non-Audited
Audit Date: 10.06.2019
Personnel: Dan Barkin (Ed.); Peter Tompkins (Adv. Dir.)
Parent company (for newspapers): The News & Observer Publishing Co.

OUTER BANKS SENTINEL

Street address 1: PO Box 546
Street address city: Nags Head
Street address state: NC
Zip/Postal code: 27959-0546
General Phone: (252) 480-2234
General Fax: (252) 480-1146
General/National Adv. E-mail: donna@obsentinel.com
Display Adv. E-mail: classifieds@obsentinel.com
Editorial e-mail: mark@obsentinel.com
Primary Website: obsentinel.com
Year Established: 1996
Avg Paid Circ: 5000
Audit By: Sworn/Estimate/Non-Audited
Audit Date: 10.06.2019
Personnel: Neel Keller (Ed.); Mark Jurkowitz (Pub.)
Parent company (for newspapers): SLAM Publications

OXFORD PUBLIC LEDGER

Street address 1: 200 W Spring St
Street address city: Oxford
Street address state: NC
Zip/Postal code: 27565-3247
General Phone: (919) 693-2646
General Fax: (919) 693-3704
General/National Adv. E-mail: oplronnieadvertising@earthlink.net
Display Adv. E-mail: oplchristyadvertising@earthlink.net
Editorial e-mail: opllynnallred@earthlink.net
Year Established: 1881
Avg Paid Circ: 6500
Avg Free Circ: 60
Audit By: Sworn/Estimate/Non-Audited
Audit Date: 10.06.2019
Personnel: Charles Critcher (Pub.); Ronald Critcher (Adv. Mgr.); Al Carson (Ed.)

PENDER-TOPSAIL POST & VOICE

Street address 1: P.O. Box 955
Street address city: Burgaw
Street address state: NC
Zip/Postal code: 28425
General Phone: (910) 259-9111
General Fax: (910) 259-9112
General/National Adv. E-mail: advertising@post-voice.com
Editorial e-mail: posteditor@post-voice.com
Primary Website: www.postvoiceonline.com
Avg Paid Circ: 5000
Avg Free Circ: 400
Audit By: Sworn/Estimate/Non-Audited
Audit Date: 10.06.2019
Personnel: Andy Pettigrew (Editor, puboisher); Brenda Todd (Ad. Director); Brenda Todd (Adv.)
Parent company (for newspapers): Post Voice LLC

PERQUIMANS WEEKLY

Street address 1: 111 W Market St
Street address city: Hertford
Street address state: NC
Zip/Postal code: 27944-1150
General Phone: (252) 426-5728
General Fax: (252) 426-4625
Advertising Phone: (252) 426-5728
Editorial Phone: (252) 426-5728
General/National Adv. E-mail: balexander@ncweeklies.com
Display Adv. E-mail: balexander@ncweeklies.com
Editorial e-mail: pwilliams@ncweeklies.com

Primary Website: dailyadvance.com/communities/perquimans
Year Established: 1932
Avg Paid Circ: 1733
Audit By: Sworn/Estimate/Non-Audited
Audit Date: 10.06.2019
Personnel: Michael Goodman (Pub.); Julian Eure (Mng Ed.); Sean O'Brian (Ad. Dir)
Parent company (for newspapers): Cooke Communications North Carolina, LLC

PRINCETON NEWS-LEADER

Street address 1: 119 W Edwards St
Street address city: Princeton
Street address state: NC
Zip/Postal code: 27569-7374
General Phone: (919) 936-9891
General Fax: (919) 936-2065
General/National Adv. E-mail: debra@kenlynews.com
Display Adv. E-mail: ads@newsleadernow.com
Editorial e-mail: kbarnes@kenlynews.com
Primary Website: johnstoniannews.com
Avg Paid Circ: 1500
Avg Free Circ: 267
Audit By: Sworn/Estimate/Non-Audited
Audit Date: 10.06.2019
Personnel: Rick Stewart (Pub.)

ROANOKE-CHOWAN NEWS-HERALD

Street address 1: 801 Parker Ave E
Street address city: Ahoskie
Street address state: NC
Zip/Postal code: 27910-3641
General Phone: (252) 332-2123
General Fax: (252) 332-3940
Advertising Phone: (252) 332-2123
Advertising Fax: (252) 332-3940
Editorial Phone: (252) 332-7207
Editorial Fax: (252) 332-3940
General/National Adv. E-mail: judy.farmer@r-cnews.com
Display Adv. E-mail: anna.phipps@r-cnews.com
Editorial e-mail: cal.bryant@r-cnews.com
Primary Website: r-cnews.com
Year Established: 1914
Avg Paid Circ: 6800
Avg Free Circ: 5000
Audit By: Sworn/Estimate/Non-Audited
Audit Date: 10.06.2019
Personnel: Cal Bryant (Ed.); Sarah Morris (Production Mgr.); Judy Farmer (Mktg. Consult.)
Parent company (for newspapers): Boone Newspapers, Inc.

ROCKINGHAM NOW

Street address 1: 1921 Vance St
Street address city: Reidsville
Street address state: NC
Zip/Postal code: 27320-3254
General Phone: (800) 323-2951
Editorial e-mail: ghunt@caswellmessenger.com
Primary Website: rockinghamnow.com
Audit By: Sworn/Estimate/Non-Audited
Audit Date: 10.06.2019
Personnel: Jeff Gauger (Pub.); Gerri Hunt (Ed)
Parent company (for newspapers): BH Media Group

RUTHERFORD WEEKLY

Street address 1: 369 Butler Rd
Street address city: Forest City
Street address state: NC
Zip/Postal code: 28043-6106
General Phone: (828) 248-1408
General Fax: (828) 245-7013
Editorial Phone: (828) 248-1496
General/National Adv. E-mail: mike@rutherfordweekly.com
Display Adv. E-mail: www.advertising@rutherfordweekly.com
Editorial e-mail: www.events@rutherfordweekly.com
Primary Website: rutherfordweekly.com
Year Established: 1991
Avg Free Circ: 15807
Audit By: Sworn/Estimate/Non-Audited
Audit Date: 10.06.2019
Personnel: Mike Marlow (Gen. Mgr.); Les Wood (Circ. Mgr); Jan Sailors (Prod. Mgr)
Parent company (for newspapers): CNHI, LLC

SMOKY MOUNTAIN NEWS

Street address 1: PO BOX 629
Street address city: Waynesville
Street address state: NC
Zip/Postal code: 28786-0629
General Phone: (828) 452-4251
General Fax: (828) 452-3585
General/National Adv. E-mail: ads@smokymountainnews.com
Display Adv. E-mail: classads@smokymountainnews.com
Editorial e-mail: info@smokymountainnews.com
Primary Website: smokymountainnews.com
Avg Paid Circ: 0
Avg Free Circ: 16260
Audit By: CVC
Audit Date: 6/31/2018
Personnel: Scott McLeod (Pub.); Greg Boothroyd (Adv. Dir.); Scott Collier (Circ. Mgr.); Becky Johnson (News Ed.)

SOUTH CHARLOTTE WEEKLY

Street address 1: 9506 Monroe Rd
Street address city: Charlotte
Street address state: NC
Zip/Postal code: 28270-1527
General Phone: (704) 849-2261
General Fax: (704) 849-2504
General/National Adv. E-mail: adsales@carolinaweeklynewspapers.com
Editorial e-mail: editor@thecharlotteweekly.com
Primary Website: thecharlotteweekly.com
Year Established: 2002
Avg Paid Circ: 5
Avg Free Circ: 23877
Audit By: CVC
Audit Date: 31.12.2016
Personnel: Justin Vick (Ed.)
Parent company (for newspapers): Carolina Media Group

SOUTHWEST WAKE NEWS

Street address 1: 122 E Chatham St
Street address 2: Ste 230
Street address city: Cary
Street address state: NC
Zip/Postal code: 27511-3360
General Phone: (919) 460-2600
General/National Adv. E-mail: placeads@newsobserver.com
Display Adv. E-mail: caryclassads@newsobserver.com
Editorial e-mail: carynews@newsobserver.com
Primary Website: southwestwakenews.com
Year Established: 2009
Avg Free Circ: 53190
Audit By: Sworn/Estimate/Non-Audited
Audit Date: 10.06.2019
Personnel: Kaki Berkeley (Adv Dir); Jessica Banov (Ed); Sara Glines (Pub.)
Parent company (for newspapers): The News & Observer Publishing Co.

TABOR-LORIS TRIBUNE

Street address 1: PO Box 67
Street address 2: 102 Avon Street
Street address city: Tabor City
Street address state: NC
Zip/Postal code: 28463-0067
General Phone: (910) 653-3153
General Fax: (910) 653-5818
Editorial Phone: (910) 653-7442
General/National Adv. E-mail: tribpenny@tabor-loris.com
Display Adv. E-mail: tribpenny@tabor-loris.com
Editorial e-mail: tribdeuce@tabor-loris.com
Primary Website: tabor-loris.com
Year Established: 1946
Avg Paid Circ: 3000
Avg Free Circ: 200
Audit By: Sworn/Estimate/Non-Audited
Audit Date: 10.06.2019
Personnel: Deuce Niven (Gen. Mgr./Ed.); Penny Holmes (Advertising Manager); Joyce Sammons (Adv./Reporter)
Parent company (for newspapers): Atlantic Corp.

THE ALAMANCE NEWS

Street address 1: 114 W Elm St
Street address city: Graham
Street address state: NC
Zip/Postal code: 27253-2802
General Phone: (336) 228-7851
General Fax: (336) 229-9602
General/National Adv. E-mail: alamanacenews@mail.com
Primary Website: alamancenews.us
Avg Paid Circ: 4000
Audit By: Sworn/Estimate/Non-Audited
Audit Date: 10.06.2019
Personnel: Thomas E. Boney (Pub./Ed.)

THE ALLEGHANY NEWS

Street address 1: 20 S Main St
Street address city: Sparta
Street address state: NC
Zip/Postal code: 28675-9643
General Phone: (336) 372-8999
General Fax: (336) 372-5707
General/National Adv. E-mail: ads@alleghanynews.com
Display Adv. E-mail: classifieds@alleghanynews.com
Editorial e-mail: news@alleghanynews.com
Primary Website: alleghanynews.com
Mthly Avg Views: 18000
Year Established: 1889
Avg Paid Circ: 3800
Avg Free Circ: 50
Audit By: Sworn/Estimate/Non-Audited
Audit Date: 10.06.2019
Personnel: Ron Brown (Gen. Mgr./Adv. Dir.); Nancy Greene (Circ. Mgr.); Coby LaRue (Ed.); Sarah Maynor (Ed Assit.); Mark Ketchum (Sports Ed.); Bob Bamberg (Ed)

THE ANSON RECORD

Street address 1: 123 E Martin St
Street address 2: Ste 400
Street address city: Wadesboro
Street address state: NC
Zip/Postal code: 28170-2276
General Phone: (704) 694-2161
General Fax: (704) 694-7060
General/National Adv. E-mail: dspencer@yourdailyjournal.com
Display Adv. E-mail: gtyson@civitasmedia.com
Editorial e-mail: ndavis@ansonrecord.com
Primary Website: ansonrecord.com
Year Established: 1881
Avg Paid Circ: 5000
Avg Free Circ: 1000
Audit By: Sworn/Estimate/Non-Audited
Audit Date: 10.06.2019
Personnel: Alan Wooten (Ed.); David Spencer (Gen. Mgr.); Gwen Tyson (Classifieds); Natalie Davis (Reporter)
Parent company (for newspapers): Champion Media

THE ASHE MOUNTAIN TIMES

Street address 1: 7 E Main St
Street address city: West Jefferson
Street address state: NC
Zip/Postal code: 28694
General Phone: (336) 246-6397
General/National Adv. E-mail: ron.brown@mountaintimes.com
Display Adv. E-mail: classifieds@mountaintimes.com
Editorial e-mail: ron.brown@mountaintimes.com
Primary Website: ashepostandtimes.com
Avg Free Circ: 9553
Audit By: Sworn/Estimate/Non-Audited
Audit Date: 10.06.2019
Personnel: Teresa Laws (Gen. Mgr./ Adv.); Ron Brown (Adv.); Tom Mayer (Ex. Ed.)
Parent company (for newspapers): Adams Publishing Group, LLC

THE AVERY JOURNAL-TIMES

Street address 1: 428 Pineola Street
Street address city: Newland
Street address state: NC
Zip/Postal code: 28657-8037
General Phone: (828) 733-2448
General/National Adv. E-mail: news@averyjournal.com
Display Adv. E-mail: henry.volk@averyjournal.com
Classified Adv. e-mail: classifieds@mountaintimes.com
Editorial e-mail: editor@averyjournal.com
Primary Website: averyjournal.com
Year Established: 1959
Avg Paid Circ: 5300
Avg Free Circ: 415
Audit By: Sworn/Estimate/Non-Audited
Audit Date: 10.06.2019
Personnel: Gene Fowler (Pub.); Brenda Minton (Class Adv. Mgr.); Mark Mitchell (Adv. Mgr)
Parent company (for newspapers): Adams Publishing Group, LLC

THE BLOWING ROCKET

Street address 1: 474 Industrial Park Drive
Street address city: Blowing Rock
Street address state: NC
Zip/Postal code: 28607
General Phone: (828) 264-6397
General Fax: (828) 262-0282
Editorial e-mail: newpaper@mountaintimes.com
Primary Website: blowingrocket.com
Year Established: 1932
Avg Paid Circ: 2700
Avg Free Circ: 36
Audit By: Sworn/Estimate/Non-Audited
Audit Date: 10.06.2019
Personnel: Tom Mayer (Exec. Ed.)
Parent company (for newspapers): Adams Publishing Group, LLC

THE BRUNSWICK BEACON

Street address 1: 208 Smith Ave
Street address city: Shallotte
Street address state: NC
Zip/Postal code: 28470-4458
General Phone: (910) 754-6890
General Fax: (910) 754-5407
General/National Adv. E-mail: addirector@brunswickbeacon.com
Display Adv. E-mail: classified@brunswickbeacon.com
Editorial e-mail: editor@brunswickbeacon.com
Primary Website: brunswickbeacon.com
Year Established: 1962
Avg Paid Circ: 17700
Avg Free Circ: 2
Audit By: Sworn/Estimate/Non-Audited
Audit Date: 10.06.2019
Personnel: Scott Harrell (Pub.); Angie Sutton (Adv. Mgr.); Stacey Manning (Ed.)
Parent company (for newspapers): Landmark Communications, Inc.; Landmark Community Newspapers, LLC

THE BUSINESS JOURNAL

Street address 1: 101 South Elm Street
Street address 2: Ste 100
Street address city: Greensboro
Street address state: NC
Zip/Postal code: 27401
General Phone: (336) 271-6539
General Fax: (336) 574-3607
General/National Adv. E-mail: amellott@bizjournals.com
Display Adv. E-mail: amellott@bizjournals.com
Editorial e-mail: lwhittington@bizjournals.com
Primary Website: bizjournals.com/triad
Year Established: 1998
Audit By: Sworn/Estimate/Non-Audited
Audit Date: 10.06.2019
Personnel: Abby Mellott (Adv. Mktg. Mgr.); Lloyd Whittington (Ed.); Margaret Moffett (Mng. Ed.); Gary Marschall (Circ. Dir.)

THE BUTNER-CREEDMOOR NEWS

Street address 1: 418 N Main St
Street address 2: Ste 20
Street address city: Creedmoor
Street address state: NC
Zip/Postal code: 27522-8809
General Phone: (919) 528-2393
General Fax: (919) 528-0288
General/National Adv. E-mail: advertising@buttercreedmoornews.com

Display Adv. E-mail: advertising@buttercreedmoornews.com
Primary Website: butnercreedmoornews.com
Avg Paid Circ: 5400
Audit By: Sworn/Estimate/Non-Audited
Audit Date: 10.06.2019
Personnel: Morgan Dickerman (CEO); Keven Zepazauer (Pub.); Logan Martinez (Ed.); Sam Register (Adv. Dir.)

THE CARY NEWS

Street address 1: 215 S McDowell St
Street address city: Raleigh
Street address state: NC
Zip/Postal code: 27601-1331
General Phone: (919) 460-2600
General/National Adv. E-mail: placeads@newsobserver.com
Editorial e-mail: carynews@newsobserver.com
Primary Website: carynews.com
Year Established: 1963
Avg Paid Circ: 6
Avg Free Circ: 55997
Audit By: Sworn/Estimate/Non-Audited
Audit Date: 10.06.2019
Personnel: Kaki Berkeley (Ad. Dir.)
Parent company (for newspapers): The McClatchy Company

THE CHARLOTTE POST

Street address 1: 1531 Camden Rd
Street address city: Charlotte
Street address state: NC
Zip/Postal code: 28203-4753
General Phone: (704) 376-0496
General Fax: (704) 342-2160
General/National Adv. E-mail: advertising@thecharlottepost.com
Display Adv. E-mail: classified@thecharlottepost.com
Editorial e-mail: herb.white@thecharlottepost.com
Primary Website: thecharlottepost.com
Year Established: 1974
Avg Paid Circ: 10695
Avg Free Circ: 6083
Audit By: Sworn/Estimate/Non-Audited
Audit Date: 10.06.2019
Personnel: Herbert White (Ed.); Jeri Thompson (Adv. Dir.); Betty Potts (Office Mgr.)

THE CHATHAM NEWS

Street address 1: 303 W Raleigh St
Street address city: Siler City
Street address state: NC
Zip/Postal code: 27344-3725
General Phone: (919) 663-3232
General Fax: (919) 663-4042
General/National Adv. E-mail: advertising@thechathamnews.com
Editorial e-mail: rigsbee@thechathamnews.com
Primary Website: thechathamnews.com
Avg Paid Circ: 9200
Avg Free Circ: 395
Audit By: Sworn/Estimate/Non-Audited
Audit Date: 10.06.2019
Personnel: Randall Rigsbee (Mng. Ed.); Steve Roberts (Prodn. Mgr.)
Parent company (for newspapers): The Chatham News Publishing Co, Inc.

THE CHATHAM RECORD

Street address 1: 19 Hillsboro Street
Street address city: Pittsboro
Street address state: NC
Zip/Postal code: 27312
General Phone: (919) 542-3013
General Fax: (919) 542-2590
General/National Adv. E-mail: jjustice@chathamnr.com
Editorial e-mail: rigsbee@chathamnr.com
Primary Website: chathamnewsrecord.com
Avg Paid Circ: 2100
Avg Free Circ: 30
Audit By: Sworn/Estimate/Non-Audited
Audit Date: 10.06.2019
Personnel: Bill Horner (Pub.); Jason Justice (Adv. Dir.); Randall Rigsbee (Mng. Ed.)
Parent company (for newspapers): The Chatham News Publishing Co, Inc.

THE CHERRYVILLE EAGLE

Street address 1: 107 E Main St
Street address 2: # 12
Street address city: Cherryville
Street address state: NC
Zip/Postal code: 28021-3406
General Phone: (704) 435-6752
General Fax: (704) 435-8293
Advertising Phone: (704) 300-3493
Editorial Phone: (704) 435-6752
Editorial Fax: (704) 435-8293
General/National Adv. E-mail: michael.cherryvilleeagle@gmail.com
Display Adv. E-mail: michael.cherryvilleeagle@gmail.com
Editorial e-mail: michael.cherryvilleeagle@gmail.com
Primary Website: cherryvilleeagle.com
Year Established: 1906
Avg Paid Circ: 2750
Audit By: Sworn/Estimate/Non-Audited
Audit Date: 10.06.2019
Personnel: Michael Powell (Ed.); Mark Blanton (Sales Rep.)
Parent company (for newspapers): Community First Media, Inc.

THE CHOWAN HERALD

Street address 1: 423 S Broad St
Street address city: Edenton
Street address state: NC
Zip/Postal code: 27932-1935
General Phone: (252) 332-2123
General Fax: (252) 482-4410
Advertising Phone: (252) 332-7203
Editorial Phone: (252) 332-7207
General/National Adv. E-mail: chowanherald@nccox.com
Display Adv. E-mail: chowanadvertising@nccox.com
Editorial e-mail: cal.bryant@r-cnews.com
Avg Paid Circ: 5000
Audit By: Sworn/Estimate/Non-Audited
Audit Date: 10.06.2019
Personnel: Cal Bryant (Ed.); Sarah Morris (Prod. Mgr.); Judy Farmer (Sales Coord.)
Parent company (for newspapers): Cooke Communications North Carolina, LLC

THE CHRONICLE

Street address 1: 1300 E. 5th St.
Street address city: Winston Salem
Street address state: NC
Zip/Postal code: 27101-2912
General Phone: (336) 722-8624
General Fax: (336) 723-9173
Primary Website: wschronicle.com
Mthly Avg Views: 40000
Mthly Avg Unique Visitors: 15000
Year Established: 1974
Avg Paid Circ: 5000
Avg Free Circ: 2000
Audit By: CVC
Personnel: James Taylor (Ed./Pub.); Bridget Elam (Assoc. Ed.); Tevin Stinson (Sr. Reporter); Timothy Ramsey (Sports/Relig. Ed.)

THE CLEMMONS COURIER

Street address 1: 3600 Clemmons Rd
Street address city: Clemmons
Street address state: NC
Zip/Postal code: 27012-9104
General Phone: (336) 766-4126
General Fax: (336) 766-7350
General/National Adv. E-mail: courier9@bellsouth.net
Primary Website: clemmonscourier.net
Avg Paid Circ: 2700
Avg Free Circ: 50
Audit By: Sworn/Estimate/Non-Audited
Audit Date: 10.06.2019
Personnel: Dwight Sparks (Pub./Ed.); Christy Clark (Adv. Mgr.)
Parent company (for newspapers): SalisburyNewsMedia; Evening Post Publishing Newspaper Group

THE COUNTY COMPASS

Street address 1: PO Box 460
Street address city: Bayboro
Street address state: NC
Zip/Postal code: 28515-0460
General Phone: (252) 745-3155
General Fax: (252) 745-3220
Advertising Phone: (252) 745-3155
Editorial Phone: (252) 670-0447
General/National Adv. E-mail: flora@compassnews360.com
Display Adv. E-mail: jeff@compassnews360.com
Editorial e-mail: jeff@compassnews360.com
Primary Website: compassnews360.com
Year Established: 2009
Avg Paid Circ: 500
Avg Free Circ: 19500
Audit By: Sworn/Estimate/Non-Audited
Audit Date: 10.06.2019
Personnel: Jeff Aydelette (Pub./Ed)

THE COURIER-TIMES

Street address 1: 109 Clayton Ave
Street address city: Roxboro
Street address state: NC
Zip/Postal code: 27573-4611
General Phone: (336) 599-0162
General Fax: (336) 597-2773
General/National Adv. E-mail: learussell@roxboro-courier.com
Display Adv. E-mail: ctreception@roxboro-courier.com
Editorial e-mail: tchandler@roxboro-courier.com
Primary Website: personcountylife.com
Year Established: 1881
Avg Paid Circ: 8509
Avg Free Circ: 95
Audit By: Sworn/Estimate/Non-Audited
Audit Date: 10.06.2019
Personnel: Brinn Clayton (Pub); Eric Whitt (Circ. Mgr.); Tim Chandler (Ed.)

THE DURHAM NEWS

Street address 1: 505 W Franklin St
Street address city: Chapel Hill
Street address state: NC
Zip/Postal code: 27516-2315
General Phone: (919) 932-2003
General Fax: (919) 932-8799
General/National Adv. E-mail: kberkeley@newsobserver.com
Display Adv. E-mail: drogers@newsobserver.com
Editorial e-mail: editor@newsobserver.com
Primary Website: thedurhamnews.com
Avg Free Circ: 75594
Audit By: Sworn/Estimate/Non-Audited
Audit Date: 10.06.2019
Personnel: Felicia Gressette (Pub.); Mark Schultz (Ed); Kaki Berkeley (Adv. Mgr.); Doug Rogers (Adv. Dir.)
Parent company (for newspapers): The News & Observer Publishing Co.

THE EDEN NEWS

Street address 1: 1921 Vance St
Street address city: Reidsville
Street address state: NC
Zip/Postal code: 27320-3254
General Phone: (336) 349-4331
General Fax: (336) 342-2513
General/National Adv. E-mail: pdurham@reidsvillereview.com
Editorial e-mail: news@reidsvillereview.com
Primary Website: rockinghamnow.com
Audit By: Sworn/Estimate/Non-Audited
Audit Date: 10.06.2019
Personnel: Amanda K Lehmert (Group Ed.); Pam Durham (Adv. Dir.); Steven W. Kaylor (Pub.)
Parent company (for newspapers): BH Media Group

THE ENQUIRER-JOURNAL

Street address 1: 1508 Skyway Dr
Street address city: Monroe
Street address state: NC
Zip/Postal code: 28110-3008
General Phone: (704) 289-1541
General Fax: (704) 289-2929
Advertising Phone: (704) 261-2208
Editorial Phone: (704) 261-2220
General/National Adv. E-mail: apurser@theej.com
Display Adv. E-mail: adcopy@theej.com
Classified Adv. e-mail: classifieds@theej.com
Editorial e-mail: jerrysnow@theej.com
Primary Website: enquirerjournal.com
Mthly Avg Views: 203000
Mthly Avg Unique Visitors: 26337
Year Established: 1873
Avg Paid Circ: 5392
Avg Free Circ: 4000
Sun. Circulation Paid: 6022
Sun. Circulation Free: 3300
Audit By: Sworn/Estimate/Non-Audited
Audit Date: 10.06.2019
Personnel: Stan Hojnacki (Mng. Ed.); Jerry Snow (Sports Ed.); Sharon Jimenez (Adv. Mgr.); Randy Lohrenz (Pub.)
Parent company (for newspapers): Paxton Media Group

THE ENTERPRISE

Street address 1: 113 N Ash St
Street address city: Spring Hope
Street address state: NC
Zip/Postal code: 27882-7711
General Phone: (252) 265-8117
Advertising Phone: (252) 243-5151
Editorial Phone: (252) 265-8117
General/National Adv. E-mail: news.enterprise@wilsontimes.com
Display Adv. E-mail: brobbins@wilsontimes.com
Classified Adv. e-mail: pgarcia@wilsontimes.com
Editorial e-mail: lkay@springhopeenterprise.com
Primary Website: springhopeenterprise.com
Year Established: 1947
Avg Paid Circ: 2400
Avg Free Circ: 600
Audit By: Sworn/Estimate/Non-Audited
Audit Date: 10.06.2019
Personnel: Ken Ripley (Editor and publisher emeritus); Corey Friedman (Editor); Keven Zepezauer (President and publisher); Joseph Conner (Circulation manager); Tracy McLamb (Director of sales and marketing); Lindell Kay (News editor); Beth Robbins (Advertising account executive)
Parent company (for newspapers): Restoration NewsMedia

THE FARMVILLE ENTERPRISE

Street address 1: 3754 S Main St
Street address city: Farmville
Street address state: NC
Zip/Postal code: 27828-8546
General Phone: (252) 753-4126
General Fax: (252) 753-4126
Editorial e-mail: farmvilleed@nccox.com
Primary Website: facebook.com/pages/The-Farmville-Enterprise/178388739633
Year Established: 1910
Avg Paid Circ: 2500
Audit By: Sworn/Estimate/Non-Audited
Audit Date: 10.06.2019
Personnel: Mitchell Oakley (Pub.)
Parent company (for newspapers): Cooke Communications North Carolina, LLC

THE FRANKLIN PRESS

Street address 1: 40 Depot St
Street address city: Franklin
Street address state: NC
Zip/Postal code: 28734-2704
General Phone: (828) 524-2010
General Fax: (828) 524-8821
Advertising Phone: (828) 524-2010
General/National Adv. E-mail: addirector@thefranklinpress.com
Display Adv. E-mail: classifieds@thefranklinpress.com
Editorial e-mail: editor@thefranklinpress.com
Primary Website: thefranklinpress.com
Year Established: 1886
Avg Paid Circ: 8524
Avg Free Circ: 21
Audit By: Sworn/Estimate/Non-Audited
Audit Date: 10.06.2019
Personnel: Rachael Hopkins (Pub.); Barbara McRae (Ed.); M.A. Lewis; Joel Jenkins (Corp. Mktg. Dir.)

Parent company (for newspapers): Community Newspapers, Inc.

THE GRAHAM STAR

Street address 1: 720 Tallulah Rd
Street address city: Robbinsville
Street address state: NC
Zip/Postal code: 28771-9461
General Phone: (828) 479-3383
General Fax: (828) 479-1044
General/National Adv. E-mail: ads@grahamstar.com
Editorial e-mail: editor@grahamstar.com
Primary Website: grahamstar.com
Year Established: 1955
Avg Paid Circ: 3500
Avg Free Circ: 24
Audit By: Sworn/Estimate/Non-Audited
Audit Date: 10.06.2019
Personnel: James Budd (Pub); Joel Jenkins (Corp. Mktg. Dir.); Sam Marlow (Ed)
Parent company (for newspapers): Community Newspapers, Inc.

THE HAVELOCK NEWS

Street address 1: 230 Stonebridge Sq
Street address city: Havelock
Street address state: NC
Zip/Postal code: 28532-9505
General Phone: (252) 444-1999
General Fax: (252) 447-0897
General/National Adv. E-mail: taylor.shannon@havenews.com
Display Adv. E-mail: havenews@havenews.com
Editorial e-mail: ken.buday@havenews.com
Primary Website: havenews.com
Year Established: 1986
Avg Paid Circ: 1200
Avg Free Circ: 21
Audit By: Sworn/Estimate/Non-Audited
Audit Date: 10.06.2019
Personnel: Ken Buday (Ed./Gen. Mgr.); Taylor Shannon (Adv. Consult.)
Parent company (for newspapers): Halifax Media

THE HIGHLANDER

Street address 1: 34 N Fifth St
Street address city: Highlands
Street address state: NC
Zip/Postal code: 28741
General Phone: (828) 526-4114
General Fax: (828) 526-3658
Advertising Phone: (828) 526-4114
General/National Adv. E-mail: ads@highlandsnews.com
Display Adv. E-mail: classifieds@highlandsnews.com
Editorial e-mail: editor@highlandsnews.com
Primary Website: highlandsnews.com
Year Established: 1958
Avg Paid Circ: 3500
Avg Free Circ: 60
Audit By: Sworn/Estimate/Non-Audited
Audit Date: 10.06.2019
Personnel: Eric Nesmith (Pub.); Joel Jenkins (Mktg. Dir.)
Parent company (for newspapers): Community Newspapers, Inc.

THE HOME NEWS

Street address 1: 123 E Union St
Street address city: Marshville
Street address state: NC
Zip/Postal code: 28103-1142
General Phone: (704) 624-5068
General Fax: (704) 624-2371
General/National Adv. E-mail: homenewseditor@aol.com
Editorial e-mail: ourhomepaper@gmail.com
Primary Website: https://ourhomepaper.wordpress.com/
Year Established: 1892
Avg Paid Circ: 2850
Audit By: Sworn/Estimate/Non-Audited
Audit Date: 10.06.2019
Personnel: John H. Edmonson (Pub.); Brenda Thomas (Office Mgr.)

THE ISLAND GAZETTE

Street address 1: 1003 Bennet Ln
Street address 2: Ste F
Street address city: Carolina Beach
Street address state: NC
Zip/Postal code: 28428-5770
General Phone: (910) 458-8156
General Fax: (910) 458-0267
General/National Adv. E-mail: islandgazette@aol.com
Editorial e-mail: editor@islandgazette.net
Primary Website: islandgazette.net
Year Established: 1978
Avg Paid Circ: 7000
Avg Free Circ: 325
Audit By: Sworn/Estimate/Non-Audited
Audit Date: 10.06.2019
Personnel: Roger McKee (Pub.); Williard H. Killough (Mng. Ed.)

THE MATTHEWS-MINT HILL

Street address 1: 9506 Monroe Rd
Street address city: Charlotte
Street address state: NC
Zip/Postal code: 28270-1527
General Phone: (704) 849-2261
General Fax: (704) 849-2504
Advertising Phone: (704) 849-2261
General/National Adv. E-mail: adsales@carolinaweeklynewspapers.com
Display Adv. E-mail: brent@cmgweekly.com
Editorial e-mail: mike@matthewsminthillweekly.com
Primary Website: matthewsminthillweekly.com
Year Established: 2007
Avg Paid Circ: 1
Avg Free Circ: 12976
Audit By: VAC
Audit Date: 31.12.2016
Personnel: Justin Vick (Ed.); Kelly Wright (Pub.)
Parent company (for newspapers): Carolina Media Group

THE MEBANE ENTERPRISE

Street address 1: 106 N Fourth St
Street address city: Mebane
Street address state: NC
Zip/Postal code: 27302-2428
General Phone: (919) 563-3555
General Fax: (919) 563-9242
General/National Adv. E-mail: j.brown@mebaneenterprise.com
Display Adv. E-mail: c.manion@mebaneenterprise.com
Editorial e-mail: editor@mebaneenterprise.com
Primary Website: mebaneenterprise.com
Year Established: 1908
Avg Paid Circ: 3100
Avg Free Circ: 81
Audit By: Sworn/Estimate/Non-Audited
Audit Date: 10.06.2019
Personnel: Jackie Brown (Adv./Gen. Mgr.); Karen Carter (Ed.)
Parent company (for newspapers): Womack Publishing Co.

THE MECKLENBURG TIMES

Street address 1: 130 N McDowell St
Street address 2: Ste B
Street address city: Charlotte
Street address state: NC
Zip/Postal code: 28204-2268
General Phone: (704) 247-2900
General Fax: (704) 377-2458
General/National Adv. E-mail: andrea.mounts@nclawyersweekly.com
Editorial e-mail: sharon.roberts@mecktimes.com
Primary Website: mecktimes.com
Year Established: 1923
Avg Paid Circ: 965
Avg Free Circ: 45
Audit By: Sworn/Estimate/Non-Audited
Audit Date: 10.06.2019
Personnel: Paul Fletcher (Pub); Andrea Mounts (Adv. Dir.)
Parent company (for newspapers): BridgeTower Media

THE MESSENGER

Street address 1: 1921 Vance St
Street address city: Reidsville
Street address state: NC
Zip/Postal code: 27320-3254
General Phone: (336) 349-4331
General Fax: (336) 342-2513
General/National Adv. E-mail: karl.miller@greensboro.com
Display Adv. E-mail: karl.miller@greensboro.com
Editorial e-mail: Gerri.Hunt@RockinghamNow.com
Primary Website: rockinghamnow.com
Year Established: 1915
Avg Paid Circ: 4475
Avg Free Circ: 75
Audit By: Sworn/Estimate/Non-Audited
Audit Date: 10.06.2019
Personnel: Gerri Hunt (Mng. Ed.); Karl Miller (Retail Adv. Mgr.)
Parent company (for newspapers): BH Media Group

THE MOUNTAINEER

Street address 1: 220 N Main St
Street address city: Waynesville
Street address state: NC
Zip/Postal code: 28786-3812
General Phone: (828) 452-0661
General Fax: (828) 452-0665
General/National Adv. E-mail: info@themountaineer.com
Editorial e-mail: news@themountaineer.com
Primary Website: http://themountaineer.com
Audit By: Sworn/Estimate/Non-Audited
Audit Date: 10.06.2019
Personnel: Susan DuFour (Adv. Dir.); Vicki Hyatt (Mng. Ed); Jonathan W. Key (Pub.)

THE NASHVILLE GRAPHIC

Street address 1: 203 W Washington St
Street address city: Nashville
Street address state: NC
Zip/Postal code: 27856-1263
General Phone: (252) 459-7101
General Fax: (252) 459-3052
General/National Adv. E-mail: ads@nashvillegraphic.com
Display Adv. E-mail: classifieds@nashvillegraphic.com
Editorial e-mail: news@nashvillegraphic.com
Primary Website: nashvillegraphic.com
Mthly Avg Views: 600000
Mthly Avg Unique Visitors: 14000
Year Established: 1895
Avg Paid Circ: 3328
Avg Free Circ: 3800
Audit By: Sworn/Estimate/Non-Audited
Audit Date: 10.06.2019
Personnel: Jo Anne Cooper (Pub./Adv. Mgr.)

THE NEWS & OBSERVER

Street address 1: 421 Fayetteville Street
Street address 2: Suite 104
Street address city: Raleigh
Street address state: NC
Zip/Postal code: 27601-1331
General Phone: (919) 829-4500
Primary Website: newsobserver.com
Year Established: 1925
Avg Paid Circ: 7
Avg Free Circ: 24416
Audit By: Sworn/Estimate/Non-Audited
Audit Date: 10.06.2019
Personnel: Sara Glines (Pub.); Robyn Tomlin (Ex. Ed.)
Parent company (for newspapers): The News & Observer Publishing Co.

THE NEWS OF ORANGE COUNTY

Street address 1: 109 E King St
Street address city: Hillsborough
Street address state: NC
Zip/Postal code: 27278-2570
General Phone: (919) 732-2171
General Fax: (919) 732-4852
General/National Adv. E-mail: k.coleman@newsoforange.com
Display Adv. E-mail: advertising@newsoforange.com
Editorial e-mail: newsoforangeeditor@yahoo.com
Primary Website: newsoforange.com
Year Established: 1893
Avg Paid Circ: 4200
Audit By: Sworn/Estimate/Non-Audited
Audit Date: 10.06.2019
Personnel: Keith Coleman (Adv./Gen. Mgr); Vanessa Shortley (Ed.)
Parent company (for newspapers): Womack Publishing Co.

THE NEWS REPORTER

Street address 1: 127 W Columbus St
Street address city: Whiteville
Street address state: NC
Zip/Postal code: 28472-4023
General Phone: (910) 642-4104
General Fax: (910) 642-1856
General/National Adv. E-mail: deanlewis@nrcolumbus.com
Display Adv. E-mail: hannerichards@nrcolumbus.com
Editorial e-mail: leshigh@nrcolumbus.com
Primary Website: nrcolumbus.com
Year Established: 1890
Avg Paid Circ: 10100
Avg Free Circ: 235
Audit By: Sworn/Estimate/Non-Audited
Audit Date: 10.06.2019
Personnel: James C. High (Pub/owner); Les High (Ed); Clara Cartrette (Ed.); Barbara Milligan; Clarissa Hamilton; Laura Worthington; Mickey Greer (Adv. Dir.)

THE NEWS-JOURNAL

Street address 1: 119 W Elwood Ave
Street address city: Raeford
Street address state: NC
Zip/Postal code: 28376-2801
General Phone: (910) 875-2121
General Fax: (910) 875-7256
General/National Adv. E-mail: ads@thenews-journal.com
Display Adv. E-mail: wendy@thenews-journal.com
Editorial e-mail: ken@thenews-journal.com
Primary Website: thenews-journal.com
Year Established: 1905
Avg Paid Circ: 3100
Avg Free Circ: 10000
Audit By: Sworn/Estimate/Non-Audited
Audit Date: 10.06.2019
Personnel: Ken MacDonald (Ed.); Sue Ogas (Sales Manager); Ashley Brock (Office Manager)
Parent company (for newspapers): Dickson Press, Inc

THE PILOT

Street address 1: 11 W. Main St.
Street address city: Pilot Mountain
Street address state: NC
Zip/Postal code: 27041
General Phone: (336) 415-4739
General/National Adv. E-mail: pilnews@civitasmedia.com
Primary Website: pilotmountainnews.com
Audit By: Sworn/Estimate/Non-Audited
Audit Date: 10.06.2019
Personnel: Sherry Stanley (Sr. Adv. Rep.); Ron Clausen (Pub.)
Parent company (for newspapers): Adams Publishing Group, LLC

THE PILOT

Street address 1: 145 W Pennsylvania Ave
Street address city: Southern Pines
Street address state: NC
Zip/Postal code: 28387-5428
General Phone: (910) 692-7271
General Fax: (910) 692-9382
Advertising Phone: (919) 693-2505
Editorial Phone: (919) 693-2462
General/National Adv. E-mail: pat@thepilot.com
Display Adv. E-mail: classified@thepilot.com
Editorial e-mail: dsinclair@thepilot.com
Primary Website: thepilot.com
Mthly Avg Views: 1400000
Mthly Avg Unique Visitors: 335000
Year Established: 1920
Avg Paid Circ: 15005
Avg Free Circ: 312
Audit By: Sworn/Estimate/Non-Audited
Audit Date: 10.06.2019
Personnel: David Woronoff (Pub.); Pat Taylor (Adv. Dir); John Nagy (Ed.); Kit McKinley (Gen. Mgr.); Darlene Stark (Circ. Dir.)

THE REIDSVILLE REVIEW

Street address 1: 1921 Vance St

Street address city: Reidsville
Street address state: NC
Zip/Postal code: 27320-3254
General Phone: (336) 349-4331
General Fax: (336) 342-2513
Advertising Phone: (434) 385-5505
Advertising Fax: (336) 342-2513
Editorial Phone: (336) 349-4331
Editorial Fax: (336) 342-2513
General/National Adv. E-mail: pdurham@reidsvillereview.com
Display Adv. E-mail: pdurham@reidsvillereview.com
Classified Adv. e-mail: pdurham@reidsvillereview.com
Editorial e-mail: news@reidsvillereview.com
Primary Website: news-record.com/rockingham_now
Year Established: 1928
Avg Paid Circ: 5195
Sun. Circulation Paid: 5195
Audit By: Sworn/Estimate/Non-Audited
Audit Date: 10.06.2019
Personnel: Steven K. Kaylor (Pub.); Amanda K Lehmert (Ed.); Pam Durham (Ad. Dir)
Parent company (for newspapers): BH Media Group

THE ROANOKE BEACON

Street address 1: 212 W Water St
Street address city: Plymouth
Street address state: NC
Zip/Postal code: 27962-1212
General Phone: (252) 793-2123
General Fax: (252) 793-2123
Advertising Phone: (252) 793-2123
General/National Adv. E-mail: sales@roanokebeacon.com
Display Adv. E-mail: circulation@roanokebeacon.com
Editorial e-mail: news@roanokebeacon.com
Primary Website: roanokebeacon.com
Year Established: 1889
Avg Paid Circ: 2226
Avg Free Circ: 334
Audit By: Sworn/Estimate/Non-Audited
Audit Date: 10.06.2019
Personnel: Mary Wayt (Pub./Ed.)
Parent company (for newspapers): Maypo Media, LLC

THE ROBESONIAN

Street address 1: 2175 N Roberts Ave
Street address city: Lumberton
Street address state: NC
Zip/Postal code: 28358
General Phone: (910) 739-4322
Editorial e-mail: ddouglas@robesonian.com
Primary Website: robesonian.com
Year Established: 1889
Avg Paid Circ: 2300
Audit By: Sworn/Estimate/Non-Audited
Audit Date: 10.06.2019
Personnel: Denise Ward (Pub.); Donnie Douglas (Ed.); Dahlia Hunt (Circ. Mgr.)

THE SMOKY MOUNTAIN TIMES

Street address 1: 1 River St
Street address 2: Ste 3
Street address city: Bryson City
Street address state: NC
Zip/Postal code: 28713-6982
General Phone: (828) 488-2189
General Fax: (828) 488-0315
General/National Adv. E-mail: adrep@thesmokymountaintimes.com
Display Adv. E-mail: classifieds@thesmokymountaintimes.com
Editorial e-mail: news@thesmokymountaintimes.com
Primary Website: thesmokymountaintimes.com
Year Established: 1883
Avg Paid Circ: 3900
Audit By: Sworn/Estimate/Non-Audited
Audit Date: 10.06.2019
Personnel: Ashley Butcher (Publisher); Jessica Webb (Ed.)
Parent company (for newspapers): Community Newspapers, Inc.

THE STANLY NEWS & PRESS

Street address 1: 237 W North St
Street address city: Albemarle
Street address state: NC
Zip/Postal code: 28001-3923
General Phone: (704) 982-2121
General Fax: (704) 986-2627
Advertising Fax: (704) 982-8736
General/National Adv. E-mail: talmond@stanlynewspress.com
Display Adv. E-mail: talmond@stanlynewspress.com
Editorial e-mail: bj@stanlynewspress.com
Primary Website: thesnaponline.com
Year Established: 1880
Avg Paid Circ: 7000
Avg Free Circ: 13000
Audit By: Sworn/Estimate/Non-Audited
Audit Date: 10.06.2019
Personnel: B.J. Drye (Editor); Sandy Selvy (Pub.); Tracey Almond (Adv. Mgr.)
Parent company (for newspapers): Boone Newspapers, Inc.

THE STATE PORT PILOT

Street address 1: 114 E Moore St
Street address city: Southport
Street address state: NC
Zip/Postal code: 28461-3926
General Phone: (910) 457-4568
General Fax: (910) 457-9427
General/National Adv. E-mail: carol@stateportpilot.com
Display Adv. E-mail: kim@stateportpilot.com
Editorial e-mail: morgan@stateportpilot.com
Primary Website: stateportpilot.com
Year Established: 1928
Avg Paid Circ: 7400
Avg Free Circ: 0
Audit By: Sworn/Estimate/Non-Audited
Audit Date: 10.06.2019
Personnel: Morgan Harper (Ed./Pub.); Terry Pope (Associate Editor); Carol Magnani (Adv. Dir.); Jan Keyes; Kim Adams; Morgan Harper
Parent company (for newspapers): The State Port Pilot

THE STOKES NEWS

Street address 1: 122 S Main St
Street address city: King
Street address state: NC
Zip/Postal code: 27021-9011
General Phone: (336) 591-8191
General Fax: (336) 591-4379
Advertising Phone: (336) 779-4036
General/National Adv. E-mail: sstanley@civitasmedia.com
Display Adv. E-mail: cmabe@civitasmedia.com
Primary Website: thestokesnews.com
Year Established: 1872
Avg Paid Circ: 8400
Avg Free Circ: 21
Audit By: Sworn/Estimate/Non-Audited
Audit Date: 10.06.2019
Personnel: Anna Holcomb (Office Mgr.); Amanda Dodson (Ed.); Robert Money (Sports Ed.)
Parent company (for newspapers): Champion Media

THE SYLVA HERALD & RURALITE

Street address 1: 539 W Main St
Street address city: Sylva
Street address state: NC
Zip/Postal code: 28779-5551
General Phone: (828) 586-2611
General Fax: (828) 586-2637
Advertising Phone: (866) 572-3150
General/National Adv. E-mail: margo@thesylvaherald.com
Display Adv. E-mail: classifieds@thesylvaherald.com
Editorial e-mail: news@thesylvaherald.com
Primary Website: thesylvaherald.com
Year Established: 1926
Avg Paid Circ: 7300
Avg Free Circ: 42
Audit By: Sworn/Estimate/Non-Audited
Audit Date: 10.06.2019
Personnel: Steven B. Gray (Pub.); Margo Gray (Adv. Mgr.); Lynn Hotaling (Ed.); Joel Jenkins (Corp. Mktg. Dir.)

THE TAYLORSVILLE TIMES

Street address 1: 24 E Main Ave
Street address city: Taylorsville
Street address state: NC
Zip/Postal code: 28681-2541
General Phone: (828) 632-2532
General Fax: (828) 632-8233
General/National Adv. E-mail: ads@taylorsvilletimes.com
Display Adv. E-mail: classifieds@taylorsvilletimes.com
Editorial e-mail: taylorsvilletimes@taylorsvilletimes.com
Primary Website: taylorsvilletimes.com
Year Established: 1886
Avg Paid Circ: 5002
Avg Free Circ: 49
Audit By: Sworn/Estimate/Non-Audited
Audit Date: 10.06.2019
Personnel: Lee Sharpe (Pub.); Micah Henry (Ed.); Steve Garland (Adv. Mgr.)

THE TIMES-LEADER

Street address 1: 574 E. Third Street
Street address city: Ayden
Street address state: NC
Zip/Postal code: 28513
General Phone: (252) 746-6261
General/National Adv. E-mail: lsimonds@ncweeklies.com
Primary Website: facebook.com/timesleader.newspaper
Mthly Avg Views: 1912
Year Established: 1912
Avg Paid Circ: 2200
Audit By: Sworn/Estimate/Non-Audited
Audit Date: 10.06.2019
Personnel: Lindsey Simonds
Parent company (for newspapers): CNHI, LLC; Cooke Communications North Carolina, LLC

THE TRANSYLVANIA TIMES

Street address 1: 37 N Broad St
Street address city: Brevard
Street address state: NC
Zip/Postal code: 28712-3725
General Phone: (828) 883-8156
General Fax: (828) 883-8158
General/National Adv. E-mail: shirsh@transylvaniatimes.com
Display Adv. E-mail: classifieds@transylvaniatimes.com
Editorial e-mail: info@transylvaniatimes.com
Primary Website: transylvaniatimes.com
Year Established: 1887
Avg Paid Circ: 8200
Avg Free Circ: 80
Audit By: Sworn/Estimate/Non-Audited
Audit Date: 10.06.2019
Personnel: Stella A. Trapp (Pub.); John Connelly (Adv. Exec.); John Lanier (Ed.)
Parent company (for newspapers): CNHI

THE TRIBUNE

Street address 1: 214 E Main St
Street address city: Elkin
Street address state: NC
Zip/Postal code: 28621-3431
General Phone: (336) 835-1513
General Fax: (336) 835-8742
General/National Adv. E-mail: hlamm@elkintribune.com
Editorial e-mail: wbyerly-wood@elkintribune.com
Primary Website: elkintribune.com
Year Established: 1911
Avg Paid Circ: 6000
Audit By: Sworn/Estimate/Non-Audited
Audit Date: 10.06.2019
Personnel: Wendy Wood (Content Mgr./Ed.); Holly Lamm (Sr. Ad. Rep); Beanie Taylor (Staff Reporter); Kristian Russell (Staff Report); Dawn Bagale (Customer Service Rep); Scott Belcher (Advertising Rep); Sandy Hurley (Publisher)

THE UNION COUNTY WEEKLY

Street address 1: 9506 Monroe Rd
Street address city: Charlotte
Street address state: NC
Zip/Postal code: 28270-1527
General Phone: (704) 849-2261
General Fax: (704) 849-2504
General/National Adv. E-mail: adrian@cmgweekly.com
Display Adv. E-mail: rjensen@cmgweekly.com
Editorial e-mail: justin@cmgweekly.com
Primary Website: unioncountyweekly.com
Year Established: 2005
Avg Free Circ: 18417
Audit By: CVC
Audit Date: 03.07.2019
Personnel: Jonathon McElvy (Pres.); Adrian Garson (Pub.); Justin Vick (Ed.)
Parent company (for newspapers): Carolina Media Group

THE WAKE WEEKLY

Street address 1: 229 E Owen Ave
Street address city: Wake Forest
Street address state: NC
Zip/Postal code: 27587-2717
General Phone: (919) 556-3182
General Fax: (919) 556-2233
General/National Adv. E-mail: advertising@wakeweekly.com
Display Adv. E-mail: classifieds@wakeweekly.com
Editorial e-mail: editor@wakeweekly.com
Primary Website: wakeweekly.com
Year Established: 1947
Avg Paid Circ: 8900
Audit By: Sworn/Estimate/Non-Audited
Audit Date: 10.06.2019
Personnel: Clellie Allen (Ed./Assit. Pub.); Todd F. Allen (Pub.); Kathleen Jackson (Ad. Dir.); Al Merritt (Prod. Mgr.)

THE WEAVERVILLE TRIBUNE

Street address 1: 113 N Main St
Street address city: Weaverville
Street address state: NC
Zip/Postal code: 28787-8444
General Phone: (828) 252-5804
Advertising Phone: (828) 252-5804
Editorial Phone: (828) 252-5804
Editorial Fax: (828) 252-5817
General/National Adv. E-mail: starnesp@att.net
Display Adv. E-mail: advertising@weavervilletribune.com
Editorial e-mail: editor@weavervilletribune.com
Primary Website: weavervilletribune.com
Year Established: 2003
Audit By: Sworn/Estimate/Non-Audited
Audit Date: 10.06.2019
Personnel: Clint Parker (Pub./Ed.); Pat Starnes (Adv. Dir.)

THE WILKES JOURNAL-PATRIOT

Street address 1: 711 Main St
Street address city: North Wilkesboro
Street address state: NC
Zip/Postal code: 28659-4211
General Phone: (336) 838-4117
General Fax: (336) 838-9864
General/National Adv. E-mail: narchibald@journalpatriot.com
Display Adv. E-mail: wjpads@wilkes.net
Editorial e-mail: wilkesjp@wilkes.net
Primary Website: journalpatriot.com
Year Established: 1906
Avg Paid Circ: 11000
Audit By: Sworn/Estimate/Non-Audited
Audit Date: 10.06.2019
Personnel: Nellie Archibald (Adv. Mgr.); Debby Church (Circ. Mgr.); Jule Hubbard (Pub.)

THE YADKIN RIPPLE

Street address 1: 115 S Jackson St
Street address city: Yadkinville
Street address state: NC
Zip/Postal code: 27055-7714
General Phone: (336) 679-2341
General Fax: (336) 679-2340
Advertising Phone: (336) 258-4030
Editorial Phone: (336) 258-4035
General/National Adv. E-mail: hlamm@civitasmedia.com
Display Adv. E-mail: kball@civitasmedia.com
Editorial e-mail: wbyerly-wood@civitasmedia.com
Primary Website: yadkinripple.com
Year Established: 1892
Avg Paid Circ: 6000
Avg Free Circ: 40
Audit By: Sworn/Estimate/Non-Audited
Audit Date: 10.06.2019
Personnel: Holly Lamm (Gen. Mgr.); Ron Clausen (Pub.)

Parent company (for newspapers): Champion Media

THOMASVILLE TIMES

Street address 1: 213 Woodbine St
Street address city: High Point
Street address state: NC
Zip/Postal code: 27260-8339
General Phone: (336) 888-3590
General Fax: (336) 888-3632
General/National Adv. E-mail: aduncan@hpenews.com
Display Adv. E-mail: classified@hpenews.com
Editorial e-mail: editor@tvilletimes.com
Primary Website: tvilletimes.com
Year Established: 1890
Avg Paid Circ: 5500
Avg Free Circ: 334
Audit By: Sworn/Estimate/Non-Audited
Audit Date: 10.06.2019
Personnel: John McClure (Adv. Mgr.); Donte Owens (Circ. Mgr.)
Parent company (for newspapers): Paxton Media Group

TIDELAND NEWS

Street address 1: 774 W Corbett Ave
Street address city: Swansboro
Street address state: NC
Zip/Postal code: 28584-8452
General Phone: (910) 326-5066
General Fax: (910) 326-1165
General/National Adv. E-mail: jennifer@tidelandnews.com
Display Adv. E-mail: michelle@tidelandnews.com
Editorial e-mail: jimmy@tidelandnews.com
Primary Website: tidelandnews.com
Year Established: 1979
Avg Paid Circ: 3000
Avg Free Circ: 500
Audit By: Sworn/Estimate/Non-Audited
Audit Date: 10.06.2019
Personnel: Walter Phillips (Pub.); Jennifer Pearce (Adv. Mgr.)
Parent company (for newspapers): Carteret Publishing Co.

TRIANGLE BUSINESS JOURNAL

Street address 1: 3515 Glenwood Avenue
Street address 2: Suite 220
Street address city: Raleigh
Street address state: NC
Zip/Postal code: 27612
General Phone: (919) 327-1000
General Fax: (919) 790-6885
Editorial Phone: (919) 327-1020
General/National Adv. E-mail: triangle@bizjournals.com
Display Adv. E-mail: rbirdwell@bizjournals.com
Editorial e-mail: sougata@bizjournals.com
Primary Website: bizjournals.com/triangle
Year Established: 1985
Audit By: Sworn/Estimate/Non-Audited
Audit Date: 10.06.2019
Personnel: Jason Christie (Publisher); Sougata Mukherjee (Editor in Chief); Dane Huffman (Managing Editor); Courtney Bode (Advertising Director); Heather Rodgers (Adv.); Saleeby Caroline (Events Director); Sophia Palles (Adv.)
Parent company (for newspapers): American City Business Journals

UP & COMING WEEKLY

Street address 1: 208 Rowan St
Street address city: Fayetteville
Street address state: NC
Zip/Postal code: 28301-4922
General Phone: (910) 484-6200
General Fax: (910) 484-9218
General/National Adv. E-mail: bbowman@upandcomingweekly.com
Display Adv. E-mail: bbowman@upandcomingweekly.com
Editorial e-mail: bbowman@upandcomingweekly.com
Primary Website: upandcomingweekly.com
Year Established: 1996
Avg Paid Circ: 0
Avg Free Circ: 8648
Audit By: CVC
Audit Date: 30.09.2017
Personnel: Bill Bowman (Pub./Adv. Mgr.); Joy G. Crowe (Associate Pub.); Janice Burton (Associate Pub.); Sam Lum (Mktg. Mgr.); Jean Bolton (Vice Pres., Opns.); Laurel Handforth (Circ. Mgr); Mary Beth Leiby (Mktg. Rep.); Tracy McCullough (Office Mgr.)

WARREN RECORD

Street address 1: 112 N Main St
Street address city: Warrenton
Street address state: NC
Zip/Postal code: 27589-1922
General Phone: (252) 257-3341
General Fax: (252) 257-1413
General/National Adv. E-mail: ads@warrenrecord.com
Editorial e-mail: news@warrenrecord.com
Primary Website: warrenrecord.com
Year Established: 1896
Avg Paid Circ: 5600
Avg Free Circ: 113
Audit By: Sworn/Estimate/Non-Audited
Audit Date: 10.06.2019
Personnel: Jennifer Harris (Ed./Gen. Mgr.); Luci Weldon (Asst. Ed.); Brandy Carter (Office Mgr.)
Parent company (for newspapers): Womack Publishing Co.

WATAUGA DEMOCRAT

Street address 1: 474 Industrial Park Dr
Street address city: Boone
Street address state: NC
Zip/Postal code: 28607-3937
General Phone: (828) 264-3612
General Fax: (828) 262-0282
General/National Adv. E-mail: charlie.price@mountaintimes.com
Display Adv. E-mail: classifieds@mountaintimes.com
Editorial e-mail: community@wataugademocrat.com
Primary Website: wataugademocrat.com
Year Established: 1888
Avg Paid Circ: 3800
Avg Free Circ: 296
Audit By: Sworn/Estimate/Non-Audited
Audit Date: 10.06.2019
Personnel: Gene Fowler (Pub.); Andy Gainey (Circ. Mgr.); Tom Mayer (Ed.); Charlie Price (Adv. Dir.)
Parent company (for newspapers): Adams Publishing Group, LLC

WEEKLY GAZETTE

Street address 1: 108 S Caswell St
Street address city: La Grange
Street address state: NC
Zip/Postal code: 28551-1794
General Phone: (252) 521-2065
General Fax: (252) 566-5318
General/National Adv. E-mail: theweeklygazette@embarqmail.com
Primary Website: facebook.com/The-Weekly-Gazette-246109135408722/?ref=page_internal
Avg Paid Circ: 1500
Avg Free Circ: 25
Audit By: Sworn/Estimate/Non-Audited
Audit Date: 10.06.2019
Personnel: Glenn Penuel (Ed.)

YANCEY COMMON TIMES JOURNAL

Street address 1: 22 N Main St
Street address city: Burnsville
Street address state: NC
Zip/Postal code: 28714-2925
General Phone: (828) 682-2120
General Fax: (828) 682-3701
General/National Adv. E-mail: pat@yanceypaper.com
Editorial e-mail: jody@yanceypaper.com
Primary Website: yanceytimesjournal.com
Audit By: Sworn/Estimate/Non-Audited
Audit Date: 10.06.2019
Personnel: Jody Higgins (Pub./Ed.); Pat Randolph (Pub./ Adv. Dir.); Audria Briggs (Circ. Mgr.)
Parent company (for newspapers): Trib Publications

YES! WEEKLY

Street address 1: 5500 Adams Farm Ln
Street address 2: Ste 204
Street address city: Greensboro
Street address state: NC
Zip/Postal code: 27407-7059
General Phone: (336) 316-1231
General Fax: (336) 316-1930
General/National Adv. E-mail: publisher@yesweekly.com
Display Adv. E-mail: publisher@yesweekly.com
Editorial e-mail: katie@yesweekly.com
Primary Website: yesweekly.com
Mthly Avg Views: 850000
Mthly Avg Unique Visitors: 65000
Year Established: 2005
Avg Free Circ: 20000
Audit By: Sworn/Estimate/Non-Audited
Audit Date: 10.06.2019
Parent company (for newspapers): Womack Newspapers, Inc

NORTH DAKOTA

ADAMS COUNTY RECORD

Street address 1: 116 S Main St
Street address city: Hettinger
Street address state: ND
Zip/Postal code: 58639-7031
General Phone: (701) 567-2424
General Fax: (701) 567-2425
General/National Adv. E-mail: adamscountyrecord@countrymedia.net
Display Adv. E-mail: adamscountyrecord@countrymedia.net
Primary Website: adamscountyextra.com
Avg Paid Circ: 1232
Audit By: Sworn/Estimate/Non-Audited
Audit Date: 10.06.2019
Personnel: Cole Benz (Ed.); Stacy Swenson (Pub.); Jayden Ragsdale (Off. Mgr.); Patricia Lewton (Ad. Mgr.)
Parent company (for newspapers): Country Media Inc.; Country Media

ADVERTIZER

Street address 1: 1815 1st St W
Street address city: Dickinson
Street address state: ND
Zip/Postal code: 58601-2463
General Phone: (701) 225-8111
General Fax: (701) 225-4205
Advertising Phone: (701) 456-1220
Editorial Phone: (701) 456-1205
Editorial Fax: (701) 225-6653
General/National Adv. E-mail: reilts@thedickinsonpress.com
Display Adv. E-mail: ssacks@thedickinsonpress.com
Editorial e-mail: DMonke@thedickinsonpress.com
Primary Website: thedickinsonpress.com
Year Established: 1980
Avg Free Circ: 25848
Audit By: Sworn/Estimate/Non-Audited
Audit Date: 10.06.2019
Personnel: Harvey Brock (Pub.); John Hodges (Cir. Mgr.); Bob Carruth (Adv. Dir.); Dustin Monke (Mng. Ed.); Joy Schoch (Bus. Mgr.)
Parent company (for newspapers): Forum Communications Co.

ANETA STAR

Street address 1: 122 Main St N
Street address city: Fordville
Street address state: ND
Zip/Postal code: 58231-3134
General Phone: (701) 229-3641
General Fax: (701) 229-3217
General/National Adv. E-mail: nesspres@polarcomm.com
Year Established: 1951
Avg Paid Circ: 350
Audit By: Sworn/Estimate/Non-Audited
Audit Date: 10.06.2019
Personnel: Truman Ness (Ad. / Cir.); Ness Press (Pub. / Ed.)

BENSON COUNTY FARMERS PRESS

Street address 1: 120 B Ave N
Street address 2: 120 B Ave N
Street address city: Minnewaukan
Street address state: ND
Zip/Postal code: 58348
General Phone: (701) 473-5436
General Fax: (701) 473-5736
General/National Adv. E-mail: farmerspress@gondtc.com
Display Adv. E-mail: farmerspress@gondtc.com
Classified Adv. e-mail: farmerspress@gondtc.com
Editorial e-mail: farmerspress@gondtc.com
Primary Website: www.bensoncountynews.com
Year Established: 1884
Avg Paid Circ: 1659
Avg Free Circ: 50
Audit By: Sworn/Estimate/Non-Audited
Audit Date: 10.06.2019
Personnel: Denise Westad (Owner/Pub.)
Parent company (for newspapers): Consolidated Newspapers Inc.

BEULAH BEACON

Street address 1: 324 2nd Ave NE
Street address city: Beulah
Street address state: ND
Zip/Postal code: 58523-6613
General Phone: (701) 873-4381
General Fax: (701) 873-2383
General/National Adv. E-mail: coalnews@westriv.com
Primary Website: bhgnews.com
Avg Paid Circ: 2000
Avg Free Circ: 81
Audit By: Sworn/Estimate/Non-Audited
Audit Date: 10.06.2019
Personnel: Mike Gackle (Pub., Owner); Ken Beauchamp (Adv. Mgr., Gen. Mgr.); Kate Johnson (Ed.)
Parent company (for newspapers): BHG, Inc.

BOTTINEAU COURANT

Street address 1: 419 Main St
Street address city: Bottineau
Street address state: ND
Zip/Postal code: 58318-1229
General Phone: (701) 228-2605
General Fax: (701) 228-5864
General/National Adv. E-mail: courant3@utma.com
Display Adv. E-mail: courant4@utma.com
Editorial e-mail: courant@utma.com
Primary Website: bottineaunewspaper.com
Avg Paid Circ: 3000
Audit By: Sworn/Estimate/Non-Audited
Audit Date: 10.06.2019

BOWMAN COUNTY PIONEER

Street address 1: 203 7th Ave NW
Street address 2: 7th Ave NW
Street address city: Bowman
Street address state: ND
Zip/Postal code: 58623-4443
General Phone: (701) 523-5623
General Fax: (701) 523-3441
Advertising Phone: (701) 523-5623
General/National Adv. E-mail: finderads@countrymedia.net
Display Adv. E-mail: pioneerinfo@countrymedia.net
Editorial e-mail: cbenz@countrymedia.net
Primary Website: bowmanextra.com
Year Established: 1907
Avg Paid Circ: 1300
Avg Free Circ: 300
Audit By: ODC
Audit Date: 08.10.2017
Personnel: Frank Perea II (Pub.); Cole Benz (Ed.)
Parent company (for newspapers): Country Media Inc.

BURKE COUNTY TRIBUNE

Street address 1: 104 Railway St. SE
Street address city: Bowbells
Street address state: ND
Zip/Postal code: 58721
General Phone: (701) 377-2626
General Fax: (701) 377-2717
General/National Adv. E-mail: tribune@nccray.net
Primary Website: online.burkecountytribune.com
Year Established: 1899
Avg Paid Circ: 900
Avg Free Circ: 30
Audit By: Sworn/Estimate/Non-Audited
Audit Date: 10.06.2019

Personnel: Kristi Bohl (Pub.); Lyann Olson (office manager); Michelle Redmer (secretary)

CARSON PRESS

Street address 1: 119 N MAIN ST
Street address city: Elgin
Street address state: ND
Zip/Postal code: 58533
General Phone: (701) 584-2900
General Fax: (701) 584-2900
General/National Adv. E-mail: gcn@westriv.com
Primary Website: carsonpressnewspaper.com
Avg Paid Circ: 1000
Audit By: Sworn/Estimate/Non-Audited
Audit Date: 10.06.2019
Personnel: Dianne Mutschelknaus (Cir. Mgr.); Jill Friesz (Ed.)

CASS COUNTY REPORTER

Street address 1: 122 6th Ave N
Street address city: Casselton
Street address state: ND
Zip/Postal code: 58012-3232
General Phone: (701) 347-4493
General Fax: (701) 347-4495
General/National Adv. E-mail: ads@ccreporter.com
Editorial e-mail: news@ccreporter.com
Primary Website: ccreporter.com
Year Established: 1880
Avg Paid Circ: 2600
Audit By: Sworn/Estimate/Non-Audited
Audit Date: 10.06.2019
Personnel: Sean W. Kelly (Pub./Ed.); Trish Priewe (Front Off.); Randy Buntrock (Cir. Mgr.); Angela Kolden (Reporter); Retta Roach (Advertising); Megan Peterson (Graphic Design); Jacqueline Baarstad (Adv. Mgr.); Angela Ecklund (Graphic Designer)

CAVALIER COUNTY REPUBLICAN

Street address 1: 618 3rd St
Street address city: Langdon
Street address state: ND
Zip/Postal code: 58249-2622
General Phone: (701) 256-5311
General Fax: (701) 256-5841
General/National Adv. E-mail: ccr@utma.com
Primary Website: cavaliercountyextra.com
Year Established: 1888
Avg Paid Circ: 1800
Audit By: Sworn/Estimate/Non-Audited
Audit Date: 10.06.2019
Personnel: Lori Peterson (Cir. Mgr.); Melissa Anderson
Parent company (for newspapers): Country Media Inc.

CENTER REPUBLICAN

Street address 1: 324 2nd Ave NE
Street address city: Beulah
Street address state: ND
Zip/Postal code: 58523-6613
General Phone: (701) 748-2255
General Fax: (701) 748-5768
General/National Adv. E-mail: star@westriv.com
Editorial e-mail: coalnews@westriv.com
Primary Website: bhgnews.com
Avg Paid Circ: 555
Avg Free Circ: 18
Audit By: Sworn/Estimate/Non-Audited
Audit Date: 10.06.2019
Personnel: Annette Tait (Ed.)
Parent company (for newspapers): BHG, Inc.

DICKEY COUNTY LEADER

Street address 1: 216 Main Ave
Street address city: Ellendale
Street address state: ND
Zip/Postal code: 58436
General Phone: (701) 349-3222
General Fax: (701) 349-3229
General/National Adv. E-mail: dcleader@drtel.net
Avg Paid Circ: 1200
Audit By: Sworn/Estimate/Non-Audited
Audit Date: 10.06.2019
Personnel: Jason Nordmark (Pub.); Roberta Johnson (Ed.)
Parent company (for newspapers): Nordmark Publishing

DUNN COUNTY HERALD

Street address 1: 26 Central Ave S
Street address city: Killdeer
Street address state: ND
Zip/Postal code: 58640-4000
General Phone: (701) 764-5312
General Fax: (701) 764-5049
General/National Adv. E-mail: dcherald@countrymedia.net
Primary Website: dunncountyextra.com
Avg Paid Circ: 1334
Audit By: Sworn/Estimate/Non-Audited
Audit Date: 10.06.2019
Personnel: Carol Hicks (Office Mgr)
Parent company (for newspapers): Country Media Inc.

EDGELEY MAIL

Street address 1: 516 MAIN ST
Street address city: Edgeley
Street address state: ND
Zip/Postal code: 58433
General Phone: (701) 493-2261
General/National Adv. E-mail: advertising@drtel.net
Display Adv. E-mail: classifieds@drtel.net
Editorial e-mail: edgeleymail@drtel.net
Primary Website: edgeleynd.com
Avg Paid Circ: 1000
Audit By: Sworn/Estimate/Non-Audited
Audit Date: 10.06.2019
Personnel: Tausha Dide (Circ. Mgr.); Patty Wood Bartle (Ed.)

EDMORE HERALD

Street address 1: 122 Main St N
Street address city: Fordville
Street address state: ND
Zip/Postal code: 58231-3134
General Phone: (701) 229-3641
General Fax: (701) 229-3217
General/National Adv. E-mail: nesspres@polarcomm.com
Year Established: 1960
Avg Paid Circ: 245
Audit By: Sworn/Estimate/Non-Audited
Audit Date: 10.06.2019
Personnel: Gunnard Ness (Pub.); Truman Ness (Ed.)

EMMONS COUNTY RECORD

Street address 1: 201 N Broadway St
Street address city: Linton
Street address state: ND
Zip/Postal code: 58552-7020
General Phone: (701) 254-4537
General Fax: (701) 254-4909
General/National Adv. E-mail: info@lintonnd.com
Editorial e-mail: info@lintonnd.com
Primary Website: ecrecord.com
Year Established: 1884
Avg Paid Circ: 3012
Avg Free Circ: 163
Audit By: Sworn/Estimate/Non-Audited
Audit Date: 10.06.2019
Personnel: Leah P. Burke (Publisher/Editor); Julie Brandner (Adv. Mgr.); Allan C. Burke (Pub. Emeritus)

ENDERLIN INDEPENDENT

Street address 1: 209 4th Ave
Street address city: Enderlin
Street address state: ND
Zip/Postal code: 58027-1300
General Phone: (701) 437-3131
General/National Adv. E-mail: enderlinindependent@mlgc.com
Primary Website: enderlinindependent.com
Avg Paid Circ: 1100
Audit By: Sworn/Estimate/Non-Audited
Audit Date: 10.06.2019
Personnel: Art Hagebock (Pub.); Diane Hagebock (Pub.)

FORDVILLE TRI-COUNTY SUN

Street address 1: 122 Main St N
Street address city: Fordville
Street address state: ND
Zip/Postal code: 58231-3134
General Phone: (701) 229-3641
General Fax: (701) 229-3217
General/National Adv. E-mail: nesspres@polarcomm.com
Year Established: 1922
Avg Paid Circ: 500
Audit By: Sworn/Estimate/Non-Audited
Audit Date: 10.06.2019
Personnel: Truman Ness (Ed.); Ness Press (Pub. / Ed.)

FOSTER COUNTY INDEPENDENT

Street address 1: 1191 Main St
Street address city: Carrington
Street address state: ND
Zip/Postal code: 58421-1523
General Phone: (701) 652-3181
General Fax: (701) 652-3286
General/National Adv. E-mail: fosterconews@daktel.com
Primary Website: fostercountyindependent.com
Year Established: 1883
Avg Paid Circ: 3000
Audit By: Sworn/Estimate/Non-Audited
Audit Date: 10.06.2019
Personnel: Pattie Stock (Circ. Mgr.); Allen Stock (Ed.)

GLEN ULLIN TIMES

Street address 1: 105 B St S
Street address city: Glen Ullin
Street address state: ND
Zip/Postal code: 58631-7110
General Phone: (701) 348-3325
General Fax: (701) 348-3325
General/National Adv. E-mail: gutimes@westriv.com
Primary Website: glenullintimes.com
Year Established: 1904
Avg Paid Circ: 1000
Avg Free Circ: 50
Audit By: Sworn/Estimate/Non-Audited
Audit Date: 10.06.2019
Personnel: Nancy Bittner (Pub. / Ed.)

GRIGGS COUNTY COURIER

Street address 1: 809 Burrel Ave NW
Street address city: Cooperstown
Street address state: ND
Zip/Postal code: 58425-7106
General Phone: (701) 797-3331
General Fax: (701) 797-3476
General/National Adv. E-mail: calbert@ncppub.com
Display Adv. E-mail: calbert@ncppub.com
Editorial e-mail: chetland@ncppub.com
Year Established: 1883
Avg Paid Circ: 1600
Avg Free Circ: 106
Audit By: Sworn/Estimate/Non-Audited
Audit Date: 10.06.2019
Personnel: Nicole Henton (Off. Mgr.); Caitlin Hetland (Ed.); Catherine Albert (Ad. Mgr.)
Parent company (for newspapers): New Century Press

HATTON FREE PRESS

Street address 1: 122 MAIN ST N
Street address city: Fordville
Street address state: ND
Zip/Postal code: 58231
General Phone: (701) 229-3641
General Fax: (701) 229-3217
General/National Adv. E-mail: nesspres@polarcomm.com
Year Established: 1910
Avg Paid Circ: 358
Audit By: Sworn/Estimate/Non-Audited
Audit Date: 10.06.2019
Personnel: Truman Ness (Ed.); Ness Press (Pub. / Ed.)

HEBRON HERALD

Street address 1: 102 S Park St
Street address city: Hebron
Street address state: ND
Zip/Postal code: 58638-0009
General Phone: (701) 878-4494
General Fax: (701) 878-4498
General/National Adv. E-mail: hherald@westriv.com
Year Established: 1898
Avg Paid Circ: 950
Avg Free Circ: 50
Audit By: Sworn/Estimate/Non-Audited
Audit Date: 26.09.2022
Personnel: Jane Brandt (Pub. / Ed.)

HILLSBORO BANNER

Street address 1: 20 W Caledonia Ave
Street address city: Hillsboro
Street address state: ND
Zip/Postal code: 58045-4205
General Phone: (701) 636-4241
General Fax: (701) 636-4245
General/National Adv. E-mail: hbanner@rrv.net
Primary Website: hillsborobanner.com
Year Established: 1879
Avg Paid Circ: 1350
Audit By: Sworn/Estimate/Non-Audited
Audit Date: 10.06.2019
Personnel: Cheryl Kelly (Pub.); Shawn Kelly (Pub.); Alyssa Short (Cir. Mgr.); Cole Short (Ed.)

KULM MESSENGER

Street address 1: 6 MAIN AVE S
Street address city: Kulm
Street address state: ND
Zip/Postal code: 58456
General Phone: (701) 647-2411
General Fax: (701) 647-2398
General/National Adv. E-mail: kulm@drtel.net
Avg Paid Circ: 900
Avg Free Circ: 37
Audit By: Sworn/Estimate/Non-Audited
Audit Date: 10.06.2019
Personnel: Art Hagebock (Pub.); Diane Hagebock (Pub.)

LA MOURE CHRONICLE

Street address 1: 20 1ST ST SW
Street address city: Lamoure
Street address state: ND
Zip/Postal code: 58458
General Phone: (701) 883-5393
General Fax: (701) 883-5076
General/National Adv. E-mail: chronicle@drtel.net
Avg Paid Circ: 2456
Avg Free Circ: 15
Audit By: Sworn/Estimate/Non-Audited
Audit Date: 10.06.2019
Personnel: Art Hagebock (Pub.); Diane Hagebock (Pub. / Cir. Mgr.)

LAKE METIGOSHE MIRROR

Street address 1: 11 1st Ave NE
Street address city: Rolla
Street address state: ND
Zip/Postal code: 58367-7125
General Phone: (866)476-5253
General Fax: (701)477-3182
Advertising Phone: (701) 477-6495
General/National Adv. E-mail: metigosh@utma.com
Year Established: 2005
Audit By: Sworn/Estimate/Non-Audited
Audit Date: 10.06.2019
Personnel: Jason Nordmark; Holly Cammack (Bus. Mgr.); Alvin LaFromboise (Cir. Mgr.); Jenee Munro (Adv. Mgr.)

LAKOTA AMERICAN

Street address 1: 120 Main St
Street address city: Lakota
Street address state: ND
Zip/Postal code: 58344-0507
General Phone: (701)247-2482
General Fax: (701)247-2483
General/National Adv. E-mail: lamerican@polarcomm.com
Display Adv. E-mail: lamerican@polarcomm.com
Classified Adv. e-mail: lamerican@polarcomm.com
Editorial e-mail: lamerican@polarcomm.com
Primary Website: www.bensoncountynews.com
Year Established: 1901
Avg Paid Circ: 801
Avg Free Circ: 10
Audit By: Sworn/Estimate/Non-Audited
Audit Date: 10.06.2019
Personnel: Denise Westad (Pub.); Sara Plum (Ed.)

Parent company (for newspapers): Consolidated Newspapers Inc.

LARIMORE LEADER-TRIBUNE

Street address 1: 2802 15th St S
Street address 2: Unit C
Street address city: Fargo
Street address state: ND
Zip/Postal code: 58103-5958
General Phone: (701) 478-0277
General Fax: (701) 478-0287
Advertising Phone: (701) 478-0277
Advertising Fax: (701) 478-0287
Editorial Phone: (701) 478-0277
Editorial Fax: (701) 478-0287
General/National Adv. E-mail: larimoreleader@cableone.net
Display Adv. E-mail: larimoreleader@cableone.net
Classified Adv. e-mail: larimoreleader@cableone.net
Editorial e-mail: larimoreleader@cableone.net
Year Established: 1969
Avg Paid Circ: 525
Avg Free Circ: 25
Audit By: Sworn/Estimate/Non-Audited
Audit Date: 10.06.2019
Personnel: Marvin Ness (Ed/Mgr.)
Parent company (for newspapers): Ness Press, Inc.

LEADER-NEWS

Street address 1: 607 Main Avenue
Street address city: Washburn
Street address state: ND
Zip/Postal code: 58577
General Phone: (701) 462-8126
General Fax: (701)462-8128
General/National Adv. E-mail: bhgnews@westriv.com
Editorial e-mail: leadernews@westriv.com
Primary Website: bhgnews.com
Avg Paid Circ: 1735
Avg Free Circ: 55
Audit By: Sworn/Estimate/Non-Audited
Audit Date: 10.06.2019
Personnel: Don Winter (Ed.); Alyssa Meier (Editor)
Parent company (for newspapers): BHG, Inc.

LEADER-TRIBUNE

Street address 1: 122 Main St N
Street address city: Fordville
Street address state: ND
Zip/Postal code: 58231-3134
General Phone: (701) 229-3641
General Fax: (701) 229-3217
General/National Adv. E-mail: nesspres@polarcomm.com
Year Established: 1978
Avg Paid Circ: 525
Audit By: Sworn/Estimate/Non-Audited
Audit Date: 10.06.2019
Personnel: Gunnard Ness (Pub.); Truman Ness (Ed.)

MANDAN NEWS

Street address 1: 414 W Main St
Street address city: Mandan
Street address state: ND
Zip/Postal code: 58554-3145
General Phone: (701) 250-8250
General Fax: (701) 223-2063
Advertising Phone: (701) 250-8805
Editorial Phone: (701) 250-8250
Editorial e-mail: editor@mandan-news.com
Primary Website: mandan-news.com
Year Established: 1976
Avg Paid Circ: 1900
Audit By: Sworn/Estimate/Non-Audited
Audit Date: 10.06.2019
Personnel: Sandra Fettig (Copy Ed.); Gary Adkisson (Pub); Steve Wallick (Ed)
Parent company (for newspapers): Dispatch-Argus

MCCLUSKY GAZETTE

Street address 1: 203 Main St
Street address city: McClusky
Street address state: ND
Zip/Postal code: 58463
General Phone: (701) 363-2492
General Fax: (701) 363-2698
General/National Adv. E-mail: gazette@westriv.com
Primary Website: nd-bhginc.com
Avg Paid Circ: 900
Avg Free Circ: 50
Audit By: Sworn/Estimate/Non-Audited
Audit Date: 10.06.2019
Personnel: Allan Tinker (Editor/Office Supervisor); Betty Jean Dockter (Ad Manager)
Parent company (for newspapers): BHG, Inc.

MCKENZIE COUNTY FARMER

Street address 1: 109 N Main St
Street address city: Watford City
Street address state: ND
Zip/Postal code: 58854-7101
General Phone: (701) 842-2351
General Fax: (701) 842-2352
General/National Adv. E-mail: ads@watfordcitynd.com
Display Adv. E-mail: ads@watfordcitynd.com
Editorial e-mail: mcf@watfordcitynd.com
Primary Website: watfordcitynd.com
Year Established: 1908
Avg Paid Circ: 2200
Avg Free Circ: 26
Audit By: Sworn/Estimate/Non-Audited
Audit Date: 10.06.2021
Personnel: Neal A. Shipman (Publisher/Editor)

MCLEAN COUNTY INDEPENDENT

Street address 1: 91 N. Main Box 309
Street address city: Garrison
Street address state: ND
Zip/Postal code: 58540
General Phone: (701) 463-2201
General Fax: (701) 463-7487
General/National Adv. E-mail: independ@restel.net
Display Adv. E-mail: bhgads@nd-bhginc.com
Editorial e-mail: editors@bhgnews.com
Primary Website: bhgnews.com
Avg Paid Circ: 3000
Audit By: Sworn/Estimate/Non-Audited
Audit Date: 10.06.2019
Personnel: Mike Gackle (Pub.); Jill Denning Gackle (Gen. Mgr.); Stu Merry (Ed.); Sarah Chase (Ad. Mgr.)
Parent company (for newspapers): BHG, Inc.

MCLEAN COUNTY JOURNAL

Street address 1: 203 Main St S
Street address city: McClusky
Street address state: ND
Zip/Postal code: 58463-4000
General Phone: (701) 363-2276
General Fax: (701) 363-2698
Advertising Phone: Same
Editorial Phone: (701) 363-2276
Editorial Fax: (701) 363-2276
General/National Adv. E-mail: turtle@westriv.com
Primary Website: bhgnews.com
Year Established: 1905
Avg Paid Circ: 700
Avg Free Circ: 46
Audit By: Sworn/Estimate/Non-Audited
Audit Date: 10.06.2019
Personnel: Allan Tinker (Ed.); Betty Jean Dockter (Ad. Mgr.)
Parent company (for newspapers): BHG, Inc.

MCVILLE MESSENGER

Street address 1: 122 Main St N
Street address city: Fordville
Street address state: ND
Zip/Postal code: 58231-3134
General Phone: (701) 229-3641
General Fax: (701) 229-3217
General/National Adv. E-mail: nesspres@polarcomm.com
Year Established: 1981
Avg Paid Circ: 220
Audit By: Sworn/Estimate/Non-Audited
Audit Date: 10.06.2019
Personnel: Truman Ness (Ad. / Cir. Mgr.); Ness Press (Pub. / Ed.)

MOUNTRAIL COUNTY PROMOTER

Street address 1: 117 S Main St
Street address city: Stanley
Street address state: ND
Zip/Postal code: 58784-4003
General Phone: (701) 628-2333
General Fax: (701) 628-2694
General/National Adv. E-mail: promoter@midstatetel.com
Primary Website: mountrailcountypromoter.com
Year Established: 1906
Avg Paid Circ: 2100
Audit By: Sworn/Estimate/Non-Audited
Audit Date: 10.06.2019
Personnel: Mary Kilen (Ed.)

MOUNTRAIL COUNTY RECORD

Street address 1: 372 Main St
Street address city: New Town
Street address state: ND
Zip/Postal code: 58763-4001
General Phone: (701) 627-4829
General Fax: (701) 627-4021
General/National Adv. E-mail: ntsales@nd-bhginc.com
Editorial e-mail: nteditor@bhgnews.com
Primary Website: bhgnews.com
Avg Paid Circ: 750
Avg Free Circ: 46
Audit By: Sworn/Estimate/Non-Audited
Audit Date: 10.06.2019
Personnel: Jodi Iberson (Adv. Mgr.); Jerry Kram (Ed.)
Parent company (for newspapers): BHG, Inc.

NAPOLEON HOMESTEAD

Street address 1: 323 Main Ave
Street address city: Napoleon
Street address state: ND
Zip/Postal code: 58561-7108
General Phone: (701) 754-2212
General Fax: (701) 754-2212
General/National Adv. E-mail: homestead@napoleonnd.com
Primary Website: centraldakotanews.com
Year Established: 1886
Avg Paid Circ: 1550
Avg Free Circ: 20
Audit By: Sworn/Estimate/Non-Audited
Audit Date: 10.06.2019
Personnel: Christine Schwartzenberger (Cir. Mgr.); Terry Schwartzenberger (Pub. / Ed.)

NELSON COUNTY ARENA

Street address 1: 122 Main St N
Street address city: Fordville
Street address state: ND
Zip/Postal code: 58231-3134
General Phone: (701) 229-3641
General Fax: (701) 229-3217
General/National Adv. E-mail: nesspres@polarcomm.com
Year Established: 1908
Avg Paid Circ: 420
Audit By: Sworn/Estimate/Non-Audited
Audit Date: 10.06.2019
Personnel: Truman Ness (Ed.); Ness Press (Pub. / Ed.)

NEW ROCKFORD TRANSCRIPT

Street address 1: 6 8th St N
Street address city: New Rockford
Street address state: ND
Zip/Postal code: 58356-1518
General Phone: (701) 947-2417
General Fax: (701) 947-2418
General/National Adv. E-mail: nrtranscript@gmail.com
Display Adv. E-mail: nrtranscript@gmail.com
Editorial e-mail: amywobbema@gmail.com
Primary Website: newrockfordtranscript.com
Year Established: 1883
Avg Paid Circ: 1000
Avg Free Circ: 2000
Audit By: Sworn/Estimate/Non-Audited
Audit Date: 10.06.2019
Personnel: Amy Wobbema (Pub. /Ed.)

NEW SALEM JOURNAL

Street address 1: 1201 N. 8th St.
Street address city: New Salem
Street address state: ND
Zip/Postal code: 58563
General Phone: (701) 843-7567
General Fax: (701) 843-7623
General/National Adv. E-mail: newsalemjournal@gmail.com
Avg Paid Circ: 900
Audit By: Sworn/Estimate/Non-Audited
Audit Date: 10.06.2019
Personnel: Robyn Thiel (Pub. / Ed.)

NEW TOWN NEWS

Street address 1: PO Box 730
Street address city: New Town
Street address state: ND
Zip/Postal code: 58763-0730
General Phone: (701) 627-4829
General Fax: (701) 627-4021
General/National Adv. E-mail: ntsales@nd-bhginc.com
Editorial e-mail: nteditor@bhgnews.com
Primary Website: bhgnews.com
Avg Paid Circ: 1047
Avg Free Circ: 37
Audit By: Sworn/Estimate/Non-Audited
Audit Date: 10.06.2019
Personnel: Jerry Kram (Editor); Jodie Iverson (Adv. Mgr.)
Parent company (for newspapers): BHG, Inc.

NEWS-MONITOR

Street address 1: 601 Dakota Ave
Street address city: Wahpeton
Street address state: ND
Zip/Postal code: 58075-4325
General Phone: (701) 642-8585
General Fax: (701) 642-6068
General/National Adv. E-mail: tarak@wahpetondailynews.com
Display Adv. E-mail: classifieds@wahpetondailynews.com
Editorial e-mail: newsmonitor@wahpetondailynews.com
Primary Website: wahpetondailynews.com/news_monitor
Year Established: 1991
Avg Paid Circ: 1750
Audit By: Sworn/Estimate/Non-Audited
Audit Date: 10.06.2019
Personnel: Ken Harty (Pub.); Tara Klostreich (Adv. Mgr.); Karen Speidel (Mng. ed.)
Parent company (for newspapers): Wick Communications

PEMBINA NEW ERA

Street address 1: 122 Main St N
Street address city: Fordville
Street address state: ND
Zip/Postal code: 58231-3134
General Phone: (701) 229-3641
General Fax: (701) 229-3217
General/National Adv. E-mail: nesspres@polarcomm.com
Year Established: 1922
Avg Paid Circ: 375
Audit By: Sworn/Estimate/Non-Audited
Audit Date: 10.06.2019
Personnel: Truman Ness (Ad. / Cir. Mgr.); Ness Press (Pub. / Ed.)

PIERCE COUNTY TRIBUNE

Street address 1: 219 S Main Ave
Street address city: Rugby
Street address state: ND
Zip/Postal code: 58368-1720
General Phone: (701) 776-5252
General Fax: (701) 776-2159
General/National Adv. E-mail: cholm@thepiercecountytribune.com
Display Adv. E-mail: business@thepiercecountytribune.com
Primary Website: thepiercecountytribune.com
Avg Paid Circ: 2700
Audit By: Sworn/Estimate/Non-Audited
Audit Date: 10.06.2019
Personnel: Cheryl Holm (Adv. Acct. Exec.); Ruby Allen (Off. Mgr.); J.T. Pelt (Ed. / Mgr.)
Parent company (for newspapers): Ogden Newspapers Inc.

RENVILLE COUNTY FARMER

Street address 1: 110 Main St E
Street address city: Mohall
Street address state: ND

Zip/Postal code: 58761-4058
General Phone: (701) 756-6363
General Fax: (701) 756-7136
General/National Adv. E-mail: rcf1@ndak.net
Year Established: 1901
Avg Paid Circ: 875
Avg Free Circ: 51
Audit By: Sworn/Estimate/Non-Audited
Audit Date: 10.06.2019
Personnel: LaVonne L. Erickson (Ed.)

RICHARDTON MERCHANT

Street address 1: 102 S Park St
Street address city: Hebron
Street address state: ND
Zip/Postal code: 58638-0009
General Phone: (701) 878-4494
General Fax: (701) 878-4498
General/National Adv. E-mail: hherald@westriv.com
Year Established: 1973
Avg Paid Circ: 75
Avg Free Circ: 1100
Audit By: Sworn/Estimate/Non-Audited
Audit Date: 10.06.2019
Personnel: Jane Brandt (Pub. / Ed.)

STEELE COUNTY PRESS

Street address 1: 215 4th St W
Street address city: Finley
Street address state: ND
Zip/Postal code: 58230-3000
General Phone: (701) 524-1640
General Fax: (701) 524-2221
General/National Adv. E-mail: calbert@ncppub.com
Editorial e-mail: ldefrang@ncppub.com
Primary Website: ncppub.com
Year Established: 1897
Avg Paid Circ: 1400
Audit By: Sworn/Estimate/Non-Audited
Audit Date: 10.06.2019
Personnel: Mara Campbell (Ed.); Lisa Midstokke (Prod.); Catherine Albert (Sales)
Parent company (for newspapers): New Century Press

STEELE OZONE AND KIDDER COUNTY PRESS

Street address 1: 115 1st Ave SE
Street address city: Steele
Street address state: ND
Zip/Postal code: 58482-7131
General Phone: (701) 475-2513
General/National Adv. E-mail: sop@bektel.com
Display Adv. E-mail: sop@bektel.com
Classified Adv. e-mail: sop@bektel.com
Primary Website: steeleozonend.com
Mthly Avg Views: 5000
Mthly Avg Unique Visitors: 2000
Year Established: 2012
Avg Paid Circ: 2000
Avg Free Circ: 100
Audit By: USPS
Audit Date: 10.10.2021
Personnel: Paul Erdelt (Ed. / Pub.)

THE ASHLEY TRIBUNE

Street address 1: 115 W Main St
Street address city: Ashley
Street address state: ND
Zip/Postal code: 58413-7003
General Phone: (701) 288-3531
General Fax: (701) 288-3532
General/National Adv. E-mail: redhead@drtel.net
Primary Website: centraldakotanews.com/newspapers/ashley-tribune
Avg Paid Circ: 1600
Audit By: Sworn/Estimate/Non-Audited
Audit Date: 10.06.2019
Personnel: Tony Bender (Ed.)

THE CAVALIER CHRONICLE

Street address 1: 207 Main St W
Street address city: Cavalier
Street address state: ND
Zip/Postal code: 58220-4503
General Phone: (701) 265-8844
General Fax: (701) 265-8089
General/National Adv. E-mail: tim@cavchronicle.com
Display Adv. E-mail: tim@cavchronicle.com
Editorial e-mail: lynn@cavchronicle.com
Primary Website: cavalierchronicle.com
Year Established: 1885
Avg Paid Circ: 2500
Audit By: Sworn/Estimate/Non-Audited
Audit Date: 10.06.2019
Personnel: Delores Kemp (Cir. Mgr.); Lynn Schroeder (Ed.); Theodore Schroeder (Pub. Emeritus)

THE GLEANER

Street address 1: 22 N Main St
Street address city: Northwood
Street address state: ND
Zip/Postal code: 58267-4005
General Phone: (701) 587-6126
General Fax: (701) 587-5219
General/National Adv. E-mail: gleaner@invisimax.com
Avg Paid Circ: 900
Audit By: Sworn/Estimate/Non-Audited
Audit Date: 10.06.2019
Personnel: Beth Johnson (Pub.); Karen Bilden (Ed.)

THE GOLDEN VALLEY NEWS

Street address 1: 22 Central Ave
Street address 2: Ste 1
Street address city: Beach
Street address state: ND
Zip/Postal code: 58621
General Phone: (701) 872-3755
General Fax: (701) 872-3756
General/National Adv. E-mail: gvnews@midstate.net
Editorial e-mail: goldenandbillings@gmail.com
Avg Paid Circ: 879
Audit By: Sworn/Estimate/Non-Audited
Audit Date: 10.06.2019
Personnel: Jason Nordmark (Pub.); Richard Volesky (Ed. / Ad Mgr.)
Parent company (for newspapers): Nordmark Publishing

THE GRANT COUNTY NEWS

Street address 1: 119 Main St.
Street address city: Elgin
Street address state: ND
Zip/Postal code: 58533
General Phone: (701) 584-2900
General Fax: (701) 584-2900
General/National Adv. E-mail: gcn@westriv.com
Primary Website: grantcountynewsnewspaper.com
Year Established: 1955
Avg Paid Circ: 1500
Audit By: Sworn/Estimate/Non-Audited
Audit Date: 10.06.2019
Personnel: Jill Friesz (Ed.); John Schultz (Circ. Mgr.)

THE HAZEN STAR

Street address 1: 26 Main Rd E
Street address city: Pick City
Street address state: ND
Zip/Postal code: 58545-7034
General Phone: (701) 748-2255
General Fax: (701) 748-5768
General/National Adv. E-mail: star@westriv.com
Primary Website: nd-bhginc.com
Avg Paid Circ: 2000
Avg Free Circ: 34
Audit By: Sworn/Estimate/Non-Audited
Audit Date: 10.06.2019
Personnel: Dareen Ost (Adv. Mgr.); Daniel Arens (Ed.); Sharon Olander (Cir. Mgr.)
Parent company (for newspapers): BHG, Inc.

THE HERALD

Street address 1: 724 Main St
Street address city: New England
Street address state: ND
Zip/Postal code: 58647-7000
General Phone: (701) 579-4530
General Fax: (701) 579-4180
General/National Adv. E-mail: therald@countrymedia.net
Primary Website: newenglandextra.com
Avg Paid Circ: 1100
Audit By: Sworn/Estimate/Non-Audited
Audit Date: 10.06.2019
Personnel: Norma Peterson (Pub.); Cole Benz (Ed.); Jaden Ragsdale (Off. Mgr)
Parent company (for newspapers): Country Media Inc.

THE HERALD-PRESS

Street address 1: 913 Lincoln Ave
Street address city: Harvey
Street address state: ND
Zip/Postal code: 58341-1523
General Phone: (701) 324-4646
General Fax: (701) 324-4647
General/National Adv. E-mail: heraldpress@gondtc.com
Editorial e-mail: heraldpress@midconetwork.com
Primary Website: heraldpressnd.com
Avg Paid Circ: 2700
Avg Free Circ: 2400
Audit By: Sworn/Estimate/Non-Audited
Audit Date: 10.06.2019
Personnel: Charles Eldredge (Pub.); Edie Schell (Gen. Mgr. / Ad. Sales); Janine Schmitz (Ed.); Peg Bell (Copy Ed.); Ruth Yoder (Cir. Mgr.)

THE JOURNAL

Street address 1: 117 North Main
Street address city: Crosby
Street address state: ND
Zip/Postal code: 58730
General Phone: (701) 965-6088
General Fax: (701) 965-6089
General/National Adv. E-mail: journalads@crosbynd.com
Display Adv. E-mail: journalads@crosbynd.com
Editorial e-mail: cecilew@crosbynd.com
Primary Website: journaltrib.com
Year Established: 1904
Avg Paid Circ: 2500
Avg Free Circ: 30
Audit By: Sworn/Estimate/Non-Audited
Audit Date: 10.06.2019
Personnel: Cecile Krimm (Pub. / Ed.); Jenny Bummer (Prod.); Holly Anderson (Cir.)
Parent company (for newspapers): Journal Publishing

THE KENMARE NEWS

Street address 1: 111 1st Ave NW
Street address city: Kenmare
Street address state: ND
Zip/Postal code: 58746-0896
General Phone: (701) 385-4275
General Fax: (701) 385-4395
General/National Adv. E-mail: news@kenmarend.com
Primary Website: kenmarend.com
Year Established: 1898
Avg Paid Circ: 1500
Avg Free Circ: 28
Audit By: Sworn/Estimate/Non-Audited
Audit Date: 01.10.2021
Personnel: Terry Froseth (Pub. / Ed.); Fay Froseth (Cir. Mgr.); Glen Froseth (Pub. Emeritus); Laura Mibeck; Elsa Condit (Prod. Asst.)

THE LITCHVILLE BULLETIN

Street address 1: 505 3RD AVE
Street address city: Litchville
Street address state: ND
Zip/Postal code: 58461
General Phone: (701) 762-4267
General Fax: (701) 762-4267
General/National Adv. E-mail: bulletin@drtel.net
Year Established: 1901
Avg Paid Circ: 1025
Audit By: Sworn/Estimate/Non-Audited
Audit Date: 10.06.2019
Personnel: Ruth E. McCleerey (Ed.); Art Hagebock (Pub.); Diane Hagebock (Pub.)

THE MOUSE RIVER JOURNAL

Street address 1: PO Box 268
Street address city: Towner
Street address state: ND
Zip/Postal code: 58788-0268
General Phone: (701) 537-5610
General Fax: (701) 537-5493
General/National Adv. E-mail: msrvrjnl@ndak.net
Editorial e-mail: msrvrjnl@srt.com
Primary Website: http://mouseriverjournal.weebly.com/
Avg Paid Circ: 1200
Audit By: Sworn/Estimate/Non-Audited
Audit Date: 10.06.2019
Personnel: Jason Nordmark (Pub.); Billy Joe Eriksmoen (Ed.)
Parent company (for newspapers): Nordmark Publishing

THE OAKES TIMES

Street address 1: 501 Main Ave
Street address city: Oakes
Street address state: ND
Zip/Postal code: 58474-1241
General Phone: (701) 742-2361
General/National Adv. E-mail: oakestms@drtel.net
Year Established: 1884
Avg Paid Circ: 2800
Avg Free Circ: 15
Audit By: Sworn/Estimate/Non-Audited
Audit Date: 10.06.2019
Personnel: Jason Nordmark (Pub.); Ethel Erickson (Editor); Dusti Farley (Production Manager); Alexis Marthaller (Adv. Mgr.)
Parent company (for newspapers): Nordmark Publishing

THE PLAINS REPORTER

Street address 1: 14 4th St W
Street address city: Williston
Street address state: ND
Zip/Postal code: 58801-5308
General Phone: (701) 572-2165
General Fax: (701) 572-1965
General/National Adv. E-mail: advertising@willistonherald.com
Editorial e-mail: news@willistonherald.com
Primary Website: willistonherald.com
Avg Free Circ: 15500
Audit By: Sworn/Estimate/Non-Audited
Audit Date: 10.06.2019
Personnel: Ken Harty (Publisher); Jamie Kelly (Managing Editor)

THE RANSOM COUNTY GAZETTE

Street address 1: 410 Main St
Street address city: Lisbon
Street address state: ND
Zip/Postal code: 58054-4142
General Phone: (701) 683-4128
General Fax: (701) 683-4129
General/National Adv. E-mail: info@rcgazette.com
Primary Website: rcgazette.com
Avg Paid Circ: 3000
Audit By: Sworn/Estimate/Non-Audited
Audit Date: 10.06.2019
Personnel: Cheryl Kelly (Adv. Mgr.); Sean W. Kelly (Ed.); Terri Barta (Mng. Ed.)

THE SARGENT COUNTY TELLER

Street address 1: PO Box 247
Street address city: Milnor
Street address state: ND
Zip/Postal code: 58060-0247
General Phone: (701)427-9472
General Fax: (701)427-9492
General/National Adv. E-mail: info@thescteller.com
Display Adv. E-mail: info@thescteller.com
Editorial e-mail: info@thescteller.com
Year Established: 1883
Avg Paid Circ: 1600
Avg Free Circ: 150
Audit By: Sworn/Estimate/Non-Audited
Audit Date: 10.06.2019
Personnel: Cheryl Kelly (Co-pub.); Sean Kelly (Pub. / Ed.)
Parent company (for newspapers): Kelly Ink, Inc.

THE WALSH COUNTY PRESS

Street address 1: 401 Briggs Ave S
Street address 2: Ste 2
Street address city: Park River
Street address state: ND
Zip/Postal code: 58270-4023
General Phone: (701) 284-6333
General Fax: (701) 284-6091
General/National Adv. E-mail: wcpress@polarcomm.com

Year Established: 1884
Avg Paid Circ: 1100
Audit By: Sworn/Estimate/Non-Audited
Audit Date: 10.06.2019
Personnel: Jason Nordmark (Pub.); Sue Steinke (Prodn. Mgr.); Kevin Skavhaug (Sports); Allison Olimb (Ed.)
Parent company (for newspapers): Nordmark Publishing

THE WALSH COUNTY RECORD

Street address 1: 402 Hill Ave
Street address city: Grafton
Street address state: ND
Zip/Postal code: 58237-1002
General Phone: (701) 352-0640
Advertising Phone: (701) 352-0640
Editorial Phone: (701) 352-0641
General/National Adv. E-mail: advertising@wcrecord.com
Display Adv. E-mail: brianl@wcrecord.com
Editorial e-mail: jackie@wcrecord.com
Primary Website: wcrecord.com
Year Established: 1923
Avg Paid Circ: 3136
Avg Free Circ: 100
Audit By: Sworn/Estimate/Non-Audited
Audit Date: 10.06.2019
Personnel: Jackie L. Thompson (Pub.); Tim Martin (Adv. Mgr.); Deb Bender (Cir. Mgr.); Todd Kjelland (Ed.); Brian LeClerc (Adv. Sales Rep.)

THE WISHEK STAR

Street address 1: 24 N Centennial St
Street address city: Wishek
Street address state: ND
Zip/Postal code: 58495-0275
General Phone: (701) 452-2331
General Fax: (701) 452-2340
General/National Adv. E-mail: wishekstar@gmail.com
Display Adv. E-mail: wishekstar@gmail.com
Classified Adv. e-mail: wishekstar@gmail.com
Editorial e-mail: wishekstar@gmail.com
Primary Website: mcintosh-star-tribune.com
Year Established: 1901
Avg Paid Circ: 1000
Audit By: Sworn/Estimate/Non-Audited
Audit Date: 10.06.2019
Personnel: Francis Materi (Editorial Dir.)
Parent company (for newspapers): Redhead Publishing, Inc

TIOGA TRIBUNE

Street address 1: 101 2nd Street
Street address city: Tioga
Street address state: ND
Zip/Postal code: 58852
General Phone: (701) 664-2222
General Fax: (701) 664-3333
General/National Adv. E-mail: advertising@tiogand.com
Editorial e-mail: cecilew@crosbynd.com
Primary Website: journaltrib.com
Year Established: 1951
Avg Paid Circ: 1400
Audit By: Sworn/Estimate/Non-Audited
Audit Date: 10.06.2019
Personnel: Cecile Krimm (Pub.)
Parent company (for newspapers): Journal Publishing

TOWNER COUNTY RECORD-HERALD

Street address 1: 423 Main St
Street address city: Cando
Street address state: ND
Zip/Postal code: 58324-6309
General Phone: (701) 968-3223
General Fax: (701) 968-3345
General/National Adv. E-mail: tcrhads@gondtc.com
Display Adv. E-mail: tcrhads@gondtc.com
Editorial e-mail: tcrheditor@gondtc.com
Audit By: Sworn/Estimate/Non-Audited
Audit Date: 10.06.2019
Personnel: Jason Nordmark (Ed.)
Parent company (for newspapers): Nordmark Publishing

TRAILL COUNTY TRIBUNE

Street address 1: 12 3rd St SE
Street address city: Mayville
Street address state: ND
Zip/Postal code: 58257-1414
General Phone: (701) 788-3281
General/National Adv. E-mail: news@tctribune.net
Editorial e-mail: news@tctribune.net
Avg Paid Circ: 2600
Audit By: Sworn/Estimate/Non-Audited
Audit Date: 10.06.2019
Personnel: Sean W. Kelly (Pub.); Kelsey Majeske (NorDak Publishing Mobridge, S.D.); Thomas A. Monilaws (Gen. Mgr.); Gail Mooney (Graph. Des. / Adv.)

TRI COUNTY NEWS

Street address 1: 321 Main St
Street address city: Gackle
Street address state: ND
Zip/Postal code: 58442-7109
General Phone: (701) 485-3550
General Fax: (701) 485-3551
Editorial Phone: (605) 999-4607
General/National Adv. E-mail: tcnews@daktel.com
Editorial e-mail: wendy@dakotafire.net
Year Established: 1970
Avg Paid Circ: 750
Audit By: Sworn/Estimate/Non-Audited
Audit Date: 10.06.2019
Personnel: Art Hagebock (Pub.); Diane Hagebock (Pub.); Wendy Royston (Mng. Ed.)

TURTLE MOUNTAIN STAR

Street address 1: 11 1st Ave NE
Street address city: Rolla
Street address state: ND
Zip/Postal code: 58367-7125
General Phone: (701) 477-6495
General Fax: (701) 477-3182
General/National Adv. E-mail: tmstar@utma.com
Avg Paid Circ: 3600
Audit By: Sworn/Estimate/Non-Audited
Audit Date: 10.06.2019
Personnel: Jason Nordmark (Pub. / Ed.)
Parent company (for newspapers): Nordmark Publishing

TURTLE MOUNTAIN TIMES

Street address 1: PO Box 1270
Street address city: Belcourt
Street address state: ND
Zip/Postal code: 58316-1270
General Phone: (701)477-6670
General Fax: (701)477-6875
General/National Adv. E-mail: thetimes@utma.com
Year Established: 1993
Avg Paid Circ: 3000
Audit By: Sworn/Estimate/Non-Audited
Audit Date: 10.06.2019
Personnel: Neva M. E. Rainey (Circ. Mgr.); Eugene L. Trottier (Gen. Mgr)

UNDERWOOD NEWS

Street address 1: P.O. Box 309
Street address city: Garrison
Street address state: ND
Zip/Postal code: 58540
General Phone: (701)463-2201
Editorial e-mail: news@bhgnews.com
Primary Website: bhgnews.com
Avg Paid Circ: 529
Avg Free Circ: 22
Audit By: Sworn/Estimate/Non-Audited
Audit Date: 10.06.2019
Personnel: Don Winter (Adv. Mgr.); Suzanne Werre (Ed.)
Parent company (for newspapers): BHG, Inc.

VALLEY NEWS & VIEWS

Street address 1: 911 N Main, Suite 2
Street address city: Drayton
Street address state: ND
Zip/Postal code: 58225
General Phone: (701) 454-6333
General/National Adv. E-mail: valleynv@polarcomm.com
Primary Website: www.valleynewsandviews.com
Year Established: 1981
Avg Paid Circ: 600
Audit By: Sworn/Estimate/Non-Audited
Audit Date: 10.06.2019
Personnel: Andrea Johnston (Publisher); Lesa Van Camp (Ed/Pub/Owner)
Parent company (for newspapers): The Borderland Press

VELVA AREA VOICE

Street address 1: 1 Main St N
Street address city: Velva
Street address state: ND
Zip/Postal code: 58790-7304
General Phone: (701) 338-2599
General Fax: (701) 338-2705
General/National Adv. E-mail: yournews@srt.com
Primary Website: nd-bhginc.com
Avg Paid Circ: 1000
Audit By: Sworn/Estimate/Non-Audited
Audit Date: 10.06.2019
Personnel: Courtney Graves (Ed.)
Parent company (for newspapers): BHG, Inc.

WALHALLA MOUNTAINEER

Street address 1: 1001 Central Ave
Street address city: Walhalla
Street address state: ND
Zip/Postal code: 58282
General Phone: (701)549-2580
General/National Adv. E-mail: mtneer@utma.com
Audit By: Sworn/Estimate/Non-Audited
Audit Date: 10.06.2019

WEST FARGO PIONEER

Street address 1: 3124 41st Street S
Street address city: West Fargo
Street address state: ND
Zip/Postal code: 58078
General Phone: (701) 451-5718
General Fax: (701) 241-5487
Editorial Phone: (701) 241-5579
General/National Adv. E-mail: news@westfargopioneer.com
Primary Website: westfargopioneer.com
Avg Paid Circ: 13135
Audit By: AAM
Audit Date: 31.03.2019
Personnel: Wendy Reuer (Assistant Ed.); Matthew Von Pinnon (Ed.)
Parent company (for newspapers): Forum Communications Co.

WESTHOPE STANDARD

Street address 1: 150 MAIN ST
Street address city: Westhope
Street address state: ND
Zip/Postal code: 58793
General Phone: (701) 245-6461
General Fax: (701) 245-6461
General/National Adv. E-mail: standard@srt.com
Primary Website: cndnews.com
Year Established: 1901
Avg Paid Circ: 800
Audit By: Sworn/Estimate/Non-Audited
Audit Date: 10.06.2019
Personnel: Ginny Heth (Ed.)

OHIO

AMHERST NEWS-TIMES

Street address 1: 42 S Main St
Street address city: Oberlin
Street address state: OH
Zip/Postal code: 44074-1627
General Phone: (440) 988-2801
General Fax: (440) 988-2802
Advertising Phone: (440) 775-1611
Advertising Fax: (440) 774-2167
Editorial Phone: (440) 775-1611
Editorial Fax: (440) 774-2167
General/National Adv. E-mail: rward@civitasmedia.com
Display Adv. E-mail: aduncan@civitasmedia.com
Editorial e-mail: news@theoberlinnews.com
Primary Website: theamherstnewstimes.com
Year Established: 1919
Avg Paid Circ: 1300
Avg Free Circ: 199
Audit By: Sworn/Estimate/Non-Audited
Audit Date: 10.06.2019
Personnel: Tom Hutson (Reg. Rev. Dir.); Jason Hawk (Ed.); Robin Ward (Bus. Mgr./Adv. Rep.)
Parent company (for newspapers): AIM Media Indiana

ANTWERP BEE-ARGUS

Street address 1: 1`13 Main
Street address city: Antwerp
Street address state: OH
Zip/Postal code: 45813
General Phone: (419) 258-8161
General Fax: (419) 258-9365
Editorial Phone: (419) 258-8161
Display Adv. E-mail: an
Editorial e-mail: antwerpbeeargus@frontier.com
Primary Website: antwerpbeeargus.com
Year Established: 1883
Audit By: Sworn/Estimate/Non-Audited
Audit Date: 10.06.2019
Personnel: June L. Temple (Pub./Ed.); Sandra K. Temple (Ed.); Rodger S. Temple (Mng. Ed.)

ARCHBOLD BUCKEYE

Street address 1: 207 N Defiance St
Street address city: Archbold
Street address state: OH
Zip/Postal code: 43502-1160
General Phone: (419) 445-4466
Advertising Phone: (419) 445-4466
Editorial Phone: (419) 445-4466
Display Adv. E-mail: advertising@archboldbuckeye.com
Classified Adv. e-mail: advertising@archboldbuckeye.com
Editorial e-mail: davidpugh@archboldbuckeye.com
Primary Website: archboldbuckeye.com
Mthly Avg Views: 35247
Mthly Avg Unique Visitors: 10264
Year Established: 1905
Avg Paid Circ: 1710
Avg Free Circ: 74
Audit By: Sworn/Estimate/Non-Audited
Audit Date: 21.09.2023
Personnel: Ross William Taylor (Pub.); Mary Huber (Adv. Dir.); David Pugh (Ed.); Brent Taylor (Prodn. Mgr.); Lynn Taylor (Circulation/Accounts Receivable)
Parent company (for newspapers): Archbold Buckeye, Inc.

ATHENS NEWS

Street address 1: 14 N. Court Street
Street address 2: Ste 1
Street address city: Athens
Street address state: OH
Zip/Postal code: 45701-2429
General Phone: (740) 594-8219
General Fax: (740) 594-8219
Advertising Phone: (740) 594-8219
General/National Adv. E-mail: hilary@athensnews.com
Display Adv. E-mail: robert@athensnews.com
Editorial e-mail: news@athensnews.com
Primary Website: athensnews.com
Mthly Avg Views: 63653
Mthly Avg Unique Visitors: 54914
Year Established: 1977
Avg Free Circ: 12000
Audit By: Sworn/Estimate/Non-Audited
Audit Date: 10.06.2019
Personnel: Terry Smith (Ed. and Pub.)
Parent company (for newspapers): APG Ohio

ATTICA HUB

Street address 1: 202 N Main St
Street address city: Attica
Street address state: OH
Zip/Postal code: 44807-9484
General Phone: (419) 426-3491
General Fax: (419) 426-2003
Advertising Phone: (419) 426-3491
Advertising Fax: (419) 426-2003
Editorial Phone: (419) 426-3491
Editorial Fax: (419) 426-2003
General/National Adv. E-mail: sales@atticahub.com
Display Adv. E-mail: auctions@atticahub.com

Editorial e-mail: news@atticahub.com
Primary Website: atticahub.com
Year Established: 1896
Avg Paid Circ: 4400
Audit By: Sworn/Estimate/Non-Audited
Audit Date: 10.06.2019
Personnel: Deb Cook (Owner/Pub.); Tammy Collins (Adv. Mgr.)

AUGLAIZE MERCHANDISER

Street address 1: 520 Industrial Dr
Street address city: Wapakoneta
Street address state: OH
Zip/Postal code: 45895-9200
General Phone: (419) 738-2128
General Fax: (419) 738-5352
General/National Adv. E-mail: marketingetc@wapakwdn.com
Display Adv. E-mail: classified@wapakwdn.com
Editorial e-mail: editor@wapakwdn.com
Primary Website: wapakdailynews.com
Year Established: 1905
Avg Free Circ: 7030
Sat. Circulation Paid: 5300
Audit By: Sworn/Estimate/Non-Audited
Audit Date: 10.06.2019
Personnel: Deb Zwez (Pub.); Gayle Masonbrink (Adv. Dir.)
Parent company (for newspapers): Horizon Publications Inc.

AURORA ADVOCATE

Street address 1: 1050 W. Main St. Kent
Street address city: Kent
Street address state: OH
Zip/Postal code: 44240
General Phone: (330) 541-9400
General Fax: (330) 296-2698
Advertising Phone: (330) 541-9400
Advertising Fax: (330) 296-2698
Editorial Phone: (330) 541-9400
Editorial Fax: (330) 296-2698
General/National Adv. E-mail: Ads@recordpub.com
Display Adv. E-mail: class@recordpub.com
Editorial e-mail: editor@recordpub.com
Primary Website: auroraadvocate.com
Year Established: 1830
Avg Paid Circ: 180
Avg Free Circ: 5720
Audit By: Sworn/Estimate/Non-Audited
Audit Date: 10.06.2019
Personnel: David E. Dix (Pub.); Ken Lahmers (Ed.); Harry Newman (Adv. Mgr.); Ron Waite (Gen. Mgr.); Joe Filippini (Prod. Mgr.)
Parent company (for newspapers): CherryRoad Media; Gannett Company Inc.

AUSTINTOWN TOWN CRIER

Street address 1: 240 Franklin St SE
Street address city: Warren
Street address state: OH
Zip/Postal code: 44483-5711
General Phone: (330) 629-6200
General Fax: (330) 629-6210
Advertising Phone: (330) 841-1620
Advertising Fax: (330) 629-6210
Editorial Phone: (330) 629-6200
Editorial Fax: (330) 629-6210
General/National Adv. E-mail: kbergman@tribtoday.com
Display Adv. E-mail: kbergman@tribtoday.com
Editorial e-mail: editor@towncrieronline.com
Primary Website: towncrieronline.com
Year Established: 1993
Avg Free Circ: 16206
Audit By: Sworn/Estimate/Non-Audited
Audit Date: 10.06.2019
Personnel: Amy Wilson (Ed./Gen. Mgr.); Kim Bergman (Adv. Dir.)
Parent company (for newspapers): Ogden Newspapers Inc.

BARNESVILLE ENTERPRISE

Street address 1: 166 E Main St
Street address city: Barnesville
Street address state: OH
Zip/Postal code: 43713-1004
General Phone: (740) 425-1912
General Fax: (740) 425-2545
Advertising Phone: (740) 425-1912
Advertising Fax: (740) 425-2545
Editorial Phone: (740) 425-1912
Editorial Fax: (740) 425-2545
General/National Adv. E-mail: bstephen@barnesville-enterprise.com
Display Adv. E-mail: enterprise@barnesville-enterprise.com
Editorial e-mail: enterprise@barnesville-enterprise.com
Primary Website: barnesville-enterprise.com
Year Established: 1866
Avg Paid Circ: 4613
Avg Free Circ: 30
Audit By: Sworn/Estimate/Non-Audited
Audit Date: 10.06.2019
Personnel: Andrew Dix (Pub.); Cathryn Stanley (Ed.); Ray Booth (Mng. Ed.); Beth Stephens (Advertising)
Parent company (for newspapers): Jeffersonian Advantage

BEAVERCREEK NEWS-CURRENT

Street address 1: 1836 W Park Sq
Street address city: Xenia
Street address state: OH
Zip/Postal code: 45385-2668
General Phone: (937) 372-4444
General Fax: (937) 372-3385
Advertising Phone: (937) 372-4444 ext 200
Advertising Fax: (937) 372-3385
Editorial Phone: (937) 372-4444
Editorial Fax: (937) 372-1951
General/National Adv. E-mail: tpease@civitasmedia.com
Display Adv. E-mail: tpease@civitasmedia.com
Classified Adv. e-mail: ttootle@civitasmedia.com
Editorial e-mail: editor@xeniagazette.com
Primary Website: beavercreeknewscurrent.com
Avg Paid Circ: 3805
Sat. Circulation Paid: 3805
Audit By: Sworn/Estimate/Non-Audited
Audit Date: 10.06.2019
Personnel: Diane Chiddister (Ed.); Robert Hasek (Adv. Mgr.)

BELLVILLE STAR & TRI-FORKS PRESS

Street address 1: 107 Main St
Street address city: Bellville
Street address state: OH
Zip/Postal code: 44813-1020
General Phone: (419) 886-2291
General Fax: (419) 886-2704
Advertising Phone: (419) 468-1117 ext. 2045
Primary Website: http://thebellvillestar.com/
Avg Paid Circ: 2100
Avg Free Circ: 16
Audit By: Sworn/Estimate/Non-Audited
Audit Date: 10.06.2019
Personnel: Russ Kent (Ed.); Kristine Collier (Adv.); Alison Allonas (Adv.); Anthony Conchel (Editorial)
Parent company (for newspapers): AIM Media Indiana

BOARDMAN NEWS

Street address 1: 8302 Southern Blvd
Street address 2: Ste 2
Street address city: Boardman
Street address state: OH
Zip/Postal code: 44512-6353
General Phone: (330) 758-6397
General Fax: (330) 758-2658
Advertising Phone: (330) 758-6397
Advertising Fax: (330) 758-2658
Editorial Phone: (330) 758-6397
Editorial Fax: (330) 758-2658
General/National Adv. E-mail: bnews@zoominternet.net
Display Adv. E-mail: bnews@zoominternet.net
Editorial e-mail: bnews@zoominternet.net
Primary Website: boardmannews.net
Year Established: 1947
Avg Paid Circ: 8000
Avg Free Circ: 100
Audit By: Sworn/Estimate/Non-Audited
Audit Date: 10.06.2019
Personnel: Jack A. Darnell (Pub. Emeritus); John A. Darnell (Ed.); Gwen Darnell (Adv. Mgr.)

BOARDMAN TOWN CRIER

Street address 1: 240 Franklin St SE
Street address city: Warren
Street address state: OH
Zip/Postal code: 44483-5711
General Phone: (330) 629-6200
General Fax: (330) 629-6210
Advertising Phone: (330) 841-1620
Advertising Fax: (330) 629-6210
Editorial Phone: (330) 629-6200
Editorial Fax: (330) 629-6210
General/National Adv. E-mail: kbergman@tribtoday.com
Display Adv. E-mail: kbergman@tribtoday.com
Editorial e-mail: editor@towncrieronline.com
Primary Website: towncrieronline.com
Year Established: 1993
Avg Free Circ: 35000
Audit By: Sworn/Estimate/Non-Audited
Audit Date: 10.06.2019
Personnel: Amy Wilson (Ed./Gen. Mgr.); Kim Bergman (Adv. Dir.)
Parent company (for newspapers): Ogden Newspapers Inc.

BROOKVILLE STAR

Street address 1: 14 Mulberry St
Street address city: Brookville
Street address state: OH
Zip/Postal code: 45309-1828
General Phone: (937) 833-2545
General Fax: (937) 833-2546
Advertising Phone: (937) 833-2545
Advertising Fax: (937) 833-2546
Editorial Phone: (937) 833-2545
Editorial Fax: (937) 833-2546
General/National Adv. E-mail: ads@brookvillestar.net
Display Adv. E-mail: ads@brookvillestar.net
Editorial e-mail: news@brookvillestar.net
Primary Website: brookvillestar.net
Year Established: 1891
Avg Paid Circ: 3500
Audit By: Sworn/Estimate/Non-Audited
Audit Date: 10.06.2019
Personnel: Jim Hoffman (Pub./Ed.); Mark Gordon (Adv. Mgr./Circ. Mgr.)

CANFIELD TOWN CRIER

Street address 1: 240 Franklin St SE
Street address city: Warren
Street address state: OH
Zip/Postal code: 44483-5711
General Phone: (330) 629-6200
General Fax: (330) 629-6210
Advertising Phone: (330) 841-1620
Advertising Fax: (330) 629-6210
Editorial Phone: (330) 629-6200
Editorial Fax: (330) 629-6210
General/National Adv. E-mail: kbergman@tribtoday.com
Display Adv. E-mail: kbergman@tribtoday.com
Editorial e-mail: editor@towncrieronline.com
Primary Website: towncrieronline.com
Year Established: 1993
Avg Free Circ: 35000
Audit By: Sworn/Estimate/Non-Audited
Audit Date: 10.06.2019
Personnel: Amy Wilson (Ed./Gen. Mgr.); Kim Bergman (Adv. Dir.)
Parent company (for newspapers): Ogden Newspapers Inc.

CHAGRIN VALLEY TIMES

Street address 1: 525 Washington St
Street address city: Chagrin Falls
Street address state: OH
Zip/Postal code: 44022-4455
General Phone: (440) 247-5335
General Fax: (440) 247-5615
Advertising Phone: (440) 247-5335
Advertising Fax: (440) 247-5615
Editorial Phone: (440) 247-5335
Editorial Fax: (440) 247-5615
General/National Adv. E-mail: sales@chagrinvalleytimes.com
Display Adv. E-mail: myad@chagrinvalleytimes.com
Editorial e-mail: editor@chagrinvalleytimes.com
Primary Website: chagrinvalleytoday.com
Year Established: 1971
Avg Paid Circ: 3764
Avg Free Circ: 5150
Audit By: AAM
Audit Date: 30.09.2017
Personnel: Harold K. Douthit (Pub.); Ellen J Kleinerman (Ed.)
Parent company (for newspapers): Sun Newspapers

CLEVELAND SCENE

Street address 1: 737 Bolivar Rd
Street address 2: Ste 4100
Street address city: Cleveland
Street address state: OH
Zip/Postal code: 44115-1259
General Phone: (216) 241-7550
General Fax: (216) 802-7212
Advertising Phone: (216) 802-7258
Advertising Fax: (216) 802-7212
Editorial Phone: (216) 802-7254
Editorial Fax: (216) 802-7212
General/National Adv. E-mail: scene@clevescene.com
Display Adv. E-mail: gkelley@clevescene.com
Editorial e-mail: vgrzegorek@clevescene.com
Primary Website: clevescene.com
Year Established: 1970
Avg Free Circ: 43359
Audit By: Sworn/Estimate/Non-Audited
Audit Date: 10.06.2019
Personnel: Chris Keating (Pub.); Vince Grzegorek (Ed.); Shayne Rose (Adv. Dir.)

COLUMBUS BUSINESS FIRST

Street address 1: 303 W Nationwide Blvd
Street address city: Columbus
Street address state: OH
Zip/Postal code: 43215-2309
General Phone: (614) 461-4040
General Fax: (614) 365-2980
Advertising Phone: (614) 461-4040
Advertising Fax: (614) 365-2980
Editorial Phone: (614) 461-4040
Editorial Fax: (614) 365-2980
General/National Adv. E-mail: ddeppero@bizjournals.com
Display Adv. E-mail: dbuchanan@bizjournals.com
Editorial e-mail: dcappa@bizjournals.com
Primary Website: bizjournals.com/columbus
Audit By: Sworn/Estimate/Non-Audited
Audit Date: 10.06.2019
Personnel: Nick Fortine (Pres./Pub.); Dominic Cappa (Ed.); Doug Buchanan (Digital/Online Mng. Ed.)

COMMUNITY JOURNAL CLERMONT

Street address 1: 312 Elm St
Street address city: Cincinnati
Street address state: OH
Zip/Postal code: 45202-2739
General Phone: (513) 248-8600
General Fax: (513) 248-1938
Advertising Phone: (513) 248-8600
Advertising Fax: (513) 248-1938
Editorial Phone: (513) 248-8600
Editorial Fax: (513) 248-1938
General/National Adv. E-mail: acumby@communitypress.com
Display Adv. E-mail: acumby@communitypress.com
Editorial e-mail: therron@communitypress.com
Primary Website: cincinnati.com
Avg Free Circ: 10835
Audit By: Sworn/Estimate/Non-Audited
Audit Date: 10.06.2019
Personnel: Richard Maloney (Editor); Margaret Buchanan (Pres./Pub.); Alison Cumby (Adv. Mgr.)
Parent company (for newspapers): Gannett

CUYAHOGA FALLS NEWS-PRESS

Street address 1: 1050 W. Main Street
Street address city: Kent
Street address state: OH
Zip/Postal code: 44240
General Phone: (330) 541-9400
General Fax: (330) 296-2698
Advertising Phone: (330) 541-9400
Advertising Fax: (330) 296-2698

Editorial Phone: (330) 541-9400
Editorial Fax: (330) 296-2698
General/National Adv. E-mail: jwilliams@recordpub.com
Display Adv. E-mail: jwilliams@recordpub.com
Editorial e-mail: hrainone@recordpub.com
Primary Website: fallsnewspress.com
Year Established: 1830
Avg Paid Circ: 342
Avg Free Circ: 21540
Audit By: AAM
Audit Date: 31.03.2016
Personnel: David E. Dix (Pub.); Heather Rainone (Mng. Ed.)
Parent company (for newspapers): CherryRoad Media; Gannett Company Inc.

DELHI PRESS

Street address 1: 312 Elm St
Street address city: Cincinnati
Street address state: OH
Zip/Postal code: 45202-2739
General Phone: (513) 923-3111
General Fax: (513) 923-1806
Advertising Phone: (513) 923-3111
Advertising Fax: (513) 923-1806
Editorial Phone: (513) 923-3111
Editorial Fax: (513) 923-1806
General/National Adv. E-mail: chahn@enquirer.com
Display Adv. E-mail: mwoodruff@enquirer.com
Editorial e-mail: memral@communitypress.com
Primary Website: cincinnati.com
Avg Paid Circ: 10091
Avg Free Circ: 8241
Audit By: Sworn/Estimate/Non-Audited
Audit Date: 10.06.2019
Personnel: Margaret Buchanan (Pres./Pub.); Carolyn Washburn (Exec. Ed.); Richard Maloney (Editor); Carol Hahn (Adv. VP); Sharon Schachleiter (Circ. Mgr.)
Parent company (for newspapers): Gannett

EASTERN HILLS JOURNAL

Street address 1: 312 Elm St
Street address city: Cincinnati
Street address state: OH
Zip/Postal code: 45202-2739
General Phone: (513) 248-8600
General Fax: (513) 248-1938
Advertising Phone: (513) 248-8600
Advertising Fax: (513) 248-1938
Editorial Phone: (513) 248-8600
Editorial Fax: (513) 248-1938
General/National Adv. E-mail: acumby@communitypress.com
Display Adv. E-mail: acumby@communitypress.com
Editorial e-mail: espangler@communitypress.com
Primary Website: cincinnati.com
Avg Free Circ: 10835
Audit By: Sworn/Estimate/Non-Audited
Audit Date: 10.06.2019
Personnel: Nancy Daly (Community Recorder Editor); Margaret Buchanan (Pres./Pub.); Alison Cumby (Adv. Mgr.)
Parent company (for newspapers): Gannett

EASTSIDE MESSENGER

Street address 1: 3500 Sullivant Ave
Street address city: Columbus
Street address state: OH
Zip/Postal code: 43204-1105
General Phone: (614) 272-5422
General Fax: (614) 272-0684
Advertising Phone: (614) 272-5422
Advertising Fax: (614) 272-0684
Editorial Phone: (614) 272-5422
Editorial Fax: (614) 272-0684
General/National Adv. E-mail: phildaubel@columbusmessenger.com
Display Adv. E-mail: phildaubel@columbusmessenger.com
Editorial e-mail: eastside@columbusmessenger.com
Primary Website: columbusmessenger.com
Year Established: 1974
Avg Paid Circ: 0
Avg Free Circ: 15405
Audit By: Sworn/Estimate/Non-Audited
Audit Date: 10.06.2019
Personnel: Philip F. Daubel (Pub./Gen. Mgr.); Fred Schenk (Adv. Mgr.); Rick Palsgrove (Ed.); Doug Henry (Circ. Mgr)
Parent company (for newspapers): Columbus Messenger Newspapers

ENGLEWOOD INDEPENDENT

Street address 1: 694 W National Rd
Street address city: Vandalia
Street address state: OH
Zip/Postal code: 45377-1032
General Phone: (937) 236-4990
General Fax: (937) 836-1940
Advertising Phone: (937) 836-2619
Advertising Fax: (937) 836-1940
Editorial Phone: (937) 836-2619
Editorial Fax: (937) 836-1940
General/National Adv. E-mail: kbelcher@civitasmedia.com
Display Adv. E-mail: pbeattie@civitasmedia.com
Editorial e-mail: Rnunnari@civitasmedia.com
Primary Website: englewoodindependent.com
Year Established: 1975
Avg Paid Circ: 5800
Avg Free Circ: 1000
Audit By: Sworn/Estimate/Non-Audited
Audit Date: 10.06.2019
Personnel: Joel Ryan (Adv.)
Parent company (for newspapers): AIM Media Indiana

FARMLAND NEWS

Street address 1: 104 Depot St
Street address city: Archbold
Street address state: OH
Zip/Postal code: 43502-1235
General Phone: (419) 445-9456
General Fax: (419) 445-4444
Advertising Phone: (419) 445-9456
Advertising Fax: (419) 445-4444
Editorial Phone: (419) 445-9456
Editorial Fax: (419) 445-4444
General/National Adv. E-mail: Ads@FarmlandNews.com
Display Adv. E-mail: Ads@FarmlandNews.com
Editorial e-mail: News1@FarmlandNews.com
Year Established: 1959
Avg Paid Circ: 2300
Avg Free Circ: 100
Audit By: Sworn/Estimate/Non-Audited
Audit Date: 10.06.2019
Personnel: Larkin Wise-Chappuis (Circulation Mgr/Sales); Dianne Lantz (Pub/Adv. Mgr.); Judy Short (Ed)

FIRELANDS FARMER

Street address 1: 43 E Main St
Street address city: New London
Street address state: OH
Zip/Postal code: 44851-1213
General Phone: (419) 929-8043
General Fax: (419) 929-8210
Advertising Phone: (419) 929-8043
Advertising Fax: (419) 929-8210
Editorial Phone: (419) 929-8043
Editorial Fax: (419) 929-8210
General/National Adv. E-mail: globe@sdgnewsgroup.com
Display Adv. E-mail: globe@sdgnewsgroup.com
Editorial e-mail: globe@sdgnewsgroup.com
Primary Website: sdgnewsgroup.com
Audit By: Sworn/Estimate/Non-Audited
Audit Date: 10.06.2019
Personnel: Scott Gove (Pub.); Karla Souslin (Adv. Dir.); Terry Wilson (Ed.)
Parent company (for newspapers): SDGNewsgroup

FOREST HILLS JOURNAL

Street address 1: 312 Elm St
Street address city: Cincinnati
Street address state: OH
Zip/Postal code: 45202-2739
General Phone: (513) 248-8600
General Fax: (513) 248-1938
Advertising Phone: (513) 248-8600
Advertising Fax: (513) 248-1938
Editorial Phone: (513) 248-8600
Editorial Fax: (513) 248-1938
General/National Adv. E-mail: acumby@communitypress.com
Display Adv. E-mail: acumby@communitypress.com
Editorial e-mail: espangler@communitypress.com
Primary Website: cincinnati.com
Avg Free Circ: 10835
Audit By: Sworn/Estimate/Non-Audited
Audit Date: 10.06.2019
Personnel: Nancy Daly (Ed.); Margaret Buchanan (Pres./Pub.); Alison Cumby (Adv. Mgr.)
Parent company (for newspapers): Gannett

FRANKLIN CHRONICLE

Street address 1: 230 S 2nd St
Street address city: Miamisburg
Street address state: OH
Zip/Postal code: 45342-2925
General Phone: (937) 866-3331
General Fax: (937) 866-6011
Advertising Phone: (937) 866-3331
Advertising Fax: (937) 866-6011
Editorial Phone: (937) 866-3331
Editorial Fax: (937) 866-6011
General/National Adv. E-mail: franklinchronicle@miller-publishing.com
Display Adv. E-mail: franklinchronicle@miller-publishing.com
Editorial e-mail: franklinchronicle@miller-publishing.com
Avg Paid Circ: 1214
Avg Free Circ: 2000
Audit By: Sworn/Estimate/Non-Audited
Audit Date: 10.06.2019
Personnel: Don Miller (Pub./Ed.); Steve Sandlin (Mng. Ed.)

FULTON COUNTY EXPOSITOR

Street address 1: 1270 N Shoop Ave
Street address 2: Ste A
Street address city: Wauseon
Street address state: OH
Zip/Postal code: 43567-2211
General Phone: (419) 335-2010
General Fax: (419) 335-2030
Advertising Phone: (419) 335-2010
Advertising Fax: (419) 335-2030
Editorial Phone: (419) 335-2010
Editorial Fax: (419) 335-2030
General/National Adv. E-mail: fceadvertising@civitasmedia.com
Display Adv. E-mail: fceadvertising@civitasmedia.com
Editorial e-mail: fcenews@civitasmedia.com
Primary Website: fcnews.org
Year Established: 1874
Avg Paid Circ: 4236
Avg Free Circ: 51
Audit By: Sworn/Estimate/Non-Audited
Audit Date: 10.06.2019
Personnel: Drew Stambaugh (Ed.); Max Householder (Sports Ed.)

GALION INQUIRER

Street address 1: 129 Harding Way E
Street address city: Galion
Street address state: OH
Zip/Postal code: 44833-1902
General Phone: (419) 468-1117
General Fax: (419) 468-7255
General/National Adv. E-mail: vtaylor@civitasmedia.com
Display Adv. E-mail: vtaylor@civitasmedia.com
Editorial e-mail: vtaylor@galnews@civitasmedia.com
Primary Website: galioninquirer.com
Avg Paid Circ: 1800
Sat. Circulation Paid: 2000
Sat. Circulation Free: 8000
Audit By: Sworn/Estimate/Non-Audited
Audit Date: 10.06.2019
Personnel: Vicki Taylor (Pub.); John Kleinknecht (Sports Ed.)
Parent company (for newspapers): AIM Media Indiana

GEAUGA COUNTY MAPLE LEAF

Street address 1: 101 South St
Street address city: Chardon
Street address state: OH
Zip/Postal code: 44024-1336
General Phone: (440) 285-2013
General Fax: (440) 285-2015
Advertising Phone: (440) 285-2013
Advertising Fax: (440) 285-2015
Editorial Phone: (440) 285-2013
Editorial Fax: (440) 285-2015
General/National Adv. E-mail: ads@geaugamapleleaf.com
Display Adv. E-mail: ads@geaugamapleleaf.com
Editorial e-mail: editor@geaugamapleleaf.com
Primary Website: geaugamapleleaf.com
Year Established: 1993
Avg Paid Circ: 4200
Avg Free Circ: 508
Audit By: Sworn/Estimate/Non-Audited
Audit Date: 10.06.2019
Personnel: Jeff Karlovec (Pub.); John Karlovec (Ed.); Cassandra Shofar (News Ed.)

GEAUGA COURIER

Street address 1: 525 Washington St
Street address city: Chagrin Falls
Street address state: OH
Zip/Postal code: 44022-4455
General Phone: (440) 247-5335
General Fax: (440) 247-5615
Advertising Phone: (440) 247-5335
Advertising Fax: (440) 247-5615
Editorial Phone: (440) 247-5335
Editorial Fax: (440) 247-5615
General/National Adv. E-mail: sales@chagrinvalleytimes.com
Display Adv. E-mail: myad@chagrinvalleytimes.com
Editorial e-mail: editor@chagrinvalleytimes.com
Primary Website: chagrinvalleytoday.com
Year Established: 1998
Avg Paid Circ: 2500
Avg Free Circ: 2500
Audit By: Sworn/Estimate/Non-Audited
Audit Date: 10.06.2019
Personnel: H. Kenneth Douthit III (Pub.); Ellen J Kleinerman (Editor)
Parent company (for newspapers): Douthit Communications, Inc.

GREENWICH ENTERPRISE REVIEW

Street address 1: 211 S Myrtle Ave
Street address city: Willard
Street address state: OH
Zip/Postal code: 44890-1407
General Phone: (419) 935-0184
General Fax: (419) 933-2031
General/National Adv. E-mail: willardtj@hmcltd.net
Display Adv. E-mail: willardtj@hmcltd.net
Editorial e-mail: willardtj@hmcltd.net
Year Established: 1950
Avg Free Circ: 14200
Audit By: Sworn/Estimate/Non-Audited
Audit Date: 10.06.2019
Personnel: Karla Souslin (Assoc. Pub.); Lynne Phillips (Ed.)

HARRISON NEWS-HERALD

Street address 1: 144 S Main St
Street address 2: Ste 1
Street address city: Cadiz
Street address state: OH
Zip/Postal code: 43907-1165
General Phone: (740) 942-2118
General Fax: (740) 942-4667
Advertising Phone: (740) 942-2118
Advertising Fax: (740) 942-4667
Editorial Phone: (740) 942-2118
Editorial Fax: (740) 942-4667
General/National Adv. E-mail: andrea@harrisonnewsherald.com
Display Adv. E-mail: andrea@harrisonnewsherald.com
Editorial e-mail: newsroom@harrisonnewsherald.com
Primary Website: harrisonnewsherald.com
Year Established: 1819
Avg Paid Circ: 6000
Avg Free Circ: 40
Audit By: Sworn/Estimate/Non-Audited
Audit Date: 10.06.2019
Personnel: David G. Schloss (Pub.); Emily J. Schloss (Ed.); Mike Sieber (Editor)
Parent company (for newspapers): Schloss Media, Inc.

HILLTOP PRESS

Street address 1: 312 Elm St
Street address city: Cincinnati
Street address state: OH
Zip/Postal code: 45202-2739
General Phone: (513) 768-8200

General Fax: (513) 923-1806
Advertising Phone: (513) 923-3111
Advertising Fax: (513) 923-1806
Editorial Phone: (513) 923-3111
Editorial Fax: (513) 923-1806
General/National Adv. E-mail: chahn@enquirer.com
Display Adv. E-mail: mwoodruff@enquirer.com
Editorial e-mail: rmaloney@communitypress.com
Primary Website: cincinnati.com
Avg Paid Circ: 10091
Avg Free Circ: 8241
Audit By: Sworn/Estimate/Non-Audited
Audit Date: 10.06.2019
Personnel: Margaret Buchanan (Pres./Pub.); Carolyn Washburn (Exec. Ed.); Richard Maloney (Mng. Ed.); Carol Hahn (Adv. VP); Sharon Schachleiter (Circ. Mgr.)
Parent company (for newspapers): Gannett

HOLLAND-SPRINGFIELD JOURNAL

Street address 1: 130 Louisiana Ave
Street address city: Perrysburg
Street address state: OH
Zip/Postal code: 43551-1457
General Phone: (419) 874-2528
General Fax: (419) 874-7311
Advertising Phone: (419) 874-4491
Advertising Fax: (419) 874-7311
Editorial Phone: (419) 874-4491
Editorial Fax: (419) 874-7311
General/National Adv. E-mail: matt@welchpublishing.com
Display Adv. E-mail: publisher@perrysburg.com
Editorial e-mail: editor@hollandsfj.us
Primary Website: hollandsfj.us
Year Established: 2003
Avg Free Circ: 5000
Audit By: Sworn/Estimate/Non-Audited
Audit Date: 10.06.2019
Personnel: Matthew H. Welch (Pres); Jane Maiolo (Ed.)
Parent company (for newspapers): Welch Publishing Company

HOLMES COUNTY JOURNAL

Street address 1: 7368 County Road 623
Street address city: Millersburg
Street address state: OH
Zip/Postal code: 44654-9256
General Phone: (330) 674-2300
General Fax: (888) 769-3960
Advertising Phone: (330) 674-2300
Advertising Fax: (888) 769-3960
Editorial Phone: (330) 674-2300
Editorial Fax: (888) 769-3960
General/National Adv. E-mail: calguire@gpubs.com
Display Adv. E-mail: calguire@gpubs.com
Editorial e-mail: tmosser@gpubs.com
Primary Website: gpubs.com
Audit By: Sworn/Estimate/Non-Audited
Audit Date: 10.06.2019
Personnel: Michael Mast (Pres.); Tami Mosser (Ed.); Clint Alguire (Adv. Dir.)
Parent company (for newspapers): Graphic Publications Inc.

HOMETOWN JOURNAL

Street address 1: P.O. Box 24
Street address city: Lowellville
Street address state: OH
Zip/Postal code: 44436
General Phone: (330) 755-2155
General/National Adv. E-mail: news@hometownjournal.biz
Display Adv. E-mail: news@hometownjournal.biz
Editorial e-mail: news@hometownjournal.biz
Primary Website: hometownjournal.biz
Year Established: 1928
Avg Paid Circ: 3000
Avg Free Circ: 1000
Audit By: Sworn/Estimate/Non-Audited
Audit Date: 10.06.2019
Personnel: Nancy Johngrass (Pub./Ed.)

HUBER HEIGHTS COURIER

Street address 1: 694 W National Rd
Street address city: Vandalia
Street address state: OH
Zip/Postal code: 45377-1032
General Phone: (937) 236-4990
General Fax: (937) 236-4176
Advertising Phone: (937) 236-4990
Advertising Fax: (937) 236-4176
Editorial Phone: (937) 236-4990
Editorial Fax: (937) 236-4176
General/National Adv. E-mail: kbelcher@civitasmedia.com
Display Adv. E-mail: kbelcher@civitasmedia.com
Editorial e-mail: dwacker@civitasmedia.com
Primary Website: hhcourier.com
Year Established: 1973
Avg Paid Circ: 6000
Avg Free Circ: 4130
Audit By: Sworn/Estimate/Non-Audited
Audit Date: 10.06.2019
Personnel: Ron Nunnari (Mng. Ed.); Pamela Beattie (Adv. Mgr.)
Parent company (for newspapers): AIM Media Indiana

HUDSON HUB-TIMES

Street address 1: 1050 W. Main Street
Street address city: Kent
Street address state: OH
Zip/Postal code: 44240
General Phone: (330) 541-9400
General Fax: (330) 296-2698
General/National Adv. E-mail: jwilliams@recordpub.com
Display Adv. E-mail: jwilliams@recordpub.com
Editorial e-mail: mshearer@recordpub.com
Primary Website: mytownneo.com
Year Established: 1830
Avg Paid Circ: 726
Audit By: AAM
Audit Date: 31.03.2018
Personnel: Michael Shearer (Ed.); Jim Williams (GM/Adv. Dir.); Gary Hurst (Circ. Dir.)
Parent company (for newspapers): CherryRoad Media; Gannett Company Inc.

INDIAN HILL JOURNAL

Street address 1: 394 Wards Corner Rd
Street address 2: Ste 170
Street address city: Loveland
Street address state: OH
Zip/Postal code: 45140-8333
General Phone: (513) 248-8600
General Fax: (513) 248-1938
Advertising Phone: (513) 248-8600
Advertising Fax: (513) 248-1938
Editorial Phone: (513) 248-8600
Editorial Fax: (513) 248-1938
General/National Adv. E-mail: acumby@communitypress.com
Display Adv. E-mail: acumby@communitypress.com
Editorial e-mail: espangler@communitypress.com
Primary Website: cincinnati.com
Avg Free Circ: 10835
Audit By: Sworn/Estimate/Non-Audited
Audit Date: 10.06.2019
Personnel: Nancy Daly (Ed.); Margaret Buchanan (Pres./Pub.); Alison Cumby (Adv. Mgr.)
Parent company (for newspapers): Gannett

LAKE COUNTY TRIBUNE

Street address 1: 46 W Jefferson St
Street address city: Jefferson
Street address state: OH
Zip/Postal code: 44047-1028
General Phone: (440) 576-9125
General Fax: (440) 576-2778
Advertising Phone: (440) 576-9125 x106
Advertising Fax: (440) 576-2778
Editorial Phone: (440) 576-9125 x107
Editorial Fax: 440-576-2778
General/National Adv. E-mail: bcreed@gazettenews.com
Display Adv. E-mail: aballard@gazettenews.com
Classified Adv. e-mail: classifieds@gazettenews.com
Editorial e-mail: tribune@gazettenews.com
Primary Website: gazettenews.com
Year Established: 1992
Avg Paid Circ: 1730
Audit By: Sworn/Estimate/Non-Audited
Audit Date: 01.10.2022
Personnel: William Creed (Pres./Pub.); Becke Creed (Director of Operations); Kathy Vaci (Editor); Stefanie Wessell (Editorial Director); Gabriel McVey (Editor); Amber Ballard (Advertising Director)
Parent company (for newspapers): Gazette Newspapers, Inc.

LOVELAND HERALD

Street address 1: 394 Wards Corner Rd
Street address 2: Ste 170
Street address city: Loveland
Street address state: OH
Zip/Postal code: 45140-8333
General Phone: (513) 248-8600
General Fax: (513) 248-1938
Advertising Phone: (513) 248-8600
Advertising Fax: (513) 248-1938
Editorial Phone: (513) 248-8600
Editorial Fax: (513) 248-1938
General/National Adv. E-mail: acumby@communitypress.com
Display Adv. E-mail: acumby@communitypress.com
Editorial e-mail: espangler@communitypress.com
Primary Website: cincinnati.com
Avg Free Circ: 10835
Audit By: Sworn/Estimate/Non-Audited
Audit Date: 10.06.2019
Personnel: Nancy Daly (Ed.); Margaret Buchanan (Pres./Pub.); Alison Cumby (Adv. Mgr.)
Parent company (for newspapers): Gannett

MADISON MESSENGER

Street address 1: 3500 Sullivant Ave
Street address city: Columbus
Street address state: OH
Zip/Postal code: 43204-1105
General Phone: (740) 852-0809
General Fax: (740) 852-0814
Advertising Phone: (740) 852-0809
Advertising Fax: (740) 852-0814
Editorial Phone: (740) 852-0809
Editorial Fax: (740) 852-0814
General/National Adv. E-mail: phildaubel@columbusmessenger.com
Display Adv. E-mail: phildaubel@columbusmessenger.com
Editorial e-mail: madison@columbusmessenger.com
Primary Website: columbusmessenger.com
Year Established: 1984
Avg Free Circ: 15095
Audit By: Sworn/Estimate/Non-Audited
Audit Date: 10.06.2019
Personnel: Philip F. Daubel (Pub./Gen. Mgr.); Fred Schenk (Adv. Mgr.); Rick Palsgrove (Ed.); Doug Henry (Circ. Mgr)
Parent company (for newspapers): Columbus Messenger Newspapers

MIAMI COUNTY ADVOCATE

Street address 1: 224 S Market St
Street address city: Troy
Street address state: OH
Zip/Postal code: 45373-3327
General Phone: (937) 440-5275
General Fax: (937) 440-5286
Advertising Phone: (937) 440-5275
Advertising Fax: (937) 440-5286
Editorial Phone: (937) 335-5634
Editorial Fax: (937) 440-5286
General/National Adv. E-mail: wrheditor@gmail.com
Display Adv. E-mail: wrheditor@gmail.com
Editorial e-mail: wrheditor@gmail.com
Year Established: 1975
Avg Free Circ: 22000
Audit By: Sworn/Estimate/Non-Audited
Audit Date: 10.06.2019
Personnel: Christina Chalmers (Editor); Joyell Nevins (Ed.); Jan Burns (News Ed.)
Parent company (for newspapers): AIM Media Indiana

MIAMISBURG NEWS

Street address 1: 230 S 2nd St
Street address city: Miamisburg
Street address state: OH
Zip/Postal code: 45342-2925
General Phone: (937) 866-3331
General Fax: (937) 866-6011
Advertising Phone: (937) 866-3331
Advertising Fax: (937) 866-6011
Editorial Phone: (937) 866-3331
Editorial Fax: (937) 866-6011
General/National Adv. E-mail: news@miamivalleynewspapers.com
Display Adv. E-mail: news@miamivalleynewspapers.com
Editorial e-mail: news@miamivalleynewspapers.com
Avg Paid Circ: 3000
Avg Free Circ: 37
Audit By: Sworn/Estimate/Non-Audited
Audit Date: 10.06.2019
Personnel: Don Miller (Pub.); Steve Sandlin (Mng. Ed.)

MILFORD-MIAMI ADVERTISER

Street address 1: 312 Elm St
Street address city: Cincinnati
Street address state: OH
Zip/Postal code: 45202-2739
General Phone: (513) 248-8600
General Fax: (513) 248-1938
Advertising Phone: (513) 248-8600
Advertising Fax: (513) 248-1938
Editorial Phone: (513) 248-8600
Editorial Fax: (513) 248-1938
General/National Adv. E-mail: acumby@communitypress.com
Display Adv. E-mail: acumby@communitypress.com
Editorial e-mail: therron@communitypress.com
Primary Website: cincinnati.com
Avg Free Circ: 10835
Audit By: Sworn/Estimate/Non-Audited
Audit Date: 10.06.2019
Personnel: Richard Maloney (Ed.); Margaret Buchanan (Pres./Pub.); Alison Cumby (Adv. Mgr.)
Parent company (for newspapers): Gannett

MONROE COUNTY BEACON

Street address 1: 103 E Court St
Street address city: Woodsfield
Street address state: OH
Zip/Postal code: 43793-1110
General Phone: (740) 472-0734
General Fax: (740) 472-0735
Advertising Phone: (740) 472-0734
Advertising Fax: (740) 472-0735
Editorial Phone: (740) 472-0734
Editorial Fax: (740) 472-0735
General/National Adv. E-mail: monroecountybeacon@sbcglobal.net
Display Adv. E-mail: monroecountybeacon@sbcglobal.net
Editorial e-mail: monroecountybeacon@sbcglobal.net
Primary Website: mcbeacon.com
Year Established: 1884
Avg Paid Circ: 4950
Avg Free Circ: 15
Audit By: Sworn/Estimate/Non-Audited
Audit Date: 10.06.2019
Personnel: Darin Brown (Ed./Gen. Mgr.); Linsey Colvin (News Ed.)
Parent company (for newspapers): Delphos Herald, Inc.

MORGAN COUNTY HERALD

Street address 1: 89 W Main St
Street address city: McConnelsville
Street address state: OH
Zip/Postal code: 43756-1264
General Phone: (740) 962-3377
General Fax: (740) 962-6861
Advertising Phone: (740) 962-3377
Advertising Fax: (740) 962-6861
Editorial Phone: (740) 962-3377
Editorial Fax: (740) 962-6861
General/National Adv. E-mail: advertising@mchnews.com
Display Adv. E-mail: classifieds@mchnews.com
Editorial e-mail: newsroom@mchnews.com
Primary Website: mchnews.com
Year Established: 1844
Avg Paid Circ: 3054
Avg Free Circ: 49
Audit By: Sworn/Estimate/Non-Audited
Audit Date: 10.06.2019
Personnel: Jack L. Barnes (Publisher); David Keller (General Manager)

NEW CONCORD AREA LEADER

Street address 1: 831 Wheeling Ave
Street address city: Cambridge

Street address state: OH
Zip/Postal code: 43725-2316
General Phone: (740) 439-3531
General Fax: (740) 432-6219
Advertising Phone: (740) 439-3531
Advertising Fax: (740) 439-3533
Editorial Phone: (740) 439-3531
Editorial Fax: (740) 432-6219
General/National Adv. E-mail: Lynn@daily-jeff.com
Display Adv. E-mail: ads@daily-jeff.com
Editorial e-mail: newsroom@daily-jeff.com
Primary Website: newconcordleader.com
Avg Paid Circ: 1150
Audit By: Sworn/Estimate/Non-Audited
Audit Date: 10.06.2019
Personnel: Andrew Dix (Pub.); Ray Booth (Exec. Ed.)
Parent company (for newspapers): Jeffersonian Advantage

NEW LONDON RECORD

Street address 1: 43 E Main St
Street address city: New London
Street address state: OH
Zip/Postal code: 44851-1213
General Phone: (419) 929-3411
General Fax: (419) 929-8210
Advertising Phone: (419) 929-3411
Advertising Fax: (419) 929-8210
Editorial Phone: (419) 929-3411
Editorial Fax: (419) 929-8210
General/National Adv. E-mail: record@sdgnewsgroup.com
Display Adv. E-mail: record@sdgnewsgroup.com
Editorial e-mail: record@sdgnewsgroup.com
Primary Website: sdgnewsgroup.com
Avg Paid Circ: 1900
Audit By: Sworn/Estimate/Non-Audited
Audit Date: 10.06.2019
Personnel: Scott Gove (Pub.); Karla Souslin (Adv. Dir.)
Parent company (for newspapers): SDGNewsgroup

NEWCOMERSTOWN NEWS

Street address 1: 140 W Main St
Street address city: Newcomerstown
Street address state: OH
Zip/Postal code: 43832-1041
General Phone: (740) 498-7117
General Fax: (740) 498-5624
Advertising Phone: (740) 498-7117
Advertising Fax: (740) 498-5624
Editorial Phone: (740) 498-7117
Editorial Fax: (740) 498-5624
General/National Adv. E-mail: gjohnson@newcomerstown-news.com
Display Adv. E-mail: jtrzop@newcomerstown-news.com
Editorial e-mail: nwolfe@newcomerstown-news.com
Primary Website: newcomerstown-news.com
Year Established: 1898
Avg Paid Circ: 3500
Avg Free Circ: 24
Audit By: Sworn/Estimate/Non-Audited
Audit Date: 10.06.2019
Personnel: Andrew Dix (Pub.); Niki Wolfe (Ed.); Ray H. Booth (Mng. Ed.); Peggy Morgatroyd (Adv. Mgr.)
Parent company (for newspapers): Jeffersonian Advantage

NEWS JOURNAL STAR

Street address 1: 761 S Nelson Ave
Street address city: Wilmington
Street address state: OH
Zip/Postal code: 45177-2517
General Phone: (937) 382-2574
General Fax: (937) 382-4392
Advertising Phone: (937) 382-2574
Advertising Fax: (937) 382-4392
Editorial Phone: (937) 382-2574
Editorial Fax: (937) 382-4392
General/National Adv. E-mail: skersey@civitasmedia.com
Display Adv. E-mail: bvandeventer@civitasmedia.com
Editorial e-mail: rgraf@civitasmedia.com
Primary Website: wnewsj.com
Year Established: 1838
Avg Free Circ: 17000
Audit By: Sworn/Estimate/Non-Audited
Audit Date: 10.06.2019
Personnel: Tom Barr (Ed.); Lane Moon (Reg. Pub.); Elizabeth Mattingly (Media Sales Dir.); Mark Huber (Sports Ed.); Dawn Gunkel (Circ. Mgr.)
Parent company (for newspapers): AIM Media Indiana

NORDONIA HILLS NEWS LEADER

Street address 1: 1050 W Main St
Street address city: Kent
Street address state: OH
Zip/Postal code: 44240-2006
General Phone: (330) 541-9400
General Fax: (330) 296-2698
General/National Adv. E-mail: jwilliams@recordpub.com
Display Adv. E-mail: jwilliams@recordpub.com
Editorial e-mail: hrainone@recordpub.com
Primary Website: the-news-leader.com
Year Established: 1830
Avg Paid Circ: 316
Avg Free Circ: 12568
Audit By: AAM
Audit Date: 31.03.2016
Personnel: Heather Rainone (Ed.); Gary Hurst (Circ. Dir.); Jim Williams (GM/Adv. Dir.)
Parent company (for newspapers): CherryRoad Media

NORTH COAST BUSINESS JOURNAL

Street address 1: 205 SE Catawba Rd
Street address 2: Ste G
Street address city: Port Clinton
Street address state: OH
Zip/Postal code: 43452
General Phone: (419) 732-2154
General/National Adv. E-mail: kwilloughby@ncbj.net
Display Adv. E-mail: kwilloughby@ncbj.net
Editorial e-mail: editor@ncbj.net
Primary Website: ncbj.net
Year Established: 1994
Avg Free Circ: 6675
Audit By: CVC
Audit Date: 30.12.2017
Personnel: John Schaffner (Pub.); Angie Zam (Ed.); Kristina Willoughby (Adv.); Bruce Dinse (Circ.)
Parent company (for newspapers): Schaffner Publications, Inc.

NORTH RIDGEVILLE PRESS

Street address 1: 158 Lear Rd
Street address city: Avon Lake
Street address state: OH
Zip/Postal code: 44012-1982
General Phone: (440) 933-5100
General Fax: (440) 933-7904
Advertising Phone: (440) 933-5100
Advertising Fax: (440) 933-7904
Editorial Phone: (440) 933-5100
Editorial Fax: (440) 933-7904
General/National Adv. E-mail: NRNews@2presspapers.com
Display Adv. E-mail: nrpclass@dceye.com
Editorial e-mail: editor@2presspapers.com
Primary Website: 2presspapers.com
Year Established: 1980
Avg Paid Circ: 2000
Avg Free Circ: 1000
Audit By: Sworn/Estimate/Non-Audited
Audit Date: 10.06.2019
Personnel: Harold K. Douthit (Pub.); Peter Comings (Ed.); Janet L. Sanner (Adv. Mgr./Gen. Mgr.)
Parent company (for newspapers): Douthit Communications, Inc.

NORTHWEST PRESS

Street address 1: 5556 Cheviot Rd
Street address 2: Ste A
Street address city: Cincinnati
Street address state: OH
Zip/Postal code: 45247-5202
General Phone: (513) 923-3111
General Fax: (513) 923-1806
Advertising Phone: (513) 923-3111
Advertising Fax: (513) 923-1806
Editorial Phone: (513) 923-3111
Editorial Fax: (513) 923-1806
General/National Adv. E-mail: chahn@enquirer.com
Display Adv. E-mail: mwoodruff@enquirer.com
Editorial e-mail: cwashburn@enquirer.com
Primary Website: cincinnati.com
Year Established: 1921
Avg Paid Circ: 12176
Audit By: Sworn/Estimate/Non-Audited
Audit Date: 10.06.2019
Personnel: Margaret Buchanan (Pres./Pub.); Carolyn Washburn (Ed.); Carol Hahn (Adv. VP); Adele Baston (Account Mgr.)
Parent company (for newspapers): Gannett

OBERLIN NEWS-TRIBUNE

Street address 1: 42 S Main St
Street address city: Oberlin
Street address state: OH
Zip/Postal code: 44074-1627
General Phone: (440) 988-2801
General Fax: (440) 988-2802
Editorial e-mail: news@lcnewspapers.com
Primary Website: theoberlinnewstribune.com
Year Established: 1930
Avg Paid Circ: 2000
Avg Free Circ: 10000
Audit By: Sworn/Estimate/Non-Audited
Audit Date: 10.06.2019
Personnel: Jason Hawk (Ed.); Jonathon Delozier; Mandy Saluk (Adv.)
Parent company (for newspapers): Schloss Media, Inc.

PERRY COUNTY TRIBUNE

Street address 1: 116 S Main St
Street address city: New Lexington
Street address state: OH
Zip/Postal code: 43764-1376
General Phone: (740) 342-4121
General Fax: (740) 342-4131
Advertising Phone: (740) 342-4121 ext. 104
Editorial Phone: (740) 342-4121 ext. 106
General/National Adv. E-mail: pdennis@perrytribune.com
Display Adv. E-mail: bcarney@perrytribune.com
Editorial e-mail: dhutmire@perrytribune.com
Primary Website: perrytribune.com
Year Established: 1893
Avg Paid Circ: 4000
Avg Free Circ: 16400
Audit By: Sworn/Estimate/Non-Audited
Audit Date: 10.06.2019
Personnel: Deb Hutmire (Ed.); Pete Dennis (Adv. Dir.)
Parent company (for newspapers): Adams Publishing Group, LLC

PERRYSBURG MESSENGER JOURNAL

Street address 1: 117 E 2nd St
Street address city: Perrysburg
Street address state: OH
Zip/Postal code: 43551-2172
General Phone: (419) 874-4491
General Fax: (419) 874-7311
Advertising Phone: (419) 874-4491
Advertising Fax: (419) 874-7311
Editorial Phone: (419) 874-4491
Editorial Fax: (419) 874-7311
General/National Adv. E-mail: matt@welchpublishing.com
Display Adv. E-mail: publisher@perrysburg.com
Editorial e-mail: editor@perrysburg.com
Primary Website: perrysburg.com
Year Established: 1853
Avg Paid Circ: 5676
Avg Free Circ: 6882
Audit By: Sworn/Estimate/Non-Audited
Audit Date: 10.06.2019
Personnel: John B. Welch (Pub.); Matthew H. Welch (Adv. Mgr.); Deb Buker (Ed.)
Parent company (for newspapers): Welch Publishing Company

POINT & SHORELAND JOURNAL

Street address 1: 130 Louisiana Ave.
Street address city: Perrysburg
Street address state: OH
Zip/Postal code: 43551
General Phone: (419) 874-4491
General/National Adv. E-mail: matt@welchpublishing.com
Display Adv. E-mail: publisher@perrysburg.com
Editorial e-mail: publisher@perrysburg.com
Primary Website: pointandshoreland.com
Avg Paid Circ: 5676
Avg Free Circ: 6882
Audit By: Sworn/Estimate/Non-Audited
Audit Date: 10.06.2019
Personnel: Adam Welch (Owner); Chet Welch (Pres./Owner)
Parent company (for newspapers): Welch Publishing Company

POLAND TOWN CRIER

Street address 1: 240 Franklin St SE
Street address city: Warren
Street address state: OH
Zip/Postal code: 44483-5711
General Phone: (330) 629-6200
General Fax: (330) 629-6210
Editorial e-mail: editor@towncrieronline.com
Primary Website: towncrieronline.com
Year Established: 1993
Avg Free Circ: 35000
Audit By: Sworn/Estimate/Non-Audited
Audit Date: 10.06.2019
Personnel: Amy Wilson (Ed./Gen. Mgr.); J.T. Whitehouse
Parent company (for newspapers): Ogden Newspapers Inc.

PRICE HILL PRESS

Street address 1: 312 Elm St
Street address city: Cincinnati
Street address state: OH
Zip/Postal code: 45202-2739
General Phone: (513) 923-3111
General Fax: (513) 923-1806
Advertising Phone: (513) 923-3111
Advertising Fax: (513) 923-1806
Editorial Phone: (513) 923-3111
Editorial Fax: (513) 923-1806
General/National Adv. E-mail: chahn@enquirer.com
Display Adv. E-mail: mwoodruff@enquirer.com
Editorial e-mail: memral@communitypress.com
Primary Website: cincinnati.com
Avg Paid Circ: 10091
Avg Free Circ: 8241
Audit By: Sworn/Estimate/Non-Audited
Audit Date: 10.06.2019
Personnel: Margaret Buchanan (Pres./Pub.); Carolyn Washburn (Exec. Ed.); Richard Maloney (Mng. Ed.); Carol Hahn (Adv. VP); Sharon Schachleiter (Circ. Mgr.)
Parent company (for newspapers): Gannett

PUTNAM COUNTY SENTINEL

Street address 1: 224 E Main St
Street address city: Ottawa
Street address state: OH
Zip/Postal code: 45875-1944
General Phone: (419) 523-5709
General Fax: (419) 523-3512
Advertising Phone: (419) 523-5709 ext. 225
Advertising Fax: (419) 523-3512
Editorial Phone: (419) 523-5709 ext. 231
Editorial Fax: (419) 523-3512
General/National Adv. E-mail: kpickens@putnamsentinel.com
Display Adv. E-mail: gbogart@putnamsentinel.com
Editorial e-mail: news@putnamsentinel.com
Primary Website: putnamsentinel.com
Year Established: 1855
Avg Paid Circ: 7800
Avg Free Circ: 107
Audit By: Sworn/Estimate/Non-Audited
Audit Date: 10.06.2019
Personnel: Doug Nutter (Pub.); Anne Coburn-Griffis (Ed.); Charlie Warnimont (Sports Ed.); Mark Ranes (Circ. Mgr.); Cheryl Andres (Adv. Mgr.); Kim Andreasen (Adv. Rep.); Crystal Dunlap (Adv. Rep.)
Parent company (for newspapers): Delphos Herald, Inc.

PUTNAM COUNTY VIDETTE

Street address 1: 224 E Main St
Street address city: Ottawa
Street address state: OH
Zip/Postal code: 45875-1944
General Phone: (419) 523-5709
General Fax: (419) 523-3512
Advertising Phone: (419) 523-5709 ext. 225
Advertising Fax: (419) 523-3512
Editorial Phone: (419) 523-5709 ext. 231

Editorial Fax: (419) 523-3512
General/National Adv. E-mail: kpickens@putnamsentinel.com
Display Adv. E-mail: gbogart@putnamsentinel.com
Editorial e-mail: news@putnamsentinel.com
Primary Website: putnamsentinel.com
Audit By: Sworn/Estimate/Non-Audited
Audit Date: 10.06.2019
Personnel: Doug Nutter (Pub.); Cheryl Andres (Adv. Mgr.)
Parent company (for newspapers): Delphos Herald, Inc.

ROSSFORD RECORD JOURNAL

Street address 1: 215 Osborne St
Street address city: Rossford
Street address state: OH
Zip/Postal code: 43460-1238
General Phone: (419) 874-4491
General Fax: (419) 874-7311
Advertising Phone: (419) 874-4491
Advertising Fax: (419) 874-7311
Editorial Phone: (419) 874-4491
Editorial Fax: (419) 874-7311
General/National Adv. E-mail: matt@welchpublishing.com
Display Adv. E-mail: publisher@perrysburg.com
Editorial e-mail: editor@rossford.com
Primary Website: rossford.com
Year Established: 1940
Avg Paid Circ: 1759
Avg Free Circ: 1800
Audit By: Sworn/Estimate/Non-Audited
Audit Date: 10.06.2019
Personnel: John B. Welch (Pub.); Matthew H. Welch (Adv. Mgr.); Beth Church (Ed.)
Parent company (for newspapers): Welch Publishing Company

SOLON TIMES

Street address 1: 525 Washington St
Street address city: Chagrin Falls
Street address state: OH
Zip/Postal code: 44022-4455
General Phone: (440) 247-5335
General Fax: (440) 247-5615
Advertising Phone: (440) 247-5335
Advertising Fax: (440) 247-5615
Editorial Phone: (440) 247-5335
Editorial Fax: (440) 247-5615
General/National Adv. E-mail: sales@chagrinvalleytimes.com
Display Adv. E-mail: myad@chagrinvalleytimes.com
Editorial e-mail: editor@chagrinvalleytimes.com
Primary Website: chagrinvalleytoday.com
Year Established: 1978
Avg Paid Circ: 1900
Avg Free Circ: 1000
Audit By: Sworn/Estimate/Non-Audited
Audit Date: 10.06.2019
Personnel: H. Kenneth Douthit III (Pub.); Ellen Kleinerman (Editor); Diana Nicolanti (Classifieds Mgr.)
Parent company (for newspapers): Douthit Communications, Inc.

SOUTHEAST MESSENGER

Street address 1: 3500 Sullivant Ave
Street address city: Columbus
Street address state: OH
Zip/Postal code: 43204-1105
General Phone: (614) 272-5422
General Fax: (614) 272-0684
Advertising Phone: (614) 272-5422
Advertising Fax: (614) 272-0684
Editorial Phone: (614) 272-5422
Editorial Fax: (614) 272-0684
General/National Adv. E-mail: phildaubel@columbusmessenger.com
Display Adv. E-mail: phildaubel@columbusmessenger.com
Editorial e-mail: southeast@columbusmessenger.com
Primary Website: columbusmessenger.com
Year Established: 1974
Avg Free Circ: 20664
Audit By: Sworn/Estimate/Non-Audited
Audit Date: 10.06.2019
Personnel: Philip F. Daubel (Pub./Gen. Mgr.); Rick Palsgrove (Ed.); Fred Schenk (Adv. Mgr.); Doug Henry (Circ. Mgr)
Parent company (for newspapers): Columbus Messenger Newspapers

SOUTHWEST MESSENGER

Street address 1: 3500 Sullivant Ave
Street address city: Columbus
Street address state: OH
Zip/Postal code: 43204-1105
General Phone: (614) 272-5422
General Fax: (614) 272-0684
Advertising Phone: (614) 272-5422
Advertising Fax: (614) 272-0684
Editorial Phone: (614) 272-5422
Editorial Fax: (614) 272-0684
General/National Adv. E-mail: phildaubel@columbusmessenger.com
Display Adv. E-mail: phildaubel@columbusmessenger.com
Editorial e-mail: southwest@columbusmessenger.com
Primary Website: columbusmessenger.com
Year Established: 1974
Avg Free Circ: 21388
Audit By: Sworn/Estimate/Non-Audited
Audit Date: 10.06.2019
Personnel: Philip F. Daubel (Pub./Gen. Mgr.); Fred Schenk (Adv. Mgr.); Rick Palsgrove (Ed.); Doug Henry (Circ. Mgr)
Parent company (for newspapers): Columbus Messenger Newspapers

STOW SENTRY

Street address 1: 1050 W. Main Street
Street address city: Kent
Street address state: OH
Zip/Postal code: 44240
General Phone: (330) 541-9400
General Fax: (330) 296-2698
Advertising Phone: (330) 673-3500
Advertising Fax: (330) 296-2698
Editorial Phone: (330) 541-9400 Ext. 4178
Editorial Fax: (330) 296-2698
General/National Adv. E-mail: Ads@recordpub.com
Display Adv. E-mail: legals@recordpub.com
Classified Adv. e-mail: class@recordpub.com
Editorial e-mail: editor@recordpub.com
Primary Website: stowsentry.com
Year Established: 1830
Avg Paid Circ: 320
Avg Free Circ: 14083
Audit By: AAM
Audit Date: 31.03.2016
Personnel: David E. Dix (Pub.); Heather Rainone (Mng. Ed.); Gary Hurst; Jim Williams (GM/Adv. Dir.)
Parent company (for newspapers): CherryRoad Media; Gannett Company Inc.

SUGARCREEK BELLBROOK TIMES

Street address 1: 1836 W Park Sq
Street address city: Xenia
Street address state: OH
Zip/Postal code: 45385-2668
General Phone: (937) 294-7000
General Fax: (937) 294-2981
Advertising Phone: (937) 294-7000
Advertising Fax: (937) 294-2981
Editorial Phone: (937) 294-7000
Editorial Fax: (937) 294-2981
General/National Adv. E-mail: jmilburn@tcnewsnet.com
Display Adv. E-mail: tcnewsnet@tcnewsnet.com
Editorial e-mail: jmilburn@tcnewsnet.com
Primary Website: bellbrooktimes.com
Audit By: Sworn/Estimate/Non-Audited
Audit Date: 10.06.2019
Personnel: Jodi Milburn (Ed.); Don Yeazell (Sales); Amber Campbell (Sales)
Parent company (for newspapers): Ohio Community Media, LLC

SUN NEWS

Street address 1: 5510 Cloverleaf Pkwy
Street address city: Cleveland
Street address state: OH
Zip/Postal code: 44125-4815
General Phone: (216) 986-2600
General Fax: (216) 986-2340
Advertising Phone: (216) 986-2460
Advertising Fax: (216) 986-2340
Editorial Phone: (216) 986-6070
Editorial Fax: (216) 986-2340
General/National Adv. E-mail: sun@sunnews.com
Display Adv. E-mail: mmorilak@sunnews.com
Editorial e-mail: ckovach@sunnews.com
Primary Website: sunnews.com
Year Established: 1969
Avg Paid Circ: 137284
Audit By: Sworn/Estimate/Non-Audited
Audit Date: 10.06.2019
Personnel: Linda Kinsey (Exec. Ed.); Mark Morilak (Ed.); Carol Kovach (Mng. Ed.); Rodney Bengston (Asst. Ed.)
Parent company (for newspapers): Advance Publications, Inc.

SUNDAY TIMES-SENTINEL

Street address 1: 825 3rd Ave
Street address city: Gallipolis
Street address state: OH
Zip/Postal code: 45631-1624
General Phone: (740) 446-2342
General Fax: (740) 446-3008
General/National Adv. E-mail: jmitchell@civitasmedia.com
Display Adv. E-mail: kcade@civitasmedia.com
Editorial e-mail: mjohnsoncivitasmedia.com
Primary Website: mydailytribune.com
Audit By: Sworn/Estimate/Non-Audited
Audit Date: 10.06.2019
Personnel: Beth Sergent (Ed.); Bud Hunt (Pub.)
Parent company (for newspapers): AIM Media Indiana

SWANTON ENTERPRISE

Street address 1: 1270 N Shoop Ave
Street address 2: Ste A
Street address city: Wauseon
Street address state: OH
Zip/Postal code: 43567-2211
General Phone: (419) 335-2010
General Fax: (419) 335-2030
Advertising Phone: (419) 335-2010
Advertising Fax: (419) 335-2030
Editorial Phone: (419) 335-2010
Editorial Fax: (419) 335-2030
General/National Adv. E-mail: TSEnews@aimmediamidwest.com
Display Adv. E-mail: TSEnews@civitasmedia.com
Editorial e-mail: dstambaugh@civitasmedia.com
Primary Website: swantonenterprise.com
Year Established: 1887
Avg Paid Circ: 810
Audit By: Sworn/Estimate/Non-Audited
Audit Date: 10.06.2019
Personnel: Drew Stambaugh (Ed.); Max Householder (Sports Ed.)
Parent company (for newspapers): AIM Media Indiana

TALLMADGE EXPRESS

Street address 1: 1050 W. Main Street
Street address city: Kent
Street address state: OH
Zip/Postal code: 44240
General Phone: (330) 541-9400
Advertising Phone: (330) 541-9400
General/National Adv. E-mail: zwickert@recordpub.com
Display Adv. E-mail: zwickert@recordpub.com
Editorial e-mail: hrainone@recordpub.com
Primary Website: mytownneo.com/tallmadgeexpress
Year Established: 1830
Avg Paid Circ: 181
Avg Free Circ: 7107
Audit By: AAM
Audit Date: 31.03.2018
Personnel: David E. Dix (Pub.); Heather Rainone (Mng. Ed.); Michael Shearer (Ed./ Gen. Mgr.); Jim Williams (Adv.); Gary Hurst (Circ. Dir.)
Parent company (for newspapers): CherryRoad Media; Gannett Company Inc.

THE ADA HERALD

Street address 1: 229 N Main St
Street address city: Ada
Street address state: OH
Zip/Postal code: 45810-1109
General Phone: (419) 634-6055
General Fax: (419) 634-0912
General/National Adv. E-mail: advertising@putnamsentinel.com
Display Adv. E-mail: classifieds@putnamsentinel.com
Editorial e-mail: news@adaherald.com
Primary Website: adaherald.com
Year Established: 1885
Avg Paid Circ: 3000
Audit By: Sworn/Estimate/Non-Audited
Audit Date: 10.06.2019
Personnel: Ray Geary (COO); Cheryl Andres (Adv.); Steven Coburn-Griffis (Ed.); Mark Ranes (Circ. Mgr.)
Parent company (for newspapers): Delphos Herald, Inc.

THE ADVERTISER

Street address 1: 10 S Main St
Street address city: West Alexandria
Street address state: OH
Zip/Postal code: 45381-1216
General Phone: (937) 839-4733
General Fax: (937) 839-5351
Advertising Phone: (937) 839-4733
Advertising Fax: (937) 839-5351
Editorial Phone: (937) 839-4733
Editorial Fax: (937) 839-5351
General/National Adv. E-mail: twinvpub@infinet.com
Display Adv. E-mail: information@onlinetvp.com
Editorial e-mail: twinvpub@infinet.com
Primary Website: twinvalleypublications.com
Year Established: 1934
Avg Paid Circ: 400
Avg Free Circ: 8000
Audit By: Sworn/Estimate/Non-Audited
Audit Date: 10.06.2019
Personnel: Sam Shortes (Pub./Ed.); Cindy Shortes (Gen. Mgr.); Angie Donohoo (Adv. Mgr.)
Parent company (for newspapers): Twin Valley Publications

THE ALLIANCE REVIEW

Street address 1: 500 Market Ave. South
Street address city: Canton
Street address state: OH
Zip/Postal code: 44702
General/National Adv. E-mail: news@the-review.com
Display Adv. E-mail: news@the-review.com
Editorial e-mail: news@the-review.com
Primary Website: the-review.com
Avg Paid Circ: 4400
Avg Free Circ: 25
Audit By: Sworn/Estimate/Non-Audited
Audit Date: 10.06.2019
Personnel: Laura Kessel (Ed.); Mindy Cannon (Adv. Dir.); Ron Hurst (Circ. Dir.); Jim Porter (GM); Patti Cochran (Adv. Acct. Dir.); Missy Beadnell (Circ.)
Parent company (for newspapers): Gannett

THE BARBERTON HERALD

Street address 1: 70 4th St NW
Street address 2: Ste 1
Street address city: Barberton
Street address state: OH
Zip/Postal code: 44203-8283
General Phone: (330) 753-1068
General Fax: (330) 753-1021
Advertising Phone: (330) 753-1068
Advertising Fax: (330) 753-1021
Editorial Phone: (330) 753-1068
Editorial Fax: (330) 753-1021
General/National Adv. E-mail: jimc@barbertonherald.com
Display Adv. E-mail: classifieds@barbertonherald.com
Editorial e-mail: news@barbertonherald.com
Primary Website: barbertonherald.com
Year Established: 1923
Avg Paid Circ: 7800
Avg Free Circ: 33618
Audit By: Sworn/Estimate/Non-Audited
Audit Date: 10.06.2019
Personnel: Cheryl Vespoint (Pub.); Jim Colombo (Adv. Dir.); Rich Muller (Ed.)

THE BEACON

Street address 1: 205 SE Catawba Rd
Street address 2: Ste G
Street address city: Port Clinton
Street address state: OH
Zip/Postal code: 43452-2669

General Phone: (419) 732-2154
General Fax: (419) 734-5382
Advertising Phone: (419) 732-2154
Advertising Fax: (419) 734-5382
Editorial Phone: (419) 732-2154
Editorial Fax: (419) 734-5382
General/National Adv. E-mail: john@thebeacon.net
Display Adv. E-mail: john@thebeacon.net
Editorial e-mail: john@thebeacon.net
Primary Website: thebeacon.net
Year Established: 1983
Avg Paid Circ: 6
Avg Free Circ: 14238
Audit By: CVC
Audit Date: 31.03.2017
Personnel: John Schaffner (Pub.); Jasmine Cupp (Ed.); Connie Roberts (Adv. Mgr.); Bruce Dinse (Circ. Mgr.)
Parent company (for newspapers): Schaffner Publications, Inc.

THE BLUFFTON NEWS

Street address 1: 101 N Main St
Street address city: Bluffton
Street address state: OH
Zip/Postal code: 45817-1245
General Phone: (419) 358-8010
General Fax: (419) 358-8020
Advertising Phone: (419) 358-8010
Advertising Fax: (419) 358-8020
Editorial Phone: (419) 358-8010
Editorial Fax: (419) 358-8020
General/National Adv. E-mail: editor@blufftonnews.com
Display Adv. E-mail: editor@blufftonnews.com
Editorial e-mail: editor@blufftonnews.com
Primary Website: blufftonnews.com
Year Established: 1876
Avg Paid Circ: 2900
Audit By: Sworn/Estimate/Non-Audited
Audit Date: 10.06.2019
Personnel: Thomas M. Edwards (Pub.); Austin Arnold (Ed.); Sean Burgie (Adv. Mgr.)

THE BROWN COUNTY PRESS

Street address 1: 219 S High St
Street address city: Mount Orab
Street address state: OH
Zip/Postal code: 45154-9039
General Phone: (937) 444-3441
General Fax: (937) 444-2652
Advertising Phone: (937) 444-3441
Advertising Fax: (937) 444-2652
Editorial Phone: (937) 444-3441
Editorial Fax: (937) 444-2652
General/National Adv. E-mail: bcpress@frontier.com
Display Adv. E-mail: bcpress@frontier.com
Editorial e-mail: asa3866@aol.com
Primary Website: browncountypress.com
Mthly Avg Views: 8448
Mthly Avg Unique Visitors: 1891
Year Established: 1973
Avg Paid Circ: 0
Avg Free Circ: 18775
Audit By: CVC
Audit Date: 31.03.2018
Personnel: Wayne Gates (Ed.); Tony Adams (Pub.); Connie Watt (Circ.); Pam Stricker (Adv.)
Parent company (for newspapers): MCM Ohio LLC

THE BUCKEYE LAKE BEACON

Street address 1: 4675 Walnut Rd
Street address city: Buckeye Lake
Street address state: OH
Zip/Postal code: 43008-7770
General Phone: (740) 928-5541
General Fax: (740) 928-7960
Advertising Phone: (740) 928-5541
Advertising Fax: (740) 928-7960
Editorial Phone: (740) 928-5541
Editorial Fax: (740) 928-7960
General/National Adv. E-mail: charlesprince@buckeyelakebeacon.net
Display Adv. E-mail: art@buckeyelakebeacon.net
Editorial e-mail: charlesprince@buckeyelakebeacon.net
Primary Website: buckeyelakebeacon.net
Year Established: 1996
Avg Free Circ: 14,7
Audit By: Sworn/Estimate/Non-Audited
Audit Date: 10.06.2019
Personnel: Charles Prince (Pub./Ed./Adv. Mgr.); Mary Prince (Bus. Mgr.)

THE BUDGET

Street address 1: 134 N Factory St
Street address city: Sugarcreek
Street address state: OH
Zip/Postal code: 44681
General Phone: (330) 852-4634
General Fax: (330) 852-4421
Advertising Phone: (330) 852-4634
Advertising Fax: (330) 852-4421
Editorial Phone: (330) 852-4634
Editorial Fax: (330) 852-4421
General/National Adv. E-mail: mmiller@thebudgetnewspaper.com
Display Adv. E-mail: classifieds@thebudgetnewspaper.com
Editorial e-mail: localnews@thebudgetnewspaper.com
Primary Website: thebudgetnewspaper.com
Year Established: 1890
Avg Paid Circ: 18875
Avg Free Circ: 1161
Audit By: Sworn/Estimate/Non-Audited
Audit Date: 10.06.2019
Personnel: Fannie Erb-Miller (National Edition Ed.); Beverly Keller (Local Edition Ed.); Miller Milo (Adv. Dir.)

THE CLERMONT SUN

Street address 1: 348 West Main St
Street address city: Williamsburg
Street address state: OH
Zip/Postal code: 45176
General Phone: (513) 732-2511
General Fax: (513) 732-6344
Advertising Phone: (513) 732-2511
Advertising Fax: (513) 732-6344
Editorial Phone: (513) 732-2511
Editorial Fax: (513) 732-6344
General/National Adv. E-mail: info@clermontsun.com
Display Adv. E-mail: info@clermontsun.com
Editorial e-mail: info@clermontsun.com
Primary Website: clermontsun.com
Year Established: 1828
Avg Paid Circ: 2500
Audit By: Sworn/Estimate/Non-Audited
Audit Date: 01.09.2022
Personnel: Tony Adams (Pub.); Scott Champion (Owner); Rod Baker (Regional Publisher)
Parent company (for newspapers): MCM Ohio LLC; Champion Media, LLC

THE COMMUNITY COMMON

Street address 1: 637 6th St
Street address city: Portsmouth
Street address state: OH
Zip/Postal code: 45662-3924
General Phone: (740) 353-1151
General Fax: (740) 353-5848
Advertising Phone: (740) 353-1151
Advertising Fax: (740) 353-5848
Editorial Phone: (740) 353-1151
Editorial Fax: (740) 353-5848
General/National Adv. E-mail: bwarnock@civitasmedia.com
Display Adv. E-mail: bwarnock@civitasmedia.com
Editorial e-mail: news@communitycommon.com
Primary Website: communitycommon.com
Year Established: 1982
Audit By: Sworn/Estimate/Non-Audited
Audit Date: 10.06.2019
Personnel: Hope Comer (Pub.)
Parent company (for newspapers): AIM Media Indiana

THE COMMUNITY POST

Street address 1: 326 N Main St Ste 200
Street address city: Minster
Street address state: OH
Zip/Postal code: 45865
General Phone: (419) 628-2369
General Fax: (419) 628-4712
Advertising Phone: (419) 628-2369
Advertising Fax: (419) 628-4712
Editorial Phone: (419) 628-2369
Editorial Fax: (419) 628-4712
General/National Adv. E-mail: publisher@nktelco.net
Display Adv. E-mail: publisher@nktelco.net
Editorial e-mail: reporter@nktelco.net
Primary Website: minstercommunitypost.com
Year Established: 1896
Avg Paid Circ: 1500
Audit By: Sworn/Estimate/Non-Audited
Audit Date: 10.06.2019
Personnel: Deb Zwez (Pub.); Carol Kohn (Adv. Mgr.)
Parent company (for newspapers): Horizon Publications Inc.

THE COURIER

Street address 1: 46 W Jefferson St
Street address city: Jefferson
Street address state: OH
Zip/Postal code: 44047-1028
General Phone: (440) 576-9125
General Fax: (440) 576-2778
Advertising Phone: (440) 576-9125 x106
Advertising Fax: (440) 576-2778
Editorial Phone: (440) 576-9125 x107
Editorial Fax: (440) 576-2778
General/National Adv. E-mail: bcreed@gazettenews.com
Display Adv. E-mail: aballard@gazettenews.com
Classified Adv. e-mail: classifieds@gazettenews.com
Editorial e-mail: courier@gazettenews.com
Primary Website: gazettenews.com
Year Established: 1992
Avg Paid Circ: 1744
Audit By: Sworn/Estimate/Non-Audited
Audit Date: 01.10.2023
Personnel: William Creed (Pres./Pub.); Becke Creed (Director of Operations); Martha Sorohan (Editor); Stefanie Wessell (Editorial Director); Amber Ballard (Advertising Director)
Parent company (for newspapers): Gazettte Newspapers Inc.

THE COURIER ADVANTAGE

Street address 1: 701 W Sandusky St
Street address city: Findlay
Street address state: OH
Zip/Postal code: 45840-2325
General Phone: (419) 422-5151
General Fax: (419) 422-2937
Advertising Phone: (419) 422-5151
Advertising Fax: (419) 422-2937
Editorial Phone: (419) 422-5151
Editorial Fax: (419) 422-2937
General/National Adv. E-mail: advertising@thecourier.com
Display Adv. E-mail: advertising@thecourier.com
Editorial e-mail: news@thecourier.com
Primary Website: thecourier.com
Year Established: 1836
Avg Free Circ: 10000
Audit By: Sworn/Estimate/Non-Audited
Audit Date: 10.06.2019
Personnel: Karl L. Heminger (Pub.); Kari May-Faulkner (Adv. Mgr.); Jim Harrold (Mng. Ed.)
Parent company (for newspapers): Findlay Publishing Co.

THE CRESTLINE ADVOCATE

Street address 1: 312 N Seltzer St
Street address city: Crestline
Street address state: OH
Zip/Postal code: 44827-1403
General Phone: (419) 683-3355
General Fax: (419) 683-0175
Advertising Phone: (419) 683-3355
Advertising Fax: (419) 683-0175
Editorial Phone: (419) 683-3355
Editorial Fax: (419) 683-0175
General/National Adv. E-mail: crestlineadvocatenews@gmail.com
Display Adv. E-mail: crestlineadvocatenews@gmail.com
Editorial e-mail: crestlineadvocate@midohio.twcbc.com
Year Established: 1869
Avg Paid Circ: 2300
Avg Free Circ: 100
Audit By: Sworn/Estimate/Non-Audited
Audit Date: 18.04.2024
Personnel: Joseph Polito (Pub./Gen. Mgr.); Terri Rieman (General Manager); Kim Ross-Polito (Ed.)

THE DAILY STANDARD

Street address 1: 123 E Market St
Street address city: Celina
Street address state: OH
Zip/Postal code: 45822-1730
General Phone: (419) 586-2371
General Fax: (419) 586-6271
Advertising Phone: (419) 584-1961
General/National Adv. E-mail: asnyder@dailystandard.com
Display Adv. E-mail: mpleiman@dailystandard.com
Classified Adv. e-mail: classad@dailystandard.com
Editorial e-mail: newsroom@dailystandard.com
Primary Website: www.dailystandard.com
Mthly Avg Views: 727000
Mthly Avg Unique Visitors: 58000
Year Established: 1848
Avg Paid Circ: 6500
Avg Free Circ: 0
Sat. Circulation Paid: 10000
Audit By: Sworn/Estimate/Non-Audited
Audit Date: 12.07.2019
Personnel: Dave Hoying (Bus. Mgr.); Aaron Snyder (Gen Manager); Frank Snyder (Publisher); Diane Buening (Circ. Mgr.); Pat Royse (Mng. Ed.); Betty Lawrence (Society/Women's Ed.); Ryan Hines (Sports Ed.); Kelly Braun (Wire Ed.); Larry Smelser (Prodn. Supt.)
Parent company (for newspapers): Snyder family

THE DALTON GAZETTE & KIDRON NEWS

Street address 1: 41 W Main St
Street address city: Dalton
Street address state: OH
Zip/Postal code: 44618
General Phone: (330) 828-8401
General Fax: (330) 828-8401
Advertising Phone: (330) 828-8401
Advertising Fax: (330) 828-8401
Editorial Phone: (330) 828-8401
Editorial Fax: (330) 828-8401
General/National Adv. E-mail: daltonkidronnews@sbcglobal.net
Display Adv. E-mail: daltonkidronnews@sbcglobal.net
Editorial e-mail: daltonkidronnews@sbcglobal.net
Primary Website: daltongazette.com
Year Established: 1875
Avg Paid Circ: 1505
Avg Free Circ: 5
Audit By: Sworn/Estimate/Non-Audited
Audit Date: 10.06.2019
Personnel: Francis Woodruff (Pub./Ed.)

THE DELTA ATLAS

Street address 1: 212 Main St
Street address city: Delta
Street address state: OH
Zip/Postal code: 43515-1312
General Phone: (419) 822-3231
General Fax: (419) 822-3289
Advertising Phone: (419) 822-3231
Advertising Fax: (419) 822-3289
Editorial Phone: (419) 822-3231
Editorial Fax: (419) 822-3289
General/National Adv. E-mail: deltaatlas@windstream.net
Display Adv. E-mail: deltaatlas@windstream.net
Editorial e-mail: deltaatlas@windstream.net
Year Established: 1898
Avg Paid Circ: 1507
Avg Free Circ: 254
Audit By: Sworn/Estimate/Non-Audited
Audit Date: 10.06.2019
Personnel: Thomas W. Mack (Pub./Ed.)

THE DESHLER FLAG

Street address 1: 107 E Main St
Street address 2: Ste A
Street address city: Deshler
Street address state: OH
Zip/Postal code: 43516-1288
General Phone: (419) 278-2816
General Fax: (419) 278-2816
Advertising Phone: (419) 278-2816
Advertising Fax: (419) 278-2816

Editorial Phone: (419) 278-2816
Editorial Fax: (419) 278-2816
General/National Adv. E-mail: dflagads@embarqmail.com
Display Adv. E-mail: dflagads@embarqmail.com
Editorial e-mail: dflagnews@embarqmail.com
Primary Website: deshlerflag.embarqspace.com
Year Established: 1876
Avg Paid Circ: 1400
Audit By: Sworn/Estimate/Non-Audited
Audit Date: 10.06.2019
Personnel: Heather Spratt (Editor); Don Mickens (Publisher/Editor)
Parent company (for newspapers): Mickens, Inc.

THE EARLY BIRD

Street address 1: 100 Washington Ave.
Street address city: Greenville
Street address state: OH
Zip/Postal code: 45331
General Phone: (937) 548-3330
General Fax: (937) 548-3376
General/National Adv. E-mail: rberry@aimmediamidwest.com
Display Adv. E-mail: crandall@aimmediamidwest.com
Editorial e-mail: rberry@aimmediamidwest.com
Primary Website: dailyadvocate.com
Year Established: 1968
Avg Paid Circ: 23
Avg Free Circ: 28087
Audit By: CVC
Audit Date: 30.09.2018
Personnel: Ryan Berry (Mng. Ed.); Annette Sanders (Mkt Dir); Keith Foutz (Pres./Pub.); Christine Randall (Advertising Manager); Christine Randall (Advertising Manager); Shannie Denny (Prod. Mgr.); Becky Snyder (Circ. Mgr); Clinton Randall (webmaster)
Parent company (for newspapers): AIM Media Texas

THE EDGERTON EARTH

Street address 1: 114 S Michigan Ave
Street address city: Edgerton
Street address state: OH
Zip/Postal code: 43517-9801
General Phone: (419) 298-2369
General Fax: (419) 386-2829
Advertising Phone: (419) 298-2369
Advertising Fax: (419) 386-2829
Editorial Phone: (419) 298-2369
Editorial Fax: (419) 386-2829
General/National Adv. E-mail: edgertonearth@edgertonearth.com
Display Adv. E-mail: edgertonearth@edgertonearth.com
Editorial e-mail: edgertonearth@edgertonearth.com
Primary Website: edgertonearth.com
Avg Paid Circ: 1301
Audit By: Sworn/Estimate/Non-Audited
Audit Date: 10.06.2019
Personnel: Cindy Thiel (Pub./Ed.); Barb Imm (Adv. Mgr.); Karrie Kimpel (Office Mgr.)

THE FOSTORIA FOCUS

Street address 1: 112 N Main St
Street address city: Fostoria
Street address state: OH
Zip/Postal code: 44830-2223
General Phone: (419) 435-6397
General Fax: (419) 435-0101
Advertising Phone: (419) 435-6397
Advertising Fax: (419) 435-0101
Editorial Phone: (419) 435-6397
Editorial Fax: (419) 435-0101
General/National Adv. E-mail: sales@fostoriafocus.com
Display Adv. E-mail: salestony@fostoriafocus.com
Editorial e-mail: news@fostoriafocus.com
Primary Website: fostoriafocus.com
Year Established: 1994
Avg Paid Circ: 5
Avg Free Circ: 10680
Audit By: Sworn/Estimate/Non-Audited
Audit Date: 10.06.2019
Personnel: Judy Miller (Pub.); Donald Miller (Pub.); Tony Klima (Adv. Mgr.); Julie Heldman (Adv. Mgr); Linda Wagner (Prod. Mgr)

THE FREE PRESS STANDARD

Street address 1: 43 E Main St
Street address city: Carrollton
Street address state: OH
Zip/Postal code: 44615-1221
General Phone: (330) 627-5591
General Fax: (330) 627-3195
Advertising Phone: (330) 627-5591
Advertising Fax: (330) 627-3195
Editorial Phone: (330) 627-5591
Editorial Fax: (330) 627-3195
General/National Adv. E-mail: adfps44615@yahoo.com
Display Adv. E-mail: ctrushel@freepressstandard.com
Editorial e-mail: fps44615@yahoo.com
Primary Website: freepressstandard.com
Mthly Avg Views: 100000
Year Established: 1831
Avg Paid Circ: 4500
Avg Free Circ: 700
Audit By: Sworn/Estimate/Non-Audited
Audit Date: 10.06.2019
Personnel: Carol McIntire (Ed.); Connie Trushel (Adv. Mgr.); David Schloss (publisher)

THE GAZETTE

Street address 1: 46 W Jefferson St
Street address city: Jefferson
Street address state: OH
Zip/Postal code: 44047-1028
General Phone: (440) 576-9125
General Fax: (440) 576-2778
Advertising Phone: (440) 576-9125 x106
Advertising Fax: (440) 576-2778
Editorial Phone: (440) 576-9125 x107
Editorial Fax: 440-576-2778
General/National Adv. E-mail: bcreed@gazettenews.com
Display Adv. E-mail: aballard@gazettenews.com
Classified Adv. e-mail: classifieds@gazettenews.com
Editorial e-mail: gazette@gazettenews.com
Primary Website: gazettenews.com
Year Established: 1876
Avg Paid Circ: 3763
Audit By: Sworn/Estimate/Non-Audited
Audit Date: 01.10.2023
Personnel: William Creed (Pres./Pub.); Stefanie Wessell (Editorial Director); Becke Creed (Director of operations); Amber Ballard (Advertising Director)
Parent company (for newspapers): Gazette Newspapers, Inc.

THE GERMANTOWN PRESS

Street address 1: 230 S 2nd St
Street address city: Miamisburg
Street address state: OH
Zip/Postal code: 45342-2925
General Phone: (937) 866-3331
General Fax: (937) 866-6011
General/National Adv. E-mail: ads@miamivalleynewspapers.com
Display Adv. E-mail: ads@miamivalleynewspapers.com
Editorial e-mail: news@miamivalleynewspapers.com
Year Established: 1874
Avg Paid Circ: 3000
Audit By: Sworn/Estimate/Non-Audited
Audit Date: 10.06.2019
Personnel: Donald Miller (Pub./Adv. Mgr.); Ben Mersch (Ed.)
Parent company (for newspapers): Miami Valley Newspapers

THE GRANVILLE SENTINEL

Street address 1: 22 N 1st St
Street address city: Newark
Street address state: OH
Zip/Postal code: 43055-5608
General Phone: (740) 587-3397
General Fax: (740) 587-3398
Advertising Phone: (740) 328-8502
Advertising Fax: (740) 587-3398
Editorial Phone: (740) 328-8820
Editorial Fax: (740) 587-3398
General/National Adv. E-mail: atrabitz@newarkadvocate.com
Display Adv. E-mail: rangreen@newarkadvocate.com
Editorial e-mail: mshearer@newarkadvocate.com
Primary Website: granvillesentinel.com
Avg Paid Circ: 2300
Audit By: Sworn/Estimate/Non-Audited
Audit Date: 10.06.2019
Personnel: Michael Shearer (Exec. Ed.); Craig McDonald (Mng. Ed.); Adam Trabitz (Adv. Dir.)
Parent company (for newspapers): Gannett

THE HARTVILLE NEWS

Street address 1: 316 E Maple St
Street address city: Hartville
Street address state: OH
Zip/Postal code: 44632-8880
General Phone: (330) 877-9345
General Fax: (330) 877-1364
General/National Adv. E-mail: knowlespres_rh@sbcglobal.net
Display Adv. E-mail: knowlespress_comp@sbcglobal.net
Editorial e-mail: knowlespress_rh@sbcglobal.net
Primary Website: knowlespress.com
Year Established: 1930
Avg Paid Circ: 2000
Avg Free Circ: 37
Audit By: Sworn/Estimate/Non-Audited
Audit Date: 10.06.2019
Personnel: Rosalee Haines (Ed.); Jackie Vaughn (Mng. Ed.); Lindalee Sourini (Circ. Mgr.)

THE HOLMES COUNTY HUB SHOPPER

Street address 1: 25 N Clay St
Street address city: Millersburg
Street address state: OH
Zip/Postal code: 44654-1117
General Phone: (330) 674-1811
General Fax: (330) 674-3780
Advertising Phone: (330) 674-1811
Advertising Fax: (330) 674-3780
Editorial Phone: (330) 674-5676
Editorial Fax: (330) 674-3780
General/National Adv. E-mail: anixon@the-daily-record.com
Display Adv. E-mail: bpolen@the-daily-record.com
Editorial e-mail: bbower@the-daily-record.com
Primary Website: holmescountyshopper.com
Avg Paid Circ: 4253
Avg Free Circ: 155
Audit By: Sworn/Estimate/Non-Audited
Audit Date: 10.06.2019
Personnel: Ted Daniels (Mng. Ed.)
Parent company (for newspapers): Wooster Republican Printing Co.

THE JACKSON COUNTY TIMES-JOURNAL

Street address 1: 1 Acy Ave
Street address 2: Ste D
Street address city: Jackson
Street address state: OH
Zip/Postal code: 45640-9563
General Phone: (740) 286-2187
General Fax: (740) 286-5854
Advertising Phone: (740) 286-2187 ext. 302
Advertising Fax: (740) 286-5854
Editorial Phone: (740) 286-2187 ext. 329
Editorial Fax: (740) 286-5854
General/National Adv. E-mail: tmaynard@timesjournal.com
Display Adv. E-mail: amontgomery@timesjournal.com
Editorial e-mail: jhughes@timesjournal.com
Primary Website: jacksoncountydaily.com
Year Established: 1847
Avg Paid Circ: 5600
Avg Free Circ: 11500
Audit By: Sworn/Estimate/Non-Audited
Audit Date: 10.06.2019
Personnel: Norman Gilliland (Pub.); Jennifer Hughes (Mng. Ed.); Teresa Bryan (Adv. Dir.); Ken Cris (Circ. Mgr.)
Parent company (for newspapers): ACM Ohio LLC

THE JOURNAL & NOBLE COUNTY LEADER

Street address 1: 309 Main St
Street address city: Caldwell
Street address state: OH
Zip/Postal code: 43724-1321
General Phone: (740) 732-2341
General Fax: (740) 732-7288
Advertising Phone: (740) 732-2341
Advertising Fax: (740) 732-7288
Editorial Phone: (740) 732-2341
Editorial Fax: (740) 732-7288
General/National Adv. E-mail: news@journal-leader.com
Display Adv. E-mail: news@journal-leader.com
Editorial e-mail: news@journal-leader.com
Primary Website: journal-leader.com
Year Established: 1859
Avg Paid Circ: 4500
Audit By: Sworn/Estimate/Non-Audited
Audit Date: 10.06.2019
Personnel: Anne Chlovechok (Pub./Ed./Adv. Dir.)

THE JOURNAL NEWS

Street address 1: PO Box 8
Street address city: Spencerville
Street address state: OH
Zip/Postal code: 45887-0008
General Phone: (419) 733-855
Advertising Phone: (419) 733-0855
Editorial Phone: (419) 733-0855
General/National Adv. E-mail: news@spencervillenews.com
Display Adv. E-mail: news@spencervillenews.com
Editorial e-mail: news@spencervillenews.com
Year Established: 1879
Avg Paid Circ: 2100
Audit By: Sworn/Estimate/Non-Audited
Audit Date: 10.06.2019
Personnel: Cassandra Helmstetter (Manager)

THE LEADER-ENTERPRISE

Street address 1: 319 W Main St
Street address city: Montpelier
Street address state: OH
Zip/Postal code: 43543-1017
General Phone: (419) 485-3113
General Fax: (419) 485-3114
Advertising Phone: (419) 485-3113
Advertising Fax: (419) 485-3114
Editorial Phone: (419) 485-3113
Editorial Fax: (419) 485-3114
General/National Adv. E-mail: leaderadvertising@frontier.com
Display Adv. E-mail: leaderenterprise@frontier.com
Editorial e-mail: jward.leaderenterprise@frontier.com
Primary Website: myplace.frontier.com
Year Established: 1923
Avg Paid Circ: 1000
Avg Free Circ: 55
Audit By: Sworn/Estimate/Non-Audited
Audit Date: 10.06.2019
Personnel: Jamie Ward (Ed.); Nancy Jackson (Asst. Ed.); Jole Hills (Adv. Mgr.)

THE LEIPSIC MESSENGER

Street address 1: 117 E Main St
Street address city: Leipsic
Street address state: OH
Zip/Postal code: 45856-1428
General Phone: (419) 943-2590
General Fax: (419) 943-2590
General/National Adv. E-mail: leipsicmessenger@gmail.com
Editorial e-mail: leipsicmessenger@gmail.com
Primary Website: leipsicmessenger.com
Avg Paid Circ: 1300
Audit By: Sworn/Estimate/Non-Audited
Audit Date: 10.06.2019
Personnel: Keith Mickens (Pub.); Susan Mickens (Adv. Mgr.)

THE LEWISBURG LEADER

Street address 1: 10 S Main St
Street address city: West Alexandria
Street address state: OH
Zip/Postal code: 45381-1216
General Phone: (937) 839-4733
General Fax: (937) 839-5351
Advertising Phone: (937) 839-4733
Advertising Fax: (937) 839-5351
Editorial Phone: (937) 839-4733
Editorial Fax: (937) 839-5351
General/National Adv. E-mail: twinvpub@infinet.com
Display Adv. E-mail: information@onlinetvp.com
Editorial e-mail: twinvpub@infinet.com
Primary Website: twinvalleypublications.com
Year Established: 1934

Avg Paid Circ: 400
Avg Free Circ: 8000
Audit By: Sworn/Estimate/Non-Audited
Audit Date: 10.06.2019
Personnel: Sam Shortes (Pub./Ed.); Cindy Shortes (Gen. Mgr.); Angie Donohoo (Adv. Mgr.)
Parent company (for newspapers): Twin Valley Publications

THE LOUDONVILLE TIMES

Street address 1: 263 W Main St
Street address city: Loudonville
Street address state: OH
Zip/Postal code: 44842-1135
General Phone: (419) 994-5600
General Fax: (419) 994-5826
General/National Adv. E-mail: advertising@theloudonvilletimes.com
Display Adv. E-mail: advertising@theloudonvilletimes.com
Editorial e-mail: news@theloudonvilletimes.com
Primary Website: theloudonvilletimes.com
Year Established: 1873
Avg Paid Circ: 2100
Avg Free Circ: 50
Audit By: Sworn/Estimate/Non-Audited
Audit Date: 10.06.2019
Personnel: Lance White (Editor)
Parent company (for newspapers): Ashland Publishing Co. LLC

THE LOUISVILLE HERALD

Street address 1: 308 S Mill St
Street address city: Louisville
Street address state: OH
Zip/Postal code: 44641-1643
General Phone: (330) 875-5610
General Fax: (330) 875-4475
Advertising Phone: (330) 875-5610
Advertising Fax: (330) 875-4475
Editorial Phone: (330) 875-5610
Editorial Fax: (330) 875-4475
General/National Adv. E-mail: jackiee.marykay@gmail.com
Display Adv. E-mail: jackiee.marykay@gmail.com
Classified Adv. e-mail: jackiee.marykay@gmail.com
Editorial e-mail: jackiee.marykay@gmail.com
Primary Website: louisvilleherald.com
Year Established: 1887
Avg Paid Circ: 2100
Avg Free Circ: 0
Audit By: Sworn/Estimate/Non-Audited
Audit Date: 10.06.2019
Personnel: Frank H. Clapper (Pub./Ed.); Jackie Clapper (Adv. Mgr.); Patti Carden (Office Manager)

THE MANCHESTER SIGNAL

Street address 1: 414 E 7th St
Street address city: Manchester
Street address state: OH
Zip/Postal code: 45144-1402
General Phone: (937) 549-2800
General Fax: (937) 549-3611
General/National Adv. E-mail: thesignal1@frontier.com
Display Adv. E-mail: thesignal1@frontier.com
Editorial e-mail: thesignal1@frontier.com
Year Established: 1883
Avg Paid Circ: 5200
Avg Free Circ: 20
Audit By: Sworn/Estimate/Non-Audited
Audit Date: 10.06.2019
Personnel: William G. Woolard (Owner/Pub./Ed.)

THE MECHANICSBURG TELEGRAM

Street address 1: 1637 E US Highway 36
Street address 2: Ste 10
Street address city: Urbana
Street address state: OH
Zip/Postal code: 43078-9156
General Phone: (937) 652-1331
General Fax: (937) 652-1336
Advertising Phone: (937) 652-1331 ext. 206
Advertising Fax: (937) 652-1336
Editorial Phone: (937) 652-1331ext. 221
Editorial Fax: (937) 652-1336
General/National Adv. E-mail: lmoon@civitasmedia.com
Display Adv. E-mail: cherring@civitasmedia.com
Editorial e-mail: jmiller@civitasmedia.com
Primary Website: burgtelegram.com
Year Established: 1902
Avg Paid Circ: 52
Avg Free Circ: 2255
Audit By: Sworn/Estimate/Non-Audited
Audit Date: 10.06.2019
Personnel: Lane Moon (Pub./Adv. Dir.); Justin Miller (Ed.); Jessica Kinzer (Retail Adv. Rep.); Carol Herring (Classified Adv. Rep.)
Parent company (for newspapers): AIM Media Indiana

THE MOHAWK LEADER

Street address 1: 1198 E Findlay St
Street address city: Carey
Street address state: OH
Zip/Postal code: 43316-9760
General Phone: (419) 396-7567
General Fax: (419) 396-7527
Advertising Phone: (419) 396-7567
Advertising Fax: (419) 396-7527
Editorial Phone: (419) 396-7567
Editorial Fax: (419) 396-7527
General/National Adv. E-mail: Ads@theprogressortimes.com
Display Adv. E-mail: Amy@theprogressortimes.com
Editorial e-mail: Steve@theprogressortimes.com
Primary Website: theprogressortimes.com
Year Established: 1894
Avg Paid Circ: 4000
Audit By: Sworn/Estimate/Non-Audited
Audit Date: 10.06.2019
Personnel: Stephen C. Zender (Pub./Ed.); Amy Yeater (Adv. Dir.); Jenny Freeman (Circ. Mgr.)

THE MORROW COUNTY SENTINEL

Street address 1: 46 S Main St
Street address city: Mount Gilead
Street address state: OH
Zip/Postal code: 43338-1433
General Phone: (419) 946-3010
General Fax: (419) 947-7241
General/National Adv. E-mail: vtaylor@civitasmedia.com
Display Adv. E-mail: vtaylor@civitasmedia.com
Classified Adv. e-mail: dsheets@civitasmedia.com
Editorial e-mail: rwagner@civitasmedia.com
Primary Website: morrowcountysentinel.com
Avg Paid Circ: 2750
Audit By: Sworn/Estimate/Non-Audited
Audit Date: 10.06.2019
Personnel: Vicki Taylor (Gen. Mgr.); Randa Wagner (Ed.); Rob Hamilton (Sports Ed.); Anthony Conchel (Ed.)
Parent company (for newspapers): AIM Media Indiana

THE NEW WASHINGTON HERALD

Street address 1: 625 S Kibler St
Street address city: New Washington
Street address state: OH
Zip/Postal code: 44854-9541
General Phone: (419) 492-2133
General Fax: (419) 492-2128
Advertising Phone: (419) 492-2133
Advertising Fax: (419) 492-2128
Editorial Phone: (419) 492-2133
Editorial Fax: (419) 492-2128
General/National Adv. E-mail: backerman@theheraldinc.com
Display Adv. E-mail: backerman@theheraldinc.com
Editorial e-mail: backerman@heraldprint.com
Primary Website: theheraldinc.com
Year Established: 1881
Avg Paid Circ: 1600
Avg Free Circ: 75
Audit By: Sworn/Estimate/Non-Audited
Audit Date: 10.06.2019
Personnel: David Stump (Pub./Ed.); Bonnie Ackerman (Adv. Dir.)

THE NEWS

Street address 1: 46 W Jefferson St
Street address city: Jefferson
Street address state: OH
Zip/Postal code: 44047-1028
General Phone: (440) 576-9125
General Fax: (440) 576-2778
Advertising Phone: (440) 576-9125 X106
Advertising Fax: (440) 576-2778
Editorial Phone: (440) 576-9125 X107
Editorial Fax: 440-576-2778
General/National Adv. E-mail: pymatuningnews@gazettenews.com
Display Adv. E-mail: aballard@gazettenews.com
Classified Adv. e-mail: classifieds@gazettenews.com
Editorial e-mail: pymatuningnews@gazettenews.com
Primary Website: gazettenews.com
Year Established: 1890
Avg Paid Circ: 1130
Audit By: Sworn/Estimate/Non-Audited
Audit Date: 01.10.2023
Personnel: William Creed (Pres./Pub.); Doris Cook (Ed.); Becke Creed (Director of Operations); Stefanie Wessell (Editorial Director); Amber Ballard (Advertising Director)
Parent company (for newspapers): Gazette Newspapers, Inc.

THE NEWS DEMOCRAT

Street address 1: 111 E State St
Street address city: Georgetown
Street address state: OH
Zip/Postal code: 45121-1412
General Phone: (937) 378-6161
General Fax: (937) 378-2004
Advertising Phone: (937) 378-6161
Advertising Fax: (937) 378-2004
Editorial Phone: (937) 378-6161
Editorial Fax: (937) 378-2004
General/National Adv. E-mail: striplett@newsdemocrat.com
Display Adv. E-mail: classifieds@newsdemocrat.com
Editorial e-mail: news@newsdemocrat.com
Primary Website: newsdemocrat.com
Year Established: 1888
Avg Paid Circ: 3200
Avg Free Circ: 17000
Audit By: Sworn/Estimate/Non-Audited
Audit Date: 10.06.2019
Personnel: Steven Triplett (Pub./Adv. Mgr.); Bryan Peck (Ed.); Julie Richmond (Bus. Mgr.); Shirley Ross (Circ. Mgr.)
Parent company (for newspapers): Champion Media

THE NEWS-TRIBUNE

Street address 1: 147 E High St
Street address city: Hicksville
Street address state: OH
Zip/Postal code: 43526-1168
General Phone: (419) 542-7764
General Fax: (419) 542-7370
Advertising Phone: (419) 542-7764
Advertising Fax: (419) 542-7370
Editorial Phone: (419) 542-7764
Editorial Fax: (419) 542-7370
General/National Adv. E-mail: maryann@hicksvillenewstribune.com
Display Adv. E-mail: maryann@hicksvillenewstribune.com
Editorial e-mail: maryann@hicksvillenewstribune.com
Primary Website: hicksvillenewstribune.com
Year Established: 1886
Avg Paid Circ: 2157
Avg Free Circ: 50
Audit By: Sworn/Estimate/Non-Audited
Audit Date: 10.06.2019
Personnel: Mary Ann Barth (Pub./Ed.); Michael G. Barth (Ed.); Jan Heffelfinger (Mng. Ed.)

THE OAKWOOD REGISTER

Street address 1: 435 Patterson Rd
Street address city: Dayton
Street address state: OH
Zip/Postal code: 45419-4309
General Phone: (937) 294-2662
Advertising Phone: (937) 294-2662
Editorial Phone: (937) 294-2662
General/National Adv. E-mail: office@oakwoodregister.com
Display Adv. E-mail: office@oakwoodregister.com
Classified Adv. e-mail: office@oakwoodregister.com
Editorial e-mail: editor@oakwoodregister.com
Primary Website: www.oakwoodregister.com
Year Established: 1992
Avg Paid Circ: 50
Avg Free Circ: 6000
Personnel: Tom Girard (Prodn. Mgr.); Dana Whitney (Publisher); Richard Brame (Advertising Sales); Vicky Holloway (Advertising Sales); Robin Burnam (Office Manager)
Parent company (for newspapers): Winkler Publishing; The Winkler Company

THE OXFORD PRESS

Street address 1: 6752 Cincinnati Dayton Road
Street address 2: Suite 205
Street address city: Liberty Township
Street address state: OH
Zip/Postal code: 45044-9374
General Phone: (513) 755-5060
General Fax: (513) 483-5252
Advertising Phone: (513) 483-5225
Advertising Fax: (513) 483-5252
Editorial Phone: (513) 755-5060
Editorial Fax: (513) 483-5252
General/National Adv. E-mail: oxfordeditor@coxinc.com
Display Adv. E-mail: oxfordeditor@coxinc.com
Editorial e-mail: oxfordeditor@coxinc.com
Primary Website: Journal-News.com
Year Established: 1932
Avg Paid Circ: 1646
Avg Free Circ: 32
Audit By: Sworn/Estimate/Non-Audited
Audit Date: 10.06.2019
Personnel: Jennifer Burcham (Editor)
Parent company (for newspapers): Cox Media Group Ohio

THE PATASKALA STANDARD

Street address 1: 22 N 1st St
Street address city: Newark
Street address state: OH
Zip/Postal code: 43055-5608
General Phone: (740) 927-2991
General Fax: (740) 927-2930
Advertising Phone: (740) 328-8502
Advertising Fax: (740) 927-2930
Editorial Phone: (740) 328-8820
Editorial Fax: (740) 927-2930
General/National Adv. E-mail: atrabitz@newarkadvocate.com
Display Adv. E-mail: rangreen@newarkadvocate.com
Editorial e-mail: mshearer@newarkadvocate.com
Primary Website: pataskalastandard.com
Avg Paid Circ: 3100
Avg Free Circ: 25
Audit By: Sworn/Estimate/Non-Audited
Audit Date: 10.06.2019
Personnel: Michael Shearer (Exec. Ed.); Craig McDonald (Mng. Ed.); Adam Trabitz (Adv. Dir.)
Parent company (for newspapers): Gannett

THE PAULDING PROGRESS

Street address 1: 113 S Williams St
Street address city: Paulding
Street address state: OH
Zip/Postal code: 45879-1429
General Phone: (419) 399-4015
General Fax: (419) 399-4030
Advertising Phone: (419) 399-4015
Advertising Fax: (419) 399-4030
Editorial Phone: (419) 399-4015
Editorial Fax: (419) 399-4030
General/National Adv. E-mail: advertising@progressnewspaper.org
Display Adv. E-mail: dnutter@progressnewspaper.org
Editorial e-mail: progress@progressnewspaper.org
Primary Website: progressnewspaper.org
Avg Paid Circ: 4000
Avg Free Circ: 10000
Audit By: Sworn/Estimate/Non-Audited
Audit Date: 10.06.2019
Personnel: Doug Nutter (Pub./Adv. Mgr.); Melinda Krick (Ed.)
Parent company (for newspapers): Delphos Herald, Inc.

THE PEOPLE'S DEFENDER

Street address 1: PO Box 308
Street address city: West Union
Street address state: OH
Zip/Postal code: 45693-0308
General Phone: (937) 544-2391

General Fax: (937) 544-2298
Advertising Phone: (937) 544-2391
Advertising Fax: (937) 544-2298
Editorial Phone: (937) 544-2391
Editorial Fax: (937) 544-2298
General/National Adv. E-mail: trigdon@peoplesdefender.com
Display Adv. E-mail: pniswander@peoplesdefender.com
Editorial e-mail: lhuffman@peoplesdefender.com
Primary Website: peoplesdefender.com
Year Established: 1866
Avg Paid Circ: 8500
Avg Free Circ: 12800
Audit By: Sworn/Estimate/Non-Audited
Audit Date: 10.06.2019
Personnel: Lee Huffman (Pub./Ed.); Terry Rigdon (Adv. Mgr.); Peggy Niswander (Bus. Mgr.)
Parent company (for newspapers): Champion Media

THE PIKE COUNTY NEWS WATCHMAN

Street address 1: 14532 US Highway 23
Street address 2: Ste A
Street address city: Waverly
Street address state: OH
Zip/Postal code: 45690-8011
General Phone: (740) 947-2149
General Fax: (740) 947-1344
Advertising Phone: (740) 947-2149 ext. 104
Advertising Fax: (740) 947-1344
Editorial Phone: (740) 947-2149 ext. 110
Editorial Fax: (740) 947-1344
General/National Adv. E-mail: ngilliland@newswatchman.com
Display Adv. E-mail: tbryan@newswatchman.com
Editorial e-mail: dmagill@newswatchman.com
Primary Website: pikecountydaily.com
Year Established: 1832
Avg Paid Circ: 3800
Avg Free Circ: 11500
Audit By: Sworn/Estimate/Non-Audited
Audit Date: 10.06.2019
Personnel: Norman Gilliland (Pub.); Matt Lucas (Ed.); Teresa Bryan (Adv. Mgr.); Ken Crisp (Circ. Mgr.); Rebecca Hedges (Media Rep.); Stephanie Stanley (Ed.)
Parent company (for newspapers): ACM Ohio LLC

THE POST NEWSPAPERS - BRUNSWICK

Street address 1: 5146 Normandy Park Dr
Street address 2: Ste 100
Street address city: Medina
Street address state: OH
Zip/Postal code: 44256-9608
General Phone: (330) 721-7678
General Fax: (330) 722-9875
Advertising Phone: (330) 721-7678
Advertising Fax: (330) 722-9875
Editorial Phone: (330) 721-7678
Editorial Fax: (330) 722-9875
General/National Adv. E-mail: sales@thepostnewspapers.com
Display Adv. E-mail: classifieds@thepostnewspapers.com
Editorial e-mail: news@thepostnewspapers.com
Primary Website: thepostnewspapers.com
Year Established: 1975
Avg Paid Circ: 41436
Avg Free Circ: 38857
Audit By: AAM
Audit Date: 30.09.2017
Personnel: Bruce M. Trogdon (Pub.); Michael Trogdon (Exec. Ed.); Michelle Farnham (Mng. Ed.); Tara Leffel (Adv. Mgr.); Tami Cassidy (Adv. Mgr); Greg Studer (Circ. Mgr)
Parent company (for newspapers): The Post Newspapers

THE POST NEWSPAPERS - EASTERN MEDINA

Street address 1: 5146 Normandy Park Dr
Street address 2: Ste 100
Street address city: Medina
Street address state: OH
Zip/Postal code: 44256-9608
General Phone: (330) 721-7678
General Fax: (330) 722-9875
Advertising Phone: (330) 721-7678
Advertising Fax: (330) 722-9875
Editorial Phone: (330) 721-7678
Editorial Fax: (330) 722-9875
General/National Adv. E-mail: sales@thepostnewspapers.com
Display Adv. E-mail: classifieds@thepostnewspapers.com
Editorial e-mail: news@thepostnewspapers.com
Primary Website: thepostnewspapers.com
Year Established: 1975
Avg Free Circ: 3611
Audit By: Sworn/Estimate/Non-Audited
Audit Date: 10.06.2019
Personnel: Bruce M. Trogdon (Pub.); Michael Trogdon (Exec. Ed.); Michelle Farnham (Mng. Ed.); Tara Leffel (Adv. Mgr.); Tami Cassidy (Adv. Mgr); Greg Studer (Circ. Mgr)
Parent company (for newspapers): The Post Newspapers

THE POST NEWSPAPERS - MEDINA

Street address 1: 5146 Normandy Park Dr
Street address 2: Ste 100
Street address city: Medina
Street address state: OH
Zip/Postal code: 44256-9608
General Phone: (330) 721-7678
General Fax: (330) 722-9875
Advertising Phone: (330) 721-7678
Advertising Fax: (330) 722-9875
Editorial Phone: (330) 721-7678
Editorial Fax: (330) 722-9875
General/National Adv. E-mail: sales@thepostnewspapers.com
Display Adv. E-mail: classifieds@thepostnewspapers.com
Editorial e-mail: news@thepostnewspapers.com
Primary Website: thepostnewspapers.com
Year Established: 1975
Avg Free Circ: 10640
Audit By: Sworn/Estimate/Non-Audited
Audit Date: 10.06.2019
Personnel: Bruce M. Trogdon (Pub.); Michael Trogdon (Exec. Ed.); Michelle Farnham (Managing Editor); Tara Leffel (Adv. Mgr.); Tami Cassidy (Adv. Mgr); Greg Studer (Circ. Mgr); Michelle Arnst (Graphic Designer); David Sickels (Managing Editor)
Parent company (for newspapers): The Post Newspapers

THE POST NEWSPAPERS - NORTHERN WAYNE

Street address 1: 5164 Normandy Park Dr
Street address city: Medina
Street address state: OH
Zip/Postal code: 44256-5901
General Phone: (330) 721-7678
General Fax: (330) 722-9875
Advertising Phone: (330) 721-7678
Advertising Fax: (330) 722-9875
Editorial Phone: (330) 721-7678
Editorial Fax: (330) 722-9875
General/National Adv. E-mail: btrogdon@thepostnewspapers.com
Display Adv. E-mail: btrogdon@thepostnewspapers.com
Editorial e-mail: btrogdon@thepostnewspapers.com
Primary Website: thepostnewspapers.com
Year Established: 1975
Avg Free Circ: 9225
Audit By: Sworn/Estimate/Non-Audited
Audit Date: 10.06.2019
Personnel: Bruce M. Trogdon (Pub.); Michael Trogdon (Exec. Ed.); Michelle Farnham (Mng. Ed.); Tara Leffel (Adv. Mgr.); Tami Cassidy (Adv. Mgr); Greg Studer (Circ. Mgr)
Parent company (for newspapers): The Post Newspapers

THE POST NEWSPAPERS - NORTON

Street address 1: 5164 Normandy Park Dr
Street address 2: Ste 100
Street address city: Medina
Street address state: OH
Zip/Postal code: 44256-5903
General Phone: (330) 721-7678
General Fax: (330) 722-9875
Advertising Phone: (330) 721-7678
Advertising Fax: (330) 722-9875
Editorial Phone: (330) 721-7678
Editorial Fax: (330) 722-9875
General/National Adv. E-mail: sales@thepostnewspapers.com
Display Adv. E-mail: classifieds@thepostnewspapers.com
Editorial e-mail: news@thepostnewspapers.com
Primary Website: thepostnewspapers.com
Year Established: 1975
Avg Free Circ: 3004
Audit By: Sworn/Estimate/Non-Audited
Audit Date: 10.06.2019
Personnel: Bruce M. Trogdon (Pub.); Michael Trogdon (Exec. Ed.); Michelle Farnham (Mng. Ed.); Tara Leffel (Adv. Mgr.)
Parent company (for newspapers): The Post Newspapers

THE POST NEWSPAPERS - SOUTHERN MEDINA

Street address 1: 5146 Normandy Park Dr
Street address 2: Ste 100
Street address city: Medina
Street address state: OH
Zip/Postal code: 44256-9608
General Phone: (330) 721-7678
General Fax: (330) 722-9875
Advertising Phone: (330) 721-7678
Advertising Fax: (330) 722-9875
Editorial Phone: (330) 721-7678
Editorial Fax: (330) 722-9875
General/National Adv. E-mail: sales@thepostnewspapers.com
Display Adv. E-mail: classifieds@thepostnewspapers.com
Editorial e-mail: news@thepostnewspapers.com
Primary Website: thepostnewspapers.com
Year Established: 1975
Avg Free Circ: 8003
Audit By: Sworn/Estimate/Non-Audited
Audit Date: 10.06.2019
Personnel: Bruce M. Trogdon (Pub.); Michael Trogdon (Exec. Ed.); Michelle Farnham (Mng. Ed.); Tara Leffel (Adv. Mgr.); Tami Cassidy (Adv. Mgr); Greg Studer (Circ. Mgr)
Parent company (for newspapers): The Post Newspapers

THE POST NEWSPAPERS - STRONGSVILLE

Street address 1: 5146 Normandy Park Dr
Street address 2: Ste 100
Street address city: Medina
Street address state: OH
Zip/Postal code: 44256-9608
General Phone: (330) 721-7678
General Fax: (330) 722-9875
Advertising Phone: (330) 721-7678
Advertising Fax: (330) 722-9875
Editorial Phone: (330) 721-7678
Editorial Fax: (330) 722-9875
General/National Adv. E-mail: sales@thepostnewspapers.com
Display Adv. E-mail: classifieds@thepostnewspapers.com
Editorial e-mail: news@thepostnewspapers.com
Primary Website: thepostnewspapers.com
Year Established: 1975
Avg Free Circ: 9095
Audit By: Sworn/Estimate/Non-Audited
Audit Date: 10.06.2019
Personnel: Bruce M. Trogdon (Pub.); Michael Trogdon (Exec. Ed.); Michelle Farnham (Mng. Ed.); Tara Leffel (Adv. Mgr.); Greg Studer (Circ. Mgr); Tami Cassidy (Adv. Mgr)
Parent company (for newspapers): The Post Newspapers

THE POST NEWSPAPERS - WADSWORTH

Street address 1: 5146 Normandy Park Dr
Street address 2: Ste 100
Street address city: Medina
Street address state: OH
Zip/Postal code: 44256-9608
General Phone: (330) 721-7678
General Fax: (330) 722-9875
Advertising Phone: (330) 721-7678
Advertising Fax: (330) 722-9875
Editorial Phone: (330) 721-7678
Editorial Fax: (330) 722-9875
General/National Adv. E-mail: sales@thepostnewspapers.com
Display Adv. E-mail: classifieds@thepostnewspapers.com
Editorial e-mail: news@thepostnewspapers.com
Primary Website: thepostnewspapers.com
Year Established: 1975
Avg Free Circ: 9066
Audit By: Sworn/Estimate/Non-Audited
Audit Date: 10.06.2019
Personnel: Bruce M. Trogdon (Pub.); Michael Trogdon (Exec. Ed.); Michelle Farnham (Mng. Ed.); Tara Leffel (Adv. Mgr.); Tami Cassidy (Adv. Mgr); Greg Studer (Circ. Mgr)
Parent company (for newspapers): The Post Newspapers

THE PRESS

Street address 1: 158 Lear Rd
Street address city: Avon Lake
Street address state: OH
Zip/Postal code: 44012-1982
General Phone: (440) 933-5100
General Fax: (440) 933-7904
Advertising Phone: (440) 933-5100
Advertising Fax: (440) 933-7904
Editorial Phone: (440) 933-5100
Editorial Fax: (440) 933-7904
General/National Adv. E-mail: advertising@2presspapers.com
Display Adv. E-mail: alpclass@dceye.com
Editorial e-mail: editor@2presspapers.com
Primary Website: 2presspapers.com
Year Established: 1951
Avg Paid Circ: 4000
Avg Free Circ: 2500
Audit By: Sworn/Estimate/Non-Audited
Audit Date: 10.06.2019
Personnel: Larry Limpf (Ed.)
Parent company (for newspapers): Douthit Communications, Inc.

THE PRESS

Street address 1: 1550 Woodville Rd
Street address city: Millbury
Street address state: OH
Zip/Postal code: 43447-9619
General Phone: (419) 836-2221
General Fax: (419) 836-1319
Advertising Phone: (419) 836-2221
Advertising Fax: (419) 836-1319
Editorial Phone: (419) 836-2221
Editorial Fax: (419) 836-1319
General/National Adv. E-mail: mperkins@presspublications.com
Display Adv. E-mail: mperkins@presspublications.com
Editorial e-mail: news@presspublications.com
Primary Website: presspublications.com
Mthly Avg Views: 40365
Mthly Avg Unique Visitors: 14852
Year Established: 1972
Avg Paid Circ: 0
Avg Free Circ: 33965
Audit By: CVC
Audit Date: 31.03.2017
Personnel: Harold K. Douthit (Pub.); Mary Perkins (General Manager); Jordan Szozda (Circ. Mgr); Tammy Payne (Prod. Mgr)
Parent company (for newspapers): Douthit Communications, Inc.

THE PRESS-NEWS

Street address 1: 604 Valley St
Street address city: Minerva
Street address state: OH
Zip/Postal code: 44657-1580
General Phone: (330) 868-3408
General Fax: (330) 868-3273
Advertising Phone: (330) 868-5222
Advertising Fax: (330) 868-3273
Editorial Phone: (330) 868-3408
Editorial Fax: (330) 868-3273
General/National Adv. E-mail: jkaplan@the-review.com
Display Adv. E-mail: ccarle@the-review.com
Editorial e-mail: kmundy@the-review.com
Primary Website: the-press-news.com
Avg Paid Circ: 2200
Audit By: Sworn/Estimate/Non-Audited

Audit Date: 10.06.2019
Personnel: G. Charles Dix (Pub.); Rob Todor (Ed.); Jeff Kaplan (Adv. Dir.)

THE PROGRESSOR TIMES

Street address 1: 1198 E Findlay St
Street address city: Carey
Street address state: OH
Zip/Postal code: 43316-9760
General Phone: (419) 396-7567
General Fax: (419) 396-7527
Advertising Phone: (419) 396-7567
Advertising Fax: (419) 396-7527
Editorial Phone: (419) 396-7567
Editorial Fax: (419) 396-7527
General/National Adv. E-mail: Ads@theprogressortimes.com
Display Adv. E-mail: Amy@theprogressortimes.com
Editorial e-mail: Steve@theprogressortimes.com
Primary Website: theprogressortimes.com
Year Established: 1873
Avg Paid Circ: 4000
Audit By: Sworn/Estimate/Non-Audited
Audit Date: 10.06.2019
Personnel: Stephen C. Zender (Pub./Ed.); Amy Yeater (Adv. Dir.); Jenny Freeman (Circ. Mgr.)

THE REGISTER-HERALD

Street address 1: 532 N Barron St
Street address 2: Ste 105
Street address city: Eaton
Street address state: OH
Zip/Postal code: 45320-1710
General Phone: (937) 456-5553
General Fax: (937) 456-3558
Advertising Phone: (937) 456-5553 ext. 120
Advertising Fax: (937) 456-3558
Editorial Phone: (937) 456-5553 ext. 130
Editorial Fax: (937) 456-3558
General/National Adv. E-mail: bkemp@civitasmedia.com
Display Adv. E-mail: lcollins@civitasmedia.com
Editorial e-mail: emowen@civitasmedia.com
Primary Website: registerherald.com
Year Established: 1918
Avg Paid Circ: 5300
Avg Free Circ: 12000
Audit By: Sworn/Estimate/Non-Audited
Audit Date: 10.06.2019
Personnel: Eddie Mowen Jr. (Ed.); Leslie Collins (Gen. Mgr.); Betsy Kemp (Adv. Mgr.); Tom Hutson (Reg. Pub.); Doug Meeks (Circ. Mgr.); Margaret Crabtree (Adv.); Kelsey Kimbler (Newsroom)
Parent company (for newspapers): AIM Media Indiana

THE RICHWOOD GAZETTE

Street address 1: PO Box 226
Street address city: Marysville
Street address state: OH
Zip/Postal code: 43040-0226
General Phone: (740) 943-2214
General Fax: (740) 943-3595
Advertising Phone: (740) 943-2214
Advertising Fax: (740) 943-3595
Editorial Phone: (740) 943-2214
Editorial Fax: (740) 943-3595
General/National Adv. E-mail: rgads@rgnews.biz
Display Adv. E-mail: slsheets@rgnews.biz
Editorial e-mail: slsheets@rgnews.biz
Primary Website: rgnews.biz
Year Established: 1872
Avg Paid Circ: 2000
Avg Free Circ: 11
Audit By: Sworn/Estimate/Non-Audited
Audit Date: 10.06.2019
Personnel: Daniel E. Behrens (Editor); Marie Woodford (Adv. Dir.); Sherryl Sheets (Office Mgr.); Kevin Behresn (Publisher)

THE RIPLEY BEE

Street address 1: 111 E State St
Street address city: Georgetown
Street address state: OH
Zip/Postal code: 45121-1412
General Phone: (937) 444-3441
Primary Website: ripleybee.com
Year Established: 1842
Avg Paid Circ: 1400
Avg Free Circ: 183
Audit By: Sworn/Estimate/Non-Audited
Audit Date: 10.06.2019
Personnel: Steven Triplett (Pub./Adv. Mgr.); Julie Richmond (Bus. Mgr.); Bryan Peck (Ed.)
Parent company (for newspapers): Champion Media

THE RURAL-URBAN RECORD

Street address 1: 24487 Squire Rd
Street address city: Columbia Station
Street address state: OH
Zip/Postal code: 44028-9672
General Phone: (440) 236-8982
General Fax: (440) 236-9198
Advertising Phone: (440) 236-8982
Advertising Fax: (440) 236-9198
Editorial Phone: (440) 236-8982
Editorial Fax: (440) 236-9198
General/National Adv. E-mail: lboise@windstream.net
Display Adv. E-mail: lboise@windstream.net
Editorial e-mail: lboise@windstream.net
Primary Website: rural-urbanrecord.com
Year Established: 1955
Avg Paid Circ: 64
Avg Free Circ: 21980
Audit By: CVC
Audit Date: 30.12.2018
Personnel: Lee Boise (Pub./Ed./Gen. Mgr.); Cheryl Mikoletic (Circ. Mgr); Randi MacWilliams (Graphic Artist/News Ed); Stephanie Sayles (Sales Rep); Stephanie Humphrey (Graphic Artist)

THE SCIOTO VOICE

Street address 1: 8366 Downtown Hayport Rd
Street address city: Wheelersburg
Street address state: OH
Zip/Postal code: 45694
General Phone: (740) 574-8494
General Fax: (740) 574-2329
Advertising Phone: (740) 574-8494
Advertising Fax: (740) 574-2329
Editorial Phone: (740) 574-8494
Editorial Fax: (740) 574-2329
General/National Adv. E-mail: info@thesciotovoice.com
Display Adv. E-mail: jessica@thesciotovoice.com
Editorial e-mail: debbie@thesciotovoice.com
Primary Website: thesciotovoice.com
Year Established: 1973
Avg Paid Circ: 3000
Audit By: Sworn/Estimate/Non-Audited
Audit Date: 10.06.2019
Personnel: Debora Allard (Pub./Ed.)

THE SHORES NEWS

Street address 1: 46 W Jefferson St
Street address city: Jefferson
Street address state: OH
Zip/Postal code: 44047-1028
General Phone: (440) 576-9125
General Fax: (440) 576-2778
Advertising Phone: (440) 576-9125 x106
Advertising Fax: (440) 576-2778
Editorial Phone: (440) 576-9125 x107
Editorial Fax: 440-576-2778
General/National Adv. E-mail: shoresnews@gazettenews.com
Display Adv. E-mail: aballard@gazettenews.com
Classified Adv. e-mail: classifieds@gazettenews.com
Editorial e-mail: shoresnews@gazettenews.com
Primary Website: gazettenews.com
Year Established: 1992
Avg Paid Circ: 1607
Audit By: Sworn/Estimate/Non-Audited
Audit Date: 01.10.2023
Personnel: William Creed (Pres./Pub.); Stefanie Wessell (Editorial Director); Becke Creed (Director of Operations); Amber Ballard (Advertising Director)
Parent company (for newspapers): Gazette Newspapers, Inc.

THE SUBURBANITE

Street address 1: 3577 S Arlington Rd
Street address 2: Ste B
Street address city: Akron
Street address state: OH
Zip/Postal code: 44312-5268
General Phone: (330) 899-2872
General Fax: (330) 896-7633
Advertising Phone: (330) 899-2872 ext. 12
Advertising Fax: (330) 896-7633
Editorial Phone: (330) 899-2872 ext. 14
Editorial Fax: (330) 896-7633
General/National Adv. E-mail: suburbanite@thesuburbanite.com
Display Adv. E-mail: suburbanite@thesuburbanite.com
Editorial e-mail: greg.kohntopp@thesuburbanite.com
Primary Website: thesuburbanite.com
Year Established: 1965
Avg Paid Circ: 69
Avg Free Circ: 33046
Audit By: Sworn/Estimate/Non-Audited
Audit Date: 10.06.2019
Personnel: Greg kohntopp (Ed.); Carol Cooney (Adv. Mgr.)
Parent company (for newspapers): CherryRoad Media

THE TELEGRAM

Street address 1: 920 Veterans Dr
Street address 2: Unit D
Street address city: Jackson
Street address state: OH
Zip/Postal code: 45640-2175
General Phone: (740) 286-3604
General Fax: (740) 286-0167
General/National Adv. E-mail: jgillum@jcbipaper.com
Display Adv. E-mail: bowens@jcbipaper.com
Editorial e-mail: skeller@jcbipaper.com
Primary Website: thetelegramnews.com
Year Established: 2005
Avg Paid Circ: 6000
Audit By: Sworn/Estimate/Non-Audited
Audit Date: 10.06.2019
Personnel: Pete Wilson (Exec. Ed.); Steven P. Keller (Mng. Ed.); Jerry Mossbarger (Gen. Mgr.); Jeanne Gillum (Adv. Mgr.); Rayanna Puckett (Admin.)

THE TRIBUNE

Street address 1: 55 W High St
Street address city: London
Street address state: OH
Zip/Postal code: 43140-1074
Avg Paid Circ: 0
Audit By: Sworn/Estimate/Non-Audited
Audit Date: 10.06.2019

THE TWIN VALLEY NEWS

Street address 1: 10 S Main St
Street address city: West Alexandria
Street address state: OH
Zip/Postal code: 45381-1293
General Phone: (937) 839-4733
General Fax: (937) 839-5351
Advertising Phone: (937) 839-4733
Advertising Fax: (937) 839-5351
Editorial Phone: (937) 839-4733
Editorial Fax: (937) 839-5351
General/National Adv. E-mail: twinvpub@infinet.com
Display Adv. E-mail: information@onlinetvp.com
Editorial e-mail: twinvpub@infinet.com
Primary Website: twinvalleypublications.com
Year Established: 1934
Avg Paid Circ: 400
Avg Free Circ: 8000
Audit By: Sworn/Estimate/Non-Audited
Audit Date: 10.06.2019
Personnel: Sam Shortes (Pub./Ed.); Cindy Shortes (Gen. Mgr.); Angie Donohoo (Adv. Mgr.)
Parent company (for newspapers): Twin Valley Publications

THE UTICA HERALD

Street address 1: 60 N Main St
Street address city: Utica
Street address state: OH
Zip/Postal code: 43080-7704
General Phone: (740) 892-2771
Advertising Phone: (740) 892-2771
Editorial Phone: (740) 892-2771
General/National Adv. E-mail: theuticaherald@Aol.com
Display Adv. E-mail: theuticaherald@aol.com
Editorial e-mail: theuticaherald@aol.com
Year Established: 1878
Avg Paid Circ: 2100
Audit By: Sworn/Estimate/Non-Audited
Audit Date: 10.06.2019
Personnel: Randy Almendinger (Pub.)
Parent company (for newspapers): Heartland Communications

THE VINTON COUNTY COURIER

Street address 1: 103 S Market St
Street address city: Mc Arthur
Street address state: OH
Zip/Postal code: 45651-1219
General Phone: (740) 596-5393
General Fax: (740) 596-4226
Advertising Phone: (740) 596-5393
Advertising Fax: (740) 596-4226
Editorial Phone: (740) 596-5393
Editorial Fax: (740) 596-4226
General/National Adv. E-mail: tfaught@timesjournal.com
Display Adv. E-mail: pjohnson@vintoncourier.com
Editorial e-mail: tbuchanan@vintoncourier.com
Primary Website: vintoncourier.com
Year Established: 1971
Avg Paid Circ: 2500
Audit By: Sworn/Estimate/Non-Audited
Audit Date: 10.06.2019
Personnel: Pam Johnson (Office Mgr.); Monica Nieporte (Pub.); Tyler Buchanan (Ed); Tonya Faught (Acct Exec)
Parent company (for newspapers): Adams Publishing Group, LLC

THE WILLARD TIMES-JUNCTION

Street address 1: 211 S Myrtle Ave
Street address city: Willard
Street address state: OH
Zip/Postal code: 44890-1407
General Phone: (419) 935-0184
General Fax: (419) 933-2031
Advertising Phone: (419) 935-0184
Advertising Fax: (419) 933-2031
Editorial Phone: (419) 935-0184
Editorial Fax: (419) 933-2031
General/National Adv. E-mail: globe@sdgnewsgroup.com
Display Adv. E-mail: globe@sdgnewsgroup.com
Editorial e-mail: globe@sdgnewsgroup.com
Primary Website: sdgnewsgroup.com
Avg Paid Circ: 2602
Avg Free Circ: 50
Audit By: Sworn/Estimate/Non-Audited
Audit Date: 10.06.2019
Personnel: Scott Gove (Pub.); Karla Souslin (Adv. Dir.)
Parent company (for newspapers): SDGNewsgroup

THE YELLOW SPRINGS NEWS

Street address 1: Post Office Box 187
Street address city: Yellow Springs
Street address state: OH
Zip/Postal code: 45387-0187
General Phone: (937) 767-7373
General Fax: (937) 767-2254
Advertising Phone: (937) 767-7373
Advertising Fax: (937) 767-2254
Editorial Phone: (937) 767-7373
Editorial Fax: (937) 767-2254
General/National Adv. E-mail: advert@ysnews.com
Display Adv. E-mail: classifieds@ysnews.com
Editorial e-mail: ysnews@ysnews.com
Primary Website: ysnews.com
Year Established: 1880
Avg Paid Circ: 1841
Avg Free Circ: 39
Audit By: Sworn/Estimate/Non-Audited
Audit Date: 10.06.2019
Personnel: Megan Bachman (Ed.); Robert Hasek (Adv. Mgr.); Suzanne Szempruch (Adv., Des., Prod.)

THISWEEK BEXLEY NEWS

Street address 1: 7801 N Central Dr
Street address city: Lewis Center
Street address state: OH
Zip/Postal code: 43035-9407
General Phone: (740) 888-6000
General Fax: (740) 888-6006
Advertising Phone: (740) 888-6007
Advertising Fax: (740) 888-6001
Editorial Phone: (740) 888-6100
Editorial Fax: (740) 888-6006
General/National Adv. E-mail: advertising@thisweeknews.com

Display Adv. E-mail: classified@thisweeknews.com
Editorial e-mail: lcochran@thisweeknews.com
Primary Website: thisweeknews.com
Year Established: 1990
Avg Free Circ: 7691
Audit By: Sworn/Estimate/Non-Audited
Audit Date: 10.06.2019
Personnel: Bradley Harmon (Pres./Pub.); Lee Cochran (Mng. Ed.); Doug Dixon (Adv. Dir.)
Parent company (for newspapers): ThisWeek Community News; Consumer News Service Inc.

THISWEEK CLINTONVILLE BOOSTER

Street address 1: 7801 N Central Dr
Street address city: Lewis Center
Street address state: OH
Zip/Postal code: 43035-9407
General Phone: (740) 888-6000
General Fax: (740) 888-6006
Advertising Phone: (740) 888-6007
Advertising Fax: (740) 888-6001
Editorial Phone: (740) 888-6100
Editorial Fax: (740) 888-6006
General/National Adv. E-mail: advertising@thisweeknews.com
Display Adv. E-mail: classified@thisweeknews.com
Editorial e-mail: editorial@thisweeknews.com
Primary Website: thisweeknews.com
Year Established: 1990
Avg Free Circ: 14250
Audit By: Sworn/Estimate/Non-Audited
Audit Date: 10.06.2019
Personnel: Bradley Harmon (Pub.); Lee Cochran (Mng. Ed.); Doug Dixon (Adv. Dir.)
Parent company (for newspapers): ThisWeek Community News; Consumer News Service Inc.

THISWEEK DELAWARE NEWS

Street address 1: 7801 N Central Dr
Street address city: Lewis Center
Street address state: OH
Zip/Postal code: 43035-9407
General Phone: (740) 888-6000
General Fax: (740) 888-6006
Advertising Phone: (740) 888-6007
Advertising Fax: (740) 888-6001
Editorial Phone: (740) 888-6100
Editorial Fax: (740) 888-6006
General/National Adv. E-mail: advertising@thisweeknews.com
Display Adv. E-mail: classified@thisweeknews.com
Editorial e-mail: editorial@thisweeknews.com
Primary Website: thisweeknews.com
Year Established: 1990
Avg Free Circ: 16520
Audit By: Sworn/Estimate/Non-Audited
Audit Date: 10.06.2019
Personnel: Bradley Harmon (Pub.); Lee Cochran (Mng. Ed.); Doug Dixon (Adv. Dir.)
Parent company (for newspapers): ThisWeek Community News; Consumer News Service Inc.

THISWEEK DUBLIN VILLAGER

Street address 1: 7801 N Central Dr
Street address city: Lewis Center
Street address state: OH
Zip/Postal code: 43035-9407
General Phone: (740) 888-6000
General Fax: (740) 888-6006
Advertising Phone: (740) 888-6007
Advertising Fax: (740) 888-6001
Editorial Phone: (740) 888-6100
Editorial Fax: (740) 888-6006
General/National Adv. E-mail: advertising@thisweeknews.com
Display Adv. E-mail: classified@thisweeknews.com
Editorial e-mail: editorial@thisweeknews.com
Primary Website: thisweeknews.com
Year Established: 1990
Avg Free Circ: 19462
Audit By: Sworn/Estimate/Non-Audited
Audit Date: 10.06.2019
Personnel: Bradley Harmon (Pub.); Doug Dixon (Adv. Dir.); Lee Cochran (Mng. Ed.)
Parent company (for newspapers): ThisWeek Community News; Consumer News Service Inc.

THISWEEK GERMAN VILLAGE GAZETTE

Street address 1: 7801 N Central Dr
Street address city: Lewis Center
Street address state: OH
Zip/Postal code: 43035-9407
General Phone: (740) 888-6000
General Fax: (740) 888-6006
Advertising Phone: (740) 888-6007
Advertising Fax: (740) 888-6001
Editorial Phone: (740) 888-6100
Editorial Fax: (740) 888-6006
General/National Adv. E-mail: advertising@thisweeknews.com
Display Adv. E-mail: classified@thisweeknews.com
Editorial e-mail: editorial@thisweeknews.com
Primary Website: thisweeknews.com
Year Established: 1990
Avg Free Circ: 4316
Audit By: Sworn/Estimate/Non-Audited
Audit Date: 10.06.2019
Personnel: Bradley Harmon (Pub.); Lee Cochran (Mng. Ed.); Doug Dixon (Adv. Dir.)
Parent company (for newspapers): ThisWeek Community News; Consumer News Service Inc.

THISWEEK GROVE CITY RECORD

Street address 1: 7801 N Central Dr
Street address city: Lewis Center
Street address state: OH
Zip/Postal code: 43035-9407
General Phone: (740) 888-6000
General Fax: (740) 888-6006
Advertising Phone: (740) 888-6007
Advertising Fax: (740) 888-6001
Editorial Phone: (740) 888-6100
Editorial Fax: (740) 888-6006
General/National Adv. E-mail: advertising@thisweeknews.com
Display Adv. E-mail: classified@thisweeknews.com
Editorial e-mail: editorial@thisweeknews.com
Primary Website: thisweeknews.com
Year Established: 1990
Avg Free Circ: 14614
Audit By: Sworn/Estimate/Non-Audited
Audit Date: 10.06.2019
Personnel: Bradley Harmon (Pub.); Lee Cochran (Mng. Ed.); Doug Dixon (Adv. Dir.)
Parent company (for newspapers): ThisWeek Community News; Consumer News Service Inc.

THISWEEK HILLIARD NORTHWEST NEWS

Street address 1: 7801 N Central Dr
Street address city: Lewis Center
Street address state: OH
Zip/Postal code: 43035-9407
General Phone: (740) 888-6000
General Fax: (740) 888-6006
Advertising Phone: (740) 888-6007
Advertising Fax: (740) 888-6001
Editorial Phone: (740) 888-6100
Editorial Fax: (740) 888-6006
General/National Adv. E-mail: advertising@thisweeknews.com
Display Adv. E-mail: classified@thisweeknews.com
Editorial e-mail: editorial@thisweeknews.com
Primary Website: thisweeknews.com
Year Established: 1990
Avg Free Circ: 21859
Audit By: Sworn/Estimate/Non-Audited
Audit Date: 10.06.2019
Personnel: Bradley Harmon (Pub.); Lee Cochran (Mng. Ed.); Doug Dixon (Adv. Dir.)
Parent company (for newspapers): ThisWeek Community News; Consumer News Service Inc.

THISWEEK JOHNSTOWN INDEPENDENT

Street address 1: 7801 N Central Dr
Street address city: Lewis Center
Street address state: OH
Zip/Postal code: 43035-9407
General Phone: (740) 888-6000
General Fax: (740) 888-6006
Advertising Phone: (740) 888-6007
Advertising Fax: (740) 888-6001
Editorial Phone: (740) 888-6100
Editorial Fax: (740) 888-6006
General/National Adv. E-mail: advertising@thisweeknews.com
Display Adv. E-mail: classified@thisweeknews.com
Editorial e-mail: editorial@thisweeknews.com
Primary Website: thisweeknews.com
Year Established: 1990
Avg Free Circ: 6448
Audit By: Sworn/Estimate/Non-Audited
Audit Date: 10.06.2019
Personnel: Bradley Harmon (Pub.); Lee Cochran (Mng. Ed.); Doug Dixon (Adv. Dir.)
Parent company (for newspapers): ThisWeek Community News; Consumer News Service Inc.

THISWEEK LICKING COUNTY NEWS

Street address 1: 7801 N Central Dr
Street address city: Lewis Center
Street address state: OH
Zip/Postal code: 43035-9407
General Phone: (740) 888-6000
General Fax: (740) 888-6006
Advertising Phone: (740) 888-6007
Advertising Fax: (740) 888-6001
Editorial Phone: (740) 888-6100
Editorial Fax: (740) 888-6006
General/National Adv. E-mail: advertising@thisweeknews.com
Display Adv. E-mail: classified@thisweeknews.com
Editorial e-mail: editorial@thisweeknews.com
Primary Website: thisweeknews.com
Year Established: 1990
Avg Free Circ: 14403
Audit By: Sworn/Estimate/Non-Audited
Audit Date: 10.06.2019
Personnel: Bradley Harmon (Pub.); Lee Cochran (Mng. Ed.); Doug Dixon (Adv. Dir.)
Parent company (for newspapers): ThisWeek Community News; Consumer News Service Inc.

THISWEEK MARYSVILLE NEWS

Street address 1: 7801 N Central Dr
Street address city: Lewis Center
Street address state: OH
Zip/Postal code: 43035-9407
General Phone: (740) 888-6000
General Fax: (740) 888-6006
Advertising Phone: (740) 888-6007
Advertising Fax: (740) 888-6001
Editorial Phone: (740) 888-6100
Editorial Fax: (740) 888-6006
General/National Adv. E-mail: advertising@thisweeknews.com
Display Adv. E-mail: classified@thisweeknews.com
Editorial e-mail: editorial@thisweeknews.com
Primary Website: thisweeknews.com
Year Established: 1990
Avg Free Circ: 10126
Audit By: Sworn/Estimate/Non-Audited
Audit Date: 10.06.2019
Personnel: Bradley Harmon (Pub.); Lee Cochran (Mng. Ed.); Doug Dixon (Adv. Dir.)
Parent company (for newspapers): ThisWeek Community News; Consumer News Service Inc.

THISWEEK NEW ALBANY NEWS

Street address 1: 7801 N Central Dr
Street address city: Lewis Center
Street address state: OH
Zip/Postal code: 43035-9407
General Phone: (740) 888-6000
General Fax: (740) 888-6006
Advertising Phone: (740) 888-6007
Advertising Fax: (740) 888-6001
Editorial Phone: (740) 888-6100
Editorial Fax: (740) 888-6006
General/National Adv. E-mail: advertising@thisweeknews.com
Display Adv. E-mail: classified@thisweeknews.com
Editorial e-mail: editorial@thisweeknews.com
Primary Website: thisweeknews.com
Year Established: 1990
Avg Free Circ: 7219
Audit By: Sworn/Estimate/Non-Audited
Audit Date: 10.06.2019
Personnel: Bradley Harmon (Pub.); Lee Cochran (Mng. Ed.); Doug Dixon (Adv. Dir.)
Parent company (for newspapers): ThisWeek Community News; Consumer News Service Inc.

THISWEEK NORTHLAND NEWS

Street address 1: 7801 N Central Dr
Street address city: Lewis Center
Street address state: OH
Zip/Postal code: 43035-9407
General Phone: (740) 888-6000
General Fax: (740) 888-6006
Advertising Phone: (740) 888-6007
Advertising Fax: (740) 888-6001
Editorial Phone: (740) 888-6100
Editorial Fax: (740) 888-6006
General/National Adv. E-mail: advertising@thisweeknews.com
Display Adv. E-mail: classified@thisweeknews.com
Editorial e-mail: editorial@thisweeknews.com
Primary Website: thisweeknews.com
Year Established: 1990
Avg Free Circ: 14294
Audit By: Sworn/Estimate/Non-Audited
Audit Date: 10.06.2019
Personnel: Bradley Harmon (Pub.); Lee Cochran (Mng. Ed.); Doug Dixon (Adv. Dir.)
Parent company (for newspapers): ThisWeek Community News; Consumer News Service Inc.

THISWEEK NORTHWEST NEWS

Street address 1: 7801 N Central Dr
Street address city: Lewis Center
Street address state: OH
Zip/Postal code: 43035-9407
General Phone: (740) 888-6000
General Fax: (740) 888-6006
Advertising Phone: (740) 888-6007
Advertising Fax: (740) 888-6001
Editorial Phone: (740) 888-6100
Editorial Fax: (740) 888-6006
General/National Adv. E-mail: advertising@thisweeknews.com
Display Adv. E-mail: classified@thisweeknews.com
Editorial e-mail: editorial@thisweeknews.com
Primary Website: thisweeknews.com
Year Established: 1990
Avg Free Circ: 3344
Audit By: AAM
Audit Date: 9/31/2017
Personnel: Bradley Harmon (Pub.); Lee Cochran (Mng. Ed.); Doug Dixon (Adv. Dir.)
Parent company (for newspapers): ThisWeek Community News; Consumer News Service Inc.

THISWEEK OLENTANGY VALLEY NEWS

Street address 1: 7801 N Central Dr
Street address city: Lewis Center
Street address state: OH
Zip/Postal code: 43035-9407
General Phone: (740) 888-6000
General Fax: (740) 888-6006
Advertising Phone: (740) 888-6007
Advertising Fax: (740) 888-6001
Editorial Phone: (740) 888-6100
Editorial Fax: (740) 888-6006
General/National Adv. E-mail: advertising@thisweeknews.com
Display Adv. E-mail: classified@thisweeknews.com
Editorial e-mail: editorial@thisweeknews.com
Primary Website: thisweeknews.com
Year Established: 1990
Avg Free Circ: 20103
Audit By: Sworn/Estimate/Non-Audited
Audit Date: 10.06.2019
Personnel: Bradley Harmon (Pub.); Lee Cochran (Mng. Ed.); Doug Dixon (Adv. Dir.)
Parent company (for newspapers): ThisWeek Community News; Consumer News Service Inc.

THISWEEK PICKERINGTON TIMES-SUN

Street address 1: 7801 N Central Dr
Street address city: Lewis Center
Street address state: OH
Zip/Postal code: 43035-9407
General Phone: (740) 888-6000

General Fax: (740) 888-6006
Advertising Phone: (740) 888-6007
Advertising Fax: (740) 888-6001
Editorial Phone: (740) 888-6100
Editorial Fax: (740) 888-6006
General/National Adv. E-mail: advertising@thisweeknews.com
Display Adv. E-mail: classified@thisweeknews.com
Editorial e-mail: editorial@thisweeknews.com
Primary Website: thisweeknews.com
Year Established: 1990
Avg Free Circ: 12805
Audit By: Sworn/Estimate/Non-Audited
Audit Date: 10.06.2019
Personnel: Bradley Harmon (Pub.); Lee Cochran (Mng. Ed.); Doug Dixon (Adv. Dir.)
Parent company (for newspapers): ThisWeek Community News; Consumer News Service Inc.

THISWEEK REYNOLDSBURG NEWS

Street address 1: 7801 N Central Dr
Street address city: Lewis Center
Street address state: OH
Zip/Postal code: 43035-9407
General Phone: (740) 888-6000
General Fax: (740) 888-6006
Advertising Phone: (740) 888-6007
Advertising Fax: (740) 888-6001
Editorial Phone: (740) 888-6100
Editorial Fax: (740) 888-6006
General/National Adv. E-mail: advertising@thisweeknews.com
Display Adv. E-mail: classified@thisweeknews.com
Editorial e-mail: editorial@thisweeknews.com
Primary Website: thisweeknews.com
Year Established: 1990
Avg Free Circ: 11110
Audit By: Sworn/Estimate/Non-Audited
Audit Date: 10.06.2019
Personnel: Bradley Harmon (Pub.); Lee Cochran (Mng. Ed.); Doug Dixon (Adv. Dir.)
Parent company (for newspapers): ThisWeek Community News; Consumer News Service Inc.

THISWEEK ROCKY FORK ENTERPRISE

Street address 1: 7801 N Central Dr
Street address city: Lewis Center
Street address state: OH
Zip/Postal code: 43035-9407
General Phone: (740) 888-6000
General Fax: (740) 888-6006
Advertising Phone: (740) 888-6007
Advertising Fax: (740) 888-6001
Editorial Phone: (740) 888-6100
Editorial Fax: (740) 888-6006
General/National Adv. E-mail: advertising@thisweeknews.com
Display Adv. E-mail: classified@thisweeknews.com
Editorial e-mail: editorial@thisweeknews.com
Primary Website: thisweeknews.com
Year Established: 1990
Avg Free Circ: 14419
Audit By: Sworn/Estimate/Non-Audited
Audit Date: 10.06.2019
Personnel: Bradley Harmon (Pub.); Lee Cochran (Mng. Ed.); Doug Dixon (Adv. Dir.)
Parent company (for newspapers): ThisWeek Community News; Consumer News Service Inc.

THISWEEK THE CANAL WINCHESTER TIMES

Street address 1: 7801 N Central Dr
Street address city: Lewis Center
Street address state: OH
Zip/Postal code: 43035-9407
General Phone: (740) 888-6000
General Fax: (740) 888-6006
Advertising Phone: (740) 888-6007
Advertising Fax: (740) 888-6001
Editorial Phone: (740) 888-6100
Editorial Fax: (740) 888-6006
General/National Adv. E-mail: advertising@thisweeknews.com
Display Adv. E-mail: classified@thisweeknews.com
Editorial e-mail: editorial@thisweeknews.com
Primary Website: thisweeknews.com
Year Established: 1990
Avg Free Circ: 9580
Audit By: Sworn/Estimate/Non-Audited
Audit Date: 10.06.2019
Personnel: Bradley Harmon (Pub.); Lee Cochran (Mng. Ed.); Doug Dixon (Adv. Dir.)
Parent company (for newspapers): ThisWeek Community News; Consumer News Service Inc.

THISWEEK TRI-VILLAGE NEWS

Street address 1: 7801 N Central Dr
Street address city: Lewis Center
Street address state: OH
Zip/Postal code: 43035-9407
General Phone: (740) 888-6000
General Fax: (740) 888-6006
Advertising Phone: (740) 888-6007
Advertising Fax: (740) 888-6001
Editorial Phone: (740) 888-6100
Editorial Fax: (740) 888-6006
General/National Adv. E-mail: advertising@thisweeknews.com
Display Adv. E-mail: classified@thisweeknews.com
Editorial e-mail: editorial@thisweeknews.com
Primary Website: thisweeknews.com
Year Established: 1990
Avg Free Circ: 4669
Audit By: Sworn/Estimate/Non-Audited
Audit Date: 10.06.2019
Personnel: Bradley Harmon (Pub.); Lee Cochran (Mng. Ed.); Doug Dixon (Adv. Dir.)
Parent company (for newspapers): ThisWeek Community News; Consumer News Service Inc.

THISWEEK UPPER ARLINGTON NEWS

Street address 1: 7801 N Central Dr
Street address city: Lewis Center
Street address state: OH
Zip/Postal code: 43035-9407
General Phone: (740) 888-6000
General Fax: (740) 888-6006
Advertising Phone: (740) 888-6007
Advertising Fax: (740) 888-6001
Editorial Phone: (740) 888-6100
Editorial Fax: (740) 888-6006
General/National Adv. E-mail: advertising@thisweeknews.com
Display Adv. E-mail: classified@thisweeknews.com
Editorial e-mail: editorial@thisweeknews.com
Primary Website: thisweeknews.com
Year Established: 1990
Avg Free Circ: 18473
Audit By: Sworn/Estimate/Non-Audited
Audit Date: 10.06.2019
Personnel: Bradley Harmon (Pub.); Lee Cochran (Mng. Ed.); Doug Dixon (Adv. Dir.)
Parent company (for newspapers): ThisWeek Community News; Consumer News Service Inc.

THISWEEK WEST SIDE NEWS

Street address 1: 7801 N Central Dr
Street address city: Lewis Center
Street address state: OH
Zip/Postal code: 43035-9407
General Phone: (740) 888-6000
General Fax: (740) 888-6006
Advertising Phone: (740) 888-6007
Advertising Fax: (740) 888-6001
Editorial Phone: (740) 888-6100
Editorial Fax: (740) 888-6006
General/National Adv. E-mail: advertising@thisweeknews.com
Display Adv. E-mail: classified@thisweeknews.com
Editorial e-mail: editorial@thisweeknews.com
Primary Website: thisweeknews.com
Year Established: 1990
Avg Free Circ: 7850
Audit By: Sworn/Estimate/Non-Audited
Audit Date: 10.06.2019
Personnel: Bradley Harmon (Pub.); Lee Cochran (Mng. Ed.); Doug Dixon (Adv. Dir.)
Parent company (for newspapers): ThisWeek Community News; Consumer News Service Inc.

THISWEEK WESTERVILLE NEWS & PUBLIC OPINION

Street address 1: 7801 N Central Dr
Street address city: Lewis Center
Street address state: OH
Zip/Postal code: 43035-9407
General Phone: (740) 888-6000
General Fax: (740) 888-6006
Advertising Phone: (740) 888-6007
Advertising Fax: (740) 888-6001
Editorial Phone: (740) 888-6100
Editorial Fax: (740) 888-6006
General/National Adv. E-mail: advertising@thisweeknews.com
Display Adv. E-mail: classified@thisweeknews.com
Editorial e-mail: editorial@thisweeknews.com
Primary Website: thisweeknews.com
Year Established: 1990
Avg Free Circ: 25825
Audit By: Sworn/Estimate/Non-Audited
Audit Date: 10.06.2019
Personnel: Bradley Harmon (Pub.); Lee Cochran (Mng. Ed.); Doug Dixon (Adv. Dir.)
Parent company (for newspapers): ThisWeek Community News; Consumer News Service Inc.

THISWEEK WHITEHALL NEWS

Street address 1: 7801 N Central Dr
Street address city: Lewis Center
Street address state: OH
Zip/Postal code: 43035-9407
General Phone: (740) 888-6000
General Fax: (740) 888-6006
Advertising Phone: (740) 888-6007
Advertising Fax: (740) 888-6001
Editorial Phone: (740) 888-6100
Editorial Fax: (740) 888-6006
General/National Adv. E-mail: advertising@thisweeknews.com
Display Adv. E-mail: classified@thisweeknews.com
Editorial e-mail: editorial@thisweeknews.com
Primary Website: thisweeknews.com
Year Established: 1990
Avg Free Circ: 5110
Audit By: Sworn/Estimate/Non-Audited
Audit Date: 10.06.2019
Personnel: Bradley Harmon (Pub.); Lee Cochran (Mng. Ed.); Doug Dixon (Adv. Dir.)
Parent company (for newspapers): ThisWeek Community News; Consumer News Service Inc.

THISWEEK WORTHINGTON NEWS

Street address 1: 7801 N Central Dr
Street address city: Lewis Center
Street address state: OH
Zip/Postal code: 43035-9407
General Phone: (740) 888-6000
General Fax: (740) 888-6006
Advertising Phone: (740) 888-6007
Advertising Fax: (740) 888-6001
Editorial Phone: (740) 888-6100
Editorial Fax: (740) 888-6006
General/National Adv. E-mail: advertising@thisweeknews.com
Display Adv. E-mail: classified@thisweeknews.com
Editorial e-mail: editorial@thisweeknews.com
Primary Website: thisweeknews.com
Year Established: 1990
Avg Free Circ: 17875
Audit By: Sworn/Estimate/Non-Audited
Audit Date: 10.06.2019
Personnel: Bradley Harmon (Pub.); Lee Cochran (Mng. Ed.); Doug Dixon (Adv. Dir.)
Parent company (for newspapers): ThisWeek Community News; Consumer News Service Inc.

TODAY'S PULSE

Street address 1: 6752 Cincinnati Dayton Road
Street address 2: Suite 205
Street address city: Liberty Township
Street address state: OH
Zip/Postal code: 45044-9168
General Phone: (513) 755-5060
General Fax: (513) 483-5252
Advertising Phone: (513) 483-5225
Advertising Fax: (513) 483-5252
Editorial Phone: (513) 755-5060
Editorial Fax: (513) 483-5252
General/National Adv. E-mail: Lisa.sherbauer@coxinc.com
Editorial e-mail: Jennifer.Burcham@coxinc.com
Primary Website: journal-news.com
Avg Free Circ: 45400
Audit By: AAM
Audit Date: 28.11.2018
Personnel: Jennifer Burcham (Editor); Jennifer Collins (Ed.)
Parent company (for newspapers): Cox Media Group Ohio

TRIBUNE COURIER & MADISON TRIBUNE

Street address 1: 347 Allen Dr
Street address city: Ontario
Street address state: OH
Zip/Postal code: 44906-1001
General Phone: (419) 529-2847
General/National Adv. E-mail: news@tribune-courier.com
Display Adv. E-mail: news@tribune-courier.com
Classified Adv. e-mail: news@tribune-courier.com
Editorial e-mail: news@tribune-courier.com
Primary Website: www.tribune-courier.com
Mthly Avg Views: 30000
Year Established: 1961
Audit By: Sworn/Estimate/Non-Audited
Audit Date: 10.06.2019
Personnel: Frank Stumbo (Pub./Ed.); Jenna Wolford (Manger/Production Manager/Photo Journalist); Betty E. Stumbo (Treasurer); Teresa Vore (Office Manager); Kim Knapp (Adv. Mgr.); Traci Little (Photo Journalist/ Advertising Manager)
Parent company (for newspapers): Stumbo Publishing Co.

TRI-COUNTY MARKETPLACE

Street address 1: 825 3rd Ave
Street address city: Gallipolis
Street address state: OH
Zip/Postal code: 45631-1624
General Phone: (740) 446-2342
General Fax: (740) 446-3008
General/National Adv. E-mail: jmitchell@civitasmedia.com
Display Adv. E-mail: kcade@civitasmedia.com
Editorial e-mail: mjohnson@civitasmedia.com
Primary Website: mydailytribune.com
Avg Free Circ: 18000
Audit By: Sworn/Estimate/Non-Audited
Audit Date: 10.06.2019
Personnel: Beth Sergent (Adv. Mgr.); Matt Rodgers (Sales)
Parent company (for newspapers): AIM Media Indiana

TRI-COUNTY PRESS

Street address 1: 312 Elm St
Street address city: Cincinnati
Street address state: OH
Zip/Postal code: 45202-2739
General Phone: (513) 248-8600
General Fax: (513) 248-1938
Advertising Phone: (513) 248-8600
Advertising Fax: (513) 248-1938
Editorial Phone: (513) 248-8600
Editorial Fax: (513) 248-1938
General/National Adv. E-mail: acumby@communitypress.com
Display Adv. E-mail: acumby@communitypress.com
Editorial e-mail: espangler@communitypress.com
Primary Website: cincinnati.com
Avg Free Circ: 10835
Audit By: Sworn/Estimate/Non-Audited
Audit Date: 10.06.2019
Personnel: Nancy Daly (Ed.); Margaret Buchanan (Pres./ Pub.); Alison Cumby (Adv. Mgr.)
Parent company (for newspapers): Gannett

TWINSBURG BULLETIN

Street address 1: 1050 W. Main Street
Street address city: Kent
Street address state: OH
Zip/Postal code: 44240
General Phone: (330) 541-9400
General Fax: (330) 296-2698
General/National Adv. E-mail: Ads@recordpub.com
Display Adv. E-mail: jgasper@recordpub.com
Classified Adv. e-mail: class@recordpub.com
Editorial e-mail: aschunk@recordpub.com
Primary Website: mytownneo.com/twinsburgbulletin
Year Established: 1830
Avg Paid Circ: 162
Avg Free Circ: 8293

Audit By: AAM
Audit Date: 31.03.2016
Personnel: Michael Shearer (Ed.); Heather Rainone (Mng. Ed.); Jim Williams (Adv. Dir. / GM); Gary Hurst
Parent company (for newspapers): CherryRoad Media; Gannett Company Inc.

VANDALIA DRUMMER NEWS

Street address 1: 694 W National Rd
Street address city: Vandalia
Street address state: OH
Zip/Postal code: 45377-1032
General Phone: (937) 236-4990
General Fax: (937) 890-9153
Advertising Phone: (937) 890-6030
Advertising Fax: (937) 890-9153
Editorial Phone: (937) 890-6030
Editorial Fax: (937) 890-9153
General/National Adv. E-mail: kbelcher@civitasmedia.com
Display Adv. E-mail: kbelcher@civitasmedia.com
Editorial e-mail: dwacker@civitasmedia.com
Primary Website: vandaliadrummernews.com
Year Established: 1979
Avg Paid Circ: 4200
Avg Free Circ: 1000
Audit By: Sworn/Estimate/Non-Audited
Audit Date: 10.06.2019
Personnel: Ron Nunnari (Mng. Ed.); Pamela Beattie (Adv. Mgr.)
Parent company (for newspapers): AIM Media Indiana

VERMILION PHOTOJOURNAL

Street address 1: 630 Main St
Street address city: Vermilion
Street address state: OH
Zip/Postal code: 44089-1047
General Phone: (440) 967-5268
General Fax: (440) 967-2535
Advertising Phone: (440) 967-5268
Advertising Fax: (440) 967-2535
Editorial Phone: (440) 967-5268
Editorial Fax: (440) 967-2535
General/National Adv. E-mail: info@vermilion-news.com
Display Adv. E-mail: info@vermilion-news.com
Editorial e-mail: info@vermilion-news.com
Avg Paid Circ: 3000
Avg Free Circ: 486
Audit By: Sworn/Estimate/Non-Audited
Audit Date: 10.06.2019
Personnel: Karen Cornelius (Ed./Gen. Mgr.); Susan Borso (Adv. Dir.); Melanie Williamson (News Ed)
Parent company (for newspapers): Douthit Communications, Inc.

VERSAILLES POLICY

Street address 1: 308 N West St
Street address city: Versailles
Street address state: OH
Zip/Postal code: 45380-1360
General Phone: (937) 526-9131
Advertising Phone: (937) 526-9131
Editorial Phone: (937) 526-9131
General/National Adv. E-mail: vpolicy@roadrunner.com
Display Adv. E-mail: vpolicy@roadrunner.com
Editorial e-mail: vpolicy@roadrunner.com
Year Established: 1875
Avg Paid Circ: 2000
Audit By: Sworn/Estimate/Non-Audited
Audit Date: 10.06.2019
Personnel: Scott Langston (Pub./Ed./Adv. Mgr.)

WEEKEND ADVOCATE

Street address 1: 428 S Broadway St
Street address city: Greenville
Street address state: OH
Zip/Postal code: 45331-1926
General Phone: (937) 548-3151
General Fax: (937) 548-3913
General/National Adv. E-mail: crandall@aimmediamidwest.com
Display Adv. E-mail: crandall@aimmediamidwest.com
Classified Adv. e-mail: info@dailyadvocate.com
Editorial e-mail: kshaner@aimmediamidwest.com
Primary Website: dailyadvocate.com
Avg Free Circ: 25296
Audit By: Sworn/Estimate/Non-Audited
Audit Date: 10.06.2019
Personnel: Kyle Shaner (Ed.); Christie Randall (Adv. Mgr.)
Parent company (for newspapers): AIM Media Texas

WEEKLY RECORD HERALD

Street address 1: 224 S Market St
Street address city: Troy
Street address state: OH
Zip/Postal code: 45373-3327
General Phone: (937) 440-5275
General Fax: (937) 440-5286
Advertising Phone: (937) 440-5275
Advertising Fax: (937) 440-5286
Editorial Phone: (937) 335-5634
Editorial Fax: (937) 440-5286
General/National Adv. E-mail: wrheditor@gmail.com
Display Adv. E-mail: wrheditor@gmail.com
Editorial e-mail: wrheditor@gmail.com
Primary Website: weeklyrecordherald.com
Year Established: 2008
Avg Paid Circ: 3000
Audit By: Sworn/Estimate/Non-Audited
Audit Date: 10.06.2019
Personnel: Joyell Nevins (Ed.); Jan Burns (News Ed.)
Parent company (for newspapers): Ohio Community Media, LLC

WELLINGTON ENTERPRISE

Street address 1: 42 S Main St
Street address city: Oberlin
Street address state: OH
Zip/Postal code: 44074-1627
General Phone: (440) 988-2801
General Fax: (440) 988-2802
Advertising Phone: (440) 775-1611
Advertising Fax: (440) 774-2167
Editorial Phone: (440) 775-1611
Editorial Fax: (440) 774-2167
General/National Adv. E-mail: rward@civitasmedia.com
Display Adv. E-mail: aduncan@civitasmedia.com
Editorial e-mail: news@theoberlinnews.com
Primary Website: thewellingtonenterprise.com
Year Established: 1864
Avg Paid Circ: 1358
Avg Free Circ: 62
Audit By: Sworn/Estimate/Non-Audited
Audit Date: 10.06.2019
Personnel: Tom Hutson (Reg. Rev. Dir.); Jason Hawk (Ed.); Robin Ward (Bus. Mgr./Adv. Rep.)
Parent company (for newspapers): Schloss Media, Inc.

WEST LIFE

Street address 1: 19071 Old Detroit Rd
Street address city: Rocky River
Street address state: OH
Zip/Postal code: 44116-1767
General Phone: (440) 871-5797
General Fax: (440) 871-3824
Advertising Phone: (440) 933-5100
Advertising Fax: (440) 871-0157
Editorial Phone: (440) 871-5797
Editorial Fax: (440) 871-3824
General/National Adv. E-mail: bkohler@2presspapers.com
Display Adv. E-mail: bkohler@westlifenews.com
Editorial e-mail: editor@westlifenews.com
Primary Website: westlifenews.com
Year Established: 1959
Avg Paid Circ: 12000
Avg Free Circ: 750
Audit By: Sworn/Estimate/Non-Audited
Audit Date: 10.06.2019
Personnel: Harold K. Douthit (Pub.); Susan Love (Managing Editor)
Parent company (for newspapers): Douthit Communications, Inc.

WESTERN HILLS PRESS

Street address 1: 312 Elm St
Street address city: Cincinnati
Street address state: OH
Zip/Postal code: 45202-2739
General Phone: (513) 923-3111
General Fax: (513) 923-1806
Advertising Phone: (513) 923-3111
Advertising Fax: (513) 923-1806
Editorial Phone: (513) 923-3111
Editorial Fax: (513) 923-1806
General/National Adv. E-mail: chahn@enquirer.com
Display Adv. E-mail: mwoodruff@enquirer.com
Editorial e-mail: memral@communitypress.com
Primary Website: cincinnati.com
Avg Paid Circ: 10091
Avg Free Circ: 8241
Audit By: Sworn/Estimate/Non-Audited
Audit Date: 10.06.2019
Personnel: Margaret Buchanan (Pres./Pub.); Carolyn Washburn (Exec. Ed.); Richard Maloney (Mng. Ed.); Carol Hahn (Adv. VP); Sharon Schachleiter (Circ. Mgr.)
Parent company (for newspapers): Gannett

WESTSIDE MESSENGER

Street address 1: 3500 Sullivant Ave
Street address city: Columbus
Street address state: OH
Zip/Postal code: 43204-1105
General Phone: (614) 272-5422
General Fax: (614) 272-0684
Advertising Phone: (614) 272-5422
Advertising Fax: (614) 272-0684
Editorial Phone: (614) 272-5422
Editorial Fax: (614) 272-0684
General/National Adv. E-mail: phildaubel@columbusmessenger.com
Display Adv. E-mail: phildaubel@columbusmessenger.com
Editorial e-mail: westside@columbusmessenger.com
Primary Website: columbusmessenger.com
Year Established: 1974
Avg Paid Circ: 0
Avg Free Circ: 22404
Audit By: Sworn/Estimate/Non-Audited
Audit Date: 10.06.2019
Personnel: Philip F. Daubel (Pub./Gen. Mgr.); Fred Schenk (Adv. Mgr.); Rick Palsgrove (Ed.); Doug Henry (Circ. Mgr)
Parent company (for newspapers): Columbus Messenger Newspapers

WILLSHIRE PHOTO STAR

Street address 1: 307 State St.
Street address city: Willshire
Street address state: OH
Zip/Postal code: 45898
General Phone: (419) 495-2696
General Fax: (419) 495-2143
Advertising Phone: (419) 495-2696
Advertising Fax: (419) 495-2143
Editorial Phone: (419) 495-2696
Editorial Fax: (419) 495-2143
General/National Adv. E-mail: photostarnews@verizon.net
Display Adv. E-mail: photostarnews@verizon.net
Editorial e-mail: photostarnews@verizon.net
Year Established: 1895
Avg Paid Circ: 165
Avg Free Circ: 11025
Audit By: Sworn/Estimate/Non-Audited
Audit Date: 10.06.2019
Personnel: Judith Bunner (Pub./Ed.); John D. Bunner (Co-Pub./Ed.)

WOOSTER WEEKLY NEWS

Street address 1: 7368 County Road 623
Street address city: Millersburg
Street address state: OH
Zip/Postal code: 44654-9256
General Phone: (330) 674-2300
General Fax: (888) 769-3960
Editorial e-mail: kvalentini@alonovus.com
Primary Website: alonovus.com
Mthly Avg Views: 12043
Mthly Avg Unique Visitors: 5027
Year Established: 2002
Avg Free Circ: 8625
Audit By: Sworn/Estimate/Non-Audited
Audit Date: 10.06.2019
Personnel: Michael Mast (Pres.); Rick Festi (Circ. Mgr)
Parent company (for newspapers): AloNovus Corp.

OKLAHOMA

ALVA REVIEW-COURIER

Street address 1: 620 Choctaw St
Street address city: Alva
Street address state: OK
Zip/Postal code: 73717-1626
General Phone: (580) 327-2200
General Fax: (580) 327-2454
General/National Adv. E-mail: sales@alvareviewcourier.net
Display Adv. E-mail: manager@alvareviewcourier.net
Classified Adv. e-mail: manager@alvareviewcourier.net
Editorial e-mail: news@alvareviewcourier.net
Primary Website: alvareviewcourier.com
Avg Paid Circ: 1300
Audit By: Sworn/Estimate/Non-Audited
Audit Date: 10.06.2019
Personnel: Marione Martin (Ed); Lynn L. Martin (Publisher); Bill Springer (Ad Rep); Amanda Galindo (Ad Rep); Linda Toone (Office Manager)

ANTLERS AMERICAN

Street address 1: 110 E Main St
Street address city: Antlers
Street address state: OK
Zip/Postal code: 74523-3254
General Phone: (580) 298-3314
General Fax: (580) 298-3316
General/National Adv. E-mail: comp.antlers.amer@sbcglobal.net
Display Adv. E-mail: class.antlers.amer@sbcglobal.net
Editorial e-mail: ed.antlersamer@sbcglobal.net
Primary Website: theantlersamerican.com
Year Established: 1895
Avg Paid Circ: 2703
Audit By: Sworn/Estimate/Non-Audited
Audit Date: 10.06.2019
Personnel: Shelley Baskin (Adv. Mgr.); Steffenson Tracy (Pub/Ed/Gen. Mgr); Van Meter Michelle (Class/ Legal Clerk)
Parent company (for newspapers): Heritage Publications (2003) Inc.; Horizon Publications Inc.

ATOKA COUNTY TIMES

Street address 1: 894 W 13th St
Street address city: Atoka
Street address state: OK
Zip/Postal code: 74525-3426
General Phone: (580) 889-3319
General Fax: (580) 889-2300
Advertising Phone: (580) 889-3310
General/National Adv. E-mail: rlinscott@atokaspeedynet.net
Editorial e-mail: dstuart@atokaspeedynet.net
Primary Website: atokacountytimes.com
Year Established: 1950
Avg Paid Circ: 3600
Audit By: Sworn/Estimate/Non-Audited
Audit Date: 10.06.2019
Personnel: Louise Cain (Pub.); Ron Linscott (Adv. Mgr.); Deanna Stuart (Ed)

BIGHEART TIMES

Street address 1: 116 N 5th St
Street address city: Barnsdall
Street address state: OK
Zip/Postal code: 74002-6616
General Phone: (918) 847-2916
General Fax: (918) 847-2654
General/National Adv. E-mail: marlyn@bigheartime.com
Editorial e-mail: louise@bigheartime.com
Primary Website: bigheartimes.com
Year Established: 1919
Avg Paid Circ: 1500
Audit By: Sworn/Estimate/Non-Audited
Audit Date: 10.06.2019
Personnel: Louise Red Corn (Owner/Pub/Ed); Marlyn Slone (Adv.)
Parent company (for newspapers): CherryRoad Media

BLACKWELL JOURNAL-TRIBUNE

Street address 1: 523 South Main St
Street address city: Blackwell
Street address state: OK

Zip/Postal code: 74631
General Phone: (580) 363-3370
General Fax: (580) 363-4415
Editorial e-mail: news@blackwelljournaltribune.net
Primary Website: blackwelljournaltribune.net
Year Established: 1915
Avg Paid Circ: 2475
Avg Free Circ: 3
Audit By: Sworn/Estimate/Non-Audited
Audit Date: 10.06.2019
Personnel: Tina Anderson (Pub.); Kris Wayman (Circ.); Charles Gerian (Staff Writer); Jordan Green (Staff Writer)
Parent company (for newspapers): American Hometown Publishing

BRISTOW NEWS

Street address 1: 112 W 6th Ave
Street address city: Bristow
Street address state: OK
Zip/Postal code: 74010-2810
General Phone: (918) 367-2282
General Fax: (918) 367-2724
General/National Adv. E-mail: bristownews@sbcglobal.net
Primary Website: bristownews.com
Year Established: 1889
Avg Paid Circ: 3000
Audit By: Sworn/Estimate/Non-Audited
Audit Date: 10.06.2019
Personnel: Tabatha Shadow (Adv.); Angie Gentry (Class Acct.); J. D. Meisner; Rick Vyper
Parent company (for newspapers): Central Oklahoma Publishing

BROKEN ARROW LEDGER

Street address 1: PO Box 1770
Street address city: Tulsa
Street address state: OK
Zip/Postal code: 74102-1770
General Phone: (918) 259-7500
General/National Adv. E-mail: melissa.lambert@baledger.com
Editorial e-mail: john.ferguson@baledger.com
Primary Website: tulsaworld.com/communities/brokenarrow
Mthly Avg Views: 77292
Mthly Avg Unique Visitors: 22449
Year Established: 1903
Avg Paid Circ: 1444
Avg Free Circ: 16424
Audit By: Sworn/Estimate/Non-Audited
Audit Date: 10.06.2019
Personnel: John Ferguson (Ed); Melissa Lambert (Mktg.)
Parent company (for newspapers): Community Publishers, Inc.

BROKEN BOW NEWS

Street address 1: 107 S Central Ave
Street address city: Idabel
Street address state: OK
Zip/Postal code: 74745-4847
General Phone: (580) 584-6210
General Fax: (580) 286-2208
General/National Adv. E-mail: ads@mccurtain.com
Editorial e-mail: paper@mccurtain.com
Primary Website: mccurtain.com
Avg Paid Circ: 1232
Audit By: Sworn/Estimate/Non-Audited
Audit Date: 10.06.2019
Personnel: Bruce Willingham (Pub.); Hallee Deramus (Adv. Dir.)

CARNEGIE HERALD

Street address 1: 8 N. Broadway
Street address city: Carnegie
Street address state: OK
Zip/Postal code: 73015
General Phone: (580) 654-1443
General Fax: (580) 654-1608
General/National Adv. E-mail: news@carnegieherald.com
Editorial e-mail: news@carnegieherald.com
Primary Website: thecarnegieherald.com
Year Established: 1903
Avg Paid Circ: 1405
Audit By: Sworn/Estimate/Non-Audited
Audit Date: 10.06.2019
Personnel: Donald Cooper (Pub./Adv. Dir./Ed.); Tommy Wells; Lori Cooper (Pub./Adv. Dir./Managing Ed.); Pattie Wells
Parent company (for newspapers): Wells Media

CATOOSA TIMES

Street address 1: 315 S Boulder Ave
Street address city: Tulsa
Street address state: OK
Zip/Postal code: 74103-3401
General Phone: (918) 272-1155
General Fax: (918) 272-0642
Advertising Phone: (918) 259-7527
Editorial Phone: (918) 272-1155 x 402
General/National Adv. E-mail: advertising@tulsaworld.com
Editorial e-mail: news@tulsaworld.com
Primary Website: CatoosaWorld.com
Avg Paid Circ: 1300
Audit By: Sworn/Estimate/Non-Audited
Audit Date: 10.06.2019
Personnel: Mike Brown (Pub.); Art Haddaway (Ed)

CHELSEA REPORTER

Street address 1: 245 W 6th St
Street address city: Chelsea
Street address state: OK
Zip/Postal code: 74016-1833
General Phone: (918) 789-2331
General Fax: (918) 789-2333
Editorial e-mail: chelsea_reporter@sbcgoble.net
Primary Website: https://facebook.com/ChelseaReporter
Avg Paid Circ: 1850
Audit By: Sworn/Estimate/Non-Audited
Audit Date: 10.06.2019
Personnel: Linda Lord (Pub.)

CHICKASHA NEWS

Street address 1: 411 W Chickasha Ave
Street address city: Chickasha
Street address state: OK
Zip/Postal code: 73018-2505
General Phone: (405) 224-2600
General/National Adv. E-mail: james@chickashanews.com
Display Adv. E-mail: james@chickashanews.com
Editorial e-mail: james@chickashanews.com
Primary Website: chickashanews.com
Audit By: Sworn/Estimate/Non-Audited
Audit Date: 10.06.2019
Personnel: Vonnie Clark (Circ. Dir.); Lindsey Palesano (Adv. Mgr); James Bright (Ed. in Chief)
Parent company (for newspapers): CNHI, LLC

COMANCHE TIMES

Street address 1: 513 Hillery Rd Ste A
Street address 2: Suite A
Street address city: Comanche
Street address state: OK
Zip/Postal code: 73529-1200
General Phone: (580) 439-6500
General Fax: (580) 439-6500
Editorial e-mail: comanchetimes@pldi.net
Primary Website: comancheok.net
Mthly Avg Views: 10000
Mthly Avg Unique Visitors: 7000
Year Established: 1992
Avg Paid Circ: 1100
Avg Free Circ: 35
Audit By: Sworn/Estimate/Non-Audited
Audit Date: 10.06.2019
Personnel: Todd Brooks (Owner/Publisher); Steve Bolton (Ed.)

COUNTYWIDE & SUN

Street address 1: 108 E Washington St
Street address 2: 108 E. Washington St.
Street address city: Tecumseh
Street address state: OK
Zip/Postal code: 74873-3242
General Phone: (405) 598-3793
General Fax: (405) 598-3891
Editorial e-mail: editor@countywidenews.com
Primary Website: countywidenews.com
Year Established: 1923
Avg Paid Circ: 1798
Avg Free Circ: 250
Audit By: Sworn/Estimate/Non-Audited
Audit Date: 29.10.2023
Personnel: Suzie Campbell (Pres./Publisher); Gloria Trotter (Co-Pub./Ed.); Suzie Campbell (Mktg. Dir.); Aaron McDonald (Advertising Executive)

CUSHING CITIZEN

Street address 1: 120 E Broadway
Street address city: Cushing
Street address state: OK
Zip/Postal code: 74023
General Phone: 918285555
General Fax: 9182855556
Advertising Phone: 918285555
Advertising Fax: 9182855556
Editorial Phone: 918285555
Editorial Fax: 9182855556
General/National Adv. E-mail: publisher@cushingcitizen.com
Display Adv. E-mail: ads@cushingcitizen.com
Classified Adv. e-mail: ads@cushingcitizen.com
Editorial e-mail: editor@cushingcitizen.com
Primary Website: www.cushingcitizen.com
Mthly Avg Views: 6000
Mthly Avg Unique Visitors: 1900
Year Established: 1898
Avg Paid Circ: 1300
Avg Free Circ: 0
Sat. Circulation Paid: 2300
Audit By: USPS
Audit Date: 26.09.2022
Personnel: J. D. Meisner (Owner/Publisher); Jim Perry (Ed.); Allie Prater (Editor); David Reid (Owner/Pub.); Sapphire Smith (Business Manager); Chris Reid (Graphics); Myra Reid (Accounting); Deanna Maddox (Reporter); Kayla Watson (Ad Director); Crissy Kindley (Receptionist)
Parent company (for newspapers): Cimarron Valley Communications, LLC

DELAWARE COUNTY JOURNAL

Street address 1: 254 N 5TH ST
Street address city: Jay
Street address state: OK
Zip/Postal code: 74346
General Phone: (918) 253-4322
General Fax: (918) 253-4380
General/National Adv. E-mail: khutchison@grovesun.com
Display Adv. E-mail: sedwards@grovesun.com
Editorial e-mail: khutson@grovesun.com
Primary Website: grandlakenews.com
Year Established: 1922
Avg Paid Circ: 2200
Avg Free Circ: 30
Audit By: Sworn/Estimate/Non-Audited
Audit Date: 10.06.2019
Personnel: Janet Barber (Ed.); Cheryl Franklin (Pub); Kaylea Hutson-Miller (Ed); Dylan Elliott (Circ. Mgr)
Parent company (for newspapers): Reid Newspapers

DRUMRIGHT GUSHER

Street address 1: 129 E Broadway St
Street address city: Drumright
Street address state: OK
Zip/Postal code: 74030-3801
General Phone: (918) 352-2284
General/National Adv. E-mail: ads@drumrightgusher.com
Editorial e-mail: pub@drumrightgusher.com, news@drumrightgusher.com
Primary Website: Drumright Gusher
Year Established: 1989
Avg Paid Circ: 1192
Audit By: Sworn/Estimate/Non-Audited
Audit Date: 10.06.2019
Personnel: Barbara Vice (Pub./Ed.)

EL RENO TRIBUNE

Street address 1: 102 E Wade St
Street address city: El Reno
Street address state: OK
Zip/Postal code: 73036-2742
General Phone: (405) 262-5180
General Fax: (405) 262-3541
Editorial e-mail: webmaster@elrenotribune.com
Primary Website: elrenotribune.com
Avg Paid Circ: 5500
Audit By: Sworn/Estimate/Non-Audited
Audit Date: 10.06.2019
Personnel: Ray T. Dyer (Ed.)

FAIRVIEW REPUBLICAN

Street address 1: 112 N Main St
Street address city: Fairview
Street address state: OK
Zip/Postal code: 73737-1621
General Phone: (580) 227-4439
General Fax: (580) 227-4430
General/National Adv. E-mail: ads@fairviewrepublican.com
Editorial e-mail: editor@fairviewrepublican.com
Primary Website: fairviewrepublican.com
Avg Paid Circ: 2850
Avg Free Circ: 45
Audit By: Sworn/Estimate/Non-Audited
Audit Date: 10.06.2019
Personnel: Jo Hammer (Adv. Mgr.); Hoby Hammer (Ed.)

FLETCHER HERALD

Street address 1: 203 W Cole Ave
Street address city: Fletcher
Street address state: OK
Zip/Postal code: 73541-9462
General Phone: (580) 549-6045
General Fax: (580) 549-4443
Editorial e-mail: lfletcherherald@aol.com
Year Established: 1912
Avg Paid Circ: 950
Audit By: Sworn/Estimate/Non-Audited
Audit Date: 10.06.2019
Personnel: Lynn Moon (Owner/Pub)

FREDERICK PRESS-LEADER

Street address 1: 102 S Main St
Street address city: Frederick
Street address state: OK
Zip/Postal code: 73542-5431
General Phone: (580) 379-0588
General Fax: (580) 335-2047
General/National Adv. E-mail: pressled@pldi.net
Editorial e-mail: press@pldi.net
Primary Website: press-leader.com
Year Established: 1904
Avg Paid Circ: 1000
Audit By: Sworn/Estimate/Non-Audited
Audit Date: 10.06.2019
Personnel: Kathleen Guill (Ed.); Bill Murphy (Pub.); Jennifer Grice (Adv. Mgr.); Ray Wallace (Mng. Ed.)

GARBER-BILLINGS NEWS

Street address 1: 516 Main St
Street address city: Garber
Street address state: OK
Zip/Postal code: 73738
General Phone: (580) 863-2240
General Fax: 5808632240
Editorial e-mail: gbnews@pldi.net
Year Established: 1899
Avg Paid Circ: 700
Audit By: Sworn/Estimate/Non-Audited
Audit Date: 10.06.2019
Personnel: Lacey Deeds (Ed.)

GEARY STAR

Street address 1: 116 S Broadway
Street address city: Geary
Street address state: OK
Zip/Postal code: 73040-2409
General Phone: (405) 884-2476
General Fax: (580) 623-4925
General/National Adv. E-mail: ads@TheGearyStar.com
Display Adv. E-mail: ads@watongarepublican.com
Editorial e-mail: Editor@TheGearyStar.com
Primary Website: thegearystar.com
Avg Paid Circ: 1250
Audit By: Sworn/Estimate/Non-Audited
Audit Date: 10.06.2019
Personnel: Eric Warsinskey (Ed); Kimberly Jenkins (Adv Rep)

GROVE SUN

Street address 1: 16 W 3rd St
Street address city: Grove

Street address state: OK
Zip/Postal code: 74344-3223
General Phone: (918) 786-2228
General Fax: (918) 786-2156
General/National Adv. E-mail: khutchison@grovesun.com
Display Adv. E-mail: sedwards@grovesun.com
Editorial e-mail: khutson@grovesun.com
Primary Website: grandlakenews.com
Year Established: 1898
Avg Paid Circ: 2800
Audit By: Sworn/Estimate/Non-Audited
Audit Date: 10.06.2019
Personnel: Cheryl Franklin (Pub.); Kaylea Hutson (Mng. Ed.); Kaylea Hutson-Miller (Ed); Dylan Elliott (Circ. Mgr)

GUTHRIE NEWS LEADER

Street address 1: PO Box 879
Street address city: Guthrie
Street address state: OK
Zip/Postal code: 73044-0879
General Phone: (405) 282-2222
General Fax: (405) 282-7378
General/National Adv. E-mail: gnlsales@guthrienewsleader.net
Display Adv. E-mail: gnlnews@yahoo.com
Editorial e-mail: publisher@guthrienewsleader.net
Primary Website: guthrienewsleader.net
Year Established: 1898
Avg Paid Circ: 5649
Sun. Circulation Paid: 5649
Audit By: Sworn/Estimate/Non-Audited
Audit Date: 10.06.2019
Personnel: Mona Robinson (Adv. Dir.); Rochelle Stidham (Pub); Kala Plagg (Office Mgr)
Parent company (for newspapers): American Hometown Publishing

HENRYETTA FREE-LANCE

Street address 1: 302 W Main St
Street address city: Henryetta
Street address state: OK
Zip/Postal code: 74437-4240
General Phone: (918) 652-3311
General Fax: (918) 652-7347
General/National Adv. E-mail: advertising@henryettanewspaper.com
Display Adv. E-mail: hflclassified@bigbasinllc.com
Editorial e-mail: news@henryettanewspaper.com
Primary Website: henryettafree-lance.com
Year Established: 1901
Avg Paid Circ: 2000
Audit By: Sworn/Estimate/Non-Audited
Audit Date: 10.06.2019
Personnel: Stephanie Grist (Adv. Dir.); Valerie Rice (Mng. Ed.)

HINTON RECORD

Street address 1: 116 W MAIN ST
Street address city: Hinton
Street address state: OK
Zip/Postal code: 73047
General Phone: (405) 542-6644
General Fax: (405) 542-3120
General/National Adv. E-mail: ads@HintonRecord.com
Editorial e-mail: Editor@HintonRecord.com
Primary Website: hintonrecord.com
Avg Paid Circ: 1025
Avg Free Circ: 6
Audit By: Sworn/Estimate/Non-Audited
Audit Date: 10.06.2019
Personnel: Eric Warsinskey (Ed); Kimberly Jenkins (Adv. Rep)

HOLDENVILLE TRIBUNE

Street address 1: 114 N Broadway St
Street address 2: PO Box 30
Street address city: Holdenville
Street address state: OK
Zip/Postal code: 74848-3248
General Phone: (405) 379-5184
General/National Adv. E-mail: bill@holdenvilletribune.com
Editorial e-mail: dayna@holdenvilletribune.com
Primary Website: holdenvilletribune.com
Audit By: Sworn/Estimate/Non-Audited
Audit Date: 10.06.2019
Personnel: Dayna Robinson (Pub./Ed); Jade Robinson (Office Mgr./Ed./Circ.); Holley Mouser (Staff Writer/ Photography)

HUGO NEWS

Street address 1: 128 E Jackson St
Street address city: Hugo
Street address state: OK
Zip/Postal code: 74743-4082
General Phone: (580) 326-3311
General Fax: (580) 326-6397
Advertising Phone: (580) 326-3311
Advertising Fax: (580) 326-6397
Editorial Phone: (580) 326-3311
Editorial Fax: (580) 326-6397
General/National Adv. E-mail: hugonews@sbcglobal.net
Display Adv. E-mail: adsolutions@sbcglobal.net
Classified Adv. e-mail: adsolutions@sbcglobal.net
Editorial e-mail: editor@sbcglobal.net
Primary Website: hugonews.com
Year Established: 1902
Avg Paid Circ: 2200
Audit By: Sworn/Estimate/Non-Audited
Audit Date: 01.10.2023
Personnel: Judy Stamper (VP, Acct.); Stan Stamper (Pres./Pub./Ed.); Krystle Taylor (Editor); Jody Rawls (Legal Publications, Circulation, Advertising Sales); Linda Packard (Adv. Dir.); Homer Garrison (Prodn. Mgr.); Krystle Taylor (Ed)
Parent company (for newspapers): Hugo Publishing Co.

INDIAN JOURNAL

Street address 1: 109 S Main St
Street address city: Eufaula
Street address state: OK
Zip/Postal code: 74432-2875
General Phone: (918) 689-2191
General Fax: (918) 689-2377
Editorial e-mail: ijdemolegals@bigbasinllc.com
Primary Website: eufaulaindianjournal.com/site
Avg Paid Circ: 3600
Audit By: Sworn/Estimate/Non-Audited
Audit Date: 10.06.2019
Personnel: Donna Pearce (Ed.)

JOHNSTON COUNTY CAPITAL-DEMOCRAT

Street address 1: 103 N Neshoba St
Street address city: Tishomingo
Street address state: OK
Zip/Postal code: 73460-1739
General Phone: (405) 371-2356
General Fax: (405) 371-9648
Editorial e-mail: ray.lokey@capital-democrat.com
Primary Website: johnstoncountycapital-democrat.com
Avg Paid Circ: 3023
Avg Free Circ: 25
Audit By: Sworn/Estimate/Non-Audited
Audit Date: 10.06.2019
Personnel: Ray Lokey (Pub); Jenny Lokey (Ed.)

KIOWA COUNTY DEMOCRAT

Street address 1: 530 E St
Street address city: Snyder
Street address state: OK
Zip/Postal code: 73566-1626
General Phone: (580) 569-2684
General Fax: (580) 569-2640
Advertising Phone: (580) 569-2684
Advertising Fax: (580) 569-2640
Editorial Phone: (580) 569-2684
Editorial Fax: (580) 569-2640
General/National Adv. E-mail: ads@kiowacountydemocrat.com
Display Adv. E-mail: ads@kiowacountydemocrat.com
Editorial e-mail: dee@kiowacountydemocrat.com
Year Established: 1905
Avg Paid Circ: 1000
Avg Free Circ: 25
Audit By: Sworn/Estimate/Non-Audited
Audit Date: 10.06.2019
Personnel: Dee Richardson (Owner/Ed./Pub.); Jenny Stouder (Office Mgr/Advertising Manager)

KONAWA LEADER

Street address 1: 102 N Broadway St
Street address city: Seminole
Street address state: OK
Zip/Postal code: 74818
General Phone: (405) 382-1100
General/National Adv. E-mail: seminolecopub@gmail.com
Editorial e-mail: seminolecopub@gmail.com
Primary Website: etypeservices.com
Avg Paid Circ: 1500
Audit By: Sworn/Estimate/Non-Audited
Audit Date: 10.06.2019
Personnel: Stu Phillips (Pub.)

LATIMER COUNTY NEWS-TRIBUNE

Street address 1: 111 W Ada Ave
Street address city: Wilburton
Street address state: OK
Zip/Postal code: 74578-2416
General Phone: (918) 465-2321
General Fax: (918) 465-3011
General/National Adv. E-mail: lcntads@att.net
Display Adv. E-mail: lcntclassifieds@att.net
Editorial e-mail: lcnt@att.net
Year Established: 1915
Avg Paid Circ: 2400
Avg Free Circ: 40
Audit By: Sworn/Estimate/Non-Audited
Audit Date: 10.06.2019
Personnel: Mark Showell (Ed.); Brenda Showell (Office Mgr); Malissa Evans (Class./Legals)

LINDSAY NEWS

Street address 1: 117 S Main St
Street address city: Lindsay
Street address state: OK
Zip/Postal code: 73052-5631
General Phone: (405) 756-4045
General Fax: (405) 756-2729
General/National Adv. E-mail: dustin@cableprinting.com
Display Adv. E-mail: dustin@cableprinting.com
Editorial e-mail: gina@cableprinting.com
Primary Website: cableprinting.com
Year Established: 1902
Avg Paid Circ: 2500
Audit By: Sworn/Estimate/Non-Audited
Audit Date: 10.06.2019
Personnel: Darrell Cable (Pub.); Gina Cable (Ed.); Dustin Hawkins (Adv./Sales)

MADILL RECORD

Street address 1: 211 Plaza
Street address city: Madill
Street address state: OK
Zip/Postal code: 73446-2250
General Phone: (580) 795-3355
General Fax: (580) 795-3530
General/National Adv. E-mail: madillrecord@sbcglobal.net
Editorial e-mail: recordeditorial@sbcglobal.net
Primary Website: madillrecord.net
Year Established: 1895
Avg Paid Circ: 3900
Avg Free Circ: 50
Audit By: Sworn/Estimate/Non-Audited
Audit Date: 10.06.2019
Personnel: Tiffani Stewart (General Manager); Lori Robinson (Advertising Specialist); Janice Jurden (Advertising Sales); Tina Firquain (Reporter)
Parent company (for newspapers): Cordell Beacon Co. Inc.

MARIETTA MONITOR

Street address 1: 104 W Main St
Street address city: Marietta
Street address state: OK
Zip/Postal code: 73448-2832
General Phone: (580) 276-3255
General Fax: (580) 276-2118
Editorial e-mail: monitorok@sbcglobal.net
Primary Website: https://facebook.com/mariettamonitor.newspaper
Year Established: 1895
Avg Paid Circ: 3000
Avg Free Circ: 30
Audit By: Sworn/Estimate/Non-Audited
Audit Date: 10.06.2019
Personnel: Willis Choate (Pub.); Norene Choate (Ed.)

MIDWEST CITY BEACON

Street address 1: 1500 S Midwest Blvd
Street address 2: Ste 202
Street address city: Midwest City
Street address state: OK
Zip/Postal code: 73110-4944
General Phone: (405) 455-1110
General Fax: (405) 455-1126
Advertising Phone: (405) 376-6688
Editorial Phone: (405) 455-1110
General/National Adv. E-mail: ads@midwestcitybeacon.com
Display Adv. E-mail: ads@midwestcitybeacon.com
Editorial e-mail: news@midwestcitybeacon.com
Primary Website: midwestcitybeacon.com
Year Established: 1936
Avg Paid Circ: 1500
Avg Free Circ: 0
Audit By: Sworn/Estimate/Non-Audited
Audit Date: 10.06.2019
Personnel: Jeff Harrison (Mng Ed)
Parent company (for newspapers): Mustang Times LLC

MOORELAND LEADER

Street address 1: 202 N Main St
Street address city: Mooreland
Street address state: OK
Zip/Postal code: 73852-9217
General Phone: (580) 994-5410
General Fax: (580) 994-5409
Editorial e-mail: leader2@pldi.net
Primary Website: mooreland leader.com
Year Established: 1903
Avg Paid Circ: 800
Avg Free Circ: 45
Audit By: Sworn/Estimate/Non-Audited
Audit Date: 10.06.2019
Personnel: Tim Schnoebelen (Ed.)

NEWCASTLE PACER

Street address 1: 120 NE 2nd St
Street address 2: Suite 102
Street address city: Newcastle
Street address state: OK
Zip/Postal code: 73065-4185
General Phone: (405) 387-5277
General Fax: (405) 387-9863
General/National Adv. E-mail: peg@newcastlepacer.com
Editorial e-mail: darla@newcastlepacer.com
Primary Website: newcastlepacer.com
Year Established: 1978
Avg Paid Circ: 1800
Avg Free Circ: 72
Audit By: Sworn/Estimate/Non-Audited
Audit Date: 10.06.2019
Personnel: Clarence Wright (Gen. Mgr.); Darla Welchel (Ed); Peggy Brian (Adv. Sales)

NORTHWEST OKLAHOMAN

Street address 1: 329 S Main St
Street address city: Shattuck
Street address state: OK
Zip/Postal code: 73858-8804
General Phone: (580) 938-2533
General Fax: (580) 938-5240
Editorial Phone: (580) 938-2533
General/National Adv. E-mail: nwopaper@pldi.net
Editorial e-mail: nwopaper@pldi.net
Primary Website: northwestoklahoman.com
Year Established: 1931
Avg Paid Circ: 1350
Audit By: Sworn/Estimate/Non-Audited
Audit Date: 10.06.2019
Personnel: Jeff Schnoebelen (Pub.)

OKEENE RECORD

Street address 1: 211 N Main St
Street address city: Okeene

Street address state: OK
Zip/Postal code: 73763-9447
General Phone: (580) 822-4401
General Fax: (877) 420-6331
Advertising Phone: (580) 822-4401
Editorial Phone: (580) 822-4401
Editorial Fax: (877) 420-6331
General/National Adv. E-mail: bcpub@pldi.net
Display Adv. E-mail: bcpub@pldi.net
Editorial e-mail: bcpub@pldi.net
Primary Website: okeenerecord.com
Year Established: 1918
Avg Paid Circ: 750
Audit By: Sworn/Estimate/Non-Audited
Audit Date: 10.06.2019
Personnel: Toni Goforth (Managing Editor)
Parent company (for newspapers): Trail Miller Co., LLC

OKEMAH NEWS LEADER

Street address 1: 115 W Broadway St
Street address city: Okemah
Street address state: OK
Zip/Postal code: 74859-2616
General Phone: (918) 623-0123
General Fax: (918) 623-1024
Advertising Phone: (918) 623-0123
Editorial Phone: (918) 623-0123
General/National Adv. E-mail: Ads@okemahnewsleader.com
Primary Website: okemahnewsleader.com
Year Established: 1921
Avg Paid Circ: 2700
Avg Free Circ: 22
Audit By: Sworn/Estimate/Non-Audited
Audit Date: 10.06.2019
Personnel: Lynn Thompson (Pub./Ed.); Roger Thompson (Ed./Adv. Dir.); Kay Thompson (Office Mgr); Shakara Shepard (Reporter); Pamela Thompson

OKLAHOMA CITY FRIDAY

Street address 1: 10801 Quail Plaza Dr
Street address city: Oklahoma City
Street address state: OK
Zip/Postal code: 73120-3118
General Phone: (405) 755-3311
General Fax: (405) 755-3315
General/National Adv. E-mail: lovina@okcfriday.com
Display Adv. E-mail: rebecca@okcfriday.com
Editorial e-mail: rose@okcfriday.com
Primary Website: okcfriday.com
Avg Paid Circ: 8200
Avg Free Circ: 100
Audit By: Sworn/Estimate/Non-Audited
Audit Date: 10.06.2019
Personnel: Vicki Gourley (CEO/Pub); Rose Lane (Ed/Co-Pub.); Rebecca Hall (Class./Legal Mgr.); Jason Jewell (Prod. Mgr); Jennifer Clark (Circ. Mgr.); Lovina Morgan (Adv. Sales)

OOLOGAH LAKE LEADER

Street address 1: 109 S Maple St
Street address city: Oologah
Street address state: OK
Zip/Postal code: 74053-3299
General Phone: (918) 443-2428
General Fax: (918) 443-2429
General/National Adv. E-mail: Carolyn.Estes@sbcglobal.net
Display Adv. E-mail: OologahInfo@sbcglobal.net
Editorial e-mail: LakeLeader@sbcglobal.net
Primary Website: oologahonline.com
Mthly Avg Views: 15000
Mthly Avg Unique Visitors: 8500
Year Established: 1982
Avg Paid Circ: 2700
Avg Free Circ: 5501
Audit By: Sworn/Estimate/Non-Audited
Audit Date: 10.06.2019
Personnel: Faith Wylie (Co-Pub./Gen. Mgr.); Carolyn Estes (Mktg. Dir.); John Wylie (Co-Pub./Ed.)
Parent company (for newspapers): Oologah Lake Leader LLC

OWASSO RAMBLER

Street address 1: 5401 S. Sheridan Rd.
Street address 2: Suite 302
Street address city: Tulsa
Street address state: OK
Zip/Postal code: 74145
General Phone: (918) 254-1515
General Fax: (918) 254-1515
Advertising Phone: (918) 254-1515
General/National Adv. E-mail: fcameron@gtrnews.com
Display Adv. E-mail: fcameron@gtrnews.com
Editorial e-mail: fcameron@gtrnews.com
Primary Website: gtrnews.com/owasso-rambler
Year Established: 1993
Avg Paid Circ: 1
Avg Free Circ: 1974
Audit By: CVC
Audit Date: 30.09.2017
Personnel: Forrest Cameron (Pub./CEO); Sharon Cameron (Adv. Dir.); Dan Cameron (Circ. Mgr)
Parent company (for newspapers): Greater Tulsa Reporter Newspapers; Union Boundry Inc.

OWASSO REPORTER

Street address 1: 202 E 2nd Ave
Street address 2: Suite 101
Street address city: Owasso
Street address state: OK
Zip/Postal code: 74055-3131
General Phone: (918) 272-1155
General Fax: (918) 272-0642
Advertising Phone: (918) 259-7527
Editorial Phone: (918) 272-1155 x 402
General/National Adv. E-mail: Aeron.Taylor@owassoreporter.com
Display Adv. E-mail: Ashley.Roop@owassoreporter.com
Editorial e-mail: art.haddaway@owassoreporter.com
Primary Website: tulsaworld.com/communities/owasso
Mthly Avg Views: 48393
Mthly Avg Unique Visitors: 14315
Year Established: 1964
Avg Paid Circ: 3934
Avg Free Circ: 348
Audit By: CVC
Audit Date: 12//2012
Personnel: Shawn Hein (Sports Ed.); Art Haddaway (Ed); Karen Bennett (Advtg.)
Parent company (for newspapers): Community Publishers, Inc.

PAULS VALLEY DEMOCRAT

Street address 1: 108 S Willow St
Street address city: Pauls Valley
Street address state: OK
Zip/Postal code: 73075-3834
General Phone: (405) 238-6464
General Fax: (405) 238-3042
General/National Adv. E-mail: jdavenport@pvdemocrat.com
Display Adv. E-mail: charris@pvdemocrat.com
Editorial e-mail: marie@pvdemocrat.com
Primary Website: paulsvalleydailydemocrat.com
Year Established: 1904
Avg Paid Circ: 2950
Sun. Circulation Paid: 2950
Audit By: Sworn/Estimate/Non-Audited
Audit Date: 10.06.2019
Personnel: Mike Arie (Ed); Christy Harris (Class./Legal); Sheila Johnson (Circ.); Sara Fisher (Gen. Mgr./ Sales)
Parent company (for newspapers): CNHI, LLC

PAWHUSKA JOURNAL-CAPITAL

Street address 1: 1020 Lynn Ave
Street address 2: # A
Street address city: Pawhuska
Street address state: OK
Zip/Postal code: 74056-3062
General Phone: (918) 335-8200
General/National Adv. E-mail: mtranquill@examiner-enterprise.com
Display Adv. E-mail: mtranquill@examiner-enterprise.com
Editorial e-mail: rsmith@pawhuskajournalcapital.com
Primary Website: pawhuskajournalcapital.com
Year Established: 1867
Avg Paid Circ: 3500
Audit By: Sworn/Estimate/Non-Audited
Audit Date: 10.06.2019
Personnel: Matthew Tranquill (Pub./Adv.); Tammy Green (Office Mgr.); Robert Dye (Circ. Mgr); Robert Smith (Ed.)

PAWNEE CHIEF

Street address 1: 556 Illinois St
Street address city: Pawnee
Street address state: OK
Zip/Postal code: 74058-2011
General Phone: (918) 762-2552
General Fax: (918) 762-2554
Editorial e-mail: news@pawneechief.net
Primary Website: pawneechief.net
Year Established: 1941
Avg Paid Circ: 2300
Avg Free Circ: 101
Audit By: Sworn/Estimate/Non-Audited
Audit Date: 10.06.2019
Personnel: Vickie Denny (Pub./Ed.)
Parent company (for newspapers): American Chief Co.

PERKINS JOURNAL

Street address 1: 222 N Main St
Street address city: Perkins
Street address state: OK
Zip/Postal code: 74059-3630
General Phone: (405) 547-2411
General Fax: (405) 547-2419
Editorial e-mail: publisher@thejournalok.com
Primary Website: thejournalok.com
Year Established: 1892
Avg Paid Circ: 3500
Audit By: Sworn/Estimate/Non-Audited
Audit Date: 10.06.2019
Personnel: David Sasser (Pub.); Rick Lomenick (Sports Ed.)

PIEDMONT SURREY GAZETTE

Street address 1: 508 W. Vandament Avenue
Street address 2: Ste. 204
Street address city: Yukon
Street address state: OK
Zip/Postal code: 73078-8521
General Phone: (405) 577-6208
General Fax: (405) 265-2931
General/National Adv. E-mail: orkarchechieftain@sbcglobal.net
Editorial e-mail: editor@piedmontnewsonline.com
Primary Website: piedmontnewsonline.com
Avg Paid Circ: 700
Avg Free Circ: 15
Audit By: Sworn/Estimate/Non-Audited
Audit Date: 10.06.2019
Personnel: Randy K. Anderson (Pub.); Valerie Anderson (Office Mgr.); Debbie Cook (Adv. Sales); Tim Farley (News Ed.); Rob Agnew (Prod. Mgr.); Trey Hunter (Sports Ed.)

SAND SPRINGS LEADER

Street address 1: PO Box 1770
Street address city: Tulsa
Street address state: OK
Zip/Postal code: 74102-1770
General Phone: (918) 245-6634
General Fax: (918) 241-3610
Advertising Phone: (918) 259-7527
General/National Adv. E-mail: samantha.ferguson@sandspringsleader.com
Editorial e-mail: kirk.mccracken@sandspringsleader.com
Primary Website: sandspringsleader.com
Mthly Avg Views: 58193
Mthly Avg Unique Visitors: 15233
Year Established: 1903
Avg Paid Circ: 929
Avg Free Circ: 10
Audit By: Sworn/Estimate/Non-Audited
Audit Date: 10.06.2019
Personnel: Mike Brown (Pub.); Chala DeSelm (CSR); Kirk McCracken (Mng. Ed.); Samantha Ferguson (Mktg.)
Parent company (for newspapers): Community Publishers, Inc.

SENTINEL LEADER

Street address 1: 307 E Main St
Street address city: Sentinel
Street address state: OK
Zip/Postal code: 73664-9800
General Phone: (580) 393-4348
General Fax: (580) 393-4349
Editorial e-mail: sleader@pldi.net
Primary Website: thesentinelleader.com
Year Established: 1902
Avg Paid Circ: 1200
Audit By: Sworn/Estimate/Non-Audited
Audit Date: 10.06.2019
Personnel: Jolene Wolfenbarger (Pub./Ed.)

SEQUOYAH COUNTY TIMES

Street address 1: 111 N Oak St
Street address city: Sallisaw
Street address state: OK
Zip/Postal code: 74955-4637
General Phone: (918) 775-4433
General Fax: (918) 775-3023
General/National Adv. E-mail: advertising@seqcotimes.com
Classified Adv. e-mail: advertising@seqcotimes.com
Editorial e-mail: news@seqcotimes.com
Primary Website: sequoyahcountytimes.com
Year Established: 1893
Avg Paid Circ: 4627
Avg Free Circ: 96
Audit By: Sworn/Estimate/Non-Audited
Audit Date: 10.06.2019
Personnel: James Mayo (Publisher); Carrie Carberry (Gen. Mgr. /Assoc. Pub.); Carrie Carberry (Advertising Manager)

SKIATOOK JOURNAL

Street address 1: 500 W Rogers Blvd
Street address city: Skiatook
Street address state: OK
Zip/Postal code: 74070-1081
General Phone: (918) 396-1616
General Fax: (918) 396-1618
Advertising Phone: (918) 259-7527
Editorial Phone: (918) 272-1155 x 402
General/National Adv. E-mail: bruce.hugill@skiatookjournal.com
Editorial e-mail: john.ferguson@baledger.com
Primary Website: skiatookjournal.com
Mthly Avg Views: 23552
Mthly Avg Unique Visitors: 5679
Year Established: 1903
Avg Paid Circ: 1965
Avg Free Circ: 126
Audit By: CVC
Audit Date: 12//2012
Personnel: Mike Brown (Pub.); Lindsey Renuard (Ed); Bruce Hugill (Mktg.)
Parent company (for newspapers): Community Publishers, Inc.

SPIRO GRAPHIC

Street address 1: 212 S Main St
Street address city: Spiro
Street address state: OK
Zip/Postal code: 74959-2506
General Phone: (918) 962-2075
General Fax: (918) 962-3531
General/National Adv. E-mail: spirographic@sbcglobal.net
Editorial e-mail: ttowner@batavianews.com
Year Established: 1962
Avg Paid Circ: 2850
Avg Free Circ: 75
Audit By: Sworn/Estimate/Non-Audited
Audit Date: 10.06.2019
Personnel: Jim Fienup (Pub.); Michael Messerly (Gen. Mgr./Ed.)

STIGLER NEWS-SENTINEL

Street address 1: 204 S Broadway St
Street address city: Stigler
Street address state: OK
Zip/Postal code: 74462-2320
General Phone: (918) 967-4655
General Fax: (918) 967-4289
General/National Adv. E-mail: summer@stiglernews.com
Editorial e-mail: editor@stiglernews.com
Primary Website: stiglernews.com
Year Established: 1980
Avg Paid Circ: 3953

Avg Free Circ: 53
Audit By: Sworn/Estimate/Non-Audited
Audit Date: 10.06.2019
Personnel: Linus G.Jr. Williams (Owner/Pub.); Summer Long (Asst. Pub./Adv. Mgr.); Anita Reding (Mng. Ed.)

STILWELL DEMOCRAT JOURNAL

Street address 1: 118 N 2nd St
Street address city: Stilwell
Street address state: OK
Zip/Postal code: 74960-3028
General Phone: (918) 696-2228
General Fax: (918) 696-7066
General/National Adv. E-mail: stilwelldj@windstream.net
Year Established: 1898
Avg Paid Circ: 5000
Audit By: Sworn/Estimate/Non-Audited
Audit Date: 10.06.2019
Personnel: Gary Jackson (Pub.); Keith Neale (Ed./Adv.); Darrell Neale (Reporter); Chris Fuson (Composing); Brittany Tatum (Office Mgr); Sydney Asbill; Noveena Littlejohn (Clerk)
Parent company (for newspapers): CNHI, LLC

STROUD AMERICAN

Street address 1: 315 W Main St
Street address city: Stroud
Street address state: OK
Zip/Postal code: 74079-3611
General Phone: (918) 968-2581
General Fax: (918) 968-3864
Advertising Phone: (918) 968-2581
Editorial Phone: (918) 968-2581
General/National Adv. E-mail: stroudamerican@brightok.net
Editorial e-mail: stroudamerican@cotc.net
Primary Website: facebook.com/stroudamerican
Year Established: 1898
Avg Paid Circ: 2100
Audit By: Sworn/Estimate/Non-Audited
Audit Date: 10.06.2019
Personnel: Michael Brown (Ed.); Alicia Brown (Office Mgr.)

SULPHUR TIMES-DEMOCRAT

Street address 1: 115 W Muskogee Ave
Street address city: Sulphur
Street address state: OK
Zip/Postal code: 73086-4809
General Phone: (580) 622-2102
General Fax: (580) 622-2937
Editorial e-mail: jcjohn@sulphurtimes.com
Primary Website: sulphurtimes.com
Avg Paid Circ: 3400
Avg Free Circ: 160
Audit By: Sworn/Estimate/Non-Audited
Audit Date: 10.06.2019
Personnel: James John (Ed.)

TALIHINA AMERICAN

Street address 1: 205 2nd St
Street address city: Talihina
Street address state: OK
Zip/Postal code: 74571-2323
General Phone: (918) 567-2390
General Fax: (918) 465-2170
General/National Adv. E-mail: tricountypubinc@sbcglobal.net
Year Established: 1918
Avg Paid Circ: 1700
Audit By: Sworn/Estimate/Non-Audited
Audit Date: 10.06.2019
Personnel: Mark Showell (Ed)

THE ALLEN ADVOCATE

Street address 1: 101 S. Easton
Street address city: Allen
Street address state: OK
Zip/Postal code: 74825
General Phone: (580) 857-2687
General Fax: (580) 857-2573
General/National Adv. E-mail: allennews@aol.com
Display Adv. E-mail: allennews@aol.com
Editorial e-mail: allennews@sbcglobal.net
Primary Website: allennewspaper.com
Avg Paid Circ: 1350
Audit By: Sworn/Estimate/Non-Audited
Audit Date: 10.06.2019
Personnel: Diane Brannan (Pub./Mng. Ed./Circ.); Cindy Davis (Adv. Mgr)

THE AMERICAN

Street address 1: 7 N Main St
Street address city: Fairland
Street address state: OK
Zip/Postal code: 74343-4744
General Phone: (918) 676-3484
General Fax: (918) 256-7100
General/National Adv. E-mail: vdj@cableone.net
Editorial e-mail: nowatastarl@sbcglobal.net
Primary Website: aftonamerican.com
Year Established: 1906
Avg Paid Circ: 1050
Avg Free Circ: 20
Audit By: Sworn/Estimate/Non-Audited
Audit Date: 10.06.2019
Personnel: John Link (Gen Mgr.); Philip Reid (Pub); Becky Clark (Ed)

THE APACHE NEWS

Street address 1: 120 E Evans Ave
Street address city: Apache
Street address state: OK
Zip/Postal code: 73006-9190
General Phone: (580) 588-3862
General Fax: (580) 588-3862
General/National Adv. E-mail: apachenews@pldi.net
Year Established: 1901
Avg Paid Circ: 1000
Audit By: Sworn/Estimate/Non-Audited
Audit Date: 10.06.2019
Personnel: Joye Wright (Ed.)

THE BECKHAM COUNTY RECORD

Street address 1: 112 E Main St
Street address city: Sayre
Street address state: OK
Zip/Postal code: 73662-2914
General Phone: (580) 928-5540
General Fax: (580) 928-5547
Advertising Phone: (580) 928-5540
Advertising Fax: (580) 928-5547
Editorial Phone: (580) 928-5540
Editorial Fax: (580) 928-5547
General/National Adv. E-mail: sayrerecord@cableone.net
Display Adv. E-mail: sayrerecord@cableone.net
Editorial e-mail: sayrerecord@cableone.net
Primary Website: sayrerecord.com
Year Established: 1987
Avg Paid Circ: 2300
Avg Free Circ: 100
Audit By: Sworn/Estimate/Non-Audited
Audit Date: 10.06.2019
Personnel: Brad Spitzer (Pub.); Connie Ferrero (Ed./Ad Mgr.); Amy Brinkley (Cric. Off. Mgr.)

THE BETHANY TRIBUNE

Street address 1: 6728 NW 38th St
Street address city: Bethany
Street address state: OK
Zip/Postal code: 73008-3360
General Phone: (405) 789-1962
General Fax: (405) 789-4253
General/National Adv. E-mail: ads@OKCTribune.com
Editorial e-mail: news@OKCTribune.com
Primary Website: bethanytribuneonline.com
Year Established: 1923
Avg Paid Circ: 3500
Audit By: Sworn/Estimate/Non-Audited
Audit Date: 10.06.2019
Personnel: Stacie Henderson-Harrington (Asst. Pub); Matt Montgomery (Ed/Adv); Teresa Wardell (Office Mgr.)

THE BOISE CITY NEWS

Street address 1: 105 W Main
Street address city: Boise City
Street address state: OK
Zip/Postal code: 73933
General Phone: (580) 544-2222
General Fax: (580) 544-3281
General/National Adv. E-mail: blackmesapub@yahoo.com
Editorial e-mail: bcnews@ptsi.net
Primary Website: boisecitynews2.wordpress.com
Avg Paid Circ: 1750
Audit By: Sworn/Estimate/Non-Audited
Audit Date: 10.06.2019
Personnel: Linda Gray (Adv. Mgr); C.F. David (Ed.)

THE CHEROKEE MESSENGER & REPUBLICAN

Street address 1: 216 S Grand Ave
Street address city: Cherokee
Street address state: OK
Zip/Postal code: 73728-2030
General Phone: (580) 596-3344
General Fax: (580) 596-2959
General/National Adv. E-mail: ads@cherokeenewspaper.com
Display Adv. E-mail: info@cherokeenewspaper.com
Editorial e-mail: news@cherokeenewspaper.com
Primary Website: cherokeemessengerrepublican.com
Year Established: 1900
Avg Paid Circ: 1900
Avg Free Circ: 250
Audit By: Sworn/Estimate/Non-Audited
Audit Date: 10.06.2019
Personnel: Marsha Tucker (Gen. Mgr.); Heather Gilley (Adv. Dir.); Kyle Spade (Ed); Hoby Hammer (Pub)

THE CITY SENTINEL

Street address 1: PO Box 60876
Street address city: Oklahoma City
Street address state: OK
Zip/Postal code: 73146-0876
General Phone: (405) 740-8687
General/National Adv. E-mail: sales@city-sentinel.com
Display Adv. E-mail: sales@city-sentinel.com
Editorial e-mail: news@city-sentinel.com
Primary Website: city-sentinel.com
Year Established: 2000
Avg Paid Circ: 10000
Avg Free Circ: 10000
Audit By: Sworn/Estimate/Non-Audited
Audit Date: 10.06.2019
Personnel: Patrick McGuigan (Pub./Ed.); Vincent Lee (Creative. Dir.)

THE CLEVELAND AMERICAN

Street address 1: 212 S Broadway St
Street address city: Cleveland
Street address state: OK
Zip/Postal code: 74020-4617
General Phone: (918) 358-2553
General Fax: (918) 358-2182
General/National Adv. E-mail: advertising@theclevelandamerican.com
Editorial e-mail: news@theclevelandamerican.com
Primary Website: theclevelandamerican.com
Year Established: 1919
Avg Paid Circ: 2150
Audit By: Sworn/Estimate/Non-Audited
Audit Date: 10.06.2019
Personnel: Rusty Ferguson (Pub./Ed.); Caleb Head (Adv. Dir)

THE COALGATE RECORD-REGISTER

Street address 1: 602 E Lafayette Ave
Street address city: Coalgate
Street address state: OK
Zip/Postal code: 74538-4018
General Phone: (580) 927-2355
General Fax: (580) 927-3800
General/National Adv. E-mail: helen@coalgaterecordregister.com
Editorial e-mail: coalgaterec@aol.com
Primary Website: coalgaterecordregister.com
Year Established: 1988
Avg Paid Circ: 1800
Audit By: Sworn/Estimate/Non-Audited
Audit Date: 10.06.2019
Personnel: Dayna Robinson (Pub.); Helen Langdon (Adv. Mgr.); Bill Robinson (Ed.)

THE CORDELL BEACON

Street address 1: 115 E Main St
Street address city: Cordell
Street address state: OK
Zip/Postal code: 73632-4897
General Phone: (580) 832-3333
General Fax: (580) 832-3335
General/National Adv. E-mail: thebeacon@cordellbeacon.com
Primary Website: cordellbeacon.com
Year Established: 1897
Avg Paid Circ: 3000
Audit By: Sworn/Estimate/Non-Audited
Audit Date: 10.06.2019
Personnel: Cindy Banks (Circ. Mgr.); Zonelle Cox Rainbolt (Ed.); Penelope Gibbons; Vicki Salley; Mary Anderson

THE DAVIS NEWS

Street address 1: 400 E Main St
Street address city: Davis
Street address state: OK
Zip/Postal code: 73030-1908
General Phone: (580) 369-2807
General Fax: (580) 369-2807
Editorial e-mail: davispaper@sbcglobal.net
Primary Website: davisnewspaper.net
Year Established: 1894
Avg Paid Circ: 1500
Avg Free Circ: 39
Audit By: Sworn/Estimate/Non-Audited
Audit Date: 10.06.2019
Personnel: Sharon R. Chadwick (Pub./Ed.)

THE DEWEY COUNTY RECORD

Street address 1: 207 N Main St
Street address city: Seiling
Street address state: OK
Zip/Postal code: 73663-6676
General Phone: (580) 922-4296
General Fax: (877) 420-6331
Advertising Phone: (580) 922-4296
Editorial Phone: (580) 922-4296
General/National Adv. E-mail: ads@trailmiller.com
Display Adv. E-mail: ads@trailmiller.com
Editorial e-mail: seilingnews@trailmiller.com
Primary Website: http://deweycountyrecord.com/
Year Established: 1972
Avg Paid Circ: 1500
Avg Free Circ: 6
Audit By: Sworn/Estimate/Non-Audited
Audit Date: 10.06.2019
Personnel: Kevin Farr (Mng. Ed.)
Parent company (for newspapers): Trail Miller Co. LLC

THE EDMOND SUN

Street address 1: 123 S Broadway
Street address city: Edmond
Street address state: OK
Zip/Postal code: 73034-3899
General Phone: (405) 341-2121
General Fax: (405) 340-7363
Advertising Phone: (405) 341-2121 x 135
Editorial Phone: (405) 341-2121 x 110
General/National Adv. E-mail: aburger@edmondsun.com
Display Adv. E-mail: terrib@edmondsun.com
Editorial e-mail: sbrackett@edmondsun.com
Primary Website: edmondsun.com
Year Established: 1889
Avg Paid Circ: 3540
Sat. Circulation Paid: 4094
Audit By: Sworn/Estimate/Non-Audited
Audit Date: 10.06.2019
Personnel: Mark Codner (Ed.); Lance Moler (Gen. Mgr.); Stephanie Brackett (Bus. Mgr.); Kari Tompkins (Dig. Cor./ Special Projects); Nancy Sade (Sales)
Parent company (for newspapers): McNaughton Newspapers; CNHI, LLC

THE FREEDOM CALL

Street address 1: 1575 Greer Rd
Street address city: Freedom
Street address state: OK
Zip/Postal code: 73842
General Phone: (580) 621-3578
General Fax: (580) 621-3472
Editorial e-mail: freedomcall@pldi.net
Year Established: 1959
Avg Paid Circ: 500
Audit By: Sworn/Estimate/Non-Audited

Audit Date: 10.06.2019
Personnel: Donna Hodgson (Ed.)

THE GARVIN COUNTY NEWS STAR

Street address 1: 402 Williams
Street address city: Maysville
Street address state: OK
Zip/Postal code: 73057-3683
General Phone: (405) 867-4457
General Fax: (405) 867-5115
General/National Adv. E-mail: news@gcnews-star.com
Display Adv. E-mail: news@gcnews-star.com
Editorial e-mail: publisher@gcnews-star.com
Primary Website: gcnews-star.com
Year Established: 2008
Avg Paid Circ: 1800
Audit By: Sworn/Estimate/Non-Audited
Audit Date: 10.06.2019
Personnel: Jeff Shultz (Co-Pub./Co-Own./Ed.); Nanette Shultz (Co-Pub./Co-Own.); Judy Baker (Office Mgr.); Tessa Widmer (Office worker)

THE HEALDTON HERALD

Street address 1: 11207 Highway 76
Street address city: Healdton
Street address state: OK
Zip/Postal code: 73438-1725
General Phone: (580) 229-0147
General Fax: (580) 229-0132
Editorial e-mail: hherald@cablerocket.com
Year Established: 1917
Avg Paid Circ: 1500
Avg Free Circ: 21
Audit By: Sworn/Estimate/Non-Audited
Audit Date: 10.06.2019
Personnel: Cindy Dickerson (Ed)

THE HEAVENER LEDGER

Street address 1: 507 E 1st St
Street address city: Heavener
Street address state: OK
Zip/Postal code: 74937-3203
General Phone: (918) 653-2425
General Fax: (918) 653-7305
Advertising Phone: (918) 653-2425
Editorial Phone: (918) 653-2425
General/National Adv. E-mail: heavenerledger@windstream.net
Display Adv. E-mail: heavenerledgerchris@windstream.net
Primary Website: ledgerlcj.com
Mthly Avg Views: 20000
Mthly Avg Unique Visitors: 7500
Year Established: 1904
Avg Paid Circ: 1200
Audit By: Sworn/Estimate/Non-Audited
Audit Date: 10.06.2019
Personnel: Karen Toney (Legals); Chris Lessley (Classified)
Parent company (for newspapers): Heavener Ledger

THE HENNESSEY CLIPPER

Street address 1: 117 S Main St
Street address city: Hennessey
Street address state: OK
Zip/Postal code: 73742-1402
General Phone: (405) 853-4888
General Fax: (405) 853-4890
General/National Adv. E-mail: tracie@hennesseyclipper.com
Display Adv. E-mail: linda@hennesseyclipper.com
Editorial e-mail: barb@hennesseyclipper.com
Primary Website: hennesseyclipper.com
Year Established: 1890
Avg Paid Circ: 1650
Avg Free Circ: 140
Audit By: Sworn/Estimate/Non-Audited
Audit Date: 10.06.2019
Personnel: Maria Laubach (Pub); Paul Laubauch (Mng. Ed.)

THE HERALD-DEMOCRAT

Street address 1: 108 Douglas Ave
Street address city: Beaver
Street address state: OK
Zip/Postal code: 73932-9620
General Phone: (580) 625-3241
General Fax: (580) 625-4269
Editorial e-mail: bvrnews@gmail.com
Primary Website: bvrcowchipnews.com
Avg Paid Circ: 1500
Audit By: Sworn/Estimate/Non-Audited
Audit Date: 10.06.2019
Personnel: Joe Lansden (Co-pub.)

THE HOLLIS NEWS

Street address 1: 204 E Vivian St
Street address city: Hollis
Street address state: OK
Zip/Postal code: 73550-1840
General Phone: (580) 688-3376
General Fax: (580) 688-2261
Editorial e-mail: hollisnews@pldi.net
Primary Website: redriversun.com/index117.htm
Year Established: 1938
Avg Paid Circ: 1200
Audit By: Sworn/Estimate/Non-Audited
Audit Date: 10.06.2019
Personnel: Everett Brazil (Ed.)
Parent company (for newspapers): Blackburn Media Group

THE HOMINY NEWS-PROGRESS

Street address 1: 115 W Main St
Street address city: Hominy
Street address state: OK
Zip/Postal code: 74035-1031
General Phone: (918) 885-2101
General Fax: (918) 885-4596
Advertising Phone: (918) 885-2101
Advertising Fax: (918) 885-4596
Editorial Phone: (918) 885-2101
Editorial Fax: (918) 885-4596
General/National Adv. E-mail: hominynews2@gmail.com
Display Adv. E-mail: hominyews2@gmail.com
Classified Adv. e-mail: hominyews2@gmail.com
Editorial e-mail: same
Primary Website: N/A
Year Established: 1918
Avg Paid Circ: 1400
Audit By: Sworn/Estimate/Non-Audited
Audit Date: 10.06.2019
Personnel: Vickie Denny (Gen Mgr); Treca Carter (Office Mgr)
Parent company (for newspapers): American Chief Co.

THE HUGHES COUNTY TIMES

Street address 1: 501 E Highway 9
Street address city: Wetumka
Street address state: OK
Zip/Postal code: 74883-6048
General Phone: (405) 452-3294
General Fax: (405) 452-3574
Advertising Phone: (405) 4523294
Editorial Phone: (405) 452-3294
General/National Adv. E-mail: hughescountytimes@sbcglobal.net
Editorial e-mail: hughescountytimes@sbcglobal.net
Primary Website: hughescountytimes.com
Year Established: 1908
Avg Paid Circ: 1500
Avg Free Circ: 20
Audit By: Sworn/Estimate/Non-Audited
Audit Date: 10.06.2019
Personnel: Jade Robinson (Off. mng.)
Parent company (for newspapers): ROBINSON PUBLISHING CO., INC.

THE KINGFISHER TIMES & FREE PRESS

Street address 1: 323 N Main St
Street address city: Kingfisher
Street address state: OK
Zip/Postal code: 73750-2749
General Phone: (405) 375-3220
General Fax: (405) 375-3222
General/National Adv. E-mail: kfrtimesads@pldi.net
Display Adv. E-mail: kfrnews@pldi.net
Editorial e-mail: editor@kingfisherpress.net
Primary Website: kingfisherpress.net
Year Established: 1889
Avg Paid Circ: 3750
Avg Free Circ: 50
Audit By: Sworn/Estimate/Non-Audited
Audit Date: 10.06.2019
Personnel: Gary Reid (Pub. Emeritus); Barry Reid (Pub.); Christine Reid (Sr. Ed.); Michael Swisher (Mng./Sports Ed.); Robin Johnston (Ad Mng.)

THE MANGUM STAR-NEWS

Street address 1: 121 S Oklahoma Ave
Street address city: Mangum
Street address state: OK
Zip/Postal code: 73554-4274
General Phone: (580) 782-3321
General Fax: (580) 782-2198
Editorial e-mail: mangumnews@gmail.com
Primary Website: mangumstarnews.net
Year Established: 1887
Avg Paid Circ: 2000
Audit By: Sworn/Estimate/Non-Audited
Audit Date: 10.06.2019
Personnel: Casey Paxton (Ed.)

THE MARLOW REVIEW

Street address 1: 316 W Main St
Street address city: Marlow
Street address state: OK
Zip/Postal code: 73055-2442
General Phone: (580) 658-6657
General Fax: (580) 658-6659
General/National Adv. E-mail: advertising@marlowreview.com
Display Adv. E-mail: classifieds@marlowreview.com
Editorial e-mail: news@marlowreview.com
Primary Website: marlowreview.com
Year Established: 1892
Avg Paid Circ: 3700
Audit By: Sworn/Estimate/Non-Audited
Audit Date: 10.06.2019
Personnel: Todd Brooks (Ed.); Judy Keller (Pub.)

THE MEDFORD PATRIOT-STAR AND GRANT COUNTY JOURNAL

Street address 1: 116 12 W CHEROKEE ST
Street address city: Medford
Street address state: OK
Zip/Postal code: 73759
General Phone: (580) 395-2212
General/National Adv. E-mail: patriotstar@att.net
Display Adv. E-mail: patriotstar@att.net
Primary Website:
Year Established: 1896
Avg Paid Circ: 1500
Avg Free Circ: 0
Audit By: Sworn/Estimate/Non-Audited
Audit Date: 10.06.2019
Personnel: Ken Kiser (Ed.)

THE MOUNTAIN VIEW NEWS

Street address 1: 319 Main St
Street address city: Mountain View
Street address state: OK
Zip/Postal code: 73062-9557
General Phone: (580) 347-2231
Editorial e-mail: news@westok.net
Primary Website: themountainviewnews.com
Audit By: Sworn/Estimate/Non-Audited
Audit Date: 10.06.2019
Personnel: Jyl Hobbs (Co-Pub.)

THE MUSTANG NEWS

Street address 1: 120 E Trade Center Ter
Street address 2: Suite #102
Street address city: Mustang
Street address state: OK
Zip/Postal code: 73064-4410
General Phone: (405) 376-4571
General Fax: (405) 376-5312
General/National Adv. E-mail: dsettle@mustangnews.info
Display Adv. E-mail: rlerma@mustangnews.info
Editorial e-mail: vmiddleton@mustangnews.info
Primary Website: theyukonreview.com/mustang-news
Year Established: 1982
Avg Paid Circ: 4000
Audit By: Sworn/Estimate/Non-Audited
Audit Date: 10.06.2019
Personnel: Victoria Middleton (Ed); John Settle (Pub); David Settle (Adv./Ops Dir.); Andrea Griffin (Office Mgr.)
Parent company (for newspapers): El Reno Tribune

THE NEWKIRK HERALD JOURNAL

Street address 1: 121 N Main St
Street address city: Newkirk
Street address state: OK
Zip/Postal code: 74647-2217
General Phone: (580) 362-2140
General Fax: (580) 362-2348
General/National Adv. E-mail: adv@newkirkherald.com
Display Adv. E-mail: class@newkirkherald.com
Editorial e-mail: news@newkirkherald.com
Primary Website: newkirkherald.com
Avg Paid Circ: 1450
Avg Free Circ: 100
Audit By: Sworn/Estimate/Non-Audited
Audit Date: 10.06.2019
Personnel: Scott Cloud (Ed./Pub.); Dixie Colquhon (Mktg. Dir.); Cindy Daigle (Class./Legal Dir.); Theda Sheets (Circ./Office Mgr.)

THE NORMAN TRANSCRIPT

Street address 1: 215 E Comanche St
Street address city: Norman
Street address state: OK
Zip/Postal code: 73069-6007
General Phone: (405) 321-1800
General Fax: (405) 366-3516
Advertising Phone: (405) 366-3503
Editorial Phone: (405) 366-3543
General/National Adv. E-mail: kmiller@normantranscript.com
Display Adv. E-mail: kmiller@normantranscript.com
Classified Adv. e-mail: jtrowbridge@normantranscript.com
Editorial e-mail: editor@normantranscript.com
Primary Website: normantranscript.com
Mthly Avg Views: 710241
Mthly Avg Unique Visitors: 337659
Year Established: 1889
Avg Paid Circ: 4600
Audit By: USPS
Audit Date: 21.10.2023
Personnel: Katherine Miller (Publisher); Rob Rasor (Production Director); Beau Simmons (Editor); Jessica Trowbridge (Customer Service Manager); Kelly Senne (Circulation Senior District Manager); Paxson Haws (Assistant Editor); Chris Hartman (Prepress Manager); Tarik Masri (Sports Reporter); Andrea Hancock (Reporter); Kyle Phillips (Photographer); Greta Samwel (Nationals/Special Projects Coordinator); Mark Millsap (Pub); Shana Adkisson (Ed); Vonnie Clark (Circ. Dir.); Tammy Griffis (Bus. Mgr.); Rob Rasor (Prod. Mgr.)
Parent company (for newspapers): CNHI, LLC

THE NOWATA STAR

Street address 1: 126 E Cherokee Ave
Street address city: Nowata
Street address state: OK
Zip/Postal code: 74048-2702
General Phone: (918) 273-2446
General Fax: (918) 273-0537
General/National Adv. E-mail: vdj@cableone.net
Editorial e-mail: nowatastar@sbcglobal.net
Primary Website: nowatastaronline.com
Year Established: 1909
Avg Paid Circ: 2800
Audit By: Sworn/Estimate/Non-Audited
Audit Date: 10.06.2019
Personnel: Michelle Milner (Advertising rep); John Link (Gen. Mgr.); Phillip Red (Pub.)

THE PAPER

Street address 1: 3 N Adair St
Street address 2: Ste 7
Street address city: Pryor
Street address state: OK
Zip/Postal code: 74361-2480
General Phone: (918) 825-2860
General Fax: (918) 825-2862
Advertising Phone: (918) 825-2860
Editorial Phone: (918) 825-2860
General/National Adv. E-mail: legals@mayescounty.com
Editorial e-mail: paull@mayescounty.com
Primary Website: thepaper.mayescounty.com
Year Established: 1999
Audit By: Sworn/Estimate/Non-Audited
Audit Date: 10.06.2019

Personnel: Paul Lewis (Ed.); Andrea Finney (Ads./Class./Legals)

THE PIEDMONT-SURREY GAZETTE

Street address 1: 109 Monroe Ave NW
Street address city: Piedmont
Street address state: OK
Zip/Postal code: 73078-8521
General Phone: (405) 373-1616
General Fax: (405) 373-1636
Editorial e-mail: piedmontgazette@sbcglobal.net
Primary Website: piedmontsurreygazette.com
Year Established: 1976
Avg Paid Circ: 1475
Avg Free Circ: 10
Audit By: Sworn/Estimate/Non-Audited
Audit Date: 10.06.2019
Personnel: Roger Pugh (Pub.); Eric Berger (Mng. Ed.)

THE PRAGUE TIMES-HERALD

Street address 1: 1123 N Jim Thorpe Blvd
Street address city: Prague
Street address state: OK
Zip/Postal code: 74864-3524
General Phone: (405) 567-3933
General Fax: (405) 567-3934
Editorial e-mail: praguetimes@windstream.net
Primary Website: facebook.com/Prague-Times-Herald-127645500614437
Year Established: 1972
Avg Paid Circ: 2500
Audit By: Sworn/Estimate/Non-Audited
Audit Date: 10.06.2019
Personnel: Sharon Lee (Pub)

THE PURCELL REGISTER

Street address 1: 225 W Main St
Street address city: Purcell
Street address state: OK
Zip/Postal code: 73080-4221
General Phone: (405) 527-2126
General Fax: (405) 527-3299
Advertising Phone: (405) 527-2126
Editorial Phone: (405) 527-2126
General/National Adv. E-mail: purcellregister@gmail.com
Display Adv. E-mail: advertising@purcellregister.com
Editorial e-mail: jdmontgomery70@gmail.com
Primary Website: purcellregister.com
Year Established: 1887
Avg Paid Circ: 2316
Avg Free Circ: 29
Audit By: VAC
Audit Date: 25.05.2018
Personnel: John D. Montgomery (Ed./Pub.)

THE RINGLING EAGLE

Street address 1: 103 E Main St
Street address city: Ringling
Street address state: OK
Zip/Postal code: 73456-1117
General Phone: (580) 662-2221
Editorial e-mail: ringlingeagle@sbcglobal.net
Primary Website: ringlingeagle.com
Year Established: 1920
Avg Paid Circ: 709
Avg Free Circ: 24
Audit By: Sworn/Estimate/Non-Audited
Audit Date: 10.06.2019
Personnel: Melissa Grace (Pub./Ed.)

THE RUSH SPRINGS GAZETTE

Street address 1: 220 W Blakely St
Street address city: Rush Springs
Street address state: OK
Zip/Postal code: 73082-1709
General Phone: (580) 476-2525
General Fax: (580) 476-2526
Editorial e-mail: rsgazette@sbcglobal.net
Avg Paid Circ: 1200
Avg Free Circ: 25
Audit By: Sworn/Estimate/Non-Audited
Audit Date: 10.06.2019
Personnel: Karen Goodwin (Ed.)

THE THOMAS TRIBUNE

Street address 1: 115 W Orient
Street address city: Thomas
Street address state: OK
Zip/Postal code: 73669
General Phone: (580) 661-3524
General Fax: (580) 661-3324
Editorial e-mail: thethomastribune@yahoo.com
Primary Website: etypeservices.com/Thomas%20TribuneID638/
Year Established: 1902
Avg Paid Circ: 1150
Audit By: Sworn/Estimate/Non-Audited
Audit Date: 10.06.2019
Personnel: Jessica Braun (Editor)

THE TONKAWA NEWS

Street address 1: 108 N 7th St
Street address city: Tonkawa
Street address state: OK
Zip/Postal code: 74653-3578
General Phone: (580) 628-2532
General Fax: (580) 628-4044
General/National Adv. E-mail: ads@tonkawanews.com
Editorial e-mail: news@tonkawanews.com
Primary Website: tonkawanews.com
Avg Paid Circ: 1708
Avg Free Circ: 23
Audit By: Sworn/Estimate/Non-Audited
Audit Date: 10.06.2019
Personnel: H. Lyle Becker (Ed.)

THE TUTTLE TIMES

Street address 1: 553 N Mustang Rd
Street address city: Mustang
Street address state: OK
Zip/Postal code: 73064-7002
General Phone: (405) 376-6688
General Fax: (405) 376-3565
General/National Adv. E-mail: mustangpublisher@sbcglobal.net
Editorial e-mail: editor@tuttletimes.com
Primary Website: mustangpaper.com/the-tuttle-times
Year Established: 1905
Avg Paid Circ: 2400
Avg Free Circ: 40
Audit By: Sworn/Estimate/Non-Audited
Audit Date: 10.06.2019
Personnel: Steven Kizzias (Pub.); Angie Russell (Circ. Mgr.); Jeff Harrison (Ed.)
Parent company (for newspapers): CNHI, LLC

THE VALLIANT LEADER

Street address 1: 119 N DALTON ST
Street address city: Valliant
Street address state: OK
Zip/Postal code: 74764
General Phone: (580) 933-4579
General Fax: (580) 933-4900
General/National Adv. E-mail: valeader@valliant.net
Year Established: 1982
Avg Paid Circ: 1800
Audit By: Sworn/Estimate/Non-Audited
Audit Date: 10.06.2019
Personnel: Peter A. Wilson (Ed.)

THE WATONGA REPUBLICAN

Street address 1: 104 E Main St
Street address city: Watonga
Street address state: OK
Zip/Postal code: 73772-3831
General Phone: (580) 623-4922
General Fax: (580) 623-4925
General/National Adv. E-mail: ian@WatongaRepublican.com
Display Adv. E-mail: ads@wrnews.net
Editorial e-mail: Editor@WatongaRepublican.com
Primary Website: thewatongarepublican.com
Year Established: 1892
Avg Paid Circ: 2950
Avg Free Circ: 17
Audit By: Sworn/Estimate/Non-Audited
Audit Date: 10.06.2019
Personnel: Eric Warsinskey (Chief Ed); Ian Pribanic (News Ed); Kimberly Jenkins (Adv)
Parent company (for newspapers): Central Oklahoma Publishing

THE YUKON REVIEW

Street address 1: 110 S 5th St
Street address city: Yukon
Street address state: OK
Zip/Postal code: 73099-2601
General Phone: (405) 354-5264
General Fax: (405) 354-3044
General/National Adv. E-mail: dsettle@theyukonreview.com
Display Adv. E-mail: rreynolds@theyukonreview.com
Editorial e-mail: editor@theyukonreview.com
Primary Website: yukonreview.net
Avg Paid Circ: 4321
Avg Free Circ: 4800
Audit By: Sworn/Estimate/Non-Audited
Audit Date: 10.06.2019
Personnel: Bart Nicholson (Gen. Mgr.); David Settle (Adv./Ops Dir.); John Settle (Pub.); Kyle Salomon (Ed.)
Parent company (for newspapers): Black Press Group Ltd.

TULSA BEACON

Street address 1: 6784 S 67th East Ave
Street address city: Tulsa
Street address state: OK
Zip/Postal code: 74133-1723
General Phone: (918) 523-4425
General Fax: (918) 523-4408
General/National Adv. E-mail: orders@tulsabeacon.com
Editorial e-mail: charlesbiggs@tulsabeacon.com
Primary Website: tulsabeacon.com
Audit By: Sworn/Estimate/Non-Audited
Audit Date: 10.06.2019
Personnel: Charles Biggs (Ed.)

TULSA COUNTY NEWS

Street address 1: 315 S Boulder Ave
Street address city: Tulsa
Street address state: OK
Zip/Postal code: 74103-3401
General Phone: (918) 582-0921
General/National Adv. E-mail: stephanie.knight@tulsaworld.com
Display Adv. E-mail: advertising@tulsaworld.com
Editorial e-mail: news@tulsaworld.com
Primary Website: tulsaworld.com/news
Year Established: 1965
Avg Paid Circ: 942
Avg Free Circ: 10
Audit By: Sworn/Estimate/Non-Audited
Audit Date: 10.06.2019
Personnel: Gary Percefull (Pub.)

WAGONER TRIBUNE

Street address 1: 221 E Cherokee St
Street address city: Wagoner
Street address state: OK
Zip/Postal code: 74467-4703
General Phone: (918) 485-5505
General Fax: (918) 485-8442
Editorial Phone: (918) 485-5505
General/National Adv. E-mail: Shelby.stockton@wagonercountyat.com
Display Adv. E-mail: Channing.Wedel@wagonercountyat.com
Editorial e-mail: christy.wheeland@wagonercountyat.com
Primary Website: wagonertribune.com
Mthly Avg Views: 44807
Mthly Avg Unique Visitors: 9215
Year Established: 1903
Avg Paid Circ: 2115
Avg Free Circ: 217
Audit By: CVC
Audit Date: 12//2012
Personnel: Christy Wheeland (Ed); Laura Schnee (Mktg.); Channing Wedel (Class./Inside Sales)
Parent company (for newspapers): Community Publishers, Inc.

WALTERS HERALD

Street address 1: 112 S Broadway St
Street address city: Walters
Street address state: OK
Zip/Postal code: 73572-2033
General Phone: (580) 875-3326
General Fax: (580) 875-3150
General/National Adv. E-mail: waltersheraldads@sbcglobal.net
Display Adv. E-mail: waltersheraldads@sbcglobal.net
Classified Adv. e-mail: waltersheraldads@sbcglobal.net
Editorial e-mail: cottoncountylegals@sbcglobal.net
Primary Website: waltersherald.com
Year Established: 1901
Avg Paid Circ: 173
Avg Free Circ: 25
Audit By: Sworn/Estimate/Non-Audited
Audit Date: 10.06.2019
Personnel: Beth Davis (Ed. Adv./Gen Mgr); Kim Hicklin (Adv. Mgr./Circ. Mgr.)

WESTVILLE REPORTER

Street address 1: 118 N 2nd St
Street address city: Stilwell
Street address state: OK
Zip/Postal code: 74960
General Phone: (918) 696-2228
General Fax: (918) 696-7066
General/National Adv. E-mail: stilwelldj@windstream.net
Editorial e-mail: westvillereporter@yahoo.com
Year Established: 1931
Avg Paid Circ: 2100
Avg Free Circ: 400
Audit By: Sworn/Estimate/Non-Audited
Audit Date: 10.06.2019
Personnel: Gary Jackson (Pub.); Keith Neale (Ed.); Darrell Neale (Editor)
Parent company (for newspapers): CNHI, LLC

WEWOKA TIMES

Street address 1: 210 S Wewoka Ave
Street address city: Wewoka
Street address state: OK
Zip/Postal code: 74884-2640
General Phone: (405) 257-3341
General Fax: (405) 257-3342
General/National Adv. E-mail: ads@seminoleproducer.com
Display Adv. E-mail: lovina@okcfriday.com
Editorial e-mail: stu@seminoleoklahoma.com
Primary Website: wewokatimes.com
Year Established: 1920
Avg Paid Circ: 1200
Audit By: Sworn/Estimate/Non-Audited
Audit Date: 10.06.2019
Personnel: Donny Cofer (Mng. Ed.); Mike Gifford (Adv. Dir); Lovina Morgan (Adv. Sales Rep.); Stu Phillips (Pub.)

WYNNEWOOD GAZETTE

Street address 1: 210 S Dean A McGee Ave
Street address city: Wynnewood
Street address state: OK
Zip/Postal code: 73098-7810
General Phone: (405) 665-4333
General Fax: (405) 665-4333
Advertising Phone: (405) 665-4333
Editorial Phone: (405) 665-4333
General/National Adv. E-mail: info@wwgazette.news
Year Established: 1902
Avg Paid Circ: 1700
Avg Free Circ: 60
Audit By: Sworn/Estimate/Non-Audited
Audit Date: 10.06.2019
Personnel: Tara Brown (Advertising Manager)
Parent company (for newspapers): Victory Publishing LLC

OREGON

APPEAL TRIBUNE

Street address 1: 340 Vista Ave SE
Street address city: Salem
Street address state: OR
Zip/Postal code: 97302-4546
General Phone: (503) 399-6611

General/National Adv. E-mail: golocal@statesmanjournal.com
Display Adv. E-mail: ads@statesmanjournal.com
Editorial e-mail: ccrosby@statesmanjournal.com
Primary Website: silvertonappeal.com
Year Established: 1880
Avg Paid Circ: 1009
Avg Free Circ: 0
Audit By: Sworn/Estimate/Non-Audited
Audit Date: 10.06.2019
Personnel: Ryan Kedzierski (Pres.); Paul Nettland (Circ. Dir.); Cherrill Crosby (Ed)
Parent company (for newspapers): Gannett

BAKER CITY HERALD

Street address 1: 1668 Resort St.
Street address city: Baker City
Street address state: OR
Zip/Postal code: 97814
General Phone: (541) 523-3673
General Fax: (541) 523-6424
General/National Adv. E-mail: kbrogoitti@lagrandeobserver.com
Display Adv. E-mail: kbrogoitti@lagrandeobserver.com
Classified Adv. e-mail: classified@bakercityherald.com
Editorial e-mail: kbrogoitti@lagrandeobserver.com
Primary Website: bakercityherald.com
Mthly Avg Views: 154900
Mthly Avg Unique Visitors: 35900
Year Established: 1870
Avg Paid Circ: 1858
Avg Free Circ: 73
Audit By: Sworn/Estimate/Non-Audited
Audit Date: 10.06.2019
Personnel: Karrine Brogoitti (Pub./Adv. Dir.); Kelli Craft (Circ. Mgr); Frank Everidge (Prodn. Mgr.)
Parent company (for newspapers): EO Media Group

BANDON WESTERN WORLD

Street address 1: 1185 BALTIMORE AVE SE
Street address city: Bandon
Street address state: OR
Zip/Postal code: 97411
General Phone: (541) 347-2423
General Fax: (541) 347-2424
General/National Adv. E-mail: kari.sholter@theworldlink.com
Display Adv. E-mail: sandy.stevens@theworldlink.com
Editorial e-mail: rjackimowicz@theworldlink.com
Primary Website: theworldlink.com
Year Established: 1912
Avg Paid Circ: 1059
Audit By: Sworn/Estimate/Non-Audited
Audit Date: 10.06.2019
Personnel: Jeff Precourt (Pub.); Amanda Johnson (Circ. Mgr.); Sandy Stevens (Class.); Ron Jackimowicz (Ed.)
Parent company (for newspapers): Southwestern Oregon Publishing Company

BLUE MOUNTAIN EAGLE

Street address 1: 195 N Canyon Blvd
Street address city: John Day
Street address state: OR
Zip/Postal code: 97845-1187
General Phone: (541) 575-0710
General Fax: (541) 575-1244
General/National Adv. E-mail: kim@bmeagle.com
Display Adv. E-mail: trista@bmeagle.com
Editorial e-mail: editor@bluemountaineagle.com
Primary Website: myeaglenews.com
Year Established: 1868
Avg Paid Circ: 3500
Avg Free Circ: 75
Audit By: Sworn/Estimate/Non-Audited
Audit Date: 10.06.2019
Personnel: Scotta Calister (Ed.); Marissa Williams (Pub.); Kim Kell (Adv. Rep); Trista Cox (Class./Circ.)
Parent company (for newspapers): East Oregonian

BOOM! BOOMERS AND BEYOND

Street address 1: 1190 NE Division St
Street address city: Gresham
Street address state: OR
Zip/Postal code: 97030-5727
General Phone: (503) 665-2181
General Fax: (503) 665-2187
Advertising Fax: (503) 669-2760
General/National Adv. E-mail: cmoore@commnewspapers.com
Editorial e-mail: jschrag@pamplinmedia.com
Primary Website: boomnw.com
Audit By: Sworn/Estimate/Non-Audited
Audit Date: 10.06.2019
Personnel: John Schrag (Ed); Kim Stephens (Circ. Mgr); Christine Moore (Adv. Dir.)

BURNS TIMES-HERALD

Street address 1: 355 N Broadway Ave
Street address city: Burns
Street address state: OR
Zip/Postal code: 97720-1704
General Phone: (541) 573-2022
General Fax: (541) 573-3915
General/National Adv. E-mail: addrop@burnstimesherald.info
Editorial e-mail: editor@burnstimesherald.info
Primary Website: burnstimesherald.info
Year Established: 1887
Avg Paid Circ: 3008
Avg Free Circ: 46
Audit By: Sworn/Estimate/Non-Audited
Audit Date: 10.06.2019
Personnel: Sue Pedersen (Gen. Mgr.); Jeff Graham (Circ. Mgr.); Jennifer Jenks (Ed.)
Parent company (for newspapers): Survival Media LLC

BUSINESS JOURNAL OF PORTLAND

Street address 1: 851 SW 6th Ave
Street address 2: Suite 500
Street address city: Portland
Street address state: OR
Zip/Postal code: 97204-1342
General Phone: (503) 274-8733
General Fax: (503) 219-3450
General/National Adv. E-mail: avangordon@bizjournals.com
Display Adv. E-mail: athomas@bizjournals.com
Editorial e-mail: sstevens@bizjournals.com
Primary Website: bizjournals.com/portland
Year Established: 1984
Audit By: Sworn/Estimate/Non-Audited
Audit Date: 10.06.2019
Personnel: Craig Wessel (Pub); Angela Thomas (Adv. Coord.); Suzanne Stevenson (Ed)

CAPITAL PRESS

Street address 1: 2870 Broadway St. NE
Street address city: Salem
Street address state: OR
Zip/Postal code: 97301
General Phone: (800) 882-6789
Advertising Phone: (800) 882-6789
Editorial Phone: (208) 914-8264
General/National Adv. E-mail: bsell@capitalpress.com
Display Adv. E-mail: bsell@capitalpress.com
Editorial e-mail: sellis@capitalpress.com
Primary Website: capitalpress.com
Mthly Avg Views: 180000
Mthly Avg Unique Visitors: 54000
Year Established: 1924
Avg Paid Circ: 24332
Avg Free Circ: 27361
Audit By: AAM
Audit Date: 31.12.2018
Personnel: Joe Beach (Ed.); Beth Sell (Adv. Dir.); Carl Sampson (Mng. Ed.); Sean Ellis (Newsroom)
Parent company (for newspapers): EO Media Group

CENTRAL OREGONIAN

Street address 1: 558 N Main St
Street address city: Prineville
Street address state: OR
Zip/Postal code: 97754-1199
General Phone: (541) 447-6205
General Fax: (541) 447-1754
General/National Adv. E-mail: advertising@centraloregonian.com
Display Adv. E-mail: classifieds@centraloregonian.com
Editorial e-mail: jchaney@centraloregonian.com
Primary Website: centraloregonian.com
Year Established: 1881
Avg Paid Circ: 3753
Audit By: Sworn/Estimate/Non-Audited
Audit Date: 10.06.2019
Personnel: Teresa Tooley (Gen. Mgr.); Tony Ahern (Pub.); Jason Chaney (Ed.)
Parent company (for newspapers): Pamplin Media Group

COLUMBIA GORGE NEWS

Street address 1: 419 State St
Street address 2: Ste 1
Street address city: Hood River
Street address state: OR
Zip/Postal code: 97031-2075
General Phone: (541) 386-1234
General Fax: (541) 386-6796
General/National Adv. E-mail: jthompson@hoodrivernews.com
Display Adv. E-mail: hrnews@hoodrivernews.com
Editorial e-mail: kneumann-rea@hoodrivernews.com
Primary Website: hoodrivernews.com
Year Established: 1905
Avg Paid Circ: 5300
Avg Free Circ: 98
Audit By: Sworn/Estimate/Non-Audited
Audit Date: 10.06.2019
Personnel: Joe Petshow (Pub.); Esther Smith (Circ. Mgr.); Kirby Neumann-Rea (Ed.); Jody Thompson (Adv. Mgr.)
Parent company (for newspapers): Eagle Newspapers, Inc.

COLUMBIA GORGE NEWS

Street address 1: 419 State St
Street address 2: Ste 1
Street address city: Hood River
Street address state: OR
Zip/Postal code: 97031-2075
General Phone: (541) 386-1234
General Fax: (541) 386-6796
General/National Adv. E-mail: jthompson@hoodrivernews.com
Display Adv. E-mail: hrnews@hoodrivernews.com
Editorial e-mail: kneumann-rea@hoodrivernews.com
Primary Website: hoodrivernews.com
Year Established: 1905
Avg Paid Circ: 5300
Avg Free Circ: 98
Audit By: Sworn/Estimate/Non-Audited
Audit Date: 10.06.2019
Personnel: Joe Petshow (Pub.); Esther Smith (Circ. Mgr.); Kirby Neumann-Rea (Ed.); Jody Thompson (Adv. Mgr.)
Parent company (for newspapers): Eagle Newspapers, Inc.

COTTAGE GROVE SENTINEL

Street address 1: 116 N 6th St
Street address city: Cottage Grove
Street address state: OR
Zip/Postal code: 97424-1601
General Phone: (541) 942-3325
General Fax: (541) 942-3328
General/National Adv. E-mail: cgnews@cgsentinel.com
Display Adv. E-mail: legals@cgsentinel.com
Editorial e-mail: cgnews@cgsentinel.com
Primary Website: cgsentinel.com
Year Established: 1889
Avg Paid Circ: 2500
Avg Free Circ: 225
Audit By: Sworn/Estimate/Non-Audited
Audit Date: 10.06.2019
Personnel: Jessica Baker (Pub.); Jon Stinnett (Ed.); Gary Manly (Gen. Mgr.); Carla Williams (Circ./Class. Mgr)
Parent company (for newspapers): San Luis Valley Publishing

CURRY COASTAL PILOT

Street address 1: 507 Chetco Ave
Street address city: Brookings
Street address state: OR
Zip/Postal code: 97415-8011
General Phone: (541) 469-3123
General Fax: (541) 469-4679
General/National Adv. E-mail: mail@currypilot.com
Display Adv. E-mail: mail@currypilot.com
Editorial e-mail: news@currypilot.com
Primary Website: currypilot.com
Year Established: 1946
Avg Paid Circ: 4759
Avg Free Circ: 87
Audit By: CVC
Audit Date: 30.09.2016
Personnel: Jenna Steineke (Circ. Mgr.); Scott Graves (Ed.); Charles Kocher (Pub); Aura Wright (Prod. Mgr.); David Jeffcoat (Circ. Mgr)
Parent company (for newspapers): Country Media, Inc.

CURRY COUNTY REPORTER

Street address 1: 29822 ELLENSBURG AVE
Street address city: Gold Beach
Street address state: OR
Zip/Postal code: 97444
General Phone: (541) 247-6643
General Fax: (541) 247-6644
General/National Adv. E-mail: micki@currycountyreporter.com
Editorial e-mail: currycountyreporter@gmail.com
Primary Website: currycountyreporter.com
Year Established: 1914
Avg Paid Circ: 2748
Audit By: Sworn/Estimate/Non-Audited
Audit Date: 10.06.2019
Personnel: Matt Hall (Co-Pub.); Molly Walker (Co-Pub/Adv.)

DAILY JOURNAL OF COMMERCE

Street address 1: 9137 Ridgeline Blvd
Street address 2: Suite 210
Street address city: Portland
Street address state: OR
Zip/Postal code: 97205-2810
General Phone: (503) 226-1311
General/National Adv. E-mail: bbeyer@djcOregon.com
Display Adv. E-mail: sales@djcoregon.com
Editorial e-mail: stephanie.basalyga@djcoregon.com
Primary Website: djcoregon.com
Year Established: 1872
Audit By: Sworn/Estimate/Non-Audited
Audit Date: 10.06.2019
Personnel: Joe Yovino (Grp Pub.); Joel Slaughter (Copy Ed.); Chuck Slothower (Reporter); Sam Tenny (Photograher); Josh Kulla (Reporter); Bill Beyer (Adv. Mgr.); David Gwynn (Adv. Acct. Mgr.); Nick Bjork (Pub.)
Parent company (for newspapers): The Dolan Company

DEAD MOUNTAIN ECHO

Street address 1: 48013 Highway 58
Street address city: Oakridge
Street address state: OR
Zip/Postal code: 97463-9523
General Phone: (541) 782-4241
General Fax: (541) 782-3323
Editorial e-mail: lroberts@efn.org
Primary Website: https://facebook.com/DeadMountainEcho
Year Established: 1973
Avg Paid Circ: 650
Avg Free Circ: 2400
Audit By: Sworn/Estimate/Non-Audited
Audit Date: 10.06.2019
Personnel: Larry D. Roberts (Ed./Pub)
Parent company (for newspapers): Echo Publishing, Inc.

ESTACADA NEWS

Street address 1: 307 SW Highway 224
Street address city: Estacada
Street address state: OR
Zip/Postal code: 97023-7026
General Phone: (503) 630-3241
General Fax: (503) 630-5840
General/National Adv. E-mail: email@estacadanews.com
Editorial e-mail: editor@estacadanews.com
Primary Website: estacadanews.com
Year Established: 1904
Avg Paid Circ: 2000
Avg Free Circ: 35
Audit By: Sworn/Estimate/Non-Audited
Audit Date: 10.06.2019
Personnel: Mark Garber (Pres.); Brian Monahan (VP); Karen Tamburina (Adv.)

Parent company (for newspapers): Pamplin Media Group

FOREST GROVE NEWS-TIMES

Street address 1: 2004 Main St.
Street address 2: Suite 309
Street address city: Forest Grove
Street address state: OR
Zip/Postal code: 97116-2357
General Phone: (503) 357-3181
Advertising Phone: (503) 357-3181
Editorial Phone: (503) 357-3181
General/National Adv. E-mail: advertising@fgnewstimes.com
Editorial e-mail: news@fgnewstimes.com
Primary Website: forestgrovenewstimes.com
Year Established: 1886
Avg Paid Circ: 3800
Avg Free Circ: 600
Audit By: Sworn/Estimate/Non-Audited
Audit Date: 10.06.2019
Personnel: Nikki DeBuse (Regional Publisher); Rebecca Mansfield (Clas. Adv.); Toni Ashby (Advertising Manager); Kim Stephens (Circ. Mgr.); Mark Miller (Regional Editor); Maureen Zoebelein (Prodn. Mgr.); Marc Caplan (Public Notice); Jill Smith (Editor)
Parent company (for newspapers): Pamplin Media Group

HEADLIGHT-HERALD

Street address 1: 1908 2nd St
Street address city: Tillamook
Street address state: OR
Zip/Postal code: 97141-2206
General Phone: (503) 842-7535
General Fax: (503) 842-8842
General/National Adv. E-mail: headlightads@countrymedia.net
Display Adv. E-mail: classifieds@orcoastnews.com
Editorial e-mail: jwolfe@countrymedia.net
Primary Website: tillamookheadlightherald.com
Year Established: 1888
Avg Paid Circ: 8500
Avg Free Circ: 86
Audit By: Sworn/Estimate/Non-Audited
Audit Date: 10.06.2019
Personnel: Joe Warren (Pub); Jordan Wolfe (Ed); Brian Humphrey (Circ. Mgr.)
Parent company (for newspapers): Country Media, Inc

HELLS CANYON JOURNAL

Street address 1: 145 N Main St
Street address city: Halfway
Street address state: OR
Zip/Postal code: 97834-2018
General Phone: (541) 742-7900
General Fax: (541) 742-7933
General/National Adv. E-mail: hcjads@pinetel.com
Display Adv. E-mail: hcjads@pinetel.com
Classified Adv. e-mail: hcj@p[netel.com
Editorial e-mail: hcj@pinetel.com
Primary Website: http://orenews.com/halfway
Year Established: 1983
Avg Paid Circ: 1000
Audit By: Sworn/Estimate/Non-Audited
Audit Date: 10.06.2019
Personnel: Cindy Thayer (Adv. Dir); Julie Bishop (Circ. Mgr.); Steve Backstrom (Pub./Ed/Prod. Mgr.)
Parent company (for newspapers): Hells Canyon Publishing, Inc.

HEPPNER GAZETTE-TIMES

Street address 1: 188 W Willow St
Street address city: Heppner
Street address state: OR
Zip/Postal code: 97836-2070
General Phone: (541) 676-9228
General Fax: (541) 676-9211
General/National Adv. E-mail: david@rapidserve.net
Editorial e-mail: editor@rapidserve.net
Primary Website: heppner.net/gazette
Year Established: 1883
Avg Paid Circ: 2000
Audit By: Sworn/Estimate/Non-Audited
Audit Date: 10.06.2019
Personnel: Andrea Di Salvo (Ed.)
Parent company (for newspapers): Sykes Publishing, LLC

ILLINOIS VALLEY NEWS

Street address 1: 221 S REDWOOD HWY
Street address city: Cave Junction
Street address state: OR
Zip/Postal code: 97523
General Phone: (541) 592-2541
General Fax: (541) 592-433
General/National Adv. E-mail: dan@illinoies-valley-news.com
Display Adv. E-mail: zbooth@illinois-valley-news.com
Editorial e-mail: newsroom1@frontiernet.net
Primary Website: illinois-valley-news.com
Year Established: 1937
Avg Paid Circ: 3500
Avg Free Circ: 25
Audit By: Sworn/Estimate/Non-Audited
Audit Date: 10.06.2019
Personnel: Dan Mancuso (Pub)
Parent company (for newspapers): W. H. Alltheway, LLC

KEIZERTIMES

Street address 1: 142 Chemawa Rd N
Street address city: Keizer
Street address state: OR
Zip/Postal code: 97303-5356
General Phone: (503) 390-1051
General Fax: (503) 390-8023
General/National Adv. E-mail: advertising@keizertimes.com; publisher@keizertimes.com
Display Adv. E-mail: classifieds@keizertimes.com
Editorial e-mail: editor@keizertimes.com
Primary Website: keizertimes.com
Year Established: 1979
Avg Paid Circ: 1900
Avg Free Circ: 0
Audit By: Sworn/Estimate/Non-Audited
Audit Date: 10.06.2019
Personnel: Lyndon Zaitz (Pub.); Laurie Painter (Legal Notices); Andrew Jackson (Prod./Clas.); Eric A. Howald (News Ed.); Derek Wiley (Assoc. Ed.); Paula Moseley (Adv. Acc. Rep.)
Parent company (for newspapers): Wheatland Publishing Corp.

LAKE COUNTY EXAMINER

Street address 1: 739 N 2nd St
Street address city: Lakeview
Street address state: OR
Zip/Postal code: 97630-1512
General Phone: (541) 947-3378
General Fax: (541) 947-4359
General/National Adv. E-mail: ads@lakecountyexam.com
Editorial e-mail: news@lakecountyexam.com
Primary Website: lakecountyexam.com
Year Established: 1880
Avg Paid Circ: 2150
Avg Free Circ: 4300
Audit By: Sworn/Estimate/Non-Audited
Audit Date: 10.06.2019
Personnel: Tillie Flynn (Ed.); Jolie Murphy (Circ. Mgr.); Kristin Keiser (Adv.)
Parent company (for newspapers): Adams Publishing Group, LLC

LEBANON EXPRESS

Street address 1: 90 E Grant St
Street address city: Lebanon
Street address state: OR
Zip/Postal code: 97355-3201
General Phone: (541) 258-3151
General Fax: (541) 259-3569
Advertising Phone: (541) 812-6073
General/National Adv. E-mail: jeff.precourt@lee.net
Display Adv. E-mail: jeff.precourt@lee.net
Editorial e-mail: news@lebanon-express.com
Primary Website: lebanon-express.com
Year Established: 1887
Avg Paid Circ: 2664
Audit By: Sworn/Estimate/Non-Audited
Audit Date: 10.06.2019
Personnel: Les Gehrett (Ed.); Jeff Precourt (Pub./Adv. Dir.); Mike McInally (Ed./Gen. Mgr.)
Parent company (for newspapers): Dispatch-Argus

MALHEUR ENTERPRISE

Street address 1: 289 A St W
Street address city: Vale
Street address state: OR
Zip/Postal code: 97918-1303
General Phone: (541) 473-3377
General Fax: (541) 473-3268
General/National Adv. E-mail: business@malheurenterprise.com
Editorial e-mail: scotta@malheurenterprise.com
Primary Website: http://malheurenterprise.com/
Year Established: 1909
Avg Paid Circ: 1300
Avg Free Circ: 40
Audit By: Sworn/Estimate/Non-Audited
Audit Date: 10.06.2019
Personnel: Scotta Callister (Pub/Ed); Lyndon Zaitz (Gen. Mgr.); Bobbi Buttice (Bus. Mgr.)

MCKENZIE RIVER REFLECTIONS

Street address 1: 59059 Old McKenzie Hwy
Street address city: McKenzie Bridge
Street address state: OR
Zip/Postal code: 97413-9615
General Phone: (541) 822-3358
General Fax: (541) 663-4550
General/National Adv. E-mail: rivref@aol.com
Display Adv. E-mail: rivref@aol.com
Editorial e-mail: rivref@aol.com
Primary Website: mckenzieriverreflectionsnewspaper.com
Year Established: 1978
Avg Paid Circ: 850
Avg Free Circ: 80
Audit By: Sworn/Estimate/Non-Audited
Audit Date: 10.06.2019
Personnel: Kenneth Engelman (Pub.); Louise Engelman (Mng. Ed.)

NEWS-REGISTER

Street address 1: 611 NE 3rd St
Street address city: McMinnville
Street address state: OR
Zip/Postal code: 97128-4518
General Phone: (503) 472-5114
General Fax: (503) 472-9151
General/National Adv. E-mail: rsudeith@oregonlitho.com
Display Adv. E-mail: classified@newsregister.com
Editorial e-mail: sbagwell@newsregister.com
Primary Website: newsregister.com
Year Established: 1866
Avg Paid Circ: 8291
Avg Free Circ: 300
Audit By: Sworn/Estimate/Non-Audited
Audit Date: 10.06.2019
Personnel: Jeb Bladine (Pres./Pub); Steve Bagwell (Mng. Ed.); Robert Sudeith (Sale/Mktg. Dir)
Parent company (for newspapers): Bladine Family

NEWS-TIMES

Street address 1: 831 NE Avery St
Street address city: Newport
Street address state: OR
Zip/Postal code: 97365-3033
General Phone: (541) 265-8571
General Fax: (541) 265-3862
General/National Adv. E-mail: bmoore@newportnewstimes.com
Display Adv. E-mail: bmoore@newportnewstimes.com
Editorial e-mail: byager@newportnewstimes.com
Primary Website: newportnewstimes.com
Year Established: 1882
Avg Paid Circ: 10100
Avg Free Circ: 301
Audit By: Sworn/Estimate/Non-Audited
Audit Date: 10.06.2019
Personnel: Jeremy Burke (Pub.); Bret Yager (Mng. Ed.); Barbara Moore (Adv. Dir.)
Parent company (for newspapers): San Luis Valley Publishing

NORTH COAST CITIZEN

Street address 1: PO Box 355
Street address city: Manzanita
Street address state: OR
Zip/Postal code: 97130-0355
General Phone: (503) 842-7535
General Fax: (503) 842-8842
Editorial Phone: editor@northcoastcitizen.com
General/National Adv. E-mail: jwarren@countrymedia.net
Primary Website: northcoastcitizen.com
Year Established: 1996
Avg Paid Circ: 1200
Avg Free Circ: 50
Audit By: Sworn/Estimate/Non-Audited
Audit Date: 10.06.2019
Personnel: Brian Cameron (Managing Editor)
Parent company (for newspapers): Country Media Inc.

OREGON CITY NEWS

Street address 1: 6605 SE Lake Rd
Street address city: Portland
Street address state: OR
Zip/Postal code: 97222-2161
General Phone: (503) 684-0360
General Fax: (503) 620-3433
General/National Adv. E-mail: kschaub@clackamasreview.com
Display Adv. E-mail: dbeauchamp@pamplinmedia.com
Editorial e-mail: rrendleman@clackamasreview.com
Primary Website: oregoncitynewsonline.com
Avg Paid Circ: 3500
Audit By: Sworn/Estimate/Non-Audited
Audit Date: 10.06.2019
Personnel: Angela Fox (Pub.); Raymond Rendleman (Ed); Kathy Schaub (Adv. Rep)
Parent company (for newspapers): Pamplin Media Group

OREGON COAST TODAY

Street address 1: 800 SE Highway 101
Street address city: Lincoln City
Street address state: OR
Zip/Postal code: 97367-2755
General Phone: (541) 921-0413
General/National Adv. E-mail: greg@oregoncoasttoday.com
Editorial e-mail: patrick@oregoncoasttoday.com
Primary Website: oregoncoasttoday.com
Avg Free Circ: 17000
Audit By: Sworn/Estimate/Non-Audited
Audit Date: 10.06.2019
Personnel: Greg Robertson (Adv. Rep.); Patrick Alexander (Ed.)
Parent company (for newspapers): EO Media Group

PORT ORFORD NEWS

Street address 1: 519 10th St
Street address city: Port Orford
Street address state: OR
Zip/Postal code: 97465-8765
General Phone: (541) 260-3638
Editorial e-mail: portorfordnews@gmail.com
Primary Website: portorfordnews.net
Year Established: 1958
Avg Paid Circ: 1200
Avg Free Circ: 9
Audit By: Sworn/Estimate/Non-Audited
Audit Date: 10.06.2019
Personnel: Matt Hall (Pub.)

PORTLAND MERCURY

Street address 1: 115 SW Ash St
Street address 2: Suite 600
Street address city: Portland
Street address state: OR
Zip/Postal code: 97204-3549
General Phone: (503) 294-0840
General Fax: (503) 294-0844
General/National Adv. E-mail: salesinfo@portlandmercury.com
Editorial e-mail: news@portlandmercury.com
Primary Website: portlandmercury.com
Year Established: 2001
Avg Paid Circ: 8
Avg Free Circ: 35645
Audit By: Sworn/Estimate/Non-Audited
Audit Date: 10.06.2019
Personnel: Rob Thomas (Pub./Adv. Mgr.); Erik Henrikson (Ed.)

Parent company (for newspapers): Index Newspapers, Inc

REGAL COURIER

Street address 1: 10170 SW Nimbus Ave
Street address city: Portland
Street address state: OR
Zip/Postal code: 97223
General Phone: (503) 639-5414
Primary Website: pamplinmedia.com/regal-courier
Year Established: 1977
Avg Free Circ: 4800
Audit By: Sworn/Estimate/Non-Audited
Audit Date: 10.06.2019
Personnel: Dana Haynes (Ed.); Christine Moore (Pub.); Katie Hickman (Adv. Sales); Kim Stephens (Circ. Mgr.)
Parent company (for newspapers): Pamplin Media Group

ROGUE RIVER PRESS

Street address 1: 8991 Rogue River Hwy
Street address city: Grants Pass
Street address state: OR
Zip/Postal code: 97527-4377
General Phone: (541) 582-1707
General Fax: (541) 582-0201
General/National Adv. E-mail: rrpress@roguerivepress.com
Display Adv. E-mail: marketing@rogueriverpress.com
Editorial e-mail: editor@rogueriverpress.com
Primary Website: rogueriverpress.com
Year Established: 1915
Avg Paid Circ: 2000
Audit By: Sworn/Estimate/Non-Audited
Audit Date: 10.06.2019
Personnel: Leif Birdsall (Circ/Web Mgr); Pam Birdsall (Admin); Brian Mortenson (Sports Ed.)
Parent company (for newspapers): Valley Pride Publications, Llc

SANDY POST

Street address 1: 584 NE 8TH ST
Street address city: Gresham
Street address state: OR
Zip/Postal code: 97030
General Phone: (503) 668-5548
General Fax: (503) 668-0748
Advertising Phone: (503) 665-2181
Advertising Fax: (503) 668-5549
General/National Adv. E-mail: aapplegate@theoutlookonline.com
Display Adv. E-mail: dbeauchamp@pamplinmedia.com
Editorial e-mail: sbrown@theoutlookonline.com
Primary Website: http://pamplinmedia.com/sandy-post-news/
Year Established: 1937
Avg Paid Circ: 3500
Avg Free Circ: 28
Audit By: Sworn/Estimate/Non-Audited
Audit Date: 10.06.2019
Personnel: Mark Garber (Pres.); Steve Brown (Pub/Ed); Alisa Applegate (Adv. Mgr.); Kim Stephens (Circ. Mgr.)
Parent company (for newspapers): Pamplin Media Group; Pamplin Media Group

SEASIDE SIGNAL

Street address 1: 949 Exchange Street
Street address city: Astoria
Street address state: OR
Zip/Postal code: 97103
General Phone: 503-738-5561
General/National Adv. E-mail: editor@seasidesignal.com
Editorial e-mail: editor@seasidesignal.com
Primary Website: seasidesignal.com
Year Established: 1905
Avg Paid Circ: 3500
Audit By: Sworn/Estimate/Non-Audited
Audit Date: 10.06.2019
Personnel: Betty Smith (Adv. Mgr.); Rebecca Herren (Office Coord.); R.J. Marx (Ed)
Parent company (for newspapers): EO Media Group; Country Media, Inc

SIUSLAW NEWS

Street address 1: 148 Maple St
Street address city: Florence
Street address state: OR
Zip/Postal code: 97439-9656
General Phone: (541) 997-3441
General Fax: (541) 997-7979
Editorial Phone: (541) 902-3520
General/National Adv. E-mail: s.gutierrez@thesiuslawnews.com
Editorial e-mail: editor@thesiuslawnews.com
Primary Website: thesiuslawnews.com
Year Established: 1890
Avg Paid Circ: 6
Avg Free Circ: 125
Audit By: Sworn/Estimate/Non-Audited
Audit Date: 10.06.2019
Personnel: Susan Gutierrez (Adv. Mgr.); Jenna Bartlett (Publisher); Jeanna Petersen (Sales person)
Parent company (for newspapers): San Luis Valley Publishing

SOURCE WEEKLY

Street address 1: 704 NW Georgia Ave
Street address city: Bend
Street address state: OR
Zip/Postal code: 97703-3243
General Phone: (541) 383-0800
General/National Adv. E-mail: amanda@bendsource.com
Editorial e-mail: editor@bendsource.com
Primary Website: bendsource.com
Year Established: 1997
Avg Paid Circ: 325
Audit By: Sworn/Estimate/Non-Audited
Audit Date: 10.06.2019
Personnel: Aaron Switzer (Pub.); Amanda Klingman (Adv. Dir.); Nicole Vulcan (Ed)

SOUTHWEST COMMUNITY CONNECTION

Street address 1: 400 2nd St
Street address city: Lake Oswego
Street address state: OR
Zip/Postal code: 97034-3127
General Phone: (503) 636-1281
Advertising Phone: (503) 546-9883
General/National Adv. E-mail: ldavis@pamplinmedia.com
Display Adv. E-mail: mjohnson@pamplinmedia.com
Editorial e-mail: cbuchanan@pamplinmedia.com
Primary Website: swcommconnection.com
Year Established: 1994
Audit By: Sworn/Estimate/Non-Audited
Audit Date: 10.06.2019
Personnel: Brian Monihan (Pub.); Corey Buchanan (Ed.); Christine Moore (Adv. Dir.); Kim Stephens (Circ. Mgr.); Bart Betz (Web Dev.)
Parent company (for newspapers): Pamplin Media Group; Pamplin Media Group

STAYTON MAIL

Street address 1: 340 Vista Ave SE
Street address city: Salem
Street address state: OR
Zip/Postal code: 97302-4546
General Phone: (503) 399-6611
General/National Adv. E-mail: golocal@statesmanjournal.com
Display Adv. E-mail: ads@statesmanjournal.com
Editorial e-mail: ccrosby@statesmanjournal.com
Primary Website: staytonmail.com
Year Established: 1894
Avg Paid Circ: 765
Avg Free Circ: 0
Audit By: AAM
Audit Date: 31.03.2017
Personnel: Ryan Kedzierski (Pres.); Paul Nettland (Circ. Dir.); Cherrill Crosby (Ed)
Parent company (for newspapers): Gannett

SUSTAINABLE LIFE

Street address 1: 6605 SE Lake Rd
Street address city: Portland
Street address state: OR
Zip/Postal code: 97222-2161
General Phone: (503) 226-6397
General Fax: (503) 546-0727
Advertising Phone: (503) 546-0771
Advertising Fax: (503) 620-3433
Editorial Phone: (503) 546-5139
Editorial Fax: (503) 546-0727
General/National Adv. E-mail: cmoore@commnewspapers.com
Display Adv. E-mail: classifiedadvertising@commnewspapers.com
Editorial e-mail: kharden@commnewspapers.com
Primary Website: http://portlandtribune.com/portland-tribune-sustainable-life
Mthly Avg Views: 69137
Mthly Avg Unique Visitors: 12643
Year Established: 2006
Avg Paid Circ: 80000
Avg Free Circ: 97000
Audit By: Sworn/Estimate/Non-Audited
Audit Date: 10.06.2019
Personnel: Mark Garber (Pres.); Christine Moore (Adv. Dir.); Kevin Harden (Exec. Ed.); Kim Stephens (Circ. Mgr)
Parent company (for newspapers): Pamplin Media Group

THE BEAVERTON VALLEY TIMES

Street address 1: 6605 SE Lake Rd
Street address city: Portland
Street address state: OR
Zip/Postal code: 97222-2161
General Phone: (503) 684-0360
General Fax: (503) 620-3433
General/National Adv. E-mail: cmoore@pamplinmedia.com
Display Adv. E-mail: rmansfield@pamplinmedia.com
Editorial e-mail: dhaynes@pamplinmedia.com
Primary Website: beavertonvalleytimes.com
Year Established: 1921
Avg Paid Circ: 7000
Audit By: Sworn/Estimate/Non-Audited
Audit Date: 10.06.2019
Personnel: Christine Moore (Adv. Dir); Kim Stephens (Circ. Mgr); Mark Garber (Pub.); Dana Haynes (Ed.)
Parent company (for newspapers): Pamplin Media Group; Pamplin Media Group

THE BEE

Street address 1: 1837 SE Harold St
Street address city: Portland
Street address state: OR
Zip/Postal code: 97202-4932
General Phone: (503) 232-2326
General Fax: (503) 232-9787
Primary Website: thebeenews.com
Year Established: ReadTheBee@myexcel.com
Audit By: Sworn/Estimate/Non-Audited
Audit Date: 10.06.2019
Personnel: J. Brian Monihan (Pub.); Eric Norberg (Ed./Gen. Mgr.)
Parent company (for newspapers): Pamplin Media Group

THE CANBY HERALD

Street address 1: 241 N Grant St
Street address city: Canby
Street address state: OR
Zip/Postal code: 97013-3629
General Phone: (503) 266-6831
General Fax: (503) 266-6836
General/National Adv. E-mail: sstorey@canbyherald.com
Primary Website: canbyherald.com
Year Established: 1906
Avg Paid Circ: 5100
Audit By: Sworn/Estimate/Non-Audited
Audit Date: 10.06.2019
Personnel: John Baker (Ed.); Sandy Storey (Adv); Georgia Newton (Pub.)
Parent company (for newspapers): Pamplin Media Group; Pamplin Media Group

THE CHIEF

Street address 1: 148 N Nehalem St
Street address city: Clatskanie
Street address state: OR
Zip/Postal code: 97016-7435
General Phone: (503) 728-3350
General Fax: (503) 308-6791
General/National Adv. E-mail: lressler@countrymedia.net
Editorial e-mail: cmann@countrymedia.net
Primary Website: thechiefnews.com
Year Established: 1891
Avg Paid Circ: 2750
Audit By: Sworn/Estimate/Non-Audited
Audit Date: 10.06.2019
Personnel: Lora Ressler (Gen. Mgr.); Cody Mann (Ed)
Parent company (for newspapers): Country Media Inc.

THE CHRONICLE

Street address 1: 1805 Columbia Blvd
Street address city: Saint Helens
Street address state: OR
Zip/Postal code: 97051-6220
General Phone: (503) 397-0116
General Fax: (503) 397-4093
General/National Adv. E-mail: chronicleads@countrymedia.net
Display Adv. E-mail: chronicleclassifieds@countrymedia.net
Editorial e-mail: dpatterson@countrymedia.net
Primary Website: thechronicleonline.com
Year Established: 1881
Avg Paid Circ: 3100
Avg Free Circ: 7349
Audit By: Sworn/Estimate/Non-Audited
Audit Date: 10.06.2019
Personnel: Don Patterson (Pub./Ed.); Amy Johnson (Adv. Sales)
Parent company (for newspapers): Country Media, Inc

THE CLACKAMAS REVIEW

Street address 1: 6605 SE Lake Rd
Street address city: Portland
Street address state: OR
Zip/Postal code: 97222-2161
General Phone: (503) 684-0360
General Fax: (503) 620-3433
General/National Adv. E-mail: kschaub@clackamasreview.com
Display Adv. E-mail: dbeauchamp@pamplinmedia.com
Editorial e-mail: RRendleman@clackamasreview.com
Primary Website: clackamasreview.com
Avg Paid Circ: 1000
Avg Free Circ: 33300
Audit By: Sworn/Estimate/Non-Audited
Audit Date: 10.06.2019
Personnel: Angela Fox (Pub.); Raymond Rendleman (Ed); Kim Stephens (Circ. Mgr.); Kathy Schaub (Adv. Rep.)
Parent company (for newspapers): Pamplin Media Group

THE COLUMBIA PRESS

Street address 1: 5 N HIGHWAY 101
Street address 2: # 500
Street address city: Warrenton
Street address state: OR
Zip/Postal code: 97146-9313
General Phone: (503) 861-3331
General Fax: (503) 861-7039
Advertising Phone: (503) 861-3331
Advertising Fax: (503) 861-7039
Editorial Phone: (503) 861-3331
Editorial Fax: (503) 861-7039
General/National Adv. E-mail: ads@thecolumbiapress.com
Display Adv. E-mail: ads@thecolumbiapress.com
Editorial e-mail: news@thecolumbiapress.com
Primary Website: thecolumbiapress.com
Year Established: 1922
Avg Paid Circ: 850
Avg Free Circ: 20
Audit By: Sworn/Estimate/Non-Audited
Audit Date: 10.06.2019
Personnel: Cindy Yingst (Pub./Ed.); D.B. Lewis (Circulation director); Peggy Yingst (Advertising director)
Parent company (for newspapers): Clatsop County Media Services LLC

THE CRESWELL CHRONICLE

Street address 1: 34 W Oregon Ave
Street address city: Creswell
Street address state: OR
Zip/Postal code: 97426-9259
General Phone: (541) 895-2197
General Fax: (541) 895-2361
General/National Adv. E-mail: olson@thecreswellchronicle.com
Primary Website: thecreswellchronicle.com
Year Established: 1965
Avg Paid Circ: 1050

Avg Free Circ: 50
Audit By: Sworn/Estimate/Non-Audited
Audit Date: 10.06.2019
Personnel: Scott Olson (Pub.)
Parent company (for newspapers): SJ Olson Publishing, Inc

THE DOUGLAS COUNTY MAIL

Street address 1: 325 NE 1st Ave
Street address city: Myrtle Creek
Street address state: OR
Zip/Postal code: 97457-9063
General Phone: (541) 863-5233
General Fax: (541) 863-5234
Editorial e-mail: dcmail@dcmail.info
Year Established: 1902
Avg Paid Circ: 2000
Avg Free Circ: 20
Audit By: Sworn/Estimate/Non-Audited
Audit Date: 10.06.2019
Personnel: Robert L. Chaney (Pub./Ed.)
Parent company (for newspapers): Myrtle Tree Press, Inc.

THE HERMISTON HERALD

Street address 1: 333 E Main St
Street address city: Hermiston
Street address state: OR
Zip/Postal code: 97838-1869
General Phone: (541) 567-6457
Editorial e-mail: jmcdowell@eastoregonian.com
Primary Website: hermistonherald.com
Year Established: 1906
Avg Paid Circ: 10000
Avg Free Circ: 156
Audit By: Sworn/Estimate/Non-Audited
Audit Date: 10.06.2019
Personnel: Christopher Rush (Reg. Pub./Revenue Officer); Jade McDowell (Ed.)
Parent company (for newspapers): EO Media Group

THE HILLSBORO TRIBUNE

Street address 1: 2038 Pacific Ave
Street address city: Forest Grove
Street address state: OR
Zip/Postal code: 97116-2357
General Phone: (503) 357-3181
General/National Adv. E-mail: info@hillsborotribune.com
Editorial e-mail: news@hillsborotribune.com
Primary Website: hillsborotribune.com
Year Established: 2012
Avg Paid Circ: 3500
Avg Free Circ: 2500
Audit By: Sworn/Estimate/Non-Audited
Audit Date: 10.06.2019
Personnel: Geoff Pursinger (Editor)
Parent company (for newspapers): Pamplin Media Group

THE LAKE OSWEGO REVIEW

Street address 1: 400 2nd St
Street address city: Lake Oswego
Street address state: OR
Zip/Postal code: 97034-3127
General Phone: (503) 635-8811
General Fax: (503) 635-8817
Advertising Phone: (503) 546-0771
General/National Adv. E-mail: cmoore@commnewspapers.com
Display Adv. E-mail: callsop@commnewspapers.com
Editorial e-mail: gstein@lakeoswegoreview.com
Primary Website: portlandtribune.com/lake-oswego-review-news
Year Established: 1920
Avg Paid Circ: 7600
Audit By: Sworn/Estimate/Non-Audited
Audit Date: 10.06.2019
Personnel: J. Brian Monihan (Pub); Christine Moore (Adv Dir); Charlotte Allsop (Class Sales Mgr.); Gini Kraemer (Circ. Mgr.); Patrick Malee (Ed.)
Parent company (for newspapers): Pamplin Media Group; Pamplin Media Group

THE MADRAS PIONEER

Street address 1: 345 SE 5th St
Street address city: Madras
Street address state: OR
Zip/Postal code: 97741-1501
General Phone: (541) 475-2275
General Fax: (541) 475-3710
General/National Adv. E-mail: tahern@eaglenewspapers.com
Primary Website: madraspioneer.com
Year Established: 1904
Avg Paid Circ: 3300
Avg Free Circ: 125
Audit By: Sworn/Estimate/Non-Audited
Audit Date: 10.06.2019
Personnel: Tony Ahern (Pub.); Susan Matheny (Ed.); Holly Gill (News Ed.); Joy DeHaan (Adv. Dir.); Joey Lantz (Circ. Dir); Becky Johnson (Comp. Supv.)
Parent company (for newspapers): Pamplin Media Group

THE NEW ERA

Street address 1: 1313 Main St
Street address city: Sweet Home
Street address state: OR
Zip/Postal code: 97386-1611
General Phone: (541) 367-2135
General Fax: (541) 367-2137
General/National Adv. E-mail: jessica@gcc-media.com
Display Adv. E-mail: advertising@sweethomenews.com
Editorial e-mail: news@sweethomenews.com
Primary Website: sweethomenews.com
Year Established: 1929
Avg Paid Circ: 2000
Avg Free Circ: 6625
Audit By: Sworn/Estimate/Non-Audited
Audit Date: 10.06.2019
Personnel: Firiel Severns (Advertising); Chris Chapman (Publisher); Miriam Swanson (Adv. Dir)

THE NEWBERG GRAPHIC

Street address 1: 1505 Portland Rd.
Street address 2: Suite 210
Street address city: Newberg
Street address state: OR
Zip/Postal code: 97132-0700
General Phone: (503) 538-2181
General Fax: (503) 538-1632
General/National Adv. E-mail: pbecker@newberggraphic.com
Display Adv. E-mail: rmansfield@pamplinmedia.com
Editorial e-mail: gallen@newberggraphic.com
Primary Website: pamplinmedia.com/newberg-graphic-home
Year Established: 1888
Avg Paid Circ: 5500
Audit By: Sworn/Estimate/Non-Audited
Audit Date: 10.06.2019
Personnel: Allen Herriges (Pub.); Gary Allen (Ed.); Paula Becker (Adv.)
Parent company (for newspapers): Pamplin Media Group; Pamplin Media Group

THE NEWS GUARD

Street address 1: 1818 N E. 21st St.
Street address city: Lincoln City
Street address state: OR
Zip/Postal code: 97367
General Phone: (541) 994-2178
General Fax: (541) 994-7613
General/National Adv. E-mail: newsguardads@countrymedia.net
Display Adv. E-mail: classifieds@thenewsguard.com
Editorial e-mail: newsguardeditor@countrymedia.net
Primary Website: thenewsguard.com
Year Established: 1927
Avg Paid Circ: 6000
Audit By: Sworn/Estimate/Non-Audited
Audit Date: 10.06.2019
Personnel: Max Kirkendall (Mng. Ed.); Frank Perea (Pub.); Nicole Clarke (Adv. Sales); Brian Humphrey (Circ. Mgr.)
Parent company (for newspapers): Country Media Inc.; Country Media, Inc

THE OBSERVER

Street address 1: 1406 5th St
Street address city: La Grande
Street address state: OR
Zip/Postal code: 97850-2402
General Phone: (541) 963-3161
General Fax: (541) 963-7804
General/National Adv. E-mail: kbrogoitti@lagrandeobserver.com
Display Adv. E-mail: kbrogoitti@lagrandeobserver.com
Classified Adv. e-mail: classifieds@lagrandeobserver.com
Editorial e-mail: kbrogoitti@lagrandeobserver.com
Primary Website: lagrandeobserver.com
Mthly Avg Views: 253700
Mthly Avg Unique Visitors: 54500
Year Established: 1896
Avg Paid Circ: 3371
Avg Free Circ: 166
Audit By: CVC
Audit Date: 31.12.2018
Personnel: Karrine Brogoitti (Pub./ Adv. Dir.); Kelli Craft (Circ. Mgr); Frank Everidge (Gen Mgr, Operations)
Parent company (for newspapers): EO Media Group

THE OUTLOOK

Street address 1: 1190 NE Division St
Street address city: Gresham
Street address state: OR
Zip/Postal code: 97030-5727
General Phone: (503) 665-2181
General Fax: (503) 665-2187
General/National Adv. E-mail: todell@theoutlookonline.com
Editorial e-mail: todell@theoutlookonline.com
Primary Website: portlandtribune.com/gresham-outlook-news/
Year Established: 1911
Audit By: Sworn/Estimate/Non-Audited
Audit Date: 10.06.2019
Personnel: J. Brian Monihan (VP); Tiffaney O'Dell (Ed.); Kim Stephens (Circ. Mgr)
Parent company (for newspapers): Pamplin Media Group

THE PENDLETON RECORD

Street address 1: 809 SE Court
Street address 2: PO Box 69
Street address city: Pendleton
Street address state: OR
Zip/Postal code: 97801-0069
General Phone: (541) 276-2853
General/National Adv. E-mail: penrecor@uci.net
Year Established: 1911
Avg Paid Circ: 1000
Audit By: Sworn/Estimate/Non-Audited
Audit Date: 10.06.2019
Personnel: Marguerite Maznaritz (Adv. Mgr.); Sam Westover (Ed.)

THE PHILOMATH EXPRESS

Street address 1: 1835 NW Circle Blvd
Street address city: Corvallis
Street address state: OR
Zip/Postal code: 97330-1310
General Phone: (541) 753-2641
Advertising Phone: (541) 758-9581
Audit By: Sworn/Estimate/Non-Audited
Audit Date: 10.06.2019
Personnel: Mike McInally (Gen. Mngr.); Doug Byers (Controller); Brad Fuqua (Ed.)
Parent company (for newspapers): Dispatch-Argus

THE POLK COUNTY ITEMIZER-OBSERVER

Street address 1: 147 SE Court St
Street address city: Dallas
Street address state: OR
Zip/Postal code: 97338-3158
General Phone: (503) 623-2373
General Fax: (503) 623-2395
Primary Website: polkio.com
Year Established: 1875
Avg Paid Circ: 4800
Avg Free Circ: 8500
Audit By: Sworn/Estimate/Non-Audited
Audit Date: 10.06.2019
Personnel: Nancy Adams (Pub); Kurt Holland (Ed.); Heidi Leppin (Adv. Leader)
Parent company (for newspapers): Eagle Newspapers, Inc.

THE PORTLAND TRIBUNE

Street address 1: 6605 SE Lake Rd
Street address city: Portland
Street address state: OR
Zip/Postal code: 97222-2161
General Phone: (503) 226-6397
General Fax: (503) 620-3433
Advertising Phone: (503) 546-0771
Editorial Phone: (503) 546-5167
General/National Adv. E-mail: cmoore@commnewspapers.com
Display Adv. E-mail: dbeauchamp@pamplinmedia.com
Editorial e-mail: jschrag@pamplinmedia.com
Primary Website: portlandtribune.com
Year Established: 2001
Audit By: Sworn/Estimate/Non-Audited
Audit Date: 10.06.2019
Personnel: Mark Garber (Pres.); John Schrag (Ed.); Christine Moore (Adv. Dir.); Kim Stephens (Circ. Mgr)
Parent company (for newspapers): Pamplin Media Group; Pamplin Media Group

THE REDMOND SPOKESMAN

Street address 1: 226 NW 6th St
Street address city: Redmond
Street address state: OR
Zip/Postal code: 97756-1718
General Phone: (541) 548-2184
General Fax: (541) 548-3203
General/National Adv. E-mail: adv@redmondspokesman.com
Display Adv. E-mail: classified@redmonspokesman.com
Editorial e-mail: news@redmondspokesman.com
Primary Website: redmondspokesman.com
Year Established: 1911
Avg Paid Circ: 1962
Avg Free Circ: 725
Audit By: CVC
Audit Date: 31.12.2018
Personnel: Betsy McCool (Pub.); Amy Husted (Circ. Mgr.); Denise Duval (Adv. Mgr.); Geoff Folsom (Senior Reporter); Colby Brown (Reporter); Debbie Coffman (Adv.); Kim Fowler (Circ.)
Parent company (for newspapers): EO Media Group

THE SOUTH COUNTY SPOTLIGHT

Street address 1: 33548 Edward Ln
Street address 2: Ste 110
Street address city: Scappoose
Street address state: OR
Zip/Postal code: 97056-3838
General Phone: (503) 543-6387
General Fax: (503) 543-6380
General/National Adv. E-mail: dswan@spotlightnews.net
Editorial e-mail: news@spotlightnews.net
Primary Website: spotlightnews.net
Year Established: 1961
Avg Paid Circ: 4500
Audit By: Sworn/Estimate/Non-Audited
Audit Date: 10.06.2019
Personnel: Darryl Swan (Pub.); Kim Stephens (Circ. Mgr.); Chelsea Tull (Graphic Designer); Nicole Thill (News Reporter); Courtney Vaughn (News Reporter); Rose Zimnicki (Office Coord); Jake McNeal (Sports Ed); Dawn Britton (Advt Sales)
Parent company (for newspapers): Pamplin Media Group; Pamplin Media Group

THE SOUTHEAST EXAMINER

Street address 1: PO Box 33663
Street address city: Portland
Street address state: OR
Zip/Postal code: 97292-3663
General Phone: (503) 254-7550
General Fax: (503) 254-7545
Editorial e-mail: examiner@inseportland.com
Primary Website: southeastexaminer.com
Year Established: 1988
Avg Free Circ: 25975
Audit By: Sworn/Estimate/Non-Audited
Audit Date: 10.06.2019
Personnel: Nancy Tannler (Pub./Circ. Mgr.)

THE TIMES

Street address 1: 343 N MAIN ST
Street address city: Brownsville
Street address state: OR
Zip/Postal code: 97327
General Phone: (541) 466-5311

General Fax: (541) 466-5312
General/National Adv. E-mail: thetimes@peak.org
Editorial e-mail: thetimes089@centurytel.net
Primary Website: thebrownsvilletimes.com
Year Established: 1888
Avg Paid Circ: 1200
Avg Free Circ: 62
Audit By: Sworn/Estimate/Non-Audited
Audit Date: 10.06.2019
Personnel: Don Ware (Ed.); Vance Parrish (Owner/Pub)

THE TIMES (TIGARD/TUALATIN TIMES)

Street address 1: 6605 SE Lake Rd
Street address city: Portland
Street address state: OR
Zip/Postal code: 97222-2161
General Phone: (503) 546-0771
General Fax: (503) 620-3433
Advertising Phone: (503) 546-0771
Editorial Phone: (503) 546-0771
General/National Adv. E-mail: cmoore@pamplinmedia.com
Display Adv. E-mail: rmanffield@pamplinmedia.com
Editorial e-mail: dhaynes@pamplinmedia.com
Primary Website: tigardtimes.com
Year Established: 1956
Avg Paid Circ: 7000
Audit By: Sworn/Estimate/Non-Audited
Audit Date: 10.06.2019
Personnel: Christine Moore (Adv. Dir); Kim Stephens (Circ. Mgr.); Dana Haynes (Ed.)
Parent company (for newspapers): Pamplin Media Group

THE TIMES-JOURNAL

Street address 1: 319 S Main St
Street address city: Condon
Street address state: OR
Zip/Postal code: 97823-7647
General Phone: (541) 384-2421
General Fax: (541) 384-2411
General/National Adv. E-mail: timesjournal1886@gmail.com
Year Established: 1886
Avg Paid Circ: 1400
Avg Free Circ: 40
Audit By: Sworn/Estimate/Non-Audited
Audit Date: 10.06.2019
Personnel: Janet L. Stinchfield (Pub.); McLaren E. Stinchfield (Ed.); Cody Bettencourt (Class. Mgr)
Parent company (for newspapers): Macro Graphics of Condon, LLC

THE UMPQUA POST

Street address 1: 350 Commercial Ave
Street address city: Coos Bay
Street address state: OR
Zip/Postal code: 97420-2269
General Phone: (541) 271-7474
General Fax: (541) 271-2821
Advertising Phone: (541) 271-7474
Editorial Phone: (541) 269-1222
General/National Adv. E-mail: amanda.johnson@theworldlink.com
Display Adv. E-mail: umpquapost@theworldlink.com
Editorial e-mail: shelby.case@theworldlink.com
Primary Website: theUmpquapost.com
Year Established: 1996
Avg Paid Circ: 750
Audit By: Sworn/Estimate/Non-Audited
Audit Date: 10.06.2019
Parent company (for newspapers): Southwestern Oregon Publishing Company

THE WORLD

Street address 1: 350 Commercial Ave
Street address city: Coos Bay
Street address state: OR
Zip/Postal code: 97420
General Phone: (541) 269-1222
General Fax: (541) 267-0294
Primary Website: theworldlink.com
Year Established: 1889
Avg Paid Circ: 2100
Audit By: Sworn/Estimate/Non-Audited
Audit Date: 10.06.2019
Personnel: Jeff Precourt; Amanda Johnson (Circ. Mgr.); Ron Jackimowicz (Ed)

TRI-COUNTY NEWS

Street address 1: 225 W 6th Ave
Street address city: Junction City
Street address state: OR
Zip/Postal code: 97448-1605
General Phone: (541) 234-2111
Editorial Phone: (541) 234-2111
General/National Adv. E-mail: ads@tctrib.com
Editorial e-mail: news@tctrib.com
Primary Website: yourtribunenews.com
Year Established: 1977
Avg Paid Circ: 2000
Audit By: Sworn/Estimate/Non-Audited
Audit Date: 10.06.2019
Personnel: Steve Rowland (Pub); Gini Barmlett (Ed); Sayde Moser (Mng. Editor); Kyle Krenik (Bus. Mgr.)

UPPER ROGUE INDEPENDENT

Street address 1: 11136 Highway 62
Street address city: Eagle Point
Street address state: OR
Zip/Postal code: 97524-9779
General Phone: (541) 826-7700
General Fax: (541) 826-1340
Editorial e-mail: editor@urindependent.com
Primary Website: urindependent.com
Year Established: 1976
Avg Paid Circ: 2000
Avg Free Circ: 0
Audit By: Sworn/Estimate/Non-Audited
Audit Date: 10.06.2019
Personnel: Ralph McKechnie (Owner/Ed)

VALLEY HERALD

Street address 1: 408 N Main St
Street address city: Milton Freewater
Street address state: OR
Zip/Postal code: 97862-1724
General Phone: (541) 938-6688
General Fax: (541) 938-6689
Editorial e-mail: s.widmer.valleyherald@gmail.com
Primary Website: mfvalleyherald.net
Year Established: 2001
Avg Paid Circ: 2500
Audit By: Sworn/Estimate/Non-Audited
Audit Date: 10.06.2019
Personnel: Melanie Hall (Circ. Mgr); Sherrie Widmer (Pub)

WALLOWA COUNTY CHIEFTAIN

Street address 1: 209 NW 1st St
Street address city: Enterprise
Street address state: OR
Zip/Postal code: 97828-1003
General Phone: (541) 426-4567
General Fax: (541) 426-3921
General/National Adv. E-mail: jsackett@wallowa.com
Display Adv. E-mail: cjenkins@wallowa.com
Editorial e-mail: editor@wallowa.com
Primary Website: wallowa.com
Year Established: 1884
Avg Paid Circ: 4000
Audit By: Sworn/Estimate/Non-Audited
Audit Date: 10.06.2019
Personnel: Marissa Williams (Pub.); Roberth Ruth (Ed.); Jim Sackett (Adv Sales); Cheryl Jenkkins (Class/ Circ. Mgr.)
Parent company (for newspapers): East Oregonian

WEST LINN TIDINGS

Street address 1: 400 2nd St
Street address city: Lake Oswego
Street address state: OR
Zip/Postal code: 97034-3127
General Phone: (503) 635-8811
General Fax: (503) 635-8817
Advertising Phone: (503) 684-0360
General/National Adv. E-mail: cmoore@commnewspapers.com
Display Adv. E-mail: bmonihan@westlinntidings.com
Editorial e-mail: gstein@lakeoswegoreview.com
Primary Website: westlinntidings.com
Year Established: 1981
Avg Paid Circ: 3750
Audit By: Sworn/Estimate/Non-Audited
Audit Date: 10.06.2019
Personnel: J. Brian Monihan (Pub); Gary Stein (Ed); Christine Moore (Adv. Dir.)
Parent company (for newspapers): Pamplin Media Group

WILSONVILLE SPOKESMAN

Street address 1: 400 2nd St
Street address city: Lake Oswego
Street address state: OR
Zip/Postal code: 97034-3127
General Phone: (503) 682-3935
General Fax: (503) 682-6265
Advertising Phone: (503) 684-0360
General/National Adv. E-mail: cmoore@commnewspapers.com
Editorial e-mail: gstein@lakeoswegoreview.com
Primary Website: wilsonvillespokesman.com
Year Established: 1985
Avg Paid Circ: 3350
Avg Free Circ: 2500
Audit By: Sworn/Estimate/Non-Audited
Audit Date: 10.06.2019
Personnel: J. Brian Monihan (Pub.); Christine Moore (Adv. Dir.); Gary Stein (Ed)
Parent company (for newspapers): Pamplin Media Group

WOODBURN INDEPENDENT

Street address 1: 650 N 1st St
Street address city: Woodburn
Street address state: OR
Zip/Postal code: 97071-4002
General Phone: (503) 981-3441
General Fax: (503) 981-1253
General/National Adv. E-mail: Klang@woodburnindependent.com
Display Adv. E-mail: Svetter@woodburnindependent.com
Editorial e-mail: Phawkins@woodburnindependent.com
Primary Website: woodburnindependent.com
Year Established: 1888
Avg Paid Circ: 4692
Avg Free Circ: 163
Audit By: Sworn/Estimate/Non-Audited
Audit Date: 10.06.2019
Personnel: Al Herriges (Pub.); Phil Hawkins (Ed.); Susan Vetter (Adv./ Sales Rep.); Kim Stephens (Circ. Mgr.)
Parent company (for newspapers): Pamplin Media Group

PENNSYLVANIA

ABINGTON JOURNAL

Street address 1: 211 S State St
Street address city: Clarks Summit
Street address state: PA
Zip/Postal code: 18411-1546
General Phone: (570) 587-1148
General Fax: (570) 586-3980
Advertising Phone: (570) 829-7293
Advertising Fax: (570) 829-2002
Editorial Phone: (570) 585-1604
Editorial Fax: (570) 829-5537
General/National Adv. E-mail: aspina@civitasmedia.com
Display Adv. E-mail: lbyrnes@civitasmedia.com
Editorial e-mail: dmartin@timesleader.com
Primary Website: theabingtonjournal.com
Year Established: 1947
Avg Paid Circ: 494
Avg Free Circ: 1
Audit By: Sworn/Estimate/Non-Audited
Audit Date: 10.06.2019
Personnel: Dotty Martin (Ed.); Anthony Spina (Media Dir.); Mike Murray (Pub.)

ADVANCE OF BUCKS COUNTY

Street address 1: 307 Derstine Ave
Street address city: Lansdale
Street address state: PA
Zip/Postal code: 19446-3532
General Phone: (215) 542-0200
General Fax: (215) 648-1120
Advertising Phone: (215) 785-5960 ext. 113
Advertising Fax: (215) 785-0283
Editorial Phone: (215) 542-0200 ext. 157
General/National Adv. E-mail: tdarmiento@buckslocalnews.com
Display Adv. E-mail: bucksclass@buckslocalnews.com
Editorial e-mail: advance@buckslocalnews.com
Primary Website: buckslocalnews.com
Avg Paid Circ: 2400
Avg Free Circ: 18
Audit By: Sworn/Estimate/Non-Audited
Audit Date: 10.06.2019
Personnel: Bill Murray (Pub.); Tammy Darmiento (Adv. Mgr.); Jeff Werner (Ed.)
Parent company (for newspapers): Digital First Media

ALLIED NEWS

Street address 1: 201 Erie St
Street address 2: Ste A
Street address city: Grove City
Street address state: PA
Zip/Postal code: 16127-1659
General Phone: (724) 458-5010
General Fax: (724) 458-1609
Advertising Phone: (724) 458-5010
Advertising Fax: (724) 458-1609
Editorial Phone: (724) 458-5010
Editorial Fax: (724) 458-1609
General/National Adv. E-mail: alliednews@gmail.com
Display Adv. E-mail: vkoper@sharonherald.com
Editorial e-mail: alliednewspaper@gmail.com
Primary Website: alliednews.com
Year Established: 1872
Avg Paid Circ: 1929
Avg Free Circ: 7665
Audit By: Sworn/Estimate/Non-Audited
Audit Date: 10.06.2019
Personnel: Sharon Sorg (Pub)
Parent company (for newspapers): CNHI, LLC

AMBLER GAZETTE

Street address 1: 307 Derstine Ave
Street address city: Lansdale
Street address state: PA
Zip/Postal code: 19446
General Phone: (215) 542-0200
General Fax: (215) 648-1120
Advertising Phone: (215) 542-0200
Editorial Phone: (215) 542-0200
General/National Adv. E-mail: bdouglas@21st-centurymedia.com
Display Adv. E-mail: classified@montgomerynews.com
Editorial e-mail: editorial@montgomerynews.com
Primary Website: montgomerynews.com
Year Established: 1957
Avg Paid Circ: 8113
Avg Free Circ: 11581
Audit By: Sworn/Estimate/Non-Audited
Audit Date: 10.06.2019
Personnel: Thomas Celona (Exec. Ed.); Beth Douglas (Adv. Mgr.); Joe Flenders (Circ. Mgr.)
Parent company (for newspapers): Montgomery Newspapers; MediaNews Group; Digital First Media

AVON GROVE SUN

Street address 1: 250 N Bradford Ave
Street address city: West Chester
Street address state: PA
Zip/Postal code: 19382-1912
General Phone: (610) 696-1775
General/National Adv. E-mail: bdouglas@21st-centurymedia.com
Display Adv. E-mail: bdouglas@21st-centurymedia.com
Editorial e-mail: fmaye@21st-centurymedia.com
Primary Website: avongrovesun.com
Avg Paid Circ: 2428
Audit By: Sworn/Estimate/Non-Audited
Audit Date: 10.06.2019
Personnel: Edward Condra (Pub.); Fran Maye (News Ed.); Beth Douglas (Adv.); Joseph Forst (Circ. Dir.)

BEDFORD GAZETTE

Street address 1: 424 W Penn St
Street address city: Bedford
Street address state: PA
Zip/Postal code: 15522-1230
General Phone: (814) 623-1151

General Fax: (814) 623-5055
General/National Adv. E-mail: sgrowden@bedfordgazette.com
Display Adv. E-mail: classifieds@bedfordgazette.com
Editorial e-mail: ecoyle@bedfordgazette.com
Primary Website: bedfordgazette.com
Year Established: 1805
Avg Paid Circ: 200
Audit By: Sworn/Estimate/Non-Audited
Audit Date: 10.06.2019
Personnel: Joseph Beegle (Pub.); Rebecca Smith (Bus. Mgr.); Elizabeth Coyle (Ed.); Susan May (Circ.)
Parent company (for newspapers): Bedford Gazette LLC

BERKSMONT NEWS

Street address 1: 390 Eagleview Blvd.
Street address city: Exton
Street address state: PA
Zip/Postal code: 19341
General Phone: (610) 970-3218
General Fax: (610) 369-0233
Editorial Phone: (610) 970-3218 ext. 625
General/National Adv. E-mail: denice@berksmontnews.com
Display Adv. E-mail: wordad@berksmontnews.com
Editorial e-mail: ethiel@berksmontnews.com
Primary Website: berksmontnews.com
Year Established: 1885
Avg Paid Circ: 395
Avg Free Circ: 5500
Audit By: Sworn/Estimate/Non-Audited
Audit Date: 10.06.2019
Personnel: Patti Paul (Gen. Mgr.); Steve Batten (Sales); Lisa Mitchell (Mng. Ed.)
Parent company (for newspapers): Berks-Mont Newspapers, Inc.; Digital First Media

BETHLEHEM PRESS

Street address 1: 1633 N 26th St
Street address 2: Ste 102
Street address city: Allentown
Street address state: PA
Zip/Postal code: 18104-1805
General Phone: (610) 625-2121
General Fax: (610) 625-2126
Advertising Phone: (610) 740-0944
Advertising Fax: (610) 740-9908
Editorial Phone: (610) 740-0944
Editorial Fax: (610) 740-0947
General/National Adv. E-mail: mstocking@tnonline.com
Editorial e-mail: gtaylor@tnonline.com
Primary Website: bethlehem.thelehighvalleypress.com
Year Established: 2005
Avg Paid Circ: 5046
Audit By: Sworn/Estimate/Non-Audited
Audit Date: 10.06.2019
Personnel: Peg Stocking (Adv. Mgr.); George Taylor (Ed.)
Parent company (for newspapers): Times News, LLC

BLAIRSVILLE DISPATCH

Street address 1: 116 E Market St
Street address city: Blairsville
Street address state: PA
Zip/Postal code: 15717-1326
General Phone: (724) 459-6100
General Fax: (724) 459-7366
Editorial Phone: (724) 459-6100 ext. 13
General/National Adv. E-mail: dfellabaum@tribweb.com
Display Adv. E-mail: jpaschl@tribweb.com
Editorial e-mail: jhimler@tribweb.com
Primary Website: tribLIVE.com
Avg Paid Circ: 16500
Avg Free Circ: 1500
Audit By: Sworn/Estimate/Non-Audited
Audit Date: 10.06.2019
Personnel: Jill Paschl (Adv. Mgr.); Jeffrey Himler (Ed.)
Parent company (for newspapers): Sample Media Group

BRADFORD JOURNAL-MINER

Street address 1: 69 Garlock Holw
Street address city: Bradford
Street address state: PA
Zip/Postal code: 16701-3420
General Phone: (814) 465-3468
General Fax: (814) 465-3468
Editorial e-mail: bradfordjournal@bradfordjournalonline.com
Primary Website: bradfordjournal.com
Year Established: 1940
Avg Paid Circ: 5500
Audit By: Sworn/Estimate/Non-Audited
Audit Date: 10.06.2019
Personnel: Grant Nichols (Pub.); Debi Nichols (Ed.)

BRISTOL PILOT

Street address 1: 220 Radcliffe St
Street address 2: St 2
Street address city: Bristol
Street address state: PA
Zip/Postal code: 19007-5014
General Phone: (215) 788-1682
General Fax: (215) 788-6328
Advertising Phone: (215) 542-0200 ext. 153
Editorial Phone: (215) 542-0200 ext. 157
General/National Adv. E-mail: mburns@buckslocalnews.com
Display Adv. E-mail: buckslass@buckslocalnews.com
Editorial e-mail: advance@buckslocalnews.com
Primary Website: bristolpilot.com
Avg Paid Circ: 1197
Avg Free Circ: 5
Audit By: Sworn/Estimate/Non-Audited
Audit Date: 10.06.2019
Personnel: Jeff Werner (Pub.); Tammy Darmiento (Adv. Mgr.); Heather Drill (Ed.)
Parent company (for newspapers): Digital First Media

BUCKS COUNTY HERALD

Street address 1: PO Box 685
Street address 2: 5761 Lower York Road
Street address city: Lahaska
Street address state: PA
Zip/Postal code: 18931-0685
General Phone: (215) 794-1096
General Fax: (215) 794-1109
Advertising Phone: (215) 794-1096
Advertising Fax: (215) 794-1109
Editorial Phone: (215) 794-1096
Editorial Fax: (215) 794-1109
General/National Adv. E-mail: jgwingert@buckscountyherald.com
Display Adv. E-mail: jgwingert@buckscountyherald.com
Classified Adv. e-mail: ken@buckscountyherald.com
Editorial e-mail: jgwingert@buckscountyherald.com
Primary Website: buckscountyherald.com
Year Established: 2002
Avg Free Circ: 25000
Audit By: Sworn/Estimate/Non-Audited
Audit Date: 10.06.2019
Personnel: Bridget Wingert (Ed.); Joseph Wingert (Publisher)

BUCKS LOCAL NEWS

Street address 1: 307 Derstine Ave
Street address city: Lansdale
Street address state: PA
Zip/Postal code: 19446-3532
General Phone: (215)Â 648-1080
General Fax: (215) 648-1120
Advertising Phone: (215) 648-1087
General/National Adv. E-mail: hdrill@montgomerynews.com
Display Adv. E-mail: hdrill@montgomerynews.com
Editorial e-mail: advance@buckslocalnews.com
Primary Website: buckslocalnews.com
Avg Paid Circ: 2400
Avg Free Circ: 18
Audit By: Sworn/Estimate/Non-Audited
Audit Date: 10.06.2019
Personnel: Jeff Werner (Ed.); Thomas Celona (Reg. Ed.); Heather Drill (Adv.)
Parent company (for newspapers): Digital First Media

BUTTERMILK FALLS

Street address 1: 460 Rodi Rd
Street address city: Pittsburgh
Street address state: PA
Zip/Postal code: 15235-4547
General Phone: (412) 871-2345
General Fax: (724) 568-1729
Advertising Phone: (724) 567-5656
General/National Adv. E-mail: jpaschl@tribweb.com
Display Adv. E-mail: mzigarovich@tribweb.com
Editorial e-mail: smcfarland@tribweb.com
Primary Website: http://tribtotalmedia.com/
Avg Free Circ: 16600
Audit By: Sworn/Estimate/Non-Audited
Audit Date: 10.06.2019
Personnel: Susan McFarland (Ed.); Jill Paschl (Adv. Dir.)
Parent company (for newspapers): Trib Total Media, Inc.

CAMERON COUNTY ECHO

Street address 1: 300 S Broad St
Street address 2: Ste 1
Street address city: Emporium
Street address state: PA
Zip/Postal code: 15834-1495
General Phone: (814) 486-3711
General Fax: (814) 486-0990
Editorial e-mail: ccecho@zitomedia.net
Primary Website: cameroncountyecho.net
Avg Paid Circ: 3761
Avg Free Circ: 48
Audit By: Sworn/Estimate/Non-Audited
Audit Date: 10.06.2019
Personnel: David A. Brown (Pub.)

CARBONDALE NEWS

Street address 1: 220 8th St
Street address city: Honesdale
Street address state: PA
Zip/Postal code: 18431-1854
General Phone: (570) 253-3055
General Fax: (570) 253-5387
Advertising Phone: (570) 253-3055 ext. 301
Advertising Fax: (570) 253-5387
Editorial Phone: (570) 253-3055 ext: 329
Editorial Fax: (570) 253-5387
General/National Adv. E-mail: mfleece@wayneindependent.com
Display Adv. E-mail: pjordan@wayneindependent.com
Editorial e-mail: mleet@wayneindependent.com
Primary Website: thecarbondalenews.com
Year Established: 1851
Avg Paid Circ: 1315
Audit By: Sworn/Estimate/Non-Audited
Audit Date: 10.06.2019
Personnel: Michelle Fleece (Pres./Pub/Adv. Sales Mgr.); Melissa Lee (Managing Editor); Marcia Barrera (Circulation Coordinator)
Parent company (for newspapers): CherryRoad Media

CATASAUQUA PRESS

Street address 1: 1633 N 26th St
Street address city: Allentown
Street address state: PA
Zip/Postal code: 18104-1805
General Phone: (610) 740-0944
General Fax: (610) 740-0947
Advertising Phone: (610) 740-0944
Advertising Fax: (610) 740-9908
Editorial Phone: (610) 740-0944
Editorial Fax: (610) 740-0947
General/National Adv. E-mail: mstocking@tnonline.com
Display Adv. E-mail: mstocking@tnonline.com
Editorial e-mail: lwojciechowski@tnonline.com
Primary Website: catasauqua.thelehighvalleypress.com
Year Established: 2003
Avg Paid Circ: 1380
Audit By: Sworn/Estimate/Non-Audited
Audit Date: 10.06.2019
Personnel: Peg Stocking (Adv. Mgr.); Scott Masenheimer (Gen. Mgr.); Linda Wojciechowski (Assoc. Ed.)
Parent company (for newspapers): Times News, LLC

CENTRAL PENN BUSINESS JOURNAL

Street address 1: 1500 Paxton St
Street address 2: Fl 3
Street address city: Harrisburg
Street address state: PA
Zip/Postal code: 17104-2626
General Phone: (717) 236-4300
General Fax: (717) 236-6803
General/National Adv. E-mail: mengle@cpbj.com
Display Adv. E-mail: mengle@cpbj.com
Editorial e-mail: jberg@cpbj.com
Primary Website: cpbj.com
Year Established: 1984
Avg Paid Circ: 3340
Avg Free Circ: 4561
Audit By: CVC
Audit Date: 09.12.2018
Personnel: Suzanne Fischer-Huettner (Group Pub.); Cathy Hirko (Assoc. Pub.); Maria Kelly (Bus. Mgr.); Joel Berg (Advisor); Michelle Engle (Sr. Adv. Acct. Exec.); Tracy Bumba (Mgr.)
Parent company (for newspapers): BridgeTower Media

CHESTER COUNTY COMMUNITY COURIER

Street address 1: 1100 Corporate BLvd
Street address city: Lancaster
Street address state: PA
Zip/Postal code: 17601
General Phone: 717-653-1833
General Fax: (717) 492-2584
Advertising Phone: 717-278-1394
General/National Adv. E-mail: jhemperly@engleonline.com
Display Adv. E-mail: jhemperly@engleonline.com
Editorial e-mail: news@engleonline.com
Primary Website: www.townlively.com
Mthly Avg Views: 16500
Mthly Avg Unique Visitors: 14350
Year Established: 1988
Avg Paid Circ: 0
Avg Free Circ: 21132
Audit By: CVC
Audit Date: 31.03.2023
Personnel: Mark Malloy (Circ. Mgr.); Jeremy Engle (VP Operations); John Hemperly
Parent company (for newspapers): Engle Printing & Publishing Co., Inc.

CHESTER COUNTY PRESS

Street address 1: 144 S Jennersville Rd
Street address city: West Grove
Street address state: PA
Zip/Postal code: 19390-9430
General Phone: (610) 869-5533
General Fax: (610) 869-9628
General/National Adv. E-mail: info@chestercounty.com
Display Adv. E-mail: adsales@chestercounty.com
Editorial e-mail: editor@chestercounty.com
Primary Website: chestercounty.com
Year Established: 1866
Avg Paid Circ: 13125
Avg Free Circ: 1441
Audit By: Sworn/Estimate/Non-Audited
Audit Date: 10.06.2019
Personnel: Randall S. Lieberman (Pub.); Alan Turns (Adv. Mgr.); Steve Hoffman (Ed.)
Parent company (for newspapers): Ad Pro Inc.

CHESTNUT HILL LOCAL

Street address 1: 8434 Germantown Ave
Street address 2: Ste 1
Street address city: Philadelphia
Street address state: PA
Zip/Postal code: 19118-3386
General Phone: (215) 248-8800
General Fax: (215) 248-8814
General/National Adv. E-mail: sonia@chestnuthilllocal.com
Display Adv. E-mail: classifieds@chestnuthilllocal.com
Editorial e-mail: pete@chestnuthilllocal.com
Primary Website: chestnuthilllocal.com
Mthly Avg Views: 130070
Mthly Avg Unique Visitors: 50000
Year Established: 1958
Avg Paid Circ: 6000
Avg Free Circ: 300
Audit By: Sworn/Estimate/Non-Audited
Audit Date: 10.06.2019
Personnel: Larry Hochberger (Assc. Pub.); Peter Mazzaccaro (Ed.); Sonia Leones (Adv. Mgr.); Cheryl Massaro (Circ. Mgr.)

CLARION NEWS

Street address 1: 860 S 5th Ave
Street address 2: Ste 4
Street address city: Clarion
Street address state: PA

Zip/Postal code: 16214-8601
General Phone: (814) 226-7000
General Fax: (814) 226-7518
General/National Adv. E-mail: clarionnews.circulation@gmail.com
Display Adv. E-mail: cnclassifieds@gmail.com
Editorial e-mail: rsherman.theclarionnews@gmail.com
Primary Website: theclarionnews.com
Year Established: 1840
Avg Paid Circ: 7000
Avg Free Circ: 64
Audit By: Sworn/Estimate/Non-Audited
Audit Date: 10.06.2019
Personnel: Patrick C. Boyle (Pub.); Rodney Sherman (Ed.); Mary Louise Loque (Adv. Mgr.); Jeff McLaughlin (Circ. Mgr.)

COUNTY PRESS

Street address 1: 639 S Chester Rd
Street address city: Swarthmore
Street address state: PA
Zip/Postal code: 19081-2315
General Phone: (610) 583-4432
General Fax: (610) 583-0503
Advertising Phone: (610) 583-4432 ext. 116
Editorial Phone: (610) 583-4432 ext. 120
General/National Adv. E-mail: rcrowe@21st-centurymedia.com
Display Adv. E-mail: classified@delconewsnetwork.com
Editorial e-mail: cparker@delconewsnetwork.com
Primary Website: delconewsnetwork.com
Year Established: 1931
Avg Paid Circ: 4375
Avg Free Circ: 450
Audit By: Sworn/Estimate/Non-Audited
Audit Date: 10.06.2019
Personnel: Richard L. Crowe (Pub./Adv. Dir.); Peg DeGrassa (Ed)
Parent company (for newspapers): Digital First Media; 21st Century Media

COURIER NEWS WEEKLY

Street address 1: 70 Souderton Hatfield Pike
Street address 2: Ste 250
Street address city: Souderton
Street address state: PA
Zip/Postal code: 18964-1939
General Phone: (267) 663-6300
General Fax: (215) 799-2226
General/National Adv. E-mail: slapp@buxmontmedia.com
Display Adv. E-mail: classifieds@buxmontmedia.com
Editorial e-mail: editorial@buxmontmedia.com
Primary Website: buxmontmedia.com
Year Established: 1947
Avg Paid Circ: 10
Avg Free Circ: 48656
Audit By: Sworn/Estimate/Non-Audited
Audit Date: 10.06.2019
Personnel: Susan Lapp (Pub.); Thomas O'Donnell (Gen. Mgr.)
Parent company (for newspapers): Buxmont Media, LLC

CRANBERRY JOURNAL

Street address 1: 535 Keystone Dr
Street address city: Warrendale
Street address state: PA
Zip/Postal code: 15086-7538
General Phone: (724) 772-8742
General Fax: (724) 779-6911
Advertising Phone: (412) 838-5131
General/National Adv. E-mail: bdawson@tribweb.com
Display Adv. E-mail: dsciotto@tribweb.com
Editorial e-mail: kpalmiero@tribweb.com
Primary Website: triblive.com/local/cranberry
Avg Paid Circ: 52
Avg Free Circ: 16295
Audit By: Sworn/Estimate/Non-Audited
Audit Date: 10.06.2019
Personnel: Jerry DeFlitch (Mng. Ed.); Susan K. McFarland (Exec. Ed.)
Parent company (for newspapers): Trib Total Media, Inc.

DILLSBURG BANNER

Street address 1: 31 S Baltimore St
Street address city: Dillsburg
Street address state: PA
Zip/Postal code: 17019-1228
General Phone: (717) 432-3456
General Fax: (717) 432-1518
General/National Adv. E-mail: sara@dillsburgbanner.net
Editorial e-mail: dillsburgbanner@dillsburgbanner.net
Primary Website: dillsburgbanner.net
Year Established: 1987
Avg Paid Circ: 3900
Audit By: Sworn/Estimate/Non-Audited
Audit Date: 10.06.2019
Personnel: Marie Chomicki (Pres./Pub./Ed.)

DUNCANNON RECORD

Street address 1: 51 Church St
Street address city: New Bloomfield
Street address state: PA
Zip/Postal code: 17068-9683
General Phone: (717) 582-4305
General Fax: (717) 582-7933
General/National Adv. E-mail: advertising@perrycountytimes.com
Display Adv. E-mail: advertising@perrycountytimes.com
Editorial e-mail: editor@perrycountytimes.com
Primary Website: pennlive.com/perry-county-times
Avg Paid Circ: 1549
Avg Free Circ: 18
Audit By: Sworn/Estimate/Non-Audited
Audit Date: 10.06.2019
Personnel: Curt Dreibelbis (Pub.); George Roche (Adv. Mgr.); Wade Fowler (Ed. Consult.); Gary Thomas (Ed.); Jennifer Hare (Circ. Dir.)
Parent company (for newspapers): Advance Publications, Inc.

EAST PENN PRESS

Street address 1: 1633 N 26th St
Street address 2: Ste 102
Street address city: Allentown
Street address state: PA
Zip/Postal code: 18104-1805
General Phone: (610) 740-0944
General Fax: (610) 740-9908
Editorial Fax: (610) 740-0947
General/National Adv. E-mail: mstocking@tnonline.com
Editorial e-mail: dgalbraith@tnonline.com
Primary Website: http://eastpenn.thelehighvalleypress.com
Year Established: 1959
Avg Paid Circ: 5159
Audit By: Sworn/Estimate/Non-Audited
Audit Date: 10.06.2019
Personnel: Debra Galbraith (Ed.); Peg Stocking (Adv. Mgr.)
Parent company (for newspapers): Times News, LLC

ENGLE - COLUMBIA / WRIGHTSVILLE MERCHANDISER

Street address 1: PO Box 500
Street address city: Mount Joy
Street address state: PA
Zip/Postal code: 17552
General Phone: (717) 653-1833
General/National Adv. E-mail: jhemperly@engleonline.com
Display Adv. E-mail: jhemperly@engleonline.com
Editorial e-mail: newsdept@engleonline.com
Primary Website: www.townlively.com
Mthly Avg Views: 16500
Mthly Avg Unique Visitors: 14350
Year Established: 1959
Avg Paid Circ: 0
Avg Free Circ: 12764
Audit By: CVC
Audit Date: 31.03.2023
Personnel: Charles A. Engle (CEO/Pres./Pub.); John Hemperly (Operations Manager); Jeremy Engle (Prod. Mgr.); Mark Malloy (Circ. Mgr.)
Parent company (for newspapers): Engle Printing & Publishing Co., Inc.

ENGLE - CONESTOGA VALLEY / PEQUEA VALLEY PENNY SAVER

Street address 1: PO Box 500
Street address city: Mount Joy
Street address state: PA
Zip/Postal code: 17552
General Phone: (717) 653-1833
General/National Adv. E-mail: jhemperly@engleonline.com
Display Adv. E-mail: jhemperly@engleonline.com
Editorial e-mail: newsdept@engleonline.com
Primary Website: www.townlively.com
Mthly Avg Views: 16500
Mthly Avg Unique Visitors: 14350
Year Established: 1959
Avg Paid Circ: 0
Avg Free Circ: 20672
Audit By: CVC
Audit Date: 31.03.2023
Personnel: Charles A. Engle (CEO/Pres./Pub.); John Hemperly (OPerations Manager); Jeremy Engle (Prod. Mgr.); Mark Malloy (Circ. Mgr.)
Parent company (for newspapers): Engle Printing & Publishing Co., Inc.

ENGLE - DONEGAL MERCHANDISER

Street address 1: 1100 Corporate Blvd
Street address city: Lancaster
Street address state: PA
Zip/Postal code: 17601
General Phone: (717) 492-2514
Advertising Phone: (717) 492-2514
Editorial Phone: 717-492-2544
General/National Adv. E-mail: jhemperly@engleonline.com
Display Adv. E-mail: jhemperly@engleonline.com
Classified Adv. e-mail: classifieds@engleonlie.com
Editorial e-mail: news@engleonline.com
Primary Website: www.engleonline.com
Year Established: 1954
Avg Paid Circ: 0
Avg Free Circ: 9780
Audit By: CVC
Audit Date: 30.03.2021
Personnel: Jocelyn Engle (Publisher); John Hemperly (Operations Manager); Mark Malloy (Circ.); Jeremy Engle (Prod.)
Parent company (for newspapers): Engle Printing & Publishing Co., Inc.

ENGLE - ELIZABETHTOWN / MOUNT JOY MERCHANDISER

Street address 1: PO Box 500
Street address city: Mount Joy
Street address state: PA
Zip/Postal code: 17552
General Phone: (717) 653-1833
Advertising Phone: 717-278-1394
General/National Adv. E-mail: jhemperly@engleonline.com
Display Adv. E-mail: jhemperly@engleonline.com
Editorial e-mail: newsdept@engleonline.com
Primary Website: www.townlively.com
Mthly Avg Views: 16500
Mthly Avg Unique Visitors: 14350
Year Established: 1959
Avg Paid Circ: 0
Avg Free Circ: 23033
Audit By: CVC
Audit Date: 31.03.2023
Personnel: Charles A. Engle (CEO/Pres./Pub.); John Hemperly (Operations Manager); Jeremy Engle (Prod. Mgr.); Mark Malloy (Circ. Mgr.); Jocelyn Engle; Greg March (Sales Manager)
Parent company (for newspapers): Engle Printing & Publishing Co., Inc.

ENGLE - GARDEN SPOT PENNYSAVER

Street address 1: 1425 W Main St
Street address city: Mount Joy
Street address state: PA
Zip/Postal code: 17552
General Phone: 717-653-1833
Advertising Phone: 717-492-2514
Editorial Phone: 717-492-2544
General/National Adv. E-mail: jhemperly@engleonline.com
Display Adv. E-mail: jhemperly@engleonline.com
Classified Adv. e-mail: classifieds@engleonline.com
Editorial e-mail: news@engleonline.com
Primary Website: engleonline.com
Year Established: 2014
Avg Paid Circ: 0
Avg Free Circ: 11137
Audit By: CVC
Audit Date: 30.03.2021
Personnel: John Hemperly (Operations Manager); Jeremy Engle (Prod.); Jocelyn Engle (Publisher); Mark Malloy (Circ.)
Parent company (for newspapers): Engle Printing & Publishing Co., Inc.

ENGLE - HEMPFIELD / MOUNTVILLE MERCHANDISER

Street address 1: PO Box 500
Street address city: Mount Joy
Street address state: PA
Zip/Postal code: 17552
General Phone: (717) 653-1833
Advertising Phone: 717-278-1394
General/National Adv. E-mail: jhemperly@engleonline.com
Display Adv. E-mail: jhemperly@engleonline.com
Editorial e-mail: newsdept@engleonline.com
Primary Website: www.townlively.com
Mthly Avg Views: 16500
Mthly Avg Unique Visitors: 14350
Year Established: 1959
Avg Paid Circ: 0
Avg Free Circ: 20373
Audit By: CVC
Audit Date: 31.03.2023
Personnel: Charles A. Engle (CEO/Pres./Pub.); John Hemperly (Operations manager); Mark Malloy (Circ. Mgr.); Jocelyn Engle; Greg March (Sales Manager); Jeremy Engle (Prod. Mgr.)
Parent company (for newspapers): Engle Printing & Publishing Co., Inc.

ENGLE - HERSHEY / HUMMELSTOWN /MIDDLETOWN COMMUNITY COURIER

Street address 1: PO Box 500
Street address city: Mount Joy
Street address state: PA
Zip/Postal code: 17552
General Phone: (717) 653-1833
Advertising Phone: 717-278-1394
General/National Adv. E-mail: jhemperly@engleonline.com
Display Adv. E-mail: jhemperly@engleonline.com
Editorial e-mail: jrengle@engleonline.com
Primary Website: www.townlively.com
Mthly Avg Views: 16500
Mthly Avg Unique Visitors: 14350
Year Established: 1959
Avg Paid Circ: 0
Avg Free Circ: 27255
Audit By: CVC
Audit Date: 31.03.2023
Personnel: Charles A. Engle (CEO/Pres./Pub.); John Hemperly; Mark Malloy (Circ. Mgr.); Jocelyn Engle; Jeremy Engle (Prod. Mgr.)
Parent company (for newspapers): Engle Printing & Publishing Co., Inc.

ENGLE - LAMPETER-STRASBURG ADVERTISER

Street address 1: 1100 Corporate Blvd
Street address city: Lancaster
Street address state: PA
Zip/Postal code: 17601
General Phone: 717-492-2514
Advertising Phone: 717-492-2514
Editorial Phone: 717-492-2544
General/National Adv. E-mail: jhemperly@engleonline.com
Display Adv. E-mail: jhemperly@engleonline.com
Classified Adv. e-mail: classifieds@engleonline.com
Editorial e-mail: news@engleonline.com
Primary Website: www.engleonline.com
Year Established: 1954
Avg Paid Circ: 0
Avg Free Circ: 8941
Audit By: CVC
Audit Date: 30.03.2021
Personnel: Jeremy Engle (Prod.); Jocelyn Engle (Publisher); John Hemperly (Operations Manager); Mark Malloy (Circ.)

Parent company (for newspapers): Engle Printing & Publishing Co., Inc.

ENGLE - MANHEIM / LITITZ MERCHANDISER

Street address 1: PO Box 500
Street address city: Mount Joy
Street address state: PA
Zip/Postal code: 17552
General Phone: (717) 653-1833
Advertising Phone: 717-278-1394
General/National Adv. E-mail: jhemperly@engleonline.com
Display Adv. E-mail: jhemperly@engleonline.com
Editorial e-mail: newsdept@engleonline.com
Primary Website: www.townlively.com
Mthly Avg Views: 16500
Mthly Avg Unique Visitors: 14350
Year Established: 1959
Avg Paid Circ: 0
Avg Free Circ: 24630
Audit By: CVC
Audit Date: 30.03.2023
Personnel: Charles A. Engle (CEO/Pres./Pub.); John Hemperly; Jeremy Engle (Prod. Mgr.); Mark Malloy (Circ. Mgr.); Jocelyn Engle
Parent company (for newspapers): Engle Printing & Publishing Co., Inc.

ENGLE - MANHEIM TOWNSHIP MERCHANDISER

Street address 1: PO Box 500
Street address city: Mount Joy
Street address state: PA
Zip/Postal code: 17552
General Phone: (717) 653-1833
Advertising Phone: 717-278-1394
General/National Adv. E-mail: jhemperly@engleonline.com
Display Adv. E-mail: jhemperly@engleonline.com
Editorial e-mail: newsdept@engleonline.com
Primary Website: www.townlively.com
Mthly Avg Views: 16500
Mthly Avg Unique Visitors: 14350
Year Established: 1959
Avg Paid Circ: 0
Avg Free Circ: 15966
Audit By: CVC
Audit Date: 31.03.2023
Personnel: Charles A. Engle (CEO/Pres./Pub.); John Hemperly (Sales Mgr.); Jeremy Engle (Prod. Mgr.); Mark Malloy (Circ. Mgr.); Jocelyn Engle; Greg March (Sales Manager)
Parent company (for newspapers): Engle Printing & Publishing Co., Inc.

ENGLE - MIDDLETOWN SHOPPER

Street address 1: PO Box 500
Street address city: Mount Joy
Street address state: PA
Zip/Postal code: 17552
General Phone: (717) 653-1833
Advertising Phone: 717-278-1394
General/National Adv. E-mail: jhemperly@engleonline.com
Display Adv. E-mail: jhemperly@engleonline.com
Editorial e-mail: newsdept@engleonline.com
Primary Website: www.townlively.com
Mthly Avg Views: 16500
Mthly Avg Unique Visitors: 14350
Year Established: 1959
Avg Paid Circ: 0
Avg Free Circ: 9166
Audit By: CVC
Audit Date: 31.03.2023
Personnel: Charles A. Engle (CEO/Pres./Pub.); John Hemperly (Sales Mgr.); Jeremy Engle (Prod. Mgr.); Mark Malloy (Circ. Mgr.); Jocelyn Engle; Greg March (Sales Manager)
Parent company (for newspapers): Engle Printing & Publishing Co., Inc.

ENGLE - MILLERSVILLE ADVERTISER

Street address 1: PO Box 500
Street address city: Mount Joy
Street address state: PA
Zip/Postal code: 17552
General Phone: (717) 653-1833
Advertising Phone: 717-278-1394
General/National Adv. E-mail: jhemperly@engleonline.com
Display Adv. E-mail: jhemperly@engleonline.com
Editorial e-mail: jpengle@engleonline.com
Primary Website: www.townlively.com
Mthly Avg Views: 16500
Mthly Avg Unique Visitors: 14350
Year Established: 1959
Avg Paid Circ: 0
Avg Free Circ: 17156
Audit By: CVC
Audit Date: 31.03.2023
Personnel: Charles A. Engle (CEO/Pres./Pub.); John Hemperly (Operations Manager); Jeremy Engle (Prod. Mgr.); Mark Malloy (Circ. Mgr.); Greg March (Sales Manager)
Parent company (for newspapers): Engle Printing & Publishing Co., Inc.

ENGLE - MORGANTOWN / HONEY BROOK COMMUNITY COURIER

Street address 1: PO Box 500
Street address city: Mount Joy
Street address state: PA
Zip/Postal code: 17552
General Phone: (717) 653-1833
General/National Adv. E-mail: jhemperly@engleonline.com
Display Adv. E-mail: jhemperly@engleonline.com
Editorial e-mail: newsdept@engleonline.com
Primary Website: www.townlively.com
Mthly Avg Views: 16500
Mthly Avg Unique Visitors: 14350
Year Established: 1959
Avg Paid Circ: 0
Avg Free Circ: 14350
Audit By: CVC
Audit Date: 31.03.2023
Personnel: Charles A. Engle (CEO/Pres./Pub.); John Hemperly (Operations Manager); Jeremy Engle (Prod. Mgr.); Mark Malloy (Circ. Mgr.); Jocelyn Engle; Greg March (Sales Manager)
Parent company (for newspapers): Engle Printing & Publishing Co., Inc.

ENGLE - NEW HOLLAND PENNYSAVER GARDEN SPOT

Street address 1: PO Box 500
Street address city: Mount Joy
Street address state: PA
Zip/Postal code: 17552
General Phone: (717) 653-1833
General/National Adv. E-mail: jhemperly@engleonline.com
Display Adv. E-mail: jhemperly@engleonline.com
Editorial e-mail: news@engleonline.com
Primary Website: www.townlively.com
Mthly Avg Views: 16500
Mthly Avg Unique Visitors: 14350
Year Established: 1959
Avg Paid Circ: 0
Avg Free Circ: 11217
Audit By: CVC
Audit Date: 31.03.2023
Personnel: Charles A. Engle (CEO/Pres./Pub.); John Hemperly (Sales Mgr.); Jeremy Engle (Prod. Mgr.); Mark Malloy (Circ. Mgr.)
Parent company (for newspapers): Engle Printing & Publishing Co., Inc.

ENGLE - OCTORARA COMMUNITY COURIER

Street address 1: 1100 Corporate Blvd
Street address city: Lancaster
Street address state: PA
Zip/Postal code: 17601
General Phone: 717-653-1833
Advertising Phone: 717-278-1394
Editorial Phone: 717-492-2544
General/National Adv. E-mail: jhemperly@engleonline.com
Display Adv. E-mail: jhemperly@engleonline.com
Classified Adv. e-mail: classifieds@engleonline.com
Editorial e-mail: newsdept@engleonline.com
Primary Website: www.townlively.com
Mthly Avg Views: 16500
Mthly Avg Unique Visitors: 14350
Year Established: 1954
Avg Free Circ: 7081
Audit By: CVC
Audit Date: 30.03.2023
Personnel: Jeremy Engle (Prod.); Jocelyn Engle (Publisher); John Hemperly (Operations Manager); Mark Malloy (Circ.)
Parent company (for newspapers): Engle Printing & Publishing Co., Inc.

ENGLE - PENN MANOR ADVERTISER

Street address 1: 1100 Corpoarte Blvd.
Street address city: Lancaster
Street address state: PA
Zip/Postal code: 17601
General Phone: (717) 492-2514
Advertising Phone: (717) 492-2514
Editorial Phone: 717-492-2544
General/National Adv. E-mail: jhemperly@engleonline.com
Display Adv. E-mail: jhemperly@engleonline.com
Classified Adv. e-mail: classifieds@engleonline.com
Editorial e-mail: news@engleonline.com
Primary Website: www.engleonline.com
Year Established: 1954
Avg Paid Circ: 0
Avg Free Circ: 17031
Audit By: CVC
Audit Date: 30.03.2021
Personnel: John Hemperly (Operations Manager); Jeremy Engle (Prod.); Jocelyn Engle (Publisher); Mark Malloy (Circ.)
Parent company (for newspapers): Engle Printing & Publishing Co., Inc.

ENGLE - QUARRYVILLE ADVERTISER

Street address 1: PO Box 500
Street address city: Mount Joy
Street address state: PA
Zip/Postal code: 17552-9589
General Phone: (717) 653-1833
General Fax: (717) 492-2580
General/National Adv. E-mail: jhemperly@engleonline.com
Display Adv. E-mail: jhemperly@engleonline.com
Editorial e-mail: news@engleonline.com
Primary Website: www.townlively.com
Mthly Avg Views: 16500
Mthly Avg Unique Visitors: 14350
Year Established: 1959
Avg Paid Circ: 0
Avg Free Circ: 11218
Audit By: CVC
Audit Date: 31.03.2023
Personnel: Charles A. Engle (CEO/Pres./Pub.); John Hemperly (Sales Mgr.); Jeremy Engle (Prod. Mgr.); Mark Malloy (Circ. Mgr.)
Parent company (for newspapers): Engle Printing & Publishing Co., Inc.

ENGLE - RED LION / DALLASTOWN COMMUNITY COURIER

Street address 1: 1425 W Main St
Street address city: Mount Joy
Street address state: PA
Zip/Postal code: 17552
Avg Paid Circ: 0
Audit By: CVC
Audit Date: 30.03.2017
Personnel: Jeremy Engle (Prod.); Jocelyn Engle; John Hemperly; Mark Malloy
Parent company (for newspapers): Engle Printing & Publishing Co., Inc.

ENGLE - SOLANCO ADVERTISER

Street address 1: 1100 Corporate Blvd
Street address city: Lancaster
Street address state: PA
Zip/Postal code: 17601
General Phone: 717-492-2514
Advertising Phone: 717-492-2514
Editorial Phone: 717-492-2544
General/National Adv. E-mail: jhemperly@engleonline.com
Display Adv. E-mail: jhemperly@engleonline.com
Classified Adv. e-mail: classifieds@engleonline.com
Editorial e-mail: news@engleonline.com
Primary Website: www.engleonline.com
Year Established: 1954
Avg Paid Circ: 0
Avg Free Circ: 11040
Audit By: CVC
Audit Date: 31.03.2021
Personnel: Jeremy Engle (Prod.); Jocelyn Engle (Publisher); John Hemperly (Operations Manager); Mark Malloy
Parent company (for newspapers): Engle Printing & Publishing Co., Inc.

ENGLE - WARWICK MERCHANDISER

Street address 1: 1100 Corporate Blvd
Street address city: Lancaster
Street address state: PA
Zip/Postal code: 17601
General Phone: (717) 492-2514
Advertising Phone: 717-492-2514
Editorial Phone: 717-492-2544
General/National Adv. E-mail: jhemperly@engleonline.com
Display Adv. E-mail: jhemperly@engleonline.com
Classified Adv. e-mail: classifieds@engleonline.com
Editorial e-mail: news@engleonline.com
Primary Website: www.engleonline.com
Year Established: 1954
Avg Paid Circ: 0
Avg Free Circ: 13038
Audit By: CVC
Audit Date: 30.03.2021
Personnel: Mark Malloy (Circ.); Jocelyn Engle (Publisher); John Hemperly (Operations Manager); Jeremy Engle (Prod.)
Parent company (for newspapers): Engle Printing & Publishing Co., Inc.

ENGLE - WILLOW STREET STRASBURG ADVERTISER (LSA)

Street address 1: PO Box 500
Street address city: Mount Joy
Street address state: PA
Zip/Postal code: 17552-9589
General Phone: (717) 653-1833
Advertising Phone: 717-278-1394
General/National Adv. E-mail: jhemperly@engleonline.com
Display Adv. E-mail: jhemperly@engleonline.com
Editorial e-mail: newsdept@engleonline.com
Primary Website: www.townlively.com
Mthly Avg Views: 16500
Mthly Avg Unique Visitors: 14350
Year Established: 1959
Avg Paid Circ: 0
Avg Free Circ: 9100
Audit By: Sworn/Estimate/Non-Audited
Audit Date: 31.03.2023
Personnel: Charles A. Engle (CEO/Pres./Pub.); John Hemperly (Operations Manager); Jeremy Engle (Prod. Mgr.); Mark Malloy (Circ. Mgr.); Greg March
Parent company (for newspapers): Engle Printing & Publishing Co., Inc.

ENGLE PRINTING & PUBLISHING CO., INC.

Street address 1: PO Box 500
Street address city: Mount Joy
Street address state: PA
Zip/Postal code: 17552
General Phone: 717-653-1833
Advertising Phone: 717-278-1394
Editorial Phone: 717-492-2544
General/National Adv. E-mail: advertising@engleonline.com
Display Adv. E-mail: jhemperly@engleonline.com
Classified Adv. e-mail: classifieds@engleonline.com
Editorial e-mail: newsdept@engleonline.com
Primary Website: www.townlively.com
Mthly Avg Views: 16500
Mthly Avg Unique Visitors: 14350
Year Established: 1954
Avg Free Circ: 230000
Audit By: CVC
Audit Date: 31.03.2023
Personnel: Jocelyn Engle (Publisher); John Hemperly (Operations Manager); Wendy Royal (Editor); ???? ????

Parent company (for newspapers): Engle Printing & Publishing Co., Inc

FOREST PRESS

Street address 1: 165 Elm St
Street address city: Tionesta
Street address state: PA
Zip/Postal code: 16353-9704
General Phone: (814) 755-4900
General Fax: (814) 755-4429
General/National Adv. E-mail: info@visitANF.com
Editorial e-mail: forestpress1@yahoo.com
Primary Website: titusvilleherald.com/eedition_myforestpress
Year Established: 1867
Avg Paid Circ: 3800
Audit By: Sworn/Estimate/Non-Audited
Audit Date: 10.06.2019
Personnel: Tina Mohrey (Adv. Mgr.); Cathy Culver (Ed.)

FREE PRESS-COURIER

Street address 1: 25 East Ave
Street address city: Wellsboro
Street address state: PA
Zip/Postal code: 16901-1618
General Phone: (814) 367-2230
General Fax: (570) 724-2278
General/National Adv. E-mail: palmer@tiogapublishing.com
Display Adv. E-mail: slapoint@tiogapublishing.com
Editorial e-mail: nkennedy@tiogapublishing.com
Primary Website: tiogapublishing.com
Avg Paid Circ: 2735
Audit By: Sworn/Estimate/Non-Audited
Audit Date: 10.06.2019
Personnel: Natalie Kennedy (Ed.); David Sullens (Ed./Pub.)
Parent company (for newspapers): Community Media Group; Tioga Publishing Company

FULTON COUNTY NEWS

Street address 1: PO Box 635
Street address 2: 417 E Market St
Street address city: Mc Connellsburg
Street address state: PA
Zip/Postal code: 17233-0635
General Phone: (717) 485-3811
General Fax: (717) 485-5187
General/National Adv. E-mail: Newsads@comcast.net
Display Adv. E-mail:
Editorial e-mail: fultoncountynews@comcast.net
Primary Website: fultoncountynews.com
Mthly Avg Views: 332733
Mthly Avg Unique Visitors: 10733
Year Established: 1899
Avg Paid Circ: 4850
Avg Free Circ: 15
Audit By: Sworn/Estimate/Non-Audited
Audit Date: 10.06.2019
Personnel: Jamie S. Greathead (Pub. / Adv. Mgr); Trudy Gelvin (Circ. Mgr.); Lindsay Mellott (Ed.); Madison Romig; Cassidy Pittman (reporter)

GLENSIDE NEWS

Street address 1: 290 Commerce Dr
Street address city: Fort Washington
Street address state: PA
Zip/Postal code: 19034-2400
General Phone: (215) 542-0200
General Fax: (215) 643-9475
Advertising Phone: (215) 542-0200 ext. 150
Editorial Phone: (215) 542-0200 ext. 264
General/National Adv. E-mail: sanderer@montgomerynews.com
Display Adv. E-mail: classified@montgomerynews.com
Editorial e-mail: editorial@montgomerynews.com
Primary Website: montgomerynews.com
Year Established: 1894
Avg Paid Circ: 573
Avg Free Circ: 62
Audit By: Sworn/Estimate/Non-Audited
Audit Date: 10.06.2019
Personnel: Joe Flenders (Circ. Mgr); Beth Douglas (Adv. Mgr); Thomas Celona (Ed)
Parent company (for newspapers): Montgomery Newspapers; Digital First Media

GREENE COUNTY MESSENGER

Street address 1: 95 E High St
Street address 2: Suite 107
Street address city: Waynesburg
Street address state: PA
Zip/Postal code: 15370-1853
General Phone: (724) 852-2251
General Fax: (724) 852-2271
Advertising Phone: (724) 425-7213
Advertising Fax: (724) 438-7528
General/National Adv. E-mail: info@greenecountymessenger.com
Display Adv. E-mail: dbehary@heraldstandard.com
Editorial e-mail: steve@greenemessenger.com
Primary Website: greenecountymessenger.com
Year Established: 1990
Avg Paid Circ: 7000
Avg Free Circ: 150
Audit By: Sworn/Estimate/Non-Audited
Audit Date: 10.06.2019
Personnel: Steve Barrett (Ed.); Jane Adams (Gen. Mgr)
Parent company (for newspapers): Calkins Media

GREENESPEAK

Street address 1: PO Box 1003
Street address city: Waynesburg
Street address state: PA
Zip/Postal code: 15370-3003
General Phone: (724) 344-7980
General Fax: (724) 267-3911
Advertising Phone: (724) 344-7980
Advertising Fax: (724) 267-3911
Editorial Phone: (724) 344-7980
Editorial Fax: (724) 267-3911
General/National Adv. E-mail: cindy@greenespeak.com
Display Adv. E-mail: cindy@greenespeak.com
Editorial e-mail: cindy@greenespeak.com
Primary Website: greenespeak.com
Year Established: 2004
Avg Free Circ: 4000
Audit By: Sworn/Estimate/Non-Audited
Audit Date: 10.06.2019
Personnel: Cindy Bailey (Pub./Ed.)

HERSHEY COMMUNITY COURIER

Street address 1: PO Box 500
Street address city: Mount Joy
Street address state: PA
Zip/Postal code: 17552-9589
General Phone: (717) 492-2514
General Fax: (717) 492-2584
Advertising Phone: (717) 492-2514
Editorial Phone: (717) 892-6018
Editorial Fax: (717) 892-6024
General/National Adv. E-mail: jhemperly@engleonline.com
Display Adv. E-mail: jhemperly@engleonline.com
Editorial e-mail: news@engleonline.com
Primary Website: www.townlively.com
Mthly Avg Views: 16500
Mthly Avg Unique Visitors: 14350
Year Established: 1954
Avg Paid Circ: 0
Avg Free Circ: 27255
Audit By: CVC
Audit Date: 30.03.2023
Personnel: John Hemperly (General Sales Manager); Greg March (Sales Manager)
Parent company (for newspapers): Engle Printing & Publishing Co., Inc.

JEFFERSONIAN DEMOCRAT

Street address 1: 301 Main St
Street address 2: Apt 1
Street address city: Brookville
Street address state: PA
Zip/Postal code: 15825-1204
General Phone: (814) 849-5339
General Fax: (814) 849-4333
Advertising Phone: (814) 849-6737 ext. 25
Editorial Phone: (814) 849-6737 ext. 28
General/National Adv. E-mail: jeffdem@windstream.net
Editorial e-mail: rbartley@thecourierexpress.com
Primary Website: thecourierexpress.com/jeffersonian_democrat
Year Established: 1873
Avg Paid Circ: 3342
Audit By: Sworn/Estimate/Non-Audited
Audit Date: 10.06.2019
Personnel: Pat Patterson (Pub); Joy Norwood (Ed.); Tammi Nogel (Display Adv.); Rich Rhoades (Sports)
Parent company (for newspapers): Community Media Group; McLean Publishing Co.

JOURNAL OF THE POCONO PLATEAU

Street address 1: Route 940
Street address city: Blakeslee
Street address state: PA
Zip/Postal code: 18610
General Phone: (570) 215-0204
General Fax: no
Advertising Phone: (570) 215-0204 ext. 1
General/National Adv. E-mail: journalnews@pa.metrocast.net
Display Adv. E-mail: journalruth@gmail.com
Editorial e-mail: journalnews@pa.metrocast.net
Primary Website: poconorewspapers.com
Year Established: 1995
Avg Paid Circ: 35
Avg Free Circ: 9465
Audit By: CVC
Audit Date: 12.12.2017
Personnel: Ruth Isenberg (Ed. & Pub.); Seth Isenberg (Gen. Mgr.)
Parent company (for newspapers): CANWIN

JUNIATA NEWS

Street address 1: E Erie Ave
Street address city: Philadelphia
Street address state: PA
Zip/Postal code: 19124
General Phone: (215) 435-3909
General Fax: (215) 887-3716
Editorial e-mail: juniatanews@comcast.net
Year Established: 1934
Audit By: Sworn/Estimate/Non-Audited
Audit Date: 10.06.2019
Personnel: Thomas Lineman (Pub./Ed.)

JUNIATA SENTINEL

Street address 1: 1806 WILLIAM PENN HWY
Street address city: Mifflintown
Street address state: PA
Zip/Postal code: 17059
General Phone: (717) 436-8206
General Fax: (717) 436-5174
Advertising Phone: (717) 582-4305
Advertising Fax: (717) 582-7933
General/National Adv. E-mail: displayads@juniata-sentinel.com
Editorial e-mail: csmith@juniata-sentinel.com
Primary Website: juniata-sentinel.com
Year Established: 1846
Avg Paid Circ: 3617
Avg Free Circ: 49
Audit By: Sworn/Estimate/Non-Audited
Audit Date: 10.06.2019
Personnel: Curt Dreibelbis (Pub.); Carol Smith (Ed.); Bryan Smith (Circ. Mgr.); Melanie Campbell (Adv.)
Parent company (for newspapers): Advance Publications, Inc.

KING OF PRUSSIA COURIER

Street address 1: 311 E Lancaster Ave
Street address city: Ardmore
Street address state: PA
Zip/Postal code: 19003
General Phone: (610) 642-4300
General Fax: (610) 645-7620
Editorial Phone: (610) 642-4300 ext. 82524
Editorial Fax: (610) 642-9704
General/National Adv. E-mail: cwert@mainlinemedianews.com
Display Adv. E-mail: brsmith@21st-centurymedia.com
Editorial e-mail: sgreenspon@mainlinemedianews.com
Primary Website: mainlinemedianews.com/kingofprussiacourier
Avg Paid Circ: 21
Avg Free Circ: 6446
Audit By: Sworn/Estimate/Non-Audited
Audit Date: 10.06.2019
Personnel: T Celona

KISKI VALLEY NEWS

Street address 1: 151 Grant Ave
Street address city: Vandergrift
Street address state: PA
Zip/Postal code: 15690-1201
General Phone: (724) 567-5656
General Fax: (724) 568-1729
General/National Adv. E-mail: dfellabaum@tribweb.com
Display Adv. E-mail: jpaschl@tribweb.com
Editorial e-mail: smcfarland@tribweb.com
Primary Website: tribLIVE.com
Audit By: Sworn/Estimate/Non-Audited
Audit Date: 10.06.2019
Personnel: Susan McFarland (Ed.); Jill Paschl (Adv. Mgr.)

LANCASTER FARMING

Street address 1: 1 E Main St
Street address city: Ephrata
Street address state: PA
Zip/Postal code: 17522-2713
General Phone: (717) 733-6397
General Fax: (717) 733-6058
Advertising Phone: (717) 733-6397
General/National Adv. E-mail: awelk@lancasterfarming.com
Display Adv. E-mail: awelk@lancasterfarming.com
Editorial e-mail: sseeber.eph@lnpnews.com
Primary Website: lancasterfarming.com
Year Established: 1955
Avg Paid Circ: 59454
Avg Free Circ: 529
Audit By: Sworn/Estimate/Non-Audited
Audit Date: 10.06.2019
Personnel: Bill Burgess (President and publisher); Peter Lindquist (Vice President); Steve Seeber (Ed.); John Wennerholt (Circ. Mgr.)
Parent company (for newspapers): LNP; LNP Media Group, Inc.; Lancaster Newspapers Inc.

LE HIGH VALLEY LIVE

Street address 1: 18 Centre Sq
Street address city: Easton
Street address state: PA
Zip/Postal code: 18042-7746
General Phone: (610) 258-7171
General Fax: (610) 559-7240
General/National Adv. E-mail: news@express-times.com
Display Adv. E-mail: advertising@express-times.com
Primary Website: lehighvalleylive.com/the-us
Year Established: 1980
Avg Free Circ: 21000
Audit By: Sworn/Estimate/Non-Audited
Audit Date: 10.06.2019
Personnel: Nick Falsone (Mng. Prod.)
Parent company (for newspapers): Advance Publications, Inc.

LEBANON VALLEY REVIEW

Street address 1: 718 Poplar St
Street address city: Lebanon
Street address state: PA
Zip/Postal code: 17042-6755
General Phone: (717) 272-5611
General Fax: (717) 274-1608
Advertising Phone: (717) 272-5611 ext. 105
Advertising Fax: (717) 270-9503
Editorial Phone: (717) 272-5611 ext. 138
General/National Adv. E-mail: trprice@mediaonepa.com
Display Adv. E-mail: eweidman@mediaonepa.com
Editorial e-mail: andrearich@ldnews.com
Primary Website: ldnews.com
Mthly Avg Views: 8137364
Mthly Avg Unique Visitors: 1603024
Year Established: 1872
Avg Free Circ: 22300
Audit By: Sworn/Estimate/Non-Audited
Audit Date: 10.06.2019
Personnel: Scott Downs (Pub.); Rahn Forney (News Ed.); Andrea Rich (Managing Ed.)

LEHIGH VALLEY BUSINESS

Street address 1: 65 E Elizabeth Ave

Street address 2: Suite 700
Street address city: Bethlehem
Street address state: PA
Zip/Postal code: 18018-6515
General Phone: (610) 807-9619
General Fax: (610) 807-9612
General/National Adv. E-mail: johnc@lvb.com
Display Adv. E-mail: johnc@lvb.com
Editorial e-mail: jberg@lvb.com
Primary Website: LVB.com
Mthly Avg Views: 150000
Mthly Avg Unique Visitors: 30000
Year Established: 2012
Avg Paid Circ: 2425
Avg Free Circ: 4244
Audit By: Sworn/Estimate/Non-Audited
Audit Date: 10.06.2019
Personnel: Michael O'Rourke (Pub.); Joel Berg (Ed.); John Coyle (Adv.)
Parent company (for newspapers): CherryRoad Media

LITITZ RECORD EXPRESS

Street address 1: 1 E Main St
Street address city: Ephrata
Street address state: PA
Zip/Postal code: 17522-2713
General Phone: (717) 733-6397
General Fax: (717) 733-6058
General/National Adv. E-mail: bkent@lnpnews.com
Display Adv. E-mail: mreidenbach.eph@lnpnews.com
Editorial e-mail: afasnacht.eph@lnpnews.com
Primary Website: lititzrecordexpress.com
Year Established: 1877
Avg Paid Circ: 8200
Audit By: Sworn/Estimate/Non-Audited
Audit Date: 10.06.2019
Personnel: Beverly Kent (Adv. Mgr); Andrew Fasnacht (Ed.)
Parent company (for newspapers): LNP; LNP Media Group, Inc.

MAIN LINE SUBURBAN LIFE

Street address 1: 110 Ardmore Ave
Street address city: Ardmore
Street address state: PA
Zip/Postal code: 19003-1339
General Phone: (610) 642-4300
General Fax: (610) 645-7620
Editorial Phone: (610) 642-4300 ext. 82523
Editorial Fax: (610) 642-9704
General/National Adv. E-mail: paadvertising@digitalfirstmedia.com
Display Adv. E-mail: brsmith@21st-centurymedia.com
Editorial e-mail: sgreenspon@mainlinemedianews.com
Primary Website: mainlinemedianews.com/mainlinesuburbanlife
Year Established: 1987
Avg Paid Circ: 2283
Avg Free Circ: 64
Audit By: CAC
Audit Date: 30.06.2017
Personnel: Andy Stettler (Exec. Ed.); Brad Smith (Adv. Mgr.); Larry Butts (Circ. Mgr.); Susan Greenspon (Ed.); Ryan Wells
Parent company (for newspapers): Digital First Media

MAIN LINE TIMES

Street address 1: 390 Eagleview Blvd
Street address city: Exton
Street address state: PA
Zip/Postal code: 19341
General Phone: (610) 642-4300
Advertising Phone: (610) 645-7620
Editorial Phone: (610) 648-1077
Editorial e-mail: crodgers@timesherald.com
Primary Website: mainlinemedianews.com
Avg Paid Circ: 3003
Avg Free Circ: 757
Audit By: AAM
Audit Date: 31.03.2019
Personnel: Edward Condra (Pub.); Cheryl Rodgers (Ed.); Beth Douglas (Adv.); Philip Metz (Circ. Dir.)
Parent company (for newspapers): Digital First Media; MediaNews Group

MAINLINE EXTRA

Street address 1: 975 Rowena Dr
Street address city: Ebensburg
Street address state: PA
Zip/Postal code: 15931-2077
General Phone: (814) 472-4110
General Fax: (814) 472-2275
Editorial e-mail: mainlinenews@verizon.net
Primary Website: mainline-news.com
Avg Free Circ: 10130
Audit By: Sworn/Estimate/Non-Audited
Audit Date: 10.06.2019
Personnel: William Anderson (Pub.); Paula Varner (Ed.)
Parent company (for newspapers): Mainline Newspapers

MERCERSBURG JOURNAL

Street address 1: 120 N Main St
Street address city: Mercersburg
Street address state: PA
Zip/Postal code: 17236-1724
General Phone: (717) 307-2430
General Fax: (717) 485-0341
Advertising Phone: (717) 307-2432
Advertising Fax: (717) 307-2240
Editorial Phone: (717) 307-2440
Editorial Fax: (717) 307-2240
General/National Adv. E-mail: ads@mercersburgjournal.com
Display Adv. E-mail: classifieds@mercersburgjournal.com
Editorial e-mail: news@mercersburgjournal.com
Year Established: 1843
Avg Paid Circ: 2700
Avg Free Circ: 5950
Audit By: Sworn/Estimate/Non-Audited
Audit Date: 10.06.2019
Personnel: Ken Bustin (Publisher & Editor); Tom Stapleford (Mng Ed.); Valerie Dykes (Office Mgr); Oram Lawry (Sales Dir.); Simon Blodgett (Circ. Mgr)

MERCURY SAMPLER

Street address 1: 24 N Hanover St
Street address city: Pottstown
Street address state: PA
Zip/Postal code: 19464-5410
General Phone: (610) 323-3000
General Fax: (610) 327-3308
Advertising Phone: (610) 970-4451
Editorial Phone: (610) 970-4455
Editorial Fax: (610) 323-0682
General/National Adv. E-mail: sbatten@pottsmerc.com
Display Adv. E-mail: classified@pottsmerc.com
Editorial e-mail: letters@pottsmerc.com
Primary Website: pottsmerc.com
Avg Free Circ: 24244
Audit By: Sworn/Estimate/Non-Audited
Audit Date: 10.06.2019
Personnel: Edward Condra (Pub.); Steve Batten (Adv. Mgr.); Nancy March (Ed.); Thomas Abbott (Pub)

MIFFLINBURG TELEGRAPH

Street address 1: 358 Walnut St
Street address city: Mifflinburg
Street address state: PA
Zip/Postal code: 17844-1123
General Phone: (570) 966-2255
General Fax: (570) 966-0062
General/National Adv. E-mail: heidi@mifflinburgtelegraph.com
Display Adv. E-mail: john@mifflinburgtelegraph.com
Editorial e-mail: heidi@mifflinburgtelegraph.com
Primary Website: mifflinburgtelegraph.com
Year Established: 1862
Avg Paid Circ: 500
Audit By: Sworn/Estimate/Non-Audited
Audit Date: 10.06.2019
Personnel: John Stamm (Pub.); Heidi Criswell (Ed.)
Parent company (for newspapers): Mifflinburg Telegraph, Inc.

MONTGOMERY LIFE

Street address 1: 290 Commerce Dr
Street address city: Fort Washington
Street address state: PA
Zip/Postal code: 19034-2400
General Phone: (215) 542-0200
General Fax: (215) 643-9475
Advertising Phone: (215) 542-0200 ext. 150
Editorial Phone: (215) 542-0200 ext. 264
General/National Adv. E-mail: sanderer@montgomerynews.com
Display Adv. E-mail: classified@montgomerynews.com
Editorial e-mail: editorial@montgomerynews.com
Primary Website: montgomerynews.com
Avg Paid Circ: 220
Avg Free Circ: 151
Audit By: Sworn/Estimate/Non-Audited
Audit Date: 10.06.2019
Personnel: Thomas Celona (Exec. Ed.); Beth Douglas (Adv. Mgr.); Joe Flenders (Circ. Mgr)
Parent company (for newspapers): Digital First Media

MONTGOMERY MEDIA

Street address 1: 307 Derstine Ave
Street address city: Lansdale
Street address state: PA
Zip/Postal code: 19446-3532
General Phone: (215) 542-0200
General Fax: (215) 648-1120
General/National Adv. E-mail: tdarmiento@buckslocalnews.com
Display Adv. E-mail: bucksclass@buckslocalnews.com
Editorial e-mail: advance@buckslocalnews.com
Primary Website: buckslocalnews.com
Avg Paid Circ: 10853
Avg Free Circ: 1129
Audit By: Sworn/Estimate/Non-Audited
Audit Date: 10.06.2019
Personnel: Jeff Werner (Ed)
Parent company (for newspapers): Digital First Media

MORGANTOWN/ HONEBROOK COMMUNITY COURIER

Street address 1: PO Box 500
Street address city: Mount Joy
Street address state: PA
Zip/Postal code: 17552
General Phone: 717-653-1833
Advertising Phone: 717-492-2514
General/National Adv. E-mail: jhemperly@engleonline.com
Display Adv. E-mail: jhemperly@engleonline.com
Editorial e-mail: newsdept@engleonline.com
Primary Website: www.townlively.com
Mthly Avg Views: 16500
Year Established: 1954
Avg Free Circ: 7500
Audit By: CVC
Audit Date: 31.03.2023
Personnel: John Hemperly (Operations Manager)
Parent company (for newspapers): Engle Printing & Publishing Co., Inc

MORRISONS COVE HERALD

Street address 1: 209 S. Walnut St.
Street address city: Martinsburg
Street address state: PA
Zip/Postal code: 16662
General Phone: (814) 793-2144
General Fax: (814) 793-4882
Advertising Phone: (814) 793-2144
Advertising Fax: (814) 793-4882
Editorial Phone: (814) 793-2144
Editorial Fax: (814) 793-4882
General/National Adv. E-mail: advertising@mcheraldonline.com
Display Adv. E-mail: advertising@mcheraldonline.com
Editorial e-mail: news@mcheraldonline.com
Primary Website: mcheraldonline.com
Year Established: 1885
Avg Paid Circ: 3100
Avg Free Circ: 50
Audit By: Sworn/Estimate/Non-Audited
Audit Date: 10.06.2019
Personnel: Allan Bassler (Publisher); Martin Bakner (Acct Mgr.)

MOUNTAINTOP EAGLE

Street address 1: 85 S Main St
Street address city: Mountain Top
Street address state: PA
Zip/Postal code: 18707-1962
General Phone: (570) 474-6397
General Fax: (570) 474-9272
General/National Adv. E-mail: mteagle@ptd.net
Display Adv. E-mail: steffie@ptd.net
Editorial e-mail: news@mteagle.com
Primary Website: mteagle.com
Year Established: 1970
Avg Paid Circ: 2500
Avg Free Circ: 3
Audit By: Sworn/Estimate/Non-Audited
Audit Date: 10.06.2019
Personnel: Stephanie Grubert (Pub.); Kathy Flower (Ed.)

MURRYSVILLE STAR

Street address 1: 460 Rodi Rd
Street address city: Pittsburgh
Street address state: PA
Zip/Postal code: 15235-4547
General Phone: (412) 856-7400
General Fax: (412) 856-7954
Advertising Phone: (724) 567-5656
General/National Adv. E-mail: jpaschl@tribweb.com
Display Adv. E-mail: mzigarovich@tribweb.com
Editorial e-mail: smcfarland@tribweb.com
Primary Website: tribLIVE.com
Avg Paid Circ: 68
Avg Free Circ: 11299
Audit By: Sworn/Estimate/Non-Audited
Audit Date: 10.06.2019
Personnel: Brian Estadt (Ed.); Jill Paschl (Adv. Dir.)
Parent company (for newspapers): Trib Total Media, Inc.

NEWS OF DELAWARE COUNTY, TOWN TALK, GARNET VALLEY PRESS, SPRINGFIELD PRESS, COUNTY PRESS

Street address 1: 21 S Swarthmore Ave
Street address 2: 5
Street address city: Swarthmore
Street address state: PA
Zip/Postal code: 19081
General Phone: (610) 915-2223
General Fax: (610) 583-0503
Advertising Phone: (610) 915-2223
Editorial Phone: (610) 306-6171
General/National Adv. E-mail: advertising@delconewsnetwork.com
Display Adv. E-mail: classified@delconewsnetwork.com
Editorial e-mail: pdegrassa@delconewsnetwork.com
Primary Website: delconewsnetwork.com
Avg Paid Circ: 137214
Audit By: Sworn/Estimate/Non-Audited
Audit Date: 10.06.2019
Personnel: Richard L. Crowe (Pub./Adv. Mgr.); David Bjorkgren (Mng. Ed.)
Parent company (for newspapers): Digital First Media; 21st Century Media

NORTH JOURNAL

Street address 1: 610 Beatty Rd
Street address city: Monroeville
Street address state: PA
Zip/Postal code: 15146-1558
General Phone: (412) 856-7400
General Fax: (412) 856-7954
Advertising Phone: (724) 567-5656
Advertising Fax: (724) 568-1729
General/National Adv. E-mail: dfellabaum@tribweb.com
Display Adv. E-mail: jpaschl@tribweb.com
Editorial e-mail: jcuddy@tribweb.com
Primary Website: tribLIVE.com
Avg Paid Circ: 59
Avg Free Circ: 18759
Audit By: Sworn/Estimate/Non-Audited
Audit Date: 10.06.2019
Personnel: Frank Craig (Ed.); Jim Cuddy (Mng. Ed.)
Parent company (for newspapers): Trib Total Media, Inc.

NORTH PENN LIFE

Street address 1: 290 Commerce Dr
Street address city: Fort Washington
Street address state: PA
Zip/Postal code: 19034-2400
General Phone: (215) 542-0200
General Fax: (215) 643-9475
Advertising Phone: (215) 542-0200 ext. 150
Editorial Phone: (215) 542-0200 ext. 264
General/National Adv. E-mail: sanderer@montgomerynews.com

Display Adv. E-mail: classified@montgomerynews.com
Editorial e-mail: dgodshalk@montgomerynews.com
Primary Website: montgomerynews.com
Avg Paid Circ: 570
Avg Free Circ: 168
Audit By: CAC
Audit Date: 30.06.2017
Personnel: Joe Flenders (Circ. Dir.); Beth Douglas (Adv. Mgr.); Thomas Celona
Parent company (for newspapers): Montgomery Newspapers; Digital First Media

NORTHAMPTON PRESS

Street address 1: 1633 N 26th St
Street address 2: Ste 102
Street address city: Allentown
Street address state: PA
Zip/Postal code: 18104-1805
General Phone: (610) 740-0944
General Fax: (610) 740-0947
Advertising Fax: (610) 740-9908
General/National Adv. E-mail: mstocking@tnonline.com
Editorial e-mail: jbillings@tnonline.com
Primary Website: http://northampton.thelehighvalleypress.com
Year Established: 1998
Avg Paid Circ: 2770
Audit By: Sworn/Estimate/Non-Audited
Audit Date: 10.06.2019
Personnel: Scott Masenheimer (Gen. Mgr.); Peg Stocking (Adv. Mgr.)
Parent company (for newspapers): Times News, LLC

NORTHEAST PENNSYLVANIA BUSINESS JOURNAL

Street address 1: 149 Penn Ave
Street address 2: Ofc
Street address city: Scranton
Street address state: PA
Zip/Postal code: 18503-2056
General Phone: (570) 207-9001
General Fax: (570) 207-3448
Editorial e-mail: BIZ570@timesshamrock.com
Primary Website: biz570.com
Audit By: Sworn/Estimate/Non-Audited
Audit Date: 10.06.2019
Personnel: Elizabeth Zygmunt (Ed.)
Parent company (for newspapers): Times Shamrock Communications

NORTHEAST TIMES

Street address 1: 3412 Progress Dr
Street address 2: Ste C
Street address city: Bensalem
Street address state: PA
Zip/Postal code: 19020-5817
General Phone: (215) 355-9009
General Fax: (215) 355-4812
Advertising Phone: (215) 354-3058
Editorial Phone: (215) 354-3030
General/National Adv. E-mail: kstuski@bsmphilly.com
Display Adv. E-mail: kstuski@bsmphilly.com
Editorial e-mail: lswanson@bsmphilly.com
Primary Website: bsmphilly.com
Year Established: 1937
Avg Paid Circ: 1025
Avg Free Circ: 109074
Audit By: Sworn/Estimate/Non-Audited
Audit Date: 10.06.2019
Personnel: Perry Corsetti (Pub.); Pearl Harta (Circ. Mgr.); Lillian Swanson (Ed)
Parent company (for newspapers): Broad Street Media

NORTHWESTERN PRESS

Street address 1: 1633 N 26th St
Street address 2: Ste 102
Street address city: Allentown
Street address state: PA
Zip/Postal code: 18104-1805
General Phone: (610) 740-0944
General Fax: (610) 740-0947
Advertising Fax: (610) 740-9908
General/National Adv. E-mail: mstocking @tnonline.com
Display Adv. E-mail: mstocking@tnonline.com
Editorial e-mail: dpalmieri@tnonline.com
Primary Website: http://northwestern.thelehighvalleypress.comhelehighvalleypress.com
Year Established: 1994
Avg Paid Circ: 2344
Audit By: Sworn/Estimate/Non-Audited
Audit Date: 10.06.2019
Personnel: Peg Stocking (Adv. Mgr.); Debbie Palmieri (Ed)
Parent company (for newspapers): Times News, LLC

NORWIN STAR

Street address 1: 460 Rodi Rd
Street address city: Pittsburgh
Street address state: PA
Zip/Postal code: 15235-4547
General Phone: (412) 856-7400
General Fax: (412) 856-7954
Advertising Phone: (724) 567-5656
Editorial Phone: (412) 856-7400 ext. 8627
General/National Adv. E-mail: jpaschl@tribweb.com
Display Adv. E-mail: mzigarovich@tribweb.com
Editorial e-mail: awallace@tribweb.com
Primary Website: tribLIVE.com
Avg Paid Circ: 134
Avg Free Circ: 16170
Audit By: Sworn/Estimate/Non-Audited
Audit Date: 10.06.2019
Personnel: Jill Paschl (Adv. Dir.); Alan Wallace (Ed.)
Parent company (for newspapers): Trib Total Media, Inc.

PARKLAND PRESS

Street address 1: 1633 N 26th St
Street address 2: Ste 102
Street address city: Allentown
Street address state: PA
Zip/Postal code: 18104-1805
General Phone: (610) 740-0944
General Fax: (610) 740-0947
Advertising Fax: (610) 740-9908
General/National Adv. E-mail: mstocking@tnonline.com
Editorial e-mail: dpalmieri@tnonline.com
Primary Website: http://parkland.thelehighvalleypress.com
Year Established: 1989
Avg Paid Circ: 4174
Audit By: Sworn/Estimate/Non-Audited
Audit Date: 10.06.2019
Personnel: Peg Stocking (Adv. Mgr.); Debbie Palmieri (Ed.)
Parent company (for newspapers): Times News, LLC

PENN FRANKLIN NEWS

Street address 1: 4021 Old William Penn Hwy
Street address city: Murrysville
Street address state: PA
Zip/Postal code: 15668-1846
General Phone: (724) 327-3471
General Fax: (724) 325-4591
General/National Adv. E-mail: admanager@penn-franklin.com
Editorial e-mail: news@penn-franklin.com
Primary Website: penn-franklin.com
Year Established: 1947
Audit By: Sworn/Estimate/Non-Audited
Audit Date: 10.06.2019
Personnel: Charlene Word (Pub./Ed.)
Parent company (for newspapers): Penn Franklin Publishing Co.

PENN-TRAFFORD STAR

Street address 1: 460 Rodi Rd
Street address city: Pittsburgh
Street address state: PA
Zip/Postal code: 15235-4547
General Phone: (412) 856-7400
General Fax: (412) 856-7954
Advertising Phone: (724) 567-5656
Editorial Phone: (412) 856-7400 ext. 8680
General/National Adv. E-mail: jpaschl@tribweb.com
Display Adv. E-mail: mzigarovich@tribweb.com
Editorial e-mail: b.estadt@gatewaynewspapers.com
Primary Website: tribLIVE.com
Avg Paid Circ: 170
Avg Free Circ: 8138
Audit By: Sworn/Estimate/Non-Audited
Audit Date: 10.06.2019
Personnel: Brian Estadt (Ed.); Jill Paschl (Adv. Dir.)
Parent company (for newspapers): Trib Total Media, Inc.

PENNYSAVER

Street address 1: 1100 Corporate Blvd
Street address city: Lancater
Street address state: PA
Zip/Postal code: 17601
General Phone: (717) 492-2514
General Fax: (717) 492-2584
Advertising Phone: (717) 492-2514
Editorial Phone: (717) 892-6018
Editorial Fax: (717) 892-6024
General/National Adv. E-mail: jhemperly@engleonline.com
Display Adv. E-mail: jhemperly@engleonline.com
Editorial e-mail: news@engleonline.com
Primary Website: www.engleonline.com
Year Established: 1963
Avg Paid Circ: 0
Avg Free Circ: 31410
Audit By: CVC
Audit Date: 30.03.2021
Personnel: Mark Malloy (Circ. Mgr.); John Hemperly (Sales Manager); Greg March (Advertising Sales Manager)
Parent company (for newspapers): Engle Printing & Publishing Co., Inc.

PERKASIE NEWS-HERALD

Street address 1: 307 Derstine Ave.
Street address city: Lansdale
Street address state: PA
Zip/Postal code: 19446
General Phone: (215) 542-0200
General Fax: (215) 643-9475
Advertising Phone: (215) 542-0200 ext. 150
Editorial Phone: (215) 542-0200 ext. 264
General/National Adv. E-mail: bdouglas@21st-centurymedia.com
Display Adv. E-mail: bdouglas@21st-centurymedia.com
Editorial e-mail: econdra@21st-centurymedia.com
Primary Website: montgomerynews.com
Avg Paid Circ: 539
Avg Free Circ: 80
Audit By: AAM
Audit Date: 31.03.2019
Personnel: Edward Condra (Pub.); Beth Douglas (Adv.); Phillip Metz (Circ. Dir.)
Parent company (for newspapers): Montgomery Newspapers; Digital First Media

PERRY COUNTY TIMES

Street address 1: 51 Church St
Street address city: New Bloomfield
Street address state: PA
Zip/Postal code: 17068-9683
General Phone: (717) 582-4305
General Fax: (717) 582-7933
General/National Adv. E-mail: advertising@perrycountytimes.com
Display Adv. E-mail: advertising@perrycountytimes.com
Editorial e-mail: editor@perrycountytimes.com
Primary Website:
Year Established: 1886
Avg Paid Circ: 3590
Avg Free Circ: 39
Audit By: Sworn/Estimate/Non-Audited
Audit Date: 10.06.2019
Personnel: Curt Dreibelbis (Pub.); George Roche (Adv. Mgr.); Wade Fowler (Editorial Consultant); Gary Thomas (Ed.); Jennifer Hare (Circulation Director); Brittany Ciccocioppo (Circulation Manager)
Parent company (for newspapers): Advance Publications, Inc.

PHILADELPHIA BUSINESS JOURNAL

Street address 1: 400 Market St
Street address 2: Suite 1200
Street address city: Philadelphia
Street address state: PA
Zip/Postal code: 19106-2501
General Phone: (215) 238-1450
General Fax: (215) 238-9489
General/National Adv. E-mail: acornelius@bizjournals.com
Display Adv. E-mail: acornelius@bizjournals.com
Editorial e-mail: cey@bizjournals.com
Primary Website: bizjournals.com/philadelphia
Year Established: 1982
Audit By: Sworn/Estimate/Non-Audited
Audit Date: 10.06.2019
Personnel: Sandy Smith (Pub.); Craig Ey (Ed.); Dell Poncet (Mng. Ed.); John Spencer (Creative Dir.)

PHILADELPHIA FREE PRESS

Street address 1: 218 S 45th St
Street address city: Philadelphia
Street address state: PA
Zip/Postal code: 19104-2919
General Phone: (215) 222-2846
General Fax: (215) 222-2378
Advertising Phone: (215) 222-2846
Advertising Fax: (215) 222-2378
Editorial Phone: (215) 222-2846
Editorial Fax: (215) 222-2378
General/National Adv. E-mail: cchristian@pressreview.net
Display Adv. E-mail: cchristian@pressreview.net
Editorial e-mail: editor@pressreview.net
Primary Website: phillyfreepress.com
Mthly Avg Views: 25200
Year Established: 1988
Avg Free Circ: 15000
Audit By: Sworn/Estimate/Non-Audited
Audit Date: 10.06.2019
Personnel: Robert Christian (Pub./Ed.); Nicole Contosta (News Reporter); Claudia Christian (Adv. Mgr); George Chavame (Circ. Mgr)
Parent company (for newspapers): University City Review, Inc.

PIKE COUNTY DISPATCH

Street address 1: 105 W Catherine St
Street address city: Milford
Street address state: PA
Zip/Postal code: 18337-1417
General Phone: (570) 296-6641
General Fax: (570) 296-2610
General/National Adv. E-mail: ads@pikedispatch.com
Display Adv. E-mail: Classifieds@pikeduspatch.com
Classified Adv. e-mail: Classifode@pikedispat.com
Editorial e-mail: editor@pikedispatch..com
Primary Website: pikedispatch.com
Mthly Avg Views: 36000
Year Established: 1826
Avg Paid Circ: 6500
Avg Free Circ: 21174
Audit By: Sworn/Estimate/Non-Audited
Audit Date: 10.06.2019
Personnel: Sue Doty-Lloyd (Pub.); Chris Jones (Ed.); Christina Holffman (Prod. Mgr)

PINE CREEK JOURNAL

Street address 1: 535 Keystone Dr
Street address city: Warrendale
Street address state: PA
Zip/Postal code: 15086-7538
General Phone: (412) 856-7400
General Fax: (412) 856-7954
Advertising Phone: (724) 567-5656
Advertising Fax: (724) 568-1729
Editorial Phone: (412) 782-2121
General/National Adv. E-mail: jpaschl@tribweb.com
Display Adv. E-mail: mzigarovich@tribweb.com
Editorial e-mail: DMcElhinny@tribweb.com
Primary Website: tribLIVE.com
Avg Paid Circ: 309
Avg Free Circ: 9619
Audit By: Sworn/Estimate/Non-Audited
Audit Date: 10.06.2019
Personnel: Dave McElhinny (Ed.); Jill Paschl (Senior Advertising Sales Director)

PITTSBURGH BUSINESS TIMES

Street address 1: 45 S. 23rd Street
Street address 2: Suite 200
Street address city: Pittsburgh
Street address state: PA
Zip/Postal code: 15203
General Phone: (412) 481-6397
General Fax: (412) 481-9956
Primary Website: bizjournals.com/pittsburgh
Year Established: 1981

Audit By: Sworn/Estimate/Non-Audited
Audit Date: 10.06.2019
Personnel: Evan Rosenberg (Pub.); Dena Trusiak (Dir. Aud. Dev.); Sheri Darpino (Sr. Sales Ex.); Stanley Malyszka (Dir. Adv.); Jennifer Beahm (Editor-In-Chief); Mike Larson (Mng. Ed.); Jim Snivley (Art Dir.)

PLUM ADVANCE LEADER

Street address 1: 460 Rodi Rd
Street address city: Pittsburgh
Street address state: PA
Zip/Postal code: 15235-4547
General Phone: (412) 856-7400
General Fax: (412) 856-7954
Advertising Phone: (724) 567-5656
General/National Adv. E-mail: jpaschl@tribweb.com
Display Adv. E-mail: mzigarovich@tribweb.com
Editorial e-mail: fcraig@tribweb.com
Primary Website: tribLIVE.com
Avg Paid Circ: 95
Avg Free Circ: 10657
Audit By: Sworn/Estimate/Non-Audited
Audit Date: 10.06.2019
Personnel: Frank Craig (Exec. Ed.); Jill Paschl (Adv. Dir/)
Parent company (for newspapers): Trib Total Media, Inc.

POTTER LEADER-ENTERPRISE

Street address 1: 6 W 2nd St
Street address city: Coudersport
Street address state: PA
Zip/Postal code: 16915-1131
General Phone: (814) 274-8044
General Fax: (814) 274-8120
Editorial Phone: 570-463-5746
General/National Adv. E-mail: leader@tiogapublishing.com
Classified Adv. e-mail: pleclassified@tiogapublishing.com
Editorial e-mail: leader@tiogapublishing.com
Primary Website: www.tiogapublishing.com
Year Established: 1874
Avg Paid Circ: 5000
Avg Free Circ: 200
Audit By: Sworn/Estimate/Non-Audited
Audit Date: 10.06.2019
Personnel: Blake Bacho (Ed); Taylor Della (Office Manager); Kennedy Natalie (General Manager, Managing Editor); Briggs Krista (Sales Rep)
Parent company (for newspapers): Community Media Group

PRESS AND JOURNAL

Street address 1: 20 S Union St
Street address city: Middletown
Street address state: PA
Zip/Postal code: 17057-1466
General Phone: (717) 944-4628
General Fax: (717) 944-2083
Advertising Phone: (717) 944-4628
Advertising Fax: (717) 944-2083
Editorial Phone: (717) 944-4628
Editorial Fax: (717) 944-2083
General/National Adv. E-mail: sales@pressandjournal.com
Display Adv. E-mail: info@pressandjournal.com
Editorial e-mail: editor@pressandjournal.com
Primary Website: pressandjournal.com
Year Established: 1854
Avg Paid Circ: 8000
Avg Free Circ: 1000
Audit By: Sworn/Estimate/Non-Audited
Audit Date: 10.06.2019
Personnel: Joseph G. Sukle (Pub.); David Brown (Adv. Mgr.); Maxine Etter (Gen. Mgr.); Sukle Louise; Jason Maddux (Editor)

PUBLIC SPIRIT

Street address 1: 290 Commerce Dr
Street address city: Fort Washington
Street address state: PA
Zip/Postal code: 19034-2400
General Phone: (215) 542-0200
General Fax: (215) 643-9475
Advertising Phone: (215) 542-0200 ext. 150
Editorial Phone: (215) 542-0200 ext. 414
General/National Adv. E-mail: sanderer@montgomerynews.com
Display Adv. E-mail: classified@montgomerynews.com
Editorial e-mail: sroman@montgomerynews.com
Primary Website: montgomerynews.com
Year Established: 1957
Avg Paid Circ: 299
Avg Free Circ: 63
Audit By: CAC
Audit Date: 30.06.2017
Personnel: Thomas Celona (Ed); Joe Flenders (Circ. Mgr.); Beth Douglas (Adv. Mgr)
Parent company (for newspapers): Digital First Media

RIDLEY PRESS

Street address 1: 3245 Garrett Rd
Street address 2: Apt 3
Street address city: Drexel Hill
Street address state: PA
Zip/Postal code: 19026-2338
General Phone: (610) 259-4141
General/National Adv. E-mail: mail@presspublishing.org
Display Adv. E-mail: mail@presspublishing.org
Editorial e-mail: mail@presspublishing.org
Year Established: 1963
Avg Free Circ: 7000
Audit By: Sworn/Estimate/Non-Audited
Audit Date: 10.06.2019
Personnel: P.A. Girard (Mng. Ed.)
Parent company (for newspapers): Press Publishing Co.

SALISBURY PRESS

Street address 1: 1633 N 26th St
Street address 2: Ste 102
Street address city: Allentown
Street address state: PA
Zip/Postal code: 18104-1805
General Phone: (610) 740-0944
General Fax: (610) 740-0947
Advertising Fax: (610) 740-9908
General/National Adv. E-mail: mstocking@tnonline.com
Editorial e-mail: dgalbraith@tnonline.com
Primary Website: http://salisbury.thelehighvalleypress.com
Year Established: 2000
Avg Paid Circ: 1868
Audit By: Sworn/Estimate/Non-Audited
Audit Date: 10.06.2019
Personnel: Peg Stocking (Adv. Mgr.); Deb Galbraith (Ed.)
Parent company (for newspapers): Times News, LLC

SCRAPBOOK

Street address 1: 200 Market St
Street address city: Sunbury
Street address state: PA
Zip/Postal code: 17801-3402
General Phone: (570) 286-5671
General Fax: (570) 286-2570
General/National Adv. E-mail: sdiads@dailyitem.com
Display Adv. E-mail: pbennett@dailyitem.com
Editorial e-mail: dhilliard@dailyitem.com
Primary Website: dailyitem.com
Mthly Avg Views: 1700000
Avg Free Circ: 24000
Audit By: Sworn/Estimate/Non-Audited
Audit Date: 10.06.2019
Personnel: Gary Grossman (Pub.); David Hilliard (Mng. Ed.); Patty Bennett (Adv. Dir.)
Parent company (for newspapers): The Daily Item

SEWICKLEY HERALD

Street address 1: 504 Beaver St
Street address city: Sewickley
Street address state: PA
Zip/Postal code: 15143-1753
General Phone: (412) 324-1400
General Fax: (412) 324-1401
General/National Adv. E-mail: jpaschl@tribweb.com
Display Adv. E-mail: mzigarovich@tribweb.com
Editorial e-mail: jcuddy@tribweb.com
Primary Website: tribLIVE.com
Year Established: 1903
Avg Paid Circ: 431
Avg Free Circ: 7981
Audit By: Sworn/Estimate/Non-Audited
Audit Date: 10.06.2019
Personnel: Jill Paschl (Adv. Dir.); Frank Craig (Ed.)
Parent company (for newspapers): Trib Total Media, Inc.

SNYDER COUNTY TIMES

Street address 1: 405 E Main St
Street address 2: PO Box 356
Street address city: Middleburg
Street address state: PA
Zip/Postal code: 17842-1215
General Phone: (570) 837-6065
General Fax: (570) 837-0776
General/National Adv. E-mail: scuc@ptd.net
Editorial e-mail: scuc@ptd.net
Primary Website: thesnydercountytimes.com
Year Established: 1997
Avg Paid Circ: 26000
Audit By: Sworn/Estimate/Non-Audited
Audit Date: 10.06.2019
Personnel: Susan Weaver (Pres./Pub./Ed.)
Parent company (for newspapers): Snyder County Times, Inc.

SOUDERTON INDEPENDENT

Street address 1: 307 Derstine Ave
Street address city: Lansdale
Street address state: PA
Zip/Postal code: 19446
General Phone: (215)542-0200
General Fax: (215) 643-9475
Advertising Phone: (215) 542-0200 ext. 150
Advertising Fax: (215) 643-9475
Editorial Phone: (215) 542-0200 ext. 414
Editorial Fax: (215) 643-9475
General/National Adv. E-mail: bdouglas@21st-centurymedia.com
Display Adv. E-mail: bdouglas@21st-centurymedia.com
Editorial e-mail: econdra@21st-centurymedia.com
Primary Website: montgomerynews.com
Year Established: 1957
Avg Paid Circ: 978
Avg Free Circ: 77
Audit By: AAM
Audit Date: 31.03.2019
Personnel: Edward Condra (Pub.); Beth Douglas (Adv.); Phillip Metz (Circ. Dir.)
Parent company (for newspapers): Media News Group; Digital First Media; Montgomery Newspapers

SOUTH HILLS RECORD

Street address 1: 503 Martindale St
Street address city: Pittsburgh
Street address state: PA
Zip/Postal code: 15212-5746
General Phone: (412) 388-5805
General Fax: (412) 388-0900
Advertising Phone: (412) 324-1400
Advertising Fax: (412) 324-1401
General/National Adv. E-mail: jpaschl@tribweb.com
Display Adv. E-mail: mzigarovich@tribweb.com
Editorial e-mail: jcuddy@tribweb.com
Primary Website: tribLIVE.com
Avg Paid Circ: 3114
Audit By: Sworn/Estimate/Non-Audited
Audit Date: 10.06.2019
Personnel: Jill Paschl (Adv. Dir.); Jim Cuddy (Mng. Ed.)
Parent company (for newspapers): Trib Total Media, Inc.

SOUTH SCHUYLKILL NEWS

Street address 1: 960 E Main St
Street address 2: Ste 1
Street address city: Schuylkill Haven
Street address state: PA
Zip/Postal code: 17972-9752
General Phone: (570) 385-3120
General Fax: (570) 385-0725
General/National Adv. E-mail: dschaeffer@southschuylkillnews.com
Display Adv. E-mail: classified@southschuylkillnews.com
Editorial e-mail: news@southschuylkill.net
Primary Website: southschuylkill.com
Year Established: 1891
Avg Paid Circ: 3140
Avg Free Circ: 8
Audit By: Sworn/Estimate/Non-Audited
Audit Date: 10.06.2019
Personnel: William K. Knecht (Pub./Ed./Adv. Dir.); Steve Batten (Adv.)
Parent company (for newspapers): MediaNews Group

SPRINGFIELD PRESS

Street address 1: 639 S Chester Rd
Street address city: Swarthmore
Street address state: PA
Zip/Postal code: 19081-2315
General Phone: (610) 583-4432
General Fax: (610) 583-0503
Advertising Phone: (610) 583-4432 ext. 108
Editorial Phone: (610) 583-4432 ext. 110
General/National Adv. E-mail: rcrowe@21st-centurymedia.com
Display Adv. E-mail: classified@delconewsnetwork.com
Editorial e-mail: awinnemore@delconewsnetwork.com
Primary Website: delconewsnetwork.com
Year Established: 1931
Avg Paid Circ: 4700
Avg Free Circ: 525
Audit By: Sworn/Estimate/Non-Audited
Audit Date: 10.06.2019
Personnel: Richard L. Crowe (Adv. Mgr.); Amy Winnemore (Mng. Ed.)

SPRINGFIELD SUN

Street address 1: 290 Commerce Dr
Street address city: Fort Washington
Street address state: PA
Zip/Postal code: 19034-2400
General Phone: (215) 542-0200
General Fax: (215) 643-9475
Advertising Phone: (215) 542-0200 ext. 150
Editorial Phone: (215) 542-0200 ext. 279
General/National Adv. E-mail: sanderer@montgomerynews.com
Display Adv. E-mail: classified@montgomerynews.com
Editorial e-mail: mross@montgomerynews.com
Primary Website: montgomerynews.com
Year Established: 1957
Avg Paid Circ: 1047
Sun. Circulation Paid: 1060
Sun. Circulation Free: 62
Audit By: CAC
Audit Date: 30.06.2017
Personnel: Joe Flenders (Circ. Mgr.); Beth Douglas (Adv. Mgr.); Thomas Celona (Ed)
Parent company (for newspapers): Montgomery Newspapers; Digital First Media

STAR COMMUNITY NEWSWEEKLY

Street address 1: 3412 Progress Dr
Street address 2: Ste C
Street address city: Bensalem
Street address state: PA
Zip/Postal code: 19020-5817
General Phone: (215) 354-3000
General Fax: (215) 244-1406
Advertising Phone: (215) 354-3070
Advertising Fax: (215) 244-1406
Editorial Phone: (215) 354-3113
Editorial Fax: (215) 244-1406
General/National Adv. E-mail: mmcdevitt@bsmphilly.com
Display Adv. E-mail: pbuzine@bsmphilly.com
Editorial e-mail: star@bsmphilly.com
Primary Website: starnewsphilly.com
Year Established: 1982
Avg Free Circ: 27275
Audit By: Sworn/Estimate/Non-Audited
Audit Date: 10.06.2019
Personnel: Perry Corsetti (Pub.); Michelle McDevitt (Adv. Sales Mgr.); Patti Buzine (Adv. Sales Rep.); Carmen Ferugean (Adv. Sales Rep.); Pearl Harta (Circ. Mgr)
Parent company (for newspapers): Broad Street Media

SUNDAY DISPATCH

Street address 1: 71 N Main St
Street address city: Pittston
Street address state: PA
Zip/Postal code: 18640-1915
General Phone: (570) 655-1418
General Fax: (570) 602-0184
Advertising Phone: (570) 829-7293
Advertising Fax: (570) 829-2002

Editorial Phone: (570) 602-0715
General/National Adv. E-mail: tspina@timesleader.com
Display Adv. E-mail: classifieds@timesleader.com
Editorial e-mail: eackerman@psdispatch.com
Primary Website: psdispatch.com
Avg Paid Circ: 2179
Audit By: AAM
Audit Date: 31.03.2019
Personnel: Mike Murray (Pub.); Dotty Martin (Ed.); Paula Hapeman (Media Sales Consult.)

SUSQUEHANNA COUNTY TRANSCRIPT

Street address 1: 1141 Oak Hill Road
Street address city: Susquehanna
Street address state: PA
Zip/Postal code: 18847-2610
General Phone: (570) 536-5794
General/National Adv. E-mail: susqtran@epix.net
Display Adv. E-mail: susqtran@gmail.com
Editorial e-mail: susqtran@epix.net
Primary Website: susquehannatranscript.com
Avg Paid Circ: 5500
Avg Free Circ: 50
Audit By: USPS
Audit Date: 28.05.2024
Personnel: Charles Ficarro (Editor)

THE ALMANAC

Street address 1: 122 S. Main St
Street address city: Washington
Street address state: PA
Zip/Postal code: 15301
General Phone: (724) 941-7725
General Fax: (724)941-8685
General/National Adv. E-mail: advertising@observer-reporter.com
Display Adv. E-mail: aanews@thealmanac.net
Editorial e-mail: aanews@thealmanac.net
Primary Website: thealmanac.net
Year Established: 1965
Avg Paid Circ: 36
Avg Free Circ: 32162
Audit By: AAM
Audit Date: 31.03.2017
Personnel: Katie Green (Ed.); Judi Smith (Circ. Mgr.); Jeannie Robinson (Prod. Mgr.); Jasmine Blussick (Adv. Mgr)
Parent company (for newspapers): Observer Publishing Co.

THE BOYERTOWN AREA TIMES

Street address 1: 24 N Hanover St
Street address city: Pottstown
Street address state: PA
Zip/Postal code: 19464-5410
General Phone: (610) 970-3218
General Fax: (610) 369-0233
Advertising Phone: (610) 970-3218 ext. 632
Editorial Phone: (610) 850-0270
General/National Adv. E-mail: denice@berksmontnews.com
Display Adv. E-mail: wordad@berksmontnews.com
Editorial e-mail: tphyrillas@pottsmerc.com
Primary Website: berksmontnews.com
Year Established: 1857
Avg Paid Circ: 5820
Avg Free Circ: 488
Audit By: Sworn/Estimate/Non-Audited
Audit Date: 10.06.2019
Personnel: Patti Paul (Pub.); Tony Phyrillas (Editor); Toni Morrissey (Advertising sales); Lisa Mitchell (Managing Editor)
Parent company (for newspapers): Berks-Mont Newspapers, Inc.; Digital First Media

THE CANTON INDEPENDENT SENTINEL

Street address 1: 10 W Main St
Street address city: Canton
Street address state: PA
Zip/Postal code: 17724-1503
General Phone: (570) 673-5151
General Fax: (570) 673-5152
General/National Adv. E-mail: advertise@myweeklysentinel.com
Display Adv. E-mail: cisnews@frontiernet.net
Editorial e-mail: editor@myweeklysentinel.com
Primary Website: thecantonsentinel.com
Year Established: 1941
Avg Paid Circ: 3700
Audit By: Sworn/Estimate/Non-Audited
Audit Date: 10.06.2019
Personnel: Andrea Sutton (News Ed.); John Shaffer (Ed); Amy Bellows (Adv.)
Parent company (for newspapers): Troy Gazette-Register

THE CITIZEN-STANDARD

Street address 1: 104 W Main St
Street address city: Valley View
Street address state: PA
Zip/Postal code: 17983-9423
General Phone: (570) 682-9081
General Fax: (570) 682-8734
General/National Adv. E-mail: ads@citizenstandard.com
Display Adv. E-mail: stacy-h@citizenstandard.com
Editorial e-mail: news@citizenstandard.com
Primary Website: citizenstandard.com
Year Established: 1929
Avg Paid Circ: 4800
Audit By: Sworn/Estimate/Non-Audited
Audit Date: 10.06.2019
Personnel: Stacy Hoover (Sales Mgr.); Rebecca Zemenick (Mng. Ed.); Vicki Terwilliger (Ed.); Jessica Witmer (Adv. Consultant)

THE COLONIAL

Street address 1: 290 Commerce Dr
Street address city: Fort Washington
Street address state: PA
Zip/Postal code: 19034-2400
General Phone: (215) 542-0200
General Fax: (215) 643-9475
Advertising Phone: (215) 542-0200 ext. 150
Editorial Phone: (215) 542-0200 ext. 279
General/National Adv. E-mail: sanderer@montgomerynews.com
Display Adv. E-mail: classified@montgomerynews.com
Editorial e-mail: tcelona@montgomerynews.com
Primary Website: montgomerynews.com
Avg Paid Circ: 791
Avg Free Circ: 125
Audit By: CAC
Audit Date: 30.06.2017
Personnel: Thomas Celona (Ed.); Beth Douglas (Adv. Mgr.); Joe Flenders (Circ. Mgr.)

THE COMMUNITY CONNECTION

Street address 1: 24 N Hanover St
Street address city: Pottstown
Street address state: PA
Zip/Postal code: 19464-5410
General Phone: (610) 970-3218
General Fax: (610) 369-0233
Advertising Phone: (610) 970-3218 ext. 632
Editorial Phone: (610) 970-3218 ext. 640
General/National Adv. E-mail: denice@berksmontnews.com
Display Adv. E-mail: wordad@berksmontnews.com
Editorial e-mail: mreichl@berksmontnews.com
Primary Website: berksmontnews.con
Avg Free Circ: 7000
Audit By: Sworn/Estimate/Non-Audited
Audit Date: 10.06.2019
Personnel: Lisa Mitchell (Ed.); Steve Batten (Gen. Mgr)
Parent company (for newspapers): Berks-Mont Newspapers, Inc.; Digital First Media

THE CRANBERRY EAGLE

Street address 1: 20701 Route 19
Street address city: Cranberry Township
Street address state: PA
Zip/Postal code: 16066-6009
General Phone: (724) 776-4270
General Fax: (724) 776-0211
Advertising Phone: (724) 776-4270, ext. 120
Editorial Phone: (724) 776-4270, ext. 116
General/National Adv. E-mail: mjurysta@butlereagle.com
Display Adv. E-mail: mjurysta@butlereagle.com
Editorial e-mail: jjohnson@butlereagle.com
Primary Website: thecranberryeagle.com
Year Established: 1987
Avg Free Circ: 21625
Audit By: AAM
Audit Date: 31.03.2018
Personnel: Alice Lunn (Circ. Dir.); Michelle Jurysta (Adv. Mgr.); J.W. Johnson (Ed.)
Parent company (for newspapers): Eagle Publications, Inc.

THE DALLAS POST

Street address 1: 15 N Main St
Street address city: Wilkes Barre
Street address state: PA
Zip/Postal code: 18701-2604
General Phone: (570) 675-5211
General Fax: (570) 675-3650
Advertising Phone: (570) 970-7153
Advertising Fax: (570) 829-2002
Editorial Phone: (570) 970-7440
General/National Adv. E-mail: advertising@timesleader.com
Display Adv. E-mail: classifieds@timesleader.com
Editorial e-mail: dmartin@mydallaspost.com
Primary Website: mydallaspost.com
Year Established: 1889
Avg Paid Circ: 4665
Avg Free Circ: 20
Audit By: Sworn/Estimate/Non-Audited
Audit Date: 10.06.2019
Personnel: Susan Kahlau (Adv. Dir.); Matt Golas (Ed.); Jayson McAree (Pub.)
Parent company (for newspapers): impreMedia LLC

THE DISPATCH

Street address 1: 975 Rowena Dr
Street address city: Ebensburg
Street address state: PA
Zip/Postal code: 15931-2077
General Phone: (814) 472-2275
General Fax: (814) 472-4110
Editorial e-mail: mainlinenews@verizon.net
Primary Website: mainline-news.com
Avg Paid Circ: 1928
Avg Free Circ: 10451
Audit By: Sworn/Estimate/Non-Audited
Audit Date: 10.06.2019
Personnel: William Anderson (Pub.); Paula Varner (Ed.)
Parent company (for newspapers): Mainline Newspapers

THE ECHO-PILOT

Street address 1: PO Box 159
Street address 2: 24 E. Baltimore St
Street address city: Greencastle
Street address state: PA
Zip/Postal code: 17225-0159
General Phone: (717) 597-2164
General Fax: (717) 597-3754
General/National Adv. E-mail: agreen@echo-pilot.com
Editorial e-mail: news@echo-pilot.com
Primary Website: echo-pilot.com
Year Established: 1849
Avg Paid Circ: 2700
Audit By: Sworn/Estimate/Non-Audited
Audit Date: 10.06.2019
Personnel: Joyce Nowell (Ed.); Alice Green (Adv. Mgr)
Parent company (for newspapers): CherryRoad Media

THE ELIZABETHTOWN ADVOCATE

Street address 1: 9 S Market St
Street address city: Elizabethtown
Street address state: PA
Zip/Postal code: 17022-2308
General Phone: (717) 361-0340
Advertising Phone: (717)481-7321
General/National Adv. E-mail: drobrish@lnpnews.com
Display Adv. E-mail: bkent.eph@lnpnews.com
Editorial e-mail: drobrish@lnpnews.com
Primary Website: etownpa.com
Year Established: 2010
Avg Paid Circ: 203
Avg Free Circ: 1237
Audit By: Sworn/Estimate/Non-Audited
Audit Date: 10.06.2019
Personnel: Dan Robrish (Editor)
Parent company (for newspapers): LNP Media Group, Inc.

THE EPHRATA REVIEW

Street address 1: 1 E Main St
Street address city: Ephrata
Street address state: PA
Zip/Postal code: 17522-2713
General Phone: (717) 733-6397
General Fax: (717) 733-6058
General/National Adv. E-mail: bkent@lnpnews.com
Display Adv. E-mail: mreidenbach.eph@lnpnews.com
Editorial e-mail: afasnacht.eph@lnpnews.com
Primary Website: ephratareview.com
Year Established: 1878
Avg Paid Circ: 1542
Audit By: Sworn/Estimate/Non-Audited
Audit Date: 10.06.2019
Personnel: Bill Burgess (Pres./Pub.); Peter Lindquist (Vice Pres./Asst. Gen. Mgr.); Andrew Fasnacht (Ed.); Beverly Kent (Adv. Mgr.)
Parent company (for newspapers): LNP; LNP Media Group, Inc.

THE EVENING SUN

Street address 1: 135 Baltimore St
Street address city: Hanover
Street address state: PA
Zip/Postal code: 17331-3142
General Phone: (717) 637-3736
General Fax: (717) 637-7730
Advertising Phone: (717) 637-3736
Advertising Fax: (717) 264-2009
Editorial Phone: (717) 637-3736
Editorial Fax: (717) 637-0900
General/National Adv. E-mail: info@eveningsun.com
Display Adv. E-mail: advertising@eveningsun.com
Classified Adv. e-mail: advertising@eveningsun.com
Editorial e-mail: ejones@eveningsun.com
Primary Website: eveningsun.com
Avg Paid Circ: 5730
Avg Free Circ: 1064
Sat. Circulation Paid: 4029
Sat. Circulation Free: 754
Sun. Circulation Paid: 9118
Sun. Circulation Free: 1136
Audit By: AAM
Audit Date: 30.06.2018
Personnel: Richard Snyder (Pres.); Tyler Murphy (Ed.); Megan Schulz (Sports Ed.); Russ Foote (Sales Mgr.); Martin Conklin (Circ.)
Parent company (for newspapers): Gannett

THE FOREST CITY NEWS

Street address 1: 636 Main St
Street address city: Forest City
Street address state: PA
Zip/Postal code: 18421-1430
General Phone: (570) 785-3800
General Fax: (570) 785-9840
General/National Adv. E-mail: jennifer@forestcitynews.com
Editorial e-mail: patricia@forestcitynews.com
Primary Website: forestcitynews.com
Year Established: 1887
Avg Paid Circ: 3500
Avg Free Circ: 140
Audit By: Sworn/Estimate/Non-Audited
Audit Date: 10.06.2019
Personnel: Patricia M. Striessky (Pub./Ed.); Jennifer Butler (Adv. Sales); Jean Matoushek (Office Mgr.)

THE GLOBE

Street address 1: 290 Commerce Dr
Street address city: Fort Washington
Street address state: PA
Zip/Postal code: 19034-2400
General Phone: (215) 542-0200
General Fax: (215) 643-9475
Advertising Phone: (215) 542-0200 ext. 150
Editorial Phone: (215) 542-0200 ext. 279
General/National Adv. E-mail: sanderer@montgomerynews.com
Display Adv. E-mail: classified@montgomerynews.com
Editorial e-mail: mross@montgomerynews.com
Primary Website: montgomerynews.com
Avg Paid Circ: 226
Avg Free Circ: 62

Audit By: CAC
Audit Date: 30.06.2017
Personnel: Joe Flenders (Circ. Mgr.); Thomas Celona (Ed); Beth Douglas (Adv. Mgr.)
Parent company (for newspapers): Digital First Media

THE GLOBE LEADER

Street address 1: 129 W Neshannock Ave
Street address 2: Ste C
Street address city: New Wilmington
Street address state: PA
Zip/Postal code: 16142-1183
General Phone: (724) 946-8098
General Fax: (724) 946-2097
General/National Adv. E-mail: globepaper@aol.com
Editorial e-mail: globeleaderparrish@gmail.com
Primary Website: globe-leader.com
Year Established: 1880
Avg Paid Circ: 2000
Audit By: Sworn/Estimate/Non-Audited
Audit Date: 10.06.2019
Personnel: Frank Parrish (Pub.); Darlinda McDonald (Mng. Ed.)

THE HERALD

Street address 1: 101 Emerson Ave
Street address 2: Suite 13
Street address city: Aspinwall
Street address state: PA
Zip/Postal code: 15215-3252
General Phone: (412) 782-2121
General Fax: (412) 782-1195
Advertising Phone: (724) 459-6100
Advertising Fax: (724) 459-7366
General/National Adv. E-mail: dfellabaum@tribweb.com
Display Adv. E-mail: jpaschl@tribweb.com
Editorial e-mail: lfabregas@tribweb.com
Primary Website: tribLIVE.com
Avg Paid Circ: 2251
Audit By: Sworn/Estimate/Non-Audited
Audit Date: 10.06.2019
Personnel: Jill Paschl (Adv. Mgr.); Frank Craig (Exec. Ed.); Luis FÃ¡bregas (Ed.)
Parent company (for newspapers): Trib Total Media, Inc.

THE HOME NEWS

Street address 1: 255 E South Best Ave.
Street address city: Walnutport
Street address state: PA
Zip/Postal code: 18088-9574
General Phone: (610) 923-0382
General Fax: (610) 923-0383
General/National Adv. E-mail: AskUs@HomeNewsPA.com
Display Adv. E-mail: AskUs@HomeNewsPA.com
Editorial e-mail: AskUs@HomeNewsPA.com
Primary Website: homenewspa.com
Year Established: 1942
Avg Paid Circ: 3500
Audit By: Sworn/Estimate/Non-Audited
Audit Date: 10.06.2019
Personnel: Paul Prass (Pub.); Lisa Prass (Pub.); William J. Halbfoerster (Ed. Em.); Catherine Stroh (Assoc. Pub.); Kristy O'Brien (Acct. Exec.); Tony Pisco (Art Dir.); Erica Montes (Dir. Creative Serv.)
Parent company (for newspapers): Innovative Designs & Publishing

THE JOHNSONBURG PRESS

Street address 1: 517 Market St
Street address city: Johnsonburg
Street address state: PA
Zip/Postal code: 15845-1294
General Phone: (814) 965-2503
General Fax: (814) 965-2504
Editorial e-mail: jbgpress@windstream.net
Primary Website: jonestownship.com/bul/jbgpress.htm
Avg Paid Circ: 2004
Avg Free Circ: 25
Audit By: Sworn/Estimate/Non-Audited
Audit Date: 10.06.2019
Personnel: John E. Fowler (Gen. Mgr.); Frances Fowler (Ed.)

THE JOURNAL

Street address 1: 975 Rowena Dr
Street address city: Ebensburg
Street address state: PA
Zip/Postal code: 15931-2077
General Phone: (814) 472-4110
General Fax: (814) 472-2275
Editorial e-mail: mainlinenews@verizon.net
Primary Website: mainline-news.com
Avg Paid Circ: 2300
Audit By: Sworn/Estimate/Non-Audited
Audit Date: 10.06.2019
Personnel: William Anderson (Pub.); Paula Varner (Ed.)
Parent company (for newspapers): Mainline Newspapers

THE JOURNAL-HERALD

Street address 1: 211 Main St
Street address city: White Haven
Street address state: PA
Zip/Postal code: 18661-1406
General Phone: (570) 215-0204
Advertising Phone: 570 215-0204 x1
Editorial Phone: (570) 215-0204 x2
General/National Adv. E-mail: journalads@pa.metrocast.net
Display Adv. E-mail: journalads@pa.metrocast.net
Editorial e-mail: journalnews@pa.metrocast.net
Primary Website: pocononewspapers.com
Year Established: 1878
Avg Paid Circ: 845
Avg Free Circ: 36
Audit By: Sworn/Estimate/Non-Audited
Audit Date: 10.06.2019
Personnel: Seth Isenberg (Ptr.); Ruth Isenberg (Ed.); Steve Stallone (sports editor); Heather Maslo
Parent company (for newspapers): CANWIN/Journal newspapers and LAKE NEWS

THE KENNETT PAPER

Street address 1: 250 N Bradford Ave
Street address city: West Chester
Street address state: PA
Zip/Postal code: 19382-1912
General Phone: (610) 430-6590
General Fax: (610) 430-1192
Advertising Phone: (610) 430-6961
Advertising Fax: (610) 430-1192
General/National Adv. E-mail: tjohnston@dailylocal.com
Display Adv. E-mail: kennettpaper@gmail.com
Editorial e-mail: andyh@dailylocal.com
Primary Website: kennettpaper.com
Avg Paid Circ: 5000
Audit By: Sworn/Estimate/Non-Audited
Audit Date: 10.06.2019
Personnel: Edward Condra (Pub.); Andrew Hachadorian (Ed.); Tricia Johnston (Adv.)

THE KUTZTOWN AREA PATRIOT

Street address 1: 24 N Hanover St
Street address city: Pottstown
Street address state: PA
Zip/Postal code: 19464-5410
General Phone: (610) 562-7515
General Fax: (610) 562-4644
General/National Adv. E-mail: denice@berksmontnews.com
Display Adv. E-mail: wordad@berksmontnews.com
Editorial e-mail: lmitchell@berksmontnews.com
Primary Website: berksmontnews.com
Year Established: 1874
Avg Paid Circ: 3100
Avg Free Circ: 336
Audit By: Sworn/Estimate/Non-Audited
Audit Date: 10.06.2019
Personnel: Patti Paul (Pub.); Denice Schaeffer (Gen. Mgr.); Lisa Mitchell (Ed.)
Parent company (for newspapers): Berks-Mont Newspapers, Inc.

THE LEADER-VINDICATOR

Street address 1: 435 Broad St
Street address city: New Bethlehem
Street address state: PA
Zip/Postal code: 16242-1194
General Phone: (814) 275-3131
General Fax: (814) 275-3531
Advertising Phone: (814) 275-3131 ext. 224
General/National Adv. E-mail: rwells@thecourierexpress.com
Display Adv. E-mail: mcraig@thecourierexpress.com
Editorial e-mail: jwalzak@thecourierexpress.com
Primary Website: thecourierexpress.com/the_leader_vindicator
Year Established: 1873
Avg Paid Circ: 4899
Avg Free Circ: 46
Audit By: Sworn/Estimate/Non-Audited
Audit Date: 10.06.2019
Personnel: Devin Hamilton (Pub.); Josh Walzak (Ed.); Randy Bartley (Gen. Mgr.)
Parent company (for newspapers): Community Media Group

THE LIGONIER ECHO

Street address 1: 112 W Main St
Street address city: Ligonier
Street address state: PA
Zip/Postal code: 15658-1243
General Phone: (724) 238-2111
General Fax: (724) 887-5115
Advertising Phone: (724) 838-5154
Advertising Fax: (724) 887-5115
General/National Adv. E-mail: dfellabaum@tribweb.com
Display Adv. E-mail: jpaschl@tribweb.com
Editorial e-mail: echo@tribweb.com
Primary Website: tribLIVE.com
Year Established: 1888
Avg Paid Circ: 3331
Audit By: Sworn/Estimate/Non-Audited
Audit Date: 10.06.2019
Personnel: Jill Paschl (Adv. Mgr.); Deborah Brehun (Ed.); Joseph F. Soforic (Pub.)
Parent company (for newspapers): Trib Total Media, Inc.

THE LUMINARY

Street address 1: 1025 Route 405 Hwy
Street address city: Hughesville
Street address state: PA
Zip/Postal code: 17737-9069
General Phone: (570) 584-0111
General Fax: (570) 584-5399
General/National Adv. E-mail: advertising@muncyluminary.com
Editorial e-mail: bbarrett@muncyluminary.com
Primary Website: muncyluminary.com
Avg Paid Circ: 1300
Avg Free Circ: 12
Audit By: Sworn/Estimate/Non-Audited
Audit Date: 10.06.2019
Personnel: Bernard Oravec (Pub.); Barbara Barrett (Mng. Ed.)
Parent company (for newspapers): Ogden Newspapers Inc.

THE MAINLINER

Street address 1: 975 Rowena Dr
Street address city: Ebensburg
Street address state: PA
Zip/Postal code: 15931-2077
General Phone: (814) 472-4110
General Fax: (814) 472-2275
Editorial e-mail: mainlinenews@verizon.net
Primary Website: mainline-news.com
Avg Paid Circ: 2700
Audit By: Sworn/Estimate/Non-Audited
Audit Date: 10.06.2019
Personnel: William Anderson (Pub.); Paula Varner (Ed.)
Parent company (for newspapers): Mainline Newspapers

THE MIDWEEK WIRE

Street address 1: 3412 Progress Dr
Street address 2: Ste C
Street address city: Bensalem
Street address state: PA
Zip/Postal code: 19020-5817
General Phone: (215) 354-3000
General Fax: (215) 355-4812
Advertising Phone: (215) 354-3058
Editorial Phone: (215) 354-3030
General/National Adv. E-mail: pawirenews@bsmphilly.com
Display Adv. E-mail: kstuski@bsmphilly.com
Editorial e-mail: pawirenews@bsmphilly.com
Primary Website: bsmphilly.com
Year Established: 1987
Avg Free Circ: 178628
Audit By: Sworn/Estimate/Non-Audited
Audit Date: 10.06.2019
Personnel: Ted Bordelon (Mng. Ed.); Perry Corsetti (Pub.); Pearl Harta (Circ. Mgr)
Parent company (for newspapers): Broad Street Media

THE MOSCOW VILLAGER

Street address 1: 220 8th St
Street address city: Honesdale
Street address state: PA
Zip/Postal code: 18431-1854
General Phone: (570) 253-3055
General Fax: (570) 253-5387
Advertising Phone: (570) 253-3055 ext. 301
Advertising Fax: (570) 253-5387
Editorial Phone: (570) 253-3055 ext: 329
Editorial Fax: (570) 253-5387
General/National Adv. E-mail: mfleece@wayneindependent.com
Display Adv. E-mail: pjordan@wayneindependent.com
Editorial e-mail: mleet@wayneindependent.com
Primary Website: moscowvillager.com
Mthly Avg Views: 19137
Mthly Avg Unique Visitors: 5318
Year Established: 1961
Avg Paid Circ: 500
Avg Free Circ: 0
Audit By: Sworn/Estimate/Non-Audited
Audit Date: 10.06.2019
Personnel: Michelle Fleece (Pres./Pub./Adv. Dir.)
Parent company (for newspapers): CherryRoad Media

THE MOUNT PLEASANT JOURNAL

Street address 1: 23 S Church St
Street address 2: # 33
Street address city: Mount Pleasant
Street address state: PA
Zip/Postal code: 15666-1831
General Phone: (724) 547-5722
General Fax: (724) 887-5115
Advertising Phone: (724) 779-6959
Advertising Fax: (724) 568-1729
General/National Adv. E-mail: jpaschl@tribweb.com
Display Adv. E-mail: mzigarovich@tribweb.com
Editorial e-mail: apanian@tribweb.com
Primary Website: tribLIVE.com
Year Established: 1873
Avg Paid Circ: 2812
Audit By: Sworn/Estimate/Non-Audited
Audit Date: 10.06.2019
Personnel: Jill Paschl (Adv. Dir.); A.J. Panian (Ed.)
Parent company (for newspapers): Trib Total Media, Inc.

THE MOUNTAINEER-HERALD

Street address 1: 975 Rowena Dr
Street address city: Ebensburg
Street address state: PA
Zip/Postal code: 15931-2077
General Phone: (814) 472-4110
General Fax: (814) 472-2275
Editorial e-mail: mainlinenews@verizon.net
Primary Website: mainline-news.com
Avg Paid Circ: 3013
Audit By: Sworn/Estimate/Non-Audited
Audit Date: 10.06.2019
Personnel: William Anderson (Pub.); Paula Varner (Ed.)
Parent company (for newspapers): Mainline Newspapers; Sample News Group LLC

THE NEW REPUBLIC

Street address 1: 145 Center St
Street address city: Meyersdale
Street address state: PA
Zip/Postal code: 15552-1320
General Phone: (814) 634-8321
General Fax: (814) 634-5556
General/National Adv. E-mail: ads@tnrnewspaper.com

Display Adv. E-mail: classifieds@tnrnewspaper.com
Editorial e-mail: editorial@tnrnewspaper.com
Primary Website: tnrnewspaper.com
Year Established: 1900
Avg Paid Circ: 5000
Audit By: Sworn/Estimate/Non-Audited
Audit Date: 10.06.2019
Personnel: Linda A. Gindlesperger (Pub./Gen. Mgr.); Denise Kester (Ed.)
Parent company (for newspapers): The New Republuc

THE NEWS AND PRESS OF DELAWARE COUNTY

Street address 1: 639 S Chester Rd
Street address city: Swarthmore
Street address state: PA
Zip/Postal code: 19081-2315
General Phone: (610) 235-2679
General Fax: (610) 622-8829
Advertising Phone: (610) 915-2223
Editorial Phone: (610) 915-2250
General/National Adv. E-mail: rcrowe@21st-centurymedia.com
Display Adv. E-mail: classified@delconewsnetwork.com
Editorial e-mail: pdegrassa@delconewsnetwork.com
Primary Website: delconewsnetwork.com
Year Established: 1992
Avg Paid Circ: 6750
Avg Free Circ: 75
Audit By: Sworn/Estimate/Non-Audited
Audit Date: 10.06.2019
Personnel: Richard L. Crowe (Adv Mgr.); Peg DeGrassa (Ed)
Parent company (for newspapers): Digital First Media; 21st Century Media

THE NEWS EAGLE

Street address 1: 8 Silk Mill Drive
Street address 2: Suite 101
Street address city: Honesdale
Street address state: PA
Zip/Postal code: 18431
General Phone: (570) 253-3055
General Fax: (570) 226-4548
Advertising Phone: (570) 253-3055 ext. 301
Advertising Fax: (570) 253-5387
Editorial Phone: (570) 226-4547 ext. 107
Editorial Fax: (570) 226-4548
General/National Adv. E-mail: mfleece@wayneindependent.com
Display Adv. E-mail: pjordan@wayneindependent.com
Editorial e-mail: pbecker@neagle.com
Primary Website: neagle.com
Year Established: 1950
Avg Paid Circ: 1294
Audit By: Sworn/Estimate/Non-Audited
Audit Date: 10.06.2019
Personnel: Michelle Fleee (Pub.); Peter Becker (Managing Editor)
Parent company (for newspapers): CherryRoad Media

THE NEWS-SUN

Street address 1: 51 Church St
Street address city: New Bloomfield
Street address state: PA
Zip/Postal code: 17068-9683
General Phone: (717) 582-4305
General Fax: (717) 582-7933
Advertising Phone: (717) 582-4305
Advertising Fax: (717) 582-7933
Editorial Phone: (717) 582-4305
Editorial Fax: (717) 582-7933
General/National Adv. E-mail: advertising@perrycountytimes.com
Display Adv. E-mail: advertising@perrycountytimes.com
Editorial e-mail: editor@perrycountytimes.com
Avg Paid Circ: 2248
Avg Free Circ: 34
Audit By: Sworn/Estimate/Non-Audited
Audit Date: 10.06.2019
Personnel: George Roche (Adv. Mgr.); Wade Fowler (Editorial Consultant); Gary Thomas (Ed.); Curt Dreibelbis (Pub.); Jennifer Hare (Circ. Dir.)
Parent company (for newspapers): Advance Publications, Inc.

THE NORTHSIDE CHRONICLE

Street address 1: 922 Middle St
Street address city: Pittsburgh
Street address state: PA
Zip/Postal code: 15212-7200
General Phone: (412) 321-3919
General Fax: (412) 321-1447
General/National Adv. E-mail: editor@thenorthsidechronicle.com
Primary Website: thenorthsidechronicle.com
Year Established: 1985
Audit By: Sworn/Estimate/Non-Audited
Audit Date: 10.06.2019
Personnel: Lauren Stauffer (Advertising Manager)

THE PATRIOT-NEWS

Street address 1: 2020 Technology Pkwy
Street address 2: Ste 300
Street address city: Mechanicsburg
Street address state: PA
Zip/Postal code: 17050-9412
General Phone: (717) 255-8100
General Fax: (717) 255-8456
Advertising Phone: (717) 255-8190
Advertising Fax: (717) 255-8450
Editorial Phone: (717) 255-4127
Editorial Fax: (717) 255-8456
General/National Adv. E-mail: verticalsupport@pennlive.com
Display Adv. E-mail: bizsupport@pennlive.com
Classified Adv. e-mail: classifieds@pennlive.com
Editorial e-mail: business@pennlive.com
Primary Website: pennlive.com
Mthly Avg Unique Visitors: 1523000
Year Established: 1852
Avg Paid Circ: 50107
Avg Free Circ: 7666
Sat. Circulation Paid: 57899
Sun. Circulation Paid: 105270
Audit By: Sworn/Estimate/Non-Audited
Audit Date: 10.06.2019
Personnel: Gwen Witman (National Advt Account Exec); Kurt Hower (Director of Operations); D. Lee Carlson (President); Susan Chieca (VP of Sales); Cate Barron (VP of Content); Dan Christ (Director of Circulation & Audience Development)
Parent company (for newspapers): Advance Publications, Inc.

THE PHILADELPHIA PUBLIC RECORD

Street address 1: 325 Chestnut St Ste 1110
Street address 2: Suite 1110
Street address city: Philadelphia
Street address state: PA
Zip/Postal code: 19106-2611
General Phone: (215) 755-2000
General Fax: (215) 689-4099
General/National Adv. E-mail: editor@phillyrecord.com
Display Adv. E-mail: mbarrett@phillyrecord.com
Primary Website: phillyrecord.com
Year Established: 1999
Avg Paid Circ: 4000
Avg Free Circ: 25000
Audit By: Sworn/Estimate/Non-Audited
Audit Date: 10.06.2019
Personnel: Melissa Barrett (Adv. Dir.)
Parent company (for newspapers): City & State PA

THE PHOENIX REPORTER & ITEM

Street address 1: 24 N Hanover St
Street address city: Pottstown
Street address state: PA
Zip/Postal code: 19464-5410
General Phone: (610) 933-8926
General Fax: (610) 933-1187
Editorial Phone: (610) 933-8926 ext. 633
General/National Adv. E-mail: ppaul@21st-centurymedia.com
Display Adv. E-mail: jfinneran@21st-centurymedia.com
Classified Adv. e-mail: classified@phoenixvillenews.com
Editorial e-mail: editor@phoenixvillenews.com
Primary Website: phoenixvillenews.com
Year Established: 2013
Avg Paid Circ: 2566
Sat. Circulation Paid: 2566
Sun. Circulation Paid: 4000
Audit By: Sworn/Estimate/Non-Audited
Audit Date: 10.06.2019
Personnel: Patricia Paul (Pub.); Leann Pettit (Ed.)
Parent company (for newspapers): Digital First Media

THE PROGRESS NEWS

Street address 1: 410 Main St
Street address city: Emlenton
Street address state: PA
Zip/Postal code: 16373
General Phone: (724) 867-1112
General Fax: (724) 867-1356
Advertising Phone: 724-867-1112
Advertising Fax: 724-867-1356
General/National Adv. E-mail: dstaab@myprogressnews.com
Display Adv. E-mail: ads@myprogressnews.com
Editorial e-mail: news@myprogressnews.com
Primary Website: myprogressnews.com
Year Established: 1885
Avg Free Circ: 14000
Audit By: Sworn/Estimate/Non-Audited
Audit Date: 10.06.2019
Personnel: David J. Staab (Pub./Ed.)
Parent company (for newspapers): Staab Typographic

THE RECORD

Street address 1: 12423 Renovo Rd
Street address city: Renovo
Street address state: PA
Zip/Postal code: 17764-1335
General Phone: (570) 923-1500
General Fax: (570) 923-1572
Advertising Phone: (570) 858-5688
General/National Adv. E-mail: clintoncountyrecord@yahoo.com
Display Adv. E-mail: lgavlock@verizon.net
Editorial e-mail: clintoncountyrecord@comcast.net
Primary Website: therecord-online.com
Year Established: 1871
Avg Paid Circ: 2000
Audit By: Sworn/Estimate/Non-Audited
Audit Date: 10.06.2019
Personnel: John Lipez (Publisher); Lynn Gavlock (Editor); Jeannine Lipez (Advertising); Tracy Embick (Billing/Subscriptions)
Parent company (for newspapers): Clinton County Publishing Company

THE REVIEW

Street address 1: 6220 Ridge Ave
Street address city: Philadelphia
Street address state: PA
Zip/Postal code: 19128-2750
General Phone: (215) 483-7300
General Fax: (215) 483-2073
Advertising Phone: (215) 483-7300 ext. 218
Editorial Phone: (215) 483-7300 ext. 210
General/National Adv. E-mail: cswider@ingnews.com
Display Adv. E-mail: noleary@ingnews.com
Editorial e-mail: review@ingnews.com
Primary Website: roxreview.com
Avg Paid Circ: 16000
Avg Free Circ: 9500
Audit By: Sworn/Estimate/Non-Audited
Audit Date: 10.06.2019
Personnel: Elizabeth Wilson (Pub.); George Beetham (Ed.); Kathy Zapp (Adv. Mgr.)
Parent company (for newspapers): Digital First Media

THE ROCKET-COURIER

Street address 1: 302 State St
Street address city: Wyalusing
Street address state: PA
Zip/Postal code: 18853
General Phone: (570) 746-1217
General Fax: (570) 746-7737
General/National Adv. E-mail: rocket@epix.net
Display Adv. E-mail: rocket@epix.net
Editorial e-mail: rocket@epix.net
Primary Website: rocket-courier.com
Year Established: 1887
Avg Paid Circ: 4000
Avg Free Circ: 100
Audit By: Sworn/Estimate/Non-Audited
Audit Date: 10.06.2019
Personnel: Cain Chamberlain (Reporter)

THE SHIPPENSBURG NEWS-CHRONICLE

Street address 1: 22 E King St
Street address city: Shippensburg
Street address state: PA
Zip/Postal code: 17257-1308
General Phone: (717) 532-4101
General Fax: (717) 532-3020
Advertising Phone: (717) 532-4101 ext. 225
Editorial Phone: (717) 532-4101 ext. 222
General/National Adv. E-mail: advertising@shipnewschronicle.com
Editorial e-mail: nceditor@gmail.com
Primary Website: shipnc.com
Year Established: 1844
Avg Paid Circ: 5100
Avg Free Circ: 100
Audit By: Sworn/Estimate/Non-Audited
Audit Date: 10.06.2019
Personnel: John Zimmerman (Gen. Mgr./Adv. Dir.); Dale Heberlig (Mng. Ed.)
Parent company (for newspapers): Sample News Group LLC

THE SHOPPING NEWS OF LANCASTER COUNTY

Street address 1: 615 E Main St
Street address city: Ephrata
Street address state: PA
Zip/Postal code: 17522-2537
General Phone: (717) 738-1151
General Fax: (717) 733-3900
Advertising Phone: (717) 738-1151 ext. 225
General/National Adv. E-mail: hwenger@snews.com
Display Adv. E-mail: hwenger@snews.com
Classified Adv. e-mail: snews@ptd.com
Editorial e-mail: hwenger@snews.com
Primary Website: snews.com
Mthly Avg Views: 62944
Mthly Avg Unique Visitors: 6230
Year Established: 1965
Avg Paid Circ: 2
Avg Free Circ: 37000
Audit By: CVC
Audit Date: 31.03.2021
Personnel: Harold Wenger (General Manager); Julie Hocking (Pub.)
Parent company (for newspapers): Hocking Printing Co., Inc.

THE SIGNAL ITEM

Street address 1: 503 Martindale St
Street address city: Pittsburgh
Street address state: PA
Zip/Postal code: 15212-5746
General Phone: (412) 388-5801
General Fax: (412) 388-0900
General/National Adv. E-mail: jpaschl@tribweb.com
Display Adv. E-mail: mzigarovich@tribweb.com
Editorial e-mail: bridgeville.news@gatewaynewspapers.com
Primary Website: tribLIVE.com
Avg Paid Circ: 270
Avg Free Circ: 8664
Audit By: Sworn/Estimate/Non-Audited
Audit Date: 10.06.2019
Personnel: Jill Paschl (Adv. Dir.); Bob Pastin (Ed.)
Parent company (for newspapers): Trib Total Media, Inc.

THE STAR-COURIER

Street address 1: 520 Philadelphia Ave
Street address city: Northern Cambria
Street address state: PA
Zip/Postal code: 15714-1630
General Phone: (814) 948-6210
General Fax: (814) 948-7563
Editorial e-mail: mainlinenews@verizon.net
Primary Website: mainline-news.com
Year Established: 1900
Avg Paid Circ: 4500
Audit By: Sworn/Estimate/Non-Audited
Audit Date: 10.06.2019
Personnel: William Anderson (Pub.); Paula Varner (Ed.); Katie Hanlon (Adv. Mgr.)

Parent company (for newspapers): Mainline Newspapers; Sample News Group LLC

THE SULLIVAN REVIEW

Street address 1: 211 Water St
Street address city: Dushore
Street address state: PA
Zip/Postal code: 18614
General Phone: (570) 928-8403
General Fax: (570) 928-8006
Advertising Phone: (570) 928-8403
Editorial Phone: (570) 928-8403
General/National Adv. E-mail: ads@thesullivanreview.com
Editorial e-mail: news@thesullivanreview.com
Primary Website: https://thesullivanreview.com
Year Established: 1878
Avg Paid Circ: 6727
Avg Free Circ: 63
Audit By: Sworn/Estimate/Non-Audited
Audit Date: 10.06.2019
Personnel: John Shoemaker (Pub.)

THE SUN

Street address 1: 18 E Main St
Street address city: Hummelstown
Street address state: PA
Zip/Postal code: 17036-1613
General Phone: (717) 566-3251
General Fax: (717) 566-6196
General/National Adv. E-mail: ads@thesunontheweb.com
Display Adv. E-mail: ads@thesunontheweb.com
Editorial e-mail: news@thesunontheweb.com
Primary Website: news.thesunontheweb.com
Year Established: 1871
Avg Paid Circ: 8000
Audit By: Sworn/Estimate/Non-Audited
Audit Date: 10.06.2019
Personnel: Amber Topper (Adv. Mgr.); Dave Buffington (Owner); Drew Weidman (Editor)

THE SUSQUEHANNA COUNTY INDEPENDENT

Street address 1: 231 Church St
Street address city: Montrose
Street address state: PA
Zip/Postal code: 18801-1272
General Phone: (570) 278-6397
General Fax: (570) 278-4305
Editorial e-mail: indynews@independentweekender.com
Primary Website: susqcoindy.com/PS/contact
Year Established: 1816
Avg Paid Circ: 3700
Avg Free Circ: 173
Audit By: Sworn/Estimate/Non-Audited
Audit Date: 10.06.2019
Personnel: Vicki Wooden (Adv. Mgr.)

THE SWARTHMOREAN

Street address 1: 112 Park Ave
Street address city: Swarthmore
Street address state: PA
Zip/Postal code: 19081-1724
General Phone: (610) 543-0900
General Fax: (610) 543-3790
General/National Adv. E-mail: diane@swarthmorean.com
Editorial e-mail: chris@swarthmorean.com
Primary Website: swarthmorean.com
Year Established: 1893
Avg Paid Circ: 2200
Audit By: Sworn/Estimate/Non-Audited
Audit Date: 10.06.2019
Personnel: Diane Madison (Adv. Mgr.); Chris Reynolds (Ed)

THE TIMES

Street address 1: 410 MILFORD ST
Street address city: Port Royal
Street address state: PA
Zip/Postal code: 17082
General Phone: (717) 436-9900
General Fax: (717) 436-8300
Editorial e-mail: thetimes@nmax.net
Primary Website: timesnewspaper.com
Avg Paid Circ: 3650
Avg Free Circ: 15
Audit By: Sworn/Estimate/Non-Audited
Audit Date: 10.06.2019
Personnel: Donna Swartz (Owner/Ed.)

THE TIMES EXPRESS

Street address 1: 460 Rodi Rd
Street address city: Pittsburgh
Street address state: PA
Zip/Postal code: 15235-4547
General Phone: (412) 856-7400
General Fax: (412) 856-7954
General/National Adv. E-mail: jpaschl@tribweb.com
Display Adv. E-mail: mzigarovich@tribweb.com
Editorial e-mail: jcuddy@tribweb.com
Primary Website: tribLIVE.com
Avg Paid Circ: 137
Avg Free Circ: 15766
Audit By: Sworn/Estimate/Non-Audited
Audit Date: 10.06.2019
Personnel: Jill Paschl (Adv. Dir); Jim Cuddy (Mng. Ed.)
Parent company (for newspapers): Trib Total Media, Inc.

THE TIMES-SUN

Street address 1: 205 E Main St
Street address city: West Newton
Street address state: PA
Zip/Postal code: 15089-1519
General Phone: (724) 872-6800
General Fax: (724) 887-5115
General/National Adv. E-mail: jpaschl@tribweb.com
Display Adv. E-mail: mzigarovich@tribweb.com
Editorial e-mail: bzirkle@tribweb.com
Primary Website: tribLIVE.com
Year Established: 1878
Avg Paid Circ: 1648
Audit By: Sworn/Estimate/Non-Audited
Audit Date: 10.06.2019
Personnel: William Zirkle (Ed.); Jill Paschl (Adv. Dir.)
Parent company (for newspapers): Trib Total Media, Inc.

THE VALLEY LOG

Street address 1: PO Box 384
Street address city: Huntingdon
Street address state: PA
Zip/Postal code: 16652-0384
General Phone: (814) 447-5506
General Fax: (814) 447-3050
General/National Adv. E-mail: ads@thevalleylog.net
Editorial e-mail: news@thevalleylog.net
Year Established: 1980
Avg Paid Circ: 2716
Avg Free Circ: 78
Audit By: Sworn/Estimate/Non-Audited
Audit Date: 10.06.2019
Personnel: C. Arnold McClure (Pub.)
Parent company (for newspapers): Joseph F. Biddle Publishing Co.

THE VALLEY MIRROR

Street address 1: 3315 Main St Ste A
Street address 2: Ste 2
Street address city: Munhall
Street address state: PA
Zip/Postal code: 15120-3200
General Phone: (412) 462-0626
General Fax: (412) 462-1847
General/National Adv. E-mail: valleymirror@comcast.net
Editorial e-mail: valleymirror@comcast.net
Year Established: 1981
Avg Paid Circ: 2000
Audit By: Sworn/Estimate/Non-Audited
Audit Date: 10.06.2019
Personnel: Marilyn Schiavoni (Owner/Publisher); Emily O'Conly (Editor-in-Chief)
Parent company (for newspapers): Laughing Dog Media LLC

THE VALLEY TIMES-STAR

Street address 1: 22 E King St
Street address city: Shippensburg
Street address state: PA
Zip/Postal code: 17257-1308
General Phone: (717) 532-4101
General Fax: (717) 532-3020
Advertising Phone: (717) 532-4101 ext. 225
Editorial Phone: (717) 532-4101 ext. 222
General/National Adv. E-mail: advertising@shipnewschronicle.com
Editorial e-mail: nceditor@gmail.com
Primary Website: shipnc.com
Avg Paid Circ: 3017
Avg Free Circ: 75
Audit By: Sworn/Estimate/Non-Audited
Audit Date: 10.06.2019
Personnel: Dale Heberlig (Mng. Ed.); John Zimmerman (Gen. Mgr./Adv. Dir.)

THE VALLEY VOICE

Street address 1: 1188 Main St
Street address city: Hellertown
Street address state: PA
Zip/Postal code: 18055-1319
General Phone: (610) 838-2066
General Fax: (610) 838-2239
Editorial e-mail: valleyvoice@verizon.net
Primary Website: hellertown.patch.com/listings/the-valley-voice
Year Established: 1988
Avg Paid Circ: 4317
Avg Free Circ: 451
Audit By: Sworn/Estimate/Non-Audited
Audit Date: 10.06.2019
Personnel: Ann Marie Gonsalves (Pub./Adv. Mgr.); Paul Bealer (Ed.)

THE WEEKLY RECORDER

Street address 1: 1056 Route 519
Street address city: Eighty Four
Street address state: PA
Zip/Postal code: 15330-2812
General Phone: (724) 884-1498
General Fax: (724) 884-0006
General/National Adv. E-mail: recorderads01@gmail.com
Display Adv. E-mail: recorderads02@gmail.com
Editorial e-mail: jessicaashley@theweeklyrecorder.com
Primary Website: theweeklyrecorder.info
Year Established: 1888
Avg Paid Circ: 3000
Avg Free Circ: 10
Audit By: Sworn/Estimate/Non-Audited
Audit Date: 10.06.2019
Personnel: Jessica Dernosek (Owner/Pub./Ed.); Christina Luna (Adv. Mgr.)

THE WELLSBORO GAZETTE

Street address 1: 25 East Ave
Street address city: Wellsboro
Street address state: PA
Zip/Postal code: 16901-1618
General Phone: (570) 724-2287
General Fax: (570) 724-2278
General/National Adv. E-mail: phusick@tiogapublishing.com
Display Adv. E-mail: slapoint@tiogapublishing.com
Editorial e-mail: nkennedy@tiogapublishing.com
Primary Website: tiogapublishing.com
Mthly Avg Views: 180000
Mthly Avg Unique Visitors: 40000
Year Established: 1874
Avg Paid Circ: 5500
Audit By: Sworn/Estimate/Non-Audited
Audit Date: 10.06.2019
Personnel: Phil Husick (Pub.)
Parent company (for newspapers): Tioga Publishing Company

THE YEADON TIMES

Street address 1: 3245 Garrett Rd
Street address 2: Apt 3
Street address city: Drexel Hill
Street address state: PA
Zip/Postal code: 19026-2338
General Phone: (610) 259-4141
General/National Adv. E-mail: mail@presspublishing.org
Display Adv. E-mail: mail@presspublishing.org
Editorial e-mail: mail@presspublishing.org
Year Established: 1929
Avg Free Circ: 2500
Audit By: Sworn/Estimate/Non-Audited
Audit Date: 10.06.2019
Personnel: Philippe A. Girard (Ed.)
Parent company (for newspapers): Press Publishing Co.

TIMES CHRONICLE

Street address 1: 290 Commerce Dr
Street address city: Fort Washington
Street address state: PA
Zip/Postal code: 19034-2400
General Phone: (215) 542-0200
General Fax: (215) 643-9475
Advertising Phone: (215) 542-0200 ext. 150
Editorial Phone: (215) 542-0200 ext. 279
General/National Adv. E-mail: sanderer@montgomerynews.com
Display Adv. E-mail: classified@montgomerynews.com
Editorial e-mail: mross@montgomerynews.com
Primary Website: montgomerynews.com
Year Established: 1957
Avg Paid Circ: 1064
Avg Free Circ: 63
Audit By: CAC
Audit Date: 30.06.2017
Personnel: Thomas Celona (Ed); Beth Douglas (Adv. Mgr.); Joe Flenders (Circ. Mgr.)
Parent company (for newspapers): Digital First Media

TIMES CHRONICLE & PUBLIC SPIRIT

Street address 1: 307 Derstine Ave
Street address city: Lansdale
Street address state: PA
Zip/Postal code: 19446
General Phone: (215) 542-0200
Primary Website: montgomerynews.com/timeschronicle
Avg Paid Circ: 1310
Avg Free Circ: 63
Audit By: AAM
Audit Date: 31.03.2019
Personnel: Edward Condra (Pub.)
Parent company (for newspapers): Montgomery Newspapers; MediaNews Group

TOWN AND COUNTRY

Street address 1: 2508 Kutztown Rd
Street address city: Pennsburg
Street address state: PA
Zip/Postal code: 18073-1914
General Phone: (215) 679-5060
General Fax: (215) 679-5077
General/National Adv. E-mail: townandcountry@upvnews.com
Display Adv. E-mail: mkoder.ljrpublishing@gmail.com
Editorial e-mail: lroeder.ljrpublishing@gmail.com
Primary Website: upvnews.com
Year Established: 1899
Avg Paid Circ: 5600
Avg Free Circ: 100
Audit By: USPS
Audit Date: 01.09.2022
Personnel: Larry Roeder (Pub./Ed.); Wayne Suhl (Adv. Mgr.); Robert Esposito (Graphics Editor); Bradlwy Schlegel (Staff Writer)

TOWN TALK NEWSPAPERS

Street address 1: 639 S Chester Rd
Street address city: Swarthmore
Street address state: PA
Zip/Postal code: 19081-2315
General Phone: (610) 915-2223
General Fax: (610) 622-8829
Advertising Phone: (610) 915-2223
Editorial Phone: (610) 915-2247
General/National Adv. E-mail: rcrowe@21st-centurymedia.com
Display Adv. E-mail: classified@delconewsnetwork.com
Primary Website: delconewsnetwork.com
Year Established: 1961
Avg Free Circ: 28500
Audit By: Sworn/Estimate/Non-Audited
Audit Date: 10.06.2019
Personnel: Margaret DeGrasssa (Ed.); Richard L. Crowe (Adv. Mgr.)

Parent company (for newspapers): 21st Century Media

TRI-COUNTY RECORD

Street address 1: 24 N Hanover St
Street address city: Pottstown
Street address state: PA
Zip/Postal code: 19464-5410
General Phone: (610) 286-0162
General Fax: (610) 369-0233
Editorial Phone: (610) 286-0162 ext. 25
General/National Adv. E-mail: denice@berksmontnews.com
Display Adv. E-mail: wordad@berksmontnews.com
Editorial e-mail: jfinneran@tricountyrecord.com
Primary Website: tricountyrecord.com
Avg Free Circ: 20100
Audit By: Sworn/Estimate/Non-Audited
Audit Date: 10.06.2019
Personnel: Patti Paul (Pub.); Steve Batten (Adv. Mgr.); Justin Finneran (Ed.)
Parent company (for newspapers): Berks-Mont Newspapers, Inc.; Digital First Media

TRI-COUNTY SUNDAY

Street address 1: 500 Jeffers St
Street address city: Du Bois
Street address state: PA
Zip/Postal code: 15801-2430
General Phone: (814) 371-4200
General Fax: (814) 371-3241
Editorial e-mail: newspaper@thecourierexpress.com
Primary Website: thecourierexpress.com/tri_county_Sunday
Year Established: 1993
Audit By: Sworn/Estimate/Non-Audited
Audit Date: 10.06.2019
Personnel: Devin Hamilton (Pub.); Joy Norwood (Ed.)
Parent company (for newspapers): Community Media Group

UNIVERSITY CITY REVIEW

Street address 1: 218 S 45th St
Street address city: Philadelphia
Street address state: PA
Zip/Postal code: 19104-2919
General Phone: (215) 222-2846
General Fax: (215) 222-2378
General/National Adv. E-mail: cchristian@pressreview.net
Editorial e-mail: editor@pressreview.net
Primary Website: ucreview.com
Mthly Avg Views: 17200
Avg Free Circ: 29467
Audit By: CVC
Audit Date: 31.03.2017
Personnel: Robert Christian (Pub./Ed.); Claudia Christian (Adv. Mgr)

UPPER DARBY PRESS

Street address 1: 3245 Garrett Rd
Street address 2: Apt 3
Street address city: Drexel Hill
Street address state: PA
Zip/Postal code: 19026-2338
General Phone: (610) 259-4141
General/National Adv. E-mail: mail@presspublishing.org
Display Adv. E-mail: mail@presspublishing.org
Editorial e-mail: mail@presspublishing.org
Year Established: 1926
Avg Free Circ: 4100
Audit By: Sworn/Estimate/Non-Audited
Audit Date: 10.06.2019
Personnel: Philippe A. Girard (Ed.)
Parent company (for newspapers): Press Publishing Co.

UPPER DAUPHIN SENTINEL

Street address 1: 510 Union St
Street address city: Millersburg
Street address state: PA
Zip/Postal code: 17061-1470
General Phone: (717) 692-4737
General Fax: (717) 692-2420
Advertising Phone: (717) 692-4737 ext. 113
Editorial Phone: (717) 692-4737 ext. 104
General/National Adv. E-mail: ads@sentinelnow.com
Display Adv. E-mail: classifieds@sentinelnow.com
Editorial e-mail: dgood@sentinelnow.com
Primary Website: sentinelnow.com
Avg Paid Circ: 8683
Audit By: Sworn/Estimate/Non-Audited
Audit Date: 10.06.2019
Personnel: Ben L. Kocher (Pub.); Duane E. Good (Ed.); Sue King (Adv. Mgr.)

WEBB WEEKLY

Street address 1: 280 Kane St
Street address 2: Ste 2
Street address city: South Williamsport
Street address state: PA
Zip/Postal code: 17702-7166
General Phone: (570) 326-9322
General Fax: (570) 326-9383
Advertising Phone: (570) 419-9826
Editorial Phone: (570) 337-0759
General/National Adv. E-mail: jwebb@webbweekly.com
Display Adv. E-mail: jwebb@webbweekly.com
Editorial e-mail: jwebb@webbweekly.com
Primary Website: webbweekly.com
Avg Paid Circ: 0
Avg Free Circ: 57940
Audit By: CVC
Audit Date: 31.03.2017
Personnel: James A. Jr. Webb (Pub.); Larry Andrews (Gen. Mgr.); Eric Nordstrom (Prod. Mgr); Steph Nordstrom (Circ.)

WHITEHALL-COPLAY PRESS

Street address 1: 1633 N 26th St
Street address 2: Ste 102
Street address city: Allentown
Street address state: PA
Zip/Postal code: 18104-1805
General Phone: (610) 740-0944
General Fax: (610) 740-0947
Advertising Fax: (610) 740-9908
General/National Adv. E-mail: mstocking@tnonline.com
Display Adv. E-mail: smasenheimer@tnonline.com
Editorial e-mail: klutterschmidt@tnonline.com
Primary Website: http://whitehallcoplay.thelehighvalleypress.com
Year Established: 1992
Avg Paid Circ: 3014
Audit By: Sworn/Estimate/Non-Audited
Audit Date: 10.06.2019
Personnel: Peg Stocking (Adv. Mgr.); Kathy Carpenter (Circ. Mgr.); Scott Masenheimer (Gen. Mgr.); Kelly Lutterschmidt (Ed)
Parent company (for newspapers): Times News, LLC

WILLOW GROVE GUIDE

Street address 1: 290 Commerce Dr
Street address city: Fort Washington
Street address state: PA
Zip/Postal code: 19034-2400
General Phone: (215) 542-0200
General Fax: (215) 643-9475
Advertising Phone: (215) 542-0200 ext. 150
Editorial Phone: (215) 542-0200 ext. 414
General/National Adv. E-mail: sanderer@montgomerynews.com
Display Adv. E-mail: classified@montgomerynews.com
Editorial e-mail: sroman@montgomerynews.com
Primary Website: montgomerynews.com
Avg Paid Circ: 144
Avg Free Circ: 62
Audit By: CAC
Audit Date: 30.06.2017
Personnel: Joe Flenders (Circ. Mgr); Thomas Celona (Ed.); Beth Douglas (Adv. Mgr)
Parent company (for newspapers): Digital First Media

WYOMING COUNTY PRESS EXAMINER

Street address 1: 16 E Tioga St
Street address city: Tunkhannock
Street address state: PA
Zip/Postal code: 18657-1599
General Phone: (570) 836-2123
General Fax: (570) 836-3378
Advertising Phone: (570) 836-2123 ext. 26
Editorial Phone: (570) 836-2123 ext. 33
General/National Adv. E-mail: bromanski@wcexaminer.com
Display Adv. E-mail: classifieds@wcexaminer.com
Editorial e-mail: bbaker@wcexaminer.com
Primary Website: wcexaminer.com
Year Established: 1865
Avg Paid Circ: 5570
Avg Free Circ: 120
Audit By: Sworn/Estimate/Non-Audited
Audit Date: 10.06.2019
Personnel: Greg Zyla (Pub.); Robert L. Baker (Ed.)
Parent company (for newspapers): Times-Shamrock Communications

RHODE ISLAND

BARRINGTON TIMES

Street address 1: 1 Bradford St
Street address city: Bristol
Street address state: RI
Zip/Postal code: 02809-1906
General Phone: (401) 253-6000
General Fax: (401) 253-6055
General/National Adv. E-mail: spickering@eastbaynewspapers.com
Display Adv. E-mail: spickering@eastbaynewspapers.com
Editorial e-mail: mhayes@eastbaynewspapers.com
Primary Website: eastbayri.com
Year Established: 1958
Avg Paid Circ: 2497
Avg Free Circ: 0
Audit By: Sworn/Estimate/Non-Audited
Audit Date: 10.06.2019
Personnel: Matthew D. Hayes (Pub.); Josh Bickford (Ed.); Scott Pickering (Adv.); Wendy Allen (Circ.)
Parent company (for newspapers): East Bay Newspapers

BRISTOL PHOENIX

Street address 1: 1 Bradford St
Street address city: Bristol
Street address state: RI
Zip/Postal code: 02809-1906
General Phone: (401) 253-6000
General Fax: (401) 253-6055
General/National Adv. E-mail: spickering@eastbaynewspapers.com
Display Adv. E-mail: spickering@eastbaynewspapers.com
Editorial e-mail: mhayes@eastbaynewspapers.com
Primary Website: eastbayri.com
Year Established: 1837
Avg Paid Circ: 3284
Avg Free Circ: 15
Audit By: CVC
Audit Date: 30.06.2018
Personnel: Matthew D. Hayes (Pub.); Josh Bickford (Ed.); Scott Pickering (Adv.); Wendy Allen (Circ.)
Parent company (for newspapers): East Bay Newspapers

CHARIHO TIMES

Street address 1: 187 Main Street
Street address city: Wakefield
Street address state: RI
Zip/Postal code: 2879
General Phone: (401) 789-9744
General Fax: (401) 789-1550
Advertising Phone: (401) 789-9744
Advertising Fax: (401) 789-1550
Editorial Phone: (401) 789-9744
Editorial Fax: (401) 789-1550
General/National Adv. E-mail: jboucher@ricentral.com
Display Adv. E-mail: jboucher@ricentral.com
Editorial e-mail: mwunsch@ricentral.com
Primary Website: ricentral.com
Year Established: 1992
Avg Paid Circ: 426
Avg Free Circ: 117
Audit By: AAM
Audit Date: 30.06.2017
Personnel: Jody Boucher (Adv. Mgr./Pub.); Matt Wunsch; Phil Rowell (Circ. Mgr.)
Parent company (for newspapers): Southern Rhode Island Newspapers; RISN Operations Inc.

CHARLESTOWN PRESS

Street address 1: 56 Main St
Street address city: Westerly
Street address state: RI
Zip/Postal code: 02891-2113
General Phone: (401) 348-1000
General Fax: (401) 348-3080
Advertising Phone: (860) 495-8265
Advertising Fax: (401) 348-3080
Editorial Phone: (860) 495-8224
Editorial Fax: (401) 348-3080
General/National Adv. E-mail: jlayton@thewesterlysun.com
Display Adv. E-mail: classified@thewesterlysun.com
Editorial e-mail: dsmith@thewesterlysun.com
Primary Website: thewesterlysun.com
Audit By: Sworn/Estimate/Non-Audited
Audit Date: 10.06.2019
Personnel: David Smith (Ed.); Kelly Tremaine (Vice Pres./Adv. Dir.)
Parent company (for newspapers): Sun Publishing Company

COVENTRY COURIER

Street address 1: 187 Main Street
Street address city: Wakefield
Street address state: RI
Zip/Postal code: 2879
General Phone: (401) 789-9744
General Fax: (401) 789-1550
Advertising Phone: (401) 789-9744
Advertising Fax: (401) 789-1550
Editorial Phone: (401) 789-9744
Editorial Fax: (401) 789-1550
General/National Adv. E-mail: jboucher@ricentral.com
Display Adv. E-mail: jboucher@ricentral.com
Editorial e-mail: jryan@ricentral.com
Primary Website: ricentral.com
Year Established: 1996
Avg Paid Circ: 282
Avg Free Circ: 58
Audit By: AAM
Audit Date: 30.06.2017
Personnel: Jody Boucher (Regional Pub./Adv. Dir.); Phil Rowell (Circ. Mgr.); Jeremiah Ryan (Ed.)
Parent company (for newspapers): Southern Rhode Island Newspapers

CRANSTON HERALD

Street address 1: 1944 Warwick Ave
Street address city: Warwick
Street address state: RI
Zip/Postal code: 02889-2448
General Phone: (401) 732-3100
General Fax: (401) 732-3110
Display Adv. E-mail: richardf@rhodybeat.com
Editorial e-mail: johnh@rhodybeat.com
Primary Website: cranstononline.com
Year Established: 1928
Avg Paid Circ: 1901
Avg Free Circ: 94
Audit By: CVC
Audit Date: 30.06.2018
Personnel: John I. Howell (Pub.); Richard G. Fleischer (Gen. Mgr.)
Parent company (for newspapers): Beacon Communications, Inc

EAST GREENWICH PENDULUM

Street address 1: 187 Main Street
Street address city: Wakefield
Street address state: RI
Zip/Postal code: 2879
General Phone: (401) 789-9744
General Fax: (401) 789-1550
Advertising Phone: (401) 789-9744
Advertising Fax: (401) 789-1550
Editorial Phone: (401) 789-9744
Editorial Fax: (401) 789-1550
General/National Adv. E-mail: jboucher@ricentral.com
Display Adv. E-mail: ediggins@ricentral.com
Editorial e-mail: mwunsch@ricentral.com
Primary Website: ricentral.com
Year Established: 1854
Avg Paid Circ: 741

Avg Free Circ: 61
Audit By: AAM
Audit Date: 30.06.2017
Personnel: Phil Rowell (Circ. Mgr.); Jody Boucher (Adv. Dir.); Matt Wunsch (Editor)
Parent company (for newspapers): Southern Rhode Island Newspapers; RISN Operations Inc.

EAST PROVIDENCE POST

Street address 1: 1 Bradford St
Street address city: Bristol
Street address state: RI
Zip/Postal code: 02809
General Phone: (401) 253-6000
General Fax: (401) 253-6055
General/National Adv. E-mail: spickering@eastbaynewspapers.com
Display Adv. E-mail: spickering@eastbaynewspapers.com
Editorial e-mail: spickering@eastbaynewspapers.com
Primary Website: eastbayri.com
Year Established: 1837
Avg Paid Circ: 0
Avg Free Circ: 7981
Audit By: CVC
Audit Date: 30.06.2018
Personnel: Scott Pickering (Pub.); Matthew D. Hayes (Adv.); Wendy Allen (Circ.)

JOHNSTON SUN RISE

Street address 1: 1944 Warwick Ave
Street address city: Warwick
Street address state: RI
Zip/Postal code: 02889-2448
General Phone: (401) 732-3100
General Fax: (401) 732-3100
General/National Adv. E-mail: LynneT@rhodybeat.com
Display Adv. E-mail: richardf@rhodybeat.com
Editorial e-mail: johnh@rhodybeat.com
Primary Website: johnstonsunrise.net
Year Established: 1998
Avg Paid Circ: 0
Avg Free Circ: 8175
Audit By: CVC
Audit Date: 30.06.2018
Personnel: John I. Howell (Pub./Ed.); Richard G. Fleischer (Gen. Mgr.); Lynne Taylor (Adv.)
Parent company (for newspapers): Beacon Communications, Inc

NARRAGANSETT TIMES

Street address 1: 187 Main Street
Street address city: Wakefield
Street address state: RI
Zip/Postal code: 2879
General Phone: (401) 789-9744
General Fax: (401) 789-1550
Advertising Phone: (401) 789-9744
Advertising Fax: (401) 789-1550
Editorial Phone: (401) 789-9744
Editorial Fax: (401) 789-1550
General/National Adv. E-mail: jboucher@ricentral.com
Display Adv. E-mail: jboucher@ricentral.com
Editorial e-mail: mwunsch@ricentral.com
Primary Website: ricentral.com
Year Established: 1855
Avg Paid Circ: 1613
Avg Free Circ: 110
Audit By: AAM
Audit Date: 31.03.2019
Personnel: Jody Boucher (Adv. Mgr./Pub.); Matt Wunsch (Ed.); Phil Rowell (Circ. Mgr.)
Parent company (for newspapers): Southern Rhode Island Newspapers

NEWPORT MERCURY

Street address 1: 101 Malbone Rd
Street address city: Newport
Street address state: RI
Zip/Postal code: 02840-1340
General Phone: (401) 849-3300
General Fax: (401) 849-3335
Advertising Phone: (401) 380-2319
Advertising Fax: (401) 849-3335
Editorial Phone: (401) 380-2371
Editorial Fax: (401) 849-3335
General/National Adv. E-mail: marketing@newportri.com
Display Adv. E-mail: mercury@newportmercury.com
Editorial e-mail: editor@newportmercury.com
Primary Website: newportmercury.com
Year Established: 1758
Audit By: Sworn/Estimate/Non-Audited
Audit Date: 10.06.2019
Personnel: William F. Lucey (Pub.); Janine Weisman (Ed.); Annemarie Brisson (Adv. Dir.)
Parent company (for newspapers): CherryRoad Media

NEWPORT NAVALOG

Street address 1: 101 Malbone Rd
Street address city: Newport
Street address state: RI
Zip/Postal code: 02840-1340
General Phone: (401) 849-3300
General Fax: (401) 849-3335
Advertising Phone: (401) 849-3300 ext. 212
Advertising Fax: (401) 849-3335
Editorial Phone: (401) 849-3300
Editorial Fax: (401) 849-3335
General/National Adv. E-mail: brisson@newportri.com
Display Adv. E-mail: marketing@newportri.com
Editorial e-mail: editor@newportri.com
Primary Website: newportri.com
Year Established: 1901
Audit By: Sworn/Estimate/Non-Audited
Audit Date: 10.06.2019
Personnel: William F. Lucey (Pub.); Sheila L. Mullowney (Exec. Ed.); Annemarie Brisson (Adv. Dir.)
Parent company (for newspapers): CherryRoad Media

NEWPORT THIS WEEK

Street address 1: 86 Broadway
Street address city: Newport
Street address state: RI
Zip/Postal code: 02840-2750
General Phone: (401) 847-7766
General Fax: (401) 846-4974
Advertising Phone: (401) 847-7766
Advertising Fax: (401) 846-4974
Editorial Phone: (401) 847-7766
Editorial Fax: (401) 846-4974
General/National Adv. E-mail: kirby@newportthisweek.net
Display Adv. E-mail: kirby@newportthisweek.net
Editorial e-mail: ltungett@cox.net
Primary Website: newportthisweek.com
Mthly Avg Views: 300000
Year Established: 1973
Avg Paid Circ: 0
Avg Free Circ: 14762
Audit By: CVC
Audit Date: 30.06.2018
Personnel: Kirby Varacalli (Adv. Dir.); Lynne Tungett (Pub.); Tom Shevlin (Web Pub.); Nila Asciolla (Adv. Exec.); Diana Oehrli (Gen. Mgr.); Lisette Prince (Ed.)

PORTSMOUTH TIMES

Street address 1: 1 Bradford St
Street address city: Bristol
Street address state: RI
Zip/Postal code: 02809-1906
General Phone: (401) 253-6000
General Fax: (401) 253-6055
Advertising Phone: (401) 424-9129
Editorial Phone: (401) 424-9144
General/National Adv. E-mail: spickering@eastbaynewspapers.com
Display Adv. E-mail: spickering@eastbaynewspapers.com
Editorial e-mail: spickering@eastbaynewspapers.com
Primary Website: eastbayri.com
Year Established: 1837
Avg Free Circ: 3814
Audit By: CVC
Audit Date: 30.06.2018
Personnel: Scott Pickering (Pub.); Matthew D. Hayes; Wendy Allen
Parent company (for newspapers): East Bay Newspapers

PROVIDENCE BUSINESS NEWS

Street address 1: 400 Westminster St
Street address 2: Ste 600
Street address city: Providence
Street address state: RI
Zip/Postal code: 02903-3222
General Phone: (401) 273-2201
General Fax: (401) 274-6580
Advertising Phone: (401) 680-4800
Advertising Fax: (401) 274-0270
Editorial Phone: (401) 680-4820
Editorial Fax: (401) 274-0670
General/National Adv. E-mail: advertising@pbn.com
Display Adv. E-mail: ahlers@pbn.com
Editorial e-mail: editor@pbn.com
Primary Website: pbn.com
Year Established: 1986
Avg Paid Circ: 4410
Avg Free Circ: 2137
Audit By: CVC
Audit Date: 22.12.2017
Personnel: Roger Bergenheim (Pub.); Mark Murphy (Ed.); Michael Mello (Mng. Ed.); Annemarie Brisson (Dir of Sales & Mktg)

SAKONNET TIMES

Street address 1: 1 Bradford St
Street address city: Bristol
Street address state: RI
Zip/Postal code: 02809-1906
General Phone: (401) 253-6000
General Fax: (401) 253-6055
Advertising Phone: (401) 424-9146
Advertising Fax: (401) 253-6055
Editorial Phone: (401) 424-9120
Editorial Fax: (401) 253-6055
General/National Adv. E-mail: tnuttall@eastbaynewspapers.com
Display Adv. E-mail: spitocchelli@eastbaynewspapers.com
Editorial e-mail: bburdett@eastbaynewspapers.com
Primary Website: eastbayri.com
Year Established: 1967
Avg Paid Circ: 2842
Avg Free Circ: 0
Audit By: CVC
Audit Date: 30.06.2016
Personnel: Matthew D. Hayes (Pub.); Bruce Burdett (Ed.); Toni Nuttall (Adv. Dir.); Steve Pitocchelli (Classified Mgr.)
Parent company (for newspapers): East Bay Newspapers

STANDARD-TIMES

Street address 1: 187 Main St
Street address city: Wakefield
Street address state: RI
Zip/Postal code: 02879-3504
General Phone: (401) 789-9744
General Fax: (401) 789-1550
Advertising Phone: (401) 789-9744
Advertising Fax: (401) 789-1550
Editorial Phone: (401) 789-9744
Editorial Fax: (401) 789-1550
General/National Adv. E-mail: jboucher@ricentral.com
Display Adv. E-mail: jboucher@ricentral.com
Editorial e-mail: pspetrini@ricentral.com
Primary Website: ricentral.com
Year Established: 1888
Avg Paid Circ: 1197
Avg Free Circ: 1205
Audit By: AAM
Audit Date: 31.03.2019
Personnel: Jody Boucher (Adv. Mgr.); Paul Spetrini (Ed.); Phil Rowell (Circ. Mgr.); Nanci Batson (Pub.)
Parent company (for newspapers): Southern Rhode Island Newspapers

THE BLOCK ISLAND TIMES

Street address 1: PO Box 278
Street address 2: Ocean Ave
Street address city: Block Island
Street address state: RI
Zip/Postal code: 02807-0278
General Phone: (401) 466-2222
General Fax: (401) 466-8804
Advertising Phone: (401) 466-2222
Advertising Fax: (401) 466-8804
Editorial Phone: (401) 466-2222
Editorial Fax: (401) 466-8804
General/National Adv. E-mail: ads@blockislandtimes.com
Display Adv. E-mail: classifieds@blockislandtimes.com
Editorial e-mail: ltrodson@blockislandtimes.com
Primary Website: blockislandtimes.com
Year Established: 1970
Avg Paid Circ: 4000
Audit By: Sworn/Estimate/Non-Audited
Audit Date: 10.06.2019
Personnel: Fraser Lang (Co-Pub.); Betty Lang (Co-Pub./Adv. Dir.); John Barry (Adv. Mgr./Prodn. Mgr.); Lars R. Trodson (Ed.); Lisa Stiepock (Ed. of Special Publications)
Parent company (for newspapers): Central Connecticut Communications LLC

THE INDEPENDENT

Street address 1: 101 Malbone Rd
Street address city: Newport
Street address state: RI
Zip/Postal code: 02840-1340
General Phone: (401) 789-6000
General Fax: (401) 849-3306
Advertising Phone: (401) 380-2317
Advertising Fax: (401) 849-3335
Editorial Phone: (401) 380-2394
Editorial Fax: (401) 849-3306
General/National Adv. E-mail: abrams@newportri.com
Display Adv. E-mail: classified@independentri.com
Editorial e-mail: editorial@scindependent.com
Primary Website: independentri.com
Year Established: 1997
Avg Paid Circ: 5907
Avg Free Circ: 510
Audit By: CVC
Audit Date: 30.06.2017
Personnel: William F. Lucey (Pub.); Lynn Abrams (Adv. Sales Mgr.); Liz Boardman (Mng. Ed.); Kevin Shoen (Circ. Mgr); Liz Boardman (Managing Editor); Annemarie Brisson (Adv. Dir.); William Geoghegan (Sports Editor)
Parent company (for newspapers): CherryRoad Media

THE JAMESTOWN PRESS

Street address 1: 45 Narragansett Ave
Street address city: Jamestown
Street address state: RI
Zip/Postal code: 02835-1150
General Phone: (401) 423-3200
General/National Adv. E-mail: production@jamestownpress.com
Display Adv. E-mail: production@jamestownpress.com
Editorial e-mail: tim@jamestownpress.com
Primary Website: jamestownpress.com
Year Established: 1989
Avg Paid Circ: 0
Avg Free Circ: 5076
Audit By: CVC
Audit Date: 19.06.2023
Personnel: Robert Berczuk (Pub.); Tim Riel (Editor); Katie Lucas (Bookkeeper)
Parent company (for newspapers): Write Way Media

THE NORTH PROVIDENCE BREEZE

Street address 1: 6 Blackstone Valley Pl
Street address 2: Ste 204
Street address city: Lincoln
Street address state: RI
Zip/Postal code: 02865-1112
General Phone: (401)334-9555
General Fax: (401)334-9994
Advertising Phone: (401)334-9555 x 153
Editorial Phone: (401)334-9555 x122
General/National Adv. E-mail: cindy@valleybreeze.com
Display Adv. E-mail: donna@valleybreeze.com
Editorial e-mail: mgreen@valleybreeze.com
Primary Website: valleybreeze.com
Avg Paid Circ: 2
Avg Free Circ: 7749
Audit By: CVC
Audit Date: 30.06.2017
Personnel: Tom Ward (Pub.); Jamie Quinn (Dep. Pub.); Barbara Phinney (Accounting/HR); Karen Buckley (Adv. Dir.); Marcia Green (Ed.-in-Chief)
Parent company (for newspapers): Breeze Publications Inc.

THE POST

Street address 1: 1 Bradford St
Street address city: Bristol
Street address state: RI
Zip/Postal code: 02809-1906
General Phone: (401) 253-6000
General Fax: (401) 253-6055

Advertising Fax: (401) 253-6055
Editorial Fax: (401) 253-6055
General/National Adv. E-mail: mnascimento@eastbaynewspapers.com
Display Adv. E-mail:
Editorial e-mail: mrego@eastbaynewspapers.com
Primary Website: eastbayri.com
Avg Free Circ: 8324
Audit By: VAC
Audit Date: 30.06.2016
Personnel: Matthew D. Hayes (Pub.); Mike Rego (Ed.); Mary Nascimento (Ad Rep)
Parent company (for newspapers): East Bay Newspapers

THE VALLEY BREEZE - CUMBERLAND/LINCOLN

Street address 1: 6 Blackstone Valley Pl
Street address 2: Ste. 204
Street address city: Lincoln
Street address state: RI
Zip/Postal code: 02865-1112
General Phone: (401) 334-9555
General Fax: (401) 334-9994
General/National Adv. E-mail: tward@valleybreeze.com
Primary Website: valleybreeze.com
Year Established: 1996
Avg Paid Circ: 9
Avg Free Circ: 17014
Audit By: VAC
Audit Date: 30.09.2017
Personnel: Thomas V. Ward (Pub.); Marcia Green (Ed.); Karen Buckley (Adv. Dir.); James E. Quinn (Prodn. Mgr.); Rhonda Hanson (Circ. Mgr)
Parent company (for newspapers): Breeze Publications Inc.

THE VALLEY BREEZE - PAWTUCKET

Street address 1: 6 Blackstone Valley Pl
Street address 2: Ste 204
Street address city: Lincoln
Street address state: RI
Zip/Postal code: 02865-1112
General Phone: (401)334-9555
General Fax: (401)334-9994
General/National Adv. E-mail: karen@valleybreeze.com
Primary Website: valleybreeze.com
Avg Paid Circ: 3
Avg Free Circ: 9083
Audit By: VAC
Audit Date: 30.06.2017
Personnel: Tom Ward (Pub.); Jamie Quinn (Dep. Pub.); Barbara Phinney (Accounting/HR); Karen Buckley (Adv. Dir.); Marcia Green (Ed.-in-Chief)

THE VALLEY BREEZE - WOONSOCKET/NORTH SMITHFIELD

Street address 1: 6 Blackstone Valley Pl
Street address 2: Suite 204
Street address city: Lincoln
Street address state: RI
Zip/Postal code: 02865-1112
General Phone: (401) 334-9555
General Fax: (401) 334-9994
Advertising Phone: (401) 334-9555 ext. 142
Editorial Phone: ((401) 334-9555 ext. 122
General/National Adv. E-mail: karen@valleybreeze.com
Display Adv. E-mail: donna@valleybreeze.com
Editorial e-mail: mgreen@valleybreeze.com
Primary Website: valleybreeze.com
Avg Paid Circ: 7
Avg Free Circ: 16421
Audit By: VAC
Audit Date: 30.06.2017
Personnel: Tom Ward (Pub.); Jamie Quinn (Dep. Pub.); Barbara Phinney (Acounting/HR); Karen Buckley (Adv. Dir.); Marcia Green (Ed.-in-Chief)

THE VALLEY BREEZE & OBSERVER

Street address 1: 6 Blackstone Valley Pl
Street address 2: Suite 204
Street address city: Lincoln
Street address state: RI
Zip/Postal code: 02865-1112
General Phone: (401)334-9555
General Fax: (401)334-9994
General/National Adv. E-mail: karen@valleybreeze.com
Primary Website: valleybreeze.com
Avg Paid Circ: 4
Avg Free Circ: 10657
Audit By: VAC
Audit Date: 30.06.2017
Personnel: Tom Ward (Pub.); Jamie Quinn (Deputy Pub.); Karen Buckley (Adv. Dir.); Marcia Green (Ed.-in-Chief); Barbara Phinney (Accounting/HR)
Parent company (for newspapers): Breeze Publications Inc.

WARREN TIMES-GAZETTE

Street address 1: 1 Bradford St
Street address city: Bristol
Street address state: RI
Zip/Postal code: 02809-1906
General Phone: (401) 253-6000
General Fax: (401) 253-6055
Advertising Phone: (401) 424-9146
Advertising Fax: (401) 253-6055
Editorial Phone: (401) 935-2738
Editorial Fax: (401) 253-6055
General/National Adv. E-mail: tnuttall@eastbaynewspapers.com
Display Adv. E-mail: spitocchelli@eastbaynewspapers.com
Editorial e-mail: spickering@eastbaynewspapers.com
Primary Website: eastbayri.com
Year Established: 1837
Avg Paid Circ: 1426
Avg Free Circ: 0
Audit By: CVC
Audit Date: 30.06.2018
Personnel: Matthew D. Hayes (Pub.); Ted Hayes (Ed.); Scott Pickering (Mng. Ed.); Toni Nuttall (Adv. Dir.); Lisa Carro (Gen. Mgr.); Jock Hayes (Prodn. Mgr.)
Parent company (for newspapers): East Bay Newspapers

WARWICK BEACON

Street address 1: 1944 Warwick Ave
Street address city: Warwick
Street address state: RI
Zip/Postal code: 02889-2400
General Phone: (401)732-3100
General Fax: (401)732-3100
General/National Adv. E-mail: lisab@rhodybeat.com
Display Adv. E-mail: richardf@rhodybeat.com
Classified Adv. e-mail: sueh@rhodybeat.com
Editorial e-mail: johnh@rhodybeat.com
Primary Website: warwickonline.com
Mthly Avg Views: 220000
Mthly Avg Unique Visitors: 17000
Year Established: 1954
Avg Paid Circ: 5275
Avg Free Circ: 423
Audit By: CVC
Audit Date: 30.06.2018
Personnel: John I. Howell (Pub./Ed.); Richard G. Fleischer (Gen. Mgr.); Lynne Taylor (CFO)
Parent company (for newspapers): Beacon Communications, Inc

WESTPORT SHORELINES

Street address 1: 1 Bradford St
Street address city: Bristol
Street address state: RI
Zip/Postal code: 02809-1906
General Phone: (401) 253-6000
General Fax: (401) 253-6055
General/National Adv. E-mail: spickering@eastbaynewspapers.com
Display Adv. E-mail: spickering@eastbaynewspapers.com
Editorial e-mail: mhayes@eastbaynewspapers.com
Primary Website: eastbayri.com
Year Established: 1837
Avg Paid Circ: 1103
Avg Free Circ: 0
Audit By: CVC
Audit Date: 30.06.2018
Personnel: Matthew D. Hayes (Pub.); Bruce Burdett (Ed.); Scott Pickering (Mng. Ed.); Toni Nuttall (Adv. Dir.); Lisa Carro (Gen. Mgr.); Jock Hayes (Prodn. Mgr.)
Parent company (for newspapers): East Bay Newspapers

WOOD RIVER PRESS

Street address 1: 56 Main St
Street address city: Westerly
Street address state: RI
Zip/Postal code: 02891-2113
General Phone: (401) 348-1000
General Fax: (401) 348-3080
Advertising Phone: (860) 495-8265
Advertising Fax: (401) 348-3080
Editorial Phone: (860) 495-8224
Editorial Fax: (401) 348-3080
General/National Adv. E-mail: jlayton@thewesterlysun.com
Display Adv. E-mail: classified@thewesterlysun.com
Editorial e-mail: dsmith@thewesterlysun.com
Primary Website: thewesterlysun.com
Audit By: Sworn/Estimate/Non-Audited
Audit Date: 10.06.2019
Personnel: David Smith (Ed.); Kelly Tremaine (Vice Pres./Adv. Dir.)
Parent company (for newspapers): Sun Publishing Company

SOUTH CAROLINA

BERKELEY INDEPENDENT

Street address 1: 104 E Doty Ave
Street address city: Summerville
Street address state: SC
Zip/Postal code: 29483-6300
General Phone: (843) 761-6397
General Fax: (843) 899-6996
Advertising Phone: (843) 873-9424
Advertising Fax: (843) 899-6996
Editorial Phone: (843) 761-6397
Editorial Fax: (843) 899-6996
General/National Adv. E-mail: amack@berkeleyind.com
Display Adv. E-mail: landerson@berkeleyind.com
Editorial e-mail: dbrown@berkeleyind.com
Primary Website: berkeleyind.com
Year Established: 1987
Avg Paid Circ: 4500
Audit By: Sworn/Estimate/Non-Audited
Audit Date: 10.06.2019
Personnel: Ellen Priest (Pub.); Frank Johnson (Ed.); Chris Zoeller (Adv. Dir.); Cheryl Cargill (Bus. Mgr.)
Parent company (for newspapers): Evening Post Publishing Newspaper Group

BLUFFTON TODAY

Street address 1: 6 Promenade St
Street address 2: Unit 1005
Street address city: Bluffton
Street address state: SC
Zip/Postal code: 29910-7051
General Phone: (843) 815-0800
General Fax: (843) 815-0828
Advertising Phone: (843) 815-0800 ext. 18
Advertising Fax: (843) 815-0828
Editorial Phone: (843) 815-0800 ext. 19
Editorial Fax: (843) 815-0828
General/National Adv. E-mail: Kathryn.goodman@blufftontoday.com
Display Adv. E-mail: Mary.Ryan@blufftontoday.com
Editorial e-mail: lawrence.conneff@blufftontoday.com
Primary Website: blufftontoday.com
Year Established: 2005
Avg Free Circ: 10663
Sun. Circulation Paid: 442
Sun. Circulation Free: 9465
Audit By: AAM
Audit Date: 31.03.2018
Personnel: Michael Traynor (Pub.); Susan Catron (Exec. Ed.)
Parent company (for newspapers): CherryRoad Media

CAROLINA FOREST CHRONICLE

Street address 1: 4761 Highway 501
Street address 2: Ste 3
Street address city: Myrtle Beach
Street address state: SC
Zip/Postal code: 29579-9457
General Phone: (843) 236-4810
General Fax: (843) 448-4860
Advertising Phone: (843) 488-7234
Advertising Fax: (843) 448-4860
Editorial Phone: (843) 488-7259
Editorial Fax: (843) 448-4860
General/National Adv. E-mail: shari.harms@myhorrynews.com
Display Adv. E-mail: shari.harms@myhorrynews.com
Editorial e-mail: michael.smith@myhorrynews.com
Primary Website: myhorrynews.com
Year Established: 2007
Avg Paid Circ: 5000
Avg Free Circ: 125
Audit By: Sworn/Estimate/Non-Audited
Audit Date: 10.06.2019
Personnel: Steve Robertson (Owner/Pub.); Betty Moses (Prod. Mgr.); charles Perry (Editor); Shari Harms (Advertising Director)
Parent company (for newspapers): Waccamaw Publishers Inc.

CHESTER NEWS & REPORTER

Street address 1: 104 York St
Street address city: Chester
Street address state: SC
Zip/Postal code: 29706-1427
General Phone: (803) 385-3177
General Fax: (803) 581-2518
Advertising Phone: (803)385-3177
Advertising Fax: (803)581-2518
Editorial Phone: (803)385-3177
Editorial Fax: (803)581-2518
General/National Adv. E-mail: addepartment@onlinechester.com
Display Adv. E-mail: addepartment@onlinechester.com
Editorial e-mail: newsdepartment@onlinechester.com
Primary Website: onlinechester.com
Year Established: 1869
Avg Paid Circ: 7175
Audit By: Sworn/Estimate/Non-Audited
Audit Date: 10.06.2019
Personnel: William J. Aultman (Pub.); Nancy Pearsons (Ed./Adv. Sales Rep.); Fran Dodds (Adv. Rep.); Karen Graham (Classified Mgr.)
Parent company (for newspapers): Landmark Communications, Inc.; Landmark Community Newspapers, LLC

CHRONICLE-INDEPENDENT

Street address 1: 909 W Dekalb St
Street address city: Camden
Street address state: SC
Zip/Postal code: 29020-4259
General Phone: (803) 432-6157
General Fax: (803) 432-7609
Advertising Phone: (803) 432-6157 ext. 127
Advertising Fax: (803) 432-7609
Editorial Phone: (803) 432-6157 ext. 115
Editorial Fax: (803) 432-7609
General/National Adv. E-mail: bgreenway@ci-camden.com
Display Adv. E-mail: csmith@ci-camden.com
Editorial e-mail: editor@ci-camden.com
Primary Website: chronicle-independent.com
Year Established: 1889
Avg Paid Circ: 6500
Audit By: Sworn/Estimate/Non-Audited
Audit Date: 10.06.2019
Personnel: Michael Mischner (Pub.); Betsy Greenway (Adv. Mgr.); Debbie Albertson (Circ. Mgr.); Martha Bruce (Ed.)
Parent company (for newspapers): Morris Multimedia, Inc.

COASTAL OBSERVER

Street address 1: 97 Commerce Dr
Street address city: Pawleys Island
Street address state: SC
Zip/Postal code: 29585-6011
General Phone: (843) 237-8438
General Fax: (843) 235-0084
Advertising Phone: (843) 237-8438
Advertising Fax: (843) 235-0084
Editorial Phone: (843) 237-8438
Editorial Fax: (843) 235-0084
General/National Adv. E-mail: coastalobserverads@gmail.com
Display Adv. E-mail: coastalobserverads@gmail.com

Editorial e-mail: editor@coastalobserver.com
Primary Website: coastalobserver.com
Year Established: 1982
Avg Paid Circ: 5000
Audit By: Sworn/Estimate/Non-Audited
Audit Date: 10.06.2019
Personnel: M.P. Swenson (Pub.); Charles R. Swenson (Ed.)

FORT MILL TIMES

Street address 1: 132 W Main St
Street address city: Rock Hill
Street address state: SC
Zip/Postal code: 29730-4430
General Phone: (803) 326-4315
Advertising Phone: (803) 326-4313
Editorial Phone: (803) 326-4315
General/National Adv. E-mail: gkerosetz@heraldonline.com
Display Adv. E-mail: myoung@heraldonline.com
Editorial e-mail: news@fortmilltimes.com
Primary Website: fortmilltimes.com
Year Established: 1892
Avg Free Circ: 24000
Audit By: Sworn/Estimate/Non-Audited
Audit Date: 10.06.2019
Personnel: Cliff Harrington (Ed.); Catherine Muccigrosso (Asst. Ed.); Bret McCormick (Sports Ed.); Greg DePaoli (Circ. Mgr.); Betty Halliday (Adv. Sales)
Parent company (for newspapers): The McClatchy Company

HAMPTON COUNTY GUARDIAN

Street address 1: 306 Lee Ave
Street address city: Hampton
Street address state: SC
Zip/Postal code: 29924-3442
General Phone: (803) 943-4645
General Fax: (803) 943-9365
Advertising Phone: (803) 943-4645
Advertising Fax: (803) 943-9365
Editorial Phone: (803) 943-4645
Editorial Fax: (803) 943-9365
General/National Adv. E-mail: ads@hamptoncountyguardian.com
Display Adv. E-mail: news@hamptoncountyguardian.com
Editorial e-mail: news@hamptoncountyguardian.com
Primary Website: hamptoncountyguardian.com
Year Established: 1879
Avg Paid Circ: 5200
Audit By: Sworn/Estimate/Non-Audited
Audit Date: 10.06.2019
Personnel: Michael DeWitt (Pub.); Angie Crosby (Circ. Mgr.); Catina Gadson (Adv. Sales)

HERALD-ADVOCATE

Street address 1: 100 Fayetteville Ave
Street address city: Bennettsville
Street address state: SC
Zip/Postal code: 29512-4022
General Phone: (843) 479-3815
General Fax: (843) 479-7671
Advertising Phone: (843) 479-3815
Advertising Fax: (843) 479-7671
Editorial Phone: (843) 479-3815
Editorial Fax: (843) 479-7671
General/National Adv. E-mail: ads@heraldadvocate.com
Display Adv. E-mail: ads@heraldadvocate.com
Editorial e-mail: news@heraldadvocate.com
Primary Website: heraldadvocate.com
Year Established: 1874
Avg Paid Circ: 6800
Audit By: Sworn/Estimate/Non-Audited
Audit Date: 10.06.2019
Personnel: Dan McNiel (Ed.); Elizabeth McNiel (Pub.)
Parent company (for newspapers): Marlboro Publishing Co.

JASPER COUNTY SUN

Street address 1: 138 S RAILROAD AVE
Street address city: Ridgeland
Street address state: SC
Zip/Postal code: 29936
General Phone: (843) 726-6161
General Fax: (843) 726-8661
Advertising Phone: (843) 726-6161
Advertising Fax: (843) 726-8661
Editorial Phone: (843) 726-6161
Editorial Fax: (843) 726-8661
General/National Adv. E-mail: news@jaspercountysun.com
Display Adv. E-mail: news@jaspercountysun.com
Editorial e-mail: news@jaspercountysun.com
Primary Website: jaspercountysun.com
Avg Paid Circ: 6000
Audit By: Sworn/Estimate/Non-Audited
Audit Date: 10.06.2019
Personnel: Anthony Garzilli (Ed.); Wanda Phillips (Sales Rep.); Nancy White (Office Mgr.)

KEOWEE COURIER

Street address 1: 118 S College St
Street address city: Walhalla
Street address state: SC
Zip/Postal code: 29691-2258
General Phone: (864) 638-5856
General Fax: (864) 638-5857
Advertising Phone: (864) 638-5856
Advertising Fax: (864) 638-5857
Editorial Phone: (864) 638-5856
Editorial Fax: (864) 638-5857
General/National Adv. E-mail: keoweecourier@bellsouth.net
Display Adv. E-mail: westnews@bellsouth.net
Editorial e-mail: westnews@bellsouth.net
Primary Website: laserbuddy.com/news/kc.htm
Year Established: 1849
Avg Paid Circ: 2300
Avg Free Circ: 206
Audit By: Sworn/Estimate/Non-Audited
Audit Date: 10.06.2019
Personnel: Candi Phillips (Mng. Ed./ Adv. Dir.)
Parent company (for newspapers): Keowee Publications, Inc.

LAKE CITY NEWS & POST

Street address 1: 310 S Dargan St
Street address city: Florence
Street address state: SC
Zip/Postal code: 29506-2537
General Phone: (843) 317-6397
Advertising Fax: (843) 317-7290
Editorial Fax: (843) 317-7292
General/National Adv. E-mail: news@scnow.com
Primary Website: scnow.com/newsandpost
Audit By: Sworn/Estimate/Non-Audited
Audit Date: 10.06.2019
Personnel: Donna Wiggins (Acct. Exec.); Shamira McCray (Ed.)
Parent company (for newspapers): BH Media Group

LANCASTER NEWS

Street address 1: 701 N White St
Street address city: Lancaster
Street address state: SC
Zip/Postal code: 29720-2174
General Phone: (803) 283-1133
General Fax: (803) 283-8969
Advertising Phone: (803) 283-1133
Advertising Fax: (803) 283-8969
Editorial Phone: (803) 283-1133
Editorial Fax: (803) 283-8969
General/National Adv. E-mail: news@thelancasternews.com
Display Adv. E-mail: news@thelancasternews.com
Editorial e-mail: news@thelancasternews.com
Primary Website: thelancasternews.com
Year Established: 1852
Avg Paid Circ: 12500
Audit By: Sworn/Estimate/Non-Audited
Audit Date: 10.06.2019
Personnel: Susan Rowell (Pub.); Jane Alford (Editor); Leigh Alrington (Adv. Mgr.); Angela Vincent (Circ. Mgr.); Barbara Howell (Ed.); Bruce Adams (Prodn. Mgr.)
Parent company (for newspapers): Paxton Media Group; Landmark Communications, Inc.; Paxton Media Group; Landmark Community Newspapers, LLC

LAURENS COUNTY ADVERTISER

Street address 1: 226 W Laurens St
Street address city: Laurens
Street address state: SC
Zip/Postal code: 29360-2960
General Phone: (864) 984-2586
General Fax: (864) 984-4039
Advertising Phone: (864) 984-2586
Advertising Fax: (864) 984-4039
Editorial Phone: (864) 984-2586
Editorial Fax: (864) 984-4039
General/National Adv. E-mail: advertising@lcadvertiser.com
Display Adv. E-mail: classifieds@lcadvertiser.com
Editorial e-mail: news@lcadvertiser.com
Primary Website: laurenscountyadvertiser.net
Avg Free Circ: 250
Audit By: Sworn/Estimate/Non-Audited
Audit Date: 10.06.2019
Personnel: James Brown (Adv. Mgr.); Marc Brown (Prodn. Mgr.)

LEE COUNTY OBSERVER

Street address 1: 218 N Main St
Street address city: Bishopville
Street address state: SC
Zip/Postal code: 29010-1416
General Phone: (803) 484-9431
General Fax: (803) 484-5055
Advertising Phone: (803) 484-9431
Advertising Fax: (803) 484-5055
Editorial Phone: (803) 484-9431
Editorial Fax: (803) 484-5055
General/National Adv. E-mail: advertise@sc.rr.com
Display Adv. E-mail: observer@sc.rr.com
Editorial e-mail: editor@sc.rr.com
Year Established: 1902
Avg Paid Circ: 3100
Avg Free Circ: 25
Audit By: Sworn/Estimate/Non-Audited
Audit Date: 10.06.2019
Personnel: Michael Mischner (Pub.); Nancy Wilson (Office Mgr.); Millie Scott (Adv. Sales Mgr.); BG Maize (Circ. Mgr.); Gee Atkinson (Mng. Ed.)
Parent company (for newspapers): Morris Multimedia, Inc.

LEXINGTON COUNTY CHRONICLE & THE DISPATCH-NEWS

Street address 1: 131 Swartz Rd
Street address city: Lexington
Street address state: SC
Zip/Postal code: 29072-3623
General Phone: (803) 359-7633
General Fax: (803) 359-2936
Advertising Phone: (803) 359-7633
Editorial Phone: (803) 359-7633
General/National Adv. E-mail: lexingtonchronicle@gmail.com
Display Adv. E-mail: lexingtonchronicle@gmail.com
Editorial e-mail: lexingtonchronicle@gmail.com
Primary Website: lexingtonchronicle.com
Year Established: 1870
Avg Paid Circ: 3500
Avg Free Circ: 6000
Audit By: Sworn/Estimate/Non-Audited
Audit Date: 10.06.2019
Personnel: MacLeod Bellune (Adv. Mgr.); Jerry Bellune (Ed. Emer.); Linda Sauls (Adv. Mgr.); Mark Bellune (Mng. Ed.); Thomas Grant (Sports Ed.); Jewel Hull (Office Manager); Rose Cisneros (Mng. Ed.); Katie Ritchie (Circ. Mgr.)
Parent company (for newspapers): Lexington Publishing Co, Inc.

MARION COUNTY NEWS JOURNAL

Street address 1: 800 N MAIN ST
Street address city: Marion
Street address state: SC
Zip/Postal code: 29571-2519
General Phone: (843) 423-7336
General Fax: (843) 423-7111
Advertising Phone: (843) 423-7336
Advertising Fax: (843) 423-7111
Editorial Phone: (843) 423-7336
Editorial Fax: (843) 423-7111
General/National Adv. E-mail: advertising@marionnewsjournal.com
Display Adv. E-mail: classifiedads@marioncountynewsjournal.com
Editorial e-mail: mcnj@marioncountynewsjournal.com
Primary Website: marioncountynewsjournal.com
Mthly Avg Views: 23458
Mthly Avg Unique Visitors: 7942
Year Established: 1996
Avg Paid Circ: 6
Avg Free Circ: 11297
Audit By: CVC
Audit Date: 30.09.2017
Personnel: Don Swartz (Pub./Ed.); Kay Byrd (Adv. Dir.); Catherine Moreno (Web Mgr.); Beth Strett (Prod. Mgr)
Parent company (for newspapers): Swartz Media, LLC

MARION STAR & MULLINS ENTERPRISE

Street address 1: 310 S Dargan St
Street address city: Florence
Street address state: SC
Zip/Postal code: 29506-2537
General Phone: (843) 317-6397
General Fax: (843) 423-2542
Advertising Phone: (843) 423-2050
Advertising Fax: (843) 423-2542
Editorial Phone: (843) 317-6397
Editorial Fax: (843) 423-2542
General/National Adv. E-mail: starandenterprise@scnow.com
Display Adv. E-mail: starandenterprise@scnow.com
Editorial e-mail: news@scnow.com
Primary Website: scnow.com/starandenterprise
Year Established: 1846
Avg Paid Circ: 4000
Avg Free Circ: 20000
Audit By: Sworn/Estimate/Non-Audited
Audit Date: 10.06.2019
Personnel: Joe Craig (Pub.); Naeem McFadden (Ed.); Kathy Sawyer (Adv. Account Exec.)

MCCORMICK MESSENGER

Street address 1: 120 S Main St
Street address city: Mc Cormick
Street address state: SC
Zip/Postal code: 29835-8345
General Phone: (864) 852-3311
General Fax: (864) 852-3528
Advertising Phone: (864) 852-3311
Advertising Fax: (864) 852-3528
Editorial Phone: (864) 852-3311
Editorial Fax: (864) 852-3528
General/National Adv. E-mail: mccmess@wctel.net
Display Adv. E-mail: mccmess@wctel.net
Editorial e-mail: mccmess@wctel.net
Primary Website: themccormickmessenger.com
Year Established: 1902
Avg Paid Circ: 2200
Audit By: Sworn/Estimate/Non-Audited
Audit Date: 10.06.2019
Personnel: Vicki Dorn (Gen. Mgr.); Ashley Creswell (Adv. Mgr.); Karen Bowick (Office Mgr.)

MOULTRIE NEWS

Street address 1: 134 Columbus St
Street address city: Charleston
Street address state: SC
Zip/Postal code: 29403-4809
General Phone: (843) 958-7480
General Fax: (843) 958-7490
Advertising Phone: (843) 958-7489
Advertising Fax: (843) 958-7490
Editorial Phone: (843) 958-7482
Editorial Fax: (843) 958-7490
General/National Adv. E-mail: advertising@moultrienews.com
Display Adv. E-mail: emailads@moultrienews.com
Editorial e-mail: editor@moultrienews.com
Primary Website: moultrienews.com
Year Established: 1964
Avg Free Circ: 28000
Audit By: Sworn/Estimate/Non-Audited
Audit Date: 10.06.2019
Personnel: Vickey Boyd (Pub.); Sully Witte (Ed.)
Parent company (for newspapers): Evening Post Publishing Newspaper Group; Island Publications, Inc.

MRS.

Street address 1: 104 E Doty Ave
Street address 2: Ste C
Street address city: Summerville
Street address state: SC
Zip/Postal code: 29483-6394
General Phone: (843) 901-9968
General Fax: (843) 873-9432
Advertising Phone: (843) 873-9424

Advertising Fax: (843) 873-9432
Editorial Phone: (843) 873-9424
Editorial Fax: (843) 873-9432
General/National Adv. E-mail: ralexander@journalscene.com
Editorial e-mail: dkennard@journalscene.com
Primary Website: journalscene.com
Year Established: 1972
Avg Paid Circ: 1500
Avg Free Circ: 20000
Audit By: Sworn/Estimate/Non-Audited
Audit Date: 10.06.2019
Personnel: Rebecca Alexander (Exec. Ed.); David Kennard (Executive Editor)
Parent company (for newspapers): Evening Post Publishing Newspaper Group

MYRTLE BEACH HERALD

Street address 1: 4761 Highway 501
Street address 2: Ste 3
Street address city: Myrtle Beach
Street address state: SC
Zip/Postal code: 29579-9457
General Phone: (843) 236-4810
General Fax: (843) 448-4860
Advertising Phone: (843) 488-7234
Advertising Fax: (843) 448-4860
Editorial Phone: (843) 488-7258
Editorial Fax: (843) 448-4860
General/National Adv. E-mail: shari.harms@myhorrynews.com
Display Adv. E-mail: shari.harms@myhorrynews.com
Editorial e-mail: charles.perry@myhorrynews.com
Primary Website: myhorrynews.com
Year Established: 2009
Avg Paid Circ: 5600
Avg Free Circ: 125
Audit By: Sworn/Estimate/Non-Audited
Audit Date: 10.06.2019
Personnel: Steve Robertson (Owner/Pub.); Tom O'Dare (Ed.); Shari Harms (Advertising Directo)
Parent company (for newspapers): Waccamaw Publishers, Inc

NEWS & POST

Street address 1: 107 N Acline St
Street address city: Lake City
Street address state: SC
Zip/Postal code: 29560-2129
General Phone: (843) 394-3571
General Fax: (843) 394-5057
Advertising Phone: (843) 394-3571
Advertising Fax: (843) 394-5057
Editorial Phone: (843) 394-3571
Editorial Fax: (843) 394-5057
General/National Adv. E-mail: newsandpost@florencenews.com
Display Adv. E-mail: newsandpost@florencenews.com
Editorial e-mail: newsandpost@florencenews.com
Primary Website: scnow.com
Avg Paid Circ: 2500
Audit By: Sworn/Estimate/Non-Audited
Audit Date: 10.06.2019
Personnel: Donna Tracy (Pub./Ed.); David Johnson (Circ. Mgr.)
Parent company (for newspapers): World Media Enterprises Inc.

NORTH MYRTLE BEACH TIMES

Street address 1: 203 Highay 17 North
Street address city: North Myrtle Beach
Street address state: SC
Zip/Postal code: 29582
General Phone: (843) 249-3525
General Fax: (843) 249-7012
General/National Adv. E-mail: nmbtimes@sc.rr.com
Display Adv. E-mail: nmbtimes@sc.rr.com
Editorial e-mail: nmbtimes@sc.rr.com
Primary Website: nmbtimes.com
Year Established: 1971
Avg Paid Circ: 12598
Avg Free Circ: 200
Audit By: Sworn/Estimate/Non-Audited
Audit Date: 10.06.2019
Personnel: Polly Lowman (Pub./Ed.)

PAGELAND PROGRESSIVE-JOURNAL

Street address 1: P.O. Box 218
Street address city: Pageland
Street address state: SC
Zip/Postal code: 29728-0218
General Phone: (843) 672-2358
General Fax: (843) 672-5593
Editorial Phone: (843) 672-3002
General/National Adv. E-mail: dstokes@thelancasternews.com
Display Adv. E-mail: mcraig@thelancasternews.com
Editorial e-mail: editor@pagelandprogressive.com
Primary Website: pagelandprogressive.com
Avg Paid Circ: 3000
Audit By: Sworn/Estimate/Non-Audited
Audit Date: 10.06.2019
Personnel: Susan Rowell (Pub.); Kimberly Harrington (Editor); Sheila Whitaker (Office manager); Donna Stokes (Sales consultant); Vanessa Brewer-Tyson (Reporter)
Parent company (for newspapers): Paxton Media Group; Landmark Communications, Inc.; Landmark Community Newspapers, LLC

PEE DEE WEEKLY

Street address 1: 310 S Dargan St
Street address city: Florence
Street address state: SC
Zip/Postal code: 29506-2537
General Phone: (843) 558-3323
General Fax: (843) 558-9601
Advertising Phone: (843) 558-3323
Advertising Fax: (843) 558-9601
Editorial Phone: (843) 558-3323
Editorial Fax: (843) 558-9601
General/National Adv. E-mail: jcomfort@florencenews.com
Display Adv. E-mail: jcomfort@florencenews.com
Editorial e-mail: bdabney@florencenews.com
Primary Website: scnow.com
Year Established: 1973
Avg Paid Circ: 0
Avg Free Circ: 53294
Audit By: CVC
Audit Date: 30.09.2018
Personnel: Bailey Dabney; Jane Comfort (Adv.); William Calcutt (Circ.)
Parent company (for newspapers): BH Media Group

SOUTH STRAND NEWS

Street address 1: 615 Front St
Street address city: Georgetown
Street address state: SC
Zip/Postal code: 29440-3623
General Phone: (843) 546-4148
General Fax: (843) 545-8928
General/National Adv. E-mail: jcioni@southstrandnews.com
Display Adv. E-mail: classifieds@southstrandnews.com
Primary Website: southstrandnews.com
Year Established: 1798
Avg Paid Circ: 6208
Avg Free Circ: 0
Audit By: Sworn/Estimate/Non-Audited
Audit Date: 10.06.2019
Personnel: John Cioni (Adv. Mgr.)
Parent company (for newspapers): Evening Post Publishing Newspaper Group

STANDARD SENTINEL

Street address 1: 302 N Main St
Street address city: Saluda
Street address state: SC
Zip/Postal code: 29138-1353
General Phone: (864) 445-2527
General Fax: (864) 445-8679
Advertising Phone: (864) 445-2527
Advertising Fax: (864) 445-8679
Editorial Phone: (864) 445-2527
Editorial Fax: (864) 445-8679
General/National Adv. E-mail: sentinel@saludasc.com
Display Adv. E-mail: sentinel@saludasc.com
Editorial e-mail: sentinel@saludasc.com
Primary Website: saludastandard-sentinel.com
Avg Paid Circ: 4200
Audit By: Sworn/Estimate/Non-Audited
Audit Date: 10.06.2019
Personnel: Ralph B. Shealy (Pub./Ed.)

THE ADVERTIZER-HERALD

Street address 1: 369 McGee St
Street address city: Bamberg
Street address state: SC
Zip/Postal code: 29003-1338
General Phone: (803) 245-5204
General Fax: (803) 245-3900
Advertising Phone: (803) 245-5204
Advertising Fax: (803) 245-3900
Editorial Phone: (803) 245-5204
Editorial Fax: (803) 245-3900
General/National Adv. E-mail: ahpublisher@bellsouth.net
Display Adv. E-mail: ahpublisher@bellsouth.net
Editorial e-mail: ahpublisher@bellsouth.net
Primary Website: advertizerherald.com
Avg Paid Circ: 2450
Audit By: Sworn/Estimate/Non-Audited
Audit Date: 10.06.2019
Personnel: Joyce Searson (Pub./Gen. Mgr.)

THE BELTON & HONEA PATH NEWS-CHRONICLE

Street address 1: 310 City Sq
Street address city: Belton
Street address state: SC
Zip/Postal code: 29627-1435
General Phone: (864) 338-6124
General Fax: (864) 338-1109
Advertising Phone: (864) 338-6124
Advertising Fax: (864) 338-1109
Editorial Phone: (864) 338-6124
Editorial Fax: (864) 338-1109
General/National Adv. E-mail: elaine@bhpnc.com
Display Adv. E-mail: elaine@bhpnc.com
Editorial e-mail: elaine@bhpnc.com
Primary Website: bhpnc.com
Year Established: 1894
Avg Paid Circ: 2500
Audit By: Sworn/Estimate/Non-Audited
Audit Date: 10.06.2019
Personnel: Lynn Robinson (Co-Pub./Bus. Mgr.); Elaine Ellison-Rider (Co-Pub./Ed.); Doris E. Ellison (Co-Pub.)

THE CALHOUN TIMES

Street address 1: 1632 Bridge St
Street address city: Saint Matthews
Street address state: SC
Zip/Postal code: 29135-1373
General Phone: (803) 874-3137
General Fax: (803) 874-1588
Advertising Phone: (803) 874-3137
Advertising Fax: (803) 874-1588
Editorial Phone: (803) 874-3137
Editorial Fax: (803) 874-1588
General/National Adv. E-mail: thecalhountimes@windstream.net
Display Adv. E-mail: thecalhountimes@windstream.net
Editorial e-mail: thecalhountimes@windstream.net
Year Established: 1929
Avg Paid Circ: 2200
Avg Free Circ: 20
Audit By: Sworn/Estimate/Non-Audited
Audit Date: 10.06.2019
Personnel: Edwin C. Morris (Pub.); Edwin C. Sr. (Ed.)
Parent company (for newspapers): Rome News-Tribune

THE CHARLESTON CHRONICLE

Street address 1: 1111 King St
Street address city: Charleston
Street address state: SC
Zip/Postal code: 29403-3761
General Phone: (843) 723-2785
General Fax: (843) 737-5443
Advertising Phone: (843) 723-2785
Advertising Fax: (843) 737-5443
Editorial Phone: (843) 723-2785
Editorial Fax: (843) 737-5443
General/National Adv. E-mail: sales@charlestonchronicle.net
Display Adv. E-mail: publisher@charlestonchronicle.net
Editorial e-mail: news@charlestonchronicle.net
Primary Website: charlestonchronicle.net
Year Established: 1971
Avg Paid Circ: 6000
Audit By: Sworn/Estimate/Non-Audited
Audit Date: 10.06.2019
Personnel: Nanette Smalls (Circ. Mgr.); James J. French (Pub.)

THE CLINTON CHRONICLE

Street address 1: 513 N Broad St
Street address city: Clinton
Street address state: SC
Zip/Postal code: 29325-1705
General Phone: (864)833-1900
General Fax: (864)833-1902
Advertising Phone: (864)833-1900
Advertising Fax: (864)833-1902
Editorial Phone: (864)833-1900
Editorial Fax: (864)833-1902
General/National Adv. E-mail: sales1@clintonchronicle.net
Display Adv. E-mail: janice@clintonchronicle.net
Editorial e-mail: news@clintonchronicle.net
Primary Website: clintonchronicle.com
Year Established: 1900
Avg Paid Circ: 3250
Avg Free Circ: 150
Audit By: Sworn/Estimate/Non-Audited
Audit Date: 10.06.2019
Personnel: Larry Franklin (Pub.); Janice Franklin (Office Mgr.); Shirley Pace (Adv. Mgr.)

THE COLUMBIA STAR

Street address 1: 723 Queen St
Street address city: Columbia
Street address state: SC
Zip/Postal code: 29205-1723
General Phone: (803) 771-0219
General Fax: (866) 608-1782
Advertising Phone: (803) 771-0219
Advertising Fax: (866) 608-1782
Editorial Phone: (803) 771-0219
Editorial Fax: (866) 608-1782
General/National Adv. E-mail: GailT@TheColumbiaStar.com
Display Adv. E-mail: Pams@TheColumbiaStar.com
Editorial e-mail: mimim@thecolumbiastar.com
Primary Website: thecolumbiastar.com
Year Established: 1963
Avg Paid Circ: 0
Avg Free Circ: 15000
Audit By: Sworn/Estimate/Non-Audited
Audit Date: 10.06.2019
Personnel: Mimi Maddock (Pub.); Mike Maedock (Exec. Ed.); Gail Trebuchon (Adv. Mgr.); Pam Clark (Office Mgr.)
Parent company (for newspapers): Star Reporter Corporation

THE DILLON HERALD

Street address 1: 505 Highway 301 N
Street address city: Dillon
Street address state: SC
Zip/Postal code: 29536-2957
General Phone: (843)774-3311
General Fax: (843)841-1930
Advertising Phone: (843)774-3311
Advertising Fax: (843)841-1930
Editorial Phone: (843)774-3311
Editorial Fax: (843)841-1930
General/National Adv. E-mail: jd@thedillonherald.com
Display Adv. E-mail: jd@thedillonherald.com
Editorial e-mail: bf@thedillonherald.com
Primary Website: thedillonherald.com
Year Established: 1894
Avg Paid Circ: 7485
Audit By: Sworn/Estimate/Non-Audited
Audit Date: 10.06.2019
Personnel: Johnnie Daniels (Gen. Mgr./Adv. Mgr.); Betsy Finklea (Pub./Ed.)

THE EAGLE-RECORD

Street address 1: 5549 Memorial Blvd
Street address city: Saint George
Street address state: SC
Zip/Postal code: 29477-2473
General Phone: (843) 563-3121
General Fax: (843) 563-5355
Advertising Phone: (843) 563-3121

Advertising Fax: (843) 563-5355
Editorial Phone: (843) 563-3121
Editorial Fax: (843) 563-5355
General/National Adv. E-mail: eaglerecord@lowcountry.com
Display Adv. E-mail: eaglerecord@lowcountry.com
Editorial e-mail: eaglerecord@lowcountry.com
Primary Website: theeaglerecord.com
Year Established: 1899
Avg Paid Circ: 3100
Audit By: Sworn/Estimate/Non-Audited
Audit Date: 10.06.2019
Personnel: Andrew Gentry (Pub./Ed.); Elizabeth Gentry (Office Mgr./Circ. Mgr.); Victoria M. Owens (Adv. Dir.); Julie McAlhany (Prod. Mgr.)

THE EASLEY PROGRESS

Street address 1: 201 W Main St
Street address city: Easley
Street address state: SC
Zip/Postal code: 29640-2040
General Phone: (864) 855-0355
General Fax: (864) 855-6825
Advertising Phone: (864) 855-0355
Advertising Fax: (864) 855-6825
Editorial Phone: (864) 855-0355
Editorial Fax: (864) 855-6825
General/National Adv. E-mail: cwyatt@civitasmedia.com
Display Adv. E-mail: ryoungblood@civitasmedia.com
Editorial e-mail: ladamson@civitasmedia.com
Primary Website: theeasleyprogress.com
Year Established: 1902
Avg Paid Circ: 7401
Audit By: Sworn/Estimate/Non-Audited
Audit Date: 10.06.2019
Personnel: Christine Wyatt (Gen. Mgr./Media Dir.); Rhonda Youngblood (Customer Ser Rep.)
Parent company (for newspapers): Champion Media

THE EDGEFIELD ADVERTISER

Street address 1: 117 Courthouse Sq
Street address city: Edgefield
Street address state: SC
Zip/Postal code: 29824-1319
General Phone: (803) 637-3540
General Fax: (803) 637-0602
Advertising Phone: (803) 637-3540
Advertising Fax: (803) 637-0602
Editorial Phone: (803) 637-3540
Editorial Fax: (803) 637-0602
General/National Adv. E-mail: sharon@edgefieldadvertiser.com
Display Adv. E-mail: sandra@edgefieldadvertiser.com
Editorial e-mail: suzanne@edgefieldadvertiser.com
Primary Website: edgefieldadvertiser.com
Year Established: 1836
Avg Paid Circ: 4000
Audit By: Sworn/Estimate/Non-Audited
Audit Date: 10.06.2019
Personnel: Suzanne Gile Mims Derrick (Owner/Pub./Ed.); Robert Norris (Online Ed.); Sandra Reece (Office Mgr.); Sharon Nunamaker (Adv. Mgr.)

THE FLORENCE NEWS JOURNAL

Street address 1: 312 Railroad Ave
Street address city: Florence
Street address state: SC
Zip/Postal code: 29506-2583
General Phone: (843) 667-9656
General Fax: (843) 661-7102
General/National Adv. E-mail: powersc@myflorencetoday.com
Display Adv. E-mail: classifieds@florencenewsjournal.com
Editorial e-mail: bharrison@florencenewsjournal.com
Primary Website: florencenewsjournal.com
Mthly Avg Views: 26037
Mthly Avg Unique Visitors: 10254
Year Established: 1982
Avg Paid Circ: 9
Avg Free Circ: 16212
Audit By: CVC
Audit Date: 30.09.2017
Personnel: Don Swartz (Pub.); Brenda Harrison (Ed.); Beth Strett (Prodn. Mgr.)
Parent company (for newspapers): Swartz Media, LLC

THE GAFFNEY LEDGER

Street address 1: 1604 W Floyd Baker Blvd
Street address city: Gaffney
Street address state: SC
Zip/Postal code: 29341-1206
General Phone: (864) 489-1131
General Fax: (864) 487-7667
General/National Adv. E-mail: cody@gaffneyledger.com
Display Adv. E-mail: wilson@gaffneyledger.com
Editorial e-mail: abbie@gaffneyledger.com
Primary Website: gaffneyledger.com
Mthly Avg Views: 93363
Mthly Avg Unique Visitors: 14858
Year Established: 1894
Avg Paid Circ: 4900
Avg Free Circ: 0
Audit By: Sworn/Estimate/Non-Audited
Audit Date: 28.09.2022
Personnel: Cody Sossamon (Pub.); Klonie Jordan (Ed.); Abbie Sossamon (Features/Lifestyles Editor); Greg Moore (Advt Mgr)

THE GAZETTE

Street address 1: 104 E Doty Ave
Street address 2: Ste C
Street address city: Summerville
Street address state: SC
Zip/Postal code: 29483-6300
General Phone: (843) 873-9424
General Fax: (843) 873-9432
Advertising Phone: (843) 873-9424
Advertising Fax: (843) 873-9432
Editorial Phone: (843) 873-9424
Editorial Fax: (843) 873-9432
General/National Adv. E-mail: czoeller@journalscene.com
Display Adv. E-mail: jasmine@ourgazette.com
Editorial e-mail: fjohnson@ourgazette.com
Primary Website: ourgazette.com
Avg Paid Circ: 77
Avg Free Circ: 15000
Audit By: Sworn/Estimate/Non-Audited
Audit Date: 10.06.2019
Personnel: Ellen Priest (Pub.); Frank Johnson (Ed.); Chris Zoeller (Adv. Dir.)
Parent company (for newspapers): Evening Post Publishing Newspaper Group

THE GEORGETOWN TIMES

Street address 1: 615 Front St
Street address city: Georgetown
Street address state: SC
Zip/Postal code: 29440-3623
General Phone: (843) 546-4148
Advertising Phone: (843) 546-4148 (Ext 235)
General/National Adv. E-mail: digital@southstrandnews.com
Display Adv. E-mail: classifieds@sothstrandnews.com
Primary Website: southstrandnews.com
Year Established: 1798
Avg Paid Circ: 9223
Avg Free Circ: 22000
Audit By: Sworn/Estimate/Non-Audited
Audit Date: 10.06.2019
Personnel: Jasmine Brown (Sales Ops. Exec.); John Cioni (Adv. Dir / Sales Mgr.); Lisa Wang (Bus. Mgr.); David Purtell (Reporter); Chris Decker (Reporter); Peter Banko (Ed., Pub.)
Parent company (for newspapers): Evening Post Publishing Newspaper Group

THE GREER CITIZEN

Street address 1: 317 Trade St
Street address city: Greer
Street address state: SC
Zip/Postal code: 29651-3431
General Phone: (864) 877-2076
General Fax: (864) 877-3563
Advertising Phone: (864) 877-2076 ext. 100
Advertising Fax: (864) 877-3563
Editorial Phone: (864) 877-2076 ext. 103
Editorial Fax: (864) 877-3563
General/National Adv. E-mail: sblackwell@greercitizen.com
Display Adv. E-mail: sreider@greercitizen.com
Editorial e-mail: billy@greercitizen.com
Primary Website: greercitizen.com
Year Established: 1918
Avg Paid Circ: 6300
Audit By: Sworn/Estimate/Non-Audited
Audit Date: 10.06.2019
Personnel: Steve Blackwell (Pub./Adv. Mgr.); Billy Cannada (Ed.)

THE HARTSVILLE MESSENGER

Street address 1: 212 Swift Creek Rd
Street address city: Hartsville
Street address state: SC
Zip/Postal code: 29550-4383
General Phone: (843) 332-6545
General Fax: (843) 332-1341
Advertising Phone: (843) 332-6545 ext. 10
Advertising Fax: (843) 332-1341
Editorial Phone: (843) 332-6545 ext. 16
Editorial Fax: (843) 332-1341
General/National Adv. E-mail: dwiggins@hartsvillemessenger.com
Display Adv. E-mail: swyatt@hartsvillemessenger.com
Editorial e-mail: rsloan@hartsvillemessenger.com
Primary Website: scnow.com
Year Established: 1893
Avg Paid Circ: 3
Avg Free Circ: 14640
Audit By: Sworn/Estimate/Non-Audited
Audit Date: 10.06.2019
Personnel: Robert Sloan (Pub./Ed.); Donna Wiggins (Account Exec.); Sara Wyatt (Account Exec.)
Parent company (for newspapers): Media General, Inc. (OOB); BH Media Group

THE HORRY INDEPENDENT

Street address 1: 2510 Main St
Street address city: Conway
Street address state: SC
Zip/Postal code: 29526-3365
General Phone: (843) 248-6671
General Fax: (843) 248-6024
Advertising Phone: (843) 488-7234
Advertising Fax: (843) 248-6024
Editorial Phone: (843) 488-7241
Editorial Fax: (843) 248-6024
General/National Adv. E-mail: shari.harms@myhorrynews.com
Display Adv. E-mail: shari.harms@myhorrynews.com
Editorial e-mail: kathy.ropp@myhorrynews.com
Primary Website: myhorrynews.com
Year Established: 1980
Avg Paid Circ: 6000
Avg Free Circ: 125
Audit By: Sworn/Estimate/Non-Audited
Audit Date: 10.06.2019
Personnel: Steve Robertson (Owner/Pub.); Kathy Ropp (Ed.); Adrian Robertson (Business Mgr.); Tom O'Dare (Editor)
Parent company (for newspapers): Waccamaw Publishers, Inc.

THE JOURNAL

Street address 1: 106 W Main St
Street address city: Williamston
Street address state: SC
Zip/Postal code: 29697-1404
General Phone: (864) 847-7361
General Fax: (864) 847-9879
Advertising Phone: (864) 847-7361
Advertising Fax: (864) 847-9879
Editorial Phone: (864) 847-7361
Editorial Fax: (864) 847-9879
General/National Adv. E-mail: tina@thejournalonline.com
Display Adv. E-mail: tina@thejournalonline.com
Editorial e-mail: editor@thejournalonline.com
Primary Website: thejournalonline.com
Year Established: 1955
Avg Paid Circ: 2500
Audit By: Sworn/Estimate/Non-Audited
Audit Date: 10.06.2019
Personnel: David C. Meade (Mng. Ed.); Richard A. Meade (Prod. Mgr.); Tina Williams (Graphics/Layout/Legal Adv. Mgr.)

THE LAKE MURRAY NEWS

Street address 1: PO Box 175
Street address city: Irmo
Street address state: SC
Zip/Postal code: 29063-0175
General Phone: (803) 772-5584
General Fax: (803) 772-7795
Advertising Phone: (803) 772-5584
Advertising Fax: (803) 772-7795
Editorial Phone: (803) 772-5584
Editorial Fax: (803) 772-7795
General/National Adv. E-mail: lakemurraynews@aol.com
Display Adv. E-mail: lakemurraynews@aol.com
Editorial e-mail: lakemurraynews@aol.com
Primary Website: thelakemurraynews.net
Avg Paid Circ: 9000
Audit By: Sworn/Estimate/Non-Audited
Audit Date: 10.06.2019
Personnel: Kirk Luther (Owner/Pub.); Rod Shealy Jr. (Co-Pub./Ed.)

THE LORIS SCENE

Street address 1: 2510 Main St
Street address city: Conway
Street address state: SC
Zip/Postal code: 29526-3365
General Phone: (843) 248-6671
General Fax: (843) 248-6024
Advertising Phone: (843) 488-7234
Advertising Fax: (843) 248-6024
Editorial Phone: (843) 488-7250
Editorial Fax: (843) 248-6024
General/National Adv. E-mail: shari.harms@myhorrynews.com
Display Adv. E-mail: shari.harms@myhorrynews.com
Editorial e-mail: annette.norris@myhorrynews.com
Primary Website: myhorrynews.com
Year Established: 190
Avg Paid Circ: 1800
Audit By: Sworn/Estimate/Non-Audited
Audit Date: 10.06.2019
Personnel: Steve Robertson (Owner/Pub.); Annette Norris (Ed.); Adrian Robertson (Business Mgr.); Shari Harms (Advertising Director)
Parent company (for newspapers): Horry News & Shopper; Waccamaw Publishers, Inc

THE MANNING TIMES

Street address 1: 230 E Boyce St
Street address city: Manning
Street address state: SC
Zip/Postal code: 29102-3441
General Phone: (803) 435-8422
General Fax: (803) 435-4189
General/National Adv. E-mail: manningsctimes@gmail.com
Display Adv. E-mail: manningsctimes@gmail.com
Editorial e-mail: editorial@manninglive.com
Primary Website: manninglive.com
Mthly Avg Views: 7000
Mthly Avg Unique Visitors: 150000
Year Established: 1882
Avg Paid Circ: 4000
Avg Free Circ: 14000
Audit By: Sworn/Estimate/Non-Audited
Audit Date: 10.06.2019
Personnel: Robert Baker (Ed.); Leigh Ann Maynard (Pub.)

THE NEWBERRY OBSERVER

Street address 1: 1716 Main St
Street address city: Newberry
Street address state: SC
Zip/Postal code: 29108-3548
General Phone: (803) 276-0625
General Fax: (803) 276-1517
Advertising Phone: (803) 276-0625
Advertising Fax: (803) 276-1517
Editorial Phone: (803) 276-0625
Editorial Fax: (803) 276-1517
General/National Adv. E-mail: news@newberryobserver.com
Display Adv. E-mail: news@newberryobserver.com
Editorial e-mail: news@newberryobserver.com
Primary Website: newberryobserver.com
Year Established: 1883
Avg Paid Circ: 7000
Audit By: Sworn/Estimate/Non-Audited
Audit Date: 10.06.2019

Personnel: Ty Ransdell (Pub.); Tiffany Lancaster (Circ. Mgr.); Holly Astwood (Ed.); Michelle Cromer (Prodn. Mgr.)
Parent company (for newspapers): Champion Media

THE NEWS

Street address 1: 511 N Longstreet St
Street address city: Kingstree
Street address state: SC
Zip/Postal code: 29556-3301
General Phone: (843) 355-6397
General Fax: (843) 355-6530
Advertising Phone: (843) 355-7454
Advertising Fax: (843) 355-6530
Editorial Phone: (843) 355-6397
Editorial Fax: (843) 355-6530
General/National Adv. E-mail: advertising@kingstreenews.com
Display Adv. E-mail: classifieds@kingstreenews.com
Editorial e-mail: trodgers@kingstreenews.com
Primary Website: kingstreenews.com
Avg Paid Circ: 4800
Audit By: Sworn/Estimate/Non-Audited
Audit Date: 10.06.2019
Personnel: Tami Rodgers (Pub./Ed.); Patricia McCrea (Circ. Mgr.); Beth Ward (Adv. Rep.)
Parent company (for newspapers): Evening Post Publishing Newspaper Group

THE NEWS & PRESS

Street address 1: 117 S MAIN ST
Street address city: Darlington
Street address state: SC
Zip/Postal code: 29532
General Phone: (843)393-3811
General Fax: (843)393-6811
General/National Adv. E-mail: ads@newsandpress.net
Display Adv. E-mail: sales@newsandpress.net
Editorial e-mail: editor@newsandpress.net
Primary Website: newsandpress.net
Year Established: 1874
Avg Paid Circ: 6200
Audit By: Sworn/Estimate/Non-Audited
Audit Date: 10.06.2019
Personnel: Bobby Bryant (Ed.); Stephan Drew (Editor); Dawson Jordan (General Manager); Glenda Atkinson (Sales Representative); Morrey Thomas (GM); Phyllis Caples (Customer Service Rep.)
Parent company (for newspapers): Herald Media Group, Inc.

THE PEOPLE-SENTINEL

Street address 1: 10481 DUNBARTON BLVD
Street address city: Barnwell
Street address state: SC
Zip/Postal code: 29812
General Phone: (803) 259-3501
General Fax: (803) 259-2703
General/National Adv. E-mail: advertise@chroniclemedia.com
Display Adv. E-mail: advertise@chroniclemedia.com
Editorial e-mail: newsroom@augustachronicle.com
Primary Website: thepeoplesentinel.com
Year Established: 1852
Avg Paid Circ: 3985
Avg Free Circ: 73
Audit By: Sworn/Estimate/Non-Audited
Audit Date: 10.06.2019
Personnel: John Gogick (Exec. Ed.); Mike Wynn (News Ed.); Tony Bernados (Pres.); James Holmes (VP, Sales)

THE PICKENS SENTINEL

Street address 1: 714-D S PENDLETON ST
Street address city: Easley
Street address state: SC
Zip/Postal code: 29640-3526
General Phone: (864) 855-0355
General Fax: (864) 855-6825
Advertising Phone: (864) 855-0355
Advertising Fax: (864) 855-6825
Editorial Phone: (864) 855-0355
Editorial Fax: (864) 855-6825
General/National Adv. E-mail: cwyatt@civitasmedia.com
Display Adv. E-mail: ryoungblood@civitasmedia.com
Editorial e-mail: ladamson@civitasmedia.com
Primary Website: pickenssentinel.com
Year Established: 1871
Avg Paid Circ: 6800
Audit By: Sworn/Estimate/Non-Audited
Audit Date: 10.06.2019
Personnel: Lonnie Adamson (Gen. Mgr./Ed.); Christine Wyatt (Adv. Mgr.); Rhonda Youngblood (Circ. Mgr./Classified)
Parent company (for newspapers): Champion Media

THE PRESS & BANNER

Street address 1: 107 W Pickens St
Street address city: Abbeville
Street address state: SC
Zip/Postal code: 29620-2415
General Phone: (864) 366-5461
General Fax: (864) 366-5463
Advertising Phone: (864) 366-5461
Advertising Fax: (864) 366-5463
Editorial Phone: (864) 366-5461
Editorial Fax: (864) 366-5463
General/National Adv. E-mail: pb@bannercorp.net
Display Adv. E-mail: pb@bannercorp.net
Editorial e-mail: pb@bannercorp.net
Year Established: 1844
Avg Paid Circ: 7000
Audit By: Sworn/Estimate/Non-Audited
Audit Date: 10.06.2019
Personnel: John R. West (Pub./Ed.); Lamar West (Prod. Mgr.)

THE PRESS AND STANDARD

Street address 1: 1025 Bells Hwy
Street address city: Walterboro
Street address state: SC
Zip/Postal code: 29488-2507
General Phone: (843) 549-2586
General Fax: (843) 549-2446
Advertising Phone: (843) 549-2586
Advertising Fax: (843) 549-2446
Editorial Phone: (843) 549-2586
Editorial Fax: (843) 549-2446
General/National Adv. E-mail: pressadvertising@lowcountry.com
Display Adv. E-mail: pressadvertising@lowcountry.com
Editorial e-mail: editor@lowcountry.com
Primary Website: walterborolive.com
Year Established: 1877
Avg Paid Circ: 4500
Audit By: Sworn/Estimate/Non-Audited
Audit Date: 10.06.2019
Personnel: Carol Haun (Pub.)

THE STAR

Street address 1: 406 West Avenue
Street address city: North Augusta
Street address state: SC
Zip/Postal code: 29841
General Phone: (803) 279-2793
General Fax: (803) 278-4070
General/National Adv. E-mail: rdallas@northaugustastar.com
Display Adv. E-mail: rdallas@northaugustastar.com
Editorial e-mail: editor@northaugustastar.com
Primary Website: northaugustastar.com
Year Established: 1954
Avg Paid Circ: 4000
Avg Free Circ: 33
Audit By: Sworn/Estimate/Non-Audited
Audit Date: 10.06.2019
Personnel: Lindsey McCullough; Diane Daniell
Parent company (for newspapers): Aiken Communications, Inc.; Evening Post Publishing Newspaper Group

THE TWIN-CITY NEWS

Street address 1: 114 E Columbia Ave
Street address city: Batesburg Leesville
Street address state: SC
Zip/Postal code: 29006-2130
General Phone: (803) 532-6203
General Fax: (803) 532-6204
Advertising Phone: (803) 532-6203
Advertising Fax: (803) 532-6204
Editorial Phone: (803) 532-6203
Editorial Fax: (803) 532-6204
General/National Adv. E-mail: bltwincitynews@gmail.com
Display Adv. E-mail: bltwincitynews@gmail.com
Classified Adv. e-mail: bltwincitynews@gmail.com
Editorial e-mail: bltwincitynews@gmail.com
Primary Website: twin-citynews.com
Year Established: 1925
Avg Paid Circ: 2675
Avg Free Circ: 39
Audit By: Sworn/Estimate/Non-Audited
Audit Date: 10.06.2019
Personnel: Douglas Bruner III (Publisher); Teresa Shealy (Office Mgr.); Leah Bruner (Editor)

THE WARE SHOALS OBSERVER

Street address 1: 730 N Greenwood Ave
Street address city: Ware Shoals
Street address state: SC
Zip/Postal code: 29692-1233
General Phone: (864) 456-7772
General Fax: (864) 456-7122
Advertising Phone: (864) 456-7772
Advertising Fax: (864) 456-7122
Editorial Phone: (864) 456-7772
Editorial Fax: (864) 456-7122
General/National Adv. E-mail: theobserver@embarqmail.com
Display Adv. E-mail: theobserver@embarqmail.com
Editorial e-mail: theobserver@embarqmail.com
Avg Paid Circ: 2950
Avg Free Circ: 50
Audit By: Sworn/Estimate/Non-Audited
Audit Date: 10.06.2019
Personnel: S. Daniel Branyon (Pub.); Faye Branyon (Ed.)

THE WESTMINSTER NEWS

Street address 1: 100 E Main St
Street address city: Westminster
Street address state: SC
Zip/Postal code: 29693-1715
General Phone: (864) 647-5404
General Fax: (864) 647-5405
Advertising Phone: (864) 647-5404
Advertising Fax: (864) 647-5405
Editorial Phone: (864) 647-5404
Editorial Fax: (864) 647-5405
General/National Adv. E-mail: westnews@bellsouth.net
Display Adv. E-mail: westnews@bellsouth.net
Editorial e-mail: westnews@bellsouth.net
Primary Website: westminstersc.com
Year Established: 1954
Avg Paid Circ: 2500
Avg Free Circ: 50
Audit By: Sworn/Estimate/Non-Audited
Audit Date: 10.06.2019
Personnel: Robert E. Tribble (Pres./Pub.); Mary Beth King (Mng. Ed.); Rolann Lee (Ed.)
Parent company (for newspapers): Trib Publications

TRIBUNE-TIMES

Street address 1: 305 S Main St
Street address city: Greenville
Street address state: SC
Zip/Postal code: 29601-2605
General Phone: (864) 298-4100
General Fax: (864) 298-4395
Advertising Phone: (864) 298-4342
Advertising Fax: (864) 298-4395
Editorial Phone: (864) 298-4100
Editorial Fax: (864) 298-4395
General/National Adv. E-mail: dfoster3@gannett.com
Display Adv. E-mail: dfoster3@gannett.com
Editorial e-mail: khardy1@greenvillenews.com
Primary Website: greenvilleonline.com
Avg Free Circ: 37674
Audit By: Sworn/Estimate/Non-Audited
Audit Date: 10.06.2019
Personnel: John S. Pittman (Exec. Ed.); Bill Fox (News Dir.); Maggie Krost (Marketing VP)
Parent company (for newspapers): Gannett

WEST WATEREE CHRONICLE

Street address 1: 909 W Dekalb St
Street address city: Camden
Street address state: SC
Zip/Postal code: 29020-4259
General Phone: (803) 432-6157
General Fax: (803) 432-7609
Advertising Phone: (803) 432-6157 ext. 127
Advertising Fax: (803) 432-7609
Editorial Phone: (803) 432-6157 ext. 115
Editorial Fax: (803) 432-7609
General/National Adv. E-mail: bgreenway@ci-camden.com
Display Adv. E-mail: csmith@ci-camden.com
Editorial e-mail: editor@ci-camden.com
Primary Website: chronicle-independent.com
Year Established: 1889
Avg Paid Circ: 6500
Audit By: Sworn/Estimate/Non-Audited
Audit Date: 10.06.2019
Personnel: Michael Mischner (Pub.); Betsy Greenway (Adv. Mgr.); Debbie Albertson (Circ. Mgr.); Martha Bruce (Ed.)

SOUTH DAKOTA

ALCESTER UNION & HUDSONITE

Street address 1: 110 E First St
Street address city: Alcester
Street address state: SD
Zip/Postal code: 57001
General Phone: (605) 934-2640
General Fax: (605) 934-2096
Advertising Phone: (605) 934-2640
Advertising Fax: (605) 934-2096
Editorial Phone: (605) 934-2640
Editorial Fax: (605) 934-2096
General/National Adv. E-mail: advertising@ahenews.com
Display Adv. E-mail: info@ahenews.com
Editorial e-mail: publisher@ahenews.com
Primary Website: ahenews.com
Year Established: 1889
Avg Paid Circ: 890
Avg Free Circ: 35
Audit By: Sworn/Estimate/Non-Audited
Audit Date: 10.06.2019
Personnel: Paul Buum (Pub./Ed.); Michele Buum (Circ. Mgr.)
Parent company (for newspapers): Paragon Publishing

AVON CLARION

Street address 1: 103 MAIN ST N
Street address city: Avon
Street address state: SD
Zip/Postal code: 57315
General Phone: (605) 286-3919
General Fax: (605) 286-3507
Advertising Phone: (605) 286-3919
Advertising Fax: (605) 286-3507
Editorial Phone: (605) 286-3919
Editorial Fax: (605) 286-3507
General/National Adv. E-mail: theavonclarion@yahoo.com
Display Adv. E-mail: theavonclarion@yahoo.com
Editorial e-mail: theavonclarion@yahoo.com
Primary Website: avonsd.com
Avg Paid Circ: 800
Audit By: Sworn/Estimate/Non-Audited
Audit Date: 10.06.2019
Personnel: Jackson S. Brodeen (Pub./Ed./Adv. Mgr.)

BALTIC BEACON

Street address 1: 414 E 4th St
Street address city: Dell Rapids
Street address state: SD
Zip/Postal code: 57022-1928
General Phone: (605) 428-5441
General Fax: (605) 428-5992
Advertising Phone: (605) 428-5441
Advertising Fax: (605) 428-5992
Editorial Phone: (605) 428-5441
Editorial Fax: (605) 428-5992
General/National Adv. E-mail: tribune@dellrapids.net
Display Adv. E-mail: tribune@dellrapids.net
Editorial e-mail: editor@dellrapidsinfo.com
Primary Website: argusleader.com/news/dell-rapids
Avg Paid Circ: 320
Avg Free Circ: 6100
Audit By: Sworn/Estimate/Non-Audited
Audit Date: 10.06.2019
Personnel: Corey Meyers (News Dir.); Brent Vell (Ed.); Rick Wagoner (Prod. Mgr.); Jane Thaden Lawson (Planning Ed.)

Parent company (for newspapers): Gannett

BENNETT COUNTY BOOSTER II

Street address 1: 502 2nd Ave
Street address city: Martin
Street address state: SD
Zip/Postal code: 57551-8502
General Phone: (605) 685-6866
General Fax: (605) 685-6535
Advertising Phone: (605) 685-6866
Advertising Fax: (605) 685-6535
Editorial Phone: (605) 685-6866
Editorial Fax: (605) 685-6535
General/National Adv. E-mail: booster@gwtc.net
Display Adv. E-mail: booster@gwtc.net
Editorial e-mail: booster@gwtc.net
Primary Website: bennettcountyboostersd.com
Avg Paid Circ: 2250
Audit By: Sworn/Estimate/Non-Audited
Audit Date: 10.06.2019
Personnel: Tim Huether (Pub./Ed.); Marj Oleske (Adv. Mgr./News Ed.); Mandy Scherer (Gen. Mgr.)

BERESFORD REPUBLIC

Street address 1: 111 N 3rd St
Street address city: Beresford
Street address state: SD
Zip/Postal code: 57004-1741
General Phone: (605) 763-2006
General Fax: (605) 763-5503
Advertising Phone: (605) 763-2006
Advertising Fax: (605) 763-5503
Editorial Phone: (605) 763-2006
Editorial Fax: (605) 763-5503
General/National Adv. E-mail: republic@bmtc.net
Display Adv. E-mail: republic@bmtc.net
Editorial e-mail: republic@bmtc.net
Year Established: 1894
Avg Paid Circ: 1200
Audit By: Sworn/Estimate/Non-Audited
Audit Date: 10.06.2019
Personnel: Shane Hill (Pub.); Allyson Hill (Pub./Ed.)
Parent company (for newspapers): Star Publishing Co.

BLACK HILLS PIONEER

Street address 1: PO Box 7
Street address 2: 315 Seaton Circle
Street address city: Spearfish
Street address state: SD
Zip/Postal code: 57783
General Phone: (605) 642-2761
General Fax: (605) 642-9060
Advertising Phone: (605) 642-2761
Advertising Fax: (605) 642-9060
Editorial Phone: (605) 642-2761
Editorial Fax: (605) 642-9060
General/National Adv. E-mail: sona@bhpioneer.com
Display Adv. E-mail: sona@bhpioneer.com
Classified Adv. e-mail: classifieds@bhpioneer.com
Editorial e-mail: news@bhpioneer.com
Primary Website: www.bhpioneer.com
Mthly Avg Views: 408333
Mthly Avg Unique Visitors: 79833
Year Established: 1876
Avg Paid Circ: 4500
Avg Free Circ: 50
Audit By: Sworn/Estimate/Non-Audited
Audit Date: 23.09.2019
Personnel: Letitia Lister (Pub.); Mark Watson (Ed.); Sona O'Connell (Ad Manager); Dru Thomas (Adv. Mgr.)
Parent company (for newspapers): Seaton Publishing Company, Inc.

BRANDON VALLEY CHALLENGER

Street address 1: 1400 E Cedar St
Street address city: Brandon
Street address state: SD
Zip/Postal code: 57005-1604
General Phone: (605) 582-6025
General Fax: (605) 582-7184
Advertising Phone: (605) 582-6025
Advertising Fax: (605) 582-7184
Editorial Phone: (605) 582-6025
Editorial Fax: (605) 582-7184
General/National Adv. E-mail: aschultz@argusleader.com
Display Adv. E-mail: aschultz@argusleader.com
Editorial e-mail: apthiele@argusleader.com
Primary Website: brandoninfo.com
Avg Paid Circ: 1200
Avg Free Circ: 5700
Audit By: Sworn/Estimate/Non-Audited
Audit Date: 10.06.2019
Personnel: Jill Meier (Ed.); Andrea Schultz (Adv. Mgr.)
Parent company (for newspapers): Gannett

BRIDGEWATER TRIBUNE

Street address 1: 440 N Main St
Street address city: Bridgewater
Street address state: SD
Zip/Postal code: 57319
General Phone: (605) 425-2361
General Fax: (605) 425-2547
Advertising Phone: (605) 425-2361
Advertising Fax: (605) 425-2547
Editorial Phone: (605) 425-2361
Editorial Fax: (605) 425-2547
General/National Adv. E-mail: tschwans@triotel.net
Display Adv. E-mail: tschwans@triotel.net
Editorial e-mail: tschwans@triotel.net
Primary Website: salemspecial.com
Avg Paid Circ: 350
Avg Free Circ: 50
Audit By: Sworn/Estimate/Non-Audited
Audit Date: 10.06.2019
Personnel: Troy Schwans (Ed.)

CANISTOTA CLIPPER

Street address 1: 210 W Main St
Street address city: Canistota
Street address state: SD
Zip/Postal code: 57012
General Phone: (605) 296-3181
General Fax: (605) 296-3289
Advertising Phone: (605) 296-3181
Advertising Fax: (605) 296-3289
Editorial Phone: (605) 296-3181
Editorial Fax: (605) 296-3289
General/National Adv. E-mail: ads@andersonpublications.com
Display Adv. E-mail: ads@andersonpublications.com
Editorial e-mail: news@andersonpublications.com
Avg Paid Circ: 625
Audit By: Sworn/Estimate/Non-Audited
Audit Date: 10.06.2019
Personnel: Matt Anderson (Pub./Ed.); Jelene Olsen (Gen. Mgr.)

CENTERVILLE JOURNAL

Street address 1: 1000 Washington St
Street address city: Centerville
Street address state: SD
Zip/Postal code: 57014-2218
General Phone: (605) 563-2351
General Fax: (605) 326-5333
Advertising Phone: (605) 563-2351
Advertising Fax: (605) 326-5333
Editorial Phone: (605) 563-2351
Editorial Fax: (605) 326-5333
General/National Adv. E-mail: journal@iw.net
Display Adv. E-mail: journal@iw.net
Editorial e-mail: journal@iw.net
Avg Paid Circ: 810
Audit By: Sworn/Estimate/Non-Audited
Audit Date: 10.06.2019
Personnel: Shane Hill (Pub.); Allyson Hill (Ed.)
Parent company (for newspapers): Star Publishing Co.

CHARLES MIX COUNTY NEWS

Street address 1: 308 Main St
Street address city: Geddes
Street address state: SD
Zip/Postal code: 57342
General Phone: (605) 337-2571
General Fax: (605) 337-2363
Advertising Phone: (605) 337-2571
Advertising Fax: (605) 337-2363
Editorial Phone: (605) 337-2571
Editorial Fax: (605) 337-2363
General/National Adv. E-mail: cmcountynews@midstatesd.net
Display Adv. E-mail: cmcountynews@midstatesd.net
Editorial e-mail: cmcountynews@midstatesd.net
Avg Paid Circ: 685
Avg Free Circ: 1
Audit By: Sworn/Estimate/Non-Audited
Audit Date: 10.06.2019
Personnel: Rhonda Blair (Pub./Ed.); Wayne Blair (Co-Pub.)

CLARK COUNTY COURIER

Street address 1: 119 1st Ave E
Street address city: Clark
Street address state: SD
Zip/Postal code: 57225-1712
General Phone: (605) 532-3654
General Fax: (605) 532-5424
Advertising Phone: (605) 532-3654
Advertising Fax: (605) 532-5424
Editorial Phone: (605) 532-3654
Editorial Fax: (605) 532-5424
General/National Adv. E-mail: courier@itctel.com
Display Adv. E-mail: courier@itctel.com
Editorial e-mail: courier@itctel.com
Primary Website: clarkcountypublishing.com
Year Established: 1885
Avg Paid Circ: 2400
Avg Free Circ: 33
Audit By: Sworn/Estimate/Non-Audited
Audit Date: 10.06.2019
Personnel: Bill Krikac (Pub./Ed.)

CLEAR LAKE COURIER

Street address 1: 416 3rd Ave S
Street address city: Clear Lake
Street address state: SD
Zip/Postal code: 57226
General Phone: (605) 874-2499
General Fax: (605) 874-2642
Advertising Phone: (605) 874-2499
Advertising Fax: (605) 874-2642
Editorial Phone: (605) 874-2499
Editorial Fax: (605) 874-2642
General/National Adv. E-mail: clprint@itctel.com
Display Adv. E-mail: clprint@itctel.com
Editorial e-mail: clprint@itctel.com
Year Established: 1883
Avg Paid Circ: 1375
Avg Free Circ: 25
Audit By: Sworn/Estimate/Non-Audited
Audit Date: 10.06.2019
Personnel: Kenneth Reiste (Pub./Ed.); Nancy A. Greene (Adv. Mgr.)

CORSON SIOUX COUNTY NEWS MESSE

Street address 1: PO Box 788
Street address 2: 202 W 1st Ave
Street address city: Mc Laughlin
Street address state: SD
Zip/Postal code: 57642-0788
General Phone: (605) 823-4490
General Fax: (605) 823-4632
Advertising Phone: (605) 823-4490
Editorial Phone: (605) 823-4490
General/National Adv. E-mail: macnews@westriv.com
Display Adv. E-mail: macnews@westriv.com
Editorial e-mail: macnews@westriv.com
Primary Website: siouxcountynewsmessenger.blogspot.com
Year Established: 1915
Avg Paid Circ: 1000
Avg Free Circ: 12
Audit By: Sworn/Estimate/Non-Audited
Audit Date: 10.06.2019
Personnel: Zach Buechler (Ed.itor)

CUSTER COUNTY CHRONICLE

Street address 1: 522 Mount Rushmore Rd
Street address city: Custer
Street address state: SD
Zip/Postal code: 57730-1930
General Phone: (605) 673-2217
General Fax: (605) 673-3321
Advertising Phone: (605) 673-2217
Advertising Fax: (605) 673-3321
Editorial Phone: (605) 673-2217
Editorial Fax: (605) 673-3321
General/National Adv. E-mail: custerchronicle@gwtc.net
Display Adv. E-mail: custerads@gwtc.net
Editorial e-mail: custernews@gwtc.net
Primary Website: custercountynews.com
Year Established: 1880
Avg Paid Circ: 1800
Audit By: Sworn/Estimate/Non-Audited
Audit Date: 10.06.2019
Personnel: Norma G. Najacht (Ed.); Jason Ferguson (Gen. Mgr.); Charles W. Najacht (Pub./Adv. Mgr.); Jacy Glazier (Reporter)

DELL RAPIDS TRIBUNE

Street address 1: 414 E 4th St
Street address city: Dell Rapids
Street address state: SD
Zip/Postal code: 57022-1928
General Phone: (605) 428-5441
Editorial e-mail: ctmyers@argusleader.com
Avg Paid Circ: 1300
Avg Free Circ: 34
Audit By: Sworn/Estimate/Non-Audited
Audit Date: 10.06.2019
Personnel: Corey Meyers (News Dir.); Luke Tatge (Ed.); Lisa Severson (Support Staff); Ron Allen (Dist. Dir.); Rick Wagoner (Prod. Mgr.)
Parent company (for newspapers): Gannett

EDGEMONT HERALD TRIBUNE

Street address 1: 410 2nd Ave
Street address city: Edgemont
Street address state: SD
Zip/Postal code: 57735-4910
General Phone: (605) 662-7201
General Fax: (605) 662-7202
Advertising Phone: (605) 662-7201
Advertising Fax: (605) 662-7202
Editorial Phone: (605) 662-7201
Editorial Fax: (605) 662-7202
General/National Adv. E-mail: tribune@gwtc.net
Display Adv. E-mail: tribune@gwtc.net
Editorial e-mail: tribune@gwtc.net
Primary Website: edgemonttribune.com
Year Established: 1923
Avg Paid Circ: 800
Audit By: Sworn/Estimate/Non-Audited
Audit Date: 10.06.2019
Personnel: Amber Schumacher (Mng. Ed.)

ESTELLINE JOURNAL

Street address 1: 214 Main St
Street address city: Estelline
Street address state: SD
Zip/Postal code: 57234
General Phone: (605) 873-2475
General Fax: (605) 793-9140
Advertising Phone: (605) 873-2475
Advertising Fax: (605) 793-9140
Editorial Phone: (605) 793-2293
Editorial Fax: (605) 793-9140
General/National Adv. E-mail: hcp@itctel.com
Display Adv. E-mail: hcp@itctel.com
Editorial e-mail: hcp@itctel.com
Primary Website: hamlincountypublishing.com
Avg Paid Circ: 650
Audit By: Sworn/Estimate/Non-Audited
Audit Date: 10.06.2019
Personnel: Lee Anne Dufek (Pub.); Jenna Aderhold (Ed.); Doug Kruiter (Adv. Mgr.)

FARM FORUM

Street address 1: 124 S 2nd St
Street address city: Aberdeen
Street address state: SD
Zip/Postal code: 57401-4010
General Phone: (605)225-4100
Advertising Phone: (605)622-2264
Editorial Phone: (605)622-2318
General/National Adv. E-mail: farmforum@aberdeennews.com
Display Adv. E-mail: farmforum@aberdeennews.com
Editorial e-mail: farmforum@aberdeennews.com
Primary Website: farmforum.net
Avg Free Circ: 35409
Audit By: Sworn/Estimate/Non-Audited
Audit Date: 10.06.2019
Personnel: Stan Wise (Ed); Christy Orwig (Adv. Dir)
Parent company (for newspapers): Schurz Communications Inc

FAULK COUNTY RECORD

Street address 1: 121 8th Ave S

Street address city: Faulkton
Street address state: SD
Zip/Postal code: 57438-2116
General Phone: (605) 598-6525
General Fax: (605) 598-4355
Advertising Phone: (605) 598-6525
Advertising Fax: (605) 598-4355
Editorial Phone: (605) 598-6525
Editorial Fax: (605) 598-4355
General/National Adv. E-mail: info@faulkcountyrecord.com
Display Adv. E-mail: info@faulkcountyrecord.com
Editorial e-mail: info@faulkcountyrecord.com
Primary Website: faulkcountyrecord.com
Year Established: 1882
Avg Paid Circ: 1420
Avg Free Circ: 8
Audit By: Sworn/Estimate/Non-Audited
Audit Date: 10.06.2019
Personnel: James Moritz (Pub./Ed.); Jennifer Miller (Owner/publisher); Jody Moritz (Co-Pub.)

GRANT COUNTY REVIEW

Street address 1: 225 S Main St
Street address city: Milbank
Street address state: SD
Zip/Postal code: 57252-1808
General Phone: (605) 432-4516
Advertising Phone: (605) 432-4516
Editorial Phone: (605) 432-4516
General/National Adv. E-mail: gcreview@itcmilbank.com
Display Adv. E-mail: gcreview@itcmilbank.com
Editorial e-mail: gcreview@itcmilbank.com
Primary Website: grantcountyreview.com
Year Established: 1880
Avg Paid Circ: 3000
Avg Free Circ: 22
Audit By: Sworn/Estimate/Non-Audited
Audit Date: 13.09.2023
Personnel: Deb Hemmer (Sportswriter, Historian); Holli Seehafer (general manager); Ashlie Schweitzer (design, bookkeeping); Phyllis Dolan Justice (Pub./Ed.); Clarence Justice (Co-Pub.); Holli Seehafer (General Manager)

GREGORY TIMES-ADVOCATE

Street address 1: 119 E 7th St
Street address city: Gregory
Street address state: SD
Zip/Postal code: 57533-1412
General Phone: (605) 835-8089
General Fax: (605) 835-8467
Advertising Phone: (605) 835-8089
Advertising Fax: (605) 835-8467
Editorial Phone: (605) 835-8089
Editorial Fax: (605) 835-8467
General/National Adv. E-mail: gregorynews@gregorynews.com
Display Adv. E-mail: gregorynews@gregorynews.com
Editorial e-mail: gregorynews@gregorynews.com
Primary Website: ainsworthnews.com
Year Established: 1904
Avg Paid Circ: 2000
Audit By: Sworn/Estimate/Non-Audited
Audit Date: 10.06.2019
Personnel: Cheryl Sperl (Pub./Ed.); Sue Brozik (Adv. Mgr.)

GROTON INDEPENDENT

Street address 1: 21 N Main St.
Street address city: Groton
Street address state: SD
Zip/Postal code: 57445
General Phone: (605) 397-6397
General Fax: (775) 459-6259
Advertising Phone: (605) 397-6397
Advertising Fax: (775) 459-6259
Editorial Phone: (605) 397-6397
Editorial Fax: (775) 459-6259
General/National Adv. E-mail: office@grotonsd.net
Display Adv. E-mail: office@grotonsd.net
Editorial e-mail: paperpaul@grotonsd.net
Primary Website: 397news.com
Year Established: 1883
Avg Paid Circ: 400
Audit By: Sworn/Estimate/Non-Audited
Audit Date: 10.06.2019
Personnel: Paul Irvin Kosel (Pub.); Tina Kosel (Office Mgr.)
Parent company (for newspapers): Next Generation Publications, Inc.; Finger Lakes Community Newspapers

HAMLIN COUNTY REPUBLICAN

Street address 1: 123 E Main St
Street address city: Castlewood
Street address state: SD
Zip/Postal code: 57223
General Phone: (605) 793-2293
General Fax: (605) 793-9140
Advertising Phone: (605) 793-2293
Advertising Fax: (605) 793-9140
Editorial Phone: (605) 793-2293
Editorial Fax: (605) 793-9140
General/National Adv. E-mail: hcp@itctel.com
Display Adv. E-mail: hcp@itctel.com
Editorial e-mail: hcp@itctel.com
Primary Website: hamlincountypublishing.com
Avg Paid Circ: 800
Audit By: Sworn/Estimate/Non-Audited
Audit Date: 10.06.2019
Personnel: LeeAnne Dufek (Pub.); Jenna Aderhold (News Ed.); Doug Kruiter (Adv. Mgr.)
Parent company (for newspapers): Hamlin County Publishing, Inc.

HERALD-ENTERPRISE

Street address 1: PO Box 207
Street address city: Hayti
Street address state: SD
Zip/Postal code: 57241-0207
General Phone: (605) 783-3636
General Fax: (605) 793-9140
Advertising Phone: (605) 783-3636
Advertising Fax: (605) 793-9140
Editorial Phone: (605) 783-3636
Editorial Fax: (605) 793-9140
General/National Adv. E-mail: hcp@itctel.com
Display Adv. E-mail: hcp@itctel.com
Editorial e-mail: hcp@itctel.com
Primary Website: hamlincountypublishing.com
Avg Paid Circ: 750
Avg Free Circ: 35
Audit By: Sworn/Estimate/Non-Audited
Audit Date: 10.06.2019
Personnel: Lee Anne Dufek (Pub./Ed./Adv. Mgr.)
Parent company (for newspapers): Hamlin County Publishing, Inc.

HIGHMORE HERALD

Street address 1: 211 Iowa Ave N
Street address city: Highmore
Street address state: SD
Zip/Postal code: 57345-2101
General Phone: (605) 852-2927
General Fax: (605) 852-2927
Advertising Phone: (605) 852-2927
Advertising Fax: (605) 852-2927
Editorial Phone: (605) 852-2927
Editorial Fax: (605) 852-2927
General/National Adv. E-mail: hiherald@venturecomm.net
Display Adv. E-mail: hiherald@venturecomm.net
Editorial e-mail: hiherald@venturecomm.net
Year Established: 1882
Avg Paid Circ: 1450
Audit By: Sworn/Estimate/Non-Audited
Audit Date: 10.06.2019
Personnel: Mary Ann Morford (Pub./Ed.); Mary Hamlin (Adv. Mgr.)

HILL CITY PREVAILER-NEWS

Street address 1: 522 Mt. Rushmore Rd.
Street address city: Custer
Street address state: SD
Zip/Postal code: 57730
General Phone: (605) 673-2217
General Fax: (605) 673-3321
Primary Website: hillcityprevailernews.blogspot.com
Year Established: 1971
Avg Paid Circ: 700
Audit By: Sworn/Estimate/Non-Audited
Audit Date: 10.06.2019
Personnel: Charles W. Najacht (Pub.); Jeff Smith (Ed.); Jeanne Fuerstenberg (Circ.); Daryl Mohr (Graphic Des.); Kate Najacht (Writer)
Parent company (for newspapers): Southern Hills Publishing, Inc.

HOT SPRINGS STAR

Street address 1: 107 N Chicago St
Street address city: Hot Springs
Street address state: SD
Zip/Postal code: 57747-1631
General Phone: (605) 745-4170
General Fax: (605) 745-3161
General/National Adv. E-mail: starads@lee.net
Display Adv. E-mail: hsstar@lee.net
Editorial e-mail: hsstar@lee.net
Primary Website: rapidcityjournal.com/community/hot-springs
Year Established: 1886
Avg Paid Circ: 1900
Avg Free Circ: 25
Audit By: Sworn/Estimate/Non-Audited
Audit Date: 10.06.2019
Personnel: Isaac Zarecki (Ed.); Mathew Tranquill (Pub.); Brad Casto (VP Adv. Mktg.); Josh Hart (Circ. Dir.)
Parent company (for newspapers): Dispatch-Argus

IPSWICH TRIBUNE

Street address 1: 419 S 5th St
Street address city: Ipswich
Street address state: SD
Zip/Postal code: 57451-2500
General Phone: (605) 426-6471
General Fax: (605) 426-6202
General/National Adv. E-mail: iptribune@valleytel.net
Display Adv. E-mail: iptribune@valleytel.net
Classified Adv. e-mail: iptribune@valleytel.net
Editorial e-mail: iptribune@valleytel.net
Avg Paid Circ: 941
Avg Free Circ: 3
Audit By: Sworn/Estimate/Non-Audited
Audit Date: 10.06.2019
Personnel: Dwain Gibson (Pub.); Tena Gibson (Managing Ed.)

KADOKA PRESS

Street address 1: 915 S Main St
Street address city: Kadoka
Street address state: SD
Zip/Postal code: 57543
General Phone: (605) 837-2259
General Fax: (605) 837-2312
Advertising Phone: (605) 837-2259
Advertising Fax: (605) 837-2312
Editorial Phone: (605) 837-2259
Editorial Fax: (605) 837-2312
General/National Adv. E-mail: press@kadokatelco.com
Display Adv. E-mail: press@kadokatelco.com
Editorial e-mail: editor@kadokatelco.com
Primary Website: ravellettepublications.com
Avg Paid Circ: 1100
Audit By: Sworn/Estimate/Non-Audited
Audit Date: 10.06.2019
Personnel: Don Ravellette (Pub.); Rhonda Dennis (Ed.)

LAKE ANDES WAVE

Street address 1: 209 S Main Ave
Street address city: Wagner
Street address state: SD
Zip/Postal code: 57380-1727
General Phone: (605) 384-5616
General Fax: (605) 384-5955
Advertising Phone: (605) 384-5616
Advertising Fax: (605) 384-5955
Editorial Phone: (605) 384-5616
Editorial Fax: (605) 384-5955
General/National Adv. E-mail: announcer@hcinet.net
Display Adv. E-mail: announcer@hcinet.net
Editorial e-mail: announcer@hcinet.net
Primary Website: thelakeandeswave.com
Avg Paid Circ: 440
Audit By: Sworn/Estimate/Non-Audited
Audit Date: 10.06.2019
Personnel: Barb Pechous (Pub./Ed.)
Parent company (for newspapers): Star Publishing Co.

LAKE PRESTON TIMES

Street address 1: 301 N Main St
Street address city: Lake Preston
Street address state: SD
Zip/Postal code: 57249
General Phone: (605) 847-4421
General Fax: (605) 847-4421
Advertising Phone: (605) 847-4421
Advertising Fax: (605) 847-4421
Editorial Phone: (605) 847-4421
Editorial Fax: (605) 847-4421
General/National Adv. E-mail: mail@lakeprestontimes.net
Display Adv. E-mail: mail@lakeprestontimes.net
Editorial e-mail: mail@lakeprestontimes.net
Primary Website: lakeprestontimes.net
Avg Paid Circ: 1104
Avg Free Circ: 37
Audit By: Sworn/Estimate/Non-Audited
Audit Date: 10.06.2019
Personnel: Dale Blegen (Pub.); Donna Palmlund (Editor)
Parent company (for newspapers): Blegen Publishing Inc.

LANGFORD BUGLE

Street address 1: 706 Seventh St
Street address city: Britton
Street address state: SD
Zip/Postal code: 57430
General Phone: (605) 448-2281
General Fax: (605) 448-2282
General/National Adv. E-mail: hgnice@brittonsd.com
Display Adv. E-mail: kbuhl@brittonsd.com
Editorial e-mail: dcard@brittonsd.com
Primary Website: marshallcountyjournal.com
Avg Paid Circ: 485
Audit By: Sworn/Estimate/Non-Audited
Audit Date: 10.06.2019
Personnel: Douglas M. Card (Pub./Ed.); Helen Nice (Adv. Mgr.)

LYMAN COUNTY HERALD

Street address 1: 223 N MAIN AVE
Street address city: Presho
Street address state: SD
Zip/Postal code: 57568
General Phone: (605) 895-6397
General Fax: (605) 895-6377
Advertising Phone: (605) 895-6397
Advertising Fax: (605) 895-6377
Editorial Phone: (605) 895-6397
Editorial Fax: (605) 895-6377
General/National Adv. E-mail: news@lcherald.com
Display Adv. E-mail: news@lcherald.com
Editorial e-mail: news@lcherald.com
Primary Website: lcherald.com
Avg Paid Circ: 962
Audit By: Sworn/Estimate/Non-Audited
Audit Date: 10.06.2019
Personnel: Lucy Halverson (Pub./Ed./Adv. Mgr.); Kim Halverson (Co-Pub.)

MARION RECORD

Street address 1: 305 N. Broadway
Street address city: Marion
Street address state: SD
Zip/Postal code: 57043-0298
General Phone: (605) 648-3821
General Fax: (605) 648-3920
General/National Adv. E-mail: mrecord@gwtc.net
Display Adv. E-mail: mrecord@gwtc.net
Editorial e-mail: mrecord@gwtc.net
Primary Website: andersonpublications.com/contact-us/marion-record
Year Established: 1900
Avg Paid Circ: 500
Audit By: Sworn/Estimate/Non-Audited
Audit Date: 10.06.2019
Personnel: Jelene Wipf (Owner/Ed.)
Parent company (for newspapers): Anderson Publications Inc

MCPHERSON COUNTY HERALD

Street address 1: 1203 Moulton St
Street address city: Leola

Street address state: SD
Zip/Postal code: 57456-2214
General Phone: (605) 439-3131
Advertising Phone: (605) 439-3131
Editorial Phone: (605) 439-3131
General/National Adv. E-mail: herald@valleytel.net
Display Adv. E-mail: herald@valleytel.net
Editorial e-mail: herald@valleytel.net
Year Established: 1890
Avg Paid Circ: 375
Audit By: Sworn/Estimate/Non-Audited
Audit Date: 10.06.2019
Personnel: Jeremy Cox (Pub./Ed.)

MEADE COUNTY TIMES-TRIBUNE

Street address 1: 1010 Ballpark Rd
Street address 2: Ste 1
Street address city: Sturgis
Street address state: SD
Zip/Postal code: 57785-2208
General Phone: (605) 347-2503
General Fax: (605) 347-2321
Advertising Phone: (605) 892-2528
Advertising Fax: (605) 347-2321
Editorial Phone: (605) 347-2503
Editorial Fax: (605) 347-2321
General/National Adv. E-mail: mona.heimbaugh@rapidcityjournal.com
Display Adv. E-mail: mona.heimbaugh@rapidcityjournal.com
Editorial e-mail: deb.holland@rapidcityjournal.com
Primary Website: meadecountytimes.com
Year Established: 1907
Avg Paid Circ: 2800
Avg Free Circ: 5000
Audit By: Sworn/Estimate/Non-Audited
Audit Date: 10.06.2019
Personnel: Deb Holland (Ed.); Alisa Harlan (Inside sales/news clerk)
Parent company (for newspapers): Dispatch-Argus

MELLETTE COUNTY NEWS

Street address 1: 416 N MAIN ST
Street address city: White River
Street address state: SD
Zip/Postal code: 57579
General Phone: (605) 259-3642
General Fax: (605) 259-3497
Advertising Phone: (605) 259-3642
Advertising Fax: (605) 259-3497
Editorial Phone: (605) 259-3642
Editorial Fax: (605) 259-3497
General/National Adv. E-mail: mcnews@gwtc.net
Display Adv. E-mail: mcnews@gwtc.net
Editorial e-mail: mcnews@gwtc.net
Primary Website: mellettecountynews.com
Year Established: 1912
Avg Paid Circ: 500
Audit By: Sworn/Estimate/Non-Audited
Audit Date: 10.06.2019
Personnel: Tim Huether (Pub.); Kristan Krogman (Ed.)

MINER COUNTY PIONEER

Street address 1: 120 S Main St
Street address city: Howard
Street address state: SD
Zip/Postal code: 57349-9058
General Phone: (605) 772-5644
General Fax: (605) 772-5645
Advertising Phone: (605) 772-5644
Advertising Fax: (605) 772-5645
Editorial Phone: (605) 772-5644
Editorial Fax: (605) 772-5645
General/National Adv. E-mail: ads@minercountypioneer.com
Display Adv. E-mail: ads@minercountypioneer.com
Editorial e-mail: news@minercountypioneer.com
Avg Paid Circ: 1902
Avg Free Circ: 65
Audit By: Sworn/Estimate/Non-Audited
Audit Date: 10.06.2019
Personnel: Carla Poulson (Pub./Ed.); Heather Poulson (Managing Editor/Office Manager)

MOBRIDGE TRIBUNE

Street address 1: 1413 E Grand Xing
Street address city: Mobridge
Street address state: SD
Zip/Postal code: 57601-2905
General Phone: (605) 845-3646
General Fax: (605) 845-7659
Advertising Phone: (605) 845-3646
Advertising Fax: (605) 845-7659
Editorial Phone: (605) 845-3646
Editorial Fax: (605) 845-7659
General/National Adv. E-mail: ads@mobridgetribune.com
Display Adv. E-mail: office@mobridgetribune.com
Editorial e-mail: news@mobridgetribune.com
Primary Website: mobridgetribune.com
Year Established: 1909
Avg Paid Circ: 2012
Avg Free Circ: 46
Audit By: Sworn/Estimate/Non-Audited
Audit Date: 10.06.2019
Personnel: Larry Atkinson (Pub); Katie Zerr (Ed.); Linda Meyer (Gen. Mgr.); Arden Nelson (Adv. Specialties/Printing Mgr.); Lance St. John (Web Printing Mgr.); Jay Davis (Sports Ed.); Risa Fryhling (Sales Mgr); Kelsey Majeski (Bus. Mgr.); Jane Bachman (Composition Mgr.); Lori Cox (Circulation Mgr.); Justin Petersen (Webmaster/Photoshop)
Parent company (for newspapers): Bridge City Publishing, Inc.

MONTROSE HERALD

Street address 1: 210 W Main St
Street address city: Canistota
Street address state: SD
Zip/Postal code: 57012
General Phone: (605) 296-3181
General Fax: (605) 296-3289
Advertising Phone: (605) 296-3181
Advertising Fax: (605) 296-3289
Editorial Phone: (605) 296-3181
Editorial Fax: (605) 296-3289
General/National Adv. E-mail: ads@andersonpublications.com
Display Adv. E-mail: ads@andersonpublications.com
Editorial e-mail: news@andersonpublications.com
Avg Paid Circ: 518
Audit By: Sworn/Estimate/Non-Audited
Audit Date: 10.06.2019
Personnel: Matt Anderson (Pub./Ed.); Jelene Olsen (Gen. Mgr.)

MOODY COUNTY ENTERPRISE

Street address 1: 107 W 2nd Ave
Street address city: Flandreau
Street address state: SD
Zip/Postal code: 57028-1149
General Phone: (605) 997-3725
General Fax: (605) 997-3194
Advertising Phone: (605) 997-3725
Advertising Fax: (605) 997-3194
Editorial Phone: (605) 997-3725
Editorial Fax: (605) 997-3194
General/National Adv. E-mail: mce6@mcisweb.com
Display Adv. E-mail: mce3@mcisweb.com
Editorial e-mail: mce6@mcisweb.com
Primary Website: moodycountyenterprise.com
Year Established: 1878
Avg Paid Circ: 3300
Avg Free Circ: 1200
Audit By: Sworn/Estimate/Non-Audited
Audit Date: 10.06.2019
Personnel: William McMacken (Pub.); M.L. Headrick (Ed.); Roger Janssen (Gen. Mgr.)
Parent company (for newspapers): San Luis Valley Publishing

MURDO COYOTE

Street address 1: 210 Main St
Street address city: Murdo
Street address state: SD
Zip/Postal code: 57559-2022
General Phone: (605) 669-2271
General Fax: (605) 669-2744
Advertising Phone: (605) 669-2271
Advertising Fax: (605) 669-2744
Editorial Phone: (605) 669-2271
Editorial Fax: (605) 669-2744
General/National Adv. E-mail: coyoteads@gwtc.net
Display Adv. E-mail: coyoteads@gwtc.net
Editorial e-mail: mcoyote@gwtc.net
Primary Website: ravellettepublications.com
Year Established: 1906
Avg Paid Circ: 550
Avg Free Circ: 10
Audit By: Sworn/Estimate/Non-Audited
Audit Date: 10.06.2019
Personnel: Don Ravellette (Pub.); Kelly Penticoff (Gen. Mgr.); Karlee Barnes (Adv. Mgr.)

NORTHWEST BLADE

Street address 1: 701 7th St.
Street address city: Eureka
Street address state: SD
Zip/Postal code: 57437
General Phone: (605) 284-2631
General/National Adv. E-mail: nwblade@valleytel.net
Display Adv. E-mail: nwblade@valleytel.net
Editorial e-mail: nwblade@valleytel.net
Avg Paid Circ: 675
Avg Free Circ: 25
Audit By: Sworn/Estimate/Non-Audited
Audit Date: 10.06.2019
Personnel: Tara Beitelspacher (Pub.)
Parent company (for newspapers): Pride Publications

ONIDA WATCHMAN

Street address 1: 106 S Main St
Street address city: Onida
Street address state: SD
Zip/Postal code: 57564-2178
General Phone: (605) 258-2604
General Fax: (605) 258-2572
Advertising Phone: (605) 258-2604
Advertising Fax: (605) 258-2572
Editorial Phone: (605) 258-2604
Editorial Fax: (605) 258-2572
General/National Adv. E-mail: amanda.fanger@onidawatchman.com
Display Adv. E-mail: curt.olson@onidawatchman.com
Editorial e-mail: marileen.tilberg@onidawatchman.com
Primary Website: onidawatchman.com
Year Established: 1883
Avg Paid Circ: 1037
Avg Free Circ: 30
Audit By: Sworn/Estimate/Non-Audited
Audit Date: 10.06.2019
Personnel: Curt Olson (Pub.); Marileen Tilberg (Ed.); Amanda Fanger (Adv. Mgr.)

POTTER COUNTY NEWS

Street address 1: 110 S Exene St
Street address city: Gettysburg
Street address state: SD
Zip/Postal code: 57442-1520
General Phone: (605) 765-2464
General Fax: (605) 765-2465
Advertising Phone: (605) 765-2464
Advertising Fax: (605) 765-2465
Editorial Phone: (605) 765-2464
Editorial Fax: (605) 765-2465
General/National Adv. E-mail: pcnews@pottercountynews.com
Display Adv. E-mail: lacey@pottercountynews.com
Editorial e-mail: pcnews@pottercountynews.com
Primary Website: pottercountynews.com
Mthly Avg Views: 13000
Year Established: 1883
Avg Paid Circ: 1600
Audit By: Sworn/Estimate/Non-Audited
Audit Date: 10.06.2019
Personnel: Larry Atkinson (Pub.); Molly McRoberts (Ed.); Lacey Johnson (Adv. Mgr.)

PRAIRIE PIONEER

Street address 1: 117 Main St
Street address city: Pollock
Street address state: SD
Zip/Postal code: 57648-8616
General Phone: (605) 889-2320
General Fax: (605) 889-2361
Advertising Phone: (605) 889-2320
Advertising Fax: (605) 889-2361
Editorial Phone: (605) 889-2320
Editorial Fax: (605) 889-2361
General/National Adv. E-mail: ads@valleytel.net
Display Adv. E-mail: ads@valleytel.net
Editorial e-mail: pioneer@valleytel.net
Primary Website: ppioneer.com
Year Established: 1883
Avg Paid Circ: 1500
Audit By: Sworn/Estimate/Non-Audited
Audit Date: 10.06.2019
Personnel: Leah P. Burke (Pub.); Julie Brandner (Adv. Dir.); Orland Geigle (Ed.); Waynette Geigle (Sports Ed.)

REPORTER & FARMER

Street address 1: 516 Main St
Street address city: Webster
Street address state: SD
Zip/Postal code: 57274-1719
General Phone: (605) 345-3356
General Fax: (605) 345-3739
Advertising Phone: (605) 345-3356
Advertising Fax: (605) 345-3739
Editorial Phone: (605) 345-3356
Editorial Fax: (605) 345-3739
General/National Adv. E-mail: news@reporterandfarmer.com
Display Adv. E-mail: sports@reporterandfarmer.com
Editorial e-mail: news@reporterandfarmer.com
Primary Website: reporterandfarmer.com
Year Established: 1881
Avg Paid Circ: 3200
Audit By: Sworn/Estimate/Non-Audited
Audit Date: 10.06.2019
Personnel: LeAnn Suhr (Pub./Ed.); John Suhr (Adv. Mgr.)

ROSCOE-HOSMER INDEPENDENT

Street address 1: 419 S 5th St
Street address city: Ipswich
Street address state: SD
Zip/Postal code: 57451-2500
General Phone: (605) 426-6471
General Fax: (605) 426-6202
General/National Adv. E-mail: iptribune@valleytel
Display Adv. E-mail: iptribune@valleytel.net
Editorial e-mail: iptribune@valleytel.net
Avg Paid Circ: 605
Audit By: Sworn/Estimate/Non-Audited
Audit Date: 10.06.2019
Personnel: Dwain Gibson (Pub.); Tena Gibson (Managing Ed.)

SALEM SPECIAL

Street address 1: 135 S Main St
Street address city: Salem
Street address state: SD
Zip/Postal code: 57058-8514
General Phone: (605) 425-2361
General Fax: (605) 425-2547
Advertising Phone: (605) 425-2361
Advertising Fax: (605) 425-2547
Editorial Phone: (605) 425-2361
Editorial Fax: (605) 425-2547
General/National Adv. E-mail: tschwans@triotel.net
Display Adv. E-mail: tschwans@triotel.net
Editorial e-mail: tschwans@triotel.net
Primary Website: salemspecial.com
Year Established: 1890
Avg Paid Circ: 1200
Audit By: Sworn/Estimate/Non-Audited
Audit Date: 10.06.2019
Personnel: Troy Schwans (Pub./Ed.); McKillop LuAnn

SANBORN WEEKLY JOURNAL

Street address 1: 506 W 6th St
Street address city: Woonsocket
Street address state: SD
Zip/Postal code: 57385
General Phone: (605) 796-4221
General Fax: (605) 796-4221
Advertising Phone: (605) 796-4221
Advertising Fax: (605) 796-4221
Editorial Phone: (605) 796-4221
Editorial Fax: (605) 796-4221
General/National Adv. E-mail: swj124@mac.com
Display Adv. E-mail: swj124@mac.com
Editorial e-mail: swj124@mac.com
Primary Website: sanbornjournal.com
Year Established: 1883
Avg Paid Circ: 1201
Avg Free Circ: 38
Audit By: Sworn/Estimate/Non-Audited
Audit Date: 10.06.2019

Personnel: Hillary Lutter (Pub./Ed.); Bryan Lutter (Mng. Ed.)

SCOTLAND JOURNAL

Street address 1: 630 1st St
Street address city: Scotland
Street address state: SD
Zip/Postal code: 57059
General Phone: (605) 583-4419
General Fax: (605) 583-4406
General/National Adv. E-mail: scotnews@gwtc.net
Display Adv. E-mail: scotnews@gwtc.net
Editorial e-mail: scotnews@gwtc.net
Year Established: 1894
Avg Paid Circ: 900
Avg Free Circ: 60
Audit By: Sworn/Estimate/Non-Audited
Audit Date: 10.06.2019
Personnel: Becky Tycz (Pub.); Peggy Schelske (Ed./Adv. Dir.); Billie Jo Hayes (Circ.)
Parent company (for newspapers): B&H Publishing, Inc.

SELBY RECORD

Street address 1: 4411 Main St
Street address city: Selby
Street address state: SD
Zip/Postal code: 57472-2010
General Phone: (605) 649-7866
General Fax: (605) 649-1126
Advertising Phone: (605) 649-7866
Advertising Fax: (605) 649-1126
Editorial Phone: (605) 649-7866
Editorial Fax: (605) 649-1126
General/National Adv. E-mail: selbyrec@venturecomm.net
Display Adv. E-mail: selbyrec@venturecomm.net
Editorial e-mail: selbyrec@venturecomm.net
Avg Paid Circ: 1000
Avg Free Circ: 10
Audit By: Sworn/Estimate/Non-Audited
Audit Date: 10.06.2019
Personnel: Sharon Wolff (Pub.); Karen Speidel (Owner/Publisher); Sandy Bond (Ed.)

SIOUX VALLEY NEWS

Street address 1: 213 E 5th St
Street address 2: P.O. Box 255
Street address city: Canton
Street address state: SD
Zip/Postal code: 57013-1733
General Phone: (605) 764-2000
General Fax: (605) 764-6397
Advertising Phone: (605) 764-2000
Advertising Fax: (605) 764-6397
Editorial Phone: (605) 764-2000
Editorial Fax: (605) 764-6397
General/National Adv. E-mail: SiouxValleynews@vastbb.net
Display Adv. E-mail: SiouxValleynews@vastbb.net
Editorial e-mail: SiouxValleynews@vastbb.net
Primary Website: siouxvalleynewsonline.com
Year Established: 1872
Avg Paid Circ: 1680
Audit By: Sworn/Estimate/Non-Audited
Audit Date: 10.06.2019
Personnel: Teresa Wilcox (Pub./Ed.); Teresa Zomer (Owner)

SISSETON COURIER

Street address 1: 117 E Oak St
Street address city: Sisseton
Street address state: SD
Zip/Postal code: 57262-1413
General Phone: (605) 698-7642
General Fax: (605) 698-3641
Advertising Phone: (605) 698-7642
Advertising Fax: (605) 698-3641
Editorial Phone: (605) 698-7642
Editorial Fax: (605) 698-3641
General/National Adv. E-mail: ads@sissetoncourier.com
Display Adv. E-mail: design@sissetoncourier.com
Editorial e-mail: news@sissetoncourier.com
Primary Website: sissetoncourier.com
Avg Paid Circ: 3201
Avg Free Circ: 90
Audit By: Sworn/Estimate/Non-Audited
Audit Date: 10.06.2019
Personnel: Kevin Deutsch (Pub./Ed.); Sylvia Deutsch (Office Mgr.); Jennie Evenson (Adv. Dir.)

SOUTH DAKOTA MAIL

Street address 1: 116 N Main St
Street address city: Plankinton
Street address state: SD
Zip/Postal code: 57368-2015
General Phone: (605) 942-7770
General Fax: (605) 942-7770
Advertising Phone: (605) 942-7770
Advertising Fax: (605) 942-7770
Editorial Phone: (605) 942-7770
Editorial Fax: (605) 942-7770
General/National Adv. E-mail: sdmail@siouxvalley.net
Display Adv. E-mail: sdmail@siouxvalley.net
Editorial e-mail: sdmail@siouxvalley.net
Avg Paid Circ: 950
Audit By: Sworn/Estimate/Non-Audited
Audit Date: 10.06.2019
Personnel: Gayle Van Genderen (Pub.); J.P. Studeny (Ed.)

SOUTHERN UNION COUNTY LEADER-COURIER

Street address 1: 108 W Main St
Street address city: Elk Point
Street address state: SD
Zip/Postal code: 57025-2314
General Phone: (605) 356-2632
General Fax: (605) 356-3626
Advertising Phone: (605) 356-2632
Advertising Fax: (605) 356-3626
Editorial Phone: (605) 356-2632
Editorial Fax: (605) 356-3626
General/National Adv. E-mail: leader2@iw.net
Display Adv. E-mail: leader2@iw.net
Editorial e-mail: leader1@iw.net
Primary Website: leadercourier-times.com
Avg Paid Circ: 1150
Avg Free Circ: 19
Audit By: Sworn/Estimate/Non-Audited
Audit Date: 10.06.2019
Personnel: Bruce Odson (Pub.); Susan Odson (Gen. Mgr.)

SPRINGFIELD TIMES

Street address 1: 712 8TH ST
Street address city: Springfield
Street address state: SD
Zip/Postal code: 57062
General Phone: (605) 369-2441
General Fax: (605) 369-2793
Advertising Phone: (605) 369-2441
Advertising Fax: (605) 369-2793
Editorial Phone: (605) 589-3242
Editorial Fax: (605) 369-2793
General/National Adv. E-mail: times@gwtc.net
Display Adv. E-mail: times@gwtc.net
Editorial e-mail: times@gwtc.net
Primary Website: facebook.com/pg/Springfield-Times
Year Established: 1871
Avg Paid Circ: 850
Audit By: Sworn/Estimate/Non-Audited
Audit Date: 10.06.2019
Personnel: Springfield News

THE (MOORHEAD, MN) EXTRA

Street address 1: 133 N Main St
Street address city: Parker
Street address state: SD
Zip/Postal code: 57053
General Phone: (605) 297-4419
General Fax: (605) 297-4015
Advertising Phone: (605) 297-4419
Advertising Fax: (605) 297-4015
Editorial Phone: (605) 297-4419
Editorial Fax: (605) 297-4015
General/National Adv. E-mail: ads@ncppub.com
Display Adv. E-mail: rschneider@ncppub.com
Editorial e-mail: sebeling@ncppub.com
Primary Website: thenewera-online.com
Year Established: 1875
Avg Paid Circ: 0
Avg Free Circ: 5635
Audit By: Sworn/Estimate/Non-Audited
Audit Date: 10.06.2019
Personnel: Michael Ohop (Pub.); Sarah Eveling (Ed.); Paul Harms (Adv. Mgr.)
Parent company (for newspapers): New Century Press

THE ALEXANDRIA HERALD

Street address 1: 531 Main St
Street address city: Alexandria
Street address state: SD
Zip/Postal code: 57311-2286
General Phone: (605) 239-4521
General Fax: (605) 449-4430
Advertising Phone: (605) 239-4521
Advertising Fax: (605) 449-4430
Editorial Phone: (605) 239-4521
Editorial Fax: (605) 449-4430
General/National Adv. E-mail: ementerprise@triotel.net
Display Adv. E-mail: ementerprise@triotel.net
Editorial e-mail: ementerprise@triotel.net
Primary Website: andersonpublications.com
Avg Paid Circ: 430
Avg Free Circ: 15
Audit By: Sworn/Estimate/Non-Audited
Audit Date: 10.06.2019
Personnel: Matt Anderson (Pub./Ed.); Terry Janssen (Mng. Ed.)

THE ARLINGTON SUN

Street address 1: 208 S Main St
Street address city: Arlington
Street address state: SD
Zip/Postal code: 57212-8000
General Phone: (605) 983-5491
General Fax: (866) 314-4217
Advertising Phone: (605) 983-5491
Advertising Fax: (866) 314-4217
Editorial Phone: (605) 983-5491
Editorial Fax: (866) 314-4217
General/National Adv. E-mail: asn@mchsi.com
Display Adv. E-mail: asn@mchsi.com
Editorial e-mail: asn@mchsi.com
Primary Website: rfdnewsgroup.com
Year Established: 1885
Avg Paid Circ: 900
Audit By: Sworn/Estimate/Non-Audited
Audit Date: 10.06.2019
Personnel: Chris Schumacher (Pub.); Linda Schumacher (Co-Pub.); Aggie Cleveland (Adv. Mgr.); Frank Crisler (Ed.)

THE ARMOUR CHRONICLE

Street address 1: 624 MAIN AVE
Street address city: Armour
Street address state: SD
Zip/Postal code: 57313
General Phone: (605) 724-2747
General Fax: (605) 724-2947
Advertising Phone: (605) 724-2747
Advertising Fax: (605) 724-2947
Editorial Phone: (605) 724-2747
Editorial Fax: (605) 724-2947
General/National Adv. E-mail: chronicle@unitelsd.com
Display Adv. E-mail: chronicle@unitelsd.com
Editorial e-mail: chronicle@unitelsd.com
Avg Paid Circ: 913
Avg Free Circ: 10
Audit By: Sworn/Estimate/Non-Audited
Audit Date: 10.06.2019
Personnel: Gerri Olson (Editor/Publisher)

THE BISON COURIER

Street address 1: 122A W Main St
Street address city: Bison
Street address state: SD
Zip/Postal code: 57620
General Phone: (605) 244-7199
General Fax: (605) 244-7198
Advertising Phone: (605) 244-7199
Advertising Fax: (605) 244-7198
Editorial Phone: (605) 244-7199
Editorial Fax: (605) 244-7198
General/National Adv. E-mail: courier@sdplains.com
Display Adv. E-mail: courier@sdplains.com
Editorial e-mail: courier@sdplains.com
Primary Website: ravellettepublications.com
Avg Paid Circ: 750
Avg Free Circ: 25
Audit By: Sworn/Estimate/Non-Audited
Audit Date: 10.06.2019
Personnel: Don Ravellette (Pub.); Marsha Veal (Gen. Mgr.)

THE BRITTON JOURNAL

Street address 1: 706 Seventh St
Street address city: Britton
Street address state: SD
Zip/Postal code: 57430
General Phone: (605) 448-2281
General Fax: (605) 448-2282
Advertising Phone: (605) 448-2281
Advertising Fax: (605) 448-2282
Editorial Phone: (605) 448-2281
Editorial Fax: (605) 448-2282
General/National Adv. E-mail: hgnice@brittonsd.com
Display Adv. E-mail: journal@brittonsd.com
Editorial e-mail: dcard@brittonsd.com
Primary Website: marshallcountyjournal.com
Avg Paid Circ: 1779
Avg Free Circ: 50
Audit By: Sworn/Estimate/Non-Audited
Audit Date: 10.06.2019
Personnel: Douglas M. Card (Pub./Ed.); Ann Stiegelmeier; Stephanie Elsaas

THE BRYANT DAKOTAN

Street address 1: 110 W Main St
Street address city: Bryant
Street address state: SD
Zip/Postal code: 57221-2058
General Phone: (605) 628-2551
General Fax: (605) 881-4008
Advertising Phone: (605) 628-2551
Advertising Fax: (605) 881-4008
Editorial Phone: (605) 628-2551
Editorial Fax: (605) 881-4008
General/National Adv. E-mail: dakotan@datatruck.com
Display Adv. E-mail: dakotan@datatruck.com
Editorial e-mail: dakotan@datatruck.com
Year Established: 1979
Avg Paid Circ: 504
Avg Free Circ: 30
Audit By: Sworn/Estimate/Non-Audited
Audit Date: 10.06.2019
Personnel: Stephanie Bawdon (Pub./Ed.)

THE BURKE GAZETTE

Street address 1: 825 Main St
Street address city: Burke
Street address state: SD
Zip/Postal code: 57523
General Phone: (605) 775-2612
General Fax: (605) 775-2612
Advertising Phone: (605) 775-2612
Advertising Fax: (605) 775-2612
Editorial Phone: (605) 775-2612
Editorial Fax: (605) 775-2612
General/National Adv. E-mail: burkegaz@gwtc.net
Display Adv. E-mail: burkegaz@gwtc.net
Editorial e-mail: burkegaz@gwtc.net
Primary Website: burkegazette.com
Year Established: 1904
Avg Paid Circ: 1250
Audit By: Sworn/Estimate/Non-Audited
Audit Date: 10.06.2019
Personnel: C.J. Fahrenbacher (Pub./Ed.)

THE CORSICA GLOBE

Street address 1: 215 Main St
Street address city: Corsica
Street address state: SD
Zip/Postal code: 57328
General Phone: (605) 946-5489
General Fax: (605) 946-5179
Advertising Phone: (605) 946-5489
Advertising Fax: (605) 946-5179
Editorial Phone: (605) 946-5489
Editorial Fax: (605) 946-5179
General/National Adv. E-mail: globe@siouxvalley.net
Display Adv. E-mail: globe@siouxvalley.net
Editorial e-mail: globe@siouxvalley.net
Primary Website: corsicaglobe.blogspot.com
Avg Paid Circ: 1093
Avg Free Circ: 51
Audit By: Sworn/Estimate/Non-Audited
Audit Date: 10.06.2019

Personnel: Mary Neugebauer (Pub./Ed./Adv. Mgr.); Dennis Neugebauer (Pub.)

THE DE SMET NEWS

Street address 1: 220 Calumet Ave SE
Street address city: De Smet
Street address state: SD
Zip/Postal code: 57231-3100
General Phone: (605) 854-3331
General Fax: (605) 854-9977
Advertising Phone: (605) 854-3331
Advertising Fax: (605) 854-9977
Editorial Phone: (605) 854-3331
Editorial Fax: (605) 854-9977
General/National Adv. E-mail: mail@desmetnews.com
Display Adv. E-mail: mail@desmetnews.com
Editorial e-mail: mail@desmetnews.com
Primary Website: desmetnews.com
Mthly Avg Views: 14000
Mthly Avg Unique Visitors: 2700
Year Established: 1880
Avg Paid Circ: 1315
Avg Free Circ: 20
Audit By: Sworn/Estimate/Non-Audited
Audit Date: 10.06.2019
Personnel: Dale Blegen (Pub.); David Tritle (Ed.); Jessica Jung (Office Mgr.)
Parent company (for newspapers): Blegen Publishing Inc.

THE DELMONT RECORD

Street address 1: 624 MAIN AVE
Street address city: Armour
Street address state: SD
Zip/Postal code: 57313
General Phone: (605) 724-2747
General Fax: (605) 724-2947
Advertising Phone: (605) 724-2747
Advertising Fax: (605) 724-2947
Editorial Phone: (605) 724-2747
Editorial Fax: (605) 724-2947
General/National Adv. E-mail: chronicle@unitelsd.com
Display Adv. E-mail: chronicle@unitelsd.com
Editorial e-mail: chronicle@unitelsd.com
Avg Paid Circ: 220
Avg Free Circ: 10
Audit By: Sworn/Estimate/Non-Audited
Audit Date: 10.06.2019
Personnel: Gerri Olson (Editor/Publisher)

THE ELKTON RECORD

Street address 1: 205 Elk St
Street address city: Elkton
Street address state: SD
Zip/Postal code: 57026-2193
General Phone: (605) 542-4831
General Fax: (605) 542-1306
Advertising Phone: (605) 542-4831
Advertising Fax: (605) 542-1306
Editorial Phone: (605) 542-4831
Editorial Fax: (605) 542-1306
General/National Adv. E-mail: ern@itctel.com
Display Adv. E-mail: ern@itctel.com
Editorial e-mail: ern@itctel.com
Primary Website: rfdnewsgroup.com
Year Established: 1884
Avg Paid Circ: 600
Avg Free Circ: 57
Audit By: Sworn/Estimate/Non-Audited
Audit Date: 10.06.2019
Personnel: Linda Schumacher (Pub./Ed.)
Parent company (for newspapers): Clear Lake Courier

THE FAITH INDEPENDENT

Street address 1: 106 Main St
Street address city: Faith
Street address state: SD
Zip/Postal code: 57626
General Phone: (605) 967-2161
General Fax: (605) 967-2160
Advertising Phone: (605) 967-2161
Advertising Fax: (605) 967-2160
Editorial Phone: (605) 967-2161
Editorial Fax: (605) 967-2160
General/National Adv. E-mail: faithind@faithsd.com
Display Adv. E-mail: faithind@faithsd.com
Editorial e-mail: faithind@faithsd.com
Primary Website: ravellettepublications.com
Avg Paid Circ: 1000
Audit By: Sworn/Estimate/Non-Audited
Audit Date: 10.06.2019
Personnel: Don Ravellette (Pub./Ed.); Diane Isaacs (Office Mgr.)

THE FREEMAN COURIER

Street address 1: 308 S Main St
Street address city: Freeman
Street address state: SD
Zip/Postal code: 57029-2302
General Phone: (605) 925-7033
General Fax: (605) 925-4684
General/National Adv. E-mail: courier@gwtc.net
Display Adv. E-mail: courier@gwtc.net
Editorial e-mail: courier@gwtc.net
Primary Website: freemansd.com
Year Established: 1901
Avg Paid Circ: 1500
Audit By: Sworn/Estimate/Non-Audited
Audit Date: 10.06.2019
Personnel: Tim Waltner (Former publisher); Jeremy Waltner (Publisher); Jason Scharberg (Adv. Mgr.); Tabitha Schoenwald (Graphic Designer); Linda VonEye (Office Manager)
Parent company (for newspapers): Second Century Publishing Inc.

THE HARTFORD AREA NEWS

Street address 1: 210 W Main St
Street address city: Canistota
Street address state: SD
Zip/Postal code: 57012
General Phone: (605) 296-3181
General Fax: (605) 296-3289
Advertising Phone: (605) 296-3181
Advertising Fax: (605) 296-3289
Editorial Phone: (605) 296-3181
Editorial Fax: (605) 296-3289
General/National Adv. E-mail: ads@andersonpublications.com
Display Adv. E-mail: ads@andersonpublications.com
Editorial e-mail: news@andersonpublications.com
Avg Paid Circ: 636
Audit By: Sworn/Estimate/Non-Audited
Audit Date: 10.06.2019
Personnel: Matt Anderson (Pub./Ed.); Jelene Olsen (Gen. Mgr.)

THE HOVEN REVIEW

Street address 1: 69 2nd Ave E
Street address city: Hoven
Street address state: SD
Zip/Postal code: 57450
General Phone: (605) 948-2110
General Fax: (605) 948-2578
Advertising Phone: (605) 948-2110
Advertising Fax: (605) 948-2578
Editorial Phone: (605) 948-2110
Editorial Fax: (605) 948-2578
General/National Adv. E-mail: hoven@venturecomm.net
Display Adv. E-mail: hoven@venturecomm.net
Editorial e-mail: hoven@venturecomm.net
Avg Paid Circ: 650
Avg Free Circ: 9
Audit By: Sworn/Estimate/Non-Audited
Audit Date: 10.06.2019
Personnel: Kyle Krueger (Pub.); Janel Lehman (Ed.)

THE HUMBOLDT JOURNAL

Street address 1: 210 W Main St
Street address city: Canistota
Street address state: SD
Zip/Postal code: 57012
General Phone: (605) 296-3181
General Fax: (605) 296-3289
Advertising Phone: (605) 296-3181
Advertising Fax: (605) 296-3289
Editorial Phone: (605) 296-3181
Editorial Fax: (605) 296-3289
General/National Adv. E-mail: ads@andersonpublications.com
Display Adv. E-mail: ads@andersonpublications.com
Editorial e-mail: news@andersonpublications.com
Avg Paid Circ: 399
Audit By: Sworn/Estimate/Non-Audited
Audit Date: 10.06.2019
Personnel: Matt Anderson (Pub./Ed.); Jelene Olsen (Gen. Mgr.)

THE HUTCHINSON HERALD

Street address 1: 203 S 5th St
Street address city: Menno
Street address state: SD
Zip/Postal code: 57045-2127
General Phone: (605) 387-5158
General Fax: (605) 387-5148
Advertising Phone: (605) 387-5158
Advertising Fax: (605) 387-5148
Editorial Phone: (605) 387-5158
Editorial Fax: (605) 387-5148
General/National Adv. E-mail: scpi.adv@gwtc.net
Display Adv. E-mail: hherald@gwpc.net
Editorial e-mail: hherald@gwpc.net
Primary Website: mennosd.com
Year Established: 1882
Avg Paid Circ: 700
Audit By: Sworn/Estimate/Non-Audited
Audit Date: 10.06.2019
Personnel: Tim Waltner (Pub.); Erik Kaufman (Ed.); Jason Scharberg (Adv. Dir.)
Parent company (for newspapers): Second Century Publishing Inc.

THE ISABEL DAKOTAN

Street address 1: 403 N Main St
Street address city: Isabel
Street address state: SD
Zip/Postal code: 57633
General Phone: (605) 466-2258
General Fax: (605) 446-2258
Advertising Phone: (605) 466-2258
Advertising Fax: (605) 446-2258
Editorial Phone: (605) 466-2258
Editorial Fax: (605) 446-2258
General/National Adv. E-mail: dakotan@lakotanetwork.com
Display Adv. E-mail: dakotan@lakotanetwork.com
Editorial e-mail: dakotan@lakotanetwork.com
Avg Paid Circ: 750
Audit By: Sworn/Estimate/Non-Audited
Audit Date: 10.06.2019
Personnel: Robert Slocum (Pub./Adv. Dir.); Barbara Begeman (Ed.)

THE LEMMON LEADER

Street address 1: 213 Main Ave
Street address city: Lemmon
Street address state: SD
Zip/Postal code: 57638-1119
General Phone: (605) 374-3751
General Fax: (605) 374-5295
Advertising Phone: (605) 374-3751
Advertising Fax: (605) 374-5295
Editorial Phone: (605) 374-3751
Editorial Fax: (605) 374-5295
General/National Adv. E-mail: leader@sdplains.com
Display Adv. E-mail: leader@sdplains.com
Editorial e-mail: leader@sdplains.com
Primary Website: lemmonleader.net
Avg Paid Circ: 604
Audit By: Sworn/Estimate/Non-Audited
Audit Date: 10.06.2019
Personnel: Tanya Mitchell (Pub./Adv. Dir.); Jamie Spainhower (Ed.); Jennifer Marxsen (Office Mgr.)

THE LENNOX INDEPENDENT

Street address 1: 116 S Main St
Street address city: Lennox
Street address state: SD
Zip/Postal code: 57039-2096
General Phone: (605) 647-2284
General Fax: (605) 647-2218
Advertising Phone: (605) 647-2284
Advertising Fax: (605) 647-2218
Editorial Phone: (605) 647-2284
Editorial Fax: (605) 647-2218
General/National Adv. E-mail: ads@lennoxnews.com
Display Adv. E-mail: ads@lennoxnews.com
Editorial e-mail: editor@lennoxnews.com
Primary Website: lennoxnews.com
Year Established: 1885
Avg Paid Circ: 1500
Avg Free Circ: 35
Audit By: Sworn/Estimate/Non-Audited
Audit Date: 10.06.2019
Personnel: Kelli Bultena (Co-Pub./Ed); Debbie Schmidt (Co-Pub./Business manager); Anne Homan (Sports Ed)
Parent company (for newspapers): Independent Publishing Co.

THE MILLER PRESS

Street address 1: 114 W 3rd St
Street address city: Miller
Street address state: SD
Zip/Postal code: 57362-1325
General Phone: (605) 853-3575
General Fax: (605) 853-2478
Advertising Phone: (605) 853-3575
Advertising Fax: (605) 853-2478
Editorial Phone: (605) 853-3575
Editorial Fax: (605) 853-2478
General/National Adv. E-mail: advertising@themillerpress.com
Display Adv. E-mail: advertising@themillerpress.com
Editorial e-mail: publisher@themillerpress.com
Primary Website: themillerpress.com
Year Established: 1882
Avg Paid Circ: 2050
Audit By: Sworn/Estimate/Non-Audited
Audit Date: 10.06.2019
Personnel: Mike Caviness (Pub./Ed.); Janice Erfman (Adv. Dir.)

THE PARKSTON ADVANCE

Street address 1: 205 W Main St
Street address city: Parkston
Street address state: SD
Zip/Postal code: 57366
General Phone: (605) 928-3111
General Fax: (605) 928-3111
Advertising Phone: (605) 928-3111
Advertising Fax: (605) 928-3111
Editorial Phone: (605) 928-3111
Editorial Fax: (605) 928-3111
General/National Adv. E-mail: advance@santel.net
Display Adv. E-mail: advance@santel.net
Editorial e-mail: advance@santel.net
Primary Website: parkstonadvance.com
Avg Paid Circ: 1100
Audit By: Sworn/Estimate/Non-Audited
Audit Date: 10.06.2019
Personnel: Scott E. Ehler (Pub.); Wendy Royston (Mng. Ed.); Kevin Geppert (Adv. Mgr.)

THE PIONEER-REVIEW

Street address 1: 105 Wood Ave
Street address city: Philip
Street address state: SD
Zip/Postal code: 57567-4100
General Phone: (605) 859-2516
General Fax: (605) 859-2410
Advertising Phone: (605) 859-2516
Advertising Fax: (605) 859-2410
Editorial Phone: (605) 859-2516
Editorial Fax: (605) 859-2410
General/National Adv. E-mail: ads@pioneer-review.com
Display Adv. E-mail: ads@pioneer-review.com
Editorial e-mail: newsdesk@pioneer-review.com
Primary Website: pioneer-review.com
Avg Paid Circ: 1650
Avg Free Circ: 35
Audit By: Sworn/Estimate/Non-Audited
Audit Date: 10.06.2019
Personnel: Don Ravellette (Pub.); Del Bartels (Ed.); Kelly Penticoff (Gen. Mgr.)

THE PLATTE ENTERPRISE

Street address 1: 511 S Main St
Street address city: Platte
Street address state: SD
Zip/Postal code: 57369-2130
General Phone: (605) 337-3101
General Fax: (605) 337-3433
General/National Adv. E-mail: eprise@midstatesd.net
Display Adv. E-mail: eprise@midstatesd.net
Editorial e-mail: eprise@midstatesd.net
Primary Website: platteenterprise.blogspot.com
Year Established: 1900
Avg Paid Circ: 1890
Audit By: Sworn/Estimate/Non-Audited
Audit Date: 10.06.2019

Personnel: Sharon Huizenga (Pub./Gen. Mgr.); Jason Huizenga (Adv. Mgr.)

THE REDFIELD PRESS

Street address 1: 16 E 7th Ave
Street address city: Redfield
Street address state: SD
Zip/Postal code: 57469-1206
General Phone: (605) 472-0822
General Fax: (605) 472-3634
Advertising Phone: (605) 472-0822
Advertising Fax: (605) 472-3634
Editorial Phone: (605) 472-0822
Editorial Fax: (605) 472-3634
General/National Adv. E-mail: psterner@redfieldpress.com
Display Adv. E-mail: psterner@redfieldpress.com
Editorial e-mail: sappel@redfieldpress.com
Primary Website: redfieldpress.com
Avg Paid Circ: 1950
Audit By: Sworn/Estimate/Non-Audited
Audit Date: 10.06.2019
Personnel: Mark Davis (Pub.); Parry Sterner (Adv. Sales Mgr.); Shiloh Appel (Editor); Kayla Understock (Office Manager)
Parent company (for newspapers): San Luis Valley Publishing

THE ROSHOLT REVIEW

Street address 1: 104 Park Place
Street address city: Rosholt
Street address state: SD
Zip/Postal code: 57260
General Phone: (605) 537-4276
General Fax: (605) 537-4858
Advertising Phone: (605) 537-4276
Advertising Fax: (605) 537-4858
Editorial Phone: (605) 537-4276
Editorial Fax: (605) 537-4858
General/National Adv. E-mail: review@tnics.com
Display Adv. E-mail: review@tnics.com
Editorial e-mail: review@tnics.com
Primary Website: rosholtreview.blogspot.com
Avg Paid Circ: 1280
Avg Free Circ: 25
Audit By: Sworn/Estimate/Non-Audited
Audit Date: 10.06.2019
Personnel: Calvin Ceroll (Pub./Ed./Adv. Dir.)

THE STICKNEY ARGUS

Street address 1: PO Box 216
Street address city: White Lake
Street address state: SD
Zip/Postal code: 57383-0216
General Phone: (605) 249-2420
General Fax: (855) 303-3153
Advertising Phone: (605) 249-2420
Editorial Phone: (605) 249-2420
General/National Adv. E-mail: info@auroracountynews.net
Display Adv. E-mail: info@auroracountynews.net
Editorial e-mail: info@auroracountynews.net
Year Established: 1906
Avg Paid Circ: 400
Avg Free Circ: 31
Audit By: Sworn/Estimate/Non-Audited
Audit Date: 10.06.2019
Personnel: Kim Ehlers (Owner)
Parent company (for newspapers): Standard Publishing Inc.

THE TRI-CITY STAR

Street address 1: PO Box 341
Street address city: White
Street address state: SD
Zip/Postal code: 57276-0341
General Phone: (605) 629-2052
General Fax: (605) 629-1303
Advertising Phone: (605) 629-2052
Advertising Fax: (605) 629-1303
Editorial Phone: (605) 629-2052
Editorial Fax: (605) 629-1303
General/National Adv. E-mail: t.c.s@mchsi.com
Display Adv. E-mail: t.c.s@mchsi.com
Editorial e-mail: t.c.s@mchsi.com
Primary Website: rfdnewsgroup.com
Year Established: 1884
Avg Paid Circ: 1800
Audit By: Sworn/Estimate/Non-Audited
Audit Date: 10.06.2019
Personnel: Chris Schumacher (Pub.); Paul Ekren (Ed.)

THE TRI-COUNTY NEWS

Street address 1: 303 W Main St
Street address city: Irene
Street address state: SD
Zip/Postal code: 57037
General Phone: (605) 263-3339
General Fax: (605) 263-2425
Advertising Phone: (605) 263-3339
Advertising Fax: (605) 263-2425
Editorial Phone: (605) 263-3339
Editorial Fax: (605) 263-2425
General/National Adv. E-mail: thenews@iw.net
Display Adv. E-mail: thenews@iw.net
Editorial e-mail: thenews@iw.net
Avg Paid Circ: 560
Avg Free Circ: 23
Audit By: Sworn/Estimate/Non-Audited
Audit Date: 10.06.2019
Personnel: Allyson Hill (Pub./Ed.); Shane Hill (Co-Pub.)
Parent company (for newspapers): Clear Lake Courier

THE VOLGA TRIBUNE

Street address 1: 207 Kasan Ave
Street address city: Volga
Street address state: SD
Zip/Postal code: 57071
General Phone: (605) 627-9471
General Fax: (605) 627-9310
Advertising Phone: (605) 627-9471
Advertising Fax: (605) 627-9310
Editorial Phone: (605) 627-9471
Editorial Fax: (605) 627-9310
General/National Adv. E-mail: chris.rfdnews@mchsi.com
Display Adv. E-mail: chris.rfdnews@mchsi.com
Editorial e-mail: rfdnews@mchsi.com
Primary Website: rfdnewsgroup.com
Year Established: 1882
Avg Paid Circ: 1800
Audit By: Sworn/Estimate/Non-Audited
Audit Date: 10.06.2019
Personnel: Chris Schumacher (Pub.); David Keith (Ed.)
Parent company (for newspapers): Clear Lake Courier

THE WAGNER POST

Street address 1: 209 S Main Ave
Street address city: Wagner
Street address state: SD
Zip/Postal code: 57380-1727
General Phone: (605) 384-5616
General Fax: (605) 384-5955
Advertising Phone: (605) 384-5616
Advertising Fax: (605) 384-5955
Editorial Phone: (605) 384-5616
Editorial Fax: (605) 384-5955
General/National Adv. E-mail: announcer@hcinet.net
Display Adv. E-mail: announcer@hcinet.net
Editorial e-mail: announcer@hcinet.net
Primary Website: postandwave.com
Avg Paid Circ: 1800
Avg Free Circ: 6500
Audit By: Sworn/Estimate/Non-Audited
Audit Date: 10.06.2019
Personnel: Barb Pechous (Pub./Ed.)

THE YANKTON COUNTY OBSERVER

Street address 1: 308 Douglas Ave
Street address city: Yankton
Street address state: SD
Zip/Postal code: 57078-4432
General Phone: (605) 665-0484
General Fax: (605) 665-2263
Advertising Phone: (605) 665-0484
Advertising Fax: (605) 665-2263
Editorial Phone: (605) 665-0484
Editorial Fax: (605) 665-2263
General/National Adv. E-mail: kathy@ycobserver.com
Display Adv. E-mail: ads@ycobserver.com
Editorial e-mail: kathy@ycobserver.com
Primary Website: ycobserver.com
Year Established: 1978
Avg Paid Circ: 2700
Avg Free Circ: 60
Audit By: Sworn/Estimate/Non-Audited
Audit Date: 10.06.2019
Personnel: Kathy Church (Editor, Publisher); Kathy Church (Pub./Ed.); Jim Anderson (Adv. Mgr.)

TIMBER LAKE TOPIC

Street address 1: 806 Main St
Street address city: Timber Lake
Street address state: SD
Zip/Postal code: 57656
General Phone: (605) 865-3546
General Fax: (605) 865-3787
Advertising Phone: (605) 865-3546
Advertising Fax: (605) 865-3787
Editorial Phone: (605) 865-3546
Editorial Fax: (605) 865-3787
General/National Adv. E-mail: timtopic@lakotanetwork.com
Display Adv. E-mail: timtopic@lakotanetwork.com
Editorial e-mail: timtopic@lakotanetwork.com
Primary Website: timberlakesouthdakota.com
Year Established: 1910
Avg Paid Circ: 1450
Avg Free Circ: 31
Audit By: Sworn/Estimate/Non-Audited
Audit Date: 10.06.2019
Personnel: Jim Nelson (Pub./Ed./Adv. Dir.); Kathy Snyder Nelson (Pub./Ed.)

TIMES-RECORD

Street address 1: 165 2nd St SW
Street address city: Conde
Street address state: SD
Zip/Postal code: 57434-2014
General Phone: (605) 382-5627
General Fax: (605) 382-5629
Advertising Phone: (605) 382-5627
Advertising Fax: (605) 382-5629
Editorial Phone: (605) 382-5627
Editorial Fax: (605) 382-5629
General/National Adv. E-mail: eastarea@nvc.net
Display Adv. E-mail: eastarea@nvc.net
Editorial e-mail: eastarea@nvc.net
Avg Paid Circ: 807
Audit By: Sworn/Estimate/Non-Audited
Audit Date: 10.06.2019
Personnel: Tina Sanderson (Pub./Ed./Adv. Mgr.); Amy Hearnen (News Ed.)

TODD COUNTY TRIBUNE

Street address 1: W Highway 18
Street address city: Mission
Street address state: SD
Zip/Postal code: 57555
General Phone: (605) 856-4469
General Fax: (605) 856-2428
Advertising Phone: (605) 856-4469
Advertising Fax: (605) 856-2428
Editorial Phone: (605) 856-4469
Editorial Fax: (605) 856-2428
General/National Adv. E-mail: tribnews@gwtc.net
Display Adv. E-mail: tribnews@gwtc.net
Editorial e-mail: tribnews@gwtc.net
Primary Website: trib-news.com
Avg Paid Circ: 2200
Audit By: Sworn/Estimate/Non-Audited
Audit Date: 10.06.2019
Personnel: Tim Huether (Pub.); Elaine Emery (Office Mgr.)

TRIPP STAR-LEDGER

Street address 1: PO Box D
Street address city: Tripp
Street address state: SD
Zip/Postal code: 57376-0454
General Phone: (605) 928-3111
General Fax: (605) 928-3111
Advertising Phone: (605) 928-3911
Advertising Fax: (605) 928-3111
Editorial Phone: (605) 928-3111
Editorial Fax: (605) 928-3111
General/National Adv. E-mail: advance@santel.net
Display Adv. E-mail: advance@santel.net
Editorial e-mail: advance@santel.net
Primary Website: parkstonadvance.com
Avg Paid Circ: 606
Audit By: Sworn/Estimate/Non-Audited
Audit Date: 10.06.2019
Personnel: Scott Ehler (Pub.); Wendy Royston (Mng. Ed.); Kevin Geppert (Adv. Dir.)

TRUE DAKOTAN

Street address 1: 113 E Main St
Street address city: Wessington Springs
Street address state: SD
Zip/Postal code: 57382
General Phone: (605) 539-1281
Advertising Phone: (605) 539-1281
Editorial Phone: (605) 539-1281
General/National Adv. E-mail: news@truedakotan.com
Display Adv. E-mail: delia@truedakotan.com
Editorial e-mail: kristi@truedakotan.com
Primary Website: truedakotan.com
Year Established: 1975
Avg Paid Circ: 1400
Audit By: Sworn/Estimate/Non-Audited
Audit Date: 10.06.2019
Personnel: Kristi Hine (Editor/Publisher)
Parent company (for newspapers): Kristi Publishing, Inc.

VERMILLION PLAIN TALK

Street address 1: 201 W Cherry St
Street address city: Vermillion
Street address state: SD
Zip/Postal code: 57069-1109
General Phone: (605) 624-2695
General Fax: (605) 624-2696
Advertising Phone: (605) 624-4429 ext. 103
Advertising Fax: (605) 624-2696
Editorial Phone: (605) 624-4429 ext. 105
Editorial Fax: (605) 624-2696
General/National Adv. E-mail: gary.wood@plaintalk.net
Display Adv. E-mail: michele.schievelbein@plaintalk.net
Editorial e-mail: david.lias@plaintalk.net
Primary Website: plaintalk.net
Year Established: 1886
Avg Paid Circ: 2275
Avg Free Circ: 30
Audit By: Sworn/Estimate/Non-Audited
Audit Date: 10.06.2019
Personnel: Gary Wood (Pub./Ed.); David Lias (Ed.); Micki Schievelbein (Adv. Dir.); Shauna Marlette (Ed.)

VIBORG ENTERPRISE/HURLEY LEADER

Street address 1: 100 N Main St
Street address city: Viborg
Street address state: SD
Zip/Postal code: 57070-2102
General Phone: (605) 766-7827
General Fax: (605) 766-7828
Advertising Phone: (605) 766-7827
Advertising Fax: (605) 766-7828
Editorial Phone: (605) 766-7827
Editorial Fax: (605) 766-7828
General/National Adv. E-mail: enterprise@iw.net
Display Adv. E-mail: enterprise@iw.net
Editorial e-mail: leader@iw.net
Avg Paid Circ: 583
Avg Free Circ: 22
Audit By: Sworn/Estimate/Non-Audited
Audit Date: 10.06.2019
Personnel: Shane Hill (Pub./Ed.); Allyson Hill (Pub./Gen. Mgr.)
Parent company (for newspapers): Star Publishing Co.

WAUBAY CLIPPER

Street address 1: 122 N Main St
Street address city: Waubay
Street address state: SD
Zip/Postal code: 57273
General Phone: (605) 947-4501
General Fax: (605) 947-4501
Advertising Phone: (605) 947-4501
Advertising Fax: (605) 947-4501
Editorial Phone: (605) 947-4501
Editorial Fax: (605) 947-4501
General/National Adv. E-mail: linda@waubayclipper.com
Display Adv. E-mail: linda@waubayclipper.com
Editorial e-mail: linda@waubayclipper.com
Primary Website: waubayclipper.blogspot.com
Year Established: 1890
Avg Paid Circ: 500

Avg Free Circ: 7
Audit By: Sworn/Estimate/Non-Audited
Audit Date: 10.09.2023
Personnel: Linda M. Walters (Pub./Ed./Adv. Dir.)

WEST RIVER EAGLE

Street address 1: 317 South Main Street
Street address city: Eagle Butte
Street address state: SD
Zip/Postal code: 57625
General Phone: (605) 964-2100
General Fax: (605) 964-2110
Advertising Phone: (605) 964-2100
Advertising Fax: (605) 964-2110
Editorial Phone: (605) 964-2100
Editorial Fax: (605) 964-2110
General/National Adv. E-mail: wreagle@westrivereagle.com
Display Adv. E-mail: wreagle@westrivereagle.com
Editorial e-mail: wreagle@westrivereagle.com
Primary Website: westrivereagle.com
Year Established: 1910
Avg Paid Circ: 2100
Audit By: Sworn/Estimate/Non-Audited
Audit Date: 10.06.2019
Personnel: Larry Atkinson (Pub.); Nancy Anderson (Gen. Mgr.); Justice Garreau (Customer Service); Cadyn Dupris (Advertising Sales); Jody Rust (Editor)
Parent company (for newspapers): Bridge City Publishing, Inc.

WILMOT ENTERPRISE

Street address 1: 805 Main St
Street address city: Wilmot
Street address state: SD
Zip/Postal code: 57279
General Phone: (605) 938-4651
General Fax: (605) 938-4683
Advertising Phone: (605) 938-4651
Advertising Fax: (605) 938-4683
Editorial Phone: (605) 938-4651
Editorial Fax: (605) 938-4683
General/National Adv. E-mail: wilnews@tnics.com
Display Adv. E-mail: wilnews@tnics.com
Editorial e-mail: wilnews@tnics.com
Primary Website: wilmotenterprise.blogspot.com
Year Established: 1884
Avg Paid Circ: 850
Audit By: Sworn/Estimate/Non-Audited
Audit Date: 10.06.2019
Personnel: Nancy Kimmel (Pub./Ed./Adv. Dir.)

WINNER ADVOCATE

Street address 1: 125 W 3rd St
Street address city: Winner
Street address state: SD
Zip/Postal code: 57580-1707
General Phone: (605) 842-1481
General Fax: (605) 842-1979
Advertising Phone: (605)842-1481
Advertising Fax: (605)842-1979
Editorial Phone: (605)842-1481
Editorial Fax: (605)842-1979
General/National Adv. E-mail: winneradvocate@hotmail.com
Display Adv. E-mail: winneradvocate@hotmail.com
Editorial e-mail: charley.najacht@thewinneradvocate.com
Primary Website: thewinneradvocate.com
Year Established: 1910
Avg Paid Circ: 2600
Audit By: Sworn/Estimate/Non-Audited
Audit Date: 10.06.2019
Personnel: Charley Najacht (Pub.); Dan Bechtold (Ed.); Rick Hoover (Gen. Mgr.); Laura Brown (Adv. Mgr.)

TENNESSEE

ASHLAND CITY TIMES

Street address 1: 202 N Main St
Street address 2: Ste A
Street address city: Ashland City
Street address state: TN
Zip/Postal code: 37015-1318
General Phone: (615) 792-4230
General Fax: (615) 792-3671
Advertising Phone: (615) 792-4230
Advertising Fax: (615) 792-3671
Editorial Phone: (615) 792-4230
Editorial Fax: (615) 792-3671
General/National Adv. E-mail: jward@tennessean.com
Display Adv. E-mail: pdyates@tennessean.com
Editorial e-mail: madowney@tennessean.com
Primary Website: ashlandcitytimes.com
Avg Paid Circ: 5000
Audit By: Sworn/Estimate/Non-Audited
Audit Date: 10.06.2019
Personnel: Meg Downey (Mng. Ed.); John Ward (Sales VP); Shirley Bradley (Circ. Mgr.)
Parent company (for newspapers): Gannett; The Tennessean; TN Media

BROWNSVILLE STATES-GRAPHIC

Street address 1: 20 N Washington Ave
Street address city: Brownsville
Street address state: TN
Zip/Postal code: 38012-2555
General Phone: (731) 772-1172
General Fax: (731) 772-8306
Advertising Phone: (731) 772-1172
Advertising Fax: (731) 772-8306
Editorial Phone: (731) 772-1172
Editorial Fax: (731) 772-8306
General/National Adv. E-mail: advertising@statesgraphic.com
Display Adv. E-mail: advertising@statesgraphic.com
Editorial e-mail: mmatlock@statesgraphic.com
Primary Website: statesgraphic.com
Year Established: 1867
Avg Paid Circ: 4600
Avg Free Circ: 50
Audit By: Sworn/Estimate/Non-Audited
Audit Date: 10.06.2019
Personnel: Jennifer Willis (Editor); Kristine Osteen (Adv. Mgr.); Jeff Ireland (Sports Ed.)
Parent company (for newspapers): American Hometown Publishing

BUFFALO RIVER REVIEW

Street address 1: 115 S Mill St
Street address city: Linden
Street address state: TN
Zip/Postal code: 37096-6457
General Phone: (931) 589-2169
General Fax: (931) 589-3858
Advertising Phone: (931) 589-2169
Advertising Fax: (931) 589-3858
Editorial Phone: (931) 589-2169
Editorial Fax: (931) 589-3858
General/National Adv. E-mail: brreview@tds.net
Display Adv. E-mail: brreview@tds.net
Editorial e-mail: brreditor@tds.net
Primary Website: buffaloriverreview.com
Year Established: 1976
Avg Paid Circ: 3000
Audit By: Sworn/Estimate/Non-Audited
Audit Date: 10.06.2019
Personnel: Sam Kennedy (Pub.); John Finney (VP); Sherri Groom (Gen. Mgr.); Randy Mackin (Ed.)
Parent company (for newspapers): Kennedy Newspapers

BULLETIN-TIMES

Street address 1: PO Box 438
Street address city: Bolivar
Street address state: TN
Zip/Postal code: 38008-0438
General Phone: (731) 658-3691
General Fax: (731) 658-7222
Advertising Phone: (731) 658-3691
Advertising Fax: (731) 658-7222
Editorial Phone: (731) 658-3691
Editorial Fax: (731) 658-7222
General/National Adv. E-mail: editor@hardemancountyjournal.com
Display Adv. E-mail: editor@hardemancountyjournal.com
Editorial e-mail: editor@hardemancountyjournal.com
Primary Website: bulletintimesnews.com
Year Established: 1865
Avg Paid Circ: 5000
Avg Free Circ: 15000
Audit By: Sworn/Estimate/Non-Audited
Audit Date: 10.06.2019
Personnel: Richard Fry (Pub./Ed.); Shasity Mynatt (Account Exec./Circ. Mgr.)
Parent company (for newspapers): Delphos Herald, Inc.

CARROLL COUNTY NEWS-LEADER

Street address 1: 165 Court Sq
Street address 2: Ste 2
Street address city: Huntingdon
Street address state: TN
Zip/Postal code: 38344-3703
General Phone: (731) 986-2253
General Fax: (731) 986-3585
Advertising Phone: (731) 986-2253
Advertising Fax: (731) 986-3585
Editorial Phone: (731) 986-2253
Editorial Fax: (731) 986-3585
General/National Adv. E-mail: daniel@newsleaderonline.com
Display Adv. E-mail: daniel@newsleaderonline.com
Editorial e-mail: daniel@newsleaderonline.com
Primary Website: magicvalleypublishing.com
Year Established: 1868
Avg Paid Circ: 2800
Audit By: Sworn/Estimate/Non-Audited
Audit Date: 10.06.2019
Personnel: Dennis M. Richardson (Owner); Shirley Nanney (Ed.); Daniel Richardson (Pub); Ron Park (Sports Ed); Lindsey Bell (Society Ed); Christy Slaman (Art Director)
Parent company (for newspapers): Magic Valley Publishing Co., Inc

CARTHAGE COURIER

Street address 1: 509 Main St N
Street address city: Carthage
Street address state: TN
Zip/Postal code: 37030-1270
General Phone: (615) 735-1110
General Fax: (615) 735-0635
Advertising Phone: (615) 735-1110
Advertising Fax: (615) 735-0635
Editorial Phone: (615) 735-1110
Editorial Fax: (615) 735-0635
General/National Adv. E-mail: advertising@carthagecourier.com
Display Adv. E-mail: production@carthagecourier.com
Editorial e-mail: news@carthagecourier.com
Primary Website: carthagecourier.com
Year Established: 1913
Avg Paid Circ: 5500
Audit By: Sworn/Estimate/Non-Audited
Audit Date: 10.06.2019
Personnel: Scott Winfree (Pub./Adv. Dir.); Eddie West (Ed.)

CHESTER COUNTY INDEPENDENT

Street address 1: 218 S Church Ave
Street address city: Henderson
Street address state: TN
Zip/Postal code: 38340-2638
General Phone: (731) 989-4624
General Fax: (731) 989-5008
Advertising Phone: (731) 989-4624
Advertising Fax: (731) 989-5008
Editorial Phone: (731) 989-4624
Editorial Fax: (731) 989-5008
General/National Adv. E-mail: mcroom@chestercountyindependent.com
Display Adv. E-mail: news@chestercountyindependent.com
Editorial e-mail: jwebb@chestercountyindependent.com
Primary Website: chestercountyindependent.com
Year Established: 1865
Avg Paid Circ: 5100
Avg Free Circ: 6
Audit By: Sworn/Estimate/Non-Audited
Audit Date: 10.06.2019
Personnel: Scott Whaley (Publisher); James A. Webb (Ed./Circ. Dir.); Marvin Croom (Adv. Dir.); Scott Whaley (Ed.)
Parent company (for newspapers): American Hometown Publishing

CLAIBORNE PROGRESS

Street address 1: 1705 Main St
Street address city: Tazewell
Street address state: TN
Zip/Postal code: 37879-3413
General Phone: (423) 254-5588
General/National Adv. E-mail: mike.grimm@claiborneprogress.net
Display Adv. E-mail: karen.rhymer@claiborneprogress.net
Editorial e-mail: marisa.anders@claiborneprogress.net
Primary Website: claiborneprogress.net
Year Established: 1887
Avg Paid Circ: 7000
Audit By: Sworn/Estimate/Non-Audited
Audit Date: 10.06.2019
Personnel: Bill Sharp (Pub.); Debbie Spears (Reg. Pub.); Marisa Anders (Ed.); Mike Grimm (Adv.); Karen Rhymer (Class & Front Desk)
Parent company (for newspapers): Boone Newspapers, Inc.

COLLIERVILLE INDEPENDENT

Street address 1: 2850 Stage Village Cv
Street address 2: Ste 5
Street address city: Bartlett
Street address state: TN
Zip/Postal code: 38134-4682
General Phone: (901) 388-1500
General Fax: (901) 529-7687
Advertising Phone: (901) 388-1500
Advertising Fax: (901) 529-7687
Editorial Phone: (901) 388-1500
Editorial Fax: (901) 529-7687
General/National Adv. E-mail: graham.sweeney@journalinc.com
Display Adv. E-mail: graham.sweeney@journalinc.com
Editorial e-mail: graham.sweeney@journalinc.com
Primary Website: colliervilleindependent.com
Avg Free Circ: 14000
Audit By: Sworn/Estimate/Non-Audited
Audit Date: 10.06.2019
Personnel: Graham Sweeney (Pub./Ed./Adv. Dir.)

CROSSVILLE CHRONICLE

Street address 1: 125 West Ave
Street address city: Crossville
Street address state: TN
Zip/Postal code: 38555-4478
General Phone: (931) 484-5145
General Fax: (931) 456-7683
Advertising Phone: (931) 484-5145
Advertising Fax: (931) 456-7683
Editorial Phone: (931) 484-5145
Editorial Fax: (931) 456-7683
General/National Adv. E-mail: batkinson@crossville-chronicle.com
Display Adv. E-mail: batkinson@crossville-chronicle.com
Editorial e-mail: mmoser@crossville-chronicle.com
Primary Website: crossville-chronicle.com
Year Established: 1886
Avg Paid Circ: 8500
Avg Free Circ: 10200
Audit By: Sworn/Estimate/Non-Audited
Audit Date: 10.06.2019
Personnel: Pauline D. Sherrer (Pub.); Mike Moser (Ed.); Heather Mullinix (Asst. Ed.); Jimmy Burks (Prodn. Mgr.); Bill Atkinson (GM/Marketing Director)
Parent company (for newspapers): CNHI, LLC

DYERSBURG NEWS

Street address 1: 294 US Highway 51 Byp N
Street address city: Dyersburg
Street address state: TN
Zip/Postal code: 38024-3659
General Phone: (731) 285-4091
General Fax: (731) 285-9747
Advertising Phone: (731) 285-4091 ext. 116
Advertising Fax: (731) 285-9747
Editorial Phone: (731) 285-4091 ext. 121
Editorial Fax: (731) 285-9747
General/National Adv. E-mail: sruse@stategazette.com
Display Adv. E-mail: cdawson@stategazette.com
Editorial e-mail: jcannon@stategazette.com
Primary Website: stategazette.com
Year Established: 1865
Avg Free Circ: 16985
Audit By: Sworn/Estimate/Non-Audited
Audit Date: 10.06.2019

Personnel: Shelia Rouse (Pub./Gen. Mgr.); Jason Cannon (Ed.); Charles Dawson (Adv. Dir.)

FAIRVIEW OBSERVER

Street address 1: 1874 Fairview Blvd
Street address 2: Ste A
Street address city: Fairview
Street address state: TN
Zip/Postal code: 37062-9412
General Phone: (615) 799-8565
General Fax: (615) 799-8728
Editorial e-mail: news@fairviewobserver.com
Primary Website: fairviewobserver.com
Year Established: 1989
Avg Paid Circ: 1350
Audit By: Sworn/Estimate/Non-Audited
Audit Date: 10.06.2019
Personnel: Laura Hollingsworth (Pres./Pub.); Becky Moran (Gen. Mgr.); Nancy Phillips Stephens (Ed.); Megan Wren (Adv. Mgr.)
Parent company (for newspapers): Gannett; The Tennessean; TN Media

FARRAGUT PRESS

Street address 1: 11863 Kingston Pike
Street address city: Farragut
Street address state: TN
Zip/Postal code: 37934-3833
General Phone: (865) 675-6397
General Fax: (865) 675-1675
Advertising Phone: (865)675-6397 ext. 8877
Advertising Fax: (865)675-1675
Editorial Phone: (865)675-6397 ext. 8876
Editorial Fax: (865)675-1675
General/National Adv. E-mail: egrove@farragutpress.com
Display Adv. E-mail: egrove@farragutpress.com
Editorial e-mail: dbarile@farragutpress.com
Primary Website: farragutpress.com
Year Established: 1988
Avg Paid Circ: 401
Avg Free Circ: 14541
Audit By: CVC
Audit Date: 31.03.2017
Personnel: Dan Barile (Pub./Ed.); Elaine Grove (Adv. Mgr.); Julie Gunter (Advertising Sales); Kathy Hartman (Advertising Sales); Laura Sayers (Advertising Sales); Lori Timmis (Receptionist); Scott Hamstead (Sales); Linda Gildner (Circ. Mgr.); Sherry Long (Advertising Sales); Shannon Diane (Adverstising Sales)
Parent company (for newspapers): Republic Newspapers, Inc.

FENTRESS COURIER

Street address 1: 114 White Oak St
Street address city: Jamestown
Street address state: TN
Zip/Postal code: 38556-4204
General Phone: (931) 879-4040
General Fax: (931) 879-7716
General/National Adv. E-mail: fencourier@twlakes.net
Display Adv. E-mail: fencourier@twlakes.net
Editorial e-mail: fencourier@twlakes.net
Primary Website: fentresscouriernews.com
Year Established: 1946
Avg Paid Circ: 4700
Audit By: Sworn/Estimate/Non-Audited
Audit Date: 10.06.2019
Personnel: Bill Bowden (Pub./Ed.)

GALLATIN NEWS EXAMINER

Street address 1: 1 Examiner Ct
Street address city: Gallatin
Street address state: TN
Zip/Postal code: 37066-7111
General Phone: (615) 452-2561
General Fax: (615) 575-7181
Advertising Phone: (615) 575-7141
Advertising Fax: (615) 575-7181
Editorial Phone: (615) 575-7161
Editorial Fax: (615) 575-7181
General/National Adv. E-mail: slupton@tennessean.com
Display Adv. E-mail: pdyates@tennessean.com
Editorial e-mail: mdevarenne@tennessean.com
Primary Website: gallatinnewsexaminer.com
Mthly Avg Views: 100000
Year Established: 1840
Audit By: Sworn/Estimate/Non-Audited
Audit Date: 10.06.2019
Personnel: Robyn Williams (Retail Adv. Mgr.); Cecil Joyce (Sports Ed.); Roger Watson (Gen. Mgr.); Mealand Ragland-Hudgins (Ed.); Josh Cross (Gen. Mgr.)
Parent company (for newspapers): Gannett; The Tennessean; TN Media

GERMANTOWN NEWS

Street address 1: 7545 North St
Street address city: Germantown
Street address state: TN
Zip/Postal code: 38138-3822
General Phone: (901) 754-0337
General Fax: (901) 754-2961
General/National Adv. E-mail: advertising@germantownnews.com
Display Adv. E-mail: classified@germantownnews.com
Editorial e-mail: news@germantownnews.com
Primary Website: germantownnews.com
Year Established: 1974
Avg Paid Circ: 7500
Audit By: Sworn/Estimate/Non-Audited
Audit Date: 10.06.2019
Personnel: Rebekah Yearout (Mng. Ed.)
Parent company (for newspapers): Crittenden Publishing Co.

GRUNDY COUNTY HERALD

Street address 1: 65 Oak St
Street address city: Tracy City
Street address state: TN
Zip/Postal code: 37387-5048
General Phone: (931) 592-2781
General Fax: (931) 598-5812
Advertising Phone: (931) 592-2781
Advertising Fax: (931) 592-9241
Editorial Phone: (931) 592-2781
Editorial Fax: (931) 598-5812
General/National Adv. E-mail: gcherald@lcs.net
Display Adv. E-mail: gcherald@lcs.net
Editorial e-mail: gcherald@lcs.net
Primary Website: grundycountyherald.com
Year Established: 1929
Avg Paid Circ: 5100
Audit By: Sworn/Estimate/Non-Audited
Audit Date: 10.06.2019
Personnel: Joy Caldwell (Pub./Ed.); Chris Cooper (Adv. Dir.); Mandy Phillips
Parent company (for newspapers): Lakeway Publishers, Inc.

HAMILTON COUNTY HERALD

Street address 1: 1412 McCallie Ave
Street address city: Chattanooga
Street address state: TN
Zip/Postal code: 37404-2935
General Phone: (423) 602-9270
General Fax: (423) 602-9269
Advertising Phone: (423) 602-9267
Editorial Phone: (423) 602-9268
General/National Adv. E-mail: gm@hamiltoncountyherald.com
Display Adv. E-mail: gm@hamiltoncountyherald.com
Editorial e-mail: editor@HamiltonCountyHerald.com
Primary Website: hamiltoncountyherald.com
Year Established: 1913
Avg Paid Circ: 3733
Audit By: Sworn/Estimate/Non-Audited
Audit Date: 10.06.2019
Personnel: Susanne Reed (Gen. Mgr./Adv. Dir.); David Laprad (Ed.); Eric Barnes (Pub, CEO)
Parent company (for newspapers): The Daily News Publishing Co., Inc

HERALD & TRIBUNE

Street address 1: 702 W Jackson Blvd
Street address city: Jonesborough
Street address state: TN
Zip/Postal code: 37659-5264
General Phone: (423) 753-3136
General Fax: (423) 753-6528
Advertising Phone: (423) 753-3136
Advertising Fax: (423) 753-6528
Editorial Phone: (423) 753-3136
Editorial Fax: (423) 753-6528
General/National Adv. E-mail: ads@heraldandtribune.com
Display Adv. E-mail: bcasey@heraldandtribune.com
Editorial e-mail: kswing@heraldandtribune.com
Primary Website: heraldandtribune.com
Year Established: 1869
Avg Paid Circ: 4500
Avg Free Circ: 195
Audit By: Sworn/Estimate/Non-Audited
Audit Date: 10.06.2019
Personnel: Krystal Hawkins; Collin Brooks (Gen Asst); Marcella Peeks (Adv Mgr); Lisa Whaley (Gen Mgr & Ed)
Parent company (for newspapers): Sandusky Newspapers, Inc.

LA FOLLETTE PRESS

Street address 1: 225 N 1st St
Street address city: La Follette
Street address state: TN
Zip/Postal code: 37766-2462
General Phone: (423) 562-8468
General Fax: (423) 566-7060
Advertising Phone: (423) 562-8468
Advertising Fax: (423) 566-7060
Editorial Phone: (423) 562-8468
Editorial Fax: (423) 566-7060
General/National Adv. E-mail: ads@lafollettepress.com
Display Adv. E-mail: classifieds@lafollettepress.com
Editorial e-mail: bschanding@lafollettepress.com
Primary Website: lafollettepress.com
Year Established: 1910
Avg Paid Circ: 10300
Avg Free Circ: 150
Audit By: Sworn/Estimate/Non-Audited
Audit Date: 10.06.2019
Personnel: Ann Rutherford (Adv. Mgr.); Linn Hudson (Pub.); Mae Clotfelter (Adv. Sales); Tilbert McCrary (Adv. Sales); Karen Cumorich (Office Mgr.)
Parent company (for newspapers): Landmark Community Newspapers, LLC

LAWRENCE COUNTY ADVOCATE

Street address 1: 121 N Military Ave
Street address city: Lawrenceburg
Street address state: TN
Zip/Postal code: 38464-3323
General Phone: (931) 762-1726
General Fax: (931) 762-7874
General/National Adv. E-mail: lawcoadv@bellsouth.net
Display Adv. E-mail: lawcoadv@bellsouth.net
Editorial e-mail: joebax1959@gmail.com
Primary Website: lawrencecountyadvocate.net
Year Established: 1984
Avg Paid Circ: 202
Avg Free Circ: 15643
Audit By: CVC
Audit Date: 30.09.2017
Personnel: Dorothy Adams (Circ. Mgr.); John Finney (Prodn. Mgr.); Joe Baxter (Pub.); Amber McIntyre (Adv.)

LEDGER - KNOXVILLE EDITION

Street address 1: 222 2nd Ave N.
Street address 2: Suite 101
Street address city: Nashville
Street address state: TN
Zip/Postal code: 37201
General Phone: (615) 254-5522
General Fax: (615) 254-5525
General/National Adv. E-mail: dchambers@TNLedger.com
Display Adv. E-mail: dchambers@TNLedger.com
Editorial e-mail: lgraves@TNLedger.com
Primary Website: tnledger.com
Year Established: 2014
Avg Free Circ: 10975
Audit By: CVC
Audit Date: 10.12.2018
Personnel: Lyle Graves (Ed.); Dianna Chambers (Adv. Sales); Donna Gosnell (Circ.); Don Fancher (Franchise Closure Announcer)

LEWIS COUNTY HERALD

Street address 1: 31 E Linden Ave
Street address city: Hohenwald
Street address state: TN
Zip/Postal code: 38462-1415
General Phone: (931) 796-3191
General Fax: (931) 796-2153
General/National Adv. E-mail: lewisherald@bellsouth.net
Display Adv. E-mail: lewisherald@bellsouth.net
Editorial e-mail: lewisherald@bellsouth.net
Primary Website: lewisherald.com
Year Established: 1898
Avg Paid Circ: 3251
Avg Free Circ: 18
Audit By: Sworn/Estimate/Non-Audited
Audit Date: 10.06.2019
Personnel: Walton Dunn (Ed./Adv. Mgr.); Hulon Dunn (Mng. Ed./Prod. Mgr.); Marne Carroll (Circ. Mgr.); Julie Reeves (Graphic Artist); Glenda Atkinson (Reporter/ Photographer); Michael Hinson (Pressman)

LEXINGTON PROGRESS

Street address 1: 508 S Broad St
Street address city: Lexington
Street address state: TN
Zip/Postal code: 38351-2211
General Phone: (731) 968-6397
General Fax: (731) 968-9560
Advertising Phone: (731) 968-6397
Advertising Fax: (731) 968-9560
Editorial Phone: (731) 968-6397
Editorial Fax: (731) 968-9560
General/National Adv. E-mail: advertising@lexingtonprogress.com
Display Adv. E-mail: advertising@lexingtonprogress.com
Editorial e-mail: news@lexingtonprogress.com
Primary Website: lexingtonprogress.com
Year Established: 1884
Avg Paid Circ: 7300
Avg Free Circ: 2000
Audit By: Sworn/Estimate/Non-Audited
Audit Date: 10.06.2019
Personnel: Tom Franklin (Pub.); Mike Reed (Ed.); Susan Small (Adv. Dir.)

MACON COUNTY TIMES

Street address 1: 200 Times Ave
Street address city: Lafayette
Street address state: TN
Zip/Postal code: 37083-1244
General Phone: (615) 666-2440
General Fax: (615) 666-4909
Advertising Phone: (615) 666-2440
Advertising Fax: (615) 666-4909
Editorial Phone: (615) 666-2440
Editorial Fax: (615) 666-4909
General/National Adv. E-mail: cturner@civitasmedia.com
Display Adv. E-mail: ldallas@civitasmedia.com
Editorial e-mail: tcryar@civitasmedia.com
Primary Website: maconcountytimes.com
Mthly Avg Views: 25000
Mthly Avg Unique Visitors: 13000
Year Established: 1919
Avg Paid Circ: 4000
Avg Free Circ: 18
Audit By: Sworn/Estimate/Non-Audited
Audit Date: 10.06.2019
Personnel: Lane Moon (Publisher)
Parent company (for newspapers): AIM Media Indiana

MANCHESTER TIMES

Street address 1: 300 N Spring St
Street address city: Manchester
Street address state: TN
Zip/Postal code: 37355-1567
General Phone: (931) 728-7577
General Fax: (931) 728-7614
Advertising Phone: (931) 728-7577
Advertising Fax: (931) 728-7614
Editorial Phone: (931) 728-7577
Editorial Fax: (931) 728-7614
General/National Adv. E-mail: mtpub@lcs.net
Display Adv. E-mail: mtclass@lcs.net
Editorial e-mail: lnunez@manchestertimes.com
Primary Website: manchestertimes.com
Year Established: 1881
Avg Paid Circ: 4880
Audit By: Sworn/Estimate/Non-Audited
Audit Date: 10.06.2019
Personnel: Josh Peterson (Pub.)

Parent company (for newspapers): Lakeway Publishers, Inc.

MARION COUNTY NEWS

Street address 1: 307 Elm Ave
Street address city: South Pittsburg
Street address state: TN
Zip/Postal code: 37380-1337
General Phone: (423) 837-6312
General/National Adv. E-mail: adsales@mcnewstn.com
Display Adv. E-mail: classifieds@mcnewstn.com
Primary Website: mcnewstn.com
Year Established: 1938
Avg Paid Circ: 2500
Audit By: Sworn/Estimate/Non-Audited
Audit Date: 10.06.2019
Personnel: David Riley (Pub.); Debbie Keahey (Circ./Class.); Christie Pitts (Adv. Sales); Christy Sacks

MARSHALL COUNTY TRIBUNE

Street address 1: 111 W Commerce St
Street address city: Lewisburg
Street address state: TN
Zip/Postal code: 37091-3343
General Phone: (931) 359-1188
General Fax: (931) 359-1847
Advertising Phone: (931) 359-1188 ext. 24
Advertising Fax: (931) 359-1847
Editorial Phone: (931) 359-1188 ext. 26
Editorial Fax: (931) 359-1847
General/National Adv. E-mail: jward@marshalltribune.com
Display Adv. E-mail: lbrown@marshalltribune.com
Editorial e-mail: mteditor@marshalltribune.com
Primary Website: marshalltribune.com
Year Established: 1873
Avg Paid Circ: 4025
Avg Free Circ: 21
Audit By: Sworn/Estimate/Non-Audited
Audit Date: 10.06.2019
Personnel: Anthony Puca (Sports Ed.); Jim Wilson (Adv. Rep.); Scott Pearson (Assoc. Ed.)
Parent company (for newspapers): Rust Communications

MCKENZIE BANNER

Street address 1: 3 Banner Row
Street address city: Mc Kenzie
Street address state: TN
Zip/Postal code: 38201-2230
General Phone: (731) 352-3323
General Fax: (731) 352-3322
Advertising Phone: (731) 352-3323
Advertising Fax: (731) 352-3322
Editorial Phone: (731) 352-3323
Editorial Fax: (731) 352-3322
General/National Adv. E-mail: jennifer@mckenziebanner.com
Display Adv. E-mail: jennifer@mckenziebanner.com
Editorial e-mail: washburn@mckenziebanner.com
Primary Website: mckenziebanner.com
Year Established: 1870
Avg Paid Circ: 4500
Audit By: Sworn/Estimate/Non-Audited
Audit Date: 10.06.2019
Personnel: Joel T. Washburn (Ed.); Jennifer Sims (Adv. Mgr.)
Parent company (for newspapers): Tri-County Publishing, Inc.

MEMPHIS BUSINESS JOURNAL

Street address 1: 80 Monroe Ave
Street address 2: Ste 600
Street address city: Memphis
Street address state: TN
Zip/Postal code: 38103-2440
General Phone: (901) 523-1000
General Fax: (901) 526-5240
Advertising Phone: (901) 523-1000
Advertising Fax: (901) 526-5240
Editorial Phone: (901) 259-1721
Editorial Fax: (901) 526-5240
General/National Adv. E-mail: schamblin@bizjournals.com
Display Adv. E-mail: thollahan@bizjournals.com
Editorial e-mail: bwellborn@bizjournals.com
Primary Website: bizjournals.com/memphis
Year Established: 1979
Avg Paid Circ: 5196
Audit By: Sworn/Estimate/Non-Audited
Audit Date: 10.06.2019
Personnel: Stuart Chamblin (Pub.); Bill Wellborn (Ed.); Mary Cashiola (Managing Editor)

MILAN MIRROR-EXCHANGE

Street address 1: 1104 S Main St
Street address city: Milan
Street address state: TN
Zip/Postal code: 38358-2726
General Phone: (731) 686-1632
General Fax: (731) 686-9005
Advertising Phone: (731) 686-1632
Advertising Fax: (731) 686-9005
Editorial Phone: (731) 686-1632
Editorial Fax: (731) 686-9005
General/National Adv. E-mail: scarlet@milanmirrorexchange.com
Display Adv. E-mail: melissa@milanmirrorexchange.com
Editorial e-mail: victor@milanmirrorexchange.com
Primary Website: milanmirrorexchange.com
Year Established: 1964
Avg Paid Circ: 5600
Audit By: Sworn/Estimate/Non-Audited
Audit Date: 10.06.2019
Personnel: Dorris Parkins (Pub.); Victor Parkins (Ed.); Melanie Day (Mng. Ed.); Scarlet Elliott (Adv. Mgr.)

MOORE COUNTY NEWS

Street address 1: 30 Hiles St
Street address city: Lynchburg
Street address state: TN
Zip/Postal code: 37352-8355
General Phone: (931) 759-7302
General Fax: (931) 759-6838
Advertising Phone: (931) 759-7302
Advertising Fax: (931) 759-6838
Editorial Phone: (931) 759-7302
Editorial Fax: (931) 759-6838
General/National Adv. E-mail: mcnpub@lcs.net
Display Adv. E-mail: mcnpub@lcs.net
Editorial e-mail: mcnpub@lcs.net
Primary Website: themoorecountynews.com
Year Established: 1928
Avg Paid Circ: 2500
Avg Free Circ: 19
Audit By: Sworn/Estimate/Non-Audited
Audit Date: 10.06.2019
Personnel: Tabitha Moore (Pub./Ed.); Barbara Green (Adv. Mgr.)
Parent company (for newspapers): Lakeway Publishers, Inc.

MORGAN COUNTY NEWS

Street address 1: 202 N MAIDEN ST
Street address city: Wartburg
Street address state: TN
Zip/Postal code: 37887
General Phone: (423) 346-6225
General Fax: (423) 346-5788
Advertising Phone: (423) 346-6225
Advertising Fax: (423) 346-5788
Editorial Phone: (423) 346-6225
Editorial Fax: (423) 346-5788
General/National Adv. E-mail: kkile@roanecounty.com
Display Adv. E-mail: kkile@roanecounty.com
Editorial e-mail: jbyrge@morgancountynews.net
Primary Website: morgancountynews.net
Year Established: 1917
Avg Paid Circ: 5377
Avg Free Circ: 49
Audit By: Sworn/Estimate/Non-Audited
Audit Date: 10.06.2019
Personnel: Johnny Teglas (Gen. Mgr.); Kevin Kile (Adv. Mgr.); John "Goose" Lindsay (Editor)
Parent company (for newspapers): Paxton Media Group; Landmark Communications, Inc.; Landmark Community Newspapers, LLC

MT. JULIET NEWS

Street address 1: 402 N Cumberland St
Street address city: Lebanon
Street address state: TN
Zip/Postal code: 37087-2306
General Phone: (615) 754-6397
General Fax: (615) 754-6398
Advertising Phone: (615) 754-6397
Advertising Fax: (615) 754-6398
Editorial Phone: (615) 754-6397
Editorial Fax: (615) 754-6398
General/National Adv. E-mail: mtjulietnews@tds.net
Display Adv. E-mail: mtjulietnews@tds.net
Editorial e-mail: mtjulietnews@tds.net
Primary Website: mtjulietnews.com
Year Established: 1987
Avg Paid Circ: 2000
Avg Free Circ: 12500
Audit By: Sworn/Estimate/Non-Audited
Audit Date: 10.06.2019
Personnel: Matt Masters (Reporter); Laurie Everett (Mng. Ed.); Roger Wells (Adv. Dir.); Mark Rogers (Prod. Mgr.)
Parent company (for newspapers): Sandusky Newspapers, Inc.

NASHVILLE BUSINESS JOURNAL

Street address 1: 1800 Church St
Street address 2: Ste 300
Street address city: Nashville
Street address state: TN
Zip/Postal code: 37203-2224
General Phone: (615) 248-2222
General Fax: (615) 248-6246
Advertising Phone: (615) 248-2222
Advertising Fax: (615) 248-6246
Editorial Phone: (615) 248-2222
Editorial Fax: (615) 248-6246
General/National Adv. E-mail: aharris@bizjournals.com
Display Adv. E-mail: mfriedenberg@bizjournals.com
Editorial e-mail: lbecker@bizjournals.com
Primary Website: bizjournals.com/nashville
Audit By: Sworn/Estimate/Non-Audited
Audit Date: 10.06.2019
Personnel: Kate Herman (Pres./Pub.); Lori Becker (Ed. in Chief); Eric Snyder (Mng. Ed.); Amy Harris (Adv. Dir.)

NASHVILLE LEDGER

Street address 1: 222 2nd Ave N
Street address 2: Ste 101
Street address city: Nashville
Street address state: TN
Zip/Postal code: 37201-1693
General Phone: (615) 254-5522
General Fax: (615) 254-5525
General/National Adv. E-mail: dchambers@TNLedger.com
Display Adv. E-mail: dchambers@TNLedger.com
Editorial e-mail: lgraves@TNLedger.com
Primary Website: tnledger.com
Year Established: 1978
Avg Paid Circ: 0
Avg Free Circ: 26723
Audit By: CVC
Audit Date: 01.06.2018
Personnel: Lyle Graves (Pub./Ed.); Dianna Chambers (Adv. Mgr.); Don Fancher (Public Notice Adv.); Donna Gosnell (Circ. Mgr.)
Parent company (for newspapers): The Daily News Publishing Co.

NEWS-HERALD

Street address 1: 201 Simpson Rd
Street address city: Lenoir City
Street address state: TN
Zip/Postal code: 37771-6567
General Phone: (865) 986-6581
General Fax: (865) 988-3261
Advertising Phone: (865) 986-6581
Advertising Fax: (865) 988-3261
Editorial Phone: (865) 986-6581
Editorial Fax: (865) 988-3261
General/National Adv. E-mail: amanda.kimbrell@news-herald.net
Display Adv. E-mail: classifieds@news-herald.net
Editorial e-mail: news@news-herald.net
Primary Website: news-herald.net
Year Established: 1885
Avg Paid Circ: 3450
Avg Free Circ: 250
Audit By: Sworn/Estimate/Non-Audited
Audit Date: 10.06.2019
Personnel: Steve Meadows (Pub./Ed.); Amanda Kimbrell (Business Manager); Jonathan Herrmann (News Editor)
Parent company (for newspapers): Adams Publishing Group, LLC

OVERTON COUNTY NEWS

Street address 1: 415 W Main St
Street address city: Livingston
Street address state: TN
Zip/Postal code: 38570-1831
General Phone: (931) 403-6397
General Fax: (931) 823-6486
Advertising Phone: (931) 823-6485
Advertising Fax: (931) 823-6486
Editorial Phone: (931) 823-6485
Editorial Fax: (931) 823-6486
General/National Adv. E-mail: ads@overtoncountynews.com
Display Adv. E-mail: ads@overtoncountynews.com
Editorial e-mail: news@overtoncountynews.com
Primary Website: overtoncountynews.com
Year Established: 1967
Avg Paid Circ: 5600
Avg Free Circ: 60
Audit By: Sworn/Estimate/Non-Audited
Audit Date: 10.06.2019
Personnel: Carson Oliver (Owner/Pub./Nat'l Adv. Mgr.); Dewain Peek (Ed.); Darren Oliver (Adv. Mgr.)

PICKETT COUNTY PRESS

Street address 1: 23 Courthouse Sq
Street address city: Byrdstown
Street address state: TN
Zip/Postal code: 38549-2253
General Phone: (931) 864-3675
General Fax: (931) 864-3695
Advertising Phone: (931) 864-3675
Advertising Fax: (931) 864-3695
Editorial Phone: (931) 864-3675
Editorial Fax: (931) 864-3695
General/National Adv. E-mail: pickettpress@twlakes.net
Display Adv. E-mail: pickettpress@twlakes.net
Editorial e-mail: pickettpress@twlakes.net
Primary Website: pickettcountypress.com
Year Established: 1962
Avg Paid Circ: 2100
Avg Free Circ: 11
Audit By: Sworn/Estimate/Non-Audited
Audit Date: 10.06.2019
Personnel: Amanda Bond (Pub./Ed.); Lora Presley (Adv. Dir./Office Mgr.); Heather Smith (Admin. Assistant)

POLK COUNTY NEWS/CITIZEN ADVANCE

Street address 1: 3 Main St
Street address city: Benton
Street address state: TN
Zip/Postal code: 37307
General Phone: (423) 338-2818
General Fax: (423) 338-4574
Advertising Phone: (423) 338-2818
Advertising Fax: (423) 338-4574
Editorial Phone: (423) 338-2818
Editorial Fax: (423) 338-4574
General/National Adv. E-mail: advertising@thepolkcountynews.com
Display Adv. E-mail: advertising@thepolkcountynews.com
Editorial e-mail: news@thepolkcountynews.com
Primary Website: polknewsonline.com
Year Established: 1883
Avg Paid Circ: 3800
Audit By: Sworn/Estimate/Non-Audited
Audit Date: 10.06.2019
Personnel: Cheryl Buehler (Pub.); Richmond Clayton (Ed.)
Parent company (for newspapers): The Newspaper Publishing Company, LLC

PULASKI CITIZEN

Street address 1: 955 W College St
Street address city: Pulaski
Street address state: TN
Zip/Postal code: 38478-3600
General Phone: (931) 363-3544
General Fax: (931) 363-4312
Advertising Phone: (931) 363-3544 ext. 115
Advertising Fax: (931) 424-2828
Editorial Phone: (931) 363-3544 ext. 131

Editorial Fax: (931) 363-8656
General/National Adv. E-mail: support@pulaskicitizen.com
Display Adv. E-mail: Kelley@pulaskicitizen.com
Classified Adv. e-mail: rebecca.brooks@pulaskicitizen.com
Editorial e-mail: cary.malone@pulaskicitizen.com
Primary Website: pulaskicitizen.com
Year Established: 1854
Avg Paid Circ: 4848
Avg Free Circ: 524
Audit By: Sworn/Estimate/Non-Audited
Audit Date: 10.06.2019
Personnel: Cary Jane Malone (EIC); Scott Stewart (Pub Circ. Mgr. Advertising Manager); Wade Neely (Sports Ed); Kelley Garrett (Advertising Manager); Margaret Campbell (Lifestyles Writer); Trea Dunnavant (Staff Writer/Photographer); Tiffany Hagood (Sales Rep)

ROANE COUNTY NEWS

Street address 1: 204 Franklin St
Street address city: Kingston
Street address state: TN
Zip/Postal code: 37763-2625
General Phone: (865) 376-3481
General Fax: (865) 376-1945
Editorial Phone: (865) 376-3481 ext. 320
General/National Adv. E-mail: kkile@roanecounty.com
Display Adv. E-mail: tyeary@roanecounty.com
Editorial e-mail: hwillett@roanecounty.com
Primary Website: roanecounty.com
Year Established: 1957
Avg Paid Circ: 8609
Avg Free Circ: 45
Audit By: Sworn/Estimate/Non-Audited
Audit Date: 10.06.2019
Personnel: Kevin Kile (Adv. Mgr.); Neva Peters (Circ. Mgr.)
Parent company (for newspapers): Paxton Media Group; Landmark Community Newspapers, LLC

ROBERTSON COUNTY TIMES

Street address 1: 200 Commerce St
Street address city: Clarksville
Street address state: TN
Zip/Postal code: 37040-5101
General Phone: (615) 384-3567
General Fax: (615) 384-1221
Advertising Phone: (615) 384-3567
Advertising Fax: (615) 384-1221
Editorial Phone: (615) 384-3567
Editorial Fax: (615) 384-1221
General/National Adv. E-mail: slupton@tennessean.com
Editorial e-mail: ebmiller@mtcngroup.com
Primary Website: tennessean.com/counties/robertson
Mthly Avg Views: 173576
Mthly Avg Unique Visitors: 47907
Year Established: 1922
Avg Paid Circ: 13946
Audit By: Sworn/Estimate/Non-Audited
Audit Date: 10.06.2019
Personnel: Laura Hollingsworth (Pub.); Jamie McPherson (VP of Advertising); Nicole Young (Editor)
Parent company (for newspapers): Gannett; The Tennessean; TN Media

SCOTT COUNTY NEWS

Street address 1: PO Box 4399
Street address city: Oneida
Street address state: TN
Zip/Postal code: 37841-4399
General Phone: (423) 569-8351
General Fax: (423) 569-4500
Advertising Phone: (423) 569-8351
Advertising Fax: (423) 569-4500
Editorial Phone: (423) 569-8351
Editorial Fax: (423) 569-4500
General/National Adv. E-mail: scn@highland.net
Display Adv. E-mail: scn@highland.net
Editorial e-mail: scn@highland.net
Primary Website: scnoneida.net
Year Established: 1916
Avg Paid Circ: 5000
Audit By: Sworn/Estimate/Non-Audited
Audit Date: 10.06.2019
Personnel: Mike Erwin (Pub.)

SHELBY SUN TIMES

Street address 1: 2850 Stage Village Cv
Street address 2: Ste 5
Street address city: Bartlett
Street address state: TN
Zip/Postal code: 38134-4682
General Phone: (901) 388-1500
General Fax: (901) 529-7687
Advertising Phone: (901) 388-1500
Advertising Fax: (901) 529-7687
Editorial Phone: (901) 388-1500
Editorial Fax: (901) 529-7687
General/National Adv. E-mail: graham.sweeney@journalinc.com
Display Adv. E-mail: graham.sweeney@journalinc.com
Editorial e-mail: graham.sweeney@journalinc.com
Primary Website: shelby-news.com
Year Established: 1987
Avg Free Circ: 30000
Audit By: Sworn/Estimate/Non-Audited
Audit Date: 10.06.2019
Personnel: Graham Sweeney (Pub./Ed./Adv. Dir.)

SMITHVILLE REVIEW

Street address 1: 106 S 1st St
Street address 2: Ste A
Street address city: Smithville
Street address state: TN
Zip/Postal code: 37166-1744
General Phone: (615) 597-5485
General Fax: (615) 597-5489
General/National Adv. E-mail: angie@smithvillereview.com
Display Adv. E-mail: angie@smithvillerevice.com
Editorial e-mail: news@smithvillereview.com
Primary Website: smithvillereview.com
Year Established: 1892
Avg Paid Circ: 3500
Avg Free Circ: 0
Audit By: Sworn/Estimate/Non-Audited
Audit Date: 10.06.2019
Personnel: Angie Meadows (Pub./Gen. Mgr./Adv. Dir.); Reed Vanderpool (Ed.)

SOUTHERN STANDARD

Street address 1: 105 College St
Street address city: McMinnville
Street address state: TN
Zip/Postal code: 37110-2573
General Phone: (931) 473-2191
General Fax: (931) 473-6823
Advertising Phone: (931) 473-2191
Advertising Fax: (931) 473-6823
Editorial Phone: (931) 473-2191
Editorial Fax: (931) 473-6823
General/National Adv. E-mail: advertising@southernstandard.com
Display Adv. E-mail: classifieds@southernstandard.com
Editorial e-mail: editor@southernstandard.com
Primary Website: southernstandard.com
Year Established: 1879
Avg Paid Circ: 9500
Avg Free Circ: 409
Audit By: Sworn/Estimate/Non-Audited
Audit Date: 10.06.2019
Personnel: Patricia Zechman (Pub.); Dale Stubblefield (Circ. Mgr.); James Clark (Ed.); Sharon Patrick (Adv. Mgr.); Bill Cathcart (Circ. Mgr.)
Parent company (for newspapers): Morris Multimedia, Inc.

STEWART-HOUSTON TIMES

Street address 1: 310 Spring St
Street address city: Dover
Street address state: TN
Zip/Postal code: 37058-3233
General Phone: (931) 232-5421
General Fax: (931) 232-8224
Advertising Phone: (931) 232-5421
Advertising Fax: (931) 232-8224
Editorial Phone: (931) 232-5421
Editorial Fax: (931) 232-8224
General/National Adv. E-mail: shirellefine@theleafchronicle.com
Display Adv. E-mail: jbolin@theleafchronicle.com
Editorial e-mail: rstevens@theleafchronicle.com
Primary Website: thestewarthoustontimes.com
Year Established: 1888
Avg Paid Circ: 6000
Avg Free Circ: 5300
Audit By: Sworn/Estimate/Non-Audited
Audit Date: 10.06.2019
Personnel: Loretta Threatt (Pub.); Richard V. Stevens (Ed./Gen. Mgr.); Shirelle Fine (Adv. Mgr.)
Parent company (for newspapers): Gannett; The Tennessean; TN Media

THE ADVOCATE & DEMOCRAT

Street address 1: 609 E North St
Street address city: Sweetwater
Street address state: TN
Zip/Postal code: 37874-3137
General Phone: (423) 337-7101
General Fax: (423) 337-5932
Advertising Phone: (423) 337-7101
Advertising Fax: (423) 337-5932
Editorial Phone: (423) 337-7101
Editorial Fax: (423) 337-5932
General/National Adv. E-mail: sharon.livingston@advocateanddemocrat.com
Display Adv. E-mail: tommy.wilson@advocateanddemocrat.com
Editorial e-mail: editor@advocateanddemocrat.com
Primary Website: advocateanddemocrat.com
Year Established: 1896
Avg Paid Circ: 4533
Avg Free Circ: 12000
Audit By: Sworn/Estimate/Non-Audited
Audit Date: 10.06.2019
Personnel: Jeff Schumacher (Pub.); Tommy Millsaps (Ed.); Sharon Livingston (Adv. Mgr.); Kevin Kiser (Sports Ed.)
Parent company (for newspapers): Adams Publishing Group, LLC

THE BARTLETT EXPRESS

Street address 1: 2850 Stage Village Cv
Street address 2: Ste 5
Street address city: Bartlett
Street address state: TN
Zip/Postal code: 38134-4682
General Phone: (901) 433-9138
General Fax: (901) 529-7687
Advertising Phone: (901) 433-9138
Advertising Fax: (901) 529-7687
Editorial Phone: (901) 433-9138
Editorial Fax: (901) 529-7687
General/National Adv. E-mail: vickie.clark@journalinc.com
Display Adv. E-mail: felicia.watkins@journalinc.com
Editorial e-mail: carolyn.bahm@journalinc.com
Primary Website: bartlett-express.com
Year Established: 1978
Avg Paid Circ: 3045
Audit By: Sworn/Estimate/Non-Audited
Audit Date: 10.06.2019
Personnel: Carolyn Bahm (Ed); Vickie Clark (Sales Mgr); Whitney Fisher (Sales); Lyn Whitson (Sales)
Parent company (for newspapers): Journal West 10 Media, LLC

THE BLEDSONIAN-BANNER

Street address 1: 399 Spring St
Street address city: Pikeville
Street address state: TN
Zip/Postal code: 37367-5624
General Phone: (423) 447-2996
General Fax: (423) 447-2997
Advertising Phone: (423) 447-2996
Advertising Fax: (423) 447-2997
Editorial Phone: (423) 447-2996
Editorial Fax: (423) 447-2997
General/National Adv. E-mail: valleypubinc@bledsoe.net
Display Adv. E-mail: valleypubincads@bledsoe.net
Classified Adv. e-mail: valleypubincads@bledsoe.net
Editorial e-mail: valleypubincnews@bledsoe.net
Primary Website: thebledsonian-banner.net
Year Established: 1891
Avg Paid Circ: 2100
Avg Free Circ: 0
Audit By: Sworn/Estimate/Non-Audited
Audit Date: 01.10.2023
Personnel: Amy Sue Hale (Pub.); Sandy Dodson (Publisher)

THE CAMDEN CHRONICLE

Street address 1: 144 W Main St
Street address city: Camden
Street address state: TN
Zip/Postal code: 38320-1786
General Phone: (731) 584-7200
General Fax: (731) 584-4943
Advertising Phone: (731) 584-7200
Advertising Fax: (731) 584-4943
Editorial Phone: (731) 584-7200
Editorial Fax: (731) 584-4943
General/National Adv. E-mail: bentonco@usit.net
Display Adv. E-mail: bentonco@usit.net
Editorial e-mail: bentonco@usit.net
Primary Website: magicvalleypublishing.com/camden-chronicle
Year Established: 1890
Avg Paid Circ: 6000
Audit By: Sworn/Estimate/Non-Audited
Audit Date: 10.06.2019
Personnel: Dennis Richardson (Pub.); Lisa Richardson (Ed.); Vanessa Witt (Prodn. Mgr.); Daniel Richardson

THE CHRONICLE OF MT. JULIET

Street address 1: 11509 Lebanon Rd
Street address city: Mount Juliet
Street address state: TN
Zip/Postal code: 37122-5500
General Phone: (615) 754-6111
General Fax: (615) 754-8203
Advertising Phone: (615) 754-6111
Advertising Fax: (615) 754-8203
Editorial Phone: (615) 754-6111
Editorial Fax: (615) 754-8203
General/National Adv. E-mail: doyle@thechronicleofmtjuliet.com
Display Adv. E-mail: thechronicle@thechronicleofmtjuliet.com
Editorial e-mail: editor@thechronicleofmtjuliet.com
Primary Website: thechronicleofmtjuliet.com
Year Established: 1980
Avg Paid Circ: 13000
Avg Free Circ: 11600
Audit By: Sworn/Estimate/Non-Audited
Audit Date: 10.06.2019
Personnel: Phyllis Robinson (Vice Pres.); Bill Robinson (Pub.); Michael Robinson (Assc. Pub.); Kenny Howell (Ed.); Doyle Wood (Sales Mgr.)

THE COLLIERVILLE HERALD

Street address 1: 165 N Main St
Street address 2: Ste 107
Street address city: Collierville
Street address state: TN
Zip/Postal code: 38017-2654
General Phone: (901) 853-2241
Advertising Phone: (901) 853-2241
Editorial Phone: (901) 853-2241 ext. 107
General/National Adv. E-mail: publisher@colliervilleherald.net
Display Adv. E-mail: ads@colliervilleherald.net
Editorial e-mail: editor@colliervilleherald.net
Primary Website: colliervilleherald.net
Year Established: 1870
Avg Paid Circ: 1575
Avg Free Circ: 300
Audit By: Sworn/Estimate/Non-Audited
Audit Date: 10.06.2019
Personnel: Toni Rowan (Pub.); Gena Bumpas (Office Manager); Kelly Josephson (Editor); Jennifer DeShazo (Production/Graphics)
Parent company (for newspapers): American Hometown Publishing

THE CONNECTION

Street address 1: 201 Simpson Rd
Street address city: Lenoir City
Street address state: TN
Zip/Postal code: 37771-6567
General Phone: (865) 986-6581
General Fax: (865) 988-3261
Advertising Phone: (865) 986-6581
Advertising Fax: (865) 988-3261
Editorial Phone: (865) 986-6581
Editorial Fax: (865) 988-3261

General/National Adv. E-mail: amanda.kimbrell@news-herald.net
Display Adv. E-mail: classifieds@news-herald.net
Editorial e-mail: news@news-herald.net
Primary Website: tellicovillageconnection.com
Year Established: 1993
Avg Free Circ: 4050
Audit By: Sworn/Estimate/Non-Audited
Audit Date: 10.06.2019
Personnel: Steve Meadows (Pub./Ed.); Jonathan Herrmann (News Ed.); Amanda Kimbrell (Business Manager)

THE COURIER

Street address 1: 375 Main St
Street address city: Savannah
Street address state: TN
Zip/Postal code: 38372-2056
General Phone: (731) 925-6397
General Fax: (731) 925-6310
Advertising Phone: (731) 925-6397
Advertising Fax: (731) 925-6310
Editorial Phone: (731) 925-6397
Editorial Fax: (731) 925-6310
General/National Adv. E-mail: advertising@courieranywhere.com
Display Adv. E-mail: advertising@courieranywhere.com
Editorial e-mail: info@courieranywhere.com
Primary Website: courieranywhere.com
Mthly Avg Views: 45000
Mthly Avg Unique Visitors: 11200
Year Established: 1884
Avg Paid Circ: 6400
Avg Free Circ: 52
Audit By: Sworn/Estimate/Non-Audited
Audit Date: 10.06.2019
Personnel: Joseph Hurd (Pub.); Ron Schaming (Ed.)

THE COURIER NEWS

Street address 1: 233 N Hicks St
Street address city: Clinton
Street address state: TN
Zip/Postal code: 37716-2919
General Phone: (865) 457-2515
General Fax: (865) 457-1586
General/National Adv. E-mail: jwright@mycouriernews.com
Display Adv. E-mail: classifieds@hometownclinton.com
Editorial e-mail: editor@hometownclinton.com
Primary Website: mycouriernews.com
Year Established: 1887
Avg Paid Circ: 4000
Audit By: Sworn/Estimate/Non-Audited
Audit Date: 10.06.2019
Personnel: Ken Leinhart (Ed.); Allison McKeehn (Retail Adv.); Penny Sullivan (Business Mgr.); Brenda Foster (Classified Adv.); Kim Webber; Richard Evans (Sports ed.); Heather Miller (Gen. Assignment Reporter); Denise Wrasman (Mailroom Supervisor); John Wright (Publisher)
Parent company (for newspapers): Republic Newspapers

THE CROCKETT COUNTY TIMES

Street address 1: 46 W Main St
Street address city: Alamo
Street address state: TN
Zip/Postal code: 38001-1614
General Phone: (731) 696-4558
General Fax: (731) 696-4550
Advertising Phone: (731) 696-4558
Advertising Fax: (731) 696-4550
Editorial Phone: (731) 696-4558
Editorial Fax: (731) 696-4550
General/National Adv. E-mail: thetimes@crockettnet.com
Display Adv. E-mail: thetimes@crockettnet.com
Editorial e-mail: thetimes@crockettnet.com
Primary Website: magicvalleypublishing.com
Year Established: 1873
Avg Paid Circ: 4200
Audit By: Sworn/Estimate/Non-Audited
Audit Date: 10.06.2019
Personnel: Dennis Richardson (Pub.); Hope Riley (Ed.); Keshia Richardson (Adv. Dir.)

THE DEMOCRAT-UNION

Street address 1: 238 Hughes St
Street address city: Lawrenceburg
Street address state: TN
Zip/Postal code: 38464-3364
General Phone: (931) 762-2222
General Fax: (931) 762-4191
Advertising Phone: (931) 762-2222
Advertising Fax: (931) 762-4191
Editorial Phone: (931) 762-2222
Editorial Fax: (931) 762-4191
General/National Adv. E-mail: duadv@bellsouth.net
Display Adv. E-mail: duadv@bellsouth.net
Editorial e-mail: dunews@bellsouth.net
Primary Website: lawrenceburg.com/du
Year Established: 1884
Avg Paid Circ: 7600
Audit By: Sworn/Estimate/Non-Audited
Audit Date: 10.06.2019
Personnel: Jim Crawford (Pub./Ed.); Bobby Crawford (Assc. Ed.); Charlie Crawford (Assc. Ed.)

THE DICKSON HERALD

Street address 1: 104 Church St
Street address city: Dickson
Street address state: TN
Zip/Postal code: 37055-1826
General Phone: (615) 446-2811
Advertising Phone: (615) 446-2811
Editorial Phone: (615) 446-2811
Editorial Fax: (615) 446-5560
General/National Adv. E-mail: slupton@tennessean.com
Display Adv. E-mail: slupton@tennessean.com
Classified Adv. e-mail: classifieds@tennessean.com
Editorial e-mail: news@dicksonherald.com
Primary Website: tennessean.com/counties/dickson
Mthly Avg Views: 122450
Mthly Avg Unique Visitors: 45001
Year Established: 1907
Avg Paid Circ: 17453
Audit By: Sworn/Estimate/Non-Audited
Audit Date: 10.06.2019
Personnel: Laura Hollingsworth (Pres./Pub.); Sean Lupton (National Adv. Mgr.); Chris Gadd (Ed.)
Parent company (for newspapers): Gannett; The Tennessean; TN Media

THE DUNLAP TRIBUNE

Street address 1: 15331 Rankin Ave
Street address city: Dunlap
Street address state: TN
Zip/Postal code: 37327-7048
General Phone: (423) 949-2505
General Fax: (423) 949-5297
Advertising Phone: (423) 949-2505
Advertising Fax: (423) 949-5297
Editorial Phone: (423) 949-2505
Editorial Fax: (423) 949-5297
General/National Adv. E-mail: valleypubinc@bledsoe.net
Display Adv. E-mail: valleypubincads@bledsoe.net
Classified Adv. e-mail: valleypubincads@bledsoe.net
Editorial e-mail: valleypubincnews@bledsoe.net
Primary Website: thedunlap-tribune.com
Year Established: 1889
Avg Paid Circ: 2100
Audit By: Sworn/Estimate/Non-Audited
Audit Date: 01.10.2022
Personnel: Sandy Dodson (Publisher); Amy S. Hale (Pub.)

THE ELK VALLEY TIMES

Street address 1: 418 Elk Ave N
Street address 2: 418 Elk Ave N
Street address city: Fayetteville
Street address state: TN
Zip/Postal code: 37334-2512
General Phone: (931) 433-6151
General Fax: (931) 433-6040
General/National Adv. E-mail: evtadmgr@lcs.net
Display Adv. E-mail: evtad1@lcs.net
Editorial e-mail: evtnews@lcs.net
Primary Website: elkvalleytimes.com
Year Established: 1850
Avg Paid Circ: 9600
Avg Free Circ: 124
Audit By: Sworn/Estimate/Non-Audited
Audit Date: 10.06.2019
Personnel: Lucy Williams (CEO/Pub./Ed.); Sandy Williams (Mng. Ed.); Janie Herrin (Advertising Manager)
Parent company (for newspapers): Lakeway Publishers, Inc.

THE ERWIN RECORD

Street address 1: 218 Gay St
Street address city: Erwin
Street address state: TN
Zip/Postal code: 37650-1230
General Phone: (423) 743-4112
General Fax: (423) 743-6125
Advertising Phone: (423) 743-4112
Advertising Fax: (423) 743-6125
Editorial Phone: (423) 743-4112
Editorial Fax: (423) 743-6125
General/National Adv. E-mail: dhiggins@erwinrecord.net
Display Adv. E-mail: dhiggins@erwinrecord.net
Editorial e-mail: kwhitson@erwinrecord.net
Primary Website: erwinrecord.net
Year Established: 1928
Avg Paid Circ: 4200
Avg Free Circ: 40
Audit By: Sworn/Estimate/Non-Audited
Audit Date: 10.06.2019
Personnel: Keith Whitson (Publisher); Keeli Parkey (Managing Editor); Damaris Higgins (Advertising Director); David Sheets (Graphic Design); Curtis Carden (Staff Writer/Sports Writer)
Parent company (for newspapers): Sandusky Newspapers, Inc.

THE EXPOSITOR

Street address 1: 34 W Bockman Way
Street address city: Sparta
Street address state: TN
Zip/Postal code: 38583-2015
General Phone: (931) 836-3284
General Fax: (931) 836-3948
Advertising Phone: (931) 836-3284
Advertising Fax: (931) 836-3948
Editorial Phone: (931) 836-3284
Editorial Fax: (931) 836-3948
General/National Adv. E-mail: kim@myspartanews.com
Display Adv. E-mail: cristie@myspartanews.com
Editorial e-mail: editor@myspartanews.com
Primary Website: spartalive.com
Year Established: 1876
Avg Paid Circ: 5000
Avg Free Circ: 6900
Audit By: Sworn/Estimate/Non-Audited
Audit Date: 10.06.2019
Personnel: Jim Shanks (Pub.); Kim Wood (Ed.); Cristie Hatmaker (Gen. Mgr.)
Parent company (for newspapers): Smith Newspaper, Inc.

THE HARTSVILLE VIDETTE

Street address 1: 206 River St
Street address city: Hartsville
Street address state: TN
Zip/Postal code: 37074-1709
General Phone: (615) 374-3556
General Fax: (615) 374-2211
Advertising Phone: (615) 374-3556
Advertising Fax: (615) 374-2211
Editorial Phone: (615) 374-3556
Editorial Fax: (615) 374-2211
General/National Adv. E-mail: thevidette@bellsouth.net
Display Adv. E-mail: thevidette@bellsouth.net
Editorial e-mail: thevidette@bellsouth.net
Primary Website: hartsvillevidette.com
Year Established: 1862
Avg Paid Circ: 2300
Audit By: Sworn/Estimate/Non-Audited
Audit Date: 10.06.2019
Personnel: Joe Adams (Pub.); Laurie Everett (Mng. Ed.); Roger Wells (Adv. Mgr.); Melanie Ray (Classified Mgr.)
Parent company (for newspapers): Sandusky Newspapers, Inc.

THE HENDERSONVILLE STAR NEWS

Street address 1: 1 Examiner Ct
Street address city: Gallatin
Street address state: TN
Zip/Postal code: 37066-7111
General Phone: (615) 824-8480
General Fax: (615) 824-3126
Advertising Phone: (615) 824-8480
Advertising Fax: (615) 824-3126
Editorial Phone: (615) 824-8480
Editorial Fax: (615) 824-3126
General/National Adv. E-mail: slupton@tennessean.com
Display Adv. E-mail: pdyates@tennessean.com
Editorial e-mail: mdevarenne@tennessean.com
Primary Website: tennessean.com/section/hendersonville
Avg Free Circ: 15850
Audit By: Sworn/Estimate/Non-Audited
Audit Date: 10.06.2019
Personnel: Laura Hollingsworth (Pres./Pub.); Maria De Varenne (Exec. Ed./Vice Pres.); Sean Lupton (National Adv. Mgr.); Rachel Biggirstaff (Adv. Dir./Gen. Mgr./Adv. Sales)
Parent company (for newspapers): Gannett; The Tennessean; TN Media

THE HERALD-NEWS

Street address 1: 3687 Rhea County Hwy
Street address city: Dayton
Street address state: TN
Zip/Postal code: 37321-5819
General Phone: (423) 775-6111
General Fax: (423) 775-8218
Advertising Phone: (423) 775-6111
Advertising Fax: (423) 775-8259
Editorial Phone: (423) 775-6111
Editorial Fax: (423) 775-8218
General/National Adv. E-mail: keith.locke@rheaheraldnews.com
Display Adv. E-mail: sarajane.locke@rheaheraldnews.com
Editorial e-mail: reed.johnson@rheaheraldnews.com
Primary Website: rheaheraldnews.com
Year Established: 1898
Avg Paid Circ: 9700
Avg Free Circ: 9
Audit By: Sworn/Estimate/Non-Audited
Audit Date: 10.06.2019
Personnel: Sara Jane Locke (Pub.); Reed Johnson (Ed.); Diane Emens (Gen. Mgr.); Kerth Locke (Adv. Mgr.); Lynne Spivey (Circ. Mgr.); June Yarbrough (Prodn. Mgr.)
Parent company (for newspapers): Adams Publishing Group, LLC

THE HUMBOLDT CHRONICLE

Street address 1: 2606 Eastend Dr
Street address 2: Ste A
Street address city: Humboldt
Street address state: TN
Zip/Postal code: 38343-2265
General Phone: (731) 784-2531
General Fax: (731) 784-2533
Advertising Phone: (731) 784-2531
Advertising Fax: (731) 784-2533
Editorial Phone: (731) 784-2531
Editorial Fax: (731) 784-2533
General/National Adv. E-mail: ads@hchronicle.net
Display Adv. E-mail: ads@hchronicle.net
Editorial e-mail: dwade@hchronicle.net
Primary Website: hchronicle.net
Year Established: 1886
Avg Paid Circ: 2000
Avg Free Circ: 400
Audit By: Sworn/Estimate/Non-Audited
Audit Date: 10.06.2019
Personnel: Danny Wade (Ed.)
Parent company (for newspapers): Gibson County Publishing

THE LAKE COUNTY BANNER

Street address 1: 315 Church St
Street address city: Tiptonville
Street address state: TN
Zip/Postal code: 38079-1147
General Phone: (731) 253-6666
General Fax: (731) 253-6667
Advertising Phone: (731) 253-6666
Advertising Fax: (731) 253-6667
Editorial Phone: (731) 253-6666
Editorial Fax: (731) 253-6667
General/National Adv. E-mail: banner@lakecountybanner.com
Display Adv. E-mail: banner@lakecountybanner.com
Editorial e-mail: wilmforr@gmail.com
Primary Website: lakecountybanner.com

Year Established: 1923
Avg Paid Circ: 3400
Avg Free Circ: 160
Audit By: Sworn/Estimate/Non-Audited
Audit Date: 10.06.2019
Personnel: Matthew Forrest (Ed., Typesetting, Photo./Reporter, Adv.); Matthew Richardson (Gen. Mgr.); Jordan Price (Office Mgr/Circ.)
Parent company (for newspapers): Magic Valley Publishing

THE LAUDERDALE COUNTY ENTERPRISE

Street address 1: 145 E Jackson Ave
Street address city: Ripley
Street address state: TN
Zip/Postal code: 38063-1556
General Phone: (731) 635-1771
General Fax: (731) 635-2111
Advertising Phone: (731) 635-1771
Advertising Fax: (731) 635-2111
Editorial Phone: (731) 635-1771
Editorial Fax: (731) 635-2111
General/National Adv. E-mail: LCENEWS@YAHOO.COM
Display Adv. E-mail: LCENEWS@YAHOO.COM
Editorial e-mail: LCENEWS@YAHOO.COM
Year Established: 1885
Avg Paid Circ: 4600
Avg Free Circ: 43
Audit By: Sworn/Estimate/Non-Audited
Audit Date: 10.06.2019
Personnel: Beverly Hutcherson (Pub./Gen. Mgr.)

THE LAUDERDALE VOICE

Street address 1: 127 N Main St
Street address city: Ripley
Street address state: TN
Zip/Postal code: 38063-1307
General Phone: (731) 635-1238
General Fax: (731) 635-3394
Advertising Phone: (731) 635-1238
Advertising Fax: (731) 635-3394
Editorial Phone: (731) 635-1238
Editorial Fax: (731) 635-3394
General/National Adv. E-mail: news@lauderdalevoice.com
Display Adv. E-mail: news@lauderdalevoice.com
Editorial e-mail: news@lauderdalevoice.com
Primary Website: facebook.com/The-Lauderdale-Voice-371515821839
Year Established: 1977
Avg Paid Circ: 3500
Avg Free Circ: 4
Audit By: Sworn/Estimate/Non-Audited
Audit Date: 10.06.2019
Personnel: Jay Heath (Ed.); Rose Heath (Adv. Dir./Circ. Dir.)

THE MEMPHIS NEWS

Street address 1: 193 Jefferson Ave
Street address city: Memphis
Street address state: TN
Zip/Postal code: 38103-2322
General Phone: (901) 528-8117
General Fax: (901) 526-5813
General/National Adv. E-mail: advertising@memphisdailynews.com
Display Adv. E-mail: advertising@memphisdailynews.com
Editorial e-mail: joverstreet@memphisdailynews.com
Primary Website: thememphisnews.com
Year Established: 2008
Avg Free Circ: 21948
Audit By: CVC
Audit Date: 31.03.2018
Personnel: Eric Barnes (Pub./CEO); James Overstreet (Assoc. Pub/Ed.); Terry Hollahan (Mng. Ed.); Pam Capshaw (CFO); Connie Rasberry (Circ.)
Parent company (for newspapers): The Daily News Publishing Co.

THE MILLINGTON STAR

Street address 1: 2850 Stage Village Cv
Street address 2: Ste 5
Street address city: Memphis
Street address state: TN
Zip/Postal code: 38134-4682
General Phone: (901) 872-2286
General Fax: (901) 872-2965
Advertising Phone: (901) 872-2286
Advertising Fax: (901) 872-2965
Editorial Phone: (901) 872-2286
Editorial Fax: (901) 872-2965
General/National Adv. E-mail: sheri.williams@journalinc.com
Display Adv. E-mail: felicia.watkins@journalinc.com
Editorial e-mail: sheri.williams@journalinc.com
Primary Website: millington-news.com
Year Established: 1950
Avg Paid Circ: 6000
Audit By: Sworn/Estimate/Non-Audited
Audit Date: 10.06.2019
Personnel: Brian Boom (Pub./Adv. Dir.); Bill Short (Copy Ed.)

THE MURFREESBORO POST

Street address 1: 307 N Walnut St
Street address 2: Ste 2
Street address city: Murfreesboro
Street address state: TN
Zip/Postal code: 37130-3656
General Phone: (615) 869-0800
General Fax: (615) 869-0849
Advertising Phone: (615) 869-0800
Advertising Fax: (615) 869-0849
Editorial Phone: (615) 869-0800
Editorial Fax: (615) 869-0849
General/National Adv. E-mail: retailads@murfreesboropost.com
Display Adv. E-mail: retailads@murfreesboropost.com
Editorial e-mail: editor@murfreesboropost.com
Primary Website: murfreesboropost.com
Year Established: 2006
Avg Paid Circ: 0
Avg Free Circ: 10000
Audit By: Sworn/Estimate/Non-Audited
Audit Date: 10.06.2019
Personnel: Zack Owensby (Ed); Cat Murphy (Asst News Ed); Monte Hale (Sports Ed); Lisa Peters (Class Mgr)
Parent company (for newspapers): Main Street Media of Tennessee

THE NEWPORT PLAIN TALK

Street address 1: 145 E Broadway
Street address city: Newport
Street address state: TN
Zip/Postal code: 37821-2324
General Phone: (423) 623-6171
General Fax: (423) 625-1995
Display Adv. E-mail: ads@newportplaintalk.com
Editorial e-mail: seth.butler@newportplaintalk.com
Primary Website: newportplaintalk.com
Mthly Avg Views: 140000
Mthly Avg Unique Visitors: 35000
Year Established: 1900
Avg Paid Circ: 6000
Sun. Circulation Paid: 6480
Audit By: Sworn/Estimate/Non-Audited
Audit Date: 10.06.2019
Personnel: Seth Butler (Pub. Ed.); Matt Winter (News Editor); Duay O'Neil (Assistant Editor); Alison Brooks (Staff Writer); Dennis Barker Jr (Sports Editor); Sharon Bryant (Advertising); Vickie Mason (Advertising); Sandy Freshour (Classifieds Manager); Larry Davis (Circulation Manager); Lynn Crum (District Manager Circulation); Claudine Harris (Business Manager)
Parent company (for newspapers): Adams Publishing Group, LLC

THE NEWS LEADER

Street address 1: 24 W Main St
Street address city: Parsons
Street address state: TN
Zip/Postal code: 38363-2012
General Phone: (731) 847-6354
General Fax: (731) 847-9120
Advertising Phone: (731) 847-6354
Advertising Fax: (731) 847-9120
Editorial Phone: (731) 847-6354
Editorial Fax: (731) 847-9120
Editorial e-mail: danny@readtheleader.com
Primary Website: readtheleader.com
Year Established: 1926
Avg Paid Circ: 3500
Audit By: Sworn/Estimate/Non-Audited
Audit Date: 10.06.2019
Personnel: Danny Haynes (Pub./Ed.)

THE NEWS-DEMOCRAT

Street address 1: 302A W Main St
Street address city: Waverly
Street address state: TN
Zip/Postal code: 37185-1513
General Phone: (931) 296-2426
General Fax: (931) 296-5156
Advertising Phone: (931) 296-2426
Advertising Fax: (931) 296-5156
Editorial Phone: (931) 296-2426
Editorial Fax: (931) 296-5156
General/National Adv. E-mail: kerrylampley@bellsouth.net
Display Adv. E-mail: newsdemocrat@bellsouth.net
Editorial e-mail: newsdemocrat@bellsouth.net
Primary Website: thenews-democrat.com
Year Established: 1871
Avg Paid Circ: 4000
Avg Free Circ: 165
Audit By: Sworn/Estimate/Non-Audited
Audit Date: 10.06.2019
Personnel: Ward Phillips (Pub.); Grey Collier (Ed.); Kerry Lamplet (Adv. Mgr.)
Parent company (for newspapers): Kennedy Newspapers Co., Inc

THE PORTLAND LEADER

Street address 1: 109 S Broadway St
Street address city: Portland
Street address state: TN
Zip/Postal code: 37148-1303
General Phone: (615) 325-9241
General Fax: (615) 325-9243
Advertising Phone: (615) 325-9241
Advertising Fax: (615) 325-9243
Editorial Phone: (615) 325-9241
Editorial Fax: (615) 325-9243
General/National Adv. E-mail: sales@portlandleader.net
Display Adv. E-mail: customerservice@portlandleader.net
Editorial e-mail: editor@portlandleader.net
Primary Website: portlandleader.net
Year Established: 1958
Avg Paid Circ: 3000
Avg Free Circ: 50
Audit By: Sworn/Estimate/Non-Audited
Audit Date: 10.06.2019
Personnel: Jamie Johnson (Pub./Gen. Mgr.); Sonya Thompson (Ed.); April Barton (Office Mgr.); Jared Wilber (Sales Mgr.)

THE ROGERSVILLE REVIEW

Street address 1: 316 E Main St
Street address 2: PO Box 100
Street address city: Rogersville
Street address state: TN
Zip/Postal code: 37857-3355
General Phone: (423) 272-7422
General Fax: (423) 272-7889
Advertising Phone: (423) 272-7422
Advertising Fax: (423) 272-7889
Editorial Phone: (423) 272-7422
Editorial Fax: (423) 272-7889
General/National Adv. E-mail: ads@therogersvillereview.com
Display Adv. E-mail: classifieds@therogersvillereview.com
Editorial e-mail: news@therogersvillereview.com
Primary Website: therogersvillereview.com
Year Established: 1885
Avg Paid Circ: 5775
Avg Free Circ: 3308
Audit By: Sworn/Estimate/Non-Audited
Audit Date: 10.06.2019
Personnel: Tommy Campbell (Pub./Ed.); Jim Beller (Adv. Exec.); Abby Swearingen (Adv. Exec.); Christy Alvis (Classified Adv. Mgr.)
Parent company (for newspapers): Adams Publishing Group, LLC

THE STANDARD BANNER

Street address 1: 122 W Old Andrew Johnson Hwy
Street address city: Jefferson City
Street address state: TN
Zip/Postal code: 37760-1996
General Phone: (865) 475-2081
General Fax: (865) 475-8539
General/National Adv. E-mail: info@standardbanner.com
Editorial e-mail: news@standardbanner.com
Primary Website: standardbanner.com
Year Established: 1928
Avg Paid Circ: 5136
Avg Free Circ: 10
Audit By: USPS
Audit Date: 07.10.2021
Personnel: Dale Gentry (Pub./Ed.); Shane Cook (Adv. Mgr.); Dave Gentry (Sports Ed.)

THE TOMAHAWK

Street address 1: 118 S Church St
Street address city: Mountain City
Street address state: TN
Zip/Postal code: 37683-1502
General Phone: (423) 727-6121
General Fax: (423) 727-4833
Advertising Phone: (423) 727-6121
Advertising Fax: (423) 727-4833
Editorial Phone: (423) 727-6121
Editorial Fax: (423) 727-4833
General/National Adv. E-mail: advertise@thetomahawk.com
Display Adv. E-mail: classifieds@thetomahawk.com
Editorial e-mail: editor@thetomahawk.com
Primary Website: thetomahawk.com
Year Established: 1874
Avg Paid Circ: 5700
Audit By: Sworn/Estimate/Non-Audited
Audit Date: 10.06.2019
Personnel: Bill Thomas (Pub.); Angie Gambill (Ed.); Ann Badal (Adv. Mgr.); Paula Walter (Classified Adv. Mgr.); David Holloway (Office Manager)
Parent company (for newspapers): Sandusky Newspapers, Inc.

THE TRI-CITY REPORTER

Street address 1: 111 East First Street
Street address city: Trenton
Street address state: TN
Zip/Postal code: 38330
General Phone: (731) 692-3506
General Fax: (731) 692-4844
Advertising Phone: (731) 855-1711
Advertising Fax: (731) 692-4844
General/National Adv. E-mail: mindy@tricityreporter.net
Display Adv. E-mail: news@tricityreporter.net
Editorial e-mail: lori@tricityreporter.net
Primary Website: milanmirrorexchange.com/tri-city-reporter
Year Established: 1892
Avg Paid Circ: 3000
Avg Free Circ: 203
Audit By: Sworn/Estimate/Non-Audited
Audit Date: 10.06.2019
Personnel: Lori Cathey; Laurin Stroud; Crystal Burns; Lee Ann Butler
Parent company (for newspapers): American Hometown Publishing

THE TULLAHOMA NEWS

Street address 1: 505 Lake Way Pl
Street address city: Tullahoma
Street address state: TN
Zip/Postal code: 37388-4710
General Phone: (931) 455-4545
General Fax: (931) 455-9299
Advertising Phone: (931) 455-4545
Advertising Fax: (931) 455-9299
Editorial Phone: (931) 455-4545
Editorial Fax: (931) 455-9299
General/National Adv. E-mail: tnads@lcs.net
Display Adv. E-mail: tnclass@lcs.net
Editorial e-mail: tnedit@lcs.net
Primary Website: tullahomanews.com
Mthly Avg Views: 1700000
Mthly Avg Unique Visitors: 76000
Year Established: 1881
Avg Paid Circ: 8252
Avg Free Circ: 9500
Audit By: Sworn/Estimate/Non-Audited
Audit Date: 10.06.2019
Personnel: Jeff Fishman (Pub.); Susan Campbell (Editor)

Parent company (for newspapers): Lakeway Publishers, Inc.

THE UNION NEWS LEADER

Street address 1: 3755 Maynardville Hwy
Street address city: Maynardville
Street address state: TN
Zip/Postal code: 37807-3437
General Phone: (865) 992-3392
General Fax: (865) 992-6861
Advertising Phone: (865) 992-3392
Advertising Fax: (865) 992-6861
Editorial Phone: (865) 992-3392
Editorial Fax: (865) 992-6861
General/National Adv. E-mail: enewspaper@aol.com
Display Adv. E-mail: enewspaper@aol.com
Editorial e-mail: enewspaper@aol.com
Primary Website: ucnewsleader.com
Year Established: 1990
Avg Paid Circ: 3000
Audit By: Sworn/Estimate/Non-Audited
Audit Date: 10.06.2019
Personnel: Chris Upton (Pub.); Elbra Davis (Mng. Ed./Adv. Dir.)

THE WILSON POST

Street address 1: 223 N Cumberland St
Street address 2: Ste A
Street address city: Lebanon
Street address state: TN
Zip/Postal code: 37087-2869
General Phone: (615) 444-6008
General Fax: (615) 444-6018
Advertising Phone: (615) 444-6008
Advertising Fax: (615) 444-6018
Editorial Phone: (615) 444-6008
Editorial Fax: (615) 444-6018
General/National Adv. E-mail: mhazelwood@mainstreetmediatn.com
Display Adv. E-mail: classifieds@wilsonpost.com
Editorial e-mail: news@wilsonpost.com
Primary Website: wilsonpost.com
Year Established: 1978
Avg Paid Circ: 10000
Audit By: Sworn/Estimate/Non-Audited
Audit Date: 10.06.2019
Personnel: Dave Gould (Pres./Pub.); Sabrina Garrett (Editor); Brian Harville (Managing Editor); Tommy Bryan (Sports Editor); Debby Mabry (Advertising Account Executive); Dallus Whitfield (Photographer); Shelley Satterfield (Office Manager); Mary Anne Ferrell (Ad Designer); Carrie Tomlin (Graphic Designer)
Parent company (for newspapers): Main Street Media of Tennessee

WEAKLEY COUNTY PRESS

Street address 1: 235 S Lindell St
Street address city: Martin
Street address state: TN
Zip/Postal code: 38237-2438
General Phone: (731) 587-3144
General Fax: (731) 587-3147
Advertising Phone: (731) 587-3144
Advertising Fax: (731) 587-3147
Editorial Phone: (731) 587-3144
Editorial Fax: (731) 587-3147
General/National Adv. E-mail: lcwagster@frontiernet.net
Display Adv. E-mail: classifieds@wcpnews.com
Editorial e-mail: editor@wcpnews.com
Primary Website: nwtntoday.com
Year Established: 1884
Avg Paid Circ: 3150
Audit By: Sworn/Estimate/Non-Audited
Audit Date: 10.06.2019
Personnel: Lynette Calhoun Wagster (Gen. Mgr.); Beth Cravens (Editorial Cartoonist Graphic Design)

TEXAS

ADVANCE NEWS JOURNAL

Street address 1: 217 W Newcombe Ave
Street address city: Pharr
Street address state: TX
Zip/Postal code: 78577-4742
General Phone: (956) 783-0036
General Fax: (956) 787-8824
Advertising Phone: (956) 783-0036
Advertising Fax: (956) 787-8824
Editorial Phone: (956) 783-0036
Editorial Fax: (956) 787-8824
General/National Adv. E-mail: advancenews@aol.com
Display Adv. E-mail: advancenews@aol.com
Editorial e-mail: advancenews@aol.com
Primary Website: anjournal.com
Year Established: 1978
Audit By: Sworn/Estimate/Non-Audited
Audit Date: 10.06.2019
Personnel: Gregg Wendorf (Pub.); Ruben Acosta (Ed.); Jan Wendorf (Adv. Dir.)

ALBANY NEWS

Street address 1: 49 S Main St
Street address city: Albany
Street address state: TX
Zip/Postal code: 76430
General Phone: (325) 762-2201
General Fax: (325) 762-3201
Advertising Phone: (325) 762-2201
Advertising Fax: (325) 762-3201
Editorial Phone: (325) 762-2201
Editorial Fax: (325) 762-3201
General/National Adv. E-mail: dlucas@thealbanynews.net
Display Adv. E-mail: ads@thealbanynews.net
Editorial e-mail: melinda@thealbanynews.net
Primary Website: thealbanynews.net
Year Established: 1875
Avg Paid Circ: 1350
Audit By: Sworn/Estimate/Non-Audited
Audit Date: 10.06.2019
Personnel: Donnie Lucas (Pub.); Melinda Lucas (Ed.)

ALICE ECHO-NEWS JOURNAL

Street address 1: 405 E Main St
Street address city: Alice
Street address state: TX
Zip/Postal code: 78332-4968
General Phone: (361) 664-6588
General Fax: (361) 668-1030
Advertising Phone: (361) 664-6588 ext. 212
Advertising Fax: (361) 668-1030
Editorial Phone: (361) 664-6588
Editorial Fax: (361) 668-1030
General/National Adv. E-mail: gdelaney@gatehousemedia.com
Display Adv. E-mail: ssalaiz@aliceechonews.com
Classified Adv. e-mail: russel.gruber@aliceechonews.com
Editorial e-mail: ohunter@aliceechonews.com
Primary Website: alicetx.com
Year Established: 1894
Avg Paid Circ: 3107
Avg Free Circ: 500
Sun. Circulation Paid: 3845
Audit By: Sworn/Estimate/Non-Audited
Audit Date: 10.06.2019
Personnel: Ofelia Hunter (Ed.); Pete Garcia (Sports Ed.); Russel Gruber (National/Major acciunts)
Parent company (for newspapers): CherryRoad Media

ALLEN AMERICAN

Street address 1: 624 Krona Dr
Street address 2: Ste 170
Street address city: Plano
Street address state: TX
Zip/Postal code: 75074-8304
General Phone: (972) 398-4200
General Fax: (972) 398-4470
General/National Adv. E-mail: jdittrich@starlocalmedia.com
Display Adv. E-mail: jdittrich@starlocalmedia.com
Editorial e-mail: lmcgathey@starlocalmedia.com
Primary Website: starlocalmedia.com
Mthly Avg Views: 546019
Mthly Avg Unique Visitors: 201046
Year Established: 1969
Avg Paid Circ: 753
Avg Free Circ: 28234
Audit By: Sworn/Estimate/Non-Audited
Audit Date: 10.06.2019
Personnel: Scott Wright (Pub.); Melissa Rougeot (Circ. Mgr); Liz McGathey (Ed. Dir.)
Parent company (for newspapers): S.A.W. Advisors, LLC; Star Community Newspapers

ALPINE AVALANCHE

Street address 1: 118 N 5th St
Street address city: Alpine
Street address state: TX
Zip/Postal code: 79830-4602
General Phone: (432) 837-3334
General Fax: (432)837-7181
Advertising Phone: (432) 837-3334
Advertising Fax: (432)837-7181
Editorial Phone: (432) 837-3334
Editorial Fax: (432)837-7181
General/National Adv. E-mail: publisher@alpineavalanche.com
Display Adv. E-mail: bookkeeping@alpineavalanche.com
Editorial e-mail: editor@alpineavalanche.com
Primary Website: alpineavalanche.com
Mthly Avg Views: 60000
Mthly Avg Unique Visitors: 19000
Year Established: 1891
Avg Paid Circ: 1930
Avg Free Circ: 373
Audit By: Sworn/Estimate/Non-Audited
Audit Date: 10.06.2019
Personnel: Gwin Grimes (Publisher and editor)

ALVIN SUN-ADVERTISER

Street address 1: 570 Dula St
Street address city: Alvin
Street address state: TX
Zip/Postal code: 77511-2942
General Phone: (281) 331-4421
General Fax: (281) 331-4424
Advertising Phone: (281) 331-4421
Advertising Fax: (281) 331-4424
Editorial Phone: (281) 331-4421
Editorial Fax: (281) 331-4424
General/National Adv. E-mail: ads@alvinsun.net
Display Adv. E-mail: ads@alvinsun.net
Editorial e-mail: publisher@alvinsun.net
Primary Website: alvinsun.net
Year Established: 1892
Avg Paid Circ: 500
Avg Free Circ: 14500
Audit By: Sworn/Estimate/Non-Audited
Audit Date: 10.06.2019
Personnel: Donna Hopkins (Bus. Mgr.); David Rupkalvis (Publisher)
Parent company (for newspapers): Hartman News LLP

ANDREWS COUNTY NEWS

Street address 1: 210 E Broadway St
Street address city: Andrews
Street address state: TX
Zip/Postal code: 79714-6586
General Phone: (432) 523-2085
General Fax: (432) 523-9492
Advertising Phone: (432) 523-2085
Advertising Fax: (432) 523-9492
Editorial Phone: (432) 523-2085
Editorial Fax: (432) 523-9492
General/National Adv. E-mail: publisher@basinbroadband.com
Display Adv. E-mail: ads@basinbroadband.com
Editorial e-mail: editor@basinbroadband.com
Primary Website: andrewscountynews.com
Year Established: 1934
Avg Paid Circ: 3100
Avg Free Circ: 135
Audit By: Sworn/Estimate/Non-Audited
Audit Date: 10.06.2019
Personnel: Kandi Roberts (Pub.); Sam Kaufman (Ed.); Priscilla Rider (Adv. Dir.)

ARANSAS PASS PROGRESS

Street address 1: 346 S Houston St
Street address city: Aransas Pass
Street address state: TX
Zip/Postal code: 78336-2515
General Phone: (361) 758-5391
General Fax: (361) 758-5393
Advertising Phone: (361) 758-5391
Advertising Fax: (361) 758-5393
Editorial Phone: (361) 758-5391
Editorial Fax: (361) 758-5393
General/National Adv. E-mail: mattie@aransaspassprogress.com
Display Adv. E-mail: classifieds@aransaspassprogress.com
Editorial e-mail: publisher@aransaspassprogress.com
Primary Website: aransaspassprogress.com
Year Established: 1909
Avg Paid Circ: 1854
Audit By: Sworn/Estimate/Non-Audited
Audit Date: 10.06.2019
Personnel: Brenda Burr (Pub./Ed./Adv. Dir.); Amanda Torres (Bus. Mgr.)

ARCHER COUNTY NEWS

Street address 1: 104 E Walnut
Street address city: Archer City
Street address state: TX
Zip/Postal code: 76351
General Phone: (940) 574-4569
General Fax: (940) 574-4234
Advertising Phone: (940) 574-4569
Advertising Fax: (940) 574-4234
Editorial Phone: (940) 574-4569
Editorial Fax: (940) 574-4234
General/National Adv. E-mail: archernews@yahoo.com
Display Adv. E-mail: archernews@yahoo.com
Editorial e-mail: acjennyg@gmail.com
Primary Website: archercountynews.com
Year Established: 1908
Avg Paid Circ: 1300
Audit By: Sworn/Estimate/Non-Audited
Audit Date: 10.06.2019
Personnel: Barbara Phillips (Pres./Ed./Adv. Dir.); Jerry Phillips (Co-Pub.); Mandy Kinnaman (Assistant Editor)

ATASCOCITA OBSERVER

Street address 1: 100 Avenue A
Street address city: Conroe
Street address state: TX
Zip/Postal code: 77301-2946
General Phone: (713) 362-1570
Editorial Phone: (281) 378-1064
Editorial Fax: (281) 446-6901
General/National Adv. E-mail: cturner@hcnonline.com
Display Adv. E-mail: cturner@hcnonline.com
Editorial e-mail: jsummer@hcnonline.com
Primary Website: asascocitaobserver.com
Year Established: 2003
Avg Paid Circ: 0
Avg Free Circ: 17998
Audit By: Sworn/Estimate/Non-Audited
Audit Date: 10.06.2019
Personnel: Chris Shelton
Parent company (for newspapers): Hearst Communications, Inc.; Times Media Group

ATLANTA CITITZENS JOURNAL

Street address 1: 306 W Main St
Street address city: Atlanta
Street address state: TX
Zip/Postal code: 75551-2523
General Phone: (903) 796-7133
General Fax: (903) 796-3294
Advertising Phone: (903) 796-7133
Advertising Fax: (903) 796-3294
Editorial Phone: (903) 796-7133
Editorial Fax: (903) 796-3294
General/National Adv. E-mail: production@casscountynow.com
Display Adv. E-mail: production@casscountynow.com
Editorial e-mail: raaron@casscountynow.com
Primary Website: casscountynow.com
Year Established: 1879
Avg Paid Circ: 3100
Avg Free Circ: 51
Audit By: Sworn/Estimate/Non-Audited
Audit Date: 10.06.2019
Personnel: Lee Ellen Benjamin (Designer); Tim Emmons (Sports Editor); Rachel Woods (Office Manager); Robin Aaron (Editor)
Parent company (for newspapers): Northeast Texas Publishing

AUSTIN BUSINESS JOURNAL

Street address 1: 111 Congress Ave
Street address 2: Ste 750
Street address city: Austin
Street address state: TX

Zip/Postal code: 78701-4074
General Phone: (512) 494-2500
General Fax: (512) 494-2525
Advertising Phone: (512) 494-2500
Advertising Fax: (512) 494-2525
Editorial Phone: (512) 494-2500
Editorial Fax: (512) 494-2525
General/National Adv. E-mail: austin@bizjournals.com
Display Adv. E-mail: austin@bizjournals.com
Editorial e-mail: austin@bizjournals.com
Primary Website: bizjournals.com/austin
Year Established: 1981
Audit By: Sworn/Estimate/Non-Audited
Audit Date: 10.06.2019
Personnel: Heather Ledage (Pub.); Colin Pope (Ed.); Doug Pogemiller (Adv. Dir.)

AZLE NEWS

Street address 1: 321 W Main St
Street address city: Azle
Street address state: TX
Zip/Postal code: 76020-2903
General Phone: (817) 270-3340
General Fax: (817) 270-5300
General/National Adv. E-mail: johnna@azlenews.net
Display Adv. E-mail: classified@azlenews.net
Editorial e-mail: markcampbell@azlenews.net
Primary Website: azlenews.net
Year Established: 1959
Avg Paid Circ: 3000
Avg Free Circ: 112
Audit By: Sworn/Estimate/Non-Audited
Audit Date: 10.06.2019
Personnel: Kim Ware (Pub./Adv. Dir.); Mark Campbell (Ed.); Johnna Bridges (Adv. Mgr.)

BAIRD BANNER

Street address 1: 312 N 1st St
Street address city: Clyde
Street address state: TX
Zip/Postal code: 79510-4729
General Phone: (325) 893-4244
General Fax: (325) 893-2780
Advertising Phone: (325) 893-4244
Editorial Phone: (325) 893-4244
General/National Adv. E-mail: clydejournal@earthlink.net
Display Adv. E-mail: clydejournal@earthlink.net
Editorial e-mail: clydejournal@earthlink.net
Primary Website: clydenewspaper.com
Year Established: 1997
Avg Paid Circ: 525
Avg Free Circ: 30
Audit By: Sworn/Estimate/Non-Audited
Audit Date: 10.06.2019
Personnel: Lyn Walker (Ed./Adv. Dir.); Danny Tabor (Editor)

BANDERA BULLETIN

Street address 1: 1110 MAIN ST
Street address city: Bandera
Street address state: TX
Zip/Postal code: 78003
General Phone: (830) 796-3718
General Fax: (830) 796-4885
Advertising Phone: (830) 796-3718
Advertising Fax: (830) 796-4885
Editorial Phone: (830) 796-3718
Editorial Fax: (830) 796-4885
General/National Adv. E-mail: jessica@banderabulletin.com
Display Adv. E-mail: jessica@banderabulletin.com
Editorial e-mail: news@banderabulletin.com
Primary Website: banderabulletin.com
Year Established: 1945
Avg Paid Circ: 2193
Audit By: Sworn/Estimate/Non-Audited
Audit Date: 10.06.2019
Personnel: Jessica Hawley-Jerome (Pub./Ed.); James Taylor (Adv. Dir.)
Parent company (for newspapers): Fenice Community Media

BANDERA COUNTY COURIER

Street address 1: 302 Dallas St
Street address city: Bandera
Street address state: TX
Zip/Postal code: 78003-5819
General Phone: (830) 796-9799
General Fax: (830) 796-9399
Advertising Phone: (830) 796-9799
Advertising Fax: (830) 796-9399
Editorial Phone: (830) 796-9799
Editorial Fax: (830) 796-9399
General/National Adv. E-mail: bccourier@sbcglobal.net
Display Adv. E-mail: bccclass@sbcglobal.net
Editorial e-mail: bcceditor@sbcglobal.net
Primary Website: bccourier.com
Year Established: 2004
Avg Paid Circ: 2000
Audit By: Sworn/Estimate/Non-Audited
Audit Date: 10.06.2019
Personnel: Gail Joiner (Pub.); Bev Barr (Editor); Dee Russ (Adv. Dir.)

BAY AREA CITIZEN

Street address 1: 12554 Highway 3
Street address city: Webster
Street address state: TX
Zip/Postal code: 77598-5426
General Phone: (281) 378-1920
General Fax: (281) 668-1103
Advertising Phone: (281) 378-1922
Advertising Fax: (281) 668-1103
Editorial Phone: (281) 378-1930
Editorial Fax: (281) 668-1103
General/National Adv. E-mail: cwentz@hcnonline.com
Display Adv. E-mail: cwentz@hcnonline.com
Editorial e-mail: jmolony@hcnonline.com
Primary Website: YourBayAreaNews.com
Year Established: 1961
Avg Free Circ: 28523
Audit By: Sworn/Estimate/Non-Audited
Audit Date: 10.06.2019
Personnel: Brenda Miller-Fergerson (Pub.); Jim Molony (Ed.); Charles Lee (Adv. Dir.); Cheryl Wentz (Advt Sales Mgr)
Parent company (for newspapers): Hearst Communications, Inc.; Times Media Group

BAYLOR COUNTY BANNER

Street address 1: 109 E Morris St
Street address city: Seymour
Street address state: TX
Zip/Postal code: 76380-2140
General Phone: (940) 889-2616
General Fax: (940) 889-3610
Advertising Phone: (940) 889-2616
Advertising Fax: (940) 889-3610
Editorial Phone: (940) 889-2616
Editorial Fax: (940) 889-3610
General/National Adv. E-mail: banner@srcaccess.net
Display Adv. E-mail: banner@srcaccess.net
Editorial e-mail: banner@srcaccess.net
Primary Website: baylorbanner.com
Year Established: 1895
Avg Paid Circ: 2500
Avg Free Circ: 26
Audit By: Sworn/Estimate/Non-Audited
Audit Date: 10.06.2019
Personnel: Suzette Gwinn (Co-Pub.); Matt Gwinn (Co-Pub./Ed.); Lisa Torrez (Adv. Dir.)

BEEVILLE BEE-PICAYUNE

Street address 1: 111 N Washington St
Street address city: Beeville
Street address state: TX
Zip/Postal code: 78102-4508
General Phone: (361) 358-2550
General Fax: (361) 358-5323
Advertising Phone: (361) 358-2550
Advertising Fax: (361) 358-5323
Editorial Phone: (361) 358-2550
Editorial Fax: (361) 358-5323
General/National Adv. E-mail: news@mysoutex.com
Display Adv. E-mail: karneseditor@mysoutex.com
Editorial e-mail: news@mysoutex.com
Primary Website: mySouTex.com
Year Established: 1886
Avg Paid Circ: 4158
Audit By: Sworn/Estimate/Non-Audited
Audit Date: 10.06.2019
Personnel: Chip Latcham (Co-Pub.); Jeff Latcham (Co-Pub.); Jason Collins (Ed.); Karl Arnst (Adv. Dir.)

BELLAIRE EXAMINER

Street address 1: 7613 Katy Fwy
Street address 2: Ste C
Street address city: Houston
Street address state: TX
Zip/Postal code: 77024-2007
General Phone: (281) 378-1900
General Fax: (713) 520-1193
Advertising Phone: (281) 378-1906
Advertising Fax: (713) 520-1193
Editorial Phone: (281) 378-1911
Editorial Fax: (713) 520-1193
General/National Adv. E-mail: rdavis@hcnonline.com
Display Adv. E-mail: pstewart@hcnonline.com
Editorial e-mail: rgraham@hcnonline.com
Primary Website: hcnonline.com/bellaire_examiner
Avg Free Circ: 13998
Audit By: Sworn/Estimate/Non-Audited
Audit Date: 10.06.2019
Personnel: Richard Davis (Pub.); Tom Legg (Major Sr. Acct. Mgr.); Charles Lee (Adv. Dir.); David Taylor (Ed.)
Parent company (for newspapers): Hearst Communications, Inc.; Times Media Group

BIG LAKE WILDCAT

Street address 1: 707 N Florida Ave
Street address city: Big Lake
Street address state: TX
Zip/Postal code: 76932-4139
General Phone: (325) 884-2215
General Fax: (325) 884-5771
Advertising Phone: (325) 884-2215
Advertising Fax: (325) 884-5771
Editorial Phone: (325) 884-2215
Editorial Fax: (325) 884-5771
General/National Adv. E-mail: editor@mybiglake.com
Display Adv. E-mail: editor@mybiglake.com
Editorial e-mail: editor@mybiglake.com
Primary Website: mybiglake.com
Year Established: 1925
Avg Paid Circ: 890
Audit By: Sworn/Estimate/Non-Audited
Audit Date: 10.06.2019
Personnel: Randy Mankin (Pub.); Marla Daugherty (Ed.); J.L. Mankin (Adv. Dir.)

BIG SANDY-HAWKINS JOURNAL

Street address 1: 102 N TYLER ST
Street address city: Big Sandy
Street address state: TX
Zip/Postal code: 75755
General Phone: (903) 636-4351
General Fax: (903) 636-5091
Advertising Phone: (903) 636-4351
Advertising Fax: (903) 636-5091
Editorial Phone: (903) 636-4351
Editorial Fax: (903) 636-5091
General/National Adv. E-mail: BSHjournal@aol.com
Display Adv. E-mail: BSHjournal@aol.com
Editorial e-mail: BSHjournal@aol.com
Primary Website: thejournal.biz
Year Established: 1949
Avg Paid Circ: 1153
Audit By: Sworn/Estimate/Non-Audited
Audit Date: 10.06.2019
Personnel: Jim Bardwell (Pub.); Vicky Himel (Adv. Dir.); Danielle Dupree (Mgr.)
Parent company (for newspapers): M. Roberts Media

BLANCO COUNTY NEWS

Street address 1: 714 4th St
Street address 2: Ste 102
Street address city: Blanco
Street address state: TX
Zip/Postal code: 78606-5569
General Phone: (830) 833-4812
General Fax: (830) 833-4246
Advertising Phone: (830) 833-4812
Advertising Fax: (830) 833-4246
Editorial Phone: (830) 833-4812
Editorial Fax: (830) 833-4246
General/National Adv. E-mail: news@blanconews.com
Display Adv. E-mail: scottwesner@hotmail.com
Editorial e-mail: editor@blanconews.com
Year Established: 1883
Avg Paid Circ: 3200
Avg Free Circ: 35
Audit By: Sworn/Estimate/Non-Audited
Audit Date: 10.06.2019
Personnel: Scott Wesner (Pub.); Charles Willgren (Ed.); Jill Hunter (Adv. Dir.)

BOERNE STAR

Street address 1: 941 N School St
Street address city: Boerne
Street address state: TX
Zip/Postal code: 78006-5922
General Phone: (830) 249-2441
General Fax: (830) 249-4607
Advertising Phone: (830) 249-2441
Advertising Fax: (830) 249-4607
Editorial Phone: (830) 249-2441
Editorial Fax: (830) 249-4607
General/National Adv. E-mail: frank@boernestar.com
Display Adv. E-mail: kolleen@boernestar.com
Editorial e-mail: briancartwright@boernestar.com
Primary Website: boernestar.com
Year Established: 1906
Avg Paid Circ: 4179
Avg Free Circ: 1401
Audit By: Sworn/Estimate/Non-Audited
Audit Date: 10.06.2019
Personnel: Jeffrey Parra (Pub.); Kit Brenner (Copy Ed.); Kerry Barboza (Sports Ed.); Rose Stewart (Adv.); Dana Smith (Circ.)
Parent company (for newspapers): Fenice Community Media

BOGATA NEWS-TALCO TIMES

Street address 1: Highway 271
Street address city: Bogata
Street address state: TX
Zip/Postal code: 75417
General Phone: (903) 632-5322
General Fax: (903) 652-6041
Advertising Phone: (903) 632-5322
Advertising Fax: (903) 652-6041
Editorial Phone: (903) 632-5322
Editorial Fax: (903) 652-6041
General/National Adv. E-mail: tppub@1starnet.com
Display Adv. E-mail: tppub@1starnet.com
Editorial e-mail: nnichols@1starnet.com
Year Established: 1910
Avg Paid Circ: 1249
Avg Free Circ: 10
Audit By: Sworn/Estimate/Non-Audited
Audit Date: 10.06.2019
Personnel: Nanalee Nichols (Pub.); Nancy Brown (Ed.); Thomas Nichols (Adv. Dir.)
Parent company (for newspapers): Thunder Prairie Publishing

BOOKER NEWS

Street address 1: PO Box 807
Street address city: Booker
Street address state: TX
Zip/Postal code: 79005-0807
General Phone: (806) 658-4732
General/National Adv. E-mail: bookernews@amaonline.com
Display Adv. E-mail: bnews@ptsi.net
Editorial e-mail: bnews@ptsi.net
Year Established: 1927
Avg Paid Circ: 758
Audit By: Sworn/Estimate/Non-Audited
Audit Date: 10.06.2019
Personnel: Kayla Parvin (Advertising Director)

BOWIE COUNTY CITIZEN TRIBUNE

Street address 1: 312 N. Center St.
Street address 2: Ste. 103
Street address city: New Boston
Street address state: TX
Zip/Postal code: 75570
General Phone: (903) 628-5801
General Fax: (903) 628-8272
Advertising Phone: (903) 628-5801
Advertising Fax: (903) 628-8272
Editorial Phone: (903) 628-5801
Editorial Fax: (903) 628-8272
General/National Adv. E-mail: alewter@bowiecountynow.com
Display Adv. E-mail: alewter@bowiecountynow.com

Editorial e-mail: tribunenews@bowiecountynow.com
Primary Website: bowiecountynow.com
Year Established: 1885
Avg Paid Circ: 5700
Audit By: Sworn/Estimate/Non-Audited
Audit Date: 10.06.2019
Personnel: Kenny Mitchell (Pub.); Sandy Tutt (Class. & Circ.)
Parent company (for newspapers): Northeast Texas Publishing

BRADY STANDARD-HERALD

Street address 1: 201 S Bridge St
Street address city: Brady
Street address state: TX
Zip/Postal code: 76825-4917
General Phone: (325) 597-2959
General Fax: (888) 908-4741
Advertising Phone: (325) 597-2959
Advertising Fax: (888) 908-4741
Editorial Phone: (325) 597-2959
Editorial Fax: (888) 908-4741
General/National Adv. E-mail: publisher@bradystandard.com
Display Adv. E-mail: advertise@bradystandard.com
Editorial e-mail: newseditor@bradystandard.com
Primary Website: bradystandard.com
Year Established: 1909
Avg Paid Circ: 3800
Avg Free Circ: 68
Audit By: Sworn/Estimate/Non-Audited
Audit Date: 10.06.2019
Personnel: James Stewart (Pub./Ed.); Larry B. Smith (Pub. Emeritus); Holly Stewart (Adv. Dir.); Kathy Smith (Office Mgr.); Amanda Howell (News Ed.)

BRECKENRIDGE AMERICAN

Street address 1: 114 E Elm Street
Street address city: Breckenridge
Street address state: TX
Zip/Postal code: 76424-3613
General Phone: (254) 559-5412
Advertising Phone: (254) 559-5412
Editorial Phone: (254) 559-5412
General/National Adv. E-mail: kbailey@grahamleader.com
Display Adv. E-mail: admgr@breckenridgeamerican.com
Classified Adv. e-mail: classified@grahamleader.com
Editorial e-mail: editor@breckenridgeamerican.com
Primary Website: www.breckenridgeamerican.com
Year Established: 1920
Avg Paid Circ: 1000
Avg Free Circ: 25
Audit By: Sworn/Estimate/Non-Audited
Audit Date: 07.09.2022
Personnel: Kylie Bailey (Editor); Kylie Bailey (Publisher/Creative Director); Kaci Funderburg (Advertising Representative); Maddison Evans (Circulation/Classified Manager)
Parent company (for newspapers): Palo Pinto Communications, LP

BRIDGEPORT INDEX

Street address 1: 916 Halsell St
Street address city: Bridgeport
Street address state: TX
Zip/Postal code: 76426-3028
General Phone: (940) 683-4021
General Fax: (940) 683-3841
Advertising Phone: (940) 683-4021
Advertising Fax: (940) 683-3841
Editorial Phone: (940) 683-4021
Editorial Fax: (940) 683-3841
General/National Adv. E-mail: bridwellk@bridgeportindex.com
Display Adv. E-mail: ads@bridgeportindex.com
Editorial e-mail: news@bridgeportindex.com
Primary Website: bridgeportindex.com
Year Established: 1894
Avg Paid Circ: 2690
Avg Free Circ: 30
Audit By: Sworn/Estimate/Non-Audited
Audit Date: 10.06.2019
Personnel: Keith Bridwell (Pub./Adv. Dir.); Jay Bridwell (Ed.); Francine West (Prodn. Dir.)

BRISCOE COUNTY NEWS

Street address 1: BOX CLOSED
Street address city: Silverton
Street address state: TX
Zip/Postal code: 79257-0130
General Phone: (806) 823-2333
Advertising Phone: (806) 823-2333
Editorial Phone: (806) 847-7803
General/National Adv. E-mail: briscoenews@gmail.com
Display Adv. E-mail: briscoenews@gmail.com
Editorial e-mail: briscoenews@gmail.com
Primary Website: caprockcourier.com
Year Established: 1912
Avg Paid Circ: 1500
Audit By: Sworn/Estimate/Non-Audited
Audit Date: 10.06.2019
Personnel: Sally Arnold (Pub./Ed.); Brenda Hutson (Mng. Ed.); Tori Fry (Reporter/Photographer)

BROOKS DISCOVERY NEWS

Street address 1: 301 Avenue E
Street address city: San Antonio
Street address state: TX
Zip/Postal code: 78205-2006
General Phone: (210) 250-3711
General Fax: (210) 250-3715
Advertising Phone: (210) 250-2500
Advertising Fax: (210) 250-2565
Editorial Phone: (210) 250-3195
Editorial Fax: (210) 250-3105
General/National Adv. E-mail: rcaplan@express-news.net
Display Adv. E-mail: communitysupport@express-news.net
Editorial e-mail: editors@express-news.net
Primary Website: express-news.com
Audit By: Sworn/Estimate/Non-Audited
Audit Date: 10.06.2019
Personnel: Fred Mergele (Vice Pres., Finance); Susan Ehrman (Vice Pres., HR); Rebecca Named Chavez-Becker (Sales Dir.); Doug Bennight (Adv. Mgr., Automotive); Roxanne Beavers (Adv. Mgr., Telemktg./Classified); Pat Harvey (Adv. Mgr., Telemktg./Retail); Dean Aitken (Vice Pres., Mktg.); Patrick Magallanes (Vice Pres., Mktg.); Liz English (Target Mktg. Mgr.); Scott Frantzen (Circ. Sr. Vice Pres.); Paul Borrego (Circ. Dir., Admin.); Sammy Aburumuh (Dir., Metro Home Delivery); Terry Scott-Bertling (New Publications & Special Projects Ed.); Michael Leary (Ed.); Jamie Stockwell (Mng. Ed)

BROWNFIELD NEWS

Street address 1: 409 W Hill St
Street address city: Brownfield
Street address state: TX
Zip/Postal code: 79316-3203
General Phone: (806) 637-4535
General Fax: (806) 637-3795
Advertising Phone: (806) 637-4535
Advertising Fax: (806) 637-3795
Editorial Phone: (806) 637-4535
Editorial Fax: (806) 637-3795
General/National Adv. E-mail: advertising@brownfieldonline.com
Display Adv. E-mail: classifieds@brownfieldonline.com
Editorial e-mail: news@brownfieldonline.com
Primary Website: brownfieldonline.com
Year Established: 1904
Avg Paid Circ: 3100
Avg Free Circ: 60
Audit By: Sworn/Estimate/Non-Audited
Audit Date: 10.06.2019
Personnel: Brian Brisendine (Pub.); Mattie Garcia (Adv. Mgr.)

BROWNWOOD BULLETIN

Street address 1: 700 Carnegie St
Street address city: Brownwood
Street address state: TX
Zip/Postal code: 76801-7040
General Phone: (325) 646-2541
General Fax: (325) 646-6835
Advertising Phone: (325)641-3122
Advertising Fax: (325)646-6835
Editorial Phone: (325) 641-3112
Editorial Fax: (325)646-6835
General/National Adv. E-mail: mhorton@gatehousemedia.com
Display Adv. E-mail: mhorton@gatehousemedia.com
Classified Adv. e-mail: trease.burke@brownwoodbulletin.com
Editorial e-mail: derrick.stuckly@brownwoodbulletin.com
Primary Website: brownwoodtx.com
Year Established: 1900
Avg Paid Circ: 3000
Sun. Circulation Paid: 3500
Audit By: Sworn/Estimate/Non-Audited
Audit Date: 10.06.2019
Personnel: Derrick Stuckly (Assistant Editor/Sports Editor)
Parent company (for newspapers): CherryRoad Media

BUFFALO EXPRESS

Street address 1: 912 E Commerce
Street address city: Buffalo
Street address state: TX
Zip/Postal code: 75831
General Phone: (903) 322-6009
General Fax: (903) 322-7215
Advertising Phone: (903) 322-6009
Advertising Fax: (903) 322-7215
Editorial Phone: (903) 322-6009
Editorial Fax: (903) 322-7215
General/National Adv. E-mail: buffaloexpress@windstream.net
Display Adv. E-mail: buffaloexpress@windstream.net
Editorial e-mail: buffaloexpress@windstream.net
Primary Website: buffaloexpressnews.com
Year Established: 2000
Avg Paid Circ: 1695
Audit By: Sworn/Estimate/Non-Audited
Audit Date: 10.06.2019
Personnel: Mary Ann Vaughn (Pub./Adv. Dir.); Lee Gayle Boettcher (Ed.)

BULLARD BANNER NEWS

Street address 1: 610 E Main St
Street address city: Kilgore
Street address state: TX
Zip/Postal code: 75662-2612
General Phone: (903) 894-9306
General Fax: (903) 894-9308
Advertising Phone: (903) 894-9306
Advertising Fax: (903) 894-9308
Editorial Phone: (903) 894-9306
Editorial Fax: (903) 894-9308
General/National Adv. E-mail: advertising@bullardnews.com
Display Adv. E-mail: classifieds@kilgorenewsherald.com
Editorial e-mail: news1@bullardnews.com
Primary Website: bullardnews.com
Year Established: 1996
Avg Paid Circ: 1800
Audit By: Sworn/Estimate/Non-Audited
Audit Date: 10.06.2019
Personnel: Bill Woodall (Pub./Ed.); Jessica Woodall (Co-Pub.); Jamie Mims (Adv. Dir.)
Parent company (for newspapers): Bluebonnet Publishing, LLC

BULVERDE NEWS

Street address 1: 301 Avenue E
Street address city: San Antonio
Street address state: TX
Zip/Postal code: 78205-2006
General Phone: (210) 250-3711
General Fax: (210) 250-3715
Advertising Phone: (210) 250-2500
Advertising Fax: (210) 250-2565
Editorial Phone: (210) 250-3195
Editorial Fax: (210) 250-3105
General/National Adv. E-mail: communitysupport@express-news.net
Display Adv. E-mail: communitysupport@express-news.net
Editorial e-mail: editors@express-news.net
Primary Website: express-news.com
Avg Paid Circ: 35
Avg Free Circ: 3285
Audit By: Sworn/Estimate/Non-Audited
Audit Date: 10.06.2019
Personnel: Thomas A. Stephenson (Pres./Pub.); Fred Mergele (Vice Pres., Finance); Susan Ehrman (Vice Pres., HR); Charlotte Aaron (Vice Pres., Classified Adv.); Rebecca Named Chavez-Becker (Sales Dir.); Doug Bennight (Adv. Mgr., Automotive); Roxanne Beavers (Adv. Mgr., Telemktg./Classified); Pat Harvey (Adv. Mgr., Telemktg./Retail); Dean Aitken (Vice Pres., Mktg.); Patrick Magallanes (Vice Pres., Mktg.); Liz English (Target Mktg. Mgr.); Scott Frantzen (Circ. Sr. Vice Pres.); Paul Borrego (Circ. Dir., Admin.); Sammy Aburumuh (Dir., Metro Home Delivery); Robert Rivard (Ed.); Brett Thacker (Mng. Ed.); Terry Scott-Bertling (Asst. Mng. Ed., Features); Hallie Paul (Asst. Mng. Ed., Graphics/Design/Photo); Craig Thomason (Asst. Mng. Ed., News)

BURKBURNETT INFORMER STAR

Street address 1: 417 Avenue C
Street address city: Burkburnett
Street address state: TX
Zip/Postal code: 76354-3424
General Phone: (940) 569-2191
General Fax: (940) 569-0704
Advertising Phone: (940) 569-2191
Advertising Fax: (940) 569-0704
Editorial Phone: (940) 569-2191
Editorial Fax: (940) 569-0704
General/National Adv. E-mail: jeff@burknews.com
Display Adv. E-mail: linda@burknews.com
Editorial e-mail: jeff@burknews.com
Primary Website: burknews.com
Year Established: 1908
Avg Paid Circ: 2850
Audit By: Sworn/Estimate/Non-Audited
Audit Date: 10.06.2019
Personnel: Bret McCormick (Pub.); Jeff Bromley (Ed.); Linda Ingram (Adv. Mgr.)

BURLESON COUNTY TRIBUNE

Street address 1: 306 W Highway 21
Street address city: Caldwell
Street address state: TX
Zip/Postal code: 77836-1122
General Phone: (979) 567-3286
General Fax: (979) 567-7898
Advertising Phone: (979)567-3286
Advertising Fax: (979) 567-7898
Editorial Phone: (979)567-3286
Editorial Fax: (979)567-7898
General/National Adv. E-mail: news@bctribune.com
Display Adv. E-mail: ads@bctribune.com
Editorial e-mail: news@bctribuine.com
Primary Website: bctribune.com
Year Established: 1884
Avg Paid Circ: 4300
Avg Free Circ: 40
Audit By: Sworn/Estimate/Non-Audited
Audit Date: 10.06.2019
Personnel: Sam Preuss (Pub.); Roy Sanders (Ed.); Amber Campise (Ad. Director)

BURLESON STAR

Street address 1: 327 N.W. Renfro St.
Street address 2: PO Box 909
Street address city: Burleson
Street address state: TX
Zip/Postal code: 76028-0909
General Phone: (817) 295-0486
General Fax: (817) 295-5278
Advertising Phone: (817) 295-0486
Editorial Phone: (817) 295-0486
General/National Adv. E-mail: graphics@thestargroup.com
Display Adv. E-mail: classified@thestargroup.com
Primary Website: burlesonstar.net
Year Established: 1993
Avg Paid Circ: 950
Avg Free Circ: 1106
Audit By: Sworn/Estimate/Non-Audited
Audit Date: 10.06.2019
Personnel: Sharon Cregg (Gen. Mgr.); Ricky Moore (Mng. Ed.); Neetish Basnet (Reporter); Duane Boyd (Graphic Des.)

BURLESON STAR

Street address 1: 327 NW Renfro St
Street address city: Burleson
Street address state: TX
Zip/Postal code: 76028-3421
General Phone: (817) 295-0486
General Fax: (817) 295-5278
Advertising Phone: (817) 295-0486
Advertising Fax: (817) 295-5278
Editorial Phone: (817) 295-0486
Editorial Fax: (817) 295-5278
General/National Adv. E-mail: ads@thestargroup.com

Display Adv. E-mail: classified@thestargroup.com
Editorial e-mail: btinsley@live.com
Primary Website: burlesonstar.net
Year Established: 1964
Avg Paid Circ: 3328
Avg Free Circ: 259
Audit By: Sworn/Estimate/Non-Audited
Audit Date: 10.06.2019
Personnel: Dan Taylor (Pub.); Brian Porter (Ed.); Cathy Smith (Adv. Dir.)
Parent company (for newspapers): Palo Pinto Communications, LP

BURNET BULLETIN

Street address 1: 220 S Main St
Street address city: Burnet
Street address state: TX
Zip/Postal code: 78611-3107
General Phone: (512) 756-6136
General Fax: (512) 756-8911
Advertising Phone: (512) 756-6136
Advertising Fax: (512) 756-8911
Editorial Phone: (512) 756-6136
Editorial Fax: (512) 756-8911
General/National Adv. E-mail: publisher@burnetbulletin.com
Display Adv. E-mail: publisher@burnetbulletin.com
Editorial e-mail: editorial@burnetbulletin.com
Primary Website: burnetbulletin.com
Mthly Avg Views: 16500
Mthly Avg Unique Visitors: 8700
Year Established: 1873
Avg Paid Circ: 5115
Audit By: Sworn/Estimate/Non-Audited
Audit Date: 10.06.2019
Personnel: Lora Cheney (Adv. Consultant); James Herbert Walker (Burnet Community Ed.); Frank Shubert (Ed. / Pub.); Sharon Pelky (Bus. Mgr.)
Parent company (for newspapers): Highland Lakes Newspapers

CALLAHAN COUNTY STAR

Street address 1: 215 S Seaman St
Street address city: Eastland
Street address state: TX
Zip/Postal code: 76448-2745
General Phone: (254) 629-1707
General Fax: (254) 629-2092
Advertising Phone: (254) 629-1707
Advertising Fax: (254) 629-2092
Editorial Phone: (254) 629-1707
Editorial Fax: (254) 629-2092
General/National Adv. E-mail: ecn@att.net
Display Adv. E-mail: ecn@att.net
Editorial e-mail: ecn@att.net
Primary Website: eastlandcountytoday.com
Year Established: 1887
Avg Paid Circ: 579
Audit By: Sworn/Estimate/Non-Audited
Audit Date: 10.06.2019
Personnel: Houston V. O'Brien (Pub./Ed.); Rebecca McCrary (Adv. Dir.)

CANTON HERALD

Street address 1: 103 E Tyler St
Street address city: Canton
Street address state: TX
Zip/Postal code: 75103-1413
General Phone: (903) 567-4000
General Fax: (903) 567-6076
Advertising Phone: (903) 567-4000
Advertising Fax: (903) 567-6076
Editorial Phone: (903) 567-4000
Editorial Fax: (903) 567-6076
General/National Adv. E-mail: business@vanzandtnews.com
Display Adv. E-mail: business@vanzandtnews.com
Editorial e-mail: editor@vanzandtnews.com
Primary Website: thecantonherald.com
Year Established: 1882
Avg Paid Circ: 5000
Audit By: Sworn/Estimate/Non-Audited
Audit Date: 30.09.2021
Personnel: Tiffany Hardy (General Manager); Karla Dunson (Advertising Manager)
Parent company (for newspapers): Van Zandt Newspapers, LLC

CANYON LAKE WEEK

Street address 1: 1850 Old Sattler Rd
Street address city: Canyon Lake
Street address state: TX
Zip/Postal code: 78132-1874
General Phone: (830) 899-3137
Advertising Phone: (830) 237-7313
Editorial Phone: (830) 899-3137
General/National Adv. E-mail: dougkirk@gvtc.com
Display Adv. E-mail: dougkirk@gvtc.com
Editorial e-mail: dougkirk@gvtc.com
Primary Website: No Website
Year Established: 1985
Avg Free Circ: 3200
Audit By: Sworn/Estimate/Non-Audited
Audit Date: 10.06.2019
Personnel: Douglas Kirk (Ed.)

CARRIZO SPRINGS JAVELIN

Street address 1: 604 N 1st St
Street address city: Carrizo Springs
Street address state: TX
Zip/Postal code: 78834-2602
General Phone: (830) 876-2318
General Fax: (830) 876-2620
Advertising Phone: (830) 876-2318
Advertising Fax: (830) 876-2620
Editorial Phone: (830) 876-2318
Editorial Fax: (830) 876-2620
General/National Adv. E-mail: csjavelin@yahoo.com
Display Adv. E-mail: csjavelin@yahoo.com
Editorial e-mail: csjdigital@yahoo.com
Primary Website: carrizospringsjavelin.com
Year Established: 1884
Avg Paid Circ: 2100
Avg Free Circ: 100
Audit By: Sworn/Estimate/Non-Audited
Audit Date: 10.06.2019
Personnel: Claudia McDaniel (Co-Pub./Ed./Adv. Dir.)

CARROLLTON LEADER

Street address 1: 624 Krona Dr
Street address 2: Ste 170
Street address city: Plano
Street address state: TX
Zip/Postal code: 75074-8304
General Phone: (972) 398-4200
General Fax: (972) 398-4470
General/National Adv. E-mail: jdittrich@starlocalmedia.com
Display Adv. E-mail: jdittrich@starlocalmedia.com
Editorial e-mail: vatterberry@starlocalmedia.com
Primary Website: starlocalmedia.com
Mthly Avg Views: 546019
Mthly Avg Unique Visitors: 201046
Year Established: 2001
Avg Paid Circ: 209
Avg Free Circ: 1813
Audit By: CVC
Audit Date: 31.12.2018
Personnel: Scott Wright (Pub.); Melissa Rougeot (Circ. Mgr); Victoria Atterberry (Reporter); Joani Dittrich (Adv. Dir.)
Parent company (for newspapers): S.A.W. Advisors, LLC; Star Community Newspapers

CASTROVILLE NEWS BULLETIN

Street address 1: 1105 Fiorella St
Street address city: Castroville
Street address state: TX
Zip/Postal code: 78009-4577
General Phone: (830) 538-2556
General Fax: (830) 931-3450
Advertising Phone: (830) 538-2556
Advertising Fax: (830) 931-3450
Editorial Phone: (830) 538-2556
Editorial Fax: (830) 931-3450
General/National Adv. E-mail: cornerstoneads@sbcglobal.net
Display Adv. E-mail: cornerstoneads@sbcglobal.net
Editorial e-mail: cornerstonenews@sbcglobal.net
Primary Website: cornerstonenewspapers.com
Year Established: 1958
Avg Paid Circ: 1991
Avg Free Circ: 9
Audit By: Sworn/Estimate/Non-Audited
Audit Date: 10.06.2019
Personnel: Natalie Spencer (Pub./Ed./Adv. Dir.); Lori Black (Adv. Mgr.); Alicia Ramirez (News Ed.)
Parent company (for newspapers): McNaughton Newspapers

CELINA RECORD

Street address 1: 624 Krona Dr
Street address 2: Ste 170
Street address city: Plano
Street address state: TX
Zip/Postal code: 75074-8304
General Phone: (972) 398-4200
General Fax: (972) 398-4470
General/National Adv. E-mail: jdittrich@starlocalmedia.com
Display Adv. E-mail: jdittrich@starlocalmedia.com
Editorial e-mail: lmcgathey@starlocalmedia.com
Primary Website: starlocalmedia.com
Mthly Avg Views: 546019
Mthly Avg Unique Visitors: 201046
Year Established: 1901
Avg Paid Circ: 284
Avg Free Circ: 87
Audit By: CVC
Audit Date: 31.12.2018
Personnel: Scott Wright (Pub.); Joani Dittrich (Adv. Dir.); Melissa Rougeot (Circ. Mgr); Liz McGathey (Ed. Dir.)
Parent company (for newspapers): S.A.W. Advisors, LLC; Star Community Newspapers

CENTERVILLE NEWS

Street address 1: 204 E Main St
Street address city: Centerville
Street address state: TX
Zip/Postal code: 75833
General Phone: (903) 536-2015
General Fax: (903) 536-2329
Advertising Phone: (903) 536-2015
Advertising Fax: (903) 536-2329
Editorial Phone: (903) 536-2015
Editorial Fax: (903) 536-2329
General/National Adv. E-mail: centervillenewspaper@gmail.com
Display Adv. E-mail: centervillenewspaper@gmail.com
Editorial e-mail: centervillenewspaper@gmail.com
Year Established: 1980
Avg Paid Circ: 1140
Avg Free Circ: 45
Audit By: Sworn/Estimate/Non-Audited
Audit Date: 10.06.2019
Personnel: Christie Stanford (Publisher)

CENTURY NEWS

Street address 1: PO Box 49
Street address city: Wimberley
Street address state: TX
Zip/Postal code: 78676-0049
General Phone: (512) 847-2202
General Fax: (512) 847-9054
Advertising Phone: (512) 847-2202
Advertising Fax: (512) 847-9054
Editorial Phone: (512) 847-2202
Editorial Fax: (512) 847-9054
General/National Adv. E-mail: dscenturynews@gmail.com
Display Adv. E-mail: dscenturynews@gmail.com
Editorial e-mail: dscenturynews@gmail.com
Avg Paid Circ: 300
Audit By: Sworn/Estimate/Non-Audited
Audit Date: 10.06.2019
Personnel: Mary V. Saunders (Pub.); Anne Drabicky (Ed.); Gina McClure (Adv. Mgr.); Jim Gore (Prodn. Mgr.)

CHANDLER & BROWNSBORO STATESMAN

Street address 1: 300 Second St
Street address city: Chandler
Street address state: TX
Zip/Postal code: 75758-2238
General Phone: (903) 849-3333
General Fax: NA
Advertising Phone: (903) 849-3333
Advertising Fax: NA
Editorial Phone: (903) 849-3333
Editorial Fax: NA
General/National Adv. E-mail: advertising@c-bstatesman.com
Display Adv. E-mail: advertising@c-bstatesman.com
Editorial e-mail: editor@c-bstatesman.com
Primary Website: c-bstatesman.com
Year Established: 1976
Avg Paid Circ: 425
Audit By: Sworn/Estimate/Non-Audited
Audit Date: 10.06.2019
Personnel: Betty Abendroth (Owner / Publisher); Amanda Wilcox (Circulation / Distribution)
Parent company (for newspapers): Faith 3 Media, LLC

CHEROKEEAN HERALD

Street address 1: 140 N Main St
Street address city: Rusk
Street address state: TX
Zip/Postal code: 75785-1326
General Phone: (903) 683-2257
General Fax: (903) 683-5104
Advertising Phone: (903) 683-2257 ext. 105
Advertising Fax: (903) 683-5104
Editorial Phone: (903) 683-2257 ext. 107
Editorial Fax: (903) 683-5104
General/National Adv. E-mail: advertising@mediactr.com
Display Adv. E-mail: classifiedads@mediactr.com
Editorial e-mail: herald@mediactr.com
Primary Website: thecherokeean.com
Year Established: 1850
Avg Paid Circ: 4500
Avg Free Circ: 200
Audit By: Sworn/Estimate/Non-Audited
Audit Date: 10.06.2019
Personnel: Marie Whitehead (Pub.); Terrie Gonzalez (Ed.); Robert Gonzalez (Adv. Dir.); Quinten Boyd (Managing Ed.)
Parent company (for newspapers): Cherokeean Herald KTLU LLC

CHICO TEXAN

Street address 1: 916 Halsell St
Street address city: Bridgeport
Street address state: TX
Zip/Postal code: 76426-3028
General Phone: (940) 683-4021
General Fax: (940) 683-3841
Advertising Phone: (940) 683-4021
Advertising Fax: (940) 683-3841
Editorial Phone: (940) 683-4021
Editorial Fax: (940) 683-3841
General/National Adv. E-mail: bridwellk@bridgeportindex.com
Display Adv. E-mail: bridwellk@bridgeportindex.com
Editorial e-mail: news@bridgeportindex.com
Primary Website: chicotexan.com
Year Established: 1894
Avg Paid Circ: 700
Audit By: Sworn/Estimate/Non-Audited
Audit Date: 10.06.2019
Personnel: Keith Bridwell (Pub./Adv. Dir.); Jay Bridwell (Ed.); Francine West (Prod. Mgr.)

CHRONICLE & DEMOCRAT-VOICE

Street address 1: 208 W Pecan St
Street address city: Coleman
Street address state: TX
Zip/Postal code: 76834-4148
General Phone: (325) 625-4128
General Fax: (325) 625-4129
Advertising Phone: (325) 625-4128
Advertising Fax: (325) 625-4129
Editorial Phone: (325) 625-4128
Editorial Fax: (325) 625-4129
General/National Adv. E-mail: mail@colemannews.com
Display Adv. E-mail: mail@colemannews.com
Editorial e-mail: mail@colemannews.com
Primary Website: colemannews.com
Year Established: 1881
Avg Paid Circ: 2945
Avg Free Circ: 80
Audit By: Sworn/Estimate/Non-Audited
Audit Date: 10.06.2019

Personnel: Brett Autry (Pub.); Amber Hardin (Ed./ Adv. Dir.)

CISCO PRESS

Street address 1: 215 S. Seaman Street
Street address city: Eastland
Street address state: TX
Zip/Postal code: 76448
General Phone: (254) 629-1707
General Fax: (254) 629-2092
Advertising Fax: (254) 629-2092
Editorial Fax: (254) 629-2092
General/National Adv. E-mail: ecnads@yahoo.com
Display Adv. E-mail: ecn@att.net
Editorial e-mail: ecn@att.net
Primary Website: eastlandcountytoday.com
Year Established: 1919
Avg Paid Circ: 965
Audit By: Sworn/Estimate/Non-Audited
Audit Date: 10.06.2019
Personnel: Houston V. O'Brien (Pub.); Amy O'Brien-Glen (Gen. Mgr.)
Parent company (for newspapers): Eastland County Newspapers

CITIZENS' ADVOCATE

Street address 1: 509 W Bethel Rd
Street address city: Coppell
Street address state: TX
Zip/Postal code: 75019-4481
General Phone: (972) 462-8192
Advertising Phone: (972) 462-8192
Editorial Phone: (972) 462-8192
General/National Adv. E-mail: citizensadvocate2000@yahoo.com
Display Adv. E-mail: citizensadvocate2000@yahoo.com
Editorial e-mail: citizensadvocate2000@yahoo.com
Primary Website: coppellcitizensadvocate.com
Year Established: 1984
Avg Paid Circ: 5000
Audit By: Sworn/Estimate/Non-Audited
Audit Date: 10.06.2019
Personnel: Jean Murph (Pub./Ed.); Kathryn Walker (Adv. Dir.)

CITIZENS GAZETTE

Street address 1: 106 Linsey Cv
Street address city: Burnet
Street address state: TX
Zip/Postal code: 78611-5886
General Phone: (512) 756-6640
General Fax: (512) 756-6640
Advertising Phone: (512) 756-6640
Advertising Fax: (512) 756-6640
Editorial Phone: (512) 756-6640
Editorial Fax: (512) 756-6640
General/National Adv. E-mail: cgazette@tstar.net
Display Adv. E-mail: cgazette@tstar.net
Editorial e-mail: cgazette@tstar.net
Year Established: 1991
Avg Paid Circ: 1000
Audit By: Sworn/Estimate/Non-Audited
Audit Date: 10.06.2019
Personnel: Rick Espitia (Ed./Pub./Adv. Dir.)

CLARENDON ENTERPRISE

Street address 1: 105 Kearney St
Street address city: Clarendon
Street address state: TX
Zip/Postal code: 79226-6051
General Phone: (806) 874-2259
General Fax: (806) 874-2423
General/National Adv. E-mail: news@clarendononline.com
Display Adv. E-mail: news@clarendononline.com
Editorial e-mail: news@clarendononline.com
Primary Website: clarendonlive.com
Year Established: 1878
Avg Paid Circ: 1125
Audit By: Sworn/Estimate/Non-Audited
Audit Date: 10.06.2019
Personnel: Roger A. Estlack (Pub./Ed.); Tara Hogan (Adv. Dir.)

CLARKSVILLE TIMES

Street address 1: 109 South Locust St.
Street address city: Clarksville
Street address state: TX
Zip/Postal code: 75426
General Phone: (903) 427-0002
General Fax: (903) 427-0003
Advertising Phone: (903) 427-0002
Advertising Fax: (903) 427-0003
Editorial Phone: (903) 427-0002
Editorial Fax: (903) 427-0003
General/National Adv. E-mail: theclarksvilletimes@gmail.com
Display Adv. E-mail: ctimesadvertising@gmail.com
Editorial e-mail: theclarksvilletimes@gmail.com
Primary Website: theclarksvilletimes.blogspot.com
Year Established: 1873
Avg Paid Circ: 1842
Avg Free Circ: 52
Audit By: Sworn/Estimate/Non-Audited
Audit Date: 10.06.2019
Personnel: Lou Antonelli (Managing Editor); Patricia Antonelli (Publisher); Connie Hernandez (General Manager)
Parent company (for newspapers): New Clarksville Times Publishing LLC

CLAY COUNTY LEADER

Street address 1: 114 W Ikard St
Street address city: Henrietta
Street address state: TX
Zip/Postal code: 76365-2827
General Phone: (940) 538-4333
General Fax: (940) 538-4542
Advertising Phone: (940) 538-4333
Advertising Fax: (940) 538-4542
Editorial Phone: (940) 538-4333
Editorial Fax: (940) 538-4542
General/National Adv. E-mail: ads@claycountyleader.com
Display Adv. E-mail: ads@claycountyleader.com
Editorial e-mail: news@claycountyleader.com
Primary Website: claycountyleader.com
Year Established: 1932
Audit By: Sworn/Estimate/Non-Audited
Audit Date: 10.06.2019
Personnel: Bret McCormick (Pub.); Mike Chacanaca (Ed.)

CLEVELAND ADVOCATE

Street address 1: 100 Avenue A
Street address 2: Ste 600
Street address city: Conroe
Street address state: TX
Zip/Postal code: 77301-2946
General Phone: (281) 592-2626
General Fax: (281) 592-2629
Advertising Phone: (281) 592-2626
Advertising Fax: (281) 592-2629
Editorial Phone: (281) 592-2626
Editorial Fax: (281) 592-2629
General/National Adv. E-mail: dbrady@hcnonline.com
Display Adv. E-mail: dbrady@hcnonline.com
Editorial e-mail: vbrashier@hcnonline.com
Primary Website: hcndaytonnews.com
Year Established: 1917
Avg Paid Circ: 4152
Audit By: Sworn/Estimate/Non-Audited
Audit Date: 10.06.2019
Personnel: Brenda Miller-Fergerson (Pub.); Vanesa Brashier (Ed.); Dianne Brady (Adv. Dir.); Jason Joseph (Pub.); Charles Lee (Adv. Mgr); Rick Flores (Circ. Mgr); Angela Hicks (Prod. Mgr)
Parent company (for newspapers): Times Media Group

CLYDE JOURNAL

Street address 1: 312 N 1st St
Street address 2: 2226 Castle Drive
Street address city: Clyde
Street address state: TX
Zip/Postal code: 79510-4729
General Phone: (325) 893-4244
General Fax: (325) 893-2780
General/National Adv. E-mail: clydejournal@earthlink.net
Display Adv. E-mail: clydejournal@earthlink.net
Editorial e-mail: clydejournal@earthlink.net
Primary Website: clydenewspaper.com
Year Established: 1972
Avg Paid Circ: 2000
Avg Free Circ: 70
Audit By: Sworn/Estimate/Non-Audited
Audit Date: 10.06.2020
Personnel: Daniel Tabor (Editor); Melinda Kevil; Lyn Walker (Adv Dir)

COLLIN COUNTY COMMERCIAL RECORD

Street address 1: 202 W Louisiana St
Street address 2: Ste 202
Street address city: McKinney
Street address state: TX
Zip/Postal code: 75069-4459
General Phone: (972) 562-0606
General Fax: (972) 562-2919
Advertising Phone: (972) 562-0606
Advertising Fax: (972) 562-2919
Editorial Phone: (972) 562-0606
Editorial Fax: (972) 562-2919
General/National Adv. E-mail: cccr@collincountycommercialrecord.com
Display Adv. E-mail: cccr@collincountycommercialrecord.com
Editorial e-mail: cccr@collincountycommercialrecord.com
Primary Website: collincountycommercialrecord.com
Year Established: 1982
Audit By: Sworn/Estimate/Non-Audited
Audit Date: 10.06.2019
Personnel: E. Nuel Cates (Pub.); Emily Cates (Ed.)

COLONY-COURIER LEADER

Street address 1: 624 Krona Dr
Street address 2: Ste 170
Street address city: Plano
Street address state: TX
Zip/Postal code: 75074-8304
General Phone: (972)398-4200
General Fax: (972)398-4470
Advertising Phone: (972) 398-4471
Advertising Fax: (972)398-4470
Editorial Phone: (972)424-9504
Editorial Fax: (972)398-4470
General/National Adv. E-mail: llibby@starlocalmedia.com
Display Adv. E-mail: dhemphill@starlocalmedia.com
Editorial e-mail: swright@starlocalnews.com
Primary Website: starlocalmedia.com
Audit By: Sworn/Estimate/Non-Audited
Audit Date: 10.06.2019
Personnel: Liz McGathey (Exec. Ed.)
Parent company (for newspapers): Times Media Group

COLORADO CITY RECORD

Street address 1: 257 E 2nd St
Street address city: Colorado City
Street address state: TX
Zip/Postal code: 79512-6431
General Phone: (325) 728-3413
General Fax: (325) 728-3414
Advertising Phone: (325) 728-3413
Advertising Fax: (325) 728-3414
Editorial Phone: (325) 728-3413
Editorial Fax: (325) 728-3414
General/National Adv. E-mail: coloradorecord@yahoo.com
Display Adv. E-mail: coloradorecord@yahoo.com
Editorial e-mail: coloradorecord@yahoo.com
Primary Website: coloradorecord.com
Year Established: 1905
Avg Paid Circ: 3000
Avg Free Circ: 100
Audit By: Sworn/Estimate/Non-Audited
Audit Date: 10.06.2019
Personnel: Earl Plagens (Adv. Mgr.); Sheila Plagens (Pub.); Stephanie Perez (Editor)

COMAL COUNTY BEACON

Street address 1: 1850 Old Sattler Rd
Street address city: Canyon Lake
Street address state: TX
Zip/Postal code: 78132-1874
General Phone: (830) 899-3137
Advertising Phone: (830) 237-7313
Editorial Phone: (830) 899-3137
General/National Adv. E-mail: dougkirk@gvtc.com
Display Adv. E-mail: dougkirk@gvtc.com
Editorial e-mail: dougkirk@gvtc.com
Primary Website: LookForMeIWillFindYou.com
Year Established: 1985
Avg Free Circ: 3500
Audit By: Sworn/Estimate/Non-Audited
Audit Date: 10.06.2019
Personnel: Douglas Kirk (Pub./Ed.)

COMMERCE JOURNAL

Street address 1: 2305 King St
Street address city: Greenville
Street address state: TX
Zip/Postal code: 75401-3257
General Phone: (903) 455-4220
General Fax: (903) 455-6281
Advertising Phone: (903) 455-4220 ext. 311
Advertising Fax: (903) 455-6281
Editorial Phone: (903) 455-4220 ext. 324
Editorial Fax: (903) 455-6281
General/National Adv. E-mail: advertising@heraldbanner.com
Display Adv. E-mail: smorgan@heraldbanner.com
Editorial e-mail: editor@heraldbanner.com
Primary Website: commercejournal.com
Year Established: 1889
Avg Paid Circ: 2000
Avg Free Circ: 67
Audit By: Sworn/Estimate/Non-Audited
Audit Date: 10.06.2019
Personnel: Lisa Chappell (Pub.); Derek Price (Ed.); Rita Haldeman (Adv. Dir.)
Parent company (for newspapers): CNHI, LLC

COOPER REVIEW

Street address 1: 50 E Side Sq
Street address city: Cooper
Street address state: TX
Zip/Postal code: 75432-1935
General Phone: (903) 395-2175
General Fax: (903) 395-0424
Advertising Phone: (903) 395-2175
Advertising Fax: (903) 395-0424
Editorial Phone: (903) 395-2175
Editorial Fax: (903) 395-0424
General/National Adv. E-mail: ads@cooperreview.com
Display Adv. E-mail: ads@cooperreview.com
Editorial e-mail: news@cooperreview.com
Primary Website: cooperreview.com
Year Established: 1880
Avg Paid Circ: 1550
Avg Free Circ: 100
Audit By: Sworn/Estimate/Non-Audited
Audit Date: 10.06.2019
Personnel: Jim Butler (Pub./Adv. Dir.); Cindy Roller (Ed.); Sally Butler (Office Mgr.)

COPPELL GAZETTE

Street address 1: 624 Krona Dr
Street address 2: Ste 170
Street address city: Plano
Street address state: TX
Zip/Postal code: 75074-8304
General Phone: (972) 398-4200
General Fax: (972) 398-4470
General/National Adv. E-mail: jdittrich@starlocalmedia.com
Display Adv. E-mail: jdittrich@starlocalmedia.com
Editorial e-mail: swright@starlocalmedia.com
Primary Website: starlocalmedia.com
Mthly Avg Views: 546019
Mthly Avg Unique Visitors: 201046
Year Established: 1981
Avg Paid Circ: 185
Avg Free Circ: 9305
Audit By: CVC
Audit Date: 31.12.2018
Personnel: Scott Wright; Melissa Rougeot (Circ. Mgr); Joani Dittrich (Adv. Dir.); Victoria Atterberry (Reporter)
Parent company (for newspapers): S.A.W. Advisors, LLC; Star Community Newspapers

COPPERAS COVE LEADER-PRESS

Street address 1: 2210 E Business 190
Street address 2: Ste 1
Street address city: Copperas Cove
Street address state: TX
Zip/Postal code: 76522-2523
General Phone: (254) 547-4207
General Fax: (254) 542-3299

Advertising Phone: (254) 547-4207
Advertising Fax: (254) 542-3299
Editorial Phone: (254) 547-4207
Editorial Fax: (254) 542-3299
General/National Adv. E-mail: advertising@coveleaderpress.com
Display Adv. E-mail: ads@coveleaderpress.com
Editorial e-mail: news@coveleaderpress.com
Primary Website: coveleaderpress.com
Year Established: 1894
Avg Paid Circ: 3650
Avg Free Circ: 56
Audit By: Sworn/Estimate/Non-Audited
Audit Date: 10.06.2019
Personnel: David Morris (Pub.)
Parent company (for newspapers): Copperas Cove Newspapers Inc.

CORRIGAN TIMES

Street address 1: 202 E Front St
Street address city: Corrigan
Street address state: TX
Zip/Postal code: 75939-2589
General Phone: (936) 398-2535
General Fax: (936) 327-7156
Advertising Phone: (936) 398-2535
Advertising Fax: (936) 327-7156
Editorial Phone: (936) 398-2535
Editorial Fax: (936) 327-7156
General/National Adv. E-mail: polknews@livingston.net
Display Adv. E-mail: polknews@livingston.net
Editorial e-mail: polknews@livingston.net
Primary Website: EastTexasNews.com
Year Established: 1953
Avg Paid Circ: 1350
Audit By: Sworn/Estimate/Non-Audited
Audit Date: 10.06.2019
Personnel: Kim Popham (Ed.); Linda Holley (Adv. Dir.)
Parent company (for newspapers): Polk County Publishing Co.

COUNTY STAR NEWS

Street address 1: 212 N Main St
Street address city: Shamrock
Street address state: TX
Zip/Postal code: 79079-2228
General Phone: (806) 256-2070
General Fax: (806) 256-2071
Advertising Phone: (806) 256-2070
Advertising Fax: (806) 256-2071
Editorial Phone: (806) 256-2070
Editorial Fax: (806) 256-2071
General/National Adv. E-mail: Jeff@countystarnews.com
Display Adv. E-mail: Jeff@countystarnews.com
Editorial e-mail: thecastrocountynews@yahoo.com
Primary Website: countystarnews.com
Year Established: 1993
Avg Paid Circ: 2400
Audit By: Sworn/Estimate/Non-Audited
Audit Date: 10.06.2019
Personnel: Jeff Blackmon (Pub./Ed./Adv. Dir.)

COW COUNTRY COURIER

Street address 1: 2652 FM 2922
Street address city: Nixon
Street address state: TX
Zip/Postal code: 78140-5245
General Phone: (830) 582-1740
General Fax: (830) 582-2123
Advertising Phone: (830) 582-1740
Advertising Fax: (830) 582-2123
Editorial Phone: (830) 582-1740
Editorial Fax: (830) 582-2123
General/National Adv. E-mail: wscott@gvec.net
Display Adv. E-mail: wscott@gvec.net
Editorial e-mail: wscott@gvec.net
Year Established: 1993
Avg Paid Circ: 850
Audit By: Sworn/Estimate/Non-Audited
Audit Date: 10.06.2019
Personnel: Scott Wendle (Pub./Ed./Owner)

CRANE NEWS

Street address 1: 401 S Gaston St
Street address city: Crane
Street address state: TX
Zip/Postal code: 79731-2621
General Phone: (432) 558-3541
General Fax: (432) 558-2676
Advertising Phone: (432) 558-3541
Advertising Fax: (432) 558-2676
Editorial Phone: (432) 558-3541
Editorial Fax: (432) 558-2676
General/National Adv. E-mail: newspub@nwol.net
Display Adv. E-mail: newspub@nwol.net
Editorial e-mail: newspub@nwol.net
Year Established: 1879
Avg Paid Circ: 1780
Avg Free Circ: 70
Audit By: Sworn/Estimate/Non-Audited
Audit Date: 10.06.2019
Personnel: Dennis Greer (Pub./Ed.); Mandy Timmons (Adv. Dir.)

CROSBY COUNTY NEWS

Street address 1: 817 Main
Street address city: Ralls
Street address state: TX
Zip/Postal code: 79357
General Phone: (806) 253-0211
General Fax: none
Advertising Phone: (806) 253-0211
Advertising Fax: none
Editorial Phone: (806) 253-0211
Editorial Fax: noine
General/National Adv. E-mail: crosbycountynews@windstream.net
Display Adv. E-mail: crosbycountynews@windstream.net
Editorial e-mail: crosbycountynews@windstream.net
Year Established: 1985
Avg Paid Circ: 1000
Audit By: Sworn/Estimate/Non-Audited
Audit Date: 10.06.2019
Personnel: John Valentine (Pub./Ed.); Brenda Valentine (Adv. Dir.)

CROSS PLAINS REVIEW

Street address 1: 116 E 1st St
Street address city: Cross Plains
Street address state: TX
Zip/Postal code: 76443-2464
General Phone: (254) 725-6111
General Fax: (254) 725-7225
General/National Adv. E-mail: clydejournal@earthlink.net
Display Adv. E-mail: clydejournal@earthlink.net
Editorial e-mail: clydejournal@earthlink.net
Year Established: 1908
Avg Paid Circ: 1300
Avg Free Circ: 35
Audit By: Sworn/Estimate/Non-Audited
Audit Date: 10.06.2019
Personnel: Betty Tabor (Pub.); Becky Tabor (Ed)

CYPRESS CREEK MIRROR

Street address 1: 21901 State Highway 249
Street address 2: Ste 500
Street address city: Houston
Street address state: TX
Zip/Postal code: 77070-1545
General Phone: (281) 378-1080
General Fax: (281) 320-2005
Advertising Phone: (281) 378-1082
Advertising Fax: (281) 320-2005
Editorial Phone: (281) 378-1087
Editorial Fax: (281) 320-2005
General/National Adv. E-mail: rdavis@hcnonline.com
Display Adv. E-mail: srovegno@hcnonline.com
Editorial e-mail: rkent@hcnonline.com
Primary Website: hcnonline.com
Year Established: 2003
Avg Paid Circ: 0
Avg Free Circ: 6750
Audit By: AAM
Audit Date: 30.09.2018
Personnel: Richard Davis (Pub.); Roy Kent (Ed.); Susan Rovegno (Sales Mgr.); Megan O'Sullivan (Mktg. Mgr.); Tom Legg (Major Sr. Acct. Mgr.); Charles Lee (Adv. Dir.)
Parent company (for newspapers): Hearst Communications, Inc.

DALHART TEXAN

Street address 1: 410 Denrock Ave
Street address city: Dalhart
Street address state: TX
Zip/Postal code: 79022-2628
General Phone: (806) 244-4511
General Fax: (806) 244-2395
Advertising Phone: (806)244-4511
Advertising Fax: (806)244-2395
Editorial Phone: (806)244-4511
Editorial Fax: (806)244-2395
General/National Adv. E-mail: advertising@thedalharttexan.com
Display Adv. E-mail: classifieds@thedalharttexan.com
Editorial e-mail: publisher@thedalharttexan.com
Primary Website: thedalharttexan.com
Year Established: 1901
Avg Paid Circ: 2300
Audit By: Sworn/Estimate/Non-Audited
Audit Date: 10.06.2019
Personnel: Scott Wood (Owner/Co-Pub.); Scott Wesner (Owner/Co-Pub.); Tammi Kate Ledford (Ed./Adv. Dir.)

DALLAS BUSINESS JOURNAL

Street address 1: 2515 McKinney Ave
Street address 2: Ste 100
Street address city: Dallas
Street address state: TX
Zip/Postal code: 75201-7675
General Phone: (214) 696-5959
General Fax: (214) 696-1486
Advertising Phone: (214) 696-5959
Advertising Fax: (214) 696-1486
Editorial Phone: (214) 696-5959
Editorial Fax: (214) 696-1486
General/National Adv. E-mail: dallas@bizjournals.com
Display Adv. E-mail: tphillips@bizjournals.com
Editorial e-mail: dallas@bizjournals.com
Primary Website: bizjournals.com/dallas
Year Established: 1977
Avg Paid Circ: 11847
Audit By: Sworn/Estimate/Non-Audited
Audit Date: 10.06.2019
Personnel: Lisa Bormaster (Pub.); Juan Elizondo Jr. (Ed.); Bob Baranski (Adv. Dir.)

DAYTON NEWS

Street address 1: 100 Avenue A
Street address city: Conroe
Street address state: TX
Zip/Postal code: 77301-2946
General Phone: (281) 592-2626
General Fax: (281) 592-2629
Advertising Phone: (281) 592-2626
Advertising Fax: (281) 592-2629
Editorial Phone: (281) 592-2626
Editorial Fax: (281) 592-2629
General/National Adv. E-mail: dbrady@hcnonline.com
Display Adv. E-mail: dbrady@hcnonline.com
Editorial e-mail: vbrashier@hcnonline.com
Primary Website: yourdaytonnews.com
Year Established: 2004
Avg Paid Circ: 0
Avg Free Circ: 6177
Audit By: Sworn/Estimate/Non-Audited
Audit Date: 10.06.2019
Personnel: Brenda Miller-Fergerson (Pub.); Vanesa Brashier (Ed.); Dianne Brady (Adv. Dir.); Angela Hicks (Prod. Mgr); Jason Joseph (Pub.); Charles Lee (Adv. Mgr); Rick Flores (Circ. Mgr); Corey Turner (Pub/Ad Dir)
Parent company (for newspapers): Times Media Group

DE LEON FREE PRESS

Street address 1: 324 S. Texas Street
Street address city: De Leon
Street address state: TX
Zip/Postal code: 76444
General Phone: (254) 893-6868
General Fax: (254) 893-3550
Advertising Phone: (254) 893-6868
Advertising Fax: (254) 893-3550
Editorial Phone: (254) 893-6868
Editorial Fax: (254) 893-3550
General/National Adv. E-mail: ads@deleonfreepress.com
Display Adv. E-mail: ads@deleonfreepress.com
Editorial e-mail: ads@deleonfreepress.com
Primary Website: deleonfreepress.com
Year Established: 1890
Avg Paid Circ: 2000
Audit By: Sworn/Estimate/Non-Audited
Audit Date: 10.06.2019
Personnel: Jon Awbrey (Pub.); Laura Kestner (Ed.); Betty Wofford (Adv. Mgr.)

DEER PARK BROADCASTER

Street address 1: 12554 Highway 3
Street address city: Webster
Street address state: TX
Zip/Postal code: 77598-5426
General Phone: (281) 378-1920
General/National Adv. E-mail: cwentz@hcnonline.com
Display Adv. E-mail: clee@hcnonline.com
Editorial e-mail: jmolony@hcnonline.com
Primary Website: yourhoustonnews.com/deer_park
Avg Free Circ: 1763
Audit By: CVC
Audit Date: 30.09.2018
Personnel: Brenda Miller-Fergerson (Pub); Cheryl Wentz (Advt Sales Mgr)
Parent company (for newspapers): Hearst Communications, Inc.

DENVER CITY PRESS

Street address 1: 321 N Main Ave
Street address city: Denver City
Street address state: TX
Zip/Postal code: 79323-3249
General Phone: (806) 592-2141
General Fax: (806) 592-8233
Advertising Phone: (806) 592-2141
Advertising Fax: (806) 592-8233
Editorial Phone: (806) 592-2141
Editorial Fax: (806) 592-8233
General/National Adv. E-mail: dcpress@midtech.net
Display Adv. E-mail: dcpress@midtech.net
Editorial e-mail: dcpress@midtech.net
Year Established: 1939
Avg Paid Circ: 1600
Avg Free Circ: 3
Audit By: Sworn/Estimate/Non-Audited
Audit Date: 10.06.2019
Personnel: John Graham (Pub.); JP Landry (Ed.)

DEPORT TIMES-BLOSSOM TIMES

Street address 1: 161 Main St
Street address city: Deport
Street address state: TX
Zip/Postal code: 75435
General Phone: (903) 652-4205
General Fax: (903) 652-6041
Advertising Phone: (903) 652-4205
Advertising Fax: (903) 652-6041
Editorial Phone: (903) 652-4205
Editorial Fax: (903) 652-6041
General/National Adv. E-mail: tppub@1starnet.com
Display Adv. E-mail: tppub@1starnet.com
Editorial e-mail: tppub@1starnet.com
Year Established: 1909
Avg Paid Circ: 783
Avg Free Circ: 10
Audit By: Sworn/Estimate/Non-Audited
Audit Date: 10.06.2019
Personnel: Nanalee Nichols (Pub./Ed.); Thomas Nichols (Adv. Mgr.); Cindy Allen (Office Mgr.)
Parent company (for newspapers): Thunder Prairie Publishing

DETROIT WEEKLY

Street address 1: 161 Main St
Street address city: Deport
Street address state: TX
Zip/Postal code: 75435
General Phone: (903) 652-4205
General Fax: (903) 652-6041
Advertising Phone: (903) 652-4205
Advertising Fax: (903) 652-6041
Editorial Phone: (903) 652-4205
Editorial Fax: (903) 652-6041
General/National Adv. E-mail: tppub@1starnet.com
Display Adv. E-mail: tppub@1starnet.com
Editorial e-mail: tppub@1starnet.com
Year Established: 1982
Avg Paid Circ: 614
Audit By: Sworn/Estimate/Non-Audited
Audit Date: 10.06.2019
Personnel: Nanalee Nichols (Pub.); Thomas Nichols (Adv. Mgr.); Liz Irwin (Ed.)

Parent company (for newspapers): Thunder Prairie Publishing

DEVIL'S RIVER NEWS

Street address 1: 224 E Main St
Street address city: Sonora
Street address state: TX
Zip/Postal code: 76950-2605
General Phone: (325) 387-2507
General Fax: (325) 387-5691
Advertising Phone: (325) 387-2507
Advertising Fax: (325) 387-5691
Editorial Phone: (325) 387-2507
Editorial Fax: (325) 387-5691
General/National Adv. E-mail: editor@sonoratx.net
Display Adv. E-mail: editor@sonoratx.net
Editorial e-mail: editor@sonoratx.net
Primary Website: devilsriver.news
Year Established: 1890
Audit By: Sworn/Estimate/Non-Audited
Audit Date: 10.06.2019
Personnel: Ben Taylor (Pub./Ed.); Rhonda Wilson (Adv. Dir.)

DEVINE NEWS

Street address 1: 216 S Bright Dr
Street address city: Devine
Street address state: TX
Zip/Postal code: 78016-3202
General Phone: (830) 665-2211
General Fax: (830) 663-3686
Advertising Phone: (830) 665-2211
Advertising Fax: (830) 663-3686
Editorial Phone: (830) 665-2211
Editorial Fax: (830) 663-3686
General/National Adv. E-mail: ads@devinenews.com
Display Adv. E-mail: kk@devinenews.com
Editorial e-mail: news@devinenews.com
Primary Website: devinenews.com
Year Established: 1897
Audit By: Sworn/Estimate/Non-Audited
Audit Date: 10.06.2019
Personnel: Kathleen DuBose Calame (Pub./Gen. Mgr.); Linda Sherrell (Adv. Sales Rep.); Kayleen Holden (Ed./ Office Mgr.)

DIBOLL FREE PRESS

Street address 1: PO Box 339
Street address city: Diboll
Street address state: TX
Zip/Postal code: 75941-0339
General Phone: (936) 829-3313
General Fax: (936) 829-3321
Advertising Phone: (936) 829-3313
Advertising Fax: (936) 829-3321
Editorial Phone: (936) 829-3313
Editorial Fax: (936) 829-3321
General/National Adv. E-mail: ads@dibollfreepress.com
Display Adv. E-mail: web@dibollfreepress.com
Editorial e-mail: editor@dibollfreepress.com
Primary Website: dibollfreepress.com
Year Established: 1952
Avg Paid Circ: 3526
Avg Free Circ: 187
Audit By: Sworn/Estimate/Non-Audited
Audit Date: 10.06.2019
Personnel: Hunter McLeroy (Online Media Dir.); Bill Woodall (Pub.); Jerry Gaudling (Ed.)
Parent company (for newspapers): Temple-Inland Forest Products Corp.

DOUBLE MOUNTAIN CHRONICLE

Street address 1: 114 E Sammy Baugh Ave
Street address city: Rotan
Street address state: TX
Zip/Postal code: 79546-4522
General Phone: (325) 735-2562
General Fax: (325) 735-2230
Advertising Phone: (325) 735-2562
Advertising Fax: (325) 735-2230
Editorial Phone: (325) 735-2562
Editorial Fax: (325) 735-2230
General/National Adv. E-mail: advertising@dmchronicle.com
Display Adv. E-mail: publisher@dmchronicle.com
Editorial e-mail: editor@dmchronicle.com
Primary Website: doublemountainchronicle.com
Year Established: 1907
Avg Paid Circ: 1038
Audit By: Sworn/Estimate/Non-Audited
Audit Date: 10.06.2019
Personnel: Jeff Hurt (Editor); Kyndra Vaught (Advertising/Reporting); Pat Porter (Business)

EAGLE LAKE HEADLIGHT

Street address 1: 220 E Main St
Street address city: Eagle Lake
Street address state: TX
Zip/Postal code: 77434-2426
General Phone: (979) 234-5521
General Fax: (979) 234-5522
Advertising Phone: (979) 234-5521
Advertising Fax: (979) 234-5522
Editorial Phone: (979) 234-5521
Editorial Fax: (979) 234-5522
General/National Adv. E-mail: eaglelakeheadlight@sbcglobal.net
Display Adv. E-mail: eaglelakeheadlight@sbcglobal.net
Editorial e-mail: eaglelakeheadlight@sbcglobal.net
Primary Website: eaglelakeheadlight.com
Year Established: 1903
Avg Paid Circ: 2057
Audit By: Sworn/Estimate/Non-Audited
Audit Date: 10.06.2019
Personnel: Doug Beal (Pub./Ed.); Alesia Davis (Adv. Dir.)

EAST BERNARD EXPRESS

Street address 1: 115 W. Burleson St.
Street address city: Wharton
Street address state: TX
Zip/Postal code: 77488
General Phone: 9795328840
General Fax: 9795328840
Advertising Phone: 9795328840
Advertising Fax: 9795328840
Editorial Phone: 9795328840
Editorial Fax: 9795328840
General/National Adv. E-mail: bwallace@journal-spectator.com
Display Adv. E-mail: bwallace@journal-spectator.com
Classified Adv. e-mail: bwallace@journal-spectator.com
Editorial e-mail: bwallace@journal-spectator.com
Year Established: 1949
Avg Paid Circ: 600
Audit By: Sworn/Estimate/Non-Audited
Audit Date: 06.10.2022
Personnel: Bill Wallace (Pub./Ed./Adv. Dir.)
Parent company (for newspapers): Hartman Newspapers LP

EAST MONTGOMERY COUNTY OBSERVER

Street address 1: 907 E Main St
Street address city: Humble
Street address state: TX
Zip/Postal code: 77338-4749
General Phone: (281) 378-1060
General Fax: (281) 446-6901
Advertising Phone: (281) 378-1071
Advertising Fax: (281) 446-6901
Editorial Phone: (281) 378-1062
Editorial Fax: (281) 446-6901
General/National Adv. E-mail: cturner@hcnonline.com
Display Adv. E-mail: cturner@hcnonline.com
Editorial e-mail: jsummer@hcnonline.com
Primary Website: chron.com/neighborhood/east-montgomery
Year Established: 1982
Avg Paid Circ: 0
Avg Free Circ: 10498
Audit By: Sworn/Estimate/Non-Audited
Audit Date: 10.06.2019
Personnel: Brenda Miller-Fergerson (Pub.); Corey Turner (Pub/Ad Dir)
Parent company (for newspapers): Hearst Communications, Inc.; Times Media Group

EASTEX ADVOCATE

Street address 1: 106 W Hanson St
Street address city: Cleveland
Street address state: TX
Zip/Postal code: 77327-4406
General Phone: (281) 592-2626
General Fax: (281) 592-2629
Advertising Phone: (281) 592-2626
Advertising Fax: (281) 592-2629
Editorial Phone: (281) 592-2626
Editorial Fax: (281) 592-2629
General/National Adv. E-mail: dbrady@hcnonline.com
Display Adv. E-mail: dbrady@hcnonline.com
Editorial e-mail: vbrashier@hcnonline.com
Primary Website: YourEastexNews.com/eastex
Year Established: 1917
Avg Free Circ: 10523
Audit By: Sworn/Estimate/Non-Audited
Audit Date: 10.06.2019
Personnel: Brenda Miller-Fergerson (Pub.); Vanesa Brashier (Ed.); Dianne Brady (Adv. Dir.); Corey Turner (Pub/Ad Dir)
Parent company (for newspapers): 1013 Communications; Hearst Communications, Inc.

EASTLAND TELEGRAM

Street address 1: 215 S Seaman St
Street address city: Eastland
Street address state: TX
Zip/Postal code: 76448-2745
General Phone: (254) 629-1707
General Fax: (254) 629-2092
Advertising Phone: (254) 629-1707
Advertising Fax: (254) 629-2092
Editorial Fax: (254) 629-2092
General/National Adv. E-mail: ecn@att.net
Display Adv. E-mail: ecn@att.net
Editorial e-mail: ecn@att.net
Primary Website: eastlandcountytoday.com
Year Established: 1925
Avg Paid Circ: 1825
Audit By: Sworn/Estimate/Non-Audited
Audit Date: 10.06.2019
Personnel: Houston V. O'Brien (Pub.); Margaret Hetrick; Sheila Hickcock
Parent company (for newspapers): Eastland County Newspapers

EDINBURG REVIEW

Street address 1: 1811 N 23rd St
Street address city: McAllen
Street address state: TX
Zip/Postal code: 78501-6121
General Phone: (956) 682-2423
General Fax: (956) 630-6371
Advertising Phone: (956) 682-2423
Editorial Phone: (956) 682-2423
General/National Adv. E-mail: lmedrano@valleytowncrier.com
Display Adv. E-mail: sales@valleytowncrier.com
Editorial e-mail: pperez@valleytowncrier.com
Primary Website: edinburgreview.com
Year Established: 1914
Avg Free Circ: 24041
Audit By: Sworn/Estimate/Non-Audited
Audit Date: 10.06.2019
Personnel: Linda Medrano (Pub./Reg. Op. Dir.); Pedro Perez (Ed.); Claudia Garcia (Majors/Nationals Representative)
Parent company (for newspapers): CherryRoad Media

EL CAMPO LEADER-NEWS

Street address 1: 203 E Jackson St
Street address city: El Campo
Street address state: TX
Zip/Postal code: 77437-4413
General Phone: (979) 543-3363
General Fax: (979) 543-0097
Advertising Phone: (979) 543-3363
Advertising Fax: (979) 543-0097
Editorial Phone: (979) 543-3363
Editorial Fax: (979) 543-0097
General/National Adv. E-mail: publisher@leader-news.com
Display Adv. E-mail: classified@leader-news.com
Editorial e-mail: publisher@leader-news.com
Primary Website: leader-news.com
Year Established: 1885
Avg Paid Circ: 4583
Avg Free Circ: 115
Audit By: Sworn/Estimate/Non-Audited
Audit Date: 10.06.2019
Personnel: Jay T. Strasner (Pub./Ed.); Diana David (Office Mgr.); Keri Mahalitc
Parent company (for newspapers): Hartman Newspapers LP

ELDORADO SUCCESS

Street address 1: 204 SW Main St
Street address city: Eldorado
Street address state: TX
Zip/Postal code: 76936
General Phone: (325) 853-3125
Advertising Phone: (325) 853-3125
Editorial Phone: (325) 853-3125
General/National Adv. E-mail: success@myeldorado.net
Display Adv. E-mail: kathy@myeldorado.net
Classified Adv. e-mail: kathy@myeldorado.net
Editorial e-mail: success@myeldorado.net
Primary Website: myeldorado.net
Mthly Avg Views: 12500
Mthly Avg Unique Visitors: 4300
Year Established: 1901
Avg Paid Circ: 1150
Audit By: Sworn/Estimate/Non-Audited
Audit Date: 10.06.2019
Personnel: Randy Mankin (Pub.); Kathy Mankin (Gen. Mgr./Adv. Dir); Lupe Elizondo (Circ. Mgr.); Mandi Umphress (Production Assistant)
Parent company (for newspapers): Masked Rider Publishing, Inc.

ELECTRA STAR-NEWS

Street address 1: 207 N Waggoner St
Street address city: Electra
Street address state: TX
Zip/Postal code: 76360-2440
General Phone: (940) 495-2149
General Fax: (940) 495-2627
Advertising Phone: (940) 495-2149
Advertising Fax: (940) 495-2627
Editorial Phone: (940) 495-2149
Editorial Fax: (940) 495-2627
General/National Adv. E-mail: electrastarnews@electratel.net
Display Adv. E-mail: electrastarnews@electratel.net
Editorial e-mail: electrastarnews@electratel.net
Year Established: 1907
Avg Paid Circ: 2000
Avg Free Circ: 79
Audit By: Sworn/Estimate/Non-Audited
Audit Date: 10.06.2019
Personnel: Ted Miller (Pub.); Jeannette Miller (Ed.); Ann Wright (Adv. Dir.)

ELGIN COURIER

Street address 1: 105 N Main St
Street address city: Elgin
Street address state: TX
Zip/Postal code: 78621-2618
General Phone: (512) 285-3333
General Fax: (512) 285-9406
Advertising Phone: (512)285-3333
Advertising Fax: (512)285-9406
Editorial Phone: (512)285-3333
Editorial Fax: (512)392-9406
General/National Adv. E-mail: publisher@elgincourier.com
Display Adv. E-mail: publisher@elgincourier.com
Editorial e-mail: elgincourier@elgincourier.com
Primary Website: elgincourier.com
Year Established: 1890
Avg Paid Circ: 2007
Avg Free Circ: 220
Audit By: Sworn/Estimate/Non-Audited
Audit Date: 10.06.2019
Personnel: Marie Ott (Adv. Mgr.); Dan Kleiner (Publisher); Charles Wood (Ed.); Heather Romine (Circ. Mgr); Patricia Finney (Prod. Mgr)
Parent company (for newspapers): Fenice Community Media

FALFURRIAS FACTS

Street address 1: 219 E Rice St
Street address city: Falfurrias
Street address state: TX
Zip/Postal code: 78355-3621
General Phone: (361) 325-2200
General Fax: (361) 325-2200
Advertising Phone: (361) 325-2200
Advertising Fax: (361) 325-2200

Editorial Phone: (361) 325-2200
Editorial Fax: (361) 325-2200
General/National Adv. E-mail: falfacts@yahoo.com
Display Adv. E-mail: falfacts@yahoo.com
Editorial e-mail: falfacts@yahoo.com
Year Established: 1906
Avg Paid Circ: 3000
Audit By: Sworn/Estimate/Non-Audited
Audit Date: 10.06.2019
Personnel: Marcelo Silva (Pub./Ed.); San Juanita Olivarez (Adv. Dir.)

FARMERSVILLE TIMES

Street address 1: 101 S Main St
Street address city: Farmersville
Street address state: TX
Zip/Postal code: 75442-2207
General Phone: (972) 784-6397
Advertising Phone: (972) 442.5515 x29
Editorial Phone: (972) 784.6397 x30
General/National Adv. E-mail: advertising@csmediatexas.com
Display Adv. E-mail: classifieds@csmediatexas.com
Editorial e-mail: news@farmersvilletimes.com
Primary Website: farmersvilletimes.com
Year Established: 1885
Avg Paid Circ: 3500
Audit By: Sworn/Estimate/Non-Audited
Audit Date: 10.06.2019
Personnel: Chad Engbrock (Pub./Ed./Adv. Mgr.)
Parent company (for newspapers): C&S Media, Inc.

FLOWER MOUND LEADER

Street address 1: 624 Krona Dr
Street address 2: Ste 170
Street address city: Plano
Street address state: TX
Zip/Postal code: 75074-8304
General Phone: (972) 398-4200
General Fax: (972) 398-4470
Advertising Phone: (972) 398-4471
General/National Adv. E-mail: jdittrich@starlocalmedia.com
Display Adv. E-mail: nsouders@starlocalmedia.com
Editorial e-mail: croark@starlocalmedia.com
Primary Website: starlocalmedia.com
Avg Paid Circ: 176
Avg Free Circ: 24867
Audit By: CVC
Audit Date: 31.12.2018
Personnel: Chris Roark (Ed.); Joani Dittrich (Adv. Dir.); Scott Wright (Pub.)
Parent company (for newspapers): S.A.W. Advisors, LLC; Star Community Newspapers

FLOYD COUNTY HESPERIAN-BEACON

Street address 1: 201 W California St
Street address 2: Ste A
Street address city: Floydada
Street address state: TX
Zip/Postal code: 79235-2700
General Phone: (806) 983-3737
General Fax: (806) 983-3141
Advertising Phone: (806) 983-3737
Advertising Fax: (806) 983-3141
Editorial Phone: (806) 983-3737
Editorial Fax: (806) 983-3141
General/National Adv. E-mail: fchb.editor@yahoo.com
Display Adv. E-mail: fchblockney@yahoo.com
Editorial e-mail: fchb.editor@yahoo.com
Primary Website: hesperianbeacononline.com
Year Established: 1896
Avg Paid Circ: 2600
Avg Free Circ: 23
Audit By: Sworn/Estimate/Non-Audited
Audit Date: 10.06.2019
Personnel: Chris Bleckburn (Owner); Jennifer Harbin (Ed.); Barbara Anderson (Adv. Dir.)

FOARD COUNTY NEWS

Street address 1: 108 S 1st St
Street address city: Crowell
Street address state: TX
Zip/Postal code: 79227
General Phone: (940) 684-1355
General Fax: (940) 684-1700
Advertising Phone: (940) 684-1355
Advertising Fax: (940) 684-1700
Editorial Phone: (940) 684-1355
Editorial Fax: (940) 684-1700
General/National Adv. E-mail: fcnews@srcaccess.net
Display Adv. E-mail: fcnews@srcaccess.net
Editorial e-mail: fcnews@srcaccess.net
Year Established: 1891
Avg Paid Circ: 727
Audit By: Sworn/Estimate/Non-Audited
Audit Date: 10.06.2019
Personnel: Leslie Hopkins (Pub./Ed./Adv. Dir.); Lisa Hopkins (Pub./Ed./Adv. Dir.)

FORNEY MESSENGER

Street address 1: 201 W Broad St
Street address 2: P. O. Box 936
Street address city: Forney
Street address state: TX
Zip/Postal code: 75126-9161
General Phone: (972) 564-3121
General Fax: (972) 552-3599
Advertising Phone: (972) 564-3121
Advertising Fax: (972) 552-3599
Editorial Phone: (972) 564-3121
Editorial Fax: (972) 552-3599
General/National Adv. E-mail: ads@forneymessenger.com
Display Adv. E-mail: ads@forneymessenger.com
Classified Adv. e-mail: messengerads@sbcglobal.net
Editorial e-mail: news@forneymessenger.com
Primary Website: forneymessenger.com
Year Established: 1896
Avg Paid Circ: 3600
Audit By: Sworn/Estimate/Non-Audited
Audit Date: 10.06.2019
Personnel: Jeff Cannon (Graphic Designer); Darrell Grooms (Publisher); Misty Holler (Accounts receivable)

FORT BEND STAR

Street address 1: 3944 Bluebonnet Dr
Street address city: Stafford
Street address state: TX
Zip/Postal code: 77477-3952
General Phone: (281) 690-4200
General Fax: (281) 690-4237
General/National Adv. E-mail: ads@fortbendstar.com
Display Adv. E-mail: starnews@fortbendstar.com
Editorial e-mail: starnews@fortbendstar.com
Primary Website: fortbendstar.com
Avg Paid Circ: 200
Avg Free Circ: 34775
Audit By: Sworn/Estimate/Non-Audited
Audit Date: 10.06.2019
Personnel: Michael Fredrickson (Pub.); Joe Southern (Ed.); B.K. Carter (Acct. Exec.)

FORT SAM NEWS LEADER

Street address 1: 301 Avenue E
Street address city: San Antonio
Street address state: TX
Zip/Postal code: 78205-2006
General Phone: (210) 250-3000
General Fax: (210) 221-1198
Advertising Phone: (210) 250-2500
Advertising Fax: (210) 250-2565
Editorial Phone: (210) 250-3195
Editorial Fax: (210) 250-3105
General/National Adv. E-mail: USAF.jbsa.502-ABW.Mbx.502-abw-pa@mail.mil
Display Adv. E-mail: communitysupport@express-news.net
Editorial e-mail: editors@express-news.net
Primary Website: express-news.com
Avg Paid Circ: 0
Avg Free Circ: 0
Audit By: VAC
Audit Date: 31.05.2017
Personnel: Thomas A. Stephenson (Pres./Pub.); Fred Mergele (Vice Pres., Finance); Susan Ehrman (Vice Pres., HR); Charlotte Aaron (Vice Pres., Classified Adv.); Rebecca Named Chavez-Becker (Sales Dir.); Doug Bennight (Adv. Mgr., Automotive); Roxanne Beavers (Adv. Mgr., Telemktg./Classified); Pat Harvey (Adv. Mgr., Telemktg./Retail); Dean Aitken (Vice Pres., Mktg.); Patrick Magallanes (Vice Pres., Mktg.); Liz English (Target Mktg. Mgr.); Scott Frantzen (Circ. Sr. Vice Pres.); Paul Borrego (Circ. Dir., Admin.); Sammy Aburumuh (Dir., Metro Home Delivery); Robert Rivard (Ed.); Brett Thacker (Mng. Ed.); Terry Scott-Bertling (Asst. Mng. Ed., Features); Hallie Paul (Asst. Mng. Ed., Graphics/Design/Photo); Craig Thomason (Asst. Mng. Ed., News)

FORT WORTH BUSINESS PRESS

Street address 1: 3509 Hulen St.
Street address 2: Suite 200
Street address city: Fort Worth
Street address state: TX
Zip/Postal code: 76107
General Phone: (817) 336-8300
General Fax: (817) 332-3038
General/National Adv. E-mail: mlester@bizpress.net
Display Adv. E-mail: mlester@bizpress.net
Editorial e-mail: rfrancis@bizpress.net
Primary Website: fortworthbusiness.com
Year Established: 1988
Avg Paid Circ: 631
Avg Free Circ: 3446
Audit By: Sworn/Estimate/Non-Audited
Audit Date: 10.06.2019
Personnel: Robert Francis (Ed.); Michelle Lester

FRANKLIN ADVOCATE

Street address 1: 114 W 4th St
Street address city: Hearne
Street address state: TX
Zip/Postal code: 77859-2506
General Phone: (979) 279-3411
General Fax: (979) 279-5401
Advertising Phone: (979)279-3411
Advertising Fax: (979) 279-5401
Editorial Phone: (979)279-3411
Editorial Fax: (979)279-5401
General/National Adv. E-mail: ads@robconews.com
Display Adv. E-mail: ads@robconews.com
Editorial e-mail: news@robconews.com
Primary Website: franklin-advocate.com
Year Established: 1982 - Reestablished 2014
Avg Paid Circ: 494
Avg Free Circ: 6
Audit By: Sworn/Estimate/Non-Audited
Audit Date: 10.06.2019
Personnel: Dennis Phillips (Publisher)
Parent company (for newspapers): Keane Media, Inc.

FRANKLIN NEWS WEEKLY

Street address 1: 107 E Decherd St
Street address city: Franklin
Street address state: TX
Zip/Postal code: 77856-3747
General Phone: (979) 828-1520
General Fax: (979) 828-1525
General/National Adv. E-mail: FranklinNewsWeekly@gmail.com
Display Adv. E-mail: FranklinNewsWeekly@gmail.com
Editorial e-mail: FranklinNewsWeekly@gmail.com
Year Established: 1970
Avg Paid Circ: 1000
Audit By: Sworn/Estimate/Non-Audited
Audit Date: 10.06.2019
Personnel: Sharon Jean Russell (Pub./Ed./Adv. Dir.)

FRANKSTON CITIZEN

Street address 1: 142 W Main St
Street address city: Frankston
Street address state: TX
Zip/Postal code: 75763-3519
General Phone: (903) 876-2218
General Fax: (903) 876-4974
Advertising Phone: (903) 876-2218
Advertising Fax: (903) 876-4974
Editorial Phone: (903) 876-2218
Editorial Fax: (903) 876-4974
General/National Adv. E-mail: sales@frankstoncitizen.com
Display Adv. E-mail: sales@frankstoncitizen.com
Editorial e-mail: news@frankstoncitizen.com
Primary Website: frankstoncitizen.com
Year Established: 1910
Avg Paid Circ: 1901
Avg Free Circ: 88
Audit By: Sworn/Estimate/Non-Audited
Audit Date: 10.06.2019
Personnel: Jay Graham (Ed.); J. Tom Graham (Adv. Dir.)

FREDERICKSBURG STANDARD-RADIO POST

Street address 1: 712 W Main St
Street address city: Fredericksburg
Street address state: TX
Zip/Postal code: 78624-3134
General Phone: (830) 997-2155
General Fax: (830) 990-0036
Advertising Phone: (830) 997-2155
Advertising Fax: (830) 990-0036
Editorial Phone: (830) 997-2155
Editorial Fax: (830) 990-0036
General/National Adv. E-mail: fbgads@fredericksburgstandard.com
Display Adv. E-mail: kim@fredericksburgstandard.com
Classified Adv. e-mail: connie@fredericksburgstandard.com
Editorial e-mail: ken@fredericksburgstandard.com
Primary Website: fredericksburgstandard.com
Year Established: 1907
Avg Paid Circ: 7999
Audit By: Sworn/Estimate/Non-Audited
Audit Date: 10.06.2019
Personnel: Ken Esten Cooke (Pub.); Kimberly Jung (Adv. Dir.); Sherrie Geistweidt (Circ. Mgr.); Yvonne Hartmann (Mng Ed)
Parent company (for newspapers): Palo Pinto Communications, LP

FREESTONE COUNTY TIMES

Street address 1: 401 E Commerce St
Street address city: Fairfield
Street address state: TX
Zip/Postal code: 75840-1603
General Phone: (903) 389-6397
General Fax: (903) 389-2636
Advertising Phone: (903) 389-6397
Advertising Fax: (903) 389-2636
Editorial Phone: (903) 389-6397
Editorial Fax: (903) 389-2636
General/National Adv. E-mail: news@freestonecountytimes.com
Display Adv. E-mail: ads@freestonecountytimes.com
Classified Adv. e-mail: ads@freestonecountytimes.com
Editorial e-mail: news@freestonecountytimes.com
Primary Website: freestonecountytimes.com
Mthly Avg Unique Visitors: 24498
Year Established: 2002
Avg Paid Circ: 2147
Avg Free Circ: 40
Audit By: Sworn/Estimate/Non-Audited
Audit Date: 28.09.2022
Personnel: Scott Marster Sr. (Pub./Adv. Dir.); Karen Leidy (Editor/Ad Design); Sherry Schoeneberg (Sales Exec.); Megan Hempel (Asst. Editor / Ad Designer); Nicole Schaefer (Reporter / Photographer)

FRIENDSWOOD JOURNAL

Street address 1: 100 Avenue A
Street address city: Conroe
Street address state: TX
Zip/Postal code: 77301-2946
General Phone: (281) 378-1920
General Fax: (281) 922-4499
Advertising Phone: (281) 378-1922
Advertising Fax: (281) 922-4499
Editorial Phone: (281) 378-1930
Editorial Fax: (281) 922-4499
General/National Adv. E-mail: cwentz@hcnonline.com
Display Adv. E-mail: cwentz@hcnonline.com
Editorial e-mail: jmolony@hcnonline.com
Primary Website: yourfriendswoodnews.com
Year Established: 1975
Avg Paid Circ: 724
Avg Free Circ: 7995
Audit By: Sworn/Estimate/Non-Audited
Audit Date: 10.06.2019
Personnel: Brenda Miller-Fergerson (Pub.); Jim Molony (Ed.); Charles Lee (Adv. Dir.); Jason Joseph (Pub.); Rick Flores (Circ. Mgr); Carol Taylor (Prod. Mgr); Cheryl Wentz (Advt Sales Mgr)
Parent company (for newspapers): Hearst Communications, Inc.; Times Media Group

FRIO-NUECES CURRENT

Street address 1: 321 E San Marcos St

Street address city: Pearsall
Street address state: TX
Zip/Postal code: 78061-3223
General Phone: (830) 334-3644
General Fax: (830) 334-3647
Advertising Phone: (830)334-3644
Advertising Fax: (830)334-3647
Editorial Phone: (830)334-3644
Editorial Fax: (830)334-3647
General/National Adv. E-mail: currentads@att.net
Display Adv. E-mail: currentads@att.net
Editorial e-mail: currenteditor@att.net
Primary Website: frio-nuecescurrent.com
Year Established: 1896
Avg Paid Circ: 3453
Avg Free Circ: 75
Audit By: Sworn/Estimate/Non-Audited
Audit Date: 10.06.2019
Personnel: Craig Garnett (Pub.); Marc Robertson (Ed.); Logan Garnett (Gen. Mgr.); Michelle Frausto (Adv. Dir.)

FRISCO ENTERPRISE

Street address 1: 624 Krona Dr
Street address 2: Ste 170
Street address city: Plano
Street address state: TX
Zip/Postal code: 75074-8304
General Phone: (972) 398-4200
General Fax: (972) 398-4470
General/National Adv. E-mail: jdittrich@starlocalmedia.com
Display Adv. E-mail: jdittrich@starlocalmedia.com
Editorial e-mail: croark@starlocalmedia.com
Primary Website: starlocalmedia.com
Mthly Avg Views: 546019
Mthly Avg Unique Visitors: 201046
Year Established: 1957
Avg Paid Circ: 534
Avg Free Circ: 26210
Audit By: CVC
Audit Date: 31.12.2018
Personnel: Scott Wright (Pub.); Chris Roark (Ed.); Melissa Rougeot (Circ. Mgr); Joani Dittrich (Adv. VP)
Parent company (for newspapers): S.A.W. Advisors, LLC; Star Community Newspapers

GAINESVILLE DAILY REGISTER

Street address 1: 306 E California St
Street address city: Gainesville
Street address state: TX
Zip/Postal code: 76240-4006
General Phone: (940) 665-5511
General Fax: 940-668-7257
Advertising Fax: (940) 665-0920
Editorial Phone: (864) 356-1036
Editorial Fax: (940) 665-1499
General/National Adv. E-mail: meads@gainesvilleregister.com
Display Adv. E-mail: sales1@gainesvilleregister.com
Classified Adv. e-mail: classifiedsgdr@ntin.net
Editorial e-mail: editor@gainesvilleregister.com
Primary Website: www.gainesvilleregister.com
Mthly Avg Views: 50000
Mthly Avg Unique Visitors: 35000
Year Established: 1890
Avg Paid Circ: 4000
Sun. Circulation Paid: 5019
Audit By: USPS
Audit Date: 30.09.2006
Personnel: Bernice Trimble (Bus. Mgr.); Jack Bills (Circ. Mgr.); Jim Perry (Pub.); Darin Allred (Managing Ed.); Lisa Chappell (Pub.)
Parent company (for newspapers): CNHI, LLC; CNHI, LLC

GATESVILLE MESSENGER AND STAR FORUM

Street address 1: 116 S 6th St
Street address city: Gatesville
Street address state: TX
Zip/Postal code: 76528-2052
General Phone: (254) 865-5212
General Fax: (254) 865-2361
Advertising Phone: (254) 865-5212
Advertising Fax: (254) 865-2361
Editorial Phone: (254) 865-5212
Editorial Fax: (254) 865-2361
General/National Adv. E-mail: advertising@gatesvillemessenger.com
Display Adv. E-mail: classifieds@gatesvillemessenger.com
Editorial e-mail: editor@gatesvillemessenger.com
Primary Website: gatesvillemessenger.com
Year Established: 1881
Avg Paid Circ: 3400
Audit By: Sworn/Estimate/Non-Audited
Audit Date: 10.06.2019
Personnel: Marshall Day (Pub.); Larry Kennedy (Ed.)

GIDDINGS TIMES & NEWS

Street address 1: 170 N Knox Ave
Street address city: Giddings
Street address state: TX
Zip/Postal code: 78942-3439
General Phone: (979) 542-2222
General Fax: (979) 542-9410
Advertising Phone: (979) 542-2222
Advertising Fax: (979) 542-9410
Editorial Phone: (979) 542-2222
Editorial Fax: (979) 542-9410
General/National Adv. E-mail: gtimes@verizon.net
Display Adv. E-mail: gtimes@verizon.net
Editorial e-mail: gtimes@verizon.net
Primary Website: giddingstimes.com
Year Established: 1888
Audit By: Sworn/Estimate/Non-Audited
Audit Date: 10.06.2019
Personnel: David True (Pub./Ed./Adv. Dir.)

GILMER MIRROR

Street address 1: 214 E Marshall St
Street address city: Gilmer
Street address state: TX
Zip/Postal code: 75644-2228
General Phone: (903) 843-2503
General Fax: (903) 843-5123
Advertising Phone: (903) 843-2503
Advertising Fax: (903) 843-5123
Editorial Phone: (903) 843-2503
Editorial Fax: (903) 843-5123
General/National Adv. E-mail: gilmermirror@yahoo.com
Display Adv. E-mail: gilmermirrorclassifieds@yahoo.com
Editorial e-mail: gilmermirror@gmail.com
Primary Website: gilmermirror.com
Year Established: 1877
Avg Paid Circ: 3500
Avg Free Circ: 23
Audit By: Sworn/Estimate/Non-Audited
Audit Date: 10.06.2019
Personnel: William R. Greene (Pub.); Suzanne Patterson (Adv. Mgr.); Tabitha McCain
Parent company (for newspapers): Greeneway Enterprises, Inc.

GLADEWATER MIRROR

Street address 1: 211 N Main St
Street address city: Gladewater
Street address state: TX
Zip/Postal code: 75647-2335
General Phone: (903) 845-2235
General Fax: (903) 845-2237
General/National Adv. E-mail: gladewatermirror@aol.com
Display Adv. E-mail: gladewatermirror@aol.com
Editorial e-mail: gladewatermirror@aol.com
Primary Website: gladewatermirror.com
Year Established: 1928
Avg Paid Circ: 1750
Audit By: Sworn/Estimate/Non-Audited
Audit Date: 10.06.2019
Personnel: Jim Bardwell (Pub./Ed.)
Parent company (for newspapers): Bardwell Ink LLC

GLEN ROSE REPORTER

Street address 1: 702 E South Loop
Street address city: Stephenville
Street address state: TX
Zip/Postal code: 76401-5314
General Phone: (254) 897-2282
General Fax: (254) 897-9423
Advertising Phone: (225)323-4383
Advertising Fax: (254)897-9423
Editorial Phone: (254)965-3124
Editorial Fax: (254)897-9423
General/National Adv. E-mail: advertising@theglenrosereporter.com
Display Adv. E-mail: advertising@theglenrosereporter.com
Editorial e-mail: news@theglenrosereporter.com
Primary Website: yourglenrosetx.com
Year Established: 1887
Avg Paid Circ: 3000
Audit By: Sworn/Estimate/Non-Audited
Audit Date: 10.06.2019
Personnel: Todd Franz (Gen. Mgr.); Tye Chandler (Sports Ed.); Haley Thompson (Adv. Exec.); Travis Smith (Mng. Ed.)
Parent company (for newspapers): CherryRoad Media

GOLDTHWAITE EAGLE

Street address 1: 1002 Fisher St
Street address city: Goldthwaite
Street address state: TX
Zip/Postal code: 76844-2159
General Phone: (325) 648-2244
General Fax: (325) 648-2024
Advertising Phone: (325) 648-2244
Advertising Fax: (325) 648-2024
Editorial Phone: (325) 648-2244
Editorial Fax: (325) 648-2024
General/National Adv. E-mail: goldnews@centex.net
Display Adv. E-mail: goldedit@centex.net
Editorial e-mail: goldpub@centex.net
Primary Website: goldthwaiteeagle.com
Year Established: 1894
Avg Paid Circ: 1975
Audit By: Sworn/Estimate/Non-Audited
Audit Date: 10.06.2019
Personnel: Steven W. Bridges (Ed./Pub./Adv. Dir.)

GOLIAD ADVANCE-GUARD

Street address 1: 202 S Commercial St
Street address city: Goliad
Street address state: TX
Zip/Postal code: 77963-4189
General Phone: (361) 645-2330
Advertising Phone: (361) 645-2330
Advertising Fax: (361) 645-2812
Editorial Phone: (361) 645-2330
General/National Adv. E-mail: advertising@mysoutex.com
Display Adv. E-mail: advertising@mysoutex.com
Classified Adv. e-mail: goliadoffice@mysoutex.com
Editorial e-mail: goliad@mysoutex.com
Primary Website: mysoutex.com
Year Established: 1913
Avg Paid Circ: 2000
Audit By: Sworn/Estimate/Non-Audited
Audit Date: 10.06.2019
Personnel: Jeff Latcham (Co-Pub.); Chip Latcham (Co-Pub.); Bill Clough (Ed)
Parent company (for newspapers): Beeville Publishing Co. Inc

GRAND SALINE SUN

Street address 1: 116 N Main St
Street address city: Grand Saline
Street address state: TX
Zip/Postal code: 75140-1844
General Phone: (903) 962-4275
General Fax: (903) 962-3660
General/National Adv. E-mail: amoore@grandsalinesun.com
Display Adv. E-mail: amoore@grandsalinesun.com
Editorial e-mail: wcallaway@grandsalinesun.com
Primary Website: grandsalinesun.com
Year Established: 1893
Avg Paid Circ: 1200
Avg Free Circ: 54
Audit By: Sworn/Estimate/Non-Audited
Audit Date: 10.06.2019
Personnel: Dan Moore (Pub.); Wendi Callaway (Ed.); Ann Moore (Adv. Dir./Bus. Mgr.)
Parent company (for newspapers): Lake Country Media, LLC

GRANDVIEW TRIBUNE

Street address 1: 104 E Criner St
Street address city: Grandview
Street address state: TX
Zip/Postal code: 76050-2179
General Phone: (817) 866-3391
General Fax: (817) 866-3869
Advertising Phone: (817) 866-3391
Advertising Fax: (817) 866-3869
Editorial Phone: (817) 866-3391
Editorial Fax: (817) 866-3869
General/National Adv. E-mail: darladudley@windstream.net
Display Adv. E-mail: tribune-sales@windstream.net
Editorial e-mail: tribune-editor@windstream.net
Year Established: 1896
Avg Paid Circ: 1200
Audit By: Sworn/Estimate/Non-Audited
Audit Date: 10.06.2019
Personnel: Darla Dudley (Owner/Pub.); Janeen Roberts (Ed.); Janet MacDonald (Adv. Dir.)

GREENWOOD RANGER

Street address 1: 10703 FM 307
Street address city: Midland
Street address state: TX
Zip/Postal code: 79706-5319
General Phone: (432) 756-2090
General Fax: (432) 756-2090
Advertising Phone: (432) 756-2090
Advertising Fax: (432) 756-2090
Editorial Phone: (432) 756-2090
Editorial Fax: (432) 756-2090
General/National Adv. E-mail: gwranger@crcom.net
Display Adv. E-mail: gwranger@crcom.net
Editorial e-mail: gwranger@crcom.net
Avg Paid Circ: 1400
Audit By: Sworn/Estimate/Non-Audited
Audit Date: 10.06.2019
Personnel: Bob Dillard (Pub.); Tate Dillard (Ed.)

GROESBECK JOURNAL

Street address 1: 115 N Ellis St
Street address city: Groesbeck
Street address state: TX
Zip/Postal code: 76642-1308
General Phone: (254) 729-5103
General Fax: (254) 729-8310
Advertising Phone: (254) 729-5103
Advertising Fax: (254) 729-8310
Editorial Phone: (254) 729-5103
Editorial Fax: (254) 729-8310
General/National Adv. E-mail: groesbeckads@groesbeckjournal.com
Display Adv. E-mail: groesbeckads@groesbeckjournal.com
Editorial e-mail: news@groesbeckjournal.com
Primary Website: groesbeckjournal.com
Year Established: 1892
Avg Paid Circ: 2550
Avg Free Circ: 50
Audit By: Sworn/Estimate/Non-Audited
Audit Date: 10.06.2019
Personnel: Kim Smith (General Manager)
Parent company (for newspapers): Palo Pinto Communications, LP

GROOM / MCLEAN / LEFORS

Street address 1: 84 BROADWAY AVE
Street address city: Groom
Street address state: TX
Zip/Postal code: 79039
General Phone: (806) 248-7333
General Fax: (806) 822-7333
Advertising Phone: (806) 248-7333
Advertising Fax: (806) 822-7333
Editorial Phone: (806) 248-7333
Editorial Fax: (806) 822-7333
General/National Adv. E-mail: thegroomnews@gmail.com
Display Adv. E-mail: thegroomnews@gmail.com
Editorial e-mail: thegroomnews@gmail.com
Year Established: 1925
Audit By: Sworn/Estimate/Non-Audited
Audit Date: 10.06.2019
Personnel: Donna Burton (Pub./Adv. Dir.); Bob Glass (Ed.); Janet Glass (Ed.)

GROVETON NEWS

Street address 1: 134 E 1st St
Street address city: Groveton
Street address state: TX
Zip/Postal code: 75845-4809
General Phone: (936) 642-1726

General Fax: (936) 642-1195
General/National Adv. E-mail: grovetonnews@gmail.com
Display Adv. E-mail: grovetonnews@gmail.com
Editorial e-mail: grovetonnews@gmail.com
Primary Website: grovetonnews.com
Year Established: 1905
Avg Paid Circ: 2000
Audit By: Sworn/Estimate/Non-Audited
Audit Date: 10.06.2019
Personnel: Alvin Holley (Pub./Adv. Dir.); Darlene Pyle (Composition/News Ed)
Parent company (for newspapers): Polk County Publishing Co.

HALE CENTER AMERICAN

Street address 1: 616 S Main St
Street address city: Hale Center
Street address state: TX
Zip/Postal code: 79041-9586
General Phone: (806) 285-7766
General Fax: (866) 641-2816
Advertising Phone: (806) 285-7766
Advertising Fax: (866) 641-2816
Editorial Phone: (806) 285-7766
Editorial Fax: (866) 641-2816
General/National Adv. E-mail: halecenterpaper@hotmail.com
Display Adv. E-mail: halecenterpaper@hotmail.com
Editorial e-mail: halecenterpaper@hotmail.com
Primary Website: southplainsplus.com
Year Established: 1922
Avg Paid Circ: 300
Audit By: Sworn/Estimate/Non-Audited
Audit Date: 10.06.2019
Personnel: Phillip Hamilton (Pub./Ed.); Ursula Hamilton (Adv. Dir.)
Parent company (for newspapers): Triple S Media

HALL COUNTY HERALD

Street address 1: 617 W Main St
Street address city: Memphis
Street address state: TX
Zip/Postal code: 79245-3303
General Phone: (806) 259-2441
General Fax: (806) 259-2798
Advertising Phone: (806) 259-2441
Advertising Fax: (806) 259-2798
Editorial Phone: (806) 259-2441
Editorial Fax: (806) 259-2798
General/National Adv. E-mail: hallcountyherald@yahoo.com
Display Adv. E-mail: hallcountyherald@yahoo.com
Editorial e-mail: editor@myhallcounty.com
Primary Website: hallcountyherald.com
Year Established: 1890
Avg Paid Circ: 2000
Avg Free Circ: 65
Audit By: Sworn/Estimate/Non-Audited
Audit Date: 10.06.2019
Personnel: Christopher Blackburn (Pub.); Ryan Mills (Ed.); Rebekah Dietrich (Adv. Dir.)

HALLETTSVILLE TRIBUNE-HERALD

Street address 1: 108 S Texana St
Street address city: Hallettsville
Street address state: TX
Zip/Postal code: 77964-2847
General Phone: (361) 798-2481
General Fax: (361) 798-9902
Advertising Phone: (361) 798-2481
Advertising Fax: (361) 798-9902
Editorial Phone: (361) 798-2481
Editorial Fax: (361) 798-9902
General/National Adv. E-mail: tribuneherald@sbcglobal.net
Display Adv. E-mail: tribuneads@sbcglobal.net
Editorial e-mail: tribuneherald@sbcglobal.net
Year Established: 1875
Avg Paid Circ: 2800
Audit By: Sworn/Estimate/Non-Audited
Audit Date: 10.06.2019
Personnel: L.M. Preuss III (Pub.); Kristie Bludau (Adv. Dir.)

HAMILTON HERALD-NEWS

Street address 1: 112 E Main St
Street address city: Hamilton
Street address state: TX
Zip/Postal code: 76531-1954
General Phone: (254) 386-3145
General Fax: (254) 386-3001
Advertising Phone: (254) 386-3145
Advertising Fax: (254) 386-3001
Editorial Phone: (254) 386-3145
Editorial Fax: (254) 386-3001
General/National Adv. E-mail: lthompson@thehamiltonherald-news.com
Display Adv. E-mail: classifieds@thehamiltonherald-news.com
Editorial e-mail: kmiller@thehamiltonherald-news.com
Primary Website: theHamiltonHerald-News.com
Year Established: 1875
Avg Paid Circ: 3200
Audit By: Sworn/Estimate/Non-Audited
Audit Date: 10.06.2019
Personnel: Kenneth Miller (Pub./Ed./Adv. Dir.)

HAMLIN HERALD

Street address 1: 350 S Central Ave
Street address city: Hamlin
Street address state: TX
Zip/Postal code: 79520-4832
General Phone: (325) 576-3606
General Fax: (325) 576-3606
General/National Adv. E-mail: pipernews@sbcglobal.net
Display Adv. E-mail: pipernews@sbcglobal.net
Editorial e-mail: pipernews@sbcglobal.net
Year Established: 1905
Avg Paid Circ: 1200
Audit By: Sworn/Estimate/Non-Audited
Audit Date: 10.06.2019
Personnel: Rudy Martinez (Owner)

HART BEAT

Street address 1: 407 Broadway
Street address city: Hart
Street address state: TX
Zip/Postal code: 79043
General Phone: (806) 938-2640
General Fax: (806) 938-2216
Advertising Phone: (806) 938-2640
Advertising Fax: (806) 938-2216
Editorial Phone: (806) 938-2640
Editorial Fax: (806) 938-2216
General/National Adv. E-mail: hbeat@amaonline.com
Display Adv. E-mail: hbeat@amaonline.com
Editorial e-mail: hbeat@amaonline.com
Year Established: 1962
Avg Paid Circ: 342
Avg Free Circ: 40
Audit By: Sworn/Estimate/Non-Audited
Audit Date: 10.06.2019
Personnel: Neoma Wall Williams (Pub./Ed./Adv. Dir.)

HAYS FREE PRESS

Street address 1: 113 W Center St
Street address city: Kyle
Street address state: TX
Zip/Postal code: 78640-9450
General Phone: (512) 268-7862
General Fax: (512) 268-0262
General/National Adv. E-mail: tracy@haysfreepress.com
Display Adv. E-mail: david@haysfreepress.com
Editorial e-mail: news@haysfreepress.com
Primary Website: haysfreepress.com
Mthly Avg Unique Visitors: 35000
Year Established: 1903
Avg Paid Circ: 3205
Avg Free Circ: 454
Audit By: Sworn/Estimate/Non-Audited
Audit Date: 10.06.2019
Personnel: Cyndy Slovak-Barton (Pub.); Moses Leos III (Ed.); Connie Brewer (Bus. Mgr.); Tracy Mack (Adv. Mgr.); Suzanne Hallam (Circ. Mgr.); David White (Prodn. Mgr.)
Parent company (for newspapers): Barton Publications, Inc.

HEBBRONVILLE VIEW

Street address 1: 212 E Galbraith St
Street address city: Hebbronville
Street address state: TX
Zip/Postal code: 78361-3404
General Phone: (361) 527-4272
General Fax: (361) 527-5271
Advertising Phone: (361) 527-4272
Advertising Fax: (361) 527-5271
Editorial Phone: (361) 527-4272
Editorial Fax: (361) 527-5271
General/National Adv. E-mail: hebview@gmail.com
Display Adv. E-mail: hebview@gmail.com
Editorial e-mail: hebview@gmail.com
Year Established: 1985
Avg Paid Circ: 1400
Audit By: Sworn/Estimate/Non-Audited
Audit Date: 10.06.2019
Personnel: Carlos Vela (Pub./Ed.); Vanessa Saenz (Adv. Dir.)

HICO NEWS REVIEW

Street address 1: 110 E Second St
Street address city: Hico
Street address state: TX
Zip/Postal code: 76457-6433
General Phone: (254) 796-4325
General Fax: (254) 796-2548
Advertising Phone: (254) 796-4325
Advertising Fax: (254) 796-2548
Editorial Phone: (254) 796-4325
Editorial Fax: (254) 796-2548
General/National Adv. E-mail: hiconews@gmail.com
Display Adv. E-mail: hiconews@gmail.com
Editorial e-mail: hiconews@gmail.com
Primary Website: thehiconewsreview.com
Year Established: 1895
Avg Paid Circ: 1550
Audit By: Sworn/Estimate/Non-Audited
Audit Date: 10.06.2019
Personnel: Jerry McAdams (Pub.); Traci Till (Managing Editor, Production Coordinator)

HIGHLANDS STAR / CROSBY COURIER

Street address 1: 5906 Star Ln
Street address city: Houston
Street address state: TX
Zip/Postal code: 77057-7118
General Phone: (281) 328-9605
General Fax: (713) 977-1188
Advertising Phone: (281) 328-9605
Advertising Fax: (713) 977-1188
Editorial Phone: (281) 328-9605
Editorial Fax: (713) 977-1188
General/National Adv. E-mail: grafikstar@aol.com
Display Adv. E-mail: grafikstar@aol.com
Editorial e-mail: grafikstar@aol.com
Primary Website: starcouriernews.com
Year Established: 1955
Avg Paid Circ: 4400
Avg Free Circ: 3400
Audit By: Sworn/Estimate/Non-Audited
Audit Date: 10.06.2019
Personnel: Gilbert Hoffman (Pub./Ed.); Lewis Spearman (Adv. Dir.)
Parent company (for newspapers): Grafikpress Corp.

HILL COUNTRY COMMUNITY JOURNAL

Street address 1: 303 Earl Garrett St
Street address city: Kerrville
Street address state: TX
Zip/Postal code: 78028-4529
General Phone: (830) 257-2828
General Fax: (830) 896-9444
Advertising Phone: (830) 257-2828
Advertising Fax: (830) 896-9444
Editorial Phone: (830) 257-2828
Editorial Fax: (830) 896-9444
General/National Adv. E-mail: journal@ktc.com
Display Adv. E-mail: journal@ktc.com
Editorial e-mail: journal@ktc.com
Primary Website: hccommunityjournal.com
Year Established: 2005
Audit By: Sworn/Estimate/Non-Audited
Audit Date: 10.06.2019
Personnel: Tammy Prout (Pub./Ed.); Linda Wise (Adv. Dir.)

HILL COUNTRY NEWS

Street address 1: 715 Discovery Blvd
Street address 2: Ste 304
Street address city: Cedar Park
Street address state: TX
Zip/Postal code: 78613-2289
General Phone: (512) 259-4449
General Fax: (512) 259-8889
General/National Adv. E-mail: publisher@hillcountrynews.com
Display Adv. E-mail: classifieds@hillcountrynews.com
Editorial e-mail: news@hillcountrynews.com
Primary Website: hillcountrynews.com
Mthly Avg Views: 546019
Mthly Avg Unique Visitors: 201046
Year Established: 1968
Avg Paid Circ: 988
Avg Free Circ: 15910
Audit By: Sworn/Estimate/Non-Audited
Audit Date: 10.06.2019
Personnel: Scott Coleman (Pub.); Shelly Stamport (Classifieds); Roger Munford (Adv.); Nick Brothers (Managing Editor); Zach Smith (Sports Editor)
Parent company (for newspapers): Fenice Community Media

HILLSBORO REPORTER

Street address 1: 335 Country Club Rd
Street address city: Hillsboro
Street address state: TX
Zip/Postal code: 76645-2318
General Phone: (254) 582-3431
General Fax: (254) 582-3800
Advertising Phone: (254) 582-3431
Advertising Fax: (254) 582-3800
Editorial Phone: (254) 582-3431
Editorial Fax: (254) 582-3800
General/National Adv. E-mail: ads@hillsbororeporter.com
Display Adv. E-mail: ads@hillsbororeporter.com
Classified Adv. e-mail: ads@hillsbororeporter.com
Primary Website: www.hillsbororeporter.com
Year Established: 1963
Avg Paid Circ: 4250
Audit By: Sworn/Estimate/Non-Audited
Audit Date: 10.08.2021
Personnel: Roger Galle (Pub./Adv. Dir.); Rick Bailey (Ed.)

HOMETOWN PRESS

Street address 1: 336 Broadway
Street address city: Winnie
Street address state: TX
Zip/Postal code: 77665-7829
General Phone: (409) 296-9988
General Fax: (409) 296-9987
Advertising Phone: (409) 296-9988
Advertising Fax: (409) 296-9987
Editorial Phone: (409) 296-9988
Editorial Fax: (409) 296-9987
General/National Adv. E-mail: htpress99@windstream.net
Display Adv. E-mail: htpress99@windstream.net
Editorial e-mail: htpress99@windstream.net
Year Established: 1991
Avg Paid Circ: 2000
Audit By: Sworn/Estimate/Non-Audited
Audit Date: 10.06.2019
Personnel: Scott Reese Willey (Pub./Ed.); Crystal Estes (Adv. Mgr.); Jennifer Brown (Gen. Mgr.)

HONDO ANVIL HERALD

Street address 1: 1601 Avenue K
Street address city: Hondo
Street address state: TX
Zip/Postal code: 78861-1838
General Phone: (830) 426-3346
General Fax: (830) 426-3348
General/National Adv. E-mail: anvil1@hondo.net
Display Adv. E-mail: anvil2@hondo.net
Editorial e-mail: anvil4@hondo.net
Primary Website: hondoanvilherald.com
Year Established: 1886
Avg Paid Circ: 4521
Avg Free Circ: 10
Audit By: Sworn/Estimate/Non-Audited
Audit Date: 10.06.2019
Personnel: Jeff Berger (Pub./Ed.); Lois Davis (Adv. Mgr.)

HOOD COUNTY NEWS

Street address 1: 1501 S Morgan St
Street address city: Granbury

Street address state: TX
Zip/Postal code: 76048-2791
General Phone: (817) 573-7066
General Fax: (817) 279-8371
Advertising Phone: (817) 573-7066 ext. 272
Advertising Fax: (817) 279-8371
Editorial Phone: (817) 573-7066 ext. 245
Editorial Fax: (817) 279-8371
General/National Adv. E-mail: advertising@hcnews.com
Display Adv. E-mail: classads@hcnews.com
Editorial e-mail: editor@hcnews.com
Primary Website: hcnews.com
Year Established: 1886
Avg Paid Circ: 8959
Audit By: Sworn/Estimate/Non-Audited
Audit Date: 10.06.2019
Personnel: Jerry Tidwell (Pub.); Roger Enlow (Ed.); Rick Craig (Adv. Dir.)

HOUSTON BUSINESS JOURNAL

Street address 1: 5444 Westheimer Rd
Street address 2: Ste 1700
Street address city: Houston
Street address state: TX
Zip/Postal code: 77056-5349
General Phone: (713) 688-8811
General Fax: (713) 963-0482
Advertising Phone: (713) 688-8811
Advertising Fax: (713) 963-0482
Editorial Phone: (713) 688-8811
Editorial Fax: (713) 963-0482
General/National Adv. E-mail: jbeddow@bizjournals.com
Display Adv. E-mail: jbeddow@bizjournals.com
Editorial e-mail: houston@bizjournals.com
Primary Website: bizjournals.com/houston
Mthly Avg Views: 1300000
Mthly Avg Unique Visitors: 300000
Year Established: 1971
Avg Paid Circ: 17000
Avg Free Circ: 3500
Audit By: Sworn/Estimate/Non-Audited
Audit Date: 10.06.2019
Personnel: John Beddow (Pub.); B. Candace Beeke (Ed.); Nancy Brown (Adv. Dir.)

HOUSTON COUNTY COURIER

Street address 1: 102 S 7th St
Street address city: Crockett
Street address state: TX
Zip/Postal code: 75835-2146
General Phone: (936) 544-2238
General Fax: (936) 544-4088
Advertising Phone: (936) 544-2238
Advertising Fax: (936) 544-4088
Editorial Phone: (936) 544-2238
Editorial Fax: (936) 544-4088
General/National Adv. E-mail: lreynolds@houstoncountycourier.com
Display Adv. E-mail: joycel@houstoncountycourier.com
Editorial e-mail: news@houstoncountycourier.com
Primary Website: houstoncountycourier.com
Year Established: 1890
Avg Paid Circ: 5763
Audit By: Sworn/Estimate/Non-Audited
Audit Date: 10.06.2019
Personnel: Alvin Holley (Owner); Larry Reynolds (Pub.); Lynda Jones (Ed.); Jeannine Rhone (Adv. Dir./Gen. Mgr.)
Parent company (for newspapers): Polk County Publishing Co.

HOUSTON FORWARD TIMES

Street address 1: 4411 Almeda Rd
Street address city: Houston
Street address state: TX
Zip/Postal code: 77004-4999
General Phone: (713) 526-4727
General Fax: (713) 526-3170
Advertising Phone: (713) 526-4727
Advertising Fax: (713) 526-3170
Editorial Phone: (713) 526-4727
Editorial Fax: (713) 526-3170
General/National Adv. E-mail: forwardtimes@forwardtimes.com
Display Adv. E-mail: forwardtimes@forwardtimes.com
Editorial e-mail: forwardtimes@forwardtimes.com
Primary Website: forwardtimes.com
Year Established: 1960
Avg Paid Circ: 35089
Audit By: Sworn/Estimate/Non-Audited
Audit Date: 10.06.2019
Personnel: Karen Carter Richards (Pub./Ed.); Henrietta Wilson (Adv. Dir.)
Parent company (for newspapers): Houston Forward Times Publishing Co.

HUBBARD CITY NEWS

Street address 1: 205 NW 6th St
Street address city: Hubbard
Street address state: TX
Zip/Postal code: 76648-2016
General Phone: (254) 576-2978
General Fax: (254) 576-5076
Advertising Phone: (254) 576-2978
Advertising Fax: (254) 576-5076
Editorial Phone: (254) 576-2978
Editorial Fax: (254) 576-5076
General/National Adv. E-mail: bminzenews@hillsboro.net
Display Adv. E-mail: bminzenews@hillsboro.net
Editorial e-mail: bminzenews@hillsboro.net
Year Established: 1881
Avg Paid Circ: 1050
Audit By: Sworn/Estimate/Non-Audited
Audit Date: 10.06.2019
Personnel: Barbara Minze (Pub./Ed./Adv. Dir.)

HUDSPETH COUNTY HERALD

Street address 1: 6560 fm 192
Street address city: Fort Hancock
Street address state: TX
Zip/Postal code: 79839
General Phone: (915) 964-2426
Advertising Phone: (915) 964-2426
Editorial Phone: (915) 964-2426
General/National Adv. E-mail: hcherald@dellcity.com
Display Adv. E-mail: hcherald@dellcity.com
Editorial e-mail: hcherald@dellcity.com
Year Established: 1956
Avg Paid Circ: 350
Audit By: Sworn/Estimate/Non-Audited
Audit Date: 10.08.2022
Personnel: James Lynch (Pub.); Guadalupe Kelly (Editor); Shannon Stewart (Editor); Shannon Martin-Stewart (Ed)

HUMBLE OBSERVER

Street address 1: 100 Avenue A
Street address 2: # B
Street address city: Conroe
Street address state: TX
Zip/Postal code: 77301-2946
General Phone: (281) 378-1060
General Fax: (281) 446-6901
Advertising Phone: (281) 378-1071
Advertising Fax: (281) 446-6901
Editorial Phone: (281) 378-1064
Editorial Fax: (281) 446-6901
General/National Adv. E-mail: cturner@hcnonline.com
Display Adv. E-mail: cturner@hcnonline.com
Editorial e-mail: jsummer@hcnonline.com
Primary Website: yourhumblenews.com
Year Established: 1975
Avg Paid Circ: 0
Avg Free Circ: 11977
Audit By: Sworn/Estimate/Non-Audited
Audit Date: 10.06.2019
Personnel: Brenda Miller-Fergerson (Pub.); Corey Turner (Gen. Sales Mgr.); Melecio C. Franco (Ed.); Jason Joseph (Pub.); Charles Lee (Adv. Mgr); Rick Flores (Circ. Mgr); Angela Hicks (Prod. Mgr)
Parent company (for newspapers): Hearst Communications, Inc.; Times Media Group

IDALOU BEACON

Street address 1: 207 Main St
Street address city: Idalou
Street address state: TX
Zip/Postal code: 79329-9127
General Phone: (806) 892-2233
General Fax: (806) 892-2233
General/National Adv. E-mail: beacon@windstream.net
Display Adv. E-mail: beacon@windstream.net
Editorial e-mail: beacon@windstream.net
Year Established: 1955
Avg Paid Circ: 800
Audit By: Sworn/Estimate/Non-Audited
Audit Date: 10.06.2019
Personnel: Jona Janet (Pub./Ed./Adv. Dir.)

IOWA PARK LEADER

Street address 1: 112 W Cash St
Street address city: Iowa Park
Street address state: TX
Zip/Postal code: 76367-2824
General Phone: (940) 592-4431
General Fax: (940) 592-4431
Advertising Phone: (940) 592-4431
Advertising Fax: (940) 592-4431
Editorial Phone: (940) 592-4431
Editorial Fax: (940) 592-4431
General/National Adv. E-mail: kcollins@iowaparkleader.com
Display Adv. E-mail: kcollins@iowaparkleader.com
Editorial e-mail: dhamilton@iowaparkleader.com
Primary Website: iowaparkleader.com
Year Established: 1969
Avg Paid Circ: 2700
Audit By: Sworn/Estimate/Non-Audited
Audit Date: 10.06.2019
Personnel: Dolores Hamilton (Ed./Pub.); Kevin Hamilton (Sports Ed.); Kari Collins (Adv. Mgr.); Sherrie Williams (reporter/photographer)

JACKSBORO HERALD-GAZETTE

Street address 1: 212 N Church Street
Street address city: Jacksboro
Street address state: TX
Zip/Postal code: 76458-1800
General Phone: (940) 567-2616
Advertising Phone: (940) 567-2616
Editorial Phone: (940) 567-2616
General/National Adv. E-mail: kbailey@grahamleader.com
Display Adv. E-mail: ads@jacksboronewspapers.com
Classified Adv. e-mail: classified@grahamleader.com
Editorial e-mail: editor@jacksboronewspapers.com
Primary Website: www.jacksboronewspapers.com
Year Established: 1880
Avg Paid Circ: 1000
Avg Free Circ: 11
Audit By: Sworn/Estimate/Non-Audited
Audit Date: 07.09.2022
Personnel: Brian Smith (Staff Writer); Mary Jo Watson (Advertising Representative); Kylie Bailey (Publisher/Creative Director); Kylie Bailey (Editor)
Parent company (for newspapers): Palo Pinto Communications, LP

JACKSON COUNTY HERALD-TRIBUNE

Street address 1: 306 N Wells St
Street address city: Edna
Street address state: TX
Zip/Postal code: 77957-2729
General Phone: (361) 782-3547
General Fax: (361) 782-6002
Advertising Phone: (361) 782-3547
Advertising Fax: (361) 782-6002
Editorial Phone: (361) 782-3547
Editorial Fax: (361) 782-6002
General/National Adv. E-mail: advertising@jacksonconews.com
Display Adv. E-mail: Sales@jacksonconews.com
Editorial e-mail: news@jacksonconews.com
Primary Website: jacksonconews.com
Year Established: 1906
Avg Paid Circ: 2700
Avg Free Circ: 410
Audit By: Sworn/Estimate/Non-Audited
Audit Date: 10.06.2019
Personnel: Chris Lundstrom (Publisher); Chelsea Slusher (Adv. Dir.)
Parent company (for newspapers): Moser community Media

JACKSONVILLE DAILY PROGRESS

Street address 1: 525 E Commerce St
Street address city: Jacksonville
Street address state: TX
Zip/Postal code: 75766-4909
General Phone: (903) 586-2236
General Fax: (903) 586-0987
Advertising Phone: (903) 586-2236
Advertising Fax: (903) 586-0987
Editorial Phone: (903) 586-2236
Editorial Fax: (903) 586-0987
General/National Adv. E-mail: publisher@jacksonvilleprogress.com
Display Adv. E-mail: publisher@jacksonvilleprogress.com
Classified Adv. e-mail: publisher@jacksonvilleprogress.com
Editorial e-mail: editor@jacksonvilleprogress.com
Primary Website: jacksonvilleprogress.com
Year Established: 1910
Avg Paid Circ: 3000
Sun. Circulation Paid: 3900
Audit By: Sworn/Estimate/Non-Audited
Audit Date: 10.06.2019
Personnel: Jay Neal (Sports Ed.); Lange Svehlak (Pub.); Sharon Claxton (Adv. Asst.); April Barbe (Ed.)
Parent company (for newspapers): CNHI, LLC; CNHI, LLC

JASPER NEWSBOY

Street address 1: 702 S Wheeler St
Street address city: Jasper
Street address state: TX
Zip/Postal code: 75951-4544
General Phone: (409) 384-3441
General Fax: (409) 384-8803
Advertising Phone: (409) 384-3441
Advertising Fax: (409) 384-8803
Editorial Phone: (409) 384-3441
Editorial Fax: (409) 384-8803
General/National Adv. E-mail: plinares@hearstnp.com
Display Adv. E-mail: jhidalgo@hearstnp.com
Editorial e-mail: tkelly@hearstnp.com
Primary Website: beaumontenterprise.com
Year Established: 1865
Avg Paid Circ: 6100
Audit By: Sworn/Estimate/Non-Audited
Audit Date: 10.06.2019
Personnel: Mark Adkins (Pub.); Timothy M. Kelly (Ed.); Sharon Friedes (Adv. Dir.)

JEFF DAVIS COUNTY MT. DISPATCH

Street address 1: 100 Court Ave
Street address city: Fort Davis
Street address state: TX
Zip/Postal code: 79734
General Phone: (432) 426-3077
General Fax: (432) 426-3077
Advertising Phone: (432) 426-3077
Advertising Fax: (432) 426-3077
Editorial Phone: (432) 426-3077
Editorial Fax: (432) 426-3077
General/National Adv. E-mail: dispatch@mztv.net
Display Adv. E-mail: dispatch@mztv.net
Editorial e-mail: dispatch@mztv.net
Primary Website: jdcmountaindispatch.com
Year Established: 1983
Avg Paid Circ: 1500
Audit By: Sworn/Estimate/Non-Audited
Audit Date: 10.06.2019
Personnel: Christi Dillard (Business Manager); Bob Dillard (Ed.); Kristi Huffman (Adv. Dir.)

JEFFERSON JIMPLECUTE

Street address 1: 120 N Vale St
Street address city: Jefferson
Street address state: TX
Zip/Postal code: 75657-2256
General Phone: (903) 665-2462
General Fax: (903) 705-4326
Advertising Phone: (903)665-2462
Advertising Fax: (903)705-4326
Editorial Phone: (903)665-2462
Editorial Fax: (903)705-4326
General/National Adv. E-mail: ads@jimplecute.com
Display Adv. E-mail: ads@jimplecute.com
Editorial e-mail: editor@jimplecute.com
Primary Website: jimplecute1848.com
Year Established: 1848
Avg Paid Circ: 2000
Avg Free Circ: 75
Audit By: Sworn/Estimate/Non-Audited
Audit Date: 10.06.2019
Personnel: Bob Palmer (Pub.); Hugh Lewis (Gen. Mgr.); Sara Whitaker (Ed.)

Parent company (for newspapers): Red River Media

JEWETT MESSENGER

Street address 1: 224 North Main Street
Street address city: Jewett
Street address state: TX
Zip/Postal code: 75846-4612
General Phone: (903) 626-4296
General Fax: (903) 626-5248
Advertising Phone: (903) 626-4296
Advertising Fax: (903) 626-5248
Editorial Phone: (903) 626-4296
Editorial Fax: (903) 626-5248
General/National Adv. E-mail: messenger3100@sbcglobal.net
Display Adv. E-mail: messenger3100@sbcglobal.net
Editorial e-mail: messenger3100@sbcglobal.net
Primary Website: jewettmessengeronline.com
Year Established: 1885
Avg Paid Circ: 1500
Avg Free Circ: 24
Audit By: Sworn/Estimate/Non-Audited
Audit Date: 10.06.2019
Personnel: David Clute (Pub./Ed./Adv. Dir.)

JEWISH HERALD-VOICE

Street address 1: 3403 Audley St
Street address city: Houston
Street address state: TX
Zip/Postal code: 77098-1923
General Phone: (713) 630-0391
General Fax: (713) 630-0404
Advertising Phone: (713) 630-0391
Advertising Fax: (713) 630-0404
Editorial Phone: (713) 630-0391
Editorial Fax: (713) 630-0404
General/National Adv. E-mail: advertising@jhvonline.com
Display Adv. E-mail: classified@jhvonline.com
Editorial e-mail: editor@jhvonline.com
Primary Website: jhvonline.com
Year Established: 1908
Avg Paid Circ: 5000
Audit By: Sworn/Estimate/Non-Audited
Audit Date: 10.06.2019
Personnel: Jeanne Samuels (Pub./Ed.); Vicki Samuels (Adv. Dir.)

JIM HOGG COUNTY ENTERPRISE

Street address 1: 304 E Galbraith St
Street address city: Hebbronville
Street address state: TX
Zip/Postal code: 78361-3402
General Phone: (361) 527-3261
General Fax: (361) 527-4545
Advertising Phone: (361) 527-3261
Advertising Fax: (361) 527-4545
Editorial Phone: (361) 527-3261
Editorial Fax: (361) 527-4545
General/National Adv. E-mail: enterprise78361@aol.com
Display Adv. E-mail: enterprise78361@aol.com
Editorial e-mail: enterprise78361@aol.com
Year Established: 1926
Audit By: Sworn/Estimate/Non-Audited
Audit Date: 10.06.2019
Personnel: Tony Salinas (Pub.); Poncho Hernandez (Ed.); Maribel Guerrero (Adv. Dir.)

JOHNSON CITY RECORD-COURIER

Street address 1: 110 E Main St
Street address 2: Ste B
Street address city: Johnson City
Street address state: TX
Zip/Postal code: 78636-4239
General Phone: (830) 868-7181
General Fax: (830) 868-7182
Advertising Phone: (830) 868-7181
Advertising Fax: (830) 868-7182
Editorial Phone: (830) 868-7181
Editorial Fax: (830) 868-7182
General/National Adv. E-mail: jcrecordcourier@verizon.net
Display Adv. E-mail: jcrecordcourier@verizon.net
Editorial e-mail: jcrecordcourier@verizon.net
Primary Website: jcrecordcourier.com
Year Established: 1880
Avg Paid Circ: 1600
Avg Free Circ: 200
Audit By: Sworn/Estimate/Non-Audited
Audit Date: 10.06.2019
Personnel: Scott Wesner (Pub.); Emily Zbytovsky (Ed./Adv. Dir.)

KATY TIMES

Street address 1: PO Box 678
Street address city: Katy
Street address state: TX
Zip/Postal code: 77492-0678
General Phone: 281-391-3141
General/National Adv. E-mail: Publisher@katytimes.com
Display Adv. E-mail: Sales@katytimes.com
Classified Adv. e-mail: Bookkeeper@katytimes.com
Editorial e-mail: Publisher@katytimes.com
Primary Website: www katytimrs.com
Mthly Avg Unique Visitors: 36000
Year Established: 1912
Avg Paid Circ: 3000
Audit By: Sworn/Estimate/Non-Audited
Audit Date: 10/
Personnel: Susan Rovegno (Publisher); Terry Schaub (Pub.); Greg Densmore (Mgr. Ed.); Quincey Prickett (Circulation)
Parent company (for newspapers): Fenice Community Media; Hartman Newspapers LP

KELLY OBSERVER

Street address 1: 301 Avenue E
Street address city: San Antonio
Street address state: TX
Zip/Postal code: 78205-2006
General Phone: (210) 250-3711
General Fax: (210) 250-3715
Advertising Phone: (210) 250-2500
Advertising Fax: (210) 250-2565
Editorial Phone: (210) 250-3195
Editorial Fax: (210) 250-3105
General/National Adv. E-mail: communitysupport@express-news.net
Display Adv. E-mail: communitysupport@express-news.net
Editorial e-mail: editors@express-news.net
Primary Website: express-news.com
Avg Paid Circ: 10
Avg Free Circ: 6934
Audit By: Sworn/Estimate/Non-Audited
Audit Date: 10.06.2019
Personnel: Thomas A. Stephenson (Pres./Pub.); Fred Mergele (Vice Pres., Finance); Susan Ehrman (Vice Pres., HR); Charlotte Aaron (Vice Pres., Classified Adv.); Rebecca Named Chavez-Becker (Sales Dir.); Doug Bennight (Adv. Mgr., Automotive); Roxanne Beavers (Adv. Mgr., Telemktg./Classified); Pat Harvey (Adv. Mgr., Telemktg./Retail); Dean Aitken (Vice Pres., Mktg.); Patrick Magallanes (Vice Pres., Mktg.); Liz English (Target Mktg. Mgr.); Scott Frantzen (Circ. Sr. Vice Pres.); Paul Borrego (Circ. Dir., Admin.); Sammy Aburumuh (Dir., Metro Home Delivery); Robert Rivard (Ed.); Brett Thacker (Mng. Ed.); Terry Scott-Bertling (Asst. Mng. Ed., Features); Hallie Paul (Asst. Mng. Ed., Graphics/Design/Photo); Craig Thomason (Asst. Mng. Ed., News)

KILGORE NEWS HERALD

Street address 1: 610 E Main St
Street address city: Kilgore
Street address state: TX
Zip/Postal code: 75662-2612
General Phone: (903) 984-2593
General Fax: (903) 984-7462
Advertising Phone: (903) 984-2593
Advertising Fax: (903) 984-7462
Editorial Phone: (903) 984-2593
Editorial Fax: (903) 984-7462
General/National Adv. E-mail: bwoodall@kilgorenewsherald.com
Display Adv. E-mail: addirector@kilgorenewsherald.com
Classified Adv. e-mail: classifieds@kilgorenewsherald.com
Editorial e-mail: news1@kilgorenewsherald.com
Primary Website: kilgorenewsherald.com
Mthly Avg Views: 161000
Mthly Avg Unique Visitors: 60000
Year Established: 1935
Avg Paid Circ: 2770
Avg Free Circ: 1200
Sat. Circulation Paid: 2850
Audit By: Sworn/Estimate/Non-Audited
Audit Date: 10.06.2019
Personnel: Bill Woodall (Co-Pub./Ed.); Jessica Woodall (Co-Pub.); James Draper (News Ed.); Mitch Lucas (Sports Ed.); Charlotte Smith (Prod. Mgr.)
Parent company (for newspapers): Bluebonnet Publishing, LLC

KINGSVILLE RECORD & BISHOP NEWS

Street address 1: 1831 W Santa Gertrudis St
Street address city: Kingsville
Street address state: TX
Zip/Postal code: 78363-3447
General Phone: (361) 592-4304
General Fax: (361) 592-1015
Advertising Phone: (361) 592-4304
Advertising Fax: (361) 592-1015
Editorial Phone: (361) 592-4304
Editorial Fax: (361) 592-1015
General/National Adv. E-mail: cjmaher@king-ranch.com
Display Adv. E-mail: cjmaher@king-ranch.com
Editorial e-mail: cjmaher@king-ranch.com
Primary Website: KingsvilleRecord.com
Year Established: 1906
Audit By: Sworn/Estimate/Non-Audited
Audit Date: 10.06.2019
Personnel: Christopher Maher (Pub./Ed.); Tracy Pena (Ad. Director)

KINGWOOD OBSERVER

Street address 1: 907 E Main St.
Street address 2: # B
Street address city: Humble
Street address state: TX
Zip/Postal code: 77338
General Phone: (281) 446-4438
Advertising Phone: (281) 446-1071
Editorial Phone: (281) 446-4438
General/National Adv. E-mail: cturner@hcnonline.com
Display Adv. E-mail: cturner@hcnonline.com
Editorial e-mail: jsummer@hcnonline.com
Primary Website: yourkingwoodnews.com
Year Established: 1977
Avg Paid Circ: 0
Avg Free Circ: 20580
Audit By: Sworn/Estimate/Non-Audited
Audit Date: 10.06.2019
Personnel: Ryan Hickman (Ed.); Trish Olivia (Adv. Mgr.)
Parent company (for newspapers): Hearst Communications, Inc.; Times Media Group

KIRBYVILLE BANNER

Street address 1: 104 N Kellie Ave
Street address city: Kirbyville
Street address state: TX
Zip/Postal code: 75956-1824
General Phone: (409) 423-2696
General Fax: (409) 423-4793
Advertising Phone: (409) 423-2696
Advertising Fax: (409) 423-4793
Editorial Phone: (409) 423-2696
Editorial Fax: (409) 423-4793
General/National Adv. E-mail: kbannerads@sbcglobal.net
Display Adv. E-mail: kbannerads@sbcglobal.net
Editorial e-mail: kbanner@sbcglobal.net
Year Established: 1906
Avg Paid Circ: 1770
Avg Free Circ: 9
Audit By: Sworn/Estimate/Non-Audited
Audit Date: 10.06.2019
Personnel: Danny Reneau (Pub); Karen Kilmer (Adv. Dir.); Sallie Solly (Reporter)

KNOX COUNTY NEWS-COURIER

Street address 1: 121 East B St
Street address city: Munday
Street address state: TX
Zip/Postal code: 76371
General Phone: (940) 422-5350
General Fax: (866) 863-1118
Advertising Phone: (940) 422-5350
Advertising Fax: (866) 400-1083
Editorial Phone: (940) 422-5350
Editorial Fax: (866) 863-1118
General/National Adv. E-mail: kcnewscourier@gmail.com
Display Adv. E-mail: kcnewscourier@gmail.com
Editorial e-mail: kcnewscourier@gmail.com
Primary Website: kcnewscourier.com
Year Established: 2011
Avg Paid Circ: 934
Audit By: Sworn/Estimate/Non-Audited
Audit Date: 10.06.2019
Personnel: Christopher Blackburn (Pub.)
Parent company (for newspapers): Blackburn Media Group

LA FERIA NEWS

Street address 1: 102 S Main St
Street address city: La Feria
Street address state: TX
Zip/Postal code: 78559-5005
General Phone: (956) 797-9920
General Fax: (956) 797-9921
Advertising Phone: (956) 797-9920
Advertising Fax: (956) 797-9921
Editorial Phone: (956) 797-9920
Editorial Fax: (956) 797-9921
General/National Adv. E-mail: drwpops@aol.com
Display Adv. E-mail: laferianews2@aol.com
Editorial e-mail: laferianews@aol.com
Primary Website: laferianews.net
Year Established: 1923
Avg Paid Circ: 5000
Audit By: Sworn/Estimate/Non-Audited
Audit Date: 10.06.2019
Personnel: Don Wright (Pub./Adv. Dir.); Mary Beth Wright (Ed.)

LAKE AREA LEADER

Street address 1: 1316 S 3rd St
Street address 2: Ste 108
Street address city: Mabank
Street address state: TX
Zip/Postal code: 75147-7680
General Phone: (903) 887-4511
General Fax: (903) 887-4510
Advertising Phone: (903) 887-4511
Advertising Fax: (903) 887-4510
Editorial Phone: (903) 887-4511
Editorial Fax: (903) 887-4510
General/National Adv. E-mail: advertising@themonitor.net
Display Adv. E-mail: advertising@themonitor.net
Editorial e-mail: publisher@themonitor.net
Primary Website: themonitor.net
Year Established: 1974
Avg Free Circ: 26000
Audit By: Sworn/Estimate/Non-Audited
Audit Date: 10.06.2019
Personnel: Susan Harrison (General Manager); Susan Harrison (Gen. Mgr.); Pearl Cantrell (Ed.)
Parent company (for newspapers): Van Zandt Newspapers LLC

LAKE CITIES SUN

Street address 1: 624 Krona Dr
Street address 2: Ste 170
Street address city: Plano
Street address state: TX
Zip/Postal code: 75074-8304
General Phone: (972) 398-4200
General Fax: (972) 398-4470
General/National Adv. E-mail: jdittrich@starlocalmedia.com
Display Adv. E-mail: jdittrich@starlocalmedia.com
Editorial e-mail: croark@starlocalmedia.com
Primary Website: starlocalmedia.com
Year Established: 1974
Avg Paid Circ: 163
Avg Free Circ: 5208
Audit By: CVC
Audit Date: 31.12.2018
Personnel: Scott Wright (Pub.); Chris Roark (Ed.); Melissa Rougeot (Circ. Mgr); Joani Dittrich (Adv. VP)
Parent company (for newspapers): S.A.W. Advisors, LLC; Star Community Newspapers

LAKE HOUSTON OBSERVER

Street address 1: 100 Avenue A
Street address city: Conroe
Street address state: TX

Zip/Postal code: 77301-2946
General Phone: (281) 378-1060
General Fax: (281) 446-6901
Advertising Phone: (281) 378-1071
Advertising Fax: (281) 446-6901
Editorial Phone: (281) 378-1064
Editorial Fax: (281) 446-6901
General/National Adv. E-mail: cturner@hcnonline.com
Display Adv. E-mail: cturner@hcnonline.com
Editorial e-mail: jsummer@hcnonline.com
Primary Website: yourlakehouston.com
Year Established: 1981
Avg Paid Circ: 0
Avg Free Circ: 7270
Audit By: Sworn/Estimate/Non-Audited
Audit Date: 10.06.2019
Personnel: Brenda Miller-Fergerson (Pub.); Corey Turner (Gen. Sales Mgr.); Angela Hicks (Prod. Mgr); Jason Joseph (Pub.); Charles Lee (Adv. Mgr); Rick Flores (Circ. Mgr)
Parent company (for newspapers): Hearst Communications, Inc.; Times Media Group

LAKE TRAVIS VIEW

Street address 1: 305 S Congress Ave
Street address city: Austin
Street address state: TX
Zip/Postal code: 78704-1200
General Phone: (512) 263-1100
General Fax: (512) 263-3583
Advertising Phone: (512) 263-1100
Advertising Fax: (512) 263-3583
Editorial Phone: (512) 263-1100
Editorial Fax: (512) 263-3583
General/National Adv. E-mail: news@statesman.com
Display Adv. E-mail: news@statesman.com
Editorial e-mail: news@statesman.com
Primary Website: statesman.com
Year Established: 1985
Avg Paid Circ: 438
Avg Free Circ: 1476
Audit By: AAM
Audit Date: 31.12.2016
Personnel: Jay Plotkin (Pub.); Ed Allen (Ed.); Ken Brown (Adv. Dir.); Danny Esposito (Adv. Mgr.); Max Thompson (Sports Ed.); Devin Monk
Parent company (for newspapers): Cox Media Group

LAMB COUNTY LEADER-NEWS

Street address 1: 313 W 4th St
Street address city: Littlefield
Street address state: TX
Zip/Postal code: 79339-3313
General Phone: (806) 385-4481
General Fax: (806) 385-4640
General/National Adv. E-mail: ads@lambcountyleadernews.com
Display Adv. E-mail: classifieds@lambcountyleadernews.com
Editorial e-mail: news@lambcountyleadernews.com
Year Established: 1918
Audit By: Sworn/Estimate/Non-Audited
Audit Date: 10.06.2019
Personnel: Grata Reber (Adv. Dir.); Brett Wesner (Pub.); Melissa Silva (Classified Adv. Mgr./Circ. Mgr.)

LAMESA PRESS REPORTER

Street address 1: 523 N 1st St
Street address city: Lamesa
Street address state: TX
Zip/Postal code: 79331-5405
General Phone: (806) 872-2177
General Fax: (806) 872-2623
General/National Adv. E-mail: adsales@pressreporter.com
Display Adv. E-mail: classifieds@pressreporter.com
Editorial e-mail: editor@pressreporter.com
Primary Website: pressreporter.com
Year Established: 1905
Avg Paid Circ: 1970
Avg Free Circ: 83
Audit By: Sworn/Estimate/Non-Audited
Audit Date: 10.06.2019
Personnel: Russel Skiles (Pub.); Herrel Hallmark (Ed.); Heather Allen (Bookkeeper); Kelsey Odom (ad manager)

LAMPASAS DISPATCH RECORD

Street address 1: 416 S Live Oak St
Street address city: Lampasas
Street address state: TX
Zip/Postal code: 76550
General Phone: (512) 556-6262
General Fax: (512) 556-3278
Advertising Phone: (512) 556-6262
Advertising Fax: (512) 556-3278
Editorial Phone: (512) 556-6262
Editorial Fax: (512) 556-3278
General/National Adv. E-mail: news@lampasas.com
Display Adv. E-mail: teresa@lampasas.com
Classified Adv. e-mail: classads@lampasas.com
Editorial e-mail: news@lampasas.com
Primary Website: lampasasdispatchrecord.com
Year Established: 1955
Avg Paid Circ: 1975
Avg Free Circ: 13
Audit By: Sworn/Estimate/Non-Audited
Audit Date: 30.09.2021
Personnel: David Lowe (Publisher); Gail Lowe (Co-Pub.); Teresa Thornton (Adv. Dir.); Gail Lowe (co-publisher)
Parent company (for newspapers): Hill Country Publishing Co. Inc.

LEADER NEWS

Street address 1: 1105 Fiorella St
Street address city: Castroville
Street address state: TX
Zip/Postal code: 78009-4577
General Phone: (830) 931-9698
General Fax: (830) 931-3450
Advertising Phone: (830) 931-9698
Advertising Fax: (830) 931-3450
Editorial Phone: (830) 931-9698
Editorial Fax: (830) 931-3450
General/National Adv. E-mail: cornerstonenews@sbcglobal.net
Display Adv. E-mail: cornerstonenews@sbcglobal.net
Editorial e-mail: cornerstonenews@sbcglobal.net
Year Established: 1999
Avg Paid Circ: 2300
Audit By: Sworn/Estimate/Non-Audited
Audit Date: 10.06.2019
Personnel: Natalie Spencer (Adv. Dir.); James La Combe (Ed.); Frank Vasquez (Pub.); Jane Broyles (Circ. Mgr.)
Parent company (for newspapers): Burge Publishing Corp.

LEONARD GRAPHIC

Street address 1: 100 E Collin St
Street address 2: Ste 201
Street address city: Leonard
Street address state: TX
Zip/Postal code: 75452-2561
General Phone: (903) 587-2850
General Fax: (903) 587-0297
Advertising Phone: (903) 587-2853
Advertising Fax: (903) 587-0297
Editorial Phone: (903) 587-2850
Editorial Fax: (903) 587-0297
General/National Adv. E-mail: ava@theleonardgraphic.com
Display Adv. E-mail: ava@theleonardgraphic.com
Editorial e-mail: betsy@theleonardgraphic.com
Primary Website: theleonardgraphic.com
Year Established: 1890
Avg Paid Circ: 724
Audit By: Sworn/Estimate/Non-Audited
Audit Date: 10.06.2019
Personnel: Betsy Blevins (Pub./Ed.); Ava Barlow (Adv. Dir.)

LEVELLAND & HOCKLEY COUNTY NEWS-PRESS

Street address 1: 711 Austin St
Street address city: Levelland
Street address state: TX
Zip/Postal code: 79336-4523
General Phone: (806) 894-3121
General Fax: (806) 894-7957
Advertising Phone: (806) 894-3121
Advertising Fax: (806) 894-7957
Editorial Phone: (806) 894-3121
Editorial Fax: (806) 894-7957
General/National Adv. E-mail: levellandads@valornet.com
Display Adv. E-mail: levclassified@valornet.com
Classified Adv. e-mail: levclassified@valornet.com
Editorial e-mail: levellandnews@valornet.com
Primary Website: levellandnews.net
Year Established: 1928
Avg Paid Circ: 4000
Avg Free Circ: 50
Sun. Circulation Paid: 4300
Sun. Circulation Free: 50
Audit By: Sworn/Estimate/Non-Audited
Audit Date: 10.06.2019
Personnel: Stephen A. Henry (Pub.); Pat Henry (Pub.); Kati Moody (News Ed); Michelle Davis (Adv. Mgr.)
Parent company (for newspapers): Stephen & Pat Enterprises

LEWISVILLE LEADER

Street address 1: 624 Krona Dr
Street address 2: Ste 170
Street address city: Plano
Street address state: TX
Zip/Postal code: 75074-8304
General Phone: (972) 398-4200
General Fax: (972) 398-4470
General/National Adv. E-mail: jdittrich@starlocalmedia.com
Display Adv. E-mail: jdittrich@starlocalmedia.com
Editorial e-mail: swright@starlocalmedia.com
Primary Website: starlocalmedia.com
Avg Paid Circ: 207
Avg Free Circ: 11345
Audit By: CVC
Audit Date: 31.12.2018
Personnel: Scott Wright (Pub.); Melissa Rougeot (Circ. Mgr); Joani Dittrich (Adv. VP); Heather Goodwin (Reporter)
Parent company (for newspapers): S.A.W. Advisors, LLC; Star Community Newspapers

LEXINGTON LEADER

Street address 1: 612 Wheatley St
Street address city: Lexington
Street address state: TX
Zip/Postal code: 78947-9401
General Phone: (979) 773-3022
General Fax: (979) 773-4125
Advertising Phone: (979) 773-3022
Advertising Fax: (979) 773-4125
Editorial Phone: (979) 773-3022
Editorial Fax: (979) 773-4125
General/National Adv. E-mail: editor@lexingtonleader.com
Display Adv. E-mail: editor@lexingtonleader.com
Editorial e-mail: editor@lexingtonleader.com
Primary Website: lexingtonleader.com
Year Established: 1997
Avg Paid Circ: 1500
Audit By: Sworn/Estimate/Non-Audited
Audit Date: 10.06.2019
Personnel: Cindy Terrell (Ed.)

LINDSAY LETTER

Street address 1: 117 E Main St
Street address city: Lindsay
Street address state: TX
Zip/Postal code: 76250-2105
General Phone: (940) 668-8788
General Fax: (940) 668-6677
Advertising Phone: (940) 668-8788
Advertising Fax: (940) 668-6677
Editorial Phone: (940) 668-8788
Editorial Fax: (940) 668-6677
General/National Adv. E-mail: news@lindsayletter.net
Display Adv. E-mail: news@lindsayletter.net
Editorial e-mail: news@lindsayletter.net
Primary Website: lindsayletter.net
Year Established: 2007
Audit By: Sworn/Estimate/Non-Audited
Audit Date: 10.06.2019
Personnel: Joe Warren (Pub./Ed.); Karen Corley (Adv. Dir.)

LITTLE ELM JOURNAL

Street address 1: 624 Krona Dr
Street address 2: Ste 170
Street address city: Plano
Street address state: TX
Zip/Postal code: 75074-8304
General Phone: (972) 398-4200
General Fax: (972) 398-4470
General/National Adv. E-mail: jdittrich@starlocalmedia.com
Display Adv. E-mail: jdittrich@starlocalmedia.com
Editorial e-mail: swright@starlocalmedia.com
Primary Website: starlocalmedia.com
Mthly Avg Views: 546019
Mthly Avg Unique Visitors: 201046
Year Established: 1993
Avg Paid Circ: 110
Avg Free Circ: 5921
Audit By: CVC
Audit Date: 31.12.2018
Personnel: Melissa Rougeot (Circ. Mgr); Scott Wright (Pub.); Joani Dittrich (Adv. VP); Heather Goodwin (Reporter); Bryan Murphy (Sports Rep.)
Parent company (for newspapers): S.A.W. Advisors, LLC; Star Community Newspapers

LOCKHART POST-REGISTER

Street address 1: 111 S Church St
Street address city: Lockhart
Street address state: TX
Zip/Postal code: 78644-2641
General Phone: (512) 398-4886
General/National Adv. E-mail: Patty@post-register.com
Display Adv. E-mail: News@post-register.com
Editorial e-mail: Editor@post-register.com
Primary Website: post-register.com
Year Established: 1872
Avg Paid Circ: 3086
Avg Free Circ: 177
Audit By: Sworn/Estimate/Non-Audited
Audit Date: 10.06.2019
Personnel: Dana Garrett (Pub.); Kathi Bliss (Mng. Ed.)

LONE STAR OUTDOOR NEWS

Street address 1: PO Box 551695
Street address city: Dallas
Street address state: TX
Zip/Postal code: 75355-1695
General Phone: (214) 361-2276
General Fax: (214) 501-0509
Advertising Phone: (214) 361-2276
Advertising Fax: (214) 501-0509
Editorial Phone: (214) 361-2276
Editorial Fax: (214) 501-0509
General/National Adv. E-mail: cnyhus@lonestaroutdoornews.com
Display Adv. E-mail: dsams@lonestaroutdoornews.com
Editorial e-mail: editor@lonestaroutdoornews.com
Primary Website: lsonews.com
Year Established: 2004
Avg Paid Circ: 5242
Avg Free Circ: 35519
Audit By: VAC
Audit Date: 31.12.2016
Personnel: David J. Sams (Founder/CEO); Craig Nyhus (Exec. Ed.); Conor Harrison (Mng. Ed.)

LYNN COUNTY NEWS

Street address 1: 1617 Main St
Street address city: Tahoka
Street address state: TX
Zip/Postal code: 79373
General Phone: (806) 561-4888
General Fax: (806) 561-6308
Advertising Phone: (806) 561-4888
Advertising Fax: (806) 561-6308
Editorial Phone: (806) 561-4888
Editorial Fax: (806) 561-6308
General/National Adv. E-mail: LCNpam@poka.com
Display Adv. E-mail: LCNpam@poka.com
Editorial e-mail: lynnconews@poka.com
Year Established: 1903
Avg Paid Circ: 1150
Avg Free Circ: 10
Audit By: Sworn/Estimate/Non-Audited
Audit Date: 10.06.2019
Personnel: Juanell Jones (Pub)

MADISONVILLE METEOR

Street address 1: 205 N Madison St
Street address city: Madisonville
Street address state: TX
Zip/Postal code: 77864-1509
General Phone: (936) 348-3505
General Fax: (936) 348-3338

General/National Adv. E-mail: classifieds@madisonvillemeteor.com
Display Adv. E-mail: classifieds@madisonvillemeteor.com
Editorial e-mail: editor@madisonvillemeteor.com
Primary Website: madisonvillemeteor.com
Year Established: 1894
Avg Paid Circ: 1197
Avg Free Circ: 37
Audit By: CVC
Audit Date: 12.12.2017
Personnel: Tony Farkas (Ed./Pub.); Tammy Farkas (Advertising Manager); Campbell Atkins (Sports writer); Kim McKee (Office Manager)
Parent company (for newspapers): Fenice Community Media

MAGNOLIA POTPOURRI

Street address 1: 100 Avenue A
Street address city: Conroe
Street address state: TX
Zip/Postal code: 77301-2946
General Phone: (281) 378-1080
General Fax: (281) 320-2005
Advertising Phone: (281) 378-1082
Advertising Fax: (281) 320-2005
Editorial Phone: (281) 378-1087
Editorial Fax: (281) 320-2005
General/National Adv. E-mail: rdavis@hcnonline.com
Display Adv. E-mail: srovegno@hcnonline.com
Editorial e-mail: rkent@hcnonline.com
Primary Website: thetomballpotpourri.com
Year Established: 1986
Avg Paid Circ: 0
Avg Free Circ: 13545
Audit By: Sworn/Estimate/Non-Audited
Audit Date: 10.06.2019
Personnel: Roy Kent (Ed.); Susan Rovegno (Sales Mgr.); Jason Joseph (Pub.); Charles Lee (Adv. Mgr); Rick Flores (Circ. Mgr); Tom Legg (Major Sr. Acct. Mgr.); Megan O'Sullivan (Mktg. Mgr.)
Parent company (for newspapers): Hearst Communications, Inc.; Times Media Group

MANSFIELD NEWS-MIRROR

Street address 1: PO Box 337
Street address city: Mansfield
Street address state: TX
Zip/Postal code: 76063-0337
General Phone: (817) 473-4451
General Fax: (817) 473-0730
Advertising Phone: (817) 987-6303
Advertising Fax: (817) 473-0730
Editorial Phone: (817) 473-4451
Editorial Fax: (817) 473-0730
General/National Adv. E-mail: kmordecai@star-telegram.com
Display Adv. E-mail: kmordecai@star-telegram.com
Editorial e-mail: arogers@mansfieldnewsmirror.com
Primary Website: star-telegram.com/mansfieldnewsmirror
Avg Free Circ: 32158
Audit By: Sworn/Estimate/Non-Audited
Audit Date: 10.06.2019
Personnel: Shelly Kofler (Op. Ed.); Steve Coffman (Exec. Ed.); Tom Johanningmeier (Mng. Ed.); Michael Currie (Mng. Ed.)
Parent company (for newspapers): The McClatchy Company

MARTIN COUNTY MESSENGER

Street address 1: 210 Saint Peter
Street address city: Stanton
Street address state: TX
Zip/Postal code: 79782
General Phone: (432) 756-2090
Advertising Phone: (432) 756-2090
Editorial Phone: (432) 756-2090
General/National Adv. E-mail: ncmessenger@crcom.net
Display Adv. E-mail: ncmessenger@crcom.net
Editorial e-mail: ncmessenger@crcom.net
Primary Website: martincountymessenger.com
Year Established: 1925
Avg Paid Circ: 1500
Audit By: Sworn/Estimate/Non-Audited
Audit Date: 10.06.2019

Personnel: Bob Dillard (Pub./Ed.); David Butler (Adv. Dir.)

MASON COUNTY NEWS

Street address 1: 122 S Live Oak
Street address city: Mason
Street address state: TX
Zip/Postal code: 76856
General Phone: (325) 347-5757
General Fax: (325) 347-5668
Advertising Phone: (325) 347-5757
Advertising Fax: (325) 347-5668
Editorial Phone: (325) 347-5757
Editorial Fax: (325) 347-5668
General/National Adv. E-mail: mcnads@hctc.net
Display Adv. E-mail: mcnads@hctc.net
Editorial e-mail: mcnnews@hctc.net
Primary Website: masoncountynews.com
Year Established: 1877
Avg Paid Circ: 2188
Audit By: Sworn/Estimate/Non-Audited
Audit Date: 10.06.2019
Personnel: Scott Wesner (Pub.); Gerry Gamel (Ed.); T.J. Schmidt (Adv. Dir.)

MCGREGOR MIRROR & CRAWFORD SUN

Street address 1: 311 S Main St
Street address city: Mc Gregor
Street address state: TX
Zip/Postal code: 76657-1608
General Phone: (254) 840-2091
General Fax: (254) 840-2097
General/National Adv. E-mail: bonnie@mcgregormirror.com
Display Adv. E-mail: bonnie@mcgregormirror.com
Editorial e-mail: charles@mcgregormirror.com
Primary Website: mcgregormirror.com
Year Established: 1892
Avg Paid Circ: 1700
Avg Free Circ: 7
Audit By: Sworn/Estimate/Non-Audited
Audit Date: 10.06.2019
Personnel: Bonnie Mullens (Co-Pub./Adv. Mgr.); Charles Mooney (Co-Pub./Ed.); Mynette Taylor (Circ. Mgr./Bus. Mgr.)

MCKINNEY COURIER GAZETTE

Street address 1: 624 Krona Dr
Street address 2: Ste 170
Street address city: Plano
Street address state: TX
Zip/Postal code: 75074-8304
General Phone: (972) 398-4200
General Fax: (972) 398-4470
General/National Adv. E-mail: jdittrich@starlocalmedia.com
Display Adv. E-mail: nsouders@starlocalmedia.com
Editorial e-mail: croark@starlocalmedia.com
Primary Website: starlocalmedia.com
Mthly Avg Views: 546019
Mthly Avg Unique Visitors: 201046
Year Established: 1991
Avg Paid Circ: 684
Avg Free Circ: 29451
Sun. Circulation Paid: 4938
Audit By: CVC
Audit Date: 14.12.2018
Personnel: Scott Wright (Pub.); Joani Dittrich (VP Adv.); Melissa Rougeot (Circ. Mgr); Liz McGathey (Ed. Dir.); Chris Roark (Ed.)
Parent company (for newspapers): S.A.W. Advisors, LLC; Star Community Newspapers

MEDICAL PATRIOT

Street address 1: 301 Avenue E
Street address city: San Antonio
Street address state: TX
Zip/Postal code: 78205-2006
General Phone: (210) 250-3711
General Fax: (210) 250-3715
Advertising Phone: (210) 250-2500
Advertising Fax: (210) 250-2565
Editorial Phone: (210) 250-3195
Editorial Fax: (210) 250-3105
General/National Adv. E-mail: communitysupport@express-news.net
Display Adv. E-mail: communitysupport@express-news.net
Editorial e-mail: editors@express-news.net
Primary Website: express-news.com
Avg Paid Circ: 10
Avg Free Circ: 4898
Audit By: Sworn/Estimate/Non-Audited
Audit Date: 10.06.2019
Personnel: Thomas A. Stephenson (Pres./Pub.); Fred Mergele (Vice Pres., Finance); Susan Ehrman (Vice Pres., HR); Charlotte Aaron (Vice Pres., Classified Adv.); Rebecca Named Chavez-Becker (Sales Dir.); Doug Bennight (Adv. Mgr., Automotive); Roxanne Beavers (Adv. Mgr., Telemktg./Classified); Pat Harvey (Adv. Mgr., Telemktg./Retail); Dean Aitken (Vice Pres., Mktg.); Patrick Magallanes (Vice Pres., Mktg.); Liz English (Target Mktg. Mgr.); Scott Frantzen (Circ. Sr. Vice Pres.); Paul Borrego (Circ. Dir., Admin.); Sammy Aburumuh (Dir., Metro Home Delivery); Robert Rivard (Ed.); Brett Thacker (Mng. Ed.); Terry Scott-Bertling (Asst. Mng. Ed., Features); Hallie Paul (Asst. Mng. Ed., Graphics/Design/Photo); Craig Thomason (Asst. Mng. Ed., News)

MEDINA VALLEY TIMES

Street address 1: 1105 Fiorella St
Street address city: Castroville
Street address state: TX
Zip/Postal code: 78009-4577
General Phone: (830) 538-2556
General Fax: (830) 931-3450
Advertising Phone: (830) 538-2556
Advertising Fax: (830) 931-3450
Editorial Phone: (830) 538-2556
Editorial Fax: (830) 931-3450
General/National Adv. E-mail: cornerstoneads@sbcglobal.net
Display Adv. E-mail: cornerstoneads@sbcglobal.net
Editorial e-mail: cornerstonenews@sbcglobal.net
Primary Website: cornerstonenewspapers.com
Year Established: 1977
Avg Paid Circ: 3255
Avg Free Circ: 44
Audit By: Sworn/Estimate/Non-Audited
Audit Date: 10.06.2019
Personnel: Natalie Spencer (Pub./Adv. Dir.); Alicia Ramirez (News Ed.)

MEMORIAL EXAMINER

Street address 1: 100 Avenue A
Street address 2: Ste 200
Street address city: Conroe
Street address state: TX
Zip/Postal code: 77301-2946
General Phone: (281) 378-1900
General Fax: (713) 520-1193
Advertising Phone: (281) 378-1904
Advertising Fax: (713) 520-1193
Editorial Phone: (281) 378-1911
Editorial Fax: (713) 520-1193
General/National Adv. E-mail: rdavis@hcnonline.com
Display Adv. E-mail: ljohnson@hcnonline.com
Editorial e-mail: rgraham@hcnonline.com
Primary Website: examinernews.com/memorial
Year Established: 2004
Avg Paid Circ: 0
Avg Free Circ: 27451
Audit By: Sworn/Estimate/Non-Audited
Audit Date: 10.06.2019
Personnel: Richard Davis (Pub.); Rusty Graham (Ed.); Jason Joseph (Pub.); Charles Lee (Adv. Mgr); Rick Flores (Circ. Mgr); Clayton Harris (Prod. Mgr); Megan O'Sullivan (Mktg. Mgr.); Tom Legg (Major Sr. Acct. Mgr.)
Parent company (for newspapers): Hearst Communications, Inc.; Times Media Group

MENARD NEWS AND MESSENGER

Street address 1: 220 Gay St
Street address city: Menard
Street address state: TX
Zip/Postal code: 76859
General Phone: (325) 396-2243
General Fax: (325) 396-2739
Advertising Phone: (325) 396-2243
Advertising Fax: (325) 396-2739
Editorial Phone: (325) 396-2243
Editorial Fax: (325) 396-2739
General/National Adv. E-mail: menardnews@verizon.net
Display Adv. E-mail: menardnews@verizon.net
Editorial e-mail: menardnews@verizon.net

Year Established: 1936
Audit By: Sworn/Estimate/Non-Audited
Audit Date: 10.06.2019
Personnel: Dan Feather Jr. (Pub./Ed./Adv. Dir.)

MERCEDES ENTERPRISE

Street address 1: 805 S Missouri Ave
Street address city: Mercedes
Street address state: TX
Zip/Postal code: 78570-3441
General Phone: (956) 565-2425
General Fax: (956) 565-2570
Advertising Phone: (956) 565-2425
Advertising Fax: (956) 565-2570
Editorial Phone: (956) 565-2425
Editorial Fax: (956) 565-2570
General/National Adv. E-mail: mercedesenterprise@sbcglobal.net
Display Adv. E-mail: mercedesenterprise@sbcglobal.net
Editorial e-mail: mercedesenterprise@sbcglobal.net
Year Established: 1907
Avg Paid Circ: 2000
Audit By: Sworn/Estimate/Non-Audited
Audit Date: 10.06.2019
Personnel: Dr. Barbara Baggerly-Hinojosa (Publisher/Owner); C.A. Hinojosa, III (Sales/Owner); Cristina Cantu-Gutierrez (Office Manager); Carlos Cardenas (Editor)
Parent company (for newspapers): Mercedes Publishing

MERIDIAN TRIBUNE

Street address 1: 114 N MAIN
Street address city: Meridian
Street address state: TX
Zip/Postal code: 76665
General Phone: (254) 435-6333
General Fax: (254) 435-6348
Advertising Phone: (254) 435-6333
Advertising Fax: (254) 435-6348
Editorial Phone: (254) 435-6333
Editorial Fax: (254) 435-6348
General/National Adv. E-mail: brett@meridiantribune.com
Display Adv. E-mail: design@meridiantribune.com
Editorial e-mail: news@meridiantribune.com
Primary Website: meridiantribune.com
Year Established: 1893
Avg Paid Circ: 1780
Audit By: Sworn/Estimate/Non-Audited
Audit Date: 10.06.2019
Personnel: Brett Voss (Pub./Ed.)

MESQUITE NEWS

Street address 1: 624 Krona Dr
Street address 2: Ste 170
Street address city: Plano
Street address state: TX
Zip/Postal code: 75074-8304
General Phone: (972) 398-4200
General Fax: (972) 398-4470
General/National Adv. E-mail: jdittrich@starlocalmedia.com
Display Adv. E-mail: jdittrich@starlocalmedia.com
Editorial e-mail: swright@starlocalmedia.com
Primary Website: starlocalmedia.com
Mthly Avg Views: 546019
Mthly Avg Unique Visitors: 201046
Year Established: 1882
Avg Paid Circ: 284
Avg Free Circ: 23353
Audit By: CVC
Audit Date: 31.12.2018
Personnel: Scott Wright (Pub.); Melissa Rougeot (Circ. Mgr); Joani Dittrich (Adv. VP); Anny Sivilay (Reporter); Devin Hasson (Sports Rep.)
Parent company (for newspapers): S.A.W. Advisors, LLC; Star Community Newspapers

MILES MESSENGER

Street address 1: 104 Robinson St
Street address city: Miles
Street address state: TX
Zip/Postal code: 76861
General Phone: (325) 468-3611
General Fax: (325) 468-3611
Advertising Phone: (325) 468-3611

Advertising Fax: (325) 468-3611
Editorial Phone: (325) 468-3611
Editorial Fax: (325) 468-3611
General/National Adv. E-mail: shortcake56@verizon.net
Display Adv. E-mail: shortcake56@verizon.net
Editorial e-mail: shortcake56@verizon.net
Year Established: 1903
Audit By: Sworn/Estimate/Non-Audited
Audit Date: 10.06.2019
Personnel: Donna Glass (Pub./Ed./Adv. Dir.)

MOTLEY COUNTY TRIBUNE

Street address 1: 904 Childress Ave
Street address city: Turkey
Street address state: TX
Zip/Postal code: 79261-2022
General Phone: (806) 402-0120
Advertising Phone: (806) 402-0120
Editorial Phone: (806) 402-0120
General/National Adv. E-mail: caprockcourier@gmail.com
Display Adv. E-mail: caprockcourier@gmail.com
Editorial e-mail: caprockcourier@gmail.com
Year Established: 1891
Avg Paid Circ: 669
Audit By: Sworn/Estimate/Non-Audited
Audit Date: 10.06.2019
Personnel: Tori Minick (Ed)

MOUNT VERNON OPTIC-HERALD

Street address 1: 108 Kaufman St S
Street address city: Mount Vernon
Street address state: TX
Zip/Postal code: 75457-2833
General Phone: (903) 537-2228
General Fax: (903) 537-2227
Advertising Phone: (903) 537-2228
Advertising Fax: (903) 537-2227
Editorial Phone: (903) 537-2228
Editorial Fax: (903) 537-2227
General/National Adv. E-mail: optic@mt-vernon.com
Display Adv. E-mail: optic@mt-vernon.com
Editorial e-mail: optic@mt-vernon.com
Primary Website: mt-vernon.com
Year Established: 1874
Avg Paid Circ: 2500
Audit By: Sworn/Estimate/Non-Audited
Audit Date: 10.06.2019
Personnel: Susan Reeves (Pub.); Lillie M. Bush-Reeves (Ed.); John Reeves; Terri Cruit

MUENSTER ENTERPRISE

Street address 1: 117 E 1st St
Street address city: Muenster
Street address state: TX
Zip/Postal code: 76252-2788
General Phone: (940) 759-4311
General Fax: (940) 759-4110
General/National Adv. E-mail: advertising@ntin.net
Display Adv. E-mail: advertising@ntin.net
Editorial e-mail: swood@ntin.net
Year Established: 1936
Avg Paid Circ: 1700
Avg Free Circ: 36
Audit By: Sworn/Estimate/Non-Audited
Audit Date: 10.06.2019
Personnel: Deborah Wood (Pub./Owner); Scott Wood (Ed.)

MULESHOE JOURNAL

Street address 1: 201 W Avenue C
Street address city: Muleshoe
Street address state: TX
Zip/Postal code: 79347-3530
General Phone: (806) 272-4536
General Fax: (806) 272-3567
Advertising Phone: (806) 272-4536
Advertising Fax: (806) 272-3567
Editorial Phone: (806) 272-4536
Editorial Fax: (806) 272-3567
General/National Adv. E-mail: adsales@muleshoejournal.com
Display Adv. E-mail: circulation@muleshoejournal.com
Editorial e-mail: editor@muleshoejournal.com
Primary Website: muleshoejournal.com
Year Established: 1924
Avg Paid Circ: 1600
Avg Free Circ: 50
Audit By: Sworn/Estimate/Non-Audited
Audit Date: 10.06.2019
Personnel: David Wedel (Pub.); Rhea Gonzales (Adv. Dir.); APRIL CISNEROS (CIRCULATON/BOOK KEEPING)
Parent company (for newspapers): Hearst Communications, Inc.

MURPHY MONITOR

Street address 1: 110 N Ballard Ave
Street address city: Wylie
Street address state: TX
Zip/Postal code: 75098-4467
General Phone: (972) 442-5515
General Fax:
Advertising Phone: (972) 442-5515
Advertising Fax:
Editorial Phone: (972) 442-5515
Editorial Fax:
General/National Adv. E-mail: news@murphymonitor.com
Display Adv. E-mail: classifieds@csmediatexas.com
Editorial e-mail: news@murphymonitor.com
Primary Website: murphymonitor.com
Year Established: 2005
Avg Paid Circ: 2568
Avg Free Circ: 0
Audit By: Sworn/Estimate/Non-Audited
Audit Date: 10.06.2019
Personnel: Chad B. Engbrock (Pub./Ed./Adv. Dir.); Sonia Duggan (Associate Publisher)
Parent company (for newspapers): C&S Media, Inc.

NEWTON COUNTY NEWS

Street address 1: 112 GLOVER DR
Street address city: Newton
Street address state: TX
Zip/Postal code: 75966
General Phone: (409) 379-2416
General Fax: (409) 379-2416
Advertising Phone: (409) 379-2416
Advertising Fax: (409) 379-2416
Editorial Phone: (409) 379-2416
Editorial Fax: (409) 379-2416
General/National Adv. E-mail: newtonnews@valornet.com
Display Adv. E-mail: newtonnews@valornet.com
Editorial e-mail: newtonnews@valornet.com
Primary Website: newtonnews.com
Year Established: 1969
Avg Paid Circ: 1500
Audit By: Sworn/Estimate/Non-Audited
Audit Date: 10.06.2019
Personnel: Jay Wilkerson (Co-Pub.); Shawn Wilkerson (Co-Pub./Adv. Dir.); Karyn Lobb (Office Mgr./Classifieds)

NOCONA NEWS

Street address 1: 115 Cooke St
Street address city: Nocona
Street address state: TX
Zip/Postal code: 76255-2107
General Phone: (940) 825-3201
General Fax: (940) 825-3202
Advertising Phone: (940) 825-3201
Advertising Fax: (940) 825-3202
Editorial Phone: (940) 825-3201
Editorial Fax: (940) 825-3202
General/National Adv. E-mail: advertising@noconanews.net
Display Adv. E-mail: advertising@noconanews.net
Editorial e-mail: news@noconanews.net
Primary Website: noconanews.net
Year Established: 1905
Audit By: Sworn/Estimate/Non-Audited
Audit Date: 10.06.2019
Personnel: Tracy Mesler (Co-Pub./Ed.); Linda Mesler (Co-Pub./Adv. Dir.)

NORTH CENTRAL NEWS

Street address 1: 301 Avenue E
Street address city: San Antonio
Street address state: TX
Zip/Postal code: 78205-2006
General Phone: (210) 250-3711
General Fax: (210) 250-3715
Advertising Phone: (210) 250-2500
Advertising Fax: (210) 250-2565
Editorial Phone: (210) 250-3195
Editorial Fax: (210) 250-3105
General/National Adv. E-mail: communitysupport@express-news.net
Display Adv. E-mail: communitysupport@express-news.net
Editorial e-mail: editors@express-news.net
Primary Website: express-news.com
Avg Paid Circ: 10
Avg Free Circ: 28141
Audit By: Sworn/Estimate/Non-Audited
Audit Date: 10.06.2019
Personnel: Thomas A. Stephenson (Pres./Pub.); Fred Mergele (Vice Pres., Finance); Susan Ehrman (Vice Pres., HR); Charlotte Aaron (Vice Pres., Classified Adv.); Rebecca Named Chavez-Becker (Sales Dir.); Doug Bennight (Adv. Mgr., Automotive); Roxanne Beavers (Adv. Mgr., Telemktg./Classified); Pat Harvey (Adv. Mgr., Telemktg./Retail); Dean Aitken (Vice Pres., Mktg.); Patrick Magallanes (Vice Pres., Mktg.); Liz English (Target Mktg. Mgr.); Scott Frantzen (Circ. Sr. Vice Pres.); Paul Borrego (Circ. Dir., Admin.); Sammy Aburumuh (Dir., Metro Home Delivery); Robert Rivard (Ed.); Brett Thacker (Mng. Ed.); Terry Scott-Bertling (Asst. Mng. Ed., Features); Hallie Paul (Asst. Mng. Ed., Graphics/Design/Photo); Craig Thomason (Asst. Mng. Ed., News)

NORTHEAST HERALD

Street address 1: 301 Avenue E
Street address city: San Antonio
Street address state: TX
Zip/Postal code: 78205-2006
General Phone: (210) 250-3711
General Fax: (210) 250-3715
Advertising Phone: (210) 250-2500
Advertising Fax: (210) 250-2565
Editorial Phone: (210) 250-3195
Editorial Fax: (210) 250-3105
General/National Adv. E-mail: communitysupport@express-news.net
Display Adv. E-mail: communitysupport@express-news.net
Classified Adv. e-mail: classifieds@express-news.net
Editorial e-mail: mleary@express-news.net
Primary Website: express-news.com
Avg Free Circ: 15428
Audit By: AAM
Audit Date: 31.12.2017
Personnel: Thomas A. Stephenson (Pres./Pub.); Fred Mergele (Vice Pres., Finance); Susan Ehrman (Vice Pres., HR); Charlotte Aaron (Vice Pres., Classified Adv.); Rebecca Named Chavez-Becker (Sales Dir.); Doug Bennight (Adv. Mgr., Automotive); Roxanne Beavers (Adv. Mgr., Telemktg./Classified); Pat Harvey (Adv. Mgr., Telemktg./Retail); Dean Aitken (Vice Pres., Mktg.); Patrick Magallanes (Vice Pres., Mktg.); Liz English (Target Mktg. Mgr.); Scott Frantzen (Circ. Sr. Vice Pres.); Paul Borrego (Circ. Dir., Admin.); Sammy Aburumuh (Dir., Metro Home Delivery); Robert Rivard (Ed.); Brett Thacker (Mng. Ed.); Terry Scott-Bertling (Asst. Mng. Ed., Features); Hallie Paul (Asst. Mng. Ed., Graphics/Design/Photo); Craig Thomason (Asst. Mng. Ed., News)
Parent company (for newspapers): Hearst Communications, Inc.

NORTHEAST NEWS

Street address 1: 5906 Star Ln
Street address city: Houston
Street address state: TX
Zip/Postal code: 77057-7118
General Phone: (281) 449-9945
General Fax: (713) 977-1188
Advertising Phone: (281) 449-9945
Advertising Fax: (713) 977-1188
Editorial Phone: (281) 449-9945
Editorial Fax: (713) 977-1188
General/National Adv. E-mail: nenewsroom@aol.com
Display Adv. E-mail: nenewsroom@aol.com
Editorial e-mail: nenewsroom@aol.com
Primary Website: nenewsroom.com
Year Established: 1977
Avg Free Circ: 30000
Audit By: Sworn/Estimate/Non-Audited
Audit Date: 10.06.2019
Personnel: Gilbert Hoffman (Pub./Gen. Mgr./Adv. Mgr.); Tom Thornburgh (Ed); Lewis Spearman
Parent company (for newspapers): Grafikpress Corp.

NORTHWEST WEEKLY

Street address 1: 301 Avenue E
Street address city: San Antonio
Street address state: TX
Zip/Postal code: 78205-2006
General Phone: (210) 250-3711
General Fax: (210) 250-3715
Advertising Phone: (210) 250-2500
Advertising Fax: (210) 250-2565
Editorial Phone: (210) 250-3195
Editorial Fax: (210) 250-3105
General/National Adv. E-mail: communitysupport@express-news.net
Display Adv. E-mail: communitysupport@express-news.net
Editorial e-mail: editors@express-news.net
Primary Website: express-news.com
Avg Paid Circ: 10
Avg Free Circ: 22617
Audit By: Sworn/Estimate/Non-Audited
Audit Date: 10.06.2019
Personnel: Thomas A. Stephenson (Pres./Pub.); Fred Mergele (Vice Pres., Finance); Susan Ehrman (Vice Pres., HR); Charlotte Aaron (Vice Pres., Classified Adv.); Rebecca Named Chavez-Becker (Sales Dir.); Doug Bennight (Adv. Mgr., Automotive); Roxanne Beavers (Adv. Mgr., Telemktg./Classified); Pat Harvey (Adv. Mgr., Telemktg./Retail); Dean Aitken (Vice Pres., Mktg.); Patrick Magallanes (Vice Pres., Mktg.); Liz English (Target Mktg. Mgr.); Scott Frantzen (Circ. Sr. Vice Pres.); Paul Borrego (Circ. Dir., Admin.); Sammy Aburumuh (Dir., Metro Home Delivery); Robert Rivard (Ed.); Brett Thacker (Mng. Ed.); Terry Scott-Bertling (Asst. Mng. Ed., Features); Hallie Paul (Asst. Mng. Ed., Graphics/Design/Photo); Craig Thomason (Asst. Mng. Ed., News)

NUECES COUNTY RECORD-STAR

Street address 1: 405 E Main St
Street address city: Alice
Street address state: TX
Zip/Postal code: 78332-4968
General Phone: (361) 664-6588
General Fax: (361) 668-1030
Advertising Phone: (361) 664-6588 ext. 214
Advertising Fax: (361) 668-1030
Editorial Phone: (361) 664-6588
Editorial Fax: (361) 668-1030
General/National Adv. E-mail: bweaver@aliceechonews.com
Display Adv. E-mail: bweaver@aliceechonews.com
Editorial e-mail: news@recordstar.com
Primary Website: recordstar.com
Year Established: 1910
Avg Paid Circ: 3100
Audit By: Sworn/Estimate/Non-Audited
Audit Date: 10.06.2019
Personnel: Russel Gruber (Pub.); Jay Landingham (Adv. Mgr.); Pete Garcia (Exec. Ed.)
Parent company (for newspapers): CherryRoad Media

O'DONNELL INDEX-PRESS

Street address 1: 1629 FM 2053
Street address city: Odonnell
Street address state: TX
Zip/Postal code: 79351-3205
General Phone: (806) 428-3591
General Fax: (806) 428-3360
Advertising Phone: (806) 428-3591
Advertising Fax: (806) 428-3360
Editorial Phone: (806) 428-3591
Editorial Fax: (806) 428-3360
General/National Adv. E-mail: indexpress@poka.com
Display Adv. E-mail: indexpress@poka.com
Editorial e-mail: indexpress@poka.com
Year Established: 1923
Avg Paid Circ: 400
Avg Free Circ: 20
Audit By: Sworn/Estimate/Non-Audited
Audit Date: 10.06.2019
Personnel: Sharon Wells (Pub./Adv. Dir.); John Wells (Ed./Adv. Dir.)

OVERTON NEWS

Street address 1: 1711 US Highway 79 S
Street address city: Henderson
Street address state: TX

Zip/Postal code: 75654-4509
General Phone: (903) 657-2501
General Fax: (903) 657-2452
Editorial Fax: (903) 657-0056
General/National Adv. E-mail: leslinebarger@hendersondailynews.com
Display Adv. E-mail: classifieds@hendersondailynews.com
Editorial e-mail: mprosser@hendersondailynews.com
Primary Website: hendersondailynews.com
Year Established: 1930
Avg Paid Circ: 7000
Avg Free Circ: 6400
Audit By: Sworn/Estimate/Non-Audited
Audit Date: 10.06.2019
Personnel: Les Linebarger (Pub.); Matthew Prosser (Ed.); John Garrison (Circ. Mgr.)

OZONA STOCKMAN

Street address 1: 1000 Avenue E
Street address city: Ozona
Street address state: TX
Zip/Postal code: 76943
General Phone: (325) 392-2551
General Fax: (325) 392-2439
Advertising Phone: (325) 392-2551
Advertising Fax: (325) 392-2439
Editorial Phone: (325) 392-2551
Editorial Fax: (325) 392-2439
General/National Adv. E-mail: susan@ozonastockman.com
Display Adv. E-mail: susan@ozonastockman.com
Editorial e-mail: publisher@ozonastockman.com
Primary Website: ozonastockman.com
Year Established: 1913
Avg Paid Circ: 1755
Avg Free Circ: 20
Audit By: Sworn/Estimate/Non-Audited
Audit Date: 10.06.2019
Personnel: Melissa Perner (Pub./Ed.); Susan Calloway (Adv. Dir.)

PADUCAH POST

Street address 1: 819 8th St
Street address city: Paducah
Street address state: TX
Zip/Postal code: 79248
General Phone: (806) 492-3585
General Fax: (806) 492-3585
Advertising Phone: (806) 492-3585
Advertising Fax: (806) 492-3585
Editorial Phone: (806) 492-3585
Editorial Fax: (806) 492-3585
General/National Adv. E-mail: jtaylor1@caprock-spur.com
Display Adv. E-mail: jtaylor1@caprock-spur.com
Editorial e-mail: jtaylor1@caprock-spur.com
Year Established: 1906
Audit By: Sworn/Estimate/Non-Audited
Audit Date: 10.06.2019
Personnel: Jimmye C. Taylor (Pub./Ed./Adv. Dir.); Chad Piper (Mng. Ed.)

PALACIOS BEACON

Street address 1: 310 5th St
Street address city: Palacios
Street address state: TX
Zip/Postal code: 77465-4702
General Phone: (361) 972-3009
General Fax: (361) 972-2610
Advertising Phone: (361) 972-3009
Advertising Fax: (361) 972-2610
Editorial Phone: (361) 972-3009
Editorial Fax: (361) 972-2610
General/National Adv. E-mail: brandi.palaciosbeacon@gmail.com
Display Adv. E-mail: carolyn.beacon@gmail.com
Editorial e-mail: ryan.palaciosbeacon@gmail.com
Primary Website: palaciosbeacon.com
Year Established: 1907
Avg Paid Circ: 1600
Audit By: Sworn/Estimate/Non-Audited
Audit Date: 10.06.2019
Personnel: Carolyn White (Adv. Mgr.); Ryan West; Brandi West; Alan Schulman

Parent company (for newspapers): City by the Sea Publishing, LLC

PANHANDLE HERALD / WHITE DEER NEWS

Street address 1: 319 Main
Street address city: Panhandle
Street address state: TX
Zip/Postal code: 79068
General Phone: (806) 537-3634
General Fax: (806) 537-3634
Advertising Phone: (806) 537-3634
Advertising Fax: (806) 537-3634
Editorial Phone: (806) 537-3634
Editorial Fax: (806) 537-3634
General/National Adv. E-mail: shaun@panhandleherald.com
Display Adv. E-mail: shaun@panhandleherald.com
Editorial e-mail: panhandleherald@hotmail.com
Primary Website: panhandleherald.com
Year Established: 1887
Avg Paid Circ: 1251
Avg Free Circ: 19
Audit By: Sworn/Estimate/Non-Audited
Audit Date: 10.06.2019
Personnel: Shaun Wink (Ed./Pub./Adv. Dir./Owner); Frank Wink (Co-Pub.)

PARK CITIES NEWS

Street address 1: 4136 Greenbrier Dr
Street address 2: Ste 575
Street address city: Dallas
Street address state: TX
Zip/Postal code: 75225-6635
General Phone: (214) 369-7570
General Fax: (214) 369-7736
Advertising Phone: (214) 369-7570
Advertising Fax: (214) 369-7736
Editorial Phone: (214) 369-7570
Editorial Fax: (214) 369-7736
General/National Adv. E-mail: advertising@peoplenewspapers.com
Display Adv. E-mail: pcn@parkcitiesnews.com
Editorial e-mail: pcn@parkcitiesnews.com
Primary Website: parkcitiesnews.com
Year Established: 1938
Avg Paid Circ: 5000
Avg Free Circ: 250
Audit By: Sworn/Estimate/Non-Audited
Audit Date: 10.06.2019
Personnel: Marjorie B. Waters (Pub.); Thomas R. Waters (Ed./Gen. Mgr.); Peter H. Waters (Ed./Adv. Dir.)

PARK CITIES PEOPLE

Street address 1: 750 N Saint Paul St
Street address 2: Ste 2100
Street address city: Dallas
Street address state: TX
Zip/Postal code: 75201-3214
General Phone: (214) 739-2244
General Fax: (214) 594-5779
Advertising Phone: (214) 739-2244
Advertising Fax: (214) 594-5779
Editorial Phone: (214) 739-2244 ext. 257
Editorial Fax: (214) 594-5779
General/National Adv. E-mail: advertising@peoplenewspapers.com
Display Adv. E-mail: advertising@peoplenewspapers.com
Editorial e-mail: editor@peoplenewspapers.com
Primary Website: peoplenewspapers.com
Mthly Avg Views: 96938
Mthly Avg Unique Visitors: 79675
Year Established: 1981
Avg Paid Circ: 290
Avg Free Circ: 45320
Audit By: CVC
Audit Date: 31.12.2017
Personnel: Patricia Martin (Publisher); William Taylor (Editor)
Parent company (for newspapers): D Magazine Partners LP

PEARLAND JOURNAL

Street address 1: 100 Avenue A
Street address city: Conroe
Street address state: TX
Zip/Postal code: 77301-2946
General Phone: (281) 378-1920
General Fax: (281) 922-4499
Advertising Phone: (281) 378-1922
Advertising Fax: (281) 922-4499
Editorial Phone: (281) 378-1930
Editorial Fax: (281) 922-4499
General/National Adv. E-mail: bmiller-fergerson@hcnonline.com
Display Adv. E-mail: bcrainer@hcnonline.com
Editorial e-mail: jmolony@hcnonline.com
Primary Website: pearlandjournal.com
Mthly Avg Views: 56000
Year Established: 1975
Avg Paid Circ: 1125
Avg Free Circ: 19330
Audit By: Sworn/Estimate/Non-Audited
Audit Date: 10.06.2019
Personnel: Brenda Miller-Fergerson (Pub.); Jim Molony (Ed.); Dean West (Sales Mgr.); Jason Joseph (Pub.); Charles Lee (Adv. Mgr); Rick Flores (Circ. Mgr); Carol Taylor (Prod. Mgr); Tom Legg (Major Sr. Acct. Mgr.); Megan O'Sullivan (Mktg. Mgr.)
Parent company (for newspapers): Times Media Group

PEARLAND REPORTER NEWS

Street address 1: 2404 Park Ave
Street address city: Pearland
Street address state: TX
Zip/Postal code: 77581-4234
General Phone: (281) 485-7501
General Fax: (281) 485-6397
Advertising Phone: (281) 485-7501
Advertising Fax: (281) 485-6397
Editorial Phone: (281) 485-7501
Editorial Fax: (281) 485-6397
General/National Adv. E-mail: laurae3009@yahoo.com
Display Adv. E-mail: laurae3009@yahoo.com
Editorial e-mail: laurae3009@yahoo.com
Year Established: 1971
Avg Paid Circ: 28000
Audit By: Sworn/Estimate/Non-Audited
Audit Date: 10.06.2019
Personnel: Laura Emmons (Pub. / Exec. Ed.); Randy Emmons (Circ. Mgr.); Kathy Pulpan (Prodn. Mgr.)

PECOS ENTERPRISE

Street address 1: 324 S Cedar St
Street address city: Pecos
Street address state: TX
Zip/Postal code: 79772-3211
General Phone: (432) 445-5475
General Fax: (432) 445-4321
Advertising Phone: (432) 445-5475
Advertising Fax: (432) 445-4321
Editorial Phone: (432) 445-5475
Editorial Fax: (432) 445-4321
General/National Adv. E-mail: smokey@pecos.net
Display Adv. E-mail: news@pecos.net
Editorial e-mail: jon@pecos.net
Primary Website: pecos.net/news
Year Established: 1887
Avg Paid Circ: 1700
Audit By: Sworn/Estimate/Non-Audited
Audit Date: 10.06.2019
Personnel: Smokey Briggs (Pub.); Jon Fulbright (Ed.); Christina Bitolas (Adv. Dir.); Lorna Navarette (Bus. Mgr.); Laura Rodriguez (Classified Adv. Mgr.)

PERRYTON HERALD

Street address 1: 401 S. Amherst
Street address 2: PO Box 989
Street address city: Perryton
Street address state: TX
Zip/Postal code: 79070-3012
General Phone: (806) 435-3631
General Fax: (806) 435-2420
Advertising Phone: (806) 435-3631
Advertising Fax: (806) 435-2420
Editorial Phone: (806) 435-3631
Editorial Fax: (806) 435-2420
General/National Adv. E-mail: dclardy@ptsi.net
Display Adv. E-mail: wiarmon@ptsi.net
Editorial e-mail: mhdudley@ptsi.net
Primary Website: perrytonherald.com
Year Established: 1917
Avg Paid Circ: 3500
Audit By: Sworn/Estimate/Non-Audited
Audit Date: 10.06.2019
Personnel: Jim Hudson (Pub.); Mary H. Dudley (Ed.); Doris Clardy (Adv. Dir.); Meagan Rogers (Classified Mgr.)

PILOT POINT POST SIGNAL

Street address 1: 111 E Main St
Street address city: Pilot Point
Street address state: TX
Zip/Postal code: 76258-4532
General Phone: (940) 686-2169
General Fax: (940) 686-2437
Advertising Phone: (940) 686-2169
Advertising Fax: (940) 686-2437
Editorial Phone: (940) 686-2169
Editorial Fax: (940) 686-2437
General/National Adv. E-mail: creid@postsignal.com
Display Adv. E-mail: rgreene@postsignal.com
Editorial e-mail: editor@postsignal.com
Primary Website: postsignal.com
Year Established: 1878
Avg Paid Circ: 2030
Audit By: Sworn/Estimate/Non-Audited
Audit Date: 10.06.2019
Personnel: Cathy Reid (Adv. Mgr.); Richard Greene (Mng. Ed.); David Lewis (Pub./Ed.)

PITTSBURG GAZETTE

Street address 1: 112 Quitman St
Street address city: Pittsburg
Street address state: TX
Zip/Postal code: 75686-1322
General Phone: (903) 856-6629
General Fax: (903) 856-0510
Advertising Phone: (903) 856-6629
Advertising Fax: (903) 856-0510
Editorial Phone: (903) 856-6629
Editorial Fax: (903) 856-0510
General/National Adv. E-mail: iperez@campcountynow.com
Display Adv. E-mail: iperez@campcountynow.com
Editorial e-mail: dknox@campcountynow.com
Primary Website: campcountynow.com
Year Established: 1884
Avg Paid Circ: 3100
Avg Free Circ: 33
Audit By: Sworn/Estimate/Non-Audited
Audit Date: 10.06.2019
Personnel: Debbie Knox (Pub.); Susan Taft (Ed.); Brittany York (Adv. Mgr.)
Parent company (for newspapers): Northeast Texas Publishing

PLANO STAR COURIER

Street address 1: 624 Krona Dr
Street address 2: Ste 170
Street address city: Plano
Street address state: TX
Zip/Postal code: 75074-8304
General Phone: (972) 398-4200
General Fax: (972) 398-4470
General/National Adv. E-mail: jdittrich@starlocalmedia.com
Display Adv. E-mail: jdittrich@starlocalmedia.com
Editorial e-mail: swright@starlocalmedia.com
Primary Website: starlocalmedia.com
Mthly Avg Views: 546019
Mthly Avg Unique Visitors: 201046
Year Established: 1889
Avg Paid Circ: 993
Avg Free Circ: 44046
Audit By: CVC
Audit Date: 31.12.2018
Personnel: Scott Wright (Pub.); Joani Dittrich (Adv. VP); Melissa Rougeot (Circ. Mgr.); Kelsey Samuels (Reporter)
Parent company (for newspapers): Star Community Newspapers; Times Media Group

PLEASANTON EXPRESS

Street address 1: 114 E Goodwin St
Street address city: Pleasanton
Street address state: TX
Zip/Postal code: 78064-4124
General Phone: (830) 281-2341
General Fax: (830) 569-6100
General/National Adv. E-mail: mgallegos@pleasantonexpress.com
Display Adv. E-mail: classifieds@pleasantonexpress.com

Editorial e-mail: sbrown@pleasantonexpress.com
Primary Website: pleasantonexpress.com
Year Established: 1909
Avg Free Circ: 8400
Audit By: Sworn/Estimate/Non-Audited
Audit Date: 10.06.2019
Personnel: Judith Wilkerson (Pub.); Sue Brown (Editor); Mary Gallegos (Adv. Dir.); Rhonda Chancellor (Business Manager, Classifieds Manager); Megan Benishek (Ad Sales); Noel Wilkerson Holmes (Associate Pub.)

POLK COUNTY ENTERPRISE

Street address 1: 100 E Calhoun St
Street address city: Livingston
Street address state: TX
Zip/Postal code: 77351-2908
General Phone: (936) 327-4357
General Fax: (936) 327-7156
Advertising Phone: (936) 327-4357
Advertising Fax: (936) 327-7156
Editorial Phone: (936) 327-4357
Editorial Fax: (936) 327-7156
General/National Adv. E-mail: enterprise@easttexasnews.com
Display Adv. E-mail: enterprise@easttexasnews.com
Editorial e-mail: enterprise@easttexasnews.com
Primary Website: easttexasnews.com
Year Established: 1904
Avg Paid Circ: 7673
Avg Free Circ: 83
Audit By: Sworn/Estimate/Non-Audited
Audit Date: 10.06.2019
Personnel: Alvin Holley (Pub.); Valerie Reddell (Ed.); Linda Holley (Adv. Mgr.)
Parent company (for newspapers): Polk County Publishing Co.

PORT ARANSAS SOUTH JETTY

Street address 1: 141 W Cotter Ave
Street address city: Port Aransas
Street address state: TX
Zip/Postal code: 78373-4034
General Phone: (361) 749-5131
General Fax: (361) 749-5137
Advertising Phone: (361) 749-5131
Advertising Fax: (361) 749-5137
Editorial Phone: (361) 749-5131
Editorial Fax: (361) 749-5137
General/National Adv. E-mail: displayads@portasouthjetty.com
Display Adv. E-mail: classifiedads@portasouthjetty.com
Editorial e-mail: southjetty@centurytel.net
Primary Website: portasouthjetty.com
Year Established: 1971
Avg Paid Circ: 3730
Avg Free Circ: 56
Audit By: Sworn/Estimate/Non-Audited
Audit Date: 10.06.2019
Personnel: Murray Judson (Co-Pub./Adv. Dir.); Mary Judson (Co-Pub./Ed.)

PORT ISABEL-SOUTH PADRE PRESS

Street address 1: 101 E Maxan St
Street address city: Port Isabel
Street address state: TX
Zip/Postal code: 78578-4504
General Phone: (956) 943-5545
General Fax: (956) 943-4782
Advertising Phone: (956) 943-5545
Advertising Fax: (956) 943-4782
Editorial Phone: (956) 943-5545
Editorial Fax: (956) 943-4782
General/National Adv. E-mail: rayq@portisabelsouthpadre.com
Display Adv. E-mail: rayq@portisabelsouthpadre.com
Editorial e-mail: editor@portisabelsouthpadre.com
Primary Website: portisabelsouthpadre.com
Year Established: 1952
Avg Paid Circ: 30000
Avg Free Circ: 0
Audit By: Sworn/Estimate/Non-Audited
Audit Date: 10.06.2019
Personnel: Ray Quiroga (Pub./Ed.)

PORT LAVACA WAVE

Street address 1: 107 E Austin St
Street address city: Port Lavaca
Street address state: TX
Zip/Postal code: 77979-4402
General Phone: (361) 552-9788
General Fax: (361) 552-3108
Advertising Phone: (361) 552-9788
Advertising Fax: (361) 552-3108
Editorial Phone: (361) 552-9788
Editorial Fax: (361) 552-3108
General/National Adv. E-mail: tfrench@plwave.com
Display Adv. E-mail: tfrench@plwave.com
Editorial e-mail: tfrench@plwave.com
Primary Website: portlavacawave.com
Year Established: 1890
Avg Paid Circ: 4200
Avg Free Circ: 2300
Audit By: Sworn/Estimate/Non-Audited
Audit Date: 10.06.2019
Personnel: Tania French (Pub./Ed.)
Parent company (for newspapers): Hartman Newspapers LP

PORTLAND NEWS

Street address 1: 1105 Railroad Dr
Street address 2: Ste B
Street address city: Portland
Street address state: TX
Zip/Postal code: 78374-1759
General Phone: (361) 643-1566
General Fax: (361) 643-1400
Advertising Phone: (361) 643-1566
Advertising Fax: (361) 643-1400
Editorial Phone: (361) 643-1566
Editorial Fax: (361) 643-1400
General/National Adv. E-mail: advertising@mysoutex.com
Display Adv. E-mail: receptionist@mysoutex.com
Editorial e-mail: editor@mysoutex.com
Year Established: 1964
Avg Paid Circ: 2500
Avg Free Circ: 50
Audit By: Sworn/Estimate/Non-Audited
Audit Date: 10.06.2019
Personnel: James F. Tracy (Co-Pub.); John H. Tracy (Co-Pub./Adv. Mgr.); Diana Stone (Ed.)
Parent company (for newspapers): San Patricio Publishing Co., Inc.

PRESTON HOLLOW PEOPLE

Street address 1: 750 N Saint Paul St
Street address 2: Ste 2100
Street address city: Dallas
Street address state: TX
Zip/Postal code: 75201-3214
General Phone: (214) 739-2244
General Fax: (214) 594-5779
General/National Adv. E-mail: advertising@peoplenewspapers.com
Display Adv. E-mail: classifieds@peoplenewspapers.com
Editorial e-mail: pat.martin@peoplenewspapers.com
Primary Website: prestonhollowpeople.com
Mthly Avg Views: 11000
Mthly Avg Unique Visitors: 4000
Year Established: 1981
Avg Paid Circ: 125
Avg Free Circ: 25963
Audit By: CVC
Audit Date: 31.12.2017
Personnel: Patricia Martin (Pub.); Gabrielle Reese (Marketing Coordinator)
Parent company (for newspapers): D Magazine Partners LP

PRINCETON HERALD

Street address 1: 101 S Main St
Street address city: Farmersville
Street address state: TX
Zip/Postal code: 75442-2207
General Phone: (972) 784-6397
General Fax: (972) 782-7023
Advertising Phone: (972) 784-6397
Advertising Fax: (972) 782-7023
Editorial Phone: (972) 784-6397
Editorial Fax: (972) 782-7023
General/National Adv. E-mail: advertising@csmediatexas.com
Display Adv. E-mail: advertising@csmediatexas.com
Editorial e-mail: news@princetonherald.com
Primary Website: princetonherald.com
Year Established: 1970
Avg Paid Circ: 1799
Avg Free Circ: 27
Audit By: Sworn/Estimate/Non-Audited
Audit Date: 10.06.2019
Personnel: Chad Engbrock (Pub./Ed./Adv. Dir.)
Parent company (for newspapers): C&S Media, Inc.

PROGRESS TIMES

Street address 1: 1217 N Conway Ave
Street address city: Mission
Street address state: TX
Zip/Postal code: 78572-4112
General Phone: (956) 585-4893
General Fax: (956) 585-2304
Advertising Phone: (956) 585-4893
Advertising Fax: (956) 585-2304
Editorial Phone: (956) 585-4893
Editorial Fax: (956) 585-2304
General/National Adv. E-mail: ads@progresstimes.net
Display Adv. E-mail: info@progresstimes.net
Editorial e-mail: news@progresstimes.net
Primary Website: progresstimes.net
Mthly Avg Views: 11011
Mthly Avg Unique Visitors: 3874
Year Established: 1972
Avg Paid Circ: 2905
Avg Free Circ: 7095
Audit By: Sworn/Estimate/Non-Audited
Audit Date: 10.06.2019
Personnel: Jim Brunson (Pub./Ed.); Sharon Sanchez (Office Mgr.); Dee Rendon (Advertising Manager); Maria Smith (Advertising Representative)
Parent company (for newspapers): Mission Publishing Co

QUANAH TRIBUNE-CHIEF

Street address 1: PO Box 481
Street address city: Quanah
Street address state: TX
Zip/Postal code: 79252-0481
General Phone: (940) 663-5333
General Fax: (940) 663-5073
General/National Adv. E-mail: editor@quanahtribunechief.com
Display Adv. E-mail: editor@quanahtribunechief.com
Editorial e-mail: editor@quanahtribunechief.com
Primary Website: quanahtribunechief.com
Year Established: 1889
Avg Paid Circ: 1500
Avg Free Circ: 19
Audit By: Sworn/Estimate/Non-Audited
Audit Date: 10.06.2019
Personnel: Bret McCormick (Pub.); Shane Lance (Editor, Publisher, Owner); Carol Whitmire (Ed.)

RAINS COUNTY LEADER

Street address 1: 239 N Texas St
Street address city: Emory
Street address state: TX
Zip/Postal code: 75440-2405
General Phone: (903) 473-2653
General Fax: (903) 473-0050
Advertising Phone: (903) 473-2653
Advertising Fax: (903) 473-0050
Editorial Phone: (903) 473-2653
Editorial Fax: (903) 473-0050
General/National Adv. E-mail: rainsleader@earthlink.net
Display Adv. E-mail: ads@rainscountyleader.com
Editorial e-mail: news@rainscountyleader.com
Primary Website: rainscountyleader.com
Year Established: 1887
Avg Paid Circ: 2400
Avg Free Circ: 79
Audit By: Sworn/Estimate/Non-Audited
Audit Date: 10.06.2019
Personnel: Earl C. Hill (Pub.); Nancy Fenter (Circ. Mgr.); Earl, III Hill (Ed.); Kay Thompson (Adv. Mgr.)

RANDOLPH WINGSPREAD

Street address 1: 301 Avenue E
Street address city: San Antonio
Street address state: TX
Zip/Postal code: 78205-2006
General Phone: (210) 250-3000
General Fax: (210) 250-3715
Advertising Phone: (210) 250-2500
Advertising Fax: (210) 250-2565
Editorial Phone: (210) 250-3195
Editorial Fax: (210) 250-3105
General/National Adv. E-mail: communitysupport@express-news.net
Display Adv. E-mail: communitysupport@express-news.net
Editorial e-mail: editors@express-news.net
Primary Website: express-news.com
Avg Paid Circ: 0
Avg Free Circ: 0
Audit By: VAC
Audit Date: 31.05.2017
Personnel: Thomas A. Stephenson (Pres./Pub.); Fred Mergele (Vice Pres., Finance); Susan Ehrman (Vice Pres., HR); Charlotte Aaron (Vice Pres., Classified Adv.); Rebecca Named Chavez-Becker (Sales Dir.); Doug Bennight (Adv. Mgr., Automotive); Roxanne Beavers (Adv. Mgr., Telemktg./Classified); Pat Harvey (Adv. Mgr., Telemktg./Retail); Dean Aitken (Vice Pres., Mktg.); Patrick Magallanes (Vice Pres., Mktg.); Liz English (Target Mktg. Mgr.); Scott Frantzen (Circ. Sr. Vice Pres.); Paul Borrego (Circ. Dir., Admin.); Sammy Aburumuh (Dir., Metro Home Delivery); Robert Rivard (Ed.); Brett Thacker (Mng. Ed.); Terry Scott-Bertling (Asst. Mng. Ed., Features); Hallie Paul (Asst. Mng. Ed., Graphics/Design/Photo); Craig Thomason (Asst. Mng. Ed., News)

RANGER TIMES

Street address 1: 215 S Seaman St
Street address city: Eastland
Street address state: TX
Zip/Postal code: 76448-2745
General Phone: (254) 629-1707
General Fax: (254) 629-2092
Advertising Phone: (254) 629-1707
Advertising Fax: (254) 629-2092
Editorial Phone: (254) 629-1707
Editorial Fax: (254) 629-2092
General/National Adv. E-mail: ecn@att.net
Display Adv. E-mail: ecn@att.net
Editorial e-mail: ecn@att.net
Primary Website: eastlandcountytoday.com
Year Established: 1919
Avg Paid Circ: 538
Audit By: Sworn/Estimate/Non-Audited
Audit Date: 10.06.2019
Personnel: Houston V. O'Brien (Pub.); Margaret Hetrick (Ed.)
Parent company (for newspapers): Eastland County Newspapers

RAYMONDVILLE CHRONICLE & WILLACY COUNTY NEWS

Street address 1: PO Box 369
Street address 2: 192 N 4th St
Street address city: Raymondville
Street address state: TX
Zip/Postal code: 78580-0369
General Phone: (956) 689-2421
General Fax: (956) 689-6575
General/National Adv. E-mail: erica@raymondvillechroniclenews.com
Display Adv. E-mail: erica@raymondvillechroniclenews.com
Editorial e-mail: chroniclenews@msn.com
Primary Website: raymondvillechroniclenews.com
Year Established: 1920
Avg Paid Circ: 2500
Audit By: Sworn/Estimate/Non-Audited
Audit Date: 10.06.2019
Personnel: Paul E. Whitworth (Pub./Ed.); Carlos Martinez (Adv. Dir.); Antonio Vindell (Reporter); Erica Ysasi (Sec./Office Mgr.); Eric Aguirre (Graphics Designer)

REFUGIO COUNTY PRESS

Street address 1: 412 N Alamo St
Street address city: Refugio
Street address state: TX
Zip/Postal code: 78377-2504
General Phone: (361) 526-2397
General Fax: (361) 526-2398
General/National Adv. E-mail: sales@mysoutex.com
Display Adv. E-mail: classifieds@mysoutex.com
Editorial e-mail: refugiocountypress@mysoutex.com
Primary Website: mySouTex.com
Year Established: 1959
Avg Paid Circ: 2200
Avg Free Circ: 0

Audit By: Sworn/Estimate/Non-Audited
Audit Date: 10.06.2019
Personnel: Jeff Latcham (Co-Pub.); Chip Latcham (Co-Pub.); Karl Arnst (Adv. Dir.); Tim Delaney (Ed.)
Parent company (for newspapers): Beeville Publishing Company, Inc.

RISING STAR

Street address 1: PO Box 29
Street address city: Eastland
Street address state: TX
Zip/Postal code: 76448-0029
General Phone: (254) 629-1707
General Fax: (254) 629-2092
Advertising Phone: (254) 629-1707
Advertising Fax: (254) 629-2092
Editorial Phone: (254) 629-1707
Editorial Fax: (254) 629-2092
General/National Adv. E-mail: ecn@att.net
Display Adv. E-mail: ecn@att.net
Editorial e-mail: ecn@att.net
Primary Website: eastlandcountytoday.com
Avg Paid Circ: 550
Avg Free Circ: 41
Audit By: Sworn/Estimate/Non-Audited
Audit Date: 10.06.2019
Personnel: Houston V. O'Brien (Pub.)
Parent company (for newspapers): Eastland County Newspapers

RIVER OAKS EXAMINER

Street address 1: 7613 Katy Fwy
Street address 2: Ste C
Street address city: Houston
Street address state: TX
Zip/Postal code: 77024-2007
General Phone: (281) 378-1900
General Fax: (713) 520-1193
Advertising Phone: (281) 378-1906
Advertising Fax: (713) 520-1193
Editorial Phone: (281) 378-1911
Editorial Fax: (713) 520-1193
General/National Adv. E-mail: rdavis@hcnonline.com
Display Adv. E-mail: pstewart@hcnonline.com
Editorial e-mail: rgraham@hcnonline.com
Primary Website: hcnonline.com/river_oaks_examiner
Avg Free Circ: 12027
Audit By: Sworn/Estimate/Non-Audited
Audit Date: 10.06.2019
Personnel: Richard Davis (Pub.); Rusty Graham (Ed.); Megan O'Sullivan (Mktg. Mgr.); Tom Legg (Major Sr. Acct. Mgr.); Charles Lee (Adv. Dir.)
Parent company (for newspapers): Times Media Group; Hearst Communications, Inc.

ROBERTSON COUNTY NEWS

Street address 1: 114 W 4th St
Street address city: Hearne
Street address state: TX
Zip/Postal code: 77859-2506
General Phone: (979) 279-3411
General Fax: (979) 279-5401
Advertising Phone: (979) 279-3411
Advertising Fax: (979) 279-5401
Editorial Phone: (979) 279-3411
Editorial Fax: (979) 279-5401
General/National Adv. E-mail: ads@robconews.com
Display Adv. E-mail: ads@robconews.com
Editorial e-mail: news@robconews.com
Primary Website: robconews.com
Year Established: 1889
Avg Paid Circ: 2146
Avg Free Circ: 92
Audit By: Sworn/Estimate/Non-Audited
Audit Date: 10.06.2019
Personnel: Dennis Phillips (Pub./Ed.); Teresa Phillips (Adv. Dir.)
Parent company (for newspapers): Moser Community Media

ROCKDALE REPORTER

Street address 1: P.O. Box 552
Street address 2: 221 E. Cameron Ave.
Street address city: Rockdale
Street address state: TX
Zip/Postal code: 76567-2972
General Phone: (512) 446-5838
General Fax: (512) 446-5317
Advertising Phone: (512) 446-5838
Advertising Fax: (512) 446-5317
Editorial Phone: (512) 446-5838
Editorial Fax: (512) 446-5317
General/National Adv. E-mail: kathy@rockdalereporter.com
Display Adv. E-mail: linda@rockdalereporter.com
Editorial e-mail: mike@rockdalereporter.com
Primary Website: rockdalereporter.com
Year Established: 1893
Audit By: Sworn/Estimate/Non-Audited
Audit Date: 10.06.2019
Personnel: Ken Esten Cooke (Pub.); Christine Granados (Pub.); Bill Cooke (Pub. Emeritus); Mike Brown (Ed.)

ROCKWALL COUNTY HERALD BANNER

Street address 1: 2305 King St
Street address city: Greenville
Street address state: TX
Zip/Postal code: 75401-3257
General Phone: (903) 455-4220
General Fax: (903) 455-6281
Advertising Phone: (903) 455-4220, Ext. 312
General/National Adv. E-mail: advertising@heraldbanner.com
Display Adv. E-mail: advertising@heraldbanner.com
Primary Website: rockwallheraldbanner.com
Audit By: Sworn/Estimate/Non-Audited
Audit Date: 10.06.2019
Personnel: Caleb Slinkard (Ed.)
Parent company (for newspapers): CNHI, LLC

ROWLETT LAKESHORE TIMES

Street address 1: 624 Krona Dr
Street address 2: Ste 170
Street address city: Plano
Street address state: TX
Zip/Postal code: 75074-8304
General Phone: (972) 398-4200
General Fax: (972) 398-4470
General/National Adv. E-mail: jdittrich@starlocalmedia.com
Display Adv. E-mail: jdittrich@starlocalmedia.com
Editorial e-mail: swright@starlocalmedia.com
Primary Website: starlocalmedia.com
Mthly Avg Views: 546019
Mthly Avg Unique Visitors: 201046
Year Established: 1982
Avg Paid Circ: 174
Avg Free Circ: 6252
Audit By: CVC
Audit Date: 31.12.2018
Personnel: Scott Wright (Pub.); Joani Dittrich (Adv. VP); Melissa Rougeot (Circ. Mgr); Anny Sivilay (Reporter); Devin Hasson (Sports Rep.)
Parent company (for newspapers): S.A.W. Advisors, LLC; Star Community Newspapers

ROYSE CITY HERALD BANNER

Street address 1: 2305 King St
Street address city: Greenville
Street address state: TX
Zip/Postal code: 75401-3257
General Phone: (903) 455-4220
General Fax: (903) 455-6281
Advertising Phone: (903) 455-4220, Ext. 312
General/National Adv. E-mail: advertising@heraldbanner.com
Display Adv. E-mail: advertising@heraldbanner.com
Primary Website: roysecityheraldbanner.com
Audit By: Sworn/Estimate/Non-Audited
Audit Date: 10.06.2019
Personnel: Caleb Slinkard; Mary Standfield
Parent company (for newspapers): CNHI, LLC

SACHSE NEWS

Street address 1: 110 N Ballard Ave
Street address city: Wylie
Street address state: TX
Zip/Postal code: 75098-4467
General Phone: (972) 442-5515
General Fax: (972) 442-4318
Advertising Phone: (972) 442-5515
Advertising Fax: (972) 442-4318
Editorial Phone: (972) 442-5515
Editorial Fax: (972) 442-4318
General/National Adv. E-mail: advertising@csmediatexas.com
Display Adv. E-mail: cengbrock@csmediatexas.com
Editorial e-mail: news@sachsenews.com
Primary Website: sachsenews.com
Year Established: 2005
Avg Paid Circ: 1533
Audit By: Sworn/Estimate/Non-Audited
Audit Date: 10.06.2019
Personnel: Chad B. Engbrock (Pub./Ed./Adv. Dir.)

SALADO VILLAGE VOICE

Street address 1: 213 Mill Creek Dr
Street address 2: Ste 125
Street address city: Salado
Street address state: TX
Zip/Postal code: 76571-4939
General Phone: (254) 947-5321
Advertising Phone: (254) 947-5321
Editorial Phone: (254) 947-5321
General/National Adv. E-mail: advertising@saladovillagevoice.com
Display Adv. E-mail: classifieds@saladovillagevoice.com
Editorial e-mail: news@saladovillagevoice.com
Primary Website: saladovillagevoice.com
Year Established: 1979
Avg Paid Circ: 1500
Audit By: Sworn/Estimate/Non-Audited
Audit Date: 10.06.2019
Personnel: Tim Fleischer (Pub./Ed.); Marilyn Fleischer (Pub./Adv. Mgr.)
Parent company (for newspapers): Salado Village Voice Inc.

SAN ANTONIO BUSINESS JOURNAL

Street address 1: 8200 W Interstate 10
Street address 2: Ste 820
Street address city: San Antonio
Street address state: TX
Zip/Postal code: 78230-3877
General Phone: (210) 341-3202
General Fax: (210) 342-4443
Advertising Phone: (210) 341-3202
Advertising Fax: (210) 342-4443
Editorial Phone: (210) 341-3202
Editorial Fax: (210) 342-4443
General/National Adv. E-mail: sanantonio@bizjournals.com
Display Adv. E-mail: sanantonio@bizjournals.com
Editorial e-mail: sanantonio@bizjournals.com
Primary Website: bizjournals.com/sanantonio
Year Established: 1987
Audit By: Sworn/Estimate/Non-Audited
Audit Date: 10.06.2019
Personnel: Kent Krauss (Pub.); Bill Conroy (Ed.); Mary Jonas (Adv. Dir.)

SAN AUGUSTINE TRIBUNE

Street address 1: 807 E Columbia St
Street address city: San Augustine
Street address state: TX
Zip/Postal code: 75972-2213
General Phone: (936) 275-2181
General Fax: (936) 275-0572
General/National Adv. E-mail: mail@sanaugustinetribune.com
Display Adv. E-mail: mail@sanaugustinetribune.com
Editorial e-mail: mail@sanaugustinetribune.com
Primary Website: sanaugustinetribune.com
Year Established: 1916
Avg Paid Circ: 3000
Avg Free Circ: 300
Audit By: Sworn/Estimate/Non-Audited
Audit Date: 10.06.2019
Personnel: Stephen Hays (Pub./Ed./Adv. Dir.)

SAN BENITO NEWS

Street address 1: PO Box 1791
Street address city: San Benito
Street address state: TX
Zip/Postal code: 78586-0017
General Phone: (956) 399-2436
General Fax: (956) 399-2430
Advertising Phone: (956) 399-2436
Advertising Fax: (956) 399-2430
Editorial Phone: (956) 399-2436
Editorial Fax: (956) 399-2430
General/National Adv. E-mail: publisher@sbnewspaper.com
Display Adv. E-mail: publisher@sbnewspaper.com
Editorial e-mail: editor@sbnewspaper.com
Primary Website: sbnewspaper.com
Year Established: 1929
Avg Paid Circ: 3933
Avg Free Circ: 231
Audit By: Sworn/Estimate/Non-Audited
Audit Date: 10.06.2019
Personnel: Rudy Pena (Adv. Dir./Circ. Mgr.); Ray Quiroga (Publisher)

SAN JACINTO NEWS-TIMES

Street address 1: 100 E Calhoun St
Street address city: Livingston
Street address state: TX
Zip/Postal code: 77351-2908
General Phone: (936) 628-6851
General Fax: (936) 327-7156
Advertising Phone: (936) 327-4357
Advertising Fax: (936) 327-7156
Editorial Phone: (936) 628-6851
Editorial Fax: (936) 327-7156
General/National Adv. E-mail: enterprise@easttexasnews.com
Display Adv. E-mail: enterprise@easttexasnews.com
Editorial e-mail: enterprise@easttexasnews.com
Primary Website: easttexasnews.com
Year Established: 1904
Avg Paid Circ: 2450
Avg Free Circ: 17
Audit By: Sworn/Estimate/Non-Audited
Audit Date: 10.06.2019
Personnel: Alvin Holley (Pub.); Martha Charrey (Ed.); Linda Holley (Adv. Dir.)
Parent company (for newspapers): Polk County Publishing Co.

SAN PATRICIO COUNTY NEWS

Street address 1: 104 N Sehorn St
Street address city: Sinton
Street address state: TX
Zip/Postal code: 78387-2550
General Phone: (361) 364-1270
General Fax: (361) 364-3833
Advertising Phone: (361) 364-1270
Advertising Fax: (361) 364-3833
Editorial Phone: (361) 364-1270
Editorial Fax: (361) 364-3833
General/National Adv. E-mail: advertishing@sanpatpublishing.com
Display Adv. E-mail: receptionist@sanpatpublishing.com
Editorial e-mail: editor@sanpatpublishing.com
Primary Website: sanpatpublishing.com
Year Established: 1901
Avg Paid Circ: 2500
Audit By: Sworn/Estimate/Non-Audited
Audit Date: 10.06.2019
Personnel: James F. Tracy (Co-Pub./Ed.); John Tracy (Co-Pub./Adv. Dir.)
Parent company (for newspapers): San Patricio Publishing Co., Inc.

SAN SABA NEWS & STAR

Street address 1: 505 E Wallace St
Street address city: San Saba
Street address state: TX
Zip/Postal code: 76877-3603
General Phone: (325) 372-5115
General Fax: (325) 372-3973
Advertising Phone: (325) 372-5115
Advertising Fax: (325) 372-3973
Editorial Phone: (325) 372-5115
Editorial Fax: (325) 372-3973
General/National Adv. E-mail: sabanews@centex.net
Display Adv. E-mail: sabanews@centex.net
Editorial e-mail: sabanews@centex.net
Primary Website: sansabanews.com
Year Established: 1873
Avg Paid Circ: 2394
Avg Free Circ: 70
Audit By: Sworn/Estimate/Non-Audited
Audit Date: 10.06.2019

Personnel: Ken Wesner (Pub.); Karen Faught (Pub./Ed.); Yvonne Contreras (Adv. Dir.)

SANGER NEWS

Street address 1: 412 Bolivar St
Street address city: Sanger
Street address state: TX
Zip/Postal code: 76266-8961
General Phone: (940) 458-8515
General Fax: (940) 458-8011
Advertising Phone: (940) 458-8515
Advertising Fax: (940) 458-8011
Editorial Phone: (940) 458-8515
Editorial Fax: (940) 458-8011
General/National Adv. E-mail: sanger@lemonspublications.com
Display Adv. E-mail: sanger@lemonspublications.com
Editorial e-mail: sanger@lemonspublications.com
Primary Website: lemonspublications.com
Year Established: 2012
Avg Paid Circ: 1513
Audit By: Sworn/Estimate/Non-Audited
Audit Date: 10.06.2019
Personnel: Blake Lemons (Pub.); Lee Ann Lemons (Ed./Adv. Dir.)
Parent company (for newspapers): Lemons Publications

SEMINOLE SENTINEL

Street address 1: 406 S Main St
Street address city: Seminole
Street address state: TX
Zip/Postal code: 79360-5058
General Phone: (432) 758-3667
General Fax: (432) 758-2136
Advertising Phone: (432) 758-3667
Advertising Fax: (432) 758-2136
Editorial Phone: (432) 758-3667
Editorial Fax: (432) 758-2136
General/National Adv. E-mail: ads@seminolesentinel.com
Display Adv. E-mail: ads@seminolesentinel.com
Editorial e-mail: news@seminolesentinel.com
Primary Website: seminolesentinel.com
Year Established: 1907
Avg Paid Circ: 2100
Audit By: Sworn/Estimate/Non-Audited
Audit Date: 10.06.2019
Personnel: Dustin Wright (Ed.); Christy Hawkins (Office Mgr.); Misty Ramirez (Adv. Dir.)
Parent company (for newspapers): Roberts Publishing

SILSBEE BEE

Street address 1: 404 Highway 96 S
Street address city: Silsbee
Street address state: TX
Zip/Postal code: 77656-4810
General Phone: (409) 385-5278
General Fax: (409) 385-5270
Advertising Phone: (409) 385-5278
Advertising Fax: (409) 385-5270
Editorial Phone: (409) 385-5278
Editorial Fax: (409) 385-5270
General/National Adv. E-mail: publisher@silsbeebee.com
Display Adv. E-mail: publisher@silsbeebee.com
Editorial e-mail: editor@silsbeebee.com
Primary Website: silsbeebee.com
Year Established: 1919
Avg Paid Circ: 4709
Avg Free Circ: 25
Audit By: Sworn/Estimate/Non-Audited
Audit Date: 10.06.2019
Personnel: Danny Reneau (Pub.); Daniel Elizondo (Ed.); Janet Reneau (Adv. Dir.)
Parent company (for newspapers): Reneau

SOUTH TEXAS REPORTER

Street address 1: 101 E La Fragua Ave
Street address city: Roma
Street address state: TX
Zip/Postal code: 78584-5593
General Phone: (956) 271-4500
General Fax: (956) 267-9322
General/National Adv. E-mail: southtexasreporter@ymail.com
Display Adv. E-mail: southtexasreporter@ymail.com
Editorial e-mail: southtexasreporter@ymail.com
Year Established: 1971
Avg Free Circ: 10000
Audit By: Sworn/Estimate/Non-Audited
Audit Date: 10.06.2019
Personnel: Raul Guerra (Pub./Ed.); Larry Hoelter (Chief Ed.)

SOUTHSIDE REPORTER

Street address 1: 301 Avenue E
Street address city: San Antonio
Street address state: TX
Zip/Postal code: 78297
General Phone: (210) 250-3000
General Fax: (210) 250-3105
Advertising Phone: (210) 250-2500
Advertising Fax: (210) 250-3360
Editorial Phone: (210) 250-3171
Editorial Fax: (210) 250-3105
General/National Adv. E-mail: dbrennan@primetimenewspapers.com
Display Adv. E-mail: dbrennan@primetimenewspapers.com
Classified Adv. e-mail: aaronc@express-news.net
Editorial e-mail: mleary@express-news.net
Primary Website: mysanantonio.com
Year Established: 1935
Avg Free Circ: 16352
Audit By: Sworn/Estimate/Non-Audited
Audit Date: 10.06.2019
Personnel: Tom Stephenson (Pres.); Johnny Flores (Vice. Pres. Sales); Aunna Wright (Prodn. Mgr.); Jamie Stockwell (Mng. Ed.)
Parent company (for newspapers): Hearst Communications, Inc.

SPRING OBSERVER

Street address 1: 100 Avenue A
Street address 2: Ste 108
Street address city: Conroe
Street address state: TX
Zip/Postal code: 77301-2946
General Phone: (936) 521-3400
General Fax: (936) 521-3392
Advertising Phone: (936) 521-3422
Advertising Fax: (936) 521-3392
Editorial Phone: (396) 521-3400
General/National Adv. E-mail: tlegg@hcnonline.com
Display Adv. E-mail: lelizade@hcnonline.com
Editorial e-mail: adubois@hcnonline.com
Primary Website: yourhoustonnews.com
Year Established: 2004
Avg Paid Circ: 0
Avg Free Circ: 18167
Audit By: Sworn/Estimate/Non-Audited
Audit Date: 10.06.2019
Personnel: Richard Davis (Pub./Adv. Dir.); Andy DuBois (Exec. Ed.); Catherine Dominguez (Mng. Ed.); Jason Joseph (Pub.); Charles Lee (Adv. Mgr); Rick Flores (Circ. Mgr); Angela Hicks (Prod. Mgr); Tom Legg (Majors Sr. Acct. Mgr.); Megan O'Sullivan (Mktg. Mgr.)
Parent company (for newspapers): Times Media Group

SPRINGTOWN EPIGRAPH

Street address 1: 109 E 1ST ST
Street address city: Springtown
Street address state: TX
Zip/Postal code: 76082
General Phone: (817) 220-7217
General Fax: (817) 523-4457
Advertising Phone: (817) 220-7217
Advertising Fax: (817) 270-5300
Editorial Phone: (817) 270-3370
Editorial Fax: (817) 270-5300
General/National Adv. E-mail: publisher@azlenews.net
Display Adv. E-mail: classified@azlenews.net
Editorial e-mail: markcampbell@azlenews.net
Primary Website: springtown-epigraph.net
Year Established: 1964
Avg Paid Circ: 1600
Audit By: Sworn/Estimate/Non-Audited
Audit Date: 10.06.2019
Personnel: Kim Ware (Pub./Adv. Dir.); Mark Campbell (Ed.)

STONEWALL COUNTY COURIER

Street address 1: 111 East B St
Street address city: Munday
Street address state: TX
Zip/Postal code: 76371
General Phone: (877) 308-9684
General Fax: (877) 811-4754
Advertising Phone: (877) 308-9684
Advertising Fax: (877) 811-4754
Editorial Phone: (877) 308-9684
Editorial Fax: (877) 811-4754
General/National Adv. E-mail: courier@westex.net
Display Adv. E-mail: courier@westex.net
Editorial e-mail: webmaster@stonewallcountycourier.com
Year Established: 1985
Avg Paid Circ: 900
Avg Free Circ: 60
Audit By: Sworn/Estimate/Non-Audited
Audit Date: 10.06.2019
Personnel: Jay White (Pub./Ed./Adv. Dir.)

STRATFORD STAR

Street address 1: 805 Purnell Ave
Street address city: Stratford
Street address state: TX
Zip/Postal code: 79084-5006
General Phone: (806) 366-5885
General Fax: (806) 366-5884
Advertising Phone: (806) 366-5885
Advertising Fax: (806) 366-5884
Editorial Phone: (806) 366-5885
Editorial Fax: (806) 366-5884
General/National Adv. E-mail: stardm@xit.net
Display Adv. E-mail: stardm@xit.net
Editorial e-mail: stardm@xit.net
Year Established: 1901
Avg Paid Circ: 529
Audit By: Sworn/Estimate/Non-Audited
Audit Date: 10.06.2019
Personnel: Martha Robertson (Pub./Ed.)

SUGAR LAND SUN

Street address 1: 4747 Southwest Freeway
Street address 2: Ste 500
Street address city: Houston
Street address state: TX
Zip/Postal code: 77027
General Phone: (281) 378-1900
General Fax: (713) 520-1193
Advertising Phone: (281) 378-1908
Advertising Fax: (713) 520-1193
Editorial Phone: (281) 378-1911
Editorial Fax: (713) 520-1193
General/National Adv. E-mail: rdavis@hcnonline.com
Display Adv. E-mail: tisaacks@hcnonline.com
Editorial e-mail: rgraham@hcnonline.com
Primary Website: yourhoustonnews.com/sugar_land
Avg Free Circ: 27081
Audit By: Sworn/Estimate/Non-Audited
Audit Date: 10.06.2019
Personnel: Richard Davis (Pub.); Rusty Graham (Ed.); Charles Lee (Adv. Dir.); Megan O'Sullivan (Mktg. Mgr.); Tom Legg (Majors Sr. Acct. Mgr.)
Parent company (for newspapers): Hearst Communications, Inc.; Times Media Group; Brumby Newspapers

SUNDAY SUN

Street address 1: 709 S Main St
Street address city: Georgetown
Street address state: TX
Zip/Postal code: 78626-5700
General Phone: (512) 930-4824
Advertising Phone: (512) 930-4824
Editorial Phone: (512) 930-4824
General/National Adv. E-mail: ads@wilcosun.com
Display Adv. E-mail: class@wilcosun.com
Editorial e-mail: editor@wilcosun.com
Primary Website: wilcosun.com
Year Established: 1974
Avg Paid Circ: 9000
Audit By: Sworn/Estimate/Non-Audited
Audit Date: 10.06.2019
Personnel: Clark Thurmond (Pub.); Linda Scarbrough (Co-Pub./Ed.); Will Anderson (Mng. Ed.); Teri Gray (Adv. Mgr.)

SUNNYVALE VIEW

Street address 1: 624 Krona Dr
Street address 2: Ste 170
Street address city: Plano
Street address state: TX
Zip/Postal code: 75074-8304
General Phone: (972) 398-4471
General Fax: (972) 398-4470
Advertising Phone: (972) 398-4471
Advertising Fax: (972) 398-4470
Editorial Phone: (972) 398-4471
Editorial Fax: (972) 398-4470
General/National Adv. E-mail: llibby@starlocalmedia.com
Display Adv. E-mail: dhemphill@starlocalmedia.com
Editorial e-mail: swright@starlocalmedia.com
Primary Website: starlocalmedia.com
Mthly Avg Views: 546019
Mthly Avg Unique Visitors: 201046
Year Established: 1998
Avg Paid Circ: 21
Avg Free Circ: 1740
Audit By: Sworn/Estimate/Non-Audited
Audit Date: 10.06.2019
Personnel: Mike Miller (Group Pub.); Danny James (National Adv. Dir.); Rick Mann (Mng. Ed.); Della Hemphill (Classifieds)
Parent company (for newspapers): American Community Newspapers LLC

SWISHER COUNTY NEWS

Street address 1: 109 S Austin Ave
Street address city: Tulia
Street address state: TX
Zip/Postal code: 79088-2802
General Phone: (806) 995-0052
Advertising Phone: (806) 995-0052
Editorial Phone: (806) 995-0052
Editorial Fax: (806) 995-0011
General/National Adv. E-mail: swishernews1@gmail.com
Display Adv. E-mail: swishernews1@gmail.com
Classified Adv. e-mail: swishernews1@gmail.com
Editorial e-mail: swishernews1@gmail.com
Primary Website: www.swishernews.com
Year Established: 2009
Avg Paid Circ: 1184
Audit By: Sworn/Estimate/Non-Audited
Audit Date: 10.06.2019
Personnel: Patrice Sims

TAYLOR PRESS

Street address 1: 211 W 3rd St
Street address city: Taylor
Street address state: TX
Zip/Postal code: 76574-3518
General Phone: (512) 3528535
General/National Adv. E-mail: publisher@taylorpress.net
Editorial e-mail: news@taylorpress.net
Primary Website: taylorpress.net
Mthly Avg Views: 110000
Mthly Avg Unique Visitors: 40000
Year Established: 1911
Avg Paid Circ: 2233
Avg Free Circ: 172
Sun. Circulation Paid: 2280
Sun. Circulation Free: 159
Audit By: CVC
Audit Date: 30.09.2016
Personnel: Grace Rangel (Prodn. Mgr., Pre-press); Scott Rucker (Adv. Mgr.); Richard Stone (Pub./Ed.); Jason Hennington (News Ed.)
Parent company (for newspapers): Fenice Community Media

TEAGUE CHRONICLE

Street address 1: 319 Main St
Street address city: Teague
Street address state: TX
Zip/Postal code: 75860-1621
General Phone: (254) 739-2141
General Fax: (254) 739-2144
Advertising Phone: (254) 739-2141
Advertising Fax: (254) 739-2144
Editorial Phone: (254) 739-2141
Editorial Fax: (254) 739-2144
General/National Adv. E-mail: teaguechronicle@sbcglobal.net
Display Adv. E-mail: teaguechronicle@sbcglobal.net
Editorial e-mail: teaguechronicle@sbcglobal.net
Primary Website: teaguechronicle.com
Year Established: 1906

Avg Paid Circ: 2500
Audit By: Sworn/Estimate/Non-Audited
Audit Date: 10.06.2019
Personnel: Steve Massey (Pub./Ed.); Paula Swinburn (Adv. Mgr.)

TEXAS JEWISH POST

Street address 1: 7920 Belt Line Rd
Street address 2: Ste 680
Street address city: Dallas
Street address state: TX
Zip/Postal code: 75254-8150
General Phone: (972) 458-7283
General Fax: (214) 466-2633
General/National Adv. E-mail: susanw@tjpnews.com
Display Adv. E-mail: susanw@tjpnews.com
Editorial e-mail: sharon@tjpnews.com
Primary Website: tjpnews.com
Year Established: 1947
Avg Paid Circ: 3569
Avg Free Circ: 455
Audit By: Sworn/Estimate/Non-Audited
Audit Date: 10.06.2019
Personnel: Sharon Wisch-Ray (Pub./Ed.); Amy Doty (VP, Sales/Mktg.); Susan Wisch (VP Sales and Circ.)
Parent company (for newspapers): Joseph Jacobs Organization

TEXAS LAWYER

Street address 1: 1412 Main St
Street address city: Dallas
Street address state: TX
Zip/Postal code: 75202-4014
General Phone: (214) 744-9300
General Fax: (214) 741-2325
Advertising Phone: (214) 744-7751
Advertising Fax: (214) 741-2325
Editorial Phone: (214) 744-7721
Editorial Fax: (214) 741-2325
General/National Adv. E-mail: ccollins@alm.com
Display Adv. E-mail: ccollins@alm.com
Editorial e-mail: ccollins@alm.com
Primary Website: texaslawyer.com
Year Established: 1985
Avg Paid Circ: 3694
Audit By: Sworn/Estimate/Non-Audited
Audit Date: 10.06.2019
Personnel: Cathy Collins (Pub.); Heather D Nevitt (Ed. in Chief)

TEXAS MOHAIR WEEKLY

Street address 1: 108 N Well St
Street address city: Rocksprings
Street address state: TX
Zip/Postal code: 78880
General Phone: (830) 683-3130
Advertising Phone: (830) 683-3130
Editorial Phone: (830) 683-3130
General/National Adv. E-mail: tmw@swtexas.net
Display Adv. E-mail: tmw@swtexas.net
Editorial e-mail: tmw@swtexas.net
Primary Website: rockspringsrecord.com
Year Established: 1893
Avg Paid Circ: 1100
Audit By: Sworn/Estimate/Non-Audited
Audit Date: 10.09.2021
Personnel: Carolyn Anderson (Co-Pub./Co-Ed./Adv. Dir.); Dean Anderson (Co-Ed./Co-Pub.)

TEXOMA MARKETING AND MEDIA GROUP, PUBLISHER OF THE VAN ALSTYNE LEADER

Street address 1: 603 S Sam Rayburn Fwy
Street address city: Sherman
Street address state: TX
Zip/Postal code: 75090-7258
General Phone: (903) 893-8181
General/National Adv. E-mail: tyoung@heralddemocrat.com
Display Adv. E-mail: tyoung@heralddemocrat.com
Editorial e-mail: svest@heralddemocrat.com
Primary Website: vanalstyneleader.com
Year Established: 1892
Avg Paid Circ: 969
Audit By: Sworn/Estimate/Non-Audited
Audit Date: 10.06.2019
Personnel: Nate Rodriguez (Sr. Grp. Pub.); Sue Vest (Mng. Ed.); William Wadsack (Sr. Mng. Ed.); Teresa Young (Adv. Mgr.)
Parent company (for newspapers): texoma marketing and media group

THE ANAHUAC PROGRESS

Street address 1: 306 Willcox St
Street address city: Anahuac
Street address state: TX
Zip/Postal code: 77514
General Phone: (409) 267-6131
General Fax: (409) 267-4157
General/National Adv. E-mail: theprogress@theanahuacprogress.com
Display Adv. E-mail: theprogress@theanahuacprogress.com
Editorial e-mail: theprogress@theanahuacprogress.com
Primary Website: theanahuacprogress.com
Year Established: 1908
Avg Paid Circ: 647
Avg Free Circ: 0
Audit By: Sworn/Estimate/Non-Audited
Audit Date: 10.06.2019
Personnel: Dayna Haynes (Mng. Ed./Gen. Mgr.)
Parent company (for newspapers): Granite Publishing Partners LLC

THE ANNA-MELISSA TRIBUNE

Street address 1: 603 S Sam Rayburn Fwy
Street address city: Sherman
Street address state: TX
Zip/Postal code: 75090-7258
General Phone: (903) 893-8181
Advertising Phone: (903) 893-8181
Editorial Phone: (903) 893-8181
General/National Adv. E-mail: gmiller@heralddemocrat.com
Display Adv. E-mail: jsewell@heralddemocrat.com
Editorial e-mail: gmiller@heralddemocrat.com
Primary Website: amtrib.com
Year Established: 2002
Avg Free Circ: 9000
Audit By: Sworn/Estimate/Non-Audited
Audit Date: 10.06.2019
Personnel: nate rodriguez (senior group publisher)
Parent company (for newspapers): CherryRoad Media

THE BALLINGER LEDGER

Street address 1: 709 Hutchins Ave
Street address city: Ballinger
Street address state: TX
Zip/Postal code: 76821-5608
General Phone: (325) 365-3501
General Fax: (325) 365-5389
Advertising Phone: (325) 365-3501
Advertising Fax: (325) 365-5389
Editorial Phone: (325) 365-3501
Editorial Fax: (325) 365-5389
General/National Adv. E-mail: news@ballingerledger.com
Display Adv. E-mail: news@ballingerledger.com
Editorial e-mail: news@ballingerledger.com
Primary Website: ballingerledger.com
Year Established: 1886
Avg Paid Circ: 2500
Avg Free Circ: 13
Audit By: Sworn/Estimate/Non-Audited
Audit Date: 10.06.2019
Personnel: Juliet LeMond (Pub.); Ruben Cantu-Rodriguez (Ed.); Brandi Rosenbaum (Adv. Dir.)

THE BANNER PRESS NEWSPAPER

Street address 1: 1217 Bowie St
Street address city: Columbus
Street address state: TX
Zip/Postal code: 78934-2343
General Phone: (979) 732-6243
General Fax: (979) 732-6245
General/National Adv. E-mail: banneroffice@sbcglobal.net
Display Adv. E-mail: london1214@sbcglobal.net
Editorial e-mail: bannercolumbus@sbcglobal.net
Primary Website: bannerpresspaper.com
Year Established: 1985
Avg Paid Circ: 4250
Avg Free Circ: 50
Audit By: Sworn/Estimate/Non-Audited
Audit Date: 10.06.2019
Personnel: Chad Ferguson (Pub./Ed.); Ramona Ferguson (Bookkeeper); London Ferguson (Classified Sales)

THE BASTROP ADVERTISER

Street address 1: 1106 College St
Street address 2: Ste C
Street address city: Bastrop
Street address state: TX
Zip/Postal code: 78602-3948
General Phone: (512) 321-2557
General Fax: (512) 321-1680
Advertising Phone: (512) 321-2557
Advertising Fax: (512) 321-1680
Editorial Phone: (512) 321-2557
Editorial Fax: (512) 321-1680
Display Adv. E-mail: classifieds@statesman.com
Editorial e-mail: asevilla@statesman.com
Primary Website: bastropadvertiser.com
Year Established: 1853
Avg Free Circ: 3091
Audit By: Sworn/Estimate/Non-Audited
Audit Date: 10.06.2019
Personnel: Patrick E. Dorsey (Pub.); Andy Sevilla (Ed.)
Parent company (for newspapers): Cox Media Group; Gannett

THE BAY CITY TRIBUNE

Street address 1: 2901 Carey Smith Boulevard
Street address city: Bay City
Street address state: TX
Zip/Postal code: 77414
General Phone: (979) 245-5555
General Fax: (979) 244-5908
Advertising Phone: (979) 245-5555
Advertising Fax: (979) 244-5908
Editorial Phone: (979) 245-5555
Editorial Fax: (979) 244-5908
General/National Adv. E-mail: brenda.burr@baycitytribune.com
Display Adv. E-mail: brenda.burr@baycitytribune.com
Editorial e-mail: brenda.burr@baycitytribune.com
Primary Website: baycitytribune.com
Year Established: 1845
Avg Paid Circ: 2385
Avg Free Circ: 708
Audit By: AAM
Audit Date: 31.03.2019
Personnel: Brenda Burr (Pub./Adv. Dir.); Jimmy Galvan (Mng. Ed.); Arthur Amenta (Circ. Mgr.)
Parent company (for newspapers): Southern Newspapers Inc.

THE BEE

Street address 1: 404 Broadnax Street
Street address 2: Suite 4
Street address city: Daingerfield
Street address state: TX
Zip/Postal code: 75638
General Phone: (903) 645-3948
Advertising Phone: (903) 645-3948
Advertising Fax: (903) 645-3731
Editorial Phone: (903) 645-3948
Editorial Fax: (903) 645-3731
General/National Adv. E-mail: thebee@etcnonline.com
Display Adv. E-mail: beenewspaper@etcnonline.com
Editorial e-mail: alewter@steelcountrybee.com
Primary Website: steelcountrybee.com
Year Established: 1965
Avg Paid Circ: 3100
Avg Free Circ: 3068
Audit By: Sworn/Estimate/Non-Audited
Audit Date: 10.06.2019
Personnel: Leslie Brosnan (Adv. Mgr.); Toni Walker (Ed.)
Parent company (for newspapers): Northeast Texas Publishing

THE BELLVILLE TIMES

Street address 1: 106 E Palm St
Street address city: Bellville
Street address state: TX
Zip/Postal code: 77418-1544
General Phone: (979) 865-3131
General Fax: (979) 865-3132
Advertising Phone: (979) 865-3131
Advertising Fax: (979) 865-3132
Editorial Phone: (979) 865-3131
Editorial Fax: (979) 865-3132
General/National Adv. E-mail: bvtimes@sbcglobal.net
Display Adv. E-mail: bvtimes@sbcglobal.net
Editorial e-mail: bvtimes@sbcglobal.net
Primary Website: bellvilletimes.com
Year Established: 1879
Avg Paid Circ: 4100
Avg Free Circ: 44
Audit By: Sworn/Estimate/Non-Audited
Audit Date: 10.06.2019
Personnel: Bruce White (Pub./Ed.); Angie Grawunder (Adv. Dir.)

THE BELTON JOURNAL

Street address 1: 210 N Penelope St
Street address city: Belton
Street address state: TX
Zip/Postal code: 76513-3159
General Phone: (254) 939-5754
General Fax: (254) 939-2333
General/National Adv. E-mail: david@beltonjournal.com
Display Adv. E-mail: david@beltonjournal.com
Editorial e-mail: editor@beltonjournal.com
Primary Website: beltonjournal.com
Year Established: 1866
Avg Paid Circ: 4090
Audit By: Sworn/Estimate/Non-Audited
Audit Date: 10.06.2019
Personnel: David Tuma (Pub.); Matthew Girard (Ed.); Susan Gibson (Adv. Dir.)

THE BIG BEND SENTINEL

Street address 1: 110 N Highland Ave
Street address city: Marfa
Street address state: TX
Zip/Postal code: 79843-6500
General Phone: (432) 729-4342
Advertising Phone: (432) 729-4342
Editorial Phone: (432) 729-4342
General/National Adv. E-mail: rosario@bigbendsentinel.com
Display Adv. E-mail: rosario@bigbendsentinel.com
Editorial e-mail: editor@bigbendsentinel.com
Primary Website: bigbendnow.com
Year Established: 1926
Avg Paid Circ: 2658
Avg Free Circ: 25
Audit By: Sworn/Estimate/Non-Audited
Audit Date: 10.06.2019
Personnel: Robert L. Halpern (Pub./Ed.); Rosario Halpern-Salgado (CFO/Adv. Dir.)

THE BOWIE NEWS

Street address 1: 200 Walnut Street
Street address city: Bowie
Street address state: TX
Zip/Postal code: 76230-5036
General Phone: (940) 872-2247
General Fax: (940) 872-4812
Advertising Phone: (940) 872-2247
Advertising Fax: (940) 872-4812
Editorial Phone: (940) 872-2247
Editorial Fax: (940) 872-4812
General/National Adv. E-mail: ads@bowienewsonline.com
Display Adv. E-mail: classifieds@bowienewsonline.com
Editorial e-mail: editor@bowienewsonline.com
Primary Website: bowienewsonline.com
Year Established: 1922
Avg Paid Circ: 4700
Avg Free Circ: 550
Audit By: Sworn/Estimate/Non-Audited
Audit Date: 10.06.2019
Personnel: Michael Winter (Owner/Pub.); Barbara Beckwith Green (Ed.)

THE BRAZORIA COUNTY NEWS

Street address 1: 113 E Bernard St
Street address city: West Columbia
Street address state: TX
Zip/Postal code: 77486-3213
General Phone: (979) 345-3127
General Fax: (979) 345-5308
Advertising Phone: (979) 345-3127
Advertising Fax: (979) 345-5308
Editorial Phone: (979) 345-3127
Editorial Fax: (979) 345-5308

General/National Adv. E-mail: thenews@brazoriacountynews.com
Display Adv. E-mail: gctribune@consolidated.net
Editorial e-mail: thenews@brazoriacountynews.com
Primary Website: brazoriacountynews.com
Year Established: 1962
Avg Free Circ: 11000
Audit By: Sworn/Estimate/Non-Audited
Audit Date: 10.06.2019
Personnel: David E. Toney (Pub.); Becky Toney Hutchinson (Ed.)

THE BREMOND PRESS

Street address 1: 301 S Main St
Street address city: Bremond
Street address state: TX
Zip/Postal code: 76629
General Phone: (254) 746-7033
General Fax: (254) 746-7089
Advertising Phone: (254) 746-7033
Advertising Fax: (254) 746-7089
Editorial Phone: (254) 746-7033
Editorial Fax: (254) 746-7089
General/National Adv. E-mail: bremondpress@earthlink.net
Display Adv. E-mail: bremondpress@earthlink.net
Editorial e-mail: bremondpress@earthlink.net
Year Established: 1922
Avg Paid Circ: 1319
Audit By: Sworn/Estimate/Non-Audited
Audit Date: 10.06.2019
Personnel: Betty Yezak (Pub./Ed.); George Yezak (Adv. Dir.)

THE BUFFALO PRESS

Street address 1: 924 W Commerce
Street address city: Buffalo
Street address state: TX
Zip/Postal code: 75831
General Phone: (903) 322-4248
General Fax: (903) 322-4023
Advertising Phone: (903) 322-4248
Advertising Fax: (903) 322-4023
Editorial Phone: (903) 322-4248
Editorial Fax: (903) 322-4023
General/National Adv. E-mail: buffalopress@gmail.com
Display Adv. E-mail: buffalopress@gmail.com
Editorial e-mail: buffalopress@gmail.com
Primary Website: leoncountytoday.com
Year Established: 1931
Avg Paid Circ: 3000
Avg Free Circ: 2500
Audit By: Sworn/Estimate/Non-Audited
Audit Date: 10.06.2019
Personnel: Mac Shadix (Pub.); Richard Moran (Sales Dir.); Linda Smith (Prodn. Mgr.)

THE BULLETIN

Street address 1: PO Box 2426
Street address city: Angleton
Street address state: TX
Zip/Postal code: 77516-2426
General Phone: (979) 849-5407
General Fax: (866) 844-5288
Advertising Phone: (979) 849-5407
Advertising Fax: (866) 844-5288
Editorial Phone: (979) 849-5407
Editorial Fax: (866) 844-5288
General/National Adv. E-mail: sharon.bulletin@gmail.com
Display Adv. E-mail: sharon.bulletin@gmail.com
Editorial e-mail: john.bulletin@gmail.com
Primary Website: mybulletinnewspaper.com
Year Established: 1994
Avg Free Circ: 6000
Audit By: Sworn/Estimate/Non-Audited
Audit Date: 10.06.2019
Personnel: Sharon Toth (Co-Publisher /Advertising Director); John Toth (Ed.)
Parent company (for newspapers): J&S Communications

THE BUNA BEACON

Street address 1: 566 TX State Highway 62
Street address city: Buna
Street address state: TX
Zip/Postal code: 77612-6472
General Phone: (409) 994-2218
General Fax: (409) 994-0228
Advertising Phone: (409) 994-2218
Advertising Fax: (409) 994-0228
Editorial Phone: (409) 994-2218
Editorial Fax: (409) 994-0228
General/National Adv. E-mail: publisher@bunabeacon.com
Display Adv. E-mail: advertising@bunabeacon.com
Editorial e-mail: editor@bunabeacon.com
Primary Website: bunabeacon.com
Year Established: 1990
Avg Paid Circ: 1601
Audit By: Sworn/Estimate/Non-Audited
Audit Date: 10.06.2019
Personnel: Barbara Davis (Co-Pub./Mng. Ed.); Terry Wells (Co-Pub./Adv. Dir.)

THE CAMERON HERALD

Street address 1: 108 E 1st St
Street address city: Cameron
Street address state: TX
Zip/Postal code: 76520-3341
General Phone: (254) 697-6671
General Fax: (254) 697-4902
Advertising Phone: (254) 697-6671
Advertising Fax: (254) 697-4902
Editorial Phone: (254) 697-6671
Editorial Fax: (254) 697-4902
General/National Adv. E-mail: herald@cameronherald.com
Display Adv. E-mail: classifieds@cameronherald.com
Editorial e-mail: publisher@cameronherald.com
Primary Website: cameronherald.com
Year Established: 1860
Avg Paid Circ: 1943
Avg Free Circ: 123
Audit By: Sworn/Estimate/Non-Audited
Audit Date: 10.06.2019
Personnel: Phil Major (Pub./Ed.); Candace Velvin (Interim Pub.); Elissa Hernandez (Adv. Mgr.); Clydell Seaton (Office Mgr.)

THE CANADIAN RECORD

Street address 1: 211 Main St
Street address city: Canadian
Street address state: TX
Zip/Postal code: 79014-2212
General Phone: (806) 323-6461
General Fax: (806) 323-5738
Advertising Phone: (806) 323-6461
Advertising Fax: (806) 323-5738
Editorial Phone: (806) 323-6461
Editorial Fax: (806) 323-5738
General/National Adv. E-mail: ray@canadianrecord.com
Display Adv. E-mail: mary@canadianrecord.com
Editorial e-mail: laurie@canadianrecord.com
Primary Website: canadianrecord.com
Year Established: 1893
Avg Paid Circ: 1750
Avg Free Circ: 35
Audit By: Sworn/Estimate/Non-Audited
Audit Date: 10.06.2019
Personnel: Laurie Ezzell Brown (Pub./Ed.); Mary L. Smithee (Bus. Mgr.); Ray Weeks (Adv. Mgr.); Jaquita Adcock (Adv. Sales); Peyton Aufill (Sports Ed); Cathy Ricketts (News Ed)

THE CANYON NEWS

Street address 1: 1500 5th Ave
Street address city: Canyon
Street address state: TX
Zip/Postal code: 79015-3830
General Phone: (806) 655-7121
General Fax: (806) 655-0823
Advertising Phone: (806) 655-7121
Advertising Fax: (806) 655-0823
Editorial Phone: (806) 655-7121
Editorial Fax: (806) 655-0823
General/National Adv. E-mail: marketing@canyonnews.com
Display Adv. E-mail: marketing@canyonnews.com
Editorial e-mail: news@canyonnews.com
Primary Website: canyonnews.com
Year Established: 1896
Avg Paid Circ: 3900
Avg Free Circ: 300
Audit By: Sworn/Estimate/Non-Audited
Audit Date: 10.06.2019
Personnel: Debbie Aylesworth (Pub.); James Barrington (Ed.)
Parent company (for newspapers): Hearst Communications, Inc.

THE CASS COUNTY SUN

Street address 1: 122 W Houston St
Street address city: Linden
Street address state: TX
Zip/Postal code: 75563-5556
General Phone: (903) 756-7396
General Fax: (903) 756-3038
Advertising Phone: (903) 756-7396
Advertising Fax: (903) 756-3038
Editorial Phone: (903) 756-7396
Editorial Fax: (903) 756-3038
General/National Adv. E-mail: aguillory@casscountynow.com
Display Adv. E-mail: aguillory@casscountynow.com
Editorial e-mail: bwoods@casscountynow.com
Primary Website: casscountynow.com
Year Established: 1876
Avg Paid Circ: 1100
Avg Free Circ: 1075
Audit By: Sworn/Estimate/Non-Audited
Audit Date: 10.06.2019
Personnel: Angela Guillory (Ad Mgr); Ben Woods (Editor); Rachel Woods (General Manager)
Parent company (for newspapers): Northeast Texas Publishing

THE CASTRO COUNTY NEWS

Street address 1: 108 W Bedford St
Street address city: Dimmitt
Street address state: TX
Zip/Postal code: 79027-2504
General Phone: (806) 647-1234
General Fax: (866) 563-8728
Advertising Phone: (806) 647-1234
Advertising Fax: (866) 563-8728
Editorial Phone: (806) 647-1234
Editorial Fax: (866) 563-8728
General/National Adv. E-mail: thecastrocountynews@yahoo.com
Display Adv. E-mail: newspaperjeff@yahoo.com
Editorial e-mail: thecastrocountynews@yahoo.com
Primary Website: thecastrocountynews.com
Year Established: 1924
Avg Paid Circ: 1500
Avg Free Circ: 62
Audit By: Sworn/Estimate/Non-Audited
Audit Date: 10.06.2019
Personnel: Jeff Blackmon (Adv. Dir.); Bill Holland (Assoc. Pub.); Brett Wesner (Pub.)

THE CLAUDE NEWS

Street address 1: 119 N Trice St
Street address city: Claude
Street address state: TX
Zip/Postal code: 79019
General Phone: (806) 226-4500
General Fax: (806) 222-0023
Advertising Phone: (806) 226-4500
Advertising Fax: (806) 222-0023
Editorial Phone: (806) 226-4500
Editorial Fax: (806) 222-0023
General/National Adv. E-mail: editor@claudenews.com
Display Adv. E-mail: editor@claudenews.com
Editorial e-mail: editor@claudenews.com
Primary Website: claudenews.com
Year Established: 1890
Avg Paid Circ: 700
Audit By: Sworn/Estimate/Non-Audited
Audit Date: 10.06.2019
Personnel: Jessica Montgomery (Co-Pub./Ed./Adv. Dir.); Will Montgomery (Co-Pub.)

THE CLIFTON RECORD

Street address 1: 310 W 5th St
Street address city: Clifton
Street address state: TX
Zip/Postal code: 76634-1611
General Phone: (254) 675-3336
General Fax: (254) 675-4090
Advertising Phone: (254) 675-3336
Advertising Fax: (254) 675-4090
Editorial Phone: (254) 675-3336
Editorial Fax: (254) 675-4090
General/National Adv. E-mail: Bvoss@cliftonrecord.com
Display Adv. E-mail: Joyce@meridiantribune.com
Editorial e-mail: Simone@cliftonrecord.com
Primary Website: cliftonrecord.com
Year Established: 1895
Avg Paid Circ: 2303
Audit By: Sworn/Estimate/Non-Audited
Audit Date: 10.06.2019
Personnel: Brett Voss (Pub./Ed.)

THE COLONY COURIER LEADER

Street address 1: 624 Krona Dr
Street address 2: Ste 170
Street address city: Plano
Street address state: TX
Zip/Postal code: 75074-8304
General Phone: (972) 398-4200
General Fax: (972) 398-4470
General/National Adv. E-mail: jdittrich@starlocalmedia.com
Display Adv. E-mail: jdittrich@starlocalmedia.com
Editorial e-mail: croark@starlocalmedia.com
Primary Website: starlocalnews.com
Mthly Avg Views: 546019
Mthly Avg Unique Visitors: 201046
Year Established: 1981
Avg Paid Circ: 223
Avg Free Circ: 6801
Audit By: CVC
Audit Date: 31.12.2018
Personnel: Scott Wright (Pub.); Chris Roark (Ed.); Melissa Rougeot (Circ. Mgr); Joani Dittrich (Adv. VP); Justin Thomas (Sports Rep.)
Parent company (for newspapers): S.A.W. Advisors, LLC; Star Community Newspapers

THE COLORADO COUNTY CITIZEN

Street address 1: 2024 Highway 71 S
Street address city: Columbus
Street address state: TX
Zip/Postal code: 78934-2820
General Phone: (979) 732-2304
General Fax: (979) 732-8804
Advertising Phone: (979) 732-2304
Advertising Fax: (979) 732-8804
Editorial Phone: (979) 732-2304
Editorial Fax: (979) 732-8804
General/National Adv. E-mail: publisher@coloradocountycitizen.com
Display Adv. E-mail: ads@coloradocountycitizen.com
Editorial e-mail: editor@coloradocountycitizen.com
Primary Website: coloradocountycitizen.com
Year Established: 1857
Avg Paid Circ: 2868
Avg Free Circ: 50
Audit By: Sworn/Estimate/Non-Audited
Audit Date: 10.06.2019
Personnel: Michelle Banse (Pub.); John Brown; Roxanne Glover (Adv. Dir.); Gina Sides (Bookkeeper)
Parent company (for newspapers): Fenice Community Media

THE COMANCHE CHIEF

Street address 1: 203 W Grand Ave
Street address city: Comanche
Street address state: TX
Zip/Postal code: 76442-2316
General Phone: (325) 356-2636
General Fax: (325) 356-5380
Advertising Phone: (325) 356-2636
Advertising Fax: (325) 356-5380
Editorial Phone: (325) 356-2636
Editorial Fax: (325) 356-5380
General/National Adv. E-mail: editor@thecomanchechief.com
Display Adv. E-mail: editor@thecomanchechief.com
Editorial e-mail: editor@thecomanchechief.com
Primary Website: thecomanchechief.com
Year Established: 1873
Avg Paid Circ: 3000
Audit By: Sworn/Estimate/Non-Audited
Audit Date: 10.06.2019

Personnel: Bradley Wilkerson (Editor); Lance Wilkerson (Editor)

THE COMFORT NEWS

Street address 1: 504B Sixth St
Street address city: Comfort
Street address state: TX
Zip/Postal code: 78013-2318
General Phone: (830) 995-3634
General Fax: (830) 995-2075
General/National Adv. E-mail: dukecomfort@hctc.net
Display Adv. E-mail: dukecomfort@hctc.net
Editorial e-mail: dukecomfort@hctc.net
Primary Website: thecomfortnews.com
Year Established: 1904
Avg Paid Circ: 1146
Audit By: Sworn/Estimate/Non-Audited
Audit Date: 10.06.2019
Personnel: Deborah Hawkins (Co-Pub.); Michael Hawkins (Co-Pub./Ed.); Bill Terry (Features editor and photographer); Michele Coover (Office Mgr.)
Parent company (for newspapers): The Comfort News & Print, Inc.

THE COMMUNITY NEWS

Street address 1: 203 Pecan Dr
Street address city: Aledo
Street address state: TX
Zip/Postal code: 76008
General Phone: (817) 441-7661
General Fax: (817) 441-5419
Advertising Phone: (817) 441-7661
Advertising Fax: (817) 441-5419
Editorial Phone: (817) 441-7661
Editorial Fax: (817) 441-5419
General/National Adv. E-mail: business@community-news.com
Display Adv. E-mail: business@community-news.com
Editorial e-mail: news@community-news.com
Primary Website: community-news.com
Year Established: 1995
Avg Paid Circ: 2244
Audit By: Sworn/Estimate/Non-Audited
Audit Date: 10.06.2019
Personnel: Randy Keck (Pub./Ed.); Loydale Schmid (Adv. Dir.); Phil Major

THE CONCHO HERALD

Street address 1: 104 Robinson St
Street address city: Miles
Street address state: TX
Zip/Postal code: 76861
General Phone: (325) 468-3611
General Fax: (325) 468-3611
Advertising Phone: (325) 468-3611
Advertising Fax: (325) 468-3611
Editorial Phone: (325) 468-3611
Editorial Fax: (325) 468-3611
General/National Adv. E-mail: shortcake56@verizon.net
Display Adv. E-mail: shortcake56@verizon.net
Editorial e-mail: shortcake56@verizon.net
Year Established: 1890
Avg Paid Circ: 200
Audit By: Sworn/Estimate/Non-Audited
Audit Date: 10.06.2019
Personnel: Donna Glass (Pub./Ed./Adv. Dir.)

THE CUERO RECORD

Street address 1: 119 E Main St
Street address city: Cuero
Street address state: TX
Zip/Postal code: 77954-3021
General Phone: (361) 275-3464
General Fax: (361) 275-3131
Advertising Phone: (361) 275-3464
Advertising Fax: (361) 275-3131
Editorial Phone: (361) 275-3464
Editorial Fax: (361) 275-3131
General/National Adv. E-mail: cuerorecord@cuerorecord.com
Display Adv. E-mail: cuerorecord@cuerorecord.com
Editorial e-mail: cuerorecord@cuerorecord.com
Primary Website: cuerorecord.com
Year Established: 1894
Avg Paid Circ: 2445
Avg Free Circ: 2685
Audit By: Sworn/Estimate/Non-Audited
Audit Date: 10.06.2019
Personnel: Glenn Rea (Pub./Ed.); Sonya Timpone (Adv. Dir.)
Parent company (for newspapers): Moser Community Media

THE DUBLIN CITIZEN

Street address 1: 938 N Patrick St
Street address city: Dublin
Street address state: TX
Zip/Postal code: 76446-1128
General Phone: (254) 445-2515
General Fax: (254) 445-4116
Advertising Phone: (254)445-2515
Advertising Fax: (254)445-4116
Editorial Phone: (254)445-2515
Editorial Fax: (254)445-4116
General/National Adv. E-mail: publisher@dublincitizen.com
Display Adv. E-mail: classifieds@dublincitizen.com
Editorial e-mail: publisher@dublincitizen.com
Primary Website: dublincitizen.com
Year Established: 1990
Avg Paid Circ: 2400
Audit By: Sworn/Estimate/Non-Audited
Audit Date: 10.06.2019
Personnel: Mac McKinnon (Pub./Ed./Owner); Cindy Combs (Bus. Mgr.)

THE EAGLE PRESS

Street address 1: None
Street address city: Fritch
Street address state: TX
Zip/Postal code: 79036
General Phone: (806) 275-0015
General/National Adv. E-mail: tara.eaglepress@ymail.com
Display Adv. E-mail: tara.eaglepress@ymail.com
Editorial e-mail: tara.eaglepress@ymail.com
Year Established: 1987
Avg Paid Circ: 808
Audit By: Sworn/Estimate/Non-Audited
Audit Date: 10.06.2019
Personnel: Tara Huff (Pub./Ed./Adv. Dir.)

THE EDEN ECHO

Street address 1: 131 Market St
Street address city: Eden
Street address state: TX
Zip/Postal code: 76837
General Phone: (325) 869-5717
Advertising Phone: (325) 869-5717
Editorial Phone: (325) 869-5717
General/National Adv. E-mail: edenecho@wcc.net
Display Adv. E-mail: edenecho@wcc.net
Editorial e-mail: edenecho@wcc.net
Primary Website: EDENECHO.NET
Year Established: 1906
Avg Paid Circ: 610
Avg Free Circ: 30
Audit By: Sworn/Estimate/Non-Audited
Audit Date: 10.06.2019
Personnel: A.J. Dolle (Pub./Ed./Adv. Dir.); Lillian Harrod (Ed.)
Parent company (for newspapers): EDEN APPLE TREE ENTERPRISES LLC

THE ELLIS COUNTY PRESS

Street address 1: 208 S Central St
Street address city: Ferris
Street address state: TX
Zip/Postal code: 75125-2622
General Phone: (972) 544-2369
General/National Adv. E-mail: press@elliscountypress.com
Display Adv. E-mail: charles@elliscountypress.com
Classified Adv. e-mail: charles@elliscountypress.com
Editorial e-mail: charles@elliscountypress.com
Primary Website: elliscountypress.com
Mthly Avg Views: 14348
Mthly Avg Unique Visitors: 10622
Year Established: 1992
Avg Paid Circ: 2500
Avg Free Circ: 500
Audit By: Sworn/Estimate/Non-Audited
Audit Date: 29.09.2022
Personnel: Charles D. Hatfield Jr. (Pub./Owner/Ed.); Shirley Habingga (Inside Ad Sales); Greg Chapman (Creative Dir.); Rita Cook (News Ed.)
Parent company (for newspapers): County Press Enterprises, LLC

THE EXAMINERS

Street address 1: 100 Avenue A
Street address 2: Ste 200
Street address city: Conroe
Street address state: TX
Zip/Postal code: 77301-2946
General Phone: (281) 378-1900
General Fax: (713) 520-1193
Advertising Phone: (281) 378-1906
Advertising Fax: (713) 520-1193
Editorial Phone: (281) 378-1911
Editorial Fax: (713) 520-1193
General/National Adv. E-mail: rdavis@hcnonline.com
Display Adv. E-mail: pstewart@hcnonline.com
Editorial e-mail: rgraham@hcnonline.com
Primary Website: Examinernews.com
Year Established: 2001
Avg Paid Circ: 0
Avg Free Circ: 33286
Audit By: Sworn/Estimate/Non-Audited
Audit Date: 10.06.2019
Personnel: Richard Davis (Pub.); Rusty Graham (Ed.); Jason Joseph (Pub.); Charles Lee (Adv. Mgr); Rick Flores (Circ. Mgr); Clayton Harris (Prod. Mgr); Tom Legg (Major Sr. Acct. Mgr.); Megan O'Sullivan (Mktg. Mgr.)
Parent company (for newspapers): Hearst Communications, Inc.

THE FAIRFIELD RECORDER

Street address 1: 101 E Commerce St
Street address city: Fairfield
Street address state: TX
Zip/Postal code: 75840-1507
General Phone: (903) 389-3334
General Fax: (903) 389-8255
General/National Adv. E-mail: office@fairfield-recorder.com
Display Adv. E-mail: classifieds@fairfield-recorder.com
Editorial e-mail: news@fairfield-recorder.com
Primary Website: fairfield-recorder.com
Year Established: 1876
Avg Paid Circ: 2000
Audit By: Sworn/Estimate/Non-Audited
Audit Date: 10.06.2019
Personnel: Laura Robinson (Bookkeeper, Advertising); April Walker (Gen. Mgr.); Timothy O'Malley (Pub.)
Parent company (for newspapers): Freestone County Publishing LP

THE FAYETTE COUNTY RECORD

Street address 1: 127 S Washington St
Street address city: La Grange
Street address state: TX
Zip/Postal code: 78945-2628
General Phone: (979) 968-3155
General Fax: (979) 968-6767
Advertising Phone: (979) 968-3155
Advertising Fax: (979) 968-6767
Editorial Phone: (979) 968-3155
Editorial Fax: (979) 968-6767
General/National Adv. E-mail: becky@fayettecountyrecord.com
Display Adv. E-mail: jackie@fayettecountyrecord.com
Editorial e-mail: regina@fayettecountyrecord.com
Primary Website: fayettecountyrecord.com
Year Established: 1922
Avg Paid Circ: 5477
Avg Free Circ: 51
Audit By: Sworn/Estimate/Non-Audited
Audit Date: 10.06.2019
Personnel: Regina Keilers (Pub.); Jeff Wick (Ed.); Becky Weise (Adv. Dir.); Jackie Daniels (Classified Mgr.); Theresia Karstedt (Circ. Mgr.); Aileen Loehr (Office Mgr.); John Castaneda (Prod. Mgr.)
Parent company (for newspapers): Fayette County Record, Inc.

THE FLATONIA ARGUS

Street address 1: 212 S Penn Ave
Street address city: Flatonia
Street address state: TX
Zip/Postal code: 78941
General Phone: (361) 865-3510
General Fax: (361) 865-3510
Advertising Phone: (361) 865-3510
Advertising Fax: (361) 865-3510
Editorial Phone: (361) 865-3510
Editorial Fax: (361) 865-3510
General/National Adv. E-mail: admanager@flatoniaargus.com
Display Adv. E-mail: admanager@flatoniaargus.com
Editorial e-mail: newspaper@flatoniaargus.com
Primary Website: flatoniaargus.com
Year Established: 1875
Avg Paid Circ: 940
Avg Free Circ: 38
Audit By: Sworn/Estimate/Non-Audited
Audit Date: 10.06.2019
Personnel: Paul A. Prause (Pub./Ed./Adv. Dir.); Melanie Berger (Office Mgr./Reporter/Photo.)

THE FORT STOCKTON PIONEER

Street address 1: 210 N Nelson St
Street address city: Fort Stockton
Street address state: TX
Zip/Postal code: 79735-6724
General Phone: (432) 336-2281
General Fax: (432) 336-6432
Advertising Phone: (432) 336-2281
Advertising Fax: (432) 336-6432
Editorial Phone: (432) 336-2281
Editorial Fax: (432) 336-6432
General/National Adv. E-mail: publisher@fspioneer.com
Display Adv. E-mail: publisher@fspioneer.com
Editorial e-mail: pioneer@fspioneer.com
Primary Website: fortstocktonpioneer.com
Year Established: 1908
Avg Paid Circ: 3365
Audit By: Sworn/Estimate/Non-Audited
Audit Date: 10.06.2019
Personnel: Pam Palileo (Pub./Adv. Dir./Ed.)
Parent company (for newspapers): Fenice Community Media

THE FRIONA STAR

Street address 1: 916 Main St
Street address city: Friona
Street address state: TX
Zip/Postal code: 79035-2042
General Phone: (806) 250-2211
General Fax: (806) 250-5127
General/National Adv. E-mail: frionastar@wtrt.net
Display Adv. E-mail: frionastar@wtrt.net
Editorial e-mail: frionastar@wtrt.net
Primary Website: frionaonline.com
Year Established: 1925
Avg Paid Circ: 1350
Audit By: Sworn/Estimate/Non-Audited
Audit Date: 10.06.2019
Personnel: Dana Jameson (Mng Ed.)

THE GONZALES CANNON

Street address 1: 901 N Saint Joseph St
Street address city: Gonzales
Street address state: TX
Zip/Postal code: 78629-3566
General Phone: (830) 672-7100
General Fax: (830) 672-7111
Advertising Phone: (830)672-7100
Advertising Fax: (830)672-7111
Editorial Phone: (830)672-7100
Editorial Fax: (830)672-7111
General/National Adv. E-mail: advertising@gonzalescannon.com
Display Adv. E-mail: subscriptions@gonzalescannon.com
Editorial e-mail: news@gonzalescannon.com
Primary Website: gonzalescannon.com
Year Established: 2009
Avg Paid Circ: 2500
Avg Free Circ: 500
Audit By: Sworn/Estimate/Non-Audited
Audit Date: 10.06.2019
Personnel: Sanya Harkey; Mark Lube; Dorothy Gast; Kathryn Penrose (News Editor); Chris Johnson (Reporter); Michael McCracken (Pub.)

THE GONZALES INQUIRER

Street address 1: 622 Saint Paul St

Street address city: Gonzales
Street address state: TX
Zip/Postal code: 78629-3552
General Phone: (830) 672-2861
General Fax: (830) 672-7029
Advertising Phone: (830) 672-2861
Advertising Fax: (830) 672-7029
Editorial Phone: (830) 672-2861
Editorial Fax: (830) 672-7029
General/National Adv. E-mail: publisher@gonzalesinquirer.com
Display Adv. E-mail: ads@gonzalesinquirer.com
Editorial e-mail: news@gonalesinquirer.com
Primary Website: gonzalesinquirer.com
Year Established: 1853
Avg Paid Circ: 1189
Avg Free Circ: 1088
Audit By: Sworn/Estimate/Non-Audited
Audit Date: 10.06.2019
Personnel: Brandi Guy (Ed./Pub.); Kim Brewer (Office Mgr.); Jessie Hott (Adv. Mgr.); Cammy Lewis (Classifieds Adv. Sales); Shane Taylor (Adv. Sales); Rob Ford (Reporter); Jose Torres; Valerie Reddell
Parent company (for newspapers): Fenice Community Media

THE GRAHAM LEADER

Street address 1: 620 Oak Street
Street address city: Graham
Street address state: TX
Zip/Postal code: 76450-3040
General Phone: 940-549-7800
Advertising Phone: 940-549-7800
Editorial Phone: 940-549-7800
General/National Adv. E-mail: kbailey@grahamleader.com
Display Adv. E-mail: admgr@grahamleader.com
Classified Adv. e-mail: classified@grahamleader.com
Editorial e-mail: editor@grahamleader.com
Primary Website: www.grahamleader.com
Year Established: 1876
Avg Paid Circ: 2000
Avg Free Circ: 50
Audit By: Sworn/Estimate/Non-Audited
Audit Date: 08.09.2022
Personnel: Thomas Wallner (Editor); Kylie Bailey (Publisher/Creative Director); Krystin Stell (Advertising Representative); Maddison Evans (Circulation/Classified Manager)
Parent company (for newspapers): Palo Pinto Communications, LP

THE GULF COAST TRIBUNE

Street address 1: 3115 School St
Street address city: Needville
Street address state: TX
Zip/Postal code: 77461-8446
General Phone: (979) 793-6560
General Fax: (979) 793-4260
Advertising Phone: (979) 793-6560
Advertising Fax: (979) 793-4260
Editorial Phone: (979) 793-6560
Editorial Fax: (979) 793-4260
General/National Adv. E-mail: advertising@consolidated.net
Display Adv. E-mail: advertising@consolidated.net
Editorial e-mail: gctribune@consolidated.net
Primary Website: fbherald.com
Year Established: 1962
Avg Paid Circ: 1200
Avg Free Circ: 67
Audit By: Sworn/Estimate/Non-Audited
Audit Date: 10.06.2019
Personnel: David E. Toney (Pub.); Rebecca Hutchinson (Ed.); Dale McFarland (Adv. Dir.)

THE HANSFORD COUNTY REPORTER-STATESMAN

Street address 1: 310 Barkley Street
Street address city: Spearman
Street address state: TX
Zip/Postal code: 79081-2065
General Phone: (806) 659-3434
Advertising Phone: (806) 659-3434
Editorial Phone: (806) 659-3434
General/National Adv. E-mail: cami.peepaw@gmail.com
Display Adv. E-mail: cami.peepaw@gmail.com
Classified Adv. e-mail: reporterstatesman@gmail.com
Editorial e-mail: cami.peepaw@gmail.com
Primary Website: reporterstatesman.com
Year Established: 1901
Avg Paid Circ: 1400
Avg Free Circ: 300
Audit By: Sworn/Estimate/Non-Audited
Audit Date: 10.06.2019
Personnel: Ernie Bowen (Ass. Ed./Phot.); Catherine Ritchie (Owner/Pub/Ed)

THE HARDIN COUNTY NEWS

Street address 1: 380 Main St
Street address city: Beaumont
Street address state: TX
Zip/Postal code: 77701-2331
General Phone: (409) 838-2872
Advertising Phone: (409) 838-2820
Editorial Phone: (409) 838-2859
General/National Adv. E-mail: jreedy@hearstnp.com
Display Adv. E-mail: jreedy@hearstnp.com
Editorial e-mail: dlisenby@beaumontenterprise.com
Primary Website: beaumontenterprise.com
Year Established: 1970
Avg Free Circ: 19000
Audit By: Sworn/Estimate/Non-Audited
Audit Date: 10.06.2019
Personnel: Mark Adkins; Paul Banister (Circ. Dir.); Craig Hatcher (CRO); Ronnie Crocker (Ed.)
Parent company (for newspapers): Hearst Communications, Inc.

THE HENDERSON NEWS

Street address 1: 1711 US Highway 79 S
Street address city: Henderson
Street address state: TX
Zip/Postal code: 75654-4509
General Phone: (903) 657-2501
General Fax: (903) 657-2452
Advertising Phone: (903) 657-2501
Advertising Fax: (903) 657-2452
Editorial Phone: (903) 657-2501
Editorial Fax: (903) 657-0056
General/National Adv. E-mail: publisher@thehendersonnews.com
Display Adv. E-mail: publisher@thehendersonnews.com
Classified Adv. e-mail: classifieds@thenedersonsonnews.com
Editorial e-mail: managingeditor@thehendersonnews.com
Primary Website: thehendersonnews.com
Mthly Avg Views: 48098
Mthly Avg Unique Visitors: 11780
Year Established: 1930
Avg Paid Circ: 4500
Sun. Circulation Paid: 5200
Audit By: Sworn/Estimate/Non-Audited
Audit Date: 10.06.2019
Personnel: Nancy Harris (Accountant); Joy Slaymaker (Prodn. Mgr.); Jade Causey (Circ. Mgr.); Dan Moore (Publisher); Ashton Griffin (Managing Editor); Andrew Burnes
Parent company (for newspapers): Hartman Newspapers LP

THE HEREFORD BRAND

Street address 1: PO Box 673
Street address city: Hereford
Street address state: TX
Zip/Postal code: 79045-0673
General Phone: (806) 364-2030
General Fax: (806) 364-8364
Advertising Phone: (806)364-2030
Advertising Fax: (806)364-8364
Editorial Phone: (806)364-2030
Editorial Fax: (806)364-8364
General/National Adv. E-mail: retail@herefordbrand.com
Display Adv. E-mail: class@herefordbrand.com
Classified Adv. e-mail: class@herefordbrand.com
Editorial e-mail: editor@herefordbrand.com
Primary Website: herefordbrand.com
Year Established: 1901
Avg Paid Circ: 2100
Sun. Circulation Paid: 2500
Audit By: Sworn/Estimate/Non-Audited
Audit Date: 10.06.2019
Personnel: Lynda Work (Editor/Gen. Mgr.); Raymond Gonzales (Adv. Dir.); John Daigle (Sports Ed.); Tyler Jameson (Lifestyle Ed.); Mary Freeman (Staff News Writer); Kaylee Sparkman (Lifestyles Writer); Laura Foster (Classifieds/Circulation); Paige Arnold (Accountant)
Parent company (for newspapers): Roberts Publishing

THE HIGHLANDER

Street address 1: 304 Highlander Cir
Street address city: Marble Falls
Street address state: TX
Zip/Postal code: 78654-6322
General Phone: (830) 693-4367
General Fax: (830) 693-3650
Advertising Phone: (830) 693-4367
Advertising Fax: (830) 693-3650
Editorial Phone: (830) 693-4367
Editorial Fax: (830) 693-3650
General/National Adv. E-mail: advertising@highlandernews.com
Display Adv. E-mail: classifieds@highlandernews.com
Editorial e-mail: roy.bode@highlandernews.com
Primary Website: highlandernews.com
Mthly Avg Views: 79800
Mthly Avg Unique Visitors: 12100
Year Established: 1959
Avg Paid Circ: 6159
Audit By: Sworn/Estimate/Non-Audited
Audit Date: 10.06.2019
Personnel: Roy Bode (Pub./Ed.); Phil Schoch (Exec. Ed.); Tina Phillips (Adv. Dir.)
Parent company (for newspapers): Highland Lakes Newspapers

THE HUTTO NEWS

Street address 1: 211 W 3rd St
Street address city: Taylor
Street address state: TX
Zip/Postal code: 76574-3518
General Phone: (512) 578-5229
General Fax: (512) 352-2227
Advertising Phone: (512)578-5229
Advertising Fax: (512)352-2227
Editorial Phone: (512)578-5229
Editorial Fax: (512)352-2227
General/National Adv. E-mail: scott@taylorpress.net
Display Adv. E-mail: classified@taylorpress.net
Editorial e-mail: scott@taylorpress.net
Primary Website: thehuttonews.com
Avg Paid Circ: 100
Avg Free Circ: 6500
Audit By: Sworn/Estimate/Non-Audited
Audit Date: 10.06.2019
Personnel: Laura Bachmeyer (Classified Adv. Mgr.); Scott Rucker (Adv.); Reagan Roehl (Sports Ed.); Richard Stone (Pub.)
Parent company (for newspapers): Fenice Community Media

THE INGLESIDE INDEX

Street address 1: 346 S Houston St
Street address city: Aransas Pass
Street address state: TX
Zip/Postal code: 78336-2515
General Phone: (361) 758-5391
General Fax: (361) 758-5393
Advertising Phone: (361) 758-5391
Advertising Fax: (361) 758-5393
Editorial Phone: (361) 758-5391
Editorial Fax: (361) 758-5393
General/National Adv. E-mail: mattie@aransaspassprogress.com
Display Adv. E-mail: classifieds@aransaspassprogress.com
Editorial e-mail: publisher@aransaspassprogress.com
Primary Website: inglesideindex.com
Year Established: 1953
Avg Paid Circ: 1500
Avg Free Circ: 46
Audit By: Sworn/Estimate/Non-Audited
Audit Date: 10.06.2019
Personnel: Brenda Burr (Pub./Ed.); Amanda Torres (Bus. Mgr.)

THE IRVING RAMBLER

Street address 1: 627 S Rogers Rd
Street address city: Irving
Street address state: TX
Zip/Postal code: 75060-3753
General Phone: (972) 870-1992
Advertising Phone: (214) 675-6493
Editorial Phone: (214) 675-6493
General/National Adv. E-mail: johns@ramblernewspapers.net
Display Adv. E-mail: laurier@ramblernewspapers.net
Editorial e-mail: staceys@ramblernewspapers.net
Primary Website: irvingrambler.com
Year Established: 2003
Avg Paid Circ: 4400
Avg Free Circ: 1900
Audit By: Sworn/Estimate/Non-Audited
Audit Date: 10.06.2019
Personnel: John Starkey (Pub.); Stacey Starkey (Ed.); Laurie Reeter-Brown (Adv. Mgr)
Parent company (for newspapers): Rambler Newspapers

THE JIM NED JOURNAL

Street address 1: 334 Butterfield Trail Rd
Street address city: Tuscola
Street address state: TX
Zip/Postal code: 79562-2566
General Phone: (325) 572-3716
General Fax: (325) 480-4196
Advertising Phone: (325) 572-3716
Advertising Fax: (325) 480-4196
Editorial Phone: (325) 572-3716
Editorial Fax: (325) 480-4196
General/National Adv. E-mail: jimnedjournal@taylortel.net
Display Adv. E-mail: jimnedjournal@taylortel.net
Editorial e-mail: jimnedjournal@taylortel.net
Year Established: 1986
Avg Paid Circ: 440
Audit By: Sworn/Estimate/Non-Audited
Audit Date: 10.06.2019
Personnel: Bill Broyles (Pub./Ed.); Grace Broyles (Adv. Dir.)

THE JUNCTION EAGLE

Street address 1: 215 N 6th St
Street address city: Junction
Street address state: TX
Zip/Postal code: 76849-4123
General Phone: (325) 446-2610
General Fax: (325) 446-4025
Advertising Phone: (325) 446-2610
Advertising Fax: (325) 446-4025
Editorial Phone: (325) 446-2610
Editorial Fax: (325) 446-4025
General/National Adv. E-mail: editor@junctioneagle.com
Display Adv. E-mail: asia@junctioneagle.com
Classified Adv. e-mail: asia@junctioneagle.com
Editorial e-mail: editor@junctioneagle.com
Primary Website: junctioneagle.com
Year Established: 1882
Avg Paid Circ: 2000
Audit By: Sworn/Estimate/Non-Audited
Audit Date: 28.09.2022
Personnel: Debbie Cooper Kistler (Pub./Ed.); Jimmy Kistler (Ed.); Asia Happner (Admin. Assistant); Ashley Lundy (Adv. Director); Kendra Powers (photographer); Kendra Powers (photographer)
Parent company (for newspapers): Junction Publishing Company, LLC

THE KARNES COUNTYWIDE

Street address 1: 106 N Esplanade St
Street address city: Karnes City
Street address state: TX
Zip/Postal code: 78377
General Phone: (830) 254-8088
General/National Adv. E-mail: karnesoffice@mysoutex.com
Display Adv. E-mail: karnesoffice@mysoutex.com
Editorial e-mail: karnesoffice@mysoutex.com
Primary Website: mysoutex.com
Year Established: 1891
Avg Paid Circ: 4000
Audit By: Sworn/Estimate/Non-Audited
Audit Date: 10.06.2019
Personnel: Joe Baker (Ed.)

THE KAUFMAN HERALD

Street address 1: 300 N Washington St
Street address city: Kaufman
Street address state: TX

Zip/Postal code: 75142-1345
General Phone: (972) 932-2171
General Fax: (972) 932-2172
Advertising Phone: (972) 932-2171
Advertising Fax: (972) 932-2172
Editorial Phone: (972) 932-2171
Editorial Fax: (972) 932-2172
General/National Adv. E-mail: sales@kaufmanherald.com
Display Adv. E-mail: classifieds@kaufmanherald.com
Editorial e-mail: mlewis@kaufmanherald.com
Primary Website: kaufmanherald.com
Year Established: 1885
Avg Paid Circ: 2972
Avg Free Circ: 277
Audit By: Sworn/Estimate/Non-Audited
Audit Date: 10.06.2019
Personnel: Monica Lewis (Pub./Ed./Adv. Dir.); Amy Fowler (Retail Adv. Mgr.); Kathy Lynn Dieken (Classified Adv. Mgr.)
Parent company (for newspapers): Hartman Newspapers LP

THE KERENS TRIBUNE

Street address 1: 1316 S 3rd St
Street address city: Mabank
Street address state: TX
Zip/Postal code: 75147-7680
General Phone: (903) 887-4511
General Fax: (903) 887-4510
Advertising Phone: (903) 887-4511
Advertising Fax: (903) 887-4510
Editorial Phone: (903) 887-4511
Editorial Fax: (903) 887-4510
General/National Adv. E-mail: kteditor07@yahoo.com
Display Adv. E-mail: kteditor07@yahoo.com
Editorial e-mail: kteditor07@yahoo.com
Year Established: 1892
Avg Paid Circ: 905
Avg Free Circ: 78
Audit By: Sworn/Estimate/Non-Audited
Audit Date: 10.06.2019
Personnel: John Buzzetta (Pub.); Erik Walsh (Ed.); Keron Walker (Adv. Dir.)

THE LEADER

Street address 1: 3500 E T C Jester Blvd
Street address 2: Ste A
Street address city: Houston
Street address state: TX
Zip/Postal code: 77018-6020
General Phone: (713) 686-8494
General Fax: (713) 686-0970
Advertising Phone: (713) 686-8494
Advertising Fax: (713) 686-0970
Editorial Phone: (713) 686-8494
Editorial Fax: (713) 686-0970
General/National Adv. E-mail: ads@theleadernews.com
Display Adv. E-mail: ads@theleadernews.com
Editorial e-mail: news@theleadernews.com
Primary Website: theleadernews.com
Mthly Avg Views: 23794
Mthly Avg Unique Visitors: 8425
Year Established: 1954
Avg Paid Circ: 17
Avg Free Circ: 33935
Audit By: Sworn/Estimate/Non-Audited
Audit Date: 10.06.2019
Personnel: Terry Burge (Pub.); Greg Densmore (Ed.); Jane Broyles (Circ. Mgr.); Jonathan McElvy (Pub.); Jake Dukate (Prod. Mgr)

THE LIBERTY HILL INDEPENDENT

Street address 1: 921 Loop 332
Street address city: Liberty Hill
Street address state: TX
Zip/Postal code: 78642-5843
General Phone: (512) 778-5577
General/National Adv. E-mail: news@LHindependent.com
Primary Website: LHindependent.com
Mthly Avg Views: 10500
Mthly Avg Unique Visitors: 7200
Year Established: 1987
Avg Paid Circ: 1850
Audit By: Sworn/Estimate/Non-Audited
Audit Date: 23.10.2021
Personnel: Shelly Wilkison (Pub./Owner)
Parent company (for newspapers): Free State Media Group; Texas Independent News Corp.

THE LIGHT & CHAMPION

Street address 1: 137 San Augustine St
Street address city: Center
Street address state: TX
Zip/Postal code: 75935-3951
General Phone: (936) 598-3377
General Fax: (936) 598-6394
Advertising Phone: (936)598-3377
Advertising Fax: (936)598-6394
Editorial Phone: (936)598-3377
Editorial Fax: (936)598-6394
General/National Adv. E-mail: steve.fountain@lightandchampion.com
Display Adv. E-mail: cgilcrease@lightandchampion.com
Editorial e-mail: steve.fountain@lightandchampion.com
Primary Website: lightandchampion.com
Year Established: 1877
Avg Paid Circ: 2496
Avg Free Circ: 29
Audit By: Sworn/Estimate/Non-Audited
Audit Date: 10.06.2019
Personnel: Dale Buie (Pub.); Leah Dolan (Managing editor)
Parent company (for newspapers): Fenice Community Media; PTS, Inc.

THE LINDALE NEWS & TIMES

Street address 1: 104 N Main St
Street address city: Lindale
Street address state: TX
Zip/Postal code: 75771-6294
General Phone: (903) 882-8880
General Fax: (903) 882-8234
General/National Adv. E-mail: mattaway@lindalenews-times.com
Display Adv. E-mail: advertising@lindalenews-times.com
Editorial e-mail: news@lindalenews-times.com
Primary Website: lindalenews-times.com
Year Established: 1900
Avg Paid Circ: 2127
Audit By: Sworn/Estimate/Non-Audited
Audit Date: 10.06.2019
Personnel: Joyce Hathcock (Pub.); Terry Cannon (Ed.); Maria Attaway (Adv. Dir.); Angela' Houston (Office Mgr.)
Parent company (for newspapers): Bluebonnet Publishing, LLC

THE LLANO NEWS

Street address 1: 813 Berry St
Street address city: Llano
Street address state: TX
Zip/Postal code: 78643-1907
General Phone: (325) 247-4433
General Fax: (325) 247-3338
Advertising Phone: (325) 247-4433
Advertising Fax: (325) 247-3338
Editorial Phone: (325) 247-4433
Editorial Fax: (325) 247-3338
General/National Adv. E-mail: thenews@verizon.net
Display Adv. E-mail: thenews@verizon.net
Editorial e-mail: thenews@verizon.net
Primary Website: llanonews.com
Year Established: 1889
Audit By: Sworn/Estimate/Non-Audited
Audit Date: 10.06.2019
Personnel: Ken Wesner (Pub.); Heather Wagner (Ed.); Scott Wesner (Adv. Dir.)

THE LULING NEWSBOY AND SIGNAL

Street address 1: 415 E Davis St
Street address city: Luling
Street address state: TX
Zip/Postal code: 78648-2316
General Phone: (830) 875-2116
General Fax: (830) 875-2124
Advertising Phone: (830)875-2116
Advertising Fax: (830)875-2124
Editorial Phone: (830)875-2116
Editorial Fax: (830)875-2124
General/National Adv. E-mail: slulingnewsboy@austin.rr.com
Display Adv. E-mail: slulingnewsboy@austin.rr.com
Editorial e-mail: slulingnewsboy@austin.rr.com
Primary Website: lulingnewsboy.com
Year Established: 1878
Avg Paid Circ: 1300
Avg Free Circ: 39
Audit By: Sworn/Estimate/Non-Audited
Audit Date: 10.06.2019
Personnel: Dayton Gonzales (Pub./Ed./Adv. Dir.)
Parent company (for newspapers): Luling Publishing Co., Inc.

THE MALAKOFF NEWS

Street address 1: 815 E Royall Blvd
Street address 2: Ste 6
Street address city: Malakoff
Street address state: TX
Zip/Postal code: 75148-9273
General Phone: (903) 887-4511
General Fax: (903) 887-4510
Advertising Phone: (903) 887-4511
Advertising Fax: (903) 887-4510
Editorial Phone: (903) 887-4511
Editorial Fax: (903) 887-4510
General/National Adv. E-mail: thenews.hendersonco@yahoo.com
Display Adv. E-mail: thenews.hendersonco@yahoo.com
Editorial e-mail: thenews.hendersonco@yahoo.com
Primary Website: malakoffnews.net
Year Established: 1903
Avg Paid Circ: 2000
Avg Free Circ: 200
Audit By: Sworn/Estimate/Non-Audited
Audit Date: 10.06.2019
Personnel: John Buzzetta (Pub.); Michael Hannigan (Ed.); Keron Walker (Adv. Dir.)

THE MARLIN DEMOCRAT

Street address 1: 211 Fortune St
Street address city: Marlin
Street address state: TX
Zip/Postal code: 76661-2799
General Phone: (254) 883-2554
General Fax: (254) 883-6553
Advertising Phone: (256) 604-7381
Editorial Phone: (256) 604-7381
General/National Adv. E-mail: advertising@marlindemocrat.com
Display Adv. E-mail: advertising@marlindemocrat.com
Editorial e-mail: publisher@marlindemocrat.com
Primary Website: marlindemocrat.com
Year Established: 1890
Avg Paid Circ: 2300
Avg Free Circ: 70
Audit By: Sworn/Estimate/Non-Audited
Audit Date: 10.06.2019
Personnel: Dennis Phillips (Publisher)
Parent company (for newspapers): Moser Community Media

THE MART MESSENGER

Street address 1: 105 S Pearl St
Street address city: Mart
Street address state: TX
Zip/Postal code: 76664-1424
General Phone: (254) 876-3939
General Fax: (254) 876-3942
Advertising Phone: (254) 876-3939
Advertising Fax: (254) 876-3942
Editorial Phone: (254) 876-3939
Editorial Fax: (254) 876-3942
General/National Adv. E-mail: lhauk@aol.com
Display Adv. E-mail: martmessenger@yahoo.com
Editorial e-mail: martmessenger@yahoo.com
Year Established: 1993
Avg Paid Circ: 1800
Audit By: Sworn/Estimate/Non-Audited
Audit Date: 10.06.2019
Personnel: Larry Hauk (Pub.); Carolyn Potts (Ed./Adv. Dir.)

THE MERKEL MAIL

Street address 1: 912 N 1st
Street address city: Merkel
Street address state: TX
Zip/Postal code: 79536-3815
General Phone: (325) 928-5712
General Fax: (325) 928-5899
Advertising Phone: (325) 928-5712
Advertising Fax: (325) 928-5899
Editorial Phone: (325) 928-5712
Editorial Fax: (325) 928-5899
General/National Adv. E-mail: merkelmail@windstream.net
Display Adv. E-mail: merkelmail@windstream.net
Editorial e-mail: merkelmail@windstream.net
Year Established: 1890
Avg Paid Circ: 1046
Avg Free Circ: 20
Audit By: Sworn/Estimate/Non-Audited
Audit Date: 10.06.2019
Personnel: John Starbuck (Pub./Ed./Adv. Dir.)

THE MESSENGER

Street address 1: 202 S Main St
Street address city: Grapeland
Street address state: TX
Zip/Postal code: 75844-2404
General Phone: (936) 687-2424
General Fax: (936) 687-3441
Advertising Phone: (936) 687-2424
Advertising Fax: (936) 687-3441
Editorial Phone: (936) 687-2424
Editorial Fax: (936) 687-3441
General/National Adv. E-mail: news@messenger-news.com
Display Adv. E-mail: news@messenger-news.com
Editorial e-mail: kboothe@messenger-news.com
Primary Website: messenger-news.com
Year Established: 1899
Avg Paid Circ: 2376
Audit By: Sworn/Estimate/Non-Audited
Audit Date: 10.06.2019
Personnel: Tom Nicol (Pub.); Kay Boothe (Ed.); Cheril Vernon (Copy Editor / Composing); Will Johnson (Reporter); Lesia Rounsavall (Office Manager/Sales); Ansel Bradshaw (Sales)
Parent company (for newspapers): Nicol Publishing

THE MEXIA NEWS

Street address 1: 214 N Railroad St
Street address city: Mexia
Street address state: TX
Zip/Postal code: 76667-2850
General Phone: (254) 562-2868
General Fax: (254) 562-3121
Advertising Phone: (254) 562-2868
Advertising Fax: (254) 562-3121
Editorial Phone: (254) 562-2868
Editorial Fax: (254) 562-3121
General/National Adv. E-mail: mike@themexianews.com
Display Adv. E-mail: classifieds@themexianews.com
Editorial e-mail: news@themexianews.com
Primary Website: mexiadailynews.com
Year Established: 1899
Avg Paid Circ: 2350
Sat. Circulation Paid: 2300
Audit By: Sworn/Estimate/Non-Audited
Audit Date: 10.06.2019
Personnel: Mike Eddleman (Pub.); Brenda Sommer (Ed.); Jennifer Bynum (Adv. Dir.)
Parent company (for newspapers): Palo Pinto Communications, LP

THE MIDLOTHIAN MIRROR

Street address 1: 200 W Marvin Ave
Street address city: Waxahachie
Street address state: TX
Zip/Postal code: 75165-3040
General Phone: (972) 775-3322
General Fax: (972) 775-4669
Advertising Phone: (972) 775-3322
Advertising Fax: (972) 775-4669
Editorial Phone: (972) 775-3322
Editorial Fax: (972) 775-4669
General/National Adv. E-mail: advertising@waxahachietx.com
Display Adv. E-mail: classifieds@waxahachietx.com
Editorial e-mail: tsmith@waxahachietx.com
Primary Website: midlothianmirror.com
Year Established: 1882
Avg Paid Circ: 6000
Audit By: Sworn/Estimate/Non-Audited
Audit Date: 10.06.2019
Personnel: Travis Smith (Mng. Ed.); Colton Crist (Adv./Ops Mgr.); Robin Fox (Circ.)

Parent company (for newspapers): CherryRoad Media

THE MID-VALLEY TOWN CRIER

Street address 1: 401 S Kansas Ave
Street address 2: Ste C2
Street address city: Weslaco
Street address state: TX
Zip/Postal code: 78596-6382
General Phone: (956) 969-2543
General Fax: (956) 968-0855
Advertising Phone: (956) 969-2543
Advertising Fax: (956) 968-0855
Editorial Phone: (956) 969-2543
Editorial Fax: (956) 968-0855
General/National Adv. E-mail: ads@mvtcnews.com
Display Adv. E-mail: ads@mvtcnews.com
Editorial e-mail: mrodriguez@mvtcnews.com
Primary Website: midvalleytowncrier.com
Year Established: 1967
Avg Free Circ: 21750
Audit By: Sworn/Estimate/Non-Audited
Audit Date: 10.06.2019
Personnel: John Greider (Pub.); Matt Lynch (Ed.); Benita Mendell (Nat'l Adv. Mgr.)
Parent company (for newspapers): Times Media Group

THE MONAHANS NEWS

Street address 1: 107 W 2nd St
Street address city: Monahans
Street address state: TX
Zip/Postal code: 79756-4235
General Phone: (432) 943-4313
General Fax: (432) 943-4314
Advertising Phone: (432) 943-4313
Advertising Fax: (432) 943-4314
Editorial Phone: (432) 943-4313
Editorial Fax: (432) 943-4314
General/National Adv. E-mail: editor@monahansnews.net
Display Adv. E-mail: editor@monahansnews.net
Editorial e-mail: editor@monahansnews.net
Year Established: 1931
Audit By: Sworn/Estimate/Non-Audited
Audit Date: 10.06.2019
Personnel: Smokey Briggs (Pub.); Paula Bard (Ed.); Bob Rice (Adv. Dir.)

THE MONITOR

Street address 1: 1316 S 3rd St
Street address 2: Ste 108
Street address city: Mabank
Street address state: TX
Zip/Postal code: 75147-7680
General Phone: (903) 887-4511
General Fax: (903) 887-4510
Advertising Phone: (903) 887-4511
Advertising Fax: (903) 887-4510
Editorial Phone: (903) 887-4511
Editorial Fax: (903) 887-4510
General/National Adv. E-mail: advertising@themonitor.net
Display Adv. E-mail: classifieds@themonitor.net
Editorial e-mail: publisher@themonitor.net
Primary Website: themonitor.net
Year Established: 1974
Audit By: Sworn/Estimate/Non-Audited
Audit Date: 10.06.2019
Personnel: Susan Harrison (Pub.); Pearl Cantrell (Ed.); Keron Walker (Adv. Dir.)

THE MONITOR

Street address 1: 110 Main St
Street address city: Naples
Street address state: TX
Zip/Postal code: 75568
General Phone: (903) 897-2281
General Fax: (903) 897-2095
Advertising Phone: (903) 897-2281
Advertising Fax: (903) 897-2095
Editorial Phone: (903) 897-2281
Editorial Fax: (903) 897-2095
General/National Adv. E-mail: themonitor@valornet.com
Display Adv. E-mail: themonitor@valornet.com
Editorial e-mail: themonitor@valornet.com
Year Established: 1886
Avg Paid Circ: 2000
Avg Free Circ: 50
Audit By: Sworn/Estimate/Non-Audited
Audit Date: 10.06.2019
Personnel: Morris Craig (Pub./Ed.); Melody Alford (Adv. Dir.); Denise Summerlin (Circ. Mgr.); Jennifer Adams (Bookkeeper); Jeremy Craig (Photographer/Reporter)

THE MOORE COUNTY NEWS-PRESS

Street address 1: 702 S Meredith Ave
Street address city: Dumas
Street address state: TX
Zip/Postal code: 79029-4444
General Phone: (806) 935-4111
General Fax: (806) 935-2348
Advertising Phone: (806) 935-4111
Advertising Fax: (806) 935-2348
Editorial Phone: (806) 935-4111
Editorial Fax: (806) 935-2348
General/National Adv. E-mail: advertising@moorenews.com
Display Adv. E-mail: classifieds@moorenews.com
Editorial e-mail: editor@moorenews.com
Primary Website: moorenews.com
Year Established: 1927
Avg Paid Circ: 3480
Sun. Circulation Paid: 3480
Audit By: Sworn/Estimate/Non-Audited
Audit Date: 10.06.2019
Personnel: Wanda Brooks (Pub.); Michael Wright (Ed.); Robin Patterson (Bus. Mgr.)
Parent company (for newspapers): Lancaster Management, Inc.

THE MOULTON EAGLE

Street address 1: 208B W Moore
Street address city: Moulton
Street address state: TX
Zip/Postal code: 77975-5513
General Phone: (361) 596-4871
General Fax: (361) 596-7562
Advertising Phone: (361) 596-4871
Advertising Fax: (361) 596-7562
Editorial Phone: (361) 596-4871
Editorial Fax: (361) 596-7562
General/National Adv. E-mail: moultoneagle@sbcglobal.net
Display Adv. E-mail: moultoneagle@sbcglobal.net
Editorial e-mail: moultoneagle@sbcglobal.net
Year Established: 1914
Avg Paid Circ: 1350
Audit By: Sworn/Estimate/Non-Audited
Audit Date: 10.06.2019
Personnel: Bob Anderson (Pub.); Kristie Bludau (Ed.); Margaret Pozzi (Adv. Mgr.); Stef Demorie (Circ. Mgr.)

THE NAVASOTA EXAMINER

Street address 1: 115 Railroad Street
Street address city: Navasota
Street address state: TX
Zip/Postal code: 77868
General Phone: (936) 825-6484
General Fax: (936) 825-2230
General/National Adv. E-mail: ads@navasotaexaminer.com
Display Adv. E-mail: ads@navasotaexaminer.com
Editorial e-mail: news@navasotaexaminer.com
Primary Website: navasotaexaminer.com
Year Established: 1894
Avg Paid Circ: 3616
Avg Free Circ: 370
Audit By: Sworn/Estimate/Non-Audited
Audit Date: 10.06.2019
Personnel: Nicole Shupe (Ed.); Ana Cosino (Pub.); Angela Scurlock (Adv. Sales); Sonya Bobo (Circ.)
Parent company (for newspapers): Fenice Community Media

THE NEW STAMFORD AMERICAN

Street address 1: 102 S Swenson St
Street address city: Stamford
Street address state: TX
Zip/Postal code: 79553-4624
General Phone: (325) 773-5550
General Fax: (325) 773-5551
Advertising Phone: (325) 773-5550
Advertising Fax: (325) 773-5551
Editorial Phone: (325) 773-5550
Editorial Fax: (325) 773-5551
General/National Adv. E-mail: ads@stamfordamerican.net
Display Adv. E-mail: cmetler@stamfordamerican.net
Editorial e-mail: editor@stamfordamerican.net
Primary Website: stamfordamerican.net
Year Established: 2009
Avg Paid Circ: 526
Audit By: Sworn/Estimate/Non-Audited
Audit Date: 10.06.2019
Personnel: Callie Metler-Smith (Pub.); Debbie Heald (Adv. Dir./Ed.); Jennifer Prichard (Ed.)

THE NEW ULM ENTERPRISE

Street address 1: 910 FM 109
Street address city: New Ulm
Street address state: TX
Zip/Postal code: 78950
General Phone: (979) 992-3351
General Fax: (979) 992-3352
Advertising Phone: (979) 992-3351
Advertising Fax: (979) 992-3352
Editorial Phone: (979) 992-3351
Editorial Fax: (979) 992-3352
General/National Adv. E-mail: nuent@industryinet.com
Display Adv. E-mail: nuent@industryinet.com
Editorial e-mail: editor@industryinet.com
Year Established: 1910
Avg Paid Circ: 1031
Avg Free Circ: 16
Audit By: Sworn/Estimate/Non-Audited
Audit Date: 10.06.2019
Personnel: Maridel Dungen (Pub.)

THE NEWS OF SAN PATRICIO

Street address 1: 104 N Sehorn St
Street address city: Sinton
Street address state: TX
Zip/Postal code: 78387
General Phone: (361) 364-1270
Advertising Phone: (361) 364-1270
Editorial Phone: (361) 364-1270
General/National Adv. E-mail: Sintonoffice@mysoutex.com
Display Adv. E-mail: Sintonoffice@mysoutex.com
Editorial e-mail: Mathisnews@mysoutex.com
Primary Website: mysoutex.com
Year Established: 1924
Avg Paid Circ: 2000
Avg Free Circ: 35
Audit By: Sworn/Estimate/Non-Audited
Audit Date: 10.06.2019
Personnel: Paul Gonzales (Ed.); Mian Contact
Parent company (for newspapers): San Patricio Publishing Co., Inc.

THE NORMANGEE STAR

Street address 1: 122 Taft St.
Street address city: Normangee
Street address state: TX
Zip/Postal code: 77871
General Phone: (936) 396-3391
General Fax: (936) 396-2478
Editorial e-mail: normangeestar@yahoo.com
Primary Website: normangeestar.com
Year Established: 1912
Avg Paid Circ: 1400
Avg Free Circ: 50
Audit By: Sworn/Estimate/Non-Audited
Audit Date: 10.06.2019
Personnel: Hank Hargrave (Pub./Ed./Adv. Dir.)

THE OBSERVER/ENTERPRISE

Street address 1: 707 Austin St
Street address city: Robert Lee
Street address state: TX
Zip/Postal code: 76945
General Phone: (325) 453-2433
General Fax: (325) 453-4643
Advertising Phone: (325) 453-2433
Advertising Fax: (325) 453-4643
Editorial Phone: (325) 453-2433
Editorial Fax: (325) 453-4643
General/National Adv. E-mail: o-e@wcc.net
Display Adv. E-mail: o-e@wcc.net
Editorial e-mail: o-e@wcc.net
Primary Website: observerenterprise.com
Year Established: 1898
Avg Paid Circ: 1553
Avg Free Circ: 32
Audit By: Sworn/Estimate/Non-Audited
Audit Date: 10.06.2019
Personnel: Melinda McCutchen (Pub./Ed./Adv. Dir.); Amber Sawyer (Classified Ed.)

THE ODEM - EDROY TIMES

Street address 1: 117 S Rachal St
Street address city: Sinton
Street address state: TX
Zip/Postal code: 78387-2545
General Phone: (361) 364-1270
General Fax: (361) 364-3833
Advertising Phone: (361) 364-1270
Advertising Fax: (361) 364-3833
Editorial Phone: (361) 364-1270
Editorial Fax: (361) 364-3833
General/National Adv. E-mail: advertising@sanpatpublishing.com
Display Adv. E-mail: receptionist@sanpatpublishing.com
Editorial e-mail: editor@sanpatpublishing.com
Primary Website: sanpatpublishing.com
Year Established: 1948
Audit By: Sworn/Estimate/Non-Audited
Audit Date: 10.06.2019
Personnel: James Tracy (Co-Pub./Ed.); John Tracy (Co-Pub./Adv. Dir.)

THE OLNEY ENTERPRISE

Street address 1: 213 E Main St
Street address city: Olney
Street address state: TX
Zip/Postal code: 76374-1923
General Phone: (940) 564-5558
General Fax: (940) 564-3992
Advertising Phone: (940) 564-5558
Advertising Fax: (940) 564-3992
Editorial Phone: (940) 564-5558
Editorial Fax: (940) 564-3992
General/National Adv. E-mail: advertising@olneyenterprise.com
Display Adv. E-mail: classified@olneyenterprise.com
Editorial e-mail: editor@olneyenterprise.com
Primary Website: olneyenterprise.com
Year Established: 1908
Avg Paid Circ: 1218
Avg Free Circ: 15
Audit By: Sworn/Estimate/Non-Audited
Audit Date: 10.06.2019
Personnel: Robb Krecklow (Group Pub.); Mindi Kimbro (Ed.); Karen Harris (Adv. Mgr.); Tommy Leeman (Circ. Mgr.); Roy G. Robinson (Pub.); Jimmy Potts (Managing Editor)
Parent company (for newspapers): Palo Pinto Communications, LP

THE OLTON ENTERPRISE

Street address 1: 520 Eighth St
Street address city: Olton
Street address state: TX
Zip/Postal code: 79064
General Phone: (806) 285-7766
General Fax: (866) 641-2816
Advertising Phone: (806) 285-7766
Advertising Fax: (866) 641-2816
Editorial Phone: (806) 285-7766
Editorial Fax: (866) 641-2816
General/National Adv. E-mail: oltonenterprise@hotmail.com
Display Adv. E-mail: oltonenterprise@hotmail.com
Editorial e-mail: oltonenterprise@hotmail.com
Primary Website: southplainsplus.com
Year Established: 1926
Avg Paid Circ: 1000
Avg Free Circ: 20
Audit By: Sworn/Estimate/Non-Audited
Audit Date: 10.06.2019
Personnel: Phillip Hamilton (Pub./Ed.); Ursula Hamilton (Adv. Dir.)
Parent company (for newspapers): Triple S Media

THE ORANGE LEADER

Street address 1: 841B Dal Sasso Dr
Street address city: Orange
Street address state: TX
Zip/Postal code: 77630-4825
General Phone: (409) 883-3571

Advertising Phone: (409) 883-3571
Editorial Phone: (409) 883-3571
General/National Adv. E-mail: candice.trahan@orangeleader.com
Display Adv. E-mail: candice.trahan@orangeleader.com
Editorial e-mail: news@orangeleader.com
Primary Website: orangeleader.com
Year Established: 1875
Avg Paid Circ: 2967
Sat. Circulation Paid: 3695
Sun. Circulation Paid: 4084
Audit By: Sworn/Estimate/Non-Audited
Audit Date: 10.06.2019
Personnel: Dawn Burleigh (Ed); Bobby Tingle (Pub); Van Wade (Sports Ed); Candice Trahan (Inside Sales)
Parent company (for newspapers): Boone's Newspapers

THE PANOLA WATCHMAN

Street address 1: 109 W Panola St
Street address city: Carthage
Street address state: TX
Zip/Postal code: 75633-2631
General Phone: (903) 693-7888
General Fax: (903) 693-5857
Advertising Phone: (903) 693-7888
Advertising Fax: (903) 693-5857
Editorial Phone: (903) 693-7888
Editorial Fax: (903) 693-5857
General/National Adv. E-mail: msweeney@panolawatchman.com
Display Adv. E-mail: tpeel@panolawatchman.com
Editorial e-mail: bbarlish@panolawatchman.com
Primary Website: panolawatchman.com
Year Established: 1873
Avg Paid Circ: 4826
Avg Free Circ: 80
Audit By: Sworn/Estimate/Non-Audited
Audit Date: 10.06.2019
Personnel: Bill Holder (Pub./Adv. Dir.); Becky Barlish (Ed.); Tammy Peel (Classified Mgr.)

THE PFLUGERVILLE PFLAG

Street address 1: 305 S Congress Ave
Street address city: Austin
Street address state: TX
Zip/Postal code: 78704-1200
General Phone: (512) 255-5827
General Fax: (512) 251-6221
Advertising Phone: (512) 255-5827
Advertising Fax: (512) 251-6221
Editorial Phone: (512) 255-5827
Editorial Fax: (512) 251-6221
General/National Adv. E-mail: communityadvertising@statesman.com
Display Adv. E-mail: classified@statesman.com
Editorial e-mail: mguajardo@archive.pflugervillepflag.com
Primary Website: statesman.com/s/news/local/pflugerville-pflag
Year Established: 1980
Avg Paid Circ: 0
Avg Free Circ: 8547
Audit By: Sworn/Estimate/Non-Audited
Audit Date: 10.06.2019
Personnel: Terry Schaub (Pub.); Marcial Guajardo (Mng. Ed.); Joe Harrington (Sports Ed.)
Parent company (for newspapers): Cox Media Group

THE PICAYUNE

Street address 1: 1007 Avenue K
Street address city: Marble Falls
Street address state: TX
Zip/Postal code: 78654-5039
General Phone: (830) 693-7152
General Fax: (830) 693-3085
General/National Adv. E-mail: advertising@thepicayune.com
Display Adv. E-mail: classifieds@thepicayune.com
Editorial e-mail: editor@thepicayune.com
Primary Website: 101highlandlakes.com
Year Established: 1991
Avg Paid Circ: 0
Avg Free Circ: 23427
Audit By: CVC
Audit Date: 30.06.2018
Personnel: Dan Alvey (Owner); Lee Alvey (Owner); Amber Weems (COO/Pub.); Mandi Wyatt (Adv. Mgr.); Thomas Edwards (Ed.); Florence Edwards (Prodn. Mgr.); Daniel Clifton (Ed.); Stacee Hopkins (Circ.)
Parent company (for newspapers): Victory Publising Co., Ltd.

THE POST DISPATCH

Street address 1: 123 E Main St
Street address city: Post
Street address state: TX
Zip/Postal code: 79356-3229
General Phone: (806) 495-2816
General Fax: (806) 495-2059
Advertising Phone: (806) 495-2816
Advertising Fax: (806) 495-2059
Editorial Phone: (806) 495-2816
Editorial Fax: (806) 495-2059
General/National Adv. E-mail: thepostcitydispatch@gmail.com
Display Adv. E-mail: thepostcitydispatch@gmail.com
Editorial e-mail: thepostcitydispatch@gmail.com
Primary Website: thepostdispatchonline.com
Year Established: 1926
Avg Paid Circ: 1550
Audit By: Sworn/Estimate/Non-Audited
Audit Date: 10.06.2019
Personnel: Christopher Blackburn (Pub.); Wayne Hodgin (Ed./Adv. Dir.)

THE PRESIDIO INTERNATIONAL

Street address 1: 110 N Highland Avenue
Street address city: Presidio
Street address state: TX
Zip/Postal code: 79845
General Phone: (432) 729-4342
Advertising Phone: (432) 729-4342
Editorial Phone: (432) 729-4342
Editorial Fax: (432) 729-4601
General/National Adv. E-mail: rosario@bigbendnow.com
Display Adv. E-mail: rosario@bigbendnow.com
Editorial e-mail: editor@bigbendnow.com
Primary Website: bigbendnow.com
Year Established: 1986
Avg Paid Circ: 900
Audit By: Sworn/Estimate/Non-Audited
Audit Date: 10.06.2019
Personnel: Robert L. Halpern (Pub./Ed.); Rosario Salgado-Halpern (Adv. Dir.)

THE PROGRESS

Street address 1: 501 N Harborth Ave.
Street address 2: Suite D
Street address city: Three Rivers
Street address state: TX
Zip/Postal code: 78071
General Phone: (361)786-3022
Advertising Phone: (361) 343-5214
Editorial Phone: (361) 786-3022
General/National Adv. E-mail: theprogress@mysoutex.com
Display Adv. E-mail: sales4@mysoutex.com
Editorial e-mail: theprogress@mysoutex.com
Primary Website: mysoutex.com
Year Established: 1928
Avg Paid Circ: 3173
Avg Free Circ: 13
Audit By: Sworn/Estimate/Non-Audited
Audit Date: 10.06.2019
Personnel: Delia Soto (Office Manager)
Parent company (for newspapers): Beeville Publishing Co. Inc.

THE PULSE

Street address 1: 407 Broadway
Street address city: Hart
Street address state: TX
Zip/Postal code: 79043
General Phone: (806) 938-2640
General Fax: (806) 938-2216
Advertising Phone: (806) 938-2640
Advertising Fax: (806) 938-2216
Editorial Phone: (806) 938-2640
Editorial Fax: (806) 938-2216
General/National Adv. E-mail: hbeat@amaonline.com
Display Adv. E-mail: hbeat@amaonline.com
Editorial e-mail: hbeat@amaonline.com
Primary Website: thepulsenews.net
Year Established: 1962
Avg Paid Circ: 185
Audit By: Sworn/Estimate/Non-Audited
Audit Date: 10.06.2019
Personnel: Neoma Wall Williams (Pub./Ed./Adv. Dir.)

THE QUINLAN-TAWAKONI NEWS

Street address 1: 103 E Tyler St
Street address city: Canton
Street address state: TX
Zip/Postal code: 75103-1413
General Phone: (903) 567-4000
General Fax: (903) 567-6076
Advertising Phone: (903) 567-4000
Advertising Fax: (903) 567-6076
Editorial e-mail: news@terrelltribune.com
Primary Website: quinlan-tawakoninews.com
Year Established: 1963
Avg Paid Circ: 3000
Audit By: Sworn/Estimate/Non-Audited
Audit Date: 10.06.2019
Personnel: Kendall Lyons (Ed.)

THE RANCHER

Street address 1: 100 Avenue A
Street address city: Conroe
Street address state: TX
Zip/Postal code: 77301-2946
General Phone: (281) 378-1900
General Fax: (713) 520-1193
Advertising Phone: (281) 378-1908
Advertising Fax: (713) 520-1193
Editorial Phone: (281) 378-1911
Editorial Fax: (713) 520-1193
General/National Adv. E-mail: rdavis@hcnonline.com
Display Adv. E-mail: tisaacks@hcnonline.com
Editorial e-mail: rgraham@hcnonline.com
Primary Website: katysun.com
Year Established: 1953
Avg Paid Circ: 0
Avg Free Circ: 26985
Audit By: Sworn/Estimate/Non-Audited
Audit Date: 10.06.2019
Personnel: Richard Davis (Pub.); Rusty Graham (Ed.); Jason Johnson (Pub.); Charles Lee (Adv. Mgr); Rick Flores (Circ. Mgr); Tom Stamper (Prod. Mgr)
Parent company (for newspapers): Hearst Communications, Inc.; Times Media Group

THE ROCKPORT PILOT

Street address 1: 1002 E Wharf St
Street address city: Rockport
Street address state: TX
Zip/Postal code: 78382-2662
General Phone: (361) 729-9900
General Fax: (361) 729-8903
Advertising Phone: (361) 729-9900
Advertising Fax: (361) 729-8903
Editorial Phone: (361) 729-9900
Editorial Fax: (361) 729-8903
General/National Adv. E-mail: displayadvertising@rockportpilot.com
Display Adv. E-mail: classifieds@rockportpilot.com
Editorial e-mail: publisher@rockportpilot.com
Primary Website: rockportpilot.com
Year Established: 1869
Audit By: Sworn/Estimate/Non-Audited
Audit Date: 10.06.2019
Personnel: Mike Probst (Pub./Ed.); Norma Martinez (Mng. Ed.); Kim Gove (Adv. Dir.)
Parent company (for newspapers): Hartman Newspapers LP

THE ROSEBUD NEWS

Street address 1: 211 Fortune St.
Street address 2: P.O. Box 112
Street address city: Marlin
Street address state: TX
Zip/Postal code: 76661
General Phone: (254) 883-2554
General Fax: (254) 883-6553
Primary Website: rosebudnews.net
Year Established: 1893
Avg Paid Circ: 1800
Avg Free Circ: 15
Audit By: Sworn/Estimate/Non-Audited
Audit Date: 10.06.2019
Personnel: Raymond Moore (Pub.); Melinda Foster (Adv.); Madisson Mahooney (Office Mgr.)

THE ROWENA PRESS

Street address 1: Robinson St
Street address city: Miles
Street address state: TX
Zip/Postal code: 76861
General Phone: (325) 468-3611
General Fax: (325) 468-3611
Advertising Phone: (325) 468-3611
Advertising Fax: (325) 468-3611
Editorial Phone: (325) 468-3611
Editorial Fax: (325) 468-3611
General/National Adv. E-mail: shortcake56@verizon.net
Display Adv. E-mail: shortcake56@verizon.net
Editorial e-mail: shortcake56@verizon.net
Year Established: 1936
Audit By: Sworn/Estimate/Non-Audited
Audit Date: 10.06.2019
Personnel: Donna Glass (Pub./Ed./Adv. Dir.)

THE SABINE COUNTY REPORTER

Street address 1: 610 Worth St
Street address city: Hemphill
Street address state: TX
Zip/Postal code: 75948-7258
General Phone: (409) 787-2172
General Fax: (409) 787-4300
General/National Adv. E-mail: screporter@yahoo.com
Primary Website: sabinecountyreporter.com
Year Established: 1883
Avg Paid Circ: 2100
Audit By: Sworn/Estimate/Non-Audited
Audit Date: 10.06.2019
Personnel: Brandy Meurer (Ed.)

THE SAINT JO TRIBUNE

Street address 1: 105 E Howell St
Street address city: Saint Jo
Street address state: TX
Zip/Postal code: 76265-2228
General Phone: (940) 995-2586
General Fax: (940) 995-2586
Advertising Phone: (940) 995-2586
Advertising Fax: (940) 995-2586
Editorial Phone: (940) 995-2586
Editorial Fax: (940) 995-2586
General/National Adv. E-mail: saintjotribune@embarqmail.com
Display Adv. E-mail: saintjotribune@embarqmail.com
Editorial e-mail: saintjotribune@embarqmail.com
Year Established: 1898
Avg Paid Circ: 832
Avg Free Circ: 51
Audit By: Sworn/Estimate/Non-Audited
Audit Date: 10.06.2019
Personnel: C.E. Cole (Co-Pub./Ed.); Dee Cole (Co-Pub./Mng. Ed.)

THE SCHULENBURG STICKER

Street address 1: 405 N Main St
Street address city: Schulenburg
Street address state: TX
Zip/Postal code: 78956-1561
General Phone: (979) 743-3450
General Fax: (979) 743-4609
General/National Adv. E-mail: ads@schulenburgsticker.com
Display Adv. E-mail: darrell@schulenburgsticker.com
Editorial e-mail: news@schulenburgsticker.com
Primary Website: schulenburgsticker.com
Year Established: 1894
Avg Paid Circ: 2823
Avg Free Circ: 34
Audit By: Sworn/Estimate/Non-Audited
Audit Date: 10.06.2019
Personnel: Carla Ricicar (Adv. Mgr.); Diane Prause (Ed.); Darrell Vyvjala (Ed.)

THE SEALY NEWS

Street address 1: 372 Fowlkes
Street address city: Sealy
Street address state: TX
Zip/Postal code: 77474-9320
General Phone: (979) 885-3562

General Fax: (979) 885-3564
Advertising Phone: (979) 885-3562
Advertising Fax: (979) 885-3564
Editorial Phone: (979) 885-3562
Editorial Fax: (979) 885-3564
General/National Adv. E-mail: advertising@sealynews.com
Display Adv. E-mail: classifieds@sealynews.com
Editorial e-mail: editor@sealynews.com
Primary Website: sealynews.com
Mthly Avg Views: 80000
Mthly Avg Unique Visitors: 40000
Year Established: 1887
Avg Paid Circ: 3972
Avg Free Circ: 94
Audit By: Sworn/Estimate/Non-Audited
Audit Date: 10.06.2019
Personnel: Karen Lopez (Executive Publisher)
Parent company (for newspapers): Fenice Community Media; Granite Media Partners

THE SHINER GAZETTE

Street address 1: 1509 North Ave E.
Street address city: Shiner
Street address state: TX
Zip/Postal code: 77984-5210
General Phone: (361) 594-3346
General Fax: (361) 594-2655
Advertising Phone: (361) 594-3346
Advertising Fax: (361) 594-2655
Editorial Phone: (361) 594-3346
Editorial Fax: (361) 594-2655
General/National Adv. E-mail: shinergazette@sbcglobal.net
Display Adv. E-mail: shinergazette@sbcglobal.net
Editorial e-mail: shinergazette@sbcglobal.net
Year Established: 1892
Avg Paid Circ: 1750
Audit By: Sworn/Estimate/Non-Audited
Audit Date: 10.06.2019
Personnel: Kristie Bludau (Gen. Mgr.)

THE SLATONITE

Street address 1: 139 S 9th St
Street address city: Slaton
Street address state: TX
Zip/Postal code: 79364-4121
General Phone: (806) 828-6201
General Fax: (806) 828-6202
Advertising Phone: (806) 828-6201
Advertising Fax: (806) 828-6202
Editorial Phone: (806) 828-6201
Editorial Fax: (806) 828-6202
General/National Adv. E-mail: slatonite@sbcglobal.net
Display Adv. E-mail: slatonite@sbcglobal.net
Editorial e-mail: slatonite@sbcglobal.net
Primary Website: slatonitenews.com
Year Established: 1911
Avg Paid Circ: 1900
Avg Free Circ: 25
Audit By: Sworn/Estimate/Non-Audited
Audit Date: 10.06.2019
Personnel: Ken Richardson (Publisher/Ed.); James Villanueva
Parent company (for newspapers): Slaton Media, LLC

THE SMITHVILLE TIMES

Street address 1: PO Box 459
Street address city: Bastrop
Street address state: TX
Zip/Postal code: 78602-0459
General Phone: (512) 237-4655
General Fax: (512) 237-5443
Advertising Phone: (512) 237-4655
Advertising Fax: (512) 237-5443
Editorial Phone: (512) 237-4655
Editorial Fax: (512) 237-5443
General/National Adv. E-mail: news@statesman.com
Display Adv. E-mail: news@statesman.com
Editorial e-mail: news@statesman.com
Primary Website: statesman.com
Year Established: 1895
Avg Free Circ: 1359
Audit By: Sworn/Estimate/Non-Audited
Audit Date: 10.06.2019
Personnel: Tammy Moore (Vice Pres.); Mark Gwin (Pub.); Cyndi Wright (Ed.)
Parent company (for newspapers): Cox Media Group

THE STAMFORD STAR

Street address 1: 202 E Hamilton St
Street address city: Stamford
Street address state: TX
Zip/Postal code: 79553-4730
General Phone: (325) 773-5100
General Fax: (325) 773-5105
Advertising Phone: (325) 773-5100
Advertising Fax: (325) 773-5105
Editorial Phone: (325) 773-5100
Editorial Fax: (325) 773-5105
General/National Adv. E-mail: audra@thestamfordstar.com
Display Adv. E-mail: cheyenne@thestamfordstar.com
Editorial e-mail: cheyenne@thestamfordstar.com
Primary Website: thestamfordstar.com
Year Established: 2006
Avg Paid Circ: 1500
Avg Free Circ: 200
Audit By: Sworn/Estimate/Non-Audited
Audit Date: 10.06.2019
Personnel: Cheyenne Bereuter (Pub./Ed.); Audra Arendall (Adv. Dir.)
Parent company (for newspapers): The Stamford Star

THE STATE LINE TRIBUNE

Street address 1: 404 3rd St
Street address city: Farwell
Street address state: TX
Zip/Postal code: 79325-4670
General Phone: (806) 481-3681
Advertising Phone: (806) 481-3681
Editorial Phone: (806) 481-3681
General/National Adv. E-mail: tribune@plateautel.net
Display Adv. E-mail: tribune@plateautel.net
Editorial e-mail: tribune@plateautel.net
Primary Website: statelinetribune.com
Year Established: 1911
Avg Paid Circ: 1500
Avg Free Circ: 0
Audit By: Sworn/Estimate/Non-Audited
Audit Date: 10.06.2019
Personnel: Rob Pomper (Pub./Ed./Adv. Dir.)

THE TERRELL TRIBUNE

Street address 1: 201 N. Rockwall Ave.
Street address city: Terrell
Street address state: TX
Zip/Postal code: 75160
General Phone: (972) 563-6476
General Fax: (972) 563-0340
Advertising Phone: (972) 563-6476
Advertising Fax: (972) 563-0340
Editorial Phone: (972) 563-6476
Editorial Fax: (972) 563-0340
General/National Adv. E-mail: mary@terrelltribune.com
Display Adv. E-mail: karla@terrelltribune.com
Classified Adv. e-mail: mary@terrelltribune.com
Editorial e-mail: editor@terrelltribune.com
Primary Website: terrelltribune.com
Year Established: 1898
Avg Paid Circ: 2300
Sun. Circulation Paid: 2950
Sun. Circulation Free: 137
Audit By: Sworn/Estimate/Non-Audited
Audit Date: 30.09.2021
Personnel: Vickie Painter (Bus Mgr/Circu/Inserts); Tiffany Hardy (General Manager); Karla Dunson (Advertising Manager); Mary Dlabaj (Office Manager / Sales Consultant); David Kapitan (Editor)
Parent company (for newspapers): Van Zandt Newspapers, LLC

THE TEXAS SPUR

Street address 1: PO Box 430
Street address city: Spur
Street address state: TX
Zip/Postal code: 79370-0430
General Phone: (806) 271-3381
General Fax: (806) 271-3966
Editorial e-mail: news@thetexasspur.com
Primary Website: thetexasspur.com
Year Established: 1909
Avg Paid Circ: 1200
Audit By: Sworn/Estimate/Non-Audited
Audit Date: 10.06.2019
Personnel: Cindi Taylor (Pub.); Kassi Atkinson (Asst. Ed./Adv. Dir.)

THE TIMES TRIBUNE

Street address 1: 921 Cooper St
Street address city: Brookshire
Street address state: TX
Zip/Postal code: 77423
General Phone: (281) 934-4949
General Fax: (281) 934-2012
Advertising Phone: (281) 934-4949
Advertising Fax: (281) 934-2012
Editorial Phone: (281) 934-4949
Editorial Fax: (281) 934-2012
General/National Adv. E-mail: news.trib@timestribune.com
Display Adv. E-mail: news.trib@timestribune.com
Editorial e-mail: news.trib@timestribune.com
Primary Website: timestribune.com
Year Established: 1993
Avg Paid Circ: 1100
Audit By: Sworn/Estimate/Non-Audited
Audit Date: 10.06.2019
Personnel: Jan Mincy (Pub./Ed.); Lillie Ruby (Adv. Dir.)
Parent company (for newspapers): CNHI, LLC

THE TRINITY STANDARD

Street address 1: 106 E Main St
Street address city: Trinity
Street address state: TX
Zip/Postal code: 75862
General Phone: (936) 594-2126
General Fax: (936) 594-7547
Advertising Phone: (936) 594-2126
Advertising Fax: (936) 594-7547
Editorial Phone: (936) 594-2126
Editorial Fax: (936) 594-7547
General/National Adv. E-mail: trinity.standard@gmail.com
Display Adv. E-mail: trinity.standard@gmail.com
Editorial e-mail: trinity.standard@gmail.com
Primary Website: easttexasnews.com
Year Established: 1928
Avg Paid Circ: 2800
Audit By: Sworn/Estimate/Non-Audited
Audit Date: 10.06.2019
Personnel: Alvin Holley (Pub.); Gregory Peak (Ed.); Linda Holley (Adv. Mgr.); Mary McClure (Office Mgr.)
Parent company (for newspapers): Polk County Publishing Co.

THE VALLEY TRIBUNE

Street address 1: 205 Cypress
Street address city: Quitaque
Street address state: TX
Zip/Postal code: 79255
General Phone: (806) 455-1101
General Fax: (806) 455-1101
General/National Adv. E-mail: thevalleytribune@yahoo.com
Display Adv. E-mail: thevalleytribune@yahoo.com
Editorial e-mail: thevalleytribune@yahoo.com
Year Established: 1926
Avg Paid Circ: 1000
Audit By: Sworn/Estimate/Non-Audited
Audit Date: 10.06.2019
Personnel: Brandei Taylor (Pub./Adv. Dir.)

THE VAN HORN ADVOCATE

Street address 1: 701 W Broadway
Street address city: Van Horn
Street address state: TX
Zip/Postal code: 79855
General Phone: (432) 283-2003
General Fax: (432) 283-1070
Advertising Phone: (432) 283-2003
Advertising Fax: (432) 283-1070
Editorial Phone: (432) 283-2003
Editorial Fax: (432) 283-1070
General/National Adv. E-mail: Lmorton@thevanhornadvocate.com
Display Adv. E-mail: Lmorton@thevanhornadvocate.com
Editorial e-mail: rmorales@thevanhornadvocate.com
Primary Website: thevanhornadvocate.com
Year Established: 1910
Avg Paid Circ: 985
Audit By: Sworn/Estimate/Non-Audited
Audit Date: 10.06.2019
Personnel: Robert Morales (Pub./Ed.); Lisa Morton (Adv. Dir.)

THE VINDICATOR

Street address 1: 1939 Trinity St
Street address 2: Ste A
Street address city: Liberty
Street address state: TX
Zip/Postal code: 77575-4851
General Phone: (936) 336-3611
General Fax: (936) 336-3345
Advertising Phone: (936) 336-3611
Advertising Fax: (936) 336-3345
Editorial Phone: (936) 336-3611
Editorial Fax: (936) 336-3345
General/National Adv. E-mail: publisher@thevindicator.com
Display Adv. E-mail: ads@thevindicator.com
Editorial e-mail: editor@thevindicator.com
Primary Website: thevindicator.com
Mthly Avg Views: 62689
Mthly Avg Unique Visitors: 25327
Year Established: 1887
Avg Paid Circ: 1019
Avg Free Circ: 732
Audit By: Sworn/Estimate/Non-Audited
Audit Date: 10.06.2019
Personnel: Carol Skewes (Pub.); Kim Marlow (Adv. Mgr.); Rodger Slusher (Circ. Mgr); Jennfier Gray (Office Mgr.); Jerry Michalsky (Sports Ed.)
Parent company (for newspapers): Fenice Community Media

THE WEEKLY GAZETTE

Street address 1: 511 5th St
Street address city: Honey Grove
Street address state: TX
Zip/Postal code: 75446-1901
General Phone: (903) 378-3558
General Fax: (903) 378-3588
Advertising Phone: (903) 378-3558
Advertising Fax: (903) 378-3588
Editorial Phone: (903) 378-3558
Editorial Fax: (903) 378-3588
General/National Adv. E-mail: hgwcnews@sbcglobal.net
Display Adv. E-mail: hgwcnews@sbcglobal.net
Editorial e-mail: hgwcnews@sbcglobal.net
Primary Website: honeygroveweeklygazette.com
Year Established: 1999
Avg Paid Circ: 1500
Audit By: Sworn/Estimate/Non-Audited
Audit Date: 10.06.2019
Personnel: Lorrie Page (Pub./Ed.); JoAnn Page (Adv. Dir.)

THE WEIMAR MERCURY

Street address 1: 200 W Main St
Street address city: Weimar
Street address state: TX
Zip/Postal code: 78962-2013
General Phone: (979) 725-9595
General Fax: (979) 725-9051
General/National Adv. E-mail: mercuryads@weimarmercury.com
Display Adv. E-mail: mercuryads@weimarmercury.com
Editorial e-mail: mercury@weimarmercury.com
Primary Website: weimarmercury.com
Year Established: 1888
Avg Paid Circ: 3205
Avg Free Circ: 146
Audit By: Sworn/Estimate/Non-Audited
Audit Date: 10.06.2019
Personnel: Bruce Beal (Pub./Ed./Adv. Dir.)

THE WEST NEWS

Street address 1: 214 W Oak St
Street address city: West
Street address state: TX
Zip/Postal code: 76691-1443
General Phone: (254) 826-3718
General Fax: (254) 826-3719
Advertising Phone: (254) 826-3718
Advertising Fax: (254) 826-3719
Editorial Phone: (254) 826-3718
Editorial Fax: (254) 826-3719

General/National Adv. E-mail: westnews@sbcglobal.net
Display Adv. E-mail: westnews@sbcglobal.net
Editorial e-mail: westnews@sbcglobal.net
Year Established: 1889
Avg Paid Circ: 3000
Audit By: Sworn/Estimate/Non-Audited
Audit Date: 10.06.2019
Personnel: Linn A. Pescaia (Pub.); Larry Knapek (Ed.); Scott Knapek (Adv. Dir.)

THE WHEELER TIMES

Street address 1: 110 E Texas Ave
Street address city: Wheeler
Street address state: TX
Zip/Postal code: 79096
General Phone: (806) 826-3123
Advertising Phone: (806) 826-3123
Editorial Phone: (806)826-3123
General/National Adv. E-mail: wtimes@windstream.net
Display Adv. E-mail: wtimes@windstream.net
Editorial e-mail: wtimes@windstream.net
Year Established: 1933
Avg Paid Circ: 973
Audit By: Sworn/Estimate/Non-Audited
Audit Date: 10.06.2019
Personnel: Louis C. Stas (Pub./Ed./Adv. Dir.)

THE WILLIAMSON COUNTY SUN

Street address 1: 709 S Main St
Street address city: Georgetown
Street address state: TX
Zip/Postal code: 78626-5700
General Phone: (512) 930-4824
Advertising Phone: (512) 930-4824
Editorial Phone: (512) 930-4824
General/National Adv. E-mail: ads@wilcosun.com
Display Adv. E-mail: ads@wilcosun.com
Classified Adv. e-mail: class@wilcosun.com
Editorial e-mail: editor@wilcosun.com
Primary Website: wilcosun.com
Year Established: 1877
Avg Paid Circ: 4700
Audit By: Sworn/Estimate/Non-Audited
Audit Date: 30.09.2023
Personnel: Clark Thurmond (Pub.); Linda Scarbrough (Co-Pub./Ed.); Nick Cicale (Editor); Teri Gray (Adv. Dir.); Will Anderson (Mng. Ed.)

THE WINKLER COUNTY NEWS

Street address 1: 109 S Poplar St
Street address city: Kermit
Street address state: TX
Zip/Postal code: 79745-3027
General Phone: (432) 586-2561
General Fax: (432) 586-2562
Advertising Phone: (432) 586-2561
Advertising Fax: (432) 586-2562
Editorial Phone: (432) 586-2561
Editorial Fax: (432) 586-2562
General/National Adv. E-mail: gfreepress@sbcglobal.net
Display Adv. E-mail: gfreepress@sbcglobal.net
Editorial e-mail: gfreepress@sbcglobal.net
Year Established: 1936
Avg Paid Circ: 1500
Audit By: Sworn/Estimate/Non-Audited
Audit Date: 10.06.2019
Personnel: Denise Hannah (Co-Pub.); Tom Beckham (Co-Pub.); Phil Parks (Ed.); Phyllis Thomas (Adv. Dir.)

THE WINNSBORO NEWS

Street address 1: 105 Locust St
Street address city: Winnsboro
Street address state: TX
Zip/Postal code: 75494-2519
General Phone: (903) 342-5247
General Fax: (903) 342-3266
Advertising Phone: (903) 342-5247
Advertising Fax: (903) 342-3266
Editorial Phone: (903) 342-5247
Editorial Fax: (903) 342-3266
General/National Adv. E-mail: winnsboronews@suddenlinkmail.com
Display Adv. E-mail: winnsboronews@suddenlinkmail.com
Editorial e-mail: winnsboronews@suddenlinkmail.com
Year Established: 1908
Avg Paid Circ: 4010
Avg Free Circ: 8
Audit By: Sworn/Estimate/Non-Audited
Audit Date: 10.06.2019
Personnel: Thomas F. Pendergast (Pub./Ed.); Karen W. Pendergast (Mng. Ed.); Linda Henry (Adv. Mgr.); Ross Hunter (Prodn. Mgr.)

THE WOODLANDS VILLAGER

Street address 1: 100 Avenue A
Street address 2: Ste 190
Street address city: Conroe
Street address state: TX
Zip/Postal code: 77301-2946
General Phone: (281) 378-1040
General Fax: (281) 363-3299
Advertising Phone: (281) 378-1042
Advertising Fax: (281) 363-3299
Editorial Phone: (281) 378-1049
Editorial Fax: (281) 363-3299
General/National Adv. E-mail: rdavis@hcnonline.com
Display Adv. E-mail: lelizade@hcnonline.com
Editorial e-mail: adubois@hcnonline.com
Primary Website: thewoodlandsvillager.com
Year Established: 1977
Avg Paid Circ: 0
Avg Free Circ: 44200
Audit By: Sworn/Estimate/Non-Audited
Audit Date: 10.06.2019
Personnel: Richard Davis (Pub./Adv. Dir.); Andy DuBois (Exec. Ed.); Catherine Dominguez (Mng. Ed.); Jason Joseph (Pub.); Charles Lee (Adv. Mgr); Rick Flores (Circ. Mgr); Megan O'Sullivan (Mktg. Mgr.); Tom Legg (Major Sr. Acct. Mgr.)
Parent company (for newspapers): Times Media Group

THE WYLIE NEWS

Street address 1: 110 N Ballard Ave
Street address city: Wylie
Street address state: TX
Zip/Postal code: 75098-4467
General Phone: (972) 442-5515
General Fax:
Advertising Phone: (972) 442-5515
Editorial Phone: (972) 442-5515
General/National Adv. E-mail: advertising@csmediatexas.com
Display Adv. E-mail: classifieds@csmediatexas.com
Editorial e-mail: cengbrock@csmediatexas.com
Primary Website: wylienews.com
Year Established: 1948
Avg Paid Circ: 6548
Audit By: Sworn/Estimate/Non-Audited
Audit Date: 10.06.2019
Personnel: Chad B. Engbrock (Pub.); Sonia Duggan (Associate Publisher)
Parent company (for newspapers): C&S Media, Inc.

THORNDALE CHAMPION

Street address 1: 108 E 1st St
Street address city: Cameron
Street address state: TX
Zip/Postal code: 76520-3341
General Phone: (254) 455-0144
General Fax: (254) 697-4902
Advertising Phone: (254) 455-0144
Advertising Fax: (254) 697-4902
Editorial Phone: (254) 455-0144
Editorial Fax: (254) 697-4902
General/National Adv. E-mail: tdchamp@cameronherald.com
Display Adv. E-mail: tdchamp@cameronherald.com
Editorial e-mail: tdchamp@cameronherald.com
Primary Website: cameronherald.com/thorndale
Year Established: 1898
Avg Paid Circ: 490
Audit By: Sworn/Estimate/Non-Audited
Audit Date: 10.06.2019
Personnel: Phil Major (Pub./Ed.); Elissa Hernandez (Adv. Dir.)

THROCKMORTON TRIBUNE

Street address 1: 140 N Minter Ave
Street address 2: Ste 109
Street address city: Throckmorton
Street address state: TX
Zip/Postal code: 76483-5344
General Phone: (940) 849-0147
General Fax: (940) 849-0149
Advertising Phone: (940) 849-0147
Advertising Fax: (940) 849-0149
Editorial Phone: (940) 849-0147
Editorial Fax: (940) 849-0149
General/National Adv. E-mail: throckmortontribune@gmail.com
Display Adv. E-mail: throckmortontribune@gmail.com
Editorial e-mail: throckmortontribune@gmail.com
Year Established: 1886
Avg Paid Circ: 1051
Avg Free Circ: 214
Audit By: Sworn/Estimate/Non-Audited
Audit Date: 10.06.2019
Personnel: Dobbi Makovy (Pub./Ed.)

TIMPSON & TENAHA NEWS

Street address 1: 150 Park Plz
Street address city: Timpson
Street address state: TX
Zip/Postal code: 75975
General Phone: (936) 254-3618
General Fax: (936) 254-3206
General/National Adv. E-mail: ttnews@ttnewsinc.com
Display Adv. E-mail: ttnews@ttnewsinc.com
Editorial e-mail: ttnews@ttnewsinc.com
Primary Website: ttnewsinc.com
Year Established: 1885
Avg Paid Circ: 2001
Avg Free Circ: 6
Audit By: Sworn/Estimate/Non-Audited
Audit Date: 10.06.2019
Personnel: Hilda Pena (Ed./Pub.); Rhonda Samford (Adv. Mgr.)

TOMBALL POTPOURRI

Street address 1: 100 Avenue A
Street address city: Conroe
Street address state: TX
Zip/Postal code: 77301-2946
General Phone: (281) 378-1080
General Fax: (281) 320-2005
Advertising Phone: (281) 378-1082
Advertising Fax: (281) 320-2005
Editorial Phone: (281) 378-1087
Editorial Fax: (281) 320-2005
General/National Adv. E-mail: rdavis@hcnonline.com
Display Adv. E-mail: srovegno@hcnonline.com
Editorial e-mail: rkent@hcnonline.com
Primary Website: hcnonline.com
Year Established: 1986
Avg Paid Circ: 0
Avg Free Circ: 17490
Audit By: Sworn/Estimate/Non-Audited
Audit Date: 10.06.2019
Personnel: Richard Davis (Pub.); Roy Kent (Ed.); Susan Rovegno (Sales Mgr.); Jason Joseph (Pub.); Charles Lee; Rick Flores (Circ. Mgr); Megan O'Sullivan (Mktg. Mgr.); Tom Legg (Major Sr. Acct. Mgr.)
Parent company (for newspapers): Hearst Communications, Inc.; Times Media Group

TRAMMEL TRACE TRIBUNE

Street address 1: 245 W Johnson St
Street address city: Tatum
Street address state: TX
Zip/Postal code: 75691
General Phone: (903) 240-9226
Advertising Phone: (903) 240-9226
Editorial Phone: (903) 240-9226
General/National Adv. E-mail: info@tatumnews.com
Display Adv. E-mail: info@tatumnews.com
Editorial e-mail: info@tatumnews.com
Year Established: 1976
Avg Paid Circ: 560
Avg Free Circ: 440
Audit By: Sworn/Estimate/Non-Audited
Audit Date: 10.06.2019
Personnel: Amy Haden (Pub.); Byron Haden (Co-Pub./Ed./Adv. Dir.)

TRENTON TRIBUNE

Street address 1: 115 Hamilton St
Street address city: Trenton
Street address state: TX
Zip/Postal code: 75490-2610
General Phone: (903) 989-2325
General Fax: (903) 989-2923
Advertising Phone: (903) 989-2325
Advertising Fax: (903) 989-2923
Editorial Phone: (903) 989-2325
Editorial Fax: (903) 989-2923
General/National Adv. E-mail: trentontribune@texoma.net
Display Adv. E-mail: trentontribune@texoma.net
Editorial e-mail: trentontribune@texoma.net
Primary Website: texomaliving.com
Avg Paid Circ: 1215
Audit By: Sworn/Estimate/Non-Audited
Audit Date: 10.06.2019
Personnel: Tom M. Holmes (Pub./Ed./Adv. Dir.)

TRI COUNTY LEADER

Street address 1: 304 State Highway 110 N
Street address city: Whitehouse
Street address state: TX
Zip/Postal code: 75791-3112
General Phone: (903) 839-2353
General Fax: (903) 839-8519
Advertising Phone: (903) 839-2353
Advertising Fax: (903) 839-8519
Editorial Phone: (903) 839-2353
Editorial Fax: (903) 839-8519
General/National Adv. E-mail: ads@tricountyleader.com
Display Adv. E-mail: classifieds@kilgorenewsherald.com
Editorial e-mail: reporter@tricountyleader.com
Primary Website: tricountyleader.com
Year Established: 1988
Avg Paid Circ: 2600
Audit By: Sworn/Estimate/Non-Audited
Audit Date: 10.06.2019
Personnel: Bill Woodall (Pub./Adv. Dir.); Jessica Woodall (Co-Pub.); Don Treul (Ed.); Suzanne Loudamy (Staff Writer)
Parent company (for newspapers): Bluebonnet Publishing

TRIBUNE-PROGRESS

Street address 1: 108 W Clark St
Street address city: Bartlett
Street address state: TX
Zip/Postal code: 76511-4371
General Phone: (254) 527-4424
General Fax: (254) 527-4333
Advertising Phone: (254) 527-4424
Advertising Fax: (254) 527-4333
Editorial Phone: (254) 527-4424
Editorial Fax: (254) 527-4333
General/National Adv. E-mail: newslady01@sbcglobal.net
Display Adv. E-mail: newslady01@sbcglobal.net
Editorial e-mail: newslady01@sbcglobal.net
Year Established: 1886
Avg Paid Circ: 1259
Audit By: Sworn/Estimate/Non-Audited
Audit Date: 10.06.2019
Personnel: Gayle Bielss (Pub./Ed./Adv. Dir.); Debbie McKeon (Office Mgr.)

TWIN CITIES NEWS

Street address 1: 111 East B St
Street address city: Munday
Street address state: TX
Zip/Postal code: 76371
General Phone: (940) 422-4314
General Fax: (940) 422-4333
Advertising Phone: (940) 422-4314
Advertising Fax: (940) 422-4333
Editorial Phone: (940) 422-4314
Editorial Fax: (940) 422-4333
General/National Adv. E-mail: mcourier@westex.net
Display Adv. E-mail: mcourier@westex.net
Editorial e-mail: mcourier@westex.net
Primary Website: smalltownpapers.com
Avg Paid Circ: 772
Avg Free Circ: 17
Audit By: Sworn/Estimate/Non-Audited
Audit Date: 10.06.2019
Personnel: Jay White (Pub./Ed./Adv. Dir.)

TYLER COUNTY BOOSTER

Street address 1: 205 W Bluff St

Street address city: Woodville
Street address state: TX
Zip/Postal code: 75979-5221
General Phone: (409) 283-2516
General Fax: (409) 283-2560
Advertising Phone: (409)283-2516
Advertising Fax: (409)283-2560
Editorial Phone: (409)283-2516
Editorial Fax: (409)283-2560
General/National Adv. E-mail: kelli@polkcountypublishing.com
Display Adv. E-mail: beth@polkcountypublishing.com
Classified Adv. e-mail: classified@tylercountybooster.com
Editorial e-mail: news@tylercountybooster.com
Primary Website: easttexasnews.com
Year Established: 1930
Avg Paid Circ: 2000
Avg Free Circ: 0
Audit By: Sworn/Estimate/Non-Audited
Audit Date: 10.11.2021
Personnel: Kelli Barnes (Publisher); Jim Powers (Ed.)
Parent company (for newspapers): Polk County Publishing Co.

UVALDE LEADER-NEWS

Street address 1: 110 N East St
Street address city: Uvalde
Street address state: TX
Zip/Postal code: 78801-5312
General Phone: (830) 278-3335
General Fax: (830) 278-9191
General/National Adv. E-mail: sbalke@uvaldeleadernews.com
Display Adv. E-mail: nybarra@uvaldeleadernews.com
Editorial e-mail: cgarnett@uvaldeleadernews.com
Primary Website: uvaldeleadernews.com
Year Established: 1879
Avg Paid Circ: 4741
Audit By: Sworn/Estimate/Non-Audited
Audit Date: 10.06.2019
Personnel: Craig Garnett (Pub./Ed.); Steve Balke (Adv. Dir.); Meghann Garcia (Managing Ed.)

VALLEY MILLS PROGRESS

Street address 1: 403 E Avenue A
Street address city: Valley Mills
Street address state: TX
Zip/Postal code: 76689-4424
General Phone: (254) 932-6450
General Fax: (254) 932-6450
Advertising Phone: (254) 932-6450
Advertising Fax: (254) 932-6450
Editorial Phone: (254) 932-6450
Editorial Fax: (254) 932-6450
General/National Adv. E-mail: vmprogress.tx@gmail.com
Display Adv. E-mail: vmprogress.tx@gmail.com
Editorial e-mail: vmprogress.tx@gmail.com
Primary Website: none
Year Established: 1989
Avg Paid Circ: 675
Audit By: Sworn/Estimate/Non-Audited
Audit Date: 10.06.2019
Personnel: Mark Grear (Pub./Ed./Adv. Dir.)

VALLEY TOWN CRIER

Street address 1: 1811 N 23rd St
Street address city: McAllen
Street address state: TX
Zip/Postal code: 78501-6196
General Phone: (956) 682-2423
General Fax: (956) 630-6371
Advertising Phone: (956)682-2423 x 260
Advertising Fax: (956)630-6371
Editorial Phone: (956)682-2423 x 220
Editorial Fax: (956)630-6371
General/National Adv. E-mail: rdeluna@valleytowncrier.com
Display Adv. E-mail: rdeluna@valleytowncrier.com
Classified Adv. e-mail: jgarcia@valleytowncrier.com
Editorial e-mail: pperez@valleytowncrier.com
Primary Website: yourvalleyvoice.com
Mthly Avg Views: 76521
Mthly Avg Unique Visitors: 11611
Year Established: 1964
Avg Free Circ: 15000
Audit By: VAC
Audit Date: 31.12.2016
Personnel: Linda Medrano (Pub./Reg. Op. Dir.); Pedro Perez (Ed.); Ernesto Sanchez (Circ. Mgr); Holly Reyes (Business Manager); Jimmy Rocha (Production Director)
Parent company (for newspapers): CherryRoad Media

VAN BANNER

Street address 1: 109 N 5th St
Street address city: Wills Point
Street address state: TX
Zip/Postal code: 75169-2058
General Phone: (903) 567-4000
General Fax: (903) 567-6076
Advertising Phone: (903) 567-4000
Advertising Fax: (903) 567-6076
Editorial Phone: (903) 567-4000
Editorial Fax: (903) 567-6076
General/National Adv. E-mail: brad@vanzandtnews.com
Display Adv. E-mail: brad@vanzandtnews.com
Editorial e-mail: brad@vanzandtnews.com
Primary Website: vanbanner.com
Year Established: 1998
Avg Paid Circ: 694
Audit By: Sworn/Estimate/Non-Audited
Audit Date: 10.06.2019
Personnel: Brad Blakemore (Pub.); Julie Vaughan (Ed.); Kelli Baxter (Adv. Dir.)

VAN ZANDT NEWS

Street address 1: 103 E. Tyler Street
Street address city: Canton
Street address state: TX
Zip/Postal code: 75103
General Phone: (903) 567-4000
General Fax: 903-567-6076
Advertising Phone: 903-567-4000
Advertising Fax: 903-567-6076
Editorial Phone: 903-567-4000
Editorial Fax: 903-567-6076
General/National Adv. E-mail: business@vanzandtnews.com
Display Adv. E-mail: sales@vanzandtnews.com
Classified Adv. e-mail: classifieds@vanzandtnews.com
Editorial e-mail: editor@vanzandtnews.com
Primary Website: vanzandtnews.com
Year Established: 1982
Avg Paid Circ: 5500
Avg Free Circ: 100
Audit By: Sworn/Estimate/Non-Audited
Audit Date: 30.09.2021
Personnel: Tiffany Hardy (General Manager)
Parent company (for newspapers): Van Zandt Newspapers LLC

VEGA ENTERPRISE

Street address 1: 116 S Main St
Street address city: Vega
Street address state: TX
Zip/Postal code: 79092
General Phone: (806)344-6892
Advertising Phone: (806) 344-6892
Editorial Phone: (806) 344-6892
General/National Adv. E-mail: vegaent@arn.net
Display Adv. E-mail: vegaent@arn.net
Editorial e-mail: vegaent@arn.net
Year Established: 1948
Avg Paid Circ: 900
Audit By: Sworn/Estimate/Non-Audited
Audit Date: 10.06.2019
Personnel: Quincy Taylor (Pub./Ed./Adv. Dir.)

VIDOR VIDORIAN

Street address 1: 450 W Bolivar St
Street address city: Vidor
Street address state: TX
Zip/Postal code: 77662-4724
General Phone: (409) 769-5428
General Fax: (409) 769-2600
Advertising Phone: (409) 769-5428
Advertising Fax: (409) 769-2600
Editorial Phone: (409) 769-5428
Editorial Fax: (409) 769-2600
General/National Adv. E-mail: vidorian1@sbcglobal.net
Display Adv. E-mail: vidorian1@sbcglobal.net
Editorial e-mail: vidorian1@sbcglobal.net
Year Established: 1959
Avg Paid Circ: 1502
Avg Free Circ: 11275
Audit By: Sworn/Estimate/Non-Audited
Audit Date: 10.06.2019
Personnel: Adair Luker (Pub.); Randall Luker (Ed./Adv. Dir.)

WALLIS NEWS-REVIEW

Street address 1: 256 Cedar St
Street address city: Wallis
Street address state: TX
Zip/Postal code: 77485-9787
General Phone: (979) 478-6412
Advertising Phone: (979) 478-6412
Editorial Phone: (979) 478-6412
Editorial Fax: (979) 478-2198
General/National Adv. E-mail: joanie@wallisnews.com
Display Adv. E-mail: joanie@wallisnews.com
Editorial e-mail: johnny@wallisnews.com
Primary Website: wallisnews.com
Year Established: 1974
Avg Paid Circ: 800
Avg Free Circ: 25
Audit By: Sworn/Estimate/Non-Audited
Audit Date: 10.06.2019
Personnel: Joanie Griffin (Pub./Adv. Dir.); Johnny Griffin (Ed.)

WEST AUSTIN NEWS

Street address 1: 5511 Parkcrest Drive
Street address 2: Ste 100
Street address city: Austin
Street address state: TX
Zip/Postal code: 78731
General Phone: (512) 459-4070
General Fax: (512) 206-0704
Advertising Phone: (512) 459-4070
Advertising Fax: (512) 206-0704
Editorial Phone: (512) 459-4070
Editorial Fax: (512) 206-0704
General/National Adv. E-mail: adsales@westaustinnews.com
Display Adv. E-mail: adsales@westaustinnews.com
Editorial e-mail: editor@westaustinnews.com
Primary Website: westaustinnews.com
Year Established: 1986
Avg Paid Circ: 1880
Audit By: Sworn/Estimate/Non-Audited
Audit Date: 10.06.2019
Personnel: Bart Stephens (Pub./Ed.); Rachelle Topete (Adv. Mgr./Office Mgr.); Kim Bader (Prodn. Mgr.)

WEST KERR CURRENT

Street address 1: 107 Highway 39
Street address 2: Ste A
Street address city: Ingram
Street address state: TX
Zip/Postal code: 78025-3286
General Phone: (830) 367-3501
General Fax: (830) 367-3064
Advertising Phone: (830) 367-3501
Advertising Fax: (830) 367-3501
Editorial Phone: (830) 367-3501
Editorial Fax: (830) 367-3501
General/National Adv. E-mail: wkcurrent@classicnet.net
Display Adv. E-mail: wkcurrent@classicnet.net
Editorial e-mail: wkcurrent@classicnet.net
Primary Website: wkcurrent.com
Year Established: 2003
Avg Paid Circ: 1400
Avg Free Circ: 25
Audit By: Sworn/Estimate/Non-Audited
Audit Date: 10.06.2019
Personnel: Clint Schroeder (Pub./Ed.); Irene Van Winkle (reporter, ad sales); Nancy Schroeder (Advertising Director)

WEST TEXAS COUNTY COURIER

Street address 1: 15344 Werling Ct
Street address city: Horizon City
Street address state: TX
Zip/Postal code: 79928-7012
General Phone: (915) 852-3235
General Fax: (915) 852-0123
Advertising Phone: (915) 852-3235
Advertising Fax: (915) 852-0123
Editorial Phone: (915) 852-3235
Editorial Fax: (915) 852-0123
General/National Adv. E-mail: wtxcc@wtxcc.com
Display Adv. E-mail: wtxcc@wtxcc.com
Editorial e-mail: wtxcc@wtxcc.com
Primary Website: wtxcc.com
Year Established: 1973
Avg Free Circ: 11000
Audit By: Sworn/Estimate/Non-Audited
Audit Date: 10.06.2019
Personnel: Rick Shrum (Pub./Ed./Adv. Dir.)

WEST UNIVERSITY EXAMINER

Street address 1: 21901 State Highway 249
Street address 2: Ste 500
Street address city: Houston
Street address state: TX
Zip/Postal code: 77070-1545
General Phone: (281) 378-1900
General Fax: (713) 520-1193
General/National Adv. E-mail: kkonter@hcnonline.com
Display Adv. E-mail: clee@hcnonline.com
Editorial e-mail: rkent@hcnonline.com
Primary Website: yourhoustonnews.com
Avg Paid Circ: 5362
Audit By: AAM
Audit Date: 30.09.2018
Personnel: Kathy Konter (Advt Sales Mgr); Roy Kent (Ed)
Parent company (for newspapers): Hearst Communications, Inc.

WESTERN OBSERVER

Street address 1: 1120 W Court Plz
Street address city: Anson
Street address state: TX
Zip/Postal code: 79501-4315
General Phone: (325) 823-3253
General Fax: (325) 823-2957
Advertising Phone: (325) 823-3253
Advertising Fax: (325) 823-2957
Editorial Phone: (325) 823-3253
Editorial Fax: (325) 823-2957
General/National Adv. E-mail: westobserver@sbcglobal.net
Display Adv. E-mail: westobserver@sbcglobal.net
Editorial e-mail: westobserver@sbcglobal.net
Year Established: 1883
Avg Paid Circ: 2100
Audit By: Sworn/Estimate/Non-Audited
Audit Date: 10.06.2019
Personnel: Tiffany Waddell (Pub./Ed./Adv. Dir.)

WESTLAKE PICAYUNE

Street address 1: 305 S Congress Ave
Street address city: Austin
Street address state: TX
Zip/Postal code: 78704-1200
General Phone: (512) 327-2990
Advertising Phone: (512) 445-3742
Editorial Phone: (512) 912-2502
General/National Adv. E-mail: communityadvertising@statesman.com
Display Adv. E-mail: classified@statesman.com
Editorial e-mail: editor@statesman.com
Primary Website: statesman.com
Year Established: 1976
Avg Paid Circ: 463
Avg Free Circ: 3415
Audit By: Sworn/Estimate/Non-Audited
Audit Date: 10.06.2019
Personnel: Ed Allen (Pub./Ed.); Habeab Kurdi (Sports Ed.)
Parent company (for newspapers): Cox Media Group

WHARTON JOURNAL-SPECTATOR

Street address 1: 115 W Burleson St
Street address city: Wharton
Street address state: TX
Zip/Postal code: 77488-5090
General Phone: (979) 532-8840
General Fax: (979) 532-8845
Advertising Phone: (979) 532-8840
Advertising Fax: (979) 532-8845
Editorial Phone: (979) 532-8840
Editorial Fax: (979) 532-8845
General/National Adv. E-mail: bwallace@journal-spectator.com
Display Adv. E-mail: bwallace@journal-spectator.com
Classified Adv. e-mail: bwallace@journal-spectator.com

Editorial e-mail: bwallace@journal-spectator.com
Primary Website: journal-spectator.com
Year Established: 1889
Avg Paid Circ: 3300
Audit By: Sworn/Estimate/Non-Audited
Audit Date: 05.10.2022
Personnel: Bill Wallace (Editor & Publisher); Keith Magee (Mng. Ed.); Joe Southern (Managing Editor); Ann Watson (Retail Adv. Mgr.); Helen Sevier (Classified Adv. Mgr.)
Parent company (for newspapers): Hartman Newspapers LP

WHITE OAK INDEPENDENT

Street address 1: 100 N White Oak Rd
Street address city: White Oak
Street address state: TX
Zip/Postal code: 75693-1243
General Phone: (903) 845-5349
General Fax: (903) 845-5349
Advertising Phone: (903) 845-5349
Advertising Fax: (903) 845-5349
Editorial Phone: (903) 845-5349
Editorial Fax: (903) 845-5349
General/National Adv. E-mail: newman5608@suddenlink.net
Display Adv. E-mail: newman5608@suddenlink.net
Editorial e-mail: newman5608@suddenlink.net
Year Established: 1990
Avg Paid Circ: 745
Audit By: Sworn/Estimate/Non-Audited
Audit Date: 10.06.2019
Personnel: Winnie Newman (Pub./Ed.); Candy Miller (Adv. Mgr.)

WHITESBORO NEWS-RECORD

Street address 1: 130 E Main St
Street address city: Whitesboro
Street address state: TX
Zip/Postal code: 76273-1705
General Phone: (903) 564-3565
General Fax: (903) 564-9655
Advertising Phone: (903) 564-3565
Advertising Fax: (903) 564-9655
Editorial Phone: (903) 564-3565
Editorial Fax: (903) 564-9655
General/National Adv. E-mail: ads@whitesboroneews.com
Display Adv. E-mail: ads@whitesboroneews.com
Editorial e-mail: news@whitesboronews.com
Primary Website: whitesboronews.com
Year Established: 1877
Avg Paid Circ: 3000
Avg Free Circ: 38
Audit By: Sworn/Estimate/Non-Audited
Audit Date: 10.06.2019
Personnel: Scott Wood (Pub./Ed.); Jaquita Lewter (Prod. Mgr.); Mary Jane Farmer (Reporter); Vic Riley (Sports writer)

WHITEWRIGHT SUN

Street address 1: PO Box 218
Street address 2: 121 W Grand
Street address city: Whitewright
Street address state: TX
Zip/Postal code: 75491-0218
General Phone: (903) 364-2276
General/National Adv. E-mail: whitewrightsun@cableone.net
Display Adv. E-mail: whitewrightsun@cableone.net
Editorial e-mail: whitewrightsun@cableone.net
Year Established: 1884
Avg Paid Circ: 1100
Avg Free Circ: 50
Audit By: Sworn/Estimate/Non-Audited
Audit Date: 10.06.2019
Personnel: Kim Palmer (Ed.)

WILLS POINT CHRONICLE

Street address 1: 109 N 5th St
Street address city: Wills Point
Street address state: TX
Zip/Postal code: 75169-2058
General Phone: (903) 873-2525
General Fax: (903) 873-4321
Advertising Phone: (903) 873-2525
Advertising Fax: (903) 873-4321
Editorial Phone: (903) 873-2525
Editorial Fax: (903) 873-4321
General/National Adv. E-mail: business@vanzandtnews.com
Display Adv. E-mail: sales@vanzandtnews.com
Classified Adv. e-mail: classifieds@vanzandtnews.com
Editorial e-mail: editor@vanzandtnews.com
Primary Website: willspointchronicle.com
Year Established: 1879
Avg Paid Circ: 3051
Avg Free Circ: 500
Audit By: Sworn/Estimate/Non-Audited
Audit Date: 10.06.2019
Personnel: Willis Editor (Ed.)

WILSON COUNTY NEWS

Street address 1: 1012 C St
Street address city: Floresville
Street address state: TX
Zip/Postal code: 78114-2224
General Phone: (830) 216-4519
General Fax: 210-855-4848
Advertising Phone: (830)216-4519
Advertising Fax: 210-855-4848
Editorial Phone: 830-216-4519
Editorial Fax: 210-855-4848
General/National Adv. E-mail: display@wcn-online.com
Display Adv. E-mail: classifieds@wcn-online.com
Editorial e-mail: editor@wcn-online.com
Primary Website: wilsoncountynews.com
Mthly Avg Views: 101000
Mthly Avg Unique Visitors: 50000
Year Established: 1973
Avg Paid Circ: 8190
Audit By: USPS
Audit Date: 10.06.2019
Personnel: Elaine Kolodziej (Publisher); Nannette Kilbey-Smith (Ed.); Kristen Weaver (Op. Dir.)
Parent company (for newspapers): WCN, Inc.

WIMBERLEY VIEW

Street address 1: 101 FM 3237
Street address 2: Ste A
Street address city: Wimberley
Street address state: TX
Zip/Postal code: 78676-5371
General Phone: (512) 847-2202
General Fax: (512) 847-9054
General/National Adv. E-mail: wimberleyview@gmail.com
Display Adv. E-mail: wimberleyview@gmail.com
Editorial e-mail: dsweat@wimberleyview.com
Primary Website: wimberleyview.com
Year Established: 1976
Avg Paid Circ: 2100
Audit By: Sworn/Estimate/Non-Audited
Audit Date: 10.06.2019
Personnel: Dalton Sweat (GM/Ed.); Susan Sisson (Sales Rep); Gary Zupancic (Reporter)
Parent company (for newspapers): San Marcos Publishing

WINTERS ENTERPRISE

Street address 1: 709 Hutchins Ave
Street address city: Ballinger
Street address state: TX
Zip/Postal code: 76821-5608
General Phone: (325) 365-3501
Editorial e-mail: chawkins@ballingerledger.com
Primary Website: wintersenterprise.com
Year Established: 1905
Avg Paid Circ: 714
Avg Free Circ: 48
Audit By: Sworn/Estimate/Non-Audited
Audit Date: 10.06.2019
Personnel: Celinda Hawkins (Ed.)

WISE COUNTY MESSENGER

Street address 1: 115 S Trinity St
Street address city: Decatur
Street address state: TX
Zip/Postal code: 76234-1819
General Phone: (940) 627-5987
General Fax: (940) 627-1004
Advertising Phone: (940) 627-5987
Advertising Fax: (940) 627-1004
Editorial Phone: (940) 627-5987
Editorial Fax: (940) 627-1004
General/National Adv. E-mail: webmaster@wcmessenger.com
Display Adv. E-mail: webmaster@wcmessenger.com
Editorial e-mail: news@wcmessenger.com
Primary Website: wcmessenger.com
Year Established: 1880
Avg Paid Circ: 7745
Avg Free Circ: 34
Audit By: Sworn/Estimate/Non-Audited
Audit Date: 10.06.2019
Personnel: Roy J. Eaton (Pres./Pub.); Bob Buckel (Exec. Ed.); Brian Knox (Sp. Project Mgr.); Lisa Davis (Adv. Mgr.); Todd Griffith (Prod. Mgr.); Mark Jordan (Gen. Mgr./VP, Adv.); Kristin Tribe (Ed.)

WOOD COUNTY MONITOR

Street address 1: 715 Mimosa Dr
Street address city: Mineola
Street address state: TX
Zip/Postal code: 75773-2611
General Phone: (903) 569-2442
General/National Adv. E-mail: publisher@wood.cm
Display Adv. E-mail: ads@wood.cm
Editorial e-mail: editor@wood.cm
Primary Website: wood.cm
Year Established: 1876
Avg Paid Circ: 2500
Audit By: Sworn/Estimate/Non-Audited
Audit Date: 30.09.2021
Personnel: Joyce Hathcock (Pub.); Phil Major (publisher); Larry Tucker (editor); Doris Newman (Ed.)
Parent company (for newspapers): Bluebonnet Publishing, LLC; Dot Gain Publications LLC

WOOD COUNTY MONITOR

Street address 1: 310 E Goode St
Street address 2: Ste C
Street address city: Quitman
Street address state: TX
Zip/Postal code: 75783-2502
General Phone: (903) 763-4522
General Fax: (903) 763-2313
Advertising Phone: (903) 763-4522
Advertising Fax: (903) 763-2313
Editorial Phone: (903) 763-4522
Editorial Fax: (903) 763-2313
General/National Adv. E-mail: advertising@thewoodcountymonitor.com
Display Adv. E-mail: classifieds@thewoodcountymonitort.com
Editorial e-mail: news@thewoodcountydemocrat.com
Primary Website: thewoodcountymonitor.com
Year Established: 1893
Avg Paid Circ: 3065
Audit By: Sworn/Estimate/Non-Audited
Audit Date: 10.06.2019
Personnel: Larry Tucker (News Editor); Maggie Fraser (Ed.); Kiki Bettis (Adv. Dir.)
Parent company (for newspapers): Bluebonnet Publishing, LLC

YOAKUM HERALD-TIMES

Street address 1: 312 Lott St
Street address city: Yoakum
Street address state: TX
Zip/Postal code: 77995-2798
General Phone: (361) 293-5266
General Fax: (361) 293-5267
Advertising Phone: (361) 293-5266
Advertising Fax: (361) 293-5267
Editorial Phone: (361) 293-5266
Editorial Fax: (361) 293-5267
General/National Adv. E-mail: heraldtimes@sbcglobal.net
Display Adv. E-mail: heraldtimes@sbcglobal.net
Editorial e-mail: heraldtimes@sbcglobal.net
Primary Website: levacacountytoday.com
Year Established: 1892
Avg Paid Circ: 3200
Audit By: Sworn/Estimate/Non-Audited
Audit Date: 10.06.2019
Personnel: Mike McCracken (Pub./Ed./Adv. Dir.)

YORKTOWN NEWS-VIEW

Street address 1: 133 E MAIN ST
Street address city: Yorktown
Street address state: TX
Zip/Postal code: 78164
General Phone: (361) 564-2242
General Fax: (361) 564-9290
Advertising Phone: (361) 564-2242
Advertising Fax: (361) 564-9290
Editorial Phone: (361) 564-2242
Editorial Fax: (361) 564-9290
General/National Adv. E-mail: yorktownnews@sbcglobal.net
Display Adv. E-mail: yorktownnews@sbcglobal.net
Editorial e-mail: yorktownnews@sbcglobal.net
Primary Website: yorktownnews-view.com
Year Established: 1895
Avg Paid Circ: 2700
Avg Free Circ: 75
Audit By: Sworn/Estimate/Non-Audited
Audit Date: 10.06.2019
Personnel: Glenn Rea (Pub./Ed.); Sonya Timpone (Adv. Dir.); Mari Gohlke (Office Mgr.); Elizabeth Rodriguez (News Ed.)

ZAPATA COUNTY NEWS

Street address 1: 2765 US Highway 83
Street address city: Zapata
Street address state: TX
Zip/Postal code: 78076-4239
General Phone: (956) 765-6931
General Fax: (956) 765-9058
General/National Adv. E-mail: zapatarates@sbcglobal.net
Display Adv. E-mail: zapatamngr@gmail.com
Editorial e-mail: zapatarates@sbcglobal.net
Year Established: 1976
Avg Paid Circ: 2500
Avg Free Circ: 66
Audit By: Sworn/Estimate/Non-Audited
Audit Date: 10.06.2019
Personnel: Karran Westerman (Pub.); Danielle Westerman (Adv. Dir.)

ZAVALA COUNTY SENTINEL

Street address 1: 202 E Nueces St
Street address city: Crystal City
Street address state: TX
Zip/Postal code: 78839-3325
General Phone: (830) 374-3465
General Fax: (830) 374-5771
Advertising Phone: (830) 374-3465
Advertising Fax: (830) 374-5771
Editorial Phone: (830) 374-3465
Editorial Fax: (830) 374-5771
General/National Adv. E-mail: zcsentinel@sbcglobal.net
Display Adv. E-mail: zcsentinel@sbcglobal.net
Editorial e-mail: zcsentinel@sbcglobal.net
Primary Website: zavalacountysentinel.net
Year Established: 1911
Avg Paid Circ: 2300
Avg Free Circ: 50
Audit By: Sworn/Estimate/Non-Audited
Audit Date: 10.06.2019
Personnel: Ricardo Sanchez (Co-Pub.); Jerry Mata (Co-Pub.); Mary Rodriquez (Managing Ed./Circ. Mgr.); Rosa Rocha (Adv. Mgr.); Tomas Aguilar (Pub.); Alberto Lira (District Mgr.)
Parent company (for newspapers): Winter Garden Publishing Co., Inc.

UTAH

BOX ELDER NEWS JOURNAL

Street address 1: 55 S 100 W
Street address city: Brigham City
Street address state: UT
Zip/Postal code: 84302-2540
General Phone: (435) 723-3471
General Fax: (435) 723-5247
Advertising Phone: (435) 723-3471
Advertising Fax: (435) 723-5247
Editorial Phone: (435) 723-3471
Editorial Fax: (435) 723-5247
General/National Adv. E-mail: casey@benewsjournal.com
Display Adv. E-mail: sales1@benewsjournal.com
Classified Adv. e-mail: classsifieds@benewsjournal.com
Editorial e-mail: editor@benewsjournal.com

Primary Website: www.benewsjournal.com
Year Established: 1896
Avg Paid Circ: 3200
Avg Free Circ: 9500
Audit By: USPS
Audit Date: 10.06.2019
Personnel: Casey Claybaugh (Pub.); Sean Hales (Ed.); Jessica Polumbo (Ad Sales); Jamie Hester (Advertising Manager); Carson Barnhart (Classifieds Manager)

MILLARD COUNTY CHRONICLE PROGRESS

Street address 1: 40 N 300 W
Street address city: Delta
Street address state: UT
Zip/Postal code: 84624-8505
General Phone: (435) 864-2400
General Fax: (775) 514-2931
Advertising Phone: (435) 864-2400
Editorial Phone: (435) 864-2400
General/National Adv. E-mail: debbie@millardccp.com
Display Adv. E-mail: debbie@millardccp.com
Editorial e-mail: chronpro@millardccp.com
Primary Website: millardccp.com
Year Established: 1910
Avg Paid Circ: 2600
Audit By: Sworn/Estimate/Non-Audited
Audit Date: 10.06.2019
Personnel: Lewis Dutson (Co-Publisher)
Parent company (for newspapers): DuMor Publishing

PARK RECORD

Street address 1: 1670 Bonanza Dr
Street address 2: Ste 202
Street address city: Park City
Street address state: UT
Zip/Postal code: 84060-7239
General Phone: (435) 649-9014
General Fax: (435) 649-4942
Advertising Phone: (435) 649-9014
Advertising Fax: (435) 649-4942
Editorial Phone: (435) 649-9014
Editorial Fax: (435) 649-4942
General/National Adv. E-mail: vdeming@parkrecord.com
Display Adv. E-mail: classads@parkrecord.com
Editorial e-mail: editor@parkrecord.com
Primary Website: parkrecord.com
Year Established: 1880
Avg Paid Circ: 7800
Avg Free Circ: 300
Audit By: Sworn/Estimate/Non-Audited
Audit Date: 10.06.2019
Personnel: Andy Bernhard (Pub.); Lacy Brundy (Circ. Mgr.); Nan Chalat-Noaker (Ed.); Valerie Spung (Adv. Dir.); Jennifer Lynch (Classified Mgr.); Lisa Powell (Production Mgr.)

RICHFIELD REAPER

Street address 1: 65 W Center St
Street address city: Richfield
Street address state: UT
Zip/Postal code: 84701-2546
General Phone: (435) 896-5476
General Fax: (435) 896-8123
Advertising Phone: (435) 896-5476 ext. 18
Advertising Fax: (435) 896-8123
Editorial Phone: (435) 896-5476 ext. 21
Editorial Fax: (435) 896-8123
General/National Adv. E-mail: reaperad@richfieldreaper.com
Display Adv. E-mail: class@richfieldreaper.com
Editorial e-mail: reapered@richfieldreaper.com
Primary Website: richfieldreaper.com
Year Established: 1888
Avg Paid Circ: 5300
Avg Free Circ: 6300
Audit By: Sworn/Estimate/Non-Audited
Audit Date: 10.06.2019
Personnel: Charles G. Hawley (Pub.); Cherry Niemeyer (Office Mgr.); Sandy Phillips (Ed.); David Anderson (Assoc. Ed.)
Parent company (for newspapers): Brehm Communications, Inc.

SALINA SUN

Street address 1: PO Box 85
Street address city: Salina
Street address state: UT
Zip/Postal code: 84654-0085
General Phone: (435) 529-6397
General Fax: (866) 492-5194
Advertising Phone: (435) 529-6397
Advertising Fax: (866) 492-5194
Editorial Phone: (435) 529-6397
Editorial Fax: (866) 492-5194
General/National Adv. E-mail: news@salinasunonline.com
Display Adv. E-mail: news@salinasunonline.com
Editorial e-mail: news@salinasunonline.com
Primary Website: salinasunonline.com
Year Established: 1911
Avg Paid Circ: 750
Avg Free Circ: 2400
Audit By: Sworn/Estimate/Non-Audited
Audit Date: 10.06.2019
Personnel: Laura Fielding (Adv. Dir./Pub.); Troy Fielding (Ed.)

SANPETE MESSENGER

Street address 1: 35 S Main St
Street address city: Manti
Street address state: UT
Zip/Postal code: 84642-1350
General Phone: (435) 835-4241
General Fax: (435) 835-1493
Advertising Phone: (435) 835-4241
Advertising Fax: (435) 835-1493
Editorial Phone: (435) 835-4241
Editorial Fax: (435) 835-1493
General/National Adv. E-mail: ads@sanpetemessenger.com
Display Adv. E-mail: ads@sanpetemessenger.com
Editorial e-mail: news@sanpetemessenger.com
Primary Website: sanpetemessenger.com
Year Established: 1893
Avg Paid Circ: 2000
Avg Free Circ: 100
Audit By: Sworn/Estimate/Non-Audited
Audit Date: 10.06.2019
Personnel: Suzanne Dean (Pub.); Robert Stevens (Mng Ed); Lloyd Call (Associate Pub and Advt Mgr); Karen Christensen (Office Mgr)

SUN ADVOCATE

Street address 1: 845 E Main St
Street address city: Price
Street address state: UT
Zip/Postal code: 84501-2708
General Phone: (435) 637-0732
General Fax: (435)ÃƒÂ‚Â 637-2716
Advertising Phone: (435) 637-0732
Advertising Fax: (435)ÃƒÂ‚Â 637-2716
Editorial Phone: (435) 637-0732
Editorial Fax: (435)ÃƒÂ‚Â 637-2716
General/National Adv. E-mail: ads@sunad.com
Display Adv. E-mail: ads@sunad.com
Editorial e-mail: editor@sunad.com
Primary Website: sunad.com
Year Established: 1891
Audit By: Sworn/Estimate/Non-Audited
Audit Date: 10.06.2019
Personnel: Richard Shaw (Pub.); Jenni Fasselin (Adv. Dir.); Lynnda Johnson (Ed.); John Serfustini (Assoc. Ed.)
Parent company (for newspapers): Brehm Communications, Inc.

THE DAVIS CLIPPER

Street address 1: 1370 S. 500 West
Street address city: Bountiful
Street address state: UT
Zip/Postal code: 84010
General Phone: (801) 295-2251
General Fax: (801) 295-3181
Advertising Phone: (801) 295-2251
Advertising Fax: (801) 295-3044
Editorial Phone: (801) 295-2251
Editorial Fax: (801) 295-3044
Editorial e-mail: news@davisclipper.com
Primary Website: davisclipper.com
Year Established: 1891
Avg Free Circ: 32633
Audit By: Sworn/Estimate/Non-Audited
Audit Date: 10.06.2019
Personnel: R. Gale Stahle (Pub.); Tom Haraldsen (Mng. Ed.); Reed Stahle (Sales Mgr.)
Parent company (for newspapers): Spectrum Press Inc.

THE LEADER

Street address 1: 119 E Main St
Street address city: Tremonton
Street address state: UT
Zip/Postal code: 84337-1645
General Phone: (435)Â 257-5182
General Fax: (435) 257-6175
Advertising Phone: (435) 257-5182
Advertising Fax: (435) 257-6175
Editorial Phone: (435) 257-5182
Editorial Fax: (435) 257-6175
General/National Adv. E-mail: jodiev@tremontonleader.com
Display Adv. E-mail: info@tremontonleader.com
Editorial e-mail: gregm@tremontonleader.com
Primary Website: tremontonleader.com
Year Established: 1914
Avg Paid Circ: 7000
Audit By: Sworn/Estimate/Non-Audited
Audit Date: 10.06.2019
Personnel: Jodie V. (Gen Mgr.); Ellen Cook (Editor)
Parent company (for newspapers): Adams Publishing Group

THE PAYSON CHRONICLE

Street address 1: 145 E Utah Ave
Street address city: Payson
Street address state: UT
Zip/Postal code: 84651-2248
General Phone: (801) 465-9221
General Fax: (801) 465-9221
Advertising Phone: (801) 465-9221
Advertising Fax: (801) 465-9221
Editorial Phone: (801) 465-9221
Editorial Fax: (801) 465-9221
General/National Adv. E-mail: thepaysonchronicle@msn.com
Display Adv. E-mail: thepaysonchronicle@msn.com
Editorial e-mail: thepaysonchronicle@msn.com
Primary Website: paysonads.com
Avg Paid Circ: 2000
Audit By: Sworn/Estimate/Non-Audited
Audit Date: 10.06.2019
Personnel: Michael Olson (Pub./Ed.); Denise Windley (Mng. Ed.)

THE TIMES-NEWS

Street address 1: 96 S Main St
Street address city: Nephi
Street address state: UT
Zip/Postal code: 84648-1708
General Phone: (435) 623-0525
General Fax: (435) 623-4735
Advertising Phone: (435) 623-0525
Advertising Fax: (435) 623-4735
Editorial Phone: (435) 623-0525
Editorial Fax: (435) 623-4735
General/National Adv. E-mail: publisher@nephitimesnews.com
Display Adv. E-mail: publisher@nephitimesnews.com
Editorial e-mail: editor@nephitimesnews.com
Primary Website: nephitimesnews.com
Avg Paid Circ: 1700
Audit By: Sworn/Estimate/Non-Audited
Audit Date: 10.06.2019
Personnel: Allan R. Gibson (Pub.); Rebecca Dopp (Ed.)

THE WASATCH WAVE

Street address 1: 165 S 100 W
Street address city: Heber City
Street address state: UT
Zip/Postal code: 84032-2001
General Phone: (435) 654-1471
General Fax: (435) 654-5085
Advertising Phone: (435) 654-1471
Advertising Fax: (435) 654-5085
Editorial Phone: (435) 654-1471
Editorial Fax: (435) 654-5085
General/National Adv. E-mail: kari@wasatchwave.com
Display Adv. E-mail: classifieds@wasatchwave.com
Editorial e-mail: editor@wasatchwave.com
Primary Website: wasatchwave.com
Year Established: 1889
Avg Paid Circ: 4200
Audit By: Sworn/Estimate/Non-Audited
Audit Date: 10.06.2019
Personnel: Paul McFee (Gen. Mgr.); Laurie Wynn (Ed./Co. Pub.); Kari McFee (Adv. Mgr.)
Parent company (for newspapers): Wave Publishing, Inc.

VERMONT

ADDISON COUNTY INDEPENDENT

Street address 1: 58 Maple St
Street address city: Middlebury
Street address state: VT
Zip/Postal code: 05753-1276
General Phone: (802) 388-4944
General Fax: (802) 388-3100
Advertising Phone: (802) 388-4944
Advertising Fax: (802) 388-3100
Editorial Phone: (802) 388-4944
Editorial Fax: (802) 388-3100
General/National Adv. E-mail: ads@addisonindependent.com
Display Adv. E-mail: classifieds@addisonindependent.com
Editorial e-mail: news@addisonindependent.com
Primary Website: addisonindependent.com
Year Established: 1946
Avg Paid Circ: 7425
Audit By: Sworn/Estimate/Non-Audited
Audit Date: 30.09.2017
Personnel: Angelo S. Lynn (Ed./Pub.); Christy Lynn (Adv. Mgr.); Susan Leggett (Prodn. Mgr.); John McCright (News Ed.)
Parent company (for newspapers): Addison County Independent

COUNTY COURIER

Street address 1: 349 Main St
Street address city: Enosburg Falls
Street address state: VT
Zip/Postal code: 05450
General Phone: (802) 933-4375
General/National Adv. E-mail: courierads@gmail.com
Display Adv. E-mail: courierads@gmail.com
Editorial e-mail: couriereditor@gmail.com
Primary Website: countycourier.net
Year Established: 1878
Avg Paid Circ: 3000
Avg Free Circ: 76
Audit By: Sworn/Estimate/Non-Audited
Audit Date: 10.06.2019
Personnel: Ed Shamy (Ed./Pub.); Dan Rico (Adv. Rep.)

GREEN MOUNTAIN OUTLOOK

Street address 1: 16 Creek Rd
Street address city: Middlebury
Street address state: VT
Zip/Postal code: 05753-1574
General Phone: (802) 388-6397
General Fax: (802) 388-6399
Advertising Phone: (802) 388-6397
Advertising Fax: (802) 388-6399
Editorial Phone: (802) 388-6397
Editorial Fax: (802) 388-6399
General/National Adv. E-mail: andy@denpubs.com
Display Adv. E-mail: andy@denpubs.com
Editorial e-mail: andy@denpubs.com
Primary Website: denpubs.com
Mthly Avg Views: 2418
Mthly Avg Unique Visitors: 1059
Year Established: 1966
Avg Paid Circ: 47
Avg Free Circ: 6766
Audit By: Sworn/Estimate/Non-Audited
Audit Date: 10.06.2019
Personnel: Edward Coats (Pres./Pub.); Mark Brady (Gen. Mgr.); Louis Varricchio (Ed.)

JOURNAL OPINION

Street address 1: 172 N Main St
Street address 2: Ste 23
Street address city: Bradford
Street address state: VT
Zip/Postal code: 05033-9290
General Phone: (802) 222-5281
General Fax: (802) 222-5438

Advertising Phone: (802) 222-5281
Advertising Fax: (802) 222-5438
Editorial Phone: (802) 222-5281
Editorial Fax: (802) 222-5438
General/National Adv. E-mail: publisher@jonews.com
Display Adv. E-mail: advertising@jonews.com
Editorial e-mail: editor@jonews.com
Primary Website: jonews.com
Year Established: 1865
Avg Paid Circ: 4000
Avg Free Circ: 200
Audit By: Sworn/Estimate/Non-Audited
Audit Date: 10.06.2019
Personnel: Connie Sanville (Owner/Pub.); Michele Sherburne (Adv. Mgr.); Alex Nuti-De Biasi (Mng. Ed.)

MANCHESTER JOURNAL

Street address 1: 3624 Main Street, Room 204
Street address city: Manchester
Street address state: VT
Zip/Postal code: 05254
Advertising Phone: (802)-855-7861
Editorial Phone: (802) 855-7861
Editorial e-mail: news@manchesterjournal.com
Primary Website: manchesterjournal.com
Year Established: 1861
Avg Free Circ: 15000
Audit By: Sworn/Estimate/Non-Audited
Audit Date: 10.06.2019
Personnel: Evan Pringle (Circ. Mgr.); Darren Marcy; Susan Plaisance (Adv. Sales Mgr.); Melodie Sinopoli (Class. Adv. Mgr.); Fredrick Rutberg (Pres./ Pub.); Greg Sukiennik (Ed.)
Parent company (for newspapers): Birdland Acquisition LLC.; Paul Belogour

MILTON INDEPENDENT

Street address 1: PO Box 163
Street address city: Milton
Street address state: VT
Zip/Postal code: 05468-0163
General Phone: (802) 893-2028
General Fax: (802) 893-7467
Advertising Phone: (802) 893-2028 ext. 103
Advertising Fax: (802) 893-7467
Editorial Phone: (802) 893-2028
Editorial Fax: (802) 893-7467
General/National Adv. E-mail: dillon@samessenger.com
Display Adv. E-mail: classifieds@samessenger.com
Editorial e-mail: courtney@miltonindependent.com
Primary Website: miltonindependent.com
Year Established: 1993
Audit By: Sworn/Estimate/Non-Audited
Audit Date: 10.06.2019
Personnel: Emerson Lynn (Pub.); Courtney Lamdin (Ed.)
Parent company (for newspapers): Addison County Independent

SHELBURNE NEWS

Street address 1: PO Box 1149
Street address 2: 233 Falls Road
Street address city: Shelburne
Street address state: VT
Zip/Postal code: 05482-1149
General Phone: (802) 985-3091
General Fax: n/a
Advertising Phone: (802) 985-3091
Advertising Fax: n/a
Editorial Phone: (802) 985-3091
Editorial Fax: n/a
General/National Adv. E-mail: wendy@sheburnenews.com
Display Adv. E-mail: wendy@sheburnenews.com
Editorial e-mail: editor@sheburnenews.com
Primary Website: shelburnenews.com
Year Established: 1982
Avg Paid Circ: 0
Avg Free Circ: 5000
Audit By: Sworn/Estimate/Non-Audited
Audit Date: 10.06.2019
Personnel: Wendy Ewing (Adv. Dir.); Lisa Scagliotti (Ed.)
Parent company (for newspapers): Stowe Reporter LLC

STOWE REPORTER

Street address 1: 49 School St
Street address city: Stowe
Street address state: VT
Zip/Postal code: 05672-4447
General Phone: (802) 253-2101
General Fax: (802) 253-8332
Advertising Phone: (802) 253-2101 ext. 13
Editorial Phone: (802) 253-2101 ext. 11
General/National Adv. E-mail: ads@stowereporter.com
Display Adv. E-mail: classified@stowereporter.com
Editorial e-mail: news@stowereporter.com
Primary Website: stowetoday.com
Year Established: 1958
Avg Paid Circ: 4700
Audit By: Sworn/Estimate/Non-Audited
Audit Date: 10.06.2019
Personnel: Greg Popa (Publisher); Tom Kearney (Ed.); Tommy Gardner
Parent company (for newspapers): Burlington Area Newspaper Group

STOWE TODAY

Street address 1: P.O. Box 489
Street address city: Stowe
Street address state: VT
Zip/Postal code: 05672
General Phone: (802) 253-2101
General Fax: (802) 888-2173
General/National Adv. E-mail: irene@newsandcitizen.com
Display Adv. E-mail: news@newsandcitizen.com
Editorial e-mail: news@stowereporter.com
Primary Website: stowetoday.com
Year Established: 1881
Avg Paid Circ: 2700
Avg Free Circ: 28
Audit By: Sworn/Estimate/Non-Audited
Audit Date: 10.06.2019
Personnel: Greg Popa (Pub.); Tommy Gardner (News Ed.); Irene Nuzzo (Dir. Adv. Sales)

THE CHRONICLE

Street address 1: 133 WATER ST
Street address city: Barton
Street address state: VT
Zip/Postal code: 5822
General Phone: (802) 525-3531
General Fax: (802) 525-3200
Advertising Phone: (802) 525-3531
Advertising Fax: (802) 525-3200
Editorial Phone: (802) 525-3531
Editorial Fax: (802) 525-3200
General/National Adv. E-mail: ads@bartonchronicle.com
Display Adv. E-mail: ads@bartonchronicle.com
Editorial e-mail: news@bartonchronicle.com
Primary Website: bartonchronicle.com
Year Established: 1974
Avg Paid Circ: 8000
Avg Free Circ: 173
Audit By: Sworn/Estimate/Non-Audited
Audit Date: 10.06.2019
Personnel: Tracy Davis Pierce (Pub.); Brianne Nichols (Production Mgr.); Tena Starr (Ed.)

THE COLCHESTER SUN

Street address 1: 462 Hegeman Ave
Street address 2: Ste 105
Street address city: Colchester
Street address state: VT
Zip/Postal code: 05446-3187
General Phone: (802) 878-5282
General Fax: (802) 651-9635
Advertising Phone: (802) 878-5282
Advertising Fax: (802) 651-9635
Editorial Phone: (802) 878-5282
Editorial Fax: (802) 651-9635
General/National Adv. E-mail: ewing@colchestersun.com
Display Adv. E-mail: kelly@colchestersun.com
Editorial e-mail: news@colchestersun.com
Primary Website: colchester.essexreporter.com
Audit By: Sworn/Estimate/Non-Audited
Audit Date: 10.06.2019
Personnel: Angelo Lynn (Co-Pub.); Emerson Lynn (Co-Pub.); Wendy Ewing (Adv. Dir.); Maria Archangelo (Editor); Colin Flanders
Parent company (for newspapers): Lynn Publications Inc.; Addison County Independent

THE COMMONS

Street address 1: 139 Main St
Street address 2: Rm 604
Street address city: Brattleboro
Street address state: VT
Zip/Postal code: 05301-2871
General Phone: (802) 246-6397
General Fax: (802) 246-1319
Advertising Phone: (802) 246-6397
Advertising Fax: (802) 246-1319
Editorial Phone: (802) 246-6397
Editorial Fax: (802) 246-1319
General/National Adv. E-mail: ads@commonsnews.org
Display Adv. E-mail: ads@commonsnews.org
Editorial e-mail: news@commonsnews.org
Primary Website: commonsnews.org
Year Established: 2006
Avg Paid Circ: 500
Avg Free Circ: 10500
Audit By: Sworn/Estimate/Non-Audited
Audit Date: 10.06.2019
Personnel: Raechel Bennett (Adv. Dir.); Mia Gannon (Mgr.); Jeff Potter (Ed.)
Parent company (for newspapers): Vermont Independent Media, Inc.

THE EAGLE

Street address 1: 16 Creek Rd
Street address 2: Ste 5A
Street address city: Middlebury
Street address state: VT
Zip/Postal code: 05753-1376
General Phone: (518) 873-6368
General Fax: (802) 388-6399
General/National Adv. E-mail: Cyndi@addison-eagle.com
Display Adv. E-mail: Cyndi@addison-eagle.com
Editorial e-mail: vermonttimes@gmail.com
Primary Website: suncommunitynews.com
Year Established: 2000
Avg Paid Circ: 176
Avg Free Circ: 12239
Audit By: Sworn/Estimate/Non-Audited
Audit Date: 10.06.2019
Personnel: Jennifer Valenze (Circ. Mgr.); Laurie Goff (Prod.); Edward Coats (Pub.)
Parent company (for newspapers): Sun Community News, Published by:Denton Publications, Inc.

THE ESSEX REPORTER

Street address 1: 281 N Main St
Street address city: Saint Albans
Street address state: VT
Zip/Postal code: 05478-2503
General Phone: (802) 878-5282
General Fax: (802) 651-9635
General/National Adv. E-mail: ewing@essexreporter.com
Display Adv. E-mail: classified@essexreporter.com
Editorial e-mail: news@essexreporter.com
Primary Website: essexreporter.com
Avg Free Circ: 8800
Audit By: Sworn/Estimate/Non-Audited
Audit Date: 10.06.2019
Personnel: Angelo Lynn (Co-Pub.); Emerson Lynn (Co-Pub.); Wendy Ewing (Adv. Man.); Maria Archangelo (Ed. and Co-publisher); Colin Flanders (Sports Ed.); Elsie Lynn (Ed.)
Parent company (for newspapers): Lynn Publications Inc.; Addison County Independent

THE HARDWICK GAZETTE

Street address 1: 42 S MAIN ST
Street address city: Hardwick
Street address state: VT
Zip/Postal code: 5843
General Phone: (802) 472-6521
General Fax: (802) 472-6522
Advertising Phone: (802) 472-6521
Advertising Fax: (802) 472-6522
Editorial Phone: (802) 472-6521
Editorial Fax: (802) 472-6522
General/National Adv. E-mail: ads@thehardwickgazette.com
Display Adv. E-mail: ads@thehardwickgazette.com
Editorial e-mail: news@thehardwickgazette.com
Year Established: 1889
Avg Paid Circ: 2300
Avg Free Circ: 35
Audit By: Sworn/Estimate/Non-Audited
Audit Date: 10.06.2019
Personnel: Ross Connelly (Pub./Ed.); Dawn Gustafson (Circ. Mgr.); Sandy Atkins (Prodn. Mgr.)

THE HERALD OF RANDOLPH

Street address 1: 30 Pleasant St
Street address city: Randolph
Street address state: VT
Zip/Postal code: 05060-1156
General Phone: (802) 728-3232
General Fax: (802) 728-9275
Advertising Phone: (802) 728-3232
Advertising Fax: (802) 728-9275
Editorial Phone: (802) 728-3232
Editorial Fax: (802) 728-9275
General/National Adv. E-mail: ads@ourherald.com
Display Adv. E-mail: ads@ourherald.com
Editorial e-mail: news@ourherald.com
Primary Website: OurHerald.com
Year Established: 1874
Avg Paid Circ: 5000
Audit By: Sworn/Estimate/Non-Audited
Audit Date: 10.06.2019
Personnel: M. Dickey Drysdale (Editor Emeritus); Sandy Cooch (Mgr Ed); Tim Calabro (Ed & Pub)

THE MOUNTAIN TIMES

Street address 1: 5465 ROUTE 4
Street address city: Killington
Street address state: VT
Zip/Postal code: 5751
General Phone: (802) 422-2399
General Fax: (802) 422-2395
Advertising Phone: (802) 422-2399
Advertising Fax: (802) 422-2395
Editorial Phone: (802) 422-2399
Editorial Fax: (802) 422-2395
General/National Adv. E-mail: jason@mountaintimes.info
Display Adv. E-mail: jason@mountaintimes.info
Editorial e-mail: editor@mountaintimes.info
Primary Website: mountaintimes.info
Avg Paid Circ: 0
Avg Free Circ: 10000
Audit By: Sworn/Estimate/Non-Audited
Audit Date: 10.06.2019
Personnel: Polly Lynn (Pub./Ed.); Jason Mikula (Sales Mgr.); Erica Harrington (Bus. Mgr.)
Parent company (for newspapers): Outer Limits Publishing

THE NORTHFIELD NEWS

Street address 1: PO Box 43
Street address city: Northfield
Street address state: VT
Zip/Postal code: 05663-0043
General Phone: (802) 485-6397
Advertising Phone: (802) 485-6397
Editorial Phone: (802) 485-6397
General/National Adv. E-mail: northfieldnewsads@gmail.com
Display Adv. E-mail: northfieldnewsads@gmail.com
Editorial e-mail: thenorthfieldnews@gmail.com
Primary Website: thenorthfieldnews.com
Year Established: 1878
Avg Paid Circ: 1600
Audit By: Sworn/Estimate/Non-Audited
Audit Date: 10.06.2019
Personnel: John Cruickshank (Ed.); Rob Wills (Adv. Dir.); Bill Croney (Sports Ed, Photographer)
Parent company (for newspapers): Northfield News Publishing, LLC.

THE OTHER PAPER

Street address 1: 1340 Williston Rd
Street address 2: Ste 201
Street address city: South Burlington
Street address state: VT
Zip/Postal code: 05403-6469
General Phone: (802) 864-6670
General Fax: (802) 864-3379
Advertising Phone: (802) 864-6670
Advertising Fax: (802) 864-3379
Editorial Phone: (802) 864-6670

Editorial Fax: (802) 864-3379
General/National Adv. E-mail: judy@otherpapersbvt.com
Display Adv. E-mail: classifieds@otherpapersbvt.com
Editorial e-mail: editor@otherpapersbvt.com
Primary Website: otherpapersbvt.com
Year Established: 1977
Audit By: Sworn/Estimate/Non-Audited
Audit Date: 10.06.2019
Personnel: Judy Kearns (Pub./Adv. Mgr.); Nina Fedrizzi (Mng. Ed.); Penne Tompkins (Ed.)
Parent company (for newspapers): Burlington Area Newspaper Group

THE TRANSCRIPT

Street address 1: 417 Brooklyn St
Street address city: Morrisville
Street address state: VT
Zip/Postal code: 05661-8510
General Phone: (802) 888-2212
General Fax: (802) 888-2173
General/National Adv. E-mail: irene@newsandcitizen.com
Display Adv. E-mail: news@newsandcitizen.com
Editorial e-mail: edit@newsandcitizen.com
Primary Website: newsandcitizen.com/transcript
Avg Free Circ: 15559
Audit By: Sworn/Estimate/Non-Audited
Audit Date: 10.06.2019
Personnel: Greg Popa (Pub.); Tommy Gardner (Ed.); Irene Nuzzo (Display Adv. Mgr.)

THE VALLEY REPORTER

Street address 1: 5222 Main St
Street address city: Waitsfield
Street address state: VT
Zip/Postal code: 05673-4445
General Phone: (802) 496-3928
General Fax: (802) 496-4703
General/National Adv. E-mail: ads@valleyreporter.com
Display Adv. E-mail: classifiedads@valleyreporter.com
Editorial e-mail: lisa@valleyreporter.com
Primary Website: thevalleyreporter.com
Year Established: 1971
Avg Paid Circ: 3200
Avg Free Circ: 98
Audit By: Sworn/Estimate/Non-Audited
Audit Date: 10.06.2019
Personnel: Patricia A. Clark (Pub.); Jeff Knight (Adv. Dir.); Lisa Loomis (Ed.)
Parent company (for newspapers): Burlington Area Newspaper Group

THE VERMONT STANDARD

Street address 1: PO Box 88
Street address 2: 43 Central Street
Street address city: Woodstock
Street address state: VT
Zip/Postal code: 05091-0088
General Phone: (802) 457-1313
General Fax: (802) 457-3639
General/National Adv. E-mail: jestey@thevermontstadard.com
Display Adv. E-mail: pwebster@thevermontstandard.com
Editorial e-mail: editor@thevermontstandard.com
Primary Website: thevermontstandard.com
Mthly Avg Unique Visitors: 14000
Year Established: 1853
Avg Paid Circ: 5400
Audit By: Sworn/Estimate/Non-Audited
Audit Date: 10.06.2019
Personnel: Phillip Camp,Sr. (Pub.); Jon Estey (Gen. Mgr.); Gareth Henderson (Ed.); Lisa Wright (Prodn. Mgr.); Jean Maynes (Bus. Mgr.); Jim Kelly (Adv. Rep.); Pattie Webster (Office Coordinator); Mary Camp (Circ./ Bus. Columnist); Kat Fulcher (Webmaster/ Calendar/eEdition); Melanie Hanson (Advertising Representative)

THE WORLD

Street address 1: 403 US Rt 302-Berlin
Street address city: Barre
Street address state: VT
Zip/Postal code: 05641
General Phone: (802) 479-2582
General Fax: (802) 479-7916
Advertising Phone: (802) 479-2582
Editorial Phone: (802) 479-2582
General/National Adv. E-mail: sales@vt-world.com
Display Adv. E-mail: sales@vt-world.com
Classified Adv. e-mail: sales@vt-world.com
Editorial e-mail: editor@vt-world.com
Primary Website: vt-world.com
Mthly Avg Views: 1000
Mthly Avg Unique Visitors: 1000
Year Established: 1972
Avg Paid Circ: 28
Avg Free Circ: 10000
Audit By: CVC
Audit Date: 01.09.2023
Personnel: Gary Hass (Co-Pub./owner); Deborah Phillips (Co-Pub./owner); Christine Richardson (Prodn. Mgr.); Aeletha Kelly (Circ.); Aaron Retherford (Ed)
Parent company (for newspapers): WORLD Publications, Inc.

TIMES ARGUS EXTRA

Street address 1: 47 N Main St
Street address 2: Ste 200
Street address city: Barre
Street address state: VT
Zip/Postal code: 05641-4168
General Phone: (802) 479-0191
General Fax: (802) 479-4096
Advertising Phone: (802) 479-0191
Advertising Fax: (802) 776-5600
Editorial Phone: (802) 479-0191
Editorial Fax: (802) 479-4096
General/National Adv. E-mail: mandy.dwinell@timesargus.com
Display Adv. E-mail: marineau@timesargus.com
Editorial e-mail: steven.pappas@timesargus.com
Primary Website: timesargus.com
Audit By: Sworn/Estimate/Non-Audited
Audit Date: 10.06.2019
Personnel: R. John Mitchell (Pres./Pub.); Sean Burke (Adv. Exec.); Steven Pappas (Ed.)

VERMONT NEWS GUIDE

Street address 1: 105A BONNET ST
Street address city: Manchester Center
Street address state: VT
Zip/Postal code: 05255-4488
General Phone: (802) 362-3535
General Fax: (802) 362-5368
General/National Adv. E-mail: jmurren@hersamacornvt.com
Display Adv. E-mail: dburgess@hersamacornvt.com
Editorial e-mail: editor@hersamacornvt.com
Primary Website: vermontnews-guide.com
Year Established: 1972
Avg Free Circ: 15419
Audit By: Sworn/Estimate/Non-Audited
Audit Date: 10.06.2019
Personnel: Liz Schafer (Ed.); Angie Leonard (General Manager)

WATERBURY RECORD

Street address 1: 49 School St
Street address city: Stowe
Street address state: VT
Zip/Postal code: 05672-4447
General Phone: (802) 253-2101
General Fax: (802) 253-8332
Advertising Phone: (802) 253-2101
Advertising Fax: (802) 253-8332
Editorial Phone: (802) 253-2101 ext. 11
Editorial Fax: (802) 253-8332
General/National Adv. E-mail: sales@stowereporter.com
Display Adv. E-mail: ads@waterburyrecord.com
Classified Adv. e-mail: classified@waterburyrecord.com
Editorial e-mail: news@waterburyrecord.com
Primary Website: waterburyrecord.com
Year Established: 2007
Avg Free Circ: 4500
Audit By: Sworn/Estimate/Non-Audited
Audit Date: 10.06.2019
Personnel: Greg Popa (Pub.)

WILLISTON OBSERVER

Street address 1: 300 Cornerstone Dr
Street address 2: Ste 330
Street address city: Williston
Street address state: VT
Zip/Postal code: 05495-4045
General Phone: (802) 872-9000
General Fax: (802) 872-0151
Advertising Phone: (802) 872-9000 ext. 118
Advertising Fax: (802) 872-0151
Editorial Phone: (802) 872-9000 ext. 117
Editorial Fax: (802) 872-0151
General/National Adv. E-mail: marianne@willistonobserver.com
Display Adv. E-mail: marianne@willistonobserver.com
Editorial e-mail: editor@willistonobserver.com
Primary Website: willistonobserver.com
Year Established: 1985
Avg Free Circ: 7000
Audit By: Sworn/Estimate/Non-Audited
Audit Date: 10.06.2019
Personnel: Marianne Apfelbaum (Sales Mgr.); Jason Starr (Editor)
Parent company (for newspapers): Williston Publishing; Burlington Area Newspaper Group

VIRGINIA

ALEXANDRIA GAZETTE PACKET

Street address 1: 1606 King St
Street address city: Alexandria
Street address state: VA
Zip/Postal code: 22314-2719
General Phone: (703) 778-9410
General Fax: (703) 778-9445
Advertising Phone: (703) 778-9444
Advertising Fax: (703) 778-9445
Editorial Phone: (703) 778-9433
Editorial Fax: (703) 778-9445
General/National Adv. E-mail: dfunk@connectionnewspapers.com
Display Adv. E-mail: sales@connectionnewspapers.com
Editorial e-mail: mkimm@connectionnewspapers.com
Primary Website: connectionnewspapers.com
Mthly Avg Views: 502543
Mthly Avg Unique Visitors: 73776
Year Established: 1784
Avg Paid Circ: 105
Avg Free Circ: 10114
Audit By: Sworn/Estimate/Non-Audited
Audit Date: 10.06.2019
Personnel: Mary Kimm (Pub./Ed.); Jerry Vernon (Exec. Vice Pres.); Debbie Funk (Adv. Dir.); Linda Pecquex (Circ. Mgr.); Steven Mauren (Editor-in-Chief); Jean Card (Prod. Mgr)
Parent company (for newspapers): Connection Publishing, Inc.

ALTAVISTA JOURNAL

Street address 1: 1007 Main St
Street address 2: # A
Street address city: Altavista
Street address state: VA
Zip/Postal code: 24517-1530
General Phone: (434) 369-6688
General Fax: (434) 369-6689
Advertising Phone: (434) 369-6688
Advertising Fax: (434) 369-6689
Editorial Phone: (434) 369-6688
Editorial Fax: (434) 369-6689
General/National Adv. E-mail: j.wood@altavistajournal.com
Display Adv. E-mail: aljournal@altavistajournal.com
Editorial e-mail: m.thomas@altavistajournal.com
Primary Website: altavistajournal.com
Year Established: 1909
Avg Paid Circ: 16200
Avg Free Circ: 120
Audit By: Sworn/Estimate/Non-Audited
Audit Date: 10.06.2019
Personnel: Chad Harrison (Pub.); Mark Thomas (Ed./ Gen. Mgr.); Jamie Glass (Adv. Mgr.)
Parent company (for newspapers): Womack Publishing Co.

AMHERST NEW ERA-PROGRESS

Street address 1: 134 2nd St
Street address city: Amherst
Street address state: VA
Zip/Postal code: 24521-2710
General Phone: (434) 946-7195
General Fax: (434) 946-2684
Advertising Phone: (434) 946-7195
Advertising Fax: (434) 946-2684
Editorial Phone: (434) 946-7196
Editorial Fax: (434) 946-2684
General/National Adv. E-mail: kmays@neweraprogress.com
Display Adv. E-mail: dsmith@newsadvance.com
Editorial e-mail: editor@nelsoncountytimes.com
Primary Website: neweraprogress.com
Avg Paid Circ: 3943
Audit By: Sworn/Estimate/Non-Audited
Audit Date: 10.06.2019
Personnel: Dean Smith (Gen. Mgr.); Kelly Mays (Adv. Dir.); Scott Marshall (Ed.)
Parent company (for newspapers): World Media Enterprises Inc.

ARLINGTON CONNECTION

Street address 1: 1606 King St
Street address city: Alexandria
Street address state: VA
Zip/Postal code: 22314-2719
General Phone: (703) 778-9410
General Fax: (703) 778-9445
Advertising Phone: (703) 778-9444
Advertising Fax: (703) 778-9445
Editorial Phone: (703) 778-9433
Editorial Fax: (703) 778-9445
General/National Adv. E-mail: dfunk@connectionnewspapers.com
Display Adv. E-mail: sales@connectionnewspapers.com
Editorial e-mail: mkimm@connectionnewspapers.com
Primary Website: connectionnewspapers.com
Mthly Avg Views: 502543
Mthly Avg Unique Visitors: 73776
Year Established: 1988
Avg Paid Circ: 0
Avg Free Circ: 5556
Audit By: Sworn/Estimate/Non-Audited
Audit Date: 10.06.2019
Personnel: Mary Kimm (Pub./Ed.); Jerry Vernon (Exec. Vice Pres.); Debbie Funk (Nat'l Adv. Sales); Linda Pecquex (Circ. Mgr.); Peter C. Labovitz (CEO/Pres.); Jean Card (Prod. Mgr)
Parent company (for newspapers): Connection Publishing, Inc.

ARMY TIMES

Street address 1: 1919 Gallows Rd
Street address 2: Ste 400
Street address city: Vienna
Street address state: VA
Zip/Postal code: 22182-4038
General Phone: (703) 642-7330
General Fax: (703) 642-7386
Advertising Phone: (703) 642-7330
Advertising Fax: (703) 642-7386
Editorial Phone: (703) 642-7330
Editorial Fax: (703) 642-7386
General/National Adv. E-mail: advertising@militarytimes.com
Display Adv. E-mail: armylet@armytimes.com
Editorial e-mail: rsandza@militarytimes.com
Primary Website: armytimes.com
Year Established: 1940
Personnel: Richard Sandza (Ed.)
Parent company (for newspapers): Gannett

BEDFORD BULLETIN

Street address 1: 233 W Depot St
Street address city: Bedford
Street address state: VA
Zip/Postal code: 24523-1935
General Phone: (540) 586-8612
General Fax: (540) 586-0834
Advertising Phone: (540) 586-8612
Advertising Fax: (540) 586-0834
Editorial Phone: (540) 586-8612
Editorial Fax: (540) 586-0834
General/National Adv. E-mail: jaybondurant@bedfordbulletin.com
Display Adv. E-mail: classified@bedfordbulletin.com
Editorial e-mail: news@bedfordbulletin.com
Primary Website: bedfordbulletin.com
Year Established: 1857
Avg Paid Circ: 4202

Audit By: Sworn/Estimate/Non-Audited
Audit Date: 10.06.2019
Personnel: Jay Bondurant (Pub./Adv. Mgr.); Tom Wilmoth (Ed.)
Parent company (for newspapers): Paxton Media Group; Landmark Community Newspapers, LLC; Landmark Media Enterprises, LLC

BLAND COUNTY MESSENGER

Street address 1: 460 W Main St
Street address city: Wytheville
Street address state: VA
Zip/Postal code: 24382-2207
General Phone: (276) 228-6611
General Fax: (276) 228-7260
Advertising Phone: (800) 655-1406 ext. 31
Advertising Fax: (276) 228-7260
Editorial Phone: (800) 655-1406 ext. 19
Editorial Fax: (276) 228-7260
General/National Adv. E-mail: bsewell@wythenews.com
Display Adv. E-mail: jsage@wythenews.com
Editorial e-mail: jsimmons@wythenews.com
Primary Website: blandcountynews.com
Avg Paid Circ: 2500
Avg Free Circ: 64
Audit By: Sworn/Estimate/Non-Audited
Audit Date: 10.06.2019
Personnel: Mark Sage (Group Ed.); Jeff Simmons (Mng. Ed.); Sam Cooper (Pub.); Linda Crigger (Adv. Dir.)
Parent company (for newspapers): BH Media Group

BRUNSWICK TIMES-GAZETTE

Street address 1: 213 N Main St
Street address city: Lawrenceville
Street address state: VA
Zip/Postal code: 23868-1807
General Phone: (434) 848-2114
General Fax: (434) 848-2115
Advertising Phone: (434) 848-2114
Advertising Fax: (434) 848-2115
Editorial Phone: (434) 848-2114
Editorial Fax: (434) 848-2115
General/National Adv. E-mail: ads@brunswicktimes-gazette.com
Display Adv. E-mail: classifieds@brunswicktimes-gazette.com
Editorial e-mail: news@brunswicktimes-gazette.com
Primary Website: brunswicktimes-gazette.com
Year Established: 1894
Audit By: Sworn/Estimate/Non-Audited
Audit Date: 10.06.2019
Personnel: Chad Harrison (Pub.); Tom Childrey (Acct. Exec.); Sylvia Allen (Ed.)
Parent company (for newspapers): Womack Publishing Co.

BURKE CONNECTION

Street address 1: 1606 King St
Street address city: Alexandria
Street address state: VA
Zip/Postal code: 22314-2719
General Phone: (703) 778-9410
General Fax: (703) 778-9445
Advertising Phone: (703) 778-9444
Advertising Fax: (703) 778-9445
Editorial Phone: (703) 778-9433
Editorial Fax: (703) 778-9445
General/National Adv. E-mail: dfunk@connectionnewspapers.com
Display Adv. E-mail: sales@connectionnewspapers.com
Editorial e-mail: mkimm@connectionnewspapers.com
Primary Website: connectionnewspapers.com
Mthly Avg Views: 502543
Mthly Avg Unique Visitors: 73776
Year Established: 1988
Avg Paid Circ: 0
Avg Free Circ: 5963
Audit By: Sworn/Estimate/Non-Audited
Audit Date: 10.06.2019
Personnel: Mary Kimm (Pub./Ed.); Jerry Vernon (Exec. Vice Pres.); Debbie Funk (Adv. Dir.); Linda Pecquex (Circ. Mgr.); Peter C. Labovitz (Pres./CEO); Jean Card (Prod. Mgr)
Parent company (for newspapers): Connection Publishing, Inc.

CENTRE VIEW

Street address 1: 1606 King St
Street address city: Alexandria
Street address state: VA
Zip/Postal code: 22314-2719
General Phone: (703) 778-9410
General Fax: (703) 778-9445
Advertising Phone: (703) 778-9444
Advertising Fax: (703) 778-9445
Editorial Phone: (703) 778-9433
Editorial Fax: (703) 778-9445
General/National Adv. E-mail: dfunk@connectionnewspapers.com
Display Adv. E-mail: sales@connectionnewspapers.com
Editorial e-mail: mkimm@connectionnewspapers.com
Primary Website: connectionnewspapers.com
Mthly Avg Views: 502543
Mthly Avg Unique Visitors: 73776
Year Established: 1988
Avg Paid Circ: 2
Avg Free Circ: 4745
Audit By: Sworn/Estimate/Non-Audited
Audit Date: 10.06.2019
Personnel: Mary Kimm (Pub./Ed.); Jerry Vernon (Exec. Vice Pres.); Debbie Funk (Adv. Dir.); Linda Pecquex (Circ. Mgr.); Peter C. Labovitz (Pres./CEO); Jean Card (Prod. Mgr)
Parent company (for newspapers): Connection Publishing, Inc.

COURIER-RECORD

Street address 1: 111 W Maple St
Street address city: Blackstone
Street address state: VA
Zip/Postal code: 23824-1707
General Phone: (434) 292-3019
General Fax: (434) 292-5966
Advertising Phone: (434) 292-3019
Advertising Fax: (434) 292-5966
Editorial Phone: (434) 292-6397
Editorial Fax: (434) 292-5966
General/National Adv. E-mail: frontoffice@courier-record.com
Display Adv. E-mail: ads@courier-record.com
Classified Adv. e-mail: ads@courier-record.com
Editorial e-mail: news@courier-record.com
Primary Website: www.courier-record.com
Mthly Avg Views: 50000
Year Established: 1890
Avg Paid Circ: 5100
Avg Free Circ: 0
Audit By: Sworn/Estimate/Non-Audited
Audit Date: 10.06.2019
Personnel: James Coleburn (Publisher); John Coleburn (Advertising Manager); William Coleburn (Editor & General Manager); Jeff Martin (Advertising Department / Graphic Designer); Scott Matthew (Advertising Representative); Jeff Clements (Advertising Representative); Donna Pridemore (Office Manager); Karlie Smith (Assistant Office Manager)
Parent company (for newspapers): Nottoway Publishing Company

CULPEPER TIMES

Street address 1: 206 S Main St
Street address 2: Ste 301
Street address city: Culpeper
Street address state: VA
Zip/Postal code: 22701-3138
General Phone: (540) 812-2282
General Fax: (540) 812-2117
Advertising Phone: (540) 812-2282
Advertising Fax: (540) 812-2117
Editorial Phone: (540) 812-2282
Editorial Fax: (540) 812-2117
General/National Adv. E-mail: tspargur@culpepertimes.com
Display Adv. E-mail: ecobert@virginianewsgroup.com
Editorial e-mail: anita@culpepertimes.com
Primary Website: culpepertimes.com
Year Established: 2006
Avg Free Circ: 11000
Audit By: Sworn/Estimate/Non-Audited
Audit Date: 10.06.2019
Personnel: Anita Sherman (Ed); Tom Spargur (Group Sales Dir)
Parent company (for newspapers): Rappahannock Media LLC

DAILY NEWS-RECORD

Street address 1: 231 S Liberty St
Street address city: Harrisonburg
Street address state: VA
Zip/Postal code: 22801-3621
General Phone: (540) 574-6265
General Fax: (540) 433-9112
Advertising Phone: (540) 574-6220
Advertising Fax: (540) 433-9112
Editorial Phone: (540) 574-6280
Editorial Fax: (540) 433-9112
Primary Website: dnronline.com
Avg Free Circ: 12500
Audit By: Sworn/Estimate/Non-Audited
Audit Date: 10.06.2019
Personnel: Craig Bartoldston (Pub.); Rhonda McNeal (Adv. Dir.); Mark Golding (Circ. Mgr.); Jeremy Hunt (Ed.); Jim Sacco (Sports Ed.)

DINWIDDIE MONITOR

Street address 1: 111 Baker Street
Street address city: Emporia
Street address state: VA
Zip/Postal code: 23847
General Phone: (434) 634-4153
General Fax: (434) 634-0783
General/National Adv. E-mail: ads@brunswicktimes-gazette.com
Display Adv. E-mail: ads@brunswicktimes-gazette.com
Editorial e-mail: mcampbell89@icloud.com
Primary Website: thedinwiddiemonitor.com
Avg Paid Circ: 5200
Avg Free Circ: 4100
Audit By: Sworn/Estimate/Non-Audited
Audit Date: 10.06.2019
Personnel: Michael Campbell (Ed.)

EASTERN SHORE NEWS

Street address 1: PO Box 288
Street address city: Tasley
Street address state: VA
Zip/Postal code: 23441-0288
General Phone: (757) 787-1200
General Fax: (757) 787-2370
General/National Adv. E-mail: mmlewis@dmg.gannett.com
Display Adv. E-mail: krowan@dmg.gannett.com
Editorial e-mail: tschockley@dmg.gannett.com
Primary Website: easternshorenews.com
Year Established: 1897
Avg Paid Circ: 8700
Avg Free Circ: 55
Audit By: Sworn/Estimate/Non-Audited
Audit Date: 10.06.2019
Personnel: Mike Kilian (Exec. Ed.); Ted Shockley (Mng. Ed.); Robb Scott (Adv. Dir.); Megan Lewis (VA Adv. Mgr.)
Parent company (for newspapers): Gannett

FAIRFAX CONNECTION

Street address 1: 1606 King St
Street address city: Alexandria
Street address state: VA
Zip/Postal code: 22314-2719
General Phone: (703) 778-9410
General Fax: (703) 778-9445
Advertising Phone: (703) 778-9444
Advertising Fax: (703) 778-9445
Editorial Phone: (703) 778-9433
Editorial Fax: (703) 778-9445
General/National Adv. E-mail: dfunk@connectionnewspapers.com
Display Adv. E-mail: sales@connectionnewspapers.com
Editorial e-mail: mkimm@connectionnewspapers.com
Primary Website: connectionnewspapers.com
Mthly Avg Views: 502543
Mthly Avg Unique Visitors: 73776
Year Established: 1986
Avg Paid Circ: 0
Avg Free Circ: 4952
Audit By: Sworn/Estimate/Non-Audited
Audit Date: 10.06.2019
Personnel: Mary Kimm (Pub./Ed.); Jerry Vernon (Exec. Vice Pres.); Debbie Funk (Adv. Dir.); Peter C. Labovitz (CEO/Pub.); Jean Card (Prod. Mgr); Linda Pecquex (Circ. Mgr)
Parent company (for newspapers): Connection Publishing, Inc.

FAIRFAX COUNTY TIMES

Street address 1: 20 Pidgeon Hill Dr
Street address 2: Ste 201
Street address city: Sterling
Street address state: VA
Zip/Postal code: 20165-6134
General Phone: (703) 437-5400
General Fax: (703) 437-6019
Advertising Phone: (571) 323-6212
Advertising Fax: (703) 437-6019
Editorial Phone: (571) 323-6224
Editorial Fax: (703) 437-6019
General/National Adv. E-mail: kwashburn@fairfaxtimes.com
Display Adv. E-mail: Pstamper@fairfaxtimes.com
Classified Adv. e-mail: pstamper@wspnet.com
Editorial e-mail: gmacdonald@fairfaxtimes.com
Primary Website: fairfaxtimes.com
Mthly Avg Views: 80000
Mthly Avg Unique Visitors: 15000
Year Established: 1964
Avg Free Circ: 102157
Audit By: Sworn/Estimate/Non-Audited
Audit Date: 10.06.2019
Personnel: Gregg MacDonald (Exec. Ed)
Parent company (for newspapers): Whip It Media, Inc.

FAIRFAX STATION/CLIFTON/LORTON CONNECTION

Street address 1: 1606 King St
Street address city: Alexandria
Street address state: VA
Zip/Postal code: 22314-2719
General Phone: (703) 778-9410
General Fax: (703) 778-9445
Advertising Phone: (703) 778-9444
Advertising Fax: (703) 778-9445
Editorial Phone: (703) 778-9433
Editorial Fax: (703) 778-9445
General/National Adv. E-mail: dfunk@connectionnewspapers.com
Display Adv. E-mail: sales@connectionnewspapers.com
Editorial e-mail: mkimm@connectionnewspapers.com
Primary Website: connectionnewspapers.com
Mthly Avg Views: 502543
Mthly Avg Unique Visitors: 73776
Year Established: 1988
Avg Paid Circ: 0
Avg Free Circ: 6594
Audit By: Sworn/Estimate/Non-Audited
Audit Date: 10.06.2019
Personnel: Mary Kimm (Pub./Ed.); Jerry Vernon (Exec. Vice Pres.); Debbie Funk (Adv. Dir.); Peter C. Labovitz (Pres./CEO); Linda Pecquex (Circ. Mgr); Jean Card (Prod. Mgr)
Parent company (for newspapers): Connection Publishing, Inc.

FALLS CHURCH NEWS-PRESS

Street address 1: 200 Little Falls St
Street address 2: Ste 508
Street address city: Falls Church
Street address state: VA
Zip/Postal code: 22046-4302
General Phone: (703) 532-3267
General Fax: (703) 342-0347
Advertising Phone: (703) 532-3267
Advertising Fax: (703) 342-0347
Editorial Phone: (703) 532-3267
Editorial Fax: (703) 342-0347
General/National Adv. E-mail: fcnp@fcnp.com
Display Adv. E-mail: ads@fcnp.com
Editorial e-mail: nfbenton@fcnp.com
Primary Website: fcnp.com
Year Established: 1991
Avg Free Circ: 15000
Audit By: Sworn/Estimate/Non-Audited
Audit Date: 10.06.2019

Personnel: Nicholas F. Benton (Owner/Pub./Ed.); Jody Fellows (Mng. Ed.); Joe Fridling (Adv. Dir.); Nick Gatz (Adv. Sales); Melissa Morse (Adv. Sales); Leslie Poster (Writer); Mike Hume (Sports Ed.)
Parent company (for newspapers): Benton Communications Inc.

FAUQUIER TIMES

Street address 1: 39 Culpeper St
Street address city: Warrenton
Street address state: VA
Zip/Postal code: 20186-3319
General Phone: (540) 347-4222
General Fax: (540) 349-8676
Advertising Phone: (540) 351-1166
Editorial Phone: (540) 351-1663
General/National Adv. E-mail: psymington@fauquier.com
Display Adv. E-mail: kgodfrey@fauquier.com
Editorial e-mail: kpugh@fauquier.com
Primary Website: fauquier.com
Year Established: 1905
Avg Paid Circ: 9447
Audit By: Sworn/Estimate/Non-Audited
Audit Date: 10.06.2019
Personnel: Peter W. Arundel (Chairman/CEO); Pamela Symington (Gen. Mgr); Kathy Godfrey (Piedmont Adv. Supervisor); Nancy Keyser (Dist. Mgr); Mark Grandstaff (Managing Ed.); Steve Campbell (Exec. Ed.)
Parent company (for newspapers): Piedmont Media

FEDERAL TIMES

Street address 1: 6883 Commercial Dr
Street address city: Springfield
Street address state: VA
Zip/Postal code: 22159-0002
General Phone: (703) 642-7330
General Fax: (703) 642-7386
Advertising Phone: (703) 642-7330
Advertising Fax: (703) 642-7386
Editorial Phone: (703) 642-7330
Editorial Fax: (703) 642-7386
General/National Adv. E-mail: advertising@federaltimes.com
Display Adv. E-mail: advertising@militarytimes.com
Editorial e-mail: swatkins@federaltimes.com
Primary Website: federaltimes.com
Year Established: 1965
Audit By: Sworn/Estimate/Non-Audited
Audit Date: 10.06.2019
Personnel: Jill Aitoro (Ed.)
Parent company (for newspapers): Gannett

FLUVANNA REVIEW

Street address 1: Crofton Plaza Building 106
Street address 2: Suite 1
Street address city: Palmyra
Street address state: VA
Zip/Postal code: 22963
General Phone: (434) 591-1000
General Fax: (434) 589-1704
General/National Adv. E-mail: sales@fluvannareview.com
Display Adv. E-mail: sales@fluvannareview.com
Editorial e-mail: editor@fluvannareview.com
Primary Website: fluvannareview.com
Mthly Avg Views: 10000
Mthly Avg Unique Visitors: 6000
Year Established: 1979
Avg Paid Circ: 15
Avg Free Circ: 6200
Audit By: CVC
Audit Date: 30.09.2018
Personnel: Carlos Santos (Pub./Ed./Circ. Mgr.); Kathy Zeek (Prod. Mgr); Christina Dimeo (Ed.); Judi Price (Adv. Mgr.)
Parent company (for newspapers): Valley Publishing

GAINESVILLE TIMES

Street address 1: 9 E MARKET ST
Street address city: LEESBURG
Street address state: VA
Zip/Postal code: 20176-3013
General Phone: (540) 351-1162
General/National Adv. E-mail: kgodfrey@timespapers.com
Display Adv. E-mail: kgodfrey@timespapers.com
Primary Website: northernvatimes.com/gainesville
Year Established: 1963
Avg Paid Circ: 291
Avg Free Circ: 13399
Audit By: Sworn/Estimate/Non-Audited
Audit Date: 10.06.2019
Personnel: Shari Keyes (Executive Assistant to Chairman/CEO); Kathy Godfrey (Adv. Mgr.)
Parent company (for newspapers): Piedmont Media

GALAX GAZETTE

Street address 1: 108 W Stuart Dr
Street address city: Galax
Street address state: VA
Zip/Postal code: 24333-2114
General Phone: (276) 236-5178
General Fax: (276) 236-0756
General/National Adv. E-mail: ads@galaxgazette.com
Display Adv. E-mail: classifieds@galaxgazette.com
Editorial e-mail: editor@galaxgazette.com
Primary Website: galaxgazette.com
Year Established: 1876
Avg Paid Circ: 7170
Audit By: Sworn/Estimate/Non-Audited
Audit Date: 10.06.2019
Personnel: Chuck Burress (Pub.); Brian Funk (Ed.); Randy Kegley (Adv. Mgr.)
Parent company (for newspapers): Landmark Community Newspapers, LLC

GOOCHLAND GAZETTE

Street address 1: 8460 Times Dispatch Boulevard
Street address city: Mechanicsville
Street address state: VA
Zip/Postal code: 23116-2029
General Phone: (804) 775-4614
General Fax: (804) 730-0476
General/National Adv. E-mail: schildrey@mechlocal.com
Display Adv. E-mail: cgrant@mechlocal.com
Editorial e-mail: jmonopoli@rsnva.com
Primary Website: richmond.com
Year Established: 1955
Avg Paid Circ: 38
Avg Free Circ: 6854
Audit By: AAM
Audit Date: 31.03.2019
Personnel: Joy Monopoli (Pub.); Melody Kinser (Managing Ed.); Charlie Leffler (Sports Ed.)
Parent company (for newspapers): BH Media Group; Lee Enterprises, Incorporated

GREAT FALLS CONNECTION

Street address 1: 1606 King St
Street address city: Alexandria
Street address state: VA
Zip/Postal code: 22314-2719
General Phone: (703) 778-9410
General Fax: (703) 778-9445
Advertising Phone: (703) 778-9444
Advertising Fax: (703) 778-9445
Editorial Phone: (703) 778-9433
Editorial Fax: (703) 778-9445
General/National Adv. E-mail: dfunk@connectionnewspapers.com
Display Adv. E-mail: sales@connectionnewspapers.com
Editorial e-mail: mkimm@connectionnewspapers.com
Primary Website: connectionnewspapers.com
Mthly Avg Views: 502543
Mthly Avg Unique Visitors: 7
Year Established: 1988
Avg Paid Circ: 1
Avg Free Circ: 6088
Audit By: Sworn/Estimate/Non-Audited
Audit Date: 10.06.2019
Personnel: Mary Kimm (Pub./Ed.); Jerry Vernon (Exec. Vice Pres.); Debbie Funk (Adv. Dir.); Peter C. Labovitz (Pres./CEO); Linda Pecquex (Circ. Mgr); Jean Card (Prod. Mgr)
Parent company (for newspapers): Connection Publishing, Inc.

HERALD-PROGRESS

Street address 1: 112 Thompson St
Street address 2: Ste C
Street address city: Ashland
Street address state: VA
Zip/Postal code: 23005-1527
General Phone: (804) 798-9031
General Fax: (804) 798-9036
Advertising Phone: (804) 798-9031 ext. 220
Advertising Fax: (804) 798-9036
Editorial Phone: (804) 798-9031 ext. 203
Editorial Fax: (804) 798-9036
General/National Adv. E-mail: hpads@lcs.net
Display Adv. E-mail: hpclassifieds@lcs.net
Editorial e-mail: hpeditor@lcs.net
Primary Website: herald-progress.com
Avg Paid Circ: 7527
Audit By: Sworn/Estimate/Non-Audited
Audit Date: 10.06.2019
Personnel: William Trimble (Pub.); Greg Glassner (Ed.); Julia Wigginton (Adv. Mgr.)
Parent company (for newspapers): Lakeway Publishers, Inc.

INSIDE BUSINESS, THE HAMPTON ROADS BUSINESS JOURNAL

Street address 1: 150 W Brambleton Ave
Street address city: Norfolk
Street address state: VA
Zip/Postal code: 23510-2018
General Phone: (757) 222-5353
General Fax: (757) 222-5359
Advertising Phone: (757) 222-3165
Advertising Fax: (757) 222-5359
Editorial Phone: (757) 222-5349
Editorial Fax: (757) 222-5359
General/National Adv. E-mail: ski.miller@insidebiz.com
Display Adv. E-mail: ski.miller@insidebiz.com
Editorial e-mail: ron.crow@insidebiz.com
Primary Website: insidebiz.com
Year Established: 1996
Avg Paid Circ: 4048
Avg Free Circ: 3468
Audit By: VAC
Audit Date: 31.12.2016
Personnel: Mike Herron (Pub.); Ron Crow (Editor)
Parent company (for newspapers): Landmark Media Enterprises, LLC; The Virginian-Pilot

MADISON COUNTY EAGLE

Street address 1: 201 N Main St
Street address city: Madison
Street address state: VA
Zip/Postal code: 22727-3053
General Phone: (540) 948-5121
General Fax: (540) 948-3045
Advertising Phone: (434) 975-7112
Advertising Fax: (540) 948-3045
Editorial Phone: (540) 948-5121
Editorial Fax: (540) 948-3045
General/National Adv. E-mail: ccullen@dailyprogress.com
Display Adv. E-mail: fkern@orangenews.com
Editorial e-mail: news@madison-news.com
Primary Website: madison-news.com
Year Established: 1910
Avg Paid Circ: 4500
Avg Free Circ: 10
Audit By: Sworn/Estimate/Non-Audited
Audit Date: 10.06.2019
Personnel: Lawrence McConnell (Pub.); Don Richeson (Ed.); Jeff Poole (Managing Editor); Carolyn Cullen (Adv. Dir.)

MARINE CORPS TIMES

Street address 1: 1919 Gallows Rd
Street address 2: Ste 400
Street address city: Vienna
Street address state: VA
Zip/Postal code: 22182-4038
General Phone: (703) 642-7330
General Fax: (703) 642-7386
Advertising Phone: (703) 642-7330
Advertising Fax: (703) 642-7386
Editorial Phone: (703) 642-7330
Editorial Fax: (703) 642-7386
General/National Adv. E-mail: advertising@militarytimes.com
Display Adv. E-mail: marinelet@marinecorpstimes.com
Editorial e-mail: adegrandpre@militarytimes.com
Primary Website: marinecorpstimes.com
Year Established: 1999
Audit By: Sworn/Estimate/Non-Audited
Audit Date: 10.06.2019
Personnel: Andrew DeGrandpre (Ed.)
Parent company (for newspapers): Gannett

MCLEAN CONNECTION

Street address 1: 1606 King St
Street address city: Alexandria
Street address state: VA
Zip/Postal code: 22314-2719
General Phone: (703) 778-9410
General Fax: (703) 778-9445
Advertising Phone: (703) 778-9444
Advertising Fax: (703) 778-9445
Editorial Phone: (703) 778-9433
Editorial Fax: (703) 778-9445
General/National Adv. E-mail: dfunk@connectionnewspapers.com
Display Adv. E-mail: sales@connectionnewspapers.com
Editorial e-mail: mkimm@connectionnewspapers.com
Primary Website: connectionnewspapers.com
Mthly Avg Views: 502543
Mthly Avg Unique Visitors: 73776
Year Established: 1988
Avg Paid Circ: 0
Avg Free Circ: 6987
Audit By: Sworn/Estimate/Non-Audited
Audit Date: 10.06.2019
Personnel: Mary Kimm (Pub./Ed.); Jerry Vernon (Exec. Vice Pres.); Debbie Funk (Adv. Dir.); Peter C. Labovitz (Pres./CEO); Jean Card (Prod. Mgr); Linda Pecquex (Circ. Mgr)
Parent company (for newspapers): Connection Publishing, Inc.

MECHANICSVILLE LOCAL

Street address 1: 8460 Times Dispatch Boulevard
Street address city: Mechanicsville
Street address state: VA
Zip/Postal code: 23116-2029
General Phone: (804) 775-4614
General Fax: (804) 730-0476
General/National Adv. E-mail: jmonopoli@rsnva.com
Editorial e-mail: jmonopoli@rsnva.com
Primary Website: richmond.com
Year Established: 1984
Avg Paid Circ: 31
Avg Free Circ: 22340
Audit By: AAM
Audit Date: 30.06.2018
Personnel: Joy Monopoli (Pub.); Melody Kinser
Parent company (for newspapers): BH Media Group; Lee Enterprises, Incorporated

MECKLENBURG REPORTER

Street address 1: PO Box 60
Street address city: South Hill
Street address state: VA
Zip/Postal code: 23970-0060
General Phone: (434) 447-3178
General Fax: (434) 447-5931
General/National Adv. E-mail: tbrowder@womackpublishing.com
Primary Website: mecklenburgreporter.com
Audit By: Sworn/Estimate/Non-Audited
Audit Date: 10.06.2019
Personnel: Randy Velvin (Gen. Mgr.); Patrick Love (Mng. Ed.); Dallas Weston (News Ed.); Tina Browder (Acct. Exec.); Teresa Elliott (Acct. Exec.)

MIDDLEBURG LIFE

Street address 1: 112 W Washington St
Street address city: Middleburg
Street address state: VA
Zip/Postal code: 20118
General Phone: (540) 687-6059
Advertising Phone: (540)687-6059
Editorial Phone: (540)687-6059
General/National Adv. E-mail: info@middleburglife.com
Display Adv. E-mail: tfields@insidenova.com
Editorial e-mail: info@middleburglife.com
Primary Website: middleburglife.com
Audit By: Sworn/Estimate/Non-Audited
Audit Date: 10.06.2019
Personnel: Vicky Moon (Advertising)

Parent company (for newspapers): Greenhill Media

MOUNT VERNON GAZETTE

Street address 1: 1606 King St
Street address city: Alexandria
Street address state: VA
Zip/Postal code: 22314-2719
General Phone: (703) 778-9410
General Fax: (703) 778-9445
Advertising Phone: (703) 778-9444
Advertising Fax: (703) 778-9445
Editorial Phone: (703) 778-9433
Editorial Fax: (703) 778-9445
General/National Adv. E-mail: dfunk@connectionnewspapers.com
Display Adv. E-mail: sales@connectionnewspapers.com
Editorial e-mail: mkimm@connectionnewspapers.com
Primary Website: connectionnewspapers.com
Mthly Avg Views: 502543
Mthly Avg Unique Visitors: 73776
Year Established: 1989
Avg Paid Circ: 27
Avg Free Circ: 8724
Audit By: Sworn/Estimate/Non-Audited
Audit Date: 10.06.2019
Personnel: Mary Kimm (Pub./Ed.); Jerry Vernon (Exec. Vice Pres.); Debbie Funk (Adv. Dir.); Peter C. Labovitz (Pres./CEO); Linda Pecquex (Circ. Mgr); Jean Card (Prod. Mgr)
Parent company (for newspapers): Connection Publishing, Inc.

NELSON COUNTY TIMES

Street address 1: 134 2nd St
Street address city: Amherst
Street address state: VA
Zip/Postal code: 24521-2710
General Phone: (434) 385-5450
General Fax: (434) 946-2684
Advertising Phone: (434) 946-7195
Advertising Fax: (434) 946-2684
Editorial Phone: (434) 946-7196
Editorial Fax: (434) 946-2684
General/National Adv. E-mail: jobrien@newsadvance.com
Display Adv. E-mail: cmarsh@neweraprogress.com
Editorial e-mail: editor@nelsoncountytimes.com
Primary Website: nelsoncountytimes.com
Audit By: Sworn/Estimate/Non-Audited
Audit Date: 10.06.2019
Personnel: Dean Smith (Gen. Mgr.); Scott Marshall (Ed.); Jeffrey O'Brien (Adv. Mgr.); Cathy Marsh (Classified Adv. Mgr.)
Parent company (for newspapers): World Media Enterprises Inc.

NORTHERN NECK NEWS

Street address 1: 132 COURT CIR
Street address city: Warsaw
Street address state: VA
Zip/Postal code: 22572
General Phone: (804) 333-6937
General Fax: (804) 333-0033
General/National Adv. E-mail: nnnclassifieds@lcs.net
Display Adv. E-mail: nnnclassifieds@lcs.net
Editorial e-mail: nnneditor@lcs.net
Primary Website: northernnecknews.com
Avg Paid Circ: 8300
Audit By: Sworn/Estimate/Non-Audited
Audit Date: 10.06.2019
Personnel: Brittlynn Powell (Ed.); Cathy Gerring (Pub.); Ali Foti
Parent company (for newspapers): Lakeway Publishers, Inc.

NORTHUMBERLAND ECHO

Street address 1: 132 COURT CIR
Street address city: Warsaw
Street address state: VA
Zip/Postal code: 22572
General Phone: (804) 333-6397
General/National Adv. E-mail: nnnclassifieds@lcs.net
Display Adv. E-mail: nnnclassifieds@lcs.net
Editorial e-mail: echo@lcs.net
Primary Website: northumberlandecho.com
Year Established: 1902
Avg Paid Circ: 2800
Audit By: Sworn/Estimate/Non-Audited
Audit Date: 10.06.2019
Personnel: Brittlynn Powell (Ed.); Cathy Gerring (Pub.)
Parent company (for newspapers): Lakeway Publishers, Inc.

OAK HILL/HERNDON CONNECTION

Street address 1: 1606 King St
Street address city: Alexandria
Street address state: VA
Zip/Postal code: 22314-2719
General Phone: (703) 778-9410
General Fax: (703) 778-9445
Advertising Phone: (703) 778-9444
Advertising Fax: (703) 778-9445
Editorial Phone: (703) 778-9433
Editorial Fax: (703) 778-9445
General/National Adv. E-mail: dfunk@connectionnewspapers.com
Display Adv. E-mail: sales@connectionnewspapers.com
Editorial e-mail: mkimm@connectionnewspapers.com
Primary Website: connectionnewspapers.com
Mthly Avg Views: 502543
Mthly Avg Unique Visitors: 73776
Year Established: 1988
Avg Paid Circ: 0
Avg Free Circ: 3450
Audit By: Sworn/Estimate/Non-Audited
Audit Date: 10.06.2019
Personnel: Mary Kimm (Pub./Ed.); Jerry Vernon (Exec. Vice Pres.); Debbie Funk (Adv. Dir.); Peter C. Labovitz (Pres./CEO); Jean Card (Prod. Mgr); Linda Pecquex (Circ. Mgr)
Parent company (for newspapers): Connection Publishing, Inc.

ORANGE COUNTY REVIEW

Street address 1: 146 Byrd St
Street address city: Orange
Street address state: VA
Zip/Postal code: 22960-1631
General Phone: (540) 672-1266
General Fax: (540) 672-7481
Advertising Phone: (540) 672-1266 ext. 14
Advertising Fax: (540) 672-7481
Editorial Phone: (540) 672-1266 ext. 23
Editorial Fax: (540) 672-7481
General/National Adv. E-mail: news@orangenews.com
Display Adv. E-mail: jstrader@orangenews.com
Editorial e-mail: jpoole@orangenews.com
Primary Website: dailyprogress.com
Avg Paid Circ: 7000
Avg Free Circ: 18
Audit By: Sworn/Estimate/Non-Audited
Audit Date: 10.06.2019
Personnel: Lawrence McConnell (Pub.); Jeff Poole (Mng. Ed.); John Strader (Adv. Mgr.)
Parent company (for newspapers): BH Media Group

PAGE NEWS & COURIER

Street address 1: 17 S Broad St
Street address city: Luray
Street address state: VA
Zip/Postal code: 22835-1904
General Phone: (540) 743-5123
General Fax: (540) 743-4779
Advertising Phone: (540) 743-5123
Advertising Fax: (540) 743-4779
Editorial Phone: (540) 743-5123
Editorial Fax: (540) 743-4779
General/National Adv. E-mail: pncads@gmail.com
Display Adv. E-mail: classified@pagenewspaper.com
Editorial e-mail: editor@pagenewspaper.com
Primary Website: ShenValleyNow.com
Year Established: 1867
Avg Paid Circ: 6746
Audit By: Sworn/Estimate/Non-Audited
Audit Date: 10.06.2019
Personnel: Randy Arrington (Ed./Gen. Mgr.); Kelli Bailey (Adv. Mgr.); China Martin (Circ. Mgr.)
Parent company (for newspapers): Ogden Newspapers Inc.

POTOMAC ALMANAC

Street address 1: 1606 King St
Street address city: Alexandria
Street address state: VA
Zip/Postal code: 22314-2719
General Phone: (703) 778-9410
General Fax: (703) 778-9445
Advertising Phone: (703) 778-9444
Advertising Fax: (703) 778-9445
Editorial Phone: (703) 778-9433
Editorial Fax: (703) 778-9445
General/National Adv. E-mail: dfunk@connectionnewspapers.com
Display Adv. E-mail: sales@connectionnewspapers.com
Editorial e-mail: mkimm@connectionnewspapers.com
Primary Website: connectionnewspapers.com
Mthly Avg Views: 502543
Mthly Avg Unique Visitors: 73776
Year Established: 1957
Avg Paid Circ: 0
Avg Free Circ: 6528
Audit By: Sworn/Estimate/Non-Audited
Audit Date: 10.06.2019
Personnel: Mary Kimm (Pub./Ed.); Jerry Vernon (Exec. Vice Pres.); Debbie Funk (Adv. Dir.); Peter C. Labovitz (Pres./CEO); Linda Pecquex (Circ. Mgr); Jean Card (Prod. Mgr)
Parent company (for newspapers): Connection Publishing, Inc.

POWHATAN TODAY

Street address 1: 3229 Anderson Hwy
Street address 2: Ste 200
Street address city: Powhatan
Street address state: VA
Zip/Postal code: 23139-7340
General Phone: (804) 598-4305
General Fax: (804) 598-7757
Advertising Phone: (804) 598-4305 ext. 14
Editorial Phone: (804) 598-4305 ext. 13
General/National Adv. E-mail: sales@powhatantoday.com
Display Adv. E-mail: bweeks@powhatantoday.com
Editorial e-mail: lmcfarland@powhatantoday.com
Primary Website: powhatantoday.com
Year Established: 1986
Avg Paid Circ: 72
Avg Free Circ: 11167
Audit By: AAM
Audit Date: 30.06.2017
Personnel: Joy Monopoli (Pub.); Melody Kinser (Ed.); Birgit Weeks (Adv. Mgr.)
Parent company (for newspapers): BH Media Group

PRINCE WILLIAM TIMES

Street address 1: 9 E Market St
Street address city: Leesburg
Street address state: VA
Zip/Postal code: 20176-3013
General Phone: (703) 777-1111
General Fax: (703) 771-1285
General/National Adv. E-mail: skeyes@virginianewsgroup.com
Primary Website: northernvatimes.com/gainesville
Year Established: 1963
Audit By: Sworn/Estimate/Non-Audited
Audit Date: 10.06.2019
Personnel: Shari Keyes (Executive Assistant to Chairman/CEO)
Parent company (for newspapers): Piedmont Media

RAPPAHANNOCK TIMES

Street address 1: 622 Charlotte St
Street address city: Tappahannock
Street address state: VA
Zip/Postal code: 22560
General Phone: (804) 443-2200
General Fax: (804) 443-9684
Advertising Phone: (804) 443-2200
Advertising Fax: (804) 443-9684
Editorial Phone: (804) 443-2200
Editorial Fax: (804) 443-9684
General/National Adv. E-mail: julie@rappnews.com
Display Adv. E-mail: julie@rappnews.com
Editorial e-mail: raptimes@verizon.net
Year Established: 1850
Avg Paid Circ: 4926
Avg Free Circ: 74
Audit By: Sworn/Estimate/Non-Audited
Audit Date: 10.06.2019
Personnel: Catherine Wells (Adv. Mgr.); Walter Nicklin (Pub./Chairman); Dennis Brack (Pres.); Jan Clatterbuck (Gen. Mgr./Circ. Mgr.); Patrice Indig (Adv. Dir.)

RESTON CONNECTION

Street address 1: 1606 King St
Street address city: Alexandria
Street address state: VA
Zip/Postal code: 22314-2719
General Phone: (703) 778-9410
General Fax: (703) 778-9445
Advertising Phone: (703) 778-9444
Advertising Fax: (703) 778-9445
Editorial Phone: (703) 778-9433
Editorial Fax: (703) 778-9445
General/National Adv. E-mail: dfunk@connectionnewspapers.com
Display Adv. E-mail: sales@connectionnewspapers.com
Editorial e-mail: mkimm@connectionnewspapers.com
Primary Website: connectionnewspapers.com
Mthly Avg Views: 502543
Mthly Avg Unique Visitors: 73776
Year Established: 1988
Avg Paid Circ: 0
Avg Free Circ: 6650
Audit By: Sworn/Estimate/Non-Audited
Audit Date: 10.06.2019
Personnel: Mary Kimm (Pub./Ed.); Jerry Vernon (Exec. Vice Pres.); Debbie Funk (Adv. Dir.); Peter C. Labovitz (Pres./CEO); Jean Card (Prod. Mgr); Linda Pecquex (Circ. Mgr)
Parent company (for newspapers): Connection Publishing, Inc.

RICHLANDS NEWS-PRESS

Street address 1: 1945 2nd St
Street address city: Richlands
Street address state: VA
Zip/Postal code: 24641-2303
General Phone: (276) 963-1081
General Fax: (276) 963-0202
Advertising Phone: (800) 655-1406 ext. 31
Advertising Fax: (276) 963-0202
Editorial Phone: (276) 963-1081
Editorial Fax: (276) 963-0202
General/National Adv. E-mail: bsewell@wythennews.com
Display Adv. E-mail: jsage@wythenews.com
Editorial e-mail: jtalbert@richlands-news-press.com
Primary Website: richlands-news-press.com
Avg Paid Circ: 7000
Avg Free Circ: 172
Audit By: Sworn/Estimate/Non-Audited
Audit Date: 10.06.2019
Personnel: Mark Sage (Pub.); Jim Talbert (Ed.); Barbara Sewell (Adv. Dir.)
Parent company (for newspapers): BH Media Group

RURAL VIRGINIAN

Street address 1: 685 Rio Rd W
Street address city: Charlottesville
Street address state: VA
Zip/Postal code: 22901-1413
General Phone: (434) 978-7216
General Fax: (434) 978-7204
Advertising Phone: (434) 978-7216
Advertising Fax: (434) 978-7204
Editorial Phone: (434) 978-7216
Editorial Fax: (434) 978-7204
General/National Adv. E-mail: srhodes@dailyprogress.com
Display Adv. E-mail: dhubbard@dailyprogress.com
Editorial e-mail: rv@dailyprogress.com
Primary Website: dailyprogress.com
Year Established: 1971
Avg Free Circ: 12000
Audit By: Sworn/Estimate/Non-Audited
Audit Date: 10.06.2019
Personnel: Aaron Richardson (Ed.); Terry Beigie (Ed.)

SALEM TIMES-REGISTER

Street address 1: 1633 W Main St
Street address city: Salem
Street address state: VA
Zip/Postal code: 24153-3115
General Phone: (540) 389-9355
General Fax: (540) 389-2930

Advertising Phone: (540) 389-9355
Advertising Fax: (540) 389-2930
Editorial Phone: (540) 389-9355
Editorial Fax: (540) 389-2930
General/National Adv. E-mail: wendicraig@gmail.com
Display Adv. E-mail: customerservice@ourvalley.org
Editorial e-mail: shawn.nowlin@ourvalley.org
Primary Website: ourvalley.org
Year Established: 1884
Avg Paid Circ: 2800
Audit By: Sworn/Estimate/Non-Audited
Audit Date: 10.06.2019
Personnel: Lynn Hurst (General Manager)
Parent company (for newspapers): Virginia Media, LLC

SCOTT COUNTY VIRGINIA STAR

Street address 1: 255 W Jackson St
Street address city: Gate City
Street address state: VA
Zip/Postal code: 24251-4129
General Phone: (276) 386-6300
General Fax: (276) 254-6011
General/National Adv. E-mail: info@virginiastar.org
Display Adv. E-mail: advertising@virginiastar.org
Classified Adv. e-mail: classifieds@virginiastar.og
Editorial e-mail: news@virginiastar.org
Primary Website: www.virginiastar.net
Year Established: 1903
Avg Paid Circ: 6500
Avg Free Circ: 103
Audit By: Sworn/Estimate/Non-Audited
Audit Date: 06.10.2023
Personnel: Terry Rose (Graphic Designer); Emily McCarty (Circ. Dir.); Rex McCarty (Advt Dir); Lisa McCarty (Publisher); Gabriel Edmunds (Advertising Representative); Sierra Lane (Advertising Representative); Maycee Christian
Parent company (for newspapers): Scott County Herald-Virginia Inc.

SMYTH COUNTY NEWS & MESSENGER

Street address 1: PO Box 640
Street address city: Marion
Street address state: VA
Zip/Postal code: 24354-2523
General Phone: (276) 228-6611
General/National Adv. E-mail: sportern@smythnews.com
Display Adv. E-mail: ashell@bristolnews.com
Classified Adv. e-mail: rguffey@bristolnews.com
Editorial e-mail: sportern@smythnews.com
Primary Website: swvatoday.com
Year Established: 1884
Avg Paid Circ: 1900
Audit By: Sworn/Estimate/Non-Audited
Audit Date: 10.[illegible]
Personnel: Stephanie Porter-Nichols (Ed.); Mark Sage (Group Ed.); Sonny Corpus (Circ. Mgr.)
Parent company (for newspapers): BH Media Group; Lee Enterprises

SOUTH HILL ENTERPRISE

Street address 1: 914 W Danville St
Street address city: South Hill
Street address state: VA
Zip/Postal code: 23970
General Phone: (434) 447-3178
General Fax: (434) 447-5931
General/National Adv. E-mail: editor@southhillenterprise.com
Primary Website: southhillenterprise.com
Audit By: Sworn/Estimate/Non-Audited
Audit Date: 10.06.2019
Personnel: Randy Velvin (Gen. Mgr.); Patrick Love (Mng. Ed.); Barbara Arthur (Office Mgr.)
Parent company (for newspapers): Womack Publishing Co.

SOUTHSIDE SENTINEL

Street address 1: 276 Virginia St
Street address city: Urbanna
Street address state: VA
Zip/Postal code: 23175-2041
General Phone: (804) 758-2328
General Fax: (804) 758-5896
Advertising Phone: (804) 758-2328 ext. 104
Advertising Fax: (804) 758-5896
Editorial Phone: (804) 758-2328 ext. 109
Editorial Fax: (804) 758-5896
General/National Adv. E-mail: wpayne@ssentinel.com
Display Adv. E-mail: classifieds@ssentinel.com
Editorial e-mail: editor@ssentinel.com
Primary Website: SSentinel.com
Year Established: 1896
Avg Paid Circ: 4394
Avg Free Circ: 141
Audit By: Sworn/Estimate/Non-Audited
Audit Date: 10.06.2019
Personnel: Frederick A. Gaskins (Pub.); John Thomas Hardin (Ed.); Wendy Payne (Adv. Dir.); Peggy Baughan (Circ. Mgr./Classified Mgr.); Julie Burwood (Art Dir.); Joseph Gaskins (IT/Web Mgr.); Geanie Longest (Customer Acct. Mgr.)

SPRINGFIELD CONNECTION

Street address 1: 1606 King St
Street address city: Alexandria
Street address state: VA
Zip/Postal code: 22314-2719
General Phone: (703) 778-9410
General Fax: (703) 778-9445
Advertising Phone: (703) 778-9444
Advertising Fax: (703) 778-9445
Editorial Phone: (703) 778-9433
Editorial Fax: (703) 778-9445
General/National Adv. E-mail: dfunk@connectionnewspapers.com
Display Adv. E-mail: sales@connectionnewspapers.com
Editorial e-mail: mkimm@connectionnewspapers.com
Primary Website: connectionnewspapers.com
Mthly Avg Views: 502543
Mthly Avg Unique Visitors: 73776
Year Established: 1995
Avg Paid Circ: 3
Avg Free Circ: 4610
Audit By: Sworn/Estimate/Non-Audited
Audit Date: 10.06.2019
Personnel: Mary Kimm (Pub./Ed.); Jerry Vernon (Exec. Vice Pres.); Debbie Funk (Adv. Dir.); Peter C. Labovitz (CEO/Pres.); Linda Pecquex (Circ. Mgr); Jean Card (Prod. Mgr)
Parent company (for newspapers): Connection Publishing, Inc.

STAR-TRIBUNE

Street address 1: 30 S Main St
Street address city: Chatham
Street address state: VA
Zip/Postal code: 24531-5436
General Phone: (434) 432-2791
General Fax: (434) 432-4033
Advertising Phone: (434) 432-2791
Advertising Fax: (434) 432-4033
Editorial Phone: (434) 432-2791
Editorial Fax: (434) 432-4033
General/National Adv. E-mail: advertising@chathamstartribune.com
Display Adv. E-mail: legals@chathamstartribune.com
Editorial e-mail: s.light@chathamstartribune.com
Primary Website: chathamstartribune.com
Year Established: 1869
Avg Paid Circ: 8217
Avg Free Circ: 275
Audit By: Sworn/Estimate/Non-Audited
Audit Date: 10.06.2019
Personnel: Chad Harrison (Pub.); Susan Light (Ed.); Johnathan Pettiford (Account Exec.); Eddy Lloyd (Sports Ed.)
Parent company (for newspapers): Womack Publishing Co.

SUN GAZETTE

Street address 1: 6704 Old McLean Village Dr
Street address 2: Ste 200
Street address city: Mc Lean
Street address state: VA
Zip/Postal code: 22101-3906
General Phone: (703) 738-2520
General Fax: (703) 738-2530
Advertising Phone: (703) 738-2523
Advertising Fax: (703) 738-2530
Editorial Phone: (703) 738-2520
Editorial Fax: (703) 738-2530
General/National Adv. E-mail: dmartin@sungazette.net
Display Adv. E-mail: tfields@sungazette.net
Editorial e-mail: smccaffrey@sungazette.net
Primary Website: sungazette.net
Year Established: 1935
Avg Paid Circ: 37
Avg Free Circ: 34420
Audit By: Sworn/Estimate/Non-Audited
Audit Date: 10.06.2019
Personnel: Norm Styer (Pub.); Scott McCaffrey (Ed.); Debbie Martin (Adv. Mgr.); Bruce Potter (COO); Paula Grose (Classified Adv. Mgr.)
Parent company (for newspapers): Northern Virginia Media Services

THE AMELIA BULLETIN MONITOR

Street address 1: 16311 Goodes Bridge Rd
Street address city: Amelia Court House
Street address state: VA
Zip/Postal code: 23002-4837
General Phone: (804) 561-3655
General Fax: (804) 561-2065
Advertising Phone: (804) 561-3655
Advertising Fax: (804) 561-2065
Editorial Phone: (804) 561-3655
Editorial Fax: (804) 561-2065
General/National Adv. E-mail: contactus@ameliamonitor.com
Display Adv. E-mail: contactus@ameliamonitor.com
Classified Adv. e-mail: contactus@ameliamonitor.com
Editorial e-mail: bekki@ameliamonitor.com
Primary Website: ameliamonitor.com
Year Established: 1973
Avg Paid Circ: 4000
Avg Free Circ: 1000
Audit By: Sworn/Estimate/Non-Audited
Audit Date: 10.07.2019
Personnel: Ann B. Morris-Salster (Pub.); Wayne Russell (Editor); Bekki Morris (Publisher); Susan Ellis (Circulation Manager); Julee McConnell (Circ. Mgr.); Cathy Banton (Business Mgr.)
Parent company (for newspapers): ABM Enterprises Inc.

THE CAROLINE PROGRESS

Street address 1: 204 N Main St
Street address city: Bowling Green
Street address state: VA
Zip/Postal code: 22427-9416
General Phone: (804) 633-5005
General Fax: (804) 633-6740
Advertising Phone: (804) 633-5005
Advertising Fax: (804) 633-6740
Editorial Phone: (804) 633-5005
Editorial Fax: (804) 633-6740
General/National Adv. E-mail: cpadvertising@lcs.net
Display Adv. E-mail: cpclassifieds@lcs.net
Editorial e-mail: cpeditor@lcs.net
Primary Website: carolineprogress.com
Avg Paid Circ: 2800
Avg Free Circ: 30
Audit By: Sworn/Estimate/Non-Audited
Audit Date: 10.06.2019
Personnel: Mosby Wigginton (Publisher); Constance Snow (Editor)
Parent company (for newspapers): Lakeway Publishers, Inc.

THE CARROLL NEWS

Street address 1: 804 N MAIN ST
Street address city: Hillsville
Street address state: VA
Zip/Postal code: 24343
General Phone: (276) 728-7311
General Fax: (276) 728-4119
Advertising Phone: (276) 728-7311
Advertising Fax: (276) 728-4119
Editorial Phone: (276) 728-7311
Editorial Fax: (276) 728-4119
General/National Adv. E-mail: sstanley@civitasmedia.com
Display Adv. E-mail: sstanley@civitasmedia.com
Editorial e-mail: aworrell@civitasmedia.com
Primary Website: thecarrollnews.com
Year Established: 1920
Avg Paid Circ: 6700
Avg Free Circ: 10
Audit By: Sworn/Estimate/Non-Audited
Audit Date: 10.06.2019
Personnel: Allen Worrell (Ed.); Sherry Stanley (Adv. Mgr.); Ron Clausen (Pub.); Amber Dowell (Class./Circ.)
Parent company (for newspapers): Champion Media

THE CENTRAL VIRGINIAN

Street address 1: 89 Rescue Ln
Street address city: Louisa
Street address state: VA
Zip/Postal code: 23093-4105
General Phone: (540) 967-0368
General Fax: (540) 967-0457
Advertising Phone: (540) 967-0368
Advertising Fax: (540) 967-0457
Editorial Phone: (540) 967-0368
Editorial Fax: (540) 967-3847
General/National Adv. E-mail: tcvads@lcs.net
Display Adv. E-mail: tcvclass@lcs.net
Classified Adv. e-mail: tcvclass@lcs.net
Editorial e-mail: tcveditor@lcs.net
Primary Website: thecentralvirginian.com
Year Established: 1912
Avg Paid Circ: 7655
Avg Free Circ: 205
Audit By: Sworn/Estimate/Non-Audited
Audit Date: 10.06.2019
Personnel: Kelly Seay (Adv. Mgr.); David Holtzman (Assoc. Ed.); Joseph Haney (Reporter); Steve Weddle (Pub.)
Parent company (for newspapers): Lakeway Publishers, Inc.

THE CHARLOTTE GAZETTE

Street address 1: 4789 Drakes Main St
Street address city: Drakes Branch
Street address state: VA
Zip/Postal code: 23937
General Phone: (434) 568-3341
General Fax: (434) 392-3366
Advertising Phone: (434) 808-0614
General/National Adv. E-mail: jackie.newman@thecharlottegazette.com
Primary Website: thecharlottegazette.com
Audit By: Sworn/Estimate/Non-Audited
Audit Date: 10.06.2019
Personnel: Betty Ramsey (Pub.); Staci Bridge (Dir. of Ops.); Jackie Newman (Adv. Dir.); Rhonda Finch (Circ. Dir.); Italia Gregory (Community Ed.)

THE COALFIELD PROGRESS

Street address 1: 725 Park Ave NE
Street address city: Norton
Street address state: VA
Zip/Postal code: 24273-1007
General Phone: (276) 679-1101
General Fax: (276) 679-5922
General/National Adv. E-mail: ktate@coalfield.com
Primary Website: thecoalfieldprogress.com
Audit By: Sworn/Estimate/Non-Audited
Audit Date: 10.06.2019
Personnel: Debbie Belcher (Office Mgr.); Becky McElroy (Circ.); Karen Tate (Adv. Mgr.); Jeff Lester (News Ed.); Sam Dixon (Sports Ed.)

THE DICKENSON STAR

Street address 1: 250 Main St
Street address city: Clintwood
Street address state: VA
Zip/Postal code: 24228
General Phone: (276) 926-8816
General Fax: (276) 926-8827
Advertising Phone: (276) 926-8816
Advertising Fax: (276) 926-8827
Editorial Phone: (276) 926-8816
Editorial Fax: (276) 926-8827
General/National Adv. E-mail: csutherland@coalfield.com
Display Adv. E-mail: dlawson@coalfield.com
Editorial e-mail: ptate@coalfield.com
Primary Website: coalfield.com
Year Established: 1982
Avg Paid Circ: 4000
Avg Free Circ: 125
Audit By: Sworn/Estimate/Non-Audited
Audit Date: 10.06.2019
Personnel: Jenay Tate (Pub.); Karen Tate (Adv. Mgr.); Paula Tate (Mng. Ed.); Becky McElroy (Circ.); Candacee Watkins (Account Exec.); Sam Dixon (Sports Ed.)

Parent company (for newspapers): American Hometown Publishing

THE ENTERPRISE

Street address 1: 129 N Main St
Street address city: Stuart
Street address state: VA
Zip/Postal code: 24171-8802
General Phone: (276) 694-3101
General Fax: (276) 694-5110
Advertising Phone: (276) 694-3101
Advertising Fax: (276) 694-5110
Editorial Phone: (276) 694-3101
Editorial Fax: (276) 694-5110
General/National Adv. E-mail: mail@theenterprise.net
Display Adv. E-mail: mail@theenterprise.net
Editorial e-mail: mail@theenterprise.net
Primary Website: theenterprise.net
Year Established: 1876
Avg Paid Circ: 5900
Audit By: Sworn/Estimate/Non-Audited
Audit Date: 10.06.2019
Personnel: Gail M. Harding (Pub.); Pam Hall (Adv. Mgr.); Nancy Lindsey (Ed.)

THE FARMVILLE HERALD

Street address 1: 114 North St
Street address city: Farmville
Street address state: VA
Zip/Postal code: 23901-1312
General Phone: (434) 392-4151
General Fax: (434) 392-3366
Advertising Phone: (434)392-4151
Editorial Phone: (434)392-4151
General/National Adv. E-mail: jackie.newman@farmvilleherald.com
Display Adv. E-mail: jackie.newman@farmvilleherald.com
Editorial e-mail: martin.cahn@farmvilleherald.com
Primary Website: farmvilleherald.com
Year Established: 1890
Audit By: Sworn/Estimate/Non-Audited
Audit Date: 10.06.2019
Personnel: Jackie Newman (Adv. Mgr.); Martin Cahn (Mng. Ed.); Staci Bridge (Dir. of Ops.); Rhonda Finch (Circ. Mgr.); Titus Mohler (Sports Ed.)
Parent company (for newspapers): Boone Newspapers, Inc.

THE FINCASTLE HERALD

Street address 1: 7 S. Roanoke St
Street address city: Fincastle
Street address state: VA
Zip/Postal code: 24090
General Phone: (540) 473-2741
General Fax: (540) 473-2742
Advertising Phone: (540) 761-7019
Advertising Fax: (540) 473-2742
Editorial Phone: (540) 473-2741
Editorial Fax: (540) 473-2742
General/National Adv. E-mail: tfrye@ourvalley.org
Display Adv. E-mail: customerservice@ourvalley.org
Editorial e-mail: edmccoy@ourvalley.org
Primary Website: fincastleherald.com
Year Established: 1866
Avg Paid Circ: 5500
Audit By: Sworn/Estimate/Non-Audited
Audit Date: 10.06.2019
Personnel: Edwin L. McCoy (Ed.); Tucker Frye (Advertising); Lynn Hurst (General Manager); Michael Stowe (Publisher)
Parent company (for newspapers): Virginia Media Inc.

THE FLOYD PRESS

Street address 1: 710 E Main St
Street address city: Floyd
Street address state: VA
Zip/Postal code: 24091-2620
General Phone: (540) 745-2127
General Fax: (540) 745-2123
Advertising Phone: (540) 745-2127
Advertising Fax: (540) 745-2123
Editorial Phone: (540) 745-2127
Editorial Fax: (540) 745-2123
General/National Adv. E-mail: bsewell@wythenews.com.com
Display Adv. E-mail: wcombs@wythenews.com
Editorial e-mail: news@floydpress.com
Primary Website: floydpress.com
Avg Paid Circ: 5200
Avg Free Circ: 63
Audit By: Sworn/Estimate/Non-Audited
Audit Date: 10.06.2019
Personnel: Samuel Cooper (Pub.); Mark Sage (Group Ed.); Wanda Combs (Ed.); Barbara Sewell (Adv. Mgr.); Kristi Griffith (Circ. Mgr.)
Parent company (for newspapers): BH Media Group

THE FRANKLIN NEWS-POST

Street address 1: 310 S Main St
Street address city: Rocky Mount
Street address state: VA
Zip/Postal code: 24151-1711
General Phone: (540) 483-5113
Advertising Phone: (540) 483-5113
Editorial Phone: (540) 483-5113
Editorial Fax: (54
General/National Adv. E-mail: classifieds@thefranklinnewspost.com
Display Adv. E-mail: classifieds@thefranklinnewspost.com
Editorial e-mail: editor@thefranklinnewspost.com
Primary Website: thefranklinnewspost.com
Year Established: 1905
Avg Paid Circ: 4500
Avg Free Circ: 6
Audit By: Sworn/Estimate/Non-Audited
Audit Date: 10.06.2019
Personnel: Patricia Heffron (Regional Circulation Office Coordinator); STEVE MARSH (SPORTS EDITOR); Mellissa Wibalda (Advertising Account Executive); Tina Angle (Advertising Account Executive); Patricia Baraty (Receptionist / Customer Service Manager)
Parent company (for newspapers): BH Media Group

THE GAZETTE-VIRGINIAN

Street address 1: 3201 Halifax Rd
Street address city: South Boston
Street address state: VA
Zip/Postal code: 24592-4907
General Phone: (434) 572-3945
General Fax: (434) 572-1173
Advertising Phone: (434) 572-3945
Advertising Fax: (434) 572-1173
Editorial Phone: (434) 572-3945
Editorial Fax: (434) 572-1173
General/National Adv. E-mail: pseat@gazettevirginian.com
Display Adv. E-mail: classifieds@gazettevirginian.com
Editorial e-mail: ahodge@gazettevirginian.com
Primary Website: yourgv.com
Avg Paid Circ: 9100
Audit By: Sworn/Estimate/Non-Audited
Audit Date: 10.06.2019
Personnel: Linda Shelton (Pub.); Ashley Conner (Ed.); Patricia Seat

THE GREENE COUNTY RECORD

Street address 1: 113 Main Street
Street address city: Stanardsville
Street address state: VA
Zip/Postal code: 22973-2970
General Phone: (434) 985-2315
General Fax: (434) 985-8356
Editorial Phone: (434) 985-2315
Display Adv. E-mail: classifieds@dailyprogress.com
Editorial e-mail: news@greene-news.com
Primary Website: dailyprogress.com
Year Established: 1895
Avg Paid Circ: 3000
Audit By: Sworn/Estimate/Non-Audited
Audit Date: 10.06.2019
Personnel: Jeff Poole (Mng. Ed.); Terrie Beigie (Reporter); Peter Yates (Pub.); Andra Landi-New (Circ.)
Parent company (for newspapers): BH Media Group

THE HOPEWELL NEWS

Street address 1: 516 E Randolph Rd
Street address city: Hopewell
Street address state: VA
Zip/Postal code: 23860-2652
General Phone: (804) 458-8511
General Fax: (804) 458-7556
Advertising Phone: (804) 458-8511
Advertising Fax: (804) 458-7556
Editorial Phone: (804) 458-8511
Editorial Fax: (804) 458-7556
General/National Adv. E-mail: advertising@hpcmedia.net
Display Adv. E-mail: classifieds@hpcmedia.net
Editorial e-mail: editor@hpcmedia.net
Primary Website: hopewellnews.com
Avg Paid Circ: 56
Avg Free Circ: 5325
Audit By: Sworn/Estimate/Non-Audited
Audit Date: 10.06.2019
Personnel: Mike Davis (Pub.); Freda Cook-Snyder (Gen. Mgr.); Pat Cook (Adv. Mgr.); Adrienne Wallace (Mng. Ed.)
Parent company (for newspapers): Lancaster Management, Inc.

THE KENBRIDGE-VICTORIA DISPATCH

Street address 1: 1404 Nottoway Boulevard
Street address city: Victoria
Street address state: VA
Zip/Postal code: 23974
General Phone: (434) 696-5550
General Fax: (434) 696-2958
General/National Adv. E-mail: jackie.newman@kenbridgevictoriadispatch.com
Primary Website: kenbridgevictoriadispatch.com
Audit By: Sworn/Estimate/Non-Audited
Audit Date: 10.06.2019
Personnel: Betty Ramsey (Pub.); Jordan Miles (Mng. Ed.); Staci Bridge (Dir. of Ops); Wanda Fix (Community Ed.); Jackie Newman (Adv. Dir.); Rhonda Finch (Circ. Dir.); Titus Mohler (Sports Ed.)

THE NEWS-GAZETTE

Street address 1: 20 W Nelson St
Street address city: Lexington
Street address state: VA
Zip/Postal code: 24450-2034
General Phone: (540) 463-3113
General Fax: (540) 463-1925
Advertising Phone: (540) 463-3113
Advertising Fax: (540) 463-1925
Editorial Phone: (540) 463-3113
Editorial Fax: (540) 463-1925
General/National Adv. E-mail: publisher@thenews-gazette.com
Display Adv. E-mail: advertising@thenews-gazette.com
Classified Adv. e-mail: classified@thenews-gazette.com
Editorial e-mail: editor@thenews-gazette.com
Primary Website: thenews-gazette.com
Mthly Avg Views: 160000
Mthly Avg Unique Visitors: 22800
Year Established: 1801
Avg Paid Circ: 5608
Avg Free Circ: 425
Audit By: USPS
Audit Date: 25.09.2022
Personnel: Tonia Watterson (Classified Adv. Dir.); Darryl Woodson (Ed.); April Mikels (Advertising Rep.); Gay Lea Goodbar (Adv. Coord.); Matthew Paxton (publisher); Jill Taylor (Circulation Manager)
Parent company (for newspapers): The News-Gazette Corp.

THE POST

Street address 1: 215 Wood Ave E
Street address city: Big Stone Gap
Street address state: VA
Zip/Postal code: 24219-2823
General Phone: (276) 523-1141
General Fax: (276) 523-1175
General/National Adv. E-mail: ktate@coalfield.com
Primary Website: thecoalfieldprogress.com
Audit By: Sworn/Estimate/Non-Audited
Audit Date: 10.06.2019
Personnel: Karen Tate (Account Exec.); Marilyn Young (Office Mgr.); Becky McElroy (Circ. Mgr.); Glen Gannaway (News Ed.); Sam Dixon (Sports Ed.)

THE PRINCE GEORGE JOURNAL

Street address 1: 111 Baker St
Street address city: Emporia
Street address state: VA
Zip/Postal code: 23847-1703
General Phone: (434) 634-4153
General Fax: (434) 634-0783
General/National Adv. E-mail: shanbury26@gmail.com
Primary Website: theprincegeorgejournal.com
Audit By: Sworn/Estimate/Non-Audited
Audit Date: 10.06.2019
Personnel: Roger Bell (Reg. Ed.); Sarah Hanbury (Adv. Mgr.)

THE RADFORD NEWS JOURNAL

Street address 1: 302 W Main St
Street address 2: Ste B
Street address city: Christiansburg
Street address state: VA
Zip/Postal code: 24073-2981
General Phone: (540) 382-6171
General Fax: (540) 382-3009
General/National Adv. E-mail: lward@ourvalley.org
Display Adv. E-mail: lward@ourvalley.org
Editorial e-mail: editor@ourvalley.org
Primary Website: ourvalley.org
Year Established: 1884
Avg Paid Circ: 3250
Audit By: Sworn/Estimate/Non-Audited
Audit Date: 10.06.2019
Personnel: Larry Ward (Adv. Mgr.); Brian Perdue (Ed.); Sam Wall (Community reporter)
Parent company (for newspapers): Mountain Media

THE SHENANDOAH VALLEY-HERALD

Street address 1: 136 W Court St
Street address city: Woodstock
Street address state: VA
Zip/Postal code: 22664-1490
General Phone: (540) 459-4078
General Fax: (540) 459-4077
Advertising Phone: (540) 459-4078
Advertising Fax: (540) 459-4077
Editorial Phone: (540) 459-4078
Editorial Fax: (540) 459-4077
General/National Adv. E-mail: editor@pagenewspaper.com
Display Adv. E-mail: svhads@dnronline.com
Editorial e-mail: editor@pagenewspaper.com
Primary Website: ShenValleyNow.com
Year Established: 1806
Avg Paid Circ: 2503
Audit By: Sworn/Estimate/Non-Audited
Audit Date: 10.06.2019
Personnel: Randy Arrington (Ed./Gen. Mgr.); Toni Allen (Advt Sales)
Parent company (for newspapers): Ogden Newspapers Inc.

THE SUSSEX-SURRY DISPATCH

Street address 1: 111 Railroad Avenue
Street address city: Wakefield
Street address state: VA
Zip/Postal code: 23888
General Phone: (757) 899-3551
General Fax: (757) 899-7312
General/National Adv. E-mail: ads@dinwiddie-monitor.com
Primary Website: sussexsurrydispatch.com
Avg Paid Circ: 6800
Audit By: Sworn/Estimate/Non-Audited
Audit Date: 10.06.2019
Personnel: Ben May (News Ed.); Evan Jones (Pub.)

THE TIDEWATER NEWS

Street address 1: 1000 Armory Dr
Street address city: Franklin
Street address state: VA
Zip/Postal code: 23851-1852
General Phone: (757) 562-3187
General Fax: (757) 562-6795
Advertising Phone: (757) 562-3187
Advertising Fax: (757) 562-6795
Editorial Phone: (757) 562-3187
Editorial Fax: (757) 562-6795
General/National Adv. E-mail: mitzi.lusk@tidewaternews.com
Display Adv. E-mail: kate.archer@tidewaternews.com
Editorial e-mail: cain.madden@tidewaternews.com
Primary Website: tidewaternews.com
Year Established: 1905
Avg Paid Circ: 5058
Avg Free Circ: 1500
Audit By: Sworn/Estimate/Non-Audited
Audit Date: 10.06.2019

Personnel: Steve Stewart (Pres./Pub.); Tony Clark (Assc. Pub.); Cain Madden (Mng. Ed.); Mitzi Lusk (Adv. Dir.); Michelle Gray (Office Mgr.)
Parent company (for newspapers): Boone Newspapers, Inc.

THE TIDEWATER REVIEW

Street address 1: 425 12th St
Street address city: West Point
Street address state: VA
Zip/Postal code: 23181
General Phone: (804) 843-2282
General Fax: (804) 843-4404
Advertising Phone: (804) 843-2282
Advertising Fax: (804) 843-4404
Editorial Phone: (804) 843-2282
Editorial Fax: (804) 843-4404
General/National Adv. E-mail: Jhaynes@tidewaterreview.com
Display Adv. E-mail: Sfrench@tidewaterreview.com
Editorial e-mail: Rlawson@tidewaterreview.com
Avg Paid Circ: 5000
Avg Free Circ: 121
Audit By: Sworn/Estimate/Non-Audited
Audit Date: 10.06.2019
Personnel: Robin Lawson (Gen. Mgr./Ed.); Jennifer Haynes (Adv. Mgr.)

THE UNION STAR

Street address 1: 241 MAIN ST
Street address city: Brookneal
Street address state: VA
Zip/Postal code: 24528
General Phone: (434) 376-2795
General Fax: (434) 376-2676
Advertising Phone: (434) 376-2795
Advertising Fax: (434) 376-2676
Editorial Phone: (434) 376-2795
Editorial Fax: (434) 376-2676
General/National Adv. E-mail: ads@altavistajournal.com
Display Adv. E-mail: ads@theunionstar.com
Editorial e-mail: news@theunionstar.com
Primary Website: theunionstar.com
Year Established: 1906
Avg Paid Circ: 2850
Avg Free Circ: 50
Audit By: Sworn/Estimate/Non-Audited
Audit Date: 10.06.2019
Parent company (for newspapers): Womack Publishing Co.

THE VALLEY BANNER

Street address 1: 157 W Spotswood Ave
Street address city: Elkton
Street address state: VA
Zip/Postal code: 22827-1118
General Phone: (540) 298-9444
General Fax: (540) 298-2560
Advertising Phone: (540) 298-9444
Advertising Fax: (540) 298-2560
Editorial Phone: (540) 298-9444
Editorial Fax: (540) 298-2560
General/National Adv. E-mail: vbads@comcast.net
Display Adv. E-mail: vbads@comcast.net
Editorial e-mail: vbnews@comcast.net
Primary Website: shenvalleynow.com
Year Established: 1966
Avg Paid Circ: 29896
Audit By: Sworn/Estimate/Non-Audited
Audit Date: 10.06.2019
Personnel: Travis Long (Ed.); Peter Yates (Gen. Mgr.); Carol Campbell (Adv. Mgr.); Tommy Bridges (Circ. Mgr.); James Deboer (Prod. Mgr.)
Parent company (for newspapers): Rockingham Publishing Co.

THE VIRGINIA GAZETTE

Street address 1: 703 Mariners Row
Street address city: Newport News
Street address state: VA
Zip/Postal code: 23606-4432
General Phone: (757) 220-1736
General Fax: (757) 220-1766
Advertising Phone: (757) 220-1736
Advertising Fax: (757) 220-1766
Editorial Phone: (757) 220-1736
Editorial Fax: (757) 220-1766
General/National Adv. E-mail: jcunnison@dailypress.com
Display Adv. E-mail: jcunnison@dailypress.com
Editorial e-mail: pbellow@vagazette.com
Primary Website: vagazette.com
Year Established: 1930
Avg Paid Circ: 14000
Audit By: Sworn/Estimate/Non-Audited
Audit Date: 10.06.2019
Personnel: Olivia Hartman (Adv. Mgr.); Jennifer Cunnison (Advertising Manager)

THE VIRGINIA MOUNTAINEER

Street address 1: 1122 Grundy Plaza Dr
Street address 2: STE 2400
Street address city: Grundy
Street address state: VA
Zip/Postal code: 24614
General Phone: (276) 935-2123
General Fax: (276) 935-2125
Advertising Phone: (276) 935-2123
Advertising Fax: (276) 935-2125
Editorial Phone: (276) 935-2123
Editorial Fax: (276) 935-2125
General/National Adv. E-mail: VirginiaMountaineer@gmail.com
Display Adv. E-mail: VirginiaMountaineer@gmail.com
Editorial e-mail: VirginiaMountaineer@gmail.com
Primary Website: virginiamountaineer.com
Year Established: 1922
Avg Paid Circ: 6300
Avg Free Circ: 100
Audit By: Sworn/Estimate/Non-Audited
Audit Date: 10.06.2019
Personnel: Sam Bartley (Pub./Ed.); Scotty Wampler (Mng. Ed.); Joe St. Clair (Gen. Mgr.)

THE WARREN SENTINEL

Street address 1: 429 N Royal Ave
Street address city: Front Royal
Street address state: VA
Zip/Postal code: 22630-2619
General Phone: (540) 635-4174
General Fax: (540) 635-7478
Advertising Phone: (540) 635-4174
Advertising Fax: (540) 635-7478
Editorial Phone: (540) 635-4174
Editorial Fax: (540) 635-7478
General/National Adv. E-mail: linda@thewarrensentinel.com
Display Adv. E-mail: heidi@thewarrensentinel.com
Editorial e-mail: kolmstead@thewarrensentinel.com
Primary Website: ShenValleyNow.com
Year Established: 1869
Avg Paid Circ: 3638
Audit By: Sworn/Estimate/Non-Audited
Audit Date: 10.06.2019
Personnel: Thomas T. Byrd (Pub.); Randy Arrington (Ed./Gen. Mgr.); Kevin Olmstead (Mng. Ed.); Heidi Anderson (Office Mgr.); Linda York (Adv. Mgr.); Todd Allen (Prod. Mgr.)
Parent company (for newspapers): Ogden Newspapers Inc.

TIMES-VIRGINIAN

Street address 1: 589 COURT ST
Street address city: Appomattox
Street address state: VA
Zip/Postal code: 24522
General Phone: (434) 352-8215
General Fax: (434) 352-2216
Advertising Phone: (434) 352-8215
Advertising Fax: (434) 352-2216
Editorial Phone: (434) 352-8215
Editorial Fax: (434) 352-2216
General/National Adv. E-mail: tvads@timesvirginian.com
Display Adv. E-mail: accounts@timesvirginian.com
Editorial e-mail: editor@timesvirginian.com
Primary Website: timesvirginian.com
Year Established: 1892
Avg Paid Circ: 4000
Avg Free Circ: 4800
Audit By: Sworn/Estimate/Non-Audited
Audit Date: 10.06.2019
Personnel: Marvin Hamlet (Ed./Gen. Mgr.); Lisa Irvin (Account Exec.); Cindy Smith (Adv. Mgr.); Chad Harrison (Pub.)
Parent company (for newspapers): Womack Publishing Co.

VIENNA/OAKTON CONNECTION

Street address 1: 1606 King St
Street address city: Alexandria
Street address state: VA
Zip/Postal code: 22314-2719
General Phone: (703) 778-9410
General Fax: (703) 778-9445
Advertising Phone: (703) 778-9444
Advertising Fax: (703) 778-9445
Editorial Phone: (703) 778-9433
Editorial Fax: (703) 778-9445
General/National Adv. E-mail: dfunk@connectionnewspapers.com
Display Adv. E-mail: sales@connectionnewspapers.com
Editorial e-mail: mkimm@connectionnewspapers.com
Primary Website: connectionnewspapers.com
Mthly Avg Views: 502543
Mthly Avg Unique Visitors: 73776
Year Established: 1988
Avg Paid Circ: 1
Avg Free Circ: 6180
Audit By: Sworn/Estimate/Non-Audited
Audit Date: 10.06.2019
Personnel: Mary Kimm (Pub./Ed.); Jerry Vernon (Exec. Vice Pres.); Debbie Funk (Adv. Dir.); Peter C. Labovitz (Pres./CEO); Linda Pecquex (Circ. Mgr); Jean Card (Prod. Mgr)
Parent company (for newspapers): Connection Publishing, Inc.

VILLAGE NEWS

Street address 1: 4709 Pwesue Street
Street address city: Chester
Street address state: VA
Zip/Postal code: 23831-1781
General Phone: (804) 751-0421
General/National Adv. E-mail: news@villagenewsonline.com
Primary Website: villagenewsonline.com
Year Established: 1998
Audit By: Sworn/Estimate/Non-Audited
Audit Date: 10.06.2019
Personnel: Linda Fausz (Pub.)

VIRGINIAN REVIEW

Street address 1: 128 N Maple Ave
Street address city: Covington
Street address state: VA
Zip/Postal code: 24426-1545
General Phone: (540) 962-2121
General Fax: (540) 962-6966
Advertising Phone: (540) 962-2121
Advertising Fax: (540) 962-6966
Editorial Phone: (540) 962-2121
Editorial Fax: (540) 962-6966
General/National Adv. E-mail: Advertising@thevirginianreview.com
Display Adv. E-mail: Classified@thevirginianreview.com
Classified Adv. e-mail: vareviewads@aol.com
Editorial e-mail: Newsroom@thevirginianreview.com
Primary Website: thevirginianreview.com
Year Established: 1914
Avg Paid Circ: 7119
Sat. Circulation Paid: 7119
Audit By: Sworn/Estimate/Non-Audited
Audit Date: 10.06.2019
Personnel: Ewell S. Beirne (Vice Pres.); Mary Ann Beirne (Adv. Dir.); Horton P. Beirne (News Ed.); Adam Crawford (Sports Ed.); David Crosier (Online Mgr.); Coite Charles Beirne (Prodn. Mgr., Pressroom)

WASHINGTON BUSINESS JOURNAL

Street address 1: 1555 Wilson Blvd
Street address 2: Ste 400
Street address city: Arlington
Street address state: VA
Zip/Postal code: 22209-2405
General Phone: (703) 258-0800
General Fax: (703) 258-0802
Advertising Phone: (703) 258-0800
Advertising Fax: (703) 258-0802
Editorial Phone: (703) 258-0820
Editorial Fax: (703) 258-0802
General/National Adv. E-mail: ssmith@bizjournals.com
Display Adv. E-mail: skaplan@bizjournals.com
Editorial e-mail: dfruehling@bizjournals.com
Primary Website: bizjournals.com/washington
Year Established: 1982
Audit By: Sworn/Estimate/Non-Audited
Audit Date: 10.06.2019
Personnel: Alex Orfinger (Pub.); Douglas Fruehling (Ed. In Chief); Robert Terry (Mng. Ed.); Sandy Smith (Adv. Dir.)

WASHINGTON COUNTY NEWS

Street address 1: 460 W Main St
Street address city: Wytheville
Street address state: VA
Zip/Postal code: 24382-2207
General Phone: (276) 628-7101
General Fax: (276) 628-1195
Advertising Phone: (276) 628-7101
Advertising Fax: (276) 628-1195
Editorial Phone: (800) 655-1406 ext. 16
Editorial Fax: (276) 628-1195
General/National Adv. E-mail: jmaxwell@bristolnews.com
Display Adv. E-mail: bsewell@wythenews.com
Editorial e-mail: jsage@wythenews.com
Primary Website: swvat.com
Avg Paid Circ: 4255
Avg Free Circ: 287
Audit By: Sworn/Estimate/Non-Audited
Audit Date: 10.06.2019
Personnel: James Maxwell (Pub.); Mark Sage (Ed.); Barbara Sewell (Adv. Mgr.); Sonny Corpus (Circ. Dir.); Hilda Foster (Production Mgr.)
Parent company (for newspapers): World Media Enterprises Inc.

WESTMORELAND NEWS

Street address 1: 15692 Kings Hwy
Street address city: Montross
Street address state: VA
Zip/Postal code: 22520
General Phone: (804) 493-8096
General Fax: (804) 493-8009
Advertising Phone: (804) 493-8096
Advertising Fax: (804) 493-8009
Editorial Phone: (804) 493-8096
Editorial Fax: (804) 493-8009
Primary Website: westmorelandnews.net
Year Established: 1948
Avg Paid Circ: 7608
Audit By: Sworn/Estimate/Non-Audited
Audit Date: 10.06.2019
Personnel: Brittiynn Powell (Ed.); Ali Foti (Adv. Rep.); Cassandra Lanier (Office Mgr.); Cathy Gerring (Pub.)
Parent company (for newspapers): Lakeway Publishers, Inc.

WYTHEVILLE ENTERPRISE

Street address 1: 460 W Main St
Street address city: Wytheville
Street address state: VA
Zip/Postal code: 24382-2207
General Phone: (276) 228-6611
General Fax: (276) 228-7260
Primary Website: swvatoday.com
Avg Paid Circ: 6700
Audit By: Sworn/Estimate/Non-Audited
Audit Date: 10.06.2019
Personnel: Mark Sage (Group Ed.); Jeff Simmons (Mng. Ed.); Curtis Hawkins (Adv. Dir.); Sonny Corpus (Circ. Dir.)
Parent company (for newspapers): BH Media Group

YORK TOWN CRIER/THE POQUOSON POST

Street address 1: 3526 George Washington Mem Hwy
Street address city: Yorktown
Street address state: VA
Zip/Postal code: 23693-3371
General Phone: (757) 766-1776
General Fax: (757) 766-1788
Advertising Phone: (757) 766-1776
Advertising Fax: (757) 766-1788
Editorial Phone: (757) 766-1776
Editorial Fax: (757) 766-1788
General/National Adv. E-mail: rob@yorktowncrier.com
Display Adv. E-mail: rob@yorktowncrier.com
Editorial e-mail: news@yorktowncrier.com
Primary Website: yorktowncrier.com

Year Established: 1978
Avg Paid Circ: 4000
Audit By: Sworn/Estimate/Non-Audited
Audit Date: 10.06.2019
Personnel: Elizabeth Meisner (Pub./Mng. Ed.); Rob Meisner (Adv. Mgr.)

WASHINGTON

ANACORTES AMERICAN

Street address 1: 901 Sixth Street
Street address city: Anacortes
Street address state: WA
Zip/Postal code: 98221
General Phone: (360) 293-3122
Advertising Phone: (360) 293-3122
Editorial Phone: (360) 293-3122 ext. 1040
General/National Adv. E-mail: ads@skagitpublishing.com
Display Adv. E-mail: classified@skagitpublishing.com
Editorial e-mail: news@goanacortes.com
Primary Website: goanacortes.com
Year Established: 1890
Avg Paid Circ: 2355
Avg Free Circ: 46
Audit By: Sworn/Estimate/Non-Audited
Audit Date: 10.06.2019
Personnel: Jack Darnton (Pub./Ed.); Colette Weeks (Ed. / Gen. Mgr); Deb Davis Bundy (Display Adv. Mgr)
Parent company (for newspapers): Adams Publishing Group, LLC; Skagit Valley Publishing Company

BAINBRIDGE ISLAND REVIEW

Street address 1: PO Box 278
Street address city: Poulsbo
Street address state: WA
Zip/Postal code: 98370-0278
General Phone: (206) 842-6613
Advertising Phone: (206) 842-6613
Editorial Phone: (206) 842-6613
General/National Adv. E-mail: tward@soundpublishing.com
Display Adv. E-mail: tward@soundpublishing.com
Editorial e-mail: bkelly@soundpublishing.com
Primary Website: bainbridgereview.com
Year Established: 1923
Avg Paid Circ: 1925
Avg Free Circ: 55
Audit By: Sworn/Estimate/Non-Audited
Audit Date: 10.06.2019
Personnel: Terry Kelly (Pub.); Brian Kelly (Ed.)
Parent company (for newspapers): Black Press Group Ltd.; Sound Publishing, Inc.

BALLARD NEWS-TRIBUNE

Street address 1: PO Box 66769
Street address city: Seattle
Street address state: WA
Zip/Postal code: 98166-0769
General Phone: (425) 238-4616
General Fax: (206) 453-5041
Advertising Phone: (206) 387-3873
Advertising Fax: (206) 453-5041
Editorial Phone: (425)-238-4616
General/National Adv. E-mail: donao@robinsonnews.com
Display Adv. E-mail: classifieds@robinsonnews.com
Editorial e-mail: kenr@robinsonnews.com
Primary Website: westsideweekly.com
Year Established: 1898
Avg Paid Circ: 10351
Audit By: Sworn/Estimate/Non-Audited
Audit Date: 10.06.2019
Personnel: Ken Robinson (Co-Pub.); Tim Robinson (Assoc. Pub.); Ken Robinson (Mng. Ed.); Dona Ozier (Adv. Mgr.)
Parent company (for newspapers): Robinson Newspapers

BASIN BUSINESS JOURNAL FARM NEWS

Street address 1: 815 W 3rd Ave
Street address city: Moses Lake
Street address state: WA
Zip/Postal code: 98837-2008
General Phone: (509) 765-8549
Advertising Phone: (509)765-8549
Editorial Phone: (509)765-8549
General/National Adv. E-mail: bbjagnews@basinbusinessjournal.com
Display Adv. E-mail: bbjagnews@basinbusinessjournal.com
Editorial e-mail: bbjagnews@basinbusinessjournal.com
Primary Website: basinbusinessjournal.com
Audit By: Sworn/Estimate/Non-Audited
Audit Date: 10.06.2019
Personnel: Judy Nelson (Pub.)
Parent company (for newspapers): Hagadone Corporation

BELLEVUE REPORTER

Street address 1: 2700 Richards Rd
Street address 2: Ste 201
Street address city: Bellevue
Street address state: WA
Zip/Postal code: 98005-4200
General Phone: (425) 453-4270
Advertising Phone: (425) 453-4623
Editorial Phone: (425) 453-4233
General/National Adv. E-mail: jgralish@bellevuereporter.com
Display Adv. E-mail: mdevere@soundpublishing.com
Editorial e-mail: editor@bellevuereporter.com
Primary Website: bellevuereporter.com
Year Established: 1930
Avg Paid Circ: 42
Avg Free Circ: 34892
Audit By: Sworn/Estimate/Non-Audited
Audit Date: 10.06.2019
Personnel: Craig Groshart (Pub./Ed.); Jen Gralish (Adv. Mgr.); Clare Ortblad (Market Develop. Admin.); Stephen Barrett (Nat'l Sales Dir.)
Parent company (for newspapers): Black Press Group Ltd.; Sound Publishing, Inc.

BELLINGHAM BUSINESS JOURNAL

Street address 1: 1909 Cornwall Ave
Street address city: Bellingham
Street address state: WA
Zip/Postal code: 98225-3659
General Phone: (360) 647-8805
General Fax: (360) 647-0502
Advertising Phone: (360) 647-8805
Advertising Fax: (360) 647-0502
Editorial Phone: (360) 647-8805
Editorial Fax: (360) 647-0502
General/National Adv. E-mail: tbouchard@bbjtoday.com
Display Adv. E-mail: sales@bbjtoday.com
Editorial e-mail: editor@bbjtoday.com
Primary Website: bbjtoday.com
Year Established: 1994
Audit By: Sworn/Estimate/Non-Audited
Audit Date: 10.06.2019
Personnel: Tony Bouchard (Adv. Mgr.); Evan Marczynski (News Ed.)
Parent company (for newspapers): Black Press Group Ltd.; Sound Publishing, Inc.

BOTHELL/KENMORE REPORTER

Street address 1: 11630 Slater Ave NE
Street address 2: Ste 9
Street address city: Kirkland
Street address state: WA
Zip/Postal code: 98034-4100
General Phone: (425) 483-3732
Advertising Phone: (425) 483-3732
Editorial Phone: (425) 483-3732 ext. 5050
General/National Adv. E-mail: sallison@soundpublishing.com
Display Adv. E-mail: sallison@soundpublishing.com
Editorial e-mail: editor@bothell-reporter.com
Primary Website: bothell-reporter.com
Avg Paid Circ: 38
Avg Free Circ: 19547
Audit By: AAM
Audit Date: 31.03.2018
Personnel: Stephen Barrett (Nat'l Sales Dir.)
Parent company (for newspapers): Black Press Group Ltd.; Sound Publishing, Inc.

CAMAS-WASHOUGAL POST RECORD

Street address 1: 425 NE 4th Ave
Street address city: Camas
Street address state: WA
Zip/Postal code: 98607-2129
General Phone: (360) 834-2141
General Fax: (360) 834-3423
Advertising Phone: (360) 735-4670
Advertising Fax: (360) 834-3423
Editorial Phone: (360) 735-4674
Editorial Fax: (360) 834-3423
General/National Adv. E-mail: heather.acheson@camaspostrecord.com
Display Adv. E-mail: shelly.atwell@camaspostrecord.com
Editorial e-mail: heather.acheson@camaspostrecord.com
Primary Website: camaspostrecord.com
Avg Paid Circ: 10000
Audit By: Sworn/Estimate/Non-Audited
Audit Date: 10.06.2019
Personnel: Mike Gallagher (Pub./Adv. Mgr.); Shelly Atwell (Circ. Mgr.); Heather Acheson (Mng. Ed.)

CASHMERE VALLEY RECORD

Street address 1: 201 Cottage Ave
Street address 2: Ste 4
Street address city: Cashmere
Street address state: WA
Zip/Postal code: 98815-1616
General Phone: (509) 782-3781
General Fax: (509) 782-9074
Advertising Phone: (509) 548-5286
Advertising Fax: (509) 548-4789
Editorial Phone: (509) 782-3781
Editorial Fax: (509) 782-9074
General/National Adv. E-mail: carol@leavenworthecho.com
Display Adv. E-mail: classifieds@leavenworthecho.com
Editorial e-mail: reporter@cashmerevalleyrecord.com
Primary Website: cashmerevalleyrecord.com
Mthly Avg Views: 7741
Mthly Avg Unique Visitors: 6834
Year Established: 1905
Avg Paid Circ: 1000
Audit By: Sworn/Estimate/Non-Audited
Audit Date: 10.06.2019
Personnel: Bill Forhan (CEO/Pub.); Carol Forhan (Adv. Mgr.)
Parent company (for newspapers): NCW Media, Inc.

CENTRAL KITSAP REPORTER

Street address 1: 19351 8th Ave NE
Street address 2: Ste 205
Street address city: Poulsbo
Street address state: WA
Zip/Postal code: 98370-8710
General Phone: (360) 308-9161
General Fax: (360) 308-9363
Advertising Phone: (360) 308-9161
Advertising Fax: (360) 308-9363
Editorial Phone: (360) 308-9161 ext. 5050
Editorial Fax: (360) 308-9363
General/National Adv. E-mail: smcdonald@soundpublishing.com
Display Adv. E-mail: rnicholson@soundpublishing.com
Editorial e-mail: editor@soundpublishing.com
Primary Website: kitsapdailynews.com
Avg Paid Circ: 271
Avg Free Circ: 14487
Audit By: AAM
Audit Date: 31.03.2018
Personnel: Terry Ward; Robert Monteith (Reg. Ed.)
Parent company (for newspapers): Black Press Group Ltd.; Sound Publishing, Inc.

CHENEY FREE PRESS

Street address 1: 1616 W 1st St
Street address city: Cheney
Street address state: WA
Zip/Postal code: 99004-8800
General Phone: (509) 235-6184
General Fax: (509) 235-2887
Advertising Phone: (509) 235-6184
Advertising Fax: (509) 235-2887
Editorial Phone: (509) 235-6184
Editorial Fax: (509) 235-2887
General/National Adv. E-mail: info@cheneyfreepress.com
Display Adv. E-mail: info@cheneyfreepress.com
Editorial e-mail: info@cheneyfreepress.com
Primary Website: cheneyfreepress.com
Year Established: 1896
Audit By: Sworn/Estimate/Non-Audited
Audit Date: 10.06.2019
Personnel: William Ifft (Pub./Ed.)

CHINOOK OBSERVER

Street address 1: 205 Bolstad Ave E
Street address 2: Ste 2
Street address city: Long Beach
Street address state: WA
Zip/Postal code: 98631-9200
General Phone: (360) 642-8181
General Fax: (360) 642-8105
Advertising Phone: (360) 642-8181
Advertising Fax: (360) 642-8105
Editorial Phone: (360) 642-8181
Editorial Fax: (360) 642-8105
General/National Adv. E-mail: advertising@chinookobserver.com
Display Adv. E-mail: classifieds@chinookobserver.com
Editorial e-mail: mwinters@chinookobserver.com
Primary Website: chinookobserver.com
Year Established: 1900
Avg Paid Circ: 6800
Audit By: Sworn/Estimate/Non-Audited
Audit Date: 10.06.2019
Personnel: Matt Winters (Pub./Ed.); Andrew Renwick (Adv. Mgr.); Marlene Quillin (Office Mgr.)
Parent company (for newspapers): EO Media Group

CITY LIVING SEATTLE

Street address 1: 636 S Alaska St
Street address city: Seattle
Street address state: WA
Zip/Postal code: 98108-1727
General Phone: (206) 461-1300
Advertising Phone: (206) 461-1322
Editorial Phone: (206) 461-1346
General/National Adv. E-mail: ppcadmanager@nwlink.com
Display Adv. E-mail: class1@nwlink.com
Editorial e-mail: CityLivingEditor@nwlink.com
Primary Website: citylivingseattle.com
Avg Paid Circ: 3500
Avg Free Circ: 18000
Audit By: Sworn/Estimate/Non-Audited
Audit Date: 10.06.2019
Personnel: Vera Chan-Pool (Ed.); Terry Fain (Adv. Mgr.)
Parent company (for newspapers): Pacific Publishing Company

COLUMBIA BASIN HERALD/ HAGADONE MEDIA WASHINGTON

Street address 1: 813 West Third Ave
Street address city: Moses Lake
Street address state: WA
Zip/Postal code: 98837
General Phone: 509-765-4561
General Fax: 509-765-8659
Advertising Phone: 509-765-4561
Advertising Fax: 509-765-8659
Editorial Phone: 509-765-4561
Editorial Fax: 509-765-8659
Display Adv. E-mail: jrountree@columbiabasinherald.com
Classified Adv. e-mail: lherbert@columbiabasinherald.com
Editorial e-mail: editor@columbiabasinherald.com
Primary Website: columbiabasinherald.com
Mthly Avg Views: 285000
Mthly Avg Unique Visitors: 90000
Year Established: 1941
Avg Paid Circ: 3500
Avg Free Circ: 2000
Audit By: Sworn/Estimate/Non-Audited
Audit Date: 12.[illegible]
Personnel: Denise Lembcke (Bus. Mgr.); Caralyn Bess (Regional Publisher); Joyce McLanahan (Nat'l Adv. Mgr.); Dave Burgess (Managing Editor); Curt Weaver (Prodn. Supt.); Bob Richardson (Advertising Director Columbia Basin Herald/Publisher Basin

Business Journal); Dana Moreno (Marketing/ Audience Development Director); Rosalie Black (Sales Manager); Emily Thornton (Assistant Managing Editor); Tom Hinde (Circ. Dir.); Bill Stevenson (Mng. Ed.); Karyll Van Ness (Circulation District Manager); Sheri Jones (HR/Business Manager)
Parent company (for newspapers): Hagadone Corporation; Hagadone Media

COVINGTON-MAPLE VALLEY-BLACK DIAMOND REPORTER

Street address 1: 19426 68th Ave S
Street address city: Kent
Street address state: WA
Zip/Postal code: 98032-1193
General Phone: (425) 432-1209
Advertising Phone: (425) 432-1209
Editorial Phone: (425) 432-1209 ext. 5050
Editorial e-mail: ahobbs@soundpublishing.com
Primary Website: maplevalleyreporter.com
Year Established: 2005
Avg Paid Circ: 11
Avg Free Circ: 24024
Audit By: AAM
Audit Date: 31.03.2018
Personnel: Polly Shepherd (Pub.); Andy Hobbs (Ed.); Sarah Brenden (Editor); Natalie Routh (Advertising Manager)
Parent company (for newspapers): Sound Publishing, Inc.

DAVENPORT TIMES

Street address 1: 506 Morgan St
Street address city: Davenport
Street address state: WA
Zip/Postal code: 99122-5213
General Phone: (509) 725-0101
General Fax: (509) 725-0009
Advertising Phone: (509) 725-0101
Advertising Fax: (509) 725-0009
Editorial Phone: (509) 725-0101
Editorial Fax: (509) 725-0009
General/National Adv. E-mail: davenporttimes@centurytel.net
Display Adv. E-mail: davenporttimes@centurytel.net
Editorial e-mail: davenporttimes@centurytel.net
Avg Paid Circ: 2200
Audit By: Sworn/Estimate/Non-Audited
Audit Date: 10.06.2019
Personnel: Bill Ifft (Pub.); Marcia Smith (Adv. Mgr.); Mark Smith (Ed.)

DAYTON CHRONICLE

Street address 1: 163 E Main St
Street address city: Dayton
Street address state: WA
Zip/Postal code: 99328-1350
General Phone: (509) 382-2221
General Fax: (509) 382-1546
Advertising Phone: (509) 382-2221
Advertising Fax: (509) 382-1546
Editorial Phone: (509) 382-2221
Editorial Fax: (509) 382-1546
General/National Adv. E-mail: daytonchronicle@hotmail.com
Display Adv. E-mail: daytonchronicle@hotmail.com
Editorial e-mail: daytonchronicle@hotmail.com
Year Established: 1878
Avg Paid Circ: 1700
Audit By: Sworn/Estimate/Non-Audited
Audit Date: 10.06.2019
Personnel: Jack Williams (Pub./Ed.)

DEER PARK TRIBUNE

Street address 1: 104 N Main St
Street address city: Deer Park
Street address state: WA
Zip/Postal code: 99006-5086
General Phone: (509) 276-5043
General Fax: (509) 276-2041
Advertising Phone: (509) 276-5043
Advertising Fax: (509) 276-2041
Editorial Phone: (509) 276-5043
Editorial Fax: (509) 276-2041
General/National Adv. E-mail: sales@dptribune.com
Display Adv. E-mail: classifieds@dptribune.com
Editorial e-mail: tom@dptribune.com
Primary Website: dptribune.biz
Year Established: 1906
Audit By: Sworn/Estimate/Non-Audited
Audit Date: 10.06.2019
Personnel: Thomas Costigan (Pub./Ed.); Theresa Douvia (Gen. Mgr.); Jeanne Flugel (Adv. Mgr.)
Parent company (for newspapers): Horizon Publications Inc.

DOUGLAS COUNTY EMPIRE PRESS

Street address 1: 2290 Grand Ave
Street address city: East Wenatchee
Street address state: WA
Zip/Postal code: 98802-8253
General Phone: (509) 886-8668
General Fax: (509) 665-1183
Advertising Phone: (509) 886-8668
Advertising Fax: (509) 665-1183
Editorial Phone: (509) 886-8668
Editorial Fax: (509) 665-1183
General/National Adv. E-mail: weekly@empire-press.com
Display Adv. E-mail: legals@empire-press.com
Editorial e-mail: weekly@empire-press.com
Primary Website: empire-press.com
Year Established: 1888
Avg Paid Circ: 925
Avg Free Circ: 10
Audit By: Sworn/Estimate/Non-Audited
Audit Date: 10.06.2019
Personnel: Joe Pitt (Pub.); Linda Barta (Ed.)

EAST WASHINGTONIAN

Street address 1: 742 Main St
Street address city: Pomeroy
Street address state: WA
Zip/Postal code: 99347
General Phone: (509) 843-1313
General Fax: (509) 843-3911
Advertising Phone: (509) 843-1313
Advertising Fax: (509) 843-3911
Editorial Phone: (509) 843-1313
Editorial Fax: (509) 843-3911
General/National Adv. E-mail: e-dub@pomeroy-wa.com
Display Adv. E-mail: e-dub@pomeroy-wa.com
Editorial e-mail: e-dub@pomeroy-wa.com
Year Established: 1882
Audit By: Sworn/Estimate/Non-Audited
Audit Date: 10.06.2019
Personnel: Mike Tom (Pub./Ed.)

EDMONDS BEACON

Street address 1: 728 3rd Street
Street address 2: Suite D
Street address city: Mukilteo
Street address state: WA
Zip/Postal code: 98275-1628
General Phone: (425) 347-5634
General Fax: (425) 347-6077
Advertising Phone: (425) 347-5634
Advertising Fax: (425) 347-6077
Editorial Phone: (425) 347-5634
Editorial Fax: (425) 347-6077
General/National Adv. E-mail: gm@yourbeacon.net
Display Adv. E-mail: edmondssales@yourbeacon.net
Classified Adv. e-mail: classifieds@yourbeacon.net
Editorial e-mail: edmondseditor@yourbeacon.net
Primary Website: edmondsbeacon.com
Mthly Avg Views: 30000
Year Established: 1986
Avg Paid Circ: 2100
Avg Free Circ: 200
Audit By: Sworn/Estimate/Non-Audited
Audit Date: 10.06.2019
Personnel: Paul Archipley (Pub./Ed.); Archipley Paul (Publisher); Barker Jenn (General Manager); Linda Chittim (Adv. Dir.); Carol Norton (Circ. Mgr.)
Parent company (for newspapers): Beacon Publishing Inc.

EVERETT NEW TRIBUNE

Street address 1: 127 Avenue C
Street address 2: Ste B
Street address city: Snohomish
Street address state: WA
Zip/Postal code: 98290-2768
General Phone: (360) 568-4121
General Fax: (360) 568-1484
Advertising Phone: (360) 568-4121
Advertising Fax: (360) 568-1484
Editorial Phone: (360) 568-4121
Editorial Fax: (360) 568-1484
General/National Adv. E-mail: becky@snoho.com
Display Adv. E-mail: classad.tribune@snoho.com
Editorial e-mail: editor.tribune@snoho.com
Primary Website: snoho.com
Year Established: 1892
Avg Paid Circ: 15000
Avg Free Circ: 3500
Audit By: Sworn/Estimate/Non-Audited
Audit Date: 10.06.2019
Personnel: Becky Reed (Pub. / Adv. Mgr.); Michael Whitney (Editor)

FEDERAL WAY MIRROR

Street address 1: 31919 1st Ave S
Street address 2: Ste. 101
Street address city: Federal Way
Street address state: WA
Zip/Postal code: 98003-5258
General Phone: (253) 925-5565
General Fax: (253) 925-5750
Editorial Phone: (253) 925-5565 ext. 5050
General/National Adv. E-mail: publisher@federalwaymirror.com
Display Adv. E-mail: janderson@federalwaymirror.com
Editorial e-mail: editor@fedwaymirror.com
Primary Website: federalwaymirror.com
Year Established: 1998
Avg Paid Circ: 918
Avg Free Circ: 27964
Audit By: AAM
Audit Date: 31.03.2018
Personnel: Carrie Rodriguez (Ed.); Andy Hobbs (Ed.)
Parent company (for newspapers): Black Press Group Ltd.; Sound Publishing, Inc.

FEDERAL WAY NEWS

Street address 1: 14006 1st Ave S
Street address 2: Ste B
Street address city: Burien
Street address state: WA
Zip/Postal code: 98168-3402
General Phone: (206) 708-1378
General Fax: (206) 453-5041
Advertising Phone: (206) 387-3873
Editorial Phone: (425)-238-4616
General/National Adv. E-mail: donao@robinsonnews.com
Display Adv. E-mail: classifieds@robinsonnews.com
Editorial e-mail: kenr@robinsonnews.com
Primary Website: federalwaynews.net
Year Established: 1953
Audit By: Sworn/Estimate/Non-Audited
Audit Date: 10.06.2019
Personnel: Tim Robinson (Assoc. Pub.); Ken Robinson (Mng. Ed.); Dona Ozier (Adv. Mgr.)
Parent company (for newspapers): Robinson Newspapers

FERNDALE RECORD

Street address 1: 2008 B Main St
Street address city: Ferndale
Street address state: WA
Zip/Postal code: 98248-9468
General Phone: (360) 384-1411
General Fax: (360) 384-1417
General/National Adv. E-mail: jan@ferndalerecord.com
Display Adv. E-mail: jan@ferndalerecord.com
Editorial e-mail: news@ferndalerecord.com
Primary Website: ferndalerecord.com
Year Established: 1885
Avg Paid Circ: 1000
Avg Free Circ: 4700
Audit By: Sworn/Estimate/Non-Audited
Audit Date: 10.06.2019
Personnel: Brent Lindquist (News Editor); Jan Brown (Adv. Mgr.); Ashley Hiruko (Reporter, Social Media editor)
Parent company (for newspapers): Lewis Publishing Co., Inc.

FORKS FORUM

Street address 1: 490 S Forks Ave
Street address city: Forks
Street address state: WA
Zip/Postal code: 98331-9155
General Phone: (360) 374-3311
General Fax: (360) 374-5739
Advertising Phone: (360) 374-3311
Advertising Fax: (360) 374-5739
Editorial Phone: (360) 374-3311
Editorial Fax: (360) 374-5739
General/National Adv. E-mail: cbaron@soundpublishing.com
Display Adv. E-mail: cbaron@soundpublishing.com
Editorial e-mail: cbaron@soundpublishing.com
Primary Website: forksforum.com
Year Established: 1930
Avg Paid Circ: 157
Avg Free Circ: 4287
Audit By: AAM
Audit Date: 31.03.2018
Personnel: Christi Baron (Ed.)
Parent company (for newspapers): Black Press Group Ltd.; Sound Publishing, Inc.

GAUGER MEDIA SERVICE, INC.

Street address 1: 1034 Bradford Street
Street address 2: P.O. Box 627
Street address city: Raymond
Street address state: WA
Zip/Postal code: 98577
General Phone: (360) 942-2661
General/National Adv. E-mail: dave@gaugermedia.com
Personnel: Dave Gauger (Now Retired)

GOLDENDALE SENTINEL

Street address 1: 117 W Main St
Street address city: Goldendale
Street address state: WA
Zip/Postal code: 98620-9526
General Phone: (509) 773-3777
Advertising Phone: (509) 773-3777
Editorial Phone: (509) 773-3777
General/National Adv. E-mail: info@goldendalesentinel.com
Display Adv. E-mail: ads@goldendalesentinel.com
Classified Adv. e-mail: classifieds@goldendalesentinel.com
Editorial e-mail: news@goldendalesentinel.com
Primary Website: goldendalesentinel.com
Mthly Avg Views: 34000
Mthly Avg Unique Visitors: 20000
Year Established: 1879
Avg Paid Circ: 3200
Audit By: Sworn/Estimate/Non-Audited
Audit Date: 10.06.2024
Personnel: Lou Marzeles (Ed./Pub.); Naomi James (Ads/ Bookkeeping); Brendan Relaford (Ad Sales Rep); Paul Gourley (Billing Specialist)
Parent company (for newspapers): Tartan Publications, Inc.

HIGHLINE TIMES

Street address 1: 14006 1st Ave S
Street address 2: Ste B
Street address city: Burien
Street address state: WA
Zip/Postal code: 98168-3402
General Phone: (425) 238-4616
General Fax: (206) 453-5041
Advertising Phone: (206) 387-3873
Advertising Fax: (206) 453-5041
Editorial Phone: (425)-238-4616
Editorial Fax: (206) 453-5041
General/National Adv. E-mail: donao@robinsonnews.com
Display Adv. E-mail: classifieds@robinsonnews.com
Editorial e-mail: kenr@robinsonnews.com
Primary Website: highlinetimes.com
Year Established: 1945
Avg Paid Circ: 15000
Audit By: Sworn/Estimate/Non-Audited
Audit Date: 10.06.2019
Personnel: Jerry Robinson (Pub.); Tim Robinson (Assoc. Pub.); Ken Robinson (Mng. Ed.); Dona Ozier (Adv. Mgr.)
Parent company (for newspapers): Robinson Newspapers

ISSAQUAH/SAMMAMISH REPORTER

Street address 1: 2700 Richards Rd
Street address 2: Ste 201

Street address city: Bellevue
Street address state: WA
Zip/Postal code: 98005-4200
General Phone: (425) 391-0363
Advertising Phone: (425) 391-0363
Editorial Phone: (425) 391-0363
General/National Adv. E-mail: scravens@issaquahreporter.com
Display Adv. E-mail: jsuman@bellevuereporter.com
Editorial e-mail: cgroshart@issaquahreporter.com
Primary Website: issaquah-reporter.com
Avg Paid Circ: 50
Avg Free Circ: 24020
Audit By: AAM
Audit Date: 31.03.2018
Personnel: William Shaw (Pub.); Craig Groshart (Ed.); Sally Cravens (Adv. Mgr.); Stephen Barrett (Nat'l Sales Dir.)
Parent company (for newspapers): Black Press Group Ltd.; Sound Publishing, Inc.

KENT REPORTER

Street address 1: 19426 68th Ave S
Street address 2: Ste A
Street address city: Kent
Street address state: WA
Zip/Postal code: 98032-1193
General Phone: (253) 872-6600
Advertising Phone: (253) 833-0218
Editorial Phone: (253) 872-6600
General/National Adv. E-mail: khenry@auburn-reporter.com
Display Adv. E-mail: dblood@auburn-reporter.com
Editorial e-mail: mklaas@auburn-reporter.com
Primary Website: auburn-reporter.com
Year Established: 1998
Avg Paid Circ: 168
Avg Free Circ: 24660
Audit By: AAM
Audit Date: 31.03.2018
Personnel: Mark Klaas (Reg. Ed.)
Parent company (for newspapers): Sound Publishing, Inc.

KINGSTON COMMUNITY NEWS

Street address 1: PO Box 278
Street address city: Poulsbo
Street address state: WA
Zip/Postal code: 98370-0278
General Phone: (360) 779-4464
Advertising Phone: (360) 779-4464
Editorial Phone: (360) 779-4464
General/National Adv. E-mail: publisher@kingstoncommunitynews.com
Display Adv. E-mail: publisher@kingstoncommunitynews.com
Editorial e-mail: rwalker@northkitsapherald.com
Primary Website: kitsapdailynews.com
Avg Free Circ: 8988
Audit By: AAM
Audit Date: 31.03.2018
Personnel: Donna Etchey (Pub.); Richard Walker (Ed.); Stephen Barrett (Nat'l Sales Dir.)
Parent company (for newspapers): Sound Publishing, Inc.

KIRKLAND REPORTER

Street address 1: 11630 Slater Ave NE
Street address 2: Ste 8-9
Street address city: Kirkland
Street address state: WA
Zip/Postal code: 98034-4100
General Phone: (425) 822-9166
Advertising Phone: (425) 822-9166
Editorial Phone: (425) 822-9166
General/National Adv. E-mail: pbrown@kirklandreporter.com
Display Adv. E-mail: pbrown@kirklandreporter.com
Editorial e-mail: editor@kirklandreporter.com
Primary Website: kirklandreporter.com
Year Established: 1978
Avg Paid Circ: 24
Avg Free Circ: 24676
Audit By: AAM
Audit Date: 31.03.2018
Personnel: Stephen Barrett (Nat'l Sales Dir.)
Parent company (for newspapers): Black Press Group Ltd.; Sound Publishing, Inc.

LA CONNER WEEKLY NEWS

Street address 1: 119 N 3rd Street
Street address city: La Conner
Street address state: WA
Zip/Postal code: 98257
General Phone: (360) 466-3315
Advertising Phone: (360) 466-3315
Editorial Phone: (360) 466-3315
General/National Adv. E-mail: editor@laconnernews.com
Display Adv. E-mail: editor@laconnernews.com
Classified Adv. e-mail: editor@laconnernews.com
Editorial e-mail: news@laconnernews.com
Primary Website: laconnerweeklynews.com
Mthly Avg Views: 5000
Mthly Avg Unique Visitors: 4800
Year Established: 2006
Avg Paid Circ: 900
Avg Free Circ: 25
Audit By: Sworn/Estimate/Non-Audited
Audit Date: 04.10.2023
Personnel: Kenneth Stern (Publisher and Editor); Kenneth Stern (Publisher and Editor); Sandy Stokes (Co-Pub./ Ed.); Cindy Vest (Gen. Mgr./Co-Pub.)
Parent company (for newspapers): La Conner News Publishing LLC

LAKE CHELAN MIRROR

Street address 1: 310 E Johnson Ave
Street address city: Chelan
Street address state: WA
Zip/Postal code: 98816
General Phone: (509) 682-2213
General Fax: (509) 682-4209
Advertising Phone: (509) 548-5286
Advertising Fax: (509) 548-4789
Editorial Phone: (509) 682-2213
Editorial Fax: (509) 682-4209
General/National Adv. E-mail: carol@leavenworthecho.com
Display Adv. E-mail: classifieds@leavenworthecho.com
Editorial e-mail: editor@lakechelanmirror.com
Primary Website: lakechelanmirror.com
Year Established: 1891
Avg Paid Circ: 1800
Audit By: Sworn/Estimate/Non-Audited
Audit Date: 10.06.2019
Personnel: Bill Forhan (Publisher/CEO); Carol Forhan (VP, Advertising Director)
Parent company (for newspapers): NCW Media, Inc.

LIBERTY LAKE SPLASH

Street address 1: 2310 N Molter Rd
Street address 2: Ste 305
Street address city: Liberty Lake
Street address state: WA
Zip/Postal code: 99019-8630
General Phone: (509) 242-7752
General Fax: (509) 927-2190
Advertising Phone: (509) 242-7752
Advertising Fax: (509) 927-2190
Editorial Phone: (509) 242-7752
Editorial Fax: (509) 927-2190
General/National Adv. E-mail: advertise@libertylakesplash.com
Display Adv. E-mail: josh@libertylakesplash.com
Editorial e-mail: editor@libertylakesplash.com
Primary Website: libertylakesplash.com
Year Established: 1999
Avg Paid Circ: 100
Avg Free Circ: 6900
Audit By: Sworn/Estimate/Non-Audited
Audit Date: 10.06.2019
Personnel: Josh Johnson (Pub./Ed.); Tammy Kimberley (Gen. Mgr.)

LYNDEN TRIBUNE

Street address 1: 113 6th St
Street address city: Lynden
Street address state: WA
Zip/Postal code: 98264-1901
General Phone: (360) 354-4444
General Fax: (360) 354-4445
General/National Adv. E-mail: mitze@lyndentribune.com
Display Adv. E-mail: mitze@lyndentribune.com
Editorial e-mail: editor@lyndentribune.com
Primary Website: lyndentribune.com
Mthly Avg Views: 34450
Mthly Avg Unique Visitors: 5100
Year Established: 1888
Avg Paid Circ: 4200
Audit By: Sworn/Estimate/Non-Audited
Audit Date: 01.10.2023
Personnel: Michael D. Lewis (Publisher); Mary Jo Lewis (Adv. Dir.); Mitze Kester (Adv. Mgr.); Bill Helm (Editor); Sharon O'Shaughnessy (Circulation); Carol Griffin (Controller); Calvin Bratt (Ed.); Brent Lindquist (Assistant Ed.); Karina Vance (Circulation Mgr); Ashley Hiruko (Reporter); Eric Trent (Sports Editor)
Parent company (for newspapers): Lewis Publishing Co., Inc.

MERCER ISLAND REPORTER

Street address 1: 11630 Slater Ave. N.E.
Street address 2: Suite 8/9
Street address city: Kirkland
Street address state: WA
Zip/Postal code: 98034
General Phone: (206) 232-1215
Editorial e-mail: spak@soundpublishing.com
Primary Website: mi-reporter.com
Year Established: 1947
Avg Paid Circ: 2613
Avg Free Circ: 0
Audit By: AAM
Audit Date: 31.03.2018
Personnel: Corey Morris (Reg. Ed.); Samantha Pak (Sr. Ed.); Andy Nystrom (Sports Ed.)
Parent company (for newspapers): Black Press Group Ltd.; Sound Publishing, Inc.

METHOW VALLEY NEWS

Street address 1: 502 Glover St S
Street address city: Twisp
Street address state: WA
Zip/Postal code: 98856-5818
General Phone: (509) 997-7011
General Fax: (509) 997-3277
Advertising Phone: (509) 997-7011
Advertising Fax: (509) 997-3277
Editorial Phone: (509) 997-7011
Editorial Fax: (509) 997-3277
General/National Adv. E-mail: sales@methowvalleynews.com
Display Adv. E-mail: advertising@methowvalleynews.com
Editorial e-mail: editor@methowvalleynews.com
Primary Website: methowvalleynews.com
Year Established: 1903
Avg Paid Circ: 3000
Avg Free Circ: 35
Audit By: Sworn/Estimate/Non-Audited
Audit Date: 10.06.2019
Personnel: Don Nelson (Pub./Ed.)
Parent company (for newspapers): MVN Publishing LLC

MUKILTEO BEACON

Street address 1: 806 5th St
Street address city: Mukilteo
Street address state: WA
Zip/Postal code: 98275-1628
General Phone: (425) 347-5634
General Fax: (425) 347-6077
Advertising Phone: (425) 347-5634
Advertising Fax: (425) 347-6077
Editorial Phone: (425) 347-5634
Editorial Fax: (425) 347-6077
General/National Adv. E-mail: mukilteosales@yourbeacon.net
Display Adv. E-mail: classifieds@yourbeacon.net
Editorial e-mail: mukilteoeditor@yourbeacon.net
Primary Website: mukilteobeacon.com
Year Established: 1991
Avg Paid Circ: 166
Avg Free Circ: 10000
Audit By: Sworn/Estimate/Non-Audited
Audit Date: 10.06.2019
Personnel: Paul Archipley (Pub.); Linda Chittim (Gen. Mgr.); Sara Bruestle (Ed.); Doug Kimball (Adv. Mgr.); Doug Warren (Graphics); Carol Norton (Circ. Mgr.)
Parent company (for newspapers): Beacon Publishing Inc.

NEWCASTLE NEWS

Street address 1: PO Box 1328
Street address city: Issaquah
Street address state: WA
Zip/Postal code: 98027-0053
General Phone: (425) 392-6434
General Fax: (425) 392-1695
Advertising Phone: (425) 392-6434
Advertising Fax: (425) 392-1695
Editorial Phone: (425) 392-6434
Editorial Fax: (425) 392-1695
General/National Adv. E-mail: admanager@isspress.com
Display Adv. E-mail: classifieds@isspress.com
Editorial e-mail: news@isspress.com
Primary Website: newcastle-news.com
Year Established: 1999
Avg Paid Circ: 46
Avg Free Circ: 5778
Audit By: Sworn/Estimate/Non-Audited
Audit Date: 10.06.2019
Personnel: Scott Stoddard (Editor)

NEWPORT MINER

Street address 1: 421 S. Spokane Ave
Street address city: Newport
Street address state: WA
Zip/Postal code: 99156-7039
General Phone: (509) 447-2433
General Fax: (509) 447-9222
General/National Adv. E-mail: minernews@povn.com
Display Adv. E-mail: mineradvertising@povn.com
Classified Adv. e-mail: minerclassifieds@povn.com
Editorial e-mail: minernews@povn.com
Primary Website: pendoreillerivervalley.com
Year Established: 1891
Avg Paid Circ: 6000
Avg Free Circ: 11000
Audit By: Sworn/Estimate/Non-Audited
Audit Date: 10.06.2019
Personnel: J. Lindsay Guscott (Adv. Mgr.); Don Gronning (Editor); Michelle Nedved (Pub.); Susan Willenbrock (Circ. Mgr.)

NISQUALLY VALLEY NEWS

Street address 1: 106 Plaza Dr SE
Street address city: Yelm
Street address state: WA
Zip/Postal code: 98597-8841
General Phone: (360) 458-2681
General Fax: (360) 458-5741
Advertising Phone: (360) 458-2681
Advertising Fax: (360) 458-5741
Editorial Phone: (360) 458-2681
Editorial Fax: (360) 458-5741
General/National Adv. E-mail: advertise@yelmonline.com
Display Adv. E-mail: class2@yelmonline.com
Editorial e-mail: mwagar@yelmonline.com
Primary Website: yelmonline.com
Year Established: 1922
Avg Paid Circ: 4000
Audit By: Sworn/Estimate/Non-Audited
Audit Date: 10.06.2019
Personnel: Michael Wagar (Pub./Ed.); Tyler Huey (Assistant Ed.); Angie Evans (Adv. Mgr.); Kim Proffit (Office Mgr.); Keven R. Graves (Pub./Ed.); Nicole Kiourkas (Production Lead)
Parent company (for newspapers): CT Publishing

NORTH COAST NEWS

Street address 1: 668 Ocean Shores Blvd NW
Street address city: Ocean Shores
Street address state: WA
Zip/Postal code: 98569-9346
General Phone: (360) 289-2441
Advertising Phone: (360) 537-3955
Editorial Phone: (360) 289-3968
General/National Adv. E-mail: editor@northcoastnews.com
Display Adv. E-mail: editor@northcoastnews.com
Editorial e-mail: editor@northcoastnews.com
Primary Website: northcoastnews.com
Year Established: 1989
Avg Paid Circ: 1224

Avg Free Circ: 21
Audit By: Sworn/Estimate/Non-Audited
Audit Date: 10.06.2019
Personnel: Angelo Bruscas (Pub./Ed.); Stanley Woody (Publisher)

NORTH COUNTY OUTLOOK

Street address 1: 1331 State Ave
Street address 2: Ste A
Street address city: Marysville
Street address state: WA
Zip/Postal code: 98270-3604
General Phone: (360) 659-1100
General Fax: (360) 658-7536
General/National Adv. E-mail: sue@northcountyoutlook.com
Display Adv. E-mail: sales@northcountyoutlook.com
Editorial e-mail: editor@northcountyoutlook.com
Primary Website: northcountyoutlook.com
Year Established: 2007
Avg Free Circ: 21337
Audit By: Sworn/Estimate/Non-Audited
Audit Date: 10.06.2019
Personnel: Sue Stevenson (Co-Pub./Adv. Mgr.)

NORTH KITSAP HERALD

Street address 1: 19351 8th Ave NE
Street address 2: Ste 205
Street address city: Poulsbo
Street address state: WA
Zip/Postal code: 98370-8710
General Phone: (360) 779-4464
General Fax: (360) 779-8276
Advertising Phone: (360) 779-4464
Advertising Fax: (360) 779-8276
Editorial Phone: (360) 779-4464
Editorial Fax: (360) 779-8276
General/National Adv. E-mail: publisher@northkitsapherald.com
Display Adv. E-mail: rwalker@northkitsapherald.com
Editorial e-mail: editor@northkitsapherald.com
Primary Website: kitsapdailynews.com
Year Established: 1901
Avg Paid Circ: 509
Avg Free Circ: 10565
Audit By: AAM
Audit Date: 31.03.2018
Personnel: Donna Etchey (Pub.); Richard Walker (Ed.); Christy Dano (Circ. Mgr.); Stephen Barrett (Nat'l Sales Dir.)
Parent company (for newspapers): Sound Publishing, Inc.

NORTHERN KITTITAS COUNTY TRIBUNE

Street address 1: 807 W Davis St
Street address 2: Ste A101
Street address city: Cle Elum
Street address state: WA
Zip/Postal code: 98922-1027
General Phone: (509) 674-2511
General Fax: (509) 674-5571
General/National Adv. E-mail: ads@nkctribune.com
Editorial e-mail: tribune@nkctribune.com
Primary Website: nkctribune.com
Year Established: 1953
Avg Paid Circ: 2300
Audit By: Sworn/Estimate/Non-Audited
Audit Date: 30.05.2024
Personnel: Jana Stoner (Pub./Ed.); Terry Hamberg (Pub.)
Parent company (for newspapers): Oahe Publishing Corporation

OKANOGAN VALLEY GAZETTE-TRIBUNE

Street address 1: 1422 Main St
Street address city: Oroville
Street address state: WA
Zip/Postal code: 98844-9385
General Phone: (509) 476-3602
General Fax: (509) 476-3602
Advertising Phone: (509) 476-3054
Advertising Fax: (509) 476-3602
Editorial Phone: (509) 476-3054
Editorial Fax: (509) 476-3602
General/National Adv. E-mail: gary@gazette-tribune.com
Display Adv. E-mail: gary@gazette-tribune.com
Editorial e-mail: editor@gazette-tribune.com
Primary Website: gazette-tribune.com
Year Established: 1905
Avg Paid Circ: 1309
Audit By: AAM
Audit Date: 31.03.2018
Personnel: Gary DeVon (Pub./Ed.); Brent Baker (Reporter); Stephen Barrett (Nat'l Sales Dir.)
Parent company (for newspapers): Black Press Group Ltd.; Sound Publishing, Inc.

OMAK-OKANOGAN COUNTY CHRONICLE

Street address 1: PO Box 553
Street address city: Omak
Street address state: WA
Zip/Postal code: 98841-0553
General Phone: (509) 826-1110
General Fax: (509) 826-5819
Advertising Phone: (509)826-1110
Advertising Fax: (509)826-5819
Editorial Phone: (509)826-1110
Editorial Fax: (509)826-5819
General/National Adv. E-mail: ads@omakchronicle.com
Display Adv. E-mail: classifieds@omakchronicle.com
Editorial e-mail: news@omakchronicle.com
Primary Website: omakchronicle.com
Year Established: 1910
Avg Paid Circ: 6600
Avg Free Circ: 300
Audit By: Sworn/Estimate/Non-Audited
Audit Date: 10.06.2019
Personnel: Roger Harnack (Publisher and editor); Howard Thompson (Mailroom Manager); Teresa Myers (Advertising Manager); Julie Bock (Circulation/classified manager)
Parent company (for newspapers): Eagle Newspapers, Inc.

PORT ORCHARD INDEPENDENT

Street address 1: 2497 Bethel Rd SE
Street address 2: Ste 102
Street address city: Port Orchard
Street address state: WA
Zip/Postal code: 98366-4889
General Phone: (360) 876-4414
General Fax: (360) 876-4458
Advertising Phone: (360) 876-4414
Advertising Fax: (360) 876-4458
Editorial Phone: (360) 876-4414
Editorial Fax: (360) 876-4458
General/National Adv. E-mail: lmay@portorchardindependent.com
Display Adv. E-mail: smcdonald@soundpublishing.com
Editorial e-mail: editor@portorchardindependent.com
Primary Website: portorchardindependent.com
Year Established: 1890
Avg Paid Circ: 837
Avg Free Circ: 16382
Audit By: AAM
Audit Date: 31.03.2018
Personnel: Sean McDonald (Pub.); Dannie Oliveaux (Ed.); Stephen Barrett (Nat'l Sales Dir.)
Parent company (for newspapers): Black Press Group Ltd.; Sound Publishing, Inc.

PORT TOWNSEND/JEFFERSON COUNTY LEADER

Street address 1: 226 Adams St
Street address city: Port Townsend
Street address state: WA
Zip/Postal code: 9838
General Phone: 360-385-2900
General Fax: 30-385-3422
Advertising Phone: 30-385-2900
Editorial Phone: 360-385-2900
General/National Adv. E-mail: detchey@ptleader.com
Display Adv. E-mail: detchey@ptleader.com
Classified Adv. e-mail: classified@ptleader.com
Editorial e-mail: news@ptleader.com
Primary Website: ptleader.com
Mthly Avg Views: 270000
Mthly Avg Unique Visitors: 75000
Year Established: 1889
Avg Paid Circ: 6200
Audit By: CAC
Personnel: Scott Wilson (Pub.); Donna Etchey (Publisher); Patrick Sullivan (Mng. Ed.); ???? ????; Catherine Brewer (Adv. Dir.); John Stanger

PROSSER RECORD-BULLETIN

Street address 1: 613 7th St
Street address city: Prosser
Street address state: WA
Zip/Postal code: 99350-1459
General Phone: (509) 786-1711
General Fax: (509) 786-1779
Advertising Phone: (509) 786-1711
Advertising Fax: (509) 786-1779
Editorial Phone: (509) 786-1711
Editorial Fax: (509) 786-1779
General/National Adv. E-mail: ads@recordbulletin.com
Display Adv. E-mail: office@recordbulletin.com
Editorial e-mail: editor@recordbulletin.com
Primary Website: thenews@valleypublishing.com
Year Established: 1920
Audit By: Sworn/Estimate/Non-Audited
Audit Date: 10.06.2019
Personnel: Danielle Fournier (Pub.); Victoria Walker (General Manager); Dianne Buxton (Adv. Mgr.)

PUGET SOUND BUSINESS JOURNAL

Street address 1: 801 2nd Ave
Street address 2: Ste 210
Street address city: Seattle
Street address state: WA
Zip/Postal code: 98104-1528
General Phone: (206) 876-5500
General Fax: (206) 447-8510
Advertising Phone: (206) 876-5450
Advertising Fax: (206) 447-8510
Editorial Phone: (206) 876-5431
Editorial Fax: (206) 447-8510
General/National Adv. E-mail: mgeoghegan@bizjournals.com
Display Adv. E-mail: mwall@bizjournals.com
Editorial e-mail: gerb@bizjournals.com
Primary Website: bizjournals.com/seattle
Year Established: 1980
Audit By: Sworn/Estimate/Non-Audited
Audit Date: 10.06.2019
Personnel: Gordon Prouty (Pub.); George Erb (Ed.); Martha Geoghegan (Adv. Mgr.)

QUAD CITY HERALD

Street address 1: 310 E Johnson Ave
Street address city: Chelan
Street address state: WA
Zip/Postal code: 98816
General Phone: (509) 682-2213
General Fax: (509) 682-4209
Advertising Phone: (509) 548-5286
Advertising Fax: (509) 682-4209
Editorial Phone: (509) 682-2213
Editorial Fax: (509) 682-4209
General/National Adv. E-mail: carol@leavenworthecho.com
Display Adv. E-mail: classifieds@leavenworthecho.com
Editorial e-mail: reporter@qcherald.com
Primary Website: qcherald.com
Year Established: 1907
Avg Paid Circ: 1000
Audit By: Sworn/Estimate/Non-Audited
Audit Date: 10.06.2019
Personnel: Carol Forhan (Advertising Director)
Parent company (for newspapers): NCW Media, Inc.

QUEEN ANNE & MAGNOLIA NEWS

Street address 1: 636 S Alaska St
Street address city: Seattle
Street address state: WA
Zip/Postal code: 98108-1727
General Phone: (206) 461-1300
General Fax: (206) 461-1285
Advertising Phone: (206) 461-1322
Advertising Fax: (206) 461-1285
Editorial Phone: (206) 461-1346
Editorial Fax: (206) 461-1285
General/National Adv. E-mail: PPCsales@nwlink.com
Display Adv. E-mail: classmgr@nwlink.com
Editorial e-mail: QAMagNews@nwlink.com
Primary Website: queenannenews.com
Year Established: 1919
Avg Paid Circ: 1898
Avg Free Circ: 5102
Audit By: Sworn/Estimate/Non-Audited
Audit Date: 10.06.2019
Personnel: Vera Chan-Pool (Ed.); Terry Fain (Sales Mgr.); Robert Munford (Gen. Mgr.)
Parent company (for newspapers): Pacific Publishing Company

REDMOND REPORTER

Street address 1: 11630 Slater Ave NE
Street address 2: Ste 8-9
Street address city: Kirkland
Street address state: WA
Zip/Postal code: 98034-4100
General Phone: (425) 867-0353
Advertising Phone: (425) 867-0353
Editorial Phone: (425) 296-3276
General/National Adv. E-mail: cfreese@redmond-reporter.com
Editorial e-mail: anystrom@redmond-reporter.com
Primary Website: redmond-reporter.com
Year Established: 2001
Avg Paid Circ: 9
Avg Free Circ: 22224
Audit By: AAM
Audit Date: 31.03.2018
Personnel: Andy Nystrom (Ed.); Aaron Kunkler; Cynthia Freese
Parent company (for newspapers): Black Press Group Ltd.; Sound Publishing, Inc.

RENTON REPORTER

Street address 1: 19426 68th Ave S
Street address city: Kent
Street address state: WA
Zip/Postal code: 98032-1193
General Phone: (253) 255-3484
Advertising Phone: (253) 255-3484
Editorial Phone: (253) 255-3484 ext. 1050
General/National Adv. E-mail: lyaskus@rentonreporter.com
Display Adv. E-mail: jhughes@soundpublishing.com
Editorial e-mail: sbrenden@rentonreporter.com
Primary Website: rentonreporter.com
Avg Paid Circ: 31
Avg Free Circ: 24257
Audit By: AAM
Audit Date: 31.03.2018
Personnel: Lisa Yaskus (Multi Media Consultant)
Parent company (for newspapers): Black Press Group Ltd.; Sound Publishing, Inc.

REVIEW INDEPENDENT

Street address 1: 218 W 1st Ave
Street address city: Toppenish
Street address state: WA
Zip/Postal code: 98948-1526
General Phone: (509) 314-6400
General Fax: (509) 314-6402
Advertising Phone: (509) 314-6400
Advertising Fax: (509) 314-6402
Editorial Phone: (509) 314-6400
Editorial Fax: (509) 314-6402
General/National Adv. E-mail: asmith3421@hotmail.com
Display Adv. E-mail: asmith3421@hotmail.com
Editorial e-mail: asmith3421@hotmail.com
Primary Website: reviewindependent.com
Year Established: 1904
Avg Paid Circ: 2000
Audit By: Sworn/Estimate/Non-Audited
Audit Date: 10.06.2019
Personnel: Bruce Smith (Pub.); Erick Peterson (Ed.)
Parent company (for newspapers): Yakima Valley Newspapers LLC

SAMMAMISH REVIEW

Street address 1: 1085 12th Ave NW
Street address 2: Ste D1
Street address city: Issaquah
Street address state: WA
Zip/Postal code: 98027-8988
General Phone: (425) 392-6434
General Fax: (425) 392-1695
Advertising Phone: (425) 392-6434 ext. 229
Advertising Fax: (425) 392-1695
Editorial Phone: (425) 392-6434 ext. 233
Editorial Fax: (425) 392-1695

General/National Adv. E-mail: admanager@isspress.com
Display Adv. E-mail: classifieds@isspress.com
Editorial e-mail: samrev@isspress.com
Primary Website: sammamishreview.com
Year Established: 1992
Avg Paid Circ: 400
Avg Free Circ: 14300
Audit By: Sworn/Estimate/Non-Audited
Audit Date: 10.06.2019
Personnel: Ari Cetron (Ed.); Dan DeLong (Adv. Mgr.)
Parent company (for newspapers): Issaquah Press Inc.

SHELTON-MASON COUNTY JOURNAL

Street address 1: 227 W Cota St
Street address city: Shelton
Street address state: WA
Zip/Postal code: 98584-2263
General Phone: (360) 426-4412
General Fax: (360) 426 9399
General/National Adv. E-mail: ads@masoncounty.com
Display Adv. E-mail: dave@masoncounty.com
Editorial e-mail: news@masoncounty.com
Primary Website: masoncounty.com
Year Established: 1887
Avg Paid Circ: 7100
Avg Free Circ: 100
Audit By: Sworn/Estimate/Non-Audited
Audit Date: 10.06.2019
Personnel: Adam Rudnick (EIC); Dave Pierik (Adv. Mgr.); Tom Mullen (Pub.)

SKAMANIA COUNTY PIONEER

Street address 1: 198 SW 2ND ST
Street address city: Stevenson
Street address state: WA
Zip/Postal code: 98648
General Phone: (509) 427-8444
General Fax: (509) 427-4229
Advertising Phone: (509) 427-8444
Advertising Fax: (509) 427-4229
Editorial Phone: (509) 427-8444
Editorial Fax: (509) 427-4229
General/National Adv. E-mail: scpioneerads@gorge.net
Display Adv. E-mail: scpioneer@gorge.net
Editorial e-mail: scpioneernews@gorge.net
Year Established: 1898
Avg Paid Circ: 2600
Audit By: Sworn/Estimate/Non-Audited
Audit Date: 10.06.2019
Personnel: Frank DeVaul (Pub.); Judy DeVaul (Pub.); Philip Watness (Ed.); Jean Foster (Office Mgr./Sports Ed.); Angela Rogers (Adv. Mgr.); Bridget Callahan (Circ. Mgr.)

SNOHOMISH COUNTY TRIBUNE

Street address 1: 127 Avenue C
Street address 2: Ste B
Street address city: Snohomish
Street address state: WA
Zip/Postal code: 98290-2768
General Phone: (360) 568-4121
General Fax: (360) 568-1484
Advertising Phone: (360) 568-4121
Advertising Fax: (360) 568-1484
Editorial Phone: (360) 568-4121
Editorial Fax: (360) 568-1484
General/National Adv. E-mail: becky@snoho.com
Display Adv. E-mail: classad.tribune@snoho.com
Editorial e-mail: editor.tribune@snoho.com
Primary Website: snoho.com
Year Established: 1892
Avg Paid Circ: 8500
Avg Free Circ: 8000
Audit By: Sworn/Estimate/Non-Audited
Audit Date: 10.06.2019
Personnel: Becky Reed (Pub. / Adv. Mgr.); Michael Whitney (Editor)

SNOQUALMIE VALLEY RECORD

Street address 1: 8124 Falls Ave SE
Street address city: Snoqualmie
Street address state: WA
Zip/Postal code: 98065
General Phone: (425) 888-2311
General Fax: (425) 888-2427
Advertising Phone: (425) 888-2311
Advertising Fax: (425) 888-2427
Editorial Phone: (425) 888-2311
Editorial Fax: (425) 888-2427
General/National Adv. E-mail: wshaw@valleyrecord.com
Display Adv. E-mail: dhamilton@soundpublishing.com
Editorial e-mail: editor@valleyrecord.com
Primary Website: valleyrecord.com
Year Established: 1913
Avg Paid Circ: 351
Avg Free Circ: 10810
Audit By: AAM
Audit Date: 31.03.2018
Personnel: William Shaw (Pub.); Seth Truscott (Ed.); Stephen Barrett (Nat'l Sales Dir.)
Parent company (for newspapers): Black Press Group Ltd.; Sound Publishing, Inc.

SNOVALLEY STAR

Street address 1: 1085 12th Ave NW
Street address 2: Ste D1
Street address city: Issaquah
Street address state: WA
Zip/Postal code: 98027-8988
General Phone: (425) 392-6434
General Fax: (425) 392-1695
Advertising Phone: (425) 392-6434 ext. 229
Advertising Fax: (425) 392-1695
Editorial Phone: (425) 392-6434 ext. 233
Editorial Fax: (425) 392-1695
General/National Adv. E-mail: admanager@isspress.com
Display Adv. E-mail: classifieds@isspress.com
Editorial e-mail: editor@snovalleystar.com
Primary Website: snovalleystar.com
Year Established: 2008
Audit By: Sworn/Estimate/Non-Audited
Audit Date: 10.06.2019
Personnel: Sherry Grindeland (Ed.); Dan DeLong (Adv. Mgr.); Joe Heslet (Gen. Mgr.)
Parent company (for newspapers): Issaquah Press Inc.

SOUTH BEACH BULLETIN

Street address 1: 114 W Pacific Ave
Street address city: Westport
Street address state: WA
Zip/Postal code: 98595-1395
General Phone: (360) 268-0156
General/National Adv. E-mail: dames@soundpublishing.com
Display Adv. E-mail: class@thedailyworld.com
Editorial e-mail: publisher@thedailyworld.com
Primary Website: southbeachbulletin.com
Year Established: 1993
Avg Paid Circ: 208
Avg Free Circ: 4243
Audit By: AAM
Audit Date: 31.03.2018
Personnel: Michael Hrycko (Pub.); Douglas Ames (Adv.); Amy Husted (Circ. Dir.)
Parent company (for newspapers): Sound Publishing Inc.

SOUTH SOUND BUSINESS

Street address 1: 2112 North 30th St
Street address 2: Suite A
Street address city: Tacoma
Street address state: WA
Zip/Postal code: 98403
General Phone: (253) 588-5340
General Fax: (253) 588-5348
General/National Adv. E-mail: aubrey@premiermedia.net
Display Adv. E-mail: aubrey@premiermedia.net
Primary Website: southsoundbiz.com
Year Established: 1985
Avg Paid Circ: 954
Avg Free Circ: 6127
Audit By: CVC
Audit Date: 31.12.2017
Personnel: Josh Dunn (Pub./CEO); Aubrey Pike (Adv.)

SOUTH WHIDBEY RECORD

Street address 1: 800 SE Barrington Drive
Street address city: Oak Harbor
Street address state: WA
Zip/Postal code: 98277
General Phone: (360) 675-6611
General Fax: (360) 221-6474
Advertising Phone: (360) 221-5300
Advertising Fax: (360) 221-6474
Editorial Phone: (360) 221-5300
Editorial Fax: (360) 221-6474
General/National Adv. E-mail: kwinjum@whidbeynewsgroup.com
Display Adv. E-mail: Classifieds@whidbeynewsgroup.com
Editorial e-mail: editor@whidbeynewsgroup.com
Primary Website: southwhidbeyrecord.com
Year Established: 1921
Avg Paid Circ: 2623
Avg Free Circ: 3
Audit By: AAM
Audit Date: 31.03.2018
Personnel: Keven R. Graves (Pub./Exec. Ed.); Jessie Stensland (Editor); Kimberly Winjum (Assc. Pub.); Justin Burnett (Ed.); Stephen Barrett (Nat'l Sales Dir.)
Parent company (for newspapers): Black Press Group Ltd.; Sound Publishing, Inc.

SPOKANE JOURNAL OF BUSINESS

Street address 1: 429 E. Third Ave.
Street address city: Spokane
Street address state: WA
Zip/Postal code: 99202-1414
General Phone: (509) 456-5257
General Fax: (509) 456-0624
General/National Adv. E-mail: info@spokanejournal.com
Display Adv. E-mail: paulr@spokanejournal.com
Classified Adv. e-mail: jenniferz@spokanejournal.com
Editorial e-mail: editor@spokanejournal.com
Primary Website: spokanejournal.com
Year Established: 1986
Avg Paid Circ: 4630
Avg Free Circ: 2500
Audit By: CVC
Audit Date: 31.12.2023
Personnel: Paul Read (Publisher); Jonelle Opitz (Bus. Mgr.); Linn Parish (Ed.); Dana Cunningham (Adv. Sales); Kathy Minor (Circ. Mgr.)
Parent company (for newspapers): Cowles Co.

SPOKANE VALLEY NEWS HERALD

Street address 1: 1616 W. First St.
Street address city: Cheney
Street address state: WA
Zip/Postal code: 99004
General Phone: (509) 235-6184
Advertising Phone: 509-235-6184
Editorial Phone: 509-235-6184
General/National Adv. E-mail: vnh@onemain.com
Display Adv. E-mail: advertising@cheneyfreepress.com
Classified Adv. e-mail: classifieds@cheneyfreepress.com
Editorial e-mail: vnh@onemain.com
Primary Website: www.cheneyfreepress.com/section/spokane_valley
Mthly Avg Views: 88000
Mthly Avg Unique Visitors: 7000
Year Established: 1920
Avg Paid Circ: 1000
Avg Free Circ: 300
Audit By: Sworn/Estimate/Non-Audited
Audit Date: 01.10.2023
Personnel: Harlan Schelleberger (Pub./Adv. Mgr.); Linda Pantzer (Advertising manager); Mike Huffman (Mng. Ed.); Dean Henrich (Reporter); Roger Harnack (Owner/Publisher)
Parent company (for newspapers): Free Press Publishing Inc.

STANWOOD CAMANO NEWS

Street address 1: 9005 271st Street NW
Street address city: Stanwood
Street address state: WA
Zip/Postal code: 98292
General Phone: (360) 629-2155
General/National Adv. E-mail: newsroom@scnews.com
Year Established: 1895
Avg Paid Circ: 2247
Audit By: AAM
Audit Date: 31.03.2017
Personnel: Kathy Boyd (Gen. Mgr/ Ed.)
Parent company (for newspapers): Skagit Publishing

STATESMAN-EXAMINER

Street address 1: 220 S Main St
Street address city: Colville
Street address state: WA
Zip/Postal code: 99114-2408
General Phone: (509) 684-4567
General Fax: (509) 684-3849
Advertising Phone: (509) 684-4567
Advertising Fax: (509) 684-3849
Editorial Phone: (509) 684-4567
Editorial Fax: (509) 684-3849
General/National Adv. E-mail: shannon@statesmanexaminer.com
Display Adv. E-mail: classified@statesmanexaminer.com
Editorial e-mail: editor@statesmanexaminer.com
Primary Website: statesmanexaminer.com
Year Established: 1948
Avg Paid Circ: 3000
Avg Free Circ: 100
Audit By: Sworn/Estimate/Non-Audited
Audit Date: 10.06.2019
Personnel: Roger Harnack (Publisher); Shannon Chapman (Advertising specialist)
Parent company (for newspapers): Horizon Publications Inc.

TACOMA WEEKLY

Street address 1: 2588 Pacific Hwy E
Street address city: Fife
Street address state: WA
Zip/Postal code: 98424-1016
General Phone: (253) 922-5317
General Fax: (253) 922-5305
Advertising Phone: (253) 922-5317
Advertising Fax: (253) 922-5305
Editorial Phone: (253) 922-5317
Editorial Fax: (253) 922-5305
General/National Adv. E-mail: rose@tacomaweekly.com
Display Adv. E-mail: cmcdonald@tacomaweekly.com
Editorial e-mail: jweymer@tacomaweekly.com
Primary Website: tacomaweekly.com
Year Established: 1986
Audit By: Sworn/Estimate/Non-Audited
Audit Date: 10.06.2019
Personnel: John Weymer (Pub./Ed.); Rose Thiele (Adv. Mgr.)
Parent company (for newspapers): Pierce County Community Newspaper Group

THE ARGUS

Street address 1: 1215 Anderson Rd
Street address city: Mount Vernon
Street address state: WA
Zip/Postal code: 98274-7615
General Phone: (360) 424-3251
General Fax: (360) 424-5300
Advertising Phone: (360) 424-3251
Advertising Fax: (360) 424-5300
Editorial Phone: (360) 424-3251
Editorial Fax: (360) 424-5300
General/National Adv. E-mail: dbundy@skagitpublishing.com
Display Adv. E-mail: mdoble@skagitpublishing.com
Editorial e-mail: kboyd@skagitpublishing.com
Primary Website: goskagit.com
Avg Paid Circ: 3200
Avg Free Circ: 6300
Audit By: Sworn/Estimate/Non-Audited
Audit Date: 10.06.2019
Personnel: Leighton Wood (Pres.); Deb Davis Bundy (Adv. Mgr.); Kathy Boyd (Ed.)
Parent company (for newspapers): Adams Publishing Group

THE ARLINGTON TIMES

Street address 1: 1085 Cedar Ave
Street address city: Marysville
Street address state: WA
Zip/Postal code: 98270-4232
General Phone: (360) 654-4157
General Fax: (360) 658-0350
Advertising Phone: (360) 659-1300
Advertising Fax: (360) 658-0350
Editorial Phone: (360) 654-4157

Editorial Fax: (360) 435-0350
General/National Adv. E-mail: jknoblich@soundpublishing.com
Display Adv. E-mail: jknoblich@soundpublishing.com
Editorial e-mail: editor@marysvilleglobe.com
Primary Website: arlingtontimes.com
Year Established: 1887
Avg Paid Circ: 137
Avg Free Circ: 4949
Audit By: AAM
Audit Date: 17.03.2016
Parent company (for newspapers): Black Press Group Ltd.; Sound Publishing, Inc.

THE CAPITOL HILL TIMES

Street address 1: 4000 Aurora Ave N
Street address 2: Ste 100
Street address city: Seattle
Street address state: WA
Zip/Postal code: 98103-7853
General Phone: (425) 213-5579
Advertising Phone: (425) 213-5579
Editorial Phone: (425) 213-5579
General/National Adv. E-mail: advertising@capitolhilltimes.com
Display Adv. E-mail: info@capitolhilltimes.com
Editorial e-mail: editor@capitolhilltimes.com
Primary Website: capitolhilltimes.com
Year Established: 1926
Audit By: Sworn/Estimate/Non-Audited
Audit Date: 10.06.2019
Personnel: Gina Luna (Ed.); Angela Nickerson (Designer/ Adv. Mgr.)
Parent company (for newspapers): RIM Publications

THE CHRONICLE

Street address 1: 321 N Pearl St
Street address city: Centralia
Street address state: WA
Zip/Postal code: 98531-4323
General Phone: (360) 736-3311
General Fax: (360)807-8258
General/National Adv. E-mail: bwatson@chronline.com
Display Adv. E-mail: classified@chronline.com
Classified Adv. e-mail: advertising@chronline.com
Editorial e-mail: letters@chronline.com
Primary Website: chronline.com
Year Established: 1966
Avg Paid Circ: 10200
Sat. Circulation Paid: 12800
Audit By: Sworn/Estimate/Non-Audited
Audit Date: 10.06.2019
Personnel: Christine Fossett (Pub.); Michael Wagar (Regional Exec. Ed.); Eric Schwartz (Editor); Aaron Van Tuyl (Sports Ed.); Anita Freeborn (Circ. Mgr.); Brian Watson (Sales Dir.); Mary Jackson (Business Mgr.)
Parent company (for newspapers): Lafromboise Communications, Inc.

THE COMMUNITY CURRENT

Street address 1: 15 E Front St
Street address city: Saint John
Street address state: WA
Zip/Postal code: 99171-8775
General Phone: (509) 648-3264
Advertising Phone: (509) 648-3264
Editorial Phone: (509) 648-3264
General/National Adv. E-mail: becky@communitycurrentnewspaper.com
Display Adv. E-mail: becky@communitycurrentnewspaper.com
Editorial e-mail: becky@communitycurrentnewspaper.com
Primary Website: communitycurrentnewspaper.com
Year Established: 1994
Audit By: Sworn/Estimate/Non-Audited
Audit Date: 10.06.2019
Personnel: Becky Dickerson (Pub./Ed.)

THE COURIER-HERALD

Street address 1: 1627 Cole St
Street address city: Enumclaw
Street address state: WA
Zip/Postal code: 98022-3509
General Phone: (360) 825-2555
Advertising Phone: (360) 825-2555
Editorial Phone: (360) 802-8205
General/National Adv. E-mail: tbeitinger@courierherald.com
Display Adv. E-mail: jtribbett@courierherald.com
Editorial e-mail: dbox@soundpublishing.com
Primary Website: courierherald.com
Year Established: 2003
Avg Paid Circ: 924
Avg Free Circ: 24468
Audit By: Sworn/Estimate/Non-Audited
Audit Date: 10.06.2019
Personnel: Dennis Box (Ed.)
Parent company (for newspapers): Sound Publishing, Inc.

THE DAILY WORLD

Street address 1: 315 S Michigan St
Street address city: Aberdeen
Street address state: WA
Zip/Postal code: 98520-6037
General Phone: (360) 532-4000
General Fax: (360) 533-1328
Advertising Phone: (360) 532-4000
Advertising Fax: (360) 533-1328
Editorial Phone: (360) 532-4000
Editorial Fax: (360) 533-6039
General/National Adv. E-mail: mspezia@thedailyworld.com
Display Adv. E-mail: advert@thedailyworld.com
Editorial e-mail: editor@thedailyworld.com
Primary Website: thedailyworld.com
Avg Paid Circ: 5422
Avg Free Circ: 222
Sat. Circulation Paid: 6966
Sat. Circulation Free: 1248
Audit By: AAM
Audit Date: 31.03.2018
Personnel: Mike Spezia (Adv. Mgr.); Gerald Atkinson (Circ. Dir.); Bill Lindstrom (City Ed.); Dan Jackson (Asst. City Ed.); Jeff Burlingame (Entertainment Ed., Preview Magazine); Kathy Quigg (Photo Dept. Mgr.); Tommi Gatlin (Religion Ed.); Rick Anderson (Sports Ed.); Ryan Parson (Mgr., Distr.); David Dutton (Prodn. Mgr., Pre Press Systems); Larry Schoening (Prodn. Foreman, Pressroom); Stanley Woody (Publisher); Doug Barker (Editor)
Parent company (for newspapers): Black Press Group Ltd.

THE EAST COUNTY JOURNAL

Street address 1: 278 W MAIN ST
Street address city: Morton
Street address state: WA
Zip/Postal code: 98356
General Phone: (360) 496-5993
General Fax: (360) 496-5110
Advertising Phone: (360) 496-5993
Advertising Fax: (360) 496-5110
Editorial Phone: (360) 496-5993
Editorial Fax: (360) 496-5110
General/National Adv. E-mail: ecjeditor@devaulpublishing.com
Display Adv. E-mail: ecjournal@devaulpublishing.com
Classified Adv. e-mail: dpiads@devaulpublishing.com
Editorial e-mail: ecjeditor@devaulpublishing.com
Primary Website: devaulpublishing.com/eastcounty
Year Established: 1936
Avg Free Circ: 7979
Audit By: AAM
Audit Date: 31.03.2016
Personnel: Frank DeVaul (Co-Pub.); Judy DeVaul (Co-Pub./Adv. Vice Pres.); Kevin Westrick (Ed.); Ric Hallock (Editor)
Parent company (for newspapers): DeVaul Publishing Inc.

THE EATONVILLE DISPATCH

Street address 1: 133 Mashell Ave N
Street address city: Eatonville
Street address state: WA
Zip/Postal code: 98328
General Phone: (360) 832-4411
Advertising Phone: (360) 832-4411
Editorial Phone: (360) 832-4411
General/National Adv. E-mail: advertising@dispatchnews.com
Display Adv. E-mail: officemanager@dispatchnews.com
Editorial e-mail: editor@dispatchnews.com
Primary Website: dispatchnews.com
Year Established: 1893
Audit By: Sworn/Estimate/Non-Audited
Audit Date: 10.06.2019
Personnel: Cliff Wright (Pub.); Pat Jenkins (Ed.); Joni L. Eades (Adv. Mgr.)

THE ENTERPRISE

Street address 1: 220 E Jewett Blvd
Street address city: White Salmon
Street address state: WA
Zip/Postal code: 98672-3000
General Phone: (509) 493-2112
General Fax: (509) 493-2399
Advertising Phone: (509) 493-2112
Advertising Fax: (509) 493-2399
Editorial Phone: (509) 493-2112
Editorial Fax: (509) 493-2399
General/National Adv. E-mail: ebakke@eaglenewspapers.com
Display Adv. E-mail: amarra@whitesalmonenterprise.com
Editorial e-mail: amarra@whitesalmonenterprise.com
Primary Website: whitesalmonenterprise.com
Year Established: 1903
Audit By: Sworn/Estimate/Non-Audited
Audit Date: 10.06.2019
Personnel: Elaine Bakke (Pub.); Sverre Bakke (Ed. / Sports Ed.); Janet Barnes (Class. / Circ. Mgr); Michelle Scott (Reporter)
Parent company (for newspapers): Eagle Newspapers, Inc.

THE ENUMCLAW COURIER-HERALD

Street address 1: 1186 Myrtle Avenue
Street address city: Enumclaw
Street address state: WA
Zip/Postal code: 98022-3509
General Phone: (360) 825-2555
Advertising Phone: (360) 825-2555
Editorial Phone: (360) 802-8220
Primary Website: courierherald.com
Avg Paid Circ: 1800
Audit By: AAM
Audit Date: 31.03.2018
Personnel: Kevin Hanson (Ed./Sr. Writer); Dennis Box (Ed.); Stephen Barrett (Nat'l Sales Dir.); Ray Miller-Still (Editor/Reporter)
Parent company (for newspapers): Sound Publishing, Inc.

THE GEM STATE MINER

Street address 1: 421 S Spokane Ave
Street address city: Newport
Street address state: WA
Zip/Postal code: 99156-7039
General Phone: (509) 447-2433
General Fax: (509) 447-9222
General/National Adv. E-mail: mineradvertising@povn.com
Display Adv. E-mail: minerclassifieds@povn.com
Editorial e-mail: minernews@povn.com
Primary Website: pendoreillerivervalley.com
Year Established: 1891
Avg Paid Circ: 6000
Avg Free Circ: 11000
Audit By: Sworn/Estimate/Non-Audited
Audit Date: 10.06.2019
Personnel: Fred J. Willenbrock (Pub.); Michelle Nedved (Mng. Ed.); Lindsay Guscott (Adv. Mgr.); Susan Willenbrock (Circ. Mgr.)

THE INDEPENDENT

Street address 1: 401 S Park St
Street address 2: Ste A
Street address city: Chewelah
Street address state: WA
Zip/Postal code: 99109-9337
General Phone: (509) 935-8422
General Fax: (509) 935-4755
Advertising Phone: (509) 935-8422
Advertising Fax: (509) 935-4755
Editorial Phone: (509) 935-8422
Editorial Fax: (509) 935-4755
General/National Adv. E-mail: theindependent@centurytel.net
Display Adv. E-mail: theindependent@centurytel.net
Editorial e-mail: theindependent@centurytel.net
Primary Website: chewelahindependent.com
Year Established: 1903
Avg Paid Circ: 2100
Avg Free Circ: 500
Audit By: Sworn/Estimate/Non-Audited
Audit Date: 10.06.2019
Personnel: Jared Arnold (Pub.); Andrea Arnold (Office Mgr.); Brandon Hansen (Managing Editor)
Parent company (for newspapers): Chewelah Independent, Inc.

THE INDEPENDENT

Street address 1: 401 S. Park St.
Street address city: Chewelah
Street address state: WA
Zip/Postal code: 99109
General Phone: 509-935-8422
General Fax: 509-935-4755
Advertising Phone: 509-935-8422
Advertising Fax: 509-935-4755
Editorial Phone: 509-935-8422
Editorial Fax: 509-935-4755
General/National Adv. E-mail: theindependent@centurytel.net
Display Adv. E-mail: publisher@chewelahindependent.com
Classified Adv. e-mail: theindependent@centurytel.net
Editorial e-mail: publisher@chewelahindependent.com
Primary Website: Chewelahindependent.com
Year Established: 1903
Avg Paid Circ: 2500
Audit By: USPS
Audit Date: 01.10.2021
Personnel: Jared Arnold (Publisher); Andrea Arnold (Office Manager); K.S. Brooks (Copy Editor, Reporter); Geno Ludwig (Sports Reporter)
Parent company (for newspapers): ()

THE ISLANDS' SOUNDER

Street address 1: 217 Main St
Street address city: Eastsound
Street address state: WA
Zip/Postal code: 98245-5510
General Phone: (360) 376-4500
General Fax: (360) 376-4501
General/National Adv. E-mail: publisher@islandssounder.com
Display Adv. E-mail: carmstrong@islandssounder.com
Editorial e-mail: cbagby@islandssounder.com
Primary Website: islandssounder.com
Year Established: 1964
Avg Paid Circ: 1269
Avg Free Circ: 8
Audit By: AAM
Audit Date: 31.03.2018
Personnel: Colleen Armstrong (Pub.); Nicole Matisse Duke (Circ. Mgr.); Stephen Barrett (Nat'l Sales Dir.)
Parent company (for newspapers): Black Press Group Ltd.; Sound Publishing, Inc.

THE ISLANDS' WEEKLY

Street address 1: 131 Weeks Rd
Street address city: Lopez Island
Street address state: WA
Zip/Postal code: 98261-5530
General Phone: (360) 376-4500
General Fax: (360) 468-4900
Advertising Phone: (360) 468-4242
Advertising Fax: (360) 468-4900
Editorial Phone: (360) 468-4242
Editorial Fax: (360) 468-4900
General/National Adv. E-mail: cbagby@islandsweekly.com
Display Adv. E-mail: cbagby@islandsweekly.com
Editorial e-mail: publisher@islandsweekly.net
Primary Website: islandsweekly.com
Year Established: 1982
Avg Paid Circ: 44
Avg Free Circ: 1863
Audit By: AAM
Audit Date: 31.03.2018
Personnel: Roxannne Angel (Pub.); Cali Bagby (Ed./Adv. Mgr.); Stephen Barrett (Nat'l Sales Dir.)
Parent company (for newspapers): Black Press Group Ltd.; Sound Publishing, Inc.

THE ISSAQUAH PRESS

Street address 1: 1085 12th Ave NW
Street address 2: Ste D1
Street address city: Issaquah
Street address state: WA
Zip/Postal code: 98027-8988

General Phone: (425) 392-6434
General Fax: (425) 392-1695
Advertising Phone: (425) 392-6434
Advertising Fax: (425) 392-1695
Editorial Phone: (425) 392-6434
Editorial Fax: (425) 392-1695
General/National Adv. E-mail: admanager@isspress.com
Display Adv. E-mail: classifieds@isspress.com
Editorial e-mail: editor@isspress.com
Primary Website: issaquahpress.com
Year Established: 1900
Avg Paid Circ: 1382
Avg Free Circ: 12738
Audit By: Sworn/Estimate/Non-Audited
Audit Date: 10.06.2019
Personnel: Scott Stoddard (Editor)

THE JOURNAL OF THE SAN JUAN ISLANDS

Street address 1: 640 Mullis St
Street address city: Friday Harbor
Street address state: WA
Zip/Postal code: 98250-7940
General Phone: (360) 378-5696
General Fax: (360) 378-5128
Advertising Phone: (360) 378-5696
Advertising Fax: (360) 378-5128
Editorial Phone: (360) 378-5696
Editorial Fax: (360) 378-5128
General/National Adv. E-mail: publisher@sanjuanjournal.com
Display Adv. E-mail: classifieds@soundpublishing.com
Editorial e-mail: editor@sanjuanjournal.com
Primary Website: sanjuanjournal.com
Mthly Avg Views: 70000
Mthly Avg Unique Visitors: 25000
Year Established: 1906
Avg Paid Circ: 1264
Avg Free Circ: 35
Audit By: AAM
Audit Date: 31.03.2018
Personnel: Roxanne Angel (Pub.); Scott Rasmussen (Ed.); Stephen Barrett (Nat'l Sales Dir.)
Parent company (for newspapers): Black Press Group Ltd.; Sound Publishing, Inc.

THE LEAVENWORTH ECHO

Street address 1: 215 14th St
Street address city: Leavenworth
Street address state: WA
Zip/Postal code: 98826-1411
General Phone: (509) 548-5286
General Fax: (509) 548-4789
Advertising Phone: (509) 548-5286
Advertising Fax: (509) 548-4789
Editorial Phone: (509) 548-5286
Editorial Fax: (509) 548-4789
General/National Adv. E-mail: carol@leavenworthecho.com
Display Adv. E-mail: classifieds@leavenworthecho.com
Editorial e-mail: editor@leavenworthecho.com
Primary Website: leavenworthecho.com
Mthly Avg Views: 11030
Mthly Avg Unique Visitors: 8189
Year Established: 1904
Avg Paid Circ: 1600
Audit By: Sworn/Estimate/Non-Audited
Audit Date: 10.06.2019
Personnel: Bill Forhan (Pub.); Carol Forhan (VP Advertising Director); Kalie Drago (Reporter); Edward Wateerman (Ad Sales Executive)
Parent company (for newspapers): NCW Media, Inc.

THE MARYSVILLE GLOBE

Street address 1: 1085 Cedar Ave
Street address city: Marysville
Street address state: WA
Zip/Postal code: 98270-4232
General Phone: (360) 654-4157
General Fax: (360) 658-0350
Advertising Phone: (360) 659-1300
Advertising Fax: (360) 658-0350
Editorial Phone: (360) 654-4157
Editorial Fax: (360) 658-0350
General/National Adv. E-mail: jknoblich@soundpublishing.com
Display Adv. E-mail: 360-654-4157
Editorial e-mail: editor@marysvilleglobe.com
Primary Website: marysvilleglobe.com
Year Established: 1892
Avg Paid Circ: 74
Avg Free Circ: 15000
Audit By: AAM
Audit Date: 16.03.2016
Personnel: Steve Powell (Managing Ed.)
Parent company (for newspapers): Black Press Group Ltd.; Sound Publishing, Inc.

THE MONROE MONITOR & VALLEY NEWS

Street address 1: PO Box 80156
Street address city: Seattle
Street address state: WA
Zip/Postal code: 98108-0156
General Phone: (360) 794-7116
General Fax: (360) 794-6202
Advertising Phone: (360) 794-7116
Advertising Fax: (360) 794-6202
Editorial Phone: (360) 794-7116
Editorial Fax: (360) 794-6202
General/National Adv. E-mail: sfreshman@monroemonitor.com
Display Adv. E-mail: kathie@monroemonitor.com
Editorial e-mail: editor@monroemonitor.com
Primary Website: monroemonitor.com
Year Established: 1899
Avg Paid Circ: 4000
Audit By: Sworn/Estimate/Non-Audited
Audit Date: 10.06.2019
Personnel: Polly Keary (Pub./Ed.); Kathie Savelesky (Office Mgr.)
Parent company (for newspapers): RIM Publications

THE NEWS & STANDARD

Street address 1: 405 W Main St
Street address city: Coulee City
Street address state: WA
Zip/Postal code: 99115
General Phone: (509) 632-5402
Advertising Phone: (509) 632-5402
Editorial Phone: (509) 632-5402
General/National Adv. E-mail: tns@accima.com
Display Adv. E-mail: tns@accima.com
Editorial e-mail: tns@accima.com
Primary Website: smalltownpapers.com
Year Established: 1890
Avg Paid Circ: 800
Audit By: Sworn/Estimate/Non-Audited
Audit Date: 10.06.2019
Personnel: Shirley Rae Maes (Ed./Pub.)

THE NORTHERN LIGHT

Street address 1: 225 Marine Dr
Street address 2: Ste 200
Street address city: Blaine
Street address state: WA
Zip/Postal code: 98230-4052
General Phone: (360) 332-1777
General Fax: (360) 332-2777
Advertising Phone: (360) 332-1777
Advertising Fax: (360) 332-2777
Editorial Phone: (360) 332-1777
Editorial Fax: (360) 332-2777
General/National Adv. E-mail: sales@thenorthernlight.com
Display Adv. E-mail: info@thenorthernlight.com
Editorial e-mail: editor@thenorthernlight.com
Primary Website: thenorthernlight.com
Year Established: 1995
Avg Paid Circ: 15
Avg Free Circ: 10460
Audit By: CVC
Audit Date: 30.09.2018
Personnel: Patrick J. Grubb (Pub./Mng. Ed.); Louise H. Mugar (Adv. Mgr.); Jeanie Luna; Ruth Lauman (Prod. Mgr)
Parent company (for newspapers): Point Roberts Press, Inc.

THE ODESSA RECORD

Street address 1: 1 W 1st Ave
Street address city: Odessa
Street address state: WA
Zip/Postal code: 99159-7004
General Phone: (509) 982-2632
General Fax: (509) 982-2651
Advertising Phone: (509) 982-2632
Advertising Fax: (509) 982-2651
Editorial Phone: (509) 982-2632
Editorial Fax: (509) 982-2651
General/National Adv. E-mail: therecordads@odessaoffice.com
Display Adv. E-mail: therecord@odessaoffice.com
Editorial e-mail: therecord@odessaoffice.com
Primary Website: odessarecord.com
Year Established: 1901
Avg Paid Circ: 1250
Audit By: Sworn/Estimate/Non-Audited
Audit Date: 10.06.2019
Personnel: Edward Crosby (Co-Pub.)

THE OTHELLO OUTLOOK

Street address 1: 10518 NE 37th Cir
Street address city: Kirkland
Street address state: WA
Zip/Postal code: 98033-7920
General Phone: (509) 488-3342
General Fax: (509) 488-3345
Advertising Phone: (509) 488-3342
Advertising Fax: (509) 488-3345
Editorial Phone: (509) 488-3342
Editorial Fax: (509) 488-3345
General/National Adv. E-mail: admanager@othellooutlook.com
Display Adv. E-mail: officemanager@othellooutlook.com
Editorial e-mail: editor@othellooutlook.com
Primary Website: othellooutlook.com
Year Established: 1947
Avg Paid Circ: 800
Avg Free Circ: 5000
Audit By: Sworn/Estimate/Non-Audited
Audit Date: 10.06.2019
Personnel: Briana Alzola (Ed.); LuAnn Morgan
Parent company (for newspapers): Basin Publishing Co.

THE PUYALLUP HERALD

Street address 1: 510 E Main
Street address city: Puyallup
Street address state: WA
Zip/Postal code: 98372-5698
General Phone: (253) 841-2481
General Fax: (253) 840-8249
Advertising Phone: (253) 841-2481
Advertising Fax: (253) 840-8249
Editorial Phone: (253) 841-2481
Editorial Fax: (253) 840-8249
General/National Adv. E-mail: jim.appelgate@gateline.com
Display Adv. E-mail: brian.mclean@puyallupherald.com
Editorial e-mail: editor@puyallupherald.com
Primary Website: thenewstribune.com
Avg Paid Circ: 27000
Audit By: Sworn/Estimate/Non-Audited
Audit Date: 10.06.2019
Personnel: Brian McLean (Pub./Ed.); Jim Appelgate (Adv. Dir.)
Parent company (for newspapers): The McClatchy Company

THE QUINCY VALLEY POST-REGISTER

Street address 1: 305 Central Ave S
Street address city: Quincy
Street address state: WA
Zip/Postal code: 98848-1227
General Phone: (509) 787-4511
General Fax: (509) 787-2682
Advertising Phone: (509) 787-4511
Advertising Fax: (509) 787-2682
Editorial Phone: (509) 787-4511
Editorial Fax: (509) 787-2682
General/National Adv. E-mail: qvprads@gmail.com
Display Adv. E-mail: qvprclassifieds@gmail.com
Editorial e-mail: qvpreditor@gmail.com
Primary Website: qvpr.com
Year Established: 1949
Audit By: Sworn/Estimate/Non-Audited
Audit Date: 10.06.2019
Parent company (for newspapers): The Wenatchee World

THE REFLECTOR

Street address 1: 208 SE 1ST ST
Street address city: Battle Ground
Street address state: WA
Zip/Postal code: 98604
General Phone: (360) 687-5151
General Fax: (360) 687-5162
General/National Adv. E-mail: ads@thereflector.com
Display Adv. E-mail: legals@thereflector.com
Editorial e-mail: news@thereflector.com
Primary Website: thereflector.com
Mthly Avg Views: 41169
Mthly Avg Unique Visitors: 11732
Year Established: 1909
Avg Paid Circ: 816
Avg Free Circ: 28206
Audit By: Sworn/Estimate/Non-Audited
Audit Date: 10.06.2019
Personnel: Laura Venneri (Pub)
Parent company (for newspapers): Lafromboise Communications, Inc.

THE RITZVILLE ADAMS COUNTY JOURNAL

Street address 1: 216 W Railroad Ave
Street address city: Ritzville
Street address state: WA
Zip/Postal code: 99169-2309
General Phone: (509) 659-1020
General Fax: (509) 659-0842
Advertising Phone: 509-235-6184
Advertising Fax: (509) 659-0842
Editorial Phone: (509) 659-1020
Editorial Fax: (509) 659-0842
General/National Adv. E-mail: editor@ritzvillejournal.com
Display Adv. E-mail: advertising@ritzvillejournal.com
Classified Adv. e-mail: classifieds@cheneyfreepress.com
Editorial e-mail: editor@ritzvillejournal.com
Primary Website: ritzvillejournal.com
Mthly Avg Views: 30000
Mthly Avg Unique Visitors: 8000
Year Established: 1886
Avg Paid Circ: 2000
Avg Free Circ: 50
Audit By: Sworn/Estimate/Non-Audited
Audit Date: 27.09.2023
Personnel: Brandon Cline (Managing Editor); Roger Harnack (Owner/Publisher); Dale Brown (Ritzville Reporter); Linda Pantzer (Advertising Manager)
Parent company (for newspapers): Free Press Publishing

THE SEQUIM GAZETTE

Street address 1: 147 W Washington St
Street address 2: Ste A
Street address city: Sequim
Street address state: WA
Zip/Postal code: 98382-3372
General Phone: (360) 683-3311
General Fax: (360) 683-6670
Advertising Phone: (360) 683-3311 ext. 1050
Advertising Fax: (360) 683-6670
Editorial Phone: (360) 683-3311 ext. 5050
Editorial Fax: (360) 683-6670
General/National Adv. E-mail: dlahmeyer@sequimgazette.com
Display Adv. E-mail: classified@sequimgazette.com
Editorial e-mail: editor@sequimgazette.com
Primary Website: sequimgazette.com
Year Established: 1988
Avg Paid Circ: 3547
Audit By: AAM
Audit Date: 31.03.2018
Personnel: Mike Dashiell (Ed.); Debi Lahmeyer (Gen. Mgr./Adv. Mgr.); Bob Morris (Circ. Mgr.); Stephen Barrett (Nat'l Sales Dir.)
Parent company (for newspapers): Black Press Group Ltd.; Sound Publishing, Inc.

THE STAR

Street address 1: 3 MIDWAY AVE
Street address city: Grand Coulee
Street address state: WA

Zip/Postal code: 99133
General Phone: (509) 633-1350
General Fax: (509) 633-3828
Advertising Phone: (509) 633-1350
Advertising Fax: (509) 633-3828
Editorial Phone: (509) 633-1350
Editorial Fax: (509) 633-3828
General/National Adv. E-mail: ads@grandcoulee.com
Display Adv. E-mail: ads@grandcoulee.com
Editorial e-mail: scott@grandcoulee.com
Primary Website: grandcoulee.com
Year Established: 1945
Avg Paid Circ: 1720
Avg Free Circ: 3000
Audit By: Sworn/Estimate/Non-Audited
Audit Date: 10.06.2019
Personnel: Scott Hunter (Ed./Pub.); Gwen Hilson (Prod. Mgr.); Roger Lucas (Reporter)
Parent company (for newspapers): Star Publishing Inc

THE SUN TRIBUNE

Street address 1: 705 E Hemlock St
Street address city: Othello
Street address state: WA
Zip/Postal code: 99344-1425
General Phone: (509) 765-8549
General Fax: (509) 765-8659
Advertising Phone: (509) 765-8549
Advertising Fax: (509) 765-8659
Editorial Phone: (509) 765-8549
Editorial Fax: (509) 765-8659
General/National Adv. E-mail: publisher@suntribunenews.com
Display Adv. E-mail: publisher@suntribunenews.com
Editorial e-mail: editor@suntribunenews.com
Primary Website: suntribunenews.com
Year Established: 2012
Avg Paid Circ: 1250
Avg Free Circ: 0
Audit By: Sworn/Estimate/Non-Audited
Audit Date: 10.06.2019
Personnel: Bob Richardson (Publisher)
Parent company (for newspapers): Hagadone Corporation

THE TENINO INDEPENDENT

Street address 1: 297 Sussex Ave W
Street address city: Tenino
Street address state: WA
Zip/Postal code: 98589-9360
General Phone: (360) 264-2500
General Fax: (360) 264-2955
Advertising Phone: (360) 748-6848
Advertising Fax: (360) 748-3666
Editorial Phone: (360) 264-2500
Editorial Fax: (360) 264-2955
General/National Adv. E-mail: independent@devaulpublishing.com
Display Adv. E-mail: sales2@devaulpublishing.com
Editorial e-mail: independent@devaulpublishing.com
Primary Website: devaulpublishing.com
Year Established: 1922
Avg Paid Circ: 1200
Audit By: Sworn/Estimate/Non-Audited
Audit Date: 10.06.2019
Personnel: Frank DeVaul (Pub.); Judy DeVaul (Pub.); Dan Fisher (Ed.)

THE TIMES

Street address 1: PO Box 97
Street address city: Waitsburg
Street address state: WA
Zip/Postal code: 99361-0097
General Phone: (509) 337-6631
General Fax: (509) 337-6045
Advertising Phone: (509) 337-6631
Advertising Fax: (509) 337-6045
Editorial Phone: (509) 337-6631
Editorial Fax: (509) 337-6045
General/National Adv. E-mail: advertising@waitsburgtimes.com
Display Adv. E-mail: publisher@waitsburgtimes.com
Editorial e-mail: editor@waitsburgtimes.com
Primary Website: waitsburgtimes.com
Year Established: 1877
Audit By: Sworn/Estimate/Non-Audited
Audit Date: 10.06.2019
Personnel: Imbert Matthee (Pub.); Ken Graham (Ed.); Larry Davidson (Adv. Mgr.)

THE VIDETTE

Street address 1: 109 W Marcy Ave
Street address city: Montesano
Street address state: WA
Zip/Postal code: 98563-3615
General Phone: (360) 249-3311
General Fax: (360) 249-5636
General/National Adv. E-mail: bhunter@thedailyworld.com
Display Adv. E-mail: class@thedailyworld.com
Editorial e-mail: mlang@thevidette.com
Primary Website: thevidette.com
Year Established: 1883
Avg Paid Circ: 5583
Avg Free Circ: 749
Audit By: AAM
Audit Date: 31.03.2016
Personnel: Michael Hrycko (Pub.); Michael Lang (Ed.); Brent Hunter (Adv.); Amy Husted (Circ. Dir.)
Parent company (for newspapers): Sound Publishing, Inc.

THE WHIDBEY EXAMINER

Street address 1: 6 NW Coveland St
Street address city: Coupeville
Street address state: WA
Zip/Postal code: 98239
General Phone: (360) 678-8060
General Fax: (360) 678-6073
Advertising Phone: (360) 678-8060
Advertising Fax: (360) 678-6073
Editorial Phone: (360) 678-8060
Editorial Fax: (360) 678-6073
General/National Adv. E-mail: news@whidbeyexaminer.com
Display Adv. E-mail: news@whidbeyexaminer.com
Editorial e-mail: editor@whidbeyexaminer.com
Primary Website: whidbeyexaminer.com
Year Established: 1994
Avg Paid Circ: 983
Avg Free Circ: 40
Audit By: Sworn/Estimate/Non-Audited
Audit Date: 10.06.2019
Personnel: Kasia Pierzga (Ed./Pub.); Stephen Barrett (Nat'l Sales Dir.); Theresa Eskridge (Nat'l/Rgl Acct. Mgr.)
Parent company (for newspapers): Black Press Group Ltd.; Sound Publishing, Inc.

THE WOODINVILLE WEEKLY

Street address 1: 16932 Wdnvl Red Rd NE
Street address 2: Ste A101
Street address city: Woodinville
Street address state: WA
Zip/Postal code: 98072-6980
General Phone: (425) 483-0606
General Fax: (425) 486-7593
Advertising Phone: (425) 483-0606
Advertising Fax: (425) 486-7593
Editorial Phone: (425) 483-0606
Editorial Fax: (425) 486-7593
General/National Adv. E-mail: sales@woodinville.com
Display Adv. E-mail: sales@woodinville.com
Editorial e-mail: editor@woodinville.com
Primary Website: nwnews.com
Year Established: 1976
Avg Free Circ: 17700
Audit By: Sworn/Estimate/Non-Audited
Audit Date: 10.06.2019
Personnel: Julie Boselly (Pub.)

TUKWILA REPORTER

Street address 1: 19426 68th Ave S
Street address 2: Ste A
Street address city: Kent
Street address state: WA
Zip/Postal code: 98032-1193
General Phone: (253) 872-6600
General/National Adv. E-mail: marketing@soundpublishing.com
Editorial e-mail: mklaas@soundpublishing.com
Primary Website: tukwilareporter.com
Avg Paid Circ: 9383
Avg Free Circ: 385
Audit By: AAM
Audit Date: 31.03.2018
Personnel: Mark Klaas (Ed.)
Parent company (for newspapers): Black Press Group Ltd.; Sound Publishing, Inc.

VASHON-MAURY ISLAND BEACHCOMBER

Street address 1: 17141 Vashon Hwy SW
Street address 2: Ste B
Street address city: Vashon
Street address state: WA
Zip/Postal code: 98070-4603
General Phone: (206) 463-9195
General Fax: (206) 673.8288
Advertising Phone: (206) 463-9195
Advertising Fax: (206) 463-6122
Editorial Phone: (206) 463-9195
Editorial Fax: (206) 673.8288
General/National Adv. E-mail: publisher@vashonbeachcomber.com
Display Adv. E-mail: sriemer@vashonbeachcomber.com
Editorial e-mail: editor@vashonbeachcomber.com
Primary Website: vashonbeachcomber.com
Year Established: 1957
Avg Paid Circ: 2606
Avg Free Circ: 30
Audit By: AAM
Audit Date: 31.03.2018
Personnel: Daralyn Anderson (Pub.); Stephen Barrett (Nat'l Sales Dir.)
Parent company (for newspapers): Black Press Group Ltd.; Sound Publishing, Inc.

VOICE OF THE VALLEY

Street address 1: 26909 206th Ave SE
Street address city: Covington
Street address state: WA
Zip/Postal code: 98042
General Phone: (425) 432-9696
General Fax: (866) 423-9203
Advertising Phone: (425) 432-9696
Advertising Fax: (866) 423-9203
Editorial Phone: (425) 432-9696
Editorial Fax: (866) 423-9203
General/National Adv. E-mail: advertising@voiceofthevalley.com
Display Adv. E-mail: advertising@voiceofthevalley.com
Editorial e-mail: news@voiceofthevalley.com
Primary Website: voiceofthevalley.com
Year Established: 1969
Audit By: Sworn/Estimate/Non-Audited
Audit Date: 10.06.2019
Personnel: Donna Hayes (Pub./Ed.)

WAHKIAKUM COUNTY EAGLE

Street address 1: 77 Main St
Street address city: Cathlamet
Street address state: WA
Zip/Postal code: 98612-4201
General Phone: (360) 795-3391
General Fax: (360) 795-3983
Advertising Phone: (360) 795-3391
Advertising Fax: (360) 795-3983
Editorial Phone: (360) 795-3391
Editorial Fax: (360) 795-3983
General/National Adv. E-mail: kathi@waheagle.com
Display Adv. E-mail: geri@waheagle.com
Editorial e-mail: ernelson@teleport.com
Primary Website: waheagle.com
Year Established: 1891
Avg Paid Circ: 1660
Avg Free Circ: 33
Audit By: Sworn/Estimate/Non-Audited
Audit Date: 10.06.2019
Personnel: Rick Nelson (Pub./Ed.); Geri R. Florek (Adv. Mgr./Prod. Mgr.); Kathi Howell (Adv. Account Mgr.)

WENATCHEE BUSINESS JOURNAL

Street address 1: 201 Cottage Ave
Street address 2: Ste 4
Street address city: Cashmere
Street address state: WA
Zip/Postal code: 98815-1616
General Phone: (509) 782-3781
General Fax: (509) 782-9074
Advertising Phone: (509) 548-5286
Advertising Fax: (509) 548-4789
Editorial Phone: (509) 782-3781
Editorial Fax: (509) 782-9074
General/National Adv. E-mail: carol@leavenworthecho.com
Display Adv. E-mail: classifieds@leavenworthecho.com
Editorial e-mail: gary@ncwmedia.net
Primary Website: ncwbusiness.com
Year Established: 1987
Avg Paid Circ: 2100
Avg Free Circ: 2200
Audit By: Sworn/Estimate/Non-Audited
Audit Date: 10.06.2019
Personnel: Gary Begin (Mng. Ed.)
Parent company (for newspapers): NCW Media, Inc.

WESTSIDE SEATTLE

Street address 1: PO Box 66769
Street address city: Seattle
Street address state: WA
Zip/Postal code: 98166-0769
General Phone: (206) 251-3220
Advertising Phone: (206) 387-3873
Editorial Phone: (425) 238-4616
General/National Adv. E-mail: donao@robinsonnews.com
Display Adv. E-mail: classifieds@robinsonnews.com
Editorial e-mail: kenr@robinsonnews.com
Primary Website: westsideseattle.com
Year Established: 1923
Audit By: Sworn/Estimate/Non-Audited
Audit Date: 10.06.2019
Personnel: Tim Robinson (Pub.); Ken Robinson (Mng. Ed.)
Parent company (for newspapers): Robinson Communications, Inc.

WHIDBEY CROSSWIND

Street address 1: 800 SE Barrington Drive
Street address city: Oak Harbor
Street address state: WA
Zip/Postal code: 98277
General Phone: (360) 675-6611
Advertising Phone: (360) 675-6611
Editorial Phone: (360) 675-6611
Editorial e-mail: editor@whidbeynewsgroup.com
Primary Website: whidbeycrosswind.com
Avg Paid Circ: 0
Avg Free Circ: 5650
Audit By: AAM
Audit Date: 31.03.2018
Personnel: Kevin Graves (Pub./Ed.); Jessie Stensland (Editor); Stephen Barrett (Nat'l Sales Dir.)
Parent company (for newspapers): Sound Publishing, Inc.

WHIDBEY NEWS TIMES

Street address 1: 800 SE Barrington Drive
Street address city: Oak Harbor
Street address state: WA
Zip/Postal code: 98277
General Phone: (360) 675-6611
Advertising Phone: (360) 675-6611
Editorial Phone: (360) 675-6611
Display Adv. E-mail: kwinjum@whidbeynewsgroup.com
Editorial e-mail: editor@whidbeynewsgroup.com
Primary Website: whidbeynewstimes.com
Mthly Avg Views: 150000
Mthly Avg Unique Visitors: 60000
Year Established: 1908
Avg Paid Circ: 3576
Avg Free Circ: 309
Sat. Circulation Paid: 6498
Sat. Circulation Free: 239
Audit By: AAM
Audit Date: 31.03.2018
Personnel: Keven R. Graves (Pub.); Jessie Stensland (Editor); Megan Hansen (Ed.); Stephen Barrett (Nat'l Sales Dir.)
Parent company (for newspapers): Black Press Group Ltd.; Sound Publishing, Inc.

WHITMAN COUNTY GAZETTE

Street address 1: 211 N Main St
Street address city: Colfax
Street address state: WA
Zip/Postal code: 99111-1816
General Phone: (509) 397-4333

General Fax: (509) 397-4527
Advertising Phone: (509) 397-4333
Advertising Fax: (509) 397-4527
Editorial Phone: (509) 397-4333
Editorial Fax: (509) 397-4527
General/National Adv. E-mail: WCGAZETTE@GMAIL.COM
Display Adv. E-mail: WCGAZETTE@GMAIL.COM
Editorial e-mail: WCGAZETTE@GMAIL.COM
Primary Website: wcgazette.com
Year Established: 1877
Audit By: Sworn/Estimate/Non-Audited
Audit Date: 10.06.2019
Personnel: Sally Ousley (News Ed.); Gordon Forgey (News Ed.)

WILBUR REGISTER

Street address 1: 110 NE Main St
Street address city: Wilbur
Street address state: WA
Zip/Postal code: 99185-5115
General Phone: (509) 647-5551
General Fax: (509) 647-5552
General/National Adv. E-mail: wilburregister@centurytel.net
Display Adv. E-mail: wilburregister@centurytel.net
Editorial e-mail: wilburregister@centurytel.net
Year Established: 1889
Avg Paid Circ: 1000
Audit By: Sworn/Estimate/Non-Audited
Audit Date: 10.06.2019
Personnel: Frank Stedman (Pub.)

YAKIMA VALLEY BUSINESS TIMES

Street address 1: 416 S 3rd St
Street address city: Yakima
Street address state: WA
Zip/Postal code: 98901-2834
General Phone: (509) 457-4886
General Fax: (509) 457-5214
Advertising Phone: (509) 457-4886
Advertising Fax: (509) 457-5214
Editorial Phone: (509) 457-4886
Editorial Fax: (509) 457-5214
General/National Adv. E-mail: sales@yvpub.com
Display Adv. E-mail: ads@yvpub.com
Editorial e-mail: news@yvpub.com
Primary Website: yvpub.com
Year Established: 1997
Audit By: Sworn/Estimate/Non-Audited
Audit Date: 10.06.2019
Personnel: Bruce Smith (Pub.); Erick Peterson (Ed.)
Parent company (for newspapers): Yakima Valley Newspapers LLC

WEST VIRGINIA

BRAXTON CITIZENS' NEWS

Street address 1: 501 Main St
Street address city: Sutton
Street address state: WV
Zip/Postal code: 26601-1320
General Phone: (304)765-5193
General Fax: (304)765-2754
Advertising Phone: (304)765-5193
Advertising Fax: (304)765-2754
Editorial Phone: (304)765-5193
Editorial Fax: (304)765-2754
General/National Adv. E-mail: editor@bcn-news.com
Display Adv. E-mail: jennifer@bcn-news.com
Classified Adv. e-mail: janet@bcn-news.com
Editorial e-mail: editor@bcn-news.com
Primary Website: bcn-news.com
Year Established: 1976
Avg Paid Circ: 6150
Audit By: Sworn/Estimate/Non-Audited
Audit Date: 10.06.2019
Personnel: Ed Given (Pub./Ed.)

BRAXTON DEMOCRAT-CENTRAL

Street address 1: 201 2nd St
Street address city: Sutton
Street address state: WV
Zip/Postal code: 26601-1349
General Phone: (304)765-5555
Advertising Phone: (304) 765-5555
Editorial Phone: (304) 765-5555
General/National Adv. E-mail: braxton@wvdsl.net
Display Adv. E-mail: braxton@wvdsl.net
Editorial e-mail: braxton@mountain.net
Year Established: 1883
Avg Paid Circ: 4900
Avg Free Circ: 100
Audit By: Sworn/Estimate/Non-Audited
Audit Date: 10.06.2019
Personnel: Craig A. Smith (Pub.); Brenda Tingler (Adv. Mgr.); Joan Bias (Ed.)

BRIDGER VALLEY PIONEER

Street address 1: 317 Bradshaw St # 2
Street address city: Lyman
Street address state: WY
Zip/Postal code: 82937
General Phone: (307)787-3229
General Fax: (307)787-6795
Advertising Phone: (307)789-6560 ext. 103
Advertising Fax: (307)787-6795
Editorial Phone: (307)789-6560
Editorial Fax: (307)787-6795
General/National Adv. E-mail: ads@bridgervalleypioneer.com
Display Adv. E-mail: ads@bridgervalleypioneer.com
Editorial e-mail: news@bridgervalleypioneer.com
Primary Website: bridgervalleypioneer.com
Avg Paid Circ: 1800
Audit By: Sworn/Estimate/Non-Audited
Audit Date: 10.06.2019
Personnel: Mark Tesoro (Pub.); Virginia Giorgis (Ed.); Jerilyn Case (Adv.)
Parent company (for newspapers): San Luis Valley Publishing

BUFFALO BULLETIN

Street address 1: 58 N Lobban Ave
Street address city: Buffalo
Street address state: WY
Zip/Postal code: 82834-1953
General Phone: (307)684-2223
General Fax: (307)684-7431
Advertising Phone: (307)684-2223
Advertising Fax: (307)684-7431
Editorial Phone: (307)684-2223
Editorial Fax: (307)684-7431
General/National Adv. E-mail: clayton@buffalobulletin.com
Display Adv. E-mail: clayton@buffalobulletin.com
Editorial e-mail: jen@buffalobulletin.com
Primary Website: buffalobulletin.com
Avg Paid Circ: 3800
Audit By: Sworn/Estimate/Non-Audited
Audit Date: 10.06.2019
Personnel: Tammy Teigen (Office Mgr.); Robert Hicks (Pub.); Jen Sieve-Hicks (News Ed.); Clayton Maynard (Adv. Sales Rep.); Evelyn Lack (Business Mgr.); Shelley Gill (Adv. Sales Rep.)

CASPER JOURNAL

Street address 1: 170 Star Ln
Street address city: Casper
Street address state: WY
Zip/Postal code: 82604-2883
General Phone: (307)265-3870
General Fax: (307)265-4616
Advertising Phone: (307)265-3870
Advertising Fax: (307)265-4616
Editorial Phone: (307)266-0516
Editorial Fax: (307)265-4616
General/National Adv. E-mail: publisher@casperjournal.com
Display Adv. E-mail: publisher@casperjournal.com
Editorial e-mail: editor@casperjournal.com
Primary Website: casperjournal.com
Year Established: 1978
Avg Paid Circ: 600
Avg Free Circ: 25000
Audit By: Sworn/Estimate/Non-Audited
Audit Date: 10.06.2019
Personnel: Dale Bohren (Pub./Ed.); Gen Cotherman (Assistant Ed.); Makayla Moore (Reporter); Janet Johnson (Adv. Sales); LeeAnn Crawley (Circ. Mgr.)
Parent company (for newspapers): Dispatch-Argus

CLAY COUNTY FREE PRESS

Street address 1: 136 MAIN ST
Street address city: Clay
Street address state: WV
Zip/Postal code: 25043
General Phone: (304) 587-4250
General Fax: (304) 587-7300
Advertising Phone: (304) 587-4250
Advertising Fax: (304) 587-7300
Editorial Phone: (304) 587-4250
Editorial Fax: (304) 587-7300
General/National Adv. E-mail: news@claycountyfreepress.com
Display Adv. E-mail: advertising@claycountyfreepress.com
Editorial e-mail: news@claycountyfreepress.com
Primary Website: claycountyfreepress.com
Avg Paid Circ: 3500
Audit By: Sworn/Estimate/Non-Audited
Audit Date: 10.06.2019
Personnel: Marti Marshall (Pub./Ed.)
Parent company (for newspapers): Mountain Media

COAL VALLEY NEWS

Street address 1: 350 Main St
Street address city: Madison
Street address state: WV
Zip/Postal code: 25130-1293
General Phone: (304)369-1165
General Fax: (304)369-1166
Advertising Phone: (304)369-1165
Advertising Fax: (304)369-1166
Editorial Phone: (304)369-1165
Editorial Fax: (304)369-1166
General/National Adv. E-mail: MBush@civitasmedia.com
Display Adv. E-mail: SChampion@civitasmedia.com
Editorial e-mail: fpace@civitasmedia.com
Primary Website: coalvalleynews.com
Year Established: 1925
Avg Paid Circ: 5000
Audit By: Sworn/Estimate/Non-Audited
Audit Date: 10.06.2019
Personnel: Fred Pace (Pub./Ed.); Jani Newan (Mng. Ed.); Angie Alexander (Gen. Mgr.)
Parent company (for newspapers): HD Media Company LLC

DUBOIS FRONTIER

Street address 1: 8 C St
Street address city: Dubois
Street address state: WY
Zip/Postal code: 82513
General Phone: (307)455-2525
Advertising Phone: (307)455-2525
Editorial Phone: (307)455-2525
General/National Adv. E-mail: frontierads@wyoming.com
Display Adv. E-mail: frontierads@wyoming.com
Editorial e-mail: duboisfrontier@wyoming.com
Primary Website: duboisfrontier.com
Year Established: 1927
Avg Paid Circ: 1200
Audit By: Sworn/Estimate/Non-Audited
Audit Date: 10.06.2019
Personnel: Christine Smith (Mng. Ed.)

GREEN RIVER STAR

Street address 1: 445 Uinta Dr
Street address city: Green River
Street address state: WY
Zip/Postal code: 82935-4815
General Phone: (307)875-3103
Advertising Phone: (307)875-3103
Editorial Phone: (307)875-3103
General/National Adv. E-mail: sales1@greenriverstar.com
Display Adv. E-mail: sales1@greenriverstar.com
Editorial e-mail: editor@greenriverstar.com
Primary Website: greenriverstar.com
Year Established: 1890
Avg Paid Circ: 3200
Audit By: Sworn/Estimate/Non-Audited
Audit Date: 10.06.2019
Personnel: J. Louis Mullen (Publisher); Sarah Wallace (Advertising); David Martin (Editor)

GUERNSEY GAZETTE

Street address 1: 40 S Wyoming St
Street address city: Guernsey
Street address state: WY
Zip/Postal code: 82214
General Phone: (307)836-2021
General Fax: (307)836-2021
Advertising Phone: (307)322-2627
Advertising Fax: (307)836-2021
Editorial Phone: (307)836-2021
Editorial Fax: (307)836-2021
General/National Adv. E-mail: kcoburn@guernseygazette.com
Display Adv. E-mail: ggads@guernseygazette.com
Editorial e-mail: ggeditor@guernseygazette.com
Primary Website: guernseygazette.com
Avg Paid Circ: 550
Audit By: Sworn/Estimate/Non-Audited
Audit Date: 10.06.2019
Personnel: Jeff Robertson (Pub.); Karry Coburn (Gen. Mgr./Account Exec.); Vicki Hood (Ed.)
Parent company (for newspapers): San Luis Valley Publishing

HD MEDIA COMPANY LLC

Street address 1: 946 5th Ave
Street address city: Huntington
Street address state: WV
Zip/Postal code: 25701-2004
General Phone: (304) 526-2753
General Fax: (304) 526-2857
General/National Adv. E-mail: brrenfroe@herald-dispatch.com
Display Adv. E-mail: brrenfroe@herald-dispatch.com
Editorial e-mail: news@herald-dispatch.com
Primary Website: herald-dispatch.com
Year Established: 1874
Avg Paid Circ: 5800
Audit By: Sworn/Estimate/Non-Audited
Audit Date: 10.06.2019
Personnel: Les Smith; Brenda Renfroe (Adv. Dir.); Misty Deere (Circ. Mgr.)

HERALD & DISPATCH

Street address 1: 946 5th Ave
Street address city: Huntington
Street address state: WV
Zip/Postal code: 25701-2004
General Phone: (304) 526-2753
General Fax: (304) 526-2857
Advertising Phone: (304) 526-6696
Advertising Fax: (304) 526-2863
Editorial Phone: (304) 526-2787
General/National Adv. E-mail: news@herald-dispatch.com
Editorial e-mail: news@herald-dispatch.com
Primary Website: herald-dispatch.com
Avg Paid Circ: 1044
Avg Free Circ: 6
Audit By: Sworn/Estimate/Non-Audited
Audit Date: 10.06.2019
Personnel: Les Smith (Ed.); Charles Jessup (Adv. Dir.); Paul Buckley (Oper. Mgr.); Misty Deere (Circ. Mgr.)

JACKSON HERALD

Street address 1: PO Box 38
Street address 2: 305 N Church St
Street address city: Ravenswood
Street address state: WV
Zip/Postal code: 26164-0038
General Phone: (304) 372-4222
General Fax: (304) 372-5544
Advertising Phone: (304) 372-4222
Advertising Fax: (304) 372-5544
Editorial Phone: (304) 372-4222
Editorial Fax: (304) 372-5544
General/National Adv. E-mail: tmandrake@jacksonnewspapers.com
Display Adv. E-mail: classified@jacksonnewspapers.com
Editorial e-mail: gmatics@jacksonnewspapers.com
Primary Website: jacksonnewspapers.com
Year Established: March 1, 1876
Avg Paid Circ: 6500
Audit By: Sworn/Estimate/Non-Audited

Audit Date: 10.06.2019
Personnel: Greg Matics (Ed/Gen Mgr); Jennifer Patterson (Website Mgr.)
Parent company (for newspapers): CherryRoad Media

JACKSON HOLE NEWS&GUIDE

Street address 1: 1225 Maple Way
Street address city: Jackson
Street address state: WY
Zip/Postal code: 83001-8567
General Phone: (307) 733-2047
General Fax: (307) 733-2138
Advertising Phone: (307) 732 7070
Advertising Fax: (307) 733-2138
Editorial Phone: (307) 732 7063
Editorial Fax: (307) 732-2138
General/National Adv. E-mail: adsales@jhnewsandguide.com
Display Adv. E-mail: adsales@jhnewsandguide.com
Classified Adv. e-mail: classifieds@jhnewsandguide.com
Editorial e-mail: editor@jhnewsandguide.com
Primary Website: jhnewsandguide.com
Mthly Avg Views: 528555
Mthly Avg Unique Visitors: 353898
Year Established: 1970
Avg Paid Circ: 7571
Audit By: USPS
Audit Date: 01.10.2021
Personnel: Kevin Olson (CEO, President); Adam Meyer (VP, COO, Publisher); Amy Golightly (Director of Business Development); John Moses (Editor)
Parent company (for newspapers): Teton Media Works, Inc.

LANDER JOURNAL

Street address 1: 332 Main St
Street address city: Lander
Street address state: WY
Zip/Postal code: 82520-3102
General Phone: (307)332-2323
General Fax: (307)332-9332
Advertising Phone: (307)332-2323
Advertising Fax: (307)332-9332
Editorial Phone: (307)332-2323
Editorial Fax: (307)332-9332
General/National Adv. E-mail: journal@wyoming.com
Display Adv. E-mail: journal@wyoming.com
Editorial e-mail: newsdepartment@wyoming.com
Primary Website: landerjournal.net
Avg Paid Circ: 4475
Avg Free Circ: 2600
Audit By: Sworn/Estimate/Non-Audited
Audit Date: 10.06.2019
Personnel: Steve Peck (Pub.)
Parent company (for newspapers): The Riverton Ranger, Inc.

MONROE WATCHMAN

Street address 1: 430 Main St
Street address city: Union
Street address state: WV
Zip/Postal code: 24983
General Phone: (304)772-3016
General Fax: (304)772-4421
Advertising Phone: (304)772-3016
Advertising Fax: (304)772-4421
Editorial Phone: (304)772-3016
Editorial Fax: (304)772-4421
General/National Adv. E-mail: watchman2@earthlink.net
Display Adv. E-mail: watchman2@earthlink.net
Classified Adv. e-mail: watchman.sales@earthlink.net
Editorial e-mail: watchman2@earthlink.net
Primary Website: www.themonroewatchman.com
Year Established: 1872
Avg Paid Circ: 2820
Avg Free Circ: 15
Audit By: Sworn/Estimate/Non-Audited
Audit Date: 23.09.2023
Personnel: Dale Mohler (Pub./Gen. Mgr.); Craig Mohler (Editor); Laura Jewell (Advertising design and classifieds); John Honaker (Advertising Manager); Jesse Willey (Classifieds and subscriptions manager); Robin Lloyd (Classifieds manager); Joe Adkins (Staff writer and page layout)

MONTGOMERY HERALD

Street address 1: 417 Main St.
Street address city: Oak Hill
Street address state: WV
Zip/Postal code: 25901
General Phone: (304) 442-4156
General Fax: (304) 442-8753
Advertising Phone: (304) 442-4156
Advertising Fax: (304) 442-8753
Editorial Phone: (304) 442-4156
Editorial Fax: (304) 442-8753
General/National Adv. E-mail: fwood@register-herald.com
Display Adv. E-mail: mhnews@register-herald.com
Editorial e-mail: ckeenan@register-herald.com
Primary Website: montgomery-herald.com
Avg Paid Circ: 1500
Avg Free Circ: 184
Audit By: Sworn/Estimate/Non-Audited
Audit Date: 10.06.2019
Personnel: Frank Wood (Pub.); Cheryl Keenan (Ed.)
Parent company (for newspapers): CNHI, LLC

MOORCROFT LEADER

Street address 1: 304 N Riley Ave
Street address city: Moorcroft
Street address state: WY
Zip/Postal code: 82721
General Phone: (307)756-3371
Editorial e-mail: moorcroftleader@gmail.com
Primary Website: moorcroftleader.com
Year Established: 1909
Avg Paid Circ: 1200
Avg Free Circ: 135
Audit By: Sworn/Estimate/Non-Audited
Audit Date: 10.06.2019
Personnel: Margaret Bauer (Pub./Ed./Adv. Mgr.); Melissa Paden (Adv. Mgr.); Grace Moore (Reporter)
Parent company (for newspapers): Moorcroft Leader

MOUNTAIN STATESMAN

Street address 1: 914 W Main St
Street address city: Grafton
Street address state: WV
Zip/Postal code: 26354-1028
General Phone: (304) 265-3333
General Fax: (304) 265-3342
Advertising Phone: (304) 265-3333 ext. 20
Advertising Fax: (304) 265-3342
Editorial Phone: (304) 265-3333
Editorial Fax: (304) 265-3342
General/National Adv. E-mail: gftemail@aol.com
Display Adv. E-mail: gftemail@aol.com
Editorial e-mail: editor@mountainstatesman.com
Primary Website: mountainstatesman.com
Avg Paid Circ: 3300
Avg Free Circ: 20
Audit By: Sworn/Estimate/Non-Audited
Audit Date: 10.06.2019
Personnel: Jean Metz (Pub.); Robert Jennings (Ed.); Monica Robinson (Circ. Mgr.)
Parent company (for newspapers): San Luis Valley Publishing

MULLENS ADVOCATE

Street address 1: 217 Moran Ave
Street address city: Mullens
Street address state: WV
Zip/Postal code: 25882-1426
General Phone: (304)294-4144
Advertising Phone: (304) 294-4144
Editorial Phone: (304)294-4144
General/National Adv. E-mail: mullensadvocate@yahoo.com
Display Adv. E-mail: mullensadvocate@yahoo.com
Editorial e-mail: mullensadvocate@yahoo.com
Year Established: 1913
Avg Paid Circ: 1700
Audit By: Sworn/Estimate/Non-Audited
Audit Date: 10.06.2019
Personnel: Melissa Nester (Publisher); Miranda Austin (Assistant Legal Editor)

NEWS LETTER JOURNAL

Street address 1: 14 West Main
Street address city: Newcastle
Street address state: WY
Zip/Postal code: 82701
General Phone: 3077468726
General Fax: 3077468726
Advertising Phone: 3077468726
Advertising Fax: 3077468726
Editorial Phone: 3077468726
Editorial Fax: 3077468726
General/National Adv. E-mail: editor@newslj.com
Display Adv. E-mail: editor@newslj.com
Classified Adv. e-mail: classifieds@newslj.com
Editorial e-mail: editor@newslj.com
Primary Website: newslj.com
Mthly Avg Views: 250000
Mthly Avg Unique Visitors: 130000
Year Established: 1890
Avg Paid Circ: 1500
Avg Free Circ: 100
Audit By: Sworn/Estimate/Non-Audited
Audit Date: 10.06.2019
Personnel: Bob Bonnar (Assc. Pub./Ed.); Becky Vodopich (Office Mgr.); Kim Dean (Circ. Mgr.); Stacy Haggerty (Adv. Sales Mgr.); Stephanie Bonnar (Graphic Designer)

PINE BLUFFS POST

Street address 1: 201 E 2nd St
Street address city: Pine Bluffs
Street address state: WY
Zip/Postal code: 82082
General Phone: (307)245-3763
General Fax: (307)245-3325
Advertising Phone: (307)245-3763
Advertising Fax: (307)245-3325
Editorial Phone: (307)245-3763
Editorial Fax: (307)245-3325
General/National Adv. E-mail: news@pinebluffspost.com
Display Adv. E-mail: pinebluffsads@rtconnect.net
Editorial e-mail: piebluffsedition@rtconnect.net
Primary Website: pinebluffspost.com
Year Established: 1908
Avg Paid Circ: 1100
Audit By: Sworn/Estimate/Non-Audited
Audit Date: 10.06.2019
Personnel: Gary W. Stevenson (Owner); Sue Stevenson (Owner); Cynthia Shroyer (Pub./Mng. Ed.); Polly Taylor (Gen. Mgr.)
Parent company (for newspapers): Stevenson Newspapers

PLEASANTS COUNTY LEADER

Street address 1: 206 George St
Street address city: Saint Marys
Street address state: WV
Zip/Postal code: 26170-1024
General Phone: (304)684-2424
Advertising Phone: (304)684-2424
Editorial Phone: (304) 684-2424
General/National Adv. E-mail: advertsing@oracleandleader.com
Display Adv. E-mail: advertsing@oracleandleader.com
Editorial e-mail: news@oracleandleader.com
Primary Website: oracleandleader.com
Year Established: 1899
Avg Paid Circ: 2100
Audit By: Sworn/Estimate/Non-Audited
Audit Date: 10.06.2019
Personnel: James McGoldrick (Pub.); Randa Gregg (Gen. Mgr.)

PRINCETON TIMES

Street address 1: 213 S Walker St
Street address city: Princeton
Street address state: WV
Zip/Postal code: 24740-2746
General Phone: (304)425-8191
General Fax: (304)487-1632
Advertising Phone: (304)327-2816
Advertising Fax: (304)487-1632
Editorial Phone: (304)425-2185
Editorial Fax: (304)487-1632
General/National Adv. E-mail: princetontimes@gmail.com
Display Adv. E-mail: princetontimes@gmail.com
Editorial e-mail: ttoler@ptonline.net
Primary Website: ptonline.net
Avg Paid Circ: 4900
Audit By: Sworn/Estimate/Non-Audited
Audit Date: 10.06.2019
Personnel: Tammie Toler (Pub./Gen. Mgr.); Terri Hale (Adv. Dir.); Darryl Husdon (Pub.)
Parent company (for newspapers): CNHI, LLC

PUTNAM HERALD

Street address 1: 946 5th Ave
Street address city: Huntington
Street address state: WV
Zip/Postal code: 25701-2004
General Phone: (304) 526-4000
General Fax: (304) 526-2858
Advertising Phone: (304) 526-2836
Advertising Fax: (304) 526-2858
Editorial Phone: (304) 526-2798
Editorial Fax: (304) 526-2858
General/National Adv. E-mail: cjessup@heralddispatch.com
Display Adv. E-mail: LWADDELL@heralddispatch.com
Editorial e-mail: news@heralddispatch.com
Primary Website: herald-dispatch.com
Avg Free Circ: 3203
Audit By: AAM
Audit Date: 31.12.2018
Personnel: Ed Dawson (Pub./Ed.); Les Smith (Mng. Ed.); Amy Howat (Adv. Dir.)
Parent company (for newspapers): HD Media Company LLC

RAWLINS TIMES

Street address 1: 522 W Buffalo St
Street address city: Rawlins
Street address state: WY
Zip/Postal code: 82301-5623
General Phone: (307) 324-3411
General Fax: (307) 324-2797
Advertising Phone: (307)324-3411
Advertising Fax: (307)324-2797
Editorial Phone: (307)324-3411
Editorial Fax: (307)324-2797
General/National Adv. E-mail: ads@rawlinstimes.com
Display Adv. E-mail: ads@rawlinstimes.com
Classified Adv. e-mail: classifieds@rawlinstimes.com
Editorial e-mail: editor@rawlinstimes.com
Primary Website: rawlinstimes.com
Year Established: 1889
Avg Paid Circ: 1600
Sat. Circulation Paid: 1600
Audit By: Sworn/Estimate/Non-Audited
Audit Date: 10.06.2019
Personnel: Ray Erku (Editor); Kellie Kemp (Advertising Rep); Stephanie Paulsen (Circulation Manager)
Parent company (for newspapers): Adams Publishing Group, LLC

RITCHIE GAZETTE & CAIRO STANDARD

Street address 1: 200 E Main St
Street address city: Harrisville
Street address state: WV
Zip/Postal code: 26362-1204
General Phone: (304) 643-2221
General Fax: (304) 643-2156
Advertising Phone: (304) 643-2221
Advertising Fax: (304) 643-2156
Editorial Phone: (304) 643-2221
Editorial Fax: (304) 643-2156
General/National Adv. E-mail: adsgazette@zoominternet.net
Display Adv. E-mail: adsgazette@zoominternet.net
Editorial e-mail: gazette@zoominternet.net
Year Established: 1873
Avg Paid Circ: 3333
Avg Free Circ: 18
Audit By: Sworn/Estimate/Non-Audited
Audit Date: 10.06.2019
Personnel: Debbie Frederick (Adv. Mgr.); Torie Knight (News Ed.); Denise Shiflet (Prodn. Mgr.)

ROANE COUNTY REPORTER

Street address 1: 210 E Main St
Street address city: Spencer
Street address state: WV
Zip/Postal code: 25276-1602
General Phone: (304)927-2360
General Fax: (304)927-2361
Advertising Phone: (304)927-2360
Advertising Fax: (304)927-2361
Editorial Phone: (304)927-2360
Editorial Fax: (304)927-2361

General/National Adv. E-mail: dhedges@thetimesrecord.net
Display Adv. E-mail: sales@thetimesrecord.net
Editorial e-mail: jcoop@thetimesrecord.net
Primary Website: smalltownpapers.com
Year Established: 1915
Avg Paid Circ: 3145
Avg Free Circ: 100
Audit By: Sworn/Estimate/Non-Audited
Audit Date: 10.06.2019
Personnel: David J. Hedges (Pub.); Jim Cooper (Ed.); Andrew Hedges (Prodn. Mgr.); Annie Hedges (Sales Mgr.); Jim Lemon (Adv. Mgr.)
Parent company (for newspapers): Spencer Newspapers Inc.

SHINNSTON NEWS & HARRISON COUNTY JOURNAL

Street address 1: 860 Court St. N
Street address city: Lewisburg
Street address state: WV
Zip/Postal code: 24901-1159
General Phone: (304) 592-1030
General Fax: (304) 592-0603
Advertising Phone: (304) 647-5724
Advertising Fax: (304) 647-5767
Editorial Phone: (304) 592-1030
Editorial Fax: (304) 592-0603
General/National Adv. E-mail: debra@mountainmedianews.com
Display Adv. E-mail: debra@mountainmedianews.com
Editorial e-mail: newsandjournal@yahoo.com
Primary Website: shinnstonnews.com
Avg Paid Circ: 1000
Audit By: Sworn/Estimate/Non-Audited
Audit Date: 15.09.2019
Personnel: Michael Showell (Pub.); Erin Beck (Editor); Leigh Merrifield (Ed.)
Parent company (for newspapers): Mountain Media, LLC

SPIRIT OF JEFFERSON

Street address 1: 114 N Charles St
Street address city: Charles Town
Street address state: WV
Zip/Postal code: 25414-1508
General Phone: (304) 725-2046
General Fax: (304) 728-6856
Advertising Phone: (304) 725-2046
Advertising Fax: (304) 728-6856
Editorial Phone: (304) 725-2046
Editorial Fax: (304) 728-6856
General/National Adv. E-mail: mary@spiritofjefferson.com
Display Adv. E-mail: ads@spiritofjefferson.com
Editorial e-mail: editor@spiritofjefferson.com
Primary Website: spiritofjefferson.com
Year Established: 1844
Avg Paid Circ: 5000
Avg Free Circ: 63
Audit By: Sworn/Estimate/Non-Audited
Audit Date: 10.06.2019
Personnel: Craig E. See (Pres./Pub.); Robert Snyder (Ed.); Mary Burns (Adv. Mgr.)
Parent company (for newspapers): Jefferson Publishing Co.

STAR VALLEY INDEPENDENT

Street address 1: 360 S Washington St
Street address city: Afton
Street address state: WY
Zip/Postal code: 83110
General Phone: (307)885-5727
General Fax: (307)885-5742
Advertising Phone: (307)885-5727
Advertising Fax: (307)885-5742
Editorial Phone: (307)885-5727
Editorial Fax: (307)885-5742
General/National Adv. E-mail: sviad1@silverstar.com
Display Adv. E-mail: sviclassifieds@silverstar.com
Editorial e-mail: svisarah@silverstar.com
Primary Website: starvalleyindependent.com
Year Established: 1902
Avg Paid Circ: 4000
Audit By: Sworn/Estimate/Non-Audited
Audit Date: 10.06.2019
Personnel: Dan Dockstader (Pub.); Sarah Hale (Managing Ed.); Paula Nield (Circ. Mgr.); Josh Hendreson (Adv. Mgr.); Dahl Erickson (Sports Ed.); Patty Taylor (Adv. Sales); Josh Henderson (Adv. Mgr.)

SUBLETTE EXAMINER

Street address 1: 219 E Pine St
Street address 2: Ste 109
Street address city: Pinedale
Street address state: WY
Zip/Postal code: 82941
General Phone: (307)367-3203
General Fax: (307)367-3209
Advertising Phone: (307)367-3203
Advertising Fax: (307)367-3209
Editorial Phone: (307)367-3203
Editorial Fax: (307)367-3209
General/National Adv. E-mail: spape@subletteexaminer.com
Display Adv. E-mail: spape@subletteexaminer.com
Editorial e-mail: mtesoro@subletteexaminer.com
Primary Website: subletteexaminer.com
Audit By: Sworn/Estimate/Non-Audited
Audit Date: 10.06.2019
Personnel: Megan Neher (Editor); Mark Tesoro (Publisher); Sharon Paper (Gen. Mgr./Adv. Dir)
Parent company (for newspapers): San Luis Valley Publishing

THE BARBOUR DEMOCRAT

Street address 1: 113 CHURCH ST
Street address city: Philippi
Street address state: WV
Zip/Postal code: 26416
General Phone: (304)457-2222
General Fax: (304)457-2235
Advertising Phone: (304)457-2222
Advertising Fax: (304)457-2235
Editorial Phone: (304)457-2222
Editorial Fax: (304)457-2235
General/National Adv. E-mail: ads@barbourdemocratwv.com
Display Adv. E-mail: ads@barbourdemocratwv.com
Editorial e-mail: news@barbourdemocratwv.com
Primary Website: barbourdemocratwv.com
Mthly Avg Views: 1000
Year Established: 1893
Avg Paid Circ: 5301
Avg Free Circ: 300
Audit By: Sworn/Estimate/Non-Audited
Audit Date: 10.06.2019
Personnel: Eric Cutright (Owner)

THE CALHOUN CHRONICLE

Street address 1: PO Box 400
Street address city: Grantsville
Street address state: WV
Zip/Postal code: 26147-0400
General Phone: (304) 354-6917
General Fax: (304) 354-6917
Advertising Phone: (304) 354-6917
Advertising Fax: (304) 354-6917
Editorial Phone: (304) 354-6917
Editorial Fax: (304) 354-6917
General/National Adv. E-mail: contact@calhounchronicle.com
Display Adv. E-mail: office@calhounchronicle.com
Editorial e-mail: contact@calhounchronicle.com
Primary Website: calhounchronicle.com
Year Established: 1883
Avg Paid Circ: 2800
Audit By: Sworn/Estimate/Non-Audited
Audit Date: 10.06.2019
Personnel: Helen Morris (Pub.); Newton Nichols (Ed.)

THE CAMPBELL COUNTY OBSERVER

Street address 1: PO Box 222
Street address city: Rozet
Street address state: WY
Zip/Postal code: 82727-0222
General Phone: (307)670-8980
General Fax: (307)670-9348
Advertising Phone: (307)670-8980
Advertising Fax: (307)670-9348
Editorial Phone: (307)670-8980
Editorial Fax: (307)670-9348
General/National Adv. E-mail: countycampbellobserver@gmail.com
Display Adv. E-mail: countycampbellobserver@gmail.com
Editorial e-mail: countycampbellobserver@gmail.com
Year Established: 2011
Avg Paid Circ: 2000
Audit By: Sworn/Estimate/Non-Audited
Audit Date: 10.06.2019
Personnel: Nicholas De Laat (Owner/Publisher/Editor); Candice De Laat (Owner/Manager); Anne Peterson (Advertising Sales Manager); Dale Russell (Advertising Sales); Owen Clarke (Advertising Design)
Parent company (for newspapers): Patriot Publishing

THE CODY ENTERPRISE

Street address 1: 3101 Big Horn Ave
Street address city: Cody
Street address state: WY
Zip/Postal code: 82414-9250
General Phone: (307) 587-2231
General Fax: (307) 587-5208
Advertising Phone: (307) 587-2231
Advertising Fax: (307) 587-5208
Editorial Phone: (307) 587-2231
Editorial Fax: (307) 587-5208
General/National Adv. E-mail: office@codyenterprise.com
Display Adv. E-mail: classified@codyenterprise.com
Editorial e-mail: amber@codyenterprise.com
Primary Website: codyenterprise.com
Year Established: 1899
Avg Paid Circ: 7050
Audit By: Sworn/Estimate/Non-Audited
Audit Date: 10.06.2019
Personnel: Bob Kennedy (Co-Pub.); John Malmberg (Publisher); John Sides (Prodn. Mgr.); Vin Cappiello (Editor)

THE DOUGLAS BUDGET

Street address 1: 310 E Center St
Street address city: Douglas
Street address state: WY
Zip/Postal code: 82633-2541
General Phone: (307)358-2965
Advertising Phone: (307)358-2965
Editorial Phone: (307)358-2965
General/National Adv. E-mail: publisher@douglas-budget.com
Display Adv. E-mail: publisher@douglas-budget.com
Classified Adv. e-mail: classifieds@douglas-budget.com
Editorial e-mail: publisher@douglas-budget.com
Primary Website: douglas-budget.com
Mthly Avg Views: 32000
Year Established: 1886
Avg Paid Circ: 3960
Avg Free Circ: 20
Audit By: Sworn/Estimate/Non-Audited
Audit Date: 25.09.2021
Personnel: Matt Adelman (Pub./Ed.)
Parent company (for newspapers): Sage Publishing

THE FAYETTE TRIBUNE

Street address 1: 417 Main St
Street address city: Oak Hill
Street address state: WV
Zip/Postal code: 25901
General Phone: (304)469-3373
General Fax: (304)469-4105
General/National Adv. E-mail: fwood@register-herald.com
Display Adv. E-mail: fwood@register-herald.com
Editorial e-mail: ckeenan@register-herald.com
Primary Website: fayettetribune.com
Avg Paid Circ: 2200
Audit By: Sworn/Estimate/Non-Audited
Audit Date: 10.06.2019
Personnel: Cheryl Keenan (Ed.); Frank Wood (Pub.); Debbie Maxwell (Retail Mgr.)
Parent company (for newspapers): CNHI, LLC

THE GLENVILLE DEMOCRAT/ PATHFINDER

Street address 1: PO Box 458
Street address 2: 208 N Court St
Street address city: Glenville
Street address state: WV
Zip/Postal code: 26351-0458
General Phone: (304) 462-7309
General Fax: (304) 462-7300
Advertising Phone: (304) 462-7309
Advertising Fax: (304) 462-7300
Editorial Phone: (304) 462-7309
Editorial Fax: (304) 462-7300
General/National Adv. E-mail: glenvillenews@gmail.com
Display Adv. E-mail: rockbender@hotmail.com
Editorial e-mail: glenvillenews@gmail.com
Primary Website: glenvillenews.com
Year Established: 1892
Avg Paid Circ: 3200
Avg Free Circ: 500
Audit By: Sworn/Estimate/Non-Audited
Audit Date: 10.06.2019
Personnel: David H. Corcoran Sr. (Pub./Sr. Ed./Owner); David Corcoran Jr. (General Manager); Patricia Golden (Bus. Mgr.); Sara Wise (Receptionist/Circulation Manager); Myra Chico-Miller (County Editor)

THE GLENVILLE PATHFINDER

Street address 1: 108 N Court St
Street address city: Glenville
Street address state: WV
Zip/Postal code: 26351-1215
General Phone: (304) 462-7309
General Fax: (304) 462-7300
Advertising Phone: (304) 462-7309
Advertising Fax: (304) 462-7300
Editorial Phone: (304) 462-7309
Editorial Fax: (304) 462-7300
General/National Adv. E-mail: glenvillenews@gmail.com
Display Adv. E-mail: glenvillenews@gmail.com
Editorial e-mail: glenvillenews@gmail.com
Primary Website: glenvillenews.com
Year Established: 1892
Avg Paid Circ: 1500
Avg Free Circ: 300
Audit By: Sworn/Estimate/Non-Audited
Audit Date: 10.06.2019
Personnel: David H. Corcoran Sr. (Pub./Sr. Ed./Owner); David Corcoran Jr. (Gen. Mgr.); Patricia Golden (Bus. Mgr.); Sara Wise (Receptionist/Circulation Clerk)

THE HERALD RECORD

Street address 1: 177 Main St
Street address city: West Union
Street address state: WV
Zip/Postal code: 26456-2019
General Phone: (304)873-1600
General Fax: (304)873-2811
Advertising Phone: (304)873-1600
Advertising Fax: (304)873-2811
Editorial Phone: (304)873-1600
Editorial Fax: (304)873-2811
General/National Adv. E-mail: theheraldrecord1@gmail.com
Display Adv. E-mail: theheraldrecord1@gmail.com
Editorial e-mail: theheraldrecord1@gmail.com
Year Established: 1878
Avg Paid Circ: 2721
Avg Free Circ: 31
Audit By: Sworn/Estimate/Non-Audited
Audit Date: 10.06.2019
Personnel: Virginia Nicholson (Pub./Ed.)

THE INDEPENDENT HERALD

Street address 1: 127 Main Ave.
Street address city: Pineville
Street address state: WV
Zip/Postal code: 24874
General Phone: (800) 888-2834
General/National Adv. E-mail: cjessup@heralddispatch.com
Display Adv. E-mail: lwaddell@heralddispatch.com
Editorial e-mail: vlovejoy@herald-dispatch.com
Primary Website: williamsondailynews.com
Year Established: 1968
Avg Paid Circ: 2500
Audit By: Sworn/Estimate/Non-Audited
Audit Date: 10.06.2019
Personnel: Melissa Blair (Adv. Mgr.)
Parent company (for newspapers): HD Media Company LLC

THE INDUSTRIAL NEWS

Street address 1: PO Box 569

Street address city: Welch
Street address state: WV
Zip/Postal code: 24801-0569
General Phone: (304)938-2142
General Fax: (304)436-3146
Advertising Phone: (304)938-2142
Advertising Fax: (304)436-3146
Editorial Phone: (304)938-2142
Editorial Fax: (304)436-3146
General/National Adv. E-mail: rubyfmccoy@yahoo.com
Display Adv. E-mail: rubyfmccoy@yahoo.com
Editorial e-mail: rubyfmccoy@yahoo.com
Year Established: 1926
Avg Paid Circ: 2000
Audit By: Sworn/Estimate/Non-Audited
Audit Date: 10.06.2019
Personnel: Ruby McCoy (Mng. Ed.); Sheila Bailey (Adv. Mgr.); Gregory Spinella (Pub.); Missy Price (Adv. Mgr.)

THE JACKSON STAR NEWS

Street address 1: 410 Race Street
Street address city: Ravenswood
Street address state: WV
Zip/Postal code: 26164
General Phone: (304) 372-4222
General Fax: (304) 372-5544
Advertising Phone: (304) 372-4222
Advertising Fax: (304) 372-5544
Editorial Phone: (304) 372-4222
Editorial Fax: (304) 372-5544
General/National Adv. E-mail: tmandrake@jacksonnewspapers.com
Display Adv. E-mail: classified@jacksonnewspapers.com
Editorial e-mail: editor@jacksonnewspapers.com
Primary Website: jacksonnewspapers.com
Year Established: January 1, 1868
Avg Paid Circ: 6000
Avg Free Circ: 50
Audit By: Sworn/Estimate/Non-Audited
Audit Date: 10.06.2019
Personnel: Roger Adkins (Ed.); Tina Mandrake (Adv. Mgr.); Teresa Elkins (Circ.)
Parent company (for newspapers): CherryRoad Media

THE KEMMERER GAZETTE

Street address 1: 708 J C Penney Dr
Street address city: Kemmerer
Street address state: WY
Zip/Postal code: 83101-2936
General Phone: (307)877-3347
General Fax: (307)877-3736
Advertising Phone: (307)877-3347
Advertising Fax: (307)877-3736
Editorial Phone: (307)877-3347
Editorial Fax: (307)877-3736
General/National Adv. E-mail: advertising@kemmerergazette.com
Display Adv. E-mail: advertising@kemmerergazette.com
Editorial e-mail: editor@kemmerergazette.com
Primary Website: kemmerergazette.com
Avg Paid Circ: 1650
Audit By: Sworn/Estimate/Non-Audited
Audit Date: 10.06.2019
Personnel: Mark Tesoro (Pub.); Ryan O'Connell (Ed.); Rose Capellen (Office Mgr.); Cortney Reed (Adv. Mgr.)
Parent company (for newspapers): San Luis Valley Publishing

THE LINCOLN JOURNAL

Street address 1: 328 Walnut St
Street address city: Hamlin
Street address state: WV
Zip/Postal code: 25523-1403
General Phone: (304) 824-5101
General Fax: (304) 824-5210
Advertising Phone: (304) 824-5101
Advertising Fax: (304) 824-5210
Editorial Phone: (304) 824-5101
Editorial Fax: (304) 824-5210
General/National Adv. E-mail: advertising@lincolnjournal.com
Display Adv. E-mail: advertising@lincolnjournal.com
Editorial e-mail: editor@lincolnjournal.com
Primary Website: lincolnjournal.com
Year Established: 1903
Avg Paid Circ: 5625
Avg Free Circ: 12875
Audit By: Sworn/Estimate/Non-Audited
Audit Date: 10.06.2019
Personnel: Thomas A. Robinson (Pub./Owner); Sean O'Donoghue (Mng. Ed.); Barbara Cummings (Adv. Mgr.); Patty Robinson (Office Mgr.); Verona Miller (Circ. Mgr.)
Parent company (for newspapers): The Lincoln Journal, Inc.

THE LINCOLN NEWS SENTINEL

Street address 1: 328 Walnut St
Street address city: Hamlin
Street address state: WV
Zip/Postal code: 25523-1403
General Phone: (304)824-5101
General Fax: (304)824-5210
Advertising Phone: (304) 824-5101
Advertising Fax: (304)824-5210
Editorial Phone: (304)824-5101
Editorial Fax: (304)824-5210
General/National Adv. E-mail: advertising@lincolnnewssentinel.com
Display Adv. E-mail: advertising@lincolnnewssentinel.com
Editorial e-mail: editor@lincolnnewssentinel.com
Primary Website: lincolnnewssentinel.com
Avg Paid Circ: 1350
Audit By: Sworn/Estimate/Non-Audited
Audit Date: 10.06.2019
Personnel: Sean O'Donoghue (Managing Editor); Barbara Cummings (Adv. Mgr.); Patty Robinson (Office Mgr.); Verona Miller (Circ. Mgr.)
Parent company (for newspapers): The Lincoln Journal, Inc.

THE LINCOLN TIMES

Street address 1: 328 Walnut St
Street address city: Hamlin
Street address state: WV
Zip/Postal code: 25523-1403
General Phone: (304)824-5101
General Fax: (304)824-5210
Advertising Phone: (304)824-5101
Advertising Fax: (304)824-5210
Editorial Phone: (304)824-5101
Editorial Fax: (304)824-5210
General/National Adv. E-mail: advertising@lincolnjournal.com
Display Adv. E-mail: advertising@lincolnjournal.com
Editorial e-mail: editor@lincolnjournal.com
Primary Website: lincolnjournal.com
Year Established: 1901
Avg Paid Circ: 5461
Avg Free Circ: 12638
Audit By: Sworn/Estimate/Non-Audited
Audit Date: 10.06.2019
Personnel: Sean O'Donoghue (Mng. Ed.); Barbara Cummings (Adv. Mgr.); Patty Robinson (Office Mgr.); Verona Miller (Circ. Mgr.); Jerry G. Leedy (Publisher)
Parent company (for newspapers): The Lincoln Journal, Inc.

THE LINGLE GUIDE

Street address 1: 228 Main St
Street address city: Lingle
Street address state: WY
Zip/Postal code: 82223
General Phone: (307)837-2255
General Fax: (307)532-2283
Advertising Phone: (307)837-2255
Advertising Fax: (307)532-2283
Editorial Phone: (307)837-2255
Editorial Fax: (307)532-2283
General/National Adv. E-mail: calbers@lingleguide.com
Display Adv. E-mail: jgood@lingleguide.com
Editorial e-mail: calbers@lingleguide.com
Primary Website: lingleguide.com
Audit By: Sworn/Estimate/Non-Audited
Audit Date: 10.06.2019
Parent company (for newspapers): San Luis Valley Publishing

THE LUSK HERALD

Street address 1: 227 S Main St
Street address city: Lusk
Street address state: WY
Zip/Postal code: 82225
General Phone: (307)334-2867
General Fax: (307)334-2514
General/National Adv. E-mail: dmaychrzak@torringtontelegram.com
Display Adv. E-mail: dmaychrzak@torringtontelegram.com
Editorial e-mail: hgoddard@luskherald.com
Primary Website: luskherald.com
Year Established: 1886
Avg Paid Circ: 1300
Audit By: Sworn/Estimate/Non-Audited
Audit Date: 10.06.2019
Personnel: Rob Mortimore (Pub.); Heather Goddard (GM/Ed.); Danielle Maychrzak (Adv. Dir.)
Parent company (for newspapers): San Luis Valley Publishing

THE MORGAN MESSENGER

Street address 1: 16 N Mercer St
Street address city: Berkeley Springs
Street address state: WV
Zip/Postal code: 25411-1587
General Phone: (304) 258-1800
General Fax: (304) 258-8441
General/National Adv. E-mail: ads@morganmessenger.com
Display Adv. E-mail: ads@morganmessenger.com
Classified Adv. e-mail: ads@morganmessenger.com
Editorial e-mail: news@morganmessenger.com
Primary Website: morganmessenger.com
Year Established: 1893
Avg Paid Circ: 4800
Audit By: Sworn/Estimate/Non-Audited
Audit Date: 10.06.2020
Personnel: Sandy Buzzerd (Adv. Mgr./Mng. Ed.); Kate Shunney (Editor); Jody Crouse (Managing Editor)

THE PENNSBORO NEWS

Street address 1: 103 N Spring St
Street address city: Harrisville
Street address state: WV
Zip/Postal code: 26362-1274
General Phone: (304)643-4947
General Fax: (304)643-4717
Advertising Phone: (304)643-4947
Advertising Fax: (304)643-4717
Editorial Phone: (304)643-4947
Editorial Fax: (304)643-4717
General/National Adv. E-mail: advertising@ritchiecountynews.com
Display Adv. E-mail: advertising@ritchiecountynews.com
Editorial e-mail: news@ritchiecountynews.com
Primary Website: ritchiecountynews.com
Year Established: 1892
Avg Paid Circ: 4800
Avg Free Circ: 32
Audit By: Sworn/Estimate/Non-Audited
Audit Date: 10.06.2019
Personnel: James McGoldrick (Pub.)

THE PINEDALE ROUNDUP

Street address 1: 219 E Pine St
Street address 2: Ste 116
Street address city: Pinedale
Street address state: WY
Zip/Postal code: 82941
General Phone: (307)367-2123
General Fax: (307)367-6623
Advertising Phone: (307)367-2123
Advertising Fax: (307)367-6623
Editorial Phone: (307)367-2123
Editorial Fax: (307)367-6623
General/National Adv. E-mail: spape@pinedaleroundup.com
Display Adv. E-mail: spape@pinedaleroundup.com
Editorial e-mail: mtesoro@uintacountyherald.com
Primary Website: pinedaleroundup.com
Year Established: 1904
Avg Paid Circ: 4000
Audit By: Sworn/Estimate/Non-Audited
Audit Date: 10.06.2019
Personnel: Megan Neher (Ed.); Kara Losik (General Mgr.)
Parent company (for newspapers): San Luis Valley Publishing

THE PLATTE COUNTY RECORD-TIMES

Street address 1: 1007 8th St
Street address city: Wheatland
Street address state: WY
Zip/Postal code: 82201-2602
General Phone: (307)322-2627
General Fax: (307)322-9612
Advertising Phone: (307)322-2627
Advertising Fax: (307)322-9612
Editorial Phone: (307)322-2627
Editorial Fax: (307)322-9612
General/National Adv. E-mail: kcoburn@pcrecordtimes.com
Display Adv. E-mail: amcdaniel@pcrecordtimes.com
Editorial e-mail: pceditor@pcrecordtimes.com
Primary Website: pcrecordtimes.com
Year Established: 1960
Avg Paid Circ: 1900
Audit By: Sworn/Estimate/Non-Audited
Audit Date: 10.06.2019
Personnel: Jeff Robertson (Pub.); Adam Louis (Ed.); Teri Cordingly (Office Mgr.); Karry Coburn (Adv. Mgr./Gen. Mgr.); Amanda McDaniel (Advertising Rep.)
Parent company (for newspapers): San Luis Valley Publishing

THE POCAHONTAS TIMES

Street address 1: 206 8th St
Street address city: Marlinton
Street address state: WV
Zip/Postal code: 24954-1031
General Phone: (304)799-4973
General Fax: (304)799-6466
Advertising Phone: (304)799-4973
Advertising Fax: (304)799-6466
Editorial Phone: (304)799-4973
Editorial Fax: (304)799-6466
General/National Adv. E-mail: jnh@pocahontastimes.com
Display Adv. E-mail: clj@pocahotnastimes.com
Editorial e-mail: jsgraham@pocahontastimes.com
Primary Website: pocahontastimes.com
Year Established: 1883
Avg Paid Circ: 4500
Audit By: Sworn/Estimate/Non-Audited
Audit Date: 10.06.2019
Personnel: Jaynell Graham (Editor)

THE POWELL TRIBUNE

Street address 1: 128 S Bent St
Street address city: Powell
Street address state: WY
Zip/Postal code: 82435-2714
General Phone: (307)754-2221
General Fax: (307)754-4873
Advertising Phone: (307)754-2221
Advertising Fax: (307)754-4873
Editorial Phone: (307)754-2221
Editorial Fax: (307)754-4873
General/National Adv. E-mail: toby@powelltribune.com
Display Adv. E-mail: fawn@powelltribune.com
Editorial e-mail: tom@powelltribune.com
Primary Website: powelltribune.com
Year Established: 1908
Avg Paid Circ: 4000
Audit By: Sworn/Estimate/Non-Audited
Audit Date: 10.06.2019
Personnel: Dave Bonner (Pub.); Toby Bonner (Adv. Mgr./Gen. Mgr.); Tom Lawrence (Mng. Ed.); Beth Cunning (Office Mgr.)

THE PRESTON COUNTY JOURNAL

Street address 1: 208 W Main St
Street address city: Kingwood
Street address state: WV
Zip/Postal code: 26537
General Phone: (304) 329-0090
General/National Adv. E-mail: advertising@prestonnj.com
Display Adv. E-mail: classified@prestonnj.com
Editorial e-mail: news@prestonnj.com
Primary Website: wvnews.com
Year Established: 1866
Avg Paid Circ: 4700
Audit By: Sworn/Estimate/Non-Audited
Audit Date: 10.06.2019
Personnel: Joseph Hauger

Parent company (for newspapers): Preston Publications, Inc.

THE RECORD DELTA

Street address 1: 2B Clarksburg Rd
Street address city: Buckhannon
Street address state: WV
Zip/Postal code: 26201-8461
General Phone: (304) 472-2800
General Fax: (304) 472-0537
Advertising Phone: (304) 472-2800
Advertising Fax: (304) 472-0537
Editorial Phone: (304) 472-2800 ext. 24
Editorial Fax: (304) 472-0537
General/National Adv. E-mail: ads@recorddeltaonline.com
Display Adv. E-mail: ads@recorddeltaonline.com
Editorial e-mail: brian@recorddeltaonline.com
Primary Website: therecorddelta.com
Avg Paid Circ: 4304
Audit By: Sworn/Estimate/Non-Audited
Audit Date: 10.06.2019
Personnel: Tammy Lyons (Pub.); Brian Bergsstrom (Ed.); Carol Atkins (Prodn. Mgr.)
Parent company (for newspapers): San Luis Valley Publishing

THE SARATOGA SUN

Street address 1: 116 E Bridge St
Street address city: Saratoga
Street address state: WY
Zip/Postal code: 82331
General Phone: (307)326-8311
General Fax: (307)326-5108
Advertising Phone: (307)326-8311
Advertising Fax: (307)326-5108
Editorial Phone: (307) 326-8311
Editorial Fax: (307) 326-5108
General/National Adv. E-mail: sunads@union-tel.com
Display Adv. E-mail: sunads@union-tel.com
Editorial e-mail: saratogasun@netcommander.com
Primary Website: saratogasun.com
Year Established: 1888
Avg Paid Circ: 1800
Avg Free Circ: 20
Audit By: Sworn/Estimate/Non-Audited
Audit Date: 10.06.2019
Personnel: Gary W. Stevenson (Pub./Owner); Joe Elder (Ed.); Liz Wood (Gen. Mgr.)

THE SHEPHERDSTOWN CHRONICLE

Street address 1: P.O. Box 2088
Street address city: Shepherdstown
Street address state: WV
Zip/Postal code: 25443-2088
General Phone: (304)876-3380
General Fax: (304)876-1957
Advertising Phone: (304)263-8931 ext. 121
Advertising Fax: (304)876-1957
Editorial Phone: (304)876-3380
Editorial Fax: (304)876-1957
General/National Adv. E-mail: kspielman@journal-news.net
Display Adv. E-mail: kcambrel@shepherdstownchronicle.com
Editorial e-mail: tmilbourne@shepherdstownchronicle.com
Primary Website: shepherdstownchronicle.com
Audit By: Sworn/Estimate/Non-Audited
Audit Date: 10.06.2019
Personnel: Tabitha Johnston (Ed.); Kelly Cambrel (Ed. Assistant); Judy Gelester (Adv. Dir.)
Parent company (for newspapers): Ogden Newspapers Inc.

THE SUNDANCE TIMES

Street address 1: 311 E Main St
Street address city: Sundance
Street address state: WY
Zip/Postal code: 82729
General Phone: (307)283-3411
General Fax: (307)283-3332
Advertising Phone: (307)283-3411
Advertising Fax: (307)283-3332
Editorial Phone: (307) 283-3411
Editorial Fax: (307) 283-3332
General/National Adv. E-mail: jeff@sundancetimes.com
Display Adv. E-mail: jeff@sundancetimes.com
Editorial e-mail: web@sundancetimes.com
Primary Website: sundancetimes.com
Year Established: 1884
Avg Paid Circ: 1800
Avg Free Circ: 35
Audit By: Sworn/Estimate/Non-Audited
Audit Date: 10.06.2019
Personnel: Jeff Moberg (Adv. Mgr./Ed.)

THE TIMES RECORD

Street address 1: 210 E Main St
Street address city: Spencer
Street address state: WV
Zip/Postal code: 25276-1602
General Phone: (304) 927-2360
General Fax: (304) 927-2361
Advertising Phone: (304) 927-2360
Advertising Fax: (304) 927-2361
Editorial Phone: (304) 927-2360
Editorial Fax: (304) 927-2361
General/National Adv. E-mail: sales@thetimesrecord.net
Display Adv. E-mail: starr@thetimesrecord.net
Editorial e-mail: jcoop@thetimesrecord.net
Year Established: 1888
Avg Paid Circ: 2075
Avg Free Circ: 25
Audit By: Sworn/Estimate/Non-Audited
Audit Date: 10.06.2019
Personnel: David J. Hedges (Pub.); Jim Cooper (Ed.); Andrew Hedges (Prod. Mgr.); Annie Hedges (Sales Mgr)

THE TORRINGTON TELEGRAM

Street address 1: 2025 Main St
Street address city: Torrington
Street address state: WY
Zip/Postal code: 82240-2708
General Phone: (307)532-2184
General Fax: (307)532-2283
Advertising Phone: (307)532-2184
Advertising Fax: (307)532-2283
Editorial Phone: (307)532-2184
Editorial Fax: (307)532-2283
General/National Adv. E-mail: rmort@torringtontelegram.com
Display Adv. E-mail: ttclass@torringtontelegram.com
Editorial e-mail: tpearson@torringtontelegram.com
Primary Website: torringtontelegram.com
Year Established: 1907
Avg Paid Circ: 2600
Avg Free Circ: 70
Audit By: Sworn/Estimate/Non-Audited
Audit Date: 10.06.2019
Personnel: Jeff Robertson (Pub.); Rob Mortimore (Gen. Mgr./Adv. Mgr.); Jean Good (Office Mgr.); Travis Pearson (Ed.)
Parent company (for newspapers): San Luis Valley Publishing

THE WELCH NEWS

Street address 1: 125 Wyoming St
Street address city: Welch
Street address state: WV
Zip/Postal code: 24801-2220
General Phone: (304)436-3144
General Fax: (304)436-3146
Advertising Phone: (304)436-3144
Advertising Fax: (304)436-3146
Editorial Phone: (304)436-3144
Editorial Fax: (304)436-3146
General/National Adv. E-mail: welchnews@frontiernet.net
Display Adv. E-mail: welchnews@frontiernet.net
Editorial e-mail: welchnews@frontiernet.net
Avg Paid Circ: 4764
Audit By: Sworn/Estimate/Non-Audited
Audit Date: 10.06.2019
Personnel: Gregory Spinella (Pub.); Andrea Moorahead (Mng. Ed.); Melissa McKinney (Adv. Dir.); Tom Molin (Circ. Mgr.)

THERMOPOLIS INDEPENDENT RECORD

Street address 1: 431 Broadway St
Street address city: Thermopolis
Street address state: WY
Zip/Postal code: 82443-2715
General Phone: (307)864-2328
General Fax: (307)864-5711
Advertising Phone: (307)864-2328
Advertising Fax: (307)864-5711
Editorial Phone: (307)864-2328
Editorial Fax: (307)864-5711
General/National Adv. E-mail: ads@thermopir.com
Display Adv. E-mail: ads@thermopir.com
Editorial e-mail: news@thermopir.com
Primary Website: thermopir.com
Year Established: 1901
Avg Paid Circ: 1700
Audit By: Sworn/Estimate/Non-Audited
Audit Date: 22.09.2022
Personnel: Amber Geis (Advertising Sales)

TYLER STAR NEWS

Street address 1: 720 Wells St
Street address city: Sistersville
Street address state: WV
Zip/Postal code: 26175-1326
General Phone: (304)652-4141
General Fax: (304)652-1454
Advertising Phone: (304)652-4141
Advertising Fax: (304)652-1454
Editorial Phone: (304)652-4141
Editorial Fax: (304)652-1454
General/National Adv. E-mail: lnorthcraft@tylerstarnews.com
Display Adv. E-mail: bclutter@tylerstarnews.com
Editorial e-mail: editor@tylerstarnews.com
Primary Website: tylerstarnews.com
Avg Paid Circ: 4000
Audit By: Sworn/Estimate/Non-Audited
Audit Date: 10.06.2019
Personnel: Brian Clutter (Pub.); Amy Witschey (Ed.); Lisa Northcraft (Adv. Mgr.)
Parent company (for newspapers): Ogden Newspapers Inc.

UINTA COUNTY HERALD

Street address 1: 849 Front St
Street address 2: Ste 101
Street address city: Evanston
Street address state: WY
Zip/Postal code: 82930-3475
General Phone: (307)789-6560
General Fax: (307)789-2700
Advertising Phone: (307)789-6560 ext. 102
Advertising Fax: (307)789-2700
Editorial Phone: (307)789-6560 ext. 110
Editorial Fax: (307)789-2700
General/National Adv. E-mail: bliechty@uintacountyherald.com
Display Adv. E-mail: mtesoro@uintacountyherald.com
Editorial e-mail: editor@uintacountyherald.com
Primary Website: uintacountyherald.com
Year Established: 1937
Avg Paid Circ: 3250
Avg Free Circ: 73
Audit By: Sworn/Estimate/Non-Audited
Audit Date: 10.06.2019
Personnel: Mark Tesoro (Pub.); Jodi Jensen (Circ. Mgr.); Matt Roberts (Ed.); Kae Ellis (Prodn. Mgr.)
Parent company (for newspapers): San Luis Valley Publishing

WEBSTER ECHO

Street address 1: 219 Back Fork St
Street address city: Webster Springs
Street address state: WV
Zip/Postal code: 26288-1034
General Phone: (304)847-5828
General Fax: (304)847-5991
Advertising Phone: (304)847-5828
Advertising Fax: (304)847-5991
Editorial Phone: (304)847-5828
Editorial Fax: (304)847-5991
General/National Adv. E-mail: websterecho@citlink.net
Display Adv. E-mail: websterecho@citlink.net
Editorial e-mail: websterecho@citlink.net
Avg Paid Circ: 2825
Audit By: Sworn/Estimate/Non-Audited
Audit Date: 10.06.2019
Personnel: Tom Clark (Ed.)

WEBSTER REPUBLICAN

Street address 1: 219 Back Fork St
Street address city: Webster Springs
Street address state: WV
Zip/Postal code: 26288-1034
General Phone: (304)847-5828
General Fax: (304)847-5991
Advertising Phone: (304)847-5828
Advertising Fax: (304)847-5991
Editorial Phone: (304)847-5828
Editorial Fax: (304)847-5991
General/National Adv. E-mail: websterecho@citlink.net
Display Adv. E-mail: websterecho@citlink.net
Editorial e-mail: websterecho@citlink.net
Avg Paid Circ: 994
Audit By: Sworn/Estimate/Non-Audited
Audit Date: 10.06.2019
Personnel: Tom Clark (Ed.)

WESTON DEMOCRAT

Street address 1: 306 Main Ave
Street address city: Weston
Street address state: WV
Zip/Postal code: 26452-2046
General Phone: (304)269-1600
General Fax: (304)269-4035
Advertising Phone: (304)269-1600
Advertising Fax: (304)269-4035
Editorial Phone: (304)269-1600
Editorial Fax: (304)269-4035
General/National Adv. E-mail: ads@westondemocrat.com
Display Adv. E-mail: classifiedlineads@westondemocrat.com
Editorial e-mail: news@westondemocrat.com
Primary Website: westondemocrat.com
Year Established: 1867
Avg Paid Circ: 7000
Avg Free Circ: 88
Audit By: Sworn/Estimate/Non-Audited
Audit Date: 10.06.2019
Personnel: Connie Posey (Adv. Mgr.); Melissa Toothman (Editor); Dusty Metzgar (Reporter); Rebecca Young (Reporter); Alli Clark (Sports Reporter); Tom Hall (Sports Reporter); Donna Prunty (Production Assistant)
Parent company (for newspapers): News Media Corp.

WETZEL CHRONICLE

Street address 1: 1100 3rd St
Street address city: New Martinsville
Street address state: WV
Zip/Postal code: 26155-1500
General Phone: (304)455-3300
General Fax: (304)455-1275
Advertising Phone: (304)455-3300
Advertising Fax: (304)455-1275
Editorial Phone: (304)455-3300
Editorial Fax: (304)455-1275
General/National Adv. E-mail: advertising@wetzelchronicle.com
Display Adv. E-mail: lnorthcraft@wetzelchronicle.com
Editorial e-mail: bclutter@wetzelchronicle.com
Primary Website: wetzelchronicle.com
Avg Paid Circ: 6000
Avg Free Circ: 106
Audit By: Sworn/Estimate/Non-Audited
Audit Date: 10.06.2019
Personnel: Brian Clutter (Pub.); Amy Witschey (Ed.); Lisa Northcraft (Adv. Mgr.)
Parent company (for newspapers): Ogden Newspapers Inc.

WIND RIVER NEWS

Street address 1: 421 E Main St
Street address city: Riverton
Street address state: WY
Zip/Postal code: 82501-4438
General Phone: (307)856-2244
General Fax: (307)856-0189
Advertising Phone: (307)856-2244
Advertising Fax: (307)856-0189
Editorial Phone: (307)856-2244
Editorial Fax: (307)856-0189
General/National Adv. E-mail: rangerads@wyoming.com
Display Adv. E-mail: luanne@dailyranger.com

Editorial e-mail: steve@dailyranger.com
Primary Website: dailyranger.com
Avg Paid Circ: 3500
Audit By: Sworn/Estimate/Non-Audited
Audit Date: 10.06.2019
Personnel: Steve Peck (Pub./Ed.); Chris Peck (Assistant Ed.); Carl Manning (Circ. Mgr.)
Parent company (for newspapers): The Riverton Ranger, Inc.

WIRT COUNTY JOURNAL

Street address 1: 1 Midway Plaza
Street address city: Elizabeth
Street address state: WV
Zip/Postal code: 26143
General Phone: (304) 275-8981
General Fax: (304) 275-8981
Advertising Phone: (304) 275-8981
Advertising Fax: (304) 275-8981
Editorial Phone: (304) 275-8981
Editorial Fax: (304) 275-8981
General/National Adv. E-mail: advertising@wirtjournal.com
Display Adv. E-mail: advertising@wirtjournal.com
Editorial e-mail: news@wirtjournal.com
Primary Website: wirtjournal.com
Year Established: 1907
Avg Paid Circ: 2600
Avg Free Circ: 60
Audit By: Sworn/Estimate/Non-Audited
Audit Date: 10.06.2019
Personnel: James McGoldrick (Pub.)

WISCONSIN

ACTION ADVERTISER

Street address 1: N6637 Rolling Meadows Dr
Street address city: Fond Du Lac
Street address state: WI
Zip/Postal code: 54937-9471
General Phone: (920) 922-4600
General Fax: (920) 922-0125
Advertising Phone: (920) 907-7901
Advertising Fax: (920) 922-0125
Editorial Phone: (920) 922-4600
Editorial Fax: (920) 922-0125
General/National Adv. E-mail: jkramer2@gannett.com
Display Adv. E-mail: jkramer2@gannett.com
Editorial e-mail: mwolcans@greenbay.gannett.com
Primary Website: actiononline.net
Year Established: 1970
Avg Free Circ: 33752
Audit By: Sworn/Estimate/Non-Audited
Audit Date: 10.06.2019
Personnel: Matthew Wolcanski (Pub.); Peggy Breister (Ed.); Tami Whicher (Admin. Assistant); Barb Rosenberger (Prod. Mgr); Jason Kramer (Adv.)
Parent company (for newspapers): Gannett

ACTION SUNDAY

Street address 1: N6637 Rolling Meadows Dr
Street address city: Fond Du Lac
Street address state: WI
Zip/Postal code: 54937-9471
General Phone: (920) 922-4600
General Fax: (920) 922-0125
Advertising Phone: (920) 907-7901
Advertising Fax: (920) 922-0125
Editorial Phone: (920) 922-8640
Editorial Fax: (920) 922-0125
General/National Adv. E-mail: jkramer2@gannett.com
Display Adv. E-mail: jkramer2@gannett.com
Editorial e-mail: mwolcans@greenbay.gannett.com
Primary Website: actiononline.net
Year Established: 1988
Avg Free Circ: 41784
Audit By: Sworn/Estimate/Non-Audited
Audit Date: 10.06.2019
Personnel: Peggy Breister (Ed.); Tami Whicher (Admin. Assistant); Heather Bradwin (Adv. Mgr.); Matthew Wolcanski (Pub.); Jason Kramer (Adv.); Barb Rosenberger (Prod.)

Parent company (for newspapers): Gannett

ADVERTISER COMMUNITY NEWS

Street address 1: 800 E Factory St
Street address city: Seymour
Street address state: WI
Zip/Postal code: 54165-1210
General Phone: (920) 833-0420
General Fax: (920) 833-0423
Advertising Phone: (920) 833-0420
Advertising Fax: (920) 833-0423
Editorial Phone: (920) 833-0420
Editorial Fax: (920) 833-0423
General/National Adv. E-mail: ken.h@adcommnews.com
Display Adv. E-mail: becky.m@adcommnews.com
Editorial e-mail: keith.s@adcommnews.com
Primary Website: advertisercommunitynews.com
Mthly Avg Views: 6811
Mthly Avg Unique Visitors: 1900
Year Established: 2009
Avg Paid Circ: 103
Avg Free Circ: 8853
Audit By: VAC
Audit Date: 31.03.2017
Personnel: Ken Hodgden (Pub./Owner); Becky Mueller (Circ. Mgr); Keith Skenadore (Ed)
Parent company (for newspapers): ()

AMERY FREE PRESS

Street address 1: 215 Keller Ave S
Street address city: Amery
Street address state: WI
Zip/Postal code: 54001-1275
General Phone: (715) 268-8101
General Fax: (715) 268-5300
Advertising Phone: (715) 268-8101
Advertising Fax: (715) 268-5300
Editorial Phone: (715) 268-8101
Editorial Fax: (715) 268-5300
General/National Adv. E-mail: phumpal@theameryfreepress.com
Display Adv. E-mail: classifieds@theameryfreepress.com
Editorial e-mail: editor@theameryfreepress.com
Primary Website: theameryfreepress.com
Year Established: 1895
Avg Paid Circ: 5000
Audit By: Sworn/Estimate/Non-Audited
Audit Date: 10.06.2019
Personnel: Steven R. Sondreal (Pub./Gen. Mgr.); Jerry Sondreal (Pub.); Pam Humpal (Adv. Mgr.)

BARRON NEWS-SHIELD

Street address 1: 219 E La Salle Ave
Street address city: Barron
Street address state: WI
Zip/Postal code: 54812-1426
General Phone: (715) 537-3117
General Fax: (715) 537-5640
Advertising Phone: (715) 537-3117
Advertising Fax: (715) 537-5640
Editorial Phone: (715) 537-3117
Editorial Fax: (715) 537-5640
General/National Adv. E-mail: ads.newsshield@chibardun.net
Display Adv. E-mail: newsshield@chibardun.net
Editorial e-mail: editor.barron@chibardun.net
Primary Website: news-shield.com
Avg Paid Circ: 4250
Audit By: Sworn/Estimate/Non-Audited
Audit Date: 10.06.2019
Personnel: Mark Bell (Pub./Sports Ed.); Jim Bell (Assoc. Pub.); Robert Zientara (Ed.); Jennifer Cox (Adv. Mgr.)

BAY VIEW NOW

Street address 1: 1741 Dolphin Dr
Street address 2: Ste A
Street address city: Waukesha
Street address state: WI
Zip/Postal code: 53186-1493
General Phone: (414) 224-2100
General Fax: (262) 446-6646
Advertising Phone: (414) 224-2498
Advertising Fax: (262) 446-6646
Editorial Phone: (414) 224-2100 ext. 5
Editorial Fax: (262) 446-6646
General/National Adv. E-mail: alaffe@jrn.com
Display Adv. E-mail: btschacher@jrn.com
Editorial e-mail: speterson@jrn.com
Primary Website: bayviewnow.com
Year Established: 1956
Audit By: Sworn/Estimate/Non-Audited
Audit Date: 10.06.2019
Personnel: Scott Peterson (Chief Ed.); Matt Newman (Design/Interactive Content Dir.); Jim Riccioli (Ed.)
Parent company (for newspapers): Community Newspapers, Inc.; Journal Media Group

BAYFIELD COUNTY JOURNAL

Street address 1: 122 3rd St W
Street address city: Ashland
Street address state: WI
Zip/Postal code: 54806-1661
General Phone: (715) 682-2313
General/National Adv. E-mail: pressclass@ashlanddailypress.net
Display Adv. E-mail: pressclass@ashlanddailypress.net
Editorial e-mail: pressclass@ashlanddailypress.net
Primary Website: apg-wi.com
Audit By: Sworn/Estimate/Non-Audited
Audit Date: 10.06.2019
Personnel: Jeff Evans; Deb Baker
Parent company (for newspapers): Adams Publishing Group, LLC

BEAVER DAM - MONDAY MINI

Street address 1: 805 Park Ave
Street address city: Beaver Dam
Street address state: WI
Zip/Postal code: 53916-2205
General Phone: (920)356-6756
General Fax: (920)887-8790
Advertising Phone: (920)356-6756
Advertising Fax: (920)887-8790
Editorial Phone: (920)356-6756
Editorial Fax: (920)887-8790
General/National Adv. E-mail: szeinemann@capitalnewspapers.com
Display Adv. E-mail: szeienmann@capitalnewspapers.com
Editorial e-mail: szeinemann@capitalnewspapers.com
Primary Website: capitalnewspapers.com
Year Established: 1986
Avg Paid Circ: 0
Avg Free Circ: 5647
Audit By: Sworn/Estimate/Non-Audited
Audit Date: 10.06.2019
Personnel: James Keish (Pub.)

BERLIN JOURNAL

Street address 1: 301 June St
Street address city: Berlin
Street address state: WI
Zip/Postal code: 54923-2147
General Phone: (920) 361-1515
General Fax: (920) 361-1518
Advertising Phone: (920) 361-1515
Advertising Fax: (920) 361-1518
Editorial Phone: (920) 361-1515
Editorial Fax: (920) 361-1518
General/National Adv. E-mail: ads@theberlinjournal.com
Display Adv. E-mail: classifieds@theberlinjournal.com
Editorial e-mail: news@theberlinjournal.com
Primary Website: theberlinjournal.com
Year Established: 1870
Avg Paid Circ: 3500
Audit By: Sworn/Estimate/Non-Audited
Audit Date: 10.06.2019
Personnel: Tyler Gonyo (Pub./Gen. Mgr.); Jason Fox (Ed.); Kristian Troudt (Adv. Mgr.); Tracy Kallas (Circ. Mgr.)
Parent company (for newspapers): Berlin Journal Newspapers

BLOOMER ADVANCE

Street address 1: 1210 15th Ave
Street address city: Bloomer
Street address state: WI
Zip/Postal code: 54724-1668
General Phone: (715) 568-3100
General Fax: (715) 568-3111
Advertising Phone: (715) 568-3100
Advertising Fax: (715) 568-3111
Editorial Phone: (715) 568-3100
Editorial Fax: (715) 568-3111
General/National Adv. E-mail: ads@bloomeradvance.com
Display Adv. E-mail: badvance@bloomer.net
Editorial e-mail: editor@bloomeradvance.com
Primary Website: bloomeradvance.com
Year Established: 1886
Avg Paid Circ: 2310
Avg Free Circ: 29
Audit By: Sworn/Estimate/Non-Audited
Audit Date: 10.06.2019
Personnel: Jim Bell (Pub.); Barry Hoff (Ed./Gen. Mgr.); Dave Boyea (Sports Ed.); Sandra Metcalf (Circ. Mgr.); Lana Durch (Adv. Production.)

BROOKFIELD-ELM GROVE NOW

Street address 1: 1741 Dolphin Dr
Street address 2: Ste A
Street address city: Waukesha
Street address state: WI
Zip/Postal code: 53186-1493
General Phone: (414) 224-2100
General Fax: (262) 446-6646
Advertising Phone: (414) 224-2498
Advertising Fax: (262) 446-6646
Editorial Phone: (414) 224-2100 ext. 5
Editorial Fax: (262) 446-6646
General/National Adv. E-mail: alaffe@jrn.com
Display Adv. E-mail: btschacher@jrn.com
Editorial e-mail: speterson@jrn.com
Primary Website: brookfieldnow.com
Year Established: 1956
Audit By: Sworn/Estimate/Non-Audited
Audit Date: 10.06.2019
Personnel: Scott Peterson (Chief Ed.); Matt Newman (Design/Interactive Content Dir.)
Parent company (for newspapers): Community Newspapers, Inc.; Journal Media Group

BURLINGTON STANDARD PRESS

Street address 1: 700 N Pine St
Street address city: Burlington
Street address state: WI
Zip/Postal code: 53105-1472
General Phone: (262) 763-3330
General Fax: (262) 763-2238
Advertising Phone: (262) 763-3330
Advertising Fax: (262) 763-2238
Editorial Phone: (262) 763-3330 ext. 148
Editorial Fax: (262) 763-2238
General/National Adv. E-mail: karend@standardpress.com
Display Adv. E-mail: dee@southernlakesnewspapers.com
Editorial e-mail: jeisenbart@southernlakesnewspapers.com
Primary Website: southernlakesnewspapers.com
Avg Paid Circ: 3900
Avg Free Circ: 4801
Audit By: Sworn/Estimate/Non-Audited
Audit Date: 10.06.2019
Personnel: Jack Cruger (Pub.); Ed Nadolski (Ed. in Chief); Jennifer Eisenbart (Mng. Ed.); Jamie Wambach (Adv. Mgr.)
Parent company (for newspapers): Southern Lakes Newspapers LLC

BURNETT COUNTY SENTINEL

Street address 1: 114 W Madison Ave
Street address city: Grantsburg
Street address state: WI
Zip/Postal code: 54840-7022
General Phone: (715) 463-2341
General Fax: (715) 463-5138
General/National Adv. E-mail: stacy@burnettcountysentinel.com
Display Adv. E-mail: stacy@burnettcountysentinel.com
Editorial e-mail: editor@burnettcountysentinel.com
Primary Website: burnettcountysentinel.com
Year Established: 1875
Avg Paid Circ: 2425
Audit By: Sworn/Estimate/Non-Audited
Audit Date: 10.06.2019
Personnel: Teresa Nordrum (Office Mgr.); Tom Stangl (Publisher); Stacy Coy (Advertising Agent); Sean Devlin (Editor)

Parent company (for newspapers): Sentinel Publications

CAMPBELLSPORT NEWS

Street address 1: 101 N Fond Du Lac Ave
Street address city: Campbellsport
Street address state: WI
Zip/Postal code: 53010-3542
General Phone: (920) 533-8338
General Fax: (920) 533-5579
Advertising Phone: (920)533-8338
Advertising Fax: (920) 533-5579
Editorial Phone: (920) 533-8338
Editorial Fax: (920) 533-5579
General/National Adv. E-mail: sales@thecampbellsportnews.com
Display Adv. E-mail: frontdesk@thecampbellsportnews.com
Editorial e-mail: editor@thecampbellsportnews.com
Primary Website: thecampbellsportnews.com
Year Established: 1906
Avg Paid Circ: 2000
Avg Free Circ: 11
Audit By: Sworn/Estimate/Non-Audited
Audit Date: 10.06.2019
Personnel: Andrew Johnson (Pub.); Andrea Hansen Abler (Ed.); Rebecca Van Beek (office/production); Tracy Dieckman (Adv.); Andrea Steger (Production)
Parent company (for newspapers): Wisconsin Free Press, Inc.

CHILTON TIMES-JOURNAL

Street address 1: 19 E Main St
Street address city: Chilton
Street address state: WI
Zip/Postal code: 53014-1427
General Phone: (920) 849-4551
General Fax: (920) 849-4651
Advertising Phone: (920) 849-4551
Advertising Fax: (920) 849-4651
Editorial Phone: (920) 849-4551
Editorial Fax: (920) 849-4651
General/National Adv. E-mail: calumetadvertiser@charter.net
Display Adv. E-mail: marilynmcgrew@yahoo.com
Editorial e-mail: timesjournal@charter.net
Primary Website: chiltontimesjournal.com
Year Established: 1857
Avg Paid Circ: 5020
Avg Free Circ: 50
Audit By: Sworn/Estimate/Non-Audited
Audit Date: 10.06.2019
Personnel: Pooja Baviskar (Ed.); Sonia Javadekar (Author)
Parent company (for newspapers): Calumet Publishing, Inc.

COLUMBUS JOURNAL

Street address 1: 805 Park Ave
Street address city: Beaver Dam
Street address state: WI
Zip/Postal code: 53916-2205
General Phone: (920) 623-3160
General Fax: (920) 623-9383
General/National Adv. E-mail: kpremo-rake@wiscnews.com
Display Adv. E-mail: kpremo-rake@wiscnews.com
Editorial e-mail: kdamask@wiscnews.com
Primary Website: wiscnews.com/columbusjournal
Year Established: 1855
Avg Paid Circ: 1736
Audit By: Sworn/Estimate/Non-Audited
Audit Date: 10.06.2019
Personnel: Kevin Damask (Ed.); Kara Premo Rake (Adv.)
Parent company (for newspapers): Capital Newspapers

COULEE NEWS

Street address 1: 401 3rd St N
Street address city: La Crosse
Street address state: WI
Zip/Postal code: 54601-3267
General Phone: (608)782-9710
General Fax: (608)786-1670
Advertising Phone: (608)791-8260
Advertising Fax: (608)786-1670
Editorial Phone: (608)791-8219
Editorial Fax: (608)786-1670
General/National Adv. E-mail: barb.formanek@lee.net
Display Adv. E-mail: ads@lacrossetribune.com
Editorial e-mail: mike.burns@lee.net
Primary Website: couleenews.com
Avg Paid Circ: 1743
Avg Free Circ: 4
Audit By: Sworn/Estimate/Non-Audited
Audit Date: 10.06.2019
Personnel: Chris Hardie (Pub.); Randy Erickson (Ed.)
Parent company (for newspapers): Dispatch-Argus

COURIER SENTINEL

Street address 1: 121 Main St
Street address city: Cornell
Street address state: WI
Zip/Postal code: 54732-8386
General Phone: (715) 239-6688
General Fax: (715) 239-6200
Advertising Phone: (715) 289-4978
Advertising Fax: (715) 239-6200
Editorial Phone: (715) 239-6688
Editorial Fax: (715) 239-6200
General/National Adv. E-mail: cornellcourier@centurytel.net
Display Adv. E-mail: cadottsentinel@centurytel.net
Editorial e-mail: cornellcourier@centurytel.net
Primary Website: couriersentinelnews.com
Year Established: 1958
Avg Paid Circ: 3200
Avg Free Circ: 59
Audit By: Sworn/Estimate/Non-Audited
Audit Date: 10.06.2019
Personnel: Trygg Hansen (Pub.); John Marder (Ed.); Monique Westaby (Cadott Mgr.); Kris O'Leary (Gen. Mgr.); Rebecca Lindquist (Business Mgr.)
Parent company (for newspapers): Trygg J. Hansen Publications Inc.

COURIER-PRESS

Street address 1: 132 S Beaumont Rd
Street address city: Prairie Du Chien
Street address state: WI
Zip/Postal code: 53821-1415
General Phone: (608)326-2441
General Fax: (608)326-2443
Advertising Phone: (608)326-2441
Advertising Fax: (608)326-2443
Editorial Phone: (608)326-2441
Editorial Fax: (608)326-2443
General/National Adv. E-mail: howeads@mhtc.net
Display Adv. E-mail: howeads@mhtc.net
Editorial e-mail: howenews@mhtc.net
Primary Website: pdccourier.com
Audit By: Sworn/Estimate/Non-Audited
Audit Date: 10.06.2019
Parent company (for newspapers): Mississippi Valley Printers

CRAWFORD COUNTY INDEPENDENT & KICKAPOO SCOUT

Street address 1: 320 Main St
Street address city: Gays Mills
Street address state: WI
Zip/Postal code: 54631-8278
General Phone: (608) 735-4413
General Fax: (608) 735-4413
Advertising Phone: (608)735-4413
Advertising Fax: (608)735-4413
Editorial Phone: (608)735-4413
Editorial Fax: (608)735-4413
General/National Adv. E-mail: jinge@tds.net
Display Adv. E-mail: jinge@tds.net
Editorial e-mail: jinge@tds.net
Primary Website: swnews4u.com
Audit By: Sworn/Estimate/Non-Audited
Audit Date: 10.06.2019
Personnel: Charley Preusser
Parent company (for newspapers): Morris Multimedia, Inc.

CUDAHY NOW

Street address 1: 1741 Dolphin Dr
Street address 2: Ste A
Street address city: Waukesha
Street address state: WI
Zip/Postal code: 53186-1493
General Phone: (414) 224-2100
General Fax: (262) 446-6646
Advertising Phone: (414) 224-2498
Advertising Fax: (262) 446-6646
Editorial Phone: (414) 224-2100 ext. 5
Editorial Fax: (262) 446-6646
General/National Adv. E-mail: alaffe@jrn.com
Display Adv. E-mail: btschacher@jrn.com
Editorial e-mail: speterson@jrn.com
Primary Website: cudahynow.com
Year Established: 1956
Audit By: Sworn/Estimate/Non-Audited
Audit Date: 10.06.2019
Personnel: Scott Peterson (Chief Ed.); Matt Newman (Design/Interactive Content Dir.)
Parent company (for newspapers): Community Newspapers, Inc.; Journal Media Group

CUMBERLAND ADVOCATE

Street address 1: 1375 2nd Ave
Street address city: Cumberland
Street address state: WI
Zip/Postal code: 54829-7211
General Phone: (715)822-4469
General Fax: (715)822-4451
Advertising Phone: (715)822-4469
Advertising Fax: (715)822-4451
Editorial Phone: (715)822-4469
Editorial Fax: (715)822-4451
General/National Adv. E-mail: news@cumberland-advocate.com
Display Adv. E-mail: news@cumberland-advocate.com
Editorial e-mail: news@cumberland-advocate.com
Year Established: 1882
Avg Paid Circ: 2550
Audit By: Sworn/Estimate/Non-Audited
Audit Date: 10.06.2019
Personnel: Paul Bucher (Pub./Adv. Mgr.)
Parent company (for newspapers): B&H Publishing, Inc.

DEFOREST TIMES-TRIBUNE

Street address 1: 105 South Street
Street address city: Waunakee
Street address state: WI
Zip/Postal code: 53597
General Phone: (608) 846-5576
General Fax: (608) 846-5757
Advertising Phone: (608) 846-5576
Advertising Fax: (608) 846-5757
Editorial Phone: (608) 846-5576
Editorial Fax: (608) 846-5757
General/National Adv. E-mail: lkanderson@hngnews.com
Display Adv. E-mail: spstar@hngnews.com
Editorial e-mail: jkurtz@hngnews.com
Primary Website: hngnews.com/deforest_times
Year Established: 1895
Avg Paid Circ: 2825
Audit By: Sworn/Estimate/Non-Audited
Audit Date: 10.06.2019
Personnel: Brian Knox (Pub.); Christine Benisch (Circ. Mgr.); Hannah Rajnicek (Ed.); Sam Rodriguez (Sports Ed.); Lisa Kueter-Anderson (Adv. Sales); Mary-Jo Curie
Parent company (for newspapers): Hometown News Group

DEMOCRAT TRIBUNE

Street address 1: 334 High St
Street address city: Mineral Point
Street address state: WI
Zip/Postal code: 53565-1219
General Phone: (608) 987-2141
General Fax: (608) 935-9531
Advertising Phone: (608) 987-2141
Advertising Fax: (608) 935-9531
Editorial Phone: (608) 987-2141
Editorial Fax: (608) 935-9531
General/National Adv. E-mail: jdoye@thedodgevillechronicle.com
Display Adv. E-mail: jdoye@thedodgevillechronicle.com
Editorial e-mail: jdoye@thedodgevillechronicle.com
Primary Website: facebook.com/pg/mpdemocrattribune/about/?ref=page_internal
Year Established: 1849
Avg Paid Circ: 1200
Avg Free Circ: 15
Audit By: Sworn/Estimate/Non-Audited
Audit Date: 10.06.2019
Personnel: Janelle Miller (Ed.)

DODGE COUNTY INDEPENDENT-NEWS

Street address 1: 122 S Main St
Street address city: Juneau
Street address state: WI
Zip/Postal code: 53039-1018
General Phone: (920)386-2421
General Fax: (920)386-2422
Advertising Phone: (920)386-2421
Advertising Fax: (920)386-2422
Editorial Phone: (920)386-2421
Editorial Fax: (920)386-2422
General/National Adv. E-mail: dcind@charterinternet.com
Display Adv. E-mail: dcind@charterinternet.com
Editorial e-mail: dcind@charterinternet.com
Avg Paid Circ: 1000
Avg Free Circ: 27
Audit By: Sworn/Estimate/Non-Audited
Audit Date: 10.06.2019
Personnel: James M. Clifford (Pub.); Kevin C. Clifford (Gen. Mgr.); Thomas L. Schultz (Ed.)
Parent company (for newspapers): Adams Publishing Group, LLC

DOOR COUNTY ADVOCATE

Street address 1: 235 N 3rd Ave
Street address city: Sturgeon Bay
Street address state: WI
Zip/Postal code: 54235-2417
General Phone: (920) 615-9592
General Fax: (920) 743-8908
General/National Adv. E-mail: spleasan@localiq.com
Display Adv. E-mail: spleasan@localiq.com
Editorial e-mail: jmaertz@localiq.com
Primary Website: doorcountyadvocate.com
Mthly Avg Views: 32482
Mthly Avg Unique Visitors: 3937
Year Established: 1862
Avg Paid Circ: 5897
Avg Free Circ: 279
Sat. Circulation Paid: 7003
Sat. Circulation Free: 250
Audit By: CVC
Audit Date: 30.09.2018
Personnel: Jen Maertz (Pub.); Scott Domalick; Stephanie Pleasants (Adv.)
Parent company (for newspapers): Gannett

ELM GROVE NOW

Street address 1: 1741 Dolphin Dr
Street address 2: Ste A
Street address city: Waukesha
Street address state: WI
Zip/Postal code: 53186-1493
General Phone: (414) 224-2100
General Fax: (262) 446-6646
Advertising Phone: (414) 224-2498
Advertising Fax: (262) 446-6646
Editorial Phone: (414) 224-2100 ext. 5
Editorial Fax: (262) 446-6646
General/National Adv. E-mail: alaffe@jrn.com
Display Adv. E-mail: btschacher@jrn.com
Editorial e-mail: speterson@jrn.com
Primary Website: elmgrovenow.com
Year Established: 1956
Audit By: Sworn/Estimate/Non-Audited
Audit Date: 10.06.2019
Personnel: Scott Peterson (Chief Ed.); Matt Newman (Design/Interactive Content Dir.)
Parent company (for newspapers): Community Newspapers, Inc.; Journal Media Group

EVANSVILLE REVIEW

Street address 1: 8409 N US Highway 14
Street address city: Evansville
Street address state: WI
Zip/Postal code: 53536-9263
General Phone: (608) 882-5220
General Fax: (608) 882-5221
Advertising Phone: (608) 882-5220
Advertising Fax: (608) 882-5221
Editorial Phone: (608) 882-5220
Editorial Fax: (608) 882-5221
General/National Adv. E-mail: gildner@litewire.net
Display Adv. E-mail: gildner@litewire.net

Editorial e-mail: gildner@litewire.net
Primary Website: evansvillereview.com
Year Established: 1862
Avg Paid Circ: 3000
Avg Free Circ: 2295
Audit By: Sworn/Estimate/Non-Audited
Audit Date: 10.06.2019
Personnel: Stan Gildner (Pub.); Kelly Gildner (Ed.)

FENNIMORE TIMES

Street address 1: 1150 Lincoln Ave
Street address city: Fennimore
Street address state: WI
Zip/Postal code: 53809-1746
General Phone: (608) 822-3912
General Fax: (608) 822-3916
Advertising Phone: (608) 822-3912
Advertising Fax: (608) 822-3916
Editorial Phone: (608) 822-3912
Editorial Fax: (608) 822-3916
General/National Adv. E-mail: tcpads@yousq.net
Display Adv. E-mail: fennimoretimes@tds.net
Editorial e-mail: timeseditor@tds.net
Primary Website: swnews4u.com
Year Established: 1889
Avg Paid Circ: 1600
Avg Free Circ: 20
Audit By: Sworn/Estimate/Non-Audited
Audit Date: 10.06.2019
Personnel: John Ingebritsen (Pub.); David Timmerman (Ed.); Heather Copus (Office Mgr.)
Parent company (for newspapers): Morris Multimedia, Inc.

FLORENCE MINING NEWS

Street address 1: 103 S Hazeldell Ave
Street address city: Crandon
Street address state: WI
Zip/Postal code: 54520-1453
General Phone: (715) 528-3276
General Fax: (715) 528-5976
Advertising Phone: (715)528-3276
Advertising Fax: (715)528-5976
Editorial Phone: (715)528-3276
Editorial Fax: (715)528-5976
General/National Adv. E-mail: upnorth2@borderlandnet.net
Display Adv. E-mail: upnorth2@borderlandnet.net
Editorial e-mail: upnorth2@borderlandnet.net
Primary Website: florence-forestnews.com
Audit By: Sworn/Estimate/Non-Audited
Audit Date: 10.06.2019
Personnel: Hank Murphy (Pub./Ed.); Dianne Olive (Ad. Design); Teresa Broullire (Adv. Mgr.)

FOTO NEWS

Street address 1: 807 E 1st St
Street address city: Merrill
Street address state: WI
Zip/Postal code: 54452-2412
General Phone: (715) 536-7121
General Fax: (715) 539-3686
General/National Adv. E-mail: tschreiber@mmclocal.com
Display Adv. E-mail: tschreiber@mmclocal.com
Editorial e-mail: tschreiber@mmclocal.com
Primary Website: merrillfotonews.com
Year Established: 1955
Avg Paid Circ: 172
Avg Free Circ: 15949
Audit By: VAC
Audit Date: 31.03.2017
Personnel: Kurt Haebig; Tim Schreiber (Gen. Mgr.)
Parent company (for newspapers): Multi Media Channels

FOX POINT NOW

Street address 1: 1741 Dolphin Dr
Street address 2: Ste A
Street address city: Waukesha
Street address state: WI
Zip/Postal code: 53186-1493
General Phone: (414) 224-2100
General Fax: (262) 446-6646
Advertising Phone: (414) 224-2498
Advertising Fax: (262) 446-6646
Editorial Phone: (414) 224-2100 ext. 5
Editorial Fax: (262) 446-6646
General/National Adv. E-mail: alaffe@jrn.com
Display Adv. E-mail: btschacher@jrn.com
Editorial e-mail: speterson@jrn.com
Primary Website: myfoxpointnow.com
Year Established: 1956
Audit By: Sworn/Estimate/Non-Audited
Audit Date: 10.06.2019
Personnel: Scott Peterson (Chief Ed.); Matt Newman (Design/Interactive Content Dir.)
Parent company (for newspapers): Community Newspapers, Inc.; Journal Media Group

FRANKLIN NOW

Street address 1: 1741 Dolphin Dr
Street address 2: Ste A
Street address city: Waukesha
Street address state: WI
Zip/Postal code: 53186-1493
General Phone: (414) 224-2100
General Fax: (262) 446-6646
Advertising Phone: (414) 224-2498
Advertising Fax: (262) 446-6646
Editorial Phone: (414) 224-2100 ext. 5
Editorial Fax: (262) 446-6646
General/National Adv. E-mail: alaffe@jrn.com
Display Adv. E-mail: btschacher@jrn.com
Editorial e-mail: speterson@jrn.com
Primary Website: franklinnow.com
Year Established: 1956
Audit By: Sworn/Estimate/Non-Audited
Audit Date: 10.06.2019
Personnel: Scott Peterson (Chief Ed.); Matt Newman (Design/Interactive Content Dir.)
Parent company (for newspapers): Community Newspapers, Inc.; Journal Media Group

GERMANTOWN EXPRESS NEWS

Street address 1: 8990 N 51st St
Street address city: Brown Deer
Street address state: WI
Zip/Postal code: 53223-2402
General Phone: (262) 238-6397
General Fax: (262) 242-9450
Advertising Phone: (262) 238-6397
Advertising Fax: (262) 242-9450
Editorial Phone: (262) 238-6397
Editorial Fax: (262) 242-9450
General/National Adv. E-mail: advertising@discoverhometown.com
Display Adv. E-mail: jonesjf@discoverhometown.com
Editorial e-mail: thomasj@discoverhometown.com
Primary Website: discoverhometown.com
Year Established: 1994
Avg Free Circ: 11006
Audit By: VAC
Audit Date: 30.06.2016
Personnel: Ken Ubert (Pres./Pub.); Thomas McKillen (Mng. Ed.); Holly Potter (Prod. Mgr./Adv. Mgr.); Russ Schliepp (Adv. Sales Rep.)
Parent company (for newspapers): Hometown Publications, Inc.

GERMANTOWN NOW

Street address 1: 1741 Dolphin Dr
Street address 2: Ste A
Street address city: Waukesha
Street address state: WI
Zip/Postal code: 53186-1493
General Phone: (414) 224-2100
General Fax: (262) 446-6646
Advertising Phone: (414) 224-2498
Advertising Fax: (262) 446-6646
Editorial Phone: (414) 224-2100 ext. 5
Editorial Fax: (262) 446-6646
General/National Adv. E-mail: alaffe@jrn.com
Display Adv. E-mail: btschacher@jrn.com
Editorial e-mail: speterson@jrn.com
Primary Website: germantownnow.com
Year Established: 1956
Audit By: Sworn/Estimate/Non-Audited
Audit Date: 10.06.2019
Personnel: Scott Peterson (Chief Ed.); Matt Newman (Design/Interactive Content Dir.)
Parent company (for newspapers): Community Newspapers, Inc.; Journal Media Group

GLENDALE NOW

Street address 1: 1741 Dolphin Dr
Street address 2: Ste A
Street address city: Waukesha
Street address state: WI
Zip/Postal code: 53186-1493
General Phone: (414) 224-2100
General Fax: (262) 446-6646
Advertising Phone: (414) 224-2498
Advertising Fax: (262) 446-6646
Editorial Phone: (414) 224-2100 ext. 5
Editorial Fax: (262) 446-6646
General/National Adv. E-mail: alaffe@jrn.com
Display Adv. E-mail: btschacher@jrn.com
Editorial e-mail: speterson@jrn.com
Primary Website: glendalenow.com
Year Established: 1956
Audit By: Sworn/Estimate/Non-Audited
Audit Date: 10.06.2019
Personnel: Scott Peterson (Chief Ed.); Matt Newman (Design/Interactive Content Dir.)
Parent company (for newspapers): Community Newspapers, Inc.; Journal Media Group

GRANT COUNTY HERALD INDEPENDENT

Street address 1: 208 W Cherry St
Street address city: Lancaster
Street address state: WI
Zip/Postal code: 53813-1629
General Phone: (608) 723-2151
General Fax: (608) 723-7272
Advertising Phone: (608) 723-2151
Advertising Fax: (608) 723-7272
Editorial Phone: (608) 723-2151
Editorial Fax: (608) 723-7272
General/National Adv. E-mail: kkads@tds.net
Display Adv. E-mail: jinge@tds.net
Editorial e-mail: newseditor@tds.net
Primary Website: swnews4u.com
Year Established: 1843
Avg Paid Circ: 3400
Audit By: Sworn/Estimate/Non-Audited
Audit Date: 10.06.2019
Personnel: John Ingebritsen (Reg. Pub.); Kevin Kelly (Reg. Adv. Dir.); David Timmerman (Ed.)

GREEN LAKE REPORTER

Street address 1: 301 June St
Street address city: Berlin
Street address state: WI
Zip/Postal code: 54923-2147
General Phone: (920) 361-1515
General Fax: (920) 361-1518
Advertising Phone: (920) 361-1515
Advertising Fax: (920) 361-1518
Editorial Phone: (920) 361-1515
Editorial Fax: (920) 361-1518
General/National Adv. E-mail: ads@theberlinjournal.com
Display Adv. E-mail: classifieds@theberlinjournal.com
Editorial e-mail: news@theberlinjournal.com
Primary Website: theberlinjournal.com
Year Established: 1870
Avg Paid Circ: 3500
Audit By: Sworn/Estimate/Non-Audited
Audit Date: 10.06.2019
Personnel: Tyler Gonyo (Pub./Gen. Mgr.); Jason Fox (Ed.); Kristian Troudt (Adv. Mgr.); Tracy Kallas (Circ. Mgr.)
Parent company (for newspapers): Berlin Journal Newspapers

GREENFIELD-WEST ALLIS NOW

Street address 1: 1741 Dolphin Dr
Street address 2: Ste A
Street address city: Waukesha
Street address state: WI
Zip/Postal code: 53186-1493
General Phone: (414) 224-2100
General Fax: (262) 446-6646
Advertising Phone: (414) 224-2498
Advertising Fax: (262) 446-6646
Editorial Phone: (414) 224-2100 ext. 5
Editorial Fax: (262) 446-6646
General/National Adv. E-mail: alaffe@jrn.com
Display Adv. E-mail: btschacher@jrn.com
Editorial e-mail: speterson@jrn.com
Primary Website: greenfieldnow.com
Year Established: 1956
Audit By: Sworn/Estimate/Non-Audited
Audit Date: 10.06.2019
Personnel: Scott Peterson (Chief Ed.); Matt Newman (Design/Interactive Content Dir.)
Parent company (for newspapers): Community Newspapers, Inc.; Journal Media Group

HALES CORNERS NOW

Street address 1: 1741 Dolphin Dr
Street address 2: Ste A
Street address city: Waukesha
Street address state: WI
Zip/Postal code: 53186-1493
General Phone: (414) 224-2100
General Fax: (262) 446-6646
Advertising Phone: (414) 224-2498
Advertising Fax: (262) 446-6646
Editorial Phone: (414) 224-2100 ext. 5
Editorial Fax: (262) 446-6646
General/National Adv. E-mail: alaffe@jrn.com
Display Adv. E-mail: btschacher@jrn.com
Editorial e-mail: speterson@jrn.com
Primary Website: myhalescornersnow.com
Year Established: 1956
Audit By: Sworn/Estimate/Non-Audited
Audit Date: 10.06.2019
Personnel: Scott Peterson (Chief Ed.); Matt Newman (Design/Interactive Content Dir.)
Parent company (for newspapers): Community Newspapers, Inc.; Journal Media Group

HARTFORD EXPRESS NEWS

Street address 1: 8990 N 51st St
Street address city: Brown Deer
Street address state: WI
Zip/Postal code: 53223-2402
General Phone: (262) 238-6397
General Fax: (262) 242-9450
Advertising Phone: (262) 238-6397
Advertising Fax: (262) 242-9450
Editorial Phone: (262) 238-6397
Editorial Fax: (262) 242-9450
General/National Adv. E-mail: advertising@discoverhometown.com
Display Adv. E-mail: jonesjf@discoverhometown.com
Editorial e-mail: thomasj@discoverhometown.com
Primary Website: discoverhometown.com
Year Established: 1994
Avg Free Circ: 3909
Audit By: VAC
Audit Date: 30.06.2016
Personnel: Ken Ubert (Pres./Pub.); Thomas McKillen (Mng. Ed.); Holly Potter (Prod. Mgr./Adv. Mgr.); Russ Schliepp (Adv. Sales Rep.)
Parent company (for newspapers): Hometown Publications, Inc.

HILLSBORO SENTRY-ENTERPRISE

Street address 1: 839 Water Ave
Street address city: Hillsboro
Street address state: WI
Zip/Postal code: 54634-6213
General Phone: (608) 489-2264
General Fax: (608) 489-2348
General/National Adv. E-mail: observerads@mwt.net
Display Adv. E-mail: observerads@mwt.net
Editorial e-mail: sentry@mwt.net
Primary Website: swnews4u.com
Year Established: 1885
Avg Paid Circ: 1694
Avg Free Circ: 108
Audit By: Sworn/Estimate/Non-Audited
Audit Date: 10.06.2019
Personnel: John Ingebritsen (Reg. Pub.); Dave McGowan (Adv. Dir.); Mary Sterba (Office Mgr.); Harvey Leverenz (Managing Editor)

HOUSTON COUNTY NEWS

Street address 1: 401 3rd St N
Street address city: La Crosse
Street address state: WI
Zip/Postal code: 54601-3267
General Phone: (608)791-8411
General Fax: (608)791-8238
Advertising Phone: (608)791-8411
Advertising Fax: (608)791-8238
Editorial Phone: (608)791-8411
Editorial Fax: (608)791-8238

General/National Adv. E-mail: Shari.Holliday@lacrossetribune.com
Display Adv. E-mail: ads@lacrossetribune.com
Editorial e-mail: mike.burns@lee.net
Primary Website: houstonconews.com
Year Established: 1968
Avg Paid Circ: 1953
Avg Free Circ: 36
Audit By: Sworn/Estimate/Non-Audited
Audit Date: 10.06.2019
Personnel: Chris Hardie (Pub.); Ryan Henry (Ed.)

INSIGHT ON BUSINESS

Street address 1: 400 N. Richmond St.
Street address 2: Suite B
Street address city: Appleton
Street address state: WI
Zip/Postal code: 54911
General Phone: (920) 882-0491
General Fax: (920) 227-4158
General/National Adv. E-mail: wgilbert@insightonbusiness.com
Display Adv. E-mail: wgilbert@insightonbusiness.com
Editorial e-mail: mmatzek@insightonbusiness.com
Year Established: 2008
Avg Paid Circ: 1
Avg Free Circ: 11231
Audit By: CVC
Audit Date: 30.12.2018
Personnel: Brian Rasmussen (Pub.); MaryBeth Matzek (Mng. Ed.); Wendy Gilbert (Adv.)

INTER-COUNTY LEADER

Street address 1: 303 Wisconsin Ave N
Street address city: Frederic
Street address state: WI
Zip/Postal code: 54837-9048
General Phone: (715) 327-4236
General Fax: (715) 327-4117
General/National Adv. E-mail: iccpaonline@centurytel.net
Editorial e-mail: editor@leaderregister.com
Primary Website: leaderregister.com
Year Established: 1933
Avg Paid Circ: 6870
Avg Free Circ: 0
Audit By: Sworn/Estimate/Non-Audited
Audit Date: 10.06.2019
Personnel: Douglas Panek (Manager); Gary B. King (Ed.)
Parent company (for newspapers): Inter-County Cooperative Publishing Association

IRON COUNTY MINER

Street address 1: 216 Copper St
Street address city: Hurley
Street address state: WI
Zip/Postal code: 54534-1339
General Phone: (715) 561-3405
General Fax: (715) 561-3799
Advertising Phone: (715) 561-3405
Advertising Fax: (715) 561-3799
Editorial Phone: (715) 561-3405
Editorial Fax: (715) 561-3799
General/National Adv. E-mail: icm@ironcountyminer.com
Display Adv. E-mail: icm@ironcountyminer.com
Editorial e-mail: icm@ironcountyminer.com
Primary Website: ironcountyminer.com
Year Established: 1884
Avg Paid Circ: 2430
Avg Free Circ: 114
Audit By: Sworn/Estimate/Non-Audited
Audit Date: 10.06.2019
Personnel: Ernest Moore (Pub./Ed.)

JACKSON EXPRESS NEWS

Street address 1: 8990 N 51st St
Street address city: Brown Deer
Street address state: WI
Zip/Postal code: 53223-2402
General Phone: (262) 238-6397
General Fax: (262) 242-9450
Advertising Phone: (262) 238-6397
Advertising Fax: (262) 242-9450
Editorial Phone: (262) 238-6397
Editorial Fax: (262) 242-9450
General/National Adv. E-mail: advertising@discoverhometown.com
Display Adv. E-mail: jonesjf@discoverhometown.com
Editorial e-mail: thomasj@discoverhometown.com
Primary Website: discoverhometown.com
Year Established: 1994
Avg Free Circ: 4878
Audit By: Sworn/Estimate/Non-Audited
Audit Date: 10.06.2019
Personnel: Ken Ubert (Pres./Pub.); Thomas McKillen (Mng. Ed.); Holly Potter (Prod. Mgr./Adv. Mgr.); Russ Schliepp (Adv. Sales Rep.)
Parent company (for newspapers): Hometown Publications, Inc.

JANESVILLE MESSENGER

Street address 1: 2208 Commerce Ct.
Street address city: Elkhorn
Street address state: WI
Zip/Postal code: 53121
General Phone: (262) 728-3424
General Fax: (262) 728-5479
Advertising Phone: (608) 752-0777
Advertising Fax: (608) 754-8038
Editorial Phone: (608) 752-0777
Editorial Fax: (608) 754-8038
General/National Adv. E-mail: ewood@communityshoppers.com
Display Adv. E-mail: kbliss@gazetteextra.com
Editorial e-mail: ewood@communityshoppers.com
Primary Website: communityshoppers.com
Mthly Avg Views: 16529
Mthly Avg Unique Visitors: 7140
Year Established: 1983
Avg Paid Circ: 0
Avg Free Circ: 64640
Audit By: CVC
Audit Date: 31.03.2017
Personnel: Ed Wood; Kyle Bliss
Parent company (for newspapers): Adams Publishing Group, LLC

JUNEAU COUNTY STAR-TIMES

Street address 1: 201 E State St
Street address city: Mauston
Street address state: WI
Zip/Postal code: 53948-1390
General Phone: (608)847-7341
General Fax: (608)847-4867
Advertising Phone: (608)847-7341 ext. 222
Advertising Fax: (608)745-3530
Editorial Phone: (608)847-7341
Editorial Fax: (608)847-4867
General/National Adv. E-mail: mmeyers@capitalnewspapers.com
Display Adv. E-mail: jcst-news@capitalnewspapers.com
Editorial e-mail: jcuevas@capitalnewspapers.com
Primary Website: wiscnews.com
Year Established: 1857
Avg Paid Circ: 2771
Audit By: Sworn/Estimate/Non-Audited
Audit Date: 10.06.2019
Personnel: Matt Meyers (Gen. Mgr.); Jason Cuevas (Ed.)
Parent company (for newspapers): Capital Newspapers

KETTLE MORAINE INDEX

Street address 1: 1010 Richards Rd
Street address city: Hartland
Street address state: WI
Zip/Postal code: 53029-8301
General Phone: (262) 367-3272
General Fax: (262) 367-7414
Advertising Phone: (262) 367-3272
Advertising Fax: (262) 367-7414
Editorial Phone: (262) 367-3272
Editorial Fax: (262) 367-1136
General/National Adv. E-mail: slyles@jrn.com
Display Adv. E-mail: mbilke@jrn.com
Editorial e-mail: lakenews@jcpgroup.com
Primary Website: livinglakecountry.com
Avg Paid Circ: 653
Avg Free Circ: 0
Audit By: AAM
Audit Date: 31.03.2016
Personnel: Steve Lyles (Pub./Adv. Dir./Gen. Mgr.); Scott Peterson (Mng. Ed.); Katie Zurn (Office Mgr.); Britani Zambo (Adv. Coord.)
Parent company (for newspapers): Lake County Publications; JCP Group

KEWAUNEE COUNTY STAR-NEWS

Street address 1: 203 Ellis St
Street address city: Kewaunee
Street address state: WI
Zip/Postal code: 54216-1051
General Phone: (920)388-3175
General Fax: (920)388-0198
Advertising Phone: (920)304-3300
Advertising Fax: (920)388-0198
Editorial Phone: (920)388-3175
Editorial Fax: (920)388-0198
General/National Adv. E-mail: pharkema@gokewauneecounty.com
Display Adv. E-mail: ddana@gokewauneecounty.com
Editorial e-mail: editorial@gokewauneecounty.com
Primary Website: gokewauneecounty.com
Year Established: 1859
Avg Free Circ: 11060
Audit By: Sworn/Estimate/Non-Audited
Audit Date: 10.06.2019
Personnel: Warren Bluhm (Assoc. Ed.); Deb Dana (Adv. Assistant); Scott Johnson (Pub.); Scott Domalick (Circ. Mgr); Diane Nolan (Prod. Mgr); Leah Clover (Adv. Sales Rep.); Laurie Bolle (Classified Mgr.)
Parent company (for newspapers): Gannett

LA CROSSE TRIBUNE

Street address 1: 401 3rd St N
Street address city: La Crosse
Street address state: WI
Zip/Postal code: 54601
General Phone: (608) 782-9710
General/National Adv. E-mail: barb.Wandling@lee.net
Editorial e-mail: Matthew.Perenchio@lee.net
Primary Website: lacrossetribune.com
Audit By: Sworn/Estimate/Non-Audited
Audit Date: 10.06.2019
Personnel: Josh Trust; Paul Fritz (Adv. Dir.); Rusty Cunningham (Ed.)
Parent company (for newspapers): Dispatch-Argus

LADYSMITH NEWS

Street address 1: 120 W 3rd St S
Street address city: Ladysmith
Street address state: WI
Zip/Postal code: 54848-1764
General Phone: (715) 532-5591
General Fax: (715) 532-6644
Advertising Phone: (715) 532-5591
Advertising Fax: (715) 532-6644
Editorial Phone: (715) 532-5591
Editorial Fax: (715) 532-6644
General/National Adv. E-mail: adsales@ladysmithnews.com
Display Adv. E-mail: advertise@ladysmithnews.com
Editorial e-mail: editor@ladysmithnews.com
Primary Website: ladysmithnews.com
Year Established: 1895
Avg Paid Circ: 5050
Audit By: Sworn/Estimate/Non-Audited
Audit Date: 10.06.2019
Personnel: James L. Bell (Pub.); Luke Klink (Editor); Brian Joles

LAKE COUNTRY REPORTER

Street address 1: 1010 Richards Rd
Street address city: Hartland
Street address state: WI
Zip/Postal code: 53029-8301
General Phone: (262) 367-3272
General Fax: (262) 367-7414
Advertising Phone: (262) 367-3272
Advertising Fax: (262) 367-7414
Editorial Phone: (262) 367-3272
Editorial Fax: (262) 367-1136
General/National Adv. E-mail: slyles@jrn.com
Display Adv. E-mail: mbilke@jrn.com
Editorial e-mail: lakenews@jcpgroup.com
Primary Website: livinglakecountry.com
Avg Paid Circ: 5050
Audit By: AAM
Audit Date: 31.03.2016
Personnel: Steve Lyles (Pub./Adv. Dir./Gen. Mgr.); Scott Peterson (Mng. Ed.); Katie Zurn (Office Mgr.); Britani Zambo (Adv. Coord.)
Parent company (for newspapers): Lake County Publications; JCP Group

LAKE GENEVA REGIONAL NEWS

Street address 1: 315 Broad St
Street address city: Lake Geneva
Street address state: WI
Zip/Postal code: 53147-1811
General Phone: (262) 248-4444
General Fax: (262) 248-4476
Advertising Phone: (262)248-4444
Advertising Fax: (262)248-4476
Editorial Phone: (262)248-8096
Editorial Fax: (242)248-4476
General/National Adv. E-mail: rireland@lakegenevanews.net
Display Adv. E-mail: sue@lakegenevanews.net
Editorial e-mail: newsroom@lakegenevanews.net
Primary Website: lakegenevanews.net
Year Established: 1872
Avg Paid Circ: 4000
Audit By: Sworn/Estimate/Non-Audited
Audit Date: 10.06.2019
Personnel: Robert Ireland (Mng. Ed.); Sue Hinske (Office Mgr.)
Parent company (for newspapers): Lee Enterprises, Incorporated

LAKE GENEVA TIMES

Street address 1: 1102 Ann St
Street address city: Delavan
Street address state: WI
Zip/Postal code: 53115-1938
General Phone: (262) 728-3411
General Fax: (262) 728-6844
Advertising Phone: (262) 763-2575 ext. 128
Advertising Fax: (262) 728-6844
Editorial Phone: (262) 763-3330 ext. 123
Editorial Fax: (262) 763-2238
General/National Adv. E-mail: dee@southernlakesnewspapers.com
Display Adv. E-mail: jstearns@southernlakesnewspapers.com
Editorial e-mail: enadolski@standardpress.com
Primary Website: standardpress.com
Avg Free Circ: 1206
Audit By: Sworn/Estimate/Non-Audited
Audit Date: 10.06.2019
Personnel: Cyndi Jensen (Pub./Gen. Mgr.); Edward Nadolski (Ed. in Chief); Dee Fladwood (Asst. Adv. Dir.); Vicki Vanderwerff (Adv. Dir); Tom Flatow (Circ. Mgr); Jessica Franzene (Prod. Mgr.)
Parent company (for newspapers): Southern Lakes Newspapers LLC

LAKE MILLS LEADER

Street address 1: 320 N Main St
Street address city: Lake Mills
Street address state: WI
Zip/Postal code: 53551-1137
General Phone: (920) 648-2334
Advertising Phone: (608) 478-2517
Editorial Phone: (920) 648-2334
General/National Adv. E-mail: mfeiler@hngnews.com
Display Adv. E-mail: classifieds@hngnews.com
Editorial e-mail: leadereditor@hngnews.com
Primary Website: lakemillsleader.com
Year Established: 1878
Avg Paid Circ: 2150
Audit By: Sworn/Estimate/Non-Audited
Audit Date: 10.06.2019
Personnel: Brian Knox (Pub); Missy Feiler (Adv. Mgr.); Chris Drake (Bus. Mgr.); Brian Knox II (Circ. Dir.); Robb Grindstaff (Gen. Mgr.); Sarah Weihert (Mng. Ed.)
Parent company (for newspapers): Hometown News Group

LAKELAND TIMES

Street address 1: 510 Chippewa St
Street address city: Minocqua
Street address state: WI
Zip/Postal code: 54548-9395
General Phone: (715) 356-5236
General Fax: (715) 358-2121
Advertising Phone: (715) 356-5236
Advertising Fax: (715) 358-2121
Editorial Phone: (715) 356-5236
Editorial Fax: (715) 358-2121

General/National Adv. E-mail: sales@lakelandtimes.com
Display Adv. E-mail: classifieds@lakelandtimes.com
Editorial e-mail: editor@lakelandtimes.com
Primary Website: lakelandtimes.com
Year Established: 1891
Avg Paid Circ: 9873
Audit By: Sworn/Estimate/Non-Audited
Audit Date: 10.06.2019
Personnel: Gregg Walker (Gen. Mgr.); Tony Loomis (Adv. Mgr.); Ray Rivard (Assoc. Ed.)

LAKESHORE CHRONICLE

Street address 1: 902 Franklin St
Street address city: Manitowoc
Street address state: WI
Zip/Postal code: 54220-4514
General Phone: (920) 431-8669
General Fax: (920) 684-4416
General/National Adv. E-mail: ljohnso2@gannett.com
Display Adv. E-mail: ljohnso2@gannett.com
Editorial e-mail: ljohnso2@gannett.com
Primary Website: htrnews.com
Year Established: 1972
Avg Free Circ: 28473
Audit By: CVC
Audit Date: 31.03.2017
Personnel: Pat Pankratz (Ed.); Lowell Johnson (Pub.); Greg Fiorito (Prod. Mgr); Amy Leitzke (Circ.)
Parent company (for newspapers): Gannett

MARKESAN REGIONAL REPORTER

Street address 1: 301 June St
Street address city: Berlin
Street address state: WI
Zip/Postal code: 54923-2147
General Phone: (920) 361-1515
General Fax: (920) 361-1518
Advertising Phone: (920) 361-1515
Advertising Fax: (920) 361-1518
Editorial Phone: (920) 361-1515
Editorial Fax: (920) 361-1518
General/National Adv. E-mail: news@theberlinjournal.com
Display Adv. E-mail: ads@theberlinjournal.com
Classified Adv. e-mail: classifieds@theberlinjournal.com
Editorial e-mail: news@theberlinjournal.com
Primary Website: theberlinjournal.com
Year Established: 1870
Avg Paid Circ: 3500
Audit By: Sworn/Estimate/Non-Audited
Audit Date: 10.06.2019
Personnel: Tyler Gonyo (Pub./Gen. Mgr.); Kristian Troudt (Adv. Mgr.); Tracy Kallas (Circ. Mgr.); Scott Mundro (Managing Editor/Editor)
Parent company (for newspapers): Berlin Journal Newspapers

MCFARLAND THISTLE

Street address 1: 213 W Cottage Grove Rd
Street address 2: Ste 9
Street address city: Cottage Grove
Street address state: WI
Zip/Postal code: 53527-9330
General Phone: (608)838-6435
Advertising Phone: (608)838-6435
Editorial Phone: (608)838-6435
General/National Adv. E-mail: pjohnson@hngnews.com
Display Adv. E-mail: pjohnson@hngnews.com
Editorial e-mail: agerber@hngnews.com
Primary Website: hngnews.com/mcfarland_thistle
Audit By: Sworn/Estimate/Non-Audited
Audit Date: 10.06.2019
Personnel: Amber Gerber (Managing Ed.); Pat Johnson (Adv. Mgr.); Luann Neabling (Circ. Mgr.)
Parent company (for newspapers): Hometown News Group

MENOMONEE FALLS EXPRESS NEWS

Street address 1: 8990 N 51st St
Street address city: Brown Deer
Street address state: WI
Zip/Postal code: 53223-2402
General Phone: (262) 238-6397
General Fax: (262) 242-9450
Advertising Phone: (262) 238-6397
Advertising Fax: (262) 242-9450
Editorial Phone: (262) 238-6397
Editorial Fax: (262) 242-9450
General/National Adv. E-mail: advertising@discoverhometown.com
Display Adv. E-mail: jonesjf@discoverhometown.com
Editorial e-mail: thomasj@discoverhometown.com
Primary Website: discoverhometown.com
Year Established: 1994
Avg Free Circ: 12496
Audit By: VAC
Audit Date: 30.06.2016
Personnel: Ken Ubert (Pres./Pub.); Thomas McKillen (Mng. Ed.); Holly Potter (Prod. Mgr./Adv. Mgr.); Russ Schliepp (Adv. Sales Rep.)
Parent company (for newspapers): Hometown Publications, Inc.

MENOMONEE FALLS-GERMANTOWN NOW

Street address 1: 1741 Dolphin Dr
Street address 2: Ste A
Street address city: Waukesha
Street address state: WI
Zip/Postal code: 53186-1493
General Phone: (414) 224-2100
General Fax: (262) 446-6646
Advertising Phone: (414) 224-2498
Advertising Fax: (262) 446-6646
Editorial Phone: (414) 224-2100 ext. 5
Editorial Fax: (262) 446-6646
General/National Adv. E-mail: alaffe@jrn.com
Display Adv. E-mail: btschacher@jrn.com
Editorial e-mail: speterson@jrn.com
Primary Website: menomoneefallsnow.com
Year Established: 1956
Audit By: Sworn/Estimate/Non-Audited
Audit Date: 10.06.2019
Personnel: Scott Peterson (Chief Ed.); Matt Newman (Design/Interactive Content Dir.)
Parent company (for newspapers): Community Newspapers, Inc.; Journal Media Group

MEQUON NOW

Street address 1: 1741 Dolphin Dr
Street address 2: Ste A
Street address city: Waukesha
Street address state: WI
Zip/Postal code: 53186-1493
General Phone: (414) 224-2100
General Fax: (262) 446-6646
Advertising Phone: (414) 224-2498
Advertising Fax: (262) 446-6646
Editorial Phone: (414) 224-2100 ext. 5
Editorial Fax: (262) 446-6646
General/National Adv. E-mail: alaffe@jrn.com
Display Adv. E-mail: btschacher@jrn.com
Editorial e-mail: speterson@jrn.com
Primary Website: mequonnow.com
Year Established: 1956
Audit By: Sworn/Estimate/Non-Audited
Audit Date: 10.06.2019
Personnel: Scott Peterson (Chief Ed.); Matt Newman (Design/Interactive Content Dir.)
Parent company (for newspapers): Community Newspapers, Inc.; Journal Media Group

MERRILL COURIER

Street address 1: 14027 E. Main St.
Street address city: Merrill
Street address state: WI
Zip/Postal code: 54452
General Phone: (715) 536-5843
General Fax: (715)539-3686
Advertising Phone: (715)536-5843
Advertising Fax: (715)539-3686
Editorial Phone: (715)536-5843
Editorial Fax: (715)339-3686
General/National Adv. E-mail: jgartman@mmclocal.com
Display Adv. E-mail: jgartman@mmclocal.com
Editorial e-mail: clueck@mmclocal.com
Primary Website: merrillcourier.net
Audit By: Sworn/Estimate/Non-Audited
Audit Date: 10.06.2019
Personnel: Susan Hovind
Parent company (for newspapers): Multi-Media Channels

MESSENGER OF JUNEAU COUNTY

Street address 1: 229 Main St
Street address city: Elroy
Street address state: WI
Zip/Postal code: 53929-1251
General Phone: (608) 462-4902
Advertising Phone: (608)462-4902
Editorial Phone: (608)462-4902
General/National Adv. E-mail: themessenger@centurytel.net
Display Adv. E-mail: themessenger@centurytel.net
Editorial e-mail: themessenger@centurytel.net
Primary Website: juneaumessenger.com
Audit By: Sworn/Estimate/Non-Audited
Audit Date: 10.06.2019

MIDDLETON TIMES-TRIBUNE

Street address 1: 1126 Mills St
Street address city: Black Earth
Street address state: WI
Zip/Postal code: 53515-9419
General Phone: (608) 836-1601
General Fax: (608) 836-3759
Advertising Phone: (608) 358-7958
General/National Adv. E-mail: khenning@newspubinc.com
Display Adv. E-mail: classifieds@newspubinc.com
Editorial e-mail: mgeiger@newspubinc.com
Primary Website: http://middletontimes.com
Avg Paid Circ: 1694
Audit By: Sworn/Estimate/Non-Audited
Audit Date: 10.06.2019
Personnel: Karin Henning (Adv. Sales); Tim Brubaker (Adv. Sales); Michelle Phillips (Editor); Rob Reischel (Sports Ed.)
Parent company (for newspapers): News Publishing, Co., Inc.

MILTON COURIER

Street address 1: 513 Vernal Ave
Street address city: Milton
Street address state: WI
Zip/Postal code: 53563-1144
General Phone: (608) 868-2442
Advertising Phone: (608) 208-1683
Editorial Phone: (608) 868-2442
General/National Adv. E-mail: courierads@hngnews.com
Display Adv. E-mail: classifieds@hngnews.com
Editorial e-mail: couriernews@hngnews.com
Primary Website: miltoncourieronline.com
Year Established: 1878
Avg Paid Circ: 2165
Avg Free Circ: 49
Audit By: Sworn/Estimate/Non-Audited
Audit Date: 10.06.2019
Personnel: Brian Knox (Pub.); Rebecca Kanable (Mng. Ed.); Ben Gauger (Sports Ed.); Renee` Ziegel (Display Adv.); Brooke Ostema (Office Mgr./Photographer); Paul McMurray (Adv. Mgr.); Barb Trimble (Gen. Mgr.); Susan Angeli (Graphics/Prod. Coord.); Michael Gouvion (Sports Ed.); Judy Lippincott (Office Clerk)
Parent company (for newspapers): Hometown News Group

MILWAUKEE BUSINESS JOURNAL

Street address 1: 825 N Jefferson St
Street address 2: Suite 200
Street address city: Milwaukee
Street address state: WI
Zip/Postal code: 53202-3720
General Phone: (414) 277-8181
General Fax: (414) 277-8191
Advertising Phone: (414) 336-7112
Editorial Phone: (414) 336-7116
General/National Adv. E-mail: jon.armstrong@biztimes.com
Display Adv. E-mail: robert.bahillo@biztimes.com
Editorial e-mail: andrew.weiland@biztimes.com
Primary Website: bizjournals.com/milwaukee
Year Established: 1995
Avg Paid Circ: 413
Avg Free Circ: 11258
Audit By: Sworn/Estimate/Non-Audited
Audit Date: 10.06.2019
Personnel: Dan Meyer (Pub.); Mark Sabljak (Pub.); Steve Jagler (Exec. Ed.); Mark Kass (Ed. in Chief); Kristy Leutermann (Adv. Mgr.)
Parent company (for newspapers): BizTimes Media LLC

MILWAUKEE EXPRESS NEWS

Street address 1: 8990 N 51st St
Street address city: Brown Deer
Street address state: WI
Zip/Postal code: 53223-2402
General Phone: (262) 238-6397
General Fax: (262) 242-9450
Advertising Phone: (262) 238-6397
Advertising Fax: (262) 242-9450
Editorial Phone: (262) 238-6397
Editorial Fax: (262) 242-9450
General/National Adv. E-mail: advertising@discoverhometown.com
Display Adv. E-mail: jonesjf@discoverhometown.com
Editorial e-mail: thomasj@discoverhometown.com
Primary Website: discoverhometown.com
Year Established: 1994
Avg Free Circ: 4878
Audit By: Sworn/Estimate/Non-Audited
Audit Date: 10.06.2019
Personnel: Ken Ubert (Pres./Pub.); Thomas McKillen (Mng. Ed.); Holly Potter (Prod. Mgr./Adv. Mgr.); Russ Schliepp (Adv. Sales Rep.)
Parent company (for newspapers): Hometown Publications, Inc.

MILWAUKEE POST

Street address 1: 3397 S Howell Ave
Street address city: Milwaukee
Street address state: WI
Zip/Postal code: 53207-2743
General Phone: (414)744-6370
General Fax: (414)375-7070
Advertising Phone: (414)744-6370
Advertising Fax: (414)375-7070
Editorial Phone: (414)744-6370
Editorial Fax: (414)375-7070
General/National Adv. E-mail: mkepost@conleynet.com
Display Adv. E-mail: mkepost@conleynet.com
Editorial e-mail: dmuck@conleynet.com
Primary Website: gmtoday.com
Audit By: Sworn/Estimate/Non-Audited
Audit Date: 10.06.2019
Personnel: Dan Muckelbauer (Ed.)
Parent company (for newspapers): Conley Media LLC

MONROE COUNTY HERALD

Street address 1: 1302 River Rd
Street address city: Sparta
Street address state: WI
Zip/Postal code: 54656-2498
General Phone: (608) 269-3186
General Fax: (608) 269-6876
Advertising Phone: (608) 269-3186
Advertising Fax: (608) 269-6876
Editorial Phone: (608) 269-3186
Editorial Fax: (608) 269-6876
General/National Adv. E-mail: kyle@monroecountyherald.com
Display Adv. E-mail: kyle@monroecountyherald.com
Editorial e-mail: pat@monroecountyherald.com
Primary Website: monroecountyherald.com
Year Established: 1857
Avg Paid Circ: 5000
Avg Free Circ: 35
Audit By: Sworn/Estimate/Non-Audited
Audit Date: 10.06.2019
Personnel: Evans Greg (Pub.)
Parent company (for newspapers): Evans Print & Media Group

MOSINEE TIMES

Street address 1: 407 3rd St
Street address city: Mosinee
Street address state: WI
Zip/Postal code: 54455-1426
General Phone: (715) 693-2300
General Fax: (715) 693-1574
General/National Adv. E-mail: motimes@mtc.net
Display Adv. E-mail: motimes@mtc.net
Editorial e-mail: motimes@mtc.net

Year Established: 1895
Avg Paid Circ: 1800
Audit By: Sworn/Estimate/Non-Audited
Audit Date: 01.09.2023
Personnel: James Kress (Pub.); Susan Durst (Publisher and Editor)

MUSKEGO-NEW BERLIN NOW

Street address 1: 1741 Dolphin Dr
Street address 2: Ste A
Street address city: Waukesha
Street address state: WI
Zip/Postal code: 53186-1493
General Phone: (414) 224-2100
General Fax: (262) 446-6646
Advertising Phone: (414) 224-2498
Advertising Fax: (262) 446-6646
Editorial Phone: (414) 224-2100 ext. 5
Editorial Fax: (262) 446-6646
General/National Adv. E-mail: alaffe@jrn.com
Display Adv. E-mail: btschacher@jrn.com
Editorial e-mail: speterson@jrn.com
Primary Website: mymuskegonow.com
Year Established: 1956
Audit By: Sworn/Estimate/Non-Audited
Audit Date: 10.06.2019
Personnel: Scott Peterson (Chief Ed.); Matt Newman (Design/Interactive Content Dir.)
Parent company (for newspapers): Community Newspapers, Inc.; Journal Media Group

NEW BERLIN NOW

Street address 1: 1741 Dolphin Dr
Street address 2: Ste A
Street address city: Waukesha
Street address state: WI
Zip/Postal code: 53186-1493
General Phone: (414) 224-2100
General Fax: (262) 446-6646
Advertising Phone: (414) 224-2498
Advertising Fax: (262) 446-6646
Editorial Phone: (414) 224-2100 ext. 5
Editorial Fax: (262) 446-6646
General/National Adv. E-mail: alaffe@jrn.com
Display Adv. E-mail: btschacher@jrn.com
Editorial e-mail: speterson@jrn.com
Primary Website: newberlinnow.com
Year Established: 1956
Audit By: Sworn/Estimate/Non-Audited
Audit Date: 10.06.2019
Personnel: Scott Peterson (Chief Ed.); Matt Newman (Design/Interactive Content Dir.)
Parent company (for newspapers): Community Newspapers, Inc.; Journal Media Group

NEW RICHMOND NEWS

Street address 1: 127 S Knowles Ave
Street address city: New Richmond
Street address state: WI
Zip/Postal code: 54017-1726
General Phone: (715) 246-6881
General Fax: (715) 246-7117
Advertising Phone: (715) 426-1052
Advertising Fax: (715) 246-7117
Editorial Phone: (715) 243-7767 ext. 241
Editorial Fax: (715) 246-7117
General/National Adv. E-mail: pfrebault@rivertowns.net
Display Adv. E-mail: classifieds@rivertowns.net
Editorial e-mail: nrneditor@rivertowns.net
Primary Website: newrichmond-news.net
Year Established: 1869
Avg Paid Circ: 5000
Avg Free Circ: 100
Audit By: Sworn/Estimate/Non-Audited
Audit Date: 10.06.2019
Personnel: Chad Richardson (Ed Dir)
Parent company (for newspapers): Forum Communications Co.

NEWS GRAPHIC

Street address 1: W61N306 Washington Ave
Street address 2: Ste 1
Street address city: Cedarburg
Street address state: WI
Zip/Postal code: 53012-2451
General Phone: (262) 375-5100
General Fax: (262) 375-5107
Advertising Phone: (262) 375-5100
Advertising Fax: (262) 375-5107
Editorial Phone: (262) 375-5100
Editorial Fax: (262) 375-5107
General/National Adv. E-mail: hrogge@conleynet.com
Display Adv. E-mail: agannon@conleynet.com
Editorial e-mail: jrockley@conleynet.com
Primary Website: gmtoday.com
Year Established: 1883
Avg Paid Circ: 7218
Avg Free Circ: 232
Audit By: Sworn/Estimate/Non-Audited
Audit Date: 10.06.2019
Personnel: Lisa Curtis (Mng. Ed.); Heather Rogge (Pub./Adv. Dir.)
Parent company (for newspapers): Conley Media LLC

NEWS-RECORD

Street address 1: 306 W Washington St
Street address city: Appleton
Street address state: WI
Zip/Postal code: 54911-5452
General Phone: (920) 996-7289
General Fax: (920) 954-1945
Editorial e-mail: sprinsen@gannett.com
Primary Website: newsrecord.net
Year Established: 1961
Avg Free Circ: 22659
Audit By: CVC
Audit Date: 30.03.2017
Personnel: Sandy Prinsen; Matthew Wolcanski
Parent company (for newspapers): Gannett

NEWS-SICKLE-ARROW

Street address 1: 1126 Mills St
Street address city: Black Earth
Street address state: WI
Zip/Postal code: 53515-9419
General Phone: (608) 767-3655
General Fax: (608) 767-2222
Advertising Phone: (608) 767-3655 ext. 242
Advertising Fax: (608)767-2222
Editorial Phone: (608) 767-4029 ext. 226
Editorial Fax: (608)767-2222
General/National Adv. E-mail: marc@newspubinc.com
Display Adv. E-mail: classifieds@newspubinc.com
Editorial e-mail: nsa@newspubinc.com
Primary Website: nsarrow.com
Avg Paid Circ: 2012
Audit By: Sworn/Estimate/Non-Audited
Audit Date: 10.06.2019
Personnel: Dan Witte (Pub.); John Donaldson (Mng. Ed.); Marc Mickelson (Adv. Mgr.)
Parent company (for newspapers): News Publishing, Co., Inc.

NORTH SHORE NOW

Street address 1: 1741 Dolphin Dr
Street address 2: Ste A
Street address city: Waukesha
Street address state: WI
Zip/Postal code: 53186-1493
General Phone: (414) 224-2100
General Fax: (262) 446-6646
Advertising Phone: (414) 224-2498
Advertising Fax: (262) 446-6646
Editorial Phone: (414) 224-2100 ext. 5
Editorial Fax: (262) 446-6646
General/National Adv. E-mail: alaffe@jrn.com
Display Adv. E-mail: btschacher@jrn.com
Editorial e-mail: speterson@jrn.com
Year Established: 1956
Audit By: Sworn/Estimate/Non-Audited
Audit Date: 10.06.2019
Personnel: Scott Peterson (Chief Ed.); Matt Newman (Design/Interactive Content Dir.)
Parent company (for newspapers): Community Newspapers, Inc.; Journal Media Group

OAK CREEK NOW

Street address 1: 1741 Dolphin Dr
Street address 2: Ste A
Street address city: Waukesha
Street address state: WI
Zip/Postal code: 53186-1493
General Phone: (414) 224-2100
General Fax: (262) 446-6646
Advertising Phone: (414) 224-2498
Advertising Fax: (262) 446-6646
Editorial Phone: (414) 224-2100 ext. 5
Editorial Fax: (262) 446-6646
General/National Adv. E-mail: alaffe@jrn.com
Display Adv. E-mail: btschacher@jrn.com
Editorial e-mail: speterson@jrn.com
Primary Website: oakcreeknow.com
Year Established: 1956
Audit By: Sworn/Estimate/Non-Audited
Audit Date: 10.06.2019
Personnel: Scott Peterson (Ed.); Matt Newman (Design/Interactive Content Dir.)
Parent company (for newspapers): Community Newspapers, Inc.; Journal Media Group

OAK CREEK-FRANKLIN-GREENDALE-HALES CORNERS NOW

Street address 1: 1741 Dolphin Dr
Street address 2: Ste A
Street address city: Waukesha
Street address state: WI
Zip/Postal code: 53186-1493
General Phone: (414) 224-2100
General Fax: (262) 446-6646
Advertising Phone: (414) 224-2498
Advertising Fax: (262) 446-6646
Editorial Phone: (414) 224-2100 ext. 5
Editorial Fax: (262) 446-6646
General/National Adv. E-mail: alaffe@jrn.com
Display Adv. E-mail: btschacher@jrn.com
Editorial e-mail: speterson@jrn.com
Primary Website: greendalenow.com
Year Established: 1956
Audit By: Sworn/Estimate/Non-Audited
Audit Date: 10.06.2019
Personnel: Scott Peterson (Chief Ed.); Matt Newman (Design/Interactive Content Dir.)
Parent company (for newspapers): Community Newspapers, Inc.; Journal Media Group

OCONOMOWOC ENTERPRISE

Street address 1: 801 N Barstow St
Street address city: Waukesha
Street address state: WI
Zip/Postal code: 53186-4801
General Phone: (262) 567-5511
General/National Adv. E-mail: jbaumgart@conleynet.com
Display Adv. E-mail: jbaumgart@conleynet.com
Primary Website: gmtoday.com
Year Established: 1888
Avg Paid Circ: 3804
Avg Free Circ: 40
Audit By: CVC
Audit Date: 31.12.2018
Personnel: Bill Yorth (Pub.); Jim Baumgart (Advertising Manager); Barb Parker (Circulation Manager); Pat School (Production Manager)
Parent company (for newspapers): Conley Media LLC

OCONOMOWOC FOCUS

Street address 1: 1010 Richards Rd
Street address city: Hartland
Street address state: WI
Zip/Postal code: 53029-8301
General Phone: (262) 367-3272
General Fax: (262) 367-7414
Advertising Phone: (262) 367-3272
Advertising Fax: (262) 367-7414
Editorial Phone: (262) 367-3272
Editorial Fax: (262) 367-1136
General/National Adv. E-mail: slyles@jrn.com
Display Adv. E-mail: mbilke@jrn.com
Editorial e-mail: lakenews@jcpgroup.com
Primary Website: livinglakecountry.com
Avg Paid Circ: 1303
Audit By: AAM
Audit Date: 31.03.2016
Personnel: Steve Lyles (Pub./Adv. Dir./Gen. Mgr.); Scott Peterson (Mng. Ed.); Katie Zurn (Office Mgr.); Britani Zambo (Adv. Coord.)
Parent company (for newspapers): Lake County Publications; JCP Group

OCONTO COUNTY REPORTER

Street address 1: PO Box 59
Street address city: Appleton
Street address state: WI
Zip/Postal code: 54912
General Phone: (920)431-8416
Advertising Phone: (888) 774-7744
Editorial Phone: (920)431-8416
General/National Adv. E-mail: editorial@goocontocounty.com
Display Adv. E-mail: baypublicationsOE@gannett.com
Editorial e-mail: editorial@goocontocounty.com
Primary Website: ocontocountyreporter.com
Year Established: 1871
Avg Paid Circ: 5000
Avg Free Circ: 50
Audit By: Sworn/Estimate/Non-Audited
Audit Date: 10.06.2019
Personnel: Kent Tempus (Reporter); Scott Johnson (Pres./Pub.); Kevin Dittman (Editor); Christina Kruse (Account executive)
Parent company (for newspapers): Gannett

OMRO HERALD

Street address 1: 301 June St
Street address city: Berlin
Street address state: WI
Zip/Postal code: 54923-2147
General Phone: (920) 361-1515
General Fax: (920) 361-1518
Advertising Phone: (920) 361-1515
Advertising Fax: (920) 361-1518
Editorial Phone: (920) 361-1515
Editorial Fax: (920) 361-1518
General/National Adv. E-mail: ads@theberlinjournal.com
Display Adv. E-mail: classifieds@theberlinjournal.com
Editorial e-mail: news@theberlinjournal.com
Primary Website: theberlinjournal.com
Year Established: 1870
Avg Paid Circ: 3500
Audit By: Sworn/Estimate/Non-Audited
Audit Date: 10.06.2019
Personnel: Tyler Gonyo (Pub./Gen. Mgr.); Jason Fox (Ed.); Kristian Troudt (Adv. Mgr.); Tracy Kallas (Circ. Mgr.)
Parent company (for newspapers): Berlin Journal Newspapers

ONALASKA HOLMEN COURIER-LIFE

Street address 1: 401 3rd St N
Street address city: La Crosse
Street address state: WI
Zip/Postal code: 54601-3267
General Phone: (608)782-9710
General Fax: (608)782-9723
Advertising Phone: (608)791-8257
Advertising Fax: (608)791-8213
Editorial Phone: (608)791-8219
Editorial Fax: (608)782-9723
General/National Adv. E-mail: barb.formanek@lee.net
Display Adv. E-mail: ads@lacrossetribune.com
Editorial e-mail: mike.burns@lee.net
Primary Website: courierlifenews.com
Year Established: 2008
Avg Paid Circ: 3026
Audit By: Sworn/Estimate/Non-Audited
Audit Date: 10.06.2019
Personnel: Randy Erickson (Ed.)
Parent company (for newspapers): Dispatch-Argus

OREGON OBSERVER

Street address 1: 125 N Main St
Street address city: Oregon
Street address state: WI
Zip/Postal code: 53575-1430
General Phone: (608) 845-9559
General Fax: (608) 835-0130
Advertising Phone: (608) 845-9559
Advertising Fax: (608) 835-0130
Editorial Phone: (608) 845-9559
Editorial Fax: (608) 835-0130
General/National Adv. E-mail: oregonsales@wcinet.com
Display Adv. E-mail: ungclassified@wcinet.com
Editorial e-mail: veronapress@wcinet.com
Primary Website: connectoregonwi.com
Year Established: 1880
Avg Paid Circ: 1987
Audit By: Sworn/Estimate/Non-Audited
Audit Date: 10.06.2019
Personnel: Jim Ferolie (Group Ed.); Lee Borkowski (General manager)

Parent company (for newspapers): Woodward Communications, Inc.; O'Rourke Media Group

OSHKOSH HERALD

Street address 1: 36 Broad St
Street address 2: Suite 300
Street address city: Oshkosh
Street address state: WI
Zip/Postal code: 54901
General Phone: 9203854512
General/National Adv. E-mail: advertise@oshkoshherald.com
Display Adv. E-mail: advertise@oshkoshherald.com
Classified Adv. e-mail: Classifieds@OshkoshHerald.com
Editorial e-mail: submit@oshkoshherald.com
Primary Website: oshkoshherald.com
Mthly Avg Views: 7000
Mthly Avg Unique Visitors: 3000
Year Established: 2017
Avg Paid Circ: 625
Avg Free Circ: 31115
Audit By: CVC
Audit Date: 31.03.2023
Personnel: Karen Schneider (Publisher)

OZAUKEE PRESS

Street address 1: 125 E Main St
Street address city: Port Washington
Street address state: WI
Zip/Postal code: 53074-1915
General Phone: (262) 284-3494
General Fax: (262) 284-0067
Advertising Phone: (262) 284-3494 ext. 1102
Advertising Fax: (262) 284-0067
Editorial Phone: (262) 284-3494
Editorial Fax: (262) 284-0067
General/National Adv. E-mail: news@ozaukeepress.com
Display Adv. E-mail: news@ozaukeepress.com
Editorial e-mail: news@ozaukeepress.com
Primary Website: ozaukeepress.com
Year Established: 1940
Avg Paid Circ: 6295
Avg Free Circ: 215
Audit By: CVC
Audit Date: 30.09.2016
Personnel: William F. Schanen (Pub./Ed.); Holly Osterman (Adv. Mgr.)

PADDOCK LAKE REPORT

Street address 1: 1102 Ann St
Street address city: Delavan
Street address state: WI
Zip/Postal code: 53115-1938
General Phone: (262) 728-3411
General Fax: (262) 728-6844
Advertising Phone: (262) 763-2575 ext. 128
Advertising Fax: (262) 728-6844
Editorial Phone: (262) 763-3330 ext. 123
Editorial Fax: (262) 763-2238
General/National Adv. E-mail: dee@southernlakesnewspapers.com
Display Adv. E-mail: jstearns@southernlakesnewspapers.com
Editorial e-mail: enadolski@standardpress.com
Primary Website: standardpress.com
Avg Free Circ: 1496
Audit By: Sworn/Estimate/Non-Audited
Audit Date: 10.06.2019
Personnel: Cyndi Jensen (Pub./Gen. Mgr.); Edward Nadolski (Ed. in Chief); Dee Fladwood (Adv. Dir.); Vicki Vanderwerff (Adv. Mgr); Tom Flatow (Circ. Mgr); Sue Lange (Prod. Mgr)
Parent company (for newspapers): Southern Lakes Newspapers LLC

PALMYRA ENTERPRISE

Street address 1: 1102 Ann St
Street address city: Delavan
Street address state: WI
Zip/Postal code: 53115-1938
General Phone: (262) 728-3411
General Fax: (262) 725-7702
Advertising Phone: (262) 728-3411
Advertising Fax: (262) 725-7702
Editorial Phone: (262) 728-3411
Editorial Fax: (262) 725-7702
General/National Adv. E-mail: cjensen@rvpublishing.com
Display Adv. E-mail: cjensen@rvpublishing.com
Editorial e-mail: cjensen@rvpublishing.com
Avg Paid Circ: 1400
Avg Free Circ: 700
Audit By: Sworn/Estimate/Non-Audited
Audit Date: 10.06.2019
Personnel: Jack Crueger (Pub.); Ed Nadolski (Ed. in Chief); Cyndi Jensen (Gen. Mgr.)
Parent company (for newspapers): Southern Lakes Newspapers LLC

PARK FALLS HERALD

Street address 1: 115 N Lake Ave
Street address city: Phillips
Street address state: WI
Zip/Postal code: 54555-1220
General Phone: (715) 339-3036
General Fax: (715) 339-4300
Advertising Phone: (715) 339-3036
Advertising Fax: (715) 339-4300
Editorial Phone: (715) 339-3036
Editorial Fax: (715) 339-4300
General/National Adv. E-mail: skelley@thephillipsbee.com
Display Adv. E-mail: lhaskins@thephillipsbee.com
Editorial e-mail: eknudson@thephillipsbee.com
Primary Website: pricecountydaily.com
Year Established: 1900
Avg Paid Circ: 4367
Avg Free Circ: 6200
Audit By: Sworn/Estimate/Non-Audited
Audit Date: 10.06.2019
Personnel: Eric Knudson (Ed.); Susan Kelley (Adv. Dir.); Linda Haskins (Circ. Mgr.); Kenneth Dischler (Pub./Gen. Mgr.)
Parent company (for newspapers): Adams Publishing Group, LLC

POST MESSENGER RECORDER

Street address 1: 109 5th Ave
Street address city: New Glarus
Street address state: WI
Zip/Postal code: 53574
General Phone: (608) 527-5252
General Fax: (608) 527-5285
Advertising Phone: (608) 358-7958
General/National Adv. E-mail: khenning@newspubinc.com
Display Adv. E-mail: pmr@newspubinc.com
Classified Adv. e-mail: pmr@newspubinc.com
Editorial e-mail: pmreditor@newspubinc.com
Primary Website: https://postmessengerrecorder.com
Avg Paid Circ: 1217
Audit By: Sworn/Estimate/Non-Audited
Audit Date: 10.06.2019
Personnel: Karin Henning (Adv. Sales); Sue Moen (Ed.); Katie Pederson (Classifieds/Subscriptions)
Parent company (for newspapers): News Publishing, Co., Inc.

POYNETTE PRESS

Street address 1: 105 S Main St
Street address 2: Ste H
Street address city: Lodi
Street address state: WI
Zip/Postal code: 53555-1140
General Phone: (606) 592-3261
Advertising Phone: (606) 592-3261
Advertising Fax: (606)592-3866
Editorial Phone: (608) 729-3366
Editorial Fax: (606)592-3866
General/National Adv. E-mail: mfeiler@hngnews.com
Display Adv. E-mail: classifieds@hngnews.com
Editorial e-mail: lpedit@hngnews.com
Primary Website: hngnews.com/poynette_press
Year Established: 1896
Avg Paid Circ: 2600
Audit By: Sworn/Estimate/Non-Audited
Audit Date: 10.06.2019
Personnel: Ryan Broege (Mng. Ed.); Sam Rodriguez; Christine Benisch
Parent company (for newspapers): Hometown News Limited Partnership

PRICE COUNTY REVIEW

Street address 1: 115 N Lake Ave
Street address city: Phillips
Street address state: WI
Zip/Postal code: 54555-1220
General Phone: (715) 339-3036
Avg Paid Circ: 100
Audit By: Sworn/Estimate/Non-Audited
Audit Date: 10.06.2019
Parent company (for newspapers): Adams Publishing Group, LLC

PRINCETON TIMES-REPUBLIC

Street address 1: 301 June St
Street address city: Berlin
Street address state: WI
Zip/Postal code: 54923-2147
General Phone: (920) 361-1515
General Fax: (920) 361-1518
Advertising Phone: (920) 361-1515
Advertising Fax: (920) 361-1518
Editorial Phone: (920) 361-1515
Editorial Fax: (920) 361-1518
General/National Adv. E-mail: ads@theberlinjournal.com
Display Adv. E-mail: classifieds@theberlinjournal.com
Editorial e-mail: news@theberlinjournal.com
Primary Website: theberlinjournal.com
Year Established: 1870
Avg Paid Circ: 3500
Audit By: Sworn/Estimate/Non-Audited
Audit Date: 10.06.2019
Personnel: Tyler Gonyo (Pub./Gen. Mgr.); Jason Fox (Ed.); Kristian Troudt (Adv. Mgr.); Tracy Kallas (Circ. Mgr.)
Parent company (for newspapers): Berlin Journal Newspapers

REEDSBURG TIMES-PRESS

Street address 1: 714 Matts Ferry Rd
Street address city: Baraboo
Street address state: WI
Zip/Postal code: 53913-3152
General Phone: (608) 356-3808
Advertising Phone: (608) 745-3500
Advertising Fax: (608) 745-3530
Editorial Phone: (608) 356-3808
General/National Adv. E-mail: nfoesch@capitalnewspapers.com
Display Adv. E-mail: jdenk@capitalnewspapers.com
Editorial e-mail: tkrysiak@capitalnewspapers.com
Primary Website: reedsburgtimespress.com
Avg Paid Circ: 966
Audit By: Sworn/Estimate/Non-Audited
Audit Date: 10.06.2019
Personnel: Todd Krysiak (Editor); Jon Denk (General Manager)
Parent company (for newspapers): Capital Newspapers

REPUBLICAN JOURNAL

Street address 1: 316 Main St
Street address city: Darlington
Street address state: WI
Zip/Postal code: 53530-1426
General Phone: (608) 776-4425
General/National Adv. E-mail: ads@myrjonline.com
Display Adv. E-mail: editor@myrjonline.com
Editorial e-mail: editor@myrjonline.com
Primary Website: swnews4u.com
Year Established: 1861
Avg Paid Circ: 2700
Audit By: USPS
Audit Date: 10.10.2023
Personnel: John Ingebritson (Pub.); Adam Ploessl (Adv. Mgr.); Kayla Barnes (Ed.); Brian Lund (Publisher)
Parent company (for newspapers): Morris Multimedia, Inc.

RICE LAKE CHRONOTYPE

Street address 1: 28 S Main St
Street address city: Rice Lake
Street address state: WI
Zip/Postal code: 54868-2232
General Phone: (715) 234-2121
General Fax: (715) 234-5232
General/National Adv. E-mail: bdorrance@chronotype.com
Editorial e-mail: bdorrance@chronotype.com
Primary Website: apg-wi.com/rice_lake_chronotype
Year Established: 1874
Avg Paid Circ: 7176
Audit By: Sworn/Estimate/Non-Audited
Audit Date: 10.06.2019
Personnel: Ryan Urban (Ed.); Dave Greschner (Sports Ed.); Pam Page (Adv.); Charlene Raley (Circ.)
Parent company (for newspapers): Adams Publishing Group, LLC

RIPON COMMONWEALTH PRESS

Street address 1: 656 S Douglas St
Street address city: Ripon
Street address state: WI
Zip/Postal code: 54971-9044
General Phone: (920) 748-3017
General Fax: (920) 748-3028
Advertising Phone: (920) 748-3017
Advertising Fax: (920) 748-3028
Editorial Phone: (920) 748-3017
Editorial Fax: (920) 748-3028
General/National Adv. E-mail: TimL@riponprinters.com
Display Adv. E-mail: rcpads@riponprinters.com
Editorial e-mail: rcpnews@riponprinters.com
Primary Website: riponpress.com
Year Established: 1864
Avg Free Circ: 3400
Audit By: Sworn/Estimate/Non-Audited
Audit Date: 10.06.2019
Personnel: Tim Lyke (Pub.); Ian Stepleton (Ed.); Bob Chikowski (Adv. Mgr.); Kelly Schmude (Circ.)

RIVER FALLS JOURNAL

Street address 1: 2815 Prairie Dr
Street address city: River Falls
Street address state: WI
Zip/Postal code: 54022-5211
General Phone: (715)425-1561
General Fax: (715)425-5666
Advertising Phone: (715)426-1052
Advertising Fax: (715)425-5666
Editorial Phone: (715)426-1050
Editorial Fax: (715)425-5666
General/National Adv. E-mail: sengelhart@rivertowns.net
Display Adv. E-mail: classifieds@rivertowns.net
Editorial e-mail: ajacboson@rivertowns.net
Primary Website: riverfallsjournal.com
Year Established: 1858
Avg Paid Circ: 2839
Audit By: Sworn/Estimate/Non-Audited
Audit Date: 10.06.2019
Personnel: Neal Ronquist (Publisher); Steve Engelhart (Advertising Director); Anne Jacobson (Editor); Dave Pevonka (Circulation Director Production Director)
Parent company (for newspapers): Forum Communications Co.

SAUK PRAIRIE EAGLE

Street address 1: 714 Matts Ferry Rd
Street address city: Baraboo
Street address state: WI
Zip/Postal code: 53913-3152
General Phone: (608) 356-4808
Advertising Phone: (608) 745-3500
Advertising Fax: (608) 745-3530
Editorial Phone: (608) 356-4808
General/National Adv. E-mail: mbudde@capitalnewspapers.com
Display Adv. E-mail: jdenk@capitalnewspapers.com
Editorial e-mail: jcuevas@wiscnews.com
Primary Website: saukprairieeagle.com
Avg Paid Circ: 2000
Audit By: Sworn/Estimate/Non-Audited
Audit Date: 10.06.2019
Personnel: Todd Krisiak (Ed.); Jon Denk (General Manager); Jason Cuevas (Weeklies Lead)
Parent company (for newspapers): Capital Newspapers

SAUK PRAIRIE STAR

Street address 1: 801 Water St
Street address city: Sauk City
Street address state: WI
Zip/Postal code: 53583-1502
General Phone: (608) 643-3444
General Fax: (608) 643-4988
Advertising Phone: (608) 643-3444
Advertising Fax: (608) 643-4988
Editorial Phone: (608) 643-3444

Editorial Fax: (608) 643-4988
General/National Adv. E-mail: homenewssales@newspubinc.com
Display Adv. E-mail: spstar@newspubinc.com
Editorial e-mail: mikesps@newspubinc.com
Primary Website: newspubinc.com
Avg Paid Circ: 2800
Avg Free Circ: 40
Audit By: Sworn/Estimate/Non-Audited
Audit Date: 10.06.2019
Personnel: Dan Witte (Pub.); Mark Witte (Pub.); Mike Carignan (Ed.)
Parent company (for newspapers): News Publishing, Co., Inc.

SAWYER COUNTY RECORD

Street address 1: 15617B US Highway 63
Street address city: Hayward
Street address state: WI
Zip/Postal code: 54843-4244
General Phone: (715) 634-4881
General Fax: (715) 634-8191
Advertising Phone: (715) 634-4881
Advertising Fax: (715) 634-8191
Editorial Phone: (715) 634-4881
Editorial Fax: (715) 634-8191
General/National Adv. E-mail: dlaporte@sawyercountyrecord.net
Display Adv. E-mail: denise.p@sawyercountyrecord.net
Editorial e-mail: akurth@sawyercountyrecord.net
Primary Website: apg-wi.com
Year Established: 1893
Avg Paid Circ: 4000
Avg Free Circ: 44
Audit By: Sworn/Estimate/Non-Audited
Audit Date: 10.06.2019
Personnel: Janet Krokson (Pub.); Anna Kurth (Mng. Ed.); David LaPorte (Adv. Mgr.)
Parent company (for newspapers): Adams Publishing Group, LLC

SLINGER EXPRESS NEWS

Street address 1: 8990 N 51st St
Street address city: Brown Deer
Street address state: WI
Zip/Postal code: 53223-2402
General Phone: (262) 238-6397
General Fax: (262) 242-9450
Advertising Phone: (262) 238-6397
Advertising Fax: (262) 242-9450
Editorial Phone: (262) 238-6397
Editorial Fax: (262) 242-9450
General/National Adv. E-mail: advertising@discoverhometown.com
Display Adv. E-mail: jonesjf@discoverhometown.com
Editorial e-mail: thomasj@discoverhometown.com
Primary Website: discoverhometown.com
Year Established: 1994
Avg Free Circ: 3909
Audit By: VAC
Audit Date: 30.06.2016
Personnel: Ken Ubert (Pres./Pub.); Thomas McKillen (Mng. Ed.); Holly Potter (Prod. Mgr./Adv. Mgr.); Russ Schliepp (Adv. Sales Rep.)
Parent company (for newspapers): Hometown Publications, Inc.

SOUTH MILWAUKEE NOW

Street address 1: 1741 Dolphin Dr
Street address 2: Ste A
Street address city: Waukesha
Street address state: WI
Zip/Postal code: 53186-1493
General Phone: (414) 224-2100
General Fax: (262) 446-6646
Advertising Phone: (414) 224-2498
Advertising Fax: (262) 446-6646
Editorial Phone: (414) 224-2100 ext. 5
Editorial Fax: (262) 446-6646
General/National Adv. E-mail: alaffe@jrn.com
Display Adv. E-mail: btschacher@jrn.com
Editorial e-mail: speterson@jrn.com
Primary Website: southmilwaukeenow.com
Year Established: 1956
Audit By: Sworn/Estimate/Non-Audited
Audit Date: 10.06.2019
Personnel: Scott Peterson (Chief Ed.); Matt Newman (Design/Interactive Content Dir.)
Parent company (for newspapers): Community Newspapers, Inc.; Journal Media Group

SPOONER ADVOCATE

Street address 1: 251 E Maple St
Street address city: Spooner
Street address state: WI
Zip/Postal code: 54801-9698
General Phone: (715) 635-2181
General Fax: (715) 635-2186
Advertising Phone: (715) 635-2181 ext. 29
Advertising Fax: (715) 635-2186
Editorial Phone: (715) 635-2181
Editorial Fax: (715) 635-2186
General/National Adv. E-mail: mcarlson@spooneradvocate.com
Display Adv. E-mail: ads@spooneradvocate.com
Editorial e-mail: news@spooneradvocate.com
Primary Website: spooneradvocate.com
Year Established: 1901
Avg Paid Circ: 3000
Audit By: Sworn/Estimate/Non-Audited
Audit Date: 10.06.2019
Personnel: Janet I. Krokson (Pub./Ed./Gen. Mgr.); Bill Thornley (Assc. Ed.); Michelle Carlson (Adv. Mgr.); Janis Redman (Prod. Mgr.); Julie Hustvet (News editor); Deb Fosberg (Advertising consultant); Kelie Kuffel (Office manager)
Parent company (for newspapers): Adams Publishing Group, LLC

SPRING GREEN HOME NEWS

Street address 1: 120 N Worcester St
Street address city: Spring Green
Street address state: WI
Zip/Postal code: 53588-8015
General Phone: (608)588-2508
General Fax: (608)588-3536
Advertising Phone: (608)588-2508
Advertising Fax: (608)588-3536
Editorial Phone: (608)588-2508
Editorial Fax: (608)588-3536
General/National Adv. E-mail: homenewssales@newspubinc.com
Display Adv. E-mail: classifieds@newspubinc.com
Editorial e-mail: nsa@newspubinc.com
Primary Website: newspubinc.com
Avg Paid Circ: 2700
Audit By: Sworn/Estimate/Non-Audited
Audit Date: 10.06.2019
Personnel: Tom Finger (CFO/Controller); John Donaldson (Mng. Ed.)
Parent company (for newspapers): News Publishing, Co., Inc.

ST. FRANCIS NOW

Street address 1: 1741 Dolphin Dr
Street address 2: Ste A
Street address city: Waukesha
Street address state: WI
Zip/Postal code: 53186-1493
General Phone: (414) 224-2100
General Fax: (262) 446-6646
Advertising Phone: (414) 224-2498
Advertising Fax: (262) 446-6646
Editorial Phone: (414) 224-2100 ext. 5
Editorial Fax: (262) 446-6646
General/National Adv. E-mail: alaffe@jrn.com
Display Adv. E-mail: btschacher@jrn.com
Editorial e-mail: speterson@jrn.com
Primary Website: stfrancisnow.com
Year Established: 1956
Audit By: Sworn/Estimate/Non-Audited
Audit Date: 10.06.2019
Personnel: Scott Peterson (Chief Ed.); Matt Newman (Design/Interactive Content Dir.)
Parent company (for newspapers): Community Newspapers, Inc.; Journal Media Group

STAR JOURNAL

Street address 1: 24 W Rives St
Street address city: Rhinelander
Street address state: WI
Zip/Postal code: 54501-3164
General Phone: (715) 369-3331
General Fax: (715) 369-4859
General/National Adv. E-mail: hodagads@mmclocal.com
Display Adv. E-mail: hodagads@mmclocal.com
Editorial e-mail: starjournal@mmclocal.com
Primary Website: starjournalnow.com
Mthly Avg Views: 21974
Mthly Avg Unique Visitors: 5083
Year Established: 1977
Avg Paid Circ: 5
Avg Free Circ: 15940
Audit By: Sworn/Estimate/Non-Audited
Audit Date: 10.06.2019
Personnel: Peter Daniels (Pub.); Cathy Oelrich (Circ. Mgr.); Ernie Neuenfeldt (Prod. Mgr)
Parent company (for newspapers): Multi Media Channels LLC

STATELINE NEWS

Street address 1: 220B Commerce Ct
Street address city: Elkhorn
Street address state: WI
Zip/Postal code: 53121-4371
General Phone: (608) 365-1663
General Fax: (608) 365-7045
Advertising Phone: (608) 365-1663
Advertising Fax: (608) 365-7045
Editorial Phone: (608) 365-1663
Editorial Fax: (608) 365-7045
General/National Adv. E-mail: kbliss@gazetteextra.com
Display Adv. E-mail: kbliss@gazetteextra.com
Editorial e-mail: ewood@communityshoppers.com
Primary Website: communityshoppers.com
Mthly Avg Views: 16529
Mthly Avg Unique Visitors: 7140
Year Established: 1968
Avg Paid Circ: 0
Avg Free Circ: 67480
Audit By: CVC
Audit Date: 4/31/2017
Personnel: Ed Wood (Pub.); Kyle Bliss (Adv.)
Parent company (for newspapers): Adams Publishing Group, LLC

STOUGHTON COURIER HUB

Street address 1: 135 W Main St
Street address 2: Ste. 102
Street address city: Stoughton
Street address state: WI
Zip/Postal code: 53589-2135
General Phone: (608)873-6671
General Fax: (608)873-3473
Advertising Phone: (608)873-6671
Advertising Fax: (608)873-3473
Editorial Phone: (608)873-6671
Editorial Fax: (608)873-3473
General/National Adv. E-mail: stoughtonsales@wcinet.com
Display Adv. E-mail: ungclassified@wcinet.com
Editorial e-mail: stoughtoneditor@wcinet.com
Primary Website: connectstoughton.com
Year Established: 1879
Avg Paid Circ: 2458
Audit By: Sworn/Estimate/Non-Audited
Audit Date: 10.06.2019
Personnel: Jim Ferolie (Group Ed.); David Enstad (Gen. Mgr.)
Parent company (for newspapers): Woodward Communications, Inc.; O'Rourke Media Group

SUN-ARGUS

Street address 1: W2855 730th Ave
Street address city: Spring Valley
Street address state: WI
Zip/Postal code: 54767-8512
General Phone: (715) 778-4990
General Fax: (715) 778-4996
Editorial Phone: (715) 778-4990
General/National Adv. E-mail: editor@mygatewaynews.com
Display Adv. E-mail: admins@mygatewaynews.com
Editorial e-mail: editor@mygatewaynews.com
Primary Website: mygatewaynews.com
Year Established: 1892
Avg Paid Circ: 800
Avg Free Circ: 2
Audit By: Sworn/Estimate/Non-Audited
Audit Date: 10.06.2019
Personnel: Paul Seeling (Ed./Pub.)
Parent company (for newspapers): Gateway Publishing, Inc.

SUPERIOR TELEGRAM

Street address 1: 1410 Tower Ave
Street address city: Superior
Street address state: WI
Zip/Postal code: 54880-1590
General Phone: (715) 395-5000
General Fax: (715) 395-5002
Advertising Phone: (715) 395-5000
Advertising Fax: (715) 395-5002
Editorial Phone: (715) 395-5000
Editorial Fax: (715) 395-5002
General/National Adv. E-mail: telegram@superiortelegram.com
Editorial e-mail: editorial@superiortelegram.com
Primary Website: superiortelegram.com
Avg Paid Circ: 2488
Avg Free Circ: 0
Sat. Circulation Paid: 8180
Audit By: Sworn/Estimate/Non-Audited
Audit Date: 10.06.2021
Personnel: Megan Keller (Adv. Dir.); Deb Williams (Human Resources Manager); Neal Ronquist (Publisher); Shelley Nelson (Editor); Rick Lubbers (Editor); Rich Roxbury (Circulation Director)
Parent company (for newspapers): Forum Communications Co.

SUSSEX EXPRESS NEWS

Street address 1: 8990 N 51st St
Street address city: Brown Deer
Street address state: WI
Zip/Postal code: 53223-2402
General Phone: (262) 238-6397
General Fax: (262) 242-9450
Advertising Phone: (262) 238-6397
Advertising Fax: (262) 242-9450
Editorial Phone: (262) 238-6397
Editorial Fax: (262) 242-9450
General/National Adv. E-mail: advertising@discoverhometown.com
Display Adv. E-mail: jonesjf@discoverhometown.com
Editorial e-mail: thomasj@discoverhometown.com
Primary Website: discoverhometown.com
Year Established: 1994
Avg Free Circ: 12496
Audit By: VAC
Audit Date: 30.06.2016
Personnel: Ken Ubert (Pres./Pub.); Thomas McKillen (Mng. Ed.); Holly Potter (Prod. Mgr./Adv. Mgr.); Russ Schliepp (Adv. Sales Rep.)
Parent company (for newspapers): Hometown Publications, Inc.

SUSSEX SUN

Street address 1: 1010 Richards Rd
Street address city: Hartland
Street address state: WI
Zip/Postal code: 53029-8301
General Phone: (262) 367-3272
General Fax: (262) 367-7414
Advertising Phone: (262) 367-3272
Advertising Fax: (262) 367-7414
Editorial Phone: (262) 367-3272
Editorial Fax: (262) 367-1136
General/National Adv. E-mail: slyles@jrn.com
Display Adv. E-mail: mbilke@jrn.com
Editorial e-mail: lakenews@jcpgroup.com
Primary Website: livinglakecountry.com
Avg Paid Circ: 1239
Audit By: AAM
Audit Date: 31.03.2016
Personnel: Steve Lyles (Pub./Adv. Dir./Gen. Mgr.); Scott Peterson (Mng. Ed.); Katie Zurn (Office Mgr.); Britani Zambo (Adv. Coord.)
Parent company (for newspapers): JCP Group

THE BALDWIN BULLETIN

Street address 1: 805 MAIN ST
Street address city: Baldwin
Street address state: WI
Zip/Postal code: 54002
General Phone: (715) 684-2484
General Fax: (715) 684-4937
Advertising Phone: (715) 684-2484
Advertising Fax: (715) 684-4937
Editorial Phone: (715) 684-2484

Editorial Fax: (715) 684-4937
General/National Adv. E-mail: pehaw@baldwin-telecom.net
Display Adv. E-mail: pehaw@baldwin-telecom.net
Editorial e-mail: pehaw@baldwin-telecom.net
Primary Website: baldwin-bulletin.com
Year Established: 1873
Avg Paid Circ: 2050
Audit By: Sworn/Estimate/Non-Audited
Audit Date: 10.06.2019
Personnel: Peter Hawley (Pub.); Thomas Hawley (Ed.)

THE BEE

Street address 1: 115 N Lake Ave
Street address city: Phillips
Street address state: WI
Zip/Postal code: 54555-1220
General Phone: (715) 339-3036
General Fax: (715) 339-4300
Advertising Phone: (715) 339-3036
Advertising Fax: (715) 339-4300
Editorial Phone: (715) 339-3036
Editorial Fax: (715) 339-4300
General/National Adv. E-mail: skelley@thephillipsbee.com
Display Adv. E-mail: lhaskins@thephillipsbee.com
Editorial e-mail: eknudson@thephillipsbee.com
Primary Website: pricecountydaily.com
Year Established: 1884
Avg Paid Circ: 4367
Avg Free Circ: 6200
Audit By: Sworn/Estimate/Non-Audited
Audit Date: 10.06.2019
Personnel: Eric Knudson (Ed.); Susan Kelley (Adv. Dir.); Linda Haskins (Circ. Mgr.)

THE BOSCOBEL DIAL

Street address 1: 901 Wisconsin Ave
Street address city: Boscobel
Street address state: WI
Zip/Postal code: 53805-1531
General Phone: (608) 375-4458
General Fax: (608) 375-2369
Advertising Phone: (608)375-4458
Advertising Fax: (608)375-2369
Editorial Phone: (608)375-4458
Editorial Fax: (608)375-2369
General/National Adv. E-mail: dialads@boscobeldial.net
Display Adv. E-mail: dialads@boscobeldial.net
Classified Adv. e-mail: dialads@boscobeldial.net
Editorial e-mail: dialeditor@boscobeldial.net
Primary Website: swnews4u.com
Year Established: 1872
Avg Paid Circ: 3100
Audit By: Sworn/Estimate/Non-Audited
Audit Date: 10.06.2019
Personnel: David Krier (Ed.); Barb Puckett (Production Manager); Jean Roth (Adv. Mgr./Gen. Mgr.); Joe Hart (Editor)
Parent company (for newspapers): Morris Multimedia, Inc.

THE BRILLION NEWS

Street address 1: 425 W Ryan St
Street address city: Brillion
Street address state: WI
Zip/Postal code: 54110-1037
General Phone: (920) 756-2222
General Fax: (920) 756-2701
Advertising Phone: (920)756-2222
Advertising Fax: (920)756-2701
Editorial Phone: (920)756-2222
Editorial Fax: (920)756-2701
General/National Adv. E-mail: kris@zanderpressinc.com
Display Adv. E-mail: lisa@zanderpressinc.com
Editorial e-mail: editor@thebrillionnews.com
Primary Website: thebrillionnews.com
Mthly Avg Views: 10000
Mthly Avg Unique Visitors: 2200
Year Established: 1894
Avg Paid Circ: 2100
Avg Free Circ: 5
Audit By: Sworn/Estimate/Non-Audited
Audit Date: 10.06.2019
Personnel: Beth Wenzel (Pub.); David Nordby (Ed.); Kris Bastian (Adv. Mgr.); Ed Byrne (Reporter)
Parent company (for newspapers): Zander Press Inc.

THE CAMBRIDGE NEWS & THE INDEPENDENT

Street address 1: 201 W North St
Street address city: Cambridge
Street address state: WI
Zip/Postal code: 53523-8714
General Phone: (608) 423-3213
General/National Adv. E-mail: LCDSales@hngnews.com
Display Adv. E-mail: classifieds@hngnews.com
Editorial e-mail: cambridge.deerfield@hngnews.com
Primary Website: cambridgeenews.com
Year Established: 1894
Avg Paid Circ: 1443
Avg Free Circ: 17
Audit By: Sworn/Estimate/Non-Audited
Audit Date: 10.06.2019
Personnel: Brian Knox (Pub.); Karyn Saemann (Ed.); Cody Ruell (Adv. /Sales); Christine Benisch (Circ.)
Parent company (for newspapers): Hometown News Group

THE CAPITAL TIMES

Street address 1: 1901 Fish Hatchery Rd
Street address city: Madison
Street address state: WI
Zip/Postal code: 53713-1248
General Phone: (608) 252-6400
General Fax: (608) 252-6445
Advertising Phone: (608) 252-6274
Advertising Fax: (608) 252-6333
Editorial Fax: (608) 252-6445
General/National Adv. E-mail: jallen@madison.com
Display Adv. E-mail: jallen@madison.com
Classified Adv. e-mail: jallen@madison.com
Editorial e-mail: citydesk@madison.com
Primary Website: http://host.madison.com/ct/
Year Established: 1917
Avg Paid Circ: 61000
Avg Free Circ: 8000
Audit By: Sworn/Estimate/Non-Audited
Audit Date: 10.06.2019
Personnel: Scott Zeinemann (Publisher); Dave Zweifel (Ed.); Lynn Danielson (Books Ed.); Paul Fanlund (Editor); Debra Carr-Elsing (Food Writer); Chris Murphy; Katie Dean; Jason Joyce; Rob Thomas; Pam Wells; Steven Elbow; Brandon Raygo; Amber Walker; Lisa Speckhard; Katelyn Ferral; Abigail Becker; Jessie Opoien; Pat Schneider; Michelle Stocker; Saiyna Bashir; John Nichols; Lindsay Christians

THE CASHTON RECORD

Street address 1: 713 Broadway St
Street address city: Cashton
Street address state: WI
Zip/Postal code: 54619-2013
General Phone: (608) 654-7330
General Fax: (608) 654-7324
Advertising Phone: (608) 654-7330
Advertising Fax: (608) 654-7324
Editorial Phone: (608) 654-7330
Editorial Fax: (608) 654-7324
General/National Adv. E-mail: cashtonrecord@mwt.net
Display Adv. E-mail: cashtonrecord@mwt.net
Editorial e-mail: cashtonrecord@mwt.net
Primary Website: cashtonrecord.com
Year Established: 1896
Avg Paid Circ: 1000
Audit By: Sworn/Estimate/Non-Audited
Audit Date: 10.06.2019
Personnel: Logan Everson (Editor); Kyle Evans (Ad Salsman); Paul Fanning (Pub.); Kim Fanning (Ed.)
Parent company (for newspapers): Evans Print + Media Group

THE CHEESE REPORTER

Street address 1: 2810 Crossroads Dr
Street address 2: Ste 3000
Street address city: Madison
Street address state: WI
Zip/Postal code: 53718-7972
General Phone: (608)246-8430
General Fax: (608)246-8431
Advertising Phone: (608)246-8430
Advertising Fax: (608)246-8431
Editorial Phone: (608)246-8430
Editorial Fax: (608)246-8431
General/National Adv. E-mail: advertisers@cheesereporter.com
Display Adv. E-mail: advertisers@cheesereporter.com
Editorial e-mail: dgroves@cheesereporter.com
Primary Website: cheesereporter.com
Audit By: Sworn/Estimate/Non-Audited
Audit Date: 10.06.2019
Personnel: Dick Groves (Pub./Ed.); Moira Crowley (Asst. Ed.); Kevin Thome (Mktg. Dir./Adv. Mgr.); Betty Merkes (Subscriptions)

THE CHETEK ALERT

Street address 1: 312 Knapp St
Street address city: Chetek
Street address state: WI
Zip/Postal code: 54728-4129
General Phone: (715) 924-4118
General Fax: (715) 924-4122
Advertising Phone: (715) 924-4118
Advertising Fax: (715) 924-4122
Editorial Phone: (715) 924-4118
Editorial Fax: (715) 924-4122
General/National Adv. E-mail: jim@thechetekalert.com
Display Adv. E-mail: julie@thechetekalert.com
Editorial e-mail: editor@thechetekalert.com
Primary Website: chetekalert.com
Year Established: 1882
Avg Paid Circ: 3000
Avg Free Circ: 20
Audit By: Sworn/Estimate/Non-Audited
Audit Date: 10.06.2019
Personnel: Jim Bell (Pub./Ed.); Ryan Urban (News Ed.); Julie LeMoine (Sales Mgr.)

THE CLINTON TOPPER

Street address 1: 407 Church St
Street address city: Clinton
Street address state: WI
Zip/Postal code: 53525-9494
General Phone: (608) 676-4111
General Fax: (608) 676-4664
Advertising Phone: (608) 676-4111
Advertising Fax: (608) 676-4664
Editorial Phone: (608) 676-4111
Editorial Fax: (608) 676-4664
General/National Adv. E-mail: theclintontopper@aol.com
Display Adv. E-mail: theclintontopper@aol.com
Editorial e-mail: theclintontopper@aol.com
Primary Website: indreg.com
Year Established: 1938
Avg Paid Circ: 1650
Avg Free Circ: 44
Audit By: Sworn/Estimate/Non-Audited
Audit Date: 10.06.2019
Personnel: Jack Cruger (Pub.); Dawn Martin (Ed.); Celesce Lightner-Greenwalt (Adv. Mgr.)
Parent company (for newspapers): Rock Valley Publishing LLC

THE COLFAX MESSENGER

Street address 1: 511 E Railroad Ave
Street address city: Colfax
Street address state: WI
Zip/Postal code: 54730-9187
General Phone: (715) 962-3535
General Fax: (715) 962-3413
Advertising Phone: (715) 962-3535
Advertising Fax: (715) 962-3413
Editorial Phone: (715) 962-3535
Editorial Fax: (715) 962-3413
General/National Adv. E-mail: messenger@dewittmedia.com
Display Adv. E-mail: messenger@dewittmedia.com
Editorial e-mail: messenger@dewittmedia.com
Primary Website: ColfaxMessenger.com
Year Established: 1897
Avg Paid Circ: 1100
Avg Free Circ: 15
Audit By: Sworn/Estimate/Non-Audited
Audit Date: 10.06.2019
Personnel: Carlton DeWitt (Pub./Ed.); Shawn DeWitt (Mng. Ed.)
Parent company (for newspapers): DeWitt Media Inc.

THE COMMONWEALTH EXPRESS

Street address 1: 656 S Douglas St
Street address city: Ripon
Street address state: WI
Zip/Postal code: 54971-9044
General Phone: (920)748-3017
General Fax: (920)748-3028
Advertising Phone: (920)748-3017
Advertising Fax: (920)748-3028
Editorial Phone: (920)748-3017
Editorial Fax: (920)748-3028
General/National Adv. E-mail: TimL@riponprinters.com
Display Adv. E-mail: TimL@riponprinters.com
Editorial e-mail: TimL@riponprinters.com
Primary Website: riponpress.com
Avg Free Circ: 17540
Audit By: Sworn/Estimate/Non-Audited
Audit Date: 10.06.2019
Personnel: Tim Lyke (Pub.)

THE COUNTRY TODAY

Street address 1: 701 S Farwell St
Street address city: Eau Claire
Street address state: WI
Zip/Postal code: 54701-3831
General Phone: (715) 833-9270
General Fax: (715) 858-7307
Advertising Phone: (715) 833-9276
Advertising Fax: (715) 858-7307
Editorial Phone: (715) 833-9275
Editorial Fax: (715) 858-7307
General/National Adv. E-mail: sue.bauer@ecpc.com
Display Adv. E-mail: mary.brownell@ecpc.com
Editorial e-mail: nathan.jackson@ecpc.com
Primary Website: thecountrytoday.com
Avg Paid Circ: 25000
Avg Free Circ: 1124
Audit By: Sworn/Estimate/Non-Audited
Audit Date: 10.06.2019
Personnel: Nate Jackson (Reg. Ed./Prod. Coord.); Sue Bauer (Adv. Mgr.)

THE COUNTY LINE

Street address 1: 207 N Garden St
Street address city: Ontario
Street address state: WI
Zip/Postal code: 54651-6532
General Phone: (608) 337-4232
General Fax: (608) 338-0472
General/National Adv. E-mail: sales@thecountyline.net
Editorial e-mail: countyline@centurytel.net
Primary Website: thecountyline.net
Year Established: 1983
Avg Paid Circ: 1200
Audit By: USPS
Audit Date: 10.06.2019

THE COURIER-WEDGE

Street address 1: 103 W Main St
Street address city: Durand
Street address state: WI
Zip/Postal code: 54736-1144
General Phone: (715) 672-4252
General Fax: (715) 672-4254
Advertising Phone: (715) 672-4252
Advertising Fax: (715) 672-4254
Editorial Phone: (715) 672-4252
Editorial Fax: (715) 672-4254
General/National Adv. E-mail: thewedge@nelson-tel.net
Display Adv. E-mail: thewedge@nelson-tel.net
Editorial e-mail: thewedge@nelson-tel.net
Avg Paid Circ: 4300
Avg Free Circ: 36
Audit By: Sworn/Estimate/Non-Audited
Audit Date: 10.06.2019
Personnel: Michael Stumpf (Pub.); Deb Claxton (Ed.)

THE DAILY PRESS: COUNTY JOURNAL

Street address 1: 122 3rd St W
Street address city: Ashland
Street address state: WI
Zip/Postal code: 54806-1661
General Phone: (715) 682-2313
General Fax: (715) 682-4699
General/National Adv. E-mail: hwesterlund@ashlanddailypress.net
Display Adv. E-mail: okillam@ashlanddailypress.net
Editorial e-mail: pwasson@ashlanddailypress.net

Primary Website: apg-wi.com
Avg Paid Circ: 3950
Avg Free Circ: 25
Audit By: Sworn/Estimate/Non-Audited
Audit Date: 10.06.2019
Personnel: Pete Wasson (Mng. Ed.); David LaPorte (GM); Bets North (Adv.); Heidi Hicks (Adv.); Oliver Killam (Circ./Class.)

THE DELAVAN ENTERPRISE

Street address 1: 1102 Ann St
Street address city: Delavan
Street address state: WI
Zip/Postal code: 53115-1938
General Phone: (262) 728-3411
General Fax: (262) 728-6844
Advertising Phone: (262) 725-7701 ext. 132
Advertising Fax: (262) 728-6844
Editorial Phone: (262) 725-7701 ext. 130
Editorial Fax: (262) 728-6844
General/National Adv. E-mail: jstearns@southernlakesnewspapers.com
Display Adv. E-mail: delavanassistant@southernlakesnewspapers.com
Editorial e-mail: delavaneditor@southernlakesnewspapers.com
Primary Website: southernlakesnewspapers.com
Year Established: 1878
Avg Paid Circ: 4500
Audit By: Sworn/Estimate/Non-Audited
Audit Date: 10.06.2019
Personnel: Vicky Wedig-Farence (Pub./Ed.); Jackie Stearns (Adv. Mgr.)
Parent company (for newspapers): Southern Lakes Newspapers LLC

THE DENMARK NEWS

Street address 1: 116 Main St
Street address city: Denmark
Street address state: WI
Zip/Postal code: 54208-9683
General Phone: (920) 863-2700
General Fax: (920) 863-2710
Advertising Phone: (920) 713-2047
Advertising Fax: (920) 863-2710
Editorial Phone: (920) 863-2700
Editorial Fax: (920) 863-2710
General/National Adv. E-mail: jc@thedenmarknews.com
Display Adv. E-mail: karen@thedenmarknews.com
Editorial e-mail: ryan@thedenmarknews.com
Primary Website: thedenmarknews.com
Year Established: 2009
Avg Paid Circ: 2900
Avg Free Circ: 43
Audit By: Sworn/Estimate/Non-Audited
Audit Date: 10.06.2019
Personnel: Ryan Radue (Pub.); JC Marquez (Adv. Mgr.); Karen Nelsen (Office Mgr.)

THE DODGE COUNTY PIONEER

Street address 1: 126 Bridge St
Street address city: Mayville
Street address state: WI
Zip/Postal code: 53050-1634
General Phone: (920) 387-2211
General Fax: (920) 387-5515
Advertising Phone: (920) 387-2211
Advertising Fax: (920) 387-5515
Editorial Phone: (920) 387-2211
Editorial Fax: (920) 387-5515
General/National Adv. E-mail: salesmgr@dodgecountypionier.com
Display Adv. E-mail: salemgr@dodgecountypionier.com
Editorial e-mail: mayville@dodgecountypionier.com
Primary Website: dodgecountypionier.com
Year Established: 1892
Avg Paid Circ: 3221
Audit By: Sworn/Estimate/Non-Audited
Audit Date: 10.06.2019
Personnel: Andrew Johnson (Pub.)

THE DODGEVILLE CHRONICLE

Street address 1: 106 W Merrimac St
Street address city: Dodgeville
Street address state: WI
Zip/Postal code: 53533-1440
General Phone: (608) 935-2331
Advertising Phone: (608) 935-2331
Editorial Phone: (608) 935-2331
General/National Adv. E-mail: ad@thedodgevillechronicle.com
Display Adv. E-mail: ad@thedodgevillechronicle.com
Editorial e-mail: preilly@thedodgevillechronicle.com
Primary Website: thedodgevillechronicle.com
Year Established: 1862
Avg Paid Circ: 4700
Avg Free Circ: 75
Audit By: Sworn/Estimate/Non-Audited
Audit Date: 24.06.2019
Personnel: pat reilly (Ed./ Co-Pub.); Michael Reilly (Co-Pub.); Shelly Roh (Adv. Mgr.); Josh Edwards (production manager); Brooke Bechen (Ed.)

THE DUNN COUNTY NEWS

Street address 1: 321 Frenette Dr
Street address city: Chippewa Falls
Street address state: WI
Zip/Postal code: 54729-3372
General Phone: (715) 738-1619
General Fax: (715) 723-9644
Advertising Phone: (715) 738-1615
Editorial Phone: (715) 450-1557
General/National Adv. E-mail: paul.pehler@lee.net
Display Adv. E-mail: ads@lacrossetribune.com
Classified Adv. e-mail: ads@lacrossetribune.com
Editorial e-mail: editor@dunnconnect.com
Primary Website: dunnconnect.com
Year Established: 1860
Avg Paid Circ: 2047
Audit By: Sworn/Estimate/Non-Audited
Audit Date: 10.06.2019
Personnel: Sarah Seifert (Ed.); Paul Pehler (Reg. Adv. Mgr.); Erin Brunke (Adv. Sales Rep.)
Parent company (for newspapers): Dispatch-Argus

THE ELKHORN INDEPENDENT

Street address 1: 812 N Wisconsin St
Street address city: Elkhorn
Street address state: WI
Zip/Postal code: 53121-1137
General Phone: (262) 723-2250
General/National Adv. E-mail: assistant@elkhornindependent.com
Display Adv. E-mail: phansen@standardpress.com
Editorial e-mail: elkinde@elkhornindependent.com
Primary Website: mywalworthcounty.com
Year Established: 1853
Avg Paid Circ: 2911
Avg Free Circ: 18
Audit By: Sworn/Estimate/Non-Audited
Audit Date: 10.06.2019
Personnel: Heather Ruenz (Ed.); Pete Hansen (Adv. Mgr.)
Parent company (for newspapers): Southern Lakes Newspapers LLC

THE FITCHBURG STAR

Street address 1: PO Box 930427
Street address 2: 133 Enterprise Drive
Street address city: Verona
Street address state: WI
Zip/Postal code: 53593-0427
General Phone: (608) 845-9559
General/National Adv. E-mail: fitchburgstar@wcinet.com
Primary Website: connectfitchburg.com
Avg Free Circ: 13277
Audit By: Sworn/Estimate/Non-Audited
Audit Date: 10.06.2019
Personnel: Lee Borkowski (Gen. Mgr.); Jim Ferolie (Ed.); Catherine Stang (Ad. Sales); Kathy Neumeister (Advertising & Marketing Manager)
Parent company (for newspapers): Unified Newspaper Group

THE FOREST REPUBLICAN

Street address 1: 103 S Hazeldell Ave
Street address city: Crandon
Street address state: WI
Zip/Postal code: 54520-1453
General Phone: (715) 478-3315
General Fax: (715) 478-5385
Advertising Phone: (715)478-3315
Advertising Fax: (715)478-5385
Editorial Phone: (715)478-3315
Editorial Fax: (715)478-5385
General/National Adv. E-mail: news@forestrepublican.com
Display Adv. E-mail: news@forestrepublican.com
Editorial e-mail: news@forestrepublican.com
Primary Website: florence-forestnews.com
Year Established: 1886
Avg Paid Circ: 2500
Avg Free Circ: 50
Audit By: Sworn/Estimate/Non-Audited
Audit Date: 10.06.2019
Personnel: Sarah Giddings (Ed.); Teresa Broullire (Adv.); Deb Siversten (Pub.)
Parent company (for newspapers): Borderland Publishing Inc.

THE FOX LAKE REPRESENTATIVE

Street address 1: 301 June St
Street address city: Berlin
Street address state: WI
Zip/Postal code: 54923-2147
General Phone: (920) 361-1515
General Fax: (920) 361-1518
Advertising Phone: (920) 361-1515
Advertising Fax: (920) 361-1518
Editorial Phone: (920) 361-1515
Editorial Fax: (920) 361-1518
General/National Adv. E-mail: ads@theberlinjournal.com
Display Adv. E-mail: classifieds@theberlinjournal.com
Editorial e-mail: news@theberlinjournal.com
Primary Website: theberlinjournal.com
Year Established: 1870
Avg Paid Circ: 3500
Audit By: Sworn/Estimate/Non-Audited
Audit Date: 10.06.2019
Personnel: Tyler Gonyo (Pub./Gen. Mgr.); Jason Fox (Ed.); Kristian Troudt (Adv. Mgr.); Tracy Kallas (Circ. Mgr.)
Parent company (for newspapers): Berlin Journal Newspapers

THE HARTFORD TIMES PRESS

Street address 1: 100 S 6th Ave
Street address city: West Bend
Street address state: WI
Zip/Postal code: 53095-3309
General Phone: (262) 375-5100
General Fax: (262) 670-6689
Advertising Phone: (262) 375-5100
Advertising Fax: (262) 670-6689
Editorial Phone: (262) 375-5100
Editorial Fax: (262) 670-6689
General/National Adv. E-mail: jvan@conleynet.com
Display Adv. E-mail: jvan@conleynet.com
Editorial e-mail: jvan@conleynet.com
Primary Website: gmtoday.com
Year Established: 1867
Avg Free Circ: 13779
Audit By: Sworn/Estimate/Non-Audited
Audit Date: 10.06.2019
Personnel: Heather Rogge (Pub.); Sarah Mann (Ed.); Mary Meyer (Adv. Mgr.); Tim Haffemann (Circ. Mgr); Scott Wiesner (Prod. Mgr)
Parent company (for newspapers): Conley Media LLC

THE INDEPENDENT REGISTER

Street address 1: 922 W Exchange St
Street address city: Brodhead
Street address state: WI
Zip/Postal code: 53520-1469
General Phone: (608) 897-2193
General Fax: (608) 897-4137
Advertising Phone: (608) 897-2193
Advertising Fax: (608) 897-4137
Editorial Phone: (608) 897-2193
Editorial Fax: (608) 897-4137
General/National Adv. E-mail: ads@indreg.com
Display Adv. E-mail: paper@indreg.com
Editorial e-mail: sschwartzlow@indreg.com
Primary Website: indreg.com
Year Established: 1860
Avg Free Circ: 5166
Audit By: Sworn/Estimate/Non-Audited
Audit Date: 10.06.2019
Personnel: Dan Moeller (Ed.); Shirley Sauer (Adv. Mgr.); Joyce Chrisbaum (Office Mgr.); Randy Johnson (Pub./Gen. Mgr.)

THE MADISON TIMES

Street address 1: 313 W Beltline Hwy
Street address 2: Ste 132
Street address city: Madison
Street address state: WI
Zip/Postal code: 53713-2679
General Phone: (608)270-9470
Advertising Phone: (608)270-9470
Editorial Phone: (608)270-9470
General/National Adv. E-mail: sales@madtimes.com
Display Adv. E-mail: sales@madtimes.com
Editorial e-mail: news@madtimes.com
Primary Website: themadisontimes.themadent.com
Year Established: 1991
Avg Paid Circ: 250
Avg Free Circ: 8750
Audit By: Sworn/Estimate/Non-Audited
Audit Date: 10.06.2019
Personnel: Bri Breunig (Sales Manager)

THE MARQUETTE COUNTY TRIBUNE

Street address 1: 120 Underwood Ave
Street address city: Montello
Street address state: WI
Zip/Postal code: 53949-9354
General Phone: (608) 297-2424
General Fax: (608) 297-9293
General/National Adv. E-mail: marquettetribune@newspubinc.com
Display Adv. E-mail: marquettetribune@newspubinc.com
Editorial e-mail: marquettetribune@newspubinc.com
Primary Website: marquettecountytribune.com
Avg Paid Circ: 3203
Avg Free Circ: 12
Audit By: Sworn/Estimate/Non-Audited
Audit Date: 10.06.2019
Personnel: Daniel Witte (Pub.); Mark Witte (Pub.); Mary Faltz (Prodn. Mgr.)
Parent company (for newspapers): News Publishing Company, Inc.

THE MONROE COUNTY HERALD

Street address 1: 1302 River Rd
Street address city: Sparta
Street address state: WI
Zip/Postal code: 54656-2498
General Phone: (608) 269-3186
General Fax: (608) 269-6876
Advertising Phone: (608) 269-3186
Advertising Fax: (608) 269-6876
Editorial Phone: (608) 269-3186
Editorial Fax: (608) 269-6876
General/National Adv. E-mail: mcp2006@centurytel.net
Display Adv. E-mail: mcp2006@centurytel.net
Editorial e-mail: sadtad@centurytel.net
Primary Website: spartanewspapers.com
Avg Paid Circ: 4650
Avg Free Circ: 35
Audit By: Sworn/Estimate/Non-Audited
Audit Date: 10.06.2019
Personnel: Pat Mulvaney (Ed.); Tim Evans (Gen. Mgr.); JP Schaller (Sports Ed.)
Parent company (for newspapers): Monroe County Publishers, Inc.

THE PLATTEVILLE JOURNAL

Street address 1: 25 E Main St
Street address city: Platteville
Street address state: WI
Zip/Postal code: 53818-3216
General Phone: (608) 348-3006
General Fax: (608) 348-7979
Advertising Phone: (608) 348-3006
Advertising Fax: (608) 348-7979
Editorial Phone: (608) 348-3006
Editorial Fax: (608) 348-7979
General/National Adv. E-mail: ads@theplattevillejournal.com
Display Adv. E-mail: ads@theplattevillejournal.com
Editorial e-mail: editor@theplattevillejournal.com
Primary Website: swnews4u.com
Year Established: 1899

Avg Paid Circ: 4300
Avg Free Circ: 17665
Audit By: Sworn/Estimate/Non-Audited
Audit Date: 10.06.2019
Personnel: John Ingebritsen (Publisher); Ann Rupp (Adv. Mgr.); Steve Prestegard (Ed.); Jason Nihles (Sports Ed.)
Parent company (for newspapers): Morris Multimedia, Inc.

THE PORTAGE COUNTY GAZETTE

Street address 1: 1024 Main St
Street address city: Stevens Point
Street address state: WI
Zip/Postal code: 54481-2859
General Phone: (715)343-8045
General Fax: (715)343-8048
Advertising Phone: (715)343-8045
Advertising Fax: (715)343-8048
Editorial Phone: (715)343-8045
Editorial Fax: (715)343-8048
General/National Adv. E-mail: ads@pcgazette.com
Display Adv. E-mail: subscriptions@pcgazette.com
Editorial e-mail: pcgazette@g2a.net
Primary Website: pcgazette.com
Year Established: 1878
Audit By: Sworn/Estimate/Non-Audited
Audit Date: 10.06.2019
Personnel: Nathanael Enwald (Managing Ed.); Joey Hetzel (Adv. Rep.); John Kemmeter (Sports Ed.); Matt Clucas (Adv. Rep.); Sarah McQueen (Assoc. Ed.); Gary Glennon (Gen. Mgr.); Paula O'Kray (Prod. Coord.); Norb Tepp (CFO); Nancy Kramer (Circ./Classifieds); Amy McKenzie (Circ./Classifieds)

THE REVIEW

Street address 1: 113 E Mill St
Street address city: Plymouth
Street address state: WI
Zip/Postal code: 53073-1703
General Phone: (920) 893-6411
General Fax: (920) 893-5505
Advertising Phone: (920) 893-6411
Advertising Fax: (920) 893-5505
Editorial Phone: (920) 893-6411
Editorial Fax: (920) 893-5505
General/National Adv. E-mail: displayads@plymouth-review.com
Display Adv. E-mail: reviewclassifieds@gmail.com
Editorial e-mail: reply@plymouth-review.com
Primary Website: plymouth-review.com
Year Established: 1895
Avg Paid Circ: 5308
Avg Free Circ: 33
Audit By: Sworn/Estimate/Non-Audited
Audit Date: 10.06.2019
Personnel: Barry S. Johanson (Pub.); M. Christine Johanson (Pub.); Ian Johanson (Assoc. Pub.); Debbie Mueller (Circ. Mgr.); Emmitt Feldner (Ed.)

THE RICHLAND OBSERVER

Street address 1: 172 E Court St
Street address city: Richland Center
Street address state: WI
Zip/Postal code: 53581-2339
General Phone: (608) 647-6141
General Fax: (608) 647-6143
Primary Website: swnews4u.com
Year Established: 1864
Audit By: Sworn/Estimate/Non-Audited
Audit Date: 10.06.2019
Parent company (for newspapers): Morris Multimedia, Inc.

THE SHEBOYGAN FALLS NEWS

Street address 1: 113 E Mill St
Street address city: Plymouth
Street address state: WI
Zip/Postal code: 53073-1703
General Phone: (920) 893-6411
General Fax: (920) 893-5505
Advertising Phone: (920) 893-6411
Advertising Fax: (920) 893-5505
Editorial Phone: (920) 893-6411
Editorial Fax: (920) 893-5505
General/National Adv. E-mail: displayads@plymouth-review.com
Display Adv. E-mail: reviewclassifieds@gmail.com
Editorial e-mail: fallsnews@plymouth-review.com
Primary Website: sheboyganfallsnews.com
Year Established: 1895
Avg Paid Circ: 2133
Audit By: Sworn/Estimate/Non-Audited
Audit Date: 10.06.2019
Personnel: Barry S. Johanson (Pub.); M. Christine Johanson (Pub.); Ian Johanson (Assoc. Pub.); Debbie Mueller (Circ. Mgr.); Jeff Pederson (Ed.)

THE SOUNDER

Street address 1: 405 2nd St
Street address city: Random Lake
Street address state: WI
Zip/Postal code: 53075-1824
General Phone: (920) 994-9244
General Fax: (920) 994-4817
Editorial e-mail: editor@thesounder.com
Primary Website: thesounder.com
Year Established: 1918
Avg Paid Circ: 2122
Audit By: Sworn/Estimate/Non-Audited
Audit Date: 10.06.2019
Personnel: Gary Feider (Ed.); Katie Cramer (Office Mgr.)

THE STANLEY REPUBLICAN

Street address 1: 131 E 1st Ave
Street address city: Stanley
Street address state: WI
Zip/Postal code: 54768-1202
General Phone: (715) 644-5452
General Fax: (715) 644-5459
Advertising Phone: (715) 644-5452
Advertising Fax: (715) 644-5459
Editorial Phone: (715) 644-5452
Editorial Fax: (715) 644-5459
General/National Adv. E-mail: therepublican@charterinternet.com
Display Adv. E-mail: therepublican@charterinternet.com
Editorial e-mail: therepublican@charterinternet.com
Avg Paid Circ: 2600
Audit By: Sworn/Estimate/Non-Audited
Audit Date: 10.06.2019
Personnel: John McLoone (Pub./Ed.)

THE STAR

Street address 1: 804 Liberty Blvd
Street address 2: Ste 201
Street address city: Sun Prairie
Street address state: WI
Zip/Postal code: 53590-4643
General Phone: (608) 837-2521
Advertising Phone: (608) 837-2521
Editorial Phone: (608) 837-2521
General/National Adv. E-mail: mfeiler@hngnews.com
Display Adv. E-mail: classifieds@hngnews.com
Editorial e-mail: spedit@hngnews.com
Primary Website: sunprairiestar.com
Year Established: 1877
Avg Paid Circ: 3750
Audit By: Sworn/Estimate/Non-Audited
Audit Date: 10.06.2019
Personnel: Chris Mertes (Mng. Ed.); Missy Feiler (Adv Mgr); Robb Grindstaff (Gen Mgr); Brian Knox (Pub)
Parent company (for newspapers): Hometown News Group

THE SUN

Street address 1: 108 N Cascade St
Street address city: Osceola
Street address state: WI
Zip/Postal code: 54020
General Phone: (715) 294-2314
General Fax: (715) 755-3314
Advertising Phone: (715) 294-2314
Advertising Fax: (715) 755-3314
Editorial Phone: (715) 294-2314
Editorial Fax: (715) 755-3314
General/National Adv. E-mail: sales@osceolasun.com
Display Adv. E-mail: office@osceolasun.com
Editorial e-mail: editor@osceolasun.com
Primary Website: osceolasun.com
Year Established: 1897
Avg Paid Circ: 1800
Audit By: Sworn/Estimate/Non-Audited
Audit Date: 10.06.2019
Personnel: Tom Stangl (Pub)
Parent company (for newspapers): Sentinel Publication

THE THREE LAKES NEWS

Street address 1: 425 W Mill St
Street address city: Eagle River
Street address state: WI
Zip/Postal code: 54521-8002
General Phone: (715) 479-4421
General Fax: (715) 479-6242
Advertising Phone: (715) 479-4421
Advertising Fax: (715) 479-6242
Editorial Phone: (715) 479-4421
Editorial Fax: (715) 479-6242
General/National Adv. E-mail: kurtk@vcnewsreview.com
Display Adv. E-mail: maryjoa@vcnewsreview.com
Editorial e-mail: michelled@vcnewsreview.com
Primary Website: vcnewsreview.com
Mthly Avg Views: 52000
Mthly Avg Unique Visitors: 9800
Year Established: 1881
Avg Paid Circ: 6000
Audit By: USPS
Audit Date: 10.06.2019
Personnel: Kurt Krueger (Pub.); Gary Ridderbusch (Ed.); Doug Etten (Assist. Editor); Michelle Drew; Liz Schmidt (Circ. Mgr.)
Parent company (for newspapers): Delphos Herald, Inc.

THE TIMES-VILLAGER

Street address 1: 1900 Crooks Ave
Street address city: Kaukauna
Street address state: WI
Zip/Postal code: 54130-3248
General Phone: (920) 759-2000
General Fax: (920) 759-7344
Advertising Phone: (920) 759-2000
Advertising Fax: (920) 759-7344
Editorial Phone: (920) 759-2000
Editorial Fax: (920) 759-7344
General/National Adv. E-mail: sales@timesvillager.com
Display Adv. E-mail: classifieds@timesvillager.com
Editorial e-mail: editor@timesvillager.com
Primary Website: timesvillager.com
Year Established: 1880
Avg Paid Circ: 5000
Avg Free Circ: 500
Audit By: Sworn/Estimate/Non-Audited
Audit Date: 10.06.2019
Personnel: Brian Roebke (Ed.); Kim Reynebeau (Sales); Trev Hurst (Sports Reporter)
Parent company (for newspapers): News Publishing Inc.

THE TOMAH JOURNAL

Street address 1: 903 Superior Ave
Street address 2: Ste 1
Street address city: Tomah
Street address state: WI
Zip/Postal code: 54660-2060
General Phone: (608)372-4123
General Fax: (608)372-2791
Advertising Phone: (608)791-8260
Advertising Fax: (608)372-2791
Editorial Phone: (608)374-7785
Editorial Fax: (608)372-2791
General/National Adv. E-mail: barb.formanek@lee.net
Display Adv. E-mail: wendy.rasmussen@lee.net
Editorial e-mail: mike.burns@lee.net
Primary Website: lacrossetribune.com
Avg Paid Circ: 5200
Audit By: Sworn/Estimate/Non-Audited
Audit Date: 10.06.2019
Personnel: Chris Hardie (Pub.); Matthew Perenchio (Exec. Ed.); Steve Rundio (Ed.); Barb Formanek (Adv. Mgr.)

THE TRIBUNE RECORD-GLEANER

Street address 1: 318 N Main St
Street address city: Loyal
Street address state: WI
Zip/Postal code: 54446-9407
General Phone: (715)255-8531
General Fax: (715)255-8357
Advertising Phone: (715)255-8531
Advertising Fax: (715)255-8357
Editorial Phone: (715)255-8531
Editorial Fax: (715)255-8357
General/National Adv. E-mail: news@trgnews.com
Display Adv. E-mail: news@trgnews.com
Editorial e-mail: news@trgnews.com
Primary Website: centralwinews.com
Year Established: 1969
Avg Paid Circ: 3100
Audit By: Sworn/Estimate/Non-Audited
Audit Date: 10.06.2019
Personnel: Dean Lesar (Ed.)

THE TRIBUNE-PHONOGRAPH

Street address 1: 318 N Main St
Street address city: Loyal
Street address state: WI
Zip/Postal code: 54446-9407
General Phone: (715)223-2342
General Fax: (715)255-8357
Advertising Phone: (715)223-2342
Advertising Fax: (715)255-8357
Editorial Phone: (715)223-2342
Editorial Fax: (715)255-8357
General/National Adv. E-mail: tpads@tpprinting.com
Display Adv. E-mail: tpads@tpprinting.com
Editorial e-mail: tp@tpprinting.com
Primary Website: centralwinews.com
Year Established: 1969
Avg Paid Circ: 3100
Audit By: Sworn/Estimate/Non-Audited
Audit Date: 10.06.2019
Personnel: Dean Lesar (Ed.)

THE VERONA PRESS

Street address 1: 133 Enterprise Dr
Street address city: Verona
Street address state: WI
Zip/Postal code: 53593-9122
General Phone: (608) 845-9559
General Fax: (608) 845-9550
Advertising Phone: (608) 845-9559
Advertising Fax: (608) 845-9550
Editorial Phone: (608) 845-9559
Editorial Fax: (608) 845-9550
General/National Adv. E-mail: kathy.neumeister@wcinet.com
Display Adv. E-mail: ungclassified@wcinet.com
Editorial e-mail: veronapress@wcinet.com
Primary Website: connectverona.com
Year Established: 1965
Avg Paid Circ: 2100
Audit By: Sworn/Estimate/Non-Audited
Audit Date: 10.06.2019
Personnel: James Ferolie (Group Ed.); David Enstad (Gen. Mgr.)
Parent company (for newspapers): Woodward Communications, Inc.

THE WATERLOO/MARSHALL COURIER

Street address 1: 123 N Monroe St
Street address city: Waterloo
Street address state: WI
Zip/Postal code: 53594-1124
General Phone: (920) 478-2188
General Fax: (920)478-3618
Advertising Phone: (608) 478-2517
Editorial Phone: (920) 478-2188
General/National Adv. E-mail: mfeiler@hngnews.com
Display Adv. E-mail: classifieds@hngnews.com
Editorial e-mail: dgraff@hngnews.com
Primary Website: courierenews.com
Year Established: 1871
Avg Paid Circ: 1500
Audit By: Sworn/Estimate/Non-Audited
Audit Date: 10.06.2019
Personnel: Diane Graff (Mng. Ed.); Missy Feiler (Adv. Mgr.); Brian Knox II (Circulation Director); Robb Grindstaff (General Manager); Brian Knox (Publisher)
Parent company (for newspapers): Hometown News Limited Partnership

THE WESTBY TIMES

Street address 1: PO Box 28
Street address city: Westby
Street address state: WI
Zip/Postal code: 54667-0028
General Phone: (608)634-4317

General Fax: (608)634-6499
Advertising Phone: (608)634-4317
Advertising Fax: (608)634-6499
Editorial Phone: (608)634-4317
Editorial Fax: (608)634-6499
General/National Adv. E-mail: barb.formanek@lee.net
Display Adv. E-mail: chardie@rivervalleynewspapers.com
Editorial e-mail: mike.burns@lee.net
Primary Website: westbytimes.com
Avg Paid Circ: 2000
Audit By: Sworn/Estimate/Non-Audited
Audit Date: 10.06.2019
Personnel: Chris Hardie (Pub.); Barb Formanek (Adv. Mgr.); Dorothy Jasperson (Ed.)

THE WINNECONNE NEWS

Street address 1: 908 E Main St
Street address 2: Ste C
Street address city: Winneconne
Street address state: WI
Zip/Postal code: 54986-9672
General Phone: (920) 582-4541
General Fax: (
General/National Adv. E-mail: beckyladue@winneconnenews.com
Editorial e-mail: beckyladue@rogerspublishing.com
Primary Website: winneconnenews.com
Year Established: 1953
Audit By: Sworn/Estimate/Non-Audited
Audit Date: 10.06.2019
Personnel: Becky LaDue (Ed.); Mary Harper (Proofreader); Kari Joas (Adv. Mgr.)
Parent company (for newspapers): Rogers Printing Solutions

THORP COURIER

Street address 1: 403 N Washington St
Street address city: Thorp
Street address state: WI
Zip/Postal code: 54771-9538
General Phone: (715) 669-5525
General Fax: (715) 669-5596
Advertising Phone: (715) 669-5525
Advertising Fax: (715) 669-5596
Editorial Phone: (715) 669-5525
Editorial Fax: (715) 669-5596
General/National Adv. E-mail: thorpcourier@centurytel.net
Display Adv. E-mail: thorpcourier@centurytel.net
Editorial e-mail: thorpcourier@centurytel.net
Year Established: 1883
Avg Paid Circ: 2100
Avg Free Circ: 35
Audit By: Sworn/Estimate/Non-Audited
Audit Date: 10.06.2019
Personnel: Mark J. LaGasse (Pub./Ed.)

TOMAHAWK LEADER

Street address 1: 315 W Wisconsin Ave
Street address city: Tomahawk
Street address state: WI
Zip/Postal code: 54487-1133
General Phone: (715) 453-2151
General Fax: (715) 453-1865
Advertising Phone: (715) 453-2151
Advertising Fax: (715) 453-1865
Editorial Phone: (715) 453-2151
Editorial Fax: (715) 453-1865
General/National Adv. E-mail: sales@tomahawkleader.com
Display Adv. E-mail: sales@tomahawkleader.com
Classified Adv. e-mail: sales@tomahawkleader.com
Editorial e-mail: news@tomahawkleader.com
Primary Website: tomahawkleader.com
Year Established: 1887
Avg Paid Circ: 3200
Avg Free Circ: 5300
Audit By: Sworn/Estimate/Non-Audited
Audit Date: 10.06.2019
Personnel: Kathleen A. Tobin (Co-Pub./Ed.); Larry Tobin (Co-Publisher); Tatum Evans (Sales Consultant)

TRIBUNE PRESS REPORTER

Street address 1: 105 Misty Ct
Street address city: Glenwood City
Street address state: WI
Zip/Postal code: 54013-8574
General Phone: (715) 265-4646
General Fax: (715) 265-7496
Advertising Phone: (715) 265-4646
Advertising Fax: (715) 265-7496
Editorial Phone: (715) 265-4646
Editorial Fax: (715) 265-7496
General/National Adv. E-mail: tribune@dewittmedia.com
Display Adv. E-mail: tribune@dewittmedia.com
Editorial e-mail: tribune@dewittmedia.com
Primary Website: dewittmedia.com
Year Established: 1889
Avg Paid Circ: 2785
Avg Free Circ: 37
Audit By: Sworn/Estimate/Non-Audited
Audit Date: 10.06.2019
Personnel: Carlton DeWitt (Pub./Ed.); Shawn DeWitt (Mng. Ed.)
Parent company (for newspapers): DeWitt Media Inc.

TRI-COUNTY NEWS

Street address 1: 123 W Main St
Street address city: Mondovi
Street address state: WI
Zip/Postal code: 54755-1523
General Phone: (715) 597-3313
General Fax: (715) 597-2705
Advertising Phone: (715) 597-3313
Advertising Fax: (715) 597-2705
Editorial Phone: (715) 597-3313
Editorial Fax: (715) 597-2705
General/National Adv. E-mail: patrick@media-md.net
Display Adv. E-mail: patrick@media-md.net
Editorial e-mail: tricountynews@media-md.net
Avg Paid Circ: 1418
Avg Free Circ: 10
Audit By: Sworn/Estimate/Non-Audited
Audit Date: 10.06.2019
Personnel: Brian Sheridan (Mng. Ed.); Erika Bjerstedt (Graphic Design); Patrick Milliren (Adv. Mng.); Michael Stumpf (Pub.)

TRI-COUNTY PRESS

Street address 1: 223 S Main St
Street address city: Cuba City
Street address state: WI
Zip/Postal code: 53807-1543
General Phone: (608) 744-2107
General Fax: (608) 744-2108
Advertising Phone: (608) 744-2107
Advertising Fax: (608) 744-2108
Editorial Phone: (608) 744-2107
Editorial Fax: (608) 744-2108
General/National Adv. E-mail: tcpads@yousq.net
Display Adv. E-mail: tcpads@yousq.net
Editorial e-mail: tcpnews@yousq.net
Primary Website: swnews4u.com
Year Established: 1894
Avg Paid Circ: 2667
Avg Free Circ: 17
Audit By: Sworn/Estimate/Non-Audited
Audit Date: 10.06.2019
Personnel: John Ingebritsen (Pub.); Brian Muldoon (Adv. Mgr.)
Parent company (for newspapers): Morris Multimedia, Inc.

VERNON COUNTY BROADCASTER

Street address 1: 124 W Court St
Street address city: Viroqua
Street address state: WI
Zip/Postal code: 54665-1505
General Phone: (608)637-3137
General Fax: (608)637-8557
Advertising Phone: (608)791-8223
Advertising Fax: (608)637-8557
Editorial Phone: (608)637-3137
Editorial Fax: (608)637-8557
General/National Adv. E-mail: barb.formanek@lee.net
Display Adv. E-mail: chardie@rivervalleynewspapers.com
Editorial e-mail: mike.burns@lee.net
Primary Website: vernonbroadcaster.com
Year Established: 1854
Avg Paid Circ: 5336
Avg Free Circ: 23
Audit By: Sworn/Estimate/Non-Audited
Audit Date: 10.06.2019
Personnel: Chris Hardie (Pub.); Barb Formanek (Adv. Mgr.); Matt Johnson (Mng. Ed.)

VILAS COUNTY NEWS-REVIEW

Street address 1: 425 W Mill St
Street address city: Eagle River
Street address state: WI
Zip/Postal code: 54521-8002
General Phone: (715) 479-4421
General Fax: (715) 479-6242
Advertising Phone: (715) 479-4421
Advertising Fax: (715) 479-6242
Editorial Phone: (715) 479-4421
Editorial Fax: (715) 479-6242
General/National Adv. E-mail: kurtk@vcnewsreview.com
Display Adv. E-mail: maryjoa@vcnewsreview.com
Editorial e-mail: michelled@vcnewsreview.com
Primary Website: vcnewsreview.com
Mthly Avg Views: 50200
Mthly Avg Unique Visitors: 9800
Year Established: 1881
Avg Paid Circ: 6000
Audit By: USPS
Audit Date: 10.09.2019
Personnel: Kurt Krueger (Pub.); Doug Etten (Assit. Editor); Gary Ridderbusch (Ed.); Kurt Krueger (Publisher); Michelle Drew (Editor); Doug Etten

WALWORTH COUNTY SUNDAY

Street address 1: 220B E. Commerce Ct.
Street address city: Elkhorn
Street address state: WI
Zip/Postal code: 53121
General Phone: (262) 728-3424
General Fax: (262) 728-5479
General/National Adv. E-mail: kbliss@gazetteextra.com
Display Adv. E-mail: kbliss@gazetteextra.com
Editorial e-mail: ewood@communityshoppers.com
Primary Website: communityshoppers.com
Year Established: 1926
Avg Paid Circ: 0
Avg Free Circ: 39009
Audit By: CVC
Audit Date: 31.03.2017
Personnel: Ed Wood (Pub.); Kyle Bliss (Adv.)
Parent company (for newspapers): CSI Media, LLC

WASHBURN COUNTY REGISTER

Street address 1: 11 5th Ave
Street address 2: Ste 103
Street address city: Shell Lake
Street address state: WI
Zip/Postal code: 54871
General Phone: (715) 468-2314
General Fax: (715) 468-4900
Advertising Phone: (715) 468-2314
Advertising Fax: (715) 468-4900
Editorial Phone: (715) 468-2314
Editorial Fax: (715) 468-4900
General/National Adv. E-mail: wcregister@centurytel.net
Display Adv. E-mail: wcregister@centurytel.net
Editorial e-mail: wcregister@centurytel.net
Primary Website: wcregister.net
Year Established: 1889
Avg Paid Circ: 1900
Avg Free Circ: 20
Audit By: Sworn/Estimate/Non-Audited
Audit Date: 10.06.2019
Personnel: Doug Panek (Pub./Gen. Mgr.); Gary B. King (Ed.); Sue Buck (Adv. Sales Coord.)

WASHINGTON COUNTY POST

Street address 1: 100 S 6th Ave
Street address city: West Bend
Street address state: WI
Zip/Postal code: 53095-3309
General Phone: (262) 306-5000
General Fax: (262) 338-1984
Advertising Phone: (262) 306-5011
Editorial Phone: (262) 306-5000
General/National Adv. E-mail: jdenk@conleynet.com
Display Adv. E-mail: jdenk@conleynet.com
Classified Adv. e-mail: sjerdee@conleynet.com
Editorial e-mail: byorth@conleynet.com
Primary Website: gmtoday.com
Mthly Avg Views: 517000
Mthly Avg Unique Visitors: 140000
Year Established: 1995
Avg Free Circ: 36618
Audit By: Sworn/Estimate/Non-Audited
Audit Date: 31.03.2021
Personnel: Jon Denk (General Manager)
Parent company (for newspapers): Conley Media LLC

WASHINGTON ISLAND OBSERVER

Street address 1: 1253 Main Rd
Street address city: Washington Island
Street address state: WI
Zip/Postal code: 54246-9009
General Phone: (920)847-2661
General Fax: (920)847-2141
Advertising Phone: (920)847-2661
Advertising Fax: (920)847-2141
Editorial Phone: (920)847-2661
Editorial Fax: (920)847-2141
General/National Adv. E-mail: ads@washingtonislandobserver.com
Display Adv. E-mail: ads@washingtonislandobserver.com
Editorial e-mail: editor@washingtonislandobserver.com
Primary Website: washingtonislandobserver.com
Audit By: Sworn/Estimate/Non-Audited
Audit Date: 10.06.2019
Personnel: Laurel Hauser (Ed.); Zuzka Krueger (Adv. Mgr.); DJ Kickbush (GM)

WATERFORD POST

Street address 1: 1102 Ann St.
Street address city: Delavan
Street address state: WI
Zip/Postal code: 53115
General Phone: (262) 728-3411
General/National Adv. E-mail: vicki@southernlakesnewspapers.com
Display Adv. E-mail: vicki@southernlakesnewspapers.com
Editorial e-mail: enadolski@standardpress.com
Primary Website: southernlakesnewspapers.com
Avg Paid Circ: 1900
Avg Free Circ: 527
Audit By: Sworn/Estimate/Non-Audited
Audit Date: 10.06.2019
Personnel: Edward Nadolski; Vicki Vanderwerff; Lindy Sweet (Circ. Dir.); Sue Lange (GM); Karen Whittington (Bus. Mgr.)
Parent company (for newspapers): Southern Lakes Newspapers LLC

WAUNAKEE TRIBUNE

Street address 1: 105 South St
Street address city: Waunakee
Street address state: WI
Zip/Postal code: 53597-1343
General Phone: (608) 849-5227
General Fax: (608) 849-4225
Advertising Phone: (608) 467-1945
Advertising Fax: (608) 849-4225
Editorial Phone: (608) 729-3697
Editorial Fax: (608) 849-4225
General/National Adv. E-mail: dmcguigan@hngnews.com
Display Adv. E-mail: classifieds@hngnews.com
Editorial e-mail: tribnews@hngnews.com
Primary Website: waunakeetribune.com
Year Established: 1920
Avg Paid Circ: 3550
Audit By: Sworn/Estimate/Non-Audited
Audit Date: 10.06.2019
Personnel: Roberta Baumann (Mng. Ed.); Dan McGuigan (Adv Rep); Robb Grindstaff (Gen. Mgr); Brian Knox (Pub.)
Parent company (for newspapers): Hometown News Group

WAUPACA COUNTY POST

Street address 1: 1990 Godfrey Dr
Street address city: Waupaca
Street address state: WI
Zip/Postal code: 54981-7908
General Phone: (920) 217-3309
General Fax: (715) 258-8162
Advertising Phone: (920) 217-3309
Editorial Phone: (920) 217-3309
General/National Adv. E-mail: dwood@mmclocal.com

Display Adv. E-mail: dwood@mmclocal.com
Editorial e-mail: dwood@mmclocal.com
Primary Website: waupacanow.com
Mthly Avg Views: 22000
Mthly Avg Unique Visitors: 10000
Year Established: 2009
Avg Paid Circ: 5054
Avg Free Circ: 16828
Audit By: CVC
Audit Date: 31.03.2017
Personnel: Robert Cloud (Ed.); Greg Seubert (Sports Ed.); Lynn Schoohs (Circ.)
Parent company (for newspapers): Multi Media Channels, LLC

WAUSHARA ARGUS

Street address 1: W7781 Hwy 21 & 73 E
Street address city: Wautoma
Street address state: WI
Zip/Postal code: 54982
General Phone: (920) 787-3334
General Fax: (920) 787-2883
Advertising Phone: (920) 787-3334
Advertising Fax: (920) 787-2883
Editorial Phone: (920) 787-3334
Editorial Fax: (920) 787-2883
General/National Adv. E-mail: argus@wausharaagrus.com
Display Adv. E-mail: argusmarge@wausharaargus.com
Editorial e-mail: argusmary@wausharaargus.com
Primary Website: wausharaargus.com
Year Established: 1859
Avg Paid Circ: 5400
Avg Free Circ: 40
Audit By: Sworn/Estimate/Non-Audited
Audit Date: 10.06.2019
Personnel: Marjorie Williams (Production Manager); Karla Perkins (Sales); Jon Gneiser (Publisher); Mary Kunasch (Senior Publisher)
Parent company (for newspapers): Delphos Herald, Inc.

WAUWATOSA EXPRESS NEWS

Street address 1: 8990 N 51st St
Street address city: Brown Deer
Street address state: WI
Zip/Postal code: 53223-2402
General Phone: (262) 238-6397
General Fax: (262) 242-9450
Advertising Phone: (262) 238-6397
Advertising Fax: (262) 242-9450
Editorial Phone: (262) 238-6397
Editorial Fax: (262) 242-9450
General/National Adv. E-mail: advertising@discoverhometown.com
Display Adv. E-mail: jonesjf@discoverhometown.com
Editorial e-mail: thomasj@discoverhometown.com
Primary Website: discoverhometown.com
Year Established: 1994
Avg Free Circ: 4878
Audit By: Sworn/Estimate/Non-Audited
Audit Date: 10.06.2019
Personnel: Ken Ubert (Pres./Pub.); Thomas McKillen (Mng. Ed.); Holly Potter (Prod. Mgr./Adv. Mgr.); Russ Schliepp (Adv. Sales Rep.)
Parent company (for newspapers): Hometown Publications, Inc.

WAUWATOSA NOW

Street address 1: 1741 Dolphin Dr
Street address 2: Ste A
Street address city: Waukesha
Street address state: WI
Zip/Postal code: 53186-1493
General Phone: (414) 224-2100
General Fax: (262) 446-6646
Advertising Phone: (414) 224-2498
Advertising Fax: (262) 446-6646
Editorial Phone: (414) 224-2100 ext. 5
Editorial Fax: (262) 446-6646
General/National Adv. E-mail: alaffe@jrn.com
Display Adv. E-mail: btschacher@jrn.com
Editorial e-mail: speterson@jrn.com
Primary Website: wauwatosanow.com
Year Established: 1956
Audit By: Sworn/Estimate/Non-Audited
Audit Date: 10.06.2019
Personnel: Scott Peterson (Chief Ed.); Matt Newman (Design/Interactive Content Dir.)
Parent company (for newspapers): Community Newspapers, Inc.; Journal Media Group

WEST ALLIS EXPRESS NEWS

Street address 1: 8990 N 51st St
Street address city: Brown Deer
Street address state: WI
Zip/Postal code: 53223-2402
General Phone: (262) 238-6397
General Fax: (262) 242-9450
Advertising Phone: (262) 238-6397
Advertising Fax: (262) 242-9450
Editorial Phone: (262) 238-6397
Editorial Fax: (262) 242-9450
General/National Adv. E-mail: advertising@discoverhometown.com
Display Adv. E-mail: jonesjf@discoverhometown.com
Editorial e-mail: thomasj@discoverhometown.com
Primary Website: discoverhometown.com
Year Established: 1994
Avg Free Circ: 4878
Audit By: Sworn/Estimate/Non-Audited
Audit Date: 10.06.2019
Personnel: Ken Ubert (Pres./Pub.); Thomas McKillen (Mng. Ed.); Holly Potter (Prod. Mgr./Adv. Mgr.); Russ Schliepp (Adv. Sales Rep.)
Parent company (for newspapers): Hometown Publications, Inc.

WEST ALLIS NOW

Street address 1: 1741 Dolphin Dr
Street address 2: Ste A
Street address city: Waukesha
Street address state: WI
Zip/Postal code: 53186-1493
General Phone: (414) 224-2100
General Fax: (262) 446-6646
Advertising Phone: (414) 224-2498
Advertising Fax: (262) 446-6646
Editorial Phone: (414) 224-2100 ext. 5
Editorial Fax: (262) 446-6646
General/National Adv. E-mail: alaffe@jrn.com
Display Adv. E-mail: btschacher@jrn.com
Editorial e-mail: speterson@jrn.com
Primary Website: westallisnow.com
Year Established: 1956
Audit By: Sworn/Estimate/Non-Audited
Audit Date: 10.06.2019
Personnel: Scott Peterson (Chief Ed.); Matt Newman (Design/Interactive Content Dir.)
Parent company (for newspapers): Community Newspapers, Inc.; Journal Media Group

WEST BEND EXPRESS NEWS

Street address 1: 8990 N 51st St
Street address city: Brown Deer
Street address state: WI
Zip/Postal code: 53223-2402
General Phone: (262) 238-6397
General Fax: (262) 242-9450
Advertising Phone: (262) 238-6397
Advertising Fax: (262) 242-9450
Editorial Phone: (262) 238-6397
Editorial Fax: (262) 242-9450
General/National Adv. E-mail: advertising@discoverhometown.com
Display Adv. E-mail: jonesjf@discoverhometown.com
Editorial e-mail: thomasj@discoverhometown.com
Primary Website: discoverhometown.com
Year Established: 1994
Avg Free Circ: 4433
Audit By: VAC
Audit Date: 30.06.2016
Personnel: Ken Ubert (Pres./Pub.); Thomas McKillen (Mng. Ed.); Holly Potter (Prod. Mgr./Adv. Mgr.); Russ Schliepp (Adv. Sales Rep.)
Parent company (for newspapers): Hometown Publications, Inc.

WESTOSHA REPORT

Street address 1: 147 E Main St
Street address city: Twin Lakes
Street address state: WI
Zip/Postal code: 53181-9679
General Phone: (262) 877-2813
General Fax: (262) 877-3619
Advertising Phone: (262) 945-5728
Advertising Fax: (262) 877-3619
Editorial Phone: (262) 877-2813
Editorial Fax: (262) 877-3619
General/National Adv. E-mail: advertising@westoshareport.com
Display Adv. E-mail: assistant@westoshareport.com
Editorial e-mail: annette@westoshareport.com
Primary Website: westoshareport.com
Avg Paid Circ: 0
Avg Free Circ: 1208
Audit By: Sworn/Estimate/Non-Audited
Audit Date: 10.06.2019
Personnel: Edward Nadolski (Ed.); Sue Z. Lange (Creative Dept. Dir.); Vicki Vanderwerff (Adv. Dir.); Cyndi Jensen (Pub.); Tom Flatow (Circ. Mgr.)
Parent company (for newspapers): Southern Lakes Newspapers LLC

WISCONSIN DELLS EVENTS

Street address 1: 201 E. State St.
Street address city: Mauston
Street address state: WI
Zip/Postal code: 53948
General Phone: (608) 847-7341
General/National Adv. E-mail: szeinemann@madison.com
Display Adv. E-mail: szeinemann@madison.com
Editorial e-mail: wde-news@wiscnews.com
Primary Website: wiscnews.com
Year Established: 1903
Avg Paid Circ: 2305
Avg Free Circ: 100
Audit By: Sworn/Estimate/Non-Audited
Audit Date: 10.06.2019
Personnel: Scott Zeinemann (Dir. Adv.); Jason Cuevas (News Staff); Todd Krysiak (Reg. Ed.)
Parent company (for newspapers): Capital Newspapers

WISCONSIN STATE FARMER

Street address 1: 600 Industrial Dr
Street address city: Waupaca
Street address state: WI
Zip/Postal code: 54981-8814
General Phone: (715)258-5546
General Fax: (844)271-6834
Advertising Phone: (920) 228-1494
Editorial Phone: (920) 517-2653
General/National Adv. E-mail: kmagrude@gannett.com
Display Adv. E-mail: wisfarmerclassifieds@gannett.com
Editorial e-mail: colleen.kottke@jrn.com
Primary Website: wisfarmer.com
Year Established: 1956
Avg Paid Circ: 16669
Avg Free Circ: 511
Audit By: Sworn/Estimate/Non-Audited
Audit Date: 10.06.2019
Personnel: Colleen Kottke (Ed.); Carol Spaeth-Bauer (Assoc. Ed.); Kristin Magruder (Adv. Sales)
Parent company (for newspapers): Journal Media Group

WOODVILLE LEADER

Street address 1: W2855 730th Ave
Street address city: Spring Valley
Street address state: WI
Zip/Postal code: 54767-8512
General Phone: (715) 778-4990
General Fax: (715) 778-4996
Editorial Phone: (715) 778-4990
General/National Adv. E-mail: editor@mygatewaynews.com
Display Adv. E-mail: admins@mygatewaynews.com
Editorial e-mail: editor@mygatewaynews.com
Primary Website: mygatewaynews.com
Year Established: 1929
Avg Paid Circ: 196
Avg Free Circ: 2
Audit By: Sworn/Estimate/Non-Audited
Audit Date: 10.06.2019
Personnel: Paul Seeling (Ed./Pub.)
Parent company (for newspapers): Gateway Publishing, Inc.

CANADIAN COMMUNITY NEWSPAPER

ALBERTA

AIRDRIE CITY VIEW

Street address 1: #403-2903 Kingsview Blvd.
Street address city: Airdrie
Province/Territory: AB
Postal code: T4A 0C4
Country: Canada
General Phone: (403) 948-1885
General Fax: (403) 948-2554
Display Adv. E-mail: rsonghurst@airdrie.greatwest.ca
Classified Adv. e-mail: classifieds@airdrie.greatwest.ca
Editorial e-mail: achorney@airdrie.greatwest.ca
Primary Website: http://www.airdriecityview.com
Published: Thur
Avg Paid Circ: 557
Avg Free Circ: 18336
Audit By: VAC
Audit Date: 31.05.2016
Personnel: Cam Christianson (Pub.); Allison Chorney (Ed)
Parent company (for newspapers): Great West Media LP

AIRDRIE ECHO

Street address 1: 112 - 1 Ave Ne
Street address city: Airdrie
Province/Territory: AB
Postal code: T4B 0R6
County: Canada
Country: Canada
General Phone: (403) 948-7280
General Fax: (403) 912-2341
General/National Adv. E-mail: airdrie.echo@shaw.ca
Display Adv. E-mail: rmackintosh@postmedia.com
Editorial e-mail: jchalmers@postmedia.com
Primary Website: www.airdrieecho.com
Published: Wed
Avg Free Circ: 18330
Audit By: VAC
Audit Date: 31.03.2016
Personnel: Ed Huculak (Pub.); John Chalmers (Ed.); Roxanne Mackintosh (Adv. Dir)
Parent company (for newspapers): Postmedia Network Inc.; Quebecor Communications, Inc.

BANNER POST

Street address 1: Po Box 686
Street address 2: Po Box 1010
Street address city: Grimshaw
Province/Territory: AB
Postal code: T0H 1W0
County: Canada
Country: Canada
General Phone: (780) 836-3588
General Fax: (780) 836-2820
Advertising Phone: (780) 332-2215
General/National Adv. E-mail: bannerpost@mackreport.ab.ca
Display Adv. E-mail: bannerpost@mrnews.ca
Editorial e-mail: publisher@mrnews.ca
Primary Website: mrnews.ca
Published: Wed
Avg Paid Circ: 0
Avg Free Circ: 45404
Audit By: CCAB
Audit Date: 31.10.2018
Personnel: Tom Mihaly (Pub/Ed); Kristin Dyck (Ed); Jillian Vandemark-Chomiak (Office/Adv. Mgr)
Parent company (for newspapers): Metroland Media Group Ltd.

BARRHEAD LEADER

Street address 1: 5015 51st St.
Street address city: Barrhead
Province/Territory: AB
Postal code: T7N 1A4
County: Barrhead
Country: Canada
General Phone: (780) 674-3823
General Fax: (780) 674-6337
General/National Adv. E-mail: leader@barrhead.greatwest.ca
Display Adv. E-mail: sales@barrhead.greatwest.ca
Editorial e-mail: lleng@barrhead.greatwest.ca
Primary Website: www.barrheadleader.com
Published: Tues
Avg Paid Circ: 3114
Avg Free Circ: 3
Audit By: VAC
Audit Date: 31.03.2016
Personnel: Lynda Leng (Pub)
Parent company (for newspapers): Glacier Media Group; Great West Media LP

BEAVER RIVER BANNER

Street address 1: 4110 51 Ave
Street address city: cold lake
Province/Territory: AB
Postal code: t9m 2a1
County: Canada
Country: Canada
General Phone: (780) 201-0623
General/National Adv. E-mail: br.banner@sasktel.net
Primary Website: www.beaverriverbanner.com
Published: Wed
Avg Free Circ: 2300
Audit By: Sworn/Estimate/Non-Audited
Audit Date: 12.07.2019
Personnel: Dan Brisebois (Ed.)

BONNYVILLE NOUVELLE

Street address 1: 5304 50th Ave.
Street address city: Bonnyville
Province/Territory: AB
Postal code: T9N 1Y4
County: Canada
Country: Canada
General Phone: (780) 826-3876
General Fax: (780) 826-7062
Advertising Phone: (780) 826-3876
Display Adv. E-mail: aclarke@bonnyville.greatwest.ca
Editorial e-mail: koelschlagel@bonnyville.greatwest.ca
Primary Website: www.bonnyvillenouvelle.ca
Published: Tues
Avg Paid Circ: 626
Avg Free Circ: 681
Audit By: VAC
Audit Date: 31.03.2016
Personnel: Cindy Coates (Circ. Mgr.); Kristen Oelschlagel (Ed); Angie Hampshire (Pub)
Parent company (for newspapers): Glacier Media Group; Great West Media LP

BOW VALLEY CRAG & CANYON

Street address 1: 201 Bear St., 2nd Fl.
Street address city: Banff
Province/Territory: AB
Postal code: T1L 1H2
County: Canada
Country: Canada
General Phone: (403) 762-2453
General Fax: (403) 762-5274
General/National Adv. E-mail: editor@thecrag.ca
Display Adv. E-mail: rmackintosh@postmedia.com
Editorial e-mail: russ.ullyot@sunmedia.ca
Primary Website: www.thecragandcanyon.ca
Published: Wed
Avg Paid Circ: 0
Avg Free Circ: 8537
Audit By: CMCA
Audit Date: 28.02.2014
Personnel: Shawn Cornell (Pub); Russ Ullyot (Ed); Roxanne Mackintosh (Adv. Dir.)
Parent company (for newspapers): Postmedia Network Inc.; Quebecor Communications, Inc.

CARSTAIRS COURIER

Street address 1: 5013 - 51 Street
Street address city: Olds
Province/Territory: AB
Postal code: T4H 1P6
County: Canada
Country: Canada
General Phone: (403) 337-2806
General Fax: (403) 556-7515
Advertising Phone: (403) 337-2806
General/National Adv. E-mail: courier@carstairs.greatwest.ca
Editorial e-mail: dsingleton@olds.greatwest.ca
Primary Website: www.carstairscourier.ca
Published: Tues
Avg Paid Circ: 12
Avg Free Circ: 3289
Audit By: CMCA
Audit Date: 30.06.2014
Personnel: Dan Singleton (Ed)
Parent company (for newspapers): Glacier Media Group; Great West Media LP

CASTOR ADVANCE

Street address 1: 5012 50 Ave.
Street address city: Castor
Province/Territory: AB
Postal code: T0C 0X0
County: Canada
Country: Canada
General Phone: (403) 882-4044
Display Adv. E-mail: admin@castoradvance.com
Editorial e-mail: editor@castoradvance.com
Published: Thur
Avg Paid Circ: 79
Avg Free Circ: 22
Audit By: VAC
Audit Date: 12.12.2017
Personnel: Mustafa Eric (Ed.)
Parent company (for newspapers): Black Press Group Ltd.

CENTRAL ALBERTA LIFE

Street address 1: 2950 Bremner Ave.
Street address city: Red Deer
Province/Territory: AB
Postal code: T4R 1M9
County: Canada
Country: Canada
General Phone: (403) 314-4373
General Fax: (403) 342-4051
Display Adv. E-mail: advertising@reddeeradvocate.com
Classified Adv. e-mail: prausch@reddeeradvocate.com
Editorial e-mail: editorial@reddeeradvocate.com
Primary Website: www.reddeeradvocate.com
Published: Thur
Avg Free Circ: 33301
Audit By: Sworn/Estimate/Non-Audited
Audit Date: 12.07.2019
Personnel: Mary Kemmis (Pub); Crystal Rhyno (Mng Ed); Wendy Moore (Adv. Mgr.); Deb Reitmeie (Circ. Mgr.)
Parent company (for newspapers): Red Deer Advocate

CLARESHOLM LOCAL PRESS

Street address 1: 4913 2nd St. W.
Street address city: Claresholm
Province/Territory: AB
Postal code: T0L 0T0
County: Canada
Country: Canada
General Phone: (403) 625-4474
General Fax: (403) 625-2828
General/National Adv. E-mail: clpress@telusplanet.net; clpsales@telus.net
Display Adv. E-mail: sales@claresholmlocalpress.ca
Classified Adv. e-mail: sales@claresholmlocalpress.ca
Editorial e-mail: rob@claresholmlocalpress.ca
Primary Website: www.claresholmlocalpress.ca
Published: Wed
Avg Paid Circ: 1429
Avg Free Circ: 19
Audit By: CMCA
Audit Date: 31.05.2018
Personnel: Roxanne Thompson (Owner/Pub.); Rob Vogt (Ed.); Amanda Zimmer (Prod. Mgr.); Brandy McLean (Sales contact); Jill Cook (Graphic Designer)
Parent company (for newspapers): EMS Press Ltd.

COCHRANE EAGLE

Street address 1: #2, 124 River Ave
Street address city: Cochrane
Province/Territory: AB
Postal code: T4C 2C2
Country: Canada
General Phone: (403) 932-6588
General Fax: (403) 851-6520
Display Adv. E-mail: btennant@cochrane.greatwest.ca
Classified Adv. e-mail: classifieds@cochrane.greatwest.ca
Editorial e-mail: cpuglia@cochrane.greatwest.ca
Primary Website: www.cochraneeagle.com
Published: Thur
Avg Free Circ: 11631
Audit By: VAC
Audit Date: 31.05.2016
Personnel: Brenda Tennant (Pub./Adv. Mgr); Chris Puglia (Ed)
Parent company (for newspapers): Great West Media LP

COCHRANE TIMES

Street address 1: Bay 8, 206 Fifth Ave. W.
Street address city: Cochrane
Province/Territory: AB
Postal code: T4C 1X3
County: Canada
Country: Canada
General Phone: (403) 932-3500
General Fax: (403) 932-3935
Display Adv. E-mail: roxanne.mackintosh@sunmedia.ca
Classified Adv. e-mail: roxanne.mackintosh@sunmedia.ca
Editorial e-mail: editor@cochranetimes.com
Primary Website: www.cochranetimes.com
Published: Wed
Avg Paid Circ: 1374
Avg Free Circ: 12378
Audit By: VAC
Audit Date: 31.12.2015
Personnel: Shawn Cornell (Pub); Noel Edey (Ed); Roxanne MacKintosh (Adv Dir)
Parent company (for newspapers): Postmedia Network Inc.; Quebecor Communications, Inc.

COLD LAKE SUN

Street address 1: 5121 50 Ave
Street address city: Cold Lake
Province/Territory: AB
Postal code: T9M 1P1
Country: Canada
General Phone: (780) 594-5881
General Fax: (780) 594-2120
Display Adv. E-mail: ljohnston@postmedia.com
Editorial e-mail: plozinski@postmedia.com
Primary Website: www.coldlakesun.com
Published: Tues
Avg Paid Circ: 71
Avg Free Circ: 7179
Audit By: VAC
Audit Date: 31.12.2015
Personnel: Mary-Ann Kostiuk (Pub); Leanne Johnson (Adv Mgr); Peter Lozinski (Ed)

Parent company (for newspapers): Postmedia Network Inc.

CONNECT

Street address 1: 208, 9715 Main Street
Street address city: Fort McMurray
Province/Territory: AB
Postal code: T9H 1T5
Country: Canada
General Phone: (780) 790-6627
General Fax: (780) 714-6485
General/National Adv. E-mail: info@macmedia.ca
Display Adv. E-mail: tim@starnews.ca
Classified Adv. e-mail: tim@starnews.ca
Editorial e-mail: dawn@starnews.ca
Primary Website: www.fortmacconnect.ca
Published: Fri
Avg Free Circ: 19992
Audit By: VAC
Audit Date: 28.02.2015
Personnel: Tim O'Rourke (Publisher/Sales Manager)
Parent company (for newspapers): Star News Publishing Inc.

CROWSNEST PASS HERALD

Street address 1: 12925 20th Ave.
Street address city: Blairmore
Province/Territory: AB
Postal code: T0K 0E0
County: Canada
Country: Canada
General Phone: (403) 562-2248
General Fax: (403) 562-8379
General/National Adv. E-mail: news@passherald.ca
Editorial e-mail: news@passherald.ca
Primary Website: www.passherald.ca
Published: Wed
Avg Paid Circ: 1361
Avg Free Circ: 235
Audit By: Sworn/Estimate/Non-Audited
Audit Date: 12.07.2019
Personnel: Lisa Sygutek (Pub.)

DEVON DISPATCH NEWS

Street address 1: 4b Saskatchewan Drive
Street address city: Devon
Province/Territory: AB
Postal code: T9G 1E7
Country: Canada
General Phone: (780) 987-3488
General Fax: (780) 987-4431
Display Adv. E-mail: jfigeat@postmedia.com
Editorial e-mail: bobby.roy@sunmedia.ca
Primary Website: www.devondispatch.ca
Published: Fri
Avg Paid Circ: 2021
Avg Free Circ: 5072
Audit By: VAC
Audit Date: 31.12.2015
Personnel: Susanne Holmlund (Pub.); Bobby Roy (Ed); Jean Figeat (Adv. Dir)
Parent company (for newspapers): Postmedia Network Inc.

DRAYTON VALLEY WESTERN REVIEW

Street address 1: 4905 52nd Ave.
Street address city: Drayton Valley
Province/Territory: AB
Postal code: T7A 1S3
County: Canada
Country: Canada
General Phone: (780) 542-5380
General Fax: (780) 542-9200
General/National Adv. E-mail: dvwr@bowesnet.com
Display Adv. E-mail: theresa.hunt@sunmedia.ca
Editorial e-mail: cweetman@postmedia.com
Primary Website: www.draytonvalleywesternreview.com
Published: Tues
Avg Paid Circ: 1132
Avg Free Circ: 5
Audit By: VAC
Audit Date: 31.12.2015
Personnel: Susanne Holmlund (Pub.); Pamela Allain (Adv. Dir); Cathy Weetman (Ed)
Parent company (for newspapers): Postmedia Network Inc.; Quebecor Communications, Inc.

DRUMHELLER MAIL

Street address 1: 515 Hwy 10 East
Street address city: Drumheller
Province/Territory: AB
Postal code: T0J 0Y0
County: Canada
Country: Canada
General Phone: (403) 823-2580
General Fax: (403) 823-3864
General/National Adv. E-mail: information@drumhellermail.com
Display Adv. E-mail: information@drumhellermail.com
Editorial e-mail: bob@drumhellermail.com
Primary Website: www.drumhellermail.com
Published: Wed
Avg Paid Circ: 4400
Avg Free Circ: 0
Audit By: CMCA
Audit Date: 30.06.2017
Personnel: Ossie Sheddy (Pub.); Bob Sheddy (Mng. Ed)

EAST CENTRAL ALBERTA REVIEW

Street address 1: 4923 Victoria Ave.
Street address city: Coronation
Province/Territory: AB
Postal code: T0C 1C0
County: Canada
Country: Canada
General Phone: (403) 578-4111
General Fax: (403) 578-2088
Advertising Phone: (403) 578-7120
General/National Adv. E-mail: publisher@ecareview.com
Display Adv. E-mail: advertise@ECAreview.com
Classified Adv. e-mail: admin@ECAreview.com
Editorial e-mail: publisher@ECAreview.com
Primary Website: www.ecareview.com
Published: Thur
Avg Paid Circ: 90
Avg Free Circ: 27075
Audit By: CMCA
Audit Date: 31.03.2017
Personnel: Joyce Webster (Pub); Yvonne Thulien (Office Mgr.); Gayle Jaraway (Adv. Rep); Lisa Joy (Marketing Rep/Reporter Photographer); Lisa Myers-Sortland (Graphic Artist)

ECKVILLE ECHO

Street address 1: Suite 103 5020-50 A St.
Street address city: Sylvan Lake
Province/Territory: AB
Postal code: T4S 1R2
Country: Canada
General Phone: (403) 887-2331
General Fax: (403) 887-2081
General/National Adv. E-mail: admin@sylvanlakenews.com
Display Adv. E-mail: admin@sylvanlakenews.com
Editorial e-mail: editor@sylvanlakenews.com
Published: Thur
Avg Paid Circ: 1077
Avg Free Circ: 2466
Audit By: VAC
Audit Date: 30.09.2016
Personnel: Cheryl Hyvonen (Admin); Randy Holt (Pub); Jenna Swan (Ed)
Parent company (for newspapers): Black Press Group Ltd.

EDMONTON EXAMINER

Street address 1: 10006 101 St
Street address city: Edmonton
Province/Territory: AB
Postal code: T5J 0S1
Country: Canada
General Phone: (780) 453-9001
General Fax: (780) 447-7333
Advertising Phone: (780) 444-5450
Display Adv. E-mail: rpaterson@postmedia.com
Classified Adv. e-mail: bob.paterson@sunmedia.ca
Editorial e-mail: dave.breakenridge@sunmedia.ca
Primary Website: www.edmontonexaminer.com
Published: Wed
Avg Paid Circ: 0
Avg Free Circ: 131000
Audit By: CCAB
Audit Date: 24.12.2017
Personnel: John Caputo (Pub); Ted Dakin (Adv. Dir); Dave Breakenridge (Ed)
Parent company (for newspapers): Postmedia Network Inc.; Quebecor Communications, Inc.

EDSON LEADER

Street address 1: 4820 3rd Ave.
Street address city: Edson
Province/Territory: AB
Postal code: T7E 1T8
County: Canada
Country: Canada
General Phone: (780) 723-3301
General Fax: (780) 723-5171
General/National Adv. E-mail: leadernews@telusplanet.net
Display Adv. E-mail: pam.thesen@sunmedia.ca
Editorial e-mail: ian.mcinnes@sunmedia.ca
Primary Website: www.edsonleader.com
Published: Mon
Avg Paid Circ: 3
Avg Free Circ: 3468
Audit By: VAC
Audit Date: 31.12.2015
Personnel: Pamela Thesen (Adv. Dir); Janice Foisy (Pub.); Ian McInnes (Ed.)
Parent company (for newspapers): Postmedia Network Inc.; Quebecor Communications, Inc.

ELK POINT REVIEW

Street address 1: 5022 - 49 Ave
Street address city: Elk Point
Province/Territory: AB
Postal code: T0A 1A0
County: Canada
Country: Canada
General Phone: (780) 724-4087
General Fax: (780) 645-2346
General/National Adv. E-mail: production@stpaul.greatwest.ca; aglaser@greatwest.ca
Display Adv. E-mail: cgauvreau@greatwest.ca
Editorial e-mail: vbrooker@stpaul.greatwest.ca
Primary Website: www.greatwest.ca
Published: Tues
Avg Paid Circ: 2950
Avg Free Circ: 0
Audit By: VAC
Audit Date: 31.12.2015
Personnel: Clare Gauvreau (Pub./Adv. Mgr.); Vicki Brooker (Ed.); Marg Smith (Prod.)
Parent company (for newspapers): Glacier Media Group; Great West Media LP

FAIRVIEW POST

Street address 1: 10118-110 St.
Street address city: Fairview
Province/Territory: AB
Postal code: T0H 1L0
Country: Canada
General Phone: (780) 835-4925
General Fax: (780) 835-4227
General/National Adv. E-mail: info@fairviewpost.com
Display Adv. E-mail: peter.meyerhoffer@sunmedia.ca
Editorial e-mail: chris.eakin@sunmedia.ca
Primary Website: www.fairviewpost.com
Published: Wed
Avg Paid Circ: 119
Avg Free Circ: 8
Audit By: VAC
Audit Date: 31.12.2015
Personnel: Peter Meyerhoffer (Adv. Dir); Chris Eakin (Ed.)
Parent company (for newspapers): Postmedia Network Inc.; Quebecor Communications, Inc.

FARM 'N' FRIENDS

Street address 1: 4720 50 Ave
Street address city: Redwater
Province/Territory: AB
Postal code: T0A 2W0
County: Sturgeon
Country: Canada
General Phone: (780) 421-9715
General Fax: (780) 942-2515
General/National Adv. E-mail: redwater@shaw.ca
Display Adv. E-mail: redwater@shaw.ca
Classified Adv. e-mail: redwater@shaw.ca
Editorial e-mail: redwater@shaw.ca
Primary Website: www.cowleynewspapers.com/farm-n-friends/
Published: Fri
Avg Free Circ: 17759
Audit By: CMCA
Audit Date: 30.04.2014
Personnel: Ed Cowley (Pub./Owner/Adv. Mgr./ Ed.)
Parent company (for newspapers): W & E Cowley Pub. Ltd.

FRIDAY FORWARD

Street address 1: 2950 Bremner Ave.
Street address city: Red Deer
Province/Territory: AB
Postal code: T4R 1M9
County: Canada
Country: Canada
General Phone: (403) 343-2400
General Fax: (403) 342-4051
Advertising Phone: (403) 314-4343
Editorial Phone: (403) 314-4325
Display Adv. E-mail: advertising@reddeeradvocate.com
Classified Adv. e-mail: classified@reddeeradvocate.com
Editorial e-mail: editorial@reddeeradvocate.com
Primary Website: www.reddeeradvocate.com
Published: Fri
Avg Paid Circ: 8500
Audit By: AAM
Audit Date: 30.06.2018
Personnel: Mary Kemmis (Pub Red Deer Advocate; Pres Prarie/ East Kootenay Division Black Press); Wendy Moore (Advt Mgr); Patricia Rausch (National Rep & Major Acct Asst); Debbie Reitmeier (Circulation Mgr); David Marsden (Managing Editor)
Parent company (for newspapers): Black Press Group Ltd.

GRANDE CACHE MOUNTAINEER

Street address 1: 1800 Pine Plaza
Street address city: Grande Cache
Province/Territory: AB
Postal code: T0E 0Y0
Country: Canada
General Phone: (780) 827-3539
General/National Adv. E-mail: gcnews@telus.net
Display Adv. E-mail: gcnews@telus.net
Editorial e-mail: pamnews@telus.net
Primary Website: http://www.grandecachemountaineer.canic.ws/
Published: Thur
Avg Paid Circ: 1060
Avg Free Circ: 36
Audit By: Sworn/Estimate/Non-Audited
Audit Date: 12.07.2019
Personnel: Pamela Brown (Pub./Ed./GM); Lisa Gould (Sales)

GRIZZLY GAZETTE

Street address 1: 5435 Plaza Ave.
Street address city: Swan Hills
Province/Territory: AB
Postal code: T0G 2C0
Country: Canada
General Phone: (780) 333-2100
General Fax: (780) 333-2111
General/National Adv. E-mail: sgazett@telusplanet.net
Display Adv. E-mail: sgazette@telusplanet.net
Classified Adv. e-mail: sgazette@telusplanet.net
Editorial e-mail: sgazette@telusplanet.net
Primary Website: thegrizzlygazette.com
Published: Tues
Avg Paid Circ: 394
Avg Free Circ: 135
Audit By: Sworn/Estimate/Non-Audited
Audit Date: 12.07.2019
Personnel: Phyllis Webster (Gen. Mgr.); Carol Webster (Ed.)

HANNA HERALD

Street address 1: 113 - 1st Ave West
Street address city: Hanna
Province/Territory: AB
Postal code: T0J 1P0
Country: Canada
General Phone: (403) 854-3366

General Fax: (403) 854-3256
Display Adv. E-mail: rmackintosh@postmedia.com
Classified Adv. e-mail: deanne.cornell@sunmedia.ca
Editorial e-mail: jackie.gold@sunmedia.ca
Primary Website: www.hannaherald.com
Published: Wed
Avg Paid Circ: 900
Avg Free Circ: 0
Audit By: CMCA
Audit Date: 30.06.2014
Personnel: Shawn Cornell (Pub); Deanne Cornell (Adv. Sales Rep.); Krista Avery (Office Mgr.); Jackie Gold (Mng. Ed.)
Parent company (for newspapers): Postmedia Network Inc.; Quebecor Communications, Inc.

INNISFAIL PROVINCE

Street address 1: 5036 - 48th St.
Street address city: Innisfail
Province/Territory: AB
Postal code: T4G 1M2
County: Innisfail Alberta
Country: Canada
General Phone: (403) 227-3477
General Fax: (403) 227-3330
Display Adv. E-mail: ddemers@innisfail.greatwest.ca
Editorial e-mail: jbachusky@innisfail.greatwest.ca
Primary Website: www.innisfailprovince.ca
Published: Tues
Avg Paid Circ: 7
Avg Free Circ: 8240
Audit By: VAC
Audit Date: 31.08.2018
Personnel: Brent Spilak (Pub/Adv. Mgr.); Johnnie Bachusky (Ed)
Parent company (for newspapers): Glacier Media Group; Great West Media LP

LA NOUVELLE BEAUMONT NEWS

Street address 1: 5021b 52 Ave.
Street address city: Beaumont
Province/Territory: AB
Postal code: T4X 1E5
Country: Canada
General Phone: (780) 929-6632
General Fax: (780) 929-6634
Display Adv. E-mail: jfigeat@postmedia.com
Editorial e-mail: bobby.roy@sunmedia.ca
Primary Website: www.thebeaumontnews.ca
Published: Fri
Avg Paid Circ: 11
Avg Free Circ: 7221
Audit By: VAC
Audit Date: 31.12.2015
Personnel: Jean Figeat (Adv. Dir.); Bobby Roy (Ed)
Parent company (for newspapers): Sun Media Corporation; Post Media

LAC LA BICHE POST

Street address 1: 10211 101st St.
Street address city: Lac La Biche
Province/Territory: AB
Postal code: T0A 2C0
Country: Canada
General Phone: (780) 623-4221
General Fax: (780) 623-4230
General/National Adv. E-mail: post@llb.greatwest.ca
Display Adv. E-mail: iwolstenholme@llb.greatwest.ca
Editorial e-mail: rmckinley@llb.greatwest.ca
Primary Website: www.laclabichepost.com
Published: Tues
Avg Paid Circ: 1123
Avg Free Circ: 1
Audit By: VAC
Audit Date: 31.03.2016
Personnel: Robert McKinley (Pub.); Iona Wolstenholme (Sales Mgr.)
Parent company (for newspapers): Glacier Media Group; Great West Media LP

LACOMBE GLOBE

Street address 1: 5019-50 St.
Street address city: Lacombe
Province/Territory: AB
Postal code: T4L 1W8
County: Canada
Country: Canada
General Phone: (403) 782-3498
General Fax: (403) 782-5850
Display Adv. E-mail: ngoetz@postmedia.com
Editorial e-mail: sswenson@postmedia.com
Primary Website: www.lacombeglobe.com
Published: Thur
Avg Paid Circ: 1507
Avg Free Circ: 8604
Audit By: VAC
Audit Date: 31.12.2015
Personnel: Nick Goetz (Adv. Dir); Sarah Swenson (Ed)
Parent company (for newspapers): Postmedia Network Inc.; Quebecor Communications, Inc.

LAKESIDE LEADER

Street address 1: 103 Third Ave. Ne
Street address city: Slave Lake
Province/Territory: AB
Postal code: T0G 2A0
Country: Canada
General Phone: (780) 849-4380
General Fax: (780) 849-3903
Advertising Phone: (780) 849-4380
General/National Adv. E-mail: lsleader@telusplanet.net
Editorial e-mail: lsleader@telusplanet.net
Primary Website: www.lakesideleader.com
Published: Wed
Avg Paid Circ: 1030
Audit By: CMCA
Audit Date: 31.12.2016
Personnel: Mary Burgar (Pub); Joe McWilliams (Ed); Tammy Leslie (Circulation Mgr/Primary Ad Contact)
Parent company (for newspapers): South Peace News(High Prairie)

LE FRANCO

Street address 1: 8627-91 St.
Street address 2: Rm 312
Street address city: Edmonton
Province/Territory: AB
Postal code: T6C 3N1
Country: Canada
General Phone: (780) 465-6581
General Fax: (780) 469-1129
General/National Adv. E-mail: journal@lefranco.ab.ca
Display Adv. E-mail: commercial@lefranco.ab.ca
Editorial e-mail: direction@lefranco.ab.ca
Primary Website: http://www.lefranco.ab.ca
Published: Thur
Avg Paid Circ: 3206
Avg Free Circ: 302
Audit By: Sworn/Estimate/Non-Audited
Audit Date: 12.07.2019
Personnel: Emma Hautecoeur (Ed.)

LEDUC REPRESENTATIVE

Street address 1: 4504 61st Ave.
Street address city: Leduc
Province/Territory: AB
Postal code: T9E 3Z1
County: Canada
Country: Canada
General Phone: (780) 986-2271
General Fax: (780) 986-6397
Display Adv. E-mail: ngoetz@postmedia.com
Editorial e-mail: bobby.roy@sunmedia.ca
Primary Website: www.leducrep.com
Published: Fri
Avg Paid Circ: 3069
Avg Free Circ: 16449
Audit By: VAC
Audit Date: 31.12.2015
Personnel: Susanne Holmlund (Pub.); Jan Eyre (Circ. Mgr.); Nick Goetz (Adv. Dir.); Bobby Roy (Ed)
Parent company (for newspapers): Postmedia Network Inc.; Quebecor Communications, Inc.

LEDUC-WETASKIWIN PIPESTONE FLYER

Street address 1: 5025 - 50 Street
Street address city: Millet
Province/Territory: AB
Postal code: T0C 1Z0
Country: Canada
General Phone: (780) 387-5797
General Fax: (780) 387-4397
Display Adv. E-mail: sales1@pipestoneflyer.ca
Editorial e-mail: editor@pipestoneflyer.ca
Primary Website: www.pipestoneflyer.ca
Published: Thur
Avg Paid Circ: 0
Avg Free Circ: 16935
Audit By: VAC
Audit Date: 31.07.2016
Personnel: Michele Rosenthal (Pub); Stu Salkeld (Ed)
Parent company (for newspapers): Black Press Group Ltd.; Black Press, Prairie Division

LETHBRIDGE SUN TIMES

Street address 1: 504 - 7th Street S
Street address city: Lethbridge
Province/Territory: AB
Postal code: T1J 2G8
Country: Canada
General Phone: (403) 328-4433
General Fax: (403) 329-9355
General/National Adv. E-mail: suntimes@lethbridgeherald.com
Editorial e-mail: ccampbell@abnewsgroup.com
Primary Website: www.lethsuntimes.com
Published: Mon`Tues`Wed`Thur`Fri`Sat`Sun
Avg Paid Circ: 19864
Audit By: AAM
Audit Date: 30.09.2017
Personnel: Coleen Campbell (Pub.)
Parent company (for newspapers): Alberta Newspaper Group LP

LLOYDMINSTER MERIDIAN BOOSTER

Street address 1: 5714 44th St.
Street address city: Lloydminster
Province/Territory: AB
Postal code: T9V 0B6
County: Canada
Country: Canada
General Phone: (780) 875-3362
General Fax: (780) 875-3423
Advertising Phone: (877) 786-8227
General/National Adv. E-mail: lisa.lamoureux@sunmedia.ca
Display Adv. E-mail: ljohnston@postmedia.com
Classified Adv. e-mail: meridianbooster.classifieds@sunmedia.ca
Editorial e-mail: tweaver@postmedia.com
Primary Website: www.meridianbooster.com
Published: Wed
Avg Paid Circ: 2653
Avg Free Circ: 14879
Audit By: VAC
Audit Date: 31.12.2015
Personnel: Mary-Ann Kostiuk (Pub); Leanne Johnson (Adv. Dir.); Taylor Weaver (Ed)
Parent company (for newspapers): Postmedia Network Inc.; Quebecor Communications, Inc.

MOUNTAIN VIEW GAZETTE

Street address 1: 5013 - 51 St
Street address city: Olds
Province/Territory: AB
Postal code: T4H 1P6
Country: Canada
General Phone: (403) 556-7510
General Fax: (403) 556-7515
General/National Adv. E-mail: gazette@olds.greatwest.ca
Editorial e-mail: dsingleton@olds.greatwest.ca
Primary Website: www.mountainviewgazette.ca/
Published: Tues
Avg Free Circ: 20000
Audit By: Sworn/Estimate/Non-Audited
Audit Date: 12.07.2019
Personnel: Murray Elliott (Grp. Pub./Gen. Mgr.); Dan Singleton (Ed)
Parent company (for newspapers): Great West Media LP

OKOTOKS WESTERN WHEEL

Street address 1: 9 Mcrae St.
Street address city: Okotoks
Province/Territory: AB
Postal code: T1S 2A2
Country: Canada
General Phone: (403) 938-6397
General Fax: (403) 938-2518
General/National Adv. E-mail: westernwheel@okotoks.greatwest.ca
Display Adv. E-mail: sjessome@greatwest.ca
Classified Adv. e-mail: classified@okotoks.greatwest.ca
Editorial e-mail: tmurphy@greatwest.ca
Primary Website: okotokstoday.ca
Published: Wed
Avg Paid Circ: 91
Avg Free Circ: 16875
Audit By: VAC
Audit Date: 24.06.2021
Personnel: Don Patterson (Ed); Shaun Jessome (Publisher); Ted Murphy (Editor); Matt Rockley (Pub)
Parent company (for newspapers): Glacier Media Group; Great West Media LP

OLDS ALBERTAN

Street address 1: 5013 51st St.
Street address city: Olds
Province/Territory: AB
Postal code: T4H 1P6
Country: Canada
General Phone: (403) 556-7510
General Fax: (403) 556-7515
General/National Adv. E-mail: albertan@olds.greatwest.ca
Display Adv. E-mail: melliott@olds.greatwest.ca
Editorial e-mail: dcollie@olds.greatwest.ca
Primary Website: www.oldsalbertan.ca
Published: Tues
Avg Paid Circ: 5
Avg Free Circ: 6933
Audit By: VAC
Audit Date: 28.02.2016
Personnel: Murray Elliott (Pub); Doug Collie (Ed)
Parent company (for newspapers): Glacier Media Group; Great West Media LP

OYEN ECHO

Street address 1: 109 Sixth Ave. E.
Street address city: Oyen
Province/Territory: AB
Postal code: T0J 2J0
County: Special Area #3
Country: Canada
General Phone: (403) 664-3622
General Fax: (403) 664-3622
General/National Adv. E-mail: oyenecho@telusplanet.net
Display Adv. E-mail: oyenecho@telusplanet.net
Classified Adv. e-mail: 88
Editorial e-mail: oyenecho@telusplanet.net
Primary Website: www.oyenecho.ca
Published: Tues
Avg Paid Circ: 986
Avg Free Circ: 22
Audit By: VAC
Audit Date: 30.06.2017
Personnel: Ronald E. Holmes (Pub.); Diana Walker (Ed.)
Parent company (for newspapers): Holmes Publishing Co. Ltd.-OOB

PINCHER CREEK ECHO

Street address 1: 714 Main St.
Street address city: Pincher Creek
Province/Territory: AB
Postal code: T0K 1W0
County: Canada
Country: Canada
General Phone: (403) 627-3252
General Fax: (403) 627-3949
General/National Adv. E-mail: pcecho@awna.com
Display Adv. E-mail: rmackintosh@postmedia.com
Editorial e-mail: cclow@postmedia.com
Primary Website: www.pinchercreekecho.com
Published: Wed
Avg Paid Circ: 1077
Avg Free Circ: 14
Audit By: CMCA
Audit Date: 30.06.2014
Personnel: Nancy Middleton (Pub); Martha Goforth (Office Mgr); Caitlin Clow (Ed); Roxanne Mackintoch (Adv. Dir)
Parent company (for newspapers): Postmedia Network Inc.; Quebecor Communications, Inc.

PONOKA NEWS

Street address 1: 5019-a 50th Ave.
Street address city: Ponoka

Province/Territory: AB
Postal code: T4J 1R6
County: Ponoka
Country: Canada
General Phone: (403) 783-3311
General Fax: (403) 783-6300
Display Adv. E-mail: judy.dick@ponokanews.com
Classified Adv. e-mail: judy.dick@ponokanews.com
Editorial e-mail: jeff.heyden-kaye@ponokanews.com
Primary Website: www.ponokanews.com
Published: Wed
Avg Paid Circ: 16
Avg Free Circ: 5856
Audit By: CMCA
Audit Date: 30.04.2018
Personnel: Mary Kemmis (Pres.)
Parent company (for newspapers): Black Press Group Ltd.

PRAIRIE POST

Street address 1: 3256 Dunmore Rd Se
Street address city: Medicine Hat
Province/Territory: AB
Postal code: T1B 3R2
Country: Canada
General Phone: (403) 528-5769
General Fax: (403) 528-2276
General/National Adv. E-mail: rdahlman@prairiepost.com
Editorial e-mail: rdahlman@prairiepost.com
Primary Website: www.prairiepost.com
Published: Fri
Avg Paid Circ: 0
Avg Free Circ: 12562
Audit By: VAC
Audit Date: 30.09.2015
Personnel: Ryan Dahlman (Mng Ed.)
Parent company (for newspapers): Alberta Newspaper Group LP

RED DEER EXPRESS

Street address 1: 121 5301-43 St.
Street address city: Red Deer
Province/Territory: AB
Postal code: T4N 1C8
County: Canada
Country: Canada
General Phone: (403) 346-3356
General Fax: (403) 347-6620
Advertising Phone: (403) 625-4474
General/National Adv. E-mail: express@reddeer.greatwest.ca
Display Adv. E-mail: publisher@reddeerexpress.com
Classified Adv. e-mail: publisher@reddeerexpress.com
Editorial e-mail: editor@reddeerexpress.com
Primary Website: www.reddeerexpress.com
Published: Wed
Avg Paid Circ: 0
Avg Free Circ: 24718
Audit By: VAC
Audit Date: 31.08.2016
Personnel: Tracey Scheveers (Pub); Mark Weber (Ed)
Parent company (for newspapers): Black Press Group Ltd.

RIMBEY REVIEW

Street address 1: 5001-50 Ave. Main St.
Street address city: Rimbey
Province/Territory: AB
Postal code: T0C 2J0
Country: Canada
General Phone: (403) 843-4909
General Fax: (403) 843-4907
General/National Adv. E-mail: admin@rimbeyreview.com
Display Adv. E-mail: sales@rimbeyreview.com
Editorial e-mail: editor@rimbeyreview.com
Primary Website: www.rimbeyreview.com
Published: Tues
Avg Paid Circ: 7
Avg Free Circ: 5136
Audit By: VAC
Audit Date: 31.05.2016
Personnel: Michele Rosenthal (Pub); Connie Johnson (Sales); Treena Mielke (Ed)
Parent company (for newspapers): Black Press Group Ltd.

ROCKY MOUNTAIN OUTLOOK

Street address 1: Box 8610
Street address 2: Suite 201 - 1001. 6th Avenue
Street address city: Canmore
Province/Territory: AB
Postal code: T1W 2V3
Country: Canada
General Phone: (403) 609-0220
General Fax: (403)609-0221
Display Adv. E-mail: clacroix@outlook.greatwest.ca
Classified Adv. e-mail: jlyon@outlook.greatwest.ca
Editorial e-mail: dwhitfield@rmoutlook.com
Primary Website: www.rmoutlook.com
Published: Thur
Avg Paid Circ: 0
Avg Free Circ: 9395
Audit By: VAC
Audit Date: 31.01.2016
Personnel: Jason Lyon (Pub/Adv. Mgr); Donna Browne (Circ. Mgr); Dave Whitfield (Ed)
Parent company (for newspapers): Glacier Media Group; Great West Media LP

ROCKY VIEW WEEKLY

Street address 1: #403 2903 Kingsview Blvd.
Street address city: Airdrie
Province/Territory: AB
Postal code: T4A 0C4
County: Canada
Country: Canada
General Phone: (403) 948-1885
General Fax: (403) 948-2554
General/National Adv. E-mail: sales@airdrie.greatwest.ca
Display Adv. E-mail: rsonghurst@airdrie.greatwest.ca
Classified Adv. e-mail: rvwclassifieds@airdrie.greatwest.ca
Editorial e-mail: achorney@airdrie.greatwest.ca
Primary Website: www.rockyviewweekly.com
Published: Tues
Avg Paid Circ: 457
Avg Free Circ: 12910
Audit By: VAC
Audit Date: 30.06.2016
Personnel: Cameron Christianson (Pub.); Lisa Gebruck (Circ. Mgr.); Allison Chorney (Ed)
Parent company (for newspapers): Glacier Media Group; Great West Media LP; Rocky View Publishing

RYCROFT CENTRAL PEACE SIGNAL

Street address 1: 47011 50th St.
Street address city: Rycroft
Province/Territory: AB
Postal code: T0H 3A0
County: Canada
Country: Canada
General Phone: (780) 765-3604
General Fax: (780) 785-2188
General/National Adv. E-mail: admin@cpsignal.com
Display Adv. E-mail: signalads@telus.net
Classified Adv. e-mail: signalads@telus.net
Editorial e-mail: signalnews@telus.net
Published: Tues
Avg Paid Circ: 2633
Avg Free Circ: 5
Audit By: CMCA
Audit Date: 30.03.2017
Personnel: Dan Zahara (Pub/Advt Mgr); Carol Grover (Circ. Mgr.); Morgan Zahara
Parent company (for newspapers): 847562 Alberta Ltd.

SHERWOOD PARK/STRATHCONA COUNTY NEWS

Street address 1: 168 Kaska Rd.
Street address 2: 168 Kaska Road
Street address city: Sherwood Park
Province/Territory: AB
Postal code: T8A 4G7
County: Strathcona
Country: Canada
General Phone: (780) 464-0033
General Fax: (780) 464-8512
Advertising Phone: (780) 464-0033 Ext 239
Editorial Phone: 780 464-0033
General/National Adv. E-mail: shelagh.pastoor@sunmedia.ca
Display Adv. E-mail: jfigeat@postmedia.com
Editorial e-mail: bproulx@postmedia.com
Primary Website: www.sherwoodparknews.com
Published: Fri
Avg Paid Circ: 1702
Avg Free Circ: 30851
Audit By: VAC
Audit Date: 31.12.2015
Personnel: Jean Figeat (Adv. Dir.); Dawn Zapatoski (Circ.); Ben Proulx (Ed)
Parent company (for newspapers): Postmedia Network Inc.; Division of Post Media

SMOKY LAKE SIGNAL

Street address 1: 4924 50th St
Street address city: Smoky Lake
Province/Territory: AB
Postal code: T0A 3C0
Country: Canada
General Phone: (780) 656-6530
Advertising Phone: (780) 656-4114
Editorial Phone: (780) 656-6530
General/National Adv. E-mail: signal@mcsnet.ca
Display Adv. E-mail: lorne_taylor@smokylake.com
Classified Adv. e-mail: lornetaylor@smokylake.com
Editorial e-mail: lornetaylor@smokylake.com
Published: Tues`Wed
Avg Paid Circ: 855
Avg Free Circ: 20
Audit By: Sworn/Estimate/Non-Audited
Audit Date: 12.07.2019
Personnel: Lorne Taylor (Ed/Pub/Owner)
Parent company (for newspapers): Smoky Lake Signal Press Ltd.

SOUTH PEACE NEWS

Street address 1: 4903 51st Ave.
Street address city: High Prairie
Province/Territory: AB
Postal code: T0G 1E0
County: Canada
Country: Canada
General Phone: (780) 523-4484
General Fax: (780) 523-3039
General/National Adv. E-mail: spn@cablecomet.com
Display Adv. E-mail: southpeacenews@hotmail.com
Classified Adv. e-mail: southpeacenews@hotmail.com
Editorial e-mail: spn@cablecomet.com
Primary Website: www.southpeacenews.com
Published: Wed
Avg Paid Circ: 1257
Avg Free Circ: 0
Audit By: CMCA
Audit Date: 30.01.2017
Personnel: Mary Burgar (Pub.); Chris Clegg (Ed.)

ST. ALBERT GAZETTE

Street address 1: 340 Carelton Drive
Street address city: St. Albert
Province/Territory: AB
Postal code: T8N 7L3
County: Canada
Country: Canada
General Phone: (780) 460-5500
General Fax: (780) 460-8220
Editorial Phone: (780) 460-5510
General/National Adv. E-mail: gazette@stalbert.greatwest.ca
Display Adv. E-mail: advertising@stalbert.greatwest.ca
Editorial e-mail: cmartindale@stalbert.greatwest.ca
Primary Website: www.stalbertgazette.com
Published: Wed`Sat
Avg Paid Circ: 1652
Avg Free Circ: 24879
Audit By: VAC
Audit Date: 30.06.2016
Personnel: Al Glaser (Adv. Mgr.); Brian Bachynski (Pub); Carolyn Martindale (Ed)
Parent company (for newspapers): Glacier Media Group; Great West Media LP

ST. PAUL JOURNAL

Street address 1: 4813 50th Ave.
Street address city: Saint Paul
Province/Territory: AB
Postal code: T0A 3A0
County: Canada
Country: Canada
General Phone: (780) 645-3342
General Fax: (780) 645-2346
General/National Adv. E-mail: production@stpaul.greatwest.ca; journal@stpaul.greatwest.ca
Display Adv. E-mail: rberlinguette@stpaul.greatwest.ca
Editorial e-mail: jhuser@stpaul.greatwest.ca
Primary Website: www.spjournal.com
Published: Tues
Avg Paid Circ: 21
Avg Free Circ: 460
Audit By: VAC
Audit Date: 31.12.2015
Personnel: Janice Huser (Ed); Janani Whitfield (Pub)
Parent company (for newspapers): Glacier Media Group; Great West Media LP

STETTLER INDEPENDENT

Street address 1: 4810 50th St.
Street address city: Stettler
Province/Territory: AB
Postal code: T0C 2L0
Country: Canada
General Phone: (403) 742-2395
General Fax: (403) 742-8050
Editorial Phone: (403) 740-4431
General/National Adv. E-mail: stetnews@telusplanet.net
Display Adv. E-mail: nicole.stratulate@stettlerindependent.com
Classified Adv. e-mail: ddoell@stettlerindependent.com
Editorial e-mail: editor@stettlerindependent.com
Primary Website: www.stettlerindependent.com
Published: Thur
Avg Paid Circ: 34
Avg Free Circ: 33
Audit By: VAC
Audit Date: 20.03.2017
Personnel: Debbie Doell (Ad control); Karen Fischer (Graphic artist); Landin Chambers (reporter)
Parent company (for newspapers): Black Press Group Ltd.

STRATHMORE STANDARD

Street address 1: Unit A-510 Hwy 1
Street address city: Strathmore
Province/Territory: AB
Postal code: T1P 1M6
County: Canada
Country: Canada
General Phone: (403) 934-3021
General Fax: (403) 934-5011
Display Adv. E-mail: rmackintosh@postmedia.com
Editorial e-mail: josh.chalmers@sunmedia.ca
Primary Website: www.strathmorestandard.com
Published: Wed
Avg Paid Circ: 3679
Avg Free Circ: 10858
Audit By: VAC
Audit Date: 31.12.2015
Personnel: Josh Chalmers (Ed); Roxanne MacKintosh (Adv. Dir)
Parent company (for newspapers): Postmedia Network Inc.; Quebecor Communications, Inc.

STRATHMORE TIMES

Street address 1: 123 2nd Avenue
Street address city: Strathmore
Province/Territory: AB
Postal code: T1P 1K1
Country: Canada
General Phone: (403) 934-5589
General Fax: (403) 934-5546
General/National Adv. E-mail: info@strathmoretimes.com
Display Adv. E-mail: rose@strathmoretimes.com
Classified Adv. e-mail: classifieds@strathmoretimes.com
Editorial e-mail: miriam@strathmoretimes.com
Primary Website: www.strathmoretimes.com
Published: Fri
Avg Free Circ: 11001
Audit By: Sworn/Estimate/Non-Audited
Audit Date: 12.07.2019

Personnel: Mario Prusina (Pub/Ed); Rose Hamrlik (Adv Mgr); Miriam Ostermann (Associate Editor)

SUNDRE ROUND-UP

Street address 1: 103 2nd St. Nw
Street address city: Sundre
Province/Territory: AB
Postal code: T0M 1X0
County: Canada
Country: Canada
General Phone: (403) 638-3577
General Fax: (403) 638-3077
General/National Adv. E-mail: roundup@sundre.greatwest.ca
Display Adv. E-mail: kcomfort@sundre.greatwest.ca
Editorial e-mail: dsingleton@olds.greatwest.ca
Primary Website: www.sundreroundup.ca
Published: Tues
Avg Paid Circ: 879
Avg Free Circ: 0
Audit By: VAC
Audit Date: 30.06.2016
Personnel: Ray Lachambre (Pub.); Dan Singleton (Ed); Kim Comfort (Sales Mgr)
Parent company (for newspapers): Glacier Media Group; Great West Media LP

SYLVAN LAKE NEWS

Street address 1: Suite 103, 5020-50a St.,
Street address city: Sylvan Lake
Province/Territory: AB
Postal code: T4S 1R2
County: Canada
Country: Canada
General Phone: (403) 887-2331
Advertising Phone: (403) 887-2331
General/National Adv. E-mail: publisher@sylvanlakenews.com
Display Adv. E-mail: sales@sylvanlakenews.com
Classified Adv. e-mail: classifieds@blackpress.ca
Editorial e-mail: editor@sylvanlakenews.com
Primary Website: www.sylvanlakenews.com
Published: Thur
Avg Paid Circ: 377
Avg Free Circ: 5200
Audit By: CMCA
Audit Date: 30.09.2023
Personnel: Cheryl Hyvonen (Admin); Barb Pettie (Regional Publisher); Sarah Baker (Reporter); Julie Daillaire (Multimedia Sales); Randy Holt (Pub); Jenna Swan (Ed)
Parent company (for newspapers): Black Press Group Ltd.

TEMPLE CITY STAR

Street address 1: 30-b 3rd Ave. West
Street address city: Cardston
Province/Territory: AB
Postal code: T0K 0K0
County: Canada
Country: Canada
General Phone: (403) 653-4664
General Fax: (403) 653-3162
Advertising Phone: (403) 653-4664
General/National Adv. E-mail: info@templecitystar.net
Display Adv. E-mail: news@templecitystar.net
Editorial e-mail: news@templecitystar.net
Primary Website: www.templecitystar.net
Published: Thur
Avg Paid Circ: 650
Avg Free Circ: 50
Audit By: Sworn/Estimate/Non-Audited
Audit Date: 12.07.2019
Personnel: Robert Smith (Owner/Pub.); Dan Burt (Office Mgr.)

THE 40-MILE COUNTY COMMENTATOR

Street address 1: 147-5 Ave. W.
Street address city: Bow Island
Province/Territory: AB
Postal code: T0K 0G0
County: County of Forty Mile No. 8
Country: Canada
General Phone: (403) 545-2258
General Fax: (403) 545-6886
General/National Adv. E-mail: tabads@tabertimes.com
Display Adv. E-mail: editor@bowislandcommentator.com
Primary Website: www.bowislandcommentator.com
Published: Tues
Avg Paid Circ: 426
Avg Free Circ: 45
Audit By: VAC
Audit Date: 30.09.2016
Personnel: Coleen Campbell (Pub.); Tom Conquergood (Adv. Mgr.); Jamie Rieger (Ed.)

THE ATHABASCA ADVOCATE

Street address 1: 4917b 49th Street
Street address city: Athabasca
Province/Territory: AB
Postal code: T9S 1C5
County: Athabasca County
Country: Canada
General Phone: (780) 675-9222
General Fax: (780) 675-3143
Advertising Phone: (780) 675-9222 ext. 24
Editorial Phone: (780) 675-9222
Display Adv. E-mail: production@athabasca.greatwest.ca
Editorial e-mail: advocate@athabasca.greatwest.ca
Primary Website: www.athabascaadvocate.com
Published: Tues
Avg Paid Circ: 41
Avg Free Circ: 106
Audit By: VAC
Audit Date: 31.03.2016
Personnel: Vanessa Annand (Ed.); Meghan McIvor (Prod. Mgr.); Mona Muzyka (Circ. Mgr.); Allendria Brunjes (Pub.)
Parent company (for newspapers): Great West Media LP

THE BASSANO TIMES

Street address 1: 402 First Ave.
Street address city: Bassano
Province/Territory: AB
Postal code: T0J 0B0
County: Canada
Country: Canada
General Phone: (403) 641-3636
General Fax: (403) 641-3952
Advertising Phone: (403) 641-3636
General/National Adv. E-mail: btymes@telus.net
Published: Mon
Avg Paid Circ: 503
Audit By: CMCA
Audit Date: 30.06.2017
Personnel: Mary Lou Brooks (Publisher/Advertising Manager)

THE BROOKS BULLETIN

Street address 1: 124-3 St. W.
Street address city: Brooks
Province/Territory: AB
Postal code: T1R 0S3
County: Canada
Country: Canada
General Phone: (403) 362-5571
General Fax: (403) 362-5080
General/National Adv. E-mail: diane@brooksbulletin.com
Display Adv. E-mail: diane@brooksbulletin.com
Classified Adv. e-mail: diane@brooksbulletin.com
Editorial e-mail: editor@brooksbulletin.com
Primary Website: www.brooksbulletin.com
Published: Wed
Avg Paid Circ: 87
Avg Free Circ: 7600
Audit By: CMCA
Audit Date: 12.07.2019
Personnel: Jamie Nesbitt (Ed./Pub.)
Parent company (for newspapers): Brooks Bulletin

THE CAMROSE BOOSTER

Street address 1: 4925 48th St.
Street address city: Camrose
Province/Territory: AB
Postal code: T4V 1L7
County: Camrose, Flagstaff and Beaver
Country: Canada
General Phone: (780) 672-3142
General Fax: (780) 672-2518
General/National Adv. E-mail: ads@camrosebooster.com
Display Adv. E-mail: ads@camrosebooster.com
Editorial e-mail: news@camrosebooster.com
Primary Website: www.camrosebooster.com
Published: Tues
Avg Paid Circ: 11
Avg Free Circ: 12062
Audit By: CVC
Audit Date: 30.09.2023
Personnel: Blain Fowler (Publisher); Don Hutchinson (Comptroller); Ronald Pilger (Associate Publisher / Sales Manager); Jeff Fowler (Sales Rep.); Mike Pioner (Sales Rep.); Kirby Fowler (Production Manager); Sharon Schwartz (Art Director); Pat Horton (Art Director); Leanne Taje (Circ. Mgr.)

THE CAMROSE CANADIAN

Street address 1: 4610 49th Ave.
Street address city: Camrose
Province/Territory: AB
Postal code: T4V 0M6
County: Camrose County
Country: Canada
General Phone: (780) 672-4421
General Fax: (780) 672-5323
Advertising Phone: (877) 786-8227
General/National Adv. E-mail: production@camrosecanadian.com
Display Adv. E-mail: ngoetz@postmedia.com
Primary Website: www.camrosecanadian.com
Published: Thur
Avg Paid Circ: 3673
Avg Free Circ: 15292
Audit By: VAC
Audit Date: 31.12.2015
Personnel: Dan Macpherson (Adv. Mgr.); Nick Goetz (Publisher); Trent Wilkie (Editor); Vince Burke (Editor(online)); Jim Clark (Publisher(online))
Parent company (for newspapers): Postmedia Network Inc.

THE CHESTERMERE ANCHOR CITY NEWS

Street address 1: P.o. Box 127
Street address city: Chestermere
Province/Territory: AB
Postal code: T1X 1K8
County: Rocky View
Country: Canada
General Phone: (403) 770-9448
Advertising Phone: (403) 774-1322
Editorial Phone: (403) 774-1322
General/National Adv. E-mail: info@anchormedia.ca
Display Adv. E-mail: ads@theanchor.ca
Classified Adv. e-mail: ads@theanchor.ca
Editorial e-mail: news@theanchor.ca
Primary Website: www.theanchor.ca
Published: Mon
Avg Free Circ: 7923
Audit By: VAC
Audit Date: 28.02.2016

THE COMMUNITY PRESS

Street address 1: 4919 - 50 St.,
Street address city: Killam
Province/Territory: AB
Postal code: T0B 2L0
County: All of Flagstaff County, Alberta: Total municipalities covered: Bawlf, Daysland, Strome, Killam, Sedgewick, Lougheed, Hardisty, Amisk, Hughenden, Czar, Forestburg, Galahad, Heisler, Alliance
Country: Canada
General Phone: (780) 385-6693
General Fax: (780) 385-3107
Advertising Phone: (780-385-6693
Display Adv. E-mail: ads@thecommunitypress.com
Classified Adv. e-mail: ads@thecommunitypress.com
Editorial e-mail: news@thecommunitypress.com
Primary Website: www.thecommunitypress.com
Published: Wed
Avg Paid Circ: 2000
Avg Free Circ: 500
Audit By: CMCA
Audit Date: 31.12.2016
Personnel: Leslie Cholowsky (Editor); Eric Anderson (Publisher/Sales/Production Manager); Jae Robbins (Sales); Ally Anderson (Production Manager)
Parent company (for newspapers): Caribou Publishing

THE CONSORT ENTERPRISE

Street address 1: 5012 - 52st.
Street address city: Consort
Province/Territory: AB
Postal code: T0C 1B0
County: Canada
Country: Canada
General Phone: (403) 577-3337
General Fax: (403) 577-3611
Advertising Phone: (403) 577-3337
Editorial Phone: (403) 577-3337
General/National Adv. E-mail: consort_enterprise@awna.com
Display Adv. E-mail: ads@consortenterprise.com
Classified Adv. e-mail: ads@consortenterprise.com
Editorial e-mail: editor@consortenterprise.com
Primary Website: www.consortenterprise.awna.com
Published: Wed
Avg Paid Circ: 2935
Audit By: CMCA
Audit Date: 12.12.2017
Personnel: Carol Bruha (Circ. Mgr./Adv. Mgr.); David Bruha (Ed.)

THE COURIER

Street address 1: Bldg. 67 Centennial Bldg., Kingsway
Street address city: Cold Lake
Province/Territory: AB
Postal code: T9M 2C5
County: Cold Lake
Country: Canada
General Phone: (780) 594-5206
General Fax: (780) 594-2139
Editorial Phone: (780) 840-8000 ext. 7854
General/National Adv. E-mail: thecourier@telus.net
Editorial e-mail: Jeff.Gaye@forces.gc.ca
Primary Website: www.thecouriernewspaper.ca
Published: Tues
Avg Paid Circ: 32
Avg Free Circ: 1995
Audit By: VAC
Audit Date: 28.02.2016
Personnel: Connie Lavigne (Mgr); Jeff Gaye (Ed); Angela Hetherington (Admin); Alina Mallais (Produc Coord)

THE ECHO-PIONEER

Street address 1: 10006 - 97th St.
Street address city: High Level
Province/Territory: AB
Postal code: T0H 1Z0
County: Canada
Country: Canada
General Phone: (780) 926-2000
General Fax: (780) 926-2001
General/National Adv. E-mail: pioneer@mackreport.ab.ca
Display Adv. E-mail: echoads1@mrnews.ca
Classified Adv. e-mail: echoads1@mrnews.ca
Editorial e-mail: echonews2@mrnews.ca
Primary Website: www.mrnews.ca
Published: Wed
Audit By: Sworn/Estimate/Non-Audited
Audit Date: 12.07.2019
Personnel: Nikki Coles (Advertising); Tom Mihaly (Pub./Mng. Ed.); Ann Bassett (Office/Adv.); Matt Marcone (Ed); Lacey Reid (Advertising)
Parent company (for newspapers): Mackenzie Report Inc.

THE FITZHUGH

Street address 1: PO Box 428
Street address city: Jasper
Province/Territory: AB
Postal code: T0E 1E0
County: Jasper
Country: Canada
General Phone: (780) 852-8423
General/National Adv. E-mail: pshokeir@greatwest.ca
Primary Website: www.fitzhugh.ca
Published: Thur
Avg Free Circ: 2400
Audit By: VAC
Audit Date: 31.07.2016
Personnel: Matt Figueira (Sales); Jeremy Derksen (Pub.); Mishelle Menzies (Prod.); Nicole Veerman (Ed.)

Parent company (for newspapers): Jasper Media Group; Great West Media

THE FORT SASKATCHEWAN RECORD

Street address 1: 10404 99 Ave
Street address 2: 168A
Street address city: Fort Saskatchewan
Province/Territory: AB
Postal code: T8L 3W2
County: Strathcona County
Country: Canada
General Phone: (780) 998-7070 Ext 724227
General Fax: (780) 998-5515
Editorial e-mail: agreen@postmedia.com
Primary Website: fortsaskatchewanrecord.com
Published: Thur
Avg Paid Circ: 9
Avg Free Circ: 8806
Audit By: Sworn/Estimate/Non-Audited
Audit Date: 12.07.2019
Personnel: A Green
Parent company (for newspapers): Postmedia Network Inc.

THE FREE PRESS

Street address 1: 10126 100 Ave.
Street address city: Morinville
Province/Territory: AB
Postal code: T8R 1R9
County: Sturgeon County
Country: Canada
General Phone: (780) 939-3309
General Fax: (780) 939-3093
Advertising Phone: (780) 939-3309
General/National Adv. E-mail: redwater@shaw.ca
Display Adv. E-mail: morinville@shaw.ca
Primary Website: www.cowleynewspapers.com
Published: Tues
Avg Paid Circ: 55
Avg Free Circ: 11996
Audit By: VAC
Audit Date: 31.07.2016
Personnel: Ed Cowley (Pub.)
Parent company (for newspapers): W & E Cowley Publishing Ltd.

THE GROVE EXAMINER

Street address 1: 420 King Street
Street address 2: #1
Street address city: Spruce Grove
Province/Territory: AB
Postal code: T7X 3B4
County: Canada
Country: Canada
General Phone: (780) 962-4257
General Fax: (780) 962-0658
Advertising Phone: (877) 786-8227
Display Adv. E-mail: matthew.maceachen@sunmedia.ca
Classified Adv. e-mail: matthew.maceachen@sunmedia.ca
Editorial e-mail: carsonm@bowesnet.com
Primary Website: www.sprucegroveexaminer.com
Published: Fri
Avg Paid Circ: 1273
Avg Free Circ: 11471
Audit By: VAC
Audit Date: 31.12.2015
Personnel: Mary Ann Kostiuk (Reg. Sales Mgr.); Janet Stace (Prodn. Mgr.); Pamela Allain (Pub.); Matthew MacEachen (Adv. Mgr.); Carson Mills (Ed.)
Parent company (for newspapers): Postmedia Network Inc.

THE HIGH RIVER TIMES

Street address 1: 618 Centre St. S.
Street address city: High River
Province/Territory: AB
Postal code: T1V 1E9
County: Canada
Country: Canada
General Phone: (403) 652-2034
General/National Adv. E-mail: info@highrivertimes.com
Display Adv. E-mail: hmorgan@postmedia.com
Classified Adv. e-mail: hmorgan@postmedia.com
Editorial e-mail: krushworth@postmedia.com
Primary Website: www.highrivertimes.com
Published: Tues`Fri
Avg Paid Circ: 0
Avg Free Circ: 6406
Audit By: VAC
Audit Date: 31.03.2017
Personnel: Kaire Davis (Admin./Office Mgr.); Kevin Rushworth (Multimedia. Ed.); Roxanne Mackintosh (Reg. Adv. Dir.); Heather Morgan (Advertising Manager)
Parent company (for newspapers): Postmedia Network Inc.

THE HINTON PARKLANDER

Street address 1: 387 Drinnan Way
Street address city: Hinton
Province/Territory: AB
Postal code: T7V 2A3
County: Canada
Country: Canada
General Phone: (780) 865-3115
General Fax: (780) 865-1252
General/National Adv. E-mail: news@hintonparklander.com
Classified Adv. e-mail: hintonparklander.classifieds@sunmedia.ca
Editorial e-mail: eric.plummer@sunmedia.ca
Primary Website: www.hintonparklander.com
Published: Mon
Avg Paid Circ: 7
Avg Free Circ: 3720
Audit By: VAC
Audit Date: 31.12.2015
Personnel: Eric Plummer (Ed.); Terry Thachuk (Pub.); Nathalie Lovoie-Murray (Nationals & Classified Booking)
Parent company (for newspapers): Postmedia Network Inc.

THE HINTON VOICE

Street address 1: 187 Pembina Ave.
Street address city: Hinton
Province/Territory: AB
Postal code: T7V 2B2
Country: Canada
General Phone: (890) 865-5688
General Fax: (780) 865-5699
General/National Adv. E-mail: news@hintonvoice.ca
Display Adv. E-mail: sales@hintonvoice.ca
Primary Website: www.hintonvoice.com
Published: Thur
Avg Free Circ: 445
Audit By: VAC
Audit Date: 31.08.2016
Personnel: Tyler Waugh (Pub.); Sarah Burns (Mktg. Specialist); Robin Garreck (Prodn./Distrib. Mgr.); Angie Still (Accounting)

THE LAMONT LEADER

Street address 1: 5038 50 Ave.
Street address city: Lamont
Province/Territory: AB
Postal code: T0B 2R0
Country: Canada
General Phone: (780) 895-2780
General Fax: (780) 895-2705
Display Adv. E-mail: lmtleader@gmail.com
Editorial e-mail: lamontnews@gmail.com
Primary Website: lamontleader.com
Published: Tues
Avg Paid Circ: 0
Avg Free Circ: 2606
Audit By: VAC
Audit Date: 30.06.2016
Personnel: Kerry Anderson (Pub.); Michelle Pinon (Ed.)
Parent company (for newspapers): Caribou Pub.

THE MACLEOD GAZETTE

Street address 1: 310 24th St.
Street address city: Fort Macleod
Province/Territory: AB
Postal code: T0L 0Z0
County: Municipal District of Willow Creek
Country: Canada
General Phone: (403) 553-3391
General Fax: (403) 553-2961
General/National Adv. E-mail: ftmgazet@telusplanet.net
Display Adv. E-mail: tmgsales@telus.net
Classified Adv. e-mail: tmgsales@telus.net
Editorial e-mail: tmgedit@telus.net
Primary Website: www.fortmacleodgazette.com
Published: Wed
Avg Paid Circ: 852
Avg Free Circ: 0
Audit By: CMCA
Audit Date: 28.02.2022
Personnel: Emily McTighe (Adv. Mgr.); Sharon Monical (Circ. Mgr.); Frank McTighe (Pub./Ed.)

THE MAYERTHORPE FREELANCER

Street address 1: 4732 - 50 Ave.
Street address city: Whitecourt
Province/Territory: AB
Postal code: T7S 1N7
County: Woodlands County
Country: Canada
General Phone: (780) 778-3977
General Fax: (780) 778-6459
General/National Adv. E-mail: info@mayerthorpefreelancer.com
Display Adv. E-mail: advertising@mayerthorpefreelancer.com
Editorial e-mail: ann.harvey@sunmedia.ca
Primary Website: www.mayerthorpefreelancer.com
Published: Wed
Avg Paid Circ: 589
Avg Free Circ: 7
Audit By: CMCA
Audit Date: 31.12.2013
Personnel: Pam Allain (Reg. Dir. of Adv.); Candice Daniels (Circ. Mgr.); Christopher King (Ed.)
Parent company (for newspapers): Quebecor Communications, Inc.

THE MILE ZERO NEWS

Street address 1: 10006-97 St.
Street address city: High Level
Province/Territory: AB
Postal code: T0H 1Z0
Country: Canada
General Phone: (780) 332-2215
General Fax: (780) 926-2001
General/National Adv. E-mail: milezeronews@mrnews.ca
Display Adv. E-mail: echo@mrnews.ca
Primary Website: www.mrnews.ca
Published: Wed
Avg Paid Circ: 0
Avg Free Circ: 1575
Audit By: VAC
Audit Date: 31.10.2016
Personnel: Carmen Kratky (Office/Advertising); Tom Mihaly (Pub.); Ann Bassett (Circ. Mgr.); Kristen Feddema (Ed.); Barb Schofield (Adv. Sales)
Parent company (for newspapers): Mackenzie Report Inc.

THE MOUNTAINEER

Street address 1: 4814 49th St.
Street address city: Rocky Mountain House
Province/Territory: AB
Postal code: T4T 1S8
Country: Canada
General Phone: (403) 845-3334
General Fax: (403) 845-5570
General/National Adv. E-mail: rocky_mountain_house@awna.com
Display Adv. E-mail: advertising@mountaineer.bz
Classified Adv. e-mail: advertising@mountaineer.bz
Editorial e-mail: editor@mountaineer.bz
Primary Website: www.mountaineer.bz
Published: Tues
Avg Paid Circ: 2264
Avg Free Circ: 53
Audit By: VAC
Audit Date: 31.03.2016
Personnel: Gail Krabben (Prodn. Mgr.); Glen Mazza (Pub.); Penny Allen (Adv. Mgr.); Laura Button (Ed.); Bernie Visotto (Office Mgr.)
Parent company (for newspapers): Mountaineer Publishing Co.

THE NANTON NEWS

Street address 1: 2019 20th Avenue
Street address city: Nanton
Province/Territory: AB
Postal code: T0L 1R0
County: Canada
Country: Canada
General Phone: (403) 646-2023
General Fax: (403) 646-2848
General/National Adv. E-mail: info@highrivertimes.com
Editorial e-mail: sheena.read@sunmedia.ca
Primary Website: www.nantonnews.com
Published: Wed
Avg Paid Circ: 592
Avg Free Circ: 8
Audit By: CMCA
Audit Date: 30.06.2014
Personnel: Nancy Middleton (Pub.); Donna Knowles (Circ. Mgr.); Shawn Cornell (Group Pub.); Lorelei Doell (Circ. Mgr.); Sheena Reed (Ed.); Roxanne Mackintosh (Reg. Adv. Dir.); Stephen Tipper (Ed.)
Parent company (for newspapers): Postmedia Network Inc.

THE PEACE RIVER RECORD-GAZETTE

Street address 1: 10002 100th St.
Street address city: Peace River
Province/Territory: AB
Postal code: T8S 1S6
County: Canada
Country: Canada
General Phone: (780) 624-2591
General Fax: (780) 624-8600
Advertising Phone: (877) 786-8227
General/National Adv. E-mail: news@prrecordgazette.com
Display Adv. E-mail: adsales@prrecordgazette.com
Editorial e-mail: erin.steele@sunmedia.ca
Primary Website: www.prrecordgazette.com
Published: Wed
Avg Paid Circ: 0
Avg Free Circ: 3
Audit By: VAC
Audit Date: 31.12.2015
Personnel: Kristjanna Grimmelt (Mng. Ed.); Peter Meyerhoffer (reg. Adv. Dir.); Lori Czoba (Sales (online)); Fred Rinne (City Ed.)
Parent company (for newspapers): Postmedia Network Inc.

THE PROVOST NEWS

Street address 1: 5111 50th St.
Street address city: Provost
Province/Territory: AB
Postal code: T0B 3S0
County: Provost M.D. No. 52
Country: Canada
General Phone: (780) 753-2564
General Fax: (780) 753-6117
General/National Adv. E-mail: advertising@provostnews.ca
Display Adv. E-mail: advertising@provostnews.ca
Editorial e-mail: rcholmes@agt.net
Primary Website: www.provostnews.ca
Published: Wed
Avg Paid Circ: 1300
Avg Free Circ: 54
Audit By: VAC
Audit Date: 30.06.2017
Personnel: Richard C. Holmes (Ed.)
Parent company (for newspapers): Holmes Publishing Co. Ltd.-OOB

THE REVIEW

Street address 1: 4720 50th Ave.
Street address city: Redwater
Province/Territory: AB
Postal code: T0A 2W0
Country: Canada
General Phone: (780) 942-2023
General Fax: (780) 942-2515
General/National Adv. E-mail: redwater@shaw.ca
Display Adv. E-mail: redwater@shaw.ca
Primary Website: www.cowleynewspapers.com
Published: Tues
Avg Free Circ: 4405
Audit By: VAC
Audit Date: 30.06.2016
Personnel: Ed Cowley (Pub./Adv. Mgr./Owner)

Parent company (for newspapers): W & E Cowley Publishing Ltd.

THE STONY PLAIN REPORTER

Street address 1: 420 King Street
Street address 2: #1
Street address city: Spruce Grove
Province/Territory: AB
Postal code: T7X 3B4
County: Canada
Country: Canada
General Phone: (780) 962-4257
General Fax: (780) 962-0658
Advertising Phone: (877) 786-8227
General/National Adv. E-mail: ex.repoffice1@bowesnet.com
Display Adv. E-mail: matthew.maceachen@sunmedia.ca
Classified Adv. e-mail: matthew.maceachen@sunmedia.ca
Editorial e-mail: thomas.miller@sunmedia.ca
Primary Website: www.stonyplainreporter.com
Published: Fri
Avg Paid Circ: 1643
Avg Free Circ: 10513
Audit By: VAC
Audit Date: 31.12.2015
Personnel: Mary-Ann Kostiuk (Circ. Mgr.); Carson Mills (Ed.); Jim Myers (Prodn. Mgr.); Pamela Allain (Pub.); Thomas Miller (CARDonline(10/31/14))
Parent company (for newspapers): Postmedia Network Inc.

THE SUNNY SOUTH NEWS

Street address 1: 1802 20th Ave.
Street address city: Coaldale
Province/Territory: AB
Postal code: T1M 1M2
Country: Canada
General Phone: (403) 345-3081
General Fax: (403) 223-5408
General/National Adv. E-mail: office@sunnysouthnews.com
Display Adv. E-mail: office@sunnysouthnews.com
Primary Website: www.sunnysouthnews.com
Published: Tues
Avg Paid Circ: 2263
Avg Free Circ: 48
Audit By: VAC
Audit Date: 30.09.2016
Personnel: Valorie Wiebe (Pub)

THE TABER TIMES

Street address 1: 4822-53 St.
Street address city: Taber
Province/Territory: AB
Postal code: T1G 1W4
County: Canada
Country: Canada
General Phone: (403) 223-2266
General Fax: (403) 223-1408
General/National Adv. E-mail: gsimmons@tabertimes.com
Display Adv. E-mail: chrissales@tabertimes.com
Primary Website: www.tabertimes.com
Published: Wed
Avg Paid Circ: 54
Avg Free Circ: 179
Audit By: VAC
Audit Date: 30.09.2016
Personnel: Valorie Wiebe (Pub.); Christine Mykytiw (Adv. Consult.); Erin Lickiss (Adv. Consult.); Greg Price (Ed.)

THE THREE HILLS CAPITAL

Street address 1: 411 Main St.
Street address city: Three Hills
Province/Territory: AB
Postal code: T0M 2A0
County: Canada
Country: Canada
General Phone: (403) 443-5133
General Fax: (403) 443-7331
General/National Adv. E-mail: info@threehillscapital.com
Display Adv. E-mail: info@threehillscapital.com
Classified Adv. e-mail: info@threehillscapital.com
Editorial e-mail: info@threehillscapital.com
Primary Website: threehillscapital.com
Published: Wed
Avg Paid Circ: 1029
Avg Free Circ: 4
Audit By: VAC
Audit Date: 31.12.2015
Personnel: Theresa Shearlaw (Adv. Mgr.); Timothy Shearlaw (Ed.); Jay Shearlaw (Produ Mgr)

THE WEEKLY ANCHOR

Street address 1: 5040 3rd Ave.
Street address city: Edson
Province/Territory: AB
Postal code: T7E 1V2
County: Canada
Country: Canada
General Phone: (780) 723-5787
General/National Adv. E-mail: anchorwk@telusplanet.net
Display Adv. E-mail: anchorwk@telusplanet.net
Classified Adv. e-mail: anchorwk@telusplanet.net
Editorial e-mail: anchorwk@telusplanet.net
Primary Website: www.weeklyanchor.com
Published: Mon
Avg Paid Circ: 50
Avg Free Circ: 6025
Audit By: CMCA
Audit Date: 31.12.2016
Personnel: Dana McArthur (Pub./Adv. Dir.)

THE WEEKLY REVIEW

Street address 1: 5208 50th Street
Street address city: Viking
Province/Territory: AB
Postal code: T0B 4N0
Country: Canada
General Phone: (780) 336-3422
General Fax: (780) 336-3223
General/National Adv. E-mail: vikingweeklyreview@gmail.com
Display Adv. E-mail: vikingreview@gmail.com
Editorial e-mail: vikingweeklyreview@gmail.com
Primary Website: www.weeklyreview.ca
Published: Tues
Avg Paid Circ: 0
Avg Free Circ: 10
Audit By: VAC
Audit Date: 30.06.2016
Personnel: Leslie Cholowsky (Ed.); Eric Anderson (Pub.); Kerry Anderson (Owner)
Parent company (for newspapers): Caribou Publishing

THE WESTLOCK NEWS

Street address 1: 9871 107th St.
Street address city: Westlock
Province/Territory: AB
Postal code: T7P 1R9
County: Canada
Country: Canada
General Phone: (780) 349-3033
General Fax: (780) 349-3677
General/National Adv. E-mail: production@westlock.greatwest.ca
Display Adv. E-mail: abaxandall@westlock.greatwest.ca
Classified Adv. e-mail: abaxandall@westlock.greatwest.ca
Editorial e-mail: dneuman@westlock.greatwest.ca
Primary Website: www.westlocknews.com
Published: Tues
Avg Paid Circ: 10
Avg Free Circ: 5
Audit By: VAC
Audit Date: 31.03.2016
Personnel: George Blais (Pub.); Louise Strehlau (Circ. Mgr.); Olivia Bako (Ed.); Connie Onyschuk (Adv.); Joyce Weber (Adv.)
Parent company (for newspapers): Glacier Media Group

THE WHITECOURT STAR

Street address 1: 4732 50th Ave.
Street address city: Whitecourt
Province/Territory: AB
Postal code: T7S 1N7
Country: Canada
General Phone: (780) 778-3977
General Fax: (780) 778-6459
General/National Adv. E-mail: wcstar.general@sunmedia.ca
Display Adv. E-mail: nikki.greening@sunmedia.ca
Editorial e-mail: wcstar.editorial@sunmedia.ca
Primary Website: www.whitecourtstar.com
Published: Wed
Avg Paid Circ: 2467
Avg Free Circ: 113
Audit By: VAC
Audit Date: 31.12.2015
Personnel: Pamela Allain (Pub.); Meghan Brown (Sales); Candice Daniels (Circ.); Nikki Greening (Sales); Tracy McKinnon (Front Office Classifieds); Christopher King (Ed.)
Parent company (for newspapers): Postmedia Network Inc.

TOFIELD MERCURY

Street address 1: 5312 50th St.
Street address city: Tofield
Province/Territory: AB
Postal code: T0B 4J0
County: Canada
Country: Canada
General Phone: (780) 662-4046
General Fax: (780) 662-3735
Advertising Phone: (780) 662-4046
General/National Adv. E-mail: adsmercury@gmail.com
Display Adv. E-mail: kamcjm@gmail.com
Classified Adv. e-mail: kamcjm@gmail.com
Editorial e-mail: tofmerc@telusplanet.net
Primary Website: www.tofieldmerc.com
Published: Wed
Avg Paid Circ: 1400
Avg Free Circ: 23
Audit By: Sworn/Estimate/Non-Audited
Audit Date: 12.07.2019
Personnel: Kerry Anderson (Pub/Advt Mgr)
Parent company (for newspapers): Caribou Publishing

TOWN & COUNTRY NEWS

Street address 1: 916 2nd Avenue
Street address city: Beaverlodge
Province/Territory: AB
Postal code: T0H 0C0
County: Canada
Country: Canada
General Phone: (780) 354-2980
General Fax: (780) 354-2460
General/National Adv. E-mail: beaverlodge.advertiser@gmail.com
Display Adv. E-mail: rebecca@nextchapterpublishing.ca
Primary Website: facebook.com/westcountynews
Published: Thur
Avg Paid Circ: 1857
Avg Free Circ: 20
Audit By: CMCA
Audit Date: 12.12.2017
Personnel: Rebecca Dika (Pub.)
Parent company (for newspapers): Next Chapter Printing & Publishing

VAUXHALL ADVANCE

Street address 1: 516 2nd Ave. N.
Street address city: Vauxhall
Province/Territory: AB
Postal code: T0K 2K0
Country: Canada
General Phone: (403) 654-2122
General Fax: (403) 654-4184
Display Adv. E-mail: tabads@tabertimes.com
Primary Website: www.vauxhalladvance.com
Published: Thur
Avg Paid Circ: 0
Avg Free Circ: 47
Audit By: VAC
Audit Date: 30.09.2016
Personnel: Greg Price (Ed.); Valorie Wiebe (Pub.); Shawna Wiestm (Office/Sales)

VERMILION STANDARD

Street address 1: 4917 50th Ave.
Street address city: Vermilion
Province/Territory: AB
Postal code: T9X 1A6
Country: Canada
General Phone: (780) 853-5344
General Fax: (780) 853-5203
Advertising Phone: (877) 786-8227
Display Adv. E-mail: ngoetz@postmedia.com
Classified Adv. e-mail: ngoetz@postmedia.com
Editorial e-mail: thermiston@postmedia.com
Primary Website: www.vermilionstandard.com
Published: Wed
Avg Paid Circ: 1250
Avg Free Circ: 3972
Audit By: VAC
Audit Date: 31.12.2015
Personnel: Trina de Regt (Circulation); Mary-Ann Kostiuk (Publisher); Pat Lavigne (Production and Circulation); Nicki Goetz (Dir. of Adv.); Taylor Hermiston (Reg. Mng. Ed. ext.4)
Parent company (for newspapers): Postmedia Network Inc.

VERMILION VOICE

Street address 1: 5006-50th Ave.
Street address city: Vermilion
Province/Territory: AB
Postal code: T9X 1A2
Country: Canada
General Phone: 7808536305
General Fax: (780) 853-5426
General/National Adv. E-mail: vermilionvoice@gmail.com
Display Adv. E-mail: vermilionvoice@gmail.com
Classified Adv. e-mail: vermilionvoice@gmail.com
Editorial e-mail: vermilionvoice@gmail.com
Primary Website: www.vermilionvoice.com
Published: Tues
Avg Free Circ: 5500
Audit By: CMCA
Audit Date: 30.06.2018
Personnel: Susan Chikie (Pub.); Lorna Hamilton (Sales, reporter, newspaper layout); Angela Mouley (Reporter and Sales); Amr Rezk (Graphics, website etc.)

VULCAN ADVOCATE

Street address 1: 112 - 3rd Ave. N
Street address city: Vulcan
Province/Territory: AB
Postal code: T0L 2B0
Country: Canada
General Phone: (403) 485-2036
General Fax: (403) 485-6938
Advertising Phone: (877) 786-8227
General/National Adv. E-mail: maureen.howard@sunmedia.ca
Display Adv. E-mail: enid.fraser@sunmedia.ca
Classified Adv. e-mail: enid.fraser@sunmedia.ca
Editorial e-mail: stephen.tipper@sunmedia.ca
Primary Website: www.vulcanadvocate.com
Published: Wed
Avg Paid Circ: 1032
Avg Free Circ: 11
Audit By: CMCA
Audit Date: 31.12.2014
Personnel: Shawn Cornell (Publisher); Stephen Tipper (Editor); Roxanne MacKintosh (Reg. Dir. of Adv.)
Parent company (for newspapers): Postmedia Network Inc.

WABASCA FEVER

Street address 1: 12015 76 Street
Street address city: Wabasca
Province/Territory: AB
Postal code: T0G 2K0
Country: Canada
General Phone: (780) 891-2108
General Fax: (888) 318-5555
General/National Adv. E-mail: wabascafever@shaw.ca
Display Adv. E-mail: wabascafever@shaw.ca
Classified Adv. e-mail: wabascafever@shaw.ca
Editorial e-mail: wabascafever@shaw.ca
Published: Thur
Avg Paid Circ: 630
Avg Free Circ: 250
Audit By: Sworn/Estimate/Non-Audited
Audit Date: 12.07.2019
Personnel: Patricia Thomas; Bruce Thomas (Pub.)
Parent company (for newspapers): Title

WAINWRIGHT STAR EDGE

Street address 1: 1027 3rd Ave
Street address city: Wainwright

Province/Territory: AB
Postal code: T9W 1T6
County: MD of Wainwright
Country: Canada
General Phone: (780) 842-4465
General Fax: (780) 842-2760
Advertising Phone: (780) 842-4465 ext.112
General/National Adv. E-mail: classifieds@starnews.ca
Display Adv. E-mail: patrick@starnews.ca
Classified Adv. e-mail: classifieds@starnews.ca
Editorial e-mail: zak@starnews.ca
Primary Website: www.starnews.ca
Published: Fri
Avg Paid Circ: 0
Avg Free Circ: 6500
Audit By: VAC
Audit Date: 6/31/2017
Personnel: Roger Holmes (Pub.); Patrick Moroz (Adv. Sales); Sherry Shatz (Sales & Promo); Zak McLachlan (Editor); Barb Tywoniuk (Graphic Design Dept. Manager)
Parent company (for newspapers): Star News Inc.

WESTWIND WEEKLY NEWS

Street address 1: 74a South - 1st Street West
Street address 2: Box 9
Street address city: Magrath
Province/Territory: AB
Postal code: T0K 1J0
Country: Canada
General Phone: (403) 758-6911
General Fax: (403) 758-3661
Display Adv. E-mail: sales@westwindweekly.com
Primary Website: www.westwindweekly.com
Published: Thur
Avg Paid Circ: 0
Avg Free Circ: 51
Audit By: VAC
Audit Date: 31.12.2015
Personnel: Valorie Wiebe (Pub.); Maggie Belisle (Adv. Sales Consult.); Joan Bly (Office Admin.); J.W Schnarr (Ed.)

WETASKIWIN TIMES

Street address 1: 5013 51 St.
Street address city: Wetaskiwin
Province/Territory: AB
Postal code: T9A 1L4
County: Canada
Country: Canada
General Phone: (780) 352-2231
General Fax: (780) 352-4333
General/National Adv. E-mail: production@wetaskiwintimes.com
Display Adv. E-mail: pam.tremaine@sunmedia.ca
Classified Adv. e-mail: pam.tremaine@sunmedia.ca
Editorial e-mail: editor@sunmedia.ca
Primary Website: www.wetaskiwintimes.com
Published: Wed
Avg Free Circ: 9957
Audit By: VAC
Audit Date: 31.12.2015
Personnel: Adam Roy (Prodn. Mgr.); Nick Goetz (Pub.); Clara Mitchell (Office Mgr.); Pam Tremaine (Adv. Mgr.); Sarah Swenson (Ed.)
Parent company (for newspapers): Postmedia Network Inc.

BRITISH COLUMBIA

100 MILE HOUSE FREE PRESS

Street address 1: #1-250 Birch Ave
Street address city: 100 Mile House
Province/Territory: BC
Postal code: V0K 2E0
Country: Canada
General Phone: (250) 395-2219
General/National Adv. E-mail: publisher@100milefreepress.net
Display Adv. E-mail: publisher@100milefreepress.net
Classified Adv. e-mail: classifieds@blackpress.ca
Editorial e-mail: newsroom@100milefreepress.net
Primary Website: www.100milefreepress.net
Published: Thur
Avg Paid Circ: 1342
Avg Free Circ: 3987
Audit By: CMCA
Audit Date: 17.08.2022
Personnel: Martina Dopf (Publisher); Debbie Theoret (Creative); Evan Fentiman (Creative); Sabrina Ede (Multi-Media Sales Consultant); Chris Nickless (Sales); Bonny Banas (Administration); Patrick Davies (Multi-Media Reporter); Fiona Grisswell (Multi-Media Reporter); Kerri Mingo (Advertising Creative); Carole Rooney (Reporter); Lori Brodie (Reception/Circulation); Max Winkelman (Ed.)
Parent company (for newspapers): Black Press Group Ltd.

ALBERNI VALLEY NEWS

Street address 1: 4918 Napier Street,
Street address city: Port Alberni
Province/Territory: BC
Postal code: V9Y 6H2

ARROW LAKES NEWS

Street address 1: 89 1st Avenue Northwest
Street address city: Nakusp
Province/Territory: BC
Postal code: V0G 1R0
County: Canada
Country: Canada
General Phone: (250) 265-3841
General/National Adv. E-mail: newsroom@arrowlakesnews.com; sales@arrowlakesnews.com
Display Adv. E-mail: sales@arrowlakesnews.com
Editorial e-mail: newsroom@arrowlakesnews.com
Primary Website: www.arrowlakenews.com
Published: Wed
Avg Paid Circ: 585
Avg Free Circ: 10
Audit By: VAC
Audit Date: 30.06.2017
Personnel: Eric Lawson (Pub.)
Parent company (for newspapers): Black Press Group Ltd.

BARRIERE STAR JOURNAL

Street address 1: 1-4353 Conner Road
Street address city: Barriere
Province/Territory: BC
Postal code: V0E 1E0
County: Canada
Country: Canada
General Phone: (250) 672-5611
General Fax: (250) 672-9900
General/National Adv. E-mail: office@starjournal.net
Display Adv. E-mail: advertising@starjournal.net
Classified Adv. e-mail: advertising@starjournal.net
Editorial e-mail: news@starjournal.net
Primary Website: www.starjournal.net
Published: Thur
Avg Paid Circ: 2043
Avg Free Circ: 37
Audit By: VAC
Audit Date: 12.12.2017
Personnel: Jill Hayward (Ed.); Lisa Quiding (Adv./Office/Production)
Parent company (for newspapers): Black Press Group Ltd.

BOWEN ISLAND UNDERCURRENT

Street address 1: 102-495 Bowen Trunk Rd.
Street address city: Bowen Island
Province/Territory: BC
Postal code: V0N 1V0
County: Canada
Country: Canada
General Phone: (604) 947-2442
General Fax: (604) 947-0148
Advertising Phone: (604) 947-2442
Editorial Phone: (604) 947-2442
General/National Adv. E-mail: publisher@bowenislandundercurrent.com
Display Adv. E-mail: ads@bowenislandundercurrent.com
Classified Adv. e-mail: ads@bowenislandundercurrent.com
Editorial e-mail: editor@bowenislandundercurrent.com
Primary Website: www.bowenislandundercurrent.com
Published: Fri
Avg Free Circ: 73
Audit By: VAC
Audit Date: 31.05.2016
Personnel: Martha Perkins (Ed.); Kaana Bjork (Prodn. Mgr.); Maureen Sawasy (Adv. Sales); Peter Kvarnstrom (Pub.)
Parent company (for newspapers): Glacier Media Group

BRIDGE RIVER LILLOOET NEWS

Street address 1: 979 Main St.
Street address city: Lillooet
Province/Territory: BC
Postal code: V0K 1V0
County: Canada
Country: Canada
General Phone: (250) 256-4219
General Fax: (250) 256-4210
Advertising Phone: (778) 773-4797
General/National Adv. E-mail: pub@lillooetnews.net
Display Adv. E-mail: sales@lillooetnews.net
Editorial e-mail: editor@lillooetnews.net
Primary Website: www.lillooetnews.net
Published: Wed
Avg Paid Circ: 1709
Avg Free Circ: 16
Audit By: VAC
Audit Date: 28.02.2016
Personnel: Wendy Fraser (Ed.); Bruce MacLennan (Publisher); Eliza Payne (Sales Associate)
Parent company (for newspapers): Glacier Media Group

BRITISH COLUMBIA/YUKON COMMUNITY NEWSPAPERS ASSOCIATION

Street address 1: #9 West Broadway
Street address city: Vancouver
Province/Territory: BC
Postal code: V5Y 1P1
Country: Canada
General Phone: (604) 669-9222
General/National Adv. E-mail: info@bccommunitynews.com
Primary Website: www.bccommunitynews.com
Personnel: George Affleck (Gen. Mgr.)

BURNABY NOW

Street address 1: 3430 Brighton Ave.
Street address 2: Ste. 201a
Street address city: Burnaby
Province/Territory: BC
Postal code: V5A 3H4
Country: Canada
General Phone: (604) 444-3451
General Fax: (604) 444-3460
Advertising Phone: (604) 444-3030
Editorial Phone: (604) 444-3007
General/National Adv. E-mail: editorial@burnabynow.com
Display Adv. E-mail: chendrix@burnabynow.com
Editorial e-mail: ptracy@royalcityrecord.com
Primary Website: burnabynow.com
Published: Wed Fri
Avg Paid Circ: 0
Avg Free Circ: 43521
Audit By: CCAB
Audit Date: 23.11.2017
Personnel: Lara Graham (Pub.); Pat Tracy (Ed.); Cynthia Hendrix (Adv.); Dan Olson (Sports Ed.)
Parent company (for newspapers): Glacier Media Group

BURNS LAKES DISTRICT NEWS

Street address 1: 23 3rd Ave.
Street address city: Burns Lake
Province/Territory: BC
Postal code: V0J 1E0
Country: Canada
General Phone: (250) 692-7526
General Fax: (250) 692-3685
General/National Adv. E-mail: newsroom@ldnews.net; advertising@ldnews.net
Display Adv. E-mail: advertising@ldnews.net
Classified Adv. e-mail: advertising@ldnews.net
Editorial e-mail: newsroom@ldnews.net
Primary Website: www.ldnews.net
Published: Wed
Avg Paid Circ: 1181
Avg Free Circ: 117
Audit By: VAC
Audit Date: 30.06.2017
Personnel: Laura Blackwell (Adv. Mgr./Pub.); Annamarie Douglas (Prod. Mgr.); Kim Piper (front office); Flavio Nienow (Editor)
Parent company (for newspapers): Black Press Group Ltd.

CALEDONIA COURIER

Street address 1: Box 1298
Street address city: Fort St. James
Province/Territory: BC
Postal code: V0J 3A0
Country: Canada
General Phone: (250) 567-9258
General Fax: (250) 567-2070
General/National Adv. E-mail: newsroom@ominecaexpress.com
Display Adv. E-mail: advertising@ominecaexpress.com
Primary Website: www.caledoniacourier.com
Published: Wed
Avg Paid Circ: 562
Avg Free Circ: 31
Audit By: VAC
Audit Date: 30.06.2016
Personnel: Pam Berger (Pub./Sales Mgr.); Ruth Lloyd (Ed.); Julia Beal (Prod.); Wendy Haslam (Prod.); Mariella Drogomatz (Circ.)
Parent company (for newspapers): Black Press Group Ltd.

CHILLIWACK TIMES

Street address 1: 45951 Trethewey Ave.
Street address city: Chilliwack
Province/Territory: BC
Postal code: V2P 1K4
Country: Canada
General Phone: (604) 792-9117
General Fax: (604) 792-9300
General/National Adv. E-mail: editor@chilliwacktimes.com
Display Adv. E-mail: nbastaja@chilliwacktimes.com
Editorial e-mail: kgoudswaard@chilliwacktimes.com
Primary Website: www.chilliwacktimes.com
Published: Thur
Avg Free Circ: 27605
Audit By: AAM
Audit Date: 30.09.2016
Personnel: Ken Goudswaard (Ed.); Jean Hincks (Pub.)

CLOVERDALE REPORTER

Street address 1: 17586 56a Ave.
Street address city: Surrey
Province/Territory: BC
Postal code: V3S 1G3
Country: Canada
General Phone: (604) 575-2400
Advertising Phone: (604) 575-2423
Display Adv. E-mail: cynthia.dunsmore@cloverdalereporter.com
Classified Adv. e-mail: bcclassifieds@blackpress.com
Editorial e-mail: editor@cloverdalereporter.com
Primary Website: www.cloverdalereporter.com
Published: Wed
Avg Free Circ: 16159
Audit By: CMCA
Audit Date: 31.03.2018
Personnel: Cynthia Dunsmore (Sales Representative); Sam Anderson (Ed.); Grace Kennedy (Reporter)
Parent company (for newspapers): Black Press Group Ltd.

COAST REPORTER

Street address 1: 5485 Wharf Road
Street address city: Sechelt
Province/Territory: BC
Postal code: V0N 3A0
Country: Canada
General Phone: (604) 885-4811
General Fax: (604) 885-4818
General/National Adv. E-mail: pkvarnstrom@coastreporter.net
Display Adv. E-mail: pat@coastreporter.net
Classified Adv. e-mail: classified@coastreporter.net
Editorial e-mail: editor@coastreporter.net
Primary Website: www.coastreporter.net
Published: Fri
Avg Paid Circ: 31
Avg Free Circ: 11639
Audit By: VAC

Audit Date: 30.06.2016
Personnel: Peter Kvarnstrom (Pub.); Christine Wood (Circ. Mgr.); John Gleeson (Ed./Assoc. Pub.); Pat Paproski (Sales Mgr.); Shelley Alleyne (Class. Supv.)
Parent company (for newspapers): Glacier Media Group

COMOX VALLEY ECHO

Street address 1: 407-e Fifth Street
Street address city: Courtenay
Province/Territory: BC
Postal code: V9N 1J7
County: Canada
Country: Canada
General Phone: (250) 334-4722
General Fax: (250) 334-3172
General/National Adv. E-mail: echo@comoxvalleyecho.com
Display Adv. E-mail: keith.currie@comoxvalleyecho.com
Classified Adv. e-mail: debra.fowler@comoxvalleyecho.com
Editorial e-mail: echo@comoxvalleyecho.com
Primary Website: www.comoxvalleyecho.com
Published: Fri
Avg Paid Circ: 50
Avg Free Circ: 23000
Audit By: CCAB
Audit Date: 17.03.2013
Personnel: Keith Currie (Publisher); Debra Martin (Mng. Ed.); Ryan Getz (Prodn. Mgr.)

COMOX VALLEY RECORD

Street address 1: 407D Fifth Street
Street address city: Courtenay
Province/Territory: BC
Postal code: V9N 1J7
Country: Canada
General Phone: (250) 338-5811
General/National Adv. E-mail: publisher@comoxvalleyrecord.com
Display Adv. E-mail: keith.currie@comoxvalleyrecord.com
Classified Adv. e-mail: keith.currie@comoxvalleyrecord.com
Editorial e-mail: terry.farrell@comoxvalleyrecord.com
Primary Website: comoxvalleyrecord.com
Published: Tues`Thur
Avg Paid Circ: 53
Avg Free Circ: 21566
Audit By: AAM
Audit Date: 31.03.2019
Personnel: Terry Marshall (Circ. Mgr.); Terry Farrell (Ed.); Susan Granberg (Prodn. Mgr.); Keith Currie (Pub.)
Parent company (for newspapers): Black Press Group Ltd.

COWICHAN VALLEY CITIZEN

Street address 1: 251 Jubilee Street
Street address city: Duncan
Province/Territory: BC
Postal code: V9L 1W8
County: Canada
Country: Canada
General Phone: (250) 748-2666
General/National Adv. E-mail: news@cowichanvalleycitizen.com
Display Adv. E-mail: warren.goulding@blackpress.ca
Classified Adv. e-mail: bcclassifieds@blackpress.ca
Editorial e-mail: editor@cowichanvalleycitizen.com
Primary Website: cowichanvalleycitizen.com
Published: Wed`Fri
Avg Free Circ: 20910
Audit By: AAM
Audit Date: 31.03.2019
Personnel: Warren Goulding (Pub./Adv. Mgr.)
Parent company (for newspapers): Torstar

CRANBROOK DAILY TOWNSMAN

Street address 1: 822 Cranbrook St. N.
Street address city: Cranbrook
Province/Territory: BC
Postal code: V1C 3R9
Country: Canada
General Phone: (250) 426-5201
General Fax: (250) 426-5003
Advertising Phone: (250) 426-5201
Editorial Phone: (250) 426-5201
General/National Adv. E-mail: sueb@blackpress.ca
Display Adv. E-mail: zena.williams@blackpress.ca
Classified Adv. e-mail: zena.williams@blackpress.ca
Editorial e-mail: barry.coulter@cranbrooktownsman.com
Primary Website: www.cranbrooktownsman.com
Published: Wed`Thur`Fri
Avg Paid Circ: 3500
Audit By: CMCA
Audit Date: 31.12.2015
Personnel: Zena Williams (Pub.); Barry Coulter (Ed.); Nicole Koran (Adv. Sales Mgr.); Jennifer Leiman (Office Mgr.)
Parent company (for newspapers): Black Press Group Ltd.

CRESTON VALLEY ADVANCE

Street address 1: 1018 Canyon St.
Street address city: Creston
Province/Territory: BC
Postal code: V0B 1G0
County: Canada
Country: Canada
General Phone: (250) 428-2266
General Fax: (250) 483-1909
Display Adv. E-mail: advertising@crestonvalleyadvance.ca
Editorial e-mail: editor@crestonvalleyadvance.ca
Primary Website: www.crestonvalleyadvance.ca
Published: Thur
Avg Paid Circ: 2
Avg Free Circ: 9
Audit By: VAC
Audit Date: 31.07.2016
Personnel: Lorne Eckersley (Pub.); Diane Audette (Circ. Mgr.); Brian Lorns (Ed.); Anita Horton (Sales Coord.); Brian Lawrence (Ed.); Jacky Smith (Prod. Department)
Parent company (for newspapers): Torstar

DELTA OPTIMIST

Street address 1: 5008-47a Avenue
Street address city: Delta
Province/Territory: BC
Postal code: V4K 1T8
Country: Canada
General Phone: (604) 946-4451
General Fax: (604) 946-5680
General/National Adv. E-mail: tsiba@delta-optimist.com
Display Adv. E-mail: dhamilton@delta-optimist.com
Editorial e-mail: editor@delta-optimist.com
Primary Website: delta-optimist.com
Published: Wed`Fri
Avg Paid Circ: 0
Avg Free Circ: 17029
Audit By: CCAB
Audit Date: 22.11.2017
Personnel: Dave Hamilton (Gen Mgr); Ted Murphy (Ed.); Alvin Brouwer (Pub)
Parent company (for newspapers): Glacier Media Group

DESIBUZZZCANADA

Street address 1: 16318 - 113B Avenue
Street address city: Surrey
Province/Territory: BC
Postal code: V4N 5A2
Country: Canada
General Phone: 16048803463
Advertising Phone: 1604-880-3463
Editorial Phone: 16047104945
General/National Adv. E-mail: news@desibuzzbc.com
Display Adv. E-mail: editorpd@hotmail.com
Classified Adv. e-mail: classifieds@desibuzzbc.com
Editorial e-mail: editor@desibuzzbc.com
Primary Website: www.desibuzzbc.com
Published: Mon`Tues`Wed`Thur`Fri`Sat`Sun`Other
Avg Paid Circ: 1000
Avg Free Circ: 18000

EAGLE VALLEY NEWS

Street address 1: 171 Shuswap St. Nw
Street address city: Salmon Arm
Province/Territory: BC
Postal code: V1E 4N7
County: Canada
Country: Canada
General Phone: (250) 832-2131
General Fax: (250) 832-5140
General/National Adv. E-mail: publisher@saobserver.net
Display Adv. E-mail: advertising@saobserver.net
Classified Adv. e-mail: classifieds@eaglevalleynews.com
Editorial e-mail: newsroom@saobserver.net
Primary Website: www.eaglevalleynews.com
Published: Wed
Avg Paid Circ: 376
Avg Free Circ: 12
Audit By: CMCA
Audit Date: 31.05.2017
Personnel: Rick Proznick (Adv. Mgr); Tracy Hughes (Ed.); Laura Lavigne (Sales); Lachian Labere (Reporter/ Columnist)
Parent company (for newspapers): Black Press Group Ltd.

GABRIOLA SOUNDER

Street address 1: 510 North Rd
Street address 2: Unit 1
Street address city: Gabriola Island
Province/Territory: BC
Postal code: V0R 1X0
Country: Canada
General Phone: (250) 247-9337
General Fax: (250) 247-8147
Advertising Phone: (250) 247-9337
Editorial Phone: (250) 247-9337
General/National Adv. E-mail: derek@soundernews.com
Display Adv. E-mail: sarah@soundernew.com
Classified Adv. e-mail: derek@soundernews.com
Editorial e-mail: derek@soundernews.com
Primary Website: www.soundernews.com
Published: Tues
Avg Paid Circ: 50
Avg Free Circ: 2750
Audit By: Sworn/Estimate/Non-Audited
Audit Date: 12.07.2019
Personnel: Sarah Holmes (Pub.); Derek Kilbourn (Ed./ Sales/Prod. Mgr.)
Parent company (for newspapers): Gabriola Sounder Media Inc.

GEORGIA STRAIGHT

Street address 1: 1635 West Broadway
Street address city: Vancouver
Province/Territory: BC
Postal code: V6J 1W9
Country: Canada
General Phone: (604) 730-7000
General Fax: (604) 730-7010
General/National Adv. E-mail: gs.info@straight.com
Display Adv. E-mail: sales@straight.com
Editorial e-mail: contact@straight.com
Primary Website: www.straight.com
Published: Thur
Avg Paid Circ: 25
Avg Free Circ: 81544
Audit By: VAC
Audit Date: 30.06.2017
Personnel: Tara Lalanne (Sales Director); Dexter Vosper (Circulation Manager); Dennis Jangula (IT Director); Charlie Smith (Editor)
Parent company (for newspapers): Vancouver Free Press Publishing Corp.

GOLDEN STAR

Street address 1: 413a N. Ninth Ave.
Street address city: Golden
Province/Territory: BC
Postal code: V0H 1H0
Country: Canada
General Phone: (250) 344-5251
General Fax: (250) 344-7344
General/National Adv. E-mail: publisher@thegoldenstar.net
Display Adv. E-mail: advertising@thegoldenstar.net
Classified Adv. e-mail: advertising@thegoldenstar.net
Editorial e-mail: editor@thegoldenstar.net
Primary Website: www.thegoldenstar.net
Published: Wed
Avg Paid Circ: 502
Avg Free Circ: 32
Audit By: VAC
Audit Date: 30.06.2016
Personnel: Sue Hein (Classified Mgr.); Michele Lapointe (Pub.); Jessica Schwitek (Ed.)
Parent company (for newspapers): Black Press Group Ltd.

GOLDSTREAM GAZETTE

Street address 1: 103-9843 Second Street
Street address city: Sidney
Province/Territory: BC
Postal code: V8L 3C6
County: Langford
Country: Canada
General Phone: 250) 656-1151
General Fax: 250) 656-5526
Display Adv. E-mail: publisher@peninsulanewsreview.com
Editorial e-mail: editor@goldstreamgazette.com
Primary Website: goldstreamgazette.com
Published: Wed`Fri
Avg Free Circ: 17257
Audit By: AAM
Audit Date: 31.03.2019
Personnel: Mellissa Mitchell (Circ. Mgr.); Michelle Cabana (Pub.); Dale Naftel (Pub.)
Parent company (for newspapers): Black Press Group Ltd.

GULF ISLANDS DRIFTWOOD

Street address 1: 328 Lower Ganges Rd.
Street address city: Salt Spring Island
Province/Territory: BC
Postal code: V8K 2V3
County: Canada
Country: Canada
General Phone: (250) 537-9933
General Fax: (250) 537-2613
General/National Adv. E-mail: inquiries@driftwoodgulfislandsmedia.com
Display Adv. E-mail: sales@driftwoodgimedia.com
Editorial e-mail: news@driftwoodgimedia.com
Primary Website: www.driftwoodgulfislandsmedia.com
Published: Wed
Avg Paid Circ: 2300
Avg Free Circ: 2200
Audit By: Sworn/Estimate/Non-Audited
Audit Date: 12.07.2019
Personnel: Gail Sjuberg (Mng. Ed.); Lorraine Sullivan (Prodn. Mgr.); Amber Ogilvie (Publisher)
Parent company (for newspapers): Driftwood Publishing Ltd.

HAIDA GWAII OBSERVER

Street address 1: 623 7th St.
Street address city: Queen Charlotte
Province/Territory: BC
Postal code: V0T 1S0
Country: Canada
General Phone: (250) 559-4680
General Fax: (250) 559-8433
Advertising Phone: (250) 559-4680
Editorial Phone: (250) 559-4680
General/National Adv. E-mail: observer@haidagwaii.ca
Display Adv. E-mail: chris.williams@haidagwaiiobserver.com
Editorial e-mail: observer@haidagwaii.ca
Primary Website: www.haidagwaiiobserver.com
Published: Fri
Avg Paid Circ: 963
Avg Free Circ: 2
Audit By: VAC
Audit Date: 31.08.2016
Personnel: Todd Hamilton (Pub./Ed.); Chris Williams (Sales Mgr.)

HOPE STANDARD

Street address 1: 540 Wallace St.
Street address city: Hope
Province/Territory: BC
Postal code: V0X 1L0
County: Canada
Country: Canada
General Phone: (604) 869-2421
General Fax: (604) 869-7351
General/National Adv. E-mail: news@hopestandard.com
Display Adv. E-mail: sales@hopestandard.com
Classified Adv. e-mail: classifieds@hopestandard.com
Primary Website: www.hopestandard.com
Published: Thur
Avg Paid Circ: 346

Avg Free Circ: 0
Audit By: VAC
Audit Date: 30.06.2016
Personnel: Patti Desjardins (Adv. Mgr.); Janice McDonald (Circ. Mgr.); Carly Ferguson (Pub.); X.Y. Zeng (Ed.)
Parent company (for newspapers): Torstar

HOUSTON TODAY

Street address 1: 3232 Hwy 16 W.
Street address city: Houston
Province/Territory: BC
Postal code: V0J 1Z1
County: Canada
Country: Canada
General Phone: (250) 845-2890
General Fax: (250) 847-2995
General/National Adv. E-mail: editor@houston-today.com
Display Adv. E-mail: advertising@houston-today.com
Primary Website: www.houston-today.com
Published: Wed
Avg Paid Circ: 983
Avg Free Circ: 305
Audit By: VAC
Audit Date: 30.06.2016
Personnel: Mary Ann Ruiter (Ed.); Todd Hamilton (Mng. Ed.); Jackie Lieuwen (Reporter)
Parent company (for newspapers): Torstar

INVERMERE VALLEY ECHO

Street address 1: 1008-8th Avenue
Street address 2: #8
Street address city: Invermere
Province/Territory: BC
Postal code: V0A 1K0
County: n/a
Country: Canada
General Phone: (250) 341-6299
General/National Adv. E-mail: general@invermerevalleyecho.com
Display Adv. E-mail: advertising@invermerevalleyecho.com
Editorial e-mail: editor@invermerevalleyecho.com
Primary Website: www.invermerevalleyecho.com
Published: Wed
Avg Free Circ: 488
Audit By: VAC
Audit Date: 30.06.2016
Personnel: Dean Midyette (Pub.); Nicole Trigg (Ed.); Amanda Nason (Adv. Sales)
Parent company (for newspapers): Torstar

KAMLOOPS THIS WEEK

Street address 1: 1365b Dalhousie Dr.
Street address city: Kamloops
Province/Territory: BC
Postal code: V2C 5P6
Country: Canada
General Phone: (250) 374-7467
General Fax: (250) 374-1033
Editorial Phone: (250) 374-7467
General/National Adv. E-mail: editor@kamloopsthisweek.com; ktw@kamloopsthisweek.com
Display Adv. E-mail: sales@kamloopsthisweek.com
Editorial e-mail: editor@kamloopsthisweek.com
Primary Website: kamloopsthisweek.com
Published: Tues`Thur`Fri
Avg Paid Circ: 0
Avg Free Circ: 30602
Audit By: CCAB
Audit Date: 23.11.2017
Personnel: Kelly Hall; Chris Foulds (Pub & Ed)
Parent company (for newspapers): Thompson River Publications

KELOWNA CAPITAL NEWS

Street address 1: 2495 Enterprise Way
Street address city: Kelowna
Province/Territory: BC
Postal code: V1X 7K2
County: Canada
Country: Canada
General Phone: (250) 763-3212
General Fax: (250) 862-5275
General/National Adv. E-mail: candy@blackpress.ca
Display Adv. E-mail: karen.hill@blackpress.ca
Classified Adv. e-mail: karen.hill@blackpress.ca
Editorial e-mail: karen.hill@blackpress.ca
Primary Website: kelownacapnews.com
Published: Tues`Thur`Fri
Avg Free Circ: 42292
Audit By: AAM
Audit Date: 31.03.2019
Personnel: Karen Hill (Pub.); Nigel Lark (Adv. Mgr.); Gary Jhonston (Sales Mgr.); Glenn Beaudry (Circ. Mgr.); Tessa Ringness (Prodn. Mgr.); Kevin Parnell (Mng. Ed.)
Parent company (for newspapers): Black Press Group Ltd.

KEREMEOS REVIEW

Street address 1: 605 7th Avenue
Street address city: Keremeos
Province/Territory: BC
Postal code: V0X 1N0
Country: Canada
General Phone: (250) 499-2653
General Fax: (250) 499-2645
General/National Adv. E-mail: dkendall@blackpress.ca
Display Adv. E-mail: publisher@keremeosreview.com
Classified Adv. e-mail: publisher@keremeosreview.com
Primary Website: www.keremeosreview.com
Published: Thur
Avg Paid Circ: 889
Avg Free Circ: 51
Audit By: VAC
Audit Date: 31.03.2016
Personnel: Don Kendall (Pub.); Tara Bowie (Ed.); Andrea DeMeer (Assoc. Pub.); Sandi Nolan (Adv. Rep.)
Parent company (for newspapers): Torstar

LAKE COUNTRY CALENDAR

Street address 1: 2495 Enterprise Way
Street address city: Kelowna
Province/Territory: BC
Postal code: V1X 7K2
County: Lake Country
Country: Canada
General Phone: (250) 763-3212
General Fax: (250) 386-2624
Display Adv. E-mail: ads4web@blackpress.ca
Editorial e-mail: newsroom@lakecountrynews.net
Primary Website: www.lakecountrycalendar.net
Published: Wed
Avg Paid Circ: 306
Avg Free Circ: 3779
Audit By: Sworn/Estimate/Non-Audited
Audit Date: 12.07.2019
Personnel: Barry Gerding (Ed.); Jonathan Lawson (Trafficking Coordinator); Kolby Solinsky (Online Editor); Mark Walker (Director of Sales and Marketing)
Parent company (for newspapers): Torstar

LANGLEY ADVANCE

Street address 1: 6375 202 St.
Street address 2: Suite 112
Street address city: Langley
Province/Territory: BC
Postal code: V2Y 1N1
County: Canada
Country: Canada
General Phone: (604) 534-8641
General Fax: (604) 534-3383
General/National Adv. E-mail: rmcadams@langleyadvance.com
Display Adv. E-mail: peggy.obrien@langleyadvance.com
Editorial e-mail: rhooper@langleyadvance.com
Primary Website: www.langleyadvance.com
Published: Tues`Thur
Avg Paid Circ: 0
Avg Free Circ: 27538
Audit By: AAM
Audit Date: 31.03.2019
Personnel: Lisa Farquharson (Pub); Peggy O'Brien (Sales Mgr.); Roxanne Hooper (Ed)
Parent company (for newspapers): Black Press Group Ltd.

LANGLEY TIMES

Street address 1: 20258 Fraser Hwy.
Street address city: Langley
Province/Territory: BC
Postal code: V3A 4E6
Country: Canada
General Phone: (604) 533-4157
General Fax: (604) 533-4623
General/National Adv. E-mail: newsroom@langleytimes.com
Display Adv. E-mail: admanager@langleytimes.com
Editorial e-mail: newsroom@langleytimes.com
Primary Website: www.langleytimes.com
Published: Tues`Thur
Avg Free Circ: 28417
Audit By: AAM
Audit Date: 31.03.2019
Personnel: Kelly Myers (Sales Mgr); Lisa Farquharson (Pub); Brenda Anderson (Ed)
Parent company (for newspapers): Black Press Group Ltd.

MERRITT HERALD

Street address 1: 2090 Granite Ave.
Street address city: Merritt
Province/Territory: BC
Postal code: V1K 1B8
Country: Canada
General Phone: (250) 378-4241
General Fax: (250) 378-6818
General/National Adv. E-mail: newsroom@merrittherald.com
Display Adv. E-mail: sales2@merrittherald.com
Classified Adv. e-mail: classifieds@merrittherald.com
Editorial e-mail: newsroom@merrittherald.com
Primary Website: www.merrittherald.com
Published: Thur
Avg Paid Circ: 1092
Avg Free Circ: 5589
Audit By: VAC
Audit Date: 30.06.2016
Personnel: Theresa Arnold (Pub.); Cole Wagner (Ed); Kenneth Couture (Office Mgr)
Parent company (for newspapers): Aberdeen Publishing; Merrit Newspapers

MISSION CITY RECORD

Street address 1: 33047 1st Ave.
Street address city: Mission
Province/Territory: BC
Postal code: V2V 1G2
County: Mission - Abbotsford
Country: Canada
General Phone: (604) 826-6221
General Fax: (604) 826-8266
Advertising Phone: (800) 363-2232
General/National Adv. E-mail: news@missioncityrecord.com
Display Adv. E-mail: karen.murtagh@missioncityrecord.com
Classified Adv. e-mail: adcontrol@missioncityrecord.com
Editorial e-mail: kevin.mills@missioncityrecord.com
Primary Website: www.missioncityrecord.com
Published: Fri
Avg Paid Circ: 21
Avg Free Circ: 10968
Audit By: AAM
Audit Date: 31.12.2018
Personnel: Carly Ferguson (Pub); Kevin Mills (Ed); Krista Stobbe (Office Mgr.)
Parent company (for newspapers): Black Press Group Ltd.

NANAIMO NEWS BULLETIN

Street address 1: 777 Poplar St.
Street address city: Nanaimo
Province/Territory: BC
Postal code: V9S 2H7
County: Canada
Country: Canada
General Phone: (250) 753-3707
General Fax: (250) 753-0788
Editorial Phone: (250) 734-4621
Display Adv. E-mail: sueb@blackpress.ca
Editorial e-mail: editor@nanaimobulletin.com
Primary Website: www.nanaimobulletin.com
Published: Mon`Fri`Sat
Avg Free Circ: 31789
Audit By: AAM
Audit Date: 31.03.2019
Personnel: Sean McCue (Pub); Melissa Fryer (Ed.); Darrell Summerfelt (Prodn. Mgr.)
Parent company (for newspapers): Black Press Group Ltd.

NELSON STAR

Street address 1: 91 Baker Street, Suite B
Street address city: Nelson
Province/Territory: BC
Postal code: V1L 4G8
Country: Canada
General Phone: (877) 365-6397
Display Adv. E-mail: advertising@nelsonstar.com
Editorial e-mail: editor@nelsonstar.com
Primary Website: www.nelsonstar.com
Published: Wed`Fri
Avg Paid Circ: 0
Avg Free Circ: 8448
Audit By: VAC
Audit Date: 31.08.2016
Personnel: Eric Lawson (Publisher)
Parent company (for newspapers): Black Press Group Ltd.

NEW WESTMINSTER RECORD

Street address 1: 201a-3430 Brighton Ave
Street address city: New Westminster
Province/Territory: BC
Postal code: V5A 3H4
Country: Canada
General Phone: (604) 444-6451
Display Adv. E-mail: kgilmour@newwestrecord.ca
Classified Adv. e-mail: mmacleod@newwestrecord.ca
Editorial e-mail: ptracy@newwestrecord.ca
Primary Website: http://www.newwestrecord.ca/
Published: Wed
Avg Paid Circ: 0
Avg Free Circ: 16290
Audit By: CCAB
Audit Date: 30.09.2015
Personnel: Lara Graham (Pub); Pat Tracy (Ed); Dale Dorsett (Circ Mgr)
Parent company (for newspapers): Glacier Media Group

NORTH ISLAND GAZETTE

Street address 1: #3-7053 Market St.
Street address city: Port Hardy
Province/Territory: BC
Postal code: V0N 2P0
Country: Canada
General Phone: (250) 949-6225
General/National Adv. E-mail: production@northislandgazette.com
Display Adv. E-mail: sales@northislandgazette.com
Classified Adv. e-mail: viads@bcclassified.com
Editorial e-mail: publisher@northislandgazette.com
Primary Website: www.northislandgazette.com
Published: Wed
Avg Paid Circ: 1065
Avg Free Circ: 500
Audit By: CMCA
Audit Date: 30.11.2018
Personnel: Lilian Meerveld; Tyson Whitney; Thomas Kervin (Reporter); Natasha Griffiths (Advertising Sale Rep)
Parent company (for newspapers): Black Press Group Ltd.

NORTH ISLAND MIDWEEK

Street address 1: 765 Mcphee Ave
Street address city: Courtenay
Province/Territory: BC
Postal code: V9N 2Z7
County: Canada
Country: Canada
General Phone: (250) 287-9227
General Fax: (250) 287-3238
General/National Adv. E-mail: publisher@comoxvalleyrecord.com
Display Adv. E-mail: sueb@blackpress.ca
Editorial e-mail: editor@comoxvalleyrecord.com
Primary Website: www.northislandmidweek.com
Published: Wed
Avg Paid Circ: 40
Avg Free Circ: 37030
Audit By: CMCA
Audit Date: 31.08.2014
Personnel: Chrissie Bowker (Pub); Terry Farrell (Ed); Susan Granberg (Prod. Mgr.); Terry Marshall (Circ Mgr.)

Parent company (for newspapers): Black Press Group Ltd.

NORTH PEACE EXPRESS

Street address 1: 9916 98th St.
Street address city: Fort Saint John
Province/Territory: BC
Postal code: V1J 3T8
Country: Canada
General Phone: (250) 785-5631
General Fax: (250) 785-3522
General/National Adv. E-mail: ahnews@awink.com
Display Adv. E-mail: wj@ahnfsj.ca
Editorial e-mail: editor@ahnfsj.ca
Published: Sun
Avg Free Circ: 10200
Audit By: Sworn/Estimate/Non-Audited
Audit Date: 12.07.2019
Personnel: William Julian (Pub); Debbie Oberlin (Circ. Mgr.)

NORTH SHORE NEWS

Street address 1: 980 1st St. West, Unit 116
Street address city: North Vancouver
Province/Territory: BC
Postal code: V7P 3N4
County: Canada
Country: Canada
General Phone: (604) 985-2131
Advertising Phone: (604) 985-2131
Editorial Phone: (604) 985-2131
General/National Adv. E-mail: dfoot@nsnews.com
Display Adv. E-mail: display@nsnews.com
Classified Adv. e-mail: classifieds@van.net
Editorial e-mail: editor@nsnews.com
Primary Website: nsnews.com
Published: Wed`Fri`Sun
Avg Paid Circ: 0
Avg Free Circ: 57636
Audit By: CCAB
Audit Date: 23.11.2017
Personnel: Peter Kvarnstrom (Pub); Layne Christensen (Ed); Vicki Magnison (Dir, Sales & Marketing)
Parent company (for newspapers): Glacier Media Group

NORTH THOMPSON TIMES

Street address 1: 74 Young Rd
Street address 2: Unit 14
Street address city: Clearwater
Province/Territory: BC
Postal code: V0E 1N2
Country: Canada
General Phone: (250) 674-3343
General Fax: (250) 674-3410
General/National Adv. E-mail: newsroom@clearwatertimes.com
Display Adv. E-mail: classifieds@clearwatertimes.com
Editorial e-mail: newsroom@clearwatertimes.com
Primary Website: www.clearwatertimes.com
Published: Thur
Avg Paid Circ: 751
Avg Free Circ: 20
Audit By: CMCA
Audit Date: 30.03.2017
Personnel: Keith McNeill (Ed.); Yevonne Cline (Admin Coord./Sales Rep); Lorie Williston (Pub)
Parent company (for newspapers): Black Press Group Ltd.

NORTH/WEST SHORE OUTLOOK

Street address 1: 116-980 West 1st Street
Street address city: North Vancouver
Province/Territory: BC
Postal code: V7P 3N4
Country: Canada
General Phone: (604) 903-1000
General/National Adv. E-mail: publisher@northshoreoutlook.com
Display Adv. E-mail: vmagnison@nsnews.com
Classified Adv. e-mail: classifieds@van.net
Editorial e-mail: lchristensen@nsnews.com
Primary Website: www.northshoreoutlook.com
Published: Thur
Avg Free Circ: 28038
Audit By: CMCA
Audit Date: 31.12.2012
Personnel: Vicki Magnison (Sales & Mktg. Dir.); Peter Kvarnstrom (Pub); Dale Dorsett (Circ. Mgr.); Layne Christensen (Ed)

NORTHERN SENTINEL - KITIMAT

Street address 1: 626 Enterprise Ave.
Street address city: Kitimat
Province/Territory: BC
Postal code: V8C 2E4
County: Canada
Country: Canada
General Phone: (250) 632-6144
General Fax: (250) 639-9373
General/National Adv. E-mail: publisher@northernsentinel.com
Display Adv. E-mail: advertising@northernsentinel.com
Primary Website: www.northernsentinel.com
Published: Wed
Avg Paid Circ: 439
Avg Free Circ: 248
Audit By: VAC
Audit Date: 31.03.2016
Personnel: Louisa Genzale (Publisher); Sarah Campbell; Devyn Ens (Editor/Reporter); Johnsen Misty (Circulation)
Parent company (for newspapers): Black Press Group Ltd.

OAK BAY NEWS

Street address 1: 207a-2187 Oak Bay Avenue
Street address city: Victoria
Province/Territory: BC
Postal code: V8R 1G1
Country: Canada
General Phone: (250) 480-3251
Advertising Phone: (250) 480-3251
Editorial Phone: (250) 480-3260
Display Adv. E-mail: jgairdner@blackpress.ca
Classified Adv. e-mail: bcclassifieds@blackpress.ca
Editorial e-mail: editor@oakbaynews.com
Primary Website: www.oakbaynews.com
Published: Wed`Fri
Avg Paid Circ: 0
Avg Free Circ: 5995
Audit By: AAM
Audit Date: 31.03.2019
Personnel: Janet Gairdner (Pub.); Christine van Reeuwyk (Editor); Lyn Quan (Prod.); John Stewart (Advertising Consultant); Keri Coles (Multimedia Journalist)
Parent company (for newspapers): Black Press Group Ltd.

OKANAGAN ADVERTISER

Street address 1: 3400 Okanagan St.
Street address city: Armstrong
Province/Territory: BC
Postal code: V0E 1B0
County: Canada
Country: Canada
General Phone: (250) 546-3121
General Fax: (250) 546-3636
General/National Adv. E-mail: info@okadvertiser.com
Primary Website: OkanaganAdvertiser.com
Published: Thur
Avg Free Circ: 4000
Audit By: Sworn/Estimate/Non-Audited
Audit Date: 12.07.2019
Personnel: Will Hansma (Pub)
Parent company (for newspapers): Okanagan Valley Newspaper Group

OLIVER CHRONICLE

Street address 1: 6379 Main Street
Street address city: Oliver
Province/Territory: BC
Postal code: V0H 1T0
County: Canada
Country: Canada
General Phone: (250) 498-3711
General Fax: (250) 498-3966
General/National Adv. E-mail: office@oliverchronicle.com
Display Adv. E-mail: sales@oliverchronicle.com
Editorial e-mail: editor@oliverchronicle.com
Primary Website: www.oliverchronicle.com
Published: Wed
Avg Paid Circ: 1723
Avg Free Circ: 0
Audit By: VAC
Audit Date: 6/31/2015
Personnel: Lyonel Doherty (Ed.); Robert Doull; Linda Bolton (Pub.)

OSOYOOS TIMES

Street address 1: 8712 Main St.
Street address city: Osoyoos
Province/Territory: BC
Postal code: V0H 1V0
Country: Canada
General Phone: (250) 495-7225
General Fax: (250) 495-6616
General/National Adv. E-mail: admin@osoyoostimes.com
Display Adv. E-mail: sales@osoyoostimes.com
Editorial e-mail: editor@osoyoostimes.com
Primary Website: www.osoyoostimes.com
Published: Wed
Avg Paid Circ: 1783
Avg Free Circ: 0
Audit By: VAC
Audit Date: 31.12.2015
Personnel: Jocelyn Merit (Office Mgr.); Ken Baker (Adv. Mgr.); Keith Lacey (Ed); Linda Bolton (Mng. Dir.)

PARKSVILLE QUALICUM BEACH NEWS

Street address 1: 1b/2a 1209 East Island Highway Parksville Heritage Centre
Street address city: Parksville
Province/Territory: BC
Postal code: V9P 1R5
County: Canada
Country: Canada
General Phone: (250) 248-4341
General Fax: (250) 248-4655
General/National Adv. E-mail: publisher@pqbnews.com
Display Adv. E-mail: bboyd@pqbnews.com
Classified Adv. e-mail: viads@bcclassified.com
Editorial e-mail: editor@pqbnews.com
Primary Website: www.pqbnews.com
Published: Tues`Fri
Avg Paid Circ: 6
Avg Free Circ: 16476
Audit By: AAM
Audit Date: 31.03.2019
Personnel: Peter McCully (Pub.); John Harding (Ed.); Brenda Boyd (Sales Mgr.); Michele Graham (Circ. Mgr.)
Parent company (for newspapers): Black Press Group Ltd.

PENTICTON WESTERN NEWS

Street address 1: 2250 Camrose St.
Street address city: Penticton
Province/Territory: BC
Postal code: V2A 8R1
County: Canada
Country: Canada
General Phone: (250) 492-3636
General Fax: (250) 492-9843
General/National Adv. E-mail: ads@pentictonwesternnews.com
Display Adv. E-mail: larry@pentictonwesternnews.com
Classified Adv. e-mail: classifieds@pentictonwesternnews.com
Editorial e-mail: kpatton@pentictonwesternnews.com
Primary Website: www.pentictonwesternnews.com
Published: Wed`Fri
Avg Free Circ: 23010
Audit By: AAM
Audit Date: 31.03.2019
Personnel: Sue Kovacs (Circ. Mgr.); Shannon Simpson (Pub); Larry Mercier (Sales Mgr.); Kristi Patton (Ed)
Parent company (for newspapers): Black Press Group Ltd.

PIQUE NEWSMAGAZINE

Street address 1: 103-1390 Alpha Lake Rd.
Street address city: Whistler
Province/Territory: BC
Postal code: V0N 1B1
Country: Canada
General Phone: (604) 938-0202
General Fax: (604) 938-0201
General/National Adv. E-mail: sarah@piquenewsmagazine.com
Display Adv. E-mail: susan@piquenewsmagazine.com
Classified Adv. e-mail: traffic@piquenewsmagazine.com
Editorial e-mail: edit@piquenewsmagazine.com
Primary Website: www.piquenewsmagazine.com
Published: Thur
Avg Paid Circ: 41
Avg Free Circ: 10997
Audit By: VAC
Audit Date: 30.06.2017
Personnel: Clare Ogilvie (Ed.); Sarah Strother (Pub); Susan Hutchinson (Sales Mgr); Katie Bechtel (Circ Mgr); Jennifer Treptow (Sales Coord)
Parent company (for newspapers): Glacier Media Group; Pique Publishing Inc.

POWELL RIVER PEAK

Street address 1: 4400 Marine Ave.
Street address city: Powell River
Province/Territory: BC
Postal code: V8A 2K1
County: Powell River Regional District
Country: Canada
General Phone: (604) 485-5313
General Fax: (604) 485-5007
General/National Adv. E-mail: publisher@prpeak.com
Display Adv. E-mail: sales@prpeak.com
Classified Adv. e-mail: cindy@prpeak.com
Editorial e-mail: publisher@prpeak.com
Primary Website: www.prpeak.com
Published: Wed
Avg Paid Circ: 2084
Avg Free Circ: 48
Audit By: VAC
Audit Date: 31.12.2016
Personnel: Michele Stewart (Circ. Dir.); Jason Schreuers (Pub/Ed); Dot Campbell (Sales)
Parent company (for newspapers): Glacier Media Group

PRINCETON SIMILKAMEEN SPOTLIGHT

Street address 1: 282 Bridge St.
Street address city: Princeton
Province/Territory: BC
Postal code: V0X 1W0
Country: Canada
General Phone: (250) 295-3535
General Fax: (250) 295-7322
Display Adv. E-mail: advertising@similkameenspotlight.com
Editorial e-mail: editor@similkameenspotlight.com
Primary Website: www.similkameenspotlight.com
Published: Wed
Avg Paid Circ: 2227
Avg Free Circ: 43
Audit By: VAC
Audit Date: 30.06.2016
Personnel: Andrea Demeer; Andrea DeMeer (Ed/Assist. Pub); Don Kendall (Pub); Sandi Nolan (Adv Mgr.)
Parent company (for newspapers): Black Press Group Ltd.

QUESNEL CARIBOO OBSERVER

Street address 1: 188 Carson Ave.
Street address city: Quesnel
Province/Territory: BC
Postal code: V2J 2A8
Country: Canada
General Phone: (250) 992-2121
General Fax: (250) 992-5229
General/National Adv. E-mail: newsroom@quesnelobserver.com
Display Adv. E-mail: advertising@quesnelobserver.com
Classified Adv. e-mail: publisher@quesnelobserver.com
Editorial e-mail: editor@quesnelobserver.com
Primary Website: www.quesnelobserver.com
Published: Wed`Fri
Avg Paid Circ: 984
Avg Free Circ: 2487
Audit By: VAC
Audit Date: 30.06.2016
Personnel: Autumn McDonald (Ed.); Tracey Roberts (Pub/Sales Mgr.)

Parent company (for newspapers): Black Press Group Ltd.

REVELSTOKE REVIEW

Street address 1: 518 2nd St.
Street address city: Revelstoke
Province/Territory: BC
Postal code: V0E 2S0
County: Canada
Country: Canada
General Phone: (250) 837-4667
General Fax: (250) 837-2003
General/National Adv. E-mail: editor@revelstoktimesreview.com
Display Adv. E-mail: mavis@revelstoketimesreview.com
Editorial e-mail: editor@revelstoketimesreview.com
Primary Website: www.revelstoketimesreview.com
Published: Wed
Avg Paid Circ: 770
Avg Free Circ: 216
Audit By: VAC
Audit Date: 30.06.2016
Personnel: Mavis Cann (Pub./Adv Mgr); Fran Carlson (Office Mgr.); Alex Cooper (Ed)
Parent company (for newspapers): Black Press Group Ltd.

RICHMOND NEWS

Street address 1: #200-8211 Ackroyd Road
Street address city: Richmond
Province/Territory: BC
Postal code: V6X 2C9
Country: Canada
General Phone: (604) 270-8031
General Fax: (604) 270-2248
General/National Adv. E-mail: editor@richmond-news.com
Display Adv. E-mail: rakimow@richmond-news.com
Classified Adv. e-mail: classifieds@van.net
Editorial e-mail: eedmonds@richmond-news.com
Primary Website: richmond-news.com
Published: Thur
Avg Paid Circ: 0
Avg Free Circ: 46113
Audit By: CCAB
Audit Date: 22.11.2017
Personnel: Pierre Pelletier (Pub); Rob Akimow (Adv Dir); Eve Edmonds (Ed); Kristene Murray (Circ Mgr)
Parent company (for newspapers): Glacier Media Group; CanWest MediaWorks Publications, Inc.

ROSSLAND NEWS

Street address 1: 1810 8th Avenue
Street address 2: Unit 2
Street address city: Castlegar
Province/Territory: BC
Postal code: V1N 2Y2
Country: Canada
General Phone: (250) 365 6497
General/National Adv. E-mail: publisher@rosslandnews.com
Display Adv. E-mail: sales@rosslandnews.com
Editorial e-mail: newsroom@castlegarnews.com
Primary Website: www.rosslandnews.com
Published: Thur
Avg Paid Circ: 7
Avg Free Circ: 1063
Audit By: VAC
Audit Date: 30.04.2017
Personnel: Eric Lawson (Pub.); Jennifer Cowan (Ed)
Parent company (for newspapers): Black Press Group Ltd.

SAANICH NEWS

Street address 1: 104b-3550 Saanich Road
Street address city: Victoria
Province/Territory: BC
Postal code: V8X 1X2
Country: Canada
General Phone: (250) 381-3484
General Fax: (250) 386-2624
Display Adv. E-mail: staylor@saanichnews.com
Classified Adv. e-mail: rod.fraser@saanichnews.com
Editorial e-mail: editor@saanichnews.com
Primary Website: www.saanichnews.com
Published: Wed'Fri
Avg Free Circ: 30360
Audit By: AAM
Audit Date: 31.03.2019
Personnel: Rod Fraser (Sales); Oliver Sommer (Pub); Dan Ebenal (Ed); Miki Speirs (Circ Mgr); Sarah Taylor (Sales)
Parent company (for newspapers): Black Press Group Ltd.

SALMON ARM OBSERVER

Street address 1: 171 Shuswap St., Nw
Street address city: Salmon Arm
Province/Territory: BC
Postal code: V1E 4N7
County: Canada
Country: Canada
General Phone: (250) 832-2131
General Fax: (250) 832-5140
General/National Adv. E-mail: advertising@saobserver.net
Display Adv. E-mail: advertising@saobserver.net
Classified Adv. e-mail: classifieds@saobserver.net
Editorial e-mail: newsroom@saobserver.net
Primary Website: www.saobserver.net
Published: Wed
Avg Paid Circ: 1951
Avg Free Circ: 50
Audit By: CMCA
Audit Date: 30.04.2017
Personnel: Rick Proznick (Pub.); Tracy Hughes (Senior Ed.)
Parent company (for newspapers): Black Press Group Ltd.

SHUSWAP MARKET NEWS

Street address 1: 171 Shuswap St. Nw
Street address city: Salmon Arm
Province/Territory: BC
Postal code: V1E 4N7
County: Canada
Country: Canada
General Phone: (250) 832-2131
General Fax: (250) 832-5140
Display Adv. E-mail: advertising@saoberver.net
Classified Adv. e-mail: classifieds@saobserver.net
Editorial e-mail: newsroom@saobserver.net
Primary Website: www.saobserver.net
Published: Fri
Avg Paid Circ: 0
Avg Free Circ: 12732
Audit By: CMCA
Audit Date: 30.06.2017
Personnel: Rick Proznick (Pub.); Tracy Hughes (Ed.)
Parent company (for newspapers): Black Press Group Ltd.

SOUTH DELTA LEADER

Street address 1: 5008 47a Ave
Street address city: Ladner
Province/Territory: BC
Postal code: V4K 1T8
General Phone: (604) 948-3640
General Fax: (604) 943-8619
General/National Adv. E-mail: publisher@southdeltaleader.com
Display Adv. E-mail: dhamilton@delta-optimist.com
Classified Adv. e-mail: classifieds@van.net
Editorial e-mail: tmurphy@delta-optimist.com
Primary Website: www.southdeltaleader.com
Published: Fri
Avg Paid Circ: 0
Avg Free Circ: 14313
Audit By: CCAB
Audit Date: 30.09.2012
Personnel: Alvin Brouwer (Pub); Ted Murphy (Ed); Dave Hamilton (Gen Mgr/Adv. Sales)

SQUAMISH CHIEF

Street address 1: 38117 Second Avenue
Street address city: Squamish
Province/Territory: BC
Postal code: V8B 0B9
Country: Canada
General Phone: (604) 892-9161
General Fax: (604) 892-8483
Display Adv. E-mail: ads@squamishchief.com
Classified Adv. e-mail: jgibson@squamishchief.com
Editorial e-mail: michaela@squamishchief.com
Primary Website: www.squamishchief.com
Published: Thur
Avg Free Circ: 794
Audit By: VAC
Audit Date: 30.04.2016
Personnel: Darren Roberts (Pub); Michaela Garstin (Ed); Tina Pisch (Mktg Coord.); Jennifer Gibson (Sales & Mktg. Mgr); Denise Conway (Circ. Mgr.)
Parent company (for newspapers): Glacier Media Group

SUMMERLAND REVIEW

Street address 1: 13226 Victoria Rd. N.
Street address city: Summerland
Province/Territory: BC
Postal code: V0H 1Z0
Country: Canada
General Phone: (250) 494-5406
General Fax: (250) 494-5453
General/National Adv. E-mail: news@summerlandreview.com
Display Adv. E-mail: rob@summerlandreview.com
Classified Adv. e-mail: class@summerlandreview.com
Editorial e-mail: news@summerlandreview.com
Primary Website: www.summerlandreview.com
Published: Thur
Avg Paid Circ: 52
Avg Free Circ: 21
Audit By: VAC
Audit Date: 30.06.2016
Personnel: John Arendt (Ed.); Shannon Simpson (Pub); Rob Murphy (Sales Mgr); Nan Cogbill (Class./Circ Mgr)
Parent company (for newspapers): Black Press Group Ltd.

SURREY NOW-LEADER

Street address 1: 102-5460 152nd St.
Street address city: Surrey
Province/Territory: BC
Postal code: V3S 5J9
County: Canada
Country: Canada
General Phone: (604) 572-0064
General Fax: (604) 575-2544
Advertising Phone: (604) 572-0064
Editorial Phone: (604)543-5816
General/National Adv. E-mail: sueb@blackpress.ca
Display Adv. E-mail: sueb@blackpress.ca
Classified Adv. e-mail: sueb@blackpress.ca
Editorial e-mail: beau.simpson@surreynowleader.com
Primary Website: www.surreynowleader.com
Published: Wed'Fri
Avg Free Circ: 54521
Audit By: AAM
Audit Date: 31.03.2019
Parent company (for newspapers): Black Press Group Ltd.

THE ABBOTSFORD NEWS

Street address 1: 34375 Gladys Ave.
Street address city: Abbotsford
Province/Territory: BC
Postal code: V2S 2H5
County: Canada
Country: Canada
General Phone: (604) 853-1144
General Fax: (604) 852-1641
General/National Adv. E-mail: publisher@abbynews.com
Display Adv. E-mail: donb@abbynews.com
Editorial e-mail: newsroom@abbynews.com
Primary Website: abbynews.com
Published: Tues'Thur'Sat
Avg Paid Circ: 45
Avg Free Circ: 38814
Audit By: AAM
Audit Date: 31.12.2018
Personnel: Kevin Hemery (Circ. Mgr.); Andrew Holota (Mng. Ed.); Carly Ferguson (Pub); Don Barbeau (Adv Mgr)
Parent company (for newspapers): Black Press Group Ltd.

THE AGASSIZ-HARRISON OBSERVER

Street address 1: 7167 Pioneer Ave
Street address city: Agassiz
Province/Territory: BC
Postal code: V0M 1A0
Country: Canada
General Phone: (604) 796-4300
General Fax: (604) 796-2081
General/National Adv. E-mail: publisher@abbynews.com
Display Adv. E-mail: ads@ahobserver.com
Classified Adv. e-mail: bcclassifieds@blackpress.ca
Editorial e-mail: news@ahobserver.com
Primary Website: www.agassizharrisonobserver.com
Published: Fri
Avg Paid Circ: 590
Avg Free Circ: 2815
Audit By: VAC
Audit Date: 30.06.2016
Personnel: Carly Ferguson (Pub.); Erin Knutson (Ed); Tanya Jeyachandran (Class. Adv); Christine Douglas (Adv, Rep)
Parent company (for newspapers): Black Press Group Ltd.

THE ALDERGROVE STAR

Street address 1: 27118 Fraser Hwy.
Street address city: Aldergrove
Province/Territory: BC
Postal code: V4W 3P6
County: Canada
Country: Canada
General Phone: (604) 514-6770
General Fax: (604) 856-5212
General/National Adv. E-mail: publisher@aldergrovestar.com
Display Adv. E-mail: sales@aldergrovestar.com
Editorial e-mail: newsroom@aldergrovestar.com
Primary Website: www.aldergrovestar.com
Published: Thur
Avg Paid Circ: 728
Avg Free Circ: 6469
Audit By: VAC
Audit Date: 30.06.2016
Personnel: Janice Reid (Adv. Sales Mgr.); Kurt Langmann (Ed.); Lisa Farquharson (Pub)
Parent company (for newspapers): Black Press Group Ltd.

THE ASHCROFT-CACHE CREEK JOURNAL

Street address 1: 120 4th Street
Street address city: Ashcroft
Province/Territory: BC
Postal code: V0K 1A0
County: Canada
Country: Canada
General Phone: (250) 453-2261
General Fax: (250) 453-9625
Editorial Phone: (250) 453-2261
General/National Adv. E-mail: sales@accjournal.ca
Display Adv. E-mail: publisher@accjournal.ca
Editorial e-mail: editorial@accjournal.ca
Primary Website: https://www.ashcroftcachecreekjournal.com/
Published: Thur
Avg Paid Circ: 850
Avg Free Circ: 87
Audit By: CMCA
Audit Date: 23.09.2018
Personnel: Barbara Roden (Editor); Christopher Roden (Salesperson); Martina Dopf (Publisher)
Parent company (for newspapers): Black Press Group Ltd.

THE BOUNDARY CREEK TIMES

Street address 1: 318 Copper St.
Street address city: Greenwood
Province/Territory: BC
Postal code: V0H 1J0
County: Canada
Country: Canada
General Phone: (250) 445-2233
General/National Adv. E-mail: bctimes@shaw.ca
Display Adv. E-mail: dyan.stoochnoff@boundarycreektimes.com
Primary Website: boundarycreektimes.ca
Published: Thur
Avg Paid Circ: 471
Avg Free Circ: 1
Audit By: CMCA
Audit Date: 30.09.2017

Personnel: Dyan Stoochnoff (Associate Publisher); Darlainea Redlack (Circulation); Kathleen Saylors (Reporter)
Parent company (for newspapers): Black Press Group Ltd.

THE CAMPBELL RIVER COURIER-ISLANDER

Street address 1: 104 - 250 Dogwood St
Street address city: Campbell River
Province/Territory: BC
Postal code: V9W 5Z5
County: Campbell River
Country: Canada
General Phone: (250) 287-9227
General Fax: (250) 287-8891
Display Adv. E-mail: jacquie.duns@campbellrivermirror.com
Classified Adv. e-mail: darceyw@campbellrivermirror.com
Editorial e-mail: editor@campbellrivermirror.com
Primary Website: www.courierislander.com
Published: Wed`Fri
Avg Paid Circ: 0
Avg Free Circ: 16561
Audit By: AAM
Audit Date: 30.09.2015
Personnel: David Hamilton (Pub); Alistair Taylor (Ed); Kevin McKinnon (Circ. Mgr)

THE CAMPBELL RIVER MIRROR

Street address 1: 104-250 Dogwood St.
Street address city: Campbell River
Province/Territory: BC
Postal code: V9W 2X9
County: Canada
Country: Canada
General Phone: (250) 287-9227
General Fax: (250) 287-3238
Editorial Phone: (250) 287-9227
General/National Adv. E-mail: publisher@campbellrivermirror.com
Editorial e-mail: editor@campbellrivermirror.com
Primary Website: campbellrivermirror.com
Published: Wed`Fri
Avg Paid Circ: 30
Avg Free Circ: 16442
Audit By: AAM
Audit Date: 31.03.2019
Personnel: Alistair Taylor (Ed.); David Hamilton (Pub.); Michelle Hueller (Prod.); Kevin McKinnon (Circ. Mgr.); Zena Williams (Publisher); Artur Ciastkowski (Publisher)
Parent company (for newspapers): Black Press Group Ltd.

THE CASTLEGAR NEWS

Street address 1: Unit 2, 1810 8th Avenue
Street address city: Castlegar
Province/Territory: BC
Postal code: V1N 2y2
Country: Canada
General Phone: (250) 365-6397
General/National Adv. E-mail: newsroom@castlegarnews.com
Display Adv. E-mail: sales@castlegarnews.com
Classified Adv. e-mail: sales@castlegarnews.com
Editorial e-mail: newsroom@castlegarnews.com
Primary Website: www.castlegarnews.com
Published: Thur
Avg Paid Circ: 0
Avg Free Circ: 6442
Audit By: VAC
Audit Date: 30.04.2017
Personnel: Eric Lawson (Pub.)
Parent company (for newspapers): Black Press Group Ltd.

THE CHILLIWACK PROGRESS

Street address 1: 45860 Spadina Ave.
Street address city: Chilliwack
Province/Territory: BC
Postal code: V2P 6H9
County: Canada
Country: Canada
General Phone: (604) 792-1931
General Fax: (604) 792-4936
General/National Adv. E-mail: publisher@theprogress.com
Display Adv. E-mail: advertising@theprogress.com
Editorial e-mail: editor@theprogress.com
Primary Website: theprogress.com
Published: Wed`Fri
Avg Paid Circ: 28
Avg Free Circ: 27657
Audit By: AAM
Audit Date: 31.12.2018
Personnel: Kyle Williams (Adv. Mgr.); Louise Meger (Circ. Mgr.); Greg Knill (Ed.); Carly Ferguson (Pub.)
Parent company (for newspapers): Black Press Group Ltd.

THE COLUMBIA VALLEY PIONEER

Street address 1: #8, 1008-8th Avenue
Street address city: Invermere
Province/Territory: BC
Postal code: V0A 1K0
Country: Canada
General Phone: (250) 341-6299
General Fax: (855) 377-0312
General/National Adv. E-mail: info@cv-pioneer.com
Display Adv. E-mail: ads@columbiavalleypioneer.com
Classified Adv. e-mail: info@columbiavalleypioneer.com
Editorial e-mail: news@columbiavalleypioneer.com
Primary Website: www.columbiavalleypioneer.com
Published: Fri
Avg Paid Circ: 499
Avg Free Circ: 6238
Audit By: VAC
Audit Date: 31.03.2016
Personnel: Steve Hubrecht (Reporter); Dean Midyette (Advertising Sales); Emily Rawbon (Graphic design); Nicole Trigg (Ed.); Amanda Murray (Admin.); Eric Elliott (Reporter)
Parent company (for newspapers): Misko Publishing

THE COWICHAN NEWS LEADER

Street address 1: 251 Jubilee St
Street address city: Duncan
Province/Territory: BC
Postal code: V9L 1W8
County: Canada
Country: Canada
General Phone: (250) 748-2666
General Fax: (250) 746-8529
General/National Adv. E-mail: publisher@cowichannewsleader.com
Editorial e-mail: editor@cowichannewsleader.com
Primary Website: www.cowichannewsleader.com
Published: Wed`Fri
Avg Paid Circ: 0
Avg Free Circ: 22430
Audit By: CMCA
Audit Date: 30.04.2013
Personnel: Lara Stuart (Circ. Mgr.); John McKinley (Ed.); Shirley Skolos (Pub)

THE FALSE CREEK NEWS

Street address 1: 661 A Market Hill
Street address city: Vancouver
Province/Territory: BC
Postal code: V5Z 4B5
Country: Canada
General Phone: (604) 875-9626
General Fax: (604) 875-0336
General/National Adv. E-mail: news@thefalsecreeknews.com
Display Adv. E-mail: adsales@thefalsecreeknews.com
Editorial e-mail: mail@thefalsecreeknews.com
Primary Website: www.thefalsecreeknews.com
Published: Fri
Avg Free Circ: 25000
Audit By: Sworn/Estimate/Non-Audited
Audit Date: 12.07.2019
Personnel: M. Juma (Adv. Sales); Stephen Bowell (Mng. Ed.)

THE FORT NELSON NEWS

Street address 1: 4448 50th Ave., Ste. 3
Street address 2: P.o. Box 600
Street address city: Fort Nelson
Province/Territory: BC
Postal code: V0C 1R0
County: Northern Rockies Regional District
Country: Canada
General Phone: (250) 774-2357
General Fax: (250) 774-3612
General/National Adv. E-mail: editorial@fnnews.ca
Display Adv. E-mail: ads@fnnews.ca
Classified Adv. e-mail: ads@fnnews.ca
Editorial e-mail: editorial@fortnelsonnews.ca
Primary Website: www.fortnelsonnews.ca
Published: Wed
Avg Paid Circ: 439
Avg Free Circ: 665
Audit By: VAC
Audit Date: 12.12.2017
Personnel: Judith A. Kenyon (Ed & Pub); Alexandra Kenyon (Mng. Ed.); Kathy Smith (reporter and photographer); Abigail Neville (Mgr)

THE FREE PRESS

Street address 1: 342 2nd Ave.
Street address city: Fernie
Province/Territory: BC
Postal code: V0B 1M0
Country: Canada
General Phone: (250) 423-4666
General/National Adv. E-mail: publisher@thefreepress.ca
Display Adv. E-mail: advertising@thefreepress.ca
Editorial e-mail: editor@thefreepress.ca
Primary Website: www.thefreepress.ca
Published: Thur
Avg Paid Circ: 234
Avg Free Circ: 5643
Audit By: VAC
Audit Date: 30.11.2015
Personnel: Andrea Horton (Pub); Katie Smith (Ed); Jennifer Cronin (Adv); Bonny McLardy (Prod Mgr.)
Parent company (for newspapers): Black Press Group Ltd.

THE GRAND FORKS GAZETTE

Street address 1: 7255 Riverside Dr.
Street address city: Grand Forks
Province/Territory: BC
Postal code: V0H 1H0
County: Canada
Country: Canada
General Phone: (250) 442-2191
General Fax: (250) 442-3336
General/National Adv. E-mail: publisher@grandforksgazette.ca
Display Adv. E-mail: advertising@grandforksgazette.ca
Editorial e-mail: editor@grandforkscagazette.ca
Primary Website: grandforksgazette.ca
Published: Wed
Avg Paid Circ: 2399
Avg Free Circ: 12
Audit By: VAC
Audit Date: 30.06.2017
Personnel: Della Mallette (Prodn. Mgr.); Dyan Stoochnoff (Advertising); Kathleen Saylors (Reporter); Dustin LaCroix (Graphic Artist); Darlainea Redlack (Circulation)
Parent company (for newspapers): Black Press Group Ltd.

THE KIMBERLEY DAILY BULLETIN

Street address 1: 335 Spokane St.
Street address city: Kimberley
Province/Territory: BC
Postal code: V1A 1Y9
Country: Canada
General Phone: (250) 427-5333
General Fax: (250) 427-5336
Advertising Phone: (250) 427-5333
Editorial Phone: (250) 427-5333
General/National Adv. E-mail: sueb@blackpress.ca
Editorial e-mail: carolyn.grant@kimberleybulletin.com
Primary Website: www.kimberleybulletin.com
Published: Wed`Thur`Fri
Avg Paid Circ: 3350
Avg Free Circ: 3350
Audit By: CMCA
Audit Date: 31.12.2015
Personnel: Zena Williams (Pub.); Carolyn Grant (Ed.); Nicole Koran
Parent company (for newspapers): Black Press Group Ltd.

THE LADYSMITH CHRONICLE

Street address 1: 940 Oyster Bay Drive
Street address city: Ladysmith
Province/Territory: BC
Postal code: V9G 1A3
County: Canada
Country: Canada
General Phone: (250) 245-2277
General Fax: (250) 245-2230
Advertising Phone: (250) 245-2277
Editorial Phone: (250) 245-2277
General/National Adv. E-mail: editor@ladysmithchronicle.com
Display Adv. E-mail: publisher@ladysmithchronicle.com
Editorial e-mail: editor@ladysmithchronicle.com
Primary Website: www.ladysmithchronicle.com
Published: Tues
Avg Paid Circ: 1348
Avg Free Circ: 3678
Audit By: VAC
Audit Date: 30.09.2016
Personnel: Douglas Kent (Prodn. Mgr.); Teresa McKinley (Pub); Craig Spence (Ed)
Parent company (for newspapers): Black Press Group Ltd.

THE LAKE COWICHAN GAZETTE

Street address 1: 251 Jubilee Street
Street address city: Duncan
Province/Territory: BC
Postal code: V9L 1W8
Country: Canada
General Phone: (250) 748-2666
Advertising Phone: (250) 748-2666
General/National Adv. E-mail: office@lakecowichangazette.com
Display Adv. E-mail: warren.goulding@blackpress.ca
Editorial e-mail: editor@lakecowichangazette.com
Primary Website: www.lakecowichangazette.com
Published: Wed
Avg Paid Circ: 430
Avg Free Circ: 26
Audit By: VAC
Audit Date: 30.09.2017
Personnel: Waren Goulding (Pub.); Classified Ads (Classifieds); Drew McLachlan (Ed)
Parent company (for newspapers): Black Press Group Ltd.

THE MAPLE RIDGE NEWS

Street address 1: 22611 Dewdney Trunk Road
Street address city: Maple Ridge
Province/Territory: BC
Postal code: V2X 3K1
Country: Canada
General Phone: (604) 467-1122
General Fax: (604) 463-4741
Advertising Phone: (604) 476-2728
General/National Adv. E-mail: publisher@mapleridgenews.com
Display Adv. E-mail: ads@mapleridgenews.com
Editorial e-mail: editor@mapleridgenews.com
Primary Website: www.mapleridgenews.com
Published: Wed`Fri
Avg Free Circ: 30223
Audit By: AAM
Audit Date: 31.03.2019
Personnel: Michael Hall (Ed.); Lisa Prophet (Pub); Brian Yip (Circ Mgr)
Parent company (for newspapers): Black Press Group Ltd.

THE MIRROR

Street address 1: 901-100th Ave.
Street address city: Dawson Creek
Province/Territory: BC
Postal code: V1G 1W2
County: Canada
Country: Canada
General Phone: (250) 782-4888
General Fax: (250) 782-6300
General/National Adv. E-mail: editor@dcdn.ca
Display Adv. E-mail: jkmet@dcdn.ca
Editorial e-mail: editor@dcdn.ca

Primary Website: http://www.dawsoncreekmirror.ca/
Published: Fri
Avg Paid Circ: 0
Avg Free Circ: 7457
Audit By: Sworn/Estimate/Non-Audited
Audit Date: 12.07.2019
Personnel: William Julian (Reg. Mgr.); Nicole Palfy (Assoc. Pub.); Rob Brown (Ed); Margot Owens (Circ Mgr)

THE MORNING STAR

Street address 1: 4407 25th Ave.
Street address city: Vernon
Province/Territory: BC
Postal code: V1T 1P5
Country: Canada
General Phone: (250) 545-3322
General Fax: (250) 542-1510
Display Adv. E-mail: stephanie@vernonmorningstar.com
Classified Adv. e-mail: Classifieds@vernonmorningstar.com
Editorial e-mail: glenn@vernonmorningstar.com
Primary Website: www.vernonmorningstar.com
Published: Wed`Fri`Sun
Avg Paid Circ: 29884
Audit By: AAM
Audit Date: 30.09.2016
Personnel: Tammy Stelmachowich (Circ. Mgr.); Glenn Mitchell (Mng. Ed.); Ian Jensen (Pub.); Carol Williment (Class. Mgr.)
Parent company (for newspapers): Torstar

THE NORTHERN HORIZON

Street address 1: 901 - 100th Ave
Street address city: Dawson Creek
Province/Territory: BC
Postal code: V1G 1W2
Country: Canada
General Phone: (250) 782-4888
General Fax: (250) 782-6300
Display Adv. E-mail: jkmet@dcdn.ca
Editorial e-mail: editor@dcdn.ca
Primary Website: http://www.northernhorizon.ca/
Published: Fri
Avg Free Circ: 16500
Audit Date: 22.07.2022
Personnel: William Julian (Pub); Nicole Palfy (Assoc. Pub.); Rob Brown (Ed); Margot Owens (Circ. Mgr)
Parent company (for newspapers): Glacier Media Group

THE NORTHERNER

Street address 1: 9916 98th St.
Street address city: Fort Saint John
Province/Territory: BC
Postal code: V1J 3T8
Country: Canada
General Phone: (250) 785-5631
General Fax: (250) 785-3522
General/National Adv. E-mail: ahnews@awink.com
Display Adv. E-mail: mhill@ahnfsj.ca
Classified Adv. e-mail: rwallace@ahnfsj.ca
Editorial e-mail: editor@ahnfsj.ca
Primary Website: www.thenortherner.ca
Published: Fri
Avg Paid Circ: 0
Avg Free Circ: 8657
Audit By: Sworn/Estimate/Non-Audited
Audit Date: 12.07.2019
Personnel: Melody Hill (Sales); William Julian (Pub.); Ryan Wallace (Sales); Debbie Oberlin (Circ.)

THE NOW NEWSPAPER

Street address 1: 102 - 5460 152 St
Street address city: Surrey
Province/Territory: BC
Postal code: V3S 5J9
County: Canada
Country: Canada
General Phone: (604) 572-0064
General Fax: (604) 572-6438
Display Adv. E-mail: dal.hothi@thenownewspaper.com
Classified Adv. e-mail: sarah.sigurdswon@thenownewspaper.com
Editorial e-mail: bsimpson@thenownewspaper.com
Primary Website: www.thenownewspaper.com
Published: Tues`Thur
Avg Free Circ: 177757
Audit By: CCAB
Audit Date: 31.03.2014
Personnel: Beau Simpson (Ed); Dwayne Weidendorf (Pub); Sarah Sigurdson (Ad Control/Admin); Dal Hothi (Sales Mgr)

THE OCEANSIDE STAR

Street address 1: 166 E. Island Hwy.
Street address city: Parksville
Province/Territory: BC
Postal code: V9P 2G3
Country: Canada
General Phone: (250) 954-0600
General Fax: (250) 954-0601
General/National Adv. E-mail: hnicholson@glaciermedia.com
Display Adv. E-mail: ads@oceansidestar.com
Editorial e-mail: bwilford@oceansidestar.com
Primary Website: www2.canada.com/oceansidestar/index.html
Published: Thur
Avg Paid Circ: 0
Avg Free Circ: 16243
Audit By: CMCA
Audit Date: 31.12.2013
Personnel: Coreen Greene (Adv. Mgr.); Michael Kelly (Circ. Mgr.); Brian Wilford (Ed.); Hugh Nicholson (Pub.)
Parent company (for newspapers): CanWest MediaWorks Publications, Inc.

THE PEACE ARCH NEWS

Street address 1: 200-2411 160 Street
Street address city: Surrey
Province/Territory: BC
Postal code: V3S 0C8
Country: Canada
General Phone: (604) 531-1711
General Fax: (604) 531-7977
Editorial e-mail: editorial@peacearchnews.com
Primary Website: www.peacearchnews.com
Published: Wed`Fri
Avg Free Circ: 37090
Audit By: AAM
Audit Date: 31.03.2019
Personnel: Lance Peverley (Ed.)
Parent company (for newspapers): Black Press Group Ltd.

THE PENINSULA NEWS REVIEW

Street address 1: 102-9830 Second Street
Street address city: Sidney
Province/Territory: BC
Postal code: V8L 3C6
County: Canada
Country: Canada
General Phone: (250) 656-1151
General Fax: (250) 656-5526
Editorial Phone: (250) 656-1151
Display Adv. E-mail: sales@peninsulanewsreview.com
Editorial e-mail: editor@peninsulanewsreview.com
Primary Website: www.peninsulanewsreview.com
Published: Wed`Fri
Avg Free Circ: 14556
Audit By: AAM
Audit Date: 31.03.2019
Personnel: Steven Heywood; Dale Naftel; Chris R Cook; Hugo Wong; Rosemarie Bandura
Parent company (for newspapers): Black Press Group Ltd.

THE RECORD

Street address 1: 201a 3430 Brighton Ave.
Street address city: Burnaby
Province/Territory: BC
Postal code: V5A 3H4
County: Canada
Country: Canada
General Phone: (604) 444-3451
General Fax: (604) 444-3460
Advertising Phone: (604)444-3030
Editorial Phone: (604) 444-3007
Display Adv. E-mail: kgilmour@newwestrecord.ca
Editorial e-mail: ptracy@newwestrecord.ca
Primary Website: royalcityrecord.com
Published: Wed`Fri
Avg Paid Circ: 0
Avg Free Circ: 16966
Audit By: CCAB
Audit Date: 23.11.2017
Personnel: Lara Graham (Pub); Pat Tracy (Ed.); Dale Dorsett (Circ. Mgr)
Parent company (for newspapers): CanWest MediaWorks Publications, Inc.

THE SMITHERS INTERIOR NEWS

Street address 1: 3764 Broadway
Street address city: Smithers
Province/Territory: BC
Postal code: V0J 2N0
County: Canada
Country: Canada
General Phone: (250) 847-3266
General Fax: (250) 847-2995
General/National Adv. E-mail: publisher@interior-news.com
Display Adv. E-mail: publisher@interior-news.com
Editorial e-mail: editor@interior-news.com
Primary Website: www.interior-news.com
Published: Wed
Avg Paid Circ: 13
Avg Free Circ: 152
Audit By: VAC
Audit Date: 30.06.2016
Personnel: Grant Harris (Pub/Sales Mgr); Chris Gareau (Ed)
Parent company (for newspapers): Black Press Group Ltd.

THE SOOKE NEWS MIRROR

Street address 1: #4 6631 Sooke Road
Street address city: Sooke
Province/Territory: BC
Postal code: V9Z 0A3
County: District of Sooke
Country: Canada
General Phone: (250) 642-5752
General Fax: (250) 642-4767
Advertising Phone: (250) 642-5752
Display Adv. E-mail: sales@sookenewsmirror.com
Editorial e-mail: editor@sookenewsmirror.com
Primary Website: www.sookenewsmirror.com
Published: Wed
Avg Paid Circ: 63
Avg Free Circ: 5713
Audit By: AAM
Audit Date: 31.03.2019
Personnel: Rod Sluggett (publisher); Laird Kevin (editor); Kelvin Phair (Advertising Sales)
Parent company (for newspapers): Black Press Group Ltd.

THE TERRACE STANDARD

Street address 1: 3210 Clinton St
Street address city: Terrace
Province/Territory: BC
Postal code: V8G5R2
County: Canada
Country: Canada
General Phone: (250) 638-7283
General Fax: (250) 638-8432
General/National Adv. E-mail: newsroom@terracestandard.com
Display Adv. E-mail: bwhusband@terracestandard.com
Classified Adv. e-mail: classifieds@terracestandard.com
Editorial e-mail: newsroom@terracestandard.com
Primary Website: www.terracestandard.com
Published: Thur
Avg Free Circ: 7729
Audit By: VAC
Audit Date: 12.12.2017
Personnel: Quinn Bender (Editor); Bert Husband (Sales)
Parent company (for newspapers): Black Press Group Ltd.

THE TIMES

Street address 1: 125-403 Mackenzie Blvd.
Street address city: Mackenzie
Province/Territory: BC
Postal code: V0J 2C0
Country: Canada
General Phone: (250) 997-6675
General Fax: (250) 997-4747
Advertising Phone: (250) 997-6675
Editorial Phone: (250) 997-6675
General/National Adv. E-mail: news@mackenzietimes.com
Display Adv. E-mail: ads@mackenzietimes.com
Editorial e-mail: news@mackenzietimes.com
Primary Website: www.sterlingnews.com/Mackenzie
Published: Wed
Avg Paid Circ: 1000
Audit By: Sworn/Estimate/Non-Audited
Audit Date: 12.07.2019
Personnel: Jackie Benton (Pub/Ed); Andrea Massicotte (Adv Mgr)

THE VALLEY SENTINEL

Street address 1: 1418 Bruce Place
Street address city: Valemount
Province/Territory: BC
Postal code: V0E 2Z0
Country: Canada
General Phone: (250) 566-4425
General Fax: (250) 566-4528
General/National Adv. E-mail: insertions@the vallysentinel.com
Display Adv. E-mail: ads@valley-sentinel.com
Editorial e-mail: articles@valley-sentinel.com
Primary Website: www.thevalleysentinel.com
Published: Thur
Avg Paid Circ: 385
Avg Free Circ: 13
Audit By: VAC
Audit Date: 31.12.2015
Personnel: Deanna Mickelow (Ad Sales); Joshua Estabroks (Pub.)
Parent company (for newspapers): Aberdeen Publishing

THE VANCOUVER COURIER

Street address 1: 303 West 5th Ave
Street address city: Vancouver
Province/Territory: BC
Postal code: V5Y 1J6
County: Canada
Country: Canada
General Phone: (604) 738-1411
General Fax: (604) 731-1474
Display Adv. E-mail: mbhatti@vancourier.com
Editorial e-mail: mperkins@vancourier.com
Primary Website: vancourier.com
Published: Wed`Fri
Avg Paid Circ: 0
Avg Free Circ: 106402
Audit By: CCAB
Audit Date: 22.11.2017
Personnel: Alvin Brouwer (Pub); Martha Perkins (Ed); Michelle Bhatti (Mktg Dir)
Parent company (for newspapers): Glacier Media Group; CanWest MediaWorks Publications, Inc.

THE WESTENDER

Street address 1: 303 West 5th Ave
Street address city: Vancouver
Province/Territory: BC
Postal code: V5Y 1J6
Country: Canada
General Phone: (604) 742-8686
Display Adv. E-mail: matty@westender.com
Editorial e-mail: editor@westender.com
Primary Website: http://www.westender.com/
Published: Thur
Avg Paid Circ: 0
Avg Free Circ: 23887
Audit By: CCAB
Audit Date: 30.09.2017
Personnel: Gail Nugent (Pub); Kelsey Klassen (Ed); Miguel Black (Circ Mgr)
Parent company (for newspapers): Glacier Media Group

THE WHISTLER QUESTION

Street address 1: 103-1390 Alpha Lake Rd
Street address city: Whistler
Province/Territory: BC
Postal code: V0N 1B4
County: Canada
Country: Canada
General Phone: (604) 932-5131
General Fax: (604) 932-2862
General/National Adv. E-mail: smatches@whistlerquestion.com

Display Adv. E-mail: susan@piquenewsmagazine.com
Classified Adv. e-mail: mail@piquenewsmagazine.com
Editorial e-mail: editor@whistlerquestion.com
Primary Website: www.whistlerquestion.com
Published: Tues
Avg Paid Circ: 433
Avg Free Circ: 5762
Audit By: VAC
Audit Date: 31.08.2016
Personnel: Sarah Strother (Pres., WPLP); Kathryn Bechtel (Office/Class. Mgr); Alyssa Noel (Ed); Susan Hutchinson (Sales Mgr)
Parent company (for newspapers): Glacier Media Group

THE WILLIAMS LAKE TRIBUNE

Street address 1: 188 N. 1st Ave.
Street address city: Williams Lake
Province/Territory: BC
Postal code: V2G 1Y8
County: Canada
Country: Canada
General Phone: (250) 392-2331
General Fax: (250) 392-7253
General/National Adv. E-mail: classifieds@wltribune.com
Display Adv. E-mail: advertising@wltribune.com
Classified Adv. e-mail: classifieds@wltribune.com
Editorial e-mail: editor@wltribune.com
Primary Website: www.wltribune.com
Published: Wed
Avg Paid Circ: 1109
Avg Free Circ: 9794
Audit By: VAC
Audit Date: 30.06.2016
Personnel: Kathy McLean (Pub); Angie Mindus (Ed); Lynn Bolt (Class. Mgr)
Parent company (for newspapers): Black Press Group Ltd.

TRI CITY NEWS

Street address 1: 118 - 1680 Broadway Street
Street address city: Port Coquitlam
Province/Territory: BC
Postal code: V3C 2M8
Country: Canada
General Phone: (604) 525-6397
Advertising Phone: (604) 472-3020
Editorial Phone: (604) 472-3030
Display Adv. E-mail: admanager@tricitynews.com
Primary Website: tricitynews.com
Published: Wed`Fri
Avg Paid Circ: 0
Avg Free Circ: 52297
Audit By: Sworn/Estimate/Non-Audited
Audit Date: 12.07.2019
Parent company (for newspapers): Glacier Media

TRI-CITY NEWS

Street address 1: 1680 Broadway Street
Street address 2: Unit 118
Street address city: Port Coquitlam
Province/Territory: BC
Postal code: V3C 2M8
County: Tri-Cities
Country: Canada
General Phone: (604) 525-6397
General/National Adv. E-mail: publisher@tricitynews.com
Display Adv. E-mail: smitchell@tricitynews.com
Editorial e-mail: newsroom@tricitynews.com
Primary Website: tricitynews.com
Published: Wed`Fri
Avg Paid Circ: 0
Avg Free Circ: 51702
Audit By: CCAB
Audit Date: 23.11.2017
Personnel: Richard Dal Monte (Ed.); Shannon Mitchell (Pub); Kim Yorston (Circ Mgr)
Parent company (for newspapers): Black Press Group Ltd.; Glacier Media Group

TUMBLER RIDGE NEWS

Street address 1: 230 Mains Street
Street address city: Tumbler Ridge
Province/Territory: BC
Postal code: V0C 2W0
Country: Canada
General Phone: (250) 242-5343
General Fax: (250) 242-5340
General/National Adv. E-mail: mail@tumblerridgenews.com
Display Adv. E-mail: advertising@tumblerridgenews.com
Editorial e-mail: editor@tumblerridgenews.com
Primary Website: www.tumblerridgenews.com
Published: Thur
Avg Paid Circ: 2
Avg Free Circ: 1179
Audit By: VAC
Audit Date: 31.12.2015
Personnel: Loraine Funk (Owner); Trent Ernst (Pub/Ed.); Lisa Allen (Sales Mgr)

VANDERHOOF OMINECA EXPRESS

Street address 1: 150 W. Columbia
Street address city: Vanderhoof
Province/Territory: BC
Postal code: V0J 3A0
Country: Canada
General Phone: (250) 567-9258
General Fax: (250) 567-2070
General/National Adv. E-mail: newsroom@ominecaexpress.com
Display Adv. E-mail: publisher@ominecaexpress.com
Editorial e-mail: newsroom@ominecaexpress.com
Primary Website: www.ominecaexpress.com
Published: Wed
Avg Paid Circ: 998
Avg Free Circ: 52
Audit By: VAC
Audit Date: 30.06.2016
Personnel: Pam Berger (Pub./Sales Mgr); Vivian Chui (Ed); Denise Smith (Office/Sales/Circ)
Parent company (for newspapers): Black Press Group Ltd.

VERNON MORNING STAR

Street address 1: 4407 25th Avenue
Street address city: Vernon
Province/Territory: BC
Postal code: V1T 1P5
County: Vernon
Country: British Columbia
General Phone: (250) 545-3322
General Fax: (250) 862-5275
Display Adv. E-mail: karen.hill@blackpress.ca
Classified Adv. e-mail: bcclassifieds@blackpress.ca
Editorial e-mail: editor@vernonmorningstar.com
Primary Website: vernonmorningstar.com
Published: Wed`Fri
Avg Free Circ: 28286
Audit By: AAM
Audit Date: 31.03.2019
Personnel: Dave Hamilton (Pres.); Karen Hill (Adv. Dir.)
Parent company (for newspapers): Black Press Group Ltd.

VICTORIA NEWS

Street address 1: 818 Broughton St.
Street address city: Victoria
Province/Territory: BC
Postal code: V8W 1E4
County: Canada
Country: Canada
General Phone: (250) 381-3484
General Fax: (250) 386-2624
Display Adv. E-mail: michelle.cabana@goldstreamgazette.com
Editorial e-mail: michelle.cabana@goldstreamgazette.com
Primary Website: vicnews.com
Published: Wed`Fri
Avg Free Circ: 24056
Audit By: AAM
Audit Date: 31.03.2019
Personnel: Mike Cowan (Pub); Pamela Roth (Ed); Michelle Cabana (Pub.)
Parent company (for newspapers): Black Press Group Ltd.

WE VANCOUVER WEEKLY

Street address 1: 303 West 5th Ave
Street address city: Vancouver
Province/Territory: BC
Postal code: V5Y 1J6
Country: Canada
General Phone: (604) 742-8686
General Fax: (604) 606-8687
Advertising Phone: (604) 742-8677
General/National Adv. E-mail: publisher@wevancouver.com
Display Adv. E-mail: matty@westender.com
Editorial e-mail: editor@westender.com
Primary Website: www.wevancouver.com
Published: Thur
Avg Paid Circ: 0
Avg Free Circ: 53671
Audit By: CMCA
Audit Date: 30.11.2013
Personnel: Gail Nugent (Pub); Kelsey Klassen (Ed); Miguel Black (Circ. Mgr.)

WESTERLY NEWS

Street address 1: 102-1801 Bay Street
Street address city: Ucluelet
Province/Territory: BC
Postal code: V0R 3A0
Country: Canada
General Phone: (250) 726-7029
General Fax: (250) 726-4282
General/National Adv. E-mail: office@westerlynews.ca
Display Adv. E-mail: office@westerlynews.ca
Editorial e-mail: andrew.bailey@westerlynews.ca
Primary Website: www.westerlynews.ca
Published: Wed
Avg Paid Circ: 7
Avg Free Circ: 0
Audit By: Sworn/Estimate/Non-Audited
Audit Date: 12.07.2019
Personnel: Andrew Bailey (Ed); Peter McCully (Pub); Nora O'Malley
Parent company (for newspapers): Black Press Group Ltd.

MANITOBA

BANNER

Street address 1: 455 Main St.
Street address city: Russell
Province/Territory: MB
Postal code: R0J 1W0
Country: Canada
General Phone: (204) 773-2069
General Fax: (204) 773-2645
General/National Adv. E-mail: rbanner@mts.net
Display Adv. E-mail: russellbannerads@mymts.net
Editorial e-mail: editor@russellbanner.com
Primary Website: russellbanner.com
Published: Tues
Avg Paid Circ: 1300
Avg Free Circ: 19
Audit By: CCAB
Audit Date: 30.11.2018
Personnel: Chantelle Senchuk (Adv); Jessica Ludvig
Parent company (for newspapers): Dauphin Herald

CARBERRY NEWS EXPRESS

Street address 1: 34 Main St. W.
Street address city: Carberry
Province/Territory: MB
Postal code: R0K 0H0
Country: Canada
General Phone: (204) 834-2153
General Fax: (204) 834-2714
General/National Adv. E-mail: info@carberrynews.ca
Display Adv. E-mail: ads@carberrynews.ca
Editorial e-mail: kathy@carberrynews.ca
Primary Website: www.carberrynews.ca
Published: Mon
Avg Paid Circ: 593
Avg Free Circ: 34
Audit By: VAC
Audit Date: 30.09.2018
Personnel: Kathy Carr (Gen. Mgr.); Eva Rutz
Parent company (for newspapers): FP Newspapers Inc.

CENTRAL PLAINS HERALD LEADER

Street address 1: 1941 Saskatchewan Ave. W.
Street address city: Portage La Prairie
Province/Territory: MB
Postal code: R1N 0R7
Country: Canada
General Phone: (204) 857-3427
General Fax: (204) 239-1270
General/National Adv. E-mail: news.dailygraphic@shawcable.com
Display Adv. E-mail: daria.zmiyiwsky@sunmedia.ca
Editorial e-mail: mickey.dumont@sunmedia.ca
Primary Website: http://www.portagedailygraphic.com/
Published: Thur
Avg Paid Circ: 4551
Avg Free Circ: 9595
Audit By: VAC
Audit Date: 30.06.2016
Personnel: Guey Fiset (Class./Circ. Mgr.); Daria Zmiyiwsky (Adv. Dir); Mickey Dumont (Ed)
Parent company (for newspapers): Postmedia Network Inc.; Quebecor Communications, Inc.

CROSSROADS THIS WEEK

Street address 1: 353 Station Road
Street address city: Shoal Lake
Province/Territory: MB
Postal code: R0J 1Z0
County: Canada
Country: Canada
General Phone: (204) 759-2644
General Fax: (204) 759-2521
Advertising Phone: (204) 759-2644
Editorial Phone: (204) 759-2644
General/National Adv. E-mail: ctwnews@mymts.net
Display Adv. E-mail: ctwdisplay@mymts.net
Classified Adv. e-mail: ctwclassified@mymts.net
Editorial e-mail: ctwnews@mymts.net
Primary Website: www.crossroadsthisweek.com
Published: Fri
Avg Paid Circ: 2294
Avg Free Circ: 25
Audit By: Sworn/Estimate/Non-Audited
Audit Date: 12.07.2019
Personnel: Connie Kay (Advertising Manager); Michelle Genslorek (Classified/Accounting); Darrell Nesbitt (News Reporter); Ryan Nesbitt (Publisher); Marcie Harrison (News Reporter)
Parent company (for newspapers): Nesbitt Publishing Ltd.

DAUPHIN HERALD

Street address 1: 120 1st Ave. Ne
Street address city: Dauphin
Province/Territory: MB
Postal code: R7N 1A5
County: Canada
Country: Canada
General Phone: (204) 638-4420
General Fax: (204) 638-8760
General/National Adv. E-mail: dherald@mts.net
Display Adv. E-mail: bwright@mymts.net
Classified Adv. e-mail: classifieds@dauphinherald.com
Editorial e-mail: psbailey@mymts.net
Primary Website: www.dauphinherald.com
Published: Tues
Avg Paid Circ: 1189
Avg Free Circ: 59
Audit By: VAC
Audit Date: 30.06.2016
Personnel: Robert F. Gilroy (Pub./Owner); Brent Wright (Adv. Mgr.); Mandy Carderry (Circ. Mgr.); Shawn Bailey (Ed.)

FLIN FLON REMINDER

Street address 1: 14 North Ave.
Street address city: Flin Flon
Province/Territory: MB
Postal code: R8A 0T2
Country: Canada
General Phone: (204) 687-3454
General Fax: (204) 687-4473
General/National Adv. E-mail: reminder@mb.sympatico.ca
Display Adv. E-mail: ads@thereminder.ca
Classified Adv. e-mail: sales@thereminder.ca
Editorial e-mail: news@thereminder.ca
Primary Website: www.thereminder.ca
Published: Wed`Fri
Avg Paid Circ: 12
Avg Free Circ: 38

Audit By: VAC
Audit Date: 30.06.2016
Personnel: Valerie Durnin (Pub); Jonathon Naylor (Ed); Shannon Thompson (Office Admin)
Parent company (for newspapers): Glacier Media Group

FREE PRESS COMMUNITY REVIEW â€" WEST EDITION

Street address 1: 1355 Mountain Ave.
Street address city: Winnipeg
Province/Territory: MB
Postal code: R2X 3B6
Country: Canada
General Phone: (204) 697-7009
Advertising Phone: (204) 697-7021
Editorial Phone: 204-697-7093
Display Adv. E-mail: CRsales@freepress.mb.ca
Classified Adv. e-mail: CRsales@freepress.mb.ca
Editorial e-mail: CRnews@freepress.mb.ca
Primary Website: www.fpcommunityreview.com
Published: Wed
Avg Paid Circ: 0
Avg Free Circ: 141425
Audit By: Sworn/Estimate/Non-Audited
Audit Date: 01.03.2023
Personnel: John Kendle (Managing Editor); Michele Prysazniuk (Vice-President, Revenue and Business Development); Monique Norbury (Advertising Co-ordinator); Barb Borden (Sales Manager)
Parent company (for newspapers): Winnipeg Free Press

FREE PRESS COMMUNITY REVIEW EAST EDITON

Street address 1: 1355 Mountain Ave.
Street address city: Winnipeg
Province/Territory: MB
Postal code: R2X 3B6
Country: Canada
General Phone: (204) 697-7009
Advertising Phone: (204) 697-7021
Editorial Phone: (204) 697-7093
General/National Adv. E-mail: CRsales@freepress.mb.ca
Display Adv. E-mail: CRsales@freepress.mb.ca
Classified Adv. e-mail: CRsales@freepress.mb.ca
Editorial e-mail: CRnews@freepress.mb.ca
Primary Website: www.fpcommunityreview.com
Published: Wed
Avg Free Circ: 93338
Audit By: Sworn/Estimate/Non-Audited
Audit Date: 01.03.2022
Personnel: John Kendle (Managing Editor); Karen Buss (Vice-President, Sales, Marketing & Creative Services); Monique Norbury; Michele Prysazniuk (Vice-President, revenue and business development); Darren Ridgley (Deputy Editor); Linda Mackenzie (Executive Assistant); Barb Borden (Sales Manager)
Parent company (for newspapers): Winnipeg Free Press

GAZETTE

Street address 1: 702 Railway Ave.
Street address city: Glenboro
Province/Territory: MB
Postal code: R0K 0X0
County: Canada
Country: Canada
General Phone: (204) 827-2343
General Fax: (204) 827-2207
General/National Adv. E-mail: gazette@mts.net
Display Adv. E-mail: gazette2@mts.net
Editorial e-mail: gazette@mts.net
Primary Website: http://www.baldur-glenborogazette.ca/
Published: Tues
Avg Paid Circ: 1557
Avg Free Circ: 0
Audit By: CMCA
Audit Date: 31.05.2014
Personnel: Mike Johnson (Ed./Pub/Adv); Travis Johnson (Ed./Pub/Adv)

KILLARNEY GUIDE

Street address 1: 336 Park St.
Street address city: Killarney
Province/Territory: MB
Postal code: R0K 1G0
Country: Canada
General Phone: (204) 523-4611
General Fax: (204) 523-4445
General/National Adv. E-mail: news@killarneyguide.ca
Display Adv. E-mail: ads@killarneyguide.ca
Editorial e-mail: news@killarneyguide.ca
Primary Website: http://new.killarneyguide.ca/
Published: Fri
Avg Paid Circ: 56
Avg Free Circ: 134
Audit By: VAC
Audit Date: 30.06.2016
Personnel: Jay Struth (Ed.); Wendy Johnston (Adv. Mgr.); Iris Krahn (Circ Mgr)

LA LIBERTE

Street address 1: Po Box 190
Street address city: Saint Boniface
Province/Territory: MB
Postal code: R2H 3B4
Country: Canada
General Phone: (204) 237-4823
General Fax: (204) 231-1998
General/National Adv. E-mail: la_liberte@la-liberte.mb.ca
Editorial e-mail: la-liberte@la-liberte.mb.ca
Primary Website: http://la-liberte.mb.ca/tag/saint-boniface
Published: Wed
Avg Paid Circ: 0
Avg Free Circ: 12
Audit By: VAC
Audit Date: 30.06.2016
Personnel: Sophie Gaulin (Dir/Ed); Bernard Bocquel (Assoc. Ed); Roxanne Bouchard (Office Admin)

MELITA NEW ERA

Street address 1: 128 Main St.
Street address city: Melita
Province/Territory: MB
Postal code: R0M 1L0
Country: Canada
General Phone: (204) 522-3491
General Fax: (204) 522-3648
General/National Adv. E-mail: newera@cpocket.mts.net
Display Adv. E-mail: ads.cpocket@mts.net
Editorial e-mail: cpocket@mts.net
Primary Website: http://www.melitanewera.ca/
Published: Fri
Avg Paid Circ: 1104
Avg Free Circ: 0
Audit By: CMCA
Audit Date: 28.02.2014
Personnel: Patty Lewis (Ed.)
Parent company (for newspapers): Glacier Media Group

MINNEDOSA TRIBUNE

Street address 1: 353 Station Rd.
Street address city: Shoal Lake
Province/Territory: MB
Postal code: R0J 1Z0
Country: Canada
General Phone: (204) 867-3816
General Fax: 204-759-2521
General/National Adv. E-mail: editor@minnedosatribune.com
Display Adv. E-mail: adsales@minnedosatribune.com
Classified Adv. e-mail: class@minnedosatribune.com
Editorial e-mail: editor@minnedosatribune.com
Primary Website: www.minnedosatribune.com
Published: Fri
Avg Paid Circ: 456
Avg Free Circ: 258
Audit By: VAC
Audit Date: 30.06.2016
Personnel: Ryan Nesbitt (Publisher); Darryl Holyk (Pub./Ed); Heather Horner (Adv); Georgia Keriuke (Office Mgr/Class.)
Parent company (for newspapers): Nesbitt Publishing Ltd.

MORDEN TIMES

Street address 1: 583 Main St.
Street address city: Winkler
Province/Territory: MB
Postal code: R6W 4B3
County: Canada
Country: Canada
General Phone: (204) 325-4771
General Fax: 204-325-8646
Display Adv. E-mail: jbilsky@postmedia.com
Editorial e-mail: gvandermeulen@postmedia.com
Primary Website: www.mordentimes.com
Published: Thur
Avg Paid Circ: 4924
Avg Free Circ: 5418
Audit By: Sworn/Estimate/Non-Audited
Audit Date: 12.07.2019
Personnel: Greg Vandermeulen (Ed); Lauren MacGill (Reporter)
Parent company (for newspapers): Postmedia Network Inc.

NEEPAWA BANNER

Street address 1: 243 Hamilton St.
Street address city: Neepawa
Province/Territory: MB
Postal code: R0J 1H0
Country: Canada
General Phone: (204) 476-3401
General Fax: (204) 476-5073
General/National Adv. E-mail: print@neepawanabanner.com
Editorial e-mail: nekwaddell@neepawabanner.com
Primary Website: www.neepawabanner.com
Published: Fri
Avg Paid Circ: 92
Avg Free Circ: 8179
Audit By: VAC
Audit Date: 30.06.2017
Personnel: Ken Waddell (Pub/Ed.)
Newspapers (for newspaper groups): Rivers Banner Gazette-reporter, Rivers

OPASQUIA TIMES

Street address 1: 352 Fischer Avenue
Street address 2: Box 750
Street address city: The Pas
Province/Territory: MB
Postal code: R9A 1K8
Country: Canada
General Phone: (204) 623-3435
General Fax: (204) 623-5601
General/National Adv. E-mail: optimes@mymts.net
Display Adv. E-mail: opads@mymts.net
Classified Adv. e-mail: opads@mymts.net
Editorial e-mail: opeditor@mymts.net
Primary Website: www.opasquiatimes.com
Published: Wed
Avg Paid Circ: 1200
Avg Free Circ: 0
Audit By: VAC
Audit Date: 31.08.2015
Personnel: Jennifer Cook (Gen. Mgr.); Trent Allen (Ed.); Jennifer Laviolette (Editor)

RIVERS BANNER GAZETTE-REPORTER

Street address 1: 529 2nd Ave.
Street address city: Rivers
Province/Territory: MB
Postal code: R0K 1X0
County: Riverdale
Country: Canada
General Phone: (204) 328-7494
General Fax: (204) 328-5212
General/National Adv. E-mail: info@riversbanner.com
Editorial e-mail: kwaddell@neepawabanner.com
Primary Website: www.riversbanner.com
Published: Fri
Avg Paid Circ: 93
Avg Free Circ: 1668
Audit By: VAC
Audit Date: 30.06.2017
Personnel: Ken Waddell (Pub/Ed.); Sheila Runions (Gen. Mgr.)
Parent company (for newspapers): Neepawa Banner

SELKIRK JOURNAL

Street address 1: 366 Main St
Street address 2: Unit 300
Street address city: Selkirk
Province/Territory: MB
Postal code: R1A 2J7
Country: Canada
General Phone: (204) 482-7402
General Fax: (204) 482-3336
General/National Adv. E-mail: sjournal@mts.net
Display Adv. E-mail: jbilsky@postmedia.com
Editorial e-mail: bjones@postmedia.com
Primary Website: http://www.interlaketoday.ca/selkirkjournal
Published: Thur
Avg Free Circ: 14334
Audit By: VAC
Audit Date: 30.06.2016
Personnel: Jenifer Bilsky (Adv Dir); Brook Jones (Ed)
Parent company (for newspapers): Postmedia Network Inc.; Quebecor Communications, Inc.

SOURIS PLAINDEALER

Street address 1: 53 Crescent Ave. W.
Street address city: Souris
Province/Territory: MB
Postal code: R0K 2C0
County: Canada
Country: Canada
General Phone: (204) 483-2070
General Fax: (204) 522-3648
General/National Adv. E-mail: spdealer@mts.net
Editorial e-mail: spdealer@mts.net
Primary Website: http://www.sourisplaindealer.ca/
Published: Fri
Avg Free Circ: 54
Audit By: VAC
Audit Date: 31.12.2015
Personnel: Darcy Semeschuk (Office Mgr.); Patti Lewis (Pub/Ed.)
Parent company (for newspapers): Glacier Media Group

SOUTH MOUNTAIN PRESS

Street address 1: 353 Station Road
Street address city: Shoal Lake
Province/Territory: MB
Postal code: R0J 1Z0
County: Yellowhead
Country: Canada
General Phone: (204) 759-2644
General Fax: (204) 759-2521
Advertising Phone: (204) 759-2644
Editorial Phone: (204) 759-2644
Display Adv. E-mail: smpdisplay@mymts.net
Classified Adv. e-mail: smpclassified@mymts.net
Editorial e-mail: smpnews@mymts.net
Published: Fri
Avg Paid Circ: 46
Avg Free Circ: 1492
Audit By: VAC
Audit Date: 19.12.2017
Personnel: Connie Kay (Advertising); Marcie Harrison (Editor); Michelle Gensiorek (Classified/Accounting); Ryan Nesbitt (Publisher); Darrell Nesbitt (Reporter/Photographer)
Parent company (for newspapers): Nesbitt Publishing Ltd.

SOUTHERN MANITOBA REVIEW

Street address 1: B-635 Bowles St.
Street address city: Cartwright
Province/Territory: MB
Postal code: R0K 0L0
Country: Canada
General Phone: (204) 529-2342
General Fax: (204) 529-2029
General/National Adv. E-mail: cartnews@mts.net
Editorial e-mail: cartnews@mts.net
Primary Website: www.southernmanitobareview.com
Published: Thur
Avg Paid Circ: 790
Avg Free Circ: 10
Audit By: CMCA
Audit Date: 31.03.2017
Personnel: Vicki Wallace (Ed.)

SWAN VALLEY STAR & TIMES

Street address 1: 704 Main St. E.
Street address city: Swan River
Province/Territory: MB
Postal code: R0L 1Z0
Country: Canada

General Phone: (204) 734-3858
General Fax: (204) 734-4935
General/National Adv. E-mail: info@starandtimes.ca
Display Adv. E-mail: info@starandtimes.ca
Classified Adv. e-mail: info@starandtimes.ca
Editorial e-mail: editor@starandtimes.ca
Primary Website: www.starandtimes.ca
Published: Tues
Avg Paid Circ: 2700
Avg Free Circ: 0
Audit By: CMCA
Audit Date: 30.01.2017
Personnel: Brian T. Gilroy (Adv. Mgr., Publ., Gen. Mgr., Owner); Danielle Gordon-Broome (Ed.)

THE BOISSEVAIN RECORDER

Street address 1: 425 South Railway Street
Street address city: Boissevain
Province/Territory: MB
Postal code: R0K 0E0
County: Canada
Country: Canada
General Phone: (204) 534-6479
General Fax: (204) 534-2977
General/National Adv. E-mail: mail@therecorder.ca
Display Adv. E-mail: ads@therecorder.ca
Classified Adv. e-mail: mail@therecorder.ca
Editorial e-mail: editor@therecorder.ca
Primary Website: www.therecorder.ca
Published: Fri
Avg Paid Circ: 3863
Avg Free Circ: 44
Audit By: VAC
Audit Date: 31.01.2016
Personnel: Lorraine E. Houston (Ed.)

THE CARILLON

Street address 1: 377 Main St.
Street address city: Steinbach
Province/Territory: MB
Postal code: R5G 1A5
County: Canada
Country: Canada
General Phone: (204) 326-3421
General Fax: (204) 326-4860
General/National Adv. E-mail: info@thecarillon.com
Display Adv. E-mail: ads@thecarillon.com
Classified Adv. e-mail: mgauthier@thecarillon.com
Editorial e-mail: gburr@thecarillon.com
Primary Website: www.thecarillon.com
Published: Thur
Avg Paid Circ: 1140
Avg Free Circ: 234
Audit By: VAC
Audit Date: 30.09.2016
Personnel: Laurie Finley (Pub/Gen. Mgr.); Grant Burr (Ed); Holly-Jaide Nickel (Circ Mgr.)

THE CLIPPER WEEKLY & LAC DU BONNET CLIPPER

Street address 1: 27a-3rd Street South
Street address city: Beausejour
Province/Territory: MB
Postal code: R0E 0C0
Country: Canada
General Phone: (204) 268-4700
General Fax: (204) 268-3858
General/National Adv. E-mail: mail@clipper.mb.ca
Primary Website: www.clipper.mb.ca
Published: Thur
Avg Paid Circ: 46
Avg Free Circ: 12340
Audit By: VAC
Audit Date: 31.03.2016
Personnel: Kim MacAulay (Publisher); Mark Buss (Editor)
Parent company (for newspapers): Clipper Publishing Corp.

THE DELORAINE TIMES AND STAR

Street address 1: 122 Broadway, N.
Street address city: Deloraine
Province/Territory: MB
Postal code: R0M 0M0
Country: Canada
General Phone: (204) 747-2249
General Fax: (204) 747-3999
General/National Adv. E-mail: deltimes@mts.net
Display Adv. E-mail: ads.cpocket@mts.net
Editorial e-mail: cpocket@mts.net
Primary Website: http://www.delorainetimes.ca
Published: Fri
Avg Paid Circ: 770
Avg Free Circ: 57
Audit By: Sworn/Estimate/Non-Audited
Audit Date: 12.07.2019
Personnel: Judy Wells (Office Mgr.)
Parent company (for newspapers): Corner Pocket Publishing Ltd.; Glacier Media Group

THE EXPONENT

Street address 1: 414 Main St.
Street address city: Grandview
Province/Territory: MB
Postal code: R0L 0Y0
Country: Canada
General Phone: (204) 546-2555
General Fax: (204) 546-3081
General/National Adv. E-mail: expos@mts.net
Editorial e-mail: expos@mts.net
Primary Website: www.grandviewexponent.com
Published: Tues
Avg Paid Circ: 1687
Avg Free Circ: 27
Audit By: VAC
Audit Date: 31.01.2016
Personnel: Clayton Chaloner (Ed.)

THE HERALD

Street address 1: 1355 Mountain Ave.
Street address city: Winnipeg
Province/Territory: MB
Postal code: R2X 3B6
Country: Canada
General Phone: (204) 697-7009
General Fax: (204) 953-4300
Advertising Phone: (204) 697-7021
Display Adv. E-mail: sales@canstarnews.com
Editorial e-mail: letters@canstarnews.com
Primary Website: www.canstarnews.com
Published: Wed
Avg Paid Circ: 984
Avg Free Circ: 43869
Audit By: VAC
Audit Date: 31.08.2016
Personnel: Linda MacKenzie (Natl. Sales Mgr.); John Kendle (Mng. Ed.); Darren Ridgley; Barb Borden (Sales Mgr)
Parent company (for newspapers): Winnipeg Free Press

THE INTERLAKE SPECTATOR

Street address 1: 3411 3rd Avenue South
Street address 2: Unit 3
Street address city: Stonewall
Province/Territory: MB
Postal code: R0C 2Z0
Country: Canada
General Phone: (204) 467-2421
General Fax: (204) 467-5967
General/National Adv. E-mail: ispec@mts.net
Display Adv. E-mail: jbilsky@postmedia.com
Editorial e-mail: bjones@postmedia.com
Primary Website: http://www.interlaketoday.ca/interlakespectator
Published: Thur
Avg Paid Circ: 1520
Avg Free Circ: 10780
Audit By: VAC
Audit Date: 30.06.2016
Personnel: Jenifer Bilsky (Adv Dir.); Brook Jones (Ed)
Parent company (for newspapers): Postmedia Network Inc.; Quebecor Communications, Inc.

THE METRO

Street address 1: 1355 Mountain Ave.
Street address city: Winnipeg
Province/Territory: MB
Postal code: R2X 3B6
Country: Canada
General Phone: (204) 697-7009
General Fax: (204) 953-4300
Display Adv. E-mail: sales@canstarnews.com
Editorial e-mail: letters@canstarnews.com
Primary Website: www.canstarnews.com
Published: Wed
Avg Paid Circ: 141
Avg Free Circ: 36979
Audit By: VAC
Audit Date: 31.08.2016
Personnel: John Kendle (Mng. Ed.); Darren Ridgley (Deputy Ed); Linda Mackenzie (Exec Asst); Barb Borden (Sales Mgr)
Parent company (for newspapers): Winnipeg Free Press

THE NEEPAWA BANNER AND PRESS

Street address 1: 423 Mountain Avw.
Street address city: Neepawa
Province/Territory: MB
Postal code: R0J 1H0
Country: Canada
General Phone: (204) 476-3401
General Fax: (204) 476-5073
General/National Adv. E-mail: office@neepawapress.com
Display Adv. E-mail: ads@neepawabanner.com
Classified Adv. e-mail: print@neepawabanner.com
Editorial e-mail: news@neepawabanner.com
Primary Website: www.neepawabanner.com
Published: Fri
Avg Paid Circ: 100
Avg Free Circ: 8200
Audit By: VAC
Audit Date: 15.02.2018
Personnel: Kate Atkinson (Ed)
Parent company (for newspapers): Neepawa Banner

THE RED RIVER VALLEY ECHO

Street address 1: 67 2nd St.
Street address city: Altona
Province/Territory: MB
Postal code: R0G 0B0
Country: Canada
General Phone: (204) 324-5001
General Fax: (204) 324-1402
General/National Adv. E-mail: altona.news@sunmedia.ca
Display Adv. E-mail: Darcie.Morris@sunmedia.ca
Editorial e-mail: winkler.news@sunmedia.ca
Primary Website: www.altonaecho.com
Published: Thur
Avg Paid Circ: 27
Avg Free Circ: 4427
Audit By: VAC
Audit Date: 30.06.2016
Personnel: Greg Vandermeulen (Ed.); Darcie Morris (Adv Dir.)
Parent company (for newspapers): Postmedia Network Inc.; Quebecor Communications, Inc.

THE RESTON RECORDER

Street address 1: 330 4th St.
Street address city: Reston
Province/Territory: MB
Postal code: R0M 1X0
County: Canada
Country: Canada
General Phone: (204) 877-3321
General Fax: (204) 522-3648
General/National Adv. E-mail: recorder@mts.net
Editorial e-mail: recorder@mts.net
Primary Website: http://www.restonrecorder.ca/
Published: Fri
Avg Paid Circ: 116
Avg Free Circ: 59
Audit By: VAC
Audit Date: 31.12.2015
Personnel: Dolores Caldwell (Office Mgr.); Patty Lewis (Pub/Ed.)
Parent company (for newspapers): Glacier Media Group

THE ROBLIN REVIEW

Street address 1: 119 First Ave. Nw
Street address city: Roblin
Province/Territory: MB
Postal code: R0L 1P0
Country: Canada
General Phone: (204) 937-8377
General Fax: (204) 937-8212
General/National Adv. E-mail: roblinreview@mts.net
Display Adv. E-mail: reviewads@mts.net
Classified Adv. e-mail: reviewads@mts.net
Editorial e-mail: rreview@mts.net
Primary Website: theroblinreview.com
Published: Tues
Avg Paid Circ: 50
Avg Free Circ: 26
Audit By: VAC
Audit Date: 30.06.2016
Personnel: Patricia Liske (Circ. Mgr.); Ed Doering (Ed.); Brent Wright (Production Mgr.); Jackie Edel (Ad. consultant)

THE SENTINEL COURIER

Street address 1: 13 Railway St.
Street address city: Pilot Mound
Province/Territory: MB
Postal code: R0G 1P0
Country: Canada
General Phone: (204) 825-2772
General Fax: (204) 825-2439
General/National Adv. E-mail: sentinel@sentinelcourier.com
Editorial e-mail: sentinel@mymts.net
Primary Website: www.sentinelcourier.com
Published: Tues
Avg Paid Circ: 1273
Avg Free Circ: 31
Audit By: VAC
Audit Date: 31.05.2016
Personnel: Susan Peterson (Ed.)

THE SOUTHEAST JOURNAL

Street address 1: 108 Church Street
Street address city: Emerson
Province/Territory: MB
Postal code: R0A 0L0
County: Manitoba
Country: Canada
General Phone: (204) 373-2493
General Fax: (204)-272-3492
Advertising Phone: (204) 373-2493
Editorial Phone: (204) 373-2493
General/National Adv. E-mail: sej@mts.net
Display Adv. E-mail: sej@mts.net
Classified Adv. e-mail: sej@mts.net
Editorial e-mail: sej@mts.net
Primary Website: www.southeastjournal.ca
Published: Thur
Avg Paid Circ: 14
Avg Free Circ: 3500
Audit By: VAC
Audit Date: 31.08.2015

THE STONEWALL ARGUS & TEULON TIMES

Street address 1: 3411 3rd Avenue South
Street address city: Stonewall
Province/Territory: MB
Postal code: R0C 2Z0
County: Canada
Country: Canada
General Phone: (204) 467-2421
General Fax: (204) 467-5967
General/National Adv. E-mail: news@stonewallteulontribune.ca
Display Adv. E-mail: jbilsky@postmedia.com
Editorial e-mail: bjones@postmedia.com
Primary Website: http://www.interlaketoday.ca/stonewallargusteulontimes
Published: Thur
Avg Paid Circ: 1219
Avg Free Circ: 6467
Audit By: VAC
Audit Date: 30.06.2016
Personnel: Brook Jones (Ed); Jenifer Bilsky (Adv Dir)
Parent company (for newspapers): Postmedia Network Inc.; Quebecor Communications, Inc.

THE TIMES

Street address 1: 1355 Mountain Ave.
Street address city: Winnipeg
Province/Territory: MB
Postal code: R2X 3B6
Country: Canada
General Phone: (204) 697-7009
General Fax: (204) 953-4300
Advertising Phone: (204) 697-7021
General/National Adv. E-mail: sales@canstarnews.com

Display Adv. E-mail: sales@canstarnews.com
Editorial e-mail: letters@canstarnews.com
Primary Website: www.canstarnews.com
Published: Wed
Avg Paid Circ: 20
Avg Free Circ: 37763
Audit By: VAC
Audit Date: 31.08.2016
Personnel: John Kendle (Mng. Ed.); Darren Ridgley; Barb Borden (Sales Mgr); Linda MacKenzie
Parent company (for newspapers): Winnipeg Free Press

THE VALLEY LEADER

Street address 1: 4 - 1st St Sw
Street address city: Carman
Province/Territory: MB
Postal code: R0G 0J0
County: Canada
Country: Canada
General Phone: (204) 745-2051
General Fax: (204) 745-3976
General/National Adv. E-mail: carmenvl@mts.net
Display Adv. E-mail: Darcie.Morris@sunmedia.ca
Editorial e-mail: winkler.news@sunmedia.ca
Primary Website: http://www.pembinatoday.ca/carmanvalleyleader
Published: Thur
Avg Paid Circ: 955
Avg Free Circ: 3872
Audit By: VAC
Audit Date: 30.06.2016
Personnel: Darcie Morris (Adv Dir); Greg Vandermeulen (Ed)
Parent company (for newspapers): Postmedia Network Inc.; Quebecor Communications, Inc.

THE WESTERN CANADIAN

Street address 1: 424 Ellis Ave. E.
Street address city: Manitou
Province/Territory: MB
Postal code: R0G 1G0
County: Canada
Country: Canada
General Phone: (204) 242-2555
General Fax: (204) 242-3137
General/National Adv. E-mail: westerncanadian@goinet.ca
Editorial e-mail: thewesterncanadian@gmail.com
Primary Website: http://www.thewesterncanadian.ca/
Published: Tues
Avg Paid Circ: 1057
Avg Free Circ: 0
Audit By: VAC
Audit Date: 31.05.2016
Personnel: Grant Howett (Ed.)

THOMPSON CITIZEN

Street address 1: 141 Commercial Pl.
Street address city: Thompson
Province/Territory: MB
Postal code: R8N 1T1
County: Canada
Country: Canada
General Phone: (204) 677-4534
General Fax: (204) 677-3681
Advertising Phone: (204) 677-4534
Editorial Phone: (204) 677-4534
General/National Adv. E-mail: generalmanager@thompsoncitizen.net
Display Adv. E-mail: ads@thompsoncitizen.net
Classified Adv. e-mail: classifieds@thompsoncitizen.net
Editorial e-mail: editor@thompsoncitizen.net
Primary Website: www.thompsoncitizen.net
Published: Fri
Avg Paid Circ: 61
Avg Free Circ: 5000
Audit By: Sworn/Estimate/Non-Audited
Audit Date: 12.07.2022
Personnel: Lynn Taylor (Publisher); Ian Graham (Ed.)
Parent company (for newspapers): Glacier Media Group

TIMES

Street address 1: 194 Broadway St.
Street address city: Treherne
Province/Territory: MB
Postal code: R0G 2V0
Country: Canada
General Phone: (204) 723-2542
General Fax: (204) 723-2754
General/National Adv. E-mail: trehernetimes@mts.net
Editorial e-mail: trehernetimes@mts.net
Primary Website: www.trehernetimes.ca
Published: Mon
Avg Free Circ: 842
Audit By: VAC
Audit Date: 30.06.2016
Personnel: Gary Lodwick (Ed.)

VIRDEN EMPIRE-ADVANCE

Street address 1: 305 Nelson Street West
Street address city: Virden
Province/Territory: MB
Postal code: R0M 2C0
County: Canada
Country: Canada
General Phone: (204) 748-3931
General Fax: (204) 748-1816
General/National Adv. E-mail: trehernetimes@mts.net
Display Adv. E-mail: virden@empireadvance.ca
Editorial e-mail: manager@empireadvance.ca
Primary Website: http://www.empireadvance.ca/
Published: Fri
Avg Free Circ: 27
Audit By: VAC
Audit Date: 30.09.2016
Personnel: Cheryl Rushing (Gen Mgr)
Parent company (for newspapers): Glacier Media Group

WESTMAN JOURNAL

Street address 1: 315 College Avenue
Street address 2: Unit D
Street address city: Brandon
Province/Territory: MB
Postal code: R7A 1E7
Country: Canada
General Phone: (204) 725-0209
General Fax: (204) 725-3021
General/National Adv. E-mail: info@wheatcityjournal.ca
Display Adv. E-mail: rthomson@wheatcityjournal.ca
Classified Adv. e-mail: agrelowshi@wheatcityjournal.ca
Editorial e-mail: newsroom@wheatcityjournal.ca
Primary Website: www.westmanjournal.com
Published: Thur
Avg Free Circ: 13500
Audit By: VAC
Audit Date: 25.11.2017
Personnel: Rick Thomson; Alida Grelowski; Adam Wilken; Jamie Polmateer; Wade Branston; Brian Aitkinson; Judy Cluff (Admin Asst.)
Parent company (for newspapers): Glacier Media Group

WINKLER TIMES

Street address 1: 583 Main St.
Street address city: Winkler
Province/Territory: MB
Postal code: R6W 4B3
County: Canada
Country: Canada
General Phone: (204) 325-4771
General Fax: (204) 325-8646
General/National Adv. E-mail: winkler.class@sunmedia.ca
Display Adv. E-mail: Darcie.Morris@sunmedia.ca
Editorial e-mail: winkler.news@sunmedia.ca
Primary Website: http://www.pembinatoday.ca/winklertimes
Published: Thur
Avg Free Circ: 7459
Audit By: VAC
Audit Date: 30.09.2016
Personnel: Darcie Morris (Adv Dir); Greg Vandermeulen (Ed)
Parent company (for newspapers): Postmedia Network Inc.; Quebecor Communications, Inc.

NEW BRUNSWICK

L' ETOILE CATARACTE

Street address 1: 229 Broadway Blvd.
Street address city: Grand Falls
Province/Territory: NB
Postal code: E3Z 2K1
Country: Canada
General Phone: (506) 473-3083
General Fax: (506) 473-3105
General/National Adv. E-mail: cataract@nb.aibn.com
Editorial e-mail: rickard.mark@victoriastar.ca
Primary Website: https://www.telegraphjournal.com/letoile/
Published: Thur
Avg Paid Circ: 0
Avg Free Circ: 6296
Audit By: CMCA
Audit Date: 30.09.2013
Personnel: Mark Rickard (Ed. English); Madeleine Leclerc (Ed., French)
Parent company (for newspapers): Brunswick News, Inc.

LE MADAWASKA

Street address 1: 20 Rue Saint Francois
Street address city: Edmundston
Province/Territory: NB
Postal code: E3V 1E3
Country: Canada
General Phone: (506) 735-5575
General Fax: (506) 735-8086
General/National Adv. E-mail: madproduction@brunswicknews.com
Editorial e-mail: madproduction@brunswicknews.com
Primary Website: https://www.telegraphjournal.com/le-madawaska/
Published: Sat
Avg Paid Circ: 2561
Avg Free Circ: 20
Audit By: VAC
Audit Date: 31.12.2015
Personnel: Hermel Volpe (Pub.)
Parent company (for newspapers): Brunswick News, Inc.

LE MONITEUR ACADIEN

Street address 1: Cp 5191 817, West Boudreau
Street address city: Shediac
Province/Territory: NB
Postal code: E4P 8T9
Country: Canada
General Phone: (506) 532-6680
General Fax: (506) 532-6681
General/National Adv. E-mail: moniteur@rogers.com
Primary Website: www.moniteuracadien.com
Published: Wed
Avg Paid Circ: 3500
Avg Free Circ: 500
Audit By: Sworn/Estimate/Non-Audited
Audit Date: 12.07.2019
Personnel: Gilles Hache (Ed.)

MIRAMICHI LEADER

Street address 1: 175 General Manson Way
Street address city: Miramichi
Province/Territory: NB
Postal code: E1N 6K7
Country: Canada
General Phone: (506) 622-2600
General Fax: (506) 622-6506
General/National Adv. E-mail: news@miramichileader.com
Editorial e-mail: cook.nancy@miramichileader.com
Primary Website: https://www.telegraphjournal.com/miramichi-leader/
Published: Mon`Wed
Avg Paid Circ: 3768
Avg Free Circ: 13
Audit By: CMCA
Audit Date: 31.12.2013
Personnel: Nancy Cook (Pub.); Christine Savoy (Circ. Mgr.)
Parent company (for newspapers): Brunswick News, Inc.

NORTHSIDE THIS WEEK

Street address 1: 984 Prospect St.
Street address city: Fredericton
Province/Territory: NB
Postal code: E3B 5A2
Country: Canada
General Phone: (506) 452-6671
General Fax: (506) 452-7405
General/National Adv. E-mail: northside@brunswicknews.com
Editorial e-mail: shelley.wood@brunswicknews.com
Published: Sat
Avg Free Circ: 9950
Audit By: Sworn/Estimate/Non-Audited
Audit Date: 12.07.2019
Personnel: Shelly Wood (Pub./Ed)
Parent company (for newspapers): Brunswick News, Inc.

ST. CROIX COURIER

Street address 1: P.O. Box 250
Street address 2: 47 Milltown Boulevard
Street address city: Saint Stephen
Province/Territory: NB
Postal code: E3L 2X2
County: Canada
Country: Canada
General Phone: (506) 466-3220
General Fax: (506) 466-9950
General/National Adv. E-mail: courier@nb.aibn.com
Display Adv. E-mail: cairns@stcroixcourier.ca
Editorial e-mail: editor@stcroixcourier.ca
Primary Website: www.stcroixcourier.com
Published: Tues
Avg Paid Circ: 1075
Avg Free Circ: 40
Audit By: VAC
Audit Date: 31.01.2016
Personnel: Leith Orr (Pub.); Shelley McKeeman (Gen. Mgr.); Krisi Marples (Ed)

THE BUGLE-OBSERVER

Street address 1: 110 Carleton St.
Street address city: Woodstock
Province/Territory: NB
Postal code: E7M 1E4
Country: Canada
General Phone: (506) 328-8863
General Fax: (506) 328-3208
General/National Adv. E-mail: news@thebugle.ca
Editorial e-mail: news@thebugle.ca
Primary Website: https://www.telegraphjournal.com/bugle-observer/
Published: Tues`Fri
Avg Paid Circ: 2693
Avg Free Circ: 56
Audit By: CMCA
Audit Date: 31.12.2013
Personnel: Peter Macingosh (Gen Mgr.); Edward Farrell (Circ. Mgr.)
Parent company (for newspapers): Brunswick News, Inc.

THE KINGS COUNTY RECORD

Street address 1: 593 Main St.
Street address city: Sussex
Province/Territory: NB
Postal code: E4E 7H5
Country: Canada
General Phone: (506) 433-1070
General Fax: (506) 432-3532
General/National Adv. E-mail: news@kingcorecord.com
Editorial e-mail: craig.victoria@kingscorecord.com
Primary Website: https://www.telegraphjournal.com/kings-county-record/
Published: Tues
Avg Paid Circ: 0
Avg Free Circ: 2
Audit By: VAC
Audit Date: 31.12.2015
Personnel: Victoria Craig (Pub./Ed); Teresa Perry (Circ. Mgr.)

Parent company (for newspapers): Brunswick News, Inc.

THE NEW FREEMAN

Street address 1: One Bayard Dr.
Street address city: Saint John
Province/Territory: NB
Postal code: E2L 3L5
County: Canada
Country: Canada
General Phone: (506) 653-6806
General Fax: (506) 653-6818
General/National Adv. E-mail: tnf@nbnet.nb.ca
Editorial e-mail: tnf@nb.aibn.com
Primary Website: http://www.dioceseofsaintjohn.org/TNF.aspx
Published: Fri
Avg Paid Circ: 7000
Audit By: Sworn/Estimate/Non-Audited
Audit Date: 12.07.2019
Personnel: Margie Trafton (Mng. Ed.)

THE NORTHERN LIGHT

Street address 1: 355 King Ave.
Street address city: Bathurst
Province/Territory: NB
Postal code: E2A 1P4
County: Canada
Country: Canada
General Phone: (506) 546-4491
General Fax: (506) 546-1491
Editorial e-mail: mulock.greg@thenorthernlight.ca
Primary Website: https://www.telegraphjournal.com/northern-light/
Published: Tues
Avg Paid Circ: 2890
Avg Free Circ: 12
Audit By: VAC
Audit Date: 31.12.2015
Personnel: Greg Mulock (Ed.)
Parent company (for newspapers): Brunswick News, Inc.

THE OBSERVER

Street address 1: 941 Industrial Dr.
Street address city: Hartland
Province/Territory: NB
Postal code: E7P 2G8
County: Canada
Country: Canada
General Phone: (506) 375-4458
General Fax: (506) 375-4281
General/National Adv. E-mail: theobserver@nb.aibn.com
Published: Wed
Avg Paid Circ: 2569
Audit By: Sworn/Estimate/Non-Audited
Audit Date: 12.07.2019
Personnel: Stewart Fairgrieve (Gen. Mgr.)

THE OROMOCTO POST-GAZETTE

Street address 1: 291 Restigouche Rd.
Street address city: Oromocto
Province/Territory: NB
Postal code: E2V 2H2
Country: Canada
General Phone: (506) 357-9813
General Fax: (506) 452-7405
General/National Adv. E-mail: allen.shari@dailygleaner.com
Display Adv. E-mail: shelley.wood@brunswicknews.com
Editorial e-mail: williams.kimberly@dailygleaner.com
Primary Website: www.brunswicknews.com
Published: Thur
Avg Paid Circ: 0
Avg Free Circ: 12844
Audit By: CMCA
Audit Date: 30.09.2013
Personnel: Shelly Wood (Adv. Mgr.); Kimberly Williams (Pub/Ed.)
Parent company (for newspapers): Brunswick News, Inc.

THE SACKVILLE TRIBUNE-POST

Street address 1: 80 Main St.
Street address city: Sackville
Province/Territory: NB
Postal code: E4L 4A7
Country: Canada
General Phone: (506) 536-2500
General Fax: (506) 536-4024
General/National Adv. E-mail: sdoherty@sackvilletribunepost.com
Editorial e-mail: sdoherty@sackvilletribunepost.com
Primary Website: www.sackvilletribunepost.com
Published: Wed
Avg Paid Circ: 2150
Avg Free Circ: 4
Audit By: VAC
Audit Date: 31.10.2015
Personnel: Richard Russell (Pub.); Scott Doherty (Ed.); Tanya Austin (Circ/Class. Mgr)
Parent company (for newspapers): Transcontinental Media

THE TRIBUNE

Street address 1: 6 Shannon St.
Street address city: Campbellton
Province/Territory: NB
Postal code: E3N 3G9
Country: Canada
General Phone: (506) 753-4413
General Fax: (506) 759-9595
General/National Adv. E-mail: tribune@tribunenb.ca
Editorial e-mail: tribune@tribunenb.ca
Primary Website: http://www.telegraphjournal.com/tribune/
Published: Fri
Avg Free Circ: 2
Audit By: VAC
Audit Date: 31.12.2015
Personnel: Peter Makintosh (Pub./Ed)

VICTORIA COUNTY STAR

Street address 1: 229 Broadway Blvd.
Street address city: Grand Falls
Province/Territory: NB
Postal code: E3Z 2K1
Country: Canada
General Phone: (506) 473-3083
General Fax: (506) 473-3105
Editorial e-mail: rickard.mark@victoriastar.ca
Primary Website: https://www.telegraphjournal.com/victoria-star/
Published: Wed
Avg Paid Circ: 2175
Avg Free Circ: 2
Audit By: VAC
Audit Date: 31.12.2015
Personnel: Mark Rickard (Ed., English); Madeleine Leclerc (Ed., French)
Parent company (for newspapers): Brunswick News, Inc.

NEWFOUNDLAND AND LABRADOR

HARBOUR BRETON COASTER

Street address 1: 30-42 Canada Drive
Street address city: Harbour Breton
Province/Territory: NL
Postal code: A0H 1P0
Country: Canada
General Phone: (709) 885-2378
General Fax: (709) 885-2393
Editorial e-mail: editor@thecoasterr.ca
Primary Website: www.thecoasterr.ca
Published: Tues
Avg Paid Circ: 1283
Avg Free Circ: 0
Audit By: CMCA
Audit Date: 30.06.2013
Personnel: Clayton Hunt (Ed.)
Parent company (for newspapers): Transcontinental Media

LE GABOTEUR

Street address 1: 65 Ridge Road
Street address city: St. John's
Province/Territory: NL
Postal code: A1B 4P5
Country: Canada
General Phone: (709) 753-9585
Display Adv. E-mail: annonces@gaboteur.ca
Editorial e-mail: redaction@gaboteur.ca
Primary Website: www.gaboteur.ca
Published: Bi-Mthly
Avg Paid Circ: 850
Avg Free Circ: 0
Audit By: CMCA
Audit Date: 31.03.2013
Personnel: Jacinthe Tremblay (Dir/Ed)

NORTHERN PEN

Street address 1: 10-12 North St.
Street address city: Saint Anthony
Province/Territory: NL
Postal code: A0K 4S0
County: Canada
Country: Canada
General Phone: (709) 454-2191
General Fax: (709) 454-3718
General/National Adv. E-mail: info@northernpen.ca
Display Adv. E-mail: kparsons@nothernpen.ca
Editorial e-mail: arandell@nothernpen.ca
Primary Website: www.northernpen.ca
Published: Mon
Avg Paid Circ: 1085
Avg Free Circ: 0
Audit By: VAC
Audit Date: 31.12.2015
Personnel: Kathy Parsons (Adv. Mgr.); Frances Reardon (Office/Circ Mgr); Adam Randell (Ed)
Parent company (for newspapers): Transcontinental Media

THE ADVERTISER

Street address 1: Po Box 129
Street address city: Grand Falls
Province/Territory: NL
Postal code: A2A 2J4
Country: Canada
General Phone: (709) 489-2162
General Fax: (709) 489-4817
General/National Adv. E-mail: editor@advertisernl.ca
Editorial e-mail: editor@advertisernl.ca
Primary Website: www.gfwadvertiser.ca
Published: Thur
Avg Paid Circ: 1600
Avg Free Circ: 0
Audit By: VAC
Audit Date: 31.12.2015
Personnel: Ron Ennis (Ed.)
Parent company (for newspapers): Transcontinental Media

THE AURORA

Street address 1: 500 Vanier Ave.
Street address city: Labrador City
Province/Territory: NL
Postal code: A2V 2K7
County: Canada
General Phone: (709) 944-2957
General Fax: (709) 944-2958
General/National Adv. E-mail: editor@theaurora.ca
Editorial e-mail: mmurphy@optipress.ca
Primary Website: www.theaurora.ca
Published: Mon
Avg Paid Circ: 1001
Audit By: VAC
Audit Date: 30.06.2016
Personnel: Shawn Woodford (Pub.); Michelle Stewart (Ed.)
Parent company (for newspapers): Transcontinental Media

THE COMPASS

Street address 1: 176 Water St.
Street address city: Carbonear
Province/Territory: NL
Postal code: A1Y 1C3
Country: Canada
General Phone: (709) 596-6458
General Fax: (709) 596-1700
General/National Adv. E-mail: editor@cbncompass.ca
Editorial e-mail: editor@cbncompass.ca
Primary Website: www.cbncompass.ca
Published: Tues
Avg Paid Circ: 2376
Avg Free Circ: 0
Audit By: VAC
Audit Date: 31.12.2015
Personnel: Bill Bowman (Ed)
Parent company (for newspapers): Transcontinental Media

THE GANDER BEACON

Street address 1: 61 Elizabeth Dr.
Street address city: Gander
Province/Territory: NL
Postal code: A1V 1W8
Country: Canada
General Phone: (709) 256-4371
General Fax: (709) 256-3826
General/National Adv. E-mail: info@ganderbeacon.ca
Primary Website: www.ganderbeacon.ca
Published: Thur
Avg Paid Circ: 929
Avg Free Circ: 0
Audit By: VAC
Audit Date: 31.12.2015
Personnel: Kevin Higgins (Gen. Mgr.)
Parent company (for newspapers): Transcontinental Media

THE GEORGIAN

Street address 1: 43 Main St.
Street address 2: 43 Main Street
Street address city: Stephenville
Province/Territory: NL
Postal code: A2N 2Z4
Country: Canada
General Phone: (709) 643-4531
General Fax: (709) 643-5041
Editorial e-mail: editor@thegeorgian.ca
Primary Website: www.thegeorgian.ca
Published: Mon
Avg Paid Circ: 1152
Avg Free Circ: 0
Audit By: CMCA
Audit Date: 30.06.2013
Personnel: Christopher Vaughan (Ed.)
Parent company (for newspapers): Transcontinental Media

THE GULF NEWS

Street address 1: Po Box 1090
Street address city: Port aux Basques
Province/Territory: NL
Postal code: A0M 1C0
County: Canada
Country: Canada
General Phone: (709) 695-3671
General Fax: (709) 695-7901
Advertising Phone: (709) 279-3188
General/National Adv. E-mail: editor@gulfnews.ca
Display Adv. E-mail: wrose@thewesternstar.com
Editorial e-mail: chantelle.macisaac@gulfnews.ca
Primary Website: www.gulfnews.ca
Published: Mon
Avg Paid Circ: 2912
Avg Free Circ: 0
Audit By: VAC
Audit Date: 31.12.2015
Personnel: Chantelle Macisaac (Ed); Wendy Rose (Adv.)
Parent company (for newspapers): Transcontinental Media

THE LABRADORIAN

Street address 1: 2 Hillcrest Rd.
Street address city: Happy Valley
Province/Territory: NL
Postal code: A0P 1E0
Country: Canada
General Phone: (709) 896-3341
General Fax: (709) 896-8781
Advertising Phone: (709) 896-3341
General/National Adv. E-mail: sgallant@thelabradorian.ca
Display Adv. E-mail: sgallant@thelabradorian.ca
Editorial e-mail: editor@thelabradorian.ca
Primary Website: www.thelabradorian.ca
Published: Mon
Avg Paid Circ: 2009
Avg Free Circ: 0
Audit By: VAC

Audit Date: 31.12.2015
Personnel: Sharon Gallant (Adv)
Parent company (for newspapers): Transcontinental Media

THE NOR'WESTER

Street address 1: Po Box 28
Street address city: Springdale
Province/Territory: NL
Postal code: A0J 1T0
County: Canada
Country: Canada
General Phone: (709) 673-3721
General Fax: (709) 673-4171
Editorial e-mail: editor@thenorwester.ca
Primary Website: www.thenorwester.ca
Published: Thur
Avg Paid Circ: 1730
Avg Free Circ: 0
Audit By: VAC
Audit Date: 31.12.2015
Personnel: Rudy Norman (Ed.)
Parent company (for newspapers): Transcontinental Media

THE PACKET

Street address 1: 8 B Thomson St.
Street address city: Clarenville
Province/Territory: NL
Postal code: A5A 1Y9
County: Canada
Country: Canada
General Phone: (709) 466-2243
General Fax: (709) 466-2717
General/National Adv. E-mail: editor@thepacket.ca
Editorial e-mail: editor@thepacket.ca
Primary Website: www.thepacket.ca
Published: Thur
Avg Paid Circ: 1109
Avg Free Circ: 0
Audit By: VAC
Audit Date: 31.12.2015
Personnel: Barbara Dean-Simmons (Ed.)
Parent company (for newspapers): Transcontinental Media

THE PILOT

Street address 1: P151 Main St
Street address city: Lewisporte
Province/Territory: NL
Postal code: A0G 3A0
County: Canada
Country: Canada
General Phone: (709) 535-6910
General Fax: (709) 535-8640
General/National Adv. E-mail: editor@pilotnl.ca
Display Adv. E-mail: pilotsales@optipress.ca
Editorial e-mail: editor@pilotnl.ca
Primary Website: http://www.lportepilot.ca/
Published: Wed
Avg Paid Circ: 312
Avg Free Circ: 0
Audit By: VAC
Audit Date: 31.12.2015
Personnel: Joanne Chaffey (Adv. Mgr.); Karen Wells (Ed.)
Parent company (for newspapers): Transcontinental Media

THE SOUTHERN GAZETTE

Street address 1: Po Box 1116
Street address city: Marystown
Province/Territory: NL
Postal code: A0E 2M0
County: Canada
Country: Canada
General Phone: (709) 279-3188
General Fax: (709) 279-2628
General/National Adv. E-mail: editor@southerngazette.ca
Editorial e-mail: editor@southerngazette.ca
Primary Website: www.southerngazette.ca
Published: Tues
Avg Paid Circ: 2231
Avg Free Circ: 0
Audit By: VAC
Audit Date: 31.12.2015
Personnel: George MacVicar (Ed.)
Parent company (for newspapers): Transcontinental Media

NORTHWEST TERRITORIES

DEH CHO DRUM

Street address 1: 5108 50th St.
Street address city: Yellowknife
Province/Territory: NT
Postal code: X1A 2R1
Country: Canada
General Phone: (867) 873-4031
General Fax: (867) 873-8507
General/National Adv. E-mail: nnsl@nnsl.com
Display Adv. E-mail: advertising@nnsl.com
Editorial e-mail: editorial@nnsl.com
Primary Website: http://www.nnsl.com/dehcho/dehcho.html
Published: Thur
Avg Free Circ: 708
Audit By: VAC
Audit Date: 31.05.2016
Personnel: Jack Sigvaldason (Pub.); Michael Scott (Gen. Mgr.); Petra Ehrke (Adv. Mgr.); Debra Davis (Circ. Mgr.); Bruce Valpy (Mng. Ed.)

INUVIK DRUM

Street address 1: Po Box 2820
Street address city: Yellowknife
Province/Territory: NT
Postal code: X1A 2R1
Country: Canada
General Phone: (867) 873-4031
General Fax: (867) 873-8507
General/National Adv. E-mail: nnsl@nnsl.com
Display Adv. E-mail: advertising@nnsl.com
Editorial e-mail: editorial@nnsl.com
Primary Website: www.nnsl.com
Published: Thur
Avg Paid Circ: 201
Avg Free Circ: 290
Audit By: VAC
Audit Date: 31.05.2016
Personnel: Jack Sigvaldason (Pub.); Michael Scott (Gen. Mgr.); Petra Ehrke (Adv. Mgr.); Debra Davis (Circ. Mgr.); Bruce Valpy (Mng. Ed.)

L'AQUILON

Street address 1: 5102-51 Street, 2nd Floor
Street address city: Yellowknife
Province/Territory: NT
Postal code: X1A 1S7
Country: Canada
General Phone: (867) 873-6603
General Fax: (867) 873-6663
General/National Adv. E-mail: direction.aquilon@northwestel.net
Display Adv. E-mail: sandra@repco-media.ca
Editorial e-mail: aquilon@internorth.com
Primary Website: www.aquilon.nt.ca
Published: Fri
Avg Free Circ: 875
Audit By: Sworn/Estimate/Non-Audited
Audit Date: 12.07.2019
Personnel: Alain Bessette (Ed.)

NEWS/NORTH

Street address 1: 5108 50th St.
Street address city: Yellowknife
Province/Territory: NT
Postal code: X1A 2R1
County: Canada
Country: Canada
General Phone: (867) 873-4031
General Fax: (867) 873-8507
General/National Adv. E-mail: nnsl@nnsl.com
Display Adv. E-mail: advertising@nnsl.com
Editorial e-mail: editorial@nnsl.com
Primary Website: www.nnsl.com
Published: Mon
Avg Paid Circ: 1922
Avg Free Circ: 2167
Audit By: VAC
Audit Date: 31.03.2016
Personnel: Jack Sigvaldason (Pub.); Michael Scott (Gen. Mgr.); Petra Ehrke (Adv. Mgr.); Debra Davis (Circ. Mgr.); Bruce Valpy (Ed.)

NORTHERN JOURNAL

Street address 1: 207 Mcdougal Rd.
Street address city: Fort Smith
Province/Territory: NT
Postal code: X0E 0P0
County: Canada
Country: Canada
General Phone: (867) 872-3000
General Fax: (867) 872-2754
General/National Adv. E-mail: don@srj.ca
Display Adv. E-mail: admin@norj.ca
Editorial e-mail: don@norj.ca
Primary Website: http://norj.ca/
Published: Other
Avg Paid Circ: 3660
Avg Free Circ: 4065
Audit By: Sworn/Estimate/Non-Audited
Audit Date: 12.07.2019
Personnel: Sandra Jaque (Mgr); Don Jaque (Ed.)
Parent company (for newspapers): Cascade Publishing Ltd.

THE HUB

Street address 1: 8-4 Courtoreille St.
Street address city: Hay River
Province/Territory: NT
Postal code: X0E 1G2
Country: Canada
General Phone: (867) 874-6577
General Fax: (867) 874-2679
General/National Adv. E-mail: hub@hayriverhub.com
Display Adv. E-mail: ads@hayriverhub.com
Editorial e-mail: web@hayriverhub.com
Primary Website: www.hayriverhub.com
Published: Wed
Avg Paid Circ: 1996
Avg Free Circ: 182
Audit By: VAC
Audit Date: 31.01.2016
Personnel: Chris Brodeur (Pub.); Lehaina Andrews (Adv. Mgr.); Lorna Desilets (Circ. Mgr.)

YELLOWKNIFER

Street address 1: 5108 50th St.
Street address city: Yellowknife
Province/Territory: NT
Postal code: X1A 2R1
Country: Canada
General Phone: (867) 873-4031
General Fax: (867) 873-8507
General/National Adv. E-mail: nnsladmin@nnsl.com
Display Adv. E-mail: advertising@nnsl.com
Editorial e-mail: editorial@nnsl.com
Primary Website: www.nnsl.com
Published: Wed`Fri
Avg Paid Circ: 2077
Avg Free Circ: 963
Audit By: VAC
Audit Date: 30.04.2016
Personnel: Jack Sigvaldason (Pub.); Michael Scott (Gen. Mgr.); Petra Ehrke (Adv.); Debra Davis (Circ. Mgr.); Bruce Valpy (Mng. Ed.)

NOVA SCOTIA

AMHERST DAILY NEWS

Street address 1: 147 S. Albion St.
Street address city: Amherst
Province/Territory: NS
Postal code: B4H 2X2
Country: Canada
General Phone: (902) 667-5102
General Fax: (902) 667-0419
Editorial Phone: (902) 661-5426
General/National Adv. E-mail: dcole@amherstdaily.com
Display Adv. E-mail: gcoish@amherstdaily.com
Editorial e-mail: darrell.cole@tc.tc
Primary Website: www.cumberlandnewsnow.com
Published: Fri
Avg Paid Circ: 4057
Avg Free Circ: 349
Audit By: VAC
Audit Date: 31.12.2015
Personnel: Richard Russell (Pub.); Greg Landry (Ops. Mgr.); Gladys Coish (Adv. Mgr.); Chuck Macinnes (Circ. Mgr.); Darrell Cole (Sr. Ed.)
Parent company (for newspapers): Transcontinental Media

BEDFORD - SACKVILLE WEEKLY NEWS

Street address 1: 211 Horseshoe Lake Dr
Street address city: Halifax
Province/Territory: NS
Postal code: B3S 0B9
Country: Canada
General Phone: (902) 426-2811
General Fax: (902) 426-1170
General/National Adv. E-mail: reception@herald.ca
Display Adv. E-mail: sales@herald.ca
Classified Adv. e-mail: classified@herald.ca
Editorial e-mail: newsroom@herald.ca
Primary Website: http://thechronicleherald.ca/community/bedfordsackvilleobserver
Published: Thur
Avg Free Circ: 29302
Audit By: CMCA
Audit Date: 28.02.2013
Personnel: Sheryl Grant (Adv. Media Dir.); Kim Moar (Mng. Ed.)

COLE HARBOUR WEEKLY

Street address 1: 211 Horseshoe Lake Dr
Street address city: Halifax
Province/Territory: NS
Postal code: B3S 0B9
Country: Canada
General Phone: (902) 426-2811
General Fax: (902) 426-1170
General/National Adv. E-mail: reception@herald.ca
Display Adv. E-mail: sales@herald.ca
Classified Adv. e-mail: classifieds@herald.ca
Editorial e-mail: newsroom@herald.ca
Primary Website: www.thechronicleherald.ca
Published: Thur
Avg Free Circ: 37643
Audit By: CMCA
Audit Date: 28.02.2013
Personnel: Fred Fiander (Pub.); Sheryl Grant (Adv. Media Dir.)

ENFIELD WEEKLY PRESS

Street address 1: 287 Highway 2
Street address city: Enfield
Province/Territory: NS
Postal code: B2T 1C9
Country: Canada
General Phone: (902) 883-3181
General Fax: (902) 883-3180
General/National Adv. E-mail: editor@enfieldweeklypress.com
Display Adv. E-mail: michelewhite@enfieldweeklypress.com
Classified Adv. e-mail: admin@enfieldweeklypress.com
Editorial e-mail: editor@enfieldweeklypress.com
Primary Website: www.enfieldweeklypress.com
Published: Wed
Avg Free Circ: 10914
Audit By: VAC
Audit Date: 30.06.2016
Personnel: Leith Orr (Pub); Michele White (Adv. Rep)

FALL RIVER LAKER

Street address 1: 287 Highway 2
Street address city: Enfield
Province/Territory: NS
Postal code: B2T 1C9
General Phone: (902) 883-3181, Ext. 3
General Fax: (902) 883-3180
Display Adv. E-mail: michelewhite@enfieldweeklypress.com
Classified Adv. e-mail: admin@enfieldweeklypress.com
Editorial e-mail: editor@enfieldweeklypress.com
Primary Website: www.thelaker.ca
Published: Thur

Avg Paid Circ: 2247
Avg Free Circ: 7703
Audit By: VAC
Audit Date: 30.04.2016
Personnel: Leith Orr (Pub); Michele White (Adv. Rep)

GUYSBOROUGH JOURNAL

Street address 1: P.O. Box 210
Street address city: Guysborough
Province/Territory: NS
Postal code: B0H 1N0
Country: Canada
General Phone: (902) 533-2851
General/National Adv. E-mail: news@guysboroughjournal.ca
Display Adv. E-mail: advertising@guysboroughjournal.ca
Classified Adv. e-mail: advertising@guysboroughjourna
Editorial e-mail: news@guysboroughjournal.ca
Primary Website: www.guysboroughjournal.com
Published: Wed
Avg Paid Circ: 1000
Avg Free Circ: 13
Audit By: Sworn/Estimate/Non-Audited
Audit Date: 30.[illegible]
Personnel: Allan Murphy (Pub); Helen Murphy (Ed/Mgr/Pub); Sharon Heighton (Office/Circ. Mgr)

HALIFAX WEST-CLAYTON PARK WEEKLY NEWS

Street address 1: 211 Horseshoe Lake Dr
Street address city: Halifax
Province/Territory: NS
Postal code: B3S 0B9
Country: Canada
General Phone: (902) 421-5888
General/National Adv. E-mail: reception@herald.ca
Display Adv. E-mail: sgrant@herald.ca
Classified Adv. e-mail: classified@herald.ca
Editorial e-mail: newsroom@herald.ca
Primary Website: www.thechronicleherald.ca
Published: Thur
Avg Free Circ: 37145
Audit By: CMCA
Audit Date: 28.02.2013
Personnel: Sheryl Grant (Adv. Media Dir.); Kim Moar (Mng. Ed.)

HANTS JOURNAL

Street address 1: 73 Gerrish St.
Street address city: Windsor
Province/Territory: NS
Postal code: B0N 2T0
Country: Canada
General Phone: (902) 798-8371
General Fax: (902) 798-5451
General/National Adv. E-mail: info@hantsjournal.ca
Primary Website: www.hantsjournal.ca
Published: Thur
Avg Paid Circ: 2233
Avg Free Circ: 15
Audit By: CMCA
Audit Date: 30.06.2014
Personnel: Ray Savage (Sales. Mgr.)
Parent company (for newspapers): Transcontinental Media

LE COURRIER DE LA NOUVELLE-ECOSSE

Street address 1: 795 Route 1
Street address city: Comeauville
Province/Territory: NS
Postal code: B0W 2Z0
County: Canada
Country: Canada
General Phone: (902) 769-3078
General Fax: (902) 769-3869
General/National Adv. E-mail: publicite@lecourrier.com
Editorial e-mail: administration@lecourrier.com,
Primary Website: www.lecourrier.com
Published: Fri
Avg Paid Circ: 1302
Avg Free Circ: 5
Audit By: ODC
Audit Date: 13.12.2011
Personnel: Stephanie LeBlanc (Prod. Mgr.); Francis Robichaud (Ed)

LIGHTHOUSE NOW

Street address 1: 353 York St.
Street address city: Bridgewater
Province/Territory: NS
Postal code: B4V 3K2
Country: Canada
General Phone: (902) 543-2457
General Fax: (902) 543-2228
Advertising Phone: (902) 543-1569
General/National Adv. E-mail: mail@southshorenow.ca
Display Adv. E-mail: daveda.savory@lighthousenow.ca
Classified Adv. e-mail: tracy.williams@lighthousenow.ca
Editorial e-mail: editorial@southshorenow.ca
Primary Website: https://lighthousenow.ca/
Published: Thur
Avg Paid Circ: 6573
Avg Free Circ: 26963
Audit By: VAC
Audit Date: 31.10.2015
Personnel: Lynn Hennigar (Pub); Laurenda Reeves (Circ. Mgr.); Emma Smith (Ed.)

MIRROR-EXAMINER

Street address 1: 87 Commercial St.
Street address city: Middleton
Province/Territory: NS
Postal code: B0S 1P0
Country: Canada
General Phone: (902) 825-3457
General Fax: (902) 825-6707
General/National Adv. E-mail: kentpub.ads@ns.sympatico.ca
Display Adv. E-mail: kentpub.ads@ns.sympatico.ca
Published: Wed
Avg Paid Circ: 3101
Audit By: Sworn/Estimate/Non-Audited
Audit Date: 12.07.2019
Personnel: Garnet Austen (Pub.); Wayne Smith (Adv. Mgr.); Lori Errington (Ed.)

REGISTER

Street address 1: 28 Aberdeen St
Street address 2: Suite 6
Street address city: Kentville
Province/Territory: NS
Postal code: B4N 2N1
Country: Canada
General Phone: (902) 538-3189
General Fax: (902) 681-0923
Display Adv. E-mail: events@kentvilleadvertiser.ca
Primary Website: http://www.kingscountynews.ca/
Published: Thur
Avg Paid Circ: 3392
Avg Free Circ: 47
Audit By: CMCA
Audit Date: 31.07.2014
Personnel: Fred Fiander (Pub.)
Parent company (for newspapers): Transcontinental Media

THE ADVANCE

Street address 1: 271 Main St.
Street address city: Liverpool
Province/Territory: NS
Postal code: B0T 1K0
Country: Canada
General Phone: (902) 354-3441
General Fax: (902) 354-2455
General/National Adv. E-mail: info@advance.ca
Editorial e-mail: ffayander@thevanguard.ca
Primary Website: http://www.theadvance.ca/
Published: Tues
Avg Paid Circ: 1573
Audit By: CMCA
Audit Date: 31.03.2013
Personnel: Fred Fayander (Pub)
Parent company (for newspapers): Transcontinental Media

THE ADVERTISER

Street address 1: 28 Aberdeen St
Street address 2: Suite 6
Street address city: Kentville
Province/Territory: NS
Postal code: B4N 2N1
County: Canada
Country: Canada
General Phone: (902) 681-2121
General Fax: (902) 681-0830
General/National Adv. E-mail: ffiander@thevanguard.ca
Display Adv. E-mail: events@kentvilleadvertiser.ca
Editorial e-mail: ffiander@thevanguard.ca
Primary Website: http://www.kingscountynews.ca/
Published: Tues
Avg Paid Circ: 3189
Avg Free Circ: 49
Audit By: CMCA
Audit Date: 31.03.2014
Personnel: Fred Fiander (Pub.)
Parent company (for newspapers): Transcontinental Media

THE AURORA

Street address 1: Po Box 99
Street address city: Greenwood
Province/Territory: NS
Postal code: B0P 1N0
County: Canada
Country: Canada
General Phone: (902) 765-1494
General Fax: (902) 765-1717
General/National Adv. E-mail: auroraeditor@ns.aliantzinc.ca
Display Adv. E-mail: auroramarketing@ns.aliantzinc.ca
Classified Adv. e-mail: auroraproduction@ns.aliantzinc.ca
Editorial e-mail: auroraeditor@ns.aliantzinc.ca
Primary Website: www.auroranewspaper.com
Published: Mon
Avg Free Circ: 4500
Audit By: Sworn/Estimate/Non-Audited
Audit Date: 22.09.2022
Personnel: Sara White (Mgr. Ed.); Diane Mestekemper (Admin Clerk); Brian Graves (Graphics designer); Christianne Robichaud (Adv)
Parent company (for newspapers): Canadian Forces Morale and Welfare Services

THE BULLETIN

Street address 1: 353 York St.
Street address city: Bridgewater
Province/Territory: NS
Postal code: B4V 3K2
County: Canada
Country: Canada
General Phone: (902) 543-2457
General Fax: (902) 543-2228
General/National Adv. E-mail: editorial@southshorenow.ca
Editorial e-mail: editorial@southshorenow.ca
Primary Website: https://lighthousenow.ca
Published: Tues
Avg Paid Circ: 7030
Avg Free Circ: 127
Audit By: Sworn/Estimate/Non-Audited
Audit Date: 12.07.2019
Personnel: Lynn Hennigar (Pub); Laurenda Reeves (Circ. Mgr.); Emma Smith (Ed.)

THE CASKET

Street address 1: 88 College St.
Street address city: Antigonish
Province/Territory: NS
Postal code: B2G 1X7
County: Canada
Country: Canada
General Phone: (902) 863-4370
General Fax: (902) 863-1943
General/National Adv. E-mail: info@thecasket.ca
Display Adv. E-mail: brianlazzuri@thecasket.ca
Classified Adv. e-mail: brianlazzuri@thecasket.ca
Editorial e-mail: editor@thecasket.ca
Primary Website: www.thecasket.ca
Published: Wed
Avg Free Circ: 27000
Audit By: Sworn/Estimate/Non-Audited
Audit Date: 12.07.2019
Personnel: Brian Lazzuri (Gen Mgr/Mng Ed/Adv Mgr)
Parent company (for newspapers): SaltWire

THE CITIZEN-RECORD

Street address 1: 147 South Albion St.
Street address city: Amherst
Province/Territory: NS
Postal code: B4H 2X2
Country: Canada
General Phone: (902) 667-5102
General Fax: (902) 667-0419
General/National Adv. E-mail: chris.gooding@tc.tc
Display Adv. E-mail: gcoish@amherstdaily.com
Editorial e-mail: darrell.cole@tc.tc
Primary Website: www.cumberlandnewsnow.com
Published: Wed
Avg Paid Circ: 4892
Avg Free Circ: 504
Audit By: VAC
Audit Date: 31.10.2014
Personnel: Richard Russell (Pub.); Gladys Coish (Adv. Mgr.); Darell Cole (Ed)
Parent company (for newspapers): Transcontinental Media

THE COAST GUARD

Street address 1: 164 Water St.
Street address city: Shelburne
Province/Territory: NS
Postal code: B0T 1W0
Country: Canada
General Phone: (902) 875-3244
General Fax: (902) 875-3454
General/National Adv. E-mail: info@thecoastguard.ca
Display Adv. E-mail: info@thecoastguard.ca
Editorial e-mail: ffaynder@transcontinental.ca
Primary Website: www.thecoastguard.ca
Published: Tues
Avg Paid Circ: 2290
Avg Free Circ: 0
Audit By: CMCA
Audit Date: 28.02.2014
Personnel: Fred Fayander (Pub.)
Parent company (for newspapers): Transcontinental Media

THE DIGBY COUNTY COURIER

Street address 1: 124 Water St.
Street address city: Digby
Province/Territory: NS
Postal code: B0V 1A0
Country: Canada
General Phone: (902) 245-4715
General Fax: (902) 245-6136
General/National Adv. E-mail: info@digbycourier.ca
Display Adv. E-mail: info@digbycourier.ca
Editorial e-mail: editor@digbycourier.ca
Primary Website: www.digbycourier.ca
Published: Thur
Avg Paid Circ: 1192
Avg Free Circ: 0
Audit By: CMCA
Audit Date: 30.06.2014
Personnel: Dave Glenen (Ed)
Parent company (for newspapers): Transcontinental Media

THE INVERNESS ORAN

Street address 1: 15767 Central Avenue
Street address city: Inverness
Province/Territory: NS
Postal code: B0E 1N0
Country: USA
General Phone: (902) 258-2253
General Fax: (902) 258-2632
Editorial e-mail: editor@oran.ca
Primary Website: www.oran.ca
Published: Wed
Avg Paid Circ: 16
Avg Free Circ: 54
Audit By: VAC
Audit Date: 30.09.2016
Personnel: Rankin MacDonald (Ed.)

THE LIGHT

Street address 1: Po Box 1000
Street address city: Tatamagouche
Province/Territory: NS

Postal code: B0K 1V0
Country: Canada
General Phone: (902) 956-8099
Display Adv. E-mail: kristinhirtle@tatamagouchelight.com
Editorial e-mail: raissatetanish@tatamagouchelight.com
Primary Website: www.tatamagouchelight.com
Published: Wed
Avg Paid Circ: 2497
Avg Free Circ: 4378
Audit By: VAC
Audit Date: 30.06.2016
Personnel: Leith Orr (Pub)

THE PICTOU ADVOCATE

Street address 1: 21 George St.
Street address city: Pictou
Province/Territory: NS
Postal code: B0K 1H0
County: Canada
Country: Canada
General Phone: (902) 485-8014
General Fax: (902) 752-4816
Advertising Phone: (902) 759-0716
General/National Adv. E-mail: pictou.advocate@ns.sympatico.ca
Display Adv. E-mail: mark@pictouadvocate.com
Editorial e-mail: editor@pictouadvocate.com
Primary Website: www.pictouadvocate.com
Published: Wed
Avg Paid Circ: 732
Avg Free Circ: 4
Audit By: VAC
Audit Date: 30.06.2016
Personnel: Jackie Jardine (Ed); Leith Orr (Pub.)

THE REPORTER

Street address 1: 2 Maclean Court
Street address city: Port Hawkesbury
Province/Territory: NS
Postal code: B9A 3K2
Country: Canada
General Phone: (902) 625-3300
General Fax: (902) 625-1701
Display Adv. E-mail: nicolefawcett@porthawkesburyreporter.com
Editorial e-mail: jake@porthawkesburyreporter.com
Primary Website: www.porthawkesburyreporter.com
Published: Wed
Avg Paid Circ: 87
Audit By: VAC
Audit Date: 30.09.2016
Personnel: Rick Cluett (Pub); Nicole Fawcett (Adv)

THE SHORELINE JOURNAL

Street address 1: Box 41
Street address city: Bass River
Province/Territory: NS
Postal code: B0M 1B0
County: Muncipality of County of Colchester
Country: Canada
General Phone: (902) 647-2968
General Fax: (902) 647-2194
Advertising Phone: (902)647-2968
Editorial Phone: (902) 647-2968
General/National Adv. E-mail: maurice@theshorelinejournal.com
Display Adv. E-mail: maurice@theshorelinejournal.com
Editorial e-mail: maurice@theshorelinejournal.com
Primary Website: www.theshorelinejournal.com
Published: Wed`Mthly
Avg Paid Circ: 1363
Avg Free Circ: 0
Audit By: CMCA
Audit Date: 31.12.2013
Personnel: Maurice Rees

THE SPECTATOR

Street address 1: 87 Commercial St.
Street address city: Middleton
Province/Territory: NS
Postal code: B0S 1P0
Country: Canada
General Phone: (902) 532-2219
General Fax: (902) 825-6707
General/National Adv. E-mail: info@annapolisspectator.ca
Display Adv. E-mail: info@annapolisspectator.ca
Editorial e-mail: editor@annapolisspectator.ca
Primary Website: www.annapoliscountyspectator.ca
Published: Thur
Avg Paid Circ: 2048
Avg Free Circ: 0
Audit By: CMCA
Audit Date: 31.01.2013
Personnel: Fred Fiander (Pub.); Lawrence Powell (Ed.)
Parent company (for newspapers): Transcontinental Media

THE VANGUARD

Street address 1: 2 Second St.
Street address city: Yarmouth
Province/Territory: NS
Postal code: B5A 4B1
County: Canada
Country: Canada
General Phone: (902) 742-7111
General Fax: (902) 742-6527
General/National Adv. E-mail: info@thevanguard.ca
Display Adv. E-mail: fred.fiander@tc.tc
Editorial e-mail: info@thevanguard.ca
Primary Website: www.thevanguard.ca
Published: Tues
Avg Paid Circ: 3485
Avg Free Circ: 52
Audit By: CMCA
Audit Date: 31.03.2014
Personnel: Fred Fiander (Pub); Fred Hatfield (Ed)
Parent company (for newspapers): Transcontinental Media

NUNAVUT

KIVALLIQ NEWS

Street address 1: Po Box 2820
Street address city: Yellowknife
Province/Territory: NU
Postal code: X1A 2R1
Country: Canada
General Phone: (867) 873-4031
General Fax: (867) 873-8507
General/National Adv. E-mail: nnsl@nnsl.com
Display Adv. E-mail: advertising@nnsl.com
Editorial e-mail: editorial@nnsl.com
Primary Website: www.nnsl.com
Published: Wed
Avg Free Circ: 935
Audit By: VAC
Audit Date: 31.03.2016
Personnel: Jack Sigvaldason (Pub)

NUNATSIAQ NEWS

Street address 1: Po Box 8
Street address city: Iqaluit
Province/Territory: NU
Postal code: X0A 0H0
Country: Canada
General Phone: (867) 979-5357
General Fax: (867) 979-4763
Advertising Phone: (800) 263-1452
General/National Adv. E-mail: adsnunatsiaqonline.ca
Display Adv. E-mail: ads@nunatsiaqonline.ca
Editorial e-mail: editor@nunatsiaq.com
Primary Website: www.nunatsiaq.com
Published: Fri
Avg Free Circ: 5388
Audit By: VAC
Audit Date: 30.06.2016
Personnel: Steven Roberts (Pub.); Bill McConkey (Adv. Mgr.); Jim Bell (Ed.)

NUNAVUT NEWS/NORTH

Street address 1: Po Box 2820
Street address city: Yellowknife
Province/Territory: NU
Postal code: X1A 2R1
Country: Canada
General Phone: (867) 873-4031
General Fax: (867) 873-8507
General/National Adv. E-mail: circulation@nnsl.com
Display Adv. E-mail: advertising@nnsl.com
Editorial e-mail: editorial@nnsl.com
Primary Website: www.nnsl.com
Published: Mon
Avg Free Circ: 4161
Audit By: VAC
Audit Date: 31.03.2016
Personnel: Jack Sigvaldason (Pub); Michael Scott (Gen Mgr)

ONTARIO

ACTION (L')

Street address 1: 920 Huron St.
Street address city: London
Province/Territory: ON
Postal code: N5Y 4K4
Country: Canada
General Phone: (519) 433-4130
General Fax: (905) 790-9127
General/National Adv. E-mail: journaliste@laction.ca
Display Adv. E-mail: marketing@laction.ca
Editorial e-mail: info@lemetropolitain.com
Primary Website: www.laction.ca
Published: Wed
Avg Paid Circ: 1648
Avg Free Circ: 812
Audit By: CMCA
Audit Date: 31.12.2012
Personnel: Denis Poirier (Ed); Richard Caumartin (Sales Dir)

ACTION LONDON SARNIA

Street address 1: Professor's Lake Parkway
Street address city: Brampton
Province/Territory: ON
Postal code: L6S 4P8
Country: Canada
General Phone: (800) 525-6752
Editorial e-mail: info@lemetropolitain.com
Primary Website: www.laction.ca
Published: Tues
Avg Paid Circ: 1907
Avg Free Circ: 1106
Audit By: ODC
Audit Date: 13.11.2011
Personnel: Denis Poirier (Ed); Richard Caumartin (Sales Dir)

ADVANCE

Street address 1: 260 Main St. E.
Street address city: Dundalk
Province/Territory: ON
Postal code: N0C 1B0
County: Southgate
Country: Canada
General Phone: (519) 923-2203
General Fax: (519) 923-2747
Display Adv. E-mail: dundalk.herald@gmail.com
Editorial e-mail: dundalk.heraldnews@gmail.com
Published: Wed
Avg Paid Circ: 1299
Audit By: Sworn/Estimate/Non-Audited
Audit Date: 12.07.2019
Personnel: Matthew Walls (Pub.)
Parent company (for newspapers): herald newspaper corp

AGRICOM

Street address 1: 2474 Rue Champlain
Street address city: Clarence Creek
Province/Territory: ON
Postal code: K0A1N0
Country: Canada
General Phone: (613) 488-2651
General Fax: (613) 488-2541
General/National Adv. E-mail: info@journalagricom.ca
Display Adv. E-mail: pub@journalagricom.ca
Editorial e-mail: redaction@journalagricom.ca
Primary Website: www.journalagricom.ca
Published: Fri`Bi-Mthly
Avg Paid Circ: 900
Avg Free Circ: 1100
Audit By: Sworn/Estimate/Non-Audited
Audit Date: 12.07.2019
Personnel: Isabelle Lessard (Ed)

AJAX-PICKERING NEWS ADVERTISER

Street address 1: 865 Farewell Ave.
Street address city: Oshawa
Province/Territory: ON
Postal code: L1H 7L5
Country: Canada
General Phone: (905) 579-4400
General Fax: (905) 579-2238
General/National Adv. E-mail: newsroom@durhamregion.com
Display Adv. E-mail: dfletcher@durhamregion.com
Editorial e-mail: jburghardt@durhamregion.com
Primary Website: durhamregion.com
Published: Wed`Thur
Avg Paid Circ: 0
Avg Free Circ: 50016
Audit By: CCAB
Audit Date: 30.09.2017
Personnel: Timothy J. Whittaker (Pub.); Duncan Fletcher (Adv. Mgr.); Abe Fackhourie (Circ. Mgr.); Joanne Burghardt (Ed.)
Parent company (for newspapers): Metroland Media Group Ltd.; Torstar

ALMAGUIN NEWS

Street address 1: 59 Ontario St.
Street address city: Burks Falls
Province/Territory: ON
Postal code: P0A 1C0
Country: Canada
General Phone: (705)382-9996
General Fax: (705) 382-9997
General/National Adv. E-mail: news@almaguinnews.com
Display Adv. E-mail: advertising@almaguinnews.com
Editorial e-mail: editor@almaguinnews.com
Primary Website: www.almaguinnews.com
Published: Thur
Avg Paid Circ: 2230
Avg Free Circ: 150
Audit By: CMCA
Audit Date: 31.12.2015
Personnel: Bill Allen (Gen. Mgr.); Twila Armstrong (Adv. Rep.); Rob Learn (News Ed.)
Parent company (for newspapers): Metroland Media Group Ltd.

ANCASTER NEWS

Street address 1: 333 Arvin Ave.
Street address city: Stoney Creek
Province/Territory: ON
Postal code: L8E 2M6
County: Ancaster
Country: Canada
General Phone: (905) 523-5800
General Fax: (905) 664-3319
General/National Adv. E-mail: editor@ancasternews.com
Display Adv. E-mail: mtherrien@metroland.com
Classified Adv. e-mail: classified@thespec.com
Editorial e-mail: mpearson@hamiltonnews.com
Primary Website: www.ancasternews.com
Published: Thur
Avg Paid Circ: 4
Avg Free Circ: 13355
Audit By: CMCA
Audit Date: 21.06.2018
Personnel: Kelly Montague (Pub.); Jason Pehora (Gen. Mgr.); Lorna Lester (Office Mgr.); Michael Pearson (News Ed.); Gordon Cameron (Mng Ed); Melinda Therrien (Dir of Advt)
Parent company (for newspapers): Metroland Media Group Ltd.; Torstar

ANGLICAN JOURNAL

Street address 1: 80 Hayden Street
Street address city: Toronto
Province/Territory: ON
Postal code: M4Y 3G2
Country: Canada
General Phone: (416) 924-9199
Advertising Phone: (226) 664-0350
General/National Adv. E-mail: editor@anglicanjournal.com
Display Adv. E-mail: advertising@national.anglican.ca

Editorial e-mail: editor@anglicanjournal.com
Primary Website: www.anglicanjournal.com
Published: Mthly
Avg Paid Circ: 123352
Avg Free Circ: 1200
Audit By: Sworn/Estimate/Non-Audited
Audit Date: 12.07.2019

ANNEX GUARDIAN

Street address 1: One River View Garden
Street address city: Toronto
Province/Territory: ON
Postal code: M6S 4E4
Country: Canada
General Phone: (416) 493-4400
General Fax: (416) 767-4880
Display Adv. E-mail: salesinfo@insidetoronto.com
Classified Adv. e-mail: classifieds@metroland.com
Editorial e-mail: gbalogiannis@insidetoronto.com
Primary Website: www.insidetoronto.ca
Published: Fri
Avg Free Circ: 55500
Audit By: Sworn/Estimate/Non-Audited
Audit Date: 12.07.2019
Personnel: Grace Peacock (Ed); Meriel Bradley (Sales Dir)
Parent company (for newspapers): Torstar

ARNPRIOR CHRONICLE GUIDE EMC

Street address 1: 8 Mcgonigal St.
Street address city: Arnprior
Province/Territory: ON
Postal code: K7S 1L8
Country: Canada
General Phone: (613) 623-6571
Display Adv. E-mail: leslie.osborne@metroland.com
Classified Adv. e-mail: christine.jarrett@metroland.com
Editorial e-mail: theresa.fritz@metroland.com
Primary Website: www.insideottawavalley.com
Published: Thur
Avg Free Circ: 8213
Audit By: CMCA
Audit Date: 30.06.2016
Personnel: Mike Tracy (Pub); Theresa Fritz (Ed)

ARNPRIOR CHRONICLE-GUIDE

Street address 1: 35 Opeongo Road
Street address city: Renfrew
Province/Territory: ON
Postal code: K7V 2T2
Country: Canada
General Phone: (800) 884-9195
Editorial e-mail: shaaima@metroland.com
Primary Website: insideottawavalley.com
Published: Thur
Avg Free Circ: 6500
Audit By: Sworn/Estimate/Non-Audited
Audit Date: 30.04.2019
Personnel: Sherry Haaima; Leslie Osborne (Adv.)
Parent company (for newspapers): Torstar

ARTHUR ENTERPRISE NEWS

Street address 1: 277 Main St. S.
Street address city: Mount Forest
Province/Territory: ON
Postal code: N0G 2L0
County: North Wellington
Country: Canada
General Phone: (519) 323-1550
General Fax: (519) 323-4548
General/National Adv. E-mail: editor@mountforest.com
Display Adv. E-mail: phaasnoot@northperth.com
Classified Adv. e-mail: classifieds@metroland.com
Editorial e-mail: sburrows@metroland.com
Primary Website: http://www.southwesternontario.ca/arthur-on/
Published: Wed
Avg Paid Circ: 2699
Avg Free Circ: 0
Audit By: VAC
Audit Date: 31.12.2015
Personnel: Shannon Burrows (Ed); Peggy Haasnoot (Adv)

Parent company (for newspapers): Metroland Media Group Ltd.; Torstar

ATIKOKAN PROGRESS

Street address 1: 109 Main St. E.
Street address city: Atikokan
Province/Territory: ON
Postal code: P0T 1C0
Country: Canada
General Phone: (807) 597-2731
General Fax: (807) 597-6103
General/National Adv. E-mail: progress@nwon.com
Editorial e-mail: progress@nwon.com
Primary Website: www.atikokanprogress.ca
Published: Mon
Avg Paid Circ: 1173
Avg Free Circ: 38
Audit By: VAC
Audit Date: 30.04.2016
Personnel: Eve Shine (Circ. Mgr.); Michael McKinnon (Ed.)

AWAAZ PUNJABI

Street address 1: 7015 Tranmere Dr. Suite #16
Street address city: Mississauga
Province/Territory: ON
Postal code: L5S 1T7
Country: Canada
General Phone: (905)795-8282
General Fax: (905) 795-9801
Advertising Phone: (416) 899 8140
Editorial Phone: (905) 795-0639
General/National Adv. E-mail: info@weeklyvoice.com
Display Adv. E-mail: marketing@weeklyvoice.com
Classified Adv. e-mail: admin@weeklyvoice.com
Editorial e-mail: pnews@weeklyvoice.com
Primary Website: www.awaazpunjabi.com
Published: Wed
Avg Free Circ: 9900
Audit By: CMCA
Audit Date: 29.02.2016
Personnel: Sudhir Anand

AYR NEWS

Street address 1: 40 Piper St.
Street address city: Ayr
Province/Territory: ON
Postal code: N0B 1E0
Country: Canada
General Phone: (519) 632-7432
General Fax: (519) 632-7743
General/National Adv. E-mail: ayrnews@golden.net
Display Adv. E-mail: hall.ayrnews@gmail.com
Primary Website: www.ayrnews.ca
Published: Wed
Avg Free Circ: 0
Audit By: VAC
Audit Date: 31.07.2017
Personnel: Heidi E. Ostner (Circ. Mgr.)

BANCROFT THIS WEEK

Street address 1: 254 Hastings St.
Street address city: Bancroft
Province/Territory: ON
Postal code: K0L 1C0
Country: Canada
General Phone: (613) 332-2002
General Fax: (613) 332-1710
General/National Adv. E-mail: curtis.armstrong@sunmedia.ca
Display Adv. E-mail: david.zilstra@gmail.com
Classified Adv. e-mail: melissa@haliburtonpress.com
Editorial e-mail: jenn@haliburtonpress.com
Primary Website: www.bancroftthisweek.com
Published: Fri
Avg Free Circ: 8962
Audit By: CMCA
Audit Date: 31.12.2015
Personnel: David Zilstra (Pub/Adv Dir); Jenn Watt (Mng. Ed); Melissa Armstong (Sales Rep)

BARRY'S BAY THIS WEEK

Street address 1: 19574 Opeongo Line
Street address city: Barry's Bay
Province/Territory: ON
Postal code: K0J 1B0
Country: Canada
General Phone: (613) 756-2944
General Fax: (613) 756-2994
General/National Adv. E-mail: newsroom@barrysbaythisweek.com
Display Adv. E-mail: michel@thevalleygazette.ca
Classified Adv. e-mail: classified@thevalleygazette.ca
Editorial e-mail: christine@thevalleygazette.ca
Primary Website: http://www.thevalleygazette.ca/node/3
Published: Wed
Avg Paid Circ: 1292
Avg Free Circ: 0
Audit By: CMCA
Audit Date: 31.12.2012
Personnel: Pete Lapinskie (Gen. Mgr.); Michel Lavigne (Owner/Pub/Adv); Christine Hudder (Ed)
Parent company (for newspapers): Quebecor Communications, Inc.

BEACH-RIVERDALE MIRROR

Street address 1: 100 Tempo Ave.
Street address city: Toronto
Province/Territory: ON
Postal code: M2H 2N8
Country: Canada
General Phone: (416) 493-4400
General Fax: (416) 493-6190
General/National Adv. E-mail: bsrm@insidetoronto.com
Display Adv. E-mail: salesinfo@insidetoronto.com
Classified Adv. e-mail: classifieds@metroland.com
Editorial e-mail: newsroom@insidetoronto.com
Primary Website: www.insidetoronto.ca
Published: Thur
Avg Paid Circ: 0
Avg Free Circ: 22241
Audit By: CCAB
Audit Date: 30.09.2015
Personnel: Betty Carr (Pub); Marg Middleton (Gen. Mgr.); Meriel Bradley (Adv. Rep)
Parent company (for newspapers): Metroland Media Group Ltd.; Torstar

BELLEVILLE NEWS

Street address 1: 250 Sidney St.
Street address city: Belleville
Province/Territory: ON
Postal code: K8P 5E0
Country: Canada
General Phone: (613) 966-2034
Advertising Phone: (613) 966-2034 ext. 504
Display Adv. E-mail: mhudgins@metroland.com
Classified Adv. e-mail: slacroix@perfprint.ca
Editorial e-mail: chris.malette@metroland.com
Primary Website: http://www.insidebelleville.com/belleville-on/
Published: Thur
Personnel: Paul Mitchell (Circ Mgr); Chris Malette (Ed); Melissa Hudgin (Adv)
Parent company (for newspapers): Metroland Media Group Ltd.

BELLEVILLE NEWS EMC

Street address 1: 244 Ashley St
Street address city: Belleville
Province/Territory: ON
Postal code: K0K 2B0
Country: Canada
General Phone: (613) 966-2034
General/National Adv. E-mail: jkearns@theemc.ca
Display Adv. E-mail: leslie.osborne@metroland.com
Classified Adv. e-mail: abarr@metroland.com
Editorial e-mail: theresa.fritz@metroland.com
Primary Website: www.insideottawavalley.com
Published: Thur
Avg Free Circ: 22549
Audit By: CMCA
Audit Date: 30.06.2016
Personnel: John Kearns (Pub.); Chris Paveley (Circ Mgr); Theresa Fritz (Ed); Leslie Osborne (Adv. Sales)
Parent company (for newspapers): Metroland Media Group Ltd.

BLENHEIM NEWS-TRIBUNE

Street address 1: 62 Talbot St. W.
Street address city: Blenheim
Province/Territory: ON
Postal code: N0P 1A0
County: Canada
Country: Canada
General Phone: (519) 676-3321
General Fax: (519) 676-3454
Advertising Phone: (519) 676-5023
Editorial Phone: (519) 676-3321
General/National Adv. E-mail: tribune@southkent.net
Editorial e-mail: pl.tribune@southkent.net
Primary Website: facebook.com/bleheimnewstribune
Published: Wed
Avg Paid Circ: 1609
Avg Free Circ: 78
Audit By: AAM
Audit Date: 31.03.2019
Personnel: Pete Laurie (Ed.); Dave Stepniak (Prod Mgr)

BLOOR WEST VILLAGER

Street address 1: 2323 Bloor St. W
Street address city: Toronto
Province/Territory: ON
Postal code: M6S 4W1
Country: Canada
General Phone: (416) 675-4390
General Fax: (416) 767-4880
General/National Adv. E-mail: metroland@insidetoronto.com
Display Adv. E-mail: mbradley@metroland.com
Editorial e-mail: gpeacock@insidetoronto.com
Primary Website: insidetoronto.com
Published: Thur
Avg Paid Circ: 0
Avg Free Circ: 39840
Audit By: CCAB
Audit Date: 30.09.2017
Personnel: Betty Carr (Pub.); Meriel Bradley (Adv. Dir.); Grace Peacock (Ed)
Parent company (for newspapers): Metroland Media Group Ltd.; Torstar

BLUE MOUNTAINS COURIER-HERALD

Street address 1: 24 Trowbridge St. West
Street address 2: Unit 6
Street address city: Meaford
Province/Territory: ON
Postal code: N4L 1Y1
Country: Canada
General Phone: (519) 538-1421
General Fax: (519) 538-5028
General/National Adv. E-mail: clamb@simcoe.com
Display Adv. E-mail: pamero@simcoe.com
Editorial e-mail: lmartin@simcoe.com
Primary Website: www.simcoe.com
Published: Wed
Avg Paid Circ: 505
Audit By: CMCA
Audit Date: 30.06.2013
Personnel: Lori Martin (Ed); Heather Harris (Circ Mgr); Pamela Amero (Adv Mgr)

BRACEBRIDGE EXAMINER

Street address 1: 34 Ep Lee Dr.
Street address city: Bracebridge
Province/Territory: ON
Postal code: P1L 1P9
County: Canada
Country: Canada
General Phone: (705) 645-8771
General Fax: (705) 645-1718
General/National Adv. E-mail: examiner@muskoka.com
Display Adv. E-mail: mbradley@metroland.com
Classified Adv. e-mail: classifieds@metroland.com
Editorial e-mail: psteel@metrolandnorthmedia.com
Primary Website: www.bracebridgeexaminer.com
Published: Thur
Avg Paid Circ: 83
Avg Free Circ: 8171
Audit By: CMCA
Audit Date: 30.04.2016
Personnel: Meriel Bradley (Adv. Mgr); Pamela Steel (Ed); Andrew Allen (Circ Mgr)
Parent company (for newspapers): Metroland Media Group Ltd.; Torstar

BRADFORD & WEST GWILLIMBURY TOPIC

Street address 1: 580b Steven Crt.
Street address city: Newmarket

Province/Territory: ON
Postal code: L3Y 4X1
Country: Canada
General Phone: (905) 775-1188
Display Adv. E-mail: asmug@metroland.com
Editorial e-mail: tmcfadden@yrmg.com
Primary Website: simcoe.com
Published: Thur
Avg Free Circ: 10538
Audit By: CCAB
Audit Date: 31.12.2017
Personnel: Amanda Sung (Adv Mgr); Ted McFadden (Ed)
Parent company (for newspapers): Metroland Media Group Ltd.

BRAMPTON GUARDIAN

Street address 1: 3145 Wolfedale Rd.
Street address city: Mississauga
Province/Territory: ON
Postal code: L5C 3A9
Country: Canada
General Phone: (905) 273-8111
General Fax: (905) 454-4385
General/National Adv. E-mail: letters@thebramptonguardian.com
Display Adv. E-mail: scotthartman@thebramptonguardian.com
Classified Adv. e-mail: classified@thebramptonguardian.com
Editorial e-mail: plonergan@metroland.com
Primary Website: thebramptonguardian.com
Published: Thur`Fri
Avg Paid Circ: 0
Avg Free Circ: 137132
Audit By: CCAB
Audit Date: 9/31/2017
Personnel: Dave Coleman (Circ. Mgr.); Dana Robbins (Pub); Bill Anderson (Gen Mgr); Patricia Lonergan (Ed)
Parent company (for newspapers): Metroland Media Group Ltd.

BRANT NEWS

Street address 1: 111 Easton Rd.
Street address city: Brantford
Province/Territory: ON
Postal code: N3P 1J4
Country: Canada
General Phone: (519) 758-1157
General Fax: (519) 753-3567
General/National Adv. E-mail: loffless@brantnews.com
Display Adv. E-mail: lbutler@brantnews.com
Classified Adv. e-mail: classified@metrolandwest.com
Editorial e-mail: sallen@brantnews.com
Primary Website: www.brantnews.com
Published: Thur
Avg Paid Circ: 0
Avg Free Circ: 48716
Audit By: CCAB
Audit Date: 30.09.2017
Personnel: Linda Hill (Circ Mgr); Sean Allen (Ed); Loren Butlet (Adv Mgr)
Parent company (for newspapers): Metroland Media Group Ltd.; Metroland Media

BROCK CITIZEN

Street address 1: 2d Cameron St. E.
Street address city: Cannington
Province/Territory: ON
Postal code: L0E 1E0
Country: Canada
General Phone: (705) 432-8842
General Fax: (705) 432-2942
General/National Adv. E-mail: bdanford@mykawartha.com
Display Adv. E-mail: btrickett@mykawartha.com
Classified Adv. e-mail: lmunro@mykawartha.com
Editorial e-mail: ltuffin@mykawartha.com
Primary Website: http://www.mykawartha.com/brocktownship-on/
Published: Thur
Avg Free Circ: 5497
Audit By: Sworn/Estimate/Non-Audited
Audit Date: 12.07.2019
Personnel: Peter Bishop (Ed); Mary Babcock (Gen. Mgr.); Lois Tuffin (Mng. Ed.); Kim Riel (Office Mgr)

Parent company (for newspapers): Metroland Media Group Ltd.; Torstar

CALEDON CITIZEN

Street address 1: 30 Martha St
Street address 2: Suite 205
Street address city: Bolton
Province/Territory: ON
Postal code: L7E 5V1
Country: Canada
General Phone: (905) 857-6626
General Fax: (905) 857-6363
General/National Adv. E-mail: admin@caledoncitizen.com
Display Adv. E-mail: erin@lpcmedia.ca
Classified Adv. e-mail: heather@caledoncitizen.com
Editorial e-mail: editor@caledoncitizen.com
Primary Website: www.caledoncitizen.com
Published: Thur
Avg Free Circ: 12240
Audit By: Sworn/Estimate/Non-Audited
Audit Date: 12.07.2019
Personnel: Alan Claridge (Pub); Mary Speck (Office Mgr); Joshua Santos
Parent company (for newspapers): Simcoe-York Group

CALEDON ENTERPRISE

Street address 1: 12612 Hwy. 50 N.
Street address city: Bolton
Province/Territory: ON
Postal code: L7E 5T1
Country: Canada
General Phone: (905) 857-3433
General Fax: (905) 857-5002
Display Adv. E-mail: mcrake@caledonenterprise.com
Classified Adv. e-mail: classifieds@metroland.com
Editorial e-mail: rwilkinson@caledonenterprise.com
Primary Website: caledonenterprise.com
Published: Tues`Thur
Avg Paid Circ: 0
Avg Free Circ: 19199
Audit By: CCAB
Audit Date: 30.09.2017
Personnel: Sheila Ogram (Circ Mgr); Robyn Wilkinson (Ed); Melinda Crake (Adv. Rep)
Parent company (for newspapers): Metroland Media Group Ltd.; Torstar

CAMBRIDGE TIMES

Street address 1: 475 Thompson Dr. Units 1-4
Street address city: Cambridge
Province/Territory: ON
Postal code: N1T 2K7
Country: Canada
General Phone: (519) 623-7395
General Fax: (519) 623-9155
Display Adv. E-mail: tanderson@cambridgetimes.ca
Classified Adv. e-mail: classified@metrolandwest.com
Editorial e-mail: rvivian@cambridgetimes.ca
Primary Website: www.cambridgetimes.ca
Published: Tues`Thur
Avg Free Circ: 31628
Audit By: CMCA
Audit Date: 30.06.2016
Personnel: Donna Luelo (Pub); Richard Vivian (Ed); Carron Woods (Prod/Circ. Mgr.); Ted Anderson (Adv. Mgr.)
Parent company (for newspapers): Metroland Media Group Ltd.; Torstar

CAMPBELLFORD/NORTHWEST NEWS EMC

Street address 1: 244 Ashley St
Street address city: Belleville
Province/Territory: ON
Postal code: K0K 2B0
Country: Canada
General Phone: (613) 966-2034
Advertising Phone: (613) 966-2034
Editorial Phone: (613) 966-2034 ext. 510
General/National Adv. E-mail: jkearns@theemc.ca
Display Adv. E-mail: jkearns@theemc.ca
Editorial e-mail: tbush@theemc.ca
Primary Website: www.insideottawavalley.com
Published: Thur
Avg Free Circ: 11630
Audit By: CMCA

Audit Date: 31.12.2012
Personnel: John Kearns (Pub.); Terry Bush (Mng. Ed.)

CANADIAN STATESMAN

Street address 1: 865 Farewell St.
Street address city: Oshawa
Province/Territory: ON
Postal code: L1H 7L5
County: Ontario
Country: Canada
General Phone: (905) 579-4400
General Fax: (416) 523-6161
Advertising Phone: (905) 215-0440
Editorial Phone: (905) 215-0462
General/National Adv. E-mail: newsroom@durhamregion.com
Editorial e-mail: mjohnston@durhamregion.com
Primary Website: www.durhamregion.com
Published: Wed`Thur`Fri
Avg Paid Circ: 104250
Audit By: Sworn/Estimate/Non-Audited
Audit Date: 12.07.2019
Personnel: Timothy J. Whittaker (Pub.); Fred Eismont (Dir. Adv.); Mike Johnston (Managing Ed.)

CHATHAM-KENT THIS WEEK

Street address 1: 138 King Street West
Street address city: Chatham
Province/Territory: ON
Postal code: N7M 1ES
County: Southwestern Ontario
Country: Canada
General Phone: (519) 351-7331
General Fax: (519) 351-7774
Editorial e-mail: peter.epp@sunmedia.ca
Primary Website: www.chathamthisweek.com
Published: Wed
Avg Free Circ: 19760
Audit By: CMCA
Audit Date: 31.12.2015
Personnel: Dean Muharrem; Aaron Rodrigues (Media Sales Mgr.); Peter Epp (Managing Ed.); Rachel Blain (Office Mgr.)
Parent company (for newspapers): Postmedia Network Inc.

CHRONICLE

Street address 1: 168 Main St.
Street address city: West Lorne
Province/Territory: ON
Postal code: N0L 2P0
County: Canada
Country: Canada
General Phone: (519) 768-2220
General Fax: (519) 768-2221
General/National Adv. E-mail: chronicle@bowesnet.com
Primary Website: www.thechronicle-online.com
Published: Thur
Avg Paid Circ: 100
Avg Free Circ: 5463
Audit By: CMCA
Audit Date: 30.06.2013
Personnel: Bev Ponton; Ian McCallum (Reg. Managing Ed.)
Parent company (for newspapers): Quebecor Communications, Inc.

CITY CENTRE MIRROR

Street address 1: 175 Gordon Baker Rd.
Street address city: Toronto
Province/Territory: ON
Postal code: M2H 2S6
Country: Canada
General Phone: (416) 774-2367
General Fax: (416) 493-6190
General/National Adv. E-mail: atedesco@insidetoronto.com
Display Adv. E-mail: mbradley@metroland.com
Classified Adv. e-mail: classifieds@metroland.com
Editorial e-mail: newsroom@insidetoronto.com
Primary Website: insidetoronto.com
Published: Thur
Avg Paid Circ: 0
Avg Free Circ: 22359
Audit By: CCAB
Audit Date: 20.12.2017
Personnel: Antoine Tedesco (Managing Ed.)

Parent company (for newspapers): Metroland Media Group Ltd.

CLARINGTON THIS WEEK

Street address 1: 865 Farewell St.
Street address city: Oshawa
Province/Territory: ON
Postal code: L1H 7L5
Country: Canada
General Phone: (905) 579-4400
General Fax: (905) 579-2238
General/National Adv. E-mail: newsroom@durhamregion.com
Primary Website: newsdurhamregion.com
Published: Wed
Avg Free Circ: 24150
Audit By: Sworn/Estimate/Non-Audited
Audit Date: 12.07.2019
Personnel: Tim Whittaker (Pub.); Lillian Hook (Office Mgr.); Fred Eismont (Adv. Dir.); Joanne Burghardt (Ed. in Chief); Mike Johnston (Mng. Ed.)
Parent company (for newspapers): Metroland Media Group Ltd.; Torstar

CLINTON NEWS-RECORD

Street address 1: 53 Albert St.
Street address city: Clinton
Province/Territory: ON
Postal code: N0M 1L0
County: Canada
Country: Canada
General Phone: (519) 482-3443
General Fax: (519) 482-7341
Display Adv. E-mail: clinton.ads@bowesnet.com
Editorial e-mail: clinton.news@bowesnet.com
Primary Website: www.clintonnewsrecord.com
Published: Wed
Avg Paid Circ: 1029
Avg Free Circ: 22
Audit By: CMCA
Audit Date: 30.06.2016
Personnel: Neil Clifford (Pub.); John Bauman (Adv. Mgr.); Cheryl Heath (Ed.)
Parent company (for newspapers): Postmedia Network Inc.; Quebecor Communications, Inc.

COCHRANE TIMES-POST

Street address 1: 143, Sixth Avenue
Street address city: Cochrane
Province/Territory: ON
Postal code: P0L 1C0
Country: Canada
General Phone: (705) 272-3344
General Fax: (705) 272-3434
General/National Adv. E-mail: wayne.major@sunmedia.ca
Display Adv. E-mail: wayne.major@sunmedia.ca
Editorial e-mail: kevin.anderson@sunmedia.ca
Primary Website: www.cochranetimespost.ca
Published: Thur
Avg Paid Circ: 1254
Audit By: CMCA
Audit Date: 30.06.2016
Personnel: Wayne Major (Pub.); Chantal Carriere (Sales Representative, print & digital); Ashley Lewis (Reporter)
Parent company (for newspapers): Postmedia Network Inc.

COLLINGWOOD CONNECTION

Street address 1: 11 Ronell Crescent, Unit B
Street address city: Collingwood
Province/Territory: ON
Postal code: L9Y 4J6
Country: Canada
General Phone: (705) 444-1875
General Fax: (705) 444-1876
Advertising Phone: (800) 387-0668
General/National Adv. E-mail: connection@simcoe.com
Editorial e-mail: editor@simcoe.com
Primary Website: simcoe.com
Published: Fri
Avg Free Circ: 11479
Audit By: CCAB
Audit Date: 29.09.2017
Personnel: Scott Woodhouse (Ed.); Stephen Hall (Prod. Mgr.); Kent Feagan (Prodn. Dir.); Carol Lamb (General Mgr.); Patsy McCarthy (Sales Mgr.)

Parent company (for newspapers): Metroland Media Group Ltd.; Torstar

CREEMORE ECHO

Street address 1: 3 Caroline St. W.
Street address city: Creemore
Province/Territory: ON
Postal code: L0M 1G0
County: Canada
Country: Canada
General Phone: (705) 466-9906
General Fax: (705) 466-9908
General/National Adv. E-mail: info@creemore.com
Primary Website: www.creemore.com
Published: Fri
Avg Paid Circ: 450
Avg Free Circ: 3396
Audit By: CMCA
Audit Date: 31.12.2015
Personnel: Sara Hershoff (Pub.); Georgi Denison (Office Mgr.); Trina Berlo (Ed.)

DELHI NEWS-RECORD

Street address 1: 237 Main St.
Street address city: Delhi
Province/Territory: ON
Postal code: N4B 2M4
County: Canada
Country: Canada
General Phone: (519) 582-2510
General Fax: (519) 582-0627
Editorial e-mail: deleditorial@bowesnet.com
Primary Website: www.delhinewsrecord.com
Published: Wed
Avg Paid Circ: 506
Audit By: CMCA
Audit Date: 31.12.2013
Personnel: Walter Keleer (Adv. Mgr.); Kim Novak (Ed.); Wayne Ward (Prodn. Mgr.); Ken Koyoma (Pub.)
Parent company (for newspapers): Postmedia Network Inc.; Quebecor Communications, Inc.

DRIFTWOOD ENTERPRISES

Street address 1: 153 Balsam
Street address city: Ignace
Province/Territory: ON
Postal code: P0T 1T0
Country: Canada
General Phone: (807) 934-6482
Published: Wed
Avg Paid Circ: 303
Audit By: CMCA
Audit Date: 31.12.2015

DRYDEN OBSERVER

Street address 1: 32 Colonization Ave.
Street address city: Dryden
Province/Territory: ON
Postal code: P8N 2Y9
Country: Canada
General Phone: (807) 223-2390
General Fax: (807) 223-2907
Advertising Phone: (807) 223-2390 ext. 35
Editorial Phone: (807) 223-2390 ext. 34
Display Adv. E-mail: lorie@drydenobserver.ca
Editorial e-mail: chrism@drydenobserver.ca
Primary Website: www.drydenobserver.ca
Published: Wed
Avg Paid Circ: 2023
Avg Free Circ: 7
Audit By: CMCA
Audit Date: 19.12.2017
Personnel: LORIE LUNDY (Adv. Mgr.); Sean Clarke (Circ. Mgr.); CHRIS MARCHAND (Ed.); Michael Christianson (Reporter); Brian Kasaboski (Prod.); Laurie Fisher (Office manager)
Parent company (for newspapers): Norwest Printing

DUNDAS STAR NEWS

Street address 1: 333 Arvin Ave.
Street address city: Stoney Creek
Province/Territory: ON
Postal code: L8E 2M6
County: Dundas
Country: Canada
General Phone: (905) 664-8800
General Fax: (905) 664-3319
General/National Adv. E-mail: editor@dundasstarnews.com
Display Adv. E-mail: mtherrien@metroland.com
Classified Adv. e-mail: classified@thespec.com
Editorial e-mail: editor@dundasstarnews.com
Primary Website: www.dundasstarnews.com
Published: Thur
Avg Paid Circ: 4
Avg Free Circ: 14302
Audit By: CMCA
Audit Date: 21.06.2018
Personnel: Montague Kelly (Pub.); Jason Pehora (Gen. Mgr.); Lorna Lester (Office Mgr.); Gord Bowes (Ed); Mike Boyle (Produ Mgr.); Gordon Cameron (Mng Ed); Holly Christofilopoulos (Dir of Advt)
Parent company (for newspapers): Metroland Media Group Ltd.; Torstar

ESSEX FREE PRESS

Street address 1: 16 Centre St.
Street address city: Essex
Province/Territory: ON
Postal code: N8M 1N9
County: Canada
Country: Canada
General Phone: (519) 776-4268
General Fax: (519) 776-4014
General/National Adv. E-mail: essexfreepress@on.aibn.com
Primary Website: www.sxfreepress.com
Published: Thur
Avg Free Circ: 9925
Audit By: CMCA
Audit Date: 30.09.2016
Personnel: Lauri Brett (Pub.)

ETOBICOKE GUARDIAN

Street address 1: 307 Humberline Dr.
Street address city: Etobicoke
Province/Territory: ON
Postal code: M9W 5V1
Country: Canada
General Phone: (416) 675-4390
General Fax: (416) 675-9296
General/National Adv. E-mail: etg@mirror-guardian.com
Primary Website: insidetoronto.ca
Published: Thur
Avg Paid Circ: 0
Avg Free Circ: 67927
Audit By: CCAB
Audit Date: 30.09.2017
Personnel: Marg Middleton (Gen. Mgr.); Betty Carr (Pub.); Cor Coran (Adv. Mgr.); Lesley Duff (Asst. Dir., Dist.); Grace Peacock (Mng. Ed.); Dave Barnett (Dir., Prodn.); Katherine Bernal (Prodn. Mgr.)
Parent company (for newspapers): Metroland Media Group Ltd.; Torstar

EXPRESS

Street address 1: 24 Trowbridge St. W Unit 6
Street address city: Meaford
Province/Territory: ON
Postal code: N4L 1Y1
Country: Canada
General Phone: (519) 538-1421
General Fax: (519) 538-5028
General/National Adv. E-mail: meafordexpress@simcoe.com
Primary Website: www.meafordexpress.com
Published: Wed
Avg Paid Circ: 544
Avg Free Circ: 96
Audit By: CMCA
Audit Date: 30.06.2016
Personnel: Scott Woodhouse (Ed.); Pamela Amero (Adv.); Chris Fell (Community Events)
Parent company (for newspapers): Metroland Media; Metroland Media Group Ltd.

EXPRESS D'ORLEANS

Street address 1: Canotek Road Unit 30
Street address 2: Unit 30
Street address city: Gloucester
Province/Territory: ON
Postal code: K1J 8R7
Country: Canada
General Phone: (613) 744-4800
Published: Wed
Avg Paid Circ: 10742
Avg Free Circ: 200
Audit By: ODC
Audit Date: 14.12.2011
Personnel: Madeleine Joanisse

FONTHILL VOICE OF PELHAM

Street address 1: 8-209 Highway 20 East
Street address city: Fonthill
Province/Territory: ON
Postal code: L0S 1E0
County: Canada
Country: Canada
General Phone: (905) 892-8690
General Fax: (905) 892-0823
General/National Adv. E-mail: office@thevoiceofpelham.ca
Display Adv. E-mail: advertising@thevoiceofpelham.ca
Editorial e-mail: editor@thevoiceofpelham.ca
Primary Website: www.thevoiceofpelham.ca
Published: Wed
Avg Free Circ: 6782
Audit By: CMCA
Audit Date: 30.09.2015
Personnel: Leslie Chiapetta (Office Mgr.); Nate Smelle (Ed.); Dave Burket (Pub.)

FOREST STANDARD

Street address 1: 1 King St. W.
Street address city: Forest
Province/Territory: ON
Postal code: N0N 1J0
Country: Canada
General Phone: (519) 786-5242
General Fax: (519) 786-4884
General/National Adv. E-mail: standard@xcelco.on.ca
Published: Thur
Avg Paid Circ: 1848
Audit By: CMCA
Audit Date: 30.06.2014
Personnel: Dale Hayter (Pub.); Gil De Schutter (Adv. Mgr.); Mavis Sanger (Circ. Mgr.); Gord Whitehead (Ed.)

FORT ERIE POST

Street address 1: 3300 Merrittville Hwy Unit 1b
Street address city: Thorold
Province/Territory: ON
Postal code: L2V 4Y6
Country: Canada
General Phone: (905) 688-2444
Primary Website: www.niagarathisweek.com/forterie-on
Published: Thur
Personnel: Dave Hawkins (Adv.)
Parent company (for newspapers): Metroland Media Group Ltd.

FORT FRANCES TIMES

Street address 1: 116 First St.
Street address city: Fort Frances
Province/Territory: ON
Postal code: P9A 3M7
County: Canada
Country: Canada
General Phone: (807) 274-5373
General Fax: (807) 274-7286
General/National Adv. E-mail: fort_frances_times@ocna.org
Display Adv. E-mail: ads@fortfrances.com
Primary Website: www.fortfrances.com
Published: Wed
Avg Paid Circ: 3134
Avg Free Circ: 130
Audit By: CMCA
Audit Date: 31.03.2016
Personnel: James R. Cumming (Pub.); Linda Plumridge (Office Mgr.); Debbie Ballare (Adv. Mgr.); Michael Behan (Ed.); Don Cumming (Prod. Mgr.)

FRONTENAC EMC

Street address 1: 375 Select Drive Unit 14
Street address city: Kingston
Province/Territory: ON
Postal code: K7M 8R1
Country: Canada
General Phone: (613) 546-8884
General Fax: (613) 546-3607
Primary Website: www.emcfrontenac.ca
Published: Thur
Avg Free Circ: 8639
Audit By: CMCA
Audit Date: 28.02.2013
Personnel: Duncan Weir (Pub.)

GERALDTON-LONGLAC TIMES STAR

Street address 1: 401 Main St.
Street address city: Geraldton
Province/Territory: ON
Postal code: P0T 1M0
Country: Canada
General Phone: (807) 854-1919
General Fax: (807) 854-1682
General/National Adv. E-mail: tstar@astrocom-on.com
Editorial e-mail: editor@thetimesstar.ca
Primary Website: www.thetimesstar.ca
Published: Wed
Avg Paid Circ: 642
Avg Free Circ: 19
Audit By: CMCA
Audit Date: 31.07.2016
Personnel: Mike Goulet (Prodn. Mgr.); Justin Saindon; Eric Pietsch (Ed.)

GLANBROOK GAZETTE

Street address 1: 3 Sutherland St. W.
Street address city: Caledonia
Province/Territory: ON
Postal code: N3W 1C1
Country: Canada
General Phone: (905) 765-4441
General Fax: (905) 765-3651
General/National Adv. E-mail: news@sachem.ca
Display Adv. E-mail: advertising@sachem.ca
Primary Website: www.sachem.ca
Published: Thur
Avg Free Circ: 9194
Audit By: CMCA
Audit Date: 31.12.2015
Parent company (for newspapers): Metroland Media Group Ltd.

GODERICH SIGNAL-STAR

Street address 1: 120 Huckins St. Industrial Park
Street address city: Goderich
Province/Territory: ON
Postal code: N7A 3X8
Country: Canada
General Phone: (519) 524-2614
General Fax: (519) 524-9175
General/National Adv. E-mail: john.bauman@sunmedia.ca
Primary Website: www.goderichsignalstar.com
Published: Wed
Avg Paid Circ: 3150
Avg Free Circ: 18
Audit By: CMCA
Audit Date: 30.06.2017
Personnel: John Bauman (Sales Mgr.)
Parent company (for newspapers): Postmedia Network Inc.

GOUT DE VIVRE

Street address 1: 343 Lafontaine St. W.
Street address city: Penetanguishene
Province/Territory: ON
Postal code: L9M 1R3
Country: Canada
General Phone: (705) 533-3349
General/National Adv. E-mail: legoutdevivre@bellnet.ca
Primary Website: www.legoutdevivre.com
Published: Thur
Avg Paid Circ: 912
Avg Free Circ: 0
Audit By: CMCA
Audit Date: 30.04.2013
Personnel: Therese Maheux

GUELPH TRIBUNE

Street address 1: 367 Woodlawn Rd. W., Unit 1
Street address city: Guelph
Province/Territory: ON
Postal code: N1H 7K9
County: Canada

Country: Canada
General Phone: (519) 763-3333
General Fax: (519) 763-4814
General/National Adv. E-mail: cclark@guelphtribune.ca
Primary Website: www.guelphtribune.ca
Published: Tues`Thur
Avg Free Circ: 41612
Audit By: VAC
Audit Date: 30.06.2016
Personnel: Peter Winkler (Pub.); Heather Dunbar (Sales Mgr.); Doug Coxson (Ed.)
Parent company (for newspapers): Metroland Media Group Ltd.; Torstar

HAMILTON MOUNTAIN NEWS

Street address 1: 333 Arvin Ave.
Street address city: Stoney Creek
Province/Territory: ON
Postal code: L8E 2M6
County: Hamilton
Country: Canada
General Phone: (905) 664-8800
General Fax: (905) 664-3319
General/National Adv. E-mail: editor@hamiltonmountainnews.com
Display Adv. E-mail: mtherrien@metroland.com
Classified Adv. e-mail: classified@thespec.com
Editorial e-mail: gordbowes@hamiltonnews.com
Primary Website: www.hamiltonnews.com
Published: Thur
Avg Paid Circ: 5
Avg Free Circ: 49048
Audit By: CMCA
Audit Date: 21.06.2018
Personnel: Jason Pehora (Gen. Mgr.); Gordon Cameron (Managing Editor); Holly Christofilopoulos (Director of Advertising)
Parent company (for newspapers): Metroland Media Group Ltd.; Torstar Corp.

HARROW NEWS

Street address 1: 5 King St.
Street address 2: P.o. Box 310
Street address city: Harrow
Province/Territory: ON
Postal code: N0R 1G0
Country: Canada
General Phone: (519) 738-2542
General Fax: (519) 738-3874
General/National Adv. E-mail: harnews@mnsi.net
Display Adv. E-mail: harnews@mnsi.net
Classified Adv. e-mail: harnews@mnsi.net
Editorial e-mail: natalie@mdirect.net
Published: Tues
Avg Paid Circ: 1221
Avg Free Circ: 3
Audit By: CMCA
Audit Date: 2/29/2017
Personnel: Natalie Koziana (Circ. Mgr.)

HAVELOCK CITIZEN

Street address 1: Po Box 239
Street address city: Marmora
Province/Territory: ON
Postal code: K0K 2M0
Country: Canada
General Phone: (613) 962-2360
General Fax: (613) 472-5026
Published: Fri
Avg Paid Circ: 35000
Avg Free Circ: 2321
Audit By: Sworn/Estimate/Non-Audited
Audit Date: 12.07.2019
Personnel: Nancy Derrer (Ed.)
Parent company (for newspapers): Shield Media

HERALD

Street address 1: 260 Main St. E.
Street address city: Dundalk
Province/Territory: ON
Postal code: N0C 1B0
Country: Canada
General Phone: (519) 923-2203
General Fax: (519) 923-2747
Display Adv. E-mail: dundalk.herald@gmail.com
Editorial e-mail: dundalk.heraldnews@gmail.com
Primary Website: www.dundalkherald.ca
Published: Wed
Avg Paid Circ: 1443
Audit By: CMCA
Audit Date: 30.06.2016
Personnel: Matthew Walls (Pub.); Cathy Walls (Adv. Mgr.)

HERALD

Street address 1: 105 Elizabeth St
Street address 2: Box 580
Street address city: Thamesville
Province/Territory: ON
Postal code: N0P 2K0
Country: Canada
General Phone: (519) 692-3825
General/National Adv. E-mail: thamesvilleherald@sympatico.ca
Published: Wed
Avg Paid Circ: 594
Audit By: CMCA
Audit Date: 29.02.2016
Personnel: Orval Schilbe (Ed.); May Schilbe (Mng. Ed.)

HUNTSVILLE FORESTER

Street address 1: 11 Main St. W.
Street address city: Huntsville
Province/Territory: ON
Postal code: P1H 2C5
Country: Canada
General Phone: (705) 789-5541
General Fax: (705) 789-9381
General/National Adv. E-mail: production@metrolandnorthmedia.com
Editorial e-mail: news@metrolandnorthmedia.com
Primary Website: www.huntsvilleforester.com
Published: Thur
Avg Paid Circ: 161
Avg Free Circ: 9177
Audit By: CMCA
Audit Date: 31.03.2016
Personnel: Bill Allen (Pub./Gen. Mgr.); Andrew Allen (Adv. Mgr.); Tamara De la Vega (News Ed.); Jack Tynan
Parent company (for newspapers): Metroland Media Group Ltd.; Torstar

HUNTSVILLE/MUSKOKA ADVANCE

Street address 1: 11 Main St. W
Street address city: Huntsville
Province/Territory: ON
Postal code: P1H 2C5
Country: Canada
General Phone: (705) 789-5541
General Fax: (705) 789-9381
General/National Adv. E-mail: production@huntsvilleforester.com; news@huntsvilleforester.com
Primary Website: www.huntsvilleforester.com
Published: Sun
Avg Paid Circ: 7100
Avg Free Circ: 23038
Audit By: Sworn/Estimate/Non-Audited
Audit Date: 12.07.2019
Personnel: Joe Anderson (Regl. Pub.); Micheal Hill (Adv. Mgr.); Brenda McGary (Circ. Mgr.); Bruce Hickey (Ed.); Paula Ashby (Prodn. Mgr.)

IN PORT NEWS

Street address 1: 228 E. Main St.
Street address city: Port Colborne
Province/Territory: ON
Postal code: L3K 1S4
Country: Canada
General Phone: (905) 732-2411
General/National Adv. E-mail: john.tobon@sunmedia.ca
Primary Website: www.inportnews.ca
Published: Wed
Avg Free Circ: 9849
Audit By: CMCA
Audit Date: 31.03.2016
Personnel: John Tobon; Julia Coles
Parent company (for newspapers): Postmedia Network Inc.

INDEPENDENT & FREE PRESS

Street address 1: 280 Guelph St., Unit 29
Street address city: Georgetown
Province/Territory: ON
Postal code: L7G 4B1
County: Canada
General Phone: (905) 873-0301
General Fax: (905) 873-0398
General/National Adv. E-mail: production@independentfreepress.com
Primary Website: independentfreepress.com
Published: Thur
Avg Free Circ: 23045
Audit By: CCAB
Audit Date: 30.09.2017
Personnel: Steve Foreman (Gen. Mgr.); Cindi Campbell (Circ. Mgr.); Nancy Geissler (Circ. Mgr.); John McGhie (Mng. Ed.); Dana Robbins (Publisher)
Parent company (for newspapers): Metroland Media Group Ltd.; Torstar

INNISFIL JOURNAL

Street address 1: 21 Patterson Rd.
Street address city: Barrie
Province/Territory: ON
Postal code: L4N 7W6
Country: Canada
General Phone: (705) 726-0573
General Fax: (705) 726-9350
General/National Adv. E-mail: eallain@simcoe.com
Editorial e-mail: rvanderlinde@simcoe.com
Primary Website: simcoe.com
Published: Thur
Avg Free Circ: 10791
Audit By: CCAB
Audit Date: 31.03.2017
Personnel: Elise Allaine (Gen. Mgr.)
Parent company (for newspapers): Metroland Media Group Ltd.

JACKFISH JOURNAL

Street address 1: 113 Herbert Ave.
Street address city: Hornepayne
Province/Territory: ON
Postal code: P0M 1Z0
General Phone: (807) 868-2381
General Fax: (807) 868-2673
General/National Adv. E-mail: Jjournal@bell.net
Primary Website: www.hornepayne.com
Published: Wed
Avg Paid Circ: 200
Avg Free Circ: 30
Audit By: CMCA
Audit Date: 30.04.2016
Personnel: Lisa Stewart (Pub./Ed.)

JOURNAL LE REFLET

Street address 1: 793 Rue Notre Dame Rr 3 # 3,
Street address city: Embrun
Province/Territory: ON
Postal code: K0A 1W1
Country: Canada
General Phone: (613) 443-2741
Primary Website: www.lereflet.qc.ca
Published: Mon
Avg Paid Circ: 29
Avg Free Circ: 18102
Audit By: ODC
Audit Date: 14.12.2011
Personnel: Roger Duplantie (Gen. Dir.)

JOURNAL LE VOYAGEUR

Street address 1: 336 Rue Pine
Street address 2: Suite 302
Street address city: Sudbury
Province/Territory: ON
Postal code: P3C 1X8
Country: Canada
General Phone: (705) 673-3377
General Fax: (705) 673-5854
General/National Adv. E-mail: administration@levoyageur.ca
Primary Website: www.lavoixdunord.ca
Published: Wed
Avg Paid Circ: 7157
Avg Free Circ: 1342
Audit By: CMCA
Audit Date: 28.02.2013
Personnel: Patrick Breton (Ed. in Chief)

KANATA KOURIER-STANDARD EMC

Street address 1: 57 Auriga Dr. Unit 103
Street address city: Ottawa
Province/Territory: ON
Postal code: K2E 8B2
Country: Canada
General Phone: (613) 723-5970
General Fax: (613)224-2265
General/National Adv. E-mail: mtracy@perfprint.ca
Primary Website: www.insideottawavalley.com
Published: Thur
Avg Free Circ: 28642
Audit By: CMCA
Audit Date: 30.06.2014
Personnel: Mike Tracy (Pub.); Theresa Fritz (Ed.)
Parent company (for newspapers): Metroland Media Group Ltd.; Runge Newspapers, Inc.

KAWARTHA LAKES THIS WEEK

Street address 1: 192 St. David St.
Street address city: Lindsay
Province/Territory: ON
Postal code: K9V 4Z4
Country: Canada
General Phone: (705) 324-8600
General Fax: (705) 324-5694
General/National Adv. E-mail: mtully@mykawartha.com
Display Adv. E-mail: mbabcock@mykawartha.com
Editorial e-mail: mtully@mykawartha.com
Primary Website: www.mykawartha.com
Published: Tues`Thur
Avg Paid Circ: 0
Avg Free Circ: 21867
Audit By: CCAB
Audit Date: 30.09.2012
Personnel: Bruce Danford (Pub.); Linda Suddes (Bus. Admin./Opns.); Kim Riel (Office Mgr.); Shane Lockyer (Adv. Mgr.); Lois Tuffin (Ed. in Chief); Marcus Tully (News Ed.); Scott Prikker (Prodn. Mgr.); Jeff Braund (Regl. Dist. Mgr.); Tracy Magee-Graham (Dir., Distr.)
Parent company (for newspapers): Metroland Media Group Ltd.; Torstar

KEMPTVILLE ADVANCE EMC

Street address 1: 65 Lorne St.
Street address city: Smiths Falls
Province/Territory: ON
Postal code: K7A 4T1
Country: Canada
General Phone: (613) 283-3181
Display Adv. E-mail: liz.gray@metroland.com
Editorial e-mail: joe.morin@metroland.com
Primary Website: www.insideottawavalley.com
Published: Thur
Avg Free Circ: 10707
Audit By: CMCA
Audit Date: 30.06.2016
Personnel: Duncan Weir (Group Pub.); Kerry Sammon (Ed.)
Parent company (for newspapers): Metroland Media Group Ltd.

KING WEEKLY SENTINEL

Street address 1: 30 Martha Streeet, Suite 205
Street address 2: Suite 205
Street address city: Bolton
Province/Territory: ON
Postal code: L7E 5V1
County: Caledon
Country: Canada
General Phone: (905) 857-6626
General Fax: (905) 857-6363
General/National Adv. E-mail: admin.syp@rogers.com
Display Adv. E-mail: zach@lpcmedia.ca
Classified Adv. e-mail: admin@caledoncitizen.com
Editorial e-mail: editor@kingsentinel.com
Primary Website: www.kingsentinel.com
Published: Thur
Avg Paid Circ: 30
Avg Free Circ: 10200
Audit By: Sworn/Estimate/Non-Audited
Audit Date: 12.07.2019
Personnel: Mark Pavilons (Editor)

KINGSTON HERITAGE EMC

Street address 1: 375 Select Dr.
Street address city: Kingston
Province/Territory: ON
Postal code: K7M 8R1

Country: Canada
General Phone: (613) 546-8885
Display Adv. E-mail: kdillon@theheritageemc.ca
Primary Website: www.insideottawavalley.com
Published: Thur
Avg Free Circ: 45862
Audit By: CMCA
Audit Date: 30.06.2016
Personnel: Donna Glasspoole (Gen. Mgr.); Kate Lawrenence (Sales Coordinator)
Parent company (for newspapers): Metroland Media Group Ltd.

KINGSTON THIS WEEK

Street address 1: 18 St. Remy Place
Street address city: Kingston
Province/Territory: ON
Postal code: K7M 6C4
Country: Canada
General Phone: (613) 389-7400
General Fax: (613) 389-7507
General/National Adv. E-mail: news@kingstonthisweek.com
Primary Website: www.kingstonthisweek.com
Published: Thur
Avg Free Circ: 48840
Audit By: CMCA
Audit Date: 31.03.2016
Personnel: Ron Drillen (Gen. Mgr.); Tracy Weaver (Mng. Ed.); Lynn Rees Lambert (News Ed.); Rob Mooy (Photo Ed.); Liza Nelson
Parent company (for newspapers): Quebecor Communications, Inc.

KITCHENER POST

Street address 1: 630 Riverbend Dr Unit 104
Street address 2: Unit 104
Street address city: Kitchener
Province/Territory: ON
Postal code: N2K 3S2
General Phone: (519) 579-7166
General Fax: (519) 579-2029
Primary Website: www.kitchenerpost.ca
Published: Fri
Avg Free Circ: 58770
Audit By: CMCA
Audit Date: 30.06.2016
Personnel: Bob Vrbanac (Managing Ed.)
Parent company (for newspapers): Metroland Media Group Ltd.

LAKE ERIE BEACON (OOB)

Street address 1: 204 A Carlow Road
Street address city: Port Stanley
Province/Territory: ON
Postal code: N5L 1C5
County: Central Elgin
Country: Canada
General Phone: (519) 782-4563
General Fax: (519) 782-4563
Advertising Phone: (519) 782-4563
Editorial Phone: (519) 782-4563
General/National Adv. E-mail: beacon@lebeacon.ca
Display Adv. E-mail: linda@lebeacon.ca
Classified Adv. e-mail: linda@lebeacon.ca
Editorial e-mail: andrew@lebeacon.ca
Primary Website: www.lebeacon.ca
Published: Fri`Bi-Mthly
Avg Free Circ: 7000
Audit By: CMCA
Audit Date: 31.12.2013
Parent company (for newspapers): Kettle Creek Publishing Ltd.

LAKE OF THE WOODS ENTERPRISE

Street address 1: 33 Main St.
Street address city: Kenora
Province/Territory: ON
Postal code: P9N 3X7
Country: Canada
General Phone: (807) 468-5555
General Fax: (807) 468-4318
General/National Adv. E-mail: lotwenterprise@bowes.com
Primary Website: www.lotwenterprise.com
Published: Thur
Avg Paid Circ: 122
Avg Free Circ: 7771
Audit By: CMCA
Audit Date: 31.08.2015
Personnel: Ted Weiss (Adv. Mgr.); Reg Clayton (Reg. Managing Ed.)
Parent company (for newspapers): Postmedia Network Inc.

LAKEFIELD HERALD

Street address 1: 74 Bridge St.
Street address city: Lakefield
Province/Territory: ON
Postal code: K0L 2H0
Country: Canada
General Phone: (705) 652-6594
General Fax: (705) 652-6912
General/National Adv. E-mail: info@lakefieldherald.com
Display Adv. E-mail: ads@lakefieldherald.com
Editorial e-mail: editor@lakefieldherald.com
Primary Website: www.lakefieldherald.com
Published: Fri
Avg Paid Circ: 937
Avg Free Circ: 39
Audit By: Sworn/Estimate/Non-Audited
Audit Date: 12.07.2019
Personnel: Terry McQuitty (Owner)

LAKESHORE ADVANCE

Street address 1: 58 Ontario St. North
Street address city: Grand Bend
Province/Territory: ON
Postal code: N0M 1T0
Country: Canada
General Phone: (519) 238-5383
General Fax: (519) 238-5131
General/National Adv. E-mail: lakeshore.advance@sunmedia.ca
Display Adv. E-mail: lakeshore.ads@sunmedia.ca
Editorial e-mail: lakeshore.advance@sunmedia.ca
Primary Website: www.lakeshoreadvance.com
Published: Wed
Avg Paid Circ: 979
Avg Free Circ: 13
Audit By: CMCA
Audit Date: 30.06.2014
Personnel: Neil Clifford (Adv. Dir.)
Parent company (for newspapers): Quebecor

LE CARILLON

Street address 1: 1100 Aberdeen St.
Street address city: Hawkesbury
Province/Territory: ON
Postal code: K6A 1K7
County: Canada
Country: Canada
General Phone: (613) 632-4155
General Fax: (613) 632-6122
Advertising Phone: (613) 632-4155
Editorial Phone: (613) 632-4155
General/National Adv. E-mail: nouvelles@eap.on.ca
Display Adv. E-mail: yvan.joly@eap.on.ca; nicole.pilon@eap.on.ca
Editorial e-mail: nouvelles@eap.on.ca
Primary Website: www.lecarillon.ca
Published: Thur
Avg Paid Circ: 30
Avg Free Circ: 15000
Audit By: Sworn/Estimate/Non-Audited
Audit Date: 12.07.2019
Personnel: Bertrand Castonguay (Pres.); Gilles Normand (Circ. Mgr.); FranÃ§ois Legault (Chief Ed.)
Parent company (for newspapers): Cie d'Edition Andre Paquette, Inc.

LE NORD

Street address 1: 1004, Rue Prince.
Street address city: Hearst
Province/Territory: ON
Postal code: P0L 1N0
County: Hearst
Country: Canada
General Phone: (705) 372-1233
General Fax: (705) 362-5954
General/National Adv. E-mail: lenord@lenord.on.ca; ocantin@lenord.on.ca
Display Adv. E-mail: lenordjournalpub@gmail.com
Classified Adv. e-mail: lenordjournalpub@gmail.com
Editorial e-mail: journalistenord@gmail.com
Primary Website: www.lenord.on.ca
Published: Wed
Avg Paid Circ: 1409
Avg Free Circ: 65
Audit By: CMCA
Audit Date: 30.06.2014
Personnel: Omer Cantin (Ed.); Steve McInnis (Gen. Mgr.); Karine Hebert (Graphic Designer)
Parent company (for newspapers): Lignes Agates Marketing

LE REGIONAL

Street address 1: 99 Professors Lake Parkway
Street address city: Brampton
Province/Territory: ON
Postal code: L6S 4P8
Country: Canada
General Phone: (905) 732-9666
General Fax: (905) 790-9127
General/National Adv. E-mail: info@leregional.com
Display Adv. E-mail: marketing@leregional.com
Classified Adv. e-mail: marketing@leregional.com
Editorial e-mail: info@leregional.cm
Primary Website: www.leregional.com
Published: Wed
Avg Paid Circ: 76
Avg Free Circ: 4164
Audit By: CMCA
Audit Date: 31.12.2012
Personnel: Christiane Beaupre

LE REMPART

Street address 1: 7515 Forest Glade Dr.
Street address city: Windsor
Province/Territory: ON
Postal code: N8T 3P5
County: Canada
Country: Canada
General Phone: (519) 948-4139
General Fax: (519) 948-0628
General/National Adv. E-mail: info@lerempart.ca
Primary Website: www.lerempart.ca
Published: Wed
Avg Paid Circ: 5735
Avg Free Circ: 802
Audit By: CMCA
Audit Date: 31.12.2012
Personnel: Dennis Poirier (Pub.); Christiane Beaupre (Gen. Mgr.); Richard Caumartin (Dir., sales)

LE/THE REGIONAL

Street address 1: 124 Rue Principale E.
Street address city: Hawkesbury
Province/Territory: ON
Postal code: K6A 1A3
Country: Canada
General Phone: (613) 632-0112
General Fax: (613) 632-0277
General/National Adv. E-mail: pub@le-regional.ca
Display Adv. E-mail: pub@le-regional.ca
Editorial e-mail: news@le-regional.ca
Primary Website: www.le-regional.ca
Published: Thur
Avg Free Circ: 34484
Audit By: Sworn/Estimate/Non-Audited
Audit Date: 12.07.2019
Personnel: Sylvain Roy (Owner)

L'EXPRESS

Street address 1: 17 Carlaw Ave.
Street address city: Toronto
Province/Territory: ON
Postal code: M4M 2R6
Country: Canada
General Phone: (416) 465-2107
General Fax: (416) 465-3778
General/National Adv. E-mail: express@lexpress.to
Primary Website: www.lexpress.to
Published: Tues
Avg Paid Circ: 20000
Avg Free Circ: 15000
Audit By: Sworn/Estimate/Non-Audited
Audit Date: 12.07.2019
Personnel: Jean Mazare (Pub.); Akli Iiu (Adv. Mgr.); Marianne Santhan (Circ. Mgr.); Francois Bergeron (Ed.)

LONDONER

Street address 1: 1147 Gainsborough Road
Street address city: London
Province/Territory: ON
Postal code: N6H 5L5
Country: Canada
General Phone: (519) 673-5005
General Fax: (519) 673-4624
General/National Adv. E-mail: linda.leblanc@sunmedia.ca
Display Adv. E-mail: linda.leblanc@sunmedia.ca
Editorial e-mail: don.biggs@sunmedia.ca
Primary Website: www.thelondoner.ca
Published: Thur
Avg Free Circ: 140111
Audit By: CMCA
Audit Date: 31.12.2015
Personnel: Linda LeBlanc (Publisher)
Parent company (for newspapers): Postmedia Network Inc.

L'ORA DI OTTAWA

Street address 1: 888 Meadowlands Dr E
Street address 2: Suite 14
Street address city: Ottawa
Province/Territory: ON
Postal code: K2C 3R2
County: Ottawa Carleton
Country: Canada
General Phone: (613) 232-5689
General Fax: (855) 596 8522
General/National Adv. E-mail: info@loradiottawa.ca
Display Adv. E-mail: annamaria@loradiottawa.ca
Classified Adv. e-mail: annamaria@loradiottawa.ca
Editorial e-mail: annamaria@loradiottawa.ca
Primary Website: loradiottawa.ca
Published: Mon
Avg Paid Circ: 954
Avg Free Circ: 49
Audit By: AAM
Audit Date: 31.03.2019
Personnel: Paolo Siraco (Managing Editor); AnnaMaria Morrone (Client Services); Cynthia Nuzzi (Assistant Editor); Olita Schultz (Accounting)

MANITOULIN EXPOSITOR

Street address 1: 1 Manitowaning Rd.
Street address city: Little Current
Province/Territory: ON
Postal code: P0P 1K0
Country: Canada
General Phone: (705) 368-2744
General Fax: (705) 368-3822
General/National Adv. E-mail: expositor@manitoulin.ca
Display Adv. E-mail: sales@manitoulin.ca
Editorial e-mail: editor@manitoulin.ca
Primary Website: www.manitoulin.ca
Published: Wed
Avg Paid Circ: 4181
Avg Free Circ: 178
Audit By: AAM
Audit Date: 31.03.2019
Personnel: Rick L. McCutcheon (Pub.); Kerrene Tilson (Gen. Mgr.); Greg Lloyd (Sales Mgr.); David Patterson (Production Manager); Alicia McCutcheon
Parent company (for newspapers): Manitoulin Publishing Co., Ltd.

MANITOULIN RECORDER

Street address 1: 37 D Meredith St.
Street address city: Gore Bay
Province/Territory: ON
Postal code: P0P 1H0
County: Canada
Country: Canada
General Phone: (705) 282-2003
General Fax: (705) 282-2432
General/National Adv. E-mail: recorder@bellnet.ca
Published: Fri
Avg Paid Circ: 997
Avg Free Circ: 72
Audit By: AAM
Audit Date: 31.03.2018

Personnel: R.L. McCutcheon (Pub.); Tom Sasvari (Ed.); Al Ryan (Prodn. Mgr.)

MANOTICK MESSENGER

Street address 1: 3201 County Road 2.
Street address city: Johnstown
Province/Territory: ON
Postal code: ON K0E 1T0
Country: Canada
General Phone: (613) 692-6000
General Fax: (616) 692-3758
Display Adv. E-mail: advert@bellnet.ca
Editorial e-mail: newsfile@bellnet.ca
Primary Website: www.manotickmessenger.on.ca
Published: Thur
Avg Free Circ: 9503
Audit By: CMCA
Audit Date: 31.03.2016
Personnel: Jeff Morris (Pub.); Gary Coulombe (Adv. Rep.)

MANOTICK NEWS EMC

Street address 1: 57 Auriga Drive Unit 103
Street address city: Ottawa
Province/Territory: ON
Postal code: K2E 8B2
Country: Canada
General Phone: (613) 723-5970
General Fax: (613) 224-2265
Display Adv. E-mail: mstoodley@theemc.ca
Editorial e-mail: joe.morin@metroland.com
Primary Website: www.insideottawavalley.com
Published: Thur
Avg Free Circ: 11392
Audit By: CMCA
Audit Date: 30.06.2014
Personnel: Mike Tracy (Pub.); Theresa Fritz (Ed.)
Parent company (for newspapers): Metroland Media Group Ltd.

MARKHAM ECONOMIST & SUN

Street address 1: 50 Mcintosh Drive Unit 115
Street address city: Markham
Province/Territory: ON
Postal code: L3R-9T3
Country: Canada
General Phone: (905) 943-6100
General Fax: (905) 943-6129
Advertising Phone: (905) 943-6100
Editorial Phone: (905) 943-6100
General/National Adv. E-mail: admin@econsun.com
Display Adv. E-mail: abeswick@yrmg.com
Editorial e-mail: boneill@yrmg.com
Primary Website: yorkregion.com
Published: Thur
Avg Free Circ: 68613
Audit By: CMCA
Audit Date: 31.12.2015
Personnel: Ian Proudfoot (Pub.); Bernie O'Neill (Ed.); John Willems (Gen. Mgr.); Meriel Bradley (Online Adv.)
Parent company (for newspapers): Metroland Media Group Ltd.; Torstar

METROPOLITAIN (LE)

Street address 1: 99 Professors Lake Pkwy
Street address city: Brampton
Province/Territory: ON
Postal code: L6S 4P8
Country: Canada
General Phone: (905) 790-3229
General Fax: (905) 790-9127
General/National Adv. E-mail: info@lemetropolitain.com
Primary Website: www.lemetropolitain.com
Published: Wed
Avg Paid Circ: 329
Avg Free Circ: 8028
Audit By: CMCA
Audit Date: 31.12.2012
Personnel: Denis Poirier (Ed.)

MILLBROOK TIMES

Street address 1: 11 Prince St.
Street address city: Millbrook
Province/Territory: ON
Postal code: L0A 1G0
County: Cavan Monaghan Twp, Peterborough County
Country: Canada
General Phone: (705) 932-3001
General Fax: n/a
General/National Adv. E-mail: thetimes@nexicom.net
Display Adv. E-mail: kgraham@nexicom.net
Classified Adv. e-mail: thetimes@nexicom.net
Editorial e-mail: thetimes@nexicom.net
Primary Website: http://themillbrooktimes.ca
Published: Thur`Mthly
Avg Paid Circ: 100
Avg Free Circ: 4000
Audit By: Sworn/Estimate/Non-Audited
Audit Date: 28.09.2022
Personnel: Karen Graham (Pub.)

MINTO EXPRESS

Street address 1: 171 William St.
Street address city: Palmerston
Province/Territory: ON
Postal code: N0G 2P0
County: Town of Minto
Country: Canada
General Phone: (519) 343-2440
General Fax: (519) 343-2267
General/National Adv. E-mail: editor@mintoexpress.com
Primary Website: www.mintoexpress.com
Published: Wed
Avg Paid Circ: 476
Avg Free Circ: 5
Audit By: CMCA
Audit Date: 30.06.2016
Personnel: Bill Heuther (Gen. Mgr.); Shannon Burrows
Parent company (for newspapers): Metroland Media Group Ltd.; Torstar

MISSISSAUGA NEWS

Street address 1: 3145 Wolfedale Road
Street address city: Mississauga
Province/Territory: ON
Postal code: L5C 3A9
Country: Canada
General Phone: (905) 273-8230
General Fax: (905) 568-0181
General/National Adv. E-mail: www.mississauga.com
Editorial e-mail: tlanks@mississauga.net
Primary Website: mississauga.com
Published: Thur`Fri
Avg Paid Circ: 0
Avg Free Circ: 153598
Audit By: CCAB
Audit Date: 30.09.2017
Personnel: Dana Robbins (Pub.); Clark Kim (Community News/Ed.)
Parent company (for newspapers): Metroland Media Group Ltd.

MUSKOKA DISTRICT WEEKENDER

Street address 1: 34 E. P. Lee Drive
Street address city: Bracebridge
Province/Territory: ON
Postal code: P1L 1V2
Country: Canada
General Phone: (705) 645-8771
General Fax: (705) 645-1718
General/National Adv. E-mail: ccunningham@metrolandnorthmedia.com
Display Adv. E-mail: ddickson@metrolandnorthmedia.com
Primary Website: www.muskokaregion.com
Published: Fri
Avg Free Circ: 26430
Audit By: CMCA
Audit Date: 30.04.2013
Personnel: Coral Brush (Sales Coordinator)

NAPANEE GUIDE

Street address 1: 2 Dairy Ave., Unit 11
Street address city: Napanee
Province/Territory: ON
Postal code: K7R 3T1
Country: Canada
General Phone: (613) 354-6648
General Fax: (613) 354-6708
General/National Adv. E-mail: news@napaneeguide.com
Display Adv. E-mail: david@napaneeguide.com
Primary Website: www.napaneeguide.com
Published: Thur
Avg Free Circ: 14962
Audit By: CMCA
Audit Date: 30.06.2016
Personnel: Liza Nelson (Group Adv. Dir.); Rob McLellan (Distribution Supervisor)
Parent company (for newspapers): Postmedia Network Inc.; Quebecor Communications, Inc.

NASHA GAZETA

Street address 1: 855 Alness Street
Street address 2: Unit #7
Street address city: Toronto
Province/Territory: ON
Postal code: M3J 2X3
Country: Canada
General Phone: (905) 738-1109
General Fax: (416) 514-0640
Primary Website: www.rcbcanada.com/broadcasting/nasha-gazeta
Published: Wed
Avg Free Circ: 2600
Audit By: AAM
Audit Date: 31.12.2018
Personnel: Garry Kukuy (Pub.)
Parent company (for newspapers): Russian Canadian Broadcasting

NEPEAN-BARRHAVEN NEWS EMC

Street address 1: 57 Auriga Drive Unit 103
Street address city: Ottawa
Province/Territory: ON
Postal code: K2E 8B2
Country: Canada
General Phone: (613) 723-5970
General Fax: (613) 224-2265
Editorial e-mail: Nevil.hunt@metroland.com
Primary Website: www.insideottawavalley.com
Published: Thur
Avg Free Circ: 50401
Audit By: CMCA
Audit Date: 30.06.2014
Personnel: Mike Tracy (Pub.); Theresa Fritz (Ed.)
Parent company (for newspapers): Metroland Media Group Ltd.

NEW HAMBURG INDEPENDENT

Street address 1: 77 Peel St.
Street address city: New Hamburg
Province/Territory: ON
Postal code: N3A 1E7
County: Township of Wilmot
Country: Canada
General Phone: (519) 662-1240
General Fax: (519) 662-3521
General/National Adv. E-mail: editor@newhamburgindependent.ca
Display Adv. E-mail: kschattner@newhamburgindependent.ca
Classified Adv. e-mail: classified@metrolandwest.com
Editorial e-mail: editor@newhamburgindependent.ca
Primary Website: www.newhamburgindependent.ca
Published: Wed
Avg Paid Circ: 1770
Audit By: CMCA
Audit Date: 30.06.2016
Personnel: Donna Luelo (Pub.); Heather Dunbar (Adv. Mgr.); Kyle Schattner (Adv. Rep.); Scott Miller Cressman (Ed); Leta Gastle (Admin/Circulation); Chris Thomson (Reporter/photographer)
Parent company (for newspapers): Metroland Media Group Ltd.; Torstar

NIAGARA THIS WEEK

Street address 1: 3300 Merrittville Hwy, Unit 1b
Street address city: Thorold
Province/Territory: ON
Postal code: L2V 4Y6
Country: Canada
General Phone: (905) 688-2444
General Fax: (905) 688-9272
General/National Adv. E-mail: letters@niagarathisweek.com
Primary Website: niagarathisweek.com
Published: Wed`Thur
Avg Paid Circ: 0
Avg Free Circ: 151084
Audit By: CCAB
Audit Date: 30.09.2017
Personnel: David Bos (Gen. Mgr.); Debbi Koppejan (Adv. Mgr.); Mike Williscraft (Editorial Dir.); Dave Hawkins (Newspaper/Online Adv.)
Parent company (for newspapers): Metroland Media Group Ltd.; Torstar

NIPIGON-RED ROCK GAZETTE

Street address 1: 155b Railway Street
Street address city: Nipigon
Province/Territory: ON
Postal code: P0T 2J0
Country: Canada
General Phone: (807) 887-3583
General Fax: (807) 887-3720
General/National Adv. E-mail: nipigongazette@shaw.ca
Published: Tues
Avg Paid Circ: 486
Avg Free Circ: 17
Audit By: CMCA
Audit Date: 30.06.2017
Personnel: Pamela Behun (Circ. Mgr./Ed.); Blair Oborne (Pub.)

NORTH HURON PUBLISHING INC.

Street address 1: 405 Queen St.
Street address 2: Po Box 429
Street address city: Blyth
Province/Territory: ON
Postal code: N0M 1H0
County: North Huron
Country: Canada
General Phone: (519) 523-4792
General Fax: (519) 523-9140
General/National Adv. E-mail: info@northhuron.on.ca
Display Adv. E-mail: deb@northhuron.on.ca
Classified Adv. e-mail: deb@northhuron.on.ca
Editorial e-mail: deb@northhuron.on.ca
Primary Website: www.huroncitizen.ca
Published: Fri
Avg Paid Circ: 1959
Avg Free Circ: 19
Audit By: CMCA
Audit Date: 31.03.2022
Personnel: Deb Sholdice (Pub.)

NORTH YORK MIRROR

Street address 1: 100 Tempo Ave.
Street address city: Toronto
Province/Territory: ON
Postal code: M2H 2N8
Country: Canada
General Phone: (416) 493-4400
General Fax: (416) 495-6629
Display Adv. E-mail: sales@insidetoronto.com
Primary Website: insidetoronto.com
Published: Thur
Avg Paid Circ: 0
Avg Free Circ: 92407
Audit By: CCAB
Audit Date: 30.09.2017
Personnel: Betty Carr (V.P.); Marg Middleton (Gen. Mgr.); Dmitry Borovik (Sales Rep.); Angela Carruthers (Sales Rep.); Paul Futhey (Mng. Ed.); Stacey Allen (Dir. Adv.)
Parent company (for newspapers): Metroland Media Group Ltd.; Torstar

NORTHERN LIFE

Street address 1: 158 Elgin St.
Street address city: Sudbury
Province/Territory: ON
Postal code: P3E 3N5
Country: Canada
General Phone: (705) 673-5667
General Fax: (705) 673-4652
Advertising Phone: (705) 673-5667 Ext. 313
Editorial Phone: (705) 673-5667 Ext. 337
Display Adv. E-mail: classify@northernlife.ca
Editorial e-mail: mgentili@sudbury.com
Primary Website: sudbury.com
Published: Tues`Thur
Avg Paid Circ: 5444
Avg Free Circ: 35536
Audit By: CCAB
Audit Date: 30.09.2017

Personnel: Abbas Homayed (Pub.); Michael R. Atkins (Pres.); Mark Gentili (Managing Ed.)

NORTHERN NEWS THIS WEEK (KIRKLAND LAKE)

Street address 1: Eight Duncan Ave.
Street address city: Kirkland Lake
Province/Territory: ON
Postal code: P2N 3L4
Country: Canada
General Phone: (705) 567-5321
General Fax: (705) 567-6162
General/National Adv. E-mail: news@northernnews.ca
Display Adv. E-mail: display@northernnews.ca
Primary Website: www.northernnews.ca
Published: Mon`Wed`Fri
Avg Paid Circ: 3122
Audit By: Sworn/Estimate/Non-Audited
Audit Date: 12.07.2019
Personnel: Tony Howell (Circ. Mgr.); Joe O'Grady (Managing Ed.); Jeff Wilkinson (Sports Ed.); Lisa Wilson (Adv. Dir.)
Parent company (for newspapers): Postmedia Network Inc.; Quebecor Communications, Inc.

NORTHUMBERLAND NEWS

Street address 1: 884 Division St., Bldg. 2, Unit 212
Street address city: Cobourg
Province/Territory: ON
Postal code: K9A 5V6
Country: Canada
General Phone: (905) 373-7355
General Fax: (905) 373-4719
Primary Website: northumberlandnews.com
Published: Thur
Avg Paid Circ: 0
Avg Free Circ: 22338
Audit By: CCAB
Audit Date: 30.09.2017
Personnel: Timothy J. Whittaker (Pub.); Lillian Hook (Office Mgr.); Abe Fakhourie (Circ. Mgr.); Joanne Burghardt (Ed. in Chief); Dwight Irwin (Mng. Ed.)
Parent company (for newspapers): Metroland Media Group Ltd.; Torstar

OAKVILLE BEAVER

Street address 1: 467 Speers Rd.
Street address city: Oakville
Province/Territory: ON
Postal code: L6K 3S4
Country: Canada
General Phone: (905) 845-3824
General Fax: (905) 337-5568
Editorial e-mail: editor@oakvillebeaver.com
Primary Website: oakvillebeaver.com
Published: Thur`Fri
Avg Paid Circ: 84
Avg Free Circ: 53165
Audit By: CCAB
Audit Date: 30.09.2017
Personnel: Neil Oliver (Pub.); Daniel Baird (Dir., Adv.); Sarah McSweeney (Circ. Mgr.); Jill Davis (Ed. in Chief); Jon Kuiperij (Sports Ed.); Manuel Garcia (Prodn. Mgr.); Angela Blackburn (Ed.)
Parent company (for newspapers): Metroland Media Group Ltd.; Torstar

OLD AUTOS

Street address 1: 348 Main St.
Street address city: Bothwell
Province/Territory: ON
Postal code: N0P 1C0
Country: Canada
General Phone: (800) 461-3457
General/National Adv. E-mail: info@oldautos.ca
Display Adv. E-mail: ads@oldautos.ca
Classified Adv. e-mail: classifieds@oldautos.ca
Editorial e-mail: maryjo@oldautos.ca
Primary Website: oldautos.ca
Published: Mon
Avg Paid Circ: 14045
Avg Free Circ: 285
Audit By: AAM
Audit Date: 31.03.2019
Personnel: Mary Jo DePelsmaeker (Publisher)

ORANGEVILLE CITIZEN

Street address 1: 10 First St.
Street address city: Orangeville
Province/Territory: ON
Postal code: L9W 2C4
Country: Canada
General Phone: (519) 941-2230
General Fax: (519) 941-9361
General/National Adv. E-mail: mail@citizen.on.ca
Primary Website: www.citizen.on.ca
Published: Thur
Avg Free Circ: 17967
Audit By: CMCA
Audit Date: 29.02.2016
Personnel: Alan M. Claridge (Pub.); Thomas M. Claridge (Ed.); Carolyn Dennis (Classifieds)

ORILLIA TODAY

Street address 1: 25 Ontario St.
Street address city: Orillia
Province/Territory: ON
Postal code: L3V 6H1
Country: Canada
General Phone: (705) 329-2058
General Fax: (705) 329-2059
General/National Adv. E-mail: orillia@simcoe.com
Primary Website: orilliatoday.com
Published: Thur
Avg Free Circ: 24164
Audit By: CCAB
Audit Date: 31.03.2017
Personnel: Joe Anderson (Pub.); Leigh Gate (Gen. Mgr.); Leigh Rourke (Adv. Mgr.); Lori Martin (Mng. Ed.); Martin Melbourne (Community/News.); Kyla Mosley (Distr. Mgr.)
Parent company (for newspapers): Metroland Media Group Ltd.; Torstar

ORLEANS NEWS EMC

Street address 1: 57 Auriga Drive Unit 103
Street address city: Ottawa
Province/Territory: ON
Postal code: K2E 8B2
Country: Canada
General Phone: (613) 723-5970
Display Adv. E-mail: dave.badham@metroland.com
Primary Website: www.insideottawavalley.com
Published: Thur
Avg Free Circ: 42273
Audit By: CMCA
Audit Date: 30.06.2014
Personnel: Mike Tracy (Pub.); Theresa Fritz (Ed.)
Parent company (for newspapers): Metroland Media Group Ltd.

ORLEANS STAR

Street address 1: Po Box 46009
Street address city: Gloucester
Province/Territory: ON
Postal code: K1J 9H7
Country: Canada
General Phone: (613) 323-2801
Advertising Phone: (613) 744-4800
General/National Adv. E-mail: orleansstar@transcontinental.ca
Primary Website: www.orleansstar.ca
Published: Thur
Avg Paid Circ: 11
Avg Free Circ: 42989
Audit By: CCAB
Audit Date: 31.03.2014

ORONO WEEKLY TIMES

Street address 1: 5310 Main St.
Street address city: Orono
Province/Territory: ON
Postal code: L0B 1M0
Country: Canada
General Phone: (905) 983-5301
Advertising Phone: (905) 983-5301
Editorial Phone: (905) 983-5301
General/National Adv. E-mail: oronotimes@rogers.com
Display Adv. E-mail: oronotimes@rogers.com
Classified Adv. e-mail: oronotimes@rogers.com
Editorial e-mail: oronotimes@rogers.com
Primary Website: www.oronoweeklytimes.com
Published: Wed
Avg Paid Circ: 1040
Audit By: CMCA
Audit Date: 30.06.2018
Personnel: Julie Cashin-Oster (Ed./Pub.)
Parent company (for newspapers): Orono Publications Inc.

OSHAWA-WHITBY THIS WEEK

Street address 1: 865 Farewell St.
Street address city: Oshawa
Province/Territory: ON
Postal code: L1H 7L5
County: Canada
Country: Canada
General Phone: (905) 579-4400
General Fax: (905) 579-2238
General/National Adv. E-mail: newsroom@durhamregion.com
Primary Website: durhamregion.com
Published: Wed`Thur
Avg Paid Circ: 0
Avg Free Circ: 100554
Audit By: CCAB
Audit Date: 06.12.2017
Personnel: Timothy J. Whittaker (Pub.); Lillian Hook (Office Mgr.); Fred Eismont (Adv. Mgr.); Tina Jennings (Adv. Coord.); Abe Fakhourie (Circ. Mgr.); Joanne Burghardt (Ed. in Chief); Mike Johnston (Mng. Ed.); Tim Kelly (Copy Ed.); Christy Chase (Entertainment Ed.); Walter Passarella (Photo Ed.); Judi Bobbitt (Regl. Ed.); Brian Legree (Sports Ed.); Janice O'Neil (Prodn. Mgr.)
Parent company (for newspapers): Metroland Media Group Ltd.; Torstar

OTTAWA EAST EMC

Street address 1: 57 Auriga Drive Unit 103
Street address city: Ottawa
Province/Territory: ON
Postal code: K2E 8B2
Country: Canada
General Phone: (613) 723-5970
General Fax: (613) 224-2265
Display Adv. E-mail: ghamilton@thenewsemc.ca
Editorial e-mail: matthew.jay@metroland.com
Primary Website: www.insideottawavalley.com
Published: Thur
Avg Free Circ: 36519
Audit By: CMCA
Audit Date: 30.06.2014
Personnel: Theresa Fritz (Ed.); Mike Tracy (Pub.)
Parent company (for newspapers): Metroland Media Group Ltd.

OTTAWA SOUTH EMC

Street address 1: 57 Auriga Drive Unit 103
Street address city: Ottawa
Province/Territory: ON
Postal code: K2E 8B2
Country: Canada
General Phone: (613) 723-5970
General Fax: (613) 224-2265
Display Adv. E-mail: cmanor@theemc.ca
Editorial e-mail: blair.edwards@metroland.com
Primary Website: www.insideottawavalley.com
Published: Thur
Avg Free Circ: 41820
Audit By: CMCA
Audit Date: 30.06.2014
Personnel: Mike Tracy (Pub.); Theresa Fritz (Ed.)
Parent company (for newspapers): Metroland Media Group Ltd.

OTTAWA WEST EMC

Street address 1: 57 Auriga Drive Unit 103
Street address city: Ottawa
Province/Territory: ON
Postal code: K2E 8B2
Country: Canada
General Phone: (613)723-5970
Display Adv. E-mail: dave.pennett@metroland.com
Primary Website: www.insideottawavalley.com
Published: Thur
Avg Free Circ: 35247
Audit By: CMCA
Audit Date: 30.06.2014
Personnel: Mike Tracy (Pub.); Theresa Fritz (Ed.)
Parent company (for newspapers): Metroland Media Group Ltd.

PARIS STAR

Street address 1: 195 Henry St
Street address 2: Building 4, Unit 1
Street address city: Brantford
Province/Territory: ON
Postal code: N3S 5C9
Country: Canada
General Phone: (519) 756-2020
General Fax: (519) 756-9470
General/National Adv. E-mail: parisstar.editorial@sunmedia.ca
Editorial e-mail: parisstar.editorial@sunmedia.ca
Primary Website: parisstaronline.com
Published: Thur
Avg Free Circ: 4877
Audit By: CMCA
Audit Date: 30.04.2019
Personnel: Ken Koyama (Pub.); Michael Peeling (Ed.)
Parent company (for newspapers): Postmedia Network Inc.; Quebecor Communications, Inc.

PARRY SOUND BEACON STAR

Street address 1: 67 James Street
Street address city: Parry Sound
Province/Territory: ON
Postal code: P2A 2X4
Country: Canada
General Phone: (705) 746-2104
General Fax: (705) 746-8369
General/National Adv. E-mail: jheidman@metrolandnorthmedia.com
Display Adv. E-mail: cbarnes@metrolandnorthmedia.com
Editorial e-mail: cpeck@metrolandnorthmedia.com
Primary Website: www.parrysound.com
Published: Fri
Avg Free Circ: 7433
Audit By: CMCA
Audit Date: 31.12.2015
Personnel: Shaun Sauve (Regional Gen. Mgr.)
Parent company (for newspapers): Metroland Media Group Ltd.

PARRY SOUND NORTH STAR

Street address 1: 67 James St.
Street address city: Parry Sound
Province/Territory: ON
Postal code: P2A 2X4
County: Canada
Country: Canada
General Phone: (705) 746-2104
General Fax: (705) 746-8369
Display Adv. E-mail: jheidman@metrolandnorthmedia.com
Editorial e-mail: jtynan@metrolandnorthmedia.com
Primary Website: www.parrysound.com
Published: Wed
Avg Paid Circ: 2081
Avg Free Circ: 125
Audit By: CMCA
Audit Date: 31.12.2015
Personnel: Bill Allen (Reg'l Gen. Mgr.); Janice Heidman Louch (Adv. Sales Mgr.); Jack Tynan (Mng. Ed.)
Parent company (for newspapers): Metroland Media Group Ltd.

PETERBOROUGH THIS WEEK

Street address 1: 884 Ford St.
Street address city: Peterborough
Province/Territory: ON
Postal code: K9J 5V4
Country: Canada
General Phone: (705) 749-3383
General Fax: (705) 749-0074
General/National Adv. E-mail: bdanford@mykawartha.com
Editorial e-mail: prellinger@mykawartha.com
Primary Website: mykawartha.com
Published: Wed`Fri
Avg Free Circ: 32354
Audit By: CCAB
Audit Date: 26.10.2017

Personnel: Bruce Danford (Pub.); Linda Sudes (Gen. Mgr.); Adam Milligan (Adv. Mgr.); Mary Babcock (Reg'l Dir., Adv.); Tracy Magee (Circ. Mgr.); Lois Tuffin (Ed. in Chief); Paul Relinger (Special Pjcts. Ed.); Mike Lacey (News Ed.); Scott Prikker (Prodn. Mgr.)
Parent company (for newspapers): Metroland Media Group Ltd.; Torstar

PORT DOVER MAPLE LEAF

Street address 1: 351 Main St.
Street address city: Port Dover
Province/Territory: ON
Postal code: N0A 1N0
County: Norfolk County
Country: Canada
General Phone: (519) 583-0112
General/National Adv. E-mail: info@portdovermapleleaf.com
Display Adv. E-mail: ads@portdovermapleleaf.com
Editorial e-mail: news@portdovermapleleaf.com
Primary Website: www.portdovermapleleaf.com
Published: Wed
Avg Paid Circ: 2904
Avg Free Circ: 15
Audit By: Sworn/Estimate/Non-Audited
Audit Date: 12.07.2019
Personnel: Paul Morris (Editor); Stan Morris (Ed.); Todd Dewell (Advertising); Beverly Snow (Accounting)

QUINTE WEST EMC

Street address 1: 250 Sidney St.
Street address city: Belleville
Province/Territory: ON
Postal code: K8P 5E0
Country: Canada
General Phone: (613) 966-2034
General/National Adv. E-mail: jkearns@theemc.ca
Primary Website: www.insideottawavalley.com
Published: Thur
Avg Free Circ: 23089
Audit By: CMCA
Audit Date: 31.12.2012
Personnel: John Kearns (Pub.); Sharon LaCroix (Community)
Parent company (for newspapers): Metroland Media Group Ltd.

RAINY RIVER RECORD

Street address 1: 312 Third St.
Street address city: Rainy River
Province/Territory: ON
Postal code: P0W 1L0
Country: Canada
General Phone: (807) 852-3366
General Fax: (807) 852-4434
Editorial Phone: (807) 852-3337
General/National Adv. E-mail: info@rainyriverrecord.com
Display Adv. E-mail: advertising@rainyriverrecord.com
Editorial e-mail: editorial@rainyriverrecord.com
Primary Website: www.rainyriverrecord.com
Published: Tues
Avg Paid Circ: 609
Audit By: CMCA
Audit Date: 31.03.2014
Personnel: Anne Mailloux (Circ. Mgr.); Melissa Hudgin (Sales); Sharon LaCroix (Ed.)

RIDEAU VALLEY MIRROR

Street address 1: 43 Bedfrod St.
Street address city: Westport
Province/Territory: ON
Postal code: K0G 1X0
Country: Canada
General Phone: (613) 273-8000
General Fax: (613) 273-8001
General/National Adv. E-mail: info@review-mirror.com
Display Adv. E-mail: advertising@review-mirror.com
Editorial e-mail: newsroom@review-mirror.com
Primary Website: www.review-mirror.com
Published: Thur
Avg Paid Circ: 1662
Avg Free Circ: 57
Audit By: CMCA
Audit Date: 28.02.2013
Personnel: Bill Ritchie (Adv. Mgr.); Louise Haughton (Circ. Mgr.); Howie Crichton (Ed.)

RIVER TOWN TIMES

Street address 1: 67 Richmond Street
Street address city: Amherstburg
Province/Territory: ON
Postal code: N9V 1G1
Country: Canada
General Phone: (519) 736-4175
General Fax: (519) 736-5420
Display Adv. E-mail: sales@rivertowntimes.com
Editorial e-mail: mail@rivertowntimes.com
Primary Website: www.rivertowntimes.com
Published: Wed
Avg Free Circ: 9183
Audit By: CMCA
Audit Date: 31.08.2016
Personnel: Ron Giofu (Ed.)

ROCKLAND VISION

Street address 1: 1315 Laurier St.
Street address city: Rockland
Province/Territory: ON
Postal code: K4K 1L5
Country: Canada
General Phone: (613) 446-6456
General Fax: (613) 446-1381
General/National Adv. E-mail: vision@eap.on.ca
Display Adv. E-mail: paulo.casimiro@eap.on.ca
Primary Website: www.facebook.com/pg/Le-journal-Vision-newspaper-199878750108078/about/?ref=page_internal
Published: Fri
Avg Paid Circ: 23297
Avg Free Circ: 39
Audit By: ODC
Audit Date: 13.12.2011
Personnel: Paulo Casimiro (Prodn. Mgr.)

SARNIA & LAMBTON COUNTY THIS WEEK

Street address 1: 140 Front St S
Street address city: Sarnia
Province/Territory: ON
Postal code: N7t2M6
County: Lambton County
Country: Canada
General Phone: (519) 336-1100
General Fax: (519) 336-1833
Advertising Phone: (519) 336-1100
Editorial Phone: (519) 336-1100
General/National Adv. E-mail: chris.courtis@sunmedia.ca
Display Adv. E-mail: stw.sales@sunmedia.ca
Editorial e-mail: stw.sales@sunmedia.ca
Primary Website: Www.sarniathisweek.ca
Published: Wed
Avg Free Circ: 41300
Audit By: Sworn/Estimate/Non-Audited
Audit Date: 12.07.2019
Personnel: Chris Courtis (Marketing Manager)
Parent company (for newspapers): Postmedia Network Inc.

SARNIA THIS WEEK

Street address 1: 140 Front St. S
Street address city: Sarnia
Province/Territory: ON
Postal code: N7T 7M8
County: Canada
Country: Canada
General Phone: (519) 336-1100
General Fax: (519) 336-1833
General/National Adv. E-mail: news@sarniamedia.com
Editorial e-mail: production@sarniamedia.com
Primary Website: www.sarniathisweek.com
Published: Thur
Avg Free Circ: 39476
Audit By: CMCA
Audit Date: 30.06.2016
Personnel: Linda LeBlanc (Pub.); Penny Churchill (Distribution Mgr.)
Parent company (for newspapers): Quebecor Communications, Inc.

SAULT STE. MARIE THIS WEEK

Street address 1: 2 Towers St.
Street address city: Sault Sainte Marie
Province/Territory: ON
Postal code: P6A 2T9
Country: Canada
General Phone: (705) 949-6111
General Fax: (705) 942-8596
Editorial Phone: (705) 759-5825
General/National Adv. E-mail: lou.maulucci@sunmedia.ca
Display Adv. E-mail: sste.advertising@sunmedia.ca
Editorial e-mail: sandra.paul@sunmedia.ca
Primary Website: www.saultthisweek.com
Published: Thur
Avg Free Circ: 31122
Audit By: CMCA
Audit Date: 30.06.2015
Personnel: Lou Maulucci (Pub.); Sandra Paul (Ed.)
Parent company (for newspapers): Postmedia Network Inc.; Quebecor Communications, Inc.

SEAFORTH HURON EXPOSITOR

Street address 1: 8 Main St. S.
Street address city: Seaforth
Province/Territory: ON
Postal code: N0K 1W0
Country: Canada
General Phone: (519) 527-0240
General Fax: (519) 527-2858
General/National Adv. E-mail: seaforth@bowesnet.com
Display Adv. E-mail: max.bickford@sunmedia.ca
Classified Adv. e-mail: seaforth.classifieds@sunmedia.ca
Editorial e-mail: seaforth.news@sunmedia.ca
Primary Website: www.seaforthhuronexpositor.com
Published: Wed
Avg Paid Circ: 1160
Avg Free Circ: 22
Audit By: CMCA
Audit Date: 30.06.2016
Personnel: Neil Clifford (Pub.); Whitney South (Multi Media Journalist)
Parent company (for newspapers): Postmedia Network Inc.; Quebecor Communications, Inc.

SEAWAY NEWS

Street address 1: 501 Campbell Street
Street address 2: Unit 6
Street address city: Cornwall
Province/Territory: ON
Postal code: K6H 6X5
County: Cornwall and SD&G
Country: Canada
General Phone: (613) 933-0014
General Fax: (613) 933-0024
General/National Adv. E-mail: info@cornwallseawaynews.com
Display Adv. E-mail: patrick.larose@tc.tc
Classified Adv. e-mail: diane.merpaw@tc.tc
Editorial e-mail: nicholas.seebruch@tc.tc
Primary Website: www.cornwallseawaynews.com
Published: Thur
Avg Free Circ: 36541
Audit By: CMCA
Audit Date: 31.12.2015
Personnel: Rick Shaver (General Manager/ Publisher); Colleen Parette (Production Coordinator); Patrick Larose (Media Strategy Manager)
Parent company (for newspapers): Transcontinental Media

SHORELINE BEACON

Street address 1: 694 Goderich St.
Street address city: Port Elgin
Province/Territory: ON
Postal code: N0H 2C0
Country: Canada
General Phone: (519) 832-9001
General Fax: (519) 389-4793
General/National Adv. E-mail: shoreline@bmts.com
Primary Website: www.shorelinebeacon.com
Published: Tues
Avg Paid Circ: 2102
Avg Free Circ: 15
Audit By: CMCA
Audit Date: 30.06.2016
Personnel: Kiera Merriam (Gen. Mgr.)
Parent company (for newspapers): Postmedia Network Inc.; Quebecor Communications, Inc.

SMITHS FALLS RECORD NEWS EMC

Street address 1: 65 Lorne St.
Street address city: Smiths Falls
Province/Territory: ON
Postal code: K7A 4T1
Country: Canada
General Phone: (613) 283-3182
General Fax: (613) 283-7480
General/National Adv. E-mail: emc@perfprint.ca
Primary Website: www.insideottawavalley.com/smithsfalls-on
Published: Thur
Avg Free Circ: 11455
Audit By: CMCA
Audit Date: 30.06.2016
Personnel: Duncan Weir (Pub.); Jason Beck (Circ. Mgr); Ryland Coyne (Ed.)
Parent company (for newspapers): Metroland Media Group Ltd.

SOUTHPOINT SUN

Street address 1: 14 Talbot Street West
Street address city: Wheatley
Province/Territory: ON
Postal code: N0P 2P0
Country: Canada
General Phone: (519) 825-4541
General Fax: (519) 825-4546
General/National Adv. E-mail: sun@southpointsun.ca
Display Adv. E-mail: journal@mnsi.net
Primary Website: www.southpointsun.ca
Published: Wed
Avg Free Circ: 10579
Audit By: CMCA
Audit Date: 28.02.2014
Personnel: Jim Heyens (Pub.); Sheila McBrayne (Ed.)

SPEAKER WEEKENDER

Street address 1: 18 Wellington St.
Street address city: New Liskeard
Province/Territory: ON
Postal code: P0J 1P0
Country: Canada
General Phone: (705) 647-6791
General Fax: (705) 647-9669
General/National Adv. E-mail: loisperry@northontario.ca
Primary Website: www.facebook.com/pages/Temiskaming-Speaker-Weekender/884448971667310
Published: Fri
Avg Free Circ: 10450
Audit By: CMCA
Audit Date: 31.03.2016
Personnel: Lois Perry (Gen. Mgr.)

SPRINGWATER NEWS

Street address 1: 9 Glenview Ave.
Street address city: Elmvale
Province/Territory: ON
Postal code: L0L 1P0
County: Simcoe County
Country: Canada
General Phone: (705) 322-2249
General Fax: (705) 322-8393
Advertising Phone: (705) 322-2249
Editorial Phone: (705) 321-2653
General/National Adv. E-mail: springwaternews@rogers.com
Display Adv. E-mail: springwaternews@rogers.com
Classified Adv. e-mail: springwaternews@rogers.com
Editorial e-mail: springwaternews@rogers.com
Primary Website: www.springwaternews.ca
Published: Thur'Other
Avg Paid Circ: 140
Avg Free Circ: 18750
Audit By: Sworn/Estimate/Non-Audited
Audit Date: 12.07.2019

Personnel: Michael Jacobs (Ed./Pub./Owner)

ST. LAWRENCE NEWS

Street address 1: 7712 Kent Blvd.
Street address city: Brockville
Province/Territory: ON
Postal code: K6V 7H6
Country: Canada
General Phone: (613) 498-0305
General Fax: (613) 498-0307
Primary Website: www.emcstlawrence.ca
Published: Thur
Avg Free Circ: 29325
Audit By: CMCA
Audit Date: 30.06.2016
Parent company (for newspapers): Metroland Media Group Ltd.

ST. MARY'S JOURNAL ARGUS

Street address 1: 11 Wellington St. N.
Street address city: St Marys
Province/Territory: ON
Postal code: N4X 1B7
Country: Canada
General Phone: (519) 284-2440
General Fax: (519) 284-3650
General/National Adv. E-mail: drowe@southwesternontario.ca
Display Adv. E-mail: ksteven@stmarys.com
Classified Adv. e-mail: csmith@stmarys.com
Editorial e-mail: sslater@stmarys.com
Primary Website: www.southwesternontario.ca
Published: Wed
Avg Paid Circ: 1354
Avg Free Circ: 110
Audit By: CMCA
Audit Date: 31.03.2016
Personnel: Anita McDonald (Business Manager); Stevens Kara (Sales Supervisor); Colleen Smith (Advertising/Circulation)
Parent company (for newspapers): Metroland Media Group Ltd.; Torstar

ST. THOMAS/ELGIN WEEKLY NEWS

Street address 1: 15 St. Catharine Street
Street address city: Saint Thomas
Province/Territory: ON
Postal code: N5P 2V7
Country: Canada
General Phone: (519) 633-1640
General Fax: (519) 633-0558
Display Adv. E-mail: geoff@theweeklynews.ca
Editorial e-mail: editor@theweeklynews.ca
Primary Website: www.theweeklynews.ca
Published: Thur
Avg Free Circ: 30393
Audit By: CMCA
Audit Date: 31.10.2017
Personnel: Geoff Rae (Office/Sales Manager)
Parent company (for newspapers): Metroland Media Group Ltd.

STIRLING/NORTHEAST NEWS EMC

Street address 1: 244 Ashley St.
Street address city: Belleville
Province/Territory: ON
Postal code: K0K 2B0
Country: Canada
General Phone: (613) 966-2034
Advertising Phone: (613) 966-2034
Editorial Phone: (613) 966-2034 ext. 510
General/National Adv. E-mail: jkearns@theemc.ca
Display Adv. E-mail: jkearns@theemc.ca
Editorial e-mail: tbush@theemc.ca
Primary Website: www.insideottawavalley.com
Published: Thur
Avg Free Circ: 11564
Audit By: CMCA
Audit Date: 31.12.2012
Personnel: John Kearns (Pub.); Terry Bush (Mng. Ed.)

STONEY CREEK NEWS

Street address 1: 333 Arvin Ave.
Street address city: Stoney Creek
Province/Territory: ON
Postal code: L8E 2M6
County: Stoney Creek
Country: Canada
General Phone: (905) 664-8800
General Fax: (905) 664-3319
Display Adv. E-mail: editor@hamiltonmountainnews.com
Classified Adv. e-mail: classified@thespec.com
Editorial e-mail: editor@stoneycreeknews.com
Primary Website: www.stoneycreeknews.com
Published: Thur
Avg Paid Circ: 4
Avg Free Circ: 30178
Audit By: CMCA
Audit Date: 21.06.2018
Personnel: Kelly Montague (Pub.); Jason Pehora (Gen. Mgr.); Michael Pearson (Ed.); Gordon Cameron (Mng Ed.); Rhonda Ridgway (Produ Mgr.); Melinda Therrien (Adv. Dir.)
Parent company (for newspapers): Metroland Media Group Ltd.

STRATFORD GAZETTE

Street address 1: 10 Downie St. Unit 207
Street address city: Stratford
Province/Territory: ON
Postal code: N5A 7K4
Country: Canada
General Phone: (519) 271-8002
General Fax: (519) 271-5636
General/National Adv. E-mail: admin@stratfordgazette.com
Display Adv. E-mail: jhaefling@stratfordgazette.com
Classified Adv. e-mail: lcarter@stratfordgazette.com
Editorial e-mail: news@stratfordgazette.com
Primary Website: www.southwesternontario.ca
Published: Thur
Avg Free Circ: 19855
Audit By: CMCA
Audit Date: 29.02.2016
Personnel: Laura Carter (Front Office/Distribution); Julie Haefling (Sales Supervisor); Anita McDonald (Business Manager)
Parent company (for newspapers): Metroland Media Group Ltd.

TAVISTOCK GAZETTE

Street address 1: 119 Woodstock St. S.
Street address city: Tavistock
Province/Territory: ON
Postal code: N0B 2R0
Country: Canada
General Phone: (519) 655-2341
Advertising Phone: (519) 655-2341
Editorial Phone: (519) 655-2341
General/National Adv. E-mail: gazette@tavistock.on.ca
Primary Website: www.tavistock.on.ca
Published: Wed
Avg Paid Circ: 1178
Avg Free Circ: 2
Audit By: CMCA
Audit Date: 31.10.2017
Personnel: Sheri Gladding (Circulation Manager); William J. Gladding (Ed.)

TECUMSEH SHORELINE WEEK

Street address 1: 1614 Lesperance Rd.
Street address city: Tecumseh
Province/Territory: ON
Postal code: N8N 1X2
Country: Canada
General Phone: (519) 735-2080
General Fax: (519) 735-2082
General/National Adv. E-mail: shorelineweek@canwest.com
Published: Fri
Avg Free Circ: 17312
Audit By: CMCA
Audit Date: 31.12.2017
Personnel: Dave Calibaba (Pub.); Rusty Wright (Mgr., Sales); William England (Ed.)
Parent company (for newspapers): Postmedia Network Inc.; CanWest MediaWorks Publications, Inc.

TEKAWENNAKE

Street address 1: Po Box 130
Street address city: Oshweken
Province/Territory: ON
Postal code: N0A 1M0
Country: Canada
General Phone: (519) 753-0077
General Fax: (519) 753-0011
General/National Adv. E-mail: teka@tekanews.com
Published: Wed
Avg Paid Circ: 2500
Audit By: Sworn/Estimate/Non-Audited
Audit Date: 12.07.2019
Personnel: G. Scott Smith (Pub.)

TEMISKAMING SPEAKER

Street address 1: 18 Wellington St. S.
Street address city: New Liskeard
Province/Territory: ON
Postal code: P0J 1P0
Country: Canada
General Phone: (705) 647-6791
General Fax: (705) 647-9669
General/National Adv. E-mail: ads@northernontario.ca
Editorial e-mail: editorial@northernontario.ca
Primary Website: www.northernontario.ca
Published: Wed
Avg Paid Circ: 3021
Avg Free Circ: 138
Audit By: CMCA
Audit Date: 31.08.2015
Personnel: Lois Perry (Gen. Mgr.); Gordon Brock (Ed.)

TERRACE BAY SCHREIBER NEWS

Street address 1: 25 Simcoe Plaza
Street address city: Terrace Bay
Province/Territory: ON
Postal code: P0T 2W0
Country: Canada
General Phone: (807) 825-9425
General Fax: (807) 825-9458
General/National Adv. E-mail: nipigongazette@shaw.ca
Published: Tues
Avg Paid Circ: 287
Avg Free Circ: 21
Audit By: CMCA
Audit Date: 30.06.2016
Personnel: Karen Schaeffer (Reporter/Photographer); Blair Oborne (Pub.); Pamela Behun (Edior)

THE ALGOMA NEWS REVIEW

Street address 1: 33 St. Marie St.
Street address city: Wawa
Province/Territory: ON
Postal code: P0S 1K0
Country: Canada
General Phone: (705) 856-2267
General Fax: (705) 856-4952
General/National Adv. E-mail: waprint2@ontera.net
Editorial e-mail: editor@thealgomanews.ca
Primary Website: www.thealgomanews.ca
Published: Wed
Avg Paid Circ: 598
Avg Free Circ: 33
Audit By: CMCA
Audit Date: 31.03.2016
Personnel: Tammy Landry (Ed.); Christel Gignac (Adv. Mgr.)

THE ALLISTON HERALD

Street address 1: 169 Dufferin St. S
Street address 2: Unit 22
Street address city: Alliston
Province/Territory: ON
Postal code: L9R 1E6
Country: Canada
General Phone: (705) 435-6228
General Fax: (705) 435-3342
Editorial e-mail: herald@simcoe.com
Primary Website: simcoe.com
Published: Thur
Avg Free Circ: 22860
Audit By: CCAB
Audit Date: 31.03.2017
Personnel: Angela Makaroff (Sales Mgr.)
Parent company (for newspapers): Metroland Media Group Ltd.

THE AURORA BANNER

Street address 1: 250 Industrial Parkway N.
Street address city: Aurora
Province/Territory: ON
Postal code: L4G 4C3
Country: Canada
General Phone: (905) 727-0819
General Fax: (905) 727-2909
Display Adv. E-mail: lmcdonald@yrmg.com
Editorial e-mail: tmcfadden@yrmg.com
Primary Website: yorkregion.com
Published: Thur`Sun
Avg Free Circ: 15943
Audit By: CCAB
Audit Date: 30.09.2018
Personnel: Ted McFadden (Managing Ed.)
Parent company (for newspapers): Metroland Media Group Ltd.

THE AURORAN

Street address 1: 15213 Yonge St Ste 8
Street address city: Aurora
Province/Territory: ON
Postal code: L4G 1L8
Country: Canada
General Phone: (905) 727-3300
General Fax: (905) 727-2620
Advertising Phone: (416) 803-9940
General/National Adv. E-mail: bob@auroran.com
Display Adv. E-mail: zach@lpcmedia.ca
Classified Adv. e-mail: cynthia@auroran.com
Editorial e-mail: brock@auroran.com
Primary Website: www.newspapers-online.com/auroran
Published: Thur
Avg Paid Circ: 15
Avg Free Circ: 20000
Audit By: CMCA
Audit Date: 2/31/2017
Personnel: Brock Weir (Ed.); Cynthia Proctor (Prod. Mgr.); Diane Buchanan (Adv. Sales); Zach Shoub (Adv. Sales)
Parent company (for newspapers): London Publishing

THE AYLMER EXPRESS

Street address 1: 390 Talbot St. E.
Street address city: Aylmer
Province/Territory: ON
Postal code: N5H 2R9
Country: Canada
General Phone: (519) 773-3126
General Fax: (519) 773-3147
General/National Adv. E-mail: info@aylmerexpress.ca
Display Adv. E-mail: advertise@aylmerexpress.ca
Primary Website: www.aylmerexpress.ca
Published: Wed
Avg Paid Circ: 13
Avg Free Circ: 14
Audit By: VAC
Audit Date: 31.03.2016
Personnel: Pam Morton (Adv. Mgr.); Wanda Kapogines (Circ. Mgr.); John Hueston (Ed.); Karen Hueston (Prodn. Mgr.)

THE BANCROFT TIMES

Street address 1: 93 Hastings St. N.
Street address city: Bancroft
Province/Territory: ON
Postal code: K0L 1C0
Country: Canada
General Phone: (613) 332-2300
General Fax: (613) 332-1894
General/National Adv. E-mail: bancroft-times@sympatico.ca
Primary Website: www.thebancrofttimes.ca
Published: Thur
Audit By: VAC
Audit Date: 30.04.2016
Personnel: Dean Walker (Owner); Jenn Watt (Managing Ed.)

THE BARRIE ADVANCE

Street address 1: 21 Patterson Rd.
Street address city: Barrie
Province/Territory: ON
Postal code: L4N 7W6
Country: Canada
General Phone: (705) 726-0573
General Fax: (705) 726-9350
Editorial e-mail: bareditor@simcoe.com
Primary Website: simcoe.com
Published: Thur

Avg Free Circ: 50827
Audit By: CCAB
Audit Date: 31.12.2017
Personnel: Shaun Sauve (Adv. Dir.); Heather Harris (Distr. Mgr.); Ian Proudfoot
Parent company (for newspapers): Metroland Media Group Ltd.

THE BAY OBSERVER

Street address 1: 140 King Street East
Street address city: Hamilton
Province/Territory: ON
Postal code: L8N 1B2
Country: USA
General Phone: (905) 522-6000
General Fax: (905) 522-5838
General/National Adv. E-mail: contact@bayobserver.ca
Primary Website: www.bayobserver.ca
Published: Thur
Avg Paid Circ: 0
Avg Free Circ: 28246
Audit By: CMCA
Audit Date: 31.01.2012
Personnel: John Best (Pub.)

THE BRUCE PENINSULA PRESS

Street address 1: 39 Legion St.
Street address city: Tobermory
Province/Territory: ON
Postal code: N0H 2R0
Country: Canada
General Phone: (519) 596-2658
General Fax: (519) 596-8030
General/National Adv. E-mail: info@tobermorypress.com
Primary Website: www.brucepeninsulapress.com
Published: Tues
Avg Paid Circ: 400
Avg Free Circ: 2235
Audit By: CMCA
Audit Date: 30.06.2017
Personnel: John Francis (Pub.); Scott McFarlane (Production Mgr./Signs); Marianne Wood (Editor)

THE BULLETIN

Street address 1: 40 Front St.
Street address city: Sioux Lookout
Province/Territory: ON
Postal code: P8T 1B9
Country: Canada
General Phone: (807) 737-3209
General Fax: (807) 737-3084
Advertising Phone: (807) 737-4207
General/National Adv. E-mail: bulletin@siouxbulletin.com
Primary Website: www.soiuxbulletin.com
Published: Wed
Avg Free Circ: 4472
Audit By: CMCA
Audit Date: 30.04.2016
Personnel: Dick MacKenzie (Ed.)

THE BULLETIN - JOURNAL OF DOWNTOWN TORONTO

Street address 1: 260 Adelaide St E Ste 121
Street address city: Toronto
Province/Territory: ON
Postal code: M5A 1N1
Country: Canada
General Phone: (416) 929-0011
General Fax: (416) 929-0011
Advertising Phone: (416) 929-0011 ext. 5
Editorial Phone: (416) 929-0011 ext. 3
Display Adv. E-mail: sales@thebulletinca
Classified Adv. e-mail: classified@thebulletin.ca
Editorial e-mail: deareditor@thebulletin.ca
Primary Website: www.thebulletin.ca
Published: Other
Avg Free Circ: 49822
Audit By: CMCA
Audit Date: 06.09.2017
Personnel: Paulette Touby (Pub.); Frank Touby (Ed.); Anisa Lancione (Mng Ed.)
Parent company (for newspapers): Community Bulletin Newspaper Group, Inc.

THE BURLINGTON POST

Street address 1: 5040 Mainway, Unit 1
Street address city: Burlington
Province/Territory: ON
Postal code: L7L 7G5
County: Canada
Country: Canada
General Phone: (905) 632-4444
General Fax: (905) 632-9162
Editorial e-mail: letters@burlingtonpost.com
Primary Website: burlingtonpost.com
Published: Thur`Fri
Avg Paid Circ: 27
Avg Free Circ: 28355
Audit By: CCAB
Audit Date: 30.09.2017
Personnel: Jill Davis (Ed. in Chief); Don Ford (Mng. Ed.); Kevin Nagel (Sports Ed.); Debbi Koppejan (Advertising Director)
Parent company (for newspapers): Metroland Media Group Ltd.; Torstar

THE CARLETON PLACE-ALMONTE CANADIAN GAZETTE EMC

Street address 1: 65 Lorne St.
Street address city: Smith Falls
Province/Territory: ON
Postal code: K7A 4T1
Country: Canada
General Phone: (613) 283-3182
Display Adv. E-mail: ssinfield@perfprint.ca
Editorial e-mail: akulp@perfprint.ca
Primary Website: www.insideottawavalley.com
Published: Thur
Avg Free Circ: 12071
Audit By: CMCA
Audit Date: 30.06.2016
Personnel: Duncan Weir (Group Pub.l); Ryland Coyne (Reg. Ed.)
Parent company (for newspapers): Metroland Media Group Ltd.

THE CHESTERVILLE RECORD

Street address 1: 7 King St.
Street address city: Chesterville
Province/Territory: ON
Postal code: K0C 1H0
County: Canada
Country: Canada
General Phone: (613) 448-2321
General Fax: (613) 448-3260
General/National Adv. E-mail: rm@agrinewsinteractive.com
Display Adv. E-mail: news@chestervillerecord.com
Editorial e-mail: editor@chestervillerecord.com
Primary Website: www.agrinewsinteractive.com
Published: Wed
Avg Paid Circ: 1456
Avg Free Circ: 2
Audit By: CMCA
Audit Date: 30.06.2016
Personnel: Robin R. Morris (Pub.); Nelson Zandbergen (Ed.)

THE CHESTERVILLE RECORD/THE VILLAGER

Street address 1: 7 King St.
Street address city: Chesterville
Province/Territory: ON
Postal code: K0C 1H0
Country: Canada
General Phone: (613) 448-2321
General Fax: (613) 448-3260
General/National Adv. E-mail: thevillager.editor@gmail.com
Primary Website: www.chestervillerecord.com; russellvillager.com
Published: Wed
Avg Paid Circ: 2600
Audit By: CMCA
Audit Date: 30.06.2013
Personnel: Muriel Carruthers (Editor)

THE COMMUNITY NEWS

Street address 1: 41 Wellington St. N.
Street address city: Drayton
Province/Territory: ON
Postal code: N0G 1P0
Country: Canada
General Phone: (519) 638-3066
General Fax: (519) 843-7606
General/National Adv. E-mail: drayton@wellingtonadvertiser.com
Editorial e-mail: editor@wellingtonadvertiser.com
Primary Website: www.wellingtonadvertiser.com
Published: Fri
Avg Paid Circ: 5
Avg Free Circ: 5152
Audit By: CMCA
Audit Date: 31.03.2016
Personnel: William Adsett (Pub.); Dave Adsett (Ed.)

THE COMMUNITY PRESS

Street address 1: 199 Front St.
Street address 2: Suite 118
Street address city: Belleville
Province/Territory: ON
Postal code: K8N 5H5
Country: Canada
General Phone: (613) 395-3015
General Fax: (613) 395-2992
Editorial Phone: (613) 392-6501
General/National Adv. E-mail: compress@redden.on.ca; general@communitypress-online.com
Display Adv. E-mail: gerry.drage@sunmedia.ca
Classified Adv. e-mail: intelligencer.classifieds@sunmedia.ca
Editorial e-mail: brice.mcvicar@sunmedia.ca
Primary Website: www.communitypress-online.com
Published: Thur
Avg Free Circ: 46476
Audit By: CMCA
Audit Date: 30.06.2016
Personnel: Brice McVicar (Ed); Gerry Drage (Adv. Dir.); Jason Hawley (Circ Mgr)

THE COMMUNITY PRESS

Street address 1: 41 Quinte St.
Street address city: Trenton
Province/Territory: ON
Postal code: K8V 5R3
Country: Canada
General Phone: (613) 395-3015
General Fax: (613) 392-0505
General/National Adv. E-mail: general@communitypress-online.com; news@communitypress-online.com
Editorial e-mail: editor@communitypress-online.com
Primary Website: www.communitypress.ca
Published: Thur
Avg Paid Circ: 0
Avg Free Circ: 45644
Audit By: CMCA
Audit Date: 30.06.2014
Personnel: John Knowles (Pub.); Chuck Parker (Gen. Mgr); Ross Lees (Mng. Ed.); John Campbell (News Ed.)

THE COUNTY WEEKLY NEWS

Street address 1: 3-252 Main St.
Street address city: Picton
Province/Territory: ON
Postal code: K0K 2T0
Country: Canada
General Phone: (613) 476-4714
General Fax: (613) 476-1281
General/National Adv. E-mail: bill.glisky@sunmedia.ca
Editorial e-mail: chris.malette@sunmedia.ca
Primary Website: www.countyweeklynews.ca
Published: Thur
Avg Free Circ: 11591
Audit By: CMCA
Audit Date: 30.06.2013
Personnel: Dave Vachon (News Ed.)
Parent company (for newspapers): Postmedia Network Inc.

THE DURHAM CHRONICLE

Street address 1: 190 Elizabeth St. E.
Street address city: Durham
Province/Territory: ON
Postal code: N0G 1R0
County: Canada
Country: Canada
General Phone: (519) 369-2504
General Fax: (519) 369-3560
General/National Adv. E-mail: themarkdalestandard@bmts.com
Published: Wed
Avg Paid Circ: 1196
Avg Free Circ: 21
Audit By: Sworn/Estimate/Non-Audited
Audit Date: 12.07.2019
Personnel: Marie David (Pub.); Bev Stoddart (Gen. Mgr.); Christine Meingast (Ed.)

THE EAST YORK MIRROR

Street address 1: 10 Tempo Ave.
Street address city: Willowdale
Province/Territory: ON
Postal code: M2H 3S5
Country: Canada
General Phone: (413) 493-4400
General Fax: (413) 495-6629
General/National Adv. E-mail: eym@mirror-guardian.com
Primary Website: www.metroland.com
Published: Thur
Avg Paid Circ: 0
Avg Free Circ: 34643
Audit By: CCAB
Audit Date: 30.09.2017
Personnel: Betty Carr (Pub.); Marg Middleton (Gen. Mgr.); Stacey Allen (Adv. Dir.); Paris Quinn (Sales Rep.); Kim Buenting (Circ. Mgr.); Deborah Bodine (Ed.); Alan Shackleton (Mng. Ed.); Katherine Bernal (Prodn. Mgr.); Dave Barnett (Prodn. Dir.)
Parent company (for newspapers): Metroland Media Group Ltd.; Torstar

THE ECHO

Street address 1: 105 Warbler
Street address city: Manitouwadge
Province/Territory: ON
Postal code: P0T 2C0
Country: Canada
General Phone: (807) 228-2333
Advertising Phone: (807) 228-2317
General/National Adv. E-mail: info@theecho.ca
Display Adv. E-mail: manitouwadgeecho@gmail.com
Editorial e-mail: news@theecho.ca
Primary Website: www.theecho.ca
Published: Wed
Avg Paid Circ: 346
Audit By: CMCA
Audit Date: 30.04.2014
Personnel: B.J. Schermann (Pub.); Scott Schermann (Prodn. Mgr.)

THE EGANVILLE LEADER

Street address 1: 150 John St.
Street address 2: P.o. Box 310
Street address city: Eganville
Province/Territory: ON
Postal code: K0J 1T0
Country: Canada
General Phone: (613) 628-2332
General Fax: (613) 628-3291
General/National Adv. E-mail: leader@nrtco.net
Display Adv. E-mail: leaderads@nrtco.net
Editorial e-mail: leader@nrtco.net
Primary Website: www.eganvilleleader.com
Published: Wed
Avg Paid Circ: 6096
Audit By: CMCA
Audit Date: 29.02.2016
Personnel: Carol Kutschke (Circ. Mgr.); Gerald J. Tracey (Ed.)

THE ENTERPRISE

Street address 1: 441 Main Street
Street address city: Iroquois Falls A
Province/Territory: ON
Postal code: P0K 1G0
Country: Canada
General Phone: (705) 232-4081
General Fax: (705) 232-4235

General/National Adv. E-mail: news@theenterprise.ca
Display Adv. E-mail: news@theenterprise.ca
Classified Adv. e-mail: news@theenterprise.ca
Editorial e-mail: editor@theenterprise.ca
Published: Thur
Avg Paid Circ: 850
Avg Free Circ: 104
Audit By: CMCA
Audit Date: 31.03.2022
Personnel: William C. Cavell (Pub); Tory Delaurier (Adv. Mgr.)

THE ENTERPRISE-BULLETIN

Street address 1: 77 Simcoe St.
Street address city: Collingwood
Province/Territory: ON
Postal code: L9Y 3Z4
Country: Canada
General Phone: (705) 445-4611
General Fax: (705) 444-6477
Editorial e-mail: editorial@theenterprisebulletin.com
Primary Website: www.theenterprisebulletin.com
Published: Fri
Avg Paid Circ: 295
Avg Free Circ: 18858
Audit By: CMCA
Audit Date: 30.06.2014
Personnel: Doreen Sykes (Pub.); April MacLean (Circ. Mgr.); J.T. McVeigh (Ed.)
Parent company (for newspapers): Postmedia Network Inc.; Sunmedia; Quebecor Communications, Inc.

THE ERIN ADVOCATE

Street address 1: 8 Thompson Crescent
Street address city: Erin
Province/Territory: ON
Postal code: N0B 1T0
Country: Canada
General Phone: (519) 833-9603
General Fax: (519) 833-9605
General/National Adv. E-mail: esales@erinadvocate.com
Published: Wed
Avg Paid Circ: 1054
Audit By: CMCA
Audit Date: 30.06.2016
Personnel: Ken Nugent (Pub.); Bill Anderson (Adv. Mgr.); Joan Murray (Ed.)
Parent company (for newspapers): Metroland Media Group Ltd.; Torstar

THE FERGUS-ELORA NEWS EXPRESS

Street address 1: 204 St. Andrew St. W
Street address city: Fergus
Province/Territory: ON
Postal code: N1M 1M7
Country: Canada
General Phone: (519) 843-1310
General Fax: (519) 323-4548
Display Adv. E-mail: ads@centrewellington.com
Editorial e-mail: editor@centrewellington.com
Primary Website: www.southwesternontario.ca/ferguselora-on
Published: Wed
Avg Paid Circ: 100
Avg Free Circ: 7850
Audit By: CMCA
Audit Date: 31.08.2014
Personnel: Shannon Burrows (Ed.)
Parent company (for newspapers): Metroland Media Group Ltd.; Torstar

THE FLAMBOROUGH REVIEW

Street address 1: 30 Main St. N.
Street address city: Waterdown
Province/Territory: ON
Postal code: L0R 2H0
Country: Canada
General Phone: (905) 689-2003
General Fax: (905) 689-3110
Advertising Phone: (905) 689-2003 ext. 272
Editorial Phone: (905) 689-2003 ext. 321
General/National Adv. E-mail: classified@haltonsearch.com
Display Adv. E-mail: tlindsay@burlingtonpost.com
Editorial e-mail: editor@flamboroughreview.com
Primary Website: flamboroughreview.com
Published: Thur
Avg Paid Circ: 0
Avg Free Circ: 14075
Audit By: CCAB
Audit Date: 30.09.2017
Personnel: Neil Oliver (Pub.); Ted Lindsay (Adv. Mgr.); Charlene Hall (Circ. Mgr.); Brenda Jefferies (Ed.); Debbi Koppejan (Advertising Director)
Parent company (for newspapers): Metroland Media Group Ltd.; Torstar

THE FORT ERIE TIMES

Street address 1: 450 Garrison Rd., Unit 1
Street address city: Fort Erie
Province/Territory: ON
Postal code: L2A 1N2
Country: Canada
General Phone: (905) 871-3100
General Fax: (905) 871-5243
Advertising Phone: (905) 871-3100 x202
Editorial Phone: (905) 871-3100 x207
General/National Adv. E-mail: myra.robertson@sunmedia.ca
Display Adv. E-mail: myra.robertson@sunmedia.ca
Editorial e-mail: kris.dube@sunmedia.com
Primary Website: www.forterietimes.com
Published: Thur
Avg Paid Circ: 9
Avg Free Circ: 12454
Audit By: CMCA
Audit Date: 31.05.2016
Personnel: Sarag Ferguson (Ed.)
Parent company (for newspapers): Postmedia Network Inc.; Quebecor Communications, Inc.

THE FRONTENAC GAZETTE

Street address 1: 375 Select Dr., Ste. 14
Street address city: Kingston
Province/Territory: ON
Postal code: K7M 8R1
Country: Canada
General Phone: (613) 546-8885
General Fax: (613) 546-3607
General/National Adv. E-mail: kingston@theritageemc.ca
Primary Website: www.whatsonkingston.com
Published: Thur
Avg Free Circ: 8220
Audit By: CMCA
Audit Date: 30.06.2016
Personnel: Darryl Cembal (Pub.)
Parent company (for newspapers): Metroland Media Group Ltd.

THE FRONTENAC NEWS

Street address 1: 1095 Garrett St.
Street address 2: Rear
Street address city: Sharbot Lake
Province/Territory: ON
Postal code: K0H 2P0
County: Central Frontenac
Country: Canada
General Phone: (613) 279-3150
General Fax: (613) 279-3172
General/National Adv. E-mail: nfnews@frontenac.net
Display Adv. E-mail: info@frontenacnews.ca
Classified Adv. e-mail: info@frontenacnews.ca
Editorial e-mail: info@frontenacnews.ca
Primary Website: Frontenacnews.ca
Published: Thur
Avg Free Circ: 12000
Audit By: Sworn/Estimate/Non-Audited
Audit Date: 12.07.2023
Personnel: Jeff Green (Publisher/Editor); Scott Cox (Designer/bookeeper)

THE GEORGINA ADVOCATE

Street address 1: 184 Simcoe Ave.
Street address city: Keswick
Province/Territory: ON
Postal code: L4P 2H7
Country: Canada
General Phone: (905) 476-7753
General Fax: (905) 476-5785
General/National Adv. E-mail: admin@georginaadvocate.com
Primary Website: yorkregion.com
Published: Thur
Avg Free Circ: 16800
Audit By: CCAB
Audit Date: 31.12.2017
Personnel: Ian Proudfoot (Pub.); Robert Lazurko (Bus. Mgr.); Neil Moore (Adv. Mgr.); Debora Kelly (Ed. in Chief); Tracy Kibble (Ed.)
Parent company (for newspapers): Metroland Media Group Ltd.

THE GLENGARRY NEWS

Street address 1: 3 Main St.
Street address city: Alexandria
Province/Territory: ON
Postal code: K0C 1A0
County: Canada
Country: Canada
General Phone: (613) 525-2020
General Fax: (613) 525-3824
General/National Adv. E-mail: gnews@glengarrynews.ca
Primary Website: www.glengarrynews.ca
Published: Wed
Avg Paid Circ: 1075
Avg Free Circ: 86
Audit By: VAC
Audit Date: 30.09.2016
Personnel: Bonnie MacDonald (Adv. Mgr.); Steven Warburton (Mng. Ed.); Sean Bray (Sports Ed.); JT Grossmith

THE GRAND RIVER SACHEM

Street address 1: 3 Sutherland St. W.
Street address city: Caledonia
Province/Territory: ON
Postal code: N3W 1C1
Country: Canada
General Phone: (905) 765-4441
General Fax: (905) 765-3651
General/National Adv. E-mail: news@sachem.ca; sachem@sachem.ca
Display Adv. E-mail: advertising@sachem.ca
Primary Website: www.sachem.ca
Published: Thur
Avg Paid Circ: 77
Avg Free Circ: 21137
Audit By: CMCA
Audit Date: 30.06.2013
Personnel: Nancy Plank (Adv. Mgr.); Georgia Mete (Adv. Mgr., Classified); Neil Dring (Ed.)
Parent company (for newspapers): Metroland Media Group Ltd.

THE GRAVENHURST BANNER

Street address 1: 140 Muskoka Rd. S.
Street address city: Gravenhurst
Province/Territory: ON
Postal code: P1P 1X2
Country: Canada
General Phone: (705) 687-6674
General Fax: (705) 687-7213
General/National Adv. E-mail: banner@muskoka.com
Primary Website: www.muskokaregion.com/gravenhurst-on
Published: Thur
Avg Paid Circ: 96
Avg Free Circ: 5237
Audit By: CMCA
Audit Date: 30.04.2016
Personnel: Bill Allen (Gen. Mgr.); Jack Tynan (Adv.)
Parent company (for newspapers): Metroland Media Group Ltd.; Torstar

THE GRIMSBY LINCOLN NEWS

Street address 1: 32 Main St. W.
Street address city: Grimsby
Province/Territory: ON
Postal code: L3M 1R4
Country: Canada
General Phone: (905) 945-8392
General Fax: (905) 945-3916
General/National Adv. E-mail: info@thegrimsbylincolnnews.com
Primary Website: www.thegrimsbylincolnnews.com
Published: Wed
Avg Free Circ: 23800
Audit By: Sworn/Estimate/Non-Audited
Audit Date: 12.07.2019
Personnel: Mike Williscraft (Editorial Mgr.); Scott Rosts (Ed.)
Parent company (for newspapers): Metroland Media Group Ltd.; Torstar

THE HALDIMAND PRESS

Street address 1: 6 Parkview Rd.
Street address city: Hagersville
Province/Territory: ON
Postal code: N0A 1H0
County: Canada
Country: Canada
General Phone: (905) 768-3111
General/National Adv. E-mail: info@haldimandpress.com
Display Adv. E-mail: advertising@haldimandpress.com
Classified Adv. e-mail: advertising@haldimandpress.com
Editorial e-mail: news@haldimandpress.com
Primary Website: www.haldimandpress.com
Published: Thur
Avg Paid Circ: 2500
Audit By: Sworn/Estimate/Non-Audited
Personnel: Jillian Zynomirski (Pub.); Kaitlyn Clark (Publisher)

THE HERITAGE

Street address 1: 375 Select Dr., Unit 14
Street address city: Kingston
Province/Territory: ON
Postal code: K7M 8R1
County: Canada
Country: Canada
General Phone: (613) 546-8885
General Fax: (613) 546-3607
General/National Adv. E-mail: kingston@theheritageemc.ca
Primary Website: www.kingstonregion.com/kingstonregion
Published: Thur
Avg Paid Circ: 12
Avg Free Circ: 38833
Audit By: Sworn/Estimate/Non-Audited
Audit Date: 12.07.2019
Personnel: Darryl Cembal (Ed.)

THE HIGHLANDER

Street address 1: 123 Maple Ave.
Street address city: Haliburton
Province/Territory: ON
Postal code: K0M 1S0
County: Haliburton County
Country: Canada
General Phone: (705) 457-2900
General/National Adv. E-mail: admin@thehighlander.ca
Display Adv. E-mail: sales@thehighlander.ca
Classified Adv. e-mail: admin@thehighlander.ca
Editorial e-mail: editor@thehighlander.ca
Primary Website: https://haliburtonhighlander.ca
Published: Thur
Avg Free Circ: 8062
Audit By: CMCA
Audit Date: 30.06.2016
Personnel: Bram Lebo (Pub.); Simon Payn (Publisher); Lisa Gervais (Editor); Dawn Poissant (Sales)

THE HILL TIMES

Street address 1: 69 Sparks St.
Street address city: Ottawa
Province/Territory: ON
Postal code: K1P 5A5
Country: Canada
General Phone: (613) 232-5952
General Fax: (613) 232-9055
General/National Adv. E-mail: news@hilltimes.com; circulation@hilltimes.com
Display Adv. E-mail: production@hilltimes.com; classified@hilltimes.com
Primary Website: www.hilltimes.com
Published: Mon`Wed
Avg Paid Circ: 3614
Avg Free Circ: 9555
Audit By: CMCA
Audit Date: 29.02.2016

Personnel: Jim Creskey (Pub.); Ross Dickson (Pub.); Andrew Morrow (Gen. Mgr.); Kate Malloy (Ed.); Benoit Deneault (Prod. Mgr.); Anne Marie Creskey (Pub.)

THE INDEPENDENT

Street address 1: 840 Queen St.
Street address city: Kincardine
Province/Territory: ON
Postal code: N2Z 2Z4
County: Canada
Country: Canada
General Phone: (519) 396-3111
General Fax: (519) 396-3899
General/National Adv. E-mail: indepen@bmts.com
Primary Website: www.independent.on.ca
Published: Wed
Avg Paid Circ: 1906
Avg Free Circ: 82
Audit By: CMCA
Audit Date: 31.12.2015
Personnel: Eric Howald (Ed.)

THE INGERSOLL TIMES

Street address 1: 16 Brock Street
Street address city: Woodstock
Province/Territory: ON
Postal code: N4S 3B4
Country: Canada
General Phone: (519) 537-2341
Display Adv. E-mail: cwetton@postmedia.com
Classified Adv. e-mail: hbrubacher@postmedia.com
Editorial e-mail: jvandermeer@postmedia.com
Primary Website: www.ingersolltimes.com
Published: Wed
Avg Paid Circ: 500
Audit By: CMCA
Audit Date: 31.12.2016
Personnel: Jennifer Vandermeer (Ed.); Ian Dowding (Group Dir., Media Sales); Claire Wetton (Media sales)
Parent company (for newspapers): Postmedia Network Inc.; Quebecor Communications, Inc.

THE KINCARDINE NEWS

Street address 1: 719 Queen St.
Street address city: Kincardine
Province/Territory: ON
Postal code: N2Z 1Z9
County: Canada
Country: Canada
General Phone: (519) 396-2963
General Fax: (519) 396-6865
General/National Adv. E-mail: kincardine.sales@sunmedia.ca
Display Adv. E-mail: kincardine.sales@sunmedia.ca
Editorial e-mail: kincardine.news@sunmedia.ca
Primary Website: www.kincardinenews.com
Published: Thur
Avg Paid Circ: 59
Avg Free Circ: 5787
Audit By: Sworn/Estimate/Non-Audited
Audit Date: 12.07.2019
Personnel: Troy Patterson (Ed.)
Parent company (for newspapers): Postmedia Network Inc.

THE KINGSVILLE REPORTER

Street address 1: 17 Chestnut St.
Street address city: Kingsville
Province/Territory: ON
Postal code: N9Y 1J9
County: Canada
Country: Canada
General Phone: (519) 733-2211
General Fax: (519) 733-6464
General/National Adv. E-mail: kingsvillereporter@canwest.com
Display Adv. E-mail: rsims@postmedia.com
Published: Tues
Avg Paid Circ: 1107
Avg Free Circ: 7
Audit By: CMCA
Audit Date: 30.06.2016
Personnel: Rita Sims (Adv. Mgr.); Nelson Santos (News Ed.); Joyce Pearce (Reception); Steve l'Anson (Associate News Editor)
Parent company (for newspapers): Postmedia Network Inc.

THE LAKESHORE NEWS

Street address 1: 1116 Lesperance Road
Street address city: Tecumseh
Province/Territory: ON
Postal code: N8N 1X2
County: Canada
Country: Canada
General Phone: (519) 735-2080
General Fax: (519) 735-2082
General/National Adv. E-mail: lakeshore@canwest.com
Primary Website: www.facebook.com/Lakeshore-News-285820481600683/?ref=page_internal
Published: Thur
Avg Free Circ: 9389
Audit By: VAC
Audit Date: 31.12.2015
Personnel: Dave Calibaba (Gen. Mgr.); Bill Harris (Ed.)
Parent company (for newspapers): Postmedia Network Inc.; CanWest MediaWorks Publications, Inc.

THE LANARK ERA

Street address 1: 66 George St.
Street address city: Lanark
Province/Territory: ON
Postal code: K0G 1K0
County: Lanark Highlands Township
Country: Canada
General Phone: (613) 259-2220
General/National Adv. E-mail: lanarkera@primus.ca
Display Adv. E-mail: kristy.gibson@lanarkera.com
Classified Adv. e-mail: lanarkera@primus.ca
Editorial e-mail: gena.gibson@lanarkera.com
Primary Website: www.lanarkera.com
Published: Tues
Avg Paid Circ: 888
Avg Free Circ: 27
Audit By: CMCA
Audit Date: 31.08.2016
Personnel: Gena Gibson (Ed./Owner)

THE LISTOWEL BANNER

Street address 1: 185 Wallace Ave. N.
Street address city: Listowel
Province/Territory: ON
Postal code: N4W 1K8
County: Canada
Country: Canada
General Phone: (519) 291-1660
General Fax: (519) 291-3771
Display Adv. E-mail: ads@northperth.com
Editorial e-mail: editor@northperth.com
Primary Website: www.northperth.com
Published: Wed
Avg Paid Circ: 1881
Avg Free Circ: 22
Audit By: CMCA
Audit Date: 30.06.2016
Personnel: Bill Huether (Gen. Mgr.); Alicia Hunter (Adv. Mgr.); Peggy Haasnoot (Circ. Mgr.); Pauline Kerr (Ed.); Terry Bridge (Sports Ed.); Marie McKertcher (Prodn. Mgr.)
Parent company (for newspapers): Metroland Media Group Ltd.; Torstar

THE LUCKNOW SENTINEL

Street address 1: 619 Campbell St.
Street address city: Lucknow
Province/Territory: ON
Postal code: N0G 2H0
Country: Canada
General Phone: (519) 528-2822
General Fax: (519) 528-3529
Advertising Phone: (519) 528-2822
Editorial Phone: (519) 528-2822
General/National Adv. E-mail: lucksent@bowesnet.com
Display Adv. E-mail: lucksentads@bowesnet.com
Editorial e-mail: lucksented@bowesnet.com
Primary Website: www.lucknowsentinel.com
Published: Wed
Avg Paid Circ: 1037
Avg Free Circ: 44
Audit By: CMCA
Audit Date: 30.06.2014
Personnel: Troy Patterson (Ed.)
Parent company (for newspapers): Postmedia Network Inc.; Quebecor Communications, Inc.

THE MARATHON MERCURY

Street address 1: 91 Peninsula Rd.
Street address city: Marathon
Province/Territory: ON
Postal code: P0T 2E0
Country: Canada
General Phone: (805) 229-1520
General Fax: (805) 229-1595
General/National Adv. E-mail: mmpl@onlink.net
Published: Tues
Avg Paid Circ: 689
Avg Free Circ: 13
Audit By: CMCA
Audit Date: 31.05.2016
Personnel: Garry R. McInnes (Adv. Mgr.); P. Douglas Gale (Ed.)

THE MATTAWA RECORDER

Street address 1: 341 Mcconnell St.
Street address city: Mattawa
Province/Territory: ON
Postal code: P0H 1V0
Country: Canada
General Phone: (705) 744-5361
General Fax: (866) 831-6626
General/National Adv. E-mail: recorder@bellnet.ca
Display Adv. E-mail: recorder@bellnet.ca
Published: Sun
Avg Paid Circ: 1100
Audit By: Sworn/Estimate/Non-Audited
Audit Date: 12.07.2019
Personnel: Tom Edwards (Pub.); Heather Edwards (Adv. Mgr.)

THE MIDDLESEX BANNER

Street address 1: 71 C Front Street West
Street address city: Strathroy
Province/Territory: ON
Postal code: N7G 1X6
Country: Canada
General Phone: (519) 245-6116
General Fax: (519) 245-6116
General/National Adv. E-mail: editor@banner.on.ca
Primary Website: www.banner.on.ca
Published: Wed
Avg Paid Circ: 1231
Avg Free Circ: 300
Audit By: CMCA
Audit Date: 21.12.2015
Personnel: Mark Holmes (Publisher)

THE MID-NORTH MONITOR

Street address 1: 14 Hillside Drive South
Street address city: Elliot Lake
Province/Territory: ON
Postal code: P5A 1M6
County: Canada
Country: Canada
General Phone: 7058661801
General Fax: (705) 869-0587
Advertising Phone: (705) 848 - 7195
General/National Adv. E-mail: mnm@sunmedia.ca
Display Adv. E-mail: kjohansen@postmedia.com
Classified Adv. e-mail: kjohansen@postmedia.com
Editorial e-mail: kjohansen@postmedia.com
Primary Website: www.midnorthmonitor.com
Published: Thur
Avg Paid Circ: 849
Audit By: Sworn/Estimate/Non-Audited
Audit Date: 12.07.2019
Personnel: Lolene Patterson (Circ. Mgr.); Kevin McSheffrey (Managing Editor)
Parent company (for newspapers): 1954; Postmedia Network Inc.

THE MILTON CANADIAN CHAMPION

Street address 1: 555 Industrial Dr.
Street address city: Milton
Province/Territory: ON
Postal code: L9T 5E1
County: Canada
Country: Canada
General Phone: (905) 878-2341
General Fax: (905) 876-2364
Editorial e-mail: editorial@miltoncanadianchampion.com
Primary Website: miltoncanadianchampion.com
Published: Tues`Thur
Avg Paid Circ: 19
Avg Free Circ: 16276
Audit By: CCAB
Audit Date: 30.09.2017
Personnel: Neil Oliver (Pub.); Karen Miceli (Ed.); Steve LeBlanc (News/Sports Ed.); Tim Coles (Prodn. Mgr.); David Harvey (Regional General Manager); Katy Letourneau (Director of Advertising); Sarah McSweeney (Circ. Manager)
Parent company (for newspapers): Metroland Media Group Ltd.; Torstar

THE MINDEN TIMES

Street address 1: 2 Iga Rd., Unit 2
Street address city: Minden
Province/Territory: ON
Postal code: K0M 2K0
County: Minden
Country: Canada
General Phone: (705) 286-1288
General Fax: (705) 286-4768
Display Adv. E-mail: jenniferm@haliburtonpress.com
Classified Adv. e-mail: classifieds@mindentimes.ca
Editorial e-mail: editor@mindentimes.ca
Primary Website: www.mindentimes.ca
Published: Thur
Avg Paid Circ: 1076
Avg Free Circ: 259
Audit By: CMCA
Audit Date: 30.06.2016
Personnel: Jenn Watt (Ed.); Jennifer McEathron (Sales); Debbie Comer (Circ., Classified)
Parent company (for newspapers): White Pine Media

THE MIRROR

Street address 1: 488 Dominion Ave.
Street address city: Midland
Province/Territory: ON
Postal code: L4R 1P6
Country: Canada
General Phone: (705) 527-5500
General Fax: (705) 527-5467
General/National Adv. E-mail: themirror@simcoe.com
Primary Website: simcoe.com
Published: Thur
Avg Paid Circ: 0
Avg Free Circ: 21435
Audit By: CCAB
Audit Date: 30.09.2017
Personnel: Joe Anderson (Pub.); Leigh Gate (Gen. Mgr.); Leigh Rourke (Adv. Mgr.); Kyla Mosley (Circ. Mgr.); Travis Mealing (Ed.); Lori Martin (Mng. Ed.)
Parent company (for newspapers): Metroland Media Group Ltd.; Torstar

THE MITCHELL ADVOCATE

Street address 1: 42 Montreal St.
Street address city: Mitchell
Province/Territory: ON
Postal code: N0K 1N0
Country: Canada
General Phone: (519) 348-8431
General Fax: (519) 348-8836
General/National Adv. E-mail: abader@bowesnet.com
Primary Website: www.mitchelladvocate.com
Published: Wed
Avg Paid Circ: 1790
Avg Free Circ: 22
Audit By: CMCA
Audit Date: 30.06.2016
Personnel: Andy Bader (Ed.); Juanita Belfour (Adv. Mgr.)
Parent company (for newspapers): Postmedia Network Inc.; Quebecor Communications, Inc.

THE MORRISBURG LEADER

Street address 1: Hwy. 2, 31 Shopping Centre, 41 Main St.
Street address city: Morrisburg
Province/Territory: ON
Postal code: K0C 1X0
Country: Canada
General Phone: (613) 543-2987
General Fax: (613) 543-3643

General/National Adv. E-mail: info@morrisburgleader.ca
Display Adv. E-mail: leaderads@vianet.ca
Primary Website: www.morrisburgleader.ca
Published: Wed
Avg Paid Circ: 1774
Avg Free Circ: 54
Audit By: CMCA
Audit Date: 30.09.2016
Personnel: Mike Laurin (Adv. Mgr.); Wanda Dawley (Circ. Mgr.); Sam Laurin (Ed.); Bonnie McNairn (Mng. Ed.); Terry Laurin (Prodn. Mgr.)

THE MOUNT FOREST CONFEDERATE

Street address 1: 277 Main St. S.
Street address city: Mount Forest
Province/Territory: ON
Postal code: N0G 2L0
County: Wellington County/ Grey County
Country: Canada
General Phone: (519) 323-1550
General Fax: (519) 323-4548
General/National Adv. E-mail: editor@mountforest.com
Display Adv. E-mail: klucas@mountforest.com
Editorial e-mail: editor@mountforest.com
Primary Website: www.mountforest.com
Published: Wed
Avg Paid Circ: 1108
Audit By: CMCA
Audit Date: 30.06.2016
Personnel: Cathy Higdon (Circ. Mgr.); Lynne Turner (Ed.); Cornelia Svela (Prodn. Mgr.); Kim Lucas (Sales)
Parent company (for newspapers): Metroland Media Group Ltd.

THE MUSKOKAN

Street address 1: 34 Ep Lee Dr.
Street address city: Bracebridge
Province/Territory: ON
Postal code: P1L 1P9
Country: Canada
General Phone: (705) 645-8771
General Fax: (705) 645-1718
General/National Adv. E-mail: muskokan@muskoka.com
Primary Website: www.muskokan.com
Published: Thur
Avg Free Circ: 24000
Audit By: Sworn/Estimate/Non-Audited
Audit Date: 12.07.2019
Personnel: Paul Drummond (Adv. Sales Mgr.); Jake Good (Editorial Coord.); Marianne Dawson (Prodn. Coord.)
Parent company (for newspapers): Metroland Media Group Ltd.; Torstar

THE NAPANEE BEAVER

Street address 1: 72 Dundas St. E.
Street address city: Napanee
Province/Territory: ON
Postal code: K7R 1H9
Country: Canada
General Phone: (613) 354-6641
General Fax: (613) 354-2622
General/National Adv. E-mail: beaver@bellnet.ca
Primary Website: www.napaneebeaver.com
Published: Thur
Avg Free Circ: 15698
Audit By: CMCA
Audit Date: 30.06.2016
Personnel: Jean M. Morrison (Pub.); Deb Mccann (Bus. Mgr.); Seth Duchene (Ed.); Michelle Bowes (Prodn. Mgr.); Scott Johnston

THE NEWMARKET ERA-BANNER

Street address 1: 580b Steven Ct
Street address city: Newmarket
Province/Territory: ON
Postal code: L3Y 4X1
Country: Canada
General Phone: (905) 773-7627
General Fax: (905) 853-5379
Advertising Phone: (416) 798-7284
General/National Adv. E-mail: admin@erabanner.com
Display Adv. E-mail: admin@erabanner.com
Editorial e-mail: newsroom@erabanner.com
Primary Website: yorkregion.com
Published: Thur
Avg Paid Circ: 0
Avg Free Circ: 24371
Audit By: CCAB
Audit Date: 31.12.2017
Personnel: Ian Proudfoot (Pub.); Gord Paolucci (Dir., Adv./Prodn./Distribution); Dave Williams (Retail Sales Mgr.); Darlene Baker (Adv. Coord.); Megan Pike (Circ. Mgr.); Teresa Mathison (Distribution Coord.); Debora Kelly (Ed. in Chief); Ted McFadden (Ed.)
Parent company (for newspapers): Metroland Media Group Ltd.; Torstar

THE NIAGARA ADVANCE

Street address 1: 1501 Niagara Stone Rd.
Street address city: Virgil
Province/Territory: ON
Postal code: L0S 1T0
County: Canada
Country: Canada
General Phone: (905) 468-3283
General Fax: (905) 468-3137
General/National Adv. E-mail: tim.dundas@sunmedia.ca
Primary Website: www.niagaraadvance.ca
Published: Thur
Avg Paid Circ: 20
Avg Free Circ: 7610
Audit By: CMCA
Audit Date: 31.05.2016
Personnel: Tim Dundas (Pub.); Penny Coles (Ed.)
Parent company (for newspapers): Postmedia Network Inc.; Quebecor Communications, Inc.

THE NORTH RENFREW TIMES

Street address 1: 21 Champlain St.
Street address city: Deep River
Province/Territory: ON
Postal code: K0J 1P0
Country: Canada
General Phone: (613) 584-4161
Advertising Phone: (613) 584-4161
Editorial Phone: (613) 584-4161
General/National Adv. E-mail: drcanrt@magma.ca; NRT@magma.ca
Display Adv. E-mail: NRT@magma.ca
Classified Adv. e-mail: NRT@magma.ca
Editorial e-mail: NRT@magma.ca
Primary Website: www.northrenfrewtimes.net
Published: Wed
Avg Paid Circ: 1661
Audit By: CMCA
Audit Date: 30.09.2016
Personnel: Kelly Lapping (Pub); Terry Myers (Editor)

THE NORTHERN SUN NEWS

Street address 1: 200 Howey Street
Street address city: Red Lake
Province/Territory: ON
Postal code: P0V 2M0
Country: Canada
General Phone: (807) 727-2888
General Fax: (807) 727-3961
Display Adv. E-mail: pamela@thenorthernsun.com
Editorial e-mail: lindsay@thenorthernsun.com
Primary Website: www.thenorthernsun.com
Published: Wed
Avg Paid Circ: 780
Audit By: CMCA
Audit Date: 31.03.2016
Personnel: Kathy Coutts (Gen Mgr.); Pamela O'Neill (Adv. Sales & Mrktg.)

THE NORTHERN TIMES

Street address 1: 51 Riverside Dr
Street address city: Kapuskasing
Province/Territory: ON
Postal code: P5N 1A7
Country: Canada
General Phone: (705) 335-2283 ext. 222
General Fax: (705) 337-1222
Advertising Phone: (705)-335-2283 ext. 230
Editorial Phone: (705)-335-2283 ext. 223
General/National Adv. E-mail: wayne.major@sunmedia.ca
Display Adv. E-mail: wayne.major@sunmedia.ca
Editorial e-mail: kevin.anderson@sunmedia.ca
Primary Website: www.kapuskasingtimes.com
Published: Wed
Avg Paid Circ: 1784
Audit By: CMCA
Audit Date: 28.02.2014
Personnel: Wayne Major (Pub.); Sylvie Genier (Senior Sales Representative); Kevin Anderson (Managing Ed.)
Parent company (for newspapers): Postmedia Network Inc.; Quebecor Communications, Inc.

THE NORWICH GAZETTE

Street address 1: 16 Brock Street
Street address city: Woodstock
Province/Territory: ON
Postal code: N4S 3B4
Country: Canada
General Phone: (519) 537-2341
General/National Adv. E-mail: norwich@bowesnet.com
Display Adv. E-mail: tleake@postmedia.com
Classified Adv. e-mail: hbrubacher@postmedia.com
Editorial e-mail: jennifer.vandermeer@sunmedia.ca
Primary Website: www.norwichgazette.ca
Published: Wed
Avg Paid Circ: 822
Audit By: CMCA
Audit Date: 31.12.2016
Personnel: Jennifer Vandermeer (Ed.); Ian Dowding (Group Director, Media Sales); Tara Leake (Media sales); John Macintosh (Media sales); Heidi Brubacher (Classified sales); Beth Faulkner (Circ.)
Parent company (for newspapers): Postmedia Network Inc.

THE OBSERVER

Street address 1: 20-B Arthur St. N
Street address city: Elmira
Province/Territory: ON
Postal code: N3B 1Z9
County: Township of Woolwich
Country: Canada
General Phone: (519) 669-5790
General Fax: (519) 669-5753
Advertising Phone: (519) 669-5790 ext. 104
Editorial Phone: (519) 669-5790 ext. 103
General/National Adv. E-mail: info@woolwichobserver.com
Display Adv. E-mail: ads@woolwichobserver.com
Classified Adv. e-mail: ads@woolwichobserver.com
Editorial e-mail: editor@woolwichobserver.com
Primary Website: www.Observerxtra.com
Published: Thur
Avg Paid Circ: 0
Avg Free Circ: 15670
Audit By: Sworn/Estimate/Non-Audited
Audit Date: 30.07.2022
Personnel: Joe Merlihan (Pub.); Steve Kannon (Ed.); Donna Rudy (Adv. Mgr.)
Parent company (for newspapers): Cathedral Communications Inc.

THE ORANGEVILLE BANNER

Street address 1: 37 Mill St.
Street address city: Orangeville
Province/Territory: ON
Postal code: L9W 2M4
Country: Canada
General Phone: (519) 941-1350
General Fax: (519) 941-9600
General/National Adv. E-mail: banner@orangevillebanner.com; info@orangevillebanner.com
Primary Website: www.orangevillebanner.com
Published: Tues`Thur
Avg Paid Circ: 85
Avg Free Circ: 20303
Audit By: CCAB
Audit Date: 31.03.2014
Personnel: Gordon Brewerton (Gen. Mgr.); Janine Taylor (Prodn. Mgr.)
Parent company (for newspapers): Metroland Media Group Ltd.; Torstar

THE PARKDALE VILLAGER

Street address 1: 175 Gordon Baker Rd
Street address city: Toronto
Province/Territory: ON
Postal code: M2H 2S6
Country: Canada
General Phone: (416) 493-4400
General Fax: (416) 493-6190
Advertising Phone: (416) 493-4400
Editorial Phone: (416) 774-2367
General/National Adv. E-mail: general@insidetoronto.com
Display Adv. E-mail: atedesco@insidetoronto.com
Editorial e-mail: atedesco@insidetoronto.com
Primary Website: www.parkdaleliberty.ca
Published: Thur
Avg Free Circ: 24917
Audit By: CCAB
Audit Date: 30.09.2015
Personnel: Ian Proudfoot (Pub.); Antoine Tedesco (Mng. Ed.)
Parent company (for newspapers): Metroland Media Group Ltd.

THE PARKHILL GAZETTE

Street address 1: 165 King St.
Street address city: Parkhill
Province/Territory: ON
Postal code: N0M 2K0
Country: Canada
General Phone: (519) 294-6264
General Fax: (519) 294-6391
General/National Adv. E-mail: gazette@execulink.com
Published: Thur
Avg Paid Circ: 860
Audit By: CMCA
Audit Date: 31.03.2014
Personnel: Melaime Carter (Adv. Mgr.); Dale Hayter (Circ. Mgr.); Gord Whitehead (Ed.)

THE PERTH COURIER EMC

Street address 1: 65 Lorne St.
Street address city: Smith Falls
Province/Territory: ON
Postal code: K7A 4T1
County: Canada
Country: Canada
General Phone: (613) 283-3180
Editorial e-mail: editor@perthcourier.com
Primary Website: www.insideottawavalley.com
Published: Thur
Avg Free Circ: 11641
Audit By: CMCA
Audit Date: 30.06.2016
Personnel: Duncan Weir (Pub.); Ryland Coyne
Parent company (for newspapers): Metroland Media Group Ltd.

THE PETROLIA TOPIC

Street address 1: 140 Front St. S
Street address city: Sarnia
Province/Territory: ON
Postal code: N7T 7M8
County: Canada
Country: Canada
General Phone: (519) 336-1100 x2230
General Fax: (519) 336-1833
Advertising Phone: (519) 882-4798
Editorial Phone: (519) 336-1100 x2230
Editorial e-mail: reporter@petroliatopic.com
Primary Website: www.petroliatopic.com
Published: Wed
Avg Paid Circ: 1309
Audit By: CMCA
Audit Date: 31.12.2012
Personnel: Linda LeBlanc (Pub.)
Parent company (for newspapers): Postmedia Network Inc.; Quebecor Communications, Inc.

THE PICTON GAZETTE

Street address 1: 100 Main St.
Street address city: Picton
Province/Territory: ON
Postal code: K0K 2T0
Country: Canada
General Phone: (613) 476-3201
Advertising Phone: (613) 476-3201 ext. 105
Editorial Phone: (613) 476-3201 ext. 110
General/National Adv. E-mail: editorial@pictongazette.ca
Editorial e-mail: editorial@pictongazette.ca
Primary Website: www.pictongazette.ca
Published: Wed
Avg Free Circ: 11450
Audit By: CMCA
Audit Date: 30.06.2016

Personnel: Karen Valihora (Pub.); Jason Parks (Ed.); Michelle Bowes (Prodn. Mgr.)

THE PORT PERRY STAR

Street address 1: 180 Mary St.
Street address 2: Unit 11
Street address city: Port Perry
Province/Territory: ON
Postal code: L9L 1C4
Country: Canada
General Phone: (905) 985-7383
General Fax: (905) 985-3708
Advertising Phone: (905) 215-0440
Editorial Phone: (905) 215-0462
General/National Adv. E-mail: chall@durhanregion.com
Display Adv. E-mail: feismont@durhamregion.com
Classified Adv. e-mail: classified@thespec.com
Editorial e-mail: chall@durhamregion.com
Primary Website: www.durhamregion.com
Published: Thur
Avg Paid Circ: 12000
Avg Free Circ: 125
Audit By: Sworn/Estimate/Non-Audited
Audit Date: 12.07.2019
Personnel: Tim Whittaker (Pub); Lisa Burgess (Sales Mgr.); Laurie Abel (Circ. Coordinator); Mike Johnston (Mng. Ed.)
Parent company (for newspapers): Metroland Media Group Ltd.

THE POST (HANOVER)

Street address 1: 413 18th Ave.
Street address city: Hanover
Province/Territory: ON
Postal code: N4N 3S5
Country: Canada
General Phone: (519) 364-2001
General Fax: (519) 364-6950
General/National Adv. E-mail: marie.david@sunmedia.ca
Display Adv. E-mail: janie.harrison@sunmedia.ca
Classified Adv. e-mail: han.classifieds@sunmedia.ca
Editorial e-mail: patrick.bales@sunmedia.ca
Primary Website: www.thepost.on.ca
Published: Thur
Avg Paid Circ: 84
Avg Free Circ: 15393
Audit By: CMCA
Audit Date: 30.06.2016
Personnel: Marie David (Gen. Mgr.); Rod Currie (Circ. Mgr.); Patrick Bales (Ed.); Kiera Merriam (Adv. Mgr.)
Parent company (for newspapers): Postmedia Network Inc.; Quebecor Communications, Inc.

THE PRESCOTT JOURNAL

Street address 1: 3201 County Rd. 2
Street address city: Prescott
Province/Territory: ON
Postal code: K0E 1T0
County: Canada
Country: Canada
General Phone: (613) 925-4265
General Fax: (613) 925-2837
Display Adv. E-mail: adsales@prescottjournal.com
Editorial e-mail: journal@stlawrenceprinting.on.ca
Primary Website: www.prescottjournal.com
Published: Wed
Avg Paid Circ: 1123
Avg Free Circ: 99
Audit By: CMCA
Audit Date: 30.06.2016
Personnel: Beth Morris (Pub.); Dave Flinn (Prodn. Mgr.); Jamie Nurse

THE RECORDER & TIMES

Street address 1: 2479 Parkedale Avenue
Street address city: Brockville
Province/Territory: ON
Postal code: K6V 3H2
County: Leeds & Grenville Counties
Country: Canada
General Phone: (613) 342-4441
General Fax: (613) 342-4456
Advertising Phone: (613) 342-4441 Ext. 500267
Editorial Phone: (613) 342-4441 Ext. 500107
General/National Adv. E-mail: newsroom@indynews.ca
Display Adv. E-mail: ksammon@postmedia.com
Editorial e-mail: dgordanier@postmedia.com
Primary Website: www.recorder.ca
Published: Wed`Thur
Avg Free Circ: 29300
Audit By: CMCA
Audit Date: 30.09.2016
Personnel: Kerry Sammon (Med. Sales Dir.)
Parent company (for newspapers): Post Media

THE RENFREW MERCURY EMC

Street address 1: 35 Opeongo Rd. W.
Street address city: Renfrew
Province/Territory: ON
Postal code: K7V 2T2
Country: Canada
General Phone: (613) 432-3655
General Fax: (613) 432-6689
General/National Adv. E-mail: mercury@renc.igs.net
Editorial e-mail: rmedit@runge.net
Primary Website: www.insideottawavalley.com/renfrew-on
Published: Thur
Avg Free Circ: 13309
Audit By: CMCA
Audit Date: 30.06.2016
Personnel: Mike Tracy (Pub.); Theresa Fritz (Ed.)
Parent company (for newspapers): Metroland Media Group Ltd.; Runge Newspapers, Inc.

THE REVIEW

Street address 1: 76 Main St. E.
Street address city: Vankleek Hill
Province/Territory: ON
Postal code: K0B 1R0
County: Champlain Township
Country: Canada
General Phone: (613) 678-3327
General Fax: (613) 937-2591
General/National Adv. E-mail: review@thereview.ca
Display Adv. E-mail: ads@thereview.ca
Classified Adv. e-mail: classifieds@thereview.ca
Editorial e-mail: editor@thereview.ca
Primary Website: www.thereview.ca
Published: Wed
Avg Paid Circ: 2785
Avg Free Circ: 727
Audit By: CMCA
Audit Date: 30.06.2016
Personnel: Irene Sensyzcyzn (Classified Adv. Mgr.); Louise Sproule (Ed.); Suzanne Tessier (Prodn. Mgr.); Diane Duval (Accounts); Shirley Shuberynski (Advertising Sales); Theresa Ketterling (Reporters/ Photographer); Tara Kirkpatrick (Advertising Sales); Sharon Graves-McRae (Website Designer); Dorothy Hodge (Graphic Designer)

THE RICHMOND HILL LIBERAL

Street address 1: 50 Mcintosh Drive Unit 115
Street address city: Markham
Province/Territory: ON
Postal code: L3R 9T3
Country: Canada
General Phone: (905) 943-6100
General Fax: (905) 943-6129
Advertising Phone: (905) 943-6095
General/National Adv. E-mail: admin@theliberal.com
Display Adv. E-mail: abeswick@yrmg.com
Classified Adv. e-mail: jkopacz@yrmg.com
Editorial e-mail: mbeck@yrmg.com
Primary Website: yorkregion.com
Published: Thur
Avg Paid Circ: 0
Avg Free Circ: 47438
Audit By: CCAB
Audit Date: 20.12.2017
Personnel: Ian Proudfoot (Pub.); Robert Lazurko (Bus. Mgr.); Anne Beswick (Retail Adv. Mgr.); Debora Kelly (Ed. in Chief); Marney Beck (Ed.); John Willems (General Manager)
Parent company (for newspapers): Metroland Media Group Ltd.; Torstar

THE RIDGETOWN INDEPENDENT NEWS

Street address 1: 1 Main St. W.
Street address city: Ridgetown
Province/Territory: ON
Postal code: N0P 2C0
General Phone: (519) 674-5205
General Fax: (519) 674-2573
Published: Wed
Avg Paid Circ: 1674
Audit By: CMCA
Audit Date: 30.04.2016
Personnel: Shelia Mcbrayne (Editor in Chief); Gordon Brown (Managing Editor)

THE SCARBOROUGH MIRROR

Street address 1: 100 Tempo Ave.
Street address city: Toronto
Province/Territory: ON
Postal code: M2H 2N8
County: Canada
Country: Canada
General Phone: (416) 493-4400
General Fax: (416) 495-6629
General/National Adv. E-mail: scm@insidetoronto.com
Primary Website: insidetoronto.com
Published: Thur`Fri
Avg Free Circ: 120479
Audit By: CCAB
Audit Date: 20.12.2017
Personnel: Betty Carr (Vice Pres./Grp. Pub.); Marg Middleton (Gen. Mgr.); Kelly Atkinson (Regl. Mgr., HR); Bruce Espey (Dir., Bus. Admin.); Tim Corcoran (Regl. Dir, Adv.); Kayland McCully (Sales Rep.); Frank Li (Sales Rep.); Shauna Paolucci (Sales Rep.); Cathie Orban (Sales Rep.); Leema Williams (Sales Rep.); Michelle King (Sales Rep.); Al Shackleton (Mng. Ed.); Dave Burnett (Dir., Prodn.); Katherine Bernal (Prodn. Mgr.)
Parent company (for newspapers): Metroland Media Group Ltd.; Torstar

THE SCOPE OF INNISFIL

Street address 1: 34 Main St. W
Street address city: Beeton
Province/Territory: ON
Postal code: L0G 1A0
Country: Canada
General Phone: (905) 729-2287
General Fax: (905) 729-2541
General/National Adv. E-mail: admin@innisfilscope.com
Display Adv. E-mail: sales@innisfilscope.com
Editorial e-mail: editor@innisfilscope.com
Primary Website: www.innisfilscope.com
Published: Wed
Avg Paid Circ: 100
Avg Free Circ: 12433
Audit By: CMCA
Audit Date: 30.04.2013
Personnel: Alex Pozdrowski (Adv.); Wendy Soloduik (Ed.)
Parent company (for newspapers): Simcoe-York Group

THE SIGNPOST

Street address 1: 15 Bridge St.
Street address city: Dorchester
Province/Territory: ON
Postal code: N0L 1G2
County: Thames Centre, Middlesex County
Country: Canada
General Phone: (519) 268-7337
General Fax: (519) 268-3260
Advertising Phone: (519) 268-7337
Editorial Phone: (519) 268-7337
General/National Adv. E-mail: signpost@on.aibn.com
Display Adv. E-mail: advertising@dorchestersignpost.com
Classified Adv. e-mail: classifieds@dorchestersignpost.com
Editorial e-mail: w.spence@on.aibn.com
Primary Website: www.dorchestersignpost.com
Published: Wed
Avg Paid Circ: 1468
Audit By: CMCA
Audit Date: 31.12.2015
Personnel: Fred Huxley (Pub.); Lyndsay Huxley (Gen. Mgr.); Wendy Spence (Ed.)

THE STANDARD NEWSPAPER

Street address 1: 94a Water St.
Street address city: Port Perry
Province/Territory: ON
Postal code: L9L 1J2
County: Durham Region
Country: Canada
General Phone: (905) 985-6985
General Fax: (905) 985-9253
General/National Adv. E-mail: production-standard@powergate.ca
Display Adv. E-mail: standardnancy@powergate.ca
Classified Adv. e-mail: office-standard@powergate.ca
Editorial e-mail: standarddarryl@powergate.ca
Primary Website: www.thestandardnewspaper.ca
Published: Thur
Avg Free Circ: 11868
Audit By: CMCA
Audit Date: 31.12.2014
Personnel: Colleen Green (Gen. Mgr.); Darryl Knight (Ed.); Nancy Lister (Adv. Rep.); Dan Cearns (Reporter)
Parent company (for newspapers): Skyline Media

THE STAR

Street address 1: 5300 Canotek Rd., Unit 30
Street address city: Ottawa
Province/Territory: ON
Postal code: K1J 8R7
Country: Canada
General Phone: (613) 744-4800
General Fax: (613) 744-0866
General/National Adv. E-mail: star@freenet.carlton.ca
Primary Website: www.eastottawa.ca
Published: Thur
Avg Free Circ: 45439
Audit By: CMCA
Audit Date: 30.04.2012
Personnel: Michael Curram (Pub.); Terry Tyo (Pub.); Patricia Lonergan (Ed.)
Parent company (for newspapers): Transcontinental Media

THE STITTSVILLE NEWS

Street address 1: 57 Auriga Drive Unit 103
Street address city: Ottawa
Province/Territory: ON
Postal code: K2E 8B2
Country: Canada
General Phone: (613) 723-5970
Display Adv. E-mail: jillmartin@theemc.ca
Editorial e-mail: theresa.fritz@metroland.com
Primary Website: www.insideottawavalley.com
Published: Thur
Avg Free Circ: 13217
Audit By: CMCA
Audit Date: 30.06.2014
Personnel: Mike Tracy (Publisher)
Parent company (for newspapers): Metroland Media Group Ltd.; Runge Newspapers, Inc.

THE STRATHROY AGE DISPATCH

Street address 1: 73 Front Street West
Street address city: Strathroy
Province/Territory: ON
Postal code: N7G 1X6
Country: Canada
General Phone: (519) 245-2370
General Fax: (519) 245-1647
General/National Adv. E-mail: news@strathroyonline.com
Primary Website: www.strathroyagedispatch.com
Published: Thur
Avg Paid Circ: 1480
Audit By: CMCA
Audit Date: 31.01.2014
Personnel: Bev Ponton (Pub.); Don Biggs (Reg. Ed.)
Parent company (for newspapers): Postmedia Network Inc.; Quebecor Communications, Inc.

THE TILBURY TIMES

Street address 1: 40 Queen St. S.
Street address city: Tilbury
Province/Territory: ON
Postal code: N0P 2L0
County: Chatham-Kent
Country: Canada
General Phone: (519) 682-0411
General Fax: (519) 682-3633
Editorial Phone: (519) 809-4347
Display Adv. E-mail: dbarnwell@tilburytimes.com
Classified Adv. e-mail: dbarnwell@tilburytimes.com
Editorial e-mail: gharvieux@tilburytimes.com
Published: Tues

Avg Paid Circ: 1100
Avg Free Circ: 50
Audit By: Sworn/Estimate/Non-Audited
Audit Date: 12.07.2019
Personnel: Bob Thwaites (Pub.); Gerry Harvieux (Ed.)
Parent company (for newspapers): Postmedia Network Inc.

THE TILLSONBURG NEWS

Street address 1: 25 Townline Rd.
Street address city: Tillsonburg
Province/Territory: ON
Postal code: N4G 4H6
Country: Canada
General Phone: (519) 688-6397
General Fax: (519) 842-3511
Advertising Phone: (519) 688-4400
General/National Adv. E-mail: tilledit@bowesnet.com
Primary Website: www.tillsonburgnews.com
Published: Fri
Avg Paid Circ: 1173
Audit By: CMCA
Audit Date: 31.12.2015
Personnel: Michael Walsh (Pub.)
Parent company (for newspapers): Postmedia Network Inc.; Quebecor Communications, Inc.

THE TIMES OF NEW TECUMSETH

Street address 1: 34 Main St. W.
Street address city: Beeton
Province/Territory: ON
Postal code: L0G 1A0
Country: Canada
General Phone: (905) 729-2287
General Fax: (905) 729-2541
General/National Adv. E-mail: admin.syp@rogers.com
Editorial e-mail: editor.syp@rogers.com
Primary Website: www.newtectimes.com
Published: Thur
Avg Paid Circ: 2230
Avg Free Circ: 100
Audit By: VAC
Audit Date: 30.04.2015
Personnel: Wendy Soloduik (Ed.); John Speziali (Production Mgr.); Annette Derraugh
Parent company (for newspapers): Simcoe-York Group

THE TRIBUNE

Street address 1: 206 King St.
Street address city: Sturgeon Falls
Province/Territory: ON
Postal code: P2B 1R7
County: Canada
Country: Canada
General Phone: (705) 753-2930
General Fax: (705) 753-5231
General/National Adv. E-mail: tribune@westnipissing.com
Primary Website: www.westnipissing.com
Published: Wed
Avg Paid Circ: 2000
Avg Free Circ: 50
Audit By: CCAB
Audit Date: 30.09.2019
Personnel: Suzanne Gammon (Ed.); Jason Steven (Prodn. Mgr.); Isabel Mosseler (Office); Linda Birmingham (Circulation and accounts)

THE TWEED NEWS

Street address 1: 242 Victoria St. N.
Street address city: Tweed
Province/Territory: ON
Postal code: K0K 3J0
County: Municpality of Tweed
Country: Canada
General Phone: (613) 478-2017
General Fax: (613) 478-2749
Advertising Phone: (613) 478-2699
Editorial Phone: (613) 478-2017
General/National Adv. E-mail: info@thetweednews.ca
Display Adv. E-mail: info@thetweednews.ca
Classified Adv. e-mail: info@thetweednews.ca
Editorial e-mail: info@thetweednews.ca
Primary Website: www.thetweednews.ca
Published: Wed
Avg Paid Circ: 8722
Avg Free Circ: 42
Audit By: CMCA
Audit Date: 26.11.2018
Personnel: Roseann Trudeau (Circ. Mgr.); Rodger Hanna (Ed./Pub.)

THE WASAGA SUN

Street address 1: 1456 Mosley St.
Street address city: Wasaga Beach
Province/Territory: ON
Postal code: L9Z 2B9
County: Wasaga
Country: Canada
General Phone: (705) 429-1688
General Fax: (705) 422-2446
General/National Adv. E-mail: sunnews@simcoe.com
Primary Website: wasagasun.ca
Published: Thur
Avg Free Circ: 13241
Audit By: CCAB
Audit Date: 20.12.2017
Personnel: Christine Brown (Adv. Mgr.); Joe Anderson (Pub.); Catherine Haller (Gen. Mgr.); Scott Woodhouse (Ed.); Craig Widdifield (Mng. Ed.); Stephen Hall (Prodn. Mgr.)
Parent company (for newspapers): Metroland Media Group Ltd.

THE WEEKENDER

Street address 1: 51 Riverside Dr
Street address city: Kapuskasing
Province/Territory: ON
Postal code: P5N 1A7
Country: Canada
General Phone: (705) 335-2283 ext. 222
General Fax: (705) 337-1222
Advertising Phone: (705) 335-2283 ext. 230
Editorial Phone: (705) 335-2283 ext. 223
General/National Adv. E-mail: wayne.major@sunmedia.ca
Display Adv. E-mail: wayne.major@sunmedia.ca
Editorial e-mail: kevin.anderson@sunmedia.ca
Primary Website: www.kapuskasingtimes.com
Published: Thur
Avg Free Circ: 8486
Audit By: CMCA
Audit Date: 30.06.2016
Personnel: Wayne Major (Pub.); Sylvie Genier (Senior Sales Representative); Kevin Anderson (Managing Ed.)
Parent company (for newspapers): Postmedia Network Inc.; Quebecor Communications, Inc.

THE WELLINGTON ADVERTISER

Street address 1: 905 Gartshore St.
Street address city: Fergus
Province/Territory: ON
Postal code: N1M 2W8
Country: Canada
General Phone: (519) 843-5410
General Fax: (519) 843-7607
General/National Adv. E-mail: news@wellingtonadvertiser.com
Display Adv. E-mail: advertising@wellingtonadvertiser.com
Editorial e-mail: editor@wellingtonadvertiser.com
Primary Website: www.wellingtonadvertiser.com
Published: Fri
Avg Paid Circ: 235
Avg Free Circ: 39898
Audit By: VAC
Audit Date: 31.03.2016
Personnel: William Adsett (Pub.); Catherine Goss (Circ. Mgr.); Dave Adsett (Ed.)

THE WIARTON ECHO

Street address 1: 573 Berford St.
Street address city: Wiarton
Province/Territory: ON
Postal code: N0H 2T0
County: Canada
Country: Canada
General Phone: (519) 534-1560
General Fax: (519) 534-4616
Advertising Phone: (519) 534-1563
Editorial Phone: (519) 534-1560
General/National Adv. E-mail: wiartonecho@bmts.com
Display Adv. E-mail: echoads@bowesnet.com
Editorial e-mail: wiartonecho@bmts.com
Primary Website: www.wiartonecho.com
Published: Tues
Avg Paid Circ: 1361
Avg Free Circ: 6
Audit By: CMCA
Audit Date: 30.06.2016
Personnel: Keith Gilbert (Ed.)
Parent company (for newspapers): Postmedia Network Inc.; Quebecor Communications, Inc.

THE WINGHAM ADVANCE-TIMES

Street address 1: 11 Veterans Rd.
Street address city: Wingham
Province/Territory: ON
Postal code: N0G 2W0
Country: Canada
General Phone: (519) 357-2320
General Fax: (519) 357-2900
General/National Adv. E-mail: advance@wcl.on.ca
Editorial e-mail: pkerr@wingham.com
Primary Website: www.wingham.com
Published: Wed
Avg Paid Circ: 862
Audit By: CMCA
Audit Date: 30.06.2016
Personnel: Sandy Woodcock (Adv. Mgr.); Bill Huether (Ed.); Dave Russell (Prodn. Mgr.)
Parent company (for newspapers): Metroland Media Group Ltd.; Torstar

THE YORK GUARDIAN

Street address 1: 100 Tempo Ave.
Street address city: Toronto
Province/Territory: ON
Postal code: M2H 2N8
County: Canada
Country: Canada
General Phone: (416) 493-4400
General Fax: (416) 495-6629
General/National Adv. E-mail: etg@insidetoronto.com
Primary Website: www.insidetoronto.com
Published: Thur
Avg Free Circ: 28544
Audit By: CCAB
Audit Date: 30.09.2017
Personnel: Betty Carr (Pub.); Marg Middleton (Gen. Mgr.); Tim Corcoran (Adv. Mgr.); Jaime Munoz (Circ. Mgr.); Paul Futhey (Mng. Ed.)
Parent company (for newspapers): Metroland Media Group Ltd.; Torstar

THOROLD NIAGARA NEWS

Street address 1: 10-1 St. Paul St.
Street address city: Saint Catharine's
Province/Territory: ON
Postal code: L2R 7L4
Country: Canada
General Phone: (905) 688-4332
General Fax: (905) 688-6313
Display Adv. E-mail: lauren.krause@sunmedia.ca
Primary Website: www.thoroldedition.ca
Published: Thur
Avg Free Circ: 7225
Audit By: CMCA
Audit Date: 31.05.2016
Personnel: Jeff Blay (Reporter); Lauren Krause (Advertising)
Parent company (for newspapers): Postmedia Network Inc.

THUNDER BAY SOURCE

Street address 1: 87 N. Hill St.
Street address city: Thunder Bay
Province/Territory: ON
Postal code: P7A 5V6
Country: Canada
General Phone: (807) 346-2650
General Fax: (807) 345-9923
Advertising Phone: (807) 346-2510
General/National Adv. E-mail: ldunick@dougallmedia.com
Primary Website: www.tbnewswatch.com
Published: Thur
Avg Free Circ: 35000
Audit By: CMCA
Audit Date: 30.06.2017
Personnel: Leith Dunick (Mng. Ed.); Doug Diaczuk (Reporter); Matt Vis (Reporter); Nicole Dixon (Content editor)
Parent company (for newspapers): T.Bay Post Inc

TIMES ADVOCATE

Street address 1: 356 Main St. S.
Street address city: Exeter
Province/Territory: ON
Postal code: N0M 1S6
Country: Canada
General Phone: (519) 235-1331
General/National Adv. E-mail: ads@southhuron.com
Display Adv. E-mail: sales@southhuron.com
Editorial e-mail: snixon@southhuron.com
Primary Website: www.southhuron.com
Published: Wed
Avg Paid Circ: 2158
Avg Free Circ: 84
Audit By: CMCA
Audit Date: 30.09.2016
Personnel: Deb Lord (Manager); Scott Nixon (Editor); Deborah Schillemore (Sales)
Parent company (for newspapers): Metroland Media Group Ltd.; Torstar

TIMES-REFORMER

Street address 1: 50 Gilbertson Dr.
Street address city: Simcoe
Province/Territory: ON
Postal code: N3Y 4L2
County: Canada
Country: Canada
General Phone: (519) 426-3528
General Fax: (519) 426-9255
General/National Adv. E-mail: sdowns@bowesnet.com
Primary Website: www.simcoereformer.ca
Published: Tues
Avg Paid Circ: 1411
Avg Free Circ: 17315
Audit By: CMCA
Audit Date: 31.12.2013
Personnel: Sue Downs (Adv. Mgr.); Kim Novak (Ed.)
Parent company (for newspapers): Postmedia Network Inc.; Quebecor Communications, Inc.

TIMMINS TIMES

Street address 1: 815 Pine St. S.
Street address city: Timmins
Province/Territory: ON
Postal code: P4N 8S3
County: Canada
Country: Canada
General Phone: (705) 268-6252
General Fax: (705) 268-2255
General/National Adv. E-mail: times@timminstimes.com
Primary Website: www.timminstimes.com
Published: Thur
Avg Free Circ: 16325
Audit By: CMCA
Audit Date: 31.12.2013
Personnel: Wayne Major (Pub.); Len Gillis (Ed.); Kevin Anderson (Regional Managing Editor)
Parent company (for newspapers): Postmedia Network Inc.; Quebecor Communications, Inc.

TOTTENHAM TIMES

Street address 1: 34 Main St. W.
Street address city: Beeton
Province/Territory: ON
Postal code: L0G 1A0
County: Canada
Country: Canada
General Phone: (905) 729-2287
General Fax: (905) 729-2541
General/National Adv. E-mail: admin.syp@rogers.com
Editorial e-mail: editor.syp@rogers.com
Primary Website: www.newtectimes.com
Published: Wed
Avg Paid Circ: 2125
Avg Free Circ: 75
Audit By: Sworn/Estimate/Non-Audited
Audit Date: 12.07.2019
Personnel: John Archibald (Adv. Mgr.); Kristen Haire (Prodn. Mgr.)

Parent company (for newspapers): Simcoe-York Group

TOWN AND COUNTRY CRIER

Street address 1: 100 Elora St.
Street address city: Mildmay
Province/Territory: ON
Postal code: N0G 2J0
Country: Canada
General Phone: (519) 367-2681
General Fax: (519) 367-5417
General/National Adv. E-mail: thecrier@wightman.ca
Published: Thur
Avg Paid Circ: 1211
Avg Free Circ: 169
Audit By: CMCA
Audit Date: 30.06.2016
Personnel: John H. Hafermehl (Pub.); Susan Bross (Ed.)

TRANSCRIPT & FREE PRESS

Street address 1: 243 Main St.
Street address city: Glencoe
Province/Territory: ON
Postal code: N0L 1M0
Country: Canada
General Phone: (519) 287-2615
General Fax: (519) 287-2408
General/National Adv. E-mail: tranfree@xcelco.on.ca
Published: Thur
Avg Paid Circ: 1033
Audit By: CMCA
Audit Date: 30.06.2014
Personnel: Dale Hayder (Circ. Mgr.)

TRENTONIAN

Street address 1: 41 Quinte St.
Street address city: Trenton
Province/Territory: ON
Postal code: K8V 5R3
Country: Canada
General Phone: (613) 392-6501
General Fax: (613) 392-0505
Display Adv. E-mail: advertising@trentonia.ca
Editorial e-mail: newsroom@trentonian.ca
Primary Website: www.trentonian.ca
Published: Thur
Avg Free Circ: 15084
Audit By: CMCA
Audit Date: 30.06.2016
Personnel: John Knowles (Pub.); Rachel Henry (Adv. Mgr.); Tim Devine (Circ. Mgr.); Ross Lees (Mng. Ed.); Sherin Tyson (Prodn. Mgr.)
Parent company (for newspapers): Postmedia Network Inc.; Quebecor Communications, Inc.

TRIBUNE EXPRESS

Street address 1: 1100 Aberdeen
Street address city: Hawkesbury
Province/Territory: ON
Postal code: K6A 1K7
County: Canada
Country: Canada
General Phone: (613) 632-4155
General Fax: (613) 632-6122
Advertising Phone: (613) 632-4155
Editorial Phone: (613) 632-4155
General/National Adv. E-mail: nouvelles@eap.on.ca
Display Adv. E-mail: yvan.joly@eap.on.ca; nicole.pilon@eap.on.ca
Editorial e-mail: nouvelles@eap.on.ca
Primary Website: www.tribune-express.ca
Published: Wed
Avg Paid Circ: 11
Avg Free Circ: 26430
Audit By: Sworn/Estimate/Non-Audited
Audit Date: 12.07.2019
Personnel: Bertrand Castonguay (President); Gilles Normand (Circ. Mgr.); Yvan Joly (Newspaper manager); Nicole Pilon (sales secretary, national, display)
Parent company (for newspapers): Cie d'Edition Andre Paquette, Inc.

TURTLE ISLAND NEWS

Street address 1: Box 329
Street address city: Ohsweken
Province/Territory: ON
Postal code: N0A 1M0
Country: Canada
General Phone: (519)445-0868
General Fax: (519) 445-0865
General/National Adv. E-mail: lynda@theturtleislandnews.com
Display Adv. E-mail: sales@theturtleislandnews.com
Primary Website: www.theturtleislandnews.com
Published: Wed
Avg Free Circ: 5000
Audit By: Sworn/Estimate/Non-Audited
Audit Date: 12.07.2019

UXBRIDGE TIMES-JOURNAL

Street address 1: 16 Bascom St.
Street address city: Uxbridge
Province/Territory: ON
Postal code: L9P 1J3
Country: Canada
General Phone: (905) 852-9141
General Fax: (905) 852-9341
Primary Website: durhamregion.com
Published: Thur
Avg Paid Circ: 0
Avg Free Circ: 8803
Audit By: CCAB
Audit Date: 15.11.2017
Personnel: Tim Whittaker (Pub.); Judy Pirone (Adv. Mgr.); Joanne Burghardt (Ed. in Chief); Judi Bobbitt (Ed.)
Parent company (for newspapers): Metroland Media Group Ltd.; Torstar

VAUGHAN CITIZEN

Street address 1: 8611 Weston Rd Unit 29
Street address city: Vaughan
Province/Territory: ON
Postal code: L4L 9P1
Country: Canada
General Phone: (905) 264-8703
General Fax: (905) 264-9453
Advertising Phone: (905) 264-8703
Editorial Phone: (905) 264-8703
General/National Adv. E-mail: john.willems@metroland.com
Display Adv. E-mail: gpaolucci@yrmg.com
Editorial e-mail: dkelly@yrmg.com
Primary Website: yorkregion.com
Published: Thur
Avg Free Circ: 57677
Audit By: CCAB
Audit Date: 20.12.2017
Personnel: Ian Proudfoot (Vice Pres./Reg. Pub.); Debora Kelly (Ed. in Chief); John Willems (Reg. Gen. Mgr.)
Parent company (for newspapers): Metroland Media Group Ltd.

WALKERTON HERALD-TIMES

Street address 1: 10 Victoria St. N.
Street address city: Walkerton
Province/Territory: ON
Postal code: N0G 2V0
County: Brockton
Country: Canada
General Phone: (519) 881-1600
General Fax: (519) 881-0276
General/National Adv. E-mail: editor@walkerton.com
Display Adv. E-mail: ads@walkerton.com
Primary Website: www.walkerton.com
Published: Thur
Avg Paid Circ: 1296
Avg Free Circ: 3
Audit By: CMCA
Audit Date: 30.06.2016
Personnel: April Wells (Adv. Sales Mgr.); Cathy Spitzig (Circ. Mgr.); John McPhee (Ed.)
Parent company (for newspapers): Metroland Media Group Ltd.; Torstar

WALLACEBURG COURIER PRESS

Street address 1: 138 King Street West
Street address city: Chatham
Province/Territory: ON
Postal code: N7M 1E3
County: Chatham Kent
Country: Canada
General Phone: (519) 354 2000
General Fax: (519) 351 7774
General/National Adv. E-mail: couriernews@kent.net
Primary Website: www.wallaceburgcourierpress.com
Published: Thur
Avg Free Circ: 8914
Audit By: CMCA
Audit Date: 30.06.2015
Personnel: Dean Muharrem (Pub.); Mary Dixon (Circ. Mgr.)
Parent company (for newspapers): Postmedia Network Inc.; Sun Media

WATERLOO CHRONICLE

Street address 1: 279 Weber St. N., Ste. 20
Street address city: Waterloo
Province/Territory: ON
Postal code: N2J 3H8
Country: Canada
General Phone: (519) 886-2830
General Fax: (519) 886-9383
General/National Adv. E-mail: classified@waterloochronicle.ca
Editorial e-mail: editorial@waterloochronicle.ca
Primary Website: www.waterloochronicle.ca
Published: Thur
Avg Free Circ: 29538
Audit By: CMCA
Audit Date: 31.03.2016
Personnel: Peter Winkler (Pub.); Gerry Mattice (Adv. Mgr., Retail Sales); Bob Vrbanac (Ed.)
Parent company (for newspapers): Metroland Media Group Ltd.; Torstar

WATFORD GUIDE-ADVOCATE

Street address 1: 5292 Nauvoo Rd.
Street address city: Watford
Province/Territory: ON
Postal code: N0M 2S0
Country: Canada
General Phone: (519) 876-2809
General Fax: (519) 876-2322
General/National Adv. E-mail: guideadvocate@execulink.com
Published: Thur
Avg Paid Circ: 1919
Audit By: CMCA
Audit Date: 29.02.2016
Personnel: Dale Hayter (Pub.); Gill Deschutter (Adv. Mgr.); Stephanie Cattryse (Ed.)

WAWATAY NEWS

Street address 1: 16 5th Ave.
Street address city: Sioux Lookout
Province/Territory: ON
Postal code: P8T 1B7
Country: Canada
General Phone: (807) 737-2951
General Fax: (807) 737-3224
General/National Adv. E-mail: editor@wawatay.on.ca
Primary Website: www.wawataynews.ca
Published: Thur
Avg Paid Circ: 399
Avg Free Circ: 5618
Audit By: CMCA
Audit Date: 31.03.2014
Personnel: Rick Garrick (Reporter)

WEEKLY JOURNAL

Street address 1: 5300 Canotek Rd., Unit 30
Street address city: Orleans
Province/Territory: ON
Postal code: K1J 8R7
Country: Canada
General Phone: (613) 744-4800
General Fax: (613) 744-0866
General/National Adv. E-mail: theweeklyjournal@transcontinental.ca
Published: Thur
Avg Free Circ: 47000
Audit By: Sworn/Estimate/Non-Audited
Audit Date: 12.07.2019
Personnel: Terry Tyo (Adv. Mgr.); Patricia Lonergan (Ed.); Sylvie Parsier (Prodn. Mgr.)

WEST CARLETON REVIEW

Street address 1: 8 Mcgonigal St.
Street address city: Arnprior
Province/Territory: ON
Postal code: K7S 1L8
Country: Canada
General Phone: (613) 623-6571
Display Adv. E-mail: leslie.osborne@metroland.com
Primary Website: www.insideottawavalley.com
Published: Thur
Avg Free Circ: 7099
Audit By: CMCA
Audit Date: 30.06.2014
Personnel: Theresa Fritz; Mike Tracy
Parent company (for newspapers): Metroland Media Group Ltd.

WHAT'S UP MUSKOKA

Street address 1: Unit 12-440 Ecclestone Drive
Street address city: Bracebridge
Province/Territory: ON
Postal code: P1L 1Z6
County: Muskoka
Country: Canada
General Phone: (705) 646-1314
General Fax: (705) 645-6424
General/National Adv. E-mail: mm.info@sunmedia.ca
Primary Website: www.whatsupmuskoka.com
Published: Wed
Avg Paid Circ: 0
Avg Free Circ: 26000
Audit By: CMCA
Audit Date: 31.07.2013
Parent company (for newspapers): Postmedia Network Inc.; Quebecor Communications, Inc.

WHEATLEY JOURNAL

Street address 1: 194 Talbot Street E.
Street address 2: Unit #5
Street address city: Leamington
Province/Territory: ON
Postal code: N8H 1M2
County: Chatham-Kent
Country: Canada
General Phone: (519) 398-9098
General Fax: (519) 398-8561
General/National Adv. E-mail: journal@mnsi.net
Published: Wed
Avg Paid Circ: 586
Avg Free Circ: 11
Audit By: CMCA
Audit Date: 30.04.2016
Personnel: Jim Heyens (Pub.)
Parent company (for newspapers): Southpoint Publishing Inc.

WINCHESTER PRESS

Street address 1: 545 St. Lawrence St.
Street address city: Winchester
Province/Territory: ON
Postal code: K0C 2K0
County: Canada
Country: Canada
General Phone: (613) 774-2524
General Fax: (613) 774-3967
General/National Adv. E-mail: news@winchesterpress.on.ca
Display Adv. E-mail: advert@winchesterpress.on.ca
Editorial e-mail: news@winchesterpress.on.ca
Primary Website: www.winchesterpress.on.ca
Published: Wed
Avg Paid Circ: 2646
Avg Free Circ: 342
Audit By: CMCA
Audit Date: 30.06.2016
Personnel: Beth Morris (Owner/Pres.); Donna Rushford (Adv. Mgr./Co. Pub.)

WING COMMANDER

Street address 1: Po Box 1000, Sta. Forces
Street address city: Astra
Province/Territory: ON
Postal code: K0K 3W0
Country: Canada
General Phone: (613) 965-7248
General Fax: (613) 965-7490
Advertising Phone: (613) 392-2811
Editorial Phone: (613) 392-2811
General/National Adv. E-mail: christopher.daniel@forces.gc.ca
Primary Website: www.forces.gc.ca
Published: Fri
Avg Free Circ: 3000

Audit By: Sworn/Estimate/Non-Audited
Audit Date: 12.07.2019
Personnel: Mark Peebles (Ed. in Chief); Andrea Steiner (Mng. Ed.); Amber Gooding (Asst. Ed.)

PRINCE EDWARD ISLAND

ATLANTIC POST CALLS

Street address 1: 567 Main Street
Street address city: Montague
Province/Territory: PE
Postal code: C0A 1R0
Country: Canada
General Phone: (902) 838-2515
General Fax: (902) 838-4392
Advertising Phone: (902) 838-4392 Ext. 203
Editorial Phone: (902) 838-2515 x 201
General/National Adv. E-mail: subscribe@peicanada.com
Display Adv. E-mail: jan@peicanada.com
Editorial e-mail: paul@peicanada.com
Primary Website: www.peicanada.com
Published: Fri
Avg Paid Circ: 752
Avg Free Circ: 625
Audit By: CMCA
Audit Date: 28.02.2014
Personnel: Paul MacNeill; Jan MacNeill

LA VOIX ACADIENNE

Street address 1: 5, Ave Maris Stella
Street address city: Summerside
Province/Territory: PE
Postal code: C1N 6M9
Country: Canada
General Phone: (902) 436-6005
General Fax: (902) 888-3976
Display Adv. E-mail: pub@lavoixacadienne.com
Editorial e-mail: texte@lavoixacadienne.com
Primary Website: www.lavoixacadienne.com
Published: Wed
Avg Paid Circ: 1517
Avg Free Circ: 20
Audit By: ODC
Audit Date: 13.12.2017
Personnel: Marcia Enman (Dir. Gen.); Jacinthe Laforest (Ed.)

THE EASTERN GRAPHIC

Street address 1: 567 Main St.
Street address city: Montague
Province/Territory: PE
Postal code: C0A 1R0
Country: Canada
General Phone: (902) 838-2515
General Fax: (902) 838-4392
General/National Adv. E-mail: subscribe@peicanada.com
Editorial e-mail: editor@peicanada.com
Primary Website: www.peicanada.com
Published: Wed
Avg Paid Circ: 4743
Avg Free Circ: 196
Audit By: CMCA
Audit Date: 30.06.2014
Personnel: Paul MacNeill (Pub.); Jan MacNeill (Adv. Mgr.); Heather Moore (Ed.); Kim Madigan (Prodn. Coord.)

WEST PRINCE GRAPHIC

Street address 1: 4 Railway St.
Street address city: Alberton
Province/Territory: PE
Postal code: C0B 1B0
Country: Canada
General Phone: (902) 853-3320
General Fax: (902) 853-3071
General/National Adv. E-mail: westgraphic@islandpress.pe.ca
Editorial e-mail: cindy@peicanada.com
Primary Website: www.peicanada.com
Published: Wed
Avg Paid Circ: 121
Avg Free Circ: 5733
Audit By: CMCA
Audit Date: 31.03.2014
Personnel: Paul MacNeill (Pub.); Jan MacNeill (Adv. Mgr.); Nicole Ford (Circ. Mgr.); Cindy Chant (Ed.)

QUEBEC

ABITIBI EXPRESS ROUYN

Street address 1: 438 Ave. Lariviere
Street address city: Rouyn-Noranda
Province/Territory: QC
Postal code: J9X 4J1
Country: Canada
General Phone: (819) 797-6776
General Fax: (819) 797-4725
Editorial Phone: (819) 767-6776
General/National Adv. E-mail: redaction.abitibi@transcontinental.ca
Primary Website: http://www.abitibiouestrouynnoranda.ca
Published: Tues
Avg Paid Circ: 18
Avg Free Circ: 29398
Audit By: CCAB
Audit Date: 31.03.2014

ABITIBI EXPRESS VAL D'OR

Street address 1: 1834 3rd Ave. 2nd Floor
Street address city: Val d'Or
Province/Territory: QC
Postal code: J9P 7A9
Country: Canada
General Phone: (819) 874-2151
General/National Adv. E-mail: redaction.abitibi@tc.tc
Primary Website: www.abitibiexpress.ca
Published: Tues
Avg Paid Circ: 22
Avg Free Circ: 31088
Audit By: CCAB
Audit Date: 31.03.2014

ACTION MERCREDI

Street address 1: 342, Beaudry Nord
Street address city: Joliette
Province/Territory: QC
Postal code: J6E 6A6
Country: Canada
General Phone: (450) 759-3664
General Fax: (450) 759-3190
General/National Adv. E-mail: infolanaudiere@tc.tc
Primary Website: www.laction.com
Published: Wed'Sun
Avg Paid Circ: 9
Avg Free Circ: 51680
Audit By: CCAB
Audit Date: 30.09.2012
Personnel: Benoit Bazinet; Benoit Bazinet

AUTRE VOIX

Street address 1: Boulevard Ste-anne Bureau 101
Street address 2: Bureau 101
Street address city: Beaupre
Province/Territory: QC
Postal code: G0A 1E0
Country: Canada
General Phone: (418) 827-1511
Published: Wed
Avg Paid Circ: 3
Avg Free Circ: 13297
Audit By: CCAB
Audit Date: 31.03.2014
Personnel: Lilianne Laprise

AVANT POSTE

Street address 1: 305, Rue De La Gare, Following 107
Street address city: Matane
Province/Territory: QC
Postal code: G4W 3J2
Country: Canada
General Phone: (418) 629-3443
General Fax: (418) 562-4607
General/National Adv. E-mail: jean.gagnon@quebecormedia.com
Primary Website: www.lavantposte.ca
Published: Wed
Avg Paid Circ: 6
Avg Free Circ: 8609
Audit By: CCAB
Audit Date: 31.03.2014
Personnel: Jean Gagnon

AVANTAGE VOTRE JOURNAL

Street address 1: 183 St-germain Ouest
Street address city: Rimouski
Province/Territory: QC
Postal code: G5L 4B8
Country: Canada
General Phone: (418) 722-0205
Primary Website: http://www.lavantage.qc.ca/
Published: Wed
Avg Paid Circ: 64
Avg Free Circ: 43009
Audit By: CCAB
Audit Date: 31.03.2014
Personnel: Lucie Moisan

BEAUCE MEDIA

Street address 1: 1147 Blvd. Vachon N.
Street address city: Sainte Marie-de-Beauce
Province/Territory: QC
Postal code: G6E 3B6
Country: Canada
General Phone: (418) 387-8000
General Fax: (418) 387-4495
General/National Adv. E-mail: smb.redaction@quebecormedia.com
Primary Website: www.beaucemedia.ca
Published: Wed
Avg Paid Circ: 3
Avg Free Circ: 25092
Audit By: CCAB
Audit Date: 31.03.2014
Personnel: Gilbert Bernier
Parent company (for newspapers): Quebecor Communications, Inc.

BEAUPORT EXPRESS

Street address 1: 710 Bouvier, Suite 107
Street address city: Beauport
Province/Territory: QC
Postal code: G2J 1C2
County: Canada
Country: Canada
General Phone: (418) 628-7460
General Fax: (418) 622-1511
General/National Adv. E-mail: redaction_quebec@tc.tc
Primary Website: www.beauportexpress.com
Published: Fri
Avg Paid Circ: 11
Avg Free Circ: 28463
Audit By: CCAB
Audit Date: 31.03.2014
Personnel: Yvan Rancourt (Pub.); Paul Lessard (Ed.); Gilles Brault (Prodn. Mgr.)

BROME COUNTY NEWS

Street address 1: 5 B Rue Victoria
Street address city: Knowlton
Province/Territory: QC
Postal code: J0E 1V0
Country: Canada
General Phone: (450) 242-1188
General Fax: (450) 243-5155
General/National Adv. E-mail: newsroom@sherbrookerecord.com
Published: Tues
Avg Free Circ: 10000
Audit By: Sworn/Estimate/Non-Audited
Audit Date: 12.07.2019
Personnel: Ken Wells (Pub.); Sharon McCully (Ed.); Richard Lessard (Prodn. Mgr.)

BROSSARD ECLAIR

Street address 1: 267 St. Charles Ouest
Street address city: Longueuil
Province/Territory: QC
Postal code: J4H 1E3
Country: Canada
General Phone: (450) 646-3333
General Fax: (450) 674-0205
General/National Adv. E-mail: lucie.masse@quebecormedia.com
Primary Website: http://www.brossardeclair.ca/
Published: Wed
Avg Free Circ: 32482
Audit By: CCAB
Audit Date: 31.03.2014
Personnel: Lucie Masse (Ed.)
Parent company (for newspapers): Reseau Select/ Select Network; Quebecor Communications, Inc.

CHAMBLY EXPRESS

Street address 1: C-1691, Boul Perigny
Street address city: Chambly
Province/Territory: QC
Postal code: J3L 1X1
Country: Canada
General Phone: (450) 658-5559
General Fax: (450) 658-1620
General/National Adv. E-mail: chamblyexpress@tc.tc
Primary Website: www.chamblyexpress.ca
Published: Tues
Avg Free Circ: 27037
Audit By: CCAB
Audit Date: 31.03.2014

CHARLESBOURG EXPRESS

Street address 1: 710 Bouvier, Suite 107
Street address city: Quebec
Province/Territory: QC
Postal code: G2J 1C2
Country: Canada
General Phone: (418) 628-7460
General Fax: (418)840-1207
General/National Adv. E-mail: redaction_quebec@tc.tc
Primary Website: www.quebechebdo.com
Published: Fri
Avg Paid Circ: 9
Avg Free Circ: 27178
Audit By: CCAB
Audit Date: 31.03.2014
Personnel: Alain LePage (Gen. Mgr.); Lilianne Laprise (Ed.)
Parent company (for newspapers): Reseau Select/ Select Network; Transcontinental Media

CHATEAUGUAY EXPRESS

Street address 1: 69, Boul St-jean-baptiste, 2nd Floor
Street address city: Chateauguay
Province/Territory: QC
Postal code: J6J 3H6
Country: Canada
General Phone: (450) 692-9111
General Fax: (450) 692-9192
General/National Adv. E-mail: redaction_chateauguayexpress@tc.tc
Primary Website: www.chateauguayexpress.ca
Published: Wed
Avg Free Circ: 40468
Audit By: CCAB
Audit Date: 31.03.2014

CITES NOUVELLES

Street address 1: 455 Boulevard Fenelon
Street address 2: Bureau 303
Street address city: Dorval
Province/Territory: QC
Postal code: H9S 5T8
Country: Canada
General Phone: (514) 636-7314
General Fax: (514) 636-7317
General/National Adv. E-mail: cites.nouvelles@tc.tc
Primary Website: www.citesnouvelles.com
Published: Wed
Avg Paid Circ: 4
Avg Free Circ: 44286
Audit By: CCAB
Audit Date: 31.03.2014
Personnel: Denis Therrien (Publisher); Joy-Ann Dempsey (Sales Support Supervisor); Robert Bourcier (Production manager); Jean Nicolas AubÃ© (News Director)

Parent company (for newspapers): Transcontinental Media

CITOYEN DE L'HARRICANA

Street address 1: 92 Rue Principale Sud
Street address city: Amos
Province/Territory: QC
Postal code: J9T 2J6
Country: Canada
General Phone: (819)732-6531
General Fax: (819) 732-3764
General/National Adv. E-mail: philippe.delachevrotiere@quebecormedia.com
Display Adv. E-mail: manon.poirier@quebecormedia.com
Editorial e-mail: caroline.couture@quebecormedia.com
Primary Website: www.lechoabitibien.ca
Published: Wed
Avg Paid Circ: 19
Avg Free Circ: 11238
Audit By: CCAB
Audit Date: 31.03.2014
Personnel: Caroline Couture

CITOYEN ROUYN NORANDA

Street address 1: 1 Rue Du Terminus
Street address city: Rouyn-Noranda
Province/Territory: QC
Postal code: J9X 3B5
Country: Canada
General Phone: (819) 762-4361 x 221
General Fax: (819) 797-2450
Advertising Phone: (819) 762-4361
Editorial Phone: (819) 279-7032
Display Adv. E-mail: stefan.baillargeon@tc.tc or marie-eve.bouchard@tc.tc
Classified Adv. e-mail: vicky.aumond@tc.tc
Editorial e-mail: joel.caya@tc.tc
Primary Website: lafrontiere.ca
Published: Wed
Avg Paid Circ: 17
Avg Free Circ: 19749
Audit By: CCAB
Audit Date: 31.03.2014
Personnel: Joel Caya (General manager)

COURRIER DE PORTNEUF

Street address 1: 276,rue Notre-dame
Street address city: Donnacona
Province/Territory: QC
Postal code: G3M 1G7
Country: Canada
General Phone: (418) 285-0211
General Fax: (418) 285-2441
General/National Adv. E-mail: josee-anne.fiset@courrierdeportneuf.com
Editorial e-mail: denise.paquin@courrierdeportneuf.com
Primary Website: www.courrierdeportneuf.com
Published: Wed
Avg Paid Circ: 31
Avg Free Circ: 34944
Audit By: CCAB
Audit Date: 30.09.2012
Personnel: Louise Latulippe (adjointe administrative)

COURRIER FRONTENAC

Street address 1: Boulevard Frontenac Est Cp 789
Street address 2: C.p. 789
Street address city: Thetford Mines
Province/Territory: QC
Postal code: G6G 5V3
Country: Canada
General Phone: (418) 338-5181
Published: Wed
Avg Paid Circ: 15
Avg Free Circ: 22826
Audit By: CCAB
Audit Date: 31.03.2014
Personnel: Lucyl Lachance

COURRIER-AHUNTSIC

Street address 1: 1500 Jules Poitras Blvd.
Street address city: Saint Laurent
Province/Territory: QC
Postal code: H4N 1X7
Country: Canada
General Phone: (514) 855-1292
General Fax: (514) 855-9916
Primary Website: www.courrierahuntsic.com; www.transcontinentalmedia.com
Published: Fri
Avg Paid Circ: 0
Avg Free Circ: 32391
Audit By: CCAB
Audit Date: 31.03.2014
Personnel: Alain De Choiniere (Gen. Mgr.); Marilaine Bolduc-Jacob (Information Dir.)
Parent company (for newspapers): Transcontinental Media

COURRIER-LAVAL

Street address 1: 2700 Francis Hughes Ave., Ste. 200
Street address city: Laval
Province/Territory: QC
Postal code: H7S 2B9
Country: Canada
General Phone: (450) 667-4360
General Fax: (450) 667-0845
General/National Adv. E-mail: redactionlaval@tc.tc
Primary Website: www.courrierlaval.com
Published: Wed`Sat
Avg Paid Circ: 8
Avg Free Circ: 12788
Audit By: CCAB
Audit Date: 30.09.2012
Personnel: Janique Duguay (Sales Dir.); Rejean Monette (Regl. Dir.); Claude Labelle (Ed.); Martine Cotton (Prodn. Mgr.)
Parent company (for newspapers): Transcontinental Media

COURRIER-SUD

Street address 1: 3255 Rte Marie-victorin
Street address city: Nicolet
Province/Territory: QC
Postal code: J3T 1X5
Country: Canada
General Phone: (819) 293-4551
General Fax: (819) 293-8758
General/National Adv. E-mail: redaction_cs@tc.tc
Editorial e-mail: redaction_cs@transcontinental.ca
Primary Website: www.lecourriersud.com
Published: Wed
Avg Paid Circ: 52
Avg Free Circ: 20758
Audit By: CCAB
Audit Date: 31.03.2014
Personnel: Claire Knight (Sales Coord.); Nancy Allaire (Ed.)
Parent company (for newspapers): Transcontinental Media

ECHO DE REPENTIGNY

Street address 1: Notre-dame Apt A
Street address 2: Apt. A
Street address city: Repentigny
Province/Territory: QC
Postal code: J6A 2T8
Country: Canada
General Phone: (450) 932-4782
General Fax: (450) 932-4794
General/National Adv. E-mail: martin.gravel@quebecormedia.com
Primary Website: www.lechoderepentigny.ca
Published: Wed
Avg Free Circ: 59248
Audit By: CCAB
Audit Date: 31.03.2014
Personnel: Martin Gravel

ECHOS VEDETTES

Street address 1: 465 Mcgill Ave.
Street address city: Montreal
Province/Territory: QC
Postal code: H2W 2H1
County: Canada
Country: Canada
General Phone: (514) 528-7111
General Fax: (514) 528-7115
General/National Adv. E-mail: redaction@echosvedettes.ca
Published: Sat
Avg Paid Circ: 54193
Avg Free Circ: 875
Audit By: Sworn/Estimate/Non-Audited
Audit Date: 12.07.2019
Personnel: Sylvie Bourgeault (Gen. Mgr.)

EDITION BEAUCE NORD

Street address 1: 691, Boul. Vachon Nord
Street address city: Sainte Marie-de-Beauce
Province/Territory: QC
Postal code: G6E 1M3
Country: Canada
General Phone: (418) 387-1205
Published: Wed
Avg Paid Circ: 2
Avg Free Circ: 24833
Audit By: CCAB
Audit Date: 31.03.2014
Personnel: Claude Grondin

ETINCELLE

Street address 1: 193 Rue Saint-georges
Street address city: Windsor
Province/Territory: QC
Postal code: J1S 1J7
Country: Canada
General Phone: (819) 845-2705
General Fax: (819) 845-5520
General/National Adv. E-mail: journal@letincelle.qc.ca
Primary Website: www.letincelle.qc.ca
Published: Wed
Avg Paid Circ: 36
Avg Free Circ: 10515
Audit By: CCAB
Audit Date: 30.09.2012
Personnel: Ralph Cote (Ed. in Chief); Genevieve Gray; Claude Frenette (Ed.)

ETOILE DE L'OUTAOUAIS ST LAURENT

Street address 1: Avenue St-charles
Street address city: Vaudreuil-Dorion
Province/Territory: QC
Postal code: J7V 2N4
Country: Canada
General Phone: (450) 455-6111
Published: Sat
Avg Paid Circ: 28
Avg Free Circ: 56711
Audit By: ODC
Audit Date: 14.12.2011
Personnel: Angele Marcoux Prevost

EVEIL

Street address 1: Rue St-eustache
Street address city: Saint Eustache
Province/Territory: QC
Postal code: J7R 2L2
Country: Canada
Published: Sat
Avg Paid Circ: 0
Avg Free Circ: 55993
Audit By: CCAB
Audit Date: 31.03.2014
Personnel: Serge Langlois

EXPRESS D'OUTREMONT

Street address 1: Jules-poitras
Street address city: Saint Laurent
Province/Territory: QC
Postal code: H4N 1X7
Country: Canada
General Phone: (514) 286-1066
General Fax: (514) 286-9310
Primary Website: www.expressoutremont.com
Published: Thur
Avg Paid Circ: 2
Avg Free Circ: 19654
Audit By: CCAB
Audit Date: 31.03.2014
Personnel: Jean Aube

EXPRESS MONTCALM

Street address 1: Rue Saint-isidore
Street address city: Saint Lin Laurentides
Province/Territory: QC
Postal code: J5M 2V4
Country: Canada
General Phone: (450) 439-2525
Published: Wed
Avg Free Circ: 20004
Audit By: CCAB
Audit Date: 31.03.2014
Personnel: Benoit Bazinet

FLAMBEAU

Street address 1: Boulevard Langelier Bureau 210
Street address 2: Bureau 210
Street address city: Montreal
Province/Territory: QC
Postal code: H1P 3C6
Country: Canada
General Phone: (514) 899-5888
Published: Tues
Avg Paid Circ: 0
Avg Free Circ: 56194
Audit By: CCAB
Audit Date: 31.03.2014
Personnel: Stephane Desjardins

GRANBY EXPRESS

Street address 1: 398 Main St., Ste 5
Street address city: Granby
Province/Territory: QC
Postal code: J2G 2W6
Country: Canada
General Phone: (450) 777-4515
General Fax: (450) 777-4516
General/National Adv. E-mail: nancy.corriveau@monjournalexpress.com
Primary Website: www.granbyexpress.com
Published: Wed
Avg Paid Circ: 3
Avg Free Circ: 41995
Audit By: CCAB
Audit Date: 31.03.2014
Personnel: Nancy Corriveau (Sales Coord.); Maritime Chagnon (Mng. Ed.); Caroline Rioux (Reg'l Ed.)

GUIDE DE MONTREAL-NORD

Street address 1: Boulevard Langelier Bureau 210
Street address 2: Bureau 210
Street address city: Montreal
Province/Territory: QC
Postal code: H1P 3C6
Country: Canada
General Phone: (514) 899-5888
Published: Tues
Avg Paid Circ: 0
Avg Free Circ: 34440
Audit By: CCAB
Audit Date: 31.03.2014
Personnel: Yannick Pinel

HAVRE

Street address 1: Rue Jacques Cartier
Street address city: Gaspe
Province/Territory: QC
Postal code: G4X 1M9
Country: Canada
General Phone: (418) 368-3242
Published: Wed
Avg Paid Circ: 6
Avg Free Circ: 8207
Audit By: CCAB
Audit Date: 31.03.2014
Personnel: Bernard Johnson

HEBDO CHARLEVOISIEN

Street address 1: 53, Rue John-nairne Ste. 100
Street address city: La Malbaie
Province/Territory: QC
Postal code: G5A 1L8
County: La Malbaie
Country: Canada
General Phone: (418) 665-1299
General Fax: (418) 453-3349
General/National Adv. E-mail: journal@hebdocharlevoisien.ca
Display Adv. E-mail: hebdo@charlevoix.net
Primary Website: www.charlevoixendirect.com
Published: Wed
Avg Paid Circ: 30
Avg Free Circ: 14487
Audit By: CCAB

Audit Date: 30.09.2012
Personnel: Charles Warren

HEBDO DU ST. MAURICE

Street address 1: 2102 Champlain Ave.
Street address city: Shawinigan
Province/Territory: QC
Postal code: G9N 6T8
County: Canada
Country: Canada
General Phone: (819) 537-5111
General Fax: (819) 537-5471
Advertising Phone: (866) 637-5236
General/National Adv. E-mail: redaction_shawinigan@transcontinental.ca
Primary Website: www.lhebdodustmaurice.com
Published: Wed
Avg Paid Circ: 24
Avg Free Circ: 36640
Audit By: CCAB
Audit Date: 31.03.2014
Personnel: Michel Matteau (Pub.); Lena Sauvageau; Gilles Guay (Adv. Mgr.); Bernard Lepage (Ed./Dir., Information)
Parent company (for newspapers): Transcontinental Media

HEBDO MEKINAC DESCHENAUX

Street address 1: C.p. 4057
Street address city: Saint Tite
Province/Territory: QC
Postal code: G0X 3H0
Country: Canada
General Phone: (819) 537-5111
Published: Sat
Avg Free Circ: 13540
Audit By: ODC
Audit Date: 14.12.2011
Personnel: Lena Sauvageau

HEBDO RIVE NORD

Street address 1: 1004 Rue Notre-dame
Street address city: Repentigny
Province/Territory: QC
Postal code: J5Y 1S9
Country: Canada
General Phone: (450) 581-5120
General Fax: (450) 581-4515
General/National Adv. E-mail: equiperedaction@transcontinental.ca
Primary Website: www.hebdorivenord.com
Published: Tues`Fri
Avg Paid Circ: 6
Avg Free Circ: 53954
Audit By: CCAB
Audit Date: 30.09.2012
Personnel: Yannick Boulanger (Chief Ed.); Sebastien Nadeau (Regl. Mgr.); Stephane Joseph (Sales Mgr.); Chantal Proulx (Prodn. Mgr.)
Parent company (for newspapers): Transcontinental Media

HUDSON GAZETTE

Street address 1: 397 Main Rd.
Street address city: Hudson
Province/Territory: QC
Postal code: J0P 1H0
County: Canada
Country: Canada
General Phone: (450) 458-5482
General Fax: (450) 458-3337
General/National Adv. E-mail: hudsongazette@videotron.ca
Primary Website: www.hudsongazette.com
Published: Wed
Avg Free Circ: 21000
Audit By: Sworn/Estimate/Non-Audited
Audit Date: 12.07.2019
Personnel: Greg Jones (Pub.); Louise Craig (Circ. Mgr.); Jim Duff (Ed.)

INFO DIMANCHE

Street address 1: Rue Fraser
Street address city: Riviere-du-Loup
Province/Territory: QC
Postal code: G5R 1C6
Country: Canada
General Phone: (418) 862-1911
General Fax: (418) 862-6165
Primary Website: www.infodimanche.com
Published: Sun
Avg Paid Circ: 106
Avg Free Circ: 31754
Audit By: CCAB
Audit Date: 30.09.2013
Personnel: Michel Chalifour

INFO WEEK-END

Street address 1: 322 Victoria St.
Street address city: Edmundston
Province/Territory: QC
Postal code: E3V 2H9
Country: Canada
General Phone: (506) 739-5083
Display Adv. E-mail: pub@infoweekend.ca
Primary Website: journaux.apf.ca/infoweekend
Published: Wed
Avg Free Circ: 21550
Audit By: CCAB
Audit Date: 30.09.2013
Personnel: Michel Chalifour

INFORMATEUR DE RIVIERE DES PRAIRIES

Street address 1: Boulevard Langelier Bureau 210
Street address 2: Bureau 210
Street address city: Montreal
Province/Territory: QC
Postal code: H1P 3C6
Country: Canada
General Phone: (514) 899-5888
Published: Tues
Avg Free Circ: 20917
Audit By: CCAB
Audit Date: 31.03.2014
Personnel: Yannick Pinel

INFORMATION DE STE JULIE

Street address 1: Rue Jules Choquet Local 2
Street address 2: Local 2
Street address city: Saint Julie
Province/Territory: QC
Postal code: J3E 1W6
Country: Canada
General Phone: (450) 649-0719
Published: Wed
Avg Paid Circ: 3
Avg Free Circ: 19435
Audit By: CCAB
Audit Date: 30.09.2012
Personnel: Serge Landry

INFORMATION DU NORD L'ANNONCIATION

Street address 1: 1107, Rue De St-jovite
Street address city: Mont-Tremblant
Province/Territory: QC
Postal code: J8E 3J9
Country: Canada
General Phone: (819) 425-8658
General Fax: (819) 425-7713
General/National Adv. E-mail: infonord.journal@quebecormedia.com
Primary Website: www.hebdosquebecor.com
Published: Thur
Avg Paid Circ: 7974
Avg Free Circ: 15500
Audit By: Sworn/Estimate/Non-Audited
Audit Date: 12.07.2019
Personnel: Josee Gauvin (Ed.); Johanne Regimbald (ÃƒÂ££££ditrice)
Parent company (for newspapers): Quebecor Communications, Inc.

INFORMATION DU NORD MONT TREMBLANT

Street address 1: 1107 Rue De St. Jovite
Street address city: Mont-Tremblant
Province/Territory: QC
Postal code: J8E 3J9
County: Canada
Country: Canada
General Phone: (819) 425-8658
General Fax: (819) 425-7713
General/National Adv. E-mail: info.nord@hebdosquebecor.com
Primary Website: www.hebdosquebecor.com
Published: Wed
Avg Paid Circ: 4
Avg Free Circ: 15029
Audit By: CCAB
Audit Date: 31.03.2014
Personnel: Michel Gareau (Adv. Mgr.); Johanne Regimbald
Parent company (for newspapers): Quebecor Communications, Inc.

INFORMATION DU NORD SAINTE-AGATHE

Street address 1: 1107 Rue De Saint Jovite
Street address city: Mont Tremblant
Province/Territory: QC
Postal code: J8E 3J9
Country: Canada
General Phone: (819) 425-8658
General Fax: (819) 425-7713
General/National Adv. E-mail: johanne.regimbald@quebecormedia.com
Primary Website: www.linformationdunordsainteagathe.ca
Published: Thur
Avg Paid Circ: 15474
Avg Free Circ: 26
Audit By: Sworn/Estimate/Non-Audited
Audit Date: 12.07.2019
Personnel: Johanne Regimbald
Parent company (for newspapers): Quebecor Communications, Inc.

INFORMATION DU NORD VALLEE DE LA ROUGE

Street address 1: Rue De St-jovite
Street address city: Mont-Tremblant
Province/Territory: QC
Postal code: J8E 3J9
Country: Canada
General Phone: (819) 425-8658
Published: Wed
Avg Paid Circ: 2
Avg Free Circ: 15487
Audit By: CCAB
Audit Date: 31.03.2014
Personnel: Johanne Regimbald

JOURNAL ACCES

Street address 1: Rue Principale
Street address city: Piedmont
Province/Territory: QC
Postal code: J0R 1K0
Country: Canada
General Phone: (450) 227-7999
Primary Website: http://www.journalacces.ca/
Published: Sat
Avg Free Circ: 25720
Audit By: ODC
Audit Date: 14.12.2011
Personnel: Josee Pilotte

JOURNAL DE CHAMBLY

Street address 1: 1685 Bourgogne Ave.
Street address city: Chambly
Province/Territory: QC
Postal code: J3L 4B3
County: Canada
Country: Canada
General Phone: (450) 658-6516
General Fax: (450) 658-3785
General/National Adv. E-mail: info@journaldechambly.com
Primary Website: www.journaldechambly.com
Published: Wed
Avg Paid Circ: 5
Avg Free Circ: 27471
Audit By: CCAB
Audit Date: 31.03.2014
Personnel: Daniel Noiseux (Mng. Ed.)
Parent company (for newspapers): Reseau Select/Select Network; Les Hebdos Monteregiens-OOB

JOURNAL DE LA BEAUCE

Street address 1: 11720 1re Rue
Street address 2: Bureau 2
Street address city: Saint Georges
Province/Territory: QC
Postal code: G5Y 2C8
Country: Canada
General Phone: (418) 220-0222
Published: Fri
Avg Free Circ: 32653
Audit By: ODC
Audit Date: 13.12.2011
Personnel: Lyne Genest

JOURNAL DE LEVIS

Street address 1: 580, Boul, Alphonse-desjardins
Street address city: Levis
Province/Territory: QC
Postal code: G6V 6R8
Country: Canada
General Phone: (418) 833-3113
General Fax: (418) 833-0890
General/National Adv. E-mail: jdl@journaldelevis.com
Primary Website: www.journaldelevis.com
Published: Wed
Avg Paid Circ: 5
Avg Free Circ: 68595
Audit By: CCAB
Audit Date: 30.09.2015
Personnel: Sandra Fontaine

JOURNAL DE MAGOG

Street address 1: Galt Ouest
Street address city: Sherbrooke
Province/Territory: QC
Postal code: J1K 2V8
Country: Canada
General Phone: (819) 575-7575
Published: Wed
Avg Free Circ: 28000
Audit By: CCAB
Audit Date: 31.03.2014
Personnel: Sarah Beaulieu

JOURNAL DE ROSEMONT / PETITE PATRIE

Street address 1: 8770 Langelier Boulevard Bureau 210
Street address city: Montreal
Province/Territory: QC
Postal code: H1P 3C6
Country: Canada
General Phone: (514) 899-5888
General Fax: (514) 899-5001
General/National Adv. E-mail: rosepatrie@tc.tc
Primary Website: www.journalderosemont.com
Published: Tues
Avg Paid Circ: 0
Avg Free Circ: 59344
Audit By: CCAB
Audit Date: 31.03.2014
Personnel: Stephane Desjardins

JOURNAL DE SHERBROOKE

Street address 1: Rue Galt Ouest
Street address city: Sherbrooke
Province/Territory: QC
Postal code: J1K 2V8
Country: Canada
General Phone: (819) 575-7575
Published: Wed
Avg Free Circ: 63500
Audit By: CCAB
Audit Date: 31.03.2014
Personnel: Sarah Beaulieu

JOURNAL DE ST MICHEL

Street address 1: Cp 50, Succ. St-michel
Street address city: Montreal
Province/Territory: QC
Postal code: H2A 3L8
Country: Canada
General Phone: (514) 721-4911
General Fax: (514) 374-4171

General/National Adv. E-mail: admin@journaldestmichel.com
Primary Website: www.journaldestmichel.com
Published: Sat
Avg Paid Circ: 20
Avg Free Circ: 24035
Audit By: ODC
Audit Date: 14.12.2011
Personnel: Claude Bricault

JOURNAL HAUTE COTE-NORD

Street address 1: 100-31 Rte. 138
Street address city: Forestville
Province/Territory: QC
Postal code: G0T 1E0
County: Canada
Country: Canada
General Phone: (418) 587-2090
General Fax: (418) 587-6407
General/National Adv. E-mail: journalhcn@globetrotter.net
Primary Website: www.journalhautecotenord.com
Published: Wed
Avg Paid Circ: 20
Avg Free Circ: 5510
Audit By: CCAB
Audit Date: 30.09.2012
Personnel: Luc Brisson (Pub.); Guylaine Boulianne (Sec.); Shirley Kennedy (Mng. Ed.)

JOURNAL LA VOIX

Street address 1: 58 Charlotte St.
Street address city: Sorel
Province/Territory: QC
Postal code: J3P 1G3
County: Canada
Country: Canada
General Phone: (450) 743-8466
General Fax: (450) 742-8567
General/National Adv. E-mail: info@journallavoix.net
Display Adv. E-mail: publicite@journallavoix.net
Editorial e-mail: redaction@journallavoix.net
Primary Website: www.journallavoix.net; monteregieweb.com
Published: Fri
Avg Free Circ: 29562
Audit By: CCAB
Audit Date: 31.03.2014
Personnel: Parise Bergeron (Adv. Rep.); Anne-Marie Nadeau (Adv. Rep.); Joey Olivier (Ed.); Johanne Berthiaume (Ed.)
Parent company (for newspapers): Les Hebdos Monteregiens-OOB

JOURNAL L'ACTUEL

Street address 1: 710 Bouvier, Suite 107
Street address city: Quebec
Province/Territory: QC
Postal code: G2J 1C2
Country: Canada
General Phone: (418) 628-7460
General Fax: (418) 622-1511
General/National Adv. E-mail: redaction_quebec@tc.tc
Primary Website: www.lactuel.com
Published: Fri
Avg Paid Circ: 5
Avg Free Circ: 57753
Audit By: CCAB
Audit Date: 31.03.2014
Personnel: Lilianne Laprese (Ed.); Alain LePage (Dir.); Lilianne Laprise (Ed.)
Parent company (for newspapers): Transcontinental Media

JOURNAL L'AVENIR & DES RIVIERES

Street address 1: 221 Main St.
Street address city: Farnham
Province/Territory: QC
Postal code: J2N 1L5
Country: Canada
General Phone: (450) 293-3138
General Fax: (450) 293-2093
General/National Adv. E-mail: caroline.dolce@tc.tc
Primary Website: www.laveniretdesrivieres.com
Published: Wed
Avg Paid Circ: 3
Avg Free Circ: 11442
Audit By: CCAB
Audit Date: 31.03.2014
Personnel: Renel Bouchard (Gen. Mgr.); Elrsa Fournyer (Pub.); Charles Couture (Circ. Mgr.)

JOURNAL L'AVENIR DE L'EST

Street address 1: 8770, Boulevard Langelier Bureau 210
Street address city: Montreal
Province/Territory: QC
Postal code: H1P 3C6
County: Canada
Country: Canada
General Phone: (514) 899-5888
General Fax: (514) 899-5001
General/National Adv. E-mail: redaction_est@tc.tc
Primary Website: http://www.avenirdelest.com
Published: Tues
Avg Paid Circ: 0
Avg Free Circ: 27818
Audit By: CCAB
Audit Date: 31.03.2014
Personnel: Paul Sauve (Ed.)

JOURNAL LE CHOIX D'ANTOINE LABELLE

Street address 1: Boulevard A.-paquette
Street address city: Mont-Laurier
Province/Territory: QC
Postal code: J9L1K5
Country: Canada
General Phone: (819) 623-3112
Published: Wed
Avg Paid Circ: 0
Avg Free Circ: 17000
Audit By: CCAB
Audit Date: 30.09.2012
Personnel: Andre Guillemette

JOURNAL LE COUP D'OEIL

Street address 1: 350 Saint Jacques St.
Street address city: Napierville
Province/Territory: QC
Postal code: J0J 1L0
County: Canada
Country: Canada
General Phone: (450) 245-3344
General Fax: (450) 245-7419
General/National Adv. E-mail: coupdoeil@tc.tc
Primary Website: www.coupdoeil.info
Published: Wed
Avg Paid Circ: 9
Avg Free Circ: 15602
Audit By: CCAB
Audit Date: 31.03.2014
Personnel: Charles Couture (Circ. Mgr.); Claude Trahan (Mng. Ed.); Jacques LaRochelle (Journalist)

JOURNAL LE COURANT DES HAUTES-LAURENTIDES

Street address 1: 534, De La Madone
Street address city: Mont-Laurier
Province/Territory: QC
Postal code: J9L 1S5
Country: Canada
General Phone: (819) 623-7374
General Fax: (819) 623-7375
Primary Website: www.lecourant.ca
Published: Thur
Avg Free Circ: 18400
Audit By: ODC
Audit Date: 14.12.2010
Personnel: Sylvie Vaillancourt

JOURNAL LE NORD

Street address 1: 393 Laurentides Blvd.
Street address city: Saint Jerome
Province/Territory: QC
Postal code: J7Z 4L9
Country: Canada
General Phone: (450) 438-8383
General Fax: (450) 438-4174
Editorial e-mail: editeur@journallenord.com
Primary Website: www.journallenord.com
Published: Wed
Avg Paid Circ: 9
Avg Free Circ: 55388
Audit By: CCAB
Audit Date: 31.03.2014
Personnel: Francois LaFerriere (Pub.); Mychel Lapointe (Ed.)

JOURNAL LE PAYS D'EN HAUT LA VALLEE

Street address 1: Rue De La Gare Bureau 104
Street address 2: Bureau 104
Street address city: Saint Sauveur-des-Monts
Province/Territory: QC
Postal code: J0R 1R6
Country: Canada
General Phone: (450) 227-4646
Published: Fri
Avg Paid Circ: 50
Avg Free Circ: 29756
Audit By: ODC
Audit Date: 14.12.2011
Personnel: Andre Guillemette

JOURNAL LE PEUPLE

Street address 1: 421 Dorimene Desjardins Rue
Street address city: Levis
Province/Territory: QC
Postal code: G6V 8V6
Country: Canada
General Phone: (418) 833-9398
General Fax: (418) 833-8177
General/National Adv. E-mail: paul.lessard@quebecormedia.com
Primary Website: http://www.hebdosregionaux.ca/chaudiere-appalaches/le-peuple-levis/
Published: Wed
Avg Paid Circ: 3
Avg Free Circ: 68451
Audit By: CCAB
Audit Date: 31.03.2014
Personnel: Paul Lessard
Parent company (for newspapers): Quebecor Communications, Inc.

JOURNAL LE RICHELIEU

Street address 1: Rue Richelieu
Street address city: Sainte Jean sur Richelieu
Province/Territory: QC
Postal code: J3B 6X3
Country: Canada
General Phone: (450) 347-0323
Published: Tues
Avg Paid Circ: 4
Avg Free Circ: 42273
Audit By: CCAB
Audit Date: 31.03.2014
Personnel: Renel Bouchard

JOURNAL L'IMPACT DE DRUMMONDVILLE

Street address 1: 2345, Rue St-pierre
Street address city: Drummondville
Province/Territory: QC
Postal code: J2C 5A7
Country: Canada
General Phone: (819) 445-7000
General Fax: (819) 445-7001
General/National Adv. E-mail: guy.levasseur@quebecormedia.com
Primary Website: www.limpact.ca
Published: Thur
Avg Paid Circ: 4
Avg Free Circ: 46173
Audit By: CCAB
Audit Date: 31.03.2014
Personnel: Jean Crepeau (Ed.)

JOURNAL OF PONTIAC

Street address 1: Unit 5
Street address 2: 289, Rue Principale
Street address city: Mansfield
Province/Territory: QC
Postal code: J0X 1R0
County: Mansfield-et-Pontefract
Country: Canada
General Phone: (819) 683-3582
General Fax: (819) 683-2977
General/National Adv. E-mail: info@journalpontiac.com
Display Adv. E-mail: journal@journalpontiac.com
Classified Adv. e-mail: notice@journalpontiac.com
Editorial e-mail: editor@journalpontiac.com
Primary Website: www.pontiacjournal.com
Published: Other
Avg Paid Circ: 70
Avg Free Circ: 9302
Audit By: Sworn/Estimate/Non-Audited
Audit Date: 12.07.2019
Personnel: Lynne Lavery (Gen. Mgr.)
Parent company (for newspapers): 155106 Canada Inc.

JOURNAL PREMIERE EDITION

Street address 1: 469 St. Charles Ave.
Street address city: Vaudreuil-Dorion
Province/Territory: QC
Postal code: J7V 2N4
Country: Canada
General Phone: (450) 455-7955
General Fax: (450) 455-3028
Advertising Phone: (450) 455-1050
General/National Adv. E-mail: webmestre@hebdosdusuroit.com
Primary Website: www.journalpremiereedition.com
Published: Sat
Avg Paid Circ: 7
Avg Free Circ: 61880
Audit By: CCAB
Audit Date: 30.09.2015

LA CONCORDE

Street address 1: 53 Rue St. Eustache
Street address city: Saint Eustache
Province/Territory: QC
Postal code: J7R 2L2
Country: Canada
General Phone: (450) 472-3440
General Fax: (450) 473-1629
Published: Wed
Avg Free Circ: 52172
Audit By: CCAB
Audit Date: 31.03.2014
Personnel: Jean-Claude Langlois (Ed.)

LA NOUVELLE

Street address 1: 43 Notre Dame St. E., Cp 130
Street address city: Victoriaville
Province/Territory: QC
Postal code: G6P 3Z4
Country: Canada
General Phone: (819) 758-6211
General Fax: (819) 758-2759
General/National Adv. E-mail: redaction_victo@transcontinental.ca
Primary Website: www.lanouvelle.net
Published: Sun
Avg Free Circ: 44008
Audit By: Sworn/Estimate/Non-Audited
Audit Date: 12.07.2019
Personnel: Pierre Gaudet (Sales Dir.); Michel Gauthier (Pub.); Ghislain Chauvette (Director de l'information); Sylvie Cote (Mng. Ed.); Danielle Deveault (Prodn. Mgr.)
Parent company (for newspapers): Transcontinental Media

LA PAROLE

Street address 1: 1050 Rue Cormier
Street address city: Drummondville
Province/Territory: QC
Postal code: J2C 2N6
County: Canada
Country: Canada
General Phone: (819) 478-8171
General Fax: (819) 393-0741
General/National Adv. E-mail: redaction@transcontinental.ca
Primary Website: www.journalexpress.ca
Published: Wed
Avg Free Circ: 46000
Audit By: Sworn/Estimate/Non-Audited
Audit Date: 12.07.2019
Personnel: Eyves Shabot (Adv. Dir.); Johanne Marceau (Ed.)

Parent company (for newspapers): Reseau Select/ Select Network

LA PENSEE DE BAGOT

Street address 1: 800 Roxton St.
Street address city: Acton Vale
Province/Territory: QC
Postal code: J0H 1A0
Country: Canada
General Phone: (450) 546-3271
General Fax: (450) 546-3491
General/National Adv. E-mail: mdorais@lapensee.qc.ca
Primary Website: www.lapensee.qc.ca
Published: Wed
Avg Paid Circ: 0
Avg Free Circ: 0
Audit By: CCAB
Audit Date: 30.09.2015
Personnel: Michel Dorais (Adv. Mgr.); Robert Beauchemin (Adv. Rep.); Jean-Francois Dorais (Adv. Rep.); Benoit Chartier (Ed.)

LA PETITE NATION

Street address 1: 3 Ste.10, Principale St.
Street address city: Saint Andre-Avellin
Province/Territory: QC
Postal code: J0V 1W0
County: Canada
Country: Canada
General Phone: (819) 983-2725
General Fax: (819) 983-6844
General/National Adv. E-mail: gessi.laslamme@transcontinental.ca
Editorial e-mail: pascal.laplante@tc.tc
Primary Website: http://www.lapetitenation.com
Published: Wed
Avg Paid Circ: 19
Avg Free Circ: 10108
Audit By: CCAB
Audit Date: 31.03.2014
Personnel: Eric Bernard (Ed.)
Parent company (for newspapers): Transcontinental Media

LA RELEVE

Street address 1: 528 St. Charles St.
Street address city: Boucherville
Province/Territory: QC
Postal code: J4B 3M5
Country: Canada
General Phone: (450) 641-4844
General Fax: (450) 641-4849
Advertising Phone: (514) 926-2354
General/National Adv. E-mail: lareleve@lareleve.qc.ca
Display Adv. E-mail: c.desmarteau@videotron.ca
Classified Adv. e-mail: classees@lareleve.qc.ca
Editorial e-mail: lareleve@lareleve.qc.ca
Primary Website: www.lareleve.qc.ca
Published: Tues
Avg Paid Circ: 0
Avg Free Circ: 59100
Audit By: Sworn/Estimate/Non-Audited
Audit Date: 12.07.2019
Personnel: Charles Desmarteau (Ed. & Gen. Mgr.)
Parent company (for newspapers): Groupe Messier
Newspapers (for newspaper groups): La Seigneurie, Boucherville

LA REVUE DE GATINEAU

Street address 1: 160 Hospital Rd., Ste. 30
Street address city: Gatineau
Province/Territory: QC
Postal code: J8T 8J1
County: Canada
Country: Canada
General Phone: (819) 568-7736
General Fax: (819) 568-8728
Editorial e-mail: pascal.laplante@tc.tc
Primary Website: www.info07.com
Published: Wed
Avg Paid Circ: 8
Avg Free Circ: 91029
Audit By: CCAB
Audit Date: 31.03.2014
Personnel: Jacques Blais (Gen. Mgr.); Martin Godcher (Ed.)
Parent company (for newspapers): Transcontinental Media

LA REVUE DE TERREBONNE

Street address 1: 231 Sainte-marie St.
Street address city: Terrebonne
Province/Territory: QC
Postal code: J6W 3E4
County: Lanaudiere
Country: Canada
General Phone: (450) 964-4444
General Fax: (450) 471-1023
General/National Adv. E-mail: larevue@larevue.qc.ca
Display Adv. E-mail: ventes@larevue.qc.ca
Classified Adv. e-mail: petitesannonces@larevue.qc.ca
Editorial e-mail: redaction@larevue.qc.ca
Primary Website: www.larevue.qc.ca
Published: Wed
Avg Paid Circ: 10
Avg Free Circ: 55990
Audit By: Sworn/Estimate/Non-Audited
Audit Date: 12.07.2019
Personnel: Gilles Bordonado (Pub./Pres./CEO.); Veronick Talbot (News Dir); Daniel Soucy (Mktg Dir); Lise Bourdages (Sales Coord)
Parent company (for newspapers): Guide Rouge; Le Trait d'Union

LA SEIGNEURIE

Street address 1: 391 Boul. De Mortagne
Street address city: Boucherville
Province/Territory: QC
Postal code: J4B 3M5
Country: Canada
General Phone: (450) 641-4844
General Fax: (450) 641-4849
General/National Adv. E-mail: info@la-seigneurie.qc.ca
Display Adv. E-mail: lareleve@lareleve.qc.ca
Editorial e-mail: redaction@la-seigneurie.qc.ca
Primary Website: www.la-seigneurie.qc.ca
Published: Wed
Avg Free Circ: 33856
Audit By: Sworn/Estimate/Non-Audited
Audit Date: 12.07.2019
Personnel: Charles Desmarteau (Pub.)
Parent company (for newspapers): La Releve

LA VOIX DE L'EST PLUS

Street address 1: 76 Dufferin St.
Street address city: Granby
Province/Territory: QC
Postal code: J2G 9L4
Country: Canada
General Phone: (450) 375-4555
General Fax: (450) 372-1308
General/National Adv. E-mail: redaction@lavoixdelest.qc.ca
Display Adv. E-mail: pub@lapresse.ca
Editorial e-mail: redaction@lavoixdelest.qc.ca
Primary Website: www.cyberpresse.ca
Published: Wed
Avg Paid Circ: 8965
Avg Free Circ: 128
Audit By: AAM
Audit Date: 31.03.2017
Personnel: Francois Beaudoin (Mng. Ed.); Daniel Touchette (Adv. Mgr.); Gilbert Arl (Dir., Finance/ Admin.); Daniel Touchet (Adv. Mgr., Sales); Christian Malo (Circ. Dir.); Guy Granger (Ed.); Haswa Budway (News Ed.); Andre Bilodeau (Sports Ed.); Claudette Ospiguy (Prodn. Mgr., Pre Press); Louisse Boisvert (Pub.); Marc Gendron (Info. Mgr.); Martyne Lessard (Adv. Mgr.)
Parent company (for newspapers): Gesca Ltd.; Reseau Select/Select Network

LA VOIX DU SUD

Street address 1: 1516 A. Rt. 277
Street address city: Lac Etchemin
Province/Territory: QC
Postal code: G0R 1S0
Country: Canada
General Phone: (418) 625-7471
General Fax: (418) 625-5200
General/National Adv. E-mail: caroline.gilbert@tc.tc
Display Adv. E-mail: caroline.gilbert@tc.tc
Classified Adv. e-mail: caroline.gilbert@tc.tc
Editorial e-mail: caroline.gilbert@tc.tc
Primary Website: www.lavoixdusud.com
Published: Wed
Avg Paid Circ: 14
Avg Free Circ: 27758
Audit By: CCAB
Audit Date: 31.03.2014
Personnel: Caroline Gilbert (Ed.); Rock Bizier (Prodn. Mgr.)
Parent company (for newspapers): Transcontinental Media

LA VOIX GASPESIENNE

Street address 1: 305 De La Gare St., Ste. 107
Street address city: Matane
Province/Territory: QC
Postal code: G4W 3J2
Country: Canada
General Phone: (418) 562-4040
General Fax: (418) 562-4607
Advertising Phone: (418) 562-0666
Editorial Phone: (418) 562-0666
Primary Website: http://www.lavantagegaspesien.com
Published: Wed
Avg Paid Circ: 13
Avg Free Circ: 17247
Audit By: CCAB
Audit Date: 31.03.2014
Personnel: Jean Gagnon ((Ed.))
Parent company (for newspapers): Quebecor Communications, Inc.

LA VOIX POPULAIRE

Street address 1: 420 La Fleur St.
Street address city: Lasalle
Province/Territory: QC
Postal code: H8R 3H6
Country: Canada
General Phone: (514) 363-5656
General Fax: (514) 363-3895
General/National Adv. E-mail: patriciaan.beaulieu@transcontinental.ca
Primary Website: www.lavoixpopulaire.com
Published: Thur
Avg Paid Circ: 4
Avg Free Circ: 29159
Audit By: CCAB
Audit Date: 31.03.2014
Personnel: Louis Mercier (Ed.); Yannick Pinel (Ed. In Chief.)
Parent company (for newspapers): Transcontinental Media

LACHINE MESSENGER

Street address 1: 455 Boulevard Fenelon, Suite 303
Street address city: Dorval
Province/Territory: QC
Postal code: H9S 5T8
Country: Canada
General Phone: (514) 636-7314
General Fax: (514) 363-7315
General/National Adv. E-mail: redaction_lachine-dorval@tc.tc
Primary Website: www.messagerlachine.com
Published: Thur
Avg Free Circ: 20000
Audit By: Sworn/Estimate/Non-Audited
Audit Date: 12.07.2019
Personnel: Patricia Ann Beaulieu (Pub.); Tina Lemelin (Adv. Mgr.); Robert Leduc (Ed.)

L'ACTION

Street address 1: 342 Beaudry N.
Street address city: Joliette
Province/Territory: QC
Postal code: J6E 6A6
County: Canada
Country: Canada
General Phone: (450) 759-3664
Advertising Phone: (450) 752-0447
Editorial Phone: (450) 759-3664
General/National Adv. E-mail: infolanaudiere@tc.tc
Display Adv. E-mail: infolanaudiere@tc.tc
Primary Website: www.laction.com
Published: Wed
Avg Free Circ: 19450
Audit By: CCAB
Audit Date: 31.03.2014
Personnel: Norman Harvey (Sales Rep.); Benoit Bazinet (Pub.); Chantal Proulx (Prodn. Mgr.); Natalie Lariviere (Pres.); Carole Bonin (Mgr.); Sebastien Nadeau (Regl. Dir.); Harvey Norman (Sales Mgr.); Andre Lafreniere (Ed.); Francine Rainville (Ed.); Chantal Troulx (Prodn. Mgr.)
Parent company (for newspapers): Transcontinental Media

L'APPEL

Street address 1: 710 Rue Bouvier Bureau 107
Street address city: Quebec
Province/Territory: QC
Postal code: G2J 1C2
Country: Canada
General Phone: (418) 628-7460
General Fax: (418) 622-1511
Advertising Phone: (418) 628-7460
Editorial Phone: (418) 628-7460
General/National Adv. E-mail: redaction_quebec@tc.tc
Display Adv. E-mail: redaction_quebec@tc.tc
Editorial e-mail: redaction_quebec@tc.tc
Primary Website: www.lappel.com
Published: Fri
Avg Paid Circ: 10
Avg Free Circ: 44099
Audit By: CCAB
Audit Date: 31.03.2014
Personnel: Michel Chalifour (Reg. Gen. Mgr.)

L'ARGENTEUIL

Street address 1: 52 Main St.
Street address city: Lachute
Province/Territory: QC
Postal code: J8H 3A8
County: Canada
Country: Canada
General Phone: (450) 562-2494
General Fax: (450) 562-1434
General/National Adv. E-mail: argenteuil@eap.on.ca
Display Adv. E-mail: francois.leblanc@eap.on.ca
Primary Website: www.largenteuil.ca
Published: Wed
Avg Paid Circ: 39
Avg Free Circ: 16540
Audit By: ODC
Audit Date: 13.12.2011
Personnel: Bertrand Castonguay (Pres.); Roger Duplantie (Dir. Gen.); Francois Leblanc (Dir., Adv.); Alain Morris (Circ. Mgr.); Robert Savard (Ed.)
Parent company (for newspapers): Reseau Select/ Select Network; Cie d'Edition Andre Paquette, Inc.

L'ARTISAN

Street address 1: 1004 Rue Nortre-dame
Street address city: Repentigny
Province/Territory: QC
Postal code: J5Y 1S9
Country: Canada
General Phone: (450) 581-5120
General Fax: (450) 581-4515
Primary Website: www.journallartisan.com
Published: Tues
Avg Free Circ: 45212
Audit By: Sworn/Estimate/Non-Audited
Audit Date: 12.07.2019
Personnel: Stephane Joseph (Adv. Mgr.); Yannick Boulanger (Ed.); Chantal Proulx (Prodn. Mgr.)
Parent company (for newspapers): Transcontinental Media

L'AVANT-POSTE GASPESIEN

Street address 1: 217 Leonidas Ave.
Street address city: Amqui
Province/Territory: QC
Postal code: G5J 2B8
Country: Canada
General Phone: (418) 629-3443
General Fax: (418)562-4607
General/National Adv. E-mail: avant-poste@hebdosquebecor.com
Display Adv. E-mail: gaby.veilleux@hebdosquebecor.com
Editorial e-mail: lucie-rose.levesque@hebdosquebecor.com
Primary Website: lavantposte.ca
Published: Wed
Avg Paid Circ: 22
Avg Free Circ: 16881

Audit By: CCAB
Audit Date: 30.09.2012
Personnel: Alain St-Amand (Regl. Dir. Gen.); Francis Desrosiers (Dir. Gen.); Lucy-Rose Levesque (Ed.)
Parent company (for newspapers): Quebecor Communications, Inc.

L'AVENIR DE BROME MISSISQUOI, INC.

Street address 1: 221 Rue Principale Est.
Street address city: Farnham
Province/Territory: QC
Postal code: J2N 1L5
Country: Canada
General Phone: (450) 293-3138
General Fax: (450) 293-2093
General/National Adv. E-mail: lavenir@canadafrancais.com
Editorial e-mail: cassandra.deblois@tc.tc
Primary Website: www.laveniretdesrivieres.com
Published: Wed
Avg Paid Circ: 34
Avg Free Circ: 8554
Audit By: Sworn/Estimate/Non-Audited
Audit Date: 12.07.2019
Personnel: Group le Canada Francais (Pub.)

L'AVENIR DE L'ERABLE

Street address 1: 1620 Saint-calixte St.
Street address city: Plessisville
Province/Territory: QC
Postal code: G6L 1P9
Country: Canada
General Phone: (819) 362-7049
General Fax: (819) 362-2216
General/National Adv. E-mail: cotes2@transcontinental.ca
Primary Website: www.lavenirdelerable.com
Published: Wed
Avg Paid Circ: 9
Avg Free Circ: 10779
Audit By: CCAB
Audit Date: 31.03.2014
Personnel: Pierre Gaudet (Dir., Sales); Sylvia Cote (Ed.); Ghislain Chauvette (Ed.)
Parent company (for newspapers): Transcontinental Media

LE BULLETIN

Street address 1: 435 Blvd Rue Principale
Street address city: Gatineau
Province/Territory: QC
Postal code: J8L 2G8
Country: Canada
General Phone: (819) 986-5089
General Fax: (819) 986-2073
Advertising Phone: (819) 986-5089
Editorial Phone: (819) 986-5089
General/National Adv. E-mail: yannick.boursier@tc.tc
Display Adv. E-mail: yannick.boursier@tc.tc
Editorial e-mail: yannick.boursier@tc.tc
Primary Website: www.lebulletin.net
Published: Wed
Avg Paid Circ: 20
Avg Free Circ: 14308
Audit By: CCAB
Audit Date: 31.03.2014
Personnel: Yannick Boursier (Pub./Ed.)

LE BULLETIN D'AYLMER

Street address 1: C-10 181 Principale St., (secteur Aylmer)
Street address city: Gatineau
Province/Territory: QC
Postal code: J9H 6A6
Country: Canada
General Phone: (819) 684-4755
General Fax: (819) 684-6428
General/National Adv. E-mail: abawqp@videotron.ca
Display Adv. E-mail: ventes.sales@bulletinaylmer.com
Editorial e-mail: abawqp@videotron.ca
Primary Website: www.bulletinaylmer.com
Published: Wed
Avg Paid Circ: 181
Avg Free Circ: 23009
Audit By: Sworn/Estimate/Non-Audited
Audit Date: 12.07.2019
Personnel: Lily Ryan (Ed.); Lynne Lavery; Sophia Ryan (Manager operations)

LE CANADA FRANCAIS

Street address 1: 84 Rue Richelieu
Street address city: Sainte Jean sur Richelieu
Province/Territory: QC
Postal code: J3B 6X3
Country: Canada
General Phone: (450) 347-0323
General Fax: (450) 347-4539
Editorial e-mail: web@tc.tc
Primary Website: www.canadafrancais.com
Published: Thur
Avg Paid Circ: 7708
Avg Free Circ: 7848
Audit By: AAM
Audit Date: 31.12.2018
Personnel: Renel Bouchard (Pres.); Charles Coutre (Adv. Mgr.); Christian Marleau (Circ. Mgr.); Robert Paradis (Ed.)

LE CITOYEN DE LA VALLEE DE L'OR

Street address 1: 1462 Rue De La Quebecoise
Street address city: Val d'Or
Province/Territory: QC
Postal code: J9P 5H4
Country: Canada
General Phone: (819) 874-4545
General Fax: (819) 874-4547
General/National Adv. E-mail: citoyens@cablevision.qc.ca
Primary Website: http://www.lechoabitibien.ca/
Published: Wed
Avg Paid Circ: 36
Avg Free Circ: 19883
Audit By: CCAB
Audit Date: 31.03.2014
Personnel: Endre Renaud (Gen. Mgr.); Carroline Couture (Adv. Mgr.); Louis Lavoie (Mng. Ed.)
Parent company (for newspapers): Quebecor Communications, Inc.

LE COURRIER

Street address 1: 190 Cure-labelle Blvd., Rm. 204
Street address city: Sainte Therese
Province/Territory: QC
Postal code: J7E 2X5
Country: Canada
General Phone: (450) 434-4144
General Fax: (450) 434-3142
Advertising Phone: (866) 637-5236
Primary Website: www.journallecourrier.com
Published: Wed
Avg Free Circ: 55014
Audit By: CCAB
Audit Date: 31.03.2014
Personnel: Louis Sauvageau (Pub./Ed.)

LE COURRIER BORDEAUX/ CARTIERVILLE

Street address 1: 1500 Jules Poitras Blvd.
Street address city: Saint Laurent
Province/Territory: QC
Postal code: H4N 1X7
Country: Canada
General Phone: (514) 855-1292
General Fax: (514) 855-9916
Primary Website: www.transcontinental.com; www.courrierbc.com
Published: Fri
Avg Paid Circ: 4
Avg Free Circ: 17925
Audit By: CCAB
Audit Date: 31.03.2014
Personnel: Alain De Choinire (Ed.)
Parent company (for newspapers): Transcontinental Media

LE COURRIER DE SAINT-HYACINTHE

Street address 1: 655 Rue St. Anne
Street address city: Saint Hyacinthe
Province/Territory: QC
Postal code: J2S 5G4
County: St. Hyacinthe
Country: Canada
General Phone: (450) 773-6028
General Fax: (450) 773-3115
Advertising Phone: (450) 771-0677
General/National Adv. E-mail: redaction@leclairon.qc.ca
Display Adv. E-mail: gbedard@courrierclairon.qc.ca
Classified Adv. e-mail: gbedard@courrierclairon.qc.ca
Primary Website: lecourrier.qc.ca/accueil
Published: Tues
Avg Paid Circ: 9352
Avg Free Circ: 142
Audit By: AAM
Audit Date: 30.09.2018
Personnel: Guillaume Bedard (Adv. Mgr.)

LE COURRIER DU SAGUENAY

Street address 1: 3635 Blvd Harvey Ste 201
Street address city: Saguenay
Province/Territory: QC
Postal code: G7X 3B2
Country: Canada
General Phone: (418) 542-2442
General Fax: (418) 542-5225
Advertising Phone: (418) 542-2442
Editorial Phone: (418) 542-2442
General/National Adv. E-mail: redaction.saguenay@tc.tc
Display Adv. E-mail: redaction.saguenay@tc.tc
Editorial e-mail: redaction.saguenay@tc.tc
Primary Website: www.courrierdusaguenay.com
Published: Wed
Avg Paid Circ: 16
Avg Free Circ: 72964
Audit By: CCAB
Audit Date: 31.03.2014
Personnel: Joan Sullivan (Ed.)

LE COURRIER DU SUD/SOUTH SHORE COURIER

Street address 1: 267 Saint Charles W
Street address city: Longueuil
Province/Territory: QC
Postal code: J4H 1E3
County: Canada
Country: Canada
General Phone: (450) 646-3333
General Fax: (450) 674-0205
Advertising Phone: (450) 646-3333
General/National Adv. E-mail: direction@courrierdusud.com
Display Adv. E-mail: journal@courrierdusud.com
Editorial e-mail: editeur@courrierdusud.com
Primary Website: http://www.lecourrierdusud.ca/
Published: Wed
Avg Free Circ: 145800
Audit By: CCAB
Audit Date: 31.03.2014
Personnel: Lucie Masse (Pub.); Jinette Claude Teron (Ed.)
Parent company (for newspapers): Quebecor Communications, Inc.

LE GATINEAU

Street address 1: 135-b, Highway 105
Street address city: Egan South
Province/Territory: QC
Postal code: J9E 3A9
Country: Canada
General Phone: (819) 449-1725
General Fax: (819) 449-5108
General/National Adv. E-mail: direction@lagatineau.com
Editorial e-mail: redaction@lagatineau.com
Primary Website: www.lagatineau.com
Published: Thur
Avg Free Circ: 11210
Audit By: CCAB
Audit Date: 31.03.2014
Personnel: Denise LacourciÃ¨re (Executive Director)

LE GROUPE JCL INC.

Street address 1: 53, Rue Saint-eustache
Street address city: Saint Eustache
Province/Territory: QC
Postal code: J7R 2L2
Country: Canada
General Phone: (450) 472-3440
General/National Adv. E-mail: leveil@groupejcl.com
Display Adv. E-mail: infojournaux@groupejcl.com
Classified Adv. e-mail: infojournaux@groupejcl.com
Editorial e-mail: infojournaux@groupejcl.com
Primary Website: www.leveil.com
Published: Sat
Avg Free Circ: 60000
Audit By: Sworn/Estimate/Non-Audited
Audit Date: 12.07.2019
Personnel: Louis Kemp (Dir., Sales); Norman Langlois (Circ. Mgr.); Claude Desjardins (Ed. in Chief); Jean Claude Langlois (Ed.); Marco Brunelle (Sports Ed.); Yves Bourbonnais (Dir., Prodn.); Serge Langlois (Dir., Dist.)

LE GUIDE DE COWANSVILLE

Street address 1: 121 Rue Principale
Street address city: Cowansville
Province/Territory: QC
Postal code: J2K 1J3
Country: Canada
General Phone: (450) 263-5288
General Fax: (450) 263-9435
General/National Adv. E-mail: leguide@tc.tc
Primary Website: http://www.journalleguide.com/
Published: Wed
Avg Paid Circ: 6
Avg Free Circ: 18340
Audit By: CCAB
Audit Date: 31.03.2014
Personnel: Cathy Bernard (Pub.); Louise Denicourt (Sec.); Caroline Rioux (Reg'l Ed.)

LE INFORMATION

Street address 1: Rue Doucet
Street address city: Mont-Joli
Province/Territory: QC
Postal code: G5H 1R6
Country: Canada
General Phone: (418) 775-4381
Published: Wed
Avg Paid Circ: 33
Avg Free Circ: 9867
Audit By: CCAB
Audit Date: 31.03.2014
Personnel: Francis Desrosiers

LE JOURNAL DE JOLIETTE

Street address 1: 1075 Blvd Firestone 5e Etage
Street address city: Joliette
Province/Territory: QC
Postal code: J6E 6X6
Country: Canada
General Phone: (450) 960-2424
General Fax: (450) 960-2626
Advertising Phone: (450) 960-2424
Editorial Phone: (450) 960-2424
General/National Adv. E-mail: janique.duguay@quebecormedia.com
Display Adv. E-mail: johanne.roussy2@quebecormedia.com
Editorial e-mail: janique.duguay@quebecormedia.com
Primary Website: www.lejournaldejoliette.ca
Published: Wed
Avg Free Circ: 60740
Audit By: CCAB
Audit Date: 30.09.2012
Personnel: Janique Duguay (Ed.); Patricia Beaulieu (Regional Director)
Parent company (for newspapers): Quebecor Communications, Inc.

LE JOURNAL DE ST-BRUNO

Street address 1: 1507 Roberval
Street address city: Saint Bruno
Province/Territory: QC
Postal code: J3V 3P8
Country: Canada
General Phone: (450) 653-3685
General Fax: (450) 653-6967
General/National Adv. E-mail: redaction@journaldest-bruno.qc.ca
Editorial e-mail: pclair@versants.com
Primary Website: http://www.journaldest-bruno.qc.ca/
Published: Fri
Avg Paid Circ: 4
Avg Free Circ: 18900
Audit By: CCAB
Audit Date: 31.03.2014

Personnel: Philippe Clair (Ed.); StÃ©phanie Lambert (Prod. Mgr.)
Parent company (for newspapers): Les Hebdos Monteregiens-OOB

LE JOURNAL DES PAYS D'EN HAUT LE VALLEE

Street address 1: 94 De La Gare St-saviour
Street address city: Sainte Adele
Province/Territory: QC
Postal code: J8B 2P7
Country: Canada
General Phone: (450) 229-6664
General Fax: (450) 227-8144
General/National Adv. E-mail: jpdh@hebdosquebecor.com
Primary Website: http://www.lejournaldespaysdenhautlavallee.ca/
Published: Wed
Avg Free Circ: 30057
Audit By: CCAB
Audit Date: 31.03.2014
Personnel: Mario Marois (Pub.)
Parent company (for newspapers): Quebecor Communications, Inc.

LE JOURNAL SAINT-FRANCOIS

Street address 1: 61 Jacques-cartier St.
Street address city: Salaberry-de-Valleyfield
Province/Territory: QC
Postal code: J6T 4R4
Country: Canada
General Phone: (450) 371-6222
General Fax: (450) 371-7254
General/National Adv. E-mail: info@st-francois.com
Primary Website: www.st-francois.com
Published: Wed
Avg Paid Circ: 36
Avg Free Circ: 34817
Audit By: CCAB
Audit Date: 31.03.2014
Personnel: Diane Dumont (Pub./Dir.); Stephane Brais (Sales Dir.); Denis Bourbonnais (Ed. in Chief)
Parent company (for newspapers): Les Hebdos Monteregiens-OOB

LE JOURNAL TEMISCAMIEN

Street address 1: 22 Rue Ste-anne
Street address city: Ville-Marie
Province/Territory: QC
Postal code: J9V 2B7
Country: Canada
General Phone: (819) 622-1313
General Fax: (819) 622-1333
Published: Wed
Avg Free Circ: 8500
Audit By: Sworn/Estimate/Non-Audited
Audit Date: 12.07.2019
Personnel: Lionel Lacasse (Ed.)

LE LAC ST. JEAN

Street address 1: 100 St. Joseph St., Locale 01
Street address city: Alma
Province/Territory: QC
Postal code: G8B 7A6
Country: Canada
General Phone: (418) 668-4545
General Fax: (418) 668-8522
General/National Adv. E-mail: redaction_alma@tc.tc
Primary Website: www.lelacstjean.com
Published: Wed
Avg Paid Circ: 80
Avg Free Circ: 23534
Audit By: CCAB
Audit Date: 31.03.2014
Personnel: Michelle Dupont (Gen. Mgr.)
Parent company (for newspapers): Transcontinental Media

LE MIRABEL

Street address 1: 179 Rue St. Georges
Street address city: Saint Jerome
Province/Territory: QC
Postal code: J7Z 4Z8
County: Canada
Country: Canada
General Phone: (450) 436-8200
General Fax: (450) 436-8912
General/National Adv. E-mail: atelier.mirabel@hebdosquebecor.com; redaction.mirabel@hebdosquebecor.com
Primary Website: www.lemirabel.com
Published: Sat
Avg Free Circ: 51862
Audit By: CCAB
Audit Date: 31.03.2014
Personnel: Marc Fradellin (Pub.); Andre Guillemette (Gen. Mgr.); Christine Leonard (Prodn. Dir.)
Parent company (for newspapers): Quebecor Communications, Inc.

LE NORD-INFO

Street address 1: 50 B Rue Turgeon
Street address city: Sainte Therese
Province/Territory: QC
Postal code: J7E 3H4
Country: Canada
General Phone: (450) 435-6537
General Fax: (450) 435-0588
General/National Adv. E-mail: nordinfo@groupgcl.com
Published: Sat
Avg Free Circ: 60079
Audit By: CCAB
Audit Date: 31.03.2014
Personnel: Serge Langlois (Gen. Mgr.); Norman Langlois (Circ. Mgr.); Jean Claude Langlois (Ed.)

LE NOUVELLES HEBDO

Street address 1: 1741 Rue Des Pins
Street address city: Dolbeau-Mistassini
Province/Territory: QC
Postal code: G8L 1J7
Country: Canada
General Phone: (418) 276-6211
General Fax: (418)276-6166
Advertising Phone: (418) 276-6211
General/National Adv. E-mail: redaction.dolbeau@tc.tc
Primary Website: http://www.nouvelleshebdo.com/
Published: Wed
Avg Paid Circ: 55
Avg Free Circ: 12594
Audit By: CCAB
Audit Date: 31.03.2014
Personnel: Michel Aub

LE PEUPLE COTE-SUD

Street address 1: 80 Boul. Tache E.
Street address city: Montmagny
Province/Territory: QC
Postal code: G5V 3S7
Country: Canada
General Phone: (418) 248-0415
General Fax: (418) 248-2377
General/National Adv. E-mail: peuple-cote-sud@globetrotter.net; vemtes.cote.sud@gmail.com
Primary Website: www.camoe.ca
Published: Wed
Avg Paid Circ: 27
Avg Free Circ: 20852
Audit By: CCAB
Audit Date: 30.09.2012
Personnel: Claueettne Tardis (Pub.)
Parent company (for newspapers): Quebecor Communications, Inc.

LE PHARILLON

Street address 1: 144 Rue De Jacques-cartier
Street address city: Gaspe
Province/Territory: QC
Postal code: G4X 1M9
County: Canada
Country: Canada
General Phone: (418) 368-3242
General Fax: (418) 368-1705
General/National Adv. E-mail: pharillon@hebdosquebecor.com
Display Adv. E-mail: gas.redaction@tc.tc
Classified Adv. e-mail: gas.redaction@tc.tc
Editorial e-mail: gas.redaction@tc.tc
Primary Website: www.lepharillon.ca
Published: Wed
Avg Paid Circ: 10
Avg Free Circ: 8720
Audit By: CCAB
Audit Date: 31.03.2014
Personnel: Alain St-Amand (Gen. Mgr.); Bernard Johnson (Mng. Ed.)
Parent company (for newspapers): Reseau Select/ Select Network; Quebecor Communications, Inc.

LE PLACOTEUX

Street address 1: 491 Ave. D'anjou
Street address city: Saint Pascal
Province/Territory: QC
Postal code: G0L 3Y0
Country: Canada
General Phone: (418) 492-2706
General Fax: (418) 492-9706
General/National Adv. E-mail: montage@leplacoteux.com
Primary Website: www.leplacoteux.com
Published: Wed
Avg Paid Circ: 75
Avg Free Circ: 18315
Audit By: CCAB
Audit Date: 31.03.2014
Personnel: Maurice Gagnon (Ed.); Raymond Freve (Adv. Mgr.)
Parent company (for newspapers): Reseau Select/ Select Network

LE POINT

Street address 1: 9085, Boul. Lacroix
Street address city: Saint-Georges
Province/Territory: QC
Postal code: G5Y 2B4
Country: Canada
General Phone: (418) 695-2601
General Fax: (418) 695-1391
General/National Adv. E-mail: ralph.pilote@quebecormedia.com
Primary Website: www.lepoint.ca
Published: Tues
Avg Free Circ: 47878
Audit By: CCAB
Audit Date: 31.03.2014
Personnel: Claude Poulin (Pres.)
Parent company (for newspapers): Quebecor Communications, Inc.

LE PORT CARTOIS

Street address 1: 365 Laure Blvd.
Street address city: Sept-Iles
Province/Territory: QC
Postal code: G4R 1X2
Country: Canada
General Phone: (418) 962-4100
General Fax: (418) 962-0439
General/National Adv. E-mail: administration.sett-iles@hebdosquebecor.com
Primary Website: www.hebdosquebecor.com
Published: Wed
Avg Paid Circ: 6
Avg Free Circ: 19072
Audit By: CCAB
Audit Date: 31.03.2014
Personnel: Isabelle Chiasson (Adv. Mgr.); Catherine Martin (Ed.)
Parent company (for newspapers): Quebecor Communications, Inc.

LE PORTAGEUR

Street address 1: 50, Chemin D'en-haut
Street address city: Natashquan
Province/Territory: QC
Postal code: G0G 2E0
Country: Canada
General Phone: (418) 726-3736
General Fax: (418) 726-3714
General/National Adv. E-mail: secom@quebectel.com
Published: Wed
Avg Free Circ: 490
Audit By: Sworn/Estimate/Non-Audited
Audit Date: 12.07.2019
Personnel: Cindy Carbonneau (Adv. Mgr.); Michel Richard (Ed.)

LE PROGRES DE COATICOOK

Street address 1: 72 Rue Child
Street address city: Coaticook
Province/Territory: QC
Postal code: J1A 2B1
Country: Canada
General Phone: (819) 849-9846
General Fax: (819) 849-1041
General/National Adv. E-mail: dany.jacques@tc.tc
Primary Website: www.leprogres.net
Published: Wed
Avg Paid Circ: 77
Avg Free Circ: 8782
Audit By: CCAB
Audit Date: 31.03.2014
Personnel: Monique Cote (Ed.)
Parent company (for newspapers): Reseau Select/ Select Network

LE PROGRES-ECHO

Street address 1: 217, Avenue LÃ£Â©onidas Sud, Bureau 6-d
Street address city: Rimouski
Province/Territory: QC
Postal code: G5L 2T5
Country: Canada
General Phone: (418) 721-1212
General/National Adv. E-mail: marc.pitre@quebecormedia.com
Primary Website: www.rimouskois.ca
Published: Sun
Avg Paid Circ: 4
Avg Free Circ: 29084
Audit By: CCAB
Audit Date: 31.03.2014
Personnel: Alain St. Amand (Pub.); Ernie Wells (Ed.)
Parent company (for newspapers): Quebecor Communications, Inc.

LE RADAR

Street address 1: 110 Chemin Gros Cap, CP 8183
Street address city: Cap-aux-Meules
Province/Territory: QC
Postal code: G4T 1R3
County: Cap-aux-Meules
Country: Canada
General Phone: (418) 986-234
General Fax: (418)986-6358
General/National Adv. E-mail: secretaire@leradar.qc.ca
Display Adv. E-mail: direction@leradar.qc.ca
Classified Adv. e-mail: direction@leradar.qc.ca
Editorial e-mail: redacteur@leradar.qc.ca
Primary Website: leradar.qc.ca
Published: Fri
Avg Paid Circ: 1512
Avg Free Circ: 1523
Audit By: AAM
Audit Date: 31.03.2019
Personnel: Hugo Miousse (Pub.); Achilles Hubert (Ed.); Lucille Tremblay (Adv. Mgr.); Francoise Decoste (Circ. Mgr.)
Parent company (for newspapers): Reseau Select/ Select Network

LE REFLET

Street address 1: 11 Rt. 132
Street address city: Delson
Province/Territory: QC
Postal code: J5B 1G9
Country: Canada
General Phone: (450) 635-9146
General Fax: (450) 635-4619
General/National Adv. E-mail: robert.fichaud@quebecormedia.com
Display Adv. E-mail: publicite@lereflet.qc.ca
Primary Website: www.lereflet.qc.ca
Published: Wed
Avg Free Circ: 49427
Audit By: CCAB
Audit Date: 31.03.2014
Personnel: Robert Fichaud (Pub./Dir.); Sandy Roy (Sales Dir.); Helene Gingras (Ed.)
Parent company (for newspapers): Les Hebdos Monteregiens-OOB

LE REGIONAL

Street address 1: 342 Beaugry N. St.
Street address city: Joliette
Province/Territory: QC
Postal code: J6E 6A6
Country: Canada
General Phone: (450) 759-3664

General Fax: (450) 759-9828
Primary Website: http://www.le-regional.ca/
Published: Wed
Avg Free Circ: 64096
Audit By: ODC
Audit Date: 13.12.2011
Personnel: Benoit Bazinet (Pub.)

LE REGIONAL DE HULL

Street address 1: 160, Boul. Hospital, Office 30
Street address city: Gatineau
Province/Territory: QC
Postal code: J8T 8J1
County: Canada
Country: Canada
General Phone: (819) 776-1063
General Fax: (819) 568-7544
General/National Adv. E-mail: boursiery@transcontinental.ca
Primary Website: www.info07.com
Published: Wed
Avg Free Circ: 11000
Audit By: Sworn/Estimate/Non-Audited
Audit Date: 12.07.2019
Personnel: Dino Roberges (Adv. Mgr.); Jacques Blais (Ed.)

LE REVEIL

Street address 1: 9085, Boul. Lacroix
Street address city: Saint-Georges
Province/Territory: QC
Postal code: G5Y 2B4
Country: Canada
General Phone: (418) 695-2601
General Fax: (418) 695-1391
General/National Adv. E-mail: lereveil@videotron.ca
Primary Website: lereveil.canoe.ca
Published: Tues
Avg Paid Circ: 0
Avg Free Circ: 73191
Audit By: CCAB
Audit Date: 30.09.2012
Personnel: Diane Audet (Pub.); Andre Rousseau (Prodn. Mgr.)
Parent company (for newspapers): Quebecor Communications, Inc.

LE RIMOUSKOIS

Street address 1: 217 Leonidas Ave, Po Box 3217, Branch A
Street address city: Rimouski
Province/Territory: QC
Postal code: G5L 9G6
Country: Canada
General Phone: (418) 721-1212
General Fax: (418) 723-1855
General/National Adv. E-mail: marc.pitre@quebecormedia.com
Primary Website: www.rimouskois.ca
Published: Wed
Avg Paid Circ: 4
Avg Free Circ: 29084
Audit By: CCAB
Audit Date: 31.03.2014
Personnel: Alain St. Amand (Pub.); Ernie Wells (Ed.)
Parent company (for newspapers): Quebecor Communications, Inc.

LE SAINT-LAURENT PORTAGE

Street address 1: 55-a, Rue De L'hotel De Ville
Street address city: Riviere-du-Loup
Province/Territory: QC
Postal code: G5R 1L4
Country: Canada
General Phone: (418) 862-1774
General Fax: (418) 862-4387
General/National Adv. E-mail: francis.desrosiers@quebecormedia.com
Primary Website: www.lesaintlaurentportage.ca
Published: Wed
Avg Paid Circ: 11
Avg Free Circ: 34286
Audit By: CCAB
Audit Date: 31.03.2014
Personnel: Gilles LeBel (Mng. Ed.); Pierre Levesque (Ed.)
Parent company (for newspapers): Quebecor Communications, Inc.

LE SOLEIL DE CHATEAUGUAY

Street address 1: 101 boulevard Saint-Jean-Baptiste
Street address 2: Suite 215
Street address city: Chateauguay
Province/Territory: QC
Postal code: J6J 3H9
Country: Canada
General Phone: (450) 692-8552
General/National Adv. E-mail: info@gravitemedia.com
Primary Website: www.monteregieweb.com
Published: Wed`Sat
Avg Paid Circ: 11
Avg Free Circ: 34473
Audit By: CCAB
Audit Date: 31.03.2019
Personnel: Julie Voyer (Pres.); Pierre Montreuil (Mktg. Strat. Mgr.); Michel Thibault (Content Mgr.); Valerie Lessard (Asst. Content Mgr.); Sophie Bayard (Sales Coor.)
Parent company (for newspapers): Les Hebdos Monteregiens-OOB

LE SOLEIL DU ST-LAURENT

Street address 1: 82 Salaberry St. S.
Street address city: Chateauguay
Province/Territory: QC
Postal code: J6J 4J6
Country: Canada
General Phone: (450) 692-8552
General Fax: (450) 692-3460
General/National Adv. E-mail: info@cybersoleil.com
Display Adv. E-mail: publicite@cybersoleil.com
Editorial e-mail: redaction@cybersoleil.com
Primary Website: www.cybersoleil.com
Published: Wed`Sat
Avg Free Circ: 32750
Audit By: Sworn/Estimate/Non-Audited
Audit Date: 12.07.2019
Personnel: Diane Cadieux (Adv. Rep.); Guylaine Mercier (Adv. Rep.); Yolaine Dorais (Adv. Rep.); Michel Thibault (Ed.); Carole Gagne (Ed.)
Parent company (for newspapers): Les Hebdos Monteregiens-OOB

LE SOLEIL DU ST-LAURENT

Street address 1: 20 Academy St.
Street address city: Salaberry-de-Valleyfield
Province/Territory: QC
Postal code: J6T 6M9
Country: Canada
General Phone: (450) 373-8555
General Fax: (450) 373-8666
General/National Adv. E-mail: info@lesoleil.qc.ca
Display Adv. E-mail: publicite@lesoleil.qc.ca
Editorial e-mail: redaction@lesoleil.qc.ca
Primary Website: www.lesoleil.qc.ca
Published: Sat
Avg Free Circ: 32750
Audit By: Sworn/Estimate/Non-Audited
Audit Date: 12.07.2019
Personnel: Andre Mooney (Dir.); Pierre Montreuil (Sales Dir.); Diane Mayer (Adv. Rep.); Serge Proulx (Adv. Rep.); Jean-Pierre Tessier (Adv. Rep.); Peter Rozon (Adv. Rep.); Mario Pitre (Ed.)
Parent company (for newspapers): Les Hebdos Monteregiens-OOB

LE TRAIT D'UNION

Street address 1: 231, Rue Sainte-marie
Street address city: Terrebonne
Province/Territory: QC
Postal code: J6W 3E4
Country: Canada
General Phone: (450) 964-4444
General Fax: (450) 471-1023
General/National Adv. E-mail: letraitdunion@transcontinental.ca
Classified Adv. e-mail: petitesannonces@larevue.qc.ca
Editorial e-mail: redaction@larevue.qc.ca
Primary Website: www.letraitdunion.com
Published: Wed
Avg Paid Circ: 10
Avg Free Circ: 49990
Audit By: ODC
Audit Date: 12.12.2017
Personnel: Gilles Bordonado (PrÃ©sident); VÃ©ronick Talbot (RÃ©dactrice en chef); Lise Bourdages (Coordonnatrice aux ventes)
Parent company (for newspapers): La Revue de Terrebonne

LE TRAIT D'UNION DU NORD

Street address 1: 850 Place Daviault
Street address city: Fermont
Province/Territory: QC
Postal code: G0G 1J0
Country: Canada
General Phone: (418) 287-3655
General Fax: (418) 287-3874
General/National Adv. E-mail: info.journaltdn@gmail.com
Display Adv. E-mail: publicite@journaltdn.ca
Classified Adv. e-mail: publicite@journaltdn.ca
Editorial e-mail: redaction@journaltdn.ca
Primary Website: www.journaltdn.ca
Published: Mon
Avg Free Circ: 1700
Audit By: Sworn/Estimate/Non-Audited
Audit Date: 12.07.2019
Personnel: Eric Cyr (Ed.); Lynda Raiche (Graphic & Adv. Consultant)

L'ECHO DE FRONTENAC

Street address 1: 5040 Blvd. Des Veterans
Street address city: Lac Megantic
Province/Territory: QC
Postal code: G6B 2G5
Country: Canada
General Phone: (819) 583-1630
General Fax: (819) 583-1124
General/National Adv. E-mail: hebdo@echodefrontenac.com
Primary Website: echodefrontenac.com
Published: Fri
Avg Paid Circ: 3904
Avg Free Circ: 3707
Audit By: CCAB
Audit Date: 31.12.2018
Personnel: Michel Pilotte (Sales Dir.); Gaetan Poulin (Ed.); Suzanne Poulin (Asst. Ed.); Remi Tremblay (Mng. Ed.)
Parent company (for newspapers): Reseau Select/Select Network

L'ECHO DE LA BAIE

Street address 1: 143 Boulevard Perron E
Street address city: New Richmond
Province/Territory: QC
Postal code: G0C 2B0
Country: Canada
General Phone: (418) 392-5083
General Fax: (418) 392-6605
General/National Adv. E-mail: bernard.johnson@quebecormedia.com
Editorial e-mail: redaction_latuque@tc.tc
Primary Website: lechodelabaie.canoe.ca
Published: Wed
Avg Paid Circ: 7
Avg Free Circ: 18364
Audit By: CCAB
Audit Date: 31.03.2014
Personnel: Bernard Johnson (Pub.)
Parent company (for newspapers): Quebecor Communications, Inc.

L'ECHO DE LA TUQUE

Street address 1: 324 St. Joseph St.
Street address city: La Tuque
Province/Territory: QC
Postal code: G9X 1L2
Country: Canada
General Phone: (819) 523-6141
General Fax: (819) 523-6143
General/National Adv. E-mail: redaction_latuque@tc.tc
Editorial e-mail: redaction_latuque@tc.tc
Primary Website: www.lechodelatuque.com
Published: Wed
Avg Paid Circ: 0
Avg Free Circ: 6406
Audit By: CCAB
Audit Date: 31.03.2014
Personnel: Michele Scarpeno (Dir.)
Parent company (for newspapers): Reseau Select/Select Network; Transcontinental Media

L'ECHO DE MASKINONGE

Street address 1: 43 Saint Louis
Street address city: Louiseville
Province/Territory: QC
Postal code: J5V 2C7
Country: Canada
General Phone: (819) 228-5532
General Fax: (819) 228-9379
General/National Adv. E-mail: redaction_em@transcontinental.ca
Primary Website: www.lechodemaskinonge.com
Published: Wed
Avg Paid Circ: 28
Avg Free Circ: 13907
Audit By: CCAB
Audit Date: 31.03.2014
Personnel: AndrÃƒÂƒ££££ Lamy (Dir.); Diane Beland (Sales Coord.)
Parent company (for newspapers): Transcontinental Media

L'ECHO DE SHAWINIGAN

Street address 1: 795 Blvd 5e Rue Local 101
Street address city: Shawinigan
Province/Territory: QC
Postal code: G9N 1G2
Country: Canada
General Phone: (819) 731-0327
General Fax: (819) 731-0328
Advertising Phone: (819) 731-0327
Editorial Phone: (819) 731-0327
General/National Adv. E-mail: jocelyn.ouellet@quebecormedia.com
Display Adv. E-mail: serge.buchanan@quebecormedia.com
Editorial e-mail: hugues.carpentier@quebecormedia.com
Primary Website: www.lechodeshawinigan.ca
Published: Wed
Avg Free Circ: 37369
Audit By: CCAB
Audit Date: 31.03.2014
Personnel: Hugues Carpentier (Ed.)

L'ECHO DE ST EUSTACHE

Street address 1: 204 Blvd Labelle Ste 208
Street address city: Sainte Therese
Province/Territory: QC
Postal code: J7E 2X7
Country: Canada
General Phone: (450) 818-7575
General Fax: (450) 818-7582
Advertising Phone: (450) 818-7575
Editorial Phone: (450) 818-7575
Published: Wed
Avg Free Circ: 57641
Audit By: CCAB
Audit Date: 31.03.2014

L'ECHO DE ST-JEAN-SUR-RICHELIEU

Street address 1: 81 Rue Richelieu Bureau 102 B
Street address city: Sainte Jean sur Richelieu
Province/Territory: QC
Postal code: J3B 6X2
Country: Canada
General Phone: (450) 376-4646
General Fax: (450) 376-4666
Advertising Phone: (450) 376-4646
Editorial Phone: (450) 376-4646
General/National Adv. E-mail: daniel.noiseux@quebecormedia.com
Display Adv. E-mail: henri-paul.raymond@quebecormedia.com
Editorial e-mail: daniel.noiseux@quebecormedia.com
Primary Website: www.lechodesaintjean.ca
Published: Wed
Avg Free Circ: 55426
Audit By: CCAB
Audit Date: 31.03.2014
Personnel: Daniel Noiseux (Ed.)

L'ECHO DE TROIS-RIVIERES

Street address 1: 3625 Blvd Du Chanoine-moreau

Street address city: Trois-Rivieres
Province/Territory: QC
Postal code: G8Y 5N6
Country: Canada
General Phone: (819) 371-4823
General Fax: (819) 371-4804
Advertising Phone: (819) 371-4823
Editorial Phone: (819) 371-4823
General/National Adv. E-mail: serge.buchanan@quebecormedia.com
Display Adv. E-mail: jocelyn.ouellet@quebecormedia.com
Editorial e-mail: serge.buchanan@quebecormedia.com
Primary Website: www.lechodetroisrivieres.ca
Published: Wed
Avg Free Circ: 68580
Audit By: CCAB
Audit Date: 31.03.2014
Personnel: Serge Buchanan (Ed.)

L'ECHO DE VICTORIAVILLE

Street address 1: 106 Blvd Bois-francs Nord
Street address city: Victoriaville
Province/Territory: QC
Postal code: G6P 1E7
Country: Canada
General Phone: (819) 604-6686
General Fax: (819) 604-6398
Advertising Phone: (819) 604-6686
Editorial Phone: (819) 604-6686
General/National Adv. E-mail: jean.crepeau@quebecormedia.com
Display Adv. E-mail: alain.saint-amand@quebecormedia.com
Editorial e-mail: jean.crepeau@quebecormedia.com
Primary Website: www.lechodevictoriaville.ca
Published: Wed
Avg Free Circ: 42844
Audit By: CCAB
Audit Date: 31.03.2014
Personnel: Jean Crepeau (Ed.)

L'ECHO DU NORD

Street address 1: 179 St. George St.
Street address city: Saint Jerome
Province/Territory: QC
Postal code: J7Z 4Z8
Country: Canada
General Phone: (450) 436-5381
General Fax: (450) 436-5904
General/National Adv. E-mail: atelier.echo@hebdosquebecor.com; redaction.echo@hebdosquebecor.com
Primary Website: http://echosdunord.com/
Published: Wed
Avg Paid Circ: 391
Avg Free Circ: 53385
Audit By: CCAB
Audit Date: 31.03.2014
Personnel: Andre Guillemette (Ed.); Jean-Paul Sauriol (Prodn. Mgr.)
Parent company (for newspapers): Quebecor Communications, Inc.

L'ECLAIREUR-PROGRES/BEAUCE NOUVELLES

Street address 1: 12625 1st Ave. E.
Street address city: Saint Georges
Province/Territory: QC
Postal code: G5Y 2E4
Country: Canada
General Phone: (418) 228-8858
General Fax: (418) 228-0268
Primary Website: leclaireurprogres.canoe.ca
Published: Wed
Avg Paid Circ: 13
Avg Free Circ: 38115
Audit By: CCAB
Audit Date: 31.03.2014
Personnel: Gilbert Bernier (Gen. Mgr.)
Parent company (for newspapers): Quebecor Communications, Inc.

LES 2 RIVES

Street address 1: 77 George St.
Street address city: Sorel-Tracy
Province/Territory: QC
Postal code: J3P 1C2
Country: Canada
General Phone: (450) 742-9408
General Fax: (450) 742-2493
General/National Adv. E-mail: pco2rives@biz.videotran.ca; info@les2rives.com
Primary Website: www.les2rives.com
Published: Tues
Avg Paid Circ: 1
Avg Free Circ: 29562
Audit By: CCAB
Audit Date: 31.03.2014
Personnel: Marcel Rainville (Gen. Mgr.); Louise Gregoire Racicot (Ed.)
Parent company (for newspapers): Les Hebdos Monteregiens-OOB

LES ACTUALITES

Street address 1: 572 1st Ave.
Street address city: Asbestos
Province/Territory: QC
Postal code: J1T 4R4
Country: Canada
General Phone: (819) 879-6681
General Fax: (819) 879-2355
General/National Adv. E-mail: carole.pellerin@quebecormedia.com
Editorial e-mail: nathalie.hurdle@quebecormedia.com
Primary Website: journallesactualites.ca
Published: Wed
Avg Paid Circ: 4
Avg Free Circ: 13160
Audit By: CCAB
Audit Date: 31.03.2014
Personnel: Carole Pellerin (ÃƒÂ©ditrice)
Parent company (for newspapers): Reseau Select/Select Network; Quebecor Communications, Inc.

LES HEBDOS MONTEREGIENS

Street address 1: 66 Chateauguay St.
Street address city: Huntingdon
Province/Territory: QC
Postal code: J0S 1H0
Country: Canada
General Phone: (450) 264-5364
General Fax: (450) 264-9521
General/National Adv. E-mail: info@gleaner-source.com; direction@gleaner-source.com
Display Adv. E-mail: petitesannonces@gleaner-source.com; pub@gleaner-source.com
Editorial e-mail: redaction@gleaner-source.com
Primary Website: www.monteregieweb.com
Published: Wed
Avg Paid Circ: 5000
Avg Free Circ: 91
Audit By: Sworn/Estimate/Non-Audited
Audit Date: 12.07.2019
Personnel: Andre Castagnier (Gen. Mgr.); Susanne J. Brown (Ed.)
Parent company (for newspapers): Hebdos Quebec

L'ETOILE DU LAC

Street address 1: 797 Blvd. Saint Joseph, Ste. 101
Street address 2: Bureau 101
Street address city: Roberval
Province/Territory: QC
Postal code: G8H 2L4
Country: Canada
General Phone: (418) 275-2911
General Fax: (418) 275-2834
General/National Adv. E-mail: redaccion_roberval@transcontinental.ca
Primary Website: www.letoiledulac.com
Published: Wed
Avg Paid Circ: 95
Avg Free Circ: 14602
Audit By: CCAB
Audit Date: 31.03.2014
Personnel: Michel Dupont (Regional Publisher); Daniel Migneault (Ed. in Chief); Claudia Turcotte (Sales manager); Michel Aub (Publisher)
Parent company (for newspapers): Transcontinental Media

L'EXPRESS

Street address 1: 1050 Cormier St.
Street address city: Drummondville
Province/Territory: QC
Postal code: J2C 2N6
Country: Canada
General Phone: (819) 478-8171
General Fax: (819) 478-4306
General/National Adv. E-mail: redaction_dr@tc.tc
Primary Website: www.journalexpress.ca
Published: Wed`Sun
Avg Paid Circ: 11
Avg Free Circ: 48116
Audit By: CCAB
Audit Date: 31.03.2014
Personnel: Johanne Marceau (Ed.)
Parent company (for newspapers): Transcontinental Media

L'HEBDO DE LAVAL

Street address 1: 3221 Hwy. 440 W., Ste. 209
Street address city: Laval
Province/Territory: QC
Postal code: H7P 5P2
Country: Canada
General Phone: (450) 681-4948
General Fax: (450) 681-2824
Published: Fri
Avg Free Circ: 84860
Audit By: Sworn/Estimate/Non-Audited
Audit Date: 12.07.2019
Personnel: Marc Ouellette (Gen. Mgr.); Francois Forget (Mng. Ed.)

L'HEBDO JOURNAL

Street address 1: 525 Barkoff St., Ste. 205
Street address 2: Bureau 205
Street address city: Trois-Rivieres
Province/Territory: QC
Postal code: G8T 2A5
Country: Canada
General Phone: (819) 379-1490
General Fax: (819) 379-0705
Advertising Phone: (866) 637-5236
Display Adv. E-mail: publicite.hj@transcontinental.ca
Editorial e-mail: redaction.hj@transcontinental.ca
Primary Website: www.lhebdojournal.com
Published: Wed
Avg Paid Circ: 30
Avg Free Circ: 60411
Audit By: CCAB
Audit Date: 31.03.2014
Personnel: Alain Bernard (Sales Mgr.); Sylviane Lussier (Pub.); Emilie Valley (Ed.)
Parent company (for newspapers): Transcontinental Media

L'HEBDO MEKINAC/DES CHENAUX

Street address 1: Cp 490
Street address city: Shawinigan
Province/Territory: QC
Postal code: G9N 6T8
Country: Canada
General Phone: (819) 537-5111
General Fax: (819) 537-5471
General/National Adv. E-mail: redaction_shawinigan@transcontinental.ca
Primary Website: www.lhebdomekinacdeschenaux.com
Published: Wed
Avg Paid Circ: 13540
Avg Free Circ: 0
Audit By: Sworn/Estimate/Non-Audited
Audit Date: 12.07.2019
Personnel: Michel Matteau (Pub.); Bernard Lepage (Dir., Information); Gilles Guay (Ed.)
Parent company (for newspapers): Transcontinental Media

L'INFORMATION

Street address 1: 55-a Rue De L'hotel De Ville
Street address city: Riviere-du-Loup
Province/Territory: QC
Postal code: G5R 1L4
County: Canada
Country: Canada
General Phone: (418) 775-4381
General Fax: (418) 862-4387
General/National Adv. E-mail: journalinformation@globetrotter.net; nsomontjoli@dosquadecoi.com
Primary Website: www.linformation.ca
Published: Wed
Avg Paid Circ: 30
Avg Free Circ: 9311
Audit By: BPA
Audit Date: 01.03.2012
Personnel: Francis Desrosiers (Ed.)
Parent company (for newspapers): Quebecor Communications, Inc.

L'INFORMATION

Street address 1: 566 Jules Choquet St., Local 2
Street address city: Sainte Julie
Province/Territory: QC
Postal code: J3E 1W6
Country: Canada
General Phone: (450) 649-0719
General Fax: (450) 649-7748
Display Adv. E-mail: l.bourdua@ infodeste-julie.qc.ca; nl.beausejour@ infodeste-julie.qc.ca
Editorial e-mail: redaction@infodeste-julie.qc.ca
Primary Website: www.monsaintejulie.ca
Published: Wed
Avg Paid Circ: 1
Avg Free Circ: 20563
Audit By: CCAB
Audit Date: 31.03.2014
Personnel: Serge Landry (Ed.); Ariane Desrochers (Ed.)

L'OEIL REGIONAL

Street address 1: 393 Laurier Blvd.
Street address city: Beloeil
Province/Territory: QC
Postal code: J3G 4H6
Country: Canada
General Phone: (450) 467-1821
General Fax: (450) 467-3087
General/National Adv. E-mail: redaction@oeilregional.com
Display Adv. E-mail: publicite@oeilregional.com
Editorial e-mail: redaction@oeilregional.com
Primary Website: www.oeilregional.com
Published: Sat
Avg Paid Circ: 8
Avg Free Circ: 34637
Audit By: CCAB
Audit Date: 31.03.2014
Personnel: Serge Landry
Parent company (for newspapers): Reseau Select/Select Network; Les Hebdos Monteregiens-OOB

L'OIE BLANCHE

Street address 1: 70 Rue De L'anse
Street address city: Montmagny
Province/Territory: QC
Postal code: G5V 1G8
Country: Canada
General Phone: (418) 248-8820
General Fax: (418) 248-4033
General/National Adv. E-mail: oieblanc@globetrotter.net
Primary Website: www.oieblanc.com
Published: Wed
Avg Paid Circ: 17
Avg Free Circ: 22533
Audit By: CCAB
Audit Date: 30.09.2015
Personnel: Yannick Patelli (Pub.)
Parent company (for newspapers): Reseau Select/Select Network

MAGAZINE DE L'ILE-DES-SOEURS

Street address 1: 455 Boulevard Fenelon
Street address city: Dorval
Province/Territory: QC
Postal code: H9S 5T8
Country: Canada
General Phone: (514) 636-7314
Published: Wed
Avg Paid Circ: 2
Avg Free Circ: 8226
Audit By: CCAB
Audit Date: 31.03.2014
Personnel: Patricia Ann Beaulieu

MAGAZINE DE SAINT LAMBERT

Street address 1: St Charles Ouest
Street address city: Longueuil
Province/Territory: QC
Postal code: J4H 1E3
Country: Canada
Published: Wed

Avg Paid Circ: 0
Avg Free Circ: 14164
Audit By: CCAB
Audit Date: 30.09.2012
Personnel: Lucie Masse (Gen. Mgr.)

MANIC

Street address 1: Rue De Bretagne
Street address city: Baie Comeau
Province/Territory: QC
Postal code: G5C 1X5
Country: Canada
General Phone: (418) 589-9990
Published: Wed
Avg Paid Circ: 4
Avg Free Circ: 14765
Audit By: CCAB
Audit Date: 30.09.2012
Personnel: Paul Brisson

MESSAGER DE LACHINE / DORVAL

Street address 1: 455 Boulevard Fenelon, Suite 303
Street address city: Dorval
Province/Territory: QC
Postal code: H9S 5T8
Country: Canada
General Phone: (514) 636-7314
General Fax: (514) 636-7315
General/National Adv. E-mail: redaction_lachine-dorval@tc.tc
Primary Website: http://www.messagerlachine.com
Published: Thur
Avg Paid Circ: 0
Avg Free Circ: 24993
Audit By: CCAB
Audit Date: 31.03.2014
Personnel: Patria Ann Beaulieu

MESSAGER DE LASALLE

Street address 1: 420 Lafleur Ave
Street address 2: Suite 303
Street address city: Lasalle
Province/Territory: QC
Postal code: H9S 5T8
Country: Canada
General Phone: (514) 636-7314
Published: Thur
Avg Paid Circ: 3
Avg Free Circ: 32736
Audit By: CCAB
Audit Date: 31.03.2014
Personnel: Patricia Ann Beaulieu

MESSAGER DE VERDUN

Street address 1: 455 Fenelon Suite 303
Street address 2: 303
Street address city: Dorval
Province/Territory: QC
Postal code: H9S 5T8
Country: Canada
General Phone: (514) 636-7314
General Fax: (514) 636-7317
General/National Adv. E-mail: redaction_verdun@tc.tc
Primary Website: www.messagerverdun.com
Published: Thur
Avg Paid Circ: 0
Avg Free Circ: 23936
Audit By: CCAB
Audit Date: 30.09.2012
Personnel: Patricia Ann Beaulieu

MISSIONS ETRANGERES

Street address 1: Place Juge-desnoyers
Street address city: Laval
Province/Territory: QC
Postal code: H7G 1A5
Country: Canada
General Phone: (450) 667-4190
Published: Wed
Avg Paid Circ: 6585
Avg Free Circ: 5647
Audit By: ODC
Audit Date: 14.12.2011
Personnel: Bertrand Roy

NIC

Street address 1: Route 138 Ste 100
Street address 2: Suite 100
Street address city: Saint Augustin de Desmaures
Province/Territory: QC
Postal code: G3A 2C6
Country: Canada
General Phone: (418) 908-3438
Published: Wed
Avg Paid Circ: 2863
Avg Free Circ: 268
Audit By: ODC
Audit Date: 14.12.2011
Personnel: Sophie Bouchard

NORD COTIER

Street address 1: Boulevard Laure
Street address city: Sept-Iles
Province/Territory: QC
Postal code: G4R 1Y2
Country: Canada
General Phone: (418) 960-2090
Published: Wed
Avg Paid Circ: 23
Avg Free Circ: 19095
Audit By: CCAB
Audit Date: 30.09.2012
Personnel: Gino Levesque

NORDEST PLUS

Street address 1: 365 Boul. Laure
Street address city: Sept-Iles
Province/Territory: QC
Postal code: G4R 1X2
Country: Canada
General Phone: (418) 962-4100
General Fax: (418) 962-0439
General/National Adv. E-mail: nordest@hebdosquebecor.com
Display Adv. E-mail: atelier.septiles@hebdosquebecor.com
Editorial e-mail: redaction.septiles @ hebdosquebecor.com
Primary Website: www.hebdosquebecor.com
Published: Wed
Avg Free Circ: 13999
Audit By: Sworn/Estimate/Non-Audited
Audit Date: 12.07.2019
Personnel: Isabelle Chiasson (Dir.); Mario Thibeault (Mng. Ed.)

NOUVELLE DE SHERBROOKE

Street address 1: Rue Roy
Street address city: Sherbrooke
Province/Territory: QC
Postal code: J1K 2X8
Country: Canada
General Phone: (819) 566-8022
Published: Sun
Avg Free Circ: 51200
Audit By: ODC
Audit Date: 14.12.2011
Personnel: Andre Custeau

NOUVELLE UNION

Street address 1: Rue Notre-dame Est
Street address city: Victoriaville
Province/Territory: QC
Postal code: G6P 3Z4
Country: Canada
General Phone: (819) 758-6211
Published: Wed`Fri
Avg Paid Circ: 13
Avg Free Circ: 38872
Audit By: CCAB
Audit Date: 31.03.2014
Personnel: Lucie Lecours

NOUVELLES HOCHELAGA MAISONNEUVE

Street address 1: Boulevard Langelier Bureau 210
Street address 2: Bureau 210
Street address city: Montreal
Province/Territory: QC
Postal code: H1P 3C6
Country: Canada
General Phone: (514) 899-5888
General/National Adv. E-mail: redactioncentre@tc.tc
Primary Website: www.nouvelleshochelagamaisonneuve.com
Published: Tues
Avg Free Circ: 22615
Audit By: CCAB
Audit Date: 31.03.2014
Personnel: Stephane Desjardins

NOUVELLES PARC EXTENSION NEWS

Street address 1: 3860 Notre-dame Blvd.
Street address 2: Suite 304
Street address city: Laval
Province/Territory: QC
Postal code: H7V 1S1
Country: Canada
General Phone: (450) 978-9999
General Fax: (450) 687-6330
Display Adv. E-mail: sales@the-news.ca
Editorial e-mail: editor@the-news.ca
Primary Website: www.px-news.com
Published: Fri
Avg Paid Circ: 0
Avg Free Circ: 9403
Audit By: Sworn/Estimate/Non-Audited
Audit Date: 12.07.2019
Personnel: George S. Guzmas (Co-Publisher); George Bakoyannis (Prodn. Mgr.)

OBJECTIF PLEIN JOUR

Street address 1: 625 Bvd., Lafleche, Ste. 309
Street address city: Baie Comeau
Province/Territory: QC
Postal code: G5C 1C5
Country: Canada
General Phone: (418) 589-5900
General Fax: (418) 589-8216
General/National Adv. E-mail: sebastien.rouillard@quebecormedia.com
Primary Website: www.pleinjourdebaiecomeau.ca
Published: Wed
Avg Free Circ: 16435
Audit By: Sworn/Estimate/Non-Audited
Audit Date: 12.07.2019
Personnel: Sebastien Rouillard
Parent company (for newspapers): Quebecor Communications, Inc.

ORATOIRE

Street address 1: Chemin Queen Mary
Street address city: Montreal
Province/Territory: QC
Postal code: H3V 1H6
Country: Canada
General Phone: (514) 733-8211
Published: Sat
Avg Paid Circ: 25131
Avg Free Circ: 4346
Audit By: ODC
Audit Date: 14.12.2011
Personnel: Claude Grou

PEUPLE DE LOTBINIERE

Street address 1: 5790, Boul. Etienne-dallaire, Suite 103 B
Street address city: Levis
Province/Territory: QC
Postal code: G6V 8V6
County: Canada
Country: Canada
General Phone: (418) 728-2131
General Fax: (418) 728-4819
General/National Adv. E-mail: peuple.lotbiniere@hebdosquebecor.com
Display Adv. E-mail: ventes.lotbiniere@hebdosquebecor.com
Editorial e-mail: redaction.lotbiniere@hebdosquebecor.com
Primary Website: www.lepeuplelotbiniere.canoe.ca
Published: Wed
Avg Paid Circ: 1
Avg Free Circ: 15029
Audit By: CCAB
Audit Date: 31.03.2014
Personnel: Lise Racette (Adv. Rep.); Paul Lessard
Parent company (for newspapers): Quebecor Communications, Inc.

PLATEAU

Street address 1: 8770 Langelier Boulevard Bureau 210
Street address city: Montreal
Province/Territory: QC
Postal code: H1P 3C6
Country: Canada
General Phone: (514) 899-5888
General Fax: (514) 899-5001
General/National Adv. E-mail: redactioncentre@tc.tc
Primary Website: www.leplateau.com
Published: Thur
Avg Free Circ: 34869
Audit By: CCAB
Audit Date: 31.03.2014
Personnel: Stephane Desjardins

PLEIN JOUR DE BAIE COMEAU

Street address 1: 625 Bvd., Lafleche, Ste. 309
Street address city: Baie Comeau
Province/Territory: QC
Postal code: G5C 1C5
Country: Canada
General Phone: (418) 589-5900
General/National Adv. E-mail: sebastien.rouillard@quebecormedia.com
Published: Wed
Avg Paid Circ: 4
Avg Free Circ: 20578
Audit By: CCAB
Audit Date: 31.03.2014
Personnel: Sebastien Rouillard

PLEIN JOUR DE CHARLEVOIX

Street address 1: 249 Rue John Nairne
Street address city: La Malbaie
Province/Territory: QC
Postal code: G5B 1M4
Country: Canada
General Phone: (418) 665-6121
General Fax: (418) 665-3105
General/National Adv. E-mail: redaction.pjc@hebdosquebecor.com
Published: Fri
Avg Free Circ: 15438
Audit By: Sworn/Estimate/Non-Audited
Audit Date: 12.07.2019
Personnel: Richard Harley (Mng. Ed.)
Parent company (for newspapers): Quebecor Communications, Inc.

PLEIN JOUR SUR MANICOUAGAN

Street address 1: 625 Bvd., Lafleche, Ste. 309
Street address city: Baie Comeau
Province/Territory: QC
Postal code: G5C 1C5
Country: Canada
General Phone: (418) 589-5900
General Fax: (418) 589-8216
General/National Adv. E-mail: sebastien.rouillard@quebecormedia.com
Display Adv. E-mail: atelier.baiecomeau@hebdosquebecor.com
Editorial e-mail: raphael.hovington@hebdosquebecor.com
Primary Website: www.pleinjourdebaiecomeau.ca
Published: Wed
Avg Paid Circ: 7
Avg Free Circ: 15628
Audit By: BPA
Audit Date: 01.03.2012
Personnel: Sebastien Rouillard
Parent company (for newspapers): Quebecor Communications, Inc.

POINT DE VUE LAURENTIDES

Street address 1: 580 Rue De Saint Jovite Ste 201
Street address city: Mont-Tremblant
Province/Territory: QC
Postal code: J8E 2Z9
Country: Canada
General Phone: (819) 425-7666
General Fax: (819) 425-9111
Advertising Phone: (819) 425-7666

Editorial Phone: (819) 425-7666
General/National Adv. E-mail: infolaurentides@transcontinental.ca
Display Adv. E-mail: infolaurentides@transcontinental.ca
Editorial e-mail: infolaurentides@transcontinental.ca
Primary Website: www.pointdevuemonttremblant.com
Published: Wed
Avg Free Circ: 31760
Audit By: CCAB
Audit Date: 31.03.2014

PROGRES DE BELLECHASSE

Street address 1: 98e Rue
Street address city: Saint Georges
Province/Territory: QC
Postal code: G5Y 8G1
Country: Canada
General Phone: (418) 228-8858
Published: Wed
Avg Paid Circ: 0
Avg Free Circ: 19789
Audit By: CCAB
Audit Date: 30.09.2012
Personnel: Gilbert Bernier

PROGRES SAINT-LEONARD

Street address 1: 8770 Langelier Blvd. Ste. 210
Street address 2: Bureau 210
Street address city: Saint Leonard
Province/Territory: QC
Postal code: H1P 3C6
Country: Canada
General Phone: (514) 899-5888
General Fax: (514) 899-5001
General/National Adv. E-mail: redaction_est@tc.tc
Primary Website: www.progresstleonard.com
Published: Wed
Avg Free Circ: 31355
Audit By: Sworn/Estimate/Non-Audited
Audit Date: 12.07.2019
Personnel: Yannick Pinel; Lucy Lecoures (Ed.)
Parent company (for newspapers): Transcontinental Media

PROGRES VILLERAY/ PARC EXTENSION

Street address 1: Jules-poitras
Street address city: Saint Laurent
Province/Territory: QC
Postal code: H4N 1X7
Country: Canada
General Phone: (514) 270-8088
Published: Tues
Avg Free Circ: 20276
Audit By: CCAB
Audit Date: 31.03.2014
Personnel: Jean Aube

PUBLIQUIP

Street address 1: Rue Gilles Villeneuve
Street address city: Berthierville
Province/Territory: QC
Postal code: J0K 1A0
Country: Canada
General Phone: (450) 836-3666
Published: Sun
Avg Paid Circ: 701
Avg Free Circ: 50494
Audit By: ODC
Audit Date: 14.12.2011
Personnel: Francoise Trepanier

QUEBEC CHRONICLE-TELEGRAPH

Street address 1: 1040 Belvedere, Suite 218
Street address city: Quebec
Province/Territory: QC
Postal code: G1S 3G3
Country: Canada
General Phone: (418) 650-1764
General Fax: (418) 650-5172
General/National Adv. E-mail: info@qctonline.com;
Display Adv. E-mail: production@qctonline.com
Editorial e-mail: editor@qctonline.com
Primary Website: www.qctonline.com
Published: Wed
Avg Paid Circ: 907
Avg Free Circ: 24
Audit By: CMCA
Audit Date: 30.09.2015
Personnel: Wendy Little (Circulation Manager); Stacie Stanton (Editor and Publisher)

QUEBEC EXPRESS

Street address 1: 710 Bouvier, Suite 107
Street address 2: Bureau 900
Street address city: Quebec
Province/Territory: QC
Postal code: G2J 1C2
Country: Canada
General Phone: (418) 628-7460
General Fax: (418) 622-1511
General/National Adv. E-mail: redaction_quebec@tc.tc
Published: Fri
Avg Paid Circ: 7
Avg Free Circ: 28899
Audit By: CCAB
Audit Date: 31.03.2014
Personnel: Lilianne Laprise (Pub./Ed.)

REFLET DU LAC

Street address 1: 53 Rue Centre
Street address 2: Bureau 300
Street address city: Magog
Province/Territory: QC
Postal code: J1X 5B6
Country: Canada
General Phone: (819) 843-3500
General Fax: (819) 843-3085
General/National Adv. E-mail: dany.jacques@tc.tc
Published: Wed
Avg Paid Circ: 0
Avg Free Circ: 24662
Audit By: CCAB
Audit Date: 30.09.2012
Personnel: Monique Cote (CEO)

REVUE DE LA MACHINERIE AGRICOLE

Street address 1: 468 Boul. Roland-therrien
Street address city: Longueuil
Province/Territory: QC
Postal code: J4H 4E3
Country: Canada
General Phone: (450) 677-2556
General Fax: (450) 677-4099
General/National Adv. E-mail: info@marevueagricole.com
Primary Website: www.marevueagricole.com
Published: Tues
Avg Paid Circ: 1300
Avg Free Circ: 33200
Audit By: ODC
Audit Date: 14.12.2011
Personnel: Martyne Simard

SAINT-LAURENT NEWS

Street address 1: 1500 Blvd. Jules Poitras
Street address city: Saint Laurent
Province/Territory: QC
Postal code: H4N 1X7
Country: Canada
General Phone: (514) 855-1292
General Fax: (514) 855-1855
General/National Adv. E-mail: hebdo.redaction@transcontinental.ca
Display Adv. E-mail: petitesannonces@journalmetro.com
Classified Adv. e-mail: petitesannonces@journalmetro.com
Primary Website: www.nouvellessaint-laurent.com
Published: Sun
Avg Free Circ: 29317
Audit By: Sworn/Estimate/Non-Audited
Audit Date: 12.07.2019
Personnel: Yannick Pinel (Ed.)
Parent company (for newspapers): Transcontinental Media

SEA-COAST PUBLICATIONS INC./ THE GASPE SPEC

Street address 1: 128 Gerard D. Levesque
Street address city: New Carlisle
Province/Territory: QC
Postal code: G0C 1Z0
Country: Canada
General Phone: (418) 752-5400
General Fax: (418) 752-6932
Editorial Phone: (418)752-5070
General/National Adv. E-mail: specs@globetrotter.net
Primary Website: www.gaspespec.com
Published: Wed
Avg Paid Circ: 2309
Audit By: CMCA
Audit Date: 31.12.2015
Personnel: Sharon Renouf-Farrell (Pub.); Joan Sawyer Imhoff (Gen. Mgr.); Robert Bradbury (Adv. Mgr.); Gilles Gagne (News Ed.)

SOLEIL DE VALLEYFIELD

Street address 1: 20 Rue De L'academie
Street address city: Salaberry-de-Valleyfield
Province/Territory: QC
Postal code: J6T 2H8
Country: Canada
General Phone: (450) 373-8555
Advertising Phone: (450) 373-8555
Editorial Phone: (450) 373-8555
General/National Adv. E-mail: diane.dumont@quebecormedia.com
Editorial e-mail: diane.dumont@quebecormedia.com
Primary Website: http://www.journalsaint-francois.ca
Published: Sat
Avg Paid Circ: 23
Avg Free Circ: 35953
Audit By: CCAB
Audit Date: 31.03.2014
Personnel: Andre Mooney (Pub.)

SOLEIL DU SAMEDI

Street address 1: Rue Salaberry Sud
Street address city: Chateauguay
Province/Territory: QC
Postal code: J6J 4J6
Country: Canada
General Phone: (450) 692-8552
Published: Sat
Avg Paid Circ: 34
Avg Free Circ: 31092
Audit By: CCAB
Audit Date: 30.09.2012
Personnel: Jeanne-d'Arc Germain

SOREL-TRACY EXPRESS

Street address 1: 100 Rue Plante
Street address city: Sorel-Tracy
Province/Territory: QC
Postal code: J3P 7P5
Country: Canada
General Phone: (450) 746-0886
General Fax: (450) 746-0801
Advertising Phone: (450) 746-0886
Editorial Phone: (450) 746-0886
General/National Adv. E-mail: sorel-tracyexpress@tc.tc
Display Adv. E-mail: sorel-tracyexpress@tc.tc
Editorial e-mail: sorel-tracyexpress@tc.tc
Primary Website: www.sorel-tracyexpress.ca
Published: Tues
Avg Free Circ: 31018
Audit By: CCAB
Audit Date: 31.03.2014
Personnel: Claude Poulin (Pres.)

THE CHRONICLE

Street address 1: 455 Boulevard Fenelon
Street address 2: Suite 303
Street address city: Dorval
Province/Territory: QC
Postal code: H9S 5T8
Country: Canada
General Phone: (514) 636-7314
General Fax: (514) 636-7317
General/National Adv. E-mail: info.chronicle@tc.tc
Primary Website: www.westislandchronicle.com
Published: Wed
Avg Paid Circ: 5
Avg Free Circ: 43393
Audit By: CMCA
Audit Date: 31.08.2013
Personnel: Denis Therrien (General Manager); Joy-Ann Dempsey (Sales Support Supervisor); Robert Bourcier (Production Manager); Jean Nicolas AubÃ© (News Director)
Parent company (for newspapers): Transcontinental Media

THE EASTERN DOOR

Street address 1: P.o. Box 1170
Street address city: Kahnawake
Province/Territory: QC
Postal code: J0L 1B0
Country: Canada
General Phone: (450) 635-3050
General Fax: (450) 635-8479
General/National Adv. E-mail: reception@easterndoor.com
Primary Website: www.easterndoor.com
Published: Fri
Avg Paid Circ: 1020
Avg Free Circ: 81
Audit By: CMCA
Audit Date: 30.06.2016
Personnel: Steve Bonspiel (Ed./Pub.)

THE EQUITY

Street address 1: 133 Center St.
Street address city: Shawville
Province/Territory: QC
Postal code: J0X 2Y0
Country: Canada
General Phone: (819) 647-2204
General Fax: (819) 647-2206
General/National Adv. E-mail: prepress@theequity.ca
Display Adv. E-mail: bonnie@theequity.ca
Classified Adv. e-mail: news@theequity.ca
Editorial e-mail: news@theequity.ca
Primary Website: www.theequity.ca
Published: Wed
Avg Paid Circ: 2429
Audit By: CMCA
Audit Date: 6/31/2022
Personnel: Charles Dickson (Publisher)
Parent company (for newspapers): Pontiac Printshop Inc.

THE LAVAL NEWS

Street address 1: 3860 Notre-dame Blvd.
Street address 2: Suite 304
Street address city: Laval
Province/Territory: QC
Postal code: H7V 1S1
Country: Canada
General Phone: (450) 978-9999
General Fax: (450) 687-6330
General/National Adv. E-mail: editor@the-news.ca
Display Adv. E-mail: sales@the-news.ca
Editorial e-mail: editor@the-news.ca
Primary Website: www.lavalnews.ca
Published: Sat
Avg Free Circ: 27982
Audit By: CMCA
Audit Date: 30.06.2016
Personnel: George S. Guzmas (Co-Publisher); George Bakoyannis (Prodn. Mgr.)
Parent company (for newspapers): Newsfirst Multi-Media

THE LOW DOWN TO HULL AND BACK NEWS

Street address 1: 815 Riverside Drive
Street address city: Wakefield
Province/Territory: QC
Postal code: J0X 3G0
County: La PÃªche, Quebec
Country: Canada
General Phone: (819) 459-2222
General Fax: (819) 459-3831
Advertising Phone: (613) 241-6767
Editorial Phone: (819) 459-2222
General/National Adv. E-mail: general@lowdownonline.com
Display Adv. E-mail: lowdowndavid1@gmail.com
Classified Adv. e-mail: classifieds@lowdownonline.com
Editorial e-mail: general@lowdownonline.com
Primary Website: www.lowdownonline.com
Published: Wed

Avg Paid Circ: 2531
Audit By: Sworn/Estimate/Non-Audited
Audit Date: 12.07.2019
Personnel: Maya Riel Lachapelle (General Manager); Heather Hopewell (Admin. Asst.); Nikki Mantell (Pub./Owner); Agnes McMillan (Circ. Mgr.); Melanie Scott (Ed.); Hunter Cresswell (Reporter); Nicole McCormick (Reporter)

THE MONITOR

Street address 1: 345 Victoria, Ste. 508
Street address city: West Mill
Province/Territory: QC
Postal code: H3Z 2M6
Country: Canada
General Phone: (514) 484-5610
General Fax: (514) 484-6028
General/National Adv. E-mail: toula.foscolos@transcontinental.ca
Primary Website: www.themonitor.ca
Published: Thur
Avg Free Circ: 35164
Audit By: Sworn/Estimate/Non-Audited
Audit Date: 12.07.2019
Personnel: Yannick Pinel (Ed.); Toula Foscolos (Ed. in Chief)

THE NORTH SHORE NEWS

Street address 1: 3860 Notre-dame Blvd.
Street address 2: Suite 304
Street address city: Laval
Province/Territory: QC
Postal code: H7V 1S1
Country: Canada
General Phone: (450) 978-9999
General Fax: (450) 678-6330
General/National Adv. E-mail: info@newsfirst.ca
Display Adv. E-mail: gg@newsfirst.ca
Editorial e-mail: editor@newsfirst.ca
Primary Website: www.ns-news.com
Published: Sat
Avg Paid Circ: 0
Avg Free Circ: 16353
Audit By: CMCA
Audit Date: 31.01.2017
Personnel: George Guzmas (Co-Pub)
Parent company (for newspapers): Newsfirst Multimedia

THE STANSTEAD JOURNAL

Street address 1: 620 Dufferin
Street address city: Stanstead
Province/Territory: QC
Postal code: J0B 3E0
County: Memphremagog
Country: Canada
General Phone: (819) 876-7514
General/National Adv. E-mail: journal@stanstead-journal.com
Display Adv. E-mail: ads@stanstead-journal.com
Editorial e-mail: communique@stanstead-journal.com
Primary Website: www.stanstead-journal.com
Published: Wed
Avg Paid Circ: 1625
Audit By: AAM
Audit Date: 31.03.2015
Personnel: Jean-Yves Durocher (Sales Mgr.); Mylene Piche (Prodn. Mgr.)
Parent company (for newspapers): Stanstead Journal Publishing

THE SUBURBAN EAST END EDITION

Street address 1: 7575 Trans Canada Highway, Suite 105
Street address city: Saint Laurent
Province/Territory: QC
Postal code: H4T 1V6
Country: Canada
General Phone: (514) 484-1107
General Fax: (514) 484-9616
General/National Adv. E-mail: suburban@thesuburban.com
Display Adv. E-mail: amanda@thesuburban.com
Editorial e-mail: editor@thesuburban.com
Primary Website: www.thesuburban.com
Published: Thur
Avg Free Circ: 26746
Audit By: CMCA
Audit Date: 31.12.2013
Personnel: Beryl Wajsman

THE SUBURBAN WEST ISLAND

Street address 1: 7575 Trans Canada Hwy, Suite 105
Street address city: Montreal
Province/Territory: QC
Postal code: H4T 1V6
General Phone: (514) 484-1107
General Fax: (514) 484-9616
General/National Adv. E-mail: suburban@thesuburban.com
Display Adv. E-mail: amanda@thesuburban.com
Editorial e-mail: editor@thesuburban.com
Primary Website: www.westislandgazette.com
Published: Wed
Avg Free Circ: 40239
Audit By: CMCA
Audit Date: 31.12.2013
Personnel: Beryl Wajsman (Editor-in-chief); Amanda Lavigne (Director of sales)

THE WESTMOUNT EXAMINER

Street address 1: 245 Victoria Street
Street address 2: Suite 210
Street address city: Westmount
Province/Territory: QC
Postal code: H3Z 2M6
Country: Canada
General Phone: (514) 484-5610
General Fax: (514) 484-6028
Advertising Phone: (514) 484-5610
Editorial Phone: 514-484-5610
General/National Adv. E-mail: examiner@tc.tc
Display Adv. E-mail: marie-france.paquette@tc.tc
Primary Website: www.westmountexaminer.com
Published: Thur
Avg Paid Circ: 2
Avg Free Circ: 9282
Audit By: CMCA
Audit Date: 28.02.2014
Personnel: Marie-France Paquette (Assistant publisher); Patricia-Ann Beaulieu (Publisher); Harvey Aisthental (Media Consultant)
Parent company (for newspapers): Transcontinental Media

THE WESTMOUNT INDEPENDENT

Street address 1: 310 Victoria Bldg. # 105
Street address city: Westmount
Province/Territory: QC
Postal code: H3Z 2M9
Country: Canada
General Fax: (514) 935-9241
Advertising Phone: (514) 223-3567
Editorial Phone: (514) 223-3578
General/National Adv. E-mail: office@westmountindependent.com
Display Adv. E-mail: advertising@westmountindependent.com
Primary Website: www.westmountindependent.com
Published: Tues
Avg Free Circ: 15057
Audit By: CMCA
Audit Date: 31.05.2015
Personnel: David Price (Pub); Arleen Candiotti (Advt Consultant)

THE WEST-QUEBEC POST

Street address 1: C-10 181 Principale St., Secteur Aylmer
Street address city: Gatineau
Province/Territory: QC
Postal code: J9H 6A6
County: Pontiac
Country: Canada
General Phone: (819) 684-4755
General Fax: (819) 684-6428
General/National Adv. E-mail: l.lavery@bulletinaylmer.com
Display Adv. E-mail: ventes.sales@bulletinaylmer.com
Editorial e-mail: abawqp@videotron.ca
Published: Fri
Avg Paid Circ: 761
Avg Free Circ: 5214
Audit By: CMCA
Audit Date: 29.02.2016
Personnel: Fred Ryan (Publisher); Lynne Lavery (General Manager); Lily Ryan (Editor); Sophia Ryan (sales manager); Nadia Paradis (Classified and subscription manager)
Parent company (for newspapers): 9040-9681 Quebec Inc.

TOURISME PLUS

Street address 1: B.p. 7 Succ Ahuntsic
Street address 2: Succ. Ahuntsic
Street address city: Montreal
Province/Territory: QC
Postal code: H3L 3N5
Country: Canada
General Phone: (514) 881-8583
Published: Wed
Avg Paid Circ: 123
Avg Free Circ: 1266
Audit By: ODC
Audit Date: 14.12.2011
Personnel: Michel Villeneuve

TRANSCONTINENTAL MEDIAS

Street address 1: 8770 Langelier
Street address 2: Suite 210
Street address city: Montreal
Province/Territory: QC
Postal code: H1P 3C6
Country: Canada
General Phone: (514) 899-5888
General/National Adv. E-mail: sdesjardins@transcontinental.ca
Primary Website: www.journalderosemont.com
Published: Tues
Avg Free Circ: 36024
Audit By: Sworn/Estimate/Non-Audited
Audit Date: 12.07.2019
Personnel: Stephane Desjardins (publisher)
Parent company (for newspapers): Transcontinental Media

VALLEE DU RICHELIEU EXPRESS

Street address 1: 4480 Chemin Chambly, Bureau 204
Street address city: Saint Hubert
Province/Territory: QC
Postal code: J3Y 3M8
Country: Canada
General Phone: (450) 678-6187
Advertising Phone: (450) 678-6187
Editorial Phone: (450) 678-6187
General/National Adv. E-mail: valleedurichelieu@tc.tc
Display Adv. E-mail: valleedurichelieu@tc.tc
Editorial e-mail: valleedurichelieu@tc.tc
Primary Website: www.valleedurichelieuexpress.ca
Published: Wed
Avg Paid Circ: 1
Avg Free Circ: 34751
Audit By: CCAB
Audit Date: 31.03.2014

VALLEYFIELD EXPRESS

Street address 1: 720 Blvd Monseigneur-langlois Ste 100
Street address city: Salaberry-de-Valleyfield
Province/Territory: QC
Postal code: J6S 5H7
Country: Canada
General Phone: (450) 371-7117
General Fax: (450) 371-7611
Advertising Phone: (450) 371-7117
Editorial Phone: (450) 371-7117
General/National Adv. E-mail: redactionvalleyfieldexpress@tc.tc
Display Adv. E-mail: redactionvalleyfieldexpress@tc.tc
Editorial e-mail: redactionvalleyfieldexpress@tc.tc
Primary Website: www.valleyfieldexpress.ca
Published: Thur
Avg Free Circ: 43310
Audit By: CCAB
Audit Date: 31.03.2014
Personnel: RÃƒÂ©seau MontÃƒÂ©rÃƒÂ©gie (Pub.)

VERDUN MESSENGER

Street address 1: 6239 Monk Blvd.
Street address city: Montreal
Province/Territory: QC
Postal code: H4E 3H8
Country: Canada
General Phone: (514) 768-1920
General Fax: (514) 768-3306
General/National Adv. E-mail: lussierp@transcontinental.ca
Published: Thur
Avg Paid Circ: 3
Avg Free Circ: 24364
Audit By: CCAB
Audit Date: 31.03.2014
Personnel: Lou Mercaer (Pub.); Pierre Lussier (Ed.)

VOIX DE LA MATANIE

Street address 1: Rue De La Gare
Street address city: Matane
Province/Territory: QC
Postal code: G4W 3J2
Country: Canada
General Phone: (418) 562-4040
General Fax: (418) 562-4607
Published: Wed
Avg Paid Circ: 11
Avg Free Circ: 17402
Audit By: CCAB
Audit Date: 31.03.2014
Personnel: Jean Gagnon

VOIX DES MILLE ILES

Street address 1: Rue Turgeon
Street address city: Sainte Therese
Province/Territory: QC
Postal code: J7E 3H4
Country: Canada
General Phone: (450) 435-6537
Primary Website: http://www.nordinfo.com/
Published: Wed
Avg Free Circ: 65177
Audit By: CCAB
Audit Date: 31.03.2014
Personnel: Serge Langlois

WEEK-END OUTAOUAIS

Street address 1: 160 Hospital Blvd., Ste. 30
Street address city: Gatineau
Province/Territory: QC
Postal code: J8T 8J1
Country: Canada
General Phone: (819) 568-7736
General Fax: (819) 568-7038
Primary Website: www.info07.com
Published: Sat
Avg Free Circ: 90000
Audit By: Sworn/Estimate/Non-Audited
Audit Date: 12.07.2019
Personnel: Jacques Blais (Pub./Gen. Mgr.)

SASKATCHEWAN

ADVANCE SOUTHWEST (FORMERLY GULL LAKE ADVANCE)

Street address 1: 1462 Conrad Ave.
Street address city: Gull Lake
Province/Territory: SK
Postal code: S0N 1A0
Country: Canada
General Phone: (306) 672-3373
Advertising Phone: (306) 741-2448
General/National Adv. E-mail: glad12@sasktel.net
Display Adv. E-mail: sales@advancesouthwest.com
Editorial e-mail: kate@advancesouthwest.com
Primary Website: www.advancesouthwest.com
Published: Mon
Avg Paid Circ: 600
Avg Free Circ: 7900
Audit By: Sworn/Estimate/Non-Audited
Audit Date: 12.07.2019
Personnel: Kate Winquist (Pub)
Parent company (for newspapers): Winquist Ventures Ltd.

ASSINIBOIA TIMES

Street address 1: 410 1st Ave. E.
Street address city: Assiniboia

Province/Territory: SK
Postal code: S0H 0B0
County: Canada
Country: Canada
General Phone: (306) 642-5901
General Fax: (306) 642-4519
General/National Adv. E-mail: heather@assiniboiatimes.ca
Editorial e-mail: joyce@assiniboiatimes.ca
Published: Fri
Avg Paid Circ: 212
Avg Free Circ: 2937
Audit By: CMCA
Audit Date: 29.02.2016
Personnel: Joyce Simard (Editor); Kevin Rasmussen (General Manager)
Parent company (for newspapers): Prairie Newspaper Group; Glacier Media Group

BATTLEFORDS NEWS-OPTIMIST

Street address 1: 892 104th St.
Street address city: North Battleford
Province/Territory: SK
Postal code: S9A 1M9
Country: Canada
General Phone: (306) 445-7261
General Fax: (306) 445-3223
General/National Adv. E-mail: battlefords.publishing@sasktel.net
Editorial e-mail: newsoptimist.news@sasktel.net
Primary Website: www.newsoptimist.ca
Published: Thur
Avg Paid Circ: 228
Avg Free Circ: 14000
Audit By: CMCA
Audit Date: 31.03.2018
Personnel: Becky Doig (Ed.)
Parent company (for newspapers): Glacier Media Group

BROADVIEW EXPRESS

Street address 1: 813 Desmond St.
Street address city: Grenfell
Province/Territory: SK
Postal code: S0G 2B0
Country: Canada
General Phone: (306) 697-2722
General Fax: (306) 697-2689
Advertising Phone: (306) 697-2722
General/National Adv. E-mail: sunnews@sasktel.net
Display Adv. E-mail: sunnews@sasktel.net
Editorial e-mail: sunnews@sasktel.net
Primary Website: www.grenfellsun.sk.ca
Published: Mon
Avg Paid Circ: 266
Avg Free Circ: 158
Audit By: CMCA
Audit Date: 31.03.2013
Personnel: Suzette Stone (Circ. Mgr.); Mariann Hughes (Sales Associate)
Parent company (for newspapers): Transcontinental Media

CANORA COURIER

Street address 1: 123 First Ave. E.
Street address city: Canora
Province/Territory: SK
Postal code: S0A 0L0
Country: Canada
General Phone: (306) 563-5131
General Fax: (306) 563-6144
General/National Adv. E-mail: canoracourier@sasktel.net
Display Adv. E-mail: sales.canoracourier@sasktel.net
Classified Adv. e-mail: office.canoracourier@sasktel.net
Editorial e-mail: canoracourier@sasktel.net
Primary Website: canoracourier.com
Published: Wed
Avg Paid Circ: 1136
Avg Free Circ: 9
Audit By: CMCA
Audit Date: 30.09.2016
Personnel: Ken Lewchuk (Pub)
Parent company (for newspapers): Glacier Media Group
Newspapers (for newspaper groups): The Kamsack Times, Canora; Preeceville Progress, Canora

CARLYLE OBSERVER

Street address 1: 132 Main St.
Street address city: Carlyle
Province/Territory: SK
Postal code: S0C 0R0
Country: Canada
General Phone: (306) 453-2525
General Fax: (306) 453-2938
General/National Adv. E-mail: observer@sasktel.net
Primary Website: www.carlyleobserver.com
Published: Fri
Avg Paid Circ: 113
Avg Free Circ: 2877
Audit By: CMCA
Audit Date: 30.06.2016
Personnel: Cindy Moffett (Pub.)
Parent company (for newspapers): Glacier Media Group

CLARK'S CROSSING GAZETTE

Street address 1: 109 Klassen Street West
Street address 2: 109 Klassen Street West
Street address city: Warman
Province/Territory: SK
Postal code: S0K 4S0
County: Corman Park
Country: Canada
General Phone: (306) 668-0575
General Fax: (306) 668-3997
General/National Adv. E-mail: tjenson@ccgazette.ca
Display Adv. E-mail: ads@ccgazette.ca
Classified Adv. e-mail: ads@ccgazette.ca
Editorial e-mail: editor@ccgazette.ca
Primary Website: http://www.ccgazette.ca
Published: Thur
Avg Paid Circ: 15
Avg Free Circ: 16500
Audit By: Sworn/Estimate/Non-Audited
Audit Date: 12.07.2019
Personnel: Terry Jenson (Publisher)
Parent company (for newspapers): JENSON PUBLISHING

CRAIK WEEKLY NEWS

Street address 1: 221 Third St.
Street address 2: Box 360
Street address city: Craik
Province/Territory: SK
Postal code: S0G 0V0
County: R.M. of Craik No. 222
Country: Canada
General Phone: (306) 734-2313
General Fax: (306) 734-2789
General/National Adv. E-mail: craiknews@sasktel.net
Display Adv. E-mail: craiknews@sasktel.net
Published: Mon
Avg Paid Circ: 880
Audit By: Sworn/Estimate/Non-Audited
Audit Date: 12.07.2019
Personnel: Harve Friedel (Ed.)

DAVIDSON LEADER

Street address 1: 205 Washington St.
Street address city: Davidson
Province/Territory: SK
Postal code: S0G 1A0
Country: Canada
General Phone: (306) 567-2047
General Fax: (306) 567-2900
General/National Adv. E-mail: davidsonleader@sasktel.net; theleaderonline@gmail.com
Primary Website: www.leaderonline.ca
Published: Mon
Avg Paid Circ: 1238
Avg Free Circ: 44
Audit By: CMCA
Audit Date: 31.03.2017
Personnel: Tara De Ryk (Publisher)
Parent company (for newspapers): Davidson Publishing Ltd.

EAST CENTRAL TRADER

Street address 1: 535 Main Street
Street address city: Humboldt
Province/Territory: SK
Postal code: S0K 2A0
Country: Canada
General Phone: (306) 682-2561
General Fax: (306) 682-3322
Display Adv. E-mail: sford@humboldtjournal.ca
Editorial e-mail: cmcrae@humboldtjournal.ca
Primary Website: www.humboldtjournal.ca
Published: Fri
Avg Paid Circ: 5
Avg Free Circ: 5443
Audit By: CMCA
Audit Date: 30.04.2016
Personnel: Becky Zimmer (Ed.); Brent Fitzpatrick (Group Publisher)

EAU VIVE (L')

Street address 1: 210-1440 9th Ave N
Street address city: Regina
Province/Territory: SK
Postal code: S4R 8B1
Country: Canada
General Phone: (306) 347-0481
General Fax: (306) 565-3450
General/National Adv. E-mail: direction@accesscomm.ca
Primary Website: http://nonprofits.accesscomm.ca/leauvive/web/
Published: Thur
Avg Paid Circ: 1046
Audit By: CMCA
Audit Date: 30.04.2014
Personnel: Jean-Pierre Picard (Publisher); Angeline Feumba (Administrative Assistant)

ESTEVAN MERCURY

Street address 1: 68 Souris Ave N.
Street address city: Estevan
Province/Territory: SK
Postal code: S4A 2M3
Country: Canada
General Phone: (306) 634-2654
General Fax: (306) 634-3934
General/National Adv. E-mail: classifieds@estevanmercury.ca
Display Adv. E-mail: adsales@estevanmercury.ca
Editorial e-mail: editor@estevanmercury.ca
Primary Website: estevanmercury.ca
Published: Wed
Avg Paid Circ: 252
Avg Free Circ: 4981
Audit By: AAM
Audit Date: 31.03.2019
Personnel: Rick Sadick (Pub.); Jihyun Choi (Prod. Mgr.); Norm Park (Ed.)
Parent company (for newspapers): Glacier Media Group

ESTON-ELROSE PRESS REVIEW

Street address 1: 108 W. Main St.
Street address city: Eston
Province/Territory: SK
Postal code: S0L 1A0
Country: Canada
General Phone: (306) 962-3221
General Fax: (306) 962-4445
General/National Adv. E-mail: estonpress@gmail.com
Published: Tues
Avg Paid Circ: 753
Audit By: CMCA
Audit Date: 30.06.2016
Personnel: Stewart Crump (Pub.); Barry Malindine (Adv. Mgr.); Tim Crump (Ed.)
Parent company (for newspapers): Jamac Publishing

FOAM LAKE REVIEW

Street address 1: 325 Main St.
Street address city: Foam Lake
Province/Territory: SK
Postal code: S0A 1A0
Country: Canada
General Phone: (306) 272-3262
General Fax: (306) 272-4521
General/National Adv. E-mail: review.foamlake@sasktel.net
Primary Website: www.foamlakereview.com
Published: Mon
Avg Paid Circ: 1123
Avg Free Circ: 3
Audit By: CMCA
Audit Date: 31.12.2015
Personnel: Bob Johnson (Ed.)

FORT QU'APPELLE TIMES

Street address 1: 141 Broadway St. W.
Street address city: Fort Qu'Appelle
Province/Territory: SK
Postal code: S0G 1S0
Country: Canada
General Phone: (306) 332-5526
General Fax: (306) 332-5414
General/National Adv. E-mail: forttimes@sasktel.net
Published: Tues
Avg Paid Circ: 837
Audit By: CMCA
Audit Date: 30.09.2016
Personnel: Sandra Huber (Pub.); Cassandra Archer (Adv. Mgr.); Linda Aspinall (Ed.)

FYI

Street address 1: 44 Fairford St W.
Street address city: Moose Jaw
Province/Territory: SK
Postal code: S6H 1V1
Country: Canada
General Phone: (306) 692-6441
General/National Adv. E-mail: editorial@mjtimes.sk.ca
Editorial e-mail: editorial@mjtimes.sk.ca
Primary Website: www.mjtimes.sk.ca
Published: Wed
Avg Free Circ: 24086
Audit By: CMCA
Audit Date: 31.12.2013

GAZETTE-POST NEWS

Street address 1: 106 Broadway
Street address city: Carnduff
Province/Territory: SK
Postal code: S0C 0S0
Country: Canada
General Phone: (306) 482-3252
General Fax: (306) 482-3373
General/National Adv. E-mail: gazettepost.news@sasktel.net; gazette_postnews@awnet.net
Published: Fri
Avg Paid Circ: 1006
Audit By: CMCA
Audit Date: 30.06.2015
Personnel: Bruce Shwanke (Pub.)

GRAVELBOURG TRIBUNE

Street address 1: 611 Main St.
Street address city: Gravelbourg
Province/Territory: SK
Postal code: S0H 1X0
County: R.M of Gravelbourg
Country: Canada
General Phone: (306) 648-3479
General Fax: (306) 648-2520
Advertising Phone: (306) 648-3479
Editorial Phone: (306) 648-3479
General/National Adv. E-mail: trib.editorial@sasktel.net
Display Adv. E-mail: trib.ads@sasktel.net
Classified Adv. e-mail: trib.ads@sasktel,net
Editorial e-mail: trib.editorial@sasktel.net
Primary Website: http://gravelbourgtribune.wixsite.com/tribune
Published: Mon
Avg Paid Circ: 875
Avg Free Circ: 30
Audit By: Sworn/Estimate/Non-Audited
Audit Date: 03.06.2024
Personnel: Paul Boisvert (Ed)

GRENFELL SUN

Street address 1: 813 Desmond St.
Street address city: Grenfell
Province/Territory: SK
Postal code: S0G 2B0
Country: Canada
General Phone: (306) 697-2722
General Fax: (306) 697-2689
General/National Adv. E-mail: sunnews@sasktel.net
Display Adv. E-mail: sunnews@sasktel.net

Editorial e-mail: sunnews@sasktel.net
Primary Website: grenfellsun.sk.ca
Published: Mon
Avg Paid Circ: 710
Avg Free Circ: 128
Audit By: CMCA
Audit Date: 30.09.2013
Personnel: Sarah Pacio (Office Manager)
Parent company (for newspapers): Transcontinental Media

HIGHWAY 40 COURIER

Street address 1: 200 Steele St.
Street address city: Cut Knife
Province/Territory: SK
Postal code: S0M 0N0
Country: Canada
General Phone: (306) 398-4901
General Fax: (306) 398-4909
General/National Adv. E-mail: ckcouriernews@sasktel.net
Published: Wed
Avg Paid Circ: 440
Avg Free Circ: 13
Audit By: CMCA
Audit Date: 31.03.2016
Personnel: Lorie Gibson (Publisher/Editor)

HUDSON BAY POST-REVIEW

Street address 1: 20 Railway Ave.
Street address city: Hudson Bay
Province/Territory: SK
Postal code: S0E 0Y0
County: Canada
Country: Canada
General Phone: (306) 865-2771
General Fax: (306) 865-2340
General/National Adv. E-mail: post.review@sasktel.net
Display Adv. E-mail: postreview3@sasktel.net
Published: Thur
Avg Paid Circ: 910
Avg Free Circ: 27
Audit By: CMCA
Audit Date: 31.03.2014
Personnel: Sherry Pilon (Mgr.)

INDIAN HEAD-WOLSELEY NEWS

Street address 1: 508 Grand Ave.
Street address city: Indian Head
Province/Territory: SK
Postal code: S0G 2K0
Country: Canada
General Phone: (306) 695-3565
General Fax: (306) 695-3448
General/National Adv. E-mail: ihwnews@sasktel.net
Published: Thur
Avg Paid Circ: 938
Avg Free Circ: 20
Audit By: CMCA
Audit Date: 29.02.2016
Personnel: Jodi Gendron (Pub.); Kerri McCabe (Circ. Mgr.); Marcel Gendron (Ed.)

KINDERSLEY CLARION

Street address 1: 919 Main St.
Street address city: Kindersley
Province/Territory: SK
Postal code: S0L 1S0
County: Kindersley
Country: Canada
General Phone: (306) 463-4611
General Fax: (306) 463-6505
General/National Adv. E-mail: editor.jamac@gmail.com
Display Adv. E-mail: ads.jamac@gmail.com
Classified Adv. e-mail: classifieds.jamac@gmail.com
Editorial e-mail: editor.jamac@gmail.com
Primary Website: theclarion.ca
Published: Wed
Avg Paid Circ: 1238
Audit By: Sworn/Estimate/Non-Audited
Audit Date: 12.07.2019
Personnel: Stewart Crump (Pub.); Kevin Mcbain (Ed.); Laurie Kelly (Salesperson)
Parent company (for newspapers): Jamac Publishing

KIPLING CITIZEN

Street address 1: #4 - 207 - 6th Avenue
Street address city: Kipling
Province/Territory: SK
Postal code: S0G 2S0
Country: Canada
General Phone: (306) 736-2535
General Fax: (306) 736-8445
Advertising Phone: (306) 736-2535
Editorial Phone: (306) 736-2535
General/National Adv. E-mail: thecitizen@sasktel.net
Display Adv. E-mail: thecitizen@sasktel.net
Classified Adv. e-mail: thecitizen@sasktel.net
Editorial e-mail: thecitizen@sasktel.net
Published: Fri
Avg Paid Circ: 730
Avg Free Circ: 13
Audit By: CMCA
Audit Date: 03.11.2017
Personnel: Laura Kish (Gen. Mgr.); Connie Schwalm (Reporter); Sean Choo-Foo (Sales Representative)
Parent company (for newspapers): Glacier Media Group

LANGENBURG FOUR-TOWN JOURNAL

Street address 1: 102 Carl Ave.
Street address city: Langenburg
Province/Territory: SK
Postal code: S0A 2A0
Country: Canada
General Phone: (306) 743-2617
General Fax: (316) 743-2299
General/National Adv. E-mail: fourtown@sasktel.net
Published: Wed
Avg Paid Circ: 1199
Audit By: CMCA
Audit Date: 31.03.2016
Personnel: Bill Johnston (Editor/Publisher)

LANIGAN ADVISOR

Street address 1: 42 Main Street
Street address city: Lanigan
Province/Territory: SK
Postal code: S0K 2M0
Country: Canada
General Phone: (306) 365-2010
General Fax: (306) 365-3388
General/National Adv. E-mail: laniganadvisor@sasktel.net
Published: Mon
Avg Paid Circ: 828
Avg Free Circ: 15
Audit By: CMCA
Audit Date: 31.01.2016
Personnel: Linda Mallett (Publisher/Editor)

LAST MOUNTAIN TIMES

Street address 1: 103 1st Ave. W.
Street address city: Nokomis
Province/Territory: SK
Postal code: S0G 3R0
County: RM Wreford
Country: Canada
General Phone: (306) 528-2020
Advertising Phone: (306) 559-0686
Editorial Phone: (306) 528-2020
General/National Adv. E-mail: inbox@lmtimes.ca
Display Adv. E-mail: advertise@lmtimes.ca
Classified Adv. e-mail: advertise@lmtimes.ca
Editorial e-mail: editor@lmtimes.ca
Primary Website: lmtimes.ca
Published: Mon
Avg Paid Circ: 100
Avg Free Circ: 4300
Audit By: Sworn/Estimate/Non-Audited
Audit Date: 12.07.2019
Personnel: Dan Degenstien (Publisher / Editor / Manager)
Parent company (for newspapers): Last Mountain Times
Newspapers (for newspaper groups): Last Mountain Times, Nokomis

LEADER NEWS

Street address 1: 919 Main St.
Street address city: Kindersley
Province/Territory: SK
Postal code: S0L 1S0
County: Canada
Country: Canada
General Phone: (306) 463-4611
General Fax: (306) 463-6505
Display Adv. E-mail: editor.jamac@gmail.com
Published: Wed
Avg Paid Circ: 710
Audit By: CMCA
Audit Date: 28.02.2014
Personnel: Stewart Crump (Pub.); Barry Malindine (Adv. Mgr.); Kevin McBain (Ed.)
Parent company (for newspapers): Jamac Publishing

LLOYDMINSTER SOURCE

Street address 1: 5921-50th Ave
Street address city: Lloydminster
Province/Territory: SK
Postal code: S9V 1W5
Country: Canada
General Phone: (306) 825-5111
General Fax: (306) 825-5147
Editorial e-mail: colin@lloydminstersource.com
Published: Tues`Thur
Avg Free Circ: 13889
Audit By: CMCA
Audit Date: 31.08.2016
Personnel: Reid Keebaugh (Publisher); Mike D'Armour (Mng. Ed.); Karrie Chang (Prod. Mgr.)

MACKLIN MIRROR

Street address 1: 4701 Herald St.
Street address city: Macklin
Province/Territory: SK
Postal code: S0L 2C0
Country: Canada
General Phone: (306) 753-2424
General Fax: (306) 753-2432
General/National Adv. E-mail: macklin.jamac@gmail.com
Display Adv. E-mail: macklin.jamac@gmail.com
Editorial e-mail: stacey.jamac@gmail.com
Published: Wed
Avg Paid Circ: 638
Avg Free Circ: 33
Audit By: CMCA
Audit Date: 30.04.2016
Personnel: Delilah Reschny (Editor/Publisher); Stacey Lavallie (Reporter)
Parent company (for newspapers): Jamac Publishing

MAPLE CREEK & SOUTHWEST ADVANCE TIMES

Street address 1: 116 Harder Street
Street address city: Maple Creek
Province/Territory: SK
Postal code: S0N 1N0
Country: Canada
General Phone: (306) 662-2100
General Fax: (306) 662-5005
General/National Adv. E-mail: classifieds@maplecreeknews.com
Display Adv. E-mail: ads@maplecreeknews.com
Editorial e-mail: editorial@maplecreeknews.com
Primary Website: www.maplecreeknews.com
Published: Tues
Avg Paid Circ: 1506
Avg Free Circ: 76
Audit By: CMCA
Audit Date: 30.04.2016
Personnel: Angela Litke (Manager); Della Fournier (Advertising Sales)

MELFORT JOURNAL

Street address 1: 901 Main St.
Street address city: Melfort
Province/Territory: SK
Postal code: S0E 1A0
Country: Canada
General Phone: (306) 752-5737
General Fax: (306) 752-5358
General/National Adv. E-mail: ads@melfortjournal.com
Primary Website: www.melfortjournal.com
Published: Tues
Avg Paid Circ: 1132
Audit By: CMCA
Audit Date: 30.06.2016
Personnel: Ken Sorensen (Pub.)
Parent company (for newspapers): Postmedia Network Inc.; Quebecor Communications, Inc.

NAICAM NEWS

Street address 1: 100-102 Main St.
Street address city: Watson
Province/Territory: SK
Postal code: S0K 4V0
County: Canada
Country: Canada
General Phone: (306) 287-4388
General Fax: (306) 287-3308
General/National Adv. E-mail: ecpress@sasktel.net
Published: Fri
Avg Paid Circ: 396
Audit By: Sworn/Estimate/Non-Audited
Audit Date: 12.07.2019
Personnel: Karen Mitchell (Pub./Gen. Mgr.)

NIPAWIN JOURNAL

Street address 1: 117 1st Ave.
Street address city: Nipawin
Province/Territory: SK
Postal code: S0E 1E0
Country: Canada
General Phone: (306) 862-4618
General Fax: (306) 862-4566
Editorial e-mail: greg.wiseman@sunmedia.ca
Primary Website: www.nipawinjournal.com
Published: Wed
Avg Paid Circ: 1093
Audit By: CMCA
Audit Date: 31.08.2014
Personnel: Ken Sorenson (Gen. Mgr.); Greg Wiseman (Managing Ed.)
Parent company (for newspapers): Postmedia Network Inc.; Quebecor Communications, Inc.

NORTH EAST SUN

Street address 1: 901 Main St.
Street address city: Melfort
Province/Territory: SK
Postal code: S0E 1A0
Country: Canada
General Phone: (306) 752-5737
General Fax: (306) 752-5358
General/National Adv. E-mail: shirley.sorensen@sunmedia.ca
Display Adv. E-mail: cassie.johnson@sunmedia.ca
Editorial e-mail: greg.wiseman@sunmedia.ca
Primary Website: www.melfortjournal.com
Published: Fri
Avg Free Circ: 21761
Audit By: CMCA
Audit Date: 30.06.2016
Personnel: Ken Sorensen

NORTHERN PRIDE

Street address 1: 219 Centre Street
Street address city: Meadow Lake
Province/Territory: SK
Postal code: S9X 1Z4
Country: Canada
General Phone: (306) 236-5353
Display Adv. E-mail: pride.terry@sasktel.net
Classified Adv. e-mail: pride.terry@sasktel.net
Editorial e-mail: pride.terry@sasktel.net
Primary Website: www.northernprideml.com
Published: Thur
Avg Paid Circ: 1638
Avg Free Circ: 4283
Audit By: CMCA
Audit Date: 31.12.2015
Personnel: Terry Villeneuve (Pub)

ORDER OF ST. BENEDICT

Street address 1: 100 College Dr.
Street address city: Muenster
Province/Territory: SK
Postal code: S0K 2Y0
Country: Canada
General Phone: (306) 682-1772
General Fax: (306) 682-5285
General/National Adv. E-mail: pm@stpeterspress.ca
Display Adv. E-mail: pm.ads@stpeterspress.ca
Editorial e-mail: pm.canadian@stpeterspress.ca
Primary Website: www.prairiemessenger.ca

Published: Wed
Avg Paid Circ: 4300
Audit By: CMCA
Audit Date: 02.09.2016
Personnel: Gail Kleefeld (Adv. Mgr.); Peter Novecosky (Ed.); Maureen Weber (Assoc. Ed.); Don Ward (Assoc. Ed.); Lucille Stewart (Layout Artist)

PARKLAND REVIEW

Street address 1: 1004-102 Ave.
Street address city: Tisdale
Province/Territory: SK
Postal code: S0E 1T0
Country: Canada
General Phone: (306) 873-4515
General Fax: (306) 873-4712
General/National Adv. E-mail: recorderoffice@sasktel.net
Display Adv. E-mail: adsrecorder@sakstel.net
Editorial e-mail: newsrecorder@sakstel.net
Published: Fri
Avg Free Circ: 11625
Audit By: CMCA
Audit Date: 31.03.2016
Personnel: August Grandguillar (Adv. Mgr.); Brent Fitzpatrick (Ed.); Gord Anderson (Prodn. Mgr.); Dan Sully (Adv. Mgr.)
Parent company (for newspapers): Glacier Media Group

PRAIRIE POST

Street address 1: 600 Chaplin Street East
Street address city: Swift Current
Province/Territory: SK
Postal code: S9H 1J3
Country: Canada
General Phone: (306) 773-8260
General Fax: (306) 773-0504
Advertising Phone: (306) 773-8260
Editorial Phone: (306) 773-8260
General/National Adv. E-mail: ppost@prairiepost.com
Display Adv. E-mail: ktumback@prairiepost.com
Editorial e-mail: mliebenberg@prairiepost.com
Primary Website: http://www.prairiepost.com
Published: Fri
Avg Free Circ: 17814
Audit By: CMCA
Audit Date: 31.03.2016
Personnel: Doug Evjen (Director of Sales and Marketing); Stacey Powell (Advertising)

PREECEVILLE PROGRESS

Street address 1: 123 First Ave. E.
Street address city: Canora
Province/Territory: SK
Postal code: S0A 0L0
Country: Canada
General Phone: (306) 563-5131
General Fax: (306) 563-6144
General/National Adv. E-mail: canoracourier@sasktel.net
Display Adv. E-mail: sales.canoracourier@sasktel.net
Classified Adv. e-mail: office.canoracourier@sasktel.net
Editorial e-mail: canoracourier@sasktel.net
Primary Website: http://www.preecevilleprogress.com/
Published: Thur
Avg Paid Circ: 971
Avg Free Circ: 4
Audit By: CMCA
Audit Date: 15.09.2014
Personnel: Ken Lewchuk
Parent company (for newspapers): Canora Courier; Glacier Media Group

PRINCE ALBERT DAILY HERALD

Street address 1: 30 10th St E
Street address city: Prince Albert
Province/Territory: SK
Postal code: S6V 0Y5
Country: Canada
General Phone: (306) 764-4276
General Fax: (306) 922-4237
Advertising Phone: (306) 764-4276
Editorial Phone: (306) 764-4276
General/National Adv. E-mail: accounting@paherald.sk.ca
Display Adv. E-mail: ebergen@paherald.sk.ca
Classified Adv. e-mail: classifieds@paherald.sk.ca
Editorial e-mail: edotorial@paherald.sk.ca
Primary Website: www.paherald.sk.ca
Published: Tues`Wed`Thur`Fri`Sat`Mthly
Avg Paid Circ: 2500
Avg Free Circ: 27525
Audit By: Sworn/Estimate/Non-Audited
Audit Date: 01.10.2011
Personnel: Donna Pfeil (Pub.); Peter Lozinski (Managing Ed.); Jason Kerr (Editor); Lucas Punkari (Sports Ed.); Erin Bergen (Marketing Mgr.)
Parent company (for newspapers): Transcontinental Media; FolioJumpline Publishing Inc.

RADVILLE DEEP SOUTH STAR

Street address 1: #1-420 Floren St.
Street address city: Radville
Province/Territory: SK
Postal code: S0C 2G0
County: Canada
Country: Canada
General Phone: (306) 869-2202
General Fax: (306) 869-2533
General/National Adv. E-mail: rstar@sasktel.net
Display Adv. E-mail: circulation@rdstar.sk.ca
Primary Website: www.rdstar.sk.ca
Published: Thur
Avg Paid Circ: 624
Audit By: CMCA
Audit Date: 31.01.2016
Personnel: Roger Holmes (Pub.)
Parent company (for newspapers): Transcontinental Media

REGIONAL OPTIMIST

Street address 1: 892-104th Street
Street address city: North Battleford
Province/Territory: SK
Postal code: S9A 3E6
Country: Canada
General Phone: (306) 445-7261
General Fax: (306) 445-3223
General/National Adv. E-mail: battlefords.publishing@sasktel.net
Editorial e-mail: newsoptimist.news@sasktel.net
Primary Website: www.newsoptimist.ca
Published: Thur
Avg Free Circ: 13514
Audit By: CMCA
Audit Date: 30.11.2016
Personnel: Becky Doig (Ed)

SHELLBROOK CHRONICLE

Street address 1: 46 Main St.
Street address city: Shellbrook
Province/Territory: SK
Postal code: S0J 2E0
County: Canada
Country: Canada
General Phone: (306) 747-2442
General Fax: (306) 747-3000
General/National Adv. E-mail: chnews@shelbrookchronicle.com
Display Adv. E-mail: chads@sbchron.com
Primary Website: http://shellbrookchronicle.com/
Published: Fri
Avg Paid Circ: 155
Avg Free Circ: 3484
Audit By: CMCA
Audit Date: 30.12.2015
Personnel: C.J. Pepper (Pub.)

SOUTHEAST LIFESTYLES

Street address 1: 300 Kensington Avenue
Street address city: Estevan
Province/Territory: SK
Postal code: S4A 2A7
Country: Canada
General Phone: (306) 634-5112
General Fax: (306) 634-2588
General/National Adv. E-mail: lifestyles@sasktel.net
Primary Website: http://www.sasklifestyles.com/
Published: Thur
Avg Paid Circ: 18
Avg Free Circ: 6585
Audit By: CMCA
Audit Date: 28.02.2014
Personnel: Rick Sadick (Pub.); Norm Park (Ed.)
Parent company (for newspapers): Glacier Media Group

SPIRITWOOD HERALD

Street address 1: 46 Main St.
Street address city: Shellbrook
Province/Territory: SK
Postal code: S0J 2E0
Country: Canada
General Phone: (306) 747-2442
General Fax: (306) 747-3000
General/National Adv. E-mail: chnews@shopperchronicle.com
Display Adv. E-mail: chads@sbchron.com
Primary Website: www.spiritwoodherald.com
Published: Fri
Avg Paid Circ: 52
Avg Free Circ: 2435
Audit By: Sworn/Estimate/Non-Audited
Audit Date: 12.07.2019
Personnel: Clark J Pepper (Publisher)

THE ADVANCE/GAZETTE

Street address 1: 301 Bosworth St.
Street address city: Wynyard
Province/Territory: SK
Postal code: S0A 4T0
County: Canada
Country: Canada
General Phone: (306) 554-2224
General Fax: (306) 554-3226
General/National Adv. E-mail: w.advance@sasktel.net
Published: Mon
Avg Paid Circ: 1211
Avg Free Circ: 18
Audit By: CMCA
Audit Date: 30.12.2015
Personnel: Bob Johnson (Ed.)

THE ESTERHAZY MINER-JOURNAL

Street address 1: 606 Veterans Ave.
Street address city: Esterhazy
Province/Territory: SK
Postal code: S0A 0X0
Country: Canada
General Phone: (306) 745-6669
General Fax: (306) 745-2699
General/National Adv. E-mail: miner.journal@sasktel.net
Primary Website: www.minerjournal.com
Published: Mon
Avg Paid Circ: 1334
Avg Free Circ: 0
Audit By: CMCA
Audit Date: 30.11.2013
Personnel: Brenda Matchett (Adv. Mgr.); Helen Solmes (Ed.)

THE HERALD

Street address 1: 716 Herbert Ave.
Street address city: Herbert
Province/Territory: SK
Postal code: S0H 2A0
County: Canada
Country: Canada
General Phone: (306) 784-2422
General Fax: (306) 784-3246
General/National Adv. E-mail: herbertherald@sasktel.net
Display Adv. E-mail: herbertherald@sasktel.net
Classified Adv. e-mail: herbertherald@sasktel.net
Editorial e-mail: herbertherald@sasktel.net
Published: Tues
Avg Paid Circ: 1442
Avg Free Circ: 5
Audit By: CMCA
Audit Date: 31.03.2017
Personnel: Rhonda J. Ens (Ed.)

THE HUMBOLDT JOURNAL

Street address 1: 535 Main St.
Street address city: Humboldt
Province/Territory: SK
Postal code: S0K 2A0
Country: Canada
General Phone: (306) 682-2561
General Fax: (306) 682-3322
General/National Adv. E-mail: humboldt.journal@sasktel.net
Display Adv. E-mail: sford@humboldtjournal.ca
Editorial e-mail: cmcrae@humboldtjournal.ca
Primary Website: www.humboldtjournal.ca
Published: Wed
Avg Paid Circ: 1765
Avg Free Circ: 29
Audit By: CMCA
Audit Date: 30.11.2016
Personnel: Becky Zimmer (Ed.)
Parent company (for newspapers): Glacier Media Group

THE INDEPENDENT

Street address 1: 102 3 Ave W
Street address city: Biggar
Province/Territory: SK
Postal code: S0K 0M0
County: Canada
Country: Canada
General Phone: (306) 948-3344
General Fax: (306) 948-2133
General/National Adv. E-mail: tip@sasktel.net
Published: Thur
Avg Paid Circ: 1310
Avg Free Circ: 538
Audit By: CMCA
Audit Date: 30.04.2016
Personnel: Margaret Hasein (Pub.); Daryl Hasein (Gen. Mgr.); Urla Tyler (Adv. Mgr.); Kevin Bratigan (Ed.)

THE ITUNA NEWS

Street address 1: 214 1st Avenue N.e.
Street address city: Ituna
Province/Territory: SK
Postal code: S0A 1N0
Country: Canada
General Phone: (306) 795-2412
General Fax: (306) 795-3621
General/National Adv. E-mail: news.ituna@sasktel.net
Primary Website: www.ituna.ca
Published: Mon
Avg Paid Circ: 578
Avg Free Circ: 1
Audit By: CMCA
Audit Date: 31.12.2015
Personnel: Bob Johnson (Prodn. Mgr.); Heidi Spilchuk (Ed)

THE KAMSACK TIMES

Street address 1: 123 First Ave. E.
Street address city: Canora
Province/Territory: SK
Postal code: S0A 0L0
Country: Canada
General Phone: (306) 563-5131
General Fax: (306) 563-6144
Advertising Phone: (306) 563-5131
Editorial Phone: (306) 542-2626
General/National Adv. E-mail: canoracourier@sasktel.net
Display Adv. E-mail: k.lewchuk@sasktel.net
Classified Adv. e-mail: office.canoracourier@sasktel.net
Editorial e-mail: kamsacktimes@sasktel.net
Primary Website: kamsacktimes.com
Published: Thur
Avg Paid Circ: 1100
Avg Free Circ: 5
Audit By: CMCA
Audit Date: 30.03.2017
Personnel: Ken Lewchuk (Publisher)
Parent company (for newspapers): Canora Courier; Glacier Media Group

THE MAPLE CREEK NEWS

Street address 1: 116 Harder St.
Street address city: Maple Creek
Province/Territory: SK
Postal code: S0N 1N0
Country: Canada
General Phone: (306) 662-2133
General Fax: (306) 662-5005
General/National Adv. E-mail: classifieds@maplecreeknews.com
Display Adv. E-mail: ads@maplecreeknews.com

Classified Adv. e-mail: classifieds@maplecreeknews.com
Editorial e-mail: editorial@maplecreeknews.com
Primary Website: www.maplecreeknews.com
Published: Thur
Avg Paid Circ: 1406
Audit By: Sworn/Estimate/Non-Audited
Audit Date: 12.07.2019
Personnel: Editorial Team (Ed.); Advertising Team (Adv.); Classifieds Team (Classifieds)
Parent company (for newspapers): Southern Alberta Newspapers

THE MELVILLE ADVANCE

Street address 1: 218 3rd Ave. W.
Street address city: Melville
Province/Territory: SK
Postal code: S0A 2P0
County: Stanley
Country: Canada
General Phone: (306) 728-5448
General Fax: (306) 728-4004
General/National Adv. E-mail: melvilleadvance@sasktel.net
Display Adv. E-mail: sales@grasslandsnews.ca
Classified Adv. e-mail: contact@grasslandsnews.ca
Editorial e-mail: editor@grasslandsnews.ca
Primary Website: www.melvilleadvance.com
Published: Fri
Avg Paid Circ: 1679
Avg Free Circ: 17
Audit By: CMCA
Audit Date: 31.05.2016
Personnel: George Brown; Chris Ashfield (Group Publisher)
Parent company (for newspapers): Grasslands News Group

THE NORTHERNER

Street address 1: 715 La Ronge Ave.
Street address city: La Ronge
Province/Territory: SK
Postal code: S0J 1L0
County: Canada
Country: Canada
General Phone: (306) 425-3344
General Fax: (306) 425-2827
General/National Adv. E-mail: ads.northerner@sasktel.net
Display Adv. E-mail: ads.northerner@sasktel.net
Classified Adv. e-mail: ads.northerner@sasktel.net
Editorial e-mail: northerner@sasktel.net
Published: Thur
Avg Paid Circ: 198
Avg Free Circ: 136
Audit By: CMCA
Audit Date: 31.07.2014
Personnel: Debra Parkinson (Office Mgr./Circ.)

THE OUTLOOK

Street address 1: 108 Saskatchewan Ave. E
Street address city: Outlook
Province/Territory: SK
Postal code: S0L 2N0
County: Canada
Country: Canada
General Phone: (306) 867-8262
General Fax: (306) 867-9556
General/National Adv. E-mail: theoutlook@sasktel.net
Published: Thur
Avg Paid Circ: 1208
Avg Free Circ: 49
Audit By: CMCA
Audit Date: 30.09.2016
Personnel: Delwyn Luedtke (General Manager)
Parent company (for newspapers): Glacier Media Group

THE OXBOW HERALD

Street address 1: Po Box 420
Street address city: Oxbow
Province/Territory: SK
Postal code: S0C 2B0
Country: Canada
General Phone: (306) 483-2323
General Fax: (306) 483-5258
General/National Adv. E-mail: oxbow.herald@sasktel.net
Display Adv. E-mail: lorena@oxbowherald.sk.ca
Editorial e-mail: liz@oxbowherald.sk.ca
Primary Website: www.SaskNewsNow.com
Published: Mon
Avg Paid Circ: 908
Audit By: CMCA
Audit Date: 30.06.2015
Personnel: Lorena Wolensky (Advertising Manger); Lizz Bottrell (Editor); Marilyn Johnson (Reporter)
Parent company (for newspapers): Transcontinental Media

THE ROSETOWN EAGLE

Street address 1: 114 2nd Ave. W.
Street address city: Rosetown
Province/Territory: SK
Postal code: S0L 2V0
County: Canada
Country: Canada
General Phone: (306) 882-4202
General Fax: (306) 882-4204
Advertising Phone: (306) 882-4202
Editorial Phone: (306) 882-4202
General/National Adv. E-mail: frontdesk.eagle@gmail.com
Display Adv. E-mail: ads.eagle@gmail.com
Classified Adv. e-mail: frontdesk.eagle@gmail.com
Editorial e-mail: editor.eagle@gmail.com
Published: Mon
Avg Paid Circ: 1100
Avg Free Circ: 38
Audit By: CMCA
Audit Date: 30.04.2017
Personnel: Stewart Crump (Owner/publisher); Simone Gaudet; David McIver; Loretta Torrence (Ads); Ian McKay (Editor); Jack Hamilton; Gerald Rogal

THE SHAUNAVON STANDARD

Street address 1: 346 Centre St.
Street address city: Shaunavon
Province/Territory: SK
Postal code: S0N 2M0
County: Canada
Country: Canada
General Phone: (306) 297-4144
General Fax: (306) 297-3357
Display Adv. E-mail: jgregoire@theshaunavonstandard.com
Editorial e-mail: standard@theshaunavonstandard.com
Published: Tues
Avg Paid Circ: 916
Audit By: CMCA
Audit Date: 30.06.2016
Personnel: Paul MacNeil (Ed.); Joanne Gregoire (Adv. Sales)

THE SOUTHWEST BOOSTER

Street address 1: 30 4th Ave. Nw
Street address city: Swift Current
Province/Territory: SK
Postal code: S9H 3X4
County: Canada
Country: Canada
General Phone: (306) 773-9321
General Fax: (306) 773-9136
General/National Adv. E-mail: msoper@swbooster.com
Display Adv. E-mail: boosterads@swbooster.com
Primary Website: www.swbooster.com
Published: Thur
Avg Free Circ: 16985
Audit By: CMCA
Audit Date: 31.10.2016
Personnel: Bob Watson (Pub.); Mark Soper (Adv. Mgr.); Ken Mattice (Circ. Mgr.); Scott Anderson (Mng. Ed.); George Driscoll (Prodn. Mgr.)
Parent company (for newspapers): Transcontinental Media

THE TISDALE RECORDER

Street address 1: 1004 102nd Ave.
Street address city: Tisdale
Province/Territory: SK
Postal code: S0E 1T0
County: Canada
Country: Canada
General Phone: (306) 873-4515
General Fax: (306) 873-4712
General/National Adv. E-mail: pub@sasktel.net
Display Adv. E-mail: recorder3@sasktel.net
Editorial e-mail: newsrecorder@sasktel.net
Published: Wed
Avg Paid Circ: 669
Avg Free Circ: 25
Audit By: CMCA
Audit Date: 31.12.2015
Personnel: Brent Fitzpatrick (Pub.); James Tarrant (Ed.); August Grandguillot (Ad.)
Parent company (for newspapers): Glacier Media Group

THE WAKAW RECORDER

Street address 1: 224 First St. S.
Street address city: Wakaw
Province/Territory: SK
Postal code: S0K 4P0
County: Canada
Country: Canada
General Phone: (306) 233-4325
General Fax: (306) 233-4386
General/National Adv. E-mail: wrecorder@sasktel.net
Published: Wed
Avg Paid Circ: 1375
Avg Free Circ: 14
Audit By: CMCA
Audit Date: 31.03.2016
Personnel: Dwayne Biccum (Ed.)

THE WATROUS MANITOU

Street address 1: 309 Main St.
Street address city: Watrous
Province/Territory: SK
Postal code: S0K 4T0
County: Canada
Country: Canada
General Phone: (306) 946-3343
General Fax: (306) 946-2026
General/National Adv. E-mail: watrous.manitou@sasktel.net
Primary Website: www.thewatrousmanitou.com
Published: Mon
Avg Paid Circ: 1387
Avg Free Circ: 21
Audit By: CMCA
Audit Date: 30.06.2016

THE WHITEWOOD HERALD

Street address 1: 708 S. Railway St.
Street address city: Whitewood
Province/Territory: SK
Postal code: S0G 5C0
County: Canada
Country: Canada
General Phone: (306) 735-2230
General Fax: (306) 735-2899
General/National Adv. E-mail: herald@whitewoodherald.com
Display Adv. E-mail: ads@whitewoodherald.com
Classified Adv. e-mail: contact@whitewoodherald.com
Editorial e-mail: herald@whitewoodherald.com
Primary Website: www.whitewoodherald.sk.ca
Published: Fri
Avg Paid Circ: 667
Avg Free Circ: 88
Audit By: CMCA
Audit Date: 30.04.2016
Personnel: Chris Ashfield (Pub)

TRIANGLE NEWS

Street address 1: 118 Centre St.
Street address city: Coronach
Province/Territory: SK
Postal code: S0H 0Z0
Country: Canada
General Phone: (306) 267-3381
General/National Adv. E-mail: trianglenews@sasktel.net
Primary Website: www.trianglenews.sk.ca
Published: Mon
Avg Paid Circ: 339
Avg Free Circ: 336
Audit By: CMCA
Audit Date: 31.10.2015
Parent company (for newspapers): Transcontinental

UNITY-WILKIE PRESS-HERALD

Street address 1: 310 Main St.
Street address city: Unity
Province/Territory: SK
Postal code: S0K 4L0
County: Canada
Country: Canada
General Phone: (306) 228-2267
General Fax: (306) 228-2767
General/National Adv. E-mail: northwest.herald@sasktel.net
Display Adv. E-mail: ads.northwest.herald@sasktel.net
Editorial e-mail: northwest.herald@sasktel.net
Primary Website: http://unitystories.com/press-herald/
Published: Fri
Avg Paid Circ: 1400
Avg Free Circ: 0
Audit By: Sworn/Estimate/Non-Audited
Audit Date: 12.07.2019
Personnel: Helena Long (Ed.); Jackie Boser (Office Manager); Tim Holtorf (ad designer)
Parent company (for newspapers): Prairie Newspaper Group

WADENA NEWS

Street address 1: 102 First St Ne
Street address city: Wadena
Province/Territory: SK
Postal code: S0A 4J0
County: Canada
Country: Canada
General Phone: (306) 338-2231
General Fax: (306) 338-3421
General/National Adv. E-mail: wadena.news@sasktel.net
Primary Website: http://wadenanews.ca/
Published: Mon
Avg Paid Circ: 1649
Avg Free Circ: 80
Audit By: Sworn/Estimate/Non-Audited
Audit Date: 12.07.2019
Personnel: Alison Squires (Pub.)

WATERFRONT PRESS

Street address 1: 635 James St. N.
Street address city: Lumsden
Province/Territory: SK
Postal code: S0G 3C0
Country: Canada
General Phone: (306) 731-3143
General Fax: (306) 731-2277
General/National Adv. E-mail: watpress@sasktel.net
Published: Thur
Avg Paid Circ: 167
Avg Free Circ: 3993
Audit By: CMCA
Audit Date: 30.06.2014
Personnel: Jacqueline Chouinard (Ed.); Lucien Chouinard (Ed.)

WEST CENTRAL CROSSROADS

Street address 1: 919 Main St.
Street address city: Kindersley
Province/Territory: SK
Postal code: S0L 1S0
Country: Canada
General Phone: (306) 463-4611
General Fax: (306) 463-6505
General/National Adv. E-mail: news_jamac@sasktel.net
Published: Fri
Avg Free Circ: 15160
Audit By: CMCA
Audit Date: 30.09.2016
Personnel: Stewart Crump (Pub.); Tim Crump (Ed.)
Parent company (for newspapers): Jamac Publishing

WEYBURN REVIEW

Street address 1: 904 East Ave.
Street address city: Weyburn
Province/Territory: SK
Postal code: S4H 2Y8
County: Canada
Country: Canada
General Phone: (306) 842-7487

General Fax: (306) 842-0282
General/National Adv. E-mail: production@weyburnreview.com
Primary Website: www.weyburnreview.com
Published: Wed
Avg Paid Circ: 2189
Avg Free Circ: 59
Audit By: CMCA
Audit Date: 30.06.2016
Personnel: Rick Major (Pub.); Patricia Ward (Mng. Ed.)
Parent company (for newspapers): Glacier Media Group

WEYBURN THIS WEEK

Street address 1: 115 2nd St Ne
Street address city: WEYBURN
Province/Territory: SK
Postal code: S4H0T7
County: Canada
Country: Canada
General Phone: (306) 842-3900
General Fax: (306) 842-2515
General/National Adv. E-mail: weyburnthisweek@sasktel.net
Primary Website: www.weyburnthisweek.com
Published: Fri
Avg Paid Circ: 3
Avg Free Circ: 5546
Audit By: CMCA
Audit Date: 31.01.2016
Personnel: Rick Major (Pub.)
Parent company (for newspapers): Glacier Media Group

WORLD-SPECTATOR

Street address 1: 714 Main Street
Street address city: Moosomin
Province/Territory: SK
Postal code: S0G 3N0
Country: Canada
General Phone: (306) 435-2445
General Fax: (306) 435-3969
General/National Adv. E-mail: world_spectator@sasktel.net
Primary Website: www.world-spectator.com
Published: Mon
Avg Paid Circ: 3609
Audit By: CMCA
Audit Date: 31.12.2015
Personnel: Kevin Weedmark (Ed.)

YORKTON THIS WEEK

Street address 1: 20 3rd Ave. N.
Street address city: YORKTON
Province/Territory: SK
Postal code: S3N 2X3
County: Canada
Country: Canada
General Phone: (306) 782-2465
General Fax: (306) 786-1898
General/National Adv. E-mail: publisher@yorktonthisweek.com
Display Adv. E-mail: classifieds@yorktonthisweek.com
Editorial e-mail: editorial@yorktonthisweek.com
Primary Website: www.yorktonthisweek.com
Published: Wed
Avg Paid Circ: 2777
Avg Free Circ: 59
Audit By: Sworn/Estimate/Non-Audited
Audit Date: 12.07.2019
Personnel: Jim Ambrose (Publisher); Debbie Barr (Prodn. Mgr.)
Parent company (for newspapers): Glacier Media Group

YUKON

YUKON NEWS

Street address 1: 3106 Third Ave.
Street address 2: Ste. 200
Street address city: Whitehorse
Province/Territory: YT
Postal code: Y1A 5G1
Country: Canada
General Phone: (867) 667-6285
Display Adv. E-mail: stephanie.simpson@yukon-news.com
Classified Adv. e-mail: wordads@yukon-news.com
Editorial e-mail: editor@yukon-news.com
Primary Website: yukon-news.com
Published: Wed`Fri
Avg Paid Circ: 1686
Avg Free Circ: 2502
Audit By: AAM
Audit Date: 31.03.2019
Personnel: Stephanie Newsome (Pub.); Stephanie Simpson (Adv.); Ashley J (Ed.)
Parent company (for newspapers): Black Press Ltd.

SHOPPER PUBLICATIONS IN THE U.S

CALIFORNIA

YUCAIPA

CENTURY GROUP NEWSPAPERS

Street address 1: 35154 Yucaipa Blvd
Street address city: Yucaipa
State: CA
Zip/Postal code: 92399-4339
County: San Bernardino
Country: USA
Mailing address: 35154 Yucaipa Blvd
Mailing city: Yucaipa
Mailing state: CA
Mailing zip: 92399-4339
General Phone: (909) 797-9101
General Fax: (909) 797-0502
General/National Adv. E-mail: tbush@centurygroup.com
Primary Website: www.centurygroup.com
Published: Fri
Avg Paid Circ: 5278
Avg Free Circ: 65861
Audit By: CVC
Audit Date: 30.09.2016
Personnel: Toebe Bush (President / CEO / Pub.); Gerald A. Bean (Owner)
State: Delaware

DELAWARE

DOVER

INDEPENDENT NEWSMEDIA INC. USA

Street address 1: 110 Galaxy Dr
Street address city: Dover
State: DE
Zip/Postal code: 19901-9262
County: Kent
Country: USA
Mailing address: 110 Galaxy Dr
Mailing city: Dover
Mailing state: DE
Mailing zip: 19901-9262
General Phone: (302) 674-3600
General Fax: (877) 377-2424
General/National Adv. E-mail: newsroom@newszap.com
Primary Website: www.newszap.com
Year Established: 1953
Avg Paid Circ: 1580
Avg Free Circ: 1939
Audit By: CAC
Audit Date: 31.12.2014
Personnel: Joe Smyth (Chrmn. of the Bd./CEO); Tamra Brittingham (Corp. Pres.); Ed Dulin (Pres., Opns.); Darel LaPrade (Vice Pres., Adv.); Chris Engel (Dir., Research/Devel.); Sheila Clendaniel (Exec. Asst.); Greg Tock (Pub.)
State: Indiana

INDIANA

PEKIN

GREEN BANNER PUBLICATIONS, INC.

Street address 1: 490 E State Road 60
Street address city: Pekin
State: IN
Zip/Postal code: 47165-7928
County: Washington
Country: USA
Mailing address: PO Box 38
Mailing city: Pekin
Mailing state: IN
Mailing zip: 47165-0038
General Phone: (812) 967-3176
General Fax: (812) 967-3194
General/National Adv. E-mail: sales@gbpnews.com
Primary Website: www.gbpnews.com
Year Established: 1933
Published: Wed
Avg Paid Circ: 0
Avg Free Circ: 62293
Audit By: CVC
Audit Date: 31.12.2015
Personnel: Joe Green (Pub.)
State: Michigan

MICHIGAN

FLASHES ADVERTISING & NEWS

Street address 1: 241 S Cochran Ave
Street address city: Charlotte
State: MI
Zip/Postal code: 48813-1584
County: Eaton
Country: USA
Mailing address: 241 S. Cochran Ave.
Mailing city: Charotte
Mailing state: MI
Mailing zip: 48813-1584
General Phone: (517) 543-1099
General Fax: (517) 543-1993
Advertising Phone: (517) 543-1099 ext 225
Advertising Fax: (517) 543-1993
Editorial Phone: (517) 543-1099 ext 227
Editorial Fax: (517) 543-1993
General/National Adv. E-mail: cgwing@county-journal.com
Display Adv. E-mail: cgwing@county-journal.com
Classified Adv. e-mail: sales@county-journal.com
Editorial e-mail: news@county-journal.com
Primary Website: www.county-journal.com
Year Established: 1945
Published: Sat
Avg Paid Circ: 15
Avg Free Circ: 5000
Audit By: CVC
Audit Date: 12.07.2020
Personnel: Cindy Gaedert (Pub./Sales/Owner); Travis Silvas (Circ. Mgr)

THE COUNTY JOURNAL

Street address 1: 241 S. Cochran Ave.
Street address city: Charlotte
State: MI
Zip/Postal code: 48813
County: Eaton
Country: United States
Mailing address: 241 S. Cochran Ave.
Mailing city: Charlotte
Mailing state: MI
Mailing zip: 48813
General Phone: (517) 543-1099
General Fax: (517) 543-1993
Advertising Phone: (517) 543-1099 ext 225
Advertising Fax: (517) 543-1993
Editorial Phone: (517) 543-1099 ext 227
Editorial Fax: (517) 543-1993
General/National Adv. E-mail: cgwing@county-journal.com
Display Adv. E-mail: cgwing@county-journal.com
Classified Adv. e-mail: sales@county-journal.com
Editorial e-mail: news@county-journal.com
Primary Website: county-journal.com
Year Established: 2006
Published: Sat
Avg Paid Circ: 28
Avg Free Circ: 15000
Audit By: CVC
Audit Date: 30.06.2020
Personnel: Cindy Gaedert (Owner, Pub. & Sales); Cindy Gaedert (Publisher/Owner); Travis Silvas (Circ. Mgr.); Denise Ensley

C & G NEWSPAPERS

Street address 1: 13650 E 11 Mile Rd
Street address city: Warren
State: MI
Zip/Postal code: 48089-1422
County: Macomb
Country: USA
Mailing address: 13650 E 11 Mile Rd
Mailing city: Warren
Mailing state: MI
Mailing zip: 48089-1422
General Phone: (586) 498-8000
General Fax: (586) 498-9631
Editorial Phone: (586) 498-1042
General/National Adv. E-mail: jdemers@candgnews.com
Display Adv. E-mail: classified@candgnews.com
Editorial e-mail: mail@candgnews.com
Primary Website: candgnews.com
Year Established: 1977
Published: Wed
Avg Free Circ: 608041
Audit By: CVC
Audit Date: 30.09.2017
Personnel: Elaine Myers (Adv. Mgr.); John Carlisle (Ed.); Gregg Demers (Editorial Dir.); Jeff Demers (Adv. Dir.)
State: Minnesota

MINNESOTA

PARK RAPIDS

PARK RAPIDS ENTERPRISE EXPRESS

Street address 1: 203 Henrietta Ave N
Street address city: Park Rapids
State: MN
Zip/Postal code: 56470-2617
County: Hubbard
Country: USA
Mailing address: PO Box 111
Mailing city: Park Rapids
Mailing state: MN
Mailing zip: 56470-0111
General Phone: (218) 732-3364
General Fax: (218) 732-8757
General/National Adv. E-mail: aerickson@parkrapidsenterprise.com
Primary Website: www.parkrapidsenterprise.com
Published: Sat
Avg Free Circ: 8599
Audit By: VAC
Audit Date: 30.09.2015
Personnel: Rory Palm (Publisher); Candy Parks (Adv. Mgr.); Vance Carlson (Sports Editor); Anna Erickson (Editor)
State: New Jersey

NEW JERSEY

BAYONNE

HUDSON REPORTER ASSOCIATES, LP

Street address 1: 447 Broadway
Street address 2: 447 Broadway
Street address city: Bayonne
State: NJ
Zip/Postal code: 07002-3623
County: Hudson
Country: USA
Mailing address: 447 Broadway
Mailing city: Bayonne
Mailing state: NJ
Mailing zip: 07002
General Phone: (201) 798-7800
General Fax: (201) 798-0018
General/National Adv. E-mail: dunger@hudsonreporter.com
Primary Website: 447 Broadway
Year Established: 1983
Published: Wed`Sun
Avg Paid Circ: 45808
Avg Free Circ: 0
Audit By: CAC
Audit Date: 30.06.2016
Personnel: Lucha Malato (Co-Pub./Gen. Mgr.); David S. Unger (Co-Pub./Adv. Dir.)
State: New Mexico

NEW MEXICO

FARMINGTON

AMERICAN CLASSIFIEDS - FARMINGTON - FOUR CORNERS

Street address 1: 928 E Main St
Street address 2: Ste C
Street address city: Farmington
State: NM
Zip/Postal code: 87401-2700
County: San Juan
Country: USA
Mailing address: 928 E Main St Ste C
Mailing city: Farmington
Mailing state: NM
Mailing zip: 87401-2700
General Phone: (505) 564-2535
General/National Adv. E-mail: 4corners@AmClass.us
Display Adv. E-mail: Allen@AmClass.us
Primary Website: www.AmClass.us
Year Established: 1985
Published: Thur
Avg Free Circ: 29000
Audit By: CVC
Audit Date: 30.09.2017
Personnel: Allen Elmore (Pres.)
State: New York

NEW YORK

GRANVILLE

MANCHESTER NEWSPAPERS, INC.

Street address 1: 14 E Main St
Street address city: Granville
State: NY
Zip/Postal code: 12832-1334
County: Washington
Country: USA
Mailing address: PO BOX 330
Mailing city: GRANVILLE
Mailing state: NY
Mailing zip: 12832-0330
General Phone: (518) 642-1234
General Fax: (518) 642-1344
General/National Adv. E-mail: publisher@manchesternewspapers.com
Display Adv. E-mail: advertising@manchesternewspapers.com
Editorial e-mail: publisher@manchesternewspapers.com
Primary Website: manchesternewspapers.com
Year Established: 1995
Published: Fri
Avg Paid Circ: 0
Avg Free Circ: 49317
Audit By: CVC
Audit Date: 30.09.2017
Personnel: John MacArthur Manchester (Pres.); Lisa Manchester (Exec. Vice Pres.); Jane Cosey (Adv.)

WILLIAMSVILLE

BEE GROUP NEWSPAPERS

Street address 1: 5564 Main St
Street address city: Williamsville
State: NY
Zip/Postal code: 14221-5410
County: Erie
Country: USA
Mailing address: 5564 Main St
Mailing city: Williamsville
Mailing state: NY
Mailing zip: 14221-5410
General Phone: (716) 632-4700
General Fax: (716) 633-8601
General/National Adv. E-mail: tmeaser@beenews.com
Display Adv. E-mail: salesdept@beenews.com
Primary Website: www.beenews.com
Year Established: 1879
Personnel: Trey Measer (Pres./Pub.); David Sherman
State: Ohio

OHIO

SUN NEWSPAPERS

Street address 1: 5510 Cloverleaf Pkwy
Street address city: Cleveland
State: OH
Zip/Postal code: 44125-4815
County: Cuyahoga
Country: USA
Mailing address: 1801 Superior Ave E
Mailing city: Cleveland
Mailing state: OH
Mailing zip: 44114-2107
General Phone: (216) 986-2600
General Fax: (216) 986-2401
General/National Adv. E-mail: sun@sunnews.com
Primary Website: www.sunnews.com
Published: Thur
Avg Paid Circ: 52097
Avg Free Circ: 39319
Audit By: AAM
Audit Date: 30.09.2016
Personnel: Keith Mathis (Pres./CEO); Donna Krause (Classified Mgr.); Cathy McBride (Circ. Mgr.); Linda Kinsey (Exec. Ed.); Bob Palmer (Mgr. Online News)
State: Pennsylvania

PENNSYLVANIA

MID-ATLANTIC COMMUNITY PAPERS ASSOCIATION

Street address 1: 16515 Pottsville Pike
Street address 2: Suite C
Street address city: Hamburg
State: PA
Zip/Postal code: 19526
County: Berks
Country: USA
Mailing address: PO Box 408
Mailing city: Hamburg
Mailing state: PA
Mailing zip: 19526-0408
General Phone: 484-709-6564
General/National Adv. E-mail: info@macpa.net
Display Adv. E-mail: Info@macnetonline.com
Primary Website: www.macpa.net
Mthly Avg Views: 3000000
Mthly Avg Unique Visitors: 800000
Year Established: 1955
Published: Mon`Tues`Wed`Thur`Fri`Sat`Sun`Mthly
Avg Free Circ: 1200000
Audit By: CVC
Audit Date: 01.01.2021
Personnel: Alyse Mitten (Exec. Dir.)

LANCASTER

CHESTER COUNTY COMMUNITY COURIER

Street address 1: 1100 Corporate BLvd
Street address city: Lancaster
State: PA
Zip/Postal code: 17601
County: Lancaster
Country: USA
Mailing address: PO Box 500
Mailing city: Mount Joy
Mailing state: PA
Mailing zip: 17552-0500
General Phone: 717-653-1833
General Fax: (717) 492-2584
Advertising Phone: 717-278-1394
General/National Adv. E-mail: jhemperly@engleonline.com
Display Adv. E-mail: jhemperly@engleonline.com
Editorial e-mail: news@engleonline.com
Primary Website: www.townlively.com
Mthly Avg Views: 16500
Mthly Avg Unique Visitors: 14350
Year Established: 1988
Published: Wed
Avg Paid Circ: 0
Avg Free Circ: 21132
Audit By: CVC
Audit Date: 31.03.2023
Personnel: Mark Malloy (Circ. Mgr.); Jeremy Engle (VP Operations); John Hemperly

ENGLE - OCTORARA COMMUNITY COURIER

Street address 1: 1100 Corporate Blvd
Street address city: Lancaster
State: PA
Zip/Postal code: 17601
County: Lancaster
Country: USA
Mailing address: PO Box 500
Mailing city: Mount Joy
Mailing state: PA
Mailing zip: 17552
General Phone: 717-653-1833
Advertising Phone: 717-278-1394
Editorial Phone: 717-492-2544
General/National Adv. E-mail: jhemperly@engleonline.com
Display Adv. E-mail: jhemperly@engleonline.com
Classified Adv. e-mail: classifieds@engleonline.com
Editorial e-mail: newsdept@engleonline.com
Primary Website: www.townlively.com
Mthly Avg Views: 16500
Mthly Avg Unique Visitors: 14350
Year Established: 1954
Published: Wed
Avg Free Circ: 7081
Audit By: CVC
Audit Date: 30.03.2023
Personnel: Jeremy Engle (Prod.); Jocelyn Engle (Publisher); John Hemperly (Operations Manager); Mark Malloy (Circ.)

LANCATER

PENNYSAVER

Street address 1: 1100 Corporate Blvd
Street address city: Lancater
State: PA
Zip/Postal code: 17601
County: Lancaster
Country: USA
Mailing address: PO Box 500
Mailing city: Mount Joy
Mailing state: PA
Mailing zip: 17552-0500
General Phone: (717) 492-2514
General Fax: (717) 492-2584
Advertising Phone: (717) 492-2514
Editorial Phone: (717) 892-6018
Editorial Fax: (717) 892-6024
General/National Adv. E-mail: jhemperly@engleonline.com
Display Adv. E-mail: jhemperly@engleonline.com
Editorial e-mail: news@engleonline.com
Primary Website: www.engleonline.com
Year Established: 1963
Published: Wed
Avg Paid Circ: 0
Avg Free Circ: 31410
Audit By: CVC
Audit Date: 30.03.2021
Personnel: Mark Malloy (Circ. Mgr.); John Hemperly (Sales Manager); Greg March (Advertising Sales Manager)

LANSDALE

MONTGOMERY NEWSPAPERS

Street address 1: 307 DERSTINE AVE
Street address city: Lansdale
State: PA
Zip/Postal code: 19446
Country: USA
Mailing address: 307 Derstine Ave
Mailing city: Lansdale
Mailing state: PA
Mailing zip: 19446-3532
General Phone: (215) 542-0200
General Fax: (215) 643-9475
General/National Adv. E-mail: pmetz@trentonian.com
Display Adv. E-mail: bdouglas@21st-centurymedia.com
Editorial e-mail: econdra@21st-centurymedia.com
Primary Website: montgomerynews.com
Year Established: 1896
Published: Sun
Avg Paid Circ: 7862
Avg Free Circ: 1756
Audit By: AAM
Audit Date: 31.03.2019
Personnel: Edward Condra (Pub.); Beth Douglas (Adv.); Philip Metz (Circ. Dir.)

MOUNT JOY

ENGLE PRINTING & PUBLISHING CO., INC.

Street address 1: PO Box 500
Street address city: Mount Joy
State: PA
Zip/Postal code: 17552
General Phone: 717-653-1833
Advertising Phone: 717-278-1394
Editorial Phone: 717-492-2544
General/National Adv. E-mail: advertising@engleonline.com
Display Adv. E-mail: jhemperly@engleonline.com
Classified Adv. e-mail: classifieds@engleonline.com
Editorial e-mail: newsdept@engleonline.com
Primary Website: www.townlively.com
Mthly Avg Views: 16500
Mthly Avg Unique Visitors: 14350
Year Established: 1954
Published: Wed
Avg Free Circ: 230000
Audit By: CVC
Audit Date: 31.03.2023
Personnel: Jocelyn Engle (Publisher); John Hemperly (Operations Manager); Wendy Royal (Editor); ???? ????

MORGANTOWN/ HONEBROOK COMMUNITY COURIER

Street address 1: PO Box 500
Street address city: Mount Joy
State: PA
Zip/Postal code: 17552
County: Berks
Country: United States
Mailing address: PO Box 500
Mailing city: Mount Joy
Mailing state: PA
Mailing zip: 17552
General Phone: 717-653-1833
Advertising Phone: 717-492-2514
General/National Adv. E-mail: jhemperly@engleonline.com
Display Adv. E-mail: jhemperly@engleonline.com
Editorial e-mail: newsdept@engleonline.com
Primary Website: www.townlively.com
Mthly Avg Views: 16500
Year Established: 1954
Published: Wed
Avg Free Circ: 7500
Audit By: CVC
Audit Date: 31.03.2023
Personnel: John Hemperly (Operations Manager)
State: Rhode Island

RHODE ISLAND

BRISTOL

EAST BAY NEWSPAPERS

Street address 1: 1 Bradford St
Street address city: Bristol
State: RI
Zip/Postal code: 02809-1906
County: Bristol
Country: USA
Mailing address: PO Box 90
Mailing city: Bristol
Mailing state: RI
Mailing zip: 02809-0090
General Phone: (401) 253-6000
General Fax: (401) 253-6055
Advertising Phone: (401) 253-1000
General/National Adv. E-mail: spickering@eastbaynewspapers.com
Display Adv. E-mail: classifieds@eastbaynewspapers.com
Editorial e-mail: spickering@eastbaynewspapers.com
Primary Website: eastbayri.com
Year Established: 1837
Published: Other
Avg Paid Circ: 11024
Avg Free Circ: 11810
Audit By: CVC
Audit Date: 30.06.2018
Personnel: Matthew D. Hayes (Pub./ Adv. Mgr.); Lisa Carro (Gen. Mgr.); Toni Nuttall (Advertising Dir.); Jim McGaw (Ed.); Scott Pickering (Mng. Ed.); Jock Hayes (Prodn. Mgr.); Dichiappari Kirsten (MANAGING DIRECTOR, ONE BRADFORD)

WAKEFIELD

SOUTHERN RHODE ISLAND NEWSPAPERS

Street address 1: 187 Main St
Street address city: Wakefield

State: RI
Zip/Postal code: 02879-3504
County: Washington
Country: USA
Mailing address: 187 Main St
Mailing city: Wakefield
Mailing state: RI
Mailing zip: 02879-3504
General Phone: (401) 789-9744
General Fax: (401) 789-1550
Primary Website: www.ricentral.com
Published: Thur
Avg Paid Circ: 1920
Avg Free Circ: 264
Audit By: CAC
Audit Date: 30.06.2017
Personnel: Nanci Batson (Publisher)
State: Virginia

VIRGINIA

WINCHESTER

BYRD NEWSPAPERS

Street address 1: 2 N Kent St
Street address city: Winchester
State: VA
Zip/Postal code: 22601-5038
County: Winchester City
Country: USA
Mailing address: 2 N. Kent St.
Mailing city: Winchester
Mailing state: VA
Mailing zip: 22601
General Phone: (540) 667-3200
State: Washington

WASHINGTON

POULSBO

SOUND PUBLISHING, INC.

Street address 1: 19351 8th Ave NE
Street address 2: Ste 106
Street address city: Poulsbo
State: WA
Zip/Postal code: 98370-8710
County: Kitsap
Country: USA
Mailing address: 19351 8th Ave NE Ste 106
Mailing city: Poulsbo
Mailing state: WA
Mailing zip: 98370-8710
General Phone: (360) 394-5800
General Fax: (360) 394-5841
General/National Adv. E-mail: marketing@soundpublishing.com
Primary Website: www.soundpublishing.com; www.bainbridgereview.com
Year Established: 1988
Avg Paid Circ: 13394
Avg Free Circ: 309003
Audit By: CAC
Audit Date: 31.03.2016
Personnel: Lori Maxim (Vice Pres.); David Theobald (CFO); Chris Allen-Hoch (Pub.); Gloria Fletcher (President); Barrett Stephen (Director, National and Regional Sales); Kurt Ploudre

GAUGER MEDIA SERVICE, INC.

Street address 1: 1034 Bradford Street
Street address 2: P.O. Box 627
Street address city: Raymond
State: WA
Zip/Postal code: 98577
County: Pacific
Country: USA
Mailing address: P.O. Box 627
Mailing city: Raymond
Mailing state: WA
Mailing zip: 98577
General Phone: (360) 942-3560
General/National Adv. E-mail: dave@gaugermedia.com
Primary Website: www.gaugermedia.com
Year Established: 1987
Personnel: Dave Gauger (Pres/Broker)
State: Wisconsin

WISCONSIN

SHEBOYGAN

THE SHEBOYGAN SUN

Street address 1: 615 S. 8th Street
Street address 2: #120
Street address city: Sheboygan
State: WI
Zip/Postal code: 53081
County: Sheboygan
Country: USA
Mailing address: 708 Erie Ave Ste 201
Mailing city: Sheboygan
Mailing state: WI
Mailing zip: 53081-4060
General Phone: (920) 803-9945
General Fax: (920) 803-9946
Advertising Phone: (920) 803-9945
Advertising Fax: (920) 803-9945
Editorial Phone: (920) 803-9945
Editorial Fax: (920) 803-9945
General/National Adv. E-mail: thesun@sheboygansun.com
Display Adv. E-mail: ads@sheboygansun.com
Editorial e-mail: gdillon@sheboygansun.com
Primary Website: sheboygansun.com
Year Established: 1999
Published: Thur
Avg Paid Circ: 0
Avg Free Circ: 48978
Audit By: VAC
Audit Date: 30.03.2015
Personnel: Greg Dillon (Publisher); Mike Walton

WEST BEND

WASHINGTON COUNTY POST

Street address 1: 100 S 6th Ave
Street address city: West Bend
State: WI
Zip/Postal code: 53095-3309
County: Washington
Country: USA
Mailing address: 100 S 6TH AVE
Mailing city: WEST BEND
Mailing state: WI
Mailing zip: 53095-3309
General Phone: (262) 306-5000
General Fax: (262) 338-1984
Advertising Phone: (262) 306-5011
Editorial Phone: (262) 306-5000
General/National Adv. E-mail: jdenk@conleynet.com
Display Adv. E-mail: jdenk@conleynet.com
Classified Adv. e-mail: sjerdee@conleynet.com
Editorial e-mail: byorth@conleynet.com
Primary Website: gmtoday.com
Mthly Avg Views: 517000
Mthly Avg Unique Visitors: 140000
Year Established: 1995
Published: Sun
Avg Free Circ: 36618
Audit By: Sworn/Estimate/Non-Audited
Audit Date: 31.03.2021
Personnel: Jon Denk (General Manager)

SHOPPER PUBLICATIONS IN CANADA

ALBERTA

EDMONTON

FLYER FORCE

Street address 1: 5637 70 Street Nw
Street address 3: Edmonton
Street address state: AB
Zip/Postal code: T6B 3P6
Country: Canada
General Phone: (780)436-8050
Published: Thur
Audit By: Sworn/Estimate/Non-Audited
Audit Date: 9/30/2017
Classified Equipment»

FALHER

SMOKY RIVER EXPRESS

Street address 1: 217 Main St. W.
Street address 3: Falher
Street address state: AB
Zip/Postal code: T0H 1M0
County: Canada
Country: Canada
Mailing address: PO Box 644
Mailing city: Falher
Mailing state: AB
Mailing zip: T0H 1M0
General Phone: (780) 837-2585
General Fax: (780) 837-2102
General/National Adv. E-mail: srexpres@telus.net
Display Adv. E-mail: srexpres@telus.net
Editorial e-mail: sreeditor@telus.net
Primary Website: www.smokyriverexpress.com
Year Established: 1967
Delivery Methods: Mail`Newsstand
Area Served - City: T0H 1M0
Own Printing Facility: Y
Commercial printers: Y
Advertising (Open Inch Rate) Weekday/Saturday: Open inch rate $.88
Mechanical specifications: Type page 10.33 x 15.5
Published: Wed
Avg Paid Circ: 2021
Audit By: CMCA
Audit Date: 12/12/2017
Classified Equipment»
Personnel: Mary Burgar (Circ. Mgr.)

PONOKA

THE BASHAW STAR

Street address 1: 5019a Chipman Ave.
Street address 3: Ponoka
Street address state: AB
Zip/Postal code: T4J 1R6
County: Bashaw
Country: Canada
Mailing address: P.O. Box 4217
Mailing city: Ponoka
Mailing state: AB
Mailing zip: T4J 1R6
General Phone: (403) 783-3311
General Fax: (403) 783 6300
General/National Adv. E-mail: manager@bashawstar.com
Advertising (Open Inch Rate) Weekday/Saturday: Open inch rate $.61
Mechanical specifications: Type page 10 1/8 x 13; E - 7 cols, 1 1/12, 3/16 between; A - 7 cols, 1 1/12, 3/16 between; C - 8 cols, 3/16 between.
Published: Wed
Avg Paid Circ: 216
Avg Free Circ: 15
Audit By: CMCA
Audit Date: 4/30/2014
Classified Equipment»
Personnel: Mustafa Eric (Ed.)
Parent company (for newspapers): Black Press Group Ltd.

MEDICINE HAT

THE MEDICINE HAT SHOPPER

Street address 1: 3257 Dunmore Rd. SE
Street address 3: Medicine Hat
Street address state: AB
Zip/Postal code: T1B 3R2
County: Canada
Country: Canada
Mailing address: 3257 Dunmore Rd. SE
Mailing city: Medicine Hat
Mailing state: AB
Mailing zip: T1B 3R2
General Phone: (403) 527-5777
General Fax: (403) 526-7352
General/National Adv. E-mail: cbrown@medicinehatnews.com
Display Adv. E-mail: cbrown@medicinehatnews.com
Primary Website: www.shoppergroup.com
Year Established: 1976
Syndicated Publications: Styles Home & Interior
Delivery Methods: Carrier
Area Served - City: T1A,T1B,T1C
Own Printing Facility: Y
Commercial printers: N
Advertising (Open Inch Rate) Weekday/Saturday: $71.40 (smallest modular rate)
Mechanical specifications: Type page 10.25 x 16; 6 cols
Published: Sat
Avg Free Circ: 26089
Audit By: CVC
Audit Date: 6/30/2015
Classified Equipment»
Personnel: Edward Thurlbeck (Sales Manager); Ron Heizelman (Ed.)

LETHBRIDGE

THE SOUTHERN SUN TIMES

Street address 1: 504 7th St., S.
Street address 3: Lethbridge
Street address state: AB
Zip/Postal code: T1J 2H1
Country: Canada
Mailing address: 504 7th St., S.
Mailing city: Lethbridge
Mailing state: AB
Mailing zip: T1J 2H1
General Phone: (403) 328-4411
General Fax: (403) 320-7539
Area Served - City: T1H 2J1
Own Printing Facility: Y
Advertising (Open Inch Rate) Weekday/Saturday: Open inch rate $.95
Published: Wed
Audit Date: 9/30/2017
Classified Equipment»
Personnel: Bob Carey (Gen. Mgr.)

VEGREVILLE

VEGREVILLE NEWS ADVERTISER

Street address 1: 5110 50th St.
Street address 3: Vegreville
Street address state: AB
Zip/Postal code: T9C 1R9
Country: Canada
Mailing address: PO Box 810
Mailing city: Vegreville
Mailing state: AB
Mailing zip: T9C 1R9
General Phone: (780) 632-2861
General Fax: (780) 632-7981
Display Adv. E-mail: ads@newsadvertiser.com
Editorial e-mail: editor@newsadvertiser.com
Primary Website: www.newsadvertiser.com
Year Established: 1950
Delivery Methods: Mail`Carrier`Racks
Area Served - City: T9C 1R9 T0B 0C0 T0B 0K0 T0b 0P0 T0B 0R0 T0B 0W0 T0B 1C0 T0B 1S0 T0B 2B0 T0B 2C0 T0B 2G0 T0B 2R0 T0B 2S0 T0B 2W0 T0B 3B0 T0B 3H0 T0B 3K0 T0B 3T0 T0B 4A0 T0A 3C0 T0B 4B0 T0B 4J0 T0B 4K0 all of T9C T0B 4N0 T0B 4R0 T0B 4S0
Own Printing Facility: Y
Commercial printers: Y
Advertising (Open Inch Rate) Weekday/Saturday: Open inch rate $15.26
Mechanical specifications: Type page 10.25" x 15.5"; 6 cols
Published: Wed
Avg Paid Circ: 50
Avg Free Circ: 11241
Audit By: Sworn/Estimate/Non-Audited
Audit Date: 9/30/2017
Classified Equipment»
Personnel: Arthur Beaudette (Gen. Mgr.); Dan Beaudette (Ed.)

IRRICANA

WHEEL & DEAL

Street address 1: Po Box 40
Street address 3: Irricana
Street address state: AB
Zip/Postal code: T0M 1B0
Country: Canada
Mailing address: PO Box 40
Mailing city: Irricana
Mailing state: AB
Mailing zip: T0M 1B0
General Phone: (204) 954-1400
General Fax: (403) 935-4981
Editorail Phone: (403) 697-4703
General/National Adv. E-mail: deal@wheel-deal.com
Primary Website: www.albertafarmexpress.ca
Year Established: 1969
Area Served - City: T0M 1B0
Advertising (Open Inch Rate) Weekday/Saturday: Open inch rate $1.90
Mechanical specifications: Type page 10 1/4 x 13; A - 6 cols, 1 1/2, 1/6 between; C - 7 cols, 1/6 between.
Published: Mon
Avg Paid Circ: 281
Avg Free Circ: 71900
Audit By: Sworn/Estimate/Non-Audited
Audit Date: 9/30/2017
Classified Equipment»
Personnel: Will Berboven (Pub.); Bob Willcox (Pub.); John Morriss (Assoc. Pub.); Donna Berting (Adv. Mgr.); Linda Tityk (Circ. Mgr.)
Parent company (for newspapers): Great West Media LP

FORT SASKATCHEWAN

THE FORT SASKATCHEWAN RECORD

Street address 1: 10404 99 Ave
Street address 2: 168A
Street address 3: Fort Saskatchewan
Street address state: AB
Zip/Postal code: T8L 3W2
County: Strathcona County
Country: Canada
Mailing address: 10404 99 Ave, 168A
Mailing city: Fort Saskatchewan
Mailing state: AB
Mailing zip: T8L 3W2
General Phone: (780) 998-7070 Ext 724227
General Fax: (780) 998-5515
Editorial e-mail: agreen@postmedia.com
Primary Website: fortsaskatchewanrecord.com
Year Established: 1922
News Services: QMI
Delivery Methods: Mail`Carrier`Racks
Area Served - City: Strathcona County
Own Printing Facility: N
Commercial printers: Y
Advertising (Open Inch Rate) Weekday/Saturday: Open inch rate $0.71
Mechanical available: mechanical info on website
Mechanical specifications: specs available on website
Published: Thur
Avg Paid Circ: 9
Avg Free Circ: 8806
Audit By: Sworn/Estimate/Non-Audited
Audit Date: 7/12/2019
Classified Equipment»
Personnel: A Green
Parent company (for newspapers): Postmedia Network Inc.
footnotes: Editorial e-mail: CARDonline; Year Established: CARDonline; Advertising (Open Inch Rate) Weekday/Saturday: CARDonline

THE LETHBRIDGE SHOPPER

Street address 1: 12th Street B North
Street address 2: 234A
Street address 3: Lethbridge
Street address state: AB
Zip/Postal code: T1H 2K7
County: Canada
Country: Canada
Mailing address: 234A 12th Street B North
Mailing city: Lethbridge
Mailing state: AB
Mailing zip: T1H 2K7
General Phone: (403) 527-5777
General Fax: (403) 526-7352
General/National Adv. E-mail: ethurlbeck@shoppergroup.com
Display Adv. E-mail: ethurlbeck@shoppergroup.com
Editorial e-mail: ethurlbeck@shoppergroup.com
Primary Website: www.shoppergroup.com
Year Established: 1976
Delivery Methods: Carrier
Area Served - City: T1A, T1B, T1C
Advertising (Open Inch Rate) Weekday/Saturday: $71.40 (smallest modular rate)
Mechanical specifications: Type page 10.25 x 16; 6 cols
Published: Sat
Avg Free Circ: 33176
Audit By: CVC
Audit Date: 6/30/2013
Classified Equipment»
Personnel: Ron Heizelman (Ed.); Edward Thurlbeck (Adv. Mgr.)

BRITISH COLUMBIA

SALMON ARM

LAKESHORE NEWS

Street address 1: 161 Hudson Ave.
Street address 3: Salmon Arm
Street address state: BC
Zip/Postal code: V1E 4N8
Country: Canada
Mailing address: PO Box 699
Mailing city: Salmon Arm
Mailing state: BC
Mailing zip: V1E 4N8
General Phone: (250) 832-9461
General Fax: (250) 832-5246

General/National Adv. E-mail: isn@lakeshorenews.bc.ca
Primary Website: lakeshorenews.bc.ca
Published: Fri
Avg Paid Circ: 0
Avg Free Circ: 13745
Audit By: Sworn/Estimate/Non-Audited
Audit Date: 9/30/2017
Classified Equipment»
Parent company (for newspapers): Black Press Group Ltd.

KASLO

PENNYWISE

Street address 1: Po Box 430
Street address 3: Kaslo
Street address state: BC
Zip/Postal code: V0G 1M0
Country: Canada
Mailing address: PO Box 430
Mailing city: Kaslo
Mailing state: BC
Mailing zip: V0G 1M0
General Phone: (250) 353-2602
General Fax: (250) 353-7444
General/National Adv. E-mail: info@pennywiseads.com
Primary Website: www.pennywiseads.com
Advertising (Open Inch Rate) Weekday/Saturday: Open inch rate $.75
Published: Tues
Avg Free Circ: 27000
Audit By: Sworn/Estimate/Non-Audited
Audit Date: 9/30/2017
Classified Equipment»
Personnel: Patricia Axen-Rotch (Pub.); Julie Wilson (Adv. Mgr.); Tania Seafoot (Ed.)

PENNYWISE - CASTLEGAR / SLOCAN VALLEY

Street address 1: Po Box 430
Street address 3: Kaslo
Street address state: BC
Zip/Postal code: V0G 1M0
Country: Canada
Mailing address: PO BOX 430
Mailing city: Kaslo
Mailing state: BC
Mailing zip: V0G 1M0
Primary Website: www.pennywiseads.com
Year Established: 1975
Delivery Methods: Racks
Area Served - City: Kalso BC
Advertising (Open Inch Rate) Weekday/Saturday: $60.12 (smallest modular rate)
Mechanical specifications: Type page 6.75" x 9.7"; 2 cols
Published: Tues
Avg Free Circ: 8515
Audit By: CVC
Audit Date: 6/30/2015
Classified Equipment»
Personnel: Patty Axenroth

PENNYWISE - KOOTENAY LAKE

Street address 1: Po Box 430
Street address 3: Kaslo
Street address state: BC
Zip/Postal code: V0G 1M0
Country: Canada
Mailing address: PO BOX 430
Mailing city: Kaslo
Mailing state: BC
Mailing zip: V0G 1M0
Primary Website: www.pennywiseads.com
Year Established: 1975
Delivery Methods: Racks
Area Served - City: Kalso, BC
Advertising (Open Inch Rate) Weekday/Saturday: $60.12 (smallest modular rate)
Mechanical specifications: Type page 6.75" x 9.7"; 2 cols
Published: Tues
Avg Free Circ: 3505
Audit By: CVC
Audit Date: 6/30/2015
Classified Equipment»
Personnel: Patty Axenroth

PENNYWISE - NELSON

Street address 1: Po Box 430
Street address 3: Kaslo
Street address state: BC
Zip/Postal code: V0G 1M0
Country: Canada
Mailing address: PO BOX 430
Mailing city: Kaslo
Mailing state: BC
Mailing zip: V0G 1M0
Primary Website: www.pennywiseads.com
Year Established: 1975
Delivery Methods: Racks
Area Served - City: Kalso, BC
Advertising (Open Inch Rate) Weekday/Saturday: $60.12 (smallest modular rate)
Mechanical specifications: Type page 6.75" x 9.7"; 2 cols
Published: Tues
Avg Paid Circ: 0
Avg Free Circ: 5661
Audit By: CVC
Audit Date: 6/30/2015
Classified Equipment»
Personnel: Patty Axenroth

PENNYWISE - TRAIL / BEAVER VALLEY / SALMO

Street address 1: Po Box 43
Street address 3: Kaslo
Street address state: BC
Zip/Postal code: V0G 1M0
Country: Canada
Mailing address: PO BOX 430
Mailing city: Kaslo
Mailing state: BC
Mailing zip: V0G 1M0
Primary Website: www.pennywiseads.com
Year Established: 1975
Delivery Methods: Racks
Area Served - City: Kalso, BC
Advertising (Open Inch Rate) Weekday/Saturday: $60.12 (smallest modular rate)
Mechanical specifications: Type page 6.75" x 9.7"; 2 cols
Published: Tues
Avg Paid Circ: 0
Avg Free Circ: 8607
Audit By: CVC
Audit Date: 6/30/2015
Classified Equipment»
Personnel: Patty Axenroth

GRAND FORKS

WEST KOOTENAY ADVERTISER

Street address 1: 7255 Riverside Dr.
Street address 3: Grand Forks
Street address state: BC
Zip/Postal code: V0H 1H0
County: Boundary
Country: Canada
Mailing address: Box 700
Mailing city: Grand Forks
Mailing state: BC
Mailing zip: V0H 1H0
General Phone: (250) 442-2191
General Fax: (866) 897-0678
General/National Adv. E-mail: publisher@grandforksgazette.ca; classifieds@grandforksgazette.ca; circulation@grandforksgazette.ca; production@grandforksgazette.ca; accounting@grandforksgazette.ca
Display Adv. E-mail: sales@grandforksgazette.ca
Editorial e-mail: editor@grandforksgazette.ca
Primary Website: www.grandforksgazette.ca
Area Served - City: v0h1h0-v0h1h9, V0H 1E0-v0h 1E3, v0h1j0,v0h1m0,v0h 1yo, v0h 1b0, v0h 2b0
Advertising (Open Inch Rate) Weekday/Saturday: Open inch rate $.88
Mechanical specifications: Type page 10 1/4 x 15 1/2; E - 5 cols, 2, 1/16 between; A - 5 cols, 2, 1/16 between; C - 5 cols, 2, 1/16 between.
Published: Thur
Avg Free Circ: 4000
Audit By: Sworn/Estimate/Non-Audited
Audit Date: 9/30/2017
Classified Equipment»
Personnel: Darlainea Redlack (Circ. Mgr.)
Parent company (for newspapers): Black Press

SURREY

THE LINK

Street address 1: 12732 80th Avenue
Street address 2: #200
Street address 3: Surrey
Street address state: BC
Zip/Postal code: V3W 3A7
County: BC
Country: Canada
Mailing address: 16318 - 113B Avenue
Mailing city: Surrey
Mailing state: BC
Mailing zip: V4N 5A2
General Phone: (604) 880-3463
General Fax: (604) 591-2113
Advertising Phone: (604) 880-3463
Editorail Phone: (604) 880-3463
General/National Adv. E-mail: editorpd@hotmail.com
Display Adv. E-mail: editorpd@hotmail.com
Editorial e-mail: editorpd@hotmail.com
Primary Website: www.thelinkpaper.ca
Year Established: 1972
Delivery Methods: Mail`Newsstand`Carrier`Racks
Own Printing Facility: Y
Advertising (Open Inch Rate) Weekday/Saturday: Open inch rate $12.00
Mechanical specifications: Type page 10 1/4 x 14 3/4; E - 6 cols, 1 7/12, 1/6 between; A - 6 cols, 1 1/3, 1/6 between.
Published: Sat
Avg Free Circ: 20000
Audit By: Sworn/Estimate/Non-Audited
Audit Date: 11/30/2018
Classified Equipment»
Personnel: Paul Dhillon (Ed.)
Parent company (for newspapers): South Asian Link Publications

BURNABY

BUY & SELL

Street address 1: 4664 Lougheed Hwy.
Street address 2: Ste. W020
Street address 3: Burnaby
Street address state: BC
Zip/Postal code: V5C 5T5
Country: Canada
Mailing address: Ste. W020 4664 Lougheed Hwy.
Mailing city: Burnaby
Mailing state: BC
Mailing zip: V5C 5T5
General Phone: (604) 540-4455
General Fax: (604) 540-6451
Advertising Phone: (604) 280-1000
Primary Website: www.buysell.com
Year Established: 1971
Area Served - City: V6X 2C9
Published: Thur
Avg Free Circ: 42005
Audit By: Sworn/Estimate/Non-Audited
Audit Date: 9/30/2017
Classified Equipment»
Personnel: Zac Goodman (Prodn. Mgr.)

NOVA SCOTIA

TRURO

WEEKEND READ

Street address 1: 6 Louise St.
Street address 3: Truro
Street address state: NS
Zip/Postal code: B2N 5C3
Country: Canada
Mailing address: PO Box 220
Mailing city: Truro
Mailing state: NS
Mailing zip: B2N 5C3
General Phone: (902) 893-9405
General Fax: (902) 895-6104
General/National Adv. E-mail: news@trurodaily.com
Primary Website: www.trurodaily.com
Area Served - City: B2N 5C3
Own Printing Facility: Y
Advertising (Open Inch Rate) Weekday/Saturday: Open inch rate $1.06
Published: Fri
Avg Free Circ: 20479
Audit By: Sworn/Estimate/Non-Audited
Audit Date: 9/30/2017
Classified Equipment»
Personnel: Richard Russell (Pub.); Carl Fleming (Ed.)

ONTARIO

CHATHAM

CHATHAM PENNYSAVER

Street address 1: 930 Richmond St.
Street address 3: Chatham
Street address state: ON
Zip/Postal code: N7M 5J5
Country: Canada
Mailing address: 930 Richmond St.
Mailing city: Chatham
Mailing state: ON
Mailing zip: N7M 5J5
General Phone: (519) 351-4362
General Fax: (519) 351-2452
Advertising Phone: (866) 541-6757
General/National Adv. E-mail: chathampennysaver@bowesnet.com
Display Adv. E-mail: placeit@classifiedextra.ca
Primary Website: www.chathampennysaver.com
Area Served - City: N7M 5J5
Own Printing Facility: Y
Mechanical specifications: Type page 10 1/4 x 12; E - 7 cols, between; A - 7 cols, between; C - 7 cols, between.
Published: Fri
Avg Free Circ: 38914
Audit By: Sworn/Estimate/Non-Audited
Audit Date: 9/30/2017
Classified Equipment»
Personnel: Dean Muharrem (Pub./Gen. Mgr.); Melissa Steele (Office Mgr.); Tracey Weaver-Curran (Sales Mgr.); Martin Steele (Supervisor)

NAPANEE

FRIDAY REGIONAL BEAVER

Street address 1: 72 Dundas St. E.
Street address 3: Napanee
Street address state: ON
Zip/Postal code: K7R 1H9
Country: Canada
Mailing address: 72 Dundas St. E.
Mailing city: Napanee
Mailing state: ON
Mailing zip: K7R 1H9
General Phone: (613) 354-6641
General Fax: (613) 354-2622
General/National Adv. E-mail: info@napaneebeaver.ca
Primary Website: napaneebeaver.ca
Year Established: 1870
Advertising (Open Inch Rate) Weekday/Saturday: Open inch rate $.70
Mechanical specifications: Type page 10 5/16 x 15 1/4; E - 6 cols, 1 9/16, 1/6 between; A - 6 cols, 1 9/16, 1/6 between; C - 6 cols, 1 9/16, 1/6 between.
Published: Fri
Audit Date: 9/30/2017
Classified Equipment»
Personnel: Jean Morrison (Pub.)

GODERICH

GODERICH SIGNAL STAR

Street address 1: 120 Huckins St.
Street address 3: Goderich
Street address state: ON
Zip/Postal code: N7A 4B6
Country: Canada
Mailing address: PO Box 220
Mailing city: Goderich
Mailing state: ON
Mailing zip: N7A 4B6
General Phone: (519) 524-2614
General Fax: (519) 524-9175
Editorial e-mail: katsmith@postmedia.com
Primary Website: goderichsignalstar.com
Area Served - City: N7A 4B6
Own Printing Facility: Y
Advertising (Open Inch Rate) Weekday/Saturday: Open inch rate $1.08
Mechanical specifications: Type page 10 3/8 x 14 7/8; E - 6 cols, 1 7/12, 1/2 between; A - 6 cols, 1 7/12, 1/2 between; C - 6 cols, 1 7/12, 1/2 between.
Published: Fri
Avg Free Circ: 20150
Audit By: Sworn/Estimate/Non-Audited
Audit Date: 3/30/2019
Classified Equipment»
Personnel: Kat Smith

GUELPH

GUELPH MERCURY TRIBUNE

Street address 1: 367 Woodlawn Rd. W., Unit 1
Street address 3: Guelph
Street address state: ON
Zip/Postal code: N1H 7K9
Country: Canada
Mailing address: 367 Woodlawn Rd. W., Unit 1
Mailing city: Guelph
Mailing state: ON
Mailing zip: N1H 7K9
General Phone: (519) 763-3333
Advertising Phone: (519) 763-3333 ext. 240
General/National Adv. E-mail: customerservice@metroland.com
Display Adv. E-mail: ccampbell@starmetrolandmedia.com
Editorial e-mail: newsroom@guelphmercurytribune.com
Primary Website: guelphmercury.com
Area Served - City: N1H 1A8
Advertising (Open Inch Rate) Weekday/Saturday: Open inch rate $1.52
Published: Fri
Avg Free Circ: 47000
Audit By: Sworn/Estimate/Non-Audited
Audit Date: 4/30/2019
Classified Equipment»
Personnel: Cindi Campbell (News/Adv.); Derek Prince-Cox (Subsc./ Circ.)

TILLSONBURG

LAKE SHORE SHOPPER (TILLSONBURG)

Street address 1: 25 Townline Rd.
Street address 3: Tillsonburg
Street address state: ON
Zip/Postal code: N4G 4H6
Country: Canada
Mailing address: PO Box 190
Mailing city: Tillsonburg
Mailing state: ON
Mailing zip: N4G 4H6
General Phone: (519) 688-1177
General Fax: (519) 688-9353
Primary Website: www.theshopper.ca
Own Printing Facility: Y
Advertising (Open Inch Rate) Weekday/Saturday: Open inch rate $.96
Mechanical specifications: Type page 10 3/8 x 15; A - 9 cols, 1 9/16, between.
Published: Fri
Avg Free Circ: 40434
Audit By: Sworn/Estimate/Non-Audited
Audit Date: 9/30/2017
Classified Equipment»
Personnel: Michael Walsh (Pub.); David Hopkins (Adv. Mgr.); Joan Tewes (Circ. Mgr.); Sharon Craig (Prodn. Mgr.)
Parent company (for newspapers): Postmedia Network Inc.; Quebecor Communications, Inc.

LEAMINGTON

LEAMINGTON SHOPPER

Street address 1: 75 Oak St.
Street address 3: Leamington
Street address state: ON
Zip/Postal code: N8H 2B2
Country: Canada
Mailing address: 75 Oak St.
Mailing city: Leamington
Mailing state: ON
Mailing zip: N8H 2B2
General Phone: (519) 326-4434
General Fax: (519) 326-2171
Display Adv. E-mail: shopper@wincom.net
Primary Website: www.leamingtonpostandshopper.com
Year Established: 1971
Delivery Methods: Carrier
Area Served - City: N8H 2X8
Advertising (Open Inch Rate) Weekday/Saturday: Open inch rate $1.02
Mechanical specifications: Type page 10 2/5 x 14; E - 9 cols, 1 1/16, 1/8 between; A - 9 cols, 1 1/16, 1/8 between.
Published: Fri
Avg Free Circ: 17400
Audit By: Sworn/Estimate/Non-Audited
Audit Date: 9/30/2017
Classified Equipment»
Note: We recently added news content and changed the name from Leamington Shopper to Tri-Town News serving the communities of Kingsville , Leamington & Wheatley
Personnel: Donald Gage (Pub.); Linda Gage (Adv. Mgr.)

ELLIOT LAKE

MARKETPLACE

Street address 1: 14 Hillside Dr. S.
Street address 3: Elliot Lake
Street address state: ON
Zip/Postal code: P5A 1M6
Country: Canada
Mailing address: 14 Hillside Dr. S.
Mailing city: Elliot Lake
Mailing state: ON
Mailing zip: P0M 3E0
General Phone: (705) 866-1801
General Fax: (705) 848-0249
General/National Adv. E-mail: kjohansen@postmedia.com
Display Adv. E-mail: kjohansen@postmedia.com
Editorial e-mail: kjohansen@postmedia.com
Primary Website: www.elliotlakestandard.ca
Year Established: 1956
Delivery Methods: Mail`Newsstand`Carrier`Racks
Own Printing Facility: Y
Commercial printers: Y
Advertising (Open Inch Rate) Weekday/Saturday: Open inch rate $9.80
Mechanical specifications: Page size - 10.25" wide X 15' tall, 9 column
Published: Thur
Avg Paid Circ: 3623
Avg Free Circ: 8000
Audit By: Sworn/Estimate/Non-Audited
Audit Date: 11/6/2018
Classified Equipment»
Personnel: Lolene Patterson (Circ. Mgr.); Kevin McSheffrey (Mng Ed.); Karsten Johansen (Gen. Mgr.)
Parent company (for newspapers): Sunmedia

NIAGARA FALLS

NIAGARA SHOPPING NEWS

Street address 1: 4949 Victoria Ave.
Street address 3: Niagara Falls
Street address state: ON
Zip/Postal code: L2E 4C7
Country: Canada
Mailing address: 4949 Victoria Ave.
Mailing city: Niagara Falls
Mailing state: ON
Mailing zip: L2E 4C7
General Phone: (905) 357-2440
General Fax: (905) 357-1620
Advertising Phone: (877) 786-8227
General/National Adv. E-mail: niagaraclassifieds@cogeco.net
Primary Website: www.ospreymedia.ca; www.niagarashoppingnews.ca
Area Served - City: L2E 4C7
Advertising (Open Inch Rate) Weekday/Saturday: Open inch rate $.68
Published: Wed`Fri
Avg Free Circ: 29250
Audit By: Sworn/Estimate/Non-Audited
Audit Date: 9/30/2017
Classified Equipment»
Personnel: Tim Dundas (Pub.)
Parent company (for newspapers): Quebecor Communications, Inc.

BURKS FALLS

OMEGA FORESTER

Street address 1: 59 Ontario St.
Street address 3: Burks Falls
Street address state: ON
Zip/Postal code: P0A 1C0
Country: Canada
Mailing address: PO Box 518
Mailing city: Burks Falls
Mailing state: ON
Mailing zip: P0A 1C0
General Phone: (705) 382-3943
General Fax: (705) 382-3440
General/National Adv. E-mail: anews@onlink.net
Primary Website: www.almaguinnews.com
Area Served - City: P0A 1C0
Advertising (Open Inch Rate) Weekday/Saturday: Open inch rate $9.00
Published: Fri
Audit Date: 9/30/2017
Classified Equipment»
Personnel: Doug Pincoee (Sales Mgr.)

LONDON

PENNYSAVER

Street address 1: 369 York St.
Street address 3: London
Street address state: ON
Zip/Postal code: N6A 4G1
Country: Canada
Mailing address: PO Box 2280
Mailing city: London
Mailing state: ON
Mailing zip: N6A 4G1
General Phone: (519) 685-2020
General Fax: (519) 649-0908
Advertising Phone: (519) 667-5472
Advertising Fax: (519) 667-4573
General/National Adv. E-mail: newsdesk@lfpress.com
Display Adv. E-mail: pennyreaderads@londonpennysaver.com
Primary Website: www.lfpress.com; www.londonpennysaver.com
Area Served - City: N5Z 3L1
Advertising (Open Inch Rate) Weekday/Saturday: Open inch rate $3.17
Published: Fri
Avg Free Circ: 159000
Audit By: Sworn/Estimate/Non-Audited
Audit Date: 9/30/2017
Classified Equipment»
Personnel: Cathy Forster (Gen. Mgr.); Nick Hawkins (Sales Rep.); Tracey Spence (Circ. Mgr.)

BELLEVILLE

SHOPPER'S MARKET

Street address 1: 365 N. Front St.
Street address 3: Belleville
Street address state: ON
Zip/Postal code: K8P 5E6
Country: Canada
Mailing address: PO Box 446
Mailing city: Belleville
Mailing state: ON
Mailing zip: K8N 5A5
General Phone: (613) 962-3422
General Fax: (613) 962-0543
Advertising Phone: (866) 541-6757
Advertising Fax: (866) 757-0227
General/National Adv. E-mail: readerads@cogeco.net
Display Adv. E-mail: placeit@classifiedextra.ca; advertise@canoe.quebecor.com
Primary Website: shoppersmarket.classifiedextra.ca
Area Served - City: K8N 5A5
Advertising (Open Inch Rate) Weekday/Saturday: Open inch rate $1.28
Mechanical specifications: Type page 10 1/4 x 12 3/10; A - 6 cols, 1 5/8, 3/16 between.
Published: Thur
Avg Free Circ: 50000
Audit By: Sworn/Estimate/Non-Audited
Audit Date: 9/30/2017
Classified Equipment»
Personnel: Charles Parker (Adv. Mgr.); Martin Courchesne (Nat'l Dir., Sales)

OTTAWA

SMART SHOPPER

Street address 1: 6 Antares Dr.
Street address 3: Ottawa
Street address state: ON
Zip/Postal code: K1G 5H7
Country: Canada
Mailing address: 6 Antares Dr.
Mailing city: Ottawa
Mailing state: ON
Mailing zip: K1G 5H7
General Phone: (613) 733-4099
General Fax: (613) 733-7107
Display Adv. E-mail: classads@ott.sunpub.com
Primary Website: www.ottawasmartshopper.ca
Area Served - City: K2E 7J6
Advertising (Open Inch Rate) Weekday/Saturday: Open inch rate $2.22
Mechanical specifications: Type page 10 1/4 x 11 1/2; A - 6 cols, 1 5/8, between.
Published: Thur
Avg Free Circ: 166000
Audit By: Sworn/Estimate/Non-Audited
Audit Date: 9/30/2017
Classified Equipment»
Personnel: Pierre Peladeau (CEO); Shane Patacairk (Adv. Mgr.); Marty Holski (Circ. Mgr.)

CORNWALL

STANDARD-FREEHOLDER COMPLIMENTARY

Street address 1: No office
Street address 3: Cornwall
Street address state: ON
Zip/Postal code: K6H1E
Country: Canada
Mailing city: Cornwall
Mailing state: ON
General Phone: (613) 933-3160
Advertising Phone: (613) 933-3160 x4
Editorail Phone: (613) 933-3160 X2
General/National Adv. E-mail: csf.news@sunmedia.ca
Display Adv. E-mail: ksammon@postmedia.com
Editorial e-mail: hrodrigues@postmedia.com
Primary Website: www.standard-freeholder.com
Year Established: 1846
Own Printing Facility: Y
Mechanical specifications: Type page 11 1/2 x 21 1/2; E - 10 cols, 1 1/10, between; A - 10 cols, 1 1/10, between; C - 10 cols, 1 1/10, between.
Published: Thur
Avg Free Circ: 24000
Audit By: Sworn/Estimate/Non-Audited
Audit Date: 9/30/2017
Classified Equipment»
Personnel: Hugo Rodrigues; Kerry Sammon; Melissa Ayerist (Circ.)

Parent company (for newspapers): Quebecor Communications, Inc.; Postmedia Network Inc.

STRATHROY

STRATHROY AGE DISPATCH

Street address 1: 73 Front St W
Street address 3: Strathroy
Street address state: ON
Zip/Postal code: N7G 1X6
Country: Canada
Mailing address: 73 Front St W
Mailing city: Strathroy
Mailing state: ON
Mailing zip: N7G 1X6
General Phone: (519) 245-2370
General/National Adv. E-mail: agedispatch@strathroyonline.com
Primary Website: www.strathroyagedispatch.com
Year Established: 1861
Area Served - City: N7G 1Y4
Advertising (Open Inch Rate) Weekday/Saturday: Open inch rate $1.12
Mechanical specifications: Type page 10 1/4 x 13; E - 8 cols, 1 3/16, 1/6 between; A - 9 cols, 1 3/16, 1/6 between; C - 8 cols, 1 3/16, 1/6 between.
Published: Wed
Avg Free Circ: 5000
Audit By: Sworn/Estimate/Non-Audited
Audit Date: 4/30/2019
Classified Equipment»
Personnel: Linda Leblanc (Pub.); Denise Armstrong (Adv. Mgr.); Cheryl Klaver (Circ. Mgr.)
Parent company (for newspapers): Postmedia Network Inc.; Quebecor Communications, Inc.

BRIGHTON

THE BRIGHTON INDEPENDENT

Street address 1: 21 Meade St
Street address 3: Brighton
Street address state: ON
Zip/Postal code: K0K 1H0
County: Canada
Country: Canada
Mailing address: PO Box 1030
Mailing city: Brighton
Mailing state: ON
Mailing zip: K0K 1H0
General Phone: (613) 475-0255
General Fax: (613) 475-4546
Advertising Phone: (613) 475-0255 X 214
Editorail Phone: (613) 966-2034
General/National Adv. E-mail: jkearns@metroland.com
Display Adv. E-mail: jkearns@metroland.com
Editorial e-mail: tbush@metroland.com
Primary Website: www.metroland.com
Year Established: 1973
Delivery Methods: Carrier`Racks
Area Served - City: K0k 1h0, K8v, K0k 1L0, K0l 1L0, K0k is0
Advertising (Open Inch Rate) Weekday/Saturday: Open inch rate $1.33
Published: Thur
Avg Free Circ: 7816
Audit By: CMCA
Audit Date: 6/30/2016
Classified Equipment»
Personnel: Benita Stansel (Circ. Mgr.); John Kearns (Publisher)
Parent company (for newspapers): Metroland Media Group Ltd.

DURHAM

THE DURHAM CHRONICLE

Street address 1: 190 Elizabeth St. E.
Street address 3: Durham
Street address state: ON
Zip/Postal code: N0G 1R0
County: Canada
Country: Canada
Mailing address: PO Box 230
Mailing city: Durham
Mailing state: ON
Mailing zip: N0G 1R0
General Phone: (519) 369-2504
General Fax: (519) 369-3560
General/National Adv. E-mail: themarkdalestandard@bmts.com
Area Served - City: Canada
Advertising (Open Inch Rate) Weekday/Saturday: Open inch rate $.37
Mechanical specifications: Type page 11 1/4 x 16 3/4; E - 5 cols, 2 1/5, between; A - 5 cols, 2 1/5, between; C - 9 cols, between.
Published: Wed
Avg Paid Circ: 1196
Avg Free Circ: 21
Audit By: Sworn/Estimate/Non-Audited
Audit Date: 7/12/2019
Classified Equipment»
Personnel: Marie David (Pub.); Bev Stoddart (Gen. Mgr.); Christine Meingast (Ed.)

PETERBOROUGH

THE EXAMINER

Street address 1: 60 Hunter Street East
Street address 3: Peterborough
Street address state: ON
Zip/Postal code: K9H 1G5
Country: Canada
Mailing address: 60 Hunter Street East
Mailing city: Peterborough
Mailing state: ON
Mailing zip: K9H 1G5
General Phone: (705) 745-4641
General/National Adv. E-mail: Circulation@peterboroughdaily.com
Display Adv. E-mail: jillian.baldwin@peterboroughdaily.com
Editorial e-mail: stefanie.lynch@peterboroughdaily.com
Primary Website: www.peterboroughexaminer.com
Year Established: 1847
Advertising (Open Inch Rate) Weekday/Saturday: Open inch rate $1.35
Published: Fri
Avg Free Circ: 49000
Audit By: Sworn/Estimate/Non-Audited
Audit Date: 4/30/2019
Classified Equipment»
Personnel: Kennedy Gordon (Mng. Ed.); Michael Everson (Mktg. Mgr.); Neil Oliver (Pub.)
Parent company (for newspapers): Quebecor Communications, Inc.

WASAGA BEACH

THE STAYNER SUN

Street address 1: 1456 Mosley St.
Street address 3: Wasaga Beach
Street address state: ON
Zip/Postal code: L9Z 2B9
County: Canada
Country: Canada
Mailing address: 1456 Mosley St.
Mailing city: Wasaga Beach
Mailing state: ON
Mailing zip: L9Z 2B9
General Phone: (705) 428-2638
General Fax: (705) 422-2446
General/National Adv. E-mail: sunnews@simcoe.com
Primary Website: www.staynersun.ca
Advertising (Open Inch Rate) Weekday/Saturday: Open inch rate $1.12
Mechanical specifications: Type page 11 1/2 x 21 1/2; E - 10 cols, 1 1/16, 3/32 between; A - 10 cols, 1 1/16, 3/32 between; C - 10 cols, 1 1/16, 3/32 between.
Published: Thur
Avg Free Circ: 4088
Audit By: CMCA
Audit Date: 6/30/2014
Classified Equipment»
Personnel: Joe Anderson (Pub.); Catherine Haller (Gen. Mgr.); Mary Ellis (Bus. Mgr.); Shaun Sauve (Adv. Dir.); Wendy Sherk (Adv. Mgr.); Scott Woodhouse (Ed.); Stephen Hall (Prodn. Mgr.)
Parent company (for newspapers): Metroland Media Group Ltd.; Torstar

BEETON

THE WOODBRIDGE ADVERTISER

Street address 1: 2 Main St. W.
Street address 3: Beeton
Street address state: ON
Zip/Postal code: L0G 1A0
Country: Canada
Mailing address: PO Box 379
Mailing city: Beeton
Mailing state: ON
Mailing zip: L0G 1A0
General Phone: (905) 729-4501
General Fax: (905) 729-3961
General/National Adv. E-mail: wa@csolve.net
Primary Website: www.ontariosauctionpaper.com
Area Served - City: L0N 1P0
Advertising (Open Inch Rate) Weekday/Saturday: Open inch rate $11.10
Published: Thur
Avg Paid Circ: 2000
Audit By: Sworn/Estimate/Non-Audited
Audit Date: 9/30/2017
Classified Equipment»
Personnel: Karl Mallette (Ed.); Tina Dedels (Editorial Mgr.)

BRANTFORD

PARIS STAR

Street address 1: 195 Henry St
Street address 2: Building 4, Unit 1
Street address 3: Brantford
Street address state: ON
Zip/Postal code: N3S 5C9
Country: Canada
Mailing address: 195 Henry St, Building 4, Unit 1
Mailing city: Brantford
Mailing state: ON
Mailing zip: N3S 5C9
General Phone: (519) 756-2020
General Fax: (519) 756-9470
General/National Adv. E-mail: parisstar.editorial@sunmedia.ca
Editorial e-mail: parisstar.editorial@sunmedia.ca
Primary Website: parisstaronline.com
Year Established: 1850
Area Served - City: Canada
Own Printing Facility: Y
Advertising (Open Inch Rate) Weekday/Saturday: Open inch rate $.72
Mechanical specifications: Type page 10 x 16; E - 5 cols, 2, 1/8 between; A - 5 cols, 2, 1/8 between; C - 6 cols, 1 3/4, 1/8 between.
Published: Thur
Avg Free Circ: 4877
Audit By: CMCA
Audit Date: 4/30/2019
Classified Equipment»
Personnel: Ken Koyama (Pub.); Michael Peeling (Ed.)
Parent company (for newspapers): Postmedia Network Inc.; Quebecor Communications, Inc.

OAKVILLE

SHOPPING NEWS

Street address 1: 2526 Speers
Street address 2: Unit 11
Street address 3: Oakville
Street address state: ON
Zip/Postal code: L6L 5M2
Country: Canada
Mailing address: 2526 Speers, Unit 11
Mailing city: Oakville
Mailing state: ON
Mailing zip: L6L 5M2
General Phone: (905) 827-2244
General Fax: (905) 827-9950
Editorial e-mail: editorial@oakvilletoday.ca
Primary Website: www.metroland.com
Area Served - City: L6C 5T7
Advertising (Open Inch Rate) Weekday/Saturday: Open inch rate $1.84
Mechanical specifications: Type page 10 7/16 x 14 1/4; E - 8 cols, 1 3/16, 1/8 between; A - 8 cols, 1 3/16, 1/8 between; C - 8 cols, 1 3/16, 1/8 between.
Published: Wed
Avg Free Circ: 49800
Audit By: Sworn/Estimate/Non-Audited
Audit Date: 9/30/2017
Classified Equipment»
Personnel: Lars Melander (Gen. Mgr.); Ian Holryd (Adv. Mgr.)
Parent company (for newspapers): Torstar

THOROLD

FORT ERIE SHOPPING TIMES

Street address 1: 3300 Merrittville Hwy
Street address 2: Unit 1B
Street address 3: Thorold
Street address state: ON
Zip/Postal code: L2V 4Y6
Country: Canada
Mailing address: 3300 Merrittville Hwy, Unit 1B
Mailing city: Thorold
Mailing state: ON
Mailing zip: L2V 4Y6
General Phone: (905) 871-3100
General Fax: (905) 871-5243
General/National Adv. E-mail: classifieds@metroland.com
Display Adv. E-mail: dhawkins@niagarathisweek.com
Editorial e-mail: letters@niagarathisweek.com
Primary Website: niagarathisweek.com
Area Served - City: L2A 5Y2
Advertising (Open Inch Rate) Weekday/Saturday: Open inch rate $.44
Published: Wed
Avg Free Circ: 11800
Audit By: Sworn/Estimate/Non-Audited
Audit Date: 3/30/2019
Classified Equipment»
Personnel: Mark Dawson; Dave Hawkins
Parent company (for newspapers): Postmedia Network Inc.; Quebecor Communications, Inc.

WINDSOR

WINDSOR SMART SHOPPER

Street address 1: 4525 Rhodes Dr.
Street address 2: Unit 400
Street address 3: Windsor
Street address state: ON
Zip/Postal code: NEW 5R8
Country: Canada
Mailing address: 4525 Rhodes Dr., Unit 400
Mailing city: Windsor
Mailing state: ON
Mailing zip: NEW 5R8
General Phone: (519) 966-4500
General Fax: (519) 966-3660
General/National Adv. E-mail: design@windsorpennysaver.com; delivery@windsorpennysaver.com; sales@windsorpennysaver.com
Display Adv. E-mail: placeit@classifiedextra.cam
Primary Website: www.windsorpennysaver.com
Area Served - City: N8T 1R1
Advertising (Open Inch Rate) Weekday/Saturday: Open inch rate $2.41
Published: Thur
Avg Free Circ: 119000
Audit By: Sworn/Estimate/Non-Audited
Audit Date: 9/30/2017
Classified Equipment»
Personnel: Shannon Ricker (Pub.); Ed Donovan (Sales Mgr)

BRANTFORD PENNYSAVER

Street address 1: 61 Dalkeith Dr.
Street address 2: Unit 5
Street address 3: Brantford
Street address state: ON
Zip/Postal code: N3P 1M1
Country: Canada
Mailing address: 61 DalKeith Dr., Unit 5
Mailing city: Brantford
Mailing state: ON
Mailing zip: N3P 1M1
General Phone: (519) 756-0076
General Fax: (519) 756-9034

General/National Adv. E-mail: classifieds@brantfordpennysaver.com
Primary Website: www.brantfordpennysaver.com
Area Served - City: N3P 1M1
Own Printing Facility: Y
Advertising (Open Inch Rate) Weekday/Saturday: Open inch rate $1.26
Mechanical specifications: Type page 10 1/4 x 11 1/4; E - 6 cols, 1 1/2, between.
Published: Fri
Audit Date: 9/30/2017
Classified Equipment»
Personnel: Andrea Demeer (Pub.); Alan Burns (Adv. Mgr.); Adrian Trombetta (Circ. Mgr.); Trudy Loslo (Prodn. Mgr.)

WELLAND

WELLAND SHOPPING NEWS

Street address 1: 440 Niagara St.
Street address 2: Unit 7
Street address 3: Welland
Street address state: ON
Zip/Postal code: L3C 1L5
Country: Canada
Mailing address: 440 Niagara St., Unit 7
Mailing city: Welland
Mailing state: ON
Mailing zip: L3C 1L5
General Phone: (905) 735-9222
General Fax: (905) 735-9224
General/National Adv. E-mail: nsncirculation@niagaracommunitynewspapers.com; wsnclassified@wellandshoppingnews.com
Primary Website: www.wellandshoppingnews.ca
Area Served - City: L3B 3W5
Own Printing Facility: Y
Advertising (Open Inch Rate) Weekday/Saturday: Open inch rate $.55
Mechanical specifications: Type page 10 3/8 x 16 3/4; E - 6 cols, 1 5/8, 1/8 between; A - 6 cols, 1 5/8, 1/8 between.
Published: Wed
Avg Free Circ: 22900
Audit By: Sworn/Estimate/Non-Audited
Audit Date: 9/30/2017
Classified Equipment»
Personnel: Timothy Dundas (Gen. Mgr.); Amanda Houser (Adv. Mgr.)
Parent company (for newspapers): Quebecor Communications, Inc.

QUEBEC

SAINT JEAN

LE GROUP CANADA FRANCAIS

Street address 1: 84 Rue Richelieu
Street address 3: Saint Jean
Street address state: QC
Zip/Postal code: J3B 6X3
Country: Canada
Mailing address: 84 rue Richelieu
Mailing city: Saint Jean
Mailing state: QC
Mailing zip: J3B 6X3
General Phone: (450) 347-0323
General Fax: (450) 347-4539
Primary Website: www.canadafrancais.com
Area Served - City: J3B 6X3
Advertising (Open Inch Rate) Weekday/Saturday: Open inch rate $1.69
Published: Wed
Avg Free Circ: 18500
Audit By: Sworn/Estimate/Non-Audited
Audit Date: 9/30/2017
Classified Equipment»
Personnel: Renel Bouchard (Circ. Mgr.); Robert Paradis (Ed.)

CHATEAUGUAY

LE SOLEIL DE CHATEAUGUAY

Street address 1: 101 boulevard Saint-Jean-Baptiste
Street address 2: Suite 215
Street address 3: Chateauguay
Street address state: QC
Zip/Postal code: J6J 3H9
Country: Canada
Mailing address: 101 boulevard Saint-Jean-Baptiste, Suite 215
Mailing city: Chateauguay
Mailing state: QC
Mailing zip: J6J 3H9
General Phone: (450) 692-8552
General/National Adv. E-mail: info@gravitemedia.com
Primary Website: www.monteregieweb.com
Area Served - City: Canada
Advertising (Open Inch Rate) Weekday/Saturday: Open inch rate $1.00
Published: Wed`Sat
Avg Paid Circ: 11
Avg Free Circ: 34473
Audit By: CCAB
Audit Date: 3/31/2019
Classified Equipment»
Personnel: Julie Voyer (Pres.); Pierre Montreuil (Mktg. Strat. Mgr.); Michel Thibault (Content Mgr.); Valerie Lessard (Asst. Content Mgr.); Sophie Bayard (Sales Coor.)
Parent company (for newspapers): Les Hebdos Monteregiens-OOB

SASKATCHEWAN

NORTH BATTLEFORD

ADVERTISER-POST

Street address 1: 892-104 St.
Street address 3: North Battleford
Street address state: SK
Zip/Postal code: S9A 3E6
Country: Canada
Mailing address: PO Box 1029
Mailing city: North Battleford
Mailing state: SK
Mailing zip: S9A 3E6
General Phone: (306) 445-7261
General Fax: (306) 445-3223
General/National Adv. E-mail: battlefords.publishing@sasktel.net
Area Served - City: S9A 3E6
Advertising (Open Inch Rate) Weekday/Saturday: Open inch rate $1.03
Mechanical specifications: Type page 10 1/4 x 15 2/3; E - 5 cols, 1 11/12, 1/6 between; A - 5 cols, 1 11/12, 1/6 between; C - 6 cols, 1 7/12, 1/6 between.
Published: Fri
Avg Free Circ: 16000
Audit By: Sworn/Estimate/Non-Audited
Audit Date: 9/30/2017
Classified Equipment»
Personnel: Alana Schweitzer (Pub.); Gary Wouters (Circ. Mgr.); Becky Doig (Ed.); Claude Paradis (Prodn. Mgr.)

TISDALE

PARKLAND REVIEW

Street address 1: 1004-102 Ave.
Street address 3: Tisdale
Street address state: SK
Zip/Postal code: S0E 1T0
Country: Canada
Mailing address: PO Box 1660
Mailing city: Tisdale
Mailing state: SK
Mailing zip: S0E 1T0
General Phone: (306) 873-4515
General Fax: (306) 873-4712
General/National Adv. E-mail: recorderoffice@sasktel.net
Display Adv. E-mail: adsrecorder@sakstel.net
Editorial e-mail: newsrecorder@sakstel.net
Delivery Methods: Mail
Area Served - City: Canada
Own Printing Facility: Y
Advertising (Open Inch Rate) Weekday/Saturday: Open inch rate $1.26
Published: Fri
Avg Free Circ: 11625
Audit By: CMCA
Audit Date: 3/31/2016
Classified Equipment»
Personnel: August Grandguillar (Adv. Mgr.); Brent Fitzpatrick (Ed.); Gord Anderson (Prodn. Mgr.); Dan Sully (Adv. Mgr.)
Parent company (for newspapers): Glacier Media Group

PRINCE ALBERT

PRINCE ALBERT SHOPPER

Street address 1: Po Box 1930
Street address 3: Prince Albert
Street address state: SK
Zip/Postal code: S6V 6J9
Country: Canada
Mailing address: PO Box 1930
Mailing city: Prince Albert
Mailing state: SK
Mailing zip: S6V 6J9
General Phone: (306) 763-8461
General Fax: (306) 763-1856
General/National Adv. E-mail: pashopper@sasktel.net
Primary Website: www.princealbertshopper.com
Area Served - City: 26V 6J9
Own Printing Facility: Y
Advertising (Open Inch Rate) Weekday/Saturday: Open inch rate $.76
Mechanical specifications: Type page 10 3/4 x 16.
Published: Mon
Avg Free Circ: 20000
Audit By: Sworn/Estimate/Non-Audited
Audit Date: 9/30/2017
Classified Equipment»
Personnel: Jerry Paskiw (Adv. Mgr.)

SHELLBROOK

SHOPPER CHRONICLE

Street address 1: 44 Main St.
Street address 3: Shellbrook
Street address state: SK
Zip/Postal code: S0J 2E0
Country: Canada
Mailing address: PO Box 10
Mailing city: Shellbrook
Mailing state: SK
Mailing zip: S0J 2E0
General Phone: (306) 747-2442
General Fax: (306) 747-3000
General/National Adv. E-mail: chnews@shellbrookchronicle.com
Advertising (Open Inch Rate) Weekday/Saturday: Open inch rate $13.72
Mechanical specifications: Type page 10 1/4 x 15; E - 6 cols, 1 7/12, 1/6 between; A - 6 cols, 1 7/12, 1/6 between; C - 6 cols, 1 7/12, 1/6 between.
Published: Fri
Avg Free Circ: 4587
Audit By: Sworn/Estimate/Non-Audited
Audit Date: 9/30/2017
Classified Equipment»
Personnel: C.J. Pepper (Pub.); Brad Dupuis (Ed.)

YORKTON

THE MARKETPLACE

Street address 1: 20 Third Ave.
Street address 3: Yorkton
Street address state: SK
Zip/Postal code: S3N 2X3
Country: Canada
Mailing address: PO Box 1300
Mailing city: Yorkton
Mailing state: SK
Mailing zip: S3N 2X3
General Phone: (306) 782-2465
General Fax: (306) 786-1898
General/National Adv. E-mail: publisher@yorktonthisweek.com
Primary Website: www.yorktonthisweek.com
Delivery Methods: Newsstand`Carrier`Racks
Area Served - City: S3N, SOA, SOE, ROJ, SOG, ROM
Advertising (Open Inch Rate) Weekday/Saturday: Open inch rate $13.86
Mechanical specifications: Type page 13 1/2 x 16; E - 5 cols, 2 1/12, 1/6 between; A - 5 cols, 2 1/12, 1/6 between; C - 5 cols, 2 1/12, 1/6 between.
Published: Fri
Avg Free Circ: 20000
Audit By: Sworn/Estimate/Non-Audited
Audit Date: 2/3/2018
Classified Equipment»
Personnel: Jim Kinaschuk (Circ. Mgr.); Jim Ambrose (Publisher); Debbie Barr (Prodn. Mgr.)

ESTEVAN

TRADER EXPRESS

Street address 1: 68 Souris Ave. N.
Street address 3: Estevan
Street address state: SK
Zip/Postal code: S4A 2A6
Country: Canada
Mailing address: PO Box 730
Mailing city: Estevan
Mailing state: SK
Mailing zip: S4A 2A6
General Phone: (306) 634-2654
General Fax: (306) 634-3934
General/National Adv. E-mail: mercury_merc1@sasktel.net; classifieds@estevanmercury.ca
Display Adv. E-mail: adsales@estevanmercury.ca
Editorial e-mail: editor@estevanmercury.ca; sports@estevanmercury.ca
Primary Website: www.estevanmercury.ca
Area Served - City: S4A 2A6
Own Printing Facility: Y
Advertising (Open Inch Rate) Weekday/Saturday: Open inch rate $.88
Mechanical specifications: Type page 11 1/2 x 13; A - 5 cols, 2, between; C - 5 cols, 2, between.
Published: Fri
Avg Free Circ: 6046
Audit By: Sworn/Estimate/Non-Audited
Audit Date: 9/30/2017
Classified Equipment»
Personnel: Peter Ng (Pub.); Janice Boyle (Adv. Mgr.); Kim Schoff (Circ. Mgr.)

WEYBURN

WEYBURN & AREA BOOSTER

Street address 1: 904 East Ave.
Street address 3: Weyburn
Street address state: SK
Zip/Postal code: S4H 2K4
Country: Canada
Mailing address: PO Box 400
Mailing city: Weyburn
Mailing state: SK
Mailing zip: S4H 2K4
General Phone: (306) 842-7487
General Fax: (306) 842-0282
General/National Adv. E-mail: production@weyburnreview.com
Primary Website: www.weyburnreview.com
Delivery Methods: Newsstand`Carrier`Racks
Area Served - City: S4H 2K4
Own Printing Facility: Y
Commercial printers: Y
Advertising (Open Inch Rate) Weekday/Saturday: Open inch rate $15.96
Mechanical specifications: 5 column tabloid 9.67" x 15.75"
Published: Sat
Published Other: Delivered Friday and Saturday
Avg Free Circ: 6280
Audit By: Sworn/Estimate/Non-Audited
Audit Date: 9/30/2017
Classified Equipment»
Personnel: Darryl D. Ward (Pub.); Patricia A. Ward (Ed.)
Parent company (for newspapers): Priaire Newspaper Group

YORKTON

YORKTON NEWS REVIEW

Street address 1: 18 1st Ave. N
Street address 3: Yorkton
Street address state: SK
Zip/Postal code: S3N 1J4
County: Canada
Country: Canada
Mailing address: 18 1st Ave. N
Mailing city: Yorkton
Mailing state: SK
Mailing zip: S3N 1J4
General Phone: (306) 783-7355
General Fax: (306) 782-9138
General/National Adv. E-mail: web@yorktonnews.com
Display Adv. E-mail: web@yorktonnews.com
Editorial e-mail: web@yorktonnews.com
Primary Website: yorktonnews.com
Year Established: 21
Delivery Methods: Newsstand`Carrier`Racks
Area Served - City: S3N
Own Printing Facility: Y
Advertising (Open Inch Rate) Weekday/Saturday: Open inch rate $14.70
Mechanical specifications: Type page 9.875 x 15 1/2; E - 6 cols, 1.5, 1/6 between; A - 6 cols, 1.5, 1/6 between; C - 6 cols, 1.5, 1/6 between.
Published: Thur
Avg Free Circ: 6797
Audit By: CMCA
Audit Date: 4/29/2019
Classified Equipment»
Personnel: Ken Chyz (Adv. Mgr.); Shannon Deveau (Ed.); Carol Melnechenko (Prodn. Mgr.)
Parent company (for newspapers): Glacier Media Group

ALTERNATIVE NEWSPAPERS IN THE U.S.

ALASKA

ANCHORAGE

ANCHORAGE PRESS

Street address 1: 731 I Street
Street address 2: Suite 102
Street address 3: Anchorage
Street address state: AK
Zip/Postal code: 99501
County: Municipality of Anchorage
General Phone: (907) 561-7737
Advertising Phone: (907) 561-7737
Editorail Phone: (907) 561-7737
General/National Adv. E-mail: matt.hickman@anchoragepress.com
Display Adv. E-mail: bridget.mackey@anchoragepress.com
Classified Adv. E-mail: robin.thompson@anchoragepress.com
Editorial e-mail: editor@anchoragepress.com
Primary Website: anchoragepress.com
Mthly Avg Views: 310000
Mthly Avg Unique Visitors: 88000
Year Established: 1992
Special Editions: Press Picks Alaska Native Quarterly Pride Guide Kickoff to the Arts
Area Served - City: Anchorage/Eagle River - all
Advertising (Open Inch Rate) Weekday/Saturday: Open inch rate $24.00
Online Advertising Rates - CPM (cost per thousand) by Size: $10 CPM
Mechanical specifications: Type page 9 3/4 x 15; E - 6 cols, 1 1/2, 1/16 between; A - 6 cols, 1 1/2, 1/16 between.
Published: Thur
Avg Paid Circ: 0
Avg Free Circ: 12000
Audit By: Sworn/Estimate/Non-Audited
Audit Date: 7/10/2020
Parent company (for newspapers): Wick Communications

ARIZONA

PHOENIX

NEW TIMES

Street address 1: 1201 E Jefferson St
Street address 3: Phoenix
Street address state: AZ
Zip/Postal code: 85034-2300
County: Maricopa
Country: USA
Mailing address: PO Box 2510
Mailing city: Phoenix
Mailing state: AZ
Mailing zip: 85002-2510
General Phone: (602) 271-0040
Advertising Phone: (602) 258-1073
Advertising Fax: (602) 495-9954
General/National Adv. E-mail: marketing@newtimes.com
Display Adv. E-mail: andrew.meister@newtimes.com
Editorial e-mail: amy.silverman@newtimes.com
Primary Website: www.phoenixnewtimes.com
Year Established: 1970
Delivery Methods: Racks
Area Served - City: Valley Wide
Advertising (Open Inch Rate) Weekday/Saturday: Open inch rate $34.00
Mechanical specifications: Ad dimensions based on column inch
Published: Thur
Avg Paid Circ: 0
Avg Free Circ: 65000
Audit By: AAM
Audit Date: 7/31/2017
Personnel: Kurtis Barton (Publisher); Jennifer Meister (Associate Publisher); Eloy Vigil (Circ. Mgr.); Rick Barrs (Editor); Amy Silverman (Mng. Editor)
Parent company (for newspapers): Voice Media Group

TUCSON

TUCSON WEEKLY

Street address 1: 7225 N Mona Lisa Rd
Street address 2: Ste 125
Street address 3: Tucson
Street address state: AZ
Zip/Postal code: 85741-2581
County: Pima
Country: USA
Mailing address: 7225 N Mona Lisa Rd Suite 125
Mailing city: Tucson
Mailing state: AZ
Mailing zip: 85741
General Phone: (520) 797-4384
General Fax: (520) 575-8891
Advertising Phone: (520) 797-4384
Advertising Fax: (520) 575-8891
Editorail Phone: (520) 797-4384
Editorial Fax: (520) 575-8891
General/National Adv. E-mail: tucsoneditor@tucsonlocalmedia.com
Display Adv. E-mail: Casey@tucsonlocalmedia.com
Editorial e-mail: TucsonEditor@tucsonlocalmedia.com
Primary Website: tucsonweekly.com
Year Established: 2017
Delivery Methods: Racks
Area Served - City: Tucson Metro
Mechanical specifications: Type page 10" x 11"
Published: Thur
Avg Free Circ: 32975
Audit By: CVC
Audit Date: 12/30/2017
Personnel: Jason Joseph (Pres/Pub); Jaime Hood (Gen Mgr); Casey Anderson (Ad. Dir.); Jim Nintzel (News Ed.); Chalo Grubb (Prod. Mgr.); Laura Horvath (Circ. Mgr. / Special Events Mgr.)
Parent company (for newspapers): Tucson Local Media, LLC; Times Media Group

ARKANSAS

FAYETTEVILLE

THE FREE WEEKLY

Street address 1: 212 N East Ave
Street address 3: Fayetteville
Street address state: AR
Zip/Postal code: 72701-5225
County: Washington
Country: USA
Mailing address: P.O. Box 1607
Mailing city: Fayetteville
Mailing state: AR
Mailing zip: 72702
General Phone: (479) 571-6486
General Fax: (479) 442-1714
General/National Adv. E-mail: tfwcalendar@nwadg.com
Display Adv. E-mail: ccotton@nwadg.com
Editorial e-mail: bmartin@nwadg.com
Primary Website: freeweekly.com
Year Established: 1994
Advertising (Open Inch Rate) Weekday/Saturday: Open inch rate $9.00
Published: Thur
Avg Paid Circ: 197
Avg Free Circ: 8000
Audit By: Sworn/Estimate/Non-Audited
Audit Date: 3/30/2019
Personnel: Becca Martin-Brown (Ed.); Casey Cotton (Display Adv.)
Parent company (for newspapers): Northwest Arkansas Newspapers LLC

CALIFORNIA

CHICO

CHICO NEWS & REVIEW

Street address 1: P.O. Box 56
Street address 3: Chico
Street address state: CA
Zip/Postal code: 95927
Mailing address: P.O. Box 56
Mailing city: Chico
Mailing state: CA
Mailing zip: 95927
General Phone: (530) 894-2300
Advertising Phone: (530) 894-2300
Editorail Phone: (530) 894-2300
Display Adv. E-mail: cnradinfo@newsreview.com
Editorial e-mail: cnrletters@newsreview.com
Primary Website: https://chico.newsreview.com/
Mthly Avg Views: 28000
Mthly Avg Unique Visitors: 16100
Year Established: 1977
Special Editions: Best of Chico Discover Butte County Chico Business issue Entrepreneur Issue Arts Issue
Area Served - City: Butte, Glenn, Tehama counties
Online Advertising Rates - CPM (cost per thousand) by Size: Newsletter ads are 970x250 px, $150/week Website 300x250 px, 150 kB max file size, $15 cpm Calendar ads available starting at $10/day
Published: Thur`Mthly
Avg Free Circ: 40070
Audit By: CVC
Audit Date: 6/30/2018
Personnel: Deborah Redmond; Jeff Vonkaenel (Publisher); Jamie DeGarmo (Adv.); Valentina Flynn (Art Director); Greg Erwin (Circ.); Ray Laager (Marketing Consultant)
Parent company (for newspapers): Chico Community Publishing, Inc.

CHICO NEWS & REVIEW

Street address 1: 353 E 2nd St
Street address 3: Chico
Street address state: CA
Zip/Postal code: 95928-5469
County: Butte
Country: USA
General Phone: (530) 894-2300
General Fax: (530) 892-1111
General/National Adv. E-mail: alecb@newsreview.com
Display Adv. E-mail: alecb@newsreview.com
Editorial e-mail: chicoeditor@newsreview.com
Primary Website: www.newsreview.com/chico/
Year Established: 1977
Delivery Methods: Racks
Area Served - City: 95928, 95926, 95965, 95969, 95973, 96080, 95929, 95966, 95954, 96021, 95988, 95948, 95963, 96055, 95951, 95968, 95938, 95953, 95917, 95974, 96035, 95913, 95925
Advertising (Open Inch Rate) Weekday/Saturday: N/A
Mechanical specifications: Type page 10" x 11.5"; 5 cols
Published: Thur
Avg Free Circ: 40441
Audit By: CVC
Audit Date: 6/30/2016
Note: The Chico News & Review is a growing newspaper in terms of year over year print ad revenue and circulation. We don't syndicate content and we are almost entirely supported by our community's vibrant and healthy local businesses. We win multiple CNPA awards every year (California Newspaper Publishers Association) against metro weeklies. In Chico, we've out-circulated the competing daily paper since the late 1980's.
Personnel: Jeff Vonkaenel (Pres.); Alec Binyon (General Manager); Mark Schuttenberg (Circ. Mgr.); Melissa Daugherty (Editor); Tina Flynn (Prodn. Mgr.)
Parent company (for newspapers): Chico Community Publishing Inc.

CULVER CITY

LA WEEKLY

Street address 1: 3861 Sepulveda Blvd
Street address 3: Culver City
Street address state: CA
Zip/Postal code: 90230-4605
County: Los Angeles
Country: USA
Mailing address: 3861 Sepulveda Blvd
Mailing city: Culver City
Mailing state: CA
Mailing zip: 90230-4605
General Phone: (310) 574-7100
General Fax: (310) 388-8702
Display Adv. E-mail: sales@laweekly.com
Editorial e-mail: editor@laweekly.com
Primary Website: www.laweekly.com
Year Established: 1978
Delivery Methods: Racks
Published: Thur
Avg Free Circ: 65128
Audit By: Sworn/Estimate/Non-Audited
Audit Date: 4/18/2019
Personnel: Erin Domash (Assoc. Pub./COO); Brian Calle (Pub./ CEO); Darrick Rainey (Ed. in Chief)
Parent company (for newspapers): Semanal Media

FOUNTAIN VALLEY

OC WEEKLY

Street address 1: 18475 Bandilier Cir
Street address 3: Fountain Valley
Street address state: CA
Zip/Postal code: 92708-7000
County: Orange
Country: USA
Mailing address: 18475 Bandilier Circle
Mailing city: Fountain Valley
Mailing state: CA
Mailing zip: 92708
General Phone: (714) 550-5900
General Fax: (714) 550-5908
General/National Adv. E-mail: letters@ocweekly.com
Primary Website: www.ocweekly.com
Mechanical specifications: Type page 10 x 13; E - 4 cols, 2 5/16, between; A - 4 cols, 2 5/16, between.
Published: Thur
Avg Paid Circ: 0
Avg Free Circ: 42490
Audit By: AAM
Audit Date: 6/30/2018
Personnel: Duncan Mcintosh (Pres./CEO.); Cynthia Rebolledo (Pub./Food Ed.); Kevin Davis (Sales Dir.); Jason Hamelburg (Sr. Sales Exec.); Jeff Fleming (V.P./ Gen. Mgr.); Federico Medina (Art Dir.); Mercedes Del Real (Layout Design/ Prod. Art.); Nate Jackson (Music Ed.); R. Scott Moxley (Sr. Ed.); Patrice Marsters (Associate Ed.); Matt Coker (Ed.)
Parent company (for newspapers): Duncan McIntosh Co., Inc.

HERMOSA BEACH

EASY READER

Street address 1: PO Box 427
Street address 2: 832 Hermosa Ave
Street address 3: Hermosa Beach
Street address state: CA

Zip/Postal code: 90254-0427
County: Los Angeles
Country: USA
Mailing address: PO Box 427
Mailing city: Hermosa Beach
Mailing state: CA
Mailing zip: 90254-0427
General Phone: (310) 372-4611
General Fax: (424) 212-6708
General/National Adv. E-mail: easyreader@easyreader.info
Display Adv. E-mail: classifiedads@easyreader.info; displayads@easyreader.info
Editorial e-mail: news@easyreader.info
Primary Website: http://www.easyreadernews.com/
Year Established: 1970
Delivery Methods: Mail`Newsstand`Carrier`Racks
Area Served - City: 90254, 90266, 90277, 90288, 90245. 90272, 90274
Advertising (Open Inch Rate) Weekday/Saturday: Open inch rate $20.00
Mechanical specifications: Type page 10 1/2 x 11 1/2; E - 4 cols, 2 1/4, 1/6 between; A - 4 cols, 2 1/4, 1/6 between; C - 7 cols, 1 1/4, 1/6 between.
Published: Thur
Avg Paid Circ: 27684
Audit By: AAM
Audit Date: 3/31/2015
Note: Easy Reader is the largest circulation, weekly newspaper serving the South Bay area of Los Angeles.
Personnel: Kevin Cody (Adv. Mgr.); Amy Berg (Dispaly Sales); Erin McCoy (Display Sales); Tami Quattrone (Classifieds); Bondo Wyszpolski (Arts/Entertainment Ed.); Mark McDermott (News Ed.); Graciela Huerta (Prodn. Dir.); Richard Budman
Parent company (for newspapers): C-VILLE Holdings LLC

IRVINE

IRVINE WEEKLY

Street address 1: 17872 Mitchell N.
Street address 3: Irvine
Street address state: CA
Zip/Postal code: 92614
County: Orange
Country: USA
General Phone: (714) 342-6892
General/National Adv. E-mail: info@irvineweekly.com
Display Adv. E-mail: publisher@irvineweekly.com
Editorial e-mail: publisher@irvineweekly.com
Primary Website: irvineweekly.com
Year Established: 2018
Delivery Methods: Newsstand`Carrier`Racks
Area Served - City: ZIP 92618 92660 92627 92706 92780 92780 92780 92705 92780 92780 92627 92661 92866 92663 92627 92612 92612 92627 92627 92627 92627 92780 92663 92660 92627 92627 92627 92660 92780 92705 92780 92780 92780 92780 92701 92618 92663 92782 92701 92780 92663 92661 92627 92780 92612 92614 92625 92780 92780 92780 92606 92606 92701 92663 92780 92625 92627 92780 92705 92780 92627 92663 92705 92627 92706 92627 92660 92663 92780 92701 92627 92618 92707 92780 92627 92780 92780 92780 92780 92780 92663 92614 92614 92627 92627 92627 92780 92660 92660 92627 92663 92730 92701 92701 92660 92663 92610 92614 92620 92780 92627 92618 92614 92660 92701 92663 92660 92660 92612 92661 92627 92627 92701 92663 92627 92701 92627 92627 92660 92780 92606 92701 92663 92627 92780 92627 92663 92625 92663 92663 92627 92612 92604 92627 92612 92663 92612 92660 92661 92660 92663 92612 92661 92701 92627 92661 92627 92612 92780 92618 92663 92625 92627 92663 92618 92663 92780 92627 92617 92627 92780 92780 92780 92614 92627 92705 92627 92612 92780 92627 92618 92705 92627 92627 92780 92701 92780 92661 92627 92660 92705 92618 92627 92627 92627 92780 92780 92705 92705 92705 92663 92663 92663 92663 92663 92663 92663 92663 92663 92663 92663 92663 92663 92663 92625 92614 92612 92614 92612 92606 92701 92612 92614 97614 92612 92618 92780 92780 92708 92701 92618 92614 92614 92614 92614 92617 92614 92617 92617 92617 92614 92614 92614 92614 92614 92614 92614 92614 92614 92614 92614 92602 92618 92618 92618 92660 92620 92702 92866 92868 92866 92868 92869 92866 92866 92869 92868 92668 92669 92669 92867 92868 92866 92868 92868 92866 92866 92866 92869 82868 92866 92866 92866 92866 92869 92867 92869 92869 92869 92869 92866 92868 92868 92866 92869 92866 92868 92869 92866 92869 92869 92868 92868 92868 92868 92866 92866 92866 92866 92866 92869 92606 92614 92614 92614 92614 92614 92614 92614 92614 92614 92606 92612 92614 92614 92612 92612 92612 92612 92614 92612 92718 92718 92718 92612 92618 92612 92612 92612 92660 90014
Advertising (Open Inch Rate) Weekday/Saturday: $2500 full page open rate
Published: Wed
Avg Free Circ: 75000
Audit By: Sworn/Estimate/Non-Audited
Audit Date: 7/12/2019
Personnel: Brian Calle (Publisher); Erin Domash

LOS ANGELES

ENTERTAINMENT TODAY INC

Street address 1: 12021 Wilshire Blvd
Street address 2: Ste 398
Street address 3: Los Angeles
Street address state: CA
Zip/Postal code: 90025-1206
County: Los Angeles
Country: USA
Mailing address: 12021 Wilshire Blvd Ste 398
Mailing city: Los Angeles
Mailing state: CA
Mailing zip: 90025-1206
General Phone: (213) 387-2060
General Fax: (310) 526-6891
Advertising Phone: (213) 387-2060
Advertising Fax: (310) 526-6891
Editorail Phone: (213) 387-2060
Editorial Fax: (310) 526-6891
General/National Adv. E-mail: editor@entertainmenttoday.net
Display Adv. E-mail: ad@entertainmenttoday.net
Editorial e-mail: editor@entertainmenttoday.net
Primary Website: www.entertainmenttoday.net
Year Established: 1967
Area Served - City: 91506
Advertising (Open Inch Rate) Weekday/Saturday: Open inch rate $62.00
Mechanical specifications: Type page 10 1/2 x 12 3/4; E - 5 cols, 2 1/16, 1/8 between; A - 5 cols, 2 1/16, 1/8 between; C - 6 cols, 1 5/8, 1/8 between.
Published: Fri
Avg Free Circ: 210000
Audit By: Sworn/Estimate/Non-Audited
Audit Date: 7/12/2019
Personnel: Katz Ueno (Pub.)

OAKLAND

EAST BAY EXPRESS

Street address 1: 318 Harrison Street
Street address 2: Suite 302
Street address 3: Oakland
Street address state: CA
Zip/Postal code: 94607
County: Alameda
Country: USA
Mailing address: 318 Harrison Street, Suite 302
Mailing city: Oakland
Mailing state: CA
Mailing zip: 94607
General Phone: (510) 879-3700
General Fax: (510) 879-3794
General/National Adv. E-mail: info@eastbayexpress.com
Primary Website: www.eastbayexpress.com
Year Established: 1978
Advertising (Open Inch Rate) Weekday/Saturday: Open inch rate $20.30
Mechanical specifications: Type page 10 3/16 x 16; E - 5 cols, 1 7/8, 1/6 between; A - 5 cols, 1 7/8, 1/6 between; C - 5 cols, 1 7/8, 1/6 between.
Published: Wed
Avg Free Circ: 50000
Audit By: Sworn/Estimate/Non-Audited
Audit Date: 4/17/2019
Personnel: Stephen Buel (Ed.); Judith Gallman (Sr. Ed.); Isreal Brown (Distr. Dir.); Andreas Jones (Production Mgr.); Justin Fanali Harris (Gen. Mgr.)

PALM SPRINGS

DESERT POST WEEKLY

Street address 1: 750 N Gene Autry Trl
Street address 3: Palm Springs
Street address state: CA
Zip/Postal code: 92262-5463
County: Riverside
Country: USA
Mailing address: 750 N Gene Autry Trail
Mailing city: Palm Springs
Mailing state: CA
Mailing zip: 92662-5463
General Phone: (760) 322-8889
Primary Website: www.desertsun.com
Own Printing Facility: Y
Commercial printers: Y
Advertising (Open Inch Rate) Weekday/Saturday: Open inch rate $13.85
Mechanical specifications: Type page 9 13/20 x 12; E - 5 cols, between; A - 5 cols, between.
Published: Thur
Audit By: Sworn/Estimate/Non-Audited
Audit Date: 3/30/2019
Personnel: Kate Franco (Mng. Ed.); Julie Makinen (Exec. Ed.)
Parent company (for newspapers): C-VILLE Holdings LLC

PALO ALTO

PALO ALTO WEEKLY

Street address 1: 450 Cambridge Ave
Street address 3: Palo Alto
Street address state: CA
Zip/Postal code: 94306-1507
County: Santa Clara
Country: USA
Mailing address: PO Box 1610
Mailing city: Palo Alto
Mailing state: CA
Mailing zip: 94302-1610
General Phone: (650) 326-8210
General Fax: (650) 326-3928
General/National Adv. E-mail: editor@paweekly.com
Display Adv. E-mail: ads@paweekly.com
Editorial e-mail: editor@paweekly.com
Primary Website: www.paloaltoonline.com
Year Established: 1979
Delivery Methods: Mail`Newsstand
Area Served - City: 94301, 94025, 94022
Advertising (Open Inch Rate) Weekday/Saturday: Open inch rate $43.65
Mechanical specifications: Type page 10 x 13.
Published: Fri
Avg Paid Circ: 33500
Avg Free Circ: 19349
Audit By: Sworn/Estimate/Non-Audited
Audit Date: 7/12/2019
Personnel: Bill Johnson (Pub.)
Parent company (for newspapers): C-VILLE Holdings LLC

SACRAMENTO

SACRAMENTO NEWS & REVIEW

Street address 1: PO Box 13370
Street address 3: Sacramento
Street address state: CA
Zip/Postal code: 95813
County: Sacramento
Country: USA
Mailing address: PO Box 13370
Mailing city: Sacramento
Mailing state: CA
Mailing zip: 95813
General Phone: (916) 498-1234
Advertising Phone: (916) 498-1234
Editorail Phone: (916) 498-1234
Display Adv. E-mail: snradinfo@newsreview.com
Editorial e-mail: sactonewstips@newsreview.com
Primary Website: https://sacramento.newsreview.com/
Mthly Avg Views: 55000
Mthly Avg Unique Visitors: 37500
Year Established: 1989
Delivery Methods: Mail`Newsstand`Racks
Area Served - City: Sacramento, Placer, Nevada, El Dorado, Amador, Yolo, Sutter, Yuba counties
Commercial printers: Y
Advertising (Open Inch Rate) Weekday/Saturday: Open inch rate $50.00
Online Advertising Rates - CPM (cost per thousand) by Size: Newsletter ads are 970x250 px, $200/week Website 300x250 px, 150 kB max file size, $15 cpm Calendar ads available starting at $10/day
Mechanical specifications: Full page 10" x 10.5", 5 column and 8 column formats available
Published Other: Online only
Audit By: CVC
Audit Date: 6/30/2018
Personnel: Jeff von Kaenel (President); Greg Erwin (Dist. Dir); Deborah Redmond (COO); Michael Gelbman (Sales Mgr.); Chris Terrazas (Design Mgr.)
Parent company (for newspapers): Chico Community Publishing, Inc.

SAN DIEGO

SAN DIEGO CITY BEAT

Street address 1: 3047 University Ave
Street address 2: Ste 202
Street address 3: San Diego
Street address state: CA
Zip/Postal code: 92104-3039
County: San Diego
Country: USA
Mailing address: 3047 University Ave Ste 202
Mailing city: San Diego
Mailing state: CA
Mailing zip: 92104-3039
General Phone: (619) 281-7526
General Fax: (619) 281-5273
General/National Adv. E-mail: editor@sdcitybeat.com
Primary Website: sdcitybeat.com
Published: Wed
Audit By: Sworn/Estimate/Non-Audited
Audit Date: 4/19/2019
Personnel: Seth Combs (Ed.); Steven Persitza (Pub.); Ryan Bradford (Web Ed.)

SAN DIEGO READER

Street address 1: 2323 Broadway
Street address 2: Ste 200
Street address 3: San Diego
Street address state: CA
Zip/Postal code: 92102-1950
County: San Diego
Country: USA
Mailing address: PO Box 85803
Mailing city: San Diego
Mailing state: CA
Mailing zip: 92102-1950
General Phone: (619) 235-3000
General Fax: (619) 231-0489
General/National Adv. E-mail: info@sdreader.com
Primary Website: www.sandiegoreader.com
Advertising (Open Inch Rate) Weekday/Saturday: Open inch rate $100.40
Mechanical specifications: Type page 10 1/4 x 13; E - 6 cols, 1 1/2, 1/4 between; A - 6 cols, 1 1/2, 1/4 between; C - 6 cols, 1 1/2, 1/4 between.
Published: Thur
Avg Paid Circ: 0
Avg Free Circ: 77417
Audit By: VAC
Audit Date: 6/30/2017
Personnel: Jim Holman (Publisher and editor); Howard Rosen (Gen. Mgr.); Linda Flounders (Adv. Mgr.); Sandy Matthews (Prodn. Mgr.)

SAN FRANCISCO

SF WEEKLY

Street address 1: 835 Market Street
Street address 2: Suite 550
Street address 3: San Francisco
Street address state: CA
Zip/Postal code: 94103-1906
County: San Francisco
Country: USA
Mailing address: 835 MARKET ST STE 550
Mailing city: SAN FRANCISCO

Mailing state: CA
Mailing zip: 94103-1906
General Phone: (415) 359-2600
General Fax: (415) 541-9096
General/National Adv. E-mail: sfweekly@sfmediaco.com
Display Adv. E-mail: advertise@sfweekly.com
Editorial e-mail: news@sfweekly.com
Primary Website: sfweekly.com
Delivery Methods: Newsstand`Racks
Advertising (Open Inch Rate) Weekday/Saturday: Open inch rate $39.00
Mechanical specifications: Type page 10 x 12 3/8; E - 4 cols, 2 2/5, 1/6 between; A - 4 cols, 2 3/8, 1/6 between; C - 8 cols, 1 1/16, between.
Published: Thur
Avg Free Circ: 68992
Audit By: Sworn/Estimate/Non-Audited
Audit Date: 4/15/2019
Personnel: SF Ed. (Ed.)
Parent company (for newspapers): San Francisco Media Company; Clint Reilly Communications

SAN JOSE

METRO

Street address 1: 380 S 1st St
Street address 3: San Jose
Street address state: CA
Zip/Postal code: 95113
County: Santa Clara
Country: USA
Mailing address: 380 S 1st St
Mailing city: San Jose
Mailing state: CA
Mailing zip: 95113-2803
General Phone: (408) 298-8000
General Fax: (408) 298-0602
Advertising Fax: (408) 298-6992
General/National Adv. E-mail: letters@metronews.com
Editorial e-mail: isawyou@metronews.com
Primary Website: metroactive.com
Advertising (Open Inch Rate) Weekday/Saturday: Open inch rate $38.00
Mechanical specifications: Type page 10 3/4 x 13 11/16; E - 4 cols, 2 5/16, 1/4 between; A - 4 cols, 2 5/16, 1/4 between; C - 8 cols, 1 1/4, between.
Published: Wed
Avg Free Circ: 77715
Audit By: Sworn/Estimate/Non-Audited
Audit Date: 3/30/2019
Personnel: Dan Pulcrano (Exec Ed. / CEO); Jorge Lopez (Circ. Dir.); Michael Gant (Arts Ed.); Kara Brown (Design Dir.)

SAN LUIS OBISPO

NEW TIMES

Street address 1: 1010 Marsh St
Street address 3: San Luis Obispo
Street address state: CA
Zip/Postal code: 93401-3630
County: San Luis Obispo
Country: USA
Mailing address: 1010 Marsh St
Mailing city: San Luis Obispo
Mailing state: CA
Mailing zip: 93401-3630
General Phone: (805) 546-8208
General Fax: (805) 546-8641
General/National Adv. E-mail: bob@newtimesslo.com
Display Adv. E-mail: advertising@newtimesslo.com
Editorial e-mail: editorial@newtimesslo.com
Primary Website: www.newtimesslo.com
Year Established: 1986
Delivery Methods: Racks
Area Served - City: 93402, 93405, 93476, 93401, 93422, 93446, 93453, 93451, 93485, 93420, 93448, 93433, 93424, 93448, 93445, 93444, 93428, 93442, 93430, 93452, 93402
Advertising (Open Inch Rate) Weekday/Saturday: Full page $1237
Mechanical specifications: Type page 10 1/4 x 12.75; E - 4 cols, 2 3/8, between; A - 4 cols, 2 3/8, between; C - 8 cols, 1 1/8, between.
Published: Thur
Avg Paid Circ: 10
Avg Free Circ: 34978
Audit By: VAC
Audit Date: 5/31/2017
Personnel: Bob Rucker (Publisher); Alex Zuniga (Arts Dir.)

SAN PEDRO

RANDOM LENGTHS NEWS

Street address 1: PO Box 731
Street address 3: San Pedro
Street address state: CA
Zip/Postal code: 90733-0731
County: Los Angeles
Country: USA
Mailing address: PO Box 731
Mailing city: San Pedro
Mailing state: CA
Mailing zip: 90733-0731
General Phone: (310) 519-1442
General Fax: (310) 832-1000
Advertising Phone: (310) 519-1442
Advertising Fax: (310) 832-1000
General/National Adv. E-mail: editor@randomlengthsnews.com
Display Adv. E-mail: reads@randomlengthnews.com
Primary Website: www.randomlengthsnews.com
Year Established: 1979
Delivery Methods: Mail`Newsstand`Racks
Area Served - City: 90731, 90732, 90733, 90275, 90274, 90744, 90745, 90717, 90710, 90806
Advertising (Open Inch Rate) Weekday/Saturday: $15.50
Published: Thur
Published Other: Every Other Thursday
Avg Paid Circ: 5000
Avg Free Circ: 22000
Audit By: Sworn/Estimate/Non-Audited
Audit Date: 7/12/2019
Personnel: James Preston Allen (Pub.)
Parent company (for newspapers): Allen Publications

RANDOM LENGTHS/HARBOR INDEPENDENT NEWS

Street address 1: 1300 S Pacific Ave
Street address 3: San Pedro
Street address state: CA
Zip/Postal code: 90731-4108
County: Los Angeles
Country: USA
Mailing address: PO Box 731
Mailing city: San Pedro
Mailing state: CA
Mailing zip: 90733-0731
General Phone: (310) 519-1442
General Fax: (310) 832-1000
Advertising Phone: (310) 561-7811
Editorail Phone: (310) 519-1016
General/National Adv. E-mail: editor@randomlengthsnews.com
Display Adv. E-mail: rlnsales@randomlengthsnews.com
Editorial e-mail: reporter@randomlengthsnews.com
Primary Website: www.randomlengthsnews.com
Year Established: 1979
Syndicated Publications: HarborLiving
Delivery Methods: Mail`Newsstand`Racks
Area Served - City: 90731, 90732, 90733, 90744, 90745, 90710, 90717, 90274, 90275, 90802-13
Own Printing Facility: Y
Commercial printers: Y
Advertising (Open Inch Rate) Weekday/Saturday: Open inch rate $15.50
Market Information: Los Angeles Harbor area
Mechanical specifications: Type page 10 1/4 x 12 3/4; E - 5 cols, 2 5/12, between; A - 5 cols, 2 5/12, between; C - 7 cols, 1 3/8, 1/16 between.
Published: Thur
Published Other: Every other Thur
Avg Paid Circ: 1000
Avg Free Circ: 22500
Audit By: Sworn/Estimate/Non-Audited
Audit Date: 7/12/2019
Personnel: James Preston Allen (Pub.); S.K. Matsumiya (Gen. Mgr.)

SAN RAFAEL

PACIFIC SUN

Street address 1: 835 4th St
Street address 2: Ste B
Street address 3: San Rafael
Street address state: CA
Zip/Postal code: 94901-3260
County: Marin
Country: USA
Mailing address: 835 4th St Ste B
Mailing city: San Rafael
Mailing state: CA
Mailing zip: 94901-3260
General Phone: (415) 485-6700
General Fax: (415) 485-6226
General/National Adv. E-mail: letters@pacificsun.com
Primary Website: www.pacificsun.com
Year Established: 1963
Advertising (Open Inch Rate) Weekday/Saturday: Open inch rate $30.58
Mechanical specifications: Type page 10 3/16 x 13 5/16; E - 4 cols, between; A - 4 cols, between; C - 8 cols, between.
Published: Fri
Audit By: Sworn/Estimate/Non-Audited
Audit Date: 7/12/2019
Personnel: Sam Chapman (Pub.)
Parent company (for newspapers): C-VILLE Holdings LLC

SANTA BARBARA

SANTA BARBARA INDEPENDENT

Street address 1: 12 E Figueroa St
Street address 3: Santa Barbara
Street address state: CA
Zip/Postal code: 93101-2709
County: Santa Barbara
Country: USA
Mailing address: 12 East Figueroa St
Mailing city: Santa Barbara
Mailing state: CA
Mailing zip: 93101-3106
General Phone: (805) 965-5205
General Fax: (805) 965-5518
General/National Adv. E-mail: admin@independent.com; sales@independent.com
Display Adv. E-mail: sales@independent.com
Editorial e-mail: news@independent.com, arts@independent.com,lisitngs@independent.com
Primary Website: www.independent.com
Year Established: 1985
Delivery Methods: Newsstand`Racks
Area Served - City: 93067, 93013, 93108, 93103, 93105, 93101, 93109, 93110, 93111, 93117, 93460, 93463, 93441, 93427, 93436
Advertising (Open Inch Rate) Weekday/Saturday: Open inch rate $30.00
Mechanical specifications: Type page 9 13/16 x 12 5/8; E - 5 cols, 1 13/16, between; A - 5 cols, 1 13/16, between; C - 7 cols, 1 5/16, between.
Published: Thur
Published Other: online daily
Avg Paid Circ: 0
Avg Free Circ: 39097
Audit By: VAC
Audit Date: 5/31/2017
Personnel: Marianne Partridge (Editor in chief.); Sarah Sinclair; Brandi Rivera (Publisher)
Parent company (for newspapers): C-VILLE Holdings LLC

SANTA CRUZ

METRO SANTA CRUZ

Street address 1: 115 Cooper St
Street address 3: Santa Cruz
Street address state: CA
Zip/Postal code: 95060-4526
County: Santa Cruz
Country: USA
Mailing address: 1205 Pacific Ave Ste 301
Mailing city: Santa Cruz
Mailing state: CA
Mailing zip: 95060-3936
General Phone: (831) 457-9000
General Fax: (831) 457-5828
Advertising Phone: (831) 457-8500
Primary Website: www.metroactive.com
Advertising (Open Inch Rate) Weekday/Saturday: Open inch rate $14.28
Mechanical specifications: Type page 10 x 12 3/4; E - 4 cols, between; A - 4 cols, between; C - 8 cols, between.
Published: Wed
Avg Free Circ: 77715
Audit By: VAC
Audit Date: 9/30/2017
Personnel: Debra Whizan (Pub.); Tracy Hukill (Ed.)

SANTA MARIA

THE SANTA MARIA SUN

Street address 1: 2540 Skyway Dr
Street address 3: Santa Maria
Street address state: CA
Zip/Postal code: 93455-1514
County: Santa Barbara
Country: USA
Mailing address: 2540 Skyway Dr
Mailing city: Santa Maria
Mailing state: CA
Mailing zip: 93455
General Phone: (805) 347-1968
General Fax: (805) 347-9889
General/National Adv. E-mail: krosa@santamariasun.com
Display Adv. E-mail: krosa@santamariasun.com
Editorial e-mail: jpayne@newtimesslo.com
Primary Website: www.santamariasun.com
Year Established: 200
Delivery Methods: Racks
Area Served - City: 93455, 93454, 93434,93444, 92436, 93437, 93440, 93427, 93463, 93460, 934401
Advertising (Open Inch Rate) Weekday/Saturday: $1033 full page
Published: Thur
Avg Paid Circ: 10
Avg Free Circ: 18000
Audit By: VAC
Audit Date: 3/30/2017
Personnel: Bob Rucker (Publisher); Alex Zuniga (Arts Dir.)

SANTA ROSA

NORTH BAY BOHEMIAN

Street address 1: 847 5th St
Street address 3: Santa Rosa
Street address state: CA
Zip/Postal code: 95404-4526
County: Sonoma
Country: USA
Mailing address: 847 5th St
Mailing city: Santa Rosa
Mailing state: CA
Mailing zip: 95404-4526
General Phone: (707) 527-1200
General Fax: (707) 527-1288
General/National Adv. E-mail: sales@bohemian.com
Primary Website: www.bohemian.com
Delivery Methods: Racks
Area Served - City: Sonoma, Napa and Marin Counties.
Mechanical specifications: Full Page 9"wide x 10" high, 300 dpi
Published: Wed
Avg Free Circ: 25000
Audit By: Sworn/Estimate/Non-Audited
Audit Date: 7/12/2019
Personnel: Rosemary Mackay Olson (Pub.); Lisa Santos (Adv. Dir.)

COLORADO

BOULDER

BOULDER WEEKLY

Street address 1: 690 S Lashley Ln
Street address 3: Boulder
Street address state: CO
Zip/Postal code: 80305-5920
County: Boulder
Country: USA
Mailing address: 690 S Lashley Ln
Mailing city: Boulder
Mailing state: CO
Mailing zip: 80305-5920
General Phone: (303) 494-5511
General Fax: (303) 494-2585
Advertising Phone: (303) 494-5511 x109
General/National Adv. E-mail: info@boulderweekly.com
Display Adv. E-mail: franzan@boulderweekly.com
Editorial e-mail: editorial@boulderweekly.com
Primary Website: www.boulderweekly.com
Year Established: 1993
Delivery Methods: Newsstand`Racks
Area Served - City: 80302, 80303, 80304, 80305, 80301, 80027, 80026, 80516, 80501, 80466
Advertising (Open Inch Rate) Weekday/Saturday: $11.72
Mechanical specifications: Full page: 9.5 x 12.5 3/4 page 7.085 x 12.336 3/4 page 9.5 x 9.2 2/3 page 9.5 x 8.178 Mini Page 7.085 x 9.2 1/2 vert 4.667 x 12.336 1/2 horizontal 9.5 x 6.076 1/4 standard 4.667 x 6.076 1/4 vert 2.25 x 12.336 1/4 horizontal 9.5 x2.953 1/6 standard 4.667 x 3.996 1/6 vert 2.25 x 8.178 1/8 vert 2.25 x 6.076 1/8 horizontal 4.667 x 2.953 1/12 vert 2.25 x 3.996 1/12 horizontal 4.667 x 1.919 1/16 2.25 x2.953
Published: Thur
Avg Free Circ: 25000
Audit By: Sworn/Estimate/Non-Audited
Audit Date: 7/12/2019
Personnel: Stewart Sallo (Pub.); Fran Zankowski (Associate Publisher)

COLORADO SPRINGS

COLORADO SPRINGS INDEPENDENT

Street address 1: 235 S Nevada Ave
Street address 3: Colorado Springs
Street address state: CO
Zip/Postal code: 80903-1906
County: El Paso
Country: USA
Mailing address: 235 S Nevada Ave
Mailing city: Colorado Springs
Mailing state: CO
Mailing zip: 80903-1906
General Phone: (719) 577-4545
General Fax: (719) 577-4107
General/National Adv. E-mail: letters@csindy.com
Primary Website: www.csindy.com
Year Established: 1993
Mechanical specifications: Type page 10 1/16 x 12 3/4; E - 4 cols, 2 3/8, 2/10 between; A - 4 cols, 2 3/8, 1/5 between; C - 8 cols, 1 1/10, 1/6 between.
Published: Thur
Avg Paid Circ: 1500
Avg Free Circ: 36000
Audit By: Sworn/Estimate/Non-Audited
Audit Date: 7/12/2019
Personnel: John Weiss (Pub.); Teri Homick (Adv. Mgr.); Carrie Simison-Bitz (Adv. Mgr., Classified); Kirk Woundy (Mng. Ed.); Kathy Conarro (Art Dir.)

DENVER

DENVER WESTWORD

Street address 1: 969 N Broadway
Street address 3: Denver
Street address state: CO
Zip/Postal code: 80203-2705
County: Denver
Country: USA
Mailing address: PO Box 5970
Mailing city: Denver
Mailing state: CO
Mailing zip: 80217-5970
General Phone: (303) 296-7744
General Fax: (303) 296-5416
General/National Adv. E-mail: retail@westword.com
Primary Website: www.westword.com
Advertising (Open Inch Rate) Weekday/Saturday: Open inch rate $37.25
Published: Thur
Avg Paid Circ: 732
Avg Free Circ: 55000
Audit By: Sworn/Estimate/Non-Audited
Audit Date: 7/12/2019
Personnel: Scott Tobias (Publisher); Tracy Kontrelos (Assoc. Pub.); Curt Sanders (Circ. Mgr.); Michael Wilson (Prodn. Mgr.)
Parent company (for newspapers): Voice Media Group

CONNECTICUT

HARTFORD

HARTFORD ADVOCATE

Street address 1: 121 Wawarme Ave
Street address 3: Hartford
Street address state: CT
Zip/Postal code: 06114-1507
County: Hartford
Country: USA
Mailing address: 285 Broad St
Mailing city: Hartford
Mailing state: CT
Mailing zip: 06115-3785
General Phone: (203) 382-9666
General Fax: (203) 382-9657
Editorial e-mail: editor@fairfieldweekly.com
Primary Website: www.fairfieldweekly.com
Year Established: 1978
Mechanical specifications: Type page 10 x 11 1/2; E - 5 cols, 1 15/16, between; A - 5 cols, 1 15/16, between; C - 8 cols, between.
Published: Thur
Avg Free Circ: 31570
Audit By: VAC
Audit Date: 9/30/2013
Personnel: Joshua Mamis (Pub.); Nick Keppler (Ed.); Susan Leighton (Adv. Dir.); Bryan Mcenery (Circ. Mgr.); Peter Uus (Prodn. Mgr.)

DISTRICT OF COLUMBIA

WASHINGTON

WASHINGTON CITY PAPER

Street address 1: 1400 I St NW
Street address 2: Ste 900
Street address 3: Washington
Street address state: DC
Zip/Postal code: 20005-6527
County: District Of Columbia
Country: USA
Mailing address: 1400 I St NW Ste 900
Mailing city: Washington
Mailing state: DC
Mailing zip: 20005-6527
General Phone: (202) 332-2100
General Fax: (202) 332-8500
General/National Adv. E-mail: mail@washingtoncitypaper.com
Primary Website: www.washingtoncitypaper.com
Advertising (Open Inch Rate) Weekday/Saturday: Open inch rate $47.37
Mechanical specifications: Type page 10 13/16 x 13 3/4; E - 5 cols, 2 1/16, 1/8 between; A - 5 cols, 2 1/16, 1/8 between; C - 5 cols, 2 1/16, 1/8 between.
Published: Thur
Avg Paid Circ: 0
Avg Free Circ: 53450
Audit By: VAC
Audit Date: 12/31/2016
Personnel: Amy Austin (Pub.); Matt Curry (Circ. Mgr.); Erik Wemple (Ed.); Eric Norwood

FLORIDA

MIAMI

MIAMI NEW TIMES

Street address 1: 2800 Biscayne Blvd
Street address 2: Ste 100
Street address 3: Miami
Street address state: FL
Zip/Postal code: 33137-4554
County: Miami-Dade
Country: USA
Mailing address: PO Box 11591
Mailing city: Miami
Mailing state: FL
Mailing zip: 33101-1591
General Phone: (305) 576-8000
Advertising Fax: (305) 571-7677
General/National Adv. E-mail: editorial@miami-newtimes.com
Editorial e-mail: chuck.striouse@miaminewtimes.com
Primary Website: www.miaminewtimes.com
Year Established: 1987
Mechanical specifications: Type page 10 x 12 7/8; E - 8 cols, between; A - 8 cols, between.
Published: Thur
Avg Free Circ: 40000
Audit By: Sworn/Estimate/Non-Audited
Audit Date: 7/12/2019
Personnel: Chuck Strouse (Mng. Ed.); Mike Lugo (Prodn. Mgr.); Adam Simon (Publisher); Russell Breiter

NEW TIMES BROWARD-PALM BEACH

Street address 1: PO Box 011591
Street address 3: Miami
Street address state: FL
Zip/Postal code: 33101-1591
Country: USA
Mailing address: PO Box 011591
Mailing city: Miami
Mailing zip: 33101-1591
Primary Website: www.browardpalmbeach.com
Year Established: 1997
Personnel: Chuck Strouse (Ed.)
Parent company (for newspapers): Voice Media Group

ORLANDO

ORLANDO WEEKLY

Street address 1: 16 W Pine St
Street address 3: Orlando
Street address state: FL
Zip/Postal code: 32801-2612
County: Orange
Country: USA
Mailing address: 16 W Pine St
Mailing city: Orlando
Mailing state: FL
Mailing zip: 32801-2612
General Phone: (407) 377-0400
General Fax: (407) 377-0420
Advertising Phone: (407) 377-0415
Editorail Phone: (407) 377-0400 ext. 232
General/National Adv. E-mail: graham@orlandoweekly.com
Editorial e-mail: jyoung@orlandoweekly.com
Primary Website: www.orlandoweekly.com
Year Established: 1990
Delivery Methods: Racks
Advertising (Open Inch Rate) Weekday/Saturday: Open inch rate $41.00
Mechanical specifications: Type page 10 x 10
Published: Wed
Avg Paid Circ: 0
Avg Free Circ: 25000
Audit By: Sworn/Estimate/Non-Audited
Audit Date: 7/12/2019
Personnel: Graham Jarrett (Pub.); Michael Wagner (Reg'l. Pub.); Jessica Bryce Young (Ed. in Cheif); Thad McCollum (Cal. Ed.); Colin Wolfe (Web Ed.); Monivette Cordeiro (Staff Writer); Melissa McHenry (Art Dir.)
Parent company (for newspapers): Euclid Media Group

GEORGIA

ATHENS

FLAGPOLE MAGAZINE

Street address 1: 112 Foundry St
Street address 3: Athens
Street address state: GA
Zip/Postal code: 30601-2672
County: Clarke
Country: USA
Mailing address: 220 Prince Ave
Mailing city: Athens
Mailing state: GA
Mailing zip: 30601-2473
General Phone: (706) 549-0301
General Fax: (706) 548-8981
General/National Adv. E-mail: mail@flagpole.com
Display Adv. E-mail: ads@flagpole.com
Editorial e-mail: editor@flagpole.com
Primary Website: flagpole.com
Year Established: 1987
Mechanical specifications: Type page 13 x 10.
Published: Wed
Avg Free Circ: 13193
Audit By: CVC
Audit Date: 3/30/2018
Personnel: Jessica Smith (Circ.); Pete McCommons (Ed.); Alicia Nickels (Adv.); Larry Tenner (Prodn. Dir.)
Parent company (for newspapers): C-VILLE Holdings LLC

HAWAII

WAILUKU

MAUI TIME WEEKLY

Street address 1: 16 S Market St
Street address 2: Ste 2K
Street address 3: Wailuku
Street address state: HI
Zip/Postal code: 96793-2201
County: Maui
Country: USA
Mailing address: 16 S Market St Ste 2K
Mailing city: Wailuku
Mailing state: HI
Mailing zip: 96793-2201
General Phone: (808) 244-0777
General Fax: (808) 244-0446
General/National Adv. E-mail: editor@mauitime.com
Primary Website: www.mauitime.com
Year Established: 1997
Delivery Methods: Racks
Published: Thur
Avg Free Circ: 18000
Audit By: Sworn/Estimate/Non-Audited
Audit Date: 7/12/2019

IDAHO

BOISE

BOISE WEEKLY

Street address 1: 523 W Broad St
Street address 3: Boise

Street address state: ID
Zip/Postal code: 83702-7642
County: Ada
Country: USA
Mailing address: 523 W Broad St
Mailing city: Boise
Mailing state: ID
Mailing zip: 83702-7642
General Phone: (208) 344-2055
General Fax: (208) 342-4733
General/National Adv. E-mail: info@boiseweekly.com
Primary Website: www.boiseweekly.com
Year Established: 1992
Mechanical specifications: Type page 9 5/8 x 12 1/2; E - 4 cols, 1/8 between; A - 4 cols, between; C - 6 cols, between.
Published: Wed
Avg Free Circ: 35000
Audit By: Sworn/Estimate/Non-Audited
Audit Date: 7/12/2019
Personnel: Stan Jackson (Circ. Dir.); Sally Freeman (Pub.)
Parent company (for newspapers): C-VILLE Holdings LLC

ILLINOIS

CHICAGO

READER

Street address 1: 11 E Illinois St
Street address 3: Chicago
Street address state: IL
Zip/Postal code: 60611-5652
County: Cook
Country: USA
Mailing address: 350 N Orleans St Fl 10
Mailing city: Chicago
Mailing state: IL
Mailing zip: 60654-1700
General Phone: (312) 828-0350
General Fax: (312) 828-0305
Editorial Fax: (312)828-9926
General/National Adv. E-mail: mail@chicagoreader.com
Primary Website: www.chicagoreader.com
Year Established: 1971
Advertising (Open Inch Rate) Weekday/Saturday: Open inch rate $76.25
Mechanical specifications: Type page 10 x 16; E - 5 cols, 1 7/8, 1/6 between; A - 5 cols, 1 7/8, 1/6 between; C - 5 cols, 1 7/8, 1/6 between.
Published: Thur
Avg Paid Circ: 329
Avg Free Circ: 100000
Audit By: Sworn/Estimate/Non-Audited
Audit Date: 7/12/2019
Personnel: Steve Timble (Assoc. Pub.); James Warren (Pub.); Brett Murphy (Adv. Mgr.); Perry A. Kim (Circ. Mgr.); Alison TRUE (Ed.); Kiki Yablon (Mng. Ed.)

SPRINGFIELD

ILLINOIS TIMES

Street address 1: 1240 S 6th St
Street address 3: Springfield
Street address state: IL
Zip/Postal code: 62703-2408
County: Sangamon
Country: USA
Mailing address: PO BOX 5256
Mailing city: SPRINGFIELD
Mailing state: IL
Mailing zip: 62705-5256
General Phone: (217) 753-2226
General Fax: (217) 753-2281
General/National Adv. E-mail: swhalen@illinoistimes.com
Primary Website: illinoistimes.com
Year Established: 1975
Area Served - City: 62701, 62702, 62703, 62704, 62706, 62707, 62563, 62568, 62650, 62629, 62675, 62684
Advertising (Open Inch Rate) Weekday/Saturday: Modular Rates: 1/8 P $295 1/4 P $575 1/2 P $900 Full $1645
Mechanical specifications: Type page 10 1/4 x 11 1/2; E - 4 cols, 2 3/8, 3/16 between; A - 4 cols, 2 3/8, 3/16 between; C - 6 cols, 1 1/2, 3/16 between.
Published: Thur
Avg Paid Circ: 20
Avg Free Circ: 27784
Audit By: CVC
Audit Date: 12/30/2018
Personnel: Michelle Ownbey (Pub.); Brenda Matheis (Bus. Mgr.); Fletcher Farrar (Ed./CEO); James Bengfort (Assoc. Pub.); Beth Parkes-Irwin (Adv.)
Parent company (for newspapers): C-VILLE Holdings LLC

INDIANA

INDIANAPOLIS

NUVO

Street address 1: 3951 N Meridian St
Street address 2: Ste 200
Street address 3: Indianapolis
Street address state: IN
Zip/Postal code: 46208-4078
County: Marion
Country: USA
Mailing address: 3951 N MERIDIAN ST STE 200
Mailing city: INDIANAPOLIS
Mailing state: IN
Mailing zip: 46208-4078
General Phone: (317) 254-2400
General Fax: (317) 254-2405
General/National Adv. E-mail: nuvo@nuvo.net
Display Adv. E-mail: advertising@nuvo.net
Editorial e-mail: editors@nuvo.net
Primary Website: www.nuvo.net
Year Established: 1990
Special Editions: City Guide Series: Annual Manual Nightlife Guide Summer Fun Guide Best of Indy Arts Guide Dining Guide Shopping Guide
Delivery Methods: Mail`Newsstand`Racks
Area Served - City: 46032 46033 46037 46038 46055 46060 46062 46074 46077 46107 46113 46123 46131 46142 46143 46168 46201 46202 46203 46204 46205 46208 46214 46216 46217 46218 46219 46220 46221 46222 46224 46225 46226 46227 46228 46229 46231 46234 46235 46236 46237 46239 46240 46241 46250 46254 46256 46260 46268 46278 46280 47405 47406
Commercial printers: Y
Advertising (Open Inch Rate) Weekday/Saturday: Open inch rate $30.00
Market Information: Indianapolis
Mechanical specifications: Type page 10 3/8 x 11 5/8; E - 5 cols, 1 7/8, 1/8 between; A - 4 cols, 2 1/2, 1/8 between; C - 8 cols, 1 1/4, 1/16 between.
Published: Wed`Other
Published Other: Bi-weekly on Wed
Avg Paid Circ: 10
Avg Free Circ: 24990
Audit By: Sworn/Estimate/Non-Audited
Audit Date: 7/12/2019
Personnel: Kathy Flahavin (Circ. Mgr.); Kevin McKinney (Publisher); McPhee Laura (Editor); Grossman Dan (Arts Editor); Rob Burgess (News Editor); Trice Rias-Thompson (Sales Manager); Charles Clark (Production Manager)

IOWA

JOHNSTON

CITYVIEW

Street address 1: 5619 NW 86th St
Street address 2: Ste 600
Street address 3: Johnston
Street address state: IA
Zip/Postal code: 50131-2955
County: Polk
Country: USA
Mailing address: 5619 N.W. 86th Street, Suite 600
Mailing city: Johnston
Mailing state: IA
Mailing zip: 50131
General Phone: (515) 953-4822
General Fax: (515) 953-1394
Advertising Phone: (515) 953-4822, ext. 303
Advertising Fax: (515) 953-1394
Editorail Phone: (515) 953-4822 ext. 305
Editorial Fax: (515) 953-1394
General/National Adv. E-mail: editor@dmcityview.com
Display Adv. E-mail: dan.juffer@dmcityview.com
Editorial e-mail: editor@dmcityview.com
Primary Website: www.dmcityview.com
Year Established: 1992
Delivery Methods: Mail`Racks
Advertising (Open Inch Rate) Weekday/Saturday: modular, call for details
Published: Wed`Mthly
Avg Paid Circ: 0
Avg Free Circ: 30000
Audit By: Sworn/Estimate/Non-Audited
Audit Date: 7/12/2019
Personnel: Shane Goodman (Publisher); Celeste Jones (Art Director)
Parent company (for newspapers): Big Green Umbrella Media

KENTUCKY

BOWLING GREEN

BOWLING GREEN PARENT

Street address 1: 1881 Mount Victor Ln
Street address 3: Bowling Green
Street address state: KY
Zip/Postal code: 42103-9043
County: Warren
Country: USA
Mailing address: 1881 Mount Victor Lane
Mailing city: Bowling Green
Mailing state: KY
Mailing zip: 42103
General Phone: (270) 535-1519
Advertising Phone: (270) 535-1519
General/National Adv. E-mail: info@bgparent.com
Display Adv. E-mail: info@bgparent.com
Editorial e-mail: info@bgparent.com
Primary Website: www.bgparent.com
Year Established: 2010
Delivery Methods: Racks
Area Served - City: 42101, 42102, 42103, 42104, 42164, 42134, 42141, 42127
Published: Bi-Mthly
Published Other: 5 times per year
Avg Free Circ: 10000
Audit By: Sworn/Estimate/Non-Audited
Audit Date: 7/12/2019
Personnel: Jennifer Simpson (Owner & Publisher)
Parent company (for newspapers): JS Publishing

LEXINGTON

BUSINESS LEXINGTON

Street address 1: 116 Cherokee Park
Street address 3: Lexington
Street address state: KY
Zip/Postal code: 40503
County: Fayette
Country: USA
General Phone: 8592666537
Advertising Phone: 8592666537
Editorail Phone: 8592666537
General/National Adv. E-mail: chris@bizlex.com
Display Adv. E-mail: chris@bizlex.com
Classified Adv. E-mail: chris@bizlex.com
Editorial e-mail: tom@bizlex
Primary Website: bizlex.com
Mthly Avg Views: 100000
Mthly Avg Unique Visitors: 39000
Year Established: 1997
Special Editions: Book of Lists
Area Served - City: Lexington, Kentucky
Published Other: monthly
Avg Paid Circ: 2500
Avg Free Circ: 6000
Audit By: Sworn/Estimate/Non-Audited
Personnel: Chris Eddie (Publisher)
Parent company (for newspapers): Smiley Pete Publishing

LOUISVILLE

LEO WEEKLEY

Street address 1: 607 W Main St
Street address 2: Ste 01
Street address 3: Louisville
Street address state: KY
Zip/Postal code: 40202-2991
County: Jefferson
Country: USA
Mailing address: 607 W Main St. Ste #001
Mailing city: Louisville
Mailing state: KY
Mailing zip: 40202-1247
General Phone: (502) 895-9770
General Fax: (502) 895-9779
General/National Adv. E-mail: leo@leoweekly.com
Display Adv. E-mail: dbrennan@leoweekly.com
Editorial e-mail: leo@leoweekly.com
Primary Website: www.leoweekly.com
Year Established: 1990
Published: Wed
Avg Free Circ: 25125
Audit By: CVC
Audit Date: 9/30/2015

LOUISVILLE ECCENTRIC OBSERVER (LEO)

Street address 1: 607 W. Main St.
Street address 3: Louisville
Street address state: KY
Zip/Postal code: 40202
County: Jefferson
Country: USA
Mailing address: 607 W. Main St.
Mailing city: Louisville
Mailing state: KY
Mailing zip: 40202
General Phone: (502) 895-9770
General Fax: (502) 895-9779
General/National Adv. E-mail: leo@leoweekly.com
Display Adv. E-mail: advertising@leoweekly.com
Editorial e-mail: kstone@leoweekly.com
Primary Website: leoweekly.com
Year Established: 1990
Delivery Methods: Racks
Area Served - City: 40202 40207 40204 40205 47130 40206 47150 40222 40217 40241 40203 40243 40220 40208 40258 40216 40292 47129 40291 40272 40214 40299 40213 40059 40219 40215 40031 40211 40245 47172 40218 40165 40014 40209 40223 40212 40242 47112 47161 40228 47119 40229
Advertising (Open Inch Rate) Weekday/Saturday: Open inch rate $32.00
Mechanical specifications: Full Page: 9.5" W x 9.75" T 1/2H page: 9.5" W x 4.7917" T 1/2V page: 4.667" W x 9.75" T 1/4V page: 2.25" W x 9.75" T 1/4S page: 4.667" W x 4.7917" T 1/8V page: 2.25" W x 4.7917" T 1/8H page: 4.667" W x 2.3125" T 1/16 page: 2.25" W x 2.3125" T
Published: Wed
Avg Free Circ: 24045
Audit By: Sworn/Estimate/Non-Audited
Audit Date: 4/15/2019
Personnel: Aaron Yarmuth (Exec. Ed.); Keith Stone (Mng. Ed.); Scott Recker (Ed. at Large); Laura Snyder (Pub.); Julie Trotter (Prod.); John Cobb (Art Dir.); Marsha Blacker (Sr. Acct. Exec.)
Parent company (for newspapers): Womack Newspapers, Inc

LOUISIANA

BATON ROUGE

THE ADVOCATE NEWSPAPER

Street address 1: 7290 Bluebonnet Blvd
Street address 3: Baton Rouge
Street address state: LA
Zip/Postal code: 70810-1611
County: East Baton Rouge
Country: USA
Mailing address: PO Box 588
Mailing city: Baton Rouge
Mailing state: LA
Mailing zip: 70821-0588
General Phone: (225) 383-1111
General Fax: (225) 388-0348
General/National Adv. E-mail: lruth@theadvocate.com
Primary Website: www.theadvocate.com
Year Established: 1992
Published: Mon`Tues`Wed`Thur`Fri`Sat`Sun
Avg Paid Circ: 43475
Avg Free Circ: 44244
Audit By: AAM
Audit Date: 3/31/2019
Personnel: Larry Ruth (Mgr., Customer Sales); Paul Fugarino (Distr. Mgr.)

LAFAYETTE

IND MONTHLY

Street address 1: 551 Jefferson St
Street address 3: Lafayette
Street address state: LA
Zip/Postal code: 70501-6905
County: Lafayette
Country: USA
Mailing address: 551 Jefferson St
Mailing city: Lafayette
Mailing state: LA
Mailing zip: 70501-6905
General Phone: (337) 988-4607
General Fax: (337) 983-0150
General/National Adv. E-mail: indbox@theind.com
Display Adv. E-mail: druek@theind.com
Editorial e-mail: walterp@theind.com
Primary Website: www.theind.com
Year Established: 2003
Published: Mthly
Avg Free Circ: 12500
Audit By: Sworn/Estimate/Non-Audited
Audit Date: 7/12/2019

TIMES OF ACADIANA

Street address 1: 1100 Bertrand Dr
Street address 3: Lafayette
Street address state: LA
Zip/Postal code: 70506-4110
County: Lafayette
Country: USA
Mailing address: 1100 Bertrand Dr
Mailing city: Lafayette
Mailing state: LA
Mailing zip: 70506-4110
General Phone: (337) 289-6300
General Fax: (337) 261-2630
General/National Adv. E-mail: timesedit@timesofacadiana.com; events@timesofacadiana.com
Primary Website: www.timesofacadiana.com
Area Served - City: 70502
Own Printing Facility: Y
Mechanical specifications: Type page 9 13/16 x 12 13/16; E - 4 cols, 2 5/16, 1 between; A - 4 cols, 2 5/16, between; C - 4 cols, 2 5/16, 1 between.
Published: Wed
Avg Free Circ: 36000
Audit By: Sworn/Estimate/Non-Audited
Audit Date: 7/12/2019
Personnel: Ted Power (Pub.); Chris Messa (Adv. Mgr.); Lisa Faust (Mng. Ed.); Melissa Herbert (Prodn. Mgr.)
Parent company (for newspapers): C-VILLE Holdings LLC

NEW ORLEANS

GAMBIT

Street address 1: 3923 Bienville St
Street address 3: New Orleans
Street address state: LA
Zip/Postal code: 70119-5102
County: Orleans
Country: USA
Mailing address: 3923 BIENVILLE ST
Mailing city: NEW ORLEANS
Mailing state: LA
Mailing zip: 70119-5146
General Phone: (504) 486-5900
General Fax: (504) 483-3159
Advertising Phone: (504) 483-3150
Advertising Fax: (504) 483-3159
Editorail Phone: (504) 483-3105
Editorial Fax: (866) 473-7199
General/National Adv. E-mail: response@gambitweekly.com
Display Adv. E-mail: sandys@gambitweekly.com
Editorial e-mail: response@gambitweekly.com
Primary Website: www.bestofneworleans.com
Year Established: 1981
Delivery Methods: Racks
Area Served - City: 80 different zip codes throughout Louisiana and other states.
Mechanical specifications: Type page 10 3/8 x 12 13/16; E - 4 cols, 2 3/8, between; A - 4 cols, 2 3/8, between.
Published: Tues
Avg Paid Circ: 15
Avg Free Circ: 37438
Audit By: VAC
Audit Date: 5/31/2017
Personnel: Jeanne Foster (Publisher); Sandy Stein (Advertising Director); Dora Sison (Production Director); Kevin Allman (Editor); Kandace Graves (Managing Editor)

MAINE

BANGOR

THE MAINE EDGE

Street address 1: 1 Cumberland Pl
Street address 2: Ste 204
Street address 3: Bangor
Street address state: ME
Zip/Postal code: 04401-5090
County: Penobscot
Country: USA
Mailing address: PO Box 2639
Mailing city: Bangor
Mailing state: ME
Mailing zip: 04402-2639
General Phone: (207) 942-2901
General Fax: (207) 942-5602
General/National Adv. E-mail: info@themaineedge.com
Display Adv. E-mail: advertising@themaineedge.com
Editorial e-mail: editorial@themaineedge.com
Primary Website: www.themaineedge.com
Year Established: 2006
Delivery Methods: Racks
Area Served - City: 04401, 04412, 04416, 04427, 04429, 04444. 04450, 04456, 04468, 04469, 04472, 04473, 04605, 04974, 04915, 04981
Advertising (Open Inch Rate) Weekday/Saturday: 24
Mechanical specifications: Format Page 10.055: x 13"; 4 cols, 2.42", 1/8" between A-6 cols, 1.5717", 1.8" between C-8 cols, 1.1475", 1.8" between.
Published: Wed
Avg Free Circ: 18500
Audit By: Sworn/Estimate/Non-Audited
Audit Date: 7/12/2019
Personnel: Allen Adams (Ed.); Matthew Fern (Adv./Ops. Mgr.); Michael Fern (Pub.)
Parent company (for newspapers): Edge Media Group

MARYLAND

BALTIMORE

CITY PAPER

Street address 1: 812 Park Ave
Street address 3: Baltimore
Street address state: MD
Zip/Postal code: 21201-4807
County: Baltimore City
Country: USA
Mailing address: 149 Penn Ave OFC
Mailing city: Scranton
Mailing state: PA
Mailing zip: 18503-2056
General Phone: (410) 523-2300
General Fax: (410) 523-1154
Advertising Phone: (410) 523-2300
Advertising Fax: (410) 523-2222
Editorail Phone: (410) 523-2300
Editorial Fax: (410) 523-1154
General/National Adv. E-mail: dfarley@citypaper.com
Display Adv. E-mail: jmarsh@citypaper.com
Editorial e-mail: lgardner@citypaper.com
Primary Website: www.citypaper.com
Year Established: 1977
Own Printing Facility: Y
Advertising (Open Inch Rate) Weekday/Saturday: Open inch rate $43.90
Mechanical specifications: Type page 10 x 12 1/2; E - 4 cols, 2 3/16, 1/6 between; A - 4 cols, 2 3/16, 1/6 between; C - 6 cols, 1 1/2, 1/6 between.
Published: Wed
Avg Free Circ: 80000
Audit By: Sworn/Estimate/Non-Audited
Audit Date: 7/12/2019
Personnel: Don Farley (Pub.); Jennifer Marsh (Adv. Mgr.); Christine Grabowski (Circ. Mgr.); Lee Gardener (Ed.)

MASSACHUSETTS

BOSTON

BOSTON'S WEEKLY DIG

Street address 1: 242 E Berkeley St
Street address 2: Ste 2
Street address 3: Boston
Street address state: MA
Zip/Postal code: 02118-2797
County: Suffolk
Country: USA
Mailing address: 242 E Berkeley St Ste 2
Mailing city: Boston
Mailing state: MA
Mailing zip: 02118-2797
General Phone: (617) 426-8942
General Fax: (617) 426-8944
Primary Website: www.weeklydig.com
Year Established: 1999
Published: Wed
Audit By: Sworn/Estimate/Non-Audited
Audit Date: 7/12/2019
Personnel: Jeff Lawrence (Pres.); Amanda Nicholson (Gen. Mgr.); Joseph B. Darby (Advisor); Alex Lapplin (Sales Mgr.); Jim Stanton (Ed.); Laura Dargus (Mng. Ed.); David Day (Arts/Music Ed.); Cara Bayles (News/ Features Ed.)

THE IMPROPER BOSTONIAN MAGAZINE

Street address 1: 142 Berkeley St
Street address 2: Ste 3
Street address 3: Boston
Street address state: MA
Zip/Postal code: 02116-5143
County: Suffolk
Country: USA
Mailing address: 142 Berkeley St Ste 3
Mailing city: Boston
Mailing state: MA
Mailing zip: 02116-5172
General Phone: (617) 859-1400
General Fax: (617) 859-1446
Display Adv. E-mail: advertising@improper.com
Primary Website: www.improper.com
Year Established: 1991
Mechanical specifications: Type page 9 1/4 x 11; E - 4 cols, 2 3/16, 1/8 between; A - 4 cols, 2, 1/8 between; C - 6 cols, 1 3/8, 1/8 between.
Published: Wed
Published Other: Every other Mon
Avg Paid Circ: 556
Avg Free Circ: 82727
Audit By: Sworn/Estimate/Non-Audited
Audit Date: 7/12/2019
Personnel: Wendy Semonian (Pub.); Gretchen Bastrom (Office Mgr.); Stacey Shane (Mktg. Dir.); Andrew Rimas (Mng. Ed.); Melinda Pattulo (Prodn. Dir.)

NORTHAMPTON

VALLEY ADVOCATE

Street address 1: 115 Conz St
Street address 3: Northampton
Street address state: MA
Zip/Postal code: 01060-4444
County: Hampshire
Country: USA
Mailing address: PO Box 477
Mailing city: Northampton
Mailing state: MA
Mailing zip: 01061-0477
General Phone: (413) 529-2840
General Fax: (413) 529-2844
Editorial e-mail: editor@valleyadvocate.com; listings@valleyadvocate.com
Primary Website: www.valleyadvocate.com
Mechanical specifications: Type page 10 3/16 x 12 9/16; E - 5 cols, 1 5/16, 1/8 between; A - 5 cols, 1 7/8, 3/16 between; C - 8 cols, 1 1/8, 1/8 between.
Published: Thur
Avg Free Circ: 26297
Audit By: VAC
Audit Date: 9/30/2015
Personnel: Aaron Julian (Pres.); Patty Desroches (Adv. Dir.); Darrell Hendrick (Circ. Mgr.); Tom Vannah (Ed. in Chief); Mark Roessler (Mng. Ed.); Tom Sturm (Listings. Ed.)
Parent company (for newspapers): Newspapers of New England; H.S. Gere & Sons
footnotes: Audit Date: Provided by VAC

WORCESTER

WORCESTER MAGAZINE

Street address 1: 72 Shrewsbury St
Street address 3: Worcester
Street address state: MA
Zip/Postal code: 01604-4625
County: Worcester
Country: USA
Mailing address: 72 Shrewsbury St.
Mailing city: Worcester
Mailing state: MA
Mailing zip: 01604
General Phone: (978) 728-4302
General Fax: (978) 534-6004
Advertising Phone: (978) 728-4302
Advertising Fax: (978) 534-6004
Editorail Phone: (978) 728-4302
Editorial Fax: (978) 534-6004
General/National Adv. E-mail: editor@worcestermag.com
Display Adv. E-mail: sales@worcestermagazine.com
Editorial e-mail: editor@worcestermag.com
Primary Website: www.worcestermag.com
Year Established: 1976
Delivery Methods: Mail`Newsstand`Racks
Area Served - City: Central Massachusetts
Advertising (Open Inch Rate) Weekday/Saturday: N/A
Mechanical specifications: Four (4) columns x 10.75 ?›???? inch column depth ; 9.5?›???? wide x 10.75?›???? depth (modular format)
Published: Thur
Avg Free Circ: 22877
Audit By: CVC
Audit Date: 9/30/2015

Personnel: Kathy Real (Pub.); Brittany Durgin (Ed.); Helen Linnehan (Sales Mgr.); Don Cloutier (Prod. Mgr.)

MICHIGAN

CHARLOTTE

FLASHES ADVERTISING & NEWS

Street address 1: 241 S Cochran Ave
Street address 3: Charlotte
Street address state: MI
Zip/Postal code: 48813-1584
County: Eaton
Country: USA
Mailing address: 241 S. Cochran Ave.
Mailing city: Charotte
Mailing state: MI
Mailing zip: 48813-1584
General Phone: (517) 543-1099
General Fax: (517) 543-1993
Advertising Phone: (517) 543-1099 ext 225
Advertising Fax: (517) 543-1993
Editorail Phone: (517) 543-1099 ext 227
Editorial Fax: (517) 543-1993
General/National Adv. E-mail: cgwing@county-journal.com
Display Adv. E-mail: cgwing@county-journal.com
Classified Adv. E-mail: sales@county-journal.com
Editorial e-mail: news@county-journal.com
Primary Website: www.county-journal.com
Year Established: 1945
Delivery Methods: Carrier
Area Served - City: 48827, 48821, 49264, 48854,
Own Printing Facility: Y
Advertising (Open Inch Rate) Weekday/Saturday: Open inch rate $8.39
Mechanical specifications: Type page 10 1/4 x 16; E - 6 cols, 1 9/16, between; A - 6 cols, 1 9/16, between.
Published: Sat
Avg Paid Circ: 15
Avg Free Circ: 6000
Audit By: CVC
Audit Date: 7/12/2020
Personnel: Cindy Gaedert (Pub./Sales/Owner); Travis Silvas (Circ. Mgr)
Parent company (for newspapers): The County Journal

THE COUNTY JOURNAL

Street address 1: 2845 Victoria Lane
Street address 3: Charlotte
Street address state: MI
Zip/Postal code: 48813
County: Eaton
Country: United States
Mailing address: 2845 Victoria Lane
Mailing city: Charlotte
Mailing state: MI
Mailing zip: 48813
General Phone: (517) 543-1099
General Fax: (517) 543-1993
Advertising Phone: (517) 543-1099 ext 225
Advertising Fax: (517) 543-1993
Editorail Phone: (517) 543-1099 ext 227
Editorial Fax: (517) 543-1993
General/National Adv. E-mail: cgwing@county-journal.com
Display Adv. E-mail: cgwing@county-journal.com
Classified Adv. E-mail: cgwing@county-journal.com
Editorial e-mail: cgwing@county-journal.com
Primary Website: county-journal.com
Year Established: 2006
Delivery Methods: Carrier
Area Served - City: 48813, 49076, 49021, 49096, 48876, 48890, 48861, 48827, 48821
Advertising (Open Inch Rate) Weekday/Saturday: Open inch rate $9.68
Mechanical specifications: Type page: 10.25 x 16; 6 col
Published: Sat
Avg Paid Circ: 28
Avg Free Circ: 16000
Audit By: CVC
Audit Date: 6/30/2020
Personnel: Cindy Gaedert (Owner, Pub. & Sales); Cindy Gaedert (Publisher/Owner); Travis Silvas (Circ. Mgr.); Denise Ensley
Parent company (for newspapers): Flashes Advertising & News

FERNDALE

METRO TIMES

Street address 1: 1200 Woodward Hts
Street address 3: Ferndale
Street address state: MI
Zip/Postal code: 48220-1427
County: Oakland
Country: USA
Mailing address: 1200 Woodward Heights
Mailing city: Ferndale
Mailing state: MI
Mailing zip: 48220
General Phone: (313) 961-4060
General Fax: (313) 964-4849
Editorail Phone: (313) 961-6598
General/National Adv. E-mail: adsales@metrotimes.com
Editorial e-mail: mjackman@metrotimes.com
Primary Website: www.metrotimes.com
Year Established: 1980
Advertising (Open Inch Rate) Weekday/Saturday: Open inch rate $39.34
Mechanical specifications: Type page 10 1/8 x 12 3/4; E - 6 cols, 1 3/8, between; A - 6 cols, 1 3/8, between; C - 6 cols, 1 3/8, between.
Published: Wed
Avg Paid Circ: 18
Avg Free Circ: 38215
Audit By: VAC
Audit Date: 3/31/2013
Personnel: Chris Keating (Pub.); Jim Nutter (Sr. Acct. Exec.); Annie O'Brien (Circ. Mgr.); Vince Grzegorek (Ed.)

LANSING

CITY PULSE

Street address 1: 1905 E Michigan Ave
Street address 3: Lansing
Street address state: MI
Zip/Postal code: 48912-2828
County: Ingham
Country: USA
Mailing address: 1905 E Michigan Ave
Mailing city: Lansing
Mailing state: MI
Mailing zip: 48912-2828
General Phone: (517) 371-5600
General Fax: (517) 999-6061
General/National Adv. E-mail: publisher@lansingcitypulse.com
Primary Website: www.lansingcitypulse.com
Published: Wed

MINNESOTA

MINNEAPOLIS

CITY PAGES

Street address 1: 800 N 1st St
Street address 2: Ste 300
Street address 3: Minneapolis
Street address state: MN
Zip/Postal code: 55401-1387
County: Hennepin
Country: USA
Mailing address: 401 N 3rd St Ste 550
Mailing city: Minneapolis
Mailing state: MN
Mailing zip: 55401-5050
General Phone: (612) 372-3700
General Fax: (612) 372-3737
General/National Adv. E-mail: adinfo@citypages.com
Primary Website: www.citypages.com
Advertising (Open Inch Rate) Weekday/Saturday: Open inch rate $61.00
Mechanical specifications: Type page 4 x 12.375; E - 4 cols, 2 2/5, 1/6 between; A - 6 cols, 1 9/16, 1/6 between; C - 8 cols, 1 3/16, 1/6 between.
Published: Wed
Avg Free Circ: 112025
Audit By: Sworn/Estimate/Non-Audited
Audit Date: 7/12/2019
Personnel: Tom Imberston (Circ. Mgr.); Kevin Hoffman (Ed. in Chief); Matt Smith (Mng. Ed.); Doug Snow (Prodn. Mgr.); Mary Erickson (Editor)

MISSOURI

KANSAS CITY

THE PITCH

Street address 1: 1701 Main St
Street address 3: Kansas City
Street address state: MO
Zip/Postal code: 64108-1368
County: Jackson
Country: USA
Mailing address: 1627 Main Ste 700
Mailing city: Kansas City
Mailing state: MO
Mailing zip: 64108-1369
General Phone: (816) 561-6061
General Fax: (816) 960-1538
Advertising Phone: (816) 218-6702
Editorail Phone: (816) 756-0502
General/National Adv. E-mail: pitch@pitch.com
Primary Website: thepitchkc.com
Year Established: 1980
Special Editions: Artopia Taste Summer Guide Music Showcase Best of Kansas City Gift
Delivery Methods: Newsstand
Area Served - City: Kansas City DMA
Own Printing Facility: N
Commercial printers: N
Advertising (Open Inch Rate) Weekday/Saturday: Open inch rate $33.00
Mechanical specifications: Type page 10 3/4 x 11; E - 4 cols, 2 3/8, 1/8 between; A - 8 cols, 1 1/8, 1/8 between; C - 8 cols, 1 1/8, 1/8 between.
Published: Wed
Avg Free Circ: 42500
Audit By: Sworn/Estimate/Non-Audited
Audit Date: 4/12/2019
Personnel: Stephanie Carey (Pub.); David Hudnall (Ed. in Chief); Jason Dockery (Mktg. Dir.); Adam Carey (CEO/ Owner)
Parent company (for newspapers): Womack Newspapers, inc

SAINT LOUIS

THE RIVERFRONT TIMES

Street address 1: 308 N 21st St
Street address 3: Saint Louis
Street address state: MO
Zip/Postal code: 63103-1642
County: Saint Louis City
Country: USA
Mailing address: 308 N. 21st Street Suite 300
Mailing city: Saint Louis
Mailing state: MO
Mailing zip: 63103
General Phone: (314) 754-5966
General Fax: (314) 754-5955
Advertising Phone: (314) 754-5932
Advertising Fax: (314) 754-6449
Editorail Phone: (314) 754-6404
Editorial Fax: (314) 754-6416
General/National Adv. E-mail: Letters@riverfronttimes.com
Display Adv. E-mail: colin.bell@riverfronttimes.com
Editorial e-mail: tips@riverfronttimes.com
Primary Website: www.riverfronttimes.com
Year Established: 1977
Delivery Methods: Mail`Racks
Area Served - City: 63101, 63102, 63103, 63104, 63105, 63106, 63107, 63108, 63109, 63110, 63111, 63112, 63113, 63114, 63115, 63116, 63118, 63120
Advertising (Open Inch Rate) Weekday/Saturday: Open inch rate $57.62
Mechanical specifications: Type page 9.72 x 10.75
Published: Wed
Avg Paid Circ: 297
Avg Free Circ: 55000
Audit By: Sworn/Estimate/Non-Audited
Audit Date: 7/12/2019
Personnel: Kevin Powers (Circ. Mgr.); Sarah Fenske (Editor in Chief); Chris Keating (Publisher)
Parent company (for newspapers): Euclid Media Group

NEBRASKA

OMAHA

THE READER

Street address 1: PO Box 7360
Street address 2: 2314 M Street
Street address 3: Omaha
Street address state: NE
Zip/Postal code: 68107-0360
County: Douglas
Country: USA
Mailing address: PO Box 7360
Mailing city: Omaha
Mailing state: NE
Mailing zip: 68107-0360
General Phone: (402) 341-7323
General Fax: (402) 341-6967
Advertising Phone: (402) 341-7323
Advertising Fax: (402) 341-6967
Editorail Phone: (402) 341-7323
General/National Adv. E-mail: help@thereader.com
Display Adv. E-mail: buildyourbusiness@thereader.com
Editorial e-mail: news@thereader.com
Primary Website: www.thereader.com
Year Established: 1994
Delivery Methods: Mail`Racks
Area Served - City: 51501,51503,68147,68005,68022,68046,68102,68105,68106,68107,68108,68110,68111,68112,68114,68116,98117,68118,68123,68124,68127,68128,68130,68131,68132,68134,68135,68137,68144,68154,68508,
Own Printing Facility: N
Commercial printers: N
Advertising (Open Inch Rate) Weekday/Saturday: Open inch rate $28.00
Mechanical specifications: Image Area 10 x 10 ; 4 cols
Published: Mthly
Avg Paid Circ: 210
Avg Free Circ: 35000
Audit By: CVC
Audit Date: 12/31/2012
Personnel: John Heaston (Publisher/Editor); Eric Stoakes (Prodn. Mgr.)
Parent company (for newspapers): Pioneer Publishing

NEVADA

HENDERSON

LAS VEGAS WEEKLY

Street address 1: 2275 Corporate Circle
Street address 2: Ste 300
Street address 3: Henderson
Street address state: NV
Zip/Postal code: 89074
County: Clark
Country: USA
Mailing address: 2275 Corporate Circle Ste 300
Mailing city: Henderson
Mailing state: NV
Mailing zip: 89074
General Phone: (702) 990-8993
General Fax: (702) 990-2424
General/National Adv. E-mail: doris.hollifield@gmgvegas.com
Display Adv. E-mail: maria.blondeaux@gmgvegas.com

Editorial e-mail: mark.depooter@gmgvegas.com
Primary Website: http://www.lasvegasweekly.com
Year Established: 1996
Advertising (Open Inch Rate) Weekday/Saturday: N/A
Mechanical specifications: Type page 10 1/2 x 13 1/2; E - 4 cols, 2 1/16, between; A - 5 cols, 2 1/16, between; C - 8 cols, between.
Published: Thur
Avg Paid Circ: 0
Avg Free Circ: 59020
Audit By: CVC
Audit Date: 12/31/2018
Personnel: Ron Gannon (Circ. Mgr.); Doris Hollifield; Mark Depooter (Pub.); Maria Blondeaux (Prod.)
Parent company (for newspapers): C-VILLE Holdings LLC

NONE

RENO NEWS & REVIEW

Street address 1: None
Street address 3: None
Street address state: NV
Zip/Postal code: 89509
Mailing address: 31855 Date Palm Drive #3-263
Mailing city: Cathedral City
Mailing state: CA
Mailing zip: 92264
General Phone: (775) 324-4440
General/National Adv. E-mail: jimmyb@renonr.com
Display Adv. E-mail: jimmyb@renonr.com
Classified Adv. E-mail: jimmyb@renonr.com
Editorial e-mail: jimmyb@renonr.com
Primary Website: renonr.com
Mthly Avg Views: 25000
Mthly Avg Unique Visitors: 20000
Year Established: 1993
Special Editions: Best of Northern Nevada--October
Area Served - City: Reno, Sparks, Carson City, Minden, Gardnerville, Truckee, Incline Village, South Lake Tahoe
Published: Mthly
Avg Free Circ: 25000
Personnel: Deborah Redmond; Jimmy Boegle; Jimmy Boegle (Publisher/executive editor); Frank Mullen (Editor); Brad Bynum (Editor); Michael Gelbman (Sales Manager); Elisabeth Bayard-Arthur (Design Manager)
Parent company (for newspapers): Coachella Valley Independent LLC; Coachella Valley Independent LLC

RENO

RENO NEWS & REVIEW

Street address 1: 760 Margrave Dr
Street address 2: Ste 100
Street address 3: Reno
Street address state: NV
Zip/Postal code: 89502
County: Washoe
Country: USA
Mailing address: 760 Margrave Dr Ste 100
Mailing city: Reno
Mailing state: NV
Mailing zip: 89502
General Phone: (775) 324-4440
General Fax: (775) 324-2515
General/National Adv. E-mail: bizmgr@newsreview.com
Display Adv. E-mail: emilyl@newsreview.com
Editorial e-mail: jeffv@newsreview.com
Primary Website: newsreview.com/reno
Area Served - City: 89503
Advertising (Open Inch Rate) Weekday/Saturday: Open inch rate $65.00
Mechanical specifications: Type page 10 13/16 x 13 1/8; E - 5 cols, 2 1/6, between; A - 5 cols, 2 1/6, between; C - 6 cols, 1 3/4, between.
Published: Thur
Avg Paid Circ: 0
Avg Free Circ: 27031
Audit By: CVC
Audit Date: 6/30/2018
Personnel: Jeff von Kaenel (CEO); John Murphy (Gen. Mgr.); Emily Litt (Adv.); Greg Erwin (Circ.)
Parent company (for newspapers): C-VILLE Holdings LLC

NEW HAMPSHIRE

MANCHESTER

THE HIPPO

Street address 1: 49 Hollis St
Street address 3: Manchester
Street address state: NH
Zip/Postal code: 03101-1239
County: Hillsborough
Country: USA
Mailing address: 49 Hollis St Ste 2
Mailing city: Manchester
Mailing state: NH
Mailing zip: 03101-1239
General Phone: (603) 625-1855
General Fax: (603) 625-2422
General/National Adv. E-mail: news@hippopress.com
Display Adv. E-mail: ccesarini@hippopress.com
Editorial e-mail: news@hippopress.com
Primary Website: hippopress.com
Year Established: 2001
Delivery Methods: Newsstand`Racks
Area Served - City: 01879 01830 01830 03275 03031 03811 03032 03110 03220 03303 03304 03033 03238 03301 03303 03038 03042 03234 03235 03249 03045 03841 03049 03106 03051 03246 03052 03053 03307 03101 03102 03103 03104 03106 03109 03253 03054 03055 03060 03062 03063 03064 03070 03256 03276 03261 03076 03263 03065 03077 03079 03885 03276 03281 03086 03087 03289
Advertising (Open Inch Rate) Weekday/Saturday: N/A
Mechanical specifications: Type page: 10.25 x 11.25; 4 col
Published: Thur
Avg Free Circ: 37860
Audit By: CVC
Audit Date: 9/6/2018
Note: We're more of a weekly magazine than an alt paper. Our coverage includes lots of information about food, arts and entertainment. Feel free to request copies or visit our website for more information.
Personnel: Jody Reese (Publisher); Doug Ladd (Circulation); Charlene Cesarini

NEW JERSEY

PLEASANTVILLE

ATLANTIC CITY WEEKLY

Street address 1: 1000 W Washington Ave
Street address 3: Pleasantville
Street address state: NJ
Zip/Postal code: 08232-3861
County: Atlantic
Country: USA
Mailing address: 1000 W Washington Ave
Mailing city: Pleasantville
Mailing state: NJ
Mailing zip: 08232-3861
General Phone: (609) 646-4848
General Fax: (609) 272-7378
Advertising Phone: (609) 646-4848
General/National Adv. E-mail: info@acweekly.com
Display Adv. E-mail: advertising@acweekly.com
Editorial e-mail: editorial@acweekly.com
Primary Website: atlanticcityweekly.com
Year Established: 1974
Delivery Methods: Mail`Newsstand`Racks
Advertising (Open Inch Rate) Weekday/Saturday: Full - $1250; 1/2 - $668; 1/4 - $370
Published: Thur
Avg Paid Circ: 44
Avg Free Circ: 34170
Audit By: Sworn/Estimate/Non-Audited
Audit Date: 4/15/2019
Personnel: Pamela Dollak (Ed.); Mike Dellavecchia (Dig. Content Mgr.); Daryl Bulthuis (Nat'l Adv.); Chris Lamy (Circ. Mgr.)
Parent company (for newspapers): BH Media Group

NEW MEXICO

ALBUQUERQUE

WEEKLY ALIBI

Street address 1: PO Box 81
Street address 3: Albuquerque
Street address state: NM
Zip/Postal code: 87103
County: Bernalillo
Country: USA
Mailing address: PO Box 81
Mailing city: Albuquerque
Mailing state: NM
Mailing zip: 87103
General Phone: (505) 346-0660
General Fax: (505) 256-9651
General/National Adv. E-mail: letters@alibi.com
Display Adv. E-mail: tierna@alibi.com
Editorial e-mail: editorial@alibi.com
Primary Website: www.alibi.com
Year Established: 1994
Delivery Methods: Racks
Area Served - City: 87048, 87114, 87113, 87122, 87120, 87107, 87109, 87111, 87104, 87110, 87112, 87120, 87121, 87106, 87108, 87116, 87123, 87117
Mechanical specifications: Type page 10 x 13; E - 4 cols, 2 7/16, between; A - 4 cols, 2 7/8, between; C - 8 cols, between.
Published: Wed
Avg Paid Circ: 0
Avg Free Circ: 32814
Audit By: VAC
Audit Date: 3/31/2019
Personnel: Constance Moss (Pub.); Devin O'Leary (Managing Editor); August March (News Ed.); Ramona Chavez (Art Dir.); Tierna Unruh-Enos (Sales Dir.); Christopher Johnson (Owner); Daniel Scott (Owner); Chris Silva (Circ. Dir.)
Parent company (for newspapers): NuCity Publications

NEW YORK

ALBANY

METROLAND

Street address 1: 419 Madison Ave
Street address 3: Albany
Street address state: NY
Zip/Postal code: 12210-1767
County: Albany
Country: USA
Mailing address: 523 Western Ave Ste 1
Mailing city: Albany
Mailing state: NY
Mailing zip: 12203-1617
General Phone: (518) 463-2500
General Fax: (518) 463-3712
General/National Adv. E-mail: metroland@metroland.net
Primary Website: www.metroland.net
Mechanical specifications: Type page 10 x 12 3/4; E - 4 cols, 2 1/4, 1/6 between; A - 4 cols, 2 1/4, 1/6 between; C - 8 cols, 1 1/8, 1/6 between.
Published: Thur
Avg Free Circ: 40000
Audit By: Sworn/Estimate/Non-Audited
Audit Date: 7/12/2019
Personnel: Stephen Leon (Pub.); John Bracchi (Art Dir.)
Parent company (for newspapers): C-VILLE Holdings LLC

BUFFALO

ART VOICE

Street address 1: 810 Main St
Street address 3: Buffalo
Street address state: NY
Zip/Postal code: 14202-1501
County: Erie
Country: USA
General Phone: (716) 881-6604
General Fax: (716) 881-6682
General/National Adv. E-mail: advertise@artvoice.com
Display Adv. E-mail: classifieds@artvoice.com
Editorial e-mail: editorial@artvoice.com
Primary Website: www.artvoice.com
Delivery Methods: Mail`Newsstand`Racks
Area Served - City: Lewiston, Lockport, Niagara Falls, North Tonawanda, Grand Island, Tonawanda, Amherst, Clarence, Buffalo, Cheektowaga, Lancaster, alden, West Seneca, Elma, East Aurora, Orchard Part, Hamburg, Angola, Springville, Derby, Dunkirk, Fredonia, Silvercreek, and West Falls
Advertising (Open Inch Rate) Weekday/Saturday: Open inch rate $65.00 (Inserts)
Mechanical specifications: Type page 10 x 11.5, 4 cols
Published: Thur
Avg Paid Circ: 55350
Audit By: Sworn/Estimate/Non-Audited
Audit Date: 7/12/2019
Personnel: Judy Sperry (Adv. Dir.); Jamie Moses (Pub.)
Parent company (for newspapers): Kahnsama Publication

ARTVOICE

Street address 1: 810812 Main St
Street address 3: Buffalo
Street address state: NY
Zip/Postal code: 14202-4006
County: Erie
Country: USA
Mailing address: 810-812 Main St
Mailing city: Buffalo
Mailing state: NY
Mailing zip: 14202
General Phone: (716) 881-6604
General Fax: (716) 881-6682
Advertising Phone: (716) 881-6604
Editorail Phone: (716) 881-6604
General/National Adv. E-mail: editorial@artvoice.com
Display Adv. E-mail: jamie@artvoice.com
Editorial e-mail: jamie@artvoice.com
Primary Website: www.artvoice.com
Year Established: 1990
Delivery Methods: Racks
Area Served - City: Buffalo-Niagara region
Published: Thur
Avg Free Circ: 55000
Audit By: Sworn/Estimate/Non-Audited
Audit Date: 7/12/2019
Personnel: Buck Quigley (Managing editor)

ITHACA

ITHACA TIMES

Street address 1: 109-111 N Cayuga St
Street address 3: Ithaca
Street address state: NY
Zip/Postal code: 14851
County: Tompkins
Country: USA
Mailing address: PO Box 27
Mailing city: Ithaca
Mailing state: NY
Mailing zip: 14851-0027
General Phone: (607) 277-7000
General Fax: (607) 277-1012
Editorial e-mail: editor@ithacatimes.com
Primary Website: www.ithacatimes.com
Year Established: 1972
Area Served - City: 14850, 14851, 14853
Mechanical specifications: sold by page fraction
Published: Wed
Avg Free Circ: 19700
Audit By: Sworn/Estimate/Non-Audited
Audit Date: 7/12/2019
Personnel: James Bilinski (Pub.); Nick Reynolds (Editor)
Parent company (for newspapers): Newski Inc

NEW YORK

NEW YORK PRESS

Street address 1: 79 Madison Ave
Street address 2: Fl 16
Street address 3: New York

Street address state: NY
Zip/Postal code: 10016-7807
County: New York
Country: USA
Mailing address: 72 Madison Ave Fl 11
Mailing city: New York
Mailing state: NY
Mailing zip: 10016-8731
General Phone: (212) 268-8600
General Fax: (212) 268-0502
Display Adv. E-mail: advertising@nypress.com
Primary Website: www.nypress.com
Advertising (Open Inch Rate) Weekday/Saturday: Open inch rate $60.00
Mechanical specifications: Type page 10 x 12 7/8; E - 6 cols, 1 1/2, 3/16 between; A - 6 cols, 1 1/2, 3/16 between; C - 7 cols, 1 1/4, 3/16 between.
Published: Wed
Avg Paid Circ: 97
Avg Free Circ: 116000
Audit By: Sworn/Estimate/Non-Audited
Audit Date: 7/12/2019
Personnel: Tom Allon (Pres.); Alex Schweitzer (Pub.); John Baxter (Circ. Mgr.); Jerry Portwood (Ed.)

PLATTSBURGH

LAKE CHAMPLAIN WEEKLY

Street address 1: 4701 State Route 9
Street address 3: Plattsburgh
Street address state: NY
Zip/Postal code: 12901-6036
County: Clinton
Country: USA
Mailing address: 4701 State Route 9
Mailing city: Plattsburgh
Mailing state: NY
Mailing zip: 12901-6036
General Phone: (518) 563-1414
General Fax: (518) 563-7060
Advertising Phone: (518) 563-1414
Advertising Fax: (518) 563-7060
Editorail Phone: (518) 563-1414
Editorial Fax: (518) 563-7060
General/National Adv. E-mail: advertising@studleyprinting.com
Display Adv. E-mail: advertising@studleyprinting.com
Editorial e-mail: editor@studleyprinting.com
Primary Website: www.lakechamplainweekly.com
Year Established: 2000
Delivery Methods: Newsstand`Racks
Area Served - City: all of 129 zip code and 12883
Advertising (Open Inch Rate) Weekday/Saturday: 12
Mechanical specifications: 1 column width-1.537"; 2 column width-3.229"; 3 column width-4.922"; 4 column width-6.615"; 5 column width-8.307:' 6 column width-10" Page height is 11.625"
Published: Wed
Avg Free Circ: 12000
Audit By: Sworn/Estimate/Non-Audited
Audit Date: 7/12/2019
Personnel: William Studley (Publisher); Bridgette Studley (Publisher)
Parent company (for newspapers): Studley Printing & Publishing, Inc.

ROCHESTER

CITY NEWSPAPER

Street address 1: 250 N Goodman St
Street address 3: Rochester
Street address state: NY
Zip/Postal code: 14607-1100
County: Monroe
Country: USA
Mailing address: 250 Goodman St N Ste 1
Mailing city: Rochester
Mailing state: NY
Mailing zip: 14607-1199
General Phone: (585) 244-3329
General Fax: (585) 244-1126
Advertising Phone: 585-244-3329 x20
Advertising Fax: (585) 244-1126
Editorail Phone: 585-244-3329 x25
Editorial Fax: (585) 244-1126
General/National Adv. E-mail: info@rochester-citynews.com
Display Adv. E-mail: ads@rochester-citynews.com
Editorial e-mail: themail@rochester-citynews.com
Primary Website: www.rochestercitynewspaper.com
Year Established: 1971
Delivery Methods: Mail`Racks
Area Served - City: Rochester metro
Advertising (Open Inch Rate) Weekday/Saturday: Modular rates (please inquire)
Mechanical specifications: Print area 9.9"w x 11.6"h.
Published: Wed
Avg Paid Circ: 31
Avg Free Circ: 32197
Audit By: VAC
Audit Date: 9/30/2016
Personnel: William Towler (co-publisher); Betsy Matthews (New Business Director); Mary Anna Towler (co-publisher/Editor); Ryan Williamson (Production Manager); Jake Clapp (Arts & Entertainment Editor)

SYRACUSE

SYRACUSE NEW TIMES

Street address 1: 1415 W Genesee St.
Street address 3: Syracuse
Street address state: NY
Zip/Postal code: 13204-2119
County: Onondaga
Country: USA
Mailing address: 1415 W Genesee St.
Mailing city: Syracuse
Mailing state: NY
Mailing zip: 13204-2119
General Phone: (315) 422-7011
General/National Adv. E-mail: tomtartaro@syracusenewtimes.com
Display Adv. E-mail: advertising@syracusenewtimes.com
Editorial e-mail: editorial@syracusenewtimes.com
Primary Website: syracusenewtimes.com
Year Established: 1969
Advertising (Open Inch Rate) Weekday/Saturday: N/A
Mechanical specifications: Type page 9.32 x 10.62; E - 4 cols, 2 1/16, 1/16 between; A - 5 cols, 2 1/16, 1/16 between; C - 7 cols, 1 1/2, 1/16 between.
Published: Wed
Avg Paid Circ: 7
Avg Free Circ: 33919
Audit By: Sworn/Estimate/Non-Audited
Audit Date: 7/12/2019
Personnel: Tom Tartaro (Circ. Dir.); William Brod (Pub./Owner); Bill DeLapp (Ed.-In-Chief); Reid Sullivan (Assoc. Ed.); Lesli Mitchell (Sr. Sales)
Parent company (for newspapers): All Times Publishing

NORTH CAROLINA

ASHEVILLE

MOUNTAIN XPRESS

Street address 1: 2 Wall St
Street address 3: Asheville
Street address state: NC
Zip/Postal code: 28801-2721
County: Buncombe
Country: USA
Mailing address: PO Box 144
Mailing city: Asheville
Mailing state: NC
Mailing zip: 28802-0144
General Phone: (828) 251-1333
General Fax: (828) 251-1311
General/National Adv. E-mail: xpress@mountainx.com
Display Adv. E-mail: advertise@mountainx.com
Editorial e-mail: news@mountainx.com
Primary Website: www.mountainx.com
Mthly Avg Views: 220076
Mthly Avg Unique Visitors: 112770
Year Established: 1994
Area Served - City: 28700 through 28999
Own Printing Facility: N
Commercial printers: N
Advertising (Open Inch Rate) Weekday/Saturday: Open inch rate $23.50
Mechanical specifications: Type page 10 1/4 x 12 3/4; E - 4 cols, 2 7/16, 1/8 between; A - 4 cols, 2 7/16, 1/8 between; C - 6 cols, 1 1/2, 1/5 between.
Published: Wed
Avg Paid Circ: 10
Avg Free Circ: 15942
Audit By: CVC
Audit Date: 6/30/2021
Personnel: Jeff Fobes (Pub.); Susan Hutchinson (Advertising Manager); Patty Levesque (Office Mgr.); Cindy Kunst (Circ Coordinator); Rebecca Sulock (Arts & Entertainment/Managing Editor); Thomas Calder (Editor); Stefan Colosimo (Techn. Mgr.); Carrie Lare (Art & Design Manager); Margaret Williams (News/ Managing Editor); Kyle Kirkpatrick (Webmaster)

BOONE

THE WATAUGA MOUNTAIN TIMES

Street address 1: 474 Industrial Park Dr
Street address 3: Boone
Street address state: NC
Zip/Postal code: 28607-3937
County: Watauga
Country: USA
Mailing address: PO BOX 1815
Mailing city: BOONE
Mailing state: NC
Mailing zip: 28607-1815
General Phone: (828) 264-3612
General Fax: (828) 262-0282
General/National Adv. E-mail: charlie.price@mountaintimes.com
Display Adv. E-mail: classifieds@mountaintimes.com
Editorial e-mail: newpaper@mountaintimes.com
Primary Website: mountaintimes.com/home
Year Established: 1978
Delivery Methods: Newsstand
Area Served - City: Watauga and Ashe 28604 Banner Elk N/A 1915 1915 28607 Boone N/A 8080 8080 28605 Blowing Rock N/A 1165 1165 28608 Boone N/A 40 40 28698 Zionville N/A 300 300 28615 Creston 780 780 28617 Crumpler 808 808 28626 Fleetwood 1024 1024 28631 Grassy Creek 291 291 28643 Lansing 1278 1278 28684 Todd 785 785 28693 Warrensville 493 493 28692 Vilas N/A 340 340 28619 Beech Mtn N/A 300 300 37683 Mountain City N/A 160 160 28679 Sugar Grove N/A 180 180 37691 Trade N/A 120 120 28657 Newland N/A 160 160 Non Alloc 0 TOTAL CIRC 18219 28604 Banner Elk N/A 1915 1915 28607 Boone N/A 8080 8080 28605 Blowing Rock N/A 1165 1165 28608 Boone N/A 40 40 28698 Zionville N/A 300 300 28615 Creston 780 780 28617 Crumpler 808 808 28626 Fleetwood 1024 1024 28631 Grassy Creek 291 291 28643 Lansing 1278 1278 28684 Todd 785 785 28693 Warrensville 493 493 28692 Vilas N/A 340 340 28619 Beech Mtn N/A 300 300 37683 Mountain City N/A 160 160 28679 Sugar Grove N/A 180 180 37691 Trade N/A 120 120 28657 Newland N/A 160 160 Non Alloc 0 TOTAL CIRC 18219 28604 Banner Elk N/A 1915 1915 28607 Boone N/A 8080 8080 28605 Blowing Rock N/A 1165 1165 28608 Boone N/A 40 40 28698 Zionville N/A 300 300 28615 Creston 780 780 28617 Crumpler 808 808 28626 Fleetwood 1024 1024 28631 Grassy Creek 291 291 28643 Lansing 1278 1278 28684 Todd 785 785 28693 Warrensville 493 493 28692 Vilas N/A 340 340 28619 Beech Mtn N/A 300 300 37683 Mountain City N/A 160 160 28679 Sugar Grove N/A 180 180 37691 Trade N/A 120 120 28657 Newland N/A 160 160 Non Alloc 0 TOTAL CIRC 18219
Advertising (Open Inch Rate) Weekday/Saturday: Open inch rate $30.24
Mechanical specifications: Type page 10 1/2 x 13; E - 6 cols, 1 9/16, 1/6 between; A - 6 cols, 1 9/16, 1/6 between; C - 6 cols, 1 9/16, 1/6 between.
Published: Wed`Thur
Avg Paid Circ: 0
Avg Free Circ: 12739
Audit By: CVC
Audit Date: 12/31/2016
Personnel: Andy Ganley (Circ. Mgr.); Gene Fowler; Charlie Price (Adv. Dir.); Tom Mayer (Ed.); Brad Miller (Lead Features Editor)
Parent company (for newspapers): Adams Publishing Group, LLC

DURHAM

THE INDEPENDENT WEEKLY

Street address 1: 302 E Pettigrew St
Street address 2: Ste 3A
Street address 3: Durham
Street address state: NC
Zip/Postal code: 27701-3712
County: Durham
Country: USA
Mailing address: PO Box 2690
Mailing city: Durham
Mailing state: NC
Mailing zip: 27715-2690
General Phone: (919) 286-1972
General Fax: (919) 286-4274
General/National Adv. E-mail: swatson@indyweek.com
Primary Website: www.indyweek.com
Year Established: 1983
Area Served - City: 27514, 27516, 27510, 27278, 27312, 27701, 27707, 27712, 27560, 27709, 27713, 27609, 27601, 27610, 27511, 27545, 27520, 27526, 27502
Mechanical specifications: Type page 9 7/8 x 11 1/2; E - 4 cols, 2 3/8, 3/16 between; A - 4 cols, 2 3/8, between; C - 6 cols, 1 1/2, 3/16 between.
Published: Wed
Avg Free Circ: 53806
Audit By: VAC
Audit Date: 12/31/2004
Personnel: Sioux Watson (Pub.); Gloria Wyly Mock (Adv. Mgr.); Robert VanVeld (Circ. Mgr.); Lisa Sorg (Ed.); Maria Shain (Prodn. Mgr.)
Parent company (for newspapers): C-VILLE Holdings LLC

GREENSBORO

YES! WEEKLY

Street address 1: 5500 Adams Farm Ln
Street address 2: Ste 204
Street address 3: Greensboro
Street address state: NC
Zip/Postal code: 27407-7059
County: Guilford
Country: USA
Mailing address: 5500 Adams Farm Ln Ste 204
Mailing city: Greensboro
Mailing state: NC
Mailing zip: 27407-7059
General Phone: (336) 316-1231
General Fax: (336) 316-1930
Advertising Phone: (336) 316-1231
Editorail Phone: (336) 316-1231
General/National Adv. E-mail: publisher@yesweekly.com
Display Adv. E-mail: publisher@yesweekly.com
Editorial e-mail: publisher@yesweekly.com
Primary Website: www.yesweekly.com
Year Established: 2005
Delivery Methods: Newsstand`Carrier`Racks
Advertising (Open Inch Rate) Weekday/Saturday: Moduler
Mechanical specifications: 9.9 x 10.2 tall
Published: Wed
Avg Free Circ: 20000
Audit By: Sworn/Estimate/Non-Audited
Audit Date: 7/12/2019
Personnel: Charles Womack (Pub.); Katie Murawski (News Ed.)
Parent company (for newspapers): Womack Newspapers, Inc

OHIO

CINCINNATI

CINCINNATI CITYBEAT

Street address 1: 811 Race St
Street address 2: Fl 5
Street address 3: Cincinnati
Street address state: OH

Zip/Postal code: 45202-2042
County: Hamilton
Country: USA
Mailing address: 811 Race St Fl 5
Mailing city: Cincinnati
Mailing state: OH
Mailing zip: 45202-2042
General Phone: (513) 665-4700
General Fax: (513) 665-4369
General/National Adv. E-mail: letters@citybeat.com
Display Adv. E-mail: ckarr@citybeat.com
Editorial e-mail: tfrank@citybeat.com
Primary Website: citybeat.com
Year Established: 1994
Delivery Methods: Carrier`Racks
Area Served - City: 45202
Advertising (Open Inch Rate) Weekday/Saturday: Open inch rate $30.00
Published: Wed
Avg Paid Circ: 13
Avg Free Circ: 30000
Audit By: Sworn/Estimate/Non-Audited
Audit Date: 3/30/2019
Personnel: Tony Frank (Ed.); Mike Zummo (Editorial); C Karr (Promotions); H Bollinger (Photo)
Parent company (for newspapers): Womack Newspapers, inc

COLUMBUS

ALIVE

Street address 1: 62 E Broad St
Street address 3: Columbus
Street address state: OH
Zip/Postal code: 43215-3500
County: Franklin
Country: USA
Mailing address: PO Box 1289
Mailing city: Columbus
Mailing state: OH
Mailing zip: 43216-1289
General Phone: (614) 221-2449
General Fax: (614) 461-8746
General/National Adv. E-mail: adowning@columbusalive.com
Display Adv. E-mail: hkritter@dispatch.com
Editorial e-mail: adowning@columbusalive.com
Primary Website: columbusalive.com
Year Established: 1983
Advertising (Open Inch Rate) Weekday/Saturday: Open inch rate $32.81
Mechanical specifications: Type page 10 1/8 x 12 1/2; E - 4 cols, 2 3/8, 1/6 between; A - 4 cols, 2 3/8, 1/6 between; C - 8 cols, 1 3/16, between.
Published: Thur
Avg Free Circ: 32421
Audit By: AAM
Audit Date: 3/31/2019
Personnel: Andy Downing (Ed.); Joel Oliphint (Asst. Ed.); Lauren Reinhard (Mktg. Mgr.); Ray Paprocki (Pub.); Rheta Gallagher (Assoc. Pub.)
Parent company (for newspapers): CherryRoad Media

DAYTON

DAYTON CITY PAPER

Street address 1: 126 N Main St
Street address 2: Ste 240
Street address 3: Dayton
Street address state: OH
Zip/Postal code: 45402-1766
County: Montgomery
Country: USA
Mailing address: PO Box 10065
Mailing city: Dayton
Mailing state: OH
Mailing zip: 45402
General Phone: (937) 222-8855
Advertising Phone: (937) 222-8855 x 603
Editorail Phone: (937) 222-8855 x 604
General/National Adv. E-mail: contactus@daytoncitypaper.com
Display Adv. E-mail: advertising@daytoncitypaper.com
Editorial e-mail: editor@daytoncitypaper.com
Primary Website: www.daytoncitypaper.com
Year Established: 2003
Delivery Methods: Carrier`Racks
Area Served - City: Entire metro Dayton Ohio region
Published: Tues
Avg Free Circ: 20120
Audit By: Sworn/Estimate/Non-Audited
Audit Date: 7/12/2019
Personnel: Paul Noah (CEO, Dayton City Media); Wanda Esken (Publisher)
Parent company (for newspapers): Dayton City Media

TOLEDO

THE TOLEDO CITY PAPER

Street address 1: 1120 Adams St
Street address 3: Toledo
Street address state: OH
Zip/Postal code: 43604-5509
County: Lucas
Country: USA
Mailing address: 1120 Adams St
Mailing city: Toledo
Mailing state: OH
Mailing zip: 43604-5509
General Phone: (419) 244-9859
General Fax: (419) 244-9871
General/National Adv. E-mail: editor@toledocitypaper.com
Primary Website: toledocitypaper.com
Year Established: 1997
Delivery Methods: Racks
Area Served - City: 43609, 43610, 43611, 43612, 43613, 43614, 43615, 43602, 43603, 43604, 43605, 43606, 43607, 43608, 43537, 43402, 43460, 43522, 43528, 43542, 43617, 43618, 43551, 43558, 43560, 43566, 43571, 43616, 43619, 43620, 43623, 43624
Advertising (Open Inch Rate) Weekday/Saturday: CP
Mechanical specifications: Type page 9 1/2 x 11 7/8; E - 4 cols, 2 1/8, 1/4 between; A - 4 cols, 2 1/8, 3/8 between; C - 5 cols, 1 3/4, 3/16 between.
Published: Wed`Other
Published Other: Bi-Weekly
Avg Paid Circ: 0
Avg Free Circ: 35897
Audit By: CVC
Audit Date: 3/30/2017
Personnel: Collette Jacobs (Publisher); Mark Jacobs (Adv. Dir.)
Parent company (for newspapers): Adams Street Publishing Co.

OKLAHOMA

OKLAHOMA CITY

OKLAHOMA GAZETTE

Street address 1: 3701 N Shartel Ave
Street address 3: Oklahoma City
Street address state: OK
Zip/Postal code: 73118-7102
County: Oklahoma
Country: USA
Mailing address: 3701 N Shartel Ave
Mailing city: Oklahoma City
Mailing state: OK
Mailing zip: 73118
General Phone: (405 605-6789
General Fax: (405) 528-4600
Display Adv. E-mail: advertising@tierramediagroup.com
Primary Website: www.okgazette.com
Year Established: 1979
Delivery Methods: Racks
Advertising (Open Inch Rate) Weekday/Saturday: Open inch rate $58
Mechanical specifications: Type page 10.25 x 12.25 Advertising - 4 columns, 2.2" wide with 1/8" between Classifeds - 6 columns, 1.5" wide with 1/16" between
Published: Wed
Avg Paid Circ: 0
Avg Free Circ: 36082
Audit By: VAC
Audit Date: 12/31/2016
Personnel: Peter Brzycki (Publisher)

TULSA

THE TULSA VOICE

Street address 1: 1603 S Boulder Ave
Street address 3: Tulsa
Street address state: OK
Zip/Postal code: 74119-4407
County: Tulsa
Country: USA
Mailing address: 1603 S. Boulder Ave
Mailing city: Tulsa
Mailing state: OK
Mailing zip: 74119
General Phone: (918)585-9924
General Fax: (918)585-9926
General/National Adv. E-mail: susie@langdonpublishing.com
Display Adv. E-mail: josh@langdonpublishing.com
Editorial e-mail: jim@langdonpublishing.com
Primary Website: thetulsavoice.com
Year Established: 2013
Delivery Methods: Newsstand
Published: Wed`Other
Published Other: Bi-Weekly
Avg Paid Circ: 2
Avg Free Circ: 20190
Audit By: CVC
Audit Date: 3/31/2018
Personnel: Jim Langdon (Pub.); Josh Kampf (Adv.); Susie Miller (Circ.); Madeline Crawford (Prod.)

OREGON

EUGENE

EUGENE WEEKLY

Street address 1: 1251 Lincoln St
Street address 3: Eugene
Street address state: OR
Zip/Postal code: 97401-3418
County: Lane
Country: USA
Mailing address: 1251 Lincoln St
Mailing city: Eugene
Mailing state: OR
Mailing zip: 97401-3418
General Phone: (541) 484-0519
General Fax: (541) 484-4044
Advertising Phone: (541) 484-0519
Editorail Phone: (541) 484-0519
General/National Adv. E-mail: office@eugeneweekly.com
Display Adv. E-mail: ads@eugeneweekly.com
Classified Adv. E-mail: office@eugeneweekly.com
Editorial e-mail: editor@eugeneweekly.com
Primary Website: www.eugeneweekly.com
Year Established: 1982
Special Editions: Best of Eugene, Chow, Back to Campus, Summer Guide, Winter Reading,
Delivery Methods: Mail`Newsstand`Carrier`Racks
Area Served - City: Lane County, Oregon; Corvallis, Oregon.
Own Printing Facility: N
Mechanical specifications: Type page 10 1/4 x 12 9/16; E - 4 cols, 2 3/8, 1/4 between; A - 4 cols, 2 3/8, 1/4 between; C - 6 cols, 1 1/2, 1/4 between.
Published: Thur
Published Other: Online several days a week.
Weekday Frequency: All day
Avg Paid Circ: 80
Avg Free Circ: 30000
Audit By: Sworn/Estimate/Non-Audited
Audit Date: 6/30/2017
Note: Print circ etc. available
Personnel: Camilla Mortensen (Editor); Rob Weiss (Director of Advertising); Todd Cooper (Head of graphics)
Parent company (for newspapers): What's Happening Inc.

PORTLAND

WILLAMETTE WEEK

Street address 1: 2220 NW Quimby St
Street address 3: Portland
Street address state: OR
Zip/Postal code: 97210-2624
County: Multnomah
Country: USA
Mailing address: 2220 NW Quimby St
Mailing city: Portland
Mailing state: OR
Mailing zip: 97210-2624
General Phone: (503) 243-2122
General Fax: (503) 243-1115
Advertising Phone: (503) 223-1500
Advertising Fax: (503) 223-0388
Display Adv. E-mail: azusman@wweek.com
Editorial e-mail: Mzusman@wweek.com
Primary Website: www.wweek.com
Mthly Avg Views: 1800000
Mthly Avg Unique Visitors: 1100000
Year Established: 1974
Special Editions: Best of Portland Restaurant Guide Drink Cheap Eats Bicycles Home Design
Syndicated Publications: Finder - August
Delivery Methods: Newsstand`Racks
Area Served - City: 97201-97245
Advertising (Open Inch Rate) Weekday/Saturday: Open inch rate $45.02
Mechanical specifications: Type page 9 3/4 x 13 1/8; E - 5 cols, 1 4/5, 1/8 between; A - 5 cols, 1 4/5, 1/8 between; C - 6 cols, 1 1/2, 1/8 between.
Published: Wed
Published Other: Wednesday
Avg Paid Circ: 100
Avg Free Circ: 50000
Audit By: Sworn/Estimate/Non-Audited
Audit Date: 7/12/2019
Personnel: Anna Zusman (Publisher); Mark Zusman (Publisher); Jane Smith (Associate Publisher)
Parent company (for newspapers): City of Roses Newspaper Company; City of Roses Newspaper Company

PENNSYLVANIA

COLUMBIA

BUSINESSWOMAN

Street address 1: 3912 Abel Dr
Street address 3: Columbia
Street address state: PA
Zip/Postal code: 17512-9031
County: Lancaster
Country: USA
Mailing address: 3912 Abel Dr
Mailing city: Columbia
Mailing state: PA
Mailing zip: 17512-9031
General Phone: (717) 285-1350
General Fax: (717) 285-1360
General/National Adv. E-mail: danderson@onlinepub.com
Primary Website: www.businesswomanpa.com
Published: Wed

PHILADELPHIA

PHILADELPHIA WEEKLY

Street address 1: 1520 Locust Street
Street address 2: Fifth Floor
Street address 3: Philadelphia
Street address state: PA
Zip/Postal code: 19102
County: Philadelphia
Country: USA
Mailing address: 1520 Locust Street, Fifth Floor
Mailing city: Philadelphia
Mailing state: PA
Mailing zip: 19102
General Phone: (215) 543-3743

General/National Adv. E-mail: mail@philadelphiaweekly.com
Display Adv. E-mail: dtangi@philadelphiaweekly.com
Editorial e-mail: kgabriel@phillyweekly.com
Primary Website: philadelphiaweekly.com
Year Established: 1981
Advertising (Open Inch Rate) Weekday/Saturday: Open inch rate $67.00
Mechanical specifications: Type page 10 x 11 5/8; E - 6 cols, 1 1/2, between; A - 6 cols, 1 1/2, between.
Published: Wed
Avg Paid Circ: 0
Avg Free Circ: 56129
Audit By: CVC
Audit Date: 3/30/2019
Personnel: Kerith Gabriel (Ed.); Daniel Tangi (Adv.)

PITTSBURGH

PITTSBURGH CITY PAPER

Street address 1: 650 Smithfield St
Street address 2: Ste 2200
Street address 3: Pittsburgh
Street address state: PA
Zip/Postal code: 15222-3925
County: Allegheny
Country: USA
General Phone: (412) 685-9009
General/National Adv. E-mail: info@pghcitypaper.com
Primary Website: www.pghcitypaper.com
Mechanical specifications: Type page 10 1/4 x 12 3/4; E - 4 cols, 2 3/8, between; A - 4 cols, 2 3/8, between.
Published: Wed
Avg Free Circ: 60627
Audit By: Sworn/Estimate/Non-Audited
Audit Date: 3/30/2019
Personnel: Lisa Cunningham (Ed. in Chief); Alex Gordon (Mng. Ed.); Justin Matase (Associate Pub.)
Parent company (for newspapers): Eagle Media

WILKES BARRE

WEEKENDER

Street address 1: 15 N Main St
Street address 3: Wilkes Barre
Street address state: PA
Zip/Postal code: 18701-2690
County: Luzerne
Country: USA
Mailing address: 15 N. Main St.
Mailing city: Wilkes-Barre
Mailing state: PA
Mailing zip: 18711
General Phone: (570) 829-7100
General Fax: (570) 831-7375
Advertising Fax: (570) 829-2002
General/National Adv. E-mail: weekender@theweekender.com
Primary Website: www.theweekender.com
Own Printing Facility: Y
Commercial printers: Y
Advertising (Open Inch Rate) Weekday/Saturday: Open inch rate $18.45
Mechanical specifications: Type page 10 1/4 x 12 3/4; E - 5 cols, 2, 1/6 between; A - 5 cols, 2, 1/6 between; C - 8 cols, 1 1/4, 1/6 between.
Published: Wed
Avg Free Circ: 41000
Audit By: AAM
Audit Date: 9/30/2014
Personnel: Rachel Hugh (Gen. Mgr.); Mike Lello (Ed.)
Parent company (for newspapers): Civitas Media, LLC

RHODE ISLAND

PAWTUCKET

MOTIF MAGAZINE

Street address 1: 65 Blackstone Ave
Street address 3: Pawtucket
Street address state: RI
Zip/Postal code: 02860-1068
County: Providence
Country: USA
Mailing address: 65 Blackstone Ave
Mailing city: Pawtucket
Mailing state: RI
Mailing zip: 02860
General Phone: (401)312+3305
General/National Adv. E-mail: news@motifri.com
Display Adv. E-mail: getout@motifri.com
Primary Website: motifri.com
Delivery Methods: Newsstand
Area Served - City: 02860
Published: Bi-Mthly
Avg Free Circ: 24328
Audit By: VAC
Audit Date: 3/31/2016

PROVIDENCE

PROVIDENCE PHOENIX

Street address 1: 150 Chestnut St
Street address 3: Providence
Street address state: RI
Zip/Postal code: 02903-4645
County: Providence
Country: USA
Mailing address: 475 Kilvert St Ste 320
Mailing city: Warwick
Mailing state: RI
Mailing zip: 02886-1360
General Phone: (401) 273-6397
General Fax: (401) 351-1399
General/National Adv. E-mail: lpapineau@phx.com
Primary Website: www.providencephoenix.com
Own Printing Facility: Y
Advertising (Open Inch Rate) Weekday/Saturday: Open inch rate $40.25
Mechanical specifications: Type page 10 x 14; E - 6 cols, 1 1/2, between; A - 6 cols, 1 1/2, between.
Published: Thur
Avg Free Circ: 68000
Audit By: Sworn/Estimate/Non-Audited
Audit Date: 7/12/2019
Personnel: Steve Brown (Associate Publisher); Stephen M. Mindich (Pub.); James Dorgan (Circ. Mgr.); Peter Kadzis (Ed.); Lou Papineau (Mng. Ed.); Stacey Congdon (Prodn. Mgr.)
Parent company (for newspapers): C-VILLE Holdings LLC

SOUTH CAROLINA

CHARLESTON

THE CHARLESTON CITY PAPER

Street address 1: 1316 Rutledge Ave
Street address 3: Charleston
Street address state: SC
Zip/Postal code: 29403-3050
County: Charleston
Country: USA
Mailing address: 1316 Rutledge Ave
Mailing city: Charleston
Mailing state: SC
Mailing zip: 29403
General Phone: (843) 577-5304
General/National Adv. E-mail: editor@charlestoncitypaper.com
Display Adv. E-mail: Sales@charlestoncitypaper.com
Primary Website: www.charlestoncitypaper.com
Year Established: 1998
Delivery Methods: Newsstand`Racks
Area Served - City: 29401 29403 29405 29406 29407 29412 29414 29418 29420 29430 29451 29455 29456 29464 29466 29482 29483 29492
Advertising (Open Inch Rate) Weekday/Saturday: $40.00
Mechanical specifications: Type page 9.5 x 10 3/4; E - 4 cols, 2 1/8, 1/8 between; A - 4 cols, 2 1/8, 1/3 between; C - 6 cols, between.
Published: Wed
Avg Free Circ: 35000
Audit By: Sworn/Estimate/Non-Audited
Audit Date: 7/12/2019
Personnel: Noel Mermer (Pub.); Blair Barna (Adv. Dir.); Scott Suchy (Arts Ed.)
Parent company (for newspapers): Jones Street Publishers, LLC

FREE TIMES

Street address 1: 1534 Main St
Street address 3: Columbia
Street address state: SC
Zip/Postal code: 29201-2808
County: Richland
Country: USA
Mailing address: PO Box 8295
Mailing city: Columbia
Mailing state: SC
Mailing zip: 29202-8295
General Phone: (803) 765-0707
General Fax: (803) 765-0727
General/National Adv. E-mail: publisher@free-times.com
Display Adv. E-mail: ads@free-times.com
Editorial e-mail: editor@free-times.com
Primary Website: www.free-times.com
Year Established: 1987
Delivery Methods: Newsstand`Racks
Area Served - City: 29169-29172, 29033, 29036, 29201-29212, 29223
Advertising (Open Inch Rate) Weekday/Saturday: N/A
Mechanical specifications: Type page 10 x 11 1/4; E - 4 cols, 2 1/3, 1/6 between; A - 6 cols, 1 1/2, 1/6 between; C - 8 cols, 1 1/12, between.
Published: Wed
Avg Paid Circ: 0
Avg Free Circ: 30753
Audit By: Sworn/Estimate/Non-Audited
Audit Date: 7/12/2019
Personnel: Lisa Heinz (Prodn. Mgr.); Eva Moore (Executive Editor); Chase Heatherly (Publisher & Advertising Director)
Parent company (for newspapers): Evening Post Publishing Company

TENNESSEE

KNOXVILLE

METRO PULSE

Street address 1: 602 S Gay St
Street address 2: Fl 2
Street address 3: Knoxville
Street address state: TN
Zip/Postal code: 37902-1605
County: Knox
Country: USA
General Phone: (865) 522-5399
General Fax: (865) 522-2955
Advertising Phone: (865) 342-6070
Editorail Phone: (865) 342-6068
Display Adv. E-mail: sales@metropulse.com
Editorial e-mail: editor@metropulse.com
Primary Website: www.metropulse.com
Year Established: 1991
Delivery Methods: Racks
Area Served - City: 37902, 37912, 37920, 37921, 37927, 37922, 37923, 37919, 37916, 37918, 37909, 37931, 37934, 37849, 37801, 37830, 37771
Advertising (Open Inch Rate) Weekday/Saturday: modular rates apply
Mechanical specifications: Type page 9 3/4 x 12 1/2; E - 4 cols, 2 1/8, 3/8 between; A - 4 cols, 2 1/8, 3/8 between; C - 8 cols, 1, 1/8 between.
Published: Thur
Avg Free Circ: 30000
Audit By: Sworn/Estimate/Non-Audited
Audit Date: 7/12/2019
Personnel: Kevin Pack (Dir. of Sales); Coury Turczyn (Ed.)
Parent company (for newspapers): E. W. Scripps Co.

MEMPHIS

MEMPHIS FLYER

Street address 1: 65 Union Ave
Street address 2: Ste 200
Street address 3: Memphis
Street address state: TN
Zip/Postal code: 38103-5131
County: Shelby
Country: USA
Mailing address: PO Box 1738
Mailing city: Memphis
Mailing state: TN
Mailing zip: 38101
General Phone: (901) 521-9000
General/National Adv. E-mail: anna@memphisflyer.com
Display Adv. E-mail: kristin@memphisflyer.com
Classified Adv. E-mail: classifieds@memphisflyer.com
Editorial e-mail: shara@memphisflyer.com
Primary Website: memphisflyer.com
Year Established: 1989
Syndicated Publications: Memphis, Memphis Parent, Inside Memphis Business
Delivery Methods: Racks
Area Served - City: 381xx
Own Printing Facility: N
Commercial printers: N
Advertising (Open Inch Rate) Weekday/Saturday: N/A
Market Information: Memphis SMA
Published: Thur
Avg Paid Circ: 0
Avg Free Circ: 28000
Audit By: CVC
Audit Date: 6/30/2021
Personnel: Bruce VanWynGarden (Ed.); Kenneth Neill (Pub.); Christopher Myers (Adv. Art. Dir.); Joseph Carey (IT Dir.); Shara Clark (Managing editor); Toby Sells (News editor); Susan Ellis (Mng. Ed.); Anna Traverse Fogle (CEO/publisher); Carrie O'Guin Hoffman (Adv. Opp. Mgr.); Brenda Ford (Class.)
Parent company (for newspapers): Contemporary Media, Inc.

NASHVILLE

NASHVILLE SCENE

Street address 1: 210 12th Ave S
Street address 2: Ste 100
Street address 3: Nashville
Street address state: TN
Zip/Postal code: 37203-4046
County: Davidson
Country: USA
Mailing address: 210 12th Ave S Ste 100
Mailing city: Nashville
Mailing state: TN
Mailing zip: 37203-4046
General Phone: (615) 844-5503
General Fax: (615) 244-8578
General/National Adv. E-mail: sales@nashvillescene.com
Primary Website: www.nashvillescene.com
Advertising (Open Inch Rate) Weekday/Saturday: Open inch rate $38.35
Mechanical specifications: Type page 9 3/4 x 12 3/8; E - 4 cols, 2 1/4, 1/4 between; A - 4 cols, 2 1/4, 1/4 between.
Published: Thur
Avg Paid Circ: 12
Avg Free Circ: 42659
Audit By: VAC
Audit Date: 6/30/2016
Personnel: Mike Smith (Pub.); Susan Torregrossa (Assoc. Pub.); Carla Holder (Mktg. Dir.); Casey Sanders (Circ. Mgr.); Jim Ridley (Ed.); Elizabeth Jones (Art Dir.)
Parent company (for newspapers): C-VILLE Holdings LLC

TEXAS

AUSTIN

AUSTIN CHRONICLE

Street address 1: 4112 Speedway
Street address 3: Austin
Street address state: TX
Zip/Postal code: 78751-4630
County: Travis
Country: USA

Mailing address: PO Box 4189
Mailing city: Austin
Mailing state: TX
Mailing zip: 78765-4189
General Phone: (512) 454-5766
General Fax: (512) 458-6910
Advertising Phone: (512) 454-5766
Editorail Phone: (512) 454-5766
General/National Adv. E-mail: mail@austinchronicle.com
Display Adv. E-mail: sales@austinchronicle.com
Editorial e-mail: kjones@austinchronicle.com
Primary Website: www.austinchronicle.com
Year Established: 1981
Delivery Methods: Racks
Area Served - City: 78601-78759
Commercial printers: Y
Advertising (Open Inch Rate) Weekday/Saturday: Open inch rate $60.00
Mechanical specifications: Type page 10 x 12 1/2; E - 4 cols, 2 3/8, between; A - 4 cols, 2 3/8, between; C - 8 cols, 1 1/8, between.
Published: Thur
Avg Paid Circ: 74
Avg Free Circ: 65932
Audit By: VAC
Audit Date: 5/31/2017
Personnel: Nick Barbaro (Pub.); Dan Hardick (Circ. Mgr.); Louis Black (Ed.); James Renovitch (Listings Ed); Marjorie Baumgarten (Film Ed); Cassidy Frazier (Sales Dir); Kimberley Jones (Ed)

THE TEXAS OBSERVER

Street address 1: 307 W 7th St
Street address 3: Austin
Street address state: TX
Zip/Postal code: 78701-2917
County: Travis
Country: USA
Mailing address: 307 W 7th St
Mailing city: Austin
Mailing state: TX
Mailing zip: 78701-2917
General Phone: (800) 939-6620
General Fax: (512) 474-1175
General/National Adv. E-mail: observer@texasobserver.org
Primary Website: www.texasobserver.org
Year Established: 1954
Mechanical specifications: Type page 8 1/2 x 11.
Published: Wed
Published Other: Every other Fri
Avg Paid Circ: 9500
Audit By: Sworn/Estimate/Non-Audited
Audit Date: 7/12/2019
Personnel: Carlton Carl (Exec. Pub.); Charlotte McCann (Pub.); Julia Austin (Assoc. Pub.); Dave Mann (Assoc. Ed.); Bob Moser (Ed.); Leah Ball (Art Dir.); Piper Nelson (Publisher)

DALLAS

DALLAS OBSERVER

Street address 1: 3800 Maple Ave
Street address 2: Ste 700
Street address 3: Dallas
Street address state: TX
Zip/Postal code: 75219-4072
County: Dallas
Country: USA
Mailing address: 2501 Oak Lawn Ave Ste 700
Mailing city: Dallas
Mailing state: TX
Mailing zip: 75219-4058
General Phone: (214) 757-9000
General Fax: (214) 757-8590
Primary Website: www.dallasobserver.com
Advertising (Open Inch Rate) Weekday/Saturday: Open inch rate $44.38
Mechanical specifications: Type page 10 x 12 1/2.
Published: Thur
Avg Free Circ: 90200
Audit By: Sworn/Estimate/Non-Audited
Audit Date: 7/12/2019
Personnel: Amy Jones (Pub.); Stephanie Riggs (Retail Sales Mgr.); Jennifer Brown (Classified Dir.); Carlos Garcia (Circ. Dir.); Mark Donald (Ed.); Patrick Williams (Mng. Ed.); Crystal Betts (Prod. Mgr.)
Parent company (for newspapers): Voice Media Group

FORT WORTH

FORT WORTH WEEKLY

Street address 1: 3311 Hamilton Ave
Street address 3: Fort Worth
Street address state: TX
Zip/Postal code: 76107-1877
County: Tarrant
Country: USA
Mailing address: 3311 Hamilton Ave
Mailing city: Fort Worth
Mailing state: TX
Mailing zip: 76107-1877
General Phone: (817) 321-9700
General Fax: (817) 321-9733
Advertising Phone: (817) 321-9700
Advertising Fax: (817) 321-9733
Editorail Phone: (817) 321-9700
Editorial Fax: (817) 321-9575
General/National Adv. E-mail: Michael.Newquist@fwweekly.com
Display Adv. E-mail: Brian.Martin@fwweekly.com
Editorial e-mail: Gayle.Reaves@fwweekly.com
Primary Website: www.fwweekly.com
Year Established: 1994
Delivery Methods: Mail`Racks
Area Served - City: Tarrant County
Advertising (Open Inch Rate) Weekday/Saturday: Open inch rate $18.25
Published: Wed
Avg Free Circ: 23064
Audit By: VAC
Audit Date: 5/31/2017
Personnel: Gayle Reaves (Ed.); Michael Newquist (Adv. Dir.); Brian Martin (Classified Adv. Dir.); Eric Griffey

HOUSTON

HOUSTON PRESS

Street address 1: 1621 Milam St
Street address 2: Ste 100
Street address 3: Houston
Street address state: TX
Zip/Postal code: 77002-8059
County: Harris
Country: USA
Mailing address: 2603 La Branch St
Mailing city: Houston
Mailing state: TX
Mailing zip: 77004-1136
General Phone: (713) 280-2400
General Fax: (713) 280-2496
Advertising Phone: (713) 280-2451
Advertising Fax: (713) 280-2444
Editorail Phone: (713) 280-2480
General/National Adv. E-mail: letters@houstonpress.com
Display Adv. E-mail: Danielle.Dalati@houstonpress.com
Primary Website: www.houstonpress.com
Year Established: 1989
Delivery Methods: Newsstand`Racks
Own Printing Facility: Y
Published: Thur
Avg Paid Circ: 85000
Audit By: Sworn/Estimate/Non-Audited
Audit Date: 7/12/2019
Personnel: Stuart Folb (Pub.); Danielle Dalati (Adv. Mgr.); Margaret Downing (Ed.); Catherine Matusow (Mng. Ed.); Monica Fuentes (Art Dir.); Daniel Ortega (Production Manager); Brenna Croom (Marketing Director); Michael McCormick (Online Director)
Parent company (for newspapers): Village Voice Media

SAN ANTONIO

LOCAL COMMUNITY NEWS

Street address 1: 4204 Gardendale Street
Street address 2: Suite 107
Street address 3: San Antonio
Street address state: TX
Zip/Postal code: 78229
County: Bexar
Country: USA
Mailing address: 4204 Gardendale Street, Suite 107
Mailing city: San Antonio
Mailing state: TX
Mailing zip: 78229
General Phone: (210) 338-8842
Editorail Phone: (210) 338-8842 ext. 212
Display Adv. E-mail: advertising@localcommunitynews.com
Editorial e-mail: tips@localcommunitynews.com
Primary Website: www.localcommunitynews.com
Year Established: 2012
Personnel: Jaselle Luna (Pub. & CEO); Thomas Edwards (Exec. Ed.)

SAN ANTONIO CURRENT

Street address 1: 915 Dallas St
Street address 3: San Antonio
Street address state: TX
Zip/Postal code: 78215-1433
County: Bexar
Country: USA
Mailing address: 915 Dallas St
Mailing city: San Antonio
Mailing state: TX
Mailing zip: 78215-1433
General Phone: (210) 227-0044
General Fax: (210) 227-7755
Primary Website: www.sacurrent.com
Year Established: 1986
Delivery Methods: Newsstand
Advertising (Open Inch Rate) Weekday/Saturday: Open inch rate $9.25
Mechanical specifications: Type page 10 x 12 1/2; E - 4 cols, 2 1/4, 1/20 between; A - 4 cols, 2 1/4, 1/20 between; C - 8 cols, 1 1/5, 1/20 between.
Published: Wed
Avg Free Circ: 19378
Audit By: VAC
Audit Date: 9/30/2015
Personnel: Michael Wagner (Publisher); Greg Harman (Advertising Director)

UTAH

SALT LAKE CITY

SALT LAKE CITY WEEKLY

Street address 1: 248 S Main St
Street address 3: Salt Lake City
Street address state: UT
Zip/Postal code: 84101-2001
County: Salt Lake
Country: USA
Mailing address: 248 S Main St.
Mailing city: Salt Lake City
Mailing state: UT
Mailing zip: 84101-2001
General Phone: (801) 575-7003
General Fax: (801) 575-6106
General/National Adv. E-mail: comments@cityweekly.net
Primary Website: www.cityweekly.net
Year Established: 1984
Delivery Methods: Racks
Area Served - City: 84101, 84102, 84103, 84104, 84105, 84106, 84107, 84108, 84109, 84110, 84111, 84112, 84113, 84114, 84115, 84116, 84117, 84118, 84119, 84120, 84121, 84122, 84123, 84124, 84125, 84126, 84127, 84128, 84130, 84131, 84132, 84133, 84134, 84135, 84136, 84137, 84138, 84139, 84140, 84141, 84142, 84143, 84144, 84145, 84147, 84148, 84150, 84151, 84152, 84153, 84157, 84158, 84165, 84170, 84171, 84180, 84184, 84185, 84189, 84190, 84199
Advertising (Open Inch Rate) Weekday/Saturday: Open inch rate $40.00
Mechanical specifications: Type page 10 x 13; E - 4 cols, 2 1/8, 1/8 between; A - 8 cols, 1 1/16, 1/8 between; C - 8 cols, 1 1/16, between.
Published: Thur
Avg Free Circ: 46467
Audit By: VAC
Audit Date: 6/30/2016
Personnel: John Saltas (Pub.); Doug Kruithof (Retail Sales Mgr.); Dylan Woolf Harris (Ed.)

VERMONT

BURLINGTON

SEVEN DAYS

Street address 1: 255 S Champlain St
Street address 3: Burlington
Street address state: VT
Zip/Postal code: 05401-4881
County: Chittenden
Country: USA
Mailing address: P.O. Box 1164
Mailing city: Burlington
Mailing state: VT
Mailing zip: 05402-1164
General Phone: (802) 864-5684
General Fax: (802) 865-1015
General/National Adv. E-mail: paula@sevendaysvt.com; cathy@sevendaysvt.com
Display Adv. E-mail: sales@sevendaysvt.com
Editorial e-mail: pamela@sevendaysvt.com (arts); matthew@sevendaysvt.com (news)
Primary Website: www.sevendaysvt.com
Year Established: 1995
Delivery Methods: Newsstand`Carrier`Racks
Area Served - City: 05001, 05031, 05041, 05047, 05060, 05061, 05091, 05401, 05403, 05404, 05405, 05408, 05439, 05441, 05443, 05444, 05445, 05446, 05450, 05451, 05452, 05454, 05456, 05458, 05461, 05462, 05463, 05464, 05465, 05466, 05468, 05469, 05470, 05471, 05472, 05473, 05474, 05477, 05478, 05479, 05482, 05486, 05487, 05489, 05491, 05494, 05495, 05602, 05640, 05461, 05648, 05651, 05655, 05656, 05658, 05660, 05661, 05663, 05667, 05671, 05673, 05674, 05676, 05701, 05733, 05734, 05735, 05740, 05743, 05753, 05760, 05766, 05770, 05819, 05826, 05828, 05843, 05873,
Own Printing Facility: N
Commercial printers: Y
Advertising (Open Inch Rate) Weekday/Saturday: Modular rates
Mechanical specifications: Type page 9.625 x 11.25; E - 4 cols, 2.3
Published: Wed
Avg Paid Circ: 3
Avg Free Circ: 35975
Audit By: CVC
Audit Date: 9/30/2018
Personnel: Pamela Polston (Assoc. Pub./Ed.); Colby Roberts (Sales Dir./Assoc. Pub.); Paula Routly (Pub./Ed.); Don Eggert (Creative Dir./Assoc. Pub.); Cathy Resmer (Assoc. Pub.); Corey Grenier (Mkt. Dir.); Ashley Cleare (Classifieds & personals manager); John James (Prodn. Mgr.); Cheryl Brownell (Bus. Mgr.); Kristen Ravin (Calendar Ed.); Paul Heintz (Political Ed.)

VIRGINIA

CHARLOTTESVILLE

C-VILLE WEEKLY

Street address 1: 308 E Main St
Street address 3: Charlottesville
Street address state: VA
Zip/Postal code: 22902-5234
County: Charlottesville City
Country: USA
Mailing address: 308 E MAIN ST
Mailing city: CHARLOTTESVILLE
Mailing state: VA
Mailing zip: 22902-5234
General Phone: (434) 817-2749
General Fax: (434) 817-2758
General/National Adv. E-mail: circulation@c-ville.com
Display Adv. E-mail: aimee@c-ville.com
Editorial e-mail: aimee@c-ville.com
Primary Website: c-ville.com
Mthly Avg Unique Visitors: 40000
Year Established: 1988
Delivery Methods: Mail`Newsstand`Racks
Area Served - City: Albemarle County
Advertising (Open Inch Rate) Weekday/Saturday: 1/8 Pg $280.00; 1/4 Pg $400.00; 3/8 Pg $510.00

Published: Wed
Avg Paid Circ: 0
Avg Free Circ: 22416
Audit By: CVC
Audit Date: 6/30/2018
Personnel: Erica Gentile (Advt Mgr); Giles Morris (Ed.); Aimee Atteberry (Pub.); Bill Dempsey (Circ.)
Parent company (for newspapers): C-VILLE Holdings LLC
footnotes: General/National Adv. E-mail: SRDS (11/26/2014); Display Adv. E-mail: SRDS (11/26/2014); Advertising (Open Inch Rate) Weekday/Saturday: SRDS (11/26/2014)

THE HOOK

Street address 1: 100 2nd St NW
Street address 3: Charlottesville
Street address state: VA
Zip/Postal code: 22902-5193
County: Charlottesville City
Country: USA
Mailing address: 308 E Main St
Mailing city: Charlottesville
Mailing state: VA
Mailing zip: 22902-5234
Primary Website: www.readthehook.com
Published: Thur
Avg Free Circ: 18999
Audit By: Sworn/Estimate/Non-Audited
Audit Date: 7/12/2019
Personnel: Hawes Spencer (Editor); Anna Harrison (Circulation)

LYNCHBURG

THE BURG

Street address 1: 101 Wyndale Dr
Street address 3: Lynchburg
Street address state: VA
Zip/Postal code: 24501-6710
County: Lynchburg City
Country: USA
Mailing address: 101 Wyndale Drive
Mailing city: Lynchburg
Mailing state: VA
Mailing zip: 24501
General Phone: (434) 385-5525
Primary Website: http://www.newsadvance.com/the_burg/
Published: Fri
Personnel: Jason McBride (Adv. Dir.)
Parent company (for newspapers): BH Media Group

RICHMOND

STYLE WEEKLY

Street address 1: 1313 E Main St
Street address 2: Apt 103
Street address 3: Richmond
Street address state: VA
Zip/Postal code: 23219-3600
County: Richmond City
Country: USA
Mailing address: 24 E 3rd St
Mailing city: Richmond
Mailing state: VA
Mailing zip: 23224-4246
General Phone: (804) 358-0825
General Fax: (804) 358-1079
General/National Adv. E-mail: info@styleweekly.com
Primary Website: www.styleweekly.com
Year Established: 1982
Own Printing Facility: Y
Mechanical specifications: Type page 9 7/8 x 13; E - 4 cols, between; A - 4 cols, between.
Published: Wed
Avg Paid Circ: 13
Avg Free Circ: 30680
Audit By: VAC
Audit Date: 12/31/2016
Personnel: Lori Waran (Publisher); Jason Roop (Editor)
Parent company (for newspapers): C-VILLE Holdings LLC

WASHINGTON

BELLVUE

SEATTLE WEEKLY

Street address 1: 2700 Richards Rd.
Street address 2: Suite 201
Street address 3: Bellvue
Street address state: WA
Zip/Postal code: 98005
Country: USA
Mailing address: 11630 Slater Ave. NE, Suite 8/9
Mailing city: Kirkland
Mailing state: WA
Mailing zip: 98034
General Phone: (206) 623-0500
Advertising Phone: (425) 453-4270
General/National Adv. E-mail: ralcott@soundpublishing.com
Display Adv. E-mail: ralcott@soundpublishing.com
Editorial e-mail: editor@seattleweekly.com
Primary Website: seattleweekly.com
Year Established: 1976
Delivery Methods: Mail`Newsstand`Racks
Own Printing Facility: N
Mechanical specifications: Type page 11 1/4 x 13 5/8; E - 4 cols, 2 5/16, 1/8 between; A - 4 cols, 2 5/16, 1/8 between; C - 4 cols, 2 5/16, 1/8 between.
Published: Wed
Avg Paid Circ: 15
Avg Free Circ: 15736
Audit By: AAM
Audit Date: 3/31/2018
Personnel: Rudi Alcott (Pub.); Andy Hobbs (Ed.); Kelley Denman (Adv. Dir.)
Parent company (for newspapers): Sound Publishing

RAYMOND

GAUGER MEDIA SERVICE, INC.

Street address 1: 1034 Bradford Street
Street address 2: P.O. Box 627
Street address 3: Raymond
Street address state: WA
Zip/Postal code: 98577
County: Pacific
Country: USA
Mailing address: P.O. Box 627
Mailing city: Raymond
Mailing state: WA
Mailing zip: 98577
General Phone: (360) 942-3560
General/National Adv. E-mail: dave@gaugermedia.com
Primary Website: www.gaugermedia.com
Year Established: 1987
Personnel: Dave Gauger (Pres/Broker)

SEATTLE

THE STRANGER

Street address 1: 800 Maynard Ave. South
Street address 2: Ste 200
Street address 3: Seattle
Street address state: WA
Zip/Postal code: 98134
County: King
Country: USA
Mailing address: 800 Maynard Ave. South, Suite 200
Mailing city: Seattle
Mailing state: WA
Mailing zip: 98134
General Phone: (206) 323-7101
Advertising Phone: (206) 323-7101
Advertising Fax: (206) 325-4865
Editorail Phone: (206) 323-7101
Editorial Fax: (206) 323-7203
General/National Adv. E-mail: press@thestranger.com
Display Adv. E-mail: adinfo@thestranger.com
Editorial e-mail: editor@thestranger.com
Primary Website: www.thestranger.com
Mthly Avg Views: 1553148
Mthly Avg Unique Visitors: 492116
Year Established: 1991
Delivery Methods: Mail`Racks
Area Served - City: 98199 98109 98119 98121 98101 98104 98134 98108 98112 98102 98122 98144 98118 98105 98195 98115 98125 98155 98103 98117 98133 98177 98107 98106 98116 98126 98136 98106 98146 98166 98028 98072 98011 98052 98033 98034 98004 98005 98006 98007 98027 98040 98108 98168 98188 98198 98178 98055 98056 98057 98030 98032 98003 98023 98422
Advertising (Open Inch Rate) Weekday/Saturday: Open inch rate $50.00
Published: Mon`Tues`Wed`Thur`Fri
Published Other: Daily, Monday-Friday, online only
Weekday Frequency: All day
Audit Date: 30-Jun
Note: The Stranger stopped publishing a print edition in March 2020 when the coronavirus hit and went online only.
Personnel: Tim Keck (Publisher); Laurie Saito (Publisher); Chase Burns (Editor); Ben Demar (Senior Account Rep); Christopher Frizzelle (Mng. Ed.); Dan Savage (Ed.); Katie Phoenix (Senior Account Rep); Rob Crocker (President); Erica Tarrant (Prodn. Mgr.)
Parent company (for newspapers): Index Newspapers LLC

SPOKANE

THE PACIFIC NORTHWEST INLANDER

Street address 1: 1227 W Summit Pkwy
Street address 3: Spokane
Street address state: WA
Zip/Postal code: 99201-7003
County: Spokane
Country: USA
Mailing address: 1227 W Summit Pkwy
Mailing city: Spokane
Mailing state: WA
Mailing zip: 99201-7003
General Phone: (509) 325-0634
General Fax: (509) 325-0638
General/National Adv. E-mail: info@inlander.com
Display Adv. E-mail: sales@inlander.com
Editorial e-mail: editor@inlander.com
Primary Website: www.inlander.com
Year Established: 1993
Delivery Methods: Mail`Racks
Area Served - City: 83814, 83822, 83835, 83843, 83852, 83854, 83855, 83856, 83857, 83858, 83860, 83861, 83864, 83869, 83870, 83876, 99001, 99003, 99004, 99005, 99006, 99009, 99011, 99016, 99019, 99021, 99022, 99027, 99030, 99036, 99037, 99163, 99201, 99202, 99203, 99204, 99205, 99206, 99207, 99208, 99212, 99216, 99217, 99218, 99223, 99224
Published: Thur
Avg Paid Circ: 50
Avg Free Circ: 52000
Audit By: Sworn/Estimate/Non-Audited
Audit Date: 7/12/2019
Personnel: Ted McGregor (Owner-Publisher); Trevor Rendall (Distribution Manager); Ted S. McGregor (Owner-Publisher); Wayne Hunt (Prodn. Mgr.); Jacob Fries (Editor)

WISCONSIN

MADISON

ISTHMUS

Street address 1: PO Box 1542
Street address 3: Madison
Street address state: WI
Zip/Postal code: 53701
Mailing address: PO Box 1542
Mailing city: Madison
Mailing state: WI
Mailing zip: 53701
General Phone: (608) 251-5627
General/National Adv. E-mail: edit@isthmus.com
Display Adv. E-mail: bbolan@isthmus.com
Editorial e-mail: edit@isthmus.com
Primary Website: isthmus.com
Year Established: 1976
Delivery Methods: Mail`Racks
Area Served - City: 53703 through 53719
Advertising (Open Inch Rate) Weekday/Saturday: Open inch rate $41.29
Mechanical specifications: Type page 10 x 12 1/2; E - 4 cols, 2 1/4, 1/4 between; A - 4 cols, 2 1/4, 1/4 between; C - 6 cols, 1 1/2, 1/4 between.
Published: Mthly
Avg Free Circ: 35000
Audit By: Sworn/Estimate/Non-Audited
Audit Date: 4/18/2019
Note: We are now a nonprofit, 501(c)(3).
Personnel: Judith Davidoff (Editor/President); Jeff Haupt (Pub.); Craig Bartlett (Asst. Pub.); Tim Henrekin (Circ. Mgr.); Jason Joyce (Publisher); Chad Hopper (Advertising Manager); Joe Tarr (News Ed.)
Parent company (for newspapers): Isthmus Community Media, Inc.

MILWAUKEE

SHEPHERD EXPRESS WEEKLY NEWS

Street address 1: 207 E Buffalo St
Street address 2: Ste 410
Street address 3: Milwaukee
Street address state: WI
Zip/Postal code: 53202-5712
County: Milwaukee
Country: USA
Mailing address: 207 E Buffalo St Ste 410
Mailing city: Milwaukee
Mailing state: WI
Mailing zip: 53202-5712
General Phone: (414) 276-2222
General Fax: (414) 276-3312
General/National Adv. E-mail: postmaster@shepherd-express.com
Primary Website: www.expressmilwaukee.com
Mechanical specifications: Type page 10 x 12 1/2; E - 4 cols, between; A - 4 cols, between.
Published: Wed
Avg Paid Circ: 15
Avg Free Circ: 57410
Audit By: VAC
Audit Date: 5/31/2017
Personnel: Joseph Porubcan (Circ. Mgr.); Louis Fortis (Ed.)

WAUSAU

CITY PAGES

Street address 1: 300 N 3rd St
Street address 2: Ste 200
Street address 3: Wausau
Street address state: WI
Zip/Postal code: 54403-5400
County: Marathon
Country: USA
Mailing address: PO Box 942
Mailing city: Wausau
Mailing state: WI
Mailing zip: 54402-0942
General Phone: (715) 845-5171
General Fax: (715) 845-5887
Advertising Phone: (715) 845-5171
Advertising Fax: (715) 848-5887
Editorail Phone: (715) 845-5171
Editorial Fax: (715) 848-5887
General/National Adv. E-mail: tammy@thecitypages.com
Display Adv. E-mail: advertising@thecitypages.com
Editorial e-mail: tammy@thecitypages.com
Primary Website: thecitypages.com
Year Established: 1993
Special Editions: Summer Fun Book- mag supplement first week June Get with the Program annual guide to Wausau area - mag supplement Thurs. after Labor Day Holiday & Winter Book - mag supplement Thurs. before Thanksgiving Abode - in paper section on house, home, living, 2nd, 3rd, 4th Thurs. of April Health & Fitness - in paper section, 2nd & 3rd Thurs. in February Kid Corner - quarterly.
Delivery Methods: Mail`Newsstand`Racks
Area Served - City: 54401, 54402, 54403, 54476, 54440, 54455, 54448, 54474, 54481, 54492
Commercial printers: N

Advertising (Open Inch Rate) Weekday/Saturday: Open inch rate $24.33
Mechanical specifications: Type page 10 x 12; E - 4 cols, 2 3/8, between; A - 4 cols, 2 3/8, between.
Published: Thur
Avg Paid Circ: 8
Avg Free Circ: 17021
Audit By: VAC
Audit Date: 5/31/2017
Note: Three magazine supplements: Summer magazine, 18K circa 'Program' year-round guide early Sept., 19K+ Holiday/winter magazine 18K week before Thanksgiving
Personnel: Tammy Stezenski (Ed/Pub); Kayla Zastrow (Administrative assistant)

WYOMING

JACKSON

BUCKRAIL

Street address 1: PO Box 10831
Street address 3: Jackson
Street address state: WY
Zip/Postal code: 83002
County: Jackson
Country: USA
Mailing address: PO Box 10831
Mailing city: Jackson
Mailing state: WY
Mailing zip: 83002
General Phone: (307) 222-8609
General/National Adv. E-mail: info@buckrail.com
Display Adv. E-mail: ads@buckrail.com
Editorial e-mail: tips@buckrail.com
Primary Website: buckrail.com
Year Established: 2002
Delivery Methods: Newsstand`Racks
Area Served - City: 83001,83002,83014,83025, 83455
Published: Wed
Avg Free Circ: 8000
Audit By: Sworn/Estimate/Non-Audited
Audit Date: 4/13/2019
Personnel: Brian Gulotta; Aaron Davis; Shannon Sollitt; Jake Nichols; Brian Modena

ALTERNATIVE NEWSPAPERS IN CANADA

ALBERTA

CALGARY

JEWISH FREE PRESS

Street address 1: 8411 Elbow Dr. SW
Street address 3: Calgary
Street address state: AB
Zip/Postal code: T2V 1K8
Country: Canada
Mailing address: 8411 Elbow Dr. SW
Mailing city: Calgary
Mailing state: AB
Mailing zip: T2V 1K8
General Phone: (403) 252-9423
General Fax: (403) 255-5640
General/National Adv. E-mail: jewishfp@tellus.net
Primary Website: www.jewishfreepress.ca
Year Established: 1990
Advertising (Open Inch Rate) Weekday/Saturday: Open inch rate $50.00
Mechanical specifications: Type page 10 1/8 x 15 1/4; E - 6 cols, 1 1/2, 1/8 between; A - 6 cols, 1 1/2, 1/8 between.
Published: Thur
Avg Paid Circ: 50
Avg Free Circ: 2100
Audit By: Sworn/Estimate/Non-Audited
Audit Date: 7/12/2019

EDMONTON

EDMONTON JEWISH LIFE

Street address 1: 7200 156th St. NE
Street address 3: Edmonton
Street address state: AB
Zip/Postal code: T5R 1X3
Country: Canada
Mailing address: 7200 156th St. NE
Mailing city: Edmonton
Mailing state: AB
Mailing zip: T5R 1X3
General Phone: (780) 487-0585
General Fax: (780) 484-4978
General/National Adv. E-mail: ejlife@shaw.ca
Primary Website: www.jewishedmonton.org
Advertising (Open Inch Rate) Weekday/Saturday: Open inch rate $1.42
Mechanical specifications: Type page 10 1/4 x 15; E - 6 cols, 1 9/16, between; A - 6 cols, 1 9/16, between.
Published: Mthly
Audit By: Sworn/Estimate/Non-Audited
Audit Date: 7/12/2019
Personnel: John Bresler (Pub.); Neil Loomer (Ed.)

VUE WEEKLY

Street address 1: Suite 200-11230 119 St NW
Street address 3: Edmonton
Street address state: AB
Zip/Postal code: T5G 2X3
Country: Canada
Mailing address: Suite 200-11230 119 St NW
Mailing city: Edmonton
Mailing state: AB
Mailing zip: T5G 2X3
General Phone: (780) 426-1996
General Fax: (780) 426-2889
Primary Website: www.vueweekly.com

BRITISH COLUMBIA

N. VANCOUVER

COMMUNITY DIGEST

Street address 1: 3707 Dollarton Hwy.
Street address 3: N. Vancouver
Street address state: BC
Zip/Postal code: V7G 1A1
County: British Columbia
Country: Canada
Mailing address: 3707 Dollarton Hwy.
Mailing city: N.Vancouver
Mailing state: BC
Mailing zip: V7G 1A1
General Phone: (604) 987-8313
General/National Adv. E-mail: mail@communitydigest.ca;
Display Adv. E-mail: adsales@communitydigest.ca
Primary Website: www.communitydigest.ca
Year Established: 1983
Delivery Methods: Mail`Newsstand`Carrier`Racks
Area Served - City: Alberta, BC , Ontario
Advertising (Open Inch Rate) Weekday/Saturday: Open inch rate $
Mechanical specifications: Type page 7 1/2 x 10; E - 5 cols, 1 3/8, 1/8 between; A - 5 cols, 1 3/8, 1/8 between.
Published: Fri
Avg Paid Circ: 2950
Avg Free Circ: 25000
Audit By: Sworn/Estimate/Non-Audited
Audit Date: 7/12/2019
Note: No phone calls will be attended. All should contact by e-mail only.
Personnel: Nick Ebrahim (Adv. Mgr.); Stephen Bowell (Managing Editor)

VANCOUVER

JEWISH INDEPENDENT

Street address 1: PO Box 47100
Street address 2: RPO City Square
Street address 3: Vancouver
Street address state: BC
Zip/Postal code: V5Z 4L6
County: Canada
Country: Canada
Mailing address: PO Box 47100 RPO City Square
Mailing city: Vancouver
Mailing state: BC
Mailing zip: V5Z 4L6
General Phone: (604) 689-1520
Display Adv. E-mail: sales@jewishindependent.ca
Editorial e-mail: editor@jewishindependent.ca
Primary Website: www.jewishindependent.ca
Year Established: 1930
Delivery Methods: Mail`Newsstand`Carrier`Racks
Area Served - City: Any
Advertising (Open Inch Rate) Weekday/Saturday: Open inch rate $30.00
Mechanical specifications: Type page 9 13/16 x 13; E - 5 cols, 1 13/16, between; A - 5 cols, 1 13/16, between; C - 5 cols, 1 13/16, between.
Published: Fri
Audit By: Sworn/Estimate/Non-Audited
Audit Date: 7/12/2019
Personnel: Leanne Jacobsen (Adv. Mgr.); Cynthia Ramsay (publisher)

VICTORIA

MONDAY MAGAZINE

Street address 1: 818 Broughton St.
Street address 3: Victoria
Street address state: BC
Zip/Postal code: V8W 1E4
County: Canada
Country: Canada
General Phone: (250) 480-3251
General Fax: (250) 386-2624
Editorail Phone: (250) 480-3247
Display Adv. E-mail: janet@mondaymag.com
Editorial e-mail: editorial@mondaymag.com
Primary Website: www.mondaymag.com
Year Established: 1975
Delivery Methods: Racks
Area Served - City: V8V
Own Printing Facility: Y
Commercial printers: Y
Advertising (Open Inch Rate) Weekday/Saturday: Open inch rate $16.00
Published: Mthly
Avg Free Circ: 18000
Audit By: Sworn/Estimate/Non-Audited
Audit Date: 7/12/2019
Personnel: Kyle Slavin; Janet Gairdner; Ruby Della-Siega
Parent company (for newspapers): Black Press Group Ltd.

MANITOBA

STEINBACH

MENNONITISCHE POST

Street address 1: 383 Main St.
Street address 3: Steinbach
Street address state: MB
Zip/Postal code: R5G 1Z4
Country: Canada
Mailing address: 383 Main St.
Mailing city: Steinbach
Mailing state: MB
Mailing zip: R5G 1Z4
General Phone: (204) 326-6790
General Fax: (204) 326-6302
General/National Adv. E-mail: office@mennpost.org
Editorial e-mail: editor@mennpost.org
Advertising (Open Inch Rate) Weekday/Saturday: Open inch rate $6.50
Mechanical specifications: Type page 10 1/4 x 15 1/2.
Published: Fri
Avg Paid Circ: 7700
Avg Free Circ: 300
Audit By: Sworn/Estimate/Non-Audited
Audit Date: 7/12/2019
Personnel: Anne Froese (Adv. Mgr.); Kennert Giesbrecht (Mng. Ed.)

WINNIPEG

KANADA KURIER

Street address 1: 955 Alexander Ave.
Street address 3: Winnipeg
Street address state: MB
Zip/Postal code: R3C 2X8
Country: Canada
Mailing address: PO Box 1054
Mailing city: Winnipeg
Mailing state: MB
Mailing zip: R3C 2X8
General Phone: (204) 774-1883
General Fax: (204) 783-5740
General/National Adv. E-mail: kanadakurier@mb.sypatico.ca
Own Printing Facility: Y
Advertising (Open Inch Rate) Weekday/Saturday: Open inch rate $61.92
Published: Sat
Avg Paid Circ: 2500
Avg Free Circ: 100
Audit By: Sworn/Estimate/Non-Audited
Audit Date: 7/12/2019
Personnel: Renee Topham (Pub.); Eva Rutzetter (Pub.); Christine Bogen (Adv. Mgr.); Marion Schirrmann (Ed.)

UKRAINSKY HOLOS

Street address 1: 842 Main St.
Street address 3: Winnipeg
Street address state: MB
Zip/Postal code: R2W 3N8
County: MB
Country: Canada
Mailing address: 842 Main St.
Mailing city: Winnipeg
Mailing state: MB
Mailing zip: R2W 3N8
General Phone: (204) 589-5871
General Fax: (204) 586-3618
Advertising Phone: (204) 589-5871
Editorail Phone: (204) 589-5871
General/National Adv. E-mail: presstr@mts.net
Display Adv. E-mail: presstr@mts.net
Editorial e-mail: presstr@mts.net
Primary Website: ukrvoice.ca
Year Established: 1910
Delivery Methods: Mail`Newsstand
Own Printing Facility: Y
Advertising (Open Inch Rate) Weekday/Saturday: Open inch rate $.58
Mechanical specifications: Type page 14 1/2 x 22 3/4; E - 6 cols, 2, 1/8 between; A - 6 cols, 2, 1/8 between; C - 6 cols, 2, 1/8 between.
Published: Mon
Published Other: 2 x Mthly
Avg Paid Circ: 1890
Avg Free Circ: 42
Audit By: Sworn/Estimate/Non-Audited
Audit Date: 7/12/2019
Personnel: Maria Bosak (Ed.)
Parent company (for newspapers): Trident Press Ltd

NOVA SCOTIA

HALIFAX

THE COAST

Street address 1: 2309 Maynard Street
Street address 3: Halifax
Street address state: NS
Zip/Postal code: B3K 3T8
County: Nova Scotia (NS)
Country: Canada
Mailing address: 2309 Maynard Street
Mailing city: Halifax
Mailing state: NS
Mailing zip: B3K 3T8
General Phone: (902) 422-6278
General Fax: (902) 425-0013
General/National Adv. E-mail: audram@thecoast.ca
Display Adv. E-mail: sales@thecoast.ca
Editorial e-mail: news@thecoast.ca
Primary Website: https://thecoast.ca
Year Established: 1993
Delivery Methods: Newsstand`Racks
Published: Thur
Avg Free Circ: 22140
Audit By: Sworn/Estimate/Non-Audited
Audit Date: 7/12/2019
Personnel: Kyle Shaw (Ed)
Parent company (for newspapers): Coast Publishing Ltd.

ONTARIO

MISSISSAUGA

EL EXPRESO

Street address 1: 1233 Nigel Road Mississauga
Street address 3: Mississauga
Street address state: ON
Zip/Postal code: M6E 2G8
County: Canada
Country: Canada
Mailing address: 1233 Nigel Road Mississauga, Ontario L5j 3S6
Mailing city: Mississauga
Mailing state: ON
Mailing zip: M6E 2G8
General Phone: 647-642-3260
General Fax: (416) 781-8420
General/National Adv. E-mail: expreso@interlog.com
Display Adv. E-mail: expreso-inter@uniserve.com
Primary Website: www.elexpresocanada.com
Year Established: 1992
Delivery Methods: Mail
Advertising (Open Inch Rate) Weekday/Saturday: Open inch rate $2.00/line/col
Mechanical specifications: Type page 14 x 22 1/2; E - 6 cols, 2 1/3, between; A - 6 cols, 2 1/3, between.
Published: Fri
Published Other: weekly
Avg Free Circ: 55000
Audit By: Sworn/Estimate/Non-Audited
Audit Date: 7/12/2019
Personnel: George Baez (Circ. Mgr.); Nabil Saad (Mng. Ed.)

KANADSKY SLOVAK / THE CANADIAN SLOVAK

Street address 1: 259 Traders Bouleward East
Street address 2: Unit 6
Street address 3: Mississauga
Street address state: ON
Zip/Postal code: L4Z 2E5
Country: Canada
Mailing address: 259 Traders Bouleward East
Mailing city: Mississauga
Mailing state: ON
Mailing zip: L4Z 2E5
General Phone: (905) 507 8004
Advertising Phone: (403) 933 2741
General/National Adv. E-mail: editor@kanadskyslovak.ca
Display Adv. E-mail: administrator@kanadskyslovak.ca
Editorial e-mail: editor@kanadskyslovak.ca
Primary Website: www.kanadskyslovak.ca
Year Established: 194
Special Editions: Christmas, Easter
Delivery Methods: Mail`Racks
Area Served - City: Globally
Commercial printers: Y
Advertising (Open Inch Rate) Weekday/Saturday: Open inch rate $2.00
Market Information: 65,000 strong community in Canada, more in the USA and Europe
Published: Sat
Avg Paid Circ: 900
Avg Free Circ: 300
Audit By: Sworn/Estimate/Non-Audited
Audit Date: 7/12/2019
Personnel: Julius Behul (Editor-in-Chief); George Frajkor (Editorial Page); Daniel Sulan (Chair, Business Committee); Paul Carnogursky (Webmaster, www.kanadskyslovak.ca); Mary Ann Doucette (President, Slovak Canadian Publishing Company); Stan Kirschbaum (Chair, Editorial Committe)

SAINT CATHARINE'S

CHRISTIAN COURIER

Street address 1: 5 Joanna Dr.
Street address 3: Saint Catharine's
Street address state: ON
Zip/Postal code: L2N 1V1
County: Niagara
Country: Canada
Mailing address: 2 Aiken St
Mailing city: St Catharines
Mailing state: ON
Mailing zip: L2N 1V8
General Phone: (905) 937-3314
General/National Adv. E-mail: admin@christiancourier.ca
Display Adv. E-mail: ads@christiancourier.ca
Editorial e-mail: editor@christiancourier.ca
Primary Website: www.christiancourier.ca
Year Established: 1945
Delivery Methods: Mail
Area Served - City: all
Advertising (Open Inch Rate) Weekday/Saturday: Open inch rate $8.00
Mechanical specifications: Type page 10 1/4 x 12 .
Published: Mon`Bi-Mthly
Published Other: second and fourth Mondays of the month
Avg Paid Circ: 2100
Avg Free Circ: 70
Audit By: Sworn/Estimate/Non-Audited
Audit Date: 7/12/2019
Personnel: Angela Reitsma-Bick (News Ed.)

SCARBOROUGH

PHILIPPINE REPORTER

Street address 1: 2682 Eglinton Ave. East
Street address 2: P.O. Box 44529
Street address 3: Scarborough
Street address state: ON
Zip/Postal code: M1K 5K2
Country: Canada
Mailing address: 2682 Eglinton Ave. East, P.O. Box 44529
Mailing city: Scarborough
Mailing state: ON
Mailing zip: M1K 5K2
General Phone: (416) 461-8694
General Fax: n/a
Advertising Phone: (416) 461-8694
Advertising Fax: n/a
General/National Adv. E-mail: philreporter@gmail.com
Display Adv. E-mail: ads@philreporter.com
Editorial e-mail: philreporter@gmail.com
Primary Website: www.philippinereporter.com
Year Established: 1989
Delivery Methods: Carrier
Area Served - City: Greater Toronto Area, Niagara Region, Peel Region, Durham Region, York Region
Advertising (Open Inch Rate) Weekday/Saturday: Open inch rate $.52
Mechanical specifications: Type page 10 1/2 x 15 3/8; E - 5 cols, 2, between; A - 5 cols, 2, between.
Published: Bi-Mthly
Published Other: 2 x Mthly
Avg Free Circ: 8000
Audit By: Sworn/Estimate/Non-Audited
Audit Date: 7/12/2019
Note: Please email ads@philreporter.com for the rate card.
Personnel: Hermie Garcia (Ed./Publisher); Norman Garcia (Account Executive)

TORONTO

BAYVIEW POST

Street address 1: 30 Lesmill Road
Street address 3: Toronto
Street address state: ON
Zip/Postal code: M3B 2T6
Country: Canada
General Phone: (416) 250-7979
General Fax: (416) 250-1737
Display Adv. E-mail: advertising@postcity.com
Editorial e-mail: concerns@postcity.com
Primary Website: www.postcity.com
Published: Mthly
Avg Free Circ: 24516
Audit By: VAC
Audit Date: 9/30/2014
Personnel: Lorne London (Publisher)

DA ZHONG BAO

Street address 1: 50 Weybright Ct., Unit 11
Street address 3: Toronto
Street address state: ON
Zip/Postal code: M1S 5A8
Country: Canada
Mailing address: 50 Weybright Ct., Unit 11
Mailing city: Toronto
Mailing state: ON
Mailing zip: M1S 5A8
General Phone: (416) 504-0761
General Fax: (416) 504-4928
General/National Adv. E-mail: cng@chinesenewsgroup.com
Primary Website: www.chinesenewsgroup.com
Advertising (Open Inch Rate) Weekday/Saturday: Open inch rate $1.68
Mechanical specifications: Type page 10 x 13 1/2.
Published: Tues`Fri`Sat
Avg Free Circ: 12000
Audit By: Sworn/Estimate/Non-Audited
Audit Date: 7/12/2019
Personnel: Jack Jia (Prodn. Mgr.)

DALIL AL ARAB

Street address 1: 368 Queen St. E.
Street address 3: Toronto
Street address state: ON
Zip/Postal code: M5A 1T1
Country: Canada
Mailing address: 368 Queen St. E.
Mailing city: Toronto
Mailing state: ON
Mailing zip: M5A 1T1
General Phone: (416) 362-0304
General Fax: (416) 861-0238
General/National Adv. E-mail: info@arabnews.ca
Editorial e-mail: arabnews@yahoo.com
Primary Website: www.arabnews.ca
Advertising (Open Inch Rate) Weekday/Saturday: Open inch rate $1.25
Published Other: 2 x Mthly
Avg Free Circ: 6000
Audit By: Sworn/Estimate/Non-Audited
Audit Date: 7/12/2019
Personnel: S. Allam (Co Pub.); Sami Zubi (Adv. Mgr.); F. Ahmed (Ed.)

EL POPULAR

Street address 1: 2413 Dundas St. W.
Street address 3: Toronto
Street address state: ON
Zip/Postal code: M6P 1X3
County: Canada
Country: Canada
Mailing address: 2413 Dundas St. W.
Mailing city: Toronto
Mailing state: ON
Mailing zip: M6P 1X3
General Phone: (416) 531-2495
General Fax: (416) 531-7187
General/National Adv. E-mail: director@diarioelpopular.com
Display Adv. E-mail: ads@diarioelpopular.com
Editorial e-mail: nixa@diarioelpopular.com
Primary Website: www.diarioelpopular.com
Year Established: 1970
Delivery Methods: Mail`Newsstand
Area Served - City: all GTA
Advertising (Open Inch Rate) Weekday/Saturday: Open inch rate $.88
Mechanical specifications: Type page 10 1/2 x 13.5; E - 6 cols, between; A - 6 cols, between; C - 6 cols, between.
Published: Mon`Wed`Fri
Published Other: 3 times per week
Avg Paid Circ: 10.5
Avg Free Circ: 200
Audit By: Sworn/Estimate/Non-Audited
Audit Date: 7/12/2019
Personnel: Eduardo Uruena (Mng. Ed.)

NORTH TORONTO POST

Street address 1: 30 Lesmill Road
Street address 3: Toronto
Street address state: ON
Zip/Postal code: M3B 2T6
Country: Canada
General Phone: (416) 250-7979
General Fax: (416) 250-1737
Display Adv. E-mail: advertising@postcity.com
Editorial e-mail: concerns@postcity.com
Primary Website: www.postcity.com
Published: Mthly
Avg Free Circ: 29392
Audit By: VAC
Audit Date: 9/1/2011
Personnel: Lorne London (Publisher)

NORTH YORK POST

Street address 1: 30 Lesmill Road
Street address 3: Toronto
Street address state: ON
Zip/Postal code: M3B 2T6
Country: Canada
General Phone: (416) 250-7979
General Fax: (416) 250-1737
Display Adv. E-mail: advertising@postcity.com
Editorial e-mail: concerns@postcity.com
Primary Website: www.postcity.com
Published: Mthly
Avg Free Circ: 24491
Audit By: VAC
Audit Date: 9/30/2014
Personnel: Lorne London (Publisher)

NOVY DOMOV 2.0 (NEW HOMELAND)

Street address 1: 450 Scarborough Golf Club Rd.
Street address 3: Toronto
Street address state: ON
Zip/Postal code: M1G 1H1
Country: Canada
Mailing address: 450 Scarborough Golf Club Rd.
Mailing city: Toronto
Mailing state: ON
Mailing zip: M1G 1H1
General Phone: (416) 439-4354
Advertising Phone: (416) 439-4354
Editorail Phone: (416) 439-4354
General/National Adv. E-mail: office@masaryktown.ca
Display Adv. E-mail: novydomoveditor@gmail.com
Editorial e-mail: office@masaryktown.ca
Primary Website: www.masaryktown.ca
Year Established: 1946
Delivery Methods: Mail`Racks
Area Served - City: Canada, USA, CZ
Own Printing Facility: N
Commercial printers: Y
Advertising (Open Inch Rate) Weekday/Saturday: Open inch rate $4.00
Published: Mthly
Avg Paid Circ: 100
Avg Free Circ: 750
Audit By: Sworn/Estimate/Non-Audited
Audit Date: 9/15/2022
Personnel: Vera Kohoutova (Editor); Karen Deschenes (Operations Manager)

NOW

Street address 1: 192 Spadina Ave
Street address 2: Ste 503
Street address 3: Toronto
Street address state: ON
Zip/Postal code: M5T 2C2
Country: Canada
Mailing address: 503-192 Spadina Ave
Mailing city: Toronto
Mailing state: ON
Mailing zip: M5T 2C2
General Phone: (416) 364-1300
General Fax: (416) 364-1166
General/National Adv. E-mail: news@nowtoronto.com
Primary Website: www.nowtoronto.com
Year Established: 1981
Delivery Methods: Mail`Newsstand`Racks
Mechanical specifications: Type page 9 13/16 x 11 1/4; E - 5 cols, 1 13/16, 3/16 between; A - 5 cols, 1 13/16, 3/16 between; C - 8 cols, 1 1/6, 1/8 between.
Published: Thur
Avg Paid Circ: 7
Avg Free Circ: 71000
Audit By: CCAB
Audit Date: 9/30/2018
Personnel: Alice Klein (Ed.); Ellie Kirzner (Sr. News Ed.); Enzo Dimatteo (Editorial Dir.); Kevin Ritchie (Sr.

Culture Ed.); Lulu El-Atab (Art Dir.); Michelle Da Silva (Life & Social Media Ed.); Glenn Sumi (Assoc. Enter. Ed.); Norman Wilner (Sr. Writer); Natalia Manzacco (Food Writer)

RICHMOND HILL POST

Street address 1: 30 Lesmill Road
Street address 3: Toronto
Street address state: ON
Zip/Postal code: M3B 2T6
Country: Canada
General Phone: (416) 250-7979
General Fax: (416) 250-1737
Display Adv. E-mail: advertising@postcity.com
Editorial e-mail: concerns@postcity.com
Primary Website: www.postcity.com
Published: Mthly
Avg Free Circ: 24970
Audit By: VAC
Audit Date: 9/30/2014
Personnel: Lorne London (Publisher)

SATELLITE 1416

Street address 1: 365 St. Clarence Ave.
Street address 3: Toronto
Street address state: ON
Zip/Postal code: M6H 3W2
County: Ontario
Country: Canada
Mailing address: P.O. Box 176, Station E
Mailing city: Toronto
Mailing state: ON
Mailing zip: M6H 4E2
General Phone: (416) 530-4222
General/National Adv. E-mail: abe@satellite1-416.com
Primary Website: www.satellite1-416.com
Year Established: 1991
Delivery Methods: Mail
Area Served - City: M6H 4E2
Advertising (Open Inch Rate) Weekday/Saturday: Open inch rate $1.65
Published: Thur
Published Other: One in month
Avg Paid Circ: 300
Avg Free Circ: 300
Audit By: Sworn/Estimate/Non-Audited
Audit Date: 7/12/2019
Personnel: Ales Brezina (Pub.)

SHARE

Street address 1: 658 Vaughan Rd.
Street address 3: Toronto
Street address state: ON
Zip/Postal code: M6E 2Y5
Country: Canada
Mailing address: 658 Vaughan Rd.
Mailing city: Toronto
Mailing state: ON
Mailing zip: M6E 2Y5
General Phone: (416) 656-3400
General Fax: (416) 656-3711
General/National Adv. E-mail: share@interlog.com
Primary Website: www.sharenews.com
Year Established: 1978
Delivery Methods: Carrier'Racks
Advertising (Open Inch Rate) Weekday/Saturday: Open inch rate $2.58
Published: Thur
Avg Free Circ: 32400
Audit By: Sworn/Estimate/Non-Audited
Audit Date: 7/12/2019
Personnel: Arnold Auguste (Pub.)

THORNHILL POST

Street address 1: 30 Lesmill Road
Street address 3: Toronto
Street address state: ON
Zip/Postal code: M3B 2T6
Country: Canada
General Phone: (416) 250-7979
General Fax: (416) 250-1737
Display Adv. E-mail: advertising@postcity.com
Editorial e-mail: concerns@postcity.com
Primary Website: www.postcity.com
Published: Mthly
Avg Free Circ: 24591
Audit By: VAC
Audit Date: 9/30/2014
Personnel: Lorne London (Publisher)

VILLAGE POST

Street address 1: 30 Lesmill Road
Street address 3: Toronto
Street address state: ON
Zip/Postal code: M3B 2T6
Country: Canada
General Phone: (416) 250-7979
General Fax: (416) 250-1737
Display Adv. E-mail: advertising@postcity.com
Editorial e-mail: concerns@postcity.com
Primary Website: www.postcity.com
Published: Mthly
Avg Free Circ: 24620
Audit By: VAC
Audit Date: 9/30/2014
Personnel: Lorne London (Publisher)

WILLOWDALE

AL-HILAL

Street address 1: 338 Hollyberry Trail
Street address 3: Willowdale
Street address state: ON
Zip/Postal code: M2H 2P6
Country: Canada
Mailing address: 338 Hollyberry Trail
Mailing city: Willowdale
Mailing state: ON
Mailing zip: M2H 2P6
General Phone: (416) 493-4374
General Fax: (416) 493-4374
General/National Adv. E-mail: lowaisi@rogers.com
Advertising (Open Inch Rate) Weekday/Saturday: Open inch rate $1.00
Mechanical specifications: Type page 9 x 13; E - 5 cols, 1 7/8, between; A - 5 cols, 1 7/8, between.
Published Other: 2 x Mthly
Audit By: Sworn/Estimate/Non-Audited
Audit Date: 7/12/2019
Personnel: L. Owaisi (Pub.); A. Raza (Adv. Mgr.); Farida Abdullah (Ed.)

QUEBEC

MONTREAL

GREEK CANADIAN TRIBUNE

Street address 1: 7835 Wiseman Ave.
Street address 3: Montreal
Street address state: QC
Zip/Postal code: H3N 2N8
Country: Canada
Mailing address: 7835 Wiseman Ave.
Mailing city: Montreal
Mailing state: QC
Mailing zip: H3N 2N8
General Phone: (514) 272-6873
General Fax: (514) 272-3157
General/National Adv. E-mail: info@bhma.net
Primary Website: www.bhma.net
Advertising (Open Inch Rate) Weekday/Saturday: Open inch rate $.86
Mechanical specifications: Type page 10 x 13 3/4.
Published: Sat
Avg Paid Circ: 1000
Avg Free Circ: 13200
Audit By: Sworn/Estimate/Non-Audited
Audit Date: 7/12/2019
Personnel: Peter Manikis (Adv. Mgr.); Christos Manikis (Ed.)

HOUR

Street address 1: 355 St. Catherine W., 7th Fl.
Street address 3: Montreal
Street address state: QC
Zip/Postal code: H3B 1A5
Country: Canada
Mailing address: 355 St. Catherine W., 7th Fl.
Mailing city: Montreal
Mailing state: QC
Mailing zip: H3B 1A5
General Phone: (514) 848-0777
General Fax: (514) 848-9004
General/National Adv. E-mail: listings@hour.ca
Primary Website: www.hour.ca
Published: Thur
Avg Paid Circ: 6
Avg Free Circ: 51700
Audit By: VAC
Audit Date: 9/30/2003
Personnel: Pierre Paquet (Pub.); Hugues Mailhot (Circ. Mgr.); Jamie O'Meara (Ed. in Chief)

IL CITTADINO CANADESE

Street address 1: 5960 Jean Talon E., Ste. 209
Street address 3: Montreal
Street address state: QC
Zip/Postal code: H1S 1M2
Country: Canada
Mailing address: 5960 Jean Talon E., Ste. 209
Mailing city: Montreal
Mailing state: QC
Mailing zip: H1S 1M2
General Phone: (514) 253-2332
General Fax: (514) 253-6574
General/National Adv. E-mail: journal@cittadinocanadese.com
Primary Website: www.cittadinocanadese.com
Advertising (Open Inch Rate) Weekday/Saturday: Open inch rate $1.55
Mechanical specifications: Type page 11 1/4 x 15; E - 6 cols, 1 7/12, between; A - 6 cols, 1 7/12, between.
Published: Wed
Avg Paid Circ: 20000
Audit By: Sworn/Estimate/Non-Audited
Audit Date: 7/12/2019
Personnel: Nina Mormina (Ed.)

LA VOZ DE MONTREAL

Street address 1: 5960 Jean Talon E., Ste. 209
Street address 3: Montreal
Street address state: QC
Zip/Postal code: H1S 1M2
Country: Canada
Mailing address: 5960 Jean Talon E., Ste. 209
Mailing city: Montreal
Mailing state: QC
Mailing zip: H1S 1M2
General Phone: (514) 253-2332
General Fax: (514) 253-6574
General/National Adv. E-mail: journal@cittadinocanadese.com
Primary Website: www.cittadinocanadese.com
Advertising (Open Inch Rate) Weekday/Saturday: Open inch rate $1.47
Mechanical specifications: Type page 11 1/4 x 15; E - 6 cols, 1 7/12, between; A - 6 cols, 1 7/12, between.
Published: Mthly
Avg Paid Circ: 13000
Audit By: Sworn/Estimate/Non-Audited
Audit Date: 7/12/2019
Personnel: Vittorio Giordano (Ed.); Basilio Giordano (Prodn. Mgr.)

L'AVENIR/AL-MOUSTAKBAL

Street address 1: 1305 Rue Mazurette, Office Ste. 206
Street address 3: Montreal
Street address state: QC
Zip/Postal code: H4N 1G8
Country: Canada
Mailing address: 1305 Rue Mazurette, Office Ste. 206
Mailing city: Montreal
Mailing state: QC
Mailing zip: H4N 1G8
General Phone: (514) 334-0909
General Fax: (514) 332-5419
General/National Adv. E-mail: journal@almustakbal.com
Primary Website: www.almustakbal.com
Mechanical specifications: Type page 17 x 11; E - 7 cols, 1 5/16, between.
Published: Tues
Avg Paid Circ: 27875
Audit By: Sworn/Estimate/Non-Audited
Audit Date: 7/12/2019
Personnel: Joseph Nakhle (Pub.); Kamal Rib (Ed.); Moe Attrach (Mng. Ed.); Mary Bitar (Prodn. Mgr.)

LE JOURNAL VOIR

Street address 1: 355 St. Catherine W., 7th Fl.
Street address 3: Montreal
Street address state: QC
Zip/Postal code: H3B 1A5
Country: Canada
Mailing address: 355 St. Catherine W., 7th Fl.
Mailing city: Montreal
Mailing state: QC
Mailing zip: H3B 1A5
General Phone: (514) 848-0805
General Fax: (514) 848-9004
General/National Adv. E-mail: courier@voir.ca
Primary Website: www.voir.ca
Advertising (Open Inch Rate) Weekday/Saturday: Open inch rate $3.28
Published: Thur
Avg Free Circ: 37292
Audit By: VAC
Audit Date: 9/1/2011
Personnel: Simon Jodoin (Ed.-in-Chief)

BLACK NEWSPAPERS IN THE U.S.

ALABAMA

EUTAW

GREENE COUNTY DEMOCRAT

Street address 1: P. O. Box 82
Street address 3: Eutaw
Street address state: AL
Zip/Postal code: 35462
County: Greene
Country: United States
Mailing address: P. O. Box 82
Mailing city: Eutaw
Mailing state: AL
Mailing zip: 35462
General Phone: (334) 372-3373
General Fax: (334) 372-3373
Advertising Phone: (334) 372-3373
Advertising Fax: (334) 372-3373
Editorail Phone: (334) 372-3373
Editorial Fax: (334) 372-3373
General/National Adv. E-mail: jzippert@aol.com
Display Adv. E-mail: jzippert@aol.com
Editorial e-mail: jzippert@aol.com
Primary Website: www.greenecodemocrat.com
Year Established: 1890
Delivery Methods: Mail`Racks
Area Served - City: 35460 to 35470
Advertising (Open Inch Rate) Weekday/Saturday: Open inch rate $10.00
Mechanical specifications: Type page 13 x 29 1/2; E - 6 cols, 2 1/16, 1/8 between; A - 6 cols, 2 1/16, 1/8 between; C - 6 cols, 2 1/16, 1/8 between.
Published: Wed
Avg Paid Circ: 4000
Avg Free Circ: 300
Audit By: Sworn/Estimate/Non-Audited
Audit Date: 7/12/2019

CLASSIFIED EQUIPMENT: HUNTSVILLE

SPEAKIN' OUT WEEKLY

Street address 1: 101 Oakwood Ave NE
Street address 3: Huntsville
Street address state: AL
Zip/Postal code: 35811-1960
County: Madison
Country: USA
Mailing address: PO Box 2826
Mailing city: Huntsville
Mailing state: AL
Mailing zip: 35804-2826
General Phone: (256) 551-1020
General Fax: (256) 551-0607
General/National Adv. E-mail: WSmoth3193@aol.com
Primary Website: www.speakinoutweeklynews.com
Year Established: 1980
Delivery Methods: Mail`Newsstand
Area Served - City: 35810 35811 35816 35806 35601 35801 35758
Advertising (Open Inch Rate) Weekday/Saturday: Open inch rate $19.84 local; $34.00 National
Mechanical specifications: Type page 10.25" by 21"
Published: Wed
Avg Paid Circ: 26000
Avg Free Circ: 1000
Audit By: Sworn/Estimate/Non-Audited
Audit Date: 7/12/2019
Classified Equipment: 75
Note: Published since 1980
Personnel: Jemeana Smothers-Roberson (Assoc. Pub.); William Smothers (Ed.)

MOBILE

MOBILE BEACON AND ALABAMA CITIZEN

Street address 1: 2311 Costarides St
Street address 3: Mobile
Street address state: AL
Zip/Postal code: 36617-2442
County: Mobile
Country: USA
Mailing address: PO Box 1407
Mailing city: Mobile
Mailing state: AL
Mailing zip: 36633-1407
General Phone: (251) 479-0629
General Fax: (251) 479-0610
General/National Adv. E-mail: mobilebeaconinc@bellsouth.net
Own Printing Facility: Y
Advertising (Open Inch Rate) Weekday/Saturday: Open inch rate $18.95
Published: Wed
Avg Paid Circ: 7000
Avg Free Circ: 20
Audit By: Sworn/Estimate/Non-Audited
Audit Date: 7/12/2019
Classified Equipment: Personnel: Cleretta T. Blackmon (Ed.)

MONTGOMERY

MONTGOMERY/TUSKEGEE TIMES

Street address 1: 525 Augusta Ave
Street address 3: Montgomery
Street address state: AL
Zip/Postal code: 36111-1315
County: Montgomery
Country: USA
Mailing address: PO Box 9133
Mailing city: Montgomery
Mailing state: AL
Mailing zip: 36108-0003
General Phone: (334) 280-2444
General Fax: (334) 280-2454
General/National Adv. E-mail: adixon711@aol.com
Advertising (Open Inch Rate) Weekday/Saturday: Open inch rate $16.54
Published: Thur
Classified Equipment: 76
Personnel: Almaria Dixon Smith (Gen. Mgr.); Daryl Watkins (Circ. Mgr.); Rev. Al Dixon (Ed.); Alphonso Dixon (Mng. Ed.); Alverene Butler (Prodn. Mgr.)

CALIFORNIA

BAKERSFIELD

BAKERSFIELD NEWS OBSERVER

Street address 1: 1219 20th St
Street address 3: Bakersfield
Street address state: CA
Zip/Postal code: 93301-4611
County: Kern
Country: USA
Mailing address: PO Box 2341
Mailing city: Bakersfield
Mailing state: CA
Mailing zip: 93303
General Phone: (661) 324-9466
General Fax: (661) 324-9472
General/National Adv. E-mail: observernews@gmail.com
Display Adv. E-mail: observeradvertising@gmail.com
Editorial e-mail: jamesluckey@thenewsobserver.net
Primary Website: theobservergroup.com
Year Established: 1977
Delivery Methods: Newsstand`Carrier`Racks
Area Served - City: 93301, 93304, 93305, 93306, 93307, 93309, 93312, 93313, 93314
Advertising (Open Inch Rate) Weekday/Saturday: Open inch rate $32.00
Mechanical specifications: Type page 13 x 21; E - 6 cols, 2, 1/4 between; A - 6 cols, 2, 1/4 between; C - 10 cols, 1 1/2, 1/4 between.
Published: Wed
Avg Free Circ: 40000
Audit By: Sworn/Estimate/Non-Audited
Audit Date: 7/12/2019
Classified Equipment: Personnel: Ellen Coley (Owner); James Luckey (Editor); Jon Coley (Owner)

EAST RANCHO DOMINGUEZ

COMPTON BULLETIN

Street address 1: 800 E Compton Blvd
Street address 3: East Rancho Dominguez
Street address state: CA
Zip/Postal code: 90221-3302
County: Los Angeles
Country: USA
Mailing address: 800 E. Compton Blvd.
Mailing city: Compton
Mailing state: CA
Mailing zip: 90221
General Phone: (310) 635-6776
General Fax: (310) 635-4045
General/National Adv. E-mail: news@thecomptonbulletin.com
Display Adv. E-mail: ads@thecomptonbulletin.com
Editorial e-mail: news@thecomptonbulletin.com
Primary Website: www.thecomptonbulletin.com
Advertising (Open Inch Rate) Weekday/Saturday: Open inch rate $45.00
Published: Wed
Avg Paid Circ: 32516
Avg Free Circ: 42484
Audit By: Sworn/Estimate/Non-Audited
Audit Date: 7/12/2019
Classified Equipment: 77
Personnel: Lisa Grace-Kellogg (Pub.); Allison Eaton (Ed.)

LOS ANGELES

LA WATTS TIMES

Street address 1: 3540 Wilshire Blvd
Street address 2: PH 3
Street address 3: Los Angeles
Street address state: CA
Zip/Postal code: 90010-2357
County: Los Angeles
Country: USA
Mailing address: PO Box 83847
Mailing city: Los Angeles
Mailing state: CA
Mailing zip: 90083-0847
General Phone: (213) 251-5700
General Fax: (213) 251-5720
General/National Adv. E-mail: LAWATTSNUS@AOL.COM
Display Adv. E-mail: advertising@lawattstimes.com
Editorial e-mail: editorial@lawattstimes.com
Primary Website: www.lawattstimes.com
Advertising (Open Inch Rate) Weekday/Saturday: Open inch rate $58.24
Mechanical specifications: Type page 10 x 16; E - 5 cols, 2, 1/8 between; A - 5 cols, 2, 1/8 between; C - 5 cols, 2, 1/8 between.
Published: Thur
Avg Paid Circ: 450
Avg Free Circ: 25000
Audit By: Sworn/Estimate/Non-Audited
Audit Date: 7/12/2019
Classified Equipment: Personnel: Melanie Polk (Pub.); Vincent Martin (Bus. Mgr.); Willa Robinson (Adv. Dir.); Sam Richard (Mng. Ed.); Issac Mctyiere (Dist. Mgr.)

LOS ANGELES SENTINEL

Street address 1: 3800 S Crenshaw Blvd
Street address 3: Los Angeles
Street address state: CA
Zip/Postal code: 90008-1813
County: Los Angeles
Country: USA
Mailing address: 3800 S Crenshaw Blvd
Mailing city: Los Angeles
Mailing state: CA
Mailing zip: 90008-1813
General Phone: (323) 299-3800
General Fax: (323) 291-6804
General/National Adv. E-mail: angela@lasentinel.net
Display Adv. E-mail: pamela@lasentinel.net
Editorial e-mail: dannyjr@lasentinel.net
Primary Website: lasentinel.net
Year Established: 1998
Own Printing Facility: Y
Advertising (Open Inch Rate) Weekday/Saturday: Open inch rate $25.00
Mechanical specifications: Type page 13 x 21 1/2; E - 6 cols, 2 1/16, 1/8 between; A - 6 cols, 2 1/16, 1/8 between; C - 10 cols, between.
Published: Thur
Avg Paid Circ: 0
Avg Free Circ: 29902
Audit By: CVC
Audit Date: 9/30/2018
Classified Equipment: 78
Personnel: Danny Bakewell (Pub.); Ken Miller (Ed.); Pamela Blackwell (Adv.); Angela Howard (Circ.)
Parent company (for newspapers): Bakewell Media LLC

OUR WEEKLY

Street address 1: 8732 S Western Ave
Street address 3: Los Angeles
Street address state: CA
Zip/Postal code: 90047-3326
County: Los Angeles
Country: USA
Mailing address: 8732 S Western Ave
Mailing city: Los Angeles
Mailing state: CA
Mailing zip: 90047-3326
General Phone: (323) 905-1316
General Fax: (323) 753-5985
Editorail Phone: 323 905 1300
General/National Adv. E-mail: Info@ourweekly.com
Display Adv. E-mail: ncole@ourweekly.com
Classified Adv. E-mail: Dmiller@ourweekly.com
Editorial e-mail: Editor@ourweekly.com
Primary Website: www.ourweekly.com
Mthly Avg Views: 500000
Mthly Avg Unique Visitors: 2500
Year Established: 2004
Area Served - City: Los Angeles, Baldwin Hills, Crenshaw District, View Park, Antelope Vallwy, Inglewood, Carson
Advertising (Open Inch Rate) Weekday/Saturday: N/A
Published: Thur`Fri
Weekday Frequency: m
Avg Paid Circ: 0
Avg Free Circ: 49975
Audit By: VAC
Audit Date: 9/31/2021
Classified Equipment: Personnel: Natalie Cole (Publisher); David Miller (Adv. Mgr.); Arnold Cole (Circ. Mgr.); Brandon Norwood

WAVE COMMUNITY NEWSPAPER

Street address 1: 1730 W Olympic Blvd
Street address 2: Ste 500
Street address 3: Los Angeles
Street address state: CA
Zip/Postal code: 90015-1008
County: Los Angeles

Country: USA
Mailing address: 3731 Wilshire Blvd Ste 840
Mailing city: Los Angeles
Mailing state: CA
Mailing zip: 90010-2851
General Phone: (323) 556-5720
General Fax: (213) 835-0584
Advertising Phone: 323-556-5720 ext.245
Advertising Fax: 213-835-0584
General/National Adv. E-mail: dwanlass@wavepublication.com
Display Adv. E-mail: rbush@wavepublication.com
Primary Website: www.wavenewspapers.com
Year Established: 1912
Delivery Methods: Newsstand`Carrier`Racks
Area Served - City: Greater Los Angels
Advertising (Open Inch Rate) Weekday/Saturday: Open inch rate $150.00
Mechanical specifications: Type page 13 x 21 1/2; E - 6 cols, 2 1/16, 1/8 between; A - 6 cols, 2 1/16, 1/8 between; C - 10 cols, between.
Published: Thur
Avg Free Circ: 150000
Audit By: AAM
Audit Date: 8/1/2012
Classified Equipment: 79
Note: African American, Hispanic, Gay and General Market Papers
Personnel: Pluria Marshall (Pub.); Andre Herndon (Ed.); Don Wanlass (Mng. Ed.); Robert Bush (Sr. VP Sales &Marketing)

PASADENA

PASADENA JOURNAL-NEWS

Street address 1: 1541 N Lake Ave
Street address 2: Ste A
Street address 3: Pasadena
Street address state: CA
Zip/Postal code: 91104-2375
County: Los Angeles
Country: USA
Mailing address: 1541 N Lake Ave Ste A
Mailing city: Pasadena
Mailing state: CA
Mailing zip: 91104-2375
General Phone: (626) 798-3972
General Fax: (626) 798-3282
General/National Adv. E-mail: pasjour@pacbell.net
Primary Website: www.pasadenajournal.com
Area Served - City: 91001, 91101, 91105, 91105, 91107, 91107, 91109, 91706, 91730, 91184, 91342, 91745, 91765, 91770, 91775, 91792, 91104, 91103, 91106, 91102, 91108, 91702, 91710, 91737, 91201, 91740, 91763, 91766, 91773, 91790, 91801
Advertising (Open Inch Rate) Weekday/Saturday: Open inch rate $18.00
Mechanical specifications: Type page 10 x 15; E - 5 cols, 1 3/4, between; A - 5 cols, 1 3/4, between; C - 5 cols, 1 3/4, between.
Published: Thur
Avg Paid Circ: 7500
Audit By: Sworn/Estimate/Non-Audited
Audit Date: 7/12/2019
Classified Equipment: Personnel: Joe C. Hopkins (Co-Pub.); Ruthie Hopkins (Ed.); Harmony Coburn (Webmaster)

RIVERSIDE

BLACK VOICE NEWS

Street address 1: 4290 Brockton Ave
Street address 3: Riverside
Street address state: CA
Zip/Postal code: 92501-3447
County: Riverside
Country: USA
Mailing address: PO Box 1581
Mailing city: Riverside
Mailing state: CA
Mailing zip: 92502-1581
General Phone: (951) 682-6070
General Fax: (951) 276-0877
General/National Adv. E-mail: cherylbrown@blackvoicenews.com
Primary Website: www.blackvoicenews.com
Year Established: 1972
Advertising (Open Inch Rate) Weekday/Saturday: Open inch rate $24.50
Mechanical specifications: Type page 13 x 21; E - 6 cols, 2, 1/6 between; C - 8 cols, 1 3/4, 1/6 between.
Published: Thur
Avg Paid Circ: 10000
Avg Free Circ: 1810
Audit By: CVC
Audit Date: 6/30/2005
Classified Equipment: 80
Personnel: Cheryl R. Brown (Co-Pub.); Hardy L. Brown (Co-Pub.); Lee Ragin (Circ. Mgr.)

SACRAMENTO

OBSERVER GROUP

Street address 1: 2330 Alhambra Blvd
Street address 3: Sacramento
Street address state: CA
Zip/Postal code: 95817-1121
County: Sacramento
Country: USA
Mailing address: PO Box 209
Mailing city: Sacramento
Mailing state: CA
Mailing zip: 95812-0209
General Phone: (916) 452-4781
General Fax: (916) 452-7744
General/National Adv. E-mail: circulation@sacobserver.com
Primary Website: www.sacobserver.com
Own Printing Facility: Y
Advertising (Open Inch Rate) Weekday/Saturday: Open inch rate $47.50
Mechanical specifications: Type page 12 15/16 x 21; E - 6 cols, between; A - 6 cols, between.
Published: Fri
Avg Paid Circ: 50000
Avg Free Circ: 100
Audit By: Sworn/Estimate/Non-Audited
Audit Date: 7/12/2019
Classified Equipment: Personnel: William H. Lee (Pub.); Joe Stinson (Circ. Mgr.); Larry Lee (Prodn. Mgr.)

SAN BERNARDINO

PRECINCT REPORTER

Street address 1: 670 N Arrowhead Ave
Street address 2: Ste B
Street address 3: San Bernardino
Street address state: CA
Zip/Postal code: 92401-1102
County: San Bernardino
Country: USA
Mailing address: 670 N Arrowhead Ave Ste B
Mailing city: San Bernardino
Mailing state: CA
Mailing zip: 92401-1102
General Phone: (909) 889-0597
General Fax: (909) 889-1706
General/National Adv. E-mail: news@precinctreporter.com
Display Adv. E-mail: sales@precinctreporter.com
Primary Website: www.precinctreporter.com
Year Established: 1965
Delivery Methods: Newsstand`Carrier`Racks
Advertising (Open Inch Rate) Weekday/Saturday: Open inch rate $35.00
Mechanical specifications: 10 x 21
Published: Thur
Audit By: Sworn/Estimate/Non-Audited
Audit Date: 7/12/2019
Classified Equipment: 81
Personnel: Brian Townsend (Ed.)

SAN DIEGO

SAN DIEGO VOICE & VIEWPOINT

Street address 1: 3619 College Ave
Street address 3: San Diego
Street address state: CA
Zip/Postal code: 92115-7041
County: San Diego
Country: USA
Mailing address: P.O. Box 120095
Mailing city: San Diego
Mailing state: CA
Mailing zip: 92112
General Phone: (619) 266-2233
General Fax: (619) 266-0533
General/National Adv. E-mail: voiceandviewpoint@gmail.com
Primary Website: www.sdvoice.com
Advertising (Open Inch Rate) Weekday/Saturday: Open inch rate $26.00
Published: Thur
Avg Paid Circ: 25000
Audit By: Sworn/Estimate/Non-Audited
Audit Date: 7/12/2019
Classified Equipment: Personnel: John Warren (Ed.); Gerri Adams-Warren (Mng. Ed.)

SAN FRANCISCO

CALIFORNIA VOICE

Street address 1: 1791 Bancroft Ave
Street address 3: San Francisco
Street address state: CA
Zip/Postal code: 94124-2644
County: San Francisco
Country: USA
Mailing address: 1791 Bancroft Ave
Mailing city: San Francisco
Mailing state: CA
Mailing zip: 94124-2644
General Phone: (415) 671-1000
General Fax: (415) 671-1005
General/National Adv. E-mail: sunmedia97@aol.com
Primary Website: www.sunreporter.com
Advertising (Open Inch Rate) Weekday/Saturday: Open inch rate $23.00
Published: Sun
Avg Paid Circ: 38840
Audit By: CVC
Audit Date: 12/31/2004
Classified Equipment: 82
Personnel: Amelia Ashley-Ward (Pub.)

METRO REPORTER

Street address 1: 1791 Bancroft Ave
Street address 3: San Francisco
Street address state: CA
Zip/Postal code: 94124-2644
County: San Francisco
Country: USA
Mailing address: 1791 Bancroft Ave
Mailing city: San Francisco
Mailing state: CA
Mailing zip: 94124-2644
General Phone: (415) 671-1000
General Fax: (415) 671-1005
General/National Adv. E-mail: sundoc97@aol.com; sunmedia97@aol.com
Primary Website: www.sunreporter.com
Own Printing Facility: Y
Advertising (Open Inch Rate) Weekday/Saturday: Open inch rate $65.00
Mechanical specifications: Type page 13 x 21; E - 6 cols, 2 1/16, between; A - 6 cols, 2 1/16, between; C - 6 cols, 2 1/16, between.
Published: Tues
Avg Free Circ: 111013
Audit By: CVC
Audit Date: 12/31/2004
Classified Equipment: Personnel: Lovie Ward (Circ. Mgr.); Amelia Ashley-Ward (Ed.)

SAN FRANCISCO BAY VIEW

Street address 1: 4917 3rd St
Street address 3: San Francisco
Street address state: CA
Zip/Postal code: 94124-2309
County: San Francisco
Country: USA
Mailing address: 4917 3rd St
Mailing city: San Francisco
Mailing state: CA
Mailing zip: 94124-2309
General Phone: (415) 671-0789
General Fax: (415) 671-0789
Advertising Phone: (415) 671-0789
Editorail Phone: (415) 671-0789
General/National Adv. E-mail: editor@sfbayview.com
Display Adv. E-mail: editor@sfbayview.com
Editorial e-mail: editor@sfbayview.com
Primary Website: www.sfbayview.com
Year Established: 1976
Delivery Methods: Mail`Newsstand`Racks
Area Served - City: 94102, 94103, 94107, 94112, 94115, 94117, 94124, 94132, 94134, 94577, 94601, 94603, 94605, 94607, 94609, 94610, 94612, 94619, 94621, 94702, 94703, 94704, 94705, 94710
Own Printing Facility: N
Commercial printers: Y
Advertising (Open Inch Rate) Weekday/Saturday: Open inch rate $15.00
Mechanical specifications: Type page 12.5 x 22.5; E - 6 cols, 2", 1/6 between; A - 6 cols, 2", 1/6 between; C - 6 cols, 2", 1/6 between.
Published: Mthly
Avg Paid Circ: 700
Avg Free Circ: 20000
Audit By: Sworn/Estimate/Non-Audited
Audit Date: 7/12/2019
Classified Equipment: 83
Personnel: Willie Ratcliff (Pub.); Mary Ratcliff (Ed.)

SUN REPORTER

Street address 1: 11286 Fillmore St
Street address 3: San Francisco
Street address state: CA
Zip/Postal code: 94115
County: San Francisco
Country: USA
Mailing address: 1791 BANCROFT AVE
Mailing city: SAN FRANCISCO
Mailing state: CA
Mailing zip: 94124-2644
General Phone: (415) 671-1000
General Fax: (415) 671-1005
General/National Adv. E-mail: sunmedia97@aol.com
Primary Website: No Website
Year Established: 1949
Area Served - City: 94124
Own Printing Facility: Y
Advertising (Open Inch Rate) Weekday/Saturday: Open inch rate $63.00
Mechanical specifications: Type page 11 x 14; E - 5 cols, 2 1/16, between; A - 5 cols, 2 1/16, between; C - 5 cols, 2 1/16, between.
Published: Thur
Avg Paid Circ: 20000
Avg Free Circ: 5000
Audit By: Sworn/Estimate/Non-Audited
Audit Date: 7/12/2019
Classified Equipment: Personnel: Amelia Ashley-Ward (Ed.); Amelia Ashley Ward (Ed.); Roslyn Gillis (Mktg./Adv. Mgr.)
footnotes: Advertising (Open Inch Rate) Weekday/Saturday: SRDS (11/13/2014)

VICTORVILLE

THE SAN BERNARDINO AMERICAN NEWS

Street address 1: 14537 Anacapa Rd
Street address 2: Ste 24
Street address 3: Victorville
Street address state: CA
Zip/Postal code: 92392-2705
County: San Bernardino
Country: USA
Mailing address: PO Box 837
Mailing city: Victorville
Mailing state: CA
Mailing zip: 92393-0837
General Phone: (909) 889-7677
General Fax: (909) 889-2882
Advertising Phone: (909) 889-7677
Advertising Fax: (909) 889-2882
Editorail Phone: (909) 889-7677
Editorial Fax: (909) 889-2882
General/National Adv. E-mail: msbamericannews@gmail.com
Display Adv. E-mail: sbamericannews@gmail.com
Editorial e-mail: samerisam1@earthlink.net
Primary Website: sbnews.us
Year Established: 1969
Delivery Methods: Mail`Carrier
Area Served - City: 92405, 92410-11, 92335-6, 92346, 92324,92392-4, 92301, 92345, 92307, 92311,91730, 92570, 92552, 92521, 92392, 92395, 91737, 92572,

Advertising (Open Inch Rate) Weekday/Saturday: Open inch rate $23.90
Published: Thur
Avg Paid Circ: 10000
Audit By: Sworn/Estimate/Non-Audited
Audit Date: 7/12/2019
Classified Equipment: 84
Personnel: Mary Harris (Pub.); Clifton Harris (Co-Pub.)
Parent company (for newspapers): Don Roberto Group Inc

CONNECTICUT

NEW HAVEN

INNER-CITY NEWS

Street address 1: 50 Fitch St
Street address 2: Ste 2
Street address 3: New Haven
Street address state: CT
Zip/Postal code: 06515-1366
County: New Haven
Country: USA
Mailing address: 50 FITCH ST.
Mailing city: NEW HAVEN
Mailing state: CT
Mailing zip: 06515
General Phone: (203) 387-0354
General Fax: (203) 387-2684
Advertising Phone: 203 387-0354
Advertising Fax: (203) 387-2684
Editorail Phone: 203 387-0354
Editorial Fax: (203) 387-2684
General/National Adv. E-mail: jthomas@penfieldcomm.com
Display Adv. E-mail: jthomas@penfieldcomm.com
Classified Adv. E-mail: jthomas@penfieldcomm.com
Editorial e-mail: jthomas@penfieldcomm.com
Primary Website: jthomas@penfieldcomm.com
Year Established: 1990
Delivery Methods: Newsstand`Racks
Area Served - City: 6515 06514, 06513, 06511, 06510, 06512, 06519,
Advertising (Open Inch Rate) Weekday/Saturday: Open inch rate $55.00
Mechanical specifications: Type page 9 3/4 x 13 5/8; E - 4 cols, 2 5/6, between; A - 4 cols, 2 5/6, between; C - 8 cols, 1 5/6, between.
Published: Thur
Published Other: WEEKLY
Avg Free Circ: 25000
Audit By: Sworn/Estimate/Non-Audited
Audit Date: 7/12/2019
Classified Equipment: Personnel: John Thomas (CEO)

DISTRICT OF COLUMBIA

WASHINGTON

DISTRICT CHRONICLES

Street address 1: 525 NW Bryant St
Street address 3: Washington
Street address state: DC
Zip/Postal code: 20059-1005
County: District Of Columbia
Country: USA
Mailing address: 525 NW Bryant St
Mailing city: Washington
Mailing state: DC
Mailing zip: 20059-1005
General Phone: 202-806-9401
Advertising Phone: 202-806-9401
Editorail Phone: 202-806-9401
General/National Adv. E-mail: lkaggwa@howard.edu
Display Adv. E-mail: lkaggwa@howard.edu
Editorial e-mail: lkaggwa@howard.edu
Primary Website: www.districtchronicles.com
Year Established: 2001
Advertising (Open Inch Rate) Weekday/Saturday: $20
Mechanical specifications: 1.94"
Published: Thur
Avg Free Circ: 9975
Audit By: Sworn/Estimate/Non-Audited
Audit Date: 7/12/2019
Classified Equipment: 85
Personnel: Lawrence Kaggwa (Publisher)

WASHINGTON AFRO-AMERICAN

Street address 1: 1917 Benning Rd NE
Street address 3: Washington
Street address state: DC
Zip/Postal code: 20002-4723
County: District Of Columbia
Country: USA
Mailing address: 1917 Benning Rd NE
Mailing city: Washington
Mailing state: DC
Mailing zip: 20002-4723
General Phone: (202) 332-0080
General Fax: (877) 570-9297
General/National Adv. E-mail: editor@afro.com
Primary Website: www.afro.com
Year Established: 1892
Delivery Methods: Mail`Newsstand`Racks
Advertising (Open Inch Rate) Weekday/Saturday: Open inch rate $46.56
Mechanical specifications: Type page 13 x 21; E - 6 cols, 2, 1/8 between; A - 6 cols, 2, between; C - 9 cols, 1, 1/8 between.
Published: Fri
Avg Paid Circ: 5463
Avg Free Circ: 649
Audit By: AAM
Audit Date: 9/30/2014
Classified Equipment: Personnel: John J. Oliver (Pub.); Edgar Brookins (Circ. Mgr.); Denise Dorsey (Prodn. Mgr.)

WASHINGTON INFORMER

Street address 1: 3117 Martin Luther King Jr Ave SE
Street address 3: Washington
Street address state: DC
Zip/Postal code: 20032-1537
County: District Of Columbia
Country: USA
Mailing address: 3117 Martin Luther King Jr Ave SE
Mailing city: Washington
Mailing state: DC
Mailing zip: 20032-1537
General Phone: (202) 888-6835
Editorail Phone: (202) 561-4100
General/National Adv. E-mail: news@washingtoninformer.com
Display Adv. E-mail: rburke@washingtoninformer.com
Editorial e-mail: news@washingtoninformer.com
Primary Website: www.washingtoninformer.com
Year Established: 1964
Delivery Methods: Mail`Carrier`Racks
Area Served - City: 20001- 22314
Advertising (Open Inch Rate) Weekday/Saturday: Open inch rate $47.10
Mechanical specifications: 1 column 1.75⊠?⊠ 2 columns 3.625⊠?⊠ 3 columns 5.625⊠?⊠ 4 columns 7.562⊠?⊠ 5 columns 9.5⊠?⊠ Page Depth 12.375 Total Inches Per Page 61.875⊠?⊠
Published: Thur
Avg Paid Circ: 153
Avg Free Circ: 16341
Audit By: CVC
Audit Date: 3/30/2017
Classified Equipment: 86
Note: ABOUT THE WASHINGTON INFORMER The Washington Informer Newspaper Co. Inc. is a multi-media company founded on October 16, 1964 by Dr Calvin Rolark, and established to report on news directly impacting African Americans in the District of Columbia and surrounding suburbs of Maryland and Virginia. The editorial content focuses on positive news, that educates, informs and empowers those members of the community who have historically been disenfranchised and ignored by local mainstream media. The Washington Informer reaches over 50,000 readers each week through our award winning newspaper print edition; a weekly average of 50,000 page views through our award winning website; 7,500 weekly subscribers through our weekly email newsletter, and growing numbers through our social media platforms including Twitter, Facebook, Instagram and LinkedIn. The Washington Informer is the official sponsor of the Annual Washington Informer Spelling Bee and African American Heritage Tour. The company recently launched WI Bridge, a monthly publication for the Washington area's thriving millenneal community, and a podcast studio is currently under construction.
Personnel: Denise Rolark Barnes (Pub.); Ron Burke (Director of Advertising); Angie Johnson (Circ. Mgr.); Kevin McNeir (Editor)

WASHINGTON SUN

Street address 1: 830 Kennedy St NW
Street address 3: Washington
Street address state: DC
Zip/Postal code: 20011-2948
County: District Of Columbia
Country: USA
Mailing address: 830 Kennedy St NW Ste B2
Mailing city: Washington
Mailing state: DC
Mailing zip: 20011-2948
General Phone: (202) 882-1021
General Fax: (202) 882-9817
General/National Adv. E-mail: thewashingtonsun@aol.com
Mechanical specifications: Type page 13 x 21 1/2; E - 6 cols, 2 1/16, 1/8 between; A - 6 cols, 2 1/16, 1/8 between.
Published: Thur
Avg Paid Circ: 55000
Audit By: Sworn/Estimate/Non-Audited
Audit Date: 7/12/2019
Classified Equipment: Personnel: Stephen Cooke (Ed.); Mae Lynn (Mng. Ed.)

FLORIDA

FORT LAUDERDALE

SOUTH FLORIDA TIMES

Street address 1: 3020 NE 32nd Ave
Street address 2: Ste 200
Street address 3: Fort Lauderdale
Street address state: FL
Zip/Postal code: 33308-7233
County: Broward
Country: USA
Mailing address: 3020 Northeast 32nd Avenue #200
Mailing city: Fort Lauderdale
Mailing state: FL
Mailing zip: 33308
General Phone: (954) 356-9360
General Fax: (954) 356-9395
Display Adv. E-mail: advertising@sfltimes.com
Primary Website: www.sfltimes.com
Advertising (Open Inch Rate) Weekday/Saturday: Open inch rate $21.18
Mechanical specifications: Type page 13 x 21; E - 6 cols, 2 1/16, 1/8 between; A - 6 cols, 2 1/16, 1/8 between.
Published: Fri
Avg Paid Circ: 20000
Audit By: Sworn/Estimate/Non-Audited
Audit Date: 7/12/2019
Classified Equipment: 87
Personnel: Robert Beatty, Esq. (Pub.); Brad Bennett (Ed.)

WESTSIDE GAZETTE

Street address 1: 545 NW 7th Ter
Street address 3: Fort Lauderdale
Street address state: FL
Zip/Postal code: 33311-8140
County: Broward
Country: USA
Mailing address: PO Box 5304
Mailing city: Fort Lauderdale
Mailing state: FL
Mailing zip: 33310-5304
General Phone: (954) 525-1489
General Fax: (954) 525-1861
General/National Adv. E-mail: wgazette@bellsouth.net
Primary Website: www.thewestsidegazette.com
Advertising (Open Inch Rate) Weekday/Saturday: Open inch rate $31.91
Mechanical specifications: Type page 13 x 21 1/2; E - 6 cols, 2 1/16, 1/8 between; A - 6 cols, 2 1/16, 1/8 between.
Published: Thur
Avg Paid Circ: 30000
Audit By: Sworn/Estimate/Non-Audited
Audit Date: 7/12/2019
Classified Equipment: Personnel: Bobby Henry (Pub.); Charles Moseley (Adv. Mgr.); Elizabeth Miller (Circ. Mgr.); Pamela Lewis (Ed.)

FORT MYERS

COMMUNITY VOICE

Street address 1: 3046 Lafayette St
Street address 3: Fort Myers
Street address state: FL
Zip/Postal code: 33916-4324
County: Lee
Country: USA
Mailing address: 3046 Lafayette St
Mailing city: Fort Myers
Mailing state: FL
Mailing zip: 33916-4324
General Phone: (239) 337-4444
General Fax: (239) 334-8289
General/National Adv. E-mail: commuvoice@aol.com
Year Established: 1987
Advertising (Open Inch Rate) Weekday/Saturday: Open inch rate $15.00
Mechanical specifications: Type page 10 5/6 x 12; E - 6 cols, 1 9/16, between; A - 6 cols, 1 9/16, between.
Published: Thur
Avg Free Circ: 12000
Audit By: Sworn/Estimate/Non-Audited
Audit Date: 7/12/2019
Classified Equipment: 88
Personnel: Corey F. Weaver (Ed.)

JACKSONVILLE

FLORIDA STAR

Street address 1: PO Box 40629
Street address 3: Jacksonville
Street address state: FL
Zip/Postal code: 32203-0629
County: Duval
Country: USA
Mailing address: PO Box 40629
Mailing city: Jacksonville
Mailing state: FL
Mailing zip: 32203-0629
General Phone: (904) 766-8834
General Fax: (904) 765-1673
General/National Adv. E-mail: info@thefloridastar.com
Display Adv. E-mail: ad@thefloridastar.com
Editorial e-mail: clara@thefloridastar.com
Primary Website: www.thefloridastar.com
Year Established: 1951
Special Editions: Black History MLK Memorial Juneteenth Black Music Month Special Events related to the Black communities of Florida and Georgia At Home (Homes of FL/GA residents
Special Weekly Sections: Crime and Justice; Youth (Prep Rap)
Delivery Methods: Mail`Newsstand`Carrier`Racks
Commercial printers: Y
Advertising (Open Inch Rate) Weekday/Saturday: Open inch rate $15.00
Mechanical specifications: Type page 13 x 21 1/2; E - 6 cols, 2 1/16, 1/8 between; A - 6 cols, 2 1/16, 1/8 between; C - 6 cols, 2 1/16, 1/8 between.
Published: Sat
Avg Paid Circ: 35000
Audit By: Sworn/Estimate/Non-Audited
Audit Date: 7/12/2019
Classified Equipment: Personnel: Clara McLaughlin (Owner/Editor-in-Chief)
Parent company (for newspapers): SCC Communications-The Florida Star Newspaper, The Georgia Star Newspaper

JACKSONVILLE FREE PRESS

Street address 1: 1122 Edgewood Ave W
Street address 3: Jacksonville
Street address state: FL
Zip/Postal code: 32208-3419

County: Duval
Country: USA
Mailing address: P.O. Box 43580
Mailing city: Jacksonville
Mailing state: FL
Mailing zip: 32203
General Phone: (904) 634-1993
General Fax: (904) 765-3803
General/National Adv. E-mail: jfreepress@aol.com
Primary Website: www.jacksonvillefreepress.com
Year Established: 1986
Delivery Methods: Mail`Newsstand
Area Served - City: All throughout Duval County, Florida
Advertising (Open Inch Rate) Weekday/Saturday: Open inch rate $30.50
Mechanical specifications: Type page 13 x 21 1/2; A - 6 cols, 2 1/8, 1/8 between.
Published: Thur
Avg Paid Circ: 43500
Audit By: Sworn/Estimate/Non-Audited
Audit Date: 7/12/2019
Classified Equipment: 89
Personnel: Brenda Burwell (Adv. Mgr.); Sylvia Perry (Ed.); Lynette Jones (Editor); Reggie Fullwood (Editorial Director); Charles Griggs (Community Relations)

MIAMI

THE MIAMI TIMES

Street address 1: 900 NW 54th St
Street address 3: Miami
Street address state: FL
Zip/Postal code: 33127-1818
County: Miami-Dade
Country: USA
Mailing address: 900 NW 54th St
Mailing city: Miami
Mailing state: FL
Mailing zip: 33127-1897
General Phone: 305-694-6210
General Fax: 305-757-5770
Advertising Phone: (305) 693-7093
Advertising Fax: (305) 694-6215
Display Adv. E-mail: advertising@miamitimesonline.com
Editorial e-mail: editorial@miamitimesonline.com
Primary Website: www.miamitimesonline.com
Year Established: 1923
Delivery Methods: Mail`Newsstand
Area Served - City: 33009 33056 33010 33125 33012 33126 33013 33127 33014 33128 33015 33130 33016 33132 33018 33133 33020 33134 33021 33135 33023 33136 33024 33137 33025 33138 33026 33139 33030 33140 33031 33141 33032 33141 33033 33142 33034 33143 33050 33144 33054 33145 33055 33146 33147 33149 33150 33153 33154 33155 33156 33157 33159 33160 33161 33162 33163 33165 33166 33167 33168 33169 33170 33172 33173 33174 33175 33176 33177 33179 33180 33181 33182 33183 33184 33185 33186 33189 33193 33196 33247 33302 33309 33311 33312 33313 33314 33317
Advertising (Open Inch Rate) Weekday/Saturday: Open inch rate $56.75
Mechanical specifications: 1 Column = 1.78" 2 Columns = 3.72" 3 Columns = 5.67" 4 Columns = 7 .61" 5 Columns = 9.56" 6 Columns = 11.50" Full Page - 6 Col (w) x 21" (h)
Published: Wed
Avg Paid Circ: 15660
Audit By: Sworn/Estimate/Non-Audited
Audit Date: 7/12/2019
Classified Equipment: Personnel: Rachel J. Reeves (Pub.); Karen Franklin (Assistant To The Publisher); Garth B. Reeves (VP Business Development); Carolyn Guniss (Executive Editor); Lorraine Cammock (Operations Manager)

ORLANDO

THE ORLANDO TIMES

Street address 1: 4403 Vineland Rd Ste B5
Street address 2: Quorum Center
Street address 3: Orlando
Street address state: FL
Zip/Postal code: 32811-7362
County: Orange
Country: USA
Mailing address: 4403 Vineland Rd. Ste B5
Mailing city: Orlando
Mailing state: FL
Mailing zip: 32811
General Phone: (407) 841-3052
General Fax: (407) 849-0434
Advertising Phone: (407) 849-0434
General/National Adv. E-mail: calvincollinsjr@aol.com
Display Adv. E-mail: calvincollinsjr@aol.com
Primary Website: www.orlando-times.com
Year Established: 1976
Delivery Methods: Mail`Newsstand`Carrier`Racks
Advertising (Open Inch Rate) Weekday/Saturday: Open inch rate $19.00
Mechanical specifications: Type page 10 x 21; E - 6 cols, between; A - 6 cols, between; C - 6 cols, between.
Published: Thur
Avg Paid Circ: 7289
Avg Free Circ: 3111
Audit By: Sworn/Estimate/Non-Audited
Audit Date: 7/12/2019
Classified Equipment: 90
Personnel: Dr. Calvin Collins (Pres./Pub.); Kevin T. Collins (Adv. Mgr.); Lottie H. Collins (Prodn. Mgr.)

SAINT PETERSBURG

WEEKLY CHALLENGER

Street address 1: 2500 Martin Luther King St S
Street address 2: Ste F
Street address 3: Saint Petersburg
Street address state: FL
Zip/Postal code: 33705-3554
County: Pinellas
Country: USA
Mailing address: 2500 Dr Martin Luther King Jr St S Ste F
Mailing city: Saint Petersburg
Mailing state: FL
Mailing zip: 33705-3554
General Phone: (727) 896-2922
General Fax: (727) 823-2568
General/National Adv. E-mail: editor@theweeklychallenger.com
Primary Website: www.theweeklychallenger.com
Advertising (Open Inch Rate) Weekday/Saturday: Open inch rate $18.00
Mechanical specifications: Type page 13 3/4 x 21; E - 8 cols, 1 1/2, 1/4 between; A - 8 cols, 1 1/2, 1/4 between; C - 8 cols, 1 1/2, 1/4 between.
Published: Thur
Avg Paid Circ: 552
Avg Free Circ: 4511
Audit By: VAC
Audit Date: 3/30/2013
Classified Equipment: Personnel: Ephel Johnson (Pub.); Dianne Speithes (Adv. Mgr.); Lorraine Bellinger (Graphic Artist)

TALLAHASSEE

CAPITAL OUTLOOK

Street address 1: 1363 E Tennessee St
Street address 3: Tallahassee
Street address state: FL
Zip/Postal code: 32308-5107
County: Leon
Country: USA
Mailing address: 1363 E Tennessee St
Mailing city: Tallahassee
Mailing state: FL
Mailing zip: 32308-5107
General Phone: (850) 877-0105
Advertising Phone: (850) 877-0105
Editorail Phone: (859) 877-0105
General/National Adv. E-mail: info@capitaloutlook.com
Display Adv. E-mail: advertising@capitaloutlook.com
Classified Adv. E-mail: advertising@capitaloutlook.com
Editorial e-mail: pressreleases@capitaloutlook.com
Primary Website: www.capitaloutlook.com
Mthly Avg Views: 25000
Mthly Avg Unique Visitors: 9800
Year Established: 1975
News Services: News Service of Florida, Trice Edney News Wire, Black PRess of America
Delivery Methods: Mail`Newsstand`Racks
Area Served - City: Multiple
Advertising (Open Inch Rate) Weekday/Saturday: Open inch rate $33.00
Online Advertising Rates - CPM (cost per thousand) by Size: $10.00 - 300x250
Mechanical specifications: Full Page: 6C (10") x 20.5" Half Page: 6C (10") x 10.25" Quarter Page: Vertical: 3C (5") x 10.25" Horizontal : 6C (10") x 5.125" Eighth Page: 3C (5") x 5.125"
Published: Thur
Avg Paid Circ: 1000
Audit By: Sworn/Estimate/Non-Audited
Audit Date: 8/26/2022
Classified Equipment: 91
Personnel: Taralisha Sanders (Gen. Mgr.); St. Clair Murraine (Ed.); Rev. Dr. R.B. Holmes, Jr. (Pub.)
Parent company (for newspapers): LIVE Communications, Inc.

TAMPA

DAYTONA TIMES

Street address 1: PO Box 48857
Street address 3: Tampa
Street address state: FL
Zip/Postal code: 33646-0124
County: Hillsborough
Country: USA
Mailing address: PO Box 48857
Mailing city: Tampa
Mailing state: FL
Mailing zip: 33646-0124
General Phone: (813) 319-0961
General Fax: (813) 628-0713
General/National Adv. E-mail: sales@flcourier.com
Display Adv. E-mail: sales@flcourier.com
Primary Website: www.daytonatimes.com
Year Established: 1977
Delivery Methods: Mail`Newsstand`Racks
Area Served - City: 32116,32117, 32118, 32119, 32122, 32114, 32115, 32120, 32121, 32124, 32125, 32126, 32198
Advertising (Open Inch Rate) Weekday/Saturday: Open inch rate $33.60
Mechanical specifications: 6C x 20" 1C =1.66"
Published: Thur
Published Other: on-line daily
Avg Free Circ: 15000
Audit By: Sworn/Estimate/Non-Audited
Audit Date: 7/12/2019
Classified Equipment: Personnel: Glenn Cherry (Circ. Mgr.); Charles W. Cherry (Ed.)

FLORIDA SENTINEL-BULLETIN

Street address 1: 2207 E 21st Ave
Street address 3: Tampa
Street address state: FL
Zip/Postal code: 33605-2043
County: Hillsborough
Country: USA
Mailing address: PO Box 3363
Mailing city: Tampa
Mailing state: FL
Mailing zip: 33601-3363
General Phone: (813) 248-1921
General Fax: (813) 248-4507
General/National Adv. E-mail: hadams@flsentinel.com
Display Adv. E-mail: bdawkins@flsentinel.com
Editorial e-mail: publisher@flsentinel.com
Primary Website: flsentinel.com
Year Established: 1945
Own Printing Facility: Y
Advertising (Open Inch Rate) Weekday/Saturday: Open inch rate $14.00
Mechanical specifications: Type page 10 x 15; E - 5 cols, 2, between; A - 5 cols, 2, between; C - 5 cols, 2, between.
Published: Tues`Fri
Avg Paid Circ: 0
Avg Free Circ: 12
Audit By: CVC
Audit Date: 6/30/2018
Classified Equipment: 92
Personnel: S. Kay Andrews Wells (Pub.); Betty Dawkins (Adv. Dir.); Gwen Hayes (Ed.); Harold Adams (Circ.)

GEORGIA

ALBANY

ALBANY SOUTHWEST GEORGIAN

Street address 1: 311 S Jackson St
Street address 2: Ste A
Street address 3: Albany
Street address state: GA
Zip/Postal code: 31701-0689
County: Dougherty
Country: USA
Mailing address: PO Box 1943
Mailing city: Albany
Mailing state: GA
Mailing zip: 31702-1943
General Phone: (229) 436-2156
General Fax: (229) 435-6860
General/National Adv. E-mail: aswgeorgian@gmail.com
Year Established: 1938
Delivery Methods: Mail`Carrier`Racks
Area Served - City: 317,013,170,531,707,000,000,000,000,000,000,000,000,000,000,000,000,000,000,000
Advertising (Open Inch Rate) Weekday/Saturday: Open inch rate $17.05
Mechanical specifications: Full page: 21x10.833,Half page: 10x10.833, 1/4 page:10x5.333
Published: Wed
Audit By: Sworn/Estimate/Non-Audited
Audit Date: 7/12/2019
Classified Equipment: Personnel: G Searles (Publisher)

ATLANTA

ATLANTA DAILY WORLD

Street address 1: 3485 N Desert Dr
Street address 2: Ste 2109
Street address 3: Atlanta
Street address state: GA
Zip/Postal code: 30344-8125
County: Fulton
Country: USA
Mailing address: 100 Hartsfield Centre Pkwy Ste 500
Mailing city: Atlanta
Mailing state: GA
Mailing zip: 30344
General Phone: 404-761-1114
General Fax: 404-761-1164
Advertising Phone: 678-515-2053
General/National Adv. E-mail: publisher@atlantadailyworld.com; adwnews@atlantadailyworld.com
Display Adv. E-mail: advertising@atlantadailyworld.com
Editorial e-mail: adwnews@atlantadailyworld.com
Primary Website: www.atlantadailyworld.com
Year Established: 1928
News Services: ap, nnpa, trice-edney
Delivery Methods: Mail`Newsstand`Carrier`Racks
Commercial printers: Y
Advertising (Open Inch Rate) Weekday/Saturday: Open inch rate $53.38
Mechanical specifications: Type page 10.5 X 13; E - 6 cols, 2, 1/8 between; A - 6 cols, 2, 1/8 between; C - 8 cols, 1 1/2, 1/16 between.
Published: Thur
Published Other: daily online
Avg Paid Circ: 0
Avg Free Circ: 3836
Audit By: VAC
Audit Date: 3/31/2016
Classified Equipment: 93
Personnel: Alexis Scott (Pub.); Michelle Gipson (Adv. Dir.); Maria Odum-Hinmon (Mng. Ed.); Wendell Scott (Prodn. Mgr.)
Parent company (for newspapers): Real Times Media, Inc.

THE ATLANTA INQUIRER

Street address 1: 947 Martin Luther King Jr Dr NW
Street address 3: Atlanta
Street address state: GA
Zip/Postal code: 30314-2947

County: Fulton
Country: USA
Mailing address: 947 Martin Luther KingJr. Dr. NW
Mailing city: Atlanta
Mailing state: GA
Mailing zip: 30314-0367
General Phone: (404) 523-6086
General Fax: (404) 523-6088
General/National Adv. E-mail: news@atlinq.com
Display Adv. E-mail: ads@atlinq.com
Editorial e-mail: news@atlinq.com
Primary Website: www.atlinq.com
Year Established: 1960
Area Served - City: 30001, 30181, 30265, 30333, 30453, 31208
Advertising (Open Inch Rate) Weekday/Saturday: Open inch rate $30.80
Mechanical specifications: Type page 11 1/2 x 21 1/2; E - 6 cols, 2 1/16, between; A - 6 cols, 2 1/16, between; C - 6 cols, 2 1/16, between.
Published: Thur
Avg Paid Circ: 0
Avg Free Circ: 0
Audit By: Sworn/Estimate/Non-Audited
Audit Date: 7/12/2019
Classified Equipment: Personnel: Sallie Pope Howard (Adv. Mgr.); Herbert Linsey (Circ. Mgr.); John B. Smith (Ed.); Kimberly Bryant (Prodn. Mgr.)

THE ATLANTA VOICE

Street address 1: 633 Pryor St SW
Street address 3: Atlanta
Street address state: GA
Zip/Postal code: 30312-2738
County: Fulton
Country: USA
Mailing address: 633 Pryor St SW
Mailing city: Atlanta
Mailing state: GA
Mailing zip: 30312-2789
General Phone: (404) 524-6426
General Fax: (404) 523-7853
Advertising Phone: (404) 524-6426 x 15
Editorail Phone: (404) 524-6426 x 13
General/National Adv. E-mail: info@theatlantavoice.com
Display Adv. E-mail: ads@theatlantavoice.com
Primary Website: www.theatlantavoice.com
Year Established: 1966
Delivery Methods: Mail`Newsstand`Racks
Own Printing Facility: Y
Advertising (Open Inch Rate) Weekday/Saturday: Open inch rate $65.17
Mechanical specifications: Type page 10 x 13 1/2; A - 6 cols, 1 1/2, 1/4 between; C - 6 cols, 1 1/2, 1/4 between.
Published: Fri
Published Other: Electronic Edition
Avg Free Circ: 17440
Audit By: AAM
Audit Date: 6/30/2018
Classified Equipment: 94
Personnel: Janis L. Ware (Pub.); James A. Washington (Editor); April Ivey (Sales Asst.); Stan Washington (Ed. in Chief.); April Armstrong (Adv./Circ. Mgr.)
Parent company (for newspapers): Voice News Network

AUGUSTA

THE METRO COURIER

Street address 1: 314 Walton Way
Street address 3: Augusta
Street address state: GA
Zip/Postal code: 30901-2436
County: Richmond
Country: USA
Mailing address: PO Box 2385
Mailing city: Augusta
Mailing state: GA
Mailing zip: 30903-2385
General Phone: (706) 724-6556
General Fax: (706) 722-7104
General/National Adv. E-mail: metrocourier@comcast.net
Advertising (Open Inch Rate) Weekday/Saturday: Open inch rate $16.50
Mechanical specifications: Type page 13 x 21; E - 6 cols, 2, 1/5 between; A - 6 cols, 2, 1/5 between; C - 6 cols, 2, 1/5 between.
Published: Thur
Avg Paid Circ: 29010
Audit By: Sworn/Estimate/Non-Audited
Audit Date: 7/12/2019
Classified Equipment: Personnel: Barbara A. Gordon (Ed.)

COLUMBUS

THE COLUMBUS TIMES

Street address 1: 2230 Buena Vista Rd
Street address 3: Columbus
Street address state: GA
Zip/Postal code: 31906-3111
County: Muscogee
Country: USA
Mailing address: 2230 Buena Vista Rd
Mailing city: Columbus
Mailing state: GA
Mailing zip: 31906-3111
General Phone: (706) 324-2404
General Fax: (706) 596-0657
General/National Adv. E-mail: columbustimes@knology.net
Primary Website: www.columbustimes.com
Advertising (Open Inch Rate) Weekday/Saturday: Open inch rate $15.00
Mechanical specifications: Type page 13 x 21 1/2; E - 6 cols, 2 1/16, between; A - 6 cols, 2 1/16, between; C - 6 cols, 2 1/16, between.
Published: Wed
Avg Paid Circ: 10000
Audit By: Sworn/Estimate/Non-Audited
Audit Date: 7/12/2019
Classified Equipment: 95
Personnel: Ophelia Devore-Mitchell (Pub.); Helmut Gertjegerdes (Mng. Ed.); Carol Gertjegerdes (News Ed.)

DECATUR

THE CHAMPION

Street address 1: 114 New St
Street address 2: Ste E
Street address 3: Decatur
Street address state: GA
Zip/Postal code: 30030-5356
County: Dekalb
Country: USA
Mailing address: PO Box 1347
Mailing city: Decatur
Mailing state: GA
Mailing zip: 30031-1347
General Phone: (404) 373-7779
General Fax: (404) 373-7721
General/National Adv. E-mail: JohnH@dekalbchamp.com
Display Adv. E-mail: JohnH@dekalbchamp.com
Editorial e-mail: Kathy@dekalbchamp.com
Primary Website: championnewspaper.com
Delivery Methods: Mail`Newsstand`Racks
Advertising (Open Inch Rate) Weekday/Saturday: Open inch rate $30.20
Mechanical specifications: Type page 10 1/4 x 14 1/4; E - 5 cols, 2, 3/16 between; A - 5 cols, 2, 3/16 between; C - 7 cols, 1 5/16, 3/16 between.
Published: Thur
Avg Paid Circ: 443
Avg Free Circ: 97
Audit By: CVC
Audit Date: 9/30/2018
Classified Equipment: Personnel: Carolyn Glenn (Pub.); John Hewitt (COO/Gen. Mgr.); Kathy Mitchell (Ed.); Gale Horton Gay (Mng. Ed.); Kemesha Hunt (Prodn. Mgr.); Travis Hutchins (Classic/Web Designer)

SAVANNAH

SAVANNAH HERALD

Street address 1: 2135 Rowland Ave
Street address 2: Ste B
Street address 3: Savannah
Street address state: GA
Zip/Postal code: 31404-4453
County: Chatham
Country: USA
Mailing address: PO Box 486
Mailing city: Savannah
Mailing state: GA
Mailing zip: 31402-0486
General Phone: (912) 356-0025
General Fax: (912) 356-0028
General/National Adv. E-mail: news@savannahherald.net
Display Adv. E-mail: sales@savannahherald.net
Editorial e-mail: news@savannahherald.net
Primary Website: www.savannahherald.net
Delivery Methods: Newsstand`Racks
Advertising (Open Inch Rate) Weekday/Saturday: Open inch rate $12.00
Mechanical specifications: Type page 10.5 x 20; E - 6 cols, between; A - 6 cols, between; C - 6 cols, between.
Published: Wed
Published Other: Weekly
Avg Free Circ: 12500
Audit By: Sworn/Estimate/Non-Audited
Audit Date: 7/12/2019
Classified Equipment: 96
Personnel: Kenneth Adams (Publisher); Khristi Chisholm (Co-Publisher)

THE SAVANNAH TRIBUNE

Street address 1: PO Box 2066
Street address 3: Savannah
Street address state: GA
Zip/Postal code: 31402-2066
County: Chatham
Country: USA
Mailing address: PO Box 2066
Mailing city: Savannah
Mailing state: GA
Mailing zip: 31402-2066
General Phone: (912) 233-6128
General Fax: (912) 233-6140
General/National Adv. E-mail: newsroom@savannahtribune.com
Display Adv. E-mail: tanyam@savannahtribune.com
Primary Website: www.savannahtribune.com
Year Established: 1875
Delivery Methods: Carrier`Racks
Area Served - City: 31401, 31404, 31405, 31406, 31419, 31411, 31410, 31314, 31409, 31415, 31408, 31407
Advertising (Open Inch Rate) Weekday/Saturday: Open inch rate $14.00
Mechanical specifications: Type page 11 5/8 x 21 1/2; E - 6 cols, 1 5/6, 1/8 between; A - 6 cols, 1 5/6, 1/8 between; C - 6 cols, 1 5/6, 1/8 between.
Published: Wed
Avg Free Circ: 15000
Audit By: Sworn/Estimate/Non-Audited
Audit Date: 7/12/2019
Classified Equipment: Personnel: Tanya Milton (Adv. Mgr.); Shirley James (Ed.); Tirany Reeves (Graphic Designer)

UNION CITY

ATLANTA-NEWS LEADER

Street address 1: 4405 Mall Blvd
Street address 2: Ste 521
Street address 3: Union City
Street address state: GA
Zip/Postal code: 30291-2083
County: Fulton
Country: USA
Mailing address: 4405 Mall Blvd Ste 521
Mailing city: Union City
Mailing state: GA
Mailing zip: 30291-2083
General Phone: (770) 969-7711
General Fax: (770) 969-7811
General/National Adv. E-mail: atlmet@bellsouth.net
Advertising (Open Inch Rate) Weekday/Saturday: Open inch rate $11.29
Mechanical specifications: Type page 13 x 21 1/2; E - 6 cols, 2 1/4, between; A - 6 cols, 2 1/4, between; C - 6 cols, 2 1/4, 1/8 between.
Published: Fri
Avg Paid Circ: 5000
Avg Free Circ: 30000
Audit By: Sworn/Estimate/Non-Audited
Audit Date: 7/12/2019
Classified Equipment: 97
Personnel: Esther Edans (Gen. Mgr.); Creed W. Pannell (Adv. Mgr.); Nicole Robinson (Ed.); Carla Harper (Assoc. Ed.)

THE ATLANTA METRO

Street address 1: 4405 Mall Blvd
Street address 2: Ste 521
Street address 3: Union City
Street address state: GA
Zip/Postal code: 30291-2083
County: Fulton
Country: USA
Mailing address: 4405 Mall Blvd Ste 521
Mailing city: Union City
Mailing state: GA
Mailing zip: 30291-2083
General Phone: (770) 969-7711
General Fax: (770) 969-7811
General/National Adv. E-mail: atlmet@bellsouth.net
Mechanical specifications: Type page 10 3/20 x 14 1/4; E - 4 cols, 2 1/8, 3/16 between; C - 4 cols, 2 1/8, 3/16 between.
Published: Fri
Avg Paid Circ: 5000
Avg Free Circ: 30000
Audit By: Sworn/Estimate/Non-Audited
Audit Date: 7/12/2019
Classified Equipment: Personnel: Willie Robinson (Circ. Mgr.); Creed W. Pannell (Ed.); Carla Harper (Assoc. Ed.)

ILLINOIS

CHICAGO

CHICAGO CRUSADER

Street address 1: 6429 S Martin Luther King Dr
Street address 3: Chicago
Street address state: IL
Zip/Postal code: 60637
County: Cook
Country: USA
Mailing address: 6429 S. Martin Luther King Dr.
Mailing city: Chicago
Mailing state: IL
Mailing zip: 60637
General Phone: (773) 752-2500
General Fax: (773) 752-2817
Advertising Phone: (773) 752-2500
Advertising Fax: (773) 752-2817
Editorail Phone: (773) 752-2500
Editorial Fax: (773) 752-2817
General/National Adv. E-mail: crusaderil@aol.com
Display Adv. E-mail: achicagocrusader@aol.com
Editorial e-mail: crusaderil@aol.com
Primary Website: www.chicagocrusader.com
Year Established: 1940
Delivery Methods: Mail`Newsstand
Area Served - City: Call (773) 752-2500 for complete list
Advertising (Open Inch Rate) Weekday/Saturday: Open inch rate $68.12
Mechanical specifications: Call (773) 752-2500
Published: Thur
Avg Paid Circ: 90661
Audit By: Sworn/Estimate/Non-Audited
Audit Date: 7/12/2019
Classified Equipment: 98
Personnel: John L. Smith (Adv. Dir.); Dorothy R. Leavell (Ed.); Erick Johnson (Ed.)

CHICAGO DEFENDER

Street address 1: 4445 S Dr Martin Luther King Dr
Street address 3: Chicago
Street address state: IL
Zip/Postal code: 60653
County: Cook
Country: USA
Mailing address: 4445 S. Dr. Martin Luther King Dr.
Mailing city: Chicago
Mailing state: IL
Mailing zip: 60653

General Phone: (312) 225-2400
General Fax: (312) 225-5659
Advertising Phone: (312) 225-2400
Advertising Fax: (312) 225-9231
Editorail Phone: (312) 225-2400
Editorial Fax: (312) 225-9231
Editorial e-mail: editorial@chicagodefender.com
Primary Website: www.chicagodefender.com
Year Established: 1905
News Services: NNPA, AP.
Special Editions: Easter Special (Apr); Back-to-School (Aug); Shopping Guide (Christmas-Kwanzaa) (Dec); African-American History Month (Feb); Dr. Martin Luther King, Jr. (Jan); Health & Fitness (Jun); Career Week (Mar); Healthcare & Wellness (Nov); Financial (Sept).
Delivery Methods: Mail`Newsstand`Racks
Commercial printers: Y
Advertising (Open Inch Rate) Weekday/Saturday: Open inch rate $97.59
Mechanical available: Offset; Black and 3 ROP colors.
Mechanical specifications: Type page 10 13/16 x 13; E - 5 cols, 2 1/16, 1/8 between; A - 5 cols, 2 1/16, 1/8 between; C - 5 cols, 2 1/16, 1/8 between.
Published: Wed
Weekday Frequency: m
Avg Paid Circ: 3178
Avg Free Circ: 7907
Audit By: VAC
Audit Date: 5/31/2017
Classified Equipment: Personnel: Michael A. House (Pres./COO); Shari Noland (Exec. Ed.); Leanne Muller-Wharton (Adv. Sr. Acct. Exec.); Kathy Chaney (Managing Editor); Carol Bell (CFO, Dir. of Fin & Bus Op)
Parent company (for newspapers): Real Times Media, Inc.

HYDE PARK CITIZEN

Street address 1: 806 E 78th St
Street address 3: Chicago
Street address state: IL
Zip/Postal code: 60619-2937
County: Cook
Country: USA
Mailing address: 806 E 78th St
Mailing city: Chicago
Mailing state: IL
Mailing zip: 60619-2937
General Phone: (773) 783-1251
General Fax: (773) 783-1301
Advertising (Open Inch Rate) Weekday/Saturday: Open inch rate $106.76
Published: Wed
Avg Free Circ: 20418
Audit By: CVC
Audit Date: 3/31/2005
Classified Equipment: 99
Personnel: William Garth (Pub.); Janice Garth (Adv. Mgr.)

N'DIGO

Street address 1: 1006 S Michigan Ave
Street address 2: Ste 200
Street address 3: Chicago
Street address state: IL
Zip/Postal code: 60605-2209
County: Cook
Country: USA
Mailing address: 1006 S Michigan Ave Ste 200
Mailing city: Chicago
Mailing state: IL
Mailing zip: 60605-2209
General Phone: (312) 822-0202
General Fax: 312 431 8893
Advertising Phone: 312 264 6272
Advertising Fax: 312 431 8893
General/National Adv. E-mail: admin@ndigo.com
Display Adv. E-mail: hhartman@ndigo.com
Editorial e-mail: dsmallwood@ndigo.com
Primary Website: www.ndigo.com
Year Established: 1989
Delivery Methods: Racks
Area Served - City: 60610, 60611, 60612, 60613, 60614, 60615, 60616, 60617, 60618, 60619, 60620, 60621, 60622, 60623, 60624, 60625, 60626, 60627, 60628, 60629, 60631, 60632, 60634, 60636, 60637, 60639, 60640, 60642, 60643, 60644, 60645, 60647, 60648, 60651, 60652, 60653, 606
Advertising (Open Inch Rate) Weekday/Saturday: Open inch rate $89.44
Mechanical specifications: Type page 10 1/8 x 12 1/2; E - 5 cols, 2 1/4, between; A - 4 cols, 2 1/2, between; C - 5 cols, 2, between.
Published: Thur
Avg Free Circ: 130000
Audit By: Sworn/Estimate/Non-Audited
Audit Date: 7/12/2019
Classified Equipment: Personnel: Hermene D. Hartman (Pub.); David Smallwood (Editor); Sylvester Cosby (Administrator); Walter Aikens (Business Development)

SOUTH SUBURBAN CITIZEN

Street address 1: 806 E 78th St
Street address 3: Chicago
Street address state: IL
Zip/Postal code: 60619-2937
County: Cook
Country: USA
Mailing address: 806 E 78th St
Mailing city: Chicago
Mailing state: IL
Mailing zip: 60619-2937
General Phone: (773) 783-1251
General Fax: (773) 783-1301
General/National Adv. E-mail: citizen_newsroom@yahoo.com
Primary Website: www.thechicagocitizen.com
Advertising (Open Inch Rate) Weekday/Saturday: Open inch rate $106.76
Published: Wed
Avg Free Circ: 20355
Audit By: CVC
Audit Date: 3/31/2005
Classified Equipment: 100
Personnel: William Garth (Pub.); Janice Garth (Adv. Mgr)

SOUTHEND CITIZEN

Street address 1: 806 E 78th St
Street address 3: Chicago
Street address state: IL
Zip/Postal code: 60619-2937
County: Cook
Country: USA
Mailing address: 806 E 78th St
Mailing city: Chicago
Mailing state: IL
Mailing zip: 60619-2937
General Phone: (773) 783-1251
General Fax: (773) 783-1301
Primary Website: www.thechicagocitizen.com
Advertising (Open Inch Rate) Weekday/Saturday: Open inch rate $129.17
Published: Wed
Avg Free Circ: 30130
Audit By: CVC
Audit Date: 3/31/2005
Classified Equipment: Personnel: William Garth (Pub.); Janice Garth (Adv. Mgr.)

EAST SAINT LOUIS

EAST ST. LOUIS MONITOR

Street address 1: 1501 State St
Street address 3: East Saint Louis
Street address state: IL
Zip/Postal code: 62205-2011
County: Saint Clair
Country: USA
Mailing address: PO Box 2137
Mailing city: East Saint Louis
Mailing state: IL
Mailing zip: 62202-2137
General Phone: (618) 271-0468
General Fax: (618) 271-8443
Advertising (Open Inch Rate) Weekday/Saturday: Open inch rate $14.60
Mechanical specifications: Type page 12 x 21 1/2; E - 6 cols, 2, between.
Published: Thur
Avg Paid Circ: 8800
Audit By: Sworn/Estimate/Non-Audited
Audit Date: 7/12/2019
Classified Equipment: 101
Personnel: George Laktzian (Adv. Mgr.); Ahmad Saae (Circ. Mgr.); Anne Jordan (Ed.); Frazier Garner (Prodn. Mgr.)

INDIANA

FORT WAYNE

FROST ILLUSTRATED

Street address 1: 3121 S Calhoun St
Street address 3: Fort Wayne
Street address state: IN
Zip/Postal code: 46807-1901
County: Allen
Country: USA
Mailing address: 3121 S Calhoun St
Mailing city: Fort Wayne
Mailing state: IN
Mailing zip: 46807-1901
General Phone: (260) 745-0552
General/National Adv. E-mail: news@frostillustrated.com
Display Adv. E-mail: fwfrostads@gmail.com
Editorial e-mail: fwfrostnews@gmail.com
Primary Website: www.frostillustrated.com
Year Established: 1968
Delivery Methods: Mail`Newsstand`Racks
Area Served - City: 46801, 46802, 46803, 46804, 45805, 46806, 46807, 46808, 46809, 46815, 46816, 46818, 46819, 46825, 46835
Advertising (Open Inch Rate) Weekday/Saturday: Open inch rate $19.00
Mechanical specifications: Type page 10 2/5 x 16; E - 5 cols, between; A - 5 cols, between; C - 8 cols, between.
Published: Wed
Avg Paid Circ: 1380
Avg Free Circ: 39
Audit By: CVC
Audit Date: 6/30/2015
Classified Equipment: Personnel: Edward N. Smith (Pub.); Michael Patterson (Managing Ed.); Andy Kurzen (Layout & Production Manager)

GARY

GARY CRUSADER

Street address 1: 1549 Broadway
Street address 3: Gary
Street address state: IN
Zip/Postal code: 46407-2240
County: Lake
Country: USA
Mailing address: 1549 Broadway
Mailing city: Gary
Mailing state: IN
Mailing zip: 46407-2240
General Phone: (219) 885-4357
General Fax: (219) 883-3317
General/National Adv. E-mail: crusaderil@aol.com
Primary Website: www.crusaderil.com
Advertising (Open Inch Rate) Weekday/Saturday: Open inch rate $32.53
Mechanical specifications: Type page 10 x 14; E - 5 cols, between; A - 5 cols, between; C - 6 cols, between.
Published: Thur
Avg Paid Circ: 44000
Audit By: Sworn/Estimate/Non-Audited
Audit Date: 7/12/2019
Classified Equipment: 102
Personnel: Dorothy R. Leavell (Ed.); David Denson (Mng. Ed.); John Smith (Prodn. Mgr.)

INDIANAPOLIS

INDIANAPOLIS RECORDER

Street address 1: 2901 N Tacoma Ave
Street address 3: Indianapolis
Street address state: IN
Zip/Postal code: 46218-2737
County: Marion
Country: USA
Mailing address: 2901 N Tacoma Ave
Mailing city: Indianapolis
Mailing state: IN
Mailing zip: 46218-2700
General Phone: (317) 924-5143
General Fax: (317) 924-5148
General/National Adv. E-mail: newsroom@indyrecorder.com
Primary Website: www.indianapolisrecorder.com
Commercial printers: Y
Advertising (Open Inch Rate) Weekday/Saturday: Open inch rate $33.00
Mechanical specifications: Type page 13 x 21; E - 6 cols, between; A - 6 cols, between; C - 9 cols, between.
Published: Fri
Avg Paid Circ: 6358
Avg Free Circ: 5257
Audit By: CVC
Audit Date: 12/31/2004
Classified Equipment: Personnel: William G. Mays (Owner/Chrmn.); Carolene Mays (Pub.); Angie Kuhn (Circ. Mgr.); Shannon Williams (Ed.); Jeana Lewis (Prodn. Mgr.)

KANSAS

LOUISVILLE

THE LOUISVILLE DEFENDER

Street address 1: 1720 Dixie Hwy
Street address 3: Louisville
Street address state: KY
Zip/Postal code: 40210-2314
County: Jefferson
Country: USA
Mailing address: PO Box 2557
Mailing city: Louisville
Mailing state: KY
Mailing zip: 40201-2557
General Phone: (502) 772-2591
General Fax: (502) 775-8655
General/National Adv. E-mail: loudefender@aol.com
Advertising (Open Inch Rate) Weekday/Saturday: Open inch rate $14.60
Mechanical specifications: Type page 13 x 21 1/2; E - 6 cols, between; A - 6 cols, between; C - 8 cols, between.
Published: Thur
Avg Paid Circ: 2615
Avg Free Circ: 73
Audit By: Sworn/Estimate/Non-Audited
Audit Date: 7/12/2019
Classified Equipment: 103
Personnel: Clarence Leslie (Adv. Mgr.); Marie Brown (Circ. Mgr.); Yvonne Coleman (Ed.)

WICHITA

THE COMMUNITY VOICE

Street address 1: 2918 E Douglas Ave
Street address 3: Wichita
Street address state: KS
Zip/Postal code: 67214-4709
County: Sedgwick
Country: USA
Mailing address: PO Box 20804
Mailing city: Wichita
Mailing state: KS
Mailing zip: 67208-6804
General Phone: (316) 681-1155
General/National Adv. E-mail: press@tcvpub.com
Display Adv. E-mail: adcopy@tcvpub.com
Editorial e-mail: press@tcvpub.com
Primary Website: tcvpub.com
Year Established: 1993
Delivery Methods: Mail`Newsstand
Area Served - City: 67214, 67219, 67220, 67226, 67203, 67208, 67206 major service area
Mechanical specifications: Tabloid. 9.90"W X 10.25"H
Published: Thur
Published Other: Every other Thurs
Avg Free Circ: 10892
Audit By: CVC
Audit Date: 3/30/2016
Classified Equipment: Personnel: Bonita Gooch (Editor-in-Chief)

LOUISIANA

ALEXANDRIA

ALEXANDRIA NEWS WEEKLY

Street address 1: 1746 Mason St
Street address 3: Alexandria
Street address state: LA
Zip/Postal code: 71301-6242
County: Rapides
Country: USA
Mailing address: 1746 Mason St
Mailing city: Alexandria
Mailing state: LA
Mailing zip: 71301-6242
General Phone: (318) 443-7664
Advertising Fax: (318) 487-1827
General/National Adv. E-mail: anwnews@bellsouth.net
Advertising (Open Inch Rate) Weekday/Saturday: Open inch rate $15.00
Mechanical specifications: Type page 14 x 21; E - 6 cols, between; A - 6 cols, between; C - 9 cols, between.
Published: Thur
Avg Paid Circ: 10000
Audit By: Sworn/Estimate/Non-Audited
Audit Date: 7/12/2019
Classified Equipment: 104
Personnel: Leon Coleman (Adv. Mgr.); Alice Coleman (Ed.)

MONROE

MONROE FREE PRESS

Street address 1: 216 Collier St
Street address 3: Monroe
Street address state: LA
Zip/Postal code: 71201-7202
County: Ouachita
Country: USA
Mailing address: PO Box 4717
Mailing city: Monroe
Mailing state: LA
Mailing zip: 71211-4717
General Phone: (318) 388-1310
General Fax: (318) 388-2911
General/National Adv. E-mail: rooseveltwright@prodigy.net
Primary Website: www.monroefreepress.com
Advertising (Open Inch Rate) Weekday/Saturday: Open inch rate $10.00
Mechanical specifications: Type page 13 x 21; E - 6 cols, 2 1/16, 1/8 between; A - 6 cols, 2 1/16, 1/8 between; C - 6 cols, 2 1/16, 1/8 between.
Published: Thur
Avg Paid Circ: 15000
Audit By: Sworn/Estimate/Non-Audited
Audit Date: 7/12/2019
Classified Equipment: Personnel: Roosevelt Wright (Ed.)

NEW ORLEANS

LOUISIANA WEEKLY

Street address 1: 2215 Pelopidas St
Street address 3: New Orleans
Street address state: LA
Zip/Postal code: 70122-4957
County: Orleans
Country: USA
Mailing address: PO Box 8628
Mailing city: New Orleans
Mailing state: LA
Mailing zip: 70182-8628
General Phone: (504) 282-3705
General Fax: (504) 282-3773
General/National Adv. E-mail: info@louisianaweekly.com
Primary Website: www.louisianaweekly.com
Advertising (Open Inch Rate) Weekday/Saturday: Open inch rate $19.41
Mechanical specifications: Type page 13 x 21 1/2; E - 6 cols, 2 1/8, between; A - 6 cols, 2 1/8, between; C - 8 cols, 1 1/2, between.
Published: Mon
Avg Paid Circ: 8300
Avg Free Circ: 1700
Audit By: Sworn/Estimate/Non-Audited
Audit Date: 7/12/2019
Classified Equipment: 105
Personnel: Chris Hall (Mktg. Mgr.); Jim Hall (Circ. Mgr.); Renette Dejoie-Hall (Exec. Ed.); Edmund W. Lewis (Ed.); David T. Baker (Webmaster)

NEW ORLEANS DATA NEWS WEEKLY

Street address 1: 3501 Napoleon Ave
Street address 3: New Orleans
Street address state: LA
Zip/Postal code: 70125-4843
County: Orleans
Country: USA
Mailing address: 3501 Napoleon Ave
Mailing city: New Orleans
Mailing state: LA
Mailing zip: 70125-4843
General Phone: (504) 821-7421
General Fax: (504) 821-7622
General/National Adv. E-mail: datanewsad@bellsouth.net
Editorial e-mail: datanewsad@bellsouth.net
Primary Website: www.ladatanews.com
Year Established: 1967
Delivery Methods: Racks
Advertising (Open Inch Rate) Weekday/Saturday: Open inch rate $74.12
Mechanical specifications: Type page 10 3/4 x 14; E - 5 cols, between; A - 5 cols, between.
Published: Sat
Avg Paid Circ: 0
Avg Free Circ: 19965
Audit By: CVC
Audit Date: 3/31/2018
Classified Equipment: Personnel: Terry B. Jones (Pub.); Terrence Lee (Circ.)
Parent company (for newspapers): New Orleans Data News Weekly
Newspaper (for newspapers group): New Orleans Data News Weekly, New Orleans

SHREVEPORT

SHREVEPORT SUN

Street address 1: 2224 Jewella Ave
Street address 3: Shreveport
Street address state: LA
Zip/Postal code: 71109-2410
County: Caddo
Country: USA
Mailing address: PO Box 3915
Mailing city: Shreveport
Mailing state: LA
Mailing zip: 71133-3915
General Phone: (318) 631-6222
General Fax: (318) 635-2822
General/National Adv. E-mail: sunweekly@aol.com
Display Adv. E-mail: sunweeklyads@aol.com
Editorial e-mail: sunweekly@aol.com
Primary Website: www.sunweeklynews.com
Year Established: 1920
Delivery Methods: Mail`Newsstand`Racks
Advertising (Open Inch Rate) Weekday/Saturday: Open inch rate $11.76
Mechanical specifications: Type page 13 x 21 1/2; E - 6 cols, 2 1/16, 1/8 between; A - 6 cols, 2 1/16, 1/8 between; C - 10 cols, between.
Published: Thur
Avg Paid Circ: 5000
Audit By: Sworn/Estimate/Non-Audited
Audit Date: 7/12/2019
Classified Equipment: 106
Personnel: Sonya C. Landry (Ed.); Larry Rogers (Advt Mgr); Brenda Demming (Circulation Mgr); Ronald Collins (Reporter)

MARYLAND

BALTIMORE

EVERY WEDNESDAY

Street address 1: 2519 N Charles St
Street address 3: Baltimore
Street address state: MD
Zip/Postal code: 21218-4602
County: Baltimore City
Country: USA
Mailing address: 2519 N Charles St
Mailing city: Baltimore
Mailing state: MD
Mailing zip: 21218-4602
General Phone: (410) 554-8200
General Fax: (410) 554-8150
Primary Website: www.afro.com
Advertising (Open Inch Rate) Weekday/Saturday: Open inch rate $25.00
Published: Wed
Classified Equipment: Personnel: John J. Oliver (Pub.); Susan Warshaw (Adv. Mgr.); Dorothy Boulware (Ed.)

PRINCE GEORGE'S COUNTY TIMES

Street address 1: 2513 N Charles St
Street address 3: Baltimore
Street address state: MD
Zip/Postal code: 21218-4602
County: Baltimore City
Country: USA
Mailing address: 2513 N Charles St
Mailing city: Baltimore
Mailing state: MD
Mailing zip: 21218-4602
General Phone: (410) 366-3900
General Fax: (410) 243-1627
General/National Adv. E-mail: btimes@btimes.com
Primary Website: www.btimes.com
Advertising (Open Inch Rate) Weekday/Saturday: Open inch rate $20.04
Published: Fri
Classified Equipment: 107
Personnel: Donnie Manuel (Adv. Sales Mgr.); Joy Bramble (Mng. Ed.); Freddie Howard (Prodn. Mgr.)

THE AFRO AMERICAN NEWSPAPER-BALTIMORE

Street address 1: 2519 N Charles St
Street address 3: Baltimore
Street address state: MD
Zip/Postal code: 21218-4602
County: Baltimore City
Country: USA
Mailing address: 2519 N Charles St
Mailing city: Baltimore
Mailing state: MD
Mailing zip: 21218-4602
General Phone: (410) 554-8200
General Fax: (877) 570-9297
General/National Adv. E-mail: adafro@afro.com
Primary Website: www.afro.com
Advertising (Open Inch Rate) Weekday/Saturday: Open inch rate $40.49
Mechanical specifications: Type page 13 x 21; E - 6 cols, 2, 1/8 between; A - 6 cols, 2, 1/8 between; C - 9 cols, 1 1/2, between.
Published: Sat
Avg Paid Circ: 5234
Avg Free Circ: 261
Audit By: AAM
Audit Date: 9/30/2014
Classified Equipment: Personnel: John J. Oliver (Pub.); Susan Warshaw (Adv. Mgr.); Sammy Graham (Circ. Mgr.); Tiffaney Ginyard (Mng. Ed.); Lenora Howze (Adv. Dir.)

THE AFRO AMERICAN NEWSPAPER-WASHINGTON

Street address 1: 2519 N Charles St
Street address 3: Baltimore
Street address state: MD
Zip/Postal code: 21218-4602
County: Baltimore City
Country: USA
Mailing address: 2519 N Charles St
Mailing city: Baltimore
Mailing state: MD
Mailing zip: 21218-4602
General Phone: (410) 554-8200
General Fax: (877) 570-9297
General/National Adv. E-mail: adafro@afro.com
Primary Website: www.afro.com
Advertising (Open Inch Rate) Weekday/Saturday: Open inch rate $46.56
Published: Sat
Classified Equipment: 108
Personnel: John J. Oliver (Pub.); Susan Warshaw (Adv. Mgr.)

THE ANNAPOLIS TIMES

Street address 1: 2513 N Charles St
Street address 3: Baltimore
Street address state: MD
Zip/Postal code: 21218-4602
County: Baltimore City
Country: USA
Mailing address: 2513 N Charles St
Mailing city: Baltimore
Mailing state: MD
Mailing zip: 21218-4602
General Phone: (410) 366-3900
General Fax: (410) 243-1627
General/National Adv. E-mail: btimes@btimes.com
Display Adv. E-mail: ads@btimes.com
Editorial e-mail: jbramble@btimes.com
Primary Website: btimes.com
Year Established: 1986
Delivery Methods: Carrier`Racks
Own Printing Facility: Y
Advertising (Open Inch Rate) Weekday/Saturday: N/A
Published: Fri
Avg Free Circ: 3975
Audit By: CVC
Audit Date: 3/30/2017
Classified Equipment: Personnel: Joy Bramble (Pub.); Ida Neal (Circ. Mgr)

THE BALTIMORE TIMES

Street address 1: 2513 N Charles St
Street address 3: Baltimore
Street address state: MD
Zip/Postal code: 21218-4602
County: Baltimore City
Country: USA
Mailing address: 2513 N Charles St
Mailing city: Baltimore
Mailing state: MD
Mailing zip: 21218-4602
General Phone: (410) 366-3900
General Fax: (410) 243-1627
General/National Adv. E-mail: ineal@btimes.com
Display Adv. E-mail: ads@btimes.com
Editorial e-mail: jbramble@btimes.com
Primary Website: baltimoretimes-online.com
Year Established: 1986
Delivery Methods: Carrier`Racks
Own Printing Facility: Y
Advertising (Open Inch Rate) Weekday/Saturday: N/A
Mechanical specifications: Type page 10 x 13; E - 5 cols, 1 19/20, between; A - 5 cols, 1 19/20, between; C - 5 cols, 1 19/20, between.
Published: Fri
Avg Free Circ: 19975
Audit By: CVC
Audit Date: 3/30/2017
Classified Equipment: 109
Personnel: Joy Bramble (Pub.); Donnie Manuel (Sales Mgr.); Dena Wane (Mng. Ed.); Freddie Howard (Prodn. Mgr.); Ida Neal (Circ. Mgr)

MASSACHUSETTS

DORCHESTER

BAY STATE BANNER

Street address 1: 1100 Washington St
Street address 3: Dorchester
Street address state: MA

Zip/Postal code: 02124-5520
County: Suffolk
Country: USA
Mailing address: 1100 Washington St
Mailing city: Dorchester
Mailing state: WA
Mailing zip: 02124-5520
General Phone: (617) 261-4600
General/National Adv. E-mail: kmiller@bannerpub.com
Display Adv. E-mail: ads@bannerpub.com
Editorial e-mail: yawu@bannerpub.com
Primary Website: baystatebanner.com
Year Established: 1965
Published: Thur
Avg Free Circ: 27400
Audit By: AAM
Audit Date: 6/30/2018
Classified Equipment: Personnel: Melvin Miller (Pub.); Yawu Miller (Ed.); Rachel Reardon (Adv. Mgr./Circ.)

MICHIGAN

DETROIT

MICHIGAN CHRONICLE

Street address 1: 479 Ledyard St
Street address 3: Detroit
Street address state: MI
Zip/Postal code: 48201-2641
County: Wayne
Country: USA
Mailing address: 479 Ledyard St
Mailing city: Detroit
Mailing state: MI
Mailing zip: 48201-2687
General Phone: (313) 963-8100
General Fax: (313) 963-8788
General/National Adv. E-mail: chronicle4@aol.com
Primary Website: www.michronicleonline.com
Year Established: 1936
Advertising (Open Inch Rate) Weekday/Saturday: Open inch rate $39.64
Mechanical specifications: Type page 11 5/8 x 21 1/4; E - 6 cols, 1 5/6, 1/8 between; A - 6 cols, 1 5/6, 1/8 between; C - 9 cols, 1 3/16, between.
Published: Wed
Avg Paid Circ: 20910
Avg Free Circ: 1321
Audit By: CVC
Audit Date: 9/30/2016
Classified Equipment: 110
Personnel: Karen A. Love (COO); Samuel Logan (Pub.); Cornelius Fortune (Mng. Ed.); Raymond Allen (Prodn. Mgr.)
Parent company (for newspapers): Real Times, Inc.

ECORSE

TELEGRAM

Street address 1: PO Box 29085
Street address 3: Ecorse
Street address state: MI
Zip/Postal code: 48229-0085
County: Wayne
Country: USA
Mailing address: PO Box 29085
Mailing city: Ecorse
Mailing state: MI
Mailing zip: 48229-0085
General Phone: (313) 928-2955
General Fax: (313) 928-3014
General/National Adv. E-mail: telegram@telegramnews.net
Primary Website: www.telegramnews.net
Advertising (Open Inch Rate) Weekday/Saturday: Open inch rate $20.50
Published: Thur
Avg Paid Circ: 35000
Audit By: Sworn/Estimate/Non-Audited
Audit Date: 7/12/2019
Classified Equipment: Personnel: Gina Wilson (Adv. Dir.)

GRAND RAPIDS

THE GRAND RAPIDS TIMES

Street address 1: 2016 Eastern Ave SE
Street address 3: Grand Rapids
Street address state: MI
Zip/Postal code: 49507-3235
County: Kent
Country: USA
Mailing address: PO Box 7258
Mailing city: Grand Rapids
Mailing state: MI
Mailing zip: 49510-7258
General Phone: (616) 245-8737
General Fax: (616) 245-1026
General/National Adv. E-mail: staff@grtimes.com
Primary Website: www.grtimes.com
Advertising (Open Inch Rate) Weekday/Saturday: Open inch rate $17.00
Mechanical specifications: Type page 10 x 15; E - 5 cols, between; A - 5 cols, between.
Published: Fri
Avg Paid Circ: 6000
Audit By: Sworn/Estimate/Non-Audited
Audit Date: 7/12/2019
Classified Equipment: 111
Personnel: Patricia Pulliam (Ed.)

MINNESOTA

MINNEAPOLIS

INSIGHT NEWS

Street address 1: 1815 Bryant Ave N
Street address 3: Minneapolis
Street address state: MN
Zip/Postal code: 55411-3212
County: Hennepin
Country: USA
Mailing address: 1815 Bryant Avenue North
Mailing city: Minneapolis
Mailing state: MN
Mailing zip: 55411
General Phone: (612) 588-1313
General Fax: (612)588-2031
General/National Adv. E-mail: info@insightnews.com
Display Adv. E-mail: selene@insightnews.com
Editorial e-mail: al@insightnews.com
Primary Website: www.insightnews.com
Year Established: 1976
Delivery Methods: Newsstand`Racks
Area Served - City: Minneapolis and St. Paul Metro Area
Commercial printers: Y
Advertising (Open Inch Rate) Weekday/Saturday: Open inch rate $69.84
Mechanical available: www.insightnews.com
Published: Mon
Avg Paid Circ: 65
Avg Free Circ: 34835
Audit By: CAC
Audit Date: 3/31/2015
Classified Equipment: Personnel: Batala McFarlane (Publisher); Jamal Mohammed (Circ. Mgr.); Al McFarlane (President); Patricia Weaver (Prodn. Mgr.)
Parent company (for newspapers): McFarlane Media Interests, Inc.

MINNESOTA SPOKESMAN-RECORDER

Street address 1: 3744 4th Ave S
Street address 2: P.O. Box 8558
Street address 3: Minneapolis
Street address state: MN
Zip/Postal code: 55409-1327
County: Hennepin
Country: USA
Mailing address: 3744 4th Ave S
Mailing city: Minneapolis
Mailing state: MN
Mailing zip: 55409-1327
General Phone: (612) 827-4021
General Fax: (612) 827-0577
Advertising Phone: 612-827-4021
Advertising Fax: 612-827-0577
Editorail Phone: 612-827-4021
Editorial Fax: 612-827-0577
General/National Adv. E-mail: display@spokesman-recorder.com
Display Adv. E-mail: display@spokesman-recorder.com
Editorial e-mail: jfreeman@spokesman-recorder.com
Primary Website: www.spokesman-recorder.com
Year Established: 1934
News Services: nnpa
Special Editions: MLK, BHM, high school gradauation, rondo days, juneteenth, education
Delivery Methods: Mail`Newsstand`Carrier`Racks
Advertising (Open Inch Rate) Weekday/Saturday: Open inch rate $55.46
Mechanical specifications: Type page 6 x 21 1/4; E - 6 cols, 2 1/16, 1/8 between; A - 6 cols, 2 1/16, 1/8 between; C - 6 cols, 2 1/16, 1/8 between.
Published: Thur
Avg Paid Circ: 9800
Avg Free Circ: 50000
Audit By: Sworn/Estimate/Non-Audited
Audit Date: 7/12/2019
Classified Equipment: 112
Personnel: Tracey Williams (CEO/Pub.); Cecelia Viel (Account rep)

MISSISSIPPI

JACKSON

JACKSON ADVOCATE

Street address 1: 100 W Hamilton St
Street address 3: Jackson
Street address state: MS
Zip/Postal code: 39202-3237
County: Hinds
Country: USA
Mailing address: PO Box 3708
Mailing city: Jackson
Mailing state: MS
Mailing zip: 39207-3708
General Phone: (601) 948-4122
General Fax: (601) 948-4125
General/National Adv. E-mail: jadvocat@aol.com
Primary Website: www.jacksonadvocate.com
Year Established: 1938
Advertising (Open Inch Rate) Weekday/Saturday: Open inch rate $22.00
Mechanical specifications: Type page 13 x 21.
Published: Thur
Avg Paid Circ: 17000
Audit By: Sworn/Estimate/Non-Audited
Audit Date: 7/12/2019
Classified Equipment: Personnel: Alice Tisdale (Adv. Mgr.)

MISSISSIPPI LINK

Street address 1: 2659 Livingston Rd
Street address 3: Jackson
Street address state: MS
Zip/Postal code: 39213-6926
County: Hinds
Country: USA
Mailing address: P.O. Box 11307
Mailing city: Jackson
Mailing state: MS
Mailing zip: 39283-1307
General Phone: (601) 896-0084
General Fax: (601) 896-0091
Advertising Phone: (601) 368-8481
Editorail Phone: (601) 896-0084
General/National Adv. E-mail: publisher@mississippilink.com
Display Adv. E-mail: jlinkads@bellsouth.net
Editorial e-mail: editor@mississippilink.com
Primary Website: www.mississippilink.com
Year Established: 1993
Delivery Methods: Mail`Newsstand`Carrier`Racks
Advertising (Open Inch Rate) Weekday/Saturday: Open inch rate $18.00
Mechanical specifications: 6 columns (11.625") X 21"
Published: Thur
Avg Paid Circ: 17000
Avg Free Circ: 150
Audit By: Sworn/Estimate/Non-Audited
Audit Date: 7/12/2019
Classified Equipment: 113
Personnel: Jackie Hampton (Pub.); Ayesha Mustafaa (Ed.)

MISSOURI

KANSAS CITY

KANSAS CITY GLOBE

Street address 1: 615 E 29th St
Street address 3: Kansas City
Street address state: MO
Zip/Postal code: 64109-1110
County: Jackson
Country: USA
Mailing address: 615 E 29th St
Mailing city: Kansas City
Mailing state: MO
Mailing zip: 64109-1110
General Phone: (816) 531-5253
General Fax: (816) 531-5256
General/National Adv. E-mail: kcglobe@swbell.net
Primary Website: www.thekcglobe.com
Own Printing Facility: Y
Advertising (Open Inch Rate) Weekday/Saturday: Open inch rate $15.80
Mechanical specifications: Type page 13 x 21; E - 6 cols, 2 1/16, 1/8 between; A - 6 cols, 2 1/16, 1/8 between.
Published: Thur
Avg Paid Circ: 10500
Audit By: Sworn/Estimate/Non-Audited
Audit Date: 7/12/2019
Classified Equipment: Personnel: Marion Jordon (Ed.); Denise Jordon (Prodn. Mgr.)

THE CALL

Street address 1: 1715 E 18th St
Street address 3: Kansas City
Street address state: MO
Zip/Postal code: 64108-1611
County: Jackson
Country: USA
Mailing address: PO Box 410-477
Mailing city: Kansas City
Mailing state: MO
Mailing zip: 64141
General Phone: (816) 842-3804
General Fax: (816) 842-4420
Advertising Phone: (816) 842-3804
Advertising Fax: (816) 842-4420
Editorail Phone: (816) 842-3804
Editorial Fax: (816) 842-4420
General/National Adv. E-mail: kccallnews@hotmail.com
Primary Website: www.kccall.com
Delivery Methods: Mail`Newsstand`Carrier`Racks
Advertising (Open Inch Rate) Weekday/Saturday: Open inch rate $15.00
Mechanical specifications: Type page 13 x 21; E - 6 cols, between; A - 6 cols, between; C - 8 cols, between.
Published: Fri
Avg Paid Circ: 16456
Audit By: Sworn/Estimate/Non-Audited
Audit Date: 7/12/2019
Classified Equipment: 114
Personnel: Donna Stewart (Pub.); Barbara Way (Circ. Mgr.); Donna F. Stewart (Mng. Ed.)

SAINT LOUIS

ST. LOUIS AMERICAN

Street address 1: 2315 Pine St
Street address 3: Saint Louis
Street address state: MO
Zip/Postal code: 63103-2218
County: Saint Louis City
Country: United States
Mailing address: 2315 Pine Street
Mailing city: St. Louis
Mailing state: MO

Mailing zip: 63103
General Phone: (314) 533-8000
General Fax: (314) 533-2332
General/National Adv. E-mail: kjones@stlamerican.com
Primary Website: www.stlamerican.com
Year Established: 1928
Delivery Methods: Newsstand`Racks
Area Served - City: 74 different throughout St. Louis
Advertising (Open Inch Rate) Weekday/Saturday: Open inch rate $51.50
Mechanical specifications: Type page 12 x 21; E - 6 cols, between; A - 6 cols, between; C - 10 cols, between.
Published: Thur
Avg Paid Circ: 60
Avg Free Circ: 56652
Audit By: AAM
Audit Date: 9/30/2018
Classified Equipment: Personnel: Donald Suggs (Pub.); Kevin Jones (COO/Adv. Dir.); Mike Terhaar (Prodn. Mgr.)

ST. LOUIS EVENING WHIRL

Street address 1: PO Box 8055
Street address 3: Saint Louis
Street address state: MO
Zip/Postal code: 63156-8055
County: Saint Louis City
Country: USA
Mailing address: PO Box 8055
Mailing city: Saint Louis
Mailing state: MO
Mailing zip: 63156
General Phone: (678) 778-2616
General Fax: N/A
Advertising Phone: N/A
Advertising Fax: N/A
General/National Adv. E-mail: tpcwhirl@aol.com
Display Adv. E-mail: tpcwhirl@aol.com
Editorial e-mail: tpcwhirl@aol.com
Primary Website: www.thewhirlonline.com
Year Established: 1938
Delivery Methods: Mail`Newsstand
Own Printing Facility: N
Commercial printers: Y
Advertising (Open Inch Rate) Weekday/Saturday: Open inch rate $30.00
Market Information: Greater St. Louis
Mechanical specifications: Type page 12 1/2 x 21 1/2; E - 7 cols, 1 5/8, 3/16 between; A - 7 cols, 1 5/8, 3/16 between; C - 9 cols, 1 1/4, 1/8 between.
Published: Mon
Avg Paid Circ: 50500
Audit By: Sworn/Estimate/Non-Audited
Audit Date: 7/12/2019
Classified Equipment: 115
Personnel: Barry R. Thomas (Pub); Anthony L. Sanders (Ed.)

NEVADA

BROOKLYN

AFRO TIMES

Street address 1: 1195 Atlantic Ave
Street address 3: Brooklyn
Street address state: NY
Zip/Postal code: 11216-2709
County: Kings
Country: USA
Mailing address: 1195 Atlantic Ave
Mailing city: Brooklyn
Mailing state: NY
Mailing zip: 11216-2709
General Phone: (718) 636-9119
General Fax: (718) 857-9115
General/National Adv. E-mail: challengegroup@yahoo.com
Advertising (Open Inch Rate) Weekday/Saturday: Open inch rate $66.65
Published: Thur
Avg Paid Circ: 57004
Audit By: Sworn/Estimate/Non-Audited
Audit Date: 7/12/2019
Classified Equipment: Personnel: Thomas H. Watkins (Pub.); Ariana Perez (Adv. Mgr.); Janel Gross (Mng. Ed.)

OUR TIME PRESS

Street address 1: 679 Lafayette Ave
Street address 3: Brooklyn
Street address state: NY
Zip/Postal code: 11216-1009
County: Kings
Country: USA
Mailing address: 679 Lafayette Ave
Mailing city: Brooklyn
Mailing state: NY
Mailing zip: 11216-1009
General Phone: (718) 599-6828
General Fax: (718) 599-6825
Editorial e-mail: editors@ourtimepress.com
Primary Website: www.ourtimepress.com
Year Established: 1995
Delivery Methods: Mail`Carrier`Racks
Area Served - City: 11201, 11205, 11207, 11212, 11213, 11216, 11217, 11221, 11225, 11233, 11238
Advertising (Open Inch Rate) Weekday/Saturday: Open inch rate $54.00
Mechanical specifications: Type page 10 x 15; E - 4 cols, 2 3/8, 1/6 between; A - 4 cols, 2 3/8, 1/6 between; C - 5 cols, 1 7/8, 1/6 between.
Published: Thur
Avg Free Circ: 20000
Audit By: Sworn/Estimate/Non-Audited
Audit Date: 7/12/2019
Classified Equipment: 116
Personnel: David Mark Greaves (Ed.); Bernice Elizabeth Green (Ed.)

THE NEW AMERICAN

Street address 1: 1195 Atlantic Ave
Street address 3: Brooklyn
Street address state: NY
Zip/Postal code: 11216-2709
County: Kings
Country: USA
Mailing address: 1195 Atlantic Ave
Mailing city: Brooklyn
Mailing state: NY
Mailing zip: 11216-2709
General Phone: (718) 636-9119
General Fax: (718) 857-9115
General/National Adv. E-mail: challengegroup@yahoo.com; newamerican@hotmail.com
Advertising (Open Inch Rate) Weekday/Saturday: Open inch rate $66.65
Published: Thur
Avg Paid Circ: 60137
Audit By: Sworn/Estimate/Non-Audited
Audit Date: 7/12/2019
Classified Equipment: Personnel: Thomas H. Watkins (Pub.); Ariana Perez (Adv. Mgr.); Tatianna Singleton (Mng. Ed.)

BUFFALO

BUFFALO CRITERION

Street address 1: 623-625 William St
Street address 3: Buffalo
Street address state: NY
Zip/Postal code: 14206
County: Erie
Country: USA
Mailing address: 623-625 William St.
Mailing city: Buffalo
Mailing state: NY
Mailing zip: 14206
General Phone: (716) 882-9570
General Fax: (716) 882-9570
General/National Adv. E-mail: criterion@apollo3.com
Primary Website: www.buffalocriterion.com
Advertising (Open Inch Rate) Weekday/Saturday: Open inch rate $13.50
Mechanical specifications: Type page 10.5 x 21; E - 6 cols, 2 1/16, 1/8 between; A - 6 cols, 2 1/16, 1/8 between; C - 8 cols, between.
Published: Sat
Avg Paid Circ: 10000
Audit By: Sworn/Estimate/Non-Audited
Audit Date: 7/12/2019
Classified Equipment: 117
Personnel: Evelyn Merriweather (Pub.); Pat Ferguson (Adv. Mgr.); Frances J. Merriweather (Ed.); Evelyn Ferguson (Prodn. Mgr.)

CHALLENGER COMMUNITY NEWS CORP.

Street address 1: 140 Linwood Ave
Street address 2: Apt C12
Street address 3: Buffalo
Street address state: NY
Zip/Postal code: 14209-2022
County: Erie
Country: USA
Mailing address: PO Box 474
Mailing city: Buffalo
Mailing state: NY
Mailing zip: 14209-0474
General Phone: (716) 881-1051
General Fax: (716) 881-1053
General/National Adv. E-mail: editor@thechallengernews.com
Display Adv. E-mail: advertising@thechallengernews.com
Editorial e-mail: editor@thechallengernews.com
Primary Website: www.challengercn.com
Year Established: 1963
Special Editions: Martin Luther King -January Black History - February Black Press Month - March Salute to Barbers and Beauticians / Mother's Day- May Juneteenth & Father's Day - June Back to School - September Black Achievers Edition - October Kwanzaa & Christmas Edition - December
Delivery Methods: Mail`Newsstand`Racks
Own Printing Facility: N
Advertising (Open Inch Rate) Weekday/Saturday: Open inch rate $19.00
Mechanical specifications: Type page 10 x 14; E - 5 cols, between; A - 5 cols, between; C - 5 cols, between.
Published: Wed
Avg Paid Circ: 12500
Audit By: Sworn/Estimate/Non-Audited
Audit Date: 7/12/2019
Classified Equipment: Personnel: Barbara Banks (Ed.)

LAS VEGAS

LAS VEGAS SENTINEL-VOICE

Street address 1: 900 E Charleston Blvd
Street address 3: Las Vegas
Street address state: NV
Zip/Postal code: 89104-1554
County: Clark
Country: USA
Mailing address: 900 E Charleston Blvd
Mailing city: Las Vegas
Mailing state: NV
Mailing zip: 89104-1554
General Phone: (702) 380-8100
General Fax: (702) 380-8102
General/National Adv. E-mail: lvsentinelvoice@earthlink.net
Advertising (Open Inch Rate) Weekday/Saturday: Open inch rate $17.00
Mechanical specifications: Type page 10 1/4 x 14; E - 6 cols, 1 5/8, between; A - 6 cols, 1 5/8, between; C - 6 cols, 1 5/8, between.
Published: Thur
Avg Free Circ: 6500
Audit By: Sworn/Estimate/Non-Audited
Audit Date: 7/12/2019
Classified Equipment: 118
Personnel: Kathi Overstreet (Assoc. Pub.); Ramon Savoy (Ed.)

NEW YORK

BLACK STAR NEWS

Street address 1: 32 Broadway
Street address 2: Ste 511
Street address 3: New York
Street address state: NY
Zip/Postal code: 10004-1665
County: New York
Country: USA
Mailing address: PO Box 1472
Mailing city: New York
Mailing state: NY
Mailing zip: 10274-1472
General Phone: (646) 261-7566
Advertising Phone: (212) 422-2352
Editorail Phone: (646) 261-7566
General/National Adv. E-mail: advertise@blackstarnews.com
Display Adv. E-mail: advertise@blackstarnews.com
Editorial e-mail: Milton@blackstarnews.com
Primary Website: www.blackstarnews.com
Year Established: 1977
Delivery Methods: Mail`Racks
Area Served - City: New York County
Published: Thur
Classified Equipment: Personnel: Milton Allimadi (Pub./Ed.-in-Chief); Neanda Salvaterra (Assistant Web Ed.)

NEW YORK AMSTERDAM NEWS

Street address 1: 2340 Frederick Douglass Blvd
Street address 3: New York
Street address state: NY
Zip/Postal code: 10027-3619
County: New York
Country: USA
Mailing address: 2340 Frederick Douglass Blvd
Mailing city: New York
Mailing state: NY
Mailing zip: 10027-3691
General Phone: (212) 932-7400
Advertising Phone: (212) 932-7498
Advertising Fax: (212) 932-7497
Editorail Phone: (212) 932-7465
Editorial Fax: (212) 932-7467
General/National Adv. E-mail: info@amsterdamnews.com
Display Adv. E-mail: penda.howell@amsterdamnews.com
Editorial e-mail: kfm@amsterdamnews.com
Primary Website: www.amsterdamnews.com
Year Established: 1909
Delivery Methods: Mail`Newsstand
Area Served - City: New York, NY
Advertising (Open Inch Rate) Weekday/Saturday: Open inch rate $62.39
Mechanical specifications: 1 column......1.342" 2 columns.....2.833" 3 columns.....4.313" 4 columns.....5.788" 6 columns.....8.75" 12 columns...18.5" Gutter space vertically and horizontally is .125" Page depth is 11.5"
Published: Thur
Avg Paid Circ: 4845
Avg Free Circ: 1480
Audit By: AAM
Audit Date: 12/31/2018
Classified Equipment: 119
Personnel: Elinor Tatum (Publisher / Editor in Chief); Penda Howell (Vice President, Advertising, Sales, Partnerships.); Nayaba Arinde (Editor); Kristin Fayne-Mulroy (Mng. Ed./ Arts/Enter. Ed.)

NEW YORK BEACON

Street address 1: 237 W 37th St
Street address 2: Rm 201
Street address 3: New York
Street address state: NY
Zip/Postal code: 10018-6958
County: New York
Country: USA
Mailing address: 237 W 37th St Rm 201
Mailing city: New York
Mailing state: NY
Mailing zip: 10018-6958
General Phone: (212) 213-8585
General Fax: (212) 213-6291
General/National Adv. E-mail: newyorkbeacon@yahoo.com
Primary Website: www.newyorkbeacon.net
Delivery Methods: Newsstand
Area Served - City: 212, 718, 646, 916' 915
Advertising (Open Inch Rate) Weekday/Saturday: Open inch rate $62.14
Mechanical specifications: Type page 10 x 14; E - 2 cols, 2, between; A - 5 cols, 2, between; C - 5 cols, between.
Published: Fri
Avg Paid Circ: 71750
Avg Free Circ: 12722
Audit By: Sworn/Estimate/Non-Audited
Audit Date: 7/12/2019
Classified Equipment: Personnel: Miatta Smith (Adv. Dir.); Walter Smith (Ed. in Chief); Willie Egyir (Mng. Ed.)

NORTH CAROLINA

CHARLOTTE

CHARLOTTE POST

Street address 1: 1531 Camden Rd
Street address 3: Charlotte
Street address state: NC
Zip/Postal code: 28203-4753
County: Mecklenburg
Country: USA
Mailing address: PO Box 30144
Mailing city: Charlotte
Mailing state: NC
Mailing zip: 28230-0144
General Phone: (704) 376-0496
General Fax: (704) 342-2160
General/National Adv. E-mail: publisher@thecharlottepost.com
Primary Website: www.thecharlottepost.com
Year Established: 1975
Advertising (Open Inch Rate) Weekday/Saturday: Open inch rate $30.00
Mechanical specifications: Type page 13 1/4 x 22; E - 6 cols, 2, 1/4 between; A - 6 cols, 2, 1/4 between; C - 9 cols, 1 1/2, 1/8 between.
Published: Thur
Avg Paid Circ: 20400
Audit By: Sworn/Estimate/Non-Audited
Audit Date: 7/12/2019
Classified Equipment: 120
Personnel: Gerald O. Johnson (Pub.); Bob Johnson (Gen. Mgr.); Betty Potts (Bus. Mgr.); Herb White (Ed.)

DAVIDSON

DENVER WEEKLY NEWS

Street address 1: 209 Delburg St
Street address 2: Ste 209
Street address 3: Davidson
Street address state: NC
Zip/Postal code: 28036
Country: USA
Mailing address: 209 Delburg St Ste 209
Mailing city: Davidson
Mailing state: NC
Mailing zip: 28036
General Phone: (704) 766-2100
General Fax: (704) 992-0801
General/National Adv. E-mail: rdiaz@lakenormanpublications.com
Display Adv. E-mail: pmoon@lakenormanpublications.com
Editorial e-mail: rdiaz@lakenormanpublications.com
Primary Website: lakenormanpublications.com
Year Established: 2011
Advertising (Open Inch Rate) Weekday/Saturday: Open inch rate $30.00
Published: Fri
Avg Paid Circ: 0
Avg Free Circ: 8182
Audit By: CVC
Audit Date: 12/30/2017
Classified Equipment: Personnel: Kelly Wright (Pub.); Richard Diaz (Circ.); Patty Moon (Adv.)

DURHAM

THE CAROLINA TIMES

Street address 1: 923 Old Fayetteville St
Street address 3: Durham
Street address state: NC
Zip/Postal code: 27701-3914
County: Durham
Country: USA
Mailing address: P.O. Box 3825
Mailing city: Durham
Mailing state: NC
Mailing zip: 27702-3825
General Phone: (919) 682-2913
General Fax: (919) 688-8434
General/National Adv. E-mail: thecarolinatimes@cs.com
Display Adv. E-mail: adstct@cs.com
Editorial e-mail: thecarolinatimes@cs.com
Year Established: 1927
Delivery Methods: Mail`Newsstand`Racks
Area Served - City: 27701, 27702, 27703, 27704, 27705, 27708, 27709, 27710, 27712, 27713, 27715, 27717, 27722; 27514, 27516, 27517;, 27601, 27601, 27603, 27604, 27605, 27606, 27607, 27608, 27610, 27611, 27612
Advertising (Open Inch Rate) Weekday/Saturday: Open inch rate $14.75
Mechanical specifications: Type page 10.75 x 21; E - 6 cols, 2 1/16, 1/8 between; A - 6 cols, 2 1/16, 1/8 between; C - 6 cols, 2 1/16, 1/8 between.
Published: Thur
Avg Paid Circ: 6100
Audit By: USPS
Audit Date: 12/12/2017
Classified Equipment: 121
Personnel: Kenneth W. Edmonds (Pub.)

THE TRIANGLE TRIBUNE

Street address 1: 5007 Southpark Drive
Street address 2: Suite 200-G
Street address 3: Durham
Street address state: NC
Zip/Postal code: 27713
County: Durham
Country: USA
Mailing state: NC
General Phone: (919) 688-9408, ext. 200
Advertising Phone: (919) 688-9086
General/National Adv. E-mail: info@triangletribune.com
Display Adv. E-mail: linda.lanel@triangletribune.com
Editorial e-mail: editor@triangletribune.com
Primary Website: www.triangletribune.com
Year Established: 1997
Delivery Methods: Mail`Newsstand`Carrier
Own Printing Facility: N
Commercial printers: Y
Advertising (Open Inch Rate) Weekday/Saturday: Open inch rate $15.00
Mechanical specifications: Type page 11 5/8 x 21; E - 6 cols, 1 5/6, between; A - 6 cols, 1 5/6, between; C - 9 cols, 1 3/20, between.
Published: Sun
Avg Paid Circ: 1000
Avg Free Circ: 6000
Audit By: Sworn/Estimate/Non-Audited
Audit Date: 7/12/2019
Classified Equipment: Note: We are a digital-first multimedia organization.
Personnel: Gerald Johnson (CEO/Pub.); Bonitta Best (Ed.)
Parent company (for newspapers): The Charlotte Post Publishing

GREENSBORO

CAROLINA PEACEMAKER

Street address 1: 807 Summit Ave
Street address 3: Greensboro
Street address state: NC
Zip/Postal code: 27405-7833
County: Guilford
Country: USA
Mailing address: PO Box 20853
Mailing city: Greensboro
Mailing state: NC
Mailing zip: 27420-0853
General Phone: (336) 274-6210
General Fax: (336) 273-5103
Display Adv. E-mail: ads@carolinapeacemaker.com
Editorial e-mail: editor@carolinapeacemaker.com
Primary Website: www.carolinapeacemaker.com
Year Established: 1967
Delivery Methods: Mail`Racks
Commercial printers: Y
Advertising (Open Inch Rate) Weekday/Saturday: Open inch rate $30.00
Mechanical specifications: Type page 11 x 20 3/4; E - 6 cols, 1 7/8, 1/4 between; A - 6 cols, between; C - 10 cols, between.
Published: Thur
Avg Paid Circ: 8100
Audit By: Sworn/Estimate/Non-Audited
Audit Date: 7/12/2019
Classified Equipment: 122
Personnel: John Marshall Kilimanjaro (Pub.); C. Vickie Kilimanjaro (Adv. Mgr.); Afraque Kilimanjaro (Ed.)

RALEIGH

THE CAROLINIAN

Street address 1: 519 S Blount St
Street address 3: Raleigh
Street address state: NC
Zip/Postal code: 27601-1827
County: Wake
Country: USA
Mailing address: PO Box 25308
Mailing city: Raleigh
Mailing state: NC
Mailing zip: 27611-5308
General Phone: (919) 834-5558
General Fax: (919) 832-3243
General/National Adv. E-mail: thecarolinian@bellsouth.net
Primary Website: www.raleighcarolinian.info
Advertising (Open Inch Rate) Weekday/Saturday: Open inch rate $22.00
Mechanical specifications: Type page 13 x 21; E - 6 cols, 2 1/16, 1/8 between; A - 6 cols, 2 1/16, 1/8 between; C - 6 cols, 2 1/16, 1/8 between.
Published: Thur
Published Other: Thur`Every other Mon
Avg Paid Circ: 15202
Audit By: Sworn/Estimate/Non-Audited
Audit Date: 7/12/2019
Classified Equipment: Personnel: Paul R. Jervay (Pub.); Paul Jervay (Adv. Mgr.); Andrew Alston (Circ. Mgr.); Evelyn Jervay (Ed.)

STATESVILLE

COUNTY NEWS

Street address 1: 211 S Center St
Street address 3: Statesville
Street address state: NC
Zip/Postal code: 28677-5873
County: Iredell
Country: USA
Mailing address: PO Box 820
Mailing city: Statesville
Mailing state: NC
Mailing zip: 28687-0820
General Phone: (704) 873-1054
General Fax: (704) 873-1054
General/National Adv. E-mail: publisher@countynews4you.com
Advertising (Open Inch Rate) Weekday/Saturday: Open inch rate $35.00
Mechanical specifications: Type page 13 x 21 1/2; E - 6 cols, 2 1/12, 1/8 between; A - 6 cols, 2 1/12, 1/8 between; C - 6 cols, 2 1/12, 1/8 between.
Published: Wed
Avg Paid Circ: 7500
Audit By: Sworn/Estimate/Non-Audited
Audit Date: 7/12/2019
Classified Equipment: 123
Personnel: Fran Farrer (Pub.)

WILMINGTON

GREATER DIVERSITY NEWS

Street address 1: 272 N Front St
Street address 2: Ste 406
Street address 3: Wilmington
Street address state: NC
Zip/Postal code: 28401-4078
County: New Hanover
Country: USA
Mailing address: PO Box 1679
Mailing city: Wilmington
Mailing state: NC
Mailing zip: 28402-1679
General Phone: (910) 762-1337
General Fax: (910) 763-6304
Primary Website: www.greaterdiversity.com
Advertising (Open Inch Rate) Weekday/Saturday: Open inch rate $15.60
Mechanical specifications: Type page 13 x 21 1/2; E - 6 cols, 2, 1/6 between; A - 6 cols, 2, 1/6 between; C - 6 cols, 2, 1/6 between.
Published: Thur
Avg Paid Circ: 2500
Avg Free Circ: 2500
Audit By: Sworn/Estimate/Non-Audited
Audit Date: 7/12/2019
Classified Equipment: Personnel: Kathy Grear (Pub.); Peter Grear (Pub.)

WILMINGTON JOURNAL

Street address 1: 412 S 7th St
Street address 3: Wilmington
Street address state: NC
Zip/Postal code: 28401-5214
County: New Hanover
Country: USA
Mailing address: PO Box 1020
Mailing city: Wilmington
Mailing state: NC
Mailing zip: 28402-1020
General Phone: (910) 762-5502
General Fax: (910) 343-1334
Advertising Phone: 910 762-5502
Advertising Fax: 910 343-1334
Editorail Phone: 910 762-5502
Editorial Fax: 910-343-1334
General/National Adv. E-mail: wilmjourn@aol.com
Display Adv. E-mail: wilmjournads@aol.com
Classified Adv. E-mail: wilmjournads@aol.com
Editorial e-mail: wilmjourn@aol.com
Primary Website: www.wilmingtonjournal.com
Area Served - City: Wilmington, NC/Southeastern NC
Advertising (Open Inch Rate) Weekday/Saturday: Open inch rate $32.00
Mechanical specifications: Type page 13 x 21; E - 6 cols, 2 1/16, 1/8 between; A - 6 cols, 2 1/16, 1/8 between.
Published: Thur
Avg Paid Circ: 7000
Avg Free Circ: 950
Audit By: USPS
Audit Date: 9/30/2021
Classified Equipment: 124
Personnel: Shawn Jervay Thatch (Office/Advertising Mgr.); Robin Allen (Adv. Exec.); Edward Crumdy (Circ. Mgr.); Mary Alice Jervay Thatch (Pub./Ed.)

WINSTON SALEM

THE CHRONICLE

Street address 1: 1300 E. Fifth St.
Street address 3: Winston Salem
Street address state: NC
Zip/Postal code: 27101
County: Forsyth
Country: USA
Mailing address: PO Box 1636
Mailing city: Winston Salem
Mailing state: NC
Mailing zip: 27102-1636
General Phone: (336) 722-8624
General Fax: (336) 723-9173
General/National Adv. E-mail: news@wschronicle.com
Display Adv. E-mail: adv@wschronicle.com
Primary Website: www.wschronicle.com
Year Established: 1974
Own Printing Facility: Y
Advertising (Open Inch Rate) Weekday/Saturday: Open inch rate $28.50
Mechanical specifications: Type page 13 x 21; E - 6 cols, 2 1/8, 1/8 between; A - 6 cols, 2 1/8, 1/8 between; C - 9 cols, 1 1/4, 1/8 between.
Published: Thur
Avg Paid Circ: 10000
Audit By: Sworn/Estimate/Non-Audited
Audit Date: 7/12/2019
Classified Equipment: Personnel: James Taylor Jr. (Publisher); Deanna Taylor (Office Manager)
Parent company (for newspapers): Chronicle Media Group

OHIO

CINCINNATI

CINCINNATI HERALD

Street address 1: 354 Hearne Ave
Street address 3: Cincinnati
Street address state: OH
Zip/Postal code: 45229-2818
County: Hamilton
Country: USA
Mailing address: 354 Hearne Ave
Mailing city: Cincinnati
Mailing state: OH
Mailing zip: 45229-2818
General Phone: (513) 961-3331
General Fax: (513) 961-0304
General/National Adv. E-mail: jmkearney@mail.com
Primary Website: www.thecincinnatiherald.com
Advertising (Open Inch Rate) Weekday/Saturday: Open inch rate $27.83
Mechanical specifications: Type page 13 x 21; E - 6 cols, 2 1/16, 1/8 between; A - 6 cols, 2 1/16, 1/8 between; C - 10 cols, between.
Published: Thur
Avg Paid Circ: 16000
Audit By: Sworn/Estimate/Non-Audited
Audit Date: 7/12/2019
Classified Equipment: 125
Personnel: Jan Michele Kearney (Pub.); Walter White (Adv. Mgr.); Dan Yount (Ed. in Chief); Wade Lacey (Prodn. Mgr.)

KING MEDIA ENTERPRISES

Street address 1: 750 E Long St
Street address 2: Ste 3000
Street address 3: Columbus
Street address state: OH
Zip/Postal code: 43203-1874
County: Franklin
Country: USA
Mailing address: 750 E Long St Ste 3000
Mailing city: Columbus
Mailing state: OH
Mailing zip: 43203-1874
General Phone: (614) 224-8123
General Fax: (216) 451-0404
General/National Adv. E-mail: info@call-post.com
Display Adv. E-mail: advertising@call-post.com; classifieds@call-post.com
Primary Website: www.cleveland.com
Advertising (Open Inch Rate) Weekday/Saturday: Open inch rate $25.88
Mechanical specifications: Type page 13 x 21; E - 6 cols, between; A - 6 cols, between; C - 6 cols, between.
Published: Wed
Classified Equipment: Personnel: Douglas Rice (Vice Pres., Mktg./Adv.); Carl Matthews (Circ. Mgr.); Gil Price (Mng. Ed.); Cheri Daniels (Vice Pres., Opns.)

TOLEDO

THE TOLEDO JOURNAL

Street address 1: 3021 Douglas Rd
Street address 3: Toledo
Street address state: OH
Zip/Postal code: 43606-3504
County: Lucas
Country: USA
Mailing address: PO Box 12559
Mailing city: Toledo
Mailing state: OH
Mailing zip: 43606-0159
General Phone: (419) 472-4521
General Fax: (419) 472-1604
General/National Adv. E-mail: toledo411@aol.com; toljour@aol.com
Primary Website: www.thetoledojournal.com
Year Established: 1975
Area Served - City: 43602, 43611, 43620, 43560
Advertising (Open Inch Rate) Weekday/Saturday: Open inch rate $28.65
Mechanical specifications: Type page 10 1/4 x 16; E - 6 cols, 1, 1/8 between; A - 6 cols, 1, between.
Published: Wed
Avg Paid Circ: 12
Avg Free Circ: 11397
Audit By: CVC
Audit Date: 9/30/2014
Classified Equipment: 126
Personnel: Sandra S. Stewart (Pub.); Myron A. Stewart (Circulation Manager); Jeff Willis (Production Manager)

YOUNGSTOWN

THE BUCKEYE REVIEW

Street address 1: 1201 Belmont Ave
Street address 3: Youngstown
Street address state: OH
Zip/Postal code: 44504-1101
County: Mahoning
Country: USA
Mailing address: 1201 Belmont Ave
Mailing city: Youngstown
Mailing state: OH
Mailing zip: 44504-1101
General Phone: (330) 743-2250
General Fax: (330) 746-2340
General/National Adv. E-mail: buckeyereview@yahoo.com
Year Established: 1927
Advertising (Open Inch Rate) Weekday/Saturday: Open inch rate $21.50
Published: Tues
Avg Free Circ: 5250
Audit By: Sworn/Estimate/Non-Audited
Audit Date: 7/12/2019
Classified Equipment: Personnel: Mike McNair (Ed.)

OKLAHOMA

OKLAHOMA CITY

BLACK CHRONICLE

Street address 1: 1528 NE 23rd St
Street address 3: Oklahoma City
Street address state: OK
Zip/Postal code: 73111-3260
County: Oklahoma
Country: USA
Mailing address: PO Box 17498
Mailing city: Oklahoma City
Mailing state: OK
Mailing zip: 73136-1498
General Phone: (405) 424-4695
General Fax: (405) 424-6708
General/National Adv. E-mail: alisdsey@blackchronicle.com
Primary Website: www.blackchronicle.com
Advertising (Open Inch Rate) Weekday/Saturday: Open inch rate $16.44
Mechanical specifications: Type page 14 1/2 x 21 1/2; E - 8 cols, 1 2/3, between; A - 8 cols, 1 2/3, between; C - 8 cols, 1 2/3, between.
Published: Thur
Avg Paid Circ: 30000
Audit By: Sworn/Estimate/Non-Audited
Audit Date: 7/12/2019
Classified Equipment: 127
Personnel: T.C. Brown (Adv. Rep.); Russell M. Perry (Ed.); Albert J. Lindsey (Mng. Ed.)

TULSA

THE OKLAHOMA EAGLE

Street address 1: 624 E Archer St
Street address 3: Tulsa
Street address state: OK
Zip/Postal code: 74120-1000
County: Tulsa
Country: USA
Mailing address: PO Box 3267
Mailing city: Tulsa
Mailing state: OK
Mailing zip: 74101-3267
General Phone: (918) 582-7124
General Fax: (918) 582-8905
General/National Adv. E-mail: editor@theoklahomaeagle.net
Advertising (Open Inch Rate) Weekday/Saturday: Open inch rate $17.02
Mechanical specifications: Type page 13 x 21; A - 6 cols, 2 1/16, between.
Published: Fri
Avg Paid Circ: 5000
Audit By: Sworn/Estimate/Non-Audited
Audit Date: 7/12/2019
Classified Equipment: Personnel: James O. Goodwin (Pub.)

OREGON

PORTLAND

PORTLAND OBSERVER

Street address 1: 4747 NE M L King Blvd
Street address 3: Portland
Street address state: OR
Zip/Postal code: 97211-3398
County: Multnomah
Country: USA
Mailing address: PO Box 3137
Mailing city: Portland
Mailing state: OR
Mailing zip: 97208-3137
General Phone: (503) 288-0033
General Fax: (503) 288-0015
General/National Adv. E-mail: news@portlandobserver.com
Primary Website: www.portlandobserver.com
Advertising (Open Inch Rate) Weekday/Saturday: Open inch rate $24.75
Mechanical specifications: Type page 13 x 21; E - 6 cols, 2 1/16, 1/8 between; A - 6 cols, 2 1/16, 1/8 between; C - 6 cols, between.
Published: Wed
Avg Paid Circ: 7000
Avg Free Circ: 30000
Audit By: Sworn/Estimate/Non-Audited
Audit Date: 7/12/2019
Classified Equipment: 128
Personnel: Mark Washington (Pub.); Mike Leighton (Ed.); Paul Newfeldt (Prodn. Mgr.)

THE SKANNER

Street address 1: 415 N Killingsworth St
Street address 3: Portland
Street address state: OR
Zip/Postal code: 97217-2440
County: Multnomah
Country: USA
Mailing address: PO Box 5455
Mailing city: Portland
Mailing state: OR
Mailing zip: 97228-5455
General Phone: (503) 285-5555
General Fax: (503) 285-3400
General/National Adv. E-mail: info@theskanner.com; adver@theskanner.com
Primary Website: www.theskanner.com
Own Printing Facility: Y
Advertising (Open Inch Rate) Weekday/Saturday: Open inch rate $69.50
Mechanical specifications: Type page 10 1/2 x 16; E - 6 cols, 1 5/8, between; A - 6 cols, 1 5/8, between.
Published: Thur
Published Other: Every other Thurs
Avg Paid Circ: 10500
Audit By: Sworn/Estimate/Non-Audited
Audit Date: 7/12/2019
Classified Equipment: Personnel: Bernie Foster (Pub.); Jerry Foster (Circ. Mgr.); Bobbie Dore Foster (Ed.); David Kidd (Prodn. Mgr.)

PENNSYLVANIA

HAMBURG

MID-ATLANTIC COMMUNITY PAPERS ASSOCIATION

Street address 1: 16515 Pottsville Pike
Street address 2: Suite C
Street address 3: Hamburg
Street address state: PA
Zip/Postal code: 19526
County: Berks
Country: USA
Mailing address: PO Box 408
Mailing city: Hamburg
Mailing state: PA
Mailing zip: 19526-0408
General Phone: 484-709-6564
General/National Adv. E-mail: info@macpa.net
Display Adv. E-mail: Info@macnetonline.com
Primary Website: www.macpa.net
Mthly Avg Views: 3000000
Mthly Avg Unique Visitors: 800000
Year Established: 1955
Published: Mon`Tues`Wed`Thur`Fri`Sat`Sun`Mthly
Avg Free Circ: 1200000
Audit By: CVC
Audit Date: 1/1/2021
Classified Equipment: 129
Personnel: Alyse Mitten (Exec. Dir.)

PHILADELPHIA

PHILADELPHIA SUNDAY SUN

Street address 1: 6661 Germantown Ave
Street address 2: Ste 63
Street address 3: Philadelphia
Street address state: PA
Zip/Postal code: 19119-2251
County: Philadelphia
Country: USA
Mailing address: 6661 GERMANTOWN AVE # 63
Mailing city: PHILADELPHIA
Mailing state: PA
Mailing zip: 19119-2251
General Phone: (215) 848-7864
General Fax: (215) 848-7893
General/National Adv. E-mail: sundaysunads@yahoo.com
Editorial e-mail: taesun@philasun.com
Primary Website: www.philasun.com
Year Established: 1992
Delivery Methods: Mail`Newsstand`Carrier`Racks
Area Served - City: Philadelphia County
Advertising (Open Inch Rate) Weekday/Saturday: Open inch rate $25.89
Mechanical specifications: Type page 10 1/4 x 14; E - 5 cols, 1 7/8, 1/6 between; A - 5 cols, 1 7/8, 1/6 between; C - 5 cols, 1 7/8, 1/6 between.
Published: Sun
Avg Paid Circ: 20000
Audit By: Sworn/Estimate/Non-Audited
Audit Date: 7/12/2019
Classified Equipment: Personnel: Teresa Emerson (Mng. Ed.); Tera Moyet (Adv.)

PHILADELPHIA TRIBUNE

Street address 1: 520 S 16th St
Street address 2: # 26
Street address 3: Philadelphia
Street address state: PA
Zip/Postal code: 19146-1565
County: Philadelphia
Country: USA
Mailing address: 520 S 16th St # 26
Mailing city: Philadelphia
Mailing state: PA
Mailing zip: 19146-1565
General Phone: (215) 893-4050
General Fax: (215) 735-3612
General/National Adv. E-mail: info@phila-tribune.com
Display Adv. E-mail: advertising@phillytrib.com
Primary Website: phillytrib.com
Advertising (Open Inch Rate) Weekday/Saturday: Open inch rate $95.95

Published: Tues`Fri`Sun
Avg Paid Circ: 3856
Avg Free Circ: 6207
Audit By: AAM
Audit Date: 3/31/2018
Classified Equipment: 130
Personnel: Al Thomas (Mktg. Dir.); Michael Levere (Circ. Mgr.); Robert W. Bogle (CEO Pres.); Irv Randolph (Mng. Ed.); John Mason (Adv. Dir.)

SCOOPUSA MEDIA

Street address 1: 1354 W. Girard Avenue, 2nd floor rear
Street address 3: Philadelphia
Street address state: PA
Zip/Postal code: 19123
County: Philadelphia
Country: USA
Mailing address: PO Box 14013
Mailing city: Philadelphia
Mailing state: PA
Mailing zip: 19122-0013
General Phone: 215 309-3139
General Fax: 267 534-2943
General/National Adv. E-mail: info@scoopusamedia.com
Display Adv. E-mail: advertisements@scoopusamedia.com
Classified Adv. E-mail: advertisements@scoopusamedia.com
Editorial e-mail: editorial@scoopusamedia.com
Primary Website: www.scoopusamedia.com
Year Established: 1960
News Services: Print, Digital, Voice (WWDB) The Inside Scoop
Special Editions: ScoopVizion Monthly; MLK Edition, Black History Month, Black. Business Month Womens Edition, October,
Delivery Methods: Mail`Newsstand`Carrier`Racks
Area Served - City: 191.. / 081.. / 190..
Advertising (Open Inch Rate) Weekday/Saturday: Open inch rate $22.00
Mechanical specifications: Type page 10 x 16; E - 6 cols, 1 1/2, 3/16 between.
Published: Mon`Fri`Mthly
Published Other: Digital Friday ScoopVizion (monthly)
Weekday Frequency: All day
Avg Free Circ: 45000
Audit By: Sworn/Estimate/Non-Audited
Audit Date: 7/12/2019
Classified Equipment: Personnel: Sherri Darden (Publisher)
Parent company (for newspapers): Scoop USA Media

PITTSBURGH

NEW PITTSBURGH COURIER

Street address 1: 315 E Carson St
Street address 3: Pittsburgh
Street address state: PA
Zip/Postal code: 15219-1202
County: Allegheny
Country: USA
Mailing address: 479 Ledyard St
Mailing city: Detroit
Mailing state: MI
Mailing zip: 15219-1278
General Phone: (412) 481-8302
General Fax: (412) 481-1360
Advertising Phone: (313) 963-8100
General/National Adv. E-mail: webmaster@newpittsburghcourier.com
Display Adv. E-mail: ads@newpittsburghcourier.com
Editorial e-mail: newsroom@newpittsburghcourier.com
Primary Website: www.newpittsburghcourieronline.com
Year Established: 1910
News Services: AP/NNPA
Delivery Methods: Mail`Newsstand`Carrier`Racks
Own Printing Facility: N
Commercial printers: Y
Advertising (Open Inch Rate) Weekday/Saturday: Open inch rate $27.31
Mechanical specifications: Type page Broadsheet 10.625 x 20 1/2; E - 6 cols, 1.667, 1/8 between
Published: Wed
Avg Paid Circ: 2014
Avg Free Circ: 593
Audit By: CVC
Audit Date: 9/30/2017
Classified Equipment: 131
Personnel: Stephan Broadus (Asst. to Pub.); Eric Gaines (Adv. Mgr.); Jeff Marion (Circ. Mgr.); Rod Doss (Editor & Publisher); Ulish Carter (Managing Editor)
Parent company (for newspapers): Real Times Media, Inc.

RHODE ISLAND

PROVIDENCE

THE PROVIDENCE AMERICAN

Street address 1: PO Box 5859
Street address 3: Providence
Street address state: RI
Zip/Postal code: 02903-0859
County: Providence
Country: USA
Mailing address: PO Box 5859
Mailing city: Providence
Mailing state: RI
Mailing zip: 02903-0859
General Phone: (401) 475-6480
General Fax: (401) 475-6254
Primary Website: The Providence American
Commercial printers: Y
Advertising (Open Inch Rate) Weekday/Saturday: Open inch rate $20.00
Mechanical specifications: Type page 10 x 16; E - 4 cols, 1 1/2, between; A - 6 cols, between; C - 6 cols, between.
Published: Mthly
Avg Free Circ: 11000
Audit By: Sworn/Estimate/Non-Audited
Audit Date: 7/12/2019
Classified Equipment: Personnel: Peter C. Wills (Pub.)

SOUTH CAROLINA

CHARLESTON

CHARLESTON CHRONICLE

Street address 1: 1111 King St
Street address 3: Charleston
Street address state: SC
Zip/Postal code: 29403-3761
County: Charleston
Country: USA
Mailing address: PO Box 20548
Mailing city: Charleston
Mailing state: SC
Mailing zip: 29413-0548
General Phone: (843) 723-2785
General Fax: (843) 577-6099
General/National Adv. E-mail: chaschron@aol.com
Advertising (Open Inch Rate) Weekday/Saturday: Open inch rate $13.00
Mechanical specifications: Type page 13 x 21; E - 6 cols, 2 1/16, 1/8 between; A - 6 cols, 2 1/16, 1/8 between; C - 6 cols, 2 1/16, 1/8 between.
Published: Wed
Avg Paid Circ: 6000
Audit By: Sworn/Estimate/Non-Audited
Audit Date: 7/12/2019
Classified Equipment: 132
Personnel: Tolbert Small (Adv. Mgr.); Jim French (Ed.)

COLUMBIA

BLACK NEWS

Street address 1: 1310 Harden St
Street address 3: Columbia
Street address state: SC
Zip/Postal code: 29204-1820
County: Richland
Country: USA
Mailing address: PO Box 11128
Mailing city: Columbia
Mailing state: SC
Mailing zip: 29211-1128
General Phone: (803) 799-5252
General Fax: (803) 799-7709
General/National Adv. E-mail: scbnews@aol.com
Primary Website: www.scblacknews.com
Advertising (Open Inch Rate) Weekday/Saturday: Open inch rate $36.91
Mechanical specifications: Type page 13 x 21 1/2; E - 6 cols, 2 1/16, 1/8 between; A - 6 cols, 2 1/16, 1/8 between; C - 9 cols, between.
Published: Thur
Avg Paid Circ: 75000
Audit By: Sworn/Estimate/Non-Audited
Audit Date: 7/12/2019
Classified Equipment: Personnel: Isaac Washington (Pres./CEO/Pub.); Clannie Washington (Gen. Mgr.); Melvin Hart (Adv. Mgr.); Benjamin Jackson (Circ. Mgr.); Wendy Brinker (Prodn.Mgr.); Ruth Carlton (Asst. Bus. Mgr.)

CAROLINA PANORAMA

Street address 1: 2346B Two Notch Road
Street address 3: Columbia
Street address state: SC
Zip/Postal code: 29204
County: Richland
Country: USA
Mailing address: P.O. Box 11205
Mailing city: Columbia
Mailing state: SC
Mailing zip: 29211
General Phone: 803-256-4015
General Fax: 803-256-6732
Advertising Phone: 803-256-4015
Advertising Fax: 803-256-6732
Editorial Phone: 803-256-4015
Editorial Fax: 803-256-6732
General/National Adv. E-mail: news@CarolinaPanorama.com
Display Adv. E-mail: ads@CarolinaPanorama.com
Classified Adv. E-mail: ads@CarolinaPanorama.com
Editorial e-mail: news@CarolinaPanorama.com
Primary Website: www.CarolinaPanorama.com
Mthly Avg Views: 15031
Mthly Avg Unique Visitors: 11931
Year Established: 1986
Special Editions: Business Profiles Travel Issue Black History Month Issue Money
Delivery Methods: Newsstand`Racks
Area Served - City: Richland, Lexington, Calhoun, Fairfield & Orangeburg counties
Advertising (Open Inch Rate) Weekday/Saturday: Open inch rate $15.00
Online Advertising Rates - CPM (cost per thousand) by Size: $15 per column inch
Mechanical specifications: Type page 11 x 21 1/2; E - 6 cols, 2 1/16, 1/8 between; A - 6 cols, 2 1/16, 1/8 between; C - 10 cols, between.
Published: Wed
Avg Free Circ: 10000
Audit By: Sworn/Estimate/Non-Audited
Classified Equipment: 133
Personnel: Nate Abraham Jr. (Publisher); Patricia Abraham (Office Manager)
Parent company (for newspapers): MBD Media, LLC

TENNESSEE

MEMPHIS

TRI STATE DEFENDER

Street address 1: 203 Beale St
Street address 2: Ste 200
Street address 3: Memphis
Street address state: TN
Zip/Postal code: 38103-3727
County: Shelby
Country: USA
Mailing address: 203 Beale St Ste 200
Mailing city: Memphis
Mailing state: TN
Mailing zip: 38103-3727
General Phone: (901) 523-1818
General Fax: (901) 578-5037
Editorial e-mail: editorial@tri-statedefender.com
Primary Website: www.tri-statedefenderonline.com
Advertising (Open Inch Rate) Weekday/Saturday: Open inch rate $23.00
Mechanical specifications: Type page 13 x 21; E - 6 cols, 2 1/16, 1/8 between; A - 6 cols, 2 1/16, 1/8 between; C - 9 cols, 1 5/16, between.
Published: Thur
Avg Paid Circ: 524
Avg Free Circ: 3709
Audit By: Sworn/Estimate/Non-Audited
Audit Date: 7/12/2019
Classified Equipment: Personnel: Karanja Ajanaku (Associate Publisher/Exec. Ed.)

NASHVILLE

CHATTANOOGA COURIER

Street address 1: 805 Bradford Ave
Street address 3: Nashville
Street address state: TN
Zip/Postal code: 37204-2105
County: Davidson
Country: USA
General Phone: (615) 292-9150
General Fax: (615) 292-9056
General/National Adv. E-mail: npnews@comcast.net
Primary Website: www.pridepublishinggroup.net
Advertising (Open Inch Rate) Weekday/Saturday: Open inch rate $24.00
Mechanical specifications: Type page 13 1/4 x 21 1/2; E - 6 cols, 2 1/8, between; A - 6 cols, 2 1/8, between; C - 6 cols, 2 1/8, between.
Published: Thur
Avg Paid Circ: 24000
Audit By: Sworn/Estimate/Non-Audited
Audit Date: 7/12/2019
Classified Equipment: 134
Personnel: Meekahl Davis (Pub.); Scott Davies (Circ. Mgr.); Geraldine D. Heath (Ed.)

MURFREESBORO VISION

Street address 1: 805 Bradford Ave
Street address 3: Nashville
Street address state: TN
Zip/Postal code: 37204-2105
County: Davidson
Country: USA
General Phone: (615) 292-9150
General Fax: (615) 292-9056
General/National Adv. E-mail: npnews@comcast.net
Primary Website: www.pridepublishinggroup.net
Advertising (Open Inch Rate) Weekday/Saturday: Open inch rate $21.00
Mechanical specifications: Type page 13 1/4 x 21 1/2; E - 6 cols, 2 1/8, between; A - 6 cols, 2 1/8, between; C - 6 cols, 2 1/8, between.
Published: Thur
Avg Paid Circ: 16000
Audit By: Sworn/Estimate/Non-Audited
Audit Date: 7/12/2019
Classified Equipment: Personnel: Meekahl Davis (Pub.); Scotty Davis (Circ. Mgr.); Geraldine Heath (Mng. Ed.)

NASHVILLE PRIDE

Street address 1: 805 Bradford Ave
Street address 3: Nashville
Street address state: TN
Zip/Postal code: 37204-2105
County: Davidson
Country: USA
General Phone: (615) 292-9150
General Fax: (615) 292-9056
General/National Adv. E-mail: npnews@comcast.net
Primary Website: www.pridepublishinggroup.com
Advertising (Open Inch Rate) Weekday/Saturday: Open inch rate $32.50
Mechanical specifications: Type page 13 x 21; E - 6 cols, between; A - 6 cols, between; C - 6 cols, between.
Published: Fri
Avg Paid Circ: 42000
Audit By: Sworn/Estimate/Non-Audited
Audit Date: 7/12/2019
Classified Equipment: 135

Personnel: Meekahl Davis (Pub.); Scott Davis (Adv. Mgr.); Geraldine Heath (Mng. Ed.); James Lewis (Prodn. Mgr.)

TENNESSEE TRIBUNE

Street address 1: 1501 Jefferson St
Street address 3: Nashville
Street address state: TN
Zip/Postal code: 37208-3016
County: Davidson
Country: USA
Mailing address: 1501 JEFFERSON ST
Mailing city: NASHVILLE
Mailing state: TN
Mailing zip: 37208-3016
General Phone: (615) 321 3268
General Fax: 1-866 694 7534
Advertising Phone: (615) 321 3268
Advertising Fax: (866) 694-7534
Editorail Phone: 615 509 3181
General/National Adv. E-mail: tennesseetribunenews@aol.com
Display Adv. E-mail: sales1501@aol.com
Editorial e-mail: tennesseetribunenews@aol.com
Primary Website: www.tntribune.com
Year Established: 1970
Delivery Methods: Mail`Newsstand`Carrier`Racks
Area Served - City: Nashville, Jackson, Memphis, Chattanooga, Knoxville
Own Printing Facility: Y
Commercial printers: Y
Advertising (Open Inch Rate) Weekday/Saturday: Open inch rate $36.00
Mechanical specifications: Type page 13 x 20 1/4; E - 6 cols, 2 1/6, between; A - 6 cols, between.
Published: Thur
Avg Paid Circ: 1200
Avg Free Circ: 24450
Audit By: CVC
Audit Date: 11/30/2017
Classified Equipment: Personnel: Rosetta Miller Perry (Pub.); William Miller III (Assoc. Pub.); Wanda Benson (Assoc. Pub.); James Artis (VP Advert.)

THE ENLIGHTENER

Street address 1: 625 Main St
Street address 3: Nashville
Street address state: TN
Zip/Postal code: 37206-3603
County: Davidson
Country: USA
Mailing address: 625 Main St
Mailing city: Nashville
Mailing state: TN
Mailing zip: 37206-3603
General Phone: (615) 292-9150
General Fax: (615) 292-9056
General/National Adv. E-mail: npnews@comcast.net
Primary Website: www.pridepublishinggroup.net
Advertising (Open Inch Rate) Weekday/Saturday: Open inch rate $28.00
Mechanical specifications: Type page 13 1/4 x 21 1/2; E - 6 cols, 2 1/8, between; A - 6 cols, 2 1/8, between; C - 6 cols, 2 1/8, between.
Published: Wed
Avg Paid Circ: 26700
Audit By: Sworn/Estimate/Non-Audited
Audit Date: 7/12/2019
Classified Equipment: 136
Personnel: Meekahl Davis (Pub.); Lisa Pate (Mng. Ed.)

TEXAS

AUSTIN

THE VILLAGER

Street address 1: 4132 E 12th St
Street address 3: Austin
Street address state: TX
Zip/Postal code: 78721-1905
County: Travis
Country: USA
Mailing address: 4132 E 12th St
Mailing city: Austin
Mailing state: TX
Mailing zip: 78721-1905
General Phone: (512) 476-0082
General Fax: (512) 476-0179
General/National Adv. E-mail: vil3202@aol.com
Display Adv. E-mail: vil3202@aol.com
Editorial e-mail: vil3202@aol.com
Primary Website: N/A
Year Established: 1973
News Services: NNPA.org
Special Weekly Sections: None
Delivery Methods: Racks
Area Served - City: 78701, 78702, 78704, 78721, 78723, 78744, 78741, 78751, 7860
Own Printing Facility: N
Commercial printers: N
Advertising (Open Inch Rate) Weekday/Saturday: Open inch rate $20.00
Mechanical specifications: Type page 11.25 x 21; E - 6 cols, 1.75 between; A - 6 cols, 2, 1/8 between; C - 6 cols, 2, 1/8 between.
Published: Fri
Avg Free Circ: 5975
Audit By: CVC
Audit Date: 12/31/2018
Classified Equipment: Personnel: T.L. Wyatt (Ed./Pub)

DALLAS

DALLAS POST TRIBUNE

Street address 1: PO Box 570769
Street address 3: Dallas
Street address state: TX
Zip/Postal code: 75357
County: Dallas
Country: USA
Mailing address: PO Box 570769
Mailing city: Dallas
Mailing state: TX
Mailing zip: 75357
General Phone: (214) 946-7678
General Fax: (214) 275-3425
Display Adv. E-mail: chloe@dallasposttrib.net
Editorial e-mail: sgray@dallasposttrib.net
Primary Website: dallasposttrib.com
Year Established: 1947
Advertising (Open Inch Rate) Weekday/Saturday: Open inch rate $35.00
Mechanical specifications: Type page 13 x 21; E - 6 cols, 2 1/16, 1/8 between; A - 6 cols, 2 1/16, 1/8 between; C - 6 cols, 2 1/16, 1/8 between.
Published: Thur
Avg Paid Circ: 60
Avg Free Circ: 3915
Audit By: CVC
Audit Date: 12/30/2018
Classified Equipment: 137
Personnel: Shirley Gray (Pub.); Chloe Buckley (Production Manager)
Parent company (for newspapers): Tribune Publishing, Inc.

DALLAS WEEKLY

Street address 1: 3101 Martin Luther King Jr Blvd
Street address 3: Dallas
Street address state: TX
Zip/Postal code: 75215-2415
County: Dallas
Country: USA
Mailing address: PO Box 151789
Mailing city: Dallas
Mailing state: TX
Mailing zip: 75315-1789
General Phone: (214) 428-8958
General Fax: (214) 428-2807
Primary Website: www.dallasweekly.com
Advertising (Open Inch Rate) Weekday/Saturday: Open inch rate $39.18
Mechanical specifications: Type page 9 7/8 x 12; A - 6 cols, 1 9/16, between; C - 6 cols, 1 9/16, between.
Published: Thur
Avg Paid Circ: 10
Avg Free Circ: 4890
Audit By: CAC
Audit Date: 6/30/2017
Classified Equipment: Personnel: James Washington (Pub.); Gordon Jackson (Ed. in chief)

GARLAND JOURNAL NEWS

Street address 1: 320 S R L Thornton Fwy
Street address 2: Ste 220
Street address 3: Dallas
Street address state: TX
Zip/Postal code: 75203-1804
County: Dallas
Country: USA
Mailing address: 320 South R L Thornton Fwy Ste 220
Mailing city: Dallas
Mailing state: TX
Mailing zip: 75203-1804
General Phone: (214) 941-0110
General/National Adv. E-mail: publisher@texasmetronews.com
Display Adv. E-mail: sales@texasmetronews.com
Editorial e-mail: editor@texasmetronews.com
Primary Website: texasmetronews.com
Year Established: 1994
Delivery Methods: Mail`Racks
Area Served - City: Dallas County Tarrant County Ellis County Denton County Wise County Hunt County Collin County
Advertising (Open Inch Rate) Weekday/Saturday: CP
Published: Other
Published Other: 1st & 15th of the month
Avg Paid Circ: 15
Avg Free Circ: 2960
Audit By: CVC
Audit Date: 12/30/2018
Classified Equipment: 138
Personnel: Cheryl Smith (Pub.); BJ Fullylove (Advertising Manger); K Davis (Circulation Manger)

IMESSENGER

Street address 1: 320 S R.L. Thornton Freeway
Street address 2: Suite 220
Street address 3: Dallas
Street address state: TX
Zip/Postal code: 75203
Country: USA
Mailing address: 320 S R.L. Thornton Freeway, Ste. 220
Mailing city: Dallas
Mailing state: TX
Mailing zip: 75203
General Phone: (214) 941-0110
Display Adv. E-mail: sales@garlandjournal.com
Editorial e-mail: editor@texasmetronews.com
Primary Website: texasmetronews.com
Year Established: 2011
Published: Wed
Avg Paid Circ: 34
Avg Free Circ: 7916
Audit By: CVC
Audit Date: 12/19/2018
Classified Equipment: Personnel: Cheryl Smith (Pub.); Stewart Curet (GM); Nina Garcia (Mkt/ Sales Mgr.); Lajuana Barton (Ed. Team)

TEXAS METRO NEWS

Street address 1: 320 S R L Thornton Fwy
Street address 2: Ste 220
Street address 3: Dallas
Street address state: TX
Zip/Postal code: 75203-1804
County: Dallas
Country: USA
Mailing address: 320 South RL Thornton Fwy Ste 220
Mailing city: Dallas
Mailing state: TX
Mailing zip: 75203-1804
General Phone: (214) 941-0110
Advertising Phone: (214) 941-0110
General/National Adv. E-mail: stewartcuret@myimessenger.com
Display Adv. E-mail: sales@garlandjournal.com
Editorial e-mail: penonfire2@gmail.com
Primary Website: texasmetronews.com
Year Established: 2012
Delivery Methods: Mail`Newsstand`Carrier`Racks
Area Served - City: Dallas County Tarrant County Ellis County Denton County Wise County Hunt County Collin County
Advertising (Open Inch Rate) Weekday/Saturday: CP
Published: Wed`Other
Published Other: Bi-Weekly (1st and 15th each month)
Avg Paid Circ: 19
Avg Free Circ: 4956
Audit By: CVC
Audit Date: 12/30/2018
Classified Equipment: 139
Personnel: Cheryl Smith (Pub./Gen. Mgr.); K Davis (Circulation Manager); Stewart Curet (Adv.)

THE DALLAS EXAMINER

Street address 1: 4510 S. Malcolm X Blvd.
Street address 3: Dallas
Street address state: TX
Zip/Postal code: 75215
County: Dallas
Country: USA
Mailing address: P.O. Box 3720
Mailing city: Dallas
Mailing state: TX
Mailing zip: 75208
General Phone: (214) 941-3100
General Fax: (214) 941-3117
General/National Adv. E-mail: jones@dallasexaminer.com
Display Adv. E-mail: advertising@dallasexaminer.com
Editorial e-mail: mbelt@dallasexaminer.com
Primary Website: dallasexaminer.com
Year Established: 1986
Special Editions: College Guide, "Putting the Pieces Together" Dallas Black History, "Black Dallas Then and Now" "Battling HIV/AIDS in Our Community" "Healthy Balance" "Diversity and Inclusion"
Delivery Methods: Mail`Newsstand`Racks
Area Served - City: Dallas Metropolitan Area
Advertising (Open Inch Rate) Weekday/Saturday: Open inch rate $36.00
Online Advertising Rates - CPM (cost per thousand) by Size: $250.00 per week
Published: Thur
Avg Paid Circ: 919
Avg Free Circ: 9055
Audit By: CVC
Audit Date: 6/30/2022
Classified Equipment: Personnel: Mollie Belt (Publisher); James Belt (Adv.); Tina Jones (Circ.); Robyn Jimenez (Prod.)

HOUSTON

AFRICAN AMERICAN NEWS & ISSUES

Street address 1: 6130 Wheatley St
Street address 3: Houston
Street address state: TX
Zip/Postal code: 77091-3947
County: Harris
Country: USA
Mailing address: 6130 Wheatley St
Mailing city: Houston
Mailing state: TX
Mailing zip: 77091-3947
General Phone: (713) 692-1892
General Fax: (713) 692-1183
General/National Adv. E-mail: news@aframnews.com
Display Adv. E-mail: sales@aframnews.com
Editorial e-mail: prod@aframnews.com
Primary Website: www.aframnews.com
Year Established: 1996
Delivery Methods: Mail`Newsstand`Carrier`Racks
Advertising (Open Inch Rate) Weekday/Saturday: Open inch rate $225.00
Mechanical specifications: Type page 11 5/8 x 21.
Published: Wed`Sun
Avg Paid Circ: 2228
Avg Free Circ: 312818
Audit By: Sworn/Estimate/Non-Audited
Audit Date: 7/12/2019
Classified Equipment: 140
Personnel: Roy Douglas Malonson (Pub.); Shirley Ann Malonson (Gen. Mgr.); Rebecca Jones (Ed.)

FORWARD TIMES

Street address 1: 4411 Almeda Rd
Street address 3: Houston
Street address state: TX
Zip/Postal code: 77004-4901
County: Harris
Country: USA
Mailing address: PO Box 8346

Mailing city: Houston
Mailing state: TX
Mailing zip: 77288-8346
General Phone: (713) 526-4727
General Fax: (713) 526-3170
General/National Adv. E-mail: forwardtimes@forwardtimes.com
Primary Website: www.forwardtimes.com
Own Printing Facility: Y
Advertising (Open Inch Rate) Weekday/Saturday: Open inch rate $28.60
Mechanical specifications: Type page 13 x 21 1/2; E - 6 cols, 2 1/16, 1/8 between; A - 6 cols, 2 1/16, 1/8 between; C - 6 cols, 2 1/16, 1/8 between.
Published: Thur
Avg Paid Circ: 64580
Audit By: Sworn/Estimate/Non-Audited
Audit Date: 7/12/2019
Classified Equipment: Personnel: Karen Carter Richards (Assoc. Pub.); Henrietta Smith (Adv. Mgr.); Lenora Carter (Ed.); Shirley Daughery (Prodn. Mgr.)

HOUSTON DEFENDER

Street address 1: 12401 S Post Oak Rd
Street address 3: Houston
Street address state: TX
Zip/Postal code: 77045-2020
County: Harris
Country: USA
Mailing address: PO Box 8005
Mailing city: Houston
Mailing state: TX
Mailing zip: 77288-8005
General Phone: (713) 663-6996
General Fax: (713) 663-7116
General/National Adv. E-mail: news@defendermediagroup.com
Display Adv. E-mail: selma@defendermediagroup.com
Editorial e-mail: news@defendermediagroup.com
Primary Website: defendernetwork.com
Year Established: 1930
Delivery Methods: Mail`Newsstand`Racks
Area Served - City: Houston Metro
Own Printing Facility: N
Commercial printers: Y
Advertising (Open Inch Rate) Weekday/Saturday: Open inch rate $35.00
Mechanical specifications: Type page Tabloid - 10.75" x 14"; Full Page: 9.75" x 13"; Half Page (h) 9.75 x 6.5"; Half Page (v) 5.78" x 11"; Qtr: 5.78" x 5.65"
Published: Thur
Avg Free Circ: 30444
Audit By: AAM
Audit Date: 9/30/2018
Classified Equipment: 141
Personnel: Sonceria Messiah-Jiles (Pub. & CEO); Von Jiles (Ed.); Selma Dodson Tyler (Adv. & Marketing Dir.); Marilyn Marshall (Print Ed.); ReShonda Billingsley (Online Ed.); LaGloria Wheatfall (Multi-media Mgr.)

HOUSTON METRO WEEKENDER

Street address 1: 4411 Almeda Rd
Street address 3: Houston
Street address state: TX
Zip/Postal code: 77004-4901
County: Harris
Country: USA
Mailing address: PO Box 8346
Mailing city: Houston
Mailing state: TX
Mailing zip: 77288-8346
General Phone: (713) 526-4727
General Fax: (713) 526-3170
General/National Adv. E-mail: fowardtimes@forwardtimes.com
Primary Website: www.forwardtimes.com
Advertising (Open Inch Rate) Weekday/Saturday: Open inch rate $36.60
Mechanical specifications: Type page 13 x 21 1/2; E - 6 cols, 2 1/16, 1/8 between; A - 6 cols, 2 1/16, 1/8 between; C - 6 cols, 2 1/16, 1/8 between.
Published: Fri
Avg Free Circ: 75000
Audit By: Sworn/Estimate/Non-Audited
Audit Date: 7/12/2019
Classified Equipment: Personnel: Karen Carter Richard (Assoc. Pub.); Henrietta Smith-Wilson (Adv. Dir.); Lenora Carter (Mng. Ed.); Shirley Daugherty (Prodn. Mgr.)

HOUSTON SUN

Street address 1: 1520 Isabella St
Street address 3: Houston
Street address state: TX
Zip/Postal code: 77004-4042
County: Harris
Country: USA
Mailing address: 1520 Isabella St
Mailing city: Houston
Mailing state: TX
Mailing zip: 77004-4042
Primary Website: www.houstonsun.com
Published: Fri
Avg Free Circ: 9925
Audit By: Sworn/Estimate/Non-Audited
Audit Date: 7/12/2019
Classified Equipment: 142
Personnel: Dorris Ellis

LONGVIEW

EAST TEXAS REVIEW

Street address 1: 517 S Mobberly Ave
Street address 3: Longview
Street address state: TX
Zip/Postal code: 75602-1827
County: Gregg
Country: USA
Mailing address: 517 S Mobberly Ave
Mailing city: Longview
Mailing state: TX
Mailing zip: 75602-1827
Primary Website: www.easttexasreview.com
Year Established: 1995
Advertising (Open Inch Rate) Weekday/Saturday: Open inch rate $19.64
Published: Thur
Avg Paid Circ: 0
Avg Free Circ: 3980
Audit By: VAC
Audit Date: 6/30/2016
Classified Equipment: Personnel: Joycelyne Fadojutimi (Publisher/General Manager); LaDana Moore (Advertising Manager); Teddy LaRose (Circulation Manager); Teresa Shearer (Production Manager)

LUBBOCK

SOUTHWEST DIGEST

Street address 1: 902 E 28th St
Street address 3: Lubbock
Street address state: TX
Zip/Postal code: 79404-1718
County: Lubbock
Country: USA
Mailing address: PO Box 2553
Mailing city: Lubbock
Mailing state: TX
Mailing zip: 79408-2553
General Phone: (806) 762-3612
General Fax: (806) 762-4605
General/National Adv. E-mail: swdigest@sbcglobal.net
Primary Website: www.southwestdigest.com
Delivery Methods: Mail`Newsstand`Racks
Area Served - City: 79401, 79403, 79404, 79413, 79414, 79423, 79424
Advertising (Open Inch Rate) Weekday/Saturday: Open inch rate $15.00
Mechanical specifications: Type page 13 x 21; E - 6 cols, 2 1/16, 1/8 between; A - 6 cols, 2 1/16, 1/8 between; C - 6 cols, 2 1/16, 1/8 between.
Published: Thur
Avg Paid Circ: 800
Avg Free Circ: 4000
Audit By: Sworn/Estimate/Non-Audited
Audit Date: 7/12/2019
Classified Equipment: 143
Personnel: T.J. Patterson (Ed.)

PLANO

NORTH DALLAS GAZETTE

Street address 1: 3401 Custer Rd
Street address 2: Ste 169
Street address 3: Plano
Street address state: TX
Zip/Postal code: 75023-7546
County: Collin
Country: USA
Mailing address: PO Box 763866
Mailing city: Dallas
Mailing state: TX
Mailing zip: 75376-3866
General Phone: (972) 432-5219
General Fax: (972) 509-9058
Display Adv. E-mail: marketing@northdallasgazette.com
Primary Website: northdallasgazette.com
Year Established: 1991
Area Served - City: 75023, 75149, 75201, 75040, 75080, 75069, 75002, 75006, 75098
Advertising (Open Inch Rate) Weekday/Saturday: N/A
Mechanical specifications: Type page 12 1/2 x 20 1/2; E - 6 cols, 2, between; A - 6 cols, 2, between; C - 6 cols, 2, between.
Published: Thur
Avg Paid Circ: 8
Avg Free Circ: 9976
Audit By: VAC
Audit Date: 12/30/2014
Classified Equipment: Personnel: Thurman R. Jones (Pub.); Ruth Ferguson (Ed.); Ana Camacho (Sales and Mktg.)

RUSK

TEXAS INFORMER

Street address 1: PO Box 332
Street address 2: 941 Loop 343
Street address 3: Rusk
Street address state: TX
Zip/Postal code: 75785-0332
County: Cherokee
Country: USA
Mailing address: PO Box 332
Mailing city: Rusk
Mailing state: TX
Mailing zip: 75785-0332
General Phone: (903) 683-5743
General Fax: (903) 683-1577
Advertising Phone: 903 721 3112
Advertising Fax: 903 683-1577
Editorial Phone: 903 721-3112
Editorial Fax: 903-683-1577
General/National Adv. E-mail: info@texasinformer.com
Display Adv. E-mail: info@texasinformer.com
Editorial e-mail: informernews08@aol.com
Primary Website: www.texasinformer.com
Year Established: 1995
Delivery Methods: Mail`Racks
Area Served - City: Cherokee County Jacksonville, Tx. - 75766 Rusk, TX. - 75785 Alto, TX. - 75925 Anderson County Palestine - 75801 Houston County Crockett, TX. - 75835 Angelina County Lufkin, TX. - 75901 Rusk County Henderson, TX. - 75652
Advertising (Open Inch Rate) Weekday/Saturday: CP
Mechanical specifications: Three (3) columns x 13-inch column depth. Full page: 10.5" wide x 13" depth. Local: $2,000.00 Full page - $250.00 1/8 page National: $2,000.00 Full page - $250.00 1/8 page Insert Open Rate: $100. per thousand Classified Rate: 15.00 for first 10 words Volume, frequency, contract, color and other rates may be available from publisher.
Published: Mthly
Avg Paid Circ: 0
Avg Free Circ: 2500
Audit By: Sworn/Estimate/Non-Audited
Audit Date: 7/12/2019
Classified Equipment: 144
Personnel: Maxine Session (Pub./Ed. Maxine Session - Co-Publisher/ Editor Walater Session -Co-Publisher)

SAN ANTONIO

SAN ANTONIO OBSERVER

Street address 1: 3427 Belgium Ln
Street address 3: San Antonio
Street address state: TX
Zip/Postal code: 78219-2501
County: Bexar
Country: USA
Mailing address: PO Box 200226
Mailing city: San Antonio
Mailing state: TX
Mailing zip: 78220-0226
General Phone: (210) 212-6397
General Fax: (210) 271-0441
General/National Adv. E-mail: taylor2039@aol.com
Advertising (Open Inch Rate) Weekday/Saturday: Open inch rate $40.00
Mechanical specifications: Type page 10 1/4 x 11 1/4; E - 4 cols, between.
Published: Wed
Avg Paid Circ: 60
Avg Free Circ: 16051
Audit By: Sworn/Estimate/Non-Audited
Audit Date: 7/12/2019
Classified Equipment: Personnel: Lanell Taylor (Pres.); Sherry Logan (Adv. Mgr.); Gus Lopez (Prodn. Mgr.)

THE SAN ANTONIO OBSERVER

Street address 1: 3427 Belgium Ln
Street address 3: San Antonio
Street address state: TX
Zip/Postal code: 78219-2501
County: Bexar
Country: USA
Mailing address: 3427 Belgium Ln
Mailing city: San Antonio
Mailing state: TX
Mailing zip: 78219-2501
Primary Website: www.saobserver.com
Year Established: 1995
Advertising (Open Inch Rate) Weekday/Saturday: Open inch rate $60.00
Published: Wed
Avg Paid Circ: 22
Avg Free Circ: 2934
Audit By: VAC
Audit Date: 12/30/2014
Classified Equipment: 145
Personnel: Fabby Ali; Sherry Logan (Publisher); Waseem Ali (Advertising Manager); Charles Jones (Production Manager)

THE SAN ANTONIO REGISTER

Street address 1: 3427 Belgium Ln
Street address 3: San Antonio
Street address state: TX
Zip/Postal code: 78219-2501
County: Bexar
Country: USA
Mailing address: 3427 Belgium Ln
Mailing city: San Antonio
Mailing state: TX
Mailing zip: 78219-2501
Primary Website: www.saregister.com
Year Established: 1931
Advertising (Open Inch Rate) Weekday/Saturday: Open inch rate $60.00
Published: Wed
Avg Paid Circ: 0
Avg Free Circ: 9486
Audit By: CVC
Audit Date: 6/30/2014
Classified Equipment: Personnel: Sherry Logan

THE TYMES

Street address 1: 3427 Belgium Ln
Street address 3: San Antonio
Street address state: TX
Zip/Postal code: 78219-2501
County: Bexar
Country: USA
Mailing address: 3427 Belgium Ln
Mailing city: San Antonio
Mailing state: TX
Mailing zip: 78219-2501
General Phone: 2102229220
Advertising Phone: 2102229220
Editorail Phone: 2102229220
General/National Adv. E-mail: Wsmali@aol.com
Display Adv. E-mail: Wsmali@aol.com
Editorial e-mail: Wsmali@aol.com
Primary Website: www.tha-tymes.com
Year Established: 2002
Delivery Methods: Mail`Newsstand`Racks

Advertising (Open Inch Rate) Weekday/Saturday: $60 per column inch
Mechanical specifications: 10.25x9.75
Published: Wed
Avg Free Circ: 10000
Audit By: CVC
Audit Date: 1/1/2012
Classified Equipment: 146
Personnel: Waseem Ali (President/CEO)

VIRGINIA

NORFOLK

JOURNAL AND GUIDE

Street address 1: 974 Norfolk Sq
Street address 3: Norfolk
Street address state: VA
Zip/Postal code: 23502-3212
County: Norfolk City
Country: USA
Mailing address: PO Box 209
Mailing city: Norfolk
Mailing state: VA
Mailing zip: 23501-0209
General Phone: (757) 543-6531
General Fax: (757) 543-7620
General/National Adv. E-mail: njguide@gmail.com
Advertising (Open Inch Rate) Weekday/Saturday: Open inch rate $18.45
Mechanical specifications: Type page 13 x 21; E - 6 cols, between; A - 6 cols, between.
Published: Thur
Avg Paid Circ: 15000
Audit By: Sworn/Estimate/Non-Audited
Audit Date: 7/12/2019
Classified Equipment: Personnel: Brenda H. Andrews (Pub.); Michael Brooks (Circ. Mgr.); David Todd (Prodn. Mgr.)

RICHMOND

RICHMOND FREE PRESS

Street address 1: 422 E Franklin St
Street address 2: Fl 2
Street address 3: Richmond
Street address state: VA
Zip/Postal code: 23219-2226
County: Richmond City
Country: USA
Mailing address: PO Box 27709
Mailing city: Richmond
Mailing state: VA
Mailing zip: 23261-7709
General Phone: (804) 644-0496
Advertising Fax: (804) 643-5436
Editorial Fax: (804) 643-7519
General/National Adv. E-mail: news@richmondfreepress.com
Display Adv. E-mail: advertising@richmondfreepress.com
Primary Website: www.richmondfreepress.com
Year Established: 1991
Delivery Methods: Newsstand`Racks
Area Served - City: 23219, 23220, 23223, 23224, 23227, 23225, 23230, 23803, 23221, 23231, 23235, 23228, 23234, 23150, 23113, 23060, 23294, 23229, 23005, 23233
Advertising (Open Inch Rate) Weekday/Saturday: Open inch rate $28.35
Mechanical specifications: Printed page area: 11" wide x 21" deep ⊠?› 126 column inchest 6 Column Width Display Measurements COLUMN SIZE 1 column 1.698" 2 columns 3.558" 3 columns 5.418" 4 columns 7.278" 5 columns 9.138" 6 columns 11" 8 Column Width Legal/ Classified Measurements COLUMN SIZE 1 column 1.223" 2 columns 2.625" 3 columns 4.02" 4 columns 5.417" 5 columns 6.813" 6 columns 8.2" 7 columns 9.593" 8 columns 11"
Published: Thur
Avg Paid Circ: 69
Avg Free Circ: 31259
Audit By: VAC
Audit Date: 12/31/2016
Classified Equipment: 147
Personnel: Jean Patterson Boone (Pres./Pub.); April A. Coleman (Prodn. Mgr.)
Parent company (for newspapers): Paradigm Communications, Inc.

THE VOICE

Street address 1: 205 E Clay St
Street address 3: Richmond
Street address state: VA
Zip/Postal code: 23219-1325
County: Richmond City
Country: USA
Mailing address: 205 E Clay St
Mailing city: Richmond
Mailing state: VA
Mailing zip: 23219-1325
General Phone: (804) 644-9060
General Fax: (804) 644-5617
General/National Adv. E-mail: info@voicenewspaper.com
Display Adv. E-mail: ads@voicenewspaper.com
Editorial e-mail: editor@voicenewspaper.com
Primary Website: www.voicenewspaper.com
Year Established: 1985
Delivery Methods: Racks
Area Served - City: 23219, 23235, 23228, 23223, 23220, 23806, 23040, 23139, 23002, 23911, 23922, 23930, 23824, 23901, 23942, 23966, 23944, 23947, 23111,
Advertising (Open Inch Rate) Weekday/Saturday: Open inch rate $24
Mechanical specifications: Type page 10.20 x 11.25; E - 4 cols, 2.375" between; A - 4 cols, 2 1/4, 1/4 between; C - 6 cols, 1 1/2, between.
Published: Wed
Avg Paid Circ: 100
Avg Free Circ: 25000
Audit By: CVC
Audit Date: 8/8/2014
Classified Equipment: Personnel: Algeree Johnson (Ed.); Marlene Jones (Executive Manager)
Parent company (for newspapers): Southside Voice, Inc.

ROANOKE

THE ROANOKE TRIBUNE

Street address 1: 2318 Melrose Ave NW
Street address 3: Roanoke
Street address state: VA
Zip/Postal code: 24017-3906
County: Roanoke City
Country: USA
Mailing address: 2318 Melrose Ave NW
Mailing city: Roanoke
Mailing state: VA
Mailing zip: 24017-3906
General Phone: (540) 343-0326
General Fax: (540) 343-7366
General/National Adv. E-mail: trib@rt.roacoxmail.com
Primary Website: www.theroanoketribune.org
Advertising (Open Inch Rate) Weekday/Saturday: Open inch rate $7.20
Mechanical specifications: Type page 13 x 21; E - 6 cols, 2 1/8, between; A - 6 cols, 2 1/8, between; C - 6 cols, 2 1/8, between.
Published: Thur
Avg Paid Circ: 6000
Audit By: Sworn/Estimate/Non-Audited
Audit Date: 7/12/2019
Classified Equipment: 148
Personnel: Claudia A. Whitworth (Ed.); Stan Hale (Assoc. Ed.)

WASHINGTON

SEATTLE

FACTS NEWS

Street address 1: 2765 E Cherry St
Street address 3: Seattle
Street address state: WA
Zip/Postal code: 98122-4900
County: King
Country: USA
Mailing address: PO Box 22015
Mailing city: Seattle
Mailing state: WA
Mailing zip: 98122-0015
General Phone: (206) 324-0552
General Fax: (206) 324-1007
General/National Adv. E-mail: seattlefacts@yahoo.com
Commercial printers: Y
Advertising (Open Inch Rate) Weekday/Saturday: Open inch rate $22.50
Mechanical specifications: Type page 9 x 17 1/2; E - 8 cols, between; A - 8 cols, between.
Published: Wed
Avg Paid Circ: 100000
Audit By: Sworn/Estimate/Non-Audited
Audit Date: 7/12/2019
Classified Equipment: Personnel: Dennis Beaver (Pub.); Marla Beaver (Adv. Mgr.); Lavonne Marla (Ed.)

SEATTLE MEDIUM

Street address 1: 2600 S Jackson St
Street address 3: Seattle
Street address state: WA
Zip/Postal code: 98144-2402
County: King
Country: USA
Mailing address: PO Box 18205
Mailing city: Seattle
Mailing state: WA
Mailing zip: 98118-0205
General Phone: (206) 323-3070
General Fax: (206) 322-6518
General/National Adv. E-mail: mediumnews@aol.com
Primary Website: www.seattlemedium.com
Own Printing Facility: Y
Advertising (Open Inch Rate) Weekday/Saturday: Open inch rate $34.00
Published: Wed
Avg Paid Circ: 13500
Audit By: Sworn/Estimate/Non-Audited
Audit Date: 7/12/2019
Classified Equipment: 149
Personnel: Chris B. Bennett (Co-Pub.); Joan Owens (Co-Pub.); Prisilla Hailey (Gen. Mgr.)

TACOMA TRUE-CITIZEN

Street address 1: 2600 S Jackson St
Street address 3: Seattle
Street address state: WA
Zip/Postal code: 98144-2402
County: King
Country: USA
Mailing address: PO Box 18205
Mailing city: Seattle
Mailing state: WA
Mailing zip: 98118-0205
General Phone: (206) 323-3070
General Fax: (206) 322-6518
General/National Adv. E-mail: mediumnews@aol.com
Primary Website: www.seattlemedium.com
Own Printing Facility: Y
Advertising (Open Inch Rate) Weekday/Saturday: Open inch rate $25.00
Mechanical specifications: Type page 13 x 21; E - 6 cols, 2 1/16, 1/8 between; A - 6 cols, 2 1/16, 1/8 between; C - 10 cols, 1 1/4, between.
Published: Thur
Avg Paid Circ: 13500
Audit By: Sworn/Estimate/Non-Audited
Audit Date: 7/12/2019
Classified Equipment: Personnel: Chris B. Bennett (Co-Pub.); Joan Owens (Co-Pub.); Pricilla Hailey (Gen. Mgr.)

WISCONSIN

GLENDALE

MILWAUKEE COURIER

Street address 1: 6310 N Port Washington Rd
Street address 3: Glendale
Street address state: WI
Zip/Postal code: 53217-4300
County: Milwaukee
Country: USA
Mailing address: PO Box 6279
Mailing city: Milwaukee
Mailing state: WI
Mailing zip: 53206-0279
General Phone: (414) 449-4860
General Fax: (414) 906-5383
General/National Adv. E-mail: milwaukeecourier@aol.com
Primary Website: milwaukeecourieronline.com
Advertising (Open Inch Rate) Weekday/Saturday: Open inch rate $18.00
Mechanical specifications: Type page 13 x 21; E - 6 cols, 2, 1/4 between; A - 6 cols, 2, 1/4 between; C - 9 cols, 1 1/4, between.
Published: Sat
Avg Paid Circ: 60000
Avg Free Circ: 60000
Audit By: Sworn/Estimate/Non-Audited
Audit Date: 7/12/2019
Classified Equipment: 150
Personnel: Sandra Robinson (Gen. Mgr.); Robert Robinson (Circ. Mgr.)

MILWAUKEE

MILWAUKEE COMMUNITY JOURNAL

Street address 1: 3612 N Martin Luther King Dr
Street address 3: Milwaukee
Street address state: WI
Zip/Postal code: 53212-4134
County: Milwaukee
Country: USA
Mailing address: 3612 N Dr Martin Luther King Dr
Mailing city: Milwaukee
Mailing state: WI
Mailing zip: 53212-4198
General Phone: (414) 265-5300
General Fax: (414) 265-6647
Display Adv. E-mail: advertising@communityjournal.net
Editorial e-mail: editorial@communityjournal.net
Primary Website: www.communityjournal.net
Commercial printers: Y
Advertising (Open Inch Rate) Weekday/Saturday: Open inch rate $37.00
Mechanical specifications: Type page 13 x 21 1/2; E - 6 cols, 2, 1/8 between; A - 6 cols, 2, 1/8 between; C - 8 cols, 1 2/3, 1/8 between.
Published: Wed`Fri
Avg Free Circ: 75000
Audit By: Sworn/Estimate/Non-Audited
Audit Date: 7/12/2019
Classified Equipment: Personnel: Patricia O. Pattillo (Pub.); Colleen Newsom (Adv. Mgr.); Robert Thomas (Circ. Mgr.); Thomas Mitchell (Ed.); Teretha Mallard (PRODN. MGR.)

THE MILWAUKEE COURIER

Street address 1: 2003 W Capitol Dr
Street address 3: Milwaukee
Street address state: WI
Zip/Postal code: 53206-1939
County: Milwaukee
Country: USA
Mailing address: PO Box 6279
Mailing city: Milwaukee
Mailing state: WI
Mailing zip: 53206-0279
General Phone: (414) 449-4860
General Fax: (414) 585-9101
General/National Adv. E-mail: milwaukeecourier@aol.com
Primary Website: www.milwaukeecourier.com
Year Established: 1964
Delivery Methods: Newsstand`Carrier`Racks
Advertising (Open Inch Rate) Weekday/Saturday: Open inch rate $21.63
Mechanical specifications: Type page full page 10"x18", half page horizontal 10"x9" half page vertical 4.9375"x18", quarter page 4.9375"x9"
Published: Sat
Avg Free Circ: 40000
Audit By: Sworn/Estimate/Non-Audited
Audit Date: 7/12/2019
Classified Equipment: 151
Personnel: Jerrel Jones (Pub)
Parent company (for newspapers): Milwaukee Courier Inc

COLLEGE/UNIVERSITY NEWSPAPER

ALASKA

ALASKA PACIFIC UNIV.

Street address 1: 4101 University Dr
Street address 2: Ste 19
Street address city: Anchorage
Street address state: AK
Zip/Postal code: 99508-4625
Country: USA
Mailing address: 4101 University Dr Ste 19
Mailing city: Anchorage
Mailing state: AK
Mailing zip: 99508-4625
General Phone: (907) 564-8297
Personnel: Rosanne Pagano (Advisor); Michelle Coles (Ed.)

UNIV. OF ALASKA ANCHORAGE

Street address 1: 3211 Providence Dr, Campus Ctr 215
Street address city: Anchorage
Street address state: AK
Zip/Postal code: 99508
Country: USA
Mailing address: 3211 Providence Dr., Campus Ctr. 215
Mailing city: Anchorage
Mailing state: AK
Mailing zip: 99508-4614
General Phone: (907) 786-1434
General Fax: (907) 786-1331
Advertising Phone: (907) 786-4690
Editorial Phone: (907) 786-1313
Display Adv. E-mail: ads@thenorthernlight.org
Editorial e-mail: editor@thenorthernlight.org
Primary Website: www.thenorthernlight.org
Year Established: 1988
Personnel: Paola Banchero (Advisor); Mariya Proskuryakova (Adv. Mgr.); Shana Roberson (Executive Editor)

UNIV. OF ALASKA FAIRBANKS

Street address 1: PO Box 756640
Street address city: Fairbanks
Street address state: AK
Zip/Postal code: 99775-6640
Country: USA
Mailing address: PO Box 756640
Mailing city: Fairbanks
Mailing state: AK
Mailing zip: 99775-6640
General Phone: (907) 474-6039
General Fax: (907) 474-5508
General/National Adv. E-mail: fystar@uaf.edu
Primary Website: www.uafsunstar.com
Published: Tues
Personnel: Chavis Lakeidra (Editor-in-Chief); Manager Advertising

UNIV. OF ALASKA SOUTHEAST

Street address 1: 11120 Glacier Hwy
Street address city: Juneau
Street address state: AK
Zip/Postal code: 99801-86
Country: USA
Mailing address: 11120 Glacier Hwy
Mailing city: Juneau
Mailing state: AK
Mailing zip: 99801-8699
General Phone: (907) 796-6434
General Fax: (907) 796-6399
General/National Adv. E-mail: uas.whalesong@gmail.com; whalesong@uas.alaska.edu
Primary Website: www.uas.alaska.edu/whalesong
Year Established: 1981
Personnel: Jeremy Hsieh (Advisor); Taylor Murph (Adv. Mgr.); Randi Spary (Ed.); Hollis Kitchin (Prodn. Mgr.)

ALABAMA

ALABAMA A&M UNIV.

Street address 1: 4900 Meridian St NW
Street address city: Normal
Street address state: AL
Zip/Postal code: 35762-7500
Country: USA
Mailing address: 4900 Meridian St.
Mailing city: Normal
Mailing state: AL
Mailing zip: 35762
Personnel: Diane Anderson (Advisor)

ALABAMA STATE UNIV.

Street address 1: 915 S Jackson St
Street address city: Montgomery
Street address state: AL
Zip/Postal code: 36104-5716
Country: USA
Mailing address: PO Box 271
Mailing city: Montgomery
Mailing state: AL
Mailing zip: 36101-0271
General Phone: (334) 229-4419
General Fax: (334) 229-4934
General/National Adv. E-mail: ayoleke@aol.com
Personnel: David Okeowo (Prof./Chair); Bryan Weaver (Exec. Ed.); E.K. Daufin (Prof.); Julian K. Johnson (Mng. Ed.); Tracy Banks (Assoc. Prof./Dir., Forensics); James B. Lucy (News Ed.); Elizabeth Fitts (Assoc. Prof.); Richard Emmanuel (Asst. Prof.); James Adams (Instr.); Coke Ellington (Instr.); Valerie Heard (Instr.); Jonathan Himsel (Instr.); John Moore (Instr.); Walter Murphy (Instr.); Larry Owens (Instr.)

ATHENS STATE UNIV.

Street address 1: 300 N Beaty St
Street address city: Athens
Street address state: AL
Zip/Postal code: 35611-1902
Country: USA
Mailing address: 300 N Beaty St
Mailing city: Athens
Mailing state: AL
Mailing zip: 35611-1999
General Phone: (256) 233-8169
Personnel: Tena Bullington (Adv. Mgr.); Aletha Pardue (Ed.)

AUBURN UNIV.

Street address 1: Student Center 1111
Street address city: Auburn University
Street address state: AL
Zip/Postal code: 1985
Country: USA
Mailing address: 255 Duncan Dr Ste 1111
Mailing city: Auburn University
Mailing state: AL
Mailing zip: 36849-0001
General Phone: (334) 844-9021
General Fax: (334) 844-9114
General/National Adv. E-mail: news@theplainsman.com
Display Adv. E-mail: advertising@theplainsman.com
Personnel: Jennifer Adams (Advisor); Tom Hopf (Bus. Mgr.); Lindsey Davidson (Ed.); Rod Guajardo (Mng. Ed.)

AUBURN UNIV.

Street address 1: 7400 East Dr
Street address 2: Rm 326
Street address city: Montgomery
Street address state: AL
Zip/Postal code: 36117-7088
Country: USA
Mailing address: PO Box 244023
Mailing city: Montgomery
Mailing state: AL
Mailing zip: 36124-4023
General Phone: (334) 244-3662
General Fax: (334) 244-3131
General/National Adv. E-mail: aumnibuseditor@yahoo.com
Personnel: Taylor Manning (Ed. in Chief); Christine Kneidter (Exec. Ed.); Amber Acker (Mng. Ed.)

BIRMINGHAM-SOUTHERN COLLEGE

Street address 1: 900 Arkadelphia Rd
Street address 2: # 549014
Street address city: Birmingham
Street address state: AL
Zip/Postal code: 35254-0002
Country: USA
Mailing address: 900 Arkadelphia Rd # 549014
Mailing city: Birmingham
Mailing state: AL
Mailing zip: 35254-0002
General Phone: (205) 226-7706
General/National Adv. E-mail: hilltop@bsc.edu
Personnel: Peter Donahue (Advisor); Kimmie Farris (Ed. in Chief); Kimmie Sarris (Ed.); Yuan Gong (Bus. Mgr.); Glorious (Adv. Mgr.)

HUNTINGDON COLLEGE

Street address 1: 1500 E Fairview Ave
Street address city: Montgomery
Street address state: AL
Zip/Postal code: 36106-2114
Country: USA
Mailing address: 1500 E Fairview Ave
Mailing city: Montgomery
Mailing state: AL
Mailing zip: 36106-2148
General Phone: (314) 833-4354
Personnel: Jackie Trimble (Advisor); Matthew Adams (Co-Ed.); Beth Woodfin (Co-Ed.)

JACKSONVILLE STATE UNIV.

Street address 1: 700 Pelham Rd N
Street address 2: Rm 180
Street address city: Jacksonville
Street address state: AL
Zip/Postal code: 36265-1602
Country: USA
Mailing address: 700 Pelham Rd N Rm 180
Mailing city: Jacksonville
Mailing state: AL
Mailing zip: 36265-1602
General Phone: (256) 782-8192
General Fax: (256) 782-5645
Advertising Phone: (256) 782-5932
Editorial Phone: (256) 782-8191
General/National Adv. E-mail: chantyeditor@gmail.com
Personnel: Mike Stedham (Advisor); Zach Childree (Ed. in Chief); Ryan Rutledge (Staff Writer)

JAMES FAULKNER STATE CMTY. COLLEGE

Street address 1: 1900 S US Highway 31
Street address city: Bay Minette
Street address state: AL
Zip/Postal code: 36507-2619
Country: USA
Mailing address: 1900 S US Highway 31
Mailing city: Bay Minette
Personnel: Margaret Strickland (Dir., College Rel.)

JOHN C. CALHOUN STATE CMTY. COLLEGE

Street address 1: PO Box 2216
Street address city: Decatur
Street address state: AL
Zip/Postal code: 35609-2216
Country: USA
Mailing address: PO Box 2216
Mailing city: Decatur
Personnel: Robin Philip (Sec.)

OAKWOOD COLLEGE

Street address 1: 7000 Adventist Blvd NW
Street address city: Huntsville
Street address state: AL
Zip/Postal code: 35896-0001
Country: USA
Mailing address: 7000 Adventist Blvd NW
Mailing city: Huntsville
Mailing state: AL
Mailing zip: 35896-0003
General Phone: (256) 726-7000
General/National Adv. E-mail: oakspread@yahoo.com
Personnel: Michael Vance (Ed.)

SAMFORD UNIV.

Street address 1: 800 Lakeshore Dr
Street address city: Birmingham
Street address state: AL
Zip/Postal code: 35229-0001
Country: USA
Mailing address: Su # 292269
Mailing city: Birmingham
Mailing state: AL
Mailing zip: 35229-0001
General Phone: (205) 726-2466
General Fax: (205) 726-2586
Editorial Phone: (205) 726-2998
General/National Adv. E-mail: crimson@samford.edu
Personnel: Jon Clemmensen (Advisor)

SPRING HILL COLLEGE

Street address 1: 4000 Dauphin St
Street address city: Mobile
Street address state: AL
Zip/Postal code: 36608-1780
County: Mobile
Country: USA
Mailing address: 4000 Dauphin St
Mailing city: Mobile
Mailing state: AL
Mailing zip: 36608-1791
General Phone: (251) 380-3850
General Fax: (251) 460-2185
General/National Adv. E-mail: shcmedia@shc.edu; sbabington@shc.edu
Display Adv. E-mail: hillian@stumail.shc.edu
Editorial e-mail: hillian@stumail.shc.edu
Primary Website: http://newswire.shc.edu/
Published: Thur
Personnel: Stuart Babington (Advisor); J.L. Stevens II (Integrated Multimedia Center (IMC) Operations Mgr and Student Media adviser)

STILLMAN COLLEGE

Street address 1: PO Box 1430
Street address city: Tuscaloosa
Street address state: AL
Zip/Postal code: 35403-1430
Country: USA
Mailing address: PO Box 1430
Mailing city: Tuscaloosa

TROY UNIVERSITY

Street address 1: Hall School of Journalism and Communication
Street address 2: 103 Wallace Hall, Troy University
Street address city: Troy
Street address state: AL
Zip/Postal code: 36082-0001
Country: USA
Mailing address: Hall School of Journalism and Communication
Mailing city: Troy
Mailing state: AL
Mailing zip: 36082-0001
General Phone: (334) 670-3583
General Fax: (334) 670-3707

Advertising Phone: (334) 670-3328
Advertising Fax: (334) 670-3707
Editorial Phone: (334) 670-3328
Editorial Fax: (334) 670-3707
General/National Adv. E-mail: sstewart71298@troy.edu
Display Adv. E-mail: sstewart71298@troy.edu
Editorial e-mail: sstewart71298@troy.edu
Primary Website: www.tropnews.com; www.troy.edu
Published: Thur
Published Other: Certain home sports game days
Personnel: Steve Stewart (Advisor)

UNIV. OF ALABAMA

Street address 1: PO Box 870170
Street address city: Tuscaloosa
Street address state: AL
Zip/Postal code: 35487-0001
Country: USA
Mailing address: PO Box 870170
Mailing city: Tuscaloosa
Mailing state: AL
Mailing zip: 35487-0170
General Phone: (205) 348-7845
General Fax: (205) 348-8036
General/National Adv. E-mail: news@cw.ua.edu
Primary Website: www.cw.ua.edu
Year Established: 1894
Personnel: Drew Gunn (Adv. Mgr.); Corey Craft (Ed. in Chief); Amanda Peterson (Ed.)

UNIV. OF ALABAMA AT BIRMINGHAM

Street address 1: 1110 12th St S
Street address city: Birmingham
Street address state: AL
Zip/Postal code: 35205-5211
Country: USA
Mailing address: 1110 12th Street South
Mailing city: Birmingham
Mailing state: AL
Mailing zip: 35205
General Phone: (205) 934-3354
General Fax: (205) 934-8050
General/National Adv. E-mail: masutton@uab.edu
Display Adv. E-mail: ads@insideuab.com
Primary Website: studentmedia.uab.edu
Year Established: 1967
Published: Tues
Avg Free Circ: 6000
Personnel: Amy Kilpatrick (Advisor./Adv. Mgr.); Daniel Twieg (Ed. in Chief); Bill Neville (Prodn. Mgr.); Marie Sutton (Director)

UNIV. OF ALABAMA HUNTSVILLE

Street address 1: 301 Sparkman Dr
Street address 2: Charger Union 201
Street address city: Huntsville
Street address state: AL
Zip/Postal code: 35805-1911
Country: USA
Mailing address: 301 Sparkman Drive
Mailing city: Huntsville
Mailing state: AL
General/National Adv. E-mail: chargertimes@uah.edu
Display Adv. E-mail: ctlayout@uah.edu
Editorial e-mail: cteditor@uah.edu
Primary Website: chargertimes.com ; chargertimes.net ; chargertimes.uah.edu
Published: Tues`Fri
Personnel: Morgan Blair (Editor-in-Chief); Amy Dunham (Managing Editor)

UNIV. OF MONTEVALLO

Street address 1: 75 College Dr
Street address 2: Station 6222
Street address city: Montevallo
Street address state: AL
Zip/Postal code: 35115-3732
Country: USA
Mailing address: 75 College Dr
Mailing city: Montevallo
Mailing state: AL
Mailing zip: 35115
General Phone: (205) 665-6222
General Fax: (205) 665-6232
General/National Adv. E-mail: alabamian@montevallo.edu
Primary Website: http://www.thealabamian.com/
Published: Bi-Mthly
Personnel: Tiffany Bunt (Adviser); Reed Strength (Editor); Stephanie Howe (Business Manager)

UNIV. OF NORTH ALABAMA

Street address 1: 1 Harrison Plz
Street address 2: # 5300
Street address city: Florence
Street address state: AL
Zip/Postal code: 35632-0002
Country: USA
Mailing address: One Harrison Plaza, UNA Box 5300
Mailing city: Florence
Mailing state: AL
Mailing zip: 35632
General Phone: (256) 765-4364
Advertising Phone: (256) 765-4427
General/National Adv. E-mail: editor@florala.net
Primary Website: www.florala.net
Year Established: 1830
Published: Thur`Other
Published Other: biweekly
Personnel: Scott Morris (Student Media Advisor)

UNIV. OF WEST ALABAMA

Street address 1: 100 US-11
Street address city: Livingston
Street address state: AL
Zip/Postal code: 35470
Country: USA
Mailing address: 100 US-11
Mailing city: Livingston
Mailing state: AL
Mailing zip: 35470
General Phone: (205) 652-3892
Personnel: Betsy Compton (Advisor)

UNIVERSITY OF SOUTH ALABAMA

Street address 1: 336 Alpha Hall South
Street address city: Mobile
Street address state: AL
Zip/Postal code: 36688-0001
Country: USA
Mailing address: 336 Alpha Hall South
Mailing city: Mobile
Mailing state: AL
Mailing zip: 36688-0001
General Phone: (251)460-6442
Primary Website: www.usavanguard.com
Year Established: 1963
Published: Mon
Avg Free Circ: 2000
Personnel: Cassie Fambro (Editor-in-Chief); Aucoin J (Adviser); Alanna Whitaker (Managing Editor)

ARKANSAS

ARKANSAS STATE UNIV.

Street address 1: 104 Cooley Drive
Street address 2: Journalism Department
Street address city: State University
Street address state: AR
Zip/Postal code: 1921
Country: USA
Mailing address: PO Box 1930
Mailing city: State University
Mailing state: AR
Mailing zip: 72467-1930
General Phone: (870) 972-3076
General Fax: (870) 972-3339
Advertising Phone: 870-972-2961
Editorial Phone: (870) 972-3076
General/National Adv. E-mail: herald@astate.edu
Display Adv. E-mail: herald@astate.edu
Editorial e-mail: herald@astate.edu
Primary Website: www.asuherald.com
Year Established: 1921
Published: Mon`Thur
Avg Free Circ: 5000
Personnel: Bonnie Thrasher (Advisor); Lindsey Blakely (Editor); Jana Waters (Advertising Manager)

ARKANSAS TECH. UNIV.

Street address 1: 1815 Coliseum Dr
Street address city: Russellville
Street address state: AR
Zip/Postal code: 72801-8820
Country: USA
Mailing address: 1815 Coliseum Drive
Mailing city: Russellville
Mailing state: AR
Mailing zip: 72801-7400
General Phone: (479) 968-0284
General Fax: (479) 964-0889
General/National Adv. E-mail: arkatech@atu.edu
Display Adv. E-mail: arkatech.ads@atu.edu
Primary Website: www.arkatechnews.com
Year Established: 1923
Published: Thur
Avg Free Circ: 2100
Personnel: Tommy Mumert (Advisor)

ARKANSAS TRAVELER

Street address 1: 119 Kimpel Hall
Street address city: Fayetteville
Street address state: AR
Zip/Postal code: 72701
Country: USA
Mailing address: 119 Kimpel Hall
Mailing city: Fayetteville
Mailing state: AR
Mailing zip: 72701
General Phone: (479) 575-3406
General Fax: (479) 575-3306
General/National Adv. E-mail: traveler@uark.edu
Personnel: Saba Naseem (Editor-in-Chief)

HARDING UNIV.

Street address 1: PO Box 11192
Street address city: Searcy
Street address state: AR
Zip/Postal code: 72149-0001
Country: USA
Mailing address: PO Box 11192
Mailing city: Searcy
Mailing state: AR
Mailing zip: 72149-0001
General Phone: (501) 279-4139
General Fax: (501) 279-4127
General/National Adv. E-mail: thebison@harding.edu
Personnel: Jermy Beauchamp (Dir., Publications); Jermy (Advisor)

HENDERSON STATE UNIV.

Street address 1: PO Box 7681
Street address 2: 1100 Henderson St.
Street address city: Arkadelphia
Street address state: AR
Zip/Postal code: 71999-7693
Country: USA
Mailing address: PO Box 7693
Mailing city: Arkadelphia
Mailing state: AR
Mailing zip: 71999-7693
General Phone: (870) 230-5221
General Fax: (870) 230-5549
Advertising Phone: (870) 230-5288
General/National Adv. E-mail: oracle@hsu.edu
Display Adv. E-mail: oracleads@hsu.edu
Primary Website: www.hsuoracle.com
Year Established: 1910
Published: Wed
Avg Free Circ: 2000
Personnel: Steve Listopad (Advisor)

HENDRIX COLLEGE

Street address 1: 1600 Washington Ave
Street address city: Conway
Street address state: AR
Zip/Postal code: 72032-4115
Country: USA
Mailing address: 1600 Washington Ave.
Mailing city: Conway
Mailing state: AR
Mailing zip: 72032
General Phone: (501) 329-6811
General/National Adv. E-mail: proed@hendrix.edu
Personnel: Alice Hines (Advisor)

JOHN BROWN UNIV.

Street address 1: 2000 W University St
Street address city: Siloam Springs
Street address state: AR
Zip/Postal code: 72761-2112
Country: USA
Mailing address: 2000 W University St
Mailing city: Siloam Springs
Mailing state: AR
Mailing zip: 72761-2121
General Phone: (479) 524-7255
General Fax: (479) 524-7394
General/National Adv. E-mail: advocate@jbu.edu
Personnel: Candy Gregor (Assistant Professor of Communication Faculty adviser for the Threefold Advocate); KJ Roh (Executive Editor of the Threefold Advocate)

LYON COLLEGE

Street address 1: PO Box 2317
Street address city: Batesville
Street address state: AR
Zip/Postal code: 72503-2317
Country: USA
Mailing address: PO Box 2317
Mailing city: Batesville
Mailing state: AR
Mailing zip: 72503-2317
General Phone: (870) 698-4288
Personnel: Gavin Johannsen (Exec. Ed.)

OUACHITA BAPTIST UNIV.

Street address 1: Obu Box 3759
Street address city: Arkadelphia
Street address state: AR
Zip/Postal code: 71998-0001
Country: USA
Mailing address: OBU Box 3759
Mailing city: Arkadelphia
Mailing state: AR
Mailing zip: 71998-0001
General Phone: (870) 245-4186
General Fax: (870) 245-5500
Advertising Phone: 870-245-4186
General/National Adv. E-mail: rootj@obu.edu
Display Adv. E-mail: rootj@obu.edu
Editorial e-mail: rootj@obu.edu
Primary Website: www.obusignal.com
Published: Thur
Published Other: twice each month while school is in session
Avg Free Circ: 1500
Personnel: Jeff Root (Advisor); Jackson Carter (Signal Online Adviser)

PHILANDER SMITH COLLEGE

Street address 1: 900 W Daisy L Gatson Bates Dr
Street address city: Little Rock
Street address state: AR
Zip/Postal code: 72202-3726
Country: USA
Mailing address: 900 W Daisy L Gatson Bates Dr
Mailing city: Little Rock
Mailing state: AR
Mailing zip: 72202-3717
Personnel: Jimmy Cheffen (Advisor)

SOUTHERN ARKANSAS UNIV.

Street address 1: PO Box 1400
Street address city: Magnolia
Street address state: AR
Zip/Postal code: 71753
Country: USA
Mailing address: P.O. Box 1400
Mailing city: Magnolia
Mailing state: AR
Mailing zip: 71753-71753
General Phone: (870) 235-4269
General Fax: (870) 235-5005
General/National Adv. E-mail: saubrayeditors@yahoo.com
Editorial e-mail: brayeditor@yahoo.com

Personnel: John Cary (Advisor); Wes Dowdy (Ed. in Chief); Terri Richardson (Asst. Ed.); Jamal Brown (Sports Ed.)

THE FORUM, UNIVERSITY OF ARKANSAS AT LITTLE ROCK

Street address 1: 2801 S University Ave
Street address 2: Ste 116
Street address city: Little Rock
Street address state: AR
Zip/Postal code: 72204-1000
Country: USA
Mailing address: 2801 S University Ave Dsc 201J
Mailing city: Little Rock
Mailing state: AR
Mailing zip: 72204-1000
General Phone: (501) 569-3319
General Fax: (501) 569-3209
Display Adv. E-mail: adman@ualr.edu
Editorial e-mail: editor@ualr.edu
Primary Website: ualr.edu/forum
Published: Bi-Mthly
Avg Free Circ: 2500
Personnel: Sonny Rhodes (Advisor); Jacob Ellerbee (Exec. Ed.)

UNIVERSITY OF ARKANSAS AT PINE BLUFF

Street address 1: 1200 Universtiy Dr
Street address city: Pine Bluff
Street address state: AR
Zip/Postal code: 71601-2799
Country: USA
Mailing address: 1200 N. University Dr.
Mailing city: Pine Bluff
Mailing state: AR
Mailing zip: 71601
General Phone: (870) 575-8427
Advertising Phone: (870) 575-8427
Editorial Phone: (870) 575-8427
General/National Adv. E-mail: arkansawyer@uapb.edu
Display Adv. E-mail: arkansawyer@uapb.edu
Editorial e-mail: arkansawyer@uapb.edu
Year Established: 1921
Published: Other
Published Other: Bi-weekly
Avg Free Circ: 1000
Personnel: Alicia Dorn (Editor)

UNIVERSITY OF CENTRAL ARKANSAS

Street address 1: 201 Donaghey Ave
Street address 2: Stanley Russ Hall 124
Street address city: Conway
Street address state: AR
Zip/Postal code: 72035-5001
Country: USA
Mailing address: PO Box 5038
Mailing city: Conway
Mailing state: AR
Mailing zip: 72035-0001
General Phone: 501-499-9822
Advertising Phone: 501-499-9822
Advertising Fax: 501-852-2375
General/National Adv. E-mail: ucaechoeditor@gmail.com
Display Adv. E-mail: echonewspaperads@gmail.com
Primary Website: www.ucaecho.net
Published: Wed
Avg Free Circ: 2500
Personnel: David Keith (Advisor); Jordan Johnson (editor); Hayley Trejo (business manager)

WESTARK CMTY. COLLEGE

Street address 1: PO Box 3649
Street address city: Fort Smith
Street address state: AR
Zip/Postal code: 72913-3649
Country: USA
Mailing address: PO Box 3649
Mailing city: Fort Smith

ARIZONA

ARIZONA STATE UNIV.

Street address 1: PO Box 871502
Street address city: Tempe
Street address state: AZ
Zip/Postal code: 85287-1502
Country: USA
Mailing address: PO Box 871502
Mailing city: Tempe
Mailing state: AZ
Mailing zip: 85287-1502
General Phone: (480) 965-7572
General Fax: (480) 965-8484
General/National Adv. E-mail: state.press@asu.edu
Personnel: Jason Manning (Advisor); Tosh Stuart (Bus. Mgr.); Leo Gonzalez (Adv. Mgr.)

EMBRY-RIDDLE AERO UNIV.

Street address 1: 3700 Willow Creek Rd
Street address city: Prescott
Street address state: AZ
Zip/Postal code: 86301-3721
Country: USA
Mailing address: 3700 Willow Creek Road
Mailing city: Prescott
Mailing state: AZ
Mailing zip: 86301
General Phone: (928) 777-3891
Advertising Phone: (928) 777-3830
General/National Adv. E-mail: prnews@erau.edu
Personnel: Alan Malnar (Advisor); Katie (Gen Mgr.)

GLENDALE CMTY. COLLEGE

Street address 1: 6000 W Olive Ave
Street address city: Glendale
Street address state: AZ
Zip/Postal code: 85302-3006
Country: USA
Mailing address: 6000 W Olive Ave
Mailing city: Glendale
Mailing state: AZ
Mailing zip: 85302-3090
General Phone: (623) 845-3820
General Fax: (623) 845-3072
General/National Adv. E-mail: ads@gccvoice.com
Personnel: Mike Mullins (Advisor); Eric Carroll (Adv. Mgr.); Michelle Tabatabai-Shab (Ed. in chief)

MESA COMMUNITY COLLEGE

Street address 1: 1833 W Southern Ave
Street address city: Mesa
Street address state: AZ
Zip/Postal code: 85202-4822
Country: USA
Mailing address: 1833 W Southern Ave
Mailing city: Mesa
Mailing state: AZ
Mailing zip: 85202-4866
General Phone: (480) 461-7270
General Fax: (480) 461-7334
General/National Adv. E-mail: jackm@mesacc.edu
Primary Website: www.mesalegend.com
Year Established: 1962
Published: Bi-Mthly
Avg Free Circ: 5000
Personnel: Jack Mullins (Advisor)

PARADISE VALLEY CMTY. COLLEGE

Street address 1: 18401 N 32nd St
Street address city: Phoenix
Street address state: AZ
Zip/Postal code: 85032-1210
Country: USA
Mailing address: 18401 N 32nd St
Mailing city: Phoenix
Mailing state: AZ
Mailing zip: 85032-1200
General Phone: (602) 787-6772
General Fax: (602) 787-7285
Advertising Phone: (602) 787-6772
Advertising Fax: (602) 787-7285
Editorial Phone: (602) 787-6772
General/National Adv. E-mail: pumapress@pvmail.maricopa.edu
Display Adv. E-mail: judy.galbraith@paradisevalley.edu
Editorial e-mail: judy.galbraith@paradisevalley.edu
Primary Website: http://nevalleynews.org/
Year Established: 1991
Published: Mthly
Avg Free Circ: 2000
Personnel: Judy Galbraith (Advisor)

PIMA COMMUNITY COLLEGE

Street address 1: 2202 W Anklam Rd
Street address city: Tucson
Street address state: AZ
Zip/Postal code: 85709-0001
Country: USA
Mailing address: 2202 W. Anklam Rd.
Mailing city: Tucson
Mailing state: AZ
Mailing zip: 85709-0001
General Phone: (520) 206-6800
General Fax: (520) 206-6834
Advertising Phone: (520) 206-6901
General/National Adv. E-mail: aztec_press@pima.edu
Display Adv. E-mail: aztecpress_ad@pima.edu
Primary Website: aztecpressonline.com
Year Established: 1970
Published: Bi-Mthly
Avg Free Circ: 5000
Personnel: Andrew Paxton (Business manager)

THE LUMBERJACK

Street address 1: 700 Knoles Dr
Street address city: Flagstaff
Street address state: AZ
Zip/Postal code: 86011-0180
County: Coconino
Country: USA
Mailing city: Flagstaff
Mailing state: AZ
General/National Adv. E-mail: lumberjack@nau.edu
Primary Website: www.jackcentral.org
Published: Fri
Personnel: Ace Mcmillin (Ed. in Cheif); Gary Sundt (Gen. Mgr.); Joshua Garcia (Adv. Dir.); Jesica Demarco (Adv. Dir.)

THUNDERBIRD SCHOOL OF GLOBAL MGMT.

Street address 1: 1 Global Pl
Street address city: Glendale
Street address state: AZ
Zip/Postal code: 85306-3216
Country: USA
Mailing address: 1 Global Pl
Mailing city: Glendale
Mailing state: AZ
Mailing zip: 85306-3216
General Phone: (602) 978-7000
General Fax: (602) 978-7971
General/National Adv. E-mail: dastor@thunderbird.edu
Personnel: Sailaja Kattubadi (Ed. in Chief)

UNIV. OF ARIZONA

Street address 1: 615 N Park Ave
Street address 2: Ste 101
Street address city: Tucson
Street address state: AZ
Zip/Postal code: 85719-5096
Country: USA
Mailing address: 615 N. Park Ave., Ste. 101
Mailing city: Tucson
Mailing state: AZ
Mailing zip: 85719-5094
General Phone: (520) 621-8659
General Fax: (520) 626-8303
Advertising Phone: (520) 621-5982
Editorial Phone: (520) 621-7879
General/National Adv. E-mail: display@wildcat.arizona.edu
Editorial e-mail: editor@wildcat.arizona.edu
Primary Website: www.wildcat.arizona.edu
Year Established: 1899
Published: Mon`Tues`Wed`Thur`Fri
Personnel: Mark Woodhams (Dir.); Brett Fera (Asst. Dir.)

WEST NEWS

Street address 1: 4701 W Thunderbird Rd
Street address 2: # 117
Street address city: Glendale
Street address state: AZ
Zip/Postal code: 85306-4900
Country: USA
Mailing address: 4701 W Thunderbird Rd # 117
Mailing city: Glendale
Mailing state: AZ
Mailing zip: 85306-4900
Year Established: 2010
Personnel: Robert Gehl (Editor-in-chief)

YAVAPAI COLLEGE

Street address 1: 1100 E Sheldon St
Street address 2: Bldg 3-118
Street address city: Prescott
Street address state: AZ
Zip/Postal code: 86301-3220
Country: USA
Mailing address: 1100 E Sheldon St Bldg 3-118
Mailing city: Prescott
Mailing state: AZ
Mailing zip: 86301-3297
General Fax: (928) 717-7678
Advertising Fax: (928) 717-7742
General/National Adv. E-mail: roughwriter.yc.edu
Display Adv. E-mail: ycwriters@yahoo.com
Personnel: Colette Strassburg (Advisor); Brandon Ross (Ed.); Elizabeth Zieche (Asst. Ed.)

CALIFORNIA

ALLIANT INTERNATIONAL UNIV.

Street address 1: 5130 E Clinton Way
Street address city: Fresno
Street address state: CA
Zip/Postal code: 93727-2014
Country: USA
Mailing address: 5130 E Clinton Way
Mailing city: Fresno
Mailing state: CA
Mailing zip: 93727-2014
General Phone: (559) 456-2777
General Fax: (858) 635-4853
Personnel: Miles Beauchamp (Advisor); Alexandria Proff (Ed.)

AMERICAN RIVER COLLEGE

Street address 1: 4700 College Oak Dr
Street address city: Sacramento
Street address state: CA
Zip/Postal code: 95841-4217
Country: USA
Mailing address: 4700 College Oak Dr
Mailing city: Sacramento
Mailing state: CA
Mailing zip: 95841-4286
General Phone: (916) 484-8653
General Fax: (916) 484-8668
General/National Adv. E-mail: current@arc.losrios.edu
Personnel: Jill Wagner (Advisor); Carol Hartman (Advisor); Andrew Clementi (Ed.)

ANTELOPE VALLEY COLLEGE

Street address 1: 3041 W Avenue K
Street address city: Lancaster
Street address state: CA
Zip/Postal code: 93536-5402
Country: USA
Mailing address: 3041 W Avenue K
Mailing city: Lancaster
Mailing state: CA
Mailing zip: 93536-5426
General Phone: (661) 722-6496
Personnel: Charles Hood (Advisor)

BAKERSFIELD COLLEGE

Street address 1: 1801 Panorama Dr
Street address city: Bakersfield
Street address state: CA
Zip/Postal code: 93305-1219
Country: USA
Mailing address: 1801 Panorama Dr
Mailing city: Bakersfield

Mailing state: CA
Mailing zip: 93305-1299
General Phone: (661) 395-4324
General Fax: (661) 395-4027
Editorial Fax: Free
General/National Adv. E-mail: ripmail@bakersfieldcollege.edu
Display Adv. E-mail: daedward@bakersfieldcollege.edu
Primary Website: www.therip.com
Year Established: 1929
Published Other: bi-weekly (once every two weeks on Wednesdays)
Avg Free Circ: 3000
Personnel: Danny Edwards (Advisor)

BIOLA UNIVERSITY

Street address 1: 13800 Biola Ave
Street address city: La Mirada
Street address state: CA
Zip/Postal code: 90639-0002
Country: USA
Mailing address: 13800 Biola Ave
Mailing city: La Mirada
Mailing state: CA
Mailing zip: 90639-0001
General Phone: (562) 906-4569
General Fax: (562) 906-4515
Advertising Phone: (562) 587-7339
General/National Adv. E-mail: lily.park@biola.edu
Display Adv. E-mail: chimes.advertising@biola.edu
Primary Website: chimes.biola.edu
Published: Thur
Personnel: Michael A. Longinow (Chair/Prof.); Sarah Sjoberg (Advertising Manager); J. Douglas Tarpley (Prof.); Michael Bower (Assoc. Prof.); Tamara Welter (Asst. Prof.); James Hirsen (Instr.); Chi-Chung Keung (Instr.); Mark Landsbaum (Instr.); Greg Schneider (Instr.); Melissa Nunnally (Instr.)

CALIFORNIA BAPTIST COLLEGE

Street address 1: 8432 Magnolia Ave
Street address city: Riverside
Street address state: CA
Zip/Postal code: 92504-3206
Country: USA
Mailing address: 8432 Magnolia Ave
Mailing city: Riverside
Mailing state: CA
Mailing zip: 92504-3297
General Phone: (951) 343-4401
Personnel: Mary Ann Pearson (Advisor); Amanda Tredinnick (Adv. Mgr.); Kendall Dewitt (Ed.)

CALIFORNIA INST. OF TECHNOLOGY

Street address 1: Caltech Msc 40-58
Street address city: Pasadena
Street address state: CA
Country: USA
Mailing address: Caltech MSC 40-58
Mailing city: Pasadena
Mailing state: CA
Mailing zip: mpearson@calbaptist.edu
General Phone: (626) 395-6154
Advertising Phone: (626) 577-1294
General/National Adv. E-mail: business@caltech.edu
Personnel: Vi Tran (Bus. Mgr.)

CALIFORNIA LUTHERAN UNIVERSITY

Street address 1: 60 W Olsen Rd
Street address city: Thousand Oaks
Street address state: CA
Zip/Postal code: 91360-2700
Country: USA
Mailing address: 60 W Olsen Rd # 4200
Mailing city: Thousand Oaks
Mailing state: CA
Mailing zip: 91360-2787
General Phone: (805) 493-3366
General Fax: (805) 493-3479
Advertising Phone: (805) 493-3327
General/National Adv. E-mail: kelley@robles.callutheran.edu
Personnel: Colleen Cason (Advisor); Sharon Docter (Chair); Jonathan Culmer (Bus. Mgr.); Margaret Nolan (Ed. in Chief)

CALIFORNIA POLYTECHNIC STATE UNIV.

Street address 1: 1 Grand Ave
Street address city: San Luis Obispo
Street address state: CA
Zip/Postal code: 93407-9000
Country: USA
Mailing address: 1 Grand Ave
Mailing city: San Luis Obispo
Mailing state: CA
Mailing zip: 93407-9000
General Phone: (805) 756-2537
General Fax: (805) 756-6784
Advertising Phone: (805) 756-1143
Advertising Fax: (805) 756-6784
Editorial Phone: (805) 756-1796
Editorial Fax: (805) 756-6784
General/National Adv. E-mail: editor@mustangnews.net
Display Adv. E-mail: advertising@mustangnews.net
Primary Website: www.mustangnews.net
Year Established: 1916
Published: Mon`Thur
Avg Free Circ: 6000
Personnel: Paul Bittick (GM)

CALIFORNIA STATE UNIV.

Street address 1: Chico Dept. of Journalism
Street address 2: Zip 600 Chico
Street address city: Chico
Street address state: CA
Zip/Postal code: 95926
Country: USA
Mailing address: Chico Dept. of Journalism
Mailing city: Chico
Mailing state: CA
Mailing zip: 95926
General Phone: (530) 898-4237
General Fax: (530) 898-4799
Editorial Fax: (530) 898-4033
Display Adv. E-mail: advertising@theorion.com
Personnel: David Waddell (Advisor); Gillian Leeds (Bus. Mgr.); Jennifer Siino (Mng. Ed.); Mike North (News Ed.)

CALIFORNIA STATE UNIV.

Street address 1: 5201 N Maple Ave
Street address 2: MS SA42
Street address city: Fresno
Street address state: CA
Zip/Postal code: 93740-0001
Country: USA
Mailing address: 5201 N Maple Ave MS SA42
Mailing city: Fresno
Mailing state: CA
Mailing zip: 93740-0001
General Phone: (559) 278-5735
General Fax: (559) 278-2679
Editorial Phone: (559) 278-5732
General/National Adv. E-mail: collegian@csufresno.edu
Personnel: Jefferson Beavers (Advisor); Virginia Sellars-Erxleben (Bus. Mgr.); Brian Maxey (Ed. in Chief)

CALIFORNIA STATE UNIV.

Street address 1: 5151 State University Dr
Street address 2: # KH-C3098
Street address city: Los Angeles
Street address state: CA
Zip/Postal code: 90032-4226
Country: USA
Mailing address: 5151 State University Dr # KH-C3098
Mailing city: Los Angeles
Mailing state: CA
Mailing zip: 90032-4226
General Phone: (323) 343-4215
General Fax: (323) 343-5337
Editorial Fax: Free
General/National Adv. E-mail: universitytimes@yahoo.com
Display Adv. E-mail: jmunson@cslanet.calstatela.edu
Editorial e-mail: universitytimes@yahoo.com
Primary Website: www.calstatela.edu
Year Established: 1947
Personnel: Jim Munson (Business, Advt. Mgr.)

CALIFORNIA STATE UNIV.

Street address 1: 5500 University Pkwy
Street address city: San Bernardino
Street address state: CA
Zip/Postal code: 92407-2318
Country: USA
Mailing address: 5500 University Pkwy
Mailing city: San Bernardino
Mailing state: CA
Mailing zip: 92407-2318
General Phone: (909) 537-5289
General Fax: (909)-537-7072
Editorial Phone: (909) 537-5815
General/National Adv. E-mail: sbchron@csusb.edu
Personnel: Jim Smart (Advisor); Linda Sand (Adv. Mgr.); Ken Dillard (Ed. in Chief)

CALIFORNIA STATE UNIV. DOMINGUEZ

Street address 1: 1000 E Victoria St
Street address 2: Dept Sac
Street address city: Carson
Street address state: CA
Zip/Postal code: 90747-0001
Country: USA
Mailing address: 1000 E Victoria St Dept Sac
Mailing city: Carson
Mailing state: CA
Mailing zip: 90747-0001
General Phone: (310) 243-2312
General Fax: (310) 217-6935
General/National Adv. E-mail: bulletin@csudh.edu
Display Adv. E-mail: Advertise@csudh.edu
Primary Website: www.csudh.edu/bulletin/
Published: Wed
Published Other: Bi-Weekly
Personnel: Catherine Risling (Advisor); Marjan Khorashadi-Zadeh (Adv. Mgr.); Karen Mossiah (Prodn. Mgr.)

CALIFORNIA STATE UNIV. LONG BEACH

Street address 1: 1250 Bellflower Blvd
Street address 2: Sppa 010B
Street address city: Long Beach
Street address state: CA
Zip/Postal code: 90840-0004
Country: USA
Mailing address: 1250 Bellflower Blvd
Mailing city: Long Beach
Mailing state: CA
Mailing zip: 90840-4601
General Phone: (562) 985-8001
General Fax: (562) 985-1740
Advertising Phone: (562)985-5736
Editorial Phone: (562)985-8000
Display Adv. E-mail: beverly.munson@csulb.edu
Editorial e-mail: eicd49er@gmail.com
Primary Website: www.daily49er.com
Year Established: 1949
Published: Mon`Tues`Wed`Thur
Avg Free Circ: 6000
Personnel: Beverly Munson (Gen. Mgr.); Barbara Kingsley-Wilson (Advisor)

CALIFORNIA STATE UNIV., FULLERTON

Street address 1: College Park Bldg Nutwood Ave
Street address 2: Ste 2600660
Street address city: Fullerton
Street address state: CA
Zip/Postal code: 1960
Country: USA
Mailing address: College Park Bldg., 2600 E. Nutwood Ave., Ste. 660
Mailing city: Fullerton
Mailing state: CA
Mailing zip: 92831-3110
General Phone: (657) 278-4411
General Fax: (657) 278-2702
Editorial Phone: (657) 278-5815
Display Adv. E-mail: ads@dailytitan.com
Editorial e-mail: editorinchief@dailytitan.com
Primary Website: www.dailytitan.com
Year Established: 1960
Published: Mon`Tues`Wed`Thur
Avg Free Circ: 6000
Personnel: Robert Sage (Bus. Mgr.)

CALIFORNIA STATE UNIVERSITY, BAKERSFIELD

Street address 1: 9001 Stockdale Hwy
Street address city: Bakersfield
Street address state: CA
Zip/Postal code: 93311-1022
Country: USA
Mailing address: 9001 Stockdale Hwy.
Mailing city: Bakersfield
Mailing state: CA
Mailing zip: 93311-1022
General Phone: (661) 654-2165
General/National Adv. E-mail: runner@csub.edu
Primary Website: http://therunneronline.com
Year Established: 1974
Published: Wed
Published Other: Back-to-School issue - 1st Day of Fall
Personnel: Jennifer Burger (Lecturer and Adviser to the Runner Student Media Center)

CALIFORNIA STATE UNIVERSITY, EAST BAY.

Street address 1: 25800 Carlos Bee Blvd
Street address city: Hayward
Street address state: CA
Zip/Postal code: 94542-3000
Country: USA
Mailing address: 25800 Carlos Bee Blvd
Mailing city: Hayward
Mailing state: CA
Mailing zip: 94542-3001
General Phone: (510) 885-3292
General Fax: (510) 885-4099
Advertising Phone: (510) 885-3526
Advertising Fax: (510) 885-2584
Editorial Phone: (510) 885-3176
Editorial Fax: (510) 885-2584
Display Adv. E-mail: pioneer.advertising@csueastbay.edu
Editorial e-mail: pioneernewspaper@sueastbay.edu
Primary Website: http://thepioneeronline.com/
Published: Thur
Avg Free Circ: 10000

CALIFORNIA STATE UNIVERSITY, NORTHRIDGE

Street address 1: 18111 Nordhoff St
Street address city: Northridge
Street address state: CA
Zip/Postal code: 91330-0001
Country: USA
Mailing address: 18111 Nordhoff St
Mailing city: Northridge
Mailing state: CA
Mailing zip: 91330-8200
General Phone: (818) 677-3135
General Fax: (818) 677-3438
Advertising Phone: 818-677-2998
Editorial Phone: (818) 677-2915
Display Adv. E-mail: ads@sundial.csun.edu
Editorial e-mail: editor@csun.edu
Primary Website: www.csun.edu
Year Established: 1957
Published: Mon`Tues`Wed`Thur
Avg Free Circ: 6000
Personnel: Kent Kirkton (Chair/Prof.); Melissa Lalum (Pub.); Susan Henry (Prof.); Jody Holcomb (Gen. Mgr.); Maureen Rubin (Prof.); Rick Marks (Assoc. Prof.); Loren Townsley (Editor); Jose Luis Benavides (Asst. Prof.); David Blumenkrantz (Asst. Prof.); Linda Bowen (Asst. Prof.); Jim Hill (Asst. Prof.); Melissa Wall (Asst. Prof.); Lori Baker-Schena (Lectr.); Jerry Jacobs (Prof. Emer.); DeWayne Johnson (Prof. Emer.); Lawrence Schneider (Prof. Emer.); Joe Giampietro (Part-time Fac.); Henrietta Charles (Part-time Fac.); Jeffrey Duclos (Part-time Fac.); Barbara Eisenstock (Part-time Fac.); Mariel Garza (Part-time Fac.); Keith Goldstein (Part-time Fac.); Lincoln Harrison (Part-time Fac.)

CALIFORNIA STATE UNIVERSITY, SAN MARCOS

Street address 1: 333 S Twin Oaks Valley Rd
Street address city: San Marcos
Street address state: CA

Zip/Postal code: 92096-0001
Country: USA
Mailing address: 333 S Twin Oaks Valley Rd
Mailing city: San Marcos
Mailing state: CA
Mailing zip: 92096-0001
General Phone: (760) 750-6099
General Fax: (760) 750-3345
Advertising Phone: (760) 750-6099
Advertising Fax: (760) 750-3345
Editorial Phone: (760) 750-6099
Editorial Fax: Free
General/National Adv. E-mail: csusm.chronicle@gmail.com
Editorial e-mail: csusm.chronicle@gmail.com
Primary Website: www.csusmchronicle.com
Year Established: 1992
Published: Wed
Avg Free Circ: 1500
Personnel: Pam Kragen (Advisor); Morgan Hall (Co-Editor-in-Chief, Editor of Design); Kristin Melody (Co-Editor-in-Chief); Rogers Jaffarian (Advertising Manager)

CALIFORNIA STATE UNIVERSITY, STANISLAUS

Street address 1: 1 University Cir
Street address city: Turlock
Street address state: CA
Zip/Postal code: 95382-3200
Country: USA
Mailing address: 1 University Cir
Mailing city: Turlock
Mailing state: CA
Mailing zip: 95382-3200
General Phone: (209) 667-3411

CERRITOS COLLEGE

Street address 1: 11110 Alondra Blvd
Street address city: Norwalk
Street address state: CA
Zip/Postal code: 90650-6203
Country: USA
Mailing address: 11110 Alondra Blvd
Mailing city: Norwalk
Mailing state: CA
Mailing zip: 90650-6298
General Phone: (562) 860-2451
General Fax: (562) 467-5044
General/National Adv. E-mail: editor@talonmarks.com
Personnel: Rich Cameron (Advisor); Elieth Koulzons (Ed. in Chief); Rick Gomez (Online Ed.); Joey Berumen (News Ed.); Joey (News Ed.); Megan (Arts Ed.)

CHABOT COLLEGE

Street address 1: 25555 Hesperian Blvd
Street address 2: Ste 1635
Street address city: Hayward
Street address state: CA
Zip/Postal code: 94545-2447
Country: USA
Mailing address: 25555 Hesperian Blvd Ste 1635
Mailing city: Hayward
Mailing state: CA
Mailing zip: 94545-2400
General Phone: (510) 723-7082
General Fax: (510) 723-6919
General/National Adv. E-mail: chabot_spectator@hotmail.com
Personnel: Jeannie Wakeland (Advisor)

CHAFFEY COLLEGE

Street address 1: 5885 Haven Ave
Street address city: Rancho Cucamonga
Street address state: CA
Zip/Postal code: 91737-3002
Country: USA
Mailing address: 5885 Haven Ave.
Mailing city: Rancho Cucamonga
Mailing state: CA
Mailing zip: 91737
General Phone: (909) 652-6934
General/National Adv. E-mail: thebreeze@chaffey.edu
Display Adv. E-mail: michelle.dowd@chaffey.edu
Primary Website: www.thebreezeonline.com
Published: Mon`Bi-Mthly
Avg Free Circ: 3000
Personnel: Michelle Dowd (Adviser)

CHAPMAN UNIV.

Street address 1: 1 University Dr
Street address city: Orange
Street address state: CA
Zip/Postal code: 92866-1005
Country: USA
Mailing address: 1 University Dr
Mailing city: Orange
Mailing state: CA
Mailing zip: 92866-1005
General Phone: (714) 997-6870
General Fax: (714) 744-7898
General/National Adv. E-mail: panthernewspaper@gmail.com
Personnel: Amber Gonzales (Ed. in Chief); Martin Syjuco (Mng. Ed.); Michelle Thomas (Opinions Ed.); Jillian Freitas (News Ed.); Jennifer (Business Mgr.); Kim (Dir., Art)

CITRUS COLLEGE

Street address 1: 1000 W Foothill Blvd
Street address city: Glendora
Street address state: CA
Zip/Postal code: 91741-1885
Country: USA
Mailing address: 1000 W Foothill Blvd
Mailing city: Glendora
Mailing state: CA
Mailing zip: 91741-1899
General Phone: (626) 914-8586
General Fax: (626) 914-8797
General/National Adv. E-mail: ccclarion@hotmail.com
Personnel: Margaret O'Neill (Advisor); Emily Rios (Ed.)

CITY COLLEGE OF SAN FRANCISCO

Street address 1: 50 Phelan Ave
Street address 2: # V67
Street address city: San Francisco
Street address state: CA
Zip/Postal code: 94112-1821
Country: USA
Mailing address: 50 Phelan Ave # V67
Mailing city: San Francisco
Mailing state: CA
Mailing zip: 94112-1898
General Phone: (415) 239-3446
General Fax: (415) 239-3884
General/National Adv. E-mail: email@theguardsman.com
Display Adv. E-mail: advertising@theguardsman.com
Editorial e-mail: editor@theguardsman.com
Primary Website: www.theguardsman.com
Year Established: 1935
Published: Wed
Published Other: Bi-Weekly
Avg Free Circ: 7000
Personnel: Juan Gonzales (Advisor)

CLAREMONT COLLEGES

Street address 1: 175 E 8th St
Street address city: Claremont
Street address state: CA
Zip/Postal code: 91711-3956
Country: USA
Mailing address: 175 E 8th St
Mailing city: Claremont
Mailing state: CA
Mailing zip: 91711-3956
Personnel: Keith Koyano (Ed.)

CLAREMONT MCKENNA COLLEGE

Street address 1: Heggblade Ctr, 500 E 9th St
Street address city: Claremont
Street address state: CA
Zip/Postal code: 91711
Country: USA
Mailing address: Heggblade Ctr., 500 E. 9th St.
Mailing city: Claremont
Mailing state: CA
Mailing zip: 91711
Personnel: Adam Sivitz (Ed.)

COLLEGE OF MARIN

Street address 1: 835 College Ave
Street address city: Kentfield
Street address state: CA
Zip/Postal code: 94904-2551
Country: USA
Mailing address: 835 College Ave
Mailing city: Kentfield
Mailing state: CA
Mailing zip: 94904-2590
General Phone: (415) 485-9690
General Fax: (415) 485-0135
General/National Adv. E-mail: echotimes@marin.cc.ca.us
Personnel: Elisa Forsgren (Adv. Mgr.); William Kennedy (Ed. in Chief); Yukie Sano (Mng. Ed.)

COLLEGE OF SAN MATEO

Street address 1: 94402 -3757
Street address city: San Mateo
Street address state: CA
Country: USA
Mailing address: 1700 W Hillsdale Blvd
Mailing city: San Mateo
Mailing state: CA
Mailing zip: 94402-3784
General Phone: (650) 574-6330
Editorial Phone: (650) 652-6721
General/National Adv. E-mail: sanmatean@smccd.edu
Primary Website: www.sanmatean.com
Year Established: 1928
Personnel: Ed Remitz (Advisor); Margeret Baum (Ed.); Sharon Ho (Mng. Ed.); Laura Babbitt (News Ed.)

COLLEGE OF THE CANYONS

Street address 1: 26455 Rockwell Canyon Rd
Street address city: Santa Clarita
Street address state: CA
Zip/Postal code: 91355-1803
Country: USA
Mailing address: 26455 Rockwell Canyon Rd
Mailing city: Santa Clarita
Mailing state: CA
Mailing zip: 91355-1899
Personnel: Jim Ruebsamen (Advisor)

COLLEGE OF THE DESERT

Street address 1: 43500 Monterey Ave
Street address city: Palm Desert
Street address state: CA
Zip/Postal code: 92260-9305
Country: USA
Mailing address: 43500 Monterey Ave
Mailing city: Palm Desert
Mailing state: CA
Mailing zip: 92260-9399
General Phone: (760) 776-7244
General Fax: (760) 862-1338
General/National Adv. E-mail: chaparral@collegeofthedesert.edu
Personnel: Aaron White (Adv. Mgr.); Edward Grofer (Co-Ed.); Sarah Wilson (Co-Ed.)

COLLEGE OF THE SEQUOIAS

Street address 1: 915 S Mooney Blvd
Street address city: Visalia
Street address state: CA
Zip/Postal code: 93277-2214
Country: USA
Mailing address: 915 S Mooney Blvd
Mailing city: Visalia
Mailing state: CA
Mailing zip: 93277-2234
General Phone: (559) 730-3844
General Fax: (559) 730-3991
General/National Adv. E-mail: campusnews@cos.edu
Display Adv. E-mail: campusads@cos.edu
Editorial e-mail: campusnews@cos.edu
Primary Website: www.coscampusonline.com

CONTRA COSTA COLLEGE

Street address 1: 2600 Mission Bell Dr
Street address city: San Pablo
Street address state: CA
Zip/Postal code: 94806-3166
Country: USA
Mailing address: 2600 Mission Bell Dr
Mailing city: San Pablo
Mailing state: CA
Mailing zip: 94806-3195
General Phone: (510) 235-7800
General Fax: (510) 235-6397
General/National Adv. E-mail: advocate@contracosta.edu
Personnel: Paul DeBlot (Advisor); Holly Pablo (Ed. in Chief); Sam Attal (Ed.)

COSUMNES RIVER COLLEGE

Street address 1: 8401 Center Pkwy
Street address city: Sacramento
Street address state: CA
Zip/Postal code: 95823-5704
Country: USA
Mailing address: 8401 Center Pkwy
Mailing city: Sacramento
Mailing state: CA
Mailing zip: 95823-5799
General Phone: (916) 691-7471
Personnel: Yvette Lessard (Ed. in Chief); Erin Bates (Features Ed.); Bhavisha Patel (Online Ed.); Lehsee Gausi (Opinion Ed.)

CUESTA COLLEGE

Street address 1: Bldg 7400, Hwy 1
Street address city: San Luis Obispo
Street address state: CA
Zip/Postal code: 93403
Country: USA
Mailing address: PO Box 8106
Mailing city: San Luis Obispo
Mailing state: CA
Mailing zip: 93403-8106
General Phone: (805) 546-3288
General Fax: (805) 546-3904
General/National Adv. E-mail: cuestonian@cuesta.edu
Personnel: Patrick Howe (Advisor); Mary Mc Corkle (Advisor); Sarah Clifford (Ed.); Bethany Fraker (Ed.)

CUYAMACA COLLEGE

Street address 1: 900 Rancho San Diego Pkwy
Street address 2: Bldg G-109
Street address city: El Cajon
Street address state: CA
Zip/Postal code: 92019-4369
Country: USA
Mailing address: 900 Rancho San Diego Pkwy Bldg G-109
Mailing city: El Cajon
Mailing state: CA
Mailing zip: 92019-4369
General Phone: (619) 660-4000
Primary Website: www.cuyamaca.edu/coyoteexpress
Year Established: 1977
Personnel: Seth Slater (Contact); Mary Graham (Contact)

CYPRESS COLLEGE CHRONICLE

Street address 1: 9200 Valley View St
Street address city: Cypress
Street address state: CA
Zip/Postal code: 90630-5805
Country: USA
Mailing address: 9200 Valley View St.
Mailing city: Cypress
Mailing state: CA
Mailing zip: 90630-5805
General Phone: 714-484-7267
General Fax: (714) 484-7466
Advertising Phone: 714-484-7268
Editorial Phone: 714-484-7269
General/National Adv. E-mail: rmercer@cypresscollege.edu
Primary Website: www.cychron.com
Year Established: 1966
Published: Mthly
Avg Free Circ: 4000
Personnel: Robert Mercer (Advisor)

DE ANZA COLLEGE

Street address 1: 21250 Stevens Creek Blvd
Street address 2: Rm L-41
Street address city: Cupertino
Street address state: CA
Zip/Postal code: 95014-5702
Country: USA
Mailing address: 21250 Stevens Creek Blvd Rm L-41
Mailing city: Cupertino

Mailing state: CA
Mailing zip: 95014-5797
General Phone: (408) 864-5626
Advertising Phone: (408) 864-5626
Editorial Fax: Free
General/National Adv. E-mail: lavoz@fhda.edu
Display Adv. E-mail: lavozadvertising@gmail.com
Editorial e-mail: lavoz@fhda.edu
Primary Website: www.lavozdeanza.com
Year Established: 1967
Published: Mon`Bi-Mthly
Published Other: 16 issues from late September to mid-June
Avg Free Circ: 2200
Personnel: Cecilia Deck (Journalism Chair)

DIABLO VALLEY COLLEGE

Street address 1: 321 Golf Club Rd
Street address city: Pleasant Hill
Street address state: CA
Zip/Postal code: 94523-1529
Country: USA
Mailing address: 321 Golf Club Rd
Mailing city: Pleasant Hill
Mailing state: CA
Mailing zip: 94523-1544
General Phone: (925) 685-1230
General Fax: (925) 681-3045
General/National Adv. E-mail: inquirer@dvc.edu
Personnel: Ann Stenmark (Adv. Mgr.); Ashley Pittson (Ed.); Catharine Ahr (Ed.); Barbara (Ed.)

DOMINICAN COLLEGE

Street address 1: 50 Acacia Ave
Street address city: San Rafael
Street address state: CA
Zip/Postal code: 94901-2230
Country: USA
Mailing address: 50 Acacia Ave
Mailing city: San Rafael
Mailing state: CA
Mailing zip: 94901-2298
General Phone: (415) 485-3204
Personnel: Melva Bealf (Advisor)

EAST LOS ANGELES COLLEGE

Street address 1: 1301 Avenida Cesar Chavez
Street address city: Monterey Park
Street address state: CA
Zip/Postal code: 91754-6001
Country: USA
Mailing address: 1301 Avenida Cesar Chavez
Mailing city: Monterey Park
Mailing state: CA
Mailing zip: 91754-6001
General Phone: (323) 265-8821
Advertising Phone: (323) 265-8821
Editorial Phone: (323) 265-8819
General/National Adv. E-mail: Elaccampusnews@gmail.com
Display Adv. E-mail: jonfanie@yahoo.com
Editorial e-mail: elaccampusnews@gmail.com
Primary Website: elaccampusnews.com
Mthly Avg Views: 19,4
Year Established: 1945
Published: Wed`Other
Published Other: Not published in summer or January. Weekly during school year.
Avg Free Circ: 2000
Personnel: Jean Stapleton (Adviser); Sylvia Rico-Sanchez (Co-Adviser)

EL CAMINO COLLEGE

Street address 1: 16007 Crenshaw Blvd
Street address 2: Rm H-113
Street address city: Torrance
Street address state: CA
Zip/Postal code: 90506-0001
County: Los Angeles
Country: USA
Mailing address: 16007 Crenshaw Blvd.
Mailing city: Torrance
Mailing state: CA
Mailing zip: 90506
General Phone: (310) 660-3328
General Fax: (310) 660-6092
Advertising Phone: (310) 660-3329
Editorial Phone: (310) 660-3328
General/National Adv. E-mail: eccunion@gmail.com
Display Adv. E-mail: elcounionads000@yahoo.com
Editorial e-mail: eccunion@gmail.com
Primary Website: eccunion.com
Year Established: 1946
Published: Wed
Published Other: Twice per month
Avg Free Circ: 5000
Personnel: Jack Mulkey (Adv. Mgr.); Kate McLaughlin (Adviser); Stefanie Frith (Adviser); Gary Kohatsu (Photo Adviser)

EVERGREEN VALLEY COLLEGE

Street address 1: 3095 Yerba Buena Rd
Street address city: San Jose
Street address state: CA
Zip/Postal code: 95135-1513
Country: USA
Mailing address: 3095 Yerba Buena Rd
Mailing city: San Jose

FOOTHILL COLLEGE

Street address 1: 12345 S El Monte Rd
Street address city: Los Altos Hills
Street address state: CA
Zip/Postal code: 94022-4504
Country: USA
Mailing address: 12345 S El Monte Rd
Mailing city: Los Altos Hills
Mailing state: CA
Mailing zip: 94022-4597
General Phone: (650) 949-7372
Personnel: Drew Dara Abrams (Ed.)

FRESNO CITY COLLEGE

Street address 1: 1101 E University Ave
Street address city: Fresno
Street address state: CA
Zip/Postal code: 93741-0001
Country: USA
Mailing address: 1101 E University Ave
Mailing city: Fresno
Mailing state: CA
Mailing zip: 93741-0002
General Phone: (559) 442-8262
General Fax: (559) 265-5783
General/National Adv. E-mail: rampage-news@fresnocitycollege.edu
Personnel: Dynpna Ugwu-Oju (Advisor); Leah Edward (Adv. Mgr.); Ramiro Gudino (Prodn. Mgr.)

FULLER THEOLOGICAL SEMINARY

Street address 1: 135 N Oakland Ave
Street address city: Pasadena
Street address state: CA
Zip/Postal code: 91182-0001
Country: USA
Mailing address: 135 N Oakland Ave
Mailing city: Pasadena
Mailing state: CA
Mailing zip: 91182-0002
Personnel: Carmen Valdez (Advisor); Eugene Suen (Adv. Mgr.); Ben Cassil (Ed.)

FULLERTON COLLEGE

Street address 1: 321 E Chapman Ave
Street address city: Fullerton
Street address state: CA
Zip/Postal code: 92832-2011
Country: USA
Mailing address: 321 E Chapman Ave
Mailing city: Fullerton
Mailing state: CA
Mailing zip: 92832-2095
General Phone: (714) 992-7154
General Fax: (714) 447-4097
General/National Adv. E-mail: hornet@fullcoll.edu
Primary Website: www.fullcoll.edu
Year Established: 1922
Published: Wed
Personnel: Jay Seidel (Advisor)

GAVILAN COLLEGE

Street address 1: 5055 Santa Teresa Blvd
Street address city: Gilroy
Street address state: CA
Zip/Postal code: 95020-9578
Country: USA
Mailing address: 5055 Santa Teresa Blvd
Mailing city: Gilroy
Mailing state: CA
Mailing zip: 95020-9599
General Phone: (408) 848-4837
Published: Bi-Mthly
Avg Free Circ: 0
Personnel: Esmeralda Montenegro (Faculty Advisor)

GLENDALE CMTY. COLLEGE

Street address 1: 1500 N Verdugo Rd
Street address 2: Rm AD212
Street address city: Glendale
Street address state: CA
Zip/Postal code: 91208-2809
Country: USA
Mailing address: 1500 N Verdugo Rd Rm AD212
Mailing city: Glendale
Mailing state: CA
Mailing zip: 91208-2809
General Phone: (818) 551-5214
Personnel: Michael Moreau (Advisor); Jeff Smith (Classified Mgr.)

GOLDEN GATE UNIV.

Street address 1: 536 Mission St
Street address city: San Francisco
Street address state: CA
Zip/Postal code: 94105-2921
Country: USA
Mailing address: 536 Mission St
Mailing city: San Francisco
Mailing state: CA
Mailing zip: 94105-2968
General Phone: (415) 442-7871
General Fax: (415) 442-7896
General/National Adv. E-mail: campuscurrent@gguol.ggu.edu
Personnel: Brian Louie (Vice Pres., PR/Mktg.); Ambrose Tse (Vice Pres., Finance/Admin.)

GOLDEN WEST COLLEGE

Street address 1: 15744 Goldenwest St
Street address 2: Rm 138
Street address city: Huntington Beach
Street address state: CA
Zip/Postal code: 92647-3103
Country: USA
Mailing address: 15744 Goldenwest St Rm 138
Mailing city: Huntington Beach
Mailing state: CA
Mailing zip: 92647-3103
General Phone: (714) 895-8786
General Fax: (714) 895-8795
Advertising Phone: 714-315-9450
Advertising Fax: (714) 895-8795
General/National Adv. E-mail: twsatgwc@aol.com
Display Adv. E-mail: gwckcumper@yahoo.com
Primary Website: www.westernsun.us; www.goldenwestcollege.edu/westernsun
Year Established: 1966
Published: Bi-Mthly
Avg Free Circ: 15000
Personnel: Jim Tortolano (Advisor); Katie Cumper (Adv. Dir.); Lanace Tonelli (Exec. Ed.); Opal McClain (Opinion Ed.); Fernando (Sports Ed.)

GROSSMONT COLLEGE

Street address 1: 8800 Grossmont College Dr
Street address city: El Cajon
Street address state: CA
Zip/Postal code: 92020-1765
Country: USA
Mailing address: 8800 Grossmont College Dr
Mailing city: El Cajon
Mailing state: CA
Mailing zip: 92020-1798
Advertising Phone: (619) 644-7271
Advertising Fax: (619) 644-7914
Editorial Phone: (619) 644-1730
General/National Adv. E-mail: summit@gcccd.edu
Primary Website: gcsummit.com
Published: Mthly

HASTINGS COLLEGE OF LAW

Street address 1: 200 McAllister St
Street address city: San Francisco
Street address state: CA
Zip/Postal code: 94102-4707
Country: USA
Mailing address: 200 McAllister St
Mailing city: San Francisco
Mailing state: CA
Mailing zip: 94102-4978
Personnel: John Hendrickson (Ed.)

HUMBOLDT STATE UNIV.

Street address 1: 1 Harpst St
Street address 2: Gist Hall 227
Street address city: Arcata
Street address state: CA
Zip/Postal code: 95521-8222
Country: USA
Mailing address: 1 Harpst Street
Mailing city: Arcata
Mailing state: CA
Mailing zip: 95521-8299
General Phone: (707) 826-3271
Advertising Phone: (707) 826-5921
General/National Adv. E-mail: thejack@humboldt.edu
Personnel: Marcy Burstiner (Advisor); Sara Wilmot (Ed.)

JOHN F. KENNEDY UNIVERSITY

Street address 1: 100 Ellinwood Way
Street address city: Pleasant Hill
Street address state: CA
Zip/Postal code: 94523-4817
Country: USA
Mailing address: 100 Ellinwood Way
Mailing city: Pleasant Hill
Mailing state: CA
Mailing zip: 94523-4817

LANEY COLLEGE

Street address 1: 900 Fallon St
Street address city: Oakland
Street address state: CA
Zip/Postal code: 94607-4808
Country: USA
Mailing address: 900 Fallon St # 160
Mailing city: Oakland
Mailing state: CA
Mailing zip: 94607-4893
General Phone: (510) 464-3460
General Fax: (510) 834-3452
General/National Adv. E-mail: laneytower@peralta.edu
Primary Website: www.laneytower.com
Published: Thur
Published Other: Every other week
Personnel: Burt Dragin (Advisor); Scott Strain (Sports Ed.); Felix Solomon (Technical Ed.)

LASSEN CMTY. COLLEGE

Street address 1: 478-200 Hwy 139
Street address city: Susanville
Street address state: CA
Zip/Postal code: 96130
Country: USA
Mailing address: PO Box 3000
Mailing city: Susanville
Mailing state: CA
Mailing zip: 96130-3000
General Phone: (530) 251-8821
General Fax: (530) 251-8839
General/National Adv. E-mail: trougar@lassen.cc.ca.us
Personnel: Andrew Owen (Ed. in Chief)

LOMA LINDA UNIV.

Street address 1: 11041 Anderson St
Street address city: Loma Linda
Street address state: CA
Zip/Postal code: 92350-1737
Country: USA
Mailing address: Anderson St Burden Hall 11041
Mailing city: Loma Linda
Mailing state: CA

Mailing zip: 92350-0001

LONG BEACH CITY COLLEGE

Street address 1: 4901 E Carson St
Street address 2: Mail Drop Y-16
Street address city: Long Beach
Street address state: CA
Zip/Postal code: 90808-1706
Country: USA
Mailing address: 4901 E Carson St Mail Drop Y-16
Mailing city: Long Beach
Mailing state: CA
Mailing zip: 90808-1780
General Phone: (562) 938-4284
General Fax: (562) 938-4948
General/National Adv. E-mail: vikingnews@lbcc.edu
Primary Website: www.lbccvikingnews.com
Year Established: 1927
Personnel: Patrick McKean (Advisor); Kori Filipek (Adv. Mgr.); Michel Simmons (Co-Ed. in Chief)

LOS ANGELES CITY COLLEGE

Street address 1: 855 N Vermont Ave
Street address city: Los Angeles
Street address state: CA
Zip/Postal code: 90029-3516
Country: USA
Mailing address: 855 N Vermont Ave
Mailing city: Los Angeles
Mailing state: CA
Mailing zip: 90029-3588
Personnel: Rhonda Guess (Advisor)

LOS ANGELES HARBOR COLLEGE

Street address 1: 1300 S Pacific Ave
Street address city: San Pedro
Street address state: CA
Zip/Postal code: 90731-4108
Country: USA
Mailing address: PO Box 731
Mailing city: San Pedro
Mailing state: CA
Mailing zip: 90733-0731
General Phone: (310) 519-1016
General Fax: (310) 832-1000
Advertising Fax: 1310 832-1000
Editorial Phone: (310) 519-1442
Display Adv. E-mail: rlnsales@randomlengthsnews.com
Editorial e-mail: editor@randomlengthsnews.com
Primary Website: www.randomlengthsnews.com
Year Established: 1979
Published: Thur`Bi-Mthly
Personnel: James Preston Allen (Pub.); Paul Rosenberg (Mng. Ed.); Terelle Jerricks (Mng Ed)

LOS ANGELES PIERCE COLLEGE

Street address 1: 6201 Winnetka Ave
Street address 2: # 8212
Street address city: Woodland Hills
Street address state: CA
Zip/Postal code: 91371-0001
Country: USA
Mailing address: 6201 Winnetka Ave # 8212
Mailing city: Woodland Hills
Mailing state: CA
Mailing zip: 91371-0001
General Phone: (818) 719-6483
General Fax: (818) 719-6447
Advertising Phone: (818) 710-2960
Advertising Fax: (818) 719-6447
Editorial Phone: (818) 719-6427
Editorial Fax: (818) 719-6447
General/National Adv. E-mail: newsroom.roundupnews@gmail.com
Display Adv. E-mail: baileyjd@piercecollege.edu
Editorial e-mail: newsroom.roundupnews@gmail.com
Primary Website: www.theroundupnews.com
Year Established: 1949
Published: Wed
Avg Free Circ: 5000
Personnel: Jill Connelly (Dept. Chrmn.); Julie Bailey (Office Mgr./Adv. Mgr.); Stefanie Frith (Adviser to the Roundup newspaper)

LOS ANGELES VALLEY COLLEGE

Street address 1: 5800 Fulton Ave
Street address city: Valley Glen
Street address state: CA
Zip/Postal code: 91401-4062
Country: USA
Mailing address: 5800 Fulton Ave
Mailing city: Valley Glen
Mailing state: CA
Mailing zip: 91401-4062
General Phone: (818) 947-2576
General Fax: (818) 947-2610
General/National Adv. E-mail: valleystar@lavalleystar.com
Personnel: Rod Lyons (Advisor); Bill Dauber (Advisor); Sarah Knowles (Ed.); Lucas Thompson (Mng. Ed.)

LOS MEDANOS COLLEGE

Street address 1: 2700 E Leland Rd
Street address city: Pittsburg
Street address state: CA
Zip/Postal code: 94565-5107
Country: USA
Mailing address: 2700 E Leland Rd
Mailing city: Pittsburg
Mailing state: CA
Mailing zip: 94565-5197
General Phone: (925) 439-2181
Primary Website: www.losmedanos.edu
Year Established: 1974
Personnel: Cindy McGrath (Advisor)

LOYOLA MARYMOUNT UNIV.

Street address 1: 1 Lmu Dr
Street address 2: Ste 8470
Street address city: Los Angeles
Street address state: CA
Zip/Postal code: 90045-2682
Country: USA
Mailing address: 1 Lmu Dr Ste 8470
Mailing city: Los Angeles
Mailing state: CA
Mailing zip: 90045-2682
General Phone: (310) 338-7509
General Fax: (310) 338-7887
General/National Adv. E-mail: loyolan@lmu.edu; editor@theloyolan.com
Personnel: Tom Nelson (Advisor); Gil Searano (Ed.); Samantha Eisner (Adv. Sales Mgr.); Jose Martinez (Ed. in Chief); Heather Chong (Managing Ed.); Emily (Mng. Ed.); Laura (News Ed.)

MENDOCINO COLLEGE

Street address 1: 1000 Hensley Creek Rd
Street address city: Ukiah
Street address state: CA
Zip/Postal code: 95482-7821
Country: USA
Mailing address: 1000 Hensley Creek Rd
Mailing city: Ukiah
Mailing state: CA
Mailing zip: 95482-3017
Personnel: Debra Wallace (Ed.)

MENLO COLLEGE

Street address 1: 1000 El Camino Real
Street address city: Atherton
Street address state: CA
Zip/Postal code: 94027-4300
County: San Mateo County
Country: USA
Mailing address: 1000 El Camino Real
Mailing city: Atherton
Mailing state: CA
Mailing zip: 94027-4301
General Phone: (650) 543-3786
General/National Adv. E-mail: pr@menlo.edu
Personnel: Priscila de Souza (Dean of Enrollment Management)

MILLS COLLEGE

Street address 1: 157 Rothwell Ctr, 5000 MacArthur Blvd
Street address city: Oakland
Street address state: CA
Zip/Postal code: 94613
Country: USA
Mailing address: 157 Rothwell Ctr., 5000 MacArthur Blvd.
Mailing city: Oakland
Mailing state: CA
Mailing zip: 94613
General Phone: (510) 430-2246
General Fax: (510) 430-3176
General/National Adv. E-mail: eic@thecampanil.com
Display Adv. E-mail: ads@thecampanil.com
Personnel: Sarah Pollock (Advisor); Jennifer Courtney (Ed. in Chief); Rashida Harmon (Mng. Ed.); Morgan Ross (News Ed.); Nicole (Opinion Ed.); Anna Belle (Features Ed.)

MIRACOSTA COLLEGE

Street address 1: 1 Barnard Dr
Street address 2: Rm 3441
Street address city: Oceanside
Street address state: CA
Zip/Postal code: 92056-3820
Country: USA
Mailing address: 1 Barnard Dr Rm 3441
Mailing city: Oceanside
Mailing state: CA
Mailing zip: 92056-3820
General Phone: (760) 757-2121
Personnel: Meghan Sills (Staff Writer)

MODESTO JUNIOR COLLEGE

Street address 1: 435 College Ave
Street address city: Modesto
Street address state: CA
Zip/Postal code: 95350-5808
Country: USA
Mailing address: 435 College Ave
Mailing city: Modesto
Mailing state: CA
Mailing zip: 95350-5800
General Phone: (209) 575-6223
General Fax: (209) 575-6612
Personnel: Laura Paull (Advisor)

MOORPARK COLLEGE

Street address 1: 7075 Campus Rd
Street address city: Moorpark
Street address state: CA
Zip/Postal code: 93021-1605
Country: USA
Mailing address: 7075 Campus Rd.
Mailing city: Moorpark
Mailing state: CA
Mailing zip: 93021-1605
General Phone: (805) 378-1552
General Fax: (805) 378-1438
General/National Adv. E-mail: studentvoice@vcccd.edu
Personnel: Joanna Miller (Advisor)

NOTRE DAME DE NAMUR UNIVERSITY

Street address 1: 1500 Ralston Ave
Street address city: Belmont
Street address state: CA
Zip/Postal code: 94002-1908
Country: USA
Mailing address: 1500 Ralston Ave
Mailing city: Belmont
Mailing state: CA
Mailing zip: 94002-1997
General Phone: (650) 508-3500
General Fax: (650) 508-3487
General/National Adv. E-mail: argonaut@ndnu.edu
Personnel: Danielle Russo (Adv. Mgr.); Victor Gonzales (Ed.)

OCCIDENTAL COLLEGE

Street address 1: 1600 Campus Rd
Street address 2: # M-40
Street address city: Los Angeles
Street address state: CA
Zip/Postal code: 90041-3314
Country: USA
Mailing address: 1600 Campus Rd # M-40
Mailing city: Los Angeles
Mailing state: CA
Mailing zip: 90041-3314
General Phone: (323) 259-2886
General Fax: (323) 341-4982
General/National Adv. E-mail: weekly@oxy.edu
Primary Website: www.oxyweekly.com
Year Established: 1893
Personnel: Riley Hooper (Ed. in Chief); Ben Dalgetty (Ed. in Chief); Ashly Burch (Mng. Ed.); Marty Cramer (Asst. Opinion Ed.); Elana (Bus. Mgr.); Tucker (Adv. Mgr.)

OHLONE COLLEGE

Street address 1: 43600 Mission Blvd
Street address city: Fremont
Street address state: CA
Zip/Postal code: 94539-5847
Country: USA
Mailing address: PO Box 3909
Mailing city: Fremont
Mailing state: CA
Mailing zip: 94539-0390
General Phone: (510) 659-6074
General Fax: (510) 659-6076
General/National Adv. E-mail: monitor@ohlone.edu; monitor@ohlone.cc.ca.us
Primary Website: www.ohlonemonitoronline.com
Published Other: Nine times per semester
Personnel: Rob Dennis (Adviser)

ORANGE COAST COLLEGE

Street address 1: 2701 Fairview Rd
Street address city: Costa Mesa
Street address state: CA
Zip/Postal code: 92626-5563
Country: USA
Mailing address: 2701 Fairview Rd
Mailing city: Costa Mesa
Mailing state: CA
Mailing zip: 92626-5561
General Phone: (714) 432-5561
General Fax: (714) 432-5978
Advertising Phone: 714-432-5978
Advertising Fax: 714-432-5673
Editorial Phone: 714-432-5561
Editorial Fax: 714-432-5673
Display Adv. E-mail: coastreportads@yahoo.com
Editorial e-mail: editor@coastreportonline.com; coastreport@yahoo.com
Primary Website: www.coastreportonline.com
Year Established: 1948
Personnel: Cathy Werblin (Advisor)

OXNARD COLLEGE

Street address 1: 4000 S Rose Ave
Street address city: Oxnard
Street address state: CA
Zip/Postal code: 93033-6699
Country: USA
Mailing address: 4000 S Rose Ave
Mailing city: Oxnard
Mailing state: CA

PACIFIC UNION COLLEGE

Street address 1: 1 Angwin Ave
Street address 2: Campus Ctr.
Street address city: Angwin
Street address state: CA
Zip/Postal code: 94508-9713
Country: USA
Mailing address: 1 Angwin Ave
Mailing city: Angwin
Mailing state: CA
Mailing zip: 94508-9797
General Phone: (707) 965-6747
General Fax: (707) 965-7123
General/National Adv. E-mail: cc@puc.edu
Personnel: Tammy McGuire (Advisor); Peter Katz (Ed.)

PALOMAR COLLEGE

Street address 1: 1140 W Mission Rd
Street address 2: Rm CH-7
Street address city: San Marcos
Street address state: CA
Zip/Postal code: 92069-1415
Country: USA
Mailing address: 1140 W Mission Rd Rm CH-7
Mailing city: San Marcos
Mailing state: CA
Mailing zip: 92069-1487
General Phone: (760) 744-1150
General Fax: (760) 744-8123

General/National Adv. E-mail: telescopead@palomar.edu
Primary Website: www.the-telescope.com
Year Established: 1946
Personnel: Erin Hiro (Advisor); Sara Burbidge (Adv. Mgr.); Kelley Foyt (Co-Ed. in Chief)

PASADENA CITY COLLEGE

Street address 1: 1570 E Colorado Blvd
Street address 2: Rm T110-A
Street address city: Pasadena
Street address state: CA
Zip/Postal code: 91106-2003
Country: USA
Mailing address: 1570 E Colorado Blvd Rm T110-A
Mailing city: Pasadena
Mailing state: CA
Mailing zip: 91106-2041
General Phone: (626) 585-7130
General Fax: (626) 585-7971
Advertising Phone: (626) 585-7979
General/National Adv. E-mail: pasadenacourier@yahoo.com
Display Adv. E-mail: courierads@yahoo.com
Personnel: Warren Swil (Advisor); John Avery (Adv. Mgr.); Barbara Beaser (Ed. in Chief)

PEPPERDINE UNIV.

Street address 1: 24255 Pacific Coast Hwy
Street address city: Malibu
Street address state: CA
Zip/Postal code: 90263-0001
Country: USA
Mailing address: 24255 Pacific Coast Hwy
Mailing city: Malibu
Mailing state: CA
Mailing zip: 90263-3999
General Phone: (310) 506-4318
General Fax: (310) 506-4411
Display Adv. E-mail: graphicadvertising@pepperdine.edu
Personnel: Elizabeth Smith (Advisor); Amanda Gordon (Adv. Dir.); Ryan Hagen (Ed. in Chief)

POINT LOMA NAZARENE UNIV.

Street address 1: 3900 Lomaland Dr
Street address city: San Diego
Street address state: CA
Zip/Postal code: 92106-2810
Country: USA
Mailing address: 3900 Lomaland Dr
Mailing city: San Diego
Mailing state: CA
Mailing zip: 92106-2899
General Phone: (619) 849-2444
General Fax: (619) 849-7009
General/National Adv. E-mail: news@pointweekly.com; sports@pointweekly.com; advertising@pointweekly.com
Personnel: Stephanie Gant (Adv. Mgr.); Dean Nelson (Journalism Dir.); Coco Jones (Ed. in Chief); Nathan Scharn (Features Ed.)

POMONA COLLEGE

Street address 1: Smith Campus Ctr.
Street address 2: Pomona College
Street address city: Claremont
Street address state: CA
Zip/Postal code: 91711
Country: USA
Mailing address: Smith Campus Ctr.
Mailing city: Claremont
Mailing state: CA
Mailing zip: 91711-7003
General Phone: (909) 607-6709
General/National Adv. E-mail: info@tsl.pomona.edu
Display Adv. E-mail: business@tsl.pomona.edu
Editorial e-mail: editor@tsl.pomona.edu
Primary Website: www.tsl.pomona.edu
Year Established: 1889
Published: Fri
Avg Free Circ: 2000
Personnel: Ian Gallogly; Adam Belzberg (Business Manager); Jeff Zalesin (Editor-in-Chief)

RANDY VANDERMEY

Street address 1: 132 Walnut Ln
Street address city: Santa Barbara
Street address state: CA
Zip/Postal code: 93111-2148
Country: (805) 683-1115
Mailing address: 132 Walnut Lane
Mailing city: Santa Barbara
Mailing state: CA
Mailing zip: 93111
General Phone: 8056831115;8054034251cell
General Fax: 8056831115;8054034251cell
Advertising Phone: (805) 683-1115
Advertising Fax: (805) 683-1115
Editorial Phone: (805) 683-1115
Editorial Fax: 8056831115;8054034251cell
General/National Adv. E-mail: vanderme@westmont.edu
Display Adv. E-mail: horizon@westmont.edu
Editorial e-mail: horizon@westmont.edu
Primary Website: http://horizon.westmont.edu/pages/contact
Year Established: c. 1945
Published: Tues
Avg Free Circ: 800
Personnel: Randy VanderMey (Advisor); M<itchell MacMahon (Editor-in-Chief)

RIO HONDO COLLEGE

Street address 1: 3600 Workman Mill Rd
Street address city: Whittier
Street address state: CA
Zip/Postal code: 90601-1616
Country: USA
Mailing address: 3600 Workman Mill Rd
Mailing city: Whittier
Mailing state: CA
Mailing zip: 90601-1699
General Phone: (562) 908-3453
General Fax: (562) 463-4641
General/National Adv. E-mail: elpaisano@riohondo.edu
Personnel: John Francis (Advisor); Mary Cowan (Ed. in Chief); Salomon Baeza (Ed. in Chief); James Tapparo (Adv. Dir.); Kathy (Exec. Dir.)

RIVERSIDE CMTY. COLLEGE

Street address 1: 4800 Magnolia Ave
Street address city: Riverside
Street address state: CA
Zip/Postal code: 92506-1201
Country: USA
Mailing address: 4800 Magnolia Ave
Mailing city: Riverside
Mailing state: CA
Mailing zip: 92506-1201
General Phone: (951) 222-8488
General Fax: (951) 328-3505
General/National Adv. E-mail: viewpoints@rcc.edu
Personnel: Allan Lovelace (Advisor); Stephanie Holland (Ed. in Chief); Chanelle Williams (Mng. Ed.); Vanessa Soto (Adv. Mgr.); Lauren (Photo Ed.)

SACRAMENTO CITY COLLEGE

Street address 1: 3835 Freeport Blvd
Street address city: Sacramento
Street address state: CA
Zip/Postal code: 95822-1318
Country: USA
Mailing address: 3835 Freeport Blvd
Mailing city: Sacramento
Mailing state: CA
Mailing zip: 95822-1386
General Phone: (916) 558-2562
General Fax: (916) 558-2282
General/National Adv. E-mail: express@scc.losrios.edu
Personnel: Dianne Heimer (Advisor); Hannah Ucol (Adv. Mgr.); Cecilio Padilla (Ed.)

SACRAMENTO STATE

Street address 1: 6000 J St
Street address city: Sacramento
Street address state: CA
Zip/Postal code: 95819-2605
Country: USA
Mailing address: 6000 J Street
Mailing city: Sacramento
Mailing state: CA
Mailing zip: 95819
General Phone: 9162786584
Advertising Phone: 9162784092
General/National Adv. E-mail: editor@statehornet.com
Display Adv. E-mail: ads@statehornet.com
Editorial e-mail: editor@statehornet.com
Primary Website: 6000 J Street
Year Established: 1949
Published: Wed
Personnel: Stu VanAirsdale (Faculty Adviser)

SADDLEBACK COLLEGE

Street address 1: 28000 Marguerite Pkwy
Street address city: Mission Viejo
Street address state: CA
Zip/Postal code: 92692-3635
Country: USA
General Phone: (626) 815-6000
Advertising Phone: (863) 604-9460
Editorial Phone: (863) 604-9460
Editorial Fax: (863) 604-9460
General/National Adv. E-mail: clause@apu.edu
Display Adv. E-mail: tim.posada@gmail.com
Editorial e-mail: tim.posada@gmail.com
Primary Website: www.lariatnews.com
Year Established: 1967
Published: Wed
Personnel: Tim Posada (Advisor)

SAINT MARY'S COLLEGE OF CALIFORNIA

Street address 1: 1928 Saint Marys Rd
Street address city: Moraga
Street address state: CA
Zip/Postal code: 94556-2715
Country: USA
Mailing address: P.O. Box 4407
Mailing city: Moraga
Mailing state: CA
Mailing zip: 94575-4407
General Phone: (925) 631-4279
Advertising Phone: (925) 421-1515
Editorial Fax: Free
General/National Adv. E-mail: staff@stmaryscollegian.com
Display Adv. E-mail: collegianads@gmail.com
Primary Website: www.stmaryscollegian.com
Year Established: 1903
Published: Tues
Avg Free Circ: 1000
Personnel: Shawny Anderson (Advisor); Charlie Guese (Co-Editor-in-Chief); Sara DeSantis (Co-Editor-in-Chief); Michael Bruer (Ed. in Chief)

SAN BERNARDINO VALLEY COLLEGE

Street address 1: 701 S Mount Vernon Ave
Street address city: San Bernardino
Street address state: CA
Zip/Postal code: 92410-2705
Country: USA
Mailing address: 701 S Mount Vernon Ave
Mailing city: San Bernardino
Mailing state: CA
Mailing zip: 92410-2798
General Phone: (909) 888-1996
Personnel: Gary Kellam (Ed.)

SAN DIEGO CITY COLLEGE

Street address 1: 1313 Park Blvd
Street address 2: Rm T-316
Street address city: San Diego
Street address state: CA
Zip/Postal code: 92101-4712
Country: USA
Mailing address: 1313 Park Blvd Rm T-316
Mailing city: San Diego
Mailing state: CA
Mailing zip: 92101-4787
General Phone: (619) 388-4026
General Fax: (619) 388-3814
General/National Adv. E-mail: citytimes@gmail.com
Display Adv. E-mail: ads.citytimes@gmail.com
Personnel: Roman Koenig (Advisor); Vanessa Gomez (Ed. in Chief)

SAN DIEGO MIRAMAR COLLEGE

Street address 1: 10440 Black Mountain Rd
Street address city: San Diego
Street address state: CA
Zip/Postal code: 92126-2910
Country: USA
Mailing address: 10440 Black Mountain Rd
Mailing city: San Diego
Mailing state: CA
Mailing zip: 92126-2999
General Phone: (619) 388-7800
Personnel: Leslie Klipper (Advisor); Sandy Treivasan (Advertisments)

SAN DIEGO STATE UNIV.

Street address 1: EBA-2
Street address city: San Diego
Street address state: CA
Zip/Postal code: 92182-0001
Country: USA
Mailing address: EBA-2
Mailing city: San Diego
Mailing state: CA
Mailing zip: 92182-0001
General Phone: (619) 594-1804
General Fax: (619) 594-1804
Advertising Phone: (619) 594-6977
General/National Adv. E-mail: daads@mail.sdsu.edu
Primary Website: 2259 Birds Nest
Year Established: 1913
Published: Wed
Avg Free Circ: 5000
Personnel: Andrew Dyer

SAN FRANCISCO STATE UNIVERSITY

Street address 1: 1600 Holloway Ave
Street address city: San Francisco
Street address state: CA
Zip/Postal code: 94132-1722
Country: USA
Mailing address: 1600 Holloway Ave # 4200
Mailing city: San Francisco
Mailing state: CA
Mailing zip: 94132-1740
General Phone: (415) 338-1689
General Fax: (415) 338-2084
General/National Adv. E-mail: jour@sfsu.edu
Primary Website: www.journalism.sfsu.edu
Year Established: 1934
Personnel: Venise Wagner (Dept. Chair/Assoc. Prof.); Jon Funabiki (Assoc. Dept. Chair/Prof.); Dottie Katzeff (Adv. Mgr.); John Burks (Prof.); Barbara Landes (Prodn. Mgr.); Nathan Codd (Ed. in Chief); Yvonne Daley (Prof.); Kenneth Kobre (Prof.); Erna R. Smith (Prof.); Rachele Kanigel (Assoc. Prof.); Austin Long-Scott (Assoc. Prof.); Cristina Azocar (Asst. Prof./Dir., Ctr. for Integration/Improvement of Journalism); Yumi Wilson (Asst. Prof.); John T. Johnson (Prof. Emer.); B.H. Liebes (Prof. Emer.); Betty Medsger (Prof. Emer.); Leonard Sellers (Prof. Emer.); Jerrold Werthimer (Prof. Emer.); Harriet Chiang (Lectr.); Roland DeWolk (Lectr.); Jesse Garnier (Lectr.); David Greene (Lectr.); Sibylla Herbrich (Lectr.)

SAN JOAQUIN DELTA COLLEGE

Street address 1: 5151 Pacific Ave
Street address 2: Shima 203
Street address city: Stockton
Street address state: CA
Zip/Postal code: 95207-6304
Country: USA
Mailing address: 5151 Pacific Ave Shima 203
Mailing city: Stockton
Mailing state: CA
Mailing zip: 95207-6370
General Phone: (209) 954-5156
General Fax: (209) 954-5288
General/National Adv. E-mail: deltacollegian@gmail.com
Personnel: Bill Davis (Advisor); Junifer Mamsaang (Ed. in Chief)

SAN JOSE CITY COLLEGE

Street address 1: 2100 Moorpark Ave
Street address city: San Jose
Street address state: CA
Zip/Postal code: 95128-2723
Country: USA
Mailing address: 2100 Moorpark Ave
Mailing city: San Jose
Mailing state: CA
Mailing zip: 95128-2799

General Phone: (408) 298-2181

SAN JOSE STATE UNIV.

Street address 1: 1 Washington Sq
Street address city: San Jose
Street address state: CA
Zip/Postal code: 95112-3613
Country: USA
Mailing address: 1 Washington Sq
Mailing city: San Jose
Mailing state: CA
Mailing zip: 95112-3613
General Phone: (408) 924-3281
General Fax: (408) 924-3282
Advertising Phone: (408) 924-3270
General/National Adv. E-mail: spartandaily@casa.sjsu.edu
Display Adv. E-mail: spartandailyads@casa.sjsu.edu
Personnel: Richard Craig (Advisor); Timothy Hendrick (Advisor); Jenny Ngo (Adv. Dir.); Joey Akeley (Exec. Ed.)

SANTA ANA COLLEGE

Street address 1: 1530 W 17th St
Street address city: Santa Ana
Street address state: CA
Zip/Postal code: 92706-3398
Country: USA
Mailing address: 1530 W 17th St
Mailing city: Santa Ana
Mailing state: CA
Mailing zip: 92706-3398
General Phone: (714) 564-5617
General Fax: (714) 564-0821
General/National Adv. E-mail: eldonbusiness@sac.edu
Personnel: Charles Little (Advisor); Allene Symons (Adv. Mgr.)

SANTA BARBARA CITY COLLEGE

Street address 1: 721 Cliff Dr
Street address 2: Rm 123
Street address city: Santa Barbara
Street address state: CA
Zip/Postal code: 93109-2312
Country: USA
Mailing address: 721 Cliff Dr Rm 123
Mailing city: Santa Barbara
Mailing state: CA
Mailing zip: 93109-2394
General Phone: (805) 965-0581
General Fax: (805) 730-3079
General/National Adv. E-mail: channels@sbcc.edu
Personnel: Patricia Stark (Advisor)

SANTA CLARA UNIVERSITY

Street address 1: Center for Student Leadership
Street address city: Santa Clara
Street address state: CA
Zip/Postal code: 95053-0001
Country: USA
Mailing address: 500 El Camino Real # 3190
Mailing city: Santa Clara
Mailing state: CA
Mailing zip: 95053-0001
General Phone: (408) 554-4849
General/National Adv. E-mail: news@thesantaclara.com
Display Adv. E-mail: advertising@thesantaclara.com
Editorial e-mail: editor@thesantaclara.com; letters@thesantaclara.com; news@thesantaclara.com
Primary Website: www.thesantaclara.com
Year Established: 1922
Published: Thur
Avg Free Circ: 1100
Personnel: Sophie Mattson

SANTA MONICA COLLEGE

Street address 1: 1900 Pico Blvd
Street address 2: # 303
Street address city: Santa Monica
Street address state: CA
Zip/Postal code: 90405-1628
Country: USA
Mailing address: 1900 Pico Blvd # 303
Mailing city: Santa Monica
Mailing state: CA
Mailing zip: 90405-1644
General Phone: (310) 434-4340
General Fax: (310) 434-3648
Editorial Fax: Free
General/National Adv. E-mail: corsair.editorinchief@gmail.com
Display Adv. E-mail: blaize_ashanti@smc.edu
Editorial e-mail: corsair.editorinchief@gmail.com
Primary Website: www.thecorsaironline.com
Year Established: 1929
Personnel: Saul Rubin (Advisor)

SANTA ROSA JUNIOR COLLEGE

Street address 1: 1501 Mendocino Ave
Street address city: Santa Rosa
Street address state: CA
Zip/Postal code: 95401-4332
Country: USA
Mailing address: 1501 Mendocino Ave.
Mailing city: Santa Rosa
Mailing state: CA
Mailing zip: 95401-4332
General Phone: (707) 527-4401
Advertising Phone: (707) 527-4254
General/National Adv. E-mail: abelden@santarosa.edu
Display Adv. E-mail: oakleaf-ads@santarosa.edu
Editorial e-mail: abelden@santarosa.edu
Primary Website: www.santarosa.edu
Year Established: 1928
Personnel: Ann Belden (Advisor)

SHASTA COLLEGE

Street address 1: 11555 Old Oregon Trl
Street address city: Redding
Street address state: CA
Zip/Postal code: 96003-7692
Country: USA
Mailing address: PO Box 496006
Mailing city: Redding
Mailing state: CA
Mailing zip: 96049-6006
General Phone: (530) 242-7729
General Fax: (530) 225-3925
General/National Adv. E-mail: editorial@sciance.com
Personnel: Craig Harrington (Advisor)

SIERRA COLLEGE

Street address 1: 5000 Rocklin Rd
Street address city: Rocklin
Street address state: CA
Zip/Postal code: 95677-3337
Country: USA
Mailing address: 5000 Rocklin Rd
Mailing city: Rocklin
Mailing state: CA
Mailing zip: 95677-3397
Personnel: Kelly Kukis (Ed.)

SOLANO COMMUNITY COLLEGE

Street address 1: 4000 Suisun Valley Rd
Street address city: Fairfield
Street address state: CA
Zip/Postal code: 94534-4017
Country: USA
Mailing address: 4000 Suisun Valley Rd
Mailing city: Fairfield
Mailing state: CA
Mailing zip: 94534-3197
General Phone: (707) 864-7000
General Fax: (707) 864-0361
General/National Adv. E-mail: tempest@solano.edu
Display Adv. E-mail: samanda.dorger@solano.edu
Editorial e-mail: tempest@solano.edu
Primary Website: www.solanotempest.net
Published: Bi-Mthly
Avg Free Circ: 1500
Personnel: Samanda Dorger (Journalism Adviser)

SONOMA STATE UNIVERSITY

Street address 1: 1801 E Cotati Ave
Street address 2: Salazar Hall 1053
Street address city: Rohnert Park
Street address state: CA
Zip/Postal code: 94928-3613
Country: USA
Mailing address: 1801 E Cotati Ave Salazar Hall 1053
Mailing city: Rohnert Park
Mailing state: CA
Mailing zip: 94928-3613
General Phone: (707) 664-2776
General Fax: (707) 664-4262
General/National Adv. E-mail: star@sonoma.edu
Display Adv. E-mail: sonomastatestar@gmail.com
Editorial e-mail: star@sonoma.edu
Primary Website: www.sonomastatestar.com
Year Established: 1979
Published: Tues
Avg Free Circ: 2000
Personnel: Dylan Sirdofsky (Editor-in-Chief); Amanda Saiki (Advertising Manager); Paul Gullixson (Faculty Advisor); Corinne Asturus

SOUTHERN CALIFORNIA UNIV. OF HEALTH SCIENCES

Street address 1: 16200 Amber Valley Dr
Street address city: Whittier
Street address state: CA
Zip/Postal code: 90604-4051
Country: USA
Mailing address: 16200 Amber Valley Dr
Mailing city: Whittier
Mailing state: CA
Mailing zip: 90604-4051
Personnel: Pam Roosevelt (Ed.)

SOUTHWESTERN COLLEGE

Street address 1: 900 Otay Lakes Rd
Street address city: Chula Vista
Street address state: CA
Zip/Postal code: 91910-7223
Country: USA
Mailing address: 900 Otay Lakes Rd
Mailing city: Chula Vista
Mailing state: CA
Mailing zip: 91910-7297
General Phone: (619) 482-6368
General Fax: (619) 482-6513
General/National Adv. E-mail: southwestern_sun@yahoo.com
Personnel: Max Branfcomb (Advisor)

THE MESA PRESS

Street address 1: 7250 Mesa College Dr
Street address 2: Room G-202
Street address city: San Diego
Street address state: CA
Zip/Postal code: 92111-4902
County: San Diego
Country: USA
Mailing address: 7250 Mesa College Dr
Mailing city: San Diego
Mailing state: CA
Mailing zip: 92111-4999
General Phone: (619) 388-2630
General Fax: (619) 388-2836
General/National Adv. E-mail: mesa.press@gmail.com
Primary Website: www.mesapress.com
Year Established: 1966
Published: Mthly
Personnel: Janna Braun (Advisor)

THE POLY POST

Street address 1: 3801 W Temple Ave
Street address 2: Bldg 1
Street address city: Pomona
Street address state: CA
Zip/Postal code: 91768-2557
Country: USA
Mailing address: 3801 W Temple Ave Bldg 1
Mailing city: Pomona
Mailing state: CA
Mailing zip: 91768-2557
General Phone: (909) 869-5483
General Fax: (909) 869-3533
Advertising Phone: (909) 869-5179
Advertising Fax: (909) 869-3863
Editorial Phone: (909) 869-3528
Editorial Fax: (909) 869-3530
General/National Adv. E-mail: advisor@thepolypost.com
Display Adv. E-mail: advertise@thepolypost.com
Personnel: Doug Spoon (Advisor); Amanda Newfield (Ed. in Chief); Aaron Castrejon (Mng. Ed.); Linda Perez (Mktg. Dir.)

THE STANFORD DAILY

Street address 1: 456 Panama Mall
Street address 2: Lorry Lokey Stanford Daily Bldg.
Street address city: Stanford
Street address state: CA
Zip/Postal code: 94305-4006
Country: USA
Mailing address: 456 Panama Mall
Mailing city: Stanford
Mailing state: CA
Mailing zip: 94305-5294
General Phone: (650) 721-5803
General Fax: (650) 725-1329
General/National Adv. E-mail: eic@stanforddaily.com
Personnel: Jason Shen (COO & Bus Mgr.); Mary Liz McCurdy (Vice Pres., Sales); Devin Banerjee (Ed. in Chief); Kamil Dada (Ed. in Chief); Eric (Sr. Mng. Ed.)

UNIV. OF CALIFORNIA BUS. SCHOOL

Street address 1: Cheit Hall, Rm 138
Street address city: Berkeley
Street address state: CA
Zip/Postal code: 94720-0001
Country: USA
Mailing address: Cheit Hall Rm 138
Mailing city: Berkeley
Mailing state: CA
Mailing zip: 94720-0001
Personnel: Joe Moss (Ed.)

UNIV. OF CALIFORNIA GRAD. SCHOOL OF MGMT.

Street address 1: 110 Westwood Plz, Rm D216
Street address city: Los Angeles
Street address state: CA
Zip/Postal code: 90095-0001
Country: USA
Mailing address: 110 Westwood Plz, Rm D216
Mailing city: Los Angeles
Mailing state: CA
Mailing zip: 90095-0001
General Phone: (310) 825-6488
General Fax: (310) 206-3981
General/National Adv. E-mail: exchange@anderson.ucla.edu
Personnel: Steve Gilison (Ed. in Chief); Daniel Gelsi (Ed. in Chief); Julie Lacouture (Ed. in Chief)

UNIV. OF CALIFORNIA IRVINE

Street address 1: 3100 Gateway Commons, 3rd Fl
Street address city: Irvine
Street address state: CA
Zip/Postal code: 92697-0001
Country: USA
Mailing address: 3100 Gateway Cmns Fl 3
Mailing city: Irvine
Mailing state: CA
Mailing zip: 92697-0001
General Phone: (949) 824-8788
General Fax: (949) 824-4828
Advertising Phone: (949) 824-4284
Editorial Phone: (949) 824-8788
General/National Adv. E-mail: eic@newuniversity.org
Display Adv. E-mail: admanager@newu.uci.edu
Editorial e-mail: eic@newuniversity.org
Primary Website: www.newuniversity.org
Avg Free Circ: 8000
Personnel: David Lumb (Ed. in Chief); Sandy Rose (Mng. Ed.)

UNIV. OF CALIFORNIA SCHOOL OF LAW

Street address 1: 400 Mrak Hall Dr
Street address city: Davis
Street address state: CA
Zip/Postal code: 95616-5203
Country: USA
Mailing address: 400 Mrak Hall Dr
Mailing city: Davis

Personnel: Heather Melton (Prodn. Ed.)

UNIV. OF CALIFORNIA, BERKELEY

Street address 1: 2483 Hearst Ave
Street address city: Berkeley
Street address state: CA
Zip/Postal code: 94709-1320
Country: USA
Mailing address: 2483 Hearst Avenue Berkeley, CA 94709
Mailing city: Berkeley
Mailing state: CA
Mailing zip: 94701-1949
General Phone: (510) 548-8300
General Fax: (510) 849-2803
General/National Adv. E-mail: dailycal@dailycal.org; dailycalifornian@dailycal.org
Display Adv. E-mail: advertising@dailycal.org
Editorial e-mail: editor@dailycal.org
Primary Website: www.dailycal.org
Year Established: 1871
Published: Mon`Tues`Thur`Fri
Personnel: Karim Doumar (Editor in Chief and President)

UNIV. OF CALIFORNIA, RIVERSIDE

Street address 1: 101 Highlander Union Bldg
Street address city: Riverside
Street address state: CA
Zip/Postal code: 92507
Country: USA
Mailing address: 101 Highlander Union Bldg.
Mailing city: Riverside
Mailing state: CA
Mailing zip: 92521-0001
General Phone: (951) 827-3617
General Fax: (951) 827-7049
Advertising Phone: (951) 827-3457
Advertising Fax: (951) 827-7049
Editorial Phone: (951) 827-2105
General/National Adv. E-mail: editorinchief@highlandernews.org
Display Adv. E-mail: highlanderads@ucr.edu
Editorial e-mail: editorinchief@highlandernews.org
Primary Website: www.highlandernews.org
Year Established: 1956
Published: Tues
Avg Free Circ: 4000
Personnel: Chris LoCascio (EIC); Kevin Keckeisen (Mgr Ed); Sandy Van (News Ed); Erin Mahoney (Advisor); Emily Wells (A&E Ed.); Kendall Petersen (Sports Ed.); Brian Tuttle (Photo Ed.); Myles Andrews-Duve (EIC); Andreas Rauch (EIC)

UNIV. OF CALIFORNIA, SANTA BARBARA

Street address 1: PO Box 13402
Street address city: Santa Barbara
Street address state: CA
Zip/Postal code: 93107-3402
Country: USA
Mailing address: PO Box 13402
Mailing city: Santa Barbara
Mailing state: CA
Mailing zip: 93107-3402
General Phone: (805) 893-3828
Advertising Phone: (805) 893-4006
General/National Adv. E-mail: production@dailynexus.com
Display Adv. E-mail: LINDA.MEYER@SA.UCSB.EDU
Editorial e-mail: EIC@DAILYNEXUS.COM
Primary Website: www.dailynexus.com
Published: Thur
Avg Free Circ: 4000
Personnel: Linda Meyer (Adv. Mgr.)

UNIV. OF CALIFORNIA-BERKELEY LAW SCHOOL

Street address 1: 215 Boalt Hall
Street address city: Berkeley
Street address state: CA
Zip/Postal code: 94720-0001
Country: USA
Mailing address: 215 Boalt Hall
Mailing city: Berkeley
Mailing state: CA
Mailing zip: 94720-0001
Personnel: Joshua Rider (Ed.)

UNIV. OF REDLANDS

Street address 1: 1200 E Colton Ave
Street address city: Redlands
Street address state: CA
Zip/Postal code: 92374-3755
Country: USA
Mailing address: PO Box 3080
Mailing city: Redlands
Personnel: Jessie Stapleton (Advisor)

UNIV. OF SAN DIEGO

Street address 1: 5998 Alcala Park
Street address city: San Diego
Street address state: CA
Zip/Postal code: 92110-8001
Country: USA
Mailing address: 5998 Alcala Park Frnt
Mailing city: San Diego
Mailing state: CA
Mailing zip: 92110-2492
General Phone: (619) 260-4714
General Fax: (619) 260-4807
Editorial Phone: (619) 260-4584
Primary Website: www.uofsdmedia.com
Published: Thur
Personnel: Brooklyn Dippo (EIC); Sarah Brewington (Associate Ed); Diego Luna (Mgr Ed)

UNIV. OF SAN DIEGO SCHOOL OF LAW

Street address 1: 5998 Alcala Park
Street address city: San Diego
Street address state: CA
Zip/Postal code: 92110-8001
Country: USA
Mailing address: 5998 Alcala Park
Mailing city: San Diego
Mailing state: CA
Mailing zip: 92110-8001
General Phone: (619) 260-4600
General Fax: (619) 260-4753
General/National Adv. E-mail: motions@sandiego.edu
Personnel: Damien Schiff (Ed.)

UNIV. OF SAN FRANCISCO

Street address 1: 2130 Fulton St
Street address city: San Francisco
Street address state: CA
Zip/Postal code: 94117-1080
Country: USA
Mailing address: 2130 Fulton St
Mailing city: San Francisco
Mailing state: CA
Mailing zip: 94117-1050
General Fax: (415) 422-2751
General/National Adv. E-mail: foghorn_ads@yahoo.com
Display Adv. E-mail: advertising@sffoghorn.info
Personnel: Theresa Moore (Advisor); Laura Plantholt (Ed. in Chief); Nicholas Muhkar (Mng. Ed.); Chelsea Sterling (News Ed.); Matt (Sports Ed.); Mark (Adv. Mgr.); Erika (Bus. Mgr.)

UNIV. OF SAN FRANCISCO LAW SCHOOL

Street address 1: 2130 Fulton St
Street address city: San Francisco
Street address state: CA
Zip/Postal code: 94117-1080
Country: USA
Mailing address: 2130 Fulton St
Mailing city: San Francisco
Mailing state: CA
Mailing zip: 94117-1050
General Phone: (415) 422-6586
Personnel: Andie Vallee (Ed.)

UNIV. OF SOUTHERN CALIFORNIA

Street address 1: Student Union 404
Street address city: Los Angeles
Street address state: CA
Zip/Postal code: 90089-0001
Country: USA
Mailing address: 404 Student Un
Mailing city: Los Angeles
Mailing state: CA
Mailing zip: 90089-0001
General Phone: (213) 740-2707
General Fax: (213) 740-5666
General/National Adv. E-mail: dtrojan@usc.edu
Editorial e-mail: editor@dailytorjan.com
Personnel: Mona Cravens (Dir., of Student Publication); Scott A. Smith (Assoc. Dir); David Khalaf (Adv. Mgr.); Sheri Brundage (Adv. Mgr.)

UNIV. OF THE PACIFIC

Street address 1: 3601 Pacific Ave
Street address city: Stockton
Street address state: CA
Zip/Postal code: 95211-0110
Country: USA
Mailing address: 3601 Pacific Ave
Mailing city: Stockton
Mailing state: CA
Mailing zip: 95211-0197
General Phone: (209) 946-2115
General Fax: (209) 946-2195
Advertising Phone: (209) 946-2114
Display Adv. E-mail: pacificanads@pacific.edu
Editorial e-mail: pacificannews@pacific.edu; pacificaneditors@pacific.edu; pacificanlifestyles@pacific.edu; pacificansports@pacific.edu
Personnel: Dave Frederickson (Advisor); Ruben Moreno (Bus. Mgr.); Devon Blount (Ed. in Chief); Andrew Mitchell (News Ed.)

UNIVERSITY OF CALIFORNIA SAN DIEGO

Street address 1: 9500 Gilman Dr
Street address 2: Dept 316
Street address city: La Jolla
Street address state: CA
Zip/Postal code: 92093-0316
Country: USA
Mailing address: 9500 Gilman Dr Dept 316
Mailing city: La Jolla
Mailing state: CA
Mailing zip: 92093-0316
General Phone: (858) 534-3466
General Fax: (858) 534-7691
Display Adv. E-mail: ads@ucsdguardian.org
Editorial e-mail: managing@ucsdguardian.org
Primary Website: www.ucsdguardian.org
Year Established: 1967
Published: Mon`Thur
Personnel: Laira Martin (Editor in Chief)

UNIVERSITY OF CALIFORNIA, DAVIS

Street address 1: 1 Shields Avenue
Street address 2: 25 Lower Freeborn Hall
Street address city: Davis
Street address state: CA
Zip/Postal code: 95616-5270
Country: USA
Mailing address: 25 Lower Freeborn Hall
Mailing city: Davis
Mailing state: CA
Mailing zip: 95616-5270
General Phone: (530) 752-9887
Advertising Phone: (530) 752-6851
Editorial Phone: (530) 752-9887
General/National Adv. E-mail: editor@theaggie.org
Display Adv. E-mail: admanager@theaggie.org
Editorial e-mail: editor@theaggie.org
Primary Website: www.theaggie.org
Year Established: 1915
Published: Thur
Personnel: Emily Stack (Editor-in-Chief); Olivia Rockeman (Managing Editor); Hannah Holzer (Campus News Editor); Kaelyn Tuermer-Lee (City News Editor); Liz Jacobson (Arts and Culture Editor); Dominic Faria (Sports Editor); Harnoor Gill (Science and Technology Editor); Olivia Luchini (Features Editor); Taryn DeOilers (Opinion Editor); Brian Landry (Photo Director); Trevor Goodman (Video Production Manager); Sydney Odman (New Media Manager); Zoe Reinhardt (Website Manager); Hali Zweigoron (Social Media Manager); Grace Simmons (Newsletter Manager); Shaelin Green (Distribution Manager); Jonathan Chen (Layout Director); Olivia Kotlarek (Design Director); Laurie Pederson (Business Development Manager); Hanna Baublitz (Copy Chief); Cecilia Morales (Copy Chief)

UNIVERSITY OF CALIFORNIA, LOS ANGELES

Street address 1: 308 Westwood Plz
Street address city: Los Angeles
Street address state: CA
Zip/Postal code: 90095-8355
Country: USA
Mailing address: 308 Westwood Plaza
Mailing city: Los Angeles
Mailing state: CA
Mailing zip: 90095-8355
General Phone: (310) 825-9898
General Fax: (310) 206-0906
Advertising Phone: (310) 825-2221
Display Adv. E-mail: ads@media.ucla.edu
Editorial e-mail: editor@media.ucla.edu
Primary Website: www.dailybruin.com
Year Established: 1919
Published: Mon`Tues`Wed`Thur`Fri
Personnel: Jeremy Wildman (Bus. Mgr.); Abigail Goldman (Media Advisor); Doria Deen (Student Media Dir); Mackenzie Possee (Editor in chief)

UNIVERSITY OF CALIFORNIA, SAN FRANCISCO

Street address 1: 500 Parnassus Ave
Street address 2: # 108W
Street address city: San Francisco
Street address state: CA
Zip/Postal code: 94143-2203
Country: USA
Mailing address: 108 W Millberry Un
Mailing city: San Francisco
Mailing state: CA
Mailing zip: 94143-0001
General Phone: (415) 476-2211
General Fax: (415) 502-4537
General/National Adv. E-mail: synapse@ucsf.edu
Display Adv. E-mail: synapse@ucsf.edu
Primary Website: synapse.ucsf.edu
Published: Thur
Personnel: Steven Chin (Managing Editor)

UNIVERSITY OF LA VERNE

Street address 1: 1950 3rd St
Street address city: La Verne
Street address state: CA
Zip/Postal code: 91750-4401
Country: USA
Mailing address: 1950 3rd St
Mailing city: La Verne
Mailing state: CA
Mailing zip: 91750-4401
General Phone: (909) 593-3511
General Fax: (909) 392-2706
Advertising Phone: 909-392-2712
General/National Adv. E-mail: ctimes@laverne.edu
Display Adv. E-mail: ctimesad@laverne.edu
Editorial e-mail: ctimes@laverne.edu
Primary Website: www.laverne.edu/campus-times
Year Established: 1919
Published: Fri
Avg Free Circ: 2000
Personnel: Elizabeth Zwerling (Faculty Advisor); Jennifer Lemus Fernandez (Adv. Mgr.); Kevin Garrity (Ed. in Chief); Eric Borer (Layout Asst.)

VANGUARD UNIV.

Street address 1: 55 Fair Dr
Street address city: Costa Mesa
Street address state: CA
Zip/Postal code: 92626-6520
Country: USA
Mailing address: 55 Fair Dr
Mailing city: Costa Mesa
Mailing state: CA
Mailing zip: 92626-6597
General Phone: (714) 662-5203
General Fax: (714) 966-5482
General/National Adv. E-mail: thevoice@vanguard.edu

Personnel: Kristy Eudy (Advisor); Hannah Petrak (Ed.)

VENTURA COLLEGE

Street address 1: 4667 Telegraph Rd
Street address city: Ventura
Street address state: CA
Zip/Postal code: 93003-3872
Country: USA
Mailing address: 4667 Telegraph Rd
Mailing city: Ventura
Mailing state: CA
Mailing zip: 93003-3899
General Phone: (805) 654-6400
Personnel: C. Weinstock (Advisor)

WEST VALLEY COLLEGE

Street address 1: 14000 Fruitvale Ave
Street address city: Saratoga
Street address state: CA
Zip/Postal code: 95070-5640
Country: USA
Mailing address: 14000 Fruitvale Ave
Mailing city: Saratoga
Mailing state: CA
Mailing zip: 95070-5698
General Phone: (408) 867-2200
Personnel: Janine Gerzanics (Advisor)

WHITTIER COLLEGE

Street address 1: 13406 Philadelphia St
Street address city: Whittier
Street address state: CA
Zip/Postal code: 90601-4446
Country: USA
Mailing address: PO Box 634
Mailing city: Whittier
Mailing state: CA
Mailing zip: 90608-0634
General Phone: (562) 907-4254
General Fax: (562) 945-5301
General/National Adv. E-mail: qc@whittier.edu
Primary Website: http://www.thequakercampus.org/
Year Established: 1914
Published: Thur
Personnel: justin dennis (EIC, Mgr Ed); matther anson

COLORADO

ARAPAHOE CMTY. COLLEGE

Street address 1: 5900 S Santa Fe Dr
Street address city: Littleton
Street address state: CO
Zip/Postal code: 80120-1801
Country: USA
Mailing address: 5900 S Santa Fe Dr
Mailing city: Littleton
Mailing state: CO
Mailing zip: 80120-1801
Personnel: Chris Ransick (Advisor); Reem Al-Omari (Ed.)

COLORADO CHRISTIAN UNIV.

Street address 1: 8787 W Alameda Ave
Street address city: Lakewood
Street address state: CO
Zip/Postal code: 80226-2824
Country: USA
Mailing address: 8787 W Alameda Ave
Mailing city: Lakewood
Mailing state: CO
Mailing zip: 80226-2824
General Phone: (303) 202-0100
General Fax: (303) 963-3001
General/National Adv. E-mail: cougartrax@ccu.edu
Personnel: Jim McCormick (Advisor); Daniel Cohrs (Bus. Mgr.)

COLORADO COLLEGE

Street address 1: 1028 N Weber St
Street address city: Colorado Springs
Street address state: CO
Zip/Postal code: 80903-2422
Country: USA
Mailing address: 1028 N. Weber St.
Mailing city: Colorado Springs
Mailing state: CO
Mailing zip: 80903
General Phone: (719) 389-6000
General Fax: (719) 389-6962
General/National Adv. E-mail: catalyst@coloradocollege.edu
Personnel: Jackson Solway (Ed.); Alex Kronman (Ed.)

COLORADO MESA UNIVERSITY

Street address 1: 1100 North Ave
Street address city: Grand Junction
Street address state: CO
Zip/Postal code: 81501-3122
Country: USA
Mailing address: PO Box 2647
Mailing city: Grand Junction
Mailing state: CO
Mailing zip: 81502-2647
General Phone: (970) 248-1570
Primary Website: www.thecrite.com
Year Established: 1934
Personnel: Eric Sandstrom (Advisor); Jamie Banks (Ed.)

COLORADO SCHOOL OF MINES

Street address 1: 1600 Maple St
Street address city: Golden
Street address state: CO
Zip/Postal code: 80401-6114
Country: USA
Mailing address: 1600 Maple St
Mailing city: Golden
Mailing state: CO
Mailing zip: 80401-6114
General Phone: (303) 384-2188
General Fax: (303) 273-3931
General/National Adv. E-mail: oredig@mines.edu
Primary Website: www.oredigger.net
Published: Mon
Personnel: Emily McNair (Managing Editor); Lucy Orsi (Editor-in-Chief); Taylor Polodna (Design Editor); Connor McDonald (Webmaster); Arnaud Filliat (Copy Editor); Karen Gilbert (Faculty Advisor); Deborah Good (Editor-in-Chief)

COLORADO STATE UNIV.

Street address 1: PO Box 13
Street address city: Fort Collins
Street address state: CO
Zip/Postal code: 80522-0013
Country: USA
Mailing address: PO Box 13
Mailing city: Fort Collins
Mailing state: CO
Mailing zip: 80522-0013
General Phone: (970) 491-1146
General Fax: (970) 491-1690
General/National Adv. E-mail: editor@collegian.com
Personnel: Holly Wolcott (Advisor); Virginia Singarayar (Ed. in Chief); Madeline Novey (News Mng. Ed.); Matt Minich (News Ed.); Matt L. (Sports Ed.); Kim (Adv. Mgr.)

COLORADO STATE UNIV. ENGINEERING COLLEGE

Street address 1: PO Box 13
Street address city: Fort Collins
Street address state: CO
Zip/Postal code: 80522-0013
Country: USA
Mailing address: PO Box 13
Mailing city: Fort Collins
Mailing state: CO
Mailing zip: 80522-0013
General Phone: (970) 491-1686
Personnel: Brandon Lowrey (Ed. in Chief)

COLORADO STATE UNIVERSITY-PUEBLO

Street address 1: 2200 Bonforte Blvd
Street address 2: # AM110
Street address city: Pueblo
Street address state: CO
Zip/Postal code: 81001-4901
Country: USA
Mailing address: 2200 Bonforte Blvd Bcc 103P
Mailing city: Pueblo
Mailing state: CO
Mailing zip: 81001-4901
General Phone: 719-549-2847
General Fax: 719-549-2977
Advertising Phone: 719-549-2812
Advertising Fax: 719-549-2977
General/National Adv. E-mail: leticia.steffen@csupueblo.edu
Primary Website: www.csupueblotoday.com
Published Other: once per semester (fall and spring)
Avg Free Circ: 3000
Personnel: Leticia L. Steffen (Advisor); Savana Charter

FRONT RANGE CMTY. COLLEGE

Street address 1: 3645 W 112th Ave
Street address city: Westminster
Street address state: CO
Zip/Postal code: 80031-2105
Country: USA
Mailing address: 3645 W 112th Ave
Mailing city: Westminster
Mailing state: CO
Mailing zip: 80031-2199
General Phone: (303) 404-5314
General Fax: (303) 404-5199
General/National Adv. E-mail: frontpage@frontrange.com
Personnel: John Heisel (Advisor); Stephanie Munger (Ed. in Chief); Jon Strungis (Ed.)

FT. LEWIS COLLEGE

Street address 1: 1000 Rim Dr
Street address 2: # 252
Street address city: Durango
Street address state: CO
Zip/Postal code: 81301-3911
Country: USA
Mailing address: 1000 Rim Dr # 252
Mailing city: Durango
Mailing state: CO
Mailing zip: 81301-3911
General Phone: (970) 247-7405
General Fax: (970) 247-7487
General/National Adv. E-mail: independent@fortlewis.edu
Personnel: Leslie Blood (Advisor); Kayala Andersen (News Ed.)

METROPOLITAN STATE COLLEGE

Street address 1: PO Box 173362
Street address city: Denver
Street address state: CO
Zip/Postal code: 80217-3362
Country: USA
Mailing address: PO Box 173362
Mailing city: Denver
Mailing state: CO
Mailing zip: 80217-3362
General Phone: (303) 556-2507
Primary Website: themet.metrostudentmedia.com; www.mscd.edu/themet
Year Established: 1979
Personnel: Dianne Harrison Miller (Dir.); Dominic Graziano (Ed.)

MORGAN CMTY. COLLEGE

Street address 1: 920 Barlow Rd
Street address city: Fort Morgan
Street address state: CO
Zip/Postal code: 80701-4371
Country: USA
Mailing address: 920 Barlow Rd
Mailing city: Fort Morgan
Mailing state: CO
Mailing zip: 80701-4371
Personnel: Jennifer Lankford (Ed.)

NORTHEASTERN JUNIOR COLLEGE

Street address 1: 100 College Ave
Street address city: Sterling
Street address state: CO
Zip/Postal code: 80751-2345
Country: USA
Mailing address: 100 College Ave
Mailing city: Sterling

Personnel: Ian Storey (Advisor); Patrick Kelling (Advisor)

PIKES PEAK CMTY. COLLEGE

Street address 1: 5675 S Academy Blvd
Street address 2: # C12
Street address city: Colorado Springs
Street address state: CO
Zip/Postal code: 80906-5422
Country: USA
Mailing address: 5675 S Academy Blvd # C12
Mailing city: Colorado Springs
Mailing state: CO
Mailing zip: 80906-5422
General Phone: (719) 502-2000
Personnel: Linda McGowan (Advisor); Sonia Gonzales (Ed.)

REGIS UNIV.

Street address 1: 3333 Regis Blvd
Street address city: Denver
Street address state: CO
Zip/Postal code: 80221-1154
Country: USA
Mailing address: 3333 Regis Blvd
Mailing city: Denver
Mailing state: CO
Mailing zip: 80221-1099
General Phone: (303) 964-5391
Personnel: Mary Beth Callie (Advisor); Maricor Coquia (Ed. in Chief)

TRINIDAD STATE JUNIOR COLLEGE

Street address 1: 600 Prospect St
Street address 2: # 182
Street address city: Trinidad
Street address state: CO
Zip/Postal code: 81082-2356
Country: USA
Mailing address: 600 Prospect St # 182
Mailing city: Trinidad
Mailing state: CO
Mailing zip: 81082-2356
Personnel: Charlene Duran (Adv. Mgr.)

UNIV. OF COLORADO

Street address 1: 1420 Austin Bluffs Pkwy
Street address city: Colorado Springs
Street address state: CO
Zip/Postal code: 80918-3733
Country: USA
Mailing address: 1420 Austin Bluffs Pkwy
Mailing city: Colorado Springs
Mailing state: CO
Mailing zip: 80918-3908
General Phone: (719) 262-3658
General Fax: (719) 262-3600
General/National Adv. E-mail: scribe@uccs.edu
Personnel: Paul Fair (Ed.)

UNIV. OF COLORADO

Street address 1: PO Box 173364
Street address city: Denver
Street address state: CO
Zip/Postal code: 80217-3364
Country: USA
Mailing address: PO Box 173364
Mailing city: Denver
Mailing state: CO
Mailing zip: 80217-3364
General Phone: (303) 556-2535
General Fax: (303) 556-3679
Display Adv. E-mail: advertising@ucdadvocate.com
Editorial e-mail: editorinchief@ucdadvocate.com
Primary Website: www.ucdadvocate.com
Year Established: 1984
Published: Wed
Personnel: Madilyn Bates (Editor in Chief); Isra Yousif (Office Coordinator)

UNIV. OF DENVER

Street address 1: 2199 S University Blvd
Street address city: Denver
Street address state: CO
Zip/Postal code: 80210-4711
Country: USA
Mailing address: 2199 S University Blvd

Mailing city: Denver
Mailing state: CO
Mailing zip: 80210-4700
General Phone: (303) 871-3131
General Fax: (303) 871-2568
General/National Adv. E-mail: duclarion@du.edu
Personnel: Arianna Ranahosseini (Ed. in Chief)

UNIV. OF NORTHERN COLORADO

Street address 1: 823 16th St
Street address city: Greeley
Street address state: CO
Zip/Postal code: 80631-5617
Country: USA
Mailing address: 823 16th St
Mailing city: Greeley
Mailing state: CO
Mailing zip: 80631-5617
General Phone: (970) 392-9270
General Fax: (970) 392-9025
Advertising Phone: (970) 392-9270
Editorial Phone: (970) 392-9270
General/National Adv. E-mail: info@uncmirror.com
Display Adv. E-mail: ads@uncmirror.com
Editorial e-mail: editor@uncmirror.com
Primary Website: www.uncmirror.com
Year Established: 1919
Published: Mon
Avg Free Circ: 4000
Personnel: Kurt Hinkle (Gen. Mgr.); Josh Espinoza (Ed. in Chief); Eric Heinz (News Ed.); Jordan Freemyer (Sports Ed.); Corey (Adv. Mgr.); Lauren (Adv. Prodn. Mgr.)

US AIR FORCE ACADEMY

Street address 1: 2304 Cadet Dr, Ste 3100
Street address city: Colorado Spgs
Street address state: CO
Zip/Postal code: 80904
Country: USA
Mailing address: 2304 Cadet Dr., Ste. 3100
Mailing city: Colorado Springs
Mailing state: CO
Mailing zip: 80904-5016
Personnel: Kim Karda (Ed. In Chief)

WESTERN STATE COLLEGE

Street address 1: 600 N Adams St
Street address city: Gunnison
Street address state: CO
Zip/Postal code: 81231-7000
Country: USA
Mailing address: 103 College Ctr
Mailing city: Gunnison
Mailing state: CO
Mailing zip: 81231-0001
General Phone: 970-943-2138
General Fax: 970-943-2702
General/National Adv. E-mail: top@western.edu
Display Adv. E-mail: topworld.ads@gmail.com
Primary Website: www.western.edu/academics/communicationtheatre/top-o-the-world
Year Established: 1921

CONNECTICUT

CENTRAL CONNECTICUT STATE UNIV.

Street address 1: 1615 Stanley St
Street address city: New Britain
Street address state: CT
Zip/Postal code: 06050-2439
Country: USA
Mailing address: 1615 Stanley St
Mailing city: New Britain
Mailing state: CT
Mailing zip: 06050-2439
General Phone: (860) 832-3744
General Fax: (860) 832-3747
General/National Adv. E-mail: ccsurecorder@gmail.com; ccsurecorder.ads@gmail.com
Personnel: Vivian B. Martin (Coord.); Melissa Traynor (Ed. in Chief); Michael Walsh (Mng. Ed.); Christopher Boulay (Sports Ed.); Christina LoBello (Opinion Ed.); Kelsey (Adv. Mgr.)

CONNECTICUT COLLEGE

Street address 1: 270 Mohegan Ave
Street address city: New London
Street address state: CT
Zip/Postal code: 06320-4125
Country: USA
Mailing address: PO Box 4970
Mailing city: New London
Mailing state: CT
Mailing zip: 06320-4196
General Phone: (860) 439-2841
General Fax: (860) 439-2843
General/National Adv. E-mail: ccvoice@conncoll.edu; contact@thecollegevoice.org
Personnel: Justin O'Shea (Bus. Mgr.); Benjamin Eagle (Ed. in Chief); Claire Gould (Mng. Ed.); CR Baker

EASTERN CONNECTICUT STATE UNIV.

Street address 1: 83 Windham St, 103 Student Ctr
Street address city: Willimantic
Street address state: CT
Zip/Postal code: 6226
Country: USA
Mailing address: 83 Windham St., 103 Student Ctr.
Mailing city: Willimantic
Mailing state: CT
Mailing zip: 06226-2211
General Phone: (860) 465-4445
General Fax: (860) 465-4685
General/National Adv. E-mail: general@campuslantern.org; lantern@stu.easternct.edu
Personnel: Edmond Chibeau (Advisor); Daniel McCue (Ed. in Chief); Christine Smith (Mng. Ed.); Michael Rouleau (News Ed.); Andrew (A&E Ed.); Zach (Sports Ed.); Jacquelyn (Opinion Ed.)

FAIRFIELD UNIV.

Street address 1: 1073 N Benson Rd
Street address city: Fairfield
Street address state: CT
Zip/Postal code: 06824-5171
Country: USA
Mailing address: PO Box AA
Mailing city: Fairfield
Mailing state: CT
Mailing zip: 06824
General Phone: (203) 254-4000
General Fax: (203) 254-4162
Display Adv. E-mail: advertising@fairfieldmirror.com
Primary Website: www.fairfieldmirror.com
Published: Wed
Avg Free Circ: 3500
Personnel: Lei Xie (Faculty adviser)

MANCHESTER COMMUNITY COLLEGE

Street address 1: 60 Bidwell St
Street address city: Manchester
Street address state: CT
Zip/Postal code: 06040-6449
Country: USA
Mailing address: 60 Bidwell Street
Mailing city: Manchester
Mailing state: CT
Mailing zip: 06045-1046
General Phone: (860) 512-3290
Editorial Phone: (860) 512-3289
General/National Adv. E-mail: livewire@manchestercc.edu
Primary Website: www.livewiremcc.org
Year Established: 1979
Published Other: Every six weeks
Avg Free Circ: 4000
Personnel: Stephania Davis (Advisor)

NAUGATUCK VALLEY COMMUNITY COLLEGE

Street address 1: 750 Chase Pkwy
Street address city: Waterbury
Street address state: CT
Zip/Postal code: 06708-3011
Country: USA
Mailing address: 750 Chase Pkwy
Mailing city: Waterbury
Mailing state: CT
Mailing zip: 06708-3089
General Phone: (203) 575-8040
General Fax: (203) 596-8721
General/National Adv. E-mail: nvcc@nvcc.commnet.edu
Primary Website: www.nvcc.commnet.edu
Published: Mthly
Personnel: Steve Parlato (Faculty Advisor); Chelsea Clow (Editor-in-Chief)

QUINNIPIAC COLLEGE SCHOOL OF LAW

Street address 1: 275 Mount Carmel Ave
Street address city: Hamden
Street address state: CT
Zip/Postal code: 06518-1905
Country: USA
Mailing address: 275 Mount Carmel Ave
Mailing city: Hamden
Mailing state: CT
Mailing zip: 06518-1908
General Phone: (203) 582-8358
General Fax: (203) 582-5203
General/National Adv. E-mail: thequchronicle@gmail.com
Personnel: Andrew Fletcher (Ed. in Chief); Joe Pelletier (Mng. Ed.)

QUINNIPIAC UNIVERSITY

Street address 1: 275 Mount Carmel Ave
Street address city: Hamden
Street address state: CT
Zip/Postal code: 06518-1905
Country: USA
Mailing address: 275 Mount Carmel Ave
Mailing city: Hamden
Mailing state: CT
Mailing zip: 06518-1908
General Phone: 8608301017
General/National Adv. E-mail: editor@quchronicle.com
Personnel: David Friedlander (Editor-in-Chief)

SACRED HEART UNIV.

Street address 1: 5151 Park Ave
Street address city: Fairfield
Street address state: CT
Zip/Postal code: 06825-1090
Country: USA
Mailing address: 5151 Park Ave
Mailing city: Fairfield
Mailing state: CT
Mailing zip: 06825-1000
General Phone: (203) 371-7966
General Fax: (203) 371-7828
Advertising Phone: (203) 371-7963
General/National Adv. E-mail: spectrum@sacredheart.edu
Display Adv. E-mail: spectrum-advertising@sacredheart.edu
Personnel: Joanne Kabak (Advisor); Lauren Sampson (Adv. Mgr.); Carli-Rae Panny (Ed. in Chief); Kate Poole (Mng. Ed.)

SOUTHERN CONNECTICUT STATE UNIV.

Street address 1: 501 Crescent St
Street address 2: # 58
Street address city: New Haven
Street address state: CT
Zip/Postal code: 06515-1330
Country: USA
Mailing address: 501 Crescent St # 58
Mailing city: New Haven
Mailing state: CT
Mailing zip: 06515-1330
General Phone: (203) 392-5804
General Fax: (203) 392-6927
General/National Adv. E-mail: snews@southernct.edu
Personnel: Frank Harris (Advisor)

TRINITY COLLEGE

Street address 1: 300 Summit St
Street address city: Hartford
Street address state: CT
Zip/Postal code: 06106-3100
Country: USA
Mailing address: 300 Summit St Ste 1
Mailing city: Hartford
Mailing state: CT
Mailing zip: 06106-3186
General Phone: (860) 297-2584
General Fax: (860) 297-5361
General/National Adv. E-mail: tripod@trincoll.edu
Primary Website: https://commons.trincoll.edu/tripod/
Year Established: 1904
Published: Tues

UNIV. OF BRIDGEPORT

Street address 1: 244 University Ave
Street address city: Bridgeport
Street address state: CT
Zip/Postal code: 06604-7775
Country: USA
Mailing address: 244 University Ave
Mailing city: Bridgeport
Mailing state: CT
Mailing zip: 06604-7775
General Phone: (203) 576-4382
General Fax: (203) 576-4493
General/National Adv. E-mail: scribe@bridgeport.edu
Personnel: Richard Unger (Ed. in Chief); Sharon Loh (Ed.)

UNIV. OF CONNECTICUT

Street address 1: 11 Dog Ln
Street address city: Storrs
Street address state: CT
Zip/Postal code: 06268-2206
Country: USA
Mailing address: 11 Dog Ln
Mailing city: Storrs
Mailing state: CT
Mailing zip: 06268-2206
General Phone: (860) 486-3407
General Fax: (860) 486-4388
General/National Adv. E-mail: advertising@dailycampus.com
Personnel: Valerie Nezvesky (Bus. Mgr./Adv. Dir.); Christopher Duray (Ed. in Chief)

UNIV. OF HARTFORD

Street address 1: 200 Bloomfield Ave
Street address 2: Rm 158
Street address city: West Hartford
Street address state: CT
Zip/Postal code: 06117-1545
Country: USA
Mailing address: 200 Bloomfield Ave Rm 158
Mailing city: West Hartford
Mailing state: CT
Mailing zip: 06117-1545
General Phone: (860) 768-4723
General Fax: (860) 768-4728
General/National Adv. E-mail: informer@hartford.edu
Personnel: Jonathan Whitson (Bus. Mgr.); Melissa O' Brien (Ed. in Chief)

UNIV. OF NEW HAVEN

Street address 1: 300 Boston Post Rd
Street address city: West Haven
Street address state: CT
Zip/Postal code: 06516-1916
Country: USA
Mailing address: 300 Boston Post Rd
Mailing city: West Haven
Mailing state: CT
Mailing zip: 06516-1999
General Phone: (203) 932-7182
General Fax: (203) 931-6037
General/National Adv. E-mail: chargerbulletin@newhaven.edu
Primary Website: www.chargerbulletin.com
Year Established: 1938
Published: Wed

Personnel: Zack Rosen (Ed. in Chief); Erin Ennis (Asst. Ed.); Sara McGuire (A&E Ed.); Michelle Blydenburg (Adv. Mgr.); Charles (Distribution Mgr.); Liana Teixeira; Elizabeth Field

WESLEYAN UNIVERSITY

Street address 1: 45 Wyllys Ave
Street address city: Middletown
Street address state: CT
Zip/Postal code: 06459-3211
Country: USA
Mailing address: 45 Wyllys Ave
Mailing city: Middletown
Mailing state: CT
Mailing zip: 06459-3211
General Phone: (860) 685-6902
General Fax: (860) 685-3411
General/National Adv. E-mail: argus@wesleyan.edu
Display Adv. E-mail: argusads@wesleyan.edu
Primary Website: www.wesleyanargus.com
Published: Tues`Fri
Personnel: Natasha Nurjadin (Editor-in-Chief); Aaron Stagoff-Belfort (Editor-in-Chief)

WESTERN CONNECTICUT STATE UNIV.

Street address 1: 181 White St
Street address city: Danbury
Street address state: CT
Zip/Postal code: 06810-6826
Country: USA
Mailing address: 181 White St
Mailing city: Danbury
Mailing state: CT
Mailing zip: 06810-6855
General Phone: (203) 837-8706
General Fax: (203) 837-8709
General/National Adv. E-mail: wcsuecho@gmail.com
Display Adv. E-mail: wcsuechoads@gmail.com
Personnel: John Birks (Advisor); Todd Passan (Bus. Mgr.); Sarah Menichelli (Adv. Mgr.); Jessylyn Foley (Ed. in Chief)

YALE UNIV.

Street address 1: 202 York St
Street address city: New Haven
Street address state: CT
Zip/Postal code: 06511-4804
Country: USA
Mailing address: PO Box 209007
Mailing city: New Haven
Mailing state: CT
Mailing zip: 06520-9007
General Phone: (203) 432-2400
General Fax: (203) 432-7425
General/National Adv. E-mail: ydn@yale.edu; ydn@yaledailynews.com
Display Adv. E-mail: business@yaledailynews.com
Personnel: Jason Chen (Pub.); Katherine Kavaler (Adv. Dir.); Thomas Kaplan (Ed. in Chief)

YALE UNIV. LAW SCHOOL

Street address 1: PO Box 208215
Street address city: New Haven
Street address state: CT
Zip/Postal code: 06520-8215
Country: USA
Mailing address: PO Box 208215
Mailing city: New Haven
Personnel: Nicola Williams (Ed.)

DELAWARE

DELAWARE STATE UNIV.

Street address 1: 1200 N Dupont Hwy
Street address city: Dover
Street address state: Delaware
Zip/Postal code: 19901-2202
Country: USA
Mailing address: 1200 N Dupont Hwy
Mailing city: Dover
Mailing state: Delaware
Mailing zip: 19901-2276
Primary Website: www.desu.edu
Published: Mthly
Personnel: Marcia Taylor (Advisor); Synquette Wilks (EIC)

THE REVIEW

Street address 1: 325 Academy St
Street address 2: Rm 250
Street address city: Newark
Street address state: Delaware
Zip/Postal code: 19716-6186
Country: USA
Mailing address: 325 Academy St Rm 250
Mailing city: Newark
Mailing state: Delaware
Mailing zip: 19716-6185
General Phone: (302) 831-1397
General Fax: (302) 831-1396
Advertising Phone: (302) 831-1398
Advertising Fax: (302) 831-1395
Editorial Phone: (302) 831-2774
General/National Adv. E-mail: business@udreview.com
Display Adv. E-mail: ads@udreview.com
Editorial e-mail: editor@udreview.com; thereview.editorial@gmail.com
Primary Website: www.udreview.com
Year Established: 1882
Personnel: Kerry Bowden (Editor-in-Chief)

WIDENER UNIV. SCHOOL OF LAW

Street address 1: PO Box 7474
Street address city: Wilmington
Street address state: Delaware
Zip/Postal code: 19803-0474
Country: USA
Mailing address: PO Box 7474
Mailing city: Wilmington
Mailing state: Delaware
Mailing zip: 19803-0474
General Phone: (302) 477-2100
Personnel: Doretta McGinnis (Advisor); Christopher Balala (Ed. in Chief); Harry Matt Taylor (Bus. Mgr.)

DISTRICT OF COLUMBIA

AMERICAN UNIV.

Street address 1: 252 Mary Graydon Ctr
Street address city: Washington
Street address state: District of Columbia
Country: USA
Mailing address: 4400 Massachusetts Ave NW
Mailing city: Washington
Mailing state: District of Columbia
Mailing zip: 20016-8003
General Phone: (202) 885-1414
General Fax: (202) 885-1428
Editorial Phone: (202) 885-1402
General/National Adv. E-mail: editor@theeagleonline.com
Personnel: Jen Calantone (Ed. in Chief); Charlie Szold (News Ed.); Andrew Tomlinson (Sports Ed.); Caitlin E. Moore (A&E Ed.); Kelsey (Photo Ed.)

CATHOLIC UNIV. OF AMERICA

Street address 1: 127 Pryzbyla Ctr
Street address city: Washington
Street address state: District of Columbia
Country: USA
Mailing address: 127 Pryzbyla Ctr
Mailing city: Washington
Mailing state: District of Columbia
Mailing zip: 20064-0001
General Phone: (202) 319-5779
Personnel: William McQuillen (Advisor.); Ben Newell (Ed.)

GALLAUDET UNIVERSITY

Street address 1: 800 Florida Ave NE
Street address city: Washington
Street address state: District of Columbia
Zip/Postal code: 20002-3600
Country: USA
Mailing address: PO Box 2334
Mailing city: Washington
Mailing state: District of Columbia
Mailing zip: 20013-2334
General Phone: (202) 651-5000
General Fax: (202) 651-5916
General/National Adv. E-mail: ursabuffinblue@gmail.comursabuffinblue
Personnel: Mary Lott (Dir.)

GEORGE WASHINGTON UNIV.

Street address 1: 2140 G St NW
Street address city: Washington
Street address state: District of Columbia
Zip/Postal code: 20052-0072
Country: USA
Mailing address: 2140 G St NW
Mailing city: Washington
Mailing state: District of Columbia
Mailing zip: 20052-0072
General Phone: (202) 994-7080
General Fax: (202) 994-1309
Advertising Fax: (202) 994-7550
General/National Adv. E-mail: news@gwhatchet.comgwhatchet
Display Adv. E-mail: ads@gwhatchet.comgwhatchet
Primary Website: www.gwhatchet.com
Year Established: 1904
Personnel: Howard Marshall (Gen. Mgr.); Arron Elkins (Adv. Mgr.); Alex Byers (Ed. in Chief); Beyers

GEORGE WASHINGTON UNIV. LAW SCHOOL

Street address 1: 2008 H St NW
Street address 2: Bsmt
Street address city: Washington
Street address state: District of Columbia
Zip/Postal code: 20052-0026
Country: USA
Mailing address: 2008 H St NW Bsmt
Mailing city: Washington
Mailing state: District of Columbia
Mailing zip: 20052-0026
General Phone: (202) 994-6261
General/National Adv. E-mail: notabene@law.gwu.edu
Personnel: Sarah Valerio (Pres.); Katie Earnest (Ed. in Chief)

GEORGETOWN UNIV. LAW CENTER

Street address 1: 600 New Jersey Ave NW
Street address city: Washington
Street address state: District of Columbia
Zip/Postal code: 20001-2022
Country: USA
Mailing address: 600 New Jersey Ave NW
Mailing city: Washington
Mailing state: District of Columbia
Mailing zip: 20001-2075
Personnel: Brett Marston (Advisor)

GEORGETOWN UNIVERSITY

Street address 1: Leavey Ctr Rm 421, 37th & O Sts NW
Street address city: Washington
Street address state: District of Columbia
Zip/Postal code: 20057-0001
Country: USA
Mailing address: PO Box 571065
Mailing city: Washington
Mailing state: District of Columbia
Mailing zip: 20057-1065
General Phone: (202) 687-3947
General Fax: (202) 687-2741
Advertising Phone: (202) 687-3947
Advertising Fax: (202) 687-2741
Editorial Phone: (202) 687-3415
General/National Adv. E-mail: gm@thehoya.com
Display Adv. E-mail: sales@thehoya.com
Editorial e-mail: editor@thehoya.com
Primary Website: www.thehoya.com
Year Established: 1920
Published: Tues`Fri
Avg Free Circ: 6500
Personnel: Roshan Vora (Advisor); Michelle Lee (Adv. Mgr.); Kaphryn Devincenzo (Ed. in chief); Eamon O' connor (Exec. Ed.); Kathryn (Mng. Ed.); Mary Nancy Walter (General Manager)

HOWARD UNIV.

Street address 1: 2251 Sherman Ave NW
Street address city: Washington
Street address state: District of Columbia
Zip/Postal code: 20001-4003
Country: USA
Mailing address: 816 Easley St Apt 805
Mailing city: Silver Spring
Mailing state: MD
Mailing zip: 20910-4581
General Phone: (202) 806-4749
General Fax: (202) 328-1681
General/National Adv. E-mail: bussinessoffice@thehilltoponline.com
Personnel: Kevin Reed (Advisor); Vanessa Rozier (Ed. in Chief)

MCDONOUGH BUS. SCHOOL/ GEORGETOWN UNIV.

Street address 1: 3520 Prospect St NW
Street address 2: Ste 215
Street address city: Washington
Street address state: District of Columbia
Zip/Postal code: 20007-2631
Country: USA
Mailing address: 3520 Prospect St NW Ste 215
Mailing city: Washington
Mailing state: District of Columbia
Mailing zip: 20007-2631
General Phone: (202) 678-0268
General Fax: (202) 678-0268
General/National Adv. E-mail: mba-globe@msb.edu
Personnel: Brenna Fleener (Ed. in Chief)

FLORIDA

BARRY UNIV.

Street address 1: 11300 NE 2nd Ave
Street address city: Miami Shores
Street address state: FL
Zip/Postal code: 33161-6628
Country: USA
Mailing address: 11300 NE 2nd Ave
Mailing city: Miami Shores
Mailing state: FL
Mailing zip: 33161-6695
General Phone: (305) 899-3093
General Fax: (305) 899-4744
General/National Adv. E-mail: buccaneer@mail.barry.edu
Personnel: Susannah Nesmith (Advisor); Amor Tagan (Adv. Dir.); Samantha Stanton (Ed. in Chief)

BETHUNE-COOKMAN COLLEGE

Street address 1: 640 Dr Mary McLeod Bethune Blvd
Street address city: Daytona Beach
Street address state: FL
Zip/Postal code: 32114-3012
Country: USA
Mailing address: 640 Dr. Mary McLeod Bethune Blvd.
Mailing city: Daytona Beach
Mailing state: FL
Mailing zip: 32114
General Phone: (386) 481-2000
General Fax: (386) 481-2701
General/National Adv. E-mail: voiceofthewildcats@gmail.edu
Display Adv. E-mail: voiceofthewildcats@gmail.com
Editorial e-mail: voiceofthewildcates@gmail.com
Primary Website: voiceofthewildcats.wordpress.com; www.cookman.edu
Year Established: 1904
Published: Mthly
Published Other: UniverCity Magazine
Avg Free Circ: 1000

Personnel: Petra Merrick (Ed); Jamie Cobb (Layout/ Paginator); Timothy White (Sports Ed); Augustinas Navickas (Columnist); Andres Whipple Girbes (Technology Writer)

CENTRAL FLORIDA CMTY. COLLEGE

Street address 1: 3001 SW College Rd
Street address city: Ocala
Street address state: FL
Zip/Postal code: 34474-4415
Country: USA
Mailing address: 3001 SW College Rd.
Mailing city: Ocala
Mailing state: FL
Mailing zip: 34474
General Phone: (352) 873-5800
General Fax: (352) 291-4450
General/National Adv. E-mail: patpress@cf.edu
Personnel: Rob Marino (Advisor)

DAYTONA STATE COLLEGE

Street address 1: 1200 W International Speedway Blvd
Street address city: Daytona Beach
Street address state: FL
Zip/Postal code: 32114-2817
Country: USA
Mailing address: 1200 W International Speedway Blvd
Mailing city: Daytona Beach
Mailing state: FL
Mailing zip: 32114-2817
General Phone: (386) 506-3268
General Fax: (386) 506-3155
Editorial Phone: (386) 506-3686
General/National Adv. E-mail: inmotion@daytonastate.edu
Display Adv. E-mail: inmotion@daytonastate.edu
Editorial e-mail: inmotion@daytonastate.edu
Primary Website: www.daytonastateinmotion.com
Year Established: 1991
Published: Mthly
Avg Free Circ: 10002000
Personnel: Elena Jarvis (Advisor)

EMBRY-RIDDLE AERONAUTICAL UNIVERSITY

Street address 1: 600 S Clyde Morris Blvd
Street address city: Daytona Beach
Street address state: FL
Zip/Postal code: 32114-3966
Country: USA
Mailing address: 600 S Clyde Morris Blvd
Mailing city: Daytona Beach
Mailing state: FL
Mailing zip: 32114-3900
General Phone: (386) 226-6049
Advertising Phone: (386) 226-6727
Advertising Fax: (386) 226-7697
Editorial Phone: (386) 226-6079
General/National Adv. E-mail: theavion@gmail.com
Display Adv. E-mail: avionadvertising@gmail.com
Primary Website: www.theavion.com
Year Established: 1969
Published: Tues
Avg Free Circ: 2000
Personnel: Jessica Searcy (Advisor)

FLAGLER COLLEGE

Street address 1: PO Box 1027
Street address city: Saint Augustine
Street address state: FL
Zip/Postal code: 32085-1027
Country: USA
Mailing address: PO Box 1027
Mailing city: Saint Augustine
Mailing state: FL
Mailing zip: 32085-1027
General Phone: (904) 819-6333
General Fax: (904) 826-3224
General/National Adv. E-mail: gargoyle@flagler.edu
Primary Website: gargoyle.flagler.edu
Year Established: 1968
Personnel: Brain Thomson (Advisor)

FLORIDA A&M UNIV.

Street address 1: 510 Orr Dr, Ste 3081
Street address city: Tallahassee
Street address state: FL
Zip/Postal code: 32307-0001
Country: USA
Mailing address: 510 Orr Dr Ste 3081
Mailing city: Tallahassee
Mailing state: FL
Mailing zip: 32307-0001
General Phone: (850) 599-3159
General Fax: (850) 561-2570
General/National Adv. E-mail: thefamuanec@gmail.com
Display Adv. E-mail: famuanads@hotmail.com
Personnel: Andrew Skeritt (Advisor); Erica Butler (Ed. in Chief)

FLORIDA ATLANTIC UNIV.

Street address 1: 777 Glades Rd
Street address city: Boca Raton
Street address state: FL
Zip/Postal code: 33431-6424
Country: USA
Mailing address: 777 Glades Rd
Mailing city: Boca Raton
Mailing state: FL
Mailing zip: 33431-6496
General Phone: (561) 297-2960
General Fax: (561) 297-2106
General/National Adv. E-mail: upress@fau.edu
Personnel: Michael Koretzky (Advisor); Devin Desjarlais (Ed. in Chief); Karla Bowsher (Mng. Ed.); Lindsey Voltoline (Art Dir.)

FLORIDA INSTITUTE OF TECHNOLOGY

Street address 1: 150 W University Blvd
Street address city: Melbourne
Street address state: FL
Zip/Postal code: 32901-6982
Country: USA
Mailing address: 150 W University Blvd Ofc
Mailing city: Melbourne
Mailing state: FL
Mailing zip: 32901-6975
General Phone: (321) 674-8024
General Fax: (321) 674-8017
General/National Adv. E-mail: crimson@fit.edu
Editorial e-mail: crimson@fit.edu
Primary Website: http://crimson@fit.edu
Year Established: 1967
Personnel: Ted Petersen (Adviser); Drew Lacy (Editor-in-Chief)

FLORIDA INTERNATIONAL UNIV.

Street address 1: University Park Campus, 11200 SW 8th St, Graham Ctr, Ste 210
Street address city: Miami
Street address state: FL
Zip/Postal code: 33174-
Country: USA
Mailing address: University Park Campus, 11200 SW 8th St., Graham Ctr., Ste. 210
Mailing city: Miami
Mailing state: FL
Mailing zip: 33174-2516
General Phone: (305) 348-6993
General Fax: (305) 348-2712
General/National Adv. E-mail: beacon@fiu.edu
Personnel: Robert jaross (Advisor); Tatiana Cantillo (Bus. Mgr.); Chris Necuze (Ed. in Chief); Jessica Maya (Prodn. Mgr.)

FLORIDA MEMORIAL COLLEGE

Street address 1: 15800 NW 42nd Ave
Street address city: Miami Gardens
Street address state: FL
Zip/Postal code: 33054-6155
Country: USA
Mailing address: 15800 NW 42nd Ave.
Mailing city: Miami Gardens
Mailing state: FL
Mailing zip: 33054
General Phone: (305) 626-3103
General Fax: (305) 626-3102
General/National Adv. E-mail: lionstal@fmuniv.edu
Personnel: Nathanael Paul (Ed.)

FLORIDA SOUTHERN COLLEGE

Street address 1: 111 Lake Hollingsworth Dr
Street address city: Lakeland
Street address state: FL
Zip/Postal code: 33801-5607
Country: USA
Mailing address: 111 Lake Hollingsworth Dr
Mailing city: Lakeland
Mailing state: FL
Mailing zip: 33801-5698
General Phone: (863) 680-4155
General Fax: (863) 680-6244
Display Adv. E-mail: mtrice@flsouthern.edu
Editorial e-mail: fscsouthern@gmail.com
Primary Website: www.fscsouthern.com
Published: Fri`Other
Published Other: every other week
Avg Free Circ: 1200
Personnel: Michael Trice (Advisor)

FLORIDA STATE COLLEGE AT JACKSONVILLE

Street address 1: 101 State St W
Street address 2: Rm C103
Street address city: Jacksonville
Street address state: FL
Zip/Postal code: 32202-3099
Country: USA
Mailing address: 101 State St W Rm C103
Mailing city: Jacksonville
Mailing state: FL
Mailing zip: 32202-3099
General Phone: (904) 633-8283
General Fax: (904) 632-3279
General/National Adv. E-mail: campusvoice@fscj.edu
Primary Website: www.campusvoiceonline.com
Published: Bi-Mthly
Personnel: Zak Gragg (Adv. Mgr.); Jocelyn Rhoten (Editor-in-Chief)

FSVIEW & FLORIDA FLAMBEAU

Street address 1: 954 W Brevard St
Street address city: Tallahassee
Street address state: FL
Zip/Postal code: 32304-7709
Country: USA
Mailing address: 277 N Magnolia Dr
Mailing city: Tallahassee
Mailing state: FL
Mailing zip: 32301-2664
General Phone: 850-561-1600
General Fax: 850-574-6578
Advertising Phone: 8505611600
Advertising Fax: 8505746578
Editorial Phone: 850-561-1606
General/National Adv. E-mail: @tallahassee.com
Display Adv. E-mail: eleporin@tallahassee.com
Editorial e-mail: eleporin@tallahassee.com
Primary Website: www.fsunews.com
Year Established: 1915
Personnel: Eliza LePorin (General Manager); Justin Dyke (Content Supervisor); Bailey Shertizinger (Editor-in-Chief); Chris Lewis (Gen. Mgr.); Liz Cox (Ed. in Chief); Arriale Douglas (Prodn. Mgr.)

HILLSBOROUGH CMTY. COLLEGE

Street address 1: 2112 N 15th St
Street address city: Ybor City
Street address state: FL
Zip/Postal code: 33605-3648
Country: USA
Mailing address: 2112 N. 15th Street
Mailing city: Ybor City
Mailing state: FL
Mailing zip: 33605
General Phone: (813) 227-7048
Personnel: Valerie Zell (Advisor)

JACKSONVILLE UNIV.

Street address 1: 2800 University Blvd N
Street address city: Jacksonville
Street address state: FL
Zip/Postal code: 32211-3321
Country: USA
Mailing address: 2800 University Blvd N
Mailing city: Jacksonville
Mailing state: FL
Mailing zip: 32211-3394
General Phone: (904) 256-7526
General Fax: (904) 256-7684
General/National Adv. E-mail: navigator@jacksonville.edu
Personnel: Peter Moberg (Advisor); Jean Sils (Adv. Mgr); Renae Ingram (Ed. in Chief)

LAKE SUMTER CMTY. COLLEGE

Street address 1: 9501 US Highway 441
Street address city: Leesburg
Street address state: FL
Zip/Postal code: 34788-3950
Country: USA
Mailing address: 9501 US Highway 441
Mailing city: Leesburg
Mailing state: FL
Mailing zip: 34788-3950
General Phone: (352) 323-3629
General Fax: (352) 435-5023
General/National Adv. E-mail: anglern@lscc.edu; angler4always@yahoo.com
Personnel: Heather Elmatti (Advisor); Gina Mussatti (Ed.)

LYNN UNIV.

Street address 1: 3601 N Military Trl
Street address city: Boca Raton
Street address state: FL
Zip/Postal code: 33431-5507
Country: USA
Mailing address: 3601 N Military Trl
Mailing city: Boca Raton
Mailing state: FL
Mailing zip: 33431-5598
General Phone: (561) 237-7463
General Fax: (561) 237-7097
General/National Adv. E-mail: advertise@lynnipulse.org
Personnel: Stefani Powers (Advisor)

MIAMI DADE COLLEGE

Street address 1: 11380 NW 27th Ave
Street address 2: Rm 4209
Street address city: Miami
Street address state: FL
Zip/Postal code: 33167-3418
Country: USA
Mailing address: 11380 NW 27th Ave., Rm. 4209
Mailing city: Miami
Mailing state: FL
Mailing zip: 33167
General Phone: (305) 237-1255
General/National Adv. E-mail: mbarco@mdc.edu
Display Adv. E-mail: thereporteradvertising@gmail.com
Primary Website: http://www.mdc.edu/main/thereporter/archive/vol02-02/
Year Established: 2010
Published: Bi-Mthly
Avg Free Circ: 10250
Personnel: Manolo Barco (Advisor)

NOVA SOUTHEASTERN UNIV.

Street address 1: 3301 College Ave
Street address 2: Modular 4
Street address city: Davie
Street address state: FL
Zip/Postal code: 33314-7721
Country: USA
Mailing address: 3301 College Ave Modular 4
Mailing city: Davie
Mailing state: FL
Mailing zip: 33314-7721
General Phone: (954) 262-8455
General Fax: (954) 262-8456
General/National Adv. E-mail: thecurrent@nova.edu; nsnews@nova.edu
Display Adv. E-mail: thecurrentad@nova.edu
Personnel: Fiona Banton

PALM BEACH ATLANTIC UNIVERSITY

Street address 1: 901 S Flagler Dr
Street address city: West Palm Beach
Street address state: FL
Zip/Postal code: 33401-6505
Country: USA
Mailing address: PO Box 24708
Mailing city: West Palm Beach
Mailing state: FL
Mailing zip: 33416-4708

General Phone: (561) 803-2566
General Fax: (561) 803-2577
General/National Adv. E-mail: beacon@pba.edu
Personnel: John Sizemore (Advisor/Exec. Ed.)

PALM BEACH CMTY. COLLEGE

Street address 1: 4200 S Congress Ave
Street address city: Lake Worth
Street address state: FL
Zip/Postal code: 33461-4705
Country: USA
Mailing address: 4200 S Congress Ave
Mailing city: Lake Worth
Mailing state: FL
Mailing zip: 33461-4796
General Phone: (561) 862-4327
Personnel: Pam Jarret (Pub.)

PENSACOLA JUNIOR COLLEGE

Street address 1: 1000 College Blvd
Street address 2: Bldg 96
Street address city: Pensacola
Street address state: FL
Zip/Postal code: 32504-8910
Country: USA
Mailing address: 1000 College Blvd Bldg 96
Mailing city: Pensacola
Mailing state: FL
Mailing zip: 32504-8910
General Phone: (850) 484-1458
General Fax: (850) 484-1149
General/National Adv. E-mail: corsair@pjc.edu
Primary Website: www.ecorsair.com
Year Established: 1949
Personnel: Christina Drain (Advisor); Audrey Davis (Adv. Mgr.); Rose Jansen (Mktg. Mgr.)

POLK CMTY. COLLEGE

Street address 1: 999 Avenue H NE
Street address city: Winter Haven
Street address state: FL
Zip/Postal code: 33881-4256
Country: USA
Mailing address: 999 Avenue H NE
Mailing city: Winter Haven
Mailing state: FL
Mailing zip: 33881-4256
Personnel: Patrick Jones (Advisor)

SAINT LEO UNIVERSITY

Street address 1: 33701 State Road 52
Street address 2: Mc 2127, Dept. of English
Street address city: Saint Leo
Street address state: FL
Zip/Postal code: 33574-9700
Country: USA
Mailing address: 33701 State Road 52
Mailing city: Saint Leo
Mailing state: FL
Mailing zip: 33574-9701
General Phone: (352) 588-7424
General Fax: (352) 588-8300
General/National Adv. E-mail: thelionspridenewspaper@gmail.com
Display Adv. E-mail: thelionspridenewspaper@gmail.com
Editorial e-mail: thelionspridenewspaper@gmail.com
Primary Website: https://prideonlinedotnet.wordpress.com/
Published: Fri
Personnel: Valerie Kasper (Advisor); Cassidy Whitaker (Editor-in-Chief)

SOUTHEASTERN UNIVERSITY

Street address 1: 1000 Longfellow Blvd
Street address city: Lakeland
Street address state: FL
Zip/Postal code: 33801-6034
Country: USA
Mailing address: 1000 Longfellow Blvd
Mailing city: Lakeland
Mailing state: FL
Mailing zip: 33801-6034
General Phone: (863) 667-5000
General Fax: (863) 667-5200
General/National Adv. E-mail: thetimes@seuniversity.edu
Personnel: Chad Neuman (Advisor)

SOUTHEASTERN UNIVERSRITY

Street address 1: 1000 Longfellow Blvd
Street address city: Lakeland
Street address state: FL
Zip/Postal code: 33801-6034
Country: USA
Mailing address: 1000 Longfellow Blvd
Mailing city: Lakeland
Mailing state: FL
Mailing zip: 33801-6034
Primary Website: www.seu.edu
Published: Mthly

ST. THOMAS UNIV.

Street address 1: 16401 NW 37th Ave
Street address city: Opa Locka
Street address state: FL
Zip/Postal code: 33054-6313
Country: USA
Mailing address: 16401 NW 37th Ave
Mailing city: Opa Locka
Mailing state: FL
Mailing zip: 33054-6313
General Phone: (305) 628-6674
General Fax: (305) 443-1210
General/National Adv. E-mail: basic@stu.edu
Personnel: Sharon Brehm (Ed.)

STETSON UNIV.

Street address 1: 421 N Woodland Blvd
Street address city: Deland
Street address state: FL
Zip/Postal code: 32723-8300
Country: USA
Mailing address: 421 N Woodland Blvd
Mailing city: Deland
Mailing state: FL
Mailing zip: 32720
General Phone: (386)-822-7100
General Fax: (904) 822-7233
Display Adv. E-mail: advertising@stetson.edu
Editorial e-mail: reporter@stetson.edu
Personnel: Andrew Davis (Commun. Coord.); Joseph O'Brien (Ed. in Chief); Jason Rickner (Mng. Ed.)

TALLAHASSEE CMTY. COLLEGE

Street address 1: 444 Appleyard Dr
Street address city: Tallahassee
Street address state: FL
Zip/Postal code: 32304-2815
Country: USA
Mailing address: 444 Appleyard Dr
Mailing city: Tallahassee
Mailing state: FL
Mailing zip: 32304-2895
General Phone: (850) 201-8035
General Fax: (850) 201-8427
Advertising Phone: (850) 201-8425
Editorial Phone: (850) 201-8525
General/National Adv. E-mail: talon@tcc.fl.edu
Display Adv. E-mail: talon@tcc.fl.edu
Editorial e-mail: talon@tcc.fl.edu
Primary Website: www.thetcctalon.com
Year Established: 1968
Published: Bi-Mthly
Avg Free Circ: 3000
Personnel: Dana Peck (Advisor)

THE CURRENT - ECKERD COLLEGE

Street address 1: 4200 54th Ave S
Street address city: Saint Petersburg
Street address state: FL
Zip/Postal code: 33711-4744
Country: USA
Mailing address: 4200 54th Ave S
Mailing city: Saint Petersburg
Mailing state: FL
Mailing zip: 33711-4700
General Phone: 610 4317931
General Fax: 610 4317931
Advertising Phone: 610 4317931
Advertising Fax: 610 4317931
Editorial Phone: 610 4317931
Editorial Fax: 610 4317931
General/National Adv. E-mail: thecurrent@eckerd.edu
Display Adv. E-mail: currentads@eckerd.edu
Editorial e-mail: danielsa1@mac.com
Primary Website: www.theonlinecurrent.com
Year Established: 2009
Personnel: Ashley Daniels (Editor-in-Chief); Max Martinez (Managing Editor)

THE SANDSPUR

Street address 1: 1000 Holt Ave
Street address 2: # 2742
Street address city: Winter Park
Street address state: FL
Zip/Postal code: 32789-4499
Country: USA
Mailing address: 1000 Holt Ave # 2742
Mailing city: Winter Park
Mailing state: FL
Mailing zip: 32789-4499
General Phone: (407) 646-2696
Advertising Phone: (407) 646-2695
Display Adv. E-mail: advertising@thesandspur.org
Editorial e-mail: staff@thesandspur.org
Primary Website: www.thesandspur.org
Year Established: 1894
Published: Thur
Avg Free Circ: 1200

UNIV. OF CENTRAL FLORIDA

Street address 1: 11825 High Tech Ave
Street address 2: Ste 100
Street address city: Orlando
Street address state: FL
Zip/Postal code: 32817-8474
Country: USA
Mailing address: 11825 High Tech Ave. Ste. 100
Mailing city: Orlando
Mailing state: FL
Mailing zip: 32817
General Phone: (407) 447-4555
General Fax: (407) 447-4556
General/National Adv. E-mail: sales@ucfnews.com
Primary Website: www.centralfloridafuture.com
Year Established: 1968
Personnel: Heissam Jebailey (Pub.); Brian Linden (Gen. Mgr.); Trisha Irwin (Office. Mgr.); Ray Bush (Adv. Mgr.)

UNIV. OF FLORIDA

Street address 1: PO Box 14257
Street address city: Gainesville
Street address state: FL
Zip/Postal code: 32604-2257
Country: USA
Mailing address: PO Box 14257
Mailing city: Gainesville
Mailing state: FL
Mailing zip: 32604-2257
General Phone: (352) 376-4458
General Fax: (352) 376-4556
General/National Adv. E-mail: advertising@alligator.org
Editorial e-mail: editor@alligator.org
Personnel: Chelsea Keenan (Ed. in Chief)

UNIV. OF MIAMI

Street address 1: 1330 Miller Rd
Street address 2: Ste 200
Street address city: Coral Gables
Street address state: FL
Zip/Postal code: 33146-2322
Country: USA
Mailing address: 1330 Miller Road, Suite 200
Mailing city: Coral Gables
Mailing state: FL
Mailing zip: 33146-2322
General Phone: (305) 284-4401
General Fax: (305) 284-4404
Advertising Phone: same
Advertising Fax: same
Editorial Phone: (305) 284-2016
Editorial Fax: (305) 284-4406
General/National Adv. E-mail: editor@themiamihurricane.com
Display Adv. E-mail: tara@themiamihurricane.com
Editorial e-mail: editor@themiamihurricane.com
Primary Website: www.themiamihurricane.com
Year Established: 1929
Published: Mon`Thur
Avg Free Circ: 10000
Personnel: Bob Radziewicz (Sr. Advisor)

UNIV. OF MIAMI SCHOOL OF LAW

Street address 1: 1311 Miller Rd
Street address city: Coral Gables
Street address state: FL
Zip/Postal code: 33146-2300
Country: USA
Mailing address: 1311 Miller Rd
Mailing city: Coral Gables
Mailing state: FL
Mailing zip: 33146-2300
General Phone: (305) 284-2339
General Fax: (305) 284-3554
General/National Adv. E-mail: resipsa@law.miami.edu
Personnel: Jennifer C. Pratt-Garces (Ed. in Chief); Alex Britell (Mng. Ed.)

UNIV. OF NORTH FLORIDA

Street address 1: 1 U N F Dr
Street address city: Jacksonville
Street address state: FL
Zip/Postal code: 32224-7699
Country: USA
Mailing address: 1 U N F Drive
Mailing city: Jacksonville
Mailing state: FL
Mailing zip: 32224
General Phone: (904) 620-2727
General Fax: (904) 620-3924
General/National Adv. E-mail: spinsads@unf.edu
Primary Website: www.espinnaker.com
Year Established: 1977
Personnel: Adina Daar (Bus. Mgr.)

UNIV. OF SOUTH FLORIDA

Street address 1: 4202 E Fowler Ave
Street address 2: Svc 2
Street address city: Tampa
Street address state: FL
Zip/Postal code: 33620-9951
Country: USA
Mailing address: 4202 E Fowler Ave Svc 2
Mailing city: Tampa
Mailing state: FL
Mailing zip: 33620-9951
General Phone: (813) 974-5190
General Fax: (813) 974-4887
Advertising Phone: (813) 974-6254
Display Adv. E-mail: ads@usforacle.com
Editorial e-mail: oraccleeditor@gmail.com
Primary Website: www.usforacle.com
Year Established: 1966
Published: Mon`Thur
Avg Free Circ: 8000
Personnel: Jay Lawrence (Advisor); Anastasia Dawson (Ed. in chief); Jimmy Geurts (Mng. Ed.)

UNIV. OF TAMPA

Street address 1: Rm 211, Vaughn Ctr, 401 W Kennedy Blvd
Street address city: Tampa
Street address state: FL
Zip/Postal code: 33606-
Country: USA
Mailing address: 401 W Kennedy Blvd
Mailing city: Tampa
Mailing state: FL
Mailing zip: 33606-1490
General Phone: (813) 257-3636
General Fax: (813) 253-6207
General/National Adv. E-mail: minaret@ut.edu; ut.minaret@gmail.com
Personnel: Stephanie Tripp (Advisor); Zoe LeCain (Adv. Mgr.); Charlie Hambos (Ed. in Chief); Kyle Bennett (Sports Ed.)

UNIV. OF WEST FLORIDA

Street address 1: 11000 University Pkwy
Street address 2: Comm Arts 36
Street address city: Pensacola
Street address state: FL
Zip/Postal code: 32514-5732
Country: USA
Mailing address: 11000 University Pkwy Comm Arts 36
Mailing city: Pensacola

Mailing state: FL

VALENCIA CMTY. COLLEGE

Street address 1: 1800 S Kirkman Rd
Street address city: Orlando
Street address state: FL
Zip/Postal code: 32811-2302
Country: USA
Mailing address: 1800 S Kirkman Rd
Mailing city: Orlando
Personnel: Ken Carpenter (Advisor)

GEORGIA

ABRAHAM BALDWIN AGRI COLLEGE

Street address 1: 2802 Moore Hwy
Street address city: Tifton
Street address state: GA
Zip/Postal code: 31793-5679
Country: USA
Mailing address: 2802 Moore Hwy
Mailing city: Tifton
Mailing state: GA
Mailing zip: 31793-5698
General Fax: (229) 391-4978
Advertising Fax: (229) 386-7158
General/National Adv. E-mail: stallion@stallion.abac.edu
Personnel: Eric Cash (Faculty Advisor)

AGNES SCOTT COLLEGE

Street address 1: 141 E College Ave
Street address city: Decatur
Street address state: GA
Zip/Postal code: 30030-3770
Country: USA
Mailing address: 141 E College Ave
Mailing city: Decatur
Personnel: Jeniffer Owen (Dir. Commun.); Josie Hoilman (Ed.)

ARMSTRONG ATLANTIC STATE UNIV.

Street address 1: Memorial College Ctr, 11935 Abercorn St, Rm 202
Street address city: Savannah
Street address state: GA
Country: USA
Mailing address: Memorial College Ctr., 11935 Abercorn St., Rm. 202
Mailing city: Savannah
Mailing state: GA
Mailing zip: 31419-1909
General Phone: (912) 344-3252
General Fax: (912) 344-3475
General/National Adv. E-mail: inkwellnews@gmail.com
Personnel: Tony Morris (Advisor); Kristin Alonso (Ed. in Chief)

ATLANTA UNIVERSITY CENTER

Street address 1: 117 Vine St SW
Street address 2: Fl 1
Street address city: Atlanta
Street address state: GA
Zip/Postal code: 30314-4205
Country: USA
Mailing address: PO Box 3191
Mailing city: Atlanta
Mailing state: GA
Mailing zip: 30302-3191
General Phone: (404) 523-6136
General/National Adv. E-mail: aucdigestmail@aol.com
Primary Website: www.aucdigest.com
Year Established: 1973
Published: Thur
Personnel: Lo Jelks (Ed.)

AUGUSTA STATE UNIV.

Street address 1: 2500 Walton Way
Street address city: Augusta
Street address state: GA
Zip/Postal code: 30904-4562
Country: USA
Mailing address: 2500 Walton Way
Mailing city: Augusta
Mailing state: GA
Mailing zip: 30904-2200
General Phone: (706) 737-1600
General Fax: (706) 729-2247
General/National Adv. E-mail: bellringerproduction@gmail.com
Personnel: Matthew Bosisio (Advisor); Kara Mauldin (Ed. in Chief); Stacie Cooper (Prodn. Mgr.); Dee Taylor (Adv. Mgr.)

BERRY COLLEGE

Street address 1: 2277 Martha Berry Hwy NW
Street address city: Mount Berry
Street address state: GA
Zip/Postal code: 30149-9707
Country: USA
Mailing address: 2277 Martha Berry Hwy NW
Mailing city: Mount Berry
Mailing state: GA
Mailing zip: 30149-9707
General Phone: (706) 238-7871
Personnel: Kevin Kleine (Advisor); Jeanne Mathews (Asst. Vice Pres., PR); Rick Woodall (Dir., News/Editorial Servs.)

BRENAU UNIV.

Street address 1: 500 Washington St SE
Street address city: Gainesville
Street address state: GA
Zip/Postal code: 30501-3628
Country: USA
Mailing address: 500 Washington St SE
Mailing city: Gainesville
Mailing state: GA
Mailing zip: 30501-3628
General Phone: (770) 538-4762
Personnel: Nathan R. Goss (Coord., Admissions)

CLARK ATLANTA UNIV.

Street address 1: 223 James P Brawley Dr SW
Street address city: Atlanta
Street address state: GA
Zip/Postal code: 30314-4358
Country: USA
Mailing address: PO Box 1523
Mailing city: Atlanta
Mailing state: GA
Mailing zip: 30301-1523
Personnel: James McJunkins (Advisor)

CLAYTON STATE UNIV.

Street address 1: 2000 Clayton State Blvd
Street address city: Morrow
Street address state: GA
Zip/Postal code: 30260-1250
Country: USA
Mailing address: 2000 Clayton State Blvd
Mailing city: Morrow
Mailing state: GA
Mailing zip: 30260-1250
General Phone: (678) 466-5436
General Fax: (678) 466-5470
General/National Adv. E-mail: info@thebenttree.org
Primary Website: www.thebenttree.org
Published: Mthly
Personnel: Randy Clark (Advisor); Sunitha Caton (Ed.)

COLUMBUS STATE UNIV.

Street address 1: 4225 University Ave
Street address city: Columbus
Street address state: GA
Zip/Postal code: 31907-5679
Country: USA
Mailing address: 4225 University Ave
Mailing city: Columbus
Mailing state: GA
Mailing zip: 31907-5645
General Phone: (706) 562-1494
General Fax: (706) 568-2434
General/National Adv. E-mail: csusaber@yahoo.com; csusaber@gmail.com; saber@colstate.edu
Primary Website: thesaber.wixsite.com/thesaber
Year Established: 1958
Published: Other
Personnel: Linda Reynold (Advisor)

COVENANT COLLEGE

Street address 1: 14049 Scenic Hwy
Street address city: Lookout Mountain
Street address state: GA
Zip/Postal code: 30750-4100
Country: USA
Mailing address: 14049 Scenic Hwy
Mailing city: Lookout Mountain
Mailing state: GA
Mailing zip: 30750-4100
General Phone: (706) 820-1560
General Fax: (706) 820-0672
General/National Adv. E-mail: bagpipe@covenant.edu
Personnel: Cliff Foreman (Faculty Advisor); Kaitlin Fender (Ed. in Chief)

DARTON COLLEGE

Street address 1: 2400 Gillionville Rd
Street address city: Albany
Street address state: GA
Zip/Postal code: 31707-3023
Country: USA
Mailing address: 2400 Gillionville Rd
Mailing city: Albany
Personnel: Roger Marietta (Advisor)

EMORY UNIV.

Street address 1: 605 Asbury Cir
Street address city: Atlanta
Street address state: GA
Zip/Postal code: 30322-1006
Country: USA
Mailing address: P.O. Box W
Mailing city: Atlanta
Mailing state: GA
Mailing zip: 30322-1006
General Phone: (404) 727-0279
Advertising Phone: (404) 727-3613
Editorial Phone: (404) 727-6178
General/National Adv. E-mail: emorywheelexec@gmail.com
Editorial e-mail: emorywheelexec@gmail.com
Primary Website: www.emorywheel.com
Year Established: 1919
Published: Tues`Fri
Personnel: Priyanka Krishnamurthy (Ed.); Sonam Vashi (Exec. Ed.); Lizzie Howell (Managing Ed.)

FT. VALLEY STATE UNIV.

Street address 1: 1005 State University Dr
Street address city: Fort Valley
Street address state: GA
Zip/Postal code: 31030-4313
Country: USA
Mailing address: 121 Huntington Chase Cir
Mailing city: Warner Robins
Mailing state: GA
Mailing zip: 31088-2675
General Phone: (478) 825-6910
Personnel: Valerie White (Advisor); Mick-Aela Nobles (Ed.)

GAINESVILLE COLLEGE

Street address 1: 3820 Mundy Mill Rd
Street address city: Oakwood
Street address state: GA
Zip/Postal code: 30566-3414
Country: USA
Mailing address: PO Box 1358
Mailing city: Gainesville
Mailing state: GA
Mailing zip: 30503-1358
General Phone: (678) 717-3820
General Fax: (678) 717-3832
General/National Adv. E-mail: compass@gsc.edu
Display Adv. E-mail: compass@gsc.edu
Editorial e-mail: compass@gsc.edu
Primary Website: www.gsccompass.org
Published: Mthly
Avg Free Circ: 1000
Personnel: Merrill Morris (Advisor); Audrey Williams (Editor in Chief); Brent VanFleet (Associate Editor)

GEORGIA COLLEGE & STATE UNIV.

Street address 1: 231 W Hancock St
Street address city: Milledgeville
Street address state: GA
Zip/Postal code: 31061-3375
Country: USA
Mailing address: 231 W. Hancock St.
Mailing city: Milledgeville
Mailing state: GA
Mailing zip: 31061
General Phone: (478) 445-4511
General Fax: (478) 445-2559
General/National Adv. E-mail: colonnade@gcsu.edu
Personnel: Macon McGinley (Advisor); Claire Dykes (Ed. in Chief); Amanda Boddy (News Ed.); Elise Colcord (Adv. Mgr.)

GEORGIA HEALTH SCIENCES UNIVERSITY (FORMERLY MEDICAL COLLEGE OF GEORGIA)

Street address state: GA
Country: USA
Mailing address: 1120 15th St
Mailing city: Augusta
Mailing state: GA
Mailing zip: 30912-0004
General Fax: (706) 721-6397
Editorial Phone: (706) 721-4410
Editorial e-mail: smcgowen@georgiahealth.edu
Personnel: Stacey Hudson (Communications Coordinator Editor, The Connection (formerly the Beeper)); Sharron Walls (Ed.)

GEORGIA HIGHLANDS COLLEGE

Street address 1: 3175 Cedartown Hwy SE
Street address city: Rome
Street address state: GA
Zip/Postal code: 30161-3897
Country: USA
Mailing address: 3175 Cedartown Highway
Mailing city: Rome
Mailing state: GA
Mailing zip: 30161
General Phone: (706) 295-6361
General Fax: (706) 295-6610
Editorial Fax: (678) 872-8040
General/National Adv. E-mail: 6mpost@highlands.edu
Display Adv. E-mail: ads6MP@student.highlands.edu
Personnel: Kristie Kemper (Advisor); Nick Godfrey (Ed.)

GEORGIA INST. OF TECHNOLOGY

Street address 1: 353 Ferst Dr
Street address 2: Rm 137
Street address city: Atlanta
Street address state: GA
Zip/Postal code: 30318-5602
Country: USA
Mailing address: 353 Ferst Dr Rm 137
Mailing city: Atlanta
Mailing state: GA
Mailing zip: 30332-0001
General Phone: (404) 894-2830
General Fax: (404) 894-1650
General/National Adv. E-mail: editor@technique.gatech.edu
Personnel: Mac Pitts (Advisor); Emily Chambers (Ed. in Chief); Jonathan Saethang (Mng. Ed.); Hahnming Lee (Bus. Mgr.)

GEORGIA PERIMETER COLLEGE

Street address 1: 555 N Indian Creek Dr
Street address city: Clarkston
Street address state: GA
Zip/Postal code: 30021-2361
Country: USA
Mailing address: 555 N Indian Creek Dr
Mailing city: Clarkston
Mailing state: GA
Mailing zip: 30021-2361
General Phone: (678)-891-3381
General Fax: (404) 298-3882
General/National Adv. E-mail: gpccollegian@gmail.com
Primary Website: www.gpc.edu

Year Established: 1986
Personnel: Alice Murray (Bus. Mgr.); Nathan Guest (Ed. in Chief)

GEORGIA SOUTHERN UNIV.

Street address 1: Williams Center Rm 2023
Street address city: Statesboro
Street address state: GA
Zip/Postal code: 30460-0001
Country: USA
Mailing address: PO Box 8001
Mailing city: Statesboro
Mailing state: GA
Mailing zip: 30460-1000
General Phone: (912) 478-5246
General Fax: (912) 478-7113
Editorial Phone: (912) 478-5418
General/National Adv. E-mail: gaeditor@georgiasouthern.edu
Display Adv. E-mail: ads1@georgiasouthern.edu
Primary Website: Georgia Southern University GSU Student Media Box 8001
Year Established: 1927
Published: Tues`Thur
Personnel: Jozsef Papp (Exec. Ed.)

GEORGIA SOUTHWESTERN STATE UNIV.

Street address 1: 800 Georgia Southwestern State University Dr
Street address city: Americus
Street address state: GA
Zip/Postal code: 31709
Country: USA
Mailing address: 800 Georgia Southwestern State University Dr.
Mailing city: Americus
Mailing state: GA
Mailing zip: 31709
General Phone: (229) 931-2003
General Fax: (229) 931-2059
General/National Adv. E-mail: gswpaper@yahoo.com; gswpaper@canes.gsw.edu
Personnel: Josh Curtin (Advisor); Emily Immke (Bus. Mgr.); Sidney Davis (Ed. in Chief)

GEORGIA STATE UNIVERSITY

Street address 1: 310 Student Center East
Street address 2: 55 Gilmer St SE
Street address city: Atlanta
Street address state: GA
Zip/Postal code: 30303
Country: USA
Mailing address: 310 Student Center East
Mailing city: Atlanta
Mailing state: GA
Mailing zip: 30303-3011
General Phone: (404) 413-1617(404) 413-1868
General Fax: 404-413-1868
Advertising Phone: 404-413-1869
Advertising Fax: 404-413-1868
Editorial Phone: 404-413-1617
General/National Adv. E-mail: signaleditor@gmail.com
Display Adv. E-mail: whenley@gsu.edu
Editorial e-mail: signaleditor@gmail.com
Primary Website: www.georgiastatesignal.com
Year Established: 1933
Published: Tues
Published Other: (Fall & Spring with summer magazine)
Avg Free Circ: 4000
Personnel: Bryce McNeil (Director, Student Media); Adam Duffy (Editor-in-Chief); Wakesha Henley (Business Coordinator); Zoana Price (Student Media Advisor, Perimeter College)

KENNESAW STATE UNIVERSITY

Street address 1: 395 Cobb Ave NW
Street address 2: Ste 274 # 501
Street address city: Kennesaw
Street address state: GA
Zip/Postal code: 30144-5660
Country: USA
Mailing address: 395 Cobb Ave NW
Mailing city: Kennesaw
Mailing state: GA
Mailing zip: 30144-5588
General Phone: (470) 578-5470
General Fax: (470) 578-9165
General/National Adv. E-mail: sentinel@ksumedia.com
Display Adv. E-mail: marketingmgr@ksumedia.com
Editorial e-mail: eic@ksusentinel.com
Primary Website: www.ksusentinel.com
Year Established: 1967
Published: Tues
Avg Free Circ: 5000
Personnel: Ed Bonza (Advisor)

LAGRANGE COLLEGE

Street address 1: 601 Broad St
Street address 2: # 1165
Street address city: Lagrange
Street address state: GA
Zip/Postal code: 30240-2955
Country: USA
Mailing address: 601 Broad St # 1165
Mailing city: Lagrange
Mailing state: GA
Mailing zip: 30240-2955
General Phone: (706) 880-8020
Personnel: John Tures (Advisor); Kate Bush (Co-Ed.); Chris Nylund (Co-Ed.)

MACON STATE COLLEGE

Street address 1: 100 University Pkwy
Street address city: Macon
Street address state: GA
Zip/Postal code: 31206-5100
Country: USA
Mailing address: 100 College Station Dr
Mailing city: Macon
Mailing state: GA
Mailing zip: 31206-5145
General Phone: (478) 471-2700
General Fax: (478) 757-2626
General/National Adv. E-mail: mscmatrix@maconstate.edu; statement@maconstate.edu
Personnel: Ray Lightner (Advisor); Glen Stone (Ed. in Chief)

MERCER UNIV.

Street address 1: PO Box 72728
Street address city: Macon
Street address state: GA
Zip/Postal code: 31207-5272
Country: USA
Mailing address: PO Box 72728
Mailing city: Macon
Mailing state: GA
Mailing zip: 31207-5272
Personnel: Lee Greenway (Advisor)

MOREHOUSE COLLEGE

Street address 1: 830 Westview Dr SW
Street address city: Atlanta
Street address state: GA
Zip/Postal code: 30314-3773
Country: USA
Mailing address: 830 Westview Dr SW
Mailing city: Atlanta
Mailing state: GA
Mailing zip: 30314-3776
General Phone: (404) 681-2800
General/National Adv. E-mail: mtiger@morehouse.edu
Personnel: Edward T. Mitchell (Ed. in Chief); Donovan Ramsey (Mng. Ed.)

NORTH GEORGIA COLLEGE

Street address 1: PO Box 5432
Street address city: Dahlonega
Street address state: GA
Zip/Postal code: 30597-0001
Country: USA
Mailing address: PO Box 5432
Mailing city: Dahlonega
Mailing state: GA
Mailing zip: 30597-0001
General Phone: (706) 864-1468
General Fax: (706) 864-1485
General/National Adv. E-mail: voice@ngcsu.edu
Personnel: Debbie Martin (Ed.)

OGLETHORPE UNIVERSITY

Street address 1: 4484 Peachtree Rd NE
Street address city: Brookhaven
Street address state: GA
Zip/Postal code: 30319-2797
Country: USA
Mailing address: 4484 Peachtree Rd. NE
Mailing city: Atlanta
Mailing state: GA
Mailing zip: 30319
General Phone: (404) 364-8425
General Fax: (404) 364-8442
General/National Adv. E-mail: stormypetrel@oglethorpe.edu
Primary Website: 3443 Somerset Trace
Published: Mthly
Personnel: Tali Schroeder (Ed.)

SAVANNAH COLLEGE OF ART/DESIGN

Street address 1: PO Box 3146
Street address city: Savannah
Street address state: GA
Zip/Postal code: 31402-3146
Country: USA
Mailing address: PO Box 3146
Mailing city: Savannah
Mailing state: GA
Mailing zip: 31402-3146
General Phone: (912) 525-5500
General Fax: (912) 525-5506
General/National Adv. E-mail: district@scad.edu
Personnel: Aisha Michael (Circ./Classified Mgr.)

SHORTER COLLEGE

Street address 1: 315 Shorter Ave SW
Street address city: Rome
Street address state: GA
Zip/Postal code: 30165-4267
Country: USA
Mailing address: 315 Shorter Ave SW
Mailing city: Rome
Mailing state: GA
Mailing zip: 30165-4267
General Phone: (706) 233-7208
General Fax: (706) 236-1515
General/National Adv. E-mail: the_periscope@hotmail.com
Personnel: Ashley Ottinger (Ed. in chief)

STATE UNIV. OF WEST GEORGIA

Street address 1: 1601 Maple St
Street address city: Carrollton
Street address state: GA
Zip/Postal code: 30118-0001
Country: USA
Mailing address: 1601 Maple St
Mailing city: Carrollton
Mailing state: GA
Mailing zip: 30118-0002
Personnel: Stephanie Smith (Adv. Mgr.)

THOMAS COLLEGE

Street address 1: 1501 Millpond Rd
Street address city: Thomasville
Street address state: GA
Zip/Postal code: 31792-7478
Country: USA
Mailing address: 1501 Millpond Rd
Mailing city: Thomasville
Mailing state: GA
Mailing zip: 31792-7636
Personnel: Charity Nixon (Ed.)

TOCCOA FALLS COLLEGE

Street address 1: 107 Kincaid Dr
Street address city: Toccoa Falls
Street address state: GA
Zip/Postal code: 30598-9602
Country: USA
Mailing address: 107 Kincaid Dr
Mailing city: Toccoa Falls
Mailing state: GA
Mailing zip: 30598-9602
General Phone: (706) 886-7299
General Fax: (706) 886-0210
General/National Adv. E-mail: talon@tfc.edu
Personnel: Christine Brubaker (Ed. in Chief)

UNIV. OF GEORGIA

Street address 1: 540 Baxter St
Street address city: Athens
Street address state: GA
Zip/Postal code: 30605-1106
Country: USA
Mailing address: 540 Baxter St
Mailing city: Athens
Mailing state: GA
Mailing zip: 30605-1106
General Phone: (706) 433-3000
General Fax: (706) 433-3033
Advertising Phone: (706) 433-3012
Editorial Phone: (706) 433-3002
General/National Adv. E-mail: news@randb.com
Personnel: Ed Morales (Editorial Adviser); Natalie McClure (General Manager)

VALDOSTA STATE UNIV.

Street address 1: 1500 N Patterson St
Street address city: Valdosta
Street address state: GA
Zip/Postal code: 31698-0100
Country: USA
Mailing address: 1500 N Patterson St
Mailing city: Valdosta
Mailing state: GA
Mailing zip: 31698-0001
General Phone: (229) 333-5686
General Fax: (229) 249-2618
General/National Adv. E-mail: spec@valdosta.edu
Personnel: Pat Miller (Advisor); John Pickworth (Adv. Mgr.); Desiree Thompson (Editor in Chief)

WESLEYAN COLLEGE

Street address 1: 4760 Forsyth Rd
Street address city: Macon
Street address state: GA
Zip/Postal code: 31210-4407
Country: USA
Mailing address: 4760 Forsyth Rd
Mailing city: Macon
Mailing state: GA
Mailing zip: 31210-4462
General Phone: (478) 757-5100
General Fax: (478) 757-4027
General/National Adv. E-mail: pioneer@wesleyancollege.edu
Personnel: Dana Amihere (Ed.)

HAWAII

BRIGHAM YOUNG UNIV.

Street address 1: 55-220 Kulanui St
Street address city: Laie
Street address state: HI
Zip/Postal code: 96762-1266
Country: USA
Mailing address: 55-220 Kulanui St Ste 1
Mailing city: Laie
Mailing state: HI
Mailing zip: 96762-1266
General Phone: (808) 675-3696
Personnel: Leeann Lambert (Advisor); Karen Hemenway (Copy Ed.)

CHAMINADE UNIV.

Street address 1: 3140 Waialae Ave
Street address city: Honolulu
Street address state: HI
Zip/Postal code: 96816-1510
Country: USA
Mailing address: 3140 Waialae Ave
Mailing city: Honolulu
Mailing state: HI
Mailing zip: 96816-1578
General Phone: (808) 739-4636
General Fax: (808) 735-4891
General/National Adv. E-mail: cuhpress@chaminade.edu

Personnel: Ashlee Duenas (Ed.)

HAWAII PACIFIC UNIVERSITY

Street address 1: 1154 Fort Street Mall
Street address 2: Ste 312
Street address city: Honolulu
Street address state: HI
Zip/Postal code: 96813-2712
Country: USA
Mailing address: 1154 Fort Street Mall Ste 312
Mailing city: Honolulu
Mailing state: HI
Mailing zip: 96813-2712
General Phone: (808) 544-9379
General Fax: (808) 566-2418
Editorial Phone: (808)687-7030
General/National Adv. E-mail: kalamalama@hpu.edu
Primary Website: http://www.hpu.edu/kalamalamaonline/index.html
Year Established: 1992
Personnel: Dayna Kalakau (Bus. Mgr.); Susanne Haala (Student Editor); Nicole Kato (Copy Editor); Kara Jernigan (Associate Editor); John Windrow (Faculty Editor); Riana Stellburg (Photo Editor); Emily Tall (Sports Editor); David Chow (Social Media Tech)

HONOLULU CMTY. COLLEGE UNIV. OF HAWAII

Street address 1: 874 Dillingham Blvd
Street address city: Honolulu
Street address state: HI
Zip/Postal code: 96817-4505
Country: USA
Mailing address: 874 Dillingham Blvd
Mailing city: Honolulu
Mailing state: HI
Mailing zip: 96817-4598
General Phone: (808) 845-9211
General Fax: (808) 847-9876
Editorial Phone: 808-227-5922
General/National Adv. E-mail: hcckala@gmail.com
Primary Website: www.thekala.net
Year Established: 1963
Published: Mthly
Avg Free Circ: 900
Personnel: Michael Leidemann (Adviser, Asst Professor of Journalism)

KA LEO O HAWAIÂ€ˇ

Street address 1: 2445 Campus Rd
Street address 2: Hemenway 107
Street address city: Honolulu
Street address state: HI
Zip/Postal code: 96822-2216
Country: USA
Mailing address: 2445 Campus Rd., Hemenway 107
Mailing city: Honolulu
Mailing state: HI
Mailing zip: 96822-2216
General Phone: (808) 956-7043
General Fax: (808) 956-9962
Advertising Phone: (808) 956-7043
Editorial Phone: (808) 956-7043
General/National Adv. E-mail: editor@kaleo.org
Display Adv. E-mail: advertising@kaleo.org
Editorial e-mail: editor@kaleo.org
Primary Website: www.kaleo.org
Year Established: 1922
Published: Mthly
Avg Free Circ: 6000
Personnel: Jay Hartwell (Ed. Advisor); Sandy Matsui (Dir)

KAPIOLANI CMTY. COLLEGE

Street address 1: 4303 Diamond Head Rd
Street address city: Honolulu
Street address state: HI
Zip/Postal code: 96816-4421
Country: USA
Mailing address: 4303 Diamond Head Rd
Mailing city: Honolulu
Mailing state: HI
Mailing zip: 96816-4496
General Phone: (808) 734-9166
General Fax: (808) 734-9287
General/National Adv. E-mail: kapio@hawaii.edu
Personnel: Catherine E. Toth (Advisor); Janell Nakahara (Adv. Mgr.)

LEEWARD CMTY. COLLEGE

Street address 1: 96-045 Ala Ike St
Street address 2: # SC-216
Street address city: Pearl City
Street address state: HI
Zip/Postal code: 96782-3366
Country: USA
Mailing address: 96-045 Ala Ike St # SC-216
Mailing city: Pearl City
Mailing state: HI
Mailing zip: 96782-3366
General Phone: (808) 455-0603
Personnel: Margaret Yasuhara (Ed.)

UNIV. OF HAWAII HILO

Street address 1: 200 W Kawili St, Campus Ctr 215
Street address city: Hilo
Street address state: HI
Zip/Postal code: 96720
Country: USA
Mailing address: 200 W. Kawili St., Campus Ctr. 215
Mailing city: Hilo
Mailing state: HI
Mailing zip: 96720-4091
General Phone: (808) 974-7504
General Fax: (808) 974-7782
General/National Adv. E-mail: kalahea@hawaii.edu
Personnel: Marc Burba (Advisor); Roxanne Yamane (Bus. Mgr.)

IOWA

BUENA VISTA UNIV.

Street address 1: 610 W 4th St
Street address city: Storm Lake
Street address state: IA
Zip/Postal code: 50588-1713
Country: USA
Mailing address: 610 W 4th St
Mailing city: Storm Lake
Mailing state: IA
Mailing zip: 50588-1798
Personnel: Jamii Claiborne (Advisor); Carly Evans (Co Ed. in Chief); Lindsey Marean (Co Ed. in Chief)

CENTRAL COLLEGE

Street address 1: 812 University St
Street address city: Pella
Street address state: IA
Zip/Postal code: 50219-1902
Country: USA
Mailing address: 812 University
Mailing city: Pella
Mailing state: IA
Mailing zip: 50219
General Phone: (877) 462-3687
General Fax: (515) 628-5316
General/National Adv. E-mail: theray@central.edu
Editorial e-mail: carmane@central.edu
Personnel: Emily Betz (Ed.)

CLARKE UNIVERSITY

Street address 1: 1550 Clarke Dr
Street address city: Dubuque
Street address state: IA
Zip/Postal code: 52001-3117
Country: USA
Mailing address: 1550 Clarke Dr
Mailing city: Dubuque
Mailing state: IA
Mailing zip: 52001-3198
General Phone: (563) 588-6335
General Fax: (563) 588-6789
General/National Adv. E-mail: abdul.sinno@clarke.edu
Personnel: Diana Russo (Advisor); Abdul Karim Sinno (Chair); Sarah Bradford (Ed.); David Deifell, Ph.D. (Assoc. Prof. Comm.)

COE COLLEGE

Street address 1: 1220 1st Ave NE
Street address city: Cedar Rapids
Street address state: IA
Zip/Postal code: 52402-5008
Country: USA
Mailing address: 1220 1st Ave NE # 1
Mailing city: Cedar Rapids
Mailing state: IA
Mailing zip: 52402-5092
General Phone: (319) 399-8646
General Fax: (319) 399-8667
General/National Adv. E-mail: cosmos@coe.edu
Primary Website: www.coe.edu
Year Established: 1889
Published: Fri
Personnel: Susanne Gubanc (Advisor)

CORNELL COLLEGE

Street address 1: 600 1st St SW
Street address city: Mount Vernon
Street address state: IA
Zip/Postal code: 52314-1006
Country: USA
Mailing address: 600 First St SW
Mailing city: Mount Vernon
Mailing state: IA
Mailing zip: 52314
General Phone: (319) 895-4430

DES MOINES AREA CMTY. COLLEGE

Street address 1: 2006 S Ankeny Blvd
Street address 2: Bldg 2
Street address city: Ankeny
Street address state: IA
Zip/Postal code: 50023-8995
Country: USA
Mailing address: 2006 S Ankeny Blvd Bldg 2
Mailing city: Ankeny
Mailing state: IA
Mailing zip: 50023-8995
General Phone: (515) 965-6425
General Fax: (515) 433-5033
General/National Adv. E-mail: chronicle@dmacc.edu
Personnel: Julie Roosa (Advisor); Julie Cahill (Adv. Mgr); Kelsey Edwards (Ed. in Chief)

DRAKE UNIV.

Street address 1: 2507 Univ, Ave 124N Meredith Hall
Street address city: Des Moines
Street address state: IA
Zip/Postal code: 50311
Country: USA
Mailing address: 2507 Univ., Ave. 124N Meredith Hall
Mailing city: Des Moines
Mailing state: IA
Mailing zip: 50311-4516
General Phone: (515) 271-3867
General Fax: (515) 271-2798
General/National Adv. E-mail: times.delphic@drake.edu
Personnel: Jill Van Wyke (Advisor); Caleb Bailey (Adv. Mgr.); Matt Vasilogambros (Ed. in Chief)

GRACELAND COLLEGE

Street address 1: 1 University Pl
Street address city: Lamoni
Street address state: IA
Zip/Postal code: 50140-1641
Country: USA
Mailing address: 1 University Pl
Mailing city: Lamoni
Mailing state: IA
Mailing zip: 50140-1684
General Phone: (641) 784-5000
General Fax: (641) 784-5480
General/National Adv. E-mail: tower@graceland.edu
Personnel: Nicky Kerr (Ed. in Chief)

GRAND VIEW UNIVERSITY

Street address 1: Cowles Communication Ctr, 1331 Grandview Ave
Street address city: Des Moines
Street address state: IA
Zip/Postal code: 50316
Country: USA
Mailing address: Cowles Communication Ctr., 1331 Grandview Ave.
Mailing city: Des Moines
Mailing state: IA
Mailing zip: 50316-1453
General Phone: (515) 263-2806
General Fax: (515) 263-2990
General/National Adv. E-mail: grandviews@grandview.edu
Primary Website: www.thegrandviews.com; www.grandview.edu
Year Established: 1949
Published: Fri
Personnel: Mark Siebert (Advisor); Stephanie Ivankovich (Editor)

GRINNELL COLLEGE

Street address 1: 1115 8th Ave
Street address city: Grinnell
Street address state: IA
Zip/Postal code: 50112-1553
Country: USA
Mailing address: P.O. Box 5886
Mailing city: Grinnell
Mailing state: IA
Mailing zip: 50112-3128
General Phone: (641) 269-3325
General Fax: (641) 269-4888
General/National Adv. E-mail: newspapr@grinnell.edu
Primary Website: www.thesandb.com
Published: Fri

IOWA CENTRAL CMTY. COLLEGE

Street address 1: 330 Avenue M
Street address city: Fort Dodge
Street address state: IA
Zip/Postal code: 50501-5739
Country: USA
Mailing address: 330 Avenue M
Mailing city: Fort Dodge
Mailing state: IA
Mailing zip: 50501-5739
General Phone: (515) 576-0099
General Fax: (515) 576-7724
General/National Adv. E-mail: mcintyre@iowacentral.com
Personnel: Bill McIntyre (Advisor); Ian Schmit (Ed.)

IOWA LAKES CMTY. COLLEGE

Street address 1: 300 S 18th St
Street address city: Estherville
Street address state: IA
Zip/Postal code: 51334-2721
Country: USA
Mailing address: 300 S 18th St
Mailing city: Estherville
Mailing state: IA
Mailing zip: 51334-2721
General Phone: (712) 362-2604
General Fax: (712) 362-8363
General/National Adv. E-mail: pbuchholz@iowalakes.edu; info@iowalakes.edu
Personnel: Pam Bushholz (Journalism Instructor/Advisor)

IOWA STATE DAILY

Street address 1: 108 Hamilton Hall
Street address city: Ames
Street address state: IA
Zip/Postal code: 50011-1180
County: Story
Country: USA
Mailing address: 108 Hamilton Hall
Mailing city: Ames
Mailing state: IA
Mailing zip: 50011-1181
General Phone: (515) 294-4120
General Fax: (515) 294-4119
Advertising Phone: (515) 294-2403
Advertising Fax: (515) 294-4119
Editorial Phone: (515) 294-5688
Editorial Fax: (515) 294-4119
General/National Adv. E-mail: ads@iowastatedaily.com
Display Adv. E-mail: ads@iowastatedaily.com

Classified Adv. e-mail: classified@iowastatedaily.com
Editorial e-mail: editor@iowastatedaily.com
Primary Website: www.iowastatedaily.com
Year Established: 1890
Published: Mon`Tues`Wed`Thur`Fri
Personnel: Laura Widmer (Gen. Mgr.); Mark Witherspoon (Ed. Advisor); Stephen Koenigsfeld (Ed.)

IOWA STATE UNIVERSITY

Street address 1: 2420 Lincoln Way
Street address 2: Ste 205
Street address city: Ames
Street address state: IA
Zip/Postal code: 50014-8340
Country: USA
Mailing address: 2420 Lincoln Way, Suite 205
Mailing city: Ames
Mailing state: IA
Mailing zip: 50014
General Phone: (515) 294-4120
General Fax: (515) 294-4119
Advertising Fax: (515) 294-4119
Editorial Phone: (515) 294-4815
Editorial Fax: (515) 294-4119
General/National Adv. E-mail: spoon@iowastatedaily.com
Display Adv. E-mail: sara.brown@iowastatedaily.com
Editorial e-mail: news@iowastatedaily.com
Primary Website: www.iowastatedaily.com
Year Established: 1890
Published: Mon`Tues`Wed`Thur`Fri
Avg Free Circ: 12500
Personnel: Mark Witherspoon (Advisor); Lawrence Cunningham (General Manager of the Iowa State Daily Media Group); Janey Nicholas (Business Manager); Sarah Lefebre (Operations manager); Sara Brown (Advertising manager); Emily Barske (Editor in chief)

IOWA WESLEYAN COLLEGE

Street address 1: 601 N Main St
Street address city: Mount Pleasant
Street address state: IA
Zip/Postal code: 52641-1348
Country: USA
Mailing address: 601 N Main St
Mailing city: Mount Pleasant
Mailing state: IA
Mailing zip: 52641-1398

IOWA WESTERN CMTY. COLLEGE

Street address 1: 2700 College Rd
Street address city: Council Bluffs
Street address state: IA
Zip/Postal code: 51503-1057
Country: USA
Mailing address: 2700 College Rd
Mailing city: Council Bluffs
Mailing state: IA
Mailing zip: 51503-1057
Personnel: Camille Steed (Advisor)

KIRKWOOD COMMUNITY COLLEGE

Street address 1: 6301 Kirkwood Blvd SW
Street address city: Cedar Rapids
Street address state: IA
Zip/Postal code: 52404-5260
Country: USA
Mailing address: 6301 Kirkwood Blvd. SW
Mailing city: Cedar Rapids
Mailing state: IA
Mailing zip: 52404
General Phone: (319) 398-5444
General Fax: (319) 398-7141
General/National Adv. E-mail: communique@kirkwood edu.
Primary Website: www.kirkwoodstudentmedia.com
Published Other: six times each semester
Personnel: Sarah Baker (Advisor); Rose Kodet (Publisher)

LORAS COLLEGE

Street address 1: 1450 Alta Vista St
Street address city: Dubuque
Street address state: IA
Zip/Postal code: 52001-4327
Country: USA
Mailing address: 1450 Alta Vista St
Mailing city: Dubuque
Mailing state: IA
Mailing zip: 52001-4399
General Phone: (563) 588-7954
General Fax: (563) 588-7339
Advertising Phone: (563) 588-7828
Editorial Phone: (563) 588-7954
General/National Adv. E-mail: lorian@loras.edu
Display Adv. E-mail: lorian@loras.edu
Editorial e-mail: lorian@loras.edu
Primary Website: myduhawk.com
Year Established: 1913
Published: Thur
Avg Free Circ: 1600
Personnel: Timothy Manning (Advisor); Anna Sweeney (Adv. Mgr.); Cassandra Busch (Co-Exec. Ed.)

MT. MERCY COLLEGE

Street address 1: 1330 Elmhurst Dr NE
Street address city: Cedar Rapids
Street address state: IA
Zip/Postal code: 52402-4763
Country: USA
Mailing address: 1330 Elmhurst Dr NE
Mailing city: Cedar Rapids
Mailing state: IA
Mailing zip: 52402-4797
General Phone: (319) 363-1323
General Fax: (319) 366-0893
General/National Adv. E-mail: mmctimes@mtmercy.edu
Personnel: Joe Sheller (Advisor); Mellette Maurice (Bus. Mgr.); Brian Heinemann (Ed.)

MUSCATINE CMTY. COLLEGE

Street address 1: 152 Colorado St
Street address city: Muscatine
Street address state: IA
Zip/Postal code: 52761-5329
Country: USA
Mailing address: 152 Colorado St
Mailing city: Muscatine
Mailing state: IA
Mailing zip: 52761-5396
Personnel: Kristina Koch (Advisor)

NORTH IOWA AREA CMTY. COLLEGE

Street address 1: 500 College Dr
Street address city: Mason City
Street address state: IA
Zip/Postal code: 50401-7213
Country: USA
Mailing address: 500 College Drive
Mailing city: Mason City
Mailing state: IA
Mailing zip: 50401
General Phone: (641) 422-4304
General Fax: (641) 422-4280
General/National Adv. E-mail: peterpau@niacc.edu
Personnel: Paul Peterson (Advisor); Emily Knoop (Adv. Mgr.); Collie Wood (Ed.)

NORTHWESTERN COLLEGE

Street address 1: 101 7th St SW
Street address city: Orange City
Street address state: IA
Zip/Postal code: 51041-1923
Country: USA
Mailing address: 101 7th St SW
Mailing city: Orange City
Mailing state: IA
Mailing zip: 51041-1996
General Phone: (712) 707-7043
General Fax: (712) 707-7345
General/National Adv. E-mail: beacon@nwciowa.edu
Personnel: Carl Vandermeulen (Advisor); Kim Eason (Ed.)

PALMER COLLEGE OF CHIROPRACTIC

Street address 1: 1000 Brady St
Street address city: Davenport
Street address state: IA
Zip/Postal code: 52803-5214
Country: USA
Mailing address: 1000 Brady St.
Mailing city: Davenport
Mailing state: IA
Mailing zip: 52803
General Phone: (563) 884-5686
General Fax: (563) 884-5719
General/National Adv. E-mail: beacon@palmer.edu
Personnel: Ramneek Bhogal (Advisor); Stephanie O'Neill (Advisor); Stewart McMillan (Ed.)

SIMPSON COLLEGE

Street address 1: 701 N C St
Street address city: Indianola
Street address state: IA
Zip/Postal code: 50125-1201
Country: USA
Mailing address: 701 N C St
Mailing city: Indianola
Mailing state: IA
Mailing zip: 50125-1202
General Phone: (515) 961-1738
General Fax: (515) 961-1350
General/National Adv. E-mail: thesimp@simpson.edu
Personnel: Emily Schettler (Ed)

UNIV. OF DUBUQUE

Street address 1: 2000 University Ave
Street address 2: # 6
Street address city: Dubuque
Street address state: IA
Zip/Postal code: 52001-5050
Country: USA
Mailing address: 2000 University Ave # 6
Mailing city: Dubuque
Mailing state: IA
Mailing zip: 52001-5050
Personnel: Laura Steinbeck (Ed.)

UNIV. OF IOWA

Street address 1: 104 West Washington St
Street address city: Iowa City
Street address state: IA
Zip/Postal code: 52240
Country: USA
Mailing address: 104 West Washington St
Mailing city: Iowa City
Mailing state: IA
Mailing zip: 52240
General Phone: (319) 335-5791
General Fax: (319) 335-6297
General/National Adv. E-mail: daily-iowan@uiowa.edu
Personnel: William Casey (Pub.); Debra Plath (Bus. Mgr.); Pete Recker (Adv./Circ. Mgr)

UNIV. OF NORTHERN IOWA

Street address 1: L011 Maucker Union
Street address city: Cedar Falls
Street address state: IA
Zip/Postal code: 50614-0001
Country: USA
Mailing address: L011 Maucker Un
Mailing city: Cedar Falls
Mailing state: IA
Mailing zip: 50614-0001
General Phone: (319) 273-2157
General Fax: (319) 273-5931
General/National Adv. E-mail: northern-iowan@uni.edu
Primary Website: www.northerniowan.com
Published: Mon`Thur
Avg Free Circ: 5000
Personnel: Michele Smith (Mgr.); Dana Klesner (Office Asst.); Seth Hadenfelt (Sales); Alex Johansen (Circ.); Jeremy (Circ.); Nikki (Exec. Ed.); Larissa (News Ed.); Anna (Prodn.)

WALDORF COLLEGE

Street address 1: 206 John K Hanson Dr
Street address city: Forest City
Street address state: IA
Zip/Postal code: 50436
Country: USA
Mailing address: 106 S 6th St
Mailing city: Forest City
Mailing state: IA
Mailing zip: 50436-1797
General Phone: (641) 585-2450
General Fax: (641) 582-8194
General/National Adv. E-mail: lobbyist@waldorf.edu
Personnel: David Damm (Advisor); Sarah Soy (Mng. Ed.); Caitlin Leitzen (Mng. Ed.); Matt Knutson (Web Ed.)

WARTBURG COLLEGE

Street address 1: 100 Wartburg Blvd
Street address city: Waverly
Street address state: IA
Zip/Postal code: 50677-2215
Country: USA
Mailing address: 100 Wartburg Blvd
Mailing city: Waverly
Mailing state: IA
Mailing zip: 50677-2200
General Phone: (319) 352-8289
General Fax: (319) 352-8242
General/National Adv. E-mail: trumpet@wartburg.edu
Personnel: Cliff Brockmen (Advisor); Luke Shanno (Ed. in Chief); Jackie Albrecht (News Ed.)

WILLIAM PENN UNIV.

Street address 1: 201 Trueblood Ave
Street address city: Oskaloosa
Street address state: IA
Zip/Postal code: 52577-1757
Country: USA
Mailing address: 201 Trueblood Ave.
Mailing city: Oskaloosa
Mailing state: IA
Mailing zip: 52577
Published: Mthly

IDAHO

BOISE STATE UNIV.

Street address 1: 1910 University Dr
Street address city: Boise
Street address state: ID
Zip/Postal code: 83725-0001
Country: USA
Mailing address: 1910 University Dr
Mailing city: Boise
Mailing state: ID
Mailing zip: 83725-0002
General Phone: (208) 426-6300
General Fax: (208) 426-3884
General/National Adv. E-mail: mcox@boisestate.edu
Personnel: Brad Arendt (Gen. Mgr.); V. Marvin Cox (Chrmn.); Steve Lyons (Advisor); Dwight Murphy (Avd. Mgr.); Shannon Morgan (Ed. in Chief)

BRIGHAM YOUNG UNIV. IDAHO

Street address 1: Spori Bldg 114B
Street address city: Rexburg
Street address state: ID
Zip/Postal code: 1908
Country: USA
Mailing address: Spori Bldg # 114B
Mailing city: Rexburg
Mailing state: ID
Mailing zip: 83460-0001
General Phone: (208) 496-2411
General Fax: (208) 496-2911
General/National Adv. E-mail: scrolleditor@byui.edu
Personnel: Jeff Hochstrasser (Advisor); John Thompson (Advisor); Ryan Hales (Advisor)

COLLEGE OF IDAHO

Street address 1: 2112 Cleveland Blvd
Street address city: Caldwell
Street address state: ID
Zip/Postal code: 83605-4432
Country: USA
Mailing address: PO Box 52
Mailing city: Caldwell
Mailing state: ID
Mailing zip: 83606-0052
General Phone: (208) 459-5509
Personnel: Danielle Blenker (Pres.); Nicole Watson (Vice Pres.); Debbie Swanson (Administrative Asst.); Colleen Smith (Ed.)

IDAHO STATE UNIV.

Street address 1: PO Box 8009

Street address city: Pocatello
Street address state: ID
Zip/Postal code: 83209-0001
Country: USA
Mailing address: PO Box 8009
Mailing city: Pocatello
Mailing state: ID
Mailing zip: 83209-0001
General Phone: (208) 282-4812
General Fax: (208) 282-5301
General/National Adv. E-mail: bgads@isu.edu
Personnel: Jerry Miller (Dir.); Clay Nelson (Ed. in Chief)

LEWIS-CLARK STATE COLLEGE

Street address 1: 500 8th Ave
Street address 2: Student Union Building Room 201
Street address city: Lewiston
Street address state: ID
Zip/Postal code: 83501-2691
Country: USA
Mailing address: 500 8th Avenue
Mailing city: Lewiston
Mailing state: ID
Mailing zip: 83501
General Phone: (208) 792-2470
General Fax: (208) 792-2082
General/National Adv. E-mail: thepathfinder@lcmail.lcsc.edu
Display Adv. E-mail: pathfinderbusmgr@lcmail.lcsc.edu
Primary Website: www.lcsc.edu/pathfinder/
Published: Wed
Avg Free Circ: 1000
Personnel: Bryce Kammers (Advisor); Kaylee Brewster (Ed.); Aaron Waits (Asst. Ed.); Ryan Grether (Business Manager)

NORTHWEST NAZARENE UNIV.

Street address 1: 623 Holly St
Street address city: Nampa
Street address state: ID
Zip/Postal code: 83686-5487
Country: USA
Mailing address: 623 Holly St
Mailing city: Nampa
Mailing state: ID
Mailing zip: 83686-5897
General Phone: (208) 467-8656
Personnel: Amber Ford (Ed.)

THE SENTINEL - NORTH IDAHO COLLEGE

Street address 1: 1000 W Garden Ave
Street address city: Coeur D Alene
Street address state: ID
Zip/Postal code: 83814-2161
County: Kootenai
Country: USA
Mailing address: North Idaho College Receiving Department (c/o Geoff Carr)
Mailing city: Coeur D Alene
Mailing state: ID
Mailing zip: 83814-2199
General Phone: (208) 769-3388
General/National Adv. E-mail: sentinel@nic.edu
Primary Website: www.nicsentinel.com
Published Other: Each semester
Avg Free Circ: 3000
Personnel: Geoff Carr (Advisor)

UNIV. OF IDAHO

Street address 1: 301 Student Union Bldg
Street address city: Moscow
Street address state: ID
Zip/Postal code: 83844-0001
Country: USA
Mailing address: 301 Student Un
Mailing city: Moscow
Mailing state: ID
Mailing zip: 83844-0001
General Phone: (208) 885-7825
General Fax: (208) 885-2222
General/National Adv. E-mail: argonaut@uidaho.edu
Personnel: Shawn O'Neal (Advisor); Hannah Liter (Adv. Mgr.); Greg Connolly (Ed. in Chief)

ILLINOIS

AUGUSTANA COLLEGE

Street address 1: 639 38th St
Street address city: Rock Island
Street address state: IL
Zip/Postal code: 61201-2210
Country: USA
Mailing address: 639 38th St
Mailing city: Rock Island
Mailing state: IL
Mailing zip: 61201-2296
General Phone: (309) 794-3460
General Fax: (309) 794-3460
Advertising Phone: (309) 794-7484
Editorial Phone: (309) 794-7485
General/National Adv. E-mail: observer@augustana.edu
Personnel: Carolyn Yaschur (Advisor); David Schwartz (Advisor)

BENEDICTINE UNIV.

Street address 1: 5700 College Rd
Street address city: Lisle
Street address state: IL
Zip/Postal code: 60532-2851
Country: USA
Mailing address: 5700 College Rd
Mailing city: Lisle
Mailing state: IL
Mailing zip: 60532-0900
General Phone: (630) 829-6252
General Fax: (630) 960-1126
General/National Adv. E-mail: thecandor@yahoo.com
Primary Website: www.thecandor.com
Year Established: 1982
Published: Wed
Avg Free Circ: 2000
Personnel: Chris Birks (Advisor)

BLACK HAWK COLLEGE

Street address 1: 6600 34th Ave
Street address 2: Bldg 4
Street address city: Moline
Street address state: IL
Zip/Postal code: 61265-5870
Country: USA
Mailing address: 6600 34th Ave Bldg 4
Mailing city: Moline
Mailing state: IL
Mailing zip: 61265-5899
General Phone: (309) 796-5477
Personnel: Tory Becht (Advisor); Thomas Cross (Ed.); David Craig (Ed.)

BRADLEY UNIVERSITY

Street address 1: 1501 W Bradley Ave
Street address city: Peoria
Street address state: IL
Zip/Postal code: 61625-0001
Country: USA
Mailing address: 1501 W Bradley Ave
Mailing city: Peoria
Mailing state: IL
Mailing zip: 61625-0003
General Phone: (309) 676-7611
General Fax: (309) 677-2609
Advertising Phone: (309) 676-7611
General/National Adv. E-mail: bradleyscout@gmail.com
Display Adv. E-mail: bradleyscout@gmail.com
Editorial e-mail: bradleyscout@gmail.com
Primary Website: www.bradleyscout.com
Year Established: 1898
Published: Fri
Avg Free Circ: 4000
Personnel: Sam Pallini (Ed.); Kristin Kreher (Managing Ed.); Travis Kelso (Adv. Mgr.)

CARL SANDBURG COLLEGE

Street address 1: 140 S Prairie St
Street address city: Galesburg
Street address state: IL
Zip/Postal code: 61401-4605
Country: USA
Mailing address: 140 S Prairie St
Mailing city: Galesburg
Mailing state: IL

CHICAGO KENT COLLEGE OF LAW

Street address 1: 565 W Adams St
Street address 2: Rm C86
Street address city: Chicago
Street address state: IL
Zip/Postal code: 60661-3652
Country: USA
Mailing address: 565 W Adams St Fl 2
Mailing city: Chicago
Mailing state: IL
Mailing zip: 60661-3652
General Phone: (312) 906-5016

COLLEGE OF DUPAGE

Street address 1: 425 Fawell Blvd
Street address city: Glen Ellyn
Street address state: IL
Zip/Postal code: 60137-6708
Country: USA
Mailing address: 425 Fawell Blvd.
Mailing city: Glen Ellyn
Mailing state: IL
Mailing zip: 60137-6599
General Phone: (630) 942-2113
Editorial e-mail: editor@cod.edu
Primary Website: www.codcourier.org
Year Established: 1967
Published: Wed
Personnel: Nick Davison (Editor-in-chief)

COLLEGE OF LAKE COUNTY

Street address 1: 19351 W Washington St
Street address city: Grayslake
Street address state: IL
Zip/Postal code: 60030-1148
Country: USA
Mailing address: 19351 W Washington St
Mailing city: Grayslake
Mailing state: IL
Mailing zip: 60030-1198
General Phone: (847) 543-2057
Personnel: John Kupetz (Faculty Advisor); Nathan Caldwell (Ed. in Chief)

COLUMBIA COLLEGE

Street address 1: 33 E Congress Pkwy
Street address city: Chicago
Street address state: IL
Zip/Postal code: 60605-1218
Country: USA
Mailing address: 600 S Michigan Ave Fl 5
Mailing city: Chicago
Mailing state: IL
Mailing zip: 60605-1996
General Phone: 312-369-8903
Advertising Phone: 312-369-8984
Editorial Phone: 312-369-8999
Editorial Fax: 312-369-8430
Editorial e-mail: jlyon@colum.edu
Primary Website: www.columbiachronicle.com
Year Established: 1965
Personnel: Jeff Lyon (Faculty advisor)

COLUMBIA COLLEGE CHICAGO

Street address 1: 33 E Congress Pkwy
Street address 2: Ste 224
Street address city: Chicago
Street address state: IL
Zip/Postal code: 60605-1237
Country: USA
Mailing address: 33 E Congress Pkwy Ste 224
Mailing city: Chicago
Mailing state: IL
Mailing zip: 60605-1237
General Phone: 312-369-8955
General Fax: (312)369-8430
Advertising Phone: 312-369-8955
Editorial Phone: (312) 369-8999
General/National Adv. E-mail: chronicle@colum.edu
Display Adv. E-mail: crichert@colum.edu
Editorial e-mail: chronicle@colum.edu
Primary Website: www.columbiachronicle.com
Year Established: 1978
Published: Mon
Avg Free Circ: 6000
Personnel: Chris Richert (General Manager)

CONCORDIA UNIV.

Street address 1: 7400 Augusta St
Street address city: River Forest
Street address state: IL
Zip/Postal code: 60305-1402
Country: USA
Mailing address: 7400 Augusta Street
Mailing city: River Forest
Mailing state: IL
Mailing zip: 60305-1499
General Phone: (708) 209-3191
General Fax: (708) 209-3176
Display Adv. E-mail: spectator@cuchicago.edu
Personnel: Melissa Williams (Advisor); Benjamin Parviz (Adv. Mgr.); Kathryn Klement (Ed.)

DEPAUL UNIVERSITY

Street address 1: 14 E Jackson Blvd
Street address 2: Fl 11
Street address city: Chicago
Street address state: IL
Zip/Postal code: 60604-2259
Country: USA
Mailing address: 14 E. Jackson Blvd.
Mailing city: Chicago
Mailing state: IL
Mailing zip: 60604
General Phone: (312) 362-7644
General/National Adv. E-mail: eic@depauliaonline.com
Display Adv. E-mail: business@depauliaonline.com
Editorial e-mail: eic@depauliaonline.com
Primary Website: www.depauliaonline.com
Year Established: 1923
Published: Mon
Avg Free Circ: 5000
Personnel: Marla Krause (Advisor)

DEVRY UNIVERSITY

Street address 1: 3300 N Campbell Ave, Campus Life Ctr
Street address city: Chicago
Street address state: IL
Zip/Postal code: 60618
Country: USA
Mailing address: 3300 N. Campbell Ave., Campus Life Ctr.
Mailing city: Chicago
Mailing state: IL
Mailing zip: 60618
General Phone: (773) 697-2089
Personnel: Joe Onorio (Assoc. Dean, Campus Life/Advisor); Marvin Cespedes (Ed.)

DOMINICAN UNIV.

Street address 1: 7900 Division St
Street address city: River Forest
Street address state: IL
Zip/Postal code: 60305-1066
Country: USA
Mailing address: 7900 Division St
Mailing city: River Forest
Mailing state: IL
Mailing zip: 60305-1066
General Phone: (708) 524-6800
Personnel: Marie Simpson (Advisor)

EASTERN ILLINOIS UNIV.

Street address 1: 600 Lincoln Ave
Street address city: Charleston
Street address state: IL
Zip/Postal code: 61920-3011
Country: USA
Mailing address: 600 Lincoln Ave.
Mailing city: Charleston
Mailing state: IL
Mailing zip: 61920
General Phone: (217) 581-2812
General Fax: (217) 581-2923
General/National Adv. E-mail: DelawareNeic@gmail.com; DelawareNnewsdesk@gmail.com; DelawareNNews.com@gmail.com

Personnel: Taylor Angelo (Ed. in chief); Lola Burnham (Advisor); Emily Steele (News Ed.); Chris Lee (Mng. Ed.); Collin (Mng. Ed.)

ELGIN COMMUNITY COLLEGE

Street address 1: 1700 Spartan Dr
Street address city: Elgin
Street address state: IL
Zip/Postal code: 60123-7189
Country: USA
Mailing address: 1700 Spartan Dr
Mailing city: Elgin
Mailing state: IL
Mailing zip: 60123-7193
General Phone: (847) 697-1000
General Fax: (847) 888-7352
General/National Adv. E-mail: elginobserver@gmail.com
Display Adv. E-mail: elgincollegeobserver@yahoo.com
Editorial e-mail: observereditorinchief@gmail.com
Primary Website: www.elgin.edu
Year Established: 1951
Published Other: Bi-weekly
Personnel: Lori Clark (Faculty Advisor); Michelle Pain (Editor-in-Chief); Fernando Chang (Managing Editor)

ELMHURST COLLEGE

Street address 1: 190 S Prospect Ave
Street address city: Elmhurst
Street address state: IL
Zip/Postal code: 60126-3271
Country: USA
Mailing address: 190 S Prospect Ave
Mailing city: Elmhurst
Mailing state: IL
Mailing zip: 60126-3296
General Phone: (630)617-3320
Advertising Phone: (630) 617-3321
General/National Adv. E-mail: leadernewsec@gmail.com
Display Adv. E-mail: advertising@ecleader.org
Editorial e-mail: leadernewsec@gmail.com
Primary Website: ecleader.org
Published: Tues
Published Other: Published bi-weekly
Personnel: Ron Wiginton (Advisor); Aaron Schroeder (Bus. Mgr.); Eric Lutz (Ed. in Chief); Haleema Shah (Editor-in-Chief)

GOVERNORS STATE UNIV.

Street address 1: 1 University Pkwy
Street address 2: E2543
Street address city: University Park
Street address state: IL
Zip/Postal code: 60484-3165
Country: USA
Mailing address: 1 University Pkwy.
Mailing city: University Park
Mailing state: IL
Mailing zip: 60484-3165
General Phone: (708) 534-4517
General Fax: (708) 534-7895
General/National Adv. E-mail: phoenix@govst.edu
Primary Website: www.gsuphoenix.com
Published: Wed
Published Other: First and third Wednesdays
Personnel: Debbie James (Faculty Advisor); Michael Purdy (Emeritus Professor)

GREENVILLE COLLEGE

Street address 1: 315 E College Ave
Street address city: Greenville
Street address state: IL
Zip/Postal code: 62246-1145
Country: USA
Mailing address: 315 E College Ave
Mailing city: Greenville
Mailing state: IL
Mailing zip: 62246-1145
General Phone: (618) 664-2800
General Fax: (618) 664-1373
General/National Adv. E-mail: papyrus@greenville.edu
Personnel: Susan Chism (Advisor)

HAROLD WASHINGTON COLLEGE

Street address 1: 30 E Lake St
Street address 2: Rm 635
Street address city: Chicago
Street address state: IL
Zip/Postal code: 60601-2408
Country: USA
Mailing address: 30 E Lake St Rm 635
Mailing city: Chicago
Mailing state: IL
Mailing zip: 60601-2449
General Phone: (312) 553-3141
General Fax: (312) 553-5647
Advertising Phone: 312-553-5631
Editorial Phone: 312-553-5630
General/National Adv. E-mail: hwc_heraldnews@ccc.edu
Primary Website: www.theheraldhwc.com
Year Established: 1979
Personnel: Molly Turner (Faculty Advisor)

HIGHLAND CMTY. COLLEGE

Street address 1: 2998 W Pearl City Rd
Street address city: Freeport
Street address state: IL
Zip/Postal code: 61032-9338
Country: USA
Mailing address: 2998 W Pearl City Rd
Mailing city: Freeport
Mailing state: IL
Mailing zip: 61032-9341
General Phone: (815) 235-6121
Personnel: Sam Tucibat (Advisor)

ILLINOIS COLLEGE

Street address 1: 1101 W College Ave
Street address city: Jacksonville
Street address state: IL
Zip/Postal code: 62650-2212
Country: USA
Mailing address: 1101 W College Ave
Mailing city: Jacksonville
Mailing state: IL
Mailing zip: 62650-2299
General Phone: (217) 245-3030
General Fax: (217) 245-3056
General/National Adv. E-mail: rambler@ic.edu
Personnel: John S. Rush (Advisor); Laurel Berkel (Ed.)

ILLINOIS INST. OF TECHNOLOGY

Street address 1: Herman Union Bldg State St
Street address 2: Rm 3201221
Street address city: Chicago
Street address state: IL
Zip/Postal code: 60616
Country: USA
Mailing address: Herman Union Bldg., 3201 S. State St., Rm. 221
Mailing city: Chicago
Mailing state: IL
Mailing zip: 60616
Personnel: Aanchal Taneja (Bus. Mgr.); Brian Wolber (Adv. Mgr.); Lory Mishra (Ed. in Chief)

ILLINOIS STATE UNIVERSITY

Street address 1: Illinois State University
Street address 2: Campus Box 0890
Street address city: Normal
Street address state: IL
Zip/Postal code: 61761
Country: USA
Mailing address: 100 North University Street
Mailing city: Normal
Mailing state: IL
Mailing zip: 61761
General Phone: (309) 438-7685
General Fax: (309) 438-5211
Advertising Phone: (309) 438-8742
Editorial Phone: (309) 438-8745
General/National Adv. E-mail: vidette@ilstu.edu
Display Adv. E-mail: vidette@ilstu.edu
Editorial e-mail: vidette@ilstu.edu
Primary Website: www.videtteonline.com
Year Established: 1888
Personnel: John Plevka (Gen. Mgr.); Brooke Goodwin (Bus. Mgr.); Amy Gorczowski (Ed.); Kristi Demonbreun (Ed.)

ILLINOIS WESLEYAN UNIVERSITY

Street address 1: 104 University Ave
Street address city: Bloomington
Street address state: IL
Zip/Postal code: 61701-1798
Country: USA
Mailing address: 104 University Ave
Mailing city: Bloomington
Mailing state: IL
General/National Adv. E-mail: argus@iwu.edu
Primary Website: www.iwuargus.com
Year Established: 1894
Published: Fri
Personnel: James Plath (Advisor)

JOHN A. LOGAN COLLEGE

Street address 1: 700 Logan College Dr
Street address city: Carterville
Street address state: IL
Zip/Postal code: 62918-2500
Country: USA
Mailing address: 700 Logan College Dr
Mailing city: Carterville
Mailing state: IL
Mailing zip: 62918-2501
General Phone: (618) 985-2828
Personnel: Matt Garrison (Advisor); Tara Fasol (Ed.)

JOLIET JUNIOR COLLEGE

Street address 1: 1215 Houbolt Rd
Street address city: Joliet
Street address state: IL
Zip/Postal code: 60431-8938
Country: USA
Mailing address: 1215 Houbolt Rd
Mailing city: Joliet
Mailing state: IL
Mailing zip: 60431-8800
General Phone: (815) 280-2313
General Fax: (815) 280-6730
Advertising Phone: (815) 280-2313
Advertising Fax: (815) 280-6730
Editorial Phone: (815) 280-2313
Editorial Fax: (815) 280-2313
General/National Adv. E-mail: blazermail@jjc.edu
Display Adv. E-mail: blazermail@jjc.edu
Editorial e-mail: blazermail@jjc.edu
Primary Website: www.jjc.edu/blazer
Published: Other
Published Other: Our frequency is tri-weekly, or 5 times per semester.
Avg Free Circ: 2000
Personnel: Robert Marcink (Advisor)

KASKASKIA COLLEGE

Street address 1: 27210 College Rd
Street address city: Centralia
Street address state: IL
Zip/Postal code: 62801-7800
Country: USA
Mailing address: 27210 College Rd
Mailing city: Centralia
Mailing state: IL
Mailing zip: 62801-7878
General Phone: (618) 545-3000
Personnel: Dale Hill (Advisor); Nathan Wilkins (Advisor); Sue Hardebeck (Advisor)

KELLOGG GRAD. SCHOOL OF MGMT.

Street address 1: 2001 Sheridan Rd
Street address city: Evanston
Street address state: IL
Zip/Postal code: 60208-0814
Country: USA
Mailing address: 2001 Sheridan Rd
Mailing city: Evanston
Mailing state: IL
Mailing zip: 60208-0814
Personnel: Nick Slater (Ed.)

KENNEDY-KING COLLEGE

Street address 1: 1751 W 47th St
Street address 2: Fl 2
Street address city: Chicago
Street address state: IL
Zip/Postal code: 60609-3825
Country: USA
Mailing city: Chicago
Mailing state: IL
Mailing zip: 60621
General Phone: (773) 602-5179
General Fax: (773) 602-5521
General/National Adv. E-mail: editor@thegatenewspaper.com
Display Adv. E-mail: editor@thegatenewspaper.com
Primary Website: www.thegatenewspaper.com
Year Established: 2010
Published: Bi-Mthly
Avg Free Circ: 13000
Personnel: Adriana Maria Cardona-Maguigad (Editor)

KISHWAUKEE COLLEGE

Street address 1: 21193 Malta Rd
Street address city: Malta
Street address state: IL
Zip/Postal code: 60150-9600
Country: USA
Mailing address: 21193 Malta Rd
Mailing city: Malta
Mailing state: IL
Mailing zip: 60150-9699
General Phone: (815) 825-2086
General Fax: (815) 825-2072
General/National Adv. E-mail: kscope@kishwaukeecollege.edu
Personnel: Melissa Blake (Advisor); John Myers (Adv. Mgr.); Andrew Hallgren (Ed. in Chief); Nelle Smith (Ed.); John (Instructor); Marissa Skonie (Ed. in Chief)

KNOX COLLEGE

Street address 1: 2 E South St
Street address 2: Knox College K-240
Street address city: Galesburg
Street address state: IL
Zip/Postal code: 61401-4938
Country: USA
Mailing address: 2 E South St Knox College K-240
Mailing city: Galesburg
Mailing state: IL
Mailing zip: 61401-4999
General Phone: (646) 784-4367
General Fax: (309) 341-7081
General/National Adv. E-mail: tks@knox.edu
Display Adv. E-mail: tksmarketing@knox.edu
Primary Website: KNOX COLLEGE BOX 2 E SOUTH ST
Year Established: 1878
Published: Thur
Personnel: Tom Martin (Advisor); Jonathan Schrag (Co-Editor-in-Chief); Lillie Chamberlin (Co-Editor-in-Chief)

LAKE FOREST COLLEGE

Street address 1: 555 N Sheridan Rd
Street address city: Lake Forest
Street address state: IL
Zip/Postal code: 60045-2338
Country: USA
Mailing address: 555 N Sheridan Rd
Mailing city: Lake Forest
Mailing state: IL
Mailing zip: 60045-2399
General Phone: (847) 735-5215
General Fax: (847) 735-6298
General/National Adv. E-mail: stentor@lakeforest.edu
Personnel: Heather Brown (Advisor); Annie Cooper (Ed. in Chief); Nate Butala (Mng. Ed.)

LAKE LAND COLLEGE

Street address 1: 5001 Lake Land Blvd
Street address city: Mattoon
Street address state: IL
Zip/Postal code: 61938-9366
Country: USA
Mailing address: 5001 Lake Land Blvd
Mailing city: Mattoon
Mailing state: IL
Mailing zip: 61938-9366
General Phone: (217) 234-5269
General Fax: (217) 234-5390
General/National Adv. E-mail: studentpublications@lakeland.cc.il.us
Primary Website: www.navigatornews.org
Published: Mthly
Personnel: Valerie Lynch (Dir of Student Life)

LEWIS AND CLARK CMTY. COLLEGE

Street address 1: 5800 Godfrey Rd

Street address city: Godfrey
Street address state: IL
Zip/Postal code: 62035-2426
Country: USA
Mailing address: 5800 Godfrey Rd
Mailing city: Godfrey
Mailing state: IL
Mailing zip: 62035-2466
General Phone: (618) 468-6042
General Fax: (618) 468-6055
Personnel: Lori Artis (Advisor); Anthony Lanham (Ed.)

LEWIS UNIV.

Street address 1: 1 University Pkwy
Street address city: Romeoville
Street address state: IL
Zip/Postal code: 60446-2200
Country: USA
Mailing address: 1 University Pkwy
Mailing city: Romeoville
Mailing state: IL
Mailing zip: 60446-1832
General Phone: (815) 836-5196
General/National Adv. E-mail: lewisflyernews@gmail.com
Personnel: Lisa O'Toole (Advisor); Adam Olszeski (Ed. in Chief)

LINCOLN LAND CMTY. COLLEGE

Street address 1: 5250 Shepherd Rd
Street address city: Springfield
Street address state: IL
Zip/Postal code: 62703-5402
Country: USA
Mailing address: 5250 Shepherd Rd
Mailing city: Springfield
Mailing state: IL
Mailing zip: 62703-5408
General Phone: (217) 786-2318
Personnel: Brenda Protz (Advisor)

LOYOLA UNIV.

Street address 1: 6525 N Sheridan Rd
Street address city: Chicago
Street address state: IL
Zip/Postal code: 60626-5761
Country: USA
Mailing address: 6525 N Sheridan Rd Ste 1
Mailing city: Chicago
Mailing state: IL
Mailing zip: 60626-5386
General Phone: (773) 508-7120
General Fax: (773) 508-7121
General/National Adv. E-mail: phoenixbusiness@luc.edu
Personnel: Kimberly Boonjathai (Bus.Mgr.); Leeann Maton (Ed. in chief)

LOYOLA UNIV. LAW SCHOOL

Street address 1: 33 N Dearborn St
Street address city: Chicago
Street address state: IL
Zip/Postal code: 60602-3102
Country: USA
Mailing address: 33 N Dearborn St
Mailing city: Chicago
Mailing state: IL
Mailing zip: 60602-3102
Personnel: Sam Puleo (Ed.)

MALCOLM X COLLEGE

Street address 1: 1900 W Van Buren St
Street address 2: Rm 2519
Street address city: Chicago
Street address state: IL
Zip/Postal code: 60612-3145
Country: USA
Mailing address: 1900 W Van Buren St Rm 2218
Mailing city: Chicago
Mailing state: IL
Mailing zip: 60612-3145
General Phone: (312) 850-7462
Personnel: Cynthia-Val Chapman (Advisor); Beth Lewis (Adv. Mgr.)

MCHENRY COUNTY COLLEGE

Street address 1: 8900 US Highway 14
Street address city: Crystal Lake
Street address state: IL
Zip/Postal code: 60012-2738
Country: USA
Mailing address: 8900 US Highway 14
Mailing city: Crystal Lake
Mailing state: IL
Mailing zip: 60012-2761
General Phone: (815) 455-8571
General Fax:
General/National Adv. E-mail: tartan@mchenry.edu
Primary Website: www.mchenry.edu; www.mcctartan.net
Published: Mthly
Avg Free Circ: 2000
Personnel: Toni Countryman (Advisor)

MCKENDREE UNIVERSITY

Street address 1: 701 College Rd
Street address city: Lebanon
Street address state: IL
Zip/Postal code: 62254-1291
Country: USA
Mailing address: 701 College Rd
Mailing city: Lebanon
Mailing state: IL
Mailing zip: 62254-1291
General Phone: (618) 537-6821
General Fax: (618) 537-2377
General/National Adv. E-mail: mckreview@mckendree.edu
Personnel: Gabe Shapiro (Faculty Advisor); Sarah Adams (Editor in Chief); Chris Moore (Associate Editor); Kevin Schaefer (Web/Design Editor); Theresa Schmidt (Ed. in Chief)

MILLIKIN UNIV.

Street address 1: 1184 W Main St
Street address city: Decatur
Street address state: IL
Zip/Postal code: 62522-2039
Country: USA
Mailing address: 1184 W Main St
Mailing city: Decatur
Mailing state: IL
Mailing zip: 62522-2084
General Phone: (217) 425-4626
General Fax: (217) 425-1687
General/National Adv. E-mail: decaturian@millikin.edu
Personnel: Priscilla Marie Meddaugh (Faculty Advisor); Caitlin Hennessy (Co-Ed. in Chief); Lauren Krage (Co-Ed. in Chief)

MONMOUTH COLLEGE

Street address 1: 700 E Broadway
Street address city: Monmouth
Street address state: IL
Zip/Postal code: 61462-1963
Country: USA
Mailing address: 700 E Broadway
Mailing city: Monmouth
Mailing state: IL
Mailing zip: 61462-1998
General Phone: (309) 457-3456
General Fax: (309) 457-2363
General/National Adv. E-mail: courier@monm.edu
Personnel: Michelle Nutting (Adv. Mgr.); Lucas Pauley (Ed. in Chief)

MORAINE VALLEY CMTY. COLLEGE

Street address 1: 9000 W College Pkwy
Street address city: Palos Hills
Street address state: IL
Zip/Postal code: 60465-1444
Country: USA
Mailing address: 9000 W. College Pkwy.
Mailing city: Palos Hills
Mailing state: IL
Mailing zip: 60465-0937
General Phone: (708) 608-4177
General Fax: (708) 974-0790
General/National Adv. E-mail: glacier@morainevalley.edu
Primary Website: www.mvccglacier.com
Published Other: Bi-Wkly
Personnel: Stacey Reichard (Advisor); William Lukitsch; Rob Peto (Ed. in Chief); Frank Florez (News Ed.)

MORTON COLLEGE

Street address 1: 3801 S Central Ave
Street address 2: Rm 328-C
Street address city: Cicero
Street address state: IL
Zip/Postal code: 60804-4300
Country: USA
Mailing address: 3801 S Central Ave Rm 328-C
Mailing city: Cicero
Mailing state: IL
Mailing zip: 60804-4398
General Phone: (708) 656-8000
General Fax: (708) 656-3924
General/National Adv. E-mail: collegian@morton.edu
Personnel: Rose Dimesio (Advisor)

NATIONAL COLLEGE OF CHIROPRACTIC

Street address 1: 200 E Roosevelt Rd
Street address city: Lombard
Street address state: IL
Zip/Postal code: 60148-4539
Country: USA
Mailing address: 200 E. Roosevelt Rd
Mailing city: Lombard
Mailing state: IL
Mailing zip: 60148-4539
Published: Mthly
Avg Free Circ: 5000
Personnel: Frank Sutter (Ed.)

NORTH CENTRAL COLLEGE

Street address 1: 31 N Loomis St
Street address city: Naperville
Street address state: IL
Zip/Postal code: 60540-4756
Country: USA
Mailing address: 31 N Loomis St
Mailing city: Naperville
Mailing state: IL
Mailing zip: 60540
General Phone: (630) 637-5422
General Fax: (630) 637-5441
General/National Adv. E-mail: chronicle@noctrl.edu
Personnel: Nancy Kirby (Faculty Advisor)

NORTH PARK UNIV.

Street address 1: 3225 W Foster Ave
Street address city: Chicago
Street address state: IL
Zip/Postal code: 60625-4823
Country: USA
Mailing address: 3225 W Foster Ave
Mailing city: Chicago
Mailing state: IL
Mailing zip: 60625-4895
General Phone: (773) 649-2816
General/National Adv. E-mail: northparkpress@gmail.com
Personnel: Casey Smagala (Adv. Dir.); Erin Hegarty (Editor-In-Chief); Kristie Vuocolo (Staff Advisory); Hannah Williams (Online Editor)

NORTHEASTERN ILLINOIS UNIVERSITY

Street address 1: 5500 N Saint Louis Ave
Street address 2: Rm E049
Street address city: Chicago
Street address state: IL
Zip/Postal code: 60625-4625
Country: USA
Mailing address: 5500 N Saint Louis Ave Rm E049
Mailing city: Chicago
Mailing state: IL
Mailing zip: 60625-4699
General Phone: (773) 442-4577
General Fax: (773) 442-4579
General/National Adv. E-mail: neiuindependent@gmail.com
Display Adv. E-mail: neiuadvertising@yahoo.com
Primary Website: www.neiuindependent.org
Year Established: 1961
Published: Tues`Bi-Mthly
Personnel: Jacklyn Nowotnik (Editor-in-Chief); Matthew Greenberg (Managing Editor)

NORTHERN ILLINOIS UNIV.

Street address 1: Northern Illinois University, Campus Life Building, Suite 130
Street address city: Dekalb
Street address state: IL
Zip/Postal code: 60115
Country: USA
Mailing address: Northern Illinois University, Campus Life Building, Suite 130
Mailing city: Dekalb
Mailing state: IL
Mailing zip: 60115
General Phone: (815) 753-4239
General Fax: (815) 753-0708
General/National Adv. E-mail: editor@northernstar.info
Display Adv. E-mail: ads@northernstar.info
Editorial e-mail: editor@northernstar.info
Primary Website: www.northernstar.info
Year Established: 1899
Personnel: Jim Killam (Advisor); Maria Krull (Bus. Advisor); Justin Weaver (Ed.)

NORTHWESTERN UNIV. SCHOOL OF LAW

Street address 1: 357 E Chicago Ave
Street address city: Chicago
Street address state: IL
Zip/Postal code: 60611-3059
Country: USA
Mailing address: 357 E Chicago Ave
Mailing city: Chicago
Personnel: Unknown Unknown (Advisor)

NORTHWESTERN UNIVERSITY

Street address 1: 1999 Campus Dr
Street address city: Evanston
Street address state: IL
Zip/Postal code: 60208-0825
Country: USA
Mailing address: 1999 Campus Dr
Mailing city: Evanston
Mailing state: IL
Mailing zip: 60208-2532
General Phone: (847) 491-3222
General Fax: (847) 491-9905
Editorial Phone: (847) 491-7206
General/National Adv. E-mail: eic@dailynorthwestern.com
Display Adv. E-mail: spc-compshop@northwestern.edu
Primary Website: www.dailynorthwestern.com
Year Established: 1881
Published: Mon`Tues`Wed`Thur`Fri

NORTHWESTERN UNIVERSITY

Street address 1: 1845 Sheridan Rd
Street address city: Evanston
Street address state: IL
Zip/Postal code: 60208-0815
Country: USA
Mailing address: 1845 Sheridan Rd
Mailing city: Evanston
Mailing state: IL
Mailing zip: 60208-0815
Personnel: John Lavine (Dean); David Abrahamson (Prof.); Martin Block (Prof.); Jack Doppelt (Prof.); Loren Ghiglione (Prof.); Alec Klein (Prof.); Donna Leff (Prof.); Frank Mulhern (Prof.); Jon Petrovich (Prof.); David Protess (Prof.); Don Schultz (Prof.); Ellen Shearer (Prof.); Clarke Caywood (Assoc. Prof.); Mary Coffman (Assoc. Prof.); Tom Collinger (Assoc. Prof.); Doug Foster (Assoc. Prof.); Jeremy Gilbert (Assoc. Prof.); Rich Gordon (Assoc. Prof.); John Greening (Assoc. Prof.); Ava Greenwell (Assoc. Prof.)

OAKTON CMTY. COLLEGE

Street address 1: 1600 E Golf Rd
Street address city: Des Plaines
Street address state: IL
Zip/Postal code: 60016-1234
Country: USA
Mailing address: 1600 E Golf Rd

Mailing city: Des Plaines
Mailing state: IL
Mailing zip: 60016-1268
General Phone: (847) 635-1678
Personnel: Sue Fox (Advisor)

OLIVET NAZARENE UNIV.

Street address 1: PO Box 592
Street address city: Bourbonnais
Street address state: IL
Zip/Postal code: 60914-0592
Country: USA
Mailing address: PO Box 592
Mailing city: Bourbonnais
Mailing state: IL
Mailing zip: 60914-0592
General Phone: (815) 939-5315
Editorial e-mail: glimmerglass@olivet.edu
Year Established: 1941
Published: Tues
Personnel: Jay Martinson (Advisor)

PARKLAND COLLEGE

Street address 1: 2400 W Bradley Ave
Street address 2: Rm X-155
Street address city: Champaign
Street address state: IL
Zip/Postal code: 61821-1806
Country: USA
Mailing address: 2400 W Bradley Ave Rm X-155
Mailing city: Champaign
Mailing state: IL
Mailing zip: 61821-1899
General Phone: (217) 351-2216
Advertising Phone: 217 351-2206
General/National Adv. E-mail: prospectus@parkland.edu
Display Adv. E-mail: prospectusads@parkland.edu
Editorial e-mail: prospectus.editor@gmail.com
Primary Website: www.prospectusnews.com
Year Established: 1969
Published: Wed
Avg Free Circ: 1000
Personnel: John Eby (Advisor); Sean Herman (Ed. in Chief)

PRAIRIE STATE COLLEGE

Street address 1: 202 S Halsted St
Street address 2: Rm 1260
Street address city: Chicago Heights
Street address state: IL
Zip/Postal code: 60411-8200
Country: USA
Mailing address: 202 S Halsted St Rm 1260
Mailing city: Chicago Heights
Mailing state: IL
Mailing zip: 60411-8226
General Phone: (708) 709-3910
General Fax: (708) 755-2587
Editorial Phone: (708) 709-3535
General/National Adv. E-mail: psc_student_review@yahoo.com
Personnel: Helen Manley (Advisor); Nike Atewologun (Adv. Mgr.); Sam Williams (Ed. in Chief)

PRINCIPIA COLLEGE

Street address 1: 1 Maybeck Pl
Street address city: Elsah
Street address state: IL
Zip/Postal code: 62028-9720
Country: USA
Mailing address: 1 Maybeck Pl
Mailing city: Elsah
Mailing state: IL
Mailing zip: 62028-9799
General Phone: (618) 374-5415
General Fax: (618) 374-5122
General/National Adv. E-mail: principia.pilot@gmail.com
Primary Website: www.prin.edu; www.principiapilot.org
Year Established: 1944
Personnel: Craig Savoye (Advisor); David Miller (Ed. in Chief); Katie Ward (Ed. in Chief); Ben Chernivsky (Photo Ed.)

QUINCY UNIV.

Street address 1: 1800 College Ave
Street address city: Quincy
Street address state: IL
Zip/Postal code: 62301-2670
Country: USA
Mailing address: 1800 College Ave
Mailing city: Quincy
Mailing state: IL
Mailing zip: 62301-2699
General Phone: (217) 228-5275
General Fax: (217) 228-5473
General/National Adv. E-mail: qufalcon@gmail.com
Primary Website: http://www.quincy.edu/information/publications-a-media/the-falcon
Year Established: 1929
Published: Mthly
Personnel: David Adam (Advisor); Barbara Schleppenbach (Chair of Fine Arts & Communication)

REND LAKE COLLEGE

Street address 1: 468 N Ken Gray Pkwy
Street address city: Ina
Street address state: IL
Zip/Postal code: 62846-2408
Country: USA
Mailing address: 468 N Ken Gray Pkwy
Mailing city: Ina
Personnel: Michael Peeples (Ed.)

RICHLAND CMTY. COLLEGE

Street address 1: 1 College Park
Street address city: Decatur
Street address state: IL
Zip/Postal code: 62521-8512
Country: USA
Mailing address: 1 College Park
Mailing city: Decatur
Mailing state: IL
Mailing zip: 62521-8513
General Phone: (217) 875-7211
General Fax: (217) 875-6961
General/National Adv. E-mail: comm@richland.edu; communicatur@richland.edu
Personnel: Marlise McDaniel (Ed. in Chief); Todd Houser (Ed.); Tina Cooper (Copy Ed.)

ROBERT MORRIS COLLEGE

Street address 1: 401 S State St
Street address city: Chicago
Street address state: IL
Zip/Postal code: 60605-1229
Country: USA
Mailing address: 401 S State St Fl 2
Mailing city: Chicago
Mailing state: IL
Mailing zip: 60605-1225
General Phone: (312) 935-6876
Personnel: Cherie Meador (Advisor); Matt Kirouac (Ed.)

ROCK VALLEY COLLEGE

Street address 1: 3301 N Mulford Rd
Street address city: Rockford
Street address state: IL
Zip/Postal code: 61114-5640
Country: USA
Mailing address: 3301 N Mulford Rd
Mailing city: Rockford
Mailing state: IL
Mailing zip: 61114-5699
Personnel: Frank Coffman (Advisor)

ROOSEVELT UNIV.

Street address 1: 430 S Michigan Ave
Street address city: Chicago
Street address state: IL
Zip/Postal code: 60605-1315
Country: USA
Mailing address: 430 S Michigan Ave
Mailing city: Chicago
Mailing state: IL
Mailing zip: 60605-1394
General Phone: (312) 281-3246
General Fax: (312) 341-3732
General/National Adv. E-mail: torchcu@roosevelt.edu
Personnel: Billy Montgomery (Advisor); Mallory Blazetic (Mng. Ed.)

SAINT XAVIER UNIVERSITY

Street address 1: 3700 W 103rd St
Street address city: Chicago
Street address state: IL
Zip/Postal code: 60655-3105
Country: USA
Mailing address: 3700 W 103rd St
Mailing city: Chicago
Mailing state: IL
Mailing zip: 60655-3199
General Phone: (773) 298-3380
General Fax: (773) 298-3381
General/National Adv. E-mail: thexavierite@yahoo.com
Display Adv. E-mail: thexavierite@yahoo.com
Editorial e-mail: thexavierite@yahoo.com
Primary Website: www.thexavierite.com
Year Established: 1935
Personnel: Peter Kreten (Asst. Dir)

SCHOOL OF THE ART INSTITUTE

Street address 1: 112 S Michigan Ave
Street address city: Chicago
Street address state: IL
Zip/Postal code: 60603-6105
Country: USA
Mailing address: 112 S Michigan Ave
Mailing city: Chicago
Mailing state: IL
Mailing zip: 60603-6105
General Phone: (312) 345-3838
General Fax: (312) 345-3839
General/National Adv. E-mail: fadvertising@saic.edu
Editorial e-mail: editors@fnewsmagazine.com
Personnel: Paul Elitzik (Advisor); Rachel Oginni (Adv. Mgr.); Natalie Edwards (Ed. in Chief)

SOUTHERN ILLINOIS UNIV.

Street address 1: 1100 Lincoln Dr
Street address city: Carbondale
Street address state: IL
Zip/Postal code: 62901-4306
Country: USA
Mailing address: Communications Bldg, 1100 Lincoln Dr
Mailing city: Carbondale
Mailing state: IL
Mailing zip: 62901
General Phone: (618) 536-3311
General Fax: (618) 453-3248
General/National Adv. E-mail: deadvert@siu.edu
Primary Website: www.siude.com
Year Established: 1916
Personnel: Eric J. Fidler (Advisor/Mng. Ed.); Jerry Bush (Bus./Adv. Dir.); Sherri Killion (Classified Mgr.); Andrea Zimmerman (Ed. in Chief); Diana (Ed. in Chief); Derek (Features Ed.); Edyta (Photo Ed.); Stile (Sports Ed.); Ashley (Webmaster)

THE ALESTLE - SOUTHERN ILLINOIS UNIVERSITY EDWARDSVILLE

Street address 1: Six Hairpin Drive, Morris University Ctr, Rm 0311
Street address city: Edwardsville
Street address state: IL
Zip/Postal code: 62026
County: Madison
Country: USA
Mailing address: Six Hairpin Drive, Box 1167
Mailing city: Edwardsville
Mailing state: IL
Mailing zip: 62026
General Phone: (618) 650-3528
General Fax: (618) 650-3514
Advertising Phone: (618) 650-3478
Display Adv. E-mail: advertising@alestlelive.com
Editorial e-mail: editor@alestlelive.com
Primary Website: www.alestlelive.com
Mthly Avg Views: 19075
Mthly Avg Unique Visitors: 14141
Year Established: 1960
Published: Tues`Thur
Published Other: Tuesdays online exclusively
Avg Free Circ: 3500
Personnel: Tammy Merrett (Program Director, Student Publications)

TRINITY CHRISTIAN COLLEGE

Street address 1: 6601 W College Dr
Street address city: Palos Heights
Street address state: IL
Zip/Postal code: 60463-1768
Country: USA
Mailing address: 6601 W College Dr
Mailing city: Palos Heights
Mailing state: IL
Mailing zip: 60463-0929
General Phone: (708) 239-4715
Personnel: Whitney Dickison (Ed. in Chief)

TRINITY INTERNATIONAL UNIV.

Street address 1: 2065 Half Day Rd
Street address city: Deerfield
Street address state: IL
Zip/Postal code: 60015-1241
Country: USA
Mailing address: 2065 Half Day Rd # T-2922
Mailing city: Deerfield
Mailing state: IL
Mailing zip: 60015-1241
Personnel: Erika Sjogren (Ed.)

TRITON COLLEGE

Street address 1: 2000 5th Ave
Street address city: River Grove
Street address state: IL
Zip/Postal code: 60171-1907
Country: USA
Mailing address: 2000 5th Ave
Mailing city: River Grove
Mailing state: IL
Mailing zip: 60171-1995
Personnel: Dawn Unger (Ed. in Chief)

UNIV. OF CHICAGO

Street address 1: 1212 E 59th St
Street address 2: Lowr Level
Street address city: Chicago
Street address state: IL
Zip/Postal code: 60637-1604
Country: USA
Mailing address: 1212 E 59th St Lowr Level
Mailing city: Chicago
Mailing state: IL
Mailing zip: 60637-1604
General Phone: (773) 702-1403
General Fax: (773) 702-3032
General/National Adv. E-mail: editor@chicagomaroon.com
Display Adv. E-mail: ads@chicagomaroon.com
Primary Website: www.chicagomaroon.com
Year Established: 1892
Published: Tues`Fri
Personnel: Rebecca Guterman (Editor-in-Chief); Sam Levine (Editor-in-Chief); Emily Wang (Managing Editor)

UNIV. OF CHICAGO LAW SCHOOL

Street address 1: 1111 E 60th St
Street address city: Chicago
Street address state: IL
Zip/Postal code: 60637-2776
Country: USA
Mailing address: 1111 E 60th St
Mailing city: Chicago
Mailing state: IL
Mailing zip: 60637-2786
General Phone: (773) 702-3164
General Fax: (773) 834-4332
General/National Adv. E-mail: phoenix@law.uchicago.edu
Primary Website: www.ÃƒÂ°law.ÃƒÂ°uchicago.ÃƒÂ°edu
Year Established: 1901
Personnel: William Weaver (Ed.); Lisa Alvarez (Contact)

UNIV. OF ILLINOIS

Street address 1: 512 E Green St
Street address city: Champaign
Street address state: IL
Zip/Postal code: 61820-6483

Country: USA
Mailing address: 512 E Green St
Mailing city: Champaign
Mailing state: IL
Mailing zip: 61820-5720
General Phone: (217) 337-8300
General Fax: (217) 337-8303
Advertising Phone: 2173378382
Advertising Fax: 2173378303
Editorial Phone: 2173378350
Editorial Fax: 2173378328
Display Adv. E-mail: adsales@illinimedia.com
Editorial e-mail: news@illinimedia.com
Primary Website: www.dailyillini.com
Year Established: 1871
Published: Mon`Tues`Wed`Thur
Avg Free Circ: 10000
Personnel: Lilyan Levant (Advisor); Nancy Elliott (Adv. Dir.); Darshan Patel (Ed. in Chief); Travis Truitt (Ad Director)

UNIV. OF ILLINOIS AT CHICAGO

Street address 1: 1212 E 59th St
Street address 2: Ida Noyes Hall
Street address city: Chicago
Street address state: IL
Zip/Postal code: 60637-1604
Country: USA
Mailing address: 1001 W Van Buren St
Mailing city: Chicago
Mailing state: IL
Mailing zip: 60607-2900
General Phone: (312) 421-0480
General Fax: (312) 421-0491
Editorial Phone: (312) 996-5421
General/National Adv. E-mail: chicagomaroon@gmail.com
Primary Website: www.chicagoflame.com
Year Established: 1988
Personnel: Darryl Brehm (Bus. Mgr.); Kate Lee (Ed.)

UNIV. OF ILLINOIS/SPRINGFIELD

Street address 1: 1 University Plz
Street address 2: Sab 20
Street address city: Springfield
Street address state: IL
Zip/Postal code: 62703-5497
Country: USA
Mailing address: 1 University Plz
Mailing city: Springfield
Mailing state: IL
Mailing zip: 62703-5407
General Phone: (217) 206-6397
General Fax: (217) 206-6048
Advertising Phone: (217) 206-7717
Advertising Fax: (217) 206-6048
Editorial Phone: (217) 206-6397
Editorial Fax: (217) 206-6048
General/National Adv. E-mail: journal@uis.edu
Display Adv. E-mail: journalmgr@uis.edu
Editorial e-mail: journal@uis.edu
Primary Website: www.uisjournal.com
Year Established: 1985
Published: Wed
Published Other: Back-to-school edition in July/mailed to newly enrolled students and circulated
Avg Free Circ: 3000
Personnel: Debra Landis (Faculty Advisor); Marc Cox (EIC)

UNIV. OF ST. FRANCIS

Street address 1: 500 Wilcox St
Street address city: Joliet
Street address state: IL
Zip/Postal code: 60435-6169
Country: USA
Mailing address: 500 Wilcox St
Mailing city: Joliet
Mailing state: IL
Mailing zip: 60435-6188
General Phone: (815) 740-3816
General Fax: (815) 740-4285
General/National Adv. E-mail: encounter@stfrancis.edu
Primary Website: http://usfencounter.stfrancis.edu
Published: Mthly
Avg Free Circ: 500

Personnel: Brien McHugh (Advisor); Mike Clinton (Editor in Chief); Thaschara VanDyke (Asst. Editor in Chief)

UNIVERSITY OF CHICAGO BOOTH SCHOOL OF BUSINESS

Street address 1: 5807 S Woodlawn Ave
Street address 2: # C26A
Street address city: Chicago
Street address state: IL
Zip/Postal code: 60637-1610
Country: USA
Mailing address: 5807 S Woodlawn Ave # C26A
Mailing city: Chicago
Mailing state: IL
Mailing zip: 60637-1610
General Phone: (773) 702-1234
General Fax: (773) 834-0628
General/National Adv. E-mail: chibusmag@gmail.com
Display Adv. E-mail: chibusmag@gmail.com
Editorial e-mail: chibusmag@gmail.com
Primary Website: www.chibus.com
Published Other: Biweekly
Avg Free Circ: 1000
Personnel: Christopher Laws (Editor in Chief); Elizabeth Oates (Editor in Chief)

WAUBONSEE CMTY. COLLEGE

Street address 1: Rt 47 at Waubonsee Dr
Street address city: Sugar Grove
Street address state: IL
Zip/Postal code: 60554
Country: USA
Mailing address: Rt. 47 at Waubonsee Dr.
Mailing city: Sugar Grove
Mailing state: IL
Mailing zip: 60554
General Phone: (630) 466-2555
General Fax: (630) 466-9102
General/National Adv. E-mail: insight@waubonsee.edu
Personnel: Gary Clarke (Advisor); DJ Terek (Ed. in Chief)

WESTERN ILLINOIS UNIVERSITY

Street address 1: 1 University Cir
Street address 2: Western Illinois University
Street address city: Macomb
Street address state: IL
Zip/Postal code: 61455-1367
Country: USA
Mailing address: 1 University Cir
Mailing city: Macomb
Mailing state: IL
Mailing zip: 61455-1390
General Phone: (309) 298-1876
General Fax: (309) 298-2309
Advertising Phone: (309) 298-1876
Advertising Fax: (309) 298-2309
Editorial Phone: (309) 298-1876
Editorial Fax: (309) 298-2309
General/National Adv. E-mail: westerncourier@wiu.edu; micour@wiu.edu
Display Adv. E-mail: westerncourier@gmail.com
Editorial e-mail: wj-buss@wiu.edu
Primary Website: www.westerncourier.com
Year Established: 1905
Published: Mon`Wed`Fri
Avg Free Circ: 4000
Personnel: Devon Greene (Editor-in-Chief); Nick Ebelhack (Editor-in-Chief); Rachel Nelson (Advertising Manager); Will Buss (Advisor)

WHEATON COLLEGE

Street address 1: 501 College Ave
Street address 2: Cpo W135
Street address city: Wheaton
Street address state: IL
Zip/Postal code: 60187-5501
Country: USA
Mailing address: 501 College Ave.
Mailing city: Wheaton
Mailing state: IL
Mailing zip: 60187
General Phone: (630) 752-5077
General/National Adv. E-mail: the.record@my.wheaton.edu
Display Adv. E-mail: ads.wheatonrecord@gmail.com
Editorial e-mail: the.record@wheaton.edu
Primary Website: http://www.wheatonrecord.com/
Year Established: 1876

Published: Thur
Personnel: Philip Kline (Co-editor in chief); Alycia Vander Vegt (Co-editor in chief)

WILBUR WRIGHT COLLEGE

Street address 1: 4300 N Narragansett Ave
Street address city: Chicago
Street address state: IL
Zip/Postal code: 60634-1591
Country: USA
Mailing address: 4300 N Narragansett Ave
Mailing city: Chicago
Mailing state: IL
Mailing zip: 60634-1500
General Phone: (773) 481-8555
General Fax: (773) 481-8555
Editorial Phone: (773) 481-8444
General/National Adv. E-mail: web.wrighttimes@yahoo.com
Personnel: Terrence Doherty (Advisor); Juan Pintor (Ed. in Chief)

WILLIAM RAINEY HARPER COLLEGE

Street address 1: 1200 W Algonquin Rd
Street address city: Palatine
Street address state: IL
Zip/Postal code: 60067-7373
Country: USA
Mailing address: 1200 W Algonquin Rd
Mailing city: Palatine
Mailing state: IL
Mailing zip: 60067-7398
General Phone: (847) 925-6460
General Fax: (847) 925-6033
General/National Adv. E-mail: harperharbinger@gmail.com
Personnel: Kent McDill (Advisor)

INDIANA

ANDERSON UNIV.

Street address 1: 1100 E 5th St
Street address city: Anderson
Street address state: IN
Zip/Postal code: 46012-3462
Country: USA
Mailing address: 1100 E 5th St
Mailing city: Anderson
Mailing state: IN
Mailing zip: 46012-3495
General Phone: (765) 641-4341
General Fax: (765) 641-3851
General/National Adv. E-mail: andersonian@anderson.edu
Personnel: David Baird (Advisor); Kayla Dunkman (Ed. in Chief); Tarah Novak (Ed.); Stacy Wood (Ed.)

BALL STATE UNIVERSITY

Street address 1: Aj 278
Street address 2: Ball State University
Street address city: Muncie
Street address state: IN
Zip/Postal code: 47306-0001
Country: USA
Mailing address: AJ 276
Mailing city: Muncie
Mailing state: IN
Mailing zip: 47306-0001
General Phone: (765) 285-8218
General/National Adv. E-mail: editor@bsudailynews.com
Primary Website: www.bsudailynews.com
Year Established: 1922
Published: Wed
Avg Free Circ: 10000
Personnel: Lisa Renze-Rhodes (Publications Adviser)

BETHEL COLLEGE

Street address 1: 1001 Bethel Cir
Street address city: Mishawaka
Street address state: IN
Zip/Postal code: 46545-2232
Country: USA
Mailing address: 1001 Bethel Cir

Mailing city: Mishawaka
Mailing state: IN
Mailing zip: 46545-5591
General Phone: (574) 257-2672
General Fax: (574) 257-2583
General/National Adv. E-mail: beacon@bethelcollege.edu
Personnel: Tim Ceravolo (Dir., Student Media); Amanda Armstrong (Ed. in Chief)

BUTLER UNIV.

Street address 1: 4600 Sunset Ave
Street address city: Indianapolis
Street address state: IN
Zip/Postal code: 46208-3443
Country: USA
Mailing address: 4600 Sunset Ave # 112
Mailing city: Indianapolis
Mailing state: IN
Mailing zip: 46208-3487
General Phone: (317) 940-9358
General Fax: (317) 940-9713
General/National Adv. E-mail: mweiteka@butler.edu
Display Adv. E-mail: advertising@butler.edu
Personnel: Kwadwo Anokwa (Dir.); Charles St. Cyr (Advisor); Lauren Fisher (Adv. Mgr); Meg Shaw (Ed.)

CALUMET COLLEGE OF ST. JOSEPH

Street address 1: 2400 New York Ave
Street address city: Whiting
Street address state: IN
Zip/Postal code: 46394-2146
Country: USA
Mailing address: 2400 New York Ave
Mailing city: Whiting
Mailing state: IN
Mailing zip: 46394-2195
General Phone: (219) 473-4322
Primary Website: www.ccsj.edu
Published: Mthly
Personnel: Mark Cassello (Director of English & Media Communications); Dawn Muhammad (PD); Daren Jasieniecki (Mktg. Mgr.)

DEPAUW UNIV.

Street address 1: 609 S Locust St
Street address city: Greencastle
Street address state: IN
Zip/Postal code: 46135-2047
Country: USA
Mailing address: 609 S Locust St
Mailing city: Greencastle
Mailing state: IN
Mailing zip: 46135-2047
General Phone: (765) 658-5972
Personnel: Lili Wright (Advisor); Samuel Autman (Advisor); Jonathan Batuello (Ed. in Chief); Alex Turco (Exec. Ed.); Macy Ayers (Mng. Ed.)

EARLHAM COLLEGE

Street address 1: PO Box 273
Street address city: Richmond
Street address state: IN
Zip/Postal code: 47375-0273
Country: USA
Mailing address: PO Box 273
Mailing city: Richmond
Mailing state: IN
Mailing zip: 47375-0273
General Phone: (765) 983-1569
Personnel: Maria Salvador (Ed. in Chief); Marisa Keller (Mng. Ed.)

FRANKLIN COLLEGE

Street address 1: 101 Branigin Blvd
Street address city: Franklin
Street address state: IN
Zip/Postal code: 46131-2598
Country: USA
Mailing address: 101 Branigin Blvd
Mailing city: Franklin
Mailing state: IN
Mailing zip: 46131-2623
General Phone: (317) 738-8191
General Fax: (317) 738-8234
General/National Adv. E-mail: thefranklin@franklincollege.edu

Personnel: Katie Coffin (Ed.)

GOSHEN COLLEGE

Street address 1: 1700 S Main St
Street address city: Goshen
Street address state: IN
Zip/Postal code: 46526-4724
Country: USA
Mailing address: 1700 S Main St
Mailing city: Goshen
Mailing state: IN
Mailing zip: 46526-4794
General Phone: (574) 535-7745
General Fax: (574) 535-7660
General/National Adv. E-mail: record@goshen.edu
Personnel: Duane Stoltzfus; Marlys Weaver (Ed. in Chief)

HANOVER COLLEGE

Street address 1: PO Box 890
Street address city: Hanover
Street address state: IN
Zip/Postal code: 47243-0890
Country: USA
Mailing address: PO Box 890
Mailing city: Hanover
Mailing state: IN
Mailing zip: 47243-0890
General Phone: (812) 866-7073
General Fax: (812) 866-7077
General/National Adv. E-mail: triangle@hanover.edu
Personnel: Kay Stokes (Fac. Advisor); Melisa Cole (Mng. Ed.)

INDIANA STATE UNIV.

Street address 1: 550 Chestnut St
Street address city: Terre Haute
Street address state: IN
Zip/Postal code: 47809-1910
Country: USA
Mailing address: 716 Hulman Memorial Student Un
Mailing city: Terre Haute
Mailing state: IN
Mailing zip: 47809-0001
General Phone: (812) 237-7629
General Fax: (812) 237-7629
Personnel: Heidi Staggs (Mng. Ed.); Caitlin Hancock (Adv.Mgr.); Daniel Greenwell (Ed. in Chief)

INDIANA UNIV.

Street address 1: 2300 S Washington St
Street address city: Kokomo
Street address state: IN
Zip/Postal code: 46902-3557
Country: USA
Mailing address: PO Box 9003
Mailing city: Kokomo
Mailing state: IN
Mailing zip: 46904-9003
General Phone: (765) 455-9280
General Fax: (765) 455-9537
General/National Adv. E-mail: paper@iuk.edu
Personnel: David Brewster (Advisor); Alyx Arnett (Entertainment Ed.); Johnathan Grant (Ed. in Chief)

INDIANA UNIV.

Street address 1: 1700 Mishawaka Ave
Street address city: South Bend
Street address state: IN
Zip/Postal code: 46615-1408
Country: USA
Mailing address: PO Box 7111
Mailing city: South Bend
Mailing state: IN
Mailing zip: 46634-7111
General Phone: (574) 520-4878
Personnel: Beth Stutsman (Ed.)

INDIANA UNIV. EAST

Street address 1: 2325 Chester Blvd
Street address city: Richmond
Street address state: IN
Zip/Postal code: 47374-1220
Country: USA
Mailing address: 2325 Chester Blvd
Mailing city: Richmond
Mailing state: IN
Mailing zip: 47374-1289
General Phone: (765) 973-8255
General Fax: (765) 973-8388
General/National Adv. E-mail: howler@iue.edu
Personnel: Belinda Wyss (Advisor); Rob Zinkan (Exec. Ed.)

INDIANA UNIV. INDIANA DAILY STUDENT

Street address 1: 601 E. Kirkwood Ave
Street address 2: Rm 130
Street address city: Bloomington
Street address state: IN
Zip/Postal code: 47405
Country: USA
General Phone: (812) 855-0763
General Fax: (812) 855-8009
General/National Adv. E-mail: ids@indiana.edu
Primary Website: www.idsnews.com
Published: Thur
Personnel: Susan McGlocklin (Advisor); Jim Rodenbush (Director)

INDIANA UNIV. KELLEY SCHOOL OF BUS.

Street address 1: 1309 E 10th St
Street address city: Bloomington
Street address state: IN
Zip/Postal code: 47405-1701
Country: USA
Mailing address: 1309 E 10th St
Mailing city: Bloomington
Mailing state: IN
Mailing zip: 47405-5308
Personnel: Chris Hildreth (Ed.)

INDIANA UNIV. NORTHWEST

Street address 1: 3400 Broadway, Moraine 110
Street address city: Gary
Street address state: IN
Zip/Postal code: 46408
Country: USA
Mailing address: 3400 Broadway, Moraine 110
Mailing city: Gary
Mailing state: IN
Mailing zip: 46408-1101
General Phone: (219) 980-6795
General Fax: (219) 980-6948
General/National Adv. E-mail: phoenixn@iun.edu
Personnel: Scott Fulk (Coordinator); Don Sjoerdsma (Ed. in Chief)

INDIANA UNIV. SOUTHEAST

Street address 1: 4201 Grant Line Rd
Street address city: New Albany
Street address state: IN
Zip/Postal code: 47150-2158
Country: USA
Mailing address: 4201 Grant Line Rd
Mailing city: New Albany
Mailing state: IN
Mailing zip: 47150-6405
General Phone: (812) 941-2253
General/National Adv. E-mail: horizon@ius.edu
Primary Website: iushorizon.com
Published: Mon
Published Other: Every two weeks
Avg Free Circ: 2000
Personnel: Adam Maksl (Adviser)

INDIANA WESLEYAN UNIVERSITY

Street address 1: 4201 S Washington St
Street address city: Marion
Street address state: IN
Zip/Postal code: 46953-4974
Country: USA
Mailing address: 4201 S Washington St
Mailing city: Marion
Mailing state: IN
Mailing zip: 46953-4974
General Phone: (765) 677-1818
General Fax: (765) 677-1755
General/National Adv. E-mail: amy.smelser@indwes.edu
Personnel: Amy Smelser (Ed.); Amy Smelser (Instructor)

INDIANA-PURDUE UNIV.

Street address 1: 2101 E Coliseum Blvd
Street address 2: Walb 215
Street address city: Fort Wayne
Street address state: IN
Zip/Postal code: 46805-1445
Country: USA
Mailing address: 2101 E Coliseum Blvd Ste 100
Mailing city: Fort Wayne
Mailing state: IN
Mailing zip: 46805-1499
General Phone: (260) 481-6583
General Fax: (260) 481-6045
General/National Adv. E-mail: publisher@ipfwcommunicator.org
Display Adv. E-mail: ads@ipfwcommunicator.org
Personnel: Matt cClure (Pub.); Kristin Conley (Adv. Mgr.); Aaron Greene (Ed. in Chief)

JOURNALISM PROGRAM, VINCENNES UNIVERSITY

Street address 1: 1002 N 1st St
Street address city: Vincennes
Street address state: IN
Zip/Postal code: 47591-1504
Country: USA
Mailing address: 1002 N 1st St
Mailing city: Vincennes
Mailing state: IN
Mailing zip: 47591-1500
General Phone: (812) 888-4551
General Fax: (812) 888-5531
General/National Adv. E-mail: trailblazer@vinu.edu
Primary Website: www.vutrailblazernews.com
Year Established: 1923
Published: Other
Personnel: Emily Taylor (Journalism Asst. Professor, Department Chair of Media Production)

MANCHESTER COLLEGE

Street address 1: 604 E College Ave
Street address 2: # 11
Street address city: North Manchester
Street address state: IN
Zip/Postal code: 46962-1276
Country: USA
Mailing address: 604 E College Ave # 11
Mailing city: North Manchester
Mailing state: IN
Mailing zip: 46962-1232
General Phone: (260) 982-5317
Personnel: Katherine Ings (Advisor); Adam King (Ed. in Chief); Cyndel Taylor (Ed. in Chief)

MARIAN COLLEGE

Street address 1: 3200 Cold Spring Rd
Street address city: Indianapolis
Street address state: IN
Zip/Postal code: 46222-1960
Country: USA
Mailing address: 3200 Cold Spring Rd
Mailing city: Indianapolis
Mailing state: IN
Mailing zip: 46222-1997
General Phone: (317) 955-6397
Personnel: Gay Lynn Crossley (Faculty Supvr.); Sarah Kreicker (Ed.)

PURDUE UNIV. NORTH CENTRAL

Street address 1: 1401 S U S 421
Street address city: Westville
Street address state: IN
Zip/Postal code: 46391
Country: USA
Mailing address: 1401 S. U.S. 421
Mailing city: Westville
Mailing state: IN
Mailing zip: 46391-9542
General Phone: (219) 785-5213
General Fax: (219) 785-5544
General/National Adv. E-mail: spectator@pnc.edu
Editorial e-mail: thevoice@pnc.edu
Personnel: Suzanne Webber (Ed.); Lyndsie Daikhi (Print Ed.)

PURDUE UNIVERSITY CALUMET

Street address 1: 2200 169th St
Street address city: Hammond
Street address state: IN
Zip/Postal code: 46323-2068
Country: USA
Mailing address: 2200 169th St
Mailing city: Hammond
Mailing state: IN
Mailing zip: 46323-2068
General Phone: (219) 989-2547
General Fax: (219) 989-2770
General/National Adv. E-mail: pucchronicle@gmail.com
Display Adv. E-mail: chronicle.businessmanager@gmail.com
Editorial e-mail: pucchronicle@gmail.com
Primary Website: pucchronicle.com
Year Established: 1982
Published: Mon
Personnel: Jessica Gerlich (Editor-in-Chief); William Koester (Sports Editor); Michelle Mullins (Entertainment Editor); Dante Vidal Silguero (Business Manager); Morgan Walker (Photo Editor); Samantha Gonzalez (Production Manager)

ROSE-HULMAN INST. OF TECHNOLOGY

Street address 1: 5500 Wabash Ave
Street address 2: # CM5037
Street address city: Terre Haute
Street address state: IN
Zip/Postal code: 47803-3920
Country: USA
Mailing address: 5500 Wabash Ave # CM5037
Mailing city: Terre Haute
Mailing state: IN
Mailing zip: 47803-3920
General Phone: (812) 877-8255
Advertising Phone: (812) 877-8255
General/National Adv. E-mail: thorn@rose-hulman.edu
Display Adv. E-mail: thorn-biz@rose-hulman.edu
Primary Website: http://thorn.rose-hulman.edu/
Published: Fri
Avg Free Circ: 1000
Personnel: Thomas Adams (Advisor); Marcus Willerscheidt (Business Manager); Katrina Brandenburg (Editor-in-Chief)

ST. JOSEPH'S COLLEGE

Street address 1: 231 US Highway
Street address city: Rensselaer
Street address state: IN
Zip/Postal code: 47978
Country: USA
Mailing address: PO Box 870
Mailing city: Rensselaer
Personnel: Charles Kerlin (Faculty Facilitator); Mike Koscielny (Ed. in Chief)

TAYLOR UNIV.

Street address 1: 236 W Reade Ave
Street address city: Upland
Street address state: IN
Zip/Postal code: 46989-1001
Country: USA
Mailing address: 236 W. Reade Ave.
Mailing city: Upland
Mailing state: IN
Mailing zip: 46989-1001
General Phone: (765) 998-5359
General/National Adv. E-mail: echo@taylor.edu
Display Adv. E-mail: echoads@taylor.edu
Primary Website: http://theechonews.com/
Year Established: 1913
Published: Fri
Personnel: Donna Downs (Ed. in Chief); Alan Blanchard (Faculty Adviser)

TAYLOR UNIV.

Street address 1: 236 W Reade Ave
Street address city: Upland
Street address state: IN
Zip/Postal code: 46989-1001

Country: USA
Mailing address: 236 W. Reade Ave
Mailing city: Upland
Mailing state: IN
Mailing zip: 46989
Published: Fri
Personnel: Alan Blanchard (Faculty Advisor)

THE PURDUE EXPONENT

Street address 1: 460 Northwestern Ave
Street address city: West Lafayette
Street address state: IN
Zip/Postal code: 47906-2966
Country: USA
Mailing address: PO Box 2506
Mailing city: West Lafayette
Mailing state: IN
Mailing zip: 47996-2506
General Phone: (765) 743-1111
General Fax: (765) 743-6087
Advertising Phone: Ext. 122
Editorial Phone: Ext. 254
General/National Adv. E-mail: help@purdueexponent.org
Display Adv. E-mail: advertising@purdueexponent.org
Primary Website: www.purdueexponent.org
Year Established: 1889
Published: Mon`Tues`Wed`Thur`Fri
Published Other: M Th during summer
Avg Free Circ: 12000
Personnel: Patirck Kuhnle (Pub.); Ingraham Vancel (Prodn. Dir.); Mindy Coddington (Advertising director)

UNIV. OF EVANSVILLE

Street address 1: 1800 Lincoln Ave
Street address city: Evansville
Street address state: IN
Zip/Postal code: 47722-1000
Country: USA
Mailing address: 1800 Lincoln Ave
Mailing city: Evansville
Mailing state: IN
Mailing zip: 47714-1506
General Phone: (812) 488-2846
General Fax: (812) 488-2224
Advertising Phone: 812-488-2221
Advertising Fax: (812) 488-2224
Editorial Phone: (812) 488-2846
Editorial Fax: (812) 488-2224
General/National Adv. E-mail: crescentmagazine@evansville.edu
Display Adv. E-mail: crescentadvertising@evansville.edu
Editorial e-mail: crescentmagazine@evansville.edu
Year Established: 2009
Published: Thur`Mthly
Avg Free Circ: 1700
Personnel: Amy Reinhart (Writing Director); Rebecca Kish (Marketing & Sales Director)

UNIV. OF INDIANAPOLIS

Street address 1: 1400 E Hanna Ave
Street address city: Indianapolis
Street address state: IN
Zip/Postal code: 46227-3630
Country: USA
Mailing address: 1400 E Hanna Ave
Mailing city: Indianapolis
Mailing state: IN
Mailing zip: 46227-3697
General Phone: (317) 788-3269
General Fax: (317) 788-3490
General/National Adv. E-mail: reflector@uindy.edu
Personnel: Jeanne Criswell (Advisor.); JP Sinclair (Bus. Mgr.); Adrian Kendrick (Ed. in Chief); Samantha Cotten (Ed.)

UNIV. OF NOTRE DAME

Street address 1: 024 S Dining Hall
Street address city: Notre Dame
Street address state: IN
Zip/Postal code: 46556
Country: USA
Mailing address: PO Box 779
Mailing city: Notre Dame
Mailing state: IN
Mailing zip: 46556-0779
General Phone: (574) 631-7471
General Fax: (574) 631-6927
Advertising Phone: (574) 631-6900
General/National Adv. E-mail: observad@nd.edu
Personnel: Theresa Bea (Adv. Mgr.); Mary Claire Rodriguez (Adv. Mgr.); Jenn Metz (Ed. in Chief); Bill Brink (Mng. Ed.)

UNIV. OF NOTRE DAME ENGINEERING SCHOOL

Street address 1: 257 Cushing Hall
Street address city: Notre Dame
Street address state: IN
Zip/Postal code: 46556
Country: USA
Mailing address: 257 Cushing Hall
Mailing city: Notre Dame
Mailing state: IN
Mailing zip: 46556
General Phone: (574) 631-5530
General Fax: (574) 631-8007
General/National Adv. E-mail: techrev@nd.edu
Personnel: Cathy Pieronek (Asst. Dean); Brandon Chynowegh (Ed.)

UNIV. OF SOUTHERN INDIANA

Street address 1: 8600 University Blvd
Street address city: Evansville
Street address state: IN
Zip/Postal code: 47712-3534
Country: USA
Mailing address: 8600 University Blvd
Mailing city: Evansville
Mailing state: IN
Mailing zip: 47712-3590
General Phone: (812) 464 8600
General Fax: (812) 465-1632
Advertising Phone: (812) 464-1870
General/National Adv. E-mail: sheild@usi.edu
Display Adv. E-mail: shieldads@gmail.com
Editorial e-mail: shieldpix@gmail.com
Personnel: Jon Webb (Ed. in Chief)

VALPARAISO UNIVERSITY

Street address 1: 1809 Chapel Dr
Street address city: Valparaiso
Street address state: IN
Zip/Postal code: 46383-4517
Country: USA
Mailing address: 1809 Chapel Dr
Mailing city: Valparaiso
Mailing state: IN
Mailing zip: 46383-4517
General Phone: (219) 464-5271
General Fax: (219) 464-6742
General/National Adv. E-mail: douglas.kocher@valpo.edu
Personnel: Douglas J. Kocher (Chair); Jason Paupore (Advisor); Andy Simmons (Bus.Mgr.); Luis Fifuentes (Adv.Mgr.); Kathryn Kattalia (Ed. in chief)

KANSAS

BAKER UNIVERSITY

Street address 1: PO Box 65
Street address city: Baldwin City
Street address state: KS
Zip/Postal code: 66006-0065
Country: USA
Mailing address: PO Box 65
Mailing city: Baldwin City
Mailing state: KS
Mailing zip: 66006-0065
General Phone: (913) 594-6451
General Fax: (913) 594-3570
General/National Adv. E-mail: bayha@harvey.bakeru.edu
Personnel: Gwyn Mellinger (Advisor); Ann Rosenthal (Chair); Dave Bostwick (Advisor); Chris Smith (Ed.)

BARTON COUNTY CMTY. COLLEGE

Street address 1: 245 NE 30 Rd
Street address city: Great Bend
Street address state: KS
Zip/Postal code: 67530-9251
Country: USA
Mailing address: 245 NE 30 Rd
Mailing city: Great Bend
Mailing state: KS
Mailing zip: 67530-9107
General Phone: (620) 792-9239
Primary Website: www.bartonccc.edu
Year Established: 1969
Published Other: Bi-weekly Print; Weekly Online
Personnel: Yvonda Acker (Advisor)

BENEDICTINE COLLEGE

Street address 1: 1020 N 2nd St
Street address city: Atchison
Street address state: KS
Zip/Postal code: 66002-1402
Country: USA
Mailing address: 1020 N 2nd St
Mailing city: Atchison
Mailing state: KS
Mailing zip: 66002-1499
General Phone: (913) 360-7390
General Fax: (913) 367-6102
General/National Adv. E-mail: circuit@benedictine.edu
Personnel: Kevin Page (Advisor)

BETHANY COLLEGE

Street address 1: PO Box 184
Street address city: Lindsborg
Street address state: KS
Zip/Postal code: 67456-0184
Country: USA
Mailing address: PO Box 184
Mailing city: Lindsborg
Mailing state: KS
Mailing zip: 67456-0184
Personnel: Joel Wiede (Ed.)

BETHEL COLLEGE

Street address 1: 300 E 27th St
Street address city: North Newton
Street address state: KS
Zip/Postal code: 67117-8061
Country: USA
Mailing address: 300 E 27th St
Mailing city: North Newton
Mailing state: KS
Mailing zip: 67117-1716
General Phone: (316) 284-5271
General Fax: (316) 284-5286
General/National Adv. E-mail: collegian@bethelks.edu
Display Adv. E-mail: collegian@bethelks.edu
Editorial e-mail: collegian@bethelks.edu
Personnel: Christine Crouse-Dick (Advisor)

BUTLER COUNTY CMTY. COLLEGE

Street address 1: 901 S Haverhill Rd
Street address city: El Dorado
Street address state: KS
Zip/Postal code: 67042-3225
Country: USA
Mailing address: 901 S Haverhill Rd
Mailing city: El Dorado
Mailing state: KS
Mailing zip: 67042-3225
General Phone: (316) 322-3170
General Fax: (316) 322-3109
General/National Adv. E-mail: lantern@butlercc.edu
Personnel: Melissa Roberts (Bus. Mgr.)

COFFEYVILLE CMTY. COLLEGE

Street address 1: 400 W 11th St
Street address city: Coffeyville
Street address state: KS
Zip/Postal code: 67337-5065
Country: USA
Mailing address: 400 W. 11th
Mailing city: Coffeyville

COLBY CMTY. COLLEGE

Street address 1: 1255 S Range Ave
Street address city: Colby
Street address state: KS
Zip/Postal code: 67701-4007
Country: USA
Mailing address: 1255 S Range Ave
Mailing city: Colby
Mailing state: KS
Mailing zip: 67701-4099
General Phone: (785) 462-3984
Personnel: Trent Rose (Advisor)

COWLEY COUNTY CMTY. COLLEGE

Street address 1: 125 S 2nd St
Street address city: Arkansas City
Street address state: KS
Zip/Postal code: 67005-2662
Country: USA
Mailing address: 125 S 2nd St
Mailing city: Arkansas City
Mailing state: KS
Mailing zip: 67005-2662
General Phone: (620) 441-5287
General Fax: (620) 441-5377
General/National Adv. E-mail: editor@cowleypress.com
Personnel: Meg Smith (Faculty Advisor); Alyssa Campbell (Adv. Mgr.); Richard Gould (Ed.)

FT. HAYS STATE UNIV.

Street address 1: 600 Park St
Street address 2: Picken 104
Street address city: Hays
Street address state: KS
Zip/Postal code: 67601-4009
Country: USA
Mailing address: 600 Park St Picken 104
Mailing city: Hays
Mailing state: KS
Mailing zip: 67601-4009
General Phone: (785) 628-3478
Personnel: Gretchen Fields (Advisor)

JOHNSON COUNTY CMTY. COLLEGE

Street address 1: 12345 College Blvd
Street address 2: # 7
Street address city: Overland Park
Street address state: KS
Zip/Postal code: 66210-1283
Country: USA
Mailing address: 12345 College Blvd # 7
Mailing city: Overland Park
Mailing state: KS
Mailing zip: 66210-1283
General Phone: (913) 469-8500
Personnel: Anne Christiansen-Bullers (Advisor); Matt Galloway (Ed. in Chief)

KANSAS CITY CMTY. COLLEGE

Street address 1: 7250 State Ave
Street address city: Kansas City
Street address state: KS
Zip/Postal code: 66112-3003
Country: USA
Mailing address: 7250 State Ave
Mailing city: Kansas City
Mailing state: KS
Mailing zip: 66112-3003
General Phone: (913) 334-1100
Personnel: Bryan Whitehead (Faculty Advisor)

KANSAS WESLEYAN UNIV.

Street address 1: 100 E Claflin Ave
Street address 2: # 87
Street address city: Salina
Street address state: KS
Zip/Postal code: 67401-6146
Country: USA
Mailing address: 100 E Claflin Ave Ste 87
Mailing city: Salina
Mailing state: KS
Mailing zip: 67401-6100
Personnel: Jack Morris (Advisor)

MCPHERSON COLLEGE

Street address 1: 1600 E Euclid St
Street address city: McPherson
Street address state: KS
Zip/Postal code: 67460-3847
Country: USA
Mailing address: PO Box 1402

Mailing city: McPherson
Mailing state: KS
Mailing zip: 67460-1402
General Phone: (620) 242-0449
Personnel: Adam Pracht (Adviser); Shannon Williams (Editor-in-Chief)

MIDAMERICA NAZARENE UNIVERSITY

Street address 1: 2030 E College Way
Street address city: Olathe
Street address state: KS
Zip/Postal code: 66062-1851
Country: USA
Mailing address: 2030 E. College Way
Mailing city: Olathe
Mailing state: KS
Mailing zip: 66062
General Phone: (913) 971-3289
General Fax: (913) 971-3421
Advertising Phone: (913) 961-8615
Editorial Phone: (913) 530-0854
Display Adv. E-mail: ehodgson@mnu.edu
Editorial e-mail: tb-edit@mnu.edu
Primary Website: www.trailblazer.mnubox.com
Year Established: 1967
Personnel: Sarah Glass (Editor-in-Chief); Molly Farnsworth (Managing Editor); Christina Wilkins (Section Editor); Melinda Smith (Faculty Advisor)

NEWMAN UNIVERSITY - THE VANTAGE

Street address 1: 3100 W McCormick St
Street address city: Wichita
Street address state: KS
Zip/Postal code: 67213-2008
Country: USA
Mailing address: 3100 W McCormick St
Mailing city: Wichita
Mailing state: KS
Mailing zip: 67213-2008
General Phone: (316) 942-4291
Personnel: Kristen McCurdy (Editor)

PRATT CMTY. COLLEGE

Street address 1: 348 NE Hwy 61
Street address city: Pratt
Street address state: KS
Zip/Postal code: 67124
Country: USA
Mailing address: 348 NE Hwy. 61
Mailing city: Pratt
Mailing state: KS

STUDENT PUBLICATIONS INC.

Street address 1: 103 Kedzie Hall
Street address city: Manhattan
Street address state: KS
Zip/Postal code: 66506-1500
Country: USA
Mailing address: 103 Kedzie Hall
Mailing city: Manhattan
Mailing state: KS
Mailing zip: 66506-1505
General Phone: (785) 532-6555
General Fax: (785) 532-6236
General/National Adv. E-mail: news@spub.ksu.edu
Display Adv. E-mail: adsales@spub.ksu.edu; classifieds@spub.ksu.edu
Primary Website: www.kstatecollegian.com
Year Established: 1896
Personnel: Steve Wolgast (Advisor); Tim Schrag (Ed.)

TABOR COLLEGE

Street address 1: 400 S Jefferson St
Street address city: Hillsboro
Street address state: KS
Zip/Postal code: 67063-1753
Country: USA
Mailing address: 400 S. Jefferson St.
Mailing city: Hillsboro
Mailing state: KS
Mailing zip: 67063-1753
General Phone: (620) 947-3121
General Fax: (620) 947-2607
General/National Adv. E-mail: theview@tabor.edu
Display Adv. E-mail: theview@tabor.edu
Editorial e-mail: theview@tabor.edu
Primary Website: https://www.facebook.com/TaborView?ref=hl
Published: Mthly
Personnel: Sara Jo Waldron (Advisor); Jared Janzen (Editor-in-Chief); Sara Sigley (Advisor); Heather Deckert (Ed.)

THE UNIVERSITY DAILY KANSAN

Street address 1: 1000 Sunnyside Ave
Street address city: Lawrence
Street address state: KS
Zip/Postal code: 66045-7599
Country: USA
Mailing address: 1000 Sunnyside Ave
Mailing city: Lawrence
Mailing state: KS
Mailing zip: 66045-7599
General Phone: (785) 864-4724
General Fax: (785) 864-5261
Advertising Phone: (785) 864-4358
Editorial Phone: (785) 864-4812
General/National Adv. E-mail: editor@kansan.com
Display Adv. E-mail: adsales@kansan.com
Editorial e-mail: editor@kansan.com
Primary Website: www.kansan.com
Year Established: 1904
Published: Mon`Tues`Wed`Thur
Published Other: Weekly in summer (June/July)
Personnel: Malcolm Gibson (Gen. Mgr./News Advisor); Jon Schlitt (Sales and Marketing Adviser)

UNIV. OF KANSAS ENGINEERING SCHOOL

Street address 1: 4010 Learned Hall
Street address city: Lawrence
Street address state: KS
Zip/Postal code: 66045-7526
Country: USA
Mailing address: 4010 Learned Hall
Mailing city: Lawrence
Personnel: Mary Jane Dunlap (News Ed.); Jill Hummels (PR Dir.)

WASHBURN UNIV.

Street address 1: 1700 SW College Ave
Street address city: Topeka
Street address state: KS
Zip/Postal code: 66621-0001
Country: USA
Mailing address: 1700 SW College Ave
Mailing city: Topeka
Mailing state: KS
Mailing zip: 66621-1101
General Phone: (785) 670-2506
General Fax: (785) 670-1035
Advertising Phone: (785) 670-1173
General/National Adv. E-mail: review@washburn.edu
Personnel: Nicole Stejskal (Ed. in Chief)

WICHITA STATE UNIV.

Street address 1: 1845 Fairmount St
Street address city: Wichita
Street address state: KS
Zip/Postal code: 67260-9700
Country: USA
Mailing address: 1845 Fairmount St
Mailing city: Wichita
Mailing state: KS
Mailing zip: 67260-0001
General Phone: (316) 978-3456
Editorial e-mail: editor@thesunflower.com; sports.editor@thesunflower.com
Personnel: Ronda Voorhis (Advisor); Candice Tullis (Ed. in Chief); Scott Elpers (Mng. Ed.); Jorge M. De Hoyos (Sports Ed.)

KENTUCKY

ASBURY COLLEGE

Street address 1: 1 Macklem Dr
Street address city: Wilmore
Street address state: KY
Zip/Postal code: 40390-1152
Country: USA
Mailing address: 1 Macklem Dr
Mailing city: Wilmore
Mailing state: KY
Mailing zip: 40390-1198
General Phone: (859) 858-3511
General Fax: (859) 858-3921
General/National Adv. E-mail: mlonginow@asbury.edu
Personnel: Deanna Morono (Exec. Ed.); James R. Owens (Chair); Kayla Dubois (Mng. Ed.); Zack Klemme (News Ed.); Morgan Schutters (Web Design)

BELLARMINE COLLEGE

Street address 1: 2001 Newburg Rd
Street address city: Louisville
Street address state: KY
Zip/Postal code: 40205-1863
Country: USA
Mailing address: 2001 Newburg Rd
Mailing city: Louisville
Mailing state: KY
Mailing zip: 40205-0671
General Phone: (502) 452-8157
Advertising Phone: (502) 452-8050
Editorial Phone: (502) 452-8157
General/National Adv. E-mail: theconcard@bellarmine.edu
Personnel: Erika Osborne (Ed. in Chief)

BEREA COLLEGE

Street address 1: Cpo 2150
Street address city: Berea
Street address state: KY
Country: USA
Mailing address: 2150 Cpo
Mailing city: Berea
Mailing state: KY
Mailing zip: 40404-0001
General Phone: (859) 985-3208
General Fax: (859) 985-3914
General/National Adv. E-mail: pinnacle@berea.edu
Personnel: Chris Lakes (Advisor); Kwadwo Juantuah (Ed.)

CAMPBELLSVILLE UNIVERSITY

Street address 1: Up 897 Campbellsville University
Street address city: Campbellsville
Street address state: KY
Zip/Postal code: 42718
County: Taylor
Country: USA
Mailing address: 1 University Dr.
Mailing city: Campbellsville
Mailing state: KY
Mailing zip: 42718
General Phone: (270) 789-5035
Primary Website: www.campbellsville.edu/campus-times
Published Other: Monthly when school is in session
Avg Free Circ: 2000

CENTRE COLLEGE

Street address 1: 600 W Walnut St
Street address city: Danville
Street address state: KY
Zip/Postal code: 40422-1309
Country: USA
Mailing address: 600 W Walnut St
Mailing city: Danville
Mailing state: KY
Mailing zip: 40422-1394
General Phone: (859) 238-5350
General/National Adv. E-mail: cento@centre.edu
Display Adv. E-mail: business@centre.edu
Editorial e-mail: ed-in-chief@centre.edu
Year Established: 1888
Personnel: Tess Simon (Ed.); Katy Meyer; Amy Senders

EASTERN KENTUCKY UNIV.

Street address 1: 521 Lancaster Ave
Street address 2: Combs Bldg. 226
Street address city: Richmond
Street address state: KY
Zip/Postal code: 40475-3100
Country: USA
Mailing address: 521 Lancaster Ave
Mailing city: Richmond
Mailing state: KY
Mailing zip: 40475-3102
General Phone: (859) 622-1881
General Fax: (859) 622-2354
General/National Adv. E-mail: progress@eku.edu
Display Adv. E-mail: progressads@eku.edu
Primary Website: www.easternprogress.com
Year Established: 1922
Published: Thur
Published Other: During semesters
Avg Free Circ: 8000
Personnel: Reggie Beehner (Advisor); Kristie Hamon (Ed.); Gina Portwood (Bus. Mgr.); Park Greer (Adv. Mgr.)

GEORGETOWN COLLEGE

Street address 1: 400 E College St
Street address 2: # 280
Street address city: Georgetown
Street address state: KY
Zip/Postal code: 40324-1628
Country: USA
Mailing address: 400 E College St Ste 1 # 280
Mailing city: Georgetown
Personnel: Whitley Arens (ed.)

HENDERSON CMTY. COLLEGE

Street address 1: 2660 S Green St
Street address city: Henderson
Street address state: KY
Zip/Postal code: 42420-4623
Country: USA
Mailing address: 2660 S Green St
Mailing city: Henderson
Mailing state: KY
Mailing zip: 42420-4699
Year Established: 1978
Personnel: Scott Taylor (Ed.)

KENTUCKY PRESS SERVICE, INC.

Street address 1: 101 Consumer Ln
Street address city: Frankfort
Street address state: KY
Zip/Postal code: 40601-8489
County: Franklin
Country: USA
Mailing address: 101 Consumer Ln
Mailing city: Frankfort
Mailing state: KY
Mailing zip: 40601-8489
General Phone: (502) 223-8821
General Fax: (502) 875-2624
General/National Adv. E-mail: dthompson@kypress.com
Display Adv. E-mail: rmccarty@kypress.com, hwillard@kypress.com
Classified Adv. e-mail: rmccarty@kypress.com, hwillard@kypress.com
Primary Website: www.kypress.com
Year Established: 1959
Published Other: Daily
Personnel: David Thompson (Exec. Dir.); Bonnie Howard (Controller)

KENTUCKY STATE UNIV.

Street address 1: 400 E Main St
Street address city: Frankfort
Street address state: KY
Zip/Postal code: 40601-2334
Country: USA
Mailing address: 400 E Main St
Mailing city: Frankfort
Mailing state: KY
Mailing zip: 40601-2355
General Phone: (502) 597-5915
Personnel: Sepricia White (Ed. in Chief); Terri McCray (Features Ed.); Cornell Ferrill (Sports Ed.)

KENTUCKY WESLEYAN COLLEGE

Street address 1: 3000 Frederica St
Street address city: Owensboro
Street address state: KY
Zip/Postal code: 42301-6057
Country: USA
Mailing address: 3000 Frederica St
Mailing city: Owensboro

Mailing state: KY
Mailing zip: 42301-6055
General Phone: (270) 852-3596
Published: Bi-Mthly
Personnel: Randall Vogt (Advisor); Devyn Lott (General Editor)

MOREHEAD STATE UNIV.

Street address 1: 150 University Blvd
Street address city: Morehead
Street address state: KY
Zip/Postal code: 40351-1684
Country: USA
Mailing address: 150 University Blvd
Mailing city: Morehead
Mailing state: KY
Mailing zip: 40351
General Phone: (606) 783-2697
General Fax: (606) 783-9113
General/National Adv. E-mail: editor@trailblazeronline.net
Personnel: Joan Atkins

MURRAY STATE UNIV.

Street address 1: 111 Wilson Hall
Street address city: Murray
Street address state: KY
Zip/Postal code: 42071-3311
Country: USA
Mailing address: 111 Wilson Hall
Mailing city: Murray
Mailing state: KY
Mailing zip: 42071-3311
General Phone: (270) 809-6877
General Fax: (270) 809-3175
General/National Adv. E-mail: news@murraystate.edu
Personnel: Mia Walters (Ed. in chief)

NORTHERN KENTUCKY UNIV.

Street address 1: University Ctr, Rm 335, Nunn Dr
Street address city: Newport
Street address state: KY
Zip/Postal code: 41099-0001
Country: USA
Mailing address: University Ctr Rm 335
Mailing city: Newport
Mailing state: KY
Mailing zip: 41099-0001
General Phone: (859) 572-5772
General Fax: (859) 572-5772
Advertising Fax: (859) 572-5232
General/National Adv. E-mail: northerner@nku.edu
Personnel: Drew Laskey (Sports Ed.)

UNIV. OF KENTUCKY

Street address 1: Grehan Journalism Bldg, Rm 026
Street address city: Lexington
Street address state: KY
Zip/Postal code: 40506-0001
Country: USA
Mailing address: Grehan Journalism Bldg Rm 26
Mailing city: Lexington
Mailing state: KY
Mailing zip: 40506-0001
General Phone: (859) 257-2872
General Fax: (859) 323-1906
General/National Adv. E-mail: features@kykernel.com
Display Adv. E-mail: news@kykernel.com
Personnel: Chris Poore (Advisor); Kenny Colston (Ed. in Chief)

UNIVERSITY OF LOUISVILLE

Street address 1: Houehens Bldg, Ste LL07
Street address city: Louisville
Street address state: KY
Zip/Postal code: 40292-0001
Country: USA
Mailing address: Houehens Bldg, Ste LL07
Mailing city: Louisville
Mailing state: KY
Mailing zip: 40292-0001
General Fax: (502) 852-0700
Advertising Phone: (502) 852-0701
Editorial Phone: (502) 852-0667
Display Adv. E-mail: advertising@louisvillecardinal.com
Editorial e-mail: editor@louisvillecardinal.com
Primary Website: www.louisvillecardinal.com
Year Established: 1926
Published: Tues
Avg Free Circ: 8000
Personnel: Simon Isham (Editor-in-Chief); Ralph Merkel (Adviser)

UNIVERSITY OF THE CUMBERLANDS

Street address 1: 6191 College Station Dr
Street address city: Williamsburg
Street address state: KY
Zip/Postal code: 40769-1372
Country: USA
Mailing address: 6191 College Station Dr
Mailing city: Williamsburg
Mailing state: KY
Mailing zip: 40769-1372

WESTERN KENTUCKY UNIVERSITY

Street address 1: 1660 Normal St
Street address 2: Western Kentucky University
Street address city: Bowling Green
Street address state: KY
Zip/Postal code: 42101-3536
Country: USA
Mailing address: 1906 College Heights Blvd # 11084
Mailing city: Bowling Green
Mailing state: KY
Mailing zip: 42101-1084
General Phone: (270) 745-2653
Advertising Phone: (270) 745-2653
Editorial Phone: (270) 745-2653
General/National Adv. E-mail: carrie.pratt@wku.edu
Display Adv. E-mail: william.hoagland@wku.edu
Editorial e-mail: herald.editor@wku.edu
Primary Website: www.wkuherald.com
Year Established: 1925
Published: Tues`Thur
Published Other: Topper Extra sports section published on home football days
Avg Free Circ: 7000
Personnel: Sherry West (Operations Mgr); Carrie Pratt (Herald Adviser, Multiplatform News Adviser); Tracy Newton (Office Associate); Will Hoagland (Advt Adviser and Sales Mgr); Chuck Clark (Dir of Student Publications); Sam Oldenburg (Talisman adviser)

LOUISIANA

BOSSIER PARISH CMTY. COLLEGE

Street address 1: 6220 E Texas St
Street address city: Bossier City
Street address state: LA
Zip/Postal code: 71111-6922
Country: USA
Mailing address: 6220 E Texas St
Mailing city: Bossier City
Mailing state: LA
Mailing zip: 71111-6922
General Phone: (318) 678-6000
General Fax: X
General/National Adv. E-mail: kaleidoscope@bpcc.edu
Personnel: Candice Gibson (Advisor); Cathy Hammel (Advisor)

CENTENARY COLLEGE

Street address 1: 2911 Centenary Blvd
Street address city: Shreveport
Street address state: LA
Zip/Postal code: 71104-3335
Country: USA
Mailing address: PO Box 41188
Mailing city: Shreveport
Mailing state: LA
Mailing zip: 71134-1188
General Phone: (318) 792-5136
General/National Adv. E-mail: paper@centenary.edu
Personnel: Mark Gruettner (Advisor); Roxie Smith (Ed. in chief)

DELGADO COMMUNITY COLLEGE

Street address 1: 615 City Park Ave
Street address city: New Orleans
Street address state: LA
Zip/Postal code: 70119-4399
Country: USA
Mailing address: 615 City Park Ave
Mailing city: New Orleans
Mailing state: LA
Mailing zip: 70119-4399
General Phone: (504) 671-6008
General Fax: (504) 483-1953
General/National Adv. E-mail: thedolphin29@gmail.com
Personnel: Susan Hague (Faculty Advisor); J.C. Romero (Ed. in Chief)

DILLARD UNIV.

Street address 1: 2601 Gentilly Blvd
Street address city: New Orleans
Street address state: LA
Zip/Postal code: 70122-3043
Country: USA
Mailing address: 2601 Gentilly Blvd
Mailing city: New Orleans
Mailing state: LA
Mailing zip: 70122-3097

GRAMBLING STATE UNIVERSITY

Street address 1: 403 Main St
Street address city: Grambling
Street address state: LA
Zip/Postal code: 71245-2715
Country: USA
Mailing address: 403 Main St
Mailing city: Grambling
Mailing state: LA
Mailing zip: 71245-2761
General Phone: (318) 247-3331
General Fax: (318) 274-3194
Editorial Phone: (318) 274-2866
General/National Adv. E-mail: mediarelations@gram.edu
Primary Website: www.thegramblinite.com
Published: Thur
Personnel: Mitzi LaSalle (Interim Director of University Communications, Marketing, and Media Relations)

LOUISIANA COLLEGE

Street address 1: 1140 College Dr
Street address 2: Dept English
Street address city: Pineville
Street address state: LA
Zip/Postal code: 71359-1000
Country: USA
Mailing address: 1140 College Dr Dept English
Mailing city: Pineville
Mailing state: LA
Mailing zip: 71359-1000
General Phone: (318) 487-7011
Personnel: Jessie Redd (Ed.)

LOUISIANA STATE UNIV.

Street address 1: 1800 Hwy 71 S
Street address city: Alexandria
Street address state: LA
Zip/Postal code: 71302
Country: USA
Mailing address: 1800 Hwy. 71 S.
Mailing city: Alexandria
Mailing state: LA
Mailing zip: 71302
Personnel: Elizabeth Beard (Advisor); Nancy Borden (Advisor); Trayce Snow (Ed.)

LOUISIANA STATE UNIV.

Street address 1: 1 University Pl
Street address 2: No 344
Street address city: Shreveport
Street address state: LA
Zip/Postal code: 71115-2301
Country: USA
Mailing address: 1 University Pl No 344
Mailing city: Shreveport
Mailing state: LA
Mailing zip: 71115-2301
General Phone: (318) 797-5328
General Fax: (318) 797-5328
Display Adv. E-mail: almagest@lsus.edu
Personnel: Rose-Marie Lillian (Advisor); Karen Wissing (Exec. Ed.)

LOUISIANA STATE UNIVERSITY

Street address 1: Office of Student Media, B-39 Hodges Hall
Street address city: Baton Rouge
Street address state: LA
Zip/Postal code: 70803-0001
Country: USA
Mailing address: Of Student Media B-39 Hodges Hall Ofc
Mailing city: Baton Rouge
Mailing state: LA
Mailing zip: 70803-0001
General Phone: (225) 578-4810
General Fax: (225) 578-1698
Advertising Phone: (225) 578-6090
Editorial Phone: (225) 578-4811
General/National Adv. E-mail: editor@lsureveille.com
Display Adv. E-mail: national@tigers.lsu.edu
Editorial e-mail: editor@lsureveille.com
Primary Website: www.lsureveille.com
Year Established: 1887
Published: Mon`Tues`Wed`Thur`Fri
Personnel: Nicholas Persac (Ed.); Kyle Whitfield (Ed.); Kodi Wilson (Adv. Mgr.); Andrea Gallo (Editor in Chief); Balkom Taylor (Editor in Chief); Chandler Rome (Editor-in-Chief)

LOYOLA UNIVERSITY NEW ORLEANS

Street address 1: 6363 Saint Charles Ave
Street address 2: Campus Box 64
Street address city: New Orleans
Street address state: LA
Zip/Postal code: 70118-6143
Country: USA
Mailing address: 6363 Saint Charles Ave
Mailing city: New Orleans
Mailing state: LA
Mailing zip: 70118-6195
General Phone: (504) 865-3535
Advertising Phone: (504) 865-3295
General/National Adv. E-mail: maroon@loyno.edu
Display Adv. E-mail: ads@loyno.edu
Primary Website: www.loyolamaroon.com
Year Established: 1923
Published: Fri
Avg Free Circ: 1000
Personnel: Michael Giusti (Advisor)

MCNEESE STATE UNIV.

Street address 1: PO Box 91375
Street address city: Lake Charles
Street address state: LA
Zip/Postal code: 70609-0001
Country: USA
Mailing address: PO Box 91375
Mailing city: Lake Charles
Mailing state: LA
Mailing zip: 70609-0001
General Phone: (337) 475-5646
General Fax: (337) 475-5259
General/National Adv. E-mail: contraband@mcneese.edu; msucontraband@gmail.com
Personnel: Candace Townsend (Advisor); Robert Teal (Ed. in Chief); Sarah Puckett (Ed.)

NICHOLLS STATE UNIV.

Street address 1: PO Box 2010
Street address city: Thibodaux
Street address state: LA
Zip/Postal code: 70310-0001
Country: USA
Mailing address: PO Box 2010
Mailing city: Thibodaux
Mailing state: LA
Mailing zip: 70310-0001
General Phone: (985) 448-4259
Personnel: Stephen Hartmann (Advisor)

NORTHWESTERN STATE UNIVERSITY

Street address 1: 225 Kyser Hall
Street address 2: Northwestern State University
Street address city: Natchitoches
Street address state: LA

Zip/Postal code: 71497-0001
Country: USA
Mailing address: The Current Sauce
Mailing city: Natchitoches
Mailing state: LA
Mailing zip: 71497
General Phone: (318) 357-5456
Advertising Phone: (318) 357-5456
Editorial Phone: (318) 357-5456
General/National Adv. E-mail: thecurrentsauce@gmail.com
Display Adv. E-mail: thecurrentsauce@gmail.com
Editorial e-mail: thecurrentsauce@gmail.com
Primary Website: www.nsulastudentmedia.com
Year Established: 1914
Published: Wed
Avg Free Circ: 1000
Personnel: Alec Horton (Editor-in-Chief); Jordan Reich (Associate Editor); Christina Arrechavala (Managing Editor); Valentina Perez (Photo Editor); Elisabeth Perez (PR Manager); Chloe' Romano (Assistant PR Manager); Julia Towry (Ad Sales Representative); Sarah Hill (Designer); Maygin Chesson (Administrative Assistant)

SOUTHEASTERN LOUISIANA UNIV.

Street address 1: 303 Texas Ave, Student Union, Rm 211D
Street address city: Hammond
Street address state: LA
Zip/Postal code: 70402-0001
Country: USA
Mailing address: Slu 10877
Mailing city: Hammond
Mailing state: LA
Mailing zip: 70402-0001
General Phone: (985) 549-3731
General Fax: (985) 549-3842
General/National Adv. E-mail: lionsroar@selu.edu
Primary Website: www.selu.edu/lionsroar
Year Established: 1929
Personnel: Lee Lind (Dir., Student Pub.); Don Aime (Ed. in Chief)

SOUTHERN UNIV. A&M COLLEGE

Street address 1: T H Harris Hall, Ste 1064
Street address city: Baton Rouge
Street address state: LA
Zip/Postal code: 70813-0001
Country: USA
Mailing address: PO Box 10180
Mailing city: Baton Rouge
Mailing state: LA
Mailing zip: 70813-0180
General Phone: (225) 771-2230
General Fax: (225) 771-3253
General/National Adv. E-mail: editor@southerndigest.com
Primary Website: www.southerndigest.com
Year Established: 1928
Personnel: Stephanie Cain (Bus./Adv. Mgr.); Derick Hackett (Dir., Student Media); Christopher Jones (Asst. Dir.); Fran Hoskins (Ed.)

SOUTHERN UNIVERSITY

Street address 1: T H Harris Hall
Street address 2: Suite 1064
Street address city: Baton Rouge
Street address state: LA
Zip/Postal code: 70813-0001
Country: USA
Mailing address: PO Box 10180
Mailing city: Baton Rouge
Mailing state: LA
Mailing zip: 70813-0180
General Phone: (225) 771-2231
General Fax: (225) 771-5840
Advertising Phone: 225-771-5833
Advertising Fax: 225-771-5840
Editorial Phone: 225-771-5829
Editorial Fax: 225-771-5840
General/National Adv. E-mail: digest@subr.edu
Display Adv. E-mail: camelia_gardner@subr.edu
Editorial e-mail: fredrick_batiste@subr.edu
Primary Website: www.southerndigest.com
Year Established: 1926
Published: Tues`Thur
Avg Free Circ: 4000
Personnel: Heather Freeman (Student Media Director); Camelia Jackson (Advertising/Business Manager); Fredrick Batiste (Publications Assistant/Advisor)

TULANE UNIVERSITY

Street address 1: Lavin-Bernick Center for University Life G06
Street address city: New Orleans
Street address state: LA
Zip/Postal code: 70118
Country: USA
Mailing address: Lavin-Bernick Center G06
Mailing city: New Orleans
Mailing state: LA
Mailing zip: 70118
General Phone: (504) 865-5657
Advertising Phone: (504) 865-5657
General/National Adv. E-mail: hull@tulane.edu
Display Adv. E-mail: hullabaloo.advertising@gmail.com
Primary Website: www.thehullabaloo.com
Year Established: 1902
Published: Thur
Published Other: Homecoming Magazine and Spring Magazine
Avg Free Circ: 4000
Personnel: Brooke Rhea (Senior Business Manager); Lily Milwit (Editor In-Chief)

UNIV. OF LOUISIANA AT LAFAYETTE THE VERMILION

Street address 1: PO Box 44813
Street address city: Lafayette
Street address state: LA
Zip/Postal code: 70504-0001
Country: USA
Mailing address: PO Box 44813
Mailing city: Lafayette
Mailing state: LA
Mailing zip: 70504-0001
General Phone: (337) 482-6110
General Fax: (337) 482-6959
Advertising Phone: (337) 482-6960
Advertising Fax: (337) 472-6959
Editorial Phone: (337) 482-6110
Editorial Fax: (337) 482-6959
General/National Adv. E-mail: vermadvertising@gmail.com
Display Adv. E-mail: vermadvertising@gmail.com
Editorial e-mail: hollyhoooot@gmail.com
Primary Website: thevermilion.com
Year Established: 1904
Published: Wed
Published Other: Aug, Sept, Oct, Nov
Personnel: Thomas Schumacher (Business Manager)

UNIV. OF LOUISIANA AT MONROE

Street address 1: 700 University Ave
Street address 2: Stubbs 131
Street address city: Monroe
Street address state: LA
Zip/Postal code: 71209-9000
Country: USA
Mailing address: 700 University Ave
Mailing city: Monroe
Mailing state: LA
Mailing zip: 71209
General Phone: (318) 342-5454
Advertising Phone: (318) 342-5453
Editorial Phone: 9318) 342-5450
General/National Adv. E-mail: ulmhawkeye@gmail.com
Display Adv. E-mail: ulmhawkeyead@gmail.com
Editorial e-mail: ulmhawkeye@gmail.com
Primary Website: www.ulmhawkeye.com
Year Established: 1934
Published: Mon
Personnel: Ethan Dennis (Editor in Chief); Clarence Nash, Jr. (Advertising Director)

UNIVERSITY OF NEW ORLEANS

Street address 1: 2000 Lakeshore Dr
Street address 2: # Ba 250/252
Street address city: New Orleans
Street address state: LA
Zip/Postal code: 70148-3520
Country: USA
Mailing address: 2000 Lakeshore Dr # UC252
Mailing city: New Orleans
Mailing state: LA
Mailing zip: 70148-0001
General Phone: (504) 280-6378
General Fax: (504) 280-6010
General/National Adv. E-mail: driftwood@uno.edu
Personnel: Edie Talley (Editor in Chief)

XAVIER UNIV. OF LOUISIANA

Street address 1: 1 Drexel Dr
Street address 2: # 299
Street address city: New Orleans
Street address state: LA
Zip/Postal code: 70125-1056
Country: USA
Mailing address: 1 Drexel Drive, Box 299
Mailing city: New Orleans
Mailing state: LA
Mailing zip: 70125-1098
General Phone: (504) 520-5092
General Fax: (504) 520-7919
Display Adv. E-mail: herald@xula.edu
Primary Website: www.xula.edu; www.xulaherald.com
Year Established: 1925
Published: Bi-Mthly
Avg Free Circ: 2000
Personnel: Melinda Shelton (Advisor)

MASSACHUSETTS

AMERICAN INTERNATIONAL COLLEGE

Street address 1: 1000 State St
Street address 2: # 4
Street address city: Springfield
Street address state: MA
Zip/Postal code: 01109-3151
Country: USA
Mailing address: 1000 State St # 4
Mailing city: Springfield
Mailing state: MA
Mailing zip: 01109-3151
General Phone: (413) 205-3265
Personnel: Will Hughes (Advisor); Brian Steele (Ed. in Chief)

AMHERST COLLEGE

Street address 1: 31 Mead Dr
Street address 2: Keefe Campus Center
Street address city: Amherst
Street address state: MA
Zip/Postal code: 01002-1786
Country: USA
Mailing address: AC#1912, Keefe Campus Center
Mailing city: Amherst
Mailing state: MA
Mailing zip: 01002-5000
General Phone: (413) 206-9319
General/National Adv. E-mail: astudent@amherst.edu
Display Adv. E-mail: astudent@amherst.edu
Primary Website: amherststudent.amherst.edu
Published: Wed
Avg Free Circ: 1600
Personnel: Christopher Friend (Publisher)

ASSUMPTION COLLEGE

Street address 1: 500 Salisbury St
Street address city: Worcester
Street address state: MA
Zip/Postal code: 01609-1265
Country: USA
Mailing address: 500 Salisbury St
Mailing city: Worcester
Mailing state: MA
Mailing zip: 01609-1296
General Phone: (508) 767-7155
General Fax: (508) 799-4401
General/National Adv. E-mail: provoc@assumption.edu
Personnel: Sara Swillo (Advisor); Greg Sebastiao (Ed. in Chief)

BABSON COLLEGE

Street address 1: 231 Forest St
Street address city: Babson Park
Street address state: MA
Country: USA
Mailing address: 231 Forest St.
Mailing city: Babson Park
Mailing state: MA
Mailing zip: 02457
General Phone: (781) 239-5541
General Fax: (781) 239-5554
General/National Adv. E-mail: freepress@babson.edu
Display Adv. E-mail: babsonfreep@babson.edu
Personnel: Anthony Micale (Ed.)

BECKER COLLEGE

Street address 1: 61 Sever St
Street address city: Worcester
Street address state: MA
Zip/Postal code: 01609-2165
Country: USA
Mailing address: 61 Sever St
Mailing city: Worcester
Mailing state: MA
Mailing zip: 01609-2195

BENTLEY UNIVERSITY

Street address 1: 175 Forest St
Street address city: Waltham
Street address state: MA
Zip/Postal code: 02452-4713
Country: USA
Mailing state: MA
General Phone: (781) 891-2921
General Fax: (781) 891-2574
Editorial Phone: (781) 891-3497
General/National Adv. E-mail: ga_vanguard@bentley.edu
Primary Website: www.bentleyvanguard.com; www.bentleyvanguardonline.com
Published: Thur
Personnel: Maria Dilorenzo (Advisor); Sindhu Palaniappan (Ed. in Chief); Greg Kokino (Adv. Mgr.)

BOSTON COLLEGE

Street address 1: McElroy Commons 113, 140 Commonwealth Ave
Street address city: Chestnut Hill
Street address state: MA
Zip/Postal code: 1919
Country: USA
Mailing address: McElroy Commons 113, 140 Commonwealth Ave.
Mailing city: Chestnut Hill
Mailing state: MA
Mailing zip: 02467-3800
General Phone: (617) 552-2221
General Fax: (617) 552-1753
Advertising Phone: (617) 552-4823
Editorial Phone: (617) 552-2220
Editorial Fax: (617) 552-2223
Display Adv. E-mail: ads@bcheights.com
Personnel: Dave Givler (Adv. Mgr.); Matt DeLuca (Ed. in chief)

BRANDEIS UNIVERSITY

Street address 1: 415 South St
Street address 2: MS 214
Street address city: Waltham
Street address state: MA
Zip/Postal code: 02453-2728
Country: USA
Mailing address: 415 South St MS 214
Mailing city: Waltham
Mailing state: MA
Mailing zip: 02453-2728
General Phone: (781) 736-3750
General Fax: (781) 736-3756
Editorial Phone: (781) 736-3751
General/National Adv. E-mail: editor@thejustice.org
Display Adv. E-mail: ads@thejustice.org
Primary Website: www.thejustice.org
Year Established: 1949
Published: Tues
Personnel: Editor (Ed.)

BRIDGEWATER STATE COLLEGE

Street address 1: Rondileau Campus Ctr, Rm.103A
Street address city: Bridgewater
Street address state: MA

Country: USA
Mailing address: Rondileau Campus Ctr Rm 103A
Mailing city: Bridgewater
Mailing state: MA
Mailing zip: 02325-0001
General Phone: (508) 531-1719
General Fax: (508) 531-6181
General/National Adv. E-mail: comment@bridgew.edu
Personnel: Justin McCauley (Advisor); Monica Monteiro (Ed. in Chief)

BRISTOL CMTY. COLLEGE

Street address 1: 777 Elsbree St
Street address city: Fall River
Street address state: MA
Zip/Postal code: 02720-7307
Country: USA
Mailing address: 777 Elsbree St
Mailing city: Fall River
Mailing state: MA
Mailing zip: 02720-7399
General Phone: (508) 678-2811
General Fax: (508) 676-7146
General/National Adv. E-mail: observer@bristolcc.edu
Personnel: Alex Potter (Ed. in Chief)

CAPE COD CMTY. COLLEGE

Street address 1: 2240 Iyannough Rd
Street address 2: North Building Room 206
Street address city: West Barnstable
Street address state: MA
Zip/Postal code: 02668-1532
Country: USA
Mailing address: 2240 Iyannough Rd
Mailing city: West Barnstable
Mailing state: MA
Mailing zip: 02668
General Phone: (508) 362-2131
General Fax: (508) 375-4116
General/National Adv. E-mail: info@capecod.edu
Primary Website: www.capecod.edu
Year Established: 1961
Personnel: James Kershner (Advisor)

CLARK UNIVERSITY

Street address 1: 950 Main St
Street address 2: # B-13
Street address city: Worcester
Street address state: MA
Zip/Postal code: 01610-1400
Country: USA
Mailing address: 950 Main St # B-13
Mailing city: Worcester
Mailing state: MA
Mailing zip: 01610-1400
General Phone: (508) 793-7508
General Fax: (508) 793-8813
General/National Adv. E-mail: scarlet@clarku.edu
Primary Website: www.clarku.edu
Published: Thur
Avg Free Circ: 700
Personnel: Jeremy Levine (Editor-in-Chief)

COLLEGE OF THE HOLY CROSS

Street address 1: 1 College St
Street address city: Worcester
Street address state: MA
Zip/Postal code: 01610-2322
County: Worcester
Country: USA
Mailing address: 1 COLLEGE ST
Mailing city: WORCESTER
Mailing state: MA
Mailing zip: 01610-2395
General Phone: (508) 293-1283
General Fax: (508) 793-3823
General/National Adv. E-mail: crusader@g.holycross.edu
Display Adv. E-mail: crusaderadvertising@gmail.com
Primary Website: www.thehccrusader.com
Published: Fri
Personnel: Steve Vineberg (Faculty Advisor); Sara Bovat (Co-Editor-in-Chief); Emily Vyse (Co-Editor-in-Chief)

DEAN COLLEGE

Street address 1: 99 Main St
Street address city: Franklin
Street address state: MA
Zip/Postal code: 02038-1941
Country: USA
Mailing address: 99 Main St
Mailing city: Franklin
Mailing state: MA

EASTERN NAZARENE COLLEGE

Street address 1: 23 E Elm Ave
Street address city: Quincy
Street address state: MA
Zip/Postal code: 02170-2905
Country: USA
Mailing address: 23 E Elm Ave
Mailing city: Quincy
Mailing state: MA
Mailing zip: 02170-2999
General Phone: (617) 745-3000
Personnel: Erica Scott Mcgrath (Advisor); Emily Prugh (Ed. in Chief)

ELMS COLLEGE

Street address 1: 291 Springfield St
Street address city: Chicopee
Street address state: MA
Zip/Postal code: 01013-2837
Country: USA
Mailing address: 291 Springfield St
Mailing city: Chicopee
Mailing state: MA
Mailing zip: 01013-2839
Personnel: James Gallant (Advisor)

EMERSON COLLEGE

Street address 1: 150 Boylston St
Street address city: Boston
Street address state: MA
Zip/Postal code: 02116-4608
Country: USA
Mailing address: 150 Boylston St
Mailing city: Boston
Mailing state: MA
Mailing zip: 02116-4608
General Phone: (617) 824-8687
General Fax: (617) 824-8908
General/National Adv. E-mail: berkeley_beacon@emerson.edu
Personnel: Ric Kahn (Advisor); Matt Byrne (Ed. in Chief); Paddy Shea (Ed. in Chief)

EMMANUEL COLLEGE

Street address 1: 400 Fenway
Street address city: Boston
Street address state: MA
Zip/Postal code: 02115-5725
Country: USA
Mailing address: 400 Fenway
Mailing city: Boston
Mailing state: MA
Mailing zip: 02115-5798
Personnel: Anne Tyson (Ed.)

ENDICOTT COLLEGE

Street address 1: 376 Hale St, Callahan Ctr
Street address city: Beverly
Street address state: MA
Zip/Postal code: 1915
Country: USA
Mailing address: 376 Hale St., Callahan Ctr.
Mailing city: Beverly
Mailing state: MA
Mailing zip: 01915-2096
General Phone: (978) 232-2050
General Fax: (978) 232-3003
General/National Adv. E-mail: observer@mail.endicott.edu
Personnel: Abigail Bottome (Advisor)

FITCHBURG STATE COLLEGE

Street address 1: 160 Pearl St
Street address city: Fitchburg
Street address state: MA
Zip/Postal code: 01420-2631
Country: USA
Mailing address: 160 Pearl St
Mailing city: Fitchburg
Mailing state: MA
Mailing zip: 01420-2697
General Phone: (978) 665-3647
Advertising Phone: (978) 665-3650
General/National Adv. E-mail: pointstorybudget@yahoo.com
Personnel: Doris Schmidt (Advisor); John McGinn (Ed.)

FRAMINGHAM STATE UNIVERSITY - THE GATEPOST

Street address 1: 100 State St
Street address 2: Rm 410
Street address city: Framingham
Street address state: MA
Zip/Postal code: 01702-2499
Country: USA
Mailing address: McCarthy Center 410
Mailing city: Framingham
Mailing state: MA
Mailing zip: 01702-2499
General Phone: (508) 626-4605
General Fax: (508) 626-4097
Advertising Phone: (508) 626-4605
Advertising Fax: (508) 626-4097
Editorial Phone: (508) 626-4605
Editorial Fax: (508) 626-4097
General/National Adv. E-mail: gatepost@framingham.edu
Display Adv. E-mail: gatepost@framingham.edu
Editorial e-mail: gatepost@framingham.edu
Primary Website: www.fsugatepost.com
Year Established: 1930
Published: Fri
Personnel: Desmond McCarthy (Advisor); Meredith O'Brien-Weiss (Advisor); Robin KurKomelis (Administrative Assistant); Kerrin Murray (Editor-in-Chief); Joe Kourieh (Associate Editor); Karin Radoc (Associate Editor)

GORDON COLLEGE

Street address 1: 255 Grapevine Rd
Street address city: Wenham
Street address state: MA
Zip/Postal code: 01984-1813
Country: USA
Mailing address: 255 Grapevine Rd
Mailing city: Wenham
Mailing state: MA
Mailing zip: 01984-1899
General Phone: (978) 927-2306
Personnel: Eric Convey (Advisor)

HAMPSHIRE COLLEGE

Street address 1: 893 West St
Street address city: Amherst
Street address state: MA
Zip/Postal code: 01002-3372
Country: USA
Mailing address: 893 West St
Mailing city: Amherst
Mailing state: MA
Mailing zip: 01002-3359
General Phone: (413) 549-4600
General Fax: (413) 559-5664
General/National Adv. E-mail: hampshireclimax@gmail.com
Personnel: Nicki Feldman (Admin. Sec.)

HARVARD BUSINESS SCHOOL

Street address 1: Gallatin Hall D Basement
Street address city: Boston
Street address state: MA
Zip/Postal code: 2163
Country: USA
General Phone: (617) 495-6528
General Fax: (617) 495-8619
General/National Adv. E-mail: general@harbus.org
Personnel: Matthew Grayson (Gen.Mgr.); Joanne Knight (Pub.)

HARVARD LAW SCHOOL

Street address 1: Harvard Law Record, Harvard Law School
Street address city: Cambridge
Street address state: MA
Zip/Postal code: 2138
Country: USA
Mailing address: Harvard Law Record, Harvard Law School
Mailing city: Cambridge
Mailing state: MA
Mailing zip: 02138-9984
General Phone: (617) 297-3590
General Fax: (617) 495-8547
General/National Adv. E-mail: record@law.harvard.edu
Personnel: Matt Hutchins (Ed. in Chief); Chris Szabla (Ed. in Chief); Rebecca Agule (News Ed.); Mark Samburg (Sports Ed.)

HARVARD UNIV.

Street address 1: 14 Plympton St
Street address city: Cambridge
Street address state: MA
Zip/Postal code: 02138-6606
Country: USA
Mailing address: 14 Plympton St
Mailing city: Cambridge
Mailing state: MA
Mailing zip: 02138-6606
General Phone: (617) 576-6600
General Fax: (617) 576-7860
General/National Adv. E-mail: ads@thecrimson.com
Personnel: Peter F. Zhu (Pres.); Julian L. Bouma (Bus. Mgr)

HARVARD UNIV./JFK SCHOOL OF GOV'T

Street address 1: 30 Jfk St
Street address city: Cambridge
Street address state: MA
Zip/Postal code: 02138-4902
Country: USA
Mailing address: 30 Jfk St
Mailing city: Cambridge
Personnel: Stephanie Geosits (Ed.)

HOLYOKE CMTY. COLLEGE

Street address 1: 303 Homestead Ave
Street address city: Holyoke
Street address state: MA
Zip/Postal code: 01040-1091
Country: USA
Mailing address: 303 Homestead Ave
Mailing city: Holyoke
Mailing state: MA
Mailing zip: 01040-1099
Personnel: Fred Cooksey (Advisor)

LASELL COLLEGE

Street address 1: 1844 Commonwealth Ave
Street address city: Auburndale
Street address state: MA
Zip/Postal code: 02466-2709
Country: USA
Mailing address: 1844 Commonwealth Ave
Mailing city: Auburndale
Mailing state: MA
Mailing zip: 02466-2716
General Phone: (617) 243-2000
Personnel: Marie C. Franklin (Advisor); Michelle McNickle (Ed. in Chief); Briana Nestor (Features Ed.)

LESLEY UNIVERSITY

Street address 1: 47 Oxford St
Street address city: Cambridge
Street address state: MA
Zip/Postal code: 02138-1902
Country: USA
Mailing address: 47 Oxford St
Mailing city: Cambridge
Mailing state: MA
Mailing zip: 02138-1972
General Phone: (617) 349-8501
Personnel: Gabriella Montell (Assoc. Ed.)

MASSACHUSETTS COLLEGE OF LIBERAL ARTS

Street address 1: 375 Church St
Street address 2: Rm 111
Street address city: North Adams
Street address state: MA
Zip/Postal code: 01247-4124
Country: USA

Mailing address: 375 Church St Rm 111
Mailing city: North Adams
Mailing state: MA
Mailing zip: 01247-4124
General Phone: (413) 662-5535
General Fax: (413) 662-5010
Editorial Phone: (413) 662-5404
General/National Adv. E-mail: beacon@mcla.edu
Primary Website: www.mclabeacon.com
Published: Wed
Avg Free Circ: 1000
Personnel: Jennifer Augur (Advisor)

MASSACHUSETTS COLLEGE OF PHARMACY

Street address 1: 179 Longwood Ave
Street address city: Boston
Street address state: MA
Zip/Postal code: 02115-5804
Country: USA
Mailing address: 179 Longwood Ave
Mailing city: Boston
Mailing state: MA
Mailing zip: 02115-5896
Personnel: Stephany Orphan (ed.)

MASSACHUSETTS INST. OF TECHNOLOGY

Street address 1: 84 Massachusetts Ave
Street address 2: Ste 483
Street address city: Cambridge
Street address state: MA
Zip/Postal code: 02139-4300
Country: USA
Mailing address: 84 Massachusetts Ave Ste 483
Mailing city: Cambridge
Mailing state: MA
Mailing zip: 02139-4300
General Phone: (617) 253 1541
General Fax: (617) 258-8226
General/National Adv. E-mail: general@tech.mit.edu; letters@the-tech.mit.edu
Display Adv. E-mail: ads@tech.mit.edu
Primary Website: thetech.com
Year Established: 1881
Published: Thur
Avg Free Circ: 8100
Personnel: Aislyn Schalck (Chrmn.); Jessica Pourian (Ed. in Chief); Karleigh Moore (Chairman)

MERRIMACK COLLEGE

Street address 1: 315 Turnpike St
Street address city: North Andover
Street address state: MA
Zip/Postal code: 01845-5806
Country: USA
Mailing address: 315 Turnpike St
Mailing city: North Andover
Mailing state: MA
Mailing zip: 01845-5800
General Phone: (978) 837-5000
Personnel: Russ Mayer (Advisor); Michael Salvucci (Ed. in Chief)

MIDDLESEX CMTY. COLLEGE

Street address 1: 591 Springs Rd
Street address city: Bedford
Street address state: MA
Zip/Postal code: 01730-1120
Country: USA
Mailing address: 591 Springs Rd
Mailing city: Bedford
Mailing state: MA
Mailing zip: 01730-1197
Personnel: Sarah Screaux (Ed.)

MOUNT HOLYOKE COLLEGE

Street address 1: 50 College St
Street address 2: Blanchard Campus Center 324
Street address city: South Hadley
Street address state: MA
Zip/Postal code: 01075-1423
Country: USA
Mailing address: 9007 Blanchard Campus Center
Mailing city: South Hadley
Mailing state: MA
Mailing zip: 01075-1423
General Phone: (413) 538-2269
General Fax: (413) 538-2476
General/National Adv. E-mail: mhnews@mtholyoke.edu
Primary Website: http://mountholyokenews.org/
Year Established: 1917
Published: Thur
Personnel: Linda Valencia Xu (Publisher); Geena Molinaro (Editor-in-Chief)

MOUNT IDA COLLEGE

Street address 1: 777 Dedham St
Street address city: Newton Center
Street address state: MA
Zip/Postal code: 02459-3323
Country: USA
Mailing address: 777 Dedham St
Mailing city: Newton Center
Mailing state: MA
Mailing zip: 02459-3310
Personnel: Melissa Constantine (Advisor); Matt Caldwell (Ed. in Chief); Jen Barrett (Asst. Ed.)

NEW ENGLAND SCHOOL OF LAW

Street address 1: 154 Stuart St
Street address city: Boston
Street address state: MA
Zip/Postal code: 02116-5616
Country: USA
Mailing address: 154 Stuart St
Mailing city: Boston
Mailing state: MA
Mailing zip: 02116-5687
General Phone: (617) 451-0010
General Fax: (617) 422-7224
General/National Adv. E-mail: dueprocess@nesl.edu
Display Adv. E-mail: dueprocess@nesl.edu
Editorial e-mail: dueprocess@nesl.edu
Primary Website: https://www.nesl.edu/students/stuorg_dp.cfm
Year Established: 2012
Published: Other
Published Other: Due Process publishes five (5) regular issues, and one (1) end of year commemorative yearbook.
Personnel: Rebecca Castaneda (Ed. in Chief); Tara Cho (Exec. Ed.); Kelly Lavari (Photo Ed.); Joe Sciabica (Editor-in-Chief); Emily White (Assistant Editor-In-Chief)

NICHOLS COLLEGE

Street address 1: 124 Center Rd
Street address city: Dudley
Street address state: MA
Zip/Postal code: 01571-6310
Country: USA
Mailing address: PO Box 5000
Mailing city: Dudley
Mailing state: MA
Mailing zip: 01571-5000
General Phone: (508) 213-1560
General Fax: (508) 943-5354
General/National Adv. E-mail: admissions@nichols.edu
Primary Website: www.nichols.edu/
Year Established: 1815
Personnel: Emily Reardon (Assistant Director of Admissions / International Students Counselor)

NORTHEASTERN UNIVERSITY

Street address 1: 295 Huntington Ave
Street address 2: Ste 208
Street address city: Boston
Street address state: MA
Zip/Postal code: 02115-4433
Country: USA
Mailing address: 295 Huntington Ave Ste 208
Mailing city: Boston
Mailing state: MA
Mailing zip: 02115-4433
General Phone: (857) 362-7325
General Fax: (857) 362-7326
General/National Adv. E-mail: editor@huntnewsnu.com
Display Adv. E-mail: advertise@huntnewsnu.com
Editorial e-mail: editorial@huntnewsnu.com
Primary Website: www.HuntNewsNU.com
Year Established: 1926
Published: Thur
Personnel: Colin Young (Editor in chief)

NORTHERN ESSEX COMMUNITY COLLEGE

Street address 1: 100 Elliott St
Street address city: Haverhill
Street address state: MA
Zip/Postal code: 01830-2306
Country: USA
Mailing address: 100 Elliott St.
Mailing city: Haverhill
Mailing state: MA
Mailing zip: 01830-2399
General Phone: (978) 556-3633
General/National Adv. E-mail: observer@necc.mass.edu
Primary Website: 100 Elliott Street
Year Established: 1962
Published: Bi-Mthly
Personnel: Amy Callahan (Professor)

QUINSIGAMOND CMTY. COLLEGE

Street address 1: 670 W Boylston St
Street address city: Worcester
Street address state: MA
Zip/Postal code: 01606-2064
Country: USA
Mailing address: 670 W Boylston St
Mailing city: Worcester
Mailing state: MA
Mailing zip: 01606-2092
General Phone: (508) 854-4285
Published: Mthly
Personnel: Pat Bisha-Valencia (Advisor)

SALEM STATE COLLEGE

Street address 1: 352 Lafayette St, Ellison Campus Ctr
Street address city: Salem
Street address state: MA
Zip/Postal code: 1970
Country: USA
Mailing address: 352 Lafayette St., Ellison Campus Ctr.
Mailing city: Salem
Mailing state: MA
Mailing zip: 01970-5348
General Phone: (978) 542-6448
General Fax: (978) 542-2077
General/National Adv. E-mail: thelog@ssclog.com
Personnel: Peggy Dillon (Advisor)

SIMMONS COLLEGE

Street address 1: 300 Fenway
Street address city: Boston
Street address state: MA
Zip/Postal code: 02115-5820
Country: USA
Mailing address: 300 The Fenway
Mailing city: Boston
Mailing state: MA
Mailing zip: 02115-5820
General Phone: (617) 521-2442
General Fax: (617) 521-3148
General/National Adv. E-mail: voice@simmons.edu
Primary Website: www.thesimmonsvoice.com
Published: Thur
Avg Free Circ: 1500
Personnel: James Corcoran (Adviser); Sarah Kinney (Advisor Editor)

SMITH COLLEGE

Street address 1: Capen Annex
Street address city: Northampton
Street address state: MA
Zip/Postal code: 01063-0001
Country: USA
Mailing address: Capen Anx
Mailing city: Northampton
Mailing state: MA
Mailing zip: 01063-0001
General Phone: (413) 585-4971
General Fax: (413) 585-2075
General/National Adv. E-mail: sophian@smith.edu
Primary Website: www.smithsophian.com
Year Established: 1911
Published: Thur
Personnel: Hira Humayun (EIC)

SPRINGFIELD COLLEGE

Street address 1: 263 Alden St
Street address city: Springfield
Street address state: MA
Zip/Postal code: 01109-3707
Country: USA
Mailing address: 263 Alden St
Mailing city: Springfield
Mailing state: MA
Mailing zip: 01109-3788
General Phone: (413) 748-3000
General Fax: (413) 748-3473
General/National Adv. E-mail: activities@spfldcol.edu
Personnel: Claire Wright (Advisor); Evin Giglio (Ed. in Cheif)

STONEHILL COLLEGE

Street address 1: 320 Washington St
Street address 2: # 1974
Street address city: North Easton
Street address state: MA
Zip/Postal code: 02357-7800
Country: USA
Mailing address: 320 Washington St # 1974
Mailing city: North Easton
Mailing state: MA
Mailing zip: 02357-0001
Personnel: Matt Gorman (News Ed.)

SUFFOLK UNIV.

Street address 1: 41 Temple St
Street address 2: Rm 428
Street address city: Boston
Street address state: MA
Zip/Postal code: 02114-4241
Country: USA
Mailing address: 41 Temple St Rm 428
Mailing city: Boston
Mailing state: MA
Mailing zip: 02114-4241
General Phone: (617) 573-8323
General Fax: (617) 994-6400
General/National Adv. E-mail: suffolkjournal@gmail.com
Primary Website: www.suffolkjournal.net; www.suffolk.edu
Year Established: 1940
Published: Wed
Personnel: Bruce Butterfield (Advisor); Melissa Hanson; Jeremy Hayes

SUFFOLK UNIV. LAW SCHOOL

Street address 1: 120 Tremont St
Street address city: Boston
Street address state: MA
Zip/Postal code: 02108-4910
Country: USA
Mailing address: 120 Tremont St
Mailing city: Boston
Mailing state: MA

THE DAILY FREE PRESS

Street address 1: 708 Commonwealth Avenue
Street address city: Boston
Street address state: MA
Zip/Postal code: 02215
Country: USA
Mailing address: P.O. Box 15655
Mailing city: Boston
Mailing state: MA
Mailing zip: 02215
General Phone: (617) 236-4433
General Fax: (617) 236-4414
General/National Adv. E-mail: editor@dailyfreepress.com
Display Adv. E-mail: ads@dailyfreepress.com
Primary Website: www.dailyfreepress.com
Year Established: 1970
Published: Mon`Tues`Wed`Thur`Fri
Published Other: Online for summer, breaking content.
Avg Free Circ: 5000

Personnel: Chloe Patel (Editor-in-Chief); Kyle Plantz (Ed.); Felicia Gans (Managing Ed.)

TUFTS UNIV.

Street address 1: PO Box 53018
Street address city: Medford
Street address state: MA
Zip/Postal code: 02153-0018
Country: USA
Mailing address: PO Box 53018
Mailing city: Medford
Mailing state: MA
Mailing zip: 02153-0018
General Phone: (617) 627-3090
Personnel: Giovanni Russonello (Ed.)

UNIV. OF MASSACHUSETTS

Street address 1: 123 S Burrowes St
Street address city: Amherst
Street address state: MA
Zip/Postal code: 1003
Country: USA
General Phone: (413) 545-3500
Editorial e-mail: editor@dailycollegian.com
Personnel: Alyssa Creamer (Ed.)

UNIV. OF MASSACHUSETTS

Street address 1: 100 William T Morrissey Blvd
Street address city: Boston
Street address state: MA
Zip/Postal code: 02125-3300
Country: USA
Mailing address: 100 Morrissey Blvd
Mailing city: Boston
Mailing state: MA
Mailing zip: 02125-3393
General Phone: (617) 287-7992
General Fax: (617) 287-7897
General/National Adv. E-mail: editor@umassmedia.com
Primary Website: www.umassmedia.com
Year Established: 1966
Personnel: Donna Neal (Advisor); Caleb Nelson (Ed.)

UNIV. OF MASSACHUSETTS

Street address 1: 285 Old Westport Rd, Campus Ctr, 2nd Fl
Street address city: North Dartmouth
Street address state: MA
Zip/Postal code: 2747
Country: USA
Mailing address: 285 Old Westport Rd., Campus Ctr., 2nd Fl.
Mailing city: North Dartmouth
Mailing state: MA
Mailing zip: 02747-2300
General Phone: (508) 999-8158
General Fax: (508) 999-8128
General/National Adv. E-mail: torch@umassd.edu
Display Adv. E-mail: TorchAds@umassd.edu
Personnel: Jason Jones (Adv. Mgr.); Chris Donovan (Ed. in Chief); Megan Gauthier (Mng. Ed.)

UNIV. OF MASSACHUSETTS LOWELL CONNECTOR

Street address 1: 71 Wilder St
Street address 2: Ste 6
Street address city: Lowell
Street address state: MA
Zip/Postal code: 01854-3096
Country: USA
Mailing address: 71 Wilder St Ste 6
Mailing city: Lowell
Mailing state: MA
Mailing zip: 01854-3096
General Phone: (978) 934-5001
General Fax: (978) 934-3072
General/National Adv. E-mail: connector@uml.edu
Primary Website: www.uml.edu/connector
Year Established: 1924
Personnel: Ruben Sanca (Office Mgr.)

WELLESLEY COLLEGE

Street address 1: 106 Central St
Street address 2: Fl 4
Street address city: Wellesley
Street address state: MA
Zip/Postal code: 02481-8203
Country: USA
Mailing address: 106 Central St
Mailing city: Wellesley
Mailing state: MA
Mailing zip: 02481-8210
General Phone: (781) 283-2689
General Fax: (781) 431-7520
General/National Adv. E-mail: thewellesleynews@gmail.com
Display Adv. E-mail: thewellesleynews@gmail.com
Editorial e-mail: thewellesleynews@gmail.com
Primary Website: www.thewellesleynews.com
Year Established: 1901
Published: Wed
Personnel: Alice Liang (Managing Editor); Stephanie Yeh (Editor-in-Chief)

WESTERN NEW ENGLAND COLLEGE

Street address 1: 1215 Wilbraham Rd
Street address city: Springfield
Street address state: MA
Zip/Postal code: 01119-2612
Country: USA
Mailing address: 1215 Wilbraham Rd
Mailing city: Springfield
Mailing state: MA
Mailing zip: 01119-2684
Personnel: Wayne Barr (Ed.)

WESTFIELD STATE UNIVERSITY

Street address 1: 577 Western Ave
Street address 2: Ely Campus Center, Room 305
Street address city: Westfield
Street address state: MA
Zip/Postal code: 01085-2580
Country: USA
Mailing address: 577 Western Avenue
Mailing city: Westfield
Mailing state: MA
Mailing zip: 01085
General Phone: (413) 572-5431
General Fax: (413) 572-5477
Advertising Phone: (413) 572-5431
Editorial Phone: (413) 572-5431
General/National Adv. E-mail: thevoice@westfield.ma.edu
Display Adv. E-mail: thevoiceadvertisement@gmail.com
Year Established: 1946
Published: Fri
Personnel: Joshua Clark (Editor-in-Chief); Andrew Burke (Editor-in-Chief); Emily Hanshaw (Managing Editor); Matthew Carlin (Assistant Managing Editor)

WILLIAMS COLLEGE

Street address 1: 209 Paresky Center
Street address city: Williamstown
Street address state: MA
Zip/Postal code: 1267
Country: USA
Mailing address: 39 Chapin Hall Dr.
Mailing city: Williamstown
Mailing state: MA
Mailing zip: 01267
General Phone: (413) 597-2289
General Fax: (413) 597-2450
General/National Adv. E-mail: williamsrecordeic@gmail.com
Display Adv. E-mail: williamsrecordadvertising@gmail.com
Editorial e-mail: williamsrecordeic@gmail.com
Primary Website: www.williamsrecord.com
Year Established: 1887
Published: Wed
Avg Free Circ: 2000
Personnel: Rachel Scharf (Editor-in-Chief); Matthew Borin (Ed. In Chief)

WORCESTER POLYTECHNIC INSTITUTE

Street address 1: 100 Institute Rd
Street address city: Worcester
Street address state: MA
Zip/Postal code: 01609-2247
Country: USA
Mailing address: 100 Institute Rd
Mailing city: Worcester
Mailing state: MA
Mailing zip: 01609-2280
General Phone: (508) 831-5464
General Fax: (508) 831-5721
General/National Adv. E-mail: technews@wpi.edu
Display Adv. E-mail: ads@wpi.edu
Personnel: Michelle Ephraim (Advisor)

WORCESTER STATE COLLEGE

Street address 1: 486 Chandler St
Street address city: Worcester
Street address state: MA
Zip/Postal code: 01602-2861
Country: USA
Mailing address: 486 Chandler St # G-209
Mailing city: Worcester
Mailing state: MA
Mailing zip: 01602-2861
General Phone: (508) 929-8589
Personnel: Elizabeth Bidinger (Advisor)

MARYLAND

ANNE ARUNDEL CMTY. COLLEGE CAMPUS CURRENT

Street address 1: 101 College Pkwy
Street address 2: Hum 206
Street address city: Arnold
Street address state: MD
Zip/Postal code: 21012-1857
Country: USA
Mailing address: 101 College Pkwy Hum 206
Mailing city: Arnold
Mailing state: MD
Mailing zip: 21012-1857
General Phone: (410) 777-2803
General Fax: (410) 777-2021
General/National Adv. E-mail: campuscurrent@aacc.edu
Primary Website: www.campus-current.com
Published: Bi-Mthly
Avg Free Circ: 2500
Personnel: Sheri Venema (Advisor)

BOWIE STATE UNIV.

Street address 1: 14000 Jericho Park Rd
Street address 2: Rm 260
Street address city: Bowie
Street address state: MD
Zip/Postal code: 20715-3319
Country: USA
Mailing address: 14000 Jericho Park Rd Rm 260
Mailing city: Bowie
Mailing state: MD
Mailing zip: 20715-3319
Personnel: Rex Martin (Advisor); Kristina Rowley (Mng. Ed.); Jocelyn Jones (Asst. Mng. Ed.)

CMTY. COLLEGE OF BALTIMORE CITY ESSEX

Street address 1: 7201 Rossville Blvd
Street address 2: Rm 116
Street address city: Baltimore
Street address state: MD
Zip/Postal code: 21237-3855
Country: USA
Mailing address: 7201 Rossville Blvd Rm 116
Mailing city: Baltimore
Mailing state: MD
Mailing zip: 21237-3855
Personnel: Jeremy Caplan (Advisor); Corey States (Ed.)

COLLEGE OF SOUTHERN MARYLAND

Street address 1: PO Box 910
Street address city: La Plata
Street address state: MD
Zip/Postal code: 20646-0910
Country: USA
Mailing address: PO Box 910
Mailing city: La Plata
Mailing state: MD
Mailing zip: 20646-0910
General Phone: (301) 934-2251
Personnel: Karen Smith-Hupp (Ed.)

COLUMBIA UNION COLLEGE

Street address 1: 7600 Flower Ave
Street address city: Takoma Park
Street address state: MD
Zip/Postal code: 20912-7744
Country: USA
Mailing address: 7600 Flower Ave
Mailing city: Takoma Park
Mailing state: MD
Mailing zip: 20912-7794
Personnel: Athina Lavinos (Pub.); Jaclyn Wile (Ed.); Heidi Lohr (News Ed.)

GOUCHER COLLEGE

Street address 1: 1021 Dulaney Valley Rd
Street address city: Towson
Street address state: MD
Zip/Postal code: 21204-2753
Country: USA
Mailing address: 1021 Dulaney Valley Rd
Mailing city: Towson
Mailing state: MD
Mailing zip: 21204-2780
General Phone: (410) 337-6322
General Fax: (410) 337-6434
General/National Adv. E-mail: quin@goucher.edu; askhd@goucher.edu
Personnel: Matt Simon (Mng. Ed.); Lori Shull (News Ed.); Ben Spangler (Photo Ed.)

HOOD COLLEGE

Street address 1: 401 Rosemont Ave
Street address city: Frederick
Street address state: MD
Zip/Postal code: 21701-8524
Country: USA
Mailing address: 401 Rosemont Ave
Mailing city: Frederick
Mailing state: MD
Mailing zip: 21701-8575
General Phone: (301) 696-3641
Personnel: Rita Davis (Ed.); Al Weinberg (Dir./Prof. of Journalism)

HOWARD CMTY. COLLEGE

Street address 1: 10901 Little Patuxent Pkwy
Street address city: Columbia
Street address state: MD
Zip/Postal code: 21044-3110
Country: USA
Mailing address: 10901 Little Patuxent Pkwy
Mailing city: Columbia
Mailing state: MD
Mailing zip: 21044-3197
General Phone: (410) 772-4937
General Fax: (410) 772-4280
General/National Adv. E-mail: newspaper@howardcc.edu
Primary Website: www.howardcc.edu
Published: Bi-Mthly
Personnel: Michelle Plummer (Advertising Manager)

LOYOLA COLLEGE

Street address 1: 4501 N Charles St
Street address 2: Bellarmine Hall 1
Street address city: Baltimore
Street address state: MD
Zip/Postal code: 21210-2601
Country: USA
Mailing address: 4501 N Charles St Bellarmine Hall 1
Mailing city: Baltimore
Mailing state: MD
Mailing zip: 21210-2694
General Phone: (410) 617-2282
General Fax: (410) 617-2982
General/National Adv. E-mail: greyhoundads@loyola.edu
Personnel: Joe Morelli (Bus. Mgr.); Kat Kienle (Ed. in Chief)

MCDANIEL COLLEGE

Street address 1: 2 College Hl

Street address city: Westminster
Street address state: MD
Zip/Postal code: 21157-4303
Country: USA
Mailing address: 2 College Hill
Mailing city: Westminster
Mailing state: MD
Mailing zip: 21157-4390
General Phone: (410) 751-8600
General Fax: (410) 857-2729
General/National Adv. E-mail: freepress@mcdaniel.edu
Primary Website: mcdanielfreepress.com
Published: Mthly
Personnel: Sarah Hull (Co-Editor-In-Chief); Daniel Valentin-Morales (Co-Editor-In-Chief)

MONTGOMERY COLLEGE

Street address 1: 51 Mannakee St
Street address city: Rockville
Street address state: MD
Zip/Postal code: 20850-1101
Country: USA
Mailing address: 51 Mannakee St
Mailing city: Rockville
Mailing state: MD
Mailing zip: 20850-1199
General Phone: (240) 567-7176
General Fax: (240) 567-5091
General/National Adv. E-mail: info@mcadvocate.com
Display Adv. E-mail: info@mcadvocate.com
Editorial e-mail: editor@mcadvocate.com
Primary Website: http://mcadvocate.com
Year Established: 1957
Personnel: Steve Thurston (Advisor)

MONTGOMERY COLLEGE

Street address 1: 7600 Takoma Ave, Commons Rm 202
Street address city: Takoma Park
Street address state: MD
Zip/Postal code: 20912
Country: USA
Mailing address: 7600 Takoma Ave., Commons Rm. 202
Mailing city: Takoma Park
Mailing state: MD
Mailing zip: 20912
General Phone: (240) 567-1490
Personnel: Angela Clubb (Ed.)

MONTGOMERY COLLEGE GERMANTOWN

Street address 1: 20200 Observation Dr
Street address city: Germantown
Street address state: MD
Zip/Postal code: 20876-4067
Country: USA
Mailing address: 20200 Observation Dr
Mailing city: Germantown
Mailing state: MD
Mailing zip: 20876-4098
General Phone: (240) 567-7840
General Fax: (240) 567-7843
General/National Adv. E-mail: theglobe@montgomerycollege.edu
Personnel: Dave Anthony (Advisor)

MOUNT ST. MARY'S UNIV.

Street address 1: 16300 Old Emmitsburg Rd
Street address city: Emmitsburg
Street address state: MD
Zip/Postal code: 21727-7700
Country: USA
Mailing address: 16300 Old Emmitsburg Rd
Mailing city: Emmitsburg
Mailing state: MD
Mailing zip: 21727-7700
General Phone: (301) 447-5246
General Fax: (301) 447-5755
General/National Adv. E-mail: echo@msmary.edu
Personnel: Sheldon Shealer (Advisor); Allison Doherty (Mng. Ed.)

NOTRE DAME OF MARYLAND UNIVERSITY

Street address 1: 4701 N Charles St
Street address city: Baltimore
Street address state: MD
Zip/Postal code: 21210-2404
Country: USA
Mailing address: 4701 N. Charles St.
Mailing city: Baltimore
Mailing state: MD
Mailing zip: 21210-2476
General Phone: (410) 532-5580
General Fax: (410) 532-5796
General/National Adv. E-mail: Columns@ndm.edu
Display Adv. E-mail: Columns@ndm.edu
Editorial e-mail: Columns@ndm.edu
Personnel: Mariel Guerrero (Editor-in-Chief); Marguerite Linz (Lead Writer/ Managing Editor)

PRINCE GEORGES CMTY. COLLEGE

Street address 1: 301 Largo Rd
Street address city: Largo
Street address state: MD
Zip/Postal code: 20774-2109
Country: USA
Mailing address: 301 Largo Rd
Mailing city: Largo
Mailing state: MD
Mailing zip: 20774-2109
General Phone: (301) 336-6000
General Fax: (301) 808-0960
General/National Adv. E-mail: theowlnewspaper@hotmail.com
Personnel: Patrick Peterson (Bus. Mgr.); Malcolm Beech (Advisor); Abelaja Obajimi (Ed. in Chief)

SALISBURY UNIV.

Street address 1: 1101 Camden Ave
Street address city: Salisbury
Street address state: MD
Zip/Postal code: 21801-6837
Country: USA
Mailing address: PO Box 3183
Mailing city: Salisbury
Mailing state: MD
Mailing zip: 21802-3183
General Phone: (410) 543-6191
General Fax: (410) 677-5359
General/National Adv. E-mail: flyer@salisbury.edu
Personnel: Leslie Pusey (Advisor.); Vanessa Junkin (Ed.)

ST. JOHNS COLLEGE

Street address 1: 60 College Ave
Street address city: Annapolis
Street address state: MD
Zip/Postal code: 21401-1687
Country: USA
Mailing address: 60 College Ave
Mailing city: Annapolis
Personnel: Ian McCracken (Ed.)

ST. MARY'S COLLEGE OF MARYLAND

Street address 1: 18952 E Fisherâ€™S Road
Street address city: Saint Marys City
Street address state: MD
Zip/Postal code: 20686
Country: USA
Mailing address: 18952 E Fisherâ€™s Road
Mailing city: Saint Mary's City
Mailing state: MD
Mailing zip: 20686
General Phone: (240) 895-4213
General Fax: (240) 895-4445
General/National Adv. E-mail: pointnews@smcm.edu
Personnel: Justin Perry (Ed. in Chief); Matt Molek (Mng. Ed.)

STEVENSON UNIVERSITY

Street address 1: 1525 Greenspring Valley Rd
Street address city: Stevenson
Street address state: MD
Zip/Postal code: 21153-0641
Country: USA
Mailing address: 1525 Greenspring Valley Rd
Mailing city: Stevenson
Mailing state: MD
Mailing zip: 21153-0641
General Phone: (443) 394-9781
General/National Adv. E-mail: suvillager@gmail.com
Primary Website: stevensonvillager.com
Year Established: 2016 online
Published: Thur
Published Other: every Thursday online
Personnel: Chip Rouse (Fac. Advisor)

THE BOTTOM LINE

Street address 1: 101 Braddock Rd
Street address 2: Lane Center 217
Street address city: Frostburg
Street address state: MD
Zip/Postal code: 21532-2303
Country: USA
Mailing address: Lane Center 217
Mailing city: Frostburg
Mailing state: MD
Mailing zip: 21532-2303
General Phone: (301) 687-4326
General Fax: (301) 687-3054
General/National Adv. E-mail: thebottomline@frostburg.edu; tblonline@gmail.comthebottomline
Primary Website: www.thebottomlineonline.org
Year Established: 1948
Personnel: Dustin Davis (Advisor); Marina Byerly (Editor-in-Chief); Michelle Giambruno (Manging Editor); Marissa Nedved (Business Manager)

THE JOHNS HOPKINS NEWS-LETTER

Street address 1: Levering Unit 102
Street address city: Baltimore
Street address state: MD
Zip/Postal code: 21218
Country: USA
Mailing address: 3400 N Charles St
Mailing city: Baltimore
Mailing state: MD
Mailing zip: 21218-2680
General Phone: (410) 516-4228
General/National Adv. E-mail: chiefs@jhunewsletter.com; business@jhunewsletter.com
Display Adv. E-mail: business@jhunewsletter.com
Primary Website: www.jhunewsletter.com
Year Established: 1896
Published: Thur
Personnel: Marie Cushing (Ed. in Chief); Leah Maniero (Mng. Ed.)

TOWSON UNIV.

Street address 1: 8000 York Rd, University Union, Rm 309
Street address city: Towson
Street address state: MD
Zip/Postal code: 21252-0001
Country: USA
Mailing address: 8000 York Rd University Un Rm 309
Mailing city: Towson
Mailing state: MD
Mailing zip: 21252-0001
General Phone: (410) 704-2288
General Fax: (410) 704-3862
General/National Adv. E-mail: towerlight@towson.edu
Display Adv. E-mail: towerlightads@yahoo.com
Editorial e-mail: towerlighteditor@gmail.com; towerlightnews@gmail.com; towerlightsports@gmail.com; towerlightarts@gmail.com
Personnel: Mike Raymond (Gen. Mgr.); Ashley Rabe (Sr. Ed.); Daniel Gross (News Ed.)

UNIV. OF MARYLAND BALTIMORE

Street address 1: PO Box 600
Street address city: Parkton
Street address state: MD
Zip/Postal code: 21120-0600
Country: USA
Mailing address: PO Box 600
Mailing city: Parkton
Mailing state: MD
Mailing zip: 21120-0600
Personnel: Susie Flaherty (Sr. Ed.); Clare Banks (Ed.)

UNIV. OF MARYLAND BALTIMORE COUNTY

Street address 1: Uc 214, 1000 Hilltop Cir
Street address city: Baltimore
Street address state: MD
Zip/Postal code: 21250-0001
Country: USA
Mailing address: Uc 214, 1000 Hilltop Cir
Mailing city: Baltimore
Mailing state: MD
Mailing zip: 21250-0001
General Phone: (410) 455-1260
General Fax: (410) 455-1265
General/National Adv. E-mail: eic@retrieverweekly.com
Personnel: Christopher Corbett (Advisor); Nimit Bhatt (Adv./Bus. Mgr.); Gaby Arevalo (Ed. in Chief)

UNIVERSITY OF MARYLAND

Street address 1: 3136 S Campus Dining Hall
Street address city: College Park
Street address state: MD
Zip/Postal code: 20742-8401
Country: USA
Mailing address: 3136 S Campus Dining Hall
Mailing city: College Park
Mailing state: MD
Mailing zip: 20742-8401
General Phone: (301) 314-8000
General Fax: (301) 314-8358
Advertising Phone: (301) 314-8000
Editorial Phone: (301) 314-8000
General/National Adv. E-mail: diamondbackeditor@gmail.com
Display Adv. E-mail: dbkadvertising@gmail.com
Editorial e-mail: newsumdbk@gmail.com
Primary Website: dbknews.com
Year Established: 1909
Published: Thur
Personnel: Mina Haq (Ed. in chief)

US NAVAL ACADEMY

Street address 1: 121 Blake Rd
Street address city: Annapolis
Street address state: MD
Zip/Postal code: 21402-1300
Country: USA
Mailing address: 121 Blake Rd
Mailing city: Annapolis
Mailing state: MD
Mailing zip: 21402-1300
General Phone: (410) 293-1536
Personnel: Jessica Clark (Ed.); Martha Thorn (Mng. Ed.)

MAINE

BATES COLLEGE

Street address 1: 2 Andrews Rd
Street address city: Lewiston
Street address state: ME
Zip/Postal code: 04240-6020
Country: USA
Mailing address: 2 Andrews Rd
Mailing city: Lewiston
Mailing state: ME
Mailing zip: 04240-6028
General Phone: (207) 795-7494
Advertising Phone: (207) 786-6035
General/National Adv. E-mail: thebatesstudent@hotmail.com
Personnel: Regina Tavani (Ed. in Chief); Zoe Rosenthal (Deputy Ed. in Chief)

BOWDOIN COLLEGE

Street address 1: 6200 College Sta
Street address city: Brunswick
Street address state: ME
Zip/Postal code: 04011-8462
Country: USA
Mailing address: 6200 College Sta
Mailing city: Brunswick
Mailing state: ME
Mailing zip: 04011-8462
General Phone: (207) 725-3300
General Fax: (207) 725-3975
General/National Adv. E-mail: orient@bowdoin.edu
Display Adv. E-mail: orientads@bowdoin.edu

Personnel: Zoe Lescaze; Lizzy Tarr (Bus. Mgr.); Will Jacob (Ed. in Chief); Gemma Leghorn (Ed. in Chief)

COLBY COLLEGE

Street address 1: 4600 Mayflower Hill Dr
Street address city: Waterville
Street address state: ME
Zip/Postal code: 4901
Country: USA
Mailing address: 4600 Mayflower Hill Dr.
Mailing city: Waterville
Mailing state: ME
Mailing zip: 04901
General Phone: (207) 859-4000
General Fax: (207) 872-3555
General/National Adv. E-mail: echo@colbyecho.com
Personnel: Peter Rummel (Bus. Mgr.); Kira Novak (Adv. Mgr); Elisabeth Ponsot (Ed. in Chief)

HUSSON COLLEGE

Street address 1: 1 College Cir
Street address city: Bangor
Street address state: ME
Zip/Postal code: 04401-2929
Country: USA
Mailing address: 1 College Cir
Mailing city: Bangor
Mailing state: ME
Mailing zip: 04401-2999
Personnel: Josh Scroggins (Ed.)

UNIV. OF MAINE

Street address 1: 181 Main St
Street address city: Presque Isle
Street address state: ME
Zip/Postal code: 04769-2844
Country: USA
Mailing address: PO Box 417
Mailing city: Presque Isle
Mailing state: ME
Mailing zip: 04769
Personnel: Tara White (Ed.)

UNIVERSITY OF MAINE

Street address 1: Memorial Union, University of Maine Rm 131
Street address 2: rm. 131
Street address city: Orono
Street address state: ME
Zip/Postal code: 04469-0001
Country: USA
Mailing address: Memorial Union, University of Maine
Mailing city: Orono
Mailing state: ME
Mailing zip: 04469-5748
General Phone: (207) 581-1273
General/National Adv. E-mail: info@mainecampus.com
Display Adv. E-mail: ads@mainecampus.com
Editorial e-mail: eic@mainecampus.com
Primary Website: www.mainecampus.com
Year Established: 1875
Published: Mon
Avg Free Circ: 1500
Personnel: Jordan Houdeshell (Ed. in Chief); Elliott Simpson (Bus. Mgr.)

UNIVERSITY OF SOUTHERN MAINE

Street address 1: 92 Bedford St 2nd Fl
Street address 2:
Street address city: Portland
Street address state: ME
Zip/Postal code: 04102-2801
Country: USA
Mailing address: PO Box 9300
Mailing city: Portland
Mailing state: ME
Mailing zip: 04104-9300
General Phone: (207) 780-4084
General Fax: N/A
Advertising Phone: 207780-4084
Advertising Fax: N/A
Editorial Phone: 207-780-4165
Editorial Fax: N/A
General/National Adv. E-mail: editor@usmfreepress.org
Display Adv. E-mail: ads@usmfreepress.org
Editorial e-mail: editor@usmfreepress.org
Primary Website: usmfreepress.org
Year Established: 1972
Published: Mon
Published Other: 10 issues per semester plus Summer orientation issues
Avg Free Circ: 2000
Personnel: Lucille Siegler (Business Manager)

MICHIGAN

ALBION COLLEGE

Street address 1: 611 E Porter St
Street address city: Albion
Street address state: MI
Zip/Postal code: 49224-1831
Country: USA
Mailing address: 611 E. Porter St.
Mailing city: Albion
Mailing state: MI
Mailing zip: 49224
General Phone: (517) 629-1315
General Fax: (517) 629-0509
General/National Adv. E-mail: pleiad@albion.edu
Display Adv. E-mail: pleaid@albion.edu
Editorial e-mail: pleiad@albion.edu
Primary Website: www.albionpleiad.com
Year Established: 1883
Published: Mon`Wed`Fri
Personnel: Glenn Deutsch (Advisor); Steve Markowski (Mng. Ed.); Beau Brockett, Jr. (Mng. Ed.); Katie Boni (Features Editor); Andrew Wittland; Morgan Garmo (Opinions editor)

ALMA COLLEGE

Street address 1: 614 W Superior St
Street address city: Alma
Street address state: MI
Zip/Postal code: 48801-1504
Country: USA
Mailing address: 614 W Superior St
Mailing city: Alma
Mailing state: MI
Mailing zip: 48801-1599
General Phone: (989) 463-7161
General Fax: (989) 463-7161
General/National Adv. E-mail: almanian@alma.edu; almanianopinion@yahoo.com; almanian@hotmail.com
Display Adv. E-mail: almanianadvert@yahoo.com
Personnel: Robert Vivian (Advisor); Brendan Guilford (Ed. in Chief); Olga Wrobel (News Ed.)

ANDREWS UNIV.

Street address 1: Student Ctr 05
Street address city: Berrien Springs
Street address state: MI
Country: USA
Mailing address: 5 Student Ctr
Mailing city: Berrien Springs
Mailing state: MI
Mailing zip: 49104-0001
General Phone: (269) 471-3385
General Fax: (269) 471-3524
General/National Adv. E-mail: smeditor@andrews.edu
Personnel: Ashleigh Burtnett (Ed. in Chief); Michele Krpalek (Ed.); Stephanie Smart (Asst. Ed.)

AQUINAS COLLEGE

Street address 1: 1700 Fulton St E
Street address city: Grand Rapids
Street address state: MI
Zip/Postal code: 49506-1801
Country: USA
Mailing address: 1607 Robinson Rd SE
Mailing city: Grand Rapids
Mailing state: MI
Mailing zip: 49506-1799
General Phone: (616) 632-2975
General Fax: (616) 732-4487
Advertising Phone: (616) 632-2975
Editorial Phone: (616) 632-2975
General/National Adv. E-mail: saint.editors@aquinas.edu
Display Adv. E-mail: saint.business@aquinas.edu
Editorial e-mail: saint.editors@aquinas.edu
Primary Website: www.aquinas.edu/thesaint
Year Established: 1980
Published: Bi-Mthly
Avg Free Circ: 1000
Personnel: Dan Brooks (Advisor); Matt Kuczynski (Editor in Chief)

CALVIN COLLEGE

Street address 1: 3201 Burton St, Student Commons
Street address city: Grand Rapids
Street address state: MI
Zip/Postal code: 49546
Country: USA
Mailing address: 3201 Burton St., Student Commons
Mailing city: Grand Rapids
Mailing state: MI
Mailing zip: 49546-4301
General Phone: (616) 819-0011
General Fax: (616) 957-8551
General/National Adv. E-mail: chimes@calvin.edu
Primary Website: http://clubs.calvin.edu/chimes
Published: Fri
Personnel: Lauren DeHaan (Ed.); Emma Slager (Ed. in Chief)

CENTRAL MICHIGAN UNIVERSITY

Street address 1: 436 Moore Hall
Street address 2: Central Michigan University
Street address city: Mount Pleasant
Street address state: MI
Zip/Postal code: 48859-0001
Country: USA
Mailing address: 436 Moore Hall
Mailing city: Mount Pleasant
Mailing state: MI
Mailing zip: 48859-0001
General Phone: (989) 774-3493
General Fax: (989) 774-7805
Advertising Phone: (989) 774-3493
Advertising Fax: (989) 774-7805
Editorial Phone: (989) 774-3493
Editorial Fax: (989) 774-7805
General/National Adv. E-mail: advertising@cm-life.com
Display Adv. E-mail: advertising@cm-life.com
Editorial e-mail: editor@cm-life.com
Primary Website: www.cm-life.com
Year Established: 1919
Published: Mon`Wed`Fri
Avg Free Circ: 10000
Personnel: Kathy Simon (Advisor); David Clark (Director, Student Publications); Catey Traylor (Editor, 2013-2014); Julie Bushart (Advertising Manager, 2013-2014)

DELTA COLLEGE

Street address 1: 1961 Delta Rd
Street address city: University Center
Street address state: MI
Zip/Postal code: 48710-1001
Country: USA
Mailing address: 1961 Delta Rd # H
Mailing city: University Center
Mailing state: MI
Mailing zip: 48710-1002
General Phone: (989) 686-9000
General/National Adv. E-mail: collegiate@delta.edu; info@delta.edu
Personnel: Kathie Bachleda (Advisor); Megan Tobias (Ed in Chief)

EASTERN MICHIGAN UNIVERSITY

Street address 1: 228 King Hall
Street address city: Ypsilanti
Street address state: MI
Zip/Postal code: 48197-2239
Country: USA
Mailing address: 228 King Hall
Mailing city: Ypsilanti
Mailing state: MI
Mailing zip: 48197-2239
General Phone: (734) 487-1026
General Fax: (734) 487-6702
Advertising Phone: (734) 748-1458
Advertising Fax: (734) 487-1241
General/National Adv. E-mail: editor@easternecho.com
Display Adv. E-mail: brian.peterson24@gmail.com
Editorial e-mail: editor@easternecho.com
Primary Website: www.easternecho.com
Year Established: 1881
Published: Mon`Thur
Personnel: Sydney Smith

FERRIS STATE TORCH.

Street address 1: 401 South St
Street address 2: Student Rec Center Room 102
Street address city: Big Rapids
Street address state: MI
Zip/Postal code: 49307-2744
Country: USA
Mailing address: 401 South St
Mailing city: Big Rapids
Mailing state: MI
Mailing zip: 49307-2744
General Phone: (231) 591-5946
General Fax: (231) 591-3617
Advertising Phone: 231-591-2609
General/National Adv. E-mail: torchads@ferris.edu
Editorial e-mail: torch@ferris.edu
Primary Website: www.fsutorch.com
Year Established: 1931
Published: Wed
Avg Free Circ: 4300
Personnel: Steve Fox (Advisor); Laura Anger (Bus. Mgr.)

GRAND RAPIDS CMTY. COLLEGE

Street address 1: 143 Bostwick Ave NE
Street address city: Grand Rapids
Street address state: MI
Zip/Postal code: 49503-3201
Country: USA
Mailing address: 143 Bostwick Ave NE
Mailing city: Grand Rapids
Mailing state: MI
Mailing zip: 49503-3201
General Phone: (616) 234-4157

GRAND VALLEY STATE UNIV.

Street address 1: 1 Campus Dr
Street address city: Allendale
Street address state: MI
Zip/Postal code: 49401-9401
Country: USA
Mailing address: 1 Campus Dr, 0051 Kirkhof Center, Grand Valley State University
Mailing city: Allendale
Mailing state: MI
Mailing zip: 49401
General Phone: (616) 331-2460
General Fax: (616) 331-2465
Advertising Phone: (616) 331-2484
General/National Adv. E-mail: lanthorn@gvsu.edu
Display Adv. E-mail: advertising@lanthorn.com
Editorial e-mail: editorial@lanthorn.com
Primary Website: www.lanthorn.com
Year Established: 1964
Published: Mon`Thur
Personnel: Shelby Carter (Business Manager); Emily Doran (Editor-and-Chief); Ian Borthwick (Advertising Manager)

HENRY FORD CMTY. COLLEGE

Street address 1: 5101 Evergreen Rd
Street address 2: # C-117
Street address city: Dearborn
Street address state: MI
Zip/Postal code: 48128-2407
Country: USA
Mailing address: 5101 Evergreen Rd # C-117
Mailing city: Dearborn
Mailing state: MI
Mailing zip: 48128-2407
General Phone: (313) 845-9639
General Fax: (313) 845-9876
General/National Adv. E-mail: mirrorbm@hfcc.edu
Personnel: Cassandra Fluker (Advisor); Joshua Gillis (Ed.)

HILLSDALE COLLEGE

Street address 1: 33 E College St
Street address city: Hillsdale
Street address state: MI
Zip/Postal code: 49242-1205

Country: USA
Mailing address: 33 E College St
Mailing city: Hillsdale
Mailing state: MI
Mailing zip: 49242-1298
General Phone: (517) 437-7341
General Fax: (517) 437-3293
General/National Adv. E-mail: collegian@hillsdale.edu
Personnel: Ingrid Jacques (Advisor)

HOPE COLLEGE

Street address 1: 141 E 12th St
Street address city: Holland
Street address state: MI
Zip/Postal code: 49423-3663
Country: USA
Mailing address: P.O. Box 9000
Mailing city: Holland
Mailing state: MI
Mailing zip: 49422-9000
General Phone: (616) 395-7877
General Fax: (616) 395-7183
General/National Adv. E-mail: anchor@hope.edu
Display Adv. E-mail: anchorads@hope.edu
Primary Website: anchor.hope.edu
Year Established: 1887
Personnel: Rosie Jahng (Advisor); Amanda Long (Co-Editor-in-Chief); James Champane (Co-Editor-in-Chief); Patterson (Co-Ed. in chief); Emily West (Co-Ed. in chief)

JACKSON CMTY. COLLEGE

Street address 1: 2111 Emmons Rd
Street address city: Jackson
Street address state: MI
Zip/Postal code: 49201-8395
Country: USA
Mailing address: 2111 Emmons Rd
Mailing city: Jackson
Mailing state: MI
Mailing zip: 49201-8399
General Phone: (517) 787-0800
General Fax: (517) 787-8663
General/National Adv. E-mail: phoenix@jccmi.edu
Personnel: Karessa E. Weir (Advisor)

KALAMAZOO COLLEGE

Street address 1: 1200 Academy St
Street address city: Kalamazoo
Street address state: MI
Zip/Postal code: 49006-3268
Country: USA
Mailing address: 1200 Academy St Ofc
Mailing city: Kalamazoo
Mailing state: MI
Mailing zip: 49006-3295
General Phone: (269) 337-7000
Personnel: Brian Ditez (Advisor)

LAKE SUPERIOR STATE UNIV.

Street address 1: 650 W Easterday Ave
Street address 2: Cisler Center 106
Street address city: Sault Sainte Marie
Street address state: MI
Zip/Postal code: 49783-1626
Country: USA
Mailing address: 650 W Easterday Ave
Mailing city: Sault Sainte Marie
Mailing state: MI
Mailing zip: 49783-1626
General Phone: (906) 635-2551
General Fax: (906) 635-7510
General/National Adv. E-mail: compass@lssu.edu
Display Adv. E-mail: compass@lssu.edu
Editorial e-mail: compass@lssu.edu
Primary Website: compass.lssu.edu
Year Established: 1946
Published: Mthly
Personnel: Asher Stephenson (Editor In Chief)

LANSING CMTY. COLLEGE

Street address 1: 411 N Grand Ave
Street address 2: Rm 351
Street address city: Lansing
Street address state: MI
Zip/Postal code: 48933-1215
Country: USA
Mailing address: Mail Code 1170
Mailing city: Lansing
Mailing state: MI
Mailing zip: 48933
General Phone: (517) 483-1291
General Fax: (517) 483-1290
Advertising Phone: (517) 483-1295
Advertising Fax: (517) 483-1290
Editorial Phone: (517) 483-1288
Editorial Fax: (517) 483-1290
General/National Adv. E-mail: hookl@lcc.edu
Display Adv. E-mail: hookl@lcc.edu
Editorial e-mail: hookl@lcc.edu
Primary Website: www.lcc.edu/lookout
Year Established: 1959
Published: Bi-Mthly
Personnel: Larry Hook (Advisor)

MICHIGAN TECHNOLOGICAL UNIV.

Street address 1: 1400 Townsend Dr
Street address 2: Mub 106
Street address city: Houghton
Street address state: MI
Zip/Postal code: 49931-1200
Country: USA
Mailing address: MUB 106 1400 Townsend Dr
Mailing city: Houghton
Mailing state: MI
Mailing zip: 49931
General Phone: (906) 487-2404
Personnel: Kara W. Sokol (Advisor); Kayla R. Herrera (Ed. in chief)

MOTT CMTY. COLLEGE

Street address 1: 1401 E Court St
Street address city: Flint
Street address state: MI
Zip/Postal code: 48503-6208
Country: USA
Mailing address: 1401 E Court St
Mailing city: Flint
Mailing state: MI
Mailing zip: 48503-2090
Personnel: Steve Bossey (Ed.)

NORTHERN MICHIGAN UNIVIVERSITY

Street address 1: 1401 Presque Isle Ave
Street address 2: 2310 University Center
Street address city: Marquette
Street address state: MI
Zip/Postal code: 49855-2818
Country: USA
Mailing address: 1401 Presque Isle Ave
Mailing city: Marquette
Mailing state: MI
Mailing zip: 49855-5301
General Phone: (906) 227-2545
General Fax: (906) 227-2449
General/National Adv. E-mail: northwind@gmail.com
Display Adv. E-mail: hkasberg@nmu.edu
Primary Website: www.thenorthwindonline.com
Year Established: 1972
Published: Thur
Personnel: Kristy Basolo (Advisor)

NORTHWESTERN MICHIGAN COLLEGE

Street address 1: 1701 E Front St
Street address city: Traverse City
Street address state: MI
Zip/Postal code: 49686-3016
Country: USA
Mailing address: 1701 E Front St
Mailing city: Traverse City
Mailing state: MI
Mailing zip: 49686-3061
General Phone: (231) 995-1173
General Fax: (231) 995-1952
General/National Adv. E-mail: whitepinepress@gmail.com
Personnel: Michael Anderson (Advisor); Nora Stone (Ed. in Chief); Jacob Bailey (Mng. Ed.)

OAKLAND UNIV.

Street address 1: 61 Oakland Ctr
Street address city: Rochester
Street address state: MI
Zip/Postal code: 48309-4409
Country: USA
Mailing address: 61 Oakland Ctr
Mailing city: Rochester
Mailing state: MI
Mailing zip: 48309-4409
General Phone: (248) 370-4268
General Fax: (248) 370-4264
General/National Adv. E-mail: editor@oaklandpostonline.com
Primary Website: www.oaklandpostonline.com
Year Established: 1957
Published: Tues
Personnel: Holly Gilbert (Advisor); Don Ritenburgh (Business Manager)

ROCHESTER COLLEGE

Street address 1: 800 W Avon Rd
Street address city: Rochester Hills
Street address state: MI
Zip/Postal code: 48307-2704
Country: USA
Mailing address: 800 W Avon Rd
Mailing city: Rochester Hills
Mailing state: MI
Mailing zip: 48307-2704
General Phone: (248) 218-2030
General Fax: (248) 218-2045
General/National Adv. E-mail: theshield@rc.edu
Primary Website: www.rcshield.com
Published: Bi-Mthly
Avg Free Circ: 550
Personnel: Liz Fulton (Mng./Design Ed.); Chelsea Hackel

SAGINAW VALLEY STATE UNIV.

Street address 1: 125 Curtiss Hall, 7400 Bay Rd
Street address city: University Center
Street address state: MI
Zip/Postal code: 48710-0001
Country: USA
Mailing address: 125 Curtiss Hall, 7400 Bay Rd
Mailing city: University Center
Mailing state: MI
Mailing zip: 48710-0001
General Phone: (989) 964-4248
General/National Adv. E-mail: vanguard@svsu.edu
Personnel: Sara Kitchen (Ed. in Chief)

SCHOOLCRAFT COLLEGE

Street address 1: 18600 Haggerty Rd
Street address 2: Rm W169
Street address city: Livonia
Street address state: MI
Zip/Postal code: 48152-3932
Country: USA
Mailing address: 18600 Haggerty Rd Rm W169
Mailing city: Livonia
Mailing state: MI
Mailing zip: 48152-2696
General Phone: (734) 462-4422
General Fax: (734) 462-4554
General/National Adv. E-mail: sao@schoolcraft.edu
Personnel: Jeffrey Petts (Advisor); Kathy Hansen (Adv. Mgr.); Ryan Russell (Ed.)

SOUTHWESTERN MICHIGAN COLLEGE

Street address 1: 58900 Cherry Grove Rd
Street address city: Dowagiac
Street address state: MI
Zip/Postal code: 49047-9726
Country: USA
Mailing address: 58900 Cherry Grove Rd
Mailing city: Dowagiac
Mailing state: MI
Mailing zip: 49047-9726
General Phone: (269) 782-1457
General Fax: (269) 782-1446
Editorial Phone: (269) 782-1457
Editorial Fax: (269) 782-1446
General/National Adv. E-mail: swester@swmich.edu
Editorial e-mail: swester@swmich.edu
Primary Website: http://southwester.swmich.edu/
Year Established: 1968
Personnel: John Eby (Senior Writer and Coordinator of Media Relations)

SPRING ARBOR UNIV.

Street address 1: 106 E Main St
Street address 2: Ste A28
Street address city: Spring Arbor
Street address state: MI
Zip/Postal code: 49283-9701
Country: USA
Mailing address: 106 E Main St Ste A28
Mailing city: Spring Arbor
Mailing state: MI
Mailing zip: 49283-9701
Personnel: Eric Platt (Ed.)

ST. CLAIR COUNTY COMMUNITY COLLEGE

Street address 1: 323 Erie St
Street address 2: # 5015
Street address city: Port Huron
Street address state: MI
Zip/Postal code: 48060-3812
Country: USA
Mailing address: 323 Erie St # 5015
Mailing city: Port Huron
Mailing state: MI
Mailing zip: 48060-3812
General Phone: (810) 989-5733
General Fax: (810) 984-4730
General/National Adv. E-mail: eriesquaregazette@gmail.com
Display Adv. E-mail: esgadvertising@gmail.com
Primary Website: www.esgonline.org
Year Established: 1931
Published Other: Bi-weekly
Personnel: John Lusk (Advisor); Erick Fredendall (Editor-in-Chief)

THE ECHO, THE UNIVERSITY OF OLIVET

Street address 1: 320 S Main St
Street address city: Olivet
Street address state: MI
Zip/Postal code: 49076-9406
County: Eaton
Country: USA
Mailing address: 320 S. Main St.
Mailing city: Olivet
Mailing state: MI
Mailing zip: 49076-9456
General Phone: (269) 749-7622
General/National Adv. E-mail: echo@uolivet.edu
Display Adv. E-mail: echo@uolivet.edu
Editorial e-mail: echo@uolivet.edu
Primary Website: www.ocecho.com
Year Established: 1888
Published: Other
Published Other: Online
Personnel: Joanne Williams (Advisor); Brian Freiberger (Editor); Bray Wright (Editor); Josh Edwards (Editor)

THE STATE NEWS/MICHIGAN STATE UNIVERSITY

Street address 1: 435 E Grand River Ave
Street address 2: Fl 2
Street address city: East Lansing
Street address state: MI
Zip/Postal code: 48823-4456
Country: USA
Mailing address: 435 E Grand River Ave
Mailing city: East Lansing
Mailing state: MI
Mailing zip: 48823-4456
General Phone: (517) 295-1680
Advertising Phone: (517) 295-1680
Editorial Phone: (517) 295-1680
General/National Adv. E-mail: feedback@statenews.com
Display Adv. E-mail: advertising@statenews.com
Editorial e-mail: editorinchief@statenews.com
Primary Website: www.statenews.com
Year Established: 1909
Published: Thur
Published Other: Digital-only during summer semester at MSU
Avg Free Circ: 7500

Personnel: Omar Sofradzija (Advisor); Marty Sturgeon (Gen. Mgr.); Mike Joseph (Webmaster); Travis Ricks (Creative Adviser)

UNIV. OF MICHIGAN

Street address 1: 420 Maynard St
Street address city: Ann Arbor
Street address state: MI
Zip/Postal code: 48109-1327
Country: USA
Mailing address: 420 Maynard St
Mailing city: Ann Arbor
Mailing state: MI
Mailing zip: 48109-1327
General Phone: (734) 763-2459
General Fax: (734) 764-4275
Advertising Phone: (734) 764-0554
General/National Adv. E-mail: news@michigandaily.com; tmdbusiness@gmail.com
Personnel: Jacob Smilovitz (Ed. in Chief); Matt Aaronson (Mng. Ed.); Dan Newman (Bus. Mgr.)

UNIV. OF MICHIGAN

Street address 1: 303 E Kearsley St
Street address city: Flint
Street address state: MI
Zip/Postal code: 48502-1907
Country: USA
Mailing address: 303 E Kearsley St
Mailing city: Flint
Mailing state: MI
Mailing zip: 48502-1907
General Phone: (810) 762-3475
General Fax: (810) 762-3023
Advertising Phone: (810) 762-0919
General/National Adv. E-mail: mtimes@hotmail.com
Personnel: Joseph Patterson (Adv. Mgr.); Jennifer Profitt (Ed. in Chief)

UNIV. OF MICHIGAN BUS. SCHOOL

Street address 1: 701 Tappan Ave
Street address 2: Ste 766
Street address city: Ann Arbor
Street address state: MI
Zip/Postal code: 48109-1234
Country: USA
Mailing address: 701 Tappan Ave Ste 766
Mailing city: Ann Arbor
Mailing state: MI
Mailing zip: 48109-1234
General Phone: (734) 764-2074
General Fax: (734) 763-6450
Display Adv. E-mail: msj.office@gmail.com
Editorial e-mail: msj.editor@gmail.com
Personnel: Robyn Katzman (Pub.); Maggie Sadowski (Ed. in Chief)

UNIVERSITY OF MICHIGAN-DEARBORN

Street address 1: 4901 Evergreen Rd
Street address 2: Ste 2130
Street address city: Dearborn
Street address state: MI
Zip/Postal code: 48128-2406
Country: USA
Mailing address: 4901 Evergreen Rd Ste 2130
Mailing city: Dearborn
Mailing state: MI
Mailing zip: 48128-2406
General Phone: (313) 593-5428
General Fax: (313) 593-5594
Advertising Phone: (313) 593-3097
General/National Adv. E-mail: themichiganj@gmail.com
Primary Website: www.michiganjournal.org
Year Established: 1971
Published: Tues
Personnel: Tim Kiska (Adviser); Ricky Lindsay (Editor-in-Chief); Kaitlynn Riley (Advertising Manager)

WASHTENAW COMMUNITY COLLEGE

Street address 1: 4800 E Huron River Dr
Street address city: Ann Arbor
Street address state: MI
Zip/Postal code: 48105-9481
Country: USA
Mailing city: Ann Arbor
Mailing state: MI
Mailing zip: 48105
General Phone: (734) 677-5125
General Fax: (734) 677-5126
Advertising Phone: (734) 973-3662
General/National Adv. E-mail: thewasntehawvoice@gmail.com
Display Adv. E-mail: ealliston@wccnet.edu
Editorial e-mail: kgave@wccnet.edu
Primary Website: www.washtenawvoice.com
Year Established: 1967
Published: Bi-Mthly
Avg Free Circ: 5000
Personnel: Keith Gave (Advisor); Becky Alliston (Adv. Mgr.); Natalie Wright (Ed.)

WAYNE STATE UNIV.

Street address 1: 5221 Gullen Mall
Street address 2: Ste 101
Street address city: Detroit
Street address state: MI
Zip/Postal code: 48202-3919
Country: USA
Mailing address: 5221 Gullen Mall, Student Center Bldg., Ste. 101
Mailing city: Detroit
Mailing state: MI
Mailing zip: 48202
General Phone: (313) 577-8067
General Fax: (313) 993-8108
Advertising Phone: (313) 577-8666
General/National Adv. E-mail: dv7262@wayne.edu
Editorial e-mail: tseletters@gmail.com
Personnel: Carolyn Chin (Mng. Ed.)

WESTERN MICHIGAN UNIV.

Street address 1: 1903 W Michigan Ave
Street address 2: 1517 Faunce Student Servs. Bldg.
Street address city: Kalamazoo
Street address state: MI
Zip/Postal code: 49008-5200
Country: USA
Mailing address: 1517 Faunce Student Servs. Bldg.
Mailing city: Kalamazoo
Mailing state: MI
Mailing zip: 49008-5363
General Phone: (269) 387-2110
General Fax: (269) 387-3820
Advertising Phone: 269-387-2107
Advertising Fax: 269-387-3820
Editorial Phone: 269-323-2101
Editorial Fax: 269-387-3820
General/National Adv. E-mail: herald-general-manager@wmich.edu
Display Adv. E-mail: herald-advertising@wmich.edu
Editorial e-mail: herald-editor@wmich.edu
Primary Website: www.westernherald.com
Year Established: 1916
Published: Bi-Mthly
Avg Free Circ: 10000
Personnel: Meghan Chandler (Editor-in-chief); Richard Junger (General Manager)

MINNESOTA

AUGSBURG COLLEGE

Street address 1: 2211 Riverside Ave
Street address city: Minneapolis
Street address state: MN
Zip/Postal code: 55454-1350
Country: USA
Mailing address: 2211 Riverside Ave
Mailing city: Minneapolis
Mailing state: MN
Mailing zip: 55454-1351
General Phone: (612) 330-1018
General Fax: (612) 330-1649
Display Adv. E-mail: echo@augsburg.edu
Personnel: Boyd Koehler (Adviser); Jenny Pinther (Editor-in-chief)

BEMIDJI STATE UNIV.

Street address 1: 1500 Birchmont Dr NE
Street address city: Bemidji
Street address state: MN
Zip/Postal code: 56601-2600
Country: USA
Mailing address: PO Box 58
Mailing city: Bemidji
Mailing state: MN
Mailing zip: 56619-0058
General Phone: (218) 755-2001
General Fax: (218) 755-2913
General/National Adv. E-mail: northernstudent@yahoo.com
Primary Website: www.northernstudent.com
Year Established: 1926
Published: Wed
Avg Free Circ: 3000
Personnel: Robby Robinson (Advisor)

BETHEL COLLEGE

Street address 1: 3900 Bethel Dr
Street address 2: Ste 1504
Street address city: Saint Paul
Street address state: MN
Zip/Postal code: 55112-6902
Country: USA
Mailing address: 3900 Bethel Dr Ste 1504
Mailing city: Saint Paul
Mailing state: MN
Mailing zip: 55112-6999
General Phone: (651) 635-8643
Personnel: Marie Wisner (Advisor)

CARLETON COLLEGE

Street address 1: 1 N College St
Street address city: Northfield
Street address state: MN
Zip/Postal code: 55057-4001
Country: USA
Mailing address: 1 N College St
Mailing city: Northfield
Mailing state: MN
Mailing zip: 55057-4044
General Fax: (507) 222-4000
General/National Adv. E-mail: carletonian@carleton.edu
Personnel: James McMenimen (Adv. Mgr); Vivyan Tran (Ed. in Chief); Emily Howell (Ed. in Chief)

COLLEGE OF ST. SCHOLASTICA

Street address 1: 1200 Kenwood Ave
Street address city: Duluth
Street address state: MN
Zip/Postal code: 55811-4199
Country: USA
Mailing address: 1200 Kenwood Ave
Mailing city: Duluth
Mailing state: MN
Mailing zip: 55811-4199
General Phone: (218) 723-6187
General Fax: (218) 723-6290
General/National Adv. E-mail: cable1@css.edu
Personnel: Joe Wicklund (Advisor); Print Corp (Pub.); Kirby Montgomery (Ed. in Chief)

CONCORDIA COLLEGE

Street address 1: 901 8th St S
Street address city: Moorhead
Street address state: MN
Zip/Postal code: 56562-0001
Country: USA
Mailing address: PO Box 104
Mailing city: Moorhead
Mailing state: MN
Mailing zip: 56561-0104
General Phone: (218) 299-3826
General Fax: (218) 299-4313
General/National Adv. E-mail: concord@cord.edu; cordadd@cord.edu
Display Adv. E-mail: cordadd@cord.edu
Editorial e-mail: concord@cord.edu
Primary Website: www.theconcordian.org
Year Established: 1920
Published: Thur
Avg Free Circ: 2000
Personnel: Cathy McMullen (Advisor); Terence Tang (Bus. Mgr.); Suzanne Maanum (Adv. Mgr.)

CONCORDIA UNIV. AT ST. PAUL

Street address 1: 275 Syndicate St N
Street address city: Saint Paul
Street address state: MN
Zip/Postal code: 55104-5436
Country: USA
Mailing address: 275 Syndicate St N
Mailing city: Saint Paul
Mailing state: MN
Mailing zip: 55104-5436
General Phone: (651) 641-8221
General Fax: (651) 659-0207
General/National Adv. E-mail: sword@csp.edu
Personnel: Eric Dregni (Advisor); Helena Woodruff (Ed. in Chief); Rachel Kuhnle (Art Ed.)

CROWN COLLEGE

Street address 1: 8700 College View Dr
Street address city: Saint Bonifacius
Street address state: MN
Zip/Postal code: 55375-9002
Country: USA
Mailing address: 8700 College View Dr
Mailing city: Saint Bonifacius
Mailing state: MN
Mailing zip: 55375-9001
General Phone: (952) 446-4100
Personnel: William Allen (Advisor)

FERGUS FALLS CMTY. COLLEGE

Street address 1: 1414 College Way
Street address city: Fergus Falls
Street address state: MN
Zip/Postal code: 56537-1009
Country: USA
Mailing address: 1414 College Way
Mailing city: Fergus Falls
Mailing state: MN
Mailing zip: 56537-1009
Personnel: Angela Schroeder (Ed.)

GUSTAVUS ADOLPHUS COLLEGE

Street address 1: 800 W College Ave
Street address city: Saint Peter
Street address state: MN
Zip/Postal code: 56082-1485
Country: USA
Mailing address: 800 W College Ave
Mailing city: Saint Peter
Mailing state: MN
Mailing zip: 56082-1498
General Phone: (507) 933-7636
General Fax: (507) 933-7633
General/National Adv. E-mail: weekly@gac.edu
Primary Website: www.gustavus.edu/weekly
Year Established: 1891
Published: Fri
Personnel: David Kogler (Advisor); Victoria Clark; Jacob Seamans (Ed.); Chelsea Johnson (Editor in Chief 2013-14); Caroline Probst (Editor-in-Chief)

HAMLINE UNIV.

Street address 1: 1536 Hewitt Ave
Street address city: Saint Paul
Street address state: MN
Zip/Postal code: 55104-1205
Country: USA
Mailing address: 1536 Hewitt Ave
Mailing city: Saint Paul
Mailing state: MN
Mailing zip: 55104-1284
General Phone: (651) 523-2268
General Fax: (651) 523-3144
General/National Adv. E-mail: oracle@hamline.edu
Primary Website: www.hamlineoracle.com
Year Established: 1888
Published: Wed
Avg Free Circ: 600
Personnel: David Hudson (Adviser); Stolz Catherine (Editor-in-Chief)

INNOTEK CORPORATION

Street address 1: 9140 Zachary Ln N

Street address city: Maple Grove
Street address state: MN
Zip/Postal code: 55369-4003
County: Hennepin
Country: USA
Mailing address: 9140 Zachary Ln N
Mailing city: Maple Grove
Mailing state: MN
Mailing zip: 55369-4003
General Phone: (763) 488 9902
General Fax: (763)488 9904
General/National Adv. E-mail: sales@innotek-ep.com
Display Adv. E-mail: www.innotek-ep.com
Primary Website: www.innotek-ep.com
Year Established: 1960
Personnel: Dennis Burns (CEO Chairman); David Kalina (Vice Pres., Finance); Tom Wiese (Vice President of Sales & Engineering)

INVER HILLS CMTY. COLLEGE

Street address 1: 2500 80th St E
Street address 2: Ste A
Street address city: Inver Grove Heights
Street address state: MN
Zip/Postal code: 55076-3224
Country: USA
Mailing address: 2500 80th St E Ste A
Mailing city: Inver Grove Heights
Mailing state: MN
Mailing zip: 55076-3224
Personnel: Dave Page (Advisor)

MACALESTER COLLEGE

Street address 1: 1600 Grand Ave
Street address city: Saint Paul
Street address state: MN
Zip/Postal code: 55105-1801
Country: USA
Mailing address: 1600 Grand Ave
Mailing city: Saint Paul
Mailing state: MN
Mailing zip: 55105-1899
General Phone: (651) 696-6212
General Fax: (651) 696-6685
Editorial Phone: (651) 696-6684
General/National Adv. E-mail: macweekly@macalester.edu
Primary Website: www.themacweekly.com
Year Established: 1914
Published: Fri
Personnel: Will Milch (Editor in Chief); Jen Katz (Editor in Cheif); Carrigan Miller (Ad Manager)

MINNEAPOLIS CMTY. & TECH. COLLEGE

Street address 1: 1501 Hennepin Ave
Street address city: Minneapolis
Street address state: MN
Zip/Postal code: 55403-1710
Country: USA
Mailing address: 1501 Hennepin Ave
Mailing city: Minneapolis
Mailing state: MN
Mailing zip: 55403-1710
General Phone: (612) 659-6796
Personnel: Ben Lathrop (Advisor); Andrea Johnson (Mng. Ed.)

MINNESOTA STATE UNIV. MANKATO

Street address 1: 293 Centennial Student Un
Street address 2: Minnesota State University, Mankato
Street address city: Mankato
Street address state: MN
Zip/Postal code: 56001-6051
Country: USA
Mailing address: Centennial Student Union 293
Mailing city: Mankato
Mailing state: MN
Mailing zip: 56001
General Phone: (507) 389-1776
General Fax: (507) 389-5812
Advertising Phone: (507)389-1079
Advertising Fax: (507)389-1595
General/National Adv. E-mail: reporter-editor@mnsu.edu
Display Adv. E-mail: reporter-ad@mnsu.edu
Personnel: Anne Schuelke (Adv.Mgr.); Nicole Smith (Ed. in Chief); Higginbotham (News Ed.); Shelly Christ (Advertising Sales Manager)

MINNESOTA STATE UNIV. MOORHEAD

Street address 1: 1104 7th Ave S
Street address city: Moorhead
Street address state: MN
Zip/Postal code: 56563-0001
Country: USA
Mailing address: PO Box 306
Mailing city: Moorhead
Mailing state: MN
Mailing zip: 56561-0306
General Phone: (218)477-2552
General Fax: (218) 477-4662
General/National Adv. E-mail: advocate@mnstate.edu
Personnel: Kristi Monson (Advisor)

NORMANDALE COMMUNITY COLLEGE

Street address 1: 9700 France Ave S
Street address city: Bloomington
Street address state: MN
Zip/Postal code: 55431-4309
Country: USA
Mailing address: 9700 France Ave S
Mailing city: Bloomington
Mailing state: MN
Mailing zip: 55431-4399
General Phone: (952) 358-8129
Advertising Phone: (952) 358-8193
General/National Adv. E-mail: lionsroar@normandale.edu
Primary Website: www.lionsroar.info
Year Established: 1969
Personnel: Mark Plenke (Advisor)

NORTH CENTRAL UNIV.

Street address 1: 910 Elliot Ave
Street address city: Minneapolis
Street address state: MN
Zip/Postal code: 55404-1322
Country: USA
Mailing address: 910 Elliot Ave
Mailing city: Minneapolis
Mailing state: MN
Mailing zip: 55404-1391
General Phone: (612) 343-4495
Personnel: Reuben David (Advisor)

NORTHLAND CMTY. & TECH. COLLEGE

Street address 1: 1101 Highway 1 E
Street address city: Thief River Falls
Street address state: MN
Zip/Postal code: 56701-2528
Country: USA
Mailing address: 1101 Highway 1 E
Mailing city: Thief River Falls
Mailing state: MN
Mailing zip: 56701-2528
General Phone: (218) 683-8801
Personnel: Adam Paulson (Contact); Elizabeth Perfecto (Ed.)

RIDGEWATER COLLEGE

Street address 1: 2101 15th Ave NW
Street address city: Willmar
Street address state: MN
Zip/Postal code: 56201-3096
Country: USA
Mailing address: 2101 15th Ave NW
Mailing city: Willmar
Mailing state: MN
Mailing zip: 56201-3096
General Phone: (320) 222-5200
General Fax: (320) 231-6602
General/National Adv. E-mail: info@ridgewater.edu
Personnel: Gregg Aamot (Advisor)

SOUTHWEST STATE UNIV.

Street address 1: 1501 State St
Street address 2: Bellows Academic 246
Street address city: Marshall
Street address state: MN
Zip/Postal code: 56258-3306
Country: USA
Mailing address: Bellows Academic 246
Mailing city: Marshall
Mailing state: MN
Mailing zip: 56258
General Phone: (507) 537-6228
General Fax: (507) 537-7359
General/National Adv. E-mail: smsuspur@yahoo.com; smsuspur@gmail.com
Personnel: Jessica Boeve (Bus. Mgr.); Jason Zahn (Ed. in Chief); McMellan Legaspi (Mng. Ed.)

ST. CLOUD STATE UNIV.

Street address 1: 720 4th Ave S
Street address city: Saint Cloud
Street address state: MN
Zip/Postal code: 56301-4442
Country: USA
Mailing address: 720 4th Ave S
Mailing city: Saint Cloud
Mailing state: MN
Mailing zip: 56301-4498
General Phone: (320) 308-4086
Advertising Phone: (320) 308-3943
General/National Adv. E-mail: editor@universitychronicle.net
Display Adv. E-mail: advertising@universitychronicle.net
Editorial e-mail: editor@universitychronicle.net
Primary Website: www.universitychronicle.net
Year Established: 1924
Published: Mon
Personnel: Sandesh Malla (Bus. Mgr.); Ashley Kalkbrenner (Adv. Mgr.); Tiffany Krupke; Jason Tham; Kamana Karki

ST. JOHNS UNIV.

Street address 1: PO Box 2000
Street address city: Collegeville
Street address state: MN
Zip/Postal code: 56321-2000
Country: USA
Mailing address: PO Box 2000
Mailing city: Collegeville
Mailing state: MN
Mailing zip: 56321-2000
General Phone: (320) 363-2540
General Fax: (320) 363-2061
General/National Adv. E-mail: record@csbsju.edu
Personnel: Kate Kompas (Advisor)

ST. MARYS UNIV. OF MINNESOTA

Street address 1: 700 Terrace Hts
Street address 2: Ste 37
Street address city: Winona
Street address state: MN
Zip/Postal code: 55987-1321
Country: USA
Mailing address: 700 Terrace Hts Ste 37
Mailing city: Winona
Mailing state: MN
Mailing zip: 55987-1321
General Phone: (507) 457-1497
Personnel: Bob Conover (Advisor)

ST. OLAF COLLEGE

Street address 1: 1520 Saint Olaf Ave
Street address city: Northfield
Street address state: MN
Zip/Postal code: 55057-1574
Country: USA
Mailing address: 1520 Saint Olaf Ave
Mailing city: Northfield
Mailing state: MN
Mailing zip: 55057-1099
General Phone: (507) 786-3275
General Fax: (507) 786-3650
General/National Adv. E-mail: manitoumessenger@stolaf.edu.com
Display Adv. E-mail: mess-advertise@stolaf.edu
Editorial e-mail: mess-exec@stolaf.edu
Personnel: Bridget Dinter (Adv. Mgr.)

THE WINONAN

Street address 1: 175 W Mark St
Street address city: Winona
Street address state: MN
Zip/Postal code: 55987-3384
Country: USA
Mailing address: 175 W Mark St
Mailing city: Winona
Mailing state: MN
General/National Adv. E-mail: winonan@winona.edu
Primary Website: https://winonan.org/
Year Established: 1919
Published: Wed
Personnel: Doug Westerman (Journalism Advisor); Tracy Rahim (Advisor); Gabriel Hathaway (Editor-in-chief)

UNIV. OF MINNESOTA

Street address 1: 2221 University Ave SE
Street address 2: Ste 450
Street address city: Minneapolis
Street address state: MN
Zip/Postal code: 55414-3077
Country: USA
Mailing address: 2221 University Ave SE Ste 450
Mailing city: Minneapolis
Mailing state: MN
Mailing zip: 55414-3077
General Phone: (612) 627-4080
General Fax: (612) 435-5865
General/National Adv. E-mail: news@mndaily.com
Personnel: Holly Miller (Ed. in Chief)

UNIV. OF MINNESOTA

Street address 1: 600 E 4th St
Street address city: Morris
Street address state: MN
Zip/Postal code: 56267-2132
Country: USA
Mailing address: 600 East Fourth Street
Mailing city: Morris
Mailing state: MN
Mailing zip: 56267
General Phone: (320) 589-6078
General Fax: (320) 589-6079
Year Established: 1987
Personnel: Ingrid Luisa AvendaÃƒÂ£Ãƒ‚Â‚Â¤o (Adv. Mgr.); Joy Heysse (Ed. in Chief); Eli Mayfield (Mng. Ed.)

UNIV. OF MINNESOTA DULUTH

Street address 1: 118 Kirby Ctr, 10 University Dr
Street address city: Duluth
Street address state: MN
Zip/Postal code: 55812
Country: USA
Mailing address: 118 Kirby Ctr., 10 University Dr.
Mailing city: Duluth
Mailing state: MN
Mailing zip: 55812-2403
General Phone: (218) 726-8154
General Fax: (218) 726-8276
General/National Adv. E-mail: statesman@d.umn.edu
Personnel: Lisa Hansen (Advisor)

UNIV. OF MINNESOTA INST. OF TECH

Street address 1: 207 Church St SE
Street address 2: Lind Hall 5
Street address city: Minneapolis
Street address state: MN
Zip/Postal code: 55455-0134
Country: USA
Mailing address: 207 Church St SE Lind Hall 5
Mailing city: Minneapolis
Mailing state: MN
Mailing zip: 55455-0134
General Phone: (612) 624-9816
General Fax: (612) 626-0261
General/National Adv. E-mail: technolog@itdean.umn.edu
Personnel: Paul Sorenson (Advisor); Nate Johnson (Ed.); Michelle Walter (Ed,)

UNIVERSITY OF NORTHWESTERN

Street address 1: 3003 Snelling Ave N

Street address city: Saint Paul
Street address state: MN
Zip/Postal code: 55113-1501
Country: USA
Mailing address: 3003 Snelling Ave N
Mailing city: Saint Paul
Mailing state: MN
Mailing zip: 55113
General Phone: (651) 631-5100
General Fax: (651) 651-5124
General/National Adv. E-mail: examiner@unwsp.edu
Display Adv. E-mail: examinerads@unwsp.edu
Primary Website: http://www.unwexaminer.com/about/
Published: Bi-Mthly
Personnel: Doug Trouten (Advisor)

WILLIAM MITCHELL COLLEGE OF LAW

Street address 1: 875 Summit Ave
Street address city: Saint Paul
Street address state: MN
Zip/Postal code: 55105-3030
Country: USA
Mailing address: 875 Summit Ave
Mailing city: Saint Paul
Personnel: Lucas Hjelle

MISSOURI

AVILA UNIVERSITY

Street address 1: 11901 Wornall Rd
Street address city: Kansas City
Street address state: MO
Zip/Postal code: 64145-1007
Country: USA
Mailing address: 11901 Wornall Rd
Mailing city: Kansas City
Mailing state: MO
Mailing zip: 64145-1007
General Phone: (816) 942-8400
General Fax: (816) 501-2459
General/National Adv. E-mail: talon@mail.avila.edu
Personnel: Joe Snorgrass (Advisor)

CROWDER COLLEGE

Street address 1: 601 Laclede Ave
Street address city: Neosho
Street address state: MO
Zip/Postal code: 64850-9165
Country: USA
Mailing address: 601 Laclede Ave
Mailing city: Neosho
Mailing state: MO
Mailing zip: 64850-9165
General Phone: (417) 451-3223
General Fax: (417) 451-4280
General/National Adv. E-mail: sentry@crowder.edu
Personnel: Leona Bailey (Advisor.); Fabian Oechsle (Ed.)

CULVER-STOCKTON COLLEGE

Street address 1: 1 College Hl
Street address city: Canton
Street address state: MO
Zip/Postal code: 63435-1257
Country: USA
Mailing address: 1 College Hl
Mailing city: Canton
Mailing state: MO
Mailing zip: 63435-1299
General Phone: (573) 231-6371
General Fax: (573) 231-6611
General/National Adv. E-mail: swiegenstein@culver.edu
Primary Website: www.culver.edu
Year Established: 1853
Personnel: Fred Berger (Asst. Prof Comm.); Tyler Tomlinson (Lecturer in Comm.)

DRURY COLLEGE

Street address 1: 900 N Benton Ave
Street address city: Springfield
Street address state: MO
Zip/Postal code: 65802-3712
Country: USA
Mailing address: 900 N Benton Ave
Mailing city: Springfield
Mailing state: MO
Mailing zip: 65802-3791
General Phone: (417) 873-7879
General Fax: (417) 873-7897
General/National Adv. E-mail: mirror@drurymirror.com
Personnel: Cristina Gilstrap (Advisor); Jeromy Layman (Ed. in Chief); Mallory Noelke (Mng. Ed.)

EVANGEL UNIVERSITY

Street address 1: 1111 N Glenstone Ave
Street address city: Springfield
Street address state: MO
Zip/Postal code: 65802-2125
Country: USA
Mailing address: 1111 N. Glenstone Ave.
Mailing city: Springfield
Mailing state: MO
Mailing zip: 65802-2125
General Phone: (417) 865-2815
Advertising Phone: (417) 865-2815, ext. 8636
Editorial Phone: (417) 865-2815, ext. 8634
General/National Adv. E-mail: evangellance@gmail.com
Editorial e-mail: evangellance@gmail.com
Primary Website: http://www.evangellance.com
Year Established: 1955
Published: Fri'Bi-Mthly
Avg Free Circ: 1500
Personnel: Melinda Booze (Advisor)

FONTBONNE COLLEGE

Street address 1: 6800 Wydown Blvd
Street address city: Clayton
Street address state: MO
Zip/Postal code: 63105-3043
Country: USA
Mailing address: 6800 Wydown Blvd
Mailing city: Clayton
Mailing state: MO
Mailing zip: 63105-3098
Personnel: Jason Sommer (Prof.); Sara Lubbes (Ed.)

LINCOLN UNIV.

Street address 1: Elliff Hall, Rm 208
Street address city: Jefferson City
Street address state: MO
Zip/Postal code: 65102
Country: USA
Mailing address: Elliff Hall, Rm. 208
Mailing city: Jefferson City
Mailing state: MO
Mailing zip: 65102
General Phone: (573) 681-5446
Personnel: Yusuf Kalyango (Advisor)

LONGVIEW CMTY. COLLEGE

Street address 1: 500 SW Longview Rd
Street address city: Lees Summit
Street address state: MO
Zip/Postal code: 64081-2105
Country: USA
Mailing address: 500 SW Longview Rd
Mailing city: Lees Summit
Mailing state: MO
Mailing zip: 64081-2100
General Phone: (816) 672-2308
General Fax: (816) 672-2025
General/National Adv. E-mail: current@mcckc.edu
Personnel: Pat Sparks (Advisor)

MISSOURI SOUTHERN UNIVERSITY

Street address 1: 3950 Newman Rd
Street address city: Joplin
Street address state: MO
Zip/Postal code: 64801-1512
Country: USA
Mailing address: 3950 Newman Rd
Mailing city: Joplin
Mailing state: MO
Mailing zip: 64801-1595
General Phone: (417) 625-9823
General Fax: (417) 625-9585
General/National Adv. E-mail: chart@mssu.edu
Primary Website: www.thechartonline.com
Year Established: 1939
Personnel: J.R. Moorman (Head); Chad Stebbins (Advisor); T.R. Hanrahan (Publications Mgr.); Alexandra Nicolas (Ed. in Chief)

MISSOURI STATE UNIV.

Street address 1: 901 S National Ave
Street address city: Springfield
Street address state: MO
Zip/Postal code: 65897-0027
Country: USA
Mailing address: 901 S National Ave
Mailing city: Springfield
Mailing state: MO
Mailing zip: 65897-0001
General Phone: (417) 836-5272
General Fax: (417) 836-6738
Editorial Phone: (417) 836-6512
General/National Adv. E-mail: standard@missouristate.edu
Personnel: Jess Rollins (Ed. in Chief)

MISSOURI UNIV. OF SCIENCE & TECHNOLOGY

Street address 1: Missouri S&T
Street address 2: Altman Hall
Street address city: Rolla
Street address state: MO
Zip/Postal code: 65401
Country: USA
Mailing address: Missouri S&T
Mailing city: Rolla
Mailing state: MO
Mailing zip: 65401-0249
General Phone: (573) 341-4312
General Fax: (573) 341-4235
General/National Adv. E-mail: miner@mst.edu
Personnel: Fred Ekstam (Advisor); Frank Sauer (Bus. Mgr.); Sarah Richmond (Ed. in Chief); Andrea Unnerstall (Mng. Ed.); Jacob (News Ed.)

MISSOURI VALLEY COLLEGE

Street address 1: 500 E College St
Street address city: Marshall
Street address state: MO
Zip/Postal code: 65340-3109
Country: USA
Mailing address: 500 E. College St.
Mailing city: Marshall
Mailing state: MO
Mailing zip: 65340-3109
General Phone: (660) 831-4214
General/National Adv. E-mail: postc@moval.edu
Display Adv. E-mail: postc@moval.edu
Personnel: Chris Post

MISSOURI WESTERN STATE UNIVERSITY

Street address 1: 4525 Downs Dr
Street address 2: Eder 221
Street address city: Saint Joseph
Street address state: MO
Zip/Postal code: 64507-2246
Country: USA
Mailing address: 4525 Downs Dr Eder 221
Mailing city: Saint Joseph
Mailing state: MO
Mailing zip: 64507-2246
General Phone: (816) 271-4412
General Fax: (816) 271-4543
General/National Adv. E-mail: bergland@missouriwestern.edu
Primary Website: www.thegriffonnews.com
Year Established: 1924
Published: Thur
Avg Free Circ: 2500
Personnel: Robert Bergland (Advisor)

NORTHWEST MISSOURI STATE UNIV.

Street address 1: 800 University Dr, Wells 4
Street address city: Maryville
Street address state: MO
Zip/Postal code: 64468
Country: USA
Mailing address: 800 University Dr., Wells 4
Mailing city: Maryville
Mailing state: MO
Mailing zip: 64468-6001
General Phone: (660) 562-1635
General Fax: (660) 562-1521
Editorial Phone: (816) 516-7030
General/National Adv. E-mail: northwestmissourian@gmail.com
Primary Website: www.nwmissourinews.com
Year Established: 1914
Published: Thur
Personnel: Steven Chappell (Advisor); Brandon Zenner (Editor-in-Chief)

ROCKHURST UNIV.

Street address 1: 1100 Rockhurst Rd
Street address city: Kansas City
Street address state: MO
Zip/Postal code: 64110-2508
Country: USA
Mailing address: 1100 Rockhurst Rd
Mailing city: Kansas City
Mailing state: MO
Mailing zip: 64110-2561
General Phone: (816) 501-4051
General Fax: (816) 501-4290
General/National Adv. E-mail: sentinel@rockhurst.edu
Personnel: Brian Roewe (Ed. in Chief)

SOUTHEAST MISSOURI STATE UNIV.

Street address 1: 1 University Plz
Street address 2: MS 2225
Street address city: Cape Girardeau
Street address state: MO
Zip/Postal code: 63701-4710
Country: USA
Mailing address: 1 University Plz MS 2225
Mailing city: Cape Girardeau
Mailing state: MO
Mailing zip: 63701-4710
General Phone: (573) 651-2540
Editorial e-mail: thearrow.news@gmail.com
Personnel: Sam Blackwell (Advisor); Erin Mustain (Ed. in Chief); Ben Marxer (Arts/Entertainment Ed.)

SOUTHWEST BAPTIST UNIV.

Street address 1: 1600 University Ave
Street address city: Bolivar
Street address state: MO
Zip/Postal code: 65613-2578
Country: USA
Mailing address: 1600 University Ave
Mailing city: Bolivar
Mailing state: MO
Mailing zip: 65613-2597
General Phone: (417) 328-1833
General Fax: (417) 328-1579
General/National Adv. E-mail: info@omnibusonline.com
Personnel: Jessica Oliver (Ed. in Chief); Nicole Heitman (Adv. Mgr.)

ST. LOUIS CMTY. COLLEGE FLORISSANT VALLEY

Street address 1: 3400 Pershall Rd
Street address city: Saint Louis
Street address state: MO
Zip/Postal code: 63135-1408
Country: USA
Mailing address: 3400 Pershall Rd
Mailing city: Saint Louis
Mailing state: MO
Mailing zip: 63135-1408
General Phone: (314) 513-4454
Advertising Phone: (314) 513-4588
General/National Adv. E-mail: fvfoumeditor@stlcc.edu
Editorial e-mail: fvforumeditor@stlcc.edu
Year Established: 1963
Published: Mthly
Personnel: Renee Thomas-Woods (Advisor); Stephan Curry (Adv. Mgr.); Joshua Schoenhoff (Ed. in Chief)

ST. LOUIS CMTY. COLLEGE FOREST PARK

Street address 1: 5600 Oakland Ave
Street address city: Saint Louis
Street address state: MO

Zip/Postal code: 63110-1316
Country: USA
Mailing address: 5600 Oakland Ave
Mailing city: Saint Louis
Mailing state: MO

ST. LOUIS CMTY. COLLEGE MERAMEC

Street address 1: 11333 Big Bend Rd
Street address city: Kirkwood
Street address state: MO
Zip/Postal code: 63122-5720
Country: USA
Mailing address: 11333 Big Bend Rd
Mailing city: Kirkwood
Mailing state: MO
Mailing zip: 63122-5799
General Phone: (314) 984-7955
General Fax: (314) 984-7947
Editorial Phone: 314-984-7857
General/National Adv. E-mail: meramecmontage@gmail.com
Primary Website: www.meramecmontage.com
Year Established: 1962
Published: Other
Published Other: bi-weekly
Personnel: Shannon Philpott-Sanders (Advisor)

ST. LOUIS UNIV.

Street address 1: 20 N Grand Blvd
Street address 2: Ste 354
Street address city: Saint Louis
Street address state: MO
Zip/Postal code: 63103-2005
Country: USA
Mailing address: 20 N Grand Blvd Ste 354
Mailing city: Saint Louis
Mailing state: MO
Mailing zip: 63103-2005
General Phone: (314) 977-2812
General Fax: (314) 977-7177
General/National Adv. E-mail: unews.slu@gmail.com
Personnel: Jason L. Young (Advisor); Peter Zagotta (Gen. Mgr); Kat Patke (Ed. in Chief)

STEPHENS COLLEGE

Street address 1: 1200 E Broadway, Campus Box 2014
Street address city: Columbia
Street address state: MO
Zip/Postal code: 65215-0001
Country: USA
Mailing address: 1200 E Broadway, Campus Box 2014
Mailing city: Columbia
Mailing state: MO
Mailing zip: 65215-0001
General Phone: (573) 876-7133
General/National Adv. E-mail: stephenslifemagazine@gmail.com
Personnel: Kathy Vogt (Bus. Mgr.); Josh Nichol-Caddy (Stephens Life Adviser)

TRUMAN STATE UNIV.

Street address 1: Barnett Hall News Ctr 1200, 100 E Normal St
Street address city: Kirksville
Street address state: MO
Zip/Postal code: 63501
Country: USA
Mailing address: Barnett Hall News Ctr. 1200, 100 E. Normal St.
Mailing city: Kirksville
Mailing state: MO
Mailing zip: 63501-4200
General Phone: (660) 785-4449
General Fax: (660) 785-7601
Advertising Phone: (660) 785-4319
General/National Adv. E-mail: indexads@truman.edu
Personnel: Don Krause (Advisor); Blake Toppmeyer (Ed. in Chief); Jessica Rapp (Mng. Ed.); Stephanie Hall (News Ed.)

UNIV. OF MISSOURI

Street address 1: 5327 Holmes St
Street address city: Kansas City
Street address state: MO
Zip/Postal code: 64110-2437
Country: USA
Mailing address: 5327 Holmes St
Mailing city: Kansas City
Mailing state: MO
Mailing zip: 64110-2437
General Phone: (816) 235-1393
Personnel: BJ Allen (Bus. Mgr.); Stefanie Crabtree (Adv. Mgr.); Hilary Hedges (Ed. in Chief)

UNIV. OF MISSOURI

Street address 1: 1 University Blvd
Street address city: Saint Louis
Street address state: MO
Zip/Postal code: 63121-4400
Country: USA
Mailing address: 1 University Blvd
Mailing city: Saint Louis
Mailing state: MO
Mailing zip: 63121-4400
General Phone: (314) 516-5174
General Fax: (314) 516-6811
General/National Adv. E-mail: thecurrent@umsl.edu
Primary Website: www.thecurrentonline.com
Published: Mon
Avg Free Circ: 5000
Personnel: Charlotte Petty (Advisor); Dan Pryor (Bus. Mgr.); Ryan Krull (Advisor)

UNIV. OF MISSOURI - THE MANEATER NEWSPAPER

Street address 1: 2509 MU Student Center
Street address city: Columbia
Street address state: MO
Zip/Postal code: 65211-0001
County: Boone
Country: USA
Mailing address: 2509 MU Student Center
Mailing city: Columbia
Mailing state: MO
Mailing zip: 65211
Editorial e-mail: editors@themaneater.com
Primary Website: www.themaneater.com
Year Established: 1955
Personnel: Becky Diehl (Coordinator)

UNIVERSITY OF CENTRAL MISSOURI

Street address 1: Martin 136, University of Central Missouri
Street address city: Warrensburg
Street address state: MO
Zip/Postal code: 64093
Country: USA
Mailing address: Martin 136, University of Central Missouri
Mailing city: Warrensburg
Mailing state: MO
Mailing zip: 64093
General Phone: (660) 543-4050
General Fax: (660) 543-8663
Advertising Phone: (660) 543-4051
General/National Adv. E-mail: muleskinner@ucmo.edu
Display Adv. E-mail: muleskinnerads@ucmo.edu
Primary Website: www.digitalburg.com
Year Established: 1906
Published: Thur
Published Other: digitalburg.com
Avg Free Circ: 3000
Personnel: Matt Bird-Meyer (Adviser); Jacque Flanagan (Managing Editor)

WASHINGTON UNIV.

Street address 1: 1 Brookings Dr
Street address 2: Campus Box 1039
Street address city: Saint Louis
Street address state: MO
Zip/Postal code: 63130-4862
Country: USA
Mailing address: 1 Brookings Dr.
Mailing city: Saint Louis
Mailing state: MO
Mailing zip: 63130-4862
General Phone: (314) 935-4240
General Fax: (314) 935-5938
Advertising Phone: (314) 935-7209
Advertising Fax: (314) 935-5938
Editorial Fax: (314) 935-5938
Display Adv. E-mail: advertising@studlife.com
Editorial e-mail: editor@studlife.com
Primary Website: www.studlife.com
Year Established: 1878
Published: Mon`Thur
Avg Free Circ: 4000
Personnel: Raymond Bush (General Manager)

WEBSTER UNIV.

Street address 1: 470 E Lockwood Ave
Street address city: Saint Louis
Street address state: MO
Zip/Postal code: 63119-3141
Country: USA
Mailing address: 470 E Lockwood Ave
Mailing city: Saint Louis
Mailing state: MO
Mailing zip: 63119-3194
General Phone: (314) 961-2660
General Fax: (314) 968-7059
Editorial Phone: (314) 968-7088
General/National Adv. E-mail: wujournal@gmail.com
Editorial e-mail: editor@webujournal.com
Primary Website: www.webujournal.com
Published: Wed
Personnel: Don Corrigan (Journ. Seq.); Kelly Kendall (Ed. in Chief)

WESTMINSTER COLLEGE

Street address 1: 501 Westminster Ave
Street address city: Fulton
Street address state: MO
Zip/Postal code: 65251-1230
Country: USA
Mailing address: 501 Westminster Ave
Mailing city: Fulton
Mailing state: MO
Mailing zip: 65251-1299
General Phone: (573) 592-5000
Personnel: Debra Brenegan (Advisor); Sarah Blackmon (Ed. in Chief); Aassan Sipra (Ed. in Chief)

WILLIAM JEWELL COLLEGE

Street address 1: 500 College Hl
Street address 2: # 1016
Street address city: Liberty
Street address state: MO
Zip/Postal code: 64068-1843
Country: USA
Mailing address: 500 College Hl # 1016
Mailing city: Liberty
Mailing state: MO
Mailing zip: 64068-1896
General Phone: (816) 781-7700
General/National Adv. E-mail: monitor@william.jewell.edu
Personnel: Samantha Sanders (Adv. Mgr.); Jessie Newman (Ed. in Chief); Trista Turley (Mng. Ed.)

MISSISSIPPI

ALCORN STATE UNIV.

Street address 1: 1000 Asu Dr, Ste 269
Street address city: Alcorn State
Street address state: MS
Country: USA
Mailing address: 1000 Alcorn Dr Ste 269
Mailing city: Lorman
Mailing state: MS
Mailing zip: 39096-7500
General Phone: (601) 877-6557
General Fax: (601) 877-2213
General/National Adv. E-mail: tnimox@lorman.alcorn.edu
Personnel: Toni Terrett (Advisor); Larry Sanders (Advisor); Erica L. Turner (Ed. in Chief)

BELHAVEN COLLEGE

Street address 1: 1500 Peachtree St
Street address city: Jackson
Street address state: MS
Zip/Postal code: 39202-1754
Country: USA
Mailing address: 1500 Peachtree St
Mailing city: Jackson
Personnel: Don Hubele (Advisor)

BULLDOG BEAT

Street address 1: 304 E Lampkin St
Street address city: Starkville
Street address state: MS
Zip/Postal code: 39759-2910
County: Oktibbeha
Country: USA
Mailing address: PO Box 1068
Mailing city: Starkville
Mailing state: MS
Mailing zip: 39760-1068
General Phone: (662) 323-1642
General Fax: (662) 323-6586
Advertising Phone: (662) 323-1642
Advertising Fax: (662) 323-6586
Editorial Phone: (662) 324-8092
Editorial Fax: (662) 323-6586
General/National Adv. E-mail: sdnads@bellsouth.net
Display Adv. E-mail: sdnads@bellsouth.net
Classified Adv. e-mail: sdnews@bellsouth.net
Editorial e-mail: sdneditor@bellsouth.net
Primary Website: www.starkvilledailynews.com
Year Established: 1875
Published: Mon`Tues`Wed`Thur`Fri`Sat`Sun
Personnel: Don Norman (Pub.); Mona Howell (Bus. Mgr.); Byron Norman (Circ. Mgr.); Larry Bost (Creative Dir.); Shea Staskowski (Educ. Ed.); Brian Hawkins (Online Ed.)

CHIEFTAIN

Street address 1: 602 W Hill St
Street address city: Fulton
Street address state: MS
Zip/Postal code: 38843-1022
County: Itawamba
Country: USA
Mailing address: 602 W. Hill St.
Mailing city: Fulton
Mailing state: MS
Mailing zip: 38843-1022
General Phone: (662) 862-8244
General/National Adv. E-mail: dsthomas@iccms.edu
Editorial e-mail: dsthomas@iccms.edu
Primary Website: www.iccms.edu
Published: Mon
Published Other: Three times each semester
Personnel: Donna Thomas (Dir., Communications)

COPIAH-LINCOLN CMTY. COLLEGE

Street address 1: Hwy 51 S
Street address city: Wesson
Street address state: MS
Zip/Postal code: 39191
Country: USA
Mailing address: PO Box 649
Mailing city: Wesson
Mailing state: MS
Mailing zip: 39191-0649
General Phone: (601) 643-8354
Personnel: Mary Warren (Advisor)

DELTA STATE UNIV.

Street address 1: 1003 W Sunflower Rd
Street address city: Cleveland
Street address state: MS
Zip/Postal code: 38733-0001
Country: USA
Mailing address: 1003 W Sunflower Rd
Mailing city: Cleveland
Mailing state: MS
Mailing zip: 38733-0002
General Phone: (662) 846-4715
General Fax: (662) 846-4737
General/National Adv. E-mail: statemnt@deltastate.edu
Personnel: Patricia Roberts (Advisor); Kaitlyn Mize (Bus. Mgr.); Ashley Robertson (Ed. in Chief)

HINDS CMTY. COLLEGE

Street address 1: PO Box 1100
Street address city: Raymond
Street address state: MS
Zip/Postal code: 39154-1100
Country: USA
Mailing address: PO Box 1100

Mailing city: Raymond
Mailing state: MS
Mailing zip: 39154-1100
Personnel: Cathy Hayden (Advisor)

HOLMES CMTY. COLLEGE

Street address 1: No 1, Hill St
Street address city: Goodman
Street address state: MS
Zip/Postal code: 39079
Country: USA
Mailing address: PO Box 369
Mailing city: Goodman
Mailing state: MS
Mailing zip: 39079-0369
General Phone: (662) 472-2312
Primary Website: www.holmescc.edu
Published Other: Twice a senester
Personnel: Steve Diffey (District Director of Communications)

JACKSON STATE UNIVERSITY

Street address 1: 1400 J R Lynch St
Street address 2: Blackburn Language Arts Building, Room 208
Street address city: Jackson
Street address state: MS
Zip/Postal code: 39217-0002
Country: USA
Mailing address: PO Box 18449
Mailing city: Jackson
Mailing state: MS
Mailing zip: 39217-0001
General Phone: (601) 979-2167
General Fax: (601) 979-2876
Advertising Phone: (601) 979-2167
Advertising Fax: (601) 979-2876
Editorial Phone: (601) 979-2167
Editorial Fax: (601) 979-2876
General/National Adv. E-mail: theflash@jsums.edu
Display Adv. E-mail: shannon.d.tatum@jsums.edu
Editorial e-mail: theflash@jsums.edu
Primary Website: www.thejsuflash.com
Published: Thur
Avg Free Circ: 3000
Personnel: Shannon Tatum (Publications Coordinator/ Ad Manager)

JONES COUNTY JUNIOR COLLEGE

Street address 1: 900 S Court St
Street address city: Ellisville
Street address state: MS
Zip/Postal code: 39437-3901
Country: USA
Mailing address: 900 S Court St
Mailing city: Ellisville
Mailing state: MS
Mailing zip: 39437-3999
General Phone: (601) 477-4084
General Fax: (601) 477-4191
General/National Adv. E-mail: radionian@jcjc.edu
Display Adv. E-mail: radionian@jcjc.edu
Editorial e-mail: radionian@jcjc.edu
Primary Website: www.jcjc.edu
Year Established: 1927
Published: Mthly
Personnel: Kelly Atwood (Newspaper Adviser)

MILLSAPS COLLEGE

Street address 1: Box 150847
Street address city: Jackson
Street address state: MS
Zip/Postal code: 39210-0001
Country: USA
Mailing address: PO Box 150847
Mailing city: Jackson
Mailing state: MS
Mailing zip: 39210-0001
Personnel: Woody Woodrick (Advisor); Kate Royals (Ed, in Chief); Kathleen Morrison (Copy Ed.)

MISSISSIPPI COLLEGE

Street address 1: 200 S Capitol St
Street address city: Clinton
Street address state: MS
Zip/Postal code: 39056-4026
Country: USA
Mailing address: 200 W College St
Mailing city: Clinton
Mailing state: MS
Mailing zip: 39058-0001
General Phone: (601) 925-3462
Personnel: Tim Nicholas (Faculty Advisor); Gabriel Winston (Adv. Mgr.); Terra Kirkland (Co. Ed.)

MISSISSIPPI STATE UNIV.

Street address 1: Henry F Meyer Student Media Ctr
Street address city: Mississippi State
Street address state: MS
Zip/Postal code: 39759
Country: USA
Mailing address: PO Box 5407
Mailing city: Mississippi State
Mailing state: MS
Mailing zip: 39762-5407
General Phone: (662) 325-2374
General Fax: (662) 325-8985
Advertising Phone: (662) 325-7907
General/National Adv. E-mail: editor@reflector.msstate.edu
Display Adv. E-mail: advertise@reflector.msstate.edu
Primary Website: www.reflector-online.com
Year Established: 1884
Published: Tues`Fri
Avg Free Circ: 10000
Personnel: Julia Langford (Adv. Mgr.)

MISSISSIPPI UNIV. FOR WOMEN

Street address 1: 1100 College St
Street address city: Columbus
Street address state: MS
Zip/Postal code: 39701-5821
Country: USA
Mailing address: 1100 College St
Mailing city: Columbus
Mailing state: MS
Mailing zip: 39701-5802
General Phone: (662) 329-7268
General Fax: (662) 329-7269
General/National Adv. E-mail: spectator@muw.edu
Personnel: Sarah Wilson (Ed. in Chief); Juna'uh Allgood (Ed.)

MISSISSIPPI VALLEY STATE UNIV.

Street address 1: 14000 Highway 82 W
Street address city: Itta Bena
Street address state: MS
Zip/Postal code: 38941-1400
County: Leflore
Country: USA
Mailing address: 14000 Highway 82 W
Mailing city: Itta Bena
Mailing state: MS
Mailing zip: 38941-1401
General Phone: (662) 254-3458
General Fax: (622) 254-6704
Advertising Phone: (662) 254-3458
Advertising Fax: (662) 254-3458
Editorial Phone: (662) 254-3458
General/National Adv. E-mail: deltadevilsgazettefacad@gmail.com
Display Adv. E-mail: ehmcclary@mvsu.edu
Editorial e-mail: deltadevilsgazettefacad@gmail.com
Primary Website: deltadevilsgazette.com
Published Other: three per semester
Avg Free Circ: 2000
Personnel: Esin C. Turk (Asst. Prof.); Samuel Osunde (Asst. Prof./Dir., Forensics); Carolyn Gordon; Zainul Abedin (Mr.)

NORTHEAST MISSISSIPPI COMMUNITY COLLEGE

Street address 1: 101 Cunningham Blvd
Street address 2: Box 67
Street address city: Booneville
Street address state: MS
Zip/Postal code: 38829-1726
Country: USA
General Phone: (662) 720-7304
General Fax: (662) 720-7216
Editorial Phone: (662) 720-7421
General/National Adv. E-mail: beacon@nemcc.edu
Display Adv. E-mail: beacon@nemcc.edu
Editorial e-mail: beacon@nemcc.edu
Year Established: 1949
Published: Other
Published Other: Two times each semester
Avg Free Circ: 3600
Personnel: Tony Finch (Advisor); Michael H Miller (Advisor)

NORTHWEST MISSISSIPPI CMTY. COLLEGE

Street address 1: 4975 Highway 51 N
Street address city: Senatobia
Street address state: MS
Zip/Postal code: 38668-1714
Country: USA
Mailing address: PO Box 7039
Mailing city: Senatobia
Mailing state: MS
Mailing zip: 38668
General Phone: (662) 562-3276
General Fax: (662) 562-3499
General/National Adv. E-mail: rangerrocket1@northwestms.edu
Primary Website: www.northwestms.edu
Year Established: 1927
Personnel: Ranate Ferreira (Advisor); Chris Creasy (Ed.)

PEARL RIVER COMMNITY COLLEGE

Street address 1: 101 Highway 11 N
Street address city: Poplarville
Street address state: MS
Zip/Postal code: 39470-2216
Country: USA
Mailing address: 101 Highway 11 N
Mailing city: Poplarville
Mailing state: MS
Mailing zip: 39470-2201
General Phone: (601) 403-1312
Editorial Phone: (601) 403-1328
General/National Adv. E-mail: cabadie@prcc.edu
Display Adv. E-mail: cabadie@prcc.edu
Editorial e-mail: cabadie@prcc.edu
Primary Website: www.prcc.edu
Year Established: 1909
Published: Mthly
Avg Free Circ: 2000
Personnel: Chuck Adadie (Ed./Advisor)

RUST COLLEGE

Street address 1: 150 Rust Ave
Street address city: Holly Springs
Street address state: MS
Zip/Postal code: 38635-2330
Country: USA
Mailing address: 150 Rust Ave
Mailing city: Holly Springs
Mailing state: MS
Mailing zip: 38635-2328
General Phone: (662) 252-8000 ext. 4553
General Fax: (662) 252-8869
General/National Adv. E-mail: rustorian_@hotmail.com
Display Adv. E-mail: rustorian_@hotmail.com
Primary Website: www.rustorian.com
Published: Mthly
Personnel: Debayo Moyo (Advisor)

THE UNIVERSITY OF MISSISSIPPI

Street address 1: 201 Bishop Hall
Street address city: Oxford
Street address state: MS
Zip/Postal code: 38677
Country: USA
Mailing address: 201 Bishop Hall
Mailing city: Oxford
Mailing state: MS
Mailing zip: 38677
General Phone: (662) 915-5503
General Fax: (662) 915-5703
General/National Adv. E-mail: studentmedia@olemiss.edu
Editorial e-mail: dmeditor@gmail.com
Primary Website: www.thedmonline.com
Year Established: 1911
Published: Mon`Tues`Wed`Thur`Fri
Avg Free Circ: 12000
Personnel: Lacey Russell (Ed.); Patricia Thompson (Dir. of Student Media/Faculty Adviser)

TOUGALOO COLLEGE

Street address 1: 500 W County Line Rd
Street address city: Tougaloo
Street address state: MS
Zip/Postal code: 39174-9700
Country: USA
Mailing address: 500 W County Line Rd
Mailing city: Tougaloo
Mailing state: MS
Mailing zip: 39174-9700
General Phone: (601) 977-6159
Personnel: Teressa Fulgham (Mng. Ed.); Colleen White (Dir. Journ. Program)

UNIV. OF SOUTHERN MISSISSIPPI

Street address 1: 118 College Dr
Street address 2: # 5121
Street address city: Hattiesburg
Street address state: MS
Zip/Postal code: 39406-0002
Country: USA
Mailing address: PO Box 5121
Mailing city: Hattiesburg
Mailing state: MS
Mailing zip: 39406-0001
General Phone: (601) 266-4288
General Fax: (601) 266-6473
Advertising Phone: (601) 266-5188
General/National Adv. E-mail: printz@usm.edu
Editorial e-mail: printzeditors@gmail.com
Primary Website: www.studentprintz.com
Year Established: 1927
Published: Wed
Avg Free Circ: 1700
Personnel: Chuck Cook (News Content Adviser)

WOOD COLLEGE

Street address 1: Weber Dr
Street address city: Mathiston
Street address state: MS
Zip/Postal code: 39752
Country: USA
Mailing address: Weber Dr.
Mailing city: Mathiston
Personnel: Jeanna Graves (Ed.)

MONTANA

CARROLL COLLEGE

Street address 1: 1601 N Benton Ave
Street address city: Helena
Street address state: MT
Zip/Postal code: 59625-0001
Country: USA
Mailing address: 1601 N Benton Ave
Mailing city: Helena
Mailing state: MT
Mailing zip: 59625-2826
General Phone: (406) 447-4300
Personnel: Brent Northup (Advisor)

MONTANA STATE UNIV. BOZEMAN

Street address 1: 305 Strand Union Bldg
Street address city: Bozeman
Street address state: MT
Zip/Postal code: 59717
Country: USA
Mailing address: P.O. Box 174140
Mailing city: Bozeman
Mailing state: MT
Mailing zip: 59717
Personnel: Amanda Larrinaga (Ed.in.Chief)

MONTANA STATE UNIV. NORTHERN

Street address 1: 300 11th St W
Street address city: Havre
Street address state: MT
Zip/Postal code: 59501-4917
Country: USA

Mailing address: PO Box 7751
Mailing city: Havre
Mailing state: MT
Mailing zip: 59501-7751
General Phone: (406) 265-4112
Personnel: Lori Renfeld (Ed.)

MONTANA TECH. UNIV.

Street address 1: 1300 W Park St
Street address city: Butte
Street address state: MT
Zip/Postal code: 59701-8932
Country: USA
Mailing address: 1300 W Park St
Mailing city: Butte
Mailing state: MT
Mailing zip: 59701-8932
General Phone: (406) 496-4241
Personnel: Patrick Munday (Advisor)

ROCKY MOUNTAIN COLLEGE

Street address 1: 1511 Poly Dr
Street address city: Billings
Street address state: MT
Zip/Postal code: 59102-1739
Country: USA
Mailing address: 1511 Poly Dr
Mailing city: Billings
Mailing state: MT
Mailing zip: 59102-1796
Personnel: Wilbur Wood (Advisor)

UNIV. OF GREAT FALLS

Street address 1: 1301 20th St S
Street address city: Great Falls
Street address state: MT
Zip/Postal code: 59405-4934
Country: USA
Mailing address: 1301 20th St S
Mailing city: Great Falls
Mailing state: MT
Mailing zip: 59405-4996
Personnel: Jerry Habets (Ed.)

UNIVERSITY OF MONTANA

Street address 1: 32 Campus Dr
Street address city: Missoula
Street address state: MT
Zip/Postal code: 59812-0003
Country: USA
Mailing address: Don Anderson Hall Ste 207
Mailing city: Missoula
Mailing state: MT
Mailing zip: 59812-0001
General Phone: (406) 243-6541
General Fax: (406) 243-5475
Advertising Phone: (406) 243-6541
Advertising Fax: (406) 243-5475
Editorial Phone: 406-243-4101
Editorial Fax: 406-243-5475
General/National Adv. E-mail: kaiminads@gmail.com
Display Adv. E-mail: kaiminads@gmail.com
Editorial e-mail: editor@montanakaimin.com
Primary Website: http://www.montanakaimin.com
Year Established: 1898
Published: Tues`Wed`Thur`Fri
Published Other: Published online daily, updated as news breaks
Avg Free Circ: 4000
Personnel: Ruth Johnson (Office manager); Nadia White (Advisor); Amy Sisk (Editor); Nick McKinney (Business manager)

NORTH CAROLINA

APPALACHIAN STATE UNIV.

Street address 1: 217 Plemmons Student Union
Street address city: Boone
Street address state: NC
Country: USA
Mailing address: Asu # 9025
Mailing city: Boone
Mailing state: NC
Mailing zip: 28608-0002
General Phone: (828) 262-6149
General Fax: (828) 262-6502
General/National Adv. E-mail: theapp@appstate.edu
Personnel: Jon LaFontaine (Ed. in Chief)

BARTON COLLEGE

Street address 1: PO Box 5000
Street address city: Wilson
Street address state: NC
Zip/Postal code: 27893-7000
Country: USA
Mailing address: PO Box 5000
Mailing city: Wilson
Mailing state: NC
Mailing zip: 27893-7000
Personnel: Rick Stewart (Advisor); Brittaney Rosencrance (Ed. in chief)

BELMONT ABBEY COLLEGE

Street address 1: 100 Belmont Mount Holly Rd
Street address city: Belmont
Street address state: NC
Zip/Postal code: 28012-2702
Country: USA
Mailing address: 100 Belmont Mount Holly Rd
Mailing city: Belmont
Mailing state: NC
General/National Adv. E-mail: albenthall@bac.edu
Display Adv. E-mail: cathycomeau@bac.edu
Editorial e-mail: anthonygwyatt@abbey.bac.edu
Primary Website: www.thecrusaderonline.com
Published: Mthly

BENNETT COLLEGE

Street address 1: 900 E Washington St
Street address city: Greensboro
Street address state: NC
Zip/Postal code: 27401-3239
Country: USA
Mailing address: 900 E Washington St
Mailing city: Greensboro
Mailing state: NC
Mailing zip: 27401-3298
General Phone: (336) 517-2305
General Fax: (336) 517-2303
General/National Adv. E-mail: banner@bennett.edu
Personnel: Yvonne Welbon (Advisor)

BREVARD COLLEGE

Street address 1: 1 Brevard Dr
Street address city: Brevard
Street address state: NC
Zip/Postal code: 28712
Country: USA
Mailing address: 1 Brevard Dr.
Mailing city: Brevard
Mailing state: NC
Mailing zip: 28712
General Phone: (828) 883-8292
General/National Adv. E-mail: clarion@brevard.edu
Display Adv. E-mail: clarion@brevard.edu
Editorial e-mail: clarion@brevard.edu
Primary Website: www.brevard.edu/clarion
Year Established: 1935
Published: Fri
Published Other: August-May (no summer publication)
Avg Free Circ: 300
Personnel: John Padgett (Advisor); Althea Dunn (Editor in Chief, 2013-2014)

CAMPBELL UNIV.

Street address 1: PO Box 130
Street address 2: 165 Dr. McKoy Drive
Street address city: Buies Creek
Street address state: NC
Zip/Postal code: 27506-0130
Country: USA
Mailing address: PO Box 130
Mailing city: Buies Creek
Mailing state: NC
Mailing zip: 27506-0130
General Phone: (910) 893-1200
Primary Website: www.campbell.edu
Published: Bi-Mthly
Personnel: Michael Smith (Advisor); Courtney Schultz (editor)

CATAWBA COLLEGE

Street address 1: 2300 W Innes St
Street address city: Salisbury
Street address state: NC
Zip/Postal code: 28144-2441
Country: USA
Mailing address: 2300 W Innes St
Mailing city: Salisbury
Mailing state: NC
Mailing zip: 28144-2488
Personnel: Cyndy Allison (Advisor)

DAVIDSON COLLEGE

Street address 1: PO Box 7182
Street address city: Davidson
Street address state: NC
Zip/Postal code: 28035-7182
Country: USA
Mailing address: PO Box 7182
Mailing city: Davidson
Mailing state: NC
General/National Adv. E-mail: davidsonian@davidson.edu
Display Adv. E-mail: davidsonian@davidson.edu
Primary Website: www.davidsonian.com
Year Established: 1914
Published: Wed
Personnel: Laura Chuckray; Caroline Queen; Lyla Halsted

DUKE UNIV. FUQUA BUS. SCHOOL

Street address 1: PO Box 90120
Street address city: Durham
Street address state: NC
Zip/Postal code: 27708-0120
Country: USA
Mailing address: PO Box 90120
Mailing city: Durham
Mailing state: NC
Mailing zip: 27708-0120
General Phone: (919) 660-7700
General Fax: (919) 684-2818
General/National Adv. E-mail: fuquatimes@gmail.com
Personnel: Mary Murphy (Ed.)

DUKE UNIVERSITY

Street address 1: 101 W Union
Street address city: Durham
Street address state: NC
Zip/Postal code: 27708-9980
Country: USA
Mailing address: PO Box 90858
Mailing city: Durham
Mailing state: NC
Mailing zip: 27708-0858
General Phone: (919) 684-8111
General Fax: (919) 668-1247
Advertising Phone: (919) 684-3811
Editorial Phone: (919) 684-2663
Primary Website: dukechronicle.com
Published: Mon`Tues`Wed`Thur`Fri
Avg Free Circ: 12000
Personnel: Yeshwanth Kandamalla (Editor)

ELIZABETH CITY STATE UNIV.

Street address 1: 1704 Weeksville Rd
Street address city: Elizabeth City
Street address state: NC
Zip/Postal code: 27909-7977
Country: USA
Mailing address: 1704 Weeksville Rd
Mailing city: Elizabeth City
Mailing state: NC
Mailing zip: 27909
Personnel: Kip Branch (Advisor)

ELON UNIVERSITY

Street address 1: 130 N Williamson Ave
Street address city: Elon
Street address state: NC
Zip/Postal code: 27244
Country: USA
Mailing address: 7012 Campus Box
Mailing city: Elon
Mailing state: NC
Mailing zip: 27244-2062
General Phone: (336) 278-7247
General Fax: (336) 278-7426
General/National Adv. E-mail: pendulum@elon.edu
Display Adv. E-mail: pendulum@elon.edu
Personnel: Colin Donohue (Advisor); Andie Diemer (Ed. in Chief); Pam Richter (Sports Ed.); Anna Johnson

FAYETTEVILLE STATE UNIV.

Street address 1: 1200 Murchison Rd
Street address city: Fayetteville
Street address state: NC
Zip/Postal code: 28301-4252
Country: USA
Mailing address: 1200 Murchison Rd
Mailing city: Fayetteville
Mailing state: NC
Mailing zip: 28301-4298
General Phone: (910) 672-2210
Personnel: Valonda Calloway (Advisor); Nathalie Rivera (Bus. Mgr.); L'Asia Brown (Ed. in Chief)

GREENSBORO COLLEGE

Street address 1: 815 W Market St
Street address city: Greensboro
Street address state: NC
Zip/Postal code: 27401-1823
Country: USA
Mailing address: 815 W Market St
Mailing city: Greensboro
Mailing state: NC
Mailing zip: 27401-1875
Personnel: L. Wayne Johns (Advisor)

GUILFORD COLLEGE

Street address 1: 5800 W Friendly Ave
Street address city: Greensboro
Street address state: NC
Zip/Postal code: 27410-4108
Country: USA
Mailing address: 5800 W Friendly Ave
Mailing city: Greensboro
Mailing state: NC
Mailing zip: 27410-4173
General Phone: (336) 316-2306
Personnel: Jeff Jeske (Advisor)

HIGH POINT UNIV.

Street address 1: 1 University Pkwy
Street address city: High Point
Street address state: NC
Zip/Postal code: 27268-0002
Country: USA
Mailing address: 833 Montlieu Ave
Mailing city: High Point
Mailing state: NC
Mailing zip: 27262-4260
General Phone: (800) 345-6993
General Fax: (336) 841-4513
General/National Adv. E-mail: news@highpoint.edu
Personnel: Bobby Hayes (Advisor); Wilfrid Tremblay (Dir./Prof.); Kate Fowkes (Prof.); Judy Isaksen (Assoc. Prof.); John Luecke (Assoc. Prof.); Nahed Eltantawy (Asst. Prof.); Jim Goodman (Asst. Prof.); Brad Lambert (Asst. Prof.); Jim Trammell (Asst. Prof.); Gerald Voorhees (Asst. Prof.); Kristina Bell (Lectr.); Don Moore (Opns. Mgr.); Martin Yount (Video Producer); Michelle Devlin (Admin. Asst.)

LENOIR-RHYNE UNIVERSITY

Street address 1: 625 7th Ave NE
Street address city: Hickory
Street address state: NC
Zip/Postal code: 28601-3984
Country: USA
Mailing address: P.O. 7341
Mailing city: Hickory
Mailing state: NC
Mailing zip: 28603
General Phone: (828) 328-7176
General/National Adv. E-mail: harrisl@lr.edu
Display Adv. E-mail: harrisl@lr.edu
Editorial e-mail: richard.gould@lr.edu
Primary Website: http://therhynean.wordpress.com/

Published: Mthly

MEREDITH COLLEGE

Street address 1: 3800 Hillsborough St
Street address city: Raleigh
Street address state: NC
Zip/Postal code: 27607-5237
Country: USA
Mailing address: 3800 Hillsborough St
Mailing city: Raleigh
Mailing state: NC
Mailing zip: 27607-5298
Personnel: Suzanne Britt (Advisor)

METHODIST UNIVERSITY

Street address 1: 5400 Ramsey St
Street address city: Fayetteville
Street address state: NC
Zip/Postal code: 28311-1420
Country: USA
Mailing address: 5400 Ramsey St
Mailing city: Fayetteville
Mailing state: NC
Mailing zip: 28311-1420
General Phone: (910) 630-7292
General Fax: (910) 630-7253
General/National Adv. E-mail: dmunoz@methodist.edu
Primary Website: www.smalltalkmu.com
Published: Bi-Mthly
Avg Free Circ: 2400
Personnel: Doris Munoz (Director of Student Life)

NORTH CAROLINA A&T STATE UNIV.

Street address 1: 1601 E Market St
Street address city: Greensboro
Street address state: NC
Zip/Postal code: 27411-0002
Country: USA
Mailing address: PO Box E25
Mailing city: Greensboro
Mailing state: NC
Mailing zip: 27411-0001
General Phone: (336) 334-7700
General Fax: (336) 334-7173
General/National Adv. E-mail: theatregister@gmail.com
Personnel: Emiley Burch Harris (Advisor); Dexter R. Mullins (Ed. in Chief)

NORTH CAROLINA CENTRAL UNIV.

Street address 1: 1801 Fayetteville St
Street address city: Durham
Street address state: NC
Zip/Postal code: 27707-3129
Country: USA
Mailing address: 1801 Fayetteville St
Mailing city: Durham
Mailing state: NC
Mailing zip: 27707-3129
General Phone: (919) 530-7116
General Fax: (919) 530-7991
General/National Adv. E-mail: campusecho@nccu.edu
Personnel: Dr. Bruce DePyssler (Advisor); Thomas Evans (Associate Professor); Carlton Koonce (Ed. in Chief)

NORTH CAROLINA STATE UNIV.

Street address 1: 323 Witherspoon Student Ctr, Ncsu Campus Box 7318
Street address city: Raleigh
Street address state: NC
Zip/Postal code: 27695-0001
Country: USA
Mailing address: 323 Witherspoon Student Ctr Ncsu Campus Box 7318
Mailing city: Raleigh
Mailing state: NC
Mailing zip: 27695-0001
General Phone: (919) 515-2411
General Fax: (919) 515-5133
General/National Adv. E-mail: editor@technicianonline.com
Display Adv. E-mail: advertising@technicianonline.com
Primary Website: www.technicianonline.com
Year Established: 1923
Personnel: Bradley Wilson (Advisor); Russell Witham (Ed. in Chief)

PEACE COLLEGE

Street address 1: 15 E Peace St
Street address city: Raleigh
Street address state: NC
Zip/Postal code: 27604-1176
Country: USA
Mailing address: 15 E Peace St
Mailing city: Raleigh
Mailing state: NC
Mailing zip: 27604-1194
General Phone: (919) 508-2214
Personnel: John Hill (Advisor)

PFEIFFER UNIV.

Street address 1: PO Box 960
Street address city: Misenheimer
Street address state: NC
Zip/Postal code: 28109-0960
Country: USA
Mailing address: PO Box 960
Mailing city: Misenheimer
Mailing state: NC
Mailing zip: 28109-0960
General Phone: (704) 463-1360
Personnel: Charisse Levine (Advisor)

QUEENS UNIVERSITY OF CHARLOTTE

Street address 1: 1900 Selwyn Ave
Street address city: Charlotte
Street address state: NC
Zip/Postal code: 28207-2450
Country: USA
Mailing address: Msc # 892
Mailing city: Charlotte
Mailing state: NC
Mailing zip: 28274-0001
General Phone: (704) 337-2220
General Fax: (704) 337-2503
General/National Adv. E-mail: quoc.chronicle@gmail.com
Primary Website: www.queens-chronicle.com
Published: Bi-Mthly
Personnel: Dustin Saunders (Editor-in-Chief)

SALEM COLLEGE

Street address 1: 601 S Church St
Street address city: Winston Salem
Street address state: NC
Zip/Postal code: 27101-5318
Country: USA
Mailing address: 601 S Church St
Mailing city: Winston Salem
Mailing state: NC
Mailing zip: 27101-5376
General Phone: (336) 917-5113
Personnel: Sarah Boyenger (Bus. Mgr.); Susan Smith (Ed. in Chief)

THE DAILY TAR HEEL

Street address 1: 151 E Rosemary St
Street address city: Chapel Hill
Street address state: NC
Zip/Postal code: 27514-3539
County: Orange
Country: USA
Mailing address: 151 E Rosemary St
Mailing city: Chapel Hill
Mailing state: NC
Mailing zip: 27514-3539
General Phone: (919) 962-1163
Advertising Phone: 919.962.1163
Editorial Phone: 919.962.0245
General/National Adv. E-mail: sales@dailytarheel.com
Display Adv. E-mail: sales@dailytarheel.com
Classified Adv. e-mail: sales@dailytarheel.com
Editorial e-mail: dth@dailytarheel.com
Primary Website: dailytarheel.com
Year Established: 1893
Personnel: Elise Young (Managing Ed.)

THE DUKE CHRONICLE

Street address 1: 301 Flowers
Street address city: Durham
Street address state: NC
Zip/Postal code: 27708-0001
County: Durham
Country: USA
Mailing address: 301 Flowers
Mailing city: Durham
Mailing state: NC
Mailing zip: 27708-0001
General Phone: 919-684-2663
General Fax: 919-684-4696
Advertising Phone: 919-684-3811
Advertising Fax: 919-668-1247
Editorial Phone: 919-684-2663
Editorial Fax: 919-684-4696
General/National Adv. E-mail: advertising@chronicle.duke.edu
Display Adv. E-mail: advertising@chronicle.duke.edu
Classified Adv. e-mail: advertising@chronicle.duke.edu
Editorial e-mail: chronicleletters@duke.edu
Primary Website: http://www.dukechronicle.com

THE EAST CAROLINIAN

Street address 1: Self Help Bldg Ecu
Street address city: Greenville
Street address state: NC
Zip/Postal code: 27858
Country: USA
Mailing address: Self Help Bldg. ECU
Mailing city: Greenville
Mailing state: NC
Mailing zip: 27858
General Phone: (252) 328-9238
General Fax: (252) 328-9143
Advertising Phone: (252) 328-9245
Advertising Fax: (252) 328-9143
Editorial Phone: (205) 328-9249
Editorial Fax: (252) 328-9143
Display Adv. E-mail: ads@theeastcarolinian.com
Editorial e-mail: editor@theeastcarolinian.com
Primary Website: www.theeastcarolinian.com
Year Established: 1925
Personnel: Paul Isom (Advisor); Caitlin Hale (Editor); Katelyn Crouse (Ed. in Chief)

UNIV. OF NORTH CAROLINA

Street address 1: 1 University Hts
Street address city: Asheville
Street address state: NC
Zip/Postal code: 28804-3251
Country: USA
Mailing address: 1 University Heights
Mailing city: Asheville
Mailing state: NC
Mailing zip: 28804-3251
General Fax: (828) 251-6591
Advertising Fax: (828) 232-2421
General/National Adv. E-mail: www.thebluebanner.net
Personnel: Michael Gouge (Advisor); Anna Kiser (Adv. Mgr.); Sam Hunt (Ed. in Chief)

UNIV. OF NORTH CAROLINA

Street address 1: Uncg, Box N1, Euc
Street address city: Greensboro
Street address state: NC
Zip/Postal code: 27412-0001
Country: USA
Mailing address: Uncg # N1
Mailing city: Greensboro
Mailing state: NC
Mailing zip: 27412-0001
General Phone: (336) 334-5752
General Fax: (336) 334-3518
General/National Adv. E-mail: the_carolinian@hotmail.com
Personnel: Y-Phuc Ayun (Bus. Mgr.); Casey Mann (Pub.); John Boschini (Ed. in Chief)

UNIV. OF NORTH CAROLINA

Street address 1: 1 University Rd
Street address city: Pembroke
Street address state: NC
Zip/Postal code: 28372-8699
Country: USA
Mailing address: PO Box 1510
Mailing city: Pembroke
Mailing state: NC
Mailing zip: 28372-1510
General Phone: (910) 521-6204
General Fax: (910) 522-5795
General/National Adv. E-mail: pineneedle@uncp.edu
Personnel: Judy Curtis (Advisor); Jodie Johnson (Adv. Mgr.); Wade Allen (Ed.)

UNIV. OF NORTH CAROLINA

Street address 1: 601 S College Rd
Street address city: Wilmington
Street address state: NC
Zip/Postal code: 28403-3201
Country: USA
Mailing address: 601 S College Rd
Mailing city: Wilmington
Mailing state: NC
Mailing zip: 28403-3201
General Phone: (910) 962-3229
Advertising Phone: (910) 962-7131
General/National Adv. E-mail: seahawk.news@uncw.edu
Editorial e-mail: seahawk.editor@gmail.com
Primary Website: www.theseahawk.org
Year Established: 1948
Personnel: Autumn Beam (Ed. in Chief); Lisa Huynh (Mng. Ed); Bethany Bestwina (Photo Ed.)

UNIV. OF NORTH CAROLINA - THE DAILY TAR HEEL

Street address 1: 151 E Rosemary St
Street address city: Chapel Hill
Street address state: NC
Zip/Postal code: 27514-3539
Country: USA
Mailing address: 151 E Rosemary St
Mailing city: Chapel Hill
Mailing state: NC
Mailing zip: 27514-3539
General Phone: (919) 962-1163
General Fax: (919) 962-1609
Editorial Phone: 919=962-0245
Display Adv. E-mail: ads@unc.edu
Editorial e-mail: dth@dailytarheel.com
Primary Website: www.dailytarheel.com
Year Established: 1893
Published: Mon`Tues`Wed`Thur`Fri
Avg Free Circ: 17000
Personnel: Erica Perel (Advisor); Megan Mcginity (Adv. Mgr.)

UNIV. OF NORTH CAROLINA AT CHARLOTTE

Street address 1: 9201 University City Blvd
Street address city: Charlotte
Street address state: NC
Zip/Postal code: 28223-0001
Country: USA
Mailing address: 9201 University City Blvd
Mailing city: Charlotte
Mailing state: NC
Mailing zip: 28223-1000
General Fax: (704) 687-3253
Advertising Phone: (704) 687-7145
Advertising Fax: (704) 687-7139
Editorial Phone: (704) 687-7148
General/National Adv. E-mail: www.nineronline.com
Display Adv. E-mail: smpads@uncc.edu
Editorial e-mail: editor@ninertimes.com
Primary Website: www.ninertimes.com
Published: Tues
Avg Free Circ: 7000
Personnel: Christine Litchfield (Ed. in Chief); Hunter Heilman (EIC)

UNIV. OF NORTH CAROLINA LAW SCHOOL

Street address 1: Cb #3380, Vanhecke-Wettach Hall
Street address city: Chapel Hill
Street address state: NC
Zip/Postal code: 27599-0001
Country: USA
Mailing address: 3380 Vanhecke-Wettach Hall
Mailing city: Chapel Hill

WAKE FOREST UNIV.

Street address 1: PO Box 7569
Street address city: Winston Salem

Street address state: NC
Zip/Postal code: 27109
Country: USA
Mailing address: PO Box 7569
Mailing city: Winston Salem
Mailing state: NC
Mailing zip: 27109-6240
General Phone: (336) 758-5279
General Fax: (336) 758-4561
General/National Adv. E-mail: ogb@wfu.edu
Personnel: Wayne King (Advisor); Tyler Kellner (Bus. Mgr.); Mariclaire Hicks (Ed. in Chief)

WESTERN CAROLINA UNIV.

Street address 1: 109A Old Student Union
Street address city: Cullowhee
Street address state: NC
Zip/Postal code: 28723
Country: USA
Mailing address: 109A Old Student Union
Mailing city: Cullowhee
Mailing state: NC
Mailing zip: 28723
General Phone: (828) 227-2694
General Fax: (828) 227-7201
General/National Adv. E-mail: jcaudell@westerncarolinian.com
Display Adv. E-mail: jcaudell@westerncarolinian.com
Editorial e-mail: amenz@westerncarolinian.com
Primary Website: www.westerncarolinian.com
Year Established: 1933
Published: Bi-Mthly
Avg Free Circ: 5000
Personnel: Justin Caudell (Ed. in Chief); Alexa Menz (Editor-in-Chief)

WINGATE UNIV.

Street address 1: PO Box 2
Street address city: Wingate
Street address state: NC
Zip/Postal code: 28174-0002
Country: USA
Mailing address: PO Box 2
Mailing city: Wingate
Mailing state: NC
Mailing zip: 28174-0002
Personnel: Keith Cannon (Advisor); Brittany Ruffner (Contact)

WINSTON-SALEM STATE UNIV.

Street address 1: 103 Old Nursing
Street address 2: 601 S. Martin Luther King Jr. Dr.
Street address city: Winston Salem
Street address state: NC
Zip/Postal code: 27110-0001
Country: USA
Mailing address: 103 Old Nursing
Mailing city: Winston Salem
Mailing state: NC
Mailing zip: 27110-0001
General Phone: 3367502327
General Fax: 3367508704
Advertising Phone: 3367508701
Advertising Fax: 3367508704
Editorial Phone: 3367508701
General/National Adv. E-mail: thenewsargus@gmail.com
Display Adv. E-mail: thenewsargus@gmail.com
Editorial e-mail: thenewsargus@gmail.com
Primary Website: www.thenewsargus.com
Year Established: 1960
Published: Mon`Bi-Mthly
Personnel: Lona D. Cobb (Advisor)

NORTH DAKOTA

BISMARCK STATE COLLEGE

Street address 1: 1500 Edwards Ave
Street address city: Bismarck
Street address state: ND
Zip/Postal code: 58501-1276
Country: USA
Mailing address: 1500 Edwards Ave
Mailing city: Bismarck
Mailing state: ND
Mailing zip: 58501-1299
General Phone: (701) 224-5467
General Fax: (701) 224-5529
Editorial Phone: (701) 224-5467
General/National Adv. E-mail: editor@mystician.org
Primary Website: www.mystician.org
Year Established: 1939
Published: Mthly
Personnel: Karen Bauer (Advisor)

JAMESTOWN COLLEGE

Street address 1: 6086 College Ln
Street address city: Jamestown
Street address state: ND
Zip/Postal code: 58405-0001
Country: USA
Mailing address: 6086 College Ln
Mailing city: Jamestown
Mailing state: ND
Mailing zip: 58405-0001
General Phone: (701) 252-3467
Personnel: Steve Listopad (Advisor); Richard Schmit (Ed. in Cheif)

MINOT STATE UNIV.

Street address 1: 500 University Ave W
Street address city: Minot
Street address state: ND
Zip/Postal code: 58707-0001
Country: USA
Mailing address: 500 University Ave W
Mailing city: Minot
Mailing state: ND
Mailing zip: 58707-0002
General Phone: (701) 858-3000
General/National Adv. E-mail: redgreen@minotstateu.edu
Personnel: Bryce Berginski (Ed.)

NORTH DAKOTA STATE COLLEGE OF SCIENCE

Street address 1: PO Box 760
Street address city: Wahpeton
Street address state: ND
Zip/Postal code: 58074-0760
Country: USA
Mailing address: c/o Daily News, PO Box 760
Mailing city: Wahpeton
Mailing state: ND
Mailing zip: 58074-0760
Personnel: Pam Marquart (Advisor)

NORTH DAKOTA STATE UNIV.

Street address 1: 254 Memorial Union
Street address city: Fargo
Street address state: ND
Zip/Postal code: 58102
Country: USA
Mailing address: P.O. Box 6050
Mailing city: Fargo
Mailing state: ND
Mailing zip: 58108-6050
General Phone: (701) 231-8929
General Fax: (701) 231-9402
Advertising Phone: (701) 231-8994
Editorial Phone: (701) 231-8629
General/National Adv. E-mail: ad.manager@ndsuspectrum.com
Display Adv. E-mail: ad.manager@ndsuspectrum.com
Editorial e-mail: editor@ndsuspectrum.com
Primary Website: www.ndsuspectrum.com
Year Established: 1896
Published: Mon`Thur
Avg Free Circ: 7000
Personnel: Andrew Pritchard (Advisor)

UNIV. OF NORTH DAKOTA

Street address 1: 2901 University Ave Stop 8385
Street address 2: University of North Dakota Memorial Union
Street address city: Grand Forks
Street address state: ND
Zip/Postal code: 58202-8385
Country: USA
Mailing address: University of North Dakota Memorial Union
Mailing city: Grand Forks
Mailing state: ND
Mailing zip: 58201
General Phone: (701) 777-2677
General Fax: (701) 777-3137
Advertising Phone: (701) 777-2677
General/National Adv. E-mail: dakotastudentmedia@gmail.com
Display Adv. E-mail: und.dakotastudent@email.und.edu
Primary Website: www.dakotastudent.com
Year Established: 1888
Published: Tues`Fri
Personnel: Carrie Sandstrom (Editor-in-Chief); Melissa Bakke (Sales and Marketing Coordinator); Adam Christianson (Managing/Opinion Editor); Kelsi Ward (Features Editor); Larry Philbin (News Editor); Elizabeth Erickson (Sports Editor); Jaye Millspaugh (Multimedia Editor); Keisuke Yoshimura (Photo Editor)

VALLEY CITY STATE UNIV.

Street address 1: Box 1431, Vcsc Student Ctr
Street address city: Valley City
Street address state: ND
Zip/Postal code: 58072
Country: USA
Mailing address: Box 1431, VCSC Student Ctr.
Mailing city: Valley City

NEBRASKA

CHADRON STATE COLLEGE

Street address 1: 1000 Main St
Street address 2: # 235
Street address city: Chadron
Street address state: NE
Zip/Postal code: 69337-2667
County: Dawes
Country: USA
Mailing address: 1000 Main St # 235
Mailing city: Chadron
Mailing state: NE
Mailing zip: 69337-2690
General Phone: (308) 432-6303
Advertising Phone: (308) 432-6304
General/National Adv. E-mail: editor@csceagle.com
Display Adv. E-mail: ads@csceagle.com
Editorial e-mail: opinion@csceagle.com
Primary Website: www.csceagle.com
Year Established: 1920
Published: Thur
Avg Free Circ: 4000
Personnel: Michael D. Kennedy (Advisor); Aubrie Lawrence (Editor-in-Chief); Jordyn Hulinsky (Mgr Ed); Mackenzie Dahlberg (Sports Editor); Janelle Kesterson (Opinion Ed); Kamryn Kozisek (Ag & Range Editor); Velvet Jessen (Opinions Editor); Rylee Greiman (Social Media Director); Angie Webb (Advt Dir); Andrew Avila (Co-Advertising Director); Preston Goehring (Sports Ed); Kinsey Smith (Co-Advertising Director); Justine Stone (Lifestyles Ed); Brendan Fangmeire (Distribution Manager); Melanie Nelson (News Ed)

CONCORDIA UNIVERSITY-NEBRASKA

Street address 1: 800 N Columbia Ave
Street address city: Seward
Street address state: NE
Zip/Postal code: 68434-1500
Country: USA
Mailing address: 800 N Columbia Ave Ste 1
Mailing city: Seward
Mailing state: NE
Mailing zip: 68434-1599
General Phone: 703-434-0355
General/National Adv. E-mail: sower@cune.org
Primary Website: www.cunesower.com
Published: Mthly
Published Other: Website updated throughout the week
Avg Free Circ: 1300
Personnel: Ellen Beck (Adviser)

CREIGHTON UNIV.

Street address 1: 2500 California Plz
Street address city: Omaha
Street address state: NE
Zip/Postal code: 68178-0133
Country: USA
Mailing address: 2500 California Plz
Mailing city: Omaha
Mailing state: NE
Mailing zip: 68178-0002
General Phone: (402) 280-4058
General Fax: (402) 280-1494
General/National Adv. E-mail: emw@creighton.edu
Personnel: Melissa Hillebrand (Ed.); Eileen M. Wirth (Chair/Prof.); Father Don Doll (Prof./Charles and Mary Heider Endowed Jesuit Chair); Kelly Fitzgerald (Asst. Ed.); Timothy S. Guthrie (Assoc. Prof.); Jeffrey Maciejewski (Assoc. Prof.); Carol Zuegner (Assoc. Prof.); Kristoffer Boyle (Asst. Prof.); Joel Davies (Asst. Prof.); Charles Heider (Asst. Prof.); Mary Heider (Asst. Prof.); Andrew Hughes (Lectr.); Kathleen Hughes (Lectr.); Richard Janda (Lectr.); Kathryn Larson (Lectr.); Brian Norton (Lectr.); Wendy Wiseman (Lectr.); Angela Zegers (Lectr.)

DOANE COLLEGE

Street address 1: 1014 Boswell Ave
Street address city: Crete
Street address state: NE
Zip/Postal code: 68333-2426
Country: USA
Mailing address: 1014 Boswell Ave Ste 289
Mailing city: Crete
Mailing state: NE
Mailing zip: 68333-2440
General Fax: (402) 826-8269
Advertising Fax: (402) 826-8600
General/National Adv. E-mail: www.doaneline.com
Personnel: David Swartzlander (Advisor); Bob Kenny (Ed.)

HASTINGS COLLEGE

Street address 1: 710 N Turner Ave
Street address city: Hastings
Street address state: NE
Zip/Postal code: 68901-7621
Country: USA
Mailing address: 710 N Turner Ave
Mailing city: Hastings
Mailing state: NE
Mailing zip: 68901-7696
Personnel: Alicia O'Donnell (Advisor); Lauren Lee (Ed.)

NEBRASKA WESLEYAN UNIV.

Street address 1: 5000 Saint Paul Ave
Street address 2: Smb 1221
Street address city: Lincoln
Street address state: NE
Zip/Postal code: 68504-2760
Country: USA
Mailing address: 5000 Saint Paul Ave Smb 1221
Mailing city: Lincoln
Mailing state: NE
Mailing zip: 68504-2760
General Phone: (402) 465-2387
General Fax: (402) 465-2179
General/National Adv. E-mail: reveille@nebrwesleyan.edu
Primary Website: www.thereveillenwu.com
Published: Bi-Mthly
Personnel: Jim Schaffer (Advisor); David Whitt (Adviser); Hannah Tangeman (Editor)

NORTHEAST CMTY. COLLEGE

Street address 1: 801 E Benjamin Ave
Street address city: Norfolk
Street address state: NE
Zip/Postal code: 68701-6831
Country: USA
Mailing address: PO Box 469
Mailing city: Norfolk
Mailing state: NE
Mailing zip: 68702-0469
Personnel: Jason Elznic (Advisor)

PERU STATE COLLEGE

Street address 1: PO Box 10
Street address city: Peru
Street address state: NE
Zip/Postal code: 68421-0010
Country: USA

Mailing address: PO Box 10
Mailing city: Peru
Mailing state: NE
Mailing zip: 68421-0010
General Phone: (402) 872-2260
Personnel: Savannah Wenzel (Adv. Mgr.)

UNIV. OF NEBRASKA

Street address 1: Mitchel Ctr 156
Street address city: Kearney
Street address state: NE
Zip/Postal code: 68847
Country: USA
Mailing address: Mitchel Ctr. 156
Mailing city: Kearney
Mailing state: NE
Mailing zip: 68847
General Phone: (308) 865-8487
Personnel: Tereca M Diffenderfer (Advisor)

UNIV. OF NEBRASKA AT OMAHA GATEWAY

Street address 1: 6001 Dodge St
Street address 2: MBSC 117H
Street address city: Omaha
Street address state: NE
Zip/Postal code: 68182-1107
Country: USA
Mailing address: 6001 Dodge St Unit 116
Mailing city: Omaha
Mailing state: NE
Mailing zip: 68182-1107
General Phone: (402) 554-2470
General Fax: (402) 554-2735
General/National Adv. E-mail: editorinchief@unothegateway.com
Editorial e-mail: jloza@unomaha.edu
Primary Website: www.unogateway.com
Year Established: 1913
Published: Tues
Avg Free Circ: 2500
Personnel: Josefina Loza (Advisor); Cody Willmer; Kate O'Dell

UNIV. OF NEBRASKA-LINCOLN

Street address 1: 1400 R St
Street address 2: 20 Nebraska Union
Street address city: Lincoln
Street address state: NE
Zip/Postal code: 68588-0007
Country: USA
Mailing address: P.O. Box 880448
Mailing city: Lincoln
Mailing state: NE
Mailing zip: 68588-0448
General Phone: (402) 472-2588
Advertising Phone: (402) 472-2589
General/National Adv. E-mail: dn@unl.edu
Display Adv. E-mail: dn@unl.edu
Editorial e-mail: news@dailynebraskan.com
Primary Website: DailyNebraskan.com
Year Established: 1901
Published: Mthly`Other
Published Other: We publish 2-3 print editions per year
Avg Free Circ: 4500
Personnel: Daniel Shattil (Gen. Mgr.); Allen Vaughan (General Manager); David Thiemann (Director of Sales and Marketing)

WAYNE STATE COLLEGE

Street address 1: 1111 Main St
Street address city: Wayne
Street address state: NE
Zip/Postal code: 68787-1181
Country: USA
Mailing address: 1111 Main St
Mailing city: Wayne
Mailing state: NE
Mailing zip: 68787-1172
General Phone: (402) 375-7324
General Fax: (402) 375-7204
Advertising Phone: (402) 375-7489
General/National Adv. E-mail: wstater@wsc.edu
Personnel: Max McElwain (Faculty Advisor); Skylar Osovski (Ed. in Chief); Katelynn Wolfe (News Ed.)

WESTERN NEBRASKA COMMUNITY COLLEGE

Street address 1: 1601 E 27th St
Street address city: Scottsbluff
Street address state: NE
Zip/Postal code: 69361-1815
Country: USA
Mailing address: 1601 E 27th St
Mailing city: Scottsbluff
Mailing state: NE
Mailing zip: 69361-1899
General Phone: (308) 635-6058
Personnel: Mark Rein (Adv. Mgr.); Jay Grote

NEW HAMPSHIRE

DARTMOUTH COLLEGE

Street address 1: 6175 Robinson Hall
Street address city: Hanover
Street address state: NH
Zip/Postal code: 03755-3507
Country: USA
Mailing address: 6175 Robinson Hall
Mailing city: Hanover
Mailing state: NH
Mailing zip: 03755-3507
General Phone: (603) 646-2600
General Fax: (603) 646-3443
General/National Adv. E-mail: publisher@dartmouth.com; thedartmouth@dartmouth.edu
Primary Website: www.thedartmouth.com
Year Established: 1799
Personnel: Ray Lu (Ed. in chief); Phil Rasansky (Pub.)

FRANKLIN PIERCE COLLEGE

Street address 1: 40 University Dr
Street address city: Rindge
Street address state: NH
Zip/Postal code: 03461-5046
Country: USA
Mailing address: 40 University Dr
Mailing city: Rindge
Mailing state: NH
Mailing zip: 03461-5045
General Phone: (603) 899-4170
Personnel: Kristen Nevious (Advisor); Tony Catinella (Ed.); Robin Michael (Mng. Ed.)

NEW ENGLAND COLLEGE

Street address 1: 98 Bridge St
Street address city: Henniker
Street address state: NH
Zip/Postal code: 03242-3292
Country: USA
Mailing address: 98 Bridge St
Mailing city: Henniker
Mailing state: NH
Mailing zip: 03242-3292
General Phone: (603) 428-2000
Personnel: William Homestead (Advisor)

PLYMOUTH STATE COLLEGE

Street address 1: Hub Ste A9
Street address city: Plymouth
Street address state: NH
Zip/Postal code: 3264
Country: USA
Mailing address: HUB Ste. A9
Mailing city: Plymouth
Mailing state: NH
Mailing zip: 03264
General Phone: (603) 535-2947
General Fax: (603) 535-2729
Editorial Phone: (603) 535-2279
Editorial e-mail: editor@clock.plymouth.edu
Personnel: Joe Mealey (Advisor); Meghan Plumpton (Adv. Mgr.); Samantha Kenney (Ed. in Chief)

SOUTHERN NEW HAMPSHIRE UNIV.

Street address 1: 2500 N River Rd
Street address 2: # 1084
Street address city: Manchester
Street address state: NH
Zip/Postal code: 03106-1018
Country: USA
Mailing address: 2500 N River Rd # 1084
Mailing city: Manchester
Mailing state: NH
General/National Adv. E-mail: Penmenpress@snhu.edu
Display Adv. E-mail: Penmenpress@snhu.edu
Primary Website: PenmenPress.com
Published: Bi-Mthly
Personnel: Jon Boroshok (Advisor)

ST. ANSELM COLLEGE

Street address 1: 100 Saint Anselm Dr
Street address city: Manchester
Street address state: NH
Zip/Postal code: 03102-1308
Country: USA
Mailing address: PO Box 1719
Mailing city: Manchester
Mailing state: NH
Mailing zip: 03102
General Phone: (603) 641-7016
General Fax: (603) 222-4289
General/National Adv. E-mail: crier@anslem.edu
Personnel: Jerome Day (Advisor)

THE NEW HAMPSHIRE

Street address 1: Memorial Union Bldg, Rm 132, 83 Main St
Street address city: Durham
Street address state: NH
Zip/Postal code: 3824
Country: USA
Mailing address: Memorial Union Bldg., Rm. 132, 83 Main St.
Mailing city: Durham
Mailing state: NH
Mailing zip: 03824-2538
General Phone: (603) 862-1323
General Fax: (603) 862-1920
General/National Adv. E-mail: tnh.news@unh.edu
Display Adv. E-mail: tnh.advertising@unh.edu
Editorial e-mail: tnh.editor@unh.edu
Primary Website: www.tnhdigital.com
Year Established: 1911
Published: Mon`Thur
Avg Free Circ: 4000
Personnel: Julie Pond (Advisor)

UNIVERSITY OF NEW HAMPSHIRE

Street address 1: 104 Hamilton Smith Hall
Street address city: Durham
Street address state: NH
Zip/Postal code: 3824
Country: USA
Mailing address: 104 Hamilton Smith Hall
Mailing city: Durham
Mailing state: NH
Mailing zip: 3824
General Phone: (603) 862-0251
Personnel: Lisa Miller (Dir.)

NEW JERSEY

ATLANTIC CAPE CMTY. COLLEGE

Street address 1: 5100 Black Horse Pike
Street address city: Mays Landing
Street address state: NJ
Zip/Postal code: 08330-2623
Country: USA
Mailing address: 5100 Black Horse Pike
Mailing city: Mays Landing
Mailing state: NJ
Mailing zip: 08330-2699
General Phone: (609) 343-5109
Personnel: Marge Nocito (Advisor); Jerry Carcache (Dir., Adv.); Anne Kemp (Ed. in Chief)

BROOKDALE CMTY. COLLEGE

Street address 1: 765 Newman Springs Rd
Street address city: Lincroft
Street address state: NJ
Zip/Postal code: 07738-1543
Country: USA
Mailing address: 765 Newman Springs Rd
Mailing city: Lincroft
Mailing state: NJ
Mailing zip: 07738-1599
General Phone: (732) 224-2266
General Fax: (732) 450-1591
General/National Adv. E-mail: stallbcc@gmail.com
Editorial e-mail: stall@brookdalecc.edu
Published: Mon`Other
Published Other: six times a semester
Personnel: Debbie Mura (Advisor)

CAMDEN COUNTY COLLEGE

Street address 1: PO Box 200
Street address city: Blackwood
Street address state: NJ
Zip/Postal code: 08012-0200
Country: USA
Mailing address: PO Box 200
Mailing city: Blackwood
Mailing state: NJ
Mailing zip: 08012-0200
General Phone: (856) 227-7200

CENTENARY COLLEGE

Street address 1: 400 Jefferson St
Street address city: Hackettstown
Street address state: NJ
Zip/Postal code: 07840-2184
Country: USA
Mailing address: 400 Jefferson St Ste 1
Mailing city: Hackettstown
Mailing state: NJ
Mailing zip: 07840-2184
General Phone: (908) 852-1400 x2243
Advertising Phone: (908) 852-1400x2243
General/National Adv. E-mail: levd@centenarycollege.edu
Display Adv. E-mail: levd@centenarycollege.edu
Primary Website: www.centenarycollege.edu
Year Established: 1991
Published: Mthly
Avg Free Circ: 1600
Personnel: Deborah Lev (Advisor)

COLLEGE OF ST. ELIZABETH

Street address 1: 2 Convent Rd
Street address city: Morristown
Street address state: NJ
Zip/Postal code: 07960-6923
Country: USA
Mailing address: 2 Convent Rd
Mailing city: Morristown
Mailing state: NJ
Mailing zip: 07960-6989
General Phone: (973) 290-4242
Personnel: Kristene Both (Ed. in Chief)

COUNTY COLLEGE OF MORRIS

Street address 1: 214 Center Grove Rd
Street address 2: Rm Scc
Street address city: Randolph
Street address state: NJ
Zip/Postal code: 07869-2007
Country: USA
Mailing address: 214 Center Grove Rd Rm Scc
Mailing city: Randolph
Mailing state: NJ
Mailing zip: 07869-2007
General Phone: (973) 328-5224
Personnel: Matthew Ayres (Advisor); Frank Blaha (Ed. in Chief)

DREW UNIV.

Street address 1: PO Box 802
Street address city: Madison

Street address state: NJ
Zip/Postal code: 07940-0802
Country: USA
Mailing address: PO Box 802
Mailing city: Madison
Mailing state: NJ
Mailing zip: 07940-0802
General Phone: (973) 408-4207
General Fax: (973) 408-3887
General/National Adv. E-mail: acorn@drew.edu
Personnel: David A.M. Wilensky (Ed. in Chief); Sheryl Mccabe (Mng. Ed.)

ESSEX COUNTY COLLEGE

Street address 1: 303 University Ave
Street address city: Newark
Street address state: NJ
Zip/Postal code: 07102-1719
Country: USA
Mailing address: 303 University Ave
Mailing city: Newark
Mailing state: NJ
Mailing zip: 07102-1798
Personnel: Kyle Miller (Ed.); Nessie Hill (Advisor)

FAIRLEIGH DICKINSON UNIV.

Street address 1: 1000 River Rd
Street address city: Teaneck
Street address state: NJ
Zip/Postal code: 07666-1914
Country: USA
Mailing address: 1000 River Rd
Mailing city: Teaneck
Mailing state: NJ
Mailing zip: 07666-1914
General Phone: (201) 692-2046
General Fax: (201) 692-2376
General/National Adv. E-mail: equinoxfdu@gmail.com
Primary Website: https://fduequinox.wordpress.com/
Published: Thur
Personnel: Bruno Battistoli (Advisor); Sarah Latson (Faculty Adviser); Kayla Hastrup (Editor-in-Chief); Miruna Seitan (Mng. Ed.); Lorena Chouza (Exec. Ed.); Melissa Hartz (News Editor)

GLOUCESTER COUNTY COLLEGE

Street address 1: 1400 Tanyard Rd
Street address city: Sewell
Street address state: NJ
Zip/Postal code: 08080-4222
Country: USA
Mailing address: 1400 Tanyard Rd
Mailing city: Sewell
Mailing state: NJ
Mailing zip: 08080-4249
General Phone: (856) 468-5000
Personnel: Brooke Hoffman (Advisor); Keesha Patterson (Advisor)

KEAN UNIV.

Street address 1: 1000 Morris Ave
Street address city: Union
Street address state: NJ
Zip/Postal code: 07083-7133
Country: USA
Mailing address: 1000 Morris Ave Ste 1
Mailing city: Union
Mailing state: NJ
Mailing zip: 07083-7131
General Phone: (908) 737-0468
General Fax: (908) 737-0465
General/National Adv. E-mail: thetower@kean.edu
Personnel: Pat Winters Lauro (Faculty Advisor); Eileen Ruf (Bus. Mgr.); Jillian Johnson (Ed. in Chief); Emannuel Urenea (Ed.)

MIDDLESEX COUNTY COLLEGE

Street address 1: 2600 Woodbridge Ave
Street address city: Edison
Street address state: NJ
Zip/Postal code: 08837-3604
Country: USA
Mailing address: 2600 Woodbridge Ave
Mailing city: Edison
Mailing state: NJ
Mailing zip: 08837-3675
General Phone: (732) 548-6000
Personnel: Melissa Edwards (Ed.)

MONMOUTH UNIVERSITY

Street address 1: 400 Cedar Ave
Street address 2: Rm 260
Street address city: West Long Branch
Street address state: NJ
Zip/Postal code: 07764-1804
Country: USA
Mailing address: 400 Cedar Ave Rm 260
Mailing city: West Long Branch
Mailing state: NJ
Mailing zip: 07764-1804
General Phone: (732) 571-3481
Advertising Phone: (732) 263-5151
General/National Adv. E-mail: outlook@monmouth.edu
Display Adv. E-mail: outlookads@monmouth.edu
Primary Website: outlook.monmouth.edu
Year Established: 1933
Published: Wed
Avg Free Circ: 5000
Personnel: John Morano (Professor of Journalism); Sandra Brown (Office Coordinator)

MONTCLAIR STATE UNIV.

Street address 1: Student Ctr. Annex Room 113
Street address 2: Room 113
Street address city: Upper Montclair
Street address state: NJ
Zip/Postal code: 7043
Country: USA
General Phone: (973) 655-5230
General Fax: (973) 655-7804
General/National Adv. E-mail: montclarioneditor@gmail.com
Personnel: Kristen Bryfogle (Ed. in Chief); Kulsoom Rizvi (News Editor); Nelson DePasquale (Sports Editor)

NEW JERSEY CITY UNIV.

Street address 1: 2039 Kennedy Blvd, Gsub 305
Street address city: Jersey City
Street address state: NJ
Zip/Postal code: 7305
Country: USA
Mailing address: 2039 Kennedy Blvd., GSUB 305
Mailing city: Jersey City
Mailing state: NJ
Mailing zip: 07305-1596
Personnel: James Broderick (Advisor); Erica Molina (Ed.); Marlen Gonzalez (Mng. Ed.)

NEW JERSEY INST. OF TECHNOLOGY

Street address 1: 150 Bleeker St
Street address city: Newark
Street address state: NJ
Zip/Postal code: 07103-3902
Country: USA
Mailing address: 150 Bleeker St
Mailing city: Newark
Mailing state: NJ
Mailing zip: 07103-3902
General Phone: (973) 596-5416
General Fax: (973) 596-3613
General/National Adv. E-mail: news@njitvector.com
Display Adv. E-mail: ads@njitvector.com
Personnel: Melissa Silderstang (Exec. Ed.)

OCEAN COUNTY COLLEGE

Street address 1: 9 East Old Whaling Lane
Street address city: Long Beach
Street address state: NJ
Zip/Postal code: 08008-2930
County: Ocean
Country: United States
Mailing address: 9 East Old Whaling Lane
Mailing city: Long Beach
Mailing state: NJ
Mailing zip: 08008-2930
General Phone: 6094920138
General Fax: 6094920138
Advertising Phone: 6094920138
General/National Adv. E-mail: kbosley@mac.com
Display Adv. E-mail: kbosley@mac.com
Classified Adv. e-mail: kbosley@mac.com
Editorial e-mail: kbosley@mac.com
Year Established: 1965
Published: Thur
Published Other: Irregularly
Personnel: Karen Bosley

PRINCETON UNIVERSITY

Street address 1: PO Box 469
Street address city: Princeton
Street address state: NJ
Zip/Postal code: 08542-0469
Country: USA
Mailing address: PO Box 469
Mailing city: Princeton
Mailing state: NJ
Mailing zip: 08542-0469
General Phone: (609) 258-3632
General/National Adv. E-mail: eic@dailyprincetonian.com
Display Adv. E-mail: bm@dailyprincetonian.com
Editorial e-mail: eic@dailyprincetonian.com
Primary Website: www.dailyprincetonian.com
Year Established: 1876
Published: Mon`Tues`Wed`Thur`Fri
Personnel: Marcelo Rochabrun (Editor in Chief)

RICHARD STOCKTON COLLEGE

Street address 1: 101 Vera King Farris Dr
Street address city: Galloway
Street address state: NJ
Zip/Postal code: 08205-9441
Country: USA
Mailing address: 101 Vera King Farris Dr
Mailing city: Galloway
Mailing state: NJ
Mailing zip: 08205-9441
General Phone: (609) 652-4296
Personnel: Craig Stambaugh (Advisor); Lina Wayman (Ed.)

ROWAN UNIV.

Street address 1: 201 Mullica Hill Rd
Street address city: Glassboro
Street address state: NJ
Zip/Postal code: 08028-1700
Country: USA
Mailing address: 201 Mullica Hill Rd
Mailing city: Glassboro
Mailing state: NJ
Mailing zip: 08028-1702
General Phone: (856) 256-4713
General Fax: (856) 256-4929
General/National Adv. E-mail: communication@rowan.edu
Personnel: Don Bagin (Prof.); Kathryn Quigley (Advisor); R. Michael Donovan (Prof.); Anthony Fulginiti (Prof.); Richard Grupenhoff (Prof.); Kenneth Kaleta (Prof.); Janice Rowan (Prof.); Edward Streb (Prof.); Julia Chang (Assoc. Prof.); Cynthia Corison (Assoc. Prof.); Edgar Eckhardt (Assoc. Prof.); Suzanne Fitzgerald (Assoc. Prof.); Carl Hausman (Assoc. Prof.); Martin Itzkowitz (Assoc. Prof.); Frances Johnson (Assoc. Prof.); Diane Penrod (Assoc. Prof.); Donald Stoll (Assoc. Prof.); Sanford Tweedie (Assoc. Prof.); Kenneth Albone (Asst. Prof.); Lorin Arnold (Asst. Prof.)

RUTGERS UNIV.

Street address 1: 326 Penn St
Street address city: Camden
Street address state: NJ
Zip/Postal code: 08102-1410
Country: USA
Mailing address: 326 Penn St
Mailing city: Camden
Mailing state: NJ
Mailing zip: 08102-1412
General Phone: (856) 225-6304
General Fax: (856) 225-6579
General/National Adv. E-mail: gleaner@camden.rutgers.edu
Personnel: Joe Capuzzo (Advisor)

RUTGERS UNIV.

Street address 1: 126 College Ave
Street address 2: Ste 431
Street address city: New Brunswick
Street address state: NJ
Zip/Postal code: 08901-1166
Country: USA
Mailing address: 126 College Ave Ste 431
Mailing city: New Brunswick
Mailing state: NJ
Mailing zip: 08901-1166
General Phone: (732) 932-7051
General Fax: (732) 932-0079
General/National Adv. E-mail: news@dailytargum.com
Personnel: John Clyde (Ed. in Cheif)

RUTGERS UNIV.

Street address 1: 350 M L King Blvd
Street address 2: Paul Robeson Campus Ctr., Rm. 237
Street address city: Newark
Street address state: NJ
Zip/Postal code: 07102-1801
Country: USA
Mailing address: 350 Martin Luther King Jr Blvd
Mailing city: Newark
Mailing state: NJ
Mailing zip: 07102-1801
General Phone: (973) 353-5023
General Fax: (973) 353-1333
General/National Adv. E-mail: observercopy@gmail.com
Personnel: Dina Sayedahmed (Executive Editor)

RUTGERS UNIV. SCHOOL OF ENVIRONMENTAL & BIOLOGICAL SCIENCES

Street address 1: 88 Lipman Dr
Street address city: New Brunswick
Street address state: NJ
Zip/Postal code: 08901-8525
Country: USA
Mailing address: 88 Lipman Dr
Mailing city: New Brunswick
Mailing state: NJ
Mailing zip: 08901-8525
Personnel: Kathryn E. Barry (Ed. in Chief)

SETON HALL UNIVERSITY

Street address 1: 400 S Orange Ave, Student Ctr, Rm 224
Street address city: South Orange
Street address state: NJ
Zip/Postal code: 7079
Country: USA
Mailing address: 400 S. Orange Ave., Student Ctr., Rm. 224
Mailing city: South Orange
Mailing state: NJ
Mailing zip: 07079
General Phone: (732) 925-7647
General Fax: (973) 761-7943
General/National Adv. E-mail: Thesetonian@gmail.com
Primary Website: www.thesetonian.com
Year Established: 1924
Published: Thur
Personnel: Amy Nyberg (Advisor); Brian Wisowaty (Mng. Ed.)

ST. PETERS COLLEGE

Street address 1: 2641 John F Kennedy Blvd
Street address city: Jersey City
Street address state: NJ
Zip/Postal code: 07306-5943
Country: USA
Mailing address: 2641 John F Kennedy Blvd
Mailing city: Jersey City
Mailing state: NJ
Mailing zip: 07306-5997
General Phone: (201) 938-1254
General Fax: (201) 938-1254
Advertising Phone: (201) 761-7378
General/National Adv. E-mail: pauwwow@hotmail.com
Display Adv. E-mail: ads@pauwwow.com
Personnel: Paul Almonte (Advisor); Frank DeMichele (Ed. in Chief); Rozen Pradhan (Mng. Ed.)

STEVENS INSTITUTE OF TECHNOLOGY

Street address 1: Stevens Institute of Technology
Street address 2: Castle Point on Hudson
Street address city: Hoboken
Street address state: NJ
Zip/Postal code: 7030
Country: USA
General Phone: (201) 216-3404

General/National Adv. E-mail: stute@stevens.edu
Display Adv. E-mail: stuteads@stevens.edu
Editorial e-mail: eboard@thestute.com
Primary Website: www.thestute.com
Year Established: 1904
Published: Fri
Personnel: Joseph Brosnan (Ed.)

THE COLLEGE OF NEW JERSEY

Street address 1: PO Box 7718
Street address city: Ewing
Street address state: NJ
Zip/Postal code: 08628-0718
Country: USA
Mailing address: PO Box 7718
Mailing city: Ewing
Mailing state: NJ
Mailing zip: 08628-0718
General Phone: (609) 771-2499
General Fax: (609) 771-3433
Advertising Phone: (609) 771-3433
Editorial Phone: (609) 771-2424
General/National Adv. E-mail: signal@tcnj.edu
Display Adv. E-mail: signalad@tcnj.edu
Primary Website: tcnjsignal.net
Year Established: 1885
Published: Wed
Personnel: Emilie Lounsberry (Advisor)

THE RIDER NEWS / RIDER UNIVERSITY

Street address 1: 2083 Lawrenceville Rd
Street address city: Lawrenceville
Street address state: NJ
Zip/Postal code: 08648-3099
Country: USA
Mailing address: 2083 Lawrenceville Rd
Mailing city: Lawrenceville
Mailing state: NJ
Mailing zip: 08648-3099
General Phone: (609) 896-5256
General Fax: (609) 895-5696
General/National Adv. E-mail: ridernews@rider.edu
Primary Website: www.theridernews.com
Year Established: 1930
Personnel: Dianne Garyantes (Co-Adviser)

UNION COUNTY COLLEGE

Street address 1: 1033 Springfield Ave
Street address city: Cranford
Street address state: NJ
Zip/Postal code: 07016-1528
Country: USA
Mailing address: 1033 Springfield Ave
Mailing city: Cranford
Mailing state: NJ
Mailing zip: 07016-1598
Personnel: John R. Farrell (Vice Pres.)

WILLIAM PATERSON UNIV.

Street address 1: 300 Pompton Rd
Street address 2: # SC329A
Street address city: Wayne
Street address state: NJ
Zip/Postal code: 07470-2103
Country: USA
Mailing address: 300 Pompton Rd # SC329A
Mailing city: Wayne
Mailing state: NJ
Mailing zip: 07470-2103
General Phone: (973) 720-3265
General Fax: (973) 720-2093
General/National Adv. E-mail: wpubeacon@hotmail.com
Personnel: Jeff Wakemen (Advisor); Tim Kauffeld (Ed. in Chief); Robin Mulder (News Ed.)

NEW MEXICO

EASTERN NEW MEXICO UNIV.

Street address 1: 1500 S Avenue K
Street address 2: Department of Communication
Street address city: Portales
Street address state: NM
Zip/Postal code: 88130-7400
Country: USA
Mailing address: Station 27
Mailing city: Portales
Mailing state: NM
Mailing zip: 88130-7400
General Phone: (575) 562-2130
General Fax: (575) 562-2847
General/National Adv. E-mail: janet.birkey@enmu.edu
Primary Website: https://www.enmuthechaseonline.com/
Published: Mon
Published Other: Hard copy published every other week; online in between
Personnel: Janet Birkey (Advisor)

NEW MEXICO DAILY LOBO

Street address 1: 1 University of New Mexico
Street address 2: MS 3
Street address city: Albuquerque
Street address state: NM
Zip/Postal code: 87131-0001
County: Bernalillo
Country: USA
Mailing address: 1 University of New Mexico MS 3
Mailing city: Albuquerque
Mailing state: NM
Mailing zip: 87131-0001
General Phone: (505) 277-7527
General Fax: (505) 277-6228
Advertising Phone: (505) 277-5656
Advertising Fax: (505) 277-7530
Editorial Phone: (505) 277-5656
Editorial Fax: (505) 277-7530
General/National Adv. E-mail: advertising@dailylobo.com
Display Adv. E-mail: advertising@dailylobo.com
Classified Adv. e-mail: classifieds@dailylobo.com
Editorial e-mail: news@dailylobo.com
Primary Website: www.dailylobo.com
Year Established: 1895
Published: Mon`Tues`Wed`Thur`Fri`Sat
Personnel: Jyllian Roach (Ed. in Chief); JR Oppenheim (Managing Ed.); Jonathan Baca (News Ed.); Daniel Montano (News Ed.); Sergio Jimenez (Photo Ed.); William Aranda (Asst. Photo Ed.); Stephen Montoya (Culture Ed.); Tomas Lujan (Asst. Culture Ed.); Thomas Romero-Salas (Sports Ed.); Jonathan Gamboa (Design Dir.); Sarah Lynas (Design Dir.); Craig Dubyk (Copy Chief); Leanne Lucero (Copy Ed.); Zach Pavlik (Ad. Mgr.); Sammy Chumpolpakdee (Sales Mgr.); Hannah Dowdy-Sue (Class. Mgr.); David Lynch (News Ed.); Nick Fojud (Photo Ed.); Veronica Munoz (Web Ed.)

NEW MEXICO INST. OF MINING & TECHNOLOGY

Street address 1: 801 Leroy Pl
Street address city: Socorro
Street address state: NM
Zip/Postal code: 87801-4681
Country: USA
Mailing address: 801 Leroy Pl
Mailing city: Socorro
Mailing state: NM
Mailing zip: 87801-4750
General Phone: (575) 835-5525
Personnel: Roger Renteria (Ed. in Chief); Rachel Armstrong (Ed.)

NEW MEXICO STATE UNIV.

Street address 1: PO Box 30001
Street address city: Las Cruces
Street address state: NM
Zip/Postal code: 88003-8001
Country: USA
Mailing address: PO Box 30001
Mailing city: Las Cruces
Mailing state: NM
Mailing zip: 88003-8001
General Phone: (575) 646-6397
General Fax: (575) 646-5557
General/National Adv. E-mail: roundup@nmsu.edu
Personnel: Jeff Hand (Advisor); Jon Blazak (Ed. in Chief)

UNIV. OF NEW MEXICO

Street address 1: 1 University of New Mexico
Street address 2: MS 3
Street address city: Albuquerque
Street address state: NM
Zip/Postal code: 87131-0001
Country: USA
Mailing address: 1 University of New Mexico MS 3
Mailing city: Albuquerque
Mailing state: NM
Mailing zip: 87131-0001
General Phone: (505) 277-5656
General Fax: (505) 277-7530
Advertising Phone: (505) 277-5656
Advertising Fax: (505) 277-7530
Editorial Phone: (505) 277-7527
General/National Adv. E-mail: advertising@dailylobo.com
Display Adv. E-mail: advertising@dailylobo.com
Editorial e-mail: editorinchief@dailylobo.com
Primary Website: www.dailylobo.com
Year Established: 1895
Published: Mon`Tues`Wed`Thur`Fri
Avg Free Circ: 9000
Personnel: Jim Fisher (Bus. Mgr.)

NEVADA

CMTY. COLLEGE OF SOUTHERN NEVADA

Street address 1: 3200 E Cheyenne Ave
Street address 2: # J2A
Street address city: North Las Vegas
Street address state: NV
Zip/Postal code: 89030-4228
Country: USA
Mailing address: 3200 E Cheyenne Ave # J2A
Mailing city: North Las Vegas
Mailing state: NV
Mailing zip: 89030-4228
General Phone: (702) 651-4339
Personnel: Arnold Vell (Advisor)

UNIV. OF NEVADA

Street address 1: the Nevada Sagebrush, Mail Stop 058
Street address city: Reno
Street address state: NV
Zip/Postal code: 89557-0001
Country: USA
Mailing address: Mill Stop 58
Mailing city: Reno
Mailing state: NV
Mailing zip: 89557-0001
General Phone: (775) 784-4033
General Fax: (775) 784-1952
Editorial e-mail: editor@nevadasagebrush.com
Personnel: Amy Koeckes (Advisor); Jessica Fryman (Ed. in Chief)

UNIVERSITY OF NEVADA, LAS VEGAS

Street address 1: 4505 S Maryland Pkwy
Street address city: Las Vegas
Street address state: NV
Zip/Postal code: 89154-9900
Country: USA
Mailing address: PO Box 2011
Mailing city: Las Vegas
Mailing state: NV
Mailing zip: 89125-2011
Advertising Phone: (702) 895-3878
General/National Adv. E-mail: chief.freepress@unlv.edu
Display Adv. E-mail: marketing.freepress@unlv.edu
Editorial e-mail: managing.freepress@unlv.edu
Primary Website: www.unlvfreepress.com
Year Established: 1955
Published: Mon
Avg Free Circ: 3800
Personnel: Bianca Cseke (Editor-in-Chief); Kathy Schreiber (Business Manager); Rick Velotta (Adviser); Blaze Lovell (Managing Editor); Nicole Gallego (Director of Marketing & Sales)

UNIVERSITY OF NEVADA, LAS VEGAS

Street address 1: 4505 S Maryland Pkwy
Street address 2: # 2011
Street address city: Las Vegas
Street address state: NV
Zip/Postal code: 89154-9900
Country: USA
Mailing address: 4505 S Maryland Pkwy
Mailing city: Las Vegas
Mailing state: NV
Mailing zip: 89154-9900
General Phone: (702) 895-2028
General Fax: (702) 895-1515
Editorial Fax: Free
General/National Adv. E-mail: chief.freepress@unlv.edu
Display Adv. E-mail: marketing.freepress@unlv.edu
Editorial e-mail: managing.freepress@unlv.edu
Primary Website: www.unlvfreepress.com
Year Established: 1955
Published: Mon
Avg Free Circ: 3800
Personnel: Rick Velotta (Adviser); Bianca Cseke (Editor-in-Chief); Blaze Lovell (Managing Editor); Nicole Gallego (Director of Marketing & Sales)

NEW YORK

ALBANY COLLEGE OF PHARMACY

Street address 1: 106 New Scotland Ave
Street address city: Albany
Street address state: NY
Zip/Postal code: 12208-3425
Country: USA
Mailing address: 106 New Scotland Ave
Mailing city: Albany
Mailing state: NY
Mailing zip: 12208-3492
Personnel: Jennie O'Rourke (Ed.)

ALFRED UNIV.

Street address 1: Powell Campus Ctr
Street address city: Alfred
Street address state: NY
Country: USA
Mailing address: Powell Campus Ctr.
Mailing city: Alfred
Mailing state: NY
Mailing zip: 14802
General Phone: (607) 871-2192
General Fax: (607) 871-3797
General/National Adv. E-mail: fiatlux@alfred.edu
Personnel: Robyn Goodman (Advisor); Nadine Titus (Adv. Mgr.); Thomas Fleming (Ed. in Chief)

BARD COLLEGE

Street address 1: PO Box 5000
Street address city: Annandale
Street address state: NY
Zip/Postal code: 12504-5000
Country: USA
Mailing address: PO Box 5000
Mailing city: Annandale
Mailing state: NY
Mailing zip: 12504-5000
General Phone: (845) 758-7131
General Fax: (845) 758-4294
General/National Adv. E-mail: observer@bard.edu
Personnel: Becca Rom Frank (Ed. in Chief); Lilian Robinson (Ed.); Christine Gehringer (Mng. Ed.)

BARNARD COLLEGE

Street address 1: 3009 Broadway
Street address city: New York
Street address state: NY
Zip/Postal code: 10027-6909
Country: USA
Mailing address: 3009 Broadway Frnt 1
Mailing city: New York
Mailing state: NY
Mailing zip: 10027-6598
General Phone: (212) 854-5262
General Fax: (212) 854-6220
General/National Adv. E-mail: bulletinedboard@gmail.com; backcover@barnardbulletin.com

Personnel: Iffat Kabeer (Adv. Mgr.); Alison Hodgson (Ed. Emer.); Meagan McElroy (Mng. Ed.)

BARUCH COLLEGE/CUNY

Street address 1: 1 Bernard Baruch Way
Street address 2: Ste 3-290
Street address city: New York
Street address state: NY
Zip/Postal code: 10010-5585
Country: USA
Mailing address: 1 Bernard Baruch Way Ste 3-290
Mailing city: New York
Mailing state: NY
Mailing zip: 10010-5585
General Phone: (646) 312-4712
Personnel: Carl Aylman (Dir., Student Lant); Jhaneel Lockhart (Ed. in Chief)

BOROUGH OF MANHATTAN CMTY. COLLEGE

Street address 1: 199 Chambers St
Street address 2: Rm S-207
Street address city: New York
Street address state: NY
Zip/Postal code: 10007-1044
Country: USA
Mailing address: 199 Chambers St Rm S-207
Mailing city: New York
Mailing state: NY
Mailing zip: 10007-1044
Personnel: Dr. Juliet Emanuel (Advisor)

BRONX CMTY. COLLEGE

Street address 1: W 181st St & University Ave
Street address city: Bronx
Street address state: NY
Zip/Postal code: 10453
Country: USA
Mailing address: W. 181st St. & University Ave.
Mailing city: Bronx
Mailing state: NY
Mailing zip: 10453-2895
General Phone: (718) 289-5445
General Fax: (718) 289-6324
General/National Adv. E-mail: communicator@bcc.cuny.edu
Personnel: Andrew Rowan (Advisor)

BROOME CMTY. COLLEGE

Street address 1: PO Box 1017
Street address city: Binghamton
Street address state: NY
Zip/Postal code: 13902-1017
Country: USA
Mailing address: PO Box 1017
Mailing city: Binghamton
Personnel: Bill Frobe (Ed.)

CANISIUS COLLEGE

Street address 1: 2001 Main St
Street address city: Buffalo
Street address state: NY
Zip/Postal code: 14208-1035
Country: USA
Mailing address: 2001 Main St
Mailing city: Buffalo
Mailing state: NY
Mailing zip: 14208-1098
General Phone: (716) 888-2115
Personnel: Barbara Irwin (Professor of Communications); Eric Koehler (Ed.); Jennifer Gorczynski (Ed.); Marisa Loffredo (News Ed.)

CARDOZO SCHOOL OF LAW/ YESHIVA

Street address 1: 55 5th Ave
Street address 2: Ste 119
Street address city: New York
Street address state: NY
Zip/Postal code: 10003-4301
Country: USA
Mailing address: 55 5th Ave Fl 6
Mailing city: New York
Mailing state: NY
Mailing zip: 10003-4301
General Phone: (212) 790-0283
Personnel: Heela Justin (Ed.)

CAYUGA COMMUNITY COLLEGE

Street address 1: 197 Franklin St
Street address city: Auburn
Street address state: NY
Zip/Postal code: 13021-3011
Country: USA
Mailing address: 197 Franklin St
Mailing city: Auburn
Mailing state: NY
Mailing zip: 13021-3011
General Phone: (315) 255-1743
General Fax: (315) 255-2117
Year Established: 1954
Published Other: ON ANNOUNCED SCHEDULE
Avg Free Circ: 1000
Personnel: Mary Gelling Merrit (Advisor)

CITY COLLEGE OF NEW YORK

Street address 1: Rm 1-119, North Academic Center Bldg, 160 Convent Ave
Street address city: New York
Street address state: NY
Zip/Postal code: 10031
Country: USA
Mailing address: Rm. 1-119, North Academic Center Bldg., 160 Convent Ave.
Mailing city: New York
Mailing state: NY
Mailing zip: 10031
General Phone: (212) 650-8177
General Fax: (212) 650-8197
General/National Adv. E-mail: ccnycampus@gmail.com
Personnel: Linda Villarosa (Advisor); Tania Bhuiyan (Bus. Mgr.)

CLARKSON UNIV.

Street address 1: PO Box 8710
Street address city: Potsdam
Street address state: NY
Zip/Postal code: 13699-0001
Country: USA
Mailing address: PO Box 8710
Mailing city: Potsdam
Mailing state: NY
Mailing zip: 13699-0001
General Phone: (315) 265-9050
General Fax: (315) 268-7661
General/National Adv. E-mail: integrat@clarkson.edu
Personnel: Mary Konecnik (Ed. in Chief); Robert Trerice (Mng. Ed.)

COLGATE UNIV.

Street address 1: 13 Oak Dr
Street address 2: Student Union
Street address city: Hamilton
Street address state: NY
Zip/Postal code: 13346-1338
Country: USA
Mailing address: Student Union
Mailing city: Hamilton
Mailing state: NY
Mailing zip: 13346
General Phone: (315) 228-7744
General Fax: (315) 228-6839
General/National Adv. E-mail: maroonnews@colgate.edu
Display Adv. E-mail: ads.maroonnews@gmail.com
Editorial e-mail: colgatemaroonnews@gmail.com
Primary Website: thecolgatemaroonnews.com
Year Established: 1868
Published: Thur
Avg Free Circ: 1600
Personnel: Matthew Knowles (Ed.); Luke Currim (Ed.); Amanda Golden (Exec. Ed.)

COLLEGE OF MT. ST. VINCENT

Street address 1: 6301 Riverdale Ave
Street address city: Bronx
Street address state: NY
Zip/Postal code: 10471-1046
Country: USA
Mailing address: The Mount Times
Mailing city: Bronx
Mailing state: NY
Mailing zip: 10471-1093
General Phone: (718) 405-3471
Editorial Phone: (516) 474-5563
General/National Adv. E-mail: mountimes@mountsaintvincent.edu
Editorial e-mail: nquaranto.student@mountsaintvincent.edu
Year Established: 1980
Published: Bi-Mthly
Personnel: Nicole Quaranto (EiC); Micheal Stephens-Emerson (Co-EIC)

COLLEGE OF NEW ROCHELLE

Street address 1: 29 Castle Pl
Street address city: New Rochelle
Street address state: NY
Zip/Postal code: 10805-2330
Country: USA
Mailing address: 29 Castle Pl Ste 1
Mailing city: New Rochelle
Mailing state: NY
Mailing zip: 10805-2339
General Phone: (914) 654-5207
Personnel: Elizabeth Brinkman (Advisor)

COLLEGE OF ST. ROSE

Street address 1: 432 Western Ave
Street address city: Albany
Street address state: NY
Zip/Postal code: 12203-1400
Country: USA
Mailing address: 432 Western Ave
Mailing city: Albany
Mailing state: NY
Mailing zip: 12203-1490
General Phone: (518) 454-5151
General Fax: (518) 454-2001
General/National Adv. E-mail: chronicle@strose.edu
Primary Website: www.strosechronicle.com
Published: Tues
Personnel: Cailin Brown (Advisor); Josh Heller (Execu Ed); Jonas Miller (Mng Ed)

COLLEGE OF STATEN ISLAND

Street address 1: 2800 Victory Blvd
Street address city: Staten Island
Street address state: NY
Zip/Postal code: 10314-6609
Country: USA
Mailing address: 2800 Victory Blvd
Mailing city: Staten Island
Mailing state: NY
Mailing zip: 10314-6600
General Phone: (718) 982-3056
Personnel: Philip Masciantonio (Gen. Mgr.)

COLUMBIA UNIV.

Street address 1: 2875 Broadway
Street address 2: Ste 3
Street address city: New York
Street address state: NY
Zip/Postal code: 10025-7847
Country: USA
Mailing address: 2875 Broadway Ste 3
Mailing city: New York
Mailing state: NY
Mailing zip: 10025-7847
General Phone: (212) 854-9550
General Fax: (212) 854-9553
General/National Adv. E-mail: info@columbiaspectator.com; spectator@columbia.edu
Personnel: Akhil Mehta (Pub.); Ben Cotton (Ed. in Chief); Thomas Rhiel (Managing Ed.); Andrew Hitti (Dir., Sales); Oscar (Dir., Fin); Yipeng (Dir.)

COLUMBIA UNIV. BUS. SCHOOL

Street address 1: 3022 Broadway
Street address 2: Rm 242
Street address city: New York
Street address state: NY
Zip/Postal code: 10027-6945
Country: USA
Mailing address: 3022 Broadway Rm 242
Mailing city: New York
Mailing state: NY
Mailing zip: 10027-6945
Personnel: Matt Wong (Bus. Mgr.)

COLUMBIA UNIV. LAW SCHOOL

Street address 1: 435 W 116th St
Street address city: New York
Street address state: NY
Zip/Postal code: 10027-7237
Country: USA
Mailing address: 435 W 116th St
Mailing city: New York
Mailing state: NY
Mailing zip: 10027-7237
General Phone: (212) 854-5833
Personnel: Matthew Dean (Ed.)

COOPER UNION

Street address 1: 30 Cooper Sq
Street address city: New York
Street address state: NY
Zip/Postal code: 10003-7120
Country: USA
Mailing address: 30 Cooper Sq Fl 3
Mailing city: New York
Mailing state: NY
Mailing zip: 10003-7120
General Phone: (212) 353-4133
Personnel: Bill McAllister (ed.)

CORNELL LAW SCHOOL

Street address 1: Myron Taylor Hall
Street address city: Ithaca
Street address state: NY
Zip/Postal code: 14853
Country: USA
Mailing address: Myron Taylor Hall
Mailing city: Ithaca
Personnel: Rick Silverman (Ed.)

CORNELL UNIV. ECONOMICS SCHOOL

Street address 1: Cornell Dept of Economics, Uris Hall, 4th Fl
Street address city: Ithaca
Street address state: NY
Zip/Postal code: 14850
Country: USA
Mailing address: Cornell Dept. of Economics, Uris Hall, 4th Fl.
Mailing city: Ithaca
Mailing state: NY
Mailing zip: 14850
Personnel: Rabia Muqaddam (Ed. in Chief)

CORNING CMTY. COLLEGE

Street address 1: 1 Academic Dr
Street address city: Corning
Street address state: NY
Zip/Postal code: 14830-3297
Country: USA
Mailing address: 1 Academic Dr
Mailing city: Corning
Mailing state: NY
Mailing zip: 14830-3299
General Phone: (607) 962-9339
Personnel: Paul McNaney (Advisor)

CULINARY INSTITUTE OF AMERICA

Street address 1: 1946 Campus Dr
Street address city: Hyde Park
Street address state: NY
Zip/Postal code: 12538-1430
Country: USA
Mailing address: 1946 Campus Dr
Mailing city: Hyde Park
Mailing state: NY
Mailing zip: 12538-1499
General Phone: (845) 452-1412
General Fax: (845) 451-1093
General/National Adv. E-mail: lapapillote@culinary.edu
Primary Website: www.ciachef.edu
Year Established: 1979
Published: Fri`Mthly

Personnel: David Whalen (Advisor)

CUNY SCHOOL OF LAW

Street address 1: 2 Court Sq
Street address city: Long Island City
Street address state: NY
Zip/Postal code: 11101-4356
Country: USA
Mailing address: 2 Court Sq
Mailing city: Long Island City
Mailing state: NY

CUNY SCHOOLS

Street address 1: 250 Bedford Park Blvd W
Street address city: Bronx
Street address state: NY
Zip/Postal code: 10468-1527
Country: USA
Mailing address: 250 Bedford Park Blvd W
Mailing city: Bronx
Mailing state: NY
Mailing zip: 10468-1527
General Phone: (718) 960-4966
Personnel: Michael Sullivan (Advisor)

CUNY/BROOKLYN COLLEGE

Street address 1: 2900 Bedford Ave
Street address city: Brooklyn
Street address state: NY
Zip/Postal code: 11210-2850
Country: USA
Mailing address: 2900 Bedford Ave
Mailing city: Brooklyn
Mailing state: NY
Mailing zip: 11210-2850
General Phone: (718) 951-5000
General Fax: (718) 434-0875
Editorial Phone: (516) 557-5714
General/National Adv. E-mail: Dylc23@gmail.com
Display Adv. E-mail: kingsman.buisness@
Editorial e-mail: Dylc23@gmail.com
Primary Website: http://kingsmanbc.com
Published: Tues
Personnel: Paul Moses (Advisor)

DOWLING COLLEGE

Street address 1: 150 Idle Hour Blvd
Street address city: Oakdale
Street address state: NY
Zip/Postal code: 11769-1906
Country: USA
Mailing address: 150 Idle Hour Blvd
Mailing city: Oakdale
Mailing state: NY
Mailing zip: 11769-1999
General Phone: (631) 244-3000
Personnel: Laura Pope Robbins (Advisor); Derek Stevens (Ed.)

DUTCHESS CMTY. COLLEGE

Street address 1: 53 Pendell Rd
Street address city: Poughkeepsie
Street address state: NY
Zip/Postal code: 12601-1512
Country: USA
Mailing address: 53 Pendell Rd
Mailing city: Poughkeepsie
Mailing state: NY
Mailing zip: 12601-1595
General Phone: (845) 431-8000
General Fax: (845) 431-8989
General/National Adv. E-mail: communityrelations@sunydutchess.edu; Helpdesk@sunydutchess.edu
Personnel: Kevin Lang (Advisor)

ELMIRA COLLEGE

Street address 1: 1 Park Pl
Street address city: Elmira
Street address state: NY
Zip/Postal code: 14901-2085
Country: USA
Mailing address: 1 Park Pl
Mailing city: Elmira
Mailing state: NY
Mailing zip: 14901-2099
General Phone: (607) 735-1800
Advertising Phone: (607) 735-1758
General/National Adv. E-mail: octagon@elmira.edu; admissions@elmira.edu
Personnel: David Williams (Advisor); Jolene Carr (Ed.)

FASHION INST. OF TECHNOLOGY

Street address 1: 227 W 27th St
Street address 2: Ste A727
Street address city: New York
Street address state: NY
Zip/Postal code: 10001-5902
Country: USA
Mailing address: 227 W 27th St Ste A727
Mailing city: New York
Mailing state: NY
Mailing zip: 10001-5902
General Phone: (212) 217-7999
General Fax: (212) 217-7144
General/National Adv. E-mail: w27newspaper@gmail.com
Personnel: Richard Baleschrino (Advisor)

FORDHAM UNIV.

Street address 1: 441 E Fordham Rd, Sta 37, Box B
Street address city: Bronx
Street address state: NY
Zip/Postal code: 10458
Country: USA
Mailing address: 441 E. Fordham Rd., Sta. 37, Box B
Mailing city: Bronx
Mailing state: NY
Mailing zip: 10458
General Phone: (718) 817-4379
General Fax: (718) 817-4319
General/National Adv. E-mail: theram@fordham.edu
Personnel: Beth Knobel (Faculty Advisor); Amanda Fiscina (Ed. in Chief); Abigail Forget (Mng. Ed.)

FORDHAM UNIV. LINCOLN CENTER

Street address 1: 140 W 62nd St
Street address 2: Rm G-32
Street address city: New York
Street address state: NY
Zip/Postal code: 10023-7407
Country: USA
Mailing address: 140 W. 62nd St., Rm. G-32
Mailing city: New York
Mailing state: NY
Mailing zip: 10023-7414
General Phone: (212) 636-6280
General Fax: (212) 636-7047
General/National Adv. E-mail: fordhamobserver@gmail.com
Display Adv. E-mail: fordhamobserveradvertising@gmail.com
Primary Website: www.fordhamobserver.com
Published: Other
Personnel: Elizabeth Stone (Advisor); Ashley WennersHerron (Ed. in Chief)

HAMILTON COLLEGE

Street address 1: 198 College Hill Rd
Street address city: Clinton
Street address state: NY
Zip/Postal code: 13323-1218
Country: USA
Mailing address: 198 College Hill Rd
Mailing city: Clinton
Mailing state: NY
Mailing zip: 13323-1295
Personnel: Erin W. Hoener (Ed. in Chief)

HARTWICK COLLEGE

Street address 1: PO Box 250
Street address city: Oneonta
Street address state: NY
Zip/Postal code: 13820-0250
Country: USA
Mailing address: c/o Daily Star, PO Box 250
Mailing city: Oneonta
Mailing state: NY
Mailing zip: 13820
General Phone: (607) 432-1000
Personnel: Bill Reeves (Advisor); Danielle Peloquin (Ed.)

HILBERT COLLEGE

Street address 1: 5200 S Park Ave
Street address city: Hamburg
Street address state: NY
Zip/Postal code: 14075-1519
Country: USA
Mailing address: 5200 S Park Ave
Mailing city: Hamburg
Mailing state: NY
Mailing zip: 14075-1597
General Phone: (716) 649-7900
General Fax: (716) 649-0702
General/National Adv. E-mail: info@hilbert.edu
Primary Website: www.hilbert.edu
Published Other: 3 months in fall & spring
Personnel: Charles A. S. Ernst (Advisor)

HOBART & WILLIAM SMITH COLLEGE

Street address 1: 300 Pulteney St
Street address city: Geneva
Street address state: NY
Zip/Postal code: 14456-3304
Country: USA
Mailing address: 300 Pulteney St
Mailing city: Geneva
Mailing state: NY
Mailing zip: 14456-3382
Personnel: Charlie Wilson (Advisor); Belinda Littlefield (Ed.)

HOFSTRA UNIV.

Street address 1: 200 Hofstra Univ, Rm 203 Student Ctr
Street address city: Hempstead
Street address state: NY
Zip/Postal code: 11550
Country: USA
Mailing address: 200 Hofstra Univ., Rm. 203 Student Ctr.
Mailing city: Hempstead
Mailing state: NY
Mailing zip: 11550-1022
General Phone: (516) 463-6965
Primary Website: www.hofstrachronicle.com
Published: Tues
Personnel: Peter Goodman (Advisor)

HOFSTRA UNIVERSITY

Street address 1: 200 Hofstra University, Student Ctr, Room 203
Street address city: Hempstead
Street address state: NY
Zip/Postal code: 48202
Country: USA
Mailing address: 200 Hofstra University, Student Ctr., Room 203
Mailing city: Hempstead
Mailing state: NY
Mailing zip: 11550
General Phone: (516) 463-6921
General/National Adv. E-mail: hofstrachronicle@gmail.com
Display Adv. E-mail: thechronicle.business@gmail.com
Primary Website: www.thehofstrachronicle.com
Year Established: 1935
Published: Thur
Avg Free Circ: 3000
Personnel: Jake Nussbaum (Business Manager)

HOUGHTON COLLEGE

Street address 1: 1 Willard Ave
Street address 2: Cpo 378
Street address city: Houghton
Street address state: NY
Zip/Postal code: 14744-8732
Country: USA
Mailing address: 1 Willard Ave Cpo 378
Mailing city: Houghton
Mailing state: NY
Mailing zip: 14744-8732
General Phone: (585) 567-9500
General Fax: (585) 567-9570
General/National Adv. E-mail: star@houghton.edu
Personnel: Joel Vanderweele (Ed. in Chief)

HUDSON VALLEY CMTY. COLLEGE

Street address 1: 80 Vandenburgh Ave
Street address city: Troy
Street address state: NY
Zip/Postal code: 12180-6037
Country: USA
Mailing address: 80 Vandenburgh Ave
Mailing city: Troy
Mailing state: NY
Mailing zip: 12180-6037
General Phone: (518) 629-7187
General Fax: (518) 629-7496
General/National Adv. E-mail: hudnews@yahoo.com
Personnel: Mat Cantore (Advisor); Nicole Monsees (Mng. Ed.)

HUNTER COLLEGE/CUNY

Street address 1: 695 Park Ave
Street address 2: Rm 211
Street address city: New York
Street address state: NY
Zip/Postal code: 10065-5024
Country: USA
Mailing address: 695 Park Ave Rm 211
Mailing city: New York
Mailing state: NY
Mailing zip: 10065-5024
General Phone: (212) 772-4251
Personnel: Joe Ireland (Ed. in Chief)

IONA COLLEGE

Street address 1: 715 North Ave, Lapenta Student Union, 2nd Fl
Street address city: New Rochelle
Street address state: NY
Zip/Postal code: 10801
Country: USA
Mailing address: 715 North Ave., LaPenta Student Union, 2nd Fl.
Mailing city: New Rochelle
Mailing state: NY
Mailing zip: 10801-1830
General Phone: (914) 633-2370
General/National Adv. E-mail: ionian@iona.edu
Personnel: Hugh Short (Moderator); James Hurley (Ed. in Chief); Alana Rome (Mng. Ed.); Heather Nannery (News Ed.)

ITHACA COLLEGE

Street address 1: 269 Park Hall
Street address city: Ithaca
Street address state: NY
Zip/Postal code: 14850-7258
Country: USA
Mailing address: 269 Park Hall
Mailing city: Ithaca
Mailing state: NY
Mailing zip: 14850-7258
General Phone: (607) 274-3208
General Fax: (607) 274-1376
Advertising Phone: (607) 274-1618
General/National Adv. E-mail: ithacan@ithaca.edu
Display Adv. E-mail: ithacanads@ithaca.edu
Primary Website: www.theithacan.org
Published: Thur
Avg Free Circ: 4000
Personnel: Michael Serino (Advisor); Kira Maddox (Ed. in Chief); Rachel Wolfgang (Mng. Ed.); Lawrence Hamacher (Advertising Sales Manager)

JEFFERSON CMTY. COLLEGE

Street address 1: 1220 Coffeen St
Street address city: Watertown
Street address state: NY
Zip/Postal code: 13601-1822
Country: USA
Mailing address: 1220 Coffeen St
Mailing city: Watertown
Mailing state: NY
Mailing zip: 13601-1897
General Phone: (315) 786-2200

Personnel: Andrea Pedrick (Advisor); Danielle Sacca (Ed.); Rachel Hunter (Ed.)

JEWISH STUDENT PRESS SERVICE

Street address 1: 114 W 26th St
Street address 2: Rm 1004
Street address city: New York
Street address state: NY
Zip/Postal code: 10001-6812
Country: USA
Mailing address: 114 W 26th St Rm 1004
Mailing city: New York
Mailing state: NY
Mailing zip: 10001-6812
General Phone: (212) 675-1168
Primary Website: www.newvoices.org
Year Established: 1970
Personnel: Ben Sales (Ed.)

JOHN JAY COLLEGE OF CRIMINAL JUSTICE

Street address 1: 899 10th Ave
Street address city: New York
Street address state: NY
Zip/Postal code: 10019-1069
Country: USA
Mailing address: 524 W 59th St
Mailing city: New York
Mailing state: NY
Mailing zip: 10019-1007
Personnel: Babafunmilayo Oke (Ed.)

KEUKA COLLEGE

Street address 1: Office of Commun
Street address city: Keuka Park
Street address state: NY
Zip/Postal code: 14478
Country: USA
Mailing address: Office of Commun.
Mailing city: Keuka Park
Mailing state: NY
Mailing zip: 14478
General Phone: (315) 279-5231
Personnel: Christen Smith (Advisor); Kilee Brown (Ed.); Chelsea DeGroote (Asst. Ed.)

KINGSBOROUGH CMTY. COLLEGE

Street address 1: 2001 Oriental Blvd
Street address 2: # M230
Street address city: Brooklyn
Street address state: NY
Zip/Postal code: 11235-2333
Country: USA
Mailing address: 2001 Oriental Blvd # M230
Mailing city: Brooklyn
Mailing state: NY
Mailing zip: 11235-2333
General Phone: (718) 368-5603
General Fax: (718) 368-4833
General/National Adv. E-mail: scepter@kingsborough.edu
Personnel: Kim Gill (Ed.)

LEHMAN COLLEGE

Street address 1: 250 Bedford Park Blvd W
Street address 2: Rm 108
Street address city: Bronx
Street address state: NY
Zip/Postal code: 10468-1527
Country: USA
Mailing address: 250 Bedford Park Blvd W Rm 108
Mailing city: Bronx
Mailing state: NY
Mailing zip: 10468-1589
General Phone: (718) 960-4966
General Fax: (718) 960-8075
General/National Adv. E-mail: lehmanmeridian@gmail.com
Primary Website: www.lcmeridian.com
Published: Mthly
Personnel: Jennifer Mackenzie (Advisor); Alisia Cordero (Ed. in Chief); Sidra Lackey (Mng. Ed.)

LONG ISLAND UNIV.

Street address 1: 1 University Plz
Street address 2: Rm S305
Street address city: Brooklyn
Street address state: NY
Zip/Postal code: 11201-5301
Country: USA
Mailing address: 1 University Plz Rm S305
Mailing city: Brooklyn
Mailing state: NY
Mailing zip: 11201-5301
General Phone: (718) 488-1591
General Fax: (718) 780-4182
General/National Adv. E-mail: seawanhakapress@yahoo.com
Personnel: Hal Bock (Advisor); Ian Smith (Ed. in Chief); Christina Long (News Ed.)

LONG ISLAND UNIV./C.W.POST

Street address 1: Hillwood Commons, Rm 199, 720 Northern Blvd (25A)
Street address city: Brookville
Street address state: NY
Zip/Postal code: 11548
Country: USA
Mailing address: Hillwood Commons, Rm. 199, 720 Northern Blvd. (25A)
Mailing city: Brookville
Mailing state: NY
Mailing zip: 11548
General Phone: (516) 299-2619
General Fax: (516) 299-2617
Year Established: 1954
Personnel: Valerie Kellogg (Advisor); Daniel Schrafel (Ed. in Chief); Lisa Martens (News Ed.)

MANHATTAN COLLEGE

Street address 1: 4513 Manhattan College Pkwy
Street address city: Bronx
Street address state: NY
Zip/Postal code: 10471-4004
Country: USA
Mailing address: 4513 Manhattan College Pkwy
Mailing city: Riverdale
Mailing state: NY
Mailing zip: 10471
General Phone: (718) 862-7270
Advertising Phone: (718) 862-8043
General/National Adv. E-mail: thequad@manhatten.edu
Personnel: Jonathan Stone (Ed. in Chief); Dom Delgardo (Exec. Ed.); Brian O'Connor (Mng. Ed.)

MANHATTANVILLE COLLEGE

Street address 1: 2900 Purchase St
Street address city: Purchase
Street address state: NY
Zip/Postal code: 10577-2131
Country: USA
Mailing address: 2900 Purchase St
Mailing city: Purchase
Mailing state: NY
Mailing zip: 10577-2132
General Phone: (914) 323-5498
General/National Adv. E-mail: touchstone@mville.edu
Personnel: Dana Schildkraut (Office Mgr.)

MARIST COLLEGE

Street address 1: 3399 North Rd
Street address 2: Lowell Thomas Communications Building Room 135-MAC Lab
Street address city: Poughkeepsie
Street address state: NY
Zip/Postal code: 12601-1350
Country: USA
Mailing address: Lowell Thomas Communications Building Room 135-Mac Lab
Mailing city: Poughkeepsie
Mailing state: NY
Mailing zip: 12601-1387
General Phone: (845) 575-3000
General/National Adv. E-mail: writethecircle@hotmail.com
Personnel: Margeaux Lippman (Ed. in Chief); Kaitlyn Smith (Mng. Ed.); Matthew Spillane (Mng. Ed.)

MEDAILLE COLLEGE

Street address 1: 18 Agassiz Cir
Street address city: Buffalo
Street address state: NY
Zip/Postal code: 14214-2601
Country: USA
Mailing address: 18 Agassiz Cir
Mailing city: Buffalo
Mailing state: NY
Mailing zip: 14214-2695
General Phone: (716) 884-3281
Personnel: Lisa Murphy (Advisor); Megan Fitzgerald (Ed.)

MEDGAR EVERS COLLEGE OF CUNY

Street address 1: 1637 Bedford Ave
Street address 2: Rm S-304
Street address city: Brooklyn
Street address state: NY
Zip/Postal code: 11225-2001
Country: USA
Mailing address: 1637 Bedford Ave Rm S-304
Mailing city: Brooklyn
Mailing state: NY
Mailing zip: 11225-2001
General Phone: (718) 270-6436
General/National Adv. E-mail: adafi@mec.cuny.edu; student-club@mec.cuny.edu
Personnel: Robin Regina Ford (Advisor); Luc Josaphat (Ed. in Chief); Samantha Sylvester (Mng. Ed.)

MERCY COLLEGE

Street address 1: 555 Broadway
Street address city: Dobbs Ferry
Street address state: NY
Zip/Postal code: 10522-1186
Country: USA
Mailing address: 555 Broadway Frnt
Mailing city: Dobbs Ferry
Mailing state: NY
Mailing zip: 10522-1189
General Phone: (914) 674-7422
General Fax: (914) 674-7433
General/National Adv. E-mail: mercyimpactnews@hotmail.com
Personnel: Michael Perrota (Advisor)

MONROE CMTY. COLLEGE

Street address 1: 1000 E Henrietta Rd
Street address city: Rochester
Street address state: NY
Zip/Postal code: 14623-5701
Country: USA
Mailing address: 1000 E Henrietta Rd
Mailing city: Rochester
Mailing state: NY
Mailing zip: 14623-5780
General Phone: (585) 292-2540
General/National Adv. E-mail: monroedoctrine@me.com
Primary Website: www.monroedoctrine.org
Year Established: 1963
Published: Other
Published Other: bi-weekly
Avg Free Circ: 3500
Personnel: Lori Moses (Advisor)

MORRISVILLE STATE COLLEGE

Street address 1: Journalism Dept
Street address city: Morrisville
Street address state: NY
Zip/Postal code: 10901
Country: USA
Mailing address: Journalism Dept.
Mailing city: Morrisville
Mailing state: NY
Mailing zip: 13408
General Phone: (315) 684-6041
General Fax: (315) 684-6247
General/National Adv. E-mail: chimes@morrisville.edu
Display Adv. E-mail: mcdowebl@morrisville.edu
Personnel: Brian McDowell (Advisor)

MT. ST. MARY COLLEGE

Street address 1: 330 Powell Ave
Street address city: Newburgh
Street address state: NY
Zip/Postal code: 12550-3412
Country: USA
Mailing address: 330 Powell Ave
Mailing city: Newburgh
Mailing state: NY
Mailing zip: 12550-3494
Personnel: Vince Begley (Advisor); Nathan Rosenblum (Ed.)

NASSAU CMTY. COLLEGE

Street address 1: College Ctr, 1 Education Dr
Street address city: Garden City
Street address state: NY
Zip/Postal code: 11530
Country: USA
Mailing address: College Ctr., 1 Education Dr.
Mailing city: Garden City
Mailing state: NY
Mailing zip: 11530-6793
General Phone: (516) 222-7071
Personnel: Richard Conway (Advisor)

NAZARETH COLLEGE OF ROCHESTER

Street address 1: 4245 East Ave
Street address city: Rochester
Street address state: NY
Zip/Postal code: 14618-3703
Country: USA
Mailing address: 4245 East Ave
Mailing city: Rochester
Mailing state: NY
Mailing zip: 14618-3790
Personnel: Halinka Spencer (Ed.)

NEW YORK INSTITUTE OF TECHNOLOGY

Street address 1: 1849 Broadway
Street address 2: Rm 212
Street address city: New York
Street address state: NY
Zip/Postal code: 10023-7602
Country: USA
Mailing address: 1849 Broadway Rm 212
Mailing city: New York
Mailing state: NY
Mailing zip: 10023-7602
Personnel: William Lawrence (Advisor)

NEW YORK INSTITUTE OF TECHNOLOGY

Street address 1: PO Box 8000
Street address city: Old Westbury
Street address state: NY
Zip/Postal code: 11568-8000
Country: USA
Mailing address: Northern Boulevard PO Box 8000
Mailing city: Old Westbury
Mailing state: NY
Mailing zip: 11568
General Phone: (516) 686-7646
General Fax: (516) 626-1290
Editorial Phone: 516-589-1615
General/National Adv. E-mail: slate@nyit.edu
Display Adv. E-mail: slate@nyit.edu
Primary Website: www.campusslate.com
Year Established: 1966
Personnel: John Hanc (Advisor); John Santamaria (Editor in Chief); Kyle Reitan (Managing Editor)

NEW YORK LAW SCHOOL

Street address 1: 57 Worth St
Street address 2: Rm L2
Street address city: New York
Street address state: NY
Zip/Postal code: 10013-2926
Country: USA
Mailing address: 57 Worth St Rm L2
Mailing city: New York
Personnel: Sally Harding (Head, Student Life)

NEW YORK METRO COMMUNITY COLLEGES

Street address 1: 39 County Route 70
Street address city: Greenwich
Street address state: NY
Zip/Postal code: 12834-6300
Country: USA
Mailing address: 39 County Route 70

Mailing city: Greenwich
Mailing state: NY
Mailing zip: 12834
General Phone: (518) 879 0965
General Fax: (518) 507 6782
Advertising Phone: (518) 879 0965
Advertising Fax: (518) 507 6782
General/National Adv. E-mail: editor@campus-news.org
Display Adv. E-mail: advertising@campus-news.org
Editorial e-mail: editor@campus-news.org
Primary Website: www.campus-news.org
Year Established: 2010
Published: Mthly`Bi-Mthly
Avg Free Circ: 10000
Personnel: Darren Johnson (Advisor)

NEW YORK UNIV.

Street address 1: 7 E 12th St
Street address 2: Ste 800
Street address city: New York
Street address state: NY
Zip/Postal code: 10003-4475
Country: USA
Mailing address: 7 E 12th St Ste 800
Mailing city: New York
Mailing state: NY
Mailing zip: 10003-4475
General Phone: (212) 998-4300
Personnel: David Cosgrove (Dir., Opns.); Julia McCarthy (Bus. Mgr.); Eric Platt (Ed. in Chief); Rachael Smith (Ed.)

NEW YORK UNIVERSITY SCHOOL OF LAW

Street address 1: 240 Mercer St Bsmt
Street address 2: Hayden Hall
Street address city: New York
Street address state: NY
Zip/Postal code: 10012-1590
Country: USA
Mailing address: 40 Washington Sq S Rm 110
Mailing city: New York
Mailing state: NY
Mailing zip: 10012-1005
General Phone: (212) 998-0564
General Fax: (212) 995-4032
General/National Adv. E-mail: Law.commentator@nyu.edu
Display Adv. E-mail: Law.commentator@nyu.edu
Editorial e-mail: Law.commentator@nyu.edu
Primary Website: www.law.nyu.edu/studentorganizations/thecommentator
Year Established: 1966
Personnel: Naeem Crawford-Muhammad (Advisor); Andrew S. Gehring (Ed. in Chief); Robert Gerrity (Sr. Mng. Ed.); Ana Namaki

NIAGARA COUNTY CMTY. COLLEGE

Street address 1: 3111 Saunders Settlement Rd
Street address city: Sanborn
Street address state: NY
Zip/Postal code: 14132-9506
Country: USA
Mailing address: 3111 Saunders Settlement Rd Ste 1
Mailing city: Sanborn
Mailing state: NY
Mailing zip: 14132-9460
General Phone: (716) 614-6259
Personnel: Amanda Pucci (Advisor)

NIAGARA UNIV.

Street address 1: Gallagher Ctr
Street address city: Niagara University
Street address state: NY
Zip/Postal code: 14109
Country: USA
Mailing address: Gallagher Ctr.
Mailing city: Niagara University
Mailing state: NY
Mailing zip: 14109-1919
General Phone: (716) 286-8512
Personnel: Bill Wolcott (Advisor); Mary Colleen Mahoney (Bus. Mgr.); Marissa Christman (Ed. in Chief)

NYACK COLLEGE

Street address 1: 1 S Boulevard
Street address city: Nyack
Street address state: NY
Zip/Postal code: 10960-3604
Country: USA
Mailing address: 1 S Boulevard
Mailing city: Nyack
Mailing state: NY
Mailing zip: 10960-3698
General Phone: (845) 358-1710
General/National Adv. E-mail: wnyk@nyack.edu; forum@nyack.edu
Personnel: Charles Beach (Advisor)

NYU STERN SCHOOL OF BUS.

Street address 1: 44 W 4th St
Street address 2: Mec 6-130
Street address city: New York
Street address state: NY
Zip/Postal code: 10012-1106
Country: USA
Mailing address: 44 W 4th St Mec 6-130
Mailing city: New York
Mailing state: NY
Mailing zip: 10012-1106
General Phone: (212) 995-4432
General Fax: (212) 995-4606
General/National Adv. E-mail: opportun@stern.nyu.edu; helpdesk@stern.nyu.edu
Personnel: Jeremy Carrine (Advisor); Deborah Garcia (Ed. in chief); Rakesh Duggal (Co-Ed.)

ONONDAGA CMTY. COLLEGE

Street address 1: Rt 173, Student Ctr G100
Street address city: Syracuse
Street address state: NY
Zip/Postal code: 13215
Country: USA
Mailing address: Rt. 173, Student Ctr. G100
Mailing city: Syracuse
Mailing state: NY
Mailing zip: 13215
Personnel: Patti Orty (Ed.)

ORANGE COUNTY CMTY. COLLEGE

Street address 1: 115 South St
Street address city: Middletown
Street address state: NY
Zip/Postal code: 10940-6404
Country: USA
Mailing address: 115 South St
Mailing city: Middletown
Mailing state: NY

PACE UNIV.

Street address 1: 41 Park Row
Street address 2: Rm 902
Street address city: New York
Street address state: NY
Zip/Postal code: 10038-1508
Country: USA
Mailing address: 41 Park Row Rm 902
Mailing city: New York
Mailing state: NY
Mailing zip: 10038-1508
General Phone: (212) 346-1553
General Fax: (212) 346-1265
General/National Adv. E-mail: editor@pacepress.org
Personnel: Mark McSherry (Advisor)

PACE UNIV.

Street address 1: 861 Bedford Rd
Street address city: Pleasantville
Street address state: NY
Zip/Postal code: 10570-2700
Country: USA
Mailing address: 861 Bedford Rd.
Mailing city: Pleasantville
Mailing state: NY
Published: Wed
Personnel: Katherine Fink

PACE UNIV. LAW SCHOOL

Street address 1: 78 N Broadway
Street address city: White Plains
Street address state: NY
Zip/Postal code: 10603-3710
Country: USA
Mailing address: 78 N Broadway
Mailing city: White Plains
Mailing state: NY
Mailing zip: 10603-3710
General Phone: (914) 422-4205
General/National Adv. E-mail: hearsay@law.case.edu
Personnel: Angela D'agostino (Dean, Student Servs.)

POLYTECHNIC INSTITUTE OF NYU

Street address 1: 6 Metrotech Ctr
Street address city: Brooklyn
Street address state: NY
Zip/Postal code: 11201-3840
Country: USA
Mailing address: 6 Metrotech Ctr
Mailing city: Brooklyn
Mailing state: NY
Mailing zip: 11201-3840
Personnel: Lowell Scheiner (Advisor); Robert Griffin (Coord.); William Modeste Jr. (Ed. in Chief); Cheryl Mcnear (Business Adviser)

PRATT INSTITUTE

Street address 1: 200 Willoughby Ave
Street address city: Brooklyn
Street address state: NY
Zip/Postal code: 11205-3802
Country: USA
Mailing address: 200 Willoughby Ave
Mailing city: Brooklyn
Mailing state: NY
Mailing zip: 11205
General Phone: 7186363600
General/National Adv. E-mail: theprattler@gmail.com
Editorial e-mail: theprattler@gmail.com
Primary Website: www.prattleronline.com
Year Established: 1940
Published: Other
Personnel: Emily Oldenquist (Ed. in Cheif)

QUEENS COLLEGE/CUNY

Street address 1: 6530 Kissena Blvd
Street address 2: Student Union Rm. LL-34
Street address city: Flushing
Street address state: NY
Zip/Postal code: 11367-1575
Country: USA
Mailing address: 6530 Kissena Blvd
Mailing city: Flushing
Mailing state: NY
Mailing zip: 11367-1597
General Phone: (718) 997-5000
Advertising Fax: (718) 997-3755
General/National Adv. E-mail: info@theknightnews.com
Primary Website: www.theknightnews.com
Published: Tues
Personnel: Gerry Solomon (Advisor); Will Sammon (Editor-in-Chief); Andrea Hardalo (Editor-In-Chief)

QUEENSBOROUGH CMTY. COLLEGE

Street address 1: 22205 56th Ave
Street address city: Bayside
Street address state: NY
Zip/Postal code: 11364-1432
Country: USA
Mailing address: 22205 56th Ave
Mailing city: Bayside
Mailing state: NY
Mailing zip: 11364-1432
General Phone: (718) 631-6262
Personnel: Andrew Levy (Advisor)

RENSSELAER POLYTECHNIC INST.

Street address 1: 110 8th St Ste 702
Street address 2: Rensselaer Union
Street address city: Troy
Street address state: NY
Zip/Postal code: 12180-3522
Country: USA
Mailing address: Rensselaer Union
Mailing city: Troy
Mailing state: NY
Mailing zip: 12180-3590
General Phone: (518) 276-6000
General Fax: (518) 276-8728
General/National Adv. E-mail: poly@rpi.edu; business@poly.rpi.edu
Display Adv. E-mail: notices@poly.rpi.edu
Editorial e-mail: editor@poly.rpi.edu; news@poly.rpi.edu; edop@poly.rpi.edu; edop@poly.rpi.edu; sports@poly.rpi.edu; photo@poly.rpi.edu; notices@poly.rpi.edu
Personnel: Richard Hartt (Advisor)

ROBERTS WESLEYAN COLLEGE

Street address 1: 2301 Westside Dr
Street address city: Rochester
Street address state: NY
Zip/Postal code: 14624-1933
Country: USA
Mailing address: 2301 Westside Dr Ofc
Mailing city: Rochester
Mailing state: NY
Mailing zip: 14624-1997
General Phone: (585) 594-6385
Published: Mthly
Personnel: Taylor Plourde (Editor-In-Chief); Elisabeth Lindke (Assistant Editor); Derick Trost (Layout Editor)

ROCHESTER INST. OF TECHNOLOGY

Street address 1: 37 Lomb Memorial Dr
Street address city: Rochester
Street address state: NY
Zip/Postal code: 14623-5602
Country: USA
Mailing address: 37 Lomb Memorial Dr
Mailing city: Rochester
Mailing state: NY
Mailing zip: 14623-5602
General Phone: (585) 475-2213
General Fax: (585) 475-2214
General/National Adv. E-mail: reporter@rit.edu
Personnel: Rudy Pugliese (Advisor); Andy Rees (Ed. in Chief)

ROCKLAND CMTY. COLLEGE

Street address 1: 145 College Rd
Street address city: Suffern
Street address state: NY
Zip/Postal code: 10901-3620
Country: USA
Mailing address: 145 College Rd
Mailing city: Suffern
Mailing state: NY
Mailing zip: 10901-3699

RUSSELL SAGE COLLEGE

Street address 1: 65 1st St
Street address city: Troy
Street address state: NY
Zip/Postal code: 12180-4013
Country: USA
Mailing address: 65 1st St
Mailing city: Troy
Mailing state: NY
Mailing zip: 12180-4003
General Phone: 518-244-2016
Editorial Phone: 518-244-2016
General/National Adv. E-mail: perkip@sage.edu
Display Adv. E-mail: perkip@sage.edu
Editorial e-mail: perkip@sage.edu
Primary Website: www.thequillrsc.com
Year Established: 1950s
Personnel: Penny Perkins (Advisor)

SCHOOL OF VISUAL ARTS

Street address 1: 209 E 23rd St
Street address city: New York
Street address state: NY
Zip/Postal code: 10010-3901
Country: USA
Mailing address: 209 E 23rd St
Mailing city: New York
Mailing state: NY
Mailing zip: 10010-3994
Personnel: Tina Crayton (Advisor); Jane Resnick (Ed.)

SIENA COLLEGE

Street address 1: 515 Loudon Rd, Student Union
Street address city: Loudonville
Street address state: NY
Zip/Postal code: 12211

Country: USA
Mailing address: 515 Loudon Rd., Student Union
Mailing city: Loudonville
Mailing state: NY
Mailing zip: 12211-1459
General Phone: (518) 783-2330
General Fax: (518) 786-5053
General/National Adv. E-mail: newspaper@siena.edu
Display Adv. E-mail: newspaper@siena.edu
Editorial e-mail: newspaper@siena.edu
Primary Website: www.siena.edu
Year Established: 1937
Published: Fri
Published Other: Published biweekly
Avg Free Circ: 500
Personnel: Emily Radigan (Editor-in-Chief)

SOUTHAMPTON COLLEGE

Street address 1: 239 Montauk Hwy
Street address city: Southampton
Street address state: NY
Zip/Postal code: 11968-4100
Country: USA
Mailing address: 239 Montauk Hwy
Mailing city: Southampton
Mailing state: NY
Mailing zip: 11968-4198
Personnel: Diane Prescott (Ed.)

ST. BONAVENTURE UNIV.

Street address 1: PO Box X
Street address city: Saint Bonaventure
Street address state: NY
Zip/Postal code: 14778-2303
Country: USA
Mailing address: PO Box X
Mailing city: Saint Bonaventure
Mailing state: NY
Mailing zip: 14778-2303
General Phone: (716) 375-2227
General Fax: (716) 375-2252
Editorial Phone: (716) 375-2128
General/National Adv. E-mail: bonavent@sbu.edu
Personnel: Carole McNall (Faculty Advisor); Samantha Berkhead (Editor in Chief); Kevin Rogers (Managing Editor)

ST. FRANCIS COLLEGE

Street address 1: 180 Remsen St
Street address city: Brooklyn
Street address state: NY
Zip/Postal code: 11201-4305
Country: USA
Mailing address: 180 Remsen St
Mailing city: Brooklyn
Mailing state: NY
Mailing zip: 11201-4398
General Phone: (718) 522-2300
Personnel: Emily Horowitz (Advisor); Kevin Korber (Ed.)

ST. JOHN FISHER COLLEGE

Street address 1: 3690 East Ave
Street address city: Rochester
Street address state: NY
Zip/Postal code: 14618-3537
Country: USA
Mailing address: 3690 East Ave
Mailing city: Rochester
Mailing state: NY
Mailing zip: 14618-3537
General Phone: (585) 385-8360
General Fax: (585) 385-7311
Advertising Phone: (585) 385-7393
General/National Adv. E-mail: cardinalcourier@sjfc.edu
Display Adv. E-mail: mvilla@sjfc.edu
Editorial e-mail: eem00114@sjfc.edu
Primary Website: www.cardinalcourieronline.com
Year Established: 2002
Published: Bi-Mthly
Personnel: Lauren Vicker (Chair/Prof.); Marie Villa (Media Adviser)

ST. JOHNS UNIV.

Street address 1: 300 Howard Ave
Street address city: Staten Island
Street address state: NY
Zip/Postal code: 10301-4450
Country: USA
Mailing address: 300 Howard Ave
Mailing city: Staten Island
Mailing state: NY
Mailing zip: 10301-4496
General Phone: (718) 390-4500
General Fax: (718) 447-0941
General/National Adv. E-mail: siadmhelp@stjohns.edu
Personnel: Crista Camerlengi (Ed.)

ST. JOHN'S UNIVERSITY

Street address 1: 8000 Utopia Pkwy
Street address city: Jamaica
Street address state: NY
Zip/Postal code: 11439-9000
Country: USA
Mailing address: 8000 Utopia Pkwy
Mailing city: Jamaica
Mailing state: NY
Mailing zip: 11439-9000
General Phone: (718) 990-6756
General Fax: (718) 990-5849
Display Adv. E-mail: torchads@gmail.com
Editorial e-mail: torchnews@gmail.com
Primary Website: www.torchonline.com
Published: Wed
Avg Free Circ: 3000
Personnel: Michael Cunniff (Editor-in-Chief)

ST. JOSEPHS COLLEGE

Street address 1: 155 W Roe Blvd
Street address city: Patchogue
Street address state: NY
Zip/Postal code: 11772-2325
Country: USA
Mailing address: 155 W Roe Blvd
Mailing city: Patchogue
Mailing state: NY
Mailing zip: 11772-2399
General Phone: (631) 447-3200
Personnel: Erin Bailey (Ed.)

ST. LAWRENCE UNIV.

Street address 1: 23 Romoda Dr
Street address city: Canton
Street address state: NY
Zip/Postal code: 13617-1423
Country: USA
Mailing address: 23 Romoda Dr
Mailing city: Canton
Mailing state: NY
Mailing zip: 13617-1501
General Phone: (315) 229-5139
General/National Adv. E-mail: hillnews@stlawu.edu
Personnel: Juri Kittler (Advisor); Rachel Barman (Ed.)

ST. THOMAS AQUINAS COLLEGE

Street address 1: 125 Route 340
Street address city: Sparkill
Street address state: NY
Zip/Postal code: 10976-1041
Country: USA
Mailing address: 125 Route 340
Mailing city: Sparkill
Mailing state: NY
Mailing zip: 10976-1050
General Phone: (845) 398-4075
General Fax: (845) 359-8136
General/National Adv. E-mail: thoma@yahoo.com; thoma@stac.edu
Personnel: Kathleen Giroux (Ed. in Chief)

STERN COLLEGE FOR WOMEN

Street address 1: 245 Lexington Ave
Street address city: New York
Street address state: NY
Zip/Postal code: 10016-4605
Country: USA
Mailing address: 245 Lexington Ave
Mailing city: New York
Mailing state: NY
Mailing zip: 10016-4699
General Phone: (212) 340-7715

SUNY COLLEGE AT GENESEO

Street address 1: 10 Macvittie Cir
Street address 2: # 42
Street address city: Geneseo
Street address state: NY
Zip/Postal code: 14454-1427
Country: USA
Mailing address: 10 Macvittie Cir # 42
Mailing city: Geneseo
Mailing state: NY
Mailing zip: 14454-1427
General Phone: (585) 245-5896
General Fax: (585) 245-5284
Advertising Phone: (585) 245-5890
General/National Adv. E-mail: lamron@geneseo.edu
Display Adv. E-mail: lamronad@geneseo.edu
Primary Website: www.thelamron.com
Year Established: 1922
Published: Thur
Avg Free Circ: 3000
Personnel: Maddy Smith (Advisor); Maria Lima (Advisor); Tom Wilder (Ed. in Chief)

SUNY COLLEGE OF TECHNOLOGY/ CANTON

Street address 1: 34 Cornell Dr
Street address 2: Ofc
Street address city: Canton
Street address state: NY
Zip/Postal code: 13617-1037
Country: USA
Mailing address: 34 Cornell Dr Ofc
Mailing city: Canton
Mailing state: NY
Mailing zip: 13617-1037
General Phone: (315) 386-7315
Personnel: Scott Quinell (Advisor)

SUNY COLLEGE OF TECHNOLOGY/ DELHI

Street address 1: 454 Delhi Dr
Street address 2: 222 Farrell Center
Street address city: Delhi
Street address state: NY
Zip/Postal code: 13753-4454
Country: USA
Mailing address: 222 Farrell Center
Mailing city: Delhi
Mailing state: NY
Mailing zip: 13753
General Phone: (607) 746-4270
General Fax: (607) 746-4323
Advertising Phone: (607) 746-4573
Advertising Fax: (607) 746-4323
Editorial Phone: (607) 746-4573
Editorial Fax: (607) 746-4323
General/National Adv. E-mail: campusvoice@delhi.edu
Display Adv. E-mail: campusvoice@delhi.edu
Editorial e-mail: campusvoice@delhi.edu
Primary Website: http://www.delhi.edu/campus-life/activities/campus-voice/index.php
Published: Mthly
Personnel: Christina Viafore (Advisor)

SUNY COLLEGE OF TECHNOLOGY/ FARMINGDALE

Street address 1: Melville Rd, Roosevelt Hall
Street address city: Farmingdale
Street address state: NY
Zip/Postal code: 11735
Country: USA
Mailing address: Melville Rd., Roosevelt Hall
Mailing city: Farmingdale
Mailing state: NY
Mailing zip: 11735
General Phone: (631) 420-2611
Personnel: Jeff Borga (Ed. in Chief)

SUNY COLLEGE/BUFFALO

Street address 1: 1300 Elmwood Ave, Student Union 414
Street address city: Buffalo
Street address state: NY
Zip/Postal code: 14222
Country: USA
Mailing address: 1300 Elmwood Ave., Student Union 414
Mailing city: Buffalo
Mailing state: NY
Mailing zip: 14222
General Phone: (716) 878-4531
General Fax: (716) 878-4532
General/National Adv. E-mail: bscrecord@gmail.com
Display Adv. E-mail: pignatelli.record@live.com
Editorial e-mail: bscrecord@gmail.com
Primary Website: www.bscrecord.com
Year Established: 1913
Published: Wed
Avg Free Circ: 1500
Personnel: Brandon Schlager (Managing Editor); Mike Meiler (Executive Editor); Brian Alexander (Opinion Editor); Michael Canfield (News Editor); Tom Gallagher (Sports Editor); Jennifer Waters (Culture Editor)

SUNY COLLEGE/CORTLAND

Street address 1: PO Box 2000
Street address city: Cortland
Street address state: NY
Zip/Postal code: 13045-0900
Country: USA
Mailing address: PO Box 2000
Mailing city: Cortland
Mailing state: NY
Mailing zip: 13045-0900

SUNY COLLEGE/NEW PALTZ

Street address 1: Rm 417, Student Union Bldg, 1 Hawk Dr
Street address city: New Paltz
Street address state: NY
Zip/Postal code: 12561
Country: USA
Mailing address: Rm. 417, Student Union Bldg., 1 Hawk Dr.
Mailing city: New Paltz
Mailing state: NY
Mailing zip: 12561
General Phone: (845) 257-3030
General Fax: (845) 257-3031
General/National Adv. E-mail: oracle@hawkmail.newpaltz.edu
Primary Website: http://oracle.newpaltz.edu
Published: Thur
Personnel: Melisa Goldman (Bus. Mgr.); Emma Boddors (Ed.); Andrew Wyrich (Editor-in-Chief)

SUNY COLLEGE/OLD WESTBURY

Street address 1: 223 Store Hill Rd
Street address city: Old Westbury
Street address state: NY
Zip/Postal code: 11568-1717
Country: USA
Mailing address: PO Box 210
Mailing city: Old Westbury
Mailing state: NY
Mailing zip: 11568-0210
Personnel: Alicia Grant (Exec.Ed.)

SUNY COLLEGE/ONEONTA

Street address 1: Ravine Pkwy
Street address city: Oneonta
Street address state: NY
Zip/Postal code: 13820
Country: USA
Mailing address: Ravine Pkwy.
Mailing city: Oneonta
Mailing state: NY
Mailing zip: 13820
Personnel: Janet Day (Advisor); Juliette Price (Mng. Ed.)

SUNY COLLEGE/OSWEGO

Street address 1: 135 A Campus Ctr
Street address city: Oswego
Street address state: NY
Zip/Postal code: 13126
Country: USA
Mailing address: 139A Campus Ctr.
Mailing city: Oswego
Mailing state: NY
Mailing zip: 13126
General Phone: (315) 312-3600

General Fax: (315) 312-3542
General/National Adv. E-mail: gonian@oswego.edu; info@oswegonian.com
Display Adv. E-mail: advertising@oswegonian.com
Primary Website: www.oswegonian.com
Year Established: 1935
Personnel: Arvin Diddi (Faculty Adviser); Adam Wolfe (Editor-in-Chief)

SUNY INST. OF TECHNOLOGY UTICA/ROME

Street address 1: PO Box 3050
Street address 2: Campus Ctr., Rm. 216
Street address city: Utica
Street address state: NY
Zip/Postal code: 13504-3050
Country: USA
Mailing address: PO Box 3050
Mailing city: Utica
Mailing state: NY
Mailing zip: 13504-3050
General Phone: (315) 792-7426
Personnel: Patricia Murphy (Advisor); Mark Ziobro (Mng. Ed.)

SUNY PLATTSBURGH

Street address 1: 101 Broad St
Street address 2: 118 Ward Hall
Street address city: Plattsburgh
Street address state: NY
Zip/Postal code: 12901-2637
Country: USA
Mailing address: 101 Broad St
Mailing city: Plattsburgh
Mailing state: NY
Mailing zip: 12901-2637
General Phone: (518) 564-2174
General Fax: (518) 564-6397
Advertising Phone: (518) 564-3173
Editorial Phone: (518) 564-2174
General/National Adv. E-mail: cp@cardinalpointsonline.com
Display Adv. E-mail: advertising@cardinalpointsonline.com
Editorial e-mail: cp@cardinalpointsonline.com
Primary Website: www.cardinalpointsonline.com
Year Established: 1969
Published: Fri
Avg Free Circ: 1300
Personnel: Shawn Murphy (Advisor); Maureen Provost (Bus Mgr)

SUNY SULLIVAN

Street address 1: 112 College Rd
Street address city: Loch Sheldrake
Street address state: NY
Zip/Postal code: 12759-5721
Country: USA
Mailing address: 112 College Rd
Mailing city: Loch Sheldrake
Mailing state: NY
Mailing zip: 12759-5721
General Phone: (845) 434-5750
Primary Website: www.sunysullivan.edu
Published: Mon
Personnel: Kathleen Birkett (Admin. Asst.)

SUNY/ALBANY

Street address 1: 353 Broadway
Street address city: Albany
Street address state: NY
Zip/Postal code: 12246-2915
Country: USA
Mailing address: 353 Broadway
Mailing city: Albany
Mailing state: NY
Mailing zip: 12246-2915
General Phone: (518) 442-5666
General Fax: (518) 442-5664
General/National Adv. E-mail: asp_online@hotmail.com
Personnel: Brett Longo (Bus. Mgr.); Ted Bean (Ed. in Chief); Jon Campbell (Mng. Ed.)

SUNY/BINGHAMTON

Street address 1: University Union Rm WB03
Street address city: Binghamton
Street address state: NY
Zip/Postal code: 13902
Country: USA
Mailing address: PO Box 6000
Mailing city: Binghamton
Mailing state: NY
Mailing zip: 13902-6000
General Phone: (607) 777-2515
Editorial e-mail: editor@bupipedream.com
Personnel: Shinsuke Kawano (Bus. Mgr.); Ashley Tarr (Ed. in Chief); Chris Carpenter (Managing Ed.); Melissa Bykofsky (News Ed.); Teressa (Photo Ed.); Marina (Opinion Ed.)

SUNY/BUFFALO

Street address 1: 132 Student Un
Street address city: Buffalo
Street address state: NY
Zip/Postal code: 14260-2100
Country: USA
Mailing address: 132 Student Un
Mailing city: Buffalo
Mailing state: NY
Mailing zip: 14260-2100
General Phone: (716) 645-2152
General Fax: (716) 645-2766
General/National Adv. E-mail: spectrum@buffalo.edu
Personnel: Debbie Smith (Bus. Mgr.); Steven Marth (Ed. in Chief)

SUNY/STONY BROOK

Street address 1: PO Box 1530
Street address city: Stony Brook
Street address state: NY
Zip/Postal code: 11790-0609
Country: USA
Mailing address: PO Box 1530
Mailing city: Stony Brook
Mailing state: NY
Mailing zip: 11790-0609
General Phone: (631) 632-6480
General Fax: (631) 632-9128
General/National Adv. E-mail: advertise@sbstatesman.org
Personnel: Frank D'alessandro (Bus. Mgr.); Bradley Donaldson (Ed. in Chief)

SYRACUSE UNIVERSITY

Street address 1: 744 Ostrom Ave
Street address city: Syracuse
Street address state: NY
Zip/Postal code: 13244-2977
Country: USA
Mailing address: 744 Ostrom Ave
Mailing city: Syracuse
Mailing state: NY
Mailing zip: 13210-2942
General Phone: (315) 443-2314
General Fax: (315) 443-3689
Advertising Phone: (315) 443-9794
General/National Adv. E-mail: ads@dailyorange.com
Display Adv. E-mail: ads@dailyorange.com
Editorial e-mail: editor@dailyorange.com
Primary Website: www.dailyorange.com
Year Established: 1903
Published: Mon`Tues`Wed`Thur`Fri
Avg Free Circ: 6000
Personnel: Peter Waack (Advisor/Gen. Mgr.)

THE COLLEGE AT BROCKPORT, SUNY

Street address 1: 350 New Campus Dr
Street address city: Brockport
Street address state: NY
Zip/Postal code: 14420-2997
Country: USA
Mailing address: 350 New Campus Dr
Mailing city: Brockport
Mailing state: NY
Mailing zip: 14420-2914
General Phone: (585) 395-2230
General/National Adv. E-mail: stylus@brockport.edu
Primary Website: www.brockportstylus.org
Year Established: 1914
Published: Wed
Personnel: Alyssa Daley (Editor-in-Chief); Kristina Livingston (Executive Editor); Victoria Martinez (Managing Editor); Breonnah Colon (Campus Talk Editor); Lou Venditti (News Editor); Alexandra Weaver (Lifestyles Editor); Panagiotis Argitis (Sports Editor)

THE CORNELL DAILY SUN

Street address 1: 139 W State St
Street address city: Ithaca
Street address state: NY
Zip/Postal code: 14850-5427
Country: USA
Mailing address: 139 W State St
Mailing city: Ithaca
Mailing state: NY
Mailing zip: 14850-5427
General Phone: (607) 273-3606
General Fax: (607) 273-0746
General/National Adv. E-mail: letters@cornelldailysun.com
Primary Website: www.cornellsun.com
Year Established: 1880
Personnel: Ben Gitlin (Editor in Chief); Michael Linhorst (Managing Editor); Dani Neuharth-Keusch (Associate Editor); Rahul Kishore (Web Editor); Chloe Gatta (Business Manager); Helene Beauchemin (Advertising Manager); Justin wheeler (Bus. Mgr.); Keenan Weatherford (Ed. in Chief); Michael J. Stratford (Managing Ed.); Sophia Qasir (Advertising Mgr.)

THE DOLPHIN

Street address 1: 1419 Salt Springs Rd
Street address city: Syracuse
Street address state: NY
Zip/Postal code: 13214-1302
Country: USA
Mailing address: 1419 Salt Springs Rd
Mailing city: Syracuse
Mailing state: NY
Mailing zip: 13214-1302
General Phone: (315) 445-4542
Advertising Phone: (607) 221-8080
Editorial Phone: (315) 445-4542
General/National Adv. E-mail: dolphin@lemoyne.edu
Display Adv. E-mail: dolphin@lemoyne.edu
Editorial e-mail: dolphin@lemoyne.edu
Personnel: Ashley Casey (Co-Executive Editor); Amy Dieffenbacher

THE EMPIRE STATE TRIBUNE

Street address 1: 56 Broadway
Street address 2: Fl 5
Street address city: New York
Street address state: NY
Zip/Postal code: 10004-1613
County: New York
Country: USA
General Phone: 212-659-0742
Advertising Phone: 212-659-0742
Editorial Phone: 212-659-0742
General/National Adv. E-mail: estribune@tkc.edu
Display Adv. E-mail: estribune@tkc.edu
Classified Adv. e-mail: estribune@tkc.edu
Editorial e-mail: estribune@tkc.edu
Primary Website: www.empirestatetribune.com
Mthly Avg Views: 8856
Mthly Avg Unique Visitors: 4124
Year Established: 2005
Published: Mon
Avg Free Circ: 100
Personnel: Clemente Lisi (Assistant Affiliate Professor of Journalism)

THE SKIDMORE NEWS

Street address 1: 815 N Broadway
Street address 2: Skidmore College
Street address city: Saratoga Springs
Street address state: NY
Zip/Postal code: 12866-1632
Country: USA
Mailing address: 815 N Broadway
Mailing city: Saratoga Springs
Mailing state: NY
Mailing zip: 12866-1632
General Phone: (518) 580-5000
General Fax: (518) 580-5188
General/National Adv. E-mail: skidnews@skidmore.edu
Primary Website: www.skidmorenews.com
Year Established: 1925
Personnel: Savannah Grier (Ed. in Chief)

TOURO COLLEGE JACOB D. FUCHSBERG LAW CENTER

Street address 1: 225 Eastview Dr
Street address city: Central Islip
Street address state: NY
Zip/Postal code: 11722-4539
Country: USA
Mailing address: 225 Eastview Dr
Mailing city: Central Islip
Mailing state: NY
Mailing zip: 11722-4539
General Phone: (631) 761-7000
Personnel: Patti Desrochers (Dir. Comm.)

UNION COLLEGE CONCORDIENSIS

Street address 1: 807 Union St
Street address city: Schenectady
Street address state: NY
Zip/Postal code: 12308-3256
Country: USA
Mailing address: 807 Union St.
Mailing city: Schenectady
Mailing state: NY
Mailing zip: 12308
General Phone: (518) 388-7128
General/National Adv. E-mail: concordy@gmail.com
Display Adv. E-mail: advertising@concordy.com
Primary Website: http://www.concordy.com/
Year Established: 1877
Personnel: Ajay Major (Ed. in Chief)

UNIV. OF ROCHESTER

Street address 1: PO Box 277086
Street address city: Rochester
Street address state: NY
Zip/Postal code: 14627-7086
Country: USA
Mailing address: CPU 277086 Campus Post Office
Mailing city: Rochester
Mailing state: NY
Mailing zip: 14627
General Phone: (585) 275-5942
General Fax: (585) 273-5303
General/National Adv. E-mail: ctads@mail.rochester.edu
Editorial e-mail: editor@campustimes.org
Personnel: Dan Wasserman (Pub.); Liz Bremer (Bus. Mgr.); Dana Hilfinger (Ed. in Chief)

UNIVERSITY AT BUFFALO SCHOOL OF LAW

Street address 1: 410 Obrian Hall
Street address city: Amherst
Street address state: NY
Zip/Postal code: 14260-1100
Country: USA
Mailing address: 410 O'Brian Hall
Mailing city: Amherst
Mailing state: NY
Mailing zip: 14260-1100
General Phone: (716) 645-3176
General Fax: (716) 645-5940
Editorial Phone: (716) 645-3176
General/National Adv. E-mail: lmueller@buffalo.edu
Editorial e-mail: lmueller@buffalo.edu
Primary Website: www.law.buffalo.edu
Year Established: 2000
Published: Mthly
Avg Free Circ: 12000
Personnel: Kristina Lively (Webmaster)

UTICA COLLEGE

Street address 1: 1600 Burrstone Rd
Street address 2: Hubbard 55
Street address city: Utica
Street address state: NY
Zip/Postal code: 13502-4857
Country: USA
Mailing address: 1600 Burrstone Rd Hubbard 55
Mailing city: Utica
Mailing state: NY
Mailing zip: 13502-4892
General Phone: (315) 792-3065

Primary Website: www.uctangerine.com
Year Established: 1946
Personnel: Christopher Cooper (Editor-in-Chief); Jonathan Monsiletto (Ed. in Chief)

VASSAR COLLEGE

Street address 1: 124 Raymond Ave
Street address 2: Box 149, Vassar College
Street address city: Poughkeepsie
Street address state: NY
Zip/Postal code: 12604-0001
Country: USA
Mailing address: Box 149, Vassar College
Mailing city: Poughkeepsie
Mailing state: NY
Mailing zip: 12604
General Phone: (518) 755-2042
General/National Adv. E-mail: misc@vassar.edu
Primary Website: PO Box 23
Published: Wed
Personnel: Talya Phelps (Editor-in-Chief)

WADE WALLERSTEIN

Street address 1: 1 Mead Way
Street address city: Bronxville
Street address state: NY
Zip/Postal code: 10708-5940
Country: USA
Mailing address: 1 Mead Way
Mailing city: Bronxville
Mailing state: NY
Mailing zip: 10708-5999
General Phone: (973) 856-2617
General Fax: (973) 856-2617
Advertising Phone: (973) 856-2617
Advertising Fax: (973) 856-2617
Editorial Phone: (973) 856-2617
Editorial Fax: (973) 856-2617
General/National Adv. E-mail: phoenix@gm.slc.edu; phoenix@slc.edu
Display Adv. E-mail: phoenix@gm.slc.edu
Editorial e-mail: wwallerstein@gm.slc.edu
Personnel: Wade Wallerstein (Editor-in-Chief)

WAGNER COLLEGE

Street address 1: 1 Campus Rd
Street address city: Staten Island
Street address state: NY
Zip/Postal code: 10301-4479
Country: USA
Mailing address: 1 Campus Rd
Mailing city: Staten Island
Mailing state: NY
Mailing zip: 10301-4495
Published: Wed
Published Other: Bi-Weekly

WATS, SIMON GRAD. SCHOOL OF BUS.

Street address 1: Schlegel Hall, University of Rochester
Street address city: Rochester
Street address state: NY
Zip/Postal code: 14627
Country: USA
Mailing address: Schlegel Hall, University of Rochester
Mailing city: Rochester
Mailing state: NY
Mailing zip: 14627
Personnel: Natalie Antal (Acting Managing Editor); Vincent Pelletier (Assignment Editor); Durba Ray (Ed. in Chief)

WESTCHESTER CMTY. COLLEGE

Street address 1: 75 Grasslands Rd
Street address city: Valhalla
Street address state: NY
Zip/Postal code: 10595-1550
Country: USA
Mailing address: 75 Grasslands Rd
Mailing city: Valhalla
Mailing state: NY
Mailing zip: 10595-1550
General Phone: (914) 606-6600
General/National Adv. E-mail: thevikingnewswcc@hotmail.com
Personnel: Craig Padawer (Advisor)

YESHIVA UNIV.

Street address 1: 500 W 185th St
Street address 2: Ste 416
Street address city: New York
Street address state: NY
Zip/Postal code: 10033-3201
Country: USA
Mailing address: 500 W 185th St Ste 416
Mailing city: New York
Mailing state: NY
Mailing zip: 10033-3201
General Phone: (212) 795-4308
General Fax: (212) 928-8637
General/National Adv. E-mail: news@yucommentator.com
Personnel: Michael Cinnamon (Ed. in Chief); Simeon Botwinick (Mng. Ed.); Isaac Silverstein (Mng. Ed.)

YORK COLLEGE OF CUNY

Street address 1: 9420 Guy R Brewer Blvd
Street address city: Jamaica
Street address state: NY
Zip/Postal code: 11451-0001
Country: USA
Mailing address: 9420 Guy R Brewer Blvd
Mailing city: Jamaica
Mailing state: NY
Mailing zip: 11451-0002
General Phone: (718) 262-2529
General Fax: (718) 262-5234
General/National Adv. E-mail: pandora@york.cuny.edu
Display Adv. E-mail: pandora@york.cuny.edu
Editorial e-mail: pandora@york.cuny.edu
Primary Website: http://pbwire.cunycampuswire.com/
Year Established: 1967
Published: Mthly
Avg Free Circ: 3000
Personnel: William Hughes (Advisor)

OHIO

ASHLAND UNIV.

Street address 1: 401 College Ave
Street address city: Ashland
Street address state: OH
Zip/Postal code: 44805-3702
Country: USA
Mailing address: 401 College Ave
Mailing city: Ashland
Mailing state: OH
Mailing zip: 44805-3799
General Phone: (419) 289-4142
General Fax: (419) 289-5604
General/National Adv. E-mail: collegian@ashland.edu
Personnel: Katie Ryder (Ed.)

BALDWIN-WALLACE COLLEGE

Street address 1: 275 Eastland Rd
Street address city: Berea
Street address state: OH
Zip/Postal code: 44017-2005
Country: USA
Mailing address: 275 Eastland Rd
Mailing city: Berea
Mailing state: OH
Mailing zip: 44017-2088
General Phone: (440) 826-2900
Personnel: Peter Kerlin (Dir.); Gerrie

BLUFFTON COLLEGE

Street address 1: 1 University Dr
Street address city: Bluffton
Street address state: OH
Zip/Postal code: 45817-2104
Country: USA
Mailing address: 1 University Dr
Mailing city: Bluffton
Mailing state: OH
Mailing zip: 45817-2104
General Phone: (419) 358-3000
General Fax: (419) 358-3356
General/National Adv. E-mail: witmarsum@bluffton.edu
Personnel: Colin Lasu (Advisor); Cyrus Weigand (Bus. Mgr.); Bethany Rayle (Ed.)

BOWLING GREEN STATE UNIV.

Street address 1: 100 Kuhlin Center
Street address city: Bowling Green
Street address state: OH
Zip/Postal code: 43403-0001
Country: USA
Mailing address: 100 Kuhlin Center
Mailing city: Bowling Green
Mailing state: OH
Mailing zip: 43403-0001
General Phone: (419) 372-0328
General Fax: (419) 372-0202
Advertising Phone: (419) 372-2606
Advertising Fax: (419) 372-9090
Editorial Phone: (419) 372-6966
Editorial Fax: (419) 372-9090
General/National Adv. E-mail: thenews@bgnews.com
Display Adv. E-mail: twhitma@bgsu.edu
Editorial e-mail: thenews@bgnews.com
Primary Website: www.bgviews.com
Year Established: 1920
Published: Mon'Thur
Avg Free Circ: 4500
Personnel: Robert Bortel (Director of Student Media); Hannah Finnerty; Holly Shively

BOWLING GREEN STATE UNIVERSITY

Street address 1: 204 West Hall
Street address city: Bowling Green
Street address state: OH
Zip/Postal code: 43403-0001
Country: USA
Mailing address: 204 W Hall
Mailing city: Bowling Green
Mailing state: OH

CAPITAL UNIV.

Street address 1: 1 College and Main
Street address city: Columbus
Street address state: OH
Zip/Postal code: 43209-7812
Country: USA
Mailing address: 1 College and Main
Mailing city: Columbus
Mailing state: OH
Mailing zip: 43209-2394
General Phone: (614) 236-6567
General Fax: (614) 236-6948
General/National Adv. E-mail: chimes@capital.edu
Primary Website: cuchimes.com
Year Established: 1926
Published: Thur
Avg Free Circ: 1200
Personnel: Kelly Messinger (Advisor)

CAPITAL UNIV. LAW SCHOOL

Street address 1: 303 E Broad St
Street address city: Columbus
Street address state: OH
Zip/Postal code: 43215-3201
Country: USA
Mailing address: 303 E Broad St
Mailing city: Columbus
Mailing state: OH
Mailing zip: 43215-3200
General Phone: (614) 236-6011
Personnel: Susan Gilles (Advisor); Sharon Simpson (Ed. in Chief); Amanda Tuttle (Ed.)

CASE WESTERN RESERVE UNIV.

Street address 1: 11111 Euclid Ave
Street address 2: Rm A09
Street address city: Cleveland
Street address state: OH
Zip/Postal code: 44106-1715
Country: USA
Mailing address: 11111 Euclid Ave Rm A09
Mailing city: Cleveland
Mailing state: OH
Mailing zip: 44106-1715
General Phone: (216) 368-6949
Personnel: Tricia Schellenbach (Advisor); Bruce Douglas (Adv. Mgr.); Bryan Bourgeois (Ed. in Chief)

CEDARVILLE UNIV.

Street address 1: 251 N Main St
Street address city: Cedarville
Street address state: OH
Zip/Postal code: 45314-8501
Country: USA
Mailing address: 251 N Main St
Mailing city: Cedarville
Mailing state: OH
Mailing zip: 45314-8564
General Phone: (937) 766-3298
General Fax: (937) 766-3456
General/National Adv. E-mail: cedars@cedarville.edu
Display Adv. E-mail: jgilbert@cedarville.edu
Primary Website: http://cedars.cedarville.edu/
Published: Mthly
Avg Free Circ: 1200
Personnel: Jeff Gilbert (Faculty adviser)

CENTRAL STATE UNIV.

Street address 1: PO Box 1004
Street address city: Wilberforce
Street address state: OH
Zip/Postal code: 45384-1004
Country: USA
Mailing address: PO Box 1004
Mailing city: Wilberforce
Mailing state: OH
Mailing zip: 45384-1004
General Phone: (937) 376-6095
General Fax: (937) 376-6530
General/National Adv. E-mail: info@centralstate.edu
Personnel: Mike Gormley (Advisor)

CLEVELAND STATE UNIV.

Street address 1: 2121 Euclid Ave
Street address 2: Student Center, Room 319
Street address city: Cleveland
Street address state: OH
Zip/Postal code: 44115-2214
Country: USA
Mailing address: 2121 Euclid Ave
Mailing city: Cleveland
Mailing state: OH
Mailing zip: 44115-2226
General Phone: (216) 687-2270
General Fax: (216) 687-5155
General/National Adv. E-mail: cauldroneditors@gmail.com
Display Adv. E-mail: cauldronadverts@gmail.com
Primary Website: www.csucauldron.com
Published: Tues
Personnel: Dan Lenhart (Advisor); Samah Assad (Editor-in-Chief)

COLLEGE OF WOOSTER

Street address 1: 1189 Beall Ave
Street address city: Wooster
Street address state: OH
Zip/Postal code: 44691-2393
Country: USA
Mailing address: Box C-1387
Mailing city: Wooster
Mailing state: OH
Mailing zip: 44691-2393
General Phone: (330) 263-2598
General Fax: (330) 263-2596
General/National Adv. E-mail: voice@wooster.edu
Display Adv. E-mail: nisles@wooster.edu
Editorial e-mail: voice@wooster.edu
Primary Website: thewoostervoice.com
Published: Tues
Personnel: Travis Marmon (Ed. in Chief); Ian Benson (Ed. in Chief)

DENISON UNIV.

Street address 1: 100 W College St
Street address city: Granville
Street address state: OH
Zip/Postal code: 43023-1100
Country: USA
Mailing address: 100 W College St
Mailing city: Granville
Mailing state: OH

Mailing zip: 43023
General Phone: (740) 587-6378
General Fax: (740) 587-6767
General/National Adv. E-mail: denisonian@denison.edu
Personnel: Alan Miller (Advisor)

FRANCISCAN UNIVERSITY OF STEUBENVILLE

Street address 1: 1235 University Blvd
Street address city: Steubenville
Street address state: OH
Zip/Postal code: 43952-1792
Country: USA
Mailing address: 1235 University Blvd
Mailing city: Steubenville
Mailing state: OH
Mailing zip: 43952-1796
General Phone: (740) 284-5014
General Fax: (740) 284-5452
General/National Adv. E-mail: troub@franciscan.edu
Personnel: Chris Pagano; Elizabeth Wong; Emily Lahr

FRANKLIN UNIVERSITY

Street address 1: 201 S Grant Ave
Street address city: Columbus
Street address state: OH
Zip/Postal code: 43215-5301
Country: USA
Mailing address: 201 S Grant Ave
Mailing city: Columbus
Mailing state: OH
Mailing zip: 43215-5399
General Phone: (614) 797-4700
General Fax: (614) 224-4025
Advertising Phone: N/A
Advertising Fax: N/A
Editorial Phone: N/A
Editorial Fax: N/A
Display Adv. E-mail: N/A
Editorial e-mail: N/A
Primary Website: www.franklin.edu
Year Established: 1902
Personnel: Sherry Mercurio (Ed.)

HEIDELBERG UNIVERSITY

Street address 1: 310 E Market St
Street address city: Tiffin
Street address state: OH
Zip/Postal code: 44883-2434
Country: USA
Mailing address: 310 E. Market St.
Mailing city: Tiffin
Mailing state: OH
Year Established: 1894
Personnel: Mary Garrison (Visiting Assistant Professor of Communication)

HIRAM COLLEGE

Street address 1: PO Box 67
Street address city: Hiram
Street address state: OH
Zip/Postal code: 44234-0067
Country: USA
Mailing address: PO Box 67
Mailing city: Hiram
Mailing state: OH
Mailing zip: 44234-0067
General Phone: (330) 569-5203
Personnel: Christopher Benek (Ed. in Chief)

JOHN CARROLL UNIVERSITY

Street address 1: 1 John Carroll Blvd
Street address city: University Heights
Street address state: OH
Zip/Postal code: 44118-4538
Country: USA
Mailing address: 1 John Carroll Blvd
Mailing city: Cleveland
Mailing state: OH
Mailing zip: 44118-4582
General Phone: (216) 397-1711
General Fax: (216) 397-1729
Advertising Phone: (216) 397-4398
Editorial Phone: (216) 397-1711
General/National Adv. E-mail: jcunews@gmail.com
Display Adv. E-mail: jcunews@gmail.com
Editorial e-mail: jcunews@gmail.com
Primary Website: www.jcunews.com
Year Established: 1925
Published: Thur
Avg Free Circ: 1600
Personnel: Mary Ann Flannery (Chair/Assoc. Prof.); Robert T. Noll (Advisor); Jacqueline J. Schmidt (Prof.); Katie Sheridan (Ed. in Chief); Bob Seeholzer (Mng. Ed.); Alan Stephenson (Prof.); Mary Beadle (Assoc. Prof.); Tim Ertle (Sports Ed.); Margaret Algren (Asst. Prof.); Richard Hendrickson (Asst. Prof.); Robert Prisco (Asst. Prof.); Bob Noll (Instr.); David Reese (Instr.); Fred Buchstein (Part-time Instr.); Mark Eden (Part-time Instr.); Bill Nichols (Part-time Instr.)

KENT STATE UNIV.

Street address 1: 201 Franklin Hall, Rm 205
Street address city: Kent
Street address state: OH
Zip/Postal code: 44242-0001
Country: USA
Mailing address: 201 Franklin Hall Rm 205
Mailing city: Kent
Mailing state: OH
Mailing zip: 44242-0001
General Phone: (330) 672-0887
General Fax: (330) 672-4880
General/National Adv. E-mail: dksads@gmail.com
Personnel: Carl Schierhorn (Advisor); Lori Cantor (Mgr.); Tami Bongiorni (Adv. Mgr.)

KENYON COLLEGE

Street address 1: Student Affairs Ctr, 100 Gaskin Ave
Street address city: Gambier
Street address state: OH
Zip/Postal code: 43022
Country: USA
Mailing address: PO Box 832
Mailing city: Gambier
Mailing state: OH
Mailing zip: 43022-0832
General Phone: (740) 427-5338
General Fax: (740) 427-5339
General/National Adv. E-mail: collegian@kenyon.edu
Personnel: Sarah Queller (Ed.)

LAKELAND CMTY. COLLEGE

Street address 1: 7700 Clocktower Dr
Street address city: Kirtland
Street address state: OH
Zip/Postal code: 44094-5198
Country: USA
Mailing address: 7700 Clocktower Dr
Mailing city: Kirtland
Mailing state: OH
Mailing zip: 44094-5198
General Phone: (440) 953-7264
General/National Adv. E-mail: lakelander@lakelandcc.edu
Personnel: Susan Zimmerman (Advisor)

LORAIN COUNTY CMTY. COLLEGE

Street address 1: 1005 Abbe Rd N
Street address city: Elyria
Street address state: OH
Zip/Postal code: 44035-1613
Country: USA
Mailing address: 1005 Abbe Rd N
Mailing city: Elyria
Mailing state: OH
Mailing zip: 44035-1692
General Phone: (440) 366-4037
General Fax: (440) 365-6519
Editorial Phone: (440) 366-7729
General/National Adv. E-mail: lcccstories@lorainccc.edu; colegian@lorainccc.edu
Primary Website: www.collegianonline.org
Published: Bi-Mthly
Personnel: Cliff Anthony (Advisor)

MALONE COLLEGE

Street address 1: 2600 Cleveland Ave NW
Street address city: Canton
Street address state: OH
Zip/Postal code: 44709-3308
Country: USA
Mailing address: 2600 Cleveland Ave NW
Mailing city: Canton
Mailing state: OH
Mailing zip: 44709-3308
General Phone: (330) 471-8212
Primary Website: www.theaviso.org
Year Established: 1958
Personnel: David Dixon (Advisor)

MALONE UNIVERSITY

Street address 1: 2600 Cleveland Ave NW
Street address city: Canton
Street address state: OH
Zip/Postal code: 44709-3308
Country: USA
Mailing address: 2600 Cleveland Ave NW
Mailing city: Canton
Mailing state: OH

MARIETTA COLLEGE

Street address 1: 215 5th St
Street address 2: # A-20
Street address city: Marietta
Street address state: OH
Zip/Postal code: 45750-4033
Country: USA
Mailing address: 215 5th St Dept 32
Mailing city: Marietta
Mailing state: OH
Mailing zip: 45750-4071
General Phone: (740) 376-4555
General Fax: (740) 376-4807
General/National Adv. E-mail: marc@marietta.edu
Personnel: Jessie Schmac (Ed. in Chief); Jamie Tidd (Mng. Ed.); Amy Bitely (Viewpoints Ed.)

MARIETTA COLLEGE

Street address 1: 215 5th St
Street address city: Marietta
Street address state: OH
Zip/Postal code: 45750-4033
Country: USA
Mailing address: 215 5th St Dept 32
Mailing city: Marietta
Mailing state: OH
Mailing zip: 45750-4071
General Phone: (740) 376-4848
General Fax: (740) 376-4807
General/National Adv. E-mail: mac@Marietta.edu
Personnel: Jack L. Hillwig (Chair)

MIAMI UNIV.

Street address 1: 4200 N University Blvd
Street address city: Middletown
Street address state: OH
Zip/Postal code: 45042-3458
Country: USA
Mailing address: 4200 N University Blvd
Mailing city: Middletown
Mailing state: OH
Mailing zip: 45042-3497
General Phone: (513) 727-3200
General Fax: (513) 727-3223
General/National Adv. E-mail: miamistudent@gmail.com; miamistudent@muohio.edu
Personnel: Catherine Couretas (Ed.); John Heyda (Advisor)

MOUNT ST. JOSEPH UNIVERSITY

Street address 1: 5701 Delhi Rd
Street address city: Cincinnati
Street address state: OH
Zip/Postal code: 45233-1669
Country: USA
Mailing address: 5701 Delhi Rd
Mailing city: Cincinnati
Mailing state: OH
Mailing zip: 45233-1670
Primary Website: www.msj.edu
Published: Mthly
Personnel: Elizabeth Barkley (Faculty Advisor)

MT. UNION COLLEGE

Street address 1: 1972 Clark Ave
Street address city: Alliance
Street address state: OH
Zip/Postal code: 44601-3929
Country: USA
Mailing address: 1972 Clark Ave
Mailing city: Alliance
Mailing state: OH
Mailing zip: 44601-3993
General Phone: (330) 823-2884
General Fax: (330) 821-0425
General/National Adv. E-mail: dynamo@muc.edu
Personnel: Len Cooper (Advisor)

MUSKINGUM COLLEGE

Street address 1: 163 Stormont St
Street address city: New Concord
Street address state: OH
Zip/Postal code: 43762-1118
Country: USA
Mailing address: 163 Stormont St
Mailing city: New Concord
Mailing state: OH
Mailing zip: 43762
General Phone: (740) 826-8296
Personnel: Vivian Wagner (Advisor); Josh Chaney (Web Ed.)

OBERLIN COLLEGE

Street address 1: 135 W Lorain St
Street address 2: # 90
Street address city: Oberlin
Street address state: OH
Zip/Postal code: 44074-1053
Country: USA
Mailing address: 135 W Lorain St # 90
Mailing city: Oberlin
Mailing state: OH
Mailing zip: 44074-1053
General Phone: (440) 775-8123
General Fax: (440) 775-6733
General/National Adv. E-mail: advertisements@oberlinreview.org
Personnel: Daniel Dudley (Bus. Mgr.); Talia Chicherio (Adv. Mgr.); Caitlin Duke (Ed. in Chief); Piper Niehaus (Ed. in Chief)

OHIO NORTHERN UNIV.

Street address 1: 525 S Main St
Street address city: Ada
Street address state: OH
Zip/Postal code: 45810-6000
Country: USA
Mailing address: 525 S Main St
Mailing city: Ada
Mailing state: OH
Mailing zip: 45810
General Phone: (419) 772-2409
General Fax: (419) 772-1880
General/National Adv. E-mail: northern-review@onu.edu
Primary Website: https://nr.onu.edu
Published: Mon`Tues`Wed`Thur`Fri`Sat`Sun
Personnel: Bill O'Connell (Advisor); Nick Dutro (Ed. in Chief)

OHIO STATE UNIV.

Street address 1: 242 W 18th Ave
Street address 2: Rm 211
Street address city: Columbus
Street address state: OH
Zip/Postal code: 43210-1107
Country: USA
Mailing address: 242 W 18th Ave Rm 211
Mailing city: Columbus
Mailing state: OH
Mailing zip: 43210-1107
General Phone: (614) 292-2031
General Fax: (614) 292-5240
Editorial Phone: (614) 292-5721
General/National Adv. E-mail: lantern@osu.edu
Editorial e-mail: lanternnewsroom@gmail.com
Primary Website: www.thelantern.com
Year Established: 1881
Personnel: Tom O'Hara (Advisor); John Milliken (Mgr.); Kevin Bruffy (Mgr., Display Adv.)

OHIO STATE UNIV. COLLEGE OF ENGINEERING

Street address 1: 2070 Neil Ave
Street address city: Columbus

Street address state: OH
Zip/Postal code: 43210-1226
Country: USA
Mailing address: 2070 Neil Ave
Mailing city: Columbus
Mailing state: OH
Mailing zip: 43210-1278
General Phone: (614) 292-7931
Personnel: Edward McCaul (Advisor)

OHIO STATE UNIV. COLLEGE OF LAW

Street address 1: 55 W 12th Ave
Street address city: Columbus
Street address state: OH
Zip/Postal code: 43210-1338
Country: USA
Mailing address: 55 W 12th Ave
Mailing city: Columbus
Mailing state: OH

OHIO STATE UNIVERSITY

Street address 1: 242 W 18th Ave
Street address city: Columbus
Street address state: OH
Zip/Postal code: 43210-1107
Country: USA
Mailing address: 242 W 18th Ave
Mailing city: Columbus
Mailing state: OH
Mailing zip: 43210-1107

OHIO UNIV.

Street address 1: 325 Baker University Center
Street address city: Athens
Street address state: OH
Zip/Postal code: 45701
Country: USA
Mailing address: 325 Baker University Center
Mailing city: Athens
Mailing state: OH
Mailing zip: 45701
General Phone: (740) 593-4011
General Fax: (740) 593-0561
Advertising Phone: (740) 593-4018
General/National Adv. E-mail: posteditorial@ohiou.edu
Personnel: Ashley Lutz (Ed. in Chief); Dave Hendricks (Managing Ed.); Ryan Dunn (Associate Ed.); Natalie Debruin (Asst. Managing Ed.); Joe (Sports Ed.); Robert (Advertising Admin.)

OHIO WESLEYAN UNIVERSITY

Street address 1: 61 S Sandusky St
Street address 2: Rm 106
Street address city: Delaware
Street address state: OH
Zip/Postal code: 43015-2333
Country: USA
Mailing address: 61 S Sandusky St Rm 106
Mailing city: Delaware
Mailing state: OH
Mailing zip: 43015-2398
General Phone: (740) 368-2911
General Fax: (740) 368-3649
General/National Adv. E-mail: owunews@owu.edu
Display Adv. E-mail: owunews@owu.edu
Editorial e-mail: owunews@owu.edu
Primary Website: transcript.owu.edu
Year Established: 1867
Published: Thur
Avg Free Circ: 1000
Personnel: Jo Ingles (Media Adviser)

OTTERBEIN UNIVERSITY

Street address 1: 1 S Grove St
Street address 2: Otterbein University
Street address city: Westerville
Street address state: OH
Zip/Postal code: 43081-2004
Country: USA
Mailing address: Communication Department
Mailing city: Westerville
Mailing state: OH
Mailing zip: 43081
General Phone: (614) 823 1159
Advertising Phone: 614 823 1159
Editorial Phone: 614 823 1159
General/National Adv. E-mail: adviser@otterbein360.com
Display Adv. E-mail: sales@otterbein360.com
Primary Website: www.otterbein360.com
Year Established: 1880
Published: Mon`Tues`Wed`Thur`Fri`Sat`Sun
Personnel: Hillary Warren (Advisor)

SHAWNEE STATE UNIV.

Street address 1: 940 2nd St
Street address city: Portsmouth
Street address state: OH
Zip/Postal code: 45662-4303
Country: USA
Mailing address: 940 2nd St
Mailing city: Portsmouth
Mailing state: OH
Mailing zip: 45662-4347
General Phone: (740) 351-3278
General Fax: (740) 351-3566
Advertising Phone: (740) 351-3502
General/National Adv. E-mail: chronicle@shawnee.edu
Personnel: Terry Hapney (Advisor)

SINCLAIR COMMUNITY COLLEGE

Street address 1: 444 W 3rd St
Street address 2: Rm 6314
Street address city: Dayton
Street address state: OH
Zip/Postal code: 45402-1421
Country: USA
Mailing address: 444 W 3rd St Rm 6314
Mailing city: Dayton
Mailing state: OH
Mailing zip: 45402-1421
General Phone: (937) 512-2744
General Fax: (937) 512-4590
Advertising Phone: (937) 512-2744
Advertising Fax: (937) 512-4590
Editorial Phone: (937) 512-2958
Editorial Fax: (937) 512-4590
General/National Adv. E-mail: clarion@sinclair.edu
Display Adv. E-mail: clarion@sinclair.edu
Editorial e-mail: clarion@sinclair.edu
Primary Website: www.sinclairclarion.com
Year Established: 1977
Published: Tues
Avg Free Circ: 4000
Personnel: Gabrielle Sharp (Exec Ed); Barton Kleen (Mng Ed); Laina Yost (Associate Ed); Susan Day (Advt Rep)

STARK STATE COLLEGE OF TECHNOLOGY

Street address 1: 6200 Frank Ave NW
Street address city: North Canton
Street address state: OH
Zip/Postal code: 44720-7228
Country: USA
Mailing address: 6200 Frank Ave NW
Mailing city: North Canton
Mailing state: OH
Mailing zip: 44720-7299
General Phone: (330) 494-6170

THE NEWS RECORD

Street address 1: Swift Hall, Ste 510
Street address city: Cincinnati
Street address state: OH
Zip/Postal code: 45221-0001
Country: USA
Mailing address: PO Box 210135
Mailing city: Cincinnati
Mailing state: OH
Mailing zip: 45221-0135
General Phone: (513) 556-5900
General Fax: (513) 556-5922
General/National Adv. E-mail: newsrecordbiz@gmail.com; chief.newsrecord@gmail.com
Editorial e-mail: chief.newsrecord@gmail.com
Primary Website: www.newsrecord.org
Year Established: 1880
Personnel: Ariel Cheung (Editor-in-chief); Kristy Conlin (Ed. in Chief)

THE UNIVERSITY OF AKRON

Street address 1: 302 Buchtel Cmn
Street address city: Akron
Street address state: OH
Zip/Postal code: 44325-0001
County: Summit
Country: USA
Mailing address: 302 Buchtel Common
Mailing city: Akron
Mailing state: OH
Mailing zip: 44325-4206
General Phone: 330-972-7919
General Fax: 330-972-7810
Advertising Phone: 330-972-5912
Advertising Fax: 330-972-7810
Editorial Phone: 330-972-6184
Editorial Fax: 330-972-7810
General/National Adv. E-mail: adviser@buchtelite.com
Display Adv. E-mail: business-manager@buchtelite.com
Classified Adv. e-mail: www.buchtelite.campusave.com
Editorial e-mail: editor-in-chief@buchtelite.com
Primary Website: buchtelite.com
Mthly Avg Views: 5100
Year Established: 1889
Published: Tues`Thur
Avg Free Circ: 2700
Personnel: Adam Bernhard (Business Manager); Zaina Salem (Editor-in-Chief)

THE UNIVERSITY OF FINDLAY

Street address 1: 1000 N Main St
Street address city: Findlay
Street address state: OH
Zip/Postal code: 45840-3653
Country: USA
Mailing address: 1000 N Main St
Mailing city: Findlay
Mailing state: OH
Mailing zip: 45840-3653
General Phone: (419) 434-5892
Advertising Phone: (419) 434-5892
Editorial Phone: (419) 434-5892
General/National Adv. E-mail: pulse@findlay.edu
Display Adv. E-mail: pulse@findlay.edu
Editorial e-mail: pulse@findlay.edu
Primary Website: www.findlay.edu/pulse
Year Established: 1986 (as the Pulse)
Published: Fri
Avg Free Circ: 1000
Personnel: Olivia Wile (Pulse Editor)

UNIV. OF AKRON

Street address 1: 303 Carroll St, Student Union, Rm 51
Street address city: Akron
Street address state: OH
Zip/Postal code: 44325-0001
Country: USA
Mailing address: 303 Carroll St Student Un Rm 51
Mailing city: Akron
Mailing state: OH
Mailing zip: 44325-0001
General Phone: (330) 972-5475
General Fax: (330) 972-7810
Advertising Phone: (330) 972-7919
Editorial Phone: (330) 972-6184
General/National Adv. E-mail: adviser@buchtelite.com
Editorial e-mail: editor@buchtelite.com
Personnel: Maryanne Bailey-Porter (Acct. Coord.); Kevin Curwin (Ed. in Chief); Allison Strouse (News Ed.)

UNIV. OF DAYTON

Street address 1: 232 Kennedy Union
Street address 2: 300 College Park
Street address city: Dayton
Street address state: OH
Zip/Postal code: 45469-0001
Country: USA
Mailing address: 232 Kennedy Union
Mailing city: Dayton
Mailing state: OH
Mailing zip: 45469-0626
General Phone: (937) 229-3226
General Fax: (937) 229-3893
Advertising Phone: (937) 229-3813
Editorial Phone: (937) 229-3878
General/National Adv. E-mail: news@flyernews.com
Display Adv. E-mail: advertising@flyernews.com
Editorial e-mail: fn.editor@udayton.edu
Primary Website: www.flyernews.com
Published: Tues
Published Other: B-Weekly (Daily online)
Avg Free Circ: 3000
Personnel: Frazier Smith (Advisor); Amy Lopez-Matthews (Co-Advisor); CC Hutten (Ed.); Matthew Worsham (Mng. Ed.); Meredith Whelchel (Mng. Ed.); Julia Hall (Print-Ed.)

UNIV. OF DAYTON LAW SCHOOL

Street address 1: 300 College Park
Street address city: Dayton
Street address state: OH
Zip/Postal code: 45469-0001
Country: USA
Mailing address: 300 College Park
Mailing city: Dayton
Personnel: Jennifer Tate (Ed.)

UNIV. OF RIO GRANDE

Street address 1: 218 N College Ave
Street address city: Rio Grande
Street address state: OH
Zip/Postal code: 45674-3100
Country: USA
Mailing address: 218 N College Ave
Mailing city: Rio Grande
Mailing state: OH
Mailing zip: 45674-3131
General Phone: (740) 245-7521
Personnel: Nick Claussen (Advisor)

UNIVERSITY OF CINCINNATI

Street address 1: PO Box 210135
Street address city: Cincinnati
Street address state: OH
Zip/Postal code: 45221-0135
Country: USA
Mailing address: PO Box 210135
Mailing city: Cincinnati
Mailing state: OH
Mailing zip: 45221-0135

UNIVERSITY OF TOLEDO

Street address 1: 2801 W Bancroft St
Street address 2: Mail Stop 530
Street address city: Toledo
Street address state: OH
Zip/Postal code: 43606-3328
Country: USA
Mailing address: 2801 W Bancroft St
Mailing city: Toledo
Mailing state: OH
Mailing zip: 43606-3390
General Phone: (419) 530-7788
General Fax: (419) 530-7770
Advertising Phone: (419) 530-7788
Advertising Fax: (419) 530-7770
Editorial Phone: (419) 530-7788
Editorial Fax: (419) 530-7770
General/National Adv. E-mail: editor@independentcollegian.com
Display Adv. E-mail: sales@independentcollegian.com
Editorial e-mail: editor@independentcollegian.com
Primary Website: www.independentcollegian.com
Year Established: 1919
Published: Wed
Avg Free Circ: 8000
Personnel: J.R. Hoppenjans (Chairman of the board of trustees); Erik Gable (Adviser); Danielle Gamble (Editor-in-Chief)

WILBERFORCE UNIV.

Street address 1: 1055 N Bickett Rd
Street address city: Wilberforce
Street address state: OH
Zip/Postal code: 45384-5801
Country: USA
Mailing address: PO Box 1001
Mailing city: Wilberforce
Mailing state: OH
Mailing zip: 45384-1001
General Phone: (937) 376-2911
General Fax: (937) 708-5793
General/National Adv. E-mail: tmorah@wilberforce.edu

Personnel: Tanya Morah (Advisor); Courtney Wiggins (Ed.)

WILMINGTON COLLEGE

Street address 1: 1870 Quaker Way
Street address city: Wilmington
Street address state: OH
Zip/Postal code: 45177-2473
Country: USA
Mailing address: 1870 Quaker Way
Mailing city: Wilmington
Mailing state: OH
Mailing zip: 45177-2499
General Phone: (937) 382-6661
Personnel: Coreen Cockerill (Advisor); Clair Green (Ed. in Chief)

WITTENBERG UNIVERSITY

Street address 1: 200 W Ward St
Street address city: Springfield
Street address state: OH
Zip/Postal code: 45504-2120
Country: USA
Mailing address: PO Box 720
Mailing city: Springfield
Mailing state: OH
Mailing zip: 45501-0720
General Phone: 512.968.4648
General/National Adv. E-mail: torch_editors@wittenberg.edu
Primary Website: www.thewittenbergtorch.com
Published: Wed
Personnel: D'Arcy Fallon (Faculty Advisor); Maggie McKune (Ed. in Chief); Tara Osborne (Bus. Mgr.)

WRIGHT STATE UNIV.

Street address 1: 014 Student Union, 3640 Colonel Glenn Hwy
Street address city: Dayton
Street address state: OH
Zip/Postal code: 45435-0001
Country: USA
Mailing address: 14 Stud Ent Union 3640 Colonel Glenn Hwy
Mailing city: Dayton
Mailing state: OH
Mailing zip: 45435-0001
General Phone: (937) 775-5534
General Fax: (937) 775-5535
Display Adv. E-mail: advertising@theguardianonline.com
Editorial e-mail: editorial@theguardianonline.com
Personnel: Tiffany Johnson (Ed. in chief)

XAVIER UNIV.

Street address 1: 3800 Victory Pkwy
Street address city: Cincinnati
Street address state: OH
Zip/Postal code: 45207-1035
Country: USA
Mailing address: 3800 Victory Pkwy Dept 156
Mailing city: Cincinnati
Mailing state: OH
Mailing zip: 45207-8010
General Phone: (513) 745-3607
General Fax: (513) 745-2898
Personnel: Kathryn Rosenbaum (Ed. in Chief); Andrew Chestnut (Mng. Ed.); Meghan Berneking (News Ed.)

YOUNGSTOWN STATE UNIV.

Street address 1: 1 University Plz
Street address city: Youngstown
Street address state: OH
Zip/Postal code: 44555-0001
Country: USA
Mailing address: 1 University Plz
Mailing city: Youngstown
Mailing state: OH
Mailing zip: 44555-0002
General Phone: (330) 941-1991
General Fax: (330) 941-2322
General/National Adv. E-mail: thejambar@gmail.com
Primary Website: www.thejambar.com
Year Established: 1931
Personnel: Mary Beth Earnheardt (Advisor); Joshua Stipanovich (Editor in Chief); Chelsea Pflugh (Ed. in Chief); Adam Rogers (Mng. Ed.)

YOUNGSTOWN STATE UNIVERSITY

Street address 1: 1 University Plz
Street address city: Youngstown
Street address state: OH
Zip/Postal code: 44555-0001
Country: USA
Mailing address: 1 University Plz
Mailing city: Youngstown
Mailing state: OH
Mailing zip: 44555-0002

OKLAHOMA

BARTLESVILLE WESLEYAN COLLEGE

Street address 1: 2201 Silver Lake Rd
Street address city: Bartlesville
Street address state: OK
Zip/Postal code: 74006-6233
Country: USA
Mailing address: 2201 Silver Lake Rd
Mailing city: Bartlesville
Mailing state: OK

CAMERON UNIV.

Street address 1: 2800 W Gore Blvd
Street address city: Lawton
Street address state: OK
Zip/Postal code: 73505-6320
Country: USA
Mailing address: 2800 W Gore Blvd
Mailing city: Lawton
Mailing state: OK
Mailing zip: 73505-6377
General Phone: (580) 581-2259
Personnel: Christopher Keller (Advisor)

CARL ALBERT STATE COLLEGE

Street address 1: 1507 S McKenna St
Street address city: Poteau
Street address state: OK
Zip/Postal code: 74953-5207
Country: USA
Mailing address: 1507 S McKenna St
Mailing city: Poteau
Mailing state: OK
Mailing zip: 74953-5207
Personnel: Marcus Blair (PR Dir.)

EAST CENTRAL UNIVERSITY

Street address 1: 1100 E 14th St
Street address city: Ada
Street address state: OK
Zip/Postal code: 74820-6915
Country: USA
Mailing address: 1100 E 14th St
Mailing city: Ada
Mailing state: OK
Mailing zip: 74820-6915
General Phone: (580) 559-5250
General Fax: (580) 559-5251
General/National Adv. E-mail: journal@ecok.edu; ecujournal@me.com
Personnel: Cathie Harding (Advisor); Melissa Hubble (Adv. Mgr.); Jonnathon Hicks (Ed. in Chief)

LANGSTON UNIV.

Street address 1: Sanford Hall Rm 308W
Street address city: Langston
Street address state: OK
Zip/Postal code: 73050
Country: USA
Mailing address: Sanford Hall Rm. 308W
Mailing city: Langston
Mailing state: OK
Mailing zip: 73050
General Phone: (405) 466-3245
General/National Adv. E-mail: lugazette@yahoo.com
Personnel: Chaz Kyser (Advisor)

NORTHEASTERN OKLAHOMA A&M COLLEGE

Street address 1: 206 I St NW
Street address city: Miami
Street address state: OK
Zip/Postal code: 74354-5630
Country: USA
Mailing address: PO Box 3988
Mailing city: Miami
Personnel: Rebecca Kirk (Advisor)

NORTHERN OKLAHOMA COLLEGE

Street address 1: 1220 E Grand Ave
Street address city: Tonkawa
Street address state: OK
Zip/Postal code: 74653-4022
Country: USA
Mailing address: PO Box 310
Mailing city: Tonkawa
Mailing state: OK
Mailing zip: 74653-0310
General Phone: (580) 628-6444
Personnel: Jeremy Stillwell (Advisor)

NORTHWESTERN OKLAHOMA STATE UNIV.

Street address 1: 709 Oklahoma Blvd
Street address city: Alva
Street address state: OK
Zip/Postal code: 73717-2749
Country: USA
Mailing address: 709 Oklahoma Blvd
Mailing city: Alva
Mailing state: OK
Mailing zip: 73717-2749
General Phone: (580) 327-8479
General Fax: (580) 327-8127
Advertising Phone: (580) 327-8479
Editorial Phone: (580) 327-8479
General/National Adv. E-mail: nwnewsroom@hotmail.com; nwnews@nwosu.edu
Display Adv. E-mail: nwnewsroom@hotmail.com
Editorial e-mail: nwnewsroom@hotmail.com
Primary Website: www.nwosu.edu/northwestern-news or www.rangerpulse.com
Year Established: 1897
Published: Thur
Avg Free Circ: 1400
Personnel: Melanie Wilderman (Advisor)

OKLAHOMA BAPTIST UNIV.

Street address 1: 500 W University St
Street address 2: Ste 61704
Street address city: Shawnee
Street address state: OK
Zip/Postal code: 74804-2522
Country: USA
Mailing address: 500 W University St Ste 61704
Mailing city: Shawnee
Mailing state: OK
Mailing zip: 74804-2522
General Phone: (405) 878-2128
General Fax: (405) 878-2113
General/National Adv. E-mail: Holly.easttom@okbu.edu
Display Adv. E-mail: Holly.easttom@okbu.edu
Primary Website: www.okbu.edu
Year Established: 1942
Published: Wed
Avg Free Circ: 1800
Personnel: Holly Easttom (Advisor); Andrew Adams (Ed. in Chief)

OKLAHOMA CHRISTIAN UNIV.

Street address 1: PO Box 11000
Street address city: Oklahoma City
Street address state: OK
Zip/Postal code: 73136-1100
Country: USA
Mailing address: PO Box 11000
Mailing city: Oklahoma City
Mailing state: OK
Mailing zip: 73136-1100
General Phone: (405) 425-5538
Personnel: Philip Patterson (Faculty Advisor); Kimberlee Rhodes (Adv. Mgr.); Will Kooi (Ed. in Chief)

OKLAHOMA CITY COMMUNITY COLLEGE

Street address 1: 7777 S May Ave
Street address city: Oklahoma City
Street address state: OK
Zip/Postal code: 73159-4419
Country: USA
Mailing address: 7777 S May Ave
Mailing city: Oklahoma City
Mailing state: OK
Mailing zip: 73159-4499
General Phone: (405) 682-1611
General/National Adv. E-mail: editor@occc.edu
Display Adv. E-mail: matthew.s.carter@occc.edu
Editorial e-mail: editor@occc.edu
Primary Website: pioineer.occc.edu
Year Established: 1978
Published: Fri
Avg Free Circ: 2500
Personnel: M Scott Carter (Advisor)

OKLAHOMA CITY UNIVERSITY

Street address 1: 2501 N Blackwelder Ave
Street address city: Oklahoma City
Street address state: OK
Zip/Postal code: 73106-1402
Country: USA
Mailing address: 2501 N Blackwelder Ave Rm 117
Mailing city: Oklahoma City
Mailing state: OK
Mailing zip: 73106-1493
General Phone: (405) 208-6068
General Fax: (405) 208-6069
Advertising Phone: (405) 208-6068
Advertising Fax: (405) 208-6069
General/National Adv. E-mail: stupub@okcu.edu
Primary Website: www.mediaocu.com
Year Established: 1907
Personnel: Kenna Griffin (Advisor)

OKLAHOMA PANHANDLE STATE UNIV.

Street address 1: PO Box 430
Street address city: Goodwell
Street address state: OK
Zip/Postal code: 73939-0430
Country: USA
Mailing address: PO Box 430
Mailing city: Goodwell
Mailing state: OK
Mailing zip: 73939-0430
General Phone: (580) 349-2611
General Fax: (580) 349-1350
General/National Adv. E-mail: collegian@opsu.edu
Personnel: Lora Hays (Advisor); Samuel Moore (Ed.)

OKLAHOMA STATE UNIV.

Street address 1: 106 Paul Miller
Street address city: Stillwater
Street address state: OK
Zip/Postal code: 74078-4050
Country: USA
Mailing address: 106 Paul Miller
Mailing city: Stillwater
Mailing state: OK
Mailing zip: 74078-4050
General Phone: (405) 744-6365
Editorial e-mail: editor@ocolly.com
Personnel: Barbara Allen (Advisor); Emily Holman (Ed. in Chief)

ORAL ROBERTS UNIV.

Street address 1: 7777 S Lewis Ave
Street address 2: Lrc 175
Street address city: Tulsa
Street address state: OK
Zip/Postal code: 74171-0003
Country: USA
Mailing address: 7777 S Lewis Ave Lrc 175
Mailing city: Tulsa
Mailing state: OK
Mailing zip: 74171-0001
General Phone: (918) 495-7080

General Fax: (918) 495-6345
Advertising Phone: (918) 495-7080
Advertising Fax: (918) 495-6345
Editorial Phone: (918) 495-7080
Editorial Fax: (918) 495-6345
General/National Adv. E-mail: oracle@oru.edu
Display Adv. E-mail: oracleads@oru.edu
Primary Website: www.oruoracle.com
Year Established: 1965
Published: Fri'Bi-Mthly
Avg Free Circ: 3500
Personnel: Kevin Armstrong (Advisor)

SOUTHEASTERN OKLAHOMA STATE UNIV.

Street address 1: 425 W University Blvd
Street address city: Durant
Street address state: OK
Zip/Postal code: 74701-3347
Country: USA
Mailing address: 425 W University Blvd.
Mailing city: Durant
Mailing state: OK
Mailing zip: 74701-0609
General Phone: (580) 745-2944
General Fax: (580) 745-7475
General/National Adv. E-mail: campuspages@gmail.com
Primary Website: www.thesoutheastern.com
Published: Mthly
Published Other: Website updated weekly. Newspaper published monthly. Magazine released once a year.
Personnel: Tascha Bond (Adviser); Kourtney Kaufman (Managing Editor)

SOUTHERN NAZARENE UNIV.

Street address 1: 6729 NW 39th Expy
Street address city: Bethany
Street address state: OK
Zip/Postal code: 73008-2605
Country: USA
Mailing address: 6729 NW 39th Expy
Mailing city: Bethany
Mailing state: OK
Mailing zip: 73008-2694
General Phone: (405) 491-6382
General Fax: (405) 491-6378
General/National Adv. E-mail: echo@snu.edu
Display Adv. E-mail: grwillia@mail.snu.edu
Editorial e-mail: kirarobe@mail.snu.edu
Primary Website: echo.snu.edu
Published: Fri
Personnel: Pam Broyles (Speech Commun. Dept.); Marcia Feisal (Yearbook); Jim Wilcox (Newspaper); Andrew Baker (Graphic Design); Les Dart (Broadcasting)

ST. GREGORY'S COLLEGE

Street address 1: 1900 W MacArthur St
Street address city: Shawnee
Street address state: OK
Zip/Postal code: 74804-2403
Country: USA
Mailing address: 1900 W MacArthur St
Mailing city: Shawnee
Mailing state: OK
Mailing zip: 74804-2499
Personnel: Andrew Sneider (Advisor)

THE CAMPUS / MEDIAOCU

Street address 1: 2501 N. Blackwelder Ave
Street address city: Oklahoma City
Street address state: OK
Zip/Postal code: 73106-1493
County: Oklahoma
General/National Adv. E-mail: TheCampus@okcu.edu
Display Adv. E-mail: thecampusads@okcu.edu
Classified Adv. e-mail: thecampusads@okcu.edu
Editorial e-mail: editor@okcu.edu
Primary Website: www.mediaocu.com
Year Established: 1906
Published: Other
Published Other: Online as updated
Avg Free Circ: 1000
Personnel: Philip Todd (Faculty adviser)

THE VISTA

Street address 1: 100 N University Dr
Street address city: Edmond
Street address state: OK
Zip/Postal code: 73034-5207
Country: USA
Mailing address: 100 N University Dr
Mailing city: Edmond
Mailing state: OK
Mailing zip: 73034-5207
General Phone: (405) 974-5123
General Fax: (405) 974-3839
Editorial Phone: (405) 974-5549
General/National Adv. E-mail: vistamedia@yahoo.com
Editorial e-mail: vista1903@gmail.com
Primary Website: www.uco360.com
Year Established: 1903
Personnel: Teddy Burch (Advisor); Nelson Solomon (Ed. in Chief)

TULSA CMTY. COLLEGE

Street address 1: 909 S Boston Ave
Street address 2: Rm G-31
Street address city: Tulsa
Street address state: OK
Zip/Postal code: 74119-2011
Country: USA
Mailing address: 909 S Boston Ave Rm G-31
Mailing city: Tulsa
Mailing state: OK
Mailing zip: 74119-2011
Personnel: Jerry Goodwin (Advisor); Eric Bruce (Ed.)

UNIV. OF OKLAHOMA

Street address 1: 860 Van Vleet
Street address 2: Rm 149A
Street address city: Norman
Street address state: OK
Zip/Postal code: 73019-2035
Country: USA
Mailing address: 860 Van Vleet Rm 149A
Mailing city: Norman
Mailing state: OK
Mailing zip: 73019-2035
General Phone: (405) 325-2521
General Fax: (405) 325-5160
Advertising Fax: (405) 325-7517
General/National Adv. E-mail: dailynews@ou.edu; studentmedia@ou.edu
Personnel: Judy Robinson (Advisor); Jamie Hughes (Ed.); Caitlin Harrison (Mng. Ed.); Michelle Gray (Photo Ed.)

UNIV. OF SCIENCE & ARTS OF OKLAHOMA

Street address 1: 1727 W Alabama Ave
Street address city: Chickasha
Street address state: OK
Zip/Postal code: 73018-5322
Country: USA
Mailing address: 1727 W Alabama Ave
Mailing city: Chickasha
Mailing state: OK
Mailing zip: 73018-5371
General Phone: (405) 224-3140
Primary Website: www.trend.usao.edu
Published: Other
Published Other: Ongoing (post several times a week)
Personnel: J. C. Casey (Faculty Advisor & Professor of Communication)

UNIV. OF TULSA

Street address 1: 800 S Tucker Dr
Street address city: Tulsa
Street address state: OK
Zip/Postal code: 74104-9700
Country: USA
Mailing address: 800 Tucker Dr
Mailing city: Tulsa
Mailing state: OK
Mailing zip: 74104-9700
General Phone: (918) 631-2259
General Fax: (918) 631-2885
General/National Adv. E-mail: collegian@utulsa.edu
Primary Website: www.utulsa.edu/collegian/
Published: Mon
Avg Free Circ: 2500
Personnel: Kendra Blevins (Advisor); J.Christopher Proctor (Editor-in-Chief); Elizabeth Cohen (Business and Advertising Manager)

OREGON

CENTRAL OREGON COMMUNITY COLLEGE

Street address 1: 2600 NW College Way
Street address city: Bend
Street address state: OR
Zip/Postal code: 97703-5933
Country: USA
Mailing address: 2600 NW College Way
Mailing city: Bend
Mailing state: OR
Mailing zip: 97701-5933
General Phone: (541) 383-7252
General Fax: (541) 383-7284
Editorial Fax: Free
General/National Adv. E-mail: broadsidemail@cocc.edu
Primary Website: broadside.cocc.edu
Published: Bi-Mthly
Personnel: Leon Pantenburg (advisor)

CHEMEKETA CMTY. COLLEGE

Street address 1: PO Box 14007
Street address city: Salem
Street address state: OR
Zip/Postal code: 97309-7070
Country: USA
Mailing address: PO Box 14007
Mailing city: Salem
Mailing state: OR
Mailing zip: 97309-7070
General Phone: (503) 399-5000
General Fax: (503) 399-2519
General/National Adv. E-mail: courier@chemeketa.edu
Display Adv. E-mail: careeradvertising@yahoo.com
Personnel: William Florence (Advisor); Gale Hann (Adv. Mgr.); Russell Vineyard (Mng.Ed.)

CLACKAMAS CMTY. COLLEGE

Street address 1: 19600 Molalla Ave
Street address city: Oregon City
Street address state: OR
Zip/Postal code: 97045-8980
Country: USA
Mailing address: 19600 Molalla Ave
Mailing city: Oregon City
Mailing state: OR
Mailing zip: 97045-7998
General Phone: (503) 657-6958
Personnel: Melissa Jones (Advisor); Kayla Berge (Ed.); John Hurlburg (Ed.)

EASTERN OREGON UNIV.

Street address 1: 1 University Blvd
Street address 2: Hoke 320
Street address city: La Grande
Street address state: OR
Zip/Postal code: 97850-2807
Country: USA
Mailing address: 1 University Blvd Hoke 320
Mailing city: La Grande
Mailing state: OR
Mailing zip: 97850-2807
General Phone: (541) 962-3386
General Fax: (541) 962-3706
General/National Adv. E-mail: thevoice@eou.edu
Personnel: Kyle Janssen (Ed. in Chief); Taylor Stanely Pawley (Adv. Mgr.)

LANE CMTY. COLLEGE

Street address 1: 4000 E 30th Ave
Street address 2: Rm 008
Street address city: Eugene
Street address state: OR
Zip/Postal code: 97405-0640
Country: USA
Mailing address: 4000 East 30th Ave. Center Building, Room 008
Mailing city: Eugene
Mailing state: OR
Mailing zip: 97405-0640
General Phone: (541) 463-5881
General Fax: (541) 463-3993
General/National Adv. E-mail: torch@lanecc.edu
Personnel: Dorothy Wearne (Advisor); Lana Boles (Ed. in Cheif); James Anderson (Ed.)

LEWIS & CLARK COLLEGE

Street address 1: 0615 SW Palatine Hill Rd
Street address city: Portland
Street address state: OR
Zip/Postal code: 97219-7879
Country: USA
Mailing address: 0615 SW Palatine Hill Rd
Mailing city: Portland
Mailing state: OR
Mailing zip: 97219-7879
General Phone: (503) 768-7146
General Fax: (503) 768-7130
Editorial Fax: Free
General/National Adv. E-mail: piolog@lclark.edu
Display Adv. E-mail: ads.piolog@gmail.com
Editorial e-mail: piolog@gmail.com
Primary Website: www.piolog.com
Year Established: 1947
Published: Fri
Avg Free Circ: 1200
Personnel: Caleb Diehl (Editor-in-Chief)

LINFIELD COLLEGE

Street address 1: 900 SE Baker St
Street address 2: Ste A518
Street address city: McMinnville
Street address state: OR
Zip/Postal code: 97128-6808
Country: USA
Mailing address: 900 SE Baker St Ste A518
Mailing city: McMinnville
Mailing state: OR
Mailing zip: 97128-6894
General Phone: (503) 883-2200
General/National Adv. E-mail: review@linfield.edu
Personnel: William Lingle (Advisor); Dominic Baez (Ed. in Chief)

LINN-BENTON CMTY. COLLEGE

Street address 1: 6500 Pacific Blvd SW
Street address city: Albany
Street address state: OR
Zip/Postal code: 97321-3755
Country: USA
Mailing address: 6500 Pacific Blvd SW
Mailing city: Albany
Mailing state: OR
Mailing zip: 97321-3774
General Phone: (541) 917-4451
General Fax: (541) 917-4454
Editorial Phone: (541) 917-4452
General/National Adv. E-mail: commuter@linnbenton.edu
Personnel: Rob Priewe (Advisor); Frank Warren (Adv. Mgr.); Ryan henson Henson (Ed. in Chief)

MT. HOOD CMTY. COLLEGE

Street address 1: 26000 SE Stark St
Street address city: Gresham
Street address state: OR
Zip/Postal code: 97030-3300
Country: USA
Mailing address: 26000 SE Stark St
Mailing city: Gresham
Mailing state: OR
Mailing zip: 97030-3300
General Phone: (503) 491-7250
Published: Fri
Personnel: Ivy Davis (EIC); Dan Ernst (Advisor)

OREGON INSTITUTE OF TECHNOLOGY

Street address 1: 3201 Campus Dr
Street address 2: # CU111C
Street address city: Klamath Falls
Street address state: OR

Zip/Postal code: 97601-8801
Country: USA
Mailing address: 3201 Campus Dr # CU111C
Mailing city: Klamath Falls
Mailing state: OR
Mailing zip: 97601-8801
General Phone: (541) 885-1371
Personnel: Steve Matthies (Advisor)

OREGON STATE UNIV.

Street address 1: 118 Memorial Un E
Street address city: Corvallis
Street address state: OR
Zip/Postal code: 97331-8592
Country: USA
Mailing address: 118 Memorial Un E
Mailing city: Corvallis
Mailing state: OR
Mailing zip: 97331-8592
General Phone: (541) 737-3374
Personnel: Brandon Southward (Ed. in chief); Taryn Luna (Ed.); Gail Cole (Ed. in Chief); Candice Ruud (Mng. Ed.)

PACIFIC UNIV.

Street address 1: 2043 College Way
Street address city: Forest Grove
Street address state: OR
Zip/Postal code: 97116-1756
Country: USA
Mailing address: 2043 College Way
Mailing city: Forest Grove
Mailing state: OR
Mailing zip: 97116
General Phone: (503) 352-2855
Advertising Phone: 503 352 2855
Advertising Fax: (503) 352-3130
Editorial Phone: 503 352 2855
General/National Adv. E-mail: index@pacificu.edu
Editorial e-mail: karissa@pacindex.com
Primary Website: www.pacindex.com
Year Established: 1897
Published: Bi-Mthly
Avg Free Circ: 1200
Personnel: Dave Cassady (Adviser); Karrisa George (Managing editor); Kathleen Rohde (Web edition editor)

PORTLAND CMTY. COLLEGE

Street address 1: 12000 SW 49th Ave
Street address city: Portland
Street address state: OR
Zip/Postal code: 97219-7132
Country: USA
Mailing address: PO Box 19000
Mailing city: Portland
Mailing state: OR
Mailing zip: 97280-0990
General Phone: (503) 977-4184
General Fax: (503) 977-4956
Year Established: 1963
Personnel: Tami Steffenhagen (Gen. Mgr.)

PORTLAND STATE UNIV.

Street address 1: PO Box 347
Street address city: Portland
Street address state: OR
Zip/Postal code: 97207-0347
Country: USA
Mailing address: PO Box 751
Mailing city: Portland
Mailing state: OR
Mailing zip: 97207-0751
General Phone: (503) 725-5691
General Fax: (503) 725-5860
General/National Adv. E-mail: vanguardadvertising@gmail.com
Primary Website: www.dailyvanguard.com
Year Established: 1948
Personnel: Judson Randall (Advisor); Matthew Kirtley (Adv. Mgr.); Sarah J. Christensen (Ed. in Chief)

REED COLLEGE

Street address 1: 3203 SE Woodstock Blvd
Street address city: Portland
Street address state: OR
Zip/Postal code: 97202-8138
Country: USA
Mailing address: 3203 SE Woodstock Blvd
Mailing city: Portland
Mailing state: OR
Mailing zip: 97202-8199

SOUTHERN OREGON UNIV.

Street address 1: Stevenson Union, Rm 336, 1250 Siskiyou Blvd
Street address city: Ashland
Street address state: OR
Zip/Postal code: 97520
Country: USA
Mailing address: Stevenson Union, Rm. 336, 1250 Siskiyou Blvd.
Mailing city: Ashland
Mailing state: OR
Mailing zip: 97520-5001
General Phone: (541) 552-6307
General Fax: (541) 552-6440
Advertising Phone: (541) 552-6306
General/National Adv. E-mail: siskiyou@students.sou.edu
Personnel: Karen Finnegan (Advisor); Dwight Melton (Ed.)

SOUTHWESTERN OREGON CMTY. COLLEGE

Street address 1: 1988 Newman Ave
Street address city: Coos Bay
Street address state: OR
Zip/Postal code: 97420
Country: USA
Mailing address: 1988 Newman Ave.
Mailing city: Coos Bay
Personnel: Bridget Hildreth (Advisor)

THE BEACON/ UNIV. OF PORTLAND

Street address 1: 5000 N Willamette Blvd
Street address 2: MS 161
Street address city: Portland
Street address state: OR
Zip/Postal code: 97203-5743
Country: USA
Mailing address: 5000 N Willamette Blvd
Mailing city: Portland
Mailing state: OR
Mailing zip: 97203-5798
General Phone: (503) 943-7376
General Fax: (503) 943-7833
General/National Adv. E-mail: beacon@up.edu
Display Adv. E-mail: beaconads@up.edu
Primary Website: www.upbeacon.com
Year Established: 1935
Published Other: We are now digital only!!!
Personnel: Nancy Copic (Advisor)

UMPQUA CMTY. COLLEGE

Street address 1: 1140 College Rd
Street address city: Roseburg
Street address state: OR
Zip/Postal code: 97470
Country: USA
Mailing address: PO Box 967
Mailing city: Roseburg
Mailing state: OR
Mailing zip: 97470-0226
General Phone: (541) 440-4687
General Fax: (541) 677-3214
General/National Adv. E-mail: uccmainstream@yahoo.com
Personnel: Melinda Benton (Advisor)

UNIV. OF OREGON

Street address 1: 1395 University St
Street address city: Eugene
Street address state: OR
Zip/Postal code: 97403-2572
Country: USA
Mailing address: PO Box 3159
Mailing city: Eugene
Mailing state: OR
Mailing zip: 97403-0159
General Phone: (541) 346-5511
General Fax: (541) 346-5821
General/National Adv. E-mail: news@dailyemerald.com
Editorial e-mail: editor@dailyemerald.com
Personnel: Allie Grasgreen (Ed. in chief); Emily E. Smith (Mng. Ed.); Ivar Vong (Photo Ed.)

WESTERN OREGON UNIV.

Street address 1: 345 Monmouth Ave N
Street address city: Monmouth
Street address state: OR
Zip/Postal code: 97361-1329
Country: USA
Mailing address: 345 Monmouth Ave N
Mailing city: Monmouth
Mailing state: OR
Mailing zip: 97361-1371
General Phone: (503) 838-9697
Personnel: Marissa Hufstader (Bus./Adv. Mgr.)

WILLAMETTE UNIV.

Street address 1: 900 State St
Street address city: Salem
Street address state: OR
Zip/Postal code: 97301-3922
Country: USA
Mailing address: 900 State St
Mailing city: Salem
Mailing state: OR
Mailing zip: 97301-3931
General Phone: (503) 370-6053
General/National Adv. E-mail: collegian-exec@willamette.edu
Display Adv. E-mail: collegian-ads@willamette.edu
Primary Website: www.willamettecollegian.com
Published: Bi-Mthly
Personnel: Avery Bento (Advisor); James Hoodecheck (Bus. Mgr.); Gianni Marabella (Ed. in Chief)

PENNSYLVANIA

ALBRIGHT COLLEGE

Street address 1: N 13th and Bern Streets
Street address city: Reading
Street address state: PA
Zip/Postal code: 19612
Country: USA
Mailing address: P.O. Box 15234
Mailing city: Reading
Mailing state: PA
Mailing zip: 19612
General Phone: (610) 921-7558
General/National Adv. E-mail: albrightian@albright.edu
Primary Website: www.albright.edu/albrightian
Published: Bi-Mthly
Personnel: Jon Bekken (Advisor); Sarah Timmons (Editor-in-chief); Megan Homsher (Assistant Editor-in-Chief)

ALLEGHENY COLLEGE

Street address 1: PO Box 12
Street address city: Meadville
Street address state: PA
Zip/Postal code: 16335-0012
Country: USA
Mailing address: PO Box 12
Mailing city: Meadville
Mailing state: PA
Mailing zip: 16335-0012
General Phone: (814) 332-2754
General Fax: (814) 724-6834
General/National Adv. E-mail: thecampus1@gmail.com
Personnel: Penny Schaefer (Advisor); Kristin Baldwin (Ed. in Chief)

ALVERNIA UNIVERSITY

Street address 1: 401 Penn Street
Street address city: Reading
Street address state: PA
Zip/Postal code: 19601-3973
County: Berks
Country: USA
Mailing address: 400 Saint Bernardine St
Mailing city: Reading
Mailing state: PA
Mailing zip: 19607-1737
General Phone: (484) 254-2114
General/National Adv. E-mail: ryan.lange@alvernia.edu
Primary Website: http://www.alvernia.edu/alvernian
Published: Mthly
Avg Free Circ: 700
Personnel: Ryan Lange (Faculty Advisor)

ARCADIA UNIV.

Street address 1: 450 S Easton Rd
Street address city: Glenside
Street address state: PA
Zip/Postal code: 19038-3215
Country: USA
Mailing address: 450 S Easton Rd
Mailing city: Glenside
Mailing state: PA
Mailing zip: 19038-3295
General Phone: (215) 572-4082
Personnel: Michele Cain (Sec)

BLOOMSBURG UNIV.

Street address 1: 400 E 2nd St
Street address city: Bloomsburg
Street address state: PA
Zip/Postal code: 17815-1301
Country: USA
Mailing address: 400 E. Second St.
Mailing city: Bloomsburg
Mailing state: PA
Mailing zip: 17815
General Phone: (570) 389-4457
Personnel: Mary Bernath (Advisor); Zach Sands (Adv. Dir.); Joe Arleth (Ed. in Chief)

BRYN MAWR-HAVERFORD COLLEGE

Street address 1: 101 N Merion Ave
Street address city: Bryn Mawr
Street address state: PA
Zip/Postal code: 19010-2859
Country: USA
Mailing address: 101 N Merion Ave
Mailing city: Bryn Mawr
Mailing state: PA
Mailing zip: 19010-2899
General Phone: (610) 526-5000
General Fax: (610) 526-7479
General/National Adv. E-mail: biconews@haverford.edu
Personnel: Eurie Kim (Bus. Mgr.); Sam Kaplan (Ed. in Chief); Dave Merrell (Ed. Emer./Web Ed.)

BUCKNELL UNIV.

Street address 1: PO Box C-3952
Street address city: Lewisburg
Street address state: PA
Zip/Postal code: 17837
Country: USA
Mailing address: PO Box C-3952
Mailing city: Lewisburg
Mailing state: PA
Mailing zip: 17837-9988
General Phone: (570) 577-1520
General Fax: (570) 577-1176
Editorial Phone: (570) 577-1085
Display Adv. E-mail: bucknellianads@bucknell.edu
Primary Website: http://bucknellian.blogs.bucknell.edu/
Year Established: 1896
Published: Fri
Avg Free Circ: 4000
Personnel: James F. Lee (Advisor); Winnie Warner (Ed. in Chief); Ben Kaufman (Editor in Chief)

BUCKNELL UNIV. COLLEGE OF ENGINEERING

Street address 1: 701 Moore Ave
Street address city: Lewisburg
Street address state: PA
Zip/Postal code: 17837-2010
Country: USA
Mailing address: 701 Moore Ave
Mailing city: Lewisburg
Mailing state: PA
Mailing zip: 17837-2010
General Phone: (570) 577-1520
General/National Adv. E-mail: bucknellian@bucknell.edu

Personnel: James Lee (Advisor); Lily Beauvilliers (Ed. in Chief)

BUCKS COUNTY CMTY. COLLEGE

Street address 1: 275 Swamp Rd
Street address city: Newtown
Street address state: PA
Zip/Postal code: 18940-4106
Country: USA
Mailing address: 275 Swamp Rd
Mailing city: Newtown
Mailing state: PA
Mailing zip: 18940-9677
General Phone: (215) 968-8379
General Fax: (215) 968-8271
Editorial Phone: (215) 968-8379
General/National Adv. E-mail: buckscenturion@gmail.com
Display Adv. E-mail: orders@mymediamate.com
Editorial e-mail: buckscenturion@gmail.com
Primary Website: www.bucks-news.com
Year Established: 1964
Published: Thur
Avg Free Circ: 2000
Personnel: Tony Rogers (Advisor)

BUTLER COUNTY CMTY. COLLEGE

Street address 1: 107 College Dr
Street address city: Butler
Street address state: PA
Zip/Postal code: 16002-3807
Country: USA
Mailing address: PO Box 1203
Mailing city: Butler
Mailing state: PA
Mailing zip: 16003-1203
General Phone: (724) 287-8711
General Fax: (724) 285-6047
General/National Adv. E-mail: cube.stass@bc3.edu
Personnel: David Moser (Advisor); Patrick Reddick (Ed.)

CABRINI UNIVERSITY LOQUITUR

Street address 1: 610 King of Prussia Rd
Street address city: Radnor
Street address state: PA
Zip/Postal code: 19087-3623
Country: USA
Mailing address: 610 King of Prussia Rd
Mailing city: Radnor
Mailing state: PA
Mailing zip: 19087-3698
General Phone: (610) 902-8360
General Fax: (610) 902-8285
General/National Adv. E-mail: loquitur@cabrini.edu
Display Adv. E-mail: loquitur@cabrini.edu
Editorial e-mail: loquitur@cabrini.edu
Primary Website: www.theloquitur.com
Year Established: 1959
Published: Thur'Bi-Mthly
Avg Free Circ: 1400
Personnel: Jerome Zurek (Chair); Angelina Miller (EIC)

CARNEGIE MELLON UNIV.

Street address 1: 5000 Forbes Ave
Street address city: Pittsburgh
Street address state: PA
Zip/Postal code: 15213-3815
Country: USA
Mailing address: Box 119
Mailing city: Pittsburgh
Mailing state: PA
Mailing zip: 15213
General Phone: (412) 268-2111
General Fax: (412) 268-1596
General/National Adv. E-mail: contact@tartan.org
Display Adv. E-mail: advertising@thetartan.org
Primary Website: www.thetartan.org
Published: Mon
Avg Free Circ: 6000

CEDAR CREST COLLEGE

Street address 1: 100 College Dr
Street address city: Allentown
Street address state: PA
Zip/Postal code: 18104-6132
Country: USA
Mailing address: 100 College Dr
Mailing city: Allentown
Mailing state: PA
Mailing zip: 18104-6196
General Phone: (610) 437-4471
General Fax: (610) 437-5955
General/National Adv. E-mail: crestiad@cedarcrest.edu
Primary Website: www.cedarcrest.edu/crestiad
Year Established: 1932
Personnel: Elizabeth Ortiz (Advisor)

CHEYNEY UNIV. OF PENNSYLVANIA

Street address 1: 1837 University Cir
Street address 2: PO Box 200
Street address city: Cheyney
Street address state: PA
Zip/Postal code: 19319-1019
Country: USA
Mailing address: 1837 University Cir
Mailing city: Cheyney
Personnel: Owens Gwen (Advisor)

CLARION UNIV. OF PENNSYLVANIA

Street address 1: 270 Gemmell Student Ctr
Street address city: Clarion
Street address state: PA
Zip/Postal code: 16214
Country: USA
Mailing address: 270 Gemmell Student Ctr.
Mailing city: Clarion
Mailing state: PA
Mailing zip: 16214
General Phone: (814) 393-2000
General Fax: (814) 393-2557
General/National Adv. E-mail: call@clarion.edu
Personnel: Laurie Miller (Advisor); Elizabeth Presutti (Adv. Mgr.); Luke Hampton (Ed. in Chief)

CMTY. COLLEGE ALLEGHENY COUNTY

Street address 1: 808 Ridge Ave
Street address city: Pittsburgh
Street address state: PA
Zip/Postal code: 15212-6003
Country: USA
Mailing address: Office of Student Life
Mailing city: Pittsburgh
Mailing state: PA
General Phone: (412) 237-2543
Personnel: Christine McQuaide (Advisor)

CMTY. COLLEGE ALLEGHENY COUNTY SOUTH

Street address 1: 1750 Clairton Rd
Street address 2: # RT885
Street address city: West Mifflin
Street address state: PA
Zip/Postal code: 15122-3029
Country: USA
Mailing address: 1750 Clairton Rd # Rt
Mailing city: West Mifflin
Mailing state: PA
Mailing zip: 15122-3029
General Phone: (412) 469-6352
Personnel: Aaron Kindeall (Ed.)

CMTY. COLLEGE OF ALLEGHENY COUNTY BOYCE

Street address 1: 595 Beatty Rd
Street address city: Monroeville
Street address state: PA
Zip/Postal code: 15146-1348
Country: USA
Mailing address: 595 Beatty Rd
Mailing city: Monroeville
Mailing state: PA
Mailing zip: 15146-1348
Personnel: Peggy Roche (Adv. Mgr.)

COMMUNITY COLLEGE OF ALLEGHENY: NORTH CAMPUS VOICE

Street address 1: 8701 Perry Hwy
Street address 2: Rm 2003
Street address city: Pittsburgh
Street address state: PA
Zip/Postal code: 15237-5353
Country: USA
Mailing address: 8701 Perry Hwy, Rm 2003 B
Mailing city: Pittsburgh
Mailing state: PA
Mailing zip: 15237

COMMUNITY COLLEGE OF ALLEGHENY:THE FORUM

Street address 1: 1750 Clourton Rd Rt 885
Street address city: West Mifflin
Street address state: PA
Zip/Postal code: 15122
Country: USA
Mailing address: 1750 Clourton Rd Rt 885
Mailing city: West Mifflin
Mailing state: PA
Mailing zip: 15122

COMMUNITY COLLEGE OF PHILADELPHIA

Street address 1: 1700 Spring Garden St
Street address city: Philadelphia
Street address state: PA
Zip/Postal code: 19130-3936
Country: USA
Mailing address: 1700 Spring Garden St.
Mailing city: Philadelphia
Mailing state: PA
Mailing zip: 19130-3936
General Phone: (215) 751-8200
Primary Website: www.thestudentvanguard.com
Year Established: 1964
Published: Bi-Mthly
Personnel: Randy LoBasso (Faculty Advisor); Michael Castaneda (Editor-In-Chief); Rachel Byrd (Associate Editor); Imzadi Davis (Managing Editor); Devonte Gillespie (Business Manager)

DELAWARE VALLEY COLLEGE

Street address 1: 700 E Butler Ave
Street address city: Doylestown
Street address state: PA
Zip/Postal code: 18901-2607
Country: USA
Mailing address: 700 E Butler Ave
Mailing city: Doylestown
Mailing state: PA
Mailing zip: 18901-2698
General Phone: (215) 489-2345
General Fax: (215) 230-2966
General/National Adv. E-mail: rampages@delval.edu
Personnel: James O'Connor (Advisor)

DESALES UNIV.

Street address 1: 2755 Station Ave
Street address city: Center Valley
Street address state: PA
Zip/Postal code: 18034-9565
Country: USA
Mailing address: 2755 Station Ave
Mailing city: Center Valley
Mailing state: PA
Mailing zip: 18034-9568
General Phone: (610) 282-1100
General Fax: (610) 282-3798
General/National Adv. E-mail: minstrel.desales@gmail.com
Primary Website: www.desalesminstrel.org
Published: Bi-Mthly
Personnel: Kellie Dietrich (Editor-in-Chief)

DICKINSON COLLEGE

Street address 1: PO Box 1773
Street address city: Carlisle
Street address state: PA
Zip/Postal code: 17013-2896
Country: USA
Mailing address: PO Box 1773
Mailing city: Carlisle
Mailing state: PA
Mailing zip: 17013-2896
General Phone: (717) 254-8434
General Fax: (717) 254-8430
General/National Adv. E-mail: dsonian@dickinson.edu
Personnel: Alec Johnson (Ed. in Chief); Eddie Small (Mng. Ed.)

DREXEL UNIV.

Street address 1: 3141 Chestnut St
Street address city: Philadelphia
Street address state: PA
Zip/Postal code: 19104-2816
Country: USA
Mailing address: 3141 Chestnut St
Mailing city: Philadelphia
Mailing state: PA
Mailing zip: 19104-2875
Primary Website: www.thetriangle.org
Year Established: 1926
Published: Fri
Personnel: David Stephenson (EIC); Keith Hobin (Mng Ed); Laura DiSanto (Staff Mgr); Alexandra Jones (EIC); Gina Vitale

DUQUESNE UNIVERSITY

Street address 1: 600 Forbes Ave
Street address 2: 113 College Hall
Street address city: Pittsburgh
Street address state: PA
Zip/Postal code: 15282-0001
Country: USA
Mailing address: 600 Forbes Ave
Mailing city: Pittsburgh
Mailing state: PA
Mailing zip: 15282-0001
General Phone: (412) 396-6629
General/National Adv. E-mail: theduke@duq.edu
Display Adv. E-mail: dukeads@yahoo.com
Primary Website: www.duqsm.com
Year Established: 1925
Published: Thur
Personnel: Bobby Kerlik (Advisor); Jess Eagle (Ed. in Chief); Brian Tierney (Associate Ed.); Matt Noonan (Managing Ed.); Shawn (News Ed.); Mickey (Advertising Mgr.)

EAST STROUDSBURG UNIV.

Street address 1: University Ctr
Street address city: East Stroudsburg
Street address state: PA
Zip/Postal code: 18301
Country: USA
Mailing address: 200 Prospect Street
Mailing city: East Stroudsburg
Mailing state: PA
Mailing zip: 18301
General Phone: (570) 422-3295
General Fax: (570) 422-3053
General/National Adv. E-mail: stroudcourier@yahoo.com
Personnel: Ryan Doyle (Adv. Mgr.); Stephanie Snyder (Ed. in Chief)

EASTERN UNIVERSITY:THE WALTONIAN

Street address 1: 1300 Eagle Rd
Street address city: St Davids
Street address state: PA
Zip/Postal code: 19087-3617
Country: USA
Mailing address: 1300 Eagle Rd
Mailing city: St Davids
Mailing state: PA
Mailing zip: 19087
General Phone: 610-341-1710

EDINBORO UNIV. OF PENNSYLVANIA

Street address 1: 119 San Antonio Hall
Street address city: Edinboro
Street address state: PA
Zip/Postal code: 16444-0001
Country: USA
Mailing address: 119 San Antonio Hall
Mailing city: Edinboro
Mailing state: PA
Mailing zip: 16444-0001
General Phone: (814) 732-2266
General Fax: (814) 732-2270
General/National Adv. E-mail: eupspectator1@yahoo.com

Personnel: Josh Tyslachney (Advisor); Carli Hoehn (Adv. Mgr.); Britney Kemp (Ed. in Chief); Canuron Ferranti (Mng. Ed.)

ELIZABETHTOWN COLLEGE

Street address 1: 1 Alpha Dr
Street address city: Elizabethtown
Street address state: PA
Zip/Postal code: 17022-2298
Country: USA
Mailing address: 1 Alpha Dr
Mailing city: Elizabethtown
Mailing state: PA
Mailing zip: 17022-2297
General Phone: (717) 361-1132
General/National Adv. E-mail: editor@etown.edu
Display Adv. E-mail: etownianads@etown.edu
Editorial e-mail: editor@etown.edu
Primary Website: www.etownian.com
Year Established: 1904
Published: Thur
Avg Free Circ: 700
Personnel: Aileen Ida (EIC); Erica Dolson (Adviser); Katie Weiler (Asst. EIC); Amanda Jobes (Mng. Ed.)

FRANKLIN & MARSHALL COLLEGE

Street address 1: PO Box 3003
Street address city: Lancaster
Street address state: PA
Zip/Postal code: 17604-3003
Country: USA
Mailing address: PO Box 3003
Mailing city: Lancaster
Mailing state: PA
Mailing zip: 17604-3003
General Phone: (717) 291-4095
General Fax: (717) 291-3886
Display Adv. E-mail: reporterads@fandm.edu
Editorial e-mail: reporter@fandm.edu
Personnel: Justin Quinn (Advisor); Patrick Bernard (Advisor); Christian Wedekind (Ed.)

GANNON UNIV.

Street address 1: 109 University Sq
Street address 2: # 2142
Street address city: Erie
Street address state: PA
Zip/Postal code: 16541-0002
Country: USA
Mailing address: 109 University Sq # 2142
Mailing city: Erie
Mailing state: PA
Mailing zip: 16541-0002
General Phone: (814) 871-7294
General Fax: (814) 871-7208
General/National Adv. E-mail: gannonknight@gannon.edu
Personnel: Frank Garland (Advisor)

GENEVA COLLEGE

Street address 1: 3200 College Ave
Street address city: Beaver Falls
Street address state: PA
Zip/Postal code: 15010-3557
Country: USA
Mailing address: 3200 College Ave
Mailing city: Beaver Falls
Mailing state: PA
Mailing zip: 15010-3599
General Phone: (724) 847-6605
General Fax: (724) 847-6772
General/National Adv. E-mail: cabinet.editor@gmail.comcabinet
Personnel: Tom Copeland (Advisor)

GETTYSBURG COLLEGE

Street address 1: PO Box 434
Street address city: Gettysburg
Street address state: PA
Zip/Postal code: 17325
Country: USA
Mailing address: PO Box 434
Mailing city: Gettysburg
Mailing state: PA
Mailing zip: 17325
General Phone: (717) 337-6449
Personnel: Joel Berg (Advisor); Sean Parke (Ed.)

GROVE CITY COLLEGE

Street address 1: 100 Campus Dr
Street address city: Grove City
Street address state: PA
Zip/Postal code: 16127-2101
Country: USA
Mailing address: 100 Campus Dr
Mailing city: Grove City
Mailing state: PA
Mailing zip: 16127-2104
General Phone: (724) 458-2193
General Fax: (724) 458-2167
Year Established: 1891
Published: Fri
Avg Free Circ: 1500
Personnel: Nick Hildebrand (Adviser); Karen Postupac (Editor-in_Chief); James Sutherland (Managing Editor)

HOLY FAMILY COLLEGE

Street address 1: 9801 Frankford Ave
Street address city: Philadelphia
Street address state: PA
Zip/Postal code: 19114-2009
Country: USA
Mailing address: 9801 Frankford Ave
Mailing city: Philadelphia
Mailing state: PA
Mailing zip: 19114
General Phone: (215) 637-5321
Personnel: Laura Wkovitz (Ed.)

INDIANA UNIV. OF PENNSYLVANIA

Street address 1: 319 Pratt Dr
Street address city: Indiana
Street address state: PA
Zip/Postal code: 15701-2954
Country: USA
Mailing address: 319 Pratt Dr
Mailing city: Indiana
Mailing state: PA
Mailing zip: 15701-2954
General Phone: (724) 357-1306
General Fax: (724) 357-0127
Advertising Phone: (724) 357-0127
Editorial Phone: (724) 357-1306
Display Adv. E-mail: the-penn@iup.edu
Personnel: Joe Lawley (Advisor); Heather Blake (Ed. in Chief); Branden Oakes (Photo Ed.)

JUNIATA COLLEGE

Street address 1: 1700 Moore St
Street address city: Huntingdon
Street address state: PA
Zip/Postal code: 16652-2119
Country: USA
Mailing address: 1700 Moore St
Mailing city: Huntingdon
Mailing state: PA
Mailing zip: 16652-2196
General Phone: (814) 641-3000
Advertising Fax: (814) 643-3620
Editorial Phone: (814) 641-3132
Primary Website: www.juniatian.com
Published: Bi-Mthly

LA ROCHE COLLEGE

Street address 1: 9000 Babcock Blvd
Street address city: Pittsburgh
Street address state: PA
Zip/Postal code: 15237-5808
Country: USA
Mailing address: 9000 Babcock Blvd
Mailing city: Pittsburgh
Mailing state: PA
Mailing zip: 15237-5898
General Phone: (412) 536-1147
General Fax: (412) 536-1067
General/National Adv. E-mail: courier@laroche.edu
Personnel: Ed Stankowski (Advisor); Rebecca Jeskey (Ed. in Chief); Maggie Kelly (Mng. Ed.)

LA SALLE UNIV.

Street address 1: 1900 W Olney Ave
Street address 2: # 417
Street address city: Philadelphia
Street address state: PA
Zip/Postal code: 19141-1108
Country: USA
Mailing address: 1900 W Olney Ave # 417
Mailing city: Philadelphia
Mailing state: PA
Mailing zip: 19141-1108
General Phone: (215) 951-1000
General Fax: (215) 763-9686
General/National Adv. E-mail: collegian@lasalle.edu
Personnel: Robert O'Brien (Advisor); Olivia Biagi (Mng. Ed.)

LAFAYETTE COLLEGE

Street address 1: 111 Quad Dr
Street address city: Easton
Street address state: PA
Zip/Postal code: 18042-1768
Country: USA
Mailing address: Farinon Center Box 9470
Mailing city: Easton
Mailing state: PA
Mailing zip: 18042
General Phone: (610) 330-5354
General Fax: (610) 330-5724
General/National Adv. E-mail: thelafayette@gmail.com
Personnel: William Gordon (EIC); Ian Morse (Mgr Ed)

LEBANON VALLEY COLLEGE

Street address 1: 101 N College Ave
Street address city: Annville
Street address state: PA
Zip/Postal code: 17003-1404
Country: USA
Mailing address: 101 N College Ave
Mailing city: Annville
Mailing state: PA
Mailing zip: 17003-1400
General Phone: (717) 867-6169
General/National Adv. E-mail: lavic@lvc.edu
Personnel: Bob Vicic (Advisor); Jake King (Co Ed. in Chief); Katie Zwiebel (Co Ed. in Chief)

LEHIGH UNIV.

Street address 1: 33 Coppee Dr
Street address city: Bethlehem
Street address state: PA
Zip/Postal code: 18015-3165
Country: USA
Mailing address: 33 Coppee Dr
Mailing city: Bethlehem
Mailing state: PA
Mailing zip: 18015-3165
General Phone: (610) 758-4454
General Fax: (610) 758-6198
General/National Adv. E-mail: bw@lehigh.edu
Personnel: Wally Trimble (Head); Julie Stewart (Ed. In Chief); Jack Lule (Ed. in Chief)

LINCOLN UNIV.

Street address 1: 1570 Baltimore Pike
Street address city: Lincoln University
Street address state: PA
Zip/Postal code: 19352-9141
Country: USA
Mailing address: 1570 Baltimore Pike
Mailing city: Lincoln University
Mailing state: PA
Mailing zip: 19352-9141
General Phone: (484) 365-7524
Personnel: Eric Watson (Advisor)

LOCK HAVEN UNIV. OF PENNSYLVANIA

Street address 1: 401 N Fairview St
Street address 2: Parsons Union Bldg.
Street address city: Lock Haven
Street address state: PA
Zip/Postal code: 17745-2342
Country: USA
General Phone: (570) 484-2334
General/National Adv. E-mail: lhueagleye@yahoo.com
Personnel: Joe Stender (Ed. in Chief); Jamie Kessinger (Mng. Ed.)

LUZERNE COUNTY CMTY. COLLEGE

Street address 1: 1333 S Prospect St
Street address city: Nanticoke
Street address state: PA
Zip/Postal code: 18634-3814
Country: USA
Mailing address: 1333 S Prospect St
Mailing city: Nanticoke
Mailing state: PA
Mailing zip: 18634-3899
Personnel: Brett Bonanny (Ed.)

LYCOMING COLLEGE

Street address 1: 700 College Pl
Street address 2: Campus Box 169
Street address city: Williamsport
Street address state: PA
Zip/Postal code: 17701-5157
Country: USA
Mailing address: 700 College Place
Mailing city: Williamsport
Mailing state: PA
Mailing zip: 17701-5192
General Phone: (570) 321-4315
General/National Adv. E-mail: lycourier@lycoming.edu
Display Adv. E-mail: lycourier@lycoming.edu
Editorial e-mail: lycourier@lycoming.edu
Primary Website: http://lycourier.lycoming.edu
Published: Other
Published Other: Bi-Wkly on Thursdays
Avg Free Circ: 800
Personnel: Dave Heemer (Advisor); Jordyn Hotchkiss (Editor-in-Chief)

MANSFIELD UNIV. OF PENNSYLVANIA

Street address 1: 202M Alumni Hall
Street address city: Mansfield
Street address state: PA
Zip/Postal code: 16933
Country: USA
Mailing address: PO Box 1
Mailing city: Mansfield
Mailing state: PA
Mailing zip: 16933-0001
General Phone: (570) 662-4986
Personnel: Daniel Mason (Advisor)

MARYWOOD UNIVERSITY

Street address 1: 2300 Adams Ave
Street address city: Scranton
Street address state: PA
Zip/Postal code: 18509-1514
Country: USA
Mailing address: 2300 Adams Ave
Mailing city: Scranton
Mailing state: PA
Mailing zip: 18509-1598
General Phone: (570) 348-6211
General Fax: (570) 961-4768
General/National Adv. E-mail: thewoodword@m.marywood.edu
Primary Website: www.thewoodword.org
Published: Mthly
Personnel: Ann Williams (Advisor); Lindsey Wotanis (Advisor)

MERCYHURST UNIVERSITY

Street address 1: 501 E 38th St
Street address city: Erie
Street address state: PA
Zip/Postal code: 16546-0002
Country: USA
Mailing address: 501 E 38th St
Mailing city: Erie
Mailing state: PA
Mailing zip: 16546-0002
General Phone: (814) 824-2376
General Fax:
General/National Adv. E-mail: editormerciad@mercyhurst.edu
Display Adv. E-mail: admerciad@mercyhurst.edu
Editorial e-mail: opinionmerciad@mercyhurst.edu
Primary Website: merciad.mercyhurst.edu

Year Established: 1929
Published: Wed
Avg Free Circ: 1200
Personnel: Bill Welch (Advisor)

MESSIAH COLLEGE

Street address 1: 1 College Ave
Street address 2: Ste 3058
Street address city: Mechanicsburg
Street address state: PA
Zip/Postal code: 17055-6806
Country: USA
Mailing address: PO Box 3043
Mailing city: Mechanicsburg
Mailing state: PA
Mailing zip: 17055
General Phone: (717) 796-5095
General Fax: (717) 796-5249
General/National Adv. E-mail: theswingingbridge@messiah.edu
Display Adv. E-mail: theswingingbridge@messiah.edu
Editorial e-mail: theswingingbridge@messiah.edu
Personnel: Ed Arke (Professor of Communications)

MILLERSVILLE UNIV. OF PENNSYLVANIA

Street address 1: 1 South George St, Rm.18
Street address city: Millersville
Street address state: PA
Zip/Postal code: 17551
Country: USA
Mailing address: PO Box 1002
Mailing city: Millersville
Mailing state: PA
Mailing zip: 17551-0302
General Phone: (717) 871-2102
General Fax: (717) 872-3515
Editorial Phone: (717) 871-2102
Editorial Fax: (717) 872-3516
General/National Adv. E-mail: snapper@marauder.millersville.edu
Personnel: Gene Ellis (Advisor); Bradley Giuranna (Ed. in Chief); Ashley Palm (News Ed.)

MISERICORDIA UNIVERSITY

Street address 1: 301 Lake St
Street address city: Dallas
Street address state: PA
Zip/Postal code: 18612-7752
Country: USA
Mailing address: 301 Lake St
Mailing city: Dallas
Mailing state: PA
Mailing zip: 18612-7752
General Phone: (570) 674-6737
General Fax: (570) 674-6751
General/National Adv. E-mail: highland@misericordia.edu
Primary Website: www.highlandernews.net
Published Other: Bi-Monthly

MONTGOMERY COUNTY CMTY. COLLEGE

Street address 1: 340 Dekalb Pike
Street address city: Blue Bell
Street address state: PA
Zip/Postal code: 19422-1412
Country: USA
Mailing address: 340 Dekalb Pike
Mailing city: Blue Bell
Mailing state: PA
Mailing zip: 19422-1400
Personnel: Brian Brendlinger (Dir., Student Activities)

MORAVIAN COLLEGE

Street address 1: 1200 Main St
Street address city: Bethlehem
Street address state: PA
Zip/Postal code: 18018-6614
Country: USA
Mailing address: 1200 Main St
Mailing city: Bethlehem
Mailing state: PA
Mailing zip: 18018-6650
General Phone: (610) 625-7509
General Fax: (610) 866-1682
General/National Adv. E-mail: comenian@moravian.edu
Primary Website: comenian.org
Published: Bi-Mthly
Personnel: Mark Harris (Advisor); Kaytlyn Gordon (Editor-in-Chief)

MUHLENBERG COLLEGE

Street address 1: 2400 Chew St
Street address city: Allentown
Street address state: PA
Zip/Postal code: 18104-5564
Country: USA
Mailing address: 2400 W. Chew Street
Mailing city: Allentown
Mailing state: PA
Mailing zip: 18104
General Phone: (484) 664-3195
General/National Adv. E-mail: weeklyeditor@gmail.com
Primary Website: www.muhlenbergweekly.com
Year Established: 1883
Published: Thur
Personnel: Gregory Kantor (Editor in Chief)

NORTHAMPTON CMTY. COLLEGE

Street address 1: 3835 Green Pond Rd
Street address city: Bethlehem
Street address state: PA
Zip/Postal code: 18020-7568
Country: USA
Mailing address: 3835 Green Pond Rd
Mailing city: Bethlehem
Mailing state: PA
Mailing zip: 18020-7599
General Phone: (610) 861-5372
General Fax: (610) 332-6163
Advertising Phone: (610) 861-5372
Editorial Phone: (610) 861-5372
General/National Adv. E-mail: thecommuter@northampton.edu
Display Adv. E-mail: thecommuter@northampton.edu
Editorial e-mail: thecommuter@northampton.edu
Primary Website: www.ncccommuter.org
Published: Mthly
Avg Free Circ: 2000
Personnel: Rob Hays (Advisor)

PENN STATE NEW KENSINGTON:COMMUNICATIONS DEPT

Street address 1: 3550 7th Street Rd
Street address city: New Kensington
Street address state: PA
Zip/Postal code: 15068-1765
Country: USA
Mailing address: 3550 Seventh St rd
Mailing city: New Kensington
Mailing state: PA
Mailing zip: 15068

PENN STATE UNIV.

Street address 1: 1600 Woodland Rd
Street address city: Abington
Street address state: PA
Zip/Postal code: 19001-3918
Country: USA
Mailing address: 1600 Woodland Rd
Mailing city: Abington
Mailing state: PA
Mailing zip: 19001-3990
General Phone: (215) 881-7507
General Fax: (215) 881-7660
General/National Adv. E-mail: fdq1@psu.edu
Personnel: Frank Quattrone (Ed.)

PENN STATE UNIV.

Street address 1: Raymond Smith Bldg
Street address city: Altoona
Street address state: PA
Zip/Postal code: 16601
Country: USA
Mailing address: Raymond Smith Bldg.
Mailing city: Altoona
Mailing state: PA
Mailing zip: 16601
Personnel: Savannah Straub (Contact); Margaret Moses (Contact)

PENN STATE UNIV.

Street address 1: 4701 College Dr
Street address city: Erie
Street address state: PA
Zip/Postal code: 16563-4117
Country: USA
Mailing address: 4701 College Dr
Mailing city: Erie
Mailing state: PA
Mailing zip: 16563-4117
General Phone: (814) 898-6488
Published: Tues
Personnel: Sarah Veslany (Editor in Chief)

PENN STATE UNIV.

Street address 1: 76 University Dr
Street address city: Hazleton
Street address state: PA
Zip/Postal code: 18202-8025
Country: USA
Mailing address: 76 University Dr
Mailing city: Hazleton
Mailing state: PA
Mailing zip: 18202-1291
Personnel: April Snyder (Advisor)

PENN STATE UNIV.

Street address 1: 4000 University Dr
Street address city: McKeesport
Street address state: PA
Zip/Postal code: 15131-7644
Country: USA
Mailing address: 4000 University Dr
Mailing city: White Oak
Personnel: Kathleen Taylor Brown (Advisor); Monica Michna (Ed. in Chief)

PENN STATE UNIV.

Street address 1: 200 University Dr
Street address city: Schuylkill Haven
Street address state: PA
Zip/Postal code: 17972-2202
Country: USA
Mailing address: 200 University Dr
Mailing city: Schuylkill Haven
Personnel: Wes Loder (Advisor)

PENN STATE UNIV.

Street address 1: 123 S Burrowes St
Street address city: State College
Street address state: PA
Zip/Postal code: 16801-3867
Country: USA
Mailing address: 123 S Burrowes St Ste 200
Mailing city: State College
Mailing state: PA
Mailing zip: 16801-3882
General Phone: (814) 865-2531
General Fax: (814) 865-3848
General/National Adv. E-mail: collegian@psu.edu
Display Adv. E-mail: mycollegianrep@gmail.com
Primary Website: www.collegian.psu.edu
Published: Mon`Tues`Wed`Thur`Fri
Personnel: Wayne Lowman (Opns. Mgr.)

PENN STATE UNIV. DELAWARE COUNTY

Street address 1: 25 Yearsley Mill Rd
Street address city: Media
Street address state: PA
Zip/Postal code: 19063-5522
Country: USA
Mailing address: 25 Yearsley Mill Rd
Mailing city: Media
Mailing state: PA
Mailing zip: 19063-5596
General Phone: (610) 892-1200
Personnel: Karrie Bowen (Ed./Advisor)

PENN STATE UNIV. HARRISBURG

Street address 1: 777 W Harrisburg Pike
Street address 2: # E-126
Street address city: Middletown
Street address state: PA
Zip/Postal code: 17057-4846
Country: USA
Mailing address: 777 W Harrisburg Pike # E-126
Mailing city: Middletown
Mailing state: PA
Mailing zip: 17057-4846
General Phone: (717) 948-6440
Personnel: Patrick Burrows (Advisor); James Speed (Adv. Mgr.); Jenna Denoyelles (Ed. in Chief)

PENN STATE UNIVERSITY: COLLEGE OF COMMUNICATIONS

Street address 1: 201 Carnegie Bldg
Street address city: University Park
Street address state: PA
Zip/Postal code: 16802-5101
Country: USA
Mailing address: 201 Carnegie Bldg
Mailing city: University Park
Mailing state: PA
Mailing zip: 16802

PHILADELPHIA NEIGHBORHOODS

Street address 1: 1515 Market St
Street address 2: Fl 1
Street address city: Philadelphia
Street address state: PA
Zip/Postal code: 19102-1904
Country: USA
Mailing address: 1515 Market St First Floor
Mailing city: Philadelphia
Mailing state: PA
Mailing zip: 19102

POINT PARK COLLEGE

Street address 1: 201 Wood St
Street address city: Pittsburgh
Street address state: PA
Zip/Postal code: 15222-1912
Country: USA
Mailing address: PO Box 627
Mailing city: Pittsburgh
Mailing state: PA
Mailing zip: 15222
General Phone: (412) 392-4740
General Fax: (412) 392-3902
General/National Adv. E-mail: theglobeadvertising@gmail.com
Editorial e-mail: szullo@pointpark.edu
Personnel: Steve Hallock (Advisor); Sara Zullo (Ed. in Chief)

READING AREA CMTY. COLLEGE

Street address 1: 10 S 2nd St
Street address city: Reading
Street address state: PA
Zip/Postal code: 19602-1014
Country: USA
Mailing address: PO Box 1706
Mailing city: Reading
Mailing state: PA
Mailing zip: 19603-1706
General Phone: (610) 607-6212
Personnel: Melissa Kushner (Mktg. PR)

ROBERT MORRIS UNIVERSITY : THE SENTRY

Street address 1: 6001 University Blvd
Street address 2: Dept of
Street address city: Moon Township
Street address state: PA
Zip/Postal code: 15108-2574
Country: USA
Mailing address: 6001 University Blvd
Mailing city: Moon Township
Mailing state: PA
Mailing zip: 15108
General Phone: 412-397-6826
General Fax: 412-397-2436
Advertising Phone: (412) 397-6826
Editorial Phone: (412) 397-6826
General/National Adv. E-mail: sentrynews@mail.rmu.edu
Display Adv. E-mail: sentrynewsads@mail.rmu.edu
Editorial e-mail: sentrynews@mail.rmu.edu

Primary Website: www.rmusentrymedia.com
Year Established: 2006
Published Other: Online only
Avg Free Circ: 500

SAINT VINCENT COLLEGE

Street address 1: 300 Fraser Purchase Rd
Street address city: Latrobe
Street address state: PA
Zip/Postal code: 15650-2667
Country: USA
Mailing address: 300 Fraser Purchase Rd
Mailing city: Latrobe
Mailing state: PA
Mailing zip: 15650-2690
General Phone: (724) 539-9761
Advertising Phone: (717)669-0703
Editorial Phone: (717)669-0703
General/National Adv. E-mail: review.stvincent@gmail.com
Editorial e-mail: bridget.fertal@stvincent.edu
Primary Website: http://www.stvincentreview.com/
Published: Wed
Personnel: Dennis McDaniel (Advisor); Bridget Fertal (Editor-in-Chief); Cheyenne Dunbar (Business Manager)

SETON HILL UNIVERSITY

Street address 1: 1 Seton Hill Dr
Street address 2: PO Box 343K
Street address city: Greensburg
Street address state: PA
Zip/Postal code: 15601-1548
Country: USA
Mailing address: PO Box 343K
Mailing city: Greensburg
Mailing state: PA
Mailing zip: 15601-1599
General Phone: (724) 830-4791
General Fax: (724) 830-4611
General/National Adv. E-mail: setonian@gmail.com
Primary Website: www.setonhill.edu
Published: Mthly
Personnel: Olivia Goudy (Editor-in-Chief)

SHIPPENSBURG UNIVERSITY:THE SLATE

Street address 1: Shippensburg University
Street address 2: Ceddia Union Bldg, Second Floor
Street address city: Shippensburg
Street address state: PA
Zip/Postal code: 17257
Country: USA
Mailing address: Shippensburg University
Mailing city: Shippensburg
Mailing state: PA
Mailing zip: 17257
General Phone: 717-477-1778
General Fax: 717-477-4022
General/National Adv. E-mail: slate@ship.edu
Personnel: Michael Drager (Advisor)

SLIPPERY ROCK UNIV.

Street address 1: 220 Eisenberg Classroom Bldg
Street address city: Slippery Rock
Street address state: PA
Zip/Postal code: 16057
Country: USA
Mailing address: 220 Eisenberg Classroom Bldg.
Mailing city: Slipper Rock
Mailing state: PA
Mailing zip: 16057
General Phone: (724) 738-2643
General Fax: (724) 738-4896
General/National Adv. E-mail: rocket.letters@sru.edu
Personnel: Joseph Harry (Advisor); Josh Rizzo (Ed. in Chief)

ST. FRANCIS UNIV.

Street address 1: PO Box 600
Street address city: Loretto
Street address state: PA
Zip/Postal code: 15940-0600
Country: USA
Mailing address: PO Box 600
Mailing city: Loretto
Mailing state: PA
Mailing zip: 15940-0600
Personnel: Dean Allison (Advisor); Andrew Maloney (Ed.)

ST. JOSEPHS UNIV.

Street address 1: 5600 City Ave, 314 Campion Ctr
Street address city: Philadelphia
Street address state: PA
Zip/Postal code: 19131
Country: USA
Mailing address: 5600 City Ave., 314 Campion Ctr.
Mailing city: Philadelphia
Mailing state: PA
Mailing zip: 19131-1395
General Phone: (610) 660-1079
General Fax: (610) 660-1089
Advertising Phone: (610) 660-1080
General/National Adv. E-mail: thehawk@sju.edu
Personnel: Dr. Jenny Spinner (Advisor); Karrin Randle (Ed. in Chief); Katy Yavorek (Bus. Mgr.)

SUSQUEHANNA UNIV.

Street address 1: 1858 Weber Way
Street address city: Selinsgrove
Street address state: PA
Zip/Postal code: 17870-1150
Country: USA
Mailing address: CA Box 18
Mailing city: Selinsgrove
Mailing state: PA
Mailing zip: 17870
General Phone: (570) 374-4298
General Fax: (570) 372-2745
General/National Adv. E-mail: suquill@susqu.edu
Primary Website: www.suquill.com
Year Established: 1896
Published: Fri
Avg Free Circ: 2200
Personnel: Catherine Hastings (Advisor)

SWARTHMORE COLLEGE

Street address 1: 500 College Ave
Street address city: Swarthmore
Street address state: PA
Zip/Postal code: 19081-1306
Country: USA
Mailing address: 500 College Ave Ste 2
Mailing city: Swarthmore
Mailing state: PA
Mailing zip: 19081-1390
General Phone: (610) 328-8000
General Fax: (208) 439-9864
General/National Adv. E-mail: phoenix@swarthmore.edu
Personnel: Mara Revkin (Ed. in Chief)

TEMPLE UNIVERSITY

Street address 1: 1755 N 13th St
Street address 2: 304 Howard Gittis Student Center
Street address city: Philadelphia
Street address state: PA
Zip/Postal code: 19122-6011
Country: USA
Mailing address: 1755 N 13th St
Mailing city: Philadelphia
Mailing state: PA
Mailing zip: 19122-6011
General Phone: 215-204-6737
General Fax: 215-204-1663
Advertising Phone: 215-204-9538
Advertising Fax: 215-204-6609
General/National Adv. E-mail: editor@temple-news.com
Display Adv. E-mail: advertising@temple-news.com
Primary Website: www.temple-news.com
Year Established: 1921
Published: Tues
Published Other: Daily online
Avg Free Circ: 5000
Personnel: John Di Carlo (Advisor)

TEPPER SCHOOL OF BUSINESS AT CARNEGIE MELLON UNIVERSITY

Street address 1: 5000 Forbes Ave
Street address city: Pittsburgh
Street address state: PA
Zip/Postal code: 15213-3815
Country: USA
Mailing address: 5000 Forbes Ave
Mailing city: Pittsburgh
Mailing state: PA
Mailing zip: 15213-3815
General Phone: (412) 268-2269
General/National Adv. E-mail: jywong@tepper.cmu.edu
Display Adv. E-mail: robberbaronstepper@gmail.com
Primary Website: http://tepper.campusgroups.com/rbp/about/
Published: Thur
Personnel: Tyson Bauer (Ed.)

THE BEHREND BEACON

Street address 1: Penn State University-Erie the Behrend College
Street address 2: 0171 Irvin Kochel Center
Street address city: Erie
Street address state: PA
Zip/Postal code: 16563-0001
Country: USA
Mailing address: Penn State University-Erie The Behrend College
Mailing city: Erie
Mailing state: PA
Mailing zip: 16563

THE FOURTH ESTATE

Street address 1: 1 Hacc Dr Cooper 110
Street address 2: Harrisburg Area Community College
Street address city: Harrisburg
Street address state: PA
Zip/Postal code: 17110-2903
Country: USA
Mailing address: Harrisburg Area Community College
Mailing city: Harrisburg
Mailing state: PA

THE JOUST

Street address 1: 1 Neumann Dr
Street address 2: Neumann University
Street address city: Aston
Street address state: PA
Zip/Postal code: 19014-1277
Country: USA
Mailing address: 1 Neumann Dr
Mailing city: Aston
Mailing state: PA
Mailing zip: 19014
General Phone: 610-358-4570

THE KEY

Street address 1: 1 College Grn
Street address 2: Keystone College
Street address city: La Plume
Street address state: PA
Zip/Postal code: 18440-1000
Country: USA
Mailing address: Keystone College
Mailing city: La Plume

THIEL COLLEGE

Street address 1: 75 College Ave
Street address city: Greenville
Street address state: PA
Zip/Postal code: 16125-2186
Country: USA
Mailing address: 75 College Ave
Mailing city: Greenville
Mailing state: PA
Mailing zip: 16125-2181
General Phone: (724)589-2416
General/National Adv. E-mail: newspaper@thiel.edu
Personnel: James Raykie (Advisor); Alivia Lapcevich (Ed. in Chief)

UNIV. OF PENNSYLVANIA ENGINEERING SCHOOL

Street address 1: 220 S 33rd St
Street address city: Philadelphia
Street address state: PA
Zip/Postal code: 19104-6315
Country: USA
Mailing address: 220 S 33rd St Rm 107
Mailing city: Philadelphia
Mailing state: PA
Mailing zip: 19104-6315
General Phone: (215) 898-1444
General Fax: (801) 469-4487
General/National Adv. E-mail: triangle@seas.upenn.edu
Personnel: Mark Smyda (Ed. in Chief); Bezhou Feng (Ed. in Chief)

UNIV. OF PENNSYLVANIA LAW SCHOOL

Street address 1: 3400 Chestnut St
Street address city: Philadelphia
Street address state: PA
Zip/Postal code: 19104-6253
Country: USA
Mailing address: 3400 Chestnut St Ste 1
Mailing city: Philadelphia
Mailing state: PA
Mailing zip: 19104-6204
Personnel: Doug Rennie (Ed.)

UNIV. OF PITTSBURGH

Street address 1: 147 Student Union, 450 School House Rd
Street address city: Johnstown
Street address state: PA
Zip/Postal code: 15904
Country: USA
Mailing address: 147 Student Union, 450 School House Rd.
Mailing city: Johnstown
Mailing state: PA
Mailing zip: 15904-1200
General Phone: (814) 269-7470
General/National Adv. E-mail: joo10@pitt.edu
Personnel: Leland Wood (Staff Advisor); Michael Cuccaro (Adv. Mgr.); Jon O' Connel (Ed. in Chief); Ryan Brown (News Ed.)

UNIV. OF PITTSBURGH

Street address 1: 434 William Pitt Un
Street address 2: University of Pittsburgh
Street address city: Pittsburgh
Street address state: PA
Zip/Postal code: 15260-5900
Country: USA
General Phone: (412) 648-7980
General Fax: (412) 648-8491
General/National Adv. E-mail: pittnews@pittnews.com
Primary Website: www.pittnews.com
Published: Mon`Tues`Wed`Thur`Fri
Personnel: Harry Kloman (Advisor); Ashwini Sivaganesh (Ed. in Chief); John Hamilton (Mng. Ed.); Victor Powell (Online Ed.)

UNIV. OF PITTSBURGH AT BRADFORD

Street address 1: 300 Campus Dr
Street address city: Bradford
Street address state: PA
Zip/Postal code: 16701-2812
Country: USA
Mailing address: 300 Campus Dr
Mailing city: Bradford
Mailing state: PA
Mailing zip: 16701-2898
General Phone: (814) 362-7682
General Fax: (814) 362-7518
General/National Adv. E-mail: source@pitt.edu
Display Adv. E-mail: tfjz@atlanticbb.net
Personnel: Tim Ziaukas (Advisor)

UNIV. OF PITTSBURGH/ GREENSBURG

Street address 1: 150 Finoli Dr
Street address 2: 122 Village Hall
Street address city: Greensburg
Street address state: PA
Zip/Postal code: 15601-5804
Country: USA
General Phone: (724) 836-7481
General Fax: (724) 836-9888
General/National Adv. E-mail: upginsider@gmail.com
Personnel: Lori Jakiela (Advisor)

UNIV. OF SCRANTON

Street address 1: 800 Linden St

Street address city: Scranton
Street address state: PA
Zip/Postal code: 18510-2429
Country: USA
Mailing address: 800 Linden St
Mailing city: Scranton
Mailing state: PA
Mailing zip: 18510
General Phone: (570) 941-7464
General Fax: (570) 941-4836
General/National Adv. E-mail: aquinas@scranton.edu
Personnel: Scott Walsh (Advisor)

UNIV. OF THE SCIENCES IN PHILADELPHIA

Street address 1: 600 S 43rd St
Street address city: Philadelphia
Street address state: PA
Zip/Postal code: 19104-4418
Country: USA
Mailing address: 600 S 43rd St
Mailing city: Philadelphia
Mailing state: PA
Mailing zip: 19104-4495
Personnel: Miriam Gilbert (Advisor); Leeann Tan (Co. Ed.); Meghan Baker (Co. Ed.)

UNIVERSITY OF PENNSYLVANIA

Street address 1: 4015 Walnut St
Street address city: Philadelphia
Street address state: PA
Zip/Postal code: 19104-3513
Country: USA
Mailing address: 4015 Walnut St. 2nd Fl
Mailing city: Philadelphia
Mailing state: PA
Mailing zip: 19104-6198
General Phone: (215) 422-4640
General Fax: (215) 422-4646
Advertising Phone: (215) 422-4640 x1
Advertising Fax: (215) 422-4646
Editorial Phone: (215) 422-4060 x2
Editorial Fax: (215) 422-4646
General/National Adv. E-mail: advertising@theDP.com
Display Adv. E-mail: advertising@theDP.com
Primary Website: www.theDP.com
Year Established: 1885
Published: Mon`Thur
Avg Free Circ: 6000
Personnel: Eric Jacobs (Gen. Mgr.); Michel Liu (Assignments Ed.); Harry Trustman (Opinions Ed.)

URSINUS COLLEGE

Street address 1: 601 E Main St
Street address city: Collegeville
Street address state: PA
Zip/Postal code: 19426-2509
Country: USA
Mailing address: PO Box 1000
Mailing city: Collegeville
Mailing state: PA
Mailing zip: 19426-1000
Personnel: Rebecca Jaroff (Advisor)

VALLEY FORGE MILITARY COLLEGE

Street address 1: 1001 Eagle Rd
Street address city: Wayne
Street address state: PA
Zip/Postal code: 19087-3613
Country: USA
Mailing address: 1001 Eagle Rd
Mailing city: Wayne
Personnel: Charles A. McGeorge (Pres.)

VILLANOVA UNIV.

Street address 1: 800 E Lancaster Ave
Street address city: Villanova
Street address state: PA
Zip/Postal code: 19085-1603
Country: USA
Mailing address: 800 E Lancaster Ave
Mailing city: Villanova
Mailing state: PA
Mailing zip: 19085-1478
General Phone: (610) 519-7207
General Fax: (610) 519-5666
General/National Adv. E-mail: business@villanovan.com
Personnel: Jessica Ramey (Bus. Mgr.); Jody Ross (Advisor); Tom Mogan (Advisor); Tim Richer (Ed. in Chief); Laura (Ed. in Chief)

WASHINGTON & JEFFERSON COLLEGE

Street address 1: 60 S Lincoln St
Street address city: Washington
Street address state: PA
Zip/Postal code: 15301-4812
Country: USA
Mailing address: 60 S Lincoln St
Mailing city: Washington
Mailing state: PA
Mailing zip: 15301-4801
General Phone: (724) 222-4400
General Fax: (724) 223-6534
General/National Adv. E-mail: redandblackstaff@jay.washjeff.edu
Primary Website: www.washjeff.edu
Year Established: 1909
Published: Thur
Personnel: Dale Lolley (Advisor)

WAYNESBURG UNIVERSITY:THE YELLOW JACKET

Street address 1: 51 W College St
Street address city: Waynesburg
Street address state: PA
Zip/Postal code: 15370-1258
Country: USA
Mailing address: 51 West College St.
Mailing city: Waynesburg
Mailing state: PA

WEST CHESTER UNIVERSITY

Street address 1: 253 Sykes Union Bldg
Street address city: West Chester
Street address state: PA
Zip/Postal code: 19383-0001
Country: USA
Mailing address: 253 Sykes Union
Mailing city: West Chester
Mailing state: PA
Mailing zip: 19383-0001
General Phone: (610) 436-2375
General Fax: (610) 436-3280
Advertising Phone: (610) 436-2375
General/National Adv. E-mail: quad@wcupa.edu
Display Adv. E-mail: quadadvertising@wcupa.edu
Editorial e-mail: quadeic@wcupa.edu
Primary Website: www.wcuquad.com
Year Established: 1934
Published: Mon
Avg Free Circ: 2500
Personnel: Philip Thompsen (Advisor); Samantha Mineroff (EIC)

WESTMINSTER COLLEGE

Street address 1: 319 S Market St
Street address city: New Wilmington
Street address state: PA
Zip/Postal code: 16172-0002
Country: USA
Mailing address: 319 S Market St
Mailing city: New Wilmington
Mailing state: PA
Mailing zip: 16172-0001
General Phone: (724) 946-7224
General/National Adv. E-mail: holcad@westminister.edu
Personnel: Shannon Richtor (Ed.)

WHARTON SCHOOL OF GRAD. BUS.

Street address 1: 3730 Walnut St
Street address 2: 330 Jon M. Huntsman Hall
Street address city: Philadelphia
Street address state: PA
Zip/Postal code: 19104-3615
Country: USA
Mailing address: 3730 Walnut St
Mailing city: Philadelphia
Mailing state: PA
Mailing zip: 19104-3615
General Phone: (215) 898-3200
General Fax: (215) 898-1200
General/National Adv. E-mail: journal@wharton.upenn.edu
Personnel: Mark Hanson (Pub.); Anix Vyas (Ed. in Chief); Gareth Keane (Mng. Ed.)

WILKES UNIV.

Street address 1: 130 S River St, Conyngham Ctr, Office 101
Street address city: Wilkes Barre
Street address state: PA
Zip/Postal code: 18701
Country: USA
Mailing address: 130 S. River St., Conyngham Ctr., Office 101
Mailing city: Wilkes-Barre
Mailing state: PA
Mailing zip: 18701
General Phone: (570) 408-5903
General Fax: (570) 408-5902
Advertising Phone: (570) 408-2962
General/National Adv. E-mail: wilkesbeacon@wilkes.edu
Personnel: Andrea Frantz (Advisor); Michele Flannery (Bus./Adv. Mgr.); Nicole Frail (Ed. in Chief)

WILSON COLLEGE

Street address 1: 1015 Philadelphia Ave
Street address city: Chambersburg
Street address state: PA
Zip/Postal code: 17201-1279
Country: USA
Mailing address: 1015 Philadelphia Ave
Mailing city: Chambersburg
Mailing state: PA
Mailing zip: 17201-1285
Personnel: Aimee-Marie Dorsten (Advisor)

YORK COLLEGE OF PENNSYLVANIA

Street address 1: 441 Country Club Rd
Street address city: York
Street address state: PA
Zip/Postal code: 17403-3614
Country: USA
Mailing address: 441 Country Club Rd
Mailing city: York
Mailing state: PA
Mailing zip: 17403-3651
General Phone: (717) 815-1312
General/National Adv. E-mail: spartan@ycp.edu
Personnel: Steven Brikowski (Advisor)

RHODE ISLAND

BROWN UNIV./RHODE ISLAND SCHOOL OF DESIGN

Street address 1: PO Box 1930
Street address city: Providence
Street address state: RI
Country: USA
Mailing address: PO Box 1930
Mailing city: Providence
Mailing state: RI
Mailing zip: 02912-1930
General Phone: (401) 863-2008
General/National Adv. E-mail: independent@brown.edu; theindyads@gmail.com
Personnel: Emily Segal (Ed.); Alex Verdolini (Mng. Ed.)

BRYANT COLLEGE

Street address 1: 1150 Douglas Pike
Street address 2: # 7
Street address city: Smithfield
Street address state: RI
Zip/Postal code: 02917-1291
Country: USA
Mailing address: 1150 Douglas Pike Ste 1
Mailing city: Smithfield
Mailing state: RI
Mailing zip: 02917-1290
General Phone: (401) 232-6028
General Fax: (401) 232-6710
General/National Adv. E-mail: archway@byrant.edu
Personnel: Meagan Sage (Advisor); Tracey Gant (Adv. Mgr.); John Crisafulli (Ed. in Chief)

JOHNSON & WALES UNIV.

Street address 1: 8 Abbott Park Pl
Street address city: Providence
Street address state: RI
Zip/Postal code: 02903-3703
Country: USA
Mailing address: 8 Abbott Park Pl
Mailing city: Providence
Mailing state: RI
Mailing zip: 02903-3775
General Phone: (401) 598-1000
General Fax: (401) 598-1171
Editorial Phone: (401) 598-1489
Editorial Fax: (401) 598-2867
General/National Adv. E-mail: campusherald@jwu.edu
Personnel: Michael Berger (Advisor); Jessica Long (Advisor); Catlin Benoit (Ed. in Chief); Samantha Krivorit (Ed. in Cheif)

PROVIDENCE COLLEGE

Street address 1: 549 River Ave
Street address city: Providence
Street address state: RI
Zip/Postal code: 02918-7000
Country: USA
Mailing address: 549 River Ave
Mailing city: Providence
Mailing state: RI
Mailing zip: 02918-0001
General Phone: (401) 865-2214
General Fax: (401) 865-1202
General/National Adv. E-mail: cowl@providence.edu
Personnel: Richard F. Kless (Advisor)

RHODE ISLAND COLLEGE

Street address 1: Student Union Plz, 600 Mt Pleasant Ave
Street address city: Providence
Street address state: RI
Zip/Postal code: 2908
Country: USA
Mailing address: Student Union Plz., 600 Mt. Pleasant Ave.
Mailing city: Providence
Mailing state: RI
Mailing zip: 02908-1940
General Phone: (401) 456-8544
General Fax: (401) 456-8792
General/National Adv. E-mail: news@anchorweb.org
Personnel: Rudy Cheeks (Professional Advisor); Ashley Dalton (Adv. Mgr.); Kameron Stualting (Ed. in Chief)

ROGER WILLIAMS UNIV.

Street address 1: 1 Old Ferry Rd
Street address city: Bristol
Street address state: RI
Zip/Postal code: 02809-2923
Country: USA
Mailing address: 1 Old Ferry Rd
Mailing city: Bristol
Mailing state: RI
Mailing zip: 02809-2921
General Phone: (401) 254-3229
General Fax: (401) 254-3355
General/National Adv. E-mail: hawksherald@gmail.com
Personnel: Ben Whitmore (Ed. in Chief); Adrianne Mukiria (Advisor); Adrianne Henderson (Advisor)

THE BROWN DAILY HERALD

Street address 1: 195 Angell St
Street address city: Providence
Street address state: RI
Zip/Postal code: 02906-1207
Country: USA
Mailing address: PO Box 2538
Mailing city: Providence
Mailing state: RI
Mailing zip: 02906-0538
General Phone: (401) 351-3260
General Fax: (401) 351-9297
General/National Adv. E-mail: herald@browndailyherald.com

Display Adv. E-mail: advertising@browndailyherald.com
Primary Website: www.browndailyherald.com
Year Established: 1891
Published: Mon`Tues`Wed`Thur`Fri
Personnel: Lauren Aratani

UNIV. OF RHODE ISLAND

Street address 1: 125 Memorial Union, 50 Lower College Rd
Street address city: Kingston
Street address state: RI
Zip/Postal code: 2881
Country: USA
Mailing address: 125 Memorial Union, 50 Lower College Rd.
Mailing city: Kingston
Mailing state: RI
Mailing zip: 02881
General Phone: (401) 874-2914
General Fax: (401) 874-5607
General/National Adv. E-mail: uricigar@gmail.com
Personnel: Lindsay Lorenz (Ed. in Chief)

SOUTH DAKOTA

BENEDICT COLLEGE

Street address 1: 1600 Harden St
Street address city: Columbia
Street address state: SC
Zip/Postal code: 29204-1058
Country: USA
Mailing address: 1600 Harden St
Mailing city: Columbia
Mailing state: SC
Mailing zip: 29204-1086
General Phone: (803) 705-4645
Personnel: Carolyn Drakeford (Chair); Momo Rogers (Ed.)

BOB JONES UNIVERSITY

Street address 1: 1700 Wade Hampton Blvd
Street address city: Greenville
Street address state: SC
Zip/Postal code: 29614-1000
Country: USA
Mailing address: 1700 Wade Hampton Blvd
Mailing city: Greenville
Mailing state: SC
Mailing zip: 29614-0001
General Phone: (864) 370-1800
General Fax: (864) 770-1307
Advertising Phone: 864-370-1800
Advertising Fax: 864-770-1307
General/National Adv. E-mail: bsolomon@bju.edu
Editorial e-mail: editor@bju.edu
Primary Website: http://www.collegianonline.com/
Year Established: 1987
Published: Fri
Personnel: David Lovegrove (Advisor); Betty Solomon (Advisor); Joanne Kappel (Adv. Coord.); Larry Stofer (Campus Media Supervisor)

CLAFLIN UNIVERSITY

Street address 1: 400 Magnolia St
Street address city: Orangeburg
Street address state: SC
Zip/Postal code: 29115-6815
Country: USA
Mailing address: 400 Magnolia Street
Mailing city: Orangeburg
Mailing state: SC
Primary Website: claflin.edu/the-panther
Published: Other
Published Other: print once per semester
Personnel: Lee Harter (Advisor)

CLEMSON UNIV.

Street address 1: 315 Hendrix Ctr
Street address city: Clemson
Street address state: SC
Zip/Postal code: 29634-0001
Country: USA
Mailing address: 315 Hendrix Ctr
Mailing city: Clemson
Mailing state: SC
Mailing zip: 29634-0001
General Phone: (864) 656-2150
Personnel: Patrich Neal (Advisor); Cory Bowers (Bus. Mgr.); Ashley Chris (Ed.)

COASTAL CAROLINA UNIV.

Street address 1: PO Box 261954
Street address city: Conway
Street address state: SC
Zip/Postal code: 29528-6054
Country: USA
Mailing address: PO Box 261954
Mailing city: Conway
Mailing state: SC
Mailing zip: 29528-6054
General Phone: (843) 349-2330
General Fax: (843) 349-2743
General/National Adv. E-mail: chanticleer@coastal.edu
Personnel: Issac Bailey (Advisor); Kyle Drapeau (Bus. Mgr.); Clarie Arambulla (Ed.)

COKER COLLEGE

Street address 1: 300 E College Ave
Street address city: Hartsville
Street address state: SC
Zip/Postal code: 29550-3742
Country: USA
Mailing address: 300 E College Ave
Mailing city: Hartsville
Mailing state: SC
Mailing zip: 29550-3797
Personnel: Dick Puffer (Advisor); Lance Player (Ed.)

COLLEGE OF CHARLESTON

Street address 1: 66 George St
Street address city: Charleston
Street address state: SC
Zip/Postal code: 29424-0001
Country: USA
Mailing address: 66 George St
Mailing city: Charleston
Mailing state: SC
Mailing zip: 29424-0001
General Phone: (843) 953-7017
General Fax: (843) 953-7037
General/National Adv. E-mail: mcgeeb@cofc.edu
Personnel: Brian McGee (Chair); Katie Orlando (Ed. in Chief)

CONVERSE COLLEGE

Street address 1: 580 E Main St
Street address city: Spartanburg
Street address state: SC
Zip/Postal code: 29302-1931
Country: USA
Mailing address: 580 E Main St
Mailing city: Spartanburg
Mailing state: SC
Mailing zip: 29302-0006
Personnel: Whitney Fisher (Advisor.)

FRANCIS MARION UNIVERSITY

Street address 1: Rm 201 University Center
Street address city: Florence
Street address state: SC
Zip/Postal code: 29506
Country: USA
Mailing address: PO Box 100547
Mailing city: Florence
Mailing state: SC
Mailing zip: 29502-0547
General Phone: (843) 661-1350
General Fax: (843) 661-1373
General/National Adv. E-mail: patriotnews@hotmail.com
Display Adv. E-mail: patriotads@hotmail.com
Primary Website: www.patriotnewsonline.com
Published: Bi-Mthly
Personnel: David Sacash (Faculty Advisor)

LANDER UNIV.

Street address 1: 320 Stanley Ave
Street address city: Greenwood
Street address state: SC
Zip/Postal code: 29649-2056
Country: USA
Mailing address: 320 Stanley Ave
Mailing city: Greenwood
Mailing state: SC
Mailing zip: 29649-2099
General Phone: (864) 388-8000
Personnel: Robert Stevenson (Advisor)

MEDICAL UNIV. OF SOUTH CAROLINA

Street address 1: PO Box 12110
Street address city: Charleston
Street address state: SC
Zip/Postal code: 29422-2110
Country: USA
Mailing address: PO Box 12110
Mailing city: Charleston
Mailing state: SC
Mailing zip: 29422-2110
General Phone: (843) 792-4107
General Fax: (843) 849-0214
General/National Adv. E-mail: catalyst@musc.edu
Personnel: Kim Draughn (Ed.)

NEWBERRY COLLEGE

Street address 1: 2100 College St
Street address city: Newberry
Street address state: SC
Zip/Postal code: 29108-2126
Country: USA
Mailing address: 2100 College St
Mailing city: Newberry
Mailing state: SC
Mailing zip: 29108-2197
General Phone: (803) 276-5010
Personnel: Jodie Peeler (Advisor)

PRESBYTERIAN COLLEGE

Street address 1: 503 S Broad St
Street address city: Clinton
Street address state: SC
Zip/Postal code: 29325-2865
Country: USA
Mailing address: 503 S Broad St
Mailing city: Clinton
Mailing state: SC
Mailing zip: 29325-2998
Year Established: 1927
Published: Mthly
Personnel: Justin Brent (Advisor); Rachel Miles (Co-Editor); Ashleigh Bethea (Co-Editor)

SOUTH CAROLINA STATE UNIV.

Street address 1: 300 College St NE
Street address city: Orangeburg
Street address state: SC
Zip/Postal code: 29117-0002
Country: USA
Mailing address: 300 College St NE
Mailing city: Orangeburg
Mailing state: SC
Mailing zip: 29117-0002
General Phone: (803) 536-7237
Personnel: Rolondo Davis (Advisor)

THE JOHNSONIAN

Street address 1: 1808 Ebenezer Rd Apt B
Street address 2: 1808-B Ebenezer Rd
Street address city: Rock Hill
Street address state: SC
Zip/Postal code: 29732-1170
Country: USA
Mailing address: 104 Digiorgio Campus Center Winthrop University
Mailing city: Rock Hill
Mailing state: SC
Mailing zip: 29733-0001
General Phone: (803) 323-3419
General Fax: (803) 323-3698
Advertising Phone: 803 984-7748
Advertising Fax: 803 984-7748
Editorial Phone: 803 984-7748
Editorial Fax: 803 984-7748
General/National Adv. E-mail: thejohnsonian@yahoo.com
Editorial e-mail: editors@mytjnow.com
Personnel: Guy Reel (Faculty Adviser)

THE PALADIN

Street address 1: 3300 Poinsett Hwy
Street address city: Greenville
Street address state: SC
Zip/Postal code: 29613-0002
County: Travelers Rest
Country: USA
Mailing address: PO Box 28584
Mailing city: Greenville
Mailing state: SC
General/National Adv. E-mail: contact-databook@thepaladin.news
Primary Website: thepaladin.news
Published: Mon`Tues`Wed`Thur`Fri`Sun`Bi-Mthly
Personnel: Tyler Sines (Circ. Mgr.); Evan Bohnenblust (Ed. in Chief); Jessica Lopez (Ed.)

UNIV. OF SOUTH CAROLINA

Street address 1: 471 University Pkwy
Street address city: Aiken
Street address state: SC
Zip/Postal code: 29801-6389
Country: USA
Mailing address: 471 University Pkwy
Mailing city: Aiken
Mailing state: SC
Mailing zip: 29801-6399
General Phone: (803) 648-6851
Personnel: Israel Butler (Ed.)

UNIV. OF SOUTH CAROLINA

Street address 1: 1400 Greene St
Street address city: Columbia
Street address state: SC
Zip/Postal code: 29225-4002
Country: USA
Mailing address: 1400 Greene St
Mailing city: Columbia
Mailing state: SC
Mailing zip: 29225-4002
General Phone: (803) 777-5064
General Fax: (803) 777-6482
Advertising Phone: (803) 777-3888
Editorial Phone: (803) 777-7182
Editorial e-mail: gamecockeditor@sc.edu
Personnel: Scott Lindenberg (Dir., Student Media); Erik Collins (Advisor); Amanda Davis (Ed. in Chief); Calli Burnett (Mng. Ed.)

UNIV. OF SOUTH CAROLINA

Street address 1: 800 University Way
Street address 2: Clc 112
Street address city: Spartanburg
Street address state: SC
Zip/Postal code: 29303-4932
Country: USA
Mailing address: 800 University Way Clc 112
Mailing city: Spartanburg
Mailing state: SC
Mailing zip: 29303-4932
General Phone: (864) 503-5138
General Fax: (864) 503-5100
General/National Adv. E-mail: carolinian@uscupstate.edu
Personnel: Chioma Ugochukwu (Advisor); India Brown (Ed.)

AUGUSTANA UNIVERSITY

Street address 1: 2001 S Summit Ave
Street address city: Sioux Falls
Street address state: SD
Zip/Postal code: 57197-0001
Country: USA
Mailing address: 2001 S Summit Ave
Mailing city: Sioux Falls
Mailing state: SD
Mailing zip: 57197-0002
General Phone: (605) 274-4423
General Fax: (605) 274-5288
Advertising Fax: (605) 274-5288
General/National Adv. E-mail: augustanamirror@gmail.com
Primary Website: www.augiemirror.com
Year Established: 1909
Published: Fri

Avg Free Circ: 1000
Personnel: Jeffrey Miller (Advisor)

BLACK HILLS STATE UNIV.

Street address 1: 1200 University St
Street address city: Spearfish
Street address state: SD
Zip/Postal code: 57799-8840
Country: USA
Mailing address: 1200 University St
Mailing city: Spearfish
Mailing state: SD
Mailing zip: 57799-0002
General Phone: (605) 642-6389
General Fax: (605) 642-6119
General/National Adv. E-mail: jacketjournal@bhsu.edu
Personnel: Mary Caton-Rosser (Advisor); Shelby Cihak (Bus. Mgr.); Kendra Bertsch (Adv. Mgr.)

DAKOTA STATE UNIV.

Street address 1: 820 N Washington Ave
Street address city: Madison
Street address state: SD
Zip/Postal code: 57042-1735
Country: USA
Mailing address: 820 N Washington Ave
Mailing city: Madison
Mailing state: SD
Mailing zip: 57042-1799
General Phone: (605) 256-5278
General Fax: (605) 256-5021
General/National Adv. E-mail: times@dsu.edu
Personnel: Justin Blessinger (Advisor); Jenny Grabinger (Adv. Mgr.); Samantha Moulton (Ed. in Chief)

MT. MARTY COLLEGE

Street address 1: 1105 W 8th St
Street address 2: Ste 564
Street address city: Yankton
Street address state: SD
Zip/Postal code: 57078-3725
Country: USA
Mailing address: 1105 W 8th St Ste 564
Mailing city: Yankton
Mailing state: SD
Mailing zip: 57078-3725
General Phone: (605) 668-1293
General Fax: (605) 668-1508
General/National Adv. E-mail: moderator@mtmc.edu
Personnel: Jill Paulson (Advisor); Lauren Donlin (Adv. Mgr.); Alicia Pick (Circ. Mgr.)

NORTHERN STATE UNIV.

Street address 1: 1200 S Jay St, Student Ctr, Rm 201
Street address city: Aberdeen
Street address state: SD
Zip/Postal code: 57401
Country: USA
Mailing address: 1200 S. Jay St., Student Ctr., Rm. 201
Mailing city: Aberdeen
Mailing state: SD
Mailing zip: 57401
General Phone: (605) 626-2534
General Fax: (605) 626-2559
General/National Adv. E-mail: stupub@northern.edu
Primary Website: www.nsuexponent.com
Published: Mthly
Personnel: Tracy Rasmussen (Advisor)

SOUTH DAKOTA SCHOOL OF MINES & TECHNOLOGY

Street address 1: 501 E Saint Joseph St
Street address city: Rapid City
Street address state: SD
Zip/Postal code: 57701-3901
Country: USA
Mailing address: 501 E Saint Joseph St
Mailing city: Rapid City
Mailing state: SD
General/National Adv. E-mail: aurum.sdsmt@gmail.com
Display Adv. E-mail: aurum.sdsmt@gmail.com
Editorial e-mail: aurum.sdsmt@gmail.com
Year Established: 1900
Published: Mthly
Avg Free Circ: 2000

Personnel: Daniel Cerfus (Business Manager); Quinn del Val (Secretary); Robin Jerman (Cuisiner Columnist); Dan Eitreim (EIC)

UNIV. OF SIOUX FALLS

Street address 1: 1101 W 22nd St
Street address city: Sioux Falls
Street address state: SD
Zip/Postal code: 57105-1600
Country: USA
Mailing address: 1101 W 22nd St
Mailing city: Sioux Falls
Mailing state: SD
Mailing zip: 57105-1699
Personnel: Tiffany Leach (Advisor); Janet Davison (Ed.)

UNIV. OF SOUTH DAKOTA

Street address 1: 555 N Dakota St
Street address city: Vermillion
Street address state: SD
Zip/Postal code: 57069-2300
Country: USA
Mailing address: 555 N Dakota St
Mailing city: Vermillion
Mailing state: SD
Mailing zip: 57069-2300
General Phone: (605) 677-5494
General Fax: (605) 677-5105

TENNESSEE

AUSTIN PEAY STATE UNIV.

Street address 1: 601 College St
Street address state: TN
Country: USA
Mailing address: PO Box 4634
Mailing city: Clarksville
Mailing state: TN
Mailing zip: 37044-0001
General Phone: (931) 221-7376
General Fax: (931) 221-7377
Editorial Phone: (931) 221-7374
General/National Adv. E-mail: theallstate@apsu.edu
Display Adv. E-mail: allstateads@apsu.edu
Personnel: Tabitha Gillaland (Advisor); Nicole June (Adv. Mgr.); Patrick Armstrong (Ed. in Chief)

BELMONT UNIV.

Street address 1: 1900 Belmont Blvd
Street address city: Nashville
Street address state: TN
Zip/Postal code: 37212-3758
Country: USA
Mailing address: 1900 Belmont Blvd
Mailing city: Nashville
Mailing state: TN
Mailing zip: 37212-3757
General Phone: (615) 460-6000
General Fax: (615) 460-5532
General/National Adv. E-mail: vision@mail.belmont.edu
Personnel: Linda Quigley (Advisor); Thom Storey (Chair); Karen Bennett (Adv. Mgr.); Bethany Brinton; Lance Conzett (Ed. in Chief)

BRYAN COLLEGE

Street address 1: 721 Bryan Dr
Street address city: Dayton
Street address state: TN
Zip/Postal code: 37321-6275
Country: USA
Mailing address: Box 7807
Mailing city: Dayton
Mailing state: TN
Mailing zip: 37321
General Phone: (423) 775-7285
General Fax: (423) 775-7330
General/National Adv. E-mail: triangle@bryan.edu; info@bryan.edu

Personnel: John Carpenter (Advisor); Allison McLean (Ed. in Chief)

CARSON-NEWMAN UNIVERSITY

Street address 1: 1646 Russell Ave
Street address city: Jefferson City
Street address state: TN
Zip/Postal code: 37760-2204
Country: USA
Mailing address: 1646 Russell Ave
Mailing city: Jefferson City
Mailing state: TN
Mailing zip: 37760
General Phone: (865) 471-3434
General Fax: (865) 471-3416
General/National Adv. E-mail: oandb@cn.edu
Personnel: Glenn Cragwall (Advisor)

CHATTANOOGA STATE TECH. CMTY. COLLEGE

Street address 1: Paul Starnes Ctr, Rm S-260, 4501 Amnicola Hwy
Street address city: Chattanooga
Street address state: TN
Country: USA
Mailing address: Paul Starnes Ctr., Rm. S-260, 4501 Amnicola Hwy.
Mailing city: Chattanooga
Mailing state: TN
Mailing zip: 37406
General Phone: (423) 697-2471
Personnel: Betty A. Proctor (Advisor); Keith Burkhalter (Ed.)

CLEVELAND STATE CMTY. COLLEGE

Street address 1: 3535 Adkisson Dr NW
Street address city: Cleveland
Street address state: TN
Zip/Postal code: 37312-2813
Country: USA
Mailing address: PO Box 3570
Mailing city: Cleveland
Mailing state: TN
Mailing zip: 37320-3570
General Phone: (423) 472-7141
General Fax: (423) 478-6255
General/National Adv. E-mail: tbartolo@clevelandstatecc.edu
Personnel: Tony Bartolo (Adv. Mgr.); Priscilla Simms (Ed.)

CUMBERLAND UNIV.

Street address 1: 1 Cumberland Sq
Street address city: Lebanon
Street address state: TN
Zip/Postal code: 37087-3408
Country: USA
Mailing address: 1 Cumberland Sq.
Mailing city: Lebanon
Mailing state: TN
Mailing zip: 37087-3408
General Phone: (615) 444-2562
General Fax: (615) 444-2569
General/National Adv. E-mail: cumberlandchronicle@gmail.com
Primary Website: www.cumberland.edu
Published: Mon`Bi-Mthly
Personnel: Michael Rex (Advisor)

EAST TENNESSEE STATE UNIV.

Street address 1: Culp Ctr, Jl Seehorn Jr Rd
Street address city: Johnson City
Street address state: TN
Zip/Postal code: 37614
Country: USA
Mailing address: PO Box 70688
Mailing city: Johnson City
Mailing state: TN
Mailing zip: 37614-1709
General Phone: (423) 439-6170
General Fax: (423) 439-8407
Editorial Phone: (423) 439-4677
General/National Adv. E-mail: etnews@etsu.edu

Personnel: Martha Milner (Advisor); Candy Naff (Office Supvr.)

FISK UNIV.

Street address 1: Humanities Div, 1000 17th Ave N
Street address city: Nashville
Street address state: TN
Zip/Postal code: 37208
Country: USA
Mailing address: Humanities Div., 1000 17th Ave. N.
Mailing city: Nashville
Mailing state: TN
Mailing zip: 37208-3045
General Phone: (615) 329-8500
Personnel: Karen Taylor (Ed.); Keen West (Ed.)

FREED-HARDEMAN UNIV.

Street address 1: 158 E Main St
Street address city: Henderson
Street address state: TN
Zip/Postal code: 38340-2306
Country: USA
Mailing address: 158 E Main St
Mailing city: Henderson
Mailing state: TN
Mailing zip: 38340-2398
General Fax: (731) 989-6000
General/National Adv. E-mail: belltower@fhu.edu
Personnel: Derrick Spradlin (Advisor); Eddie Eaton (Ed.)

KING COLLEGE

Street address 1: 1350 King College Rd
Street address city: Bristol
Street address state: TN
Zip/Postal code: 37620-2632
Country: USA
Mailing address: 1350 King College Rd
Mailing city: Bristol
Mailing state: TN
Mailing zip: 37620-2649
Personnel: Katie Vandebrake (Advisor)

LEE UNIV.

Street address 1: 1120 N Ocoee St
Street address city: Cleveland
Street address state: TN
Zip/Postal code: 37311-4458
Country: USA
Mailing address: 1120 N Ocoee St
Mailing city: Cleveland
Mailing state: TN
Mailing zip: 37311-4475
General Phone: (423) 614-8489
General Fax: (423) 614-8341
General/National Adv. E-mail: news@leeclarion.com
Personnel: Kevin Trowbridge (Advisor); Michelle Bouman (Ed.)

LEMOYNE-OWEN COLLEGE

Street address 1: 807 Walker Ave
Street address city: Memphis
Street address state: TN
Zip/Postal code: 38126-6510
Country: USA
Mailing address: 807 Walker Ave
Mailing city: Memphis
Mailing state: TN
Mailing zip: 38126-6595
General Phone: (901) 435-1309
General Fax: (901) 435-1349
Editorial Phone: (901) 435-1318
General/National Adv. E-mail: magican@loc.edu
Personnel: Lydia Lay (Instructor)

LIPSCOMB UNIV.

Street address 1: 3901 Granny White Pike
Street address 2: # 4126
Street address city: Nashville
Street address state: TN
Zip/Postal code: 37204-3903
Country: USA
Mailing address: 1 University Park Dr
Mailing city: Nashville
Mailing state: TN
Mailing zip: 37204-3956
General Phone: (615) 966-6604

General Fax: (615) 966-6605
General/National Adv. E-mail: babbler@lipscomb.edu
Display Adv. E-mail: babbleradvertising@lipscomb.edu
Personnel: Jimmy McCollum (Advisor); Michael Gilbert (Adv. Mgr.); Kaitie McDermott (Ed. in Chief)

MARYVILLE COLLEGE

Street address 1: 502 E Lamar Alexander Pkwy
Street address city: Maryville
Street address state: TN
Zip/Postal code: 37804-5907
Country: USA
Mailing address: 502 E Lamar Alexander Pkwy
Mailing city: Maryville
Mailing state: TN
Mailing zip: 37804-5919
General Phone: (865) 981-8241
General/National Adv. E-mail: highland.echo@gmail.com
Personnel: Kim Trevathan (Advisor)

MIDDLE TENNESSEE STATE UNIV.

Street address 1: 1301 E Main St
Street address city: Murfreesboro
Street address state: TN
Zip/Postal code: 37132-0002
Country: USA
Mailing address: 1301 East Main Street, Box 36
Mailing city: Murfreesboro
Mailing state: TN
Mailing zip: 37132-0001
General Phone: (615) 904-8357
General Fax: (615) 494-7648
Editorial Phone: 6156924488
General/National Adv. E-mail: editor@mtsusidelines.com
Display Adv. E-mail: editor@mtsusidelines.com
Editorial e-mail: editor@mtsusidelines.com
Primary Website: www.mtsusidelines.com
Year Established: 1925
Published: Mthly
Avg Free Circ: 4000
Personnel: Meagan White (Editor-in-chief); Dylan Aycock (Managing Editor); Sarah Taylor (News Editor); Rhiannon Gilbert (Lifestyles Editor); Ethan Clark (Assistant Lifestyles Editor); Michael Ward (Sports Editor); Connor Ulrey (Assistant Sports Editor); Grant Massey (Multimedia Editor); Darian Lindsay (Chief Videographer); Austin Lewis (Photography Editor); Anna Claire Farmer (Design Editor); Justin Morales (Design Editor); Savannah Hazlewood (Assistant News Editor)

MILLIGAN COLLEGE

Street address 1: 1 Blowers Blvd
Street address city: Milligan College
Street address state: TN
Zip/Postal code: 37682
Country: USA
Mailing address: PO Box 500
Mailing city: Milligan College
Mailing state: TN
Mailing zip: 37682-0500
General Phone: (423) 461-8995
General Fax: (423) 461-8965
General/National Adv. E-mail: stampede@milligan.edu
Primary Website: www.milliganstampede.com
Year Established: 1866
Personnel: Jim Dahlman (Advisor); Kalee Nagel (Ed.)

RHODES COLLEGE

Street address 1: 2000 N Parkway
Street address city: Memphis
Street address state: TN
Zip/Postal code: 38112-1624
Country: USA
Mailing address: PO Box 3010
Mailing city: Memphis
Mailing state: TN
Mailing zip: 38173-0010
General Phone: (901) 843-3885
General Fax: (901) 843-3576
General/National Adv. E-mail: Souwester souwester@rhodes.edu
Personnel: John Blaisdell

SOUTHWEST TENNESSEE CMTY. COLLEGE

Street address 1: 5983 Macon Cv
Street address city: Memphis
Street address state: TN
Zip/Postal code: 38134-7642
Country: USA
Mailing address: 5983 Macon Cv
Mailing city: Memphis
Mailing state: TN
Mailing zip: 38134-7693
General Phone: (901) 333-4196
General Fax: (901) 333-4995
General/National Adv. E-mail: pworthy@southwest.tn.edu
Display Adv. E-mail: cherron@southwest.tn.edu
Primary Website: southwest.tn.edu/clubs
Year Established: 2000
Personnel: Phoenix Worthy (Advisor); Connie Herron (Coorindator)

THE ORACLE

Street address 1: 1000 N Dixie Ave
Street address 2: Ruc 376
Street address city: Cookeville
Street address state: TN
Zip/Postal code: 38505-0001
County: Putnam
Country: USA
Mailing address: PO Box 5072
Mailing city: Cookeville
Mailing state: TN
Mailing zip: 38505-0001
General Phone: (931) 372-3060
General Fax: (931) 372-6225
Advertising Phone: (931) 372-3031
Advertising Fax: (931) 372-6225
Editorial Phone: (931) 372-3285
Editorial Fax: (931) 372-6225
General/National Adv. E-mail: oracle@tntech.edu
Display Adv. E-mail: tburch@tntech.edu
Editorial e-mail: oracle@tntech.edu
Primary Website: www.tntechoracle.com
Year Established: 1924
Published: Tues
Published Other: 6 editions during Fall and Spring semesters
Avg Free Circ: 3000
Personnel: Teddy Burch (Assistant Professor of Journalism); Jon Ezell (Advisor / Assistant Professor)

TRUE NORTH CUSTOM PUBLISHING

Street address state: TN
Country: USA
Mailing address: 5600 Brainerd Rd Ste 1
Mailing city: Chattanooga
Mailing state: TN
Mailing zip: 37411-5373
Personnel: Emily Young (Ed.); Tim Lale (Advisor); Katie Hammond (Managing Ed.); Alison Quiring (News Ed.); Stephanie (Opinion Ed.)

TUSCULUM COLLEGE

Street address 1: 60 Shiloh Rd
Street address city: Greeneville
Street address state: TN
Zip/Postal code: 37745-0595
Country: USA
Mailing address: PO Box 5098
Mailing city: Greeneville
Mailing state: TN
Mailing zip: 37743-0001
General Phone: (423) 636-7300
Personnel: Barth Cox (Advisor)

UNION UNIV.

Street address 1: 1050 Union University Dr
Street address 2: Dept Jenningshall
Street address city: Jackson
Street address state: TN
Zip/Postal code: 38305-3656
Country: USA
Mailing address: 1050 Union University Dr Dept Jenningshall
Mailing city: Jackson
Mailing state: TN
Mailing zip: 38305-3656
General Phone: (731) 668-1818
Personnel: Michael Chute (Advisor); Gray Coyner (Adv. Mgr.); Andrea Turner (Ed. in Chief)

UNIV. OF MEMPHIS

Street address 1: 113 Meeman Journalism Bldg
Street address city: Memphis
Street address state: TN
Zip/Postal code: 38152-3290
Country: USA
Mailing address: 113 Meeman Journalism Bldg
Mailing city: Memphis
Mailing state: TN
Mailing zip: 38152-3290
General Phone: (901) 678-5474
General Fax: (901) 678-0882
Display Adv. E-mail: rlwillis@memphis.edu
Primary Website: www.dailyhelmsman.com
Published: Tues`Wed`Thur`Fri
Avg Free Circ: 6500
Personnel: Bob Willis (Bus. Mgr.)

UNIV. OF TENNESSEE CHATTANOOGA

Street address 1: 615 McCallie Ave
Street address city: Chattanooga
Street address state: TN
Zip/Postal code: 37403-2504
Country: USA
Mailing address: 615 McCallie Ave
Mailing city: Chattanooga
Mailing state: TN
Mailing zip: 37403-2504
General Phone: (423) 425-4298
General Fax: (423) 425-8100
Advertising Phone: (423) 425-8101
General/National Adv. E-mail: echo@utcecho.com
Personnel: Holly Cowart (Advisor); Alexa Branblet (Adv. Mgr.); Paige Gabriel (Ed. in Chief); Kate Bissinger (Mng. Ed.); Hayley (Features Ed.); Rachel (News Ed.); Michael (Sports Ed.)

UNIV. OF TENNESSEE MARTIN

Street address 1: 314 Gooch Hall
Street address city: Martin
Street address state: TN
Zip/Postal code: 38238-0001
Country: USA
Mailing address: 314 Gooch Hall
Mailing city: Martin
Mailing state: TN
Mailing zip: 38238-0001
General Phone: (731) 881-7780
General Fax: (731) 881-7791
General/National Adv. E-mail: pacer@ut.utm.edu
Personnel: Tomi McCutchen Parrish (Advisor); Josh Lemons (Ed.); Spencer Taylor (Mgr./News Ed.)

UNIV. OF THE SOUTH

Street address 1: 735 University Ave
Street address city: Sewanee
Street address state: TN
Zip/Postal code: 37383-2000
Country: USA
Mailing address: 735 University Ave
Mailing city: Sewanee
Mailing state: TN
Mailing zip: 37383-1000
General Phone: (931) 598-1204
General/National Adv. E-mail: spurple@sewanee.edu
Personnel: Virginia Craighll (Advisor)

UT DAILY BEACON (UNIVERSITY OF TENNESSEE)

Street address 1: 11 Communications Bldg
Street address 2: 1345 Circle Park Dr.
Street address city: Knoxville
Street address state: TN
Zip/Postal code: 37996-0001
Country: USA
Mailing address: 11 Communications Bldg.
Mailing city: Knoxville
Mailing state: TN
Mailing zip: 37996-0314
General Phone: (865) 974-5206
General Fax: (865) 974-5569
Editorial Phone: (865) 974-3226
General/National Adv. E-mail: editorinchief@utdailybeacon.com
Display Adv. E-mail: beaconads@utk.edu
Editorial e-mail: letters@utdailybeacon.com
Primary Website: utdailybeacon.com
Year Established: 1906
Published: Mon`Thur
Published Other: Special issues (See Rate Card above)
Avg Free Circ: 6000
Personnel: Jerry Bush (Dir. of Student Media)

VANDERBILT UNIV.

Street address 1: 2301 Vanderbilt Pl
Street address 2: # 351504
Street address city: Nashville
Street address state: TN
Zip/Postal code: 37235-0002
Country: USA
Mailing address: 2301 Vanderbilt Place Vu Sta B351504
Mailing city: Nashville
Mailing state: TN
Mailing zip: 37235-0001
General Phone: (615) 322-4705
General Fax: (615) 343-4969
General/National Adv. E-mail: advertising@vanderbilthustler.com
Editorial e-mail: editor@vanderbilthustler.com
Personnel: Chris Carroll (Advisor); George Fischer (Dir. Mktg.); Carolyn Fischer (Adv. Mgr.); Hannah Twillman (Ed.)

VOLUNTEER STATE CMTY. COLLEGE

Street address 1: 1480 Nashville Pike
Street address city: Gallatin
Street address state: TN
Zip/Postal code: 37066-3148
Country: USA
Mailing address: 1480 Nashville Pike
Mailing city: Gallatin
Mailing state: TN
Mailing zip: 37066-3148
General Phone: (615) 452-8600
General Fax: (615) 230-3481
General/National Adv. E-mail: thesettler@allstate.edu
Personnel: Clay Scott (Advisor); Amy Webb (Ed.)

WALTERS STATE CMTY. COLLEGE

Street address 1: 500 S Davy Crockett Pkwy
Street address city: Morristown
Street address state: TN
Zip/Postal code: 37813-1908
Country: USA
Mailing address: 500 S Davy Crockett Pkwy
Mailing city: Morristown
Personnel: Dianna Pearson (Contact)

TEXAS

ABILENE CHRISTIAN UNIV.

Street address 1: PO Box 27892
Street address city: Abilene
Street address state: TX
Country: USA
Mailing address: PO Box 27892
Mailing city: Abilene
Mailing state: TX
Mailing zip: 79699-0001
General Fax: (325) 674-2463
Advertising Fax: (325) 674-2139
General/National Adv. E-mail: christi.stark@acu.edu
Personnel: Colter Hettich (Ed.)

AMARILLO COLLEGE

Street address 1: 2201 S Washington St
Street address city: Amarillo
Street address state: TX
Zip/Postal code: 79109-2411
Country: USA
Mailing address: PO Box 447
Mailing city: Amarillo

Mailing state: TX
Mailing zip: 79178-0001
General Phone: (806) 371-5283
General Fax: (806) 371-5398
General/National Adv. E-mail: therangereditor@gmail.com
Display Adv. E-mail: jlgibson@actx.edu
Editorial e-mail: therangereditor@gmail.com
Primary Website: www.acranger.com
Year Established: 1930
Published: Thur
Published Other: biweekly
Avg Free Circ: 2500
Personnel: Jill Gibson (Student Media Adviser Matney Mass Media Program Coord); Maddisun Fowler (Student Media Coord)

ANGELINA COLLEGE

Street address 1: 3500 S 1st St
Street address city: Lufkin
Street address state: TX
Zip/Postal code: 75901-7328
Country: USA
Mailing address: PO Box 1768
Mailing city: Lufkin
Mailing state: TX
Mailing zip: 75902-1768
Year Established: 1968
Published: Bi-Mthly
Avg Free Circ: 1500
Personnel: Libby Stapleton (Advisor)

ANGELO STATE UNIV.

Street address 1: 2601 W Avenue N
Street address city: San Angelo
Street address state: TX
Zip/Postal code: 76909-2601
Country: USA
Mailing address: PO Box 10895
Mailing city: San Angelo
Mailing state: TX
Mailing zip: 76909-0001
General Phone: (325) 942-2040
General/National Adv. E-mail: rampage@angelo.edu
Personnel: Leah Cooper (Ed. in Chief)

AUSTIN COLLEGE

Street address 1: 900 N Grand Ave
Street address 2: Ste 6J
Street address city: Sherman
Street address state: TX
Zip/Postal code: 75090-4440
Country: USA
Mailing address: 900 N Grand Ave Ste 6J
Mailing city: Sherman
Mailing state: TX
Mailing zip: 75090-4400
General Phone: (903) 813-2296
Personnel: Felecia Garvin (Advisor); Lauren Chiodo (Ed. in Chief)

BAYLOR UNIVERSITY

Street address 1: 1 Bear Pl
Street address 2: Unit 97330
Street address city: Waco
Street address state: TX
Zip/Postal code: 76798-7330
Country: USA
Mailing address: 1 Bear Pl Unit 97330
Mailing city: Waco
Mailing state: TX
Mailing zip: 76798-7330
General Phone: (254) 710-3407
General Fax: (254) 710-1714
Advertising Phone: (254) 710-3407
Advertising Fax: (254) 710-1714
Editorial Fax: (254) 710-1714
General/National Adv. E-mail: lariat@baylor.edu
Display Adv. E-mail: Lariat_Ads@baylor.edu
Editorial e-mail: Lariat-Letters@baylor.edu
Primary Website: www.baylorlariat.com
Year Established: 1900
Published: Tues`Wed`Thur`Fri
Avg Free Circ: 4000
Personnel: Paul Carr (Dir., Mktg. Information); Jamile Yglecias (Advertising Sales and Marketing Manager); Julie Freeman (Asst. Media Adviser)

BROOKHAVEN COLLEGE

Street address 1: 3939 Valley View Ln
Street address city: Farmers Branch
Street address state: TX
Zip/Postal code: 75244-4906
Country: USA
Mailing address: 3939 Valley View Ln
Mailing city: Farmers Branch
Mailing state: TX
Mailing zip: 75244-4997
General Phone: (972) 860-4700
General Fax: (972) 860-4142
General/National Adv. E-mail: bhc2110@dcccd.edu
Personnel: Wendy Moore (Advisor); Daniel Rodrigue (Advisor)

CENTRAL TEXAS COLLEGE

Street address 1: 6200 W Central Texas Expy
Street address city: Killeen
Street address state: TX
Zip/Postal code: 76549-1272
Country: USA
Mailing address: 6200 W Central Texas Expy
Mailing city: Killeen
Mailing state: TX

DEL MAR COLLEGE FOGHORN

Street address 1: 101 Baldwin Blvd
Street address 2: # HC210
Street address city: Corpus Christi
Street address state: TX
Zip/Postal code: 78404-3805
Country: USA
Mailing address: 101 Baldwin Blvd # HC210
Mailing city: Corpus Christi
Mailing state: TX
Mailing zip: 78404-3805
General Phone: 361/698-1390
General Fax: (361/698-2153
Advertising Phone: 361/698-1246
Advertising Fax: 361/698-2153
Editorial Phone: 361/698-1390
Editorial Fax: 361/698-2153
General/National Adv. E-mail: editor@delmar.edu
Display Adv. E-mail: rmuilenburg@delmar.edu
Editorial e-mail: editor@delmar.edu
Primary Website: www.foghornnews.com
Year Established: 1935
Published: Tues`Bi-Mthly
Published Other: Tuesday every two weeks; no issues in summer
Avg Free Circ: 2500
Personnel: Robert Muilenburg (Advisor); Donna Strong (Adv. Mgr.)

EASTFIELD COLLEGE

Street address 1: 3737 Motley Dr
Street address city: Mesquite
Street address state: TX
Zip/Postal code: 75150-2033
Country: USA
Mailing address: 3737 Motley Dr
Mailing city: Mesquite
Mailing state: TX
Mailing zip: 75150-2099
General Phone: (972) 860-7130
General Fax: (972) 860-7040
General/National Adv. E-mail: etc4640@dcccd.edu
Primary Website: www.eastfieldnews.com
Year Established: 1970
Personnel: Sabine Winter (Faculty)

EL PASO CMTY. COLLEGE

Street address 1: PO Box 20500
Street address city: El Paso
Street address state: TX
Zip/Postal code: 79998-0500
Country: USA
Mailing address: PO Box 20500
Mailing city: El Paso
Mailing state: TX
Mailing zip: 79998-0500
General Phone: (915) 831-2500
Personnel: Steve Escajeda (Contact); Joe Old (Advisor)

HARDIN-SIMMONS UNIV.

Street address 1: 2200 Hickory St
Street address city: Abilene
Street address state: TX
Zip/Postal code: 79601-2345
Country: USA
Mailing address: 2200 Hickory St
Mailing city: Abilene
Mailing state: TX
Mailing zip: 79601-2345
General Phone: (325) 670-1438
General Fax: (325) 677-8351
General/National Adv. E-mail: brand@hsutx.edu
Display Adv. E-mail: brandadv@hsutx.edu
Personnel: Adriel Wong (Ed. in. Chief)

HOUSTON BAPTIST UNIV.

Street address 1: 7502 Fondren Rd
Street address city: Houston
Street address state: TX
Zip/Postal code: 77074-3200
Country: USA
Mailing address: 7502 Fondren Rd
Mailing city: Houston
Mailing state: TX
Mailing zip: 77074-3298
General Phone: (281) 649-3670
General Fax: (281) 649-3246
Advertising Phone: (281) 649-3668
Editorial Phone: (281) 649-3670
General/National Adv. E-mail: thecollegian@hbucollegian.com
Display Adv. E-mail: ads@hbucollegian.com
Primary Website: www.hbucollegian.com
Year Established: 1963
Published: Bi-Mthly
Personnel: Jeffrey Wilkinson (Faculty Adviser); Katie Brown (Editor in Chief); Tabatha Trapp (Advertising Manager)

HUSTON TILLOTSON COLLEGE

Street address 1: 900 Chicon St
Street address city: Austin
Street address state: TX
Zip/Postal code: 78702-2753
Country: USA
Mailing address: 900 Chicon St
Mailing city: Austin

KILGORE COLLEGE

Street address 1: 1100 Broadway Blvd
Street address city: Kilgore
Street address state: TX
Zip/Postal code: 75662-3204
Country: USA
Mailing address: 1100 Broadway Blvd
Mailing city: Kilgore
Mailing state: TX
Mailing zip: 75662-3299
General Phone: (903) 983-8194
General Fax: (903) 983-8193
General/National Adv. E-mail: kc_flare@yahoo.com
Personnel: Betty Craddock (Advisor); christian Keit (Ed. in Chief)

LAMAR UNIV.

Street address 1: 200 Setzer Student Ctr
Street address city: Beaumont
Street address state: TX
Zip/Postal code: 77710
Country: USA
Mailing address: PO Box 10055
Mailing city: Beaumont
Mailing state: TX
Mailing zip: 77710-0055
General Phone: (409) 880-8102
General Fax: (409) 880-8735
General/National Adv. E-mail: advertising@lamaruniversitypress.com
Primary Website: www.lamaruniversitypress.com
Published: Thur
Published Other: end of semester special editions, seasonal editions
Personnel: Andy Coughlan (Advisor); Linda Barrett (Adv. Mgr.)

LETOURNEAU UNIV.

Street address 1: 2100 S Mobberly Ave
Street address city: Longview
Street address state: TX
Zip/Postal code: 75602-3564
Country: USA
Mailing address: PO Box 7001
Mailing city: Longview
Mailing state: TX

MCLENNAN CMTY. COLLEGE

Street address 1: 1400 College Dr
Street address city: Waco
Street address state: TX
Zip/Postal code: 76708-1402
Country: USA
Mailing address: 1400 College Dr
Mailing city: Waco
Mailing state: TX

MCMURRY UNIV.

Street address 1: PO Box 277
Street address city: Abilene
Street address state: TX
Zip/Postal code: 79604-0277
Country: USA
Mailing address: Box 277, McMurry Sta.
Mailing city: Abilene
Mailing state: TX

MIDLAND COLLEGE

Street address 1: 3600 N Garfield St
Street address city: Midland
Street address state: TX
Zip/Postal code: 79705-6329
Country: USA
Mailing address: 3600 N Garfield St
Mailing city: Midland
Mailing state: TX
Mailing zip: 79705-6397
General Phone: (432) 685-4768
General Fax: (432) 685-4769
General/National Adv. E-mail: studentpublications@midland.edu
Personnel: Karen Lenier (Instructor)

MIDWESTERN STATE UNIVERSITY

Street address 1: 3410 Taft Blvd
Street address city: Wichita Falls
Street address state: TX
Zip/Postal code: 76308-2036
Country: USA
Mailing address: 3410 Taft Blvd
Mailing city: Wichita Falls
Mailing state: TX
Mailing zip: 76307-0014
General Phone: (940) 397-4704
Advertising Phone: (940) 397-4704
Editorial Phone: (940) 397-4704
General/National Adv. E-mail: wichitan@msutexas.edu
Display Adv. E-mail: wichitan@msutexas.edu
Editorial e-mail: wichitan@msutexas.edu
Primary Website: http://thewichitan.com/
Year Established: 1935
Published: Wed
Avg Free Circ: 1000
Personnel: Bradley Wilson (Adviser)

NORTH LAKE COLLEGE

Street address 1: 5001 N MacArthur Blvd
Street address 2: Rm A-234
Street address city: Irving
Street address state: TX
Zip/Postal code: 75038-3804
Country: USA
Mailing address: 5001 N MacArthur Blvd Rm A-234
Mailing city: Irving
Mailing state: TX
Mailing zip: 75038-3804
General Phone: (972) 273-3057
General Fax: (972) 273-3441
Advertising Phone: 972-273-3498
General/National Adv. E-mail: nnr7420@dcccd.edu

Primary Website: www.newsregisteronline.com
Published: Mthly
Personnel: Kathleen Stockmier (Advisor); Grant V. Ziegler (Editor-in-Chief); Joanna Mikolajczak (Photography Editor)

NORTHEAST TEXAS CMTY. COLLEGE

Street address 1: PO Box 1307
Street address city: Mount Pleasant
Street address state: TX
Zip/Postal code: 75456-9991
Country: USA
Mailing address: PO Box 1307
Mailing city: Mount Pleasant
Mailing state: TX
Mailing zip: 75456-9991
General Phone: (903) 434-8232
General Fax: (903) 572-6712
General/National Adv. E-mail: eagle@ntcc.edu
Personnel: Mandy Smith (Advisor); Daniel Lockler (Mng. Ed.)

OUR LADY OF THE LAKE UNIV.

Street address 1: 411 SW 24th St
Street address 2: Ste 105
Street address city: San Antonio
Street address state: TX
Zip/Postal code: 78207-4617
Country: USA
Mailing address: 411 SW 24th St Ste 105
Mailing city: San Antonio
Mailing state: TX
Mailing zip: 78207-4617
General Phone: (210) 434-6711
General Fax: (210) 436-0824
General/National Adv. E-mail: lakefront@lake.ollusa.edu; lakefrontads@lake.ollusa.edu
Personnel: Kay O'Donnell (Advisor); Tessa Benavides (Ed.)

PALO ALTO COLLEGE

Street address 1: 1400 W Villaret Blvd
Street address city: San Antonio
Street address state: TX
Zip/Postal code: 78224-2417
Country: USA
Mailing address: 1400 W Villaret Blvd
Mailing city: San Antonio
Mailing state: TX
Mailing zip: 78224-2499
General Phone: (210) 486-3880
General Fax: (210) 486-9271
Editorial Phone: 210-486-3237
General/National Adv. E-mail: pac-info@alamo.edu
Primary Website: alamo.edu/pac
Year Established: 1983
Published: Bi-Mthly

PANOLA COLLEGE

Street address 1: 1109 W Panola St
Street address city: Carthage
Street address state: TX
Zip/Postal code: 75633-2341
Country: USA
Mailing address: 1109 W Panola St
Mailing city: Carthage
Mailing state: TX
Mailing zip: 75633-2397
General Phone: (903) 693-2079
Personnel: Teresa Beasley (Advisor)

PARIS JUNIOR COLLEGE

Street address 1: 2400 Clarksville St
Street address city: Paris
Street address state: TX
Zip/Postal code: 75460-6258
Country: USA
Mailing address: 2400 Clarksville St
Mailing city: Paris
Mailing state: TX
Mailing zip: 75460-6298
General Phone: (903) 785-7661
Personnel: Sharon Dennehy (Advisor)

PAUL QUINN COLLEGE

Street address 1: 3837 Simpson Stuart Rd
Street address city: Dallas
Street address state: TX
Zip/Postal code: 75241-4331
Country: USA
Mailing address: 3837 Simpson Stuart Rd
Mailing city: Dallas

PRAIRIE VIEW A&M UNIV.

Street address 1: PO Box 519
Street address city: Prairie View
Street address state: TX
Zip/Postal code: 77446-0519
Country: USA
Mailing address: PO Box 519
Mailing city: Prairie View
Mailing state: TX
Mailing zip: 77446-0519
General Phone: (936) 261-1353
General Fax: (936) 261-1365
General/National Adv. E-mail: panther@pvamu.edu
Personnel: Lewis Smith (Advisor); Whitney Harris (Ed. in chief)

RICE UNIV.

Street address 1: 6100 Main St
Street address 2: Fl 2MS-524
Street address city: Houston
Street address state: TX
Zip/Postal code: 77005-1827
Country: USA
Mailing address: 6100 Main St., MS-524
Mailing city: Houston
Mailing state: TX
Mailing zip: 77251-1892
General Phone: (713) 348-4801
General/National Adv. E-mail: thresher@rice.edu
Personnel: Kelley Callaway (Advisor)

RICHLAND COLLEGE

Street address 1: 12800 Abrams Rd
Street address city: Dallas
Street address state: TX
Zip/Postal code: 75243-2104
Country: USA
Mailing address: 12800 Abrams Rd.
Mailing city: Dallas
Mailing state: TX
Mailing zip: 75243-2199
General Phone: (972) 238-6079
General Fax: (972) 238-6037
Advertising Phone: (972) 238-6068
Display Adv. E-mail: advertise@dcccd.edu
Primary Website: www.richlandchronicle.com
Published: Tues
Published Other: Weekly on Tuesday
Avg Free Circ: 3000

SAM HOUSTON STATE UNIVERSITY

Street address 1: 1804 Ave J
Street address city: Huntsville
Street address state: TX
Zip/Postal code: 77341-0001
Country: USA
Mailing address: PO Box 2207SHSU
Mailing city: Huntsville
Mailing state: TX
Mailing zip: 77341-0001
Personnel: Janet A. Bridges (Chair/Prof.); Michael L. Blackman (Philip J. Warner Chair in Journ.); Mickey Herskowitz (Philip J. Warner Chair in Journ.); Tony R. DeMars (Assoc. Prof.); Anthony Friedmann (Assoc. Prof.); Hugh S. Fullerton (Assoc. Prof.); Christopher White (Assoc. Prof.); Rene Qun Chen (Asst. Prof.); Wanda Reyes Velazquez (Asst. Prof.); Ruth M. Pate (Instr.); Richard O. Kosuowei (Lectr.); Mel Strait (Lectr.); Patsy K. Ziegler (Lectr.)

SAM HOUSTON STATE UNIVERSITY

Street address 1: 1804 Ave J, Dan Rather Communications Bldg, Ste 210
Street address city: Huntsville
Street address state: TX
Zip/Postal code: 77341-0001
Country: USA
Mailing address: PO Box 2178
Mailing city: Huntsville
Mailing state: TX
Mailing zip: 77341-0001
General Phone: (936) 294-1505
General Fax: (936) 294-1888
Advertising Phone: (936) 294-1500
Advertising Fax: (936) 294-1888
Editorial Phone: (936) 294-1505
Editorial Fax: (936) 294-1888
General/National Adv. E-mail: pcm009@shsu.edu
Display Adv. E-mail: advertise@houstonianonline.com
Editorial e-mail: eic@houstonianonline.com
Primary Website: www.houstonianonline.com
Year Established: 1913
Published: Wed
Published Other: Orientation Edition, Student Guide
Avg Free Circ: 2500
Personnel: Paty Mason (Business Manager); Dr. Marcus Funk (Faculty Advisor); Carlos Medina (Advertising Manager)

SAN ANTONIO COLLEGE

Street address 1: 1300 San Pedro Ave
Street address city: San Antonio
Street address state: TX
Zip/Postal code: 78212-4201
Country: USA
Mailing address: 1300 San Pedro Ave
Mailing city: San Antonio
Mailing state: TX
Mailing zip: 78212-4299
General Phone: (210) 486-1765
General Fax: (210) 486-9239
Advertising Phone: (210) 486-1786
Advertising Fax: (210) 486-9239
Editorial Phone: (210) 486-1773
Editorial Fax: (210) 486-9292
General/National Adv. E-mail: sac-ranger@alamo.edu
Primary Website: www.theranger.org
Year Established: 1926
Personnel: Marianne Odom (Advisor)

SAN JACINTO COLLEGE

Street address 1: 8060 Spencer Hwy
Street address city: Pasadena
Street address state: TX
Zip/Postal code: 77505-5903
Country: USA
Mailing address: 8060 Spencer Hwy
Mailing city: Pasadena
Mailing state: TX
Mailing zip: 77505-5998
General Phone: (281) 478-2752
General Fax: (281) 478-2703
General/National Adv. E-mail: rsaldivar88@yahoo.com
Personnel: Fred F. Faour (Advisor)

SOUTH PLAINS COLLEGE

Street address 1: 1401 College Ave
Street address city: Levelland
Street address state: TX
Zip/Postal code: 79336-6503
Country: USA
Mailing address: PO Box 46
Mailing city: Levelland
Mailing state: TX
Mailing zip: 79336-0046
General Phone: (806) 894-9611
General Fax: (806) 894-5274
General/National Adv. E-mail: ppress@southplainscollege.edu
Primary Website: http://www.southplainscollege.edu/ppress/News.html
Published Other: Bi-weekly
Personnel: Charles Ehrenfeld (Advisor); Jayme Wheeler

SOUTHERN METHODIST UNIV.

Street address 1: 3140 Dyer St
Street address 2: Ste 315
Street address city: Dallas
Street address state: TX
Zip/Postal code: 75205-1977
Country: USA
Mailing address: 3140 Dyer St Ste 315
Mailing city: Dallas
Mailing state: TX
Mailing zip: 75205-1977
General Phone: (214) 768-4555
General Fax: (214) 768-4573
Advertising Phone: (214) 768-4111
Advertising Fax: (214) 768-4573
Editorial Phone: (214) 768-4111
Display Adv. E-mail: dcads@smu.edu
Primary Website: www.smudailycampus.com
Year Established: 1915
Published: Thur
Avg Free Circ: 3000
Personnel: Jay Miller (Exec. Dir./Editorial Advisor); Dyann Slosar (Assoc. Dir.); Candace Barnhill (Int. Exec. Dir.)

SOUTHWEST TEXAS JUNIOR COLLEGE

Street address 1: 2401 Garner Field Rd
Street address city: Uvalde
Street address state: TX
Zip/Postal code: 78801-6221
Country: USA
Mailing address: 2401 Garner Field Rd
Mailing city: Uvalde
Mailing state: TX
Mailing zip: 78801-6221
General Phone: (830) 591-7350
Personnel: Terrie Wilson (Advisor/Journalism Instructor)

SOUTHWESTERN ADVENTIST UNIV.

Street address 1: 100 W Hillcrest St
Street address city: Keene
Street address state: TX
Zip/Postal code: 76059-1922
Country: USA
Mailing address: 100 W Hillcrest St
Mailing city: Keene
Mailing state: TX
Mailing zip: 76059-1922
General Phone: (817) 645-3921
General Fax: (817) 202-6790
General/National Adv. E-mail: southwesterner@swau.edu
Primary Website: southwesterner.swau.edu
Year Established: 1958
Personnel: Glen Robinson (Ed.); Julena Allen (Associate Editor); Sierra Hernandez

ST. EDWARDS UNIV.

Street address 1: 3001 S Congress Ave
Street address 2: Campus Mailox #964
Street address city: Austin
Street address state: TX
Zip/Postal code: 78704-6425
Country: USA
Mailing address: PO Box 1033
Mailing city: Austin
Mailing state: TX
Mailing zip: 78767-1033
General Phone: (512) 448-8426
General Fax: (512) 428-1084
General/National Adv. E-mail: hilltopviewsonline@gmail.com
Display Adv. E-mail: hilltopviewsads@gmail.com
Editorial e-mail: hilltopviewseditors@gmail.com
Primary Website: hilltopviewsonline.com
Published: Wed
Personnel: Andrea Guzman (Editor-In-Chief); Gabrielle Wilkosz (Editor-In-Chief); Amanda Gonzalez (Managing Editor)

ST. MARY'S UNIV. OF SAN ANTONIO

Street address 1: 1 Camino Santa Maria St
Street address 2: University Center Room 258
Street address city: San Antonio
Street address state: TX
Zip/Postal code: 78228-5433
Country: USA
Mailing address: 1 Camino Santa Maria
Mailing city: San Antonio
Mailing state: TX
Mailing zip: 78228
General Phone: (210) 436-3401
General Fax: (210) 431-4307
General/National Adv. E-mail: rattlernews@stmarytx.edu

Personnel: Patrica R. Garcia (Advisor); Leo Reyes (Adv. Mgr.); Sarah Mills (Ed.)

STEPHEN F. AUSTIN UNIV.

Street address 1: 1936 North St, Baker Center Rm 2.308
Street address city: Nacogdoches
Street address state: TX
Zip/Postal code: 75962-0001
Country: USA
Mailing address: PO Box 13049, Sfa Station
Mailing city: Nacogdoches
Mailing state: TX
Mailing zip: 75962-0001
General Phone: (936) 468-4703
General Fax: (936) 468-1016
General/National Adv. E-mail: pinelog@sfasu.edu
Primary Website: www.thepinelog.com
Year Established: 1924
Personnel: Pat Spence (Dir.); Mark Rhoudes (Editor in Cheif)

SUL ROSS STATE UNIV.

Street address 1: PO Box C-112
Street address city: Alpine
Street address state: TX
Zip/Postal code: 79832-0001
Country: USA
Mailing address: PO Box C112
Mailing city: Alpine
Mailing state: TX
Mailing zip: 79832-0001
General Phone: (432) 837-8011
General Fax: (432) 837-8664
General/National Adv. E-mail: skyline@sulross.edu
Personnel: Cheryl Zinsmeyer (Student Publications Advisor)

TARLETON STATE UNIVERSITY

Street address 1: 201 St Felix
Street address city: Stephenville
Street address state: TX
Zip/Postal code: 76401
Country: USA
Mailing address: Box T-0440
Mailing city: Stephenville
Mailing state: TX
Mailing zip: 76402
General Phone: (254) 968-9056
General Fax: (254) 968-9709
Advertising Phone: (254) 968-9057
Advertising Fax: (254) 968-9709
Editorial Phone: (254) 968-9058
Editorial Fax: (254) 968-9709
General/National Adv. E-mail: jtac@tarleton.edu
Display Adv. E-mail: jtac_ads@tarleton.edu
Editorial e-mail: jtac@tarleton.edu
Primary Website: www.jtacnews.com
Year Established: 1919
Published: Wed
Avg Free Circ: 1000
Personnel: Caleb Chapman (Dir.)

TARRANT COUNTY COLLEGE

Street address 1: 828 W Harwood Rd
Street address 2: Cab 1124A
Street address city: Hurst
Street address state: TX
Zip/Postal code: 76054-3219
Country: USA
Mailing address: 828 W Harwood Rd Cab 1124A
Mailing city: Hurst
Mailing state: TX
Mailing zip: 76054-3219
General Phone: (817) 515-6391
General Fax: (817) 515-6767
Editorial Phone: (817) 515-6392
Editorial e-mail: tcceditor@lycos.com
Personnel: Eddye Gallagher (Dir.); Chris Webb (Ed. in Chief)

TEXARKANA COLLEGE

Street address 1: 2500 N Robison Rd
Street address city: Texarkana
Street address state: TX
Zip/Postal code: 75599-0002
Country: USA
Mailing address: 2500 N Robison Rd
Mailing city: Texarkana
Mailing state: TX
Mailing zip: 75599-0001
General Phone: (903) 838-4541
General Fax: (903) 832-5030
Personnel: Jean Cotten (Advisor); Caitlin Williams (Ed.)

TEXAS A&M UNIV.

Street address 1: the Grove Bldg 8901, 215 Limar St
Street address city: College Station
Street address state: TX
Zip/Postal code: 77843-0001
Country: USA
Mailing address: the Grove Bldg 8901, 215 Limar St
Mailing city: College Station
Mailing state: TX
Mailing zip: 77843-0001
General Phone: (979) 845-3313
General Fax: (979) 845-2647
Advertising Phone: (979) 845-0569
Advertising Fax: (979) 845-2678
Editorial Phone: (979) 845-3315
General/National Adv. E-mail: editor@thebatt.com
Display Adv. E-mail: battads@thebatt.com
Personnel: Cheri Shipman (News Advisor); Amanda Casanova (Ed. in Chief)

TEXAS A&M UNIV. COMMERCE

Street address 1: PO Box 4104
Street address city: Commerce
Street address state: TX
Zip/Postal code: 75429-4104
Country: USA
Mailing address: PO Box 4104
Mailing city: Commerce
Mailing state: TX
Mailing zip: 75429-4104
General Phone: (903) 886-5985
General Fax: (903) 468-3128
Advertising Phone: (903) 886-5231
General/National Adv. E-mail: theeasttexan@gmail.com
Primary Website: www.theeasttexan.com
Year Established: 1915
Published: Bi-Mthly
Avg Free Circ: 1000
Personnel: Fred Stewart (Fac. Advisor)

TEXAS A&M UNIV. CORPUS CHRISTI

Street address 1: 6300 Ocean Dr
Street address city: Corpus Christi
Street address state: TX
Zip/Postal code: 78412-5503
Country: USA
Mailing address: 6300 Ocean Dr
Mailing city: Corpus Christi
Mailing state: TX
Mailing zip: 78412-5599
General Phone: (361) 825-7024
General Fax: (361) 825-3931
Display Adv. E-mail: islandwaves.ads@tamucc.edu
Editorial e-mail: editor-in-chief.islandwaves@tamucc.edu
Personnel: Rob Boscamp (Advisor); Brittnye Screws (Adv. Mgr.)

TEXAS A&M UNIV. GALVESTON

Street address 1: PO Box 1675
Street address city: Galveston
Street address state: TX
Zip/Postal code: 77553-1675
Country: USA
Mailing address: PO Box 1675
Mailing city: Galveston
Mailing state: TX
Mailing zip: 77553-1675
General Phone: (409) 740-4420
General Fax: (409) 740-4775
General/National Adv. E-mail: nautilus@tamug.edu
Personnel: Kayce Peirce (Ed. in Chief)

TEXAS A&M UNIV. KINGSVILLE

Street address 1: 700 N University Blvd
Street address city: Kingsville
Street address state: TX
Zip/Postal code: 78363-8202
Country: USA
Mailing address: MSC 123
Mailing state: TX
Mailing zip: 78363
General Phone: (361) 593-2111
General Fax: (361) 593-4046
General/National Adv. E-mail: thesouthtexan@yahoo.com
Personnel: Manuel Flores (Advisor); Jaime Gonzalez (Mng. Ed.); Amanda Marcum (Ed. in Chief)

TEXAS A&M UNIVERSITY

Street address 1: 107 Scoates Hall
Street address city: College Station
Street address state: TX
Zip/Postal code: 77843-0001
Country: USA
Mailing address: 107 Scoates Hall
Mailing city: College Station
Mailing state: TX
Mailing zip: 77843-0001
General Phone: (979) 862-3003
Personnel: Deborah Dunsford (Program Coord.)

TEXAS A&M UNIVERSITY

Street address 1: 4234 Tamu
Street address city: College Station
Street address state: TX
Zip/Postal code: 77843-0001
Country: USA
Mailing address: 4234 Tamu
Mailing city: College Station
Mailing state: TX
Mailing zip: 77843-0001
General Phone: (979) 458-1802
Personnel: Randall S. Sumpter (Dir., Journ. Studies/ Assoc. Prof., Commun.); Roberto Farias (Program Asst.); Edward L. Walraven (Sr. Lectr.); Dale A. Rice (Lectr.)

TEXAS CHRISTIAN UNIVERSITY

Street address 1: 2805 S University Dr
Street address 2: Moudy South Rm. 215
Street address city: Fort Worth
Street address state: TX
Zip/Postal code: 76129-0001
Country: USA
Mailing address: TCU Box 298050
Mailing city: Fort Worth
Mailing state: TX
Mailing zip: 76129-0001
General Phone: (817) 257-7428
General Fax: (817) 257-7133
Advertising Phone: (817) 257-7426
Advertising Fax: 8172577133
Editorial Phone: 8172573600
Editorial Fax: 8172577133
General/National Adv. E-mail: 360@tcu360.com
Display Adv. E-mail: ads@tcu360.com
Editorial e-mail: 360@tcu360.com
Primary Website: www.tcu360.com
Year Established: 1902
Published: Thur
Published Other: IMAGE Magazine
Avg Free Circ: 2000
Personnel: Leah Griffin (Manager of Student Media Sales and Marketing); Jean Marie Brown (Assistant Professor of Professional Practice)

TEXAS LUTHERAN UNIV.

Street address 1: 1000 W Court St
Street address city: Seguin
Street address state: TX
Zip/Postal code: 78155-5978
Country: USA
Mailing address: 1000 W Court St
Mailing city: Seguin
Mailing state: TX
Mailing zip: 78155-9996
General Phone: (830) 372-8073
General Fax: (830) 372-8074
General/National Adv. E-mail: lonestarlutheran@tlu.edu
Personnel: Robin Bisha (Advisor); Steven S. Vrooman (Chair); Kristi Quiros (Pub.); Emmalee Drummond (Ed. in Chief); Naomi Urquiza (Mng. Ed.)

TEXAS SOUTHERN UNIV.

Street address 1: 3100 Cleburne Ave, Student Ctr
Street address city: Houston
Street address state: TX
Zip/Postal code: 77004
Country: USA
Mailing address: 3100 Cleburne Ave., Student Ctr.
Mailing city: Houston
Mailing state: TX
Mailing zip: 77004-4501
General Phone: (713) 313-1976
Personnel: Alice Rogers (Advisor)

TEXAS STATE UNIV.

Street address 1: 601 University Dr Bldg Trinity
Street address 2: 203 Pleasant Street
Street address city: San Marcos
Street address state: TX
Zip/Postal code: 78666-4684
Country: USA
Mailing address: 601 University Dr Bldg Trinity
Mailing city: San Marcos
Mailing state: TX
Mailing zip: 78666-4684
General Phone: (512) 245-3487
General Fax: (512) 245-3708
Advertising Phone: (512 245-2261
Advertising Fax: (512) 245-3708
General/National Adv. E-mail: stareditor@txstate.edu
Display Adv. E-mail: starad1@txstate.edu
Editorial e-mail: stareditor@txstate.edu
Primary Website: www.universitystar.com
Year Established: 1911
Published: Mon`Wed`Thur
Personnel: Bob Bajackson (Advisor)

TEXAS STUDENT MEDIA

Street address 1: 2500 Whitis Ave
Street address city: Austin
Street address state: TX
Zip/Postal code: 78712-1502
Country: USA
Mailing address: PO Box D
Mailing city: Austin
Mailing state: TX
Mailing zip: 78713-8904
General Phone: (512) 471-4591
General Fax: (512) 471-2952
Advertising Phone: (512) 471-1865
Editorial Phone: (512) 232-2207
Primary Website: www.dailytexanonline.com
Year Established: 1900
Published: Mon`Tues`Wed`Thur`Fri
Avg Free Circ: 13000
Personnel: Doug Warren (Advisor)

TEXAS TECH UNIVERSITY

Street address 1: 3003 15th St
Street address 2: Texas Tech Media & Comm. Bldg., Room 180
Street address city: Lubbock
Street address state: TX
Zip/Postal code: 79409
County: Lubbock
Country: USA
Mailing address: Box 43081
Mailing city: Lubbock
Mailing state: TX
Mailing zip: 79409-3081
General Phone: (806) 742-3388
General/National Adv. E-mail: dailytoreador@ttu.edu
Display Adv. E-mail: dawn.zuerker@ttu.edu
Primary Website: www.dailytoreador.com
Year Established: 1925
Published: Mthly
Personnel: Sheri Lewis (Director, Toreador Media); Dawn Zuerker (Advertising manager); Kristi Deitiker (Business manager); Sheri Lewis (Asst. Dir./Editorial/ Broadcasting Advisor); Andrea Watson (Asst Dir/Media Advisor); Amie Ward

TEXAS WOMAN'S UNIV.

Street address 1: PO Box 425828

Street address city: Denton
Street address state: TX
Zip/Postal code: 76204-5828
Country: USA
Mailing address: PO Box 425828
Mailing city: Denton
Mailing state: TX
Mailing zip: 76204-5828
General Phone: (940) 898-2191
General Fax: (940) 898-2188
Advertising Phone: (940) 898-2183
General/National Adv. E-mail: twu_lasso@yahoo.com
Personnel: Alejandro Barrientos (Bus. Mgr.); Luis Rendon (Ed. in Chief); Rhonda Ross (Advisor)

THE BATTALION

Street address 1: Grove 215 Lamar St Bldg 8901
Street address city: College Station
Street address state: TX
Zip/Postal code: 77843-0001
County: Brazos
Country: USA
Mailing address: 1111 Tamu
Mailing city: College Station
Mailing state: TX
Mailing zip: 77843-0001
General Phone: 979-845-3313
General Fax: 979-845-2647
General/National Adv. E-mail: editor@thebatt.com
Primary Website: http://thebatt.com/
Year Established: 1893
Published: Mon`Tues`Wed`Thur`Fri

THE RAM PAGE - ANGELO STATE UNIVERSITY

Street address 1: 2601 W Avenue N
Street address city: San Angelo
Street address state: TX
Zip/Postal code: 76909-2601
County: Tom Green
Country: USA
Mailing address: PO Box 10895
Mailing city: San Angelo
Mailing state: TX
Mailing zip: 76909-0001
General Phone: (325) 942-2323
General/National Adv. E-mail: rampage@angelo.edu
Primary Website: www.asurampage.com
Mthly Avg Views: 2000
Mthly Avg Unique Visitors: 800
Year Established: 1936
Published: Other
Published Other: Online
Personnel: Jack C. Eli (Prof./Head); Eilada Gamreklidze (Adviser)

THE RAMBLER

Street address 1: 1201 Wesleyan St
Street address city: Fort Worth
Street address state: TX
Zip/Postal code: 76105-1536
Country: USA
Mailing address: 1201 Wesleyan St
Mailing city: Fort Worth
Mailing state: TX
Mailing zip: 76105-1536
General Phone: (817) 531-7552
General Fax: (817) 531-4878
Advertising Phone: (817) 531-6526
Advertising Fax: 817-531-4878
Editorial Phone: 817-531-7552
Editorial Fax: 817-531-4878
General/National Adv. E-mail: twurambler@yahoo.com
Display Adv. E-mail: rambleradvertising@yahoo.com
Editorial e-mail: twurambler@yahoo.com
Primary Website: www.therambler.org
Year Established: 1917
Published Other: online only
Avg Free Circ: 800
Personnel: Jenny Dean (Adviser); Kelli Lamers (Advisor); Ashely Oldham (Adv. Mgr.); Ngozi Akinro; Tiara Nugent (Ed. in Chief); Martin Garcia (News Ed.); Kay Colley (Student Media Director)

TRAILBLAZER

Street address 1: 1900 W 7th St
Street address 2: # 1271
Street address city: Plainview
Street address state: TX
Zip/Postal code: 79072-6900
County: Hale
Country: USA
Mailing address: 1900 W 7th St # 1271
Mailing city: Plainview
Mailing state: TX
Mailing zip: 79072-6900
General Phone: (806) 291-1088
General/National Adv. E-mail: trailblazer@wbu.edu
Primary Website: www.wbu.edu/trailblazer
Mthly Avg Views: 550
Year Established: 1950
Published: Sun
Published Other: Weekly
Avg Free Circ: 4000
Personnel: Steven Long (Advisor)

TRINITY UNIV.

Street address 1: 1 Trinity Pl
Street address city: San Antonio
Street address state: TX
Zip/Postal code: 78212-4674
Country: USA
Mailing address: 1 Trinity Pl
Mailing city: San Antonio
Mailing state: TX
Mailing zip: 78212-7201
General Phone: (210) 999-8555
General Fax: (210) 999-7034
General/National Adv. E-mail: trinitonian-adv@trinity.edu
Personnel: Kathryn Martin (Advisor); Jordan Krueger (Ed.)

TRINITY VALLEY CMTY. COLLEGE

Street address 1: 100 Cardinal St
Street address city: Athens
Street address state: TX
Zip/Postal code: 75751-3243
Country: USA
Mailing address: 100 Cardinal St
Mailing city: Athens
Mailing state: TX
Mailing zip: 75751-3243
General Phone: (903) 675-6302
General Fax: (903) 675-6316
General/National Adv. E-mail: journalstaff@tvcc.edu
Primary Website: www.tvccnewsjournal.com
Year Established: 1972
Personnel: Danny Teague (Advisor); Judy Greenlee (Asst. Advisor); Melisa Boon (Ed.); Deidre Jones (Media Instructor/Adviser)

TYLER JUNIOR COLLEGE

Street address 1: 1400 E Devine St
Street address 2: # 204
Street address city: Tyler
Street address state: TX
Zip/Postal code: 75701-2207
Country: USA
Mailing address: 1400 E Devine St # 204
Mailing city: Tyler
Mailing state: TX
Mailing zip: 75701-2207
General Phone: (903) 510-2335
Personnel: Laura Krantz (Advisor)

UNIV. OF DALLAS

Street address 1: 1845 E Northgate Dr
Street address 2: # 732
Street address city: Irving
Street address state: TX
Zip/Postal code: 75062-4736
Country: USA
Mailing address: 1845 E Northgate Dr # 732
Mailing city: Irving
Mailing state: TX
Mailing zip: 75062-4736
General Phone: (972) 721-4070
General Fax: (972) 721-4136
Advertising Phone: (972) 721-5142
Editorial Phone: 972-721-5089
General/National Adv. E-mail: udnews1@yahoo.com
Primary Website: www.udallasnews.com
Year Established: 1993
Personnel: Raymond Wilkerson (Fac. Adviser)

UNIV. OF HOUSTON

Street address 1: Rm 7, Uc Satellite, Student Publications
Street address city: Houston
Street address state: TX
Zip/Postal code: 77204-0001
Country: USA
Mailing address: 7 Uc Satellite Student Publications
Mailing city: Houston
Mailing state: TX
Mailing zip: 77204-0001
General Phone: (713) 743-5350
General Fax: (713) 743-5384
Editorial Phone: (713) 743-5360
General/National Adv. E-mail: news@thedailycougar.com
Display Adv. E-mail: ads@thedailycougar.com
Personnel: Ronnie Turner (Ed. in Chief); Matthew Keever (Managing Ed.); Hiba Adi (News Ed.); Patricia Estrada (News Ed.); Alan (Opinion Ed.)

UNIV. OF HOUSTON CLEAR LAKE

Street address 1: 2700 Bay Area Blvd
Street address city: Houston
Street address state: TX
Zip/Postal code: 77058-1002
Country: USA
Mailing address: 2700 Bay Area Blvd
Mailing city: Houston
Mailing state: TX
Mailing zip: 77058-1002
General Phone: (281) 283-2569
General Fax: (281) 283-2569
Advertising Phone: (281) 283-3975
Editorial Phone: (281) 283-2570
General/National Adv. E-mail: thesignal@uhcl.edu
Personnel: Taleen Washington (Advisor); Lindsay Humphrey (Adv. Mgr./Prodn. Asst.); Matt Griesmyer (Ed.)

UNIV. OF HOUSTON DOWNTOWN

Street address 1: 1 Main St
Street address 2: S-260
Street address city: Houston
Street address state: TX
Zip/Postal code: 77002-1014
Country: USA
Mailing address: 1 Main St
Mailing city: Houston
Mailing state: TX
Mailing zip: 77002-1014
General Phone: (713) 221-8569
General Fax: (713) 221-8119
Advertising Phone: (832) 533-7659
Editorial Phone: (832) 495-5381
General/National Adv. E-mail: datelinedowntownhtx@gmail.com
Display Adv. E-mail: editor@dateline-downtown.com
Editorial e-mail: editor@dateline-downtown.com
Primary Website: 2103 Hickory Trail Place
Year Established: 1973
Published: Mon
Published Other: bi-weekly
Personnel: Joe Sample (Associate Prof.)

UNIV. OF MARY HARDIN-BAYLOR

Street address 1: 900 College St
Street address 2: # 8012
Street address city: Belton
Street address state: TX
Zip/Postal code: 76513-2578
Country: USA
Mailing address: 900 College St # 8012
Mailing city: Belton
Mailing state: TX
Mailing zip: 76513-2578
Personnel: Crystal Donahue (Ed.)

UNIV. OF NORTH TEXAS

Street address 1: 225 S Ave B, Gab Room 117
Street address city: Denton
Street address state: TX
Zip/Postal code: 76201
Country: USA
Mailing address: 225 S Ave B, GAB Room 117
Mailing city: Denton
Mailing state: TX
Mailing zip: 76201
General Phone: (940) 565-2851
General Fax: (940) 565-3573
Advertising Phone: (940) 565-3989
Editorial Phone: (940) 565-2353
General/National Adv. E-mail: editor@ntdaily.com
Personnel: Allie Durham (Adv. Mgr.); Kerry Solan (Ed. in Chief); Courtney Roberts (Mng. Ed.)

UNIV. OF ST. THOMAS

Street address 1: 3800 Montrose Blvd
Street address city: Houston
Street address state: TX
Zip/Postal code: 77006-4626
Country: USA
Mailing address: 3800 Montrose Blvd
Mailing city: Houston
Mailing state: TX
Mailing zip: 77006-4626
Personnel: Michelle Gautreau (Ed.)

UNIV. OF TEXAS

Street address 1: 14545 Roadrunner Way
Street address city: San Antonio
Street address state: TX
Zip/Postal code: 78249-1515
Country: USA
Mailing address: 14545 Roadrunner Way
Mailing city: San Antonio
Mailing state: TX
Mailing zip: 78249-1515
General Phone: (210) 690-9301
General Fax: (210) 690-3423
General/National Adv. E-mail: paisanoeditor@sbcglobal.net
Personnel: Rachel Hill (Ed.)

UNIV. OF TEXAS AT TYLER

Street address 1: 3900 University Blvd
Street address city: Tyler
Street address state: TX
Zip/Postal code: 75799-6600
Country: USA
Mailing address: 3900 University Blvd
Mailing city: Tyler
Mailing state: TX
Mailing zip: 75799-0001
General Phone: (903) 565-7131
Advertising Phone: (903) 566-5536
Editorial Phone: (903) 566-7131
Display Adv. E-mail: ads@patriottalon.com
Editorial e-mail: editor@patriottalon.com
Primary Website: www.patriottalon.com
Year Established: 1976
Published: Bi-Mthly
Avg Free Circ: 2000
Personnel: Lorri Allen (Adviser); Nathan Wright (Editor in Chief)

UNIV. OF TEXAS COLLEGE OF BUS.

Street address 1: Cba 3.328 A
Street address city: Austin
Street address state: TX
Zip/Postal code: 78712
Country: USA
Mailing address: CBA 3.328 A
Mailing city: Austin
Personnel: Sunio Varghese (Ed.)

UNIV. OF TEXAS COLLEGE OF ENGINEERING

Street address 1: 301 E Dean Keeton St
Street address city: Austin
Street address state: TX
Zip/Postal code: 78712-1476
Country: USA
Mailing address: 301 E. Dean Keeton St. C2100
Mailing city: Austin
Mailing state: TX
Mailing zip: 78712-2100
General Phone: (512) 471-3003
General Fax: (512) 471-4304
General/National Adv. E-mail: vector.ut@gmail.com

Personnel: An Nguyen (Ed.)

UNIV. OF TEXAS DALLAS

Street address 1: PO Box 830688
Street address city: Richardson
Street address state: TX
Zip/Postal code: 75083-0688
Country: USA
Mailing address: PO Box 830688
Mailing city: Richardson
Mailing state: TX
Mailing zip: 75083-0688
General Phone: (972) 883-2286
General Fax: (972) 883-2772
Editorial Phone: (972) 883-2210
General/National Adv. E-mail: mercury@utdallas.edu
Display Adv. E-mail: ads@mercury.utdallas.edu
Primary Website: www.utdmercury.com
Year Established: 1980
Personnel: James Wooley (Adv. Mgr.); Lauren Buell (Ed.)

UNIV. OF TEXAS EL PASO

Street address 1: 105 Union East
Street address 2: 500 W. University Ave.
Street address city: El Paso
Street address state: TX
Zip/Postal code: 79968-0001
Country: USA
Mailing address: 105 Union East
Mailing city: El Paso
Mailing state: TX
Mailing zip: 79968-0622
General Phone: (915) 747-5161
General Fax: (915) 747-8031
Advertising Phone: (915) 747-7434
Editorial Phone: (915) 747-7446
General/National Adv. E-mail: studentpublications@utep.edu
Display Adv. E-mail: prospectorads@utep.edu
Editorial e-mail: theprospector1@gmail.com
Primary Website: www.theprospectordaily.com
Year Established: 1914
Published: Tues
Published Other: www.theprospectordaily.com
Avg Free Circ: 5000
Personnel: Kathleen Flores (Dir); Veronica Gonzalez (Asst. Adv. Dir.)

UNIV. OF TEXAS PAN AMERICAN

Street address 1: 1201 W University Dr
Street address city: Edinburg
Street address state: TX
Zip/Postal code: 78539-2909
Country: USA
Mailing address: 1201 W. University Dr.
Mailing city: Edinburg
Mailing state: TX
Mailing zip: 78539
General Phone: (956) 381-2541
General Fax: (956) 316-7122
General/National Adv. E-mail: spubs@utpa.edu
Personnel: Gregory M. Selber (Advisor); Mariel Cantu (Adv. Mgr.); Brian Silva (Ed. in chief)

UNIV. OF TEXAS PERMIAN BASIN

Street address 1: 4901 E University Blvd
Street address 2: Rm MB
Street address city: Odessa
Street address state: TX
Zip/Postal code: 79762-8122
Country: USA
Mailing address: 4901 E University Blvd Rm MB2215A
Mailing city: Odessa
Mailing state: TX
Mailing zip: 79762-8122
General Phone: (432) 552-2659
General Fax: (432) 552-3654
General/National Adv. E-mail: mesajournal@utpb.edu
Primary Website: mesajournalnews.com
Year Established: 1975
Published: Mon`Tues`Wed`Thur`Sat
Avg Free Circ: 6000
Personnel: myra Salcedo (Advisor)

UNIVERSITY OF TEXAS AT ARLINGTON

Street address 1: University Ctr, Lower Level, 300 W 1st St
Street address 2: B100
Street address city: Arlington
Street address state: TX
Zip/Postal code: 76019-0001
Country: USA
Mailing address: P.O. Box 19038
Mailing city: Arlington
Mailing state: TX
Mailing zip: 76019-0001
General Phone: (817) 272-3188
General Fax: (817) 272-5009
Editorial Phone: (817) 272-3205
General/National Adv. E-mail: editor.shorthorn@uta.edu
Display Adv. E-mail: ads.shorthorn@uta.edu
Editorial e-mail: editor.shorthorn@uta.edu; calendar.shorthorn@uta.edu
Primary Website: www.theshorthorn.com
Year Established: 1919
Published: Wed
Published Other: Daily online
Personnel: Brian Schopf (Office Mgr.); Tammy Skrehart (Adv. Mgr./Asst. Dir.); Adam Drew (Production Mgr.); Beth Francesco (Dir. of Student Pubs.); Laurie Fox (Newsroom advisor); Lori Doskocil (Bus Mgr)

UNIVERSITY OF TEXAS AT BROWNSVILLE

Street address 1: 1 W University Blvd
Street address 2: Student Union 1.16
Street address city: Brownsville
Street address state: TX
Zip/Postal code: 78520-4933
Country: USA
Mailing address: 1 West University Boulevard
Mailing city: Brownsville
Mailing state: TX
Mailing zip: 78520-4956
General Phone: (956) 882-5143
General Fax: (956) 882-5176
General/National Adv. E-mail: collegian@utb.edu
Display Adv. E-mail: collegian.advertising@utb.edu
Editorial e-mail: collegian@utb.edu
Primary Website: utbcollegian.com
Published: Mon
Avg Free Circ: 4000
Personnel: Azenett Cornejo (Advisor); Cleiri Quezada (Editor)

UNIVERSITY OF THE INCARNATE WORD

Street address 1: 4301 Broadway, Cpo 494
Street address city: San Antonio
Street address state: TX
Zip/Postal code: 78209
Country: USA
Mailing address: 4301 Broadway, CPO 494
Mailing city: San Antonio
Mailing state: TX
Mailing zip: 78209-6318
General Phone: (210) 829-3964
General Fax: (210) 283-5005
Advertising Phone: (210) 829-6069
Advertising Fax: (210) 283-5005
Editorial Phone: (210) 829-6069
Editorial Fax: (210) 283-5005
General/National Adv. E-mail: mercer@uiwtx.edu
Display Adv. E-mail: mercer@uiwtx.edu
Editorial e-mail: mercer@uiwtx.edu
Primary Website: www.uiw.edu/logos
Year Established: 1935
Published: Mthly
Personnel: Michael L. Mercer (Advisor)

WEST TEXAS A&M UNIV.

Street address 1: PO Box 60747
Street address city: Canyon
Street address state: TX
Zip/Postal code: 79016-0001
Country: USA
Mailing address: PO Box 60747
Mailing city: Canyon
Mailing state: TX
Mailing zip: 79016-0001
General Phone: (806) 651-2410
General Fax: (806) 651-2818
Advertising Phone: (806) 651-2413
General/National Adv. E-mail: bleschper@mail.wtamu.edu; theprairiemail@yahoo.com
Personnel: Christaan Eayrs (Advisor); Joe Dowd (Bus. Mgr.); Kayla Goodman (Ed.)

WILEY COLLEGE

Street address 1: 711 Wiley Ave
Street address city: Marshall
Street address state: TX
Zip/Postal code: 75670-5151
Country: USA
Mailing address: 711 Wiley Ave
Mailing city: Marshall

UTAH

BRIGHAM YOUNG UNIVERSITY

Street address 1: 152 Brmb
Street address city: Provo
Street address state: UT
Zip/Postal code: 84602-3701
Country: USA
Mailing address: 152 BRMB
Mailing city: Provo
Mailing state: UT
Mailing zip: 84602-3701
General Phone: (801) 422-2957
General/National Adv. E-mail: dureceptionist@gmail.com
Display Adv. E-mail: ellen_hernandez@byu.edu
Editorial e-mail: universe.ideas@gmail.com
Primary Website: universe.byu.edu
Published: Tues
Personnel: Steve Fidel (Director)

DIXIE STATE COLLEGE

Street address 1: 225 S 700 E
Street address city: Saint George
Street address state: UT
Zip/Postal code: 84770-3875
Country: USA
Mailing address: 225 S. 700 E. JEN
Mailing city: Saint George
Mailing state: UT
Mailing zip: 84770
General Phone: (435) 652-7818
General Fax: (435) 656-4019
Advertising Phone: (435) 652-7818
Advertising Fax: (435) 656-4019
General/National Adv. E-mail: dixiesun@dixie.edu
Display Adv. E-mail: dixiesunads@dixie.edu
Editorial e-mail: dixiesun@dixie.edu
Personnel: Rhiannon Bent (Advisor); Taylor Forbes (Adv. Mgr.); Rachel Tanner (Ed. in Chief)

SNOW COLLEGE

Street address 1: 150 College Ave
Street address city: Ephraim
Street address state: UT
Zip/Postal code: 84627-1550
Country: USA
Mailing address: 150 College Ave
Mailing city: Ephraim
Mailing state: UT
Mailing zip: 84627-1299
General Phone: (435) 283-7385
General/National Adv. E-mail: snowdrift@snow.edu
Personnel: Greg Dart (Advisor); Justin Albee (Bus. Mgr.); Kelly Peterson (Ed. in Chief)

SOUTHERN UTAH UNIV.

Street address 1: 351 W University Blvd
Street address 2: University Journal
Street address city: Cedar City
Street address state: UT
Zip/Postal code: 84720-2415
Country: USA
Mailing address: 351 W University Blvd
Mailing city: Cedar City
Mailing state: UT
Mailing zip: 84720-2415
General Phone: (435) 865-8226
Advertising Phone: 435-704-4733
Editorial Phone: 435-865-8226
General/National Adv. E-mail: journal@suu.edu
Display Adv. E-mail: Gholdston@suuews.com
Editorial e-mail: journal@suu.edu
Primary Website: www.suunews.com
Year Established: 1937
Published: Mon`Thur
Avg Free Circ: 2000
Personnel: John Gholdston (Advisor)

UNIV. OF UTAH

Street address 1: 200 Central Campus Dr
Street address 2: Rm 234
Street address city: Salt Lake City
Street address state: UT
Zip/Postal code: 84112-9110
Country: USA
Mailing address: 200 Central Campus Dr Rm 234
Mailing city: Salt Lake City
Mailing state: UT
Mailing zip: 84112-9110
General Phone: (801) 581-2788
Editorial e-mail: news@chronicle.utah.edu; press@chronicle.utah.edu
Personnel: Rachel Hanson (Chief Ed.); Michael Mcfall (Ed.)

UTAH STATE UNIV.

Street address 1: Taggart Ctr 105
Street address city: Logan
Street address state: UT
Zip/Postal code: 84322-0001
Country: USA
Mailing address: PO Box 1249
Mailing city: Logan
Mailing state: UT
Mailing zip: 84322-0001
General Phone: (435) 797-6397
General Fax: (435) 797-1760
General/National Adv. E-mail: statesmanoffice@aggiemail.com
Primary Website: www.utahstatesman.com
Year Established: 1902
Personnel: Jay Wamsley (Advisor)

UTAH STATE UNIVERSITY EASTERN

Street address 1: 451 N 400 E St
Street address city: Price
Street address state: UT
Zip/Postal code: 84501
County: Carbon
Country: USA
Mailing address: 451 N. 400 E. St.
Mailing city: Price
Mailing state: UT
Mailing zip: 84501-3315
General Phone: (435) 613-5123
Advertising Phone: (435) 613-5213
General/National Adv. E-mail: Susan.polster@usu.edu
Primary Website: Usueagle.com
Mthly Avg Views: 900
Mthly Avg Unique Visitors: 600
Year Established: 1937
Published: Thur`Other
Avg Free Circ: 1000
Personnel: Susan Polster (Adviser)

UTAH VALLEY UNIVERSITY

Street address 1: 800 W University Pkwy
Street address city: Orem
Street address state: UT
Zip/Postal code: 84058-6703
Country: USA
Mailing address: 800 W University Pkwy # Mt
Mailing city: Orem
Mailing state: UT
Mailing zip: 84058-6703
General Phone: (801) 863-8688
General Fax: (801) 863-8601
Display Adv. E-mail: robbina@uvu.edu
Primary Website: www.uvureview.com
Published: Mon

Personnel: Robbin Anthony (Bus. Mgr.); Brent Sumner (Advisor)

WEBER STATE UNIVERSITY

Street address 1: 3910 W Campus Dr
Street address 2: Dept 2110
Street address city: Ogden
Street address state: UT
Zip/Postal code: 84408-2110
Country: USA
Mailing address: 3910 West Campus Drive Dept 2110
Mailing city: Ogden
Mailing state: UT
Mailing zip: 84408-2110
General Phone: (801) 626-7526
General Fax: (801) 626-7401
Advertising Phone: (801) 626-6359
Advertising Fax: (801) 626-7401
Editorial Phone: (801) 626-7121
Editorial Fax: (801) 626-7401
General/National Adv. E-mail: thesignpost@weber.edu
Display Adv. E-mail: Kcsanders@weber.edu
Editorial e-mail: Kcsanders@weber.edu
Primary Website: MyWeberMedia.com
Year Established: 1937
Published: Mon`Thur
Published Other: 8 issues (once a week) during the summer semester
Avg Free Circ: 2000
Personnel: KC Sanders (Advt Mgr); Georgia Edwards (Office Mgr); Jean Norman (Signpost Adviser)

WESTMINSTER COLLEGE

Street address 1: 1840 S 1300 E
Street address city: Salt Lake City
Street address state: UT
Zip/Postal code: 84105-3617
Country: USA
Mailing address: 1840 S 1300 E
Mailing city: Salt Lake City
Mailing state: UT
Mailing zip: 84105-3697
General Phone: (801) 832-2320
General Fax: (801) 466-6916
General/National Adv. E-mail: forum@wesminstercollege.edu
Editorial e-mail: forumeditor@westminstercollege.edu
Personnel: Ann Green (Bus. Mgr.); Fred Fogo (Advisor); Kimberly Zarkin (Advisor)

VIRGINIA

BLUEFIELD COLLEGE

Street address 1: 3000 College Dr
Street address city: Bluefield
Street address state: VA
Zip/Postal code: 24605-1737
Country: USA
Mailing address: 3000 College Dr
Mailing city: Bluefield
Mailing state: VA
Mailing zip: 24605-1799
General Phone: (276) 326-3682
Personnel: Mimi Merritt (Advisor)

BRIDGEWATER COLLEGE

Street address 1: 101 N 3rd St
Street address city: Bridgewater
Street address state: VA
Zip/Postal code: 22812-1714
Country: USA
Mailing address: PO Box 193
Mailing city: Bridgewater
Mailing state: VA
Mailing zip: 22812-0193
General Phone: (540) 828-5329
General Fax: (540) 828-5479
Advertising Phone: (540) 828-5329
Editorial Phone: (540) 828-5329
General/National Adv. E-mail: veritas@bridgewater.edu
Display Adv. E-mail: veritas@bridgewater.edu
Editorial e-mail: veritas@bridgewater.edu
Primary Website: http://veritas.bridgewater.edu/
Published: Wed
Avg Free Circ: 1700
Personnel: Bernardo Motta (Assistant Professor of Communication Studies)

CHRISTOPHER NEWPORT UNIV.

Street address 1: 1 University Pl
Street address city: Newport News
Street address state: VA
Zip/Postal code: 23606-2949
Country: USA
Mailing address: 1 University Pl
Mailing city: Newport News
Mailing state: VA
Mailing zip: 23606-2949
General Phone: (757) 594-7196
General/National Adv. E-mail: desk@thecaptainslog.org
Primary Website: www.thecaptainslog.org
Published: Wed
Personnel: Terry Lee (Faculty Advisor); Ben Leistensnider (Ed. in Chief); Nicole Emmelhainz (Faculty advisor)

COLGATE DARDEN GRAD. SCHOOL OF BUS.

Street address 1: 100 Darden Blvd
Street address city: Charlottesville
Street address state: VA
Zip/Postal code: 22903-1760
Country: USA
Mailing address: 100 Darden Blvd
Mailing city: Charlottesville
Mailing state: VA
Mailing zip: 22903-1760
General Phone: (434) 982-2395
General/National Adv. E-mail: ccchronicle@darden.virginia.edu
Personnel: Sarah Yoder (Pub.); Laura Dart (Adv. Mgr.); Tyler Lifton (Ed.)

COLLEGE OF WILLIAM AND MARY

Street address 1: Campus Ctr, Jamestown Rd
Street address city: Williamsburg
Street address state: VA
Zip/Postal code: 23187
Country: USA
Mailing address: PO Box 8795
Mailing city: Williamsburg
Mailing state: VA
General/National Adv. E-mail: flathat.editor@gmail.com
Display Adv. E-mail: flathatads@gmail.com
Editorial e-mail: fhnews@gmail.com
Primary Website: www.flathatnews.com
Year Established: 1911
Published: Tues
Personnel: Trici Fredrick (Advisor); Tucker Higgins (Editor-in-chief)

EMORY & HENRY COLLEGE

Street address 1: PO Box 947
Street address city: Emory
Street address state: VA
Zip/Postal code: 24327-0947
Country: USA
Mailing address: PO Box 947
Mailing city: Emory
Mailing state: VA
Mailing zip: 24327-0947
General Phone: (276) 944-6870
Personnel: Kathy Borterfield (Advisor)

FERRUM COLLEGE

Street address 1: PO Box 1000
Street address city: Ferrum
Street address state: VA
Zip/Postal code: 24088-9001
Country: USA
Mailing address: PO Box 1000
Mailing city: Ferrum
Mailing state: VA
Mailing zip: 24088-9001
General Phone: (540) 365-4334
Personnel: Dr. Lana Whited (Advisor)

GEORGE MASON UNIVERSITY

Street address 1: 4400 University Dr
Street address 2: MS 2C5
Street address city: Fairfax
Street address state: VA
Zip/Postal code: 22030-4422
Country: USA
Mailing address: 4400 University Dr MS 2C5
Mailing city: Fairfax
Mailing state: VA
Mailing zip: 22030-4444
General Phone: (703) 993-2947
General Fax: (703) 993-2948
Advertising Phone: (703) 993-2942
Editorial Phone: (703) 993-2944
General/National Adv. E-mail: cwilso12@gmu.edu
Primary Website: gmufourthestate.com
Published: Mon
Avg Free Circ: 6000
Personnel: Kathryn Mangus (Advisor)

HAMPDEN-SYDNEY COLLEGE

Street address 1: 1 College Rd
Street address city: Hampden Sydney
Street address state: VA
Zip/Postal code: 23943
Country: USA
Mailing address: PO Box 127
Mailing city: Hampden Sydney
Mailing state: VA
Mailing zip: 23943-0127
General Phone: (434) 223-6000
General Fax: (434) 223-6345
Year Established: 1920
Published: Bi-Mthly
Personnel: Max Dash (Editor-in-Chief)

HOLLINS UNIV.

Street address 1: PO Box 9707
Street address city: Roanoke
Street address state: VA
Zip/Postal code: 24020-1707
Country: USA
Mailing address: PO Box 9707
Mailing city: Roanoke
Mailing state: VA
Mailing zip: 24020-1707
General Phone: (540) 362-6000
General Fax: (540) 362-6642
General/National Adv. E-mail: hollinscolumns@hollins.edu
Personnel: Emileigh Clare (Ed. in Chief); Julie Abernethy (Ed.); KaRenda J. LaPrade (Copy Ed.)

JAMES MADISON UNIVERSITY

Street address 1: 1598 S Main St
Street address city: Harrisonburg
Street address state: VA
Zip/Postal code: 22807-1025
Country: USA
Mailing address: 1598 South Main Street
Mailing city: Harrisonburg
Mailing state: VA
Mailing zip: 22807
General Phone: (540) 568-6127
General Fax: (540) 568-6736
Advertising Phone: (540) 568-6127
Editorial Phone: (540) 568-6127
General/National Adv. E-mail: breezeeditor@gmail.com
Display Adv. E-mail: thebreezeads@gmail.com
Editorial e-mail: breezeeditor@gmail.com
Primary Website: www.breezejmu.org
Year Established: 1922
Published: Thur
Avg Free Circ: 5000
Personnel: Brad Jenkins (General Manager); Blake Shepherd (Advertising and Marketing Coordinator)

LIBERTY UNIV.

Street address 1: 1971 University Blvd
Street address city: Lynchburg
Street address state: VA
Zip/Postal code: 24515-0002
Country: USA
Mailing address: 1971 University Blvd
Mailing city: Lynchburg
Mailing state: VA
Mailing zip: 24515-0002
General Phone: (434) 582-2128
General Fax: (434) 582-2420
Editorial Phone: (434) 582-2128
General/National Adv. E-mail: advertising@liberty.edu
Primary Website: www.liberty.edu/champion
Year Established: 1971
Personnel: William Gribbin (Dean, School of Commun.); Debra Huff (Advisor); Cecil V. Kramer (Jr. Assoc. Dean); Benjamin Lesley (Adv. Dir.); William Mullen (Chrmn.); Amanda Sullivan (Ed. in Chief)

LONGWOOD COLLEGE

Street address 1: PO Box 2901
Street address city: Farmville
Street address state: VA
Zip/Postal code: 23909-0001
Country: USA
Mailing address: PO Box 2901
Mailing city: Farmville
Mailing state: VA
Mailing zip: 23909-0001
General Phone: (434) 395-2120
Personnel: Ramesh Rao (Advisor); Emily Grove (Ed. in Chief); Benjamin Byrnes (Mng. Ed.)

LYNCHBURG COLLEGE

Street address 1: 1501 Lakeside Dr
Street address city: Lynchburg
Street address state: VA
Zip/Postal code: 24501-3113
Country: USA
Mailing address: 1501 Lakeside Dr
Mailing city: Lynchburg
Mailing state: VA
Mailing zip: 24501-3113
General Phone: (434) 544-8301
General Fax: (804) 544-8661
General/National Adv. E-mail: critograph@lynchburg.edu
Display Adv. E-mail: critograph@lynchburg.edu
Editorial e-mail: critograph@lynchburg.edu
Primary Website: www.critograph.com
Published: Tues
Personnel: Rachad Davis (Editor-in-Chief); Heywood Greenberg (Dena/Prof., Journ.); Wayne Garret (Copy Desk Chief)

MARY BALDWIN COLLEGE

Street address 1: PO Box 1500
Street address city: Staunton
Street address state: VA
Zip/Postal code: 24402-1500
Country: USA
Mailing address: PO Box 1500
Mailing city: Staunton
Mailing state: VA
Mailing zip: 24402-1500
General Phone: (540) 887-7112
Personnel: Bruce Dorries (Advisor); Dawn Medley (Advisor); Hannah Barrow (Ed. in Chief)

MARYMOUNT UNIV.

Street address 1: 2807 N Glebe Rd
Street address city: Arlington
Street address state: VA
Zip/Postal code: 22207-4224
Country: USA
Mailing address: 2807 N Glebe Rd
Mailing city: Arlington
Mailing state: VA
Mailing zip: 22207-4299
General Phone: (703) 522-5600
General Fax: (703) 284-3817
General/National Adv. E-mail: banner@marymount.edu
Personnel: Paul Byers (Mass Commun. Coord.); Vincent Stovall (Dir., Student Activities); Ralph Frasca (Mass Commun. Coord.)

NORFOLK STATE UNIVERSITY

Street address 1: 700 Park Ave
Street address 2: Student Activities
Street address city: Norfolk

Street address state: VA
Zip/Postal code: 23504-8050
Country: USA
Mailing address: 700 Park Ave.
Mailing city: Norfolk
Mailing state: VA
Mailing zip: 23504-8090
General Phone: (757) 823-8200
Advertising Phone: (757) 823-8200
Editorial Phone: (757) 823-8200
General/National Adv. E-mail: spartanecho@nsu.edu
Display Adv. E-mail: spartanecho@nsu.edu
Editorial e-mail: spartanecho@nsu.edu
Primary Website: www.spartanecho.org
Year Established: 1952
Published: Bi-Mthly
Avg Free Circ: 1000
Personnel: Tarrye Venable (Student Activities Director)

OLD DOMINION UNIVERSITY

Street address 1: 1051 Webb Center
Street address city: Norfolk
Street address state: VA
Zip/Postal code: 23529-0001
Country: USA
Mailing address: 1051 Webb Center
Mailing city: Norfolk
Mailing state: VA
Mailing zip: 23529
General Phone: (757) 683-3452
Advertising Phone: (757) 683-4773
General/National Adv. E-mail: editorinchief@maceandcrown.com
Display Adv. E-mail: advertising@maceandcrown.com
Editorial e-mail: editorinchief@maceandcrown.com
Primary Website: http://www.maceandcrown.com
Year Established: 1930
Published: Wed
Personnel: Adam Flores (Editor-in-Chief); Kavita Butani (Advertising & Business Manager)

RADFORD UNIV.

Street address 1: PO Box 6985
Street address city: Radford
Street address state: VA
Zip/Postal code: 24142-6985
Country: USA
Mailing address: PO Box 6985
Mailing city: Radford
Mailing state: VA
Mailing zip: 24142-6985
General Phone: (540) 831-5474
General Fax: (540) 831-6725
Advertising Fax: (540) 831-6051
General/National Adv. E-mail: tartan@radford.edu
Personnel: Matt Labelle (Ed. in chief); Justin Ward (Mng. Ed.); Colin Daileda (News Ed.)

RANDOLPH-MACON COLLEGE

Street address 1: 204 Henry St
Street address city: Ashland
Street address state: VA
Zip/Postal code: 23005-1634
Country: USA
Mailing address: PO Box 5005
Mailing city: Ashland
Mailing state: VA
Mailing zip: 23005-5505
General Phone: (804) 752-7200
General Fax: (804) 752-3748
General/National Adv. E-mail: yellowjacket@rmc.edu
Personnel: Robert Thomas (Bus. Mgr.); Derek Gayle (News Ed.); Lara O'Brien (Sports Ed.)

RANDOLPH-MACON WOMAN'S COLLEGE

Street address 1: 2500 Rivermont Ave
Street address city: Lynchburg
Street address state: VA
Zip/Postal code: 24503-1555
Country: USA
Mailing address: 2500 Rivermont Ave
Mailing city: Lynchburg
Mailing state: VA
Mailing zip: 24503-1526
General Phone: (434) 947-8000
Personnel: Dawn Linsner (Ed.)

ROANOKE COLLEGE

Street address 1: 221 College Ln
Street address 2: Ofc Studentactivities
Street address city: Salem
Street address state: VA
Zip/Postal code: 24153-3747
Country: USA
Mailing address: 221 College Ln Ofc Studentactivities
Mailing city: Salem
Mailing state: VA
Mailing zip: 24153-3794
General Phone: (540) 375-2327
General Fax: (540) 378-5129
General/National Adv. E-mail: bracketyack@roanoke.edu
Personnel: Daniel Sarabia (Ed.)

SOUTHWEST VIRGINIA CMTY. COLLEGE

Street address 1: PO Box Svcc
Street address city: Richlands
Street address state: VA
Zip/Postal code: 24641
Country: USA
Mailing address: PO Box SVCC
Mailing city: Richlands
Mailing state: VA
Mailing zip: 24641
Personnel: Pat Bussard (Advisor)

SWEET BRIAR COLLEGE

Street address 1: PO Box H
Street address city: Sweet Briar
Street address state: VA
Zip/Postal code: 24595-1058
Country: USA
Mailing address: PO Box 1058
Mailing city: Sweet Briar
Mailing state: VA
Mailing zip: 24595-1058
General Phone: (434) 381-6100
General Fax: (434) 381-6132
General/National Adv. E-mail: sbvoice@sbc.edu
Personnel: Katy Johnstone (Ed. in chief); Carinna Finn (Mng. Ed.)

UNIV. OF RICHMOND

Street address 1: 40 W Hampton Way, North Ct, Rm B1
Street address city: Richmond
Street address state: VA
Zip/Postal code: 23173-0001
Country: USA
Mailing address: 40 W Hampton Way North Ct Rm B1
Mailing city: Richmond
Mailing state: VA
Mailing zip: 23173-0001
General Phone: (804) 289-8483
Editorial e-mail: collegianstories@gmail.com
Primary Website: www.thecollegianur.com
Year Established: 1914
Published: Mon`Tues`Wed`Thur`Fri`Sat`Sun
Personnel: Claire Comey (Editor in Chief); Liza David (Managing Editor)

UNIV. OF VIRGINIA

Street address 1: PO Box 400703
Street address city: Charlottesville
Street address state: VA
Zip/Postal code: 22904-4703
Country: USA
Mailing address: PO Box 400703
Mailing city: Charlottesville
Mailing state: VA
Mailing zip: 22904-4703
General Fax: (434) 924-7290
General/National Adv. E-mail: editor@cavalierdaily.com
Primary Website: www.cavalierdaily.com
Year Established: 1890
Published: Mon`Thur
Avg Free Circ: 10000
Personnel: Karoline Komolafe (Editor-in-chief)

UNIV. OF VIRGINIA

Street address 1: 1 College Ave
Street address city: Wise
Street address state: VA
Zip/Postal code: 24293-4400
Country: USA
Mailing address: PO Box 3043
Mailing city: Wise
Mailing state: VA
Mailing zip: 24293-3043
General Fax: (276) 328-0212
General/National Adv. E-mail: info@uvawise.edu
Personnel: Michael McGill (Adv. Mgr.)

UNIV. OF VIRGINIA SCHOOL OF LAW

Street address 1: 580 Massie Rd
Street address city: Charlottesville
Street address state: VA
Zip/Postal code: 22903-1738
Country: USA
Mailing address: 580 Massie Rd
Mailing city: Charlottesville
Mailing state: VA
Mailing zip: 22903-1789
General Phone: (434) 924-3070
General Fax: (434) 924-7536
General/National Adv. E-mail: editor@lawweekly.org
Primary Website: www.lawweekly.org
Year Established: 1948
Published: Wed
Personnel: Jenna Goldman (Editor-in-Chief)

UNIVERSITY OF MARY WASHINGTON

Street address 1: 1301 College Ave
Street address city: Fredericksburg
Street address state: VA
Zip/Postal code: 22401-5300
Country: USA
Mailing address: 1301 College Ave
Mailing city: Fredericksburg
Mailing state: VA
Mailing zip: 22401-5300
Display Adv. E-mail: blueandgray.eic@gmail.com
Personnel: Michael McCarthy (Advisor)

VIRGINIA COMMONWEALTH UNIV.

Street address 1: 817 W Broad St
Street address city: Richmond
Street address state: VA
Zip/Postal code: 23284-9104
Country: USA
Mailing address: PO Box 842010
Mailing city: Richmond
Mailing state: VA
Mailing zip: 23284-2010
General Phone: (804) 828-1058
Editorial e-mail: editor@commonwealthtimes.com
Personnel: Greg Weatherford (Student Media Dir.); Lauren Geerdes (Bus. Mgr.)

VIRGINIA MILITARY INSTITUTE

Street address 1: PO Box 7
Street address city: Lexington
Street address state: VA
Zip/Postal code: 24450-0007
Country: USA
Mailing address: PO Box 7
Mailing city: Lexington
Mailing state: VA
Mailing zip: 24450-0007
General Phone: (540) 464-7326
General Fax: (540) 463-5679
General/National Adv. E-mail: vmicadet@vmi.edu
Personnel: Captain Christopher Perry (Advisor); Nick Weishar (Ed. in Chief)

VIRGINIA POLYTECHNIC INSTITUTE

Street address 1: 365 Squires Student Ctr
Street address city: Blacksburg
Street address state: VA
Zip/Postal code: 24061-1000
Country: USA
Mailing address: 365 Squires Student Ctr
Mailing city: Blacksburg
Mailing state: VA
Mailing zip: 24061-1000
General Phone: (540) 231-9870
General Fax: (540) 231-9151
Advertising Phone: (540) 961-9860
Display Adv. E-mail: advertising@collegemedia.com
Editorial e-mail: campuseditor@collegiatetimes.com; editor@collegiatetimes.com
Primary Website: www.collegiatetimes.com
Year Established: 1903
Published: Tues`Fri
Personnel: Kiley Thompson (General Manager)

VIRGINIA STATE UNIV.

Street address 1: 402 Foster Hall, Box 9063
Street address city: Petersburg
Street address state: VA
Zip/Postal code: 23806-0001
Country: USA
Mailing address: 402 Foster Hall # 9063
Mailing city: Petersburg
Mailing state: VA
Mailing zip: 23806-0001
Personnel: Howard Hall (Advisor); Thysha Shabazz (Ed.)

VIRGINIA UNION UNIV.

Street address 1: 1500 N Lombardy St
Street address city: Richmond
Street address state: VA
Zip/Postal code: 23220-1711
Country: USA
Mailing address: 1500 N Lombardy St
Mailing city: Richmond
Mailing state: VA
Mailing zip: 23220-1784
Personnel: Gloria D. Brogdon (Dept. Chair); Peter S. Tahsoh (Advisor)

WASHINGTON AND LEE UNIV.

Street address 1: 204 W Washington St
Street address city: Lexington
Street address state: VA
Zip/Postal code: 24450-2116
Country: USA
Mailing address: 204 West Washington Street
Mailing city: Lexington
Mailing state: VA
Mailing zip: 24450
General Phone: (540) 458-4060
Personnel: David Seifert (Bus. Mgr.)

VERMONT

BENNINGTON COLLEGE

Street address 1: 1 College Dr
Street address city: Bennington
Street address state: VT
Zip/Postal code: 05201-6003
Country: USA
Mailing address: 1 College Dr
Mailing city: Bennington
Mailing state: VT
Mailing zip: 05201-6004
Personnel: Veronica Jorgensen (Asst.Dean of Student)

JOHNSON STATE COLLEGE

Street address 1: 337 College Hl
Street address city: Johnson
Street address state: VT
Zip/Postal code: 05656-9741
Country: USA
Mailing address: 337 College Hl
Mailing city: Johnson
Mailing state: VT
Mailing zip: 05656-9898
Personnel: Nathan Burgess (Ed.)

MIDDLEBURY COLLEGE

Street address 1: PO Box 30
Street address city: Middlebury
Street address state: VT

Zip/Postal code: 05753-0030
Country: USA
Mailing address: PO Box 30
Mailing city: Middlebury
Mailing state: VT
Mailing zip: 05753-0030
General Phone: (802) 443-4827
General Fax: (802) 443-2068
General/National Adv. E-mail: campus@middlebury.edu
Personnel: Zachary Karst (Bus. Mgr.); Brian Fung (Ed. in Chief); Tess Russell (Mng. Ed.)

NORWICH UNIV.

Street address 1: Communications Ctr
Street address city: Northfield
Street address state: VT
Zip/Postal code: 5663
Country: USA
Mailing address: 158 Harmon Dr
Mailing city: Northfield
Mailing state: VT
Mailing zip: 05663-1097
General Phone: (802) 485-2763
Personnel: Susan Youngwood (Advisor)

SOUTHERN VERMONT COLLEGE

Street address 1: 982 Mansion Dr
Street address city: Bennington
Street address state: VT
Zip/Postal code: 05201-9269
Country: USA
Mailing address: 982 Mansion Dr
Mailing city: Bennington
Mailing state: VT
Mailing zip: 05201-6002
General Phone: (802) 447-6347
Personnel: Peter Seward (Advisor)

ST. MICHAEL'S COLLEGE

Street address 1: 1 Winooski Park
Street address city: Colchester
Street address state: VT
Zip/Postal code: 05439-1000
Country: USA
Mailing address: 1 Winooski Park
Mailing city: Colchester
Mailing state: VT
Mailing zip: 05439-1000
General Phone: (802) 654-2421
Personnel: Paul Beique; Andrew Dennett (Ed.)

THE CRITIC

Street address 1: 1001 College Rd
Street address city: Lyndonville
Street address state: VT
Zip/Postal code: 5851
County: Caledonia
Country: USA
Mailing address: PO Box 919
Mailing city: Lyndonville
Mailing state: VT
Mailing zip: 05851-0919
General Phone: (802) 626-6353
General/National Adv. E-mail: thecritic@northernvermont.edu
Primary Website: https://www.nvulyndoncritic.com/
Year Established: 1965
Personnel: Bryanna Smith (Editor-in-Chief for 2018-2019 Academic Year.); Alexandra Huff (Editor-in-Chief)

UNIVERSITY OF VERMONT

Street address 1: Uvm Student Life
Street address 2: 590 Main St. #310
Street address city: Burlington
Street address state: VT
Zip/Postal code: 05405-0001
Country: USA
Mailing address: UVM Student Life
Mailing city: Burlington
Mailing state: VT
Mailing zip: 05405
General Phone: (802) 656-4412
General Fax: (802) 656-8482
General/National Adv. E-mail: crevans@uvm.edu
Display Adv. E-mail: crevans@uvm.edu
Editorial e-mail: crevans@uvm.edu
Primary Website: https://vtcynic.com/
Year Established: 1883
Published: Wed
Avg Free Circ: 5000
Personnel: Chris Evans (Adv.)

VERMONT LAW SCHOOL

Street address 1: PO Box 96
Street address city: South Royalton
Street address state: VT
Zip/Postal code: 05068-0096
Country: USA
Mailing address: PO Box 96
Mailing city: South Royalton
Mailing state: VT
Mailing zip: 05068-0096
General Phone: (802) 831-1299
General Fax: (802) 763-7159
General/National Adv. E-mail: forum@vermontlaw.edu
Personnel: Sean Williams (Adv. Mgr.); Kevin Schrems (Ed. in Chief)

WASHINGTON

BELLEVUE CMTY. COLLEGE

Street address 1: 3000 Landerholm Cir SE
Street address city: Bellevue
Street address state: WA
Zip/Postal code: 98007-6406
Country: USA
Mailing address: 3000 Landerholm Cir SE
Mailing city: Bellevue
Mailing state: WA
Mailing zip: 98007-6484
General Phone: (425) 564-2434
General Fax: (425) 564-4152
General/National Adv. E-mail: ataylor@bellevuecollege.edu
Display Adv. E-mail: advertising@thejibsheet.com
Personnel: Katherine Oleson (Pub.); Janelle Gardener (Advisor); Anne Taylor (Adv. Mgr.)

CENTRAL WASHINGTON UNIV.

Street address 1: 400 E University Way
Street address 2: Mail Stop 7435, Bouillon 222
Street address city: Ellensburg
Street address state: WA
Zip/Postal code: 98926-7502
Country: USA
Mailing address: 400 E University Way Rm 222
Mailing city: Ellensburg
Mailing state: WA
Mailing zip: 98926-7502
General Phone: (509) 963-1026
General Fax: (509) 963-1027
Advertising Phone: 509-963-1095
Advertising Fax: 509-963-1027
Editorial Phone: (509) 963-1073
Editorial Fax: Free
General/National Adv. E-mail: cwuobserver@gmail.com
Display Adv. E-mail: gaskillk@cwu.edu
Editorial e-mail: cwuobserver@gmail.com
Primary Website: www.cwuobserver.com
Published: Thur
Avg Free Circ: 6000

CLARK COLLEGE

Street address 1: 1933 Fort Vancouver Way
Street address city: Vancouver
Street address state: WA
Zip/Postal code: 98663-3529
Country: USA
Mailing address: 1933 Fort Vancouver Way # 124
Mailing city: Vancouver
Mailing state: WA
Mailing zip: 98663-3598
General Phone: (360) 992-2159
Personnel: Audrey McDougal (Ed. in Chief); Nick Jensen (Mng. Ed.); Daniel Hampton (News Ed.)

EDMONDS CMTY. COLLEGE

Street address 1: 20000 68th Ave W
Street address city: Lynnwood
Street address state: WA
Zip/Postal code: 98036-5912
Country: USA
Mailing address: 20000 68th Ave W
Mailing city: Lynnwood
Mailing state: WA
Mailing zip: 98036-5999
General Phone: (425) 640-1315
General/National Adv. E-mail: revedic@edcc.edu
Primary Website: thetritonreview.com
Published: Other
Published Other: Twice per quarter during the academic year.
Personnel: Rob Harrill (Advisor); Madeleine Jenness (Editor in Chief)

EVERETT COMMUNITY COLLEGE

Street address 1: 2000 Tower St
Street address 2: Whitehorse Hall 265-268
Street address city: Everett
Street address state: WA
Zip/Postal code: 98201-1352
Country: USA
Mailing address: 2000 Tower St.
Mailing city: Everett
Mailing state: WA
Mailing zip: 98201-1390
General Phone: (425) 388-9522
General/National Adv. E-mail: clipper@everettcc.edu
Primary Website: www.everettclipper.com
Year Established: 1943
Published: Other
Published Other: Every three weeks
Avg Free Circ: 2500
Personnel: T. Andrew Wahl (Adviser); Terresa King (Business & Circulation Director); Nataya Foss (Editor-in-chief)

GONZAGA UNIVERSITY

Street address 1: 502 E Boone Ave
Street address city: Spokane
Street address state: WA
Zip/Postal code: 99258-1774
Country: USA
Mailing address: Msc # 2477
Mailing city: Spokane
Mailing state: WA
Mailing zip: 99258-0001
General Phone: (509) 313-6826
General Fax: (509) 313-5848
Advertising Phone: (509) 313-6839
Advertising Fax: (509) 313-5848
Editorial Phone: (509) 313-6826
Editorial Fax: (509) 313-5848
General/National Adv. E-mail: bulletin@zagmail.gonzaga.edu
Display Adv. E-mail: adoffice@gonzaga.edu
Editorial e-mail: bulletin@zagmail.gonzaga.edu
Primary Website: www.gonzagabulletin.com
Published: Thur
Avg Free Circ: 3000
Personnel: Tom Miller (Advisor); Susan English (Adviser); John Kafentzis (Adviser); Joanne Shiosaki (Student Publications Manager); Chris Wheatley (Student Publications Assistant Manager)

GRAYS HARBOR COLLEGE

Street address 1: 1620 Edward P Smith Dr
Street address city: Aberdeen
Street address state: WA
Zip/Postal code: 98520-7500
Country: USA
Mailing address: 1620 Edward P Smith Dr
Mailing city: Aberdeen
Mailing state: WA
Mailing zip: 98520-7599

GREEN RIVER COMMUNITY COLLEGE

Street address 1: 12401 SE 320th St
Street address city: Auburn
Street address state: WA
Zip/Postal code: 98092-3622
Country: USA
Mailing address: 12401 SE 320th St
Mailing city: Auburn
Mailing state: WA
Mailing zip: 98092-3699
General Phone: (253) 833-9111 x2375
General Fax: (253) 288-3457
Advertising Phone: (253) 833-9111 x2376
Editorial Phone: (253) 833-9111 x2375
General/National Adv. E-mail: thecurrent@greenriver.edu
Primary Website: http://www.thecurrentonline.net
Published Other: Every two weeks (approximately), excluding summer
Avg Free Circ: 1200
Personnel: Brian Schraum (Adviser)

HIGHLINE COLLEGE

Street address 1: 2400 S 240th St
Street address city: Des Moines
Street address state: WA
Zip/Postal code: 98198-2714
Country: USA
Mailing address: PO Box 98000
Mailing city: Des Moines
Mailing state: WA
Mailing zip: 98198-9800
General Phone: (206) 592-3291
General Fax: (206) 870-3771
Advertising Phone: (206) 592-3292
Editorial Phone: (206) 592-3317
General/National Adv. E-mail: tword@highline.edu; thunderword@highline.edu
Display Adv. E-mail: thunderword@highline.edu
Primary Website: https://thunderword.highline.edu/
Year Established: 1961
Published: Thur
Avg Free Circ: 2000
Personnel: T.M. Sell (Advisor)

LOWER COLUMBIA COLLEGE

Street address 1: 1600 Maple St
Street address city: Longview
Street address state: WA
Zip/Postal code: 98632-3907
Country: USA
Mailing address: PO Box 3010
Mailing city: Longview
Mailing state: WA
Mailing zip: 98632-0310
General Phone: (360) 442-2311
Personnel: Jill Homme (Ed.)

OLYMPIC COLLEGE

Street address 1: 1600 Chester Ave
Street address city: Bremerton
Street address state: WA
Zip/Postal code: 98337-1600
Country: USA
Mailing address: 1600 Chester Ave
Mailing city: Bremerton
Mailing state: WA
Mailing zip: 98337-1699
General Phone: (360) 792-6050
General Fax: (360) 475-7684
General/National Adv. E-mail: olyeditor@olympic.edu
Personnel: Michael Prince (Advisor); Jon Miller (Ed.); Josh Nothnagle (Mng. Ed.)

PACIFIC LUTHERAN UNIV.

Street address 1: the Mooring Mast Pacific Lutheran University 1010 122nd Street
Street address city: Tacoma
Street address state: WA
Zip/Postal code: 98447-0001
Country: USA
Mailing address: the Mooring Mast Pacific Lutheran University 1010 122nd Street S
Mailing city: Tacoma
Mailing state: WA
Mailing zip: 98447-0001
General Phone: (253) 535-7492
General Fax: (253) 536-5067
Advertising Phone: (425) 622-2693
General/National Adv. E-mail: mast@plu.edu
Display Adv. E-mail: mastads@plu.edu
Primary Website: www.plu.edu/~mast
Year Established: 1924
Published: Fri
Avg Free Circ: 3500

Personnel: Winston Alder (Business and Ads Manager); Jessica Trondsen (Editor-in-Chief)

PIERCE COLLEGE

Street address 1: 9401 Farwest Dr SW
Street address city: Lakewood
Street address state: WA
Zip/Postal code: 98498-1919
Country: USA
Mailing address: 9401 Farwest Dr SW
Mailing city: Lakewood
Mailing state: WA
Mailing zip: 98498-1999
General Phone: (253) 964-6604
General Fax: (253) 964-6764
General/National Adv. E-mail: pioneer@pierce.ctc.edu
Personnel: Michael Parks (Advisor); Blake York (Ed. in chief)

SEATTLE CENTRAL CMTY. COLLEGE

Street address 1: 1701 Broadway
Street address 2: # BE1145
Street address city: Seattle
Street address state: WA
Zip/Postal code: 98122-2413
Country: USA
Mailing address: 1701 Broadway # BE1145
Mailing city: Seattle
Mailing state: WA
Mailing zip: 98122-2413
General Phone: (206) 587-6959
Personnel: Rachel Swedish (Ed. in Chief)

SEATTLE PACIFIC UNIV.

Street address 1: 3307 3rd Ave W
Street address city: Seattle
Street address state: WA
Zip/Postal code: 98119-1940
Country: USA
Mailing address: 3307 3rd Ave W
Mailing city: Seattle
Mailing state: WA
Mailing zip: 98119-1997
General Phone: (206) 281-2913
General Fax: (206) 378-5003
General/National Adv. E-mail: falcon-ads@spu.edu
Editorial e-mail: falcon-online@spu.edu; falcon-news@spu.edu; falcon-sports@spu.edu; falcon-features@spu.edu; falcon-opinions@spu.edu
Personnel: Katie-Joy Blanksma (Ed. in Chief); Haley Libak (Layout Ed.); Madeline Tremain (Layout Ed.)

SEATTLE UNIVERSITY

Street address 1: 901 12th Ave
Street address city: Seattle
Street address state: WA
Zip/Postal code: 98122-4411
Country: USA
Mailing address: PO Box 222000
Mailing city: Seattle
Mailing state: WA
Mailing zip: 98122-1090
General Phone: (206) 296-6470
General Fax: (206) 296-2163
Editorial e-mail: editor@su-spectator.com; support@collegepublisher.com
Primary Website: www.seattlespectator.com
Year Established: 1933
Published: Wed
Personnel: Sonora Jha (Advisor)

SHORELINE CMTY. COLLEGE

Street address 1: 16101 Greenwood Ave N
Street address 2: Rm 9101
Street address city: Shoreline
Street address state: WA
Zip/Postal code: 98133-5667
Country: USA
Mailing address: 16101 Greenwood Ave N Rm 9101
Mailing city: Shoreline
Mailing state: WA
Mailing zip: 98133-5667
General Phone: (206) 546-4730
General Fax: (206) 546-5869
General/National Adv. E-mail: webbtide@yahoo.com
Personnel: Patti Jones (Advisor); Amelia Rivera (Ed. in Chief); Daniel Demay (Copy Ed.); Sean Sherman (Photo Ed.)

SKAGIT VALLEY CMTY. COLLEGE

Street address 1: 2405 E College Way
Street address city: Mount Vernon
Street address state: WA
Zip/Postal code: 98273-5821
Country: USA
Mailing address: 2405 E College Way
Mailing city: Mount Vernon
Mailing state: WA
Mailing zip: 98273-5899
General Phone: (360) 416-7710
Personnel: Beverly Saxon (Advisor)

SOUTH PUGET SOUND CMTY. COLLEGE

Street address 1: 2011 Mottman Rd SW
Street address city: Tumwater
Street address state: WA
Zip/Postal code: 98512-6218
Country: USA
Mailing address: 2011 Mottman Rd SW
Mailing city: Tumwater
Mailing state: WA
Mailing zip: 98512-6218
General Phone: (360) 754-7711
General Fax: (360) 596-5708
General/National Adv. E-mail: soundsnewspaper@spscc.ctc.edu
Personnel: Steve Valandra (Advisor); Erin Landgraf (Ed. in Chief)

SOUTH SEATTLE CMTY. COLLEGE

Street address 1: 6000 16th Ave SW
Street address 2: Jmb 135
Street address city: Seattle
Street address state: WA
Zip/Postal code: 98106-1401
Country: USA
Mailing address: 6000 16th Ave SW Jmb 135
Mailing city: Seattle
Mailing state: WA
Mailing zip: 98106-1401
General Phone: (206) 764-5335
General Fax: (206) 764-7936
Advertising Phone: (206) 764-5335
Editorial Phone: (206) 764-5333
General/National Adv. E-mail: sentinelads@sccd.ctc.edu
Editorial e-mail: sentineleditor@sccd.ctc.edu
Personnel: Betsy Berger (Advisor)

SPOKANE CMTY. COLLEGE

Street address 1: 1810 N Greene St
Street address city: Spokane
Street address state: WA
Zip/Postal code: 99217-5320
Country: USA
Mailing address: 1810 N Greene St
Mailing city: Spokane
Mailing state: WA
Mailing zip: 99217-5399
General Phone: (509) 533-7000
Personnel: Rob Vogel (Advisor); Danie Eile (Ed.)

SPOKANE FALLS CMTY. COLLEGE

Street address 1: 3410 W Fort George Wright Dr
Street address 2: MS 3180
Street address city: Spokane
Street address state: WA
Zip/Postal code: 99224-5204
Country: USA
Mailing address: 3410 W Fort George Wright Dr MS 3180
Mailing city: Spokane
Mailing state: WA
Mailing zip: 99224-5204
General Phone: (509) 533-3246
General Fax: (509) 533-3856
General/National Adv. E-mail: communicator@spokanefalls.edu
Personnel: Jason Nix (Advisor); Sarah Radmer (Mng. Ed.); Madison Mccord (Ed.); Wendy Gaskill (Ed.)

TACOMA CMTY. COLLEGE

Street address 1: 6501 S 19th St
Street address 2: Bldg 216
Street address city: Tacoma
Street address state: WA
Zip/Postal code: 98466-6139
Country: USA
Mailing address: 6501 S 19th St Bldg 216
Mailing city: Tacoma
Mailing state: WA
Mailing zip: 98466-6139
General Phone: (253) 566-6045
Personnel: Serrell Collins (Advisor); Kathy Tavia (Ed.)

THE EASTERNER

Street address 1: 102 Isle Hall
Street address city: Cheney
Street address state: WA
Zip/Postal code: 99004-2417
Country: USA
Mailing address: 102 Isle Hall
Mailing city: Cheney
Mailing state: WA
Mailing zip: 99004-2417
General Phone: (509) 359-6737
Advertising Phone: (509) 359-7010
Display Adv. E-mail: advertising@ewu.edu
Editorial e-mail: easterner.editor@ewu.edu
Primary Website: www.easterneronline.com
Year Established: 1916
Published: Wed
Avg Free Circ: 2500
Personnel: Contact Us (Contact Us); Carleigh Hill (Dir.)

THE EVERGREEN STATE COLLEGE

Street address 1: 2700 Evergreen Pkwy
Street address 2: Cab 316
Street address city: Olympia
Street address state: WA
Zip/Postal code: 98505-0001
Country: USA
Mailing address: 2700 Evergreen Pkwy Cab 316
Mailing city: Olympia
Mailing state: WA
Mailing zip: 98505-0005
General Phone: (360) 867-6213
General Fax: (360) 867-6685
General/National Adv. E-mail: cpj@evergreen.edu
Personnel: Dianne Conrad (Advisor); Madeline Berman (Mng. Ed.); Jason Slotkin (Ed. in Chief)

THE UNIVERSITY OF WASHINGTON TACOMA LEDGER STUDENT NEWSPAPER

Street address 1: 1900 Commerce St
Street address 2: Mat 151
Street address city: Tacoma
Street address state: WA
Zip/Postal code: 98402-3112
Country: USA
Mailing address: 1900 Commerce St Mat 151
Mailing city: Tacoma
Mailing state: WA
Mailing zip: 98402-3112
General Phone: (253) 692-4428
General Fax: (253) 692-5602
Advertising Phone: (253) 692-4529
General/National Adv. E-mail: ledger@uw.edu
Display Adv. E-mail: ledger@u.washington.edu
Editorial e-mail: ledger@u.washington.edu
Primary Website: www.thetacomaledger.com
Published: Mon
Personnel: Daniel Nash (Publications Manager); Kelsie Abram (Editor-in-Chief)

UNIV. OF PUGET SOUND

Street address 1: 1500 N Warner St
Street address 2: Stop 1095
Street address city: Tacoma
Street address state: WA
Zip/Postal code: 98416-1095
Country: USA
Mailing address: 1500 N Warner St Stop 1095
Mailing city: Tacoma
Mailing state: WA
Mailing zip: 98416-1095
General Phone: (253) 879-3100
General Fax: (253) 879-3645
General/National Adv. E-mail: trail@pugetsound.edu
Personnel: Anna Marie Ausnes (Contact)

UNIV. OF WASHINGTON

Street address 1: 144 Communications Bldg
Street address 2: Box 353720
Street address city: Seattle
Street address state: WA
Zip/Postal code: 98195-0001
Country: USA
Mailing address: 132 Communications
Mailing city: Seattle
Mailing state: WA
Mailing zip: 98195-0001
General Phone: (206) 543-2336
General Fax: (206) 543-2345
Advertising Phone: (206) 543-2335
Editorial Phone: 206-543-2700
Display Adv. E-mail: ads@dailyuw.com
Editorial e-mail: editor@dailyuw.com
Primary Website: www.dailyuw.com
Year Established: 1891
Published: Mon`Tues`Wed`Thur`Fri
Avg Free Circ: 7500
Personnel: Diana Kramer (Dir., Student Publications); Andreas Redd (Editor-in-Chief)

WALLA WALLA COLLEGE

Street address 1: 204 S College Ave
Street address city: College Place
Street address state: WA
Zip/Postal code: 99324-1139
Country: USA
Mailing address: 204 S College Ave
Mailing city: College Place
Mailing state: WA
Mailing zip: 99324-1198
General Phone: (509) 527-2971
Personnel: Ross Brown (Ed.); Pamela Harris (Chair)

WASHINGTON STATE UNIVERSITY, DAILY EVERGREEN

Street address 1: 455 NE Veterans Way
Street address city: Pullman
Street address state: WA
Zip/Postal code: 99164-0001
Country: USA
Mailing address: PO Box 642510
Mailing city: Pullman
Mailing state: WA
Mailing zip: 99164-2510
General Phone: (509) 335-4573
General Fax: (509) 335-7401
Advertising Phone: (509) 335-1572
Editorial Phone: (509) 335-3194
Display Adv. E-mail: advertise@dailyevergreen.com
Editorial e-mail: news@dailyevergreen.com
Primary Website: www.dailyevergreen.com
Year Established: 1895
Published: Mon`Tues`Wed`Thur`Fri
Avg Free Circ: 5945
Personnel: Tracy Milano (Program Coord.); Richard Miller (Dir of Student Media); K. Denise Boyd (Fiscal Officer); Jacob Jones (Content Adviser)

WESTERN WASHINGTON UNIV.

Street address 1: 516 High St
Street address 2: # CF230
Street address city: Bellingham
Street address state: WA
Zip/Postal code: 98225-5946
Country: USA
Mailing address: 516 High St # CF230
Mailing city: Bellingham
Mailing state: WA
Mailing zip: 98225-5946
General Phone: (360) 650-3160
General Fax: (360) 650-7775
Advertising Phone: (360) 650-3160
General/National Adv. E-mail: editor@westernfrontonline.net; thewesternfronteditor@yahoo.com
Primary Website: www.westernfrontonline.net
Year Established: 1899

Personnel: Carolyn Nielsen (Advisor); Aletha Macomber (Bus. Mgr.); Michele Anderson (Advertising Mgr.); Nicholas Johnson (Ed. in Chief); Katie (Managing Ed.); Alex (Online Ed.)

WHATCOM CMTY. COLLEGE

Street address 1: Syre Student Ctr Rm 202 237 W Kellogg Rd
Street address city: Bellingham
Street address state: WA
Zip/Postal code: 98226
Country: USA
Mailing address: Syre Student Ctr. Rm. 202 237 W. Kellogg Rd.
Mailing city: Bellingham
Mailing state: WA
Mailing zip: 98226
General Phone: (360) 383-3101
General Fax: (360) 676-2171
General/National Adv. E-mail: horizonads@hotmail.com; admanager@whatcomhorizon.com
Editorial e-mail: editor@whatcomhorizon.com
Primary Website: www.whatcomhorizon.com
Year Established: 1972
Published: Bi-Mthly
Avg Free Circ: 1000
Personnel: Toby Sonneman (Faculty Advisor)

WHITWORTH UNIVERSITY

Street address 1: 300 W Hawthorne Rd
Street address city: Spokane
Street address state: WA
Zip/Postal code: 99251-2515
Country: USA
Mailing address: 300 W Hawthorne Rd
Mailing city: Spokane
Mailing state: WA
Mailing zip: 99251-2515
General Phone: (509) 777-3248
General Fax: (509) 777-3710
Editorial Fax: Free
Editorial e-mail: editor@whitworthian.com
Primary Website: www.thewhitworthian.com
Year Established: 1905
Published: Wed
Personnel: Jim McPherson (Advisor); Rebekah Bresee (Editor-in-Chief)

YAKIMA VALLEY CMTY. COLLEGE

Street address 1: PO Box 22520
Street address city: Yakima
Street address state: WA
Zip/Postal code: 98907-2520
Country: USA
Mailing address: PO Box 22520
Mailing city: Yakima
Mailing state: WA
Mailing zip: 98907-2520
General Phone: (509) 574-4600
General Fax: (509) 574-6860
Advertising Phone: 509-574-6870
Advertising Fax: 509-574-6870
Display Adv. E-mail: nhopkins@yvcc.edu
Primary Website: www.yvcc.edu
Year Established: 1928
Personnel: Niki Hopkins (Ed.)

WISCONSIN

BELOIT COLLEGE

Street address 1: 700 College St
Street address city: Beloit
Street address state: WI
Zip/Postal code: 53511-5509
Country: USA
Mailing address: 700 College St
Mailing city: Beloit
Mailing state: WI
Mailing zip: 53511-5595
General Phone: (608) 363-2000
General Fax: (608) 363-2718
General/National Adv. E-mail: admiss@beloit.edu
Personnel: India John (Co Editor-in-Chief); Steven Jackson (Co Editor-in-Chief)

BLACKHAWK TECHNICAL COLLEGE

Street address 1: 6004 Prairie Rd
Street address city: Janesville
Street address state: WI
Country: USA
Mailing address: PO Box 5009
Mailing city: Janesville
Mailing state: WI
Mailing zip: 53547-5009
Personnel: Amber Feibel (Advisor)

CARDINAL STRITCH UNIV.

Street address 1: 6801 N Yates Rd
Street address city: Milwaukee
Street address state: WI
Zip/Postal code: 53217-3945
Country: USA
Mailing address: 6801 N Yates Rd
Mailing city: Milwaukee
Mailing state: WI
Mailing zip: 53217-3985
Personnel: Mary Carson (Advisor)

CARTHAGE COLLEGE

Street address 1: 2001 Alford Park Dr
Street address city: Kenosha
Street address state: WI
Zip/Postal code: 53140-1929
Country: USA
Mailing address: 2001 Alford Park Dr
Mailing city: Kenosha
Mailing state: WI
Mailing zip: 53140-1994
General Phone: (262) 551-5800
Personnel: Meg Durbin (Ed. in Chief); Carmelo Chimera (Mng. Ed.); Lauren Hansen (Bus. Mng.)

CONCORDIA UNIV. OF WISCONSIN

Street address 1: 12800 N Lake Shore Dr
Street address city: Mequon
Street address state: WI
Zip/Postal code: 53097-2418
Country: USA
Mailing address: 12800 N Lake Shore Dr
Mailing city: Mequon
Mailing state: WI
Mailing zip: 53097-2402
Personnel: Sarah Holtan (Faculty Advisor); Alax Tomter (Exec. Ed.)

LAKELAND COLLEGE

Street address 1: PO Box 359
Street address city: Sheboygan
Street address state: WI
Zip/Postal code: 53082-0359
Country: USA
Mailing address: PO Box 359
Mailing city: Sheboygan
Mailing state: WI
Mailing zip: 53082-0359
General Phone: (920) 565-1316
General Fax: (920) 565-1344
General/National Adv. E-mail: mirror@lakeland.edu
Personnel: Becky Meyer (Author); Ashley Paulson (Adv. Mgr.)

LAWRENCE UNIVERSITY

Street address 1: 711 E Boldt Way
Street address 2: Spc 51
Street address city: Appleton
Street address state: WI
Zip/Postal code: 54911-5699
Country: USA
Mailing address: 711 E Boldt Way Spc 51
Mailing city: Appleton
Mailing state: WI
Mailing zip: 54911-5699
General Phone: (920) 832-6768
General Fax: (920) 832-7031
General/National Adv. E-mail: lawrentian@lawrence.edu
Primary Website: www.lawrentian.com
Year Established: 1884
Published: Fri
Avg Free Circ: 1000
Personnel: Emily Zawacki (Editor-in-Chief); Nathan Lawrence (Copy Chief)

MADISON AREA TECHNICAL COLLEGE

Street address 1: 3550 Anderson St
Street address city: Madison
Street address state: WI
Zip/Postal code: 53704-2520
Country: USA
Mailing address: 1701 Wright St
Mailing city: Madison
Mailing state: WI
Mailing zip: 53704-2599
General Phone: (608) 243-4809
General Fax: (608) 246-6488
General/National Adv. E-mail: clarioned@matcmadison.edu
Personnel: Doug Kirchberg (Advisor); Vishmaa Ramsaroop Briggs (Ed.)

MARIAN UNIVERSITY

Street address 1: 45 S National Ave
Street address city: Fond Du Lac
Street address state: WI
Zip/Postal code: 54935-4621
Country: USA
Mailing address: 45 S National Ave
Mailing city: Fond Du Lac
Mailing state: WI
Mailing zip: 54935-4621
General Phone: (920) 923-8776
Personnel: Vicky Hildebrandt (Advisor); Katie Leist (Ed.)

MARQUETTE UNIV.

Street address 1: 1131 W Wisconsin Ave
Street address city: Milwaukee
Street address state: WI
Zip/Postal code: 53233-2313
Country: USA
Mailing address: 1131 W Wisconsin Ave
Mailing city: Milwaukee
Mailing state: WI
Mailing zip: 53233-2313
General Phone: (414) 288-1739
General Fax: (414) 288-5896
General/National Adv. E-mail: student.media@mu.edu; viewpoints@marquettetribune.org
Personnel: Kim Zawada (Advisor); Lauren Frey (Adv. Dir.); Jim McLaughlin (Ed. in Chief)

MILWAUKEE AREA TECH. COLLEGE

Street address 1: 700 W State St
Street address 2: Rm S220
Street address city: Milwaukee
Street address state: WI
Zip/Postal code: 53233-1419
Country: USA
Mailing address: 700 W State St Rm S220
Mailing city: Milwaukee
Mailing state: WI
Mailing zip: 53233-1419
General Phone: (414) 297-6250
General Fax: (414) 297-7925
General/National Adv. E-mail: matctimes@gmail.com
Primary Website: www.matctimes.com
Year Established: 1959
Published Other: bi-weekly
Avg Free Circ: 2500
Personnel: Bob Hanson (Faculty Adviser)

MILWAUKEE SCHOOL OF ENGINEERING

Street address 1: 1025 N Milwaukee St
Street address city: Milwaukee
Street address state: WI
Zip/Postal code: 53202
Country: USA
Mailing address: 1025 N. Milwaukee St.
Mailing city: Milwaukee
Mailing state: WI
Mailing zip: 53202-3109
Personnel: Nicholas Petrovits (Ed.)

MOUNT MARY COLLEGE

Street address 1: 2900 N Menomonee River Pkwy
Street address city: Milwaukee
Street address state: WI
Zip/Postal code: 53222-4545
Country: USA
Mailing address: 2900 N Menomonee River Pkwy
Mailing city: Milwaukee
Mailing state: WI
Mailing zip: 53222-4597
General Phone: (414) 258-4810
Personnel: Heather Schroeder (Advisor); Laura Otto (Ed. in Chief); Elaina Meier (Ed.)

RIPON COLLEGE

Street address 1: 300 W Seward St
Street address city: Ripon
Street address state: WI
Zip/Postal code: 54971-1477
Country: USA
Mailing address: PO Box 248
Mailing city: Ripon
Mailing state: WI
Mailing zip: 54971-0248
General Phone: (920) 748-8126
Personnel: Jonathan Bailey (Ed. in Chief); John Bailey (Asst. Ed.)

SOUTHWEST WISCONSIN TECH. COLLEGE

Street address 1: 1800 Bronson Blvd
Street address city: Fennimore
Street address state: WI
Zip/Postal code: 53809-9778
Country: USA
Mailing address: 1800 Bronson Blvd
Mailing city: Fennimore
Mailing state: WI
Mailing zip: 53809-9778
General Phone: (608) 822-3262
General Fax: (608) 822-6019
General/National Adv. E-mail: jcullen@swtc.edu
Personnel: Jackie Cullen (Advisor)

ST. NORBERT COLLEGE

Street address 1: 100 Grant St
Street address 2: Ste 320
Street address city: De Pere
Street address state: WI
Zip/Postal code: 54115-2002
Country: USA
Mailing address: 100 Grant St Ste 320
Mailing city: De Pere
Mailing state: WI
Mailing zip: 54115-2002
General Phone: (920) 403-3268
Personnel: John Pennington (Advisor); Samantha Christian (Ed. in Chief)

THE NEW PERSPECTIVE

Street address 1: 100 N East Ave
Street address city: Waukesha
Street address state: WI
Zip/Postal code: 53186-3103
Country: USA
Mailing address: 1111 Sentry Dr
Mailing city: Waukesha
Mailing state: WI
Mailing zip: 53186-5965
General Phone: (262) 524-7351
General/National Adv. E-mail: perspect@carrollu.edu
Display Adv. E-mail: npadvertising@gmail.com
Editorial e-mail: persepct@carrollu.edu
Primary Website: www.thedigitalnp.com

UNIV. OF WISCONSIN CENTER

Street address 1: 705 Viebahn St
Street address city: Manitowoc
Street address state: WI
Zip/Postal code: 54220-6601
Country: USA
Mailing address: 705 Viebahn St
Mailing city: Manitowoc
Mailing state: WI

Mailing zip: 54220-6601
Personnel: Larry Desch (Advisor)

UNIV. OF WISCONSIN CENTER MARATHON

Street address 1: 518 S 7th Ave
Street address city: Wausau
Street address state: WI
Zip/Postal code: 54401-5362
Country: USA
Mailing address: 518 S 7th Ave
Mailing city: Wausau
Mailing state: WI
Mailing zip: 54401-5362
General Phone: (715) 261-6264
General Fax: (715) 261-6333
General/National Adv. E-mail: theforumuwmc@gmail.com
Personnel: Mark Parman (Advisor); Haley Zblewski (Ed. in Chief)

UNIV. OF WISCONSIN EAU CLAIRE

Street address 1: 105 Garfield Ave
Street address city: Eau Claire
Street address state: WI
Zip/Postal code: 54701-4811
Country: USA
Mailing address: 104B Hibbard Hall, 105 Garfield Ave
Mailing city: Eau Claire
Mailing state: WI
Mailing zip: 54701
General Phone: (715) 836-5618
General Fax: (715) 836-3829
Advertising Phone: (715) 836-4366
Editorial Phone: (715) 836-4416
General/National Adv. E-mail: spectator@uwec.edu
Personnel: John Cayer (Adv. Mgr.); Scott Hansen (Ed. in Cheif); Breann Schossow (Mng. Ed.); Frank Pellegrino (News Ed.)

UNIV. OF WISCONSIN GREEN BAY

Street address 1: 2420 Nicolet Dr
Street address city: Green Bay
Street address state: WI
Zip/Postal code: 54311-7003
Country: USA
Mailing address: 2420 Nicolet Dr
Mailing city: Green Bay
Mailing state: WI
Mailing zip: 54311-7003
General Phone: (920) 465-2719
General Fax: (920) 465-2895
Advertising Phone: (920) 465-2719
Advertising Fax: (920) 465-2895
Editorial Phone: (920) 465-2719
Editorial Fax: (920) 465-2895
General/National Adv. E-mail: 4e@uwgb.edu
Display Adv. E-mail: 4e@uwgb.edu
Editorial e-mail: 4e@uwgb.edu
Primary Website: www.fourthestatenewspaper.com
Published: Thur
Avg Free Circ: 6600
Personnel: Victoria Goff (Advisor); Nicole Angelucci (Adv. Mgr.); Maureen Malone (Ed. in chief)

UNIV. OF WISCONSIN LA CROSSE

Street address 1: 1725 State St
Street address city: La Crosse
Street address state: WI
Zip/Postal code: 54601-3742
Country: USA
Mailing address: 1725 State St
Mailing city: La Crosse
Mailing state: WI
Mailing zip: 54601-3788
General Phone: (608) 785-8378
General Fax: (608) 785-6575
General/National Adv. E-mail: racquet@uwlax.edu
Personnel: Chris Rochester (Ed in Chief); Mary Beth Valhalla (Advisor)

UNIV. OF WISCONSIN MARSHFIELD

Street address 1: 2000 W 5th St
Street address city: Marshfield
Street address state: WI
Zip/Postal code: 54449-3310
Country: USA
Mailing city: Marshfield
Mailing state: WI
Mailing zip: 54449
General Phone: (715) 389-6545
General Fax: (715) 389-6517
General/National Adv. E-mail: msfur@uwc.edu
Editorial e-mail: insight@uwc.edu
Personnel: Stacey Oelrich (Contact)

UNIV. OF WISCONSIN MILWAUKEE

Street address 1: 2200 E Kenwood Blvd
Street address 2: Ste EG80
Street address city: Milwaukee
Street address state: WI
Zip/Postal code: 53211-3361
Country: USA
Mailing address: PO Box 413
Mailing city: Milwaukee
Mailing state: WI
Mailing zip: 53201-0413
General Phone: (414) 229-4578
General Fax: (414) 229-4579
Advertising Phone: (414) 229-5969
General/National Adv. E-mail: post@uwm.edu; post@uwmpost.com
Personnel: Simon Bouwman (Bus. Mgr.); Kurt Raether (Adv. Mgr.); Kevin Lessmiller (Ed. in Chief)

UNIV. OF WISCONSIN OSHKOSH

Street address 1: 800 Algoma Blvd
Street address city: Oshkosh
Street address state: WI
Zip/Postal code: 54901-3551
Country: USA
Mailing address: 800 Algoma Blvd
Mailing city: Oshkosh
Mailing state: WI
Mailing zip: 54901-8651
General Phone: (920) 424-3048
Primary Website: www.advancetitan.com
Published: Thur
Personnel: Vince Filak (Advisor)

UNIV. OF WISCONSIN PARKSIDE

Street address 1: 900 Wood Rd
Street address city: Kenosha
Street address state: WI
Zip/Postal code: 53144-1133
Country: USA
Mailing address: PO Box 2000
Mailing city: Kenosha
Mailing state: WI
Mailing zip: 53141-2000
General Phone: (262) 595-2287
General Fax: (262) 595-2295
General/National Adv. E-mail: rangernews@uwp.edu
Display Adv. E-mail: advertising@therangernews.com
Personnel: Jo Kirst (Ed.)

UNIV. OF WISCONSIN PLATTEVILLE

Street address 1: 1 University Plz
Street address 2: 618 Pioneer Tower
Street address city: Platteville
Street address state: WI
Zip/Postal code: 53818-3001
Country: USA
Mailing address: 1 University Plz Stop 1
Mailing city: Platteville
Mailing state: WI
Mailing zip: 53818-3001
General Phone: (608) 342-1471
General Fax: (608) 342-1671
General/National Adv. E-mail: exponent@uwplatt.edu
Primary Website: www.uwpexponent.org
Year Established: 1889
Published: Thur
Avg Free Circ: 3600
Personnel: Becky Troy (Administrative assistant); Arthur Ranney (Advisor)

UNIV. OF WISCONSIN SHEBOYGAN

Street address 1: 1 University Dr
Street address city: Sheboygan
Street address state: WI
Zip/Postal code: 53081-4760
Country: USA
Mailing address: 1 University Dr
Mailing city: Sheboygan
Mailing state: WI
Mailing zip: 53081-4789
General Phone: (920) 459-6600
General Fax: (920) 459-6602
General/National Adv. E-mail: shbinfo@uwc.edu
Editorial e-mail: shbvoice@uwc.edu

UNIV. OF WISCONSIN STEVENS POINT

Street address 1: 1101 Reserve St
Street address 2: # 104
Street address city: Stevens Point
Street address state: WI
Zip/Postal code: 54481-3868
Country: USA
Mailing address: 1101 Reserve Street 104 CAC
Mailing city: Stevens Point
Mailing state: WI
Mailing zip: 54481-3897
General Phone: (715) 346-3707
General Fax: (715) 346-4712
General/National Adv. E-mail: pointer@uwsp.edu
Personnel: Liz Fakazis (Advisor); Steve Roeland (Ed. in Chief)

UNIV. OF WISCONSIN SUPERIOR

Street address 1: 1600 Catlin Ave
Street address city: Superior
Street address state: WI
Zip/Postal code: 54880-2953
Country: USA
Mailing address: 1600 Catlin Ave
Mailing city: Superior
Mailing state: WI
Mailing zip: 54880-2954
General Phone: (715) 394-8438
General Fax: (715) 394-8454
General/National Adv. E-mail: stinger@uwsuper.edu
Personnel: Joel Anderson (Advisor)

UNIV. OF WISCONSIN WHITEWATER

Street address 1: 800 W Main St
Street address 2: 66 University Ctr.
Street address city: Whitewater
Street address state: WI
Zip/Postal code: 53190-1705
Country: USA
Mailing address: 66 University Ctr.
Mailing city: Whitewater
Mailing state: WI
Mailing zip: 53190
General Phone: (262) 472-5100
General Fax: (262) 472-5101
Display Adv. E-mail: rpads@uww.edu
Editorial e-mail: rp@uww.edu
Primary Website: www.royalpurplenews.com
Year Established: 1901
Personnel: Sam Martino (Advisor); Kyle Geissler (Adviser)

UNIVERSITY OF WISCONSIN MADISON

Street address 1: 152 W Johnson St
Street address 2: Ste 202
Street address city: Madison
Street address state: WI
Zip/Postal code: 53703-2296
Country: USA
Mailing address: 152 West Johnson Street
Mailing city: Madison
Mailing state: WI
Mailing zip: 53703-2017
General Phone: (608) 257-4712
General Fax: (608) 258-3029
Advertising Phone: (608) 257-4712
Editorial Phone: (608) 257-4712
General/National Adv. E-mail: publisher@badgerherald.com
Display Adv. E-mail: addirector@badgerherald.com
Editorial e-mail: editor@badgerherald.com
Primary Website: www.badgerherald.com
Year Established: 1969
Published: Tues
Personnel: Alice Vagun (Editor-in-Chief)

UNIVERSITY OF WISCONSIN, FOX VALLEY

Street address 1: 1478 Midway Rd
Street address city: Menasha
Street address state: WI
Zip/Postal code: 54952-1224
Country: USA
Mailing address: 1478 Midway Rd
Mailing city: Menasha
Mailing state: WI
Mailing zip: 54952-1224
General Phone: (920) 832-2810
General Fax: (920) 832-2674
General/National Adv. E-mail: foxjournal@uwc.edu
Personnel: Paula Lovell (Advisor)

UNIVERSITY OF WISCONSIN-RIVER FALLS

Street address 1: 410 S 3rd St
Street address 2: 310 North Hall
Street address city: River Falls
Street address state: WI
Zip/Postal code: 54022-5010
County: Pierce
Country: USA
Mailing address: 410 S. Third St.
Mailing city: River Falls
Mailing state: WI
Mailing zip: 54022
General Phone: (715) 425-3169
General Fax: (715) 425-0658
General/National Adv. E-mail: journalism@uwrf.edu
Display Adv. E-mail: advertising@uwrfvoice.com
Editorial e-mail: editor@uwrfvoice.com
Primary Website: uwrfvoice.com
Year Established: 1916
Published: Fri
Avg Free Circ: 1000
Personnel: Andris Straumanis (Advisor); Sandra Ellis (Chair)

UNIVERSITY OF WISCONSIN-STOUT

Street address 1: 712 Broadway St S
Street address 2: Memorial Student Center
Street address city: Menomonie
Street address state: WI
Zip/Postal code: 54751-2458
Country: USA
Mailing address: 712 Broadway St S
Mailing city: Menomonie
Mailing state: WI
Mailing zip: 54751
General Phone: (715) 232-1141
General/National Adv. E-mail: stoutonia@uwstout.edu
Display Adv. E-mail: stoutoniaads@uwstout.edu
Editorial e-mail: stoutonia@uwstout.edu
Primary Website: www.stoutonia.com
Year Established: 1915
Published Other: Every two weeks (7 issues per semester). Not published during the summer.
Avg Free Circ: 2700
Personnel: Kate Edenborg (Advisor); Shaun Dudek

VITERBO COLLEGE

Street address 1: 900 Viterbo Dr
Street address city: La Crosse
Street address state: WI
Zip/Postal code: 54601-8804
Country: USA
Mailing address: 900 Viterbo Dr
Mailing city: La Crosse
Mailing state: WI
Mailing zip: 54601-8804
General Phone: (608) 796-3046
General Fax: (608) 796-3050
Advertising Phone: (608) 796-3041
General/National Adv. E-mail: communication@viterbo.edu
Personnel: Pat Kerrigan (Vice Pres., Commun.); Jessica Weber (Ed.)

WISCONSIN ENGINEER MAGAZINE

Street address 1: Room M1066, Engineering Centers Bldg
Street address city: Madison
Street address state: WI
Zip/Postal code: 53706
Country: USA
Mailing address: 1550 Engineering Dr.
Mailing city: Madison
Mailing state: WI
Mailing zip: 53706
General Phone: (608) 262-3494
General Fax: (608) 262-3494
General/National Adv. E-mail: wiscengr@cae.wisc.edu
Primary Website: www.wisconsinengineer.com
Year Established: 1912

Personnel: Steven Zwickel (Advisor)

WEST VIRGINIA

ALDERSON-BROADDUS COLLEGE

Street address 1: 101 College Hill Dr
Street address city: Philippi
Street address state: WV
Zip/Postal code: 26416-4600
Country: USA
Mailing address: 101 College Hill Dr
Mailing city: Philippi
Mailing state: WV
Mailing zip: 26416
General Phone: (304) 457-6357
Personnel: Jim Wilkie (Advisor); Melissa Riffle (Asst. Ed.)

BETHANY COLLEGE

Street address 1: 31 E Campus Dr
Street address city: Bethany
Street address state: WV
Zip/Postal code: 26032-3002
Country: USA
Mailing address: 31 E Campus Dr
Mailing city: Bethany
Mailing state: WV
Mailing zip: 26032-3002
General Phone: (304) 829-7951
General Fax: (304) 829-7950
General/National Adv. E-mail: tower@bethanywv.edu
Personnel: Mike King (Advisor)

CONCORD COLLEGE

Street address 1: PO Box 1000
Street address city: Athens
Street address state: WV
Zip/Postal code: 24712-1000
Country: USA
Mailing address: PO Box 1000
Mailing city: Athens
Mailing state: WV
Mailing zip: 24712-1000
General Phone: (304) 384-5364
General/National Adv. E-mail: concordian@concord.edu
Personnel: Lindsey Mullins (Advisor); Wendy Holdren (Ed. in Chief)

GLENVILLE STATE COLLEGE

Street address 1: 200 High St
Street address city: Glenville
Street address state: WV
Zip/Postal code: 26351-1200
Country: USA
General Phone: (304) 462-4133
General Fax: (304) 462-4407
General/National Adv. E-mail: news.paper@glenville.edu
Primary Website: www.glenville.edu/life/phoenix.php
Published: Thur
Published Other: Print edition twice a semester
Personnel: Marjorie Stewart (Assistant Professor of English)

MARSHALL UNIVERSITY

Street address 1: 109 Communications Bldg
Street address 2: 1 John Marshall Dr.
Street address city: Huntington
Street address state: WV
Zip/Postal code: 25755-0001
Country: USA
Mailing address: 109 Communications Building
Mailing city: Huntington
Mailing state: WV
Mailing zip: 25755-0001
General Phone: (304) 696-6696
General Fax: (304) 696-2732
Advertising Phone: (304) 526-2836
Editorial Phone: (304) 696-6696
Editorial Fax: (304) 696-2732
General/National Adv. E-mail: parthenon@marshall.edu
Display Adv. E-mail: parthenon@marshall.edu
Editorial e-mail: parthenon@marshall.edu
Primary Website: www.marshallparthenon.com
Year Established: 1898
Published: Tues`Fri
Published Other: Print Tuesday and Friday, online 24-7.
Avg Free Circ: 6000
Personnel: Sandy York (Adviser)

OHIO VALLEY UNIVERSITY

Street address 1: 1 Campus View Dr
Street address city: Vienna
Street address state: WV
Zip/Postal code: 26105-8000
Country: USA
Mailing address: 1 Campus View Dr
Mailing city: Vienna
Mailing state: WV
Mailing zip: 26105-8000
Personnel: Philip Sturm (Advisor)

SALEM INTERNATIONAL UNIV.

Street address 1: 223 W Main St
Street address city: Salem
Street address state: WV
Zip/Postal code: 26426-1227
Country: USA
Mailing address: 223 W Main St
Mailing city: Salem
Mailing state: WV
Mailing zip: 26426-1227
Personnel: Nicole Michaelas (Advisor)

SHEPHERD UNIVERSITY

Street address 1: PO Box 3210
Street address city: Shepherdstown
Street address state: WV
Zip/Postal code: 25443-3210
Country: USA
Mailing address: PO Box 3210
Mailing city: Shepherdstown
Mailing state: WV
Mailing zip: 25443-3210
General Phone: (304) 876-5100
General Fax: (304) 876-5100
Advertising Phone: (304) 876-5687
Editorial Phone: (304) 876-5377
General/National Adv. E-mail: pickweb@shepherd.edu
Personnel: Jim Lewin (Advisor); Jeb Inge (Ed. in Chief)

UNIV. OF CHARLESTON

Street address 1: 2300 Maccorkle Ave SE
Street address city: Charleston
Street address state: WV
Zip/Postal code: 25304-1045
Country: USA
Mailing address: 2300 Maccorkle Ave SE
Mailing city: Charleston
Mailing state: WV
Mailing zip: 25304-1099
Personnel: Andy Spradling (Advisor); Ginny Bennett Helmick (Ed.)

WEST LIBERTY UNIVERSITY

Street address 1: 208 Faculty Drive
Street address 2: Cub 153
Street address city: West Liberty
Street address state: WV
Zip/Postal code: 26074
Country: USA
Mailing address: 208 Faculty Drive
Mailing city: West Liberty
Mailing state: WV
Mailing zip: 26074
General Phone: (304) 336-8873
General Fax: (304) 336-8323
Editorial Phone: (304) 336-8213
General/National Adv. E-mail: wltrumpet@wlsc.edu
Primary Website: westlibertylive.com/thetrumpet
Year Established: 1922
Published: Wed
Avg Free Circ: 1500
Personnel: Tammie Beagle (Advisor)

WEST VIRGINIA STATE UNIV.

Street address 1: 214 Wilson Student Union
Street address city: Institute
Street address state: WV
Zip/Postal code: 25112
Country: USA
Mailing address: 214 Wilson Student Union
Mailing city: Institute
Mailing state: WV
Mailing zip: 25112-1000
General Phone: (304) 766-3212
Personnel: Robin Broughton (Advisor); Mary Casto (Ed. in Chief); Patrick Felton (Ed. in Chief)

WEST VIRGINIA UNIV.

Street address 1: 284 Prospect St
Street address city: Morgantown
Street address state: WV
Zip/Postal code: 26505-5021
Country: USA
Mailing address: PO Box 6427
Mailing city: Morgantown
Mailing state: WV
Mailing zip: 26506-6427
General Phone: (304) 293-2540
General Fax: (304) 293-6857
Editorial Phone: (304) 293-5092
General/National Adv. E-mail: da-mail@mail.wvu.edu
Personnel: Alan R. Waters (Advisor)

WEST VIRGINIA UNIV. INST. OF TECHNOLOGY

Street address 1: PO Box 1
Street address city: Montgomery
Street address state: WV
Zip/Postal code: 25136-0001
Country: USA
Mailing address: PO Box 1
Mailing city: Montgomery
Mailing state: WV
Mailing zip: 25136-0001
General Phone: (304) 442-3180
General Fax: (304) 442-3838
General/National Adv. E-mail: collegianwv@hotmail.com
Personnel: Jim Kerrigan (Advisor); Emily Wilkinson (Ed.)

WEST VIRGINIA UNIV. PARKERSBURG

Street address 1: 300 Campus Dr
Street address city: Parkersburg
Street address state: WV
Zip/Postal code: 26104-8647
Country: USA
Mailing address: 300 Campus Dr
Mailing city: Parkersburg
Mailing state: WV
Mailing zip: 26104-8647
General Phone: (304) 424-8247
General Fax: (304) 424-8315
Advertising Phone: (304) 424-8247
Editorial Phone: (304) 424-8247
General/National Adv. E-mail: chronicle@wvup.edu
Display Adv. E-mail: chronicle@wvup.edu
Editorial e-mail: chronicle@wvup.edu
Primary Website: http://issuu.com/wvuparkersburgchronicle
Year Established: 1969
Published: Thur
Avg Free Circ: 3500
Personnel: Torie Jackson (Advisor)

WHEELING JESUIT UNIV.

Street address 1: 316 Washington Ave
Street address city: Wheeling
Street address state: WV
Zip/Postal code: 26003-6243
Country: USA
Mailing address: 316 Washington Ave
Mailing city: Wheeling
Mailing state: WV
Mailing zip: 26003-6295
Editorial e-mail: news@wju.edu
Personnel: Becky Forney (Advisor)

WYOMING

CASPER COLLEGE

Street address 1: 125 College Dr
Street address 2: # CE-109
Street address city: Casper
Street address state: WY
Zip/Postal code: 82601-4612
Country: USA
Mailing address: 125 College Dr # CE-109
Mailing city: Casper
Mailing state: WY
Mailing zip: 82601-4699
Personnel: Pete Vanhouten (Advisor); Derek Schroder (Ed.)

LARAMIE COUNTY CMTY. COLLEGE

Street address 1: 1400 E College Dr
Street address city: Cheyenne
Street address state: WY
Zip/Postal code: 82007-3204
Country: USA
Mailing address: 1400 E. College Dr.
Mailing city: Cheyenne
Mailing state: WY
Mailing zip: 82007-3204
Year Established: 1976
Published: Mthly
Avg Free Circ: 1000
Personnel: J.L. O'Brien (Advisor); Jake Sherlock (Adviser)

NORTHERN WYOMING DAILY NEWS

Street address 1: 201 N 8th St
Street address city: Worland
Street address state: WY
Zip/Postal code: 82401-2614
County: Washakie
Country: USA
Mailing address: PO BOX 508
Mailing city: WORLAND
Mailing state: WY
Mailing zip: 82401-0508
General Phone: (307) 347-3241
General Fax: (307) 347-4267
Advertising Phone: (307) 347-3241
Advertising Fax: (307) 347-4267
Editorial Phone: (307)347-3241
Editorial Fax: (307)347-4267
General/National Adv. E-mail: editor@wyodaily.com
Display Adv. E-mail: adsales@wyodaily.com
Classified Adv. e-mail: classads@wyodaily.com
Editorial e-mail: editor@wyodaily.com
Primary Website: www.wyodaily.com
Year Established: 1905
Published: Thur`Fri
Personnel: Jane Elliott (Production manager); Dustin Fuller (Adv. Mgr.); Mindy Shaw (Circulation Manager/ Bookkeeper); Lee Lockhart (Pub.); Alex Kuhn (Sports Editor); Karla Pomeroy (General Manager/Editor); Dennis Koch (Office Mgr./Circ. Mgr.); Christine Weber (People Page Ed.); Susan Lockhart (Special Projects Ed.); John Elliott (Prodn. Supt.)

NORTHWEST COLLEGE

Street address 1: 231 W 6th St
Street address city: Powell
Street address state: WY
Zip/Postal code: 82435-1898
Country: USA
Mailing address: 231 W 6th St Bldg 3
Mailing city: Powell
Mailing state: WY
Mailing zip: 82435-1898
General Phone: (307) 754-6438
Personnel: Rob Breeding (Advisor); Kayla Dumas (Ed.)

UNIV. OF WYOMING

Street address 1: 1000 E University Ave
Street address 2: Dept 3625
Street address city: Laramie
Street address state: WY
Zip/Postal code: 82071-2000
Country: USA
Mailing address: 1000 E University Ave Dept 3625
Mailing city: Laramie
Mailing state: WY
Mailing zip: 82071-2000
General Phone: (307) 766-6190
General Fax: (307) 766-4027
Advertising Phone: (307) 766-6336
General/National Adv. E-mail: bi@uwyo.edu
Editorial e-mail: letters@brandingirononline.info
Personnel: Carry Berry-Smith (Advisor); Sasha Fahrenkops (Ed. in Chief)

ETHNIC UNITED STATES NEWSPAPERS

ALABAMA

BATH

FRANCE TODAY

Street address 1: Cambridge House
Street address 2: 6 Gay Street
Street address city: Bath
State: AL
Zip/Postal code: BA1 2PH
County: Bath
Country: UK
Mailing address: IMS Mailing
Mailing city: Virginia Beach
Mailing state: VA
General Phone: 0044 1225 463 752
Advertising Phone: 0044 1225 463 752
Editorial Phone: 0044 1225 463 752
General/National Adv. E-mail: info@francetoday.com
Display Adv. E-mail: ben@francetoday.com
Primary Website: www.francetoday.com
Year Established: 1985
Published: Bi-Mthly
Avg Paid Circ: 50000
Avg Free Circ: 20000
Audit By: Sworn/Estimate/Non-Audited
Audit Date: 12.07.2019
Personnel: Ben Stephens (Pub.)
Parent company (for newspapers): France Media Group
State: Arizona

ARIZONA

CHANDLER

ASIAN AMERICAN TIMES

Street address 1: 3821 S vista Place
Street address city: Chandler
State: AZ
Zip/Postal code: 85248
County: AZ
Country: United States
Mailing address: 3821 S vista Place
Mailing city: Chandler
Mailing state: AZ
Mailing zip: 85248
General Phone: (602) 670-4588
Advertising Phone: (602) 670-4588
General/National Adv. E-mail: zhangfutao@hotmail.com
Display Adv. E-mail: zhangfutao@hotmail.com
Editorial e-mail: zhangfutao@hotmail.com
Primary Website: www.asianamericantimes.us
Year Established: 1990
Published: Thur
Avg Paid Circ: 2000
Audit By: Sworn/Estimate/Non-Audited
Audit Date: 12.07.2019
Personnel: Futao Zhang (Pub.); Leung Eng (Ed.)
Parent company (for newspapers): Z & H LLC

FLAGSTAFF

NAVAJO-HOPI OBSERVER

Street address 1: 2717 N 4th St
Street address 2: Ste 110
Street address city: Flagstaff
State: AZ
Zip/Postal code: 86004-1813
County: Coconino
Country: USA
General Phone: (928) 635-4426
General Fax: (928) 226-1115
Advertising Phone: (928) 226-9696
Advertising Fax: (928) 226-1115
Editorial Phone: (800) 408-4726
Editorial Fax: (928) 635-4887
General/National Adv. E-mail: rsmart@nhonews.com
Display Adv. E-mail: nhographics@nhonews.com
Editorial e-mail: nhoeditorial@nhonews.com
Primary Website: www.nhonews.com
Year Established: 1981
Published: Wed
Avg Paid Circ: 25
Avg Free Circ: 13757
Audit By: VAC
Audit Date: 30.06.2013
Personnel: Debbie White-Hoel (Pub.); Ryan Williams (Ed.); Robb Smart (Adv. Exec.); Mike Carroll (Prodn. Mgr.); Connie Freson
Parent company (for newspapers): Western News&Info, Inc.

WINDOW ROCK

NAVAJO TIMES PUBLISHING COMPANY, INC.

Street address 1: Jct of Hwy 264 & Navajo Rt 12
Street address city: Window Rock
State: AZ
Zip/Postal code: 86515
County: Apache
Country: USA
Mailing address: PO Box 310
Mailing city: Window Rock
Mailing state: AZ
Mailing zip: 86515-0310
General Phone: (928) 871-1130
General Fax: (928) 871-1159
Advertising Phone: (928) 871-1145
Advertising Fax: (928) 871-1159
Editorial Phone: (928) 871-1136
Editorial Fax: (928) 871-1159
General/National Adv. E-mail: obenally@ntpc.biz
Display Adv. E-mail: vernon@ntpc.biz
Classified Adv. e-mail: legals@ntpc.biz
Editorial e-mail: editor@ntpc.biz
Primary Website: www.navajotimes.com
Year Established: 1960
Published: Thur
Avg Paid Circ: 11500
Audit By: USPS
Audit Date: 30.09.2017
Personnel: Vernon Yazzie (Display Adv Mgr); Rhonda Joe (Circulation Mgr); Olivia Benally (Controller); Olivia Benally (CEO/ Publisher); Bobby Martin (Production Mgr); Josephine Carl (Class/Legals Mgr); Duane Beyal (Editor)
State: California

CALIFORNIA

BURBANK

IL CORRIERE DI LOS ANGELES

Street address 1: 360 W Alameda
Street address 2: Ste B
Street address city: Burbank
State: CA
Zip/Postal code: 91506
County: Los Angeles
Country: USA
Mailing address: 360 W Alameda Ste B
Mailing city: Burbank
Mailing state: CA
Mailing zip: 91506
General Phone: (818) 260-9318
Year Established: 1997
Published: Bi-Mthly
Avg Paid Circ: 0
Avg Free Circ: 1900
Audit By: CVC
Audit Date: 30.12.2018
Personnel: Franco Brescia

BURLINGAME

PHILIPPINE NEWS

Street address 1: 1818 Gilbreth Rd
Street address 2: Ste 240
Street address city: Burlingame
State: CA
Zip/Postal code: 94010-1217
County: San Mateo
Country: USA
Mailing address: 1415 Rollins Rd Ste 202
Mailing city: Burlingame
Mailing state: CA
Mailing zip: 94010-2300
General Phone: (650) 552-9775
General Fax: (650) 552-9778
General/National Adv. E-mail: info@philippinenews.com
Primary Website: www.philippinenews.com
Published: Fri
Avg Paid Circ: 47000
Avg Free Circ: 2000
Audit By: Sworn/Estimate/Non-Audited
Audit Date: 12.07.2019
Personnel: John B. Espiritu (Chrmn.); Danilo Gozo (Pub.); Margarita Argente (Exec. Vice Pres., Sales/ Mktg.); Christina Pastor (Ed.)

GLENDALE

ASIAN JOURNAL

Street address 1: 1210 S Brand Blvd
Street address city: Glendale
State: CA
Zip/Postal code: 91204-2615
County: Los Angeles
Country: USA
Mailing address: 1210 S Brand Blvd
Mailing city: Glendale
Mailing state: CA
Mailing zip: 91204-2615
General Phone: (213) 250-9797
General Fax: (213) 481-0854
General/National Adv. E-mail: info@asianjournalinc.com
Primary Website: asianjournal.com
Published: Wed`Sat
Avg Free Circ: 31159
Audit By: VAC
Audit Date: 30.06.2017
Personnel: Stephen Padilla (Ed.)

CALIFORNIA COURIER

Street address 1: PO Box 5390
Street address city: Glendale
State: CA
Zip/Postal code: 91221-5390
County: Los Angeles
Country: USA
Mailing address: PO Box 5390
Mailing city: Glendale
Mailing state: CA
Mailing zip: 91207
General Phone: (818) 424-9049
General/National Adv. E-mail: sassoun@pacbell.net
Year Established: 1958
Published: Thur
Avg Paid Circ: 1000
Avg Free Circ: 200
Audit By: Sworn/Estimate/Non-Audited
Audit Date: 12.07.2019
Personnel: Harut Sassounian (Pub.)

WEEKEND BALITA/MIDWEEK BALITA

Street address 1: 520 E Wilson Ave
Street address 2: Ste 210
Street address city: Glendale
State: CA
Zip/Postal code: 91206-4374
County: Los Angeles
Country: USA
Mailing address: 520 E Wilson Ave Ste 210
Mailing city: Glendale
Mailing state: CA
Mailing zip: 91206-4374
General Phone: (818) 552-4503
General Fax: (818) 550-7635
General/National Adv. E-mail: communitynews@balita.com
Editorial e-mail: editor@balita.com
Primary Website: www.balita.com
Published: Wed`Sat
Avg Free Circ: 40000
Audit By: Sworn/Estimate/Non-Audited
Audit Date: 12.07.2019
Personnel: Luchie Mendoza Allen (Pub.); Lyn Mendoza (Office Mgr.); Gary Escarilla (Sales Mgr.); Carmen Vergara (Adv. Coord.); Rhony Laigo (Ed. in Chief); Jojo Margen (Prodn. Mgr.)

HAWTHORNE

THE AFRICAN TIMES/USA

Street address 1: 5155 W Rosecrans Ave
Street address 2: Ste 213
Street address city: Hawthorne
State: CA
Zip/Postal code: 90250-6652
County: Los Angeles
Country: USA
Mailing address: 5155 W Rosecrans Ave Ste 213
Mailing city: Hawthorne
Mailing state: CA
Mailing zip: 90250-6652
General Phone: (213) 924-8166
General Fax: (310) 644-5507
Advertising Phone: (213) 924-8166
Advertising Fax: (310) 644-5507
Editorial Phone: (213) 924-8166
Editorial Fax: (310) 644-5507
General/National Adv. E-mail: editor@theafricantimes.com
Display Adv. E-mail: africantimes-usa@mindspring.com
Editorial e-mail: editor@theafricantimes.com
Primary Website: www.theafricantimes.com
Year Established: 1989
Published: Bi-Mthly
Avg Paid Circ: 12000
Avg Free Circ: 48000
Audit By: Sworn/Estimate/Non-Audited
Audit Date: 12.07.2019
Personnel: Ronald Mracky (Mktg. Dir.); Charles Anyiam (Ed.)

LA MESA

UNION JACK

Street address 1: 8080 La Mesa Blvd
Street address 2: Ste 203
Street address city: La Mesa
State: CA
Zip/Postal code: 91942-0362
County: San Diego
Country: USA
Mailing address: PO Box 1823
Mailing city: La Mesa
Mailing state: CA
Mailing zip: 91944-1823

General Phone: (619) 466-3129
General Fax: (619) 337-1103
General/National Adv. E-mail: ujnews@ujnews.com
Primary Website: www.ujnews.com
Year Established: 1982
Published: Mthly
Avg Paid Circ: 10000
Avg Free Circ: 100000
Audit By: Sworn/Estimate/Non-Audited
Audit Date: 12.07.2019
Personnel: Jeff & Ron Choularton (Owners-Publishers); Ronald Choularton (Ed.)

LOS ANGELES

ASBAREZ DAILY

Street address 1: 1203 N Vermont Ave
Street address city: Los Angeles
State: CA
Zip/Postal code: 90029-1703
County: Los Angeles
Country: USA
Mailing address: 1203 N. Vermont Ave
Mailing city: Little Armenia
Mailing state: CA
Mailing zip: 90029
General Phone: (323) 284-0088
General Fax: (323) 284-0080
Advertising Phone: (818) 500-9555
Editorial Phone: (818) 500-0609
Editorial Fax: (818) 956-1106
General/National Adv. E-mail: editor@asbarez.com
Primary Website: www.asbarez.com
Published Other: Daily
Avg Paid Circ: 12000
Avg Free Circ: 500
Audit By: Sworn/Estimate/Non-Audited
Audit Date: 12.07.2019
Personnel: Armik Daghlian (Adv. Mgr.); Sossi Atamian (Circ. Mgr.); Ara Khachatourian (Ed.)

CALIFORNIA-STAATS ZEITUNG

Street address 1: 5750 Wilshire Blvd
Street address 2: Ste 100
Street address city: Los Angeles
State: CA
Zip/Postal code: 90036-3642
County: Los Angeles
Country: USA
Mailing address: P.O. Box 18508
Mailing city: Sarasota
Mailing state: FL
Mailing zip: 34276
General Phone: (213) 413-5500
General Fax: (213) 413-5469
General/National Adv. E-mail: CaliforniaGermans@gmail.com
Primary Website: http://californiagermans.com/
Published: Thur
Personnel: Stephanie Teichmann (Pub.); Erika Bartschat (Adv. Mgr.); Hans Reisch (Prodn. Mgr.)

JAPANESE AMERICAN CITIZENS LEAGUE

Street address 1: 250 E 1st St
Street address 2: Ste 301
Street address city: Los Angeles
State: CA
Zip/Postal code: 90012-3819
County: Los Angeles
Country: USA
Mailing address: 250 E 1st St Ste 301
Mailing city: Los Angeles
Mailing state: CA
Mailing zip: 90012-3819
General Phone: (213) 620-1767
General Fax: (213) 620-1768
General/National Adv. E-mail: pc@pacificcitizen.org; marketing @ pacificcitizen.org
Display Adv. E-mail: busmgr@pacificcitizen.org
Editorial e-mail: circulation @ pacificcitizen.org
Primary Website: www.pacificcitizen.org
Year Established: 1929
Published Other: Every other Fri
Avg Paid Circ: 23946
Avg Free Circ: 287
Audit By: Sworn/Estimate/Non-Audited
Audit Date: 12.07.2019
Personnel: Eva Ting (Circ. Dept.); Caroline Aoyagi Stom (Ed.); Lynda Lin (Asst. Ed.); Nalea Ko (Reporter); Staci Hisayasu (Business Manager)

KOREA TIMES

Street address 1: 4525 Wilshire Blvd
Street address city: Los Angeles
State: CA
Zip/Postal code: 90010-3837
County: Los Angeles
Country: USA
Mailing address: 4525 Wilshire Blvd
Mailing city: Los Angeles
Mailing state: CA
Mailing zip: 90010-3837
General Phone: (323) 692-2000
General Fax: (323) 692-2020
General/National Adv. E-mail: info@koreatimes.com; opinion@koreatimes.com
Primary Website: www.koreatimes.com
Published Other: Daily
Avg Paid Circ: 75000
Avg Free Circ: 250
Audit By: Sworn/Estimate/Non-Audited
Audit Date: 12.07.2019
Personnel: Jae Min Chang (Pub.); Grant Chang (Gen. Mgr.); Michael Hon (Adv. Mgr); Brian Jan (Cir. Mgr.); Ki Kwon (Ed.); Brian Jon (Pdn. Mgr.)
Parent company (for newspapers): Admarket International (Div. of Marcom International, Inc.)

TAIWAN JOURNAL

Street address 1: 6300 Wilshire Blvd
Street address 2: Ste 1510A
Street address city: Los Angeles
State: CA
Zip/Postal code: 90048-5217
County: Los Angeles
Country: USA
Mailing address: 6300 Wilshire Blvd Ste 1510A
Mailing city: Los Angeles
Mailing state: CA
Mailing zip: 90048-5217
General Phone: (323) 782-8770
General Fax: (323) 782-8761
General/National Adv. E-mail: tj@mail.gio.gov.tw
Primary Website: www.taiwanjournal.nat.gov.tw
Published: Fri
Personnel: Pasuya Wen-Chih Yao (Pub.); Steven Lai (Ed.)

THE RAFU SHIMPO

Street address 1: 701 E 3rd St
Street address 2: Ste 130
Street address city: Los Angeles
State: CA
Zip/Postal code: 90013-1789
County: Los Angeles
Country: USA
Mailing address: 701 E 3rd St Ste 130
Mailing city: Los Angeles
Mailing state: CA
Mailing zip: 90013-1789
General Phone: (213) 629-2231
General Fax: (213) 687-0737
Advertising Phone: (213) 453-9396
Editorial Phone: (213) 453-9396
General/National Adv. E-mail: info@rafu.com
Display Adv. E-mail: ads4rafu@earthlink.net
Primary Website: www.rafu.com
Year Established: 1903
Published: Mon`Tues`Wed`Thur`Fri`Sat
Published Other: Daily
Avg Paid Circ: 9500
Audit By: Sworn/Estimate/Non-Audited
Audit Date: 12.07.2019
Personnel: Gail Miyasaki (Circ. Mgr.; advertising); Gwen Muranaka (Ed., English); Michael Komai (Publisher)

MONROVIA

LÂ€™ITALO AMERICANO

Street address 1: 610 W Foothill Blvd
Street address 2: Unit D
Street address city: Monrovia
State: CA
Zip/Postal code: 91016
Country: USA
Mailing address: 610 W Foothill Blvd Unit D
Mailing city: Monrovia
Mailing state: CA
Mailing zip: 91016
General Phone: (626) 359-7715
Editorial e-mail: robert.barbera@italoamericano.org
Primary Website: italoamericano.org
Year Established: 1908
Published: Thur`Other
Avg Paid Circ: 980
Avg Free Circ: 7207
Audit By: CVC
Audit Date: 30.12.2018
Personnel: Patrick Abbate (Acct.); Robert Barbera (Pub.)

PASADENA

BEIRUT TIMES

Street address 1: PO Box 40277
Street address city: Pasadena
State: CA
Zip/Postal code: 91114-7277
County: Los Angeles
Country: USA
Mailing address: PO Box 40277
Mailing city: Pasadena
Mailing state: CA
Mailing zip: 91114-7277
General Phone: (626) 844-7777
General Fax: (626) 795-2222
General/National Adv. E-mail: 4beirut@gmail.com
Display Adv. E-mail: beiruttimes@yahoo.com
Editorial e-mail: beiruttimes@yahoo.com
Primary Website: www.beiruttimes.com
Year Established: 1985
Published: Thur
Published Other: Weekly
Avg Free Circ: 28000
Audit By: Sworn/Estimate/Non-Audited
Audit Date: 12.07.2019
Personnel: George Badir (Adv. Mgr.); Michel Abssi (Ed.)

ROSEMEAD

PACIFIC TIMES

Street address 1: 3001 Walnut Grove Ave
Street address 2: Ste 8
Street address city: Rosemead
State: CA
Zip/Postal code: 91770-2785
County: Los Angeles
Country: USA
Mailing address: 3001 Walnut Grove Ave Ste 8
Mailing city: Rosemead
Mailing state: CA
Mailing zip: 91770-2785
General Phone: (626) 573-4831
General Fax: (626) 573-4897
General/National Adv. E-mail: pacific@ix.netcom.com
Primary Website: www.pacific-times.com
Published: Wed
Avg Paid Circ: 15000
Avg Free Circ: 20000
Audit By: Sworn/Estimate/Non-Audited
Audit Date: 12.07.2019
Personnel: Wencheng Lin (Pres.)

SAN DIEGO

SAN DIEGO YU YU

Street address 1: 4655 Ruffner St
Street address 2: Ste 290
Street address city: San Diego
State: CA
Zip/Postal code: 92111-2270
County: San Diego
Country: USA
Mailing address: 4655 Ruffner St.
Mailing city: San Diego
Mailing state: CA
Mailing zip: 92111
General Phone: (858) 576-9016
General Fax: (858) 576-7294
Advertising Phone: (858) 576-9016 x110
Advertising Fax: (858) 576-7294
Editorial Phone: (858) 576-9016 x116
Editorial Fax: (858) 576-7294
General/National Adv. E-mail: info@sandiegoyuyu.com
Display Adv. E-mail: info@sandiegoyuyu.com
Editorial e-mail: news@sandiegoyuyu.com
Primary Website: www.sandiegoyuyu.com
Year Established: 1987
Published: Bi-Mthly
Avg Free Circ: 7000
Audit By: CVC
Audit Date: 12.12.2017
Personnel: Noriko Sato (Pres.)

SAN FRANCISCO

JOURNAL FRANCAIS

Street address 1: 944 Market St
Street address 2: Ste 210
Street address city: San Francisco
State: CA
Zip/Postal code: 94102-4025
County: San Francisco
Country: USA
Mailing address: 944 Market St Ste 210
Mailing city: San Francisco
Mailing state: CA
Mailing zip: 94102-4025
General Phone: (415) 981-9088
General Fax: (415) 981-9177
General/National Adv. E-mail: info@francetoday.com
Primary Website: www.journalfrancais.com
Published: Mthly
Personnel: Louis Kyle (Pub.); Rovi Nett (Office Mgr.); Vanessa Lotoux (Adv. Mgr.); Ame Senten (Ed.); Linda Conner (Prodn. Mgr.)

RUSSIAN LIFE

Street address 1: 2460 Sutter St
Street address city: San Francisco
State: CA
Zip/Postal code: 94115-3016
County: San Francisco
Country: USA
Mailing address: 2460 Sutter St
Mailing city: San Francisco
Mailing state: CA
Mailing zip: 94115-3016
General Phone: (415) 921-5380
General Fax: (415) 921-8726
General/National Adv. E-mail: russlife_news@yahoo.com
Published: Sat
Avg Paid Circ: 600
Audit By: Sworn/Estimate/Non-Audited
Audit Date: 13.03.2019
Personnel: Anatol Shmelev (President)

SAN JOSE

NIKKEIWEST

Street address 1: 2050 Gateway Pl.
Street address 2: Ste 100-241
Street address city: San Jose
State: CA
Zip/Postal code: 95110
County: Santa Clara
Country: USA
General Phone: (408) 998-0920
Editorial Phone: (916) 837-4178
General/National Adv. E-mail: questions@nikkeiwest.com
Display Adv. E-mail: adsales@nikkeiwest.com
Editorial e-mail: editor@nikkeiwest.com
Primary Website: www.nikkeiwest.com
Year Established: 1992
Published Other: Bi-Wkly
Avg Paid Circ: 3800
Avg Free Circ: 4200
Audit By: Sworn/Estimate/Non-Audited
Audit Date: 12.07.2019
Personnel: Ron Sakai (Adv. Mgr.); Jeffrey Kimoto (Ed.); John Sammon (Reporter)
Parent company (for newspapers): OtomikMedia Corp.

VIET MERCURY

Street address 1: 750 Ridder Park Dr

Street address city: San Jose
State: CA
Zip/Postal code: 95131-2432
County: Santa Clara
Country: USA
Mailing address: 750 Ridder Park Dr
Mailing city: San Jose
Mailing state: CA
Mailing zip: 95190-0001
General Phone: (408) 920-5000
General Fax: (408) 920-2748
General/National Adv. E-mail: letters@mercurynews.com
Primary Website: www.mercurynews.com/mld/vietmerc
Published: Fri
Personnel: Ham Xuan Nguyen (Adv. Mgr.); Terry Thompson (Circ. Mgr.); De Tren (Ed.); Hoan Nguyen (Mng. Ed.)

SAN LEANDRO

INDIA-WEST

Street address 1: 933 MacArthur Blvd
Street address city: San Leandro
State: CA
Zip/Postal code: 94577-3062
County: Alameda
Country: USA
Mailing address: 933 MacArthur Blvd
Mailing city: San Leandro
Mailing state: CA
Mailing zip: 94577-3062
General Phone: (510) 383-1140
General Fax: (510) 383-1154
Advertising Phone: (510) 383-1147
Advertising Fax: (510) 383-1154
Editorial Phone: (510) 383-1140
Editorial Fax: (510) 383-1154
General/National Adv. E-mail: editor@indiawest.com
Display Adv. E-mail: dyana@indiawest.com
Editorial e-mail: editor@indiawest.com
Primary Website: www.indiawest.com
Year Established: 1975
Published: Fri
Avg Paid Circ: 24000
Avg Free Circ: 2000
Audit By: Sworn/Estimate/Non-Audited
Audit Date: 12.07.2019
Personnel: Ramesh P. Murarka (Pub.); Rashmi Gupte (Circ. Mgr); Bina A. Murarka (Ed.); Dyana Bhandari

WESTMINSTER

NGUOI VIET NEWS

Street address 1: 14771 Moran St
Street address city: Westminster
State: CA
Zip/Postal code: 92683-5553
County: Orange
Country: USA
Mailing address: 14771 Moran St
Mailing city: Westminster
Mailing state: CA
Mailing zip: 92683-5553
General Phone: (714) 892-9414
General Fax: (714) 894-1381
General/National Adv. E-mail: news@nguoi-viet.com
Primary Website: www.nguoi-viet.com
Year Established: 1978
Published: Mon`Tues`Wed`Thur`Fri`Sat`Sun
Avg Paid Circ: 9762
Avg Free Circ: 0
Audit By: VAC
Audit Date: 30.06.2017
Personnel: Do Baohanah (Pub.); Pham Phu Thien Giao; Ngo Nhan Dung (Ed. in Chief)
State: Colorado

COLORADO

DENVER

COLORADO CHINESE NEWS

Street address 1: 1548 W Alameda Ave
Street address 2: Ste A
Street address city: Denver
State: CO
Zip/Postal code: 80223-1973
County: Denver
Country: USA
Mailing address: 1548 W Alameda Ave Ste A
Mailing city: Denver
Mailing state: CO
Mailing zip: 80223-1973
General Phone: (303) 722-8268
General Fax: (303) 722-7861
General/National Adv. E-mail: editor@cocnews.com
Primary Website: www.cocnews.com
Year Established: 1994
Published: Fri
Avg Paid Circ: 913
Avg Free Circ: 6500
Audit By: Sworn/Estimate/Non-Audited
Audit Date: 12.07.2019
Personnel: Wendy Y. Chao (Mng. Ed.)
State: Florida

FLORIDA

HOLLYWOOD

THE SEMINOLE TRIBUNE

Street address 1: 3560 N State Road 7
Street address city: Hollywood
State: FL
Zip/Postal code: 33021-2105
County: Broward
Country: USA
Mailing address: 3560 N. State Road 7
Mailing city: Hollywood
Mailing state: FL
Mailing zip: 33024-2198
General Phone: (954) 966-6300
General Fax: (954) 965-2937
General/National Adv. E-mail: tribune@semtribe.com
Display Adv. E-mail: tribune@semtribe.com
Editorial e-mail: tribune@semtribe.com
Primary Website: www.seminoletribune.org
Published: Mthly
Avg Paid Circ: 4000
Avg Free Circ: 2000
Audit By: Sworn/Estimate/Non-Audited
Audit Date: 12.07.2019
Personnel: Kevin Johnson (Senior Ed)
Parent company (for newspapers): The Seminole Tribe of Florida

JACKSONVILLE

THE SYRIAN-LEBANESE STAR

Street address 1: 4251 University Blvd S
Street address 2: Ste 201
Street address city: Jacksonville
State: FL
Zip/Postal code: 32216-4981
County: Duval
Country: USA
Mailing address: 4251 University Blvd S Ste 201
Mailing city: Jacksonville
Mailing state: FL
Mailing zip: 32216-4981
General Phone: (904) 737-6996
General Fax: (904) 636-0150
Primary Website: www.syrianlebanesestar.com
Published: Mthly
Avg Paid Circ: 22000
Avg Free Circ: 7000
Audit By: Sworn/Estimate/Non-Audited
Audit Date: 12.07.2019
Personnel: Alvin M. Coplan (Prodn. Mgr.)

MIAMI

FLORIDA REVIEW

Street address 1: 905 Brickell Bay Dr
Street address 2: Ste 2CL23
Street address city: Miami
State: FL
Zip/Postal code: 33131-2935
County: Miami-Dade
Country: USA
Mailing address: 800 Brickell Ave Ste 701
Mailing city: Miami
Mailing state: FL
Mailing zip: 33131-2967
General Phone: (305) 400-2168
General Fax: (305) 358-9456
General/National Adv. E-mail: editor@floridareview.com
Display Adv. E-mail: marketing@floridareview.com
Editorial e-mail: editor@floridareview.com
Primary Website: floridareview.com
Year Established: 1985
Published: Mon`Tues`Wed`Thur`Fri`Sat`Sun
Avg Free Circ: 32000
Audit By: Sworn/Estimate/Non-Audited
Audit Date: 12.07.2019
Personnel: Marcos Ommati (Ed. in Chief); Iaido Belo (Publisher); Marco A. Laureti (Mng. Ed.)

MINNEOLA

NORDSTJERNAN

Street address 1: 131 W Washington St
Street address 2: Suite 680
Street address city: Minneola
State: FL
Zip/Postal code: 34755
County: Lake
Country: USA
Mailing address: PO Box 680
Mailing city: Minneola
Mailing state: FL
Mailing zip: 34755
General Phone: (203) 299-0380
Advertising Phone: (800) 827-9333
General/National Adv. E-mail: info@nordstjernan.com
Primary Website: www.nordstjernan.com
Year Established: 1872
Published Other: 2 x Mthly
Avg Paid Circ: 27000
Avg Free Circ: 300
Audit By: Sworn/Estimate/Non-Audited
Audit Date: 12.07.2021
Personnel: Mette Barslund (Circ. Mgr.); Ulf E. Barslund Martensson (Ed.); Amanda Olson Robison (Copy proof)
State: Hawaii

HAWAII

HONOLULU

THE HAWAII HOCHI

Street address 1: 917 Kokea St
Street address city: Honolulu
State: HI
Zip/Postal code: 96817-4528
County: Honolulu
Country: USA
Mailing address: PO Box 17430
Mailing city: Honolulu
Mailing state: HI
Mailing zip: 96817-0430
General Phone: (808) 845-2255
General Fax: (808) 847-7215
Editorial e-mail: kanaizumi@thehawaiihochi.com
Primary Website: www.thehawaiihochi.com
Year Established: 1912
Published: Mon`Tues`Wed`Thur`Fri
Published Other: Daily
Avg Paid Circ: 2000
Audit By: Sworn/Estimate/Non-Audited
Audit Date: 12.07.2019
Personnel: Noriyoshi Kanaizumi (Editor, Hawaii Hochi); Milton Yamamoto (Production Manager, Vice President); Keiichi Tagata (President and Publisher)
Parent company (for newspapers): The Shizuoka Shimbun (Japan)
State: Idaho

IDAHO

FORT HALL

SHO-BAN NEWS

Street address 1: PO Box 900
Street address 2: Hrdc, Pima Drive
Street address city: Fort Hall
State: ID
Zip/Postal code: 83203-0900
County: Bingham
Country: USA
Mailing address: PO Box 900
Mailing city: Fort Hall
Mailing state: ID
Mailing zip: 83203-0900
General Phone: (208) 478-3701
General Fax: (208) 478-3702
Advertising Phone: (208) 478-3810
Advertising Fax: (208) 478-3702
Editorial Phone: (208) 478-3701
Editorial Fax: (208) 478-3702
General/National Adv. E-mail: shobnews@ida.net
Display Adv. E-mail: brappenay@sbtribes.com
Primary Website: www.shobannews.com
Year Established: 1970
Published: Thur
Avg Paid Circ: 1750
Avg Free Circ: 50
Audit By: Sworn/Estimate/Non-Audited
Audit Date: 12.07.2019
Personnel: Lori Edmo-Suppah (Ed.)
State: Illinois

ILLINOIS

CHICAGO

CHICAGO SHIMPO

Street address 1: 4670 N Manor Ave
Street address city: Chicago
State: IL
Zip/Postal code: 60625-3718
County: Cook
Country: USA
Mailing address: 4670 N Manor Ave
Mailing city: Chicago
Mailing state: IL
Mailing zip: 60625-3791
General Phone: (773) 478-6170
General Fax: (773) 478-9360
General/National Adv. E-mail: emailishimpo@mc.net
Year Established: 1945
Published: Fri
Avg Paid Circ: 5000
Audit By: Sworn/Estimate/Non-Audited
Audit Date: 12.07.2019
Personnel: Yoshiko Urayama (Pub.)

DRAUGAS

Street address 1: 4545 W 63rd St
Street address city: Chicago
State: IL
Zip/Postal code: 60629-5532
County: Cook
Country: USA
Mailing address: 4545 W 63rd St Ste 2

Mailing city: Chicago
Mailing state: IL
Mailing zip: 60629-5589
General Phone: (773) 585-9500
General Fax: (773) 585-8284
General/National Adv. E-mail: administrator@draugas.org
Primary Website: www.draugas.org
Published Other: Daily
Avg Paid Circ: 4800
Avg Free Circ: 100
Audit By: Sworn/Estimate/Non-Audited
Audit Date: 12.07.2019
Personnel: Danga MacKericiene (Adv. Mgr.); Dalia Cidzikaite (Ed. in Chief)

DZIENNIK ZWAIZKOWY

Street address 1: 5711 N Milwaukee Ave
Street address city: Chicago
State: IL
Zip/Postal code: 60646-6215
County: Cook
Country: USA
Mailing address: 5711 N Milwaukee Ave
Mailing city: Chicago
Mailing state: IL
Mailing zip: 60646-6215
General Phone: (773) 763-3343
General Fax: (773) 763-3825
General/National Adv. E-mail: polish@popmailinsnet.com
Published: Mon`Tues`Wed`Thur`Fri
Avg Paid Circ: 33000
Avg Free Circ: 1110
Audit By: Sworn/Estimate/Non-Audited
Audit Date: 12.07.2019
Personnel: Frank Spula (Pub.); Emily Leszczynski (Gen. Mgr.); Bogdan Mazur (Adv. Mgr.); Phil Chiaro (Circ. Mgr.); Wojciech Bialasiewicz (Ed.)

GREEK STAR

Street address 1: 4159 N Western Ave
Street address 2: Fl 2
Street address city: Chicago
State: IL
Zip/Postal code: 60618-2813
County: Cook
Country: USA
Mailing address: 44 Green Bay Rd
Mailing city: Winnetka
Mailing state: IL
Mailing zip: 60093-4006
General Phone: (773) 989-7211
General Fax: (773) 313-2006
General/National Adv. E-mail: greek@britsys.net
Primary Website: www.thegreekstar.com
Published: Thur
Avg Paid Circ: 2000
Audit By: Sworn/Estimate/Non-Audited
Audit Date: 12.07.2019
Personnel: Maria Bappert (Circ. Mgr.); Diane Adam (Prodn. Mgr.)

POLONIA TODAY

Street address 1: 6348 N Milwaukee Ave
Street address 2: Ste 360
Street address city: Chicago
State: IL
Zip/Postal code: 60646-3728
County: Cook
Country: USA
Mailing address: 6348 N Milwaukee Ave Ste 360
Mailing city: Chicago
Mailing state: IL
Mailing zip: 60646-3728
General Phone: (773) 763-1646
General Fax: (773) 763-1796
Display Adv. E-mail: sales@poloniatoday.com
Editorial e-mail: editor@poloniatoday.com
Primary Website: www.poloniatoday.com
Year Established: 1911
Published: Mthly
Avg Free Circ: 300000
Audit By: Sworn/Estimate/Non-Audited
Audit Date: 12.07.2019
Personnel: T. Ron Jasinski-Herbert (Ed.)
Parent company (for newspapers): Ameripol Corporation

ZGODA

Street address 1: 6100 N Cicero Ave
Street address city: Chicago
State: IL
Zip/Postal code: 60646-4304
County: Cook
Country: USA
Mailing address: 6100 N Cicero Ave
Mailing city: Chicago
Mailing state: IL
Mailing zip: 60646-4304
General Phone: (773) 286-0500
General Fax: (773) 286-0842
General/National Adv. E-mail: pnazgoda@pna-znp.org
Primary Website: www.pna-znp.org
Published Other: 2 x Mthly
Avg Free Circ: 65847
Audit By: Sworn/Estimate/Non-Audited
Audit Date: 12.07.2019
Personnel: Frank J. Spula (Pres.); Emily Leszczyaski (Gen. Mgr.)

HOFFMAN ESTATES

THE DANISH PIONEER NEWSPAPER

Street address 1: 1582 Glen Lake Rd
Street address city: Hoffman Estates
State: IL
Zip/Postal code: 60169-4023
County: Cook
Country: USA
Mailing address: 1582 Glen Lake Rd
Mailing city: Hoffman Estates
Mailing state: IL
Mailing zip: 60169-4023
General Phone: (847) 882-2552
General Fax: (847) 882-7082
General/National Adv. E-mail: dpioneer@aol.com
Primary Website: www.thedanishpioneer.com
Year Established: 1872
Published: Mon
Published Other: Every other Monday
Avg Paid Circ: 3200
Audit By: Sworn/Estimate/Non-Audited
Audit Date: 12.07.2019
Personnel: Linda Steffensen (Ed)

JOLIET

KSKJ VOICE

Street address 1: 2439 Glenwood Ave
Street address city: Joliet
State: IL
Zip/Postal code: 60435-5478
County: Will
Country: USA
Mailing address: 2439 Glenwood Ave
Mailing city: Joliet
Mailing state: IL
Mailing zip: 60435-5490
General Phone: (800) 843-5755
General Fax: (815) 741-2002
General/National Adv. E-mail: janice@kskjlife.com; news@kskjlife.com
Primary Website: www.kskjlife.org
Personnel: Al Kath (Mng. Ed.); Janice Frantz (Ed., English)

LINCOLNWOOD

KOREA TIMES

Street address 1: 3720 W Devon Ave
Street address city: Lincolnwood
State: IL
Zip/Postal code: 60712-1102
County: Cook
Country: USA
Mailing address: 3720 W Devon Ave
Mailing city: Lincolnwood
Mailing state: IL
Mailing zip: 60712-1102
General Phone: (847) 626-0370
General Fax: (847) 626-0351
General/National Adv. E-mail: koreatimes@irisnet.com
Primary Website: www.koreatimes.com
Published Other: Daily
Avg Paid Circ: 50000
Avg Free Circ: 100
Audit By: Sworn/Estimate/Non-Audited
Audit Date: 12.07.2019
Personnel: Inkyu Kim (Pres.); Tustin Lee (Ed. in Chief)

ZION

IRISH AMERICAN NEWS

Street address 1: PO Box 7
Street address city: Zion
State: IL
Zip/Postal code: 60099-0007
County: Lake
Country: USA
Mailing address: PO Box 7
Mailing city: Zion
Mailing state: IL
Mailing zip: 60099
General Phone: 312-498-1337
Advertising Phone: 312-498-1337
Editorial Phone: 312-498-1337
General/National Adv. E-mail: cliff@irishamericannews.com
Display Adv. E-mail: cliff@irishamericannews.com
Classified Adv. e-mail: cliff@irishamericannews.com
Editorial e-mail: cliff@irishamericannews.com
Primary Website: www.irishamericannews.com
Year Established: 1977
Published: Mthly
Avg Paid Circ: 7000
Avg Free Circ: 5000
Audit By: Sworn/Estimate/Non-Audited
Audit Date: 12.07.2019
Personnel: Cliff Carlson (publisher)
Parent company (for newspapers): Irish News Inc
State: Indiana

INDIANA

FORT WAYNE

MACEDONIAN TRIBUNE

Street address 1: 124 W Wayne St
Street address city: Fort Wayne
State: IN
Zip/Postal code: 46802-2500
County: Allen
Country: USA
Mailing address: 124 W Wayne St Ste 204
Mailing city: Fort Wayne
Mailing state: IN
Mailing zip: 46802-2505
General Phone: (260) 422-5900
General Fax: (260) 422-1348
General/National Adv. E-mail: mtfw@macedonian.org
Primary Website: www.macedonian.org
Year Established: 1927
Published: Mthly
Avg Paid Circ: 1320
Avg Free Circ: 64
Audit By: Sworn/Estimate/Non-Audited
Audit Date: 12.07.2019
Personnel: STEPHANIE GRIFFIN (Office Manager); Martha Haag (Circ. Mgr.); Virginia Surso (Ed.)
State: Massachusetts

MASSACHUSETTS

BOSTON

SAMPAN NEWSPAPER

Street address 1: 87 Tyler St
Street address 2: 5F
Street address city: Boston
State: MA
Zip/Postal code: 02111-1833
County: Suffolk
Country: USA
Mailing address: 87 Tyler Street, 5th Floor
Mailing city: Boston
Mailing state: MA
Mailing zip: 02111-1833
General Phone: (617) 426-9492 x 208
General Fax: (617) 482-2316
Advertising Phone: (617) 426-9492 x 206
General/National Adv. E-mail: editor@sampan.org
Display Adv. E-mail: ads@sampan.org
Editorial e-mail: editor@sampan.org
Primary Website: www.sampan.org
Year Established: 1972
Published: Bi-Mthly
Published Other: 2 x Mthly
Avg Paid Circ: 680
Avg Free Circ: 10000
Audit By: Sworn/Estimate/Non-Audited
Audit Date: 12.07.2019
Personnel: Mary Chin (Exec. Dir., Asian American Civic Association); Ling-Mei Wong (Ed.); Emma Le (Mktg. & Bus. Dev.)
Parent company (for newspapers): Asian American Civic Association

FALL RIVER

O JORNAL

Street address 1: 10 Purchase St
Street address city: Fall River
State: MA
Zip/Postal code: 02720-3100
County: Bristol
Country: USA
Mailing address: 10 Purchase St Ste 1
Mailing city: Fall River
Mailing state: MA
Mailing zip: 02720-3100
General Phone: (508) 678-3844
General Fax: (508) 678-1798
Display Adv. E-mail: advertising@ojornal.com
Editorial e-mail: editorial@ojornal.com
Primary Website: www.ojornal.com
Published: Fri
Avg Paid Circ: 10971
Avg Free Circ: 51
Audit By: CAC
Audit Date: 30.06.2017
Personnel: Ric Oliveira (Ed.); Lourdes DaSilva (Mng. Ed.); Tom Talbot (Adv. Dir.)

FITCHBURG

RAIVAAJA

Street address 1: 164 Elm St
Street address city: Fitchburg
State: MA
Zip/Postal code: 01420-3192
County: Worcester
Country: USA
Mailing address: PO Box 200
Mailing city: Fitchburg
Mailing state: MA
Mailing zip: 01420-0002
General Phone: (978) 343-3822
General Fax: (978) 343-8147
General/National Adv. E-mail: office@raivaaja.org; editor@raivaaja.org
Primary Website: www.raivaaja.org
Year Established: 1905
Published Other: Every other Wed
Avg Paid Circ: 2000
Audit By: Sworn/Estimate/Non-Audited
Audit Date: 12.07.2019
Personnel: Jonathan Ratila (Bus. Mgr.); Marita Cauthen (Ed.)

PITTSFIELD

BERKSHIRE JEWISH VOICE

Street address 1: 196 South Street

Street address 2: Jewish Federation of the Berkshires
Street address city: Pittsfield
State: MA
Zip/Postal code: 01201
County: Berkshire
Mailing state: MA
General Phone: 413-442-4360
Advertising Phone: 413-442-4360
Editorial Phone: 413-442-4360
General/National Adv. E-mail: astern@jewishberkshires.org
Editorial e-mail: astern@jewishberkshires.org
Primary Website: https://jewishberkshires.org/community-events/berkshire-jewish-voice/berkshire-jewish-voice-highlights
Year Established: 1989
Published Other: 9x per year
Avg Free Circ: 5000
Personnel: Dara Kaufman (Exec. Dir.); Albert Stern (Editor); Jenny Greenfield (Office Mgr.)
Parent company (for newspapers): Jewish Federation of the Berkshires; Joseph Jacobs Organization

WATERTOWN

ARMENIAN MIRROR-SPECTATOR

Street address 1: 755 Mount Auburn St
Street address city: Watertown
State: MA
Zip/Postal code: 02472-1509
County: Middlesex
Country: USA
Mailing address: 755 Mount Auburn St
Mailing city: Watertown
Mailing state: MA
Mailing zip: 02472-1509
General Phone: (617) 924-4420
General Fax: (617) 924-2887
General/National Adv. E-mail: armenmirr@aol.com
Primary Website: www.mirrorspectator.com
Published: Wed
Avg Paid Circ: 2600
Audit By: Sworn/Estimate/Non-Audited
Audit Date: 12.07.2019
Personnel: Kevork Marachlian (Gen. Mgr.); Alin Gregorian (Ed.); Mark McKertich (Computer Designer)

ARMENIAN WEEKLY

Street address 1: 80 Bigelow Ave
Street address city: Watertown
State: MA
Zip/Postal code: 02472-2012
County: Middlesex
Country: USA
Mailing address: 80 Bigelow Ave
Mailing city: Watertown
Mailing state: MA
Mailing zip: 02472-2012
General Phone: (617) 926-3974
General Fax: (617) 926-1750
General/National Adv. E-mail: manager@hairenik.com
Primary Website: www.hairenik.com
Published: Sat
Avg Paid Circ: 2000
Avg Free Circ: 550
Audit By: Sworn/Estimate/Non-Audited
Audit Date: 12.07.2019
Personnel: Lala Emirdjiin (Adv. Mgr.); Khapchig Mouradian (Ed.)

HAIRENIK WEEKLY

Street address 1: 80 Bigelow Ave
Street address city: Watertown
State: MA
Zip/Postal code: 02472-2012
County: Middlesex
Country: USA
Mailing address: 80 Bigelow Ave
Mailing city: Watertown
Mailing state: MA
Mailing zip: 02472-2012
General Phone: (617) 926-3974
General Fax: (617) 926-1750
General/National Adv. E-mail: manager@hairenik.com
Primary Website: www.hairenik.com
Published: Sat
Avg Paid Circ: 1500
Avg Free Circ: 200
Audit By: Sworn/Estimate/Non-Audited
Audit Date: 12.07.2019
Personnel: Lala Emirdjiin (Adv. Mgr.); Khajag Mgrditchian (Ed.)
State: Michigan

MICHIGAN

ROCHESTER

ALTAD, INC.

Street address 1: PO Box 80790
Street address city: Rochester
State: MI
Zip/Postal code: 48308-0790
County: Oakland
Country: USA
Mailing address: PO Box 80790
Mailing city: Rochester
Mailing state: MI
Mailing zip: 48308-0790
General Phone: (313) 365-1990
Advertising Phone: (313) 365 - 1990
General/National Adv. E-mail: polishweekly@comcast.net
Display Adv. E-mail: alicjakarlic@gmail.com
Editorial e-mail: alicjakarlic@gmail.com
Primary Website: www.polishweekly.com
Year Established: 1904
Published: Wed
Published Other: bi weekly
Avg Paid Circ: 1200
Avg Free Circ: 200
Audit By: Sworn/Estimate/Non-Audited
Audit Date: 12.07.2019
Personnel: Alicja Karlic (Ed, in Chief Publisher)

WARREN

NORDAMERIKANICHE WOCHENPOST

Street address 1: 12200 E 13 Mile Rd
Street address 2: Ste 140
Street address city: Warren
State: MI
Zip/Postal code: 48093
County: Macomb
Country: USA
Mailing address: 12200 E 13 mile Road
Mailing city: Warren
Mailing state: MI
Mailing zip: 48093
General Phone: (586) 486-5496
Advertising Phone: (586) 486-5496
Editorial Phone: (586) 486-5496
General/National Adv. E-mail: info@wochenpostusa.com
Display Adv. E-mail: sales@wochenpostusa.com
Editorial e-mail: ingrid@wochenpostusa.com
Primary Website: www.wochenpostusa.com
Year Established: 1854
Published: Sat
Avg Paid Circ: 30000
Audit By: Sworn/Estimate/Non-Audited
Audit Date: 12.07.2019
Personnel: Wilfried Mozer (Pub.); Ingrid Grotloh (Gen. Mgr.); Ingrid Stein (Adv. Mgr.); Birgit Kroon (Ed.); Kenneth Burney (Sports Ed.)
State: Minnesota

MINNESOTA

WHITE EARTH

ANISHINAABEG TODAY

Street address 1: PO Box 418
Street address city: White Earth
State: MN
Zip/Postal code: 56591-0418
County: Becker
Country: USA
Mailing address: PO Box 418
Mailing city: White Earth
Mailing state: MN
Mailing zip: 56591-0418
General Phone: (218) 983-3285
General Fax: (218) 983-3641
General/National Adv. E-mail: today@whiteearth.com
Primary Website: www.whiteearth.com
Published: Mthly
Avg Free Circ: 9988
Audit By: Sworn/Estimate/Non-Audited
Audit Date: 12.07.2019
Personnel: Gary Padrta (Ed.)
State: Missouri

MISSOURI

SAINT LOUIS

IL PENSIERO

Street address 1: 10001 Stonell Dr
Street address city: Saint Louis
State: MO
Zip/Postal code: 63123-5213
County: Saint Louis
Country: USA
Mailing address: 10001 Stonell Dr
Mailing city: Saint Louis
Mailing state: MO
Mailing zip: 63123-5213
General Phone: (314) 638-3446
General Fax: (314) 638-8222
General/National Adv. E-mail: ilpensiero@charter.net
Primary Website: www.ilpensierostl.com
Published Other: 2 x Mthly
Avg Paid Circ: 20000
Avg Free Circ: 5000
Audit By: Sworn/Estimate/Non-Audited
Audit Date: 12.07.2019
Personnel: Antonio Lombardo (Pub.); Linda Marino (Circ. Mgr.); A. Gandolfo (Ed.); Lina Lombardo (Mng. Ed.)
State: Montana

MONTANA

PABLO

CHAR-KOOSTA NEWS

Street address 1: 51396 Hwy, 93 N
Street address city: Pablo
State: MT
Zip/Postal code: 59855
County: Lake
Country: USA
Mailing address: PO Box 98
Mailing city: Pablo
Mailing state: MT
Mailing zip: 59855-0098
General Phone: (406) 275-2830
General/National Adv. E-mail: charkoosta@cskt.org
Primary Website: www.charkoosta.com
Year Established: 1955
Published: Thur
Avg Paid Circ: 3300
Avg Free Circ: 151
Audit By: Sworn/Estimate/Non-Audited
Audit Date: 12.07.2019
Personnel: Robert V. Fyant (Office/Dist. Mgr.); Sam Sandoval (Editor); Bernard Azure (Reporter); Leslie Camel (Sales Rep.); Kim Swaney (Ed.); Liz Dempsey (Reporter); Felicia Matt (Ad Sales Representative); Marlene McDanal (Business Manager)
Parent company (for newspapers): Confederated Salish and Kootenai Tribes
State: New Jersey

NEW JERSY

BOONTON

SOKOL TIMES

Street address 1: 301 Pine Street
Street address 2: PO Box 677
Street address city: Boonton
State: NJ
Zip/Postal code: 07005-0677
County: Morris
Country: USA
Mailing address: PO Box 677
Mailing city: Boonton
Mailing state: NJ
Mailing zip: 07005-0677
General Phone: (973) 676-0281
General/National Adv. E-mail: sokolusahqs@aol.com
Display Adv. E-mail: None Accepted
Year Established: 1905
Published: Mthly`Other
Published Other: every other month
Avg Free Circ: 2000
Audit By: Sworn/Estimate/Non-Audited
Audit Date: 12.07.2019
Personnel: Edward Bohon (Fraternal Secretary)

CLIFTON

THE POST EAGLE

Street address 1: 800 Van Houten Ave
Street address city: Clifton
State: NJ
Zip/Postal code: 07013-2035
County: Passaic
Country: USA
Mailing address: PO Box 109
Mailing city: Clifton
Mailing state: NJ
Mailing zip: 07015-0109
General Phone: (973) 473-5414
General Fax: (973) 473-3211
General/National Adv. E-mail: posteagle@aol.com
Primary Website: www.posteaglenewspaper.com
Year Established: 1963
Published: Wed
Avg Paid Circ: 14000
Audit By: Sworn/Estimate/Non-Audited
Audit Date: 12.07.2019
Personnel: Christine Witmyer (Ed.)
Parent company (for newspapers): Post Publishing Co.

GARFIELD

NOWY DZIENNIK

Street address 1: 70 Outwater Ln
Street address 2: Ste 402
Street address city: Garfield
State: NJ
Zip/Postal code: 07026-3867
County: Bergen
Country: USA
Mailing address: 70 Outwater Ln Ste 402
Mailing city: Garfield
Mailing state: NJ
Mailing zip: 07026-3867
General Phone: (212) 594-2266
General Fax: (212) 594-2383
General/National Adv. E-mail: listy@dziennik.com
Primary Website: www.dziennik.com
Year Established: 1971
Published: Wed
Published Other: Weekly
Avg Paid Circ: 7650
Avg Free Circ: 250
Audit By: Sworn/Estimate/Non-Audited
Audit Date: 12.07.2019
Personnel: Tom Deptula (Commentator); Tom Bagnowski; Nick Sadowski (EIC/Partner)
Parent company (for newspapers): Outwater Media Group, LLC

JERSEY CITY

FILIPINO EXPRESS

Street address 1: 2711 John F Kennedy Blvd
Street address city: Jersey City
State: NJ
Zip/Postal code: 07306-5712
County: Hudson
Country: USA
Mailing address: 2711 John F Kennedy Blvd
Mailing city: Jersey City
Mailing state: NJ
Mailing zip: 07306-5712
General Phone: (201) 434-1114
General Fax: (201) 434-0880
General/National Adv. E-mail: filexpress@aol.com
Primary Website: www.filipinoexpress.com
Published: Fri
Avg Paid Circ: 21700
Avg Free Circ: 3000
Audit By: Sworn/Estimate/Non-Audited
Audit Date: 12.07.2019
Personnel: Lito A. Gajilan (Adv. Mgr.)

NEWARK

24 HORAS

Street address 1: 68 Madison St
Street address city: Newark
State: NJ
Zip/Postal code: 07105-7109
County: Essex
Country: USA
General Phone: (973) 817-7400
General Fax: (973) 817-8383
Display Adv. E-mail: advertising@24horasnewspaper.com
Editorial e-mail: news@24horasnewspaper.com
Primary Website: www.24horasnewspaper.com
Year Established: 1998
Published: Mon`Tues`Wed`Thur`Fri`Sat
Avg Paid Circ: 12000
Avg Free Circ: 1000
Audit By: Sworn/Estimate/Non-Audited
Audit Date: 12.07.2019
Personnel: Joao Santos Matos (News Ed.); Sonia Paula Alves (Ad. Director); Igor M. Alves (Marketing Director)

LUSO AMERICANO

Street address 1: 88 Ferry St
Street address city: Newark
State: NJ
Zip/Postal code: 07105-1817
County: Essex
Country: USA
Mailing address: 88 Ferry St
Mailing city: Newark
Mailing state: NJ
Mailing zip: 07105-1817
General Phone: (973) 589-4600
General Fax: (973) 589-3848
General/National Adv. E-mail: lusoamerican@earthlink.net
Primary Website: www.lusoamericano.com
Published: Wed`Fri
Avg Paid Circ: 33460
Audit By: Sworn/Estimate/Non-Audited
Audit Date: 12.07.2019
Personnel: A.S. Matinho (Ed. in Chief); Paul Matinho (Opns. Dir.)

NORWOOD

AMERICA OGGI

Street address 1: 475 Walnut St
Street address city: Norwood
State: NJ
Zip/Postal code: 07648-1318
County: Bergen
Country: USA
Mailing address: 475 Walnut St
Mailing city: Norwood
Mailing state: NJ
Mailing zip: 07648-1318
General Phone: (201) 358-6697
General Fax: (201) 358-9212
Advertising Phone: (201)358-6692
Advertising Fax: (201) 358-9212
Editorial Phone: 212-268-0250
Editorial Fax: (201) 358-9212
General/National Adv. E-mail: americoggi@aol.com
Display Adv. E-mail: americoggi@aol.com
Editorial e-mail: americoggi@aol.com
Primary Website: www.americaoggi.it
Year Established: 1988
Published: Mon`Tues`Wed`Thur`Fri`Sat`Sun
Avg Paid Circ: 19750
Avg Free Circ: 2500
Audit By: Sworn/Estimate/Non-Audited
Audit Date: 12.07.2019
Personnel: Andrea Mantineo (President/Ed.); Enzo De Blasio (Executive consultant); Domenico Delli Carpini (Vice President)
Parent company (for newspapers): JB Offset Printing Co.

PARAMUS

ARMENIAN REPORTER INTERNATIONAL, INC.

Street address 1: PO Box 129
Street address city: Paramus
State: NJ
Zip/Postal code: 07653-0129
County: Bergen
Country: USA
Mailing address: 15 S 5th St Ste 900
Mailing city: Minneapolis
Mailing state: MN
Mailing zip: 55402-1060
General Phone: (201) 226-1995
General Fax: (201) 226-1660
General/National Adv. E-mail: armenianreporter@msn.com
Primary Website: www.armenianreporteronline.com
Year Established: 1967
Published: Tues`Thur`Sat
Avg Paid Circ: 10000
Avg Free Circ: 100
Audit By: Sworn/Estimate/Non-Audited
Audit Date: 12.07.2019
Personnel: Vincent Lima (Ed.); Sylva A. Boghossian (Prodn. Mgr.)

PARSIPPANY

SVOBODA

Street address 1: 2200 State Rt 10
Street address city: Parsippany
State: NJ
Zip/Postal code: 07054-5304
County: Morris
Country: USA
Mailing address: 2200 State Rt 10
Mailing city: Parsippany
Mailing state: NJ
Mailing zip: 07054-5304
General Phone: (973) 292-9800
General Fax: (973) 644-9510
Advertising Phone: (973) 292-9800 x3040
Advertising Fax: (973) 644-9510
Editorial Phone: (973) 292-9800 x3049
Editorial Fax: (973) 644-9510
General/National Adv. E-mail: svoboda@svoboda-news.com
Display Adv. E-mail: adukr@optonline.net
Editorial e-mail: svoboda@svoboda-news.com
Primary Website: www.svoboda-news.com
Year Established: 1893
Published: Fri
Avg Paid Circ: 7524
Avg Free Circ: 170
Audit By: Sworn/Estimate/Non-Audited
Audit Date: 12.07.2019
Parent company (for newspapers): Ukrainian National Association

THE UKRAINIAN WEEKLY

Street address 1: 2200 State Rt 10
Street address city: Parsippany
State: NJ
Zip/Postal code: 07054-5304
County: Morris
Country: USA
Mailing address: PO Box 280
Mailing city: Parsippany
Mailing state: NJ
Mailing zip: 07054-0280
General Phone: (973) 292-9800
General Fax: (973) 644-9510
General/National Adv. E-mail: staff@ukrweekly.com
Editorial e-mail: staff@ukrweekly.com
Primary Website: www.ukrweekly.com
Year Established: 1933
Published: Sun
Avg Paid Circ: 5000
Audit By: Sworn/Estimate/Non-Audited
Audit Date: 12.07.2019
Personnel: Walter Honcharyk (Adv./Circ. Mgr.); Romana Hadzewycz (Ed. in Chief); Andrew Nynka (Editor-in-chief)
Parent company (for newspapers): Ukrainian National Association

PASSAIC

SLOVAK CATHOLIC FALCON

Street address 1: 205 Madison St
Street address city: Passaic
State: NJ
Zip/Postal code: 07055-5224
County: Passaic
Country: USA
Mailing address: PO Box 899
Mailing city: Passaic
Mailing state: NJ
Mailing zip: 07055-0899
General Phone: (973) 777-4010
General Fax: (973) 779-8245
General/National Adv. E-mail: sokol205@aol.com
Primary Website: www.slovakcatholicsokol.org
Published Other: Every other Wed
Avg Paid Circ: 11200
Audit By: Sworn/Estimate/Non-Audited
Audit Date: 12.07.2019
Personnel: Daniel F. Tanzone (Ed.)

WEST ORANGE

ITALIAN TRIBUNE

Street address 1: 271 Mt. Pleasant Ave.
Street address 2: Suite 4
Street address city: West Orange
State: NJ
Zip/Postal code: 07052
County: Essex
Country: USA
Mailing address: 271 Mt. Pleasant Ave, Suite 4
Mailing city: West Orange
Mailing state: NJ
Mailing zip: 07052
General Phone: (973) 860-0101
General Fax: (973) 860-0106
General/National Adv. E-mail: mail@italiantribune.com
Primary Website: www.italiantribune.com
Year Established: 1931
Published: Thur
Avg Paid Circ: 95000
Audit By: Sworn/Estimate/Non-Audited
Audit Date: 12.07.2019
Personnel: Buddy Fortunato (Pub.); Carl Houser (Adv. Mgr.); Marion Fortunato (Ed.); Joan Alagna (Managing Editor); David Cavaliere (Editor)
State: Nevada

NEVADA

LAS VEGAS

LAS VEGAS ISRAELITE

Street address 1: PO Box 14096
Street address city: Las Vegas
State: NV
Zip/Postal code: 89114
County: Clark
Country: USA
Mailing address: PO Box 29240
Mailing city: Las Vegas
Mailing state: NV
Mailing zip: 89126-3240
General Phone: (702) 876-1255
General Fax: (702) 364-1009
General/National Adv. E-mail: Lasvegasisraelite@cox.net
Primary Website: Lvisraelite.com
Year Established: 1964
Published Other: 2 x Mthly
Avg Paid Circ: 10000
Avg Free Circ: 33000
Audit By: Sworn/Estimate/Non-Audited
Audit Date: 12.07.2019
Personnel: Michael Tell (Prodn. Mgr.)
Parent company (for newspapers): Joseph Jacobs Organization
State: New York

NEW YORK

ASTORIA

GREEK NEWS

Street address 1: 3507 23rd Ave
Street address city: Astoria
State: NY
Zip/Postal code: 11105-2204
County: Queens
Country: USA
Mailing address: 3507 23rd Ave
Mailing city: Astoria
Mailing state: NY
Mailing zip: 11105-2204
General Phone: (718) 545-4888
General Fax: (718) 545-4884
Advertising Phone: (718) 545-4888
Advertising Fax: (718) 545-4884
Editorial Phone: (718) 545-4888
Editorial Fax: (718) 545-4884
General/National Adv. E-mail: info@greeknewsonline.com
Display Adv. E-mail: info@greeknewsonline.com
Editorial e-mail: info@greeknewsonline.com
Primary Website: www.greeknewsonline.com
Published: Mon
Personnel: Apostolos Zoupaniotis (Ed.)

BROOKLYN

CARIBBEAN LIFE

Street address 1: 1 N Metrotech Ctr
Street address 2: Ste 1001
Street address city: Brooklyn
State: NY
Zip/Postal code: 11201-3949
County: Kings
Country: USA
Mailing address: One N Metrotech Center
Mailing city: Brooklyn
Mailing state: NY
Mailing zip: 11201
General Phone: (718) 260-2500
General Fax: 718-260-2579
General/National Adv. E-mail: CaribbeanLife@SchnepsMedia.com
Display Adv. E-mail: Ads@SchnepsMedia.com
Editorial e-mail: MWilliams@SchnepsMedia.com
Primary Website: caribbeanlifenews.com
Year Established: 1990
Published: Fri
Avg Free Circ: 44609
Audit By: CVC
Audit Date: 30.09.2018
Personnel: Clifford Luster (Pub.); Ralph D'onofrio (Assoc. Pub.); Michael Kevin Williams (Ed.)

Parent company (for newspapers): Schneps Media

KURIER

Street address 1: 145 Java St
Street address city: Brooklyn
State: NY
Zip/Postal code: 11222-1602
County: Kings
Country: USA
Mailing address: 145 Java St.
Mailing city: Brooklyn
Mailing state: NY
Mailing zip: 11222
General Phone: (718) 389-3018
General Fax: (718) 389-3140
General/National Adv. E-mail: kurier@kurierplus.com
Primary Website: http://kurierplus.com/
Published: Fri
Avg Paid Circ: 30000
Audit By: Sworn/Estimate/Non-Audited
Audit Date: 12.07.2019
Personnel: Michael Milochnikov (Gen. Mgr.)

NOVOYE RUSSKOYE SLOVO

Street address 1: 861 Bay Ridge Avenue
Street address 2: Ste. 6
Street address city: Brooklyn
State: NY
Zip/Postal code: 11220
County: New York
Country: USA
Mailing address: 861 Bay Ridge Avenue, Ste. 6
Mailing city: Brooklyn
Mailing state: NY
Mailing zip: 11220
General Phone: (718) 648-3511
General Fax: (718) 648-3047
Primary Website: inforeklama.com
Year Established: 1910
Published: Fri
Avg Paid Circ: 40000
Avg Free Circ: 3250
Audit By: Sworn/Estimate/Non-Audited
Audit Date: 12.07.2019
Personnel: Vladimir Sagal (Exec. Dir.); Valery Weinsberg (Ed.)

RUSSIAN ADVERTISER

Street address 1: 2699 Coney Island Ave
Street address city: Brooklyn
State: NY
Zip/Postal code: 11235-5004
County: Kings
Country: USA
Mailing address: 2699 Coney Island Ave
Mailing city: Brooklyn
Mailing state: NY
Mailing zip: 11235-5004
General Phone: (718) 769-3000
General Fax: (718) 769-4700
General/National Adv. E-mail: reklama2000@online.net
Primary Website: www.rusrek.com
Published: Fri
Avg Paid Circ: 20000
Audit By: Sworn/Estimate/Non-Audited
Audit Date: 12.07.2019
Personnel: Michael Trepolskey (Ed. in Chief)

RUSSKAYA REKLAMA

Street address 1: 2699 Coney Island Ave
Street address city: Brooklyn
State: NY
Zip/Postal code: 11235-5004
County: Kings
Country: USA
Mailing address: 2699 Coney Island Ave
Mailing city: Brooklyn
Mailing state: NY
Mailing zip: 11235-5004
General Phone: (718) 769-3000
General Fax: (718) 769-4700
General/National Adv. E-mail: reklama2000@yahoo.com
Primary Website: www.rronline.ws
Published: Fri
Avg Paid Circ: 3000
Audit By: Sworn/Estimate/Non-Audited
Audit Date: 12.07.2019
Personnel: Guily Gurevich (Adv. Mgr.); Michael Trepolskey (Ed. in Chief)

VECHERNIY NEW YORK

Street address 1: 1529 Voorhies Ave
Street address city: Brooklyn
State: NY
Zip/Postal code: 11235-3912
County: Kings
Country: USA
Mailing address: 1529 Voorhies Ave
Mailing city: Brooklyn
Mailing state: NY
Mailing zip: 11235-3912
General Phone: (718) 615-1210
General Fax: (718) 615-1244
General/National Adv. E-mail: vechny@yahoo.com
Primary Website: www.vechny.com
Published: Fri
Avg Paid Circ: 15000
Avg Free Circ: 5000
Audit By: Sworn/Estimate/Non-Audited
Audit Date: 12.07.2019
Personnel: Irena Zolotora (COO); Boris Zaturenskiy (Circ. Mgr.); Nargis Shekinskaya (Entertainment Ed.); Vseslav Tkachenko (News Ed.)

CANASTOTA

INDIAN COUNTRY TODAY

Street address 1: 3059 Seneca Tpke
Street address city: Canastota
State: NY
Zip/Postal code: 13032-3532
County: Madison
Country: USA
Mailing address: 2037 Dream Catcher Plz
Mailing city: Oneida
Mailing state: NY
Mailing zip: 13421-2710
General Phone: (315) 829-8355
Advertising Fax: (315) 829-8028
Editorial Fax: (315) 829-8393
Display Adv. E-mail: sales@indiancountry.com
Editorial e-mail: editor@indiancountry.com
Primary Website: www.indiancountry.com
Published: Wed
Avg Paid Circ: 13000
Audit By: Sworn/Estimate/Non-Audited
Audit Date: 12.07.2019
Personnel: Ray Haldritter (Pub.); Heather Donovan (Sales Mgr.); Pete Wiezalis (Dir., Mktg.); Sabrina Sharkey (Circ. Mgr.); Ken Polisse (Mng. Ed.)

FLUSHING

THE HERALD MONTHLY

Street address 1: 15603 Horace Harding Expy
Street address city: Flushing
State: NY
Zip/Postal code: 11367-1250
County: Queens
Country: USA
Mailing address: 15603 Horace Harding Expy
Mailing city: Flushing
Mailing state: NY
Mailing zip: 11367-1250
General Phone: (718) 359-2030
General Fax: (718) 359-2130
General/National Adv. E-mail: herald@cchc.org
Primary Website: www.cchc.org
Published: Mthly
Avg Paid Circ: 120000
Avg Free Circ: 120000
Audit By: Sworn/Estimate/Non-Audited
Audit Date: 12.07.2019
Personnel: Ruth Lee (Adv. Mgr.); Katie Chau (Exec. Ed.)

LONG ISLAND CITY

THE KOREA TIMES

Street address 1: 4222 27th St
Street address city: Long Island City
State: NY
Zip/Postal code: 11101-4107
County: Queens
Country: USA
Mailing address: 4222 27th St
Mailing city: Long Island City
Mailing state: NY
Mailing zip: 11101-4107
General Phone: (718) 482-1111
General Fax: (718) 784-7381
General/National Adv. E-mail: hankuk97@aol.com
Primary Website: www.koreatimes.com
Published Other: Daily
Avg Paid Circ: 30000
Audit By: Sworn/Estimate/Non-Audited
Audit Date: 12.07.2019
Personnel: Hak Y. Shin (Pres.); Jaemin Chang (Pub.)

THE NATIONAL HERALD

Street address 1: 3710 30th St
Street address city: Long Island City
State: NY
Zip/Postal code: 11101-2614
County: Queens
Country: USA
Mailing address: 3710 30th St
Mailing city: Long Island City
Mailing state: NY
Mailing zip: 11101-2614
General Phone: (718) 784-5255
General Fax: (718) 472-0510
General/National Adv. E-mail: publisher@ekirikas.com
Primary Website: www.thenationalherald.com
Published: Mon`Tues`Wed`Thur`Fri`Sat
Avg Paid Circ: 100000
Audit By: Sworn/Estimate/Non-Audited
Audit Date: 12.07.2019
Personnel: Victoria Diamataris (Asst. to Pub.); Demetrios Paregoris (Circ. Mgr.); Anthony H. Diamataris (Ed.); Chrysoula Karametros (Prodn. Mgr.)

MIDDLE VILLAGE

NEW YORK MAGAZIN

Street address 1: 6442 84th St
Street address city: Middle Village
State: NY
Zip/Postal code: 11379-2424
County: Queens
Country: USA
Mailing address: 6442 84th St
Mailing city: Middle Village
Mailing state: NY
Mailing zip: 11379-2424
General Phone: (718) 896-8383
General Fax: (718) 896-8383
General/National Adv. E-mail: nymagazin@aol.com
Primary Website: www.nymagazin.com
Published: Wed
Avg Free Circ: 5000
Audit By: Sworn/Estimate/Non-Audited
Audit Date: 12.07.2019
Personnel: Andreea M. Culian (Gen. Mgr.); Grigore L. Culian (Ed.)

NEW YORK

CARIB NEWS

Street address 1: 35 W 35th St
Street address 2: Ste 705
Street address city: New York
State: NY
Zip/Postal code: 10001-2205
County: New York
Country: USA
Mailing address: 1745 Broadway Fl 17
Mailing city: New York
Mailing state: NY
Mailing zip: 10019-4642
General Phone: (212) 944-1991
General Fax: (212) 944-2089
General/National Adv. E-mail: info@nycaribnews.com
Display Adv. E-mail: info@nycaribnews.com
Primary Website: www.nycaribnews.com
Published: Wed
Personnel: Karlisa Rodney (Ed.)

CHINA DAILY DISTRIBUTION CORP.

Street address 1: 1500 Broadway
Street address 2: Ste 2800
Street address city: New York
State: NY
Zip/Postal code: 10036-4097
County: New York
Country: USA
Mailing address: 1500 Broadway
Mailing city: New York
Mailing state: NY
Mailing zip: 10036
General Phone: (212) 537-8888
General Fax: (212) 537-8898
Advertising Phone: (212) 537-8900
General/National Adv. E-mail: readers@chinadailyusa.com
Primary Website: http://www.chinadaily.com.cn/cd/usa.html
Personnel: Lingling Sun (Adv. Mgr.); Yinghuang Zhu (Ed.); Thomoson Chen (Prodn. Mgr.)

CHINESE CHRISTIAN HERALD CRUSADES, INC.

Street address 1: 48 Allen St
Street address city: New York
State: NY
Zip/Postal code: 10002-5304
County: New York
Country: USA
Mailing address: 48 Allen St
Mailing city: New York
Mailing state: NY
Mailing zip: 10002-5304
General Phone: (212) 334-2033
Editorial Fax: (212) 334-2062
General/National Adv. E-mail: herald@cchc.org
Personnel: Katie Chau (Exec. Ed.)

FREE ESTONIAN WORD

Street address 1: 243 E 34th St
Street address city: New York
State: NY
Zip/Postal code: 10016-4852
County: New York
Country: USA
Mailing address: 243 E 34th St
Mailing city: New York
Mailing state: NY
Mailing zip: 10016-4852
General Phone: (212) 686-3356
General Fax: (212) 689-2939
General/National Adv. E-mail: talitus@vabaeestisona.com
Primary Website: www.vabaeestisona.com
Published: Thur
Avg Paid Circ: 1400
Audit By: Sworn/Estimate/Non-Audited
Audit Date: 12.07.2019
Personnel: Reet Karu (Adv. Mgr.); Kart Ulmans (Ed.)

HAITI PROGRES

Street address 1: 555 Main Street
Street address city: New York
State: NY
Zip/Postal code: 10044-0294
County: New York
Country: USA
Mailing address: PO Box 30273
Mailing city: Brooklyn
Mailing state: NY
Mailing zip: 11203-0273
General Phone: (212) 750-3411
General Fax: (718) 284-6968
Advertising Phone: (917) 548-5568
Advertising Fax: (718) 284-6968
General/National Adv. E-mail: editor@haiti-progres.com
Display Adv. E-mail: sales@haitiprogres.com
Primary Website: www.haiti-progres.com
Year Established: 1983
Published: Wed
Avg Paid Circ: 5000
Audit By: Sworn/Estimate/Non-Audited
Audit Date: 12.07.2019

Personnel: Maude LeBlanc (Prodn. Mgr.)

HELLENIC TIMES

Street address 1: 823 11th Ave
Street address city: New York
State: NY
Zip/Postal code: 10019-3557
County: New York
Country: USA
Mailing address: 823 11th Ave Fl 5
Mailing city: New York
Mailing state: NY
Mailing zip: 10019-3557
General Phone: (212) 986-6881
General Fax: (212) 977-3662
General/National Adv. E-mail: helnctimes@aol.com
Primary Website: www.thehellenictimes.com
Published: Mthly
Avg Paid Circ: 11500
Avg Free Circ: 2000
Audit By: Sworn/Estimate/Non-Audited
Audit Date: 12.07.2019
Personnel: John Catsimatidis (Pub.); Margo Catsimatidis (Adv. Mgr.); Jimmy Kapsalis (Ed.)

IMPACTO LATIN NEWS

Street address 1: 5 Penn Plaza
Street address 2: Ste 1915
Street address city: New York
State: NY
Zip/Postal code: 85261
County: New York
Country: USA
Mailing address: P.O. Box 5316
Mailing city: Scottsdale
Mailing state: AZ
Mailing zip: 10001-3437
General Phone: (212) 807-0400
General Fax: (212) 807-0408
General/National Adv. E-mail: media@impactony.com
Display Adv. E-mail: gsmith@impactolatino.com
Classified Adv. e-mail: gsmith@impactolatino.com
Editorial e-mail: jsmith@impactolatino.com
Primary Website: impactolatino.com
Year Established: 1967
Published: Thur
Avg Free Circ: 57000
Audit By: Sworn/Estimate/Non-Audited
Audit Date: 31.03.2014
Personnel: Gail M Smith (Pub.); Jason. K Smith (Ed.); Vanessa. M Smith (VP, Adv./Mktg.); Mar Verdugo (Market Research Analyst)
Parent company (for newspapers): Impacto Latin News Publishing; Impacto Latin News, Inc.

INDIA ABROAD

Street address 1: 42 Broadway
Street address 2: Ste 1836
Street address city: New York
State: NY
Zip/Postal code: 10004-3855
County: New York
Country: USA
Mailing address: 42 Broadway Ste 1836
Mailing city: New York
Mailing state: NY
Mailing zip: 10004-3855
General Phone: (877) 463-4222
General Fax: (212) 627-9503
Advertising Phone: (877) 463-4222 ext. 2
Advertising Fax: (212) 627-9503
Editorial Phone: (877) 463-4222 ext. 6045
Editorial Fax: (212) 627-9503
General/National Adv. E-mail: advertise@indiaabroad.com
Display Adv. E-mail: classified@indiaabroad.com
Editorial e-mail: editorial@indiaabroad.com
Primary Website: www.indiaabroad.com
Year Established: 1970
Published: Fri
Avg Paid Circ: 20251
Avg Free Circ: 720
Audit By: AAM
Audit Date: 19.10.2017
Personnel: Ajit Balakrishnan (Pub.); Nikhil Laksham (Ed.); Anjali Maniam (Circ. Dir.); Anjali Subramaniam (Adv. Dir.); Rajeev Bhambri (COO - US Media)

IRISH ECHO

Street address 1: 165 Madison Ave
Street address 2: Rm 302
Street address city: New York
State: NY
Zip/Postal code: 10016-5431
County: New York
Country: USA
Mailing address: 165 Madison Ave Rm 302
Mailing city: New York
Mailing state: NY
Mailing zip: 10016-5431
General Phone: (212) 482-4818
General Fax: (212) 482-6569
Editorial e-mail: letters@irishecho.com
Primary Website: www.irishecho.com
Year Established: 1928
Published: Wed
Avg Paid Circ: 60000
Avg Free Circ: 350
Audit By: Sworn/Estimate/Non-Audited
Audit Date: 12.07.2019
Personnel: Mairtin O Muilleoir (Pub.); Ray O'Hanlon (Ed.); Eileen Murphy (Prodn. Mgr.)

IRISH VOICE

Street address 1: 875 Avenue of the Americas
Street address 2: Rm 2100
Street address city: New York
State: NY
Zip/Postal code: 10001-3586
County: New York
Country: USA
Mailing address: 875 Avenue of the Americas Rm 200
Mailing city: New York
Mailing state: NY
Mailing zip: 10001-3570
General Phone: (212) 684-3366
General Fax: (212) 244-3344
Advertising Phone: (800) 582-6642
General/National Adv. E-mail: irvce@aol.com
Primary Website: www.irishvoice.com
Year Established: 1987
Published: Wed
Avg Paid Circ: 65000
Audit By: Sworn/Estimate/Non-Audited
Audit Date: 12.07.2019
Personnel: Niall O'Dowd (Pub.); Robert Hogan (Adv. Dir.); Ronan Creaney (Adv. Mgr.); Naela El Assad (Classified Mgr.); Kevin Mangan (Circ. Mgr.); Debbie McGoldrick (Ed.); Genevieve McCarthy (Prodn. Mgr.)

NEWS INDIA-TIMES

Street address 1: 115 W 30th St
Street address 2: Rm 1206
Street address city: New York
State: NY
Zip/Postal code: 10001-4043
County: New York
Country: USA
Mailing address: 115 W 30th St., Suite 1206
Mailing city: New York
Mailing state: NY
Mailing zip: 10001
General Phone: 212-675-7515
General Fax: (212) 675-7624
Advertising Phone: (212) 675-7515
Display Adv. E-mail: advertising@newsindia-times.com
Editorial e-mail: editor@newsindia-times.com
Primary Website: www.newsindia-times.com
Published: Fri
Avg Paid Circ: 39070
Audit By: AAM
Audit Date: 19.10.2017
Personnel: Shomik Chodhuri (COO); Sudhir Parikh (Pub.); Ilayas Quraishi (Sales Exec.)

THE FILIPINO REPORTER

Street address 1: 350 5th Ave
Street address 2: Bldg 601
Street address city: New York
State: NY
Zip/Postal code: 10118-0110
County: New York
Country: USA
Mailing address: 350 5th Ave Ste 601
Mailing city: New York
Mailing state: NY
Mailing zip: 10118-0601
General Phone: (212) 967-5784
General Fax: (212) 967-5848
General/National Adv. E-mail: info@filipinoreporter.com
Primary Website: www.filipinoreporter.us
Year Established: 1972
Published: Fri
Avg Paid Circ: 47000
Avg Free Circ: 2000
Audit By: Sworn/Estimate/Non-Audited
Audit Date: 12.07.2019
Personnel: Tony Campo (Mktg. Mgr.); Albert Ignacio (Circ. Mgr.); Libertito Pelayo (Ed.)

THE JERUSALEM POST INTERNATIONAL EDITION

Street address 1: 80 Wall St
Street address 2: Ste 715
Street address city: New York
State: NY
Zip/Postal code: 10005-3662
County: New York
Country: USA
Mailing address: 8690 188th St
Mailing city: Hollis
Mailing state: NY
Mailing zip: 11423-1110
General Phone: (212) 742-0505
General Fax: (212) 742-0880
General/National Adv. E-mail: sigaln@jpost.com
Primary Website: www.jpost.com
Year Established: 1932
Published: Sun
Avg Paid Circ: 50000
Audit By: Sworn/Estimate/Non-Audited
Audit Date: 12.07.2019
Personnel: Mark Ziman (Pub.); David Horovitz (Ed. in Chief); Steve Linde (Mng. Ed.)

VABA EESTI SONA

Street address 1: 243 E 34th St
Street address city: New York
State: NY
Zip/Postal code: 10016-4852
County: New York
Country: USA
Mailing address: 243 E 34th St
Mailing city: New York
Mailing state: NY
Mailing zip: 10016-4852
General Phone: (212) 686-3356
General Fax: (212) 689-2939
General/National Adv. E-mail: talitus@vabaeestisona.com
Editorial e-mail: toimetus@vabaeestisona.com
Primary Website: www.vabaeestisona.com
Year Established: 1949
Published: Thur
Audit By: Sworn/Estimate/Non-Audited
Audit Date: 12.07.2019
Personnel: Kart Ulman (Ed.)
Parent company (for newspapers): The Nordic Press, Inc

NORTH BOSTON

POLISH AMERICAN JOURNAL

Street address 1: PO Box 271
Street address city: North Boston
State: NY
Zip/Postal code: 14110-0271
County: Erie
Country: USA
Mailing address: PO Box 271
Mailing city: North Boston
Mailing state: NY
Mailing zip: 14110-0271
General Phone: (800) 422-1275
Advertising Phone: (800) 422-1275
Editorial Phone: (716) 312-8088
General/National Adv. E-mail: info@polamjournal.com
Display Adv. E-mail: editor@polamjournal.com
Editorial e-mail: editor@polamjournal.com
Primary Website: www.polamjournal.com
Year Established: 1911
Published: Bi-Mthly
Published Other: 6 issues per year
Avg Paid Circ: 5700
Avg Free Circ: 300
Audit By: Sworn/Estimate/Non-Audited
Audit Date: 01.09.2022
Personnel: Mark A. Kohan (Ed.); Thomas Tarapacki (Asst. Ed.); Kathy Bruno (Acct.); Michelle Kisluk (Director of Advertising Sales)
Parent company (for newspapers): Panagraphics, Inc.

WHITESTONE

WORLD JOURNAL

Street address 1: 14107 20th Ave
Street address city: Whitestone
State: NY
Zip/Postal code: 11357-3062
County: Queens
Country: USA
Mailing address: 14107 20th Ave Fl 2
Mailing city: Whitestone
Mailing state: NY
Mailing zip: 11357-6093
General Phone: (718) 746-8889
General Fax: (718) 445-5257
General/National Adv. E-mail: webmaster@worldjournal.com
Display Adv. E-mail: nysales@worldjournal.com
Editorial e-mail: citydesk@worldjournal.com
Primary Website: www.worldjournal.com
Year Established: 1976
Published: Mon`Tues`Wed`Thur`Fri`Sat`Sun
Published Other: Daily
Avg Paid Circ: 100000
Avg Free Circ: 2500
Audit By: Sworn/Estimate/Non-Audited
Audit Date: 12.07.2019
Personnel: Tyson Won (Ed. in Chief); Wen-Te Ling (Prodn. Mgr.); James Yang (President)
State: Ohio

OHIO

CLEVELAND

DIRVA

Street address 1: 19807 Cherokee Ave
Street address city: Cleveland
State: OH
Zip/Postal code: 44119-2825
County: Cuyahoga
Country: USA
Mailing address: PO Box 19010
Mailing city: Cleveland
Mailing state: OH
Mailing zip: 44119-0010
General Phone: (216) 531-8150
General Fax: (216) 531-8428
General/National Adv. E-mail: dirva@ix.netcom.com
Display Adv. E-mail: dirva@ix.netcom.com
Editorial e-mail: dirva@ix.netcom.com
Year Established: 1915
Published: Tues
Published Other: Every other Tues
Avg Paid Circ: 700
Avg Free Circ: 65
Audit By: Sworn/Estimate/Non-Audited
Audit Date: 12.07.2019
Personnel: A.V. Matulionis (Pres of Viltis Inc. Pub of Dirva); G. Kijauskas (Circ. Mgr.)
State: Oklahoma

OKLAHOMA

ADA

CHICKASAW TIMES

Street address 1: 2612 Arlington St
Street address 2: Ste B
Street address city: Ada
State: OK
Zip/Postal code: 74820-2905
County: Pontotoc
Country: USA
Mailing address: PO Box 1548
Mailing city: Ada
Mailing state: OK
Mailing zip: 74821-1548
General Phone: (580) 332-2977
General Fax: (580) 332-3949
General/National Adv. E-mail: times.chickasaw@chickasaw.net
Primary Website: www.chickasaw.net
Published: Mthly
Avg Free Circ: 24000
Audit By: Sworn/Estimate/Non-Audited
Audit Date: 12.07.2019
Personnel: Vicky Gold (Office Mgr.); Tom Bolitho (Ed.)
State: Pennsylvania

PENNSYLVANIA

CONCORDVILLE

HELLENIC NEWS OF AMERICA

Street address 1: P.O. Box 465
Street address city: Concordville
State: PA
Zip/Postal code: 19331-0465
County: Delaware
Country: USA
Mailing address: P.O. BOX 465
Mailing city: Concordville
Mailing state: PA
Mailing zip: 19331-0465
General Phone: (610) 446-1463
General/National Adv. E-mail: info@hellenicnews.com
Display Adv. E-mail: paul@hellenicnews.com
Editorial e-mail: aphrodite@hellenicnews.com
Primary Website: www.hellenicnews.com
Year Established: 1987
Published: Mthly
Published Other: Bilingual Monthly Review
Avg Paid Circ: 65
Avg Free Circ: 35
Audit By: Sworn/Estimate/Non-Audited
Audit Date: 12.07.2019
Personnel: Paul Kotrotsios (Adv. Mgr.); Linda Kotrotsios (Circ. Mgr.); Aphrodite Kotrotsios (CO-Publisher)

IMPERIAL

PROSVETA

Street address 1: 247 W Allegheny Rd
Street address city: Imperial
State: PA
Zip/Postal code: 15126-9786
County: Allegheny
Country: USA
Mailing address: 247 W Allegheny Rd
Mailing city: Imperial
Mailing state: PA
Mailing zip: 15126-9786
General Phone: (724) 695-1100
General Fax: (724) 695-1555
General/National Adv. E-mail: snpj@snpj.com
Primary Website: www.snpj.org
Published Other: Every other Wed
Avg Paid Circ: 50000
Audit By: Sworn/Estimate/Non-Audited
Audit Date: 12.07.2019
Personnel: Jay Sedmak (Prodn. Mgr.); Kim Gonzalez (Assoc. Ed.)

MCMURRAY

NARODNE NOVINY

Street address 1: 351 Valley Brook Rd
Street address city: McMurray
State: PA
Zip/Postal code: 15317-3337
County: Washington
Country: USA
Mailing address: 351 Valley Brook Rd
Mailing city: McMurray
Mailing state: PA
Mailing zip: 15317-3337
General Phone: (724) 731-0094
General Fax: (724) 731-0145
General/National Adv. E-mail: info@nsslife.org
Primary Website: www.nsslife.org
Published: Mthly
Avg Free Circ: 12000
Audit By: Sworn/Estimate/Non-Audited
Audit Date: 12.07.2019
Personnel: David Blazek (Circ. Mgr.); Lori Crawley (Prodn. Mgr.)

MIDDLETOWN

JEDNOTA

Street address 1: 1001 Rosedale Ave
Street address city: Middletown
State: PA
Zip/Postal code: 17057-4835
County: Dauphin
Country: USA
Mailing address: 1001 Rosedale Ave
Mailing city: Middletown
Mailing state: PA
Mailing zip: 17057-4835
General Phone: (717) 944-0461
General Fax: (717) 944-3107
Editorial e-mail: editorjednota@yahoo.com
Primary Website: www.fcsu.com
Published Other: Every other Wed
Avg Paid Circ: 500
Avg Free Circ: 16000
Audit By: Sworn/Estimate/Non-Audited
Audit Date: 12.07.2019
Personnel: Andrew Rajec (Pub.); Anthony X. Sutherland (Ed.)

ORELAND

IRISH EDITION, INC.

Street address 1: 1506 Walnut Ave
Street address city: Oreland
State: PA
Zip/Postal code: 19075-1714
County: Montgomery
Country: USA
Mailing address: 1506 Walnut Ave
Mailing city: Oreland
Mailing state: PA
Mailing zip: 19075
General Phone: (215) 886-4900
Advertising Phone: (215) 886-4900
Editorial Phone: (215) 886-4900
General/National Adv. E-mail: info@irishedition.com
Display Adv. E-mail: ads@irishedition.com
Editorial e-mail: info@irishedition.com
Primary Website: www.irishedition.com
Year Established: 1981
Published: Mthly
Avg Paid Circ: 15000
Audit By: Sworn/Estimate/Non-Audited
Audit Date: 12.07.2019
Personnel: A.R. Byrne (Pub.); Jane M. Duffin (Ed.)

PHILADELPHIA

THE TIMES

Street address 1: 170 S Independence Mall W
Street address 2: Ste 718E
Street address city: Philadelphia
State: PA
Zip/Postal code: 19106-3302
County: Philadelphia
Country: USA
Mailing address: 601 Walnut Street Suite 718E
Mailing city: Philadelphia
Mailing state: PA
Mailing zip: 19106
General Phone: (215) 592-1713
General Fax: (215) 592-9152
General/National Adv. E-mail: info@sonsofitalypa.org
Primary Website: www.sonsofitalypa.org
Year Established: 1905
Published: Bi-Mthly
Avg Paid Circ: 15000
Audit By: Sworn/Estimate/Non-Audited
Audit Date: 12.07.2019
Personnel: Michael Paolucci (Executive Director)

PILGRIM GARDENS

EL HISPANO

Street address 1: PO Box 396
Street address city: Pilgrim Gardens
State: PA
Zip/Postal code: 19026-0396
County: Delaware
Country: USA
Mailing address: PO Box 396
Mailing city: Pilgrim Gardens
Mailing state: PA
Mailing zip: 19026-0396
General Phone: (484) 472-6059
General Fax: (484) 472-8153
Advertising Phone: 484 4726059
Advertising Fax: 484 4728153
Editorial Phone: 484 4726059
Editorial Fax: 484 4728153
General/National Adv. E-mail: hispads@aol.com
Primary Website: www.el-hispano.com
Year Established: 1976
Published: Thur
Avg Free Circ: 16390
Audit By: Sworn/Estimate/Non-Audited
Audit Date: 12.07.2019
Personnel: Sara Lopez (Co-pub.); Madelyn Madary (Ad. Director); Phillip Madary (Marketing Director)

PITTSBURGH

ZAJEDNICAR

Street address 1: 100 Delaney Dr
Street address city: Pittsburgh
State: PA
Zip/Postal code: 15235-5416
County: Allegheny
Country: USA
Mailing address: 100 Delaney Dr
Mailing city: Pittsburgh
Mailing state: PA
Mailing zip: 15235-5416
General Phone: (412) 351-3909
General Fax: (412) 823-1594
Editorial e-mail: editor@croatianfraternalunion.org
Primary Website: www.croatianfraternalunion.org
Published: Wed
Avg Free Circ: 36000
Audit By: Sworn/Estimate/Non-Audited
Audit Date: 12.07.2019
Personnel: Lauren Turkall (Prodn. Mgr.); Ivan Begg (Prodn. Mgr.)

SCRANTON

STRAZ

Street address 1: 1006 Pittston Ave
Street address city: Scranton
State: PA
Zip/Postal code: 18505-4109
County: Lackawanna
Country: USA
Mailing address: 1006 Pittston Ave
Mailing city: Scranton
Mailing state: PA
Mailing zip: 18505-4109
General Phone: (570) 344-1513
General Fax: (570) 961-5961
General/National Adv. E-mail: straz@pnu.org
Primary Website: www.pnu.org
Published: Mthly
Personnel: Irene Jugan (Ed.)
State: South Carolina

SOUTH CAROLINA

MOUNT PLEASANT

EL INFORMADOR NEWSPAPER

Street address 1: 222 W Coleman Blvd
Street address 2: Suite 111
Street address city: Mount Pleasant
State: SC
Zip/Postal code: 29464
County: Charleston
Country: EEUU
General Phone: 843-817-2896
Advertising Phone: 843-817-2896
Editorial Phone: 843-817-2896
Editorial Fax: 843-352-4506
General/National Adv. E-mail: pedro@elinformador.us
Display Adv. E-mail: pedro@elinformador.us
Editorial e-mail: pedro@elinformador.us
Primary Website: https://www.elinformador.us/
Mthly Avg Views: 90000
Mthly Avg Unique Visitors: 7000
Year Established: 2008
Published: Wed
Audit By: CVC
Personnel: Lisa De Armas (Administration)
State: South Dakota

SOUTH DAKOTA

WILMOT

SISSETON-WAHPETON SIOUX TRIBE

Street address 1: PO Box 5
Street address city: Wilmot
State: SD
Zip/Postal code: 57279-0005
County: Roberts
Country: USA
Mailing address: PO Box 5
Mailing city: Wilmot
Mailing state: SD
Mailing zip: 57279-0005
General Phone: (605) 938-4452
General Fax: (605) 938-4676
General/National Adv. E-mail: earthskyweb@cs.com
Primary Website: www.earthskyweb.com/sota.html
Year Established: 1968
Published: Wed
Avg Paid Circ: 4088
Avg Free Circ: 0
Audit By: VAC
Audit Date: 30.09.2016
Personnel: Charles D. Floro (Prodn. Mgr.)
State: Texas

TEXAS

HOUSTON

INDO AMERICAN NEWS

Street address 1: 7457 Harwin Dr
Street address 2: Ste 262
Street address city: Houston
State: TX

Zip/Postal code: 77036-2025
County: Harris
Country: USA
Mailing address: 7457 Harwin Dr Ste 262
Mailing city: Houston
Mailing state: TX
Mailing zip: 77036-2025
Primary Website: www.indoamerican-news.com
Year Established: 1982
Published: Fri
Avg Paid Circ: 0
Avg Free Circ: 6952
Audit By: CVC
Audit Date: 30.03.2018
Personnel: Jawahar Malhotra

LA PRENSA DE HOUSTON

Street address 1: 7100 Regency Square Blvd. Ste 217
Street address city: Houston
State: TX
Zip/Postal code: 77036
County: Harris
Country: United States
General Phone: 713-334-4959
Advertising Phone: 713-334-4959
Editorial Phone: 713-334-4959
General/National Adv. E-mail: ecastro@prensadehouston.com
Display Adv. E-mail: info@prensadehouston.com
Classified Adv. e-mail: ecastro@prensadehouston.com
Editorial e-mail: editorial@prensadehouston.com
Primary Website: https://prensadehouston.com/
Year Established: 2001
Published: Sun
Avg Free Circ: 106000
Sun. Circulation Free: 106000
Personnel: Evelyn Castro (Vice President)

SOUTHERN CHINESE DAILY NEWS

Street address 1: 11122 Bellaire Blvd
Street address city: Houston
State: TX
Zip/Postal code: 77072-2608
County: Harris
Country: USA
Mailing address: 11122 Bellaire Blvd
Mailing city: Houston
Mailing state: TX
Mailing zip: 77072-2608
General Phone: (281) 498-4310
General Fax: (281) 498-2728
Primary Website: www.scdaily.com
Year Established: 1979
Published: Mon`Tues`Wed`Thur`Fri`Sat`Sun
Published Other: Daily
Avg Free Circ: 4075
Audit By: CVC
Audit Date: 19.06.2018
Personnel: Jennifer Lopez; Jean Lin (Pub. Asst.); Sandy Lee (Pub.); Feelie Wan (Adv.); Nicole Chiu (Class.)

U.S. ASIA NEWS

Street address 1: 11122 Bellaire Blvd
Street address city: Houston
State: TX
Zip/Postal code: 77072-2608
County: Harris
Country: USA
Mailing address: 11122 Bellaire Blvd
Mailing city: Houston
Mailing state: TX
Mailing zip: 77072-2608
General Phone: (281) 498-4310
General Fax: (281) 498-2724
General/National Adv. E-mail: wealee@scdaily.com
Primary Website: www.scdaily.com
Published: Mthly
Avg Paid Circ: 25000
Audit By: Sworn/Estimate/Non-Audited
Audit Date: 12.07.2019
Personnel: Emerson Chu (Gen. Mgr.)

VOICE OF ASIA

Street address 1: 6200 Highway 6 S
Street address 2: Ste 225
Street address city: Houston
State: TX
Zip/Postal code: 77083-1539
County: Harris
Country: USA
Mailing address: 8303 Southwest Fwy Ste 325
Mailing city: Houston
Mailing state: TX
Mailing zip: 77074-1621
General Phone: (713) 774-5140
General/National Adv. E-mail: voiceasia@aol.com
Display Adv. E-mail: ads@voiceofasiagroup.com
Editorial e-mail: koshyvoa@aol.com
Primary Website: www.voiceofasiaonline.com
Year Established: 1987
Published: Fri
Avg Paid Circ: 0
Avg Free Circ: 9900
Audit By: CVC
Audit Date: 30.06.2018
Personnel: Koshy Thomas (Publisher)
State: Virginia

VIRGINIA

HAYMARKET

ASIAN FORTUNE

Street address 1: PO Box 578
Street address city: Haymarket
State: VA
Zip/Postal code: 20168-0578
County: Prince William
Country: USA
Mailing address: 8070 Criaza Branch Ct
Mailing city: Vienna
Mailing state: VA
Mailing zip: 22182-4056
General Phone: (703) 753-8295
General/National Adv. E-mail: info@asianfortune.com
Primary Website: www.asianfortunenews.com
Published: Mthly
Avg Paid Circ: 1000
Avg Free Circ: 30000
Audit By: Sworn/Estimate/Non-Audited
Audit Date: 12.07.2019
Personnel: Jay Chen (Pres.); Jizeng Chen (Adv. Mgr.); Jennie Ilustre (Ed.)
State: Washington

WASHINGTON

LYNDEN

THE WINDMILL HERALD

Street address 1: PO Box 313
Street address city: Lynden
State: WA
Zip/Postal code: 98264-0313
County: Whatcom
Country: USA
Mailing address: PO Box 313
Mailing city: Lynden
Mailing state: WA
Mailing zip: 98264-0313
General Phone: (604) 532-1733
General Fax: (604) 532-1734
General/National Adv. E-mail: windmill@godutch.com
Primary Website: www.godutch.com
Published Other: 2 x Mthly
Avg Paid Circ: 10400
Audit By: Sworn/Estimate/Non-Audited
Audit Date: 12.07.2019

RAYMOND

GAUGER MEDIA SERVICE, INC.

Street address 1: 1034 Bradford Street
Street address 2: P.O. Box 627
Street address city: Raymond
State: WA
Zip/Postal code: 98577
County: Pacific
Country: USA
Mailing address: P.O. Box 627
Mailing city: Raymond
Mailing state: WA
Mailing zip: 98577
General Phone: (360) 942-3560
General/National Adv. E-mail: dave@gaugermedia.com
Primary Website: www.gaugermedia.com
Year Established: 1987
Personnel: Dave Gauger (Pres/Broker)

SEATTLE

NORTHWEST ASIAN WEEKLY

Street address 1: 412 Maynard Ave S
Street address city: Seattle
State: WA
Zip/Postal code: 98104-2917
County: King
Country: USA
Mailing address: PO Box 3468
Mailing city: Seattle
Mailing state: WA
Mailing zip: 98114-3468
General Phone: (206) 223-5559
General Fax: (206) 223-0626
General/National Adv. E-mail: info@nwasianweekly.com
Primary Website: www.nwasianweekly.com
Year Established: 1982
Published: Thur
Avg Paid Circ: 2000
Avg Free Circ: 14000
Audit By: Sworn/Estimate/Non-Audited
Audit Date: 12.07.2019
Personnel: Assunta Ng (Pub.); Rebecca Yip (Adv. Mgr.); George Liu (Circ. Mgr.)

NORTHWEST VIETNAMESE NEWS

Street address 1: 6951 Martin Luther King Jr Way S
Street address 2: Ste 205
Street address city: Seattle
State: WA
Zip/Postal code: 98118-354
County: King
Country: USA
Mailing address: 6951 Martin Luther King Jr Way S Ste 205
Mailing city: Seattle
Mailing state: WA
Mailing zip: 98118-3545
General Phone: (206) 722-6984
Primary Website: www.nvnorthwest.com

NORWEGIAN AMERICAN WEEKLY

Street address 1: 7301 5th Ave NE
Street address 2: Ste A
Street address city: Seattle
State: WA
Zip/Postal code: 98115-8601
County: King
Country: USA
Mailing address: 7301 5th Ave NE Ste A
Mailing city: Seattle
Mailing state: WA
Mailing zip: 98115-8601
General Phone: (206) 784-4617
General/National Adv. E-mail: naw@na-weekly.com
Display Adv. E-mail: evan@na-weekly.com
Editorial e-mail: emily@na-weekly.com
Primary Website: www.na-weekly.com
Year Established: 1889
Published: Fri
Avg Paid Circ: 3500
Audit By: Sworn/Estimate/Non-Audited
Audit Date: 12.07.2019
Personnel: Emily Skaftun (Editor-in-chief); Molly Jones (Ed. Asst.); Evan Deam (Adv. Mgr.)

SEATTLE CHINESE POST

Street address 1: 412 Maynard Ave S
Street address city: Seattle
State: WA
Zip/Postal code: 98104-2917
County: King
Country: USA
Mailing address: 412 Maynard Ave S
Mailing city: Seattle
Mailing state: WA
Mailing zip: 98104-2917
General Phone: (206) 223-0623
General Fax: (206) 223-0626
General/National Adv. E-mail: info@nwasianweekly.com
Primary Website: www.nwasianweekly.com
Published: Thur
Avg Paid Circ: 5000
Avg Free Circ: 1000
Audit By: Sworn/Estimate/Non-Audited
Audit Date: 12.07.2019
Personnel: Assunta Ng (Pub.); Han Bui (Layout & Web Ed.); Ruth Bayang (Ed.)

THE NORTH AMERICAN POST (HOKUBEI HOCHI)

Street address 1: 519 6th Ave S
Street address 2: Ste 200
Street address city: Seattle
State: WA
Zip/Postal code: 98104-2878
County: King
Country: USA
Mailing address: PO Box 3173
Mailing city: Seattle
Mailing state: WA
Mailing zip: 98114-3173
General Phone: (206) 623-0100
General Fax:
General/National Adv. E-mail: info@napost.com
Display Adv. E-mail: business@napost.com
Classified Adv. e-mail: community@napost.com
Editorial e-mail: editor@napost.com
Primary Website: www.napost.com
Year Established: 1902
Published: Thur
Avg Free Circ: 5000
Audit By: Sworn/Estimate/Non-Audited
Audit Date: 28.09.2022
Personnel: Tomio Moriguchi (Pub.); David Yamaguchi (Editor); Shihou Sasaki (Editor); Ako Mizoe (Sales Representative); Hikari Kono (Editor, Japanese section); Shigeki Kajita (General Manager); Miwa Watanabe (Designer)
State: Wisconsin

WISCONSIN

KESHENA

MENOMINEE NATION NEWS

Street address 1: PO Box 910
Street address city: Keshena
State: WI
Zip/Postal code: 54135-0910
County: Menominee
Country: USA
Mailing address: P.O. Box 910
Mailing city: Keshena
Mailing state: WI
Mailing zip: 54135
General Phone: (715) 799-5167
General Fax: (715) 799-5250
General/National Adv. E-mail: derdmann@mitw.org
Display Adv. E-mail: mnnads@mitw.org
Editorial e-mail: DErdmann@mitw.org
Primary Website: https://www.menominee-nsn.gov
Year Established: 1976
Published: Bi-Mthly
Avg Paid Circ: 1300
Audit By: Sworn/Estimate/Non-Audited
Audit Date: 12.07.2019
Personnel: Devan Erdmann (Ed.)
Parent company (for newspapers): Menominee Indian Tribe of Wisconsin

LAC DU FLAMBEAU

OUR VOICE NEWSPAPER

Street address 1: 602 Peacepipe Rd
Street address city: Lac Du Flambeau
State: WI
Zip/Postal code: 54538
County: Vilas
Country: USA
Mailing address: PO Box 67
Mailing city: Lac Du Flambeau
Mailing state: WI
Mailing zip: 54538-0067
General Phone: (715) 588-3303
General Fax: (715) 588-7930
General/National Adv. E-mail: info@ldftribe.com
Primary Website: www.ldftribe.com
Published: Mthly
Avg Paid Circ: 300
Avg Free Circ: 10000
Audit By: Sworn/Estimate/Non-Audited
Audit Date: 12.07.2019
Personnel: Abbey Thompson (Adv. Sales); Greg Johnson (Ed.)

MILWAUKEE

ITALIAN TIMES

Street address 1: 631 E Chicago St
Street address city: Milwaukee
State: WI
Zip/Postal code: 53202-5914
County: Milwaukee
Country: USA
Mailing address: 631 E Chicago St
Mailing city: Milwaukee
Mailing state: WI
Mailing zip: 53202-5916
General Phone: (414) 223-2180
General Fax: (414) 223-2187
Advertising Phone: (414) 223-2189
Advertising Fax: (414) 223-2187
Editorial Phone: (414) 223-2189
Editorial Fax: (414) 223-2187
General/National Adv. E-mail: themman@italiancc.org
Display Adv. E-mail: themman@italiancc.org
Editorial e-mail: themman@italiancc.org
Primary Website: www.ICCMilwaukee.com
Year Established: 1979
Avg Paid Circ: 12000
Audit By: Sworn/Estimate/Non-Audited
Audit Date: 12.07.2019
Personnel: Thomas Hemman (Editor); Patrick Morgan (Gen. Mgr.)

STEVENS POINT

GWIAZDA POLARNA

Street address 1: 2804 Post Rd
Street address city: Stevens Point
State: WI
Zip/Postal code: 54481-6415
County: Portage
Country: USA
Mailing address: 2804 Post Rd
Mailing city: Stevens Point
Mailing state: WI
Mailing zip: 54481-6415
General Phone: (715) 345-0744
General Fax: (715) 345-1913
General/National Adv. E-mail: pointpub@sbcglobal.net
Primary Website: www.gwiazda-polarna.com
Published Other: Every other Sat
Avg Paid Circ: 4632
Audit By: Sworn/Estimate/Non-Audited
Audit Date: 12.07.2019
Personnel: Monica Pawlack (Pub.); Jacek Hilgier (Ed. in Chief); Jerry Stolarek (Ed.)

LGBTQ NEWSPAPERS IN THE U.S.

CALIFORNIA

SAN DIEGO

GAY SAN DIEGO

Street address 1: 444 Camino del Rio South #102
Street address 3: San Diego
Street address state: CA
Zip/Postal code: 92108
County: San Diego
Country: USA
Mailing address: 444 Camino del Rio South #102
Mailing city: San Diego
Mailing state: CA
Mailing zip: 92108
General Phone: (619) 519-7775
General/National Adv. E-mail: david@sdcnn.com
Display Adv. E-mail: mike@sdcnn.com
Editorial e-mail: albert@sdcnn.com
Primary Website: gay-sd.com
Year Established: 2010
Delivery Methods: Mail`Carrier`Racks
Area Served - City: San Diego County
Advertising (Open Inch Rate) Weekday/Saturday: $80 (smallest modular rate)
Mechanical specifications: Type page 10" x 14.58"; 5 cols
Published: Fri
Published Other: biweekly, every other Friday
Avg Paid Circ: 25
Avg Free Circ: 12533
Audit By: CVC
Audit Date: 12/31/2016
Classified Equipment»
Parent company (for newspapers): San Diego Community News Netwrok

SAN FRANCISCO

BAY AREA REPORTER

Street address 1: 44 Gough St.
Street address 2: #204
Street address 3: San Francisco
Street address state: CA
Zip/Postal code: 94103
County: San Francisco
Country: USA
Mailing address: 44 Gough St. #204
Mailing city: San Francisco
Mailing state: CA
Mailing zip: 94103
General Phone: (415) 861-5019
General Fax: (415) 861-8144
General/National Adv. E-mail: information@ebar.com
Primary Website: www.ebar.com
Year Established: 1971
Advertising (Open Inch Rate) Weekday/Saturday: Open inch rate $26.50
Mechanical specifications: Type page 10 x 16; E - 5 cols, 1 7/8, 1/8 between; A - 5 cols, 1 7/8, 1/8 between; C - 5 cols, 1 7/8, 1/8 between.
Published: Thur
Avg Paid Circ: 47
Avg Free Circ: 26163
Audit By: VAC
Audit Date: 5/31/2017
Classified Equipment»
Personnel: Michael Yamashita (Pub.); Robert Friedman (Arts Ed.); Cynthia Laird (Ed.); Colleen Small Bogitini (Adv./Admin.); Scott Wazlowski

COLORADO

DENVER

OUT FRONT

Street address 1: 3535 Walnut St
Street address 3: Denver
Street address state: CO
Zip/Postal code: 80205-2433
County: Denver
Country: USA
General Phone: (303) 477-4000
General Fax: 303-325-2642
General/National Adv. E-mail: info@outfrontonline.com
Display Adv. E-mail: advertising@outfrontonline.com
Editorial e-mail: editorial@outfrontonline.com
Primary Website: http://www.outfrontonline.com/
Year Established: 1976
Delivery Methods: Mail`Racks
Published: Wed
Published Other: First & Third Wednesdays
Avg Paid Circ: 1000
Avg Free Circ: 20000
Audit By: Sworn/Estimate/Non-Audited
Audit Date: 7/12/2019
Classified Equipment»
Personnel: Jerry Cunningham (Pub.); Berlin Sylvestre (Ed.); Colby Brumit (Art Dir.); Jay Duque (Marketing); Dustin Krier (Sales); Jordan Jacobs (Sales); Ryan King (Associate Pub.)

DISTRICT OF COLUMBIA

WASHINGTON

WASHINGTON BLADE

Street address 1: 1712 14th St NW
Street address 3: Washington
Street address state: DC
Zip/Postal code: 20009-5070
County: District Of Columbia
Country: USA
General Phone: (202) 747-2077
General Fax: (202) 747-2070
General/National Adv. E-mail: info@washblade.com
Display Adv. E-mail: lbrown@washblade.com
Editorial e-mail: knaff@washblade.com
Primary Website: www.washblade.com
Year Established: 1969
Own Printing Facility: Y
Mechanical specifications: Type page 9 3/4 x 11 1/2; E - 4 cols, 2 1/4, 1/6 between; A - 4 cols, 2 1/4, 1/6 between; C - 4 cols, 2 1/4, 1/6 between.
Audit By: Sworn/Estimate/Non-Audited
Audit Date: 7/12/2019
Classified Equipment»
Personnel: Scott Gartey (Circ. Mgr.); Kevin Naff (Editor); Rob Boeger (Art Dir.); Michael Key; Lynn Brown (Publisher); Lou Chibbaro (Sr. News Editor); Stephen Rutgers (Dir Sales & Mktg); Phillip G Rockstroh (Classified Advertising)

FLORIDA

ORLANDO

WATERMARK MEDIA

Street address 1: 414 N Ferncreek Ave
Street address 3: Orlando
Street address state: FL
Zip/Postal code: 32803-5432
County: Orange
Country: USA
Mailing address: PO Box 533655
Mailing city: Orlando
Mailing state: FL
Mailing zip: 32853-3655
General Phone: (407) 481-2243
General Fax: (407) 481-2246
General/National Adv. E-mail: editor@watermarkonline.com; sales@watermarkonline.com
Primary Website: www.watermarkonline.com
Year Established: 1994
Published: Thur
Published Other: Every other Thur
Avg Free Circ: 20000
Audit By: Sworn/Estimate/Non-Audited
Audit Date: 7/12/2019
Classified Equipment»
Personnel: Tom Dyer (Pub.); Rick Claggett (CFO); Don Williams (Sales Acct. Mgr.); Steve Blanchard (Ed.)

WILTON MANORS

SOUTH FLORIDA GAY NEWS

Street address 1: 2520 N Dixie Hwy
Street address 3: Wilton Manors
Street address state: FL
Zip/Postal code: 33305-1247
County: Broward
Country: USA
Mailing address: 2520 N Dixie Hwy
Mailing city: Wilton Manors
Mailing state: FL
Mailing zip: 33305-1247
General Phone: 954-530-4970
General Fax: 954-530-7943
Primary Website: www.southfloridagaynews.com
Year Established: 2010
Published: Wed
Avg Paid Circ: 0
Avg Free Circ: 10
Audit By: Sworn/Estimate/Non-Audited
Audit Date: 7/12/2019
Classified Equipment»
Personnel: Norm Kent (Publisher)

ILLINOIS

CHICAGO

BLACK LINES

Street address 1: 5315 N Clark St
Street address 2: Ste 192
Street address 3: Chicago
Street address state: IL
Zip/Postal code: 60640-2290
County: Cook
Country: USA
Mailing address: 5315 N Clark St Ste 192
Mailing city: Chicago
Mailing state: IL
Mailing zip: 60640-2290
General Phone: (773) 871-7610
General Fax: (773) 871-7609
Editorial e-mail: editor@windycitymediagroup.com
Primary Website: www.windycitymediagroup.com
Commercial printers: Y
Mechanical specifications: Type page 8 x 10 1/2.
Audit By: Sworn/Estimate/Non-Audited
Audit Date: 7/12/2019
Classified Equipment»
Personnel: Rob Olson (Office Mgr.); Terri Klinsky (Adv. Mgr.); Tracy Baim (Ed.)

EN LA VIDA

Street address 1: 5443 N Broadway St
Street address 2: Ste 101
Street address 3: Chicago
Street address state: IL
Zip/Postal code: 60640-1703
County: Cook
Country: USA
Mailing address: 5443 N Broadway St Ste 101
Mailing city: Chicago
Mailing state: IL
Mailing zip: 60640-1703
General Phone: (773) 871-7610
General Fax: (773) 871-7609
Editorial e-mail: editor@windycitymediagroup.com
Primary Website: www.windycitymediagroup.com
Mechanical specifications: Type page 8 x 10 1/2.
Audit By: Sworn/Estimate/Non-Audited
Audit Date: 7/12/2019
Classified Equipment»
Personnel: Tracy Baim (Ed.)

NIGHTSPOTS

Street address 1: 5315 N Clark St
Street address 2: Ste 192
Street address 3: Chicago
Street address state: IL
Zip/Postal code: 60640-2290
County: Cook
Country: USA
Mailing address: 5315 N Clark St Ste 192
Mailing city: Chicago
Mailing state: IL
Mailing zip: 60640-2290
General Phone: (773) 871-7610
General Fax: (773) 871-7609
General/National Adv. E-mail: nightspots@windycitymediagroup.com
Display Adv. E-mail: advertising@windycitymediagroup.com
Editorial e-mail: nightspots@windycitymediagroup.com
Primary Website: www.windycitymediagroup.com
Year Established: 1990
Mechanical specifications: Type page 5 1/2 x 8.
Published: Wed
Avg Free Circ: 5000
Audit By: Sworn/Estimate/Non-Audited
Audit Date: 7/12/2019
Classified Equipment»
Personnel: Tracy Baim (Pub.); Kirk Williamson (Mng. Ed.)

WINDY CITY TIMES

Street address 1: 5315 N Clark St
Street address 2: Ste 192
Street address 3: Chicago
Street address state: IL
Zip/Postal code: 60640-2290
County: Cook
Country: USA
Mailing address: 5315 N Clark St Ste 192
Mailing city: Chicago
Mailing state: IL
Mailing zip: 60640-2290
General Phone: (773) 871-7610
General Fax: (773) 871-7609
General/National Adv. E-mail: publisher@windycitymediagroup.com
Display Adv. E-mail: advertising@windycitymediagroup.com

Editorial e-mail: editor@windycitymediagroup.com; calendar@windycitymediagroup.com; theater@windycitymediagroup.com; graphics@windycitymediagroup.com
Primary Website: www.windycitymediagroup.com
Year Established: 1985
Delivery Methods: Racks
Area Served - City: Chicago and Cook County, including 60640, 60613, 60660, 60614, 60616, etc.
Mechanical specifications: Type page 10 inch x 10 inch full page
Published: Wed
Published Other: Daily online
Avg Paid Circ: 0
Avg Free Circ: 10000
Audit By: Sworn/Estimate/Non-Audited
Audit Date: 7/12/2019
Classified Equipment»
Personnel: Terri Klinsky (Adv. Pub.); Jean Albright (Circ. Dir.); Tracy Baim (Publisher, Exec. Ed.); Andrew Davis (Mng. Ed)

MASSACHUSETTS

NANTUCKET

BAY WINDOWS

Street address 1: 13 Maclean Lane
Street address 3: Nantucket
Street address state: MA
Zip/Postal code: 02554
County: Suffolk
Country: USA
Mailing address: PO Box 13
Mailing city: Boston
Mailing state: MA
Mailing zip: 02127
General Phone: 617-464-7280
Advertising Phone: 617-974-8078
General/National Adv. E-mail: jcoakley@baywindows.com
Display Adv. E-mail: jcoakley@baywindows.com
Classified Adv. E-mail: jcoakley@baywindows.com
Editorial e-mail: sue.baywindows@gmail.com
Primary Website: www.baywindows.com
Year Established: 1983
Delivery Methods: Mail`Racks
Area Served - City: New England
Advertising (Open Inch Rate) Weekday/Saturday: Open inch rate $14.75
Mechanical specifications: Type page 10 x 12.75
Published: Thur`Other
Published Other: Bi-Weekly
Avg Paid Circ: 125
Avg Free Circ: 20000
Audit By: Sworn/Estimate/Non-Audited
Audit Date: 9/28/2022
Classified Equipment»
Personnel: Jeff Coakley (Co-Pub.); Sue O'Connell (Co-Pub.)

MICHIGAN

LIVONIA

BETWEEN THE LINES

Street address 1: 11920 Farmington Rd
Street address 3: Livonia
Street address state: MI
Zip/Postal code: 48150-1724
County: Wayne
Country: USA
Mailing address: 20222 Farmington Rd
Mailing city: Livonia
Mailing state: MI
Mailing zip: 48152-1412
General Phone: (734) 293-7200
General Fax: (734) 293-7201
General/National Adv. E-mail: info@pridesource.com
Display Adv. E-mail: sales@pridesource.com
Editorial e-mail: editor@pridesource.com; editor@pridesource.com
Primary Website: www.pridesource.com
Year Established: 1993
Delivery Methods: Racks
Area Served - City: 48150
Own Printing Facility: N
Commercial printers: Y
Advertising (Open Inch Rate) Weekday/Saturday: Open inch rate $95.00
Published: Thur
Avg Free Circ: 17000
Audit By: Sworn/Estimate/Non-Audited
Audit Date: 7/12/2019
Classified Equipment»
Personnel: Susan Horowitz (Publisher/Editor in Chief); Jan Stevenson (Adv. Dir.); Chris Azzopardi (Entertainment Ed.); Kevin Bryant (Webmaster/IT Mgr.)
Parent company (for newspapers): Pride Source Media Group

MINNESOTA

EDINA

LAVENDER

Street address 1: 5100 Eden Ave
Street address 2: Ste 107
Street address 3: Edina
Street address state: MN
Zip/Postal code: 55436
County: Hennepin
Country: USA
General Phone: (612) 436-4660
General/National Adv. E-mail: info@lavendermagazine.com
Primary Website: www.lavendermagazine.com
Mechanical specifications: Type page 8 1/16 x 10 5/16; E - 3 cols, 2 1/4, 1/8 between; A - 3 cols, 2 1/4, 1/8 between; C - 4 cols, 1 5/6, 1/8 between.
Audit By: Sworn/Estimate/Non-Audited
Audit Date: 7/12/2019
Classified Equipment»
Personnel: Stephen J. Rocheford (President and CEO); Barry Leavitt (Adv. Sales Dir.); Stephen Boatner (Mng. Ed.)

NORTH CAROLINA

CHARLOTTE

Q NOTES

Street address 1: 920 Central Ave
Street address 3: Charlotte
Street address state: NC
Zip/Postal code: 28204-2028
County: Mecklenburg
Country: USA
Mailing address: PO Box 221841
Mailing city: Charlotte
Mailing state: NC
Mailing zip: 28222-1841
General Phone: (704) 531-9988
General Fax: (704) 531-1361
General/National Adv. E-mail: info@goqnotes.com
Editorial e-mail: editor@goqnotes.com
Primary Website: goqnotes.com
Year Established: 1986
Delivery Methods: Mail`Newsstand`Carrier`Racks
Area Served - City: Most of NC & part of SC
Advertising (Open Inch Rate) Weekday/Saturday: Open inch rate $7.00
Mechanical specifications: Type page 10 1/4 x 12 1/4; E - 4 cols, 2 3/8, 3/16 between; A - 4 cols, 2 3/8, 3/16 between; C - 4 cols, 2 3/8, 3/16 between.
Published: Sat
Avg Free Circ: 9000
Audit By: Sworn/Estimate/Non-Audited
Audit Date: 7/12/2019
Classified Equipment»
Personnel: Jim Yarbrough (Pub.); Matt Comer (Ed.); Lainey Millen (Prodn. Mgr.)

NEW YORK

NEW YORK

GAY CITY NEWS

Street address 1: 515 Canal St
Street address 3: New York
Street address state: NY
Zip/Postal code: 10013-1330
County: New York
Country: USA
Mailing address: 515 Canal St Fl 1
Mailing city: New York
Mailing state: NY
Mailing zip: 10013-1330
General Phone: 212-229-1890
General Fax: 2152-229-2790
General/National Adv. E-mail: editor@gaycitynews.com
Display Adv. E-mail: ads@communitymediallc.com
Primary Website: www.gaycitynews.com
Year Established: 2002
Delivery Methods: Racks
Area Served - City: 10013, 10024, 10009, 10014
Mechanical specifications: Type page 10 x 14; E - 4 cols, 2 1/4, between; A - 6 cols, 2 1/2, between; C - 6 cols, 1 1/2, between.
Published: Thur
Avg Free Circ: 47000
Audit By: Sworn/Estimate/Non-Audited
Audit Date: 7/12/2019
Classified Equipment»
Personnel: Jennifer Goodstein (Publisher); Troy Masters (Assoc. Pub.); Paul Schindler (Ed. in Chief)
Parent company (for newspapers): NYC Community Media, LLC

ROCHESTER

GAY ALLIANCE

Street address 1: 100 College Ave
Street address 2: Ste 100
Street address 3: Rochester
Street address state: NY
Zip/Postal code: 14607-1073
County: Monroe
Country: United States
Mailing address: 100 College Ave
Mailing city: Rochester
Mailing state: NY
Mailing zip: 14607
General Phone: 5852448640
General Fax: (585) 244-8246
Advertising Phone: 5852448640
Editorail Phone: 5852448640
General/National Adv. E-mail: jeffreym@gayalliance.org
Display Adv. E-mail: jeffm@gayalliance.org
Editorial e-mail: jeffm@gayalliance.org
Primary Website: www.gayalliance.org
Year Established: 1971
Delivery Methods: Mail`Racks
Commercial printers: Y
Mechanical specifications: Type page 10 x 15; E - 4 cols, 2 1/4, between; A - 4 cols, 2 1/4, between; C - 5 cols, 2, between.
Published: Mthly
Avg Paid Circ: 680
Avg Free Circ: 5500
Audit By: Sworn/Estimate/Non-Audited
Audit Date: 7/12/2019
Classified Equipment»
Personnel: Susan Jordan (Ed.); Jim Anderson (Graphic Designer); Jeff Myers
Parent company (for newspapers): Gay Alliance of the Genesee Valley

OHIO

COLUMBUS

STONEWALL COLUMBUS

Street address 1: 1160 N High St
Street address 3: Columbus
Street address state: OH
Zip/Postal code: 43201-2411
County: Franklin
Country: USA
Mailing address: 1160 N High St
Mailing city: Columbus
Mailing state: OH
Mailing zip: 43201-2411
General Phone: (614) 299-7764
General Fax: (614) 299-4408
Advertising Phone: (614) 930-2262
Advertising Fax: (614) 299-4408
Editorail Phone: (614) 930-2264
Editorial Fax: (614) 299-4408
General/National Adv. E-mail: info@stonewallcolumbus.org
Display Adv. E-mail: info@lavenderlistings.com
Editorial e-mail: info@stonewallcolumbus.org
Primary Website: www.stonewallcolumbus.org
Year Established: 1981
Area Served - City: 43201-99 43001-99
Published: Tues
Avg Free Circ: 4000
Audit By: Sworn/Estimate/Non-Audited
Audit Date: 7/12/2019
Classified Equipment»
Personnel: Karla Rothan (Executive Director); Michele Fregonas (Adv. Mgr.); Herman John (Ed.)

PENNSYLVANIA

MIDDLETOWN

CENTRAL VOICE

Street address 1: 20 S Union St
Street address 3: Middletown
Street address state: PA
Zip/Postal code: 17057-1445
County: Dauphin
Country: USA
Mailing address: 20 S Union St
Mailing city: Middletown
Mailing state: PA
Mailing zip: 17110
General Phone: (717) 839-9788
General Fax: (717) 944-2083
General/National Adv. E-mail: frankpizzoli@gmail.com
Display Adv. E-mail: frankpizzoli@gmail.com
Editorial e-mail: frankpizzoli@gmail.com
Primary Website: www.thecentralvoice.com
Year Established: 2003
Delivery Methods: Racks
Published: Bi-Mthly
Audit By: Sworn/Estimate/Non-Audited
Audit Date: 7/12/2019
Classified Equipment»
Personnel: Frank Pizzoli

PHILADELPHIA

PHILADELPHIA GAY NEWS

Street address 1: 505 S 4th St
Street address 3: Philadelphia
Street address state: PA
Zip/Postal code: 19147-1506
County: Philadelphia
Country: USA
Mailing address: 505 S 4th St
Mailing city: Philadelphia
Mailing state: PA
Mailing zip: 19147-1506
General Phone: (215) 625-8501 ext 200

General Fax: (215) 925-6437
Advertising Phone: (215) 625-8501 ext 212
Advertising Fax: (215) 925-6437
Editorail Phone: (215) 625-8501 ext 206
Editorial Fax: (215) 925-6437
General/National Adv. E-mail: pgn@epgn.com
Display Adv. E-mail: prab@epgn.com
Editorial e-mail: jen@epgn.com
Primary Website: www.epgn.com
Year Established: 1976
Delivery Methods: Mail`Racks
Area Served - City: various
Own Printing Facility: Y
Commercial printers: N
Advertising (Open Inch Rate) Weekday/Saturday: NA
Mechanical specifications: 10.125x11.35
Published: Fri
Avg Free Circ: 17000
Audit By: Sworn/Estimate/Non-Audited
Audit Date: 7/12/2019
Classified Equipment»
Personnel: Mark Segal (Pub.); Don Pignolet (Officer Manager); Prab Sandhu (Advertising Manager)

TENNESSEE

NASHVILLE

OUT & ABOUT NASHVILLE

Street address 1: 3951 Moss Rose Dr
Street address 3: Nashville
Street address state: TN
Zip/Postal code: 37216-2925
County: Davidson
Country: USA
Mailing address: 3951 Moss Rose Dr
Mailing city: Nashville
Mailing state: TN
Mailing zip: 37216-2925
General Phone: (615) 596-6210
General Fax: 615-246-2787
General/National Adv. E-mail: sales@outandaboutnashville.com
Display Adv. E-mail: sales@outandaboutnashville.com
Editorial e-mail: editor@outandaboutnashville.com
Primary Website: www.outandaboutnashville.com
Year Established: 2002
Delivery Methods: Mail`Racks
Area Served - City: Nashville
Mechanical specifications: Type page 10 x 11 1/4; E - 4 cols, 2 1/2, 1/4 between.
Published: Mthly
Avg Free Circ: 15000
Audit By: Sworn/Estimate/Non-Audited
Audit Date: 7/12/2019
Classified Equipment»
Personnel: Jerry Jones (Pub.); James Grady (Managing Print Editor); Joe Brant (Managing Digital Editor)
Parent company (for newspapers): Out & About Nashville, Inc

TEXAS

DALLAS

DALLAS VOICE

Street address 1: 4145 Travis St
Street address 2: Fl 3
Street address 3: Dallas
Street address state: TX
Zip/Postal code: 75204-1840
County: Dallas
Country: USA
Mailing address: 4145 Travis St Ste 300
Mailing city: Dallas
Mailing state: TX
Mailing zip: 75204-1830
General Phone: (214) 754-8710
General Fax: (214) 969-7271
General/National Adv. E-mail: editor@dallasvoice.com; advertising@dallasvoice.com
Display Adv. E-mail: advertising@dallasvoice.com
Editorial e-mail: editor@dallasvoice.com; advertising@dallasvoice.com
Primary Website: www.dallasvoice.com
Year Established: 1984
Delivery Methods: Mail`Newsstand
Own Printing Facility: Y
Commercial printers: N
Mechanical specifications: Type page 10 3/8 x 12 1/2; E - 4 cols, between; A - 4 cols, between; C - 5 cols, between.
Published: Fri
Avg Free Circ: 13357
Audit By: Sworn/Estimate/Non-Audited
Audit Date: 7/12/2019
Classified Equipment»
Personnel: Robert Moore (Pub.); Leo Cusimano (Adv. Dir.); Tammey Nish (Ed.); Maryann Ramirez (Circ. Mgr.)

VERMONT

BENSON

OUT IN THE MOUNTAINS

Street address 1: PO Box 287
Street address 3: Benson
Street address state: VT
Zip/Postal code: 05731-0287
County: Rutland
Country: USA
Mailing address: PO Box 287
Mailing city: Benson
Mailing state: VT
Mailing zip: 05731
General Phone: (802) 275-5027
General/National Adv. E-mail: editor@oitm.org
Primary Website: www.oitm.org
Audit By: Sworn/Estimate/Non-Audited
Audit Date: 7/12/2019
Classified Equipment»
Personnel: John Fedor-Cunningham; Gabe Christian

WASHINGTON

RAYMOND

GAUGER MEDIA SERVICE, INC.

Street address 1: 1034 Bradford Street
Street address 2: P.O. Box 627
Street address 3: Raymond
Street address state: WA
Zip/Postal code: 98577
County: Pacific
Country: USA
Mailing address: P.O. Box 627
Mailing city: Raymond
Mailing state: WA
Mailing zip: 98577
General Phone: (360) 942-3560
General/National Adv. E-mail: dave@gaugermedia.com
Primary Website: www.gaugermedia.com
Year Established: 1987
Classified Equipment»
Personnel: Dave Gauger (Pres/Broker)

SEATTLE

SEATTLE GAY NEWS

Street address 1: 1605 12th Ave
Street address 2: Ste 31
Street address 3: Seattle
Street address state: WA
Zip/Postal code: 98122-2487
County: King
Country: USA
Mailing address: 1605 12th Ave Ste 31
Mailing city: Seattle
Mailing state: WA
Mailing zip: 98122-2487
General Phone: (206) 324-4297
General Fax: (206) 322-7188
General/National Adv. E-mail: sgn2@sgn.org
Primary Website: www.sgn.org
Delivery Methods: Newsstand`Racks
Advertising (Open Inch Rate) Weekday/Saturday: Open inch rate $30.00
Mechanical specifications: Type page 11 x 17.
Published: Fri
Avg Free Circ: 13500
Audit By: Sworn/Estimate/Non-Audited
Audit Date: 7/12/2019
Classified Equipment»
Personnel: George Bakan (Pub.); Rick McKinnon (Circ. Mgr.)

HISPANIC NEWSPAPER

ARKANSAS

FAYETTEVILLE

LA PRENSA LIBRE

Street address 1: 212 N East Ave
Street address city: Fayetteville
State: AR
Zip/Postal code: 72701-5225
County: Washington
Country: USA
General Phone: (479) 530-9313
General Fax: (479) 684-5570
Advertising Fax: (479) 251-8206
General/National Adv. E-mail: acueva@nwaonline.com
Display Adv. E-mail: acueva@nwaonline.com
Editorial e-mail: lpleditor@nwaonline.com
Year Established: 1996
Published: Thur
Avg Free Circ: 15000
Audit By: Sworn/Estimate/Non-Audited
Audit Date: 12.07.2019
Personnel: Jenser Morales (Ed.); Ariana Cisneros (Acct. Exec.); Hector Cueva (Gen. Mgr.)

LITTLE ROCK

EL LATINO

Street address 1: 201 E Markham St
Street address 2: Fl 2
Street address city: Little Rock
State: AR
Zip/Postal code: 72201-1627
County: Pulaski
Country: USA
Mailing address: 201 East Markham, 2nd floor
Mailing city: Little Rock
Mailing state: AR
Mailing zip: 72201
General Phone: (501)-375-2985
Published: Thur
Avg Paid Circ: 7
Avg Free Circ: 4605
Audit By: VAC
Audit Date: 30.06.2017
State: Arizona

ARIZONA

PHOENIX

LA VOZ ARIZONA

Street address 1: 7600 N 16th St
Street address 2: Ste 150
Street address city: Phoenix
State: AZ
Zip/Postal code: 85020-4487
County: Maricopa
Country: USA
Mailing address: 7600 N 16th St Ste 150
Mailing city: Phoenix
Mailing state: AZ
Mailing zip: 85004-2238
General Phone: (602) 252-5331
General Fax: (602) 444-3894
Advertising Phone: (602) 444-3800
Advertising Fax: (602) 444-3999
Editorial Phone: (602) 444-3800
Editorial Fax: (602) 444-3893
Display Adv. E-mail: lisa.simpson@lavozarizona.com
Year Established: 2000
Published: Wed
Avg Paid Circ: 0
Avg Free Circ: 58277
Audit By: VAC
Audit Date: 30.03.2015
Personnel: Elvira Diaz (Gen. Mgr.); Nadia Cantu (Ed.); Javier Arce (Dig. Prod.); Mi-Ai Parrish (Pres./Pub.)

PRENSA HISPANA

Street address 1: 809 E Washington St
Street address 2: Ste 209
Street address city: Phoenix
State: AZ
Zip/Postal code: 85034-1018
County: Maricopa
Country: USA
Mailing address: 809 E Washington St Ste 209
Mailing city: Phoenix
Mailing state: AZ
Mailing zip: 85034-1018
General Phone: (602) 256-2443
General Fax: (602) 256-2644
General/National Adv. E-mail: prensahispana@qwest.net
Published: Wed
Avg Free Circ: 65000
Audit By: Sworn/Estimate/Non-Audited
Audit Date: 12.07.2019
Personnel: Manny Garcia (Pres.); Lety Miranda-Garcia (Adv. Mgr., Classified)

YUMA

BAJO EL SOL

Street address 1: 2055 S Arizona Ave
Street address city: Yuma
State: AZ
Zip/Postal code: 85364-6549
County: Yuma
Country: USA
Mailing address: PO BOX 271
Mailing city: YUMA
Mailing state: AZ
Mailing zip: 85366-0271
General Phone: (928) 539-6800
General Fax: (928) 343-1009
Advertising Phone: (928) 539-6829
Advertising Fax: (928) 343-6928
Editorial Phone: (928) 539-6850
Editorial Fax: (928) 782-7369
General/National Adv. E-mail: nationals@yumasun.com
Display Adv. E-mail: nationals@yumasun.com
Editorial e-mail: jvaughn@yumasun.com
Year Established: 1991
Published: Fri
Avg Free Circ: 15002
Audit By: AAM
Audit Date: 30.06.2018
Personnel: Darlene Firestone (Ntl. Acct Mgr.)
State: California

CALIFORNIA

ACTON

ACTON-AGUA DULCE NEWS

Street address 1: 3413 Soledad Canyon Rd
Street address city: Acton
State: CA
Zip/Postal code: 93510-1974
County: Los Angeles
Country: USA
Mailing address: PO Box 57
Mailing city: Acton
Mailing state: CA
Mailing zip: 93510-0057
General Phone: (661) 269-1169
General Fax: (661) 269-2139
General/National Adv. E-mail: aadnews@joycemediainc.com; help@joycemediainc.com
Year Established: 1969
Published: Mon
Avg Paid Circ: 1000
Avg Free Circ: 575
Audit By: Sworn/Estimate/Non-Audited
Audit Date: 12.07.2019
Personnel: John Joyce (Pub.); M. Gayle Joyce (Ed.); Micah Joyce (Mng. Ed.); Jana Miranda (Data Supvr.)

BAKERSFIELD

EL POPULAR

Street address 1: 404 Truxtun Ave
Street address city: Bakersfield
State: CA
Zip/Postal code: 93301-5316
County: Kern
Country: USA
Mailing address: 404 Truxtun Ave
Mailing city: Bakersfield
Mailing state: CA
Mailing zip: 93301-5316
General Phone: (661) 325-7725
General Fax: (661) 325-1351
Advertising Phone: (661) 325-1351
Advertising Fax: (661) 325-1351
Editorial Phone: (661) 325-1351
Editorial Fax: (661) 325-1351
General/National Adv. E-mail: pub@elpopularnews.com
Display Adv. E-mail: ads@elpopularnews.com
Editorial e-mail: news@elpopularnews.com
Year Established: 1983
Published: Fri
Avg Paid Circ: 100
Avg Free Circ: 23000
Audit By: CVC
Audit Date: 30.12.2015
Personnel: George Camacho (President/Publisher); Raul Camacho (Founding Publisher/Editor); Lupe Medina (Associate Editor)

CAMARILLO

SIGLO 21

Street address 1: 550 Paseo Camarillo
Street address city: Camarillo
State: CA
Zip/Postal code: 93010-5900
County: Ventura
Country: USA
Published: Wed
Avg Free Circ: 16361
Audit By: VAC
Audit Date: 11.03.2012

CHULA VISTA

EL LATINO

Street address 1: 1105 Broadway
Street address 2: Ste 206
Street address city: Chula Vista
State: CA
Zip/Postal code: 91911-4091
County: San Diego
Country: USA
Mailing address: PO Box 120550
Mailing city: San Diego
Mailing state: CA
Mailing zip: 92112-0550
General Phone: (619) 426-1491
General Fax: (619) 426-3206
General/National Adv. E-mail: fanny@ellatino.net
Display Adv. E-mail: sales@ellatino.net
Classified Adv. e-mail: sales@ellatino.net
Editorial e-mail: editor@ellatino.net
Year Established: 1988
Published: Fri
Avg Free Circ: 80000
Audit By: Sworn/Estimate/Non-Audited
Audit Date: 12.07.2019
Personnel: Fanny Miller (Pub./Pres.)

ESCONDIDO

HISPANOS UNIDOS

Street address 1: 411 W 9th Ave
Street address city: Escondido
State: CA
Zip/Postal code: 92025-5034
County: San Diego
Country: USA
Mailing address: PO Box 462016
Mailing city: Escondido
Mailing state: CA
Mailing zip: 92046-2016
General Phone: (760) 740-9561
General Fax: (760) 737-3035
General/National Adv. E-mail: info@hispanosnews.com
Published: Fri
Avg Free Circ: 26000
Audit By: Sworn/Estimate/Non-Audited
Audit Date: 12.07.2019
Personnel: Ana Hannagan (Pub.); Jaime A. Castaneda (Prodn. Mgr.)

FRESNO

VIDA EN EL VALLE

Street address 1: 1626 E St
Street address city: Fresno
State: CA
Zip/Postal code: 93786
County: Fresno
Country: USA
Mailing address: 1626 E St
Mailing city: Fresno
Mailing state: CA
Mailing zip: 93786
General Phone: (559) 441-6780
General Fax: (559) 441-6790
Advertising Phone: (559) 441-6769
Advertising Fax: (559) 441-6790
Editorial Phone: (559) 441-6781
Editorial Fax: (559) 441-6790
General/National Adv. E-mail: aguajardo@vidaenelvalle.com
Display Adv. E-mail: bgutierrez@vidaenelvalle.com
Editorial e-mail: jesparza@vidaenelvalle.com
Year Established: 1990
Published: Wed
Avg Free Circ: 35584
Audit By: AAM
Audit Date: 31.03.2019
Personnel: Monica Stevens (Pub.); Morgie Rice (Office Mgr.); Juan Esparza Loera (Ed.); Anna Ramseier (Prodn. Mgr.); John Coakley (Vp, Sales/Mktg)

BELL GARDENS SUN

Street address 1: 111 S Avenue 59
Street address city: Los Angeles
State: CA
Zip/Postal code: 90042-4211
County: Los Angeles
Country: USA
General Phone: (323) 341-7970
General Fax: (323) 341-7976
General/National Adv. E-mail: service@egpnews.com
Display Adv. E-mail: advertise@egpnews.com
Editorial e-mail: editorial@egpnews.com

Year Established: 1945
Published: Thur
Avg Paid Circ: 2
Avg Free Circ: 6973
Audit By: CVC
Audit Date: 30.09.2014
Personnel: Dolores Sanchez (Pub.); Jonathan M. Sanchez (Adv. Mgr.); Bianca Sanchez (Circ. Mgr.); Gloria Alvarez (Mng. Ed.); Elizabeth Chou (Prodn. Mgr.)

CITY TERRACE COMET

Street address 1: 111 S Avenue 59
Street address city: Los Angeles
State: CA
Zip/Postal code: 90042-4211
County: Los Angeles
Country: USA
General Phone: (323) 341-7970
General Fax: (323) 341-7976
General/National Adv. E-mail: service@egpnews.com
Display Adv. E-mail: advertise@egpnews.com
Editorial e-mail: editorial@egpnews.com
Year Established: 1945
Published: Thur
Avg Paid Circ: 4
Avg Free Circ: 2971
Audit By: CVC
Audit Date: 30.09.2014
Personnel: Dolores Sanchez (Pub.); Jonathan M. Sanchez (Adv. Mgr.); Bianca Sanchez (Circ. Mgr.); Gloria Alvarez (Mng. Ed.); Elizabeth Chou (Prodn. Mgr.)

COMMERCE COMET

Street address 1: 111 S Avenue 59
Street address city: Los Angeles
State: CA
Zip/Postal code: 90042-4211
County: Los Angeles
Country: USA
General Phone: (323) 341-7970
General Fax: (323) 341-7976
General/National Adv. E-mail: service@egpnews.com
Display Adv. E-mail: advertise@egpnews.com
Editorial e-mail: editorial@egpnews.com
Year Established: 1945
Published: Thur
Avg Paid Circ: 5
Avg Free Circ: 6475
Audit By: CVC
Audit Date: 30.09.2014
Personnel: Dolores Sanchez (Pub.); Jonathan M. Sanchez (Adv. Mgr.); Bianca Sanchez (Circ. Mgr.); Gloria Alvarez (Mng. Ed.); Elizabeth Chou (Prodn. Mgr.)

EASTSIDE SUN

Street address 1: 161 S Avenue 24
Street address city: Los Angeles
State: CA
Zip/Postal code: 90031-2247
County: Los Angeles
Country: USA
General Phone: (323) 221-1092
General Fax: (323) 221-1096
Advertising Phone: (323) 221-1090
Editorial Phone: (323) 221-1092
General/National Adv. E-mail: service@egpnews.com
Display Adv. E-mail: advertise@egpnews.com
Editorial e-mail: editorial@egpnews.com
Year Established: 1945
Published: Thur
Avg Paid Circ: 131
Avg Free Circ: 43944
Audit By: CVC
Audit Date: 12.12.2017
Personnel: Dolores Sanchez (Pub.); Gloria Alvarez (Mng. Ed.); Bianca Preciado (Advertising/Office Manager)

ELA BROOKLYN-BELVEDERE COMET

Street address 1: 111 S Avenue 59
Street address city: Los Angeles
State: CA
Zip/Postal code: 90042-4211
County: Los Angeles
Country: USA
General Phone: (323) 341-7970
General Fax: (323) 341-7976
General/National Adv. E-mail: service@egpnews.com
Display Adv. E-mail: advertise@egpnews.com
Editorial e-mail: editorial@egpnews.com
Year Established: 1945
Published: Thur
Avg Paid Circ: 4
Avg Free Circ: 2971
Audit By: CVC
Audit Date: 30.09.2014
Personnel: Dolores Sanchez (Pub.); Jonathan M. Sanchez (Adv. Mgr.); Bianca Sanchez (Circ. Mgr.); Gloria Alvarez (Mng. Ed.); Elizabeth Chou (Prodn. Mgr.)

EXCELSIOR LOS ANGELES

Street address 1: 523 N Grand Ave
Street address city: Los Angeles
State: CA
Zip/Postal code: 90012-2149
County: Los Angeles
Country: USA
Mailing address: 523 N GRAND AVE
Mailing city: SANTA ANA
Mailing state: CA
Mailing zip: 92701-4345
General Phone: (714) 796-4300
General Fax: (714) 796-4316
Advertising Fax: (714) 796-4316
Editorial Fax: (714) 796-4319
General/National Adv. E-mail: adesantos@ocregister.com
Display Adv. E-mail: excelsiorads@ocregister.com
Published: Fri
Avg Free Circ: 52529
Audit By: Sworn/Estimate/Non-Audited
Audit Date: 12.07.2019
Personnel: Carlos Aviles (Pub.); Angelica De Santos; Trinidad Verduzco (Ed.)

HOY FIN DE SEMANA

Street address 1: 202 W 1st St
Street address city: Los Angeles
State: CA
Zip/Postal code: 90012-4299
County: Los Angeles
Country: USA
Advertising Phone: (213) 237-3453
Display Adv. E-mail: hcabral@hoyllc.com
Published: Sat
Avg Free Circ: 813384
Audit By: CAC
Audit Date: 30.09.2016
Personnel: Hector Cabral (Adv. Dir.); Ronaldo Moran (Pub.); Deborah Albright (Division Mgr.)

HOY LLC

Street address 1: 145 S Spring St
Street address 2: Fl 2
Street address city: Los Angeles
State: CA
Zip/Postal code: 90012-4053
County: Los Angeles
Country: USA
General Phone: (213) 237-4388
Advertising Phone: (213) 237-3453
Editorial Phone: (213) 237-3374
General/National Adv. E-mail: amaciel@hoyllc.com
Display Adv. E-mail: hcabral@hoyllc.com
Editorial e-mail: jmaciel@vivelohoy.com
Year Established: 2004
Published: Mon`Fri`Sat
Published Other: weekly
Avg Free Circ: 1000400
Audit By: Sworn/Estimate/Non-Audited
Audit Date: 12.07.2019
Personnel: John Trainor (Gen. Mgr); Michael Roenna (Sales Director); Fernando Diaz (Managing Editor); Kim Benz (Director of Sales Strategy); Roaldo Moran (General Manager Hoy Los Angeles); Alejandro Maciel (Director Editorial Hoy/ Los Angeles); Javier T. Calle (Editor Adjunto Hoy/ Los Angeles)

HOY LOS ANGELES

Street address 1: 202 W 1st St
Street address city: Los Angeles
State: CA
Zip/Postal code: 90012-4299
County: Los Angeles
Country: USA
Advertising Phone: (213) 237-3453
Display Adv. E-mail: hcabral@hoyllc.com
Published: Mon`Fri
Avg Free Circ: 130813
Audit By: CAC
Audit Date: 30.09.2018
Personnel: Hector Cabral (Adv. Dir.); Deborah Albright (Division Mgr.); Ronaldo Moran (Pub.)

LA OPINION - CONTIGO

Street address 1: 700 S Flower St
Street address city: Los Angeles
State: CA
Zip/Postal code: 90017-4101
County: Los Angeles
Country: USA
Published: Mon`Wed`Thur`Fri`Sat`Sun
Avg Paid Circ: 0
Avg Free Circ: 581129
Audit By: AAM
Audit Date: 31.03.2015
Personnel: Patricia Prieto (Adv. Dir.); Damian Mazzotta (Gen. Mgr,); Greg Hatch (Circ. Dir.)

LA PRENSA DE LOS ANGELES

Street address 1: 5554 Carlton Way
Street address 2: Apt 4
Street address city: Los Angeles
State: CA
Zip/Postal code: 90028-6847
County: Los Angeles
Country: USA
General Phone: (323) 572-0106
General/National Adv. E-mail: laprensa@laprensadelosangeles.com
Display Adv. E-mail: sales@laprensadelosangeles.com
Editorial e-mail: comentarios@laprensadelosangeles.com
Year Established: 1999
Published: Sat
Published Other: once a month
Avg Paid Circ: 10000
Avg Free Circ: 30000
Audit By: Sworn/Estimate/Non-Audited
Audit Date: 12.07.2019
Personnel: Carlos Groppa (Ed.)

MEXICAN AMERICAN SUN

Street address 1: 111 S Avenue 59
Street address city: Los Angeles
State: CA
Zip/Postal code: 90042-4211
County: Los Angeles
Country: USA
Mailing address: 111 S Avenue 59
Mailing city: Los Angeles
Mailing state: CA
Mailing zip: 90042-4211
General Phone: (323) 341-7970
General Fax: (323) 341-7976
General/National Adv. E-mail: service@egpnews.com
Display Adv. E-mail: advertise@egpnews.com
Editorial e-mail: editorial@egpnews.com
Year Established: 1945
Published: Thur
Avg Paid Circ: 186
Avg Free Circ: 15789
Audit By: CVC
Audit Date: 30.09.2014
Personnel: Dolores Sanchez (Pub.); Jonathan M. Sanchez (Adv. Mgr.); Bianca Sanchez (Circ. Mgr.); Gloria Alvarez (Mng. Ed.); Elizabeth Chou (Prodn. Mgr.)

MONTEBELLO COMET

Street address 1: 111 S Avenue 59
Street address city: Los Angeles
State: CA
Zip/Postal code: 90042-4211
County: Los Angeles
Country: USA
Mailing address: 111 S Avenue 59
Mailing city: Los Angeles
Mailing state: CA
Mailing zip: 90042-4211
General Phone: (323) 341-7970
General Fax: (323) 341-7976
General/National Adv. E-mail: service@egpnews.com
Display Adv. E-mail: advertise@egpnews.com
Editorial e-mail: editorial@egpnews.com
Year Established: 1945
Published: Thur
Avg Paid Circ: 4
Avg Free Circ: 16971
Audit By: CVC
Audit Date: 30.09.2014
Personnel: Dolores Sanchez (Pub.); Jonathan M. Sanchez (Adv. Mgr.); Bianca Sanchez (Circ. Mgr.); Gloria Alvarez (Mng. Ed.); Elizabeth Chou (Prodn. Mgr.)

MONTEREY PARK COMET

Street address 1: 111 S Avenue 59
Street address city: Los Angeles
State: CA
Zip/Postal code: 90042-4211
County: Los Angeles
Country: USA
Mailing address: 111 S Avenue 59
Mailing city: Los Angeles
Mailing state: CA
Mailing zip: 90042-4211
General Phone: (323) 341-7970
General Fax: (323) 341-7976
General/National Adv. E-mail: service@egpnews.com
Display Adv. E-mail: advertise@egpnews.com
Editorial e-mail: editorial@egpnews.com
Year Established: 1945
Published: Thur
Avg Paid Circ: 4
Avg Free Circ: 6971
Audit By: CVC
Audit Date: 30.09.2014
Personnel: Dolores Sanchez (Pub.); Jonathan M. Sanchez (Adv. Mgr.); Bianca Sanchez (Circ. Mgr.); Gloria Alvarez (Mng. Ed.); Elizabeth Chou (Prodn. Mgr.)

NORTHEAST SUN

Street address 1: 111 S Avenue 59
Street address city: Los Angeles
State: CA
Zip/Postal code: 90042-4211
County: Los Angeles
Country: USA
General Phone: (323) 341-7970
General Fax: (323) 341-7976
General/National Adv. E-mail: service@egpnews.com
Display Adv. E-mail: advertise@egpnews.com
Editorial e-mail: editorial@egpnews.com
Year Established: 1945
Published: Thur
Avg Paid Circ: 10
Avg Free Circ: 18465
Audit By: CVC
Audit Date: 30.09.2014
Personnel: Dolores Sanchez (Pub.); Jonathan M. Sanchez (Adv. Mgr.); Bianca Sanchez (Circ. Mgr.); Gloria Alvarez (Mng. Ed.); Elizabeth Chou (Prodn. Mgr.)

VERNON SUN

Street address 1: 111 S Avenue 59
Street address city: Los Angeles
State: CA
Zip/Postal code: 90042-4211
County: Los Angeles
Country: USA
General Phone: (323) 341-7970
General Fax: (323) 341-7976
General/National Adv. E-mail: service@egpnews.com
Display Adv. E-mail: advertise@egpnews.com
Editorial e-mail: editorial@egpnews.com
Year Established: 1945
Published: Thur
Avg Paid Circ: 4
Avg Free Circ: 2471
Audit By: CVC
Audit Date: 30.09.2014
Personnel: Dolores Sanchez (Pub.); Jonathan M. Sanchez (Adv. Mgr.); Bianca Sanchez (Circ. Mgr.); Gloria Alvarez (Mng. Ed.); Elizabeth Chou (Prodn. Mgr.)

WAVE PUBLICATIONS

Street address 1: 3731 W Olympic Blvd
Street address 2: Ste 840
Street address city: Los Angeles
State: CA
Zip/Postal code: 90019-2030
County: Los Angeles
Country: USA
Mailing address: 3731 Wilshire Blvd Ste 840

Mailing city: Los Angeles
Mailing state: CA
Mailing zip: 90010-2851
General Phone: (323) 556-5720
General Fax: (213) 835-0584
General/National Adv. E-mail: newsroom@wavepublication.com
Year Established: 1912
Published: Thur
Avg Free Circ: 100000
Audit By: Sworn/Estimate/Non-Audited
Audit Date: 12.07.2019
Personnel: Pluria Marshall (Pub.)

WYVERNWOOD CHRONICLE

Street address 1: 111 S Avenue 59
Street address city: Los Angeles
State: CA
Zip/Postal code: 90042-4211
County: Los Angeles
Country: USA
General Phone: (323) 341-7970
General Fax: (323) 341-7976
General/National Adv. E-mail: service@egpnews.com
Display Adv. E-mail: advertise@egpnews.com
Editorial e-mail: editorial@egpnews.com
Year Established: 1945
Published: Thur
Avg Free Circ: 1975
Audit By: CVC
Audit Date: 30.09.2014
Personnel: Dolores Sanchez (Pub.); Jonathan M. Sanchez (Adv. Mgr.); Bianca Sanchez (Circ. Mgr.); Gloria Alvarez (Mng. Ed.); Elizabeth Chou (Prodn. Mgr.)

NORWALK

EL CLASIFICADO

Street address 1: 11205 Imperial Hwy
Street address city: Norwalk
State: CA
Zip/Postal code: 90650-2229
County: Los Angeles
Country: USA
Mailing address: 11205 Imperial Hwy
Mailing city: Norwalk
Mailing state: CA
Mailing zip: 90650-2229
General Phone: 1800-242-2527
Advertising Phone: 866-893-0028
Editorial Phone: 888-261-9772
Year Established: 1988
Published: Tues`Wed
Avg Free Circ: 486626
Audit By: CVC
Audit Date: 30.03.2018
Personnel: Martha C. De la Torre; Joe Badame

RIVERSIDE

LA PRENSA

Street address 1: 1825 Chicago Avenue
Street address 2: Suite 100
Street address city: Riverside
State: CA
Zip/Postal code: 92507
County: Riverside
Country: USA
Mailing address: 1825 Chicago Avenue, Ste. 100
Mailing city: Anaheim
Mailing state: CA
Mailing zip: 92507
General Phone: (909) 806-3201
General/National Adv. E-mail: oramirez@pe.com
Published: Fri
Avg Free Circ: 95478
Audit By: VAC
Audit Date: 31.03.2013
Personnel: Carlos Aviles (Mng. Ed.); Jose Fuentes (Ed.); Angelica De Santos (Local Sales); Trinidad Verduzco (Local Sales)

SACRAMENTO

EL HISPANO

Street address 1: 1903 21st St
Street address city: Sacramento
State: CA
Zip/Postal code: 95811-6813
County: Sacramento
Country: USA
Mailing address: PO Box 2856
Mailing city: Sacramento
Mailing state: CA
Mailing zip: 95812-2856
General Phone: (916) 442-0267
General Fax: (916) 442-2818
General/National Adv. E-mail: plarenas2@yahoo.com
Published: Wed
Avg Free Circ: 15000
Audit By: Sworn/Estimate/Non-Audited
Audit Date: 12.07.2019
Personnel: Patrick Larenas (Ed.)

SALINAS

EL SOL

Street address 1: 1093 S Main St Suite 101
Street address city: Salinas
State: CA
Zip/Postal code: 93901
County: Monterey
Country: USA
Mailing address: 1093 S Main St Suite 101
Mailing city: Salinas
Mailing state: CA
Mailing zip: 93901
General Phone: (831) 424-2221
General Fax: (831) 754-4286
Editorial Phone: (831) 754-4272
General/National Adv. E-mail: jbrooks@usatoday.com
Display Adv. E-mail: tdean@gannett.com
Editorial e-mail: pgoudreau@gannett.com
Year Established: 1968
Published: Sat
Avg Free Circ: 29980
Audit By: CVC
Audit Date: 30.03.2018
Personnel: Terry Feinberg (Gen. Mgr.); Silvia Sancen (Ed.); Theresa Simpson; Paula Goudreau (Pub.); Trey Dean (Adv.); John Brooks (Circ.)

EL SOL DE SAN DIEGO

Street address 1: 2629 National Ave
Street address city: San Diego
State: CA
Zip/Postal code: 92113-3617
County: San Diego
Country: USA
Mailing address: PO Box 13447
Mailing city: San Diego
Mailing state: CA
Mailing zip: 92170-3447
General Phone: (619) 233-8496
General Fax: (619) 233-5017
General/National Adv. E-mail: elsolsd@aol.com
Audit By: Sworn/Estimate/Non-Audited
Audit Date: 12.07.2019
Personnel: Lynn Johansen (Adv. Mgr.); Julie J. Rocha (Ed.)

HOY SAN DIEGO - THE SAN DIEGO UNION TRIBUNE

Street address 1: 600 B St
Street address 2: Ste 1201
Street address city: San Diego
State: CA
Zip/Postal code: 92101-4505
County: San Diego
Country: USA
Mailing address: P.O. Box 120191
Mailing city: San Diego
Mailing state: CA
Mailing zip: 92112
General Phone: 619-299-4141
Published: Sat
Avg Paid Circ: 80920
Audit By: AAM
Audit Date: 31.12.2015
Personnel: Jeff Light (Publisher and Editor); Phyllis Pfeiffer (President and General Manager); Lora Cicalo (Managing Editor)

LA PRENSA SAN DIEGO

Street address 1: 1712 Logan Avenue
Street address city: San Diego
State: CA
Zip/Postal code: 92113
County: San Diego
Country: USA
Mailing address: 1712 Logan Avenue
Mailing city: San Diego
Mailing state: CA
Mailing zip: 92113
General Phone: (619) 425-7400
General/National Adv. E-mail: laprensasd@gmail.com
Year Established: 1976
Published: Fri
Avg Free Circ: 25000
Audit By: Sworn/Estimate/Non-Audited
Audit Date: 12.07.2019
Personnel: Art Castanares (Publisher)

VIDA LATINA - THE SAN DIEGO UNION TRIBUNE

Street address 1: 600 B St
Street address 2: Ste 1201
Street address city: San Diego
State: CA
Zip/Postal code: 92101-4505
County: San Diego
Country: USA
Mailing address: P.O. Box 120191
Mailing city: San Diego
Mailing state: CA
Mailing zip: 92112
General Phone: (619)299-4141
Published: Fri
Avg Paid Circ: 30500
Audit By: AAM
Audit Date: 31.12.2015
Personnel: Jeff Light (Pub. & Ed.); Phyllis Pfeiffer (Pres. & Gen. Mgr.); Paul Ingegneri (V. Pres. Adv.)

EL BOHEMIO NEWS

Street address 1: 3288 21st St
Street address 2: # 116
Street address city: San Francisco
State: CA
Zip/Postal code: 94110-2423
County: San Francisco
Country: USA
Mailing address: 3288 21st Street #116
Mailing city: San Francisco
Mailing state: CA
Mailing zip: 94110
General Phone: (415) 469-9579
General Fax: (415) 970-8853
General/National Adv. E-mail: bohemio@ix.netcom.com
Published: Fri
Avg Free Circ: 22472
Audit By: CVC
Audit Date: 31.03.2006
Personnel: Rosalina Contreras (Adv. Mgr.); Benny Velarde (Circ. Mgr.); Fernando Rosado (Ed.)

EL MENSAJERO

Street address 1: 333 Valencia St
Street address 2: Ste. 410
Street address city: San Francisco
State: CA
Zip/Postal code: 94103-3500
County: San Francisco
Country: USA
Mailing address: 333 Valencia St., Ste. 400
Mailing city: LOS ANGELES
Mailing state: CA
Mailing zip: 90017
General Phone: (415) 206-7230
General Fax: (415) 206-7238
Advertising Phone: (415) 206-7230
Editorial Phone: (415) 206-7230
General/National Adv. E-mail: comentarios@elmensajero.com
Display Adv. E-mail: michael.howard@elmensajero.com
Editorial e-mail: comentarios@elmensajero.com
Year Established: 1987
Published: Sun
Avg Paid Circ: 0
Avg Free Circ: 103800
Audit By: CAC
Audit Date: 30.09.2014
Personnel: Gabriel Guthellez (Nat'l Sales Dir.); Madia Mejia (Ed.); Damian Mazzotta (Gen. Mgr./West, IM Corp); Greg Hatch (Circ. Dir.)

EL TECOLOTE

Street address 1: 2958 24th St
Street address city: San Francisco
State: CA
Zip/Postal code: 94110-4132
County: San Francisco
Country: USA
Mailing address: 2958 24th St
Mailing city: San Francisco
Mailing state: CA
Mailing zip: 94110-4132
General Phone: (415) 648-1045
General Fax: (415) 648-1046
Editorial e-mail: editor@accionlatina.org
Year Established: 1970
Published Other: 2 x Mthly
Avg Paid Circ: 250
Avg Free Circ: 10000
Audit By: Sworn/Estimate/Non-Audited
Audit Date: 12.07.2019
Personnel: Roberto Daza (Ed.)

ALIANZA METROPOLITAN NEWS

Street address 1: 1090 Lincoln Ave
Street address 2: Ste 8
Street address city: San Jose
State: CA
Zip/Postal code: 95125-3156
County: Santa Clara
Country: USA
Mailing address: 3290 Cuesta Dr
Mailing city: San Jose
Mailing state: CA
Mailing zip: 95148-1601
General Phone: (408) 272-9394
General Fax: (408) 272-9395
Published Other: Every other Thur
Avg Free Circ: 40000
Audit By: Sworn/Estimate/Non-Audited
Audit Date: 12.07.2019
Personnel: Rosana Drumond (Pub.); Manuel Ortiz (Ed.)

EL OBSERVADOR

Street address 1: 1042 W Hedding St
Street address 2: Ste 250
Street address city: San Jose
State: CA
Zip/Postal code: 95126-1206
County: Santa Clara
Country: USA
Mailing address: 1042 W. Hedding St. #250
Mailing city: San Jose
Mailing state: CA
Mailing zip: 95126
General Phone: (408) 938-1700
General Fax: (408) 938-1705
Advertising Fax: 408 938 1700
Editorial Fax: 408-938-1705
General/National Adv. E-mail: angelica@el-observador.com
Display Adv. E-mail: angelica@el-observador.com
Editorial e-mail: arturo@el-observador.com
Year Established: 1980
Published: Fri
Avg Free Circ: 34500
Audit By: Sworn/Estimate/Non-Audited
Audit Date: 12.07.2019
Personnel: Angelica Rossi (Pres./Pub.); Justin Rossi (Sales); Arturo Hilario (Ed.); Leila Velasco (Graphic

Des.); Erica Medrano (Office Manager); Arturo Hilario (Managing Editor); Hilbert Morales (Pub.); Monica Amador (Adv./Mktg. Dir.); Angelica Rossi (Acct. Rep.); Roberto Romo (Graphics Design)

LA OFERTA REVIEW

Street address 1: 1009 E. Capitol Expwy
Street address 2: # 525
Street address city: San Jose
State: CA
Zip/Postal code: 95121
County: Santa Clara
Country: USA
Mailing address: 1009 E. Capitol Expwy # 525
Mailing city: San Jose
Mailing state: CA
Mailing zip: 95121
General Phone: (408)-436-7850
General Fax: (408) 436-7861
General/National Adv. E-mail: info@laoferta.com
Year Established: 1978
Published: Fri
Avg Free Circ: 21000
Audit By: Sworn/Estimate/Non-Audited
Audit Date: 12.07.2019
Personnel: Franklin G. Andrade (Co Pub.); Tatiana Andrade (Adv. Dir.); Mary J. Andrade (Ed.)

NUEVO MUNDO

Street address 1: 750 Ridder Park Dr
Street address city: San Jose
State: CA
Zip/Postal code: 95131-2432
County: Santa Clara
Country: USA
Mailing address: 750 Ridder Park Dr
Mailing city: San Jose
Mailing state: CA
Mailing zip: 95190-0001
General Phone: (408) 920-5843
General Fax: (408) 271-3732
Audit By: Sworn/Estimate/Non-Audited
Audit Date: 12.07.2019
Personnel: Rosaura Miramontes (Adv. Mgr., Natl' Sales); Marina Hinestrosa (Ed.)

SAN YSIDRO

AHORA NOW

Street address 1: 378 E San Ysidro Blvd
Street address city: San Ysidro
State: CA
Zip/Postal code: 92173-2722
County: San Diego
Country: USA
Mailing address: 378 E San Ysidro Blvd
Mailing city: Dan Ysidro
Mailing state: CA
Mailing zip: 92173-2722
General Phone: (619) 428-2277
General Fax: (619) 428-0871
General/National Adv. E-mail: ahoranow2008@hotmail.com
Published: Thur
Avg Free Circ: 20000
Audit By: Sworn/Estimate/Non-Audited
Audit Date: 12.07.2019
Personnel: Juan Manuel Torres (Adv. Mgr.); Bertha Alicia Gonzalez (Ed.)

SANTA ANA

AZTECA NEWS

Street address 1: 1823 E 17th St
Street address 2: Ste 312
Street address city: Santa Ana
State: CA
Zip/Postal code: 92705-8630
County: Orange
Country: USA
General Phone: (714) 972-9912
Advertising Phone: (714) 760-4939
General/National Adv. E-mail: aztecanews@aol.com
Display Adv. E-mail: fvelo@aztecanews.com
Editorial e-mail: rromano@aztecanews.com
Year Established: 1980
Published: Wed
Published Other: weekly
Avg Free Circ: 42
Audit By: Sworn/Estimate/Non-Audited
Audit Date: 12.07.2019
Personnel: Fernando Velo (Pub.); Alessandro Hernandez (Adv. Mgr.); Rosanna Romano (Mng. Ed.)

SANTA ROSA

LA PRENSA SONOMA

Street address 1: 427 Mendocino Ave
Street address city: Santa Rosa
State: CA
Zip/Postal code: 95401-6313
County: Sonoma
Country: USA
Mailing address: ricardo.ibarra@pressdemocrat.com
General Phone: (707) 526-8501
Advertising Phone: 707-521-5342
Display Adv. E-mail: jose.delcastillo@pressdemocrat.com
Editorial e-mail: ricardo.ibarra@pressdemocrat.com
Year Established: 2016
Published: Mthly
Avg Free Circ: 30000
Audit By: Sworn/Estimate/Non-Audited
Audit Date: 12.07.2019
Personnel: Ricardo Ibarra

LA VOZ BILINGUAL NEWSPAPER

Street address 1: PO Box 3688
Street address city: Santa Rosa
State: CA
Zip/Postal code: 95402
County: Berks
Country: USA
Mailing address: PO Box 3688
Mailing city: Santa Rosa
Mailing state: CA
Mailing zip: 95402
General Phone: (707) 538-1812
General/National Adv. E-mail: ads@lavoz.us.com
Published: Wed
Avg Free Circ: 3986
Audit By: Sworn/Estimate/Non-Audited
Audit Date: 12.07.2019
Personnel: Ani Weaver (Pub./Ed./Owner)

TORRANCE

IMPACTO USA

Street address 1: 21250 Hawthorne Blvd
Street address city: Torrance
State: CA
Zip/Postal code: 90503-5506
County: Los Angeles
Country: USA
Mailing address: 21250 Hawthorne Blvd Ste 170
Mailing city: Torrance
Mailing state: CA
Mailing zip: 90503-5514
General Phone: (562) 499-1415
General Fax: (562) 499-1484
Published: Fri
Avg Paid Circ: 207248
Audit By: AAM
Audit Date: 31.03.2015
Personnel: RaÃºl MartÃnez (Dsgn. Mgr.); Trinidad Verduzco (Ed.)

TUSTIN

MINIONDAS

Street address 1: 17291 Irvine Blvd
Street address 2: Ste 225
Street address city: Tustin
State: CA
Zip/Postal code: 92780-2941
County: Orange
Country: USA
Mailing zip: 93510-005
General Phone: (714) 668-1010
Year Established: 1975
Published: Thur
Personnel: Sandra Cervantes (Pub.)
State: Colorado

COLORADO

LA VOZ NEWSPAPER

Street address 1: 4047 Tejon St
Street address 2: # 202
Street address city: Denver
State: CO
Zip/Postal code: 80211-2214
County: Denver
Country: USA
Mailing address: PO Box 11398
Mailing city: Denver
Mailing state: CO
Mailing zip: 80211-0398
General Phone: (303) 936-8556
General Fax: (720) 889-2455
Display Adv. E-mail: advertising@lavozcolorado.com; classifieds@lavozcolorado.com
Editorial e-mail: news@lavozcolorado.com
Year Established: 1974
Published: Wed
Avg Paid Circ: 596
Avg Free Circ: 25778
Audit By: CAC
Audit Date: 30.09.2012
Personnel: Pauline Rivera (Pub.); Romelia Ulibarri (Sales Mgr.); Emma Lynch (Entertainment Ed.); Charles Corrales (Prodn. Coord.)

THORNTON

LA VOZ BILINGUE

Street address 1: 12021 Pennsylvania St Ste 201
Street address 2: #201
Street address city: Thornton
State: CO
Zip/Postal code: 80241-3152
County: Adams
Country: USA
General Phone: (303) 936-8556
General Fax: (720) 889-2455
Advertising Phone: (303) 936-8556
General/National Adv. E-mail: privera@lavozcolorado.com
Display Adv. E-mail: privera@lavozcolorado.com
Editorial e-mail: news@lavozcolorado.com
Published: Wed
Avg Free Circ: 32000
Audit By: AAM
Audit Date: 31.12.2018
Personnel: Pauline Rivera (Pub./Adv. Dir.); Romelia Ulibarri (Classified Mgr.); Jim Koucherik (Circ. Mgr.); Charles Corrales (Prod. Coord.)
State: Connecticut

CONNECTICUT

HARTFORD

EXPRESO LATINO

Street address 1: 293 Franklin Ave
Street address city: Hartford
State: CT
Zip/Postal code: 06114
Country: USA
Mailing address: 293 Franklin Ave
Mailing city: Hartford
Mailing state: CT
Mailing zip: 06114
Published: Fri
Avg Free Circ: 8322
Audit By: CAC
Audit Date: 30.09.2008
Personnel: Expresso Latino (Pub.)
State: District of Columbia

DISTRICT OF COLUMBIA

WASHINGTON

EL TIEMPO LATINO

Street address 1: 1150 15th St
Street address city: Washington
State: DC
Zip/Postal code: 20071-0001
County: District Of Columbia
Country: USA
Mailing address: 1150 15th St NW
Mailing city: Washington
Mailing state: DC
Mailing zip: 20071-0001
General Phone: 202-334-9100
General Fax: 202-496-3599
Advertising Phone: 202-334-9146
Advertising Fax: 202-496-3599
Editorial Phone: 202-334-9159
Editorial Fax: 202-496-3599
Display Adv. E-mail: zulema@eltiempolatino.com
Editorial e-mail: paula@eltiempolatino.com
Year Established: 1991
Published: Fri
Avg Free Circ: 50000
Audit By: AAM
Audit Date: 15.01.2012
Personnel: Alberto Avendano (Director of Business Development); Kris Holmes (Office Mgr.); Zulema Tijero (Adv. Mgr.)
State: Florida

FLORIDA

DORAL

EL NUEVO HERALD

Street address 1: 3511 NW 91st Ave
Street address city: Doral
State: FL
Zip/Postal code: 33172-1216
County: Miami-Dade
Country: USA
Mailing address: 3511 NW 91 Avenue
Mailing city: Miami
Mailing state: FL
Mailing zip: 33172
General Phone: (305) 376-3535
General Fax: (305) 376-2138
Published Other: Daily
Avg Paid Circ: 382896
Audit By: Sworn/Estimate/Non-Audited
Audit Date: 12.07.2019
Personnel: Aminda Marquez Gonzalez (Exec Ed); Maru AntuÃ±ano (Ed., Prod. Spec.)

FORT LAUDERDALE

EL HERALDO DE BROWARD

Street address 1: 1975 E Sunrise Blvd
Street address 2: Ste 540
Street address city: Fort Lauderdale
State: FL
Zip/Postal code: 33304-1453
County: Broward
Country: USA
Mailing address: 2600 NE 9th St
Mailing city: Fort Lauderdale
Mailing state: FL
Mailing zip: 33304-3610
General Phone: (954) 527-0627
General Fax: (954) 792-7402

General/National Adv. E-mail: elheralbroward@aol.com
Audit By: Sworn/Estimate/Non-Audited
Audit Date: 12.07.2019
Personnel: Elaine Vasquez (Pub.); Elaine Miceli-Vasquez (Ed.); Lisa Miceli (Prodn. Mgr.)

EL NOTICIERO

Street address 1: PO Box 480729
Street address city: Fort Lauderdale
State: FL
Zip/Postal code: 33348-0729
County: Broward
Country: USA
Mailing address: PO Box 480729
Mailing city: Fort Lauderdale
Mailing state: FL
Mailing zip: 33348-0729
General Phone: (954) 766-4492
General Fax: (954) 766-4492
General/National Adv. E-mail: elnoti2@aol.com
Published Other: Every other Week
Avg Free Circ: 15000
Audit By: Sworn/Estimate/Non-Audited
Audit Date: 12.07.2019
Personnel: Lilia Mantilla (Ed.); Rodrigo Martinez (Director)

LONGWOOD

LA PRENSA

Street address 1: 685 S Ronald Reagan Blvd
Street address 2: Ste 1001
Street address city: Longwood
State: FL
Zip/Postal code: 32750-6435
County: Seminole
Country: USA
Mailing address: 685 S RONALD REAGAN BLVD STE 200
Mailing city: LONGWOOD
Mailing state: FL
Mailing zip: 32750-6435
General Phone: (407) 767-0070
General Fax: (407) 767-5478
Advertising Phone: (407) 767-0070
Editorial Phone: (407) 767-0070
General/National Adv. E-mail: dora.toro@laprensaorlando.com
Display Adv. E-mail: vicky.llevada@laprensaorlando.com
Editorial e-mail: jesus.deltoro@impremedia.com
Year Established: 1981
Published: Thur
Avg Paid Circ: 35000
Audit By: CAC
Audit Date: 30.06.2015
Personnel: Dora Casanova de Toro (Pub./CEO); Julia Torres (Office Mgr.); Adalgiza Zouain (Sales); Milly Colon (Sales); Liza Ordonez (Sales); Vicky Llevada (Calssified / Display Classifieds); Jesus Del Toro (EIC)

DIARIO LAS AMERICAS

Street address 1: 888 Brickell Ave
Street address 2: Fl 5
Street address city: Miami
State: FL
Zip/Postal code: 33131-2913
County: Miami-Dade
Country: USA
Mailing address: 888 Brickell Ave 5th
Mailing city: Miami
Mailing state: FL
Mailing zip: 33131
General Phone: (305) 633-3341
General Fax: (305) 635-7668
Advertising Phone: (305) 633-3341
Advertising Fax: (305) 635-4002
Editorial Phone: (305) 633-3341
Editorial Fax: (305) 635-7668
General/National Adv. E-mail: contacto@diariolasamericas.com
Display Adv. E-mail: advertising@diariolasamericas.com
Editorial e-mail: editorial@diariolasamericas.com
Year Established: 1953
Published: Sun
Weekday Frequency: m
Avg Paid Circ: 5692
Avg Free Circ: 30453
Sat. Circulation Paid: 69132
Sun. Circulation Paid: 69132
Audit By: VAC
Audit Date: 30.09.2014
Personnel: Maribel Suarez (Asst. Pub.); Victor M. Vega (Bus. Mgr./Controller); Ariel Martinez (Prodn. Mgr.); Daniel Medina (Credit Mgr.); Alejandro Aguirre (Adv. Dir.); Bertha V. Enriquez (Adv. Mgr., Nat'l); Jose A. Yuste (Adv. Mgr., Classified); Horacio Aguirre (Ed.); Alejandro J. Aguirre (Deputy Ed.); Virginia Godoy (Food Ed.); Gustavo Pena (News Ed.); Luis David Rodriguez (Society Ed.); Jesus Hernandez (Data Processing Mgr.); Gustavo De La Osa (Prod. Mgr.)

EL ARGENTINO NEWSPAPER

Street address 1: PO Box 802133
Street address city: Miami
State: FL
Zip/Postal code: 33280-2133
County: Miami-Dade
Country: USA
Mailing address: PO Box 802133
Mailing city: Miami
Mailing state: FL
Mailing zip: 33280-2133
General Fax: (305) 371-1656
General/National Adv. E-mail: showmgz@gate.net; info@elargentino.com
Audit By: Sworn/Estimate/Non-Audited
Audit Date: 12.07.2019
Personnel: Grace Micheli (Adv. Mgr.); Alberto Micheli (Ed.)

EL NUEVO HERALD

Street address 1: 1 Herald Plz
Street address city: Miami
State: FL
Zip/Postal code: 33132-1609
County: Miami-Dade
Country: USA
Mailing address: 1 Herald Plz
Mailing city: Miami
Mailing state: FL
Mailing zip: 33132-1609
General Phone: 1-800-843-4372
Published: Mon`Tues`Wed`Thur`Fri`Sun
Weekday Frequency: m
Saturday Frequency: m
Avg Paid Circ: 45526
Sat. Circulation Paid: 50436
Sun. Circulation Paid: 68781
Audit By: AAM
Audit Date: 30.06.2017

EL NUEVO PATRIA

Street address 1: 425 NW 27th Ave Ste 2
Street address 2: Jose Marti Station
Street address city: Miami
State: FL
Zip/Postal code: 33135-4767
County: Miami-Dade
Country: USA
Mailing address: PO Box 350002
Mailing city: Miami
Mailing state: FL
Mailing zip: 33135
General Phone: (305) 530-8787
Advertising Phone: (786) 286-8787
Advertising Fax: (305) 698-8787
General/National Adv. E-mail: patrianews@aol.com
Editorial e-mail: enpnews@aol.com
Year Established: 1959
Published: Wed
Avg Paid Circ: 7180
Avg Free Circ: 22820
Audit By: Sworn/Estimate/Non-Audited
Audit Date: 12.07.2019
Personnel: Maria Laura Figueroa (Gen. Mgr.); Dr. Carlos Diaz Lujan (Ed.); Omar R. Rosa (Prodn. Mgr.); Sara P. Armesto (Associate Ed.); Eladio Jose Armesto (Publisher); Sandra Baroja (Food & Wine Editor); Ralph Garcia (Book Editor); Madeline Sandoval (Feature Editor)

LIBRE

Street address 1: 2700 SW 8th St
Street address city: Miami
State: FL
Zip/Postal code: 33135-4619
County: Miami-Dade
Country: USA
Mailing address: 2700 SW 8th St
Mailing city: Miami
Mailing state: FL
Mailing zip: 33135-4619
General Phone: (305) 643-2947
General Fax: (305) 649-2767
General/National Adv. E-mail: main@libreonline.com
Year Established: 1966
Published: Wed
Avg Paid Circ: 1100
Avg Free Circ: 3850
Audit By: Sworn/Estimate/Non-Audited
Audit Date: 12.07.2019
Personnel: Demetrio Perez (Pub.)

TAMPA

LA GACETA

Street address 1: 3210 E 7th Ave
Street address city: Tampa
State: FL
Zip/Postal code: 33605-4302
County: Hillsborough
Country: USA
Mailing address: PO Box 5536
Mailing city: Tampa
Mailing state: FL
Mailing zip: 33675-5536
General Phone: (813) 248-3921
General Fax: (813) 247-5357
General/National Adv. E-mail: lagaceta@tampabay.rr.com
Display Adv. E-mail: lagaceta@tampabay.rr.com
Editorial e-mail: lagaceta@tampabay.rr.com
Year Established: 1922
Published: Fri
Avg Paid Circ: 18000
Audit By: Sworn/Estimate/Non-Audited
Audit Date: 12.07.2019
Personnel: Peggy Schmechel (Adv. Mgr.); Gene Siudut (Circ. Mgr.); Patrick Manteiga (Ed.); Angela Manteiga (Mng. Ed.); Angie Manteiga (Prodn. Mgr.)

NUEVO SIGLO

Street address 1: 7137 N Armenia Ave
Street address 2: Ste B
Street address city: Tampa
State: FL
Zip/Postal code: 33604-5263
County: Hillsborough
Country: USA
Mailing address: 100 Rose Way
Mailing city: Tullahoma
Mailing state: TN
Mailing zip: 37388-9545
General Phone: (813) 932-7181
General Fax: (813) 932-8202
General/National Adv. E-mail: n.siglo@verizon.net
Published: Thur
Avg Paid Circ: 3000
Avg Free Circ: 24000
Audit By: Sworn/Estimate/Non-Audited
Audit Date: 12.07.2019
Personnel: Neris Ramon Palacios (Pub.); Rosmeli Palacios (Gen. Mgr.); Griseldis Palacios (Adv. Mgr.); Ledis Palacios (Mng. Ed.)

WEST PALM BEACH

EL LATINO NEWSPAPER

Street address 1: 4404 Georgia Ave
Street address city: West Palm Beach
State: FL
Zip/Postal code: 33405-2500
County: Palm Beach
Country: USA
Mailing address: 4404 Georgia Ave.
Mailing city: West Palm Beach
Mailing state: FL
Mailing zip: 33405-2524
General Phone: (561) 835-4913
General Fax: (561) 655-5059
General/National Adv. E-mail: ellatino@msn.com
Published: Fri
Avg Free Circ: 39000
Audit By: Sworn/Estimate/Non-Audited
Audit Date: 12.07.2019
Personnel: Miguel A. Lavin (Pub.); Eduardo Monzon (Adv. Mgr.); Jose Uzal (Ed.)
State: Georgia

GEORGIA

ATLANTA

ATLANTA LATINO

Street address 1: 2865 Amwiler Rd
Street address 2: Ste 100
Street address city: Atlanta
State: GA
Zip/Postal code: 30360-2827
County: Gwinnett
Country: USA
Mailing address: 2865 Amwiler Rd Ste 100
Mailing city: Atlanta
Mailing state: GA
Mailing zip: 30360-2827
General Phone: (770) 416-7570
General Fax: (770) 416-7991
Display Adv. E-mail: sales@atlantalatino.com
Editorial e-mail: editor@atlantalatino.com
Published Other: Every other Thur
Avg Free Circ: 20000
Audit By: Sworn/Estimate/Non-Audited
Audit Date: 12.07.2019
Personnel: Farid Sadri (Adv. Mgr.); Judith Martinez (Ed. in Chief)

MUNDO HISPÃ¡NICO NEWSPAPER

Street address 1: 5269 Buford Highway
Street address city: Atlanta
State: GA
Zip/Postal code: 30340
Country: USA
Mailing address: 5269 Buford Highway
Mailing city: Atlanta
Mailing state: GA
Mailing zip: 30340
General Phone: (404) 881-0441
General Fax: (404) 881-6085
General/National Adv. E-mail: mbesares@mundohispanico.com
Editorial e-mail: gdelaney@mundohispanico.com
Year Established: 1979
Published: Thur
Avg Paid Circ: 20
Avg Free Circ: 70955
Audit By: CVC
Audit Date: 30.12.2018
Personnel: Melvin Besares; Gerard Delaney (Pub.); Jimmy Vega (Circ.); Marcelo Wheelock (Prod.)
State: Illinois

ILLINOIS

ARLINGTON HEIGHTS

REFLEJOS BILINGUAL PUBLICATIONS

Street address 1: 155 E Algonquin Rd
Street address 2:
Street address city: Arlington Heights
State: IL
Zip/Postal code: 60005-4617
County: Cook
Country: USA
Mailing address: 155 E. Algonquin Road
Mailing city: Arlington Heights
Mailing state: IL
Mailing zip: 60005
General Phone: (847) 806-1111

General Fax: (847) 806-1112
Advertising Phone: (847)806-1411
Editorial Phone: (847) 806-1171
General/National Adv. E-mail: lsiete@reflejos.com
Display Adv. E-mail: lsiete@reflejos.com
Editorial e-mail: mortiz@reflejos.com
Year Established: 1990
Published: Fri
Avg Paid Circ: 5
Avg Free Circ: 32549
Audit By: CVC
Audit Date: 30.12.2018
Personnel: Linda Siete (Pub./Adv. Mgr.); John Janos (Circ.); Hector Gomez (Prod.)

BROOKFIELD

CHICAGO DEPORTIVO

Street address 1: PO Box 411
Street address city: Brookfield
State: IL
Zip/Postal code: 60513
Country: USA
Mailing address: PO Box 411
Mailing city: Brookfield
Mailing state: IL
Mailing zip: 60513
General Phone: (312) 375-8979
Advertising Phone: (312) 375-8979
Editorial Phone: (312) 375-8979
General/National Adv. E-mail: eparrdeportivo@yahoo.com
Display Adv. E-mail: eparrdeportivo@yahoo.com
Editorial e-mail: eparrdeportivo@yahoo.com
Year Established: 1988
Personnel: Julio Parrales (Ed./Pub.); Julie Parrales Cisneros (Office Mgr.); Chris Parrales Gonzalez (Media/Pub. Rel. Dir.); Edward Parrales (Mktg./Sales Dir.)

COLOMBIA HOY NEWSPAPER

Street address 1: Please fill in*
Street address city: Chicago
State: IL
Zip/Postal code: 12345
Country: USA
Mailing city: Chicago
Mailing state: IL
General Phone: (800) 344 0538
Editorial e-mail: editor@colombiahoy.net
Personnel: Margarita Mendoza (Dir.); Isabella Recio (Collaborator); Mercedes Jimenez (Collaborator)

EXTRA BILINGUAL COMMUNITY NEWSPAPER

Street address 1: 3906 W North Ave
Street address city: Chicago
State: IL
Zip/Postal code: 60647-4618
County: Cook
Country: USA
Mailing address: 3906 W North Ave
Mailing city: Chicago
Mailing state: IL
Mailing zip: 60647-4618
General Phone: (773) 252-3534
General Fax: (773) 252-4073
Display Adv. E-mail: sales@extranews.net
Editorial e-mail: editor@extranews.net
Year Established: 1980
Published: Fri
Avg Free Circ: 66
Audit By: CVC
Audit Date: 30.09.2011
Personnel: Mila Tellez (Pub.); Nile Wendorf (Assoc. Pub./Gen. Mgr.); Christina Elizabeth Rodriguez (Managing Editor)

LA PRENSA DE CHICAGO

Street address 1: 4518 W. Fullerton
Street address city: Chicago
State: IL
Zip/Postal code: 60639
Country: USA
Mailing address: 4518 W. Fullerton
Mailing city: Chicago
Mailing state: IL
Mailing zip: 60639
General Phone: (773) 521-7286
General Fax: (773) 486-9877
General/National Adv. E-mail: laprensaus@gmail.com
Display Adv. E-mail: laprensachicago@hotmail.com
Personnel: Contact Us

LA RAZA NEWSPAPER

Street address 1: 605 N Michigan Ave
Street address 2: 4th Fl
Street address city: Chicago
State: IL
Zip/Postal code: 60611
County: Cook
Country: USA
Mailing address: 605 N Michigan Ave, 4th Fl
Mailing city: Chicago
Mailing state: IL
Mailing zip: 60611
General Phone: (312) 870-7000
Display Adv. E-mail: advertising@impremedia.com
Editorial e-mail: agenda@laraza.com
Year Established: 1970
Published: Sun
Avg Free Circ: 35000
Audit By: Sworn/Estimate/Non-Audited
Audit Date: 31.[illegible]
Personnel: Martha DeLuna (Nat'l Acct. Exec.); Brian Baase (Nat'l Acct. Exec.); Jimena Catarivas Corbett (Adv. Dir./Gen. Mgr.); Jesus Del Toro (Director General / General Manager); Fabiola Pomareda (Managing d.); Tatiana Canaval (Mktg. Mgr.); Hugo Jordan (Sr. Account Mgr., Local Sales)

NEGOCIOS NOW

Street address 1: 70 W Madison St
Street address 2: Ste 1400
Street address city: Chicago
State: IL
Zip/Postal code: 60602
Mailing address: 70 W Madison St, Ste 1400
Mailing city: Chicago
Mailing state: IL
Mailing zip: 60602
General Phone: (773) 942-7410
General/National Adv. E-mail: info@negociosnow.com
Personnel: Contact Us

CICERO

TELE GUIA DE CHICAGO

Street address 1: 3116 S Austin Blvd
Street address city: Cicero
State: IL
Zip/Postal code: 60804-3729
County: Cook
Country: USA
Mailing address: 3116 S Austin Blvd
Mailing city: Cicero
Mailing state: IL
Mailing zip: 60804-3729
General Phone: 708-656-6666
General Fax: 866-4156776
Advertising Phone: 708-656-6666 x1080
Advertising Fax: 866-4156776
Editorial Phone: 708-656-6666 x1074
Editorial Fax: 866-4156776
Display Adv. E-mail: rosemontes@aol.com
Editorial e-mail: avazquez@teleguia.us
Year Established: 1985
Published: Sun
Avg Paid Circ: 7481
Avg Free Circ: 20692
Audit By: CVC
Audit Date: 19.10.2017
Personnel: Zeke Montes

THE LAWNDALE NEWS/SU NOTICIERO BILINGUE

Street address 1: 5533 W 25th St
Street address city: Cicero
State: IL
Zip/Postal code: 60804-3319
County: Cook
Country: USA
Mailing address: 5533 W 25th St
Mailing city: Cicero
Mailing state: IL
Mailing zip: 60804-3319
General Phone: (708) 656-6400
General Fax: (708) 656-2433
Advertising Phone: (708) 656-6400
Advertising Fax: (708) 656-2433
General/National Adv. E-mail: printing@lawndalenews.com
Display Adv. E-mail: pilar@lawndalenews.com
Editorial e-mail: mandou@lawndalenews.com
Year Established: 1940
Published: Thur`Sun
Published Other: Twice a month
Audit By: Sworn/Estimate/Non-Audited
Audit Date: 12.07.2019
Personnel: JamesL. Nardini (VP); Lynda Nardini (Pub.); Gary Miller (Adv. Mgr.); Robert Nardini (Gen. Mgr.); Pilar Merino (Prodn. Mgr.); Ashmar Mandou (Ed.)

EVANSTON

EL CHICAGO HISPANO

Street address 1: 701 Main St.
Street address city: Evanston
State: IL
Zip/Postal code: 60202
Mailing address: PO Box 268722
Mailing city: Chicago
Mailing state: IL
Mailing zip: 60626
General Phone: (312) 593-2557
Advertising Phone: (773) 942-7410
Editorial Phone: (312) 593-2557
General/National Adv. E-mail: editor@elchicagohispano.com
Display Adv. E-mail: acano@elchicagohispano.com
Year Established: 2010
Personnel: Alejandra Cano (Sales); Kelly Yelmene (Mktg.)

PALATINE

NUEVA SEMANA

Street address 1: 1180 E Dundee Rd
Street address city: Palatine
State: IL
Zip/Postal code: 60074-8305
County: Cook
Country: USA
Mailing address: 1180 E Dundee Rd
Mailing city: Palatine
Mailing state: IL
Mailing zip: 60074
General Phone: (847) 239-4815
General Fax: (847) 890-6327
General/National Adv. E-mail: info@lanuevasemana.com
Editorial e-mail: ealegria@lanuevasemana.com
Year Established: 1999
Published: Fri
Avg Free Circ: 9000
Audit By: Sworn/Estimate/Non-Audited
Audit Date: 12.07.2019
Personnel: Rober Reyes (Pub.)
State: Indiana

INDIANA

GOSHEN

EL PUENTE

Street address 1: 1906 W Clinton St
Street address city: Goshen
State: IN
Zip/Postal code: 46526-1618
County: Elkhart
Country: USA
Mailing address: PO Box 553
Mailing city: Goshen
Mailing state: IN
Mailing zip: 46527-0553
General Phone: (574) 533-9082
General Fax: (574) 537-0552
Advertising Phone: (574) 533-9082
Editorial Phone: (574) 533-9082
General/National Adv. E-mail: mail@webelpuente.com
Display Adv. E-mail: design@webelpuente.com
Editorial e-mail: mail@webelpuente.com
Year Established: 1992
Published: Tues
Published Other: 1st & 3rd Tuesday of the month (24 yearly issues)
Avg Free Circ: 9000
Audit By: Sworn/Estimate/Non-Audited
Audit Date: 12.07.2019
Personnel: Yizzar Prieto (Production Director. Marketing.); Jimmer Prieto (Editor); Zulma Prieto (Editor)
State: Kansas

KANSAS

GARDEN CITY

LA SEMANA EN EL SUROESTE DE KANSAS

Street address 1: 310 N 7th St
Street address city: Garden City
State: KS
Zip/Postal code: 67846-5521
County: Finney
Country: USA
Mailing address: PO Box 958
Mailing city: Garden City
Mailing state: KS
Mailing zip: 67846-0958
General Phone: (620) 275-8500
General Fax: (620) 275-5165
General/National Adv. E-mail: lasemana@gctelegram.com
Published: Fri
Avg Free Circ: 3000
Audit By: Sworn/Estimate/Non-Audited
Audit Date: 12.07.2019
Personnel: Dena Sattler (Pub.); Charity Ochs (Adv. Mgr.); Jeremy Banwell (Circ. Mgr.); Brett Riggs (Mng. Ed.)

KANSAS CITY

DOS MUNDOS

Street address 1: 1701 S 55th St
Street address city: Kansas City
State: KS
Zip/Postal code: 66106-2241
County: Wyandotte
Country: USA
Mailing address: 1701 S. 55th. Street
Mailing city: Kansas City
Mailing state: KS
Mailing zip: 66106
General Phone: (816) 221-4747
General Fax: (816) 221-4894
Advertising Phone: (816)221-4747
General/National Adv. E-mail: newstaff@dosmundos.com
Editorial e-mail: CREYES@DOSMUNDOS.COM
Year Established: 1981
Published: Thur
Weekday Frequency: e
Avg Paid Circ: 20000
Avg Free Circ: 7000
Audit By: Sworn/Estimate/Non-Audited
Audit Date: 12.07.2019
Personnel: Manuel Reyes (Pub.); Diana Raymer (Adv. Mgr.); Clara Reyes (Ed.)
State: Massachusetts

MASSACHUSETTS

EL MUNDO

Street address 1: 408 S Huntington Ave

Street address city: Boston
State: MA
Zip/Postal code: 02130-4814
County: Suffolk
Country: USA
Mailing address: 408 S Huntington Ave
Mailing city: Boston
Mailing state: MA
Mailing zip: 02130-4814
General Phone: (617) 522-5060
General Fax: (617) 524-5886
Display Adv. E-mail: sales@elmundoboston.com
Editorial e-mail: editor@elmundoboston.com
Year Established: 1972
Published: Thur
Avg Paid Circ: 38000
Audit By: Sworn/Estimate/Non-Audited
Audit Date: 12.07.2019
Personnel: Jay Cosmopoulos (Adv. Mgr.); Alberto Vasallo (Ed.); Elvis Jocol (CMO)

EL PLANETA PUBLISHING

Street address 1: 126 Brookline Ave
Street address 2: Ste 3
Street address city: Boston
State: MA
Zip/Postal code: 02215-3920
County: Suffolk
Country: USA
Mailing address: 126 Brookline Ave Ste 3
Mailing city: Boston
Mailing state: MA
Mailing zip: 02215-3920
General Phone: (617) 937-5900
General Fax: (617) 536-1463
Display Adv. E-mail: sales@elplaneta.com
Editorial e-mail: editor@elplaneta.com
Year Established: 2004
Published: Fri
Avg Free Circ: 50000
Audit By: Sworn/Estimate/Non-Audited
Audit Date: 12.07.2019
Personnel: Marcela Garcia (Ed.)

LA SEMANA

Street address 1: 903 Albany St
Street address city: Boston
State: MA
Zip/Postal code: 02119-2534
County: Suffolk
Country: USA
Mailing address: 903 Albany St
Mailing city: Boston
Mailing state: MA
Mailing zip: 02119-2534
General Phone: (617) 541-2222
General Fax: (617) 427-6227
General/National Adv. E-mail: wcea2000@aol.com
Year Established: 1978
Published: Thur
Avg Free Circ: 10000
Audit By: Sworn/Estimate/Non-Audited
Audit Date: 12.07.2019
Personnel: Nicolas Cuenca (Adv. Mgr.); Peter N. Cuenca (Ed.)
State: Maryland

MARYLAND

HYATTSVILLE

EL PREGONERO

Street address 1: 5001 Eastern Ave
Street address city: Hyattsville
State: MD
Zip/Postal code: 20782-3447
County: Prince Georges
Country: USA
Mailing address: PO Box 4464
Mailing city: Washington
Mailing state: DC
Mailing zip: 20017-0464
General Phone: (202) 281-2404
General Fax: (202) 281-2448
Advertising Phone: (202) 281-2406
Editorial Phone: (202) 281-2442
General/National Adv. E-mail: rafael@elpreg.org
Display Adv. E-mail: irieska@elpreg.org
Editorial e-mail: rafael@elpreg.org
Year Established: 1977
Published: Thur
Avg Free Circ: 24993
Audit By: AAM
Audit Date: 30.06.2018
Personnel: Rafael Roncal (Ed.); Irieska D. Caetano (Circ. Mgr.)

SILVER SPRING

WASHINGTON HISPANIC

Street address 1: 8455 Colesville Rd
Street address city: Silver Spring
State: MD
Zip/Postal code: 20910-7600
County: Montgomery
Country: USA
Mailing address: 8455 Colesville Rd
Mailing city: Washington
Mailing state: DC
Mailing zip: 20910
General Phone: (202) 667-8881
General Fax: (202) 667-8902
General/National Adv. E-mail: info@washingtonhispanic.com
Audit By: Sworn/Estimate/Non-Audited
Audit Date: 12.07.2019
Personnel: Johnny Yataco (Adv. Mgr.)
State: Michgan

MICHGAN

DETROIT

EL CENTRAL

Street address 1: 4124 W Vernor Hwy
Street address city: Detroit
State: MI
Zip/Postal code: 48209-2145
County: Wayne
Country: USA
Mailing address: 4124 W Vernor Hwy
Mailing city: Detroit
Mailing state: MI
Mailing zip: 48209-2145
General Phone: (313) 841-0100
General Fax: (313) 841-0155
General/National Adv. E-mail: elcentral1@aol.com
Display Adv. E-mail: elcentralads@aol.com
Published: Thur
Avg Free Circ: 14000
Audit By: Sworn/Estimate/Non-Audited
Audit Date: 12.07.2019
Personnel: Dolores Sanchez (Ed.)

LATINO PRESS

Street address 1: 6301 Michigan Ave
Street address city: Detroit
State: MI
Zip/Postal code: 48210-2954
County: Wayne
Country: USA
Mailing address: 6301 Michigan Ave
Mailing city: Detroit
Mailing state: MI
Mailing zip: 48210-2954
General Phone: (313) 361-3000
General Fax: (313) 361-3001
Advertising Phone: (313) 361-3000
Editorial Phone: (313) 361-3002
General/National Adv. E-mail: clau@latinodetroit.com
Display Adv. E-mail: marketing@latinodetroit.com
Classified Adv. e-mail: clau@latinodetroit.com
Editorial e-mail: editorial@latinodetroit.com
Year Established: 1993
Published: Fri
Avg Paid Circ: 2500
Avg Free Circ: 15000
Audit By: Sworn/Estimate/Non-Audited
Audit Date: 12.07.2019
Personnel: Elias M. Gutierrez (President)
State: Minnesota

MINNESOTA

MINNEAPOLIS

LA PRENSA DE MINNESOTA

Street address 1: 1516 E Lake St
Street address 2: Ste 200
Street address city: Minneapolis
State: MN
Zip/Postal code: 55407-3579
County: Hennepin
Country: USA
Mailing address: 2909 Bryant Ave. S.
Mailing city: Minneapolis
Mailing state: MN
Mailing zip: 55408
General Phone: (612) 729-5900
General Fax: (612) 729-5999
General/National Adv. E-mail: marian@lcnmedia.com
Published: Thur
Avg Free Circ: 15000
Audit By: Sworn/Estimate/Non-Audited
Audit Date: 12.07.2019
Personnel: Mario Duarte (Pub.); Lorena Duarte (Ed.)
State: North Carolina

NORTH CAROLINA

CHARLOTTE

HOLA NOTICIAS

Street address 1: 4801 E Independence Blvd
Street address 2: Ste 815
Street address city: Charlotte
State: NC
Zip/Postal code: 28212-5490
County: Mecklenburg
Country: USA
Mailing address: 4801 E Independence Blvd Ste 815
Mailing city: Charlotte
Mailing state: NC
Mailing zip: 28212-5490
Published: Tues
Audit By: Sworn/Estimate/Non-Audited
Audit Date: 12.07.2019
Personnel: Judy Galindo

LA NOTICIA

Street address 1: 5936 Monroe Rd
Street address city: Charlotte
State: NC
Zip/Postal code: 28212-6106
County: Mecklenburg
Country: USA
Mailing address: 5936 Monroe Rd
Mailing city: Charlotte
Mailing state: NC
Mailing zip: 28212-6106
General Phone: (704) 568-6966
General Fax: (704) 568-8936
General/National Adv. E-mail: hgurdian@lanoticia.com
Display Adv. E-mail: hgurdian@lanoticia.com
Editorial e-mail: editor@lanoticia.com
Year Established: 1992
Published: Wed
Avg Free Circ: 26000
Audit By: Sworn/Estimate/Non-Audited
Audit Date: 12.07.2019
Personnel: Hilda Gurdian (Pub.)

MI GENTE

Street address 1: 4801 E Independence Blvd
Street address 2: Ste 800
Street address city: Charlotte
State: NC
Zip/Postal code: 28212-5408
County: Mecklenburg
Country: USA
Mailing address: PO Box 12876
Mailing city: Winston Salem
Mailing state: NC
Mailing zip: 27117-2876
General Phone: (704) 319-5044
Advertising Phone: (704) 449-0769
Published: Tues
Avg Free Circ: 20873
Audit By: Sworn/Estimate/Non-Audited
Audit Date: 12.07.2019
Personnel: Rafael Prieto

RALEIGH

QUE PASA - RALEIGH

Street address 1: 4801 Glenwood Ave
Street address 2: Suite 200
Street address city: Raleigh
State: NC
Zip/Postal code: 27612
Country: USA
Mailing address: 4801 Glenwood Ave Ste. 200
Mailing city: Raleigh
Mailing state: NC
Mailing zip: 27612
General Phone: (919) 645-1680
Advertising Phone: (336) 935-9673
General/National Adv. E-mail: distribution@quepasamedia.com
Display Adv. E-mail: sales@quepasamedia.com
Editorial e-mail: editor@quepasamedia.com
Year Established: 1994
Published: Thur
Avg Paid Circ: 0
Avg Free Circ: 11336
Audit By: CVC
Audit Date: 31.12.2018
Personnel: Jose Isasi; Amith Arrieta; Marina Aleman (Adv.); Hernando Ramirez (Ed.)

WINSTON SALEM

QUE PASA - CHARLOTTE

Street address 1: 7520 East Independence Blvd.
Street address 2: Suite 255
Street address city: Winston Salem
State: NC
Zip/Postal code: 28227
County: Forsyth
Country: USA
Mailing address: 3025 Waughtown St Ste G
Mailing city: Winston Salem
Mailing state: NC
Mailing zip: 27107-1679
General Phone: (704) 319-5044
General/National Adv. E-mail: distribution@quepasamedia.com
Display Adv. E-mail: sales@quepasamedia.com
Editorial e-mail: editor@quepasamedia.com
Year Established: 1994
Published: Thur
Avg Paid Circ: 0
Avg Free Circ: 37078
Audit By: CVC
Audit Date: 31.12.2018
Personnel: Amith Arrieta; Jose Isasi (Pub.); Marina Aleman (Adv.); Hernando Ramirez (Ed.)

QUE PASA - WINSTON-SALEM

Street address 1: 3067 Waughtown St
Street address city: Winston Salem
State: NC
Zip/Postal code: 27107-1679
Country: USA
Mailing address: 3067 Waughtown St
Mailing city: Winston Salem

Mailing state: NC
Mailing zip: 27107
General Phone: (336) 784-9004
General/National Adv. E-mail: distribution@quepasamedia.com
Display Adv. E-mail: sales@quepasamedia.com
Editorial e-mail: editor@quepasamedia.com
Year Established: 1994
Published: Wed
Avg Paid Circ: 0
Avg Free Circ: 12698
Audit By: CVC
Audit Date: 31.12.2018
Personnel: Amith Arrieta; Jose Isasi (Pub.); Marina Aleman (Adv.)
State: New Jersey

NEW JERSEY

ELIZABETH

LA VOZ

Street address 1: PO Box 899
Street address city: Elizabeth
State: NJ
Zip/Postal code: 07207-0899
County: Union
Country: USA
Mailing address: PO Box 899
Mailing city: Elizabeth
Mailing state: NJ
Mailing zip: 07207-0899
General Phone: (908) 352-6654
General Fax: (908) 352-9735
General/National Adv. E-mail: lavoznj@aol.com
Published Other: 2 x Mthly
Avg Free Circ: 38000
Audit By: Sworn/Estimate/Non-Audited
Audit Date: 12.07.2019
Personnel: Abel Berry (Pub.); Daniel Garcia (Adv. Mgr.)

UNION CITY

CONTINENTAL NEWSPAPER

Street address 1: 212 48th St
Street address city: Union City
State: NJ
Zip/Postal code: 07087-6436
County: Hudson
Country: USA
Mailing address: 212 48th St Ste A
Mailing city: Union City
Mailing state: NJ
Mailing zip: 07087-6436
General Phone: (201) 864-9505
General Fax: (201) 864-9456
General/National Adv. E-mail: continews@aol.com
Published: Fri
Avg Paid Circ: 38000
Audit By: Sworn/Estimate/Non-Audited
Audit Date: 12.07.2019
Personnel: M. Ofelia Dones (Pres.); Mario Ciria (Exec. Dir.); Veronica Romero (Mng. Ed.)

EL ESPECIALITO

Street address 1: 3711 Hudson Ave
Street address city: Union City
State: NJ
Zip/Postal code: 07087-6015
County: Hudson
Country: USA
Mailing address: 3711 Hudson Ave
Mailing city: Union City
Mailing state: NJ
Mailing zip: 07087
General Phone: (201) 348-1959
General Fax: (201) 348-3385
General/National Adv. E-mail: anthony@elespecial.com
Display Adv. E-mail: anthony@elespecial.com
Editorial e-mail: jsibaja@elespecial.com
Year Established: 1985
Published: Fri
Published Other: Weekly
Avg Free Circ: 251339
Audit By: AAM
Audit Date: 30.06.2018
Personnel: John Ibarria (VP); Anthony Ibarria (Adv. Mgr.); Jose Sibaja (Ed. Dir.)

LA TRIBUNA PUBLICATION

Street address 1: 300 36th St
Street address city: Union City
State: NJ
Zip/Postal code: 07087-4724
County: Hudson
Country: USA
Mailing address: PO Box 805
Mailing city: Union City
Mailing state: NJ
Mailing zip: 07087-0805
General Phone: (201) 863-3310
General Fax: (201) 617-0042
General/National Adv. E-mail: info@latribuna.com
Audit By: Sworn/Estimate/Non-Audited
Audit Date: 12.07.2019
Personnel: Ruth Molenaar (Pub.); Soraya Molenaar (Adv. Mgr.); Rosario Tineo (Circ. Mgr.); Lionel Rodriquez (Ed.)
State: New Mexico

NEW MEXICO

ESPANOLA

RIO GRANDE SUN

Street address 1: 123 N Railroad Ave
Street address city: Espanola
State: NM
Zip/Postal code: 87532-2627
County: Rio Arriba
Country: USA
Mailing address: PO Box 790
Mailing city: Espanola
Mailing state: NM
Mailing zip: 87532-0790
General Phone: (505) 753-2126
General Fax: (505) 753-2140
Advertising Phone: 505-753-2126
Advertising Fax: 505-753-2140
General/National Adv. E-mail: rgsun@cybermesa.com
Display Adv. E-mail: rgsunads@cybermesa.com
Editorial e-mail: rgsun@cybermesa.com
Year Established: 1956
Published: Thur
Avg Paid Circ: 10000
Audit By: USPS
Audit Date: 12.10.2021
Personnel: Maria Garcia (General Manager); Robert Trapp (Publisher)
State: Nevada

NEVADA

BLOQUE LATINO AMERICANO DE PRENSA EL EXITO LATIN AMERICAN PRESS

Street address 1: PO Box 12599
Street address city: Las Vegas
State: NV
Zip/Postal code: 89112-0599
County: Clark
Country: USA
Mailing address: PO Box 12599
Mailing city: Las Vegas
Mailing state: NV
Mailing zip: 89112-0599
General Phone: (702) 431-1904
General Fax: (702) 431-3339
General/National Adv. E-mail: elexito2@cox.net
Display Adv. E-mail: elexito2@cox.net
Year Established: 1988
Published: Fri
Avg Free Circ: 50662
Audit By: Sworn/Estimate/Non-Audited
Audit Date: 12.07.2019
Personnel: Maggy Ruiz (Adv. Mgr.); Luz Delgado (Circ. Mgr.); Magaly Ruiz (Ed.); Tirso Del Pozo (Prodn. Mgr.)

EL MUNDO

Street address 1: 760 N Eastern Ave
Street address 2: Ste 110
Street address city: Las Vegas
State: NV
Zip/Postal code: 89101-2888
County: Clark
Country: USA
Mailing address: 760 N Eastern Ave Ste 110
Mailing city: Las Vegas
Mailing state: NV
Mailing zip: 89101-2888
General Phone: (702) 649-8553
General Fax: (702) 649-7429
General/National Adv. E-mail: distribution@elmundo.net
Display Adv. E-mail: advertising@elmundo.net
Editorial e-mail: hescobedo@elmundo.net
Year Established: 1980
Published: Fri
Avg Free Circ: 29975
Audit By: CVC
Audit Date: 31.12.2018
Personnel: Hilda Escobedo (Pub.); Nick Escobedo (Circ.); Flora Hernandez (Prodn. Mgr.)

EL TIEMPO

Street address 1: 1111 W Bonanza Rd
Street address city: Las Vegas
State: NV
Zip/Postal code: 89106-3545
County: Clark
Country: USA
Mailing address: PO BOX 70
Mailing city: LAS VEGAS
Mailing state: NV
Mailing zip: 89125-0070
General Phone: (702) 477-3845
Advertising Phone: (702) 477-3845
Editorial Phone: (702) 47-3846
General/National Adv. E-mail: gjuricad@reviewjournal.com
Display Adv. E-mail: ddyer@reviewjournal.com
Editorial e-mail: mcmatta@reviewjournal.com
Year Established: 1994
Published: Fri
Avg Paid Circ: 0
Avg Free Circ: 51878
Audit By: CAC
Audit Date: 30.09.2014
Personnel: Maria Cristina Matta-Caro (Pub./Ed.)

EL TIEMPO

Street address 1: 1111 W Bonanza Rd
Street address city: Las Vegas
State: NV
Zip/Postal code: 89106-3545
County: Clark
Country: USA
Mailing address: 1111 W Bonanza Rd
Mailing city: Las Vegas
Mailing state: NV
Mailing zip: 89106-3545
General Phone: 702-383-0300
General Fax: 702-383-0402
Advertising Phone: (702) 477-3846
Advertising Fax: (702) 387-2981
Editorial Phone: 702-387-2972
Editorial Fax: 702-251-0736
General/National Adv. E-mail: anahangi@reviewjournal.com
Display Adv. E-mail: gjurica@reviewjournal.com
Editorial e-mail: hamaya@reviewjournal.com
Year Established: 1994
Published: Fri
Avg Paid Circ: 94128
Audit By: AAM
Audit Date: 30.06.2018
Personnel: Maria Cristina Matta-Caro (Pub./Ed.); Anthony Avelleneda (Reporter); Jorge Betancourt (Graphic Des.); Eddie Corrarrubias (Sr. Account Ex.)

RENO

AHORA LATINO JOURNAL

Street address 1: 605 S Wells Ave
Street address city: Reno
State: NV
Zip/Postal code: 89502-1825
County: Washoe
Country: USA
Mailing address: 9584 Autumn Leaf Way
Mailing city: Reno
Mailing state: NV
Mailing zip: 89506-4502
General Phone: (775) 677-9694
Advertising Phone: 775-378-7025
Editorial Phone: 775-378-7025
General/National Adv. E-mail: marioreno@live.com
Display Adv. E-mail: marioreno@live.com
Editorial e-mail: adelitazapata@live.com
Year Established: 2010
Published: Tues`Wed`Other
Published Other: Bi-weekly
Avg Free Circ: 8000
Audit By: Sworn/Estimate/Non-Audited
Audit Date: 12.07.2019
State: New York

NEW YORK

EL DIARIO LA PRENSA

Street address 1: 1 Metrotech Ctr
Street address 2: Fl 18
Street address city: Brooklyn
State: NY
Zip/Postal code: 11201-3948
County: Kings
Country: USA
Mailing address: 1 Metrotech Ctr Fl 18
Mailing city: Brooklyn
Mailing state: NY
Mailing zip: 11201-3949
General Phone: (212) 807-4662
General Fax: (212) 807-4746
General/National Adv. E-mail: editorial@eldiariolaprensa.com
Display Adv. E-mail: communications@impremedia.com
Year Established: 1913
Published Other: Daily
Avg Paid Circ: 134696
Audit By: Sworn/Estimate/Non-Audited
Audit Date: 12.07.2019
Personnel: Denny PeÃ±a (Circ. Dir.); Francisco Seghezzo (CEO); Ivan Adaime (General Mgr Digital); Juan Varela (Content Dir.); Jorge Ayala (VP of Adv.); Fernando Lang (Director, Ad Rev/Operations); Angel Vazquez; Lizbeth Rodriguez (Marketing Dir.)

HEMPSTEAD

LA TRIBUNA HISPANA-USA

Street address 1: 48 Main St
Street address 2: Fl 2
Street address city: Hempstead
State: NY
Zip/Postal code: 11550-4052
County: Nassau
Country: USA
Mailing address: PO Box 186
Mailing city: Hempstead
Mailing state: NY
Mailing zip: 11551-0186
General Phone: (516) 486-6457
General Fax: (866) 215-5982
General/National Adv. E-mail: editorial@tribunahispana.com
Published: Wed
Avg Free Circ: 49000
Audit By: Sworn/Estimate/Non-Audited
Audit Date: 12.07.2019
Personnel: Dora Escobar (Gen. Mgr.); Emilio A. Ruiz (Adv. Mgr.); Luis Aguilar (Ed.)

JAMAICA

RESUMEN NEWSPAPER

Street address 1: 13842 90th Ave
Street address 2: Apt F1
Street address city: Jamaica
State: NY
Zip/Postal code: 11435-4104
County: Queens
Country: USA
Mailing address: 13842 90th Ave Apt F1
Mailing city: Jamaica
Mailing state: NY
Mailing zip: 11435-4104
General Phone: (718) 899-8603
Advertising Phone: 718-424-7976
General/National Adv. E-mail: rojas123@aol.com
Display Adv. E-mail: rojas123@aol.com
Editorial e-mail: TRACEMYMOVES@GMAIL.COM
Year Established: 1971
Published Other: Daily
Avg Paid Circ: 8000
Avg Free Circ: 32000
Audit By: Sworn/Estimate/Non-Audited
Audit Date: 12.07.2019
Personnel: Fernando F. Rojas (Pub.); Jasmina Abril (Gen. Mgr.); Fernando J. Rojas (Ed.)

DIARIO DE MEXICO USA

Street address 1: 106 32nd Street New York
Street address 2: Suite 160
Street address city: New York
State: NY
Zip/Postal code: 01001
County: New York
Country: USA
Mailing address: 106 32nd Street New York, Suite 160
Mailing city: New York
Mailing state: NY
Mailing zip: 01001
General Phone: (212) 725-1521
General/National Adv. E-mail: contacto@diariodemexicousa.com
Published: Mon`Tues`Wed`Thur`Fri
Weekday Frequency: m
Avg Paid Circ: 12181
Audit By: AAM
Audit Date: 30.09.2011
Personnel: Contact Us

IMPACTO LATIN NEWS

Street address 1: 5 Penn Plaza
Street address 2: Ste 1915
Street address city: New York
State: NY
Zip/Postal code: 85261
County: New York
Country: USA
Mailing address: P.O. Box 5316
Mailing city: Scottsdale
Mailing state: AZ
Mailing zip: 10001-3437
General Phone: (212) 807-0400
General Fax: (212) 807-0408
General/National Adv. E-mail: media@impactony.com
Display Adv. E-mail: gsmith@impactolatino.com
Classified Adv. e-mail: gsmith@impactolatino.com
Editorial e-mail: jsmith@impactolatino.com
Year Established: 1967
Published: Thur
Avg Free Circ: 57000
Audit By: Sworn/Estimate/Non-Audited
Audit Date: 31.03.2014
Personnel: Gail M Smith (Pub.); Jason. K Smith (Ed.); Vanessa. M Smith (VP, Adv./Mktg.); Mar Verdugo (Market Research Analyst)

LA VOZ HISPANA NEWSPAPER

Street address 1: 159 E 116th St
Street address city: New York
State: NY
Zip/Postal code: 10029-1399
County: New York
Country: USA
Mailing address: 159 E 116th St Fl 2
Mailing city: New York
Mailing state: NY
Mailing zip: 10029-1399
General Phone: (212) 348-8270
General Fax: (212) 348-4469
Advertising Phone: (212) 348-8270
Editorial Phone: (917) 225-8576
Editorial Fax: (212) 348-4469
General/National Adv. E-mail: discomund@aol.com
Year Established: 1970
Published: Thur
Avg Paid Circ: 61879
Avg Free Circ: 9200
Audit By: Sworn/Estimate/Non-Audited
Audit Date: 12.07.2019
Personnel: Nick Lugo (Pub.); Joaquin Del Rio (Exec. Ed.)

NUESTRO MUNDO

Street address 1: 235 W 23rd St
Street address city: New York
State: NY
Zip/Postal code: 10011-2371
County: New York
Country: USA
Mailing address: 235 W 23rd St
Mailing city: New York
Mailing state: NY
Mailing zip: 10011-2302
General Phone: (212) 924-2523
General Fax: (212) 229-1713
General/National Adv. E-mail: pww@pww.org; contact@peoplesworld.org
Published: Sat
Avg Paid Circ: 15000
Avg Free Circ: 10000
Audit By: Sworn/Estimate/Non-Audited
Audit Date: 12.07.2019
Personnel: Jose Cruz (Ed.)
State: Ohio

OHIO

BLUE ASH

LA JORNADA LATINA

Street address 1: 4412 Carver Woods Dr
Street address 2: Ste 200
Street address city: Blue Ash
State: OH
Zip/Postal code: 45242-5539
County: Hamilton
Country: USA
Mailing address: 4412 Carver Woods Dr Ste 200
Mailing city: Blue Ash
Mailing state: OH
Mailing zip: 45242-5539
Published: Fri
Avg Paid Circ: 25
Avg Free Circ: 8933
Audit By: Sworn/Estimate/Non-Audited
Audit Date: 12.07.2019
Personnel: Jason Riveiro; Josh Guttman (General Adv.)
State: Oregon

OREGON

PORTLAND

EL HISPANIC NEWS

Street address 1: 6700 N New York Ave
Street address 2: Ste 212
Street address city: Portland
State: OR
Zip/Postal code: 97203-2836
County: Multnomah
Country: USA
Mailing address: PO Box 306
Mailing city: Portland
Mailing state: OR
Mailing zip: 97207-0306
General Phone: (503) 228-3139
General Fax: (503) 228-3384
General/National Adv. E-mail: info@elhispanicnews.com
Published: Thur
Avg Free Circ: 20000
Audit By: CVC
Audit Date: 31.12.2003
Personnel: Clara Padilla Andrews (Pub.); Melanie Davis (Mng. Partner); Maria Perry Crawshaw (Adv. Mgr.); Julie Cortez (Ed.); Christopher Alvarez (Prodn. Mgr.)
State: Pennsylvania

PENNSYLVANIA

GETTYSBURG

EL DAIRIO LATINO

Street address 1: 1570 Fairfield Rd
Street address city: Gettysburg
State: PA
Zip/Postal code: 17325-7252
County: Adams
Country: USA
Mailing address: PO Box 3669
Mailing city: Gettysburg
Mailing state: PA
Mailing zip: 17325-0669

HAMBURG

MID-ATLANTIC COMMUNITY PAPERS ASSOCIATION

Street address 1: 16515 Pottsville Pike
Street address 2: Suite C
Street address city: Hamburg
State: PA
Zip/Postal code: 19526
County: Berks
Country: USA
Mailing address: PO Box 408
Mailing city: Hamburg
Mailing state: PA
Mailing zip: 19526-0408
General Phone: 484-709-6564
General/National Adv. E-mail: info@macpa.net
Display Adv. E-mail: info@macnetonline.com
Year Established: 1955
Published: Mon`Tues`Wed`Thur`Fri`Sat`Sun`Mthly
Avg Free Circ: 1200000
Audit By: CVC
Audit Date: 01.01.2021
Personnel: Alyse Mitten (Exec. Dir.)

AL DIA NEWS MEDIA

Street address 1: 1835 Market St
Street address 2: Fl 4
Street address city: Philadelphia
State: PA
Zip/Postal code: 19103-2968
County: Philadelphia
Country: USA
Mailing address: 1835 Market St Ste 450
Mailing city: Philadelphia
Mailing state: PA
Mailing zip: 19103-2939
General Phone: (215) 569-4666
General Fax: (215) 569-2721
Advertising Phone: (215) 789-6975
Advertising Fax: (215) 569-2721
Editorial Phone: (215) 789-6973
General/National Adv. E-mail: adsales@aldiainc.com
Display Adv. E-mail: ads@aldiainc.com
Editorial e-mail: editor@aldiainc.com
Year Established: 1992
Published: Sun
Avg Free Circ: 42425
Audit By: CAC
Audit Date: 30.09.2014
Personnel: Gaby Guaracao (Strategy & Operations); Hernan Guaracao (Founder & CEO); Sabrina Vourvoulias (Managing Editor); Yesid Vargas (Art Dir.)

EL HISPANO

Street address 1: PO Box 396
Street address city: Pilgrim Gardens
State: PA
Zip/Postal code: 19026-0396
County: Delaware
Country: USA
Mailing address: PO Box 396
Mailing city: Pilgrim Gardens
Mailing state: PA
Mailing zip: 19026-0396
General Phone: 484-472-6059
General Fax: 484-472-8153
Advertising Phone: 484-472-6059
Advertising Fax: 474-472-8153
General/National Adv. E-mail: alopez5268@aol.com
Display Adv. E-mail: hispads@aol.com
Editorial e-mail: alopez5268@aol.com
Published: Wed
Avg Paid Circ: 500
Avg Free Circ: 18000
Audit By: CVC
Audit Date: 30.06.2011
Personnel: Aaron G. Lopez; Madelyn Madary

UPPER DARBY

EL HISPANO

Street address 1: 8605 W Chester Pike
Street address city: Upper Darby
State: PA
Zip/Postal code: 19082-1101
County: Delaware
Country: USA
Mailing address: 8605 W Chester Pike
Mailing city: Upper Darby
Mailing state: PA
Mailing zip: 19082-1101
General Phone: (610) 789-5512
General Fax: (610) 789-5524
General/National Adv. E-mail: alopez5268@aol.com; hispads@aol.com
Year Established: 1976
Published: Wed
Avg Paid Circ: 100
Avg Free Circ: 40000
Audit By: Sworn/Estimate/Non-Audited
Audit Date: 12.07.2019
Personnel: Madelyn Madary (Adv. Mgr.); Philip Madary (Circ. Mgr.); Aaron G. Lopez (Mng. Ed.); Sara Lopez (Ed.); Aaron Galicia (Prodn. Mgr.)

WEST GROVE

UNIDAD LATINA

Street address 1: 144 S Jennersville Rd
Street address city: West Grove
State: PA
Zip/Postal code: 19390-9430
County: Chester
Country: USA
Mailing address: PO Box 150
Mailing city: Kelton
Mailing state: PA
Mailing zip: 19346-0150
General Phone: (610) 869-5553
General Fax: (610) 869-9628
General/National Adv. E-mail: info@chestercounty.com
Year Established: 1995
Audit By: Sworn/Estimate/Non-Audited
Audit Date: 12.07.2019
Personnel: Randall S. Lieberman (Pub.); Alan Turns (Adv. Mgr.); Steve Hoffman (Mng. Ed.)
State: Puerto Rico

PUERTO RICO

CAGUAS

LA SEMANA

Street address 1: Calle Crista Bai Colafan
Street address 2: Esquina Ponce De Leafan
Street address city: Caguas
State: PR
Zip/Postal code: 725
County: Caguas
Country: Puerto Rico
Mailing address: PO Box 6537
Mailing city: Caguas
Mailing state: PR
Mailing zip: 00726-6537
General Phone: (787) 743-5606
General Fax: (787) 743-5100
General/National Adv. E-mail: lasemanaelpionero@gmail.com
Editorial e-mail: redaccion@periodicolasemana.net
Published: Thur
Avg Free Circ: 80060
Audit By: AAM
Audit Date: 31.03.2015

CAROLINA

PERIODICO PRESENCIA

Street address 1: PO Box 1928
Street address city: Carolina
State: PR
Zip/Postal code: 00984-1928
County: Carolina
Country: USA
Mailing address: P.O. Box 1928
Mailing city: Carolina
Mailing state: PR
Mailing zip: 00984-1928
General Phone: (787)-946-1391
General Fax: (787) 946-1392
General/National Adv. E-mail: ernestoalmodovarlopez@gmail.com
Display Adv. E-mail: ingrid.vicente@prenciapr.com
Editorial e-mail: dcamara@presenciapr.com
Year Established: 2013
Published: Thur
Avg Free Circ: 69414
Audit By: CVC
Audit Date: 30.06.2018
Personnel: Diana Camara Santiago (Pub.); Ingrid Vincente (Adv.); Ernesto Almodovar (Circ.); Hector Alvarez (Prod.)

DORADO

EL EXPRESSO DE PUERTO RICO

Street address 1: PO Box 465
Street address city: Dorado
State: PR
Zip/Postal code: 00646-0465
County: Dorado
Country: Puerto Rico
Mailing address: PO Box 465
Mailing city: Dorado
Mailing state: PR
Mailing zip: 00646-0465
General Phone: 787-794-2000
General Fax: 787-794-2273
Advertising Phone: 787-794-2000
Advertising Fax: 787-794-2273
Editorial Phone: 787-794-2006
Editorial Fax: 787-794-2716
General/National Adv. E-mail: info@elexpresso.com
Display Adv. E-mail: anuncios@elexpresso.com
Editorial e-mail: redaccion@elexpresso.com
Year Established: 1995
Published: Thur
Avg Paid Circ: 0
Avg Free Circ: 74900
Audit By: VAC
Audit Date: 30.03.2016
Personnel: Angel Fret (Publisher)

GUAYNABO

PERIODICO METRO PUERTO RICO

Street address 1: Carazo St
Street address city: Guaynabo
State: PR
Zip/Postal code: 969
County: Guaynabo
Country: USA
General Phone: (787)705-0920
General Fax: (787)705-0926
Display Adv. E-mail: multimedia@metro.pr
Editorial e-mail: multimedia@metro.pr
Published: Mon`Tues`Wed`Thur`Fri
Avg Free Circ: 83793
Audit By: CAC
Audit Date: 31.12.2017

PRIMERA HORA

Street address 1: A 16 Genoa Street
Street address 2: Extension Villa Caparra
Street address city: Guaynabo
State: PR
Zip/Postal code: 965
County: Guaynabo
Country: Puerto Rico
Mailing address: PO Box 2009
Mailing city: Catano
Mailing state: PR
Mailing zip: 00963-2009
General Phone: 787-641-4475
General Fax: 787-641-4473
Advertising Phone: 787-641-4469
Advertising Fax: 787-641-4470
Published: Mon`Tues`Wed`Thur`Fri`Sat
Weekday Frequency: m
Saturday Frequency: m
Avg Paid Circ: 152295
Sat. Circulation Paid: 57099
Audit By: AAM
Audit Date: 31.12.2018
State: Rhode Island

RHODE ISLAND

NORTH PROVIDENCE

PROVIDENCE EN ESPANOL

Street address 1: 45 Meadow View Blvd
Street address city: North Providence
State: RI
Zip/Postal code: 02904-2916
County: Providence
Country: USA
General Phone: 401.834.5552
General Fax: 401.233.7500
Display Adv. E-mail: ads@providenceenespanol.com
Editorial e-mail: news@providenceenespanol.com
Year Established: 1999
Published: Mon`Tues`Wed`Thur`Fri`Sat`Sun
Published Other: daily updates
Personnel: Arelis Pena (Ed.); Vivian Cuenca; Victor Cuenca
State: South Carolina

SOUTH CAROLINA

EL INFORMADOR NEWSPAPER

Street address 1: 222 W Coleman Blvd
Street address 2: Suite 111
Street address city: Mount Pleasant
State: SC
Zip/Postal code: 29464
County: Charleston
Country: EEUU
General Phone: 843-817-2896
Advertising Phone: 843-817-2896
Editorial Phone: 843-817-2896
Editorial Fax: 843-352-4506
General/National Adv. E-mail: pedro@elinformador.us
Display Adv. E-mail: pedro@elinformador.us
Editorial e-mail: pedro@elinformador.us
Year Established: 2008
Published: Wed
Audit By: CVC
Personnel: Lisa De Armas (Administration)

EL INFORMADOR SPANISH LANGUAGE NEWSPAPER

Street address 1: PO Box 2458
Street address city: Mount Pleasant
State: SC
Zip/Postal code: 29465-2458
County: Charleston
Country: USA
Mailing address: PO Box 2458
Mailing city: Mount Pleasant
Mailing state: SC
Mailing zip: 29465-2458
General Phone: 843-693-1116
General Fax: 843-352-4506
Advertising Phone: 843-817-2896
Advertising Fax: 843-352-4506
Editorial Phone: 843-693-1116
Editorial Fax: 843-352-4506
General/National Adv. E-mail: lisa@elinformadornewspaper.com
Display Adv. E-mail: sales@elinformadornewspaper.com
Editorial e-mail: lisa@elinformadornewspaper.com
Year Established: 2008
Published: Wed
Published Other: Biweekly
Avg Free Circ: 10000
Audit By: Sworn/Estimate/Non-Audited
Audit Date: 12.07.2019
Personnel: Lisa De Armas (Director); Pedro De Armas (Publisher)
State: Texas

TEXAS

ABILENE

ABILENE HISPANIC GUIDE

Street address 1: 122 McGlothlin Campus Center
Street address 2: Acu Box 29004
Street address city: Abilene
State: TX
Zip/Postal code: 79699-0001
County: Taylor
Country: USA
Mailing address: ACU Box 29004
Mailing city: Abilene
Mailing state: TX
Mailing zip: 79699
General Phone: (325) 674-2067
General Fax: (325) 674-6475
Year Established: 1992
Published: Thur
Avg Free Circ: 6000
Audit By: Sworn/Estimate/Non-Audited
Audit Date: 12.07.2019
Personnel: Patricia Olvera (Owner)

AUSTIN

AHORA SI!

Street address 1: 305 S Congress Ave
Street address city: Austin
State: TX
Zip/Postal code: 78704-1200
County: Travis
Country: USA
Mailing address: 305 S Congress Ave
Mailing city: Austin
Mailing state: TX
Mailing zip: 78704-1200
General Phone: (512) 445-3500
General Fax: n/a
Advertising Phone: (512) 912-2949
Editorial Phone: (512) 445-3500
General/National Adv. E-mail: eventos@ahorasi.com
Display Adv. E-mail: Johnny.Flores@coxinc.com
Editorial e-mail: jcasati@ahorasi.com
Year Established: 2004
Published: Thur
Published Other: on web, daily
Avg Free Circ: 37535
Audit By: Sworn/Estimate/Non-Audited
Audit Date: 12.07.2019
Personnel: Josefina Villicana Casati (Ed.)

EL MUNDO - AUSTIN / SAN ANTONIO

Street address 1: 2116 E Cesar Chavez St
Street address city: Austin
State: TX
Zip/Postal code: 78702-4514
County: Travis
Country: USA
Mailing address: PO Box 6519
Mailing city: Austin
Mailing state: TX
Mailing zip: 78762-6519
General Phone: 512-476-8636
General Fax: 512-476-6402
Editorial Phone: 512-474-8535
Editorial Fax: 512-476-6402
General/National Adv. E-mail: info@elmundonewspaper.com
Display Adv. E-mail: angela@elmundonewspaper.com
Editorial e-mail: jg@elmundonewspaper.com
Year Established: 1989
Published: Thur
Avg Paid Circ: 0
Avg Free Circ: 45000
Audit By: CVC
Audit Date: 30.03.2013
Personnel: Alba Angulo (Publisher)

PERIODICO BUENA SUERTE - AUSTIN

Street address 1: 6901 N Lamar Blvd
Street address 2: Ste 139
Street address city: Austin
State: TX
Zip/Postal code: 78752-3532
County: Travis
Country: USA
Mailing address: 7324 Southwest Fwy Ste 1720
Mailing city: Houston
Mailing state: TX
Mailing zip: 77074-2058
General Phone: (512) 345-0101
Year Established: 1986
Published: Thur
Avg Paid Circ: 0
Avg Free Circ: 6180
Audit By: Sworn/Estimate/Non-Audited
Audit Date: 12.07.2019
Personnel: Emilio Martinez

BROWNSVILLE

EL NUEVO HERALDO

Street address 1: 1135 E Van Buren St
Street address city: Brownsville
State: TX
Zip/Postal code: 78520-7055
County: Cameron
Country: USA
Mailing address: PO Box 351
Mailing city: Brownsville
Mailing state: TX
Mailing zip: 78522-0351
General Phone: (956) 542-4301
General Fax: (956) 504-1119
Advertising Phone: (956) 982-6636
Advertising Fax: (956) 982-4201
Editorial Phone: (956) 982-6625
Editorial Fax: (956) 430-6233
General/National Adv. E-mail: tbhpress@brownsvilleherald.com
Published: Mon`Tues`Wed`Thur`Fri`Sat`Sun
Weekday Frequency: m
Saturday Frequency: m
Avg Paid Circ: 20575

Sun. Circulation Paid: 4593
Audit By: AAM
Audit Date: 31.03.2017
Personnel: R. Daniel Cavazos (Pub.); Karen Ashanholtzer (Adv. Dir.); Abe Gonzalez (Circ. Dir.); Rachel Benavides (Ed.); Marci Ponce (Ed.); Gary Long (News Ed.); Brad Doherty (Photo Ed.); Speedy Aldape (Prodn. Mgr., Systems)

CARRIZO SPRINGS

THE CARRIZO SPRINGS JAVELIN

Street address 1: 610 N 1st St
Street address city: Carrizo Springs
State: TX
Zip/Postal code: 78834-2602
County: Dimmit
Country: USA
Mailing address: PO Box 1046
Mailing city: Carrizo Springs
Mailing state: TX
Mailing zip: 78834-7046
General Phone: (830) 876-2318
General Fax: (830) 876-2620
General/National Adv. E-mail: csjaveline@yahoo.com
Published: Thur
Avg Paid Circ: 2000
Avg Free Circ: 100
Audit By: Sworn/Estimate/Non-Audited
Audit Date: 12.07.2019
Personnel: Howard McDaniel (Pub.); Claudia McDaniel (Ed.)

DALLAS

AL DIA DALLAS

Street address 1: 1954 Commerce St.
Street address 2: 3rd floor
Street address city: Dallas
State: TX
Zip/Postal code: 75201
County: Dallas
Country: USA
Mailing address: 1954 Commerce St. 3rd floor
Mailing city: Dallas
Mailing state: TX
Mailing zip: 75201
General Phone: (469) 977-3740
General/National Adv. E-mail: preguntas@aldiatx.com; circulation@aldiatx.com
Published: Wed`Sat
Weekday Frequency: m
Avg Free Circ: 20059
Sat. Circulation Paid: 31784
Audit By: AAM
Audit Date: 31.03.2018
Personnel: Alvin Hysong (Pub.); Alfredo Carbajal (Ed./ Mktg.); Silvana Pagliuca (Ed. Entertainment); Juan F. Jaramillo (Ed. Local); Lorena Flores (Web Ed.); Yadira Gonzalez (Cliente Serv. Coord.); Alfredo Carbajal (Ed. in Chief); Anthony Trejo (Online Ed.); Mauro Diaz (Sports Ed.)

EL EXTRA NEWSPAPER

Street address 1: 1214 Gardenview Dr
Street address city: Dallas
State: TX
Zip/Postal code: 75217-4311
County: Dallas
Country: USA
Mailing address: PO Box 270432
Mailing city: Dallas
Mailing state: TX
Mailing zip: 75227-0432
General Phone: 214-309-0990
General Fax: 214-309-0204
Advertising Phone: 214-309-0990
Advertising Fax: 214-309-0204
Editorial Phone: 214-309-0990
General/National Adv. E-mail: pressrelease@elextranewspaper.com
Display Adv. E-mail: clasificados@elextranewspaper.com
Editorial e-mail: pressrelease@elextranewspaper.com
Year Established: 1987
Published: Thur
Avg Paid Circ: 34095
Audit By: AAM
Audit Date: 31.12.2018
Personnel: Emmy Silva (Publisher/Editor Advertising Manager)

EL HERALDO

Street address 1: PO Box 141354
Street address city: Dallas
State: TX
Zip/Postal code: 75214
Country: USA
Mailing address: PO Box 141354
Mailing city: Dallas
Mailing state: TX
Mailing zip: 75214
General Phone: (214) 827-9700
Advertising Phone: (214) 827-9700
Editorial Phone: (214) 827-9700
General/National Adv. E-mail: ellie@elheraldonews.com
Published: Bi-Mthly
Avg Paid Circ: 0
Avg Free Circ: 1000
Audit By: Sworn/Estimate/Non-Audited
Audit Date: 12.07.2019
Personnel: Marta Foster (Adv. Mgr.); Gonzalo Sanchez (Ed.)

EL HERALDO NEWS

Street address 1: 4532 Columbia Ave
Street address city: Dallas
State: TX
Zip/Postal code: 75226-1016
County: Dallas
Country: USA
Mailing address: 4532 Columbia Ave
Mailing city: Dallas
Mailing state: TX
Mailing zip: 75226-1016
General Phone: (214) 827-9700
General Fax: (214) 827-8200
General/National Adv. E-mail: ellie@elheraldonews.com
Published: Fri
Avg Paid Circ: 2
Avg Free Circ: 17998
Audit By: CAC
Audit Date: 30.09.2013
Personnel: Ellie Byrd (Adv. Mgr.); Francisco Rayo (Ed.)

EL HISPANO NEWS

Street address 1: 2102 Empire Central
Street address city: Dallas
State: TX
Zip/Postal code: 75235-4302
County: Dallas
Country: USA
Mailing address: 2102 Empire Central
Mailing city: Dallas
Mailing state: TX
Mailing zip: 75235
General Phone: (214) 357-2186
General Fax: (214) 357-2195
Advertising Phone: (214) 357-2186 ext. 202
Editorial Phone: (214) 357-2186 ext. 225
General/National Adv. E-mail: editor@elhispanonews.com
Display Adv. E-mail: lupita@elhispanonews.com
Editorial e-mail: reynaldo@elhispanonews.com
Year Established: 1986
Published: Thur
Avg Free Circ: 20390
Audit By: CAC
Audit Date: 31.12.2016
Personnel: Lupita Colmenero (Adv. Mgr., Nat'l); Ruben Colmenero (Circ. Mgr.); Roxanna Lopez (Office Mgr); Einer Agredo (Graphics); Reynaldo Mena (Managing Ed); Beana Ramirez; Rodolfo Bustillos (Marketing Mgr)

LA SUBASTA DE DALLAS

Street address 1: 502 N Haskell ave
Street address city: Dallas
State: TX
Zip/Postal code: 75246
County: TX
Country: United States
Mailing address: 6120 tarnef dr
Mailing city: Houston
Mailing state: TX
Mailing zip: 77074
General Phone: (713) 777-1010
General Fax: (214) 951-9400
Advertising Phone: (713) 777-1010
General/National Adv. E-mail: sales@lasubasta.com
Display Adv. E-mail: cynthial@lasubasta.com
Editorial e-mail: cynthial@lasubasta.com
Year Established: 1981
Published: Tues`Fri
Avg Free Circ: 67000
Audit By: VAC
Audit Date: 30.09.2018
Personnel: cynthia aristizabal (Sales Director)

PERIODICO BUENA SUERTE - DALLAS

Street address 1: 1545 W Mockingbird Ln
Street address 2: Ste 1012
Street address city: Dallas
State: TX
Zip/Postal code: 75235-5014
County: Dallas
Country: USA
Mailing address: 7324 Southwest Fwy Ste 1720
Mailing city: Houston
Mailing state: TX
Mailing zip: 77074-2058
General Phone: (214) 575-4545
Display Adv. E-mail: sales@buenasuerte.com
Year Established: 2010
Published: Wed`Thur
Avg Paid Circ: 0
Avg Free Circ: 15051
Audit By: Sworn/Estimate/Non-Audited
Audit Date: 12.07.2019
Personnel: Emilio Martinez

DUNCANVILLE

NOVEDADES NEWS

Street address 1: 1019 N. Duncanville Rd.
Street address city: Duncanville
State: TX
Zip/Postal code: 75116
County: Dallas
Country: USA
Mailing address: PO Box 4752
Mailing city: Dallas
Mailing state: TX
Mailing zip: 75208-0752
General Phone: (214) 943-2932
General Fax: (214) 943-7352
Advertising Phone: (214) 943-2932
Advertising Fax: (214) 943-7352
Editorial Phone: (214) 943-2932
Editorial Fax: (214) 943-7352
General/National Adv. E-mail: editorial@novedadesnews.com
Display Adv. E-mail: editorial@novedadesnews.com
Classified Adv. e-mail: editorial@novedadesnews.com
Editorial e-mail: editorial@novedadesnews.com
Year Established: 1986
Published: Wed
Published Other: novedadesnews.com
Weekday Frequency: All day
Avg Paid Circ: 0
Avg Free Circ: 38000
Audit By: Sworn/Estimate/Non-Audited
Audit Date: 12.07.2019
Personnel: Sergio Puerto (Mktg. Dir.); Sergio Puerto Sr. (Pres./CEO); Estela Ortiz (Chief Writter); Mike Garza (Marketing Director, Ass.); Angel Puerto (Distribution Manager); Miriam Puerto (Public Relations, Director); Hassel Luzanilla (Accountant); Ellie Byrd (Sales Person)

EAGLE PASS

THE NEWS GRAM/THE GRAM

Street address 1: 2543 Del Rio Blvd
Street address city: Eagle Pass
State: TX
Zip/Postal code: 78852-3627
County: Maverick
Country: USA
Mailing address: 2543 Del Rio Blvd
Mailing city: Eagle Pass
Mailing state: TX
Mailing zip: 78852-3627
General Phone: (830) 773-8610
General Fax: (830) 773-1641
General/National Adv. E-mail: elgram@hilconet.com
Published: Tues`Wed`Thur`Fri`Sun
Avg Free Circ: 23000
Audit By: Sworn/Estimate/Non-Audited
Audit Date: 12.07.2019
Personnel: Ruben Carrillo Mazuka (Pub.); Celina Ramos (Adv. Mgr.); Jesus Maldonado (Ed.)

EL PASO

EL PASO Y MAS

Street address 1: 500 W Overland Ave
Street address 2: Ste 150
Street address city: El Paso
State: TX
Zip/Postal code: 79901-1108
County: El Paso
Country: USA
Mailing address: 500 W. Overland Ave.
Mailing city: El Paso
Mailing state: TX
Mailing zip: 79901
General Phone: (915) 546-6300
General Fax: (915) 546-6284
Advertising Phone: (915) 542-6066
Editorial Phone: (915) 546-6149
Display Adv. E-mail: jmolina@elpasotimes.com
Editorial e-mail: bmoore@elpasotimes.com
Published: Sun
Avg Free Circ: 72750
Audit By: AAM
Audit Date: 30.09.2017
Personnel: Sergio H. Salinas (CEO/President & Publisher); Malena Field (Dir., HR); Cecilia Uebel (Senior VP of Advertising and Marketing); Jim Weddell (VP of Online/Digital); Phillip Cortez (Mktg. Dir.); Jim Dove (Circ. Dir.); Craig Pogorzelski (Circ. Mgr., City Home Delivery); Randy Waldrop (Circ. Mgr., Transportation); Ramon Bracamontes (Bus. Ed.); Armando V. Durazo (City/Metro Ed.); Carlita Costello (Design Ed.); Charlie Edgren (Editorial Page Ed.); Melissa Martinez (Features Ed.); Mario Ontiveros (Online Sales Mgr.); Paz Garcia (Information Technolgy Dir.); Patsy Hernandez (VP of Production); Margaret Gallardo (Sports Editor); Robert Moore (Ed.)

FORT WORTH

LA ESTRELLA

Street address 1: 400 W 7th St
Street address city: Fort Worth
State: TX
Zip/Postal code: 76102-4701
County: Tarrant
Country: USA
Mailing address: 400 W 7th St
Mailing city: Fort Worth
Mailing state: TX
Mailing zip: 76102-4701
General Phone: (817) 390-7180
General Fax: (817) 390-7280
General/National Adv. E-mail: jaramos@laestrelladigital.com
Published: Sat
Avg Free Circ: 123150
Audit By: AAM
Audit Date: 30.06.2015
Personnel: Baker Haymes (Adv. Mgr.); Juan Antonio Ramos (Ed.); Raul Caballero (Mng. Ed.)

PANORAMA DE NUEVOS HORIZONTES

Street address 1: 3501 Williams Rd
Street address city: Fort Worth
State: TX
Zip/Postal code: 76116-7029
County: Tarrant
Country: USA
Mailing address: 3501 Williams Rd
Mailing city: Fort Worth
Mailing state: TX
Mailing zip: 76116-7029

Year Established: 2002
Published: Sat
Avg Paid Circ: 0
Avg Free Circ: 15450
Audit By: CVC
Audit Date: 31.12.2014
Personnel: Julia Martinez-Smit

ENFOQUE DEPORTIVO

Street address 1: 13227 Noblecrest Dr
Street address city: Houston
State: TX
Zip/Postal code: 77041-1871
County: Harris
Country: USA
Mailing address: 13227 Noblecrest Dr
Mailing city: Houston
Mailing state: TX
Mailing zip: 77041-1871
General Phone: (713) 785-7191
General Fax: (832) 467-9792
General/National Adv. E-mail: enfoque@sbcglobal.net
Audit By: Sworn/Estimate/Non-Audited
Audit Date: 12.07.2019
Personnel: William Jose Reyes (Pub.); Juana Reyes (Adv. Mgr.); Maritza Reyes (Ed.)

LA PRENSA DE HOUSTON

Street address 1: 7100 Regency Square Blvd. Ste 217
Street address city: Houston
State: TX
Zip/Postal code: 77036
County: Harris
Country: United States
General Phone: 713-334-4959
Advertising Phone: 713-334-4959
Editorial Phone: 713-334-4959
General/National Adv. E-mail: ecastro@prensadehouston.com
Display Adv. E-mail: info@prensadehouston.com
Classified Adv. e-mail: ecastro@prensadehouston.com
Editorial e-mail: editorial@prensadehouston.com
Year Established: 2001
Published: Sun
Avg Free Circ: 106000
Sun. Circulation Free: 106000
Personnel: Evelyn Castro (Vice President)

LA SUBASTA

Street address 1: 6120 Tarnef Dr
Street address 2: Ste 110
Street address city: Houston
State: TX
Zip/Postal code: 77074-3754
County: Harris
Country: USA
Mailing address: 6120 Tarnef Dr Ste 110
Mailing city: Houston
Mailing state: TX
Mailing zip: 77074-3754
General Phone: (713) 772-8900
General Fax: (713) 772-8999
Audit By: Sworn/Estimate/Non-Audited
Audit Date: 12.07.2019
Personnel: German Arango (Pub.)

LA VOZ DE HOUSTON

Street address 1: 4747 Southwest Fwy
Street address city: Houston
State: TX
Zip/Postal code: 77027-6901
County: Harris
Country: USA
Mailing address: 4747 Southwest Fwy
Mailing city: Houston
Mailing state: TX
Mailing zip: 77027-6901
General Phone: (713) 362-8100
General Fax: (713) 362-8630
General/National Adv. E-mail: aurora.losada@chron.com
Published: Wed
Avg Free Circ: 271040
Audit By: AAM
Audit Date: 30.09.2018
Personnel: Loida Ruiz (Mgr.); Craig Hurluy (Adv. Sales Mgr.); Aurora Losada (Ed.)

MERCADO LATINO

Street address 1: 5327 Aldine Mail Route Rd
Street address city: Houston
State: TX
Zip/Postal code: 77039-4919
County: Harris
Country: USA
Mailing address: 5327 Aldine Mail Rd
Mailing city: Houston
Mailing state: TX
Mailing zip: 77039-4919
General Phone: (281) 449-9945
General Fax: (713) 977-1188
General/National Adv. E-mail: nenewsroom@aol.com
Published: Tues
Avg Free Circ: 30000
Audit By: Sworn/Estimate/Non-Audited
Audit Date: 12.07.2019
Personnel: Gil Hoffman (Editor/PUblisher)

PERIODICO BUENA SUERTE - HOUSTON

Street address 1: 7324 Southwest Fwy
Street address 2: Ste 1720
Street address city: Houston
State: TX
Zip/Postal code: 77074-2058
County: Harris
Country: USA
Mailing address: 7324 Southwest Fwy Ste 1720
Mailing city: Houston
Mailing state: TX
Mailing zip: 77074-2058
General Phone: 713-272-0101
Display Adv. E-mail: sales@buenasuerte.com
Year Established: 1986
Published: Tues`Wed`Thur`Fri
Avg Free Circ: 84918
Audit By: Sworn/Estimate/Non-Audited
Audit Date: 12.07.2019
Personnel: Emilio Martinez

LA OPINION

Street address 1: 404 College Ave
Street address city: Jacksonville
State: TX
Zip/Postal code: 75766-2244
County: Cherokee
Country: USA
Mailing address: 404 College Ave
Mailing city: Jacksonville
Mailing state: TX
Mailing zip: 75766-2244
Year Established: 1989
Published: Other
Published Other: Bi-Weekly (Every Other Wednesday)
Avg Paid Circ: 0
Avg Free Circ: 0
Audit By: VAC
Audit Date: 30.09.2015
Personnel: Judith Cantua

LAREDO

EL TIEMPO DE LAREDO

Street address 1: 111 Esperanza Dr
Street address city: Laredo
State: TX
Zip/Postal code: 78041-2607
County: Webb
Country: USA
Mailing address: PO Box 2129
Mailing city: Laredo
Mailing state: TX
Mailing zip: 78044-2129
General Phone: (956) 728-2500
General Fax: (956) 724-3036
Audit By: Sworn/Estimate/Non-Audited
Audit Date: 12.07.2019
Personnel: William B. Green (Pub.); Adriana DeVally (Gen. Mgr.); Christian Cruz (Circ. Mgr.); Melva Lavin (Ed.); Diana Fuentes (Ed.); Raul Cruz (Creative Dir.)

LUBBOCK

EL EDITOR-LUBBOCK

Street address 1: 1502 Avenue M
Street address city: Lubbock
State: TX
Zip/Postal code: 79401-4950
County: Lubbock
Country: USA
Mailing address: PO Box 11250
Mailing city: Lubbock
Mailing state: TX
Mailing zip: 79408-7250
General Phone: (806) 763-3841
General Fax: (806) 741-1110
General/National Adv. E-mail: eleditor@sbcglobal.net
Display Adv. E-mail: eleditorsales@sbcglobal.net
Year Established: 1977
Published: Thur
Avg Paid Circ: 0
Avg Free Circ: 4017
Audit By: VAC
Audit Date: 30.12.2015
Personnel: Olga Riojas-Aguero (Owner)

EL EDITOR-PERMIAN BASIN

Street address 1: 1502 Avenue M
Street address city: Lubbock
State: TX
Zip/Postal code: 79401-4950
County: Lubbock
Country: USA
Mailing address: PO Box 11250
Mailing city: Lubbock
Mailing state: TX
Mailing zip: 79408-7250
General Phone: (806) 763-3841
General Fax: (806) 741-1110
General/National Adv. E-mail: eleditor@sbcglobal.net
Published: Wed
Avg Free Circ: 15000
Audit By: Sworn/Estimate/Non-Audited
Audit Date: 12.07.2019
Personnel: Gilbert Acuna (Circ. Mgr.); Bidal Aguero (Ed.); Olga Aguero (Prodn. Mgr.)

MCALLEN

EL PERIODICO USA

Street address 1: 801 E Fir Ave
Street address city: McAllen
State: TX
Zip/Postal code: 78501-9320
County: Hidalgo
Country: USA
Mailing address: 801 E Fir Ave
Mailing city: McAllen
Mailing state: TX
Mailing zip: 78501-9320
General Phone: (956) 631-5628
General Fax: (956) 631-0832
Advertising Phone: 956-631-5628
Advertising Fax: 956-631-0832
Editorial Phone: 956-631-5628
Editorial Fax: 956-631-0832
General/National Adv. E-mail: subscribe@elperiodicousa.com
Year Established: 1986
Published: Wed
Avg Free Circ: 38502
Audit By: CAC
Audit Date: 30.09.2018
Personnel: Jose B. Garza (Ed.); Kathy Letelier (Pub.)

PRESIDIO

THE PRESIDIO INTERNATIONAL

Street address 1: Market @ Ralph England Streets
Street address city: Presidio
State: TX
Zip/Postal code: 79845
County: Presidio
Country: USA
Mailing address: PO Box P
Mailing city: Marfa
Mailing state: TX
Mailing zip: 79843
General Phone: (432) 729-4342
General/National Adv. E-mail: editor@bigbendnow.com
Year Established: 1986
Published: Thur
Avg Paid Circ: 900
Avg Free Circ: 100
Audit By: USPS
Audit Date: 16.10.2017
Personnel: Robert L. Halpern (Ed.); Rosario Salgado-Halpern (Mng. Ed.)

SAN ANTONIO

PERIODICO BUENA SUERTE - SAN ANTONIO

Street address 1: 1804 NE Interstate 410 Loop
Street address 2: Suite #280A
Street address city: San Antonio
State: TX
Zip/Postal code: 78217
County: Bexar
Country: USA
Mailing address: 7324 Southwest Fwy Ste 1720
Mailing city: Houston
Mailing state: TX
Mailing zip: 77074-2058
General Phone: (210) 444-0001
Display Adv. E-mail: sales@BuenaSuerte.com
Year Established: 1986
Published: Fri
Avg Paid Circ: 0
Avg Free Circ: 14004
Audit By: Sworn/Estimate/Non-Audited
Audit Date: 12.07.2019
Personnel: Emilio Martinez
State: Utah

UTAH

OGDEN

EL ESTANDAR

Street address 1: 332 Standard Way
Street address city: Ogden
State: UT
Zip/Postal code: 84404-1371
County: Weber
Country: USA
Mailing address: 332 Standard Way
Mailing city: Ogden
Mailing state: UT
Mailing zip: 84404-1371
General Phone: (801) 625-4400
Advertising Phone: (801) 625-4333
Editorial Phone: (801) 625-4225
Published: Wed
Avg Free Circ: 15625
Audit By: Sworn/Estimate/Non-Audited
Audit Date: 12.07.2019
Personnel: Jordan Carroll (Ex. Ed.); Becky Cairns (TX Section Coordinator); Patrick Carr (Sports Rep.); Ryan Christner (Print Admin.); Ryan Comer (Copy Ed.)
State: Washington

WASHINGTON

KIRKLAND

EL MUNDO - WA

Street address 1: 11410 NE 124th St
Street address 2: # 441
Street address city: Kirkland
State: WA
Zip/Postal code: 98034-4399
County: King

Country: USA
Mailing address: 11410 NE 124th St # 441
Mailing city: Kirkland
Mailing state: WA
Mailing zip: 98034-4399
Year Established: 1989
Published: Thur
Avg Paid Circ: 500
Avg Free Circ: 14113
Audit By: CVC
Audit Date: 30.06.2013
Personnel: Martha Montoya

LAKEWOOD

FRONTERAS

Street address 1: 8312 Custer Rd SW
Street address city: Lakewood
State: WA
Zip/Postal code: 98499-2526
County: Pierce
Country: USA
Mailing address: PO Box 98801
Mailing city: Lakewood
Mailing state: WA
Mailing zip: 98496-8801
General Phone: (253) 584-1212
General Fax: (253) 581-5962
General/National Adv. E-mail: swarnerkm@aol.com
Year Established: 2007
Audit By: Sworn/Estimate/Non-Audited
Audit Date: 12.07.2019
Personnel: Bill White (Adv. Mgr.); Ken Swarner (Ed.)

GAUGER MEDIA SERVICE, INC.

Street address 1: 1034 Bradford Street
Street address 2: P.O. Box 627
Street address city: Raymond
State: WA
Zip/Postal code: 98577
County: Pacific
Country: USA
Mailing address: P.O. Box 627
Mailing city: Raymond
Mailing state: WA
Mailing zip: 98577
General Phone: (360) 942-3560
General/National Adv. E-mail: dave@gaugermedia.com
Year Established: 1987
Personnel: Dave Gauger (Pres/Broker)
State: Alabama
Street address city: Raymond
State: WA
Zip/Postal code: 98577
County: Pacific
Country: USA
Mailing address: P.O. Box 627
Mailing city: Raymond
Mailing state: WA
Mailing zip: 98577
General Phone: (360) 942-3560
General/National Adv. E-mail: dave@gaugermedia.com
Primary Website: 1987
Personnel: Dave Gauger (Pres/Broker)
State: Wisconsin

WISCONSIN

THE WISCONSIN JEWISH CHRONICLE

Street address 1: 1360 N Prospect Ave
Street address city: Milwaukee
State: WI
Zip/Postal code: 53202-3056
County: Milwaukee
Country: USA
Mailing address: 1360 N Prospect Ave Ste 2
Mailing city: Milwaukee
Mailing state: WI
Mailing zip: 53202-3090
General Phone: (414) 390-5770
General Fax: (414) 390-5766
Advertising Phone: (414) 390-5765
General/National Adv. E-mail: chronicle@milwaukeejewish.org
Primary Website: 1921
Year Established: Mthly
Avg Free Circ: 8000
Audit By: Sworn/Estimate/Non-Audited
Audit Date: 12.07.2019
Personnel: Yvonne Chapman (Production Manager); Leon Cohen (Editor)
State: Arizona

JEWISH NEWSPAPER

ALABAMA

SOUTHERN JEWISH LIFE

Street address 1: 2179 Highland Ave
Street address city: Birmingham
Street address state: AL
Zip/Postal code: 35205
County: Jefferson
Country: USA
Mailing address: PO Box 130052
Mailing city: Birmingham
Mailing state: AL
Mailing zip: 35213-0052
General Phone: (205) 870-7889
Advertising Phone: (205) 870-7889
General/National Adv. E-mail: connect@sjlmag.com
Display Adv. E-mail: lee@sjlmag.com
Editorial e-mail: editor@sjlmag.com
Primary Website: www.sjlmag.com
Year Established: 1990
Delivery Methods: Mail
Areas Served - City/County or Portion Thereof, or Zip codes: 324-325, 350-368, 386-397, 700-714
Published: Mthly
Avg Free Circ: 9500
Audit By: USPS
Audit Date: 25.06.2018
Note: Formerly Deep South Jewish Voice, became Southern Jewish Life in August 2009. Official publication of the New Orleans Jewish community.
Personnel: Lee Green (Adv. Mgr.); Larry Brook (Ed/Pub); Annetta Dolowitz (Advertising); Jeff Pizzo (V.P. Sales and Marketing, New Orleans)

ARIZONA

ARIZONA JEWISH POST

Street address 1: 3822 E River Rd
Street address 2: Ste 300
Street address city: Tucson
Street address state: AZ
Zip/Postal code: 85718-6635
County: Pima
Country: USA
General Phone: (520)319-1112
General Fax: (520) 319-1118
Advertising Phone: (520) 319-1112 ext. 136
Editorial Phone: (520) 319-1112 ext. 135
General/National Adv. E-mail: office@azjewishpost.com
Display Adv. E-mail: berti@azjewishpost.com
Editorial e-mail: localnews@azjewishpost.com
Primary Website: www.azjewishpost.com
Year Established: 1946
Delivery Methods: Mail`Carrier`Racks
Areas Served - City/County or Portion Thereof, or Zip codes: 85614, 85641, 85653, 85658, 85701, 85702, 85704, 85705, 85706, 8576, 85710, 85711, 85712, 85713, 85715, 85716, 85718, 85719, 85730, 85737, 85739, 85741
Published: Fri
Published Other: 24x per year
Avg Paid Circ: 2063
Avg Free Circ: 4314
Audit By: CVC
Audit Date: 30.06.2018
Personnel: Phyllis Braun (Exec. Ed.); Berti Brodsky (Pub.); Maris Finley (Account Executive); April Bauer (Circ.); Michelle Shapiro (Adv.)
Parent company (for newspapers): Jewish Federation of Southern Arizona

JEWISH NEWS

Street address 1: 12701 N. Scottsdale Rd.
Street address 2: Ste. 206
Street address city: Scottsdale
Street address state: AZ
Zip/Postal code: 85254
County: Maricopa
Country: USA
Mailing address: 12701 N. Scottsdale Rd. Ste. 206
Mailing city: Scottsdale
Mailing state: AZ
Mailing zip: 85254
General Phone: (602) 870-9470
General Fax: (602) 870-0426
General/National Adv. E-mail: publisher@jewishaz.com
Editorial e-mail: editor@jewishaz.com
Primary Website: www.jewishaz.com
Year Established: 1948
Delivery Methods: Mail`Newsstand
Published: Fri
Published Other: annual Community Directory, annual Best of Jewish Phoenix magazine
Avg Free Circ: 4870
Audit By: CVC
Audit Date: 30.06.2016
Personnel: Janet Perez (Mng. Ed.); Jodi Lipson (Adv. Acc. Exec.); Sandra Goldberg (Adv. Acc. Exec.); Nick Enquist (Staff Writer)
Parent company (for newspapers): Jewish Community Foundation

CALIFORNIA

J. THE JEWISH NEWS WEEKLY OF NORTHERN CALIFONIA

Street address 1: 225 Bush St
Street address 2: Ste 1480
Street address city: San Francisco
Street address state: CA
Zip/Postal code: 94104-4216
County: San Francisco
Country: USA
Mailing address: 225 Bush St Ste 1480
Mailing city: San Francisco
Mailing state: CA
Mailing zip: 94104-4216
General Phone: (415) 263-7200
General Fax: (415) 263-7222
Advertising Phone: (415) 263-7200
Advertising Fax: (415) 263-7222
General/National Adv. E-mail: info@jweekly.com
Display Adv. E-mail: nora@jweekly.com
Editorial e-mail: editors@jweekly.com
Primary Website: www.jweekly.com
Year Established: 1946
Delivery Methods: Mail
Areas Served - City/County or Portion Thereof, or Zip codes: SF Bay Area
Published: Fri
Avg Paid Circ: 17000
Avg Free Circ: 1000
Audit By: Sworn/Estimate/Non-Audited
Audit Date: 12.07.2019
Personnel: Nora Contini (Publisher); Cathleen Maclearie (Art Dir.); Sue Fishkoff (Editor)

JEWISH COMMUNITY CHRONICLE

Street address 1: 3801 E Willow St
Street address city: Long Beach
Street address state: CA
Zip/Postal code: 90815-1734
County: Los Angeles
Country: USA
Mailing address: 3801 E Willow St
Mailing city: Long Beach
Mailing state: CA
Mailing zip: 90815-1792
General Phone: (562) 426-7601
General Fax: (562) 424-3915
General/National Adv. E-mail: chronicle@jewishlongbeach.org
Primary Website: www.jewishlongbeach.org
Year Established: 1947
Delivery Methods: Mail`Newsstand`Racks
Published: Mthly
Avg Free Circ: 6300
Audit By: Sworn/Estimate/Non-Audited
Audit Date: 12.07.2019
Personnel: Deborah Goldfarb (CEO); Danny Levy (Director of Development)
Parent company (for newspapers): Jewish Federation of Greater Long Beach & West Orange County

JEWISH COMMUNITY NEWS

Street address 1: 14855 Oka Rd
Street address 2: Ste 202
Street address city: Los Gatos
Street address state: CA
Zip/Postal code: 95032-1957
County: Santa Clara
Country: USA
Mailing address: PO Box 320070
Mailing city: Los Gatos
Mailing state: CA
Mailing zip: 95032-0101
General Phone: (408) 556-0600
General/National Adv. E-mail: jfs@jfssv.org
Primary Website: www.jfssv.org
Personnel: Lori Cinnamon (Adv. Mgr.); Amanda Glincher (Ed.)
Parent company (for newspapers): Joseph Jacobs Organization

JEWISH NEWS

Street address 1: 16501 Ventura Blvd
Street address 2: Ste 504
Street address city: Encino
Street address state: CA
Zip/Postal code: 91436-2047
County: Los Angeles
Country: USA
Mailing address: 16501 Ventura Blvd Ste 504
Mailing city: Encino
Mailing state: CA
Mailing zip: 91436-2047
General Phone: (818) 786-4000
General Fax: (818) 380-9232
General/National Adv. E-mail: info@jewishlifetv.com
Primary Website: www.jewishlifetv.com
Published: Mthly
Avg Paid Circ: 106000
Audit By: Sworn/Estimate/Non-Audited
Audit Date: 12.07.2019
Personnel: Phil Blazer (Ed.)

SAN DIEGO JEWISH TIMES

Street address 1: 4731 Palm Ave
Street address city: La Mesa
Street address state: CA
Zip/Postal code: 91941-5221
County: San Diego
Country: USA
Mailing address: 4731 Palm Ave
Mailing city: La Mesa
Mailing state: CA
Mailing zip: 91941-5221
General Phone: (619) 463-5515
General Fax: (619) 463-1309
General/National Adv. E-mail: sdjt@sdjewishtimes.com
Display Adv. E-mail: kgreen@sdjewishtimes.com
Editorial e-mail: msirota@sdjewishtimes.com
Primary Website: www.sdjewishtimes.com
Year Established: 1980
Personnel: Michael Schwarz (Pub.); Michael Sirota (Ed.); Leslie Pebley (Prodn. Mgr.)

THE JEWISH JOURNAL OF GREATER LOS ANGELES

Street address 1: 3580 Wilshire Blvd
Street address 2: Ste 1510
Street address city: Los Angeles
Street address state: CA
Zip/Postal code: 90010-2516
County: Los Angeles
Country: USA
Mailing address: 3580 Wilshire Blvd Ste 1510
Mailing city: Los Angeles
Mailing state: CA
Mailing zip: 90010-2516
General Phone: (213) 368-1661
General Fax: (213) 368-1684
General/National Adv. E-mail: marketing@jewishjournal.com
Display Adv. E-mail: advertising@jewishjournal.com
Primary Website: jewishjournal.com
Year Established: 1986
Published: Fri
Avg Paid Circ: 0
Avg Free Circ: 49975
Audit By: CVC
Audit Date: 30.06.2015
Personnel: Matthew Tenney (Circ. Mgr.); Rob Eshman (Ed. in Chief); Adam Wills (Sr. Ed.); Susan Freudenheim (Mng. Ed.); Lionel Ochoa (Prodn. Dir.)

COLORADO

INTERMOUNTAIN JEWISH NEWS

Street address 1: 1177 N Grant St
Street address 2: Ste 200
Street address city: Denver
Street address state: CO
Zip/Postal code: 80203-2362
County: Denver
Country: USA
Mailing address: 1177 Grant St Ste 200
Mailing city: Denver
Mailing state: CO
Mailing zip: 80203-2362
General Phone: (303) 861-2234
General Fax: (303) 832-6942
General/National Adv. E-mail: email@ijn.com
Primary Website: www.ijn.com
Published: Fri
Avg Paid Circ: 3000
Avg Free Circ: 287
Audit By: Sworn/Estimate/Non-Audited
Audit Date: 12.07.2019
Personnel: Rabbi Hillel Goldberg (Gen. Mgr.); Lori Aron (Adv. Mgr.); Miriam Goldberg (Ed.); Larry Hankin (Mng. Ed.); Judy Waldren (Prodn. Mgr.)
Parent company (for newspapers): Joseph Jacobs Organization

CONNECTICUT

CONNECTICUT JEWISH LEDGER

Street address 1: 740 N Main St
Street address 2: Ste W
Street address city: West Hartford
Street address state: CT
Zip/Postal code: 06117-2403
County: Hartford
Country: USA
Mailing address: 36 Woodland St Ste 1
Mailing city: Hartford
Mailing state: CT
Mailing zip: 06105-2328
General Phone: (860) 231-2424
General Fax: (860) 231-2485
Editorial Fax: (860) 231-2428
Display Adv. E-mail: advertising@jewishledger.com
Editorial e-mail: editorial@jewishledger.com
Primary Website: www.jewishledger.com
Published: Fri
Avg Paid Circ: 35000

Audit By: Sworn/Estimate/Non-Audited
Audit Date: 12.07.2019
Personnel: N. Richard Greenfield (Pub.); Leslie Iarusso (Prodn. Mgr.); Judie Jacobson (Mng. Ed.)
Parent company (for newspapers): Joseph Jacobs Organization

THE JEWISH LEADER

Street address 1: 28 Channing St
Street address city: New London
Street address state: CT
Zip/Postal code: 06320-5756
County: New London
Country: USA
General Phone: (860) 442-7395
General Fax: (860) 443-4175
General/National Adv. E-mail: office.jfec@gmail.com
Display Adv. E-mail: office.jfec@gmail.com
Editorial e-mail: office.jfec@gmail.com
Primary Website: www.jfec.com
Year Established: 1970
Delivery Methods: Mail
Areas Served - City/County or Portion Thereof, or Zip codes: 06320, 06360, 06385, 06333, 06357, 06340, 06415, 06226, 06260, 06475, 02891
Published: Other
Published Other: Twice a month on Fridays
Avg Paid Circ: 400
Avg Free Circ: 1075
Audit By: Sworn/Estimate/Non-Audited
Audit Date: 12.07.2019
Personnel: Mimi Perl (Ed.)
Parent company (for newspapers): Jewish Federation of Eastern CT

DELAWARE

JEWISH LIVING DELAWARE

Street address 1: 101 Garden of Eden Rd
Street address city: Wilmington
Street address state: Delaware
Zip/Postal code: 19803-1511
County: New Castle
Country: USA
Mailing address: 101 Garden of Eden Rd
Mailing city: Wilmington
Mailing state: Delaware
Mailing zip: 19803-1511
General Phone: (302) 427-2100
General Fax: (302) 427-2438
General/National Adv. E-mail: seth@shalomdel.org
Display Adv. E-mail: rachel@shalomdel.org
Editorial e-mail: emma@shalomdel.org
Primary Website: www.shalomdelaware.org
Mthly Avg Views: 1200
Mthly Avg Unique Visitors: 800
Year Established: 1951
Delivery Methods: Mail
Areas Served - City/County or Portion Thereof, or Zip codes: Throughout Delaware and the Brandywine Valley - 19801, 19803, 19806, 19809, 19810
Published: Mthly
Avg Paid Circ: 1700
Avg Free Circ: 300
Audit By: Sworn/Estimate/Non-Audited
Audit Date: 9/31/2023
Note: https://www.shalomdelaware.org/publications/jewish-living-delaware/jewish-living-delaware-media-kit.html
Personnel: Shoshana Martyniak (Editor); Emma Driban (Editor)
Parent company (for newspapers): Jewish Federation of Delaware

FLORIDA

HERITAGE FLORIDA JEWISH NEWS

Street address 1: 207 Obrien Rd
Street address 2: Ste 101
Street address city: Fern Park
Street address state: FL
Zip/Postal code: 32730-2838
County: Seminole
Country: USA
Mailing address: PO Box 300742
Mailing city: Fern Park
Mailing state: FL
Mailing zip: 32730-0742
General Phone: (407) 834-8787
General Fax: (407) 831-0507
General/National Adv. E-mail: news@orlandoheritage.com
Display Adv. E-mail: jeff@orlandoheritage.com
Primary Website: www.heritagefl.com
Year Established: 1976
Delivery Methods: Mail`Newsstand`Racks
Published: Fri
Avg Paid Circ: 5200
Audit By: Sworn/Estimate/Non-Audited
Audit Date: 12.07.2019
Personnel: Jeffrey Gaeser (Ed.)

JEWISH JOURNAL

Street address 1: 333 SW 12th Ave.
Street address city: Deerfiled Beach
Street address state: FL
Zip/Postal code: 33442
County: Broward
Country: USA
Mailing address: 333 SW 12th Ave.
Mailing city: Deerfield Beach
Mailing state: FL
Mailing zip: 33442
General Phone: (954) 572-2050
Editorial Phone: (954) 596-5648
General/National Adv. E-mail: rdaley@tribune.com
Display Adv. E-mail: gbehar@tribune.com
Editorial e-mail: ctouey@tribune.com
Primary Website: www.sun-sentinel.com/florida-jewish-journal
Year Established: 1973
Delivery Methods: Mail`Racks
Areas Served - City/County or Portion Thereof, or Zip codes: Broward County
Published: Mthly
Avg Paid Circ: 0
Avg Free Circ: 30531
Audit By: CVC
Audit Date: 31.12.2012
Personnel: Tom Adams (Pub./Gen. Mgr.); Tracy Kolody (Mng. Ed.); Ed Wilder (Circ. Mgr.); Ray Daley (Adv. Mgr.); Stewart Cady (Prodn. Mgr.)
Parent company (for newspapers): Sun-Sentinel Co.

JEWISH PRESS OF PINELLAS COUNTY

Street address 1: 1101 S Belcher Rd, Ste H
Street address city: Clearwater
Street address state: FL
Zip/Postal code: 33758
County: Pinellas
Country: USA
Mailing address: PO Box 6970
Mailing city: Clearwater
Mailing state: FL
Mailing zip: 33758-6970
General Phone: (727) 535-4400
General Fax: (727) 530-3039
General/National Adv. E-mail: jewishpress@aol.com
Year Established: 1985
Areas Served - City/County or Portion Thereof, or Zip codes: 34664, 34689, 33701, 33728, 33729, 33789
Personnel: Jim Dawkins (Adv. Mgr.); Karen Dawkins (Mng. Ed.)

JEWISH PRESS OF TAMPA

Street address 1: 1101 Belcher Rd S
Street address 2: Ste H
Street address city: Largo
Street address state: FL
Zip/Postal code: 33771-3356
County: Pinellas
Country: USA
Mailing address: PO Box 6970
Mailing city: Clearwater
Mailing state: FL
Mailing zip: 33758-6970
General Phone: (727) 535-4400
General Fax: (727) 530-3039
General/National Adv. E-mail: jewishpress@aol.com
Display Adv. E-mail: jewishpressads@aol.com
Editorial e-mail: Jewishpressnews@aol.com
Primary Website: www.jewishpresstampabay.com
Year Established: 1988
News Services: Jewish Telegraphic Agency
Delivery Methods: Mail
Areas Served - City/County or Portion Thereof, or Zip codes: 337s, 336s, 346s
Published: Bi-Mthly
Published Other: Every other Friday
Avg Free Circ: 11500
Audit By: Sworn/Estimate/Non-Audited
Audit Date: 12.07.2019
Personnel: Jim Dawkins (Pub.); Karen Dawkins (Mng. Ed.); Harold Wolfson (Prodn. Mgr.)

SHALOM - BROWARD

Street address 1: 500 E Broward Blvd
Street address city: Fort Lauderdale
Street address state: FL
Zip/Postal code: 33394-3000
County: Broward
Country: USA
Mailing address: 500 E. Broward Blvd.
Mailing city: Fort Lauderdale
Mailing state: FL
Mailing zip: 33394
General Phone: (954) 536-4000
General Fax: (954) 429-1207
Advertising Phone: (954) 698-6397
Advertising Fax: (954) 429-1207
Editorial Phone: (954) 698-6397
Editorial Fax: (954) 429-1207
General/National Adv. E-mail: rdaley@tribune.com
Display Adv. E-mail: ewilder@tribune.com
Editorial e-mail: ctouey@tribune.com
Primary Website: www.forumpubs.com
Year Established: 1973
Delivery Methods: Mail`Racks
Areas Served - City/County or Portion Thereof, or Zip codes: Broward County
Published: Mthly
Avg Paid Circ: 0
Avg Free Circ: 25448
Audit By: CVC
Audit Date: 31.12.2012
Personnel: Tom Adams (Pub./Gen. Mgr.); Tracy Kolody (Mng. Ed.); Ed Wilder (Circ. Mgr.); Ray Daley (Adv. Mgr.); Stewart Cady (Prodn. Mgr.)
Parent company (for newspapers): Sun-Sentinel Co.

GEORGIA

ATLANTA JEWISH TIMES

Street address 1: 270 Carpenter Dr
Street address 2: Ste 320
Street address city: Atlanta
Street address state: GA
Zip/Postal code: 30328-4933
County: Fulton
Country: USA
Mailing address: 270 Carpenter Dr Ste 320
Mailing city: Atlanta
Mailing state: GA
Mailing zip: 30328
General Phone: (404) 883-2130
General Fax: (404) 883-2136
General/National Adv. E-mail: kaylene@atljewishtimes.com
Display Adv. E-mail: kaylene@atljewishtimes.com
Editorial e-mail: mjacobs@atljewishtimes.com
Primary Website: www.atlantajewishtimes.com
Year Established: 1925
News Services: Jewish Telegraphic Agency
Delivery Methods: Mail`Newsstand`Carrier`Racks
Published: Fri
Published Other: weekly
Avg Paid Circ: 3500
Avg Free Circ: 11500
Audit By: Sworn/Estimate/Non-Audited
Audit Date: 12.07.2019
Personnel: Kaylene Ladinsky (Assoc. Pub.); Michael Morris (Pub.); Michael Jacobs (Ed.)
Parent company (for newspapers): Southern Israelite LLC

ILLINOIS

CHICAGO JEWISH NEWS

Street address 1: 5301 Dempster St
Street address 2: Ste 100
Street address city: Skokie
Street address state: IL
Zip/Postal code: 60077-1800
County: Cook
Country: USA
Mailing address: 5301 Dempster St., Suite 100
Mailing city: Skokie
Mailing state: IL
Mailing zip: 60077-1800
General Phone: (847) 966-0606
General Fax: (847) 966-1656
Display Adv. E-mail: info@chicagojewishnews.com
Primary Website: www.chicagojewishnews.com
Year Established: 1994
Delivery Methods: Mail`Racks
Published: Fri
Avg Paid Circ: 10468
Avg Free Circ: 2422
Audit By: Sworn/Estimate/Non-Audited
Audit Date: 12.07.2019
Personnel: Joseph Aaron (Ed. and Pub.); Denise Kus (Production Manager)

CHICAGO JEWISH STAR

Street address 1: PO Box 268
Street address city: Skokie
Street address state: IL
Zip/Postal code: 60076-0268
County: Cook
Country: USA
Mailing address: PO Box 268
Mailing city: Skokie
Mailing state: IL
Mailing zip: 60076-0268
General Phone: (847) 674-7827
General Fax: (847) 674-0014
General/National Adv. E-mail: chicagojewishstar@comcast.net
Published Other: 2 x Mthly
Avg Paid Circ: 100
Avg Free Circ: 17500
Audit By: Sworn/Estimate/Non-Audited
Audit Date: 12.07.2019
Personnel: Doug Wertheimer (Ed./Pub.)

JEWISH UNITED FUND

Street address 1: 30 S. Wells St.
Street address city: Chicago
Street address state: IL
Zip/Postal code: 60606
County: Cook
Country: USA
Mailing address: 30 S. Wells St.
Mailing city: Chicago
Mailing state: IL
Mailing zip: 60606
General Phone: (312) 346-6700
General Fax: (312) 855-2470
Editorial e-mail: editorial@juf.org
Primary Website: www.juf.org
Personnel: Kathleen Evans-Mazur (Gen. Mgr.); Robert Feiger (Adv. Mgr.); Aaron Cohen (Ed.)

INDIANA

NATIONAL JEWISH POST & OPINION

Street address 1: 1427 W 86th St
Street address 2: # 228
Street address city: Indianapolis
Street address state: IN
Zip/Postal code: 46260-2103
County: Marion
Country: USA
Mailing address: 1427 W 86th St # 228
Mailing city: Indianapolis
Mailing state: IN
Mailing zip: 46260-2103

General Phone: (317) 405-8084
General Fax: (317) 405-8084
General/National Adv. E-mail: jpostopinion@gmail.com
Primary Website: www.jewishpostopinion.com
Year Established: 1935
Delivery Methods: Mail`Newsstand
Areas Served - City/County or Portion Thereof, or Zip codes: 46260, 46032, 46033, 47401,
Published Other: Monthly
Avg Paid Circ: 10000
Audit By: Sworn/Estimate/Non-Audited
Audit Date: 12.07.2019
Personnel: Jennie Cohen (Ed.)

THE INDIANA JEWISH POST & OPINION

Street address 1: 1427 W 86th St
Street address 2: # 228
Street address city: Indianapolis
Street address state: IN
Zip/Postal code: 46260-2103
County: Marion
Country: USA
Mailing address: 1427 W 86th St # 228
Mailing city: Indianapolis
Mailing state: IN
Mailing zip: 46260-2103
General Phone: (317) 405-8084
General/National Adv. E-mail: jpostopinion@gmail.com
Primary Website: www.jewishpostopinion.com
Year Established: 1935
Areas Served - City/County or Portion Thereof, or Zip codes: 46260, 46032, 46033, 46260, 46240, 46038, 46268, and others
Published: Wed
Published Other: Every other Wed
Avg Paid Circ: 5200
Audit By: Sworn/Estimate/Non-Audited
Audit Date: 12.07.2019
Personnel: Jennie Cohen (Ed.)

KANSAS

THE KANSAS CITY JEWISH CHRONICLE

Street address 1: 4210 Shawnee Mission Pkwy
Street address 2: Ste 314A
Street address city: Fairway
Street address state: KS
Zip/Postal code: 66205-2546
County: Johnson
Country: USA
Mailing address: 4210 Shawnee Mission Parkway, Suite 314A
Mailing city: Fairway
Mailing state: KS
Mailing zip: 66205
General Phone: (913) 648-4620
General Fax: (913) 381-1402
General/National Adv. E-mail: chronicle@sunpublications.com
Primary Website: www.kcjc.com
Year Established: 1920
Published: Fri
Avg Paid Circ: 4000
Audit By: Sworn/Estimate/Non-Audited
Audit Date: 12.07.2019
Personnel: David Small (Pub.); David Nevels (Circ. Mgr.); Rick Hellman (Ed.)

KENTUCKY

JEWISH LOUISVILLE COMMUNITY

Street address 1: 3600 Dutchmans Ln
Street address city: Louisville
Street address state: KY
Zip/Postal code: 40205-3302
County: Jefferson
Country: USA
General Phone: (502) 459-0660
General Fax: (502) 238-2724
Advertising Phone: (502) 418-5845
General/National Adv. E-mail: lchottiner@jewishlouisville.org
Display Adv. E-mail: lsinger@jewishlouisville.org
Primary Website: www.jewishlouisville.org
Year Established: 1975
News Services: JTA
Delivery Methods: Mail`Racks
Areas Served - City/County or Portion Thereof, or Zip codes: 40200-40299
Published: Mthly
Avg Paid Circ: 6472
Avg Free Circ: 515
Audit By: Sworn/Estimate/Non-Audited
Audit Date: 12.07.2019
Note: Community is published Monthly
Personnel: Shiela Steinman Wallace (Ed.); Larry Singer (Adv Sales); Misty Hamilton (Graphic Artist)
Parent company (for newspapers): Jewish Community of Louisville

LOUISIANA

JEWISH NEWS

Street address 1: 3747 W Esplanade Ave N
Street address city: Metairie
Street address state: LA
Zip/Postal code: 70002-3145
County: Jefferson
Country: USA
Mailing address: 3747 W Esplanade Ave N
Mailing city: Metairie
Mailing state: LA
Mailing zip: 70002-3145
General Phone: (504) 780-5600
General Fax: (504) 780-5601
General/National Adv. E-mail: jewishnews@jewishnola.com
Primary Website: www.jewishnola.com
Year Established: 1995
Published: Mthly
Avg Free Circ: 4563
Audit By: CVC
Audit Date: 31.12.2004
Personnel: Cait Muldoon (Prodn. Mgr.)
Parent company (for newspapers): Joseph Jacobs Organization

MARYLAND

JEWISH TIMES

Street address 1: 1040 Park Ave
Street address 2: Ste 200
Street address city: Baltimore
Street address state: MD
Zip/Postal code: 21201-5634
County: Baltimore City
Country: USA
Mailing address: 11459 Cronhill Dr Ste A
Mailing city: Owings Mills
Mailing state: MD
Mailing zip: 21117-6280
General Phone: (410) 752-3504
General/National Adv. E-mail: information@jewishtimes.com
Primary Website: www.jewishtimes.com
Published: Fri
Avg Paid Circ: 35000
Audit By: Sworn/Estimate/Non-Audited
Audit Date: 12.07.2019
Personnel: Maayan Jaffe (Pub.); Claudia Meyers (Gen. Mgr.); Phil Jacobs (Ed.); Erin Clare (Prodn. Mgr.)

WASHINGTON JEWISH WEEK

Street address 1: 11426 Rockville Pike
Street address 2: Ste 236
Street address city: Rockville
Street address state: MD
Zip/Postal code: 20852-3075
County: Montgomery
Country: USA
Mailing address: 11900 Parklawn Dr Ste 300
Mailing city: Rockville
Mailing state: MD
Mailing zip: 20852-2768
General Phone: 301-230-0474
General Fax: (301) 881-6362
General/National Adv. E-mail: editorial@washingtonjewishweek.com
Primary Website: www.washingtonjewishweek.com
Year Established: 1965
Published: Thur
Avg Paid Circ: 10000
Audit By: Sworn/Estimate/Non-Audited
Audit Date: 12.07.2019
Personnel: Larry Fishbein (Pub.); Debra Rubin (Ed.); Patrick Fisher (Prodn. Mgr.)
Parent company (for newspapers): Joseph Jacobs Organization

MASSACHUSETTS

BERKSHIRE JEWISH VOICE

Street address 1: 196 South Street
Street address 2: Jewish Federation of the Berkshires
Street address city: Pittsfield
Street address state: MA
Zip/Postal code: 01201
County: Berkshire
Mailing state: MA
General Phone: 413-442-4360
Advertising Phone: 413-442-4360
Editorial Phone: 413-442-4360
General/National Adv. E-mail: astern@jewishberkshires.org
Editorial e-mail: astern@jewishberkshires.org
Primary Website: https://jewishberkshires.org/community-events/berkshire-jewish-voice/berkshire-jewish-voice-highlights
Year Established: 1989
Published Other: 9x per year
Avg Free Circ: 5000
Personnel: Dara Kaufman (Exec. Dir.); Albert Stern (Editor); Jenny Greenfield (Office Mgr.)
Parent company (for newspapers): Jewish Federation of the Berkshires; Joseph Jacobs Organization

METROWEST JEWISH REPORTER

Street address 1: 29 Upper Joclyn Ave
Street address city: Framingham
Street address state: MA
Zip/Postal code: 01701-4400
County: Middlesex
Country: USA
Mailing address: 126 High St Ste 1
Mailing city: Boston
Mailing state: MA
Mailing zip: 02110-2776
General Phone: (508) 879-3300
General Fax: (508) 879-5856
General/National Adv. E-mail: jewishreporter@aol.com
Published: Mthly
Avg Free Circ: 10500
Audit By: Sworn/Estimate/Non-Audited
Audit Date: 12.07.2019
Personnel: Nancy Atlas (Mng. Ed.); Wendy Davis (Asst. Mng. Ed.)

NORTH SHORE JEWISH PRESS

Street address 1: 27 Congress St
Street address 2: Ste 501
Street address city: Salem
Street address state: MA
Zip/Postal code: 01970-5577
County: Essex
Country: USA
Mailing address: 27 Congress Street, Suite 501
Mailing city: Salem
Mailing state: MA
Mailing zip: 01970
General Phone: (978) 745-4111
General Fax: (978) 745-5333
Advertising Phone: (978) 745-4111X114
Editorial Phone: (978) 745-4111X140
General/National Adv. E-mail: business@jewishjournal.org
Primary Website: www.jewishjournal.org
Year Established: 1976
Published: Thur
Avg Free Circ: 16000
Audit By: Sworn/Estimate/Non-Audited
Audit Date: 12.07.2019
Personnel: Barbara Schneider (Pub.); Susan Jacobs (Editor); Bette Keva (Ed.)

THE JEWISH ADVOCATE

Street address 1: 15 School St
Street address city: Boston
Street address state: MA
Zip/Postal code: 02108-4307
County: Suffolk
Country: USA
General Phone: (617) 367-9100
General Fax: (617) 367-9310
General/National Adv. E-mail: sharonh@thejewishadvocate.com
Display Adv. E-mail: business@thejewishadvocate.com
Editorial e-mail: editorial@thejewishadvocate.com
Primary Website: www.thejewishadvocate.com
Year Established: 1902
Delivery Methods: Mail`Newsstand
Published: Fri
Avg Paid Circ: 30000
Audit By: Sworn/Estimate/Non-Audited
Audit Date: 12.07.2019
Personnel: Grand Rabbi Y. A. Korff (Pub.); Michael Whalen (Ed.); Sharon Harrau (Administrator); Ian Thal

THE JEWISH CHRONICLE

Street address 1: 131 Lincoln St
Street address city: Worcester
Street address state: MA
Zip/Postal code: 01605-2408
County: Worcester
Country: USA
Mailing address: 131 Lincoln St
Mailing city: Worcester
Mailing state: MA
Mailing zip: 01605-2421
General Phone: (508) 752-2512
General Fax: (508) 752-9057
General/National Adv. E-mail: chronicle.sales@verizon.net
Areas Served - City/County or Portion Thereof, or Zip codes: 1605
Published: Thur
Avg Paid Circ: 1000
Avg Free Circ: 4000
Audit By: Sworn/Estimate/Non-Audited
Audit Date: 12.07.2019
Personnel: Sondra Shapiro (Pub.); Reva Catellari (Adv. Mgr.); Ellen Weingart (Ed.)

THE JEWISH REPORTER

Street address 1: 29 Upper Joclyn Ave
Street address city: Framingham
Street address state: MA
Zip/Postal code: 01701-4400
County: Middlesex
Country: USA
Mailing address: 126 High St Ste 1
Mailing city: Boston
Mailing state: MA
Mailing zip: 02110-2776
General Phone: (508) 872-4808
General Fax: (508) 879-5856
General/National Adv. E-mail: jewishreporter@aol.com
Published: Mthly
Avg Free Circ: 6500
Audit By: Sworn/Estimate/Non-Audited
Audit Date: 12.07.2019
Personnel: Nancy Atlas (Ed.)
Parent company (for newspapers): Joseph Jacobs Organization

MICHIGAN

THE DETROIT JEWISH NEWS

Street address 1: 29200 Northwestern Hwy
Street address 2: Ste 110
Street address city: Southfield
Street address state: MI
Zip/Postal code: 48034-1055

County: Oakland
Country: USA
Mailing address: 29200 Northwestern Hwy Ste 110
Mailing city: Southfield
Mailing state: MI
Mailing zip: 48034-1055
General Phone: (248) 354-6060
Editorial Fax: (248) 304-0032
Primary Website: www.thejewishnews.com
Published: Thur
Avg Paid Circ: 17134
Avg Free Circ: 54
Audit By: Sworn/Estimate/Non-Audited
Audit Date: 12.07.2019
Personnel: Arthur Horwitz (Pub.); Kevin Browett (COO); Keith Farber (Adv. Mgr.); Zina Davis (Circ. Mgr.); Robert Sklar (Ed.); Alan Hitsky (Assoc. Ed.)
Parent company (for newspapers): Joseph Jacobs Organization

MINNESOTA

AMERICAN JEWISH WORLD

Street address 1: 4820 Minnetonka Blvd
Street address 2: Ste 104
Street address city: Minneapolis
Street address state: MN
Zip/Postal code: 55416-2278
County: Hennepin
Country: USA
Mailing address: 4820 Minnetonka Blvd Ste 104
Mailing city: Minneapolis
Mailing state: MN
Mailing zip: 55416-2278
General Phone: (952) 259-5237
General Fax: (952) 920-6205
Advertising Phone: (952) 259-5234
Advertising Fax: (952) 920-6205
Editorial Phone: (952) 259-5239
Editorial Fax: (952) 920-6205
General/National Adv. E-mail: news@ajwnews.com
Display Adv. E-mail: editor@ajwnews.com
Editorial e-mail: community@ajwnews.com
Primary Website: www.ajwnews.com
Year Established: 1912
Delivery Methods: Mail
Areas Served - City/County or Portion Thereof, or Zip codes: 55401, 55402, 55118, 55416, 55426, 55105, 55116
Published: Bi-Mthly
Published Other: Every other Fri
Avg Paid Circ: 3500
Audit By: Sworn/Estimate/Non-Audited
Audit Date: 12.07.2019
Personnel: Mordecai Specktor (Ed.)
Parent company (for newspapers): Minnesota Jewish Media, LLC

MISSOURI

SAINT LOUIS JEWISH LIGHT

Street address 1: 6 Millstone Campus Dr
Street address 2: Ste 3010
Street address city: Saint Louis
Street address state: MO
Zip/Postal code: 63146-6603
County: Saint Louis
Country: USA
Mailing address: 6 Millstone Campus Dr Ste 3010
Mailing city: Saint Louis
Mailing state: MO
Mailing zip: 63146-6603
General Phone: (314) 743-3600
General Fax: (314) 743-3690
Advertising Phone: (314) 743-3677
Advertising Fax: (314) 743-3690
Editorial Phone: (314) 743-3669
Editorial Fax: (314) 743-3690
General/National Adv. E-mail: office@thejewishlight.com
Display Adv. E-mail: jschack@thejewishlight.com
Editorial e-mail: msherwin@thejewishlight.com
Primary Website: www.stljewishlight.com
Year Established: 1947
Delivery Methods: Mail`Racks
Published: Wed
Published Other: Quarterly Oy! Magazine, 24/7 website, weekly e-newsletter
Avg Paid Circ: 5000
Avg Free Circ: 4000
Audit By: Sworn/Estimate/Non-Audited
Audit Date: 12.07.2019
Personnel: Robert A. Cohn (CEO/Pub.)

ST. LOUIS JEWISH LIGHT

Street address 1: 6 Millstone Campus Drive
Street address 2: Ste 3010
Street address city: Saint Louis
Street address state: MO
Zip/Postal code: 63146-6603
County: Saint Louis
Country: USA
Mailing address: 6 Millstone Campus Drive, Suite 3010
Mailing city: Saint Louis
Mailing state: MO
Mailing zip: 63146-6603
General Phone: (314) 743-3660
General Fax: (314) 743-3690
Advertising Phone: (314) 743-3677
Advertising Fax: (314) 743-3690
Editorial Phone: (314) 743-3669
Editorial Fax: (314) 743-3690
General/National Adv. E-mail: office@thejewishlight.com
Display Adv. E-mail: advertising@thejewishlight.com
Editorial e-mail: news@thejewishlight.com
Primary Website: www.stljewishlight.com
Year Established: 1963
Delivery Methods: Mail`Racks
Areas Served - City/County or Portion Thereof, or Zip codes: 63xxx (St. Louis Metro)
Published: Wed
Published Other: Quarterly magazine, 24/7 website, weekly email blast
Avg Paid Circ: 4813
Avg Free Circ: 4097
Audit By: CVC
Audit Date: 01.06.2012
Note: The Jewish Light is the nonprofit news organization of the St. Louis Jewish community.
Personnel: Robert A. Cohn (Ed. in Chief); Scott Berzon (Exec. Dir.)

NEBRASKA

JEWISH PRESS

Street address 1: 333 S 132nd St
Street address city: Omaha
Street address state: NE
Zip/Postal code: 68154-2106
County: Douglas
Country: USA
Mailing address: 333 S 132nd St
Mailing city: Omaha
Mailing state: NE
Mailing zip: 68154-2198
General Phone: (402) 334-6448
General Fax: (402) 334-5422
General/National Adv. E-mail: jpress@jewishomaha.org
Primary Website: www.jewishomaha.org
Year Established: 1920
Published: Fri
Avg Paid Circ: 67409
Avg Free Circ: 1875
Audit By: Sworn/Estimate/Non-Audited
Audit Date: 12.07.2019
Personnel: Allan Handleman (Adv. Mgr.); Carol Katzman (Ed.); Richard Busse (Mng. Ed.)
Parent company (for newspapers): Joseph Jacobs Organization

NEVADA

JEWISH REPORTER

Street address 1: 2317 Renaissance Dr
Street address city: Las Vegas
Street address state: NV
Zip/Postal code: 89119-6191
County: Clark
Country: USA
Mailing address: 2317 Renaissance Dr
Mailing city: Las Vegas
Mailing state: NV
Mailing zip: 89119-6191
General Phone: (702) 732-0556
General Fax: (702) 732-3228
General/National Adv. E-mail: info@jewishlasvegas.com
Display Adv. E-mail: ads@jewishlasvegas.com
Editorial e-mail: editor@jewishlasvegas.com
Primary Website: www.jewishlasvegas.com
Areas Served - City/County or Portion Thereof, or Zip codes: 89119
Personnel: Joanne Friedland (Adv. Sales Dir.); Leah Brown (Ed.); Arthur Bloberger (Ed.); Andrew Bemson (Graphics/Layout Artist)
Parent company (for newspapers): Joseph Jacobs Organization

NEW JERSEY

JEWISH STANDARD

Street address 1: 1086 Teaneck Rd
Street address city: Teaneck
Street address state: NJ
Zip/Postal code: 07666-4854
County: Bergen
Country: USA
Mailing address: 1086 Teaneck Rd Ste 2F
Mailing city: Teaneck
Mailing state: NJ
Mailing zip: 07666-4839
General Phone: (201) 837-8818
General Fax: (201) 833-4959
Display Adv. E-mail: ads@jewishmediagroup.com
Primary Website: www.jstandard.com
Published: Fri
Avg Paid Circ: 24000
Audit By: Sworn/Estimate/Non-Audited
Audit Date: 12.07.2019
Personnel: James Janoff (Pub.); Rebecca Boroson (Ed.)
Parent company (for newspapers): Joseph Jacobs Organization

JEWISH TIMES

Street address 1: 21 W Delilah Rd
Street address city: Pleasantville
Street address state: NJ
Zip/Postal code: 08232-1403
County: Atlantic
Country: USA
Mailing address: 21 W Delilah Rd
Mailing city: Pleasantville
Mailing state: NJ
Mailing zip: 08232-1403
General Phone: (609) 407-0909
General Fax: (609) 407-0999
General/National Adv. E-mail: jwishtimes@aol.com
Primary Website: www.jewishtimes-sj.com
Published: Fri
Avg Paid Circ: 4000
Avg Free Circ: 1000
Audit By: Sworn/Estimate/Non-Audited
Audit Date: 12.07.2019
Personnel: Shy Kramer (Pub.); Bonnie La Roche (Adv. Mgr.); Gerald Etter (Mng. Ed.)
Parent company (for newspapers): Joseph Jacobs Organization

JEWISH VOICE

Street address 1: 1301 Springdale Rd
Street address 2: Ste 250
Street address city: Cherry Hill
Street address state: NJ
Zip/Postal code: 08003-2763
County: Camden
Country: USA
Mailing address: 1301 Springdale Road
Mailing city: Cherry Hill
Mailing state: NJ
Mailing zip: 08003-2762
General Phone: (856) 751-9500 x1217
General Fax: (856) 489-8253
Editorial Phone: (856) 751-9500 x1237
General/National Adv. E-mail: jvoice@jfedsnj.org
Editorial e-mail: dportnoe@jfedsnj.org
Primary Website: jewishvoicesnj.org
Areas Served - City/County or Portion Thereof, or Zip codes: 7723
Audit By: Sworn/Estimate/Non-Audited
Audit Date: 10.06.2019
Personnel: Stuart Abraham (Pub.); Howard Gases (Pub.); Judy Robinowitz (Adv. Mgr.); Lauren Silver (Ed.); Oscar Trugler (Prodn. Mgr.)
Parent company (for newspapers): Joseph Jacobs Organization

JEWISH VOICE AND OPINION

Street address 1: PO Box 8097
Street address city: Englewood
Street address state: NJ
Zip/Postal code: 07631-8097
County: Bergen
Country: USA
Mailing address: PO Box 8097
Mailing city: Englewood
Mailing state: NJ
Mailing zip: 07631
General Phone: (201) 569-2845
Advertising Phone: (201) 569-2845
Editorial Phone: (201) 569-2845
General/National Adv. E-mail: susan@JewishVoiceAndOpinion.com
Display Adv. E-mail: susan@JewishVoiceAndOpinion.com
Editorial e-mail: susan@JewishVoiceAndOpinion.com
Primary Website: TheJewishVoiceAndOpinion.com
Year Established: 1987
Delivery Methods: Mail`Racks
Areas Served - City/County or Portion Thereof, or Zip codes: 07010, 07011, 07012, 07013, 07014, 07024, 07036, 07039, 07047, 07052, 07055, 07078, 07079, 07081, 07087, 07094, 07202, 07205, 07208, 07302, 07304, 07305, 07306, 07307, 07410, 07470, 07605, 07621, 06531, 07632, 07646, 07652, 07666, 07670, 07726, 07747, 07866, 07960, 07962, 08002, 08003, 08034, 08402, 08406, 08816, 08817, 08820, 08901, 08902, 08904, 10461, 10463, 10467, 10471, 10475, 10901, 10952, 10956, 10977
Published: Mthly
Avg Paid Circ: 20000
Avg Free Circ: 18000
Audit By: Sworn/Estimate/Non-Audited
Audit Date: 12.07.2019
Personnel: Susan L. Rosenbluth (Editor)
Parent company (for newspapers): The Jewish Voice and Opinion

NEW JERSEY JEWISH NEWS

Street address 1: 901 State Route 10
Street address city: Whippany
Street address state: NJ
Zip/Postal code: 07981-1105
County: Morris
Country: USA
Mailing address: 901 State Route 10
Mailing city: Whippany
Mailing state: NJ
Mailing zip: 07981-1157
General Phone: (973) 887-8500
General Fax: (973) 887-4152
Editorial Fax: (973) 887-5999
General/National Adv. E-mail: info@njjewishnews.com
Primary Website: www.njjewishnews.com
Delivery Methods: Mail
Published: Thur
Avg Paid Circ: 50000
Audit By: Sworn/Estimate/Non-Audited
Audit Date: 12.07.2019
Personnel: Andrew Silow-Carroll (Editor in Chief/CEO); Rick Kestenbaum

NEW MEXICO

NEW MEXICO JEWISH LINK

Street address 1: 5520 Wyoming Blvd NE
Street address city: Albuquerque
Street address state: NM
Zip/Postal code: 87109-3238
County: Bernalillo
Country: USA
Mailing address: 5520 Wyoming Blvd NE
Mailing city: Albuquerque
Mailing state: NM
Mailing zip: 87109-3238
General Phone: (505) 821-3214
General Fax: (505) 821-3351
General/National Adv. E-mail: news@nmjlink.org
Primary Website: www.jewishnewmexico.org
Areas Served - City/County or Portion Thereof, or Zip codes: 87109
Published: Mthly
Avg Free Circ: 6500
Audit By: Sworn/Estimate/Non-Audited
Audit Date: 12.07.2019
Personnel: Erin Tarica (Dir.); Jen Dennis (Sr. Serv. Mgr.); Rabbi Art Flicker (Chaplain)

NEW YORK

ALGEMEINER JOURNAL

Street address 1: 508 Montgomery St
Street address city: Brooklyn
Street address state: NY
Zip/Postal code: 11225-3023
County: Kings
Country: USA
Mailing address: 508 Montgomery St
Mailing city: Brooklyn
Mailing state: NY
Mailing zip: 11225-3023
General Phone: (347) 741-7830
General Fax: (718) 771-0308
General/National Adv. E-mail: algemeiner@aol.com
Primary Website: www.algemeiner.com
Published: Wed
Avg Paid Circ: 30000
Avg Free Circ: 28000
Audit By: Sworn/Estimate/Non-Audited
Audit Date: 12.07.2019
Personnel: Simon Jacobson (Pub.); Dovid Efune (Dir.); Moshe Hecht (Adv. Mgr.); Yosef Jacobson (Ed.)
Parent company (for newspapers): Joseph Jacobs Organization

BUFFALO JEWISH REVIEW

Street address 1: 964 Kenmore Ave
Street address city: Buffalo
Street address state: NY
Zip/Postal code: 14216-1450
County: Erie
Country: USA
Mailing address: 964 Kenmore Ave.
Mailing city: Buffalo
Mailing state: NY
Mailing zip: 14216
General Phone: (716) 854-2192
General Fax: (716) 854-2198
General/National Adv. E-mail: buffjewrev@aol.com
Primary Website: http://www.buffalojewishreview.com/
Published: Fri
Avg Paid Circ: 3500
Audit By: Sworn/Estimate/Non-Audited
Audit Date: 12.07.2019
Personnel: Arnold Weiss (Pub.); Rita Weiss (Ed.)
Parent company (for newspapers): Joseph Jacobs Organization

DER YID

Street address 1: 191 Rodney St
Street address city: Brooklyn
Street address state: NY
Zip/Postal code: 11211-7787
County: Kings
Country: USA
Mailing address: 191 rodney St
Mailing city: Brooklyn
Mailing state: NY
Mailing zip: 11211
General Phone: (718) 797-3900
General Fax: (718) 797-1985
General/National Adv. E-mail: adv@deryid.org
Primary Website: deryid.org
Delivery Methods: Mail`Newsstand`Racks
Published: Thur
Audit By: Sworn/Estimate/Non-Audited
Audit Date: 12.07.2019
Personnel: Herman Friedman (Gen. Mgr.); Aron Friedman (Ed.)
Parent company (for newspapers): Joseph Jacobs Organization

JEWISH JOURNAL

Street address 1: 11 Sunrise Plz
Street address city: Valley Stream
Street address state: NY
Zip/Postal code: 11580-6170
County: Nassau
Country: USA
Mailing address: 11 Sunrise Plz
Mailing city: Valley Stream
Mailing state: NY
Mailing zip: 11580-6170
General Phone: (516) 561-6900
General Fax: (516) 561-3529
Published: Fri
Avg Paid Circ: 47000
Avg Free Circ: 33000
Audit By: Sworn/Estimate/Non-Audited
Audit Date: 12.07.2019
Personnel: Paul Rubin (Ed.)
Parent company (for newspapers): Joseph Jacobs Organization

JEWISH TELEGRAPHIC AGENCY DAILY NEWS BULLETIN

Street address 1: 330 7th Ave
Street address 2: Fl 17
Street address city: New York
Street address state: NY
Zip/Postal code: 10001-5010
County: New York
Country: USA
Mailing address: 24 W 30th St Fl 4
Mailing city: New York
Mailing state: NY
Mailing zip: 10001-4443
General Phone: (212) 643-1890
General Fax: (212) 643-8499
General/National Adv. E-mail: info@jta.org
Primary Website: www.jta.org
Published Other: Daily
Avg Paid Circ: 1200
Avg Free Circ: 50
Audit By: Sworn/Estimate/Non-Audited
Audit Date: 12.07.2019
Personnel: Mark J. Joffe (Pub.); Lenore A. Silverstein (Gen. Mgr.); Ami Eden (Mng. Ed.)

JEWISH TRIBUNE OF ROCKLAND COUNTY

Street address 1: 1525 Central Ave
Street address city: Far Rockaway
Street address state: NY
Zip/Postal code: 11691-4019
County: Queens
Country: USA
Mailing address: 511 Hempstead Ave Ste 1
Mailing city: West Hempstead
Mailing state: NY
Mailing zip: 11552-2737
General Phone: (516) 829-4000
General Fax: (516) 594-4900
General/National Adv. E-mail: lijeworld@aol.com
Published: Fri
Avg Paid Circ: 7541
Avg Free Circ: 750
Audit By: Sworn/Estimate/Non-Audited
Audit Date: 12.07.2019
Personnel: Jerome W. Lippman (Mng. Ed.)

JEWISH WEEK

Street address 1: 1501 Broadway
Street address 2: Ste 505
Street address city: New York
Street address state: NY
Zip/Postal code: 10036-5501
County: New York
Country: USA
Mailing address: 1501 Broadway Ste 505
Mailing city: New York
Mailing state: NY
Mailing zip: 10036-5504
General Phone: (212) 921-7822
General Fax: (212) 921-8420
Primary Website: www.thejewishweek.com
Published: Thur
Avg Paid Circ: 74000
Audit By: Sworn/Estimate/Non-Audited
Audit Date: 12.07.2019
Personnel: Richard Waloff (Assoc. Pub.); Gershon Fastow (Adv. Coord.); Ruth Rothseid (Sales Mgr.); Paul Bukzin (Circ. Mgr.); Gary Rosenblatt (Ed.); Robert Goldblum (Mng. Ed.)
Parent company (for newspapers): Joseph Jacobs Organization

LONG ISLAND JEWISH WORLD

Street address 1: 1525 Central Ave
Street address city: Far Rockaway
Street address state: NY
Zip/Postal code: 11691-4019
County: Queens
Country: USA
Mailing address: 511 Hempstead Ave Ste 1
Mailing city: West Hempstead
Mailing state: NY
Mailing zip: 11552-2737
General Phone: (516) 829-4000
General Fax: (516) 594-4900
General/National Adv. E-mail: lijeworld@aol.com
Published: Fri
Avg Paid Circ: 15284
Avg Free Circ: 1159
Audit By: Sworn/Estimate/Non-Audited
Audit Date: 12.07.2019
Personnel: Jerome W. Lippman (Mng. Ed.)

MANHATTAN JEWISH SENTINEL

Street address 1: 1525 Central Ave
Street address city: Far Rockaway
Street address state: NY
Zip/Postal code: 11691-4019
County: Queens
Country: USA
Mailing address: 511 Hempstead Ave Ste 1
Mailing city: West Hempstead
Mailing state: NY
Mailing zip: 11552-2737
General Phone: (516) 829-4000
General Fax: (516) 594-4900
General/National Adv. E-mail: lijeworld@aol.com
Personnel: Jerome W. Lippman (Ed.)
Parent company (for newspapers): Joseph Jacobs Organization

MANHATTAN/WESTCHESTER JEWISH WEEK

Street address 1: 1501 Broadway
Street address 2: Ste 505
Street address city: New York
Street address state: NY
Zip/Postal code: 10036-5501
County: New York
Country: USA
Mailing address: 1501 Broadway Ste 505
Mailing city: New York
Mailing state: NY
Mailing zip: 10036-5504
General Phone: (212) 921-7822
General Fax: (212) 921-8420
Advertising Phone: (212) 921-7822 x254
Editorial Phone: (212) 921-7822 x213
General/National Adv. E-mail: ruth@jewishweek.org
Editorial e-mail: robert@jewishweek.org
Primary Website: www.thejewishweek.com
Mthly Avg Views: 400000
Mthly Avg Unique Visitors: 145000
Published: Fri
Personnel: Robert Goldblum (Managing Ed.); Ruth Rothseid (Sales Dir.); Gary Rosenblatt (Ed. & Pub.)

THE FORWARD

Street address 1: 125 Maiden Ln
Street address 2: Fl 8
Street address city: New York
Street address state: NY
Zip/Postal code: 10038-5015
County: New York
Country: USA
Mailing address: 125 Maiden Ln Fl 8
Mailing city: New York
Mailing state: NY
Mailing zip: 10038-5015
General Phone: (212) 889-8200
General Fax: (212) 689-4255
Display Adv. E-mail: advertising@forward.com
Primary Website: www.forward.com
Published: Fri
Avg Paid Circ: 14222
Avg Free Circ: 10701
Audit By: AAM
Audit Date: 31.03.2015
Personnel: Jerry Koenig (Adv. Mgr.); Jane Eisner (Ed. in Chief); Lil Swanson (Mng. Ed.)

THE JEWISH LEDGER

Street address 1: 2535 Brighton Henrietta Tl Rd
Street address city: Rochester
Street address state: NY
Zip/Postal code: 14623-2711
County: Monroe
Country: USA
Mailing address: 2535 Brighton-Henrietta TL Rd.
Mailing city: Rochester
Mailing state: NY
Mailing zip: 14623
General Phone: (585) 427-2434
General Fax: (585) 427-8521
Advertising Phone: (585) 427-2468
Editorial Phone: 5854272434
General/National Adv. E-mail: info@thejewishledger.com
Display Adv. E-mail: info@the jewishledger.com
Editorial e-mail: info@thejewishledger.com
Primary Website: www.thejewishledger.com
Year Established: 1924
Delivery Methods: Mail`Newsstand
Areas Served - City/County or Portion Thereof, or Zip codes: 146 171 461 814 620 000 000 000 000 000
Published: Thur
Published Other: Weekly
Avg Paid Circ: 6500
Avg Free Circ: 1000
Audit By: USPS
Audit Date: 09.11.2017
Personnel: George Morgenstern (Gen. Mgr.); Barbara G. Morgenstern (Ed.)

THE JEWISH OBSERVER

Street address 1: 5655 Thompson Rd
Street address city: Syracuse
Street address state: NY
Zip/Postal code: 13214-1234
County: Onondaga
Country: USA
Mailing address: 5655 Thompson Rd
Mailing city: Syracuse
Mailing state: NY
Mailing zip: 13214-1234
General Phone: (315) 445-0161
General Fax: (315) 445-1559
Advertising Phone: (800) 779-7896 ext 244
Editorial Phone: (315) 445-0161
Editorial Fax: (315) 445-1559
General/National Adv. E-mail: jewishobservercny@gmail.com
Display Adv. E-mail: jewishobserversyr@gmail.com
Editorial e-mail: jewishobservercny@gmail.com
Primary Website: www.jewishfederationcnyp.org
Year Established: 1976
Delivery Methods: Mail
Areas Served - City/County or Portion Thereof, or Zip codes: 01701-97201
Published: Thur
Published Other: bii-weekly
Avg Paid Circ: 3000
Audit By: Sworn/Estimate/Non-Audited

Audit Date: 12.07.2019
Personnel: Bette Siegel (Ed.)

THE JEWISH PRESS

Street address 1: 3692 Bedford Avenue
Street address city: Brooklyn
Street address state: NY
Zip/Postal code: 11229
County: Kings
Country: U.S.
General Phone: 718-330-1100
General Fax: 718/624-4106
Advertising Phone: 718-645-7297
Editorial Phone: 718-330-1100
General/National Adv. E-mail: editor@jewishpress.com
Display Adv. E-mail: arthurklass@jewishpress.com
Classified Adv. e-mail: arthurklass@jewishpress.com
Editorial e-mail: editor@jewishpress.com
Primary Website: www.jewishpress.com
Mthly Avg Views: 300000
Year Established: 1959
News Services: JNS
Areas Served - City/County or Portion Thereof, or Zip codes: National, New York metro, South Florida, L.A.
Published: Fri
Avg Paid Circ: 96000
Audit By: Sworn/Estimate/Non-Audited
Audit Date: 15.10.2020
Note: The Jewish Press is an English language ethnic weekly newspaper together with an associated digital edition website
Personnel: Irene Klass (Pub.); Arthur Klass (Director of Business Development); Heshy Kornblit (Display Dept. Mgr.); Joseph Hochberg (Circ. Mgr.); Jason Maoz (Sr. Ed.); Jerry Greenwald (Mng. Ed.)

THE JEWISH WEEK

Street address 1: 1501 Broadway
Street address 2: Ste 505
Street address city: New York
Street address state: NY
Zip/Postal code: 10036-5501
County: New York
Country: USA
Mailing address: 1501 Broadway Ste 505
Mailing city: New York
Mailing state: NY
Mailing zip: 10036-5504
General Phone: (212) 921-7822
General Fax: (212) 921-8420
Advertising Phone: (212) 997-2954
General/National Adv. E-mail: editor@jewishweek.org
Display Adv. E-mail: ruth@jewishweek.org
Editorial e-mail: editor@jewishweek.org
Primary Website: www.thejewishweek.com
Year Established: 1979
Delivery Methods: Mail`Newsstand`Carrier
Areas Served - City/County or Portion Thereof, or Zip codes: 10001 through 11999, primarily
Published: Fri
Avg Paid Circ: 44731
Avg Free Circ: 6289
Audit By: AAM
Audit Date: 31.12.2004
Personnel: Gary Rosenblatt (Pub.); Richard Waloff (Assoc. Pub.); Robert Goldblum (Mng. Ed.); Ruth Rothseid (Sales Manager)

THE JEWISH WORLD

Street address 1: 1635 Eastern Pkwy
Street address city: Schenectady
Street address state: NY
Zip/Postal code: 12309-6011
County: Schenectady
Country: USA
Mailing address: 1635 Eastern Pkwy
Mailing city: Schenectady
Mailing state: NY
Mailing zip: 12309-6011
General Phone: (518) 344-7018
General Fax: (518) 713-2137
General/National Adv. E-mail: news@jewishworldnews.org
Primary Website: www.jewishworldnews.org
Year Established: 1965
Delivery Methods: Mail`Newsstand
Published: Thur`Other
Published Other: twice a month
Avg Paid Circ: 8500
Audit By: Sworn/Estimate/Non-Audited
Audit Date: 12.07.2019
Note: serving Albany,Schenectady, Troy,all northeastern NY, western Mass, and south Vt
Personnel: Laurie Clevenson (editor.)

THE LONG ISLAND JEWISH WEEK

Street address 1: 1501 Broadway
Street address 2: Ste 505
Street address city: New York
Street address state: NY
Zip/Postal code: 10036-5501
County: New York
Country: USA
Mailing address: 1501 Broadway Ste 505
Mailing city: New York
Mailing state: NY
Mailing zip: 10036-5504
General Phone: (212) 921-7822
General Fax: (212) 921-8420
Primary Website: www.thejewishweek.com
Published: Fri
Avg Paid Circ: 90000
Avg Free Circ: 259
Audit By: Sworn/Estimate/Non-Audited
Audit Date: 12.07.2019
Personnel: Richard Waloff (Pub.); Robert Goldblum (Mng. Ed.); Gary Rosenblatt (Ed.)

THE QUEENS JEWISH WEEK

Street address 1: 1501 Broadway
Street address 2: Ste 505
Street address city: New York
Street address state: NY
Zip/Postal code: 10036-5501
County: New York
Country: USA
Mailing address: 1501 Broadway Ste 505
Mailing city: New York
Mailing state: NY
Mailing zip: 10036-5504
General Phone: (212) 921-7822
General Fax: (212) 921-8420
Primary Website: www.thejewishweek.com
Published: Fri
Avg Paid Circ: 14500
Avg Free Circ: 116
Audit By: Sworn/Estimate/Non-Audited
Audit Date: 12.07.2019
Personnel: Gary Rosenblatt (Pub.); Richard Waloff (Adv. Mgr.); Robert Goldblum (Mng. Ed.)

THE REPORTER

Street address 1: 500 Clubhouse Rd
Street address city: Vestal
Street address state: NY
Zip/Postal code: 13850-4700
County: Broome
Country: USA
Mailing address: 500 Clubhouse Rd Ste 2
Mailing city: Vestal
Mailing state: NY
Mailing zip: 13850-3734
General Phone: (607) 724-2360
General Fax: (607) 724-2311
General/National Adv. E-mail: treporter@aol.com
Primary Website: www.thereportergroup.org
Year Established: 1971
Published: Fri
Avg Paid Circ: 2400
Audit By: Sworn/Estimate/Non-Audited
Audit Date: 12.07.2019
Personnel: Bonnie Rosen (Adv. Mgr.); Diana sochor (Layout Ed.); Jenn DePersis (Prodn. Coord.)

THE VOICE

Street address 1: 500 Clubhouse Rd
Street address city: Vestal
Street address state: NY
Zip/Postal code: 13850-4700
County: Broome
Country: USA
Mailing address: 500 Clubhouse Rd
Mailing city: Vestal
Mailing state: NY
Mailing zip: 13850-4700
General Phone: (607) 724-2360
General Fax: (607) 724-2311
General/National Adv. E-mail: treporter@aol.com
Primary Website: www.thereportergroup.org
Year Established: 1989
Published: Mthly
Avg Paid Circ: 3000
Audit By: Sworn/Estimate/Non-Audited
Audit Date: 12.07.2019
Personnel: Dan Springer (Bus. Mgr.); Jenn DePersis (Prodn. Mgr.)

THE WESTCHESTER JEWISH WEEK

Street address 1: 1501 Broadway
Street address 2: Ste 505
Street address city: New York
Street address state: NY
Zip/Postal code: 10036-5501
County: New York
Country: USA
Mailing address: 1501 Broadway Ste 505
Mailing city: New York
Mailing state: NY
Mailing zip: 10036-5504
General Phone: (212) 921-7822
General Fax: (212) 921-8420
Primary Website: www.thejewishweek.com
Published: Fri
Avg Paid Circ: 15661
Avg Free Circ: 192
Audit By: Sworn/Estimate/Non-Audited
Audit Date: 12.07.2019
Personnel: Gary Rosenblatt (Pub.); Richard Waloff (Adv. Mgr.); Robert Goldblum (Mng. Ed.)

WESTCHESTER JEWISH LIFE

Street address 1: 629 Fifth Ave
Street address city: Pelham
Street address state: NY
Zip/Postal code: 10803-1251
County: Westchester
Country: USA
Mailing address: 629 Fifth Ave
Mailing city: Pelham
Mailing state: NY
Mailing zip: 10803-1251
General Phone: (914) 738-7869
General Fax: (914) 738-7876
General/National Adv. E-mail: hp@shorelinepub.com
Display Adv. E-mail: hp@shorelinepub.com
Editorial e-mail: hp@shorelinepub.com
Primary Website: www.shorelinepub.com
Year Established: 1996
Delivery Methods: Newsstand
Areas Served - City/County or Portion Thereof, or Zip codes: All Westchester County
Published: Mthly
Avg Paid Circ: 500
Avg Free Circ: 24000
Audit By: Sworn/Estimate/Non-Audited
Audit Date: 12.07.2019
Personnel: Edward Shapiro (Adv. Mgr.); Helene Pollack (Editor and Publisher)
Parent company (for newspapers): Shoreline Publishing

NORTH CAROLINA

CHARLOTTE JEWISH NEWS

Street address 1: 5007 Providence Rd
Street address city: Charlotte
Street address state: NC
Zip/Postal code: 28226-5849
County: Mecklenburg
Country: USA
Mailing address: 5007 Providence Rd Ste 112
Mailing city: Charlotte
Mailing state: NC
Mailing zip: 28226-5907
General Phone: (704) 944-6757
General Fax: (704) 944-6766
General/National Adv. E-mail: info@jewishcharlotte.org
Editorial e-mail: amontoni@shalomcharlotte.org
Primary Website: www.jewishcharlotte.org
Year Established: 1979
Published: Mthly
Avg Free Circ: 4200
Audit By: Sworn/Estimate/Non-Audited
Audit Date: 12.07.2019
Personnel: Rita Mond (Adv. Mgr.); Amy Montoni (Ed.)
Parent company (for newspapers): Joseph Jacobs Organization

OHIO

CLEVELAND JEWISH NEWS

Street address 1: 23880 Commerce Park
Street address 2: Ste 1
Street address city: Beachwood
Street address state: OH
Zip/Postal code: 44122-5830
County: Cuyahoga
Country: USA
General Phone: (216)454-8300
General Fax: (216)454-8100
Advertising Phone: (216)342-5191
Advertising Fax: (216)454-8100
Editorial Phone: (216)342-5207
Editorial Fax: (216)454-8200
General/National Adv. E-mail: info@cjn.org
Display Adv. E-mail: amandell@cjn.org
Classified Adv. e-mail: classified@cjn.org
Editorial e-mail: editorial@cjn.org
Primary Website: www.cjn.org
Mthly Avg Views: 144173
Mthly Avg Unique Visitors: 55152
Year Established: 1964
Delivery Methods: Mail`Newsstand
Areas Served - City/County or Portion Thereof, or Zip codes: Cleveland and suburbs
Published: Fri
Avg Paid Circ: 4548
Avg Free Circ: 674
Audit By: USPS
Audit Date: 24.09.2021
Personnel: Kevin Adelstein (Pres., Pub. & CEO); Adam Mandell (VP of Sales); Bob Jacob (Mng. Ed.); Tracy DiDomenico (Controller)
Parent company (for newspapers): Cleveland Jewish Publication Company

OHIO JEWISH CHRONICLE

Street address 1: 2862 Johnstown Rd
Street address city: Columbus
Street address state: OH
Zip/Postal code: 43219-1793
County: Franklin
Country: USA
Mailing address: PO Box 30965
Mailing city: Columbus
Mailing state: OH
Mailing zip: 43230-0965
General Phone: (614) 337-2055
General Fax: (614) 337-2059
General/National Adv. E-mail: ojc@insight.rr.com
Published: Thur
Avg Paid Circ: 2481
Avg Free Circ: 322
Audit By: Sworn/Estimate/Non-Audited
Audit Date: 12.07.2019
Personnel: Angela Miller (Adv. Mgr.); Stephen Pinsky (Mng. Ed.)
Parent company (for newspapers): Joseph Jacobs Organization

STARK JEWISH NEWS

Street address 1: 2631 Harvard Ave NW
Street address city: Canton
Street address state: OH
Zip/Postal code: 44709-3147
County: Stark
Country: USA
Mailing address: 432 30th St NW
Mailing city: Canton
Mailing state: OH
Mailing zip: 44709-3108
General Phone: (330) 452-6444
General Fax: (330) 452-4487
General/National Adv. E-mail: starkjewishnews@aol.com
Primary Website: www.jewishcanton.org

Areas Served - City/County or Portion Thereof, or Zip codes: 44709
Published: Mthly
Avg Paid Circ: 500
Avg Free Circ: 1500
Audit By: Sworn/Estimate/Non-Audited
Audit Date: 12.07.2019
Personnel: Bonnie Manello (CEO)
Parent company (for newspapers): Joseph Jacobs Organization

THE AMERICAN ISRAELITE

Street address 1: 18 W 9th St
Street address 2: Ste 2
Street address city: Cincinnati
Street address state: OH
Zip/Postal code: 45202-2037
County: Hamilton
Country: USA
Mailing address: 18 W 9th St Ste 2
Mailing city: Cincinnati
Mailing state: OH
Mailing zip: 45202-2037
General Phone: (513) 621-3145
General Fax: (513) 621-3744
General/National Adv. E-mail: publisher@americanisraelite.com
Primary Website: www.americanisraelite.com
Published: Thur
Avg Paid Circ: 6522
Avg Free Circ: 461
Audit By: Sworn/Estimate/Non-Audited
Audit Date: 12.07.2019
Personnel: Ted Deutsch (Pub.); Sauni Lerner (Mng. Ed.)
Parent company (for newspapers): Joseph Jacobs Organization

THE DAYTON JEWISH OBSERVER

Street address 1: 525 Versailles Dr
Street address city: Dayton
Street address state: OH
Zip/Postal code: 45459-6074
County: Montgomery
Country: USA
Mailing address: 525 Versailles Dr
Mailing city: Dayton
Mailing state: OH
Mailing zip: 45459-6074
General Phone: (937) 610-1555
General Fax: (937) 853-0378
General/National Adv. E-mail: mweiss@jfgd.net
Primary Website: www.jewishdayton.org
Year Established: 1996
Delivery Methods: Mail`Newsstand`Racks
Areas Served - City/County or Portion Thereof, or Zip codes: Southwest Ohio
Published: Mthly
Avg Free Circ: 3232
Audit By: Sworn/Estimate/Non-Audited
Audit Date: 12.07.2019
Personnel: Marshall Weiss (Ed./Pub.)
Parent company (for newspapers): Jewish Federation of Greater Dayton

TOLEDO JEWISH NEWS

Street address 1: 6465 Sylvania Ave
Street address city: Sylvania
Street address state: OH
Zip/Postal code: 43560-3916
County: Lucas
Country: USA
Mailing address: 6465 Sylvania Ave
Mailing city: Sylvania
Mailing state: OH
Mailing zip: 43560-3916
General Phone: (419) 724-0318
General Fax: (419) 885-3207
General/National Adv. E-mail: paul@jewishtoledo.org
Primary Website: www.jewishtoledo.org
Delivery Methods: Mail`Racks
Published: Mthly
Avg Paid Circ: 2000
Audit By: Sworn/Estimate/Non-Audited
Audit Date: 12.07.2019
Personnel: Paul Causman (Marketing Manager and Editor); Emily Gordon (Staff writer, Marketing Associate)
Parent company (for newspapers): Jewish Federation of Greater Toledo

PENNSYLVANIA

COMMUNITY REVIEW

Street address 1: 3301 N Front St
Street address city: Harrisburg
Street address state: PA
Zip/Postal code: 17110-1436
County: Dauphin
Country: USA
Mailing address: 3301 N. Front St.
Mailing city: Harrisburg
Mailing state: PA
Mailing zip: 17110
General Phone: (717) 236-9555
General Fax: (717) 236-8104
General/National Adv. E-mail: a.grobman@jewishfedhbg.org
Display Adv. E-mail: a.grobman@jewishfedhbg.org
Editorial e-mail: a.grobman@jewishfedhbg.org
Primary Website: www.jewishharrisburg.org
Year Established: 1925
Areas Served - City/County or Portion Thereof, or Zip codes: 17013-17112
Published: Fri`Bi-Mthly
Avg Paid Circ: 2100
Audit By: Sworn/Estimate/Non-Audited
Audit Date: 12.07.2019
Personnel: Adam Grobman (Director of Marketing); Jennifer Ross (Pres./CEO); Lorissa Delaney (COO)
Parent company (for newspapers): Jewish Federation of Greater Harrisburg

JEWISH EXPONENT

Street address 1: 2100 Arch Street
Street address 2: 4th Floor
Street address city: Philadelphia
Street address state: PA
Zip/Postal code: 19103
County: Philadelphia
Country: USA
General Phone: 215-832-0700
Advertising Phone: 215-832-0753
Editorial Phone: 215-832-0797
General/National Adv. E-mail: mcostello@jewishexponent.com
Display Adv. E-mail: sales@jewishexponent.com
Classified Adv. e-mail: classified@jewishexponent.com
Editorial e-mail: news@jewishexponent.com
Primary Website: www.jewishexponent.com
Mthly Avg Views: 113980
Mthly Avg Unique Visitors: 64997
Year Established: 1887
News Services: Mid-Atlantic Media
Areas Served - City/County or Portion Thereof, or Zip codes: Southeastern PA - Philadelphia-Bucks-Chester-Delaware-Montgomery (PA)
Published: Thur
Avg Paid Circ: 20000
Avg Free Circ: 0
Audit By: USPS
Audit Date: 31.10.2021
Personnel: Steve Rosenburg (Pub. Rep./Gen. Mgr.); Michael Costello (Finance & Operations Director); Joshua Runyan (Ed.-In-Chief); Cheryl Lutz (Dir. Bus. Ops.); Nicole McNally (Classifieds); Andy Gotlieb (Mng. Ed.); Liz Spikol (Sr. Staff Writer); Marissa Stern (Staff Writer); Steve Burke (Art/Prod. Coor.); Sharon Schmuckler (Dir. Sales/Adv.)
Parent company (for newspapers): Joseph Jacobs Organization; Jewish Federation of Greater Philadelphia

SHALOM NEWSPAPER

Street address 1: 223 Hawthorne Ct N
Street address city: Wyomissing
Street address state: PA
Zip/Postal code: 19610-1064
County: Berks
Country: USA
Mailing address: 223 Hawthorne Ct N
Mailing city: Wyomissing
Mailing state: PA
Mailing zip: 19610-1064
General Phone: (610) 921-0624
General Fax: (610) 929-0886
General/National Adv. E-mail: joan@friedman.net
Primary Website: www.readingjewishcommunity.org
Published: Mthly
Avg Paid Circ: 3000
Audit By: Sworn/Estimate/Non-Audited
Audit Date: 12.07.2019

THE JEWISH CHRONICLE

Street address 1: 5915 Beacon St
Street address 2: Fl 3
Street address city: Pittsburgh
Street address state: PA
Zip/Postal code: 15217-2005
County: Allegheny
Country: USA
Mailing address: 5915 Beacon St Fl 3
Mailing city: Pittsburgh
Mailing state: PA
Mailing zip: 15217-2005
General Phone: (412) 687-1000
General Fax: (412) 521-0154
General/National Adv. E-mail: newsdesk@thejewishchronicle.net
Display Adv. E-mail: advertising@thejewishchronicle.net
Editorial e-mail: newsdesk@thejewishchronicle.net
Primary Website: www.thejewishchronicle.net
Year Established: 1962
Delivery Methods: Mail
Areas Served - City/County or Portion Thereof, or Zip codes: All
Published: Thur
Avg Paid Circ: 3800
Avg Free Circ: 300
Audit By: Sworn/Estimate/Non-Audited
Audit Date: 12.07.2019
Personnel: Lee Chottiner (Exec. Ed.); Dawn Wanninger (Prodn. Mgr.); Jim Busis (Interim CEO)

RHODE ISLAND

JEWISH VOICE OF RHODE ISLAND

Street address 1: 130 Sessions St
Street address city: Providence
Street address state: RI
Zip/Postal code: 02906-3444
County: Providence
Country: USA
Mailing address: 130 Sessions St
Mailing city: Providence
Mailing state: RI
Mailing zip: 02906-3444
General Phone: (401) 421-4111
General Fax: (410) 331-7961
General/National Adv. E-mail: editor@jewishallianceri.org
Editorial e-mail: editor@jewishallianceri.org
Primary Website: www.jvhri.org
Delivery Methods: Mail`Racks
Areas Served - City/County or Portion Thereof, or Zip codes: all Rhode Island and Southeastern Mass.
Published: Other
Published Other: 2 x Mthly
Avg Free Circ: 10000
Audit By: Sworn/Estimate/Non-Audited
Audit Date: 12.07.2019
Personnel: Leah Camara (Prodn. Mgr.)

THE JEWISH VOICE

Street address 1: 401 Elmgrove Ave
Street address city: Providence
Street address state: RI
Zip/Postal code: 02906-3451
County: Providence
Country: USA
Mailing address: 401 Elmgrove Avenue
Mailing city: Providence
Mailing state: RI
Mailing zip: 02906-3444
General Phone: (401) 421-4111
General Fax: (401) 331-7961
General/National Adv. E-mail: editor@jewishallianceri.org
Editorial e-mail: editor@jewishallianceri.org
Primary Website: www.jvhri.org
Published Other: Every other Fri
Avg Free Circ: 9000
Audit By: Sworn/Estimate/Non-Audited
Audit Date: 12.07.2019
Personnel: Chris Westerkamp (Adv. Mgr.); Fran Ostendorf (Exec. Ed)
Parent company (for newspapers): Jewish Alliance of Greater Rhode Island

TENNESSEE

HEBREW WATCHMAN

Street address 1: 4646 Poplar Ave
Street address 2: Ste 232
Street address city: Memphis
Street address state: TN
Zip/Postal code: 38117-4426
County: Shelby
Country: USA
Mailing address: PO Box 770846
Mailing city: Memphis
Mailing state: TN
Mailing zip: 38177-0846
General Phone: (901) 763-2215
General Fax: (901) 763-2216
General/National Adv. E-mail: hebwat@bellsouth.net
Year Established: 1925
Delivery Methods: Mail
Published: Thur
Avg Paid Circ: 3000
Audit By: Sworn/Estimate/Non-Audited
Audit Date: 12.07.2019
Personnel: Herman I. Goldberger (Ed.)

THE JEWISH OBSERVER

Street address 1: 801 Percy Warner Blvd
Street address 2: Ste 102
Street address city: Nashville
Street address state: TN
Zip/Postal code: 37205-4128
County: Davidson
Country: USA
Mailing address: 801 Percy Warner Blvd Ste 102
Mailing city: Nashville
Mailing state: TN
Mailing zip: 37205-4128
General Phone: (615) 354-1653
General Fax: (615) 352-0056
Advertising Phone: (615) 354-1699
Editorial Phone: (615) 354-1653
General/National Adv. E-mail: info@jewishnashville.org
Display Adv. E-mail: carrie@nashvillejcc.org
Editorial e-mail: charles@jewishnashville.org
Primary Website: www.jewishobservernashville.org
Year Established: 1937
Delivery Methods: Mail
Areas Served - City/County or Portion Thereof, or Zip codes: Nashville - Middle Tennessee
Published: Mthly
Avg Free Circ: 4000
Audit By: Sworn/Estimate/Non-Audited
Audit Date: 12.07.2019
Personnel: Carrie Mills (Adv. Mgr.); Charles Bernsen (Editor)
Parent company (for newspapers): Jewish Federation of Nashville and Middle Tennessee

TEXAS

JEWISH HERALD-VOICE

Street address 1: 3403 Audley St
Street address city: Houston
Street address state: TX
Zip/Postal code: 77098-1923
County: Harris
Country: USA
Mailing address: 3403 Audley St
Mailing city: Houston
Mailing state: TX
Mailing zip: 77098-1923
General Phone: (713) 630-0391
General Fax: (713) 630-0404
Advertising Phone: (713) 630-0391
Advertising Fax: (713) 630-0404

Editorial Phone: (713) 630-0391
Editorial Fax: (713) 630-0404
General/National Adv. E-mail: news@jhvonline.com
Display Adv. E-mail: advertising@jhvonline.com
Editorial e-mail: editor@jhvonline.com
Primary Website: www.jhvonline.com
Year Established: 1908
News Services: JTA
Delivery Methods: Mail
Areas Served - City/County or Portion Thereof, or Zip codes: All
Published: Thur
Avg Paid Circ: 5000
Avg Free Circ: 200
Audit By: Sworn/Estimate/Non-Audited
Audit Date: 12.07.2019
Personnel: Vicki Samuels (Advertising Manager); Jeanne F. Samuels (Editor); Aaron Poscovsky (Production Manager); Levy Lawrence (Circulation)

THE JEWISH JOURNAL OF SAN ANTONIO

Street address 1: 12500 NW Military Hwy
Street address 2: Ste 200
Street address city: San Antonio
Street address state: TX
Zip/Postal code: 78231-1868
County: Bexar
Country: USA
General Phone: (210) 302-6960
General Fax: (210) 408-2332
General/National Adv. E-mail: jewishj@jfsatx.org
Display Adv. E-mail: advertising@jfsatx.org
Primary Website: www.jfsatx.org
Delivery Methods: Mail`Racks
Published: Mthly
Avg Free Circ: 4000
Audit By: Sworn/Estimate/Non-Audited
Audit Date: 12.07.2019
Personnel: Leslie Ausburn (Ed.)
Parent company (for newspapers): Jewish Federation of San Antonio

VIRGINIA

VIRGINIA JEWISH LIFE

Street address 1: 212 N Gaskins Rd
Street address city: Richmond
Street address state: VA
Zip/Postal code: 23238-5526
County: Henrico
Country: USA
Mailing address: 212 N Gaskins Rd
Mailing city: Richmond
Mailing state: VA
Mailing zip: 23238-5526
General Phone: (804) 740-2000
General Fax: (804) 750-1341
Editorial e-mail: editor@virginiajewishlife.com
Primary Website: www.virginiajewishlife.com
Year Established: 1977
Personnel: Dana Zedd (Adv. Rep.); Allie Vered (Mng. Ed.)

WASHINGTON

GAUGER MEDIA SERVICE, INC.

Street address 1: 1034 Bradford Street
Street address 2: P.O. Box 627
Street address city: Raymond
Street address state: WA
Zip/Postal code: 98577
County: Pacific
Country: USA
Mailing city: Raymond
Mailing state: WA
Mailing zip: 98577
General Phone: (360) 942-2661
General/National Adv. E-mail: dave@gaugermedia.com
Personnel: Dave Gauger (Now Retired)

WISCONSIN

THE WISCONSIN JEWISH CHRONICLE

Street address 1: 1360 N Prospect Ave
Street address city: Milwaukee
Street address state: WI
Zip/Postal code: 53202-3056
County: Milwaukee
Country: USA
Mailing address: 1360 N Prospect Ave Ste 2
Mailing city: Milwaukee
Mailing state: WI
Mailing zip: 53202-3090
General Phone: (414) 390-5770
General Fax: (414) 390-5766
Advertising Phone: (414) 390-5765
General/National Adv. E-mail: chronicle@milwaukeejewish.org
Primary Website: www.jewishchronicle.org
Year Established: 1921
Published: Mthly
Avg Free Circ: 8000
Audit By: Sworn/Estimate/Non-Audited
Audit Date: 12.07.2019
Personnel: Yvonne Chapman (Production Manager); Leon Cohen (Editor)
Parent company (for newspapers): Milwaukee Jewish Federation

MILITARY NEWSPAPERS IN THE U.S.

ALABAMA

FORT RUCKER

ARMY FLIER

Street address 1: 453 S Novasel St
Street address 2: Bldg 112
Street address 3: Fort Rucker
Street address state: AL
Zip/Postal code: 36362-5109
County: Dale
Country: USA
Mailing address: 453 S Novasel St Bldg 112
Mailing city: Fort Rucker
Mailing state: AL
Mailing zip: 36362-5109
General Phone: (334) 255-2613
General Fax: (334) 255-1004
Primary Website: www.armyflier.com
Own Printing Facility: Y
Advertising (Open Inch Rate) Weekday/Saturday: Open inch rate $10.00
Mechanical specifications: Type page 13 x 21 1/2; E - 6 cols, 2 1/8, between; A - 6 cols, 2 1/8, between; C - 9 cols, 1 9/20, between.
Published: Thur
Avg Free Circ: 10000
Audit By: Sworn/Estimate/Non-Audited
Audit Date: 7/12/2019
Classified Equipment»
Personnel: Marty Gatlin (Ed.)
Parent company (for newspapers): BH Media Group

ARIZONA

DESERT WARRIOR

Street address 1: PO Box 99113
Street address 3: Yuma
Street address state: AZ
Zip/Postal code: 85369-9113
County: Yuma
Country: USA
Mailing address: PO Box 99113
Mailing city: Yuma
Mailing state: AZ
Mailing zip: 85369-9113
General Phone: (928) 269-2275
General/National Adv. E-mail: shelby.shields@usmc.mil
Primary Website: www.yuma.usmc.mil
Area Served - City: 85369
Advertising (Open Inch Rate) Weekday/Saturday: Open inch rate $15.47
Mechanical specifications: Type page 11 13/16 x 21; E - 6 cols, 1 7/8, 1/16 between; A - 6 cols, 1 7/8, 1/16 between; C - 6 cols, 1 7/8, 1/16 between.
Published: Thur
Avg Free Circ: 3300
Audit By: Sworn/Estimate/Non-Audited
Audit Date: 7/12/2019
Classified Equipment»
Personnel: Shelby Shields (Ed.)

CALIFORNIA

BARSTOW

BARSTOW LOG

Street address 1: Marine Corps Logistics Base, Bldg 204
Street address 3: Barstow
Street address state: CA
Zip/Postal code: 92311
County: San Bernardino
Country: USA
Mailing address: PO Box 110130
Mailing city: Barstow
Mailing state: CA
Mailing zip: 92311-5050
General Phone: (760) 577-6430
General Fax: (760) 577-6350
General/National Adv. E-mail: robert.l.jackson@usmc.mil
Advertising (Open Inch Rate) Weekday/Saturday: Open inch rate $6.00
Mechanical specifications: Type page 10 1/4 x 13; E - 5 cols, 1 11/12, 1/8 between; A - 5 cols, 1 11/12, 1/8 between; C - 5 cols, 1 11/12, 1/8 between.
Published: Thur
Avg Free Circ: 3700
Audit By: Sworn/Estimate/Non-Audited
Audit Date: 7/12/2019
Classified Equipment»
Personnel: Rob L. Jackson (Pub. Affairs Officer); Quentin Grogan (Ed.)
Parent company (for newspapers): Brehm Communications, Inc.

EL CENTRO

SANDPAPER

Street address 1: 1500 8th St
Street address 3: El Centro
Street address state: CA
Zip/Postal code: 92243-5041
County: Imperial
Country: USA
Mailing address: 1500 8th St
Mailing city: El Centro
Mailing state: CA
Mailing zip: 92243-5041
General Phone: (760) 339-2519
General Fax: (760) 339-2699
General/National Adv. E-mail: elcnpao@navy.mil
Primary Website: www.nafec.navy.mil
Audit By: Sworn/Estimate/Non-Audited
Audit Date: 7/12/2019
Classified Equipment»
Personnel: Michelle Dee (Ed.)

LANCASTER

AEROTECH NEWS & REVIEW

Street address 1: 456 E Avenue K4
Street address 2: Ste 8
Street address 3: Lancaster
Street address state: CA
Zip/Postal code: 93535-4642
County: Los Angeles
Country: USA
Mailing address: 456 E Avenue K4 Ste 8
Mailing city: Lancaster
Mailing state: CA
Mailing zip: 93535-4642
General Phone: (661) 945-5634
General Fax: (661) 723-7757
General/National Adv. E-mail: aerotech@aerotechnews.com
Primary Website: www.aerotechnews.com
Advertising (Open Inch Rate) Weekday/Saturday: Open inch rate $15.70
Mechanical specifications: Type page 10 1/4 x 13; E - 5 cols, 1 11/12, 1/8 between; A - 5 cols, 1 11/12, 1/8 between; C - 5 cols, 1 11/12, 1/8 between.
Published: Fri
Avg Free Circ: 15000
Audit By: Sworn/Estimate/Non-Audited
Audit Date: 7/12/2019
Classified Equipment»
Personnel: Paul J. Kinison (Pub.); Gail Ellis (Adv. Mgr.); Stewart Ibberson (Ed.)

RIDGECREST

ON TARGET

Street address 1: 1 Administration Cir
Street address 2: Stop 1014
Street address 3: Ridgecrest
Street address state: CA
Zip/Postal code: 93555-6104
County: Kern
Country: USA
Mailing address: 1 Administration Cir Stop 1014
Mailing city: Ridgecrest
Mailing state: CA
Mailing zip: 93555-6104
General Phone: (760) 939-3354
General Fax: (760) 939-2796
Advertising (Open Inch Rate) Weekday/Saturday: Open inch rate $14.60
Published Other: Every other Thur
Avg Free Circ: 5000
Audit By: Sworn/Estimate/Non-Audited
Audit Date: 7/12/2019
Classified Equipment»
Personnel: Dee Rorex (Ed.)

COMPASS

Street address 1: 937 N Harbor Dr
Street address 3: San Diego
Street address state: CA
Zip/Postal code: 92132-5001
County: San Diego
Country: USA
Mailing address: 937 N Harbor Dr
Mailing city: San Diego
Mailing state: CA
Mailing zip: 92132-5001
General Phone: (619) 532-1434
General Fax: (619) 532-4537
General/National Adv. E-mail: johnb@navycompass.com
Primary Website: www.navycompass.com
Advertising (Open Inch Rate) Weekday/Saturday: Open inch rate $25.00
Published: Thur
Avg Free Circ: 43000
Audit By: Sworn/Estimate/Non-Audited
Audit Date: 7/12/2019
Classified Equipment»
Personnel: Jim Missit (Adv. Mgr.); Jess Levens (Ed.)

YUCCA VALLEY

OBSERVATION POST

Street address 1: 56445 29 Palms Hwy
Street address 3: Yucca Valley
Street address state: CA
Zip/Postal code: 92284-2861
County: San Bernardino
Country: USA
Mailing address: PO Box 880
Mailing city: Yucca Valley
Mailing state: CA
Mailing zip: 92286-0880
General Phone: (760) 365-3315
General Fax: (760) 365-4181
Display Adv. E-mail: advertising@hidesertstar.com
Editorial e-mail: editor@hidesertstar.com
Primary Website: www.hidesertstar.com
Delivery Methods: Carrier'Racks
Area Served - City: 92278 and 92277
Own Printing Facility: Y
Advertising (Open Inch Rate) Weekday/Saturday: Open inch rate $15.00
Mechanical specifications: Type page 10 x 21 ; E - 6 cols, 1 3/4, 1/8 between; A - 6 cols, 1 3/4, 1/8 between; C - 9 cols, 1 3/16, 1/8 between.
Published: Fri
Avg Free Circ: 6500
Audit By: Sworn/Estimate/Non-Audited
Audit Date: 7/12/2019
Classified Equipment»
Personnel: Cindy Melland (Pub.)
Parent company (for newspapers): Brehm Communications, Inc.; Hi-Desert Publishing Co., Inc.

COLORADO

COLORADO SPRINGS

MOUNTAINEER

Street address 1: 31 E Platte Ave
Street address 2: Ste 300
Street address 3: Colorado Springs
Street address state: CO
Zip/Postal code: 80903-1246
County: El Paso
Country: USA
Mailing address: 31 E Platte Ave Ste 300
Mailing city: Colorado Springs
Mailing state: CO
Mailing zip: 80903-1246
General Phone: (719) 634-1593
General Fax: (719) 632-0265
General/National Adv. E-mail: advertising@gowdyprint.com
Area Served - City: 80903
Own Printing Facility: Y
Commercial printers: Y
Advertising (Open Inch Rate) Weekday/Saturday: Open inch rate $13.00
Mechanical specifications: Type page 10 7/8 x 15 5/8; E - 6 cols, 1 1/2, between; A - 6 cols, 1 1/2, between.
Published: Fri
Avg Free Circ: 75000
Audit By: Sworn/Estimate/Non-Audited
Audit Date: 7/12/2019
Classified Equipment»
Personnel: Tex Stewart (Pub.); Barbara Hedges (Adv. Mgr.)

CONNECTICUT

GROTON

THE DOLPHIN

Street address 1: PO Box 44
Street address 2: Naval Submarine Base New London
Street address 3: Groton
Street address state: CT
Zip/Postal code: 06349-5044
County: New London
Country: USA
Mailing address: SUBASE NLON PAO PO Box 44
Mailing city: Groton
Mailing state: CT
Mailing zip: 06349-5044
General Phone: (860) 694-3514
General Fax: (860) 694-5012
Advertising Phone: (203) 680-9935
General/National Adv. E-mail: nhr.dolphin@hearstmediact.com
Display Adv. E-mail: betsy.lemkin@hearstmediact.com
Editorial e-mail: nhr.dolphin@hearstmediact.com
Primary Website: www.dolphin-news.com
Year Established: 1918

Delivery Methods: Racks
Area Served - City: 06340
Own Printing Facility: N
Commercial printers: N
Advertising (Open Inch Rate) Weekday/Saturday: Open inch rate $11.62
Mechanical specifications: Type page 12 x 21; E - 6 cols, 2, 1/6 between; A - 6 cols, 1 5/8, 1/6 between; C - 6 cols, 1 5/8, 1/6 between.
Published: Thur
Avg Free Circ: 6600
Audit By: Sworn/Estimate/Non-Audited
Audit Date: 7/12/2019
Classified Equipment»
Personnel: Sheryl Walsh (Ed.)
Parent company (for newspapers): Hearst Communications, Inc.

FLORIDA

JAX AIR NEWS

Street address 1: PO Box 2
Street address 3: Jacksonville
Street address state: FL
Zip/Postal code: 32212-0002
County: Duval
Country: USA
Mailing address: Code 00G, Box 2
Mailing city: Jacksonville
Mailing state: FL
Mailing zip: 32212-5000
General Phone: (904) 542-3531
General Fax: (904) 542-1534
Advertising Phone: (904) 359-4168
General/National Adv. E-mail: jaxairnews@comcast.net
Primary Website: jaxairnews.com
Year Established: 1940
Delivery Methods: Newsstand`Racks
Area Served - City: 32,202,322,033,220,400,000,000,000,000,000,000,000,000,000,000,000
Advertising (Open Inch Rate) Weekday/Saturday: Open inch rate $16.55
Published: Thur
Avg Free Circ: 10000
Audit By: Sworn/Estimate/Non-Audited
Audit Date: 7/12/2019
Classified Equipment»
Personnel: Clark Pierce (Ed.)

THE MIRROR

Street address 1: Massey Avenue
Street address 3: Jacksonville
Street address state: FL
Zip/Postal code: 32228
County: Duval
Country: USA
Mailing address: PO Box 280032
Mailing city: Jacksonville
Mailing state: FL
Mailing zip: 32228-0032
General Phone: (904) 270-7817
General Fax: (904) 270-5329
General/National Adv. E-mail: mayportmirror@comcast.net
Primary Website: www.mayportmirror.com
Area Served - City: 32228
Own Printing Facility: Y
Advertising (Open Inch Rate) Weekday/Saturday: Open inch rate $14.00
Published: Thur
Avg Free Circ: 10000
Audit By: Sworn/Estimate/Non-Audited
Audit Date: 7/12/2019
Classified Equipment»
Personnel: Ellen S. Rykert (Pub.); Paige Gnann (Adv. Mgr.)

MELBOURNE

MISSILEER

Street address 1: PO Box 419000
Street address 3: Melbourne
Street address state: FL
Zip/Postal code: 32941-9000
County: Brevard
Country: USA
Mailing address: PO Box 419000
Mailing city: Melbourne
Mailing state: FL
Mailing zip: 32941-9000
General Phone: (321) 242-3500
General Fax: (321) 242-6618
Primary Website: www.floridatoday.com
Year Established: 1966
Own Printing Facility: Y
Advertising (Open Inch Rate) Weekday/Saturday: Open inch rate $11.91
Mechanical specifications: Type page 9 2/3 x 11 1/2; E - 5 cols, 1 5/6, 1/8 between; A - 5 cols, 1 5/6, 1/8 between; C - 80 cols, 1 1/10, 1/16 between.
Audit By: Sworn/Estimate/Non-Audited
Audit Date: 7/12/2019
Classified Equipment»
Personnel: Mark Mikolajczyk (Pub.); John Vizzini (Opns. Dir.); Bob Stover (Exec. Ed.); John Kelly (Mng. Ed.); Chris Wood (Adv. Dir.)

MILTON

WHITING TOWER

Street address 1: Whiting Field, 7550 USS Essex St, Ste 109
Street address 3: Milton
Street address state: FL
Zip/Postal code: 32570
County: Santa Rosa
Country: USA
Mailing address: Whiting Field, 7550 USS Essex St., Ste. 109
Mailing city: Milton
Mailing state: FL
Mailing zip: 32570-6155
General Phone: (850) 665-6121
General Fax: (850) 623-7601
Advertising Phone: N/A
Editorail Phone: (850) 665-6121
Editorial Fax: (850) 623-7601
General/National Adv. E-mail: jay.cope@navy.mil
Display Adv. E-mail: N/A
Editorial e-mail: jay.cope@navy.mil
Year Established: 1943
Commercial printers: N
Published: Wed
Avg Free Circ: 3000
Audit By: Sworn/Estimate/Non-Audited
Audit Date: 7/12/2019
Classified Equipment»
Personnel: Jay Cope (Ed.)

PANAMA CITY

GULF DEFENDER

Street address 1: 501 W 11th St
Street address 3: Panama City
Street address state: FL
Zip/Postal code: 32401-2330
County: Bay
Country: USA
Mailing address: PO Box 1940
Mailing city: Panama City
Mailing state: FL
Mailing zip: 32402-1940
General Phone: (850) 747-5005
General Fax: (850) 763-4636
General/National Adv. E-mail: phgregory@pcnh.com
Primary Website: www.newsherald.com
Area Served - City: 32403
Own Printing Facility: Y
Advertising (Open Inch Rate) Weekday/Saturday: Open inch rate $18.00
Mechanical specifications: Type page 10 1/4 x 11 1/4; E - 6 cols, 2 1/16, 1/8 between; A - 6 cols, 2 1/16, 1/8 between.
Published Other: 2 x Mthly
Avg Free Circ: 12000
Audit By: Sworn/Estimate/Non-Audited
Audit Date: 7/12/2019
Classified Equipment»
Personnel: Karen E. Hanes (Pub./Reg'l Vice Pres.); Wayne Kight (Adv. Mgr.); Pam Gregory (Adv. Dir.); Mike Miller (Reg'l Circ. Dir.); Ron Smith (Opns. Dir.)

PENSACOLA

GOSPORT

Street address 1: 41 N Jefferson St
Street address 3: Pensacola
Street address state: FL
Zip/Postal code: 32502-5681
County: Escambia
Country: USA
Mailing address: 41 N Jefferson St
Mailing city: Pensacola
Mailing state: FL
Mailing zip: 32502-5681
General Phone: (850) 202-2242
General Fax: (850) 202-2248
Advertising Phone: (850) 433-1166
Editorail Phone: (850) 452-4466
Editorial e-mail: scott.hallford@navy.mil
Primary Website: www.ballingerpublishing.com
Year Established: 1921
Delivery Methods: Mail`Racks
Area Served - City: 32501,02,03,04,05,06,07,08,09
Own Printing Facility: Y
Advertising (Open Inch Rate) Weekday/Saturday: Open inch rate $20.30
Mechanical specifications: Type page 10 x 16; E - 5 cols, 2, 1/4 between.
Published: Fri
Avg Free Circ: 25000
Audit By: Sworn/Estimate/Non-Audited
Audit Date: 7/12/2019
Classified Equipment»
Personnel: Malcolm Ballinger (Pub.); Scott Hallford (Ed.); Mike O'Connor (Assoc. Ed.); Simone Sands; Janet Thomas
Parent company (for newspapers): U.S. Navy

GEORGIA

FORT BENNING

THE BAYONET

Street address 1: 6460 Way Ave
Street address 2: Ste 102
Street address 3: Fort Benning
Street address state: GA
Zip/Postal code: 31905-3771
County: Chattahoochee
Country: USA
Mailing address: 6460 Way St., Suite 102
Mailing city: Fort Benning
Mailing state: GA
Mailing zip: 31905-4584
General Phone: (706) 545-4622
Advertising Phone: (706) 576-6239
Primary Website: www.thebayonet.com
Delivery Methods: Mail`Newsstand`Carrier`Racks
Area Served - City: 31905
Own Printing Facility: Y
Advertising (Open Inch Rate) Weekday/Saturday: Open inch rate $21.00
Mechanical specifications: Type page 13 x 20 1/2; E - 6 cols, 2 1/16, 1/6 between; A - 6 cols, 2 1/16, 1/6 between; C - 6 cols, 2 1/16, 1/6 between.
Published: Wed
Avg Free Circ: 22000
Audit By: Sworn/Estimate/Non-Audited
Audit Date: 7/12/2019
Classified Equipment»
Personnel: Lori Egan (Ed.)

HINESVILLE

THE FRONTLINE

Street address 1: 125 S Main St
Street address 3: Hinesville
Street address state: GA
Zip/Postal code: 31313-3217
County: Liberty
Country: USA
Mailing address: 125 S Main St
Mailing city: Hinesville
Mailing state: GA
Mailing zip: 31313-3217
General Phone: (912) 876-0156
General Fax: (912) 368-6329
Primary Website: www.coastalcourier.com
Advertising (Open Inch Rate) Weekday/Saturday: Open inch rate $11.10
Mechanical specifications: Type page 11 3/4 x 21 1/2; E - 6 cols, 2 1/16, between; A - 6 cols, 2 1/16, between; C - 6 cols, 2 1/16, between.
Published: Thur
Avg Free Circ: 17000
Audit By: Sworn/Estimate/Non-Audited
Audit Date: 7/12/2019
Classified Equipment»
Personnel: Denise Ethridge (Ed.); Patty Leon (Gen. Mgr.)
Parent company (for newspapers): Morris Multimedia, Inc.

MACON

THE TELEGRAPH

Street address 1: 487 Cherry St
Street address 3: Macon
Street address state: GA
Zip/Postal code: 31201-7972
County: Bibb
Country: USA
Mailing address: P.O. Box 4167
Mailing city: Macon
Mailing state: GA
Mailing zip: 31208
General Phone: (478) 744-4200
Advertising Phone: (478) 744-4245
Editorail Phone: (478) 744-4411
Primary Website: www.macon.com
Delivery Methods: Newsstand`Carrier`Racks
Own Printing Facility: Y
Published: Mon`Tues`Wed`Thur`Fri`Sat`Sun
Avg Free Circ: 18000
Audit By: AAM
Audit Date: 6/19/2013
Classified Equipment»
Personnel: Crystal Ragan (Local Adv. Mgr.)
Parent company (for newspapers): The McClatchy Company

WAYNESBORO

THE SIGNAL

Street address 1: Nelson Hall Rm 215
Street address 3: Waynesboro
Street address state: GA
Zip/Postal code: 30830
County: Burke
Country: USA
Mailing address: PO Box 948
Mailing city: Waynesboro
Mailing state: GA
Mailing zip: 30830-0948
General Phone: (706) 791-7069
General Fax: (706) 791-5463
General/National Adv. E-mail: thesignal@conus.army.mil
Primary Website: www.fortgordonsignal.com
Own Printing Facility: Y
Advertising (Open Inch Rate) Weekday/Saturday: Open inch rate $11.97
Mechanical specifications: Type page 13 x 21 1/2; E - 4 cols, 3 1/6, 1/6 between; A - 6 cols, 2 1/12, 1/6 between; C - 6 cols, 2 1/12, 1/6 between.
Published: Fri
Avg Free Circ: 18600
Audit By: Sworn/Estimate/Non-Audited
Audit Date: 7/12/2019
Classified Equipment»
Personnel: Roy F. Chalker (Pub.); Bonnie Taylor (Gen. Mgr.); Deborah Kitchens (Adv. Mgr.); Jill Dumars (Prodn. Mgr.)

IDAHO

MOUNTAIN HOME

MOUNTAIN HOME PATRIOT

Street address 1: PO Box 1330
Street address 3: Mountain Home
Street address state: ID
Zip/Postal code: 83647-1330
County: Elmore
Country: USA
Mailing address: PO Box 1330
Mailing city: Mountain Home
Mailing state: ID
Mailing zip: 83647-1330
General Phone: (208) 587-3331
General Fax: (208) 587-9205
General/National Adv. E-mail: bfincher@mountainhomenews.com
Primary Website: www.mountainhomenews.com
Year Established: 1888
Delivery Methods: Mail`Racks
Area Served - City: 83648/47
Own Printing Facility: Y
Advertising (Open Inch Rate) Weekday/Saturday: 10.55 thur 10/31/14 call for current pricing
Mechanical specifications: 13x21.5
Published: Fri
Avg Free Circ: 4500
Audit By: Sworn/Estimate/Non-Audited
Audit Date: 7/12/2019
Classified Equipment»
Personnel: Brenda Fincher (Business Manager); Kelly Everitt (Ed.)

ILLINOIS

GRAYSLAKE

LAKE COUNTY SUBURBAN LIFE

Street address 1: 1100 E Washington St
Street address 2: Ste 101
Street address 3: Grayslake
Street address state: IL
Zip/Postal code: 60030-7963
County: Lake
Country: USA
Mailing address: 1100 Washington St., Suite 101
Mailing city: Grayslake
Mailing state: IL
Mailing zip: 60030-0268
General Phone: (847) 223-8161
General Fax: (847) 223-8810
General/National Adv. E-mail: edit@lakelandmedia.com
Primary Website: www.lakecountyjournals.com
Advertising (Open Inch Rate) Weekday/Saturday: Open inch rate $16.00
Mechanical specifications: Type page 10 1/4 x 16; E - 5 cols, 1 11/12, 1/4 between; A - 5 cols, 1 11/12, 1/4 between; C - 7 cols, 1 1/3, 1/6 between.
Published: Fri
Avg Free Circ: 22000
Audit By: Sworn/Estimate/Non-Audited
Audit Date: 7/12/2019
Classified Equipment»
Personnel: Jill McDermott (VP of Adv.); Paul Engstrom (Ed.); Ryan Wells

MASCOUTAH

SCOTT FLIER

Street address 1: 314 E Church St
Street address 3: Mascoutah
Street address state: IL
Zip/Postal code: 62258-2100
County: Saint Clair
Country: USA
Mailing address: PO Box C
Mailing city: Mascoutah
Mailing state: IL
Mailing zip: 62258-0189
General Phone: (618) 566-8282
General Fax: (618) 566-8283
General/National Adv. E-mail: heraldpubs@cbnstl.com
Primary Website: www.heraldpubs.com
Advertising (Open Inch Rate) Weekday/Saturday: Open inch rate $9.31
Published: Thur
Avg Free Circ: 8000
Audit By: Sworn/Estimate/Non-Audited
Audit Date: 7/12/2019
Classified Equipment»
Personnel: Greg Hoskins (Pub.); Keith Gillette (Mng. Ed.)

KANSAS

FORT LEAVENWORTH

FORT LEAVENWORTH LAMP

Street address 1: 290 Grant Ave
Street address 2: Ste 6
Street address 3: Fort Leavenworth
Street address state: KS
Zip/Postal code: 66027-1292
County: Leavenworth
Country: USA
Mailing address: 290 Grant Ave Unit 6
Mailing city: Fort Leavenworth
Mailing state: KS
Mailing zip: 66027-1292
General Phone: (913) 682-0305
General Fax: (913) 682-1089
Advertising Phone: (913) 682-0305
Advertising Fax: (913) 682-1089
Editorial Phone: (913) 684-1728
Display Adv. E-mail: shattock@leavenworthtimes.com
Editorial e-mail: editor@ftleavenworthlamp.com
Primary Website: www.ftleavenworthlamp.com
Year Established: 1971
Special Editions: Back-to-school Medical supplements
Delivery Methods: Newsstand`Carrier`Racks
Area Served - City: 66027, 66048, 66043
Commercial printers: N
Advertising (Open Inch Rate) Weekday/Saturday: Open inch rate $9.70
Mechanical specifications: Type page 10 x 16; E - 5 cols, 2, between; A - 5 cols, 2, between; C - 5 cols, 2, between.
Published: Thur
Avg Free Circ: 8000
Audit By: Sworn/Estimate/Non-Audited
Audit Date: 7/12/2019
Classified Equipment»
Personnel: Jeffery Wingo (Public Affairs Officer); Sandy Hattock (Adv. Mgr.); Robert Kerr (Ed.)
Parent company (for newspapers): CherryRoad Media

KENTUCKY

FORT KNOX

TURRET

Street address 1: Bldg 1109, Wing D, Sixth St
Street address 3: Fort Knox
Street address state: KY
Zip/Postal code: 40121-
County: Hardin
Country: USA
Mailing address: PO Box 995
Mailing city: Fort Knox
Mailing state: KY
Mailing zip: 40121-0995
General Phone: (502) 624-6517
General Fax: (502) 624-2096
Advertising Phone: (270) 769-1200
Primary Website: www.turret.com; www.newsenterpriseonline.com
Advertising (Open Inch Rate) Weekday/Saturday: Open inch rate $9.49
Mechanical specifications: Type page 13 1/2 x 21 1/2; E - 6 cols, 2 1/8, between; A - 6 cols, 2 1/8, between.
Published: Thur
Avg Free Circ: 20896
Audit By: Sworn/Estimate/Non-Audited
Audit Date: 7/12/2019
Classified Equipment»
Personnel: Larry Barnes (Ed.); Maureen Rose (Assoc. Ed.); Kellie Etheridge (Leisure Ed.); Ally Rogers (Sports Ed.)

HOPKINSVILLE

FORT CAMPBELL COURIER

Street address 1: 1618 E 9th St
Street address 3: Hopkinsville
Street address state: KY
Zip/Postal code: 42240-4430
County: Christian
Country: USA
Mailing address: PO Box 729
Mailing city: Hopkinsville
Mailing state: KY
Mailing zip: 42241-0729
General Phone: (270) 887-3220
General Fax: (270) 887-3222
Advertising Phone: (270) 887-3270
General/National Adv. E-mail: editor@kentuckynewera.com
Primary Website: www.kentuckynewera.com
Own Printing Facility: Y
Advertising (Open Inch Rate) Weekday/Saturday: Open inch rate $15.20
Mechanical specifications: Type page 13 x 21 1/2; E - 6 cols, 2 1/30, 1/6 between; A - 6 cols, 2 1/30, 1/6 between; C - 8 cols, 1 1/3, 1/6 between.
Published: Thur
Avg Free Circ: 23000
Audit By: Sworn/Estimate/Non-Audited
Audit Date: 7/12/2019
Classified Equipment»
Personnel: Taylor Wood Hayes (Pub.); Charles A. Henderson (Gen. Mgr.); Sheryl Ellis (Bus. Mgr.); Nancy Reese (Classified Mgr.); Ted Jatczak (Sales/Mktg. Dir.); George McCouch (Circ. Mgr.); Jennifer Brown (Ed.); Joe Wilson (Sports Ed.); Chris Hollis (Prodn. Mgr.)

LOUISIANA

FORT POLK

GUARDIAN

Street address 1: 7033 Magnolia Dr
Street address 3: Fort Polk
Street address state: LA
Zip/Postal code: 71459-3495
County: Vernon
Country: USA
Mailing address: 7033 Magnolia Dr.
Mailing city: Fort Polk
Mailing state: LA
Mailing zip: 71459
General Phone: (337) 462-0616
Advertising Phone: (337) 462-0616
Advertising Fax: (337) 463-5347
Editorial Phone: (337) 531-4033
Editorial Fax: (337) 531-1401
General/National Adv. E-mail: guardian@wnonline.net
Primary Website: www.thefortpolkguardian.com
Own Printing Facility: Y
Advertising (Open Inch Rate) Weekday/Saturday: Open inch rate $15.05
Published: Fri
Avg Free Circ: 13000
Audit By: Sworn/Estimate/Non-Audited
Audit Date: 7/12/2019
Classified Equipment»
Personnel: Theresa Larue (Adv. Mgr.); Kimberly Reischling (Command Info., Media Rel. Chief)

GRETNA

THE CURRENTS

Street address 1: 359 Fairfield Ave
Street address 3: Gretna
Street address state: LA
Zip/Postal code: 70056-7004
County: Jefferson
Country: USA
Mailing address: 359 Fairfield Ave
Mailing city: Gretna
Mailing state: LA
Mailing zip: 70056-7004
General Phone: (504) 363-9010
General Fax: (504) 366-4826
General/National Adv. E-mail: polov13@aol.com
Year Established: 1989
Advertising (Open Inch Rate) Weekday/Saturday: Open inch rate $15.75
Mechanical specifications: Type page 10 1/4 x 13 3/8; E - 4 cols, between; A - 6 cols, between.
Audit By: Sworn/Estimate/Non-Audited
Audit Date: 7/12/2019
Classified Equipment»
Personnel: Vicki A. Polo (Pres.); Samuel F. Polo (Pub.); Gina D. Polo (Adv. Mgr.); David P. Leger (Circ. Mgr.); Donnie R. Ryan (Ed.); Roy P. Griggs (Mng. Ed.); Carolyn R. Cuccia (Prodn. Mgr.)

MASSACHUSETTS

COTUIT

OTIS NOTICE

Street address 1: 4507 Falmouth Rd
Street address 3: Cotuit
Street address state: MA
Zip/Postal code: 02635-2652
County: Barnstable
Country: USA
Mailing address: PO Box 571
Mailing city: Osterville
Mailing state: MA
Mailing zip: 02655-0571
General Phone: (508) 428-8700
General Fax: (508) 428-8524
General/National Adv. E-mail: L.printing@comcast.net
Editorial e-mail: otis@lujeanprinting.com
Primary Website: www.lujeanprinting.com
Year Established: 1963
Delivery Methods: Mail`Carrier`Racks
Area Served - City: 2,536,025,590,253,200,000
Mechanical specifications: Type page 10 1/4 x 16; E - 6 cols, 1 5/8, 1/8 between; A - 6 cols, 1 5/8, 1/8 between.
Published: Mthly
Avg Free Circ: 5000
Audit By: Sworn/Estimate/Non-Audited
Audit Date: 7/12/2019
Classified Equipment»
Personnel: Michael Lally (Pub.); Gerry Lynn Galati (Graphic Manager)

MARYLAND

FORT MEADE

SOUNDOFF!

Street address 1: 4409 Llewellyn Avenue
Street address 3: Fort Meade
Street address state: MD
Zip/Postal code: 20755
County: Anne Arundel
Country: USA
Mailing address: 4409 Llewellyn Avenue
Mailing city: Fort Meade
Mailing state: MD
Mailing zip: 20755-5025

General Phone: (301) 677-5602
Advertising Phone: (410) 332-6300
Editorail Phone: (301) 677-6806
Editorial Fax: 301- 677-1305
General/National Adv. E-mail: soundoff@conus.army.mil
Display Adv. E-mail: advertise@baltsun.com
Editorial e-mail: rhirsch@tribune.com
Delivery Methods: Carrier`Racks
Published: Thur
Avg Paid Circ: 263
Avg Free Circ: 12031
Audit By: CAC
Audit Date: 9/30/2017
Classified Equipment»
Personnel: Dijon Rolle (Editor)
Parent company (for newspapers): Tribune Publishing, Inc.

GAITHERSBURG

ANDREWS GAZETTE

Street address 1: 9030 Comprint Ct
Street address 3: Gaithersburg
Street address state: MD
Zip/Postal code: 20877-1307
County: Montgomery
Country: USA
Mailing address: 9030 Comprint Ct
Mailing city: Gaithersburg
Mailing state: MD
Mailing zip: 20877-1307
Published: Wed`Thur`Fri
Avg Paid Circ: 14350
Avg Free Circ: 5734
Audit By: Sworn/Estimate/Non-Audited
Audit Date: 7/12/2019
Classified Equipment»

CAPITAL FLYER

Street address 1: 9030 Comprint Ct
Street address 3: Gaithersburg
Street address state: MD
Zip/Postal code: 20877-1307
County: Montgomery
Country: USA
Mailing address: 9030 Comprint Ct
Mailing city: Gaithersburg
Mailing state: MD
Mailing zip: 20877-1307
General Phone: (301) 921-2800
General Fax: (301) 948-2787
General/National Adv. E-mail: jrives@gazette.net
Own Printing Facility: Y
Advertising (Open Inch Rate) Weekday/Saturday: Open inch rate $18.20
Mechanical specifications: Type page 9 5/8 x 13 1/2; E - 6 cols, between; A - 6 cols, between; C - 7 cols, between.
Published: Fri
Avg Free Circ: 15000
Audit By: Sworn/Estimate/Non-Audited
Audit Date: 7/12/2019
Classified Equipment»
Personnel: John Rives (Pub.); Matt Dunigan (Adv. Mgr.)

FORT DETRICK STANDARD

Street address 1: 9030 Comprint Ct
Street address 3: Gaithersburg
Street address state: MD
Zip/Postal code: 20877-1307
County: Montgomery
Country: USA
Mailing address: 9030 Comprint Ct
Mailing city: Gaithersburg
Mailing state: MD
Mailing zip: 20877-1307
General Phone: (301) 921-2800
General Fax: (301) 948-2787
Primary Website: www.dcmilitary.com
Own Printing Facility: Y
Advertising (Open Inch Rate) Weekday/Saturday: Open inch rate $12.85
Mechanical specifications: Type page 9 5/8 x 13 1/2; E - 6 cols, between; A - 6 cols, between; C - 7 cols, between.
Published Other: Every other Thur
Avg Free Circ: 4100
Audit By: Sworn/Estimate/Non-Audited
Audit Date: 7/12/2019
Classified Equipment»
Personnel: John Rives (Adv. Mgr.); Jean Casey (Circ. Mgr.); Ann Duble (Ed.)

HENDERSON HALL NEWS

Street address 1: 9030 Comprint Ct
Street address 3: Gaithersburg
Street address state: MD
Zip/Postal code: 20877-1307
County: Montgomery
Country: USA
Mailing address: 9030 Comprint Ct
Mailing city: Gaithersburg
Mailing state: MD
Mailing zip: 20877-1307
General Phone: (301) 921-2800
General Fax: (301) 948-2787
Primary Website: www.dcmilitary.com
Own Printing Facility: Y
Advertising (Open Inch Rate) Weekday/Saturday: Open inch rate $12.47
Mechanical specifications: Type page 9 5/8 x 13 1/2; E - 6 cols, between; A - 6 cols, between; C - 7 cols, between.
Audit By: Sworn/Estimate/Non-Audited
Audit Date: 7/12/2019
Classified Equipment»
Personnel: Brent Wucher (Ed.)

JOINT BASE JOURNAL

Street address 1: 9030 Comprint Ct
Street address 3: Gaithersburg
Street address state: MD
Zip/Postal code: 20877-1307
County: Montgomery
Country: USA
Mailing address: 9030 Comprint Ct
Mailing city: Gaithersburg
Mailing state: MD
Mailing zip: 20877-1307
General Phone: (301) 921-2800
General Fax: (301) 948-2787
Primary Website: www.dcmilitary.com
Own Printing Facility: Y
Advertising (Open Inch Rate) Weekday/Saturday: Open inch rate $29.62
Mechanical specifications: Type page 9 5/8 x 13 1/2; E - 6 cols, between; A - 6 cols, between; C - 7 cols, between.
Published: Wed`Thur
Avg Free Circ: 24000
Audit By: Sworn/Estimate/Non-Audited
Audit Date: 7/12/2019
Classified Equipment»
Personnel: John Rives (Adv. Mgr.)

PENTAGRAM

Street address 1: 9030 Comprint Ct
Street address 3: Gaithersburg
Street address state: MD
Zip/Postal code: 20877-1307
County: Montgomery
Country: USA
Mailing address: 9030 Comprint Ct
Mailing city: Gaithersburg
Mailing state: MD
Mailing zip: 20877-1307
General Phone: (301) 921-2800
General Fax: (301) 948-2787
Primary Website: www.dcmilitary.com
Own Printing Facility: Y
Advertising (Open Inch Rate) Weekday/Saturday: Open inch rate $29.62
Mechanical specifications: Type page 9 5/8 x 13 1/2; E - 6 cols, between; A - 6 cols, between; C - 7 cols, between.
Published: Wed`Thur
Avg Free Circ: 24000
Audit By: Sworn/Estimate/Non-Audited
Audit Date: 7/12/2019
Classified Equipment»
Personnel: John Rives (Adv. Mgr.)

SOUTH POTOMAC PILOT

Street address 1: 9030 Comprint Ct
Street address 3: Gaithersburg
Street address state: MD
Zip/Postal code: 20877-1307
County: Montgomery
Country: USA
Mailing address: 9030 Comprint Ct
Mailing city: Gaithersburg
Mailing state: MD
Mailing zip: 20877-1307
General Phone: (301) 921-2800
General Fax: (301) 948-2787
Primary Website: www.dcmilitary.com
Own Printing Facility: Y
Advertising (Open Inch Rate) Weekday/Saturday: Open inch rate $29.62
Mechanical specifications: Type page 9 5/8 x 13 1/2; E - 6 cols, between; A - 6 cols, between; C - 7 cols, between.
Published: Wed`Thur
Avg Free Circ: 24000
Audit By: Sworn/Estimate/Non-Audited
Audit Date: 7/12/2019
Classified Equipment»
Personnel: John Rives (Adv. Mgr.)

TESTER

Street address 1: 9030 Comprint Ct
Street address 3: Gaithersburg
Street address state: MD
Zip/Postal code: 20877-1307
County: Montgomery
Country: USA
Mailing address: 9030 Comprint Ct
Mailing city: Gaithersburg
Mailing state: MD
Mailing zip: 20877-1307
General Phone: (301) 921-2800
General Fax: (301) 948-2787
Primary Website: www.dcmilitary.com
Own Printing Facility: Y
Advertising (Open Inch Rate) Weekday/Saturday: Open inch rate $17.17
Mechanical specifications: Type page 13 1/4 x 21; E - 8 cols, between; A - 8 cols, between; C - 9 cols, between.
Published: Thur
Avg Free Circ: 15000
Audit By: Sworn/Estimate/Non-Audited
Audit Date: 7/12/2019
Classified Equipment»
Personnel: Matt Dunigan (Adv. Mgr.); John Rives (Ed.)

THE NNMC JOURNAL

Street address 1: 9030 Comprint Ct
Street address 3: Gaithersburg
Street address state: MD
Zip/Postal code: 20877-1307
County: Montgomery
Country: USA
Mailing address: 9030 Comprint Ct
Mailing city: Gaithersburg
Mailing state: MD
Mailing zip: 20877-1307
General Phone: (301) 921-2800
General Fax: (301) 948-2787
Primary Website: www.dcmilitary.com
Own Printing Facility: Y
Advertising (Open Inch Rate) Weekday/Saturday: Open inch rate $14.37
Mechanical specifications: Type page 9 5/8 x 13 1/2; E - 4 cols, between; A - 6 cols, between; C - 7 cols, between.
Published: Thur
Avg Free Circ: 7000
Audit By: Sworn/Estimate/Non-Audited
Audit Date: 7/12/2019
Classified Equipment»
Personnel: Matt Dunigan (Gen. Mgr.); John Rives (Adv. Mgr.)

THE WATER LINE

Street address 1: 9030 Comprint Ct
Street address 3: Gaithersburg
Street address state: MD
Zip/Postal code: 20877-1307
County: Montgomery
Country: USA
Mailing address: 9030 Comprint Ct
Mailing city: Gaithersburg
Mailing state: MD
Mailing zip: 20877-1307
General Phone: (301) 921-2800
General Fax: (301) 948-2787
Primary Website: www.dcmilitary.com
Own Printing Facility: Y
Advertising (Open Inch Rate) Weekday/Saturday: Open inch rate $15.85
Mechanical specifications: Type page 9 5/8 x 13 1/2; E - 6 cols, between; A - 6 cols, between; C - 7 cols, between.
Published: Thur
Avg Free Circ: 9000
Audit By: Sworn/Estimate/Non-Audited
Audit Date: 7/12/2019
Classified Equipment»
Personnel: John Rives (Pub.); Matt Dunigan (Adv. Mgr.); Jake Joy (Ed.)

THE WATERLINE

Street address 1: 9030 Comprint Ct
Street address 3: Gaithersburg
Street address state: MD
Zip/Postal code: 20877-1307
County: Montgomery
Country: USA
Mailing address: 9030 Comprint Ct
Mailing city: Gaithersburg
Mailing state: MD
Mailing zip: 20877-1307
General Phone: 301-921-2800
General Fax: (301) 948-2787
General/National Adv. E-mail: jrives@gazette.net
Primary Website: www.dcmilitary.com
Year Established: 1984
Classified Equipment»
Personnel: John Rives (Publisher)

MAINE

BRUNSWICK

THE PATROLLER

Street address 1: 3 Business Pkwy
Street address 3: Brunswick
Street address state: ME
Zip/Postal code: 04011-7390
County: Cumberland
Country: USA
Mailing address: PO Box 10
Mailing city: Brunswick
Mailing state: ME
Mailing zip: 04011-1302
General Phone: (207) 729-3311
General Fax: (207) 729-5728
Display Adv. E-mail: adsales@timesrecord.com
Primary Website: www.timesrecord.com
Own Printing Facility: Y
Advertising (Open Inch Rate) Weekday/Saturday: Open inch rate $6.95
Mechanical specifications: Type page 10 1/8 x 15 1/4; E - 5 cols, between; A - 5 cols, between; C - 6 cols, between.
Published: Thur
Avg Free Circ: 3500
Audit By: Sworn/Estimate/Non-Audited
Audit Date: 7/12/2019
Classified Equipment»
Personnel: Chris Miles (Pub.); John Bamford (Adv. Dir.)

MISSOURI

SAINT ROBERT

GUIDON

Street address 1: 394 Old Route 66
Street address 3: Saint Robert
Street address state: MO
Zip/Postal code: 65584-3829
County: Pulaski
Country: USA

General Phone: (573) 336-0061
General Fax: (573) 336-5487
General/National Adv. E-mail: guidon_staff@myguidon.com
Primary Website: www.myguidon.com
Own Printing Facility: Y
Advertising (Open Inch Rate) Weekday/Saturday: Open inch rate $10.40
Mechanical specifications: Type page 13 1/2 x 21 1/2; E - 4 cols, 3 1/12, 1/6 between; A - 6 cols, 2 1/12, 1/6 between; C - 6 cols, 2 1/12, 1/6 between.
Published: Thur
Avg Free Circ: 10000
Audit By: Sworn/Estimate/Non-Audited
Audit Date: 7/12/2019
Classified Equipment»
Personnel: Mike Bowers (Adv. Mgr.); Robert Johnson (Ed.)

WHITEMAN AFB

WHITEMAN WARRIOR

Street address 1: 1081 Arnold Ave
Street address 3: Whiteman Afb
Street address state: MO
Zip/Postal code: 65305-5108
County: Johnson
Country: USA
Mailing address: 509th Bomb Wing, 1081 Arnold Ave., Bldg. 59
Mailing city: Whiteman AFB
Mailing state: MO
Mailing zip: 65305
General Phone: (660) 826-1000
General Fax: (660) 826-2413
Display Adv. E-mail: advertising@sedaliademocrat.com
Delivery Methods: Mail`Racks
Area Served - City: 65305
Own Printing Facility: Y
Advertising (Open Inch Rate) Weekday/Saturday: Open inch rate $8.75
Mechanical specifications: Type page 10 1/4 x 14; E - 6 cols, 1 7/12, between; A - 6 cols, 1 7/12, between; C - 7 cols, 1 1/3, 1/6 between.
Published: Fri
Avg Free Circ: 4800
Audit By: Sworn/Estimate/Non-Audited
Audit Date: 7/12/2019
Classified Equipment»
Personnel: Will Weibert (Publisher)
Parent company (for newspapers): Phillips Media

MISSISSIPPI

GULFPORT

SUNHERALD

Street address 1: 205 Debuys Rd
Street address 3: Gulfport
Street address state: MS
Zip/Postal code: 39507-2838
County: Harrison
Country: USA
Mailing address: PO Box 4567
Mailing city: Biloxi
Mailing state: MS
Mailing zip: 39535-4567
General Phone: (228) 896-2100
General Fax: (228) 896-2362
Advertising Phone: (228) 896-2463
Advertising Fax: (228) 896-0516
Editorail Phone: (228) 377-3163
General/National Adv. E-mail: specialpublications@sunherald.com
Display Adv. E-mail: cbiasi@sunherald.com
Editorial e-mail: stephen.hoffmann.ctr@us.af.mil
Primary Website: www.sunherald.com
Year Established: 1974
Delivery Methods: Mail`Newsstand`Carrier`Racks
Area Served - City: 39534 39531 39532 39535
Own Printing Facility: Y
Advertising (Open Inch Rate) Weekday/Saturday: Open inch rate $14.69
Mechanical specifications: Type page 10 x 11; A - 5 cols,
Published: Thur
Avg Free Circ: 8500
Audit By: Sworn/Estimate/Non-Audited
Audit Date: 7/12/2019
Classified Equipment»
Note: Published weekly by Sun Herald MultiMedia for Keesler Air Force Base under contract with the Department of the Air Force
Personnel: Sandi Menendez (Adv. Mgr.); Glen Nardi (Publisher); Susan Griggs (Ed.); John McFarland (Special Publications Manager); Stephen Hoffmann (Editor)
Parent company (for newspapers): The McClatchy Company

MERIDIAN

SKYLINE

Street address 1: 814 22nd Ave
Street address 3: Meridian
Street address state: MS
Zip/Postal code: 39301-5023
County: Lauderdale
Country: USA
Mailing address: PO Box 1591
Mailing city: Meridian
Mailing state: MS
Mailing zip: 39302-1591
General Phone: (601) 693-1551
General Fax: (601) 485-1229
General/National Adv. E-mail: info@themeridianstar.com
Display Adv. E-mail: eryan@themeridianstar.com
Primary Website: www.meridianstar.com
Own Printing Facility: Y
Advertising (Open Inch Rate) Weekday/Saturday: Open inch rate $9.18
Mechanical specifications: Type page 9 11/16 x 11 3/4; E - 5 cols, 1 13/16, between; A - 5 cols, 1 11/16, between.
Published: Thur
Published Other: Every other Thur
Avg Free Circ: 1800
Audit By: Sworn/Estimate/Non-Audited
Audit Date: 7/12/2019
Classified Equipment»
Personnel: Timothy Holder (Publisher); Michael Stewart (Editor for The Meridian Star); Elizabeth Ryan (Skyline Advertising)
Parent company (for newspapers): Community Newspaper Holdings, Inc.

NORTH CAROLINA

CAROLINA FLYER

Street address 1: PO Box 849
Street address 3: Fayetteville
Street address state: NC
Zip/Postal code: 28302-0849
County: Cumberland
Country: USA
Mailing address: PO Box 849
Mailing city: Fayetteville
Mailing state: NC
Mailing zip: 28302-0849
General Phone: (910) 323-4848
General Fax: (910) 486-3544
Primary Website: www.fayobserver.com
Own Printing Facility: Y
Advertising (Open Inch Rate) Weekday/Saturday: Open inch rate $7.13
Mechanical specifications: Type page 12 1/2 x 22; E - 6 cols, 1 5/6, 1/6 between; A - 6 cols, 1 5/6, 1/6 between; C - 10 cols, 1, 1/10 between.
Published: Fri
Avg Free Circ: 4019
Audit By: Sworn/Estimate/Non-Audited
Audit Date: 7/12/2019
Classified Equipment»
Personnel: Charles W. Broadwell (Pub.); Brad Parker (Weekly Sales Mgr.); Jim Adkins (Circ. Dir.); Brian Tolley (Exec. Ed.)

FORT BRAGG PARAGLIDE

Street address 1: 458 Whitfield St
Street address 3: Fayetteville
Street address state: NC
Zip/Postal code: 28306-1614
County: Cumberland
Country: USA
Mailing address: PO Box 849
Mailing city: Fayetteville
Mailing state: NC
Mailing zip: 28302-0849
General Phone: (910) 396-6817
General Fax: (910) 396-9629
Advertising Phone: (910) 323-4848
General/National Adv. E-mail: paraglidebragg@gmail.com
Primary Website: www.paraglideonline.net
Area Served - City: 28307
Own Printing Facility: Y
Commercial printers: Y
Advertising (Open Inch Rate) Weekday/Saturday: Open inch rate $25.00
Mechanical specifications: Type page 12 1/2 x 22; E - 6 cols, 1 5/6, 1/6 between; A - 6 cols, 1 5/6, 1/6 between; C - 10 cols, 1, 1/10 between.
Published: Thur
Avg Free Circ: 25000
Audit By: Sworn/Estimate/Non-Audited
Audit Date: 7/12/2019
Classified Equipment»
Personnel: Charles W. Broadwell (Pub.); Brad Parker (Mgr., Adv. Sales); James Adkins (Circ. Mgr.)

HAVELOCK

HAVELOCK NEWS

Street address 1: 230 Stonebridge Sq
Street address 3: Havelock
Street address state: NC
Zip/Postal code: 28532-9505
County: Craven
Country: USA
Mailing address: PO Box 777
Mailing city: Havelock
Mailing state: NC
Mailing zip: 28532-0777
General Phone: (252) 444-1999
General Fax: (252) 447-0897
Primary Website: www.havenews.com
Advertising (Open Inch Rate) Weekday/Saturday: Open inch rate $12.70
Mechanical specifications: Type page 13 x 21 1/2; E - 6 cols, 2 1/16, 1/6 between; A - 6 cols, 2 1/16, 1/6 between; C - 9 cols, 1 5/16, between.
Published: Thur
Avg Free Circ: 11500
Audit By: Sworn/Estimate/Non-Audited
Audit Date: 7/12/2019
Classified Equipment»
Personnel: Taylor Shannon (Adv. Media Consult.); Roxanne Smith (Circ. Mgr.); Ken Buday (Ed.); Drew Wilson (Reporter)

ROTOVUE

Street address 1: 149 Rea St
Street address 2: Ste 100
Street address 3: Jacksonville
Street address state: NC
Zip/Postal code: 28546-5717
County: Onslow
Country: USA
Mailing address: 149 Rea St., Suite #100
Mailing city: Jacksonville
Mailing state: NC
Mailing zip: 28546
General Phone: (910) 347-9624
General Fax: (910) 347-9628
Primary Website: www.newriverrotovue.com
Advertising (Open Inch Rate) Weekday/Saturday: Open inch rate $11.59
Mechanical specifications: Type page 9 9/16 x 11 1/2; E - 5 cols, 1 25/32, between; A - 5 cols, 1 25/32, between; C - 5 cols, 1 25/32, between.
Published Other: Every other Wed
Avg Free Circ: 8600
Audit By: Sworn/Estimate/Non-Audited
Audit Date: 7/12/2019
Classified Equipment»
Personnel: Jim Connors (Pub.); Heather Miller (Adv. Mgr.); Ena Sellers (Ed)

NORTH DAKOTA

MINOT

THE NORTHERN SENTRY

Street address 1: 15-1 Ave SE
Street address 3: Minot
Street address state: ND
Zip/Postal code: 58701
County: Ward
Country: USA
Mailing address: PO Box 2183
Mailing city: Minot
Mailing state: ND
Mailing zip: 58702-2183
General Phone: (701) 839-0946
General Fax: (701) 839-1867
Display Adv. E-mail: nsads@srt.com
Advertising (Open Inch Rate) Weekday/Saturday: Open inch rate $8.00
Mechanical specifications: Type page 10 x 16; E - 5 cols, 2, between; A - 5 cols, 2, between.
Published: Fri
Avg Free Circ: 6000
Audit By: Sworn/Estimate/Non-Audited
Audit Date: 7/12/2019
Classified Equipment»
Personnel: Michael W. Gackle (Pub.); Sharon Olson (Adv. Mgr.)
Parent company (for newspapers): BHG, Inc.

NEBRASKA

BELLEVUE

AIR PULSE

Street address 1: 604 Fort Crook Rd N
Street address 3: Bellevue
Street address state: NE
Zip/Postal code: 68005-4557
County: Sarpy
Country: USA
Mailing address: 604 Fort Crook Rd N
Mailing city: Bellevue
Mailing state: NE
Mailing zip: 68005-4557
General Phone: (402) 733-7300
General Fax: (402) 733-9116
Editorial e-mail: news@bellevueleader.com
Primary Website: www.omahanewsstand.com
Year Established: 1946
Advertising (Open Inch Rate) Weekday/Saturday: Open inch rate $16.22
Mechanical specifications: Type page 9 3/4 x 11 1/2; E - 6 cols, 1 1/2, between; A - 6 cols, 1 1/2, between.
Published: Thur
Avg Free Circ: 9500
Audit By: Sworn/Estimate/Non-Audited
Audit Date: 7/12/2019
Classified Equipment»
Personnel: Shon Barenklau (Pub.); Paul Swanson (Adv. Mgr.); Mellissa Vanek (Circ. Mgr.); Amy Corrigan (Prodn. Mgr.)

NEW MEXICO

WHITE SANDS MISSILE

RANGE

WHITE SANDS MISSILE RANGER

Street address 1: Public Affairs Office
Street address 3: White Sands Missile Range
Street address state: NM
Zip/Postal code: 88002
County: Dona Ana
Country: USA
Mailing address: Bldg. 1782
Mailing city: White Sands
Mailing state: NM
Mailing zip: 88002
General Phone: (575) 678-2716
General Fax: (575) 678-8814
General/National Adv. E-mail: wsmrranger@conus.army.mil
Primary Website: www.missileranger.com
Own Printing Facility: Y
Advertising (Open Inch Rate) Weekday/Saturday: Open inch rate $7.65
Mechanical specifications: Type page 11 x 11 3/4; E - 5 cols, 2 1/16, 1/8 between; A - 5 cols, 2 1/16, 1/8 between; C - 5 cols, 1/8 between.
Published: Thur
Avg Free Circ: 6000
Audit By: Sworn/Estimate/Non-Audited
Audit Date: 7/12/2019
Classified Equipment»
Personnel: Miriam U. Rodriguez (Ed.)

NEW YORK

FORT DRUM

THE MOUNTAINEER

Street address 1: 10012 S Riva Ridge Loop
Street address 3: Fort Drum
Street address state: NY
Zip/Postal code: 13602-5492
County: Jefferson
Country: USA
Mailing address: 10012 S. Riva Ridge Loop
Mailing city: Fort Drum
Mailing state: NY
Mailing zip: 13602
General Phone: (315) 772-5469
General Fax: (315) 772-8295
Published: Thur
Avg Free Circ: 10000
Audit By: Sworn/Estimate/Non-Audited
Audit Date: 7/12/2019
Classified Equipment»
Personnel: Lisa Albrecht (Managing editor)

OKLAHOMA

FORT SILL

THE CANNONEER

Street address 1: 455 McNair Hall, Ste 118
Street address 3: Fort Sill
Street address state: OK
Zip/Postal code: 73503
County: Comanche
Country: USA
Mailing address: 455 McNair Hall, Ste. 118
Mailing city: Fort Sill
Mailing state: OK
Mailing zip: 73503-5100
General Phone: (580) 442-5150
General Fax: (580) 585-5103
General/National Adv. E-mail: cannoneersill@conus.army.mil
Primary Website: www.woknews.com
Own Printing Facility: Y
Advertising (Open Inch Rate) Weekday/Saturday: Open inch rate $7.25
Mechanical specifications: Type page 13 x 21 1/6; E - 6 cols, 2 1/16, 1/8 between; A - 6 cols, 2 1/16, 1/8 between; C - 9 cols, 1 1/4, 1/8 between.
Published: Thur
Avg Free Circ: 12000
Audit By: Sworn/Estimate/Non-Audited
Audit Date: 7/12/2019
Classified Equipment»
Personnel: James Brabanec; Jeff Crawley; Marie Berberea

RHODE ISLAND

NEWPORT

NEWPORT NAVALOG

Street address 1: 101 Malbone Rd
Street address 3: Newport
Street address state: RI
Zip/Postal code: 02840-1340
County: Newport
Country: USA
Mailing address: PO Box 420
Mailing city: Newport
Mailing state: RI
Mailing zip: 02840-0936
General Phone: (401) 849-3300
General Fax: (401) 849-3335
General/National Adv. E-mail: prepress@newportri.com
Primary Website: www.newportdailynews.com
Advertising (Open Inch Rate) Weekday/Saturday: Open inch rate $16.50
Published: Fri
Avg Free Circ: 4400
Audit By: Sworn/Estimate/Non-Audited
Audit Date: 7/12/2019
Classified Equipment»
Personnel: Albert K. Sherman (Pub.); William F. Lucey (Gen. Mgr.); Ann Marie Brisson (Adv. Mgr.); Richard Alexander (Ed.); Kevin Schoen (Prodn. Mgr.)

SOUTH CAROLINA

CAMDEN

THE SHAW NEWS

Street address 1: 909 W Dekalb St
Street address 3: Camden
Street address state: SC
Zip/Postal code: 29020-4259
County: Kershaw
Country: USA
Mailing address: 909 W Dekalb St
Mailing city: Camden
Mailing state: SC
Mailing zip: 29020-4259
General Phone: (803) 432-6157
Advertising Phone: (803) 432-6157
Advertising Fax: (803) 432-7609
Editorail Phone: (803) 236-8425
General/National Adv. E-mail: mmischner@ci-camden.com
Primary Website: www.ci-camden.com
Advertising (Open Inch Rate) Weekday/Saturday: Open inch rate $13.15
Mechanical specifications: Type page 10 x 14.
Published: Fri
Avg Free Circ: 7200
Audit By: Sworn/Estimate/Non-Audited
Audit Date: 7/12/2019
Classified Equipment»
Personnel: Michael Mischner (Pub.); Betsy Greenway (Adv. Mgr.)
Parent company (for newspapers): Morris Multimedia, Inc.

TENNESSEE

MILLINGTON

THE BLUEJACKET

Street address 1: 5107 Easley Ave
Street address 3: Millington
Street address state: TN
Zip/Postal code: 38053-2107
County: Shelby
Country: USA
Mailing address: PO Box 305
Mailing city: Millington
Mailing state: TN
Mailing zip: 38083-0305
General Phone: (901) 872-2286
General Fax: (901) 872-2965
General/National Adv. E-mail: mstar@bigriver.net
Primary Website: www.nsamidsouth.navy.mil/news-bj.htm
Advertising (Open Inch Rate) Weekday/Saturday: Open inch rate $8.40
Mechanical specifications: Type page 13 x 21 1/4; E - 6 cols, 2, between; A - 6 cols, 2, between; C - 9 cols, between.
Published: Thur
Avg Free Circ: 6100
Audit By: Sworn/Estimate/Non-Audited
Audit Date: 7/12/2019
Classified Equipment»
Personnel: John Fee (Pub.); Julia A. Wallis (Ed.)

TEXAS

SOUND OF FREEDOM

Street address 1: 101 Cypress St
Street address 3: Abilene
Street address state: TX
Zip/Postal code: 79601-5816
County: Taylor
Country: USA
Mailing address: PO Box 30
Mailing city: Abilene
Mailing state: TX
Mailing zip: 79604-0030
General Phone: (325) 673-4271
General Fax: (325) 670-5222
Display Adv. E-mail: ads@reporternews.com
Primary Website: www.reporternews.com
Year Established: 1984
Own Printing Facility: Y
Advertising (Open Inch Rate) Weekday/Saturday: Open inch rate $7.99
Mechanical specifications: Type page 9 5/8 x 11 5/8; E - 5 cols, 1 5/6, between; A - 5 cols, 1 5/6, between; C - 7 cols, 1 1/16, between.
Published: Fri
Avg Free Circ: 7500
Audit By: Sworn/Estimate/Non-Audited
Audit Date: 7/12/2019
Classified Equipment»
Personnel: Kim Nussbaum (Pub.); Stephanie Boggins (Adv. Mgr.); Barton Cromeens (Ed.); Mike Hall (Opns Dir.)

FORT BLISS MONITOR

Street address 1: 1420 Geronimo Dr
Street address 2: Bldg E
Street address 3: El Paso
Street address state: TX
Zip/Postal code: 79925-1855
County: El Paso
Country: USA
Mailing address: 5959 Gateway Blvd W Ste 450
Mailing city: El Paso
Mailing state: TX
Mailing zip: 79925-3396
General Phone: (915) 772-0934
General Fax: (915) 772-1594
General/National Adv. E-mail: sflav@whc.net
Primary Website: www.lavenpublishing.com
Year Established: 1985
Area Served - City: 79906, 79924, 79925, 79936, 79902
Advertising (Open Inch Rate) Weekday/Saturday: Open inch rate $13.60
Mechanical specifications: Type page 10 1/8 x 16; E - 4 cols, 2 1/4, 1/2 between; A - 4 cols, 2 1/4, 1/2 between; C - 7 cols, 1 1/4, 1/4 between.
Published: Thur
Avg Free Circ: 20000
Audit By: Sworn/Estimate/Non-Audited
Audit Date: 7/12/2019
Classified Equipment»
Personnel: Mike Laven (Vice Pres., Sales); Skip Laven (Adv. Mgr.); Susan Laven (Vice Pres., Prodn.)

FORT HOOD

FORT HOOD SENTINEL

Street address 1: 761 Tank Battalion
Street address 2: Bldg W105
Street address 3: Fort Hood
Street address state: TX
Zip/Postal code: 76544-4906
County: Bell
Country: USA
General Phone: (254) 287-9495
Advertising Phone: (254) 634-6666
Editorail Phone: (254) 287-9495
Display Adv. E-mail: advertise@forthoodsentinel.com
Editorial e-mail: todd.pruden@forthoodsentinel.com
Primary Website: www.forthoodsentinel.com
Year Established: 1942
Delivery Methods: Mail`Newsstand`Carrier`Racks
Area Served - City: 76541, 76544
Advertising (Open Inch Rate) Weekday/Saturday: Open inch rate $12.50
Mechanical specifications: Type page 12 x 21 1/2; E - 6 cols, 1 4/5, 1/8 between; A - 6 cols, 1 4/5, 1/8 between; C - 9 cols, 1 1/5, 1/16 between.
Published: Thur
Avg Free Circ: 25000
Audit By: Sworn/Estimate/Non-Audited
Audit Date: 7/12/2019
Classified Equipment»
Personnel: Sue Mayborn (Pub.); Ray Reed (Gen. Mgr.)
Parent company (for newspapers): Frank Mayborn Enterprises, Inc.

UTAH

HILLTOP TIMES

Street address 1: 332 Standard Way
Street address 3: Ogden
Street address state: UT
Zip/Postal code: 84404-1371
County: Weber
Country: USA
Mailing address: PO Box 12790
Mailing city: Ogden
Mailing state: UT
Mailing zip: 84412-2790
General Phone: (801) 625-4310
General Fax: (801) 625-4508
Advertising Phone: (801) 625-4333
Advertising Fax: (801) 625-4508
Editorail Phone: (801) 777-7322
Editorial Fax: (801) 625-4299
General/National Adv. E-mail: hilltoptimes@standard.net
Display Adv. E-mail: advertise@standard.net
Primary Website: www.hilltoptimes.com
Year Established: 1966
Delivery Methods: Newsstand`Carrier`Racks
Area Served - City: 84056, 84041, 84015, 84040, 84067
Own Printing Facility: Y
Commercial printers: Y
Advertising (Open Inch Rate) Weekday/Saturday: Open inch rate $18.36
Mechanical specifications: 6 col. (11") x 20.5". One col. = 1.74"; gutter = .125"
Published: Thur
Avg Free Circ: 12000
Audit By: Sworn/Estimate/Non-Audited
Audit Date: 7/12/2019

Classified Equipment»
Personnel: Brad Roghaar (Adv. Dir.); Vaughn Jacobsen (Circ. Mgr.)
Parent company (for newspapers): Sandusky Newspapers, Inc.

VIRGINIA

LEESBURG

QUANTICO SENTRY

Street address 1: 19 N King St
Street address 3: Leesburg
Street address state: VA
Zip/Postal code: 20176-2819
County: Loudoun
Country: USA
Mailing address: 19 N. King St.
Mailing city: Leesburg
Mailing state: VA
Mailing zip: 20176
General Phone: 703-771-8800
General Fax: (540) 659-0039
Advertising Phone: (703) 771-8800
General/National Adv. E-mail: Jlesh@insidenova.com
Display Adv. E-mail: bpowell@staffordcountysun.com
Editorial e-mail: adolzenko@staffordcountysun.com
Primary Website: http://www.quanticosentryonline.com/
Delivery Methods: Carrier
Own Printing Facility: Y
Advertising (Open Inch Rate) Weekday/Saturday: Open inch rate $21.50
Mechanical specifications: Type page 6 x 21; E - 6 cols, 2 1/16, 1/6 between; A - 6 cols, 2 1/16, 1/6 between.
Published: Thur
Avg Free Circ: 8500
Audit By: Sworn/Estimate/Non-Audited
Audit Date: 7/12/2019
Classified Equipment»
Personnel: Tom Spargur (GM/Sales mgr)
Parent company (for newspapers): Northern Virginia Media Services

NORFOLK

FLAGSHIP

Street address 1: 150 W Brambleton Ave
Street address 3: Norfolk
Street address state: VA
Zip/Postal code: 23510-2018
County: Norfolk City
Country: USA
Mailing address: 150 W Brambleton Ave
Mailing city: Norfolk
Mailing state: VA
Mailing zip: 23510-2018
General Phone: (757) 222-3990
General Fax: (757) 622-6885
General/National Adv. E-mail: laura.baxter@militarynews.com
Primary Website: www.norfolknavyflagship.com
Own Printing Facility: Y
Commercial printers: Y
Advertising (Open Inch Rate) Weekday/Saturday: Open inch rate $20.50
Mechanical specifications: Type page 11 1/2 x 21 1/2; E - 6 cols, 1 3/4, 1/8 between; A - 6 cols, 1 3/4, 1/8 between; C - 10 cols, 1 1/10, 1/16 between.
Published: Thur
Avg Free Circ: 35000
Audit By: Sworn/Estimate/Non-Audited
Audit Date: 7/12/2019
Classified Equipment»

PENINSULA WARRIOR- AIR FORCE

Street address 1: 150 W Brambleton Ave
Street address 3: Norfolk
Street address state: VA
Zip/Postal code: 23510-2018
County: Norfolk City
Country: USA
Mailing address: 150 W Brambleton Ave
Mailing city: Norfolk
Mailing state: VA
Mailing zip: 23510-2018
General Phone: (757) 222-3990
General Fax: (757) 622-6885
General/National Adv. E-mail: sales@militarynews.com
Primary Website: www.militarynews.com
Delivery Methods: Racks
Own Printing Facility: Y
Commercial printers: N
Advertising (Open Inch Rate) Weekday/Saturday: Open rate $18.85
Mechanical specifications: Type page 9 7/8 x 14; E - 6 cols, 1 1/2, between; A - 6 cols, 1 1/2, between; C - 6 cols, 1 1/2, between.
Published: Fri
Avg Free Circ: 14000
Audit By: Sworn/Estimate/Non-Audited
Audit Date: 7/12/2019
Classified Equipment»
Personnel: Laura Baxter (Pub.)

SOUNDINGS

Street address 1: 10 W Brambleton Ave
Street address 3: Norfolk
Street address state: VA
Zip/Postal code: 23510
County: Norfolk City
Country: USA
General Phone: (757) 222-3990
General Fax: (757) 853-1634
General/National Adv. E-mail: sales@militarynews.com
Primary Website: www.militarynews.com
Own Printing Facility: Y
Advertising (Open Inch Rate) Weekday/Saturday: Open inch rate $26.97
Mechanical specifications: Type page 9 7/8 x 14; E - 6 cols, 1 1/2, between; A - 6 cols, 1 1/2, between; C - 6 cols, 1 1/2, between.
Audit By: Sworn/Estimate/Non-Audited
Audit Date: 7/12/2019
Classified Equipment»
Personnel: Laura Baxter (Pub.); Jim Van Slyke (Ed.); Reagan Haynes

THE WHEEL

Street address 1: 258 Granby St
Street address 3: Norfolk
Street address state: VA
Zip/Postal code: 23510-1812
County: Norfolk City
Country: USA
Mailing address: 150 W Brambleton Ave
Mailing city: Norfolk
Mailing state: VA
Mailing zip: 23510-2018
General Phone: (757) 222-3990
General Fax: (757) 853-1634
Primary Website: www.militarynews.com
Year Established: 1970
Own Printing Facility: Y
Advertising (Open Inch Rate) Weekday/Saturday: Open inch rate $15.98
Mechanical specifications: Type page 9 7/8 x 14; E - 6 cols, 1 1/2, between; A - 6 cols, 1 1/2, between; C - 6 cols, 1 1/2, between.
Published: Thur
Avg Free Circ: 10500
Audit By: Sworn/Estimate/Non-Audited
Audit Date: 7/12/2019
Classified Equipment»
Personnel: Laura Baxter (Adv. Mgr.); Zack Shelby (Ed.)

SPRINGFIELD

DEFENSE NEWS

Street address 1: 6883 Commercial Dr
Street address 3: Springfield
Street address state: VA
Zip/Postal code: 22159-0002
County: Fairfax
Country: USA
Mailing address: 6883 Commercial Dr
Mailing city: Springfield
Mailing state: VA
Mailing zip: 22159-0002
General Phone: (703) 642-7330
General Fax: (703) 642-7386
General/National Adv. E-mail: cust-svc@atpco.com
Primary Website: www.defensenews.com
Advertising (Open Inch Rate) Weekday/Saturday: Open inch rate $200.00
Published: Mon
Avg Paid Circ: 7319
Avg Free Circ: 30822
Audit By: Sworn/Estimate/Non-Audited
Audit Date: 7/12/2019
Classified Equipment»
Personnel: Donna Peterson (Vice Pres., Adv.); Vago Muradian (Ed.)

NAVY TIMES

Street address 1: 6883 Commercial Dr
Street address 3: Springfield
Street address state: VA
Zip/Postal code: 22159-0002
County: Fairfax
Country: USA
Mailing address: 6883 Commercial Dr
Mailing city: Springfield
Mailing state: VA
Mailing zip: 22159-0002
General Phone: (703) 750-8636
General Fax: (703) 750-8767
General/National Adv. E-mail: navylet@atpco.com
Primary Website: www.navytimes.com
Advertising (Open Inch Rate) Weekday/Saturday: Open inch rate $25.96
Mechanical specifications: Type page 21 1/2 x 12 1/4.
Published: Mon
Avg Paid Circ: 79500
Avg Free Circ: 2400
Audit By: Sworn/Estimate/Non-Audited
Audit Date: 7/12/2019
Classified Equipment»
Personnel: Elaine Howard (Pres./Pub.); Dick Howlett (Circ. Mgr.); Christopher P. Cavas (Ed.); Christopher Lawson (Mng. Ed.); Phil Rose (Prodn. Mgr.)

VIENNA

AIR FORCE TIMES

Street address 1: 1919 Gallows Rd
Street address 2: 4th Floor
Street address 3: Vienna
Street address state: VA
Zip/Postal code: 22182-4038
County: Fairfax
Country: USA
Mailing address: 1919 Gallows Road, 4th Floor
Mailing city: VIENNA
Mailing state: VA
Mailing zip: 22182-4038
General Phone: (703) 642-7330
General Fax: (703) 642-7386
Advertising Phone: (703) 642-7330
Advertising Fax: (703) 642-7386
Editorail Phone: (703) 642-7330
Editorial Fax: (703) 642-7386
General/National Adv. E-mail: Cust-svc@airforcetimes.com
Display Adv. E-mail: advertisingsales@sightlinemg.com
Editorial e-mail: tips@airforcetimes.com
Primary Website: www.airforcetimes.com
Year Established: 1947
Delivery Methods: Mail`Newsstand`Racks
Area Served - City: Fairfax County
Advertising (Open Inch Rate) Weekday/Saturday: Open inch rate $7,680.00 (Full-Page)
Published: Mon
Classified Equipment»
Personnel: Kent Miller (Ed.); Andrew Tilghman (Exec. Ed.); Michelle Tan (Mng. Ed.)
Parent company (for newspapers): Gannett

WASHINGTON

NORTHWEST AIRLIFTER

Street address 1: 8312 Custer Rd SW
Street address 3: Lakewood
Street address state: WA
Zip/Postal code: 98499-2526
County: Pierce
Country: USA
Mailing address: PO Box 98801
Mailing city: Lakewood
Mailing state: WA
Mailing zip: 98496-8801
General Phone: (253) 584-1212
General Fax: (253) 581-5962
Editorial e-mail: editor@ftlewisranger.com
Primary Website: www.ftlewisranger.com
Mechanical specifications: Type page 10 1/2 x 16; A - 7 cols, between; C - 8 cols, between.
Published: Thur
Avg Free Circ: 8200
Audit By: Sworn/Estimate/Non-Audited
Audit Date: 7/12/2019
Classified Equipment»
Personnel: Ken Swarner (Pub.); Bill White (Circ. Mgr.)

STEILACOOM

THE RANGER

Street address 1: 218 Wilkes St
Street address 3: Steilacoom
Street address state: WA
Zip/Postal code: 98388-2122
County: Pierce
Country: USA
Mailing address: 218 Wilkes
Mailing city: Steilacoom
Mailing state: WA
Mailing zip: 98388
General Phone: (253) 584-1212
General Fax: (253) 581-5962
Display Adv. E-mail: sales@northwestmilitary.com
Editorial e-mail: publisher@northwestmilitary.com
Primary Website: www.northwestmilitary.com
Year Established: 1951
Delivery Methods: Mail`Racks
Area Served - City: Pierce & Thurston counties
Advertising (Open Inch Rate) Weekday/Saturday: $85 a unit
Mechanical specifications: 24 units to the page. 4 units across by 6 units deep
Published: Thur
Avg Free Circ: 23000
Audit By: VAC
Audit Date: 6/30/2017
Classified Equipment»
Personnel: Bill White (Circ. Mgr.); Ken Swarner (Ed.); Diana Halstead (Prodn. Mgr.)

WYOMING

CHEYENNE

WARREN SENTINEL

Street address 1: 307 E 20th St
Street address 3: Cheyenne
Street address state: WY
Zip/Postal code: 82001-3705
County: Laramie
Country: USA
Mailing address: 307 E 20th St
Mailing city: Cheyenne
Mailing state: WY
Mailing zip: 82001-3705
General Phone: (307) 632-5666
General Fax: (307) 632-1554
General/National Adv. E-mail: graphics@warrensentinel.com
Display Adv. E-mail: ads@warrensentinel.com
Primary Website: www.warrensentinel.com
Own Printing Facility: Y
Advertising (Open Inch Rate) Weekday/Saturday: Open inch rate $9.00
Mechanical specifications: Type page 9 3/4 x 13; E - 6 cols, 1 1/2, 1/6 between; A - 6 cols, 1 1/2, 1/6 between; C - 6 cols, 1 1/2, 1/6 between.
Published: Fri
Avg Free Circ: 5200
Audit By: Sworn/Estimate/Non-Audited

Audit Date: 7/12/2019
Classified Equipment»

Personnel: Jim Wood (Pub.); Kelly Sebastian (Sales Mgr.); Barbara Coursey (Inside Adv. Sales); Monica Valdez (Prodn. Mgr./Graphics)

PARENTING PUBLICATION IN THE U.S.

ARIZONA

ARIZONA PARENTING

Street address 1: 4848 E Cactus Rd
Street address 2: Ste 110
Street address city: Scottsdale
Street address state: AZ
Zip/Postal code: 85254-4127
County: Maricopa
Published: Mthly
Avg Free Circ: 60000
Audit By: Sworn/Estimate/Non-Audited
Audit Date: 12.07.2019
Personnel: Todd Fisher (Pub.); Chris Neiman (Circ. Mgr.); Kimberley Fischer (Adv. Rep.); Todd Fischer (Ed.)

CALIFORNIA

BAY AREA PARENT

Street address 1: 901 Campisi Way
Street address 2: Ste 300
Street address city: Campbell
Street address state: CA
Zip/Postal code: 95008-2376
County: Santa Clara
Country: USA
Mailing address: 901 Campisi Way #300
Mailing city: Campbell
Mailing state: CA
Mailing zip: 95008-2087
General Phone: (408) 533-4413
General Fax: (408) 963-6124
General/National Adv. E-mail: dawn.hall@parenthood.com
Display Adv. E-mail: dawn.hall@parenthood.com
Editorial e-mail: jill.wolfson@parenthood.com
Primary Website: www.bayareaparent.com
Year Established: 1983
Published: Mthly
Published Other: Five print special editions plus 16 special digital-only magazines
Avg Paid Circ: 0
Avg Free Circ: 122000
Audit By: CVC
Audit Date: 12.12.2017
Personnel: Jill Wolfson (Editor); Daniel Payomo Jr (Group Publisher)

FAMILY-LIFE MAGAZINE

Street address 1: 134 Lystra Ct
Street address city: Santa Rosa
Street address state: CA
Zip/Postal code: 95403-8076
County: Sonoma
Country: USA
Mailing address: PO Box 351
Mailing city: Philo
Mailing state: CA
Mailing zip: 95466-0351
General Phone: (707) 305 1539
General Fax: (707) 895-2154
Advertising Phone: (707) 205-1539
Advertising Fax: (707) 586-9571
Editorial Phone: (707) 205-1544
Editorial Fax: (707) 586-9571
General/National Adv. E-mail: info@family-life.us
Display Adv. E-mail: Sales@family-life.us
Editorial e-mail: Editor@family-life.us
Primary Website: www.sonomafamilylife.com
Year Established: 1989
Published: Mthly
Published Other: Weekly E-newsletters.
Avg Free Circ: 46000
Audit By: VAC
Audit Date: 27.12.2012
Personnel: Sharon Gowan (Publisher/Editor)

KERN COUNTY FAMILY MAGAZINE

Street address 1: 1400 Easton Dr
Street address 2: Ste 112
Street address city: Bakersfield
Primary Website: www.kerncountyfamily.com
Year Established: 1996
Published: Mthly
Avg Paid Circ: 9
Avg Free Circ: 28207
Audit By: CVC
Audit Date: 31.12.2014
Personnel: L.J. Corby (Ed.)

LA PARENT MAGAZINE

Street address 1: PO Box 8275
Street address city: Calabasas
Street address state: CA
Zip/Postal code: 91372
General Phone: (818) 264-2222
Advertising Phone: Ext 221
Editorial Phone: Ext 222
General/National Adv. E-mail: ron.epstein@laparent,com
Display Adv. E-mail: ron.epstein@laparent,com
Editorial e-mail: cassandra.lane@laparent,com
Primary Website: www.laparent.com
Mthly Avg Views: 46000
Mthly Avg Unique Visitors: 25
Year Established: 1980
Published: Bi-Mthly
Avg Free Circ: 15000
Audit By: Sworn/Estimate/Non-Audited
Audit Date: 12.07.2019
Personnel: Elena Epstien (Creative Director); Christina Elston (Ed); Cassandra Lane (Editor in Chief)
Parent company (for newspapers): Epstein Custom Media Inc.

PARENTING MAGAZINE OF ORANGE COUNTY

Street address 1: 172 N Tustin St
Street address 2: Ste 304
Street address city: Orange
Street address state: CA
Zip/Postal code: 92867-7780
County: Orange
Published: Mthly
Avg Paid Circ: 108
Avg Free Circ: 80000
Audit By: Sworn/Estimate/Non-Audited
Audit Date: 12.07.2019
Personnel: Randall Tierney (Ed. in Chief); Bahram Fattahinia (Art Dir.)

PARENTS' PRESS

Street address 1: 875-A Island Dr. Ste 421
Street address city: Alameda
Street address state: CA
Zip/Postal code: 94502
Country: USA
Mailing address: 875-A Island Dr. Ste 421
Mailing city: Alameda
Mailing state: CA
Primary Website: www.parentspress.com
Year Established: 1980
Published: Mthly
Avg Free Circ: 62000
Audit By: CVC
Audit Date: 08.12.2014
Personnel: Tracy McKean (Pub.)

SACRAMENTO PARENT

Street address 1: 457 Grass Valley Hwy
Street address 2: Ste 5
Street address city: Auburn
Street address state: CA
Zip/Postal code: 95603-3725
County: Placer
Country: USA
Mailing address: 457 Grass Valley Hwy Ste 5
Mailing city: Auburn
Mailing state: CA
Primary Website: www.sacramentoparent.com
Year Established: 1992
Published: Mthly
Avg Free Circ: 44975
Audit By: CVC

SAN DIEGO FAMILY MAGAZINE

Street address 1: 1475 6th Ave
Street address 2: #500
Street address city: San Diego
Street address state: CA
Zip/Postal code: 92101-3245
County: San Diego
Country: USA
Mailing address: 1475 6th Ave, #500
Mailing city: San Diego
Mailing state: CA
Mailing zip: 92101
General/National Adv. E-mail: family@sandiegofamily.com
Display Adv. E-mail: sharon@sandiegofamily.com
Editorial e-mail: sharon@sandiegofamily.com
Primary Website: www.sandiegofamily.com
Year Established: 1982
Published: Mthly
Avg Paid Circ: 24
Avg Free Circ: 75000
Audit By: Sworn/Estimate/Non-Audited
Audit Date: 12.07.2019
Personnel: Sharon Bay (Pub); Michele Hancock (Mktg. Coord.)

SONOMA FAMILY-LIFE MAGAZINE

Street address 1: 100 Professional Center Dr
Street address 2: Ste 104
Street address city: Rohnert Park
Street address state: CA
Zip/Postal code: 94928-2137
County: Sonoma
Country: USA
Mailing address: PO Box 351
Mailing city: Philo
Published: Mthly
Avg Free Circ: 23000
Audit By: Sworn/Estimate/Non-Audited
Audit Date: 12.07.2019
Personnel: Sharon Gowan (Ed.)

THE PARENT CONNECTION/SCRIPPS MEMORIAL HOSPITAL

Street address 1: 4275 Campus Point Ct # CP10
Street address 2: Scripps Memorial Hospital
Street address city: San Diego
Street address state: CA
Zip/Postal code: 92121-1513
County: San Diego
Country: USA
Mailing address: 4275 Campus Pt. Ct. CP10
Mailing city: San Diego
General/National Adv. E-mail: info@sandiegoparent.com
Display Adv. E-mail: info@sandiegoparent.com
Primary Website: www.sandiegoparent.com
Year Established: 1980
Published: Mthly
Avg Paid Circ: 1500
Avg Free Circ: 1000
Audit By: Sworn/Estimate/Non-Audited
Audit Date: 12.07.2019
Personnel: Pam Nagata (Coord); Martha Stillwell (Adv. Mgr.); Alison Rob (Circ. Mgr.); Colleen McNatt (Ed.); Angel Salazar (Prodn. Mgr.)
Parent company (for newspapers): Parent Connection

COLORADO

COLORADO PARENT

Primary Website: www.coloradoparent.com
Mthly Avg Views: 20000
Mthly Avg Unique Visitors: 8000
Year Established: 1986
Published: Mthly
Avg Free Circ: 45133
Audit By: CVC
Audit Date: 30.06.2015
Personnel: Deborah Mock (Ed.); Christina Cook (Assoc. Ed.); Lydia Rueger (Copy Ed.); Heather Gott (Art Dir.)
Parent company (for newspapers): 5280 Publishing, Inc.

DALLASCHILD

Street address 1: 825 Laporte Ave
Street address 2: STE 146
Street address city: Fort Collins
Street address state: CO
Zip/Postal code: 80521-2520
County: Larimer
Country: USA
Mailing address: 4275 Kellway Cir Ste 146
Mailing city: Addison
Mailing state: TX
Mailing zip: 75001-5731
General Phone: (972) 447-9188
General Fax: (972) 447-0633
Advertising Phone: (972) 447-9188
Editorial Phone: (972) 447-9188
General/National Adv. E-mail: Joy@dfwchild.com
Display Adv. E-mail: advertising@dfwchild.com
Editorial e-mail: editorial@dfwchild.com
Primary Website: www.dfwchild.com
Year Established: 1986
Published: Mthly
Avg Free Circ: 60000
Audit By: CAC
Audit Date: 30.06.2017
Personnel: Joylyn Niebes (Pub.); Susan Horn (Prodn. Mgr.); Alison Davis (Sales Director); Lauren Niebes (Creative Director)
Parent company (for newspapers): Lauren Publications

CONNECTICUT

CONNECTICUT PARENT MAGAZINE

Street address 1: 420 E Main St
Street address 2: Ste 18
Street address city: Branford
Street address state: CT
Zip/Postal code: 06405-2942
County: New Haven
Country: USA
Mailing address: 420 E Main St Ste 18
Mailing city: Branford
Mailing state: CT
Mailing zip: 06405-2942
General Phone: (203) 483-1700
Advertising Fax: (203) 483-0522
General/National Adv. E-mail: joel.macclaren@ctparent.com
Display Adv. E-mail: joel.macclaren@ctparent.com
Editorial e-mail: editorial@ctparent.com
Primary Website: www.ctparent.com
Year Established: 1984
Published: Mthly
Avg Paid Circ: 0
Avg Free Circ: 47239
Audit By: Sworn/Estimate/Non-Audited
Audit Date: 12.07.2019
Personnel: Joel MacClaren (Ed./Pub.)
Parent company (for newspapers): Choice Media, LLC

FLORIDA

CINCINNATI PARENT

Street address 1: 1 Gannett Plaza
Street address city: Melbourne
Street address state: FL
Zip/Postal code: 32940
County: Brevard
Country: USA
Mailing address: 9435 Waterstone Blvd Ste 140
Mailing city: Cincinnati
Mailing state: OH
Mailing zip: 45249-8229
General Phone: (513) 444-2015
Advertising Phone: (317) 710-6622
Editorial Phone: (317) 722-8500, ext. 164
General/National Adv. E-mail: mary@cincinnatiparent.com
Display Adv. E-mail: mary@cincinnatiparent.com
Editorial e-mail: susan@cincinnatiparent.com
Primary Website: www.cincinnatiparent.com
Year Established: 1986
Published: Mthly
Avg Free Circ: 44000
Audit By: CVC
Audit Date: 01.07.2016
Personnel: Mary Wynne Cox (Publisher)
Parent company (for newspapers): Midwest Parenting Publications

FORT WORTH CHILD MAGAZINE

Street address 1: 6501 Nob Hill Rd
Street address city: Tamarac
Street address state: FL
Zip/Postal code: 33321-6422
County: Broward
Country: USA
Mailing address: 4275 Kellway Cir Ste 146
Mailing city: Addison
Mailing state: TX
Mailing zip: 75001-5731
General/National Adv. E-mail: support@dfwchild.com
Display Adv. E-mail: advertising@dfwchild.com
Editorial e-mail: editorial@dfwchild.com
Primary Website: www.dfwchild.com/fortworth
Year Established: 1992
Published: Mthly
Published Other: monthly
Avg Free Circ: 40000
Audit By: CVC
Audit Date: 30.06.2017
Personnel: Joylyn Niebes (Pub.); Susan Horn (Graphics Designer)
Parent company (for newspapers): Lauren Publications

GEORGIA

ATLANTA PARENT

Street address 1: 2346 Perimeter Park Dr
Street address 2: Ste 101
Street address city: Atlanta
Street address state: GA
Zip/Postal code: 30341-1319
County: Dekalb
Country: USA
Mailing address: 2346 Perimeter Park Dr Ste 101
Mailing city: Atlanta
Mailing state: GA
Mailing zip: 30341-1319
General/National Adv. E-mail: atlantaparent@atlantaparent.com
Display Adv. E-mail: calendar@atlantaparent.com; advertising@atlantaparent.com
Editorial e-mail: editor@atlantaparent.com
Published: Mthly
Avg Free Circ: 99900
Audit By: CVC
Audit Date: 30.06.2014
Personnel: Michelle McGunagle (Asst. Pub.); Amy Smith (Bus. Devel. Mgr.); Liz White (Adv. Sales Dir.); Kate Parrott (Mng. Ed.); Neal Wilkes (Prodn. Mgr.)

GEORGIA FAMILY MAGAZINE

Street address 1: 523 Sioux Dr
Street address city: Macon
Street address state: GA
Zip/Postal code: 31210-4217
County: Bibb
Country: USA
Mailing address: 523 Sioux Dr
Mailing city: Macon
Mailing state: GA
Mailing zip: 31210-4217
General Phone: (478) 471-7393
Advertising Phone: (478) 471-7393
Editorial Phone: 478 471-7393
General/National Adv. E-mail: publisher@georgiafamily.com
Display Adv. E-mail: publisher@georgiafamily.com
Editorial e-mail: editorial.gfm@gmail.com
Primary Website: www.GeorgiaFamily.com
Year Established: 1992
Published: Mthly
Published Other: Monthly
Avg Paid Circ: 105
Avg Free Circ: 55000
Audit By: CVC
Audit Date: 30.06.2011
Personnel: Olya Fessard (Ed. in Chief); Veronique Saiya (Mng. Ed.)

HAWAII

ISLAND FAMILY

Street address 1: 1000 Bishop St
Street address 2: Ste 405
Street address city: Honolulu
Street address state: HI
Zip/Postal code: 96813-4204
County: Honolulu
Country: USA
Mailing address: 1000 Bishop St.
Mailing city: Honolulu
Mailing state: HI
Mailing zip: 96813
General Phone: (808) 534-7544
General Fax: (808) 537-6455
Advertising Phone: (808) 534-7501
Editorial Phone: (808) 534-7105
General/National Adv. E-mail: chuckt@pacificbasin.net
Display Adv. E-mail: Donnaky@honolulumagazine.com
Editorial e-mail: Christiy@honolulufamily.com
Published: Mthly
Avg Free Circ: 40000
Audit By: Sworn/Estimate/Non-Audited
Audit Date: 12.07.2019
Personnel: Lennie Omalza (Adv. Mgr.); Helen McNeil (Ed.)

ILLINOIS

CHICAGO PARENT

Street address 1: 141 S Oak Park Ave
Street address city: Oak Park
Street address state: IL
Zip/Postal code: 60302-2972
County: Cook
Country: USA
Mailing address: 141 S Oak Park Ave Ste 1
Mailing city: Oak Park
Mailing state: IL
Primary Website: www.chicagoparent.com
Year Established: 1984
Published: Mthly
Avg Paid Circ: 13
Avg Free Circ: 125000
Audit By: Sworn/Estimate/Non-Audited
Audit Date: 12.07.2019
Personnel: Dan Haley (Pub.); Kathy Hansen (Circ. Mgr.); Tamara O'Shaughnessy (Ed.)

INDIANA

INDY'S CHILD

Street address 1: 6340 E Westfield Blvd
Street address 2: Ste 200
Street address city: Indianapolis
Street address state: IN
Zip/Postal code: 46220-1746
County: Marion
Country: USA
Mailing address: 6340 Westfield Blvd.
Mailing city: Indianapolis
Mailing state: IN
Mailing zip: 48220
General/National Adv. E-mail: indyschild@indyschild.com
Editorial e-mail: susan@indyschild.com
Primary Website: www.indyschild.com
Mthly Avg Views: 180876
Mthly Avg Unique Visitors: 8705
Year Established: 1984
Published: Wed'Mthly
Avg Paid Circ: 0
Avg Free Circ: 45278
Audit By: Sworn/Estimate/Non-Audited
Audit Date: 12.07.2019
Personnel: Mary Cox (Pub.); Roxanne Burns (Circ. Mgr.); Mike Hussey (Adv. Mgr.); Lynette Rowland (Ed.)
Parent company (for newspapers): Midwest Parenting Publications

KANSAS

NEW YORK FAMILY

Street address 1: 11936 W 119th St
Street address 2: Ste 335
Street address city: Overland Park
Street address state: KS
Zip/Postal code: 66213-2216
County: Johnson
Personnel: Cate Sanderson (Pub.); Sherine R. Chenault-Usher (Adv. Coord.); Thomas Butcher (Circ. Mgr.); Heather Hart (Sr. Ed.); Larissa Phillips (Ed.); Carolyn Rogalsky (Calendar Ed.)

KENTUCKY

LEXINGTON FAMILY MAGAZINE

Street address 1: 138 E Reynolds Rd
Street address 2: Ste 201
Street address city: Lexington
Street address state: KY
Zip/Postal code: 40517-1259
County: Fayette
Country: USA
Primary Website: www.lexingtonfamily.com
Year Established: 1996
Published: Mthly
Avg Free Circ: 28539
Audit By: CVC
Audit Date: 30.06.2015
Personnel: Dana Tackett (Pub.); Karyn Potts (Adv. Rep.); John Lynch (Ed.)

TODAY'S FAMILY

Street address 1: 9750 Ormsby Station Rd
Street address 2: Ste 307
Street address city: Louisville
Street address state: KY
Zip/Postal code: 40223-4064
County: Jefferson
Country: USA
Mailing address: 9750 Ormsby Station Rd Ste 307
Mailing city: Louisville
Mailing state: KY
Mailing zip: 40223-4064
General Phone: (502) 327-8855
Advertising Phone: (502) 327-8855
Editorial Phone: (502) 327-8855
General/National Adv. E-mail: info@todaysmedianow.com
Display Adv. E-mail: advertising@todaysmedianow.com
Editorial e-mail: editor@todaysmedianow.com
Primary Website: www.todaysfamilynow.com
Year Established: 1982
Published: Other
Published Other: Semi-Annual -- Spring & Fall
Avg Free Circ: 34975
Audit By: CVC
Audit Date: 30.06.2018
Personnel: Cathy Zion (Owner/Pub); Anita Oldham (Ed.); Susan Allen (Ad. Dir.)
Parent company (for newspapers): Zion Publications, LLC

CHESAPEAKE FAMILY LIFE

Street address 1: 121 Cathedral St
Street address 2: #3A
Street address city: Annapolis
Street address state: MD
Zip/Postal code: 21401-2777
County: Anne Arundel
Country: USA
Mailing address: 13 Southgate Ave
Mailing city: Annapolis
General/National Adv. E-mail: dj@jecoannapolis.com
Display Adv. E-mail: dj@jecoannapolis.com
Editorial e-mail: editor@chesapeakefamily.com
Primary Website: www.chesapeakefamily.com
Mthly Avg Views: 50000
Mthly Avg Unique Visitors: 45000
Year Established: 1990
Published: Mthly
Avg Free Circ: 34641
Audit By: Sworn/Estimate/Non-Audited
Audit Date: 12.07.2019
Personnel: Donna Jefferson (Publisher); Jeanne Slaughter (Mktg. Mgr.); Kristen Page-Kirby (Ed.)
Parent company (for newspapers): Jefferson Communications

MARYLAND FAMILY MAGAZINE

Street address 1: 409 Washington Ave
Street address 2: Ste 400
Street address city: Towson
Street address state: MD
Zip/Postal code: 21204-4919
County: Baltimore
Published: Bi-Mthly
Avg Paid Circ: 0
Avg Free Circ: 43645
Audit By: CAC
Audit Date: 31.03.2015
Personnel: Cheryl Clemens (Ed.); Kristine Henry (Ed.)

PARENT LINE

Street address 1: 11135 Beacon Way
Street address city: Lusby
Street address state: MD
Zip/Postal code: 20657-2449
County: Calvert
Published: Mthly
Avg Free Circ: 25000
Audit By: Sworn/Estimate/Non-Audited
Audit Date: 12.07.2019
Personnel: Kelly Wilder (Pub.)

WASHINGTON FAMILY MAGAZINE

Street address 1: 11900 Parklawn Dr.
Street address 2: Ste. 300
Street address city: Rockville
Street address state: MD
Zip/Postal code: 20852
Country: USA
Mailing address: 11900 Parklawn Dr., Ste. 300
Mailing city: Rockville
Mailing state: MD
Mailing zip: 20852
General Phone: (301) 230-2222
Advertising Phone: (301) 230-0819
Editorial Phone: (301) 230-6696
General/National Adv. E-mail: info@washingtonfamily.com
Display Adv. E-mail: advertising@washingtonfamily.com
Editorial e-mail: editor@washingtonfamily.com
Primary Website: www.washingtonfamily.com

Year Established: 1992
Published: Mthly
Avg Paid Circ: 7
Avg Free Circ: 53500
Audit By: CVC
Audit Date: 31.03.2017
Personnel: Craig Burke (Chief Operating Officer); Sylvia Witaschek (Assoc. Pub.)
Parent company (for newspapers): Northern Virginia Media Services

WASHINGTON PARENT MAGAZINE

Street address 1: 4701 Sangamore Rd
Street address 2: Ste N270
Street address city: Bethesda
Street address state: MD
Zip/Postal code: 20816-2528
County: Montgomery
Country: USA
Mailing address: 5825 Highland Dr
Mailing city: Chevy Chase
Mailing state: MD
Primary Website: www.washingtonparent.com
Year Established: 1996
Published: Mthly
Avg Paid Circ: 36
Avg Free Circ: 66939
Audit By: CVC
Audit Date: 30.06.2012
Personnel: Deborah Benke (Pub.); Mary Fran Gildea (Adv. Mgr.); George Benke (Circ. Mgr.); Margaret Hut (Ed.); Jane MacNealy (Prodn. Mgr.)

MICHIGAN

METRO PARENT MAGAZINE

Street address 1: 22041 Woodward Ave
Street address city: Ferndale
Street address state: MI
Zip/Postal code: 48220-2520
County: Oakland
Country: USA
Mailing address: 22041 Woodward Ave
Mailing city: Ferndale
Published: Mthly
Avg Free Circ: 59753
Audit By: CVC
Audit Date: 30.06.2015
Personnel: Alyssa Martina (Pub.); Alexis Bourkoulas (Gen. Mgr.); Tracy Connelly (Office Mgr.); Ruth Robbins (Assoc. Pub.); Julia Elliott (Ed.)

MISSOURI

PARENT TO PARENT

Street address 1: 2464 Taylor Rd
Street address 2: Ste 131
Street address city: Wildwood
Street address state: MO
Zip/Postal code: 63040-1222
County: St. Louis
Country: USA
Mailing address: 2464 Taylor Rd Ste 131
Mailing city: Wildwood
Mailing state: MO
Mailing zip: 63040-1222
General/National Adv. E-mail: editor@parenttoparent.com
Editorial e-mail: emparenttoparent@gmail.com
Primary Website: www.parenttoparent.com
Year Established: 1996
Personnel: Jodie Lynn (Owner); Kyle Johnson (Personal Assistant Assistant Editor)

SAVVY FAMILY

Street address 1: 14522 S Outer 40 Rd
Street address city: Chesterfield
Personnel: Mary Ann Wagner (Pub.)

NEW HAMPSHIRE

PARENTING NEW HAMPSHIRE

Street address 1: 150 Dow St
Street address city: Manchester
Street address state: NH
Zip/Postal code: 03101-1227
County: Hillsborough
Country: USA
Mailing address: 150 Dow St Ste 202
Mailing city: Manchester
Mailing state: NH
Mailing zip: 03101-1227
General Phone: (603) 624-1310
Primary Website: http://www.parentingnh.com/
Year Established: 1993
Published: Mthly
Avg Free Circ: 27303
Audit By: CVC
Audit Date: 30.06.2005
Personnel: Sharron Mccarthy (Pub.); David Kruger (Adv. Dir.); Shannon Spiliotis (Circ. Mgr.); Melanie Hitchcock (Ed.)

NEW JERSEY

KANSAS CITY PARENT

Street address 1: 1122 US Highway 22
Street address city: Mountainside
Street address state: NJ
Zip/Postal code: 07092-2812
County: Union
Country: USA
Mailing address: 11936 W 119th St Ste 335
Mailing city: Overland Park
Mailing state: KS
Mailing zip: 66213-2216
General/National Adv. E-mail: kcparent@mindspring.com
Display Adv. E-mail: advertising@kcparent.com
Editorial e-mail: editor@kcparent.com
Primary Website: www.kcparent.com
Year Established: 1985
Published: Mthly
Avg Free Circ: 26200
Audit By: CVC
Audit Date: 30.06.2014
Personnel: L. Richard Bruursema (Pub.)

MORRIS COUNTY FAMILY

Street address 1: 480 Morris Ave.
Street address city: Summit
Street address state: NJ
Zip/Postal code: 07901
Country: USA
Mailing address: 480 Morris Ave.
Mailing city: Summit
General/National Adv. E-mail: publisher@njfamily.com
Editorial e-mail: editor@njfamily.com
Published: Mthly
Avg Free Circ: 30000
Audit By: Sworn/Estimate/Non-Audited
Audit Date: 12.07.2019
Personnel: Cindy Mironovich (Pub.); Mary Lucid (Bus. Mgr.); Linda Galli (Dir., Adv.); Dina El Nabli (Ed. Dir.); Angel Madison (Mng. Ed.)

NEW JERSEY FAMILY

Street address 1: 1122 Rt. 22 W.
Street address city: Mountainside
Street address state: NJ
Zip/Postal code: 07092-2812
Country: USA
Mailing address: 1122 US Highway 22 Ste 204
Mailing city: Mountainside
Mailing state: NJ
Mailing zip: 07092-2813
General/National Adv. E-mail: publisher@njfamily.com
Editorial e-mail: editor@njfamily.com
Primary Website: www.njfamily.com
Year Established: 1991
Published: Mthly
Avg Free Circ: 126000
Audit By: Sworn/Estimate/Non-Audited
Audit Date: 12.07.2019
Personnel: Cindy Mironovich (Pub.); Bonnie Vohden (Assoc. Pub.); Linda Galli (Dir., Adv.); Farn Dupre (Ed.); Lucy Banta (Mng. Ed.)

NEW JERSEY FAMILY

Street address 1: 480 Morris Ave
Street address city: Summit
Street address state: NJ
Zip/Postal code: 07901-1523
County: Union
Country: USA
Mailing address: 480 Morris Ave.
Mailing city: Summit
Mailing state: NJ
Mailing zip: 07901
General Phone: 9082771919
General Fax: 9082771977
Advertising Phone: 9082771919x110
Editorial Phone: 9082771919
General/National Adv. E-mail: publisher@njfamily.com
Display Adv. E-mail: sales@njfamily.com
Editorial e-mail: dina@njfamily.com
Primary Website: www.njfamily.com
Year Established: 1990
Published: Mthly
Avg Paid Circ: 8
Avg Free Circ: 134221
Audit By: CVC
Audit Date: 30.06.2017
Personnel: Cindy Mironovich (Co-Pub.); Mary Lucid (Bus. Mgr.); Marcy Holeton (Advertising Director); Dina El Nabli (Editorial Director)

NEW YORK

CAPITAL DISTRICT PARENT

Street address 1: 595 New Loudon Rd
Street address 2: Ste 102
Street address city: Latham
Street address state: NY
Zip/Postal code: 12110-4063
County: Albany
Country: USA
Mailing address: 595 New Loudon Rd Ste 102
Mailing city: Latham
Mailing state: NY
Personnel: Terrie Goldstein (Adv. Mgr.); Leah Black (Ed.); Lisa Jabbour (Art Dir.)

CONNECTICUT FAMILY

Street address 1: 141 Halstead Ave
Street address 2: Ste 3D
Street address city: Mamaroneck
Street address state: NY
Zip/Postal code: 10543-2607
County: Westchester
Personnel: Thomas Butcher (Circ. Mgr.); Heather Hart (Ed.)

HUDSON VALLEY PARENT

Street address 1: 174 South St
Street address city: Newburgh
Street address state: NY
Zip/Postal code: 12550-4546
County: Orange
Country: USA
Mailing address: 174 South St
Mailing city: Newburgh
Mailing state: NY
Mailing zip: 12550-4546
General/National Adv. E-mail: publisher@excitingread.com
Display Adv. E-mail: sales@excitingread.com
Editorial e-mail: editor@excitingread.com
Primary Website: www.hvparent.com
Year Established: 1994
Published: Mthly
Avg Free Circ: 36000
Audit By: Sworn/Estimate/Non-Audited
Audit Date: 12.07.2019
Personnel: Terrie Goldstein (Pub.); Felicia Hodges (Editor)

NEW YORK PARENTING - BROOKLYN FAMILY/MANHATTAN FAMILY/QUEENS FAMILY/BRONX-RIVERDALE FAMILY/WESTCHESTER FAMILY

Street address 1: 1 Metrotech Ctr N
Street address 2: Fl 10
Street address city: Brooklyn
Street address state: NY
Zip/Postal code: 11201-3875
County: Kings
Country: USA
Mailing address: 1 Metrotech Ctr N Fl 10
Mailing city: Brooklyn
Mailing state: NY
Mailing zip: 11201-3875
General Phone: (718) 260-4554
General Fax: (718) 260-2568
Advertising Phone: (718) 260-4554
Editorial Phone: (718) 260-2587
General/National Adv. E-mail: Susank@NYParenting.com
Display Adv. E-mail: Family@NYParenting.com
Editorial e-mail: Susan@NYParenting.com
Primary Website: www.nyparenting.com
Year Established: 1999
Published: Mthly
Published Other: Special Child magazines - Bi-Annual
Avg Free Circ: 167500
Audit By: CVC
Audit Date: 30.06.2017
Personnel: Susan Weiss (Publisher/Exec. Editor); Clifford Luster (Pub./Bus. Mgr.); Vincent Dimecili (Ed.)
Parent company (for newspapers): CNG

NY METRO PARENTS

Street address 1: 498 Seventh Avenue, 10th Floor
Street address city: New York
Street address state: NY
Zip/Postal code: 10018
County: New York
Country: USA
Mailing address: 498 Seventh Avenue, 10th Floor
Mailing city: New York
Mailing state: NY
Mailing zip: 10018-2385
General Phone: (212) 315-0800
General Fax: (212) 271-2239
Advertising Phone: (212) 315-0800
Editorial Phone: (646) 652-7516
Editorial Fax: (212) 271-2239
General/National Adv. E-mail: info@nymetroparents.com
Display Adv. E-mail: info@nymetroparents.com
Editorial e-mail: dskolnik@davlermedia.com
Primary Website: www.nymetroparents.com
Year Established: 1985
Published: Mthly
Avg Paid Circ: 0
Avg Free Circ: 335000
Audit By: CVC
Audit Date: 15.10.2017
Personnel: David Miller (CEO)
Parent company (for newspapers): Davler Media Group

SPACE COAST PARENT

Street address 1: 498 Seventh Ave, 10th Floor
Street address city: New York
Street address state: NY
Zip/Postal code: 10018
County: New York
Country: USA
Mailing address: 1 Gannett Plaza
Mailing city: Melbourne
Published: Mthly
Avg Free Circ: 29950
Audit By: Sworn/Estimate/Non-Audited
Audit Date: 12.07.2019

Personnel: Ann Greeville (Adv. Mgr.); Kim Lyons (Adv. Mgr.); Sharon Kindred (Ed.); Corinne Ishler (Prodn. Mgr.)

SYRACUSE PARENT

Street address 1: 5910 Firestone Dr
Street address city: Syracuse
Street address state: NY
Zip/Postal code: 13206-1103
County: Onondaga
Country: USA
Mailing address: 5910 Firestone Dr
Mailing city: Syracuse
Mailing state: NY
Mailing zip: 13206-1103
General/National Adv. E-mail: syracuseparent@yahoo.com
Editorial e-mail: editor@syracuseparent.net
Published: Mthly
Avg Free Circ: 26500
Audit By: Sworn/Estimate/Non-Audited
Audit Date: 12.07.2019
Personnel: Linda Tocci (Adv. Mgr.); Colleen Kompf (Adv. Sales); Rachel Gillette (Prodn. Mgr.)

WESTCHESTER FAMILY

Street address 1: 1872 Pleasantville Road, Suite 173
Street address city: Braircliff Manor
Street address state: NY
Zip/Postal code: 10510
County: Westchester
Country: USA
Mailing address: 1872 Pleasantville Road
Mailing city: Braircliff Manor
Published: Mthly
Avg Paid Circ: 0
Avg Free Circ: 35000
Audit By: Sworn/Estimate/Non-Audited
Audit Date: 12.07.2019
Personnel: Jean Sheff (Ed./Co-Pub)

WESTCHESTER PARENT

Street address 1: 1872 Pleasantville Rd
Street address 2: Ste 173
Street address city: Briarcliff Manor
Street address state: NY
Zip/Postal code: 10510-1051
County: Westchester
Published: Mthly
Avg Free Circ: 55004
Audit By: CVC
Audit Date: 30.06.2014
Personnel: David Miller (Pub.); Phyllis Singer (Ed. Dir.); Christine Tarulli (Mng. Ed.)

WESTERN NEW YORK FAMILY

Street address 1: 3147 Delaware Ave
Street address 2: Ste B
Street address city: Buffalo
Street address state: NY
Zip/Postal code: 14217-2002
County: Erie
Country: USA
Mailing address: 3147 Delaware Ave Ste B
Mailing city: Buffalo
Mailing state: NY
Mailing zip: 14217-2002
General/National Adv. E-mail: feedback@wnyfamilymagazine.com
Display Adv. E-mail: advertising@wnyfamilymagazine.com
Editorial e-mail: michele@wnyfamilymagazine.com
Primary Website: www.wnyfamilymagazine.com
Year Established: 1984
Published: Mthly
Avg Paid Circ: 0
Avg Free Circ: 20000
Audit By: CVC
Audit Date: 30.06.2017
Personnel: Michele Miller (Editor & Publisher)

NORTH CAROLINA

CAROLINA PARENT

Street address 1: 5716 Fayetteville Rd.
Street address 2: Suite 201
Street address city: Durham
Street address state: NC
Zip/Postal code: 27713
County: Westchester
Country: USA
Mailing address: 5716 Fayetteville Rd., Suite 201
Mailing city: Durham
Mailing state: NC
Mailing zip: 27713
General/National Adv. E-mail: info@carolinaparent.com
Display Adv. E-mail: cgriffin@carolinaparent.com
Editorial e-mail: bshugg@carolinaparent.com
Primary Website: www.carolinaparent.com
Year Established: 1988
Published: Mthly
Avg Free Circ: 37044
Audit By: CVC
Audit Date: 30.06.2015
Personnel: Julianne Clune (Adv. Serv. Coor.); Beth Shugg (Ed.); Katie Reeves (Pub.); Lauren Isaacs (Dig & Social Media Specialist); Janice Lewine (Assoc. Ed.)
Parent company (for newspapers): Morris Media Network/Morris Visitor Publications

CHARLOTTE PARENT

Street address 1: 214 W Tremont Ave
Street address 2: Ste 302
Street address city: Charlotte
Street address state: NC
Zip/Postal code: 28203-5161
County: Mecklenburg
Country: USA
Mailing address: 214 W Tremont Ave Ste 302
Mailing city: Charlotte
Mailing state: NC
Mailing zip: 28203-5161
General Phone: (704) 344-1980
General Fax: (704) 344-1983
Advertising Phone: (704) 248-5221
Editorial Phone: (704) 248-5225
General/National Adv. E-mail: info@charlotteparent.com; promo@charlotteparent.com
Display Adv. E-mail: advertising@charlotteparent.com
Editorial e-mail: editor@charlotteparent.com
Primary Website: www.charlotteparent.com
Year Established: 1987
Published: Mthly
Avg Paid Circ: 0
Avg Free Circ: 39900
Audit By: CVC
Audit Date: 30.06.2015
Personnel: Michelle Huggins (Ed.); Allison Hollins (Dig. Dir.)

PIEDMONT PARENT

Street address 1: PO Box 530
Street address city: King
Street address state: NC
Zip/Postal code: 27021-0530
County: Stokes
Country: USA
Mailing address: PO Box 530
Mailing city: King
Published: Mthly
Avg Paid Circ: 1
Avg Free Circ: 30766
Audit By: CVC
Audit Date: 30.09.2014
Personnel: Sharon Havranek (Pub.); Myra Wrigh (Ed.)

SOUTH FLORIDA PARENTING MAGAZINE

Street address 1: 5716 Fayetteville Rd
Street address 2: Ste 201
Street address city: Durham
Street address state: NC
Zip/Postal code: 27713-9662
County: Durham
Country: USA
Mailing address: 6501 Nob Hill Rd
Mailing city: Tamarac
Published: Mthly
Avg Free Circ: 91546
Audit By: CVC
Audit Date: 31.12.2012
Personnel: Lisa Goodlin (Pub.); Angela Bartolone (Adv. Mgr.)
Parent company (for newspapers): Forum Publishing Group

OHIO

ANN ARBOR FAMILY PRESS

Street address 1: 1120 Adams St
Street address city: Toledo
Street address state: OH
Zip/Postal code: 43604-5509
County: Lucas
Country: USA
Mailing address: 1120 Adams St
Mailing city: Toledo
Mailing state: OH
Mailing zip: 43604-5509
General/National Adv. E-mail: cjacobs@adamsstreetpublishing.com
Display Adv. E-mail: sales@adamsstreetpublishing.com
Editorial e-mail: editor@adamsstreetpublishing.com
Primary Website: www.annarborfamily.com
Year Established: 1998
Published: Mthly
Avg Paid Circ: 0
Avg Free Circ: 21708
Audit By: CVC
Audit Date: 16.03.2013
Personnel: Robin Armstrong (Accounting); Collette Jacobs (Ed. in Chief)
Parent company (for newspapers): Adams Street Publishing Co.

COLUMBUS PARENT

Street address 1: 62 E. Broad St.
Street address city: Columbus
Street address state: OH
Zip/Postal code: 43215
General Phone: (614) 461-8878
Advertising Phone: (614) 461-8878
Editorial Phone: (614) 461-8878
General/National Adv. E-mail: contact@columbusparent.com
Display Adv. E-mail: advertise@columbusparent.com
Classified Adv. e-mail: advertise@columbusparent.com
Editorial e-mail: contact@columbusparent.com
Primary Website: www.columbusparent.com
Year Established: 1989
Published: Other
Published Other: quarterly in print, updated regularly online
Avg Free Circ: 26000
Audit By: CVC
Personnel: Rheta Gallagher (Assoc. Pub.); Ray Paprocki (Publisher); Julanne Hohbach (Ed.)

LAKE COUNTY KIDS

Street address 1: 7085 Mentor Ave
Street address city: Willoughby
Street address state: OH
Zip/Postal code: 44094-7948
County: Lake
Country: USA
Mailing address: 7085 Mentor Ave.
Mailing city: Willoughby
Mailing state: OH
Mailing zip: 44094
General Phone: (440) 951-0000
General Fax: (440) 951-0917
General/National Adv. E-mail: countykids@news-herald.com
Editorial e-mail: tambrose@news-herald.com
Published: Mthly
Avg Free Circ: 13000
Audit By: Sworn/Estimate/Non-Audited
Audit Date: 12.07.2019
Personnel: Steve Roszczyk (Pub.); Rachel DiBiasio (Gen. Mgr.); Tricia Ambrose (Ed.)

MAHONING VALLEY PARENT MAGAZINE

Street address 1: 240 Franklin St SE
Street address city: Warren
Street address state: OH
Zip/Postal code: 44483-5711
County: Trumbull
Country: USA
Mailing address: 240 Franklin St SE
Mailing city: Warren
Mailing state: OH
Mailing zip: 44483-5711
General Phone: (330) 629-6229
General/National Adv. E-mail: editor@mvparentmagazine.com
Display Adv. E-mail: advertising@forparentsonline.com
Editorial e-mail: editor@mvparentmagazine.com
Primary Website: www.forparentsonline.com
Year Established: 1989
Published: Mthly
Avg Free Circ: 36830
Audit By: CVC
Audit Date: 30.06.2012
Personnel: Robert Kurtz (Adv. Sales); Amy Leigh Wilson (Ed.)
Parent company (for newspapers): Ogden Newspapers Inc.

ROCKY MOUNTAIN PARENT MAGAZINE

Street address 1: 224 S Market St
Street address city: Troy
Street address state: OH

OKLAHOMA

METROFAMILY MAGAZINE

Street address 1: 318 NW 13th St
Street address 2: Ste 101
Street address city: Oklahoma City
Street address state: OK
Zip/Postal code: 73103-3709
County: Oklahoma
Country: USA
Mailing address: 318 NW 13th Street
Mailing city: Oklahoma City
Mailing state: OK
Mailing zip: 73103-3709
General/National Adv. E-mail: sarah@metrofamilymagazine.com
Display Adv. E-mail: sarah@metrofamilymagazine.com
Editorial e-mail: hannah@metrofamilymagazine.com
Primary Website: www.metrofamilymagazine.com
Year Established: 1998
Published: Mthly
Avg Paid Circ: 20
Avg Free Circ: 30000
Audit By: CVC
Audit Date: 30.09.2018
Personnel: Kathy Alberty (Dist. Mgr.); Sarah Taylor (Publisher); Hannah Schmitt (Editor)

TULSAKIDS

Street address 1: 1622 S Denver Ave
Street address city: Tulsa
Personnel: Chuck Foshee (Pub.); Betty Casey (Mng. Ed.)

OREGON

OREGON FAMILY MAGAZINE

Street address 1: PO Box 21732
Street address city: Eugene
Street address state: OR
Zip/Postal code: 97402-0411
County: Lane
Country: USA

Mailing address: PO Box 21732
Mailing city: Eugene
Mailing state: OR
Mailing zip: 97402-0411
General Phone: (541) 683-7452
Advertising Phone: (541) 683-7452
Editorial Phone: (541) 683-7452
General/National Adv. E-mail: info@oregonfamily.com
Display Adv. E-mail: sandy@oregonfamily.com
Editorial e-mail: info@oregonfamily.com
Primary Website: www.oregonfamily.com
Mthly Avg Views: 1500
Year Established: 1994
Published: Mthly
Avg Paid Circ: 0
Avg Free Circ: 8000
Audit By: Sworn/Estimate/Non-Audited
Audit Date: 12.07.2019
Personnel: Sandra Kauten (Owner/Publisher); Christi Kessler (Advt Acct Mgr)
Parent company (for newspapers): Pacific Parents Publishing

PENNSYLVANIA

ABOUT FAMILIES PARENTING NEWSPAPER

Street address 1: 100 E Cumberland St
Street address city: Lebanon
Street address state: PA
Zip/Postal code: 17042-5400
County: Lebanon
Country: USA
Mailing address: PO Box 840
Editorial e-mail: editor@aboutfamiliespa.com
Primary Website: www.aboutfamiliespa.com
Year Established: 1995
Published: Mthly
Avg Free Circ: 42390
Audit By: CVC
Audit Date: 31.03.2015
Personnel: Judy Fetterolf (Publication Coord.); James Snyder (Adv. Mgr.); Susan Zeller (Ed.)

BALTIMORE'S CHILD

Street address 1: 1414 Pine St
Street address city: Philadelphia
Street address state: PA
Zip/Postal code: 19102-4603
County: Philadelphia
Country: USA
Mailing address: 11 Dutton Ct
Mailing city: Baltimore
Mailing state: MD
Primary Website: www.baltimoreschild.com
Year Established: 1983
Published: Mthly
Avg Free Circ: 45000
Audit By: Sworn/Estimate/Non-Audited
Audit Date: 12.07.2019
Personnel: Joanne Giza (Pub.); Sharon Keech (Mng. Ed.); Jen Perkins Frantz (Prodn. Mgr.)

CENTRAL PENN PARENT

Street address 1: 1500 Paxton St
Street address city: Harrisburg
Street address state: PA
Zip/Postal code: 17104-2615
County: Dauphin
Country: USA
Mailing address: 1500 Paxton St
Mailing city: Harrisburg
Mailing state: PA
Mailing zip: 17104-2615
General Phone: (717) 236-4300
Editorial Fax: (717) 909-0538
General/National Adv. E-mail: annas@journalpub.com
Editorial e-mail: editor@centralpennparent.com
Primary Website: www.centralpennparent.com
Year Established: 1996
Published: Mthly
Avg Paid Circ: 0
Avg Free Circ: 40325
Audit By: CVC
Audit Date: 01.06.2012
Personnel: ShaunJude McCoach (Pub.); Carley Lucas (Adv. Acct. Exec.); Leslie Penkunas (Ed.); Tracy Bumba (Aud. Dev. Mgr.)

METROKIDS DELAWARE

Street address 1: 1412-1414 Pine St
Street address city: Philadelphia
Street address state: PA
Zip/Postal code: 19102
County: Philadelphia
Country: USA
Mailing address: 1412-1414 Pine St.
Mailing city: Philadelphia
Mailing state: PA
Mailing zip: 19102-4603
General/National Adv. E-mail: info@metrokids.com
Display Adv. E-mail: sales@metrokids.com
Personnel: Darlene Weinmann (Adv. Mgr.); Andrea Spiegel (Circ. Mgr.); Nancy Lisagor (Ed. in Chief); Tom Livingston (Exec. Ed.); Tracie Rucker (Prod. Mgr.)

METROKIDS SOUTH JERSEY

Street address 1: 1412-1414 Pine St
Street address city: Philadelphia
Street address state: PA
Zip/Postal code: 19102
County: Philadelphia
Country: USA
Mailing address: 1412-1414 Pine St.
Mailing city: Philadelphia
Mailing state: PA
Personnel: Darlene Weinmann (Adv. Mgr.); Andrea Miller (Circ. Mgr.); Nancy Lisagor (Ed. in Chief); Tom Livingston (Exec. Ed.); Tracie Rucker (Prod. Mgr.)

MID-ATLANTIC COMMUNITY PAPERS ASSOCIATION

Street address 1: 16515 Pottsville Pike
Street address 2: Suite C
Street address city: Hamburg
Street address state: PA
Zip/Postal code: 19526
County: Berks
Country: USA
Mailing address: PO Box 408
Mailing city: Hamburg
General/National Adv. E-mail: info@macpa.net
Display Adv. E-mail: Info@macnetonline.com
Primary Website: www.macpa.net
Mthly Avg Views: 3000000
Mthly Avg Unique Visitors: 800000
Year Established: 1955
Published: Mon`Tues`Wed`Thur`Fri`Sat`Sun`Mthly
Avg Free Circ: 1200000
Audit By: CVC
Audit Date: 01.01.2021
Personnel: Alyse Mitten (Exec. Dir.)

PITTSBURGH PARENT

Street address 1: 1126 Pittsburgh Rd
Street address 2: # RT8
Street address city: Valencia
Street address state: PA
Zip/Postal code: 16059-1930
County: Butler
Country: USA
Mailing address: PO Box 674
Mailing city: Valencia
Mailing state: PA
Mailing zip: 16059-0674
General/National Adv. E-mail: manager@pittsburghparent.com
Display Adv. E-mail: manager@pittsburghparent.com
Editorial e-mail: editor@pittsburghparent.com
Primary Website: www.pittsburghparent.com
Year Established: 1988
Published: Mthly
Avg Paid Circ: 32
Avg Free Circ: 45728
Audit By: VAC
Audit Date: 30.09.2016
Personnel: Lynn Honeywill (Circ. Mgr.)
Parent company (for newspapers): Honey Hill Publishing

SOUTH JERSEY PARENTS EXPRESS

Street address 1: 290 Commerce Dr
Street address city: Fort Washington
Street address state: PA
Zip/Postal code: 19034-2400
Personnel: John Bell (Adv. Mgr.); Daniel Kaye (Ed.)

SOUTH DAKOTA

LOWCOUNTRY PARENT MAGAZINE

Street address 1: 134 Columbus St
Street address city: Charleston
Street address state: SC
Zip/Postal code: 29403-4809
County: Charleston
Country: USA
Mailing address: 134 Columbus St
Mailing city: Charleston
Mailing state: SC
Mailing zip: 29403-4809
General Phone: (843) 577-7111
General Fax: (843) 937-5579
Advertising Phone: (843) 958-7394
Advertising Fax: (843) 937-5579
Editorial Phone: (843) 958-7393
Editorial Fax: (843) 937-5579
General/National Adv. E-mail: info@lowcountryparent.com
Display Adv. E-mail: dkifer@postandcourier.com
Editorial e-mail: editor@lowcountryparent.com
Primary Website: www.lowcountryparent.com
Year Established: 1997
Published: Mthly
Avg Free Circ: 41000
Audit By: Sworn/Estimate/Non-Audited
Audit Date: 12.07.2019
Personnel: Doug Kifer (Adv. Sales Mgr.); Shannon Brigham (Ed.)
Parent company (for newspapers): The Post and Courier

TENNESSEE

DAY COM MEDIA

Street address 1: 3212 West End Ave
Street address 2: #201
Street address city: Nashville
Street address state: TN
Zip/Postal code: 37203
County: Davidson
Country: USA
Mailing address: 2200 Rosa L Parks Blvd
Mailing city: Nashville
Mailing state: TN
Mailing zip: 37228-1306
General/National Adv. E-mail: stewart@daycommedia.com
Editorial e-mail: susan@daycommedia.com
Primary Website: www.parentworld.com
Year Established: 1993
Published: Mthly
Avg Paid Circ: 10
Avg Free Circ: 50000
Audit By: Sworn/Estimate/Non-Audited
Audit Date: 12.07.2019
Personnel: Stewart Day (Pub.); Susan Day (Ed.); Chad Young (Mng. Ed.); Tim Henard (Prodn. Mgr.)
Parent company (for newspapers): Day Communications Inc

MEMPHIS PARENT

Street address 1: 65 Union Avenue
Street address 2: 2nd Floor
Street address city: Memphis
Street address state: TN
Zip/Postal code: 38103
County: Shelby
Country: USA
Mailing address: 65 Union Avenue, 2nd Floor
Mailing city: Memphis
Published: Mthly
Avg Free Circ: 34975
Audit By: CVC
Audit Date: 30.06.2015
Personnel: Kenneth Neill (Pub./CEO); Bryan Rollins (Art Dir.); Shara Clark (Mng. Ed.); Sheryl Butler (Adv. Dir.)

NASHVILLE PARENT MAGAZINE

Street address 1: 1129 Lakeview Dr
Street address city: Franklin
Street address state: TN
Primary Website: www.nashvilleparent.com
Mthly Avg Views: 300000
Mthly Avg Unique Visitors: 86000
Year Established: 1993
Published: Mon`Tues`Wed`Thur`Fri`Mthly
Avg Free Circ: 25000
Audit By: CVC
Audit Date: 23.06.2023
Personnel: Stewart Day (Adv. Mgr.); Tom Guardino (Circ. Mgr.); Susan Day (Ed. in Chief.); Chad Young (Mng. Ed.); Tim Henard (Prodn. Mgr.)

TEXAS

AUSTIN FAMILY

Street address 1: PO Box 7559
Street address city: Round Rock
Street address state: TX
Zip/Postal code: 78683-7559
County: Williamson
Country: USA
Mailing address: PO Box 7559
Display Adv. E-mail: kaye2003@austinfamily.com
Editorial e-mail: editor2003@austinfamily.com
Primary Website: www.austinfamily.com
Year Established: 1991
Published: Mthly
Avg Free Circ: 35000
Audit By: Sworn/Estimate/Non-Audited
Audit Date: 12.07.2019
Personnel: Kaye Kemper (Pub.); Melanie Dunham (Ed.); Dr. Betty Kehl Richardson (Advising Ed.); John Faranzetti (Art Dir.); Betty Kemper (Calendar Ed.)

DALLASCHILD

Street address 1: 4275 Kellway Cir
Street address 2: Ste 146
Street address city: Addison
Street address state: TX
Zip/Postal code: 75001-5731
County: Dallas
Country: USA
Mailing address: 4275 Kellway Circle
Mailing city: Addison
Mailing state: TX
Mailing zip: 75001
General Phone: (972) 447-9188
Advertising Phone: (214) 707-6174
Editorial Phone: (214) 707-6174
General/National Adv. E-mail: publishing@dfwchild.com
Display Adv. E-mail: advertising@dfwchild.com
Editorial e-mail: editorial@dfwchild.com
Primary Website: dfwchild.com
Year Established: 1984
Published: Mthly
Avg Free Circ: 55000
Audit By: CVC
Audit Date: 18.12.2017
Personnel: Joylyn Niebes (Publisher); Lauren Niebes-Piccirillo (Creative & Content Director)
Parent company (for newspapers): Lauren Publications

HOUSTON FAMILY MAGAZINE

Street address 1: 5131 Braesvalley Dr
Street address city: Houston
Street address state: TX
Zip/Postal code: 77096-2609
County: Harris
Country: USA
Mailing address: 5131 Braesvalley Dr
Mailing city: Houston
Mailing state: TX
Mailing zip: 77096-2609
General/National Adv. E-mail: dana@houstonfamilymagazine.com
Display Adv. E-mail: kim@houstonfamilymagazine.com

Editorial e-mail: dana@houstonfamilymagazine.com
Published: Mthly
Avg Free Circ: 60000
Audit By: Sworn/Estimate/Non-Audited
Audit Date: 12.07.2019
Personnel: Kimberly Davis-Guerra (Publisher); Wendy Jackson-Slaton (Ed. in Chief); Casey Johnson (Creative Dir.); Gayle Wheeler-Lesuer (Graphic Des.)

METROKIDS MAGAZINE

Street address 1: 4275 Kellway Cir
Street address 2: Ste 146
Street address city: Addison
Street address state: TX
Zip/Postal code: 75001-5731
County: Dallas
Country: USA
Mailing address: 1414 Pine Street
Mailing city: Philadelphia
Mailing state: PA
Mailing zip: 19112-1202
General/National Adv. E-mail: info@metrokids.com
Display Adv. E-mail: sales@metrokids.com
Editorial e-mail: editor@metrokids.com
Primary Website: www.metrokids.com
Year Established: 1991
Published: Mthly
Published Other: Special Editions Annually, Bi Annually
Avg Free Circ: 90
Audit By: Sworn/Estimate/Non-Audited
Audit Date: 12.07.2019
Personnel: Darlene Weinmann (Publisher); Nancy Lisagor (Ed. in Chief); Sara Murphy (Managing Editor)

OUR KIDS SAN ANTONIO

Street address 1: 8400 Blanco Rd
Street address 2: Ste 300
Street address city: San Antonio
Street address state: TX
Zip/Postal code: 78216-3055
County: Bexar
Country: USA
Mailing address: PO Box 1809
Mailing city: Castroville
Mailing state: TX
Mailing zip: 78009
General Phone: (210) 349-6667
General Fax: (210) 349-5618
General/National Adv. E-mail: sanantonio.parenting@parenthood.com
Published: Wed
Avg Free Circ: 50000
Audit By: Sworn/Estimate/Non-Audited
Audit Date: 12.07.2019
Personnel: Rudy Riojas (Pub.); Cynthia Ladson (Ed.)

QUEENS PARENT

Street address 1: 4275 Kellway Cir
Street address 2: Ste 146
Street address city: Addison
Street address state: TX
Zip/Postal code: 75001-5731
Primary Website: www.nymetroparents.com
Year Established: 1985
Published: Mthly
Avg Free Circ: 54910
Audit By: CVC

SUBURBAN PARENT

Street address 1: 8344 Sterling Street
Street address city: Irving
Street address state: TX
Zip/Postal code: 75063
County: Middlesex
Country: USA
Mailing address: 8344 Sterling Street
Display Adv. E-mail: advertising@suburbanparent.com
Editorial e-mail: editor@suburbanparent.com
Published: Mthly
Avg Free Circ: 300000
Audit By: Sworn/Estimate/Non-Audited
Audit Date: 12.07.2019
Personnel: Dave Gauger (Now Retired)

PARENTMAP

Street address 1: 7683 SE 27th St
Street address city: Mercer Island
Street address state: WA
Zip/Postal code: 98040-2804
County: King
Country: USA
Mailing address: PMB #190 7683 SE 27th Street
Mailing city: Mercer Island
Mailing state: WA
Mailing zip: 98040
General Phone: (206) 709-9026
General Fax: (206) 455-7984
General/National Adv. E-mail: admin@parentmap.com
Display Adv. E-mail: jess@parentmap.com
Editorial e-mail: jody@parentmap.com
Primary Website: https://www.parentmap.com/
Year Established: 2003
Published: Mthly
Avg Paid Circ: 120
Avg Free Circ: 45000
Audit By: Sworn/Estimate/Non-Audited
Audit Date: 12.07.2019
Personnel: Ida Wicklund (Advertising & Partnerships, Manager); Danielle Sackett (Circ. Mgr.); Karen Matthee (Ed.); Anton Hafele (Prodn. Mgr.)

SEATTLE'S CHILD

Street address 1: 4303 198th St SW
Street address city: Lynnwood
Street address state: WA
Zip/Postal code: 98036-6777
County: Snohomish
Country: USA
Mailing address: 4303 198th St SW
Editorial e-mail: editor@seattleschild.com
Published: Mthly
Avg Free Circ: 80000
Audit By: Sworn/Estimate/Non-Audited
Audit Date: 12.07.2019
Personnel: Mary Armstrong (Pub. Asst.); Ann Bergman (Ed.)

WISCONSIN

DANE COUNTY KIDS

Street address 1: 2420 Evans Rd
Street address city: Mc Farland
Street address state: WI
Zip/Postal code: 53558-9043
County: Dane
Mailing zip: 53744-505
General Phone: (608) 444-0654
Advertising Phone: (608) 444-0654
Editorial Phone: same
General/National Adv. E-mail: kerickson@ericksonpublishing.com
Display Adv. E-mail: same
Editorial e-mail: same
Primary Website: tbd...revising
Year Established: 1992
Published: Mthly
Avg Free Circ: 50000
Audit By: Sworn/Estimate/Non-Audited
Audit Date: 12.07.2019
Personnel: Kristin Erickson (Pres./Pub.); Lynn Wittsell (Assoc. Editor)

METROPARENT

Street address 1: 333 W State St
Street address city: Milwaukee
Street address state: WI
Zip/Postal code: 53203-1305
County: Milwaukee
Country: USA
Mailing address: 333 W State St
Mailing city: Milwaukee
Mailing state: WI
Mailing zip: 53203-1305
General Phone: (414) 647-2478
General Fax: (414) 224-7690
Advertising Phone: 414-647-4734
Advertising Fax: 414-224-7690
General/National Adv. E-mail: info@metroparentmagazine.com
Display Adv. E-mail: bsteimle@journalsentinel.com
Editorial e-mail: rchristman@metroparentmagazine.com
Primary Website: www.jsonline.com/life/wisconsin-family
Year Established: 1986
Published: Mthly
Avg Free Circ: 42233
Audit By: CVC
Audit Date: 30.06.2004
Personnel: George Stanley (Ed./Sr. VP); Chuck Melvin (Asst. Mng. Ed.); Steve Jagler (Bus. Ed.)
Parent company (for newspapers): Journal Media Group

REAL ESTATE PUBLICATIONS IN THE U.S.

CALIFORNIA

ALTA LOMA

THE HOMES MAGAZINE

Street address 1: 6683 Capitol Pl
Street address 3: Alta Loma
Street address state: CA
Zip/Postal code: 91701-7784
County: San Bernardino
Country: USA
Mailing address: 6683 Capitol Pl
Mailing city: Alta Loma
Mailing state: CA
Mailing zip: 91701-7784
General Phone: (909) 948-7255
General Fax: (909) 948-7258
General/National Adv. E-mail: homemag@earthlink.net
Primary Website: www.thehomesmagazine.com
Published: Mthly
Avg Free Circ: 25500
Audit By: Sworn/Estimate/Non-Audited
Audit Date: 07.12.2019
Classified Equipment»
Personnel: Connie Endter (Pub.); Dave Endter (Gen. Mgr.)

ATASCADERO

CENTRAL COAST HOMES MAGAZINE

Street address 1: 7544 Morro Rd
Street address 3: Atascadero
Street address state: CA
Zip/Postal code: 93422-4404
County: San Luis Obispo
Country: USA
Mailing address: PO Box 657
Mailing city: Atascadero
Mailing state: CA
Mailing zip: 93423-0657
General Phone: (805) 461-7898
General Fax: (805) 466-8359
General/National Adv. E-mail: mraike@homesmagazine.com; sales@globalhomes.com
Primary Website: www.globalhomes.com
Published: Mthly
Avg Free Circ: 30000
Audit By: Sworn/Estimate/Non-Audited
Audit Date: 07.12.2019
Classified Equipment»
Personnel: Mike Raike (Pub.)

NAPA

NAPA VALLEY REGISTER

Street address 1: 1615 2nd St
Street address 3: Napa
Street address state: CA
Zip/Postal code: 94559-2818
County: Napa
Country: USA
Mailing address: 1615 Second St
Mailing city: Napa
Mailing state: CA
Mailing zip: 94559
General Phone: (707) 256-2244
General Fax: (707) 252-6047
Advertising Phone: (707) 256-2244
Editorail Phone: (707) 256-2244
General/National Adv. E-mail: jfawkes@napanews.com
Display Adv. E-mail: jfawkes@napanews.com
Editorial e-mail: jfawkes@napanews.com
Primary Website: napavalleyregister.com
Delivery Methods: Racks
Area Served - City: 9 455 994 558 945 740 000 000 000 000 000 000 000 000 000 000 000 000 000 000
Advertising (Open Inch Rate) Weekday/Saturday: Open inch rate $11.15
Mechanical specifications: Type page 7 1/2 x 9 3/4.
Published: Mthly
Avg Free Circ: 5000
Audit By: Sworn/Estimate/Non-Audited
Audit Date: 07.12.2019
Classified Equipment»
Personnel: Sean Scully (Ed.); Henry Lutz (Wine Reporter/Copy Ed.); Barry Eberling (Napa County Reporter); Sasha Paulsen (Features Ed.)
Parent company (for newspapers): Dispatch-Argus

WINE COUNTRY WEEKLY REAL ESTATE READER

Street address 1: 1436 2nd St
Street address 2: Unit 182
Street address 3: Napa
Street address state: CA
Zip/Postal code: 94559-5005
County: Napa
Country: USA
Mailing address: 1436 Second St.
Mailing city: Napa
Mailing state: CA
Mailing zip: 94558
General Phone: (707) 258-6150
General Fax: (707) 258-6152
Advertising Phone: (707) 258-6150
General/National Adv. E-mail: publisher@rereader.com
Display Adv. E-mail: support@rereader.com
Primary Website: www.rereader.com
Year Established: 1987
Area Served - City: 94558
Advertising (Open Inch Rate) Weekday/Saturday: Open inch rate $30.00
Mechanical specifications: Type page 10 1/4 x 13; E - 5 cols, 2, 1/8 between; C - 6 cols, 1 1/4, 1/8 between.
Published: Fri
Avg Paid Circ: 9500
Avg Free Circ: 57000
Audit By: Sworn/Estimate/Non-Audited
Audit Date: 07.12.2019
Classified Equipment»
Personnel: Teresa M. Galligan (Pub.); Charles Kamins (Mng. Ed.); Heather N. Hayne (Prodn. Mgr.)

PALM SPRINGS

HOMEFINDER

Street address 1: 750 N Gene Autry Trl
Street address 3: Palm Springs
Street address state: CA
Zip/Postal code: 92262-5463
County: Riverside
Country: USA
Mailing address: PO Box 2734
Mailing city: Palm Springs
Mailing state: CA
Mailing zip: 92263-2734
General Phone: (760) 322-8889
General Fax: (760) 778-4560
Advertising Fax: (760) 778-4528
Editorial Fax: (760) 778-4654
General/National Adv. E-mail: mwinkler@gannet.com
Display Adv. E-mail: sbweaver@gannett.com
Editorial e-mail: grburton@gannett.com
Primary Website: www.mydesert.com
Year Established: 1927
Delivery Methods: Carrier`Racks
Area Served - City: 92262, 92234, 92240, 92264, 92210, 92211, 92260, 92270, 92276, 92236, 92201, 92203, 92253
Own Printing Facility: Y
Commercial printers: Y
Advertising (Open Inch Rate) Weekday/Saturday: Open inch rate $46.00
Published: Sat
Avg Paid Circ: 52213
Avg Free Circ: 50000
Audit By: Sworn/Estimate/Non-Audited
Audit Date: 07.12.2019
Classified Equipment»
Personnel: Greg Castro (Circ. Mgr.)

CONNECTICUT

FOR SALE BY OWNER CONNECTION

Street address 1: PO Box 602
Street address 3: Canton
Street address state: CT
Zip/Postal code: 06019-0602
County: Hartford
Country: USA
Mailing address: PO Box 602
Mailing city: Canton
Mailing state: CT
Mailing zip: 6019
General Phone: (860) 659-3726
General Fax: (860) 633-1850
General/National Adv. E-mail: info@cutthecommission.com
Primary Website: www.cutthecommission.com
Area Served - City: 6019
Published: Mthly
Avg Free Circ: 60000
Audit By: Sworn/Estimate/Non-Audited
Audit Date: 07.12.2019
Classified Equipment»
Personnel: Carol York (Ed.)

NORWICH

HALLMARK HOMES

Street address 1: PO Box 626
Street address 3: Norwich
Street address state: CT
Zip/Postal code: 06360-0626
County: New London
Country: USA
Mailing address: 193 Camp Moween Rd
Mailing city: Lebanon
Mailing state: CT
Mailing zip: 06249-2705
General Phone: (860) 886-5245
General Fax: (860) 886-5244
Display Adv. E-mail: hhhomesmag@aol.com
Primary Website: http://www.hallmarkct.com/
Delivery Methods: Carrier
Published Other: Every other Wed
Avg Free Circ: 23000
Audit By: Sworn/Estimate/Non-Audited
Audit Date: 07.12.2019
Classified Equipment»
Personnel: Mike Connell (Pub.)

FLORIDA

NORTH PORT

FLORIDA MARINER/GULF MARINER

Street address 1: PO Box 8070
Street address 3: North Port
Street address state: FL
Zip/Postal code: 34290-8070
County: Sarasota
Country: USA
Mailing address: PO Box 8070
Mailing city: North Port
Mailing state: FL
Mailing zip: 34290
General Phone: (941) 488-9307
General Fax: (941) 488-9309
General/National Adv. E-mail: flmariner@floridamariner.com
Editorial e-mail: cjones@floridamariner.com
Primary Website: www.floridamariner.com
Advertising (Open Inch Rate) Weekday/Saturday: Open inch rate $39.95
Published Other: Every other Sun
Avg Free Circ: 23500
Audit By: Sworn/Estimate/Non-Audited
Audit Date: 07.12.2019
Classified Equipment»
Personnel: Michael Jones (Publisher); Stacey Fulgieri (Ed.)

GEORGIA

MARTINEZ

HOME GUIDE

Street address 1: 109 Camilla Ave
Street address 3: Martinez
Street address state: GA
Zip/Postal code: 30907-3406
County: Columbia
Country: USA
Mailing address: 109 Camilla Ave
Mailing city: Martinez
Mailing state: GA
Mailing zip: 30907-3406
General Phone: (706) 868-8544
General Fax: (706) 868-8381
General/National Adv. E-mail: handl@augustashomes.com
Primary Website: www.augustashomes.com
Published: Mthly
Audit By: Sworn/Estimate/Non-Audited
Audit Date: 07.12.2019
Classified Equipment»
Personnel: Larry Boerckel (Ed.)

HOMES & LAND OF AUGUSTA

Street address 1: 109 Camilla Ave
Street address 3: Martinez
Street address state: GA
Zip/Postal code: 30907-3406
County: Columbia
Country: USA
Mailing address: 109 Camilla Ave
Mailing city: Martinez
Mailing state: GA
Mailing zip: 30907-3406
General Phone: (706) 868-8544
General Fax: (706) 868-8381
General/National Adv. E-mail: handl@augustashomes.com
Primary Website: www.augustashomes.com
Area Served - City: 30907
Published: Mthly
Avg Free Circ: 22000
Audit By: Sworn/Estimate/Non-Audited
Audit Date: 07.12.2019
Classified Equipment»
Personnel: Larry Boerckel (Ed.)

KANSAS

KANSAS HOMES

Street address 1: 1533 NE Rice Rd
Street address 3: Kansas City
Street address state: KS

Zip/Postal code: 66103
County: Wyandotte
Country: USA
Mailing address: 1533 NE Rice Rd
Mailing city: Kansas City
Mailing state: KS
Mailing zip: 66103
General Phone: (816) 738-3633
Primary Website: www.kchomes.com
Area Served - City: 64103
Published Other: Every other Thur
Avg Free Circ: 15000
Audit By: Sworn/Estimate/Non-Audited
Audit Date: 07.12.2019
Classified Equipment»
Personnel: Crystal The Realtor (Pub.)

WICHITA

REAL ESTATE BOOK

Street address 1: PO Box 1897
Street address 3: Wichita
Street address state: KS
Zip/Postal code: 67201-1897
County: Sedgwick
Country: USA
Mailing address: PO Box 1897
Mailing city: Wichita
Mailing state: KS
Mailing zip: 67201-1897
General Phone: (316) 788-0191
General Fax: (316) 794-8767
General/National Adv. E-mail: jstebens@aol.com
Published: Mthly
Audit By: Sworn/Estimate/Non-Audited
Audit Date: 07.12.2019
Classified Equipment»
Personnel: Jim Stebens (Ed.); Nikki Stebens (Ed.)

KENTUCKY

ELIZABETHTOWN

CENTRAL KENTUCKY HOMES REAL ESTATE

Street address 1: 408 W Dixie Ave
Street address 3: Elizabethtown
Street address state: KY
Zip/Postal code: 42701-2455
County: Hardin
Country: USA
Mailing address: 408 W Dixie Ave
Mailing city: Elizabethtown
Mailing state: KY
Mailing zip: 42701-2455
General Phone: (270) 769-1200
General Fax: (270) 765-7318
Display Adv. E-mail: Ljobe@thenewsenterprise.com
Primary Website: www.newsenterpriseonline.com
Delivery Methods: Racks
Area Served - City: 42701
Published: Mthly
Avg Free Circ: 10000
Audit By: Sworn/Estimate/Non-Audited
Audit Date: 07.12.2019
Classified Equipment»
Personnel: Chris Ordway (Pub.); Ben Sheroan (Ed.); Portia Oldham (Circ. Mgr.); Larry Jobe (Advertising Director)

MASSACHUSETTS

FALL RIVER

REAL ESTATE GUIDE

Street address 1: 207 Pocasset St
Street address 3: Fall River
Street address state: MA
Zip/Postal code: 02721-1532
County: Bristol
Country: USA
Mailing address: 207 Pocasset St
Mailing city: Fall River
Mailing state: MA
Mailing zip: 02721-1532
General Phone: (508) 676-8211
General Fax: (508) 676-2588
General/National Adv. E-mail: news@heraldnews.com
Primary Website: www.heraldnews.com
Own Printing Facility: Y
Advertising (Open Inch Rate) Weekday/Saturday: Open inch rate $17.50
Mechanical specifications: Type page 10 1/2 x 12; E - 7 cols, 1 7/16, between; C - 7 cols, 1 7/16, between.
Published: Fri
Avg Paid Circ: 32173
Audit By: Sworn/Estimate/Non-Audited
Audit Date: 07.12.2019
Classified Equipment»
Personnel: Sean Burke (Pub.); Tom Booth (Adv. Dir.); Tom Amato (Circ. Dir.); Linda Murphy (Mng. Ed.); Jon Root (Mng. Ed.); Mike Niland (Prodn. Mgr.)

NEEDHAM

BOSTON HOMES

Street address 1: 254 2nd Ave
Street address 3: Needham
Street address state: MA
Zip/Postal code: 02494-2829
County: Norfolk
Country: USA
General Phone: (617) 262-0444
General Fax: (617) 266-7333
Advertising Phone: (888) 828-1515
Editorail Phone: (781) 433-8323
Primary Website: http://www.linkbostonhomes.com
Classified Equipment»
Personnel: David Petruska (Pub.); Marilyn Jackson (Ed.)

PEABODY

BANKER & TRADESMAN

Street address 1: 2 Corporation Way
Street address 2: Suite 250
Street address 3: Peabody
Street address state: MA
Zip/Postal code: 1960
County: Suffolk
Country: USA
Mailing address: 280 Summer St Fl 8
Mailing city: Boston
Mailing state: MA
Mailing zip: 02210-1130
General Phone: (617) 428-5100
Advertising Phone: (617) 896-5357
Editorail Phone: (617) 896-5313
General/National Adv. E-mail: editorial@thewarrengroup.com
Display Adv. E-mail: advertising@thewarrengroup.com
Editorial e-mail: editorial@thewarrengroup.com
Primary Website: www.bankerandtradesman.com
Year Established: 1872
Delivery Methods: Mail
Published: Mon
Avg Free Circ: 7000
Audit By: Sworn/Estimate/Non-Audited
Audit Date: 07.12.2019
Classified Equipment»
Personnel: David Lovins (Pres./COO); Cassidy Murphy (Associate Publisher); Timothy Warren (Publisher/CEO)
Parent company (for newspapers): The Warren Group

APARTMENTS

Street address 1: 525 Belmont Ave
Street address 3: Springfield
Street address state: MA
Zip/Postal code: 01108-1789
County: Hampden
Country: USA
Mailing address: 525 Belmont Ave
Mailing city: Springfield
Mailing state: MA
Mailing zip: 01108-1789
General Phone: (413) 734-3411
General Fax: (413) 734-0099
General/National Adv. E-mail: tomgreen@apt-4-rent.com, info@apt-4-rent.com
Primary Website: www.apt-4-rent.com
Area Served - City: 1108
Published: Mthly
Avg Free Circ: 30000
Audit By: Sworn/Estimate/Non-Audited
Audit Date: 07.12.2019
Classified Equipment»
Personnel: Tom Green (Pub.); Tom Savoy (Dir., Mktg.)

MICHIGAN

NORTHERN MICHIGAN REAL ESTATE MARKETPLACE

Street address 1: 711 W Pickard St
Street address 3: Mount Pleasant
Street address state: MI
Zip/Postal code: 48858-1585
County: Isabella
Country: USA
Mailing address: 311 1/2 E Mitchell St
Mailing city: Petoskey
Mailing state: MI
Mailing zip: 49770-2615
General Phone: (989) 779-6000
General Fax: (989) 779-6162
General/National Adv. E-mail: news@michigannewspapers.com
Primary Website: www.themorningsun.com
Published: Mthly
Avg Free Circ: 25000
Audit By: Sworn/Estimate/Non-Audited
Audit Date: 07.12.2019
Classified Equipment»
Personnel: Al Frattura (Pub.); Don Negus (Adv. Dir.); Donna Pung (Adv. Mgr.); Rick Mills (Exec. Ed.)

THE REAL ESTATE REVIEW

Street address 1: 711 W Pickard St
Street address 3: Mount Pleasant
Street address state: MI
Zip/Postal code: 48858-1585
County: Isabella
Country: USA
Mailing address: 711 W Pickard St
Mailing city: Mount Pleasant
Mailing state: MI
Mailing zip: 48858-1585
General Phone: (800) 616-6397
General Fax: (989) 779-6009
Primary Website: http://www.myhomemi.com/
Mechanical specifications: Type page 7 1/4 x 9 1/2; A - 4 cols, 1 5/8, 1/8 between.
Published: Mthly
Avg Free Circ: 15000
Audit By: Sworn/Estimate/Non-Audited
Audit Date: 07.12.2019
Classified Equipment»
Personnel: Christine Fox (Circ. Mgr.); Angel Norbury (Mktg. Cood.)

PONTIAC

HOMES FOR SALE

Street address 1: 48 W Huron St
Street address 3: Pontiac
Street address state: MI
Zip/Postal code: 48342-2101
County: Oakland
Country: USA
Mailing address: 48 W Huron St
Mailing city: Pontiac
Mailing state: MI
Mailing zip: 48342-2101
General Phone: (248) 745-4794
General Fax: (248) 332-3003
Primary Website: www.theoaklandpress.com
Published: Thur
Avg Free Circ: 17000
Audit By: Sworn/Estimate/Non-Audited
Audit Date: 07.12.2019
Classified Equipment»
Personnel: Jeannie Parent (Pub.)

NORTH CAROLINA

HOMES & LAND OF METRO CHARLOTTE

Street address 1: 4525 Park Rd
Street address 2: Ste B202
Street address 3: Charlotte
Street address state: NC
Zip/Postal code: 28209-3704
County: Mecklenburg
Country: USA
Mailing address: 4525 Park Rd Ste 202
Mailing city: Charlotte
Mailing state: NC
Mailing zip: 28209-3834
General Phone: (704) 527-6553
General Fax: (704) 527-6118
General/National Adv. E-mail: clthomes@attglobal.net
Primary Website: www.homesandland.com
Published: Mthly
Avg Free Circ: 40000
Audit By: Sworn/Estimate/Non-Audited
Audit Date: 07.12.2019
Classified Equipment»
Personnel: Jeff P. Cathey (Pub.)

NEW JERSEY

COLTS NECK

HOME IMPROVEMENT GUIDE

Street address 1: 440 State Route 34
Street address 3: Colts Neck
Street address state: NJ
Zip/Postal code: 07722-2525
County: Monmouth
Country: USA
Mailing address: 440 State Route 34
Mailing city: Colts Neck
Mailing state: NJ
Mailing zip: 07722-2513
General Phone: (732) 780-7474
General Fax: (732) 414-1736
General/National Adv. E-mail: info@homeimprovementguides.com
Primary Website: www.homeimprovementguides.com
Year Established: 2003
Delivery Methods: Mail`Racks
Advertising (Open Inch Rate) Weekday/Saturday: see website
Mechanical specifications: see website
Published: Mthly
Avg Free Circ: 95000
Audit By: Sworn/Estimate/Non-Audited
Audit Date: 07.12.2019
Classified Equipment»
Personnel: Nick Montalbano (Circ. Mgr.)

MORRISTOWN

HOMES & ESTATES MAGAZINE

Street address 1: 173 Morris St
Street address 3: Morristown
Street address state: NJ
Zip/Postal code: 07960-4332
County: Morris
Country: USA
Mailing address: PO Box 525
Mailing city: Ridgewood
Mailing state: NJ
Mailing zip: 7451
General Phone: (201) 394-3084
General Fax: (973) 264-1153
General/National Adv. E-mail: gene@homesandestatesonline.com
Primary Website: http://www.homesandestatesonline.com/skins/housemagazine/

Mechanical specifications: Type page 6 3/4 x 9 3/8.
Published: Wed
Avg Free Circ: 35000
Audit By: Sworn/Estimate/Non-Audited
Audit Date: 07.12.2019
Classified Equipment»
Personnel: Peter Best (Pub.); Gene Petraglia (Pub.)

NEW MEXICO

LAS CRUCES

REAL ESTATE PRESS OF LAS CRUCES

Street address 1: 256 W Las Cruces Ave
Street address 3: Las Cruces
Street address state: NM
Zip/Postal code: 88005-1804
County: Dona Ana
Country: USA
Mailing address: PO Box 1244
Mailing city: Las Cruces
Mailing state: NM
Mailing zip: 88004-1244
General Phone: (575) 541-5467
General Fax: (575) 541-5499
General/National Adv. E-mail: mderk@lcsun-news.com
Primary Website: lcsun-news.com/marketplace/real-estate
Delivery Methods: Racks
Area Served - City: 88001, 88005, 88007, 88011, 88012
Published: Mthly
Classified Equipment»
Personnel: Maria Derk

SANTA FE

HOME|SANTA FE REAL ESTATE GUIDE

Street address 1: 202 E Marcy St
Street address 3: Santa Fe
Street address state: NM
Zip/Postal code: 87501-2021
County: Santa Fe
Country: USA
Mailing address: PO Box 2048
Mailing city: Santa Fe
Mailing state: NM
Mailing zip: 87504-2048
General Phone: (505) 983-3303
General Fax: (505) 995-3875
Advertising Phone: (505) 986-3007
Advertising Fax: (505) 984-1785
Editorail Phone: (505) 986-3043
Editorial Fax: (505) 995-3875
General/National Adv. E-mail: reguide@sfnewmexican.com
Display Adv. E-mail: wortega@sfnewmexican.com
Editorial e-mail: pweideman@sfnewmexican.com
Primary Website: www.santafenewmexican.com
Year Established: 1997
Delivery Methods: Mail`Newsstand`Carrier`Racks
Area Served - City: 87501, 87502, 87504, 87505, 87508, 87544, 87532, 87507, 87010
Own Printing Facility: Y
Commercial printers: Y
Mechanical specifications: Type page 9 3/4 x 11 1/2; E - 4 cols, 1 1/5, between; A - 4 cols, 1 1/5, between.
Published: Sun`Mthly
Avg Paid Circ: 18000
Audit By: Sworn/Estimate/Non-Audited
Audit Date: 07.12.2019
Classified Equipment»
Personnel: Paul Weideman (Ed.); Wendy Ortega (Advertising AE)
Parent company (for newspapers): The New Mexican, Inc.

NEW YORK

BOHEMIA

FSBO

Street address 1: 3140 Veterans Memorial Hwy
Street address 3: Bohemia
Street address state: NY
Zip/Postal code: 11716-1039
County: Suffolk
Country: USA
Mailing address: 3140 Veterans Memorial Hwy
Mailing city: Bohemia
Mailing state: NY
Mailing zip: 11716-1039
General Phone: (800) 584-3726
General Fax: (631) 928-1755
General/National Adv. E-mail: info@lifsbo.com
Year Established: 1988
Own Printing Facility: Y
Mechanical specifications: Type page 7 x 10.
Published Other: 17 x a year
Avg Free Circ: 50000
Audit By: Sworn/Estimate/Non-Audited
Audit Date: 07.12.2019
Classified Equipment»
Personnel: Kevin C. Wood (Pub.); Craig Martin (Adv. Mgr.); Renee Alborelli (Prodn. Mgr.)

PLATTSBURGH

ADIRONDACK PROPERTIES

Street address 1: 177 Margaret St
Street address 3: Plattsburgh
Street address state: NY
Zip/Postal code: 12901-1837
County: Clinton
Country: USA
Mailing address: 177 Margaret St
Mailing city: Plattsburgh
Mailing state: NY
Mailing zip: 12901-1837
General Phone: (518) 563-0100
General Fax: (518) 562-0303
General/National Adv. E-mail: pennysaver@westelcom.com
Primary Website: www.adkpennysaver.com
Advertising (Open Inch Rate) Weekday/Saturday: Open inch rate $15.00
Published: Mthly
Classified Equipment»
Personnel: Mark Rigby (Pub.); Carol VanHise (Adv. Mgr.); John Bruno (Prodn. Mgr.)

REAL ESTATE ADVERTISER

Street address 1: 177 Margaret St
Street address 3: Plattsburgh
Street address state: NY
Zip/Postal code: 12901-1837
County: Clinton
Country: USA
Mailing address: 177 Margaret St
Mailing city: Plattsburgh
Mailing state: NY
Mailing zip: 12901-1837
General Phone: (518) 563-0100
General Fax: (518) 562-0303
General/National Adv. E-mail: mail@adkpennysaver.com
Primary Website: www.adkpennysaver.com
Advertising (Open Inch Rate) Weekday/Saturday: Open inch rate $15.00
Published Other: 4 x a year
Avg Free Circ: 18000
Audit By: Sworn/Estimate/Non-Audited
Audit Date: 07.12.2019
Classified Equipment»
Personnel: Mark Rigby (Pub.); Carol VanHise (Adv. Mgr.); John Bruno (Prodn. Mgr.)

CAPITAL REGION REAL ESTATE GUIDE

Street address 1: 270 River Triangle
Street address 2: Ste 202B
Street address 3: Troy
Street address state: NY
Zip/Postal code: 12180
County: Rensselaer
Country: USA
Mailing address: 270 River Triangle, Ste. 202B
Mailing city: Troy
Mailing state: NY
Mailing zip: 12180
General Phone: (518) 270-1200
General Fax: (518) 270-1251
General/National Adv. E-mail: newsroom@troyrecord.com
Primary Website: www.troyrecord.com
Own Printing Facility: Y
Mechanical specifications: Type page 5 1/4 x 9 1/2; E - 4 cols, 1 3/16, 1/8 between; A - 4 cols, 1 3/16, 1/8 between; C - 4 cols, 1 3/16, 1/8 between.
Published Other: 2 x Mthly
Avg Paid Circ: 25946
Audit By: Sworn/Estimate/Non-Audited
Audit Date: 07.12.2019
Classified Equipment»
Personnel: Kevin Corrado (Pub.); Karen Alvord (Adv. Dir.)

OHIO

HOLMESVILLE

HOMESELLER MAGAZINE

Street address 1: 8068 Township Road 574
Street address 3: Holmesville
Street address state: OH
Zip/Postal code: 44633-9751
County: Holmes
Country: USA
Mailing address: PO Box 87
Mailing city: Millersburg
Mailing state: OH
Mailing zip: 44654-0087
General Phone: (330) 674-7653
General Fax: (330) 674-7653
Editorial e-mail: editor@homesellermagazine.com
Primary Website: tdn.com/eedition/homeseller
Year Established: 1988
Area Served - City: 44691, 44654, 44256
Published: Mthly
Avg Free Circ: 9000
Audit By: Sworn/Estimate/Non-Audited
Audit Date: 07.12.2019
Classified Equipment»
Personnel: David Thornberry (Pub.)

OREGON

MEDFORD

PROFESSIONAL IMAGE PUBLISHING

Street address 1: 3350 1/2 W Main St
Street address 3: Medford
Street address state: OR
Zip/Postal code: 97501-2132
County: Jackson
Country: USA
Mailing address: 3350 1/2 W Main St
Mailing city: Medford
Mailing state: OR
Mailing zip: 97501-2132
General Phone: (541) 773-5744
General Fax: (541) 776-0445
General/National Adv. E-mail: office@move2oregon.com
Primary Website: www.move2oregon.com
Advertising (Open Inch Rate) Weekday/Saturday: Open inch rate $12.50
Published: Mthly
Audit By: Sworn/Estimate/Non-Audited
Audit Date: 07.12.2019
Classified Equipment»
Personnel: Cynthia Rucklos (Pub.)

PENNSYLVANIA

CONYNGHAM

REAL ESTATE JOURNAL

Street address 1: PO Box 482
Street address 3: Conyngham
Street address state: PA
Zip/Postal code: 18219
County: Luzerne
Country: USA
Mailing address: PO Box 482
Mailing city: Conyngham
Mailing state: PA
Mailing zip: 18219
General Phone: (570) 233-5652
General Fax: (570) 371-4433
General/National Adv. E-mail: rej1@ptd.net
Primary Website: www.therealestatejournal.com
Published: Mthly
Avg Free Circ: 15000
Audit By: Sworn/Estimate/Non-Audited
Audit Date: 07.12.2019
Classified Equipment»
Personnel: Nick Walser (Co-Pub.); Steve Walser (Co-Pub.); Craig Baker (Administrator)

WEST CHESTER

HOMES MAGAZINE

Street address 1: 250 N Bradford Ave
Street address 3: West Chester
Street address state: PA
Zip/Postal code: 19382-1912
County: Chester
Country: USA
Mailing address: 250 N Bradford Ave
Mailing city: West Chester
Mailing state: PA
Mailing zip: 19382-1912
General Phone: (610) 430-6961
General Fax: (610) 430-1190
Editorail Phone: (610) 430-1116
General/National Adv. E-mail: advertising@dailylocal.com
Primary Website: www.dailylocal.com
Area Served - City: 19382
Own Printing Facility: Y
Advertising (Open Inch Rate) Weekday/Saturday: Open inch rate $2.75
Mechanical specifications: Type page 6 x 10.
Published: Mthly
Audit By: Sworn/Estimate/Non-Audited
Audit Date: 07.12.2019
Classified Equipment»
Personnel: Shelly Meenan (Pub.); Andy Hachadorian (Ed.)

TENNESSEE

CHATTANOOGA

BUY A HOME

Street address 1: 3407 Fleeta Ln
Street address 3: Chattanooga
Street address state: TN
Zip/Postal code: 37416-2802
County: Hamilton
Country: USA
Mailing address: 3407 Fleeta Ln
Mailing city: Chattanooga
Mailing state: TN
Mailing zip: 37416-2802
General Phone: (423) 855-1831
General Fax: (423) 499-8543
Published: Mthly

Avg Free Circ: 18000
Audit By: Sworn/Estimate/Non-Audited
Audit Date: 07.12.2019
Classified Equipment»
Personnel: Randy Harden (Pub.); Tammy Harden (Adv. Mgr.)

REAL ESTATE REVIEW

Street address 1: 3415 Fleeta Ln
Street address 3: Chattanooga
Street address state: TN
Zip/Postal code: 37416-2802
County: Hamilton
Country: USA
Mailing address: PO Box 25218
Mailing city: Chattanooga
Mailing state: TN
Mailing zip: 37422-5218
General Phone: (423) 855-1831
General Fax: (423) 499-8543
General/National Adv. E-mail: r4rrpub@aol.com
Primary Website: www.rivercountiesrealestatereview.com
Published: Mthly
Avg Free Circ: 15000
Audit By: Sworn/Estimate/Non-Audited
Audit Date: 07.12.2019
Classified Equipment»
Personnel: Tammy Harden (Adv. Mgr.); Randy Harden (Prodn. Mgr.)

TEXAS

REAL ESTATE WEEKLY

Street address 1: 6006 N Mesa St
Street address 2: Ste 600
Street address 3: El Paso
Street address state: TX
Zip/Postal code: 79912-4655
County: El Paso
Country: USA
Mailing address: 6006 N Mesa St Ste 600
Mailing city: El Paso
Mailing state: TX
Mailing zip: 79912-4655
General Phone: (915) 585-1000
General Fax: (915) 261-0234
General/National Adv. E-mail: sandy@mesapub.com
Primary Website: www.mesapublishing.com
Year Established: 1988
Area Served - City: 79901, 79999
Mechanical specifications: Type page 9 3/4 x 11 3/4.
Published: Thur
Avg Free Circ: 10000
Audit By: Sworn/Estimate/Non-Audited
Audit Date: 07.12.2019
Classified Equipment»
Personnel: Riley R. Stephens (Ed.); Ceci Marquez (Mng. Ed.); Nancy Wiseman (Prodn. Mgr.)
Parent company (for newspapers): Mesa Publishing Corp.

TYLER

HOMES & LAND OF TYLER & EAST TEXAS

Street address 1: 5604 Old Bullard Rd
Street address 2: Ste 101
Street address 3: Tyler
Street address state: TX
Zip/Postal code: 75703-4359
County: Smith
Country: USA
Mailing address: 5604 Old Bullard Rd Ste 101
Mailing city: Tyler
Mailing state: TX
Mailing zip: 75703-4359
General Phone: (903) 509-2339
General Fax: (903) 509-2326
Advertising Phone: (903) 509-2339
Advertising Fax: (903) 509-2326
General/National Adv. E-mail: psager@tyler.net
Display Adv. E-mail: psager@tyler.net
Editorial e-mail: psager&tyler.net
Primary Website: www.tyleretex.com
Year Established: 1977
Own Printing Facility: Y
Commercial printers: Y
Published: Mthly
Avg Free Circ: 20000
Audit By: Sworn/Estimate/Non-Audited
Audit Date: 07.12.2019
Classified Equipment»
Personnel: Pat Sager (OWNER/PUBLISHER); Tom Sager (Pub.)

VERMONT

BRATTLEBORO

NEW ENGLAND SHOWCASE

Street address 1: 14 Noahs Lane
Street address 2: P.O. Box 996
Street address 3: Brattleboro
Street address state: VT
Zip/Postal code: 05302-0996
County: Windham
Country: USA
Mailing address: 14 Noahs Lane, P.O. Box 996
Mailing city: Brattleboro
Mailing state: VT
Mailing zip: 05302-0996
General Phone: (802) 257-4387
General Fax: (802) 257-1453
General/National Adv. E-mail: info@newenglandshowcase.com
Editorial e-mail: editor@newenglandshowcase.com
Primary Website: www.newenglandshowcase.com
Area Served - City: 5303
Published Other: 3 x Mthly
Avg Free Circ: 20000
Audit By: Sworn/Estimate/Non-Audited
Audit Date: 07.12.2019
Classified Equipment»
Personnel: Donna McElligott (Marketing Mgr.)

RUTLAND

PREFERRED PROPERTIES REAL ESTATE GUIDE

Street address 1: 27 Wales St
Street address 3: Rutland
Street address state: VT
Zip/Postal code: 05701-4027
County: Rutland
Country: USA
Mailing address: PO Box 668
Mailing city: Rutland
Mailing state: VT
Mailing zip: 05702-0668
General Phone: (800) 776-5512
General Fax: (802) 775-2423
General/National Adv. E-mail: glenda.hawley@aol.com
Primary Website: www.vermontclassifieds.com; www.rutlandherald.com
Area Served - City: 5701
Advertising (Open Inch Rate) Weekday/Saturday: Open inch rate $17.61
Mechanical specifications: Type page 9 11/16 x 12; E - 5 cols, 1 13/16, 1/4 between; A - 5 cols, 1 13/16, 1/4 between.
Published: Mthly
Avg Free Circ: 22500
Audit By: Sworn/Estimate/Non-Audited
Audit Date: 07.12.2019
Classified Equipment»
Personnel: R. John Mitchell (Pub.); Catherine Nelson (Gen. Mgr.); Sean Bruke (Adv. Mgr.); Christina Mahoney (Adv. Design Mgr.)

WASHINGTON

GAUGER MEDIA SERVICE, INC.

Street address 1: 1034 Bradford Street
Street address 2: P.O. Box 627
Street address 3: Raymond
Street address state: WA
Zip/Postal code: 98577
County: Pacific
Country: USA
Mailing address: P.O. Box 627
Mailing city: Raymond
Mailing state: WA
Mailing zip: 98577
General Phone: (360) 942-3560
General/National Adv. E-mail: dave@gaugermedia.com
Primary Website: www.gaugermedia.com
Year Established: 1987
Classified Equipment»
Personnel: Dave Gauger (Pres/Broker)

WISCONSIN

GREEN BAY

GREEN BAY REAL ESTATE GUIDE

Street address 1: PO Box 2467
Street address 3: Green Bay
Street address state: WI
Zip/Postal code: 54306-2467
County: Brown
Country: USA
Mailing address: P.O. Box 23430
Mailing city: Green Bay
Mailing state: WI
Mailing zip: 54305-3430
General Phone: (920) 432-2941
General Fax: (920) 432-8581
General/National Adv. E-mail: chronicle@gogreenbay.com
Primary Website: www.greenbaypressgazette.com
Year Established: 1990
Area Served - City: 54301, 54302, 54303, 54304, 54311, 54115
Advertising (Open Inch Rate) Weekday/Saturday: Open inch rate $17.00
Mechanical specifications: Type page 7 1/4 x 9 3/4.
Published: Mthly
Audit By: Sworn/Estimate/Non-Audited
Audit Date: 07.12.2019
Classified Equipment»
Personnel: Al Rasmussen (Gen. Mgr.)

MADISON

START RENTING MAGAZINE

Street address 1: 102 N Franklin St
Street address 3: Madison
Street address state: WI
Zip/Postal code: 53703-2376
County: Dane
Country: USA
Mailing address: 102 N Franklin St Frnt
Mailing city: Madison
Mailing state: WI
Mailing zip: 53703-4610
General Phone: (608) 257-4990
General Fax: (608) 257-6896
General/National Adv. E-mail: info@startrenting.com
Primary Website: www.startrenting.com
Published: Mthly
Audit By: Sworn/Estimate/Non-Audited
Audit Date: 07.12.2019
Classified Equipment»
Personnel: Dennis Barber (Adv.Mgr); Shawn Bacon (Acct. Exec.); Melissa Schwefel (Acct. Exec.)

WYOMING

PREVIEW REAL ESTATE GUIDE

Street address 1: 2021 Warren Ave
Street address 3: Cheyenne
Street address state: WY
Zip/Postal code: 82001-3725
County: Laramie
Country: USA
Mailing address: 2021 Warren Ave
Mailing city: Cheyenne
Mailing state: WY
Mailing zip: 82001-3725
General Phone: (307) 634-8895
General Fax: (307) 634-8530
General/National Adv. E-mail: publisher@wyopreview.com
Primary Website: www.wyopreview.com
Year Established: 1984
Mechanical specifications: Type page 7 x 9 3/4.
Published: Mthly
Avg Free Circ: 8000
Audit By: Sworn/Estimate/Non-Audited
Audit Date: 07.12.2019
Classified Equipment»
Personnel: Patrick Rice (Pub.); Bob Johnigan (Gen. Mgr.); Jeff Hite (Circ. Mgr.); Will Perrell (Ed.)

RELIGIOUS UNITED STATES NEWSPAPER

ALABAMA

ONE VOICE

Street address 1: 2121 3rd Ave N
Street address city: Birmingham
Street address state: AL
Zip/Postal code: 35203-3314
County: Jefferson
Country: USA
Mailing address: PO Box 10822
Mailing city: Birmingham
Mailing state: AL
Mailing zip: 35202-0822
General Phone: (205) 838-8305
General Fax: (205) 838-8319
General/National Adv. E-mail: onevoice@bhmdiocese.org
Avg Paid Circ: 19800
Avg Free Circ: 293
Audit By: Sworn/Estimate/Non-Audited
Audit Date: 12.07.2019
Personnel: Bishop Robert Baker (Pub.); Ann Lanzi (Circ. Mgr.); Mary Alice Crockett (Mng. Ed.)

THE CATHOLIC WEEK

Street address 1: 356 Government St
Street address city: Mobile
Street address state: AL
Zip/Postal code: 36602-2316
County: Mobile
Country: USA
Mailing address: PO Box 349
Mailing city: Mobile
Mailing state: AL
Mailing zip: 36601-0349
General Phone: (251) 434-1544
General Fax: (251) 434-1547
Advertising Phone: (251) 434-1543
General/National Adv. E-mail: thecatholicweek@bellsouth.net
Display Adv. E-mail: cwadvertising@bellsouth.net
Primary Website: www.mobilearchdiocese.org/catholicweek
Year Established: 1934
Delivery Methods: Mail
Avg Paid Circ: 20000
Avg Free Circ: 362
Audit By: Sworn/Estimate/Non-Audited
Audit Date: 12.07.2019
Personnel: Thomas J. Rodi (Pub.); Mary Ann Stevens (Adv. Mgr.); Larry Wahl (Ed.); Pamela Wheeler (Production Manager)

ARKANSAS CATHOLIC

Street address 1: 2500 N Tyler St
Street address city: Little Rock
Street address state: AR
Zip/Postal code: 72207-3743
County: Pulaski
Country: USA
Mailing address: PO Box 7417
Mailing city: Little Rock
Mailing state: AR
Mailing zip: 72205
General Phone: (501)664-0125
General Fax: (501) 664-6572
Advertising Phone: (501)664-0125
Editorial Phone: (501)664-0125
General/National Adv. E-mail: mhargett@dolr.org
Display Adv. E-mail: mbrasfield@dolr.org
Editorial e-mail: mhargett@dolr.org
Primary Website: www.arkansas-catholic.org
Mthly Avg Views: 20787
Mthly Avg Unique Visitors: 13367
Year Established: 1911
Delivery Methods: Mail
Areas Served - City/County or Portion Thereof, or Zip codes: All in Arkansas
Avg Paid Circ: 3900
Avg Free Circ: 500
Audit By: Sworn/Estimate/Non-Audited
Audit Date: 24.09.2022
Personnel: Malea Hargett (Ed.); Emily Roberts (Prodn. Mgr.); Pete Stabnick (advertising manager); Aprille Hanson (associate editor)

BAPTIST TRUMPET

Street address 1: 10712 Interstate 30
Street address city: Little Rock
Street address state: AR
Zip/Postal code: 72209-5835
County: Pulaski
Country: USA
Mailing address: PO Box 192208
Mailing city: Little Rock
Mailing state: AR
Mailing zip: 72219-2208
General Phone: (501) 565-4601
General/National Adv. E-mail: editor@baptisttrumpet.com
Editorial e-mail: editor@baptisttrumpet.com
Primary Website: www.baptisttrumpet.com
Year Established: 1939
Avg Paid Circ: 6318
Avg Free Circ: 236
Audit By: Sworn/Estimate/Non-Audited
Audit Date: 04.10.2023
Personnel: Jeff Herring (Executive Editor); Diane Spriggs (Editor/Business Manager); Allan Eakin (Associate Editor)

GOOD NEWS, ETC.

Street address 1: PO Box 2660
Street address city: Vista
Street address state: CA
Zip/Postal code: 92085-2660
County: San Diego
Country: USA
Mailing address: PO Box 2660
Mailing city: Vista
Mailing state: CA
Mailing zip: 92085-2660
General Phone: (760) 724-3075
General/National Adv. E-mail: goodnewseditor@cox.net
Display Adv. E-mail: goodnewseditor@cox.net
Editorial e-mail: goodnewseditor@cox.net
Primary Website: www.goodnewsetc.com
Year Established: 1984
Delivery Methods: Racks
Avg Paid Circ: 32000
Avg Free Circ: 32000
Audit By: Sworn/Estimate/Non-Audited
Audit Date: 12.07.2019
Personnel: Colleen Monroe (Adv. Mgr.); Rick Monroe (Ed.)

ORANGE COUNTY CATHOLIC

Street address 1: 13280 Chapman Ave
Street address city: Garden Grove
Street address state: CA
Zip/Postal code: 92840-4414
County: Orange
Country: USA
General Phone: (714) 282-3075
Advertising Phone: (714) 881-1622
General/National Adv. E-mail: calmanza@rcbo.org
Display Adv. E-mail: ads@occatholic.com
Editorial e-mail: pmott@rcbo.org
Primary Website: http://occatholic.com/
Delivery Methods: Mail`Newsstand
Areas Served - City/County or Portion Thereof, or Zip codes: Orange County
Personnel: Hank Evers (Editor)
Parent company (for newspapers): Times Media Group

THE SOUTHERN CROSS

Street address 1: 3888 Paducah Dr
Street address city: San Diego
Street address state: CA
Zip/Postal code: 92117-5349
County: San Diego
Country: USA
Mailing address: PO Box 81869
Mailing city: San Diego
Mailing state: CA
Mailing zip: 92138-1869
General Phone: (858) 490-8266
General Fax: (858) 490-8355
Advertising Phone: (858) 490-8266
General/National Adv. E-mail: socross@sdcatholic.org
Display Adv. E-mail: dlightsey@sdcatholic.org
Editorial e-mail: cfuld@sdcatholic.org
Primary Website: www.thesoutherncross.org
Year Established: 1912
News Services: CNS
Delivery Methods: Mail`Racks
Areas Served - City/County or Portion Thereof, or Zip codes: 91901-92299 (MAINLY)
Avg Paid Circ: 34800
Avg Free Circ: 3200
Audit By: Sworn/Estimate/Non-Audited
Audit Date: 12.07.2019
Personnel: Rev. Charles L. Fuld (Mng. Ed.); Denis Grasska (Asst. Ed.); Lucas Turnbloom (Art Dir.); Donna Lightsey (Advertising/Administrative Coordinator); Bishop Robert McElroy; Aida Bustos (Staff Writer (Spanish))

THE TIDINGS

Street address 1: 3424 Wilshire Blvd
Street address 2: Fl 3
Street address city: Los Angeles
Street address state: CA
Zip/Postal code: 90010-2262
County: Los Angeles
Country: USA
Mailing address: 3424 Wilshire Blvd Fl 3
Mailing city: Los Angeles
Mailing state: CA
Mailing zip: 90010-2262
General Phone: (213) 637-7360
General Fax: (213) 637-6360
Advertising Phone: (213) 637-7590
Editorial Phone: (213) 637-7327
General/National Adv. E-mail: info@the-tidings.com
Display Adv. E-mail: otorres@the-tidings.com
Editorial e-mail: pkay@the-tidings.com
Primary Website: www.angelusnews.com
Year Established: 1865
Delivery Methods: Mail
Areas Served - City/County or Portion Thereof, or Zip codes: 90001Â£90899, 91001Â£93599,93001-9300993101-93109
Avg Paid Circ: 50000
Avg Free Circ: 372
Audit By: Sworn/Estimate/Non-Audited
Audit Date: 12.07.2019
Personnel: David Moore (Pub.); Chris Krause (Circulation)
Parent company (for newspapers): Archdiocese of Los Angeles

DENVER CATHOLIC REGISTER

Street address 1: 1300 S Steele St
Street address city: Denver
Street address state: CO
Zip/Postal code: 80210-2526
County: Denver
Country: USA
Mailing address: 1300 S Steele St
Mailing city: Denver
Mailing state: CO
Mailing zip: 80210-2526
General Phone: (303) 722-4687
General Fax: (303) 715-2045
Advertising Phone: (303) 715-3212
General/National Adv. E-mail: dcrads@archden.org; info@archden.org
Primary Website: www.archden.org
Year Established: 1900
Avg Paid Circ: 91165
Avg Free Circ: 379
Audit By: Sworn/Estimate/Non-Audited
Audit Date: 12.07.2019
Personnel: Charles J. Chaput (Pub.); Jeanette DeMelo (Gen. Mgr.); Chad Andrzejewski (Adv. Mgr.); Karen Mendoza (Circ. Mgr.); Roxanne King (Ed.)

EL PUEBLO CATOLICO

Street address 1: 1300 S Steele St
Street address city: Denver
Street address state: CO
Zip/Postal code: 80210-2526
County: Denver
Country: USA
Mailing address: 1300 S Steele St
Mailing city: Denver
Mailing state: CO
Mailing zip: 80210-2526
General Phone: (303) 715-3219
General Fax: (303) 715-2045
Audit By: Sworn/Estimate/Non-Audited
Audit Date: 12.07.2019
Personnel: Archbishop Charles J. Chaput (Pub.); Jeanette DeMelo (Gen. Mgr.); Ann Bush (Adv. Mgr.); Rosanna Goni (Ed.); Filippo Piccone (Prodn. Mgr.)

THE CATHOLIC TRANSCRIPT

Street address 1: 467 Bloomfield Ave
Street address city: Bloomfield
Street address state: CT
Zip/Postal code: 06002-2903
County: Hartford
Country: USA
Mailing address: 467 Bloomfield Ave
Mailing city: Bloomfield
Mailing state: CT
Mailing zip: 06002-2903
General Phone: (860) 286-2828
Advertising Phone:
Editorial Phone:
General/National Adv. E-mail: info@catholictranscript.org
Editorial e-mail: swolf@catholictranscript.org
Primary Website: www.catholictranscript.org
Year Established: 1898
Delivery Methods: Mail
Areas Served - City/County or Portion Thereof, or Zip codes: Hartford, Litchfield and New Haven County
Avg Free Circ: 174000
Audit By: Sworn/Estimate/Non-Audited
Audit Date: 12.07.2019
Personnel: Shelley Wolf (Ed.); Mary Chalupsky (Reporter); Leslie DiVinere (Design/Adv.); P. Blair (Archbishop/Pub.)

DISTRICT OF COLUMBIA

CATHOLIC STANDARD

Street address 1: 145 Taylor St NE
Street address city: Washington
Street address state: District of Columbia
Zip/Postal code: 20017-1008
County: District Of Columbia
Country: USA
Mailing address: PO Box 4464
Mailing city: Washington
Mailing state: District of Columbia
Mailing zip: 20017-0464
General Phone: (202) 281-2410
Avg Paid Circ: 46000
Avg Free Circ: 368
Audit By: Sworn/Estimate/Non-Audited
Audit Date: 12.07.2019

Personnel: Thomas H. Schmidt (Gen. Mgr.); Alan Hay (Dir., Sales/Mktg.); Irieska D. Caetano (Circ. Mgr.); Mark V. Zimmermann (Ed.)

THE FLORIDA CATHOLIC

Street address 1: 50 E Robinson St
Street address city: Orlando
Street address state: FL
Zip/Postal code: 32801-1619
County: Orange
Country: USA
Mailing address: PO Box 4993
Mailing city: Orlando
Mailing state: FL
Mailing zip: 32802-4993
General Phone: (407) 373-0075
General Fax: (407) 373-0087
General/National Adv. E-mail: info@thefloridacatholic.org
Avg Paid Circ: 59000
Avg Free Circ: 60000
Audit By: Sworn/Estimate/Non-Audited
Audit Date: 12.07.2019
Personnel: Ann Borowski Slade (Pub.); Tim Shea (Adv. Sales Dir.); Tammy Osburne (Circ. Mgr.); Jean Gonzales (Ed. Dir.); Michael Jimenez (Adv. Graphic Des.)

THE FLORIDA CATHOLIC

Street address 1: 11 N B St
Street address city: Pensacola
Street address state: FL
Zip/Postal code: 32502-4601
County: Escambia
Country: USA
Mailing address: 11 N B St
Mailing city: Pensacola
Mailing state: FL
Mailing zip: 32502-4601
Audit By: Sworn/Estimate/Non-Audited
Audit Date: 12.07.2019
Personnel: Christopher Gunty (Assoc. Pub.); David O'Leary (Adv. Sales Dir.); Maureen Neder (Circ. Mgr.)

THE FLORIDA CATHOLIC

Street address 1: 1000 Pinebrook Rd
Street address city: Venice
Street address state: FL
Zip/Postal code: 34285-6426
County: Sarasota
Country: USA
Mailing address: 1000 Pinebrook Rd
Mailing city: Venice
Mailing state: FL
Mailing zip: 34285-6426
General Phone: (941) 484-9543
General Fax: (941) 486-4763
General/National Adv. E-mail: peace&justice@dioceseofvenice.org
Avg Paid Circ: 16250
Audit By: Sworn/Estimate/Non-Audited
Audit Date: 19.10.2017
Personnel: Mark Caruso (Adv. Sales Mgr.); Kristie Nguyen (Ed.)

GEORGIA

SOUTHERN CROSS

Street address 1: 601 E Liberty St
Street address city: Savannah
Street address state: GA
Zip/Postal code: 31401-5118
County: Chatham
Country: USA
Mailing address: 601 E Liberty St
Mailing city: Savannah
Mailing state: GA
Mailing zip: 31401-5118
General Phone: (912) 201-4100
General Fax: (912) 201-4101
General/National Adv. E-mail: southerncross@diosav.org
Display Adv. E-mail: 2cents@diosav.org
Editorial e-mail: editor@diosav.org
Primary Website: www.diosav.org
Year Established: 1963
Delivery Methods: Mail
Avg Paid Circ: 27600
Avg Free Circ: 100
Audit By: Sworn/Estimate/Non-Audited
Audit Date: 12.07.2019
Personnel: Gregory J. Hartmayer (Publisher); Michael J. Johnson (Editor)

THE GEORGIA BULLETIN

Street address 1: 2401 Lake Park Dr SE
Street address city: Smyrna
Street address state: GA
Zip/Postal code: 30080-8862
County: Cobb
Country: USA
Mailing address: 2401 Lake Park Dr SE Ste 175
Mailing city: Smyrna
Mailing state: GA
Mailing zip: 30080-8815
General Phone: (404) 920-7430
General Fax: (404) 920-7431
Advertising Phone: (404) 920-7441
Advertising Fax: (404) 920-7431
Editorial Phone: (404) 920-7430
Editorial Fax: (404) 920-7431
General/National Adv. E-mail: editor@georgiabulletin.org
Display Adv. E-mail: ads@georgiabulletin.org
Editorial e-mail: editor@georgiabulletin.org
Primary Website: www.georgiabulletin.org
Year Established: 1963
Delivery Methods: Mail
Areas Served - City/County or Portion Thereof, or Zip codes: 30002-33065
Avg Paid Circ: 74000
Audit By: Sworn/Estimate/Non-Audited
Audit Date: 12.07.2019
Personnel: Archbishop Wilton Gregory (Pub.); Tom Aisthorpe (Adv. Mgr.); Mary Anne Castranio (Exec. Ed.); Gretchen R. Keiser (Ed.); Tom Schulte (Graphic Artist)

HAWAII

HAWAII CATHOLIC HERALD

Street address 1: 1184 Bishop St
Street address city: Honolulu
Street address state: HI
Zip/Postal code: 96813-2859
County: Honolulu
Country: USA
Mailing address: 1184 Bishop St Ste A
Mailing city: Honolulu
Mailing state: HI
Mailing zip: 96813-2859
General Phone: (808) 585-3300
General Fax: (808) 585-3381
Editorial Phone: (808) 585-3317
Editorial e-mail: herald@rcchawaii.org
Primary Website: www.hawaiicatholicherald.org
Year Established: 1936
News Services: Catholic News Service
Delivery Methods: Mail
Audit By: Sworn/Estimate/Non-Audited
Audit Date: 12.07.2019
Personnel: Clarence Silva (Pub.); Donna Aquino (Circ. Mgr.); Patrick Downes (Ed.)
Parent company (for newspapers): Roman Catholic Church in the State of Hawaii

IDAHO

IDAHO CATHOLIC REGISTER

Street address 1: 1501 S Federal Way
Street address city: Boise
Street address state: ID
Zip/Postal code: 83705-2588
County: Ada
Country: USA
Mailing address: 1501 S Federal Way Ste 450
Mailing city: Boise
Mailing state: ID
Mailing zip: 83705-2589
General Phone: (208) 342-1311
General Fax: (208) 342-0224
General/National Adv. E-mail: idcathreg@rcdb.org
Avg Paid Circ: 16700
Audit By: Sworn/Estimate/Non-Audited
Audit Date: 12.07.2019
Personnel: Bishop Michael P. Driscoll (Pub.); Ann Bixby (Adv. Mgr.); Michael Brown (Ed.)

CATHOLIC TIMES

Street address 1: 1615 W Washington St
Street address city: Springfield
Street address state: IL
Zip/Postal code: 62702-4757
County: Sangamon
Country: USA
Mailing address: 1615 W Washington St
Mailing city: Springfield
Mailing state: IL
Mailing zip: 62702-4757
General Phone: (217) 698-8500
General Fax: (217) 698-0802
General/National Adv. E-mail: catholictimes@dio.org
Primary Website: www.dio.org
Delivery Methods: Mail
Avg Paid Circ: 44980
Avg Free Circ: 115
Audit By: USPS
Audit Date: 27.09.2012
Personnel: Paula Ruot (Adv. Mgr.); Laura Weakley (Circ. Mgr.); Kathie Sass (Ed.); Cathy Locher (Reporter); Diane Schlindwein (Reporter)

CHICAGO CATÃ“LICO

Street address 1: 835 N. Rush St.
Street address city: Chicago
Street address state: IL
Zip/Postal code: 60611-2030
Country: USA
Mailing address: 835 N. Rush St.
Mailing city: Chicago
Mailing state: IL
Display Adv. E-mail: ccazares@archchicago.org
Editorial e-mail: editorial@catholicnewworld.com
Primary Website: www.catolicoperiodico.com/publicidad
Year Established: 1985
Areas Served - City/County or Portion Thereof, or Zip codes: Throughout Cook and Lake counties.
Personnel: Cesar Cazares (Adv. Mgr.)

THE CATHOLIC NEW WORLD

Street address 1: 835 N Rush St
Street address city: Chicago
Street address state: IL
Zip/Postal code: 60611-2030
County: Cook
Country: USA
General Phone: (312) 534-7777
General Fax: (312) 534-7350
General/National Adv. E-mail: editorial@catholicnewworld.com
Primary Website: www.catholicnewworld.com
Year Established: 1892
Delivery Methods: Mail
Areas Served - City/County or Portion Thereof, or Zip codes: Cook and Lake counties
Avg Paid Circ: 55000
Audit By: Sworn/Estimate/Non-Audited
Audit Date: 12.07.2019
Personnel: Cardinal Francis E. George (Pub.); Dawn Vidmar (Adv. Mgr.); Joyce Duriga (Ed.); Tony Rodriguez (Prodn. Mgr.)

THE CATHOLIC POST

Street address 1: 419 NE Madison Ave
Street address city: Peoria
Street address state: IL
Zip/Postal code: 61603-3719
County: Peoria
Country: USA
Mailing address: P.O. Box 1722
Mailing city: Peoria
Mailing state: IL
Mailing zip: 61656-1722
General Phone: (309) 671-1550
General Fax: (309) 671-1579
General/National Adv. E-mail: cathpost@cdop.org
Display Adv. E-mail: sknelson@cdop.org
Primary Website: www.thecatholicpost.com
Year Established: 1934
Delivery Methods: Mail
Areas Served - City/County or Portion Thereof, or Zip codes: Dozens throughout 26 counties in central Illinois
Avg Paid Circ: 12000
Audit By: Sworn/Estimate/Non-Audited
Audit Date: 12.07.2019
Personnel: Bishop Daniel R. Jenky (Pub.); Sonia Nelson (Adv. Mgr.); Tom Dermody (Ed.); Jennifer Willems; Theresa Lindley (Production assistant)

THE MESSENGER

Street address 1: 2620 Lebanon Ave
Street address city: Belleville
Street address state: IL
Zip/Postal code: 62221-3002
County: Saint Clair
Country: USA
Mailing address: 2620 Lebanon Ave Stop 2
Mailing city: Belleville
Mailing state: IL
Mailing zip: 62221-3001
General Phone: (618) 235-9601
General Fax: (618) 235-9605
General/National Adv. E-mail: cathnews@bellevillemessenger.org
Primary Website: www.bellevillemessenger.org
Year Established: 1808
Avg Paid Circ: 10500
Audit By: Sworn/Estimate/Non-Audited
Audit Date: 19.10.2017
Personnel: Bernadette Middeke (Adv. Mgr.); Liz Quirin (Ed.)

NORTHWEST INDIANA CATHOLIC

Street address 1: 9292 Broadway
Street address city: Merrillville
Street address state: IN
Zip/Postal code: 46410-7047
County: Lake
Country: USA
Mailing address: 9292 Broadway
Mailing city: Merrillville
Mailing state: IN
Mailing zip: 46410-7088
General Phone: (219) 769-9292
General Fax: (219) 736-6577
General/National Adv. E-mail: nwic@dcgary.org
Primary Website: www.nwicatholic.com
Year Established: 1987
Delivery Methods: Mail
Audit By: Sworn/Estimate/Non-Audited
Audit Date: 12.07.2019
Personnel: Carol Macinga (Circulation/Administrative Assistant/Accounts Receivable); Marlene Zloza (Staff writer); Doris LaFauci (Page and graphic designer); Anthony Alonzo (Photojournalist); Erin Ciszczon (Advertising Representative); ????
Parent company (for newspapers): Roman Catholic Diocese of Gary

OUR SUNDAY VISITOR

Street address 1: 200 Noll Plz
Street address city: Huntington
Street address state: IN
Zip/Postal code: 46750-4310
County: Huntington
Country: USA
General Phone: (260) 356-8400
General Fax: (260) 356-8472
Advertising Phone: (260) 359-2578
Advertising Fax: (260) 359-2578
Editorial Phone: (260) 359-2546
Editorial Fax: (260) 359-6446
General/National Adv. E-mail: oursunvis@osv.com
Display Adv. E-mail: tcalouette@osv.com
Editorial e-mail: gcrowe@osv.com
Primary Website: www.osv.com
Year Established: 1912
Delivery Methods: Mail
Areas Served - City/County or Portion Thereof, or Zip codes: All/any
Avg Paid Circ: 43000
Avg Free Circ: 4000
Audit By: Sworn/Estimate/Non-Audited

Audit Date: 12.07.2019
Personnel: Greg R. Erlandson (Pres./Pub.); Therese Calouette (Adv. Mgr.); John Christensen (Strategic Mktg. Dir.); Gretchen Crowe (Ed.); Chris Rice (Prodn. Mgr.)

THE CATHOLIC MOMENT

Street address 1: 610 Lingle Ave
Street address city: Lafayette
Street address state: IN
Zip/Postal code: 47901-1740
County: Tippecanoe
Country: USA
Mailing address: PO Box 1603
Mailing city: Lafayette
Mailing state: IN
Mailing zip: 47902-1603
General Phone: (765) 742-2050
General Fax: (765) 269-4615
General/National Adv. E-mail: moment@dol-in.org
Primary Website: dol-in.org/catholic-moment
Year Established: 1945
Delivery Methods: Mail
Areas Served - City/County or Portion Thereof, or Zip codes: Several
Avg Paid Circ: 28500
Avg Free Circ: 264
Audit By: USPS
Audit Date: 01.10.2013
Personnel: Most Rev. Timothy L. Doherty (Pub.); Carolyn McKinney (Circ. Mgr.); Laurie Cullen (Mng. Ed.); Kevin Cullen (Ed.)

THE CRITERION

Street address 1: 1400 N Meridian St
Street address city: Indianapolis
Street address state: IN
Zip/Postal code: 46202-2305
County: Marion
Country: USA
Mailing address: PO Box 1717
Mailing city: Indianapolis
Mailing state: IN
Mailing zip: 46206-1717
General Phone: (317) 236-7325
General Fax: (317) 236-1593
Audit By: Sworn/Estimate/Non-Audited
Audit Date: 12.07.2019
Personnel: Daniel Mark Buechlein (Pub.); Greg A. Otolski (Asst. Pub.); Ron Massey (Exec. Asst.); Mike Krokos (Ed.); John Shaughnessy (Asst. Ed.); Brandon A. Evans (Online Ed.)

THE MESSAGE

Street address 1: 4200 N Kentucky Ave
Street address city: Evansville
Street address state: IN
Zip/Postal code: 47711-2752
County: Vanderburgh
Country: USA
Mailing address: PO Box 4169
Mailing city: Evansville
Mailing state: IN
Mailing zip: 47724-0169
General Phone: (812) 424-5536
General Fax: (812) 424-0972
General/National Adv. E-mail: message@evido.org
Display Adv. E-mail: messagead@evdio.org
Editorial e-mail: message@evdio.org
Primary Website: www.themessageonline.org
Year Established: 1970
Delivery Methods: Mail
Avg Paid Circ: 5000
Audit By: Sworn/Estimate/Non-Audited
Audit Date: 12.07.2019
Personnel: Tim Lilley (Ed.); Sheila Barclay (Prod. Tech.); Trisha Smith (Assist. Ed.)

TODAYS CATHOLIC

Street address 1: 915 S Clinton St
Street address city: Fort Wayne
Street address state: IN
Zip/Postal code: 46802-2601
County: Allen
Country: USA
Mailing address: PO Box 11169
Mailing city: Fort Wayne
Mailing state: IN
Mailing zip: 46856-1169
General Phone: (260) 456-2824
General Fax: (260) 744-1473
Display Adv. E-mail: jparker@diocesefwsb.org
Editorial e-mail: editor@diocesefwsb.org
Primary Website: www.diocesefwsb.org; www.todayscatholicnews.org
Year Established: 1926
Delivery Methods: Mail`Racks
Areas Served - City/County or Portion Thereof, or Zip codes: 14 counties in northeastern Indiana
Avg Paid Circ: 207
Avg Free Circ: 10000
Audit By: Sworn/Estimate/Non-Audited
Audit Date: 12.07.2019
Personnel: Kevin Rhoades (Pub.); Stephanie Patka (Dir. of Comm.); Jodi Marlin (Ed.)

THE CATHOLIC MESSENGER

Street address 1: 780 W Central Park Ave
Street address city: Davenport
Street address state: IA
Zip/Postal code: 52804-1901
County: Scott
Country: USA
Mailing address: 780 W. Central Park Ave.
Mailing city: Davenport
Mailing state: IA
Mailing zip: 52804
General Phone: (563) 323-9959
General Fax: (563) 323-6612
Advertising Phone: (563) 323-9959
Editorial Phone: (563) 888-4246
General/National Adv. E-mail: messenger@davenportdiocese.org
Display Adv. E-mail: hart@davenportdiocese.org
Editorial e-mail: arland-fye@davenportdiocese.org
Primary Website: www.catholicmessenger.net
Year Established: 1882
Delivery Methods: Mail
Areas Served - City/County or Portion Thereof, or Zip codes: Multiple
Avg Paid Circ: 17100
Avg Free Circ: 200
Audit By: Sworn/Estimate/Non-Audited
Audit Date: 12.07.2019
Personnel: Barb Arland-Fye (Mng. Ed.); Anne Marie Amacher (Asst. Ed.); Duane Freund (Circulation/Business Office Coordinator); Jill Henderson (Circulation/Business Office Coordinator)

THE GLOBE

Street address 1: 1825 Jackson St
Street address city: Sioux City
Street address state: IA
Zip/Postal code: 51105-1055
County: Woodbury
Country: USA
Mailing address: PO Box 5079
Mailing city: Sioux City
Mailing state: IA
Mailing zip: 51102-5079
General Phone: (712) 255-2550
General Fax: (712) 255-4901
General/National Adv. E-mail: rwebb@catholicglobe.org
Avg Paid Circ: 25268
Avg Free Circ: 500
Audit By: Sworn/Estimate/Non-Audited
Audit Date: 12.07.2019
Personnel: Bishop R. Walker Nickless (Pub.); Renee Webb (Ed.)

THE WITNESS

Street address 1: 1229 Mount Loretta Ave
Street address 2: Box 917
Street address city: Dubuque
Street address state: IA
Zip/Postal code: 52004-0917
County: Dubuque
Country: USA
Mailing address: PO Box 917
Mailing city: Dubuque
Mailing state: IA
Mailing zip: 52004-0917
General Phone: (563) 588-0556
General Fax: (563) 588-0557
General/National Adv. E-mail: dbqcwo@arch.pvt.k12.ia.us
Avg Paid Circ: 14000
Audit By: Sworn/Estimate/Non-Audited
Audit Date: 12.07.2019
Personnel: Jerome Hanus (Pub.); Bret Fear (Adv. Mgr.); Catherine White (Circ. Mgr.); Sister Carol Hoverman (Ed.)

MENNONITE WORLD REVIEW

Street address 1: 129 W 6th St
Street address city: Newton
Street address state: KS
Zip/Postal code: 67114-2117
County: Harvey
Country: USA
Mailing address: PO Box 568
Mailing city: Newton
Mailing state: KS
Mailing zip: 67114-0568
General Phone: (316) 283-3670
Editorial e-mail: editor@mennoweekly.org
Primary Website: mennoworld.org
Year Established: 1923
Avg Paid Circ: 10200
Avg Free Circ: 751
Audit By: Sworn/Estimate/Non-Audited
Audit Date: 12.07.2019
Personnel: Robert Schrag (Pub.); Paul Schrag (Ed.)

THE CATHOLIC ADVANCE

Street address 1: 424 N Broadway Ave
Street address city: Wichita
Street address state: KS
Zip/Postal code: 67202-2310
County: Sedgwick
Country: USA
Mailing address: 424 N Broadway St
Mailing city: Wichita
Mailing state: KS
Mailing zip: 67202-2310
General Phone: (316) 269-3965
General Fax: (316) 269-3902
General/National Adv. E-mail: advancenews@catholicdioceseofwichita.org
Display Adv. E-mail: advanceads@cdowk.org
Primary Website: www.catholicadvance.org
Delivery Methods: Mail
Avg Paid Circ: 35500
Avg Free Circ: 93
Audit By: Sworn/Estimate/Non-Audited
Audit Date: 12.07.2019
Personnel: Christopher M. Riggs (Ed.); Donald G. McClane (Prodn. Mgr.)
Parent company (for newspapers): Catholic Diocese of Wichita

THE SOUTHWEST KANSAS CATHOLIC

Street address 1: 910 Central Ave
Street address city: Dodge City
Street address state: KS
Zip/Postal code: 67801-4905
County: Ford
Country: USA
Mailing address: PO Box 137
Mailing city: Dodge City
Mailing state: KS
Mailing zip: 67801-0137
General Phone: (620) 227-1519
General Fax: (620) 227-1545
Advertising Phone: (620) 227-1556
Advertising Fax: (620) 227-1545
Editorial Phone: (620) 227-1519
Editorial Fax: (620) 227-1545
General/National Adv. E-mail: skregister@dcdiocese.org
Display Adv. E-mail: twenzl@dcdiocese.org
Editorial e-mail: skregister@dcdiocese.org
Primary Website: www.dcdiocese.org/swkscatholic
Year Established: 1966
Delivery Methods: Mail`Racks
Areas Served - City/County or Portion Thereof, or Zip codes: Southwest Quarter of Kansas
Avg Free Circ: 6000
Audit By: Sworn/Estimate/Non-Audited
Audit Date: 12.07.2019
Personnel: David Myers (Ed); Tim Wenzl (Adv Rep); Brungardt Bishop John (Pub)
Parent company (for newspapers): Catholic Diocese of Dodge City

SOUTHEAST OUTLOOK

Street address 1: 920 Blankenbaker Pkwy
Street address city: Louisville
Street address state: KY
Zip/Postal code: 40243-1845
County: Jefferson
Country: USA
Mailing address: 920 Blankenbaker Pkwy
Mailing city: Louisville
Mailing state: KY
Mailing zip: 40243-1845
General Phone: (502) 253-8650

THE MESSENGER

Street address 1: 402 E 21st St
Street address city: Covington
Street address state: KY
Zip/Postal code: 41014-1588
County: Kenton
Country: USA
Mailing address: PO Box 15550
Mailing city: Covington
Mailing state: KY
Mailing zip: 41015-0550
General Phone: (859) 392-1500
General/National Adv. E-mail: mifcic@covingtondiocese.org
Avg Paid Circ: 27000
Avg Free Circ: 75
Audit By: Sworn/Estimate/Non-Audited
Audit Date: 12.07.2019
Personnel: Roger Foys (Pub.); Michael Ifcic (Adv. Mgr.); Judy Russo (Circ. Mgr.); Tim Fitzgerald (Ed.); Laura Keener (Asst. Ed.)

THE RECORD

Street address 1: 1200 S Shelby St
Street address city: Louisville
Street address state: KY
Zip/Postal code: 40203-2627
County: Jefferson
Country: USA
Mailing address: 1200 S Shelby St
Mailing city: Louisville
Mailing state: KY
Mailing zip: 40203-2627
General Phone: (502) 471-2125
General Fax: (502) 636-2379
Advertising Phone: (502) 471-2125
General/National Adv. E-mail: record@archlou.org
Display Adv. E-mail: record@archlou.org
Editorial e-mail: record@archlou.org
Primary Website: www.therecordnewspaper.org
Year Established: 1879
Delivery Methods: Mail
Avg Paid Circ: 59708
Audit By: Sworn/Estimate/Non-Audited
Audit Date: 12.07.2019
Personnel: Marnie McAllister (Ed.); Jennifer Jenkins (Adv. Mgr.)
Parent company (for newspapers): Paxton Media Group; Archdiocese of Louisville

WESTERN RECORDER

Street address 1: 13420 Eastpoint Centre Dr
Street address city: Louisville
Street address state: KY
Zip/Postal code: 40223-4160
County: Jefferson
Country: USA
Mailing address: PO Box 43969
Mailing city: Louisville
Mailing state: KY
Mailing zip: 40253-0969
General Phone: (502) 489-3535
General Fax: (502) 489-3565
Advertising Phone: (502) 489-3428
Advertising Fax: (502) 489-3228
Editorial Phone: (502) 489-3442
Primary Website: www.westernrecorder.org
Year Established: 1826
Delivery Methods: Mail
Areas Served - City/County or Portion Thereof, or Zip codes: Kentucky
Avg Paid Circ: 24000

Avg Free Circ: 1384
Audit By: Sworn/Estimate/Non-Audited
Audit Date: 12.07.2019
Personnel: Tom Townsend (Mktg. Mgr.)

LOUISIANA

BAPTIST MESSAGE

Street address 1: PO Box 311
Street address city: Alexandria
Street address state: LA
Zip/Postal code: 71309-0311
County: Rapides
Country: USA
Mailing address: PO Box 311
Mailing city: Alexandria
Mailing state: LA
Mailing zip: 71309-0311
General Phone: (318) 442-7728
General Fax: (318) 445-8328
General/National Adv. E-mail: info@baptistmessage.com
Display Adv. E-mail: advertising@baptistmessage.com
Editorial e-mail: editor@baptistmessage.com

CLARION HERALD

Street address 1: 7887 Walmsley Ave.
Street address city: New Orleans
Street address state: LA
Zip/Postal code: 70125
County: Orleans
Country: USA
Mailing address: PO Box 53247
Mailing city: New Orleans
Mailing state: LA
Mailing zip: 70153-3247
General Phone: (504) 596-3035
General Fax: (504) 596-3020
Advertising Phone: (504)596-3034
Advertising Fax: (504) 596-3039
Editorial Phone: (504) 596-3030
Editorial Fax: (504) 596-3020
General/National Adv. E-mail: clarionherald@clarionherald.org
Display Adv. E-mail: adsales@clarionherald.org
Editorial e-mail: clarionherald@clarionherald.org
Primary Website: www.clarionherald.org
Year Established: 1963
Delivery Methods: Carrier'Racks
Areas Served - City/County or Portion Thereof, or Zip codes: Southeast Louisiana
Avg Paid Circ: 50000
Avg Free Circ: 400
Audit By: Sworn/Estimate/Non-Audited
Audit Date: 01.10.2021
Personnel: M.J. Cahill (Adv. Dir.); Peter Finney (Exec. Ed.)

THE BAYOU CATHOLIC

Street address 1: 2779 Highway 311
Street address city: Schriever
Street address state: LA
Zip/Postal code: 70395-3273
County: Terrebonne
Country: USA
Mailing address: PO Box 505
Mailing city: Schriever
Mailing state: LA
Mailing zip: 70395-0505
General Phone: (985) 850-3132
General Fax: (985) 850-3232
General/National Adv. E-mail: bc@mobiletel.com
Avg Paid Circ: 32000
Audit By: Sworn/Estimate/Non-Audited
Audit Date: 12.07.2019
Personnel: Pat Keese (Sec.); Peggy Adams (Adv. Mgr.); Louis G. Aguirre (Ed.)

THE CATHOLIC COMMENTATOR

Street address 1: 1800 S Acadian Thruway
Street address city: Baton Rouge
Street address state: LA
Zip/Postal code: 70808-1663
County: East Baton Rouge
Country: USA
Mailing address: PO Box 2028
Mailing city: Baton Rouge
Mailing state: LA
Mailing zip: 70821-2028
Personnel: Lisa Disney (Circulation)

CHURCH WORLD

Street address 1: 510 Ocean Ave
Street address city: Portland
Street address state: ME
Zip/Postal code: 04103-4936
County: Cumberland
Country: USA
Mailing address: PO Box 11559
Mailing city: Portland
Mailing state: ME
Mailing zip: 04104-7559
General Phone: (207) 773-6471
General Fax: (207) 773-0182
General/National Adv. E-mail: churchworld@portlanddiocese.net
Primary Website: www.portlanddiocese.org
Year Established: 1930
Areas Served - City/County or Portion Thereof, or Zip codes: 04001, 04999
Audit By: Sworn/Estimate/Non-Audited
Audit Date: 12.07.2019
Personnel: Bishop Richard J. Malone (Pub.); Norman F. LeBlanc (Adv. Mgr.); Rita Coulombe (Circ. Mgr.); Thomas J. Kardos (Ed.)

ADVENTIST REVIEW

Street address 1: 12501 Old Columbia Pike
Street address city: Silver Spring
Street address state: MD
Zip/Postal code: 20904-6601
County: Montgomery
Country: USA
Mailing address: 12501 Old Columbia Pike
Mailing city: Silver Spring
Mailing state: MD
Mailing zip: 20904-6601
General Phone: (301) 680-6560
General Fax: (301) 680-6638
Advertising Phone: (301) 393-3054
General/National Adv. E-mail: letters@adventistreview.com
Primary Website: www.adventistreview.org
Year Established: 1849
Delivery Methods: Mail
Areas Served - City/County or Portion Thereof, or Zip codes: all
Avg Paid Circ: 23500
Avg Free Circ: 700
Audit By: Sworn/Estimate/Non-Audited
Audit Date: 12.07.2019
Personnel: Bill Knott (Ed.); Stephen Chavez (Mng. Ed.); Merle Poirier (Tech. Pjcts. Coord.); Lael Caesar (associate editor); Gerald Klingbeil (associate editor); Wilona Karimabadi (assistant editor); Costin Jordache (Communication Director and News Editor)

EL PREGONERO

Street address 1: 5001 Eastern Ave
Street address city: Hyattsville
Street address state: MD
Zip/Postal code: 20782-3447
County: Prince Georges
Country: USA
Mailing address: PO Box 4464
Mailing city: Washington
Mailing state: District of Columbia
Mailing zip: 20017-0464
General Phone: (202) 281-2404
General Fax: (202) 281-2448
Advertising Phone: (202) 281-2406
Editorial Phone: (202) 281-2442
General/National Adv. E-mail: rafael@elpreg.org
Display Adv. E-mail: irieska@elpreg.org
Editorial e-mail: rafael@elpreg.org
Primary Website: elpreg.org
Year Established: 1977
Delivery Methods: Newsstand'Carrier
Avg Free Circ: 24993
Audit By: AAM
Audit Date: 30.06.2018
Personnel: Rafael Roncal (Ed.); Irieska D. Caetano (Circ. Mgr.)

THE CATHOLIC REVIEW

Street address 1: 880 Park Ave
Street address city: Baltimore
Street address state: MD
Zip/Postal code: 21201-4822
County: Baltimore City
Country: USA
Mailing address: PO Box 777
Mailing city: Baltimore
Mailing state: MD
Mailing zip: 21203-0777
General Phone: (443) 524-3150
General Fax: (443) 524-3155
Advertising Phone: (443) 263-0247
Advertising Fax: (443) 524-3155
Editorial Phone: (443) 263-0259
Editorial Fax: (443) 524-3160
General/National Adv. E-mail: mail@catholicreview.org
Display Adv. E-mail: mail@catholicreview.org
Editorial e-mail: mail@catholicreview.org
Primary Website: www.catholicreview.org
Year Established: 1914
Delivery Methods: Mail'Racks
Areas Served - City/County or Portion Thereof, or Zip codes: 206XX-219XX
Avg Paid Circ: 47843
Avg Free Circ: 172
Audit By: USPS
Audit Date: 27.10.2011
Personnel: Paul McMullen (Managing Ed.); Christopher Gunty (Assoc. Pub./Editor); Jeff Stintz (Advertising Mgr.)
Parent company (for newspapers): CR Media

UNITED METHODIST CONNECTION

Street address 1: 7178 Columbia Gateway Dr
Street address 2: Ste D
Street address city: Columbia
Street address state: MD
Zip/Postal code: 21046-2581
County: Howard
Country: USA
Mailing address: 7178 Columbia Gateway Dr Ste D
Mailing city: Columbia
Mailing state: MD
Mailing zip: 21046-2581
General Phone: (410) 309-3400
General Fax: (410) 309-9794
General/National Adv. E-mail: connection@bwcumc.org
Avg Paid Circ: 10000
Audit By: Sworn/Estimate/Non-Audited
Audit Date: 12.07.2019
Personnel: Melissa Lauber (Ed.)

MASSACHUSETTS

THE ANCHOR

Street address 1: 887 Highland Ave
Street address city: Fall River
Street address state: MA
Zip/Postal code: 02720-3820
County: Bristol
Country: USA
Mailing address: PO Box 7
Mailing city: Fall River
Mailing state: MA
Mailing zip: 02722-0007
General Phone: (508) 675-7151
General Fax: (508) 675-7048
Audit By: Sworn/Estimate/Non-Audited
Audit Date: 12.07.2019
Personnel: Most Rev. George W. Coleman (Pub.); Rev. Roger Landry (Exec. Ed.)

THE CATHOLIC FREE PRESS

Street address 1: 49 Elm St
Street address city: Worcester
Street address state: MA
Zip/Postal code: 01609-2514
County: Worcester
Country: USA
Mailing address: 49 Elm St
Mailing city: Worcester
Mailing state: MA
Mailing zip: 01609-2598
General Phone: (508) 757-6387
General Fax: (508) 756-8315
General/National Adv. E-mail: cpfnews@catholicfreepress.org
Display Adv. E-mail: advertising@catholicfreepress.org
Editorial e-mail: editor@catholicfreepress.org
Primary Website: www.catholicfreepress.org
Year Established: 1951
News Services: Catholic News Service
Delivery Methods: Mail
Areas Served - City/County or Portion Thereof, or Zip codes: 01401-01790
Avg Paid Circ: 11000
Avg Free Circ: 660
Audit By: Sworn/Estimate/Non-Audited
Audit Date: 12.07.2019
Personnel: Bishop Robert J. McManus (Pub.); Robert C. Ballantine (Adv. Mgr.); Margaret M. Russell (Ed.)
Parent company (for newspapers): The Roman Catholic Diocese of Worcester

THE PILOT

Street address 1: 66 Brooks Dr
Street address city: Braintree
Street address state: MA
Zip/Postal code: 02184-3839
County: Norfolk
Country: USA
Mailing address: 66 Brooks Dr
Mailing city: Braintree
Mailing state: MA
Mailing zip: 02184-3839
General Phone: (617) 779-3780
General Fax: (617) 779-4562
Advertising Phone: (617) 779-3788
Editorial Phone: (617) 779-3782
General/National Adv. E-mail: editorial@TheBostonPilot.com
Display Adv. E-mail: advertising@TheBostonPilot.com
Editorial e-mail: editorial@TheBostonPilot.com
Primary Website: www.TheBostonPilot.com.com
Year Established: 1829
Delivery Methods: Mail'Racks
Areas Served - City/County or Portion Thereof, or Zip codes: 01462-02494
Avg Paid Circ: 21150
Avg Free Circ: 300
Audit By: USPS
Audit Date: 13.10.2012
Personnel: Larry Ricardo (Adv. Mgr.); Antonio Enrique (Ed.); Gregory Tracy (Mng. Ed.); Nan Wilkins (Prodn. Mgr.); Ernesto Cuevas (Bus. Mgr.); Jon Tan (Coord., Mktg./Circ.)
Parent company (for newspapers): iCatholic Media, Inc.

THE BANNER

Street address 1: 1700 28th St SE
Street address city: Grand Rapids
Street address state: MI
Zip/Postal code: 49508-1407
County: Kent
Country: USA
Mailing address: 1700 28th St. SE
Mailing city: Grand Rapids
Mailing state: MI
Mailing zip: 49508-1407
General Phone: (616) 224-0732
General Fax: (616) 224-0834
Advertising Phone: (616) 224-5882
Editorial Phone: (616) 224-0824
General/National Adv. E-mail: info@thebanner.org
Display Adv. E-mail: ads@thebanner.org
Primary Website: www.thebanner.org
Delivery Methods: Mail
Avg Free Circ: 83500
Audit By: Sworn/Estimate/Non-Audited
Audit Date: 12.07.2019

Personnel: Shiao Chong (Editor in chief); Judy Hardy (Assoc. Ed.); Alissa Vernon (News Ed.); Gayla Postma (News Ed.); Kristy Quist (Mixed Media); Dean Heetderks (Art Dir.)

THE CATHOLIC TIMES

Street address 1: PO Box 1405
Street address city: Saginaw
Street address state: MI
Zip/Postal code: 48605-1405
County: Saginaw
Country: USA
Mailing address: PO Box 1405
Mailing city: Saginaw
Mailing state: MI
Mailing zip: 48605-1405
General Phone: (989) 793-7661
Avg Paid Circ: 8660
Avg Free Circ: 114
Audit By: Sworn/Estimate/Non-Audited
Audit Date: 12.07.2019
Personnel: Mark A. Myczkowiak (Pub.); Julie Root (Adv. Mgr.); Chris Brass (Circ. Mgr.); Mark Haney (Ed.)

THE CATHOLIC WEEKLY

Street address 1: 1520 Court St
Street address city: Saginaw
Street address state: MI
Zip/Postal code: 48602-4067
County: Saginaw
Country: USA
Mailing address: PO Box 1405
Mailing city: Saginaw
Mailing state: MI
Mailing zip: 48605-1405
General Phone: (989) 793-7661
General Fax: (989) 793-7663
General/National Adv. E-mail: catholicweekly@sbcglobal.net
Primary Website: www.catholicweekly.org
Year Established: 1942
News Services: CNS
Avg Paid Circ: 13173
Avg Free Circ: 637
Audit By: Sworn/Estimate/Non-Audited
Audit Date: 12.07.2019
Personnel: Mark A. Myczkowiak (Gen. Mgr./Adv. Mgr.); Chris Brass (Book Keeper); Mark Haney (Mng. Ed.); Julie Root
Parent company (for newspapers): G.L.S. Diocesan Reports, Inc.

THE MICHIGAN CATHOLIC

Street address 1: 305 Michigan Ave
Street address city: Detroit
Street address state: MI
Zip/Postal code: 48226-2631
County: Wayne
Country: USA
Mailing address: 305 Michigan Ave Ste 400A
Mailing city: Detroit
Mailing state: MI
Mailing zip: 48226-2698
General Phone: (313) 224-8000
Avg Paid Circ: 25000
Audit By: Sworn/Estimate/Non-Audited
Audit Date: 19.10.2017
Personnel: Michael Stechschulte (Managing Ed.)
Parent company (for newspapers): Archdiocese of Detroit

ST. CLOUD VISITOR

Street address 1: 305 7th Ave N
Street address 2: Ste 206
Street address city: Saint Cloud
Street address state: MN
Zip/Postal code: 56303-3633
County: Stearns
Country: USA
Mailing address: PO Box 1068
Mailing city: Saint Cloud
Mailing state: MN
Mailing zip: 56302-1068
General Phone: (320) 251-3022
General Fax: (320) 251-0424
General/National Adv. E-mail: news@stcloudvisitor.org
Primary Website: www.stclouddiocese.org
Year Established: 1938
Avg Paid Circ: 45000
Avg Free Circ: 125
Audit By: Sworn/Estimate/Non-Audited
Audit Date: 12.07.2019
Personnel: Bishop John Kinney (Pub.); Rose Kruger Fuchs (Adv. Mgr.); Paula Lemke (Circ. Mgr.); Joe Towalski (Ed.)

THE CATHOLIC SPIRIT

Street address 1: 244 Dayton Ave
Street address city: Saint Paul
Street address state: MN
Zip/Postal code: 55102-1802
County: Ramsey
Country: USA
Mailing address: 244 Dayton Ave
Mailing city: Saint Paul
Mailing state: MN
Mailing zip: 55102-1802
General Phone: (651) 291-4444
General Fax: (651) 291-4460
General/National Adv. E-mail: catholicspirit@archspm.org
Primary Website: www.thecatholicspirit.com
Year Established: 1911
Areas Served - City/County or Portion Thereof, or Zip codes: 55100, 55400, 55300, 56000
Avg Paid Circ: 85000
Avg Free Circ: 106
Audit By: Sworn/Estimate/Non-Audited
Audit Date: 12.07.2019
Personnel: Archbishop John Nienstedt (Pub.); Bob Zyskowski (Assoc. Pub.); Martie McMahon (Acct. Supvr.); Joe Towalski (Ed.); Pat Norby (Mng. Ed.); John Wolszon (Prodn. Mgr.)

MISSISSIPPI

GULF PINE CATHOLIC

Street address 1: 1790 Popps Ferry Rd
Street address city: Biloxi
Street address state: MS
Zip/Postal code: 39532-2118
County: Harrison
Country: USA
Mailing address: 1790 Popps Ferry Rd
Mailing city: Biloxi
Mailing state: MS
Mailing zip: 39532-2118
General Phone: (228) 702-2126
General Fax: (228) 702-2128
General/National Adv. E-mail: gulfpinecatholic&biloxidiocese.org
Display Adv. E-mail: gulfpinecatholic@biloxidiocese.org
Primary Website: www.gulfpinecatholic.com
Year Established: 1983
Delivery Methods: Mail
Avg Paid Circ: 17800
Audit By: Sworn/Estimate/Non-Audited
Audit Date: 12.07.2019
Personnel: Deborah Mowrey (Circ. Mgr.); Shirley M. Henderson (Ed.); Terrance Dickson (Reporter); Roger Morin (Bishop of Biloxi); Most Rev. Thomas J. Rodi (Pub.)

MISSISSIPPI CATHOLIC

Street address 1: 237 E Amite St
Street address city: Jackson
Street address state: MS
Zip/Postal code: 39201-2405
County: Hinds
Country: USA
Mailing address: PO Box 2130
Mailing city: Jackson
Mailing state: MS
Mailing zip: 39225-2130
General Phone: (601) 969-3581
General Fax: (601) 960-8455
General/National Adv. E-mail: editor@mississippicatholic.com
Editorial e-mail: editor@mississippicatholic.com
Primary Website: www.mississippicatholic.com
Year Established: 1954
News Services: Catholic News Service
Delivery Methods: Mail
Avg Paid Circ: 13112
Audit By: Sworn/Estimate/Non-Audited
Audit Date: 12.07.2019
Personnel: Joseph N. Latino (Pub.); Elsa Baughman (Adv. Mgr.); Pamela Butler (Circ. Mgr.); Janna Avalon (Ed.); Tyna McNealy (Prodn. Mgr.)

THE BAPTIST RECORD

Street address 1: 515 Mississippi Street
Street address city: Jackson
Street address state: MS
Zip/Postal code: 39205-0530
County: Hinds
Country: USA
Mailing address: PO Box 530
Mailing city: Jackson
Mailing state: MS
Mailing zip: 39205-0530
General Phone: (601) 968-3800
General Fax: (601) 292-3330
General/National Adv. E-mail: baptistrecord@mbcb.org
Primary Website: www.mbcb.org
Year Established: 1877
Delivery Methods: Mail
Avg Paid Circ: 57000
Avg Free Circ: 31
Audit By: Sworn/Estimate/Non-Audited
Audit Date: 12.07.2019
Personnel: Dana Richardson (Adv. Coord.); William H. Perkins (Ed.); Tony Martin (Assoc. Ed.); DeAnna Burgess (Circ. Mgr.)
Parent company (for newspapers): Mississippi Baptist Convention Board

NATIONAL CATHOLIC REPORTER

Street address 1: 115 E Armour Blvd
Street address city: Kansas City
Street address state: MO
Zip/Postal code: 64111-1203
County: Jackson
Country: USA
Mailing address: 115 E Armour Blvd
Mailing city: Kansas City
Mailing state: MO
Mailing zip: 64111
General Phone: (816) 531-0538
Advertising Phone: (816) 531-0538 opt 4
Editorial Phone: (816) 531-0538 opt 5
General/National Adv. E-mail: support@ncronline.org
Display Adv. E-mail: ncrad@ncronline.org
Classified Adv. e-mail: ncrad@ncronline.org
Editorial e-mail: ncr_editor@ncronline.org
Primary Website: www.ncronline.org
Year Established: 1964
Delivery Methods: Mail
Areas Served - City/County or Portion Thereof, or Zip codes: National and International
Avg Paid Circ: 25000
Avg Free Circ: 150
Audit By: Sworn/Estimate/Non-Audited
Audit Date: 01.08.2021
Personnel: Wally Reiter (CFO/Bus. Mgr.); Toni-Ann Ortiz (Art Dir.); Kim Rea (Adv Mgr); Jo Schierhoff (Circ Mgr); Tony Hernandez (Audience Engagement Director); Nancy Browne (Chief Advancement Officer); Sara Wiercinski (Aud Engagement Dir); Marge Gasnick (Director of Development Operations); Joe Ferullo (CEO/Publisher); Bill Mitchell (CEO/Publisher); Heidi Schlumpf (VP & Executive Editor); Tom Fox (President & CEO); Tom Roberts (Executive Editor)

REPORTER

Street address 1: 1333 S Kirkwood Rd
Street address city: Saint Louis
Street address state: MO
Zip/Postal code: 63122-7226
County: Saint Louis
Country: USA
Mailing address: 1333 S Kirkwood Rd
Mailing city: Saint Louis
Mailing state: MO
Mailing zip: 63122-7226
General Phone: (314) 996-1231
General Fax: (314) 996-1126
General/National Adv. E-mail: adriane.dorr@lcms.org
Display Adv. E-mail: kathryn.gritts@lcms.org
Editorial e-mail: joe.isenhower@lcms.org
Primary Website: www.reporter.lcms.org
Year Established: 1974
Delivery Methods: Mail
Avg Free Circ: 35000
Audit By: USPS
Audit Date: 01.10.2012
Personnel: David Strand (Executive Director); Joe Isenhower (Executive Editor, News & Information); Adriane Dorr (Executive Editor)
Parent company (for newspapers): The Lutheran Church--Missouri Synod

ST. LOUIS REVIEW

Street address 1: 20 Archbishop May Dr
Street address city: Saint Louis
Street address state: MO
Zip/Postal code: 63119-5738
County: Saint Louis
Country: USA
Mailing address: 20 Archbishop May Dr
Mailing city: Saint Louis
Mailing state: MO
Mailing zip: 63119-5738
General Phone: (314) 792-7500
General Fax: (314) 792-7534
General/National Adv. E-mail: slreview@stlouisreview.com
Avg Paid Circ: 72000
Audit By: Sworn/Estimate/Non-Audited
Audit Date: 12.07.2019
Personnel: Teak Phillips (Ed.)

THE CATHOLIC MISSOURIAN

Street address 1: PO Box 104900
Street address city: Jefferson City
Street address state: MO
Zip/Postal code: 65110-4900
County: Cole
Country: USA
Mailing address: PO Box 104900
Mailing city: Jefferson City
Mailing state: MO
Mailing zip: 65110-4900
General Phone: (573) 635-9127
General Fax: (573) 635-2286
General/National Adv. E-mail: cathmo@diojeffcity.org
Primary Website: www.diojeffcity.org
Year Established: 1957
Avg Paid Circ: 20578
Avg Free Circ: 755
Audit By: Sworn/Estimate/Non-Audited
Audit Date: 12.07.2019
Personnel: Bishop John R. Gaydos (Pub.); Kelly Martin (Adv. Dir.); Jay Nies (Ed.)

THE MIRROR

Street address 1: 601 S Jefferson Ave
Street address city: Springfield
Street address state: MO
Zip/Postal code: 65806-3107
County: Greene
Country: USA
Mailing address: 601 S Jefferson Ave
Mailing city: Springfield
Mailing state: MO
Mailing zip: 65806-3107
General Phone: (417) 866-0841
Primary Website: www.the-mirror.org
Year Established: 1956
Delivery Methods: Mail
Avg Paid Circ: 17000
Audit By: Sworn/Estimate/Non-Audited
Audit Date: 12.07.2019
Personnel: Angie Toben (Administrative Assistant/ Circulation Manager); Leslie Eidson (Ed.); Glenn Eckl (Production/Web)

THE PATHWAY

Street address 1: 400 E High St
Street address city: Jefferson City
Street address state: MO
Zip/Postal code: 65101-3215
County: Cole
Country: USA
Mailing address: 400 E High St
Mailing city: Jefferson City
Mailing state: MO
Mailing zip: 65101-3215
General Phone: (573) 636-0400
General Fax: (573) 635-5631
Advertising Phone: (573) 636-0400
General/National Adv. E-mail: dhinkle@mobaptist.org

Display Adv. E-mail: bpeeper@mobaptist.org
Editorial e-mail: dhinkle@mobaptist.org
Primary Website: www.mbcpathway.com
Year Established: 2002
Delivery Methods: Mail
Areas Served - City/County or Portion Thereof, or Zip codes: All
Avg Paid Circ: 29400
Audit By: Sworn/Estimate/Non-Audited
Audit Date: 21.10.2021
Personnel: Don Hinkle (Editor); Brian Koonce (News Writer); Ben Hawkins
Parent company (for newspapers): Missouri Baptist Convention

SOUTHERN NEBRASKA REGISTER

Street address 1: 3700 Sheridan Blvd
Street address city: Lincoln
Street address state: NE
Zip/Postal code: 68506-6100
County: Lancaster
Country: USA
Mailing address: PO Box 80329
Mailing city: Lincoln
Mailing state: NE
Mailing zip: 68501-0329
Avg Paid Circ: 25000
Audit By: Sworn/Estimate/Non-Audited
Audit Date: 12.07.2019
Personnel: James Conley (Pub.); Kim Breitfelder (Circ. Mgr.); Nick Kipper (Editor)

THE CATHOLIC VOICE

Street address 1: 2222 N. 111th St.
Street address city: Omaha
Street address state: NE
Zip/Postal code: 68164
County: Douglas
Country: USA
Mailing address: 2222 N. 111th St.
Mailing city: Omaha
Mailing state: NE
Mailing zip: 68164
Audit Date: 19.10.2017
Personnel: Most Rev. George J. Lucas (Pub.); Randy Grosse (Adv. Mgr.); Mike May (Editor)

WEST NEBRASKA REGISTER

Street address 1: 2708 Old Fair Rd
Street address city: Grand Island
Street address state: NE
Zip/Postal code: 68803-5221
County: Hall
Country: USA
Mailing address: PO Box 608
Mailing city: Grand Island
Mailing state: NE
Mailing zip: 68802-0608
General Phone: (308) 382-4660
Primary Website: www.gidiocese.org
Delivery Methods: Mail
Areas Served - City/County or Portion Thereof, or Zip codes: 688, 689, 691, 692, 693, 686,
Avg Paid Circ: 17153
Audit By: Sworn/Estimate/Non-Audited
Audit Date: 12.07.2019
Personnel: Mary Parlin (Ed.); Colleen Gallion (Assoc. Ed.)

CATHOLIC STAR HERALD

Street address 1: Pastoral Ctr 15 N Seventh St
Street address city: Camden
Street address state: NJ
Zip/Postal code: 8102
County: Camden
Country: USA
Mailing address: Pastoral Ctr. 15 N. Seventh St.
Mailing city: Camden
Mailing state: NJ
Mailing zip: 08102
General Phone: (856) 583-6142
General Fax: (856) 756-7938
Advertising Phone: (856) 583-6166
Advertising Fax: (856) 756-7938
Editorial Phone: (856) 583-6147
Display Adv. E-mail: pwothington@camdendiocese.org
Editorial e-mail: cpeters@camdendiocese.org
Primary Website: www.catholicstarherald.org
Year Established: 1951
Delivery Methods: Mail
Audit By: Sworn/Estimate/Non-Audited
Audit Date: 12.07.2019

THE BEACON

Street address 1: 775 Valley Rd
Street address city: Clifton
Street address state: NJ
Zip/Postal code: 07013-2205
County: Passaic
Country: USA
Mailing address: PO Box 1887
Mailing city: Clifton
Mailing state: NJ
Mailing zip: 07015-1887
General Phone: (973) 279-8845
General Fax: (973) 279-2265
General/National Adv. E-mail: catholicbeacon@patersondiocese.org; msbeacon@optonline.net
Primary Website: www.patersondiocese.org
Year Established: 1967
Delivery Methods: Mail
Areas Served - City/County or Portion Thereof, or Zip codes: All of Passaic, Morris and Sussex Counties in Northern New Jersey
Avg Paid Circ: 28750
Avg Free Circ: 200
Audit By: Sworn/Estimate/Non-Audited
Audit Date: 12.07.2019
Personnel: Arthur Serratelli (Pub.); Joyce DeCeglie (Circ. Mgr.); Richard Sokerka (Ed.)

THE MONITOR

Street address 1: 701 Lawrence Rd
Street address city: Trenton
Street address state: NJ
Zip/Postal code: 08648-4209
County: Mercer
Country: USA
Mailing address: PO Box 5147
Mailing city: Trenton
Mailing state: NJ
Mailing zip: 08638-0147
General Phone: (609) 406-7404
General Fax: (609) 406-7423
Advertising Phone: (609) 403-7117
General/National Adv. E-mail: monitor@dioceseoftrenton.org; info@dioceseoftrenton.org
Display Adv. E-mail: monitor-advertising@dioceseoftrenton.org
Editorial e-mail: monitor-news@dioceseoftrenton.org
Primary Website: www.TrentonMonitor.com
Year Established: 1953
Delivery Methods: Mail
Avg Paid Circ: 15000
Audit By: Sworn/Estimate/Non-Audited
Audit Date: 12.07.2019
Personnel: Rayanne Bennett (Assoc. Pub.); George Stevenson (Bus. Dir.); Mary Stadnyk (Associate Ed); David M. O'Connell (Bishop); Mary Morrell (Mng Ed.)

AMERICA

Street address 1: 106 W 56th St
Street address city: New York
Street address state: NY
Zip/Postal code: 10019-3866
County: New York
Country: USA
Mailing address: 106 W 56th St
Mailing city: New York
Mailing state: NY
Mailing zip: 10019-3893
General Phone: (212) 581-4640
General Fax: (212) 399-3596
General/National Adv. E-mail: america@americamagazine.org
Avg Paid Circ: 46000
Avg Free Circ: 283
Audit By: Sworn/Estimate/Non-Audited
Audit Date: 12.07.2019
Personnel: Rew Christiansen (Ed.); Robert C. Collins (Mng. Ed.)

CATHOLIC COURIER

Street address 1: 1150 Buffalo Rd
Street address city: Rochester
Street address state: NY
Zip/Postal code: 14624-1823
County: Monroe
Country: USA
Mailing address: PO Box 24379
Mailing city: Rochester
Mailing state: NY
Mailing zip: 14624-0379
General Phone: (585) 529-9530
General Fax: (585)529-9532
Editorial Fax: (585) 529-9509
General/National Adv. E-mail: info@catholiccourier.com
Display Adv. E-mail: ads@catholiccourier.com
Editorial e-mail: newsroom@catholiccourier.com
Primary Website: www.catholiccourier.com
Year Established: 1889
News Services: CNS
Delivery Methods: Mail
Areas Served - City/County or Portion Thereof, or Zip codes: Generally 13021-14905 with some exceptions; specific circulation by zip code data available from circ. mgr.
Avg Paid Circ: 104812
Avg Free Circ: 0
Audit By: USPS
Audit Date: 07.10.2014
Personnel: Karen M. Franz (GM/Editor); Jennifer Ficcaglia (Asst. Ed.); Donna Stubbings (Circ. Mgr.); Bishop Salvatore. R Matano (President & Publisher); Matt Saxon (Graphics Mgr.); Angela Visconte (Advertising)
Parent company (for newspapers): Rochester Catholic Press Association, Inc

CATHOLIC SUN

Street address 1: 420 Montgomery St
Street address city: Syracuse
Street address state: NY
Zip/Postal code: 13202-2920
County: Onondaga
Country: USA
Mailing address: 420 Montgomery St
Mailing city: Syracuse
Mailing state: NY
Mailing zip: 13202-2920
General Phone: (315) 422-8153
General Fax: (315) 422-7549
General/National Adv. E-mail: catholicsun@yahoo.com
Avg Paid Circ: 28000
Avg Free Circ: 348
Audit By: Sworn/Estimate/Non-Audited
Audit Date: 12.07.2019
Personnel: James Moynihan (Pres.); Katherine Long (Ed. in Chief)

NORTH COUNTRY CATHOLIC

Street address 1: 622 Washington St
Street address city: Ogdensburg
Street address state: NY
Zip/Postal code: 13669-1724
County: Saint Lawrence
Country: USA
Mailing address: PO Box 326
Mailing city: Ogdensburg
Mailing state: NY
Mailing zip: 13669-0326
General Phone: (315) 608-7556
General Fax: 866-314-7296
General/National Adv. E-mail: news@northcountrycatholic.org
Primary Website: www.northcountrycatholic.org
Year Established: 1946
Delivery Methods: Mail
Areas Served - City/County or Portion Thereof, or Zip codes: 12883 through 13690
Avg Paid Circ: 4000
Avg Free Circ: 25
Audit By: Sworn/Estimate/Non-Audited
Audit Date: 12.07.2019
Personnel: Mary Lou (Kilian)

THE CATHOLIC SUN

Street address 1: 424 Montgomery St
Street address city: Syracuse
Street address state: NY
Zip/Postal code: 13202-2920
County: Onondaga
Country: USA
Mailing address: 240 E ONONDAGA ST
Mailing city: SYRACUSE
Mailing state: NY
Mailing zip: 13202-2608
General Phone: (315) 422-8153
General Fax: (315) 422-7549
Advertising Phone: (315) 579-0001
General/National Adv. E-mail: mklenz@syracusediocese.org
Editorial e-mail: info@thecatholicsun.com
Primary Website: www.thecatholicsun.com
Year Established: 1892
Delivery Methods: Mail
Areas Served - City/County or Portion Thereof, or Zip codes: Broome, Cortland, Chenango, Madison, Oneida, Onondaga, Oswego Counties
Audit By: Sworn/Estimate/Non-Audited
Audit Date: 12.07.2019
Personnel: Katherine Long (Ed.); Mark Klenz (Ad. Director)

THE EVANGELIST

Street address 1: 40 N Main Ave
Street address city: Albany
Street address state: NY
Zip/Postal code: 12203-1481
County: Albany
Country: USA
Mailing address: 40 N Main Ave Ste 2
Mailing city: Albany
Mailing state: NY
Mailing zip: 12203-1483
General Phone: (518) 453-6688
General Fax: (518) 453-8448
Advertising Phone: (518) 453-6696
Advertising Fax: (518) 453-8448
Editorial Phone: (518) 453-6688
Editorial Fax: (518) 453-8448
General/National Adv. E-mail: christopher.ringwald@rcpa.org
Display Adv. E-mail: john.salvione@rcda.org
Primary Website: www.evangelist.org
Year Established: 1926
Avg Paid Circ: 50000
Avg Free Circ: 280
Audit By: Sworn/Estimate/Non-Audited
Audit Date: 12.07.2019
Personnel: Kate Blain (Ed.); John Salvione (Adv. Rep.)

THE FORWARD

Street address 1: 45 E 33rd St
Street address city: New York
Street address state: NY
Zip/Postal code: 10016-5336
County: New York
Country: USA
Mailing address: 45 E 33rd St
Mailing city: New York
Mailing state: NY
Mailing zip: 10016-5336
General Phone: (212) 889-8200
General Fax: (212) 689-4255
Audit By: Sworn/Estimate/Non-Audited
Audit Date: 12.07.2019
Personnel: Jerome Koenig (Adv. Mgr.); Lori Weinberg (Circ. Mgr.); J.J. Goldberg (Ed.); Wayne Hoffman (Mng. Ed.); Kurt Hoffman (Prodn. Mgr.)
Parent company (for newspapers): Joseph Jacobs Organization

THE JEWISH PRESS

Street address 1: 3692 Bedford Avenue
Street address city: Brooklyn
Street address state: NY
Zip/Postal code: 11229
County: Kings
Country: U.S.
General Phone: 718-330-1100
General Fax: 718/624-4106
Advertising Phone: 718-645-7297
Editorial Phone: 718-330-1100
General/National Adv. E-mail: editor@jewishpress.com
Display Adv. E-mail: arthurklass@jewishpress.com
Classified Adv. e-mail: arthurklass@jewishpress.com
Editorial e-mail: editor@jewishpress.com
Primary Website: www.jewishpress.com
Mthly Avg Views: 300000
Year Established: 1959
News Services: JNS
Areas Served - City/County or Portion Thereof, or Zip codes: National, New York metro, South Florida, L.A.

Avg Paid Circ: 96000
Audit By: Sworn/Estimate/Non-Audited
Audit Date: 15.10.2020
Personnel: Irene Klass (Pub.); Arthur Klass (Director of Business Development); Heshy Kornblit (Display Dept. Mgr.); Joseph Hochberg (Circ. Mgr.); Jason Maoz (Sr. Ed.); Jerry Greenwald (Mng. Ed.)

THE LONG ISLAND CATHOLIC

Street address 1: 200 W Centennial Ave
Street address 2: Ste 201
Street address city: Roosevelt
Street address state: NY
Zip/Postal code: 11575-1937
County: Nassau
Country: USA
Mailing address: PO Box 9000
Mailing city: Roosevelt
Mailing state: NY
Mailing zip: 11575-9000
General Phone: (516) 594-1000
Editorial e-mail: editor@licatholic.org
Primary Website: www.licatholic.org
Year Established: 1962
Avg Paid Circ: 103000
Avg Free Circ: 899
Audit By: Sworn/Estimate/Non-Audited
Audit Date: 12.07.2019
Personnel: Art O'Brien (Adv. Mgr.); Mary Salegna (Opns. Mgr.)

THE TABLET

Street address 1: 310 Prospect Park W
Street address city: Brooklyn
Street address state: NY
Zip/Postal code: 11215-6214
County: Kings
Country: USA
General Phone: (718) 499-9705
Advertising Phone: (718) 517-3131
Advertising Fax: (718) 965-7338
General/National Adv. E-mail: jdinapoli@desalesmedia.org
Display Adv. E-mail: jdinapoli@desalesmedia.org
Primary Website: www.thetablet.org
Year Established: 1908
Avg Free Circ: 67910
Audit By: AAM
Audit Date: 31.03.2019
Personnel: Bishop Robert Brennan (Pub.); Father Kieran E. Harrington (Assoc. Pub.); Ed Wilkinson (Ed.); James Caragiulo (Circ. Mgr.); JoAnn DiNapoli (Dir. Sales)

BIBLICAL RECORDER

Street address 1: 205 Convention Dr
Street address city: Cary
Street address state: NC
Zip/Postal code: 27511-4257
County: Wake
Country: USA
Mailing address: P.O. Box 1185
Mailing city: Cary
Mailing state: NC
Mailing zip: 27512-1185
General Phone: (919) 847-2127
General Fax: (919) 467-6180
General/National Adv. E-mail: editor@BRnow.org
Display Adv. E-mail: alison@BRnow.org
Editorial e-mail: editor@brnow.org
Primary Website: www.BRnow.org
Year Established: 1833
Delivery Methods: Mail
Avg Paid Circ: 9000
Avg Free Circ: 4000
Audit By: Sworn/Estimate/Non-Audited
Audit Date: 15.03.2022
Personnel: Alison McKinney (Bus. Mgr.); Allan Blume (Editor/President)
Parent company (for newspapers): Baptist State Convention of North Carolina

THE NORTH CAROLINA CATHOLIC

Street address 1: 715 Nazareth St
Street address city: Raleigh
Street address state: NC
Zip/Postal code: 27606-2187
County: Wake
Country: USA
Mailing address: 715 Nazareth St
Mailing city: Raleigh
Mailing state: NC
Mailing zip: 27606-2187
General Phone: (919) 821-9730
Editorial e-mail: reece@raldioc.org
Primary Website: www.nccatholics.org
Year Established: 1946
Audit By: Sworn/Estimate/Non-Audited
Audit Date: 12.07.2019
Personnel: Michael F. Burbidge (Pub.); Holly Stringer (Adv. Mgr.); Richard Reece (Ed.)

CATHOLIC CHRONICLE

Street address 1: 1933 Spielbusch Ave
Street address city: Toledo
Street address state: OH
Zip/Postal code: 43604-5360
County: Lucas
Country: USA
General Phone: (419) 244-6711
General Fax: (419) 244-0468
General/National Adv. E-mail: ccnews@toledodiocese.org
Display Adv. E-mail: ncooke@toledodiocese.org
Primary Website: www.catholicchronicle.org
Year Established: 1934
Delivery Methods: Mail`Racks
Areas Served - City/County or Portion Thereof, or Zip codes: 41017 13316 13402 43410 43420 43430 43431 43435 43440 43449 43445 43450 43452 43456 43460 43465 43502 43506 43511 43512 43516 43517 43521 43522 43524 43526 43527 43528 43537 43543 43545 43548 43551 43552 43558 43560 43566 43567 43571 43602 43604 43605 43606 43607 43608 43609 43610 43611 43612 43613 43614 43615 43616 43620 43623 43624 44089 44807 44809 44811 44820 44827 44830 44833 44839 44846 44847 44851 44853 44854 44857 44865 44870 44875 44882 44883 44889 44890 44902 44904 44905 45699 45801 15805 45817 45827 45830 45833 45840 45844 45848 45853 45856 45864 45872 45875 45876 45879 45887 45891 46225
Avg Paid Circ: 500
Avg Free Circ: 31000
Audit By: Sworn/Estimate/Non-Audited
Audit Date: 12.07.2019
Personnel: Nancy Cooke (Adv. Sales Rep.); Sally Oberski (Commun. Dir.); Angela Kessler (Ed.); Rose Anne Conrad (Circ. Coord.); Keith Tarjanyi (Graphic Artist); Cherie Spino (Staff Writer); Bishop Daniel Thomas (Pub.)

CATHOLIC DIGEST MAGAZINE

Street address 1: PO Box 291826
Street address city: Kettering
Street address state: OH
Zip/Postal code: 45429
County: New Haven
Country: USA
Mailing address: PO Box 291826
Mailing city: Kettering
Mailing state: OH
Mailing zip: 45429
General Phone: (203) 985-4450
General/National Adv. E-mail: catholicdigest@sfsdayton.com
Display Adv. E-mail: michelle.kopfmann@bayard-inc.com
Editorial e-mail: pmckibben@bayard-inc.com
Primary Website: http://www.catholicdigest.com/
Areas Served - City/County or Portion Thereof, or Zip codes: 6514
Audit By: Sworn/Estimate/Non-Audited
Audit Date: 12.07.2019
Personnel: Paul Mckibben (Ed.); Michelle Kopfmann (Adv.)

CHRISTIAN STANDARD

Street address 1: 8805 Governors Hill Dr
Street address 2: Ste 400
Street address city: Cincinnati
Street address state: OH
Zip/Postal code: 45249-3319
County: Hamilton
Country: USA
Mailing address: 8805 Governors Hill Dr Ste 400
Mailing city: Cincinnati
Mailing state: OH
Mailing zip: 45249-3319
General Phone: (513) 931-4050
General Fax: (877) 867-5751
General/National Adv. E-mail: christianstd@standardpub.com
Primary Website: www.standardpub.com
Year Established: 1866
Delivery Methods: Mail
Audit By: Sworn/Estimate/Non-Audited
Audit Date: 12.07.2019
Personnel: Mark A. Taylor (Pub.); Jim Nieman (Mng. Ed.); Paul Williams (Ed.)

THE CATHOLIC TELEGRAPH

Street address 1: 100 E 8th St
Street address city: Cincinnati
Street address state: OH
Zip/Postal code: 45202-2129
County: Hamilton
Country: USA
Mailing address: 100 E 8th St
Mailing city: Cincinnati
Mailing state: OH
Mailing zip: 45202-2129
General Phone: (513) 421-3131
General Fax: (513) 381-2242
General/National Adv. E-mail: thempel@catholiccincinnati.org
Avg Paid Circ: 85000
Avg Free Circ: 400
Audit By: Sworn/Estimate/Non-Audited
Audit Date: 12.07.2019
Personnel: Daniel E. Pilarczyk (Pub.); Tim Mayer (Adv. Mgr.); Greg Hartman (Circ. Mgr.); Tricia Hempel (Ed.); Rick Barr (Prodn. Mgr.); Steve Trosley

THE CATHOLIC TIMES

Street address 1: 197 E Gay St
Street address city: Columbus
Street address state: OH
Zip/Postal code: 43215-3229
County: Franklin
Country: USA
Mailing address: 197 E Gay St Ste 1
Mailing city: Columbus
Mailing state: OH
Mailing zip: 43215-3229
General Phone: (614) 224-5195
Avg Paid Circ: 18000
Audit By: Sworn/Estimate/Non-Audited
Audit Date: 19.10.2017
Personnel: Frederick Campbell (Pub.); Deacon Steve Demers (Adv. Mgr.); Jodie Shreddo (Circ. Mgr.); David Garick (Ed.)

OKLAHOMA

BAPTIST MESSENGER

Street address 1: 3800 N May Ave
Street address city: Oklahoma City
Street address state: OK
Zip/Postal code: 73112-6639
County: Oklahoma
Country: USA
Mailing address: PO Box 12130
Mailing city: Oklahoma City
Mailing state: OK
Mailing zip: 73157-2130
General Phone: (405) 942-3800
General Fax: (405) 942-3075
Advertising Phone: (405) 942-3800 ext 4360
Advertising Fax: 405-942-3075
Editorial Phone: (405) 942-3800 ext 4361
Editorial Fax: 405-942-3075
General/National Adv. E-mail: baptistmessenger@okbaptist.net
Display Adv. E-mail: baptistmessenger@okbaptist.net
Editorial e-mail: baptist messenger@okbaptist.net
Primary Website: www.baptistmessenger.com
Year Established: 1912
Delivery Methods: Mail`Racks
Areas Served - City/County or Portion Thereof, or Zip codes: 730-749; various other US zip codes
Avg Paid Circ: 55670
Audit By: Sworn/Estimate/Non-Audited
Audit Date: 12.07.2019
Personnel: Dana Williamson (Assoc. Ed.); Karen Kinnaird (Account Manager); Ricardo Herrera (Art Director); Brian Hobbs (Editor); Bob Nigh (Managing Editor)

THE CHRISTIAN CHRONICLE

Street address 1: 2801 E Memorial Rd
Street address city: Edmond
Street address state: OK
Zip/Postal code: 73013-6474
County: Oklahoma
Country: USA
Mailing address: PO Box 11000
Mailing city: Oklahoma City
Mailing state: OK
Mailing zip: 73136-1100
General Phone: (405) 425-5070
General Fax: (405) 425-5076
Advertising Phone: (405) 425-5071
Advertising Fax: (405) 425-5076
Editorial Phone: (405) 425-5070
General/National Adv. E-mail: lynn.mcmillon@christianchronicle.org
Display Adv. E-mail: tonya.patton@christianchronicle.org
Editorial e-mail: erik@christianchronicle.org
Primary Website: www.christianchronicle.org.net
Year Established: 1943
Delivery Methods: Mail
Audit By: Sworn/Estimate/Non-Audited
Audit Date: 12.07.2019
Parent company (for newspapers): Oklahoma Christian University

OREGON

CATHOLIC SENTINEL

Street address 1: 5536 NE Hassalo St
Street address city: Portland
Street address state: OR
Zip/Postal code: 97213-3638
County: Multnomah
Country: USA
Mailing address: PO Box 18030
Mailing city: Portland
Mailing state: OR
Mailing zip: 97218-0030
General Phone: (503) 281-1191
General Fax: (503) 460-5496
General/National Adv. E-mail: sentinel@ocp.org
Avg Paid Circ: 3000
Avg Free Circ: 25000
Audit By: Sworn/Estimate/Non-Audited
Audit Date: 12.07.2019
Personnel: John Limb (Pub.); Ed Langlois (Managing editor)

PITTSBURGH CATHOLIC

Street address 1: 135 1st Ave
Street address 2: Ste 200
Street address city: Pittsburgh
Street address state: PA
Zip/Postal code: 15222-1529
County: Allegheny
Country: USA
Mailing address: 135 1st Ave Ste 200
Mailing city: Pittsburgh
Mailing state: PA
Mailing zip: 15222-1513
General Phone: (412) 471-1252
General Fax: (412) 471-4228
General/National Adv. E-mail: info@pittsburghcatholic.org
Display Adv. E-mail: jconnolly@pittsburghcatholic.org
Editorial e-mail: wcone@pittsburghcatholic.org
Primary Website: www.pittsburghcatholic.com
Year Established: 1844
News Services: CNS
Delivery Methods: Mail
Avg Paid Circ: 96000
Avg Free Circ: 7687
Audit By: Sworn/Estimate/Non-Audited
Audit Date: 12.07.2019

Personnel: John Connolly (Dir. of Adv.); Peggy Zezza (Circ. Mgr.); William Cone (Ed.); Carmella Weismantle (Prodn. Mgr.)

THE CATHOLIC ACCENT

Street address 1: 725 E Pittsburgh St
Street address city: Greensburg
Street address state: PA
Zip/Postal code: 15601-2660
County: Westmoreland
Country: USA
Mailing address: 725 E Pittsburgh St
Mailing city: Greensburg
Mailing state: PA
Mailing zip: 15601-2660
General Phone: (724) 834-4010
General Fax: (724) 836-5650
General/National Adv. E-mail: news@dioceseofgreensburg.org
Primary Website: www.dioceseofgreensburg.org
Year Established: 1961
Delivery Methods: Mail
Areas Served - City/County or Portion Thereof, or Zip codes: 4 counties of the diocese (multiple)
Avg Paid Circ: 46500
Avg Free Circ: 924
Audit By: Sworn/Estimate/Non-Audited
Audit Date: 12.07.2019
Personnel: Lawrence E. Brandt (Chief Executive Officer and Publisher); Rose Govi (Adv. Mgr.); Nancy Balfe (Circulation Coordinator); Jerome M. Zufelt (Editor, The Catholic Accent); Elizabeth Fazzini (Assistant Editor, The Catholic Accent); Valerie Rodell (Production Coordinator)

RHODE ISLAND CATHOLIC

Street address 1: 1 Cathedral Sq
Street address city: Providence
Street address state: RI
Zip/Postal code: 02903-3601
County: Providence
Country: USA
Mailing address: 1 CATHEDRAL SQ
Mailing city: PROVIDelawareNCE
Mailing state: RI
Mailing zip: 02903-3601
General Phone: (401) 272-1010
General Fax: (401) 421-8418
Advertising Phone: (401) 272-1010
Advertising Fax: (401) 421-8418
Editorial Phone: (401) 272-1010
Editorial Fax: (401) 421-8418
General/National Adv. E-mail: editor@thericatholic.com
Display Adv. E-mail: srichard@thericatholic.com
Editorial e-mail: rsnizek@thericatholic.com
Primary Website: www.thericatholic.com
Year Established: 1875
Delivery Methods: Mail`Newsstand
Areas Served - City/County or Portion Thereof, or Zip codes: Providence County
Avg Paid Circ: 27000
Avg Free Circ: 422
Audit By: Sworn/Estimate/Non-Audited
Audit Date: 12.07.2019
Personnel: Rev. Thomas J. Tobin (Pub.); Rick Snizek (Executive Editor); Richard Lafond (Display Advertising Manager); Laura Kilgus (Assistant Editor/Production Manager)

SOUTH DAKOTA

SOUTH CAROLINA UNITED METHODIST ADVOCATE

Street address 1: 4908 Colonial Dr
Street address 2: Ste 207
Street address city: Columbia
Street address state: SC
Zip/Postal code: 29203-6080
County: Richland
Country: USA
Mailing address: 4908 Colonial Dr Ste 207
Mailing city: Columbia
Mailing state: SC
Mailing zip: 29203-6080
General Phone: (803) 786-9486
General Fax: (803) 735-8168
General/National Adv. E-mail: advocate@umcsc.org
Primary Website: www.advocatesc.org
Year Established: 1836
Avg Paid Circ: 10000
Avg Free Circ: 1000
Audit By: Sworn/Estimate/Non-Audited
Audit Date: 12.07.2019
Personnel: Allison Trussell (Circ. Mgr.); Jessica Connor (Editor); Emily Cooper (Ed.)

THE BAPTIST COURIER

Street address 1: 100 Manly St
Street address city: Greenville
Street address state: SC
Zip/Postal code: 29601-3025
County: Greenville
Country: USA
Mailing address: 100 Manly St
Mailing city: Greenville
Mailing state: SC
Mailing zip: 29601-3025
General Phone: (864) 232-8736
General Fax: (864) 232-8488
General/National Adv. E-mail: news@baptistcourier.com
Avg Paid Circ: 75000
Avg Free Circ: 2000
Audit By: Sworn/Estimate/Non-Audited
Audit Date: 12.07.2019
Personnel: Debbie Grooms (Bus. Mgr.); Butch Blame (Mng. Ed.); Don Kirkland (Ed.)

THE CATHOLIC MISCELLANY

Street address 1: 119 Broad St
Street address city: Charleston
Street address state: SC
Zip/Postal code: 29401-2435
County: Charleston
Country: USA
Mailing address: PO Box 818
Mailing city: Charleston
Mailing state: SC
Mailing zip: 29402-0818
General Phone: (843) 724-8375
Editorial e-mail: editor@catholic-doc.org
Avg Paid Circ: 29000
Avg Free Circ: 247
Audit By: Sworn/Estimate/Non-Audited
Audit Date: 12.07.2019
Personnel: Deirdre C. Mays (Ed.); Karla Consroe (Circ./Adv. Coord.)

TENNESSEE REGISTER

Street address 1: 2400 21st Ave S
Street address city: Nashville
Street address state: TN
Zip/Postal code: 37212-5302
County: Davidson
Country: USA
Mailing address: 2400 21st Ave S
Mailing city: Nashville
Mailing state: TN
Mailing zip: 37212-5302
General Phone: (615)783-0750
General Fax: (615) 783-0285
Audit By: Sworn/Estimate/Non-Audited
Audit Date: 12.07.2019
Personnel: Byron Warner (Adv. Mgr.); Rick Musacchio (Ed. in Chief); Andy Telli (Mng. Ed.); Debbie Lane (Prodn. Mgr.)

THE UNITED METHODIST REPORTER

Street address 1: 1300 Old Hickory Blvd
Street address city: Nashville
Street address state: TN
Zip/Postal code: 37207-1417
County: Davidson
Country: USA
Mailing address: 1300 Old Hickory Blvd
Mailing city: Nashville
Mailing state: TN
Mailing zip: 37207-1417
General Phone: (615) 673-4236
General/National Adv. E-mail: news@circuitwritermedia.com
Display Adv. E-mail: cherrie@circuitwritermedia.com
Editorial e-mail: news@circuitwritermedia.com
Primary Website: www.unitedmethodistreporter.org
Year Established: 1847
Areas Served - City/County or Portion Thereof, or Zip codes: Nationwide
Audit By: Sworn/Estimate/Non-Audited
Audit Date: 12.07.2019
Personnel: Jay Vorhees (Executive Editor)
Parent company (for newspapers): UMR Communications; CircuitWriter Media LLC

THE WEST TENNESSEE CATHOLIC

Street address 1: 5825 Shelby Oaks Dr
Street address 2: Catholic Center
Street address city: Memphis
Street address state: TN
Zip/Postal code: 38134-7316
County: Shelby
Country: USA
Mailing address: PO Box 341669
Mailing city: Memphis
Mailing state: TN
Mailing zip: 38184-1669
General Phone: (901) 373-1231
General Fax: (901) 373-1269
Advertising Phone: (901) 373-1209
General/National Adv. E-mail: fwt.editor@cc.cdom.org
Display Adv. E-mail: lorena.monge@cc.cdom.org
Editorial e-mail: fwt.editor@cc.cdom.org
Primary Website: www.cdom.org
Year Established: 1972
Avg Paid Circ: 0
Avg Free Circ: 1000
Audit By: Sworn/Estimate/Non-Audited
Audit Date: 12.07.2019
Personnel: Martin D. Bishop Holley (Pub.); Suzanne Aviles (Editor); Lorena Monge (Ads and subscriptions)
Parent company (for newspapers): Catholic Diocese of Memphis

BAPTIST STANDARD

Street address 1: 7161 Bishop Rd
Street address 2: Ste 200
Street address city: Plano
Street address state: TX
Zip/Postal code: 75024-3646
County: Collin
Country: USA
Mailing address: PO Box 259019
Mailing city: Plano
Mailing state: TX
Mailing zip: 75025-9019
General Phone: (214) 630-4571
General Fax: (214) 638-8535
General/National Adv. E-mail: bapstand@baptiststandard.com
Primary Website: www.baptiststandard.com
Year Established: 1888
Avg Paid Circ: 90000
Avg Free Circ: 2104
Audit By: Sworn/Estimate/Non-Audited
Audit Date: 12.07.2019
Personnel: Kayla Andrews (Bus. Mgr.); Lance Freeman (Bus. Mgr.); Marv Knox (Ed.); Ken Camp (Mng. Ed.)

CATHOLIC EAST TEXAS

Street address 1: 1015 E Southeast Loop 323
Street address city: Tyler
Street address state: TX
Zip/Postal code: 75701-9656
County: Smith
Country: USA
General Phone: (903) 534-1077
General Fax: (903) 534-1370
Editorial Phone: (903) 266-2144
General/National Adv. E-mail: editorcet3@excite.com
Editorial e-mail: editorcet3@excite.com
Primary Website: www.dioceseoftyler.org
Year Established: 1987
Delivery Methods: Mail
Avg Paid Circ: 17000
Avg Free Circ: 400
Audit By: Sworn/Estimate/Non-Audited
Audit Date: 12.07.2019
Personnel: Jim D'Avignon (Ed.)

LETTERS FROM NORTH AMERICA

Street address 1: 2002 N Greens Blvd
Street address city: Richmond
Street address state: TX
Zip/Postal code: 77406-6673
County: FORT BEND
Country: USA
Mailing address: 2002 N. Greens Blvd
Mailing city: Richmond
Mailing state: TX
Mailing zip: 77406
General Phone: (512) 653-8545
General Fax: 832-201-9818
General/National Adv. E-mail: pperry@pearyperry.com
Primary Website: www.pearyperry.com
Mthly Avg Views: 5000
Mthly Avg Unique Visitors: 1000
Year Established: 1993
Avg Free Circ: 1000
Audit By: USPS
Personnel: Peary Perry (Self-Synd/Columnist)
Parent company (for newspapers): P.PERRY&ASSOCIATES

NORTH TEXAS CATHOLIC

Street address 1: 800 W Loop 820 S
Street address city: Fort Worth
Street address state: TX
Zip/Postal code: 76108-2936
County: Tarrant
Country: USA
Mailing address: 800 W Loop 820 S
Mailing city: Fort Worth
Mailing state: TX
Mailing zip: 76108-2936
General Phone: (817) 560-3300
General Fax: (817) 244-8839
General/National Adv. E-mail: jrusseau@fwdioc.org
Display Adv. E-mail: jrusseau@fwdioc.org
Editorial e-mail: jhensley@fwdioc.org
Primary Website: www.fwdioc.org
Delivery Methods: Mail
Areas Served - City/County or Portion Thereof, or Zip codes: 76108
Avg Paid Circ: 27000
Avg Free Circ: 82000
Audit By: Sworn/Estimate/Non-Audited
Audit Date: 12.07.2019
Personnel: Judy Russeau (Adv. Mgr.); Jeff Hensley (Ed)

SOUTH TEXAS CATHOLIC

Street address 1: 620 Lipan St
Street address city: Corpus Christi
Street address state: TX
Zip/Postal code: 78401-2434
County: Nueces
Country: USA
Mailing address: 620 Lipan St
Mailing city: Corpus Christi
Mailing state: TX
Mailing zip: 78401-2434
General Phone: (361) 882-6191
General Fax: (361) 693-6701
Advertising Phone: (361) 693-6605
Advertising Fax: (361) 693-6701
Editorial Phone: (361) 693-6609
Editorial Fax: (361) 693-6701
General/National Adv. E-mail: stc@dicesecc.org
Primary Website: www.southtexascatholic.com
News Services: CNS
Delivery Methods: Mail
Avg Paid Circ: 43000
Audit By: Sworn/Estimate/Non-Audited
Audit Date: 12.07.2019
Personnel: Mary Cottingham (Mng. Ed.); Wm. Michael Mulvey (Bishop); Alfredo Cardenas (Editor); Adel Rivera (Office Mgr.); Father Joseph Lopez (Theological Consultant)

THE TEXAS CATHOLIC

Street address 1: 3725 Blackburn St
Street address city: Dallas
Street address state: TX
Zip/Postal code: 75219-4404
County: Dallas
Country: USA
Mailing address: PO Box 190347
Mailing city: Dallas
Mailing state: TX
Mailing zip: 75219-0347
General Phone: (214) 528-8792
General Fax: (214) 528-3411

General/National Adv. E-mail: texascatholic@msn.com
Avg Paid Circ: 54000
Avg Free Circ: 857
Audit By: Sworn/Estimate/Non-Audited
Audit Date: 12.07.2019
Personnel: Kevin Farrell (Pub.); Tony Ramirez (Adv. Mgr.); Rosemary Allen (Circ. Mgr.); David Sedeno (Exec. Ed.)

THE TEXAS CATHOLIC HERALD

Street address 1: 1700 San Jacinto St
Street address city: Houston
Street address state: TX
Zip/Postal code: 77002-8216
County: Harris
Country: USA
Mailing address: 1700 San Jacinto St
Mailing city: Houston
Mailing state: TX
Mailing zip: 77002-8216
General Phone: (713) 659-5461
General Fax: (713) 659-3444
General/National Adv. E-mail: tch@archgh.org
Display Adv. E-mail: ads@archgh.org
Classified Adv. e-mail: ads@archgh.org
Editorial e-mail: tch@archgh.org
Primary Website: www.archgh.org/tch
Year Established: 1964
Areas Served - City/County or Portion Thereof, or Zip codes: Austin, Brazoria, Fort Bend, Galveston, Grimes, Harris, Montgomery, San Jacinto, Walker, and Waller Counties
Avg Paid Circ: 72000
Avg Free Circ: 1680
Audit By: Sworn/Estimate/Non-Audited
Audit Date: 12.07.2019
Personnel: Daniel DiNardo (Pub.)

TODAY'S CATHOLIC

Street address 1: 2718 W Woodlawn Ave
Street address city: San Antonio
Street address state: TX
Zip/Postal code: 78228-5124
County: Bexar
Country: USA
Mailing address: PO Box 28410
Mailing city: San Antonio
Mailing state: TX
Mailing zip: 78228-0410
General Phone: (210) 734-2620
General Fax: (210) 734-2939
Advertising Phone: (210) 734-2620
Advertising Fax: (210) 734-2939
Editorial Phone: (210) 734-1634
Editorial Fax: (210) 734-2939
General/National Adv. E-mail: tcpaper@archsa.org
Display Adv. E-mail: tcpaper@archsa.org
Classified Adv. e-mail: tcpaper@archsa.org
Editorial e-mail: tcpaper@archsa.org
Primary Website: www.satodayscatholic.org
Year Established: 1892
Areas Served - City/County or Portion Thereof, or Zip codes: Archdiocese of San Antonio
Avg Paid Circ: 26000
Avg Free Circ: 467
Audit By: Sworn/Estimate/Non-Audited
Audit Date: 12.07.2019
Personnel: Jordan McMorrough (Editor); Kevin Rhoades (Publisher); Jodi Martin (Editor); Francis Hogan (Page Designer); Mark Weber (News Specialist); Emily Mae Schmid (Social Media Manager); Jackie Parker (Advertising Sales); Geoff Frank (Accounting/ Circulation); Stephanie A. Patka (Business Mgr)
Parent company (for newspapers): Archdiocese of San Antonio

UTAH

INTERMOUNTAIN CATHOLIC

Street address 1: 27 C St
Street address city: Salt Lake City
Street address state: UT
Zip/Postal code: 84103-2302
County: Salt Lake
Country: USA
Mailing address: PO Box 2489
Mailing city: Salt Lake City
Mailing state: UT
Mailing zip: 84110-2489
General Phone: (801) 328-8641
General Fax: (801) 537-1667
General/National Adv. E-mail: icnews@icnp.com
Display Adv. E-mail: advertising@icatholic.org
Primary Website: www.icatholic.org
Areas Served - City/County or Portion Thereof, or Zip codes: All Utah Zip codes
Avg Paid Circ: 14500
Avg Free Circ: 24
Audit By: Sworn/Estimate/Non-Audited
Audit Date: 12.07.2019
Personnel: Bishop John Charles Wester (Pub.); Arthur Heredia (Circ. Mgr.); Marie Mischel (Ed.); Christine Young (Assoc. Ed.)

ALL NEWS

Street address 1: 1179 Courthouse Rd
Street address city: Stafford
Street address state: VA
Zip/Postal code: 22554-7106
County: Stafford
Country: USA
Mailing address: 1179 Courthouse Rd
Mailing city: Stafford
Delivery Methods: Mail
Areas Served - City/County or Portion Thereof, or Zip codes: all
Personnel: Robert Gasper (Editor); Michael Hichborn (Contributing Author)
Parent company (for newspapers): American Life League

ARLINGTON CATHOLIC HERALD

Street address 1: 200 N Glebe Rd
Street address 2: Suite 615
Street address city: Arlington
Street address state: VA
Zip/Postal code: 22203-3763
County: Arlington
Country: USA
Mailing address: 200 N Glebe Rd Ste 600
Mailing city: Arlington
Mailing state: VA
Mailing zip: 22203-3728
General Phone: (703) 841-2590
General Fax: (703) 524-2782
Advertising Phone: (703) 841-2598
General/National Adv. E-mail: editorial@catholicherald.com
Display Adv. E-mail: csalinas@catholicherald.com
Classified Adv. e-mail: csalinas@catholicherald.com
Editorial e-mail: editorial@catholicherald.com
Primary Website: www.catholicherald.com
Mthly Avg Views: 108664
Mthly Avg Unique Visitors: 65532
Year Established: 1976
Delivery Methods: Mail`Racks
Areas Served - City/County or Portion Thereof, or Zip codes: 21 counties, including Fairfax & Loudoun.
Avg Paid Circ: 100000
Avg Free Circ: 1500
Audit By: USPS
Audit Date: 12.12.2017
Personnel: Carlos Salinas (Adverting Director); Ann Augherton (Mng. Ed.); Joe Miller (Circ. Mgr.); Rev. Michael F. Burbidge; Michael Flach (Ed.); Kevin Schweers (Executive Editor of Content); Stacy Rausch (Prodn. Coord.)

THE PRESBYTERIAN OUTLOOK

Street address 1: 1 N 5th St
Street address 2: Ste 500
Street address city: Richmond
Street address state: VA
Zip/Postal code: 23219-2231
County: Richmond City
Country: USA
Mailing address: 1 N 5th St Ste 500
Mailing city: Richmond
Mailing state: VA
Mailing zip: 23219-2231
General Phone: (804) 359-8442
General Fax: (804) 353-6369
Advertising Fax: (804) 353-6369
Display Adv. E-mail: gwhipple@pres-outlook.org
Editorial e-mail: jhaberer@pres-outlook.org
Primary Website: www.pres-outlook.org
Year Established: 1819
Delivery Methods: Mail
Areas Served - City/County or Portion Thereof, or Zip codes: We serve the entire U.S., Canada, and clergy,missionary, chaplains, serving in foreign countries.
Avg Paid Circ: 7434
Avg Free Circ: 876
Audit By: USPS
Audit Date: 30.09.2012
Personnel: Patricia Gresham (Bus. Mgr.); George Whipple (Adv. Mgr.); Stan Bailey (Prodn. Mgr.); Jack Haberer (Editor/CEO)

THE RELIGIOUS HERALD

Street address 1: 2828 Emerywood Pkwy
Street address city: Richmond
Street address state: VA
Zip/Postal code: 23294-3718
County: Henrico
Country: USA
Mailing address: 2828 Emerywood Pkwy
Mailing city: Richmond
Mailing state: VA
Mailing zip: 23294-3718
General Phone: (804) 672-1973
General Fax: (804) 672-8323
General/National Adv. E-mail: rdilday@religiousherald.org
Primary Website: www.religiousherald.org
Year Established: 1808
Avg Paid Circ: 21000
Audit By: Sworn/Estimate/Non-Audited
Audit Date: 12.07.2019
Personnel: Barbara Francis (Adv. Mgr.); James White (Ed.)

CATHOLIC HERALD

Street address 1: 3501 S Lake Dr
Street address city: Saint Francis
Street address state: WI
Zip/Postal code: 53235-0900
County: Milwaukee
Country: USA
Mailing address: PO Box 070913
Mailing city: Milwaukee
Mailing state: WI
Mailing zip: 53207-0913
General Phone: (414) 769-3500
General Fax: (414) 769-3468
General/National Adv. E-mail: catholicherald@archmil.org
Primary Website: catholicherald.org
Delivery Methods: Mail
Avg Paid Circ: 15000
Audit By: Sworn/Estimate/Non-Audited
Audit Date: 12.07.2019
Personnel: Brian Olszewski (Gen. Mgr.); Maryangela Layman Roman
Parent company (for newspapers): Milwaukee Catholic Press Apstolate

CATHOLIC HERALD

Street address 1: 1201 Hughitt Ave
Street address city: Superior
Street address state: WI
Zip/Postal code: 54880-1631
County: Douglas
Country: USA
Mailing address: PO Box 969
Mailing city: Superior
Mailing state: WI
Mailing zip: 54880-0017
General Phone: (715) 392-8268
General Fax: (715) 392-8656
General/National Adv. E-mail: catholicherald@gmail.com
Primary Website: www.superiorcatholicherald.org
Mthly Avg Unique Visitors: 7000
Year Established: 1953
News Services: Catholic News Service
Delivery Methods: Mail
Avg Paid Circ: 7800
Audit By: Sworn/Estimate/Non-Audited
Audit Date: 12.07.2019
Personnel: Bishop James P. Powers (Publisher)
Parent company (for newspapers): Wisconsin Catholic Media Apostolate

CATHOLIC HERALD NEWSPAPER

Street address 1: 702 S High Point Rd
Street address city: Madison
Street address state: WI
Zip/Postal code: 53719-4925
County: Dane
Country: USA
Mailing address: 702 S High Point Rd
Mailing city: Madison
Mailing state: WI
Mailing zip: 53719-3522
General Phone: (608) 821-3070
General Fax: (608) 821-3071
General/National Adv. E-mail: info@madisoncatholicherald.org
Primary Website: www.madisoncatholicherald.org
Year Established: 1948
Avg Paid Circ: 26000
Audit By: Sworn/Estimate/Non-Audited
Audit Date: 12.07.2019
Personnel: Robert Morlino (Pub.); Steve Hefty (Adv. Mgr.); Mary Uhler (Ed.); Pamela Payne (Assoc. Ed.)

THE CATHOLIC LIFE

Street address 1: 3710 East Ave S
Street address city: La Crosse
Street address state: WI
Zip/Postal code: 54601-7215
County: La Crosse
Country: USA
Mailing address: PO Box 4004
Mailing city: La Crosse
Mailing state: WI
Mailing zip: 54602-4004
General Phone: (608) 788-1524
General Fax: (608) 788-0932
General/National Adv. E-mail: catholictimes@dioceseoflacrosse.com
Avg Paid Circ: 31000
Avg Free Circ: 193
Audit By: Sworn/Estimate/Non-Audited
Audit Date: 12.07.2019
Personnel: Pamela Willer (Circ. Mgr.); Pam Willer (Subs./ Adv.); Denis Downey (Associate Editor); Danelle Bjornson (Graphic Designer)

COLLEGE AND UNIVERSITY NEWSPAPERS

ALASKA

ANCHORAGE

ALASKA PACIFIC UNIV.

Street address 1: 4101 University Dr
Street address 2: Ste 19
Street address 3: Anchorage
Street address state: AK
Zip/Postal code: 99508-4625
Country: USA
Mailing address: 4101 University Dr Ste 19
Mailing city: Anchorage
Mailing state: AK
Mailing zip: 99508-4625
General Phone: (907) 564-8297
General Fax: (907) 564-8236
General/National Adv. E-mail: journal@alaskapacific.edu
Classified Equipment»
Personnel: Rosanne Pagano (Advisor); Michelle Coles (Ed.)

UNIV. OF ALASKA ANCHORAGE

Street address 1: 3211 Providence Dr, Campus Ctr 215
Street address 3: Anchorage
Street address state: AK
Zip/Postal code: 99508
Country: USA
Mailing address: 3211 Providence Dr., Campus Ctr. 215
Mailing city: Anchorage
Mailing state: AK
Mailing zip: 99508-4614
General Phone: (907) 786-1434
General Fax: (907) 786-1331
Advertising Phone: (907) 786-4690
Editorail Phone: (907) 786-1313
Display Adv. E-mail: ads@thenorthernlight.org
Editorial e-mail: editor@thenorthernlight.org
Primary Website: www.thenorthernlight.org
Year Established: 1988
Special Weekly Sections: Motion (Arts & Sports)
Commercial printers: Y
Classified Equipment»
Personnel: Paola Banchero (Advisor); Mariya Proskuryakova (Adv. Mgr.); Shana Roberson (Executive Editor)

FAIRBANKS

UNIV. OF ALASKA FAIRBANKS

Street address 1: PO Box 756640
Street address 3: Fairbanks
Street address state: AK
Zip/Postal code: 99775-6640
Country: USA
Mailing address: PO Box 756640
Mailing city: Fairbanks
Mailing state: AK
Mailing zip: 99775-6640
General Phone: (907) 474-6039
General Fax: (907) 474-5508
General/National Adv. E-mail: fystar@uaf.edu
Primary Website: www.uafsunstar.com
Published: Tues
Classified Equipment»
Personnel: Chavis Lakeidra (Editor-in-Chief); Manager Advertising

JUNEAU

UNIV. OF ALASKA SOUTHEAST

Street address 1: 11120 Glacier Hwy
Street address 3: Juneau
Street address state: AK
Zip/Postal code: 99801-86
Country: USA
Mailing address: 11120 Glacier Hwy
Mailing city: Juneau
Mailing state: AK
Mailing zip: 99801-8699
General Phone: (907) 796-6434
General Fax: (907) 796-6399
General/National Adv. E-mail: uas.whalesong@gmail.com; whalesong@uas.alaska.edu
Primary Website: www.uas.alaska.edu/whalesong
Year Established: 1981
Classified Equipment»
Personnel: Jeremy Hsieh (Advisor); Taylor Murph (Adv. Mgr.); Randi Spary (Ed.); Hollis Kitchin (Prodn. Mgr.)

ALABAMA

ATHENS

ATHENS STATE UNIV.

Street address 1: 300 N Beaty St
Street address 3: Athens
Street address state: AL
Zip/Postal code: 35611-1902
Country: USA
Mailing address: 300 N Beaty St
Mailing city: Athens
Mailing state: AL
Mailing zip: 35611-1999
General Phone: (256) 233-8169
General Fax: (256) 233-8128
General/National Adv. E-mail: the.athenian@athens.edu.
Classified Equipment»
Personnel: Tena Bullington (Adv. Mgr.); Aletha Pardue (Ed.)

AUBURN UNIVERSITY

AUBURN UNIV.

Street address 1: Student Center 1111
Street address 3: Auburn University
Street address state: AL
Zip/Postal code: 1985
Country: USA
Mailing address: 255 Duncan Dr Ste 1111
Mailing city: Auburn University
Mailing state: AL
Mailing zip: 36849-0001
General Phone: (334) 844-9021
General Fax: (334) 844-9114
General/National Adv. E-mail: news@theplainsman.com
Display Adv. E-mail: advertising@theplainsman.com
Primary Website: www.theplainsman.com
Classified Equipment»
Personnel: Jennifer Adams (Advisor); Tom Hopf (Bus. Mgr.); Lindsey Davidson (Ed.); Rod Guajardo (Mng. Ed.)

BAY MINETTE

JAMES FAULKNER STATE CMTY. COLLEGE

Street address 1: 1900 S US Highway 31
Street address 3: Bay Minette
Street address state: AL
Zip/Postal code: 36507-2619
Country: USA
Mailing address: 1900 S US Highway 31
Mailing city: Bay Minette
Mailing state: AL
Mailing zip: 36507-2698
General Phone: (251) 580-2100
Classified Equipment»
Personnel: Margaret Strickland (Dir., College Rel.)

BIRMINGHAM-SOUTHERN COLLEGE

Street address 1: 900 Arkadelphia Rd
Street address 2: # 549014
Street address 3: Birmingham
Street address state: AL
Zip/Postal code: 35254-0002
Country: USA
Mailing address: 900 Arkadelphia Rd # 549014
Mailing city: Birmingham
Mailing state: AL
Mailing zip: 35254-0002
General Phone: (205) 226-7706
General/National Adv. E-mail: hilltop@bsc.edu
Primary Website: www.bsc.edu
Classified Equipment»
Personnel: Peter Donahue (Advisor); Kimmie Farris (Ed. in Chief); Kimmie Sarris (Ed.); Yuan Gong (Bus. Mgr.); Glorious (Adv. Mgr.)

SAMFORD UNIV.

Street address 1: 800 Lakeshore Dr
Street address 3: Birmingham
Street address state: AL
Zip/Postal code: 35229-0001
Country: USA
Mailing address: Su # 292269
Mailing city: Birmingham
Mailing state: AL
Mailing zip: 35229-0001
General Phone: (205) 726-2466
General Fax: (205) 726-2586
Editorail Phone: (205) 726-2998
General/National Adv. E-mail: crimson@samford.edu
Primary Website: www.samfordcrimson.com
Classified Equipment»
Personnel: Jon Clemmensen (Advisor)

UNIV. OF ALABAMA AT BIRMINGHAM

Street address 1: 1110 12th St S
Street address 3: Birmingham
Street address state: AL
Zip/Postal code: 35205-5211
Country: USA
Mailing address: 1110 12th Street South
Mailing city: Birmingham
Mailing state: AL
Mailing zip: 35205
General Phone: (205) 934-3354
General Fax: (205) 934-8050
General/National Adv. E-mail: masutton@uab.edu
Display Adv. E-mail: ads@insideuab.com
Primary Website: studentmedia.uab.edu
Year Established: 1967
Advertising (Open Inch Rate) Weekday/Saturday: Local $8 col. in.; National $12 col. in.
Published: Tues
Avg Free Circ: 6000
Classified Equipment»
Personnel: Amy Kilpatrick (Advisor./Adv. Mgr.); Daniel Twieg (Ed. in Chief); Bill Neville (Prodn. Mgr.); Marie Sutton (Director)

DECATUR

JOHN C. CALHOUN STATE CMTY. COLLEGE

Street address 1: PO Box 2216
Street address 3: Decatur
Street address state: AL
Zip/Postal code: 35609-2216
Country: USA
Mailing address: PO Box 2216
Mailing city: Decatur
Mailing state: AL
Mailing zip: 35609-2216
General Phone: (256) 306-2500
Classified Equipment»
Personnel: Robin Philip (Sec.)

FLORENCE

UNIV. OF NORTH ALABAMA

Street address 1: 1 Harrison Plz
Street address 2: # 5300
Street address 3: Florence
Street address state: AL
Zip/Postal code: 35632-0002
Country: USA
Mailing address: One Harrison Plaza, UNA Box 5300
Mailing city: Florence
Mailing state: AL
Mailing zip: 35632
General Phone: (256) 765-4364
Advertising Phone: (256) 765-4427
General/National Adv. E-mail: editor@florala.net
Primary Website: www.florala.net
Year Established: 1830
Published: Thur'Other
Published Other: biweekly
Classified Equipment»
Personnel: Scott Morris (Student Media Advisor)

HUNTSVILLE

OAKWOOD COLLEGE

Street address 1: 7000 Adventist Blvd NW
Street address 3: Huntsville
Street address state: AL
Zip/Postal code: 35896-0001
Country: USA
Mailing address: 7000 Adventist Blvd NW
Mailing city: Huntsville
Mailing state: AL
Mailing zip: 35896-0003
General Phone: (256) 726-7000
General/National Adv. E-mail: oakspread@yahoo.com
Primary Website: www.oakwood.edu
Classified Equipment»
Personnel: Michael Vance (Ed.)

UNIV. OF ALABAMA HUNTSVILLE

Street address 1: 301 Sparkman Dr
Street address 2: Charger Union 201
Street address 3: Huntsville
Street address state: AL
Zip/Postal code: 35805-1911
Country: USA
Mailing address: 301 Sparkman Drive
Mailing city: Huntsville
Mailing state: AL
Mailing zip: 35899-0001
General/National Adv. E-mail: chargertimes@uah.edu
Display Adv. E-mail: ctlayout@uah.edu
Editorial e-mail: cteditor@uah.edu
Primary Website: chargertimes.com ; chargertimes.net ; chargertimes.uah.edu
Published: Tues'Fri
Classified Equipment»
Personnel: Morgan Blair (Editor-in-Chief); Amy Dunham (Managing Editor)

JACKSONVILLE STATE UNIV.

Street address 1: 700 Pelham Rd N
Street address 2: Rm 180
Street address 3: Jacksonville
Street address state: AL
Zip/Postal code: 36265-1602
Country: USA
Mailing address: 700 Pelham Rd N Rm 180
Mailing city: Jacksonville

Mailing state: AL
Mailing zip: 36265-1602
General Phone: (256) 782-8192
General Fax: (256) 782-5645
Advertising Phone: (256) 782-5932
Editorail Phone: (256) 782-8191
General/National Adv. E-mail: chantyeditor@gmail.com
Primary Website: www.thechanticleeronline.com
Classified Equipment»
Personnel: Mike Stedham (Advisor); Zach Childree (Ed. in Chief); Ryan Rutledge (Staff Writer)

LIVINGSTON

UNIV. OF WEST ALABAMA

Street address 1: 100 US-11
Street address 3: Livingston
Street address state: AL
Zip/Postal code: 35470
Country: USA
Mailing address: 100 US-11
Mailing city: Livingston
Mailing state: AL
Mailing zip: 35470
General Phone: (205) 652-3892
General Fax: (205) 652-3586
Primary Website: www.uwa.edu/thelife
Classified Equipment»
Personnel: Betsy Compton (Advisor)

SPRING HILL COLLEGE

Street address 1: 4000 Dauphin St
Street address 3: Mobile
Street address state: AL
Zip/Postal code: 36608-1780
County: Mobile
Country: USA
Mailing address: 4000 Dauphin St
Mailing city: Mobile
Mailing state: AL
Mailing zip: 36608-1791
General Phone: (251) 380-3850
General Fax: (251) 460-2185
General/National Adv. E-mail: shcmedia@shc.edu; sbabington@shc.edu
Display Adv. E-mail: hillian@stumail.shc.edu
Editorial e-mail: hillian@stumail.shc.edu
Primary Website: http://newswire.shc.edu/
Delivery Methods: Racks
Commercial printers: Y
Published: Thur
Classified Equipment»
Personnel: Stuart Babington (Advisor); J.L. Stevens II (Integrated Multimedia Center (IMC) Operations Mgr and Student Media adviser)

UNIVERSITY OF SOUTH ALABAMA

Street address 1: 336 Alpha Hall South
Street address 3: Mobile
Street address state: AL
Zip/Postal code: 36688-0001
Country: USA
Mailing address: 336 Alpha Hall South
Mailing city: Mobile
Mailing state: AL
Mailing zip: 36688-0001
General Phone: (251)460-6442
General Fax: (251) 414-8293
Primary Website: www.usavanguard.com
Year Established: 1963
Published: Mon
Avg Free Circ: 2000
Classified Equipment»
Personnel: Cassie Fambro (Editor-in-Chief); Aucoin J (Adviser); Alanna Whitaker (Managing Editor)
Parent company (for newspapers): University of South Alabama

MONTEVALLO

UNIV. OF MONTEVALLO

Street address 1: 75 College Dr
Street address 2: Station 6222
Street address 3: Montevallo
Street address state: AL
Zip/Postal code: 35115-3732
Country: USA
Mailing address: 75 College Dr
Mailing city: Montevallo
Mailing state: AL
Mailing zip: 35115
General Phone: (205) 665-6222
General Fax: (205) 665-6232
General/National Adv. E-mail: alabamian@montevallo.edu
Primary Website: http://www.thealabamian.com/
Published: Bi-Mthly
Classified Equipment»
Personnel: Tiffany Bunt (Adviser); Reed Strength (Editor); Stephanie Howe (Business Manager)

MONTGOMERY

ALABAMA STATE UNIV.

Street address 1: 915 S Jackson St
Street address 3: Montgomery
Street address state: AL
Zip/Postal code: 36104-5716
Country: USA
Mailing address: PO Box 271
Mailing city: Montgomery
Mailing state: AL
Mailing zip: 36101-0271
General Phone: (334) 229-4419
General Fax: (334) 229-4934
General/National Adv. E-mail: ayoleke@aol.com
Primary Website: www.thehornettribune.com
Classified Equipment»
Personnel: David Okeowo (Prof./Chair); Bryan Weaver (Exec. Ed.); E.K. Daufin (Prof.); Julian K. Johnson (Mng. Ed.); Tracy Banks (Assoc. Prof./Dir., Forensics); James B. Lucy (News Ed.); Elizabeth Fitts (Assoc. Prof.); Richard Emmanuel (Asst. Prof.); James Adams (Instr.); Coke Ellington (Instr.); Valerie Heard (Instr.); Jonathan Himsel (Instr.); John Moore (Instr.); Walter Murphy (Instr.); Larry Owens (Instr.)

AUBURN UNIV.

Street address 1: 7400 East Dr
Street address 2: Rm 326
Street address 3: Montgomery
Street address state: AL
Zip/Postal code: 36117-7088
Country: USA
Mailing address: PO Box 244023
Mailing city: Montgomery
Mailing state: AL
Mailing zip: 36124-4023
General Phone: (334) 244-3662
General Fax: (334) 244-3131
General/National Adv. E-mail: aumnibuseditor@yahoo.com
Primary Website: aumnews.squarespace.com
Classified Equipment»
Personnel: Taylor Manning (Ed. in Chief); Christine Kneidter (Exec. Ed.); Amber Acker (Mng. Ed.)

HUNTINGDON COLLEGE

Street address 1: 1500 E Fairview Ave
Street address 3: Montgomery
Street address state: AL
Zip/Postal code: 36106-2114
Country: USA
Mailing address: 1500 E Fairview Ave
Mailing city: Montgomery
Mailing state: AL
Mailing zip: 36106-2148
General Phone: (314) 833-4354
General Fax: (334) 264-2951
General/National Adv. E-mail: gargoyle@huntingdon.edu
Classified Equipment»
Personnel: Jackie Trimble (Advisor); Matthew Adams (Co-Ed.); Beth Woodfin (Co-Ed.)

NORMAL

ALABAMA A&M UNIV.

Street address 1: 4900 Meridian St NW
Street address 3: Normal
Street address state: AL
Zip/Postal code: 35762-7500
Country: USA
Mailing address: 4900 Meridian St.
Mailing city: Normal
Mailing state: AL
Mailing zip: 35762
General Phone: (256) 372-5385
General Fax: (256) 372-8795
Classified Equipment»
Personnel: Diane Anderson (Advisor)

TROY UNIVERSITY

Street address 1: Hall School of Journalism and Communication
Street address 2: 103 Wallace Hall, Troy University
Street address 3: Troy
Street address state: AL
Zip/Postal code: 36082-0001
Country: USA
Mailing address: Hall School of Journalism and Communication
Mailing city: Troy
Mailing state: AL
Mailing zip: 36082-0001
General Phone: (334) 670-3583
General Fax: (334) 670-3707
Advertising Phone: (334) 670-3328
Advertising Fax: (334) 670-3707
Editorail Phone: (334) 670-3328
Editorial Fax: (334) 670-3707
General/National Adv. E-mail: sstewart71298@troy.edu
Display Adv. E-mail: sstewart71298@troy.edu
Editorial e-mail: sstewart71298@troy.edu
Primary Website: www.tropnews.com; www.troy.edu
Delivery Methods: Mail`Racks
Commercial printers: N
Published: Thur
Published Other: Certain home sports game days
Classified Equipment»
Personnel: Steve Stewart (Advisor)

TUSCALOOSA

STILLMAN COLLEGE

Street address 1: PO Box 1430
Street address 3: Tuscaloosa
Street address state: AL
Zip/Postal code: 35403-1430
Country: USA
Mailing address: PO Box 1430
Mailing city: Tuscaloosa
Mailing state: AL
Mailing zip: 35403-1430
General Phone: (205) 349-4240
Classified Equipment»

UNIV. OF ALABAMA

Street address 1: PO Box 870170
Street address 3: Tuscaloosa
Street address state: AL
Zip/Postal code: 35487-0001
Country: USA
Mailing address: PO Box 870170
Mailing city: Tuscaloosa
Mailing state: AL
Mailing zip: 35487-0170
General Phone: (205) 348-7845
General Fax: (205) 348-8036
General/National Adv. E-mail: news@cw.ua.edu
Primary Website: www.cw.ua.edu
Year Established: 1894
Classified Equipment»
Personnel: Drew Gunn (Adv. Mgr.); Corey Craft (Ed. in Chief); Amanda Peterson (Ed.)

ARKANSAS

ARKADELPHIA

HENDERSON STATE UNIV.

Street address 1: PO Box 7681
Street address 2: 1100 Henderson St.
Street address 3: Arkadelphia
Street address state: AR
Zip/Postal code: 71999-7693
Country: USA
Mailing address: PO Box 7693
Mailing city: Arkadelphia
Mailing state: AR
Mailing zip: 71999-7693
General Phone: (870) 230-5221
General Fax: (870) 230-5549
Advertising Phone: (870) 230-5288
General/National Adv. E-mail: oracle@hsu.edu
Display Adv. E-mail: oracleads@hsu.edu
Primary Website: www.hsuoracle.com
Year Established: 1910
Advertising (Open Inch Rate) Weekday/Saturday: www.hsuoracle.com/advertising
Published: Wed
Avg Free Circ: 2000
Classified Equipment»
Personnel: Steve Listopad (Advisor)

OUACHITA BAPTIST UNIV.

Street address 1: Obu Box 3759
Street address 3: Arkadelphia
Street address state: AR
Zip/Postal code: 71998-0001
Country: USA
Mailing address: OBU Box 3759
Mailing city: Arkadelphia
Mailing state: AR
Mailing zip: 71998-0001
General Phone: (870) 245-4186
General Fax: (870) 245-5500
Advertising Phone: 870-245-4186
General/National Adv. E-mail: rootj@obu.edu
Display Adv. E-mail: rootj@obu.edu
Editorial e-mail: rootj@obu.edu
Primary Website: www.obusignal.com
Published: Thur
Published Other: twice each month while school is in session
Avg Free Circ: 1500
Classified Equipment»
Note: Online Edition: carterj@obu.edu
Personnel: Jeff Root (Advisor); Jackson Carter (Signal Online Adviser)
Parent company (for newspapers): Ouachita Baptist University

BATESVILLE

LYON COLLEGE

Street address 1: PO Box 2317
Street address 3: Batesville
Street address state: AR
Zip/Postal code: 72503-2317
Country: USA
Mailing address: PO Box 2317
Mailing city: Batesville
Mailing state: AR
Mailing zip: 72503-2317
General Phone: (870) 698-4288
General Fax: (870) 698-4622
General/National Adv. E-mail: highlander@lyon.edu
Classified Equipment»
Personnel: Gavin Johannsen (Exec. Ed.)

CONWAY

HENDRIX COLLEGE

Street address 1: 1600 Washington Ave
Street address 3: Conway
Street address state: AR
Zip/Postal code: 72032-4115
Country: USA
Mailing address: 1600 Washington Ave.
Mailing city: Conway
Mailing state: AR
Mailing zip: 72032
General Phone: (501) 329-6811
General/National Adv. E-mail: proed@hendrix.edu
Primary Website: www.theprofileonline.com
Classified Equipment»

Personnel: Alice Hines (Advisor)

UNIVERSITY OF CENTRAL ARKANSAS

Street address 1: 201 Donaghey Ave
Street address 2: Stanley Russ Hall 124
Street address 3: Conway
Street address state: AR
Zip/Postal code: 72035-5001
Country: USA
Mailing address: PO Box 5038
Mailing city: Conway
Mailing state: AR
Mailing zip: 72035-0001
General Phone: 501-499-9822
Advertising Phone: 501-499-9822
Advertising Fax: 501-852-2375
General/National Adv. E-mail: ucaechoeditor@gmail.com
Display Adv. E-mail: echonewspaperads@gmail.com
Primary Website: www.ucaecho.net
Published: Wed
Avg Free Circ: 2500
Classified Equipment»
Personnel: David Keith (Advisor); Jordan Johnson (editor); Hayley Trejo (business manager)

ARKANSAS TRAVELER

Street address 1: 119 Kimpel Hall
Street address 3: Fayetteville
Street address state: AR
Zip/Postal code: 72701
Country: USA
Mailing address: 119 Kimpel Hall
Mailing city: Fayetteville
Mailing state: AR
Mailing zip: 72701
General Phone: (479) 575-3406
General Fax: (479) 575-3306
General/National Adv. E-mail: traveler@uark.edu
Primary Website: http://www.uatrav.com/
Classified Equipment»
Personnel: Saba Naseem (Editor-in-Chief)

FORT SMITH

WESTARK CMTY. COLLEGE

Street address 1: PO Box 3649
Street address 3: Fort Smith
Street address state: AR
Zip/Postal code: 72913-3649
Country: USA
Mailing address: PO Box 3649
Mailing city: Fort Smith
Mailing state: AR
Mailing zip: 72913-3649
General Phone: (501) 788-7261
Classified Equipment»

PHILANDER SMITH COLLEGE

Street address 1: 900 W Daisy L Gatson Bates Dr
Street address 3: Little Rock
Street address state: AR
Zip/Postal code: 72202-3726
Country: USA
Mailing address: 900 W Daisy L Gatson Bates Dr
Mailing city: Little Rock
Mailing state: AR
Mailing zip: 72202-3717
General Phone: (501) 370-5354
General/National Adv. E-mail: jcheffen@philander.edu
Classified Equipment»
Personnel: Jimmy Cheffen (Advisor)

THE FORUM, UNIVERSITY OF ARKANSAS AT LITTLE ROCK

Street address 1: 2801 S University Ave
Street address 2: Ste 116
Street address 3: Little Rock
Street address state: AR
Zip/Postal code: 72204-1000
Country: USA
Mailing address: 2801 S University Ave Dsc 201J
Mailing city: Little Rock
Mailing state: AR
Mailing zip: 72204-1000
General Phone: (501) 569-3319
General Fax: (501) 569-3209
Display Adv. E-mail: adman@ualr.edu
Editorial e-mail: editor@ualr.edu
Primary Website: ualr.edu/forum
Published: Bi-Mthly
Avg Free Circ: 2500
Classified Equipment»
Personnel: Sonny Rhodes (Advisor); Jacob Ellerbee (Exec. Ed.)

MAGNOLIA

SOUTHERN ARKANSAS UNIV.

Street address 1: PO Box 1400
Street address 3: Magnolia
Street address state: AR
Zip/Postal code: 71753
Country: USA
Mailing address: P.O. Box 1400
Mailing city: Magnolia
Mailing state: AR
Mailing zip: 71753-71753
General Phone: (870) 235-4269
General Fax: (870) 235-5005
General/National Adv. E-mail: saubrayeditors@yahoo.com
Editorial e-mail: brayeditor@yahoo.com
Primary Website: www.saumag.edu
Classified Equipment»
Personnel: John Cary (Advisor); Wes Dowdy (Ed. in Chief); Terri Richardson (Asst. Ed.); Jamal Brown (Sports Ed.)

PINE BLUFF

UNIVERSITY OF ARKANSAS AT PINE BLUFF

Street address 1: 1200 Universtiy Dr
Street address 3: Pine Bluff
Street address state: AR
Zip/Postal code: 71601-2799
Country: USA
Mailing address: 1200 N. University Dr.
Mailing city: Pine Bluff
Mailing state: AR
Mailing zip: 71601
General Phone: (870) 575-8427
Advertising Phone: (870) 575-8427
Editorail Phone: (870) 575-8427
General/National Adv. E-mail: arkansawyer@uapb.edu
Display Adv. E-mail: arkansawyer@uapb.edu
Editorial e-mail: arkansawyer@uapb.edu
Year Established: 1921
Advertising (Open Inch Rate) Weekday/Saturday: Rate card available
Published: Other
Published Other: Bi-weekly
Avg Free Circ: 1000
Classified Equipment»
Note: Advertising color positions available. All ads sold by contract by the semester or the year.
Personnel: Alicia Dorn (Editor)
Parent company (for newspapers): University of Arkansas at Pine Bluff

RUSSELLVILLE

ARKANSAS TECH. UNIV.

Street address 1: 1815 Coliseum Dr
Street address 3: Russellville
Street address state: AR
Zip/Postal code: 72801-8820
Country: USA
Mailing address: 1815 Coliseum Drive
Mailing city: Russellville
Mailing state: AR
Mailing zip: 72801-7400
General Phone: (479) 968-0284
General Fax: (479) 964-0889
General/National Adv. E-mail: arkatech@atu.edu
Display Adv. E-mail: arkatech.ads@atu.edu
Primary Website: www.arkatechnews.com
Year Established: 1923
Delivery Methods: Newsstand
Commercial printers: N
Advertising (Open Inch Rate) Weekday/Saturday: $3 per col. inch
Published: Thur
Avg Free Circ: 2100
Classified Equipment»
Personnel: Tommy Mumert (Advisor)

SEARCY

HARDING UNIV.

Street address 1: PO Box 11192
Street address 3: Searcy
Street address state: AR
Zip/Postal code: 72149-0001
Country: USA
Mailing address: PO Box 11192
Mailing city: Searcy
Mailing state: AR
Mailing zip: 72149-0001
General Phone: (501) 279-4139
General Fax: (501) 279-4127
General/National Adv. E-mail: thebison@harding.edu
Primary Website: thebison.harding.edu
Classified Equipment»
Personnel: Jermy Beauchamp (Dir., Publications); Jermy (Advisor)

SILOAM SPRINGS

JOHN BROWN UNIV.

Street address 1: 2000 W University St
Street address 3: Siloam Springs
Street address state: AR
Zip/Postal code: 72761-2112
Country: USA
Mailing address: 2000 W University St
Mailing city: Siloam Springs
Mailing state: AR
Mailing zip: 72761-2121
General Phone: (479) 524-7255
General Fax: (479) 524-7394
General/National Adv. E-mail: advocate@jbu.edu
Primary Website: advoacte.jbu.edu
Classified Equipment»
Personnel: Candy Gregor (Assistant Professor of Communication Faculty adviser for the Threefold Advocate); KJ Roh (Executive Editor of the Threefold Advocate)

STATE UNIVERSITY

ARKANSAS STATE UNIV.

Street address 1: 104 Cooley Drive
Street address 2: Journalism Department
Street address 3: State University
Street address state: AR
Zip/Postal code: 1921
Country: USA
Mailing address: PO Box 1930
Mailing city: State University
Mailing state: AR
Mailing zip: 72467-1930
General Phone: (870) 972-3076
General Fax: (870) 972-3339
Advertising Phone: 870-972-2961
Editorail Phone: (870) 972-3076
General/National Adv. E-mail: herald@astate.edu
Display Adv. E-mail: herald@astate.edu
Editorial e-mail: herald@astate.edu
Primary Website: www.asuherald.com
Year Established: 1921
Delivery Methods: Racks
Commercial printers: N
Published: Mon`Thur
Avg Free Circ: 5000
Classified Equipment»
Personnel: Bonnie Thrasher (Advisor); Lindsey Blakely (Editor); Jana Waters (Advertising Manager)

ARIZONA

FLAGSTAFF

THE LUMBERJACK

Street address 1: 700 Knoles Dr
Street address 3: Flagstaff
Street address state: AZ
Zip/Postal code: 86011-0180
County: Coconino
Country: USA
Mailing city: Flagstaff
Mailing state: AZ
Mailing zip: 86011-0180
General/National Adv. E-mail: lumberjack@nau.edu
Primary Website: www.jackcentral.org
Published: Fri
Classified Equipment»
Personnel: Ace Mcmillin (Ed. In Cheif); Gary Sundt (Gen. Mgr.); Joshua Garcia (Adv. Dir.); Jesica Demarco (Adv. Dir.)

GLENDALE

GLENDALE CMTY. COLLEGE

Street address 1: 6000 W Olive Ave
Street address 3: Glendale
Street address state: AZ
Zip/Postal code: 85302-3006
Country: USA
Mailing address: 6000 W Olive Ave
Mailing city: Glendale
Mailing state: AZ
Mailing zip: 85302-3090
General Phone: (623) 845-3820
General Fax: (623) 845-3072
General/National Adv. E-mail: ads@gccvoice.com
Primary Website: www.gccvoice.com
Classified Equipment»
Personnel: Mike Mullins (Advisor); Eric Carroll (Adv. Mgr.); Michelle Tabatabai-Shab (Ed. in chief)

THUNDERBIRD SCHOOL OF GLOBAL MGMT.

Street address 1: 1 Global Pl
Street address 3: Glendale
Street address state: AZ
Zip/Postal code: 85306-3216
Country: USA
Mailing address: 1 Global Pl
Mailing city: Glendale
Mailing state: AZ
Mailing zip: 85306-3216
General Phone: (602) 978-7000
General Fax: (602) 978-7971
General/National Adv. E-mail: dastor@thunderbird.edu
Primary Website: www.thunderbird.edu
Classified Equipment»
Personnel: Sailaja Kattubadi (Ed. in Chief)

WEST NEWS

Street address 1: 4701 W Thunderbird Rd
Street address 2: # 117
Street address 3: Glendale
Street address state: AZ
Zip/Postal code: 85306-4900
Country: USA
Mailing address: 4701 W Thunderbird Rd # 117
Mailing city: Glendale
Mailing state: AZ
Mailing zip: 85306-4900
General Phone: 602-543-8575
Editorial Fax: Free
Year Established: 2010
Classified Equipment»
Personnel: Robert Gehl (Editor-in-chief)

MESA

MESA COMMUNITY COLLEGE

Street address 1: 1833 W Southern Ave

Street address 3: Mesa
Street address state: AZ
Zip/Postal code: 85202-4822
Country: USA
Mailing address: 1833 W Southern Ave
Mailing city: Mesa
Mailing state: AZ
Mailing zip: 85202-4866
General Phone: (480) 461-7270
General Fax: (480) 461-7334
General/National Adv. E-mail: jackm@mesacc.edu
Primary Website: www.mesalegend.com
Year Established: 1962
Advertising (Open Inch Rate) Weekday/Saturday: display
Published: Bi-Mthly
Avg Free Circ: 5000
Classified Equipment»
Personnel: Jack Mullins (Advisor)

PARADISE VALLEY CMTY. COLLEGE

Street address 1: 18401 N 32nd St
Street address 3: Phoenix
Street address state: AZ
Zip/Postal code: 85032-1210
Country: USA
Mailing address: 18401 N 32nd St
Mailing city: Phoenix
Mailing state: AZ
Mailing zip: 85032-1200
General Phone: (602) 787-6772
General Fax: (602) 787-7285
Advertising Phone: (602) 787-6772
Advertising Fax: (602) 787-7285
Editorail Phone: (602) 787-6772
General/National Adv. E-mail: pumapress@pvmail.maricopa.edu
Display Adv. E-mail: judy.galbraith@paradisevalley.edu
Editorial e-mail: judy.galbraith@paradisevalley.edu
Primary Website: http://nevalleynews.org/
Year Established: 1991
Advertising (Open Inch Rate) Weekday/Saturday: 602-787-6772
Published: Mthly
Avg Free Circ: 2000
Classified Equipment»
Note: Paradise Valley Community College is converged online media with Scottsdale Community College to form the Northeast Valley News.
Personnel: Judy Galbraith (Advisor)
Parent company (for newspapers): Paradise Valley Community College

PRESCOTT

EMBRY-RIDDLE AERO UNIV.

Street address 1: 3700 Willow Creek Rd
Street address 3: Prescott
Street address state: AZ
Zip/Postal code: 86301-3721
Country: USA
Mailing address: 3700 Willow Creek Road
Mailing city: Prescott
Mailing state: AZ
Mailing zip: 86301
General Phone: (928) 777-3891
Advertising Phone: (928) 777-3830
General/National Adv. E-mail: prnews@erau.edu
Primary Website: www.erau.edu/
Classified Equipment»
Personnel: Alan Malnar (Advisor); Katie (Gen Mgr.)

YAVAPAI COLLEGE

Street address 1: 1100 E Sheldon St
Street address 2: Bldg 3-118
Street address 3: Prescott
Street address state: AZ
Zip/Postal code: 86301-3220
Country: USA
Mailing address: 1100 E Sheldon St Bldg 3-118
Mailing city: Prescott
Mailing state: AZ
Mailing zip: 86301-3297
General Fax: (928) 717-7678
Advertising Fax: (928) 717-7742
General/National Adv. E-mail: roughwriter.yc.edu
Display Adv. E-mail: ycwriters@yahoo.com
Primary Website: http://roughwriter.yc.edu/
Classified Equipment»
Personnel: Colette Strassburg (Advisor); Brandon Ross (Ed.); Elizabeth Zieche (Asst. Ed.)

TEMPE

ARIZONA STATE UNIV.

Street address 1: PO Box 871502
Street address 3: Tempe
Street address state: AZ
Zip/Postal code: 85287-1502
Country: USA
Mailing address: PO Box 871502
Mailing city: Tempe
Mailing state: AZ
Mailing zip: 85287-1502
General Phone: (480) 965-7572
General Fax: (480) 965-8484
General/National Adv. E-mail: state.press@asu.edu
Primary Website: www.statepress.com
Classified Equipment»
Personnel: Jason Manning (Advisor); Tosh Stuart (Bus. Mgr.); Leo Gonzalez (Adv. Mgr.)

PIMA COMMUNITY COLLEGE

Street address 1: 2202 W Anklam Rd
Street address 3: Tucson
Street address state: AZ
Zip/Postal code: 85709-0001
Country: USA
Mailing address: 2202 W. Anklam Rd.
Mailing city: Tucson
Mailing state: AZ
Mailing zip: 85709-0001
General Phone: (520) 206-6800
General Fax: (520) 206-6834
Advertising Phone: (520) 206-6901
General/National Adv. E-mail: aztec_press@pima.edu
Display Adv. E-mail: aztecpress_ad@pima.edu
Primary Website: aztecpressonline.com
Year Established: 1970
Published: Bi-Mthly
Avg Paid Circ: 0
Avg Free Circ: 5000
Classified Equipment»
Personnel: Andrew Paxton (Business manager)

UNIV. OF ARIZONA

Street address 1: 615 N Park Ave
Street address 2: Ste 101
Street address 3: Tucson
Street address state: AZ
Zip/Postal code: 85719-5096
Country: USA
Mailing address: 615 N. Park Ave., Ste. 101
Mailing city: Tucson
Mailing state: AZ
Mailing zip: 85719-5094
General Phone: (520) 621-8659
General Fax: (520) 626-8303
Advertising Phone: (520) 621-5982
Editorail Phone: (520) 621-7879
General/National Adv. E-mail: display@wildcat.arizona.edu
Editorial e-mail: editor@wildcat.arizona.edu
Primary Website: www.wildcat.arizona.edu
Year Established: 1899
Published: Mon`Tues`Wed`Thur`Fri
Classified Equipment»
Personnel: Mark Woodhams (Dir.); Brett Fera (Asst. Dir.)

CALIFORNIA

ANGWIN

PACIFIC UNION COLLEGE

Street address 1: 1 Angwin Ave
Street address 2: Campus Ctr.
Street address 3: Angwin
Street address state: CA
Zip/Postal code: 94508-9713
Country: USA
Mailing address: 1 Angwin Ave
Mailing city: Angwin
Mailing state: CA
Mailing zip: 94508-9797
General Phone: (707) 965-6747
General Fax: (707) 965-7123
General/National Adv. E-mail: cc@puc.edu
Primary Website: c2.puc.edu
Classified Equipment»
Personnel: Tammy McGuire (Advisor); Peter Katz (Ed.)

ARCATA

HUMBOLDT STATE UNIV.

Street address 1: 1 Harpst St
Street address 2: Gist Hall 227
Street address 3: Arcata
Street address state: CA
Zip/Postal code: 95521-8222
Country: USA
Mailing address: 1 Harpst Street
Mailing city: Arcata
Mailing state: CA
Mailing zip: 95521-8299
General Phone: (707) 826-3271
Advertising Phone: (707) 826-5921
General/National Adv. E-mail: thejack@humboldt.edu
Primary Website: www.thejackonline.org
Classified Equipment»
Personnel: Marcy Burstiner (Advisor); Sara Wilmot (Ed.)

ATHERTON

MENLO COLLEGE

Street address 1: 1000 El Camino Real
Street address 3: Atherton
Street address state: CA
Zip/Postal code: 94027-4300
County: San Mateo County
Country: USA
Mailing address: 1000 El Camino Real
Mailing city: Atherton
Mailing state: CA
Mailing zip: 94027-4301
General Phone: (650) 543-3786
General/National Adv. E-mail: pr@menlo.edu
Primary Website: www.menlo.edu
Classified Equipment»
Personnel: Priscila de Souza (Dean of Enrollment Management)

BAKERSFIELD COLLEGE

Street address 1: 1801 Panorama Dr
Street address 3: Bakersfield
Street address state: CA
Zip/Postal code: 93305-1219
Country: USA
Mailing address: 1801 Panorama Dr
Mailing city: Bakersfield
Mailing state: CA
Mailing zip: 93305-1299
General Phone: (661) 395-4324
General Fax: (661) 395-4027
Editorial Fax: Free
General/National Adv. E-mail: ripmail@bakersfieldcollege.edu
Display Adv. E-mail: daedward@bakersfieldcollege.edu
Primary Website: www.therip.com
Year Established: 1929
Advertising (Open Inch Rate) Weekday/Saturday: Take ROP advertising
Published Other: bi-weekly (once every two weeks on Wednesdays)
Avg Free Circ: 3000
Classified Equipment»
Personnel: Danny Edwards (Advisor)

CALIFORNIA STATE UNIVERSITY, BAKERSFIELD

Street address 1: 9001 Stockdale Hwy
Street address 3: Bakersfield
Street address state: CA
Zip/Postal code: 93311-1022
Country: USA
Mailing address: 9001 Stockdale Hwy.
Mailing city: Bakersfield
Mailing state: CA
Mailing zip: 93311-1022
General Phone: (661) 654-2165
General/National Adv. E-mail: runner@csub.edu
Primary Website: http://therunneronline.com
Year Established: 1974
Advertising (Open Inch Rate) Weekday/Saturday: $800/page, $400/half page, $200/quarter page, etc.
Published: Wed
Published Other: Back-to-School issue - 1st Day of Fall
Classified Equipment»
Personnel: Jennifer Burger (Lecturer and Adviser to the Runner Student Media Center)

BELMONT

NOTRE DAME DE NAMUR UNIVERSITY

Street address 1: 1500 Ralston Ave
Street address 3: Belmont
Street address state: CA
Zip/Postal code: 94002-1908
Country: USA
Mailing address: 1500 Ralston Ave
Mailing city: Belmont
Mailing state: CA
Mailing zip: 94002-1997
General Phone: (650) 508-3500
General Fax: (650) 508-3487
General/National Adv. E-mail: argonaut@ndnu.edu
Primary Website: www.theargonaut.net
Classified Equipment»
Personnel: Danielle Russo (Adv. Mgr.); Victor Gonzales (Ed.)

BERKELEY

UNIV. OF CALIFORNIA BUS. SCHOOL

Street address 1: Cheit Hall, Rm 138
Street address 3: Berkeley
Street address state: CA
Zip/Postal code: 94720-0001
Country: USA
Mailing address: Cheit Hall Rm 138
Mailing city: Berkeley
Mailing state: CA
Mailing zip: 94720-0001
General Phone: (510) 642-7480
General Fax: (510) 643-8764
Classified Equipment»
Personnel: Joe Moss (Ed.)

UNIV. OF CALIFORNIA, BERKELEY

Street address 1: 2483 Hearst Ave
Street address 3: Berkeley
Street address state: CA
Zip/Postal code: 94709-1320
Country: USA
Mailing address: 2483 Hearst Avenue Berkeley, CA 94709
Mailing city: Berkeley
Mailing state: CA
Mailing zip: 94701-1949
General Phone: (510) 548-8300
General Fax: (510) 849-2803
General/National Adv. E-mail: dailycal@dailycal.org; dailycalifornian@dailycal.org
Display Adv. E-mail: advertising@dailycal.org
Editorial e-mail: editor@dailycal.org
Primary Website: www.dailycal.org
Year Established: 1871
Published: Mon`Tues`Thur`Fri
Avg Paid Circ: 10000
Classified Equipment»
Personnel: Karim Doumar (Editor in Chief and President)

UNIV. OF CALIFORNIA-BERKELEY LAW SCHOOL

Street address 1: 215 Boalt Hall
Street address 3: Berkeley
Street address state: CA
Zip/Postal code: 94720-0001
Country: USA
Mailing address: 215 Boalt Hall

Mailing city: Berkeley
Mailing state: CA
Mailing zip: 94720-0001
General Phone: (510) 642-6483
General Fax: (510) 642-9893
Commercial printers: N
Classified Equipment»
Personnel: Joshua Rider (Ed.)

CARSON

CALIFORNIA STATE UNIV. DOMINGUEZ

Street address 1: 1000 E Victoria St
Street address 2: Dept Sac
Street address 3: Carson
Street address state: CA
Zip/Postal code: 90747-0001
Country: USA
Mailing address: 1000 E Victoria St Dept Sac
Mailing city: Carson
Mailing state: CA
Mailing zip: 90747-0001
General Phone: (310) 243-2312
General Fax: (310) 217-6935
General/National Adv. E-mail: bulletin@csudh.edu
Display Adv. E-mail: Advertise@csudh.edu
Primary Website: www.csudh.edu/bulletin/
Published: Wed
Published Other: Bi-Weekly
Classified Equipment»
Personnel: Catherine Risling (Advisor); Marjan Khorashadi-Zadeh (Adv. Mgr.); Karen Mossiah (Prodn. Mgr.)

CHICO

CALIFORNIA STATE UNIV.

Street address 1: Chico Dept. of Journalism
Street address 2: Zip 600 Chico
Street address 3: Chico
Street address state: CA
Zip/Postal code: 95926
Country: USA
Mailing address: Chico Dept. of Journalism
Mailing city: Chico
Mailing state: CA
Mailing zip: 95926
General Phone: (530) 898-4237
General Fax: (530) 898-4799
Editorial Fax: (530) 898-4033
Display Adv. E-mail: advertising@theorion.com
Primary Website: www.theorion.com
Classified Equipment»
Personnel: David Waddell (Advisor); Gillian Leeds (Bus. Mgr.); Jennifer Siino (Mng. Ed.); Mike North (News Ed.)

SOUTHWESTERN COLLEGE

Street address 1: 900 Otay Lakes Rd
Street address 3: Chula Vista
Street address state: CA
Zip/Postal code: 91910-7223
Country: USA
Mailing address: 900 Otay Lakes Rd
Mailing city: Chula Vista
Mailing state: CA
Mailing zip: 91910-7297
General Phone: (619) 482-6368
General Fax: (619) 482-6513
General/National Adv. E-mail: southwestern_sun@yahoo.com
Primary Website: www.southwesterncollegesun.com
Classified Equipment»
Personnel: Max Branfcomb (Advisor)

CLAREMONT

CLAREMONT COLLEGES

Street address 1: 175 E 8th St
Street address 3: Claremont
Street address state: CA
Zip/Postal code: 91711-3956
Country: USA
Mailing address: 175 E 8th St
Mailing city: Claremont
Mailing state: CA
Mailing zip: 91711-3956
General Phone: (909) 621-8000
General Fax: (909) 607-7825
Classified Equipment»
Personnel: Keith Koyano (Ed.)

CLAREMONT MCKENNA COLLEGE

Street address 1: Heggblade Ctr, 500 E 9th St
Street address 3: Claremont
Street address state: CA
Zip/Postal code: 91711
Country: USA
Mailing address: Heggblade Ctr., 500 E. 9th St.
Mailing city: Claremont
Mailing state: CA
Mailing zip: 91711
General Phone: (909) 607-6709
General Fax: (909) 607-9489
Classified Equipment»
Personnel: Adam Sivitz (Ed.)

POMONA COLLEGE

Street address 1: Smith Campus Ctr.
Street address 2: Pomona College
Street address 3: Claremont
Street address state: CA
Zip/Postal code: 91711
Country: USA
Mailing address: Smith Campus Ctr.
Mailing city: Claremont
Mailing state: CA
Mailing zip: 91711-7003
General Phone: (909) 607-6709
General/National Adv. E-mail: info@tsl.pomona.edu
Display Adv. E-mail: business@tsl.pomona.edu
Editorial e-mail: editor@tsl.pomona.edu
Primary Website: www.tsl.pomona.edu
Year Established: 1889
Delivery Methods: Mail`Racks
Commercial printers: Y
Published: Fri
Avg Paid Circ: 50
Avg Free Circ: 2000
Classified Equipment»
Personnel: Ian Gallogly; Adam Belzberg (Business Manager); Jeff Zalesin (Editor-in-Chief)

COSTA MESA

ORANGE COAST COLLEGE

Street address 1: 2701 Fairview Rd
Street address 3: Costa Mesa
Street address state: CA
Zip/Postal code: 92626-5563
Country: USA
Mailing address: 2701 Fairview Rd
Mailing city: Costa Mesa
Mailing state: CA
Mailing zip: 92626-5561
General Phone: (714) 432-5561
General Fax: (714) 432-5978
Advertising Phone: 714-432-5978
Advertising Fax: 714-432-5673
Editorail Phone: 714-432-5561
Editorial Fax: 714-432-5673
Display Adv. E-mail: coastreportads@yahoo.com
Editorial e-mail: editor@coastreportonline.com; coastreport@yahoo.com
Primary Website: www.coastreportonline.com
Year Established: 1948
Classified Equipment»
Personnel: Cathy Werblin (Advisor)

VANGUARD UNIV.

Street address 1: 55 Fair Dr
Street address 3: Costa Mesa
Street address state: CA
Zip/Postal code: 92626-6520
Country: USA
Mailing address: 55 Fair Dr
Mailing city: Costa Mesa
Mailing state: CA
Mailing zip: 92626-6597
General Phone: (714) 662-5203
General Fax: (714) 966-5482
General/National Adv. E-mail: thevoice@vanguard.edu
Primary Website: www.vanguard.edu
Classified Equipment»
Personnel: Kristy Eudy (Advisor); Hannah Petrak (Ed.)

CUPERTINO

DE ANZA COLLEGE

Street address 1: 21250 Stevens Creek Blvd
Street address 2: Rm L-41
Street address 3: Cupertino
Street address state: CA
Zip/Postal code: 95014-5702
Country: USA
Mailing address: 21250 Stevens Creek Blvd Rm L-41
Mailing city: Cupertino
Mailing state: CA
Mailing zip: 95014-5797
General Phone: (408) 864-5626
Advertising Phone: (408) 864-5626
Editorial Fax: Free
General/National Adv. E-mail: lavoz@fhda.edu
Display Adv. E-mail: lavozadvertising@gmail.com
Editorial e-mail: lavoz@fhda.edu
Primary Website: www.lavozdeanza.com
Year Established: 1967
Advertising (Open Inch Rate) Weekday/Saturday: https://issuu.com/lavozweekly/docs/mediakit2017-18
Published: Mon`Bi-Mthly
Published Other: 16 issues from late September to mid-June
Avg Free Circ: 2200
Classified Equipment»
Note: Student newspaper for De Anza College, Cupertino, CA
Personnel: Cecilia Deck (Journalism Chair)

CYPRESS

CYPRESS COLLEGE CHRONICLE

Street address 1: 9200 Valley View St
Street address 3: Cypress
Street address state: CA
Zip/Postal code: 90630-5805
Country: USA
Mailing address: 9200 Valley View St.
Mailing city: Cypress
Mailing state: CA
Mailing zip: 90630-5805
General Phone: 714-484-7267
General Fax: (714) 484-7466
Advertising Phone: 714-484-7268
Editorail Phone: 714-484-7269
General/National Adv. E-mail: rmercer@cypresscollege.edu
Primary Website: www.cychron.com
Year Established: 1966
Delivery Methods: Newsstand
Commercial printers: N
Advertising (Open Inch Rate) Weekday/Saturday: http://www.cychron.com/adverstising
Published: Mthly
Avg Free Circ: 4000
Classified Equipment»
Note: Hosted on WordPress software on own server
Personnel: Robert Mercer (Advisor)

DAVIS

UNIV. OF CALIFORNIA SCHOOL OF LAW

Street address 1: 400 Mrak Hall Dr
Street address 3: Davis
Street address state: CA
Zip/Postal code: 95616-5203
Country: USA
Mailing address: 400 Mrak Hall Dr
Mailing city: Davis
Mailing state: CA
Mailing zip: 95616-5203
General Phone: (530) 752-0243
Classified Equipment»
Personnel: Heather Melton (Prodn. Ed.)

UNIVERSITY OF CALIFORNIA, DAVIS

Street address 1: 1 Shields Avenue
Street address 2: 25 Lower Freeborn Hall
Street address 3: Davis
Street address state: CA
Zip/Postal code: 95616-5270
Country: USA
Mailing address: 25 Lower Freeborn Hall
Mailing city: Davis
Mailing state: CA
Mailing zip: 95616-5270
General Phone: (530) 752-9887
Advertising Phone: (530) 752-6851
Editorail Phone: (530) 752-9887
General/National Adv. E-mail: editor@theaggie.org
Display Adv. E-mail: admanager@theaggie.org
Editorial e-mail: editor@theaggie.org
Primary Website: www.theaggie.org
Year Established: 1915
Published: Thur
Classified Equipment»
Personnel: Emily Stack (Editor-in-Chief); Olivia Rockeman (Managing Editor); Hannah Holzer (Campus News Editor); Kaelyn Tuermer-Lee (City News Editor); Liz Jacobson (Arts and Culture Editor); Dominic Faria (Sports Editor); Harnoor Gill (Science and Technology Editor); Olivia Luchini (Features Editor); Taryn DeOliers (Opinion Editor); Brian Landry (Photo Director); Trevor Goodman (Video Production Manager); Sydney Odman (New Media Manager); Zoe Reinhardt (Website Manager); Hali Zweigoron (Social Media Manager); Grace Simmons (Newsletter Manager); Shaelin Green (Distribution Manager); Jonathan Chen (Layout Director); Olivia Kotlarek (Design Director); Laurie Pederson (Business Development Manager); Hanna Baublitz (Copy Chief); Cecilia Morales (Copy Chief)

EL CAJON

CUYAMACA COLLEGE

Street address 1: 900 Rancho San Diego Pkwy
Street address 2: Bldg G-109
Street address 3: El Cajon
Street address state: CA
Zip/Postal code: 92019-4369
Country: USA
Mailing address: 900 Rancho San Diego Pkwy Bldg G-109
Mailing city: El Cajon
Mailing state: CA
Mailing zip: 92019-4369
General Phone: (619) 660-4000
General Fax: (619) 660-4399
Primary Website: www.cuyamaca.edu/coyoteexpress
Year Established: 1977
Classified Equipment»
Personnel: Seth Slater (Contact); Mary Graham (Contact)

GROSSMONT COLLEGE

Street address 1: 8800 Grossmont College Dr
Street address 3: El Cajon
Street address state: CA
Zip/Postal code: 92020-1765
Country: USA
Mailing address: 8800 Grossmont College Dr
Mailing city: El Cajon
Mailing state: CA
Mailing zip: 92020-1798
Advertising Phone: (619) 644-7271
Advertising Fax: (619) 644-7914
Editorail Phone: (619) 644-1730
General/National Adv. E-mail: summit@gcccd.edu
Primary Website: gcsummit.com
Published: Mthly
Classified Equipment»

FAIRFIELD

SOLANO COMMUNITY COLLEGE

Street address 1: 4000 Suisun Valley Rd
Street address 3: Fairfield
Street address state: CA
Zip/Postal code: 94534-4017
Country: USA
Mailing address: 4000 Suisun Valley Rd

Mailing city: Fairfield
Mailing state: CA
Mailing zip: 94534-3197
General Phone: (707) 864-7000
General Fax: (707) 864-0361
General/National Adv. E-mail: tempest@solano.edu
Display Adv. E-mail: samanda.dorger@solano.edu
Editorial e-mail: tempest@solano.edu
Primary Website: www.solanotempest.net
Published: Bi-Mthly
Avg Free Circ: 1500
Classified Equipment»
Personnel: Samanda Dorger (Journalism Adviser)

FREMONT

OHLONE COLLEGE

Street address 1: 43600 Mission Blvd
Street address 3: Fremont
Street address state: CA
Zip/Postal code: 94539-5847
Country: USA
Mailing address: PO Box 3909
Mailing city: Fremont
Mailing state: CA
Mailing zip: 94539-0390
General Phone: (510) 659-6074
General Fax: (510) 659-6076
General/National Adv. E-mail: monitor@ohlone.edu; monitor@ohlone.cc.ca.us
Primary Website: www.ohlonemonitoronline.com
Published Other: Nine times per semester
Classified Equipment»
Personnel: Rob Dennis (Adviser)

ALLIANT INTERNATIONAL UNIV.

Street address 1: 5130 E Clinton Way
Street address 3: Fresno
Street address state: CA
Zip/Postal code: 93727-2014
Country: USA
Mailing address: 5130 E Clinton Way
Mailing city: Fresno
Mailing state: CA
Mailing zip: 93727-2014
General Phone: (559) 456-2777
General Fax: (858) 635-4853
Editorail Phone: (858) 635-4540
General/National Adv. E-mail: envoy@alliant.edu; envoy.alliant@gmail.com
Classified Equipment»
Personnel: Miles Beauchamp (Advisor); Alexandria Proff (Ed.)

CALIFORNIA STATE UNIV.

Street address 1: 5201 N Maple Ave
Street address 2: MS SA42
Street address 3: Fresno
Street address state: CA
Zip/Postal code: 93740-0001
Country: USA
Mailing address: 5201 N Maple Ave MS SA42
Mailing city: Fresno
Mailing state: CA
Mailing zip: 93740-0001
General Phone: (559) 278-5735
General Fax: (559) 278-2679
Editorail Phone: (559) 278-5732
General/National Adv. E-mail: collegian@csufresno.edu
Primary Website: www.csufresno.edu/collegian
Classified Equipment»
Personnel: Jefferson Beavers (Advisor); Virginia Sellars-Erxleben (Bus. Mgr.); Brian Maxey (Ed. in Chief)

FRESNO CITY COLLEGE

Street address 1: 1101 E University Ave
Street address 3: Fresno
Street address state: CA
Zip/Postal code: 93741-0001
Country: USA
Mailing address: 1101 E University Ave
Mailing city: Fresno
Mailing state: CA
Mailing zip: 93741-0002
General Phone: (559) 442-8262
General Fax: (559) 265-5783
General/National Adv. E-mail: rampage-news@fresnocitycollege.edu
Primary Website: www.fresnocitycollegerampage.com
Classified Equipment»
Personnel: Dynpna Ugwu-Oju (Advisor); Leah Edward (Adv. Mgr.); Ramiro Gudino (Prodn. Mgr.)

FULLERTON

CALIFORNIA STATE UNIV., FULLERTON

Street address 1: College Park Bldg Nutwood Ave
Street address 2: Ste 2600660
Street address 3: Fullerton
Street address state: CA
Zip/Postal code: 1960
Country: USA
Mailing address: College Park Bldg., 2600 E. Nutwood Ave., Ste. 660
Mailing city: Fullerton
Mailing state: CA
Mailing zip: 92831-3110
General Phone: (657) 278-4411
General Fax: (657) 278-2702
Editorail Phone: (657) 278-5815
Display Adv. E-mail: ads@dailytitan.com
Editorial e-mail: editorinchief@dailytitan.com
Primary Website: www.dailytitan.com
Year Established: 1960
News Services: MCT
Delivery Methods: Newsstand`Racks
Commercial printers: Y
Advertising (Open Inch Rate) Weekday/Saturday: $9.80 pci
Published: Mon`Tues`Wed`Thur
Avg Free Circ: 6000
Classified Equipment»
Personnel: Robert Sage (Bus. Mgr.)

FULLERTON COLLEGE

Street address 1: 321 E Chapman Ave
Street address 3: Fullerton
Street address state: CA
Zip/Postal code: 92832-2011
Country: USA
Mailing address: 321 E Chapman Ave
Mailing city: Fullerton
Mailing state: CA
Mailing zip: 92832-2095
General Phone: (714) 992-7154
General Fax: (714) 447-4097
General/National Adv. E-mail: hornet@fullcoll.edu
Primary Website: www.fullcoll.edu
Year Established: 1922
Published: Wed
Classified Equipment»
Personnel: Jay Seidel (Advisor)

GILROY

GAVILAN COLLEGE

Street address 1: 5055 Santa Teresa Blvd
Street address 3: Gilroy
Street address state: CA
Zip/Postal code: 95020-9578
Country: USA
Mailing address: 5055 Santa Teresa Blvd
Mailing city: Gilroy
Mailing state: CA
Mailing zip: 95020-9599
General Phone: (408) 848-4837
General Fax: (408) 848-4801
Editorial Fax: Free
Published: Bi-Mthly
Avg Paid Circ: 0
Avg Free Circ: 0
Classified Equipment»
Note: This publication is in transition. More information will be available when the fall semester begins.
Personnel: Esmeralda Montenegro (Faculty Advisor)

GLENDALE CMTY. COLLEGE

Street address 1: 1500 N Verdugo Rd
Street address 2: Rm AD212
Street address 3: Glendale
Street address state: CA
Zip/Postal code: 91208-2809
Country: USA
Mailing address: 1500 N Verdugo Rd Rm AD212
Mailing city: Glendale
Mailing state: CA
Mailing zip: 91208-2809
General Phone: (818) 551-5214
General Fax: (818) 551-5278
Primary Website: www.elvaq.com
Classified Equipment»
Personnel: Michael Moreau (Advisor); Jeff Smith (Classified Mgr.)

GLENDORA

CITRUS COLLEGE

Street address 1: 1000 W Foothill Blvd
Street address 3: Glendora
Street address state: CA
Zip/Postal code: 91741-1885
Country: USA
Mailing address: 1000 W Foothill Blvd
Mailing city: Glendora
Mailing state: CA
Mailing zip: 91741-1899
General Phone: (626) 914-8586
General Fax: (626) 914-8797
General/National Adv. E-mail: ccclarion@hotmail.com
Primary Website: www.theclariononline.com
Classified Equipment»
Personnel: Margaret O'Neill (Advisor); Emily Rios (Ed.)

HAYWARD

CALIFORNIA STATE UNIVERSITY, EAST BAY.

Street address 1: 25800 Carlos Bee Blvd
Street address 3: Hayward
Street address state: CA
Zip/Postal code: 94542-3000
Country: USA
Mailing address: 25800 Carlos Bee Blvd
Mailing city: Hayward
Mailing state: CA
Mailing zip: 94542-3001
General Phone: (510) 885-3292
General Fax: (510) 885-4099
Advertising Phone: (510) 885-3526
Advertising Fax: (510) 885-2584
Editorail Phone: (510) 885-3176
Editorial Fax: (510) 885-2584
Display Adv. E-mail: pioneer.advertising@csueastbay.edu
Editorial e-mail: pioneernewspaper@sueastbay.edu
Primary Website: http://thepioneeronline.com/
Published: Thur
Avg Free Circ: 10000
Classified Equipment»

CHABOT COLLEGE

Street address 1: 25555 Hesperian Blvd
Street address 2: Ste 1635
Street address 3: Hayward
Street address state: CA
Zip/Postal code: 94545-2447
Country: USA
Mailing address: 25555 Hesperian Blvd Ste 1635
Mailing city: Hayward
Mailing state: CA
Mailing zip: 94545-2400
General Phone: (510) 723-7082
General Fax: (510) 723-6919
General/National Adv. E-mail: chabot_spectator@hotmail.com
Primary Website: www.chabotspectator.com
Classified Equipment»
Personnel: Jeannie Wakeland (Advisor)

HUNTINGTON BEACH

GOLDEN WEST COLLEGE

Street address 1: 15744 Goldenwest St
Street address 2: Rm 138
Street address 3: Huntington Beach
Street address state: CA
Zip/Postal code: 92647-3103
Country: USA
Mailing address: 15744 Goldenwest St Rm 138
Mailing city: Huntington Beach
Mailing state: CA
Mailing zip: 92647-3103
General Phone: (714) 895-8786
General Fax: (714) 895-8795
Advertising Phone: 714-315-9450
Advertising Fax: (714) 895-8795
General/National Adv. E-mail: twsatgwc@aol.com
Display Adv. E-mail: gwckcumper@yahoo.com
Primary Website: www.westernsun.us; www.goldenwestcollege.edu/westernsun
Year Established: 1966
Advertising (Open Inch Rate) Weekday/Saturday: Information on website: westernsun.us
Published: Bi-Mthly
Avg Free Circ: 15000
Classified Equipment»
Note: Westernsun.us (website)
Personnel: Jim Tortolano (Advisor); Katie Cumper (Adv. Dir.); Lanace Tonelli (Exec. Ed.); Opal McClain (Opinion Ed.); Fernando (Sports Ed.)

IRVINE

UNIV. OF CALIFORNIA IRVINE

Street address 1: 3100 Gateway Commons, 3rd Fl
Street address 3: Irvine
Street address state: CA
Zip/Postal code: 92697-0001
Country: USA
Mailing address: 3100 Gateway Cmns Fl 3
Mailing city: Irvine
Mailing state: CA
Mailing zip: 92697-0001
General Phone: (949) 824-8788
General Fax: (949) 824-4828
Advertising Phone: (949) 824-4284
Editorail Phone: (949) 824-8788
General/National Adv. E-mail: eic@newuniversity.org
Display Adv. E-mail: admanager@newu.uci.edu
Editorial e-mail: eic@newuniversity.org
Primary Website: www.newuniversity.org
Avg Paid Circ: 0
Avg Free Circ: 8000
Classified Equipment»
Personnel: David Lumb (Ed. in Chief); Sandy Rose (Mng. Ed.)

KENTFIELD

COLLEGE OF MARIN

Street address 1: 835 College Ave
Street address 3: Kentfield
Street address state: CA
Zip/Postal code: 94904-2551
Country: USA
Mailing address: 835 College Ave
Mailing city: Kentfield
Mailing state: CA
Mailing zip: 94904-2590
General Phone: (415) 485-9690
General Fax: (415) 485-0135
General/National Adv. E-mail: echotimes@marin.cc.ca.us
Primary Website: www.theechotimes.com
Classified Equipment»
Personnel: Elisa Forsgren (Adv. Mgr.); William Kennedy (Ed. in Chief); Yukie Sano (Mng. Ed.)

LA JOLLA

UNIVERSITY OF CALIFORNIA SAN DIEGO

Street address 1: 9500 Gilman Dr
Street address 2: Dept 316
Street address 3: La Jolla
Street address state: CA
Zip/Postal code: 92093-0316
Country: USA
Mailing address: 9500 Gilman Dr Dept 316

Mailing city: La Jolla
Mailing state: CA
Mailing zip: 92093-0316
General Phone: (858) 534-3466
General Fax: (858) 534-7691
Display Adv. E-mail: ads@ucsdguardian.org
Editorial e-mail: managing@ucsdguardian.org
Primary Website: www.ucsdguardian.org
Year Established: 1967
Special Editions: Back to school, restaurant guide, Best of San Diego, Sun God Festival, local music, holiday and Valentine's gift guides
Delivery Methods: Mail`Racks
Commercial printers: Y
Published: Mon`Thur
Classified Equipment»
Personnel: Laira Martin (Editor in Chief)

LA MIRADA

BIOLA UNIVERSITY

Street address 1: 13800 Biola Ave
Street address 3: La Mirada
Street address state: CA
Zip/Postal code: 90639-0002
Country: USA
Mailing address: 13800 Biola Ave
Mailing city: La Mirada
Mailing state: CA
Mailing zip: 90639-0001
General Phone: (562) 906-4569
General Fax: (562) 906-4515
Advertising Phone: (562) 587-7339
General/National Adv. E-mail: lily.park@biola.edu
Display Adv. E-mail: chimes.advertising@biola.edu
Primary Website: chimes.biola.edu
Published: Thur
Classified Equipment»
Personnel: Michael A. Longinow (Chair/Prof.); Sarah Sjoberg (Advertising Manager); J. Douglas Tarpley (Prof.); Michael Bower (Assoc. Prof.); Tamara Welter (Asst. Prof.); James Hirsen (Instr.); Chi-Chung Keung (Instr.); Mark Landsbaum (Instr.); Greg Schneider (Instr.); Melissa Nunnally (Instr.)

LA VERNE

UNIVERSITY OF LA VERNE

Street address 1: 1950 3rd St
Street address 3: La Verne
Street address state: CA
Zip/Postal code: 91750-4401
Country: USA
Mailing address: 1950 3rd St
Mailing city: La Verne
Mailing state: CA
Mailing zip: 91750-4401
General Phone: (909) 593-3511
General Fax: (909) 392-2706
Advertising Phone: 909-392-2712
General/National Adv. E-mail: ctimes@laverne.edu
Display Adv. E-mail: ctimesad@laverne.edu
Editorial e-mail: ctimes@laverne.edu
Primary Website: www.laverne.edu/campus-times
Year Established: 1919
Published: Fri
Avg Free Circ: 2000
Classified Equipment»
Personnel: Elizabeth Zwerling (Faculty Advisor); Jennifer Lemus Fernandez (Adv. Mgr.); Kevin Garrity (Ed. in Chief); Eric Borer (Layout Asst.)

ANTELOPE VALLEY COLLEGE

Street address 1: 3041 W Avenue K
Street address 3: Lancaster
Street address state: CA
Zip/Postal code: 93536-5402
Country: USA
Mailing address: 3041 W Avenue K
Mailing city: Lancaster
Mailing state: CA
Mailing zip: 93536-5426
General Phone: (661) 722-6496
General Fax: (661) 943-5573
Primary Website: www.avc.edu
Classified Equipment»
Personnel: Charles Hood (Advisor)

LOMA LINDA

LOMA LINDA UNIV.

Street address 1: 11041 Anderson St
Street address 3: Loma Linda
Street address state: CA
Zip/Postal code: 92350-1737
Country: USA
Mailing address: Anderson St Burden Hall 11041
Mailing city: Loma Linda
Mailing state: CA
Mailing zip: 92350-0001
General Phone: (909) 558-4526
General Fax: (909) 558-4181
Primary Website: www.llu.edu/news/today
Classified Equipment»

CALIFORNIA STATE UNIV. LONG BEACH

Street address 1: 1250 Bellflower Blvd
Street address 2: Sppa 010B
Street address 3: Long Beach
Street address state: CA
Zip/Postal code: 90840-0004
Country: USA
Mailing address: 1250 Bellflower Blvd
Mailing city: Long Beach
Mailing state: CA
Mailing zip: 90840-4601
General Phone: (562) 985-8001
General Fax: (562) 985-1740
Advertising Phone: (562)985-5736
Editorail Phone: (562)985-8000
Display Adv. E-mail: beverly.munson@csulb.edu
Editorial e-mail: eicd49er@gmail.com
Primary Website: www.daily49er.com
Year Established: 1949
Published: Mon`Tues`Wed`Thur
Avg Free Circ: 6000
Classified Equipment»
Personnel: Beverly Munson (Gen. Mgr.); Barbara Kingsley-Wilson (Advisor)

LONG BEACH CITY COLLEGE

Street address 1: 4901 E Carson St
Street address 2: Mail Drop Y-16
Street address 3: Long Beach
Street address state: CA
Zip/Postal code: 90808-1706
Country: USA
Mailing address: 4901 E Carson St Mail Drop Y-16
Mailing city: Long Beach
Mailing state: CA
Mailing zip: 90808-1780
General Phone: (562) 938-4284
General Fax: (562) 938-4948
General/National Adv. E-mail: vikingnews@lbcc.edu
Primary Website: www.lbccvikingnews.com
Year Established: 1927
Classified Equipment»
Personnel: Patrick McKean (Advisor); Kori Filipek (Adv. Mgr.); Michel Simmons (Co-Ed. in Chief)

LOS ALTOS HILLS

FOOTHILL COLLEGE

Street address 1: 12345 S El Monte Rd
Street address 3: Los Altos Hills
Street address state: CA
Zip/Postal code: 94022-4504
Country: USA
Mailing address: 12345 S El Monte Rd
Mailing city: Los Altos Hills
Mailing state: CA
Mailing zip: 94022-4597
General Phone: (650) 949-7372
General Fax: (650) 949-7375
Primary Website: www.foothillsentinel.org
Classified Equipment»
Personnel: Drew Dara Abrams (Ed.)

CALIFORNIA STATE UNIV.

Street address 1: 5151 State University Dr
Street address 2: # KH-C3098
Street address 3: Los Angeles
Street address state: CA
Zip/Postal code: 90032-4226
Country: USA
Mailing address: 5151 State University Dr # KH-C3098
Mailing city: Los Angeles
Mailing state: CA
Mailing zip: 90032-4226
General Phone: (323) 343-4215
General Fax: (323) 343-5337
Editorial Fax: Free
General/National Adv. E-mail: universitytimes@yahoo.com
Display Adv. E-mail: jmunson@cslanet.calstatela.edu
Editorial e-mail: universitytimes@yahoo.com
Primary Website: www.calstatela.edu
Year Established: 1947
News Services: AP, Uwire, United Features
Syndicated Publications: NA
Delivery Methods: Racks
Commercial printers: Y
Advertising (Open Inch Rate) Weekday/Saturday: BW & Color
Market Information: Available
Mechanical available: On request
Mechanical specifications: 11X16; RGB
Classified Equipment»
Personnel: Jim Munson (Business, Advt. Mgr.)
Parent company (for newspapers): California State University, Los Angeles

LOS ANGELES CITY COLLEGE

Street address 1: 855 N Vermont Ave
Street address 3: Los Angeles
Street address state: CA
Zip/Postal code: 90029-3516
Country: USA
Mailing address: 855 N Vermont Ave
Mailing city: Los Angeles
Mailing state: CA
Mailing zip: 90029-3588
General Phone: (323) 953-4000
Primary Website: wwwa.lacitycollege.edu
Classified Equipment»
Personnel: Rhonda Guess (Advisor)

LOYOLA MARYMOUNT UNIV.

Street address 1: 1 Lmu Dr
Street address 2: Ste 8470
Street address 3: Los Angeles
Street address state: CA
Zip/Postal code: 90045-2682
Country: USA
Mailing address: 1 Lmu Dr Ste 8470
Mailing city: Los Angeles
Mailing state: CA
Mailing zip: 90045-2682
General Phone: (310) 338-7509
General Fax: (310) 338-7887
General/National Adv. E-mail: loyolan@lmu.edu; editor@theloyolan.com
Primary Website: www.laloyolan.com
Classified Equipment»
Personnel: Tom Nelson (Advisor); Gil Searano (Ed.); Samantha Eisner (Adv. Sales Mgr.); Jose Martinez (Ed. in Chief); Heather Chong (Managing Ed.); Emily (Mng. Ed.); Laura (News Ed.)

OCCIDENTAL COLLEGE

Street address 1: 1600 Campus Rd
Street address 2: # M-40
Street address 3: Los Angeles
Street address state: CA
Zip/Postal code: 90041-3314
Country: USA
Mailing address: 1600 Campus Rd # M-40
Mailing city: Los Angeles
Mailing state: CA
Mailing zip: 90041-3314
General Phone: (323) 259-2886
General Fax: (323) 341-4982
General/National Adv. E-mail: weekly@oxy.edu
Primary Website: www.oxyweekly.com
Year Established: 1893
Classified Equipment»

Personnel: Riley Hooper (Ed. in Chief); Ben Dalgetty (Ed. in Chief); Ashly Burch (Mng. Ed.); Marty Cramer (Asst. Opinion Ed.); Elana (Bus. Mgr.); Tucker (Adv. Mgr.)

UNIV. OF CALIFORNIA GRAD. SCHOOL OF MGMT.

Street address 1: 110 Westwood Plz, Rm D216
Street address 3: Los Angeles
Street address state: CA
Zip/Postal code: 90095-0001
Country: USA
Mailing address: 110 Westwood Plz, Rm D216
Mailing city: Los Angeles
Mailing state: CA
Mailing zip: 90095-0001
General Phone: (310) 825-6488
General Fax: (310) 206-3981
General/National Adv. E-mail: exchange@anderson.ucla.edu
Primary Website: andersonexchange.collegepublisher.com
Classified Equipment»
Personnel: Steve Gilison (Ed. in Chief); Daniel Gelsi (Ed. in Chief); Julie Lacouture (Ed. in Chief)

UNIV. OF SOUTHERN CALIFORNIA

Street address 1: Student Union 404
Street address 3: Los Angeles
Street address state: CA
Zip/Postal code: 90089-0001
Country: USA
Mailing address: 404 Student Un
Mailing city: Los Angeles
Mailing state: CA
Mailing zip: 90089-0001
General Phone: (213) 740-2707
General Fax: (213) 740-5666
General/National Adv. E-mail: dtrojan@usc.edu
Editorial e-mail: editor@dailytorjan.com
Primary Website: www.dailytrojan.com
Classified Equipment»
Personnel: Mona Cravens (Dir., of Student Publication); Scott A. Smith (Assoc. Dir); David Khalaf (Adv. Mgr.); Sheri Brundage (Adv. Mgr.)

UNIVERSITY OF CALIFORNIA, LOS ANGELES

Street address 1: 308 Westwood Plz
Street address 3: Los Angeles
Street address state: CA
Zip/Postal code: 90095-8355
Country: USA
Mailing address: 308 Westwood Plaza
Mailing city: Los Angeles
Mailing state: CA
Mailing zip: 90095-8355
General Phone: (310) 825-9898
General Fax: (310) 206-0906
Advertising Phone: (310) 825-2221
Display Adv. E-mail: ads@media.ucla.edu
Editorial e-mail: editor@media.ucla.edu
Primary Website: www.dailybruin.com
Year Established: 1919
Delivery Methods: Newsstand
Published: Mon`Tues`Wed`Thur`Fri
Classified Equipment»
Personnel: Jeremy Wildman (Bus. Mgr.); Abigail Goldman (Media Advisor); Doria Deen (Student Media Dir); Mackenzie Possee (Editor in chief)

MALIBU

PEPPERDINE UNIV.

Street address 1: 24255 Pacific Coast Hwy
Street address 3: Malibu
Street address state: CA
Zip/Postal code: 90263-0001
Country: USA
Mailing address: 24255 Pacific Coast Hwy
Mailing city: Malibu
Mailing state: CA
Mailing zip: 90263-3999
General Phone: (310) 506-4318
General Fax: (310) 506-4411
Display Adv. E-mail: graphicadvertising@pepperdine.edu

Primary Website: www.pepperdine-graphic.com
Classified Equipment»
Personnel: Elizabeth Smith (Advisor); Amanda Gordon (Adv. Dir.); Ryan Hagen (Ed. in Chief)

MISSION VIEJO

SADDLEBACK COLLEGE

Street address 1: 28000 Marguerite Pkwy
Street address 3: Mission Viejo
Street address state: CA
Zip/Postal code: 92692-3635
Country: USA
General Phone: (626) 815-6000
Advertising Phone: (863) 604-9460
Editorail Phone: (863) 604-9460
Editorial Fax: (863) 604-9460
General/National Adv. E-mail: clause@apu.edu
Display Adv. E-mail: tim.posada@gmail.com
Editorial e-mail: tim.posada@gmail.com
Primary Website: www.lariatnews.com
Year Established: 1967
Published: Wed
Classified Equipment»
Personnel: Tim Posada (Advisor)

MODESTO

MODESTO JUNIOR COLLEGE

Street address 1: 435 College Ave
Street address 3: Modesto
Street address state: CA
Zip/Postal code: 95350-5808
Country: USA
Mailing address: 435 College Ave
Mailing city: Modesto
Mailing state: CA
Mailing zip: 95350-5800
General Phone: (209) 575-6223
General Fax: (209) 575-6612
Editorail Phone: (209) 575-6224
Primary Website: www.pirateslog.org
Classified Equipment»
Personnel: Laura Paull (Advisor)

MONTEREY PARK

EAST LOS ANGELES COLLEGE

Street address 1: 1301 Avenida Cesar Chavez
Street address 3: Monterey Park
Street address state: CA
Zip/Postal code: 91754-6001
Country: USA
Mailing address: 1301 Avenida Cesar Chavez
Mailing city: Monterey Park
Mailing state: CA
Mailing zip: 91754-6001
General Phone: (323) 265-8821
General Fax: (323) 415-4190
Advertising Phone: (323) 265-8821
Advertising Fax: (323) 425-4190
Editorail Phone: (323) 265-8819
Editorial Fax: (323) 425-4190
General/National Adv. E-mail: Elaccampusnews@gmail.com
Display Adv. E-mail: jonfanie@yahoo.com
Editorial e-mail: elaccampusnews@gmail.com
Primary Website: elaccampusnews.com
Year Established: 1945
Delivery Methods: Mail`Racks
Advertising (Open Inch Rate) Weekday/Saturday: call for rates
Published: Wed`Other
Published Other: Not published in summer or January. Weekly during school year.
Avg Free Circ: 4800
Classified Equipment»
Personnel: Jean Stapleton (Adviser); Sylvia Rico-Sanchez (Co-Adviser)

MOORPARK

MOORPARK COLLEGE

Street address 1: 7075 Campus Rd
Street address 3: Moorpark
Street address state: CA
Zip/Postal code: 93021-1605
Country: USA
Mailing address: 7075 Campus Rd.
Mailing city: Moorpark
Mailing state: CA
Mailing zip: 93021-1605
General Phone: (805) 378-1552
General Fax: (805) 378-1438
General/National Adv. E-mail: studentvoice@vcccd.edu
Primary Website: www.studentvoiceonline.com
Classified Equipment»
Personnel: Joanna Miller (Advisor)

MORAGA

SAINT MARY'S COLLEGE OF CALIFORNIA

Street address 1: 1928 Saint Marys Rd
Street address 3: Moraga
Street address state: CA
Zip/Postal code: 94556-2715
Country: USA
Mailing address: P.O. Box 4407
Mailing city: Moraga
Mailing state: CA
Mailing zip: 94575-4407
General Phone: (925) 631-4279
Advertising Phone: (925) 421-1515
Editorial Fax: Free
General/National Adv. E-mail: staff@stmaryscollegian.com
Display Adv. E-mail: collegianads@gmail.com
Primary Website: www.stmaryscollegian.com
Year Established: 1903
Advertising (Open Inch Rate) Weekday/Saturday: Yes
Published: Tues
Avg Paid Circ: 0
Avg Free Circ: 1000
Classified Equipment»
Personnel: Shawny Anderson (Advisor); Charlie Guese (Co-Editor-in-Chief); Sara DeSantis (Co-Editor-in-Chief); Michael Bruer (Ed. In Chief)

NORTHRIDGE

CALIFORNIA STATE UNIVERSITY, NORTHRIDGE

Street address 1: 18111 Nordhoff St
Street address 3: Northridge
Street address state: CA
Zip/Postal code: 91330-0001
Country: USA
Mailing address: 18111 Nordhoff St
Mailing city: Northridge
Mailing state: CA
Mailing zip: 91330-8200
General Phone: (818) 677-3135
General Fax: (818) 677-3438
Advertising Phone: 818-677-2998
Editorail Phone: (818) 677-2915
Display Adv. E-mail: ads@sundial.csun.edu
Editorial e-mail: editor@csun.edu
Primary Website: www.csun.edu
Year Established: 1957
Delivery Methods: Racks
Published: Mon`Tues`Wed`Thur
Avg Free Circ: 6000
Classified Equipment»
Personnel: Kent Kirkton (Chair/Prof.); Melissa Lalum (Pub.); Susan Henry (Prof.); Jody Holcomb (Gen. Mgr.); Maureen Rubin (Prof.); Rick Marks (Assoc. Prof.); Loren Townsley (Editor); Jose Luis Benavides (Asst. Prof.); David Blumenkrantz (Asst. Prof.); Linda Bowen (Asst. Prof.); Jim Hill (Asst. Prof.); Melissa Wall (Asst. Prof.); Lori Baker-Schena (Lectr.); Jerry Jacobs (Prof. Emer.); DeWayne Johnson (Prof. Emer.); Lawrence Schneider (Prof. Emer.); Joe Giampietro (Part-time Fac.); Henrietta Charles (Part-time Fac.); Jeffrey Duclos (Part-time Fac.); Barbara Eisenstock (Part-time Fac.); Mariel Garza (Part-time Fac.); Keith Goldstein (Part-time Fac.); Lincoln Harrison (Part-time Fac.)

CERRITOS COLLEGE

Street address 1: 11110 Alondra Blvd
Street address 3: Norwalk
Street address state: CA
Zip/Postal code: 90650-6203
Country: USA
Mailing address: 11110 Alondra Blvd
Mailing city: Norwalk
Mailing state: CA
Mailing zip: 90650-6298
General Phone: (562) 860-2451
General Fax: (562) 467-5044
General/National Adv. E-mail: editor@talonmarks.com
Primary Website: www.talonmarks.com
Classified Equipment»
Personnel: Rich Cameron (Advisor); Elieth Koulzons (Ed. in Chief); Rick Gomez (Online Ed.); Joey Berumen (News Ed.); Joey (News Ed.); Megan (Arts Ed.)

OAKLAND

LANEY COLLEGE

Street address 1: 900 Fallon St
Street address 3: Oakland
Street address state: CA
Zip/Postal code: 94607-4808
Country: USA
Mailing address: 900 Fallon St # 160
Mailing city: Oakland
Mailing state: CA
Mailing zip: 94607-4893
General Phone: (510) 464-3460
General Fax: (510) 834-3452
General/National Adv. E-mail: laneytower@peralta.edu
Primary Website: www.laneytower.com
Published: Thur
Published Other: Every other week
Classified Equipment»
Personnel: Burt Dragin (Advisor); Scott Strain (Sports Ed.); Felix Solomon (Technical Ed.)

MILLS COLLEGE

Street address 1: 157 Rothwell Ctr, 5000 MacArthur Blvd
Street address 3: Oakland
Street address state: CA
Zip/Postal code: 94613
Country: USA
Mailing address: 157 Rothwell Ctr., 5000 MacArthur Blvd.
Mailing city: Oakland
Mailing state: CA
Mailing zip: 94613
General Phone: (510) 430-2246
General Fax: (510) 430-3176
General/National Adv. E-mail: eic@thecampanil.com
Display Adv. E-mail: ads@thecampanil.com
Primary Website: www.thecampanil.com
Classified Equipment»
Personnel: Sarah Pollock (Advisor); Jennifer Courtney (Ed. in Chief); Rashida Harmon (Mng. Ed.); Morgan Ross (News Ed.); Nicole (Opinion Ed.); Anna Belle (Features Ed.)

OCEANSIDE

MIRACOSTA COLLEGE

Street address 1: 1 Barnard Dr
Street address 2: Rm 3441
Street address 3: Oceanside
Street address state: CA
Zip/Postal code: 92056-3820
Country: USA
Mailing address: 1 Barnard Dr Rm 3441
Mailing city: Oceanside
Mailing state: CA
Mailing zip: 92056-3820
General Phone: (760) 757-2121
General Fax: (760) 757-8209
General/National Adv. E-mail: www.mccechariot.com
Classified Equipment»
Personnel: Meghan Sills (Staff Writer)

CHAPMAN UNIV.

Street address 1: 1 University Dr
Street address 3: Orange
Street address state: CA
Zip/Postal code: 92866-1005
Country: USA
Mailing address: 1 University Dr
Mailing city: Orange
Mailing state: CA
Mailing zip: 92866-1005
General Phone: (714) 997-6870
General Fax: (714) 744-7898
General/National Adv. E-mail: panthernewspaper@gmail.com
Primary Website: www.thepantheronline.com; www.chapman.edu/panthernewspaper
Classified Equipment»
Personnel: Amber Gonzales (Ed. in Chief); Martin Syjuco (Mng. Ed.); Michelle Thomas (Opinions Ed.); Jillian Freitas (News Ed.); Jennifer (Business Mgr.); Kim (Dir., Art)

OXNARD

OXNARD COLLEGE

Street address 1: 4000 S Rose Ave
Street address 3: Oxnard
Street address state: CA
Zip/Postal code: 93033-6699
Country: USA
Mailing address: 4000 S Rose Ave
Mailing city: Oxnard
Mailing state: CA
Mailing zip: 93033-6699
General Phone: (805) 986-5836
General Fax: (805) 986-5806
Classified Equipment»

PALM DESERT

COLLEGE OF THE DESERT

Street address 1: 43500 Monterey Ave
Street address 3: Palm Desert
Street address state: CA
Zip/Postal code: 92260-9305
Country: USA
Mailing address: 43500 Monterey Ave
Mailing city: Palm Desert
Mailing state: CA
Mailing zip: 92260-9399
General Phone: (760) 776-7244
General Fax: (760) 862-1338
General/National Adv. E-mail: chaparral@collegeofthedesert.edu
Primary Website: www.thechaparral.com
Classified Equipment»
Personnel: Aaron White (Adv. Mgr.); Edward Grofer (Co-Ed.); Sarah Wilson (Co-Ed.)

PASADENA

CALIFORNIA INST. OF TECHNOLOGY

Street address 1: Caltech Msc 40-58
Street address 3: Pasadena
Street address state: CA
Country: USA
Mailing address: Caltech MSC 40-58
Mailing city: Pasadena
Mailing state: CA
Mailing zip: mpearson@calbaptist.edu
General Phone: (626) 395-6154
Advertising Phone: (626) 577-1294
General/National Adv. E-mail: business@caltech.edu
Primary Website: tech.caltech.edu
Classified Equipment»
Personnel: Vi Tran (Bus. Mgr.)

FULLER THEOLOGICAL SEMINARY

Street address 1: 135 N Oakland Ave
Street address 3: Pasadena
Street address state: CA

Zip/Postal code: 91182-0001
Country: USA
Mailing address: 135 N Oakland Ave
Mailing city: Pasadena
Mailing state: CA
Mailing zip: 91182-0002
General Phone: (626) 584-5430
General Fax: (626) 304-3730
Classified Equipment»
Personnel: Carmen Valdez (Advisor); Eugene Suen (Adv. Mgr.); Ben Cassil (Ed.)

PASADENA CITY COLLEGE

Street address 1: 1570 E Colorado Blvd
Street address 2: Rm T110-A
Street address 3: Pasadena
Street address state: CA
Zip/Postal code: 91106-2003
Country: USA
Mailing address: 1570 E Colorado Blvd Rm T110-A
Mailing city: Pasadena
Mailing state: CA
Mailing zip: 91106-2041
General Phone: (626) 585-7130
General Fax: (626) 585-7971
Advertising Phone: (626) 585-7979
General/National Adv. E-mail: pasadenacourier@yahoo.com
Display Adv. E-mail: courierads@yahoo.com
Primary Website: www.pcccourier.com
Classified Equipment»
Personnel: Warren Swil (Advisor); John Avery (Adv. Mgr.); Barbara Beaser (Ed. in Chief)

PITTSBURG

LOS MEDANOS COLLEGE

Street address 1: 2700 E Leland Rd
Street address 3: Pittsburg
Street address state: CA
Zip/Postal code: 94565-5107
Country: USA
Mailing address: 2700 E Leland Rd
Mailing city: Pittsburg
Mailing state: CA
Mailing zip: 94565-5197
General Phone: (925) 439-2181
General Fax: (925) 427-1599
Primary Website: www.losmedanos.edu
Year Established: 1974
Classified Equipment»
Personnel: Cindy McGrath (Advisor)

PLEASANT HILL

DIABLO VALLEY COLLEGE

Street address 1: 321 Golf Club Rd
Street address 3: Pleasant Hill
Street address state: CA
Zip/Postal code: 94523-1529
Country: USA
Mailing address: 321 Golf Club Rd
Mailing city: Pleasant Hill
Mailing state: CA
Mailing zip: 94523-1544
General Phone: (925) 685-1230
General Fax: (925) 681-3045
General/National Adv. E-mail: inquirer@dvc.edu
Primary Website: www.dvc.edu/journalism
Classified Equipment»
Personnel: Ann Stenmark (Adv. Mgr.); Ashley Pittson (Ed.); Catharine Ahr (Ed.); Barbara (Ed.)

JOHN F. KENNEDY UNIVERSITY

Street address 1: 100 Ellinwood Way
Street address 3: Pleasant Hill
Street address state: CA
Zip/Postal code: 94523-4817
Country: USA
Mailing address: 100 Ellinwood Way
Mailing city: Pleasant Hill
Mailing state: CA
Mailing zip: 94523-4817
General Phone: 925.969.3584
General Fax: 925.969.3136
Primary Website: www.jfku.edu
Classified Equipment»

POMONA

THE POLY POST

Street address 1: 3801 W Temple Ave
Street address 2: Bldg 1
Street address 3: Pomona
Street address state: CA
Zip/Postal code: 91768-2557
Country: USA
Mailing address: 3801 W Temple Ave Bldg 1
Mailing city: Pomona
Mailing state: CA
Mailing zip: 91768-2557
General Phone: (909) 869-5483
General Fax: (909) 869-3533
Advertising Phone: (909) 869-5179
Advertising Fax: (909) 869-3863
Editorail Phone: (909) 869-3528
Editorial Fax: (909) 869-3530
General/National Adv. E-mail: advisor@thepolypost.com
Display Adv. E-mail: advertise@thepolypost.com
Primary Website: www.thepolypost.com
Delivery Methods: Racks
Commercial printers: Y
Classified Equipment»
Personnel: Doug Spoon (Advisor); Amanda Newfield (Ed. in Chief); Aaron Castrejon (Mng. Ed.); Linda Perez (Mktg. Dir.)

RANCHO CUCAMONGA

CHAFFEY COLLEGE

Street address 1: 5885 Haven Ave
Street address 3: Rancho Cucamonga
Street address state: CA
Zip/Postal code: 91737-3002
Country: USA
Mailing address: 5885 Haven Ave.
Mailing city: Rancho Cucamonga
Mailing state: CA
Mailing zip: 91737
General Phone: (909) 652-6934
General/National Adv. E-mail: thebreeze@chaffey.edu
Display Adv. E-mail: michelle.dowd@chaffey.edu
Primary Website: www.thebreezeonline.com
Published: Mon`Bi-Mthly
Avg Free Circ: 3000
Classified Equipment»
Personnel: Michelle Dowd (Adviser)

REDDING

SHASTA COLLEGE

Street address 1: 11555 Old Oregon Trl
Street address 3: Redding
Street address state: CA
Zip/Postal code: 96003-7692
Country: USA
Mailing address: PO Box 496006
Mailing city: Redding
Mailing state: CA
Mailing zip: 96049-6006
General Phone: (530) 242-7729
General Fax: (530) 225-3925
General/National Adv. E-mail: editorial@sclance.com
Primary Website: www.sclance.com
Classified Equipment»
Personnel: Craig Harrington (Advisor)

REDLANDS

UNIV. OF REDLANDS

Street address 1: 1200 E Colton Ave
Street address 3: Redlands
Street address state: CA
Zip/Postal code: 92374-3755
Country: USA
Mailing address: PO Box 3080
Mailing city: Redlands
Mailing state: CA
Mailing zip: 92373-0999
General Phone: (909) 748-8880
Classified Equipment»
Personnel: Jessie Stapleton (Advisor)

CALIFORNIA BAPTIST COLLEGE

Street address 1: 8432 Magnolia Ave
Street address 3: Riverside
Street address state: CA
Zip/Postal code: 92504-3206
Country: USA
Mailing address: 8432 Magnolia Ave
Mailing city: Riverside
Mailing state: CA
Mailing zip: 92504-3297
General Phone: (951) 343-4401
General Fax: (951) 351-1808
General/National Adv. E-mail: banner@calbaptist.edu
Classified Equipment»
Personnel: Mary Ann Pearson (Advisor); Amanda Tredinnick (Adv. Mgr.); Kendall Dewitt (Ed.)

RIVERSIDE CMTY. COLLEGE

Street address 1: 4800 Magnolia Ave
Street address 3: Riverside
Street address state: CA
Zip/Postal code: 92506-1201
Country: USA
Mailing address: 4800 Magnolia Ave
Mailing city: Riverside
Mailing state: CA
Mailing zip: 92506-1201
General Phone: (951) 222-8488
General Fax: (951) 328-3505
General/National Adv. E-mail: viewpoints@rcc.edu
Primary Website: www.viewpointsonline.org
Classified Equipment»
Personnel: Allan Lovelace (Advisor); Stephanie Holland (Ed. in Chief); Chanelle Williams (Mng. Ed.); Vanessa Soto (Adv. Mgr.); Lauren (Photo Ed.)

UNIV. OF CALIFORNIA, RIVERSIDE

Street address 1: 101 Highlander Union Bldg
Street address 3: Riverside
Street address state: CA
Zip/Postal code: 92507
Country: USA
Mailing address: 101 Highlander Union Bldg.
Mailing city: Riverside
Mailing state: CA
Mailing zip: 92521-0001
General Phone: (951) 827-3617
General Fax: (951) 827-7049
Advertising Phone: (951) 827-3457
Advertising Fax: (951) 827-7049
Editorail Phone: (951) 827-2105
General/National Adv. E-mail: editorinchief@highlandernews.org
Display Adv. E-mail: highlanderads@ucr.edu
Editorial e-mail: editorinchief@highlandernews.org
Primary Website: www.highlandernews.org
Year Established: 1956
Delivery Methods: Newsstand
Published: Tues
Avg Free Circ: 4000
Classified Equipment»
Personnel: Chris LoCascio (EIC); Kevin Keckeisen (Mgr Ed); Sandy Van (News Ed); Erin Mahoney (Advisor); Emily Wells (A&E Ed.); Kendall Petersen (Sports Ed.); Brian Tuttle (Photo Ed.); Myles Andrews-Duve (EIC); Andreas Rauch (EIC)

ROCKLIN

SIERRA COLLEGE

Street address 1: 5000 Rocklin Rd
Street address 3: Rocklin
Street address state: CA
Zip/Postal code: 95677-3337
Country: USA
Mailing address: 5000 Rocklin Rd
Mailing city: Rocklin
Mailing state: CA
Mailing zip: 95677-3397
General Phone: (916) 789-2699
General Fax: (916) 789-2854
Classified Equipment»
Personnel: Kelly Kukis (Ed.)

SONOMA STATE UNIVERSITY

Street address 1: 1801 E Cotati Ave
Street address 2: Salazar Hall 1053
Street address 3: Rohnert Park
Street address state: CA
Zip/Postal code: 94928-3613
Country: USA
Mailing address: 1801 E Cotati Ave Salazar Hall 1053
Mailing city: Rohnert Park
Mailing state: CA
Mailing zip: 94928-3613
General Phone: (707) 664-2776
General Fax: (707) 664-4262
General/National Adv. E-mail: star@sonoma.edu
Display Adv. E-mail: sonomastatestar@gmail.com
Editorial e-mail: star@sonoma.edu
Primary Website: www.sonomastatestar.com
Year Established: 1979
Published: Tues
Avg Free Circ: 2000
Classified Equipment»
Personnel: Dylan Sirdofsky (Editor-in-Chief); Amanda Saiki (Advertising Manager); Paul Gullixson (Faculty Advisor); Corinne Asturus

AMERICAN RIVER COLLEGE

Street address 1: 4700 College Oak Dr
Street address 3: Sacramento
Street address state: CA
Zip/Postal code: 95841-4217
Country: USA
Mailing address: 4700 College Oak Dr
Mailing city: Sacramento
Mailing state: CA
Mailing zip: 95841-4286
General Phone: (916) 484-8653
General Fax: (916) 484-8668
General/National Adv. E-mail: current@arc.losrios.edu
Primary Website: www.americanrivercurrent.com
Classified Equipment»
Personnel: Jill Wagner (Advisor); Carol Hartman (Advisor); Andrew Clementi (Ed.)

COSUMNES RIVER COLLEGE

Street address 1: 8401 Center Pkwy
Street address 3: Sacramento
Street address state: CA
Zip/Postal code: 95823-5704
Country: USA
Mailing address: 8401 Center Pkwy
Mailing city: Sacramento
Mailing state: CA
Mailing zip: 95823-5799
General Phone: (916) 691-7471
General Fax: (916) 688-7181
Primary Website: www.crcconnection.com
Classified Equipment»
Personnel: Yvette Lessard (Ed. in Chief); Erin Bates (Features Ed.); Bhavisha Patel (Online Ed.); Lehsee Gausi (Opinion Ed.)

SACRAMENTO CITY COLLEGE

Street address 1: 3835 Freeport Blvd
Street address 3: Sacramento
Street address state: CA
Zip/Postal code: 95822-1318
Country: USA
Mailing address: 3835 Freeport Blvd
Mailing city: Sacramento
Mailing state: CA
Mailing zip: 95822-1386
General Phone: (916) 558-2562
General Fax: (916) 558-2282
General/National Adv. E-mail: express@scc.losrios.edu
Primary Website: www.scc.losrios.edu/express
Classified Equipment»
Personnel: Dianne Heimer (Advisor); Hannah Ucol (Adv. Mgr.); Cecilio Padilla (Ed.)

SACRAMENTO STATE

Street address 1: 6000 J St
Street address 3: Sacramento
Street address state: CA
Zip/Postal code: 95819-2605
Country: USA

Mailing address: 6000 J Street
Mailing city: Sacramento
Mailing state: CA
Mailing zip: 95819
General Phone: 9162786584
Advertising Phone: 9162784092
General/National Adv. E-mail: editor@statehornet.com
Display Adv. E-mail: ads@statehornet.com
Editorial e-mail: editor@statehornet.com
Primary Website: 6000 J Street
Year Established: 1949
Published: Wed
Classified Equipment»
Personnel: Stu VanAirsdale (Faculty Adviser)

SAN BERNARDINO

CALIFORNIA STATE UNIV.

Street address 1: 5500 University Pkwy
Street address 3: San Bernardino
Street address state: CA
Zip/Postal code: 92407-2318
Country: USA
Mailing address: 5500 University Pkwy
Mailing city: San Bernardino
Mailing state: CA
Mailing zip: 92407-2318
General Phone: (909) 537-5289
General Fax: (909)-537-7072
Editorail Phone: (909) 537-5815
General/National Adv. E-mail: sbchron@csusb.edu
Primary Website: www.coyotechronicle.com
Classified Equipment»
Personnel: Jim Smart (Advisor); Linda Sand (Adv. Mgr.); Ken Dillard (Ed. in Chief)

SAN BERNARDINO VALLEY COLLEGE

Street address 1: 701 S Mount Vernon Ave
Street address 3: San Bernardino
Street address state: CA
Zip/Postal code: 92410-2705
Country: USA
Mailing address: 701 S Mount Vernon Ave
Mailing city: San Bernardino
Mailing state: CA
Mailing zip: 92410-2798
General Phone: (909) 888-1996
General Fax: (909) 381-4604
Primary Website: www.sbvcarrowhead.com
Classified Equipment»
Personnel: Gary Kellam (Ed.)

POINT LOMA NAZARENE UNIV.

Street address 1: 3900 Lomaland Dr
Street address 3: San Diego
Street address state: CA
Zip/Postal code: 92106-2810
Country: USA
Mailing address: 3900 Lomaland Dr
Mailing city: San Diego
Mailing state: CA
Mailing zip: 92106-2899
General Phone: (619) 849-2444
General Fax: (619) 849-7009
General/National Adv. E-mail: news@pointweekly.com; sports@pointweekly.com; advertising@pointweekly.com
Primary Website: www.pointweekly.com
Classified Equipment»
Personnel: Stephanie Gant (Adv. Mgr.); Dean Nelson (Journalism Dir.); Coco Jones (Ed. in Chief); Nathan Scharn (Features Ed.)

SAN DIEGO CITY COLLEGE

Street address 1: 1313 Park Blvd
Street address 2: Rm T-316
Street address 3: San Diego
Street address state: CA
Zip/Postal code: 92101-4712
Country: USA
Mailing address: 1313 Park Blvd Rm T-316
Mailing city: San Diego
Mailing state: CA
Mailing zip: 92101-4787
General Phone: (619) 388-4026
General Fax: (619) 388-3814
General/National Adv. E-mail: citytimes@gmail.com
Display Adv. E-mail: ads.citytimes@gmail.com
Primary Website: www.sdcitytimes.com
Classified Equipment»
Personnel: Roman Koenig (Advisor); Vanessa Gomez (Ed. in Chief)

SAN DIEGO MIRAMAR COLLEGE

Street address 1: 10440 Black Mountain Rd
Street address 3: San Diego
Street address state: CA
Zip/Postal code: 92126-2910
Country: USA
Mailing address: 10440 Black Mountain Rd
Mailing city: San Diego
Mailing state: CA
Mailing zip: 92126-2999
General Phone: (619) 388-7800
General Fax: (619)-388-7900
Primary Website: www.sdmiramar.edu
Classified Equipment»
Personnel: Leslie Klipper (Advisor); Sandy Treivasan (Advertisments)

SAN DIEGO STATE UNIV.

Street address 1: EBA-2
Street address 3: San Diego
Street address state: CA
Zip/Postal code: 92182-0001
Country: USA
Mailing address: EBA-2
Mailing city: San Diego
Mailing state: CA
Mailing zip: 92182-0001
General Phone: (619) 594-1804
General Fax: (619) 594-1804
Advertising Phone: (619) 594-6977
General/National Adv. E-mail: daads@mail.sdsu.edu
Primary Website: 2259 Birds Nest
Year Established: 1913
Published: Wed
Avg Free Circ: 5000
Classified Equipment»
Personnel: Andrew Dyer

THE MESA PRESS

Street address 1: 7250 Mesa College Dr
Street address 2: Room G-202
Street address 3: San Diego
Street address state: CA
Zip/Postal code: 92111-4902
County: San Diego
Country: USA
Mailing address: 7250 Mesa College Dr
Mailing city: San Diego
Mailing state: CA
Mailing zip: 92111-4999
General Phone: (619) 388-2630
General Fax: (619) 388-2836
General/National Adv. E-mail: mesa.press@gmail.com
Primary Website: www.mesapress.com
Year Established: 1966
Area Served - City: San Diego Mesa College
Published: Mthly
Classified Equipment»
Personnel: Janna Braun (Advisor)
Parent company (for newspapers): San Diego Mesa College

UNIV. OF SAN DIEGO

Street address 1: 5998 Alcala Park
Street address 3: San Diego
Street address state: CA
Zip/Postal code: 92110-8001
Country: USA
Mailing address: 5998 Alcala Park Frnt
Mailing city: San Diego
Mailing state: CA
Mailing zip: 92110-2492
General Phone: (619) 260-4714
General Fax: (619) 260-4807
Editorail Phone: (619) 260-4584
Primary Website: www.uofsdmedia.com
Published: Thur
Classified Equipment»
Personnel: Brooklyn Dippo (EIC); Sarah Brewington (Associate Ed); Diego Luna (Mgr Ed)

UNIV. OF SAN DIEGO SCHOOL OF LAW

Street address 1: 5998 Alcala Park
Street address 3: San Diego
Street address state: CA
Zip/Postal code: 92110-8001
Country: USA
Mailing address: 5998 Alcala Park
Mailing city: San Diego
Mailing state: CA
Mailing zip: 92110-8001
General Phone: (619) 260-4600
General Fax: (619) 260-4753
General/National Adv. E-mail: motions@sandiego.edu
Primary Website: www.sandiego.edu/motions
Classified Equipment»
Personnel: Damien Schiff (Ed.)

CITY COLLEGE OF SAN FRANCISCO

Street address 1: 50 Phelan Ave
Street address 2: # V67
Street address 3: San Francisco
Street address state: CA
Zip/Postal code: 94112-1821
Country: USA
Mailing address: 50 Phelan Ave # V67
Mailing city: San Francisco
Mailing state: CA
Mailing zip: 94112-1898
General Phone: (415) 239-3446
General Fax: (415) 239-3884
General/National Adv. E-mail: email@theguardsman.com
Display Adv. E-mail: advertising@theguardsman.com
Editorial e-mail: editor@theguardsman.com
Primary Website: www.theguardsman.com
Year Established: 1935
Delivery Methods: Racks
Commercial printers: N
Published: Wed
Published Other: Bi-Weekly
Avg Free Circ: 7000
Classified Equipment»
Note: Also available on Pulse and Issuu.com/theguardsman.com
Personnel: Juan Gonzales (Advisor)

GOLDEN GATE UNIV.

Street address 1: 536 Mission St
Street address 3: San Francisco
Street address state: CA
Zip/Postal code: 94105-2921
Country: USA
Mailing address: 536 Mission St
Mailing city: San Francisco
Mailing state: CA
Mailing zip: 94105-2968
General Phone: (415) 442-7871
General Fax: (415) 442-7896
General/National Adv. E-mail: campuscurrent@gguol.ggu.edu
Primary Website: www.ggu.edu
Classified Equipment»
Personnel: Brian Louie (Vice Pres., PR/Mktg.); Ambrose Tse (Vice Pres., Finance/Admin.)

HASTINGS COLLEGE OF LAW

Street address 1: 200 McAllister St
Street address 3: San Francisco
Street address state: CA
Zip/Postal code: 94102-4707
Country: USA
Mailing address: 200 McAllister St
Mailing city: San Francisco
Mailing state: CA
Mailing zip: 94102-4978
General Phone: (415) 565-4786
General Fax: (707) 313-0161
Classified Equipment»
Personnel: John Hendrickson (Ed.)

SAN FRANCISCO STATE UNIVERSITY

Street address 1: 1600 Holloway Ave
Street address 3: San Francisco
Street address state: CA
Zip/Postal code: 94132-1722
Country: USA
Mailing address: 1600 Holloway Ave # 4200
Mailing city: San Francisco
Mailing state: CA
Mailing zip: 94132-1740
General Phone: (415) 338-1689
General Fax: (415) 338-2084
General/National Adv. E-mail: jour@sfsu.edu
Primary Website: www.journalism.sfsu.edu
Year Established: 1934
Classified Equipment»
Personnel: Venise Wagner (Dept. Chair/Assoc. Prof.); Jon Funabiki (Assoc. Dept. Chair/Prof.); Dottie Katzeff (Adv. Mgr.); John Burks (Prof.); Barbara Landes (Prodn. Mgr.); Nathan Codd (Ed. in Chief); Yvonne Daley (Prof.); Kenneth Kobre (Prof.); Erna R. Smith (Prof.); Rachele Kanigel (Assoc. Prof.); Austin Long-Scott (Assoc. Prof.); Cristina Azocar (Asst. Prof./Dir., Ctr. for Integration/Improvement of Journalism); Yumi Wilson (Asst. Prof.); John T. Johnson (Prof. Emer.); B.H. Liebes (Prof. Emer.); Betty Medsger (Prof. Emer.); Leonard Sellers (Prof. Emer.); Jerrold Werthimer (Prof. Emer.); Harriet Chiang (Lectr.); Roland DeWolk (Lectr.); Jesse Garnier (Lectr.); David Greene (Lectr.); Sibylla Herbrich (Lectr.)

UNIV. OF SAN FRANCISCO

Street address 1: 2130 Fulton St
Street address 3: San Francisco
Street address state: CA
Zip/Postal code: 94117-1080
Country: USA
Mailing address: 2130 Fulton St
Mailing city: San Francisco
Mailing state: CA
Mailing zip: 94117-1050
General Fax: (415) 422-2751
General/National Adv. E-mail: foghorn_ads@yahoo.com
Display Adv. E-mail: advertising@sffoghorn.info
Primary Website: foghorn.usfca.edu/
Classified Equipment»
Personnel: Theresa Moore (Advisor); Laura Plantholt (Ed. in Chief); Nicholas Muhkar (Mng. Ed.); Chelsea Sterling (News Ed.); Matt (Sports Ed.); Mark (Adv. Mgr.); Erika (Bus. Mgr.)

UNIV. OF SAN FRANCISCO LAW SCHOOL

Street address 1: 2130 Fulton St
Street address 3: San Francisco
Street address state: CA
Zip/Postal code: 94117-1080
Country: USA
Mailing address: 2130 Fulton St
Mailing city: San Francisco
Mailing state: CA
Mailing zip: 94117-1050
General Phone: (415) 422-6586
General Fax: (415) 666-6433
General/National Adv. E-mail: theforumusf@gmail.com
Classified Equipment»
Personnel: Andie Vallee (Ed.)

UNIVERSITY OF CALIFORNIA, SAN FRANCISCO

Street address 1: 500 Parnassus Ave
Street address 2: # 108W
Street address 3: San Francisco
Street address state: CA
Zip/Postal code: 94143-2203
Country: USA
Mailing address: 108 W Millberry Un
Mailing city: San Francisco
Mailing state: CA
Mailing zip: 94143-0001
General Phone: (415) 476-2211
General Fax: (415) 502-4537
General/National Adv. E-mail: synapse@ucsf.edu
Display Adv. E-mail: synapse@ucsf.edu
Primary Website: synapse.ucsf.edu
Published: Thur
Classified Equipment»

Personnel: Steven Chin (Managing Editor)

EVERGREEN VALLEY COLLEGE

Street address 1: 3095 Yerba Buena Rd
Street address 3: San Jose
Street address state: CA
Zip/Postal code: 95135-1513
Country: USA
Mailing address: 3095 Yerba Buena Rd
Mailing city: San Jose
Mailing state: CA
Mailing zip: 95135-1598
General Phone: (408) 274-7900
Classified Equipment»

SAN JOSE CITY COLLEGE

Street address 1: 2100 Moorpark Ave
Street address 3: San Jose
Street address state: CA
Zip/Postal code: 95128-2723
Country: USA
Mailing address: 2100 Moorpark Ave
Mailing city: San Jose
Mailing state: CA
Mailing zip: 95128-2799
General Phone: (408) 298-2181
General Fax: (408) 288-6331
General/National Adv. E-mail: thesjcctimes@hotmail.com
Primary Website: www.sjcc.edu
Classified Equipment»

SAN JOSE STATE UNIV.

Street address 1: 1 Washington Sq
Street address 3: San Jose
Street address state: CA
Zip/Postal code: 95112-3613
Country: USA
Mailing address: 1 Washington Sq
Mailing city: San Jose
Mailing state: CA
Mailing zip: 95112-3613
General Phone: (408) 924-3281
General Fax: (408) 924-3282
Advertising Phone: (408) 924-3270
General/National Adv. E-mail: spartandaily@casa.sjsu.edu
Display Adv. E-mail: spartandailyads@casa.sjsu.edu
Primary Website: www.thespartandaily.com
Classified Equipment»
Personnel: Richard Craig (Advisor); Timothy Hendrick (Advisor); Jenny Ngo (Adv. Dir.); Joey Akeley (Exec. Ed.)

SAN LUIS OBISPO

CALIFORNIA POLYTECHNIC STATE UNIV.

Street address 1: 1 Grand Ave
Street address 3: San Luis Obispo
Street address state: CA
Zip/Postal code: 93407-9000
Country: USA
Mailing address: 1 Grand Ave
Mailing city: San Luis Obispo
Mailing state: CA
Mailing zip: 93407-9000
General Phone: (805) 756-2537
General Fax: (805) 756-6784
Advertising Phone: (805) 756-1143
Advertising Fax: (805) 756-6784
Editorail Phone: (805) 756-1796
Editorial Fax: (805) 756-6784
General/National Adv. E-mail: editor@mustangnews.net
Display Adv. E-mail: advertising@mustangnews.net
Primary Website: www.mustangnews.net
Year Established: 1916
Special Editions: Freshman Week of Welcome Back to School Fall Graduation Best for Cal Poly Housing Fair Open House Spring Graduation Summer Orientation, Advising and Registration (SOAR)
Delivery Methods: Newsstand`Racks
Commercial printers: N
Advertising (Open inch Rate) Weekday/Saturday: 10 pci
Published: Mon`Thur
Avg Free Circ: 6000
Classified Equipment»
Personnel: Paul Bittick (GM)

CUESTA COLLEGE

Street address 1: Bldg 7400, Hwy 1
Street address 3: San Luis Obispo
Street address state: CA
Zip/Postal code: 93403
Country: USA
Mailing address: PO Box 8106
Mailing city: San Luis Obispo
Mailing state: CA
Mailing zip: 93403-8106
General Phone: (805) 546-3288
General Fax: (805) 546-3904
General/National Adv. E-mail: cuestonian@cuesta.edu
Primary Website: www.cuestonian.cuesta.edu; www.cuesta.edu
Classified Equipment»
Personnel: Patrick Howe (Advisor); Mary Mc Corkle (Advisor); Sarah Clifford (Ed.); Bethany Fraker (Ed.)

SAN MARCOS

CALIFORNIA STATE UNIVERSITY, SAN MARCOS

Street address 1: 333 S Twin Oaks Valley Rd
Street address 3: San Marcos
Street address state: CA
Zip/Postal code: 92096-0001
Country: USA
Mailing address: 333 S Twin Oaks Valley Rd
Mailing city: San Marcos
Mailing state: CA
Mailing zip: 92096-0001
General Phone: (760) 750-6099
General Fax: (760) 750-3345
Advertising Phone: (760) 750-6099
Advertising Fax: (760) 750-3345
Editorail Phone: (760) 750-6099
Editorial Fax: Free
General/National Adv. E-mail: csusm.chronicle@gmail.com
Editorial e-mail: csusm.chronicle@gmail.com
Primary Website: www.csusmchronicle.com
Year Established: 1992
Delivery Methods: Newsstand
Published: Wed
Avg Paid Circ: 0
Avg Free Circ: 1500
Classified Equipment»
Personnel: Pam Kragen (Advisor); Morgan Hall (Co-Editor-in-Chief, Editor of Design); Kristin Melody (Co-Editor-in-Chief); Rogers Jaffarian (Advertising Manager)

PALOMAR COLLEGE

Street address 1: 1140 W Mission Rd
Street address 2: Rm CH-7
Street address 3: San Marcos
Street address state: CA
Zip/Postal code: 92069-1415
Country: USA
Mailing address: 1140 W Mission Rd Rm CH-7
Mailing city: San Marcos
Mailing state: CA
Mailing zip: 92069-1487
General Phone: (760) 744-1150
General Fax: (760) 744-8123
General/National Adv. E-mail: telescopead@palomar.edu
Primary Website: www.the-telescope.com
Year Established: 1946
Classified Equipment»
Personnel: Erin Hiro (Advisor); Sara Burbidge (Adv. Mgr.); Kelley Foyt (Co-Ed. in Chief)

SAN MATEO

COLLEGE OF SAN MATEO

Street address 1: 94402 -3757
Street address 3: San Mateo
Street address state: CA
Country: USA
Mailing address: 1700 W Hillsdale Blvd
Mailing city: San Mateo
Mailing state: CA
Mailing zip: 94402-3784
General Phone: (650) 574-6330
Editorail Phone: (650) 652-6721
General/National Adv. E-mail: sanmatean@smccd.edu
Primary Website: www.sanmatean.com
Year Established: 1928
Classified Equipment»
Personnel: Ed Remitz (Advisor); Margeret Baum (Ed.); Sharon Ho (Mng. Ed.); Laura Babbitt (News Ed.)

SAN PABLO

CONTRA COSTA COLLEGE

Street address 1: 2600 Mission Bell Dr
Street address 3: San Pablo
Street address state: CA
Zip/Postal code: 94806-3166
Country: USA
Mailing address: 2600 Mission Bell Dr
Mailing city: San Pablo
Mailing state: CA
Mailing zip: 94806-3195
General Phone: (510) 235-7800
General Fax: (510) 235-6397
General/National Adv. E-mail: advocate@contracosta.edu
Primary Website: www.contracosta.edu; www.accentadvocate.com
Classified Equipment»
Personnel: Paul DeBlot (Advisor); Holly Pablo (Ed. in Chief); Sam Attal (Ed.)

SAN PEDRO

LOS ANGELES HARBOR COLLEGE

Street address 1: 1300 S Pacific Ave
Street address 3: San Pedro
Street address state: CA
Zip/Postal code: 90731-4108
Country: USA
Mailing address: PO Box 731
Mailing city: San Pedro
Mailing state: CA
Mailing zip: 90733-0731
General Phone: (310) 519-1016
General Fax: (310) 832-1000
Advertising Fax: 1310 832-1000
Editorail Phone: (310) 519-1442
Display Adv. E-mail: rlnsales@randomlengthsnews.com
Editorial e-mail: editor@randomlengthsnews.com
Primary Website: www.randomlengthsnews.com
Year Established: 1979
Published: Thur`Bi-Mthly
Classified Equipment»
Personnel: James Preston Allen (Pub.); Paul Rosenberg (Mng. Ed.); Terelle Jerricks (Mng Ed)

SAN RAFAEL

DOMINICAN COLLEGE

Street address 1: 50 Acacia Ave
Street address 3: San Rafael
Street address state: CA
Zip/Postal code: 94901-2230
Country: USA
Mailing address: 50 Acacia Ave
Mailing city: San Rafael
Mailing state: CA
Mailing zip: 94901-2298
General Phone: (415) 485-3204
General Fax: (415) 485-3205
Primary Website: www.dominican.edu
Classified Equipment»
Personnel: Melva Bealf (Advisor)

SANTA ANA COLLEGE

Street address 1: 1530 W 17th St
Street address 3: Santa Ana
Street address state: CA
Zip/Postal code: 92706-3398
Country: USA
Mailing address: 1530 W 17th St
Mailing city: Santa Ana
Mailing state: CA
Mailing zip: 92706-3398
General Phone: (714) 564-5617
General Fax: (714) 564-0821
General/National Adv. E-mail: eldonbusiness@sac.edu
Primary Website: www.eldononline.org
Classified Equipment»
Personnel: Charles Little (Advisor); Allene Symons (Adv. Mgr.)

SANTA BARBARA

RANDY VANDERMEY

Street address 1: 132 Walnut Ln
Street address 3: Santa Barbara
Street address state: CA
Zip/Postal code: 93111-2148
Country: USA
Mailing address: 132 Walnut Lane
Mailing city: Santa Barbara
Mailing state: CA
Mailing zip: 93111
General Phone: 8056831115;8054034251cell
General Fax: 8056831115;8054034251cell
Advertising Phone: (805) 683-1115
Advertising Fax: (805) 683-1115
Editorail Phone: (805) 683-1115
Editorial Fax: 8056831115;8054034251cell
General/National Adv. E-mail: vanderme@westmont.edu
Display Adv. E-mail: horizon@westmont.edu
Editorial e-mail: horizon@westmont.edu
Primary Website: http://horizon.westmont.edu/pages/contact
Year Established: c. 1945
Published: Tues
Avg Paid Circ: 300
Avg Free Circ: 800
Classified Equipment»
Personnel: Randy VanderMey (Advisor); M<itchell MacMahon (Editor-in-Chief)

SANTA BARBARA CITY COLLEGE

Street address 1: 721 Cliff Dr
Street address 2: Rm 123
Street address 3: Santa Barbara
Street address state: CA
Zip/Postal code: 93109-2312
Country: USA
Mailing address: 721 Cliff Dr Rm 123
Mailing city: Santa Barbara
Mailing state: CA
Mailing zip: 93109-2394
General Phone: (805) 965-0581
General Fax: (805) 730-3079
General/National Adv. E-mail: channels@sbcc.edu
Primary Website: www.thechannelsonline.com
Classified Equipment»
Personnel: Patricia Stark (Advisor)

UNIV. OF CALIFORNIA, SANTA BARBARA

Street address 1: PO Box 13402
Street address 3: Santa Barbara
Street address state: CA
Zip/Postal code: 93107-3402
Country: USA
Mailing address: PO Box 13402
Mailing city: Santa Barbara
Mailing state: CA
Mailing zip: 93107-3402
General Phone: (805) 893-3828
Advertising Phone: (805) 893-4006
General/National Adv. E-mail: production@dailynexus.com
Display Adv. E-mail: LINDA.MEYER@SA.UCSB.EDU
Editorial e-mail: EIC@DAILYNEXUS.COM
Primary Website: www.dailynexus.com
Published: Thur
Avg Free Circ: 4000
Classified Equipment»
Personnel: Linda Meyer (Adv. Mgr.)

SANTA CLARA

SANTA CLARA UNIVERSITY

Street address 1: Center for Student Leadership
Street address 3: Santa Clara
Street address state: CA
Zip/Postal code: 95053-0001
Country: USA
Mailing address: 500 El Camino Real # 3190
Mailing city: Santa Clara
Mailing state: CA
Mailing zip: 95053-0001
General Phone: (408) 554-4849
General/National Adv. E-mail: news@thesantaclara.com
Display Adv. E-mail: advertising@thesantaclara.com
Editorial e-mail: editor@thesantaclara.com; letters@thesantaclara.com; news@thesantaclara.com
Primary Website: www.thesantaclara.com
Year Established: 1922
Published: Thur
Avg Free Circ: 1100
Classified Equipment»
Personnel: Sophie Mattson

SANTA CLARITA

COLLEGE OF THE CANYONS

Street address 1: 26455 Rockwell Canyon Rd
Street address 3: Santa Clarita
Street address state: CA
Zip/Postal code: 91355-1803
Country: USA
Mailing address: 26455 Rockwell Canyon Rd
Mailing city: Santa Clarita
Mailing state: CA
Mailing zip: 91355-1899
General Phone: (661) 259-7800
General Fax: (661) 362-3043
Classified Equipment»
Personnel: Jim Ruebsamen (Advisor)

SANTA MONICA

SANTA MONICA COLLEGE

Street address 1: 1900 Pico Blvd
Street address 2: # 303
Street address 3: Santa Monica
Street address state: CA
Zip/Postal code: 90405-1628
Country: USA
Mailing address: 1900 Pico Blvd # 303
Mailing city: Santa Monica
Mailing state: CA
Mailing zip: 90405-1644
General Phone: (310) 434-4340
General Fax: (310) 434-3648
Editorial Fax: Free
General/National Adv. E-mail: corsair.editorinchief@gmail.com
Display Adv. E-mail: blaize_ashanti@smc.edu
Editorial e-mail: corsair.editorinchief@gmail.com
Primary Website: www.thecorsaironline.com
Year Established: 1929
Delivery Methods: Mail`Newsstand`Racks
Commercial printers: Y
Advertising (Open Inch Rate) Weekday/Saturday: blaize_ashanti@smc.edu
Classified Equipment»
Personnel: Saul Rubin (Advisor)

SANTA ROSA JUNIOR COLLEGE

Street address 1: 1501 Mendocino Ave
Street address 3: Santa Rosa
Street address state: CA
Zip/Postal code: 95401-4332
Country: USA
Mailing address: 1501 Mendocino Ave.
Mailing city: Santa Rosa
Mailing state: CA
Mailing zip: 95401-4332
General Phone: (707) 527-4401
Advertising Phone: (707) 527-4254
General/National Adv. E-mail: abelden@santarosa.edu
Display Adv. E-mail: oakleaf-ads@santarosa.edu
Editorial e-mail: abelden@santarosa.edu
Primary Website: www.santarosa.edu
Year Established: 1928
Classified Equipment»
Personnel: Ann Belden (Advisor)

SARATOGA

WEST VALLEY COLLEGE

Street address 1: 14000 Fruitvale Ave
Street address 3: Saratoga
Street address state: CA
Zip/Postal code: 95070-5640
Country: USA
Mailing address: 14000 Fruitvale Ave
Mailing city: Saratoga
Mailing state: CA
Mailing zip: 95070-5698
General Phone: (408) 867-2200
General Fax: (408) 741-4040
Primary Website: www.westvalley.edu
Classified Equipment»
Personnel: Janine Gerzanics (Advisor)

STANFORD

THE STANFORD DAILY

Street address 1: 456 Panama Mall
Street address 2: Lorry Lokey Stanford Daily Bldg.
Street address 3: Stanford
Street address state: CA
Zip/Postal code: 94305-4006
Country: USA
Mailing address: 456 Panama Mall
Mailing city: Stanford
Mailing state: CA
Mailing zip: 94305-5294
General Phone: (650) 721-5803
General Fax: (650) 725-1329
General/National Adv. E-mail: eic@stanforddaily.com
Primary Website: www.stanforddaily.com
Classified Equipment»
Personnel: Jason Shen (COO & Bus Mgr.); Mary Liz McCurdy (Vice Pres., Sales); Devin Banerjee (Ed. in Chief); Kamil Dada (Ed. in Chief); Eric (Sr. Mng. Ed.)

STOCKTON

SAN JOAQUIN DELTA COLLEGE

Street address 1: 5151 Pacific Ave
Street address 2: Shima 203
Street address 3: Stockton
Street address state: CA
Zip/Postal code: 95207-6304
Country: USA
Mailing address: 5151 Pacific Ave Shima 203
Mailing city: Stockton
Mailing state: CA
Mailing zip: 95207-6370
General Phone: (209) 954-5156
General Fax: (209) 954-5288
General/National Adv. E-mail: deltacollegian@gmail.com
Primary Website: www.deltacollegian.com
Classified Equipment»
Personnel: Bill Davis (Advisor); Junifer Mamsaang (Ed. in Chief)

UNIV. OF THE PACIFIC

Street address 1: 3601 Pacific Ave
Street address 3: Stockton
Street address state: CA
Zip/Postal code: 95211-0110
Country: USA
Mailing address: 3601 Pacific Ave
Mailing city: Stockton
Mailing state: CA
Mailing zip: 95211-0197
General Phone: (209) 946-2115
General Fax: (209) 946-2195
Advertising Phone: (209) 946-2114
Display Adv. E-mail: pacificanads@pacific.edu
Editorial e-mail: pacificannews@pacific.edu; pacificaneditors@pacific.edu; pacificanlifestyles@pacific.edu; pacificansports@pacific.edu
Primary Website: www.thepacificanonline.com
Classified Equipment»
Personnel: Dave Frederickson (Advisor); Ruben Moreno (Bus. Mgr.); Devon Blount (Ed. in Chief); Andrew Mitchell (News Ed.)

SUSANVILLE

LASSEN CMTY. COLLEGE

Street address 1: 478-200 Hwy 139
Street address 3: Susanville
Street address state: CA
Zip/Postal code: 96130
Country: USA
Mailing address: PO Box 3000
Mailing city: Susanville
Mailing state: CA
Mailing zip: 96130-3000
General Phone: (530) 251-8821
General Fax: (530) 251-8839
General/National Adv. E-mail: trougar@lassen.cc.ca.us
Primary Website: www.lassencougar.com; www.lassen.cc.ca.us
Classified Equipment»
Personnel: Andrew Owen (Ed. in Chief)

THOUSAND OAKS

CALIFORNIA LUTHERAN UNIVERSITY

Street address 1: 60 W Olsen Rd
Street address 3: Thousand Oaks
Street address state: CA
Zip/Postal code: 91360-2700
Country: USA
Mailing address: 60 W Olsen Rd # 4200
Mailing city: Thousand Oaks
Mailing state: CA
Mailing zip: 91360-2787
General Phone: (805) 493-3366
General Fax: (805) 493-3479
Advertising Phone: (805) 493-3327
General/National Adv. E-mail: kelley@robles.callutheran.edu
Editorial e-mail: echo@clunet.edu
Classified Equipment»
Personnel: Colleen Cason (Advisor); Sharon Docter (Chair); Jonathan Culmer (Bus. Mgr.); Margaret Nolan (Ed. in Chief)

EL CAMINO COLLEGE

Street address 1: 16007 Crenshaw Blvd
Street address 2: Rm H-113
Street address 3: Torrance
Street address state: CA
Zip/Postal code: 90506-0001
Country: USA
Mailing address: 16007 Crenshaw Blvd.
Mailing city: Torrance
Mailing state: CA
Mailing zip: 90506
General Phone: (310) 660-3328
General Fax: (310) 660-6092
Advertising Phone: (310) 660-3329
Editorail Phone: (310) 660-3328
General/National Adv. E-mail: elcounionads000@yahoo.com
Display Adv. E-mail: elcounionads000@yahoo.com
Editorial e-mail: eccunion@gmail.com
Primary Website: eccunion.com
Year Established: 1946
Published: Bi-Mthly
Published Other: Twice per month
Avg Free Circ: 5000
Classified Equipment»
Personnel: Jack Mulkey (Adv. Mgr.); Kate McLaughlin (Adviser); Stefanie Frith (Adviser); Gary Kohatsu (Photo Adviser)

TURLOCK

CALIFORNIA STATE UNIVERSITY, STANISLAUS

Street address 1: 1 University Cir
Street address 3: Turlock
Street address state: CA
Zip/Postal code: 95382-3200
Country: USA
Mailing address: 1 University Cir
Mailing city: Turlock
Mailing state: CA
Mailing zip: 95382-3200
General Phone: (209) 667-3411
General Fax: (209) 667-3868
General/National Adv. E-mail: sstevens2@csustan.edu
Primary Website: www.csusignal.com
Classified Equipment»

UKIAH

MENDOCINO COLLEGE

Street address 1: 1000 Hensley Creek Rd
Street address 3: Ukiah
Street address state: CA
Zip/Postal code: 95482-7821
Country: USA
Mailing address: 1000 Hensley Creek Rd
Mailing city: Ukiah
Mailing state: CA
Mailing zip: 95482-3017
General Phone: (707) 468-3096
General Fax: (707) 468-3120
Classified Equipment»
Personnel: Debra Wallace (Ed.)

VALLEY GLEN

LOS ANGELES VALLEY COLLEGE

Street address 1: 5800 Fulton Ave
Street address 3: Valley Glen
Street address state: CA
Zip/Postal code: 91401-4062
Country: USA
Mailing address: 5800 Fulton Ave
Mailing city: Valley Glen
Mailing state: CA
Mailing zip: 91401-4062
General Phone: (818) 947-2576
General Fax: (818) 947-2610
General/National Adv. E-mail: valleystar@lavalleystar.com
Primary Website: www.lavalleystar.com
Classified Equipment»
Personnel: Rod Lyons (Advisor); Bill Dauber (Advisor); Sarah Knowles (Ed.); Lucas Thompson (Mng. Ed.)

VENTURA

VENTURA COLLEGE

Street address 1: 4667 Telegraph Rd
Street address 3: Ventura
Street address state: CA
Zip/Postal code: 93003-3872
Country: USA
Mailing address: 4667 Telegraph Rd
Mailing city: Ventura
Mailing state: CA
Mailing zip: 93003-3899
General Phone: (805) 654-6400
General Fax: (805) 654-6466
Primary Website: www.venturacollegepress.com
Classified Equipment»
Personnel: C. Weinstock (Advisor)

VISALIA

COLLEGE OF THE SEQUOIAS

Street address 1: 915 S Mooney Blvd
Street address 3: Visalia
Street address state: CA

Zip/Postal code: 93277-2214
Country: USA
Mailing address: 915 S Mooney Blvd
Mailing city: Visalia
Mailing state: CA
Mailing zip: 93277-2234
General Phone: (559) 730-3844
General Fax: (559) 730-3991
General/National Adv. E-mail: campusnews@cos.edu
Display Adv. E-mail: campusads@cos.edu
Editorial e-mail: campusnews@cos.edu
Primary Website: www.coscampusonline.com
Year Established: 1933
Classified Equipment»

WHITTIER

RIO HONDO COLLEGE

Street address 1: 3600 Workman Mill Rd
Street address 3: Whittier
Street address state: CA
Zip/Postal code: 90601-1616
Country: USA
Mailing address: 3600 Workman Mill Rd
Mailing city: Whittier
Mailing state: CA
Mailing zip: 90601-1699
General Phone: (562) 908-3453
General Fax: (562) 463-4641
General/National Adv. E-mail: elpaisano@riohondo.edu
Primary Website: www.elpaisanonewspaper.com
Classified Equipment»
Personnel: John Francis (Advisor); Mary Cowan (Ed. in Chief); Salomon Baeza (Ed. in Chief); James Tapparo (Adv. Dir.); Kathy (Exec. Dir.)

SOUTHERN CALIFORNIA UNIV. OF HEALTH SCIENCES

Street address 1: 16200 Amber Valley Dr
Street address 3: Whittier
Street address state: CA
Zip/Postal code: 90604-4051
Country: USA
Mailing address: 16200 Amber Valley Dr
Mailing city: Whittier
Mailing state: CA
Mailing zip: 90604-4051
General Phone: (562) 947-8755
General Fax: (562) 902-3321
Classified Equipment»
Personnel: Pam Roosevelt (Ed.)

WHITTIER COLLEGE

Street address 1: 13406 Philadelphia St
Street address 3: Whittier
Street address state: CA
Zip/Postal code: 90601-4446
Country: USA
Mailing address: PO Box 634
Mailing city: Whittier
Mailing state: CA
Mailing zip: 90608-0634
General Phone: (562) 907-4254
General Fax: (562) 945-5301
General/National Adv. E-mail: qc@whittier.edu
Primary Website: http://www.thequakercampus.org/
Year Established: 1914
Published: Thur
Classified Equipment»
Personnel: justin dennis (EIC, Mgr Ed); matther anson

LOS ANGELES PIERCE COLLEGE

Street address 1: 6201 Winnetka Ave
Street address 2: # 8212
Street address 3: Woodland Hills
Street address state: CA
Zip/Postal code: 91371-0001
Country: USA
Mailing address: 6201 Winnetka Ave # 8212
Mailing city: Woodland Hills
Mailing state: CA
Mailing zip: 91371-0001
General Phone: (818) 719-6483
General Fax: (818) 719-6447
Advertising Phone: (818) 710-2960
Advertising Fax: (818) 719-6447
Editorail Phone: (818) 719-6427
Editorial Fax: (818) 719-6447
General/National Adv. E-mail: newsroom.roundupnews@gmail.com
Display Adv. E-mail: baileyjd@piercecollege.edu
Editorial e-mail: newsroom.roundupnews@gmail.com
Primary Website: www.theroundupnews.com
Year Established: 1949
Syndicated Publications: The BULL
Delivery Methods: Newsstand
Commercial printers: Y
Advertising (Open Inch Rate) Weekday/Saturday: $7 per col inch less discounts
Mechanical available: Yes
Mechanical specifications: Call office or email advertising
Published: Wed
Avg Free Circ: 5000
Classified Equipment»
Personnel: Jill Connelly (Dept. Chrmn.); Julie Bailey (Office Mgr./Adv. Mgr.); Stefanie Frith (Adviser to the Roundup newspaper)

COLORADO

COLORADO SPGS

US AIR FORCE ACADEMY

Street address 1: 2304 Cadet Dr, Ste 3100
Street address 3: Colorado Spgs
Street address state: CO
Zip/Postal code: 80904
Country: USA
Mailing address: 2304 Cadet Dr., Ste. 3100
Mailing city: Colorado Springs
Mailing state: CO
Mailing zip: 80904-5016
General Phone: (719) 333-7731
General Fax: (719) 333-4094
Classified Equipment»
Personnel: Kim Karda (Ed. in Chief)

COLORADO COLLEGE

Street address 1: 1028 N Weber St
Street address 3: Colorado Springs
Street address state: CO
Zip/Postal code: 80903-2422
Country: USA
Mailing address: 1028 N. Weber St.
Mailing city: Colorado Springs
Mailing state: CO
Mailing zip: 80903
General Phone: (719) 389-6000
General Fax: (719) 389-6962
General/National Adv. E-mail: catalyst@coloradocollege.edu
Primary Website: www.coloradocollege.edu
Classified Equipment»
Personnel: Jackson Solway (Ed.); Alex Kronman (Ed.)

PIKES PEAK CMTY. COLLEGE

Street address 1: 5675 S Academy Blvd
Street address 2: # C12
Street address 3: Colorado Springs
Street address state: CO
Zip/Postal code: 80906-5422
Country: USA
Mailing address: 5675 S Academy Blvd # C12
Mailing city: Colorado Springs
Mailing state: CO
Mailing zip: 80906-5422
General Phone: (719) 502-2000
General Fax: (719) 579-3015
Primary Website: www.ppcc.edu
Classified Equipment»
Personnel: Linda McGowan (Advisor); Sonia Gonzales (Ed.)

UNIV. OF COLORADO

Street address 1: 1420 Austin Bluffs Pkwy
Street address 3: Colorado Springs
Street address state: CO
Zip/Postal code: 80918-3733
Country: USA
Mailing address: 1420 Austin Bluffs Pkwy
Mailing city: Colorado Springs
Mailing state: CO
Mailing zip: 80918-3908
General Phone: (719) 262-3658
General Fax: (719) 262-3600
General/National Adv. E-mail: scribe@uccs.edu
Primary Website: www.uccs.edu/scribe
Classified Equipment»
Personnel: Paul Fair (Ed.)

METROPOLITAN STATE COLLEGE

Street address 1: PO Box 173362
Street address 3: Denver
Street address state: CO
Zip/Postal code: 80217-3362
Country: USA
Mailing address: PO Box 173362
Mailing city: Denver
Mailing state: CO
Mailing zip: 80217-3362
General Phone: (303) 556-2507
General Fax: (303) 556-3421
Primary Website: themet.metrostudentmedia.com; www.mscd.edu/themet
Year Established: 1979
Classified Equipment»
Personnel: Dianne Harrison Miller (Dir.); Dominic Graziano (Ed.)

REGIS UNIV.

Street address 1: 3333 Regis Blvd
Street address 3: Denver
Street address state: CO
Zip/Postal code: 80221-1154
Country: USA
Mailing address: 3333 Regis Blvd
Mailing city: Denver
Mailing state: CO
Mailing zip: 80221-1099
General Phone: (303) 964-5391
General Fax: (303) 964-5530
Primary Website: www.regishighlander.com
Classified Equipment»
Personnel: Mary Beth Callie (Advisor); Maricor Coquia (Ed. in Chief)

UNIV. OF COLORADO

Street address 1: PO Box 173364
Street address 3: Denver
Street address state: CO
Zip/Postal code: 80217-3364
Country: USA
Mailing address: PO Box 173364
Mailing city: Denver
Mailing state: CO
Mailing zip: 80217-3364
General Phone: (303) 556-2535
General Fax: (303) 556-3679
Display Adv. E-mail: advertising@ucdadvocate.com
Editorial e-mail: editorinchief@ucdadvocate.com
Primary Website: www.ucdadvocate.com
Year Established: 1984
Published: Wed
Classified Equipment»
Personnel: Madilyn Bates (Editor in Chief); Isra Yousif (Office Coordinator)

UNIV. OF DENVER

Street address 1: 2199 S University Blvd
Street address 3: Denver
Street address state: CO
Zip/Postal code: 80210-4711
Country: USA
Mailing address: 2199 S University Blvd
Mailing city: Denver
Mailing state: CO
Mailing zip: 80210-4700
General Phone: (303) 871-3131
General Fax: (303) 871-2568
General/National Adv. E-mail: duclarion@du.edu
Primary Website: www.duclarion.com
Classified Equipment»
Personnel: Arianna Ranahosseini (Ed. in Chief)

DURANGO

FT. LEWIS COLLEGE

Street address 1: 1000 Rim Dr
Street address 2: # 252
Street address 3: Durango
Street address state: CO
Zip/Postal code: 81301-3911
Country: USA
Mailing address: 1000 Rim Dr # 252
Mailing city: Durango
Mailing state: CO
Mailing zip: 81301-3911
General Phone: (970) 247-7405
General Fax: (970) 247-7487
General/National Adv. E-mail: independent@fortlewis.edu
Primary Website: www.flcindependent.com
Classified Equipment»
Personnel: Leslie Blood (Advisor); Kayala Andersen (News Ed.)

COLORADO STATE UNIV.

Street address 1: PO Box 13
Street address 3: Fort Collins
Street address state: CO
Zip/Postal code: 80522-0013
Country: USA
Mailing address: PO Box 13
Mailing city: Fort Collins
Mailing state: CO
Mailing zip: 80522-0013
General Phone: (970) 491-1146
General Fax: (970) 491-1690
General/National Adv. E-mail: editor@collegian.com
Primary Website: www.collegian.com
Classified Equipment»
Personnel: Holly Wolcott (Advisor); Virginia Singarayar (Ed. in Chief); Madeline Novey (News Mng. Ed.); Matt Minich (News Ed.); Matt L. (Sports Ed.); Kim (Adv. Mgr.)

COLORADO STATE UNIV. ENGINEERING COLLEGE

Street address 1: PO Box 13
Street address 3: Fort Collins
Street address state: CO
Zip/Postal code: 80522-0013
Country: USA
Mailing address: PO Box 13
Mailing city: Fort Collins
Mailing state: CO
Mailing zip: 80522-0013
General Phone: (970) 491-1686
General Fax: (970) 491-1690
Primary Website: www.collegian.com
Classified Equipment»
Personnel: Brandon Lowrey (Ed. in Chief)

FORT MORGAN

MORGAN CMTY. COLLEGE

Street address 1: 920 Barlow Rd
Street address 3: Fort Morgan
Street address state: CO
Zip/Postal code: 80701-4371
Country: USA
Mailing address: 920 Barlow Rd
Mailing city: Fort Morgan
Mailing state: CO
Mailing zip: 80701-4371
General Phone: (970) 542-3170
General Fax: (970) 867-3084
Classified Equipment»
Personnel: Jennifer Lankford (Ed.)

GOLDEN

COLORADO SCHOOL OF MINES

Street address 1: 1600 Maple St
Street address 3: Golden
Street address state: CO
Zip/Postal code: 80401-6114
Country: USA

Mailing address: 1600 Maple St
Mailing city: Golden
Mailing state: CO
Mailing zip: 80401-6114
General Phone: (303) 384-2188
General Fax: (303) 273-3931
General/National Adv. E-mail: oredig@mines.edu
Primary Website: www.oredigger.net
Delivery Methods: Racks
Commercial printers: Y
Published: Mon
Classified Equipment»
Personnel: Emily McNair (Managing Editor); Lucy Orsi (Editor-in-Chief); Taylor Polodna (Design Editor); Connor McDonald (Webmaster); Arnaud Filliat (Copy Editor); Karen Gilbert (Faculty Advisor); Deborah Good (Editor-in-Chief)

GRAND JUNCTION

COLORADO MESA UNIVERSITY

Street address 1: 1100 North Ave
Street address 3: Grand Junction
Street address state: CO
Zip/Postal code: 81501-3122
Country: USA
Mailing address: PO Box 2647
Mailing city: Grand Junction
Mailing state: CO
Mailing zip: 81502-2647
General Phone: (970) 248-1570
General Fax: (970) 248-1708
Primary Website: www.thecrite.com
Year Established: 1934
Commercial printers: Y
Classified Equipment»
Personnel: Eric Sandstrom (Advisor); Jamie Banks (Ed.)

GREELEY

UNIV. OF NORTHERN COLORADO

Street address 1: 823 16th St
Street address 3: Greeley
Street address state: CO
Zip/Postal code: 80631-5617
Country: USA
Mailing address: 823 16th St
Mailing city: Greeley
Mailing state: CO
Mailing zip: 80631-5617
General Phone: (970) 392-9270
General Fax: (970) 392-9025
Advertising Phone: (970) 392-9270
Editorail Phone: (970) 392-9270
General/National Adv. E-mail: info@uncmirror.com
Display Adv. E-mail: ads@uncmirror.com
Editorial e-mail: editor@uncmirror.com
Primary Website: www.uncmirror.com
Year Established: 1919
Delivery Methods: Newsstand`Racks
Commercial printers: N
Published: Mon
Avg Free Circ: 4000
Classified Equipment»
Personnel: Kurt Hinkle (Gen. Mgr.); Josh Espinoza (Ed. in Chief); Eric Heinz (News Ed.); Jordan Freemyer (Sports Ed.); Corey (Adv. Mgr.); Lauren (Adv. Prodn. Mgr.)

GUNNISON

WESTERN STATE COLLEGE

Street address 1: 600 N Adams St
Street address 3: Gunnison
Street address state: CO
Zip/Postal code: 81231-7000
Country: USA
Mailing address: 103 College Ctr
Mailing city: Gunnison
Mailing state: CO
Mailing zip: 81231-0001
General Phone: 970-943-2138
General Fax: 970-943-2702
General/National Adv. E-mail: top@western.edu
Display Adv. E-mail: topworld.ads@gmail.com
Primary Website: www.western.edu/academics/communicationtheatre/top-o-the-world
Year Established: 1921
Classified Equipment»

COLORADO CHRISTIAN UNIV.

Street address 1: 8787 W Alameda Ave
Street address 3: Lakewood
Street address state: CO
Zip/Postal code: 80226-2824
Country: USA
Mailing address: 8787 W Alameda Ave
Mailing city: Lakewood
Mailing state: CO
Mailing zip: 80226-2824
General Phone: (303) 202-0100
General Fax: (303) 963-3001
General/National Adv. E-mail: cougartrax@ccu.edu
Primary Website: http://luke.ccu.edu/; www.ccu.edu
Classified Equipment»
Personnel: Jim McCormick (Advisor); Daniel Cohrs (Bus. Mgr.)

LITTLETON

ARAPAHOE CMTY. COLLEGE

Street address 1: 5900 S Santa Fe Dr
Street address 3: Littleton
Street address state: CO
Zip/Postal code: 80120-1801
Country: USA
Mailing address: 5900 S Santa Fe Dr
Mailing city: Littleton
Mailing state: CO
Mailing zip: 80120-1801
General Phone: (303) 797-5666
General Fax: (303) 797-5650
Classified Equipment»
Personnel: Chris Ransick (Advisor); Reem Al-Omari (Ed.)

PUEBLO

COLORADO STATE UNIVERSITY-PUEBLO

Street address 1: 2200 Bonforte Blvd
Street address 2: # AM110
Street address 3: Pueblo
Street address state: CO
Zip/Postal code: 81001-4901
Country: USA
Mailing address: 2200 Bonforte Blvd Bcc 103P
Mailing city: Pueblo
Mailing state: CO
Mailing zip: 81001-4901
General Phone: 719-549-2847
General Fax: 719-549-2977
Advertising Phone: 719-549-2812
Advertising Fax: 719-549-2977
General/National Adv. E-mail: leticia.steffen@csupueblo.edu
Primary Website: www.csupueblotoday.com
Published Other: once per semester (fall and spring)
Avg Free Circ: 3000
Classified Equipment»
Personnel: Leticia L. Steffen (Advisor); Savana Charter

STERLING

NORTHEASTERN JUNIOR COLLEGE

Street address 1: 100 College Ave
Street address 3: Sterling
Street address state: CO
Zip/Postal code: 80751-2345
Country: USA
Mailing address: 100 College Ave
Mailing city: Sterling
Mailing state: CO
Mailing zip: 80751-2399
General Phone: (970) 521-6796
Classified Equipment»
Personnel: Ian Storey (Advisor); Patrick Kelling (Advisor)

TRINIDAD

TRINIDAD STATE JUNIOR COLLEGE

Street address 1: 600 Prospect St
Street address 2: # 182
Street address 3: Trinidad
Street address state: CO
Zip/Postal code: 81082-2356
Country: USA
Mailing address: 600 Prospect St # 182
Mailing city: Trinidad
Mailing state: CO
Mailing zip: 81082-2356
General Phone: (719) 846-5011
General Fax: (719) 846-5667
Classified Equipment»
Personnel: Charlene Duran (Adv. Mgr.)

WESTMINSTER

FRONT RANGE CMTY. COLLEGE

Street address 1: 3645 W 112th Ave
Street address 3: Westminster
Street address state: CO
Zip/Postal code: 80031-2105
Country: USA
Mailing address: 3645 W 112th Ave
Mailing city: Westminster
Mailing state: CO
Mailing zip: 80031-2199
General Phone: (303) 404-5314
General Fax: (303) 404-5199
General/National Adv. E-mail: frontpage@frontrange.com
Primary Website: www.frontrange.edu
Classified Equipment»
Personnel: John Heisel (Advisor); Stephanie Munger (Ed. in Chief); Jon Strungis (Ed.)

CONNECTICUT

BRIDGEPORT

UNIV. OF BRIDGEPORT

Street address 1: 244 University Ave
Street address 3: Bridgeport
Street address state: CT
Zip/Postal code: 06604-7775
Country: USA
Mailing address: 244 University Ave
Mailing city: Bridgeport
Mailing state: CT
Mailing zip: 06604-7775
General Phone: (203) 576-4382
General Fax: (203) 576-4493
General/National Adv. E-mail: scribe@bridgeport.edu
Primary Website: www.thescribeonline.com
Classified Equipment»
Personnel: Richard Unger (Ed. in Chief); Sharon Loh (Ed.)

DANBURY

WESTERN CONNECTICUT STATE UNIV.

Street address 1: 181 White St
Street address 3: Danbury
Street address state: CT
Zip/Postal code: 06810-6826
Country: USA
Mailing address: 181 White St
Mailing city: Danbury
Mailing state: CT
Mailing zip: 06810-6855
General Phone: (203) 837-8706
General Fax: (203) 837-8709
General/National Adv. E-mail: wcsuecho@gmail.com
Display Adv. E-mail: wcsuechoads@gmail.com
Primary Website: http://wcsuecho.com/news/
Classified Equipment»
Personnel: John Birks (Advisor); Todd Passan (Bus. Mgr.); Sarah Menichelli (Adv. Mgr.); Jessylyn Foley (Ed. in Chief)

FAIRFIELD UNIV.

Street address 1: 1073 N Benson Rd
Street address 3: Fairfield
Street address state: CT
Zip/Postal code: 06824-5171
Country: USA
Mailing address: PO Box AA
Mailing city: Fairfield
Mailing state: CT
Mailing zip: 06824
General Phone: (203) 254-4000
General Fax: (203) 254-4162
Display Adv. E-mail: advertising@fairfieldmirror.com
Primary Website: www.fairfieldmirror.com
Published: Wed
Avg Free Circ: 3500
Classified Equipment»
Personnel: Lei Xie (Faculty adviser)

SACRED HEART UNIV.

Street address 1: 5151 Park Ave
Street address 3: Fairfield
Street address state: CT
Zip/Postal code: 06825-1090
Country: USA
Mailing address: 5151 Park Ave
Mailing city: Fairfield
Mailing state: CT
Mailing zip: 06825-1000
General Phone: (203) 371-7966
General Fax: (203) 371-7828
Advertising Phone: (203) 371-7963
General/National Adv. E-mail: spectrum@sacredheart.edu
Display Adv. E-mail: spectrum-advertising@sacredheart.edu
Primary Website: www.shuspectrum.wordpress.com
Classified Equipment»
Personnel: Joanne Kabak (Advisor); Lauren Sampson (Adv. Mgr.); Carli-Rae Panny (Ed. in Chief); Kate Poole (Mng. Ed.)

HAMDEN

QUINNIPIAC COLLEGE SCHOOL OF LAW

Street address 1: 275 Mount Carmel Ave
Street address 3: Hamden
Street address state: CT
Zip/Postal code: 06518-1905
Country: USA
Mailing address: 275 Mount Carmel Ave
Mailing city: Hamden
Mailing state: CT
Mailing zip: 06518-1908
General Phone: (203) 582-8358
General Fax: (203) 582-5203
General/National Adv. E-mail: thequchronicle@gmail.com
Primary Website: www.quchronicle.com
Classified Equipment»
Personnel: Andrew Fletcher (Ed. in Chief); Joe Pelletier (Mng. Ed.)

QUINNIPIAC UNIVERSITY

Street address 1: 275 Mount Carmel Ave
Street address 3: Hamden
Street address state: CT
Zip/Postal code: 06518-1905
Country: USA
Mailing address: 275 Mount Carmel Ave
Mailing city: Hamden
Mailing state: CT
Mailing zip: 06518-1908
General Phone: 8608301017
General/National Adv. E-mail: editor@quchronicle.com
Primary Website: www.quinnipiac.edu; quchronicle.com
Classified Equipment»

Personnel: David Friedlander (Editor-in-Chief)

TRINITY COLLEGE

Street address 1: 300 Summit St
Street address 3: Hartford
Street address state: CT
Zip/Postal code: 06106-3100
Country: USA
Mailing address: 300 Summit St Ste 1
Mailing city: Hartford
Mailing state: CT
Mailing zip: 06106-3186
General Phone: (860) 297-2584
General Fax: (860) 297-5361
General/National Adv. E-mail: tripod@trincoll.edu
Primary Website: https://commons.trincoll.edu/tripod/
Year Established: 1904
Delivery Methods: Newsstand
Published: Tues
Classified Equipment»

MANCHESTER COMMUNITY COLLEGE

Street address 1: 60 Bidwell St
Street address 3: Manchester
Street address state: CT
Zip/Postal code: 06040-6449
Country: USA
Mailing address: 60 Bidwell Street
Mailing city: Manchester
Mailing state: CT
Mailing zip: 06045-1046
General Phone: (860) 512-3290
Editorail Phone: (860) 512-3289
General/National Adv. E-mail: livewire@manchestercc.edu
Primary Website: www.livewiremcc.org
Year Established: 1979
Published Other: Every six weeks
Avg Free Circ: 4000
Classified Equipment»
Personnel: Stephania Davis (Advisor)

WESLEYAN UNIVERSITY

Street address 1: 45 Wyllys Ave
Street address 3: Middletown
Street address state: CT
Zip/Postal code: 06459-3211
Country: USA
Mailing address: 45 Wyllys Ave
Mailing city: Middletown
Mailing state: CT
Mailing zip: 06459-3211
General Phone: (860) 685-6902
General Fax: (860) 685-3411
General/National Adv. E-mail: argus@wesleyan.edu
Display Adv. E-mail: argusads@wesleyan.edu
Primary Website: www.wesleyanargus.com
Published: Tues`Fri
Classified Equipment»
Personnel: Natasha Nurjadin (Editor-in-Chief); Aaron Stagoff-Belfort (Editor-in-Chief)

NEW BRITAIN

CENTRAL CONNECTICUT STATE UNIV.

Street address 1: 1615 Stanley St
Street address 3: New Britain
Street address state: CT
Zip/Postal code: 06050-2439
Country: USA
Mailing address: 1615 Stanley St
Mailing city: New Britain
Mailing state: CT
Mailing zip: 06050-2439
General Phone: (860) 832-3744
General Fax: (860) 832-3747
General/National Adv. E-mail: ccsurecorder@gmail.com; ccsurecorder.ads@gmail.com
Primary Website: www.centralrecorder.com
Classified Equipment»
Personnel: Vivian B. Martin (Coord.); Melissa Traynor (Ed. in Chief); Michael Walsh (Mng. Ed.); Christopher Boulay (Sports Ed.); Christina LoBello (Opinion Ed.); Kelsey (Adv. Mgr.)

NEW HAVEN

SOUTHERN CONNECTICUT STATE UNIV.

Street address 1: 501 Crescent St
Street address 2: # 58
Street address 3: New Haven
Street address state: CT
Zip/Postal code: 06515-1330
Country: USA
Mailing address: 501 Crescent St # 58
Mailing city: New Haven
Mailing state: CT
Mailing zip: 06515-1330
General Phone: (203) 392-5804
General Fax: (203) 392-6927
General/National Adv. E-mail: snews@southernct.edu
Primary Website: snews.southernct.edu
Classified Equipment»
Personnel: Frank Harris (Advisor)

YALE UNIV.

Street address 1: 202 York St
Street address 3: New Haven
Street address state: CT
Zip/Postal code: 06511-4804
Country: USA
Mailing address: PO Box 209007
Mailing city: New Haven
Mailing state: CT
Mailing zip: 06520-9007
General Phone: (203) 432-2400
General Fax: (203) 432-7425
General/National Adv. E-mail: ydn@yale.edu; ydn@yaledailynews.com
Display Adv. E-mail: business@yaledailynews.com
Primary Website: www.yaledailynews.com
Classified Equipment»
Personnel: Jason Chen (Pub.); Katherine Kavaler (Adv. Dir.); Thomas Kaplan (Ed. in Chief)

YALE UNIV. LAW SCHOOL

Street address 1: PO Box 208215
Street address 3: New Haven
Street address state: CT
Zip/Postal code: 06520-8215
Country: USA
Mailing address: PO Box 208215
Mailing city: New Haven
Mailing state: CT
Mailing zip: 06520-8215
General Fax: (203) 432-1666
Classified Equipment»
Personnel: Nicola Williams (Ed.)

CONNECTICUT COLLEGE

Street address 1: 270 Mohegan Ave
Street address 3: New London
Street address state: CT
Zip/Postal code: 06320-4125
Country: USA
Mailing address: PO Box 4970
Mailing city: New London
Mailing state: CT
Mailing zip: 06320-4196
General Phone: (860) 439-2841
General Fax: (860) 439-2843
General/National Adv. E-mail: ccvoice@conncoll.edu; contact@thecollegevoice.org
Primary Website: thecollegevoice.org
Classified Equipment»
Personnel: Justin O'Shea (Bus. Mgr.); Benjamin Eagle (Ed. in Chief); Claire Gould (Mng. Ed.); CR Baker

STORRS

UNIV. OF CONNECTICUT

Street address 1: 11 Dog Ln
Street address 3: Storrs
Street address state: CT
Zip/Postal code: 06268-2206
Country: USA
Mailing address: 11 Dog Ln
Mailing city: Storrs
Mailing state: CT
Mailing zip: 06268-2206
General Phone: (860) 486-3407
General Fax: (860) 486-4388
General/National Adv. E-mail: advertising@dailycampus.com
Primary Website: www.dailycampus.com
Classified Equipment»
Personnel: Valerie Nezvesky (Bus. Mgr./Adv. Dir.); Christopher Duray (Ed. in Chief)

WATERBURY

NAUGATUCK VALLEY COMMUNITY COLLEGE

Street address 1: 750 Chase Pkwy
Street address 3: Waterbury
Street address state: CT
Zip/Postal code: 06708-3011
Country: USA
Mailing address: 750 Chase Pkwy
Mailing city: Waterbury
Mailing state: CT
Mailing zip: 06708-3089
General Phone: (203) 575-8040
General Fax: (203) 596-8721
General/National Adv. E-mail: nvcc@nvcc.commnet.edu
Primary Website: www.nvcc.commnet.edu
Published: Mthly
Classified Equipment»
Personnel: Steve Parlato (Faculty Advisor); Chelsea Clow (Editor-in-Chief)

UNIV. OF HARTFORD

Street address 1: 200 Bloomfield Ave
Street address 2: Rm 158
Street address 3: West Hartford
Street address state: CT
Zip/Postal code: 06117-1545
Country: USA
Mailing address: 200 Bloomfield Ave Rm 158
Mailing city: West Hartford
Mailing state: CT
Mailing zip: 06117-1545
General Phone: (860) 768-4723
General Fax: (860) 768-4728
General/National Adv. E-mail: informer@hartford.edu
Primary Website: www.hartfordinformer.com
Classified Equipment»
Personnel: Jonathan Whitson (Bus. Mgr.); Melissa O' Brien (Ed. in Chief)

WEST HAVEN

UNIV. OF NEW HAVEN

Street address 1: 300 Boston Post Rd
Street address 3: West Haven
Street address state: CT
Zip/Postal code: 06516-1916
Country: USA
Mailing address: 300 Boston Post Rd
Mailing city: West Haven
Mailing state: CT
Mailing zip: 06516-1999
General Phone: (203) 932-7182
General Fax: (203) 931-6037
General/National Adv. E-mail: chargerbulletin@newhaven.edu
Primary Website: www.chargerbulletin.com
Year Established: 1938
Published: Wed
Classified Equipment»
Personnel: Zack Rosen (Ed. in Chief); Erin Ennis (Asst. Ed.); Sara McGuire (A&E Ed.); Michelle Blydenburg (Adv. Mgr.); Charles (Distribution Mgr.); Liana Teixeira; Elizabeth Field

WILLIMANTIC

EASTERN CONNECTICUT STATE UNIV.

Street address 1: 83 Windham St, 103 Student Ctr
Street address 3: Willimantic
Street address state: CT
Zip/Postal code: 6226
Country: USA
Mailing address: 83 Windham St., 103 Student Ctr.
Mailing city: Willimantic
Mailing state: CT
Mailing zip: 06226-2211
General Phone: (860) 465-4445
General Fax: (860) 465-4685
General/National Adv. E-mail: general@campuslantern.org; lantern@stu.easternct.edu
Primary Website: www.campuslantern.org
Classified Equipment»
Personnel: Edmond Chibeau (Advisor); Daniel McCue (Ed. in Chief); Christine Smith (Mng. Ed.); Michael Rouleau (News Ed.); Andrew (A&E Ed.); Zach (Sports Ed.); Jacquelyn (Opinion Ed.)

DISTRICT OF COLUMBIA

AMERICAN UNIV.

Street address 1: 252 Mary Graydon Ctr
Street address 3: Washington
Street address state: DC
Country: USA
Mailing address: 4400 Massachusetts Ave NW
Mailing city: Washington
Mailing state: DC
Mailing zip: 20016-8003
General Phone: (202) 885-1414
General Fax: (202) 885-1428
Editorail Phone: (202) 885-1402
General/National Adv. E-mail: editor@theeagleonline.com
Primary Website: www.theeagleonline.com
Classified Equipment»
Personnel: Jen Calantone (Ed. in Chief); Charlie Szold (News Ed.); Andrew Tomlinson (Sports Ed.); Caitlin E. Moore (A&E Ed.); Kelsey (Photo Ed.)

CATHOLIC UNIV. OF AMERICA

Street address 1: 127 Pryzbyla Ctr
Street address 3: Washington
Street address state: DC
Country: USA
Mailing address: 127 Pryzbyla Ctr
Mailing city: Washington
Mailing state: DC
Mailing zip: 20064-0001
General Phone: (202) 319-5779
General Fax: (202) 319-6675
Primary Website: www.cuatower.com
Classified Equipment»
Personnel: William McQuillen (Advisor.); Ben Newell (Ed.)

GALLAUDET UNIVERSITY

Street address 1: 800 Florida Ave NE
Street address 3: Washington
Street address state: DC
Zip/Postal code: 20002-3600
Country: USA
Mailing address: PO Box 2334
Mailing city: Washington
Mailing state: DC
Mailing zip: 20013-2334
General Phone: (202) 651-5000
General Fax: (202) 651-5916
General/National Adv. E-mail: ursabuffinblue@gmail.comursabuffinblue
Primary Website: www.gallaudet.edu
Classified Equipment»
Personnel: Mary Lott (Dir.)

GEORGE WASHINGTON UNIV.

Street address 1: 2140 G St NW
Street address 3: Washington
Street address state: DC
Zip/Postal code: 20052-0072
Country: USA
Mailing address: 2140 G St NW
Mailing city: Washington
Mailing state: DC

Mailing zip: 20052-0072
General Phone: (202) 994-7080
General Fax: (202) 994-1309
Advertising Fax: (202) 994-7550
General/National Adv. E-mail: news@gwhatchet.comgwhatchet
Display Adv. E-mail: ads@gwhatchet.comgwhatchet
Primary Website: www.gwhatchet.com
Year Established: 1904
Classified Equipment»
Personnel: Howard Marshall (Gen. Mgr.); Arron Elkins (Adv. Mgr.); Alex Byers (Ed. in Chief); Beyers

GEORGE WASHINGTON UNIV. LAW SCHOOL

Street address 1: 2008 H St NW
Street address 2: Bsmt
Street address 3: Washington
Street address state: DC
Zip/Postal code: 20052-0026
Country: USA
Mailing address: 2008 H St NW Bsmt
Mailing city: Washington
Mailing state: DC
Mailing zip: 20052-0026
General Phone: (202) 994-6261
General/National Adv. E-mail: notabene@law.gwu.edu
Primary Website: http://notabene.gwsba.com
Classified Equipment»
Personnel: Sarah Valerio (Pres.); Katie Earnest (Ed. in Chief)

GEORGETOWN UNIV. LAW CENTER

Street address 1: 600 New Jersey Ave NW
Street address 3: Washington
Street address state: DC
Zip/Postal code: 20001-2022
Country: USA
Mailing address: 600 New Jersey Ave NW
Mailing city: Washington
Mailing state: DC
Mailing zip: 20001-2075
General Phone: (202) 662-9357
General Fax: (202) 662-9491
Classified Equipment»
Personnel: Brett Marston (Advisor)

GEORGETOWN UNIVERSITY

Street address 1: Leavey Ctr Rm 421, 37th & O Sts NW
Street address 3: Washington
Street address state: DC
Zip/Postal code: 20057-0001
Country: USA
Mailing address: PO Box 571065
Mailing city: Washington
Mailing state: DC
Mailing zip: 20057-1065
General Phone: (202) 687-3947
General Fax: (202) 687-2741
Advertising Phone: (202) 687-3947
Advertising Fax: (202) 687-2741
Editorail Phone: (202) 687-3415
General/National Adv. E-mail: gm@thehoya.com
Display Adv. E-mail: sales@thehoya.com
Editorial e-mail: editor@thehoya.com
Primary Website: www.thehoya.com
Year Established: 1920
Published: Tues`Fri
Avg Free Circ: 6500
Classified Equipment»
Personnel: Roshan Vora (Advisor); Michelle Lee (Adv. Mgr.); Kaphryn Devincenzo (Ed. in chief); Eamon O' connor (Exec. Ed.); Kathryn (Mng. Ed.); Mary Nancy Walter (General Manager)

MCDONOUGH BUS. SCHOOL/ GEORGETOWN UNIV.

Street address 1: 3520 Prospect St NW
Street address 2: Ste 215
Street address 3: Washington
Street address state: DC
Zip/Postal code: 20007-2631
Country: USA
Mailing address: 3520 Prospect St NW Ste 215
Mailing city: Washington
Mailing state: DC
Mailing zip: 20007-2631
General Phone: (202) 678-0268
General Fax: (202) 678-0268
General/National Adv. E-mail: mba-globe@msb.edu
Primary Website: www.georgetownglobe.com
Classified Equipment»
Personnel: Brenna Fleener (Ed. in Chief)

HOWARD UNIV.

Street address 1: 2251 Sherman Ave NW
Street address 3: Washington
Street address state: DC
Zip/Postal code: 20001-4003
Country: USA
Mailing address: 816 Easley St Apt 805
Mailing city: Silver Spring
Mailing state: MD
Mailing zip: 20910-4581
General Phone: (202) 806-4749
General Fax: (202) 328-1681
General/National Adv. E-mail: bussinessoffice@thehilltoponline.com
Primary Website: www.thehilltoponline.com
Classified Equipment»
Personnel: Kevin Reed (Advisor); Vanessa Rozier (Ed. in Chief)

DELAWARE

DOVER

DELAWARE STATE UNIV.

Street address 1: 1200 N Dupont Hwy
Street address 3: Dover
Street address state: DE
Zip/Postal code: 19901-2202
Country: USA
Mailing address: 1200 N Dupont Hwy
Mailing city: Dover
Mailing state: DE
Mailing zip: 19901-2276
General Phone: (302) 857-6290
Primary Website: www.desu.edu
Published: Mthly
Classified Equipment»
Personnel: Marcia Taylor (Advisor); Synquette Wilks (EIC)

NEWARK

THE REVIEW

Street address 1: 325 Academy St
Street address 2: Rm 250
Street address 3: Newark
Street address state: DE
Zip/Postal code: 19716-6186
Country: USA
Mailing address: 325 Academy St Rm 250
Mailing city: Newark
Mailing state: DE
Mailing zip: 19716-6185
General Phone: (302) 831-1397
General Fax: (302) 831-1396
Advertising Phone: (302) 831-1398
Advertising Fax: (302) 831-1395
Editorail Phone: (302) 831-2774
General/National Adv. E-mail: business@udreview.com
Display Adv. E-mail: ads@udreview.com
Editorial e-mail: editor@udreview.com; thereview.editorial@gmail.com
Primary Website: www.udreview.com
Year Established: 1882
Delivery Methods: Newsstand
Classified Equipment»
Personnel: Kerry Bowden (Editor-in-Chief)

WIDENER UNIV. SCHOOL OF LAW

Street address 1: PO Box 7474
Street address 3: Wilmington
Street address state: DE
Zip/Postal code: 19803-0474
Country: USA
Mailing address: PO Box 7474
Mailing city: Wilmington
Mailing state: DE
Mailing zip: 19803-0474
General Phone: (302) 477-2100
General Fax: (302) 478-3495
General/National Adv. E-mail: widenerlawforum@yahoo.com
Classified Equipment»
Personnel: Doretta McGinnis (Advisor); Christopher Balala (Ed. in Chief); Harry Matt Taylor (Bus. Mgr.)

FLORIDA

BOCA RATON

FLORIDA ATLANTIC UNIV.

Street address 1: 777 Glades Rd
Street address 3: Boca Raton
Street address state: FL
Zip/Postal code: 33431-6424
Country: USA
Mailing address: 777 Glades Rd
Mailing city: Boca Raton
Mailing state: FL
Mailing zip: 33431-6496
General Phone: (561) 297-2960
General Fax: (561) 297-2106
General/National Adv. E-mail: upress@fau.edu
Primary Website: www.upressonline.com
Classified Equipment»
Personnel: Michael Koretzky (Advisor); Devin Desjarlais (Ed. in Chief); Karla Bowsher (Mng. Ed.); Lindsey Voltoline (Art Dir.)

LYNN UNIV.

Street address 1: 3601 N Military Trl
Street address 3: Boca Raton
Street address state: FL
Zip/Postal code: 33431-5507
Country: USA
Mailing address: 3601 N Military Trl
Mailing city: Boca Raton
Mailing state: FL
Mailing zip: 33431-5598
General Phone: (561) 237-7463
General Fax: (561) 237-7097
General/National Adv. E-mail: advertise@lynnipulse.org
Primary Website: www.lynnipulse.org
Classified Equipment»
Personnel: Stefani Powers (Advisor)

CORAL GABLES

UNIV. OF MIAMI

Street address 1: 1330 Miller Rd
Street address 2: Ste 200
Street address 3: Coral Gables
Street address state: FL
Zip/Postal code: 33146-2322
Country: USA
Mailing address: 1330 Miller Road, Suite 200
Mailing city: Coral Gables
Mailing state: FL
Mailing zip: 33146-2322
General Phone: (305) 284-4401
General Fax: (305) 284-4404
Advertising Phone: same
Advertising Fax: same
Editorail Phone: (305) 284-2016
Editorial Fax: (305) 284-4406
General/National Adv. E-mail: editor@themiamihurricane.com
Display Adv. E-mail: tara@themiamihurricane.com
Editorial e-mail: editor@themiamihurricane.com
Primary Website: www.themiamihurricane.com
Year Established: 1929
Delivery Methods: Mail`Racks
Commercial printers: Y
Published: Mon`Thur
Avg Free Circ: 10000
Classified Equipment»
Personnel: Bob Radziewicz (Sr. Advisor)
Parent company (for newspapers): University of Miami

UNIV. OF MIAMI SCHOOL OF LAW

Street address 1: 1311 Miller Rd
Street address 3: Coral Gables
Street address state: FL
Zip/Postal code: 33146-2300
Country: USA
Mailing address: 1311 Miller Rd
Mailing city: Coral Gables
Mailing state: FL
Mailing zip: 33146-2300
General Phone: (305) 284-2339
General Fax: (305) 284-3554
General/National Adv. E-mail: resipsa@law.miami.edu
Primary Website: www.law.miami.edu
Classified Equipment»
Personnel: Jennifer C. Pratt-Garces (Ed. in Chief); Alex Britell (Mng. Ed.)

DAVIE

NOVA SOUTHEASTERN UNIV.

Street address 1: 3301 College Ave
Street address 2: Modular 4
Street address 3: Davie
Street address state: FL
Zip/Postal code: 33314-7721
Country: USA
Mailing address: 3301 College Ave Modular 4
Mailing city: Davie
Mailing state: FL
Mailing zip: 33314-7721
General Phone: (954) 262-8455
General Fax: (954) 262-8456
General/National Adv. E-mail: thecurrent@nova.edu; nsnews@nova.edu
Display Adv. E-mail: thecurrentad@nova.edu
Primary Website: www.nsucurrent.com
Classified Equipment»
Personnel: Fiona Banton

DAYTONA BEACH

BETHUNE-COOKMAN COLLEGE

Street address 1: 640 Dr Mary McLeod Bethune Blvd
Street address 3: Daytona Beach
Street address state: FL
Zip/Postal code: 32114-3012
Country: USA
Mailing address: 640 Dr. Mary McLeod Bethune Blvd.
Mailing city: Daytona Beach
Mailing state: FL
Mailing zip: 32114
General Phone: (386) 481-2000
General Fax: (386) 481-2701
General/National Adv. E-mail: voiceofthewildcats@gmail.edu
Display Adv. E-mail: voiceofthewildcats@gmail.com
Editorial e-mail: voiceofthewildcates@gmail.com
Primary Website: voiceofthewildcats.wordpress.com; www.cookman.edu
Year Established: 1904
Delivery Methods: Newsstand
Commercial printers: Y
Advertising (Open Inch Rate) Weekday/Saturday: Refuel Advertising Agency
Published: Mthly
Published Other: UniverCity Magazine
Avg Free Circ: 1000
Classified Equipment»
Personnel: Petra Merrick (Ed); Jamie Cobb (Layout/ Paginator); Timothy White (Sports Ed); Augustinas Navickas (Columnist); Andres Whipple Girbes (Technology Writer)
Parent company (for newspapers): Bethune-Cookman University

DAYTONA STATE COLLEGE

Street address 1: 1200 W International Speedway Blvd
Street address 3: Daytona Beach
Street address state: FL
Zip/Postal code: 32114-2817
Country: USA
Mailing address: 1200 W International Speedway Blvd
Mailing city: Daytona Beach

Mailing state: FL
Mailing zip: 32114-2817
General Phone: (386) 506-3268
General Fax: (386) 506-3155
Editorail Phone: (386) 506-3686
General/National Adv. E-mail: inmotion@daytonastate.edu
Display Adv. E-mail: inmotion@daytonastate.edu
Editorial e-mail: inmotion@daytonastate.edu
Primary Website: www.daytonastateinmotion.com
Year Established: 1991
Published: Mthly
Avg Free Circ: 10002000
Classified Equipment»
Personnel: Elena Jarvis (Advisor)
Parent company (for newspapers): Daytona State College

EMBRY-RIDDLE AERONAUTICAL UNIVERSITY

Street address 1: 600 S Clyde Morris Blvd
Street address 3: Daytona Beach
Street address state: FL
Zip/Postal code: 32114-3966
Country: USA
Mailing address: 600 S Clyde Morris Blvd
Mailing city: Daytona Beach
Mailing state: FL
Mailing zip: 32114-3900
General Phone: (386) 226-6049
Advertising Phone: (386) 226-6727
Advertising Fax: (386) 226-7697
Editorail Phone: (386) 226-6079
General/National Adv. E-mail: theavion@gmail.com
Display Adv. E-mail: avionadvertising@gmail.com
Primary Website: www.theavion.com
Year Established: 1969
Advertising (Open Inch Rate) Weekday/Saturday: Available
Published: Tues
Avg Free Circ: 2000
Classified Equipment»
Personnel: Jessica Searcy (Advisor)

DELAND

STETSON UNIV.

Street address 1: 421 N Woodland Blvd
Street address 3: Deland
Street address state: FL
Zip/Postal code: 32723-8300
Country: USA
Mailing address: 421 N Woodland Blvd
Mailing city: Deland
Mailing state: FL
Mailing zip: 32720
General Phone: (386)-822-7100
General Fax: (904) 822-7233
Display Adv. E-mail: advertising@stetson.edu
Editorial e-mail: reporter@stetson.edu
Primary Website: www.stetsonreporter.com
Classified Equipment»
Personnel: Andrew Davis (Commun. Coord.); Joseph O'Brien (Ed. in Chief); Jason Rickner (Mng. Ed.)

GAINESVILLE

UNIV. OF FLORIDA

Street address 1: PO Box 14257
Street address 3: Gainesville
Street address state: FL
Zip/Postal code: 32604-2257
Country: USA
Mailing address: PO Box 14257
Mailing city: Gainesville
Mailing state: FL
Mailing zip: 32604-2257
General Phone: (352) 376-4458
General Fax: (352) 376-4556
General/National Adv. E-mail: advertising@alligator.org
Editorial e-mail: editor@alligator.org
Primary Website: www.alligator.org
Classified Equipment»
Personnel: Chelsea Keenan (Ed. in Chief)

FLORIDA STATE COLLEGE AT JACKSONVILLE

Street address 1: 101 State St W
Street address 2: Rm C103
Street address 3: Jacksonville
Street address state: FL
Zip/Postal code: 32202-3099
Country: USA
Mailing address: 101 State St W Rm C103
Mailing city: Jacksonville
Mailing state: FL
Mailing zip: 32202-3099
General Phone: (904) 633-8283
General Fax: (904) 632-3279
General/National Adv. E-mail: campusvoice@fscj.edu
Primary Website: www.campusvoiceonline.com
Published: Bi-Mthly
Classified Equipment»
Personnel: Zak Gragg (Adv. Mgr.); Jocelyn Rhoten (Editor-in-Chief)

JACKSONVILLE UNIV.

Street address 1: 2800 University Blvd N
Street address 3: Jacksonville
Street address state: FL
Zip/Postal code: 32211-3321
Country: USA
Mailing address: 2800 University Blvd N
Mailing city: Jacksonville
Mailing state: FL
Mailing zip: 32211-3394
General Phone: (904) 256-7526
General Fax: (904) 256-7684
General/National Adv. E-mail: navigator@jacksonville.edu
Primary Website: navigator.ju.edu
Classified Equipment»
Personnel: Peter Moberg (Advisor); Jean Sils (Adv. Mgr); Renae Ingram (Ed. in Chief)

UNIV. OF NORTH FLORIDA

Street address 1: 1 U N F Dr
Street address 3: Jacksonville
Street address state: FL
Zip/Postal code: 32224-7699
Country: USA
Mailing address: 1 U N F Drive
Mailing city: Jacksonville
Mailing state: FL
Mailing zip: 32224
General Phone: (904) 620-2727
General Fax: (904) 620-3924
General/National Adv. E-mail: spinsads@unf.edu
Primary Website: www.espinnaker.com
Year Established: 1977
Classified Equipment»
Personnel: Adina Daar (Bus. Mgr.)

LAKE WORTH

PALM BEACH CMTY. COLLEGE

Street address 1: 4200 S Congress Ave
Street address 3: Lake Worth
Street address state: FL
Zip/Postal code: 33461-4705
Country: USA
Mailing address: 4200 S Congress Ave
Mailing city: Lake Worth
Mailing state: FL
Mailing zip: 33461-4796
General Phone: (561) 862-4327
General Fax: (561) 439-8210
General/National Adv. E-mail: beachcomber@pbcc.edu.campus
Classified Equipment»
Personnel: Pam Jarret (Pub.)

LAKELAND

FLORIDA SOUTHERN COLLEGE

Street address 1: 111 Lake Hollingsworth Dr
Street address 3: Lakeland
Street address state: FL
Zip/Postal code: 33801-5607
Country: USA
Mailing address: 111 Lake Hollingsworth Dr
Mailing city: Lakeland
Mailing state: FL
Mailing zip: 33801-5698
General Phone: (863) 680-4155
General Fax: (863) 680-6244
Display Adv. E-mail: mtrice@flsouthern.edu
Editorial e-mail: fscsouthern@gmail.com
Primary Website: www.fscsouthern.com
Published: Fri'Other
Published Other: every other week
Avg Free Circ: 1200
Classified Equipment»
Personnel: Michael Trice (Advisor)

SOUTHEASTERN UNIVERSITY

Street address 1: 1000 Longfellow Blvd
Street address 3: Lakeland
Street address state: FL
Zip/Postal code: 33801-6034
Country: USA
Mailing address: 1000 Longfellow Blvd
Mailing city: Lakeland
Mailing state: FL
Mailing zip: 33801-6034
General Phone: (863) 667-5000
General Fax: (863) 667-5200
General/National Adv. E-mail: thetimes@seuniversity.edu
Primary Website: www.seuniversity.edu
Classified Equipment»
Personnel: Chad Neuman (Advisor)

SOUTHEASTERN UNIVERSRITY

Street address 1: 1000 Longfellow Blvd
Street address 3: Lakeland
Street address state: FL
Zip/Postal code: 33801-6034
Country: USA
Mailing address: 1000 Longfellow Blvd
Mailing city: Lakeland
Mailing state: FL
Mailing zip: 33801-6034
General Phone: 8005008760
Primary Website: www.seu.edu
Published: Mthly
Classified Equipment»

LAKE SUMTER CMTY. COLLEGE

Street address 1: 9501 US Highway 441
Street address 3: Leesburg
Street address state: FL
Zip/Postal code: 34788-3950
Country: USA
Mailing address: 9501 US Highway 441
Mailing city: Leesburg
Mailing state: FL
Mailing zip: 34788-3950
General Phone: (352) 323-3629
General Fax: (352) 435-5023
General/National Adv. E-mail: anglern@lscc.edu; angler4always@yahoo.com
Primary Website: www.lscc.edu
Delivery Methods: Racks
Commercial printers: Y
Classified Equipment»
Personnel: Heather Elmatti (Advisor); Gina Mussatti (Ed.)

FLORIDA INSTITUTE OF TECHNOLOGY

Street address 1: 150 W University Blvd
Street address 3: Melbourne
Street address state: FL
Zip/Postal code: 32901-6982
Country: USA
Mailing address: 150 W University Blvd Ofc
Mailing city: Melbourne
Mailing state: FL
Mailing zip: 32901-6975
General Phone: (321) 674-8024
General Fax: (321) 674-8017
General/National Adv. E-mail: crimson@fit.edu
Editorial e-mail: crimson@fit.edu
Primary Website: http://crimson@fit.edu
Year Established: 1967
Delivery Methods: Racks
Classified Equipment»
Personnel: Ted Petersen (Adviser); Drew Lacy (Editor-in-Chief)

FLORIDA INTERNATIONAL UNIV.

Street address 1: University Park Campus, 11200 SW 8th St, Graham Ctr, Ste 210
Street address 3: Miami
Street address state: FL
Zip/Postal code: 33174-
Country: USA
Mailing address: University Park Campus, 11200 SW 8th St., Graham Ctr., Ste. 210
Mailing city: Miami
Mailing state: FL
Mailing zip: 33174-2516
General Phone: (305) 348-6993
General Fax: (305) 348-2712
General/National Adv. E-mail: beacon@fiu.edu
Primary Website: fiusm.com
Classified Equipment»
Personnel: Robert jaross (Advisor); Tatiana Cantillo (Bus. Mgr.); Chris Necuze (Ed. in Chief); Jessica Maya (Prodn. Mgr.)

MIAMI DADE COLLEGE

Street address 1: 11380 NW 27th Ave
Street address 2: Rm 4209
Street address 3: Miami
Street address state: FL
Zip/Postal code: 33167-3418
Country: USA
Mailing address: 11380 NW 27th Ave., Rm. 4209
Mailing city: Miami
Mailing state: FL
Mailing zip: 33167
General Phone: (305) 237-1255
General/National Adv. E-mail: mbarco@mdc.edu
Display Adv. E-mail: thereporteradvertising@gmail.com
Primary Website: http://www.mdc.edu/main/thereporter/archive/vol02-02/
Year Established: 2010
Advertising (Open Inch Rate) Weekday/Saturday: http://www.mdc.edu/main/images/The%20Reporter%20MEDIA%20KIT%20NEW%20(1)_tcm6-89417.pdf
Published: Bi-Mthly
Avg Free Circ: 10250
Classified Equipment»
Personnel: Manolo Barco (Advisor)

MIAMI GARDENS

FLORIDA MEMORIAL COLLEGE

Street address 1: 15800 NW 42nd Ave
Street address 3: Miami Gardens
Street address state: FL
Zip/Postal code: 33054-6155
Country: USA
Mailing address: 15800 NW 42nd Ave.
Mailing city: Miami Gardens
Mailing state: FL
Mailing zip: 33054
General Phone: (305) 626-3103
General Fax: (305) 626-3102
General/National Adv. E-mail: lionstal@fmuniv.edu
Primary Website: www.fmuniv.edu
Classified Equipment»
Personnel: Nathanael Paul (Ed.)

MIAMI SHORES

BARRY UNIV.

Street address 1: 11300 NE 2nd Ave
Street address 3: Miami Shores
Street address state: FL
Zip/Postal code: 33161-6628
Country: USA
Mailing address: 11300 NE 2nd Ave
Mailing city: Miami Shores
Mailing state: FL
Mailing zip: 33161-6695
General Phone: (305) 899-3093
General Fax: (305) 899-4744

General/National Adv. E-mail: buccaneer@mail.barry.edu
Primary Website: http://student.barry.edu/buccaneer
Classified Equipment»
Personnel: Susannah Nesmith (Advisor); Amor Tagan (Adv. Dir.); Samantha Stanton (Ed. in Chief)

OCALA

CENTRAL FLORIDA CMTY. COLLEGE

Street address 1: 3001 SW College Rd
Street address 3: Ocala
Street address state: FL
Zip/Postal code: 34474-4415
Country: USA
Mailing address: 3001 SW College Rd.
Mailing city: Ocala
Mailing state: FL
Mailing zip: 34474
General Phone: (352) 873-5800
General Fax: (352) 291-4450
General/National Adv. E-mail: patpress@cf.edu
Primary Website: patpress.cf.edu; www.cfcc.cc.fl.us
Classified Equipment»
Personnel: Rob Marino (Advisor)

OPA LOCKA

ST. THOMAS UNIV.

Street address 1: 16401 NW 37th Ave
Street address 3: Opa Locka
Street address state: FL
Zip/Postal code: 33054-6313
Country: USA
Mailing address: 16401 NW 37th Ave
Mailing city: Opa Locka
Mailing state: FL
Mailing zip: 33054-6313
General Phone: (305) 628-6674
General Fax: (305) 443-1210
General/National Adv. E-mail: basic@stu.edu
Primary Website: www.stu.edu
Classified Equipment»
Personnel: Sharon Brehm (Ed.)

UNIV. OF CENTRAL FLORIDA

Street address 1: 11825 High Tech Ave
Street address 2: Ste 100
Street address 3: Orlando
Street address state: FL
Zip/Postal code: 32817-8474
Country: USA
Mailing address: 11825 High Tech Ave. Ste. 100
Mailing city: Orlando
Mailing state: FL
Mailing zip: 32817
General Phone: (407) 447-4555
General Fax: (407) 447-4556
General/National Adv. E-mail: sales@ucfnews.com
Primary Website: www.centralfloridafuture.com
Year Established: 1968
Classified Equipment»
Personnel: Heissam Jebailey (Pub.); Brian Linden (Gen. Mgr.); Trisha Irwin (Office. Mgr.); Ray Bush (Adv. Mgr.)

VALENCIA CMTY. COLLEGE

Street address 1: 1800 S Kirkman Rd
Street address 3: Orlando
Street address state: FL
Zip/Postal code: 32811-2302
Country: USA
Mailing address: 1800 S Kirkman Rd
Mailing city: Orlando
Mailing state: FL
Mailing zip: 32811-2302
General Phone: (407) 582-1572
Classified Equipment»
Personnel: Ken Carpenter (Advisor)

PENSACOLA JUNIOR COLLEGE

Street address 1: 1000 College Blvd
Street address 2: Bldg 96
Street address 3: Pensacola
Street address state: FL
Zip/Postal code: 32504-8910
Country: USA
Mailing address: 1000 College Blvd Bldg 96
Mailing city: Pensacola
Mailing state: FL
Mailing zip: 32504-8910
General Phone: (850) 484-1458
General Fax: (850) 484-1149
General/National Adv. E-mail: corsair@pjc.edu
Primary Website: www.ecorsair.com
Year Established: 1949
Classified Equipment»
Personnel: Christina Drain (Advisor); Audrey Davis (Adv. Mgr.); Rose Jansen (Mktg. Mgr.)

UNIV. OF WEST FLORIDA

Street address 1: 11000 University Pkwy
Street address 2: Comm Arts 36
Street address 3: Pensacola
Street address state: FL
Zip/Postal code: 32514-5732
Country: USA
Mailing address: 11000 University Pkwy Comm Arts 36
Mailing city: Pensacola
Mailing state: FL
Mailing zip: 32514-5732
General Phone: (850) 474-2193
General/National Adv. E-mail: mdp17@students.uwf.edu
Classified Equipment»

SAINT AUGUSTINE

FLAGLER COLLEGE

Street address 1: PO Box 1027
Street address 3: Saint Augustine
Street address state: FL
Zip/Postal code: 32085-1027
Country: USA
Mailing address: PO Box 1027
Mailing city: Saint Augustine
Mailing state: FL
Mailing zip: 32085-1027
General Phone: (904) 819-6333
General Fax: (904) 826-3224
General/National Adv. E-mail: gargoyle@flagler.edu
Primary Website: gargoyle.flagler.edu
Year Established: 1968
Classified Equipment»
Personnel: Brain Thomson (Advisor)

SAINT LEO

SAINT LEO UNIVERSITY

Street address 1: 33701 State Road 52
Street address 2: Mc 2127, Dept. of English
Street address 3: Saint Leo
Street address state: FL
Zip/Postal code: 33574-9700
Country: USA
Mailing address: 33701 State Road 52
Mailing city: Saint Leo
Mailing state: FL
Mailing zip: 33574-9701
General Phone: (352) 588-7424
General Fax: (352) 588-8300
General/National Adv. E-mail: thelionspridenewspaper@gmail.com
Display Adv. E-mail: thelionspridenewspaper@gmail.com
Editorial e-mail: thelionspridenewspaper@gmail.com
Primary Website: https://prideonlinedotnet.wordpress.com/
Published: Fri
Classified Equipment»
Personnel: Valerie Kasper (Advisor); Cassidy Whitaker (Editor-in-Chief)

SAINT PETERSBURG

THE CURRENT - ECKERD COLLEGE

Street address 1: 4200 54th Ave S
Street address 3: Saint Petersburg
Street address state: FL
Zip/Postal code: 33711-4744
Country: USA
Mailing address: 4200 54th Ave S
Mailing city: Saint Petersburg
Mailing state: FL
Mailing zip: 33711-4700
General Phone: 610 4317931
General Fax: 610 4317931
Advertising Phone: 610 4317931
Advertising Fax: 610 4317931
Editorail Phone: 610 4317931
Editorial Fax: 610 4317931
General/National Adv. E-mail: thecurrent@eckerd.edu
Display Adv. E-mail: currentads@eckerd.edu
Editorial e-mail: danielsa1@mac.com
Primary Website: www.theonlinecurrent.com
Year Established: 2009
Delivery Methods: Mail
Commercial printers: Y
Classified Equipment»
Personnel: Ashley Daniels (Editor-in-Chief); Max Martinez (Managing Editor)

TALLAHASSEE

FLORIDA A&M UNIV.

Street address 1: 510 Orr Dr, Ste 3081
Street address 3: Tallahassee
Street address state: FL
Zip/Postal code: 32307-0001
Country: USA
Mailing address: 510 Orr Dr Ste 3081
Mailing city: Tallahassee
Mailing state: FL
Mailing zip: 32307-0001
General Phone: (850) 599-3159
General Fax: (850) 561-2570
General/National Adv. E-mail: thefamuanec@gmail.com
Display Adv. E-mail: famuanads@hotmail.com
Primary Website: www.thefamuan.com
Classified Equipment»
Personnel: Andrew Skeritt (Advisor); Erica Butler (Ed. in Chief)

FSVIEW & FLORIDA FLAMBEAU

Street address 1: 954 W Brevard St
Street address 3: Tallahassee
Street address state: FL
Zip/Postal code: 32304-7709
Country: USA
Mailing address: 277 N Magnolia Dr
Mailing city: Tallahassee
Mailing state: FL
Mailing zip: 32301-2664
General Phone: 850-561-1600
General Fax: 850-574-6578
Advertising Phone: 8505611600
Advertising Fax: 8505746578
Editorail Phone: 850-561-1606
General/National Adv. E-mail: @tallahassee.com
Display Adv. E-mail: eleporin@tallahassee.com
Editorial e-mail: eleporin@tallahassee.com
Primary Website: www.fsunews.com
Year Established: 1915
Special Editions: All FSU Home Games Football Previews Student Living Guides 3X a year
Delivery Methods: Mail`Newsstand`Racks
Commercial printers: N
Classified Equipment»
Personnel: Eliza LePorin (General Manager); Justin Dyke (Content Supervisor); Bailey Shertizinger (Editor-in-Chief); Chris Lewis (Gen. Mgr.); Liz Cox (Ed. In Chief); Arriale Douglas (Prodn. Mgr.)
Parent company (for newspapers): Tallahassee Democrat

TALLAHASSEE CMTY. COLLEGE

Street address 1: 444 Appleyard Dr
Street address 3: Tallahassee
Street address state: FL
Zip/Postal code: 32304-2815
Country: USA
Mailing address: 444 Appleyard Dr
Mailing city: Tallahassee
Mailing state: FL
Mailing zip: 32304-2895
General Phone: (850) 201-8035
General Fax: (850) 201-8427
Advertising Phone: (850) 201-8425
Editorail Phone: (850) 201-8525
General/National Adv. E-mail: talon@tcc.fl.edu
Display Adv. E-mail: talon@tcc.fl.edu
Editorial e-mail: talon@tcc.fl.edu
Primary Website: www.thetcctalon.com
Year Established: 1968
Published: Bi-Mthly
Avg Free Circ: 3000
Classified Equipment»
Personnel: Dana Peck (Advisor)

UNIV. OF SOUTH FLORIDA

Street address 1: 4202 E Fowler Ave
Street address 2: Svc 2
Street address 3: Tampa
Street address state: FL
Zip/Postal code: 33620-9951
Country: USA
Mailing address: 4202 E Fowler Ave Svc 2
Mailing city: Tampa
Mailing state: FL
Mailing zip: 33620-9951
General Phone: (813) 974-5190
General Fax: (813) 974-4887
Advertising Phone: (813) 974-6254
Display Adv. E-mail: ads@usforacle.com
Editorial e-mail: oraccleeditor@gmail.com
Primary Website: www.usforacle.com
Year Established: 1966
Delivery Methods: Racks
Published: Mon`Thur
Avg Free Circ: 8000
Classified Equipment»
Personnel: Jay Lawrence (Advisor); Anastasia Dawson (Ed. in chief); Jimmy Geurts (Mng. Ed.)

UNIV. OF TAMPA

Street address 1: Rm 211, Vaughn Ctr, 401 W Kennedy Blvd
Street address 3: Tampa
Street address state: FL
Zip/Postal code: 33606-
Country: USA
Mailing address: 401 W Kennedy Blvd
Mailing city: Tampa
Mailing state: FL
Mailing zip: 33606-1490
General Phone: (813) 257-3636
General Fax: (813) 253-6207
General/National Adv. E-mail: minaret@ut.edu; ut.minaret@gmail.com
Primary Website: www.theminaretonline.com
Classified Equipment»
Personnel: Stephanie Tripp (Advisor); Zoe LeCain (Adv. Mgr.); Charlie Hambos (Ed. in Chief); Kyle Bennett (Sports Ed.)

PALM BEACH ATLANTIC UNIVERSITY

Street address 1: 901 S Flagler Dr
Street address 3: West Palm Beach
Street address state: FL
Zip/Postal code: 33401-6505
Country: USA
Mailing address: PO Box 24708
Mailing city: West Palm Beach
Mailing state: FL
Mailing zip: 33416-4708
General Phone: (561) 803-2566
General Fax: (561) 803-2577
General/National Adv. E-mail: beacon@pba.edu
Primary Website: readmybeacon.com
Classified Equipment»
Personnel: John Sizemore (Advisor/Exec. Ed.)

WINTER HAVEN

POLK CMTY. COLLEGE

Street address 1: 999 Avenue H NE
Street address 3: Winter Haven
Street address state: FL
Zip/Postal code: 33881-4256
Country: USA
Mailing address: 999 Avenue H NE
Mailing city: Winter Haven
Mailing state: FL

Mailing zip: 33881-4256
General Phone: (863) 297-1000
General Fax: (863) 297-1037
Classified Equipment»
Personnel: Patrick Jones (Advisor)

WINTER PARK

THE SANDSPUR

Street address 1: 1000 Holt Ave
Street address 2: # 2742
Street address 3: Winter Park
Street address state: FL
Zip/Postal code: 32789-4499
Country: USA
Mailing address: 1000 Holt Ave # 2742
Mailing city: Winter Park
Mailing state: FL
Mailing zip: 32789-4499
General Phone: (407) 646-2696
Advertising Phone: (407) 646-2695
Display Adv. E-mail: advertising@thesandspur.org
Editorial e-mail: staff@thesandspur.org
Primary Website: www.thesandspur.org
Year Established: 1894
Published: Thur
Avg Paid Circ: 0
Avg Free Circ: 1200
Classified Equipment»

YBOR CITY

HILLSBOROUGH CMTY. COLLEGE

Street address 1: 2112 N 15th St
Street address 3: Ybor City
Street address state: FL
Zip/Postal code: 33605-3648
Country: USA
Mailing address: 2112 N. 15th Street
Mailing city: Ybor City
Mailing state: FL
Mailing zip: 33605
General Phone: (813) 227-7048
General Fax: (813) 253-7760
Primary Website: www.hccfl.edu
Classified Equipment»
Personnel: Valerie Zell (Advisor)

GEORGIA

DARTON COLLEGE

Street address 1: 2400 Gillionville Rd
Street address 3: Albany
Street address state: GA
Zip/Postal code: 31707-3023
Country: USA
Mailing address: 2400 Gillionville Rd
Mailing city: Albany
Mailing state: GA
Mailing zip: 31707-3098
General Phone: (229) 317-6808
Classified Equipment»
Personnel: Roger Marietta (Advisor)

AMERICUS

GEORGIA SOUTHWESTERN STATE UNIV.

Street address 1: 800 Georgia Southwestern State University Dr
Street address 3: Americus
Street address state: GA
Zip/Postal code: 31709
Country: USA
Mailing address: 800 Georgia Southwestern State University Dr.
Mailing city: Americus
Mailing state: GA
Mailing zip: 31709
General Phone: (229) 931-2003
General Fax: (229) 931-2059
General/National Adv. E-mail: gswpaper@yahoo.com; gswpaper@canes.gsw.edu
Primary Website: www.gsw.edu
Classified Equipment»
Personnel: Josh Curtin (Advisor); Emily Immke (Bus. Mgr.); Sidney Davis (Ed. in Chief)

UNIV. OF GEORGIA

Street address 1: 540 Baxter St
Street address 3: Athens
Street address state: GA
Zip/Postal code: 30605-1106
Country: USA
Mailing address: 540 Baxter St
Mailing city: Athens
Mailing state: GA
Mailing zip: 30605-1106
General Phone: (706) 433-3000
General Fax: (706) 433-3033
Advertising Phone: (706) 433-3012
Editorall Phone: (706) 433-3002
General/National Adv. E-mail: news@randb.com
Primary Website: www.redandblack.com
Classified Equipment»
Personnel: Ed Morales (Editorial Adviser); Natalie McClure (General Manager)

ATLANTA UNIVERSITY CENTER

Street address 1: 117 Vine St SW
Street address 2: Fl 1
Street address 3: Atlanta
Street address state: GA
Zip/Postal code: 30314-4205
Country: USA
Mailing address: PO Box 3191
Mailing city: Atlanta
Mailing state: GA
Mailing zip: 30302-3191
General Phone: (404) 523-6136
General/National Adv. E-mail: aucdigestmail@aol.com
Primary Website: www.aucdigest.com
Year Established: 1973
Advertising (Open Inch Rate) Weekday/Saturday: see rates/aucdigest.com/nationalrates
Published: Thur
Classified Equipment»
Personnel: Lo Jelks (Ed.)
Parent company (for newspapers): Collegiate Broadcasting Group, Inc.

CLARK ATLANTA UNIV.

Street address 1: 223 James P Brawley Dr SW
Street address 3: Atlanta
Street address state: GA
Zip/Postal code: 30314-4358
Country: USA
Mailing address: PO Box 1523
Mailing city: Atlanta
Mailing state: GA
Mailing zip: 30301-1523
General Phone: (404) 880-6219
General/National Adv. E-mail: caunews05@yahoo.com
Delivery Methods: Mail
Classified Equipment»
Personnel: James McJunkins (Advisor)

EMORY UNIV.

Street address 1: 605 Asbury Cir
Street address 3: Atlanta
Street address state: GA
Zip/Postal code: 30322-1006
Country: USA
Mailing address: P.O. Box W
Mailing city: Atlanta
Mailing state: GA
Mailing zip: 30322-1006
General Phone: (404) 727-0279
Advertising Phone: (404) 727-3613
Editorall Phone: (404) 727-6178
General/National Adv. E-mail: emorywheelexec@gmail.com
Editorial e-mail: emorywheelexec@gmail.com
Primary Website: www.emorywheel.com
Year Established: 1919
Published: Tues`Fri
Classified Equipment»
Personnel: Priyanka Krishnamurthy (Ed.); Sonam Vashi (Exec. Ed.); Lizzie Howell (Managing Ed.)

GEORGIA INST. OF TECHNOLOGY

Street address 1: 353 Ferst Dr
Street address 2: Rm 137
Street address 3: Atlanta
Street address state: GA
Zip/Postal code: 30318-5602
Country: USA
Mailing address: 353 Ferst Dr Rm 137
Mailing city: Atlanta
Mailing state: GA
Mailing zip: 30332-0001
General Phone: (404) 894-2830
General Fax: (404) 894-1650
General/National Adv. E-mail: editor@technique.gatech.edu
Primary Website: www.nique.net
Classified Equipment»
Personnel: Mac Pitts (Advisor); Emily Chambers (Ed. in Chief); Jonathan Saethang (Mng. Ed.); Hahnming Lee (Bus. Mgr.)

GEORGIA STATE UNIVERSITY

Street address 1: 310 Student Center East
Street address 2: 55 Gilmer St SE
Street address 3: Atlanta
Street address state: GA
Zip/Postal code: 30303
Country: USA
Mailing address: 310 Student Center East
Mailing city: Atlanta
Mailing state: GA
Mailing zip: 30303-3011
General Phone: (404) 413-1617(404) 413-1868
General Fax: 404-413-1868
Advertising Phone: 404-413-1869
Advertising Fax: 404-413-1868
Editorall Phone: 404-413-1617
General/National Adv. E-mail: signaleditor@gmail.com
Display Adv. E-mail: whenley@gsu.edu
Editorial e-mail: signaleditor@gmail.com
Primary Website: www.georgiastatesignal.com
Year Established: 1933
Published: Tues
Published Other: (Fall & Spring with summer magazine)
Avg Free Circ: 4000
Classified Equipment»
Personnel: Bryce McNeil (Director, Student Media); Adam Duffy (Editor-in-Chief); Wakesha Henley (Business Coordinator); Zoana Price (Student Media Advisor, Perimeter College)

MOREHOUSE COLLEGE

Street address 1: 830 Westview Dr SW
Street address 3: Atlanta
Street address state: GA
Zip/Postal code: 30314-3773
Country: USA
Mailing address: 830 Westview Dr SW
Mailing city: Atlanta
Mailing state: GA
Mailing zip: 30314-3776
General Phone: (404) 681-2800
General/National Adv. E-mail: mtiger@morehouse.edu
Primary Website: www.morehouse.edu/themaroontiger/
Classified Equipment»
Personnel: Edward T. Mitchell (Ed. in Chief); Donovan Ramsey (Mng. Ed.)

AUGUSTA

AUGUSTA STATE UNIV.

Street address 1: 2500 Walton Way
Street address 3: Augusta
Street address state: GA
Zip/Postal code: 30904-4562
Country: USA
Mailing address: 2500 Walton Way
Mailing city: Augusta
Mailing state: GA
Mailing zip: 30904-2200
General Phone: (706) 737-1600
General Fax: (706) 729-2247
General/National Adv. E-mail: bellringerproduction@gmail.com
Primary Website: www.asubellringer.com
Delivery Methods: Racks
Classified Equipment»
Personnel: Matthew Bosisio (Advisor); Kara Mauldin (Ed. in Chief); Stacie Cooper (Prodn. Mgr.); Dee Taylor (Adv. Mgr.)

BROOKHAVEN

OGLETHORPE UNIVERSITY

Street address 1: 4484 Peachtree Rd NE
Street address 3: Brookhaven
Street address state: GA
Zip/Postal code: 30319-2797
Country: USA
Mailing address: 4484 Peachtree Rd. NE
Mailing city: Atlanta
Mailing state: GA
Mailing zip: 30319
General Phone: (404) 364-8425
General Fax: (404) 364-8442
General/National Adv. E-mail: stormypetrel@oglethorpe.edu
Primary Website: 3443 Somerset Trace
Published: Mthly
Classified Equipment»
Personnel: Tali Schroeder (Ed.)

CARROLLTON

STATE UNIV. OF WEST GEORGIA

Street address 1: 1601 Maple St
Street address 3: Carrollton
Street address state: GA
Zip/Postal code: 30118-0001
Country: USA
Mailing address: 1601 Maple St
Mailing city: Carrollton
Mailing state: GA
Mailing zip: 30118-0002
General Phone: (678) 839-5000
Primary Website: www.westga.edu
Classified Equipment»
Personnel: Stephanie Smith (Adv. Mgr.)

CLARKSTON

GEORGIA PERIMETER COLLEGE

Street address 1: 555 N Indian Creek Dr
Street address 3: Clarkston
Street address state: GA
Zip/Postal code: 30021-2361
Country: USA
Mailing address: 555 N Indian Creek Dr
Mailing city: Clarkston
Mailing state: GA
Mailing zip: 30021-2361
General Phone: (678)-891-3381
General Fax: (404) 298-3882
General/National Adv. E-mail: gpccollegian@gmail.com
Primary Website: www.gpc.edu
Year Established: 1986
Classified Equipment»
Personnel: Alice Murray (Bus. Mgr.); Nathan Guest (Ed. in Chief)

COLUMBUS STATE UNIV.

Street address 1: 4225 University Ave
Street address 3: Columbus
Street address state: GA
Zip/Postal code: 31907-5679
Country: USA
Mailing address: 4225 University Ave
Mailing city: Columbus
Mailing state: GA
Mailing zip: 31907-5645
General Phone: (706) 562-1494
General Fax: (706) 568-2434
General/National Adv. E-mail: csusaber@yahoo.com; csusaber@gmail.com; saber@colstate.edu
Primary Website: thesaber.wixsite.com/thesaber

Year Established: 1958
Published: Other
Classified Equipment»
Personnel: Linda Reynold (Advisor)

DAHLONEGA

NORTH GEORGIA COLLEGE

Street address 1: PO Box 5432
Street address 3: Dahlonega
Street address state: GA
Zip/Postal code: 30597-0001
Country: USA
Mailing address: PO Box 5432
Mailing city: Dahlonega
Mailing state: GA
Mailing zip: 30597-0001
General Phone: (706) 864-1468
General Fax: (706) 864-1485
General/National Adv. E-mail: voice@ngcsu.edu
Primary Website: www.ngcsu.edu/voice
Classified Equipment»
Personnel: Debbie Martin (Ed.)

AGNES SCOTT COLLEGE

Street address 1: 141 E College Ave
Street address 3: Decatur
Street address state: GA
Zip/Postal code: 30030-3770
Country: USA
Mailing address: 141 E College Ave
Mailing city: Decatur
Mailing state: GA
Mailing zip: 30030-3797
General Phone: (404) 471-6000
Classified Equipment»
Personnel: Jeniffer Owen (Dir. Commun.); Josie Hoilman (Ed.)

FORT VALLEY

FT. VALLEY STATE UNIV.

Street address 1: 1005 State University Dr
Street address 3: Fort Valley
Street address state: GA
Zip/Postal code: 31030-4313
Country: USA
Mailing address: 121 Huntington Chase Cir
Mailing city: Warner Robins
Mailing state: GA
Mailing zip: 31088-2675
General Phone: (478) 825-6910
General Fax: (478) 825-6140
General/National Adv. E-mail: peachite@fvsu.edu.
Classified Equipment»
Personnel: Valerie White (Advisor); Mick-Aela Nobles (Ed.)

BRENAU UNIV.

Street address 1: 500 Washington St SE
Street address 3: Gainesville
Street address state: GA
Zip/Postal code: 30501-3628
Country: USA
Mailing address: 500 Washington St SE
Mailing city: Gainesville
Mailing state: GA
Mailing zip: 30501-3628
General Phone: (770) 538-4762
General Fax: (770) 538-4558
General/National Adv. E-mail: alchemist@brenau.edu
Classified Equipment»
Personnel: Nathan R. Goss (Coord., Admissions)

KENNESAW

KENNESAW STATE UNIVERSITY

Street address 1: 395 Cobb Ave NW
Street address 2: Ste 274 # 501
Street address 3: Kennesaw
Street address state: GA
Zip/Postal code: 30144-5660
Country: USA
Mailing address: 395 Cobb Ave NW
Mailing city: Kennesaw
Mailing state: GA
Mailing zip: 30144-5588
General Phone: (470) 578-5470
General Fax: (470) 578-9165
General/National Adv. E-mail: sentinel@ksumedia.com
Display Adv. E-mail: marketingmgr@ksumedia.com
Editorial e-mail: eic@ksusentinel.com
Primary Website: www.ksusentinel.com
Year Established: 1967
Published: Tues
Avg Free Circ: 5000
Classified Equipment»
Personnel: Ed Bonza (Advisor)

LAGRANGE

LAGRANGE COLLEGE

Street address 1: 601 Broad St
Street address 2: # 1165
Street address 3: Lagrange
Street address state: GA
Zip/Postal code: 30240-2955
Country: USA
Mailing address: 601 Broad St # 1165
Mailing city: Lagrange
Mailing state: GA
Mailing zip: 30240-2955
General Phone: (706) 880-8020
General Fax: (706) 880-8920
General/National Adv. E-mail: hilltopnews@laagrange.edu
Classified Equipment»
Personnel: John Tures (Advisor); Kate Bush (Co-Ed.); Chris Nylund (Co-Ed.)

LOOKOUT MOUNTAIN

COVENANT COLLEGE

Street address 1: 14049 Scenic Hwy
Street address 3: Lookout Mountain
Street address state: GA
Zip/Postal code: 30750-4100
Country: USA
Mailing address: 14049 Scenic Hwy
Mailing city: Lookout Mountain
Mailing state: GA
Mailing zip: 30750-4100
General Phone: (706) 820-1560
General Fax: (706) 820-0672
General/National Adv. E-mail: bagpipe@covenant.edu
Primary Website: www.bagpipeonline.com
Classified Equipment»
Personnel: Cliff Foreman (Faculty Advisor); Kaitlin Fender (Ed. in Chief)

MACON STATE COLLEGE

Street address 1: 100 University Pkwy
Street address 3: Macon
Street address state: GA
Zip/Postal code: 31206-5100
Country: USA
Mailing address: 100 College Station Dr
Mailing city: Macon
Mailing state: GA
Mailing zip: 31206-5145
General Phone: (478) 471-2700
General Fax: (478) 757-2626
General/National Adv. E-mail: mscmatrix@maconstate.edu; statement@maconstate.edu
Primary Website: www.maconstatement.com
Classified Equipment»
Personnel: Ray Lightner (Advisor); Glen Stone (Ed. in Chief)

MERCER UNIV.

Street address 1: PO Box 72728
Street address 3: Macon
Street address state: GA
Zip/Postal code: 31207-5272
Country: USA
Mailing address: PO Box 72728
Mailing city: Macon
Mailing state: GA
Mailing zip: 31207-5272
General Phone: (478) 301-2871
General Fax: (478) 301-2977
Classified Equipment»
Personnel: Lee Greenway (Advisor)

WESLEYAN COLLEGE

Street address 1: 4760 Forsyth Rd
Street address 3: Macon
Street address state: GA
Zip/Postal code: 31210-4407
Country: USA
Mailing address: 4760 Forsyth Rd
Mailing city: Macon
Mailing state: GA
Mailing zip: 31210-4462
General Phone: (478) 757-5100
General Fax: (478) 757-4027
General/National Adv. E-mail: pioneer@wesleyancollege.edu
Primary Website: www.wesleyancollege.edu
Classified Equipment»
Personnel: Dana Amihere (Ed.)

MILLEDGEVILLE

GEORGIA COLLEGE & STATE UNIV.

Street address 1: 231 W Hancock St
Street address 3: Milledgeville
Street address state: GA
Zip/Postal code: 31061-3375
Country: USA
Mailing address: 231 W. Hancock St.
Mailing city: Milledgeville
Mailing state: GA
Mailing zip: 31061
General Phone: (478) 445-4511
General Fax: (478) 445-2559
General/National Adv. E-mail: colonnade@gcsu.edu
Primary Website: www.gcsunade.com
Classified Equipment»
Personnel: Macon McGinley (Advisor); Claire Dykes (Ed. in Chief); Amanda Boddy (News Ed.); Elise Colcord (Adv. Mgr.)

MORROW

CLAYTON STATE UNIV.

Street address 1: 2000 Clayton State Blvd
Street address 3: Morrow
Street address state: GA
Zip/Postal code: 30260-1250
Country: USA
Mailing address: 2000 Clayton State Blvd
Mailing city: Morrow
Mailing state: GA
Mailing zip: 30260-1250
General Phone: (678) 466-5436
General Fax: (678) 466-5470
General/National Adv. E-mail: info@thebenttree.org
Primary Website: www.thebenttree.org
Published: Mthly
Classified Equipment»
Personnel: Randy Clark (Advisor); Sunitha Caton (Ed.)

MOUNT BERRY

BERRY COLLEGE

Street address 1: 2277 Martha Berry Hwy NW
Street address 3: Mount Berry
Street address state: GA
Zip/Postal code: 30149-9707
Country: USA
Mailing address: 2277 Martha Berry Hwy NW
Mailing city: Mount Berry
Mailing state: GA
Mailing zip: 30149-9707
General Phone: (706) 238-7871
General Fax: (706) 238-5846
General/National Adv. E-mail: campus_carrier@berry.edu
Classified Equipment»
Personnel: Kevin Kleine (Advisor); Jeanne Mathews (Asst. Vice Pres., PR); Rick Woodall (Dir., News/Editorial Servs.)

OAKWOOD

GAINESVILLE COLLEGE

Street address 1: 3820 Mundy Mill Rd
Street address 3: Oakwood
Street address state: GA
Zip/Postal code: 30566-3414
Country: USA
Mailing address: PO Box 1358
Mailing city: Gainesville
Mailing state: GA
Mailing zip: 30503-1358
General Phone: (678) 717-3820
General Fax: (678) 717-3832
General/National Adv. E-mail: compass@gsc.edu
Display Adv. E-mail: compass@gsc.edu
Editorial e-mail: compass@gsc.edu
Primary Website: www.gsccompass.org
Published: Mthly
Avg Free Circ: 1000
Classified Equipment»
Personnel: Merrill Morris (Advisor); Audrey Williams (Editor in Chief); Brent VanFleet (Associate Editor)

ROME

GEORGIA HIGHLANDS COLLEGE

Street address 1: 3175 Cedartown Hwy SE
Street address 3: Rome
Street address state: GA
Zip/Postal code: 30161-3897
Country: USA
Mailing address: 3175 Cedartown Highway
Mailing city: Rome
Mailing state: GA
Mailing zip: 30161
General Phone: (706) 295-6361
General Fax: (706) 295-6610
Editorial Fax: (678) 872-8040
General/National Adv. E-mail: 6mpost@highlands.edu
Display Adv. E-mail: ads6MP@student.highlands.edu
Primary Website: www.sixmilepost.com
Classified Equipment»
Personnel: Kristie Kemper (Advisor); Nick Godfrey (Ed.)

SHORTER COLLEGE

Street address 1: 315 Shorter Ave SW
Street address 3: Rome
Street address state: GA
Zip/Postal code: 30165-4267
Country: USA
Mailing address: 315 Shorter Ave SW
Mailing city: Rome
Mailing state: GA
Mailing zip: 30165-4267
General Phone: (706) 233-7208
General Fax: (706) 236-1515
General/National Adv. E-mail: the_periscope@hotmail.com
Primary Website: www.theperiscope.org
Classified Equipment»
Personnel: Ashley Ottinger (Ed. in chief)

ARMSTRONG ATLANTIC STATE UNIV.

Street address 1: Memorial College Ctr, 11935 Abercorn St, Rm 202
Street address 3: Savannah
Street address state: GA
Country: USA
Mailing address: Memorial College Ctr., 11935 Abercorn St., Rm. 202
Mailing city: Savannah
Mailing state: GA
Mailing zip: 31419-1909
General Phone: (912) 344-3252
General Fax: (912) 344-3475
General/National Adv. E-mail: inkwellnews@gmail.com
Primary Website: www.theinkwellonline.com
Classified Equipment»

Personnel: Tony Morris (Advisor); Kristin Alonso (Ed. in Chief)

SAVANNAH COLLEGE OF ART/ DESIGN

Street address 1: PO Box 3146
Street address 3: Savannah
Street address state: GA
Zip/Postal code: 31402-3146
Country: USA
Mailing address: PO Box 3146
Mailing city: Savannah
Mailing state: GA
Mailing zip: 31402-3146
General Phone: (912) 525-5500
General Fax: (912) 525-5506
General/National Adv. E-mail: district@scad.edu
Primary Website: www.scaddistrict.com
Classified Equipment»
Personnel: Aisha Michael (Circ./Classified Mgr.)

STATESBORO

GEORGIA SOUTHERN UNIV.

Street address 1: Williams Center Rm 2023
Street address 3: Statesboro
Street address state: GA
Zip/Postal code: 30460-0001
Country: USA
Mailing address: PO Box 8001
Mailing city: Statesboro
Mailing state: GA
Mailing zip: 30460-1000
General Phone: (912) 478-5246
General Fax: (912) 478-7113
Editorail Phone: (912) 478-5418
General/National Adv. E-mail: gaeditor@georgiasouthern.edu
Display Adv. E-mail: ads1@georgiasouthern.edu
Primary Website: Georgia Southern University GSU Student Media Box 8001
Year Established: 1927
Published: Tues`Thur
Classified Equipment»
Personnel: Jozsef Papp (Exec. Ed.)
Parent company (for newspapers): Student Media at Georgia Southern

THOMASVILLE

THOMAS COLLEGE

Street address 1: 1501 Millpond Rd
Street address 3: Thomasville
Street address state: GA
Zip/Postal code: 31792-7478
Country: USA
Mailing address: 1501 Millpond Rd
Mailing city: Thomasville
Mailing state: GA
Mailing zip: 31792-7636
General Phone: (229) 226-1621
General Fax: (229) 226-1653
Classified Equipment»
Personnel: Charity Nixon (Ed.)

TIFTON

ABRAHAM BALDWIN AGRI COLLEGE

Street address 1: 2802 Moore Hwy
Street address 3: Tifton
Street address state: GA
Zip/Postal code: 31793-5679
Country: USA
Mailing address: 2802 Moore Hwy
Mailing city: Tifton
Mailing state: GA
Mailing zip: 31793-5698
General Fax: (229) 391-4978
Advertising Fax: (229) 386-7158
General/National Adv. E-mail: stallion@stallion.abac.edu
Primary Website: www.thestalliononline.com
Classified Equipment»
Personnel: Eric Cash (Faculty Advisor)

TOCCOA FALLS

TOCCOA FALLS COLLEGE

Street address 1: 107 Kincaid Dr
Street address 3: Toccoa Falls
Street address state: GA
Zip/Postal code: 30598-9602
Country: USA
Mailing address: 107 Kincaid Dr
Mailing city: Toccoa Falls
Mailing state: GA
Mailing zip: 30598-9602
General Phone: (706) 886-7299
General Fax: (706) 886-0210
General/National Adv. E-mail: talon@tfc.edu
Primary Website: www.tfc.edu
Classified Equipment»
Personnel: Christine Brubaker (Ed. in Chief)

VALDOSTA

VALDOSTA STATE UNIV.

Street address 1: 1500 N Patterson St
Street address 3: Valdosta
Street address state: GA
Zip/Postal code: 31698-0100
Country: USA
Mailing address: 1500 N Patterson St
Mailing city: Valdosta
Mailing state: GA
Mailing zip: 31698-0001
General Phone: (229) 333-5686
General Fax: (229) 249-2618
General/National Adv. E-mail: spec@valdosta.edu
Primary Website: www.vsuspectator.com
Classified Equipment»
Personnel: Pat Miller (Advisor); John Pickworth (Adv. Mgr.); Desiree Thompson (Editor in Chief)

GEORGIA HEALTH SCIENCES UNIVERSITY (FORMERLY MEDICAL COLLEGE OF GEORGIA)

Street address state: GA
Country: USA
Mailing address: 1120 15th St
Mailing city: Augusta
Mailing state: GA
Mailing zip: 30912-0004
General Fax: (706) 721-6397
Editorail Phone: (706) 721-4410
Editorial e-mail: smcgowen@georgiahealth.edu
Primary Website: http://connection.georgiahealth.edu/
Delivery Methods: Racks
Commercial printers: Y
Classified Equipment»
Personnel: Stacey Hudson (Communications Coordinator Editor, The Connection (formerly the Beeper)); Sharron Walls (Ed.)

HAWAII

HILO

UNIV. OF HAWAII HILO

Street address 1: 200 W Kawili St, Campus Ctr 215
Street address 3: Hilo
Street address state: HI
Zip/Postal code: 96720
Country: USA
Mailing address: 200 W. Kawili St., Campus Ctr. 215
Mailing city: Hilo
Mailing state: HI
Mailing zip: 96720-4091
General Phone: (808) 974-7504
General Fax: (808) 974-7782
General/National Adv. E-mail: kalahea@hawaii.edu
Primary Website: www.uhh.hawaii.edu/news/kekalahea
Classified Equipment»
Personnel: Marc Burba (Advisor); Roxanne Yamane (Bus. Mgr.)

CHAMINADE UNIV.

Street address 1: 3140 Waialae Ave
Street address 3: Honolulu
Street address state: HI
Zip/Postal code: 96816-1510
Country: USA
Mailing address: 3140 Waialae Ave
Mailing city: Honolulu
Mailing state: HI
Mailing zip: 96816-1578
General Phone: (808) 739-4636
General Fax: (808) 735-4891
General/National Adv. E-mail: cuhpress@chaminade.edu
Primary Website: www.cuhnews.com; www.chaminade.edu
Classified Equipment»
Personnel: Ashlee Duenas (Ed.)

HAWAII PACIFIC UNIVERSITY

Street address 1: 1154 Fort Street Mall
Street address 2: Ste 312
Street address 3: Honolulu
Street address state: HI
Zip/Postal code: 96813-2712
Country: USA
Mailing address: 1154 Fort Street Mall Ste 312
Mailing city: Honolulu
Mailing state: HI
Mailing zip: 96813-2712
General Phone: (808) 544-9379
General Fax: (808) 566-2418
Editorail Phone: (808)687-7030
General/National Adv. E-mail: kalamalama@hpu.edu
Primary Website: http://www.hpu.edu/kalamalamaonline/index.html
Year Established: 1992
Classified Equipment»
Personnel: Dayna Kalakau (Bus. Mgr.); Susanne Haala (Student Editor); Nicole Kato (Copy Editor); Kara Jernigan (Associate Editor); John Windrow (Faculty Editor); Riana Stellburg (Photo Editor); Emily Tall (Sports Editor); David Chow (Social Media Tech)

HONOLULU CMTY. COLLEGE UNIV. OF HAWAII

Street address 1: 874 Dillingham Blvd
Street address 3: Honolulu
Street address state: HI
Zip/Postal code: 96817-4505
Country: USA
Mailing address: 874 Dillingham Blvd
Mailing city: Honolulu
Mailing state: HI
Mailing zip: 96817-4598
General Phone: (808) 845-9211
General Fax: (808) 847-9876
Editorail Phone: 808-227-5922
General/National Adv. E-mail: hcckala@gmail.com
Primary Website: www.thekala.net
Year Established: 1963
Published: Mthly
Avg Free Circ: 900
Classified Equipment»
Personnel: Michael Leidemann (Adviser, Asst Professor of Journalism)

KA LEO O HAWAI⊠??I

Street address 1: 2445 Campus Rd
Street address 2: Hemenway 107
Street address 3: Honolulu
Street address state: HI
Zip/Postal code: 96822-2216
Country: USA
Mailing address: 2445 Campus Rd., Hemenway 107
Mailing city: Honolulu
Mailing state: HI
Mailing zip: 96822-2216
General Phone: (808) 956-7043
General Fax: (808) 956-9962
Advertising Phone: (808) 956-7043
Editorail Phone: (808) 956-7043
General/National Adv. E-mail: editor@kaleo.org
Display Adv. E-mail: advertising@kaleo.org
Editorial e-mail: editor@kaleo.org
Primary Website: www.kaleo.org
Year Established: 1922
Delivery Methods: Racks
Commercial printers: N
Published: Mthly
Avg Free Circ: 6000
Classified Equipment»
Personnel: Jay Hartwell (Ed. Advisor); Sandy Matsui (Dir)
Parent company (for newspapers): Student Media Board, University of Hawaii at Manoa

KAPIOLANI CMTY. COLLEGE

Street address 1: 4303 Diamond Head Rd
Street address 3: Honolulu
Street address state: HI
Zip/Postal code: 96816-4421
Country: USA
Mailing address: 4303 Diamond Head Rd
Mailing city: Honolulu
Mailing state: HI
Mailing zip: 96816-4496
General Phone: (808) 734-9166
General Fax: (808) 734-9287
General/National Adv. E-mail: kapio@hawaii.edu
Primary Website: www.kapiolani.hawaii.edu/
Classified Equipment»
Personnel: Catherine E. Toth (Advisor); Janell Nakahara (Adv. Mgr.)

LAIE

BRIGHAM YOUNG UNIV.

Street address 1: 55-220 Kulanui St
Street address 3: Laie
Street address state: HI
Zip/Postal code: 96762-1266
Country: USA
Mailing address: 55-220 Kulanui St Ste 1
Mailing city: Laie
Mailing state: HI
Mailing zip: 96762-1266
General Phone: (808) 675-3696
General Fax: (808) 675-3491
Primary Website: kealakai.byuh.edu
Classified Equipment»
Personnel: Leeann Lambert (Advisor); Karen Hemenway (Copy Ed.)

PEARL CITY

LEEWARD CMTY. COLLEGE

Street address 1: 96-045 Ala Ike St
Street address 2: # SC-216
Street address 3: Pearl City
Street address state: HI
Zip/Postal code: 96782-3366
Country: USA
Mailing address: 96-045 Ala Ike St # SC-216
Mailing city: Pearl City
Mailing state: HI
Mailing zip: 96782-3366
General Phone: (808) 455-0603
General Fax: (808) 455-0471
Primary Website: emedia.leeward.hawaii.edu/kamanao/
Classified Equipment»
Personnel: Margaret Yasuhara (Ed.)

IOWA

AMES

IOWA STATE DAILY

Street address 1: 108 Hamilton Hall
Street address 3: Ames
Street address state: IA
Zip/Postal code: 50011-1180
County: Story

Country: USA
Mailing address: 108 Hamilton Hall
Mailing city: Ames
Mailing state: IA
Mailing zip: 50011-1181
General Phone: (515) 294-4120
General Fax: (515) 294-4119
Advertising Phone: (515) 294-2403
Advertising Fax: (515) 294-4119
Editorail Phone: (515) 294-5688
Editorial Fax: (515) 294-4119
General/National Adv. E-mail: ads@iowastatedaily.com
Display Adv. E-mail: ads@iowastatedaily.com
Classified Adv. E-mail: classified@iowastatedaily.com
Editorial e-mail: editor@iowastatedaily.com
Primary Website: www.iowastatedaily.com
Year Established: 1890
News Services: AP
Special Editions: Wellness Fair (Jan); Games Book (Jan); Spring Career Guide (Feb); Valentine's Section (Feb); Student Choice (Feb); Nightlife (Mar); Celebrate Summer (Jun); Unions (Jun)
Special Weekly Sections: Sports; Arts & Entertainment; Fashion; Food
Delivery Methods: Mail`Newsstand`Carrier
Own Printing Facility: Y
Commercial printers: Y
Advertising (Open Inch Rate) Weekday/Saturday: Open inch rate $105.30 (3x3 Modular rates)
Online Advertising Rates - CPM (cost per thousand) by Size: 1 Medium Rectangle & 1 Half-Page for $70.00 per week
Market Information: TMC.
Published: Mon`Tues`Wed`Thur`Fri
Weekday Frequency: e
Classified Equipment»
Personnel: Laura Widmer (Gen. Mgr.); Mark Witherspoon (Ed. Advisor); Stephen Koenigsfeld (Ed.)

IOWA STATE UNIVERSITY

Street address 1: 2420 Lincoln Way
Street address 2: Ste 205
Street address 3: Ames
Street address state: IA
Zip/Postal code: 50014-8340
Country: USA
Mailing address: 2420 Lincoln Way, Suite 205
Mailing city: Ames
Mailing state: IA
Mailing zip: 50014
General Phone: (515) 294-4120
General Fax: (515) 294-4119
Advertising Fax: (515) 294-4119
Editorail Phone: (515) 294-4815
Editorial Fax: (515) 294-4119
General/National Adv. E-mail: spoon@iowastatedaily.com
Display Adv. E-mail: sara.brown@iowastatedaily.com
Editorial e-mail: news@iowastatedaily.com
Primary Website: www.iowastatedaily.com
Year Established: 1890
Published: Mon`Tues`Wed`Thur`Fri
Avg Free Circ: 12500
Classified Equipment»
Personnel: Mark Witherspoon (Advisor); Lawrence Cunningham (General Manager of the Iowa State Daily Media Group); Janey Nicholas (Business Manager); Sarah Lefebre (Operations manager); Sara Brown (Advertising manager); Emily Barske (Editor in chief)
Parent company (for newspapers): Iowa State Daily Media Group

ANKENY

DES MOINES AREA CMTY. COLLEGE

Street address 1: 2006 S Ankeny Blvd
Street address 2: Bldg 2
Street address 3: Ankeny
Street address state: IA
Zip/Postal code: 50023-8995
Country: USA
Mailing address: 2006 S Ankeny Blvd Bldg 2
Mailing city: Ankeny
Mailing state: IA
Mailing zip: 50023-8995
General Phone: (515) 965-6425
General Fax: (515) 433-5033
General/National Adv. E-mail: chronicle@dmacc.edu
Primary Website: www.campuschronicle.net
Classified Equipment»
Personnel: Julie Roosa (Advisor); Julie Cahill (Adv. Mgr); Kelsey Edwards (Ed. in Chief)

CEDAR FALLS

UNIV. OF NORTHERN IOWA

Street address 1: L011 Maucker Union
Street address 3: Cedar Falls
Street address state: IA
Zip/Postal code: 50614-0001
Country: USA
Mailing address: L011 Maucker Un
Mailing city: Cedar Falls
Mailing state: IA
Mailing zip: 50614-0001
General Phone: (319) 273-2157
General Fax: (319) 273-5931
General/National Adv. E-mail: northern-iowan@uni.edu
Primary Website: www.northerniowan.com
Advertising (Open Inch Rate) Weekday/Saturday: $8.55 per column inch
Published: Mon`Thur
Avg Free Circ: 5000
Classified Equipment»
Note: App is the Northern Iowan Facebook and Twitter let us know if you want price sheet and publication schedule
Personnel: Michele Smith (Mgr.); Dana Klesner (Office Asst.); Seth Hadenfelt (Sales); Alex Johansen (Circ.); Jeremy (Circ.); Nikki (Exec. Ed.); Larissa (News Ed.); Anna (Prodn.)

CEDAR RAPIDS

COE COLLEGE

Street address 1: 1220 1st Ave NE
Street address 3: Cedar Rapids
Street address state: IA
Zip/Postal code: 52402-5008
Country: USA
Mailing address: 1220 1st Ave NE # 1
Mailing city: Cedar Rapids
Mailing state: IA
Mailing zip: 52402-5092
General Phone: (319) 399-8646
General Fax: (319) 399-8667
General/National Adv. E-mail: cosmos@coe.edu
Primary Website: www.coe.edu
Year Established: 1889
Published: Fri
Classified Equipment»
Personnel: Susanne Gubanc (Advisor)

KIRKWOOD COMMUNITY COLLEGE

Street address 1: 6301 Kirkwood Blvd SW
Street address 3: Cedar Rapids
Street address state: IA
Zip/Postal code: 52404-5260
Country: USA
Mailing address: 6301 Kirkwood Blvd. SW
Mailing city: Cedar Rapids
Mailing state: IA
Mailing zip: 52404
General Phone: (319) 398-5444
General Fax: (319) 398-7141
General/National Adv. E-mail: communique@kirkwood.edu.
Primary Website: www.kirkwoodstudentmedia.com
Published Other: six times each semester
Classified Equipment»
Personnel: Sarah Baker (Advisor); Rose Kodet (Publisher)

MT. MERCY COLLEGE

Street address 1: 1330 Elmhurst Dr NE
Street address 3: Cedar Rapids
Street address state: IA
Zip/Postal code: 52402-4763
Country: USA
Mailing address: 1330 Elmhurst Dr NE
Mailing city: Cedar Rapids
Mailing state: IA
Mailing zip: 52402-4797
General Phone: (319) 363-1323
General Fax: (319) 366-0893
General/National Adv. E-mail: mmctimes@mtmercy.edu
Primary Website: times.mtmercy.edu
Classified Equipment»
Personnel: Joe Sheller (Advisor); Mellette Maurice (Bus. Mgr.); Brian Heinemann (Ed.)

COUNCIL BLUFFS

IOWA WESTERN CMTY. COLLEGE

Street address 1: 2700 College Rd
Street address 3: Council Bluffs
Street address state: IA
Zip/Postal code: 51503-1057
Country: USA
Mailing address: 2700 College Rd
Mailing city: Council Bluffs
Mailing state: IA
Mailing zip: 51503-1057
General Phone: (712) 325-3200
Primary Website: iwccrover.wordpress.com
Classified Equipment»
Personnel: Camille Steed (Advisor)

PALMER COLLEGE OF CHIROPRACTIC

Street address 1: 1000 Brady St
Street address 3: Davenport
Street address state: IA
Zip/Postal code: 52803-5214
Country: USA
Mailing address: 1000 Brady St.
Mailing city: Davenport
Mailing state: IA
Mailing zip: 52803
General Phone: (563) 884-5686
General Fax: (563) 884-5719
General/National Adv. E-mail: beacon@palmer.edu
Primary Website: www.palmerbeacon.com
Classified Equipment»
Personnel: Ramneek Bhogal (Advisor); Stephanie O'Neill (Advisor); Stewart McMillan (Ed.)

DES MOINES

DRAKE UNIV.

Street address 1: 2507 Univ, Ave 124N Meredith Hall
Street address 3: Des Moines
Street address state: IA
Zip/Postal code: 50311
Country: USA
Mailing address: 2507 Univ., Ave. 124N Meredith Hall
Mailing city: Des Moines
Mailing state: IA
Mailing zip: 50311-4516
General Phone: (515) 271-3867
General Fax: (515) 271-2798
General/National Adv. E-mail: times.delphic@drake.edu
Primary Website: www.timesdelphic.com
Classified Equipment»
Personnel: Jill Van Wyke (Advisor); Caleb Bailey (Adv. Mgr.); Matt Vasilogambros (Ed. in Chief)

GRAND VIEW UNIVERSITY

Street address 1: Cowles Communication Ctr, 1331 Grandview Ave
Street address 3: Des Moines
Street address state: IA
Zip/Postal code: 50316
Country: USA
Mailing address: Cowles Communication Ctr., 1331 Grandview Ave.
Mailing city: Des Moines
Mailing state: IA
Mailing zip: 50316-1453
General Phone: (515) 263-2806
General Fax: (515) 263-2990
General/National Adv. E-mail: grandviews@grandview.edu
Primary Website: www.thegrandviews.com; www.grandview.edu
Year Established: 1949
Published: Fri
Classified Equipment»
Personnel: Mark Siebert (Advisor); Stephanie Ivankovich (Editor)

CLARKE UNIVERSITY

Street address 1: 1550 Clarke Dr
Street address 3: Dubuque
Street address state: IA
Zip/Postal code: 52001-3117
Country: USA
Mailing address: 1550 Clarke Dr
Mailing city: Dubuque
Mailing state: IA
Mailing zip: 52001-3198
General Phone: (563) 588-6335
General Fax: (563) 588-6789
General/National Adv. E-mail: abdul.sinno@clarke.edu
Primary Website: clarke.edu
Classified Equipment»
Personnel: Diana Russo (Advisor); Abdul Karim Sinno (Chair); Sarah Bradford (Ed.); David Deifell, Ph.D. (Assoc. Prof. Comm.)

LORAS COLLEGE

Street address 1: 1450 Alta Vista St
Street address 3: Dubuque
Street address state: IA
Zip/Postal code: 52001-4327
Country: USA
Mailing address: 1450 Alta Vista St
Mailing city: Dubuque
Mailing state: IA
Mailing zip: 52001-4399
General Phone: (563) 588-7954
General Fax: (563) 588-7339
Advertising Phone: (563) 588-7828
Editorail Phone: (563) 588-7954
General/National Adv. E-mail: lorian@loras.edu
Display Adv. E-mail: lorian@loras.edu
Editorial e-mail: lorian@loras.edu
Primary Website: myduhawk.com
Year Established: 1913
Advertising (Open Inch Rate) Weekday/Saturday: $6 per column inch
Published: Thur
Avg Free Circ: 1600
Classified Equipment»
Personnel: Timothy Manning (Advisor); Anna Sweeney (Adv. Mgr.); Cassandra Busch (Co-Exec. Ed.)
Parent company (for newspapers): Loras College
Newspaper (for newspapers group): Loras College, Dubuque

UNIV. OF DUBUQUE

Street address 1: 2000 University Ave
Street address 2: # 6
Street address 3: Dubuque
Street address state: IA
Zip/Postal code: 52001-5050
Country: USA
Mailing address: 2000 University Ave # 6
Mailing city: Dubuque
Mailing state: IA
Mailing zip: 52001-5050
General Phone: (563) 589-3369
General Fax: (319) 589-3419
Classified Equipment»
Personnel: Laura Steinbeck (Ed.)

ESTHERVILLE

IOWA LAKES CMTY. COLLEGE

Street address 1: 300 S 18th St
Street address 3: Estherville
Street address state: IA
Zip/Postal code: 51334-2721
Country: USA
Mailing address: 300 S 18th St
Mailing city: Estherville
Mailing state: IA
Mailing zip: 51334-2721
General Phone: (712) 362-2604
General Fax: (712) 362-8363
General/National Adv. E-mail: pbuchholz@iowalakes.edu; info@iowalakes.edu
Primary Website: www.iowalakes.edu

Classified Equipment»
Personnel: Pam Bushholz (Journalism Instructor/Advisor)

FOREST CITY

WALDORF COLLEGE

Street address 1: 206 John K Hanson Dr
Street address 3: Forest City
Street address state: IA
Zip/Postal code: 50436
Country: USA
Mailing address: 106 S 6th St
Mailing city: Forest City
Mailing state: IA
Mailing zip: 50436-1797
General Phone: (641) 585-2450
General Fax: (641) 582-8194
General/National Adv. E-mail: lobbyist@waldorf.edu
Primary Website: lobbyist.waldorf.edu
Classified Equipment»
Personnel: David Damm (Advisor); Sarah Soy (Mng. Ed.); Caitlin Leitzen (Mng. Ed.); Matt Knutson (Web Ed.)

FORT DODGE

IOWA CENTRAL CMTY. COLLEGE

Street address 1: 330 Avenue M
Street address 3: Fort Dodge
Street address state: IA
Zip/Postal code: 50501-5739
Country: USA
Mailing address: 330 Avenue M
Mailing city: Fort Dodge
Mailing state: IA
Mailing zip: 50501-5739
General Phone: (515) 576-0099
General Fax: (515) 576-7724
General/National Adv. E-mail: mcintyre@iowacentral.com
Primary Website: http://www.iccc.cc.ia.us/collegian/staff.htm
Classified Equipment»
Personnel: Bill McIntyre (Advisor); Ian Schmit (Ed.)

GRINNELL

GRINNELL COLLEGE

Street address 1: 1115 8th Ave
Street address 3: Grinnell
Street address state: IA
Zip/Postal code: 50112-1553
Country: USA
Mailing address: P.O. Box 5886
Mailing city: Grinnell
Mailing state: IA
Mailing zip: 50112-3128
General Phone: (641) 269-3325
General Fax: (641) 269-4888
General/National Adv. E-mail: newspapr@grinnell.edu
Primary Website: www.thesandb.com
Published: Fri
Classified Equipment»

INDIANOLA

SIMPSON COLLEGE

Street address 1: 701 N C St
Street address 3: Indianola
Street address state: IA
Zip/Postal code: 50125-1201
Country: USA
Mailing address: 701 N C St
Mailing city: Indianola
Mailing state: IA
Mailing zip: 50125-1202
General Phone: (515) 961-1738
General Fax: (515) 961-1350
General/National Adv. E-mail: thesimp@simpson.edu
Primary Website: www.thesimpsonian.com
Classified Equipment»
Personnel: Emily Schettler (Ed)

IOWA CITY

UNIV. OF IOWA

Street address 1: 104 West Washington St
Street address 3: Iowa City
Street address state: IA
Zip/Postal code: 52240
Country: USA
Mailing address: 104 West Washington St
Mailing city: Iowa City
Mailing state: IA
Mailing zip: 52240
General Phone: (319) 335-5791
General Fax: (319) 335-6297
General/National Adv. E-mail: daily-iowan@uiowa.edu
Primary Website: www.dailyiowan.com
Classified Equipment»
Personnel: William Casey (Pub.); Debra Plath (Bus. Mgr.); Pete Recker (Adv./Circ. Mgr)

LAMONI

GRACELAND COLLEGE

Street address 1: 1 University Pl
Street address 3: Lamoni
Street address state: IA
Zip/Postal code: 50140-1641
Country: USA
Mailing address: 1 University Pl
Mailing city: Lamoni
Mailing state: IA
Mailing zip: 50140-1684
General Phone: (641) 784-5000
General Fax: (641) 784-5480
General/National Adv. E-mail: tower@graceland.edu
Primary Website: www.graceland.edu
Classified Equipment»
Personnel: Nicky Kerr (Ed. in Chief)

MASON CITY

NORTH IOWA AREA CMTY. COLLEGE

Street address 1: 500 College Dr
Street address 3: Mason City
Street address state: IA
Zip/Postal code: 50401-7213
Country: USA
Mailing address: 500 College Drive
Mailing city: Mason City
Mailing state: IA
Mailing zip: 50401
General Phone: (641) 422-4304
General Fax: (641) 422-4280
General/National Adv. E-mail: peterpau@niacc.edu
Primary Website: www.niacc.edu/logos
Classified Equipment»
Personnel: Paul Peterson (Advisor); Emily Knoop (Adv. Mgr.); Collie Wood (Ed.)

IOWA WESLEYAN COLLEGE

Street address 1: 601 N Main St
Street address 3: Mount Pleasant
Street address state: IA
Zip/Postal code: 52641-1348
Country: USA
Mailing address: 601 N Main St
Mailing city: Mount Pleasant
Mailing state: IA
Mailing zip: 52641-1398
General Phone: (319) 385-8021
General Fax: (319) 385-6363
Primary Website: www.iwc.edu
Classified Equipment»

MOUNT VERNON

CORNELL COLLEGE

Street address 1: 600 1st St SW
Street address 3: Mount Vernon
Street address state: IA
Zip/Postal code: 52314-1006
Country: USA
Mailing address: 600 First St SW
Mailing city: Mount Vernon
Mailing state: IA
Mailing zip: 52314
General Phone: (319) 895-4430
General Fax: (319) 895-5264
General/National Adv. E-mail: cornellian@cornellcollege.edu
Primary Website: www.thecornellian.com
Delivery Methods: Mail
Commercial printers: Y
Classified Equipment»

MUSCATINE

MUSCATINE CMTY. COLLEGE

Street address 1: 152 Colorado St
Street address 3: Muscatine
Street address state: IA
Zip/Postal code: 52761-5329
Country: USA
Mailing address: 152 Colorado St
Mailing city: Muscatine
Mailing state: IA
Mailing zip: 52761-5396
General Phone: (563) 288-6053
General Fax: (563) 264-6074
Classified Equipment»
Personnel: Kristina Koch (Advisor)

ORANGE CITY

NORTHWESTERN COLLEGE

Street address 1: 101 7th St SW
Street address 3: Orange City
Street address state: IA
Zip/Postal code: 51041-1923
Country: USA
Mailing address: 101 7th St SW
Mailing city: Orange City
Mailing state: IA
Mailing zip: 51041-1996
General Phone: (712) 707-7043
General Fax: (712) 707-7345
General/National Adv. E-mail: beacon@nwciowa.edu
Primary Website: beacon.nwciowa.edu
Classified Equipment»
Personnel: Carl Vandermeulen (Advisor); Kim Eason (Ed.)

OSKALOOSA

WILLIAM PENN UNIV.

Street address 1: 201 Trueblood Ave
Street address 3: Oskaloosa
Street address state: IA
Zip/Postal code: 52577-1757
Country: USA
Mailing address: 201 Trueblood Ave.
Mailing city: Oskaloosa
Mailing state: IA
Mailing zip: 52577
General Phone: (641) 673-2170
Display Adv. E-mail: chronicle@wmpenn.edu
Published: Mthly
Classified Equipment»

PELLA

CENTRAL COLLEGE

Street address 1: 812 University St
Street address 3: Pella
Street address state: IA
Zip/Postal code: 50219-1902
Country: USA
Mailing address: 812 University
Mailing city: Pella
Mailing state: IA
Mailing zip: 50219
General Phone: (877) 462-3687
General Fax: (515) 628-5316
General/National Adv. E-mail: theray@central.edu
Editorial e-mail: carmane@central.edu
Primary Website: www.central.edu
Classified Equipment»
Personnel: Emily Betz (Ed.)

STORM LAKE

BUENA VISTA UNIV.

Street address 1: 610 W 4th St
Street address 3: Storm Lake
Street address state: IA
Zip/Postal code: 50588-1713
Country: USA
Mailing address: 610 W 4th St
Mailing city: Storm Lake
Mailing state: IA
Mailing zip: 50588-1798
General Phone: (712) 749-1247
General/National Adv. E-mail: ucbvu@bvu.edu
Classified Equipment»
Personnel: Jamii Claiborne (Advisor); Carly Evans (Co Ed. in Chief); Lindsey Marean (Co Ed. in Chief)

WAVERLY

WARTBURG COLLEGE

Street address 1: 100 Wartburg Blvd
Street address 3: Waverly
Street address state: IA
Zip/Postal code: 50677-2215
Country: USA
Mailing address: 100 Wartburg Blvd
Mailing city: Waverly
Mailing state: IA
Mailing zip: 50677-2200
General Phone: (319) 352-8289
General Fax: (319) 352-8242
General/National Adv. E-mail: trumpet@wartburg.edu
Primary Website: www.wartburg.edu/trumpet
Classified Equipment»
Personnel: Cliff Brockmen (Advisor); Luke Shanno (Ed. in Chief); Jackie Albrecht (News Ed.)

IDAHO

BOISE STATE UNIV.

Street address 1: 1910 University Dr
Street address 3: Boise
Street address state: ID
Zip/Postal code: 83725-0001
Country: USA
Mailing address: 1910 University Dr
Mailing city: Boise
Mailing state: ID
Mailing zip: 83725-0002
General Phone: (208) 426-6300
General Fax: (208) 426-3884
General/National Adv. E-mail: mcox@boisestate.edu
Primary Website: www.arbiteronline.com
Classified Equipment»
Personnel: Brad Arendt (Gen. Mgr.); V. Marvin Cox (Chrmn.); Steve Lyons (Advisor); Dwight Murphy (Avd. Mgr.); Shannon Morgan (Ed. in Chief)

CALDWELL

COLLEGE OF IDAHO

Street address 1: 2112 Cleveland Blvd
Street address 3: Caldwell
Street address state: ID
Zip/Postal code: 83605-4432
Country: USA
Mailing address: PO Box 52
Mailing city: Caldwell
Mailing state: ID
Mailing zip: 83606-0052
General Phone: (208) 459-5509
General Fax: (208) 459-5849
Primary Website: www.collegeofidaho.edu/media/phonebooks/default.asp?dpt=COYN
Delivery Methods: Carrier

Commercial printers: N
Classified Equipment»
Personnel: Danielle Blenker (Pres.); Nicole Watson (Vice Pres.); Debbie Swanson (Administrative Asst.); Colleen Smith (Ed.)

COEUR D ALENE

NORTH IDAHO COLLEGE

Street address 1: 1000 W Garden Ave
Street address 3: Coeur D Alene
Street address state: ID
Zip/Postal code: 83814-2161
Country: USA
Mailing address: North Idaho College Receiving Department (c/o Geoff Carr)
Mailing city: Coeur D Alene
Mailing state: ID
Mailing zip: 83814-2199
General Phone: (208) 769-3388
General Fax: (208) 769-3361
General/National Adv. E-mail: sentinel@nic.edu
Primary Website: www.nicsentinel.com
Published Other: Tri-weekly
Avg Paid Circ: 3000
Avg Free Circ: 3000
Classified Equipment»
Personnel: Geoff Carr (Advisor)

LEWISTON

LEWIS-CLARK STATE COLLEGE

Street address 1: 500 8th Ave
Street address 2: Student Union Building Room 201
Street address 3: Lewiston
Street address state: ID
Zip/Postal code: 83501-2691
Country: USA
Mailing address: 500 8th Avenue
Mailing city: Lewiston
Mailing state: ID
Mailing zip: 83501
General Phone: (208) 792-2470
General Fax: (208) 792-2082
General/National Adv. E-mail: thepathfinder@lcmail.lcsc.edu
Display Adv. E-mail: pathfinderbusmgr@lcmail.lcsc.edu
Primary Website: www.lcsc.edu/pathfinder/
Published: Wed
Avg Paid Circ: 0
Avg Free Circ: 1000
Classified Equipment»
Personnel: Bryce Kammers (Advisor); Kaylee Brewster (Ed.); Aaron Waits (Asst. Ed.); Ryan Grether (Business Manager)

MOSCOW

UNIV. OF IDAHO

Street address 1: 301 Student Union Bldg
Street address 3: Moscow
Street address state: ID
Zip/Postal code: 83844-0001
Country: USA
Mailing address: 301 Student Un
Mailing city: Moscow
Mailing state: ID
Mailing zip: 83844-0001
General Phone: (208) 885-7825
General Fax: (208) 885-2222
General/National Adv. E-mail: argonaut@uidaho.edu
Primary Website: www.uiargonaut.com
Classified Equipment»
Personnel: Shawn O'Neal (Advisor); Hannah Liter (Adv. Mgr.); Greg Connolly (Ed. in Chief)

NAMPA

NORTHWEST NAZARENE UNIV.

Street address 1: 623 Holly St
Street address 3: Nampa
Street address state: ID
Zip/Postal code: 83686-5487
Country: USA
Mailing address: 623 Holly St
Mailing city: Nampa
Mailing state: ID
Mailing zip: 83686-5897
General Phone: (208) 467-8656
General Fax: (208) 467-8468
General/National Adv. E-mail: crusader@nnu.edu
Classified Equipment»
Personnel: Amber Ford (Ed.)

POCATELLO

IDAHO STATE UNIV.

Street address 1: PO Box 8009
Street address 3: Pocatello
Street address state: ID
Zip/Postal code: 83209-0001
Country: USA
Mailing address: PO Box 8009
Mailing city: Pocatello
Mailing state: ID
Mailing zip: 83209-0001
General Phone: (208) 282-4812
General Fax: (208) 282-5301
General/National Adv. E-mail: bgads@isu.edu
Primary Website: www.isubengal.com
Classified Equipment»
Personnel: Jerry Miller (Dir.); Clay Nelson (Ed. in Chief)

REXBURG

BRIGHAM YOUNG UNIV. IDAHO

Street address 1: Spori Bldg 114B
Street address 3: Rexburg
Street address state: ID
Zip/Postal code: 1908
Country: USA
Mailing address: Spori Bldg # 114B
Mailing city: Rexburg
Mailing state: ID
Mailing zip: 83460-0001
General Phone: (208) 496-2411
General Fax: (208) 496-2911
General/National Adv. E-mail: scrolleditor@byui.edu
Primary Website: www.byui.edu/scroll; www.byuicomm.net
Classified Equipment»
Personnel: Jeff Hochstrasser (Advisor); John Thompson (Advisor); Ryan Hales (Advisor)

ILLINOIS

BLOOMINGTON

ILLINOIS WESLEYAN UNIVERSITY

Street address 1: 104 University Ave
Street address 3: Bloomington
Street address state: IL
Zip/Postal code: 61701-1798
Country: USA
Mailing address: 104 University Ave
Mailing city: Bloomington
Mailing state: IL
Mailing zip: 61701-1798
General/National Adv. E-mail: argus@iwu.edu
Primary Website: www.iwuargus.com
Year Established: 1894
Advertising (Open Inch Rate) Weekday/Saturday: Online and paper advertising available
Published: Fri
Classified Equipment»
Personnel: James Plath (Advisor)

BOURBONNAIS

OLIVET NAZARENE UNIV.

Street address 1: PO Box 592
Street address 3: Bourbonnais
Street address state: IL
Zip/Postal code: 60914-0592
Country: USA
Mailing address: PO Box 592
Mailing city: Bourbonnais
Mailing state: IL
Mailing zip: 60914-0592
General Phone: (815) 939-5315
General Fax: (815) 928-5549
Editorial e-mail: glimmerglass@olivet.edu
Year Established: 1941
Published: Tues
Classified Equipment»
Personnel: Jay Martinson (Advisor)

CARBONDALE

SOUTHERN ILLINOIS UNIV.

Street address 1: 1100 Lincoln Dr
Street address 3: Carbondale
Street address state: IL
Zip/Postal code: 62901-4306
Country: USA
Mailing address: Communications Bldg, 1100 Lincoln Dr
Mailing city: Carbondale
Mailing state: IL
Mailing zip: 62901
General Phone: (618) 536-3311
General Fax: (618) 453-3248
General/National Adv. E-mail: deadvert@siu.edu
Primary Website: www.siude.com
Year Established: 1916
Classified Equipment»
Personnel: Eric J. Fidler (Advisor/Mng. Ed.); Jerry Bush (Bus./Adv. Dir.); Sherri Killion (Classified Mgr.); Andrea Zimmerman (Ed. in Chief); Diana (Ed. in Chief); Derek (Features Ed.); Edyta (Photo Ed.); Stile (Sports Ed.); Ashley (Webmaster)

CARTERVILLE

JOHN A. LOGAN COLLEGE

Street address 1: 700 Logan College Dr
Street address 3: Carterville
Street address state: IL
Zip/Postal code: 62918-2500
Country: USA
Mailing address: 700 Logan College Dr
Mailing city: Carterville
Mailing state: IL
Mailing zip: 62918-2501
General Phone: (618) 985-2828
General Fax: (618) 985-4654
General/National Adv. E-mail: volunteernews@jalc.edu
Classified Equipment»
Personnel: Matt Garrison (Advisor); Tara Fasol (Ed.)

CENTRALIA

KASKASKIA COLLEGE

Street address 1: 27210 College Rd
Street address 3: Centralia
Street address state: IL
Zip/Postal code: 62801-7800
Country: USA
Mailing address: 27210 College Rd
Mailing city: Centralia
Mailing state: IL
Mailing zip: 62801-7878
General Phone: (618) 545-3000
General Fax: (618) 532-2365
Primary Website: scroll.kaskaskia.edu
Classified Equipment»
Personnel: Dale Hill (Advisor); Nathan Wilkins (Advisor); Sue Hardebeck (Advisor)

CHAMPAIGN

PARKLAND COLLEGE

Street address 1: 2400 W Bradley Ave
Street address 2: Rm X-155
Street address 3: Champaign
Street address state: IL
Zip/Postal code: 61821-1806
Country: USA
Mailing address: 2400 W Bradley Ave Rm X-155
Mailing city: Champaign
Mailing state: IL
Mailing zip: 61821-1899
General Phone: (217) 351-2216
Advertising Phone: 217 351-2206
General/National Adv. E-mail: prospectus@parkland.edu
Display Adv. E-mail: prospectusads@parkland.edu
Editorial e-mail: prospectus.editor@gmail.com
Primary Website: www.prospectusnews.com
Year Established: 1969
Published: Wed
Avg Free Circ: 1000
Classified Equipment»
Personnel: John Eby (Advisor); Sean Herman (Ed. in Chief)

UNIV. OF ILLINOIS

Street address 1: 512 E Green St
Street address 3: Champaign
Street address state: IL
Zip/Postal code: 61820-6483
Country: USA
Mailing address: 512 E Green St
Mailing city: Champaign
Mailing state: IL
Mailing zip: 61820-5720
General Phone: (217) 337-8300
General Fax: (217) 337-8303
Advertising Phone: 2173378382
Advertising Fax: 2173378303
Editorail Phone: 2173378350
Editorial Fax: 2173378328
Display Adv. E-mail: adsales@illinimedia.com
Editorial e-mail: news@illinimedia.com
Primary Website: www.dailyillini.com
Year Established: 1871
Published: Mon`Tues`Wed`Thur
Avg Free Circ: 10000
Classified Equipment»
Personnel: Lilyan Levant (Advisor); Nancy Elliott (Adv. Dir.); Darshan Patel (Ed. in Chief); Travis Truitt (Ad Director)
Parent company (for newspapers): Illini Media Company

EASTERN ILLINOIS UNIV.

Street address 1: 600 Lincoln Ave
Street address 3: Charleston
Street address state: IL
Zip/Postal code: 61920-3011
Country: USA
Mailing address: 600 Lincoln Ave.
Mailing city: Charleston
Mailing state: IL
Mailing zip: 61920
General Phone: (217) 581-2812
General Fax: (217) 581-2923
General/National Adv. E-mail: DENeic@gmail.com; DENnewsdesk@gmail.com; DENNews.com@gmail.com
Primary Website: http://www.dailyeasternnews.com/
Classified Equipment»
Personnel: Taylor Angelo (Ed. In chief); Lola Burnham (Advisor); Emily Steele (News Ed.); Chris Lee (Mng. Ed.); Collin (Mng. Ed.)

CHICAGO KENT COLLEGE OF LAW

Street address 1: 565 W Adams St
Street address 2: Rm C86
Street address 3: Chicago
Street address state: IL
Zip/Postal code: 60661-3652
Country: USA
Mailing address: 565 W Adams St Fl 2
Mailing city: Chicago
Mailing state: IL
Mailing zip: 60661-3652
General Phone: (312) 906-5016
General Fax: (312) 906-5280
General/National Adv. E-mail: comment@kentlaw.edu
Primary Website: http://www.kentlaw.edu/student_orgs/commentator

Classified Equipment»

COLUMBIA COLLEGE

Street address 1: 33 E Congress Pkwy
Street address 3: Chicago
Street address state: IL
Zip/Postal code: 60605-1218
Country: USA
Mailing address: 600 S Michigan Ave Fl 5
Mailing city: Chicago
Mailing state: IL
Mailing zip: 60605-1996
General Phone: 312-369-8903
Advertising Phone: 312-369-8984
Editorail Phone: 312-369-8999
Editorial Fax: 312-369-8430
Editorial e-mail: jlyon@colum.edu
Primary Website: www.columbiachronicle.com
Year Established: 1965
News Services: AP, MCT
Special Editions: Yes
Special Weekly Sections: Yes
Delivery Methods: Racks
Commercial printers: Y
Classified Equipment»
Personnel: Jeff Lyon (Faculty advisor)

COLUMBIA COLLEGE CHICAGO

Street address 1: 33 E Congress Pkwy
Street address 2: Ste 224
Street address 3: Chicago
Street address state: IL
Zip/Postal code: 60605-1237
Country: USA
Mailing address: 33 E Congress Pkwy Ste 224
Mailing city: Chicago
Mailing state: IL
Mailing zip: 60605-1237
General Phone: 312-369-8955
General Fax: (312)369-8430
Advertising Phone: 312-369-8955
Editorail Phone: (312) 369-8999
General/National Adv. E-mail: chronicle@colum.edu
Display Adv. E-mail: crichert@colum.edu
Editorial e-mail: chronicle@colum.edu
Primary Website: www.columbiachronicle.com
Year Established: 1978
Advertising (Open Inch Rate) Weekday/Saturday: Special Pricing for each client.
Published: Mon
Avg Free Circ: 6000
Classified Equipment»
Personnel: Chris Richert (General Manager)

DEPAUL UNIVERSITY

Street address 1: 14 E Jackson Blvd
Street address 2: Fl 11
Street address 3: Chicago
Street address state: IL
Zip/Postal code: 60604-2259
Country: USA
Mailing address: 14 E. Jackson Blvd.
Mailing city: Chicago
Mailing state: IL
Mailing zip: 60604
General Phone: (312) 362-7644
General/National Adv. E-mail: eic@depauliaonline.com
Display Adv. E-mail: business@depauliaonline.com
Editorial e-mail: eic@depauliaonline.com
Primary Website: www.depauliaonline.com
Year Established: 1923
News Services: AP
Delivery Methods: Newsstand
Commercial printers: Y
Advertising (Open Inch Rate) Weekday/Saturday: see online media kit
Published: Mon
Avg Free Circ: 5000
Classified Equipment»
Personnel: Maria Krause (Advisor)

DEVRY UNIVERSITY

Street address 1: 3300 N Campbell Ave, Campus Life Ctr
Street address 3: Chicago
Street address state: IL
Zip/Postal code: 60618
Country: USA
Mailing address: 3300 N. Campbell Ave., Campus Life Ctr.
Mailing city: Chicago
Mailing state: IL
Mailing zip: 60618
General Phone: (773) 697-2089
General Fax: (773) 697-2706
General/National Adv. E-mail: dvu.chi.hardcopy@gmail.com
Classified Equipment»
Personnel: Joe Onorio (Assoc. Dean, Campus Life/Advisor); Marvin Cespedes (Ed.)

HAROLD WASHINGTON COLLEGE

Street address 1: 30 E Lake St
Street address 2: Rm 635
Street address 3: Chicago
Street address state: IL
Zip/Postal code: 60601-2408
Country: USA
Mailing address: 30 E Lake St Rm 635
Mailing city: Chicago
Mailing state: IL
Mailing zip: 60601-2449
General Phone: (312) 553-3141
General Fax: (312) 553-5647
Advertising Phone: 312-553-5631
Editorail Phone: 312-553-5630
General/National Adv. E-mail: hwc_heraldnews@ccc.edu
Primary Website: www.theheraldhwc.com
Year Established: 1979
News Services: none
Delivery Methods: Mail`Newsstand`Racks
Commercial printers: Y
Classified Equipment»
Personnel: Molly Turner (Faculty Advisor)

ILLINOIS INST. OF TECHNOLOGY

Street address 1: Herman Union Bldg State St
Street address 2: Rm 3201221
Street address 3: Chicago
Street address state: IL
Zip/Postal code: 60616
Country: USA
Mailing address: Herman Union Bldg., 3201 S. State St., Rm. 221
Mailing city: Chicago
Mailing state: IL
Mailing zip: 60616
General Phone: (312) 567-3085
General/National Adv. E-mail: technews@iit.edu
Classified Equipment»
Personnel: Aanchal Taneja (Bus. Mgr.); Brian Wolber (Adv. Mgr.); Lory Mishra (Ed. in Chief)

KENNEDY-KING COLLEGE

Street address 1: 1751 W 47th St
Street address 2: Fl 2
Street address 3: Chicago
Street address state: IL
Zip/Postal code: 60609-3825
Country: USA
Mailing city: Chicago
Mailing state: IL
Mailing zip: 60621
General Phone: (773) 602-5179
General Fax: (773) 602-5521
General/National Adv. E-mail: editor@thegatenewspaper.com
Display Adv. E-mail: editor@thegatenewspaper.com
Primary Website: www.thegatenewspaper.com
Year Established: 2010
Published: Bi-Mthly
Avg Free Circ: 13000
Classified Equipment»
Personnel: Adriana Maria Cardona-Maguigad (Editor)

LOYOLA UNIV.

Street address 1: 6525 N Sheridan Rd
Street address 3: Chicago
Street address state: IL
Zip/Postal code: 60626-5761
Country: USA
Mailing address: 6525 N Sheridan Rd Ste 1
Mailing city: Chicago
Mailing state: IL
Mailing zip: 60626-5386
General Phone: (773) 508-7120
General Fax: (773) 508-7121
General/National Adv. E-mail: phoenixbusiness@luc.edu
Primary Website: www.loyolaphoenix.com
Classified Equipment»
Personnel: Kimberly Boonjathai (Bus.Mgr.); Leeann Maton (Ed. in chief)

LOYOLA UNIV. LAW SCHOOL

Street address 1: 33 N Dearborn St
Street address 3: Chicago
Street address state: IL
Zip/Postal code: 60602-3102
Country: USA
Mailing address: 33 N Dearborn St
Mailing city: Chicago
Mailing state: IL
Mailing zip: 60602-3102
General Phone: (312) 346-3191
General Fax: (312) 915-7201
Classified Equipment»
Personnel: Sam Puleo (Ed.)

MALCOLM X COLLEGE

Street address 1: 1900 W Van Buren St
Street address 2: Rm 2519
Street address 3: Chicago
Street address state: IL
Zip/Postal code: 60612-3145
Country: USA
Mailing address: 1900 W Van Buren St Rm 2218
Mailing city: Chicago
Mailing state: IL
Mailing zip: 60612-3145
General Phone: (312) 850-7462
General Fax: (312) 850-7323
Editorail Phone: (312) 850-7462
Delivery Methods: Racks
Commercial printers: Y
Classified Equipment»
Personnel: Cynthia-Val Chapman (Advisor); Beth Lewis (Adv. Mgr.)

NORTH PARK UNIV.

Street address 1: 3225 W Foster Ave
Street address 3: Chicago
Street address state: IL
Zip/Postal code: 60625-4823
Country: USA
Mailing address: 3225 W Foster Ave
Mailing city: Chicago
Mailing state: IL
Mailing zip: 60625-4895
General Phone: (773) 649-2816
General/National Adv. E-mail: northparkpress@gmail.com
Primary Website: www.northparkpress.com
Delivery Methods: Racks
Classified Equipment»
Personnel: Casey Smagala (Adv. Dir.); Erin Hegarty (Editor-In-Chief); Kristie Vuocolo (Staff Advisory); Hannah Williams (Online Editor)

NORTHEASTERN ILLINOIS UNIVERSITY

Street address 1: 5500 N Saint Louis Ave
Street address 2: Rm E049
Street address 3: Chicago
Street address state: IL
Zip/Postal code: 60625-4625
Country: USA
Mailing address: 5500 N Saint Louis Ave Rm E049
Mailing city: Chicago
Mailing state: IL
Mailing zip: 60625-4699
General Phone: (773) 442-4577
General Fax: (773) 442-4579
General/National Adv. E-mail: neiuindependent@gmail.com
Display Adv. E-mail: neiuadvertising@yahoo.com
Primary Website: www.neiuindependent.org
Year Established: 1961
Advertising (Open Inch Rate) Weekday/Saturday: Call for more information
Published: Tues`Bi-Mthly
Classified Equipment»
Personnel: Jacklyn Nowotnik (Editor-in-Chief); Matthew Greenberg (Managing Editor)

NORTHWESTERN UNIV. SCHOOL OF LAW

Street address 1: 357 E Chicago Ave
Street address 3: Chicago
Street address state: IL
Zip/Postal code: 60611-3059
Country: USA
Mailing address: 357 E Chicago Ave
Mailing city: Chicago
Mailing state: IL
Mailing zip: 60611-3069
General Phone: (312) 503-4714
Classified Equipment»
Personnel: Unknown Unknown (Advisor)

ROBERT MORRIS COLLEGE

Street address 1: 401 S State St
Street address 3: Chicago
Street address state: IL
Zip/Postal code: 60605-1229
Country: USA
Mailing address: 401 S State St Fl 2
Mailing city: Chicago
Mailing state: IL
Mailing zip: 60605-1225
General Phone: (312) 935-6876
General Fax: (312) 935-6880
General/National Adv. E-mail: eaglenews@robertmorris.edu; eagle@robertmorris.edu
Classified Equipment»
Personnel: Cherie Meador (Advisor); Matt Kirouac (Ed.)

ROOSEVELT UNIV.

Street address 1: 430 S Michigan Ave
Street address 3: Chicago
Street address state: IL
Zip/Postal code: 60605-1315
Country: USA
Mailing address: 430 S Michigan Ave
Mailing city: Chicago
Mailing state: IL
Mailing zip: 60605-1394
General Phone: (312) 281-3246
General Fax: (312) 341-3732
General/National Adv. E-mail: torchcu@roosevelt.edu
Primary Website: www.roosevelttorch.com
Classified Equipment»
Personnel: Billy Montgomery (Advisor); Mallory Blazetic (Mng. Ed.)

SAINT XAVIER UNIVERSITY

Street address 1: 3700 W 103rd St
Street address 3: Chicago
Street address state: IL
Zip/Postal code: 60655-3105
Country: USA
Mailing address: 3700 W 103rd St
Mailing city: Chicago
Mailing state: IL
Mailing zip: 60655-3199
General Phone: (773) 298-3380
General Fax: (773) 298-3381
General/National Adv. E-mail: thexavierite@yahoo.com
Display Adv. E-mail: thexavierite@yahoo.com
Editorial e-mail: thexavierite@yahoo.com
Primary Website: www.thexavierite.com
Year Established: 1935
Commercial printers: Y
Classified Equipment»
Personnel: Peter Kreten (Asst. Dir)

SCHOOL OF THE ART INSTITUTE

Street address 1: 112 S Michigan Ave
Street address 3: Chicago
Street address state: IL
Zip/Postal code: 60603-6105
Country: USA
Mailing address: 112 S Michigan Ave
Mailing city: Chicago
Mailing state: IL
Mailing zip: 60603-6105
General Phone: (312) 345-3838
General Fax: (312) 345-3839
General/National Adv. E-mail: fadvertising@saic.edu

Editorial e-mail: editors@fnewsmagazine.com
Primary Website: www.fnewsmagazine.com
Classified Equipment»
Personnel: Paul Elitzik (Advisor); Rachel Oginni (Adv. Mgr.); Natalie Edwards (Ed. in Chief)

UNIV. OF CHICAGO

Street address 1: 1212 E 59th St
Street address 2: Lowr Level
Street address 3: Chicago
Street address state: IL
Zip/Postal code: 60637-1604
Country: USA
Mailing address: 1212 E 59th St Lowr Level
Mailing city: Chicago
Mailing state: IL
Mailing zip: 60637-1604
General Phone: (773) 702-1403
General Fax: (773) 702-3032
General/National Adv. E-mail: editor@chicagomaroon.com
Display Adv. E-mail: ads@chicagomaroon.com
Primary Website: www.chicagomaroon.com
Year Established: 1892
Published: Tues`Fri
Classified Equipment»
Personnel: Rebecca Guterman (Editor-in-Chief); Sam Levine (Editor-in-Chief); Emily Wang (Managing Editor)

UNIV. OF CHICAGO LAW SCHOOL

Street address 1: 1111 E 60th St
Street address 3: Chicago
Street address state: IL
Zip/Postal code: 60637-2776
Country: USA
Mailing address: 1111 E 60th St
Mailing city: Chicago
Mailing state: IL
Mailing zip: 60637-2786
General Phone: (773) 702-3164
General Fax: (773) 834-4332
General/National Adv. E-mail: phoenix@law.uchicago.edu
Primary Website: www.?⊠?⊠law.?⊠?⊠uchicago.?⊠?⊠edu
Year Established: 1901
Classified Equipment»
Personnel: William Weaver (Ed.); Lisa Alvarez (Contact)

UNIV. OF ILLINOIS AT CHICAGO

Street address 1: 1212 E 59th St
Street address 2: Ida Noyes Hall
Street address 3: Chicago
Street address state: IL
Zip/Postal code: 60637-1604
Country: USA
Mailing address: 1001 W Van Buren St
Mailing city: Chicago
Mailing state: IL
Mailing zip: 60607-2900
General Phone: (312) 421-0480
General Fax: (312) 421-0491
Editorail Phone: (312) 996-5421
General/National Adv. E-mail: chicagomaroon@gmail.com
Primary Website: www.chicagoflame.com
Year Established: 1988
Classified Equipment»
Personnel: Darryl Brehm (Bus. Mgr.); Kate Lee (Ed.)

UNIVERSITY OF CHICAGO BOOTH SCHOOL OF BUSINESS

Street address 1: 5807 S Woodlawn Ave
Street address 2: # C26A
Street address 3: Chicago
Street address state: IL
Zip/Postal code: 60637-1610
Country: USA
Mailing address: 5807 S Woodlawn Ave # C26A
Mailing city: Chicago
Mailing state: IL
Mailing zip: 60637-1610
General Phone: (773) 702-1234
General Fax: (773) 834-0628
General/National Adv. E-mail: chibusmag@gmail.com
Display Adv. E-mail: chibusmag@gmail.com
Editorial e-mail: chibusmag@gmail.com
Primary Website: www.chibus.com
Published Other: Biweekly
Avg Free Circ: 1000
Classified Equipment»
Personnel: Christopher Laws (Editor in Chief); Elizabeth Oates (Editor in Chief)

WILBUR WRIGHT COLLEGE

Street address 1: 4300 N Narragansett Ave
Street address 3: Chicago
Street address state: IL
Zip/Postal code: 60634-1591
Country: USA
Mailing address: 4300 N Narragansett Ave
Mailing city: Chicago
Mailing state: IL
Mailing zip: 60634-1500
General Phone: (773) 481-8555
General Fax: (773) 481-8555
Editorail Phone: (773) 481-8444
General/National Adv. E-mail: web.wrighttimes@yahoo.com
Primary Website: www.wrighttimes.net; wright.ccc.edu
Classified Equipment»
Personnel: Terrence Doherty (Advisor); Juan Pintor (Ed. in Chief)

CHICAGO HEIGHTS

PRAIRIE STATE COLLEGE

Street address 1: 202 S Halsted St
Street address 2: Rm 1260
Street address 3: Chicago Heights
Street address state: IL
Zip/Postal code: 60411-8200
Country: USA
Mailing address: 202 S Halsted St Rm 1260
Mailing city: Chicago Heights
Mailing state: IL
Mailing zip: 60411-8226
General Phone: (708) 709-3910
General Fax: (708) 755-2587
Editorail Phone: (708) 709-3535
General/National Adv. E-mail: psc_student_review@yahoo.com
Primary Website: www.prairiestate.edu/studentreview
Classified Equipment»
Personnel: Helen Manley (Advisor); Nike Atewologun (Adv. Mgr.); Sam Williams (Ed. in Chief)

MORTON COLLEGE

Street address 1: 3801 S Central Ave
Street address 2: Rm 328-C
Street address 3: Cicero
Street address state: IL
Zip/Postal code: 60804-4300
Country: USA
Mailing address: 3801 S Central Ave Rm 328-C
Mailing city: Cicero
Mailing state: IL
Mailing zip: 60804-4398
General Phone: (708) 656-8000
General Fax: (708) 656-3924
General/National Adv. E-mail: collegian@morton.edu
Primary Website: www.morton.edu
Classified Equipment»
Personnel: Rose Dimesio (Advisor)

CRYSTAL LAKE

MCHENRY COUNTY COLLEGE

Street address 1: 8900 US Highway 14
Street address 3: Crystal Lake
Street address state: IL
Zip/Postal code: 60012-2738
Country: USA
Mailing address: 8900 US Highway 14
Mailing city: Crystal Lake
Mailing state: IL
Mailing zip: 60012-2761
General Phone: (815) 455-8571
General Fax:
General/National Adv. E-mail: tartan@mchenry.edu
Primary Website: www.mchenry.edu; www.mcctartan.net
Published: Mthly
Avg Free Circ: 2000
Classified Equipment»
Personnel: Toni Countryman (Advisor)

MILLIKIN UNIV.

Street address 1: 1184 W Main St
Street address 3: Decatur
Street address state: IL
Zip/Postal code: 62522-2039
Country: USA
Mailing address: 1184 W Main St
Mailing city: Decatur
Mailing state: IL
Mailing zip: 62522-2084
General Phone: (217) 425-4626
General Fax: (217) 425-1687
General/National Adv. E-mail: decaturian@millikin.edu
Primary Website: www.thedeconline.com
Classified Equipment»
Personnel: Priscilla Marie Meddaugh (Faculty Advisor); Caitlin Hennessy (Co-Ed. in Chief); Lauren Krage (Co-Ed. in Chief)

RICHLAND CMTY. COLLEGE

Street address 1: 1 College Park
Street address 3: Decatur
Street address state: IL
Zip/Postal code: 62521-8512
Country: USA
Mailing address: 1 College Park
Mailing city: Decatur
Mailing state: IL
Mailing zip: 62521-8513
General Phone: (217) 875-7211
General Fax: (217) 875-6961
General/National Adv. E-mail: comm@richland.edu; communicatur@richland.edu
Primary Website: www.richland.edu
Classified Equipment»
Personnel: Marlise McDaniel (Ed. in Chief); Todd Houser (Ed.); Tina Cooper (Copy Ed.)

DEERFIELD

TRINITY INTERNATIONAL UNIV.

Street address 1: 2065 Half Day Rd
Street address 3: Deerfield
Street address state: IL
Zip/Postal code: 60015-1241
Country: USA
Mailing address: 2065 Half Day Rd # T-2922
Mailing city: Deerfield
Mailing state: IL
Mailing zip: 60015-1241
General Phone: (847) 317-8155
General Fax: (847) 317-8142
Classified Equipment»
Personnel: Erika Sjogren (Ed.)

DEKALB

NORTHERN ILLINOIS UNIV.

Street address 1: Northern Illinois University, Campus Life Building, Suite 130
Street address 3: Dekalb
Street address state: IL
Zip/Postal code: 60115
Country: USA
Mailing address: Northern Illinois University, Campus Life Building, Suite 130
Mailing city: Dekalb
Mailing state: IL
Mailing zip: 60115
General Phone: (815) 753-4239
General Fax: (815) 753-0708
General/National Adv. E-mail: editor@northernstar.info
Display Adv. E-mail: ads@northernstar.info
Editorial e-mail: editor@northernstar.info
Primary Website: www.northernstar.info
Year Established: 1899
News Services: AP
Commercial printers: N
Classified Equipment»
Personnel: Jim Killam (Advisor); Maria Krull (Bus. Advisor); Justin Weaver (Ed.)

DES PLAINES

OAKTON CMTY. COLLEGE

Street address 1: 1600 E Golf Rd
Street address 3: Des Plaines
Street address state: IL
Zip/Postal code: 60016-1234
Country: USA
Mailing address: 1600 E Golf Rd
Mailing city: Des Plaines
Mailing state: IL
Mailing zip: 60016-1268
General Phone: (847) 635-1678
General Fax: (847) 635-2610
General/National Adv. E-mail: occurrence@oakton.edu
Classified Equipment»
Personnel: Sue Fox (Advisor)

EDWARDSVILLE

SOUTHERN ILLINOIS UNIVERSITY EDWARDSVILLE

Street address 1: One Hairpin Drive, Morris University Ctr, Rm 2022
Street address 3: Edwardsville
Street address state: IL
Zip/Postal code: 6202
Country: USA
Mailing address: One Hairpin Drive, Morris University Ctr, Rm 2022
Mailing city: Edwardsville
Mailing state: IL
Mailing zip: 62026
General Phone: (618) 650-3528
General Fax: (618) 650-3514
Display Adv. E-mail: advertising@alestlelive.com
Editorial e-mail: editor@alestlelive.com
Primary Website: www.alestlelive.com
Year Established: 1959
Published: Tues`Thur
Published Other: Tuesdays online exclusively
Avg Free Circ: 3500
Classified Equipment»
Personnel: Tammy Merrett (Advisor)
Parent company (for newspapers): Southern Illinois University Edwardsville

ELGIN

ELGIN COMMUNITY COLLEGE

Street address 1: 1700 Spartan Dr
Street address 3: Elgin
Street address state: IL
Zip/Postal code: 60123-7189
Country: USA
Mailing address: 1700 Spartan Dr
Mailing city: Elgin
Mailing state: IL
Mailing zip: 60123-7193
General Phone: (847) 697-1000
General Fax: (847) 888-7352
General/National Adv. E-mail: elginobserver@gmail.com
Display Adv. E-mail: elgincollegeobserver@yahoo.com
Editorial e-mail: observereditorinchief@gmail.com
Primary Website: www.elgin.edu
Year Established: 1951
Delivery Methods: Racks
Published Other: Bi-weekly
Avg Paid Circ: 1000
Classified Equipment»
Personnel: Lori Clark (Faculty Advisor); Michelle Pain (Editor-in-Chief); Fernando Chang (Managing Editor)

ELMHURST

ELMHURST COLLEGE

Street address 1: 190 S Prospect Ave
Street address 3: Elmhurst
Street address state: IL
Zip/Postal code: 60126-3271
Country: USA
Mailing address: 190 S Prospect Ave
Mailing city: Elmhurst

Mailing state: IL
Mailing zip: 60126-3296
General Phone: (630)617-3320
Advertising Phone: (630) 617-3321
General/National Adv. E-mail: leadernewsec@gmail.com
Display Adv. E-mail: advertising@ecleader.org
Editorial e-mail: leadernewsec@gmail.com
Primary Website: ecleader.org
Published: Tues
Published Other: Published bi-weekly
Classified Equipment»
Personnel: Ron Wiginton (Advisor); Aaron Schroeder (Bus. Mgr.); Eric Lutz (Ed. in Chief); Haleema Shah (Editor-in-Chief)

ELSAH

PRINCIPIA COLLEGE

Street address 1: 1 Maybeck Pl
Street address 3: Elsah
Street address state: IL
Zip/Postal code: 62028-9720
Country: USA
Mailing address: 1 Maybeck Pl
Mailing city: Elsah
Mailing state: IL
Mailing zip: 62028-9799
General Phone: (618) 374-5415
General Fax: (618) 374-5122
General/National Adv. E-mail: principia.pilot@gmail.com
Primary Website: www.prin.edu; www.principiapilot.org
Year Established: 1944
Classified Equipment»
Personnel: Craig Savoye (Advisor); David Miller (Ed. in Chief); Katie Ward (Ed. in Chief); Ben Chernivsky (Photo Ed.)

KELLOGG GRAD. SCHOOL OF MGMT.

Street address 1: 2001 Sheridan Rd
Street address 3: Evanston
Street address state: IL
Zip/Postal code: 60208-0814
Country: USA
Mailing address: 2001 Sheridan Rd
Mailing city: Evanston
Mailing state: IL
Mailing zip: 60208-0814
General Phone: (847) 491-3924
General Fax: (847) 467-6173
Classified Equipment»
Personnel: Nick Slater (Ed.)

NORTHWESTERN UNIVERSITY

Street address 1: 1999 Campus Dr
Street address 3: Evanston
Street address state: IL
Zip/Postal code: 60208-0825
Country: USA
Mailing address: 1999 Campus Dr
Mailing city: Evanston
Mailing state: IL
Mailing zip: 60208-2532
General Phone: (847) 491-3222
General Fax: (847) 491-9905
Editorail Phone: (847) 491-7206
General/National Adv. E-mail: eic@dailynorthwestern.com
Display Adv. E-mail: spc-compshop@northwestern.edu
Primary Website: www.dailynorthwestern.com
Year Established: 1881
Published: Mon`Tues`Wed`Thur`Fri
Classified Equipment»
Parent company (for newspapers): Students Publishing Company

NORTHWESTERN UNIVERSITY

Street address 1: 1845 Sheridan Rd
Street address 3: Evanston
Street address state: IL
Zip/Postal code: 60208-0815
Country: USA
Mailing address: 1845 Sheridan Rd
Mailing city: Evanston
Mailing state: IL
Mailing zip: 60208-0815
General Phone: (847) 467-1882
General Fax: (847) 491-5565
Classified Equipment»
Personnel: John Lavine (Dean); David Abrahamson (Prof.); Martin Block (Prof.); Jack Doppelt (Prof.); Loren Ghiglione (Prof.); Alec Klein (Prof.); Donna Leff (Prof.); Frank Mulhern (Prof.); Jon Petrovich (Prof.); David Protess (Prof.); Don Schultz (Prof.); Ellen Shearer (Prof.); Clarke Caywood (Assoc. Prof.); Mary Coffman (Assoc. Prof.); Tom Collinger (Assoc. Prof.); Doug Foster (Assoc. Prof.); Jeremy Gilbert (Assoc. Prof.); Rich Gordon (Assoc. Prof.); John Greening (Assoc. Prof.); Ava Greenwell (Assoc. Prof.)

FREEPORT

HIGHLAND CMTY. COLLEGE

Street address 1: 2998 W Pearl City Rd
Street address 3: Freeport
Street address state: IL
Zip/Postal code: 61032-9338
Country: USA
Mailing address: 2998 W Pearl City Rd
Mailing city: Freeport
Mailing state: IL
Mailing zip: 61032-9341
General Phone: (815) 235-6121
General Fax: (815) 235-6130
General/National Adv. E-mail: highland.chronicle@highland.edu
Classified Equipment»
Personnel: Sam Tucibat (Advisor)

GALESBURG

CARL SANDBURG COLLEGE

Street address 1: 140 S Prairie St
Street address 3: Galesburg
Street address state: IL
Zip/Postal code: 61401-4605
Country: USA
Mailing address: 140 S Prairie St
Mailing city: Galesburg
Mailing state: IL
Mailing zip: 61401-4605
General Phone: (309) 344-2518
General Fax: (309) 342-5171
Classified Equipment»

KNOX COLLEGE

Street address 1: 2 E South St
Street address 2: Knox College K-240
Street address 3: Galesburg
Street address state: IL
Zip/Postal code: 61401-4938
Country: USA
Mailing address: 2 E South St Knox College K-240
Mailing city: Galesburg
Mailing state: IL
Mailing zip: 61401-4999
General Phone: (646) 784-4367
General Fax: (309) 341-7081
General/National Adv. E-mail: tks@knox.edu
Display Adv. E-mail: tksmarketing@knox.edu
Primary Website: KNOX COLLEGE BOX 2 E SOUTH ST
Year Established: 1878
Published: Thur
Classified Equipment»
Personnel: Tom Martin (Advisor); Jonathan Schrag (Co-Editor-in-Chief); Lillie Chamberlin (Co-Editor-in-Chief)

GLEN ELLYN

COLLEGE OF DUPAGE

Street address 1: 425 Fawell Blvd
Street address 3: Glen Ellyn
Street address state: IL
Zip/Postal code: 60137-6708
Country: USA
Mailing address: 425 Fawell Blvd.
Mailing city: Glen Ellyn
Mailing state: IL
Mailing zip: 60137-6599
General Phone: (630) 942-2113
General Fax: (630) 942-3747
Editorial e-mail: editor@cod.edu
Primary Website: www.codcourier.org
Year Established: 1967
Delivery Methods: Newsstand
Commercial printers: Y
Published: Wed
Classified Equipment»
Personnel: Nick Davison (Editor-in-chief)

GODFREY

LEWIS AND CLARK CMTY. COLLEGE

Street address 1: 5800 Godfrey Rd
Street address 3: Godfrey
Street address state: IL
Zip/Postal code: 62035-2426
Country: USA
Mailing address: 5800 Godfrey Rd
Mailing city: Godfrey
Mailing state: IL
Mailing zip: 62035-2466
General Phone: (618) 468-6042
General Fax: (618) 468-6055
Editorail Phone: (618) 468-6044
General/National Adv. E-mail: bridge@lc.edu
Classified Equipment»
Personnel: Lori Artis (Advisor); Anthony Lanham (Ed.)

COLLEGE OF LAKE COUNTY

Street address 1: 19351 W Washington St
Street address 3: Grayslake
Street address state: IL
Zip/Postal code: 60030-1148
Country: USA
Mailing address: 19351 W Washington St
Mailing city: Grayslake
Mailing state: IL
Mailing zip: 60030-1198
General Phone: (847) 543-2057
Advertising Phone: (847) 543-2362
Primary Website: www.clcillinois.edu/activities/chronicle.asp
Classified Equipment»
Personnel: John Kupetz (Faculty Advisor); Nathan Caldwell (Ed. in Chief)

GREENVILLE COLLEGE

Street address 1: 315 E College Ave
Street address 3: Greenville
Street address state: IL
Zip/Postal code: 62246-1145
Country: USA
Mailing address: 315 E College Ave
Mailing city: Greenville
Mailing state: IL
Mailing zip: 62246-1145
General Phone: (618) 664-2800
General Fax: (618) 664-1373
General/National Adv. E-mail: papyrus@greenville.edu
Primary Website: www.greenville.edu
Classified Equipment»
Personnel: Susan Chism (Advisor)

INA

REND LAKE COLLEGE

Street address 1: 468 N Ken Gray Pkwy
Street address 3: Ina
Street address state: IL
Zip/Postal code: 62846-2408
Country: USA
Mailing address: 468 N Ken Gray Pkwy
Mailing city: Ina
Mailing state: IL
Mailing zip: 62846-2408
General Phone: (618) 437-5321
Classified Equipment»
Personnel: Michael Peeples (Ed.)

ILLINOIS COLLEGE

Street address 1: 1101 W College Ave
Street address 3: Jacksonville
Street address state: IL
Zip/Postal code: 62650-2212
Country: USA
Mailing address: 1101 W College Ave
Mailing city: Jacksonville
Mailing state: IL
Mailing zip: 62650-2299
General Phone: (217) 245-3030
General Fax: (217) 245-3056
General/National Adv. E-mail: rambler@ic.edu
Primary Website: www.ic.edu
Classified Equipment»
Personnel: John S. Rush (Advisor); Laurel Berkel (Ed.)

JOLIET

JOLIET JUNIOR COLLEGE

Street address 1: 1215 Houbolt Rd
Street address 3: Joliet
Street address state: IL
Zip/Postal code: 60431-8938
Country: USA
Mailing address: 1215 Houbolt Rd
Mailing city: Joliet
Mailing state: IL
Mailing zip: 60431-8800
General Phone: (815) 280-2313
General Fax: (815) 280-6730
Advertising Phone: (815) 280-2313
Advertising Fax: (815) 280-6730
Editorail Phone: (815) 280-2313
Editorial Fax: (815) 280-2313
General/National Adv. E-mail: blazermail@jjc.edu
Display Adv. E-mail: blazermail@jjc.edu
Editorial e-mail: blazermail@jjc.edu
Primary Website: www.jjc.edu/blazer
News Services: None
Special Editions: None
Special Weekly Sections: None
Delivery Methods: Racks
Advertising (Open Inch Rate) Weekday/Saturday: $6 per column inch
Published: Other
Published Other: Our frequency is tri-weekly, or 5 times per semester.
Avg Free Circ: 2000
Classified Equipment»
Personnel: Robert Marcink (Advisor)

UNIV. OF ST. FRANCIS

Street address 1: 500 Wilcox St
Street address 3: Joliet
Street address state: IL
Zip/Postal code: 60435-6169
Country: USA
Mailing address: 500 Wilcox St
Mailing city: Joliet
Mailing state: IL
Mailing zip: 60435-6188
General Phone: (815) 740-3816
General Fax: (815) 740-4285
General/National Adv. E-mail: encounter@stfrancis.edu
Primary Website: http://usfencounter.stfrancis.edu
Published: Mthly
Avg Free Circ: 500
Classified Equipment»
Personnel: Brien McHugh (Advisor); Mike Clinton (Editor in Chief); Thaschara VanDyke (Asst. Editor in Chief)

LAKE FOREST

LAKE FOREST COLLEGE

Street address 1: 555 N Sheridan Rd
Street address 3: Lake Forest
Street address state: IL
Zip/Postal code: 60045-2338
Country: USA
Mailing address: 555 N Sheridan Rd
Mailing city: Lake Forest
Mailing state: IL
Mailing zip: 60045-2399
General Phone: (847) 735-5215
General Fax: (847) 735-6298
General/National Adv. E-mail: stentor@lakeforest.edu
Primary Website: www.thestentor.com
Classified Equipment»

Personnel: Heather Brown (Advisor); Annie Cooper (Ed. in Chief); Nate Butala (Mng. Ed.)

MCKENDREE UNIVERSITY

Street address 1: 701 College Rd
Street address 3: Lebanon
Street address state: IL
Zip/Postal code: 62254-1291
Country: USA
Mailing address: 701 College Rd
Mailing city: Lebanon
Mailing state: IL
Mailing zip: 62254-1291
General Phone: (618) 537-6821
General Fax: (618) 537-2377
General/National Adv. E-mail: mckreview@mckendree.edu
Primary Website: lance.mckendree.edu/review/
Classified Equipment»
Personnel: Gabe Shapiro (Faculty Advisor); Sarah Adams (Editor in Chief); Chris Moore (Associate Editor); Kevin Schaefer (Web/Design Editor); Theresa Schmidt (Ed. in Chief)

LISLE

BENEDICTINE UNIV.

Street address 1: 5700 College Rd
Street address 3: Lisle
Street address state: IL
Zip/Postal code: 60532-2851
Country: USA
Mailing address: 5700 College Rd
Mailing city: Lisle
Mailing state: IL
Mailing zip: 60532-0900
General Phone: (630) 829-6252
General Fax: (630) 960-1126
General/National Adv. E-mail: thecandor@yahoo.com
Primary Website: www.thecandor.com
Year Established: 1982
Published: Wed
Avg Free Circ: 2000
Classified Equipment»
Note: Digital only
Personnel: Chris Birks (Advisor)

LOMBARD

NATIONAL COLLEGE OF CHIROPRACTIC

Street address 1: 200 E Roosevelt Rd
Street address 3: Lombard
Street address state: IL
Zip/Postal code: 60148-4539
Country: USA
Mailing address: 200 E. Roosevelt Rd
Mailing city: Lombard
Mailing state: IL
Mailing zip: 60148-4539
General Phone: (630) 889-6628
General Fax: (630) 889-6554
Published: Mthly
Avg Free Circ: 5000
Classified Equipment»
Personnel: Frank Sutter (Ed.)

MACOMB

WESTERN ILLINOIS UNIVERSITY

Street address 1: 1 University Cir
Street address 2: Western Illinois University
Street address 3: Macomb
Street address state: IL
Zip/Postal code: 61455-1367
Country: USA
Mailing address: 1 University Cir
Mailing city: Macomb
Mailing state: IL
Mailing zip: 61455-1390
General Phone: (309) 298-1876
General Fax: (309) 298-2309
Advertising Phone: (309) 298-1876
Advertising Fax: (309) 298-2309
Editorail Phone: (309) 298-1876
Editorial Fax: (309) 298-2309
General/National Adv. E-mail: westerncourier@wiu.edu; micour@wiu.edu
Display Adv. E-mail: westerncourier@gmail.com
Editorial e-mail: wj-buss@wiu.edu
Primary Website: www.westerncourier.com
Year Established: 1905
Delivery Methods: Carrier
Commercial printers: N
Advertising (Open Inch Rate) Weekday/Saturday: $5.50 per column inch (B/W); $7.50 per col. inch (color)
Published: Mon`Wed`Fri
Avg Free Circ: 4000
Classified Equipment»
Personnel: Devon Greene (Editor-in-Chief); Nick Ebelhack (Editor-in-Chief); Rachel Nelson (Advertising Manager); Will Buss (Advisor)

MALTA

KISHWAUKEE COLLEGE

Street address 1: 21193 Malta Rd
Street address 3: Malta
Street address state: IL
Zip/Postal code: 60150-9600
Country: USA
Mailing address: 21193 Malta Rd
Mailing city: Malta
Mailing state: IL
Mailing zip: 60150-9699
General Phone: (815) 825-2086
General Fax: (815) 825-2072
General/National Adv. E-mail: kscope@kishwaukeecollege.edu
Primary Website: www.kishkscope.com
Classified Equipment»
Personnel: Melissa Blake (Advisor); John Myers (Adv. Mgr.); Andrew Hallgren (Ed. in Chief); Nelle Smith (Ed.); John (Instructor); Marissa Skonie (Ed. In Chief)

MATTOON

LAKE LAND COLLEGE

Street address 1: 5001 Lake Land Blvd
Street address 3: Mattoon
Street address state: IL
Zip/Postal code: 61938-9366
Country: USA
Mailing address: 5001 Lake Land Blvd
Mailing city: Mattoon
Mailing state: IL
Mailing zip: 61938-9366
General Phone: (217) 234-5269
General Fax: (217) 234-5390
General/National Adv. E-mail: studentpublications@lakeland.cc.il.us
Primary Website: www.navigatornews.org
Published: Mthly
Classified Equipment»
Personnel: Valerie Lynch (Dir of Student Life)

MOLINE

BLACK HAWK COLLEGE

Street address 1: 6600 34th Ave
Street address 2: Bldg 4
Street address 3: Moline
Street address state: IL
Zip/Postal code: 61265-5870
Country: USA
Mailing address: 6600 34th Ave Bldg 4
Mailing city: Moline
Mailing state: IL
Mailing zip: 61265-5899
General Phone: (309) 796-5477
General Fax: (309) 792-5976
General/National Adv. E-mail: chieftain@bhc.edu
Classified Equipment»
Personnel: Tory Becht (Advisor); Thomas Cross (Ed.); David Craig (Ed.)

MONMOUTH

MONMOUTH COLLEGE

Street address 1: 700 E Broadway
Street address 3: Monmouth
Street address state: IL
Zip/Postal code: 61462-1963
Country: USA
Mailing address: 700 E Broadway
Mailing city: Monmouth
Mailing state: IL
Mailing zip: 61462-1998
General Phone: (309) 457-3456
General Fax: (309) 457-2363
General/National Adv. E-mail: courier@monm.edu
Primary Website: www.monm.edu/courier
Classified Equipment»
Personnel: Michelle Nutting (Adv. Mgr.); Lucas Pauley (Ed. in Chief)

NAPERVILLE

NORTH CENTRAL COLLEGE

Street address 1: 31 N Loomis St
Street address 3: Naperville
Street address state: IL
Zip/Postal code: 60540-4756
Country: USA
Mailing address: 31 N Loomis St
Mailing city: Naperville
Mailing state: IL
Mailing zip: 60540
General Phone: (630) 637-5422
General Fax: (630) 637-5441
General/National Adv. E-mail: chronicle@noctrl.edu
Primary Website: orgs.noctrl.edu/chronicle
Classified Equipment»
Personnel: Nancy Kirby (Faculty Advisor)

ILLINOIS STATE UNIVERSITY

Street address 1: Illinois State University
Street address 2: Campus Box 0890
Street address 3: Normal
Street address state: IL
Zip/Postal code: 61761
Country: USA
Mailing address: 100 North University Street
Mailing city: Normal
Mailing state: IL
Mailing zip: 61761
General Phone: (309) 438-7685
General Fax: (309) 438-5211
Advertising Phone: (309) 438-8742
Editorail Phone: (309) 438-8745
General/National Adv. E-mail: vidette@ilstu.edu
Display Adv. E-mail: vidette@ilstu.edu
Editorial e-mail: vidette@ilstu.edu
Primary Website: www.videtteonline.com
Year Established: 1888
Delivery Methods: Racks
Classified Equipment»
Personnel: John Plevka (Gen. Mgr.); Brooke Goodwin (Bus. Mgr.); Amy Gorczowski (Ed.); Kristi Demonbreun (Ed.)

WILLIAM RAINEY HARPER COLLEGE

Street address 1: 1200 W Algonquin Rd
Street address 3: Palatine
Street address state: IL
Zip/Postal code: 60067-7373
Country: USA
Mailing address: 1200 W Algonquin Rd
Mailing city: Palatine
Mailing state: IL
Mailing zip: 60067-7398
General Phone: (847) 925-6460
General Fax: (847) 925-6033
General/National Adv. E-mail: harperharbinger@gmail.com
Primary Website: www.harpercollege.edu
Classified Equipment»
Personnel: Kent McDill (Advisor)

PALOS HEIGHTS

TRINITY CHRISTIAN COLLEGE

Street address 1: 6601 W College Dr
Street address 3: Palos Heights
Street address state: IL
Zip/Postal code: 60463-1768
Country: USA
Mailing address: 6601 W College Dr
Mailing city: Palos Heights
Mailing state: IL
Mailing zip: 60463-0929
General Phone: (708) 239-4715
General Fax: (708) 385-5665
General/National Adv. E-mail: www.trnty.edu
Classified Equipment»
Personnel: Whitney Dickison (Ed. in Chief)

PALOS HILLS

MORAINE VALLEY CMTY. COLLEGE

Street address 1: 9000 W College Pkwy
Street address 3: Palos Hills
Street address state: IL
Zip/Postal code: 60465-1444
Country: USA
Mailing address: 9000 W. College Pkwy.
Mailing city: Palos Hills
Mailing state: IL
Mailing zip: 60465-0937
General Phone: (708) 608-4177
General Fax: (708) 974-0790
General/National Adv. E-mail: glacier@morainevalley.edu
Primary Website: www.mvccglacier.com
Published Other: Bi-Wkly
Classified Equipment»
Personnel: Stacey Reichard (Advisor); William Lukitsch; Rob Peto (Ed. in Chief); Frank Florez (News Ed.)

BRADLEY UNIVERSITY

Street address 1: 1501 W Bradley Ave
Street address 3: Peoria
Street address state: IL
Zip/Postal code: 61625-0001
Country: USA
Mailing address: 1501 W Bradley Ave
Mailing city: Peoria
Mailing state: IL
Mailing zip: 61625-0003
General Phone: (309) 676-7611
General Fax: (309) 677-2609
Advertising Phone: (309) 676-7611
General/National Adv. E-mail: bradleyscout@gmail.com
Display Adv. E-mail: bradleyscout@gmail.com
Editorial e-mail: bradleyscout@gmail.com
Primary Website: www.bradleyscout.com
Year Established: 1898
Commercial printers: N
Published: Fri
Avg Free Circ: 4000
Classified Equipment»
Personnel: Sam Pallini (Ed.); Kristin Kreher (Managing Ed.); Travis Kelso (Adv. Mgr.)

QUINCY

QUINCY UNIV.

Street address 1: 1800 College Ave
Street address 3: Quincy
Street address state: IL
Zip/Postal code: 62301-2670
Country: USA
Mailing address: 1800 College Ave
Mailing city: Quincy
Mailing state: IL
Mailing zip: 62301-2699
General Phone: (217) 228-5275
General Fax: (217) 228-5473
General/National Adv. E-mail: qufalcon@gmail.com
Primary Website: http://www.quincy.edu/information/publications-a-media/the-falcon
Year Established: 1929

Published: Mthly
Classified Equipment»
Personnel: David Adam (Advisor); Barbara Schleppenbach (Chair of Fine Arts & Communication)

RIVER FOREST

CONCORDIA UNIV.

Street address 1: 7400 Augusta St
Street address 3: River Forest
Street address state: IL
Zip/Postal code: 60305-1402
Country: USA
Mailing address: 7400 Augusta Street
Mailing city: River Forest
Mailing state: IL
Mailing zip: 60305-1499
General Phone: (708) 209-3191
General Fax: (708) 209-3176
Display Adv. E-mail: spectator@cuchicago.edu
Primary Website: www.cuchicago.edu/student_life/spectator
Classified Equipment»
Personnel: Melissa Williams (Advisor); Benjamin Parviz (Adv. Mgr.); Kathryn Klement (Ed.)

DOMINICAN UNIV.

Street address 1: 7900 Division St
Street address 3: River Forest
Street address state: IL
Zip/Postal code: 60305-1066
Country: USA
Mailing address: 7900 Division St
Mailing city: River Forest
Mailing state: IL
Mailing zip: 60305-1066
General Phone: (708) 524-6800
General Fax: (708) 524-5900
General/National Adv. E-mail: domadmis@dom.edu
Classified Equipment»
Personnel: Marie Simpson (Advisor)

RIVER GROVE

TRITON COLLEGE

Street address 1: 2000 5th Ave
Street address 3: River Grove
Street address state: IL
Zip/Postal code: 60171-1907
Country: USA
Mailing address: 2000 5th Ave
Mailing city: River Grove
Mailing state: IL
Mailing zip: 60171-1995
General Phone: (708) 456-0300
Primary Website: www.triton.edu
Classified Equipment»
Personnel: Dawn Unger (Ed. in Chief)

ROCK ISLAND

AUGUSTANA COLLEGE

Street address 1: 639 38th St
Street address 3: Rock Island
Street address state: IL
Zip/Postal code: 61201-2210
Country: USA
Mailing address: 639 38th St
Mailing city: Rock Island
Mailing state: IL
Mailing zip: 61201-2296
General Phone: (309) 794-3460
General Fax: (309) 794-3460
Advertising Phone: (309) 794-7484
Editorail Phone: (309) 794-7485
General/National Adv. E-mail: observer@augustana.edu
Primary Website: www.augustana.edu
Classified Equipment»
Personnel: Carolyn Yaschur (Advisor); David Schwartz (Advisor)

ROCKFORD

ROCK VALLEY COLLEGE

Street address 1: 3301 N Mulford Rd
Street address 3: Rockford
Street address state: IL
Zip/Postal code: 61114-5640
Country: USA
Mailing address: 3301 N Mulford Rd
Mailing city: Rockford
Mailing state: IL
Mailing zip: 61114-5699
General Phone: (815) 921-7821
General Fax: (815) 921-3333
Classified Equipment»
Personnel: Frank Coffman (Advisor)

ROMEOVILLE

LEWIS UNIV.

Street address 1: 1 University Pkwy
Street address 3: Romeoville
Street address state: IL
Zip/Postal code: 60446-2200
Country: USA
Mailing address: 1 University Pkwy
Mailing city: Romeoville
Mailing state: IL
Mailing zip: 60446-1832
General Phone: (815) 836-5196
General/National Adv. E-mail: lewisflyernews@gmail.com
Primary Website: www.thelewisflyer.com
Classified Equipment»
Personnel: Lisa O'Toole (Advisor); Adam Olszeski (Ed. in Chief)

LINCOLN LAND CMTY. COLLEGE

Street address 1: 5250 Shepherd Rd
Street address 3: Springfield
Street address state: IL
Zip/Postal code: 62703-5402
Country: USA
Mailing address: 5250 Shepherd Rd
Mailing city: Springfield
Mailing state: IL
Mailing zip: 62703-5408
General Phone: (217) 786-2318
General Fax: (217) 786-2340
Primary Website: www.llcc.edu
Classified Equipment»
Personnel: Brenda Protz (Advisor)

UNIV. OF ILLINOIS/SPRINGFIELD

Street address 1: 1 University Plz
Street address 2: Sab 20
Street address 3: Springfield
Street address state: IL
Zip/Postal code: 62703-5497
Country: USA
Mailing address: 1 University Plz
Mailing city: Springfield
Mailing state: IL
Mailing zip: 62703-5407
General Phone: (217) 206-6397
General Fax: (217) 206-6048
Advertising Phone: (217) 206-7717
Advertising Fax: (217) 206-6048
Editorail Phone: (217) 206-6397
Editorial Fax: (217) 206-6048
General/National Adv. E-mail: journal@uis.edu
Display Adv. E-mail: journalmgr@uis.edu
Editorial e-mail: journal@uis.edu
Primary Website: www.uisjournal.com
Year Established: 1985
Advertising (Open Inch Rate) Weekday/Saturday: $7 per column inch
Published: Wed
Published Other: Back-to-school edition in July/mailed to newly enrolled students and circulated
Avg Free Circ: 3000
Classified Equipment»
Note: www.uisjournal.com Web provider: Student Newspapers Online
Personnel: Debra Landis (Faculty Advisor); Marc Cox (EIC)

SUGAR GROVE

WAUBONSEE CMTY. COLLEGE

Street address 1: Rt 47 at Waubonsee Dr
Street address 3: Sugar Grove
Street address state: IL
Zip/Postal code: 60554
Country: USA
Mailing address: Rt. 47 at Waubonsee Dr.
Mailing city: Sugar Grove
Mailing state: IL
Mailing zip: 60554
General Phone: (630) 466-2555
General Fax: (630) 466-9102
General/National Adv. E-mail: insight@waubonsee.edu
Primary Website: www.waubonsee.edu
Classified Equipment»
Personnel: Gary Clarke (Advisor); DJ Terek (Ed. in Chief)

UNIVERSITY PARK

GOVERNORS STATE UNIV.

Street address 1: 1 University Pkwy
Street address 2: E2543
Street address 3: University Park
Street address state: IL
Zip/Postal code: 60484-3165
Country: USA
Mailing address: 1 University Pkwy.
Mailing city: University Park
Mailing state: IL
Mailing zip: 60484-3165
General Phone: (708) 534-4517
General Fax: (708) 534-7895
General/National Adv. E-mail: phoenix@govst.edu
Primary Website: www.gsuphoenix.com
Published: Wed
Published Other: First and third Wednesdays
Classified Equipment»
Personnel: Debbie James (Faculty Advisor); Michael Purdy (Emeritus Professor)

WHEATON

WHEATON COLLEGE

Street address 1: 501 College Ave
Street address 2: Cpo W135
Street address 3: Wheaton
Street address state: IL
Zip/Postal code: 60187-5501
Country: USA
Mailing address: 501 College Ave.
Mailing city: Wheaton
Mailing state: IL
Mailing zip: 60187
General Phone: (630) 752-5077
General/National Adv. E-mail: the.record@my.wheaton.edu
Display Adv. E-mail: ads.wheatonrecord@gmail.com
Editorial e-mail: the.record@wheaton.edu
Primary Website: http://www.wheatonrecord.com/
Year Established: 1876
Delivery Methods: Mail`Racks
Advertising (Open Inch Rate) Weekday/Saturday: Yes
Published: Thur
Classified Equipment»
Personnel: Philip Kline (Co-editor in chief); Alycia Vander Vegt (Co-editor in chief)

INDIANA

ANDERSON

ANDERSON UNIV.

Street address 1: 1100 E 5th St
Street address 3: Anderson
Street address state: IN
Zip/Postal code: 46012-3462
Country: USA
Mailing address: 1100 E 5th St
Mailing city: Anderson
Mailing state: IN
Mailing zip: 46012-3495
General Phone: (765) 641-4341
General Fax: (765) 641-3851
General/National Adv. E-mail: andersonian@anderson.edu
Primary Website: www.anderson.edu/andersonian/
Classified Equipment»
Personnel: David Baird (Advisor); Kayla Dunkman (Ed. in Chief); Tarah Novak (Ed.); Stacy Wood (Ed.)

INDIANA UNIV. KELLEY SCHOOL OF BUS.

Street address 1: 1309 E 10th St
Street address 3: Bloomington
Street address state: IN
Zip/Postal code: 47405-1701
Country: USA
Mailing address: 1309 E 10th St
Mailing city: Bloomington
Mailing state: IN
Mailing zip: 47405-5308
General Phone: (812) 855-8100
General Fax: (812) 855-9039
Classified Equipment»
Personnel: Chris Hildreth (Ed.)

INDIANA UNIV. INDIANA DAILY STUDENT

Street address 1: 601 E. Kirkwood Ave
Street address 2: Rm 130
Street address 3: Bloomington
Street address state: IN
Zip/Postal code: 47405
Country: USA
General Phone: (812) 855-0763
General Fax: (812) 855-8009
General/National Adv. E-mail: ids@indiana.edu
Primary Website: www.idsnews.com
Published: Thur
Classified Equipment»
Personnel: Susan McGlocklin (Advisor); Jim Rodenbush (Director)

UNIV. OF EVANSVILLE

Street address 1: 1800 Lincoln Ave
Street address 3: Evansville
Street address state: IN
Zip/Postal code: 47722-1000
Country: USA
Mailing address: 1800 Lincoln Ave
Mailing city: Evansville
Mailing state: IN
Mailing zip: 47714-1506
General Phone: (812) 488-2846
General Fax: (812) 488-2224
Advertising Phone: 812-488-2221
Advertising Fax: (812) 488-2224
Editorail Phone: (812) 488-2846
Editorial Fax: (812) 488-2224
General/National Adv. E-mail: crescentmagazine@evansville.edu
Display Adv. E-mail: crescentadvertising@evansville.edu
Editorial e-mail: crescentmagazine@evansville.edu
Year Established: 2009
Advertising (Open Inch Rate) Weekday/Saturday: yes
Published: Thur`Mthly
Avg Free Circ: 1700
Classified Equipment»
Note: We no longer offer a weekly newspaper. We switched format in fall 2009. We are now a monthly magazine.
Personnel: Amy Reinhart (Writing Director); Rebecca Kish (Marketing & Sales Director)

UNIV. OF SOUTHERN INDIANA

Street address 1: 8600 University Blvd
Street address 3: Evansville
Street address state: IN
Zip/Postal code: 47712-3534
Country: USA
Mailing address: 8600 University Blvd
Mailing city: Evansville
Mailing state: IN
Mailing zip: 47712-3590
General Phone: (812) 464 8600

General Fax: (812) 465-1632
Advertising Phone: (812) 464-1870
General/National Adv. E-mail: sheild@usi.edu
Display Adv. E-mail: shieldads@gmail.com
Editorial e-mail: shieldpix@gmail.com
Primary Website: www.usishield.com; www.usi.edu
Classified Equipment»
Personnel: Jon Webb (Ed. in Chief)

INDIANA-PURDUE UNIV.

Street address 1: 2101 E Coliseum Blvd
Street address 2: Walb 215
Street address 3: Fort Wayne
Street address state: IN
Zip/Postal code: 46805-1445
Country: USA
Mailing address: 2101 E Coliseum Blvd Ste 100
Mailing city: Fort Wayne
Mailing state: IN
Mailing zip: 46805-1499
General Phone: (260) 481-6583
General Fax: (260) 481-6045
General/National Adv. E-mail: publisher@ipfwcommunicator.org
Display Adv. E-mail: ads@ipfwcommunicator.org
Primary Website: www.ipfwcommunicator.org
Classified Equipment»
Personnel: Matt cClure (Pub.); Kristin Conley (Adv. Mgr.); Aaron Greene (Ed. in Chief)

FRANKLIN

FRANKLIN COLLEGE

Street address 1: 101 Branigin Blvd
Street address 3: Franklin
Street address state: IN
Zip/Postal code: 46131-2598
Country: USA
Mailing address: 101 Branigin Blvd
Mailing city: Franklin
Mailing state: IN
Mailing zip: 46131-2623
General Phone: (317) 738-8191
General Fax: (317) 738-8234
General/National Adv. E-mail: thefranklin@franklincollege.edu
Primary Website: www.thefranklinonline.com
Classified Equipment»
Personnel: Katie Coffin (Ed.)

GARY

INDIANA UNIV. NORTHWEST

Street address 1: 3400 Broadway, Moraine 110
Street address 3: Gary
Street address state: IN
Zip/Postal code: 46408
Country: USA
Mailing address: 3400 Broadway, Moraine 110
Mailing city: Gary
Mailing state: IN
Mailing zip: 46408-1101
General Phone: (219) 980-6795
General Fax: (219) 980-6948
General/National Adv. E-mail: phoenixn@iun.edu
Primary Website: www.iun.edu/~phoenixn
Classified Equipment»
Personnel: Scott Fulk (Coordinator); Don Sjoerdsma (Ed. in Chief)

GOSHEN COLLEGE

Street address 1: 1700 S Main St
Street address 3: Goshen
Street address state: IN
Zip/Postal code: 46526-4724
Country: USA
Mailing address: 1700 S Main St
Mailing city: Goshen
Mailing state: IN
Mailing zip: 46526-4794
General Phone: (574) 535-7745
General Fax: (574) 535-7660
General/National Adv. E-mail: record@goshen.edu
Primary Website: record.goshen.edu
Classified Equipment»
Personnel: Duane Stoltzfus; Marlys Weaver (Ed. in Chief)

GREENCASTLE

DEPAUW UNIV.

Street address 1: 609 S Locust St
Street address 3: Greencastle
Street address state: IN
Zip/Postal code: 46135-2047
Country: USA
Mailing address: 609 S Locust St
Mailing city: Greencastle
Mailing state: IN
Mailing zip: 46135-2047
General Phone: (765) 658-5972
General Fax: (765) 658-5991
Primary Website: www.thedepauw.com
Classified Equipment»
Personnel: Lili Wright (Advisor); Samuel Autman (Advisor); Jonathan Batuello (Ed. in Chief); Alex Turco (Exec. Ed.); Macy Ayers (Mng. Ed.)

HAMMOND

PURDUE UNIVERSITY CALUMET

Street address 1: 2200 169th St
Street address 3: Hammond
Street address state: IN
Zip/Postal code: 46323-2068
Country: USA
Mailing address: 2200 169th St
Mailing city: Hammond
Mailing state: IN
Mailing zip: 46323-2068
General Phone: (219) 989-2547
General Fax: (219) 989-2770
General/National Adv. E-mail: pucchronicle@gmail.com
Display Adv. E-mail: chronicle.businessmanager@gmail.com
Editorial e-mail: pucchronicle@gmail.com
Primary Website: pucchronicle.com
Year Established: 1982
Published: Mon
Classified Equipment»
Personnel: Jessica Gerlich (Editor-in-Chief); William Koester (Sports Editor); Michelle Mullins (Entertainment Editor); Dante Vidal Silguero (Business Manager); Morgan Walker (Photo Editor); Samantha Gonzalez (Production Manager)

HANOVER

HANOVER COLLEGE

Street address 1: PO Box 890
Street address 3: Hanover
Street address state: IN
Zip/Postal code: 47243-0890
Country: USA
Mailing address: PO Box 890
Mailing city: Hanover
Mailing state: IN
Mailing zip: 47243-0890
General Phone: (812) 866-7073
General Fax: (812) 866-7077
General/National Adv. E-mail: triangle@hanover.edu
Primary Website: www.hanovertriangle.com
Classified Equipment»
Personnel: Kay Stokes (Fac. Advisor); Melisa Cole (Mng. Ed.)

BUTLER UNIV.

Street address 1: 4600 Sunset Ave
Street address 3: Indianapolis
Street address state: IN
Zip/Postal code: 46208-3443
Country: USA
Mailing address: 4600 Sunset Ave # 112
Mailing city: Indianapolis
Mailing state: IN
Mailing zip: 46208-3487
General Phone: (317) 940-9358
General Fax: (317) 940-9713
General/National Adv. E-mail: mweiteka@butler.edu
Display Adv. E-mail: advertising@butler.edu
Primary Website: dawgnet.butler.edu
Classified Equipment»
Personnel: Kwadwo Anokwa (Dir.); Charles St. Cyr (Advisor); Lauren Fisher (Adv. Mgr); Meg Shaw (Ed.)

MARIAN COLLEGE

Street address 1: 3200 Cold Spring Rd
Street address 3: Indianapolis
Street address state: IN
Zip/Postal code: 46222-1960
Country: USA
Mailing address: 3200 Cold Spring Rd
Mailing city: Indianapolis
Mailing state: IN
Mailing zip: 46222-1997
General Phone: (317) 955-6397
General Fax: (317) 955-6448
Primary Website: www.marian.edu
Classified Equipment»
Personnel: Gay Lynn Crossley (Faculty Supvr.); Sarah Kreicker (Ed.)

UNIV. OF INDIANAPOLIS

Street address 1: 1400 E Hanna Ave
Street address 3: Indianapolis
Street address state: IN
Zip/Postal code: 46227-3630
Country: USA
Mailing address: 1400 E Hanna Ave
Mailing city: Indianapolis
Mailing state: IN
Mailing zip: 46227-3697
General Phone: (317) 788-3269
General Fax: (317) 788-3490
General/National Adv. E-mail: reflector@uindy.edu
Primary Website: www.reflector.uindy.edu
Classified Equipment»
Personnel: Jeanne Criswell (Advisor.); JP Sinclair (Bus. Mgr.); Adrian Kendrick (Ed. in Chief); Samantha Cotten (Ed.)

KOKOMO

INDIANA UNIV.

Street address 1: 2300 S Washington St
Street address 3: Kokomo
Street address state: IN
Zip/Postal code: 46902-3557
Country: USA
Mailing address: PO Box 9003
Mailing city: Kokomo
Mailing state: IN
Mailing zip: 46904-9003
General Phone: (765) 455-9280
General Fax: (765) 455-9537
General/National Adv. E-mail: paper@iuk.edu
Primary Website: www.kokomocorrespondent.com
Classified Equipment»
Personnel: David Brewster (Advisor); Alyx Arnett (Entertainment Ed.); Johnathan Grant (Ed. in Chief)

MARION

INDIANA WESLEYAN UNIVERSITY

Street address 1: 4201 S Washington St
Street address 3: Marion
Street address state: IN
Zip/Postal code: 46953-4974
Country: USA
Mailing address: 4201 S Washington St
Mailing city: Marion
Mailing state: IN
Mailing zip: 46953-4974
General Phone: (765) 677-1818
General Fax: (765) 677-1755
General/National Adv. E-mail: amy.smelser@indwes.edu
Primary Website: https://www.indwes.edu/undergraduate/majors/division-of-communication-and-theatre/
Classified Equipment»
Personnel: Amy Smelser (Ed.); Amy Smelser (Instructor)

MISHAWAKA

BETHEL COLLEGE

Street address 1: 1001 Bethel Cir
Street address 3: Mishawaka
Street address state: IN
Zip/Postal code: 46545-2232
Country: USA
Mailing address: 1001 Bethel Cir
Mailing city: Mishawaka
Mailing state: IN
Mailing zip: 46545-5591
General Phone: (574) 257-2672
General Fax: (574) 257-2583
General/National Adv. E-mail: beacon@bethelcollege.edu
Primary Website: www.bethelcollege.edu/studentlife/media/beacon/
Classified Equipment»
Personnel: Tim Ceravolo (Dir., Student Media); Amanda Armstrong (Ed. in Chief)

MUNCIE

BALL STATE UNIVERSITY

Street address 1: Aj 278
Street address 2: Ball State University
Street address 3: Muncie
Street address state: IN
Zip/Postal code: 47306-0001
Country: USA
Mailing address: AJ 276
Mailing city: Muncie
Mailing state: IN
Mailing zip: 47306-0001
General Phone: (765) 285-8218
General/National Adv. E-mail: editor@bsudailynews.com
Primary Website: www.bsudailynews.com
Year Established: 1922
Published: Wed
Avg Free Circ: 10000
Classified Equipment»
Personnel: Lisa Renze-Rhodes (Publications Adviser)

NEW ALBANY

INDIANA UNIV. SOUTHEAST

Street address 1: 4201 Grant Line Rd
Street address 3: New Albany
Street address state: IN
Zip/Postal code: 47150-2158
Country: USA
Mailing address: 4201 Grant Line Rd
Mailing city: New Albany
Mailing state: IN
Mailing zip: 47150-6405
General Phone: (812) 941-2253
General/National Adv. E-mail: horizon@ius.edu
Primary Website: iushorizon.com
Published: Mon
Published Other: Every two weeks
Avg Free Circ: 2000
Classified Equipment»
Personnel: Adam Maksl (Adviser)

NORTH MANCHESTER

MANCHESTER COLLEGE

Street address 1: 604 E College Ave
Street address 2: # 11
Street address 3: North Manchester
Street address state: IN
Zip/Postal code: 46962-1276
Country: USA
Mailing address: 604 E College Ave # 11
Mailing city: North Manchester
Mailing state: IN
Mailing zip: 46962-1232
General Phone: (260) 982-5317
General Fax: (260) 982-5043
Primary Website: www.manchester.edu/OSD/OakLeaves/index.htm

Classified Equipment»
Personnel: Katherine Ings (Advisor); Adam King (Ed. in Chief); Cyndel Taylor (Ed. in Chief)

NOTRE DAME

UNIV. OF NOTRE DAME

Street address 1: 024 S Dining Hall
Street address 3: Notre Dame
Street address state: IN
Zip/Postal code: 46556
Country: USA
Mailing address: PO Box 779
Mailing city: Notre Dame
Mailing state: IN
Mailing zip: 46556-0779
General Phone: (574) 631-7471
General Fax: (574) 631-6927
Advertising Phone: (574) 631-6900
General/National Adv. E-mail: observad@nd.edu
Primary Website: www.ndsmcobserver.com
Classified Equipment»
Personnel: Theresa Bea (Adv. Mgr.); Mary Claire Rodriguez (Adv. Mgr.); Jenn Metz (Ed. in Chief); Bill Brink (Mng. Ed.)

UNIV. OF NOTRE DAME ENGINEERING SCHOOL

Street address 1: 257 Cushing Hall
Street address 3: Notre Dame
Street address state: IN
Zip/Postal code: 46556
Country: USA
Mailing address: 257 Cushing Hall
Mailing city: Notre Dame
Mailing state: IN
Mailing zip: 46556
General Phone: (574) 631-5530
General Fax: (574) 631-8007
General/National Adv. E-mail: techrev@nd.edu
Primary Website: www.nd.edu
Classified Equipment»
Personnel: Cathy Pieronek (Asst. Dean); Brandon Chynowegh (Ed.)

RENSSELAER

ST. JOSEPH'S COLLEGE

Street address 1: 231 US Highway
Street address 3: Rensselaer
Street address state: IN
Zip/Postal code: 47978
Country: USA
Mailing address: PO Box 870
Mailing city: Rensselaer
Mailing state: IN
Mailing zip: 47978-0870
General Phone: (219) 866-6224
Classified Equipment»
Personnel: Charles Kerlin (Faculty Facilitator); Mike Koscielny (Ed. in Chief)

EARLHAM COLLEGE

Street address 1: PO Box 273
Street address 3: Richmond
Street address state: IN
Zip/Postal code: 47375-0273
Country: USA
Mailing address: PO Box 273
Mailing city: Richmond
Mailing state: IN
Mailing zip: 47375-0273
General Phone: (765) 983-1569
General Fax: (765) 983-1641
Primary Website: ecword.org
Classified Equipment»
Personnel: Maria Salvador (Ed. in Chief); Marisa Keller (Mng. Ed.)

INDIANA UNIV. EAST

Street address 1: 2325 Chester Blvd
Street address 3: Richmond
Street address state: IN
Zip/Postal code: 47374-1220
Country: USA
Mailing address: 2325 Chester Blvd
Mailing city: Richmond
Mailing state: IN
Mailing zip: 47374-1289
General Phone: (765) 973-8255
General Fax: (765) 973-8388
General/National Adv. E-mail: howler@iue.edu
Primary Website: www.iue.edu
Classified Equipment»
Personnel: Belinda Wyss (Advisor); Rob Zinkan (Exec. Ed.)

SOUTH BEND

INDIANA UNIV.

Street address 1: 1700 Mishawaka Ave
Street address 3: South Bend
Street address state: IN
Zip/Postal code: 46615-1408
Country: USA
Mailing address: PO Box 7111
Mailing city: South Bend
Mailing state: IN
Mailing zip: 46634-7111
General Phone: (574) 520-4878
General Fax: (574) 237-4599
Primary Website: www.iusb.edu
Classified Equipment»
Personnel: Beth Stutsman (Ed.)

TERRE HAUTE

INDIANA STATE UNIV.

Street address 1: 550 Chestnut St
Street address 3: Terre Haute
Street address state: IN
Zip/Postal code: 47809-1910
Country: USA
Mailing address: 716 Hulman Memorial Student Un
Mailing city: Terre Haute
Mailing state: IN
Mailing zip: 47809-0001
General Phone: (812) 237-7629
General Fax: (812) 237-7629
Editorail Phone: (812) 237-3025
Primary Website: www.indianastatesman.com
Classified Equipment»
Personnel: Heidi Staggs (Mng. Ed.); Caitlin Hancock (Adv.Mgr.); Daniel Greenwell (Ed. in Chief)

ROSE-HULMAN INST. OF TECHNOLOGY

Street address 1: 5500 Wabash Ave
Street address 2: # CM5037
Street address 3: Terre Haute
Street address state: IN
Zip/Postal code: 47803-3920
Country: USA
Mailing address: 5500 Wabash Ave # CM5037
Mailing city: Terre Haute
Mailing state: IN
Mailing zip: 47803-3920
General Phone: (812) 877-8255
Advertising Phone: (812) 877-8255
General/National Adv. E-mail: thorn@rose-hulman.edu
Display Adv. E-mail: thorn-biz@rose-hulman.edu
Primary Website: http://thorn.rose-hulman.edu/
Delivery Methods: Racks
Commercial printers: Y
Advertising (Open Inch Rate) Weekday/Saturday: $6.50/(column-inch)
Published: Fri
Avg Paid Circ: 0
Avg Free Circ: 1000
Classified Equipment»
Personnel: Thomas Adams (Advisor); Marcus Willerscheidt (Business Manager); Katrina Brandenburg (Editor-in-Chief)

UPLAND

TAYLOR UNIV.

Street address 1: 236 W Reade Ave
Street address 3: Upland
Street address state: IN
Zip/Postal code: 46989-1001
Country: USA
Mailing address: 236 W. Reade Ave
Mailing city: Upland
Mailing state: IN
Mailing zip: 46989
General Phone: (765) 998-5359
General/National Adv. E-mail: echo@taylor.edu
Published: Fri
Classified Equipment»
Personnel: Alan Blanchard (Faculty Advisor)

TAYLOR UNIV.

Street address 1: 236 W Reade Ave
Street address 3: Upland
Street address state: IN
Zip/Postal code: 46989-1001
Country: USA
Mailing address: 236 W. Reade Ave.
Mailing city: Upland
Mailing state: IN
Mailing zip: 46989-1001
General Phone: (765) 998-5359
General/National Adv. E-mail: echo@taylor.edu
Display Adv. E-mail: echoads@taylor.edu
Primary Website: http://theechonews.com/
Year Established: 1913
Published: Fri
Classified Equipment»
Personnel: Donna Downs (Ed. in Chief); Alan Blanchard (Faculty Adviser)

VALPARAISO

VALPARAISO UNIVERSITY

Street address 1: 1809 Chapel Dr
Street address 3: Valparaiso
Street address state: IN
Zip/Postal code: 46383-4517
Country: USA
Mailing address: 1809 Chapel Dr
Mailing city: Valparaiso
Mailing state: IN
Mailing zip: 46383-4517
General Phone: (219) 464-5271
General Fax: (219) 464-6742
General/National Adv. E-mail: douglas.kocher@valpo.edu
Primary Website: www.valpo.edu/torch
Classified Equipment»
Personnel: Douglas J. Kocher (Chair); Jason Paupore (Advisor); Andy Simmons (Bus.Mgr.); Luis Fifuentes (Adv.Mgr.); Kathryn Kattalia (Ed. in chief)

VINCENNES

JOURNALISM PROGRAM, VINCENNES UNIVERSITY

Street address 1: 1002 N 1st St
Street address 3: Vincennes
Street address state: IN
Zip/Postal code: 47591-1504
Country: USA
Mailing address: 1002 N 1st St
Mailing city: Vincennes
Mailing state: IN
Mailing zip: 47591-1500
General Phone: (812) 888-4551
General Fax: (812) 888-5531
General/National Adv. E-mail: trailblazer@vinu.edu
Primary Website: www.vutrailblazernews.com
Year Established: 1923
Published: Other
Classified Equipment»
Personnel: Emily Taylor (Journalism Asst. Professor, Department Chair of Media Production)

WEST LAFAYETTE

THE PURDUE EXPONENT

Street address 1: 460 Northwestern Ave
Street address 3: West Lafayette
Street address state: IN
Zip/Postal code: 47906-2966
Country: USA
Mailing address: PO Box 2506
Mailing city: West Lafayette
Mailing state: IN
Mailing zip: 47996-2506
General Phone: (765) 743-1111
General Fax: (765) 743-6087
Advertising Phone: Ext. 122
Editorail Phone: Ext. 254
General/National Adv. E-mail: help@purdueexponent.org
Display Adv. E-mail: advertising@purdueexponent.org
Primary Website: www.purdueexponent.org
Year Established: 1889
Delivery Methods: Carrier
Commercial printers: Y
Advertising (Open Inch Rate) Weekday/Saturday: 12.8
Published: Mon`Tues`Wed`Thur`Fri
Published Other: M Th during summer
Avg Free Circ: 12000
Classified Equipment»
Personnel: Patirck Kuhnle (Pub.); Ingraham Vancel (Prodn. Dir.); Mindy Coddington (Advertising director)
Parent company (for newspapers): Purdue Student Publishing Foundation

WESTVILLE

PURDUE UNIV. NORTH CENTRAL

Street address 1: 1401 S U S 421
Street address 3: Westville
Street address state: IN
Zip/Postal code: 46391
Country: USA
Mailing address: 1401 S. U.S. 421
Mailing city: Westville
Mailing state: IN
Mailing zip: 46391-9542
General Phone: (219) 785-5213
General Fax: (219) 785-5544
General/National Adv. E-mail: spectator@pnc.edu
Editorial e-mail: thevoice@pnc.edu
Primary Website: www.pnc.edu
Classified Equipment»
Personnel: Suzanne Webber (Ed.); Lyndsie Daikhi (Print Ed.)

WHITING

CALUMET COLLEGE OF ST. JOSEPH

Street address 1: 2400 New York Ave
Street address 3: Whiting
Street address state: IN
Zip/Postal code: 46394-2146
Country: USA
Mailing address: 2400 New York Ave
Mailing city: Whiting
Mailing state: IN
Mailing zip: 46394-2195
General Phone: (219) 473-4322
General Fax: (219) 473-4219
Primary Website: www.ccsj.edu
Published: Mthly
Classified Equipment»
Personnel: Mark Cassello (Director of English & Media Communications); Dawn Muhammad (PD); Daren Jasieniecki (Mktg. Mgr.)

KANSAS

ARKANSAS CITY

COWLEY COUNTY CMTY. COLLEGE

Street address 1: 125 S 2nd St
Street address 3: Arkansas City
Street address state: KS
Zip/Postal code: 67005-2662
Country: USA
Mailing address: 125 S 2nd St

Mailing city: Arkansas City
Mailing state: KS
Mailing zip: 67005-2662
General Phone: (620) 441-5287
General Fax: (620) 441-5377
General/National Adv. E-mail: editor@cowleypress.com
Primary Website: www.cowleypress.com
Classified Equipment»
Personnel: Meg Smith (Faculty Advisor); Alyssa Campbell (Adv. Mgr.); Richard Gould (Ed.)

ATCHISON

BENEDICTINE COLLEGE

Street address 1: 1020 N 2nd St
Street address 3: Atchison
Street address state: KS
Zip/Postal code: 66002-1402
Country: USA
Mailing address: 1020 N 2nd St
Mailing city: Atchison
Mailing state: KS
Mailing zip: 66002-1499
General Phone: (913) 360-7390
General Fax: (913) 367-6102
General/National Adv. E-mail: circuit@benedictine.edu
Primary Website: www.bccircuit.com
Classified Equipment»
Personnel: Kevin Page (Advisor)

BALDWIN CITY

BAKER UNIVERSITY

Street address 1: PO Box 65
Street address 3: Baldwin City
Street address state: KS
Zip/Postal code: 66006-0065
Country: USA
Mailing address: PO Box 65
Mailing city: Baldwin City
Mailing state: KS
Mailing zip: 66006-0065
General Phone: (913) 594-6451
General Fax: (913) 594-3570
General/National Adv. E-mail: bayha@harvey.bakeru.edu
Primary Website: www.thebakerorange.com
Classified Equipment»
Personnel: Gwyn Mellinger (Advisor); Ann Rosenthal (Chair); Dave Bostwick (Advisor); Chris Smith (Ed.)

COFFEYVILLE

COFFEYVILLE CMTY. COLLEGE

Street address 1: 400 W 11th St
Street address 3: Coffeyville
Street address state: KS
Zip/Postal code: 67337-5065
Country: USA
Mailing address: 400 W. 11th
Mailing city: Coffeyville
Mailing state: KS
Mailing zip: 67337
General Phone: (316) 252-7137
Classified Equipment»

COLBY

COLBY CMTY. COLLEGE

Street address 1: 1255 S Range Ave
Street address 3: Colby
Street address state: KS
Zip/Postal code: 67701-4007
Country: USA
Mailing address: 1255 S Range Ave
Mailing city: Colby
Mailing state: KS
Mailing zip: 67701-4099
General Phone: (785) 462-3984
General Fax: (785) 460-4699
Primary Website: www.freewebs.com/trojanexpress
Classified Equipment»
Personnel: Trent Rose (Advisor)

EL DORADO

BUTLER COUNTY CMTY. COLLEGE

Street address 1: 901 S Haverhill Rd
Street address 3: El Dorado
Street address state: KS
Zip/Postal code: 67042-3225
Country: USA
Mailing address: 901 S Haverhill Rd
Mailing city: El Dorado
Mailing state: KS
Mailing zip: 67042-3225
General Phone: (316) 322-3170
General Fax: (316) 322-3109
General/National Adv. E-mail: lantern@butlercc.edu
Primary Website: www.lanternonline.com; www.butlercc.edu
Classified Equipment»
Personnel: Melissa Roberts (Bus. Mgr.)

GREAT BEND

BARTON COUNTY CMTY. COLLEGE

Street address 1: 245 NE 30 Rd
Street address 3: Great Bend
Street address state: KS
Zip/Postal code: 67530-9251
Country: USA
Mailing address: 245 NE 30 Rd
Mailing city: Great Bend
Mailing state: KS
Mailing zip: 67530-9107
General Phone: (620) 792-9239
General Fax: 6207861157
Primary Website: www.bartonccc.edu
Year Established: 1969
Delivery Methods: Mail`Newsstand`Racks
Commercial printers: N
Advertising (Open Inch Rate) Weekday/Saturday: $5 column inch
Published Other: Bi-weekly Print; Weekly Online
Classified Equipment»
Personnel: Yvonda Acker (Advisor)

HAYS

FT. HAYS STATE UNIV.

Street address 1: 600 Park St
Street address 2: Picken 104
Street address 3: Hays
Street address state: KS
Zip/Postal code: 67601-4009
Country: USA
Mailing address: 600 Park St Picken 104
Mailing city: Hays
Mailing state: KS
Mailing zip: 67601-4009
General Phone: (785) 628-3478
General Fax: (785) 628-4004
Primary Website: www.fhsu.edu
Classified Equipment»
Personnel: Gretchen Fields (Advisor)

HILLSBORO

TABOR COLLEGE

Street address 1: 400 S Jefferson St
Street address 3: Hillsboro
Street address state: KS
Zip/Postal code: 67063-1753
Country: USA
Mailing address: 400 S. Jefferson St.
Mailing city: Hillsboro
Mailing state: KS
Mailing zip: 67063-1753
General Phone: (620) 947-3121
General Fax: (620) 947-2607
General/National Adv. E-mail: theview@tabor.edu
Display Adv. E-mail: theview@tabor.edu
Editorial e-mail: theview@tabor.edu
Primary Website: https://www.facebook.com/TaborView?ref=hl
Published: Mthly
Classified Equipment»
Personnel: Sara Jo Waldron (Advisor); Jared Janzen (Editor-in-Chief); Sara Sigley (Advisor); Heather Deckert (Ed.)

KANSAS CITY CMTY. COLLEGE

Street address 1: 7250 State Ave
Street address 3: Kansas City
Street address state: KS
Zip/Postal code: 66112-3003
Country: USA
Mailing address: 7250 State Ave
Mailing city: Kansas City
Mailing state: KS
Mailing zip: 66112-3003
General Phone: (913) 334-1100
General Fax: (913) 288-7617
Primary Website: kckcc.edu
Classified Equipment»
Personnel: Bryan Whitehead (Faculty Advisor)

LAWRENCE

THE UNIVERSITY DAILY KANSAN

Street address 1: 1000 Sunnyside Ave
Street address 3: Lawrence
Street address state: KS
Zip/Postal code: 66045-7599
Country: USA
Mailing address: 1000 Sunnyside Ave
Mailing city: Lawrence
Mailing state: KS
Mailing zip: 66045-7599
General Phone: (785) 864-4724
General Fax: (785) 864-5261
Advertising Phone: (785) 864-4358
Editorail Phone: (785) 864-4812
General/National Adv. E-mail: editor@kansan.com
Display Adv. E-mail: adsales@kansan.com
Editorial e-mail: editor@kansan.com
Primary Website: www.kansan.com
Year Established: 1904
Special Editions: Sex on the Hill; Jayhawker magazine; football and basketball special editions
Special Weekly Sections: Jayplay (weekly entertainment)
Delivery Methods: Newsstand`Racks
Published: Mon`Tues`Wed`Thur
Published Other: Weekly in summer (June/July)
Avg Paid Circ: 11000
Classified Equipment»
Personnel: Malcolm Gibson (Gen. Mgr./News Advisor); Jon Schlitt (Sales and Marketing Adviser)

UNIV. OF KANSAS ENGINEERING SCHOOL

Street address 1: 4010 Learned Hall
Street address 3: Lawrence
Street address state: KS
Zip/Postal code: 66045-7526
Country: USA
Mailing address: 4010 Learned Hall
Mailing city: Lawrence
Mailing state: KS
Mailing zip: 66045-7526
General Phone: (785) 864-8853
Classified Equipment»
Personnel: Mary Jane Dunlap (News Ed.); Jill Hummels (PR Dir.)

LINDSBORG

BETHANY COLLEGE

Street address 1: PO Box 184
Street address 3: Lindsborg
Street address state: KS
Zip/Postal code: 67456-0184
Country: USA
Mailing address: PO Box 184
Mailing city: Lindsborg
Mailing state: KS
Mailing zip: 67456-0184
General Phone: (785) 227-8234
General Fax: (785) 227-2004
Classified Equipment»
Personnel: Joel Wiede (Ed.)

MANHATTAN

STUDENT PUBLICATIONS INC.

Street address 1: 103 Kedzie Hall
Street address 3: Manhattan
Street address state: KS
Zip/Postal code: 66506-1500
Country: USA
Mailing address: 103 Kedzie Hall
Mailing city: Manhattan
Mailing state: KS
Mailing zip: 66506-1505
General Phone: (785) 532-6555
General Fax: (785) 532-6236
General/National Adv. E-mail: news@spub.ksu.edu
Display Adv. E-mail: adsales@spub.ksu.edu; classifieds@spub.ksu.edu
Primary Website: www.kstatecollegian.com
Year Established: 1896
Classified Equipment»
Personnel: Steve Wolgast (Advisor); Tim Schrag (Ed.)

MCPHERSON

MCPHERSON COLLEGE

Street address 1: 1600 E Euclid St
Street address 3: McPherson
Street address state: KS
Zip/Postal code: 67460-3847
Country: USA
Mailing address: PO Box 1402
Mailing city: McPherson
Mailing state: KS
Mailing zip: 67460-1402
General Phone: (620) 242-0449
General Fax: (620) 241-8443
Primary Website: spectator.mcpherson.edu
Classified Equipment»
Personnel: Adam Pracht (Adviser); Shannon Williams (Editor-in-Chief)

NORTH NEWTON

BETHEL COLLEGE

Street address 1: 300 E 27th St
Street address 3: North Newton
Street address state: KS
Zip/Postal code: 67117-8061
Country: USA
Mailing address: 300 E 27th St
Mailing city: North Newton
Mailing state: KS
Mailing zip: 67117-1716
General Phone: (316) 284-5271
General Fax: (316) 284-5286
General/National Adv. E-mail: collegian@bethelks.edu
Display Adv. E-mail: collegian@bethelks.edu
Editorial e-mail: collegian@bethelks.edu
Primary Website: www.bethelks.edu/collegian
Classified Equipment»
Personnel: Christine Crouse-Dick (Advisor)

OLATHE

MIDAMERICA NAZARENE UNIVERSITY

Street address 1: 2030 E College Way
Street address 3: Olathe
Street address state: KS
Zip/Postal code: 66062-1851
Country: USA
Mailing address: 2030 E. College Way
Mailing city: Olathe
Mailing state: KS
Mailing zip: 66062
General Phone: (913) 971-3289
General Fax: (913) 971-3421

Advertising Phone: (913) 961-8615
Editorail Phone: (913) 530-0854
Display Adv. E-mail: ehodgson@mnu.edu
Editorial e-mail: tb-edit@mnu.edu
Primary Website: www.trailblazer.mnubox.com
Year Established: 1967
Classified Equipment»
Personnel: Sarah Glass (Editor-in-Chief); Molly Farnsworth (Managing Editor); Christina Wilkins (Section Editor); Melinda Smith (Faculty Advisor)

JOHNSON COUNTY CMTY. COLLEGE

Street address 1: 12345 College Blvd
Street address 2: # 7
Street address 3: Overland Park
Street address state: KS
Zip/Postal code: 66210-1283
Country: USA
Mailing address: 12345 College Blvd # 7
Mailing city: Overland Park
Mailing state: KS
Mailing zip: 66210-1283
General Phone: (913) 469-8500
General Fax: (913) 469-2577
Primary Website: www.campusledger.com
Classified Equipment»
Personnel: Anne Christiansen-Bullers (Advisor); Matt Galloway (Ed. in Chief)

PRATT

PRATT CMTY. COLLEGE

Street address 1: 348 NE Hwy 61
Street address 3: Pratt
Street address state: KS
Zip/Postal code: 67124
Country: USA
Mailing address: 348 NE Hwy. 61
Mailing city: Pratt
Mailing state: KS
Mailing zip: 67124
General Phone: (316) 672-5641
General Fax: (316) 672-5641
Classified Equipment»

SALINA

KANSAS WESLEYAN UNIV.

Street address 1: 100 E Claflin Ave
Street address 2: # 87
Street address 3: Salina
Street address state: KS
Zip/Postal code: 67401-6146
Country: USA
Mailing address: 100 E Claflin Ave Ste 87
Mailing city: Salina
Mailing state: KS
Mailing zip: 67401-6100
General Phone: (785) 827-5541
General Fax: (785) 827-0927
Classified Equipment»
Personnel: Jack Morris (Advisor)

TOPEKA

WASHBURN UNIV.

Street address 1: 1700 SW College Ave
Street address 3: Topeka
Street address state: KS
Zip/Postal code: 66621-0001
Country: USA
Mailing address: 1700 SW College Ave
Mailing city: Topeka
Mailing state: KS
Mailing zip: 66621-1101
General Phone: (785) 670-2506
General Fax: (785) 670-1035
Advertising Phone: (785) 670-1173
General/National Adv. E-mail: review@washburn.edu
Primary Website: www.washburnreview.org
Classified Equipment»
Personnel: Nicole Stejskal (Ed. in Chief)

NEWMAN UNIVERSITY - THE VANTAGE

Street address 1: 3100 W McCormick St
Street address 3: Wichita
Street address state: KS
Zip/Postal code: 67213-2008
Country: USA
Mailing address: 3100 W McCormick St
Mailing city: Wichita
Mailing state: KS
Mailing zip: 67213-2008
General Phone: (316) 942-4291
General Fax: (316) 942-4483
General/National Adv. E-mail: vantage@newmanu.edu
Delivery Methods: Newsstand`Racks
Classified Equipment»
Personnel: Kristen McCurdy (Editor)

WICHITA STATE UNIV.

Street address 1: 1845 Fairmount St
Street address 3: Wichita
Street address state: KS
Zip/Postal code: 67260-9700
Country: USA
Mailing address: 1845 Fairmount St
Mailing city: Wichita
Mailing state: KS
Mailing zip: 67260-0001
General Phone: (316) 978-3456
General Fax: (316) 978-3778
Editorial e-mail: editor@thesunflower.com; sports.editor@thesunflower.com
Primary Website: www.thesunflower.com
Classified Equipment»
Personnel: Ronda Voorhis (Advisor); Candice Tullis (Ed. in Chief); Scott Elpers (Mng. Ed.); Jorge M. De Hoyos (Sports Ed.)

KENTUCKY

BEREA

BEREA COLLEGE

Street address 1: Cpo 2150
Street address 3: Berea
Street address state: KY
Country: USA
Mailing address: 2150 Cpo
Mailing city: Berea
Mailing state: KY
Mailing zip: 40404-0001
General Phone: (859) 985-3208
General Fax: (859) 985-3914
General/National Adv. E-mail: pinnacle@berea.edu
Primary Website: www.bereacollegepinnacle.com
Classified Equipment»
Personnel: Chris Lakes (Advisor); Kwadwo Juantuah (Ed.)

BOWLING GREEN

WESTERN KENTUCKY UNIVERSITY

Street address 1: 1660 Normal St
Street address 2: Western Kentucky University
Street address 3: Bowling Green
Street address state: KY
Zip/Postal code: 42101-3536
Country: USA
Mailing address: 1906 College Heights Blvd # 11084
Mailing city: Bowling Green
Mailing state: KY
Mailing zip: 42101-1084
General Phone: (270) 745-2653
Advertising Phone: (270) 745-2653
Editorail Phone: (270) 745-2653
General/National Adv. E-mail: carrie.pratt@wku.edu
Display Adv. E-mail: william.hoagland@wku.edu
Editorial e-mail: herald.editor@wku.edu
Primary Website: www.wkuherald.com
Year Established: 1925
Advertising (Open Inch Rate) Weekday/Saturday: Call for information
Published: Tues`Thur
Published Other: Topper Extra sports section published on home football days
Avg Free Circ: 7000
Classified Equipment»
Personnel: Sherry West (Operations Mgr); Carrie Pratt (Herald Adviser, Multiplatform News Adviser); Tracy Newton (Office Associate); Will Hoagland (Advt Adviser and Sales Mgr); Chuck Clark (Dir of Student Publications); Sam Oldenburg (Talisman adviser)
Parent company (for newspapers): WKU Student Publications

CAMPBELLSVILLE

CAMPBELLSVILLE UNIVERSITY

Street address 1: Up 897 Campbellsville University
Street address 3: Campbellsville
Street address state: KY
Zip/Postal code: 42718
County: Taylor
Country: USA
Mailing address: 1 University Dr.
Mailing city: Campbellsville
Mailing state: KY
Mailing zip: 42718
General Phone: (270) 789-5035
General Fax: (270)789-5145
Primary Website: www.campbellsville.edu/campus-times
Published Other: Monthly when school is in session
Avg Free Circ: 2000
Classified Equipment»

DANVILLE

CENTRE COLLEGE

Street address 1: 600 W Walnut St
Street address 3: Danville
Street address state: KY
Zip/Postal code: 40422-1309
Country: USA
Mailing address: 600 W Walnut St
Mailing city: Danville
Mailing state: KY
Mailing zip: 40422-1394
General Phone: (859) 238-5350
General/National Adv. E-mail: cento@centre.edu
Display Adv. E-mail: business@centre.edu
Editorial e-mail: ed-in-chief@centre.edu
Year Established: 1888
Classified Equipment»
Personnel: Tess Simon (Ed.); Katy Meyer; Amy Senders

FRANKFORT

KENTUCKY STATE UNIV.

Street address 1: 400 E Main St
Street address 3: Frankfort
Street address state: KY
Zip/Postal code: 40601-2334
Country: USA
Mailing address: 400 E Main St
Mailing city: Frankfort
Mailing state: KY
Mailing zip: 40601-2355
General Phone: (502) 597-5915
General Fax: (502) 597-5927
Primary Website: http://www.ksuthorobreds.com/
Classified Equipment»
Personnel: Sepricia White (Ed. in Chief); Terri McCray (Features Ed.); Cornell Ferrill (Sports Ed.)

GEORGETOWN

GEORGETOWN COLLEGE

Street address 1: 400 E College St
Street address 2: # 280
Street address 3: Georgetown
Street address state: KY
Zip/Postal code: 40324-1628
Country: USA
Mailing address: 400 E College St Ste 1 # 280
Mailing city: Georgetown
Mailing state: KY
Mailing zip: 40324-1628
General Fax: (502) 863-8150
Classified Equipment»
Personnel: Whitley Arens (ed.)

HENDERSON

HENDERSON CMTY. COLLEGE

Street address 1: 2660 S Green St
Street address 3: Henderson
Street address state: KY
Zip/Postal code: 42420-4623
Country: USA
Mailing address: 2660 S Green St
Mailing city: Henderson
Mailing state: KY
Mailing zip: 42420-4699
General Phone: (270) 827-1867
Advertising Phone: 270-831-9770
Year Established: 1978
Classified Equipment»
Personnel: Scott Taylor (Ed.)

UNIV. OF KENTUCKY

Street address 1: Grehan Journalism Bldg, Rm 026
Street address 3: Lexington
Street address state: KY
Zip/Postal code: 40506-0001
Country: USA
Mailing address: Grehan Journalism Bldg Rm 26
Mailing city: Lexington
Mailing state: KY
Mailing zip: 40506-0001
General Phone: (859) 257-2872
General Fax: (859) 323-1906
General/National Adv. E-mail: features@kykernel.com
Display Adv. E-mail: news@kykernel.com
Primary Website: www.kykernel.com
Classified Equipment»
Personnel: Chris Poore (Advisor); Kenny Colston (Ed. in Chief)

BELLARMINE COLLEGE

Street address 1: 2001 Newburg Rd
Street address 3: Louisville
Street address state: KY
Zip/Postal code: 40205-1863
Country: USA
Mailing address: 2001 Newburg Rd
Mailing city: Louisville
Mailing state: KY
Mailing zip: 40205-0671
General Phone: (502) 452-8157
Advertising Phone: (502) 452-8050
Editorail Phone: (502) 452-8157
General/National Adv. E-mail: theconcard@bellarmine.edu
Primary Website: www.theconcordonline.com
Classified Equipment»
Personnel: Erika Osborne (Ed. in Chief)

UNIVERSITY OF LOUISVILLE

Street address 1: Houehens Bldg, Ste LL07
Street address 3: Louisville
Street address state: KY
Zip/Postal code: 40292-0001
Country: USA
Mailing address: Houehens Bldg, Ste LL07
Mailing city: Louisville
Mailing state: KY
Mailing zip: 40292-0001
General Fax: (502) 852-0700
Advertising Phone: (502) 852-0701
Editorail Phone: (502) 852-0667
Display Adv. E-mail: advertising@louisvillecardinal.com
Editorial e-mail: editor@louisvillecardinal.com
Primary Website: www.louisvillecardinal.com
Year Established: 1926
Published: Tues
Avg Free Circ: 8000
Classified Equipment»

Personnel: Simon Isham (Editor-in-Chief); Ralph Merkel (Adviser)

MOREHEAD

MOREHEAD STATE UNIV.

Street address 1: 150 University Blvd
Street address 3: Morehead
Street address state: KY
Zip/Postal code: 40351-1684
Country: USA
Mailing address: 150 University Blvd
Mailing city: Morehead
Mailing state: KY
Mailing zip: 40351
General Phone: (606) 783-2697
General Fax: (606) 783-9113
General/National Adv. E-mail: editor@trailblazeronline.net
Primary Website: www.trailblazeronline.net
Classified Equipment»
Personnel: Joan Atkins

MURRAY

MURRAY STATE UNIV.

Street address 1: 111 Wilson Hall
Street address 3: Murray
Street address state: KY
Zip/Postal code: 42071-3311
Country: USA
Mailing address: 111 Wilson Hall
Mailing city: Murray
Mailing state: KY
Mailing zip: 42071-3311
General Phone: (270) 809-6877
General Fax: (270) 809-3175
General/National Adv. E-mail: news@murraystate.edu
Primary Website: www.thenews.org
Classified Equipment»
Personnel: Mia Walters (Ed. in chief)

NORTHERN KENTUCKY UNIV.

Street address 1: University Ctr, Rm 335, Nunn Dr
Street address 3: Newport
Street address state: KY
Zip/Postal code: 41099-0001
Country: USA
Mailing address: University Ctr Rm 335
Mailing city: Newport
Mailing state: KY
Mailing zip: 41099-0001
General Phone: (859) 572-5772
General Fax: (859) 572-5772
Advertising Fax: (859) 572-5232
General/National Adv. E-mail: northerner@nku.edu
Primary Website: www.thenortherner.com
Classified Equipment»
Personnel: Drew Laskey (Sports Ed.)

OWENSBORO

KENTUCKY WESLEYAN COLLEGE

Street address 1: 3000 Frederica St
Street address 3: Owensboro
Street address state: KY
Zip/Postal code: 42301-6057
Country: USA
Mailing address: 3000 Frederica St
Mailing city: Owensboro
Mailing state: KY
Mailing zip: 42301-6055
General Phone: (270) 852-3596
General Fax: (270) 852-3597
General/National Adv. E-mail: panogram@kwc.edu
Published: Bi-Mthly
Classified Equipment»
Personnel: Randall Vogt (Advisor); Devyn Lott (General Editor)

EASTERN KENTUCKY UNIV.

Street address 1: 521 Lancaster Ave
Street address 2: Combs Bldg. 226
Street address 3: Richmond
Street address state: KY
Zip/Postal code: 40475-3100
Country: USA
Mailing address: 521 Lancaster Ave
Mailing city: Richmond
Mailing state: KY
Mailing zip: 40475-3102
General Phone: (859) 622-1881
General Fax: (859) 622-2354
General/National Adv. E-mail: progress@eku.edu
Display Adv. E-mail: progressads@eku.edu
Primary Website: www.easternprogress.com
Year Established: 1922
Published: Thur
Published Other: During semesters
Avg Free Circ: 8000
Classified Equipment»
Personnel: Reggie Beehner (Advisor); Kristie Hamon (Ed.); Gina Portwood (Bus. Mgr.); Park Greer (Adv. Mgr.)

WILLIAMSBURG

UNIVERSITY OF THE CUMBERLANDS

Street address 1: 6191 College Station Dr
Street address 3: Williamsburg
Street address state: KY
Zip/Postal code: 40769-1372
Country: USA
Mailing address: 6191 College Station Dr
Mailing city: Williamsburg
Mailing state: KY
Mailing zip: 40769-1372
General Phone: 606.539.4172
General/National Adv. E-mail: thepatriot@ucumberlands.edu
Primary Website: www.thepatriot.ucumberlands.ed
Classified Equipment»

WILMORE

ASBURY COLLEGE

Street address 1: 1 Macklem Dr
Street address 3: Wilmore
Street address state: KY
Zip/Postal code: 40390-1152
Country: USA
Mailing address: 1 Macklem Dr
Mailing city: Wilmore
Mailing state: KY
Mailing zip: 40390-1198
General Phone: (859) 858-3511
General Fax: (859) 858-3921
General/National Adv. E-mail: mlonginow@asbury.edu
Primary Website: collegian.asbury.edu
Classified Equipment»
Personnel: Deanna Morono (Exec. Ed.); James R. Owens (Chair); Kayla Dubois (Mng. Ed.); Zack Klemme (News Ed.); Morgan Schutters (Web Design)

LOUISIANA

LOUISIANA STATE UNIV.

Street address 1: 1800 Hwy 71 S
Street address 3: Alexandria
Street address state: LA
Zip/Postal code: 71302
Country: USA
Mailing address: 1800 Hwy. 71 S.
Mailing city: Alexandria
Mailing state: LA
Mailing zip: 71302
General Phone: (318) 767-2602
General/National Adv. E-mail: sentrynews@lsua.edu
Classified Equipment»
Personnel: Elizabeth Beard (Advisor); Nancy Borden (Advisor); Trayce Snow (Ed.)

LOUISIANA STATE UNIVERSITY

Street address 1: Office of Student Media, B-39 Hodges Hall
Street address 3: Baton Rouge
Street address state: LA
Zip/Postal code: 70803-0001
Country: USA
Mailing address: Of Student Media B-39 Hodges Hall Ofc
Mailing city: Baton Rouge
Mailing state: LA
Mailing zip: 70803-0001
General Phone: (225) 578-4810
General Fax: (225) 578-1698
Advertising Phone: (225) 578-6090
Editorail Phone: (225) 578-4811
General/National Adv. E-mail: editor@lsureveille.com
Display Adv. E-mail: national@tigers.lsu.edu
Editorial e-mail: editor@lsureveille.com
Primary Website: www.lsureveille.com
Year Established: 1887
Published: Mon`Tues`Wed`Thur`Fri
Classified Equipment»
Personnel: Nicholas Persac (Ed.); Kyle Whitfield (Ed.); Kodi Wilson (Adv. Mgr.); Andrea Gallo (Editor in Chief); Baikom Taylor (Editor in Chief); Chandler Rome (Editor-in-Chief)

SOUTHERN UNIV. A&M COLLEGE

Street address 1: T H Harris Hall, Ste 1064
Street address 3: Baton Rouge
Street address state: LA
Zip/Postal code: 70813-0001
Country: USA
Mailing address: PO Box 10180
Mailing city: Baton Rouge
Mailing state: LA
Mailing zip: 70813-0180
General Phone: (225) 771-2230
General Fax: (225) 771-3253
General/National Adv. E-mail: editor@southerndigest.com
Primary Website: www.southerndigest.com
Year Established: 1928
Classified Equipment»
Personnel: Stephanie Cain (Bus./Adv. Mgr.); Derick Hackett (Dir., Student Media); Christopher Jones (Asst. Dir.); Fran Hoskins (Ed.)

SOUTHERN UNIVERSITY

Street address 1: T H Harris Hall
Street address 2: Suite 1064
Street address 3: Baton Rouge
Street address state: LA
Zip/Postal code: 70813-0001
Country: USA
Mailing address: PO Box 10180
Mailing city: Baton Rouge
Mailing state: LA
Mailing zip: 70813-0180
General Phone: (225) 771-2231
General Fax: (225) 771-5840
Advertising Phone: 225-771-5833
Advertising Fax: 225-771-5840
Editorail Phone: 225-771-5829
Editorial Fax: 225-771-5840
General/National Adv. E-mail: digest@subr.edu
Display Adv. E-mail: camelia_gardner@subr.edu
Editorial e-mail: fredrick_batiste@subr.edu
Primary Website: www.southerndigest.com
Year Established: 1926
Advertising (Open Inch Rate) Weekday/Saturday: Please call
Published: Tues`Thur
Avg Free Circ: 4000
Classified Equipment»
Personnel: Heather Freeman (Student Media Director); Camelia Jackson (Advertising/Business Manager); Fredrick Batiste (Publications Assistant/Advisor)

BOSSIER CITY

BOSSIER PARISH CMTY. COLLEGE

Street address 1: 6220 E Texas St
Street address 3: Bossier City
Street address state: LA
Zip/Postal code: 71111-6922
Country: USA
Mailing address: 6220 E Texas St
Mailing city: Bossier City
Mailing state: LA
Mailing zip: 71111-6922
General Phone: (318) 678-6000
General Fax: X
General/National Adv. E-mail: kaleidoscope@bpcc.edu
Primary Website: www.bpcc.edu
Classified Equipment»
Personnel: Candice Gibson (Advisor); Cathy Hammel (Advisor)

GRAMBLING

GRAMBLING STATE UNIVERSITY

Street address 1: 403 Main St
Street address 3: Grambling
Street address state: LA
Zip/Postal code: 71245-2715
Country: USA
Mailing address: 403 Main St
Mailing city: Grambling
Mailing state: LA
Mailing zip: 71245-2761
General Phone: (318) 247-3331
General Fax: (318) 274-3194
Editorail Phone: (318) 274-2866
General/National Adv. E-mail: mediarelations@gram.edu
Primary Website: www.thegramblinite.com
Published: Thur
Classified Equipment»
Personnel: Mitzi LaSalle (Interim Director of University Communications, Marketing, and Media Relations)

SOUTHEASTERN LOUISIANA UNIV.

Street address 1: 303 Texas Ave, Student Union, Rm 211D
Street address 3: Hammond
Street address state: LA
Zip/Postal code: 70402-0001
Country: USA
Mailing address: Slu 10877
Mailing city: Hammond
Mailing state: LA
Mailing zip: 70402-0001
General Phone: (985) 549-3731
General Fax: (985) 549-3842
General/National Adv. E-mail: lionsroar@selu.edu
Primary Website: www.selu.edu/lionsroar
Year Established: 1929
Classified Equipment»
Personnel: Lee Lind (Dir., Student Pub.); Don Aime (Ed. in Chief)

UNIV. OF LOUISIANA AT LAFAYETTE THE VERMILION

Street address 1: PO Box 44813
Street address 3: Lafayette
Street address state: LA
Zip/Postal code: 70504-0001
Country: USA
Mailing address: PO Box 44813
Mailing city: Lafayette
Mailing state: LA
Mailing zip: 70504-0001
General Phone: (337) 482-6110
General Fax: (337) 482-6959
Advertising Phone: (337) 482-6960
Advertising Fax: (337) 472-6959
Editorail Phone: (337) 482-6110
Editorial Fax: (337) 482-6959
General/National Adv. E-mail: vermadvertising@gmail.com
Display Adv. E-mail: vermadvertising@gmail.com
Editorial e-mail: hollyhoooot@gmail.com
Primary Website: thevermilion.com
Year Established: 1904
Delivery Methods: Newsstand`Carrier`Racks
Commercial printers: Y
Advertising (Open Inch Rate) Weekday/Saturday: $7.50 / Column Inch
Published: Wed
Published Other: Aug, Sept, Oct, Nov
Classified Equipment»
Personnel: Thomas Schumacher (Business Manager)
Parent company (for newspapers): Vermilion Communication Committee of UL Lafayette

LAKE CHARLES

MCNEESE STATE UNIV.

Street address 1: PO Box 91375
Street address 3: Lake Charles
Street address state: LA
Zip/Postal code: 70609-0001
Country: USA
Mailing address: PO Box 91375
Mailing city: Lake Charles
Mailing state: LA
Mailing zip: 70609-0001
General Phone: (337) 475-5646
General Fax: (337) 475-5259
General/National Adv. E-mail: contraband@mcneese.edu; msucontraband@gmail.com
Primary Website: www.msucontraband.com
Classified Equipment»
Personnel: Candace Townsend (Advisor); Robert Teal (Ed. in Chief); Sarah Puckett (Ed.)

MONROE

UNIV. OF LOUISIANA AT MONROE

Street address 1: 700 University Ave
Street address 2: Stubbs 131
Street address 3: Monroe
Street address state: LA
Zip/Postal code: 71209-9000
Country: USA
Mailing address: 700 University Ave
Mailing city: Monroe
Mailing state: LA
Mailing zip: 71209
General Phone: (318) 342-5454
Advertising Phone: (318) 342-5453
Editorail Phone: 9318) 342-5450
General/National Adv. E-mail: ulmhawkeye@gmail.com
Display Adv. E-mail: ulmhawkeyead@gmail.com
Editorial e-mail: ulmhawkeye@gmail.com
Primary Website: www.ulmhawkeye.com
Year Established: 1934
Advertising (Open Inch Rate) Weekday/Saturday: https://ulmhawkeyeonline.com/contact/advertising/
Published: Mon
Classified Equipment»
Personnel: Ethan Dennis (Editor in Chief); Clarence Nash, Jr. (Advertising Director)
Parent company (for newspapers): University of Louisiana Monroe

NATCHITOCHES

NORTHWESTERN STATE UNIVERSITY

Street address 1: 225 Kyser Hall
Street address 2: Northwestern State University
Street address 3: Natchitoches
Street address state: LA
Zip/Postal code: 71497-0001
Country: USA
Mailing address: The Current Sauce
Mailing city: Natchitoches
Mailing state: LA
Mailing zip: 71497
General Phone: (318) 357-5456
Advertising Phone: (318) 357-5456
Editorail Phone: (318) 357-5456
General/National Adv. E-mail: thecurrentsauce@gmail.com
Display Adv. E-mail: thecurrentsauce@gmail.com
Editorial e-mail: thecurrentsauce@gmail.com
Primary Website: www.nsulastudentmedia.com
Year Established: 1914
Published: Wed
Avg Free Circ: 1000
Classified Equipment»
Personnel: Alec Horton (Editor-in-Chief); Jordan Reich (Associate Editor); Christina Arrechavala (Managing Editor); Valentina Perez (Photo Editor); Elisabeth Perez (PR Manager); Chloe' Romano (Assistant PR Manager); Julia Towry (Ad Sales Representative); Sarah Hill (Designer); Maygin Chesson (Administrative Assistant)

DELGADO COMMUNITY COLLEGE

Street address 1: 615 City Park Ave
Street address 3: New Orleans
Street address state: LA
Zip/Postal code: 70119-4399
Country: USA
Mailing address: 615 City Park Ave
Mailing city: New Orleans
Mailing state: LA
Mailing zip: 70119-4399
General Phone: (504) 671-6008
General Fax: (504) 483-1953
General/National Adv. E-mail: thedolphin29@gmail.com
Primary Website: www.dcc.edu
Classified Equipment»
Personnel: Susan Hague (Faculty Advisor); J.C. Romero (Ed. in Chief)

DILLARD UNIV.

Street address 1: 2601 Gentilly Blvd
Street address 3: New Orleans
Street address state: LA
Zip/Postal code: 70122-3043
Country: USA
Mailing address: 2601 Gentilly Blvd
Mailing city: New Orleans
Mailing state: LA
Mailing zip: 70122-3097
General Phone: (504) 283-8822
General Fax: (504) 816-4107
Primary Website: www.dillard.edu
Classified Equipment»

LOYOLA UNIVERSITY NEW ORLEANS

Street address 1: 6363 Saint Charles Ave
Street address 2: Campus Box 64
Street address 3: New Orleans
Street address state: LA
Zip/Postal code: 70118-6143
Country: USA
Mailing address: 6363 Saint Charles Ave
Mailing city: New Orleans
Mailing state: LA
Mailing zip: 70118-6195
General Phone: (504) 865-3535
General Fax: (504) 865-3534
Advertising Phone: (504) 865-3536
General/National Adv. E-mail: maroon@loyno.edu
Display Adv. E-mail: ads@loyno.edu
Primary Website: www.loyolamaroon.com
Year Established: 1923
Advertising (Open Inch Rate) Weekday/Saturday: $5 per column inch
Published: Fri
Avg Free Circ: 2750
Classified Equipment»
Personnel: Michael Giusti (Advisor)

TULANE UNIVERSITY

Street address 1: Lavin-Bernick Center for University Life G06
Street address 3: New Orleans
Street address state: LA
Zip/Postal code: 70118
Country: USA
Mailing address: Lavin-Bernick Center G06
Mailing city: New Orleans
Mailing state: LA
Mailing zip: 70118
General Phone: (504) 865-5657
Advertising Phone: (504) 865-5657
General/National Adv. E-mail: hull@tulane.edu
Display Adv. E-mail: hullabaloo.advertising@gmail.com
Primary Website: www.thehullabaloo.com
Year Established: 1902
Published: Thur
Published Other: Homecoming Magazine and Spring Magazine
Avg Free Circ: 4000
Classified Equipment»
Personnel: Brooke Rhea (Senior Business Manager); Lily Milwit (Editor In-Chief)

UNIVERSITY OF NEW ORLEANS

Street address 1: 2000 Lakeshore Dr
Street address 2: # Ba 250/252
Street address 3: New Orleans
Street address state: LA
Zip/Postal code: 70148-3520
Country: USA
Mailing address: 2000 Lakeshore Dr # UC252
Mailing city: New Orleans
Mailing state: LA
Mailing zip: 70148-0001
General Phone: (504) 280-6378
General Fax: (504) 280-6010
General/National Adv. E-mail: driftwood@uno.edu
Primary Website: driftwood.uno.edu
Classified Equipment»
Personnel: Edie Talley (Editor in Chief)

XAVIER UNIV. OF LOUISIANA

Street address 1: 1 Drexel Dr
Street address 2: # 299
Street address 3: New Orleans
Street address state: LA
Zip/Postal code: 70125-1056
Country: USA
Mailing address: 1 Drexel Drive, Box 299
Mailing city: New Orleans
Mailing state: LA
Mailing zip: 70125-1098
General Phone: (504) 520-5092
General Fax: (504) 520-7919
Display Adv. E-mail: herald@xula.edu
Primary Website: www.xula.edu; www.xulaherald.com
Year Established: 1925
Commercial printers: Y
Published: Bi-Mthly
Avg Free Circ: 2000
Classified Equipment»
Note: online version; printed edition 6x per semester; 2,000 each printing
Personnel: Melinda Shelton (Advisor)

PINEVILLE

LOUISIANA COLLEGE

Street address 1: 1140 College Dr
Street address 2: Dept English
Street address 3: Pineville
Street address state: LA
Zip/Postal code: 71359-1000
Country: USA
Mailing address: 1140 College Dr Dept English
Mailing city: Pineville
Mailing state: LA
Mailing zip: 71359-1000
General Phone: (318) 487-7011
General Fax: (318) 487-7310
General/National Adv. E-mail: wildcat@lacollege.edu
Classified Equipment»
Personnel: Jessie Redd (Ed.)

SHREVEPORT

CENTENARY COLLEGE

Street address 1: 2911 Centenary Blvd
Street address 3: Shreveport
Street address state: LA
Zip/Postal code: 71104-3335
Country: USA
Mailing address: PO Box 41188
Mailing city: Shreveport
Mailing state: LA
Mailing zip: 71134-1188
General Phone: (318) 792-5136
General/National Adv. E-mail: paper@centenary.edu
Primary Website: www.centenary.edu/life/congo
Classified Equipment»
Personnel: Mark Gruettner (Advisor); Roxie Smith (Ed. in chief)

LOUISIANA STATE UNIV.

Street address 1: 1 University Pl
Street address 2: No 344
Street address 3: Shreveport
Street address state: LA
Zip/Postal code: 71115-2301
Country: USA
Mailing address: 1 University Pl No 344
Mailing city: Shreveport
Mailing state: LA
Mailing zip: 71115-2301
General Phone: (318) 797-5328
General Fax: (318) 797-5328
Display Adv. E-mail: almagest@lsus.edu
Primary Website: www.thealmagest.com
Classified Equipment»
Personnel: Rose-Marie Lillian (Advisor); Karen Wissing (Exec. Ed.)

THIBODAUX

NICHOLLS STATE UNIV.

Street address 1: PO Box 2010
Street address 3: Thibodaux
Street address state: LA
Zip/Postal code: 70310-0001
Country: USA
Mailing address: PO Box 2010
Mailing city: Thibodaux
Mailing state: LA
Mailing zip: 70310-0001
General Phone: (985) 448-4259
General Fax: (985) 448-4267
Primary Website: www.thenichollsworth.com
Classified Equipment»
Personnel: Stephen Hartmann (Advisor)

MASSACHUSETTS

AMHERST

AMHERST COLLEGE

Street address 1: 31 Mead Dr
Street address 2: Keefe Campus Center
Street address 3: Amherst
Street address state: MA
Zip/Postal code: 01002-1786
Country: USA
Mailing address: AC#1912, Keefe Campus Center
Mailing city: Amherst
Mailing state: MA
Mailing zip: 01002-5000
General Phone: (413) 206-9319
General/National Adv. E-mail: astudent@amherst.edu
Display Adv. E-mail: astudent@amherst.edu
Primary Website: amherststudent.amherst.edu
Advertising (Open Inch Rate) Weekday/Saturday: Yes
Published: Wed
Avg Free Circ: 1600
Classified Equipment»
Personnel: Christopher Friend (Publisher)

HAMPSHIRE COLLEGE

Street address 1: 893 West St
Street address 3: Amherst
Street address state: MA
Zip/Postal code: 01002-3372
Country: USA
Mailing address: 893 West St
Mailing city: Amherst
Mailing state: MA
Mailing zip: 01002-3359
General Phone: (413) 549-4600
General Fax: (413) 559-5664
General/National Adv. E-mail: hampshireclimax@gmail.com
Primary Website: climax.hampshire.edu
Classified Equipment»

Personnel: Nicki Feldman (Admin. Sec.)

UNIV. OF MASSACHUSETTS

Street address 1: 123 S Burrowes St
Street address 3: Amherst
Street address state: MA
Zip/Postal code: 1003
Country: USA
General Phone: (413) 545-3500
General Fax: (413) 545-3699
Editorial e-mail: editor@dailycollegian.com
Primary Website: www.dailycollegian.com; www.umass.edu
Classified Equipment»
Personnel: Alyssa Creamer (Ed.)

AUBURNDALE

LASELL COLLEGE

Street address 1: 1844 Commonwealth Ave
Street address 3: Auburndale
Street address state: MA
Zip/Postal code: 02466-2709
Country: USA
Mailing address: 1844 Commonwealth Ave
Mailing city: Auburndale
Mailing state: MA
Mailing zip: 02466-2716
General Phone: (617) 243-2000
General Fax: (617) 243-2480
General/National Adv. E-mail: newspaper@lasell.edu
Classified Equipment»
Personnel: Marie C. Franklin (Advisor); Michelle McNickle (Ed. in Chief); Briana Nestor (Features Ed.)

BABSON PARK

BABSON COLLEGE

Street address 1: 231 Forest St
Street address 3: Babson Park
Street address state: MA
Country: USA
Mailing address: 231 Forest St.
Mailing city: Babson Park
Mailing state: MA
Mailing zip: 02457
General Phone: (781) 239-5541
General Fax: (781) 239-5554
General/National Adv. E-mail: freepress@babson.edu
Display Adv. E-mail: babsonfreep@babson.edu
Primary Website: www.babsonfreep.com
Classified Equipment»
Personnel: Anthony Micale (Ed.)

BEDFORD

MIDDLESEX CMTY. COLLEGE

Street address 1: 591 Springs Rd
Street address 3: Bedford
Street address state: MA
Zip/Postal code: 01730-1120
Country: USA
Mailing address: 591 Springs Rd
Mailing city: Bedford
Mailing state: MA
Mailing zip: 01730-1197
General Phone: (781) 280-3769
General Fax: (781) 275-4396
Classified Equipment»
Personnel: Sarah Screaux (Ed.)

BEVERLY

ENDICOTT COLLEGE

Street address 1: 376 Hale St, Callahan Ctr
Street address 3: Beverly
Street address state: MA
Zip/Postal code: 1915
Country: USA
Mailing address: 376 Hale St., Callahan Ctr.
Mailing city: Beverly
Mailing state: MA
Mailing zip: 01915-2096
General Phone: (978) 232-2050
General Fax: (978) 232-3003
General/National Adv. E-mail: observer@mail.endicott.edu
Primary Website: www.endicott.edu
Classified Equipment»
Personnel: Abigail Bottome (Advisor)

BOSTON UNIV.

Street address 1: 648 Beacon St
Street address 3: Boston
Street address state: MA
Zip/Postal code: 02215-2013
Country: USA
Mailing address: 648 Beacon St
Mailing city: Boston
Mailing state: MA
Mailing zip: 02215-2013
General Phone: (617) 236-4433
General Fax: (617) 236-4414
General/National Adv. E-mail: editor@dailyfreepress.com
Display Adv. E-mail: ads@dailyfreepress.com
Primary Website: www.dailyfreepress.com
Year Established: 1970
Published: Mon`Tues`Wed`Thur
Published Other: Online for summer, breaking content.
Avg Free Circ: 5000
Classified Equipment»
Personnel: Kyle Plantz (Ed.); Felicia Gans (Managing Ed.)

EMERSON COLLEGE

Street address 1: 150 Boylston St
Street address 3: Boston
Street address state: MA
Zip/Postal code: 02116-4608
Country: USA
Mailing address: 150 Boylston St
Mailing city: Boston
Mailing state: MA
Mailing zip: 02116-4608
General Phone: (617) 824-8687
General Fax: (617) 824-8908
General/National Adv. E-mail: berkeley_beacon@emerson.edu
Primary Website: www.berkeleybeacon.com
Classified Equipment»
Personnel: Ric Kahn (Advisor); Matt Byrne (Ed. in Chief); Paddy Shea (Ed. in Chief)

EMMANUEL COLLEGE

Street address 1: 400 Fenway
Street address 3: Boston
Street address state: MA
Zip/Postal code: 02115-5725
Country: USA
Mailing address: 400 Fenway
Mailing city: Boston
Mailing state: MA
Mailing zip: 02115-5798
General Phone: (617) 735-9715
General/National Adv. E-mail: editors@emmanuel.edu
Classified Equipment»
Personnel: Anne Tyson (Ed.)

MASSACHUSETTS COLLEGE OF PHARMACY

Street address 1: 179 Longwood Ave
Street address 3: Boston
Street address state: MA
Zip/Postal code: 02115-5804
Country: USA
Mailing address: 179 Longwood Ave
Mailing city: Boston
Mailing state: MA
Mailing zip: 02115-5896
General Phone: (617) 732-2800
Primary Website: www.mcphs.edu
Classified Equipment»
Personnel: Stephany Orphan (ed.)

NEW ENGLAND SCHOOL OF LAW

Street address 1: 154 Stuart St
Street address 3: Boston
Street address state: MA
Zip/Postal code: 02116-5616
Country: USA
Mailing address: 154 Stuart St
Mailing city: Boston
Mailing state: MA
Mailing zip: 02116-5687
General Phone: (617) 451-0010
General Fax: (617) 422-7224
General/National Adv. E-mail: dueprocess@nesl.edu
Display Adv. E-mail: dueprocess@nesl.edu
Editorial e-mail: dueprocess@nesl.edu
Primary Website: https://www.nesl.edu/students/stuorg_dp.cfm
Year Established: 2012
Published: Other
Published Other: Due Process publishes five (5) regular issues, and one (1) end of year commemorative yearbook.
Classified Equipment»
Personnel: Rebecca Castaneda (Ed. in Chief); Tara Cho (Exec. Ed.); Kelly Lavari (Photo Ed.); Joe Sciabica (Editor-in-Chief); Emily White (Assistant Editor-In-Chief)

NORTHEASTERN UNIVERSITY

Street address 1: 295 Huntington Ave
Street address 2: Ste 208
Street address 3: Boston
Street address state: MA
Zip/Postal code: 02115-4433
Country: USA
Mailing address: 295 Huntington Ave Ste 208
Mailing city: Boston
Mailing state: MA
Mailing zip: 02115-4433
General Phone: (857) 362-7325
General Fax: (857) 362-7326
General/National Adv. E-mail: editor@huntnewsnu.com
Display Adv. E-mail: advertise@huntnewsnu.com
Editorial e-mail: editorial@huntnewsnu.com
Primary Website: www.HuntNewsNU.com
Year Established: 1926
Published: Thur
Classified Equipment»
Personnel: Colin Young (Editor in chief)
Parent company (for newspapers): World Series Way Publishing Co., Inc.

SIMMONS COLLEGE

Street address 1: 300 Fenway
Street address 3: Boston
Street address state: MA
Zip/Postal code: 02115-5820
Country: USA
Mailing address: 300 The Fenway
Mailing city: Boston
Mailing state: MA
Mailing zip: 02115-5820
General Phone: (617) 521-2442
General Fax: (617) 521-3148
General/National Adv. E-mail: voice@simmons.edu
Primary Website: www.thesimmonsvoice.com
Published: Thur
Avg Free Circ: 1500
Classified Equipment»
Personnel: James Corcoran (Adviser); Sarah Kinney (Advisor Editor)

SUFFOLK UNIV.

Street address 1: 41 Temple St
Street address 2: Rm 428
Street address 3: Boston
Street address state: MA
Zip/Postal code: 02114-4241
Country: USA
Mailing address: 41 Temple St Rm 428
Mailing city: Boston
Mailing state: MA
Mailing zip: 02114-4241
General Phone: (617) 573-8323
General Fax: (617) 994-6400
General/National Adv. E-mail: suffolkjournal@gmail.com
Primary Website: www.suffolkjournal.net; www.suffolk.edu
Year Established: 1940
Published: Wed
Classified Equipment»
Personnel: Bruce Butterfield (Advisor); Melissa Hanson; Jeremy Hayes

SUFFOLK UNIV. LAW SCHOOL

Street address 1: 120 Tremont St
Street address 3: Boston
Street address state: MA
Zip/Postal code: 02108-4910
Country: USA
Mailing address: 120 Tremont St
Mailing city: Boston
Mailing state: MA
Mailing zip: 02108-4977
General Phone: (617) 305-3011
General Fax: (617) 573-8706
Classified Equipment»

UNIV. OF MASSACHUSETTS

Street address 1: 100 William T Morrissey Blvd
Street address 3: Boston
Street address state: MA
Zip/Postal code: 02125-3300
Country: USA
Mailing address: 100 Morrissey Blvd
Mailing city: Boston
Mailing state: MA
Mailing zip: 02125-3393
General Phone: (617) 287-7992
General Fax: (617) 287-7897
General/National Adv. E-mail: editor@umassmedia.com
Primary Website: www.umassmedia.com
Year Established: 1966
Delivery Methods: Newsstand
Commercial printers: N
Classified Equipment»
Personnel: Donna Neal (Advisor); Caleb Nelson (Ed.)

HARVARD BUSINESS SCHOOL

Street address 1: Gallatin Hall D Basement
Street address 3: Boston
Street address state: MA
Zip/Postal code: 2163
Country: USA
General Phone: (617) 495-6528
General Fax: (617) 495-8619
General/National Adv. E-mail: general@harbus.org
Primary Website: www.harbus.org
Classified Equipment»
Personnel: Matthew Grayson (Gen.Mgr.); Joanne Knight (Pub.)

BRIDGEWATER

BRIDGEWATER STATE COLLEGE

Street address 1: Rondileau Campus Ctr, Rm.103A
Street address 3: Bridgewater
Street address state: MA
Country: USA
Mailing address: Rondileau Campus Ctr Rm 103A
Mailing city: Bridgewater
Mailing state: MA
Mailing zip: 02325-0001
General Phone: (508) 531-1719
General Fax: (508) 531-6181
General/National Adv. E-mail: comment@bridgew.edu
Primary Website: www.bsccomment.com
Classified Equipment»
Personnel: Justin McCauley (Advisor); Monica Monteiro (Ed. in Chief)

CAMBRIDGE

HARVARD LAW SCHOOL

Street address 1: Harvard Law Record, Harvard Law School
Street address 3: Cambridge
Street address state: MA
Zip/Postal code: 2138
Country: USA
Mailing address: Harvard Law Record, Harvard Law School
Mailing city: Cambridge
Mailing state: MA
Mailing zip: 02138-9984

General Phone: (617) 297-3590
General Fax: (617) 495-8547
General/National Adv. E-mail: record@law.harvard.edu
Primary Website: www.hlrecord.org
Classified Equipment»
Personnel: Matt Hutchins (Ed. in Chief); Chris Szabla (Ed. in Chief); Rebecca Agule (News Ed.); Mark Samburg (Sports Ed.)

HARVARD UNIV.

Street address 1: 14 Plympton St
Street address 3: Cambridge
Street address state: MA
Zip/Postal code: 02138-6606
Country: USA
Mailing address: 14 Plympton St
Mailing city: Cambridge
Mailing state: MA
Mailing zip: 02138-6606
General Phone: (617) 576-6600
General Fax: (617) 576-7860
General/National Adv. E-mail: ads@thecrimson.com
Primary Website: www.thecrimson.com
Classified Equipment»
Personnel: Peter F. Zhu (Pres.); Julian L. Bouma (Bus. Mgr)

HARVARD UNIV./JFK SCHOOL OF GOV'T

Street address 1: 30 Jfk St
Street address 3: Cambridge
Street address state: MA
Zip/Postal code: 02138-4902
Country: USA
Mailing address: 30 Jfk St
Mailing city: Cambridge
Mailing state: MA
Mailing zip: 02138-4902
General Phone: (617) 495-5969
Classified Equipment»
Personnel: Stephanie Geosits (Ed.)

LESLEY UNIVERSITY

Street address 1: 47 Oxford St
Street address 3: Cambridge
Street address state: MA
Zip/Postal code: 02138-1902
Country: USA
Mailing address: 47 Oxford St
Mailing city: Cambridge
Mailing state: MA
Mailing zip: 02138-1972
General Phone: (617) 349-8501
General Fax: (617) 349-8558
Primary Website: www.chronicle.com
Classified Equipment»
Personnel: Gabriella Montell (Assoc. Ed.)

MASSACHUSETTS INST. OF TECHNOLOGY

Street address 1: 84 Massachusetts Ave
Street address 2: Ste 483
Street address 3: Cambridge
Street address state: MA
Zip/Postal code: 02139-4300
Country: USA
Mailing address: 84 Massachusetts Ave Ste 483
Mailing city: Cambridge
Mailing state: MA
Mailing zip: 02139-4300
General Phone: (617) 253 1541
General Fax: (617) 258-8226
General/National Adv. E-mail: general@tech.mit.edu; letters@the-tech.mit.edu
Display Adv. E-mail: ads@tech.mit.edu
Primary Website: thetech.com
Year Established: 1881
Commercial printers: Y
Published: Thur
Avg Free Circ: 8100
Classified Equipment»
Personnel: Aislyn Schalck (Chrmn.); Jessica Pourian (Ed. in Chief); Karleigh Moore (Chairman)

CHESTNUT HILL

BOSTON COLLEGE

Street address 1: McElroy Commons 113, 140 Commonwealth Ave
Street address 3: Chestnut Hill
Street address state: MA
Zip/Postal code: 1919
Country: USA
Mailing address: McElroy Commons 113, 140 Commonwealth Ave.
Mailing city: Chestnut Hill
Mailing state: MA
Mailing zip: 02467-3800
General Phone: (617) 552-2221
General Fax: (617) 552-1753
Advertising Phone: (617) 552-4823
Editorail Phone: (617) 552-2220
Editorial Fax: (617) 552-2223
Display Adv. E-mail: ads@bcheights.com
Primary Website: www.bcheights.com
Classified Equipment»
Personnel: Dave Givler (Adv. Mgr.); Matt DeLuca (Ed. in chief)

CHICOPEE

ELMS COLLEGE

Street address 1: 291 Springfield St
Street address 3: Chicopee
Street address state: MA
Zip/Postal code: 01013-2837
Country: USA
Mailing address: 291 Springfield St
Mailing city: Chicopee
Mailing state: MA
Mailing zip: 01013-2839
General Phone: (413) 594-2761
Primary Website: www.elms.edu
Classified Equipment»
Personnel: James Gallant (Advisor)

DUDLEY

NICHOLS COLLEGE

Street address 1: 124 Center Rd
Street address 3: Dudley
Street address state: MA
Zip/Postal code: 01571-6310
Country: USA
Mailing address: PO Box 5000
Mailing city: Dudley
Mailing state: MA
Mailing zip: 01571-5000
General Phone: (508) 213-1560
General Fax: (508) 943-5354
General/National Adv. E-mail: admissions@nichols.edu
Primary Website: www.nichols.edu/
Year Established: 1815
Commercial printers: N
Classified Equipment»
Personnel: Emily Reardon (Assistant Director of Admissions / International Students Counselor)

BRISTOL CMTY. COLLEGE

Street address 1: 777 Elsbree St
Street address 3: Fall River
Street address state: MA
Zip/Postal code: 02720-7307
Country: USA
Mailing address: 777 Elsbree St
Mailing city: Fall River
Mailing state: MA
Mailing zip: 02720-7399
General Phone: (508) 678-2811
General Fax: (508) 676-7146
General/National Adv. E-mail: observer@bristolcc.edu
Primary Website: www.bristolcc.edu/Students/observer/index.cfm
Classified Equipment»
Personnel: Alex Potter (Ed. in Chief)

FITCHBURG

FITCHBURG STATE COLLEGE

Street address 1: 160 Pearl St
Street address 3: Fitchburg
Street address state: MA
Zip/Postal code: 01420-2631
Country: USA
Mailing address: 160 Pearl St
Mailing city: Fitchburg
Mailing state: MA
Mailing zip: 01420-2697
General Phone: (978) 665-3647
Advertising Phone: (978) 665-3650
General/National Adv. E-mail: pointstorybudget@yahoo.com
Primary Website: www.thepointfsc.com; www.fsc.edu
Classified Equipment»
Personnel: Doris Schmidt (Advisor); John McGinn (Ed.)

FRAMINGHAM STATE UNIVERSITY - THE GATEPOST

Street address 1: 100 State St
Street address 2: Rm 410
Street address 3: Framingham
Street address state: MA
Zip/Postal code: 01702-2499
Country: USA
Mailing address: McCarthy Center 410
Mailing city: Framingham
Mailing state: MA
Mailing zip: 01702-2499
General Phone: (508) 626-4605
General Fax: (508) 626-4097
Advertising Phone: (508) 626-4605
Advertising Fax: (508) 626-4097
Editorail Phone: (508) 626-4605
Editorial Fax: (508) 626-4097
General/National Adv. E-mail: gatepost@framingham.edu
Display Adv. E-mail: gatepost@framingham.edu
Editorial e-mail: gatepost@framingham.edu
Primary Website: www.fsugatepost.com
Year Established: 1930
Delivery Methods: Mail`Racks
Published: Fri
Classified Equipment»
Personnel: Desmond McCarthy (Advisor); Meredith O'Brien-Weiss (Advisor); Robin KurKomelis (Administrative Assistant); Kerrin Murray (Editor-in-Chief); Joe Kourieh (Associate Editor); Karin Radoc (Associate Editor)

DEAN COLLEGE

Street address 1: 99 Main St
Street address 3: Franklin
Street address state: MA
Zip/Postal code: 02038-1941
Country: USA
Mailing address: 99 Main St
Mailing city: Franklin
Mailing state: MA
Mailing zip: 02038-1994
General Phone: (508) 541-1630
General Fax: (508) 541-1946
Classified Equipment»

HAVERHILL

NORTHERN ESSEX COMMUNITY COLLEGE

Street address 1: 100 Elliott St
Street address 3: Haverhill
Street address state: MA
Zip/Postal code: 01830-2306
Country: USA
Mailing address: 100 Elliott St.
Mailing city: Haverhill
Mailing state: MA
Mailing zip: 01830-2399
General Phone: (978) 556-3633
General/National Adv. E-mail: observer@necc.mass.edu
Primary Website: 100 Elliott Street
Year Established: 1962
Published: Bi-Mthly
Classified Equipment»
Personnel: Amy Callahan (Professor)

HOLYOKE

HOLYOKE CMTY. COLLEGE

Street address 1: 303 Homestead Ave
Street address 3: Holyoke
Street address state: MA
Zip/Postal code: 01040-1091
Country: USA
Mailing address: 303 Homestead Ave
Mailing city: Holyoke
Mailing state: MA
Mailing zip: 01040-1099
General Phone: (413) 538-7000
General Fax: (413) 552-2045
Classified Equipment»
Personnel: Fred Cooksey (Advisor)

LOWELL

UNIV. OF MASSACHUSETTS LOWELL CONNECTOR

Street address 1: 71 Wilder St
Street address 2: Ste 6
Street address 3: Lowell
Street address state: MA
Zip/Postal code: 01854-3096
Country: USA
Mailing address: 71 Wilder St Ste 6
Mailing city: Lowell
Mailing state: MA
Mailing zip: 01854-3096
General Phone: (978) 934-5001
General Fax: (978) 934-3072
General/National Adv. E-mail: connector@uml.edu
Primary Website: www.uml.edu/connector
Year Established: 1924
Classified Equipment»
Personnel: Ruben Sanca (Office Mgr.)

TUFTS UNIV.

Street address 1: PO Box 53018
Street address 3: Medford
Street address state: MA
Zip/Postal code: 02153-0018
Country: USA
Mailing address: PO Box 53018
Mailing city: Medford
Mailing state: MA
Mailing zip: 02153-0018
General Phone: (617) 627-3090
General Fax: (617) 627-3910
Primary Website: www.tuftsdaily.com
Classified Equipment»
Personnel: Giovanni Russonello (Ed.)

NEWTON CENTER

MOUNT IDA COLLEGE

Street address 1: 777 Dedham St
Street address 3: Newton Center
Street address state: MA
Zip/Postal code: 02459-3323
Country: USA
Mailing address: 777 Dedham St
Mailing city: Newton Center
Mailing state: MA
Mailing zip: 02459-3310
General Phone: (617) 928-4754
General Fax: (617) 928-4766
Classified Equipment»
Personnel: Melissa Constantine (Advisor); Matt Caldwell (Ed. in Chief); Jen Barrett (Asst. Ed.)

NORTH ADAMS

MASSACHUSETTS COLLEGE OF LIBERAL ARTS

Street address 1: 375 Church St

Street address 2: Rm 111
Street address 3: North Adams
Street address state: MA
Zip/Postal code: 01247-4124
Country: USA
Mailing address: 375 Church St Rm 111
Mailing city: North Adams
Mailing state: MA
Mailing zip: 01247-4124
General Phone: (413) 662-5535
General Fax: (413) 662-5010
Editorail Phone: (413) 662-5404
General/National Adv. E-mail: beacon@mcla.edu
Primary Website: www.mclabeacon.com
Published: Wed
Avg Free Circ: 1000
Classified Equipment»
Personnel: Jennifer Augur (Advisor)

NORTH ANDOVER

MERRIMACK COLLEGE

Street address 1: 315 Turnpike St
Street address 3: North Andover
Street address state: MA
Zip/Postal code: 01845-5806
Country: USA
Mailing address: 315 Turnpike St
Mailing city: North Andover
Mailing state: MA
Mailing zip: 01845-5800
General Phone: (978) 837-5000
General Fax: (978) 837-5004
Primary Website: www.merrimack.edu
Classified Equipment»
Personnel: Russ Mayer (Advisor); Michael Salvucci (Ed. in Chief)

NORTH DARTMOUTH

UNIV. OF MASSACHUSETTS

Street address 1: 285 Old Westport Rd, Campus Ctr, 2nd Fl
Street address 3: North Dartmouth
Street address state: MA
Zip/Postal code: 2747
Country: USA
Mailing address: 285 Old Westport Rd., Campus Ctr., 2nd Fl.
Mailing city: North Dartmouth
Mailing state: MA
Mailing zip: 02747-2300
General Phone: (508) 999-8158
General Fax: (508) 999-8128
General/National Adv. E-mail: torch@umassd.edu
Display Adv. E-mail: TorchAds@umassd.edu
Primary Website: www.umasstorch.com
Classified Equipment»
Personnel: Jason Jones (Adv. Mgr.); Chris Donovan (Ed. in Chief); Megan Gauthier (Mng. Ed.)

NORTH EASTON

STONEHILL COLLEGE

Street address 1: 320 Washington St
Street address 2: # 1974
Street address 3: North Easton
Street address state: MA
Zip/Postal code: 02357-7800
Country: USA
Mailing address: 320 Washington St # 1974
Mailing city: North Easton
Mailing state: MA
Mailing zip: 02357-0001
General Phone: (508) 565-1000
General Fax: (508) 565-1794
Classified Equipment»
Personnel: Matt Gorman (News Ed.)

NORTHAMPTON

SMITH COLLEGE

Street address 1: Capen Annex
Street address 3: Northampton
Street address state: MA
Zip/Postal code: 01063-0001
Country: USA
Mailing address: Capen Anx
Mailing city: Northampton
Mailing state: MA
Mailing zip: 01063-0001
General Phone: (413) 585-4971
General Fax: (413) 585-2075
General/National Adv. E-mail: sophian@smith.edu
Primary Website: www.smithsophian.com
Year Established: 1911
Published: Thur
Classified Equipment»
Personnel: Hira Humayun (EIC)

EASTERN NAZARENE COLLEGE

Street address 1: 23 E Elm Ave
Street address 3: Quincy
Street address state: MA
Zip/Postal code: 02170-2905
Country: USA
Mailing address: 23 E Elm Ave
Mailing city: Quincy
Mailing state: MA
Mailing zip: 02170-2999
General Phone: (617) 745-3000
General Fax: (617) 745-3490
Primary Website: www1.enc.edu
Classified Equipment»
Personnel: Erica Scott Mcgrath (Advisor); Emily Prugh (Ed. in Chief)

SALEM STATE COLLEGE

Street address 1: 352 Lafayette St, Ellison Campus Ctr
Street address 3: Salem
Street address state: MA
Zip/Postal code: 1970
Country: USA
Mailing address: 352 Lafayette St., Ellison Campus Ctr.
Mailing city: Salem
Mailing state: MA
Mailing zip: 01970-5348
General Phone: (978) 542-6448
General Fax: (978) 542-2077
General/National Adv. E-mail: thelog@ssclog.com
Primary Website: www.salemstate.edu/log
Classified Equipment»
Personnel: Peggy Dillon (Advisor)

SOUTH HADLEY

MOUNT HOLYOKE COLLEGE

Street address 1: 50 College St
Street address 2: Blanchard Campus Center 324
Street address 3: South Hadley
Street address state: MA
Zip/Postal code: 01075-1423
Country: USA
Mailing address: 9007 Blanchard Campus Center
Mailing city: South Hadley
Mailing state: MA
Mailing zip: 01075-1423
General Phone: (413) 538-2269
General Fax: (413) 538-2476
General/National Adv. E-mail: mhnews@mtholyoke.edu
Primary Website: http://mountholyokenews.org/
Year Established: 1917
Published: Thur
Classified Equipment»
Personnel: Linda Valencia Xu (Publisher); Geena Molinaro (Editor-in-Chief)

AMERICAN INTERNATIONAL COLLEGE

Street address 1: 1000 State St
Street address 2: # 4
Street address 3: Springfield
Street address state: MA
Zip/Postal code: 01109-3151
Country: USA
Mailing address: 1000 State St # 4
Mailing city: Springfield
Mailing state: MA
Mailing zip: 01109-3151
General Phone: (413) 205-3265
General Fax: (413) 205-3955
Editorial e-mail: yellowjacket@aic.edu
Classified Equipment»
Personnel: Will Hughes (Advisor); Brian Steele (Ed. in Chief)

SPRINGFIELD COLLEGE

Street address 1: 263 Alden St
Street address 3: Springfield
Street address state: MA
Zip/Postal code: 01109-3707
Country: USA
Mailing address: 263 Alden St
Mailing city: Springfield
Mailing state: MA
Mailing zip: 01109-3788
General Phone: (413) 748-3000
General Fax: (413) 748-3473
General/National Adv. E-mail: activities@spfldcol.edu
Primary Website: www.spsldcol.edu
Classified Equipment»
Personnel: Claire Wright (Advisor); Evin Giglio (Ed. in Cheif)

WESTERN NEW ENGLAND COLLEGE

Street address 1: 1215 Wilbraham Rd
Street address 3: Springfield
Street address state: MA
Zip/Postal code: 01119-2612
Country: USA
Mailing address: 1215 Wilbraham Rd
Mailing city: Springfield
Mailing state: MA
Mailing zip: 01119-2684
General Phone: (413) 782-1580
General Fax: (413) 796-2008
Classified Equipment»
Personnel: Wayne Barr (Ed.)

WALTHAM

BRANDEIS UNIVERSITY

Street address 1: 415 South St
Street address 2: MS 214
Street address 3: Waltham
Street address state: MA
Zip/Postal code: 02453-2728
Country: USA
Mailing address: 415 South St MS 214
Mailing city: Waltham
Mailing state: MA
Mailing zip: 02453-2728
General Phone: (781) 736-3750
General Fax: (781) 736-3756
Editorail Phone: (781) 736-3751
General/National Adv. E-mail: editor@thejustice.org
Display Adv. E-mail: ads@thejustice.org
Primary Website: www.thejustice.org
Year Established: 1949
Published: Tues
Classified Equipment»
Personnel: Editor (Ed.)

BENTLEY UNIVERSITY

Street address 1: 175 Forest St
Street address 3: Waltham
Street address state: MA
Zip/Postal code: 02452-4713
Country: USA
Mailing state: MA
General Phone: (781) 891-2921
General Fax: (781) 891-2574
Editorail Phone: (781) 891-3497
General/National Adv. E-mail: ga_vanguard@bentley.edu
Primary Website: www.bentleyvanguard.com; www.bentleyvanguardonline.com
Published: Thur
Classified Equipment»
Personnel: Maria DiIorenzo (Advisor); Sindhu Palaniappan (Ed. in Chief); Greg Kokino (Adv. Mgr.)

WELLESLEY

WELLESLEY COLLEGE

Street address 1: 106 Central St
Street address 2: Fl 4
Street address 3: Wellesley
Street address state: MA
Zip/Postal code: 02481-8203
Country: USA
Mailing address: 106 Central St
Mailing city: Wellesley
Mailing state: MA
Mailing zip: 02481-8210
General Phone: (781) 283-2689
General Fax: (781) 431-7520
General/National Adv. E-mail: thewellesleynews@gmail.com
Display Adv. E-mail: thewellesleynews@gmail.com
Editorial e-mail: thewellesleynews@gmail.com
Primary Website: www.thewellesleynews.com
Year Established: 1901
Published: Wed
Classified Equipment»
Personnel: Alice Liang (Managing Editor); Stephanie Yeh (Editor-in-Chief)

WENHAM

GORDON COLLEGE

Street address 1: 255 Grapevine Rd
Street address 3: Wenham
Street address state: MA
Zip/Postal code: 01984-1813
Country: USA
Mailing address: 255 Grapevine Rd
Mailing city: Wenham
Mailing state: MA
Mailing zip: 01984-1899
General Phone: (978) 927-2306
General Fax: (978) 524-3300
General/National Adv. E-mail: tartan@gordon.edu
Classified Equipment»
Personnel: Eric Convey (Advisor)

WEST BARNSTABLE

CAPE COD CMTY. COLLEGE

Street address 1: 2240 Iyannough Rd
Street address 2: North Building Room 206
Street address 3: West Barnstable
Street address state: MA
Zip/Postal code: 02668-1532
Country: USA
Mailing address: 2240 Iyannough Rd
Mailing city: West Barnstable
Mailing state: MA
Mailing zip: 02668
General Phone: (508) 362-2131
General Fax: (508) 375-4116
General/National Adv. E-mail: info@capecod.edu
Primary Website: www.capecod.edu
Year Established: 1961
Classified Equipment»
Personnel: James Kershner (Advisor)

WESTFIELD

WESTFIELD STATE UNIVERSITY

Street address 1: 577 Western Ave
Street address 2: Ely Campus Center, Room 305
Street address 3: Westfield
Street address state: MA
Zip/Postal code: 01085-2580
Country: USA
Mailing address: 577 Western Avenue
Mailing city: Westfield
Mailing state: MA
Mailing zip: 01085
General Phone: (413) 572-5431
General Fax: (413) 572-5477
Advertising Phone: (413) 572-5431
Editorail Phone: (413) 572-5431

General/National Adv. E-mail: thevoice@westfield.ma.edu
Display Adv. E-mail: thevoiceadvertisement@gmail.com
Year Established: 1946
Published: Fri
Classified Equipment»
Personnel: Joshua Clark (Editor-in-Chief); Andrew Burke (Editor-in-Chief); Emily Hanshaw (Managing Editor); Matthew Carlin (Assistant Managing Editor)

WILLIAMSTOWN

WILLIAMS COLLEGE

Street address 1: 209 Paresky Center
Street address 3: Williamstown
Street address state: MA
Zip/Postal code: 1267
Country: USA
Mailing address: 39 Chapin Hall Dr.
Mailing city: Williamstown
Mailing state: MA
Mailing zip: 01267
General Phone: (413) 597-2289
General Fax: (413) 597-2450
General/National Adv. E-mail: williamsrecordeic@gmail.com
Display Adv. E-mail: williamsrecordadvertising@gmail.com
Editorial e-mail: williamsrecordeic@gmail.com
Primary Website: www.williamsrecord.com
Year Established: 1887
Advertising (Open Inch Rate) Weekday/Saturday: $6/column inch
Published: Wed
Avg Free Circ: 2000
Classified Equipment»
Personnel: Rachel Scharf (Editor-in-Chief); Matthew Borin (Ed. in Chief)

COLLEGE OF THE HOLY CROSS

Street address 1: 1 College St
Street address 3: Worcester
Street address state: MA
Zip/Postal code: 01610-2322
County: Worcester
Country: USA
Mailing address: 1 COLLEGE ST
Mailing city: WORCESTER
Mailing state: MA
Mailing zip: 01610-2395
General Phone: (508) 293-1283
General Fax: (508) 793-3823
General/National Adv. E-mail: crusader@g.holycross.edu
Display Adv. E-mail: crusaderadvertising@gmail.com
Primary Website: www.thehccrusader.com
Published: Fri
Classified Equipment»
Personnel: Steve Vineberg (Faculty Advisor); Sara Bovat (Co-Editor-in-Chief); Emily Vyse (Co-Editor-in-Chief)

ASSUMPTION COLLEGE

Street address 1: 500 Salisbury St
Street address 3: Worcester
Street address state: MA
Zip/Postal code: 01609-1265
Country: USA
Mailing address: 500 Salisbury St
Mailing city: Worcester
Mailing state: MA
Mailing zip: 01609-1296
General Phone: (508) 767-7155
General Fax: (508) 799-4401
General/National Adv. E-mail: provoc@assumption.edu
Primary Website: www.leprovoc.com
Classified Equipment»
Personnel: Sara Swillo (Advisor); Greg Sebastiao (Ed. in Chief)

BECKER COLLEGE

Street address 1: 61 Sever St
Street address 3: Worcester
Street address state: MA
Zip/Postal code: 01609-2165
Country: USA
Mailing address: 61 Sever St
Mailing city: Worcester
Mailing state: MA
Mailing zip: 01609-2195
General Phone: (508) 791-9241
General Fax: (508) 831-7505
General/National Adv. E-mail: info@becker.edu
Classified Equipment»

CLARK UNIVERSITY

Street address 1: 950 Main St
Street address 2: # B-13
Street address 3: Worcester
Street address state: MA
Zip/Postal code: 01610-1400
Country: USA
Mailing address: 950 Main St # B-13
Mailing city: Worcester
Mailing state: MA
Mailing zip: 01610-1400
General Phone: (508) 793-7508
General Fax: (508) 793-8813
General/National Adv. E-mail: scarlet@clarku.edu
Primary Website: www.clarku.edu
Published: Thur
Avg Free Circ: 700
Classified Equipment»
Personnel: Jeremy Levine (Editor-in-Chief)

QUINSIGAMOND CMTY. COLLEGE

Street address 1: 670 W Boylston St
Street address 3: Worcester
Street address state: MA
Zip/Postal code: 01606-2064
Country: USA
Mailing address: 670 W Boylston St
Mailing city: Worcester
Mailing state: MA
Mailing zip: 01606-2092
General Phone: (508) 854-4285
General Fax: (508) 852-6943
General/National Adv. E-mail: opendoor@qcc.mass.edu
Published: Mthly
Classified Equipment»
Personnel: Pat Bisha-Valencia (Advisor)

WORCESTER POLYTECHNIC INSTITUTE

Street address 1: 100 Institute Rd
Street address 3: Worcester
Street address state: MA
Zip/Postal code: 01609-2247
Country: USA
Mailing address: 100 Institute Rd
Mailing city: Worcester
Mailing state: MA
Mailing zip: 01609-2280
General Phone: (508) 831-5464
General Fax: (508) 831-5721
General/National Adv. E-mail: technews@wpi.edu
Display Adv. E-mail: ads@wpi.edu
Primary Website: www.wpi.edu/News/TechNews
Classified Equipment»
Personnel: Michelle Ephraim (Advisor)

WORCESTER STATE COLLEGE

Street address 1: 486 Chandler St
Street address 3: Worcester
Street address state: MA
Zip/Postal code: 01602-2861
Country: USA
Mailing address: 486 Chandler St # G-209
Mailing city: Worcester
Mailing state: MA
Mailing zip: 01602-2861
General Phone: (508) 929-8589
General Fax: (508) 756-8210
General/National Adv. E-mail: studentvoice@worcester.edu
Classified Equipment»
Personnel: Elizabeth Bidinger (Advisor)

MARYLAND

ST. JOHNS COLLEGE

Street address 1: 60 College Ave
Street address 3: Annapolis
Street address state: MD
Zip/Postal code: 21401-1687
Country: USA
Mailing address: 60 College Ave
Mailing city: Annapolis
Mailing state: MD
Mailing zip: 21401-1655
General Phone: (410) 263-2212
Classified Equipment»
Personnel: Ian McCracken (Ed.)

US NAVAL ACADEMY

Street address 1: 121 Blake Rd
Street address 3: Annapolis
Street address state: MD
Zip/Postal code: 21402-1300
Country: USA
Mailing address: 121 Blake Rd
Mailing city: Annapolis
Mailing state: MD
Mailing zip: 21402-1300
General Phone: (410) 293-1536
General Fax: (410) 293-3133
Primary Website: www.dcmilitary.com
Classified Equipment»
Personnel: Jessica Clark (Ed.); Martha Thorn (Mng. Ed.)

ARNOLD

ANNE ARUNDEL CMTY. COLLEGE CAMPUS CURRENT

Street address 1: 101 College Pkwy
Street address 2: Hum 206
Street address 3: Arnold
Street address state: MD
Zip/Postal code: 21012-1857
Country: USA
Mailing address: 101 College Pkwy Hum 206
Mailing city: Arnold
Mailing state: MD
Mailing zip: 21012-1857
General Phone: (410) 777-2803
General Fax: (410) 777-2021
General/National Adv. E-mail: campuscurrent@aacc.edu
Primary Website: www.campus-current.com
Commercial printers: Y
Published: Bi-Mthly
Avg Free Circ: 2500
Classified Equipment»
Personnel: Sheri Venema (Advisor)

CMTY. COLLEGE OF BALTIMORE CITY ESSEX

Street address 1: 7201 Rossville Blvd
Street address 2: Rm 116
Street address 3: Baltimore
Street address state: MD
Zip/Postal code: 21237-3855
Country: USA
Mailing address: 7201 Rossville Blvd Rm 116
Mailing city: Baltimore
Mailing state: MD
Mailing zip: 21237-3855
General Phone: (443) 840-1576
General Fax: (410) 780-6209
Classified Equipment»
Personnel: Jeremy Caplan (Advisor); Corey States (Ed.)

LOYOLA COLLEGE

Street address 1: 4501 N Charles St
Street address 2: Bellarmine Hall 1
Street address 3: Baltimore
Street address state: MD
Zip/Postal code: 21210-2601
Country: USA
Mailing address: 4501 N Charles St Bellarmine Hall 1
Mailing city: Baltimore
Mailing state: MD
Mailing zip: 21210-2694
General Phone: (410) 617-2282
General Fax: (410) 617-2982
General/National Adv. E-mail: greyhoundads@loyola.edu
Primary Website: www.loyolagreyhound.com
Classified Equipment»
Personnel: Joe Morelli (Bus. Mgr.); Kat Kienle (Ed. in Chief)

NOTRE DAME OF MARYLAND UNIVERSITY

Street address 1: 4701 N Charles St
Street address 3: Baltimore
Street address state: MD
Zip/Postal code: 21210-2404
Country: USA
Mailing address: 4701 N. Charles St.
Mailing city: Baltimore
Mailing state: MD
Mailing zip: 21210-2476
General Phone: (410) 532-5580
General Fax: (410) 532-5796
General/National Adv. E-mail: Columns@ndm.edu
Display Adv. E-mail: Columns@ndm.edu
Editorial e-mail: Columns@ndm.edu
Primary Website: www.ndmcolumns.com
Classified Equipment»
Personnel: Mariel Guerrero (Editor-in-Chief); Marguerite Linz (Lead Writer/ Managing Editor)

THE JOHNS HOPKINS NEWS-LETTER

Street address 1: Levering Unit 102
Street address 3: Baltimore
Street address state: MD
Zip/Postal code: 21218
Country: USA
Mailing address: 3400 N Charles St
Mailing city: Baltimore
Mailing state: MD
Mailing zip: 21218-2680
General Phone: (410) 516-4228
General/National Adv. E-mail: chiefs@jhunewsletter.com; business@jhunewsletter.com
Display Adv. E-mail: business@jhunewsletter.com
Primary Website: www.jhunewsletter.com
Year Established: 1896
Published: Thur
Classified Equipment»
Personnel: Marie Cushing (Ed. in Chief); Leah Maniero (Mng. Ed.)

UNIV. OF MARYLAND BALTIMORE COUNTY

Street address 1: Uc 214, 1000 Hilltop Cir
Street address 3: Baltimore
Street address state: MD
Zip/Postal code: 21250-0001
Country: USA
Mailing address: Uc 214, 1000 Hilltop Cir
Mailing city: Baltimore
Mailing state: MD
Mailing zip: 21250-0001
General Phone: (410) 455-1260
General Fax: (410) 455-1265
General/National Adv. E-mail: eic@retrieverweekly.com
Primary Website: www.retrieverweekly.com
Classified Equipment»
Personnel: Christopher Corbett (Advisor); Nimit Bhatt (Adv./Bus. Mgr.); Gaby Arevalo (Ed. in Chief)

BOWIE

BOWIE STATE UNIV.

Street address 1: 14000 Jericho Park Rd
Street address 2: Rm 260
Street address 3: Bowie
Street address state: MD
Zip/Postal code: 20715-3319
Country: USA
Mailing address: 14000 Jericho Park Rd Rm 260
Mailing city: Bowie
Mailing state: MD

Mailing zip: 20715-3319
General Phone: (301) 860-3729
General Fax: (301) 860-3714
Classified Equipment»
Personnel: Rex Martin (Advisor); Kristina Rowley (Mng. Ed.); Jocelyn Jones (Asst. Mng. Ed.)

COLLEGE PARK

UNIVERSITY OF MARYLAND

Street address 1: 3136 S Campus Dining Hall
Street address 3: College Park
Street address state: MD
Zip/Postal code: 20742-8401
Country: USA
Mailing address: 3136 S Campus Dining Hall
Mailing city: College Park
Mailing state: MD
Mailing zip: 20742-8401
General Phone: (301) 314-8000
General Fax: (301) 314-8358
Advertising Phone: (301) 314-8000
Editorail Phone: (301) 314-8000
General/National Adv. E-mail: diamondbackeditor@gmail.com
Display Adv. E-mail: dbkadvertising@gmail.com
Editorial e-mail: newsumdbk@gmail.com
Primary Website: dbknews.com
Year Established: 1909
Published: Thur
Classified Equipment»
Personnel: Mina Haq (Ed. in chief)

HOWARD CMTY. COLLEGE

Street address 1: 10901 Little Patuxent Pkwy
Street address 3: Columbia
Street address state: MD
Zip/Postal code: 21044-3110
Country: USA
Mailing address: 10901 Little Patuxent Pkwy
Mailing city: Columbia
Mailing state: MD
Mailing zip: 21044-3197
General Phone: (410) 772-4937
General Fax: (410) 772-4280
General/National Adv. E-mail: newspaper@howardcc.edu
Primary Website: www.howardcc.edu
Published: Bi-Mthly
Classified Equipment»
Personnel: Michelle Plummer (Advertising Manager)

EMMITSBURG

MOUNT ST. MARY'S UNIV.

Street address 1: 16300 Old Emmitsburg Rd
Street address 3: Emmitsburg
Street address state: MD
Zip/Postal code: 21727-7700
Country: USA
Mailing address: 16300 Old Emmitsburg Rd
Mailing city: Emmitsburg
Mailing state: MD
Mailing zip: 21727-7700
General Phone: (301) 447-5246
General Fax: (301) 447-5755
General/National Adv. E-mail: echo@msmary.edu
Primary Website: www.themountainecho.com
Classified Equipment»
Personnel: Sheldon Shealer (Advisor); Allison Doherty (Mng. Ed.)

FREDERICK

HOOD COLLEGE

Street address 1: 401 Rosemont Ave
Street address 3: Frederick
Street address state: MD
Zip/Postal code: 21701-8524
Country: USA
Mailing address: 401 Rosemont Ave
Mailing city: Frederick
Mailing state: MD
Mailing zip: 21701-8575
General Phone: (301) 696-3641
General Fax: (301) 696-3578
General/National Adv. E-mail: weinberg@hood.edu
Classified Equipment»
Personnel: Rita Davis (Ed.); Al Weinberg (Dir./Prof. of Journalism)

FROSTBURG

THE BOTTOM LINE

Street address 1: 101 Braddock Rd
Street address 2: Lane Center 217
Street address 3: Frostburg
Street address state: MD
Zip/Postal code: 21532-2303
Country: USA
Mailing address: Lane Center 217
Mailing city: Frostburg
Mailing state: MD
Mailing zip: 21532-2303
General Phone: (301) 687-4326
General Fax: (301) 687-3054
General/National Adv. E-mail: thebottomline@frostburg.edu; tblonline@gmail.comthebottomline
Primary Website: www.thebottomlineonline.org
Year Established: 1948
Delivery Methods: Newsstand
Commercial printers: Y
Advertising (Open inch Rate) Weekday/Saturday: varies
Classified Equipment»
Personnel: Dustin Davis (Advisor); Marina Byerly (Editor-in-Chief); Michelle Giambruno (Manging Editor); Marissa Nedved (Business Manager)

GERMANTOWN

MONTGOMERY COLLEGE GERMANTOWN

Street address 1: 20200 Observation Dr
Street address 3: Germantown
Street address state: MD
Zip/Postal code: 20876-4067
Country: USA
Mailing address: 20200 Observation Dr
Mailing city: Germantown
Mailing state: MD
Mailing zip: 20876-4098
General Phone: (240) 567-7840
General Fax: (240) 567-7843
General/National Adv. E-mail: theglobe@montgomerycollege.edu
Primary Website: www.montgomerycollege.edu
Classified Equipment»
Personnel: Dave Anthony (Advisor)

LA PLATA

COLLEGE OF SOUTHERN MARYLAND

Street address 1: PO Box 910
Street address 3: La Plata
Street address state: MD
Zip/Postal code: 20646-0910
Country: USA
Mailing address: PO Box 910
Mailing city: La Plata
Mailing state: MD
Mailing zip: 20646-0910
General Phone: (301) 934-2251
General Fax: (301) 934-7680
General/National Adv. E-mail: hawkeye@csmd.edu
Classified Equipment»
Personnel: Karen Smith-Hupp (Ed.)

PRINCE GEORGES CMTY. COLLEGE

Street address 1: 301 Largo Rd
Street address 3: Largo
Street address state: MD
Zip/Postal code: 20774-2109
Country: USA
Mailing address: 301 Largo Rd
Mailing city: Largo
Mailing state: MD
Mailing zip: 20774-2109
General Phone: (301) 336-6000
General Fax: (301) 808-0960
General/National Adv. E-mail: theowlnewspaper@hotmail.com
Primary Website: www.pgcc.edu
Classified Equipment»
Personnel: Patrick Peterson (Bus. Mgr.); Malcolm Beech (Advisor); Abelaja Obajimi (Ed. in Chief)

PARKTON

UNIV. OF MARYLAND BALTIMORE

Street address 1: PO Box 600
Street address 3: Parkton
Street address state: MD
Zip/Postal code: 21120-0600
Country: USA
Mailing address: PO Box 600
Mailing city: Parkton
Mailing state: MD
Mailing zip: 21120-0600
General Phone: (410) 706-7820
General Fax: (410) 343-3371
Classified Equipment»
Personnel: Susie Flaherty (Sr. Ed.); Clare Banks (Ed.)

MONTGOMERY COLLEGE

Street address 1: 51 Mannakee St
Street address 3: Rockville
Street address state: MD
Zip/Postal code: 20850-1101
Country: USA
Mailing address: 51 Mannakee St
Mailing city: Rockville
Mailing state: MD
Mailing zip: 20850-1199
General Phone: (240) 567-7176
General Fax: (240) 567-5091
General/National Adv. E-mail: info@mcadvocate.com
Display Adv. E-mail: info@mcadvocate.com
Editorial e-mail: editor@mcadvocate.com
Primary Website: http://mcadvocate.com
Year Established: 1957
Classified Equipment»
Note: We are online only. We do not publish a paper.
Personnel: Steve Thurston (Advisor)

SAINT MARYS CITY

ST. MARY'S COLLEGE OF MARYLAND

Street address 1: 18952 E Fisher??S Road
Street address 3: Saint Marys City
Street address state: MD
Zip/Postal code: 20686
Country: USA
Mailing address: 18952 E Fisher??s Road
Mailing city: Saint Mary's City
Mailing state: MD
Mailing zip: 20686
General Phone: (240) 895-4213
General Fax: (240) 895-4445
General/National Adv. E-mail: pointnews@smcm.edu
Primary Website: www.smcm.edu/PointNews
Classified Equipment»
Personnel: Justin Perry (Ed. in Chief); Matt Molek (Mng. Ed.)

SALISBURY

SALISBURY UNIV.

Street address 1: 1101 Camden Ave
Street address 3: Salisbury
Street address state: MD
Zip/Postal code: 21801-6837
Country: USA
Mailing address: PO Box 3183
Mailing city: Salisbury
Mailing state: MD
Mailing zip: 21802-3183
General Phone: (410) 543-6191
General Fax: (410) 677-5359
General/National Adv. E-mail: flyer@salisbury.edu
Primary Website: www.suflyerblog.blogspot.com
Classified Equipment»
Personnel: Leslie Pusey (Advisor.); Vanessa Junkin (Ed.)

STEVENSON

STEVENSON UNIVERSITY

Street address 1: 1525 Greenspring Valley Rd
Street address 3: Stevenson
Street address state: MD
Zip/Postal code: 21153-0641
Country: USA
Mailing address: 1525 Greenspring Valley Rd
Mailing city: Stevenson
Mailing state: MD
Mailing zip: 21153-0641
General Phone: (443) 394-9781
General/National Adv. E-mail: suvillager@gmail.com
Primary Website: stevensonvillager.com
Year Established: 2016 online
Advertising (Open inch Rate) Weekday/Saturday: rate sheet available
Published: Thur
Published Other: every Thursday online
Avg Paid Circ: 0
Classified Equipment»
Personnel: Chip Rouse (Fac. Advisor)

TAKOMA PARK

COLUMBIA UNION COLLEGE

Street address 1: 7600 Flower Ave
Street address 3: Takoma Park
Street address state: MD
Zip/Postal code: 20912-7744
Country: USA
Mailing address: 7600 Flower Ave
Mailing city: Takoma Park
Mailing state: MD
Mailing zip: 20912-7794
General Phone: (301) 891-4118
General/National Adv. E-mail: cj@cuc.edu
Classified Equipment»
Personnel: Athina Lavinos (Pub.); Jaclyn Wile (Ed.); Heidi Lohr (News Ed.)

MONTGOMERY COLLEGE

Street address 1: 7600 Takoma Ave, Commons Rm 202
Street address 3: Takoma Park
Street address state: MD
Zip/Postal code: 20912
Country: USA
Mailing address: 7600 Takoma Ave., Commons Rm. 202
Mailing city: Takoma Park
Mailing state: MD
Mailing zip: 20912
General Phone: (240) 567-1490
General Fax: (301) 650-1334
General/National Adv. E-mail: excaliburnewspaper@montgomerycollege.edu
Classified Equipment»
Personnel: Angela Clubb (Ed.)

GOUCHER COLLEGE

Street address 1: 1021 Dulaney Valley Rd
Street address 3: Towson
Street address state: MD
Zip/Postal code: 21204-2753
Country: USA
Mailing address: 1021 Dulaney Valley Rd
Mailing city: Towson
Mailing state: MD
Mailing zip: 21204-2780
General Phone: (410) 337-6322
General Fax: (410) 337-6434
General/National Adv. E-mail: quin@goucher.edu; askhd@goucher.edu
Primary Website: www.thequindecim.com
Classified Equipment»

Personnel: Matt Simon (Mng. Ed.); Lori Shull (News Ed.); Ben Spangler (Photo Ed.)

TOWSON UNIV.

Street address 1: 8000 York Rd, University Union, Rm 309
Street address 3: Towson
Street address state: MD
Zip/Postal code: 21252-0001
Country: USA
Mailing address: 8000 York Rd University Un Rm 309
Mailing city: Towson
Mailing state: MD
Mailing zip: 21252-0001
General Phone: (410) 704-2288
General Fax: (410) 704-3862
General/National Adv. E-mail: towerlight@towson.edu
Display Adv. E-mail: towerlightads@yahoo.com
Editorial e-mail: towerlighteditor@gmail.com; towerlightnews@gmail.com; towerlightsports@gmail.com; towerlightarts@gmail.com
Primary Website: www.thetowerlight.com
Classified Equipment»
Personnel: Mike Raymond (Gen. Mgr.); Ashley Rabe (Sr. Ed.); Daniel Gross (News Ed.)

MCDANIEL COLLEGE

Street address 1: 2 College Hl
Street address 3: Westminster
Street address state: MD
Zip/Postal code: 21157-4303
Country: USA
Mailing address: 2 College Hill
Mailing city: Westminster
Mailing state: MD
Mailing zip: 21157-4390
General Phone: (410) 751-8600
General Fax: (410) 857-2729
General/National Adv. E-mail: freepress@mcdaniel.edu
Primary Website: mcdanielfreepress.com
Published: Mthly
Classified Equipment»
Personnel: Sarah Hull (Co-Editor-In-Chief); Daniel Valentin-Morales (Co-Editor-In-Chief)

MAINE

BANGOR

HUSSON COLLEGE

Street address 1: 1 College Cir
Street address 3: Bangor
Street address state: ME
Zip/Postal code: 04401-2929
Country: USA
Mailing address: 1 College Cir
Mailing city: Bangor
Mailing state: ME
Mailing zip: 04401-2999
General Phone: (207) 941-7700
General Fax: (207) 941-7190
Classified Equipment»
Personnel: Josh Scroggins (Ed.)

BOWDOIN COLLEGE

Street address 1: 6200 College Sta
Street address 3: Brunswick
Street address state: ME
Zip/Postal code: 04011-8462
Country: USA
Mailing address: 6200 College Sta
Mailing city: Brunswick
Mailing state: ME
Mailing zip: 04011-8462
General Phone: (207) 725-3300
General Fax: (207) 725-3975
General/National Adv. E-mail: orient@bowdoin.edu
Display Adv. E-mail: orientads@bowdoin.edu
Primary Website: orient.bowdoin.edu/orient
Classified Equipment»
Personnel: Zoe Lescaze; Lizzy Tarr (Bus. Mgr.); Will Jacob (Ed. in Chief); Gemma Leghorn (Ed. in Chief)

BATES COLLEGE

Street address 1: 2 Andrews Rd
Street address 3: Lewiston
Street address state: ME
Zip/Postal code: 04240-6020
Country: USA
Mailing address: 2 Andrews Rd
Mailing city: Lewiston
Mailing state: ME
Mailing zip: 04240-6028
General Phone: (207) 795-7494
Advertising Phone: (207) 786-6035
General/National Adv. E-mail: thebatesstudent@hotmail.com
Primary Website: www.batesstudent.com
Classified Equipment»
Personnel: Regina Tavani (Ed. in Chief); Zoe Rosenthal (Deputy Ed. in Chief)

ORONO

UNIVERSITY OF MAINE

Street address 1: Memorial Union, University of Maine Rm 131
Street address 2: rm. 131
Street address 3: Orono
Street address state: ME
Zip/Postal code: 04469-0001
Country: USA
Mailing address: Memorial Union, University of Maine
Mailing city: Orono
Mailing state: ME
Mailing zip: 04469-5748
General Phone: (207) 581-1273
General/National Adv. E-mail: info@mainecampus.com
Display Adv. E-mail: ads@mainecampus.com
Editorial e-mail: eic@mainecampus.com
Primary Website: www.mainecampus.com
Year Established: 1875
Published: Mon
Avg Free Circ: 1500
Classified Equipment»
Personnel: Jordan Houdeshell (Ed. in Chief); Elliott Simpson (Bus. Mgr.)

UNIVERSITY OF SOUTHERN MAINE

Street address 1: 92 Bedford St 2nd Fl
Street address 2:
Street address 3: Portland
Street address state: ME
Zip/Postal code: 04102-2801
Country: USA
Mailing address: PO Box 9300
Mailing city: Portland
Mailing state: ME
Mailing zip: 04104-9300
General Phone: (207) 780-4084
General Fax: N/A
Advertising Phone: 207780-4084
Advertising Fax: N/A
Editorail Phone: 207-780-4165
Editorial Fax: N/A
General/National Adv. E-mail: editor@usmfreepress.org
Display Adv. E-mail: ads@usmfreepress.org
Editorial e-mail: editor@usmfreepress.org
Primary Website: usmfreepress.org
Year Established: 1972
News Services: news@usmfreepress.org
Delivery Methods: Newsstand`Racks
Advertising (Open Inch Rate) Weekday/Saturday: download rate card from our website usmfreepress.org
Published: Mon
Published Other: 10 issues per semester plus Summer orientation issues
Avg Free Circ: 2000
Classified Equipment»
Personnel: Lucille Siegler (Business Manager)

PRESQUE ISLE

UNIV. OF MAINE

Street address 1: 181 Main St
Street address 3: Presque Isle
Street address state: ME
Zip/Postal code: 04769-2844
Country: USA
Mailing address: PO Box 417
Mailing city: Presque Isle
Mailing state: ME
Mailing zip: 04769
General Phone: (207) 768-9400
General/National Adv. E-mail: utimes@maine.edu
Classified Equipment»
Personnel: Tara White (Ed.)

WATERVILLE

COLBY COLLEGE

Street address 1: 4600 Mayflower Hill Dr
Street address 3: Waterville
Street address state: ME
Zip/Postal code: 4901
Country: USA
Mailing address: 4600 Mayflower Hill Dr.
Mailing city: Waterville
Mailing state: ME
Mailing zip: 04901
General Phone: (207) 859-4000
General Fax: (207) 872-3555
General/National Adv. E-mail: echo@colbyecho.com
Primary Website: www.colbyecho.com
Classified Equipment»
Personnel: Peter Rummel (Bus. Mgr.); Kira Novak (Adv. Mgr); Elisabeth Ponsot (Ed. in Chief)

MICHIGAN

ALBION

ALBION COLLEGE

Street address 1: 611 E Porter St
Street address 3: Albion
Street address state: MI
Zip/Postal code: 49224-1831
Country: USA
Mailing address: 611 E. Porter St.
Mailing city: Albion
Mailing state: MI
Mailing zip: 49224
General Phone: (517) 629-1315
General Fax: (517) 629-0509
General/National Adv. E-mail: pleiad@albion.edu
Display Adv. E-mail: pleaid@albion.edu
Editorial e-mail: pleiad@albion.edu
Primary Website: www.albionpleiad.com
Year Established: 1883
Advertising (Open Inch Rate) Weekday/Saturday: City of Albion Business only
Published: Mon`Wed`Fri
Classified Equipment»
Note: Publishes three days a week online and three times a school semester in print.
Personnel: Glenn Deutsch (Advisor); Steve Markowski (Mng. Ed.); Beau Brockett, Jr. (Mng. Ed.); Katie Boni (Features Editor); Andrew Wittland; Morgan Garmo (Opinions editor)

ALLENDALE

GRAND VALLEY STATE UNIV.

Street address 1: 1 Campus Dr
Street address 3: Allendale
Street address state: MI
Zip/Postal code: 49401-9401
Country: USA
Mailing address: 1 Campus Dr, 0051 Kirkhof Center, Grand Valley State University
Mailing city: Allendale
Mailing state: MI
Mailing zip: 49401
General Phone: (616) 331-2460
General Fax: (616) 331-2465
Advertising Phone: (616) 331-2484
General/National Adv. E-mail: lanthorn@gvsu.edu
Display Adv. E-mail: advertising@lanthorn.com
Editorial e-mail: editorial@lanthorn.com
Primary Website: www.lanthorn.com
Year Established: 1964
Published: Mon`Thur
Classified Equipment»
Personnel: Shelby Carter (Business Manager); Emily Doran (Editor-and-Chief); Ian Borthwick (Advertising Manager)

ALMA

ALMA COLLEGE

Street address 1: 614 W Superior St
Street address 3: Alma
Street address state: MI
Zip/Postal code: 48801-1504
Country: USA
Mailing address: 614 W Superior St
Mailing city: Alma
Mailing state: MI
Mailing zip: 48801-1599
General Phone: (989) 463-7161
General Fax: (989) 463-7161
General/National Adv. E-mail: almanian@alma.edu; almanianopinion@yahoo.com; almanian@hotmail.com
Display Adv. E-mail: almanianadvert@yahoo.com
Primary Website: students.alma.edu/organizations/almanian
Classified Equipment»
Personnel: Robert Vivian (Advisor); Brendan Guilford (Ed. in Chief); Olga Wrobel (News Ed.)

ANN ARBOR

UNIV. OF MICHIGAN

Street address 1: 420 Maynard St
Street address 3: Ann Arbor
Street address state: MI
Zip/Postal code: 48109-1327
Country: USA
Mailing address: 420 Maynard St
Mailing city: Ann Arbor
Mailing state: MI
Mailing zip: 48109-1327
General Phone: (734) 763-2459
General Fax: (734) 764-4275
Advertising Phone: (734) 764-0554
General/National Adv. E-mail: news@michigandaily.com; tmdbusiness@gmail.com
Primary Website: www.michigandaily.com
Classified Equipment»
Personnel: Jacob Smilovitz (Ed. in Chief); Matt Aaronson (Mng. Ed.); Dan Newman (Bus. Mgr.)

UNIV. OF MICHIGAN BUS. SCHOOL

Street address 1: 701 Tappan Ave
Street address 2: Ste 766
Street address 3: Ann Arbor
Street address state: MI
Zip/Postal code: 48109-1234
Country: USA
Mailing address: 701 Tappan Ave Ste 766
Mailing city: Ann Arbor
Mailing state: MI
Mailing zip: 48109-1234
General Phone: (734) 764-2074
General Fax: (734) 763-6450
Display Adv. E-mail: msj.office@gmail.com
Editorial e-mail: msj.editor@gmail.com
Primary Website: www.themsj.com
Classified Equipment»
Personnel: Robyn Katzman (Pub.); Maggie Sadowski (Ed. In Chief)

WASHTENAW COMMUNITY COLLEGE

Street address 1: 4800 E Huron River Dr

Street address 3: Ann Arbor
Street address state: MI
Zip/Postal code: 48105-9481
Country: USA
Mailing city: Ann Arbor
Mailing state: MI
Mailing zip: 48105
General Phone: (734) 677-5125
General Fax: (734) 677-5126
Advertising Phone: (734) 973-3662
General/National Adv. E-mail: thewasntehawvoice@gmail.com
Display Adv. E-mail: ealliston@wccnet.edu
Editorial e-mail: kgave@wccnet.edu
Primary Website: www.washtenawvoice.com
Year Established: 1967
Advertising (Open Inch Rate) Weekday/Saturday: www.washtenawvoice.com
Published: Bi-Mthly
Avg Free Circ: 5000
Classified Equipment»
Personnel: Keith Gave (Advisor); Becky Alliston (Adv. Mgr.); Natalie Wright (Ed.)

BERRIEN SPRINGS

ANDREWS UNIV.

Street address 1: Student Ctr 05
Street address 3: Berrien Springs
Street address state: MI
Country: USA
Mailing address: 5 Student Ctr
Mailing city: Berrien Springs
Mailing state: MI
Mailing zip: 49104-0001
General Phone: (269) 471-3385
General Fax: (269) 471-3524
General/National Adv. E-mail: smeditor@andrews.edu
Primary Website: www.andrews.edu/sm
Classified Equipment»
Personnel: Ashleigh Burtnett (Ed. in Chief); Michele Krpalek (Ed.); Stephanie Smart (Asst. Ed.)

BIG RAPIDS

FERRIS STATE TORCH.

Street address 1: 401 South St
Street address 2: Student Rec Center Room 102
Street address 3: Big Rapids
Street address state: MI
Zip/Postal code: 49307-2744
Country: USA
Mailing address: 401 South St
Mailing city: Big Rapids
Mailing state: MI
Mailing zip: 49307-2744
General Phone: (231) 591-5946
General Fax: (231) 591-3617
Advertising Phone: 231-591-2609
General/National Adv. E-mail: torchads@ferris.edu
Editorial e-mail: torch@ferris.edu
Primary Website: www.fsutorch.com
Year Established: 1931
Special Editions: Welcome Back Orientation Housing Guide
Delivery Methods: Newsstand`Racks
Commercial printers: N
Advertising (Open Inch Rate) Weekday/Saturday: $6.25 pci
Market Information: College
Mechanical specifications: Tabloid 9.75 x 15.0
Published: Wed
Avg Free Circ: 4300
Classified Equipment»
Personnel: Steve Fox (Advisor); Laura Anger (Bus. Mgr.)

DEARBORN

HENRY FORD CMTY. COLLEGE

Street address 1: 5101 Evergreen Rd
Street address 2: # C-117
Street address 3: Dearborn
Street address state: MI
Zip/Postal code: 48128-2407
Country: USA
Mailing address: 5101 Evergreen Rd # C-117
Mailing city: Dearborn
Mailing state: MI
Mailing zip: 48128-2407
General Phone: (313) 845-9639
General Fax: (313) 845-9876
General/National Adv. E-mail: mirrorbm@hfcc.edu
Primary Website: www.hfccmirror.com
Classified Equipment»
Personnel: Cassandra Fluker (Advisor); Joshua Gillis (Ed.)

UNIVERSITY OF MICHIGAN-DEARBORN

Street address 1: 4901 Evergreen Rd
Street address 2: Ste 2130
Street address 3: Dearborn
Street address state: MI
Zip/Postal code: 48128-2406
Country: USA
Mailing address: 4901 Evergreen Rd Ste 2130
Mailing city: Dearborn
Mailing state: MI
Mailing zip: 48128-2406
General Phone: (313) 593-5428
General Fax: (313) 593-5594
Advertising Phone: (313) 593-3097
General/National Adv. E-mail: themichiganj@gmail.com
Primary Website: www.michiganjournal.org
Year Established: 1971
Published: Tues
Classified Equipment»
Personnel: Tim Kiska (Adviser); Ricky Lindsay (Editor-in-Chief); Kaitlynn Riley (Advertising Manager)

WAYNE STATE UNIV.

Street address 1: 5221 Gullen Mall
Street address 2: Ste 101
Street address 3: Detroit
Street address state: MI
Zip/Postal code: 48202-3919
Country: USA
Mailing address: 5221 Gullen Mall, Student Center Bldg., Ste. 101
Mailing city: Detroit
Mailing state: MI
Mailing zip: 48202
General Phone: (313) 577-8067
General Fax: (313) 993-8108
Advertising Phone: (313) 577-8666
General/National Adv. E-mail: dv7262@wayne.edu
Editorial e-mail: tseletters@gmail.com
Primary Website: www.thesouthendnews.com
Classified Equipment»
Personnel: Carolyn Chin (Mng. Ed.)

DOWAGIAC

SOUTHWESTERN MICHIGAN COLLEGE

Street address 1: 58900 Cherry Grove Rd
Street address 3: Dowagiac
Street address state: MI
Zip/Postal code: 49047-9726
Country: USA
Mailing address: 58900 Cherry Grove Rd
Mailing city: Dowagiac
Mailing state: MI
Mailing zip: 49047-9726
General Phone: (269) 782-1457
General Fax: (269) 782-1446
Editorail Phone: (269) 782-1457
Editorial Fax: (269) 782-1446
General/National Adv. E-mail: swester@swmich.edu
Editorial e-mail: swester@swmich.edu
Primary Website: http://southwester.swmich.edu/
Year Established: 1968
Advertising (Open Inch Rate) Weekday/Saturday: no
Classified Equipment»
Note: We no longer offer a journalism program so the newspaper became a college publication rather than a student publication and discontinued a printed product at the beginning of 2014. It's updated as new content becomes available.
Personnel: John Eby (Senior Writer and Coordinator of Media Relations)

EAST LANSING

THE STATE NEWS/MICHIGAN STATE UNIVERSITY

Street address 1: 435 E Grand River Ave
Street address 2: Fl 2
Street address 3: East Lansing
Street address state: MI
Zip/Postal code: 48823-4456
Country: USA
Mailing address: 435 E Grand River Ave
Mailing city: East Lansing
Mailing state: MI
Mailing zip: 48823-4456
General Phone: (517) 295-1680
Advertising Phone: (517) 295-1680
Editorail Phone: (517) 295-1680
General/National Adv. E-mail: feedback@statenews.com
Display Adv. E-mail: advertising@statenews.com
Editorial e-mail: editorinchief@statenews.com
Primary Website: www.statenews.com
Year Established: 1909
Special Editions: Welcome week, housing guide, new students mail-home, international students, finals week
Delivery Methods: Mail`Newsstand`Carrier`Racks
Published: Thur
Published Other: Digital-only during summer semester at MSU
Avg Free Circ: 7500
Classified Equipment»
Note: The State News/statenews.com is the independent student-run newspaper/news Web site at Michigan State University. It is a private non-profit entity spun off from the school in 1972.
Personnel: Omar Sofradzija (Advisor); Marty Sturgeon (Gen. Mgr.); Mike Joseph (Webmaster); Travis Ricks (Creative Adviser)
Parent company (for newspapers): State News, Inc.

FLINT

MOTT CMTY. COLLEGE

Street address 1: 1401 E Court St
Street address 3: Flint
Street address state: MI
Zip/Postal code: 48503-6208
Country: USA
Mailing address: 1401 E Court St
Mailing city: Flint
Mailing state: MI
Mailing zip: 48503-2090
General Phone: (810) 762-5616
General Fax: (810) 762-5646
Classified Equipment»
Personnel: Steve Bossey (Ed.)

UNIV. OF MICHIGAN

Street address 1: 303 E Kearsley St
Street address 3: Flint
Street address state: MI
Zip/Postal code: 48502-1907
Country: USA
Mailing address: 303 E Kearsley St
Mailing city: Flint
Mailing state: MI
Mailing zip: 48502-1907
General Phone: (810) 762-3475
General Fax: (810) 762-3023
Advertising Phone: (810) 762-0919
General/National Adv. E-mail: mtimes@hotmail.com
Primary Website: www.themichigantimes.com
Classified Equipment»
Personnel: Joseph Patterson (Adv. Mgr.); Jennifer Profitt (Ed. in Chief)

AQUINAS COLLEGE

Street address 1: 1700 Fulton St E
Street address 3: Grand Rapids
Street address state: MI
Zip/Postal code: 49506-1801
Country: USA
Mailing address: 1607 Robinson Rd SE
Mailing city: Grand Rapids
Mailing state: MI
Mailing zip: 49506-1799
General Phone: (616) 632-2975
General Fax: (616) 732-4487
Advertising Phone: (616) 632-2975
Editorail Phone: (616) 632-2975
General/National Adv. E-mail: saint.editors@aquinas.edu
Display Adv. E-mail: saint.business@aquinas.edu
Editorial e-mail: saint.editors@aquinas.edu
Primary Website: www.aquinas.edu/thesaint
Year Established: 1980
Advertising (Open Inch Rate) Weekday/Saturday: full $425 half $340 quarter $225
Published: Bi-Mthly
Avg Free Circ: 1000
Classified Equipment»
Personnel: Dan Brooks (Advisor); Matt Kuczynski (Editor in Chief)

CALVIN COLLEGE

Street address 1: 3201 Burton St, Student Commons
Street address 3: Grand Rapids
Street address state: MI
Zip/Postal code: 49546
Country: USA
Mailing address: 3201 Burton St., Student Commons
Mailing city: Grand Rapids
Mailing state: MI
Mailing zip: 49546-4301
General Phone: (616) 819-0011
General Fax: (616) 957-8551
General/National Adv. E-mail: chimes@calvin.edu
Primary Website: http://clubs.calvin.edu/chimes
Published: Fri
Classified Equipment»
Personnel: Lauren DeHaan (Ed.); Emma Slager (Ed. in Chief)

GRAND RAPIDS CMTY. COLLEGE

Street address 1: 143 Bostwick Ave NE
Street address 3: Grand Rapids
Street address state: MI
Zip/Postal code: 49503-3201
Country: USA
Mailing address: 143 Bostwick Ave NE
Mailing city: Grand Rapids
Mailing state: MI
Mailing zip: 49503-3201
General Phone: (616) 234-4157
General Fax: (616) 234-4158
General/National Adv. E-mail: grcc_collegiate@yahoo.com
Primary Website: www.thecollegiatelive.com
Classified Equipment»

HILLSDALE

HILLSDALE COLLEGE

Street address 1: 33 E College St
Street address 3: Hillsdale
Street address state: MI
Zip/Postal code: 49242-1205
Country: USA
Mailing address: 33 E College St
Mailing city: Hillsdale
Mailing state: MI
Mailing zip: 49242-1298
General Phone: (517) 437-7341
General Fax: (517) 437-3293
General/National Adv. E-mail: collegian@hillsdale.edu
Primary Website: www.hillsdale.edu
Classified Equipment»
Personnel: Ingrid Jacques (Advisor)

HOLLAND

HOPE COLLEGE

Street address 1: 141 E 12th St
Street address 3: Holland
Street address state: MI
Zip/Postal code: 49423-3663
Country: USA
Mailing address: P.O. Box 9000
Mailing city: Holland
Mailing state: MI
Mailing zip: 49422-9000

General Phone: (616) 395-7877
General Fax: (616) 395-7183
General/National Adv. E-mail: anchor@hope.edu
Display Adv. E-mail: anchorads@hope.edu
Primary Website: anchor.hope.edu
Year Established: 1887
Classified Equipment»
Personnel: Rosie Jahng (Advisor); Amanda Long (Co-Editor-in-Chief); James Champane (Co-Editor-in-Chief); Patterson (Co-Ed. in chief); Emily West (Co-Ed. in chief)

HOUGHTON

MICHIGAN TECHNOLOGICAL UNIV.

Street address 1: 1400 Townsend Dr
Street address 2: Mub 106
Street address 3: Houghton
Street address state: MI
Zip/Postal code: 49931-1200
Country: USA
Mailing address: MUB 106 1400 Townsend Dr
Mailing city: Houghton
Mailing state: MI
Mailing zip: 49931
General Phone: (906) 487-2404
General Fax: (906) 487-3125
Primary Website: www.mtulode.com
Classified Equipment»
Personnel: Kara W. Sokol (Advisor); Kayla R. Herrera (Ed. in chief)

JACKSON CMTY. COLLEGE

Street address 1: 2111 Emmons Rd
Street address 3: Jackson
Street address state: MI
Zip/Postal code: 49201-8395
Country: USA
Mailing address: 2111 Emmons Rd
Mailing city: Jackson
Mailing state: MI
Mailing zip: 49201-8399
General Phone: (517) 787-0800
General Fax: (517) 787-8663
General/National Adv. E-mail: phoenix@jccmi.edu
Primary Website: www.jccmi.edu
Classified Equipment»
Personnel: Karessa E. Weir (Advisor)

KALAMAZOO

KALAMAZOO COLLEGE

Street address 1: 1200 Academy St
Street address 3: Kalamazoo
Street address state: MI
Zip/Postal code: 49006-3268
Country: USA
Mailing address: 1200 Academy St Ofc
Mailing city: Kalamazoo
Mailing state: MI
Mailing zip: 49006-3295
General Phone: (269) 337-7000
General Fax: (269) 337-7216
Primary Website: www.kzoo.edu
Classified Equipment»
Personnel: Brian Ditez (Advisor)

WESTERN MICHIGAN UNIV.

Street address 1: 1903 W Michigan Ave
Street address 2: 1517 Faunce Student Servs. Bldg.
Street address 3: Kalamazoo
Street address state: MI
Zip/Postal code: 49008-5200
Country: USA
Mailing address: 1517 Faunce Student Servs. Bldg.
Mailing city: Kalamazoo
Mailing state: MI
Mailing zip: 49008-5363
General Phone: (269) 387-2110
General Fax: (269) 387-3820
Advertising Phone: 269-387-2107
Advertising Fax: 269-387-3820
Editorail Phone: 269-323-2101
Editorial Fax: 269-387-3820
General/National Adv. E-mail: herald-general-manager@wmich.edu
Display Adv. E-mail: herald-advertising@wmich.edu
Editorial e-mail: herald-editor@wmich.edu
Primary Website: www.westernherald.com
Year Established: 1916
Advertising (Open Inch Rate) Weekday/Saturday: $12.05 per column inch -- discounts available
Published: Bi-Mthly
Avg Free Circ: 10000
Classified Equipment»
Note: $150 online display ad
Personnel: Meghan Chandler (Editor-in-chief); Richard Junger (General Manager)

LANSING

LANSING CMTY. COLLEGE

Street address 1: 411 N Grand Ave
Street address 2: Rm 351
Street address 3: Lansing
Street address state: MI
Zip/Postal code: 48933-1215
Country: USA
Mailing address: Mail Code 1170
Mailing city: Lansing
Mailing state: MI
Mailing zip: 48933
General Phone: (517) 483-1291
General Fax: (517) 483-1290
Advertising Phone: (517) 483-1295
Advertising Fax: (517) 483-1290
Editorail Phone: (517) 483-1288
Editorial Fax: (517) 483-1290
General/National Adv. E-mail: hookl@lcc.edu
Display Adv. E-mail: hookl@lcc.edu
Editorial e-mail: hookl@lcc.edu
Primary Website: www.lcc.edu/lookout
Year Established: 1959
Published: Bi-Mthly
Classified Equipment»
Personnel: Larry Hook (Advisor)

SCHOOLCRAFT COLLEGE

Street address 1: 18600 Haggerty Rd
Street address 2: Rm W169
Street address 3: Livonia
Street address state: MI
Zip/Postal code: 48152-3932
Country: USA
Mailing address: 18600 Haggerty Rd Rm W169
Mailing city: Livonia
Mailing state: MI
Mailing zip: 48152-2696
General Phone: (734) 462-4422
General Fax: (734) 462-4554
General/National Adv. E-mail: sao@schoolcraft.edu
Primary Website: www.schoolcraft.edu; sao.schoolcraft.edu
Classified Equipment»
Personnel: Jeffrey Petts (Advisor); Kathy Hansen (Adv. Mgr.); Ryan Russell (Ed.)

MARQUETTE

NORTHERN MICHIGAN UNIVIVERSITY

Street address 1: 1401 Presque Isle Ave
Street address 2: 2310 University Center
Street address 3: Marquette
Street address state: MI
Zip/Postal code: 49855-2818
Country: USA
Mailing address: 1401 Presque Isle Ave
Mailing city: Marquette
Mailing state: MI
Mailing zip: 49855-5301
General Phone: (906) 227-2545
General Fax: (906) 227-2449
General/National Adv. E-mail: northwind@gmail.com
Display Adv. E-mail: hkasberg@nmu.edu
Primary Website: www.thenorthwindonline.com
Year Established: 1972
Delivery Methods: Mail`Racks
Commercial printers: N
Published: Thur
Classified Equipment»
Personnel: Kristy Basolo (Advisor)

CENTRAL MICHIGAN UNIVERSITY

Street address 1: 436 Moore Hall
Street address 2: Central Michigan University
Street address 3: Mount Pleasant
Street address state: MI
Zip/Postal code: 48859-0001
Country: USA
Mailing address: 436 Moore Hall
Mailing city: Mount Pleasant
Mailing state: MI
Mailing zip: 48859-0001
General Phone: (989) 774-3493
General Fax: (989) 774-7805
Advertising Phone: (989) 774-3493
Advertising Fax: (989) 774-7805
Editorail Phone: (989) 774-3493
Editorial Fax: (989) 774-7805
General/National Adv. E-mail: advertising@cm-life.com
Display Adv. E-mail: advertising@cm-life.com
Editorial e-mail: editor@cm-life.com
Primary Website: www.cm-life.com
Year Established: 1919
Advertising (Open Inch Rate) Weekday/Saturday: $14.95 per column inch
Published: Mon`Wed`Fri
Avg Paid Circ: 150
Avg Free Circ: 10000
Classified Equipment»
Personnel: Kathy Simon (Advisor); David Clark (Director, Student Publications); Catey Traylor (Editor, 2013-2014); Julie Bushart (Advertising Manager, 2013-2014)

OLIVET

OLIVET COLLEGE

Street address 1: 320 S Main St
Street address 3: Olivet
Street address state: MI
Zip/Postal code: 49076-9406
County: Eaton
Country: USA
Mailing address: 320 S. Main St.
Mailing city: Olivet
Mailing state: MI
Mailing zip: 49076-9456
General Phone: (269) 749-7622
General/National Adv. E-mail: echo@olivetcollege.edu
Display Adv. E-mail: echo@olivetcollege.edu
Editorial e-mail: echo@olivetcollege.edu
Primary Website: www.ocecho.com
Year Established: 1888
Delivery Methods: Newsstand
Published Other: Online
Avg Free Circ: 1100
Classified Equipment»
Personnel: Joanne Williams (Advisor); Brian Freiberger (Editor); Bray Wright (Editor)

PORT HURON

ST. CLAIR COUNTY COMMUNITY COLLEGE

Street address 1: 323 Erie St
Street address 2: # 5015
Street address 3: Port Huron
Street address state: MI
Zip/Postal code: 48060-3812
Country: USA
Mailing address: 323 Erie St # 5015
Mailing city: Port Huron
Mailing state: MI
Mailing zip: 48060-3812
General Phone: (810) 989-5733
General Fax: (810) 984-4730
General/National Adv. E-mail: eriesquaregazette@gmail.com
Display Adv. E-mail: esgadvertising@gmail.com
Primary Website: www.esgonline.org
Year Established: 1931
Published Other: Bi-weekly
Classified Equipment»
Personnel: John Lusk (Advisor); Erick Fredendall (Editor-in-Chief)

OAKLAND UNIV.

Street address 1: 61 Oakland Ctr
Street address 3: Rochester
Street address state: MI
Zip/Postal code: 48309-4409
Country: USA
Mailing address: 61 Oakland Ctr
Mailing city: Rochester
Mailing state: MI
Mailing zip: 48309-4409
General Phone: (248) 370-4268
General Fax: (248) 370-4264
General/National Adv. E-mail: editor@oaklandpostonline.com
Primary Website: www.oaklandpostonline.com
Year Established: 1957
Published: Tues
Classified Equipment»
Personnel: Holly Gilbert (Advisor); Don Ritenburgh (Business Manager)
Parent company (for newspapers): Oakland Sail

ROCHESTER HILLS

ROCHESTER COLLEGE

Street address 1: 800 W Avon Rd
Street address 3: Rochester Hills
Street address state: MI
Zip/Postal code: 48307-2704
Country: USA
Mailing address: 800 W Avon Rd
Mailing city: Rochester Hills
Mailing state: MI
Mailing zip: 48307-2704
General Phone: (248) 218-2030
General Fax: (248) 218-2045
General/National Adv. E-mail: theshield@rc.edu
Primary Website: www.rcshield.com
Commercial printers: N
Published: Bi-Mthly
Avg Free Circ: 550
Classified Equipment»
Personnel: Liz Fulton (Mng./Design Ed.); Chelsea Hackel

SAULT SAINTE MARIE

LAKE SUPERIOR STATE UNIV.

Street address 1: 650 W Easterday Ave
Street address 2: Cisler Center 106
Street address 3: Sault Sainte Marie
Street address state: MI
Zip/Postal code: 49783-1626
Country: USA
Mailing address: 650 W Easterday Ave
Mailing city: Sault Sainte Marie
Mailing state: MI
Mailing zip: 49783-1626
General Phone: (906) 635-2551
General Fax: (906) 635-7510
General/National Adv. E-mail: compass@lssu.edu
Display Adv. E-mail: compass@lssu.edu
Editorial e-mail: compass@lssu.edu
Primary Website: compass.lssu.edu
Year Established: 1946
Delivery Methods: Mail`Newsstand`Racks
Commercial printers: Y
Published: Mthly
Classified Equipment»
Personnel: Asher Stephenson (Editor In Chief)
Parent company (for newspapers): Lake Superior State University; LSSU Student Assembly

SPRING ARBOR

SPRING ARBOR UNIV.

Street address 1: 106 E Main St
Street address 2: Ste A28
Street address 3: Spring Arbor
Street address state: MI
Zip/Postal code: 49283-9701
Country: USA
Mailing address: 106 E Main St Ste A28

Mailing city: Spring Arbor
Mailing state: MI
Mailing zip: 49283-9701
General Phone: (517) 523-3616
General Fax: (517) 750-2108
Classified Equipment»
Personnel: Eric Platt (Ed.)

TRAVERSE CITY

NORTHWESTERN MICHIGAN COLLEGE

Street address 1: 1701 E Front St
Street address 3: Traverse City
Street address state: MI
Zip/Postal code: 49686-3016
Country: USA
Mailing address: 1701 E Front St
Mailing city: Traverse City
Mailing state: MI
Mailing zip: 49686-3061
General Phone: (231) 995-1173
General Fax: (231) 995-1952
General/National Adv. E-mail: whitepinepress@gmail.com
Primary Website: www.whitepinepress.org
Classified Equipment»
Personnel: Michael Anderson (Advisor); Nora Stone (Ed. in Chief); Jacob Bailey (Mng. Ed.)

UNIVERSITY CENTER

DELTA COLLEGE

Street address 1: 1961 Delta Rd
Street address 3: University Center
Street address state: MI
Zip/Postal code: 48710-1001
Country: USA
Mailing address: 1961 Delta Rd # H
Mailing city: University Center
Mailing state: MI
Mailing zip: 48710-1002
General Phone: (989) 686-9000
General/National Adv. E-mail: collegiate@delta.edu; info@delta.edu
Primary Website: www.delta.edu/collegiate
Classified Equipment»
Personnel: Kathie Bachleda (Advisor); Megan Tobias (Ed in Chief)

SAGINAW VALLEY STATE UNIV.

Street address 1: 125 Curtiss Hall, 7400 Bay Rd
Street address 3: University Center
Street address state: MI
Zip/Postal code: 48710-0001
Country: USA
Mailing address: 125 Curtiss Hall, 7400 Bay Rd
Mailing city: University Center
Mailing state: MI
Mailing zip: 48710-0001
General Phone: (989) 964-4248
General/National Adv. E-mail: vanguard@svsu.edu
Primary Website: www.thevalleyvanguard.com
Classified Equipment»
Personnel: Sara Kitchen (Ed. in Chief)

YPSILANTI

EASTERN MICHIGAN UNIVERSITY

Street address 1: 228 King Hall
Street address 3: Ypsilanti
Street address state: MI
Zip/Postal code: 48197-2239
Country: USA
Mailing address: 228 King Hall
Mailing city: Ypsilanti
Mailing state: MI
Mailing zip: 48197-2239
General Phone: (734) 487-1026
General Fax: (734) 487-6702
Advertising Phone: (734) 748-1458
Advertising Fax: (734) 487-1241
General/National Adv. E-mail: editor@easternecho.com
Display Adv. E-mail: brian.peterson24@gmail.com
Editorial e-mail: editor@easternecho.com
Primary Website: www.easternecho.com
Year Established: 1881
Published: Mon`Thur
Classified Equipment»
Personnel: Sydney Smith

MINNESOTA

BEMIDJI

BEMIDJI STATE UNIV.

Street address 1: 1500 Birchmont Dr NE
Street address 3: Bemidji
Street address state: MN
Zip/Postal code: 56601-2600
Country: USA
Mailing address: PO Box 58
Mailing city: Bemidji
Mailing state: MN
Mailing zip: 56619-0058
General Phone: (218) 755-2001
General Fax: (218) 755-2913
General/National Adv. E-mail: northernstudent@yahoo.com
Primary Website: www.northernstudent.com
Year Established: 1926
Published: Wed
Avg Paid Circ: 111
Avg Free Circ: 3000
Classified Equipment»
Personnel: Robby Robinson (Advisor)

NORMANDALE COMMUNITY COLLEGE

Street address 1: 9700 France Ave S
Street address 3: Bloomington
Street address state: MN
Zip/Postal code: 55431-4309
Country: USA
Mailing address: 9700 France Ave S
Mailing city: Bloomington
Mailing state: MN
Mailing zip: 55431-4399
General Phone: (952) 358-8129
Advertising Phone: (952) 358-8193
General/National Adv. E-mail: lionsroar@normandale.edu
Primary Website: www.lionsroar.info
Year Established: 1969
News Services: MCT Campus
Commercial printers: N
Classified Equipment»
Personnel: Mark Plenke (Advisor)

COLLEGEVILLE

ST. JOHNS UNIV.

Street address 1: PO Box 2000
Street address 3: Collegeville
Street address state: MN
Zip/Postal code: 56321-2000
Country: USA
Mailing address: PO Box 2000
Mailing city: Collegeville
Mailing state: MN
Mailing zip: 56321-2000
General Phone: (320) 363-2540
General Fax: (320) 363-2061
General/National Adv. E-mail: record@csbsju.edu
Primary Website: www.users.csbsju.edu/record
Classified Equipment»
Personnel: Kate Kompas (Advisor)

DULUTH

COLLEGE OF ST. SCHOLASTICA

Street address 1: 1200 Kenwood Ave
Street address 3: Duluth
Street address state: MN
Zip/Postal code: 55811-4199
Country: USA
Mailing address: 1200 Kenwood Ave
Mailing city: Duluth
Mailing state: MN
Mailing zip: 55811-4199
General Phone: (218) 723-6187
General Fax: (218) 723-6290
General/National Adv. E-mail: cable1@css.edu
Primary Website: www.css.edu
Classified Equipment»
Personnel: Joe Wicklund (Advisor); Print Corp (Pub.); Kirby Montgomery (Ed. in Chief)

UNIV. OF MINNESOTA DULUTH

Street address 1: 118 Kirby Ctr, 10 University Dr
Street address 3: Duluth
Street address state: MN
Zip/Postal code: 55812
Country: USA
Mailing address: 118 Kirby Ctr., 10 University Dr.
Mailing city: Duluth
Mailing state: MN
Mailing zip: 55812-2403
General Phone: (218) 726-8154
General Fax: (218) 726-8276
General/National Adv. E-mail: statesman@d.umn.edu
Primary Website: www.umdstatesman.com
Classified Equipment»
Personnel: Lisa Hansen (Advisor)

FERGUS FALLS

FERGUS FALLS CMTY. COLLEGE

Street address 1: 1414 College Way
Street address 3: Fergus Falls
Street address state: MN
Zip/Postal code: 56537-1009
Country: USA
Mailing address: 1414 College Way
Mailing city: Fergus Falls
Mailing state: MN
Mailing zip: 56537-1009
General Phone: (877) 450-3322
General Fax: (218) 736-1510
Classified Equipment»
Personnel: Angela Schroeder (Ed.)

INVER GROVE HEIGHTS

INVER HILLS CMTY. COLLEGE

Street address 1: 2500 80th St E
Street address 2: Ste A
Street address 3: Inver Grove Heights
Street address state: MN
Zip/Postal code: 55076-3224
Country: USA
Mailing address: 2500 80th St E Ste A
Mailing city: Inver Grove Heights
Mailing state: MN
Mailing zip: 55076-3224
General Phone: (651) 450-8563
General Fax: (651) 450-8679
Classified Equipment»
Personnel: Dave Page (Advisor)

MANKATO

MINNESOTA STATE UNIV. MANKATO

Street address 1: 293 Centennial Student Un
Street address 2: Minnesota State University, Mankato
Street address 3: Mankato
Street address state: MN
Zip/Postal code: 56001-6051
Country: USA
Mailing address: Centennial Student Union 293
Mailing city: Mankato
Mailing state: MN
Mailing zip: 56001
General Phone: (507) 389-1776
General Fax: (507) 389-5812
Advertising Phone: (507)389-1079
Advertising Fax: (507)389-1595
General/National Adv. E-mail: reporter-editor@mnsu.edu
Display Adv. E-mail: reporter-ad@mnsu.edu
Primary Website: www.msureporter.com
Delivery Methods: Newsstand`Racks
Classified Equipment»
Personnel: Anne Schuelke (Adv.Mgr.); Nicole Smith (Ed. in Chief); Higginbotham (News Ed.); Shelly Christ (Advertising Sales Manager)

MARSHALL

SOUTHWEST STATE UNIV.

Street address 1: 1501 State St
Street address 2: Bellows Academic 246
Street address 3: Marshall
Street address state: MN
Zip/Postal code: 56258-3306
Country: USA
Mailing address: Bellows Academic 246
Mailing city: Marshall
Mailing state: MN
Mailing zip: 56258
General Phone: (507) 537-6228
General Fax: (507) 537-7359
General/National Adv. E-mail: smsuspur@yahoo.com; smsuspur@gmail.com
Primary Website: www.smsuspur.net
Classified Equipment»
Personnel: Jessica Boeve (Bus. Mgr.); Jason Zahn (Ed. in Chief); McMellan Legaspi (Mng. Ed.)

AUGSBURG COLLEGE

Street address 1: 2211 Riverside Ave
Street address 3: Minneapolis
Street address state: MN
Zip/Postal code: 55454-1350
Country: USA
Mailing address: 2211 Riverside Ave
Mailing city: Minneapolis
Mailing state: MN
Mailing zip: 55454-1351
General Phone: (612) 330-1018
General Fax: (612) 330-1649
Display Adv. E-mail: echo@augsburg.edu
Primary Website: www.augsburg.edu/organizations/descriptions/echo.html
Classified Equipment»
Personnel: Boyd Koehler (Adviser); Jenny Pinther (Editor-in-chief)

MINNEAPOLIS CMTY. & TECH. COLLEGE

Street address 1: 1501 Hennepin Ave
Street address 3: Minneapolis
Street address state: MN
Zip/Postal code: 55403-1710
Country: USA
Mailing address: 1501 Hennepin Ave
Mailing city: Minneapolis
Mailing state: MN
Mailing zip: 55403-1710
General Phone: (612) 659-6796
General Fax: (612) 659-6825
Primary Website: www.citycollegenews.com
Classified Equipment»
Personnel: Ben Lathrop (Advisor); Andrea Johnson (Mng. Ed.)

NORTH CENTRAL UNIV.

Street address 1: 910 Elliot Ave
Street address 3: Minneapolis
Street address state: MN
Zip/Postal code: 55404-1322
Country: USA
Mailing address: 910 Elliot Ave
Mailing city: Minneapolis
Mailing state: MN
Mailing zip: 55404-1391
General Phone: (612) 343-4495
General Fax: (612) 343-4780
Primary Website: www.ncunortherner.com
Classified Equipment»

Personnel: Reuben David (Advisor)

UNIV. OF MINNESOTA

Street address 1: 2221 University Ave SE
Street address 2: Ste 450
Street address 3: Minneapolis
Street address state: MN
Zip/Postal code: 55414-3077
Country: USA
Mailing address: 2221 University Ave SE Ste 450
Mailing city: Minneapolis
Mailing state: MN
Mailing zip: 55414-3077
General Phone: (612) 627-4080
General Fax: (612) 435-5865
General/National Adv. E-mail: news@mndaily.com
Primary Website: www.mndaily.com
Classified Equipment»
Personnel: Holly Miller (Ed. in Chief)

UNIV. OF MINNESOTA INST. OF TECH

Street address 1: 207 Church St SE
Street address 2: Lind Hall 5
Street address 3: Minneapolis
Street address state: MN
Zip/Postal code: 55455-0134
Country: USA
Mailing address: 207 Church St SE Lind Hall 5
Mailing city: Minneapolis
Mailing state: MN
Mailing zip: 55455-0134
General Phone: (612) 624-9816
General Fax: (612) 626-0261
General/National Adv. E-mail: technolog@itdean.umn.edu
Primary Website: technolog.it.umn.edu/technolog
Classified Equipment»
Personnel: Paul Sorenson (Advisor); Nate Johnson (Ed.); Michelle Walter (Ed,)

MOORHEAD

CONCORDIA COLLEGE

Street address 1: 901 8th St S
Street address 3: Moorhead
Street address state: MN
Zip/Postal code: 56562-0001
Country: USA
Mailing address: PO Box 104
Mailing city: Moorhead
Mailing state: MN
Mailing zip: 56561-0104
General Phone: (218) 299-3826
General Fax: (218) 299-4313
General/National Adv. E-mail: concord@cord.edu; cordadd@cord.edu
Display Adv. E-mail: cordadd@cord.edu
Editorial e-mail: concord@cord.edu
Primary Website: www.theconcordian.org
Year Established: 1920
Published: Thur
Avg Free Circ: 2000
Classified Equipment»
Personnel: Cathy McMullen (Advisor); Terence Tang (Bus. Mgr.); Suzanne Maanum (Adv. Mgr.)

MINNESOTA STATE UNIV. MOORHEAD

Street address 1: 1104 7th Ave S
Street address 3: Moorhead
Street address state: MN
Zip/Postal code: 56563-0001
Country: USA
Mailing address: PO Box 306
Mailing city: Moorhead
Mailing state: MN
Mailing zip: 56561-0306
General Phone: (218)477-2552
General Fax: (218) 477-4662
General/National Adv. E-mail: advocate@mnstate.edu
Primary Website: www.mnstate.edu/advocate
Classified Equipment»
Personnel: Kristi Monson (Advisor)

MORRIS

UNIV. OF MINNESOTA

Street address 1: 600 E 4th St
Street address 3: Morris
Street address state: MN
Zip/Postal code: 56267-2132
Country: USA
Mailing address: 600 East Fourth Street
Mailing city: Morris
Mailing state: MN
Mailing zip: 56267
General Phone: (320) 589-6078
General Fax: (320) 589-6079
General/National Adv. E-mail: register@mrs.umn.edu
Year Established: 1987
Classified Equipment»
Personnel: Ingrid Luisa Avenda?⊠?⊠£?⊠?????o (Adv. Mgr.); Joy Heysse (Ed. in Chief); Eli Mayfield (Mng. Ed.)

NORTHFIELD

CARLETON COLLEGE

Street address 1: 1 N College St
Street address 3: Northfield
Street address state: MN
Zip/Postal code: 55057-4001
Country: USA
Mailing address: 1 N College St
Mailing city: Northfield
Mailing state: MN
Mailing zip: 55057-4044
General Fax: (507) 222-4000
General/National Adv. E-mail: carletonian@carleton.edu
Primary Website: www.carleton.edu/carletonian
Classified Equipment»
Personnel: James McMenimen (Adv. Mgr); Vivyan Tran (Ed. in Chief); Emily Howell (Ed. in Chief)

ST. OLAF COLLEGE

Street address 1: 1520 Saint Olaf Ave
Street address 3: Northfield
Street address state: MN
Zip/Postal code: 55057-1574
Country: USA
Mailing address: 1520 Saint Olaf Ave
Mailing city: Northfield
Mailing state: MN
Mailing zip: 55057-1099
General Phone: (507) 786-3275
General Fax: (507) 786-3650
General/National Adv. E-mail: manitoumessenger@stolaf.edu.com
Display Adv. E-mail: mess-advertise@stolaf.edu
Editorial e-mail: mess-exec@stolaf.edu
Primary Website: www.manitoumessenger.com
Classified Equipment»
Personnel: Bridget Dinter (Adv. Mgr.)

SAINT BONIFACIUS

CROWN COLLEGE

Street address 1: 8700 College View Dr
Street address 3: Saint Bonifacius
Street address state: MN
Zip/Postal code: 55375-9002
Country: USA
Mailing address: 8700 College View Dr
Mailing city: Saint Bonifacius
Mailing state: MN
Mailing zip: 55375-9001
General Phone: (952) 446-4100
General Fax: (952) 446-4149
Primary Website: www.crown.edu
Classified Equipment»
Personnel: William Allen (Advisor)

ST. CLOUD STATE UNIV.

Street address 1: 720 4th Ave S
Street address 3: Saint Cloud
Street address state: MN
Zip/Postal code: 56301-4442
Country: USA
Mailing address: 720 4th Ave S
Mailing city: Saint Cloud
Mailing state: MN
Mailing zip: 56301-4498
General Phone: (320) 308-4086
Advertising Phone: (320) 308-3943
General/National Adv. E-mail: editor@universitychronicle.net
Display Adv. E-mail: advertising@universitychronicle.net
Editorial e-mail: editor@universitychronicle.net
Primary Website: www.universitychronicle.net
Year Established: 1924
Special Editions: End of the year review issue, beginning of the year orientation issue
Delivery Methods: Newsstand`Carrier`Racks
Published: Mon
Classified Equipment»
Personnel: Sandesh Malla (Bus. Mgr.); Ashley Kalkbrenner (Adv. Mgr.); Tiffany Krupke; Jason Tham; Kamana Karki

BETHEL COLLEGE

Street address 1: 3900 Bethel Dr
Street address 2: Ste 1504
Street address 3: Saint Paul
Street address state: MN
Zip/Postal code: 55112-6902
Country: USA
Mailing address: 3900 Bethel Dr Ste 1504
Mailing city: Saint Paul
Mailing state: MN
Mailing zip: 55112-6999
General Phone: (651) 635-8643
General Fax: (651) 635-8650
General/National Adv. E-mail: bethelclarion@gmail.com
Classified Equipment»
Personnel: Marie Wisner (Advisor)

CONCORDIA UNIV. AT ST. PAUL

Street address 1: 275 Syndicate St N
Street address 3: Saint Paul
Street address state: MN
Zip/Postal code: 55104-5436
Country: USA
Mailing address: 275 Syndicate St N
Mailing city: Saint Paul
Mailing state: MN
Mailing zip: 55104-5436
General Phone: (651) 641-8221
General Fax: (651) 659-0207
General/National Adv. E-mail: sword@csp.edu
Primary Website: www.csp.edu/sword
Classified Equipment»
Personnel: Eric Dregni (Advisor); Helena Woodruff (Ed. in Chief); Rachel Kuhnle (Art Ed.)

HAMLINE UNIV.

Street address 1: 1536 Hewitt Ave
Street address 3: Saint Paul
Street address state: MN
Zip/Postal code: 55104-1205
Country: USA
Mailing address: 1536 Hewitt Ave
Mailing city: Saint Paul
Mailing state: MN
Mailing zip: 55104-1284
General Phone: (651) 523-2268
General Fax: (651) 523-3144
General/National Adv. E-mail: oracle@hamline.edu
Primary Website: www.hamlineoracle.com
Year Established: 1888
Published: Wed
Avg Free Circ: 600
Classified Equipment»
Personnel: David Hudson (Adviser); Stolz Catherine (Editor-in-Chief)

MACALESTER COLLEGE

Street address 1: 1600 Grand Ave
Street address 3: Saint Paul
Street address state: MN
Zip/Postal code: 55105-1801
Country: USA
Mailing address: 1600 Grand Ave
Mailing city: Saint Paul
Mailing state: MN
Mailing zip: 55105-1899
General Phone: (651) 696-6212
General Fax: (651) 696-6685
Editorail Phone: (651) 696-6684
General/National Adv. E-mail: macweekly@macalester.edu
Primary Website: www.themacweekly.com
Year Established: 1914
Published: Fri
Classified Equipment»
Personnel: Will Milch (Editor in Chief); Jen Katz (Editor in Cheif); Carrigan Miller (Ad Manager)

UNIVERSITY OF NORTHWESTERN

Street address 1: 3003 Snelling Ave N
Street address 3: Saint Paul
Street address state: MN
Zip/Postal code: 55113-1501
Country: USA
Mailing address: 3003 Snelling Ave N
Mailing city: Saint Paul
Mailing state: MN
Mailing zip: 55113
General Phone: (651) 631-5100
General Fax: (651) 651-5124
General/National Adv. E-mail: examiner@unwsp.edu
Display Adv. E-mail: examinerads@unwsp.edu
Primary Website: http://www.unwexaminer.com/about/
Published: Bi-Mthly
Classified Equipment»
Personnel: Doug Trouten (Advisor)

WILLIAM MITCHELL COLLEGE OF LAW

Street address 1: 875 Summit Ave
Street address 3: Saint Paul
Street address state: MN
Zip/Postal code: 55105-3030
Country: USA
Mailing address: 875 Summit Ave
Mailing city: Saint Paul
Mailing state: MN
Mailing zip: 55105-3076
General/National Adv. E-mail: theopinion@wmitchell.edu
Classified Equipment»
Personnel: Lucas Hjelle

SAINT PETER

GUSTAVUS ADOLPHUS COLLEGE

Street address 1: 800 W College Ave
Street address 3: Saint Peter
Street address state: MN
Zip/Postal code: 56082-1485
Country: USA
Mailing address: 800 W College Ave
Mailing city: Saint Peter
Mailing state: MN
Mailing zip: 56082-1498
General Phone: (507) 933-7636
General Fax: (507) 933-7633
General/National Adv. E-mail: weekly@gac.edu
Primary Website: www.gustavus.edu/weekly
Year Established: 1891
Commercial printers: Y
Published: Fri
Classified Equipment»
Personnel: David Kogler (Advisor); Victoria Clark; Jacob Seamans (Ed.); Chelsea Johnson (Editor In Chief 2013-14); Caroline Probst (Editor-in-Chief)

THIEF RIVER FALLS

NORTHLAND CMTY. & TECH. COLLEGE

Street address 1: 1101 Highway 1 E
Street address 3: Thief River Falls
Street address state: MN
Zip/Postal code: 56701-2528
Country: USA
Mailing address: 1101 Highway 1 E
Mailing city: Thief River Falls
Mailing state: MN

Mailing zip: 56701-2528
General Phone: (218) 683-8801
General Fax: (218) 683-8980
Primary Website: www.northlandcollege.edu
Classified Equipment»
Personnel: Adam Paulson (Contact); Elizabeth Perfecto (Ed.)

WILLMAR

RIDGEWATER COLLEGE

Street address 1: 2101 15th Ave NW
Street address 3: Willmar
Street address state: MN
Zip/Postal code: 56201-3096
Country: USA
Mailing address: 2101 15th Ave NW
Mailing city: Willmar
Mailing state: MN
Mailing zip: 56201-3096
General Phone: (320) 222-5200
General Fax: (320) 231-6602
General/National Adv. E-mail: info@ridgewater.edu
Primary Website: www.ridgewater.edu
Classified Equipment»
Personnel: Gregg Aamot (Advisor)

WINONA

ST. MARYS UNIV. OF MINNESOTA

Street address 1: 700 Terrace Hts
Street address 2: Ste 37
Street address 3: Winona
Street address state: MN
Zip/Postal code: 55987-1321
Country: USA
Mailing address: 700 Terrace Hts Ste 37
Mailing city: Winona
Mailing state: MN
Mailing zip: 55987-1321
General Phone: (507) 457-1497
General Fax: (507) 457-6967
Primary Website: www.smumn.edu
Commercial printers: N
Classified Equipment»
Personnel: Bob Conover (Advisor)

THE WINONAN

Street address 1: 175 W Mark St
Street address 3: Winona
Street address state: MN
Zip/Postal code: 55987-3384
Country: USA
Mailing address: 175 W Mark St
Mailing city: Winona
Mailing state: MN
Mailing zip: 55987
General/National Adv. E-mail: winonan@winona.edu
Primary Website: https://winonan.org/
Year Established: 1919
Published: Wed
Classified Equipment»
Personnel: Doug Westerman (Journalism Advisor); Tracy Rahim (Advisor); Gabriel Hathaway (Editor-in-chief)

MISSOURI

BOLIVAR

SOUTHWEST BAPTIST UNIV.

Street address 1: 1600 University Ave
Street address 3: Bolivar
Street address state: MO
Zip/Postal code: 65613-2578
Country: USA
Mailing address: 1600 University Ave
Mailing city: Bolivar
Mailing state: MO
Mailing zip: 65613-2597
General Phone: (417) 328-1833
General Fax: (417) 328-1579
General/National Adv. E-mail: info@omnibusonline.com
Primary Website: www.omnibusonline.com
Classified Equipment»
Personnel: Jessica Oliver (Ed. in Chief); Nicole Heitman (Adv. Mgr.)

CULVER-STOCKTON COLLEGE

Street address 1: 1 College Hl
Street address 3: Canton
Street address state: MO
Zip/Postal code: 63435-1257
Country: USA
Mailing address: 1 College Hl
Mailing city: Canton
Mailing state: MO
Mailing zip: 63435-1299
General Phone: (573) 231-6371
General Fax: (573) 231-6611
General/National Adv. E-mail: swiegenstein@culver.edu
Primary Website: www.culver.edu
Year Established: 1853
Classified Equipment»
Personnel: Fred Berger (Asst. Prof Comm.); Tyler Tomlinson (Lecturer in Comm.)

CAPE GIRARDEAU

SOUTHEAST MISSOURI STATE UNIV.

Street address 1: 1 University Plz
Street address 2: MS 2225
Street address 3: Cape Girardeau
Street address state: MO
Zip/Postal code: 63701-4710
Country: USA
Mailing address: 1 University Plz MS 2225
Mailing city: Cape Girardeau
Mailing state: MO
Mailing zip: 63701-4710
General Phone: (573) 651-2540
General Fax: (573) 651-2825
Editorial e-mail: thearrow.news@gmail.com
Primary Website: www.capahaarrow.com
Classified Equipment»
Personnel: Sam Blackwell (Advisor); Erin Mustain (Ed. in Chief); Ben Marxer (Arts/Entertainment Ed.)

CLAYTON

FONTBONNE COLLEGE

Street address 1: 6800 Wydown Blvd
Street address 3: Clayton
Street address state: MO
Zip/Postal code: 63105-3043
Country: USA
Mailing address: 6800 Wydown Blvd
Mailing city: Clayton
Mailing state: MO
Mailing zip: 63105-3098
General Phone: (314) 889-1477
General Fax: (314) 889-1451
Classified Equipment»
Personnel: Jason Sommer (Prof.); Sara Lubbes (Ed.)

STEPHENS COLLEGE

Street address 1: 1200 E Broadway, Campus Box 2014
Street address 3: Columbia
Street address state: MO
Zip/Postal code: 65215-0001
Country: USA
Mailing address: 1200 E Broadway, Campus Box 2014
Mailing city: Columbia
Mailing state: MO
Mailing zip: 65215-0001
General Phone: (573) 876-7133
General/National Adv. E-mail: stephenslifemagazine@gmail.com
Primary Website: http://www.stephens.edu/stephenslife
Classified Equipment»
Personnel: Kathy Vogt (Bus. Mgr.); Josh Nichol-Caddy (Stephens Life Adviser)

UNIV. OF MISSOURI - THE MANEATER NEWSPAPER

Street address 1: 2509 MU Student Center
Street address 3: Columbia
Street address state: MO
Zip/Postal code: 65211-0001
Country: USA
Mailing address: 2509 MU Student Center
Mailing city: Columbia
Mailing state: MO
Mailing zip: 65211
General Phone: (573) 882-6288
Display Adv. E-mail: advertising@themaneater.com
Editorial e-mail: editors@themaneater.com
Primary Website: www.themaneater.com
Year Established: 1955
Delivery Methods: Racks
Commercial printers: N
Advertising (Open Inch Rate) Weekday/Saturday: $10/pci
Published: Wed`Mthly
Avg Free Circ: 4000
Classified Equipment»
Personnel: Becky Diehl (Coordinator)

FULTON

WESTMINSTER COLLEGE

Street address 1: 501 Westminster Ave
Street address 3: Fulton
Street address state: MO
Zip/Postal code: 65251-1230
Country: USA
Mailing address: 501 Westminster Ave
Mailing city: Fulton
Mailing state: MO
Mailing zip: 65251-1299
General Phone: (573) 592-5000
General Fax: (573) 642-2699
Primary Website: www.westminster-mo.edu
Classified Equipment»
Personnel: Debra Brenegan (Advisor); Sarah Blackmon (Ed. in Chief); Aassan Sipra (Ed. in Chief)

LINCOLN UNIV.

Street address 1: Elliff Hall, Rm 208
Street address 3: Jefferson City
Street address state: MO
Zip/Postal code: 65102
Country: USA
Mailing address: Elliff Hall, Rm. 208
Mailing city: Jefferson City
Mailing state: MO
Mailing zip: 65102
General Phone: (573) 681-5446
General Fax: (573) 681-5438
Primary Website: www.lincolnu.edu
Classified Equipment»
Personnel: Yusuf Kalyango (Advisor)

JOPLIN

MISSOURI SOUTHERN UNIVERSITY

Street address 1: 3950 Newman Rd
Street address 3: Joplin
Street address state: MO
Zip/Postal code: 64801-1512
Country: USA
Mailing address: 3950 Newman Rd
Mailing city: Joplin
Mailing state: MO
Mailing zip: 64801-1595
General Phone: (417) 625-9823
General Fax: (417) 625-9585
General/National Adv. E-mail: chart@mssu.edu
Primary Website: www.thechartonline.com
Year Established: 1939
Classified Equipment»
Personnel: J.R. Moorman (Head); Chad Stebbins (Advisor); T.R. Hanrahan (Publications Mgr.); Alexandra Nicolas (Ed. in Chief)

AVILA UNIVERSITY

Street address 1: 11901 Wornall Rd
Street address 3: Kansas City
Street address state: MO
Zip/Postal code: 64145-1007
Country: USA
Mailing address: 11901 Wornall Rd
Mailing city: Kansas City
Mailing state: MO
Mailing zip: 64145-1007
General Phone: (816) 942-8400
General Fax: (816) 501-2459
General/National Adv. E-mail: talon@mail.avila.edu
Primary Website: www.thetalon-online.com
Classified Equipment»
Personnel: Joe Snorgrass (Advisor)

ROCKHURST UNIV.

Street address 1: 1100 Rockhurst Rd
Street address 3: Kansas City
Street address state: MO
Zip/Postal code: 64110-2508
Country: USA
Mailing address: 1100 Rockhurst Rd
Mailing city: Kansas City
Mailing state: MO
Mailing zip: 64110-2561
General Phone: (816) 501-4051
General Fax: (816) 501-4290
General/National Adv. E-mail: sentinel@rockhurst.edu
Primary Website: www.rockhurstsentinel.com
Classified Equipment»
Personnel: Brian Roewe (Ed. in Chief)

UNIV. OF MISSOURI

Street address 1: 5327 Holmes St
Street address 3: Kansas City
Street address state: MO
Zip/Postal code: 64110-2437
Country: USA
Mailing address: 5327 Holmes St
Mailing city: Kansas City
Mailing state: MO
Mailing zip: 64110-2437
General Phone: (816) 235-1393
General Fax: (816) 235-6514
Primary Website: www.unews.com
Classified Equipment»
Personnel: BJ Allen (Bus. Mgr.); Stefanie Crabtree (Adv. Mgr.); Hilary Hedges (Ed. in Chief)

KIRKSVILLE

TRUMAN STATE UNIV.

Street address 1: Barnett Hall News Ctr 1200, 100 E Normal St
Street address 3: Kirksville
Street address state: MO
Zip/Postal code: 63501
Country: USA
Mailing address: Barnett Hall News Ctr. 1200, 100 E. Normal St.
Mailing city: Kirksville
Mailing state: MO
Mailing zip: 63501-4200
General Phone: (660) 785-4449
General Fax: (660) 785-7601
Advertising Phone: (660) 785-4319
General/National Adv. E-mail: indexads@truman.edu
Primary Website: www.trumanindex.com
Classified Equipment»
Personnel: Don Krause (Advisor); Blake Toppmeyer (Ed. in Chief); Jessica Rapp (Mng. Ed.); Stephanie Hall (News Ed.)

KIRKWOOD

ST. LOUIS CMTY. COLLEGE MERAMEC

Street address 1: 11333 Big Bend Rd

Street address 3: Kirkwood
Street address state: MO
Zip/Postal code: 63122-5720
Country: USA
Mailing address: 11333 Big Bend Rd
Mailing city: Kirkwood
Mailing state: MO
Mailing zip: 63122-5799
General Phone: (314) 984-7955
General Fax: (314) 984-7947
Editorail Phone: 314-984-7857
General/National Adv. E-mail: meramecmontage@gmail.com
Primary Website: www.meramecmontage.com
Year Established: 1962
Published: Other
Published Other: bi-weekly
Classified Equipment»
Personnel: Shannon Philpott-Sanders (Advisor)

LEES SUMMIT

LONGVIEW CMTY. COLLEGE

Street address 1: 500 SW Longview Rd
Street address 3: Lees Summit
Street address state: MO
Zip/Postal code: 64081-2105
Country: USA
Mailing address: 500 SW Longview Rd
Mailing city: Lees Summit
Mailing state: MO
Mailing zip: 64081-2100
General Phone: (816) 672-2308
General Fax: (816) 672-2025
General/National Adv. E-mail: current@mcckc.edu
Primary Website: www.longviewcurrent.com
Classified Equipment»
Personnel: Pat Sparks (Advisor)

LIBERTY

WILLIAM JEWELL COLLEGE

Street address 1: 500 College Hl
Street address 2: # 1016
Street address 3: Liberty
Street address state: MO
Zip/Postal code: 64068-1843
Country: USA
Mailing address: 500 College Hl # 1016
Mailing city: Liberty
Mailing state: MO
Mailing zip: 64068-1896
General Phone: (816) 781-7700
General/National Adv. E-mail: monitor@william.jewell.edu
Primary Website: www.thehilltopmonitor.com
Classified Equipment»
Personnel: Samantha Sanders (Adv. Mgr.); Jessie Newman (Ed. in Chief); Trista Turley (Mng. Ed.)

MISSOURI VALLEY COLLEGE

Street address 1: 500 E College St
Street address 3: Marshall
Street address state: MO
Zip/Postal code: 65340-3109
Country: USA
Mailing address: 500 E. College St.
Mailing city: Marshall
Mailing state: MO
Mailing zip: 65340-3109
General Phone: (660) 831-4214
General/National Adv. E-mail: postc@moval.edu
Display Adv. E-mail: postc@moval.edu
Primary Website: www.mvcdelta.com
Classified Equipment»
Personnel: Chris Post

MARYVILLE

NORTHWEST MISSOURI STATE UNIV.

Street address 1: 800 University Dr, Wells 4
Street address 3: Maryville
Street address state: MO
Zip/Postal code: 64468
Country: USA
Mailing address: 800 University Dr., Wells 4
Mailing city: Maryville
Mailing state: MO
Mailing zip: 64468-6001
General Phone: (660) 562-1635
General Fax: (660) 562-1521
Editorail Phone: (816) 516-7030
General/National Adv. E-mail: northwestmissourian@gmail.com
Primary Website: www.nwmissourinews.com
Year Established: 1914
Published: Thur
Classified Equipment»
Personnel: Steven Chappell (Advisor); Brandon Zenner (Editor-in-Chief)

NEOSHO

CROWDER COLLEGE

Street address 1: 601 Laclede Ave
Street address 3: Neosho
Street address state: MO
Zip/Postal code: 64850-9165
Country: USA
Mailing address: 601 Laclede Ave
Mailing city: Neosho
Mailing state: MO
Mailing zip: 64850-9165
General Phone: (417) 451-3223
General Fax: (417) 451-4280
General/National Adv. E-mail: sentry@crowder.edu
Primary Website: www.crowder.edu
Classified Equipment»
Personnel: Leona Bailey (Advisor.); Fabian Oechsle (Ed.)

ROLLA

MISSOURI UNIV. OF SCIENCE & TECHNOLOGY

Street address 1: Missouri S&T
Street address 2: Altman Hall
Street address 3: Rolla
Street address state: MO
Zip/Postal code: 65401
Country: USA
Mailing address: Missouri S&T
Mailing city: Rolla
Mailing state: MO
Mailing zip: 65401-0249
General Phone: (573) 341-4312
General Fax: (573) 341-4235
General/National Adv. E-mail: miner@mst.edu
Primary Website: mominer.mst.edu
Classified Equipment»
Personnel: Fred Ekstam (Advisor); Frank Sauer (Bus. Mgr.); Sarah Richmond (Ed. in Chief); Andrea Unnerstall (Mng. Ed.); Jacob (News Ed.)

SAINT JOSEPH

MISSOURI WESTERN STATE UNIVERSITY

Street address 1: 4525 Downs Dr
Street address 2: Eder 221
Street address 3: Saint Joseph
Street address state: MO
Zip/Postal code: 64507-2246
Country: USA
Mailing address: 4525 Downs Dr Eder 221
Mailing city: Saint Joseph
Mailing state: MO
Mailing zip: 64507-2246
General Phone: (816) 271-4412
General Fax: (816) 271-4543
General/National Adv. E-mail: bergland@missouriwestern.edu
Primary Website: www.thegriffonnews.com
Year Established: 1924
Published: Thur
Avg Free Circ: 2500
Classified Equipment»
Personnel: Robert Bergland (Advisor)

ST. LOUIS CMTY. COLLEGE FLORISSANT VALLEY

Street address 1: 3400 Pershall Rd
Street address 3: Saint Louis
Street address state: MO
Zip/Postal code: 63135-1408
Country: USA
Mailing address: 3400 Pershall Rd
Mailing city: Saint Louis
Mailing state: MO
Mailing zip: 63135-1408
General Phone: (314) 513-4454
Advertising Phone: (314) 513-4588
General/National Adv. E-mail: fvfoumeditor@stlcc.edu
Editorial e-mail: fvforumeditor@stlcc.edu
Year Established: 1963
Published: Mthly
Classified Equipment»
Note: Forum Newspaper blog address: fvforumflo.blogspot.com
Personnel: Renee Thomas-Woods (Advisor); Stephan Curry (Adv. Mgr.); Joshua Schoenhoff (Ed. in Chief)

ST. LOUIS CMTY. COLLEGE FOREST PARK

Street address 1: 5600 Oakland Ave
Street address 3: Saint Louis
Street address state: MO
Zip/Postal code: 63110-1316
Country: USA
Mailing address: 5600 Oakland Ave
Mailing city: Saint Louis
Mailing state: MO
Mailing zip: 63110-1393
General Phone: (314) 644-9140
General/National Adv. E-mail: the_scene_fp@yahoo.com
Classified Equipment»

ST. LOUIS UNIV.

Street address 1: 20 N Grand Blvd
Street address 2: Ste 354
Street address 3: Saint Louis
Street address state: MO
Zip/Postal code: 63103-2005
Country: USA
Mailing address: 20 N Grand Blvd Ste 354
Mailing city: Saint Louis
Mailing state: MO
Mailing zip: 63103-2005
General Phone: (314) 977-2812
General Fax: (314) 977-7177
General/National Adv. E-mail: unews.slu@gmail.com
Primary Website: www.unewsonline.com
Classified Equipment»
Personnel: Jason L. Young (Advisor); Peter Zagotta (Gen. Mgr); Kat Patke (Ed. in Chief)

UNIV. OF MISSOURI

Street address 1: 1 University Blvd
Street address 3: Saint Louis
Street address state: MO
Zip/Postal code: 63121-4400
Country: USA
Mailing address: 1 University Blvd
Mailing city: Saint Louis
Mailing state: MO
Mailing zip: 63121-4400
General Phone: (314) 516-5174
General Fax: (314) 516-6811
General/National Adv. E-mail: thecurrent@umsl.edu
Primary Website: www.thecurrentonline.com
Published: Mon
Avg Free Circ: 5000
Classified Equipment»
Personnel: Charlotte Petty (Advisor); Dan Pryor (Bus. Mgr.); Ryan Krull (Advisor)

WASHINGTON UNIV.

Street address 1: 1 Brookings Dr
Street address 2: Campus Box 1039
Street address 3: Saint Louis
Street address state: MO
Zip/Postal code: 63130-4862
Country: USA
Mailing address: 1 Brookings Dr.
Mailing city: Saint Louis
Mailing state: MO
Mailing zip: 63130-4862
General Phone: (314) 935-4240
General Fax: (314) 935-5938
Advertising Phone: (314) 935-7209
Advertising Fax: (314) 935-5938
Editorial Fax: (314) 935-5938
Display Adv. E-mail: advertising@studlife.com
Editorial e-mail: editor@studlife.com
Primary Website: www.studlife.com
Year Established: 1878
Advertising (Open Inch Rate) Weekday/Saturday: www.studlife.com/advertising
Published: Mon`Thur
Avg Free Circ: 4000
Classified Equipment»
Personnel: Raymond Bush (General Manager)
Parent company (for newspapers): Washington University Student Media, Inc.

WEBSTER UNIV.

Street address 1: 470 E Lockwood Ave
Street address 3: Saint Louis
Street address state: MO
Zip/Postal code: 63119-3141
Country: USA
Mailing address: 470 E Lockwood Ave
Mailing city: Saint Louis
Mailing state: MO
Mailing zip: 63119-3194
General Phone: (314) 961-2660
General Fax: (314) 968-7059
Editorail Phone: (314) 968-7088
General/National Adv. E-mail: wujournal@gmail.com
Editorial e-mail: editor@webujournal.com
Primary Website: www.webujournal.com
Published: Wed
Classified Equipment»
Personnel: Don Corrigan (Journ. Seq.); Kelly Kendall (Ed. in Chief)

DRURY COLLEGE

Street address 1: 900 N Benton Ave
Street address 3: Springfield
Street address state: MO
Zip/Postal code: 65802-3712
Country: USA
Mailing address: 900 N Benton Ave
Mailing city: Springfield
Mailing state: MO
Mailing zip: 65802-3791
General Phone: (417) 873-7879
General Fax: (417) 873-7897
General/National Adv. E-mail: mirror@drurymirror.com
Primary Website: www.drurymirror.com
Classified Equipment»
Personnel: Cristina Gilstrap (Advisor); Jeromy Layman (Ed. in Chief); Mallory Noelke (Mng. Ed.)

EVANGEL UNIVERSITY

Street address 1: 1111 N Glenstone Ave
Street address 3: Springfield
Street address state: MO
Zip/Postal code: 65802-2125
Country: USA
Mailing address: 1111 N. Glenstone Ave.
Mailing city: Springfield
Mailing state: MO
Mailing zip: 65802-2125
General Phone: (417) 865-2815
Advertising Phone: (417) 865-2815, ext. 8636
Editorail Phone: (417) 865-2815, ext. 8634
General/National Adv. E-mail: evangellance@gmail.com
Editorial e-mail: evangellance@gmail.com
Primary Website: http://www.evangellance.com
Year Established: 1955
Delivery Methods: Racks
Commercial printers: Y
Published: Fri`Bi-Mthly
Avg Free Circ: 1500
Classified Equipment»
Personnel: Melinda Booze (Advisor)

MISSOURI STATE UNIV.

Street address 1: 901 S National Ave

Street address 3: Springfield
Street address state: MO
Zip/Postal code: 65897-0027
Country: USA
Mailing address: 901 S National Ave
Mailing city: Springfield
Mailing state: MO
Mailing zip: 65897-0001
General Phone: (417) 836-5272
General Fax: (417) 836-6738
Editorail Phone: (417) 836-6512
General/National Adv. E-mail: standard@missouristate.edu
Primary Website: www.the-standard.org
Classified Equipment»
Personnel: Jess Rollins (Ed. in Chief)

WARRENSBURG

UNIVERSITY OF CENTRAL MISSOURI

Street address 1: Martin 136, University of Central Missouri
Street address 3: Warrensburg
Street address state: MO
Zip/Postal code: 64093
Country: USA
Mailing address: Martin 136, University of Central Missouri
Mailing city: Warrensburg
Mailing state: MO
Mailing zip: 64093
General Phone: (660) 543-4050
General Fax: (660) 543-8663
Advertising Phone: (660) 543-4051
General/National Adv. E-mail: muleskinner@ucmo.edu
Display Adv. E-mail: muleskinnerads@ucmo.edu
Primary Website: www.digitalburg.com
Year Established: 1906
News Services: Associated Press
Delivery Methods: Racks
Published: Thur
Published Other: digitalburg.com
Avg Free Circ: 3000
Classified Equipment»
Personnel: Matt Bird-Meyer (Adviser); Jacque Flanagan (Managing Editor)

MISSISSIPPI

ALCORN STATE

ALCORN STATE UNIV.

Street address 1: 1000 Asu Dr, Ste 269
Street address 3: Alcorn State
Street address state: MS
Country: USA
Mailing address: 1000 Alcorn Dr Ste 269
Mailing city: Lorman
Mailing state: MS
Mailing zip: 39096-7500
General Phone: (601) 877-6557
General Fax: (601) 877-2213
General/National Adv. E-mail: tnimox@lorman.alcorn.edu
Primary Website: www.alcornchronicle.com
Classified Equipment»
Personnel: Toni Terrett (Advisor); Larry Sanders (Advisor); Erica L. Turner (Ed. in Chief)

BOONEVILLE

NORTHEAST MISSISSIPPI COMMUNITY COLLEGE

Street address 1: 101 Cunningham Blvd
Street address 2: Box 67
Street address 3: Booneville
Street address state: MS
Zip/Postal code: 38829-1726
Country: USA
General Phone: (662) 720-7304
General Fax: (662) 720-7216
Editorail Phone: (662) 720-7421
General/National Adv. E-mail: beacon@nemcc.edu
Display Adv. E-mail: beacon@nemcc.edu
Editorial e-mail: beacon@nemcc.edu
Year Established: 1949
Advertising (Open Inch Rate) Weekday/Saturday: $75 for 1/4th page, $150 for 1/2 page, $300 for full page
Published: Other
Published Other: Two times each semester
Avg Free Circ: 3600
Classified Equipment»
Personnel: Tony Finch (Advisor); Michael H Miller (Advisor)

CLEVELAND

DELTA STATE UNIV.

Street address 1: 1003 W Sunflower Rd
Street address 3: Cleveland
Street address state: MS
Zip/Postal code: 38733-0001
Country: USA
Mailing address: 1003 W Sunflower Rd
Mailing city: Cleveland
Mailing state: MS
Mailing zip: 38733-0002
General Phone: (662) 846-4715
General Fax: (662) 846-4737
General/National Adv. E-mail: statemnt@deltastate.edu
Primary Website: www.deltastate.edu
Classified Equipment»
Personnel: Patricia Roberts (Advisor); Kaitlyn Mize (Bus. Mgr.); Ashley Robertson (Ed. in Chief)

CLINTON

MISSISSIPPI COLLEGE

Street address 1: 200 S Capitol St
Street address 3: Clinton
Street address state: MS
Zip/Postal code: 39056-4026
Country: USA
Mailing address: 200 W College St
Mailing city: Clinton
Mailing state: MS
Mailing zip: 39058-0001
General Phone: (601) 925-3462
General Fax: (601) 925-3804
Primary Website: news.mc.edu/~collegian/
Classified Equipment»
Personnel: Tim Nicholas (Faculty Advisor); Gabriel Winston (Adv. Mgr.); Terra Kirkland (Co. Ed.)

MISSISSIPPI UNIV. FOR WOMEN

Street address 1: 1100 College St
Street address 3: Columbus
Street address state: MS
Zip/Postal code: 39701-5821
Country: USA
Mailing address: 1100 College St
Mailing city: Columbus
Mailing state: MS
Mailing zip: 39701-5802
General Phone: (662) 329-7268
General Fax: (662) 329-7269
General/National Adv. E-mail: spectator@muw.edu
Primary Website: www.muw.edu/spectator
Classified Equipment»
Personnel: Sarah Wilson (Ed. in Chief); Juna'uh Allgood (Ed.)

ELLISVILLE

JONES COUNTY JUNIOR COLLEGE

Street address 1: 900 S Court St
Street address 3: Ellisville
Street address state: MS
Zip/Postal code: 39437-3901
Country: USA
Mailing address: 900 S Court St
Mailing city: Ellisville
Mailing state: MS
Mailing zip: 39437-3999
General Phone: (601) 477-4084
General Fax: (601) 477-4191
General/National Adv. E-mail: radionian@jcjc.edu
Display Adv. E-mail: radionian@jcjc.edu
Editorial e-mail: radionian@jcjc.edu
Primary Website: www.jcjc.edu
Year Established: 1927
Published: Mthly
Classified Equipment»
Personnel: Kelly Atwood (Newspaper Adviser)

CHIEFTAIN

Street address 1: 602 W Hill St
Street address 3: Fulton
Street address state: MS
Zip/Postal code: 38843-1022
County: Itawamba
Country: USA
Mailing address: 602 W. Hill St.
Mailing city: Fulton
Mailing state: MS
Mailing zip: 38843-1022
General Phone: (662) 862-8244
General/National Adv. E-mail: dsthomas@iccms.edu
Editorial e-mail: dsthomas@iccms.edu
Primary Website: www.iccms.edu
Delivery Methods: Racks
Published: Mon
Published Other: Three times each semester
Classified Equipment»
Personnel: Donna Thomas (Dir., Communications)

GOODMAN

HOLMES CMTY. COLLEGE

Street address 1: No 1, Hill St
Street address 3: Goodman
Street address state: MS
Zip/Postal code: 39079
Country: USA
Mailing address: PO Box 369
Mailing city: Goodman
Mailing state: MS
Mailing zip: 39079-0369
General Phone: (662) 472-2312
General Fax: (662) 472-0012
Primary Website: www.holmescc.edu
Published Other: Twice a senester
Classified Equipment»
Personnel: Steve Diffey (District Director of Communications)

HATTIESBURG

UNIV. OF SOUTHERN MISSISSIPPI

Street address 1: 118 College Dr
Street address 2: # 5121
Street address 3: Hattiesburg
Street address state: MS
Zip/Postal code: 39406-0002
Country: USA
Mailing address: PO Box 5121
Mailing city: Hattiesburg
Mailing state: MS
Mailing zip: 39406-0001
General Phone: (601) 266-4288
General Fax: (601) 266-6473
Advertising Phone: (601) 266-5188
General/National Adv. E-mail: printz@usm.edu
Editorial e-mail: printzeditors@gmail.com
Primary Website: www.studentprintz.com
Year Established: 1927
News Services: MC-T
Commercial printers: N
Published: Wed
Avg Free Circ: 1700
Classified Equipment»
Personnel: Chuck Cook (News Content Adviser)

HOLLY SPRINGS

RUST COLLEGE

Street address 1: 150 Rust Ave
Street address 3: Holly Springs
Street address state: MS
Zip/Postal code: 38635-2330
Country: USA
Mailing address: 150 Rust Ave
Mailing city: Holly Springs
Mailing state: MS
Mailing zip: 38635-2328
General Phone: (662) 252-8000 ext. 4553
General Fax: (662) 252-8869
General/National Adv. E-mail: rustorian_@hotmail.com
Display Adv. E-mail: rustorian_@hotmail.com
Primary Website: www.rustorian.com
Delivery Methods: Racks
Published: Mthly
Classified Equipment»
Personnel: Debayo Moyo (Advisor)

ITTA BENA

MISSISSIPPI VALLEY STATE UNIV.

Street address 1: 14000 Highway 82 W
Street address 3: Itta Bena
Street address state: MS
Zip/Postal code: 38941-1400
County: Leflore
Country: USA
Mailing address: 14000 Highway 82 W
Mailing city: Itta Bena
Mailing state: MS
Mailing zip: 38941-1401
General Phone: (662) 254-3458
General Fax: (622) 254-6704
Advertising Phone: (662) 254-3458
Advertising Fax: (662) 254-3458
Editorail Phone: (662) 254-3458
General/National Adv. E-mail: deltadevilsgazettefacad@gmail.com
Display Adv. E-mail: ehmcclary@mvsu.edu
Editorial e-mail: deltadevilsgazettefacad@gmail.com
Primary Website: deltadevilsgazette.com
Advertising (Open Inch Rate) Weekday/Saturday: $100.00 full page & 150.00 back or behind cover,FP
Published Other: three per semester
Avg Free Circ: 2000
Classified Equipment»
Personnel: Esin C. Turk (Asst. Prof.); Samuel Osunde (Asst. Prof./Dir., Forensics); Carolyn Gordon; Zainul Abedin (Mr.)

BELHAVEN COLLEGE

Street address 1: 1500 Peachtree St
Street address 3: Jackson
Street address state: MS
Zip/Postal code: 39202-1754
Country: USA
Mailing address: 1500 Peachtree St
Mailing city: Jackson
Mailing state: MS
Mailing zip: 39202-1789
General Phone: (601) 968-8702
Classified Equipment»
Personnel: Don Hubele (Advisor)

JACKSON STATE UNIVERSITY

Street address 1: 1400 J R Lynch St
Street address 2: Blackburn Language Arts Building, Room 208
Street address 3: Jackson
Street address state: MS
Zip/Postal code: 39217-0002
Country: USA
Mailing address: PO Box 18449
Mailing city: Jackson
Mailing state: MS
Mailing zip: 39217-0001
General Phone: (601) 979-2167
General Fax: (601) 979-2876
Advertising Phone: (601) 979-2167
Advertising Fax: (601) 979-2876
Editorail Phone: (601) 979-2167
Editorial Fax: (601) 979-2876
General/National Adv. E-mail: theflash@jsums.edu
Display Adv. E-mail: shannon.d.tatum@jsums.edu
Editorial e-mail: theflash@jsums.edu
Primary Website: www.thejsuflash.com
Advertising (Open Inch Rate) Weekday/Saturday: Varies by ad size
Published: Thur

Avg Free Circ: 3000
Classified Equipment»
Personnel: Shannon Tatum (Publications Coordinator/ Ad Manager)

MILLSAPS COLLEGE

Street address 1: Box 150847
Street address 3: Jackson
Street address state: MS
Zip/Postal code: 39210-0001
Country: USA
Mailing address: PO Box 150847
Mailing city: Jackson
Mailing state: MS
Mailing zip: 39210-0001
General Phone: (601) 974-1211
General Fax: (601) 974-1229
Classified Equipment»
Personnel: Woody Woodrick (Advisor); Kate Royals (Ed, in Chief); Kathleen Morrison (Copy Ed.)

MATHISTON

WOOD COLLEGE

Street address 1: Weber Dr
Street address 3: Mathiston
Street address state: MS
Zip/Postal code: 39752
Country: USA
Mailing address: Weber Dr.
Mailing city: Mathiston
Mailing state: MS
Mailing zip: 39752
General Phone: (662) 263-5352
Classified Equipment»
Personnel: Jeanna Graves (Ed.)

MISSISSIPPI STATE

MISSISSIPPI STATE UNIV.

Street address 1: Henry F Meyer Student Media Ctr
Street address 3: Mississippi State
Street address state: MS
Zip/Postal code: 39759
Country: USA
Mailing address: PO Box 5407
Mailing city: Mississippi State
Mailing state: MS
Mailing zip: 39762-5407
General Phone: (662) 325-2374
General Fax: (662) 325-8985
Advertising Phone: (662) 325-7907
General/National Adv. E-mail: editor@reflector.msstate.edu
Display Adv. E-mail: advertise@reflector.msstate.edu
Primary Website: www.reflector-online.com
Year Established: 1884
Published: Tues`Fri
Avg Free Circ: 10000
Classified Equipment»
Personnel: Julia Langford (Adv. Mgr.)

OXFORD

THE UNIVERSITY OF MISSISSIPPI

Street address 1: 201 Bishop Hall
Street address 3: Oxford
Street address state: MS
Zip/Postal code: 38677
Country: USA
Mailing address: 201 Bishop Hall
Mailing city: Oxford
Mailing state: MS
Mailing zip: 38677
General Phone: (662) 915-5503
General Fax: (662) 915-5703
General/National Adv. E-mail: studentmedia@olemiss.edu
Editorial e-mail: dmeditor@gmail.com
Primary Website: www.thedmonline.com
Year Established: 1911
Published: Mon`Tues`Wed`Thur`Fri
Avg Free Circ: 12000
Classified Equipment»
Personnel: Lacey Russell (Ed.); Patricia Thompson (Dir. of Student Media/Faculty Adviser)

POPLARVILLE

PEARL RIVER COMMNITY COLLEGE

Street address 1: 101 Highway 11 N
Street address 3: Poplarville
Street address state: MS
Zip/Postal code: 39470-2216
Country: USA
Mailing address: 101 Highway 11 N
Mailing city: Poplarville
Mailing state: MS
Mailing zip: 39470-2201
General Phone: (601) 403-1312
Editorail Phone: (601) 403-1328
General/National Adv. E-mail: cabadie@prcc.edu
Display Adv. E-mail: cabadie@prcc.edu
Editorial e-mail: cabadie@prcc.edu
Primary Website: www.prcc.edu
Year Established: 1909
Advertising (Open Inch Rate) Weekday/Saturday: $3 an inch
Published: Mthly
Avg Free Circ: 2000
Classified Equipment»
Personnel: Chuck Adadie (Ed./Advisor)

HINDS CMTY. COLLEGE

Street address 1: PO Box 1100
Street address 3: Raymond
Street address state: MS
Zip/Postal code: 39154-1100
Country: USA
Mailing address: PO Box 1100
Mailing city: Raymond
Mailing state: MS
Mailing zip: 39154-1100
General Phone: (601) 857-3323
Primary Website: www.hindscc.edu
Classified Equipment»
Personnel: Cathy Hayden (Advisor)

SENATOBIA

NORTHWEST MISSISSIPPI CMTY. COLLEGE

Street address 1: 4975 Highway 51 N
Street address 3: Senatobia
Street address state: MS
Zip/Postal code: 38668-1714
Country: USA
Mailing address: PO Box 7039
Mailing city: Senatobia
Mailing state: MS
Mailing zip: 38668
General Phone: (662) 562-3276
General Fax: (662) 562-3499
General/National Adv. E-mail: rangerrocket1@northwestms.edu
Primary Website: www.northwestms.edu
Year Established: 1927
Classified Equipment»
Personnel: Ranate Ferreira (Advisor); Chris Creasy (Ed.)

STARKVILLE

BULLDOG BEAT

Street address 1: 304 E Lampkin St
Street address 3: Starkville
Street address state: MS
Zip/Postal code: 39759-2910
County: Oktibbeha
Country: USA
Mailing address: PO Box 1068
Mailing city: Starkville
Mailing state: MS
Mailing zip: 39760-1068
General Phone: (662) 323-1642
General Fax: (662) 323-6586
Advertising Phone: (662) 323-1642
Advertising Fax: (662) 323-6586
Editorail Phone: (662) 324-8092
Editorial Fax: (662) 323-6586
General/National Adv. E-mail: sdnads@bellsouth.net
Display Adv. E-mail: sdnads@bellsouth.net
Classified Adv. E-mail: sdnews@bellsouth.net
Editorial e-mail: sdneditor@bellsouth.net
Primary Website: www.starkvilledailynews.com
Year Established: 1875
News Services: AP.
Special Editions: Bulldog Weekend (Apr); Welcome Back Miss. State (Aug); Progress (Feb); Christmas Gift Guide (Nov).
Special Weekly Sections: Entertainment (Fri); Weddings (S); Religion (Sat); Agriculture (Thur); Business (Tues); Education (Wed).
Syndicated Publications: American Profile (S).
Delivery Methods: Mail`Carrier
Advertising (Open Inch Rate) Weekday/Saturday: Open inch rate $13.72
Market Information: TMC.
Mechanical available: Offset; Black and 3 ROP colors; insert accepted; page cutoffs - 22 3/4.
Mechanical specifications: Type page 10 x 21 1/2; E - 6 cols, 1 9/16, 1/8 between; A - 6 cols, 1 9/16, 1/8 between; C - 9 cols, 1 1/32, 1/8 between.
Published: Mon`Tues`Wed`Thur`Fri`Sat`Sun
Weekday Frequency: m
Saturday Frequency: m
Avg Paid Circ: 7071
Sat. Circulation Paid: 7071
Sun. Circulation Paid: 7071
Audit By: Sworn/Estimate/Non-Audited
Audit Date: 10/1/2013
Buisness Equipment: PC
Classified Equipment: Hardware -- APP/Mac Quadra 605;
Classified Software: Baseview.
Display Equipment: Hardware -- APP/Mac Quadra 660, APP/Mac Quadra 650, Umax, APP/Power Mac, APP/Mac G3, APP/Mac G4; Printers -- GCC/Elite XL; Other Hardware -- Canon/Scanner, Microtek/Scanner, Polaroid/Scanner.
Display Software: Ad Make-up Applications -- QPS/ QuarkXPress 4.2;
Editorial Equipment: Hardware -- APP/Power Mac, APP/ Mac Quadra 605, APP/Mac G3, APP/Mac G4; Printers -- APP/Mac LaserWriter II, GCC/Elite XL
Editorial Software: Baseview.
Production Equipment: Hardware -- QPS/QuarkXPress 4.2.
Note: For detailed production information, see West Point Daily Times Leader.
Personnel: Don Norman (Pub.); Mona Howell (Bus. Mgr.); Byron Norman (Circ. Mgr.); Larry Bost (Creative Dir.); Shea Staskowski (Educ. Ed.); Brian Hawkins (Online Ed.)
Parent company (for newspapers): Horizon Publications Inc.

TOUGALOO

TOUGALOO COLLEGE

Street address 1: 500 W County Line Rd
Street address 3: Tougaloo
Street address state: MS
Zip/Postal code: 39174-9700
Country: USA
Mailing address: 500 W County Line Rd
Mailing city: Tougaloo
Mailing state: MS
Mailing zip: 39174-9700
General Phone: (601) 977-6159
General Fax: (601) 977-6160
General/National Adv. E-mail: cwhite@tougaloo.edu
Classified Equipment»
Personnel: Teressa Fulgham (Mng. Ed.); Colleen White (Dir. Journ. Program)

WESSON

COPIAH-LINCOLN CMTY. COLLEGE

Street address 1: Hwy 51 S
Street address 3: Wesson
Street address state: MS
Zip/Postal code: 39191
Country: USA
Mailing address: PO Box 649
Mailing city: Wesson
Mailing state: MS
Mailing zip: 39191-0649
General Phone: (601) 643-8354
General Fax: (601) 643-8226
Primary Website: www.colin.edu
Classified Equipment»
Personnel: Mary Warren (Advisor)

MONTANA

BILLINGS

ROCKY MOUNTAIN COLLEGE

Street address 1: 1511 Poly Dr
Street address 3: Billings
Street address state: MT
Zip/Postal code: 59102-1739
Country: USA
Mailing address: 1511 Poly Dr
Mailing city: Billings
Mailing state: MT
Mailing zip: 59102-1796
General Phone: (406) 657-1093
General Fax: (406) 259-9751
Classified Equipment»
Personnel: Wilbur Wood (Advisor)

BOZEMAN

MONTANA STATE UNIV. BOZEMAN

Street address 1: 305 Strand Union Bldg
Street address 3: Bozeman
Street address state: MT
Zip/Postal code: 59717
Country: USA
Mailing address: P.O. Box 174140
Mailing city: Bozeman
Mailing state: MT
Mailing zip: 59717
General Phone: (406) 994-3976
General Fax: (406) 994-2253
Classified Equipment»
Personnel: Amanda Larrinaga (Ed.in.Chief)

BUTTE

MONTANA TECH. UNIV.

Street address 1: 1300 W Park St
Street address 3: Butte
Street address state: MT
Zip/Postal code: 59701-8932
Country: USA
Mailing address: 1300 W Park St
Mailing city: Butte
Mailing state: MT
Mailing zip: 59701-8932
General Phone: (406) 496-4241
General Fax: (406) 496-4702
General/National Adv. E-mail: technocrat@mtech.edu
Classified Equipment»
Personnel: Patrick Munday (Advisor)

GREAT FALLS

UNIV. OF GREAT FALLS

Street address 1: 1301 20th St S
Street address 3: Great Falls
Street address state: MT
Zip/Postal code: 59405-4934
Country: USA
Mailing address: 1301 20th St S
Mailing city: Great Falls
Mailing state: MT
Mailing zip: 59405-4996
General Phone: (406) 791-5231
General Fax: (406) 791-5220
Classified Equipment»
Personnel: Jerry Habets (Ed.)

HAVRE

MONTANA STATE UNIV. NORTHERN

Street address 1: 300 11th St W
Street address 3: Havre
Street address state: MT
Zip/Postal code: 59501-4917
Country: USA
Mailing address: PO Box 7751
Mailing city: Havre
Mailing state: MT
Mailing zip: 59501-7751
General Phone: (406) 265-4112
General Fax: (406) 265-3777
Primary Website: www.msun.edu
Classified Equipment»
Personnel: Lori Renfeld (Ed.)

HELENA

CARROLL COLLEGE

Street address 1: 1601 N Benton Ave
Street address 3: Helena
Street address state: MT
Zip/Postal code: 59625-0001
Country: USA
Mailing address: 1601 N Benton Ave
Mailing city: Helena
Mailing state: MT
Mailing zip: 59625-2826
General Phone: (406) 447-4300
General Fax: (406) 447-4533
Primary Website: www.carroll.edu
Classified Equipment»
Personnel: Brent Northup (Advisor)

MISSOULA

UNIVERSITY OF MONTANA

Street address 1: 32 Campus Dr
Street address 3: Missoula
Street address state: MT
Zip/Postal code: 59812-0003
Country: USA
Mailing address: Don Anderson Hall Ste 207
Mailing city: Missoula
Mailing state: MT
Mailing zip: 59812-0001
General Phone: (406) 243-6541
General Fax: (406) 243-5475
Advertising Phone: (406) 243-6541
Advertising Fax: (406) 243-5475
Editorail Phone: 406-243-4101
Editorial Fax: 406-243-5475
General/National Adv. E-mail: kaiminads@gmail.com
Display Adv. E-mail: kaiminads@gmail.com
Editorial e-mail: editor@montanakaimin.com
Primary Website: http://www.montanakaimin.com
Year Established: 1898
News Services: AP
Special Editions: Football specials sections for home games
Delivery Methods: Mail`Racks
Commercial printers: N
Published: Tues`Wed`Thur`Fri
Published Other: Published online daily, updated as news breaks
Avg Free Circ: 4000
Classified Equipment»
Personnel: Ruth Johnson (Office manager); Nadia White (Advisor); Amy Sisk (Editor); Nick McKinney (Business manager)

NORTH CAROLINA

ASHEVILLE

UNIV. OF NORTH CAROLINA

Street address 1: 1 University Hts
Street address 3: Asheville
Street address state: NC
Zip/Postal code: 28804-3251
Country: USA
Mailing address: 1 University Heights
Mailing city: Asheville
Mailing state: NC
Mailing zip: 28804-3251
General Fax: (828) 251-6591
Advertising Fax: (828) 232-2421
General/National Adv. E-mail: www.thebluebanner.net
Display Adv. E-mail: banner@unca.edu
Classified Equipment»
Personnel: Michael Gouge (Advisor); Anna Kiser (Adv. Mgr.); Sam Hunt (Ed. in Chief)

BELMONT ABBEY COLLEGE

Street address 1: 100 Belmont Mount Holly Rd
Street address 3: Belmont
Street address state: NC
Zip/Postal code: 28012-2702
Country: USA
Mailing address: 100 Belmont Mount Holly Rd
Mailing city: Belmont
Mailing state: NC
Mailing zip: 28012-1802
General/National Adv. E-mail: albenthall@bac.edu
Display Adv. E-mail: cathycomeau@bac.edu
Editorial e-mail: anthonygwyatt@abbey.bac.edu
Primary Website: www.thecrusaderonline.com
Published: Mthly
Classified Equipment»

BOONE

APPALACHIAN STATE UNIV.

Street address 1: 217 Plemmons Student Union
Street address 3: Boone
Street address state: NC
Country: USA
Mailing address: Asu # 9025
Mailing city: Boone
Mailing state: NC
Mailing zip: 28608-0002
General Phone: (828) 262-6149
General Fax: (828) 262-6502
General/National Adv. E-mail: theapp@appstate.edu
Primary Website: www.theapp.appstate.edu
Classified Equipment»
Personnel: Jon LaFontaine (Ed. in Chief)

BREVARD

BREVARD COLLEGE

Street address 1: 1 Brevard Dr
Street address 3: Brevard
Street address state: NC
Zip/Postal code: 28712
Country: USA
Mailing address: 1 Brevard Dr.
Mailing city: Brevard
Mailing state: NC
Mailing zip: 28712
General Phone: (828) 883-8292
General/National Adv. E-mail: clarion@brevard.edu
Display Adv. E-mail: clarion@brevard.edu
Editorial e-mail: clarion@brevard.edu
Primary Website: www.brevard.edu/clarion
Year Established: 1935
Published: Fri
Published Other: August-May (no summer publication)
Avg Paid Circ: 0
Avg Free Circ: 300
Classified Equipment»
Personnel: John Padgett (Advisor); Althea Dunn (Editor in Chief, 2013-2014)

BUIES CREEK

CAMPBELL UNIV.

Street address 1: PO Box 130
Street address 2: 165 Dr. McKoy Drive
Street address 3: Buies Creek
Street address state: NC
Zip/Postal code: 27506-0130
Country: USA
Mailing address: PO Box 130
Mailing city: Buies Creek
Mailing state: NC
Mailing zip: 27506-0130
General Phone: (910) 893-1200
General Fax: (910) 893-1924
Primary Website: www.campbell.edu
Published: Bi-Mthly
Classified Equipment»
Personnel: Michael Smith (Advisor); Courtney Schultz (editor)

CHAPEL HILL

THE DAILY TAR HEEL

Street address 1: 151 E Rosemary St
Street address 3: Chapel Hill
Street address state: NC
Zip/Postal code: 27514-3539
County: Orange
Country: USA
Mailing address: 151 E Rosemary St
Mailing city: Chapel Hill
Mailing state: NC
Mailing zip: 27514-3539
General Phone: (919) 962-1163
Advertising Phone: 919.962.1163
Editorail Phone: 919.962.0245
General/National Adv. E-mail: sales@dailytarheel.com
Display Adv. E-mail: sales@dailytarheel.com
Classified Adv. E-mail: sales@dailytarheel.com
Editorial e-mail: dth@dailytarheel.com
Primary Website: dailytarheel.com
Year Established: 1893
Classified Equipment»
Personnel: Elise Young (Managing Ed.)

UNIV. OF NORTH CAROLINA - THE DAILY TAR HEEL

Street address 1: 151 E Rosemary St
Street address 3: Chapel Hill
Street address state: NC
Zip/Postal code: 27514-3539
Country: USA
Mailing address: 151 E Rosemary St
Mailing city: Chapel Hill
Mailing state: NC
Mailing zip: 27514-3539
General Phone: (919) 962-1163
General Fax: (919) 962-1609
Editorail Phone: 919=962-0245
Display Adv. E-mail: ads@unc.edu
Editorial e-mail: dth@dailytarheel.com
Primary Website: www.dailytarheel.com
Year Established: 1893
Delivery Methods: Newsstand
Commercial printers: N
Published: Mon`Tues`Wed`Thur`Fri
Avg Free Circ: 17000
Classified Equipment»
Personnel: Erica Perel (Advisor); Megan Mcginity (Adv. Mgr.)

UNIV. OF NORTH CAROLINA LAW SCHOOL

Street address 1: Cb #3380, Vanhecke-Wettach Hall
Street address 3: Chapel Hill
Street address state: NC
Zip/Postal code: 27599-0001
Country: USA
Mailing address: 3380 Vanhecke-Wettach Hall
Mailing city: Chapel Hill
Mailing state: NC
Mailing zip: 27599-0001
General Phone: (919) 962-6200
Classified Equipment»

QUEENS UNIVERSITY OF CHARLOTTE

Street address 1: 1900 Selwyn Ave
Street address 3: Charlotte
Street address state: NC
Zip/Postal code: 28207-2450
Country: USA
Mailing address: Msc # 892
Mailing city: Charlotte
Mailing state: NC
Mailing zip: 28274-0001
General Phone: (704) 337-2220
General Fax: (704) 337-2503
General/National Adv. E-mail: quoc.chronicle@gmail.com
Primary Website: www.queens-chronicle.com
Published: Bi-Mthly
Classified Equipment»
Personnel: Dustin Saunders (Editor-in-Chief)

UNIV. OF NORTH CAROLINA AT CHARLOTTE

Street address 1: 9201 University City Blvd
Street address 3: Charlotte
Street address state: NC
Zip/Postal code: 28223-0001
Country: USA
Mailing address: 9201 University City Blvd
Mailing city: Charlotte
Mailing state: NC
Mailing zip: 28223-1000
General Fax: (704) 687-3253
Advertising Phone: (704) 687-7145
Advertising Fax: (704) 687-7139
Editorail Phone: (704) 687-7148
General/National Adv. E-mail: www.nineronline.com
Display Adv. E-mail: smpads@uncc.edu
Editorial e-mail: editor@ninertimes.com
Primary Website: www.ninertimes.com
Advertising (Open inch Rate) Weekday/Saturday: smpads@uncc.edu
Published: Tues
Avg Free Circ: 7000
Classified Equipment»
Personnel: Christine Litchfield (Ed. in Chief); Hunter Heilman (EIC)

CULLOWHEE

WESTERN CAROLINA UNIV.

Street address 1: 109A Old Student Union
Street address 3: Cullowhee
Street address state: NC
Zip/Postal code: 28723
Country: USA
Mailing address: 109A Old Student Union
Mailing city: Cullowhee
Mailing state: NC
Mailing zip: 28723
General Phone: (828) 227-2694
General Fax: (828) 227-7201
General/National Adv. E-mail: jcaudell@westerncarolinian.com
Display Adv. E-mail: jcaudell@westerncarolinian.com
Editorial e-mail: amenz@westerncarolinian.com
Primary Website: www.westerncarolinian.com
Year Established: 1933
Delivery Methods: Mail`Newsstand`Racks
Published: Bi-Mthly
Avg Paid Circ: 100
Avg Free Circ: 5000
Classified Equipment»
Personnel: Justin Caudell (Ed. in Chief); Alexa Menz (Editor-in-Chief)

DAVIDSON

DAVIDSON COLLEGE

Street address 1: PO Box 7182
Street address 3: Davidson
Street address state: NC
Zip/Postal code: 28035-7182
Country: USA
Mailing address: PO Box 7182
Mailing city: Davidson
Mailing state: NC
Mailing zip: 28035-7182
General/National Adv. E-mail: davidsonian@davidson.edu
Display Adv. E-mail: davidsonian@davidson.edu
Primary Website: www.davidsonian.com
Year Established: 1914
Delivery Methods: Mail`Newsstand`Racks
Published: Wed

Classified Equipment»
Note: Website www.davidsonian.com
Personnel: Laura Chuckray; Caroline Queen; Lyla Halsted

DUKE UNIV. FUQUA BUS. SCHOOL

Street address 1: PO Box 90120
Street address 3: Durham
Street address state: NC
Zip/Postal code: 27708-0120
Country: USA
Mailing address: PO Box 90120
Mailing city: Durham
Mailing state: NC
Mailing zip: 27708-0120
General Phone: (919) 660-7700
General Fax: (919) 684-2818
General/National Adv. E-mail: fuquatimes@gmail.com
Primary Website: www.axml.net/fuquatimes
Classified Equipment»
Personnel: Mary Murphy (Ed.)

DUKE UNIVERSITY

Street address 1: 101 W Union
Street address 3: Durham
Street address state: NC
Zip/Postal code: 27708-9980
Country: USA
Mailing address: PO Box 90858
Mailing city: Durham
Mailing state: NC
Mailing zip: 27708-0858
General Phone: (919) 684-8111
General Fax: (919) 668-1247
Advertising Phone: (919) 684-3811
Editorail Phone: (919) 684-2663
Primary Website: dukechronicle.com
Published: Mon`Tues`Wed`Thur`Fri
Avg Free Circ: 12000
Classified Equipment»
Personnel: Yeshwanth Kandamalla (Editor)

NORTH CAROLINA CENTRAL UNIV.

Street address 1: 1801 Fayetteville St
Street address 3: Durham
Street address state: NC
Zip/Postal code: 27707-3129
Country: USA
Mailing address: 1801 Fayetteville St
Mailing city: Durham
Mailing state: NC
Mailing zip: 27707-3129
General Phone: (919) 530-7116
General Fax: (919) 530-7991
General/National Adv. E-mail: campusecho@nccu.edu
Primary Website: www.campusecho.com
Classified Equipment»
Personnel: Dr. Bruce DePyssler (Advisor); Thomas Evans (Associate Professor); Carlton Koonce (Ed. in Chief)

THE DUKE CHRONICLE

Street address 1: 301 Flowers
Street address 3: Durham
Street address state: NC
Zip/Postal code: 27708-0001
County: Durham
Country: USA
Mailing address: 301 Flowers
Mailing city: Durham
Mailing state: NC
Mailing zip: 27708-0001
General Phone: 919-684-2663
General Fax: 919-684-4696
Advertising Phone: 919-684-3811
Advertising Fax: 919-668-1247
Editorail Phone: 919-684-2663
Editorial Fax: 919-684-4696
General/National Adv. E-mail: advertising@chronicle.duke.edu
Display Adv. E-mail: advertising@chronicle.duke.edu
Classified Adv. E-mail: advertising@chronicle.duke.edu
Editorial e-mail: chronicleletters@duke.edu
Primary Website: http://www.dukechronicle.com
Year Established: 1905
Classified Equipment»

ELIZABETH CITY

ELIZABETH CITY STATE UNIV.

Street address 1: 1704 Weeksville Rd
Street address 3: Elizabeth City
Street address state: NC
Zip/Postal code: 27909-7977
Country: USA
Mailing address: 1704 Weeksville Rd
Mailing city: Elizabeth City
Mailing state: NC
Mailing zip: 27909
General Phone: (252) 335-3343
General Fax: (252) 335-3795
Classified Equipment»
Personnel: Kip Branch (Advisor)

ELON

ELON UNIVERSITY

Street address 1: 130 N Williamson Ave
Street address 3: Elon
Street address state: NC
Zip/Postal code: 27244
Country: USA
Mailing address: 7012 Campus Box
Mailing city: Elon
Mailing state: NC
Mailing zip: 27244-2062
General Phone: (336) 278-7247
General Fax: (336) 278-7426
General/National Adv. E-mail: pendulum@elon.edu
Display Adv. E-mail: pendulum@elon.edu
Primary Website: elonpendulum.com
Classified Equipment»
Personnel: Colin Donohue (Advisor); Andie Diemer (Ed. in Chief); Pam Richter (Sports Ed.); Anna Johnson

FAYETTEVILLE STATE UNIV.

Street address 1: 1200 Murchison Rd
Street address 3: Fayetteville
Street address state: NC
Zip/Postal code: 28301-4252
Country: USA
Mailing address: 1200 Murchison Rd
Mailing city: Fayetteville
Mailing state: NC
Mailing zip: 28301-4298
General Phone: (910) 672-2210
General Fax: (910) 672-1964
Primary Website: www.fsuvoice.com
Classified Equipment»
Personnel: Valonda Calloway (Advisor); Nathalie Rivera (Bus. Mgr.); L'Asia Brown (Ed. in Chief)

METHODIST UNIVERSITY

Street address 1: 5400 Ramsey St
Street address 3: Fayetteville
Street address state: NC
Zip/Postal code: 28311-1420
Country: USA
Mailing address: 5400 Ramsey St
Mailing city: Fayetteville
Mailing state: NC
Mailing zip: 28311-1420
General Phone: (910) 630-7292
General Fax: (910) 630-7253
General/National Adv. E-mail: dmunoz@methodist.edu
Primary Website: www.smalltalkmu.com
Published: Bi-Mthly
Avg Free Circ: 2400
Classified Equipment»
Personnel: Doris Munoz (Director of Student Life)

GREENSBORO

BENNETT COLLEGE

Street address 1: 900 E Washington St
Street address 3: Greensboro
Street address state: NC
Zip/Postal code: 27401-3239
Country: USA
Mailing address: 900 E Washington St
Mailing city: Greensboro
Mailing state: NC
Mailing zip: 27401-3298
General Phone: (336) 517-2305
General Fax: (336) 517-2303
General/National Adv. E-mail: banner@bennett.edu
Primary Website: www.bennettbanner.com
Classified Equipment»
Personnel: Yvonne Welbon (Advisor)

GREENSBORO COLLEGE

Street address 1: 815 W Market St
Street address 3: Greensboro
Street address state: NC
Zip/Postal code: 27401-1823
Country: USA
Mailing address: 815 W Market St
Mailing city: Greensboro
Mailing state: NC
Mailing zip: 27401-1875
General Phone: (336) 272-7102
General Fax: (336) 271-6634
Classified Equipment»
Personnel: L. Wayne Johns (Advisor)

GUILFORD COLLEGE

Street address 1: 5800 W Friendly Ave
Street address 3: Greensboro
Street address state: NC
Zip/Postal code: 27410-4108
Country: USA
Mailing address: 5800 W Friendly Ave
Mailing city: Greensboro
Mailing state: NC
Mailing zip: 27410-4173
General Phone: (336) 316-2306
Advertising Phone: (336) 316-2306
Primary Website: www.guilfordian.com
Commercial printers: Y
Classified Equipment»
Personnel: Jeff Jeske (Advisor)

NORTH CAROLINA A&T STATE UNIV.

Street address 1: 1601 E Market St
Street address 3: Greensboro
Street address state: NC
Zip/Postal code: 27411-0002
Country: USA
Mailing address: PO Box E25
Mailing city: Greensboro
Mailing state: NC
Mailing zip: 27411-0001
General Phone: (336) 334-7700
General Fax: (336) 334-7173
General/National Adv. E-mail: theatregister@gmail.com
Primary Website: www.ncatregister.com
Classified Equipment»
Personnel: Emiley Burch Harris (Advisor); Dexter R. Mullins (Ed. in Chief)

UNIV. OF NORTH CAROLINA

Street address 1: Uncg, Box N1, Euc
Street address 3: Greensboro
Street address state: NC
Zip/Postal code: 27412-0001
Country: USA
Mailing address: Uncg # N1
Mailing city: Greensboro
Mailing state: NC
Mailing zip: 27412-0001
General Phone: (336) 334-5752
General Fax: (336) 334-3518
General/National Adv. E-mail: the_carolinian@hotmail.com
Primary Website: www.carolinianonline.com
Classified Equipment»
Personnel: Y-Phuc Ayun (Bus. Mgr.); Casey Mann (Pub.); John Boschini (Ed. in Chief)

THE EAST CAROLINIAN

Street address 1: Self Help Bldg Ecu
Street address 3: Greenville
Street address state: NC
Zip/Postal code: 27858
Country: USA
Mailing address: Self Help Bldg. ECU
Mailing city: Greenville
Mailing state: NC
Mailing zip: 27858
General Phone: (252) 328-9238
General Fax: (252) 328-9143
Advertising Phone: (252) 328-9245
Advertising Fax: (252) 328-9143
Editorail Phone: (205) 328-9249
Editorial Fax: (252) 328-9143
Display Adv. E-mail: ads@theeastcarolinian.com
Editorial e-mail: editor@theeastcarolinian.com
Primary Website: www.theeastcarolinian.com
Year Established: 1925
News Services: AP, MCT
Special Editions: Housing guide
Delivery Methods: Newsstand`Carrier`Racks
Commercial printers: Y
Classified Equipment»
Personnel: Paul Isom (Advisor); Caitlin Hale (Editor); Katelyn Crouse (Ed. in Chief)
Parent company (for newspapers): ECU Media Board

HICKORY

LENOIR-RHYNE UNIVERSITY

Street address 1: 625 7th Ave NE
Street address 3: Hickory
Street address state: NC
Zip/Postal code: 28601-3984
Country: USA
Mailing address: P.O. 7341
Mailing city: Hickory
Mailing state: NC
Mailing zip: 28603
General Phone: (828) 328-7176
General/National Adv. E-mail: harrisl@lr.edu
Display Adv. E-mail: harrisl@lr.edu
Editorial e-mail: richard.gould@lr.edu
Primary Website: http://therhynean.wordpress.com/
Delivery Methods: Newsstand
Published: Mthly
Classified Equipment»

HIGH POINT

HIGH POINT UNIV.

Street address 1: 1 University Pkwy
Street address 3: High Point
Street address state: NC
Zip/Postal code: 27268-0002
Country: USA
Mailing address: 833 Montlieu Ave
Mailing city: High Point
Mailing state: NC
Mailing zip: 27262-4260
General Phone: (800) 345-6993
General Fax: (336) 841-4513
General/National Adv. E-mail: news@highpoint.edu
Primary Website: www.highpoint.edu
Classified Equipment»
Personnel: Bobby Hayes (Advisor); Wilfrid Tremblay (Dir./Prof.); Kate Fowkes (Prof.); Judy Isaksen (Assoc. Prof.); John Luecke (Assoc. Prof.); Nahed Eltantawy (Asst. Prof.); Jim Goodman (Asst. Prof.); Brad Lambert (Asst. Prof.); Jim Trammell (Asst. Prof.); Gerald Voorhees (Asst. Prof.); Kristina Bell (Lectr.); Don Moore (Opns. Mgr.); Martin Yount (Video Producer); Michelle Devlin (Admin. Asst.)

MISENHEIMER

PFEIFFER UNIV.

Street address 1: PO Box 960
Street address 3: Misenheimer
Street address state: NC
Zip/Postal code: 28109-0960
Country: USA
Mailing address: PO Box 960
Mailing city: Misenheimer
Mailing state: NC
Mailing zip: 28109-0960
General Phone: (704) 463-1360
General Fax: (704) 463-1363
Primary Website: www.pfeiffer.edu
Classified Equipment»
Personnel: Charisse Levine (Advisor)

PEMBROKE

UNIV. OF NORTH CAROLINA

Street address 1: 1 University Rd
Street address 3: Pembroke
Street address state: NC
Zip/Postal code: 28372-8699
Country: USA
Mailing address: PO Box 1510
Mailing city: Pembroke
Mailing state: NC
Mailing zip: 28372-1510
General Phone: (910) 521-6204
General Fax: (910) 522-5795
General/National Adv. E-mail: pineneedle@uncp.edu
Primary Website: www.uncp.edu/pineneedle
Classified Equipment»
Personnel: Judy Curtis (Advisor); Jodie Johnson (Adv. Mgr.); Wade Allen (Ed.)

MEREDITH COLLEGE

Street address 1: 3800 Hillsborough St
Street address 3: Raleigh
Street address state: NC
Zip/Postal code: 27607-5237
Country: USA
Mailing address: 3800 Hillsborough St
Mailing city: Raleigh
Mailing state: NC
Mailing zip: 27607-5298
General Phone: (919) 760-8600
General/National Adv. E-mail: herald@meredith.edu
Classified Equipment»
Personnel: Suzanne Britt (Advisor)

NORTH CAROLINA STATE UNIV.

Street address 1: 323 Witherspoon Student Ctr, Ncsu Campus Box 7318
Street address 3: Raleigh
Street address state: NC
Zip/Postal code: 27695-0001
Country: USA
Mailing address: 323 Witherspoon Student Ctr Ncsu Campus Box 7318
Mailing city: Raleigh
Mailing state: NC
Mailing zip: 27695-0001
General Phone: (919) 515-2411
General Fax: (919) 515-5133
General/National Adv. E-mail: editor@technicianonline.com
Display Adv. E-mail: advertising@technicianonline.com
Primary Website: www.technicianonline.com
Year Established: 1923
Classified Equipment»
Personnel: Bradley Wilson (Advisor); Russell Witham (Ed. in Chief)

PEACE COLLEGE

Street address 1: 15 E Peace St
Street address 3: Raleigh
Street address state: NC
Zip/Postal code: 27604-1176
Country: USA
Mailing address: 15 E Peace St
Mailing city: Raleigh
Mailing state: NC
Mailing zip: 27604-1194
General Phone: (919) 508-2214
General Fax: (919) 508-2326
Primary Website: peace.edu
Classified Equipment»
Personnel: John Hill (Advisor)

CATAWBA COLLEGE

Street address 1: 2300 W Innes St
Street address 3: Salisbury
Street address state: NC
Zip/Postal code: 28144-2441
Country: USA
Mailing address: 2300 W Innes St
Mailing city: Salisbury
Mailing state: NC
Mailing zip: 28144-2488
General Phone: (704) 637-4257
Primary Website: www.catawba.edu
Classified Equipment»
Personnel: Cyndy Allison (Advisor)

UNIV. OF NORTH CAROLINA

Street address 1: 601 S College Rd
Street address 3: Wilmington
Street address state: NC
Zip/Postal code: 28403-3201
Country: USA
Mailing address: 601 S College Rd
Mailing city: Wilmington
Mailing state: NC
Mailing zip: 28403-3201
General Phone: (910) 962-3229
Advertising Phone: (910) 962-7131
General/National Adv. E-mail: seahawk.news@uncw.edu
Editorial e-mail: seahawk.editor@gmail.com
Primary Website: www.theseahawk.org
Year Established: 1948
Classified Equipment»
Personnel: Autumn Beam (Ed. in Chief); Lisa Huynh (Mng. Ed); Bethany Bestwina (Photo Ed.)

WILSON

BARTON COLLEGE

Street address 1: PO Box 5000
Street address 3: Wilson
Street address state: NC
Zip/Postal code: 27893-7000
Country: USA
Mailing address: PO Box 5000
Mailing city: Wilson
Mailing state: NC
Mailing zip: 27893-7000
General Phone: (252) 399-6370
General Fax: (252) 399-6572
Classified Equipment»
Personnel: Rick Stewart (Advisor); Brittaney Rosencrance (Ed. in chief)

WINGATE

WINGATE UNIV.

Street address 1: PO Box 2
Street address 3: Wingate
Street address state: NC
Zip/Postal code: 28174-0002
Country: USA
Mailing address: PO Box 2
Mailing city: Wingate
Mailing state: NC
Mailing zip: 28174-0002
General Phone: (704) 233-8163
General Fax: (704) 233-8285
Classified Equipment»
Personnel: Keith Cannon (Advisor); Brittany Ruffner (Contact)

SALEM COLLEGE

Street address 1: 601 S Church St
Street address 3: Winston Salem
Street address state: NC
Zip/Postal code: 27101-5318
Country: USA
Mailing address: 601 S Church St
Mailing city: Winston Salem
Mailing state: NC
Mailing zip: 27101-5376
General Phone: (336) 917-5113
General Fax: (336) 917-5117
Primary Website: www.thesalemite.com
Classified Equipment»
Personnel: Sarah Boyenger (Bus. Mgr.); Susan Smith (Ed. in Chief)

WAKE FOREST UNIV.

Street address 1: PO Box 7569
Street address 3: Winston Salem
Street address state: NC
Zip/Postal code: 27109
Country: USA
Mailing address: PO Box 7569
Mailing city: Winston Salem
Mailing state: NC
Mailing zip: 27109-6240
General Phone: (336) 758-5279
General Fax: (336) 758-4561
General/National Adv. E-mail: ogb@wfu.edu
Primary Website: www.oldgoldandblack.com
Classified Equipment»
Personnel: Wayne King (Advisor); Tyler Kellner (Bus. Mgr.); Mariclaire Hicks (Ed. in Chief)

WINSTON-SALEM STATE UNIV.

Street address 1: 103 Old Nursing
Street address 2: 601 S. Martin Luther King Jr. Dr.
Street address 3: Winston Salem
Street address state: NC
Zip/Postal code: 27110-0001
Country: USA
Mailing address: 103 Old Nursing
Mailing city: Winston Salem
Mailing state: NC
Mailing zip: 27110-0001
General Phone: 3367502327
General Fax: 3367508704
Advertising Phone: 3367508701
Advertising Fax: 3367508704
Editorail Phone: 3367508701
General/National Adv. E-mail: thenewsargus@gmail.com
Display Adv. E-mail: thenewsargus@gmail.com
Editorial e-mail: thenewsargus@gmail.com
Primary Website: www.thenewsargus.com
Year Established: 1960
Published: Mon`Bi-Mthly
Classified Equipment»
Personnel: Lona D. Cobb (Advisor)

NORTH DAKOTA

BISMARCK

BISMARCK STATE COLLEGE

Street address 1: 1500 Edwards Ave
Street address 3: Bismarck
Street address state: ND
Zip/Postal code: 58501-1276
Country: USA
Mailing address: 1500 Edwards Ave
Mailing city: Bismarck
Mailing state: ND
Mailing zip: 58501-1299
General Phone: (701) 224-5467
General Fax: (701) 224-5529
Editorail Phone: (701) 224-5467
General/National Adv. E-mail: editor@mystician.org
Primary Website: www.mystician.org
Year Established: 1939
Delivery Methods: Racks
Advertising (Open Inch Rate) Weekday/Saturday: available rates upon request
Published: Mthly
Classified Equipment»
Note: We also have a news video broadcast: MystiCast and internet radio: The MYX
Personnel: Karen Bauer (Advisor)

FARGO

NORTH DAKOTA STATE UNIV.

Street address 1: 254 Memorial Union
Street address 3: Fargo
Street address state: ND
Zip/Postal code: 58102
Country: USA
Mailing address: P.O. Box 6050
Mailing city: Fargo
Mailing state: ND
Mailing zip: 58108-6050
General Phone: (701) 231-8929
General Fax: (701) 231-9402
Advertising Phone: (701) 231-8994
Editorail Phone: (701) 231-8629
General/National Adv. E-mail: ad.manager@ndsuspectrum.com
Display Adv. E-mail: ad.manager@ndsuspectrum.com
Editorial e-mail: editor@ndsuspectrum.com
Primary Website: www.ndsuspectrum.com
Year Established: 1896
News Services: AP
Delivery Methods: Racks
Commercial printers: Y
Published: Mon`Thur
Avg Free Circ: 7000
Classified Equipment»
Personnel: Andrew Pritchard (Advisor)

GRAND FORKS

UNIV. OF NORTH DAKOTA

Street address 1: 2901 University Ave Stop 8385
Street address 2: University of North Dakota Memorial Union
Street address 3: Grand Forks
Street address state: ND
Zip/Postal code: 58202-8385
Country: USA
Mailing address: University of North Dakota Memorial Union
Mailing city: Grand Forks
Mailing state: ND
Mailing zip: 58201
General Phone: (701) 777-2677
General Fax: (701) 777-3137
Advertising Phone: (701) 777-2677
General/National Adv. E-mail: dakotastudentmedia@gmail.com
Display Adv. E-mail: und.dakotastudent@email.und.edu
Primary Website: www.dakotastudent.com
Year Established: 1888
Published: Tues`Fri
Classified Equipment»
Personnel: Carrie Sandstrom (Editor-in-Chief); Melissa Bakke (Sales and Marketing Coordinator); Adam Christianson (Managing/Opinion Editor); Kelsi Ward (Features Editor); Larry Philbin (News Editor); Elizabeth Erickson (Sports Editor); Jaye Millspaugh (Multimedia Editor); Keisuke Yoshimura (Photo Editor)

JAMESTOWN

JAMESTOWN COLLEGE

Street address 1: 6086 College Ln
Street address 3: Jamestown
Street address state: ND
Zip/Postal code: 58405-0001
Country: USA
Mailing address: 6086 College Ln
Mailing city: Jamestown
Mailing state: ND
Mailing zip: 58405-0001
General Phone: (701) 252-3467
General Fax: (701) 253-4318
Primary Website: www.jc.edu
Classified Equipment»
Personnel: Steve Listopad (Advisor); Richard Schmit (Ed. in Cheif)

MINOT STATE UNIV.

Street address 1: 500 University Ave W
Street address 3: Minot
Street address state: ND
Zip/Postal code: 58707-0001
Country: USA
Mailing address: 500 University Ave W
Mailing city: Minot
Mailing state: ND
Mailing zip: 58707-0002
General Phone: (701) 858-3000
General/National Adv. E-mail: redgreen@minotstateu.edu
Primary Website: www.minotstateu.edu
Classified Equipment»
Personnel: Bryce Berginski (Ed.)

VALLEY CITY

VALLEY CITY STATE UNIV.

Street address 1: Box 1431, Vcsc Student Ctr

Street address 3: Valley City
Street address state: ND
Zip/Postal code: 58072
Country: USA
Mailing address: Box 1431, VCSC Student Ctr.
Mailing city: Valley City
Mailing state: ND
Mailing zip: 58072
General Phone: (701) 845-7722
Classified Equipment»

WAHPETON

NORTH DAKOTA STATE COLLEGE OF SCIENCE

Street address 1: PO Box 760
Street address 3: Wahpeton
Street address state: ND
Zip/Postal code: 58074-0760
Country: USA
Mailing address: c/o Daily News, PO Box 760
Mailing city: Wahpeton
Mailing state: ND
Mailing zip: 58074-0760
General Phone: (701) 642-8585
General Fax: (701) 642-6068
Classified Equipment»
Personnel: Pam Marquart (Advisor)

NEBRASKA

CHADRON

CHADRON STATE COLLEGE

Street address 1: 1000 Main St
Street address 2: # 235
Street address 3: Chadron
Street address state: NE
Zip/Postal code: 69337-2667
County: Dawes
Country: USA
Mailing address: 1000 Main St # 235
Mailing city: Chadron
Mailing state: NE
Mailing zip: 69337-2690
General Phone: (308) 432-6303
Advertising Phone: (308) 432-6304
General/National Adv. E-mail: editor@csceagle.com
Display Adv. E-mail: ads@csceagle.com
Editorial e-mail: opinion@csceagle.com
Primary Website: www.csceagle.com
Year Established: 1920
Published: Thur
Avg Free Circ: 4000
Classified Equipment»
Personnel: Michael D. Kennedy (Advisor); Aubrie Lawrence (Editor-in-Chief); Jordyn Hulinsky (Mgr Ed); Mackenzie Dahlberg (Sports Editor); Janelle Kesterson (Opinion Ed); Kamryn Kozisek (Ag & Range Editor); Velvet Jessen (Opinions Editor); Rylee Greiman (Social Media Director); Angie Webb (Advt Dir); Andrew Avila (Co-Advertising Director); Preston Goehring (Sports Ed); Kinsey Smith (Co-Advertising Director); Justine Stone (Lifestyles Ed); Brendan Fangmeire (Distribution Manager); Melanie Nelson (News Ed)

CRETE

DOANE COLLEGE

Street address 1: 1014 Boswell Ave
Street address 3: Crete
Street address state: NE
Zip/Postal code: 68333-2426
Country: USA
Mailing address: 1014 Boswell Ave Ste 289
Mailing city: Crete
Mailing state: NE
Mailing zip: 68333-2440
General Fax: (402) 826-8269
Advertising Fax: (402) 826-8600
General/National Adv. E-mail: www.doaneline.com
Display Adv. E-mail: owl@doane.edu
Classified Equipment»
Personnel: David Swartzlander (Advisor); Bob Kenny (Ed.)

HASTINGS

HASTINGS COLLEGE

Street address 1: 710 N Turner Ave
Street address 3: Hastings
Street address state: NE
Zip/Postal code: 68901-7621
Country: USA
Mailing address: 710 N Turner Ave
Mailing city: Hastings
Mailing state: NE
Mailing zip: 68901-7696
General Phone: (402) 461-7399
General Fax: (402) 461-7442
Classified Equipment»
Personnel: Alicia O'Donnell (Advisor); Lauren Lee (Ed.)

KEARNEY

UNIV. OF NEBRASKA

Street address 1: Mitchel Ctr 156
Street address 3: Kearney
Street address state: NE
Zip/Postal code: 68847
Country: USA
Mailing address: Mitchel Ctr. 156
Mailing city: Kearney
Mailing state: NE
Mailing zip: 68847
General Phone: (308) 865-8487
General Fax: (308) 865-1537
Display Adv. E-mail: antelopeads@unk.edu
Classified Equipment»
Personnel: Tereca M Diffenderfer (Advisor)

NEBRASKA WESLEYAN UNIV.

Street address 1: 5000 Saint Paul Ave
Street address 2: Smb 1221
Street address 3: Lincoln
Street address state: NE
Zip/Postal code: 68504-2760
Country: USA
Mailing address: 5000 Saint Paul Ave Smb 1221
Mailing city: Lincoln
Mailing state: NE
Mailing zip: 68504-2760
General Phone: (402) 465-2387
General Fax: (402) 465-2179
General/National Adv. E-mail: reveille@nebrwesleyan.edu
Primary Website: www.thereveillenwu.com
Published: Bi-Mthly
Classified Equipment»
Personnel: Jim Schaffer (Advisor); David Whitt (Adviser); Hannah Tangeman (Editor)

UNIV. OF NEBRASKA-LINCOLN

Street address 1: 1400 R St
Street address 2: 20 Nebraska Union
Street address 3: Lincoln
Street address state: NE
Zip/Postal code: 68588-0007
Country: USA
Mailing address: P.O. Box 880448
Mailing city: Lincoln
Mailing state: NE
Mailing zip: 68588-0448
General Phone: (402) 472-2588
Advertising Phone: (402) 472-2589
General/National Adv. E-mail: dn@unl.edu
Display Adv. E-mail: dn@unl.edu
Editorial e-mail: news@dailynebraskan.com
Primary Website: DailyNebraskan.com
Year Established: 1901
Delivery Methods: Racks
Commercial printers: N
Advertising (Open Inch Rate) Weekday/Saturday: $900/full page; $275/1/8 page, $600/1/2 page, $425/ 1/4 pg.
Published: Mthly`Other
Published Other: We publish 2-3 print editions per year
Avg Free Circ: 4500
Classified Equipment»
Personnel: Daniel Shattil (Gen. Mgr.); Allen Vaughan (General Manager); David Thiemann (Director of Sales and Marketing)

NORTHEAST CMTY. COLLEGE

Street address 1: 801 E Benjamin Ave
Street address 3: Norfolk
Street address state: NE
Zip/Postal code: 68701-6831
Country: USA
Mailing address: PO Box 469
Mailing city: Norfolk
Mailing state: NE
Mailing zip: 68702-0469
General Phone: (402) 844-7352
Primary Website: www.neaccviewpoint.com
Classified Equipment»
Personnel: Jason Elznic (Advisor)

CREIGHTON UNIV.

Street address 1: 2500 California Plz
Street address 3: Omaha
Street address state: NE
Zip/Postal code: 68178-0133
Country: USA
Mailing address: 2500 California Plz
Mailing city: Omaha
Mailing state: NE
Mailing zip: 68178-0002
General Phone: (402) 280-4058
General Fax: (402) 280-1494
General/National Adv. E-mail: emw@creighton.edu
Primary Website: www.creightonian.com
Classified Equipment»
Personnel: Melissa Hillebrand (Ed.); Eileen M. Wirth (Chair/Prof.); Father Don Doll (Prof./Charles and Mary Heider Endowed Jesuit Chair); Kelly Fitzgerald (Asst. Ed.); Timothy S. Guthrie (Assoc. Prof.); Jeffrey Maciejewski (Assoc. Prof.); Carol Zuegner (Assoc. Prof.); Kristoffer Boyle (Asst. Prof.); Joel Davies (Asst. Prof.); Charles Heider (Asst. Prof.); Mary Heider (Asst. Prof.); Andrew Hughes (Lectr.); Kathleen Hughes (Lectr.); Richard Janda (Lectr.); Kathryn Larson (Lectr.); Brian Norton (Lectr.); Wendy Wiseman (Lectr.); Angela Zegers (Lectr.)

UNIV. OF NEBRASKA AT OMAHA GATEWAY

Street address 1: 6001 Dodge St
Street address 2: MBSC 117H
Street address 3: Omaha
Street address state: NE
Zip/Postal code: 68182-1107
Country: USA
Mailing address: 6001 Dodge St Unit 116
Mailing city: Omaha
Mailing state: NE
Mailing zip: 68182-1107
General Phone: (402) 554-2470
General Fax: (402) 554-2735
General/National Adv. E-mail: editorinchief@unothegateway.com
Editorial e-mail: jloza@unomaha.edu
Primary Website: www.unogateway.com
Year Established: 1913
Advertising (Open Inch Rate) Weekday/Saturday: $7/inch
Published: Tues
Avg Free Circ: 2500
Classified Equipment»
Personnel: Josefina Loza (Advisor); Cody Willmer; Kate O'Dell

PERU

PERU STATE COLLEGE

Street address 1: PO Box 10
Street address 3: Peru
Street address state: NE
Zip/Postal code: 68421-0010
Country: USA
Mailing address: PO Box 10
Mailing city: Peru
Mailing state: NE
Mailing zip: 68421-0010
General Phone: (402) 872-2260
General Fax: (402) 872-2302
General/National Adv. E-mail: psctimes@yahoo.com
Classified Equipment»
Personnel: Savannah Wenzel (Adv. Mgr.)

SCOTTSBLUFF

WESTERN NEBRASKA COMMUNITY COLLEGE

Street address 1: 1601 E 27th St
Street address 3: Scottsbluff
Street address state: NE
Zip/Postal code: 69361-1815
Country: USA
Mailing address: 1601 E 27th St
Mailing city: Scottsbluff
Mailing state: NE
Mailing zip: 69361-1899
General Phone: (308) 635-6058
Advertising Phone: 308-636-6057
General/National Adv. E-mail: spectator@wncc.edu
Delivery Methods: Mail`Racks
Commercial printers: Y
Classified Equipment»
Personnel: Mark Rein (Adv. Mgr.); Jay Grote

SEWARD

CONCORDIA UNIVERSITY-NEBRASKA

Street address 1: 800 N Columbia Ave
Street address 3: Seward
Street address state: NE
Zip/Postal code: 68434-1500
Country: USA
Mailing address: 800 N Columbia Ave Ste 1
Mailing city: Seward
Mailing state: NE
Mailing zip: 68434-1599
General Phone: 703-434-0355
General/National Adv. E-mail: sower@cune.org
Primary Website: www.cunesower.com
Delivery Methods: Carrier`Racks
Commercial printers: N
Advertising (Open Inch Rate) Weekday/Saturday: Please request media kit for ad prices
Published: Mthly
Published Other: Website updated throughout the week
Avg Paid Circ: 0
Avg Free Circ: 1300
Classified Equipment»
Personnel: Ellen Beck (Adviser)

WAYNE

WAYNE STATE COLLEGE

Street address 1: 1111 Main St
Street address 3: Wayne
Street address state: NE
Zip/Postal code: 68787-1181
Country: USA
Mailing address: 1111 Main St
Mailing city: Wayne
Mailing state: NE
Mailing zip: 68787-1172
General Phone: (402) 375-7324
General Fax: (402) 375-7204
Advertising Phone: (402) 375-7489
General/National Adv. E-mail: wstater@wsc.edu
Primary Website: wildcat.wsc.edu/stater/
Classified Equipment»
Personnel: Max McElwain (Faculty Advisor); Skylar Osovski (Ed. in Chief); Katelynn Wolfe (News Ed.)

NEW HAMPSHIRE

THE NEW HAMPSHIRE

Street address 1: Memorial Union Bldg, Rm 132, 83 Main St

Street address 3: Durham
Street address state: NH
Zip/Postal code: 3824
Country: USA
Mailing address: Memorial Union Bldg., Rm. 132, 83 Main St.
Mailing city: Durham
Mailing state: NH
Mailing zip: 03824-2538
General Phone: (603) 862-1323
General Fax: (603) 862-1920
General/National Adv. E-mail: tnh.news@unh.edu
Display Adv. E-mail: tnh.advertising@unh.edu
Editorial e-mail: tnh.editor@unh.edu
Primary Website: www.tnhdigital.com
Year Established: 1911
Special Weekly Sections: Arts on Fridays
Delivery Methods: Racks
Commercial printers: N
Advertising (Open Inch Rate) Weekday/Saturday: 11.75pci National, 9.25 pci Local
Published: Mon`Thur
Avg Free Circ: 4000
Classified Equipment»
Personnel: Julie Pond (Advisor)
Parent company (for newspapers): University of New Hampshire

UNIVERSITY OF NEW HAMPSHIRE

Street address 1: 104 Hamilton Smith Hall
Street address 3: Durham
Street address state: NH
Zip/Postal code: 3824
Country: USA
Mailing address: 104 Hamilton Smith Hall
Mailing city: Durham
Mailing state: NH
Mailing zip: 3824
General Phone: (603) 862-0251
General Fax: (603) 862-3563
General/National Adv. E-mail: lcm@cisunix.unh.edu
Classified Equipment»
Personnel: Lisa Miller (Dir.)
Newspaper (for newspapers group): The New Hampshire, Durham

DARTMOUTH COLLEGE

Street address 1: 6175 Robinson Hall
Street address 3: Hanover
Street address state: NH
Zip/Postal code: 03755-3507
Country: USA
Mailing address: 6175 Robinson Hall
Mailing city: Hanover
Mailing state: NH
Mailing zip: 03755-3507
General Phone: (603) 646-2600
General Fax: (603) 646-3443
General/National Adv. E-mail: publisher@dartmouth.com; thedartmouth@dartmouth.edu
Primary Website: www.thedartmouth.com
Year Established: 1799
Classified Equipment»
Personnel: Ray Lu (Ed. in chief); Phil Rasansky (Pub.)

HENNIKER

NEW ENGLAND COLLEGE

Street address 1: 98 Bridge St
Street address 3: Henniker
Street address state: NH
Zip/Postal code: 03242-3292
Country: USA
Mailing address: 98 Bridge St
Mailing city: Henniker
Mailing state: NH
Mailing zip: 03242-3292
General Phone: (603) 428-2000
General Fax: (603) 428-7230
Primary Website: www.nec.edu
Classified Equipment»
Personnel: William Homestead (Advisor)

SOUTHERN NEW HAMPSHIRE UNIV.

Street address 1: 2500 N River Rd
Street address 2: # 1084
Street address 3: Manchester
Street address state: NH
Zip/Postal code: 03106-1018
Country: USA
Mailing address: 2500 N River Rd # 1084
Mailing city: Manchester
Mailing state: NH
Mailing zip: 03106-1018
General/National Adv. E-mail: Penmenpress@snhu.edu
Display Adv. E-mail: Penmenpress@snhu.edu
Primary Website: PenmenPress.com
Published: Bi-Mthly
Classified Equipment»
Personnel: Jon Boroshok (Advisor)

ST. ANSELM COLLEGE

Street address 1: 100 Saint Anselm Dr
Street address 3: Manchester
Street address state: NH
Zip/Postal code: 03102-1308
Country: USA
Mailing address: PO Box 1719
Mailing city: Manchester
Mailing state: NH
Mailing zip: 03102
General Phone: (603) 641-7016
General Fax: (603) 222-4289
General/National Adv. E-mail: crier@anslem.edu
Primary Website: www.saintanselmcrier.com
Classified Equipment»
Personnel: Jerome Day (Advisor)

PLYMOUTH

PLYMOUTH STATE COLLEGE

Street address 1: Hub Ste A9
Street address 3: Plymouth
Street address state: NH
Zip/Postal code: 3264
Country: USA
Mailing address: HUB Ste. A9
Mailing city: Plymouth
Mailing state: NH
Mailing zip: 03264
General Phone: (603) 535-2947
General Fax: (603) 535-2729
Editorail Phone: (603) 535-2279
Editorial e-mail: editor@clock.plymouth.edu
Primary Website: www.theclockonline.com
Classified Equipment»
Personnel: Joe Mealey (Advisor); Meghan Plumpton (Adv. Mgr.); Samantha Kenney (Ed. in Chief)

RINDGE

FRANKLIN PIERCE COLLEGE

Street address 1: 40 University Dr
Street address 3: Rindge
Street address state: NH
Zip/Postal code: 03461-5046
Country: USA
Mailing address: 40 University Dr
Mailing city: Rindge
Mailing state: NH
Mailing zip: 03461-5045
General Phone: (603) 899-4170
General Fax: (603) 899-1077
Primary Website: http://www.franklinpierce.edu/
Classified Equipment»
Personnel: Kristen Nevious (Advisor); Tony Catinella (Ed.); Robin Michael (Mng. Ed.)

NEW JERSEY

BLACKWOOD

CAMDEN COUNTY COLLEGE

Street address 1: PO Box 200
Street address 3: Blackwood
Street address state: NJ
Zip/Postal code: 08012-0200
Country: USA
Mailing address: PO Box 200
Mailing city: Blackwood
Mailing state: NJ
Mailing zip: 08012-0200
General Phone: (856) 227-7200
General Fax: (856) 227-3541
General/National Adv. E-mail: campuspress@camdencc.edu
Primary Website: www.camdencc.edu/campuspress
Classified Equipment»

RUTGERS UNIV.

Street address 1: 326 Penn St
Street address 3: Camden
Street address state: NJ
Zip/Postal code: 08102-1410
Country: USA
Mailing address: 326 Penn St
Mailing city: Camden
Mailing state: NJ
Mailing zip: 08102-1412
General Phone: (856) 225-6304
General Fax: (856) 225-6579
General/National Adv. E-mail: gleaner@camden.rutgers.edu
Primary Website: gleaner.camden.rutgers.edu
Classified Equipment»
Personnel: Joe Capuzzo (Advisor)

CRANFORD

UNION COUNTY COLLEGE

Street address 1: 1033 Springfield Ave
Street address 3: Cranford
Street address state: NJ
Zip/Postal code: 07016-1528
Country: USA
Mailing address: 1033 Springfield Ave
Mailing city: Cranford
Mailing state: NJ
Mailing zip: 07016-1598
General Phone: (908) 709-7000
Primary Website: www.ucc.edu
Classified Equipment»
Personnel: John R. Farrell (Vice Pres.)

EDISON

MIDDLESEX COUNTY COLLEGE

Street address 1: 2600 Woodbridge Ave
Street address 3: Edison
Street address state: NJ
Zip/Postal code: 08837-3604
Country: USA
Mailing address: 2600 Woodbridge Ave
Mailing city: Edison
Mailing state: NJ
Mailing zip: 08837-3675
General Phone: (732) 548-6000
General Fax: (732) 906-4167
General/National Adv. E-mail: quovadis_newspaper@hotmail.com
Classified Equipment»
Personnel: Melissa Edwards (Ed.)

EWING

THE COLLEGE OF NEW JERSEY

Street address 1: PO Box 7718
Street address 3: Ewing
Street address state: NJ
Zip/Postal code: 08628-0718
Country: USA
Mailing address: PO Box 7718
Mailing city: Ewing
Mailing state: NJ
Mailing zip: 08628-0718
General Phone: (609) 771-2499
General Fax: (609) 771-3433
Advertising Phone: (609) 771-3433
Editorail Phone: (609) 771-2424
General/National Adv. E-mail: signal@tcnj.edu
Display Adv. E-mail: signalad@tcnj.edu
Primary Website: tcnjsignal.net
Year Established: 1885
Published: Wed
Classified Equipment»
Personnel: Emilie Lounsberry (Advisor)

GALLOWAY

RICHARD STOCKTON COLLEGE

Street address 1: 101 Vera King Farris Dr
Street address 3: Galloway
Street address state: NJ
Zip/Postal code: 08205-9441
Country: USA
Mailing address: 101 Vera King Farris Dr
Mailing city: Galloway
Mailing state: NJ
Mailing zip: 08205-9441
General Phone: (609) 652-4296
General Fax: (609) 748-5565
Display Adv. E-mail: argoadvertising@yahoo.com
Classified Equipment»
Personnel: Craig Stambaugh (Advisor); Lina Wayman (Ed.)

GLASSBORO

ROWAN UNIV.

Street address 1: 201 Mullica Hill Rd
Street address 3: Glassboro
Street address state: NJ
Zip/Postal code: 08028-1700
Country: USA
Mailing address: 201 Mullica Hill Rd
Mailing city: Glassboro
Mailing state: NJ
Mailing zip: 08028-1702
General Phone: (856) 256-4713
General Fax: (856) 256-4929
General/National Adv. E-mail: communication@rowan.edu
Primary Website: www.thewhitonline.com
Classified Equipment»
Personnel: Don Bagin (Prof.); Kathryn Quigley (Advisor); R. Michael Donovan (Prof.); Anthony Fulginiti (Prof.); Richard Grupenhoff (Prof.); Kenneth Kaleta (Prof.); Janice Rowan (Prof.); Edward Streb (Prof.); Julia Chang (Assoc. Prof.); Cynthia Corison (Assoc. Prof.); Edgar Eckhardt (Assoc. Prof.); Suzanne Fitzgerald (Assoc. Prof.); Carl Hausman (Assoc. Prof.); Martin Itzkowitz (Assoc. Prof.); Frances Johnson (Assoc. Prof.); Diane Penrod (Assoc. Prof.); Donald Stoll (Assoc. Prof.); Sanford Tweedie (Assoc. Prof.); Kenneth Albone (Asst. Prof.); Lorin Arnold (Asst. Prof.)

HACKETTSTOWN

CENTENARY COLLEGE

Street address 1: 400 Jefferson St
Street address 3: Hackettstown
Street address state: NJ
Zip/Postal code: 07840-2184
Country: USA
Mailing address: 400 Jefferson St Ste 1
Mailing city: Hackettstown
Mailing state: NJ
Mailing zip: 07840-2184
General Phone: (908) 852-1400 x2243
Advertising Phone: (908) 852-1400x2243
General/National Adv. E-mail: levd@centenarycollege.edu
Display Adv. E-mail: levd@centenarycollege.edu
Primary Website: www.centenarycollege.edu
Year Established: 1991
Advertising (Open Inch Rate) Weekday/Saturday: on request
Published: Mthly
Avg Free Circ: 1600
Classified Equipment»
Personnel: Deborah Lev (Advisor)

HOBOKEN

STEVENS INSTITUTE OF TECHNOLOGY

Street address 1: Stevens Institute of Technology
Street address 2: Castle Point on Hudson
Street address 3: Hoboken
Street address state: NJ
Zip/Postal code: 7030
Country: USA
General Phone: (201) 216-3404
General/National Adv. E-mail: stute@stevens.edu
Display Adv. E-mail: stuteads@stevens.edu
Editorial e-mail: eboard@thestute.com
Primary Website: www.thestute.com
Year Established: 1904
Published: Fri
Classified Equipment»
Personnel: Joseph Brosnan (Ed.)

JERSEY CITY

NEW JERSEY CITY UNIV.

Street address 1: 2039 Kennedy Blvd, Gsub 305
Street address 3: Jersey City
Street address state: NJ
Zip/Postal code: 7305
Country: USA
Mailing address: 2039 Kennedy Blvd., GSUB 305
Mailing city: Jersey City
Mailing state: NJ
Mailing zip: 07305-1596
General Phone: (201) 200-3575
Primary Website: www.njcu.edu
Classified Equipment»
Personnel: James Broderick (Advisor); Erica Molina (Ed.); Marlen Gonzalez (Mng. Ed.)

ST. PETERS COLLEGE

Street address 1: 2641 John F Kennedy Blvd
Street address 3: Jersey City
Street address state: NJ
Zip/Postal code: 07306-5943
Country: USA
Mailing address: 2641 John F Kennedy Blvd
Mailing city: Jersey City
Mailing state: NJ
Mailing zip: 07306-5997
General Phone: (201) 938-1254
General Fax: (201) 938-1254
Advertising Phone: (201) 761-7378
General/National Adv. E-mail: pauwwow@hotmail.com
Display Adv. E-mail: ads@pauwwow.com
Primary Website: pauwwow.com
Classified Equipment»
Personnel: Paul Almonte (Advisor); Frank DeMichele (Ed. in Chief); Rozen Pradhan (Mng. Ed.)

LAWRENCEVILLE

THE RIDER NEWS / RIDER UNIVERSITY

Street address 1: 2083 Lawrenceville Rd
Street address 3: Lawrenceville
Street address state: NJ
Zip/Postal code: 08648-3099
Country: USA
Mailing address: 2083 Lawrenceville Rd
Mailing city: Lawrenceville
Mailing state: NJ
Mailing zip: 08648-3099
General Phone: (609) 896-5256
General Fax: (609) 895-5696
General/National Adv. E-mail: ridernews@rider.edu
Primary Website: www.theridernews.com
Year Established: 1930
Commercial printers: Y
Classified Equipment»
Personnel: Dianne Garyantes (Co-Adviser)

LINCROFT

BROOKDALE CMTY. COLLEGE

Street address 1: 765 Newman Springs Rd
Street address 3: Lincroft
Street address state: NJ
Zip/Postal code: 07738-1543
Country: USA
Mailing address: 765 Newman Springs Rd
Mailing city: Lincroft
Mailing state: NJ
Mailing zip: 07738-1599
General Phone: (732) 224-2266
General Fax: (732) 450-1591
General/National Adv. E-mail: stallbcc@gmail.com
Editorial e-mail: stall@brookdalecc.edu
Published: Mon`Other
Published Other: six times a semester
Classified Equipment»
Personnel: Debbie Mura (Advisor)

OCEAN COUNTY COLLEGE

Street address 1: 9 East Old Whaling Lane
Street address 3: Long Beach
Street address state: NJ
Zip/Postal code: 08008-2930
County: Ocean
Country: USA
Mailing address: 9 East Old Whaling Lane
Mailing city: Long Beach
Mailing state: NJ
Mailing zip: 08008-2930
General Phone: 6094920138
General Fax: 6094920138
Advertising Phone: 6094920138
General/National Adv. E-mail: kbosley@mac.com
Display Adv. E-mail: kbosley@mac.com
Classified Adv. E-mail: kbosley@mac.com
Editorial e-mail: kbosley@mac.com
Year Established: 1965
Delivery Methods: Racks
Area Served - City: 08008-2930
Commercial printers: Y
Published: Thur
Published Other: Irregularly
Classified Equipment»
Personnel: Karen Bosley

DREW UNIV.

Street address 1: PO Box 802
Street address 3: Madison
Street address state: NJ
Zip/Postal code: 07940-0802
Country: USA
Mailing address: PO Box 802
Mailing city: Madison
Mailing state: NJ
Mailing zip: 07940-0802
General Phone: (973) 408-4207
General Fax: (973) 408-3887
General/National Adv. E-mail: acorn@drew.edu
Primary Website: www.drewacorn.com
Classified Equipment»
Personnel: David A.M. Wilensky (Ed. in Chief); Sheryl Mccabe (Mng. Ed.)

MAYS LANDING

ATLANTIC CAPE CMTY. COLLEGE

Street address 1: 5100 Black Horse Pike
Street address 3: Mays Landing
Street address state: NJ
Zip/Postal code: 08330-2623
Country: USA
Mailing address: 5100 Black Horse Pike
Mailing city: Mays Landing
Mailing state: NJ
Mailing zip: 08330-2699
General Phone: (609) 343-5109
General Fax: (609) 343-5030
Editorial e-mail: atlanticcapereview9@gmail.com
Classified Equipment»
Personnel: Marge Nocito (Advisor); Jerry Carcache (Dir., Adv.); Anne Kemp (Ed. in Chief)

COLLEGE OF ST. ELIZABETH

Street address 1: 2 Convent Rd
Street address 3: Morristown
Street address state: NJ
Zip/Postal code: 07960-6923
Country: USA
Mailing address: 2 Convent Rd
Mailing city: Morristown
Mailing state: NJ
Mailing zip: 07960-6989
General Phone: (973) 290-4242
General Fax: (973) 290-4389
General/National Adv. E-mail: thestation@cse.edu
Classified Equipment»
Personnel: Kristene Both (Ed. in Chief)

NEW BRUNSWICK

RUTGERS UNIV.

Street address 1: 126 College Ave
Street address 2: Ste 431
Street address 3: New Brunswick
Street address state: NJ
Zip/Postal code: 08901-1166
Country: USA
Mailing address: 126 College Ave Ste 431
Mailing city: New Brunswick
Mailing state: NJ
Mailing zip: 08901-1166
General Phone: (732) 932-7051
General Fax: (732) 932-0079
General/National Adv. E-mail: news@dailytargum.com
Primary Website: www.dailytargum.com
Classified Equipment»
Personnel: John Clyde (Ed. in Cheif)

RUTGERS UNIV. SCHOOL OF ENVIRONMENTAL & BIOLOGICAL SCIENCES

Street address 1: 88 Lipman Dr
Street address 3: New Brunswick
Street address state: NJ
Zip/Postal code: 08901-8525
Country: USA
Mailing address: 88 Lipman Dr
Mailing city: New Brunswick
Mailing state: NJ
Mailing zip: 08901-8525
General Phone: (732) 932-3000
General Fax: (732) 932-8526
Classified Equipment»
Personnel: Kathryn E. Barry (Ed. in Chief)

ESSEX COUNTY COLLEGE

Street address 1: 303 University Ave
Street address 3: Newark
Street address state: NJ
Zip/Postal code: 07102-1719
Country: USA
Mailing address: 303 University Ave
Mailing city: Newark
Mailing state: NJ
Mailing zip: 07102-1798
General Phone: (973) 877-3559
General Fax: (973) 877-3488
Classified Equipment»
Personnel: Kyle Miller (Ed.); Nessie Hill (Advisor)

NEW JERSEY INST. OF TECHNOLOGY

Street address 1: 150 Bleeker St
Street address 3: Newark
Street address state: NJ
Zip/Postal code: 07103-3902
Country: USA
Mailing address: 150 Bleeker St
Mailing city: Newark
Mailing state: NJ
Mailing zip: 07103-3902
General Phone: (973) 596-5416
General Fax: (973) 596-3613
General/National Adv. E-mail: news@njitvector.com
Display Adv. E-mail: ads@njitvector.com
Primary Website: www.njitvector.com
Classified Equipment»
Personnel: Melissa Silderstang (Exec. Ed.)

RUTGERS UNIV.

Street address 1: 350 M L King Blvd
Street address 2: Paul Robeson Campus Ctr., Rm. 237
Street address 3: Newark
Street address state: NJ
Zip/Postal code: 07102-1801
Country: USA
Mailing address: 350 Martin Luther King Jr Blvd
Mailing city: Newark
Mailing state: NJ
Mailing zip: 07102-1801
General Phone: (973) 353-5023
General Fax: (973) 353-1333
General/National Adv. E-mail: observercopy@gmail.com
Primary Website: www.rutgersobserver.com
Classified Equipment»
Personnel: Dina Sayedahmed (Executive Editor)

PRINCETON

PRINCETON UNIVERSITY

Street address 1: PO Box 469
Street address 3: Princeton
Street address state: NJ
Zip/Postal code: 08542-0469
Country: USA
Mailing address: PO Box 469
Mailing city: Princeton
Mailing state: NJ
Mailing zip: 08542-0469
General Phone: (609) 258-3632
General/National Adv. E-mail: eic@dailyprincetonian.com
Display Adv. E-mail: bm@dailyprincetonian.com
Editorial e-mail: eic@dailyprincetonian.com
Primary Website: www.dailyprincetonian.com
Year Established: 1876
Published: Mon`Tues`Wed`Thur`Fri
Classified Equipment»
Personnel: Marcelo Rochabrun (Editor in Chief)

RANDOLPH

COUNTY COLLEGE OF MORRIS

Street address 1: 214 Center Grove Rd
Street address 2: Rm Scc
Street address 3: Randolph
Street address state: NJ
Zip/Postal code: 07869-2007
Country: USA
Mailing address: 214 Center Grove Rd Rm Scc
Mailing city: Randolph
Mailing state: NJ
Mailing zip: 07869-2007
General Phone: (973) 328-5224
General Fax: (973) 361-4031
General/National Adv. E-mail: theyoungtownedition@yahoo.com
Classified Equipment»
Personnel: Matthew Ayres (Advisor); Frank Blaha (Ed. in Chief)

SEWELL

GLOUCESTER COUNTY COLLEGE

Street address 1: 1400 Tanyard Rd
Street address 3: Sewell
Street address state: NJ
Zip/Postal code: 08080-4222
Country: USA
Mailing address: 1400 Tanyard Rd
Mailing city: Sewell
Mailing state: NJ
Mailing zip: 08080-4249
General Phone: (856) 468-5000
General Fax: (856) 464-9153
General/National Adv. E-mail: gazette@gccnj.edu
Commercial printers: Y

Advertising (Open Inch Rate) Weekday/Saturday: $60-$200 per ad
Classified Equipment»
Personnel: Brooke Hoffman (Advisor); Keesha Patterson (Advisor)

SOUTH ORANGE

SETON HALL UNIVERSITY

Street address 1: 400 S Orange Ave, Student Ctr, Rm 224
Street address 3: South Orange
Street address state: NJ
Zip/Postal code: 7079
Country: USA
Mailing address: 400 S. Orange Ave., Student Ctr., Rm. 224
Mailing city: South Orange
Mailing state: NJ
Mailing zip: 07079
General Phone: (732) 925-7647
General Fax: (973) 761-7943
General/National Adv. E-mail: Thesetonian@gmail.com
Primary Website: www.thesetonian.com
Year Established: 1924
Published: Thur
Classified Equipment»
Personnel: Amy Nyberg (Advisor); Brian Wisowaty (Mng. Ed.)

FAIRLEIGH DICKINSON UNIV.

Street address 1: 1000 River Rd
Street address 3: Teaneck
Street address state: NJ
Zip/Postal code: 07666-1914
Country: USA
Mailing address: 1000 River Rd
Mailing city: Teaneck
Mailing state: NJ
Mailing zip: 07666-1914
General Phone: (201) 692-2046
General Fax: (201) 692-2376
General/National Adv. E-mail: equinoxfdu@gmail.com
Primary Website: https://fduequinox.wordpress.com/
Published: Thur
Classified Equipment»
Personnel: Bruno Battistoli (Advisor); Sarah Latson (Faculty Adviser); Kayla Hastrup (Editor-in-Chief); Miruna Seitan (Mng. Ed.); Lorena Chouza (Exec. Ed.); Melissa Hartz (News Editor)

UNION

KEAN UNIV.

Street address 1: 1000 Morris Ave
Street address 3: Union
Street address state: NJ
Zip/Postal code: 07083-7133
Country: USA
Mailing address: 1000 Morris Ave Ste 1
Mailing city: Union
Mailing state: NJ
Mailing zip: 07083-7131
General Phone: (908) 737-0468
General Fax: (908) 737-0465
General/National Adv. E-mail: thetower@kean.edu
Primary Website: www.kean.edu/~thetower
Classified Equipment»
Personnel: Pat Winters Lauro (Faculty Advisor); Eileen Ruf (Bus. Mgr.); Jillian Johnson (Ed. in Chief); Emannuel Urenea (Ed.)

UPPER MONTCLAIR

MONTCLAIR STATE UNIV.

Street address 1: Student Ctr. Annex Room 113
Street address 2: Room 113
Street address 3: Upper Montclair
Street address state: NJ
Zip/Postal code: 7043
Country: USA
General Phone: (973) 655-5230
General Fax: (973) 655-7804
General/National Adv. E-mail: montclarioneditor@gmail.com
Primary Website: www.themontclarion.org
Classified Equipment»
Personnel: Kristen Bryfogle (Ed. in Chief); Kulsoom Rizvi (News Editor); Nelson DePasquale (Sports Editor)

WILLIAM PATERSON UNIV.

Street address 1: 300 Pompton Rd
Street address 2: # SC329A
Street address 3: Wayne
Street address state: NJ
Zip/Postal code: 07470-2103
Country: USA
Mailing address: 300 Pompton Rd # SC329A
Mailing city: Wayne
Mailing state: NJ
Mailing zip: 07470-2103
General Phone: (973) 720-3265
General Fax: (973) 720-2093
General/National Adv. E-mail: wpubeacon@hotmail.com
Primary Website: www.wpubeacon.com
Classified Equipment»
Personnel: Jeff Wakemen (Advisor); Tim Kauffeld (Ed. in Chief); Robin Mulder (News Ed.)

WEST LONG BRANCH

MONMOUTH UNIVERSITY

Street address 1: 400 Cedar Ave
Street address 2: Rm 260
Street address 3: West Long Branch
Street address state: NJ
Zip/Postal code: 07764-1804
Country: USA
Mailing address: 400 Cedar Ave Rm 260
Mailing city: West Long Branch
Mailing state: NJ
Mailing zip: 07764-1804
General Phone: (732) 571-3481
Advertising Phone: (732) 263-5151
General/National Adv. E-mail: outlook@monmouth.edu
Display Adv. E-mail: outlookads@monmouth.edu
Primary Website: outlook.monmouth.edu
Year Established: 1933
Published: Wed
Avg Free Circ: 5000
Classified Equipment»
Personnel: John Morano (Professor of Journalism); Sandra Brown (Office Coordinator)

NEW MEXICO

NEW MEXICO DAILY LOBO

Street address 1: 1 University of New Mexico
Street address 2: MS 3
Street address 3: Albuquerque
Street address state: NM
Zip/Postal code: 87131-0001
County: Bernalillo
Country: USA
Mailing address: 1 University of New Mexico MS 3
Mailing city: Albuquerque
Mailing state: NM
Mailing zip: 87131-0001
General Phone: (505) 277-7527
General Fax: (505) 277-6228
Advertising Phone: (505) 277-5656
Advertising Fax: (505) 277-7530
Editorail Phone: (505) 277-5656
Editorial Fax: (505) 277-7530
General/National Adv. E-mail: advertising@dailylobo.com
Display Adv. E-mail: advertising@dailylobo.com
Classified Adv. E-mail: classifieds@dailylobo.com
Editorial e-mail: news@dailylobo.com
Primary Website: www.dailylobo.com
Year Established: 1895
Delivery Methods: Mail`Newsstand
Area Served - City: Bernalillo County
Advertising (Open Inch Rate) Weekday/Saturday: Open inch rate $15.50
Online Advertising Rates - CPM (cost per thousand) by Size: $15.50 cpm
Published: Mon`Tues`Wed`Thur`Fri`Sat
Weekday Frequency: m
Saturday Frequency: m
Classified Equipment»
Personnel: Jyllian Roach (Ed. in Chief); JR Oppenheim (Managing Ed.); Jonathan Baca (News Ed.); Daniel Montano (News Ed.); Sergio Jimenez (Photo Ed.); William Aranda (Asst. Photo Ed.); Stephen Montoya (Culture Ed.); Tomas Lujan (Asst. Culture Ed.); Thomas Romero-Salas (Sports Ed.); Jonathan Gamboa (Design Dir.); Sarah Lynas (Design Dir.); Craig Dubyk (Copy Chief); Leanne Lucero (Copy Ed.); Zach Pavlik (Ad. Mgr.); Sammy Chumpolpakdee (Sales Mgr.); Hannah Dowdy-Sue (Class. Mgr.); David Lynch (News Ed.); Nick Fojud (Photo Ed.); Veronica Munoz (Web Ed.)

UNIV. OF NEW MEXICO

Street address 1: 1 University of New Mexico
Street address 2: MS 3
Street address 3: Albuquerque
Street address state: NM
Zip/Postal code: 87131-0001
Country: USA
Mailing address: 1 University of New Mexico MS 3
Mailing city: Albuquerque
Mailing state: NM
Mailing zip: 87131-0001
General Phone: (505) 277-5656
General Fax: (505) 277-7530
Advertising Phone: (505) 277-5656
Advertising Fax: (505) 277-7530
Editorail Phone: (505) 277-7527
General/National Adv. E-mail: advertising@dailylobo.com
Display Adv. E-mail: advertising@dailylobo.com
Editorial e-mail: editorinchief@dailylobo.com
Primary Website: www.dailylobo.com
Year Established: 1895
News Services: AP
Delivery Methods: Mail`Racks
Commercial printers: N
Advertising (Open Inch Rate) Weekday/Saturday: National Rate $15.50
Published: Mon`Tues`Wed`Thur`Fri
Avg Free Circ: 9000
Classified Equipment»
Personnel: Jim Fisher (Bus. Mgr.)

NEW MEXICO STATE UNIV.

Street address 1: PO Box 30001
Street address 3: Las Cruces
Street address state: NM
Zip/Postal code: 88003-8001
Country: USA
Mailing address: PO Box 30001
Mailing city: Las Cruces
Mailing state: NM
Mailing zip: 88003-8001
General Phone: (575) 646-6397
General Fax: (575) 646-5557
General/National Adv. E-mail: roundup@nmsu.edu
Primary Website: www.roundupnews.com
Classified Equipment»
Personnel: Jeff Hand (Advisor); Jon Blazak (Ed. in Chief)

PORTALES

EASTERN NEW MEXICO UNIV.

Street address 1: 1500 S Avenue K
Street address 2: Department of Communication
Street address 3: Portales
Street address state: NM
Zip/Postal code: 88130-7400
Country: USA
Mailing address: Station 27
Mailing city: Portales
Mailing state: NM
Mailing zip: 88130-7400
General Phone: (575) 562-2130
General Fax: (575) 562-2847
General/National Adv. E-mail: janet.birkey@enmu.edu
Primary Website: https://www.enmuthechaseonline.com/
Advertising (Open Inch Rate) Weekday/Saturday: janet.birkey@enmu.edu
Published: Mon
Published Other: Hard copy published every other week; online in between
Classified Equipment»
Personnel: Janet Birkey (Advisor)

SOCORRO

NEW MEXICO INST. OF MINING & TECHNOLOGY

Street address 1: 801 Leroy Pl
Street address 3: Socorro
Street address state: NM
Zip/Postal code: 87801-4681
Country: USA
Mailing address: 801 Leroy Pl
Mailing city: Socorro
Mailing state: NM
Mailing zip: 87801-4750
General Phone: (575) 835-5525
General Fax: (505) 835-6364
General/National Adv. E-mail: paydirt@nmt.edu; paydirt-editor@nmt.edu; paydirt-ads@nmt.edu
Classified Equipment»
Personnel: Roger Renteria (Ed. in Chief); Rachel Armstrong (Ed.)

NEVADA

UNIVERSITY OF NEVADA, LAS VEGAS

Street address 1: 4505 S Maryland Pkwy
Street address 2: # 2011
Street address 3: Las Vegas
Street address state: NV
Zip/Postal code: 89154-9900
Country: USA
Mailing address: 4505 S Maryland Pkwy
Mailing city: Las Vegas
Mailing state: NV
Mailing zip: 89154-9900
General Phone: (702) 895-2028
General Fax: (702) 895-1515
Editorial Fax: Free
General/National Adv. E-mail: chief.freepress@unlv.edu
Display Adv. E-mail: marketing.freepress@unlv.edu
Editorial e-mail: managing.freepress@unlv.edu
Primary Website: www.unlvfreepress.com
Year Established: 1955
Advertising (Open Inch Rate) Weekday/Saturday: http://www.unlvfreepress.com/advertise-with-us/
Published: Mon
Avg Paid Circ: 0
Avg Free Circ: 3800
Classified Equipment»
Personnel: Rick Velotta (Adviser); Bianca Cseke (Editor-in-Chief); Blaze Lovell (Managing Editor); Nicole Gallego (Director of Marketing & Sales)

UNIVERSITY OF NEVADA, LAS VEGAS

Street address 1: 4505 S Maryland Pkwy
Street address 3: Las Vegas
Street address state: NV
Zip/Postal code: 89154-9900
Country: USA
Mailing address: PO Box 2011
Mailing city: Las Vegas
Mailing state: NV
Mailing zip: 89125-2011
Advertising Phone: (702) 895-3878
General/National Adv. E-mail: chief.freepress@unlv.edu
Display Adv. E-mail: marketing.freepress@unlv.edu
Editorial e-mail: managing.freepress@unlv.edu
Primary Website: www.unlvfreepress.com
Year Established: 1955
Published: Mon
Avg Free Circ: 3800
Classified Equipment»
Personnel: Bianca Cseke (Editor-in-Chief); Kathy Schreiber (Business Manager); Rick Velotta (Adviser); Blaze Lovell (Managing Editor); Nicole Gallego (Director of Marketing & Sales)

NORTH LAS VEGAS

CMTY. COLLEGE OF SOUTHERN NEVADA

Street address 1: 3200 E Cheyenne Ave
Street address 2: # J2A
Street address 3: North Las Vegas
Street address state: NV
Zip/Postal code: 89030-4228
Country: USA
Mailing address: 3200 E Cheyenne Ave # J2A
Mailing city: North Las Vegas
Mailing state: NV
Mailing zip: 89030-4228
General Phone: (702) 651-4339
General Fax: (702) 643-6427
General/National Adv. E-mail: coyotepressonline@yahoo.com
Classified Equipment»
Personnel: Arnold Vell (Advisor)

UNIV. OF NEVADA

Street address 1: the Nevada Sagebrush, Mail Stop 058
Street address 3: Reno
Street address state: NV
Zip/Postal code: 89557-0001
Country: USA
Mailing address: Mill Stop 58
Mailing city: Reno
Mailing state: NV
Mailing zip: 89557-0001
General Phone: (775) 784-4033
General Fax: (775) 784-1952
Advertising Phone: (775) 784-7773
Editorial e-mail: editor@nevadasagebrush.com
Primary Website: www.nevadasagebrush.com
Classified Equipment»
Personnel: Amy Koeckes (Advisor); Jessica Fryman (Ed. in Chief)

ALBANY COLLEGE OF PHARMACY

Street address 1: 106 New Scotland Ave
Street address 3: Albany
Street address state: NY
Zip/Postal code: 12208-3425
Country: USA
Mailing address: 106 New Scotland Ave
Mailing city: Albany
Mailing state: NY
Mailing zip: 12208-3492
General Phone: (518) 445-7200
General Fax: (518) 445-7202
Classified Equipment»
Personnel: Jennie O'Rourke (Ed.)

COLLEGE OF ST. ROSE

Street address 1: 432 Western Ave
Street address 3: Albany
Street address state: NY
Zip/Postal code: 12203-1400
Country: USA
Mailing address: 432 Western Ave
Mailing city: Albany
Mailing state: NY
Mailing zip: 12203-1490
General Phone: (518) 454-5151
General Fax: (518) 454-2001
General/National Adv. E-mail: chronicle@strose.edu
Primary Website: www.strosechronicle.com
Delivery Methods: Racks
Published: Tues
Classified Equipment»
Personnel: Cailin Brown (Advisor); Josh Heller (Execu Ed); Jonas Miller (Mng Ed)

SUNY/ALBANY

Street address 1: 353 Broadway
Street address 3: Albany
Street address state: NY
Zip/Postal code: 12246-2915
Country: USA
Mailing address: 353 Broadway
Mailing city: Albany
Mailing state: NY
Mailing zip: 12246-2915
General Phone: (518) 442-5666
General Fax: (518) 442-5664
General/National Adv. E-mail: asp_online@hotmail.com
Primary Website: www.albanystudentpress.org
Classified Equipment»
Personnel: Brett Longo (Bus. Mgr.); Ted Bean (Ed. in Chief); Jon Campbell (Mng. Ed.)

ALFRED

ALFRED UNIV.

Street address 1: Powell Campus Ctr
Street address 3: Alfred
Street address state: NY
Country: USA
Mailing address: Powell Campus Ctr.
Mailing city: Alfred
Mailing state: NY
Mailing zip: 14802
General Phone: (607) 871-2192
General Fax: (607) 871-3797
General/National Adv. E-mail: fiatlux@alfred.edu
Primary Website: www.thefiatlux.com/
Classified Equipment»
Personnel: Robyn Goodman (Advisor); Nadine Titus (Adv. Mgr.); Thomas Fleming (Ed. in Chief)

UNIVERSITY AT BUFFALO SCHOOL OF LAW

Street address 1: 410 Obrian Hall
Street address 3: Amherst
Street address state: NY
Zip/Postal code: 14260-1100
Country: USA
Mailing address: 410 O'Brian Hall
Mailing city: Amherst
Mailing state: NY
Mailing zip: 14260-1100
General Phone: (716) 645-3176
General Fax: (716) 645-5940
Editorail Phone: (716) 645-3176
General/National Adv. E-mail: lmueller@buffalo.edu
Editorial e-mail: lmueller@buffalo.edu
Primary Website: www.law.buffalo.edu
Year Established: 2000
Published: Mthly
Avg Free Circ: 12000
Classified Equipment»
Note: This is a HTML-formatted email
Personnel: Kristina Lively (Webmaster)
Parent company (for newspapers): University at Buffalo

ANNANDALE

BARD COLLEGE

Street address 1: PO Box 5000
Street address 3: Annandale
Street address state: NY
Zip/Postal code: 12504-5000
Country: USA
Mailing address: PO Box 5000
Mailing city: Annandale
Mailing state: NY
Mailing zip: 12504-5000
General Phone: (845) 758-7131
General Fax: (845) 758-4294
General/National Adv. E-mail: observer@bard.edu
Primary Website: observer.bard.edu/index.shtml
Classified Equipment»
Personnel: Becca Rom Frank (Ed. in Chief); Lilian Robinson (Ed.); Christine Gehringer (Mng. Ed.)

CAYUGA COMMUNITY COLLEGE

Street address 1: 197 Franklin St
Street address 3: Auburn
Street address state: NY
Zip/Postal code: 13021-3011
Country: USA
Mailing address: 197 Franklin St
Mailing city: Auburn
Mailing state: NY
Mailing zip: 13021-3011
General Phone: (315) 255-1743
General Fax: (315) 255-2117
General/National Adv. E-mail: cayugacollegian@gmail.com
Year Established: 1954
Delivery Methods: Newsstand
Commercial printers: Y
Advertising (Open Inch Rate) Weekday/Saturday: EMAIL FOR RATE SHEET AND POLICY
Published Other: ON ANNOUNCED SCHEDULE
Avg Free Circ: 1000
Classified Equipment»
Personnel: Mary Gelling Merrit (Advisor)

BAYSIDE

QUEENSBOROUGH CMTY. COLLEGE

Street address 1: 22205 56th Ave
Street address 3: Bayside
Street address state: NY
Zip/Postal code: 11364-1432
Country: USA
Mailing address: 22205 56th Ave
Mailing city: Bayside
Mailing state: NY
Mailing zip: 11364-1432
General Phone: (718) 631-6262
General Fax: (718) 631-6637
Primary Website: www.qcc.cuny.edu
Classified Equipment»
Personnel: Andrew Levy (Advisor)

BINGHAMTON

BROOME CMTY. COLLEGE

Street address 1: PO Box 1017
Street address 3: Binghamton
Street address state: NY
Zip/Postal code: 13902-1017
Country: USA
Mailing address: PO Box 1017
Mailing city: Binghamton
Mailing state: NY
Mailing zip: 13902-1017
General Phone: (607) 778-5110
Classified Equipment»
Personnel: Bill Frobe (Ed.)

SUNY/BINGHAMTON

Street address 1: University Union Rm WB03
Street address 3: Binghamton
Street address state: NY
Zip/Postal code: 13902
Country: USA
Mailing address: PO Box 6000
Mailing city: Binghamton
Mailing state: NY
Mailing zip: 13902-6000
General Phone: (607) 777-2515
General Fax: (607) 777-2600
Editorial e-mail: editor@bupipedream.com
Primary Website: www.bupipedream.com
Classified Equipment»
Personnel: Shinsuke Kawano (Bus. Mgr.); Ashley Tarr (Ed. in Chief); Chris Carpenter (Managing Ed.); Melissa Bykofsky (News Ed.); Teressa (Photo Ed.); Marina (Opinion Ed.)

BROCKPORT

THE COLLEGE AT BROCKPORT, SUNY

Street address 1: 350 New Campus Dr
Street address 3: Brockport
Street address state: NY
Zip/Postal code: 14420-2997
Country: USA
Mailing address: 350 New Campus Dr
Mailing city: Brockport
Mailing state: NY
Mailing zip: 14420-2914
General Phone: (585) 395-2230
General/National Adv. E-mail: stylus@brockport.edu
Primary Website: www.brockportstylus.org
Year Established: 1914
Published: Wed
Classified Equipment»
Personnel: Alyssa Daley (Editor-in-Chief); Kristina Livingston (Executive Editor); Victoria Martinez (Managing Editor); Breonnah Colon (Campus Talk Editor); Lou Venditti (News Editor); Alexandra Weaver (Lifestyles Editor); Panagiotis Argitis (Sports Editor)

BRONX

BRONX CMTY. COLLEGE

Street address 1: W 181st St & University Ave
Street address 3: Bronx
Street address state: NY
Zip/Postal code: 10453
Country: USA
Mailing address: W. 181st St. & University Ave.
Mailing city: Bronx
Mailing state: NY
Mailing zip: 10453-2895
General Phone: (718) 289-5445
General Fax: (718) 289-6324
General/National Adv. E-mail: communicator@bcc.cuny.edu
Primary Website: www.bcc.cuny.edu
Classified Equipment»
Personnel: Andrew Rowan (Advisor)

COLLEGE OF MT. ST. VINCENT

Street address 1: 6301 Riverdale Ave
Street address 3: Bronx
Street address state: NY
Zip/Postal code: 10471-1046
Country: USA
Mailing address: The Mount Times
Mailing city: Bronx
Mailing state: NY
Mailing zip: 10471-1093
General Phone: (718) 405-3471
Editorail Phone: (516) 474-5563
General/National Adv. E-mail: mountimes@mountsaintvincent.edu
Editorial e-mail: nquaranto.student@mountsaintvincent.edu
Year Established: 1980
Published: Bi-Mthly
Classified Equipment»
Personnel: Nicole Quaranto (EIC); Micheal Stephens-Emerson (Co-EIC)

CUNY SCHOOLS

Street address 1: 250 Bedford Park Blvd W
Street address 3: Bronx
Street address state: NY
Zip/Postal code: 10468-1527
Country: USA
Mailing address: 250 Bedford Park Blvd W
Mailing city: Bronx
Mailing state: NY
Mailing zip: 10468-1527
General Phone: (718) 960-4966
General Fax: (718) 960-7848
General/National Adv. E-mail: lehmanmeridian@gmail.com
Classified Equipment»
Personnel: Michael Sullivan (Advisor)

FORDHAM UNIV.

Street address 1: 441 E Fordham Rd, Sta 37, Box B
Street address 3: Bronx
Street address state: NY
Zip/Postal code: 10458
Country: USA
Mailing address: 441 E. Fordham Rd., Sta. 37, Box B
Mailing city: Bronx
Mailing state: NY
Mailing zip: 10458
General Phone: (718) 817-4379
General Fax: (718) 817-4319
General/National Adv. E-mail: theram@fordham.edu
Primary Website: www.theramonline.com
Classified Equipment»
Personnel: Beth Knobel (Faculty Advisor); Amanda Fiscina (Ed. in Chief); Abigail Forget (Mng. Ed.)

LEHMAN COLLEGE

Street address 1: 250 Bedford Park Blvd W

Street address 2: Rm 108
Street address 3: Bronx
Street address state: NY
Zip/Postal code: 10468-1527
Country: USA
Mailing address: 250 Bedford Park Blvd W Rm 108
Mailing city: Bronx
Mailing state: NY
Mailing zip: 10468-1589
General Phone: (718) 960-4966
General Fax: (718) 960-8075
General/National Adv. E-mail: lehmanmeridian@gmail.com
Primary Website: www.lcmeridian.com
Published: Mthly
Classified Equipment»
Personnel: Jennifer Mackenzie (Advisor); Alisia Cordero (Ed. in Chief); Sidra Lackey (Mng. Ed.)

MANHATTAN COLLEGE

Street address 1: 4513 Manhattan College Pkwy
Street address 3: Bronx
Street address state: NY
Zip/Postal code: 10471-4004
Country: USA
Mailing address: 4513 Manhattan College Pkwy
Mailing city: Riverdale
Mailing state: NY
Mailing zip: 10471
General Phone: (718) 862-7270
Advertising Phone: (718) 862-8043
General/National Adv. E-mail: thequad@manhatten.edu
Primary Website: www.mcquadrangle.org
Classified Equipment»
Personnel: Jonathan Stone (Ed. in Chief); Dom Delgardo (Exec. Ed.); Brian O'Connor (Mng. Ed.)

BRONXVILLE

WADE WALLERSTEIN

Street address 1: 1 Mead Way
Street address 3: Bronxville
Street address state: NY
Zip/Postal code: 10708-5940
Country: USA
Mailing address: 1 Mead Way
Mailing city: Bronxville
Mailing state: NY
Mailing zip: 10708-5999
General Phone: (973) 856-2617
General Fax: (973) 856-2617
Advertising Phone: (973) 856-2617
Advertising Fax: (973) 856-2617
Editorail Phone: (973) 856-2617
Editorial Fax: (973) 856-2617
General/National Adv. E-mail: phoenix@gm.slc.edu; phoenix@slc.edu
Display Adv. E-mail: phoenix@gm.slc.edu
Editorial e-mail: wwallerstein@gm.slc.edu
Primary Website: sarahlawrencephoenix.com
Classified Equipment»
Personnel: Wade Wallerstein (Editor-in-Chief)

CUNY/BROOKLYN COLLEGE

Street address 1: 2900 Bedford Ave
Street address 3: Brooklyn
Street address state: NY
Zip/Postal code: 11210-2850
Country: USA
Mailing address: 2900 Bedford Ave
Mailing city: Brooklyn
Mailing state: NY
Mailing zip: 11210-2850
General Phone: (718) 951-5000
General Fax: (718) 434-0875
Editorail Phone: (516) 557-5714
General/National Adv. E-mail: Dylc23@gmail.com
Display Adv. E-mail: kingsman.buisness@
Editorial e-mail: Dylc23@gmail.com
Primary Website: http://kingsmanbc.com
Advertising (Open Inch Rate) Weekday/Saturday: DEPENDS
Published: Tues
Classified Equipment»
Personnel: Paul Moses (Advisor)

KINGSBOROUGH CMTY. COLLEGE

Street address 1: 2001 Oriental Blvd
Street address 2: # M230
Street address 3: Brooklyn
Street address state: NY
Zip/Postal code: 11235-2333
Country: USA
Mailing address: 2001 Oriental Blvd # M230
Mailing city: Brooklyn
Mailing state: NY
Mailing zip: 11235-2333
General Phone: (718) 368-5603
General Fax: (718) 368-4833
General/National Adv. E-mail: scepter@kingsborough.edu
Primary Website: www.kbcc.cuny.edu/aboutKCC/Scepter
Classified Equipment»
Personnel: Kim Gill (Ed.)

LONG ISLAND UNIV.

Street address 1: 1 University Plz
Street address 2: Rm S305
Street address 3: Brooklyn
Street address state: NY
Zip/Postal code: 11201-5301
Country: USA
Mailing address: 1 University Plz Rm S305
Mailing city: Brooklyn
Mailing state: NY
Mailing zip: 11201-5301
General Phone: (718) 488-1591
General Fax: (718) 780-4182
General/National Adv. E-mail: seawanhakapress@yahoo.com
Primary Website: seawanhakapress.blogspot.com
Classified Equipment»
Personnel: Hal Bock (Advisor); Ian Smith (Ed. in Chief); Christina Long (News Ed.)

MEDGAR EVERS COLLEGE OF CUNY

Street address 1: 1637 Bedford Ave
Street address 2: Rm S-304
Street address 3: Brooklyn
Street address state: NY
Zip/Postal code: 11225-2001
Country: USA
Mailing address: 1637 Bedford Ave Rm S-304
Mailing city: Brooklyn
Mailing state: NY
Mailing zip: 11225-2001
General Phone: (718) 270-6436
General/National Adv. E-mail: adafi@mec.cuny.edu; student-club@mec.cuny.edu
Primary Website: www.adafi.org
Classified Equipment»
Personnel: Robin Regina Ford (Advisor); Luc Josaphat (Ed. in Chief); Samantha Sylvester (Mng. Ed.)

POLYTECHNIC INSTITUTE OF NYU

Street address 1: 6 Metrotech Ctr
Street address 3: Brooklyn
Street address state: NY
Zip/Postal code: 11201-3840
Country: USA
Mailing address: 6 Metrotech Ctr
Mailing city: Brooklyn
Mailing state: NY
Mailing zip: 11201-3840
General Phone: (718) 260-3600
Primary Website: www.poly.edu
Classified Equipment»
Personnel: Lowell Scheiner (Advisor); Robert Griffin (Coord.); William Modeste Jr. (Ed. in Chief); Cheryl Mcnear (Business Adviser)

PRATT INSTITUTE

Street address 1: 200 Willoughby Ave
Street address 3: Brooklyn
Street address state: NY
Zip/Postal code: 11205-3802
Country: USA
Mailing address: 200 Willoughby Ave
Mailing city: Brooklyn
Mailing state: NY
Mailing zip: 11205
General Phone: 7186363600
General/National Adv. E-mail: theprattler@gmail.com
Editorial e-mail: theprattler@gmail.com
Primary Website: www.prattleronline.com
Year Established: 1940
Published: Other
Classified Equipment»
Personnel: Emily Oldenquist (Ed. in Cheif)

ST. FRANCIS COLLEGE

Street address 1: 180 Remsen St
Street address 3: Brooklyn
Street address state: NY
Zip/Postal code: 11201-4305
Country: USA
Mailing address: 180 Remsen St
Mailing city: Brooklyn
Mailing state: NY
Mailing zip: 11201-4398
General Phone: (718) 522-2300
General Fax: (718) 522-1274
General/National Adv. E-mail: sscvoice@gmail.com
Classified Equipment»
Personnel: Emily Horowitz (Advisor); Kevin Korber (Ed.)

BROOKVILLE

LONG ISLAND UNIV./C.W.POST

Street address 1: Hillwood Commons, Rm 199, 720 Northern Blvd (25A)
Street address 3: Brookville
Street address state: NY
Zip/Postal code: 11548
Country: USA
Mailing address: Hillwood Commons, Rm. 199, 720 Northern Blvd. (25A)
Mailing city: Brookville
Mailing state: NY
Mailing zip: 11548
General Phone: (516) 299-2619
General Fax: (516) 299-2617
General/National Adv. E-mail: pioneer@cwpost.liu.edu
Year Established: 1954
Classified Equipment»
Personnel: Valerie Kellogg (Advisor); Daniel Schrafel (Ed. in Chief); Lisa Martens (News Ed.)

CANISIUS COLLEGE

Street address 1: 2001 Main St
Street address 3: Buffalo
Street address state: NY
Zip/Postal code: 14208-1035
Country: USA
Mailing address: 2001 Main St
Mailing city: Buffalo
Mailing state: NY
Mailing zip: 14208-1098
General Phone: (716) 888-2115
General Fax: (716) 888-3118
General/National Adv. E-mail: Irwin@canisius.edu
Classified Equipment»
Personnel: Barbara Irwin (Professor of Communications); Eric Koehler (Ed.); Jennifer Gorczynski (Ed.); Marisa Loffredo (News Ed.)

MEDAILLE COLLEGE

Street address 1: 18 Agassiz Cir
Street address 3: Buffalo
Street address state: NY
Zip/Postal code: 14214-2601
Country: USA
Mailing address: 18 Agassiz Cir
Mailing city: Buffalo
Mailing state: NY
Mailing zip: 14214-2695
General Phone: (716) 884-3281
General Fax: (716) 884-0291
Primary Website: www.medailleperspective.com
Classified Equipment»
Personnel: Lisa Murphy (Advisor); Megan Fitzgerald (Ed.)

SUNY COLLEGE/BUFFALO

Street address 1: 1300 Elmwood Ave, Student Union 414
Street address 3: Buffalo
Street address state: NY
Zip/Postal code: 14222
Country: USA
Mailing address: 1300 Elmwood Ave., Student Union 414
Mailing city: Buffalo
Mailing state: NY
Mailing zip: 14222
General Phone: (716) 878-4531
General Fax: (716) 878-4532
General/National Adv. E-mail: bscrecord@gmail.com
Display Adv. E-mail: pignatelli.record@live.com
Editorial e-mail: bscrecord@gmail.com
Primary Website: www.bscrecord.com
Year Established: 1913
Published: Wed
Avg Free Circ: 1500
Classified Equipment»
Personnel: Brandon Schlager (Managing Editor); Mike Meiler (Executive Editor); Brian Alexander (Opinion Editor); Michael Canfield (News Editor); Tom Gallagher (Sports Editor); Jennifer Waters (Culture Editor)

SUNY/BUFFALO

Street address 1: 132 Student Un
Street address 3: Buffalo
Street address state: NY
Zip/Postal code: 14260-2100
Country: USA
Mailing address: 132 Student Un
Mailing city: Buffalo
Mailing state: NY
Mailing zip: 14260-2100
General Phone: (716) 645-2152
General Fax: (716) 645-2766
General/National Adv. E-mail: spectrum@buffalo.edu
Primary Website: www.ubspectrum.com
Classified Equipment»
Personnel: Debbie Smith (Bus. Mgr.); Steven Marth (Ed. in Chief)

ST. LAWRENCE UNIV.

Street address 1: 23 Romoda Dr
Street address 3: Canton
Street address state: NY
Zip/Postal code: 13617-1423
Country: USA
Mailing address: 23 Romoda Dr
Mailing city: Canton
Mailing state: NY
Mailing zip: 13617-1501
General Phone: (315) 229-5139
General/National Adv. E-mail: hillnews@stlawu.edu
Primary Website: www.blogs.stlawu.edu/thehillnews
Classified Equipment»
Personnel: Juri Kittler (Advisor); Rachel Barman (Ed.)

SUNY COLLEGE OF TECHNOLOGY/ CANTON

Street address 1: 34 Cornell Dr
Street address 2: Ofc
Street address 3: Canton
Street address state: NY
Zip/Postal code: 13617-1037
Country: USA
Mailing address: 34 Cornell Dr Ofc
Mailing city: Canton
Mailing state: NY
Mailing zip: 13617-1037
General Phone: (315) 386-7315
General Fax: (315) 386-7962
General/National Adv. E-mail: quinells@canton.edu
Classified Equipment»
Personnel: Scott Quinell (Advisor)

CENTRAL ISLIP

TOURO COLLEGE JACOB D. FUCHSBERG LAW CENTER

Street address 1: 225 Eastview Dr
Street address 3: Central Islip
Street address state: NY
Zip/Postal code: 11722-4539
Country: USA
Mailing address: 225 Eastview Dr

Mailing city: Central Islip
Mailing state: NY
Mailing zip: 11722-4539
General Phone: (631) 761-7000
General Fax: (631) 761-7009
Primary Website: www.tourolaw.edu
Classified Equipment»
Personnel: Patti Desrochers (Dir. Comm.)

HAMILTON COLLEGE

Street address 1: 198 College Hill Rd
Street address 3: Clinton
Street address state: NY
Zip/Postal code: 13323-1218
Country: USA
Mailing address: 198 College Hill Rd
Mailing city: Clinton
Mailing state: NY
Mailing zip: 13323-1295
General Phone: (315) 859-4011
General Fax: (315) 859-4563
Classified Equipment»
Personnel: Erin W. Hoener (Ed. in Chief)

CORNING

CORNING CMTY. COLLEGE

Street address 1: 1 Academic Dr
Street address 3: Corning
Street address state: NY
Zip/Postal code: 14830-3297
Country: USA
Mailing address: 1 Academic Dr
Mailing city: Corning
Mailing state: NY
Mailing zip: 14830-3299
General Phone: (607) 962-9339
General Fax: (607) 962-9008
General/National Adv. E-mail: criernewspaper@yahoo.com
Classified Equipment»
Personnel: Paul McNaney (Advisor)

CORTLAND

SUNY COLLEGE/CORTLAND

Street address 1: PO Box 2000
Street address 3: Cortland
Street address state: NY
Zip/Postal code: 13045-0900
Country: USA
Mailing address: PO Box 2000
Mailing city: Cortland
Mailing state: NY
Mailing zip: 13045-0900
General Phone: (607) 753-2803
General/National Adv. E-mail: dragonchronicle@cortland.edu
Primary Website: www.cortland.edu
Classified Equipment»

DELHI

SUNY COLLEGE OF TECHNOLOGY/DELHI

Street address 1: 454 Delhi Dr
Street address 2: 222 Farrell Center
Street address 3: Delhi
Street address state: NY
Zip/Postal code: 13753-4454
Country: USA
Mailing address: 222 Farrell Center
Mailing city: Delhi
Mailing state: NY
Mailing zip: 13753
General Phone: (607) 746-4270
General Fax: (607) 746-4323
Advertising Phone: (607) 746-4573
Advertising Fax: (607) 746-4323
Editorail Phone: (607) 746-4573
Editorial Fax: (607) 746-4323
General/National Adv. E-mail: campusvoice@delhi.edu
Display Adv. E-mail: campusvoice@delhi.edu
Editorial e-mail: campusvoice@delhi.edu
Primary Website: http://www.delhi.edu/campus-life/activities/campus-voice/index.php
Published: Mthly
Classified Equipment»
Personnel: Christina Viafore (Advisor)

DOBBS FERRY

MERCY COLLEGE

Street address 1: 555 Broadway
Street address 3: Dobbs Ferry
Street address state: NY
Zip/Postal code: 10522-1186
Country: USA
Mailing address: 555 Broadway Frnt
Mailing city: Dobbs Ferry
Mailing state: NY
Mailing zip: 10522-1189
General Phone: (914) 674-7422
General Fax: (914) 674-7433
General/National Adv. E-mail: mercyimpactnews@hotmail.com
Primary Website: www.theimpactnews.com
Classified Equipment»
Personnel: Michael Perrota (Advisor)

ELMIRA

ELMIRA COLLEGE

Street address 1: 1 Park Pl
Street address 3: Elmira
Street address state: NY
Zip/Postal code: 14901-2085
Country: USA
Mailing address: 1 Park Pl
Mailing city: Elmira
Mailing state: NY
Mailing zip: 14901-2099
General Phone: (607) 735-1800
Advertising Phone: (607) 735-1758
General/National Adv. E-mail: octagon@elmira.edu; admissions@elmira.edu
Primary Website: www.elmira.edu
Classified Equipment»
Personnel: David Williams (Advisor); Jolene Carr (Ed.)

FARMINGDALE

SUNY COLLEGE OF TECHNOLOGY/FARMINGDALE

Street address 1: Melville Rd, Roosevelt Hall
Street address 3: Farmingdale
Street address state: NY
Zip/Postal code: 11735
Country: USA
Mailing address: Melville Rd., Roosevelt Hall
Mailing city: Farmingdale
Mailing state: NY
Mailing zip: 11735
General Phone: (631) 420-2611
General Fax: (631) 420-2692
General/National Adv. E-mail: rambler@farmingdale.edu
Classified Equipment»
Personnel: Jeff Borga (Ed. in Chief)

FLUSHING

QUEENS COLLEGE/CUNY

Street address 1: 6530 Kissena Blvd
Street address 2: Student Union Rm. LL-34
Street address 3: Flushing
Street address state: NY
Zip/Postal code: 11367-1575
Country: USA
Mailing address: 6530 Kissena Blvd
Mailing city: Flushing
Mailing state: NY
Mailing zip: 11367-1597
General Phone: (718) 997-5000
Advertising Fax: (718) 997-3755
General/National Adv. E-mail: info@theknightnews.com
Primary Website: www.theknightnews.com
Published: Tues
Classified Equipment»
Personnel: Gerry Solomon (Advisor); Will Sammon (Editor-in-Chief); Andrea Hardalo (Editor-in-Chief)

NASSAU CMTY. COLLEGE

Street address 1: College Ctr, 1 Education Dr
Street address 3: Garden City
Street address state: NY
Zip/Postal code: 11530
Country: USA
Mailing address: College Ctr., 1 Education Dr.
Mailing city: Garden City
Mailing state: NY
Mailing zip: 11530-6793
General Phone: (516) 222-7071
General Fax: (516) 572-3566
General/National Adv. E-mail: informationservices@ncc.edu; vignetters@yahoo.com
Classified Equipment»
Personnel: Richard Conway (Advisor)

GENESEO

SUNY COLLEGE AT GENESEO

Street address 1: 10 Macvittie Cir
Street address 2: # 42
Street address 3: Geneseo
Street address state: NY
Zip/Postal code: 14454-1427
Country: USA
Mailing address: 10 Macvittie Cir # 42
Mailing city: Geneseo
Mailing state: NY
Mailing zip: 14454-1427
General Phone: (585) 245-5896
General Fax: (585) 245-5284
Advertising Phone: (585) 245-5890
General/National Adv. E-mail: lamron@geneseo.edu
Display Adv. E-mail: lamronad@geneseo.edu
Primary Website: www.thelamron.com
Year Established: 1922
Published: Thur
Avg Free Circ: 3000
Classified Equipment»
Personnel: Maddy Smith (Advisor); Maria Lima (Advisor); Tom Wilder (Ed. in Chief)

GENEVA

HOBART & WILLIAM SMITH COLLEGE

Street address 1: 300 Pulteney St
Street address 3: Geneva
Street address state: NY
Zip/Postal code: 14456-3304
Country: USA
Mailing address: 300 Pulteney St
Mailing city: Geneva
Mailing state: NY
Mailing zip: 14456-3382
General Phone: (315) 781-3857
General/National Adv. E-mail: herald@hws.edu
Classified Equipment»
Personnel: Charlie Wilson (Advisor); Belinda Littlefield (Ed.)

GREENWICH

NEW YORK METRO COMMUNITY COLLEGES

Street address 1: 39 County Route 70
Street address 3: Greenwich
Street address state: NY
Zip/Postal code: 12834-6300
Country: USA
Mailing address: 39 County Route 70
Mailing city: Greenwich
Mailing state: NY
Mailing zip: 12834
General Phone: (518) 879 0965
General Fax: (518) 507 6782
Advertising Phone: (518) 879 0965
Advertising Fax: (518) 507 6782
General/National Adv. E-mail: editor@campus-news.org
Display Adv. E-mail: advertising@campus-news.org
Editorial e-mail: editor@campus-news.org
Primary Website: www.campus-news.org
Year Established: 2010
Advertising (Open Inch Rate) Weekday/Saturday: Available
Published: Mthly`Bi-Mthly
Avg Free Circ: 10000
Classified Equipment»
Note: Community College Campus News hits 37 2-year colleges in the Northeast; mostly in the New York Metro region.
Personnel: Darren Johnson (Advisor)

HILBERT COLLEGE

Street address 1: 5200 S Park Ave
Street address 3: Hamburg
Street address state: NY
Zip/Postal code: 14075-1519
Country: USA
Mailing address: 5200 S Park Ave
Mailing city: Hamburg
Mailing state: NY
Mailing zip: 14075-1597
General Phone: (716) 649-7900
General Fax: (716) 649-0702
General/National Adv. E-mail: info@hilbert.edu
Primary Website: www.hilbert.edu
Published Other: 3 months in fall & spring
Classified Equipment»
Personnel: Charles A. S. Ernst (Advisor)

HAMILTON

COLGATE UNIV.

Street address 1: 13 Oak Dr
Street address 2: Student Union
Street address 3: Hamilton
Street address state: NY
Zip/Postal code: 13346-1338
Country: USA
Mailing address: Student Union
Mailing city: Hamilton
Mailing state: NY
Mailing zip: 13346
General Phone: (315) 228-7744
General Fax: (315) 228-6839
General/National Adv. E-mail: maroonnews@colgate.edu
Display Adv. E-mail: ads.maroonnews@gmail.com
Editorial e-mail: colgatemaroonnews@gmail.com
Primary Website: thecolgatemaroonnews.com
Year Established: 1868
Published: Thur
Avg Free Circ: 1600
Classified Equipment»
Personnel: Matthew Knowles (Ed.); Luke Currim (Ed.); Amanda Golden (Exec. Ed.)

HOFSTRA UNIV.

Street address 1: 200 Hofstra Univ, Rm 203 Student Ctr
Street address 3: Hempstead
Street address state: NY
Zip/Postal code: 11550
Country: USA
Mailing address: 200 Hofstra Univ., Rm. 203 Student Ctr.
Mailing city: Hempstead
Mailing state: NY
Mailing zip: 11550-1022
General Phone: (516) 463-6965
General Fax: (516) 463-6977
Primary Website: www.hofstrachronicle.com
Published: Tues
Classified Equipment»
Personnel: Peter Goodman (Advisor)

HOFSTRA UNIVERSITY

Street address 1: 200 Hofstra University, Student Ctr, Room 203
Street address 3: Hempstead
Street address state: NY
Zip/Postal code: 48202

Country: USA
Mailing address: 200 Hofstra University, Student Ctr., Room 203
Mailing city: Hempstead
Mailing state: NY
Mailing zip: 11550
General Phone: (516) 463-6921
General/National Adv. E-mail: hofstrachronicle@gmail.com
Display Adv. E-mail: thechronicle.business@gmail.com
Primary Website: www.thehofstrachronicle.com
Year Established: 1935
Published: Thur
Avg Free Circ: 3000
Classified Equipment»
Personnel: Jake Nussbaum (Business Manager)

HOUGHTON COLLEGE

Street address 1: 1 Willard Ave
Street address 2: Cpo 378
Street address 3: Houghton
Street address state: NY
Zip/Postal code: 14744-8732
Country: USA
Mailing address: 1 Willard Ave Cpo 378
Mailing city: Houghton
Mailing state: NY
Mailing zip: 14744-8732
General Phone: (585) 567-9500
General Fax: (585) 567-9570
General/National Adv. E-mail: star@houghton.edu
Primary Website: www.houghtonstar.com
Classified Equipment»
Personnel: Joel Vanderweele (Ed. in Chief)

HYDE PARK

CULINARY INSTITUTE OF AMERICA

Street address 1: 1946 Campus Dr
Street address 3: Hyde Park
Street address state: NY
Zip/Postal code: 12538-1430
Country: USA
Mailing address: 1946 Campus Dr
Mailing city: Hyde Park
Mailing state: NY
Mailing zip: 12538-1499
General Phone: (845) 452-1412
General Fax: (845) 451-1093
General/National Adv. E-mail: lapapillote@culinary.edu
Primary Website: www.ciachef.edu
Year Established: 1979
Published: Fri`Mthly
Classified Equipment»
Personnel: David Whalen (Advisor)

ITHACA

CORNELL LAW SCHOOL

Street address 1: Myron Taylor Hall
Street address 3: Ithaca
Street address state: NY
Zip/Postal code: 14853
Country: USA
Mailing address: Myron Taylor Hall
Mailing city: Ithaca
Mailing state: NY
Mailing zip: 14853
General Phone: (607) 255-0565
Classified Equipment»
Personnel: Rick Silverman (Ed.)

CORNELL UNIV. ECONOMICS SCHOOL

Street address 1: Cornell Dept of Economics, Uris Hall, 4th Fl
Street address 3: Ithaca
Street address state: NY
Zip/Postal code: 14850
Country: USA
Mailing address: Cornell Dept. of Economics, Uris Hall, 4th Fl.
Mailing city: Ithaca
Mailing state: NY
Mailing zip: 14850
General Phone: (607) 255-8501
Primary Website: www.rso.cornell.edu/ces
Classified Equipment»
Personnel: Rabia Muqaddam (Ed. in Chief)

ITHACA COLLEGE

Street address 1: 269 Park Hall
Street address 3: Ithaca
Street address state: NY
Zip/Postal code: 14850-7258
Country: USA
Mailing address: 269 Park Hall
Mailing city: Ithaca
Mailing state: NY
Mailing zip: 14850-7258
General Phone: (607) 274-3208
General Fax: (607) 274-1376
Advertising Phone: (607) 274-1618
General/National Adv. E-mail: ithacan@ithaca.edu
Display Adv. E-mail: ithacanads@ithaca.edu
Primary Website: www.theithacan.org
Advertising (Open Inch Rate) Weekday/Saturday: $7.50 per column inch
Published: Thur
Avg Free Circ: 4000
Classified Equipment»
Personnel: Michael Serino (Advisor); Kira Maddox (Ed. in Chief); Rachel Wolfgang (Mng. Ed.); Lawrence Hamacher (Advertising Sales Manager)

THE CORNELL DAILY SUN

Street address 1: 139 W State St
Street address 3: Ithaca
Street address state: NY
Zip/Postal code: 14850-5427
Country: USA
Mailing address: 139 W State St
Mailing city: Ithaca
Mailing state: NY
Mailing zip: 14850-5427
General Phone: (607) 273-3606
General Fax: (607) 273-0746
General/National Adv. E-mail: letters@cornelldailysun.com
Primary Website: www.cornellsun.com
Year Established: 1880
Classified Equipment»
Personnel: Ben Gitlin (Editor in Chief); Michael Linhorst (Managing Editor); Dani Neuharth-Keusch (Associate Editor); Rahul Kishore (Web Editor); Chloe Gatta (Business Manager); Helene Beauchemin (Advertising Manager); Justin wheeler (Bus. Mgr.); Keenan Weatherford (Ed. in Chief); Michael J. Stratford (Managing Ed.); Sophia Qasir (Advertising Mgr.)

ST. JOHN'S UNIVERSITY

Street address 1: 8000 Utopia Pkwy
Street address 3: Jamaica
Street address state: NY
Zip/Postal code: 11439-9000
Country: USA
Mailing address: 8000 Utopia Pkwy
Mailing city: Jamaica
Mailing state: NY
Mailing zip: 11439-9000
General Phone: (718) 990-6756
General Fax: (718) 990-5849
Display Adv. E-mail: torchads@gmail.com
Editorial e-mail: torchnews@gmail.com
Primary Website: www.torchonline.com
Published: Wed
Avg Free Circ: 3000
Classified Equipment»
Personnel: Michael Cunniff (Editor-in-Chief)

YORK COLLEGE OF CUNY

Street address 1: 9420 Guy R Brewer Blvd
Street address 3: Jamaica
Street address state: NY
Zip/Postal code: 11451-0001
Country: USA
Mailing address: 9420 Guy R Brewer Blvd
Mailing city: Jamaica
Mailing state: NY
Mailing zip: 11451-0002
General Phone: (718) 262-2529
General Fax: (718) 262-5234
General/National Adv. E-mail: pandora@york.cuny.edu
Display Adv. E-mail: pandora@york.cuny.edu
Editorial e-mail: pandora@york.cuny.edu
Primary Website: http://pbwire.cunycampuswire.com/
Year Established: 1967
Published: Mthly
Avg Paid Circ: 0
Avg Free Circ: 3000
Classified Equipment»
Personnel: William Hughes (Advisor)

KEUKA PARK

KEUKA COLLEGE

Street address 1: Office of Commun
Street address 3: Keuka Park
Street address state: NY
Zip/Postal code: 14478
Country: USA
Mailing address: Office of Commun.
Mailing city: Keuka Park
Mailing state: NY
Mailing zip: 14478
General Phone: (315) 279-5231
General Fax: (315) 279-5281
Primary Website: www.keukonian.keuka.edu
Classified Equipment»
Personnel: Christen Smith (Advisor); Kilee Brown (Ed.); Chelsea DeGroote (Asst. Ed.)

LOCH SHELDRAKE

SUNY SULLIVAN

Street address 1: 112 College Rd
Street address 3: Loch Sheldrake
Street address state: NY
Zip/Postal code: 12759-5721
Country: USA
Mailing address: 112 College Rd
Mailing city: Loch Sheldrake
Mailing state: NY
Mailing zip: 12759-5721
General Phone: (845) 434-5750
General Fax: (914) 434-4806
Primary Website: www.sunysullivan.edu
Published: Mon
Classified Equipment»
Personnel: Kathleen Birkett (Admin. Asst.)

LONG ISLAND CITY

CUNY SCHOOL OF LAW

Street address 1: 2 Court Sq
Street address 3: Long Island City
Street address state: NY
Zip/Postal code: 11101-4356
Country: USA
Mailing address: 2 Court Sq
Mailing city: Long Island City
Mailing state: NY
Mailing zip: 11101-4356
General Phone: (718) 340-4222
Primary Website: www.law.cuny.edu
Classified Equipment»
Parent company (for newspapers): City University of New York

LOUDONVILLE

SIENA COLLEGE

Street address 1: 515 Loudon Rd, Student Union
Street address 3: Loudonville
Street address state: NY
Zip/Postal code: 12211
Country: USA
Mailing address: 515 Loudon Rd., Student Union
Mailing city: Loudonville
Mailing state: NY
Mailing zip: 12211-1459
General Phone: (518) 783-2330
General Fax: (518) 786-5053
General/National Adv. E-mail: newspaper@siena.edu
Display Adv. E-mail: newspaper@siena.edu
Editorial e-mail: newspaper@siena.edu
Primary Website: www.siena.edu
Year Established: 1937
Advertising (Open Inch Rate) Weekday/Saturday: Yes
Published: Fri
Published Other: Published biweekly
Avg Paid Circ: 0
Avg Free Circ: 500
Classified Equipment»
Personnel: Emily Radigan (Editor-in-Chief)

ORANGE COUNTY CMTY. COLLEGE

Street address 1: 115 South St
Street address 3: Middletown
Street address state: NY
Zip/Postal code: 10940-6404
Country: USA
Mailing address: 115 South St
Mailing city: Middletown
Mailing state: NY
Mailing zip: 10940-6404
General Phone: (845) 341-4240
General Fax: (845) 341-4238
Classified Equipment»

MORRISVILLE

MORRISVILLE STATE COLLEGE

Street address 1: Journalism Dept
Street address 3: Morrisville
Street address state: NY
Zip/Postal code: 10901
Country: USA
Mailing address: Journalism Dept.
Mailing city: Morrisville
Mailing state: NY
Mailing zip: 13408
General Phone: (315) 684-6041
General Fax: (315) 684-6247
General/National Adv. E-mail: chimes@morrisville.edu
Display Adv. E-mail: mcdowebl@morrisville.edu
Primary Website: thechimes.morrisville.edu
Classified Equipment»
Personnel: Brian McDowell (Advisor)

NEW PALTZ

SUNY COLLEGE/NEW PALTZ

Street address 1: Rm 417, Student Union Bldg, 1 Hawk Dr
Street address 3: New Paltz
Street address state: NY
Zip/Postal code: 12561
Country: USA
Mailing address: Rm. 417, Student Union Bldg., 1 Hawk Dr.
Mailing city: New Paltz
Mailing state: NY
Mailing zip: 12561
General Phone: (845) 257-3030
General Fax: (845) 257-3031
General/National Adv. E-mail: oracle@hawkmail.newpaltz.edu
Primary Website: http://oracle.newpaltz.edu
Published: Thur
Classified Equipment»
Personnel: Melisa Goldman (Bus. Mgr.); Emma Boddors (Ed.); Andrew Wyrich (Editor-in-Chief)

NEW ROCHELLE

COLLEGE OF NEW ROCHELLE

Street address 1: 29 Castle Pl
Street address 3: New Rochelle
Street address state: NY
Zip/Postal code: 10805-2330
Country: USA
Mailing address: 29 Castle Pl Ste 1
Mailing city: New Rochelle
Mailing state: NY
Mailing zip: 10805-2339
General Phone: (914) 654-5207
General Fax: (914) 654-5866
General/National Adv. E-mail: tatler@cnr.edu

Classified Equipment»
Personnel: Elizabeth Brinkman (Advisor)

IONA COLLEGE

Street address 1: 715 North Ave, Lapenta Student Union, 2nd Fl
Street address 3: New Rochelle
Street address state: NY
Zip/Postal code: 10801
Country: USA
Mailing address: 715 North Ave., LaPenta Student Union, 2nd Fl.
Mailing city: New Rochelle
Mailing state: NY
Mailing zip: 10801-1830
General Phone: (914) 633-2370
General/National Adv. E-mail: ionian@iona.edu
Primary Website: www.iona.edu
Classified Equipment»
Personnel: Hugh Short (Moderator); James Hurley (Ed. in Chief); Alana Rome (Mng. Ed.); Heather Nannery (News Ed.)

BARNARD COLLEGE

Street address 1: 3009 Broadway
Street address 3: New York
Street address state: NY
Zip/Postal code: 10027-6909
Country: USA
Mailing address: 3009 Broadway Frnt 1
Mailing city: New York
Mailing state: NY
Mailing zip: 10027-6598
General Phone: (212) 854-5262
General Fax: (212) 854-6220
General/National Adv. E-mail: bulletinedboard@gmail.com; backcover@barnardbulletin.com
Primary Website: barnardbulletin.com
Classified Equipment»
Personnel: Iffat Kabeer (Adv. Mgr.); Alison Hodgson (Ed. Emer.); Meagan McElroy (Mng. Ed.)

BARUCH COLLEGE/CUNY

Street address 1: 1 Bernard Baruch Way
Street address 2: Ste 3-290
Street address 3: New York
Street address state: NY
Zip/Postal code: 10010-5585
Country: USA
Mailing address: 1 Bernard Baruch Way Ste 3-290
Mailing city: New York
Mailing state: NY
Mailing zip: 10010-5585
General Phone: (646) 312-4712
General Fax: (646) 312-4711
Primary Website: www.theticker.org
Classified Equipment»
Personnel: Carl Aylman (Dir., Student Lant); Jhaneel Lockhart (Ed. in Chief)

BOROUGH OF MANHATTAN CMTY. COLLEGE

Street address 1: 199 Chambers St
Street address 2: Rm S-207
Street address 3: New York
Street address state: NY
Zip/Postal code: 10007-1044
Country: USA
Mailing address: 199 Chambers St Rm S-207
Mailing city: New York
Mailing state: NY
Mailing zip: 10007-1044
General Phone: (212) 220-8000
Primary Website: www.bmcc.cuny.edu
Classified Equipment»
Personnel: Dr. Juliet Emanuel (Advisor)

CARDOZO SCHOOL OF LAW/ YESHIVA

Street address 1: 55 5th Ave
Street address 2: Ste 119
Street address 3: New York
Street address state: NY
Zip/Postal code: 10003-4301
Country: USA
Mailing address: 55 5th Ave Fl 6
Mailing city: New York
Mailing state: NY
Mailing zip: 10003-4301
General Phone: (212) 790-0283
General Fax: (212) 790-0345
General/National Adv. E-mail: cardozoinsider@att.net
Classified Equipment»
Personnel: Heela Justin (Ed.)

CITY COLLEGE OF NEW YORK

Street address 1: Rm 1-119, North Academic Center Bldg, 160 Convent Ave
Street address 3: New York
Street address state: NY
Zip/Postal code: 10031
Country: USA
Mailing address: Rm. 1-119, North Academic Center Bldg., 160 Convent Ave.
Mailing city: New York
Mailing state: NY
Mailing zip: 10031
General Phone: (212) 650-8177
General Fax: (212) 650-8197
General/National Adv. E-mail: ccnycampus@gmail.com
Primary Website: www.ccnycampus.com
Classified Equipment»
Personnel: Linda Villarosa (Advisor); Tania Bhuiyan (Bus. Mgr.)

COLUMBIA UNIV.

Street address 1: 2875 Broadway
Street address 2: Ste 3
Street address 3: New York
Street address state: NY
Zip/Postal code: 10025-7847
Country: USA
Mailing address: 2875 Broadway Ste 3
Mailing city: New York
Mailing state: NY
Mailing zip: 10025-7847
General Phone: (212) 854-9550
General Fax: (212) 854-9553
General/National Adv. E-mail: info@columbiaspectator.com; spectator@columbia.edu
Primary Website: www.columbiaspectator.com
Classified Equipment»
Personnel: Akhil Mehta (Pub.); Ben Cotton (Ed. in Chief); Thomas Rhiel (Managing Ed.); Andrew Hitti (Dir., Sales); Oscar (Dir., Fin); Yipeng (Dir.)

COLUMBIA UNIV. BUS. SCHOOL

Street address 1: 3022 Broadway
Street address 2: Rm 242
Street address 3: New York
Street address state: NY
Zip/Postal code: 10027-6945
Country: USA
Mailing address: 3022 Broadway Rm 242
Mailing city: New York
Mailing state: NY
Mailing zip: 10027-6945
General Phone: (212) 854-8396
General Fax: (212) 854-7557
Classified Equipment»
Personnel: Matt Wong (Bus. Mgr.)

COLUMBIA UNIV. LAW SCHOOL

Street address 1: 435 W 116th St
Street address 3: New York
Street address state: NY
Zip/Postal code: 10027-7237
Country: USA
Mailing address: 435 W 116th St
Mailing city: New York
Mailing state: NY
Mailing zip: 10027-7237
General Phone: (212) 854-5833
General Fax: (212) 854-1229
General/National Adv. E-mail: jar2045@columbia.edu
Classified Equipment»
Personnel: Matthew Dean (Ed.)

COOPER UNION

Street address 1: 30 Cooper Sq
Street address 3: New York
Street address state: NY
Zip/Postal code: 10003-7120
Country: USA
Mailing address: 30 Cooper Sq Fl 3
Mailing city: New York
Mailing state: NY
Mailing zip: 10003-7120
General Phone: (212) 353-4133
General Fax: (212) 353-4343
Editorial e-mail: Cooperpioneer@gmail.com
Classified Equipment»
Personnel: Bill McAllister (ed.)

FASHION INST. OF TECHNOLOGY

Street address 1: 227 W 27th St
Street address 2: Ste A727
Street address 3: New York
Street address state: NY
Zip/Postal code: 10001-5902
Country: USA
Mailing address: 227 W 27th St Ste A727
Mailing city: New York
Mailing state: NY
Mailing zip: 10001-5902
General Phone: (212) 217-7999
General Fax: (212) 217-7144
General/National Adv. E-mail: w27newspaper@gmail.com
Primary Website: www.fitnyc.edu
Classified Equipment»
Personnel: Richard Baleschrino (Advisor)

FORDHAM UNIV. LINCOLN CENTER

Street address 1: 140 W 62nd St
Street address 2: Rm G-32
Street address 3: New York
Street address state: NY
Zip/Postal code: 10023-7407
Country: USA
Mailing address: 140 W. 62nd St., Rm. G-32
Mailing city: New York
Mailing state: NY
Mailing zip: 10023-7414
General Phone: (212) 636-6280
General Fax: (212) 636-7047
General/National Adv. E-mail: fordhamobserver@gmail.com
Display Adv. E-mail: fordhamobserveradvertising@gmail.com
Primary Website: www.fordhamobserver.com
Published: Other
Classified Equipment»
Personnel: Elizabeth Stone (Advisor); Ashley WennersHerron (Ed. in Chief)

HUNTER COLLEGE/CUNY

Street address 1: 695 Park Ave
Street address 2: Rm 211
Street address 3: New York
Street address state: NY
Zip/Postal code: 10065-5024
Country: USA
Mailing address: 695 Park Ave Rm 211
Mailing city: New York
Mailing state: NY
Mailing zip: 10065-5024
General Phone: (212) 772-4251
General Fax: (212) 772-5539
Primary Website: www.thehunterenvoy.com
Classified Equipment»
Personnel: Joe Ireland (Ed. in Chief)

JEWISH STUDENT PRESS SERVICE

Street address 1: 114 W 26th St
Street address 2: Rm 1004
Street address 3: New York
Street address state: NY
Zip/Postal code: 10001-6812
Country: USA
Mailing address: 114 W 26th St Rm 1004
Mailing city: New York
Mailing state: NY
Mailing zip: 10001-6812
General Phone: (212) 675-1168
General Fax: (212) 929-3459
Primary Website: www.newvoices.org
Year Established: 1970
Classified Equipment»
Personnel: Ben Sales (Ed.)

JOHN JAY COLLEGE OF CRIMINAL JUSTICE

Street address 1: 899 10th Ave
Street address 3: New York
Street address state: NY
Zip/Postal code: 10019-1069
Country: USA
Mailing address: 524 W 59th St
Mailing city: New York
Mailing state: NY
Mailing zip: 10019-1007
General Phone: (212) 237-8308
General Fax: (212) 237-8036
Classified Equipment»
Personnel: Babafunmilayo Oke (Ed.)

NEW YORK INSTITUTE OF TECHNOLOGY

Street address 1: 1849 Broadway
Street address 2: Rm 212
Street address 3: New York
Street address state: NY
Zip/Postal code: 10023-7602
Country: USA
Mailing address: 1849 Broadway Rm 212
Mailing city: New York
Mailing state: NY
Mailing zip: 10023-7602
General Phone: (212) 261-1693
General/National Adv. E-mail: chronicle@nyit.edu
Classified Equipment»
Personnel: William Lawrence (Advisor)

NEW YORK LAW SCHOOL

Street address 1: 57 Worth St
Street address 2: Rm L2
Street address 3: New York
Street address state: NY
Zip/Postal code: 10013-2926
Country: USA
Mailing address: 57 Worth St Rm L2
Mailing city: New York
Mailing state: NY
Mailing zip: 10013-2926
General Phone: (212) 431-2100
Classified Equipment»
Personnel: Sally Harding (Head, Student Life)

NEW YORK UNIV.

Street address 1: 7 E 12th St
Street address 2: Ste 800
Street address 3: New York
Street address state: NY
Zip/Postal code: 10003-4475
Country: USA
Mailing address: 7 E 12th St Ste 800
Mailing city: New York
Mailing state: NY
Mailing zip: 10003-4475
General Phone: (212) 998-4300
General Fax: (212) 995-3790
Primary Website: www.nyunews.com
Classified Equipment»
Personnel: David Cosgrove (Dir., Opns.); Julia McCarthy (Bus. Mgr.); Eric Platt (Ed. in Chief); Rachael Smith (Ed.)

NEW YORK UNIVERSITY SCHOOL OF LAW

Street address 1: 240 Mercer St Bsmt
Street address 2: Hayden Hall
Street address 3: New York
Street address state: NY
Zip/Postal code: 10012-1590
Country: USA
Mailing address: 40 Washington Sq S Rm 110
Mailing city: New York
Mailing state: NY
Mailing zip: 10012-1005
General Phone: (212) 998-0564
General Fax: (212) 995-4032
General/National Adv. E-mail: Law.commentator@nyu.edu
Display Adv. E-mail: Law.commentator@nyu.edu

Editorial e-mail: Law.commentator@nyu.edu
Primary Website: www.law.nyu.edu/studentorganizations/thecommentator
Year Established: 1966
Classified Equipment»
Personnel: Naeem Crawford-Muhammad (Advisor); Andrew S. Gehring (Ed. in Chief); Robert Gerrity (Sr. Mng. Ed.); Ana Namaki
Parent company (for newspapers): New York University School of Law Student Bar Association

NYU STERN SCHOOL OF BUS.

Street address 1: 44 W 4th St
Street address 2: Mec 6-130
Street address 3: New York
Street address state: NY
Zip/Postal code: 10012-1106
Country: USA
Mailing address: 44 W 4th St Mec 6-130
Mailing city: New York
Mailing state: NY
Mailing zip: 10012-1106
General Phone: (212) 995-4432
General Fax: (212) 995-4606
General/National Adv. E-mail: opportun@stern.nyu.edu; helpdesk@stern.nyu.edu
Primary Website: www.sternopportunity.com
Classified Equipment»
Personnel: Jeremy Carrine (Advisor); Deborah Garcia (Ed. in chief); Rakesh Duggal (Co-Ed.)

PACE UNIV.

Street address 1: 41 Park Row
Street address 2: Rm 902
Street address 3: New York
Street address state: NY
Zip/Postal code: 10038-1508
Country: USA
Mailing address: 41 Park Row Rm 902
Mailing city: New York
Mailing state: NY
Mailing zip: 10038-1508
General Phone: (212) 346-1553
General Fax: (212) 346-1265
General/National Adv. E-mail: editor@pacepress.org
Primary Website: www.pacepress.org
Classified Equipment»
Personnel: Mark McSherry (Advisor)

SCHOOL OF VISUAL ARTS

Street address 1: 209 E 23rd St
Street address 3: New York
Street address state: NY
Zip/Postal code: 10010-3901
Country: USA
Mailing address: 209 E 23rd St
Mailing city: New York
Mailing state: NY
Mailing zip: 10010-3994
General Phone: (212) 592-2280
General Fax: (212) 725-3587
Classified Equipment»
Personnel: Tina Crayton (Advisor); Jane Resnick (Ed.)

STERN COLLEGE FOR WOMEN

Street address 1: 245 Lexington Ave
Street address 3: New York
Street address state: NY
Zip/Postal code: 10016-4605
Country: USA
Mailing address: 245 Lexington Ave
Mailing city: New York
Mailing state: NY
Mailing zip: 10016-4699
General Phone: (212) 340-7715
General Fax: (212) 340-7773
General/National Adv. E-mail: scwobserver@gmail.com
Primary Website: www.yuobserver.com
Classified Equipment»

YESHIVA UNIV.

Street address 1: 500 W 185th St
Street address 2: Ste 416
Street address 3: New York
Street address state: NY
Zip/Postal code: 10033-3201
Country: USA
Mailing address: 500 W 185th St Ste 416
Mailing city: New York
Mailing state: NY
Mailing zip: 10033-3201
General Phone: (212) 795-4308
General Fax: (212) 928-8637
General/National Adv. E-mail: news@yucommentator.com
Primary Website: www.yucommentator.com
Classified Equipment»
Personnel: Michael Cinnamon (Ed. in Chief); Simeon Botwinick (Mng. Ed.); Isaac Silverstein (Mng. Ed.)

THE EMPIRE STATE TRIBUNE

Street address 1: 56 Broadway
Street address 2: Fl 5
Street address 3: New York
Street address state: NY
Zip/Postal code: 10004-1613
County: New York
Country: USA
General Phone: 212-659-0742
Advertising Phone: 212-659-0742
Editorail Phone: 212-659-0742
General/National Adv. E-mail: estribune@tkc.edu
Display Adv. E-mail: estribune@tkc.edu
Classified Adv. E-mail: estribune@tkc.edu
Editorial e-mail: estribune@tkc.edu
Primary Website: www.empirestatetribune.com
Mthly Avg Views: 8856
Mthly Avg Unique Visitors: 4124
Year Established: 2005
Delivery Methods: Racks
Area Served - City: 10004
Own Printing Facility: Y
Commercial printers: N
Published: Mon
Weekday Frequency: m
Avg Free Circ: 100
Audit By: Sworn/Estimate/Non-Audited
Audit Date: 2/16/2018
Classified Equipment»
Product or Service: Editorial
Personnel: Clemente Lisi (Assistant Affiliate Professor of Journalism)

MT. ST. MARY COLLEGE

Street address 1: 330 Powell Ave
Street address 3: Newburgh
Street address state: NY
Zip/Postal code: 12550-3412
Country: USA
Mailing address: 330 Powell Ave
Mailing city: Newburgh
Mailing state: NY
Mailing zip: 12550-3494
General Phone: (845) 569-3100
General Fax: (845) 561-6762
Classified Equipment»
Personnel: Vince Begley (Advisor); Nathan Rosenblum (Ed.)

NIAGARA UNIVERSITY

NIAGARA UNIV.

Street address 1: Gallagher Ctr
Street address 3: Niagara University
Street address state: NY
Zip/Postal code: 14109
Country: USA
Mailing address: Gallagher Ctr.
Mailing city: Niagara University
Mailing state: NY
Mailing zip: 14109-1919
General Phone: (716) 286-8512
General Fax: (716) 286-8542
General/National Adv. E-mail: theniagaraindex@yahoo.com
Classified Equipment»
Personnel: Bill Wolcott (Advisor); Mary Colleen Mahoney (Bus. Mgr.); Marissa Christman (Ed. in Chief)

NYACK

NYACK COLLEGE

Street address 1: 1 S Boulevard
Street address 3: Nyack
Street address state: NY
Zip/Postal code: 10960-3604
Country: USA
Mailing address: 1 S Boulevard
Mailing city: Nyack
Mailing state: NY
Mailing zip: 10960-3698
General Phone: (845) 358-1710
General/National Adv. E-mail: wnyk@nyack.edu; forum@nyack.edu
Primary Website: www.nyack.edu
Classified Equipment»
Personnel: Charles Beach (Advisor)

OAKDALE

DOWLING COLLEGE

Street address 1: 150 Idle Hour Blvd
Street address 3: Oakdale
Street address state: NY
Zip/Postal code: 11769-1906
Country: USA
Mailing address: 150 Idle Hour Blvd
Mailing city: Oakdale
Mailing state: NY
Mailing zip: 11769-1999
General Phone: (631) 244-3000
General Fax: (631) 244-3028
Primary Website: lionsvoice.dowling.edu
Classified Equipment»
Personnel: Laura Pope Robbins (Advisor); Derek Stevens (Ed.)

OLD WESTBURY

NEW YORK INSTITUTE OF TECHNOLOGY

Street address 1: PO Box 8000
Street address 3: Old Westbury
Street address state: NY
Zip/Postal code: 11568-8000
Country: USA
Mailing address: Northern Boulevard PO Box 8000
Mailing city: Old Westbury
Mailing state: NY
Mailing zip: 11568
General Phone: (516) 686-7646
General Fax: (516) 626-1290
Editorail Phone: 516-589-1615
General/National Adv. E-mail: slate@nyit.edu
Display Adv. E-mail: slate@nyit.edu
Primary Website: www.campusslate.com
Year Established: 1966
Classified Equipment»
Personnel: John Hanc (Advisor); John Santamaria (Editor in Chief); Kyle Reitan (Managing Editor)

SUNY COLLEGE/OLD WESTBURY

Street address 1: 223 Store Hill Rd
Street address 3: Old Westbury
Street address state: NY
Zip/Postal code: 11568-1717
Country: USA
Mailing address: PO Box 210
Mailing city: Old Westbury
Mailing state: NY
Mailing zip: 11568-0210
General Phone: (516) 876-3000
General/National Adv. E-mail: owcatalyst@gmail.com
Classified Equipment»
Personnel: Alicia Grant (Exec.Ed.)

ONEONTA

HARTWICK COLLEGE

Street address 1: PO Box 250
Street address 3: Oneonta
Street address state: NY
Zip/Postal code: 13820-0250
Country: USA
Mailing address: c/o Daily Star, PO Box 250
Mailing city: Oneonta
Mailing state: NY
Mailing zip: 13820
General Phone: (607) 432-1000
General Fax: (607) 432-5847
General/National Adv. E-mail: breeves@thedailystar.com; hilltops@hartwick.edu
Classified Equipment»
Personnel: Bill Reeves (Advisor); Danielle Peloquin (Ed.)

SUNY COLLEGE/ONEONTA

Street address 1: Ravine Pkwy
Street address 3: Oneonta
Street address state: NY
Zip/Postal code: 13820
Country: USA
Mailing address: Ravine Pkwy.
Mailing city: Oneonta
Mailing state: NY
Mailing zip: 13820
General Phone: (607) 436-2492
General Fax: (607) 436-2002
Classified Equipment»
Personnel: Janet Day (Advisor); Juliette Price (Mng. Ed.)

OSWEGO

SUNY COLLEGE/OSWEGO

Street address 1: 135 A Campus Ctr
Street address 3: Oswego
Street address state: NY
Zip/Postal code: 13126
Country: USA
Mailing address: 139A Campus Ctr.
Mailing city: Oswego
Mailing state: NY
Mailing zip: 13126
General Phone: (315) 312-3600
General Fax: (315) 312-3542
General/National Adv. E-mail: gonian@oswego.edu; info@oswegonian.com
Display Adv. E-mail: advertising@oswegonian.com
Primary Website: www.oswegonian.com
Year Established: 1935
Commercial printers: N
Classified Equipment»
Personnel: Arvin Diddi (Faculty Adviser); Adam Wolfe (Editor-in-Chief)

PATCHOGUE

ST. JOSEPHS COLLEGE

Street address 1: 155 W Roe Blvd
Street address 3: Patchogue
Street address state: NY
Zip/Postal code: 11772-2325
Country: USA
Mailing address: 155 W Roe Blvd
Mailing city: Patchogue
Mailing state: NY
Mailing zip: 11772-2399
General Phone: (631) 447-3200
General Fax: (631) 654-1782
General/National Adv. E-mail: talon.li@student.sjcny.edu
Classified Equipment»
Personnel: Erin Bailey (Ed.)

SUNY PLATTSBURGH

Street address 1: 101 Broad St
Street address 2: 118 Ward Hall
Street address 3: Plattsburgh
Street address state: NY
Zip/Postal code: 12901-2637
Country: USA
Mailing address: 101 Broad St
Mailing city: Plattsburgh
Mailing state: NY
Mailing zip: 12901-2637
General Phone: (518) 564-2174
General Fax: (518) 564-6397
Advertising Phone: (518) 564-3173

Editorail Phone: (518) 564-2174
General/National Adv. E-mail: cp@cardinalpointsonline.com
Display Adv. E-mail: advertising@cardinalpointsonline.com
Editorial e-mail: cp@cardinalpointsonline.com
Primary Website: www.cardinalpointsonline.com
Year Established: 1969
Advertising (Open Inch Rate) Weekday/Saturday: $10 per column inch for national ad, discounts for size and frequency and for local advertisers (see website for full rate card)
Published: Fri
Avg Paid Circ: 1700
Avg Free Circ: 1300
Classified Equipment»
Personnel: Shawn Murphy (Advisor); Maureen Provost (Bus Mgr)
Parent company (for newspapers): Plattsburgh State Media Inc.

PACE UNIV.

Street address 1: 861 Bedford Rd
Street address 3: Pleasantville
Street address state: NY
Zip/Postal code: 10570-2700
Country: USA
Mailing address: 861 Bedford Rd.
Mailing city: Pleasantville
Mailing state: NY
Mailing zip: 10570-2799
General/National Adv. E-mail: pacechronicle@pace.edu
Published: Wed
Classified Equipment»
Personnel: Katherine Fink

POTSDAM

CLARKSON UNIV.

Street address 1: PO Box 8710
Street address 3: Potsdam
Street address state: NY
Zip/Postal code: 13699-0001
Country: USA
Mailing address: PO Box 8710
Mailing city: Potsdam
Mailing state: NY
Mailing zip: 13699-0001
General Phone: (315) 265-9050
General Fax: (315) 268-7661
General/National Adv. E-mail: integrat@clarkson.edu
Primary Website: www.clarksonintegrator.com
Classified Equipment»
Personnel: Mary Konecnik (Ed. in Chief); Robert Trerice (Mng. Ed.)

POUGHKEEPSIE

DUTCHESS CMTY. COLLEGE

Street address 1: 53 Pendell Rd
Street address 3: Poughkeepsie
Street address state: NY
Zip/Postal code: 12601-1512
Country: USA
Mailing address: 53 Pendell Rd
Mailing city: Poughkeepsie
Mailing state: NY
Mailing zip: 12601-1595
General Phone: (845) 431-8000
General Fax: (845) 431-8989
General/National Adv. E-mail: communityrelations@sunydutchess.edu; Helpdesk@sunydutchess.edu
Primary Website: www.sunydutchess.edu
Classified Equipment»
Personnel: Kevin Lang (Advisor)

MARIST COLLEGE

Street address 1: 3399 North Rd
Street address 2: Lowell Thomas Communications Building Room 135-MAC Lab
Street address 3: Poughkeepsie
Street address state: NY
Zip/Postal code: 12601-1350
Country: USA
Mailing address: Lowell Thomas Communications Building Room 135-Mac Lab
Mailing city: Poughkeepsie
Mailing state: NY
Mailing zip: 12601-1387
General Phone: (845) 575-3000
General/National Adv. E-mail: writethecircle@hotmail.com
Primary Website: www.maristcircle.com
Classified Equipment»
Personnel: Margeaux Lippman (Ed. in Chief); Kaitlyn Smith (Mng. Ed.); Matthew Spillane (Mng. Ed.)

VASSAR COLLEGE

Street address 1: 124 Raymond Ave
Street address 2: Box 149, Vassar College
Street address 3: Poughkeepsie
Street address state: NY
Zip/Postal code: 12604-0001
Country: USA
Mailing address: Box 149, Vassar College
Mailing city: Poughkeepsie
Mailing state: NY
Mailing zip: 12604
General Phone: (518) 755-2042
General/National Adv. E-mail: misc@vassar.edu
Primary Website: PO Box 23
Published: Wed
Classified Equipment»
Personnel: Talya Phelps (Editor-in-Chief)

PURCHASE

MANHATTANVILLE COLLEGE

Street address 1: 2900 Purchase St
Street address 3: Purchase
Street address state: NY
Zip/Postal code: 10577-2131
Country: USA
Mailing address: 2900 Purchase St
Mailing city: Purchase
Mailing state: NY
Mailing zip: 10577-2132
General Phone: (914) 323-5498
General/National Adv. E-mail: touchstone@mville.edu
Primary Website: http://mvilletouchstone.com/
Classified Equipment»
Personnel: Dana Schildkraut (Office Mgr.)

MONROE CMTY. COLLEGE

Street address 1: 1000 E Henrietta Rd
Street address 3: Rochester
Street address state: NY
Zip/Postal code: 14623-5701
Country: USA
Mailing address: 1000 E Henrietta Rd
Mailing city: Rochester
Mailing state: NY
Mailing zip: 14623-5780
General Phone: (585) 292-2540
General/National Adv. E-mail: monroedoctrine@me.com
Primary Website: www.monroedoctrine.org
Year Established: 1963
News Services: MCT campus
Delivery Methods: Racks
Commercial printers: Y
Published: Other
Published Other: bi-weekly
Avg Free Circ: 3500
Classified Equipment»
Note: www.monroedoctrine.org
Personnel: Lori Moses (Advisor)

NAZARETH COLLEGE OF ROCHESTER

Street address 1: 4245 East Ave
Street address 3: Rochester
Street address state: NY
Zip/Postal code: 14618-3703
Country: USA
Mailing address: 4245 East Ave
Mailing city: Rochester
Mailing state: NY
Mailing zip: 14618-3790
General Phone: (585) 389-2525
General Fax: (585) 586-2452
Classified Equipment»
Personnel: Halinka Spencer (Ed.)

ROBERTS WESLEYAN COLLEGE

Street address 1: 2301 Westside Dr
Street address 3: Rochester
Street address state: NY
Zip/Postal code: 14624-1933
Country: USA
Mailing address: 2301 Westside Dr Ofc
Mailing city: Rochester
Mailing state: NY
Mailing zip: 14624-1997
General Phone: (585) 594-6385
General Fax: (585) 594-6567
General/National Adv. E-mail: beacon@roberts.edu
Published: Mthly
Classified Equipment»
Personnel: Taylor Plourde (Editor-In-Chief); Elisabeth Lindke (Assistant Editor); Derick Trost (Layout Editor)

ROCHESTER INST. OF TECHNOLOGY

Street address 1: 37 Lomb Memorial Dr
Street address 3: Rochester
Street address state: NY
Zip/Postal code: 14623-5602
Country: USA
Mailing address: 37 Lomb Memorial Dr
Mailing city: Rochester
Mailing state: NY
Mailing zip: 14623-5602
General Phone: (585) 475-2213
General Fax: (585) 475-2214
General/National Adv. E-mail: reporter@rit.edu
Primary Website: www.reportermag.com
Classified Equipment»
Personnel: Rudy Pugliese (Advisor); Andy Rees (Ed. in Chief)

ST. JOHN FISHER COLLEGE

Street address 1: 3690 East Ave
Street address 3: Rochester
Street address state: NY
Zip/Postal code: 14618-3537
Country: USA
Mailing address: 3690 East Ave
Mailing city: Rochester
Mailing state: NY
Mailing zip: 14618-3537
General Phone: (585) 385-8360
General Fax: (585) 385-7311
Advertising Phone: (585) 385-7393
General/National Adv. E-mail: cardinalcourier@sjfc.edu
Display Adv. E-mail: mvilla@sjfc.edu
Editorial e-mail: eem00114@sjfc.edu
Primary Website: www.cardinalcourieronline.com
Year Established: 2002
Published: Bi-Mthly
Classified Equipment»
Personnel: Lauren Vicker (Chair/Prof.); Marie Villa (Media Adviser)

UNIV. OF ROCHESTER

Street address 1: PO Box 277086
Street address 3: Rochester
Street address state: NY
Zip/Postal code: 14627-7086
Country: USA
Mailing address: CPU 277086 Campus Post Office
Mailing city: Rochester
Mailing state: NY
Mailing zip: 14627
General Phone: (585) 275-5942
General Fax: (585) 273-5303
General/National Adv. E-mail: ctads@mail.rochester.edu
Editorial e-mail: editor@campustimes.org
Primary Website: www.campustimes.org
Classified Equipment»
Personnel: Dan Wasserman (Pub.); Liz Bremer (Bus. Mgr.); Dana Hilfinger (Ed. in Chief)

WATS, SIMON GRAD. SCHOOL OF BUS.

Street address 1: Schlegel Hall, University of Rochester
Street address 3: Rochester
Street address state: NY
Zip/Postal code: 14627
Country: USA
Mailing address: Schlegel Hall, University of Rochester
Mailing city: Rochester
Mailing state: NY
Mailing zip: 14627
General Phone: (585) 275-9287
General/National Adv. E-mail: wats@simon.rochester.edu
Delivery Methods: Racks
Commercial printers: Y
Classified Equipment»
Personnel: Natalie Antal (Acting Managing Editor); Vincent Pelletier (Assignment Editor); Durba Ray (Ed. in Chief)

SAINT BONAVENTURE

ST. BONAVENTURE UNIV.

Street address 1: PO Box X
Street address 3: Saint Bonaventure
Street address state: NY
Zip/Postal code: 14778-2303
Country: USA
Mailing address: PO Box X
Mailing city: Saint Bonaventure
Mailing state: NY
Mailing zip: 14778-2303
General Phone: (716) 375-2227
General Fax: (716) 375-2252
Editorail Phone: (716) 375-2128
General/National Adv. E-mail: bonavent@sbu.edu
Primary Website: www.thebv.org
Classified Equipment»
Personnel: Carole McNall (Faculty Advisor); Samantha Berkhead (Editor in Chief); Kevin Rogers (Managing Editor)

SANBORN

NIAGARA COUNTY CMTY. COLLEGE

Street address 1: 3111 Saunders Settlement Rd
Street address 3: Sanborn
Street address state: NY
Zip/Postal code: 14132-9506
Country: USA
Mailing address: 3111 Saunders Settlement Rd Ste 1
Mailing city: Sanborn
Mailing state: NY
Mailing zip: 14132-9460
General Phone: (716) 614-6259
General Fax: (716) 614-6264
General/National Adv. E-mail: spirit@niagaracc.suny.edu
Classified Equipment»
Personnel: Amanda Pucci (Advisor)

SARATOGA SPRINGS

THE SKIDMORE NEWS

Street address 1: 815 N Broadway
Street address 2: Skidmore College
Street address 3: Saratoga Springs
Street address state: NY
Zip/Postal code: 12866-1632
Country: USA
Mailing address: 815 N Broadway
Mailing city: Saratoga Springs
Mailing state: NY
Mailing zip: 12866-1632
General Phone: (518) 580-5000
General Fax: (518) 580-5188
General/National Adv. E-mail: skidnews@skidmore.edu
Primary Website: www.skidmorenews.com
Year Established: 1925
Classified Equipment»
Personnel: Savannah Grier (Ed. in Chief)

UNION COLLEGE CONCORDIENSIS

Street address 1: 807 Union St
Street address 3: Schenectady
Street address state: NY

Zip/Postal code: 12308-3256
Country: USA
Mailing address: 807 Union St.
Mailing city: Schenectady
Mailing state: NY
Mailing zip: 12308
General Phone: (518) 388-7128
General/National Adv. E-mail: concordy@gmail.com
Display Adv. E-mail: advertising@concordy.com
Primary Website: http://www.concordy.com/
Year Established: 1877
Commercial printers: N
Classified Equipment»
Personnel: Ajay Major (Ed. in Chief)

SOUTHAMPTON

SOUTHAMPTON COLLEGE

Street address 1: 239 Montauk Hwy
Street address 3: Southampton
Street address state: NY
Zip/Postal code: 11968-4100
Country: USA
Mailing address: 239 Montauk Hwy
Mailing city: Southampton
Mailing state: NY
Mailing zip: 11968-4198
General Phone: (631) 287-8239
General Fax: (631) 287-5147
Classified Equipment»
Personnel: Diane Prescott (Ed.)

SPARKILL

ST. THOMAS AQUINAS COLLEGE

Street address 1: 125 Route 340
Street address 3: Sparkill
Street address state: NY
Zip/Postal code: 10976-1041
Country: USA
Mailing address: 125 Route 340
Mailing city: Sparkill
Mailing state: NY
Mailing zip: 10976-1050
General Phone: (845) 398-4075
General Fax: (845) 359-8136
General/National Adv. E-mail: thoma@yahoo.com; thoma@stac.edu
Primary Website: www.stac.edu
Classified Equipment»
Personnel: Kathleen Giroux (Ed. in Chief)

STATEN ISLAND

COLLEGE OF STATEN ISLAND

Street address 1: 2800 Victory Blvd
Street address 3: Staten Island
Street address state: NY
Zip/Postal code: 10314-6609
Country: USA
Mailing address: 2800 Victory Blvd
Mailing city: Staten Island
Mailing state: NY
Mailing zip: 10314-6600
General Phone: (718) 982-3056
General Fax: (718) 982-3087
Primary Website: www.csi.cuny.edu
Classified Equipment»
Personnel: Philip Masciantonio (Gen. Mgr.)

ST. JOHNS UNIV.

Street address 1: 300 Howard Ave
Street address 3: Staten Island
Street address state: NY
Zip/Postal code: 10301-4450
Country: USA
Mailing address: 300 Howard Ave
Mailing city: Staten Island
Mailing state: NY
Mailing zip: 10301-4496
General Phone: (718) 390-4500
General Fax: (718) 447-0941
General/National Adv. E-mail: siadmhelp@stjohns.edu
Primary Website: www.stjohns.edu
Classified Equipment»
Personnel: Crista Camerlengl (Ed.)

WAGNER COLLEGE

Street address 1: 1 Campus Rd
Street address 3: Staten Island
Street address state: NY
Zip/Postal code: 10301-4479
Country: USA
Mailing address: 1 Campus Rd
Mailing city: Staten Island
Mailing state: NY
Mailing zip: 10301-4495
General Phone: (718) 390-3110
General/National Adv. E-mail: wagnerian@wagner.edu
Published: Wed
Published Other: Bi-Weekly
Classified Equipment»

STONY BROOK

SUNY/STONY BROOK

Street address 1: PO Box 1530
Street address 3: Stony Brook
Street address state: NY
Zip/Postal code: 11790-0609
Country: USA
Mailing address: PO Box 1530
Mailing city: Stony Brook
Mailing state: NY
Mailing zip: 11790-0609
General Phone: (631) 632-6480
General Fax: (631) 632-9128
General/National Adv. E-mail: advertise@sbstatesman.org
Primary Website: www.sbstatesman.com
Classified Equipment»
Personnel: Frank D'alessandro (Bus. Mgr.); Bradley Donaldson (Ed. in Chief)

SUFFERN

ROCKLAND CMTY. COLLEGE

Street address 1: 145 College Rd
Street address 3: Suffern
Street address state: NY
Zip/Postal code: 10901-3620
Country: USA
Mailing address: 145 College Rd
Mailing city: Suffern
Mailing state: NY
Mailing zip: 10901-3699
General Phone: (845) 574-4389
General/National Adv. E-mail: outlookpress@gmail.com
Primary Website: www.sunyrockland.edu
Classified Equipment»

THE DOLPHIN

Street address 1: 1419 Salt Springs Rd
Street address 3: Syracuse
Street address state: NY
Zip/Postal code: 13214-1302
Country: USA
Mailing address: 1419 Salt Springs Rd
Mailing city: Syracuse
Mailing state: NY
Mailing zip: 13214-1302
General Phone: (315) 445-4542
Advertising Phone: (607) 221-8080
Editorail Phone: (315) 445-4542
General/National Adv. E-mail: dolphin@lemoyne.edu
Display Adv. E-mail: dolphin@lemoyne.edu
Editorial e-mail: dolphin@lemoyne.edu
Primary Website: http://www.lemoyne.edu/DOING/CLUBS/TheDolphin/tabid/1959/Default.aspx
Delivery Methods: Newsstand`Racks
Commercial printers: N
Classified Equipment»
Personnel: Ashley Casey (Co-Executive Editor); Amy Dieffenbacher

ONONDAGA CMTY. COLLEGE

Street address 1: Rt 173, Student Ctr G100
Street address 3: Syracuse
Street address state: NY
Zip/Postal code: 13215
Country: USA
Mailing address: Rt. 173, Student Ctr. G100
Mailing city: Syracuse
Mailing state: NY
Mailing zip: 13215
General Phone: (315) 498-2278
General Fax: (315) 498-2001
Classified Equipment»
Personnel: Patti Orty (Ed.)

SYRACUSE UNIVERSITY

Street address 1: 744 Ostrom Ave
Street address 3: Syracuse
Street address state: NY
Zip/Postal code: 13244-2977
Country: USA
Mailing address: 744 Ostrom Ave
Mailing city: Syracuse
Mailing state: NY
Mailing zip: 13210-2942
General Phone: (315) 443-2314
General Fax: (315) 443-3689
Advertising Phone: (315) 443-9794
General/National Adv. E-mail: ads@dailyorange.com
Display Adv. E-mail: ads@dailyorange.com
Editorial e-mail: editor@dailyorange.com
Primary Website: www.dailyorange.com
Year Established: 1903
Delivery Methods: Mail`Newsstand`Racks
Commercial printers: N
Advertising (Open Inch Rate) Weekday/Saturday: $16.4 per column inch
Published: Mon`Tues`Wed`Thur`Fri
Avg Paid Circ: 5
Avg Free Circ: 6000
Classified Equipment»
Note: Voted the #1 college paper in 2012 by The Society of Professional Journalists. Voted #1 College Newspaper Website in 2013 by Editor and Publisher.
Personnel: Peter Waack (Advisor/Gen. Mgr.)

HUDSON VALLEY CMTY. COLLEGE

Street address 1: 80 Vandenburgh Ave
Street address 3: Troy
Street address state: NY
Zip/Postal code: 12180-6037
Country: USA
Mailing address: 80 Vandenburgh Ave
Mailing city: Troy
Mailing state: NY
Mailing zip: 12180-6037
General Phone: (518) 629-7187
General Fax: (518) 629-7496
General/National Adv. E-mail: hudnews@yahoo.com
Primary Website: www.hvcc.edu
Classified Equipment»
Personnel: Mat Cantore (Advisor); Nicole Monsees (Mng. Ed.)

RENSSELAER POLYTECHNIC INST.

Street address 1: 110 8th St Ste 702
Street address 2: Rensselaer Union
Street address 3: Troy
Street address state: NY
Zip/Postal code: 12180-3522
Country: USA
Mailing address: Rensselaer Union
Mailing city: Troy
Mailing state: NY
Mailing zip: 12180-3590
General Phone: (518) 276-6000
General Fax: (518) 276-8728
General/National Adv. E-mail: poly@rpi.edu; business@poly.rpi.edu
Display Adv. E-mail: notices@poly.rpi.edu
Editorial e-mail: editor@poly.rpi.edu; news@poly.rpi.edu; edop@poly.rpi.edu; edop@poly.rpi.edu; sports@poly.rpi.edu; photo@poly.rpi.edu; notices@poly.rpi.edu
Primary Website: www.poly.rpi.edu
Classified Equipment»
Personnel: Richard Hartt (Advisor)

RUSSELL SAGE COLLEGE

Street address 1: 65 1st St
Street address 3: Troy
Street address state: NY
Zip/Postal code: 12180-4013
Country: USA
Mailing address: 65 1st St
Mailing city: Troy
Mailing state: NY
Mailing zip: 12180-4003
General Phone: 518-244-2016
Editorail Phone: 518-244-2016
General/National Adv. E-mail: perkip@sage.edu
Display Adv. E-mail: perkip@sage.edu
Editorial e-mail: perkip@sage.edu
Primary Website: www.thequillrsc.com
Year Established: 1950s
Classified Equipment»
Personnel: Penny Perkins (Advisor)

UTICA

SUNY INST. OF TECHNOLOGY UTICA/ROME

Street address 1: PO Box 3050
Street address 2: Campus Ctr., Rm. 216
Street address 3: Utica
Street address state: NY
Zip/Postal code: 13504-3050
Country: USA
Mailing address: PO Box 3050
Mailing city: Utica
Mailing state: NY
Mailing zip: 13504-3050
General Phone: (315) 792-7426
General Fax: (315) 734-4198
General/National Adv. E-mail: factorytimes@gmail.com
Classified Equipment»
Personnel: Patricia Murphy (Advisor); Mark Ziobro (Mng. Ed.)

UTICA COLLEGE

Street address 1: 1600 Burrstone Rd
Street address 2: Hubbard 55
Street address 3: Utica
Street address state: NY
Zip/Postal code: 13502-4857
Country: USA
Mailing address: 1600 Burrstone Rd Hubbard 55
Mailing city: Utica
Mailing state: NY
Mailing zip: 13502-4892
General Phone: (315) 792-3065
General Fax: (315) 792-3173
Primary Website: www.uctangerine.com
Year Established: 1946
Delivery Methods: Newsstand
Commercial printers: Y
Classified Equipment»
Personnel: Christopher Cooper (Editor-in-Chief); Jonathan Monsiletto (Ed. in Chief)

VALHALLA

WESTCHESTER CMTY. COLLEGE

Street address 1: 75 Grasslands Rd
Street address 3: Valhalla
Street address state: NY
Zip/Postal code: 10595-1550
Country: USA
Mailing address: 75 Grasslands Rd
Mailing city: Valhalla
Mailing state: NY
Mailing zip: 10595-1550
General Phone: (914) 606-6600
General/National Adv. E-mail: thevikingnewswcc@hotmail.com
Primary Website: www.sunywcc.edu
Classified Equipment»
Personnel: Craig Padawer (Advisor)

WATERTOWN

JEFFERSON CMTY. COLLEGE

Street address 1: 1220 Coffeen St
Street address 3: Watertown
Street address state: NY

Zip/Postal code: 13601-1822
Country: USA
Mailing address: 1220 Coffeen St
Mailing city: Watertown
Mailing state: NY
Mailing zip: 13601-1897
General Phone: (315) 786-2200
General Fax: (315) 788-0716
Primary Website: www.sunyjefferson.edu
Classified Equipment»
Personnel: Andrea Pedrick (Advisor); Danielle Sacca (Ed.); Rachel Hunter (Ed.)

WHITE PLAINS

PACE UNIV. LAW SCHOOL

Street address 1: 78 N Broadway
Street address 3: White Plains
Street address state: NY
Zip/Postal code: 10603-3710
Country: USA
Mailing address: 78 N Broadway
Mailing city: White Plains
Mailing state: NY
Mailing zip: 10603-3710
General Phone: (914) 422-4205
General/National Adv. E-mail: hearsay@law.case.edu
Primary Website: www.law.pace.edu
Classified Equipment»
Personnel: Angela D'agostino (Dean, Student Servs.)

OHIO

ADA

OHIO NORTHERN UNIV.

Street address 1: 525 S Main St
Street address 3: Ada
Street address state: OH
Zip/Postal code: 45810-6000
Country: USA
Mailing address: 525 S Main St
Mailing city: Ada
Mailing state: OH
Mailing zip: 45810
General Phone: (419) 772-2409
General Fax: (419) 772-1880
General/National Adv. E-mail: northern-review@onu.edu
Primary Website: https://nr.onu.edu
Published: Mon`Tues`Wed`Thur`Fri`Sat`Sun
Classified Equipment»
Personnel: Bill O'Connell (Advisor); Nick Dutro (Ed. in Chief)

AKRON

THE UNIVERSITY OF AKRON

Street address 1: 302 Buchtel Cmn
Street address 3: Akron
Street address state: OH
Zip/Postal code: 44325-0001
County: Summit
Country: USA
Mailing address: 302 Buchtel Common
Mailing city: Akron
Mailing state: OH
Mailing zip: 44325-4206
General Phone: 330-972-7919
General Fax: 330-972-7810
Advertising Phone: 330-972-5912
Advertising Fax: 330-972-7810
Editorail Phone: 330-972-6184
Editorial Fax: 330-972-7810
General/National Adv. E-mail: adviser@buchtelite.com
Display Adv. E-mail: business-manager@buchtelite.com
Classified Adv. E-mail: www.buchtelite.campusave.com
Editorial e-mail: editor-in-chief@buchtelite.com
Primary Website: buchtelite.com
Mthly Avg Views: 5100
Year Established: 1889
Delivery Methods: Newsstand
Area Served - City: 44325
Own Printing Facility: N
Commercial printers: Y
Published: Tues`Thur
Weekday Frequency: m
Avg Free Circ: 2700
Audit By: Sworn/Estimate/Non-Audited
Classified Equipment»
Personnel: Adam Bernhard (Business Manager); Zaina Salem (Editor-in-Chief)

UNIV. OF AKRON

Street address 1: 303 Carroll St, Student Union, Rm 51
Street address 3: Akron
Street address state: OH
Zip/Postal code: 44325-0001
Country: USA
Mailing address: 303 Carroll St Student Un Rm 51
Mailing city: Akron
Mailing state: OH
Mailing zip: 44325-0001
General Phone: (330) 972-5475
General Fax: (330) 972-7810
Advertising Phone: (330) 972-7919
Editorail Phone: (330) 972-6184
General/National Adv. E-mail: adviser@buchtelite.com
Editorial e-mail: editor@buchtelite.com
Primary Website: www.buchtelite.com
Classified Equipment»
Personnel: Maryanne Bailey-Porter (Acct. Coord.); Kevin Curwin (Ed. in Chief); Allison Strouse (News Ed.)

ALLIANCE

MT. UNION COLLEGE

Street address 1: 1972 Clark Ave
Street address 3: Alliance
Street address state: OH
Zip/Postal code: 44601-3929
Country: USA
Mailing address: 1972 Clark Ave
Mailing city: Alliance
Mailing state: OH
Mailing zip: 44601-3993
General Phone: (330) 823-2884
General Fax: (330) 821-0425
General/National Adv. E-mail: dynamo@muc.edu
Primary Website: www.mucdynamo.com
Classified Equipment»
Personnel: Len Cooper (Advisor)

ASHLAND

ASHLAND UNIV.

Street address 1: 401 College Ave
Street address 3: Ashland
Street address state: OH
Zip/Postal code: 44805-3702
Country: USA
Mailing address: 401 College Ave
Mailing city: Ashland
Mailing state: OH
Mailing zip: 44805-3799
General Phone: (419) 289-4142
General Fax: (419) 289-5604
General/National Adv. E-mail: collegian@ashland.edu
Primary Website: www.ashland.edu/collegian
Classified Equipment»
Personnel: Katie Ryder (Ed.)

OHIO UNIV.

Street address 1: 325 Baker University Center
Street address 3: Athens
Street address state: OH
Zip/Postal code: 45701
Country: USA
Mailing address: 325 Baker University Center
Mailing city: Athens
Mailing state: OH
Mailing zip: 45701
General Phone: (740) 593-4011
General Fax: (740) 593-0561
Advertising Phone: (740) 593-4018
General/National Adv. E-mail: posteditorial@ohiou.edu
Primary Website: www.thepost.ohiou.edu
Classified Equipment»
Personnel: Ashley Lutz (Ed. in Chief); Dave Hendricks (Managing Ed.); Ryan Dunn (Associate Ed.); Natalie Debruin (Asst. Managing Ed.); Joe (Sports Ed.); Robert (Advertising Admin.)

BALDWIN-WALLACE COLLEGE

Street address 1: 275 Eastland Rd
Street address 3: Berea
Street address state: OH
Zip/Postal code: 44017-2005
Country: USA
Mailing address: 275 Eastland Rd
Mailing city: Berea
Mailing state: OH
Mailing zip: 44017-2088
General Phone: (440) 826-2900
General Fax: (440) 826-8581
General/National Adv. E-mail: exponent@bw.edu
Classified Equipment»
Personnel: Peter Kerlin (Dir.); Gerrie

BLUFFTON

BLUFFTON COLLEGE

Street address 1: 1 University Dr
Street address 3: Bluffton
Street address state: OH
Zip/Postal code: 45817-2104
Country: USA
Mailing address: 1 University Dr
Mailing city: Bluffton
Mailing state: OH
Mailing zip: 45817-2104
General Phone: (419) 358-3000
General Fax: (419) 358-3356
General/National Adv. E-mail: witmarsum@bluffton.edu
Primary Website: www.witmarsum.org
Classified Equipment»
Personnel: Colin Lasu (Advisor); Cyrus Weigand (Bus. Mgr.); Bethany Rayle (Ed.)

BOWLING GREEN STATE UNIV.

Street address 1: 100 Kuhlin Center
Street address 3: Bowling Green
Street address state: OH
Zip/Postal code: 43403-0001
Country: USA
Mailing address: 100 Kuhlin Center
Mailing city: Bowling Green
Mailing state: OH
Mailing zip: 43403-0001
General Phone: (419) 372-0328
General Fax: (419) 372-0202
Advertising Phone: (419) 372-2606
Advertising Fax: (419) 372-9090
Editorail Phone: (419) 372-6966
Editorial Fax: (419) 372-9090
General/National Adv. E-mail: thenews@bgnews.com
Display Adv. E-mail: twhitma@bgsu.edu
Editorial e-mail: thenews@bgnews.com
Primary Website: www.bgviews.com
Year Established: 1920
Advertising (Open Inch Rate) Weekday/Saturday: 12.50 open rate
Published: Mon`Thur
Avg Free Circ: 4500
Classified Equipment»
Personnel: Robert Bortel (Director of Student Media); Hannah Finnerty; Holly Shively

BOWLING GREEN STATE UNIVERSITY

Street address 1: 204 West Hall
Street address 3: Bowling Green
Street address state: OH
Zip/Postal code: 43403-0001
Country: USA
Mailing address: 204 W Hall
Mailing city: Bowling Green
Mailing state: OH
Mailing zip: 43403-0001
General Phone: (419) 372-2607
General/National Adv. E-mail: thenews@bgnews.com
Classified Equipment»

MALONE COLLEGE

Street address 1: 2600 Cleveland Ave NW
Street address 3: Canton
Street address state: OH
Zip/Postal code: 44709-3308
Country: USA
Mailing address: 2600 Cleveland Ave NW
Mailing city: Canton
Mailing state: OH
Mailing zip: 44709-3308
General Phone: (330) 471-8212
General Fax: (330) 454-6977
Primary Website: www.theaviso.org
Year Established: 1958
Classified Equipment»
Personnel: David Dixon (Advisor)

MALONE UNIVERSITY

Street address 1: 2600 Cleveland Ave NW
Street address 3: Canton
Street address state: OH
Zip/Postal code: 44709-3308
Country: USA
Mailing address: 2600 Cleveland Ave NW
Mailing city: Canton
Mailing state: OH
Mailing zip: 44709-3897
General Phone: 330-471-8277
Primary Website: http://theaviso.org/
Classified Equipment»

CEDARVILLE

CEDARVILLE UNIV.

Street address 1: 251 N Main St
Street address 3: Cedarville
Street address state: OH
Zip/Postal code: 45314-8501
Country: USA
Mailing address: 251 N Main St
Mailing city: Cedarville
Mailing state: OH
Mailing zip: 45314-8564
General Phone: (937) 766-3298
General Fax: (937) 766-3456
General/National Adv. E-mail: cedars@cedarville.edu
Display Adv. E-mail: jgilbert@cedarville.edu
Primary Website: http://cedars.cedarville.edu/
Advertising (Open Inch Rate) Weekday/Saturday: Yes
Published: Mthly
Avg Free Circ: 1200
Classified Equipment»
Personnel: Jeff Gilbert (Faculty adviser)

MOUNT ST. JOSEPH UNIVERSITY

Street address 1: 5701 Delhi Rd
Street address 3: Cincinnati
Street address state: OH
Zip/Postal code: 45233-1669
Country: USA
Mailing address: 5701 Delhi Rd
Mailing city: Cincinnati
Mailing state: OH
Mailing zip: 45233-1670
General Phone: (513) 244-4200
Primary Website: www.msj.edu
Published: Mthly
Classified Equipment»
Personnel: Elizabeth Barkley (Faculty Advisor)

THE NEWS RECORD

Street address 1: Swift Hall, Ste 510
Street address 3: Cincinnati
Street address state: OH
Zip/Postal code: 45221-0001
Country: USA
Mailing address: PO Box 210135
Mailing city: Cincinnati
Mailing state: OH
Mailing zip: 45221-0135
General Phone: (513) 556-5900
General Fax: (513) 556-5922

General/National Adv. E-mail: newsrecordbiz@gmail.com; chief.newsrecord@gmail.com
Editorial e-mail: chief.newsrecord@gmail.com
Primary Website: www.newsrecord.org
Year Established: 1880
Special Weekly Sections: TNR Extra
Delivery Methods: Newsstand`Racks
Classified Equipment»
Personnel: Ariel Cheung (Editor-in-chief); Kristy Conlin (Ed. in Chief)

UNIVERSITY OF CINCINNATI

Street address 1: PO Box 210135
Street address 3: Cincinnati
Street address state: OH
Zip/Postal code: 45221-0135
Country: USA
Mailing address: PO Box 210135
Mailing city: Cincinnati
Mailing state: OH
Mailing zip: 45221-0135
General Phone: (513) 556-5912
General Fax: (513) 556??5922
Primary Website: www.newsrecord.org
Classified Equipment»

XAVIER UNIV.

Street address 1: 3800 Victory Pkwy
Street address 3: Cincinnati
Street address state: OH
Zip/Postal code: 45207-1035
Country: USA
Mailing address: 3800 Victory Pkwy Dept 156
Mailing city: Cincinnati
Mailing state: OH
Mailing zip: 45207-8010
General Phone: (513) 745-3607
General Fax: (513) 745-2898
Advertising Phone: (513) 745-3561
Primary Website: www.xavier.edu/newswire
Classified Equipment»
Personnel: Kathryn Rosenbaum (Ed. in Chief); Andrew Chestnut (Mng. Ed.); Meghan Berneking (News Ed.)

CASE WESTERN RESERVE UNIV.

Street address 1: 11111 Euclid Ave
Street address 2: Rm A09
Street address 3: Cleveland
Street address state: OH
Zip/Postal code: 44106-1715
Country: USA
Mailing address: 11111 Euclid Ave Rm A09
Mailing city: Cleveland
Mailing state: OH
Mailing zip: 44106-1715
General Phone: (216) 368-6949
General Fax: (216) 368-2914
Primary Website: www.cwruobserver.com
Classified Equipment»
Personnel: Tricia Schellenbach (Advisor); Bruce Douglas (Adv. Mgr.); Bryan Bourgeois (Ed. in Chief)

CLEVELAND STATE UNIV.

Street address 1: 2121 Euclid Ave
Street address 2: Student Center, Room 319
Street address 3: Cleveland
Street address state: OH
Zip/Postal code: 44115-2214
Country: USA
Mailing address: 2121 Euclid Ave
Mailing city: Cleveland
Mailing state: OH
Mailing zip: 44115-2226
General Phone: (216) 687-2270
General Fax: (216) 687-5155
General/National Adv. E-mail: cauldroneditors@gmail.com
Display Adv. E-mail: cauldronadverts@gmail.com
Primary Website: www.csucauldron.com
Published: Tues
Classified Equipment»
Personnel: Dan Lenhart (Advisor); Samah Assad (Editor-in-Chief)

CAPITAL UNIV.

Street address 1: 1 College and Main
Street address 3: Columbus
Street address state: OH
Zip/Postal code: 43209-7812
Country: USA
Mailing address: 1 College and Main
Mailing city: Columbus
Mailing state: OH
Mailing zip: 43209-2394
General Phone: (614) 236-6567
General Fax: (614) 236-6948
General/National Adv. E-mail: chimes@capital.edu
Primary Website: cuchimes.com
Year Established: 1926
Special Editions: freshmen orientation
Advertising (Open Inch Rate) Weekday/Saturday: yes
Published: Thur
Avg Free Circ: 1200
Classified Equipment»
Personnel: Kelly Messinger (Advisor)

CAPITAL UNIV. LAW SCHOOL

Street address 1: 303 E Broad St
Street address 3: Columbus
Street address state: OH
Zip/Postal code: 43215-3201
Country: USA
Mailing address: 303 E Broad St
Mailing city: Columbus
Mailing state: OH
Mailing zip: 43215-3200
General Phone: (614) 236-6011
General Fax: (614) 445-7125
General/National Adv. E-mail: resipsa@law.capital.edu
Classified Equipment»
Personnel: Susan Gilles (Advisor); Sharon Simpson (Ed. in Chief); Amanda Tuttle (Ed.)

FRANKLIN UNIVERSITY

Street address 1: 201 S Grant Ave
Street address 3: Columbus
Street address state: OH
Zip/Postal code: 43215-5301
Country: USA
Mailing address: 201 S Grant Ave
Mailing city: Columbus
Mailing state: OH
Mailing zip: 43215-5399
General Phone: (614) 797-4700
General Fax: (614) 224-4025
Advertising Phone: N/A
Advertising Fax: N/A
Editorail Phone: N/A
Editorial Fax: N/A
Display Adv. E-mail: N/A
Editorial e-mail: N/A
Primary Website: www.franklin.edu
Year Established: 1902
Commercial printers: N
Advertising (Open Inch Rate) Weekday/Saturday: N/A
Classified Equipment»
Note: This is an internal newsletter only. Outside content or ads are not permitted.
Personnel: Sherry Mercurio (Ed.)

OHIO STATE UNIV.

Street address 1: 242 W 18th Ave
Street address 2: Rm 211
Street address 3: Columbus
Street address state: OH
Zip/Postal code: 43210-1107
Country: USA
Mailing address: 242 W 18th Ave Rm 211
Mailing city: Columbus
Mailing state: OH
Mailing zip: 43210-1107
General Phone: (614) 292-2031
General Fax: (614) 292-5240
Editorail Phone: (614) 292-5721
General/National Adv. E-mail: lantern@osu.edu
Editorial e-mail: lanternnewsroom@gmail.com
Primary Website: www.thelantern.com
Year Established: 1881
Classified Equipment»
Personnel: Tom O'Hara (Advisor); John Milliken (Mgr.); Kevin Bruffy (Mgr., Display Adv.)

OHIO STATE UNIV. COLLEGE OF ENGINEERING

Street address 1: 2070 Neil Ave
Street address 3: Columbus
Street address state: OH
Zip/Postal code: 43210-1226
Country: USA
Mailing address: 2070 Neil Ave
Mailing city: Columbus
Mailing state: OH
Mailing zip: 43210-1278
General Phone: (614) 292-7931
General Fax: (614) 688-3805
Primary Website: www.engineering.osu.edu
Classified Equipment»
Personnel: Edward McCaul (Advisor)

OHIO STATE UNIV. COLLEGE OF LAW

Street address 1: 55 W 12th Ave
Street address 3: Columbus
Street address state: OH
Zip/Postal code: 43210-1338
Country: USA
Mailing address: 55 W 12th Ave
Mailing city: Columbus
Mailing state: OH
Mailing zip: 43210-1391
General Phone: (614) 292-2631
Advertising Phone: (614) 292-3202
Classified Equipment»

OHIO STATE UNIVERSITY

Street address 1: 242 W 18th Ave
Street address 3: Columbus
Street address state: OH
Zip/Postal code: 43210-1107
Country: USA
Mailing address: 242 W 18th Ave
Mailing city: Columbus
Mailing state: OH
Mailing zip: 43210-1107
General Phone: 614-292-5721
General Fax: 614-292-3722
Primary Website: www.thelantern.com
Classified Equipment»

SINCLAIR COMMUNITY COLLEGE

Street address 1: 444 W 3rd St
Street address 2: Rm 6314
Street address 3: Dayton
Street address state: OH
Zip/Postal code: 45402-1421
Country: USA
Mailing address: 444 W 3rd St Rm 6314
Mailing city: Dayton
Mailing state: OH
Mailing zip: 45402-1421
General Phone: (937) 512-2744
General Fax: (937) 512-4590
Advertising Phone: (937) 512-2744
Advertising Fax: (937) 512-4590
Editorail Phone: (937) 512-2958
Editorial Fax: (937) 512-4590
General/National Adv. E-mail: clarion@sinclair.edu
Display Adv. E-mail: clarion@sinclair.edu
Editorial e-mail: clarion@sinclair.edu
Primary Website: www.sinclairclarion.com
Year Established: 1977
Delivery Methods: Racks
Commercial printers: Y
Advertising (Open Inch Rate) Weekday/Saturday: see rate card on website
Published: Tues
Avg Free Circ: 4000
Classified Equipment»
Personnel: Gabrielle Sharp (Exec Ed); Barton Kleen (Mng Ed); Laina Yost (Associate Ed); Susan Day (Advt Rep)

UNIV. OF DAYTON

Street address 1: 232 Kennedy Union
Street address 2: 300 College Park
Street address 3: Dayton
Street address state: OH
Zip/Postal code: 45469-0001
Country: USA
Mailing address: 232 Kennedy Union
Mailing city: Dayton
Mailing state: OH
Mailing zip: 45469-0626
General Phone: (937) 229-3226
General Fax: (937) 229-3893
Advertising Phone: (937) 229-3813
Editorail Phone: (937) 229-3878
General/National Adv. E-mail: news@flyernews.com
Display Adv. E-mail: advertising@flyernews.com
Editorial e-mail: fn.editor@udayton.edu
Primary Website: www.flyernews.com
Published: Tues
Published Other: B-Weekly (Daily online)
Avg Free Circ: 3000
Classified Equipment»
Note: Flyer News now has a print editor in chief and an online editor in chief. This is the second year for this set up.
Personnel: Frazier Smith (Advisor); Amy Lopez-Matthews (Co-Advisor); CC Hutten (Ed.); Matthew Worsham (Mng. Ed.); Meredith Whelchel (Mng. Ed.); Julia Hall (Print-Ed.)

UNIV. OF DAYTON LAW SCHOOL

Street address 1: 300 College Park
Street address 3: Dayton
Street address state: OH
Zip/Postal code: 45469-0001
Country: USA
Mailing address: 300 College Park
Mailing city: Dayton
Mailing state: OH
Mailing zip: 45469-0002
General Phone: (937) 229-3211
Classified Equipment»
Personnel: Jennifer Tate (Ed.)

WRIGHT STATE UNIV.

Street address 1: 014 Student Union, 3640 Colonel Glenn Hwy
Street address 3: Dayton
Street address state: OH
Zip/Postal code: 45435-0001
Country: USA
Mailing address: 14 Stud Ent Union 3640 Colonel Glenn Hwy
Mailing city: Dayton
Mailing state: OH
Mailing zip: 45435-0001
General Phone: (937) 775-5534
General Fax: (937) 775-5535
Display Adv. E-mail: advertising@theguardianonline.com
Editorial e-mail: editorial@theguardianonline.com
Primary Website: www.theguardianonline.com
Classified Equipment»
Personnel: Tiffany Johnson (Ed. in chief)

DELAWARE

OHIO WESLEYAN UNIVERSITY

Street address 1: 61 S Sandusky St
Street address 2: Rm 106
Street address 3: Delaware
Street address state: OH
Zip/Postal code: 43015-2333
Country: USA
Mailing address: 61 S Sandusky St Rm 106
Mailing city: Delaware
Mailing state: OH
Mailing zip: 43015-2398
General Phone: (740) 368-2911
General Fax: (740) 368-3649
General/National Adv. E-mail: owunews@owu.edu
Display Adv. E-mail: owunews@owu.edu
Editorial e-mail: owunews@owu.edu
Primary Website: transcript.owu.edu
Year Established: 1867
Delivery Methods: Newsstand
Commercial printers: Y
Advertising (Open Inch Rate) Weekday/Saturday: http://transcript.owu.edu/advertisingInformation.html
Published: Thur
Avg Paid Circ: 5
Avg Free Circ: 1000
Classified Equipment»
Personnel: Jo Ingles (Media Adviser)

ELYRIA

LORAIN COUNTY CMTY. COLLEGE

Street address 1: 1005 Abbe Rd N
Street address 3: Elyria
Street address state: OH
Zip/Postal code: 44035-1613
Country: USA
Mailing address: 1005 Abbe Rd N
Mailing city: Elyria
Mailing state: OH
Mailing zip: 44035-1692
General Phone: (440) 366-4037
General Fax: (440) 365-6519
Editorail Phone: (440) 366-7729
General/National Adv. E-mail: lcccstories@lorainccc.edu; colegian@lorainccc.edu
Primary Website: www.collegianonline.org
Published: Bi-Mthly
Classified Equipment»
Personnel: Cliff Anthony (Advisor)
Parent company (for newspapers): Lorain County Community College

FINDLAY

THE UNIVERSITY OF FINDLAY

Street address 1: 1000 N Main St
Street address 3: Findlay
Street address state: OH
Zip/Postal code: 45840-3653
Country: USA
Mailing address: 1000 N Main St
Mailing city: Findlay
Mailing state: OH
Mailing zip: 45840-3653
General Phone: (419) 434-5892
Advertising Phone: (419) 434-5892
Editorial Phone: (419) 434-5892
General/National Adv. E-mail: pulse@findlay.edu
Display Adv. E-mail: pulse@findlay.edu
Editorial e-mail: pulse@findlay.edu
Primary Website: www.findlay.edu/pulse
Year Established: 1986 (as the Pulse)
Advertising (Open Inch Rate) Weekday/Saturday: $4/inch
Published: Fri
Avg Free Circ: 1000
Classified Equipment»
Note: We have a digital platform.
Personnel: Olivia Wile (Pulse Editor)

GAMBIER

KENYON COLLEGE

Street address 1: Student Affairs Ctr, 100 Gaskin Ave
Street address 3: Gambier
Street address state: OH
Zip/Postal code: 43022
Country: USA
Mailing address: PO Box 832
Mailing city: Gambier
Mailing state: OH
Mailing zip: 43022-0832
General Phone: (740) 427-5338
General Fax: (740) 427-5339
General/National Adv. E-mail: collegian@kenyon.edu
Primary Website: www. kenyoncollegian.com
Classified Equipment»
Personnel: Sarah Queller (Ed.)

GRANVILLE

DENISON UNIV.

Street address 1: 100 W College St
Street address 3: Granville
Street address state: OH
Zip/Postal code: 43023-1100
Country: USA
Mailing address: 100 W College St
Mailing city: Granville
Mailing state: OH
Mailing zip: 43023
General Phone: (740) 587-6378
General Fax: (740) 587-6767
General/National Adv. E-mail: denisonian@denison.edu
Primary Website: www.denisonian.com
Classified Equipment»
Personnel: Alan Miller (Advisor)

HIRAM

HIRAM COLLEGE

Street address 1: PO Box 67
Street address 3: Hiram
Street address state: OH
Zip/Postal code: 44234-0067
Country: USA
Mailing address: PO Box 67
Mailing city: Hiram
Mailing state: OH
Mailing zip: 44234-0067
General Phone: (330) 569-5203
General Fax: (330) 569-5479
General/National Adv. E-mail: advance@hiram.edu
Classified Equipment»
Personnel: Christopher Benek (Ed. in Chief)

KENT

KENT STATE UNIV.

Street address 1: 201 Franklin Hall, Rm 205
Street address 3: Kent
Street address state: OH
Zip/Postal code: 44242-0001
Country: USA
Mailing address: 201 Franklin Hall Rm 205
Mailing city: Kent
Mailing state: OH
Mailing zip: 44242-0001
General Phone: (330) 672-0887
General Fax: (330) 672-4880
General/National Adv. E-mail: dksads@gmail.com
Primary Website: www.kent.edu
Classified Equipment»
Personnel: Carl Schierhorn (Advisor); Lori Cantor (Mgr.); Tami Bongiorni (Adv. Mgr.)

KIRTLAND

LAKELAND CMTY. COLLEGE

Street address 1: 7700 Clocktower Dr
Street address 3: Kirtland
Street address state: OH
Zip/Postal code: 44094-5198
Country: USA
Mailing address: 7700 Clocktower Dr
Mailing city: Kirtland
Mailing state: OH
Mailing zip: 44094-5198
General Phone: (440) 953-7264
General/National Adv. E-mail: lakelander@lakelandcc.edu
Primary Website: www.lakelandcc.edu
Classified Equipment»
Personnel: Susan Zimmerman (Advisor)

MARIETTA

MARIETTA COLLEGE

Street address 1: 215 5th St
Street address 2: # A-20
Street address 3: Marietta
Street address state: OH
Zip/Postal code: 45750-4033
Country: USA
Mailing address: 215 5th St Dept 32
Mailing city: Marietta
Mailing state: OH
Mailing zip: 45750-4071
General Phone: (740) 376-4555
General Fax: (740) 376-4807
General/National Adv. E-mail: marc@marietta.edu
Primary Website: www.marcolian.com
Classified Equipment»
Personnel: Jessie Schmac (Ed. in Chief); Jamie Tidd (Mng. Ed.); Amy Bitely (Viewpoints Ed.)

MARIETTA COLLEGE

Street address 1: 215 5th St
Street address 3: Marietta
Street address state: OH
Zip/Postal code: 45750-4033
Country: USA
Mailing address: 215 5th St Dept 32
Mailing city: Marietta
Mailing state: OH
Mailing zip: 45750-4071
General Phone: (740) 376-4848
General Fax: (740) 376-4807
General/National Adv. E-mail: mac@Marietta.edu
Primary Website: www.marcolian.com/
Classified Equipment»
Personnel: Jack L. Hillwig (Chair)

MIAMI UNIV.

Street address 1: 4200 N University Blvd
Street address 3: Middletown
Street address state: OH
Zip/Postal code: 45042-3458
Country: USA
Mailing address: 4200 N University Blvd
Mailing city: Middletown
Mailing state: OH
Mailing zip: 45042-3497
General Phone: (513) 727-3200
General Fax: (513) 727-3223
General/National Adv. E-mail: miamistudent@gmail.com; miamistudent@muohio.edu
Primary Website: www.mid.muohio.edu/orgs/hawkseye/
Classified Equipment»
Personnel: Catherine Couretas (Ed.); John Heyda (Advisor)

NEW CONCORD

MUSKINGUM COLLEGE

Street address 1: 163 Stormont St
Street address 3: New Concord
Street address state: OH
Zip/Postal code: 43762-1118
Country: USA
Mailing address: 163 Stormont St
Mailing city: New Concord
Mailing state: OH
Mailing zip: 43762
General Phone: (740) 826-8296
General Fax: (740) 826-8404
Primary Website: www.bandmonline.com
Classified Equipment»
Personnel: Vivian Wagner (Advisor); Josh Chaney (Web Ed.)

NORTH CANTON

STARK STATE COLLEGE OF TECHNOLOGY

Street address 1: 6200 Frank Ave NW
Street address 3: North Canton
Street address state: OH
Zip/Postal code: 44720-7228
Country: USA
Mailing address: 6200 Frank Ave NW
Mailing city: North Canton
Mailing state: OH
Mailing zip: 44720-7299
General Phone: (330) 494-6170
General Fax: (330) 497-6313
General/National Adv. E-mail: studentinformer@starkstate.edu
Primary Website: www.starkstate.edu/studentinformer
Classified Equipment»

OBERLIN

OBERLIN COLLEGE

Street address 1: 135 W Lorain St
Street address 2: # 90
Street address 3: Oberlin
Street address state: OH
Zip/Postal code: 44074-1053
Country: USA
Mailing address: 135 W Lorain St # 90
Mailing city: Oberlin
Mailing state: OH
Mailing zip: 44074-1053
General Phone: (440) 775-8123
General Fax: (440) 775-6733
General/National Adv. E-mail: advertisements@oberlinreview.org
Primary Website: www.oberlin.edu
Classified Equipment»
Personnel: Daniel Dudley (Bus. Mgr.); Talia Chicherio (Adv. Mgr.); Caitlin Duke (Ed. in Chief); Piper Niehaus (Ed. in Chief)

PORTSMOUTH

SHAWNEE STATE UNIV.

Street address 1: 940 2nd St
Street address 3: Portsmouth
Street address state: OH
Zip/Postal code: 45662-4303
Country: USA
Mailing address: 940 2nd St
Mailing city: Portsmouth
Mailing state: OH
Mailing zip: 45662-4347
General Phone: (740) 351-3278
General Fax: (740) 351-3566
Advertising Phone: (740) 351-3502
General/National Adv. E-mail: chronicle@shawnee.edu
Primary Website: www.shawnee.edu/pub/chrn
Classified Equipment»
Personnel: Terry Hapney (Advisor)

RIO GRANDE

UNIV. OF RIO GRANDE

Street address 1: 218 N College Ave
Street address 3: Rio Grande
Street address state: OH
Zip/Postal code: 45674-3100
Country: USA
Mailing address: 218 N College Ave
Mailing city: Rio Grande
Mailing state: OH
Mailing zip: 45674-3131
General Phone: (740) 245-7521
General Fax: (740) 245-7239
General/National Adv. E-mail: signals@rio.edu
Classified Equipment»
Personnel: Nick Claussen (Advisor)

WITTENBERG UNIVERSITY

Street address 1: 200 W Ward St
Street address 3: Springfield
Street address state: OH
Zip/Postal code: 45504-2120
Country: USA
Mailing address: PO Box 720
Mailing city: Springfield
Mailing state: OH
Mailing zip: 45501-0720
General Phone: 512.968.4648
General/National Adv. E-mail: torch_editors@wittenberg.edu
Primary Website: www.thewittenbergtorch.com
Published: Wed
Classified Equipment»
Personnel: D'Arcy Fallon (Faculty Advisor); Maggie McKune (Ed. in Chief); Tara Osborne (Bus. Mgr.)

STEUBENVILLE

FRANCISCAN UNIVERSITY OF STEUBENVILLE

Street address 1: 1235 University Blvd
Street address 3: Steubenville
Street address state: OH
Zip/Postal code: 43952-1792
Country: USA
Mailing address: 1235 University Blvd
Mailing city: Steubenville
Mailing state: OH
Mailing zip: 43952-1796
General Phone: (740) 284-5014
General Fax: (740) 284-5452
General/National Adv. E-mail: troub@franciscan.edu
Primary Website: www.troubonline.com
Classified Equipment»
Personnel: Chris Pagano; Elizabeth Wong; Emily Lahr

TIFFIN

HEIDELBERG UNIVERSITY

Street address 1: 310 E Market St
Street address 3: Tiffin
Street address state: OH
Zip/Postal code: 44883-2434
Country: USA
Mailing address: 310 E. Market St.
Mailing city: Tiffin
Mailing state: OH
Mailing zip: 44883-2462
General Phone: (419) 448-2180
Year Established: 1894
Classified Equipment»
Note: We are in the process of rebuilding and investigating the possibility of going to an online format in addition to rebooting the print edition into a monthly.
Personnel: Mary Garrison (Visiting Assistant Professor of Communication)

UNIVERSITY OF TOLEDO

Street address 1: 2801 W Bancroft St
Street address 2: Mail Stop 530
Street address 3: Toledo
Street address state: OH
Zip/Postal code: 43606-3328
Country: USA
Mailing address: 2801 W Bancroft St
Mailing city: Toledo
Mailing state: OH
Mailing zip: 43606-3390
General Phone: (419) 530-7788
General Fax: (419) 530-7770
Advertising Phone: (419) 530-7788
Advertising Fax: (419) 530-7770
Editorail Phone: (419) 530-7788
Editorial Fax: (419) 530-7770
General/National Adv. E-mail: editor@independentcollegian.com
Display Adv. E-mail: sales@independentcollegian.com
Editorial e-mail: editor@independentcollegian.com
Primary Website: www.independentcollegian.com
Year Established: 1919
Special Editions: Back to school edition-August 22nd and August 25
Published: Wed
Avg Free Circ: 8000
Classified Equipment»
Personnel: J.R. Hoppenjans (Chairman of the board of trustees); Erik Gable (Adviser); Danielle Gamble (Editor-in-Chief)
Parent company (for newspapers): Collegian Media Foundation

UNIVERSITY HEIGHTS

JOHN CARROLL UNIVERSITY

Street address 1: 1 John Carroll Blvd
Street address 3: University Heights
Street address state: OH
Zip/Postal code: 44118-4538
Country: USA
Mailing address: 1 John Carroll Blvd
Mailing city: Cleveland
Mailing state: OH
Mailing zip: 44118-4582
General Phone: (216) 397-1711
General Fax: (216) 397-1729
Advertising Phone: (216) 397-4398
Editorail Phone: (216) 397-1711
General/National Adv. E-mail: jcunews@gmail.com
Display Adv. E-mail: jcunews@gmail.com
Editorial e-mail: jcunews@gmail.com
Primary Website: www.jcunews.com
Year Established: 1925
Published: Thur
Avg Free Circ: 1600
Classified Equipment»
Personnel: Mary Ann Flannery (Chair/Assoc. Prof.); Robert T. Noll (Advisor); Jacqueline J. Schmidt (Prof.); Katie Sheridan (Ed. in Chief); Bob Seeholzer (Mng. Ed.); Alan Stephenson (Prof.); Mary Beadle (Assoc. Prof.); Tim Ertle (Sports Ed.); Margaret Algren (Asst. Prof.); Richard Hendrickson (Asst. Prof.); Robert Prisco (Asst. Prof.); Bob Noll (Instr.); David Reese (Instr.); Fred Buchstein (Part-time Instr.); Mark Eden (Part-time Instr.); Bill Nichols (Part-time Instr.)

WESTERVILLE

OTTERBEIN UNIVERSITY

Street address 1: 1 S Grove St
Street address 2: Otterbein University
Street address 3: Westerville
Street address state: OH
Zip/Postal code: 43081-2004
Country: USA
Mailing address: Communication Department
Mailing city: Westerville
Mailing state: OH
Mailing zip: 43081
General Phone: (614) 823 1159
Advertising Phone: 614 823 1159
Editorail Phone: 614 823 1159
General/National Adv. E-mail: adviser@otterbein360.com
Display Adv. E-mail: sales@otterbein360.com
Primary Website: www.otterbein360.com
Year Established: 1880
Published: Mon`Tues`Wed`Thur`Fri`Sat`Sun
Classified Equipment»
Note: The Tan and Cardinal Newspaper has become a daily website, otterbein360.com, and a quarterly magazine, T&C.
Personnel: Hillary Warren (Advisor)

WILBERFORCE

CENTRAL STATE UNIV.

Street address 1: PO Box 1004
Street address 3: Wilberforce
Street address state: OH
Zip/Postal code: 45384-1004
Country: USA
Mailing address: PO Box 1004
Mailing city: Wilberforce
Mailing state: OH
Mailing zip: 45384-1004
General Phone: (937) 376-6095
General Fax: (937) 376-6530
General/National Adv. E-mail: info@centralstate.edu
Primary Website: www.centralstate.edu
Classified Equipment»
Personnel: Mike Gormley (Advisor)

WILBERFORCE UNIV.

Street address 1: 1055 N Bickett Rd
Street address 3: Wilberforce
Street address state: OH
Zip/Postal code: 45384-5801
Country: USA
Mailing address: PO Box 1001
Mailing city: Wilberforce
Mailing state: OH
Mailing zip: 45384-1001
General Phone: (937) 376-2911
General Fax: (937) 708-5793
General/National Adv. E-mail: tmorah@wilberforce.edu
Primary Website: www.wilberforce.edu
Classified Equipment»
Personnel: Tanya Morah (Advisor); Courtney Wiggins (Ed.)

WILMINGTON COLLEGE

Street address 1: 1870 Quaker Way
Street address 3: Wilmington
Street address state: OH
Zip/Postal code: 45177-2473
Country: USA
Mailing address: 1870 Quaker Way
Mailing city: Wilmington
Mailing state: OH
Mailing zip: 45177-2499
General Phone: (937) 382-6661
General Fax: (937) 382-7077
Primary Website: www2.wilmington.edu; www.wilmington.edu
Classified Equipment»
Personnel: Coreen Cockerill (Advisor); Clair Green (Ed. in Chief)

WOOSTER

COLLEGE OF WOOSTER

Street address 1: 1189 Beall Ave
Street address 3: Wooster
Street address state: OH
Zip/Postal code: 44691-2393
Country: USA
Mailing address: Box C-1387
Mailing city: Wooster
Mailing state: OH
Mailing zip: 44691-2393
General Phone: (330) 263-2598
General Fax: (330) 263-2596
General/National Adv. E-mail: voice@wooster.edu
Display Adv. E-mail: nisles@wooster.edu
Editorial e-mail: voice@wooster.edu
Primary Website: thewoostervoice.com
Published: Tues
Classified Equipment»
Personnel: Travis Marmon (Ed. in Chief); Ian Benson (Ed. in Chief)

YOUNGSTOWN

YOUNGSTOWN STATE UNIV.

Street address 1: 1 University Plz
Street address 3: Youngstown
Street address state: OH
Zip/Postal code: 44555-0001
Country: USA
Mailing address: 1 University Plz
Mailing city: Youngstown
Mailing state: OH
Mailing zip: 44555-0002
General Phone: (330) 941-1991
General Fax: (330) 941-2322
General/National Adv. E-mail: thejambar@gmail.com
Primary Website: www.thejambar.com
Year Established: 1931
Delivery Methods: Newsstand`Racks
Classified Equipment»
Personnel: Mary Beth Earnheardt (Advisor); Joshua Stipanovich (Editor in Chief); Chelsea Pflugh (Ed. in Chief); Adam Rogers (Mng. Ed.)

YOUNGSTOWN STATE UNIVERSITY

Street address 1: 1 University Plz
Street address 3: Youngstown
Street address state: OH
Zip/Postal code: 44555-0001
Country: USA
Mailing address: 1 University Plz
Mailing city: Youngstown
Mailing state: OH
Mailing zip: 44555-0002
General Phone: (330) 941-3095
General Fax: (330) 941-2322
Primary Website: www.thejambar.com
Classified Equipment»

OKLAHOMA

EAST CENTRAL UNIVERSITY

Street address 1: 1100 E 14th St
Street address 3: Ada
Street address state: OK
Zip/Postal code: 74820-6915
Country: USA
Mailing address: 1100 E 14th St
Mailing city: Ada
Mailing state: OK
Mailing zip: 74820-6915
General Phone: (580) 559-5250
General Fax: (580) 559-5251
General/National Adv. E-mail: journal@ecok.edu; ecujournal@me.com
Primary Website: www.ecujournal.com
Classified Equipment»
Personnel: Cathie Harding (Advisor); Melissa Hubble (Adv. Mgr.); Jonnathon Hicks (Ed. in Chief)

ALVA

NORTHWESTERN OKLAHOMA STATE UNIV.

Street address 1: 709 Oklahoma Blvd
Street address 3: Alva
Street address state: OK
Zip/Postal code: 73717-2749
Country: USA
Mailing address: 709 Oklahoma Blvd
Mailing city: Alva
Mailing state: OK
Mailing zip: 73717-2749
General Phone: (580) 327-8479
General Fax: (580) 327-8127
Advertising Phone: (580) 327-8479
Editorail Phone: (580) 327-8479
General/National Adv. E-mail: nwnewsroom@hotmail.com; nwnews@nwosu.edu
Display Adv. E-mail: nwnewsroom@hotmail.com
Editorial e-mail: nwnewsroom@hotmail.com
Primary Website: www.nwosu.edu/northwestern-news or www.rangerpulse.com
Year Established: 1897
Published: Thur
Avg Paid Circ: 200
Avg Free Circ: 1400
Classified Equipment»
Note: Northwestern News and rangerpulse.com are sister publications, but rangerpulse.com does carry content from both the newspaper and original content.
Personnel: Melanie Wilderman (Advisor)

BARTLESVILLE

BARTLESVILLE WESLEYAN COLLEGE

Street address 1: 2201 Silver Lake Rd
Street address 3: Bartlesville
Street address state: OK
Zip/Postal code: 74006-6233
Country: USA
Mailing address: 2201 Silver Lake Rd
Mailing city: Bartlesville
Mailing state: OK
Mailing zip: 74006-6299
General Phone: (918) 335-6200
Primary Website: www.okwu.edu
Classified Equipment»

BETHANY

SOUTHERN NAZARENE UNIV.

Street address 1: 6729 NW 39th Expy
Street address 3: Bethany
Street address state: OK
Zip/Postal code: 73008-2605
Country: USA
Mailing address: 6729 NW 39th Expy
Mailing city: Bethany
Mailing state: OK
Mailing zip: 73008-2694

General Phone: (405) 491-6382
General Fax: (405) 491-6378
General/National Adv. E-mail: echo@snu.edu
Display Adv. E-mail: grwillia@mail.snu.edu
Editorial e-mail: kirarobe@mail.snu.edu
Primary Website: echo.snu.edu
Published: Fri
Classified Equipment»
Personnel: Pam Broyles (Speech Commun. Dept.); Marcia Feisal (Yearbook); Jim Wilcox (Newspaper); Andrew Baker (Graphic Design); Les Dart (Broadcasting)

CHICKASHA

UNIV. OF SCIENCE & ARTS OF OKLAHOMA

Street address 1: 1727 W Alabama Ave
Street address 3: Chickasha
Street address state: OK
Zip/Postal code: 73018-5322
Country: USA
Mailing address: 1727 W Alabama Ave
Mailing city: Chickasha
Mailing state: OK
Mailing zip: 73018-5371
General Phone: (405) 224-3140
General Fax: (405) 521-6244
Primary Website: www.trend.usao.edu
Published: Other
Published Other: Ongoing (post several times a week)
Classified Equipment»
Personnel: J. C. Casey (Faculty Advisor & Professor of Communication)
Parent company (for newspapers): University of Science & Arts of Oklahoma

DURANT

SOUTHEASTERN OKLAHOMA STATE UNIV.

Street address 1: 425 W University Blvd
Street address 3: Durant
Street address state: OK
Zip/Postal code: 74701-3347
Country: USA
Mailing address: 425 W University Blvd.
Mailing city: Durant
Mailing state: OK
Mailing zip: 74701-0609
General Phone: (580) 745-2944
General Fax: (580) 745-7475
General/National Adv. E-mail: campuspages@gmail.com
Primary Website: www.thesoutheastern.com
Published: Mthly
Published Other: Website updated weekly. Newspaper published monthly. Magazine released once a year.
Classified Equipment»
Personnel: Tascha Bond (Adviser); Kourtney Kaufman (Managing Editor)
Parent company (for newspapers): Southeastern Oklahoma State University

THE VISTA

Street address 1: 100 N University Dr
Street address 3: Edmond
Street address state: OK
Zip/Postal code: 73034-5207
Country: USA
Mailing address: 100 N University Dr
Mailing city: Edmond
Mailing state: OK
Mailing zip: 73034-5207
General Phone: (405) 974-5123
General Fax: (405) 974-3839
Editorail Phone: (405) 974-5549
General/National Adv. E-mail: vistamedia@yahoo.com
Editorial e-mail: vista1903@gmail.com
Primary Website: www.uco360.com
Year Established: 1903
Classified Equipment»
Personnel: Teddy Burch (Advisor); Nelson Solomon (Ed. in Chief)

GOODWELL

OKLAHOMA PANHANDLE STATE UNIV.

Street address 1: PO Box 430
Street address 3: Goodwell
Street address state: OK
Zip/Postal code: 73939-0430
Country: USA
Mailing address: PO Box 430
Mailing city: Goodwell
Mailing state: OK
Mailing zip: 73939-0430
General Phone: (580) 349-2611
General Fax: (580) 349-1350
General/National Adv. E-mail: collegian@opsu.edu
Primary Website: www.opsu.edu
Classified Equipment»
Personnel: Lora Hays (Advisor); Samuel Moore (Ed.)

LANGSTON

LANGSTON UNIV.

Street address 1: Sanford Hall Rm 308W
Street address 3: Langston
Street address state: OK
Zip/Postal code: 73050
Country: USA
Mailing address: Sanford Hall Rm. 308W
Mailing city: Langston
Mailing state: OK
Mailing zip: 73050
General Phone: (405) 466-3245
General/National Adv. E-mail: lugazette@yahoo.com
Primary Website: www.lugazette.com
Classified Equipment»
Personnel: Chaz Kyser (Advisor)

LAWTON

CAMERON UNIV.

Street address 1: 2800 W Gore Blvd
Street address 3: Lawton
Street address state: OK
Zip/Postal code: 73505-6320
Country: USA
Mailing address: 2800 W Gore Blvd
Mailing city: Lawton
Mailing state: OK
Mailing zip: 73505-6377
General Phone: (580) 581-2259
Advertising Phone: (580) 581-2897
General/National Adv. E-mail: collegian@cameron.edu
Classified Equipment»
Personnel: Christopher Keller (Advisor)

NORTHEASTERN OKLAHOMA A&M COLLEGE

Street address 1: 206 I St NW
Street address 3: Miami
Street address state: OK
Zip/Postal code: 74354-5630
Country: USA
Mailing address: PO Box 3988
Mailing city: Miami
Mailing state: OK
Mailing zip: 74354
General Phone: (918) 542-8441
Classified Equipment»
Personnel: Rebecca Kirk (Advisor)

NORMAN

UNIV. OF OKLAHOMA

Street address 1: 860 Van Vleet
Street address 2: Rm 149A
Street address 3: Norman
Street address state: OK
Zip/Postal code: 73019-2035
Country: USA
Mailing address: 860 Van Vleet Rm 149A
Mailing city: Norman
Mailing state: OK
Mailing zip: 73019-2035
General Phone: (405) 325-2521
General Fax: (405) 325-5160
Advertising Fax: (405) 325-7517
General/National Adv. E-mail: dailynews@ou.edu; studentmedia@ou.edu
Primary Website: www.oudaily.com; www.ou.edu
Classified Equipment»
Personnel: Judy Robinson (Advisor); Jamie Hughes (Ed.); Caitlin Harrison (Mng. Ed.); Michelle Gray (Photo Ed.)

THE CAMPUS / MEDIAOCU

Street address 1: 2501 N. Blackwelder Ave
Street address 3: Oklahoma City
Street address state: OK
Zip/Postal code: 73106-1493
County: Oklahoma
Country: USA
General/National Adv. E-mail: TheCampus@okcu.edu
Display Adv. E-mail: thecampusads@okcu.edu
Classified Adv. E-mail: thecampusads@okcu.edu
Editorial e-mail: editor@okcu.edu
Primary Website: www.mediaocu.com
Year Established: 1906
Area Served - City: Oklahoma City University
Published: Other
Published Other: Online as updated
Weekday Frequency: All day
Avg Free Circ: 1000
Audit By: Sworn/Estimate/Non-Audited
Classified Equipment»
Personnel: Philip Todd (Faculty adviser)
Parent company (for newspapers): Oklahoma City University

OKLAHOMA CHRISTIAN UNIV.

Street address 1: PO Box 11000
Street address 3: Oklahoma City
Street address state: OK
Zip/Postal code: 73136-1100
Country: USA
Mailing address: PO Box 11000
Mailing city: Oklahoma City
Mailing state: OK
Mailing zip: 73136-1100
General Phone: (405) 425-5538
General Fax: (405) 425-5351
Editorial e-mail: talon.letter@oc.edu
Classified Equipment»
Personnel: Philip Patterson (Faculty Advisor); Kimberlee Rhodes (Adv. Mgr.); Will Kooi (Ed. in Chief)

OKLAHOMA CITY COMMUNITY COLLEGE

Street address 1: 7777 S May Ave
Street address 3: Oklahoma City
Street address state: OK
Zip/Postal code: 73159-4419
Country: USA
Mailing address: 7777 S May Ave
Mailing city: Oklahoma City
Mailing state: OK
Mailing zip: 73159-4499
General Phone: (405) 682-1611
General/National Adv. E-mail: editor@occc.edu
Display Adv. E-mail: matthew.s.carter@occc.edu
Editorial e-mail: editor@occc.edu
Primary Website: pioneer.occc.edu
Year Established: 1978
Advertising (Open Inch Rate) Weekday/Saturday: Yes
Published: Fri
Avg Free Circ: 2500
Classified Equipment»
Personnel: M Scott Carter (Advisor)
Parent company (for newspapers): Oklahoma City Community College

OKLAHOMA CITY UNIVERSITY

Street address 1: 2501 N Blackwelder Ave
Street address 3: Oklahoma City
Street address state: OK
Zip/Postal code: 73106-1402
Country: USA
Mailing address: 2501 N Blackwelder Ave Rm 117
Mailing city: Oklahoma City
Mailing state: OK
Mailing zip: 73106-1493
General Phone: (405) 208-6068
General Fax: (405) 208-6069
Advertising Phone: (405) 208-6068
Advertising Fax: (405) 208-6069
General/National Adv. E-mail: stupub@okcu.edu
Primary Website: www.mediaocu.com
Year Established: 1907
Delivery Methods: Newsstand
Commercial printers: Y
Classified Equipment»
Personnel: Kenna Griffin (Advisor)

POTEAU

CARL ALBERT STATE COLLEGE

Street address 1: 1507 S McKenna St
Street address 3: Poteau
Street address state: OK
Zip/Postal code: 74953-5207
Country: USA
Mailing address: 1507 S McKenna St
Mailing city: Poteau
Mailing state: OK
Mailing zip: 74953-5207
General Phone: (918) 647-1200
General Fax: (918) 647-1266
Classified Equipment»
Personnel: Marcus Blair (PR Dir.)

SHAWNEE

OKLAHOMA BAPTIST UNIV.

Street address 1: 500 W University St
Street address 2: Ste 61704
Street address 3: Shawnee
Street address state: OK
Zip/Postal code: 74804-2522
Country: USA
Mailing address: 500 W University St Ste 61704
Mailing city: Shawnee
Mailing state: OK
Mailing zip: 74804-2522
General Phone: (405) 878-2128
General Fax: (405) 878-2113
General/National Adv. E-mail: Holly.easttom@okbu.edu
Display Adv. E-mail: Holly.easttom@okbu.edu
Primary Website: www.okbu.edu
Year Established: 1942
Advertising (Open Inch Rate) Weekday/Saturday: Varies
Published: Wed
Avg Paid Circ: 22
Avg Free Circ: 1800
Classified Equipment»
Personnel: Holly Easttom (Advisor); Andrew Adams (Ed. in Chief)

ST. GREGORY'S COLLEGE

Street address 1: 1900 W MacArthur St
Street address 3: Shawnee
Street address state: OK
Zip/Postal code: 74804-2403
Country: USA
Mailing address: 1900 W MacArthur St
Mailing city: Shawnee
Mailing state: OK
Mailing zip: 74804-2499
General Phone: (405) 878-5100
General Fax: (405) 878-5198
Classified Equipment»
Personnel: Andrew Sneider (Advisor)

STILLWATER

OKLAHOMA STATE UNIV.

Street address 1: 106 Paul Miller
Street address 3: Stillwater
Street address state: OK
Zip/Postal code: 74078-4050
Country: USA
Mailing address: 106 Paul Miller
Mailing city: Stillwater
Mailing state: OK

Mailing zip: 74078-4050
General Phone: (405) 744-6365
General Fax: (405) 744-7936
Editorial e-mail: editor@ocolly.com
Primary Website: www.ocolly.com
Classified Equipment»
Personnel: Barbara Allen (Advisor); Emily Holman (Ed. in Chief)

TONKAWA

NORTHERN OKLAHOMA COLLEGE

Street address 1: 1220 E Grand Ave
Street address 3: Tonkawa
Street address state: OK
Zip/Postal code: 74653-4022
Country: USA
Mailing address: PO Box 310
Mailing city: Tonkawa
Mailing state: OK
Mailing zip: 74653-0310
General Phone: (580) 628-6444
General Fax: (580) 628-6209
Primary Website: www.north-ok.edu
Classified Equipment»
Personnel: Jeremy Stillwell (Advisor)

ORAL ROBERTS UNIV.

Street address 1: 7777 S Lewis Ave
Street address 2: Lrc 175
Street address 3: Tulsa
Street address state: OK
Zip/Postal code: 74171-0003
Country: USA
Mailing address: 7777 S Lewis Ave Lrc 175
Mailing city: Tulsa
Mailing state: OK
Mailing zip: 74171-0001
General Phone: (918) 495-7080
General Fax: (918) 495-6345
Advertising Phone: (918) 495-7080
Advertising Fax: (918) 495-6345
Editorail Phone: (918) 495-7080
Editorial Fax: (918) 495-6345
General/National Adv. E-mail: oracle@oru.edu
Display Adv. E-mail: oracleads@oru.edu
Primary Website: www.oruoracle.com
Year Established: 1965
News Services: Religion News Service
Delivery Methods: Carrier`Racks
Commercial printers: Y
Advertising (Open Inch Rate) Weekday/Saturday: $550 full page (b&w) to $75 one-eighth page (b&w) with color available for additional charge
Published: Fri`Bi-Mthly
Avg Paid Circ: 0
Avg Free Circ: 3500
Classified Equipment»
Note: Website only
Personnel: Kevin Armstrong (Advisor)

TULSA CMTY. COLLEGE

Street address 1: 909 S Boston Ave
Street address 2: Rm G-31
Street address 3: Tulsa
Street address state: OK
Zip/Postal code: 74119-2011
Country: USA
Mailing address: 909 S Boston Ave Rm G-31
Mailing city: Tulsa
Mailing state: OK
Mailing zip: 74119-2011
General Phone: (918) 595-7388
General Fax: (918) 595-7308
Classified Equipment»
Personnel: Jerry Goodwin (Advisor); Eric Bruce (Ed.)

UNIV. OF TULSA

Street address 1: 800 S Tucker Dr
Street address 3: Tulsa
Street address state: OK
Zip/Postal code: 74104-9700
Country: USA
Mailing address: 800 Tucker Dr
Mailing city: Tulsa
Mailing state: OK
Mailing zip: 74104-9700
General Phone: (918) 631-2259
General Fax: (918) 631-2885
General/National Adv. E-mail: collegian@utulsa.edu
Primary Website: www.utulsa.edu/collegian/
Published: Mon
Avg Free Circ: 2500
Classified Equipment»
Note: Please contact Elizabeth Cohen about advertising by email at collegian@utulsa.edu or elizabeth-cohen@utulsa.edu
Personnel: Kendra Blevins (Advisor); J.Christopher Proctor (Editor-in-Chief); Elizabeth Cohen (Business and Advertising Manager)

OREGON

LINN-BENTON CMTY. COLLEGE

Street address 1: 6500 Pacific Blvd SW
Street address 3: Albany
Street address state: OR
Zip/Postal code: 97321-3755
Country: USA
Mailing address: 6500 Pacific Blvd SW
Mailing city: Albany
Mailing state: OR
Mailing zip: 97321-3774
General Phone: (541) 917-4451
General Fax: (541) 917-4454
Editorail Phone: (541) 917-4452
General/National Adv. E-mail: commuter@linnbenton.edu
Primary Website: www.commuter.linnbenton.edu
Classified Equipment»
Personnel: Rob Priewe (Advisor); Frank Warren (Adv. Mgr.); Ryan henson Henson (Ed. in Chief)

SOUTHERN OREGON UNIV.

Street address 1: Stevenson Union, Rm 336, 1250 Siskiyou Blvd
Street address 3: Ashland
Street address state: OR
Zip/Postal code: 97520
Country: USA
Mailing address: Stevenson Union, Rm. 336, 1250 Siskiyou Blvd.
Mailing city: Ashland
Mailing state: OR
Mailing zip: 97520-5001
General Phone: (541) 552-6307
General Fax: (541) 552-6440
Advertising Phone: (541) 552-6306
General/National Adv. E-mail: siskiyou@students.sou.edu
Primary Website: www.sou.edu/su/siskiyou
Classified Equipment»
Personnel: Karen Finnegan (Advisor); Dwight Melton (Ed.)

BEND

CENTRAL OREGON COMMUNITY COLLEGE

Street address 1: 2600 NW College Way
Street address 3: Bend
Street address state: OR
Zip/Postal code: 97703-5933
Country: USA
Mailing address: 2600 NW College Way
Mailing city: Bend
Mailing state: OR
Mailing zip: 97701-5933
General Phone: (541) 383-7252
General Fax: (541) 383-7284
Editorial Fax: Free
General/National Adv. E-mail: broadsidemail@cocc.edu
Primary Website: broadside.cocc.edu
Published: Bi-Mthly
Classified Equipment»
Personnel: Leon Pantenburg (advisor)

COOS BAY

SOUTHWESTERN OREGON CMTY. COLLEGE

Street address 1: 1988 Newman Ave
Street address 3: Coos Bay
Street address state: OR
Zip/Postal code: 97420
Country: USA
Mailing address: 1988 Newman Ave.
Mailing city: Coos Bay
Mailing state: OR
Mailing zip: 97420-2956
General Phone: (541) 888-7442
Classified Equipment»
Personnel: Bridget Hildreth (Advisor)

CORVALLIS

OREGON STATE UNIV.

Street address 1: 118 Memorial Un E
Street address 3: Corvallis
Street address state: OR
Zip/Postal code: 97331-8592
Country: USA
Mailing address: 118 Memorial Un E
Mailing city: Corvallis
Mailing state: OR
Mailing zip: 97331-8592
General Phone: (541) 737-3374
General Fax: (541) 737-4999
Primary Website: www.dailybarometer.com
Classified Equipment»
Personnel: Brandon Southward (Ed. in chief); Taryn Luna (Ed.); Gail Cole (Ed. in Chief); Candice Ruud (Mng. Ed.)

LANE CMTY. COLLEGE

Street address 1: 4000 E 30th Ave
Street address 2: Rm 008
Street address 3: Eugene
Street address state: OR
Zip/Postal code: 97405-0640
Country: USA
Mailing address: 4000 East 30th Ave. Center Building, Room 008
Mailing city: Eugene
Mailing state: OR
Mailing zip: 97405-0640
General Phone: (541) 463-5881
General Fax: (541) 463-3993
General/National Adv. E-mail: torch@lanecc.edu
Primary Website: www.lcctorch.com
Classified Equipment»
Personnel: Dorothy Wearne (Advisor); Lana Boles (Ed. in Cheif); James Anderson (Ed.)

UNIV. OF OREGON

Street address 1: 1395 University St
Street address 3: Eugene
Street address state: OR
Zip/Postal code: 97403-2572
Country: USA
Mailing address: PO Box 3159
Mailing city: Eugene
Mailing state: OR
Mailing zip: 97403-0159
General Phone: (541) 346-5511
General Fax: (541) 346-5821
General/National Adv. E-mail: news@dailyemerald.com
Editorial e-mail: editor@dailyemerald.com
Primary Website: www.dailyemerald.com
Classified Equipment»
Personnel: Allie Grasgreen (Ed. in chief); Emily E. Smith (Mng. Ed.); Ivar Vong (Photo Ed.)

FOREST GROVE

PACIFIC UNIV.

Street address 1: 2043 College Way
Street address 3: Forest Grove
Street address state: OR
Zip/Postal code: 97116-1756
Country: USA
Mailing address: 2043 College Way
Mailing city: Forest Grove
Mailing state: OR
Mailing zip: 97116
General Phone: (503) 352-2855
Advertising Phone: 503 352 2855
Advertising Fax: (503) 352-3130
Editorail Phone: 503 352 2855
General/National Adv. E-mail: index@pacificu.edu
Editorial e-mail: karissa@pacindex.com
Primary Website: www.pacindex.com
Year Established: 1897
Delivery Methods: Newsstand
Advertising (Open Inch Rate) Weekday/Saturday: $5.50/ column inch net
Published: Bi-Mthly
Avg Free Circ: 1200
Classified Equipment»
Personnel: Dave Cassady (Adviser); Karrisa George (Managing editor); Kathleen Rohde (Web edition editor)

GRESHAM

MT. HOOD CMTY. COLLEGE

Street address 1: 26000 SE Stark St
Street address 3: Gresham
Street address state: OR
Zip/Postal code: 97030-3300
Country: USA
Mailing address: 26000 SE Stark St
Mailing city: Gresham
Mailing state: OR
Mailing zip: 97030-3300
General Phone: (503) 491-7250
General Fax: (503) 491-6064
General/National Adv. E-mail: advocatt@mhcc.edu
Published: Fri
Classified Equipment»
Personnel: Ivy Davis (EIC); Dan Ernst (Advisor)

KLAMATH FALLS

OREGON INSTITUTE OF TECHNOLOGY

Street address 1: 3201 Campus Dr
Street address 2: # CU111C
Street address 3: Klamath Falls
Street address state: OR
Zip/Postal code: 97601-8801
Country: USA
Mailing address: 3201 Campus Dr # CU111C
Mailing city: Klamath Falls
Mailing state: OR
Mailing zip: 97601-8801
General Phone: (541) 885-1371
General Fax: (541) 885-1024
General/National Adv. E-mail: edge@oit.edu
Classified Equipment»
Personnel: Steve Matthies (Advisor)

LA GRANDE

EASTERN OREGON UNIV.

Street address 1: 1 University Blvd
Street address 2: Hoke 320
Street address 3: La Grande
Street address state: OR
Zip/Postal code: 97850-2807
Country: USA
Mailing address: 1 University Blvd Hoke 320
Mailing city: La Grande
Mailing state: OR
Mailing zip: 97850-2807
General Phone: (541) 962-3386
General Fax: (541) 962-3706
General/National Adv. E-mail: thevoice@eou.edu
Primary Website: www.eou.edu/thevoice
Classified Equipment»
Personnel: Kyle Janssen (Ed. in Chief); Taylor Stanely Pawley (Adv. Mgr.)

MCMINNVILLE

LINFIELD COLLEGE

Street address 1: 900 SE Baker St
Street address 2: Ste A518
Street address 3: McMinnville
Street address state: OR
Zip/Postal code: 97128-6808
Country: USA
Mailing address: 900 SE Baker St Ste A518
Mailing city: McMinnville
Mailing state: OR
Mailing zip: 97128-6894
General Phone: (503) 883-2200
General/National Adv. E-mail: review@linfield.edu
Primary Website: www.linfield.edu/linfield-review
Classified Equipment»
Personnel: William Lingle (Advisor); Dominic Baez (Ed. in Chief)

WESTERN OREGON UNIV.

Street address 1: 345 Monmouth Ave N
Street address 3: Monmouth
Street address state: OR
Zip/Postal code: 97361-1329
Country: USA
Mailing address: 345 Monmouth Ave N
Mailing city: Monmouth
Mailing state: OR
Mailing zip: 97361-1371
General Phone: (503) 838-9697
General Fax: (503) 838-8616
Advertising Phone: (503) 838-8836
Classified Equipment»
Personnel: Marissa Hufstader (Bus./Adv. Mgr.)

OREGON CITY

CLACKAMAS CMTY. COLLEGE

Street address 1: 19600 Molalla Ave
Street address 3: Oregon City
Street address state: OR
Zip/Postal code: 97045-8980
Country: USA
Mailing address: 19600 Molalla Ave
Mailing city: Oregon City
Mailing state: OR
Mailing zip: 97045-7998
General Phone: (503) 657-6958
General Fax: (503) 650-7350
General/National Adv. E-mail: chiefed@clackamus.edu
Classified Equipment»
Personnel: Melissa Jones (Advisor); Kayla Berge (Ed.); John Hurlburg (Ed.)

LEWIS & CLARK COLLEGE

Street address 1: 0615 SW Palatine Hill Rd
Street address 3: Portland
Street address state: OR
Zip/Postal code: 97219-7879
Country: USA
Mailing address: 0615 SW Palatine Hill Rd
Mailing city: Portland
Mailing state: OR
Mailing zip: 97219-7879
General Phone: (503) 768-7146
General Fax: (503) 768-7130
Editorial Fax: Free
General/National Adv. E-mail: piolog@lclark.edu
Display Adv. E-mail: ads.piolog@gmail.com
Editorial e-mail: piolog@gmail.com
Primary Website: www.piolog.com
Year Established: 1947
Special Editions: New Student Orientation, April Fool's
Delivery Methods: Mail`Racks
Commercial printers: N
Published: Fri
Avg Free Circ: 1200
Classified Equipment»
Personnel: Caleb Diehl (Editor-in-Chief)

PORTLAND CMTY. COLLEGE

Street address 1: 12000 SW 49th Ave
Street address 3: Portland
Street address state: OR
Zip/Postal code: 97219-7132
Country: USA
Mailing address: PO Box 19000
Mailing city: Portland
Mailing state: OR
Mailing zip: 97280-0990
General Phone: (503) 977-4184
General Fax: (503) 977-4956
General/National Adv. E-mail: tsteffen@pcc.edu
Year Established: 1963
Classified Equipment»
Personnel: Tami Steffenhagen (Gen. Mgr.)

PORTLAND STATE UNIV.

Street address 1: PO Box 347
Street address 3: Portland
Street address state: OR
Zip/Postal code: 97207-0347
Country: USA
Mailing address: PO Box 751
Mailing city: Portland
Mailing state: OR
Mailing zip: 97207-0751
General Phone: (503) 725-5691
General Fax: (503) 725-5860
General/National Adv. E-mail: vanguardadvertising@gmail.com
Primary Website: www.dailyvanguard.com
Year Established: 1948
Classified Equipment»
Personnel: Judson Randall (Advisor); Matthew Kirtley (Adv. Mgr.); Sarah J. Christensen (Ed. in Chief)

REED COLLEGE

Street address 1: 3203 SE Woodstock Blvd
Street address 3: Portland
Street address state: OR
Zip/Postal code: 97202-8138
Country: USA
Mailing address: 3203 SE Woodstock Blvd
Mailing city: Portland
Mailing state: OR
Mailing zip: 97202-8199
General Phone: (503) 777-7707
General Fax: (503) 788-6657
General/National Adv. E-mail: quest@reed.edu
Classified Equipment»

THE BEACON/ UNIV. OF PORTLAND

Street address 1: 5000 N Willamette Blvd
Street address 2: MS 161
Street address 3: Portland
Street address state: OR
Zip/Postal code: 97203-5743
Country: USA
Mailing address: 5000 N Willamette Blvd
Mailing city: Portland
Mailing state: OR
Mailing zip: 97203-5798
General Phone: (503) 943-7376
General Fax: (503) 943-7833
General/National Adv. E-mail: beacon@up.edu
Display Adv. E-mail: beaconads@up.edu
Primary Website: www.upbeacon.com
Year Established: 1935
Delivery Methods: Racks
Commercial printers: Y

PUBLISHED OTHER: WE ARE NOW DIGITAL ONLY

~~Classified Equipment»~~
Personnel: Nancy Copic (Advisor)

ROSEBURG

UMPQUA CMTY. COLLEGE

Street address 1: 1140 College Rd
Street address 3: Roseburg
Street address state: OR
Zip/Postal code: 97470
Country: USA
Mailing address: PO Box 967
Mailing city: Roseburg
Mailing state: OR
Mailing zip: 97470-0226
General Phone: (541) 440-4687
General Fax: (541) 677-3214
General/National Adv. E-mail: uccmainstream@yahoo.com
Primary Website: www.mainstreamonline.org
Classified Equipment»
Personnel: Melinda Benton (Advisor)

CHEMEKETA CMTY. COLLEGE

Street address 1: PO Box 14007
Street address 3: Salem
Street address state: OR
Zip/Postal code: 97309-7070
Country: USA
Mailing address: PO Box 14007
Mailing city: Salem
Mailing state: OR
Mailing zip: 97309-7070
General Phone: (503) 399-5000
General Fax: (503) 399-2519
General/National Adv. E-mail: courier@chemeketa.edu
Display Adv. E-mail: careeradvertising@yahoo.com
Primary Website: www.chemeketa.edu/collegelife/newspaper/index.html
Classified Equipment»
Personnel: William Florence (Advisor); Gale Hann (Adv. Mgr.); Russell Vineyard (Mng.Ed.)

WILLAMETTE UNIV.

Street address 1: 900 State St
Street address 3: Salem
Street address state: OR
Zip/Postal code: 97301-3922
Country: USA
Mailing address: 900 State St
Mailing city: Salem
Mailing state: OR
Mailing zip: 97301-3931
General Phone: (503) 370-6053
General/National Adv. E-mail: collegian-exec@willamette.edu
Display Adv. E-mail: collegian-ads@willamette.edu
Primary Website: www.willamettecollegian.com
Published: Bi-Mthly
Classified Equipment»
Personnel: Avery Bento (Advisor); James Hoodecheck (Bus. Mgr.); Gianni Marabella (Ed. in Chief)

PENNSYLVANIA

ABINGTON

PENN STATE UNIV.

Street address 1: 1600 Woodland Rd
Street address 3: Abington
Street address state: PA
Zip/Postal code: 19001-3918
Country: USA
Mailing address: 1600 Woodland Rd
Mailing city: Abington
Mailing state: PA
Mailing zip: 19001-3990
General Phone: (215) 881-7507
General Fax: (215) 881-7660
General/National Adv. E-mail: fdq1@psu.edu
Primary Website: www.abington.psu.edu
Classified Equipment»
Personnel: Frank Quattrone (Ed.)

ALLENTOWN

CEDAR CREST COLLEGE

Street address 1: 100 College Dr
Street address 3: Allentown
Street address state: PA
Zip/Postal code: 18104-6132
Country: USA
Mailing address: 100 College Dr
Mailing city: Allentown
Mailing state: PA
Mailing zip: 18104-6196
General Phone: (610) 437-4471
General Fax: (610) 437-5955
General/National Adv. E-mail: crestiad@cedarcrest.edu
Primary Website: www.cedarcrest.edu/crestiad
Year Established: 1932
Commercial printers: Y
Classified Equipment»
Personnel: Elizabeth Ortiz (Advisor)

MUHLENBERG COLLEGE

Street address 1: 2400 Chew St
Street address 3: Allentown
Street address state: PA
Zip/Postal code: 18104-5564
Country: USA
Mailing address: 2400 W. Chew Street
Mailing city: Allentown
Mailing state: PA
Mailing zip: 18104
General Phone: (484) 664-3195
General/National Adv. E-mail: weeklyeditor@gmail.com
Primary Website: www.muhlenbergweekly.com
Year Established: 1883
Published: Thur
Classified Equipment»
Personnel: Gregory Kantor (Editor in Chief)

ALTOONA

PENN STATE UNIV.

Street address 1: Raymond Smith Bldg
Street address 3: Altoona
Street address state: PA
Zip/Postal code: 16601
Country: USA
Mailing address: Raymond Smith Bldg.
Mailing city: Altoona
Mailing state: PA
Mailing zip: 16601
General Phone: (814) 940-4658
General Fax: (814) 949-5007
Classified Equipment»
Personnel: Savannah Straub (Contact); Margaret Moses (Contact)

ANNVILLE

LEBANON VALLEY COLLEGE

Street address 1: 101 N College Ave
Street address 3: Annville
Street address state: PA
Zip/Postal code: 17003-1404
Country: USA
Mailing address: 101 N College Ave
Mailing city: Annville
Mailing state: PA
Mailing zip: 17003-1400
General Phone: (717) 867-6169
General/National Adv. E-mail: lavic@lvc.edu
Primary Website: lavieonline.lvc.edu
Classified Equipment»
Personnel: Bob Vicic (Advisor); Jake King (Co Ed. in Chief); Katie Zwiebel (Co Ed. in Chief)

ASTON

THE JOUST

Street address 1: 1 Neumann Dr
Street address 2: Neumann University
Street address 3: Aston
Street address state: PA
Zip/Postal code: 19014-1277
Country: USA
Mailing address: 1 Neumann Dr
Mailing city: Aston
Mailing state: PA
Mailing zip: 19014
General Phone: 610-358-4570

General Fax: 610-361-5314
General/National Adv. E-mail: glassj@neumann.edu
Primary Website: www.neumann.edu
Classified Equipment»

BEAVER FALLS

GENEVA COLLEGE

Street address 1: 3200 College Ave
Street address 3: Beaver Falls
Street address state: PA
Zip/Postal code: 15010-3557
Country: USA
Mailing address: 3200 College Ave
Mailing city: Beaver Falls
Mailing state: PA
Mailing zip: 15010-3599
General Phone: (724) 847-6605
General Fax: (724) 847-6772
General/National Adv. E-mail: cabinet.editor@gmail.comcabinet
Primary Website: www.geneva.edu
Classified Equipment»
Personnel: Tom Copeland (Advisor)

BETHLEHEM

LEHIGH UNIV.

Street address 1: 33 Coppee Dr
Street address 3: Bethlehem
Street address state: PA
Zip/Postal code: 18015-3165
Country: USA
Mailing address: 33 Coppee Dr
Mailing city: Bethlehem
Mailing state: PA
Mailing zip: 18015-3165
General Phone: (610) 758-4454
General Fax: (610) 758-6198
General/National Adv. E-mail: bw@lehigh.edu
Primary Website: www.thebrownandwhite.com
Classified Equipment»
Personnel: Wally Trimble (Head); Julie Stewart (Ed. In Chief); Jack Lule (Ed. in Chief)

MORAVIAN COLLEGE

Street address 1: 1200 Main St
Street address 3: Bethlehem
Street address state: PA
Zip/Postal code: 18018-6614
Country: USA
Mailing address: 1200 Main St
Mailing city: Bethlehem
Mailing state: PA
Mailing zip: 18018-6650
General Phone: (610) 625-7509
General Fax: (610) 866-1682
General/National Adv. E-mail: comenian@moravian.edu
Primary Website: comenian.org
Published: Bi-Mthly
Classified Equipment»
Personnel: Mark Harris (Advisor); Kaytlyn Gordon (Editor-in-Chief)

NORTHAMPTON CMTY. COLLEGE

Street address 1: 3835 Green Pond Rd
Street address 3: Bethlehem
Street address state: PA
Zip/Postal code: 18020-7568
Country: USA
Mailing address: 3835 Green Pond Rd
Mailing city: Bethlehem
Mailing state: PA
Mailing zip: 18020-7599
General Phone: (610) 861-5372
General Fax: (610) 332-6163
Advertising Phone: (610) 861-5372
Editorail Phone: (610) 861-5372
General/National Adv. E-mail: thecommuter@northampton.edu
Display Adv. E-mail: thecommuter@northampton.edu
Editorial e-mail: thecommuter@northampton.edu
Primary Website: www.ncccommuter.org
Advertising (Open Inch Rate) Weekday/Saturday: Yes
Published: Mthly
Avg Paid Circ: 0
Avg Free Circ: 2000
Classified Equipment»
Note: Website under development; operational fall 2012
Personnel: Rob Hays (Advisor)

BLOOMSBURG

BLOOMSBURG UNIV.

Street address 1: 400 E 2nd St
Street address 3: Bloomsburg
Street address state: PA
Zip/Postal code: 17815-1301
Country: USA
Mailing address: 400 E. Second St.
Mailing city: Bloomsburg
Mailing state: PA
Mailing zip: 17815
General Phone: (570) 389-4457
General Fax: (570) 389-3905
Primary Website: www.bloomu.edu/voice/index.php
Classified Equipment»
Personnel: Mary Bernath (Advisor); Zach Sands (Adv. Dir.); Joe Arieth (Ed. in Chief)

BLUE BELL

MONTGOMERY COUNTY CMTY. COLLEGE

Street address 1: 340 Dekalb Pike
Street address 3: Blue Bell
Street address state: PA
Zip/Postal code: 19422-1412
Country: USA
Mailing address: 340 Dekalb Pike
Mailing city: Blue Bell
Mailing state: PA
Mailing zip: 19422-1400
General Phone: (215) 619-7306
General Fax: (215) 619-7191
Classified Equipment»
Personnel: Brian Brendlinger (Dir., Student Activities)

BRADFORD

UNIV. OF PITTSBURGH AT BRADFORD

Street address 1: 300 Campus Dr
Street address 3: Bradford
Street address state: PA
Zip/Postal code: 16701-2812
Country: USA
Mailing address: 300 Campus Dr
Mailing city: Bradford
Mailing state: PA
Mailing zip: 16701-2898
General Phone: (814) 362-7682
General Fax: (814) 362-7518
General/National Adv. E-mail: source@pitt.edu
Display Adv. E-mail: tfjz@atlanticbb.net
Editorial e-mail: tfjz@atlanticbb.net
Classified Equipment»
Personnel: Tim Ziaukas (Advisor)

BRYN MAWR

BRYN MAWR-HAVERFORD COLLEGE

Street address 1: 101 N Merion Ave
Street address 3: Bryn Mawr
Street address state: PA
Zip/Postal code: 19010-2859
Country: USA
Mailing address: 101 N Merion Ave
Mailing city: Bryn Mawr
Mailing state: PA
Mailing zip: 19010-2899
General Phone: (610) 526-5000
General Fax: (610) 526-7479
General/National Adv. E-mail: biconews@haverford.edu
Primary Website: www.biconews.com
Classified Equipment»
Personnel: Eurie Kim (Bus. Mgr.); Sam Kaplan (Ed. in Chief); Dave Merrell (Ed. Emer./Web Ed.)

BUTLER

BUTLER COUNTY CMTY. COLLEGE

Street address 1: 107 College Dr
Street address 3: Butler
Street address state: PA
Zip/Postal code: 16002-3807
Country: USA
Mailing address: PO Box 1203
Mailing city: Butler
Mailing state: PA
Mailing zip: 16003-1203
General Phone: (724) 287-8711
General Fax: (724) 285-6047
General/National Adv. E-mail: cube.stass@bc3.edu
Primary Website: www.bc3.edu
Classified Equipment»
Personnel: David Moser (Advisor); Patrick Reddick (Ed.)

CARLISLE

DICKINSON COLLEGE

Street address 1: PO Box 1773
Street address 3: Carlisle
Street address state: PA
Zip/Postal code: 17013-2896
Country: USA
Mailing address: PO Box 1773
Mailing city: Carlisle
Mailing state: PA
Mailing zip: 17013-2896
General Phone: (717) 254-8434
General Fax: (717) 254-8430
General/National Adv. E-mail: dsonian@dickinson.edu
Primary Website: www.dickinson.edu/dickinsonian
Classified Equipment»
Personnel: Alec Johnson (Ed. in Chief); Eddie Small (Mng. Ed.)

CENTER VALLEY

DESALES UNIV.

Street address 1: 2755 Station Ave
Street address 3: Center Valley
Street address state: PA
Zip/Postal code: 18034-9565
Country: USA
Mailing address: 2755 Station Ave
Mailing city: Center Valley
Mailing state: PA
Mailing zip: 18034-9568
General Phone: (610) 282-1100
General Fax: (610) 282-3798
General/National Adv. E-mail: minstrel.desales@gmail.com
Primary Website: www.desalesminstrel.org
Published: Bi-Mthly
Classified Equipment»
Personnel: Kellie Dietrich (Editor-in-Chief)

CHAMBERSBURG

WILSON COLLEGE

Street address 1: 1015 Philadelphia Ave
Street address 3: Chambersburg
Street address state: PA
Zip/Postal code: 17201-1279
Country: USA
Mailing address: 1015 Philadelphia Ave
Mailing city: Chambersburg
Mailing state: PA
Mailing zip: 17201-1285
General Phone: (717) 264-4141
General Fax: (717) 264-1578
Classified Equipment»
Personnel: Aimee-Marie Dorsten (Advisor)

CHEYNEY

CHEYNEY UNIV. OF PENNSYLVANIA

Street address 1: 1837 University Cir
Street address 2: PO Box 200
Street address 3: Cheyney
Street address state: PA
Zip/Postal code: 19319-1019
Country: USA
Mailing address: 1837 University Cir
Mailing city: Cheyney
Mailing state: PA
Mailing zip: 19319-1019
General Phone: (610) 399-2121
Classified Equipment»
Note: Online version published once a semester.
Personnel: Owens Gwen (Advisor)

CLARION

CLARION UNIV. OF PENNSYLVANIA

Street address 1: 270 Gemmell Student Ctr
Street address 3: Clarion
Street address state: PA
Zip/Postal code: 16214
Country: USA
Mailing address: 270 Gemmell Student Ctr.
Mailing city: Clarion
Mailing state: PA
Mailing zip: 16214
General Phone: (814) 393-2000
General Fax: (814) 393-2557
General/National Adv. E-mail: call@clarion.edu
Primary Website: www.clarioncallnews.com
Classified Equipment»
Personnel: Laurie Miller (Advisor); Elizabeth Presutti (Adv. Mgr.); Luke Hampton (Ed. in Chief)

URSINUS COLLEGE

Street address 1: 601 E Main St
Street address 3: Collegeville
Street address state: PA
Zip/Postal code: 19426-2509
Country: USA
Mailing address: PO Box 1000
Mailing city: Collegeville
Mailing state: PA
Mailing zip: 19426-1000
General Phone: (610) 409-2448
General/National Adv. E-mail: grizzly@ursinus.edu
Classified Equipment»
Personnel: Rebecca Jaroff (Advisor)

MISERICORDIA UNIVERSITY

Street address 1: 301 Lake St
Street address 3: Dallas
Street address state: PA
Zip/Postal code: 18612-7752
Country: USA
Mailing address: 301 Lake St
Mailing city: Dallas
Mailing state: PA
Mailing zip: 18612-7752
General Phone: (570) 674-6737
General Fax: (570) 674-6751
General/National Adv. E-mail: highland@misericordia.edu
Primary Website: www.highlandernews.net
Published Other: Bi-Monthly
Classified Equipment»

DOYLESTOWN

DELAWARE VALLEY COLLEGE

Street address 1: 700 E Butler Ave
Street address 3: Doylestown
Street address state: PA
Zip/Postal code: 18901-2607
Country: USA
Mailing address: 700 E Butler Ave
Mailing city: Doylestown
Mailing state: PA
Mailing zip: 18901-2698

General Phone: (215) 489-2345
General Fax: (215) 230-2966
General/National Adv. E-mail: rampages@delval.edu
Primary Website: www.delvalrampages.com
Classified Equipment»
Personnel: James O'Connor (Advisor)

EAST STROUDSBURG

EAST STROUDSBURG UNIV.

Street address 1: University Ctr
Street address 3: East Stroudsburg
Street address state: PA
Zip/Postal code: 18301
Country: USA
Mailing address: 200 Prospect Street
Mailing city: East Stroudsburg
Mailing state: PA
Mailing zip: 18301
General Phone: (570) 422-3295
General Fax: (570) 422-3053
General/National Adv. E-mail: stroudcourier@yahoo.com
Primary Website: www.stroudcourier.com
Classified Equipment»
Personnel: Ryan Doyle (Adv. Mgr.); Stephanie Snyder (Ed. in Chief)

EASTON

LAFAYETTE COLLEGE

Street address 1: 111 Quad Dr
Street address 3: Easton
Street address state: PA
Zip/Postal code: 18042-1768
Country: USA
Mailing address: Farinon Center Box 9470
Mailing city: Easton
Mailing state: PA
Mailing zip: 18042
General Phone: (610) 330-5354
General Fax: (610) 330-5724
General/National Adv. E-mail: thelafayette@gmail.com
Primary Website: www.lafayettestudentnews.com
Classified Equipment»
Personnel: William Gordon (EIC); Ian Morse (Mgr Ed)

EDINBORO

EDINBORO UNIV. OF PENNSYLVANIA

Street address 1: 119 San Antonio Hall
Street address 3: Edinboro
Street address state: PA
Zip/Postal code: 16444-0001
Country: USA
Mailing address: 119 San Antonio Hall
Mailing city: Edinboro
Mailing state: PA
Mailing zip: 16444-0001
General Phone: (814) 732-2266
General Fax: (814) 732-2270
General/National Adv. E-mail: eupspectator1@yahoo.com
Primary Website: www.eupspectator.com
Classified Equipment»
Personnel: Josh Tysiachney (Advisor); Carli Hoehn (Adv. Mgr.); Britney Kemp (Ed. in Chief); Canuron Ferranti (Mng. Ed.)

ELIZABETHTOWN COLLEGE

Street address 1: 1 Alpha Dr
Street address 3: Elizabethtown
Street address state: PA
Zip/Postal code: 17022-2298
Country: USA
Mailing address: 1 Alpha Dr
Mailing city: Elizabethtown
Mailing state: PA
Mailing zip: 17022-2297
General Phone: (717) 361-1132
General/National Adv. E-mail: editor@etown.edu
Display Adv. E-mail: etownianads@etown.edu
Editorial e-mail: editor@etown.edu
Primary Website: www.etownian.com
Year Established: 1904
Published: Thur
Avg Paid Circ: 50
Avg Free Circ: 700
Classified Equipment»
Personnel: Aileen Ida (EIC); Erica Dolson (Adviser); Katie Weller (Asst. EIC); Amanda Jobes (Mng. Ed.)

ERIE

GANNON UNIV.

Street address 1: 109 University Sq
Street address 2: # 2142
Street address 3: Erie
Street address state: PA
Zip/Postal code: 16541-0002
Country: USA
Mailing address: 109 University Sq # 2142
Mailing city: Erie
Mailing state: PA
Mailing zip: 16541-0002
General Phone: (814) 871-7294
General Fax: (814) 871-7208
General/National Adv. E-mail: gannonknight@gannon.edu
Primary Website: www.gannon.edu
Classified Equipment»
Personnel: Frank Garland (Advisor)

MERCYHURST UNIVERSITY

Street address 1: 501 E 38th St
Street address 3: Erie
Street address state: PA
Zip/Postal code: 16546-0002
Country: USA
Mailing address: 501 E 38th St
Mailing city: Erie
Mailing state: PA
Mailing zip: 16546-0002
General Phone: (814) 824-2376
General Fax:
General/National Adv. E-mail: editormerciad@mercyhurst.edu
Display Adv. E-mail: admerciad@mercyhurst.edu
Editorial e-mail: opinionmerciad@mercyhurst.edu
Primary Website: merciad.mercyhurst.edu
Year Established: 1929
Delivery Methods: Racks
Commercial printers: Y
Advertising (Open Inch Rate) Weekday/Saturday: Yes
Mechanical available: Offset
Published: Wed
Avg Free Circ: 1200
Classified Equipment»
Personnel: Bill Welch (Advisor)

PENN STATE UNIV.

Street address 1: 4701 College Dr
Street address 3: Erie
Street address state: PA
Zip/Postal code: 16563-4117
Country: USA
Mailing address: 4701 College Dr
Mailing city: Erie
Mailing state: PA
Mailing zip: 16563-4117
General Phone: (814) 898-6488
General Fax: (814) 898-6019
General/National Adv. E-mail: www.pserie.psu.edu
Published: Tues
Classified Equipment»
Personnel: Sarah Veslany (Editor in Chief)

THE BEHREND BEACON

Street address 1: Penn State University-Erie the Behrend College
Street address 2: 0171 Irvin Kochel Center
Street address 3: Erie
Street address state: PA
Zip/Postal code: 16563-0001
Country: USA
Mailing address: Penn State University-Erie The Behrend College
Mailing city: Erie
Mailing state: PA
Mailing zip: 16563
General Phone: 814-898-6488
General/National Adv. E-mail: editor@psu.edu
Primary Website: www.thebehrendbeacon.com
Classified Equipment»

GETTYSBURG COLLEGE

Street address 1: PO Box 434
Street address 3: Gettysburg
Street address state: PA
Zip/Postal code: 17325
Country: USA
Mailing address: PO Box 434
Mailing city: Gettysburg
Mailing state: PA
Mailing zip: 17325
General Phone: (717) 337-6449
General Fax: (717) 337-6463
Primary Website: www.thegettysburgian.com
Classified Equipment»
Personnel: Joel Berg (Advisor); Sean Parke (Ed.)

GLENSIDE

ARCADIA UNIV.

Street address 1: 450 S Easton Rd
Street address 3: Glenside
Street address state: PA
Zip/Postal code: 19038-3215
Country: USA
Mailing address: 450 S Easton Rd
Mailing city: Glenside
Mailing state: PA
Mailing zip: 19038-3295
General Phone: (215) 572-4082
General Fax: (215) 881-8781
Primary Website: www.arcadia.edu; www.thetoweronline.com
Classified Equipment»
Personnel: Michele Cain (Sec)

SETON HILL UNIVERSITY

Street address 1: 1 Seton Hill Dr
Street address 2: PO Box 343K
Street address 3: Greensburg
Street address state: PA
Zip/Postal code: 15601-1548
Country: USA
Mailing address: PO Box 343K
Mailing city: Greensburg
Mailing state: PA
Mailing zip: 15601-1599
General Phone: (724) 830-4791
General Fax: (724) 830-4611
General/National Adv. E-mail: setonian@gmail.com
Primary Website: www.setonhill.edu
Published: Mthly
Classified Equipment»
Personnel: Olivia Goudy (Editor-in-Chief)

UNIV. OF PITTSBURGH/ GREENSBURG

Street address 1: 150 Finoli Dr
Street address 2: 122 Village Hall
Street address 3: Greensburg
Street address state: PA
Zip/Postal code: 15601-5804
Country: USA
General Phone: (724) 836-7481
General Fax: (724) 836-9888
General/National Adv. E-mail: upginsider@gmail.com
Primary Website: www.upginsider.com
Classified Equipment»
Personnel: Lori Jakiela (Advisor)

THIEL COLLEGE

Street address 1: 75 College Ave
Street address 3: Greenville
Street address state: PA
Zip/Postal code: 16125-2186
Country: USA
Mailing address: 75 College Ave
Mailing city: Greenville
Mailing state: PA
Mailing zip: 16125-2181
General Phone: (724)589-2416
General/National Adv. E-mail: newspaper@thiel.edu
Primary Website: www.thiel.edu/thielensian
Classified Equipment»
Personnel: James Raykie (Advisor); Alivia Lapcevich (Ed. in Chief)

GROVE CITY

GROVE CITY COLLEGE

Street address 1: 100 Campus Dr
Street address 3: Grove City
Street address state: PA
Zip/Postal code: 16127-2101
Country: USA
Mailing address: 100 Campus Dr
Mailing city: Grove City
Mailing state: PA
Mailing zip: 16127-2104
General Phone: (724) 458-2193
General Fax: (724) 458-2167
General/National Adv. E-mail: collegian@gcc.edu
Year Established: 1891
Published: Fri
Avg Free Circ: 1500
Classified Equipment»
Note: The Collegian is produced by students and published by Grove City College.
Personnel: Nick Hildebrand (Adviser); Karen Postupac (Editor-in_Chief); James Sutherland (Managing Editor)

THE FOURTH ESTATE

Street address 1: 1 Hacc Dr Cooper 110
Street address 2: Harrisburg Area Community College
Street address 3: Harrisburg
Street address state: PA
Zip/Postal code: 17110-2903
Country: USA
Mailing address: Harrisburg Area Community College
Mailing city: Harrisburg
Mailing state: PA
Mailing zip: 17110
General Phone: 717-780-2582
General/National Adv. E-mail: 4estate@hacc.edu
Classified Equipment»

HAZLETON

PENN STATE UNIV.

Street address 1: 76 University Dr
Street address 3: Hazleton
Street address state: PA
Zip/Postal code: 18202-8025
Country: USA
Mailing address: 76 University Dr
Mailing city: Hazleton
Mailing state: PA
Mailing zip: 18202-1291
General Phone: (570) 450-3131
General Fax: (570) 450-3182
Classified Equipment»
Personnel: April Snyder (Advisor)

HUNTINGDON

JUNIATA COLLEGE

Street address 1: 1700 Moore St
Street address 3: Huntingdon
Street address state: PA
Zip/Postal code: 16652-2119
Country: USA
Mailing address: 1700 Moore St
Mailing city: Huntingdon
Mailing state: PA
Mailing zip: 16652-2196
General Phone: (814) 641-3000
Advertising Fax: (814) 643-3620
Editorail Phone: (814) 641-3132
Primary Website: www.juniatian.com
Delivery Methods: Racks
Commercial printers: Y
Published: Bi-Mthly
Classified Equipment»

INDIANA

INDIANA UNIV. OF PENNSYLVANIA

Street address 1: 319 Pratt Dr
Street address 3: Indiana
Street address state: PA
Zip/Postal code: 15701-2954
Country: USA
Mailing address: 319 Pratt Dr
Mailing city: Indiana
Mailing state: PA
Mailing zip: 15701-2954
General Phone: (724) 357-1306
General Fax: (724) 357-0127
Advertising Phone: (724) 357-0127
Editorail Phone: (724) 357-1306
Display Adv. E-mail: the-penn@iup.edu
Primary Website: www.thepenn.org
Classified Equipment»
Personnel: Joe Lawley (Advisor); Heather Blake (Ed. in Cheif); Branden Oakes (Photo Ed.)

JOHNSTOWN

UNIV. OF PITTSBURGH

Street address 1: 147 Student Union, 450 School House Rd
Street address 3: Johnstown
Street address state: PA
Zip/Postal code: 15904
Country: USA
Mailing address: 147 Student Union, 450 School House Rd.
Mailing city: Johnstown
Mailing state: PA
Mailing zip: 15904-1200
General Phone: (814) 269-7470
General/National Adv. E-mail: joo10@pitt.edu
Primary Website: www.upjadvocate.com
Classified Equipment»
Personnel: Leland Wood (Staff Advisor); Michael Cuccaro (Adv. Mgr.); Jon O' Connel (Ed. in Chief); Ryan Brown (News Ed.)

LA PLUME

THE KEY

Street address 1: 1 College Grn
Street address 2: Keystone College
Street address 3: La Plume
Street address state: PA
Zip/Postal code: 18440-1000
Country: USA
Mailing address: Keystone College
Mailing city: La Plume
Mailing state: PA
Mailing zip: 18440
General Phone: 570-945-8449
Classified Equipment»

FRANKLIN & MARSHALL COLLEGE

Street address 1: PO Box 3003
Street address 3: Lancaster
Street address state: PA
Zip/Postal code: 17604-3003
Country: USA
Mailing address: PO Box 3003
Mailing city: Lancaster
Mailing state: PA
Mailing zip: 17604-3003
General Phone: (717) 291-4095
General Fax: (717) 291-3886
Display Adv. E-mail: reporterads@fandm.edu
Editorial e-mail: reporter@fandm.edu
Primary Website: thediplomat.fandm.edu
Classified Equipment»
Personnel: Justin Quinn (Advisor); Patrick Bernard (Advisor); Christian Wedekind (Ed.)

LATROBE

SAINT VINCENT COLLEGE

Street address 1: 300 Fraser Purchase Rd
Street address 3: Latrobe
Street address state: PA
Zip/Postal code: 15650-2667
Country: USA
Mailing address: 300 Fraser Purchase Rd
Mailing city: Latrobe
Mailing state: PA
Mailing zip: 15650-2690
General Phone: (724) 539-9761
Advertising Phone: (717)669-0703
Editorail Phone: (717)669-0703
General/National Adv. E-mail: review.stvincent@gmail.com
Editorial e-mail: bridget.fertal@stvincent.edu
Primary Website: http://www.stvincentreview.com/
Advertising (Open Inch Rate) Weekday/Saturday: Email review.stvincent@gmail.com for advertising details
Published: Wed
Classified Equipment»
Personnel: Dennis McDaniel (Advisor); Bridget Fertal (Editor-in-Chief); Cheyenne Dunbar (Business Manager)

LEWISBURG

BUCKNELL UNIV. COLLEGE OF ENGINEERING

Street address 1: 701 Moore Ave
Street address 3: Lewisburg
Street address state: PA
Zip/Postal code: 17837-2010
Country: USA
Mailing address: 701 Moore Ave
Mailing city: Lewisburg
Mailing state: PA
Mailing zip: 17837-2010
General Phone: (570) 577-1520
General/National Adv. E-mail: bucknellian@bucknell.edu
Primary Website: www.bucknell.edu/bucknellian
Classified Equipment»
Personnel: James Lee (Advisor); Lily Beauvilliers (Ed. in Chief)

BUCKNELL UNIV.

Street address 1: PO Box C-3952
Street address 3: Lewisburg
Street address state: PA
Zip/Postal code: 17837
Country: USA
Mailing address: PO Box C-3952
Mailing city: Lewisburg
Mailing state: PA
Mailing zip: 17837-9988
General Phone: (570) 577-1520
General Fax: (570) 577-1176
Editorail Phone: (570) 577-1085
Display Adv. E-mail: bucknellianads@bucknell.edu
Primary Website: http://bucknellian.blogs.bucknell.edu/
Year Established: 1896
Published: Fri
Avg Paid Circ: 550
Avg Free Circ: 4000
Classified Equipment»
Personnel: James F. Lee (Advisor); Winnie Warner (Ed. in Chief); Ben Kaufman (Editor in Chief)

LINCOLN UNIVERSITY

LINCOLN UNIV.

Street address 1: 1570 Baltimore Pike
Street address 3: Lincoln University
Street address state: PA
Zip/Postal code: 19352-9141
Country: USA
Mailing address: 1570 Baltimore Pike
Mailing city: Lincoln University
Mailing state: PA
Mailing zip: 19352-9141
General Phone: (484) 365-7524
General Fax: (610) 932-1256
Primary Website: www.thelincolnianonline.com
Classified Equipment»
Personnel: Eric Watson (Advisor)

LOCK HAVEN

LOCK HAVEN UNIV. OF PENNSYLVANIA

Street address 1: 401 N Fairview St
Street address 2: Parsons Union Bldg.
Street address 3: Lock Haven
Street address state: PA
Zip/Postal code: 17745-2342
Country: USA
General Phone: (570) 484-2334
General/National Adv. E-mail: lhueagleye@yahoo.com
Primary Website: www.lhueagleye.com
Classified Equipment»
Personnel: Joe Stender (Ed. in Chief); Jamie Kessinger (Mng. Ed.)

LORETTO

ST. FRANCIS UNIV.

Street address 1: PO Box 600
Street address 3: Loretto
Street address state: PA
Zip/Postal code: 15940-0600
Country: USA
Mailing address: PO Box 600
Mailing city: Loretto
Mailing state: PA
Mailing zip: 15940-0600
General Phone: (814) 472-3038
General Fax: (814) 472-3358
Classified Equipment»
Personnel: Dean Allison (Advisor); Andrew Maloney (Ed.)

MANSFIELD

MANSFIELD UNIV. OF PENNSYLVANIA

Street address 1: 202M Alumni Hall
Street address 3: Mansfield
Street address state: PA
Zip/Postal code: 16933
Country: USA
Mailing address: PO Box 1
Mailing city: Mansfield
Mailing state: PA
Mailing zip: 16933-0001
General Phone: (570) 662-4986
General Fax: (570) 662-4386
General/National Adv. E-mail: flashlit@mnsfld.edu
Classified Equipment»
Personnel: Daniel Mason (Advisor)

MCKEESPORT

PENN STATE UNIV.

Street address 1: 4000 University Dr
Street address 3: McKeesport
Street address state: PA
Zip/Postal code: 15131-7644
Country: USA
Mailing address: 4000 University Dr
Mailing city: White Oak
Mailing state: PA
Mailing zip: 15131-7644
General Phone: (412) 675-9143
Classified Equipment»
Personnel: Kathleen Taylor Brown (Advisor); Monica Michna (Ed. in Chief)

MEADVILLE

ALLEGHENY COLLEGE

Street address 1: PO Box 12
Street address 3: Meadville
Street address state: PA
Zip/Postal code: 16335-0012
Country: USA
Mailing address: PO Box 12
Mailing city: Meadville
Mailing state: PA
Mailing zip: 16335-0012
General Phone: (814) 332-2754
General Fax: (814) 724-6834
General/National Adv. E-mail: thecampus1@gmail.com
Primary Website: www.alleghenycampus.com
Classified Equipment»
Personnel: Penny Schaefer (Advisor); Kristin Baldwin (Ed. in Chief)

MECHANICSBURG

MESSIAH COLLEGE

Street address 1: 1 College Ave
Street address 2: Ste 3058
Street address 3: Mechanicsburg
Street address state: PA
Zip/Postal code: 17055-6806
Country: USA
Mailing address: PO Box 3043
Mailing city: Mechanicsburg
Mailing state: PA
Mailing zip: 17055
General Phone: (717) 796-5095
General Fax: (717) 796-5249
General/National Adv. E-mail: theswingingbridge@messiah.edu
Display Adv. E-mail: theswingingbridge@messiah.edu
Editorial e-mail: theswingingbridge@messiah.edu
Primary Website: www.messiahsb.com
Delivery Methods: Newsstand
Commercial printers: Y
Classified Equipment»
Personnel: Ed Arke (Professor of Communications)

MEDIA

PENN STATE UNIV. DELAWARE COUNTY

Street address 1: 25 Yearsley Mill Rd
Street address 3: Media
Street address state: PA
Zip/Postal code: 19063-5522
Country: USA
Mailing address: 25 Yearsley Mill Rd
Mailing city: Media
Mailing state: PA
Mailing zip: 19063-5596
General Phone: (610) 892-1200
General Fax: (610) 892-1357
General/National Adv. E-mail: kab4@psu.edu
Classified Equipment»
Personnel: Karrie Bowen (Ed./Advisor)

PENN STATE UNIV. HARRISBURG

Street address 1: 777 W Harrisburg Pike
Street address 2: # E-126
Street address 3: Middletown
Street address state: PA
Zip/Postal code: 17057-4846
Country: USA
Mailing address: 777 W Harrisburg Pike # E-126
Mailing city: Middletown
Mailing state: PA
Mailing zip: 17057-4846
General Phone: (717) 948-6440
General Fax: (717) 948-6724
General/National Adv. E-mail: captimes@psu.edu
Classified Equipment»
Personnel: Patrick Burrows (Advisor); James Speed (Adv. Mgr.); Jenna Denoyelles (Ed. in Chief)

MILLERSVILLE

MILLERSVILLE UNIV. OF PENNSYLVANIA

Street address 1: 1 South George St, Rm.18
Street address 3: Millersville
Street address state: PA
Zip/Postal code: 17551
Country: USA
Mailing address: PO Box 1002
Mailing city: Millersville

Mailing state: PA
Mailing zip: 17551-0302
General Phone: (717) 871-2102
General Fax: (717) 872-3515
Editorail Phone: (717) 871-2102
Editorial Fax: (717) 872-3516
General/National Adv. E-mail: snapper@marauder.millersville.edu
Primary Website: thesnapper.com
Classified Equipment»
Personnel: Gene Ellis (Advisor); Bradley Giuranna (Ed. in Chief); Ashley Palm (News Ed.)

MONROEVILLE

CMTY. COLLEGE OF ALLEGHENY COUNTY BOYCE

Street address 1: 595 Beatty Rd
Street address 3: Monroeville
Street address state: PA
Zip/Postal code: 15146-1348
Country: USA
Mailing address: 595 Beatty Rd
Mailing city: Monroeville
Mailing state: PA
Mailing zip: 15146-1348
General Phone: (724) 325-6730
General Fax: (724) 325-6799
Classified Equipment»
Personnel: Peggy Roche (Adv. Mgr.)

MOON TOWNSHIP

ROBERT MORRIS UNIVERSITY : THE SENTRY

Street address 1: 6001 University Blvd
Street address 2: Dept of
Street address 3: Moon Township
Street address state: PA
Zip/Postal code: 15108-2574
Country: USA
Mailing address: 6001 University Blvd
Mailing city: Moon Township
Mailing state: PA
Mailing zip: 15108
General Phone: 412-397-6826
General Fax: 412-397-2436
Advertising Phone: (412) 397-6826
Editorail Phone: (412) 397-6826
General/National Adv. E-mail: sentrynews@mail.rmu.edu
Display Adv. E-mail: sentrynewsads@mail.rmu.edu
Editorial e-mail: sentrynews@mail.rmu.edu
Primary Website: www.rmusentrymedia.com
Year Established: 2006
Published Other: Online only
Avg Free Circ: 500
Classified Equipment»

NANTICOKE

LUZERNE COUNTY CMTY. COLLEGE

Street address 1: 1333 S Prospect St
Street address 3: Nanticoke
Street address state: PA
Zip/Postal code: 18634-3814
Country: USA
Mailing address: 1333 S Prospect St
Mailing city: Nanticoke
Mailing state: PA
Mailing zip: 18634-3899
General Phone: (570) 740-0638
General Fax: (570) 740-0605
Classified Equipment»
Personnel: Brett Bonanny (Ed.)

NEW KENSINGTON

PENN STATE NEW KENSINGTON:COMMUNICATIONS DEPT

Street address 1: 3550 7th Street Rd
Street address 3: New Kensington
Street address state: PA
Zip/Postal code: 15068-1765
Country: USA
Mailing address: 3550 Seventh St rd
Mailing city: New Kensington
Mailing state: PA
Mailing zip: 15068
General Phone: 724-334-6713
General/National Adv. E-mail: aka11@psu.edu
Primary Website: http://nk.psu.edu
Classified Equipment»
Parent company (for newspapers): Tribune-Review Publishing Co.

NEW WILMINGTON

WESTMINSTER COLLEGE

Street address 1: 319 S Market St
Street address 3: New Wilmington
Street address state: PA
Zip/Postal code: 16172-0002
Country: USA
Mailing address: 319 S Market St
Mailing city: New Wilmington
Mailing state: PA
Mailing zip: 16172-0001
General Phone: (724) 946-7224
General/National Adv. E-mail: holcad@westminister.edu
Primary Website: www.theholcad.com
Classified Equipment»
Personnel: Shannon Richtor (Ed.)

NEWTOWN

BUCKS COUNTY CMTY. COLLEGE

Street address 1: 275 Swamp Rd
Street address 3: Newtown
Street address state: PA
Zip/Postal code: 18940-4106
Country: USA
Mailing address: 275 Swamp Rd
Mailing city: Newtown
Mailing state: PA
Mailing zip: 18940-9677
General Phone: (215) 968-8379
General Fax: (215) 968-8271
Editorail Phone: (215) 968-8379
General/National Adv. E-mail: buckscenturion@gmail.com
Display Adv. E-mail: orders@mymediamate.com
Editorial e-mail: buckscenturion@gmail.com
Primary Website: www.bucks-news.com
Year Established: 1964
Delivery Methods: Newsstand
Commercial printers: Y
Published: Thur
Avg Free Circ: 2000
Classified Equipment»
Personnel: Tony Rogers (Advisor)

COMMUNITY COLLEGE OF PHILADELPHIA

Street address 1: 1700 Spring Garden St
Street address 3: Philadelphia
Street address state: PA
Zip/Postal code: 19130-3936
Country: USA
Mailing address: 1700 Spring Garden St.
Mailing city: Philadelphia
Mailing state: PA
Mailing zip: 19130-3936
General Phone: (215) 751-8200
General Fax: (215) 972-6201
Primary Website: www.thestudentvanguard.com
Year Established: 1964
Delivery Methods: Newsstand`Racks
Commercial printers: Y
Published: Bi-Mthly
Classified Equipment»
Personnel: Randy LoBasso (Faculty Advisor); Michael Castaneda (Editor-In-Chief); Rachel Byrd (Associate Editor); Imzadi Davis (Managing Editor); Devonte Gillespie (Business Manager)

DREXEL UNIV.

Street address 1: 3141 Chestnut St
Street address 3: Philadelphia
Street address state: PA
Zip/Postal code: 19104-2816
Country: USA
Mailing address: 3141 Chestnut St
Mailing city: Philadelphia
Mailing state: PA
Mailing zip: 19104-2875
General Phone: (215) 895-2585
Primary Website: www.thetriangle.org
Year Established: 1926
Commercial printers: Y
Published: Fri
Classified Equipment»
Personnel: David Stephenson (EIC); Keith Hobin (Mng Ed); Laura DiSanto (Staff Mgr); Alexandra Jones (EIC); Gina Vitale

HOLY FAMILY COLLEGE

Street address 1: 9801 Frankford Ave
Street address 3: Philadelphia
Street address state: PA
Zip/Postal code: 19114-2009
Country: USA
Mailing address: 9801 Frankford Ave
Mailing city: Philadelphia
Mailing state: PA
Mailing zip: 19114
General Phone: (215) 637-5321
General Fax: (215) 824-2438
Primary Website: www.tri-liteonline.com
Classified Equipment»
Personnel: Laura Wkovitz (Ed.)

LA SALLE UNIV.

Street address 1: 1900 W Olney Ave
Street address 2: # 417
Street address 3: Philadelphia
Street address state: PA
Zip/Postal code: 19141-1108
Country: USA
Mailing address: 1900 W Olney Ave # 417
Mailing city: Philadelphia
Mailing state: PA
Mailing zip: 19141-1108
General Phone: (215) 951-1000
General Fax: (215) 763-9686
General/National Adv. E-mail: collegian@lasalle.edu
Primary Website: www.lasalle.edu/collegian
Classified Equipment»
Personnel: Robert O'Brien (Advisor); Olivia Biagi (Mng. Ed.)

PHILADELPHIA NEIGHBORHOODS

Street address 1: 1515 Market St
Street address 2: Fl 1
Street address 3: Philadelphia
Street address state: PA
Zip/Postal code: 19102-1904
Country: USA
Mailing address: 1515 Market St First Floor
Mailing city: Philadelphia
Mailing state: PA
Mailing zip: 19102
General Phone: 315-729-9020
General/National Adv. E-mail: charper@temple.edu
Primary Website: www.philadelphianeighborhoods.com
Classified Equipment»

ST. JOSEPHS UNIV.

Street address 1: 5600 City Ave, 314 Campion Ctr
Street address 3: Philadelphia
Street address state: PA
Zip/Postal code: 19131
Country: USA
Mailing address: 5600 City Ave., 314 Campion Ctr.
Mailing city: Philadelphia
Mailing state: PA
Mailing zip: 19131-1395
General Phone: (610) 660-1079
General Fax: (610) 660-1089
Advertising Phone: (610) 660-1080
General/National Adv. E-mail: thehawk@sju.edu
Primary Website: www.sjuhawknews.com
Classified Equipment»
Personnel: Dr. Jenny Spinner (Advisor); Karrin Randle (Ed. in Chief); Katy Yavorek (Bus. Mgr.)

TEMPLE UNIVERSITY

Street address 1: 1755 N 13th St
Street address 2: 304 Howard Gittis Student Center
Street address 3: Philadelphia
Street address state: PA
Zip/Postal code: 19122-6011
Country: USA
Mailing address: 1755 N 13th St
Mailing city: Philadelphia
Mailing state: PA
Mailing zip: 19122-6011
General Phone: 215-204-6737
General Fax: 215-204-1663
Advertising Phone: 215-204-9538
Advertising Fax: 215-204-6609
General/National Adv. E-mail: editor@temple-news.com
Display Adv. E-mail: advertising@temple-news.com
Primary Website: www.temple-news.com
Year Established: 1921
Published: Tues
Published Other: Daily online
Avg Free Circ: 5000
Classified Equipment»
Personnel: John Di Carlo (Advisor)

UNIV. OF PENNSYLVANIA ENGINEERING SCHOOL

Street address 1: 220 S 33rd St
Street address 3: Philadelphia
Street address state: PA
Zip/Postal code: 19104-6315
Country: USA
Mailing address: 220 S 33rd St Rm 107
Mailing city: Philadelphia
Mailing state: PA
Mailing zip: 19104-6315
General Phone: (215) 898-1444
General Fax: (801) 469-4487
General/National Adv. E-mail: triangle@seas.upenn.edu
Primary Website: www.seas.upenn.edu/~triangle/
Classified Equipment»
Personnel: Mark Smyda (Ed. in Chief); Bezhou Feng (Ed. in Chief)

UNIV. OF PENNSYLVANIA LAW SCHOOL

Street address 1: 3400 Chestnut St
Street address 3: Philadelphia
Street address state: PA
Zip/Postal code: 19104-6253
Country: USA
Mailing address: 3400 Chestnut St Ste 1
Mailing city: Philadelphia
Mailing state: PA
Mailing zip: 19104-6204
General Phone: (215) 898-7483
General Fax: (215) 573-2025
Classified Equipment»
Personnel: Doug Rennie (Ed.)

UNIV. OF THE SCIENCES IN PHILADELPHIA

Street address 1: 600 S 43rd St
Street address 3: Philadelphia
Street address state: PA
Zip/Postal code: 19104-4418
Country: USA
Mailing address: 600 S 43rd St
Mailing city: Philadelphia
Mailing state: PA
Mailing zip: 19104-4495
General Phone: (215) 596-8800
Primary Website: www.usp.edu
Classified Equipment»

Personnel: Miriam Gilbert (Advisor); Leeann Tan (Co. Ed.); Meghan Baker (Co. Ed.)

UNIVERSITY OF PENNSYLVANIA

Street address 1: 4015 Walnut St
Street address 3: Philadelphia
Street address state: PA
Zip/Postal code: 19104-3513
Country: USA
Mailing address: 4015 Walnut St. 2nd Fl
Mailing city: Philadelphia
Mailing state: PA
Mailing zip: 19104-6198
General Phone: (215) 422-4640
General Fax: (215) 422-4646
Advertising Phone: (215) 422-4640 x1
Advertising Fax: (215) 422-4646
Editorail Phone: (215) 422-4060 x2
Editorial Fax: (215) 422-4646
General/National Adv. E-mail: advertising@theDP.com
Display Adv. E-mail: advertising@theDP.com
Primary Website: www.theDP.com
Year Established: 1885
Advertising (Open Inch Rate) Weekday/Saturday: Yes; contact us
Published: Mon`Thur
Avg Free Circ: 6000
Classified Equipment»
Personnel: Eric Jacobs (Gen. Mgr.); Michel Liu (Assignments Ed.); Harry Trustman (Opinions Ed.)

WHARTON SCHOOL OF GRAD. BUS.

Street address 1: 3730 Walnut St
Street address 2: 330 Jon M. Huntsman Hall
Street address 3: Philadelphia
Street address state: PA
Zip/Postal code: 19104-3615
Country: USA
Mailing address: 3730 Walnut St
Mailing city: Philadelphia
Mailing state: PA
Mailing zip: 19104-3615
General Phone: (215) 898-3200
General Fax: (215) 898-1200
General/National Adv. E-mail: journal@wharton.upenn.edu
Primary Website: www.whartonjournal.com
Classified Equipment»
Personnel: Mark Hanson (Pub.); Anix Vyas (Ed. in Chief); Gareth Keane (Mng. Ed.)

CARNEGIE MELLON UNIV.

Street address 1: 5000 Forbes Ave
Street address 3: Pittsburgh
Street address state: PA
Zip/Postal code: 15213-3815
Country: USA
Mailing address: Box 119
Mailing city: Pittsburgh
Mailing state: PA
Mailing zip: 15213
General Phone: (412) 268-2111
General Fax: (412) 268-1596
General/National Adv. E-mail: contact@tartan.org
Display Adv. E-mail: advertising@thetartan.org
Primary Website: www.thetartan.org
Published: Mon
Avg Free Circ: 6000
Classified Equipment»

CMTY. COLLEGE ALLEGHENY COUNTY

Street address 1: 808 Ridge Ave
Street address 3: Pittsburgh
Street address state: PA
Zip/Postal code: 15212-6003
Country: USA
Mailing address: Office of Student Life
Mailing city: Pittsburgh
Mailing state: PA
General Phone: (412) 237-2543
General Fax: (412) 237-6548
Primary Website: www.ccac.edu
Classified Equipment»

Personnel: Christine McQuaide (Advisor)

COMMUNITY COLLEGE OF ALLEGHENY: NORTH CAMPUS VOICE

Street address 1: 8701 Perry Hwy
Street address 2: Rm 2003
Street address 3: Pittsburgh
Street address state: PA
Zip/Postal code: 15237-5353
Country: USA
Mailing address: 8701 Perry Hwy, Rm 2003 B
Mailing city: Pittsburgh
Mailing state: PA
Mailing zip: 15237
General Phone: 412-369-4156
General/National Adv. E-mail: rbeighey@ccac.edu
Primary Website: ccac.edu
Classified Equipment»

DUQUESNE UNIVERSITY

Street address 1: 600 Forbes Ave
Street address 2: 113 College Hall
Street address 3: Pittsburgh
Street address state: PA
Zip/Postal code: 15282-0001
Country: USA
Mailing address: 600 Forbes Ave
Mailing city: Pittsburgh
Mailing state: PA
Mailing zip: 15282-0001
General Phone: (412) 396-6629
General/National Adv. E-mail: theduke@duq.edu
Display Adv. E-mail: dukeads@yahoo.com
Primary Website: www.duqsm.com
Year Established: 1925
Published: Thur
Classified Equipment»
Personnel: Bobby Kerlik (Advisor); Jess Eagle (Ed. in Chief); Brian Tierney (Associate Ed.); Matt Noonan (Managing Ed.); Shawn (News Ed.); Mickey (Advertising Mgr.)

LA ROCHE COLLEGE

Street address 1: 9000 Babcock Blvd
Street address 3: Pittsburgh
Street address state: PA
Zip/Postal code: 15237-5808
Country: USA
Mailing address: 9000 Babcock Blvd
Mailing city: Pittsburgh
Mailing state: PA
Mailing zip: 15237-5898
General Phone: (412) 536-1147
General Fax: (412) 536-1067
General/National Adv. E-mail: courier@laroche.edu
Primary Website: www.larochecourier.com
Classified Equipment»
Personnel: Ed Stankowski (Advisor); Rebecca Jeskey (Ed. in Chief); Maggie Kelly (Mng. Ed.)

POINT PARK COLLEGE

Street address 1: 201 Wood St
Street address 3: Pittsburgh
Street address state: PA
Zip/Postal code: 15222-1912
Country: USA
Mailing address: PO Box 627
Mailing city: Pittsburgh
Mailing state: PA
Mailing zip: 15222
General Phone: (412) 392-4740
General Fax: (412) 392-3902
General/National Adv. E-mail: theglobeadvertising@gmail.com
Editorial e-mail: szullo@pointpark.edu
Primary Website: www.pointparkglobe.com
Classified Equipment»
Personnel: Steve Hallock (Advisor); Sara Zullo (Ed. in Chief)

TEPPER SCHOOL OF BUSINESS AT CARNEGIE MELLON UNIVERSITY

Street address 1: 5000 Forbes Ave
Street address 3: Pittsburgh
Street address state: PA
Zip/Postal code: 15213-3815
Country: USA
Mailing address: 5000 Forbes Ave
Mailing city: Pittsburgh
Mailing state: PA
Mailing zip: 15213-3815
General Phone: (412) 268-2269
General/National Adv. E-mail: jywong@tepper.cmu.edu
Display Adv. E-mail: robberbaronstepper@gmail.com
Primary Website: http://tepper.campusgroups.com/rbp/about/
Published: Thur
Classified Equipment»
Note: No Advertisements Being Accepted for 2012-2013 School Year
Personnel: Tyson Bauer (Ed.)

UNIV. OF PITTSBURGH

Street address 1: 434 William Pitt Un
Street address 2: University of Pittsburgh
Street address 3: Pittsburgh
Street address state: PA
Zip/Postal code: 15260-5900
Country: USA
General Phone: (412) 648-7980
General Fax: (412) 648-8491
General/National Adv. E-mail: pittnews@pittnews.com
Primary Website: www.pittnews.com
Published: Mon`Tues`Wed`Thur`Fri
Classified Equipment»
Personnel: Harry Kloman (Advisor); Ashwini Sivaganesh (Ed. in Chief); John Hamilton (Mng. Ed.); Victor Powell (Online Ed.)

RADNOR

CABRINI UNIVERSITY LOQUITUR

Street address 1: 610 King of Prussia Rd
Street address 3: Radnor
Street address state: PA
Zip/Postal code: 19087-3623
Country: USA
Mailing address: 610 King of Prussia Rd
Mailing city: Radnor
Mailing state: PA
Mailing zip: 19087-3698
General Phone: (610) 902-8360
General Fax: (610) 902-8285
General/National Adv. E-mail: loquitur@cabrini.edu
Display Adv. E-mail: loquitur@cabrini.edu
Editorial e-mail: loquitur@cabrini.edu
Primary Website: www.theloquitur.com
Year Established: 1959
News Services: MCT
Delivery Methods: Racks
Commercial printers: Y
Published: Thur`Bi-Mthly
Avg Free Circ: 1400
Classified Equipment»
Personnel: Jerome Zurek (Chair); Angelina Miller (EIC)

READING

ALBRIGHT COLLEGE

Street address 1: N 13th and Bern Streets
Street address 3: Reading
Street address state: PA
Zip/Postal code: 19612
Country: USA
Mailing address: P.O. Box 15234
Mailing city: Reading
Mailing state: PA
Mailing zip: 19612
General Phone: (610) 921-7558
General/National Adv. E-mail: albrightian@albright.edu
Primary Website: www.albright.edu/albrightian
Published: Bi-Mthly
Classified Equipment»
Personnel: Jon Bekken (Advisor); Sarah Timmons (Editor-in-chief); Megan Homsher (Assistant Editor-in-Chief)

ALVERNIA UNIVERSITY

Street address 1: 400 Saint Bernardine St
Street address 3: Reading
Street address state: PA
Zip/Postal code: 19607-1737
Country: USA
Mailing address: 400 Saint Bernardine St
Mailing city: Reading
Mailing state: PA
Mailing zip: 19607-1737
General Phone: (610) 568-1557
Editorail Phone: 610.796.8358
General/National Adv. E-mail: ryan.lange@alvernia.edu
Primary Website: http://www.alvernia.edu/alvernian
Advertising (Open Inch Rate) Weekday/Saturday: Yes
Published: Mthly
Avg Free Circ: 700
Classified Equipment»
Personnel: Ryan Lange (Faculty Advisor)

READING AREA CMTY. COLLEGE

Street address 1: 10 S 2nd St
Street address 3: Reading
Street address state: PA
Zip/Postal code: 19602-1014
Country: USA
Mailing address: PO Box 1706
Mailing city: Reading
Mailing state: PA
Mailing zip: 19603-1706
General Phone: (610) 607-6212
General Fax: (610) 375-8255
Primary Website: racc.edu
Classified Equipment»
Personnel: Melissa Kushner (Mktg. PR)

SCHUYLKILL HAVEN

PENN STATE UNIV.

Street address 1: 200 University Dr
Street address 3: Schuylkill Haven
Street address state: PA
Zip/Postal code: 17972-2202
Country: USA
Mailing address: 200 University Dr
Mailing city: Schuylkill Haven
Mailing state: PA
Mailing zip: 17972-2208
General Phone: (570) 385-6000
Classified Equipment»
Personnel: Wes Loder (Advisor)

SCRANTON

MARYWOOD UNIVERSITY

Street address 1: 2300 Adams Ave
Street address 3: Scranton
Street address state: PA
Zip/Postal code: 18509-1514
Country: USA
Mailing address: 2300 Adams Ave
Mailing city: Scranton
Mailing state: PA
Mailing zip: 18509-1598
General Phone: (570) 348-6211
General Fax: (570) 961-4768
General/National Adv. E-mail: thewoodword@m.marywood.edu
Primary Website: www.thewoodword.org
Published: Mthly
Classified Equipment»
Personnel: Ann Williams (Advisor); Lindsey Wotanis (Advisor)

UNIV. OF SCRANTON

Street address 1: 800 Linden St
Street address 3: Scranton
Street address state: PA
Zip/Postal code: 18510-2429
Country: USA
Mailing address: 800 Linden St
Mailing city: Scranton
Mailing state: PA
Mailing zip: 18510
General Phone: (570) 941-7464
General Fax: (570) 941-4836
General/National Adv. E-mail: aquinas@scranton.edu
Primary Website: academic.scranton.edu/organization/aquinas
Classified Equipment»
Personnel: Scott Walsh (Advisor)

SELINSGROVE

SUSQUEHANNA UNIV.

Street address 1: 1858 Weber Way
Street address 3: Selinsgrove
Street address state: PA
Zip/Postal code: 17870-1150
Country: USA
Mailing address: CA Box 18
Mailing city: Selinsgrove
Mailing state: PA
Mailing zip: 17870
General Phone: (570) 374-4298
General Fax: (570) 372-2745
General/National Adv. E-mail: suquill@susqu.edu
Primary Website: www.suquill.com
Year Established: 1896
Published: Fri
Avg Free Circ: 2200
Classified Equipment»
Personnel: Catherine Hastings (Advisor)

SHIPPENSBURG

SHIPPENSBURG UNIVERSITY:THE SLATE

Street address 1: Shippensburg University
Street address 2: Ceddia Union Bldg, Second Floor
Street address 3: Shippensburg
Street address state: PA
Zip/Postal code: 17257
Country: USA
Mailing address: Shippensburg University
Mailing city: Shippensburg
Mailing state: PA
Mailing zip: 17257
General Phone: 717-477-1778
General Fax: 717-477-4022
General/National Adv. E-mail: slate@ship.edu
Primary Website: www.theslateonline.com
Classified Equipment»
Personnel: Michael Drager (Advisor)

SLIPPERY ROCK

SLIPPERY ROCK UNIV.

Street address 1: 220 Eisenberg Classroom Bldg
Street address 3: Slippery Rock
Street address state: PA
Zip/Postal code: 16057
Country: USA
Mailing address: 220 Eisenberg Classroom Bldg.
Mailing city: Slipper Rock
Mailing state: PA
Mailing zip: 16057
General Phone: (724) 738-2643
General Fax: (724) 738-4896
General/National Adv. E-mail: rocket.letters@sru.edu
Primary Website: www.theonlinerocket.com
Classified Equipment»
Personnel: Joseph Harry (Advisor); Josh Rizzo (Ed. in Chief)

ST DAVIDS

EASTERN UNIVERSITY:THE WALTONIAN

Street address 1: 1300 Eagle Rd
Street address 3: St Davids
Street address state: PA
Zip/Postal code: 19087-3617
Country: USA
Mailing address: 1300 Eagle Rd
Mailing city: St Davids
Mailing state: PA
Mailing zip: 19087
General Phone: 610-341-1710
General Fax: 610-225-5255
General/National Adv. E-mail: wtonline@eastern.edu
Primary Website: www.waltonian.com
Classified Equipment»

STATE COLLEGE

PENN STATE UNIV.

Street address 1: 123 S Burrowes St
Street address 3: State College
Street address state: PA
Zip/Postal code: 16801-3867
Country: USA
Mailing address: 123 S Burrowes St Ste 200
Mailing city: State College
Mailing state: PA
Mailing zip: 16801-3882
General Phone: (814) 865-2531
General Fax: (814) 865-3848
General/National Adv. E-mail: collegian@psu.edu
Display Adv. E-mail: mycollegianrep@gmail.com
Primary Website: www.collegian.psu.edu
Published: Mon`Tues`Wed`Thur`Fri
Classified Equipment»
Personnel: Wayne Lowman (Opns. Mgr.)

SWARTHMORE

SWARTHMORE COLLEGE

Street address 1: 500 College Ave
Street address 3: Swarthmore
Street address state: PA
Zip/Postal code: 19081-1306
Country: USA
Mailing address: 500 College Ave Ste 2
Mailing city: Swarthmore
Mailing state: PA
Mailing zip: 19081-1390
General Phone: (610) 328-8000
General Fax: (208) 439-9864
General/National Adv. E-mail: phoenix@swarthmore.edu
Primary Website: www.swarthmorephoenix.com
Classified Equipment»
Personnel: Mara Revkin (Ed. in Chief)

PENN STATE UNIVERSITY: COLLEGE OF COMMUNICATIONS

Street address 1: 201 Carnegie Bldg
Street address 3: University Park
Street address state: PA
Zip/Postal code: 16802-5101
Country: USA
Mailing address: 201 Carnegie Bldg
Mailing city: University Park
Mailing state: PA
Mailing zip: 16802
General Phone: 814-863-1484
General Fax: 814-863-8044
Primary Website: http://comm.psu.edu
Classified Equipment»

VILLANOVA

VILLANOVA UNIV.

Street address 1: 800 E Lancaster Ave
Street address 3: Villanova
Street address state: PA
Zip/Postal code: 19085-1603
Country: USA
Mailing address: 800 E Lancaster Ave
Mailing city: Villanova
Mailing state: PA
Mailing zip: 19085-1478
General Phone: (610) 519-7207
General Fax: (610) 519-5666
General/National Adv. E-mail: business@villanovan.com
Primary Website: www.villanovan.com
Classified Equipment»
Personnel: Jessica Ramey (Bus. Mgr.); Jody Ross (Advisor); Tom Mogan (Advisor); Tim Richer (Ed. in Chief); Laura (Ed. in Chief)

WASHINGTON & JEFFERSON COLLEGE

Street address 1: 60 S Lincoln St
Street address 3: Washington
Street address state: PA
Zip/Postal code: 15301-4812
Country: USA
Mailing address: 60 S Lincoln St
Mailing city: Washington
Mailing state: PA
Mailing zip: 15301-4801
General Phone: (724) 222-4400
General Fax: (724) 223-6534
General/National Adv. E-mail: redandblackstaff@jay.washjeff.edu
Primary Website: www.washjeff.edu
Year Established: 1909
Published: Thur
Classified Equipment»
Note: Currently developing a website to host The Red&Black online.
Personnel: Dale Lolley (Advisor)

VALLEY FORGE MILITARY COLLEGE

Street address 1: 1001 Eagle Rd
Street address 3: Wayne
Street address state: PA
Zip/Postal code: 19087-3613
Country: USA
Mailing address: 1001 Eagle Rd
Mailing city: Wayne
Mailing state: PA
Mailing zip: 19087-3695
General Phone: (610) 989-1403
Classified Equipment»
Personnel: Charles A. McGeorge (Pres.)

WAYNESBURG

WAYNESBURG UNIVERSITY:THE YELLOW JACKET

Street address 1: 51 W College St
Street address 3: Waynesburg
Street address state: PA
Zip/Postal code: 15370-1258
Country: USA
Mailing address: 51 West College St.
Mailing city: Waynesburg
Mailing state: PA
Mailing zip: 15370
General Phone: 724-627-8191
General/National Adv. E-mail: jacket@waynesburg.edu
Classified Equipment»

WEST CHESTER UNIVERSITY

Street address 1: 253 Sykes Union Bldg
Street address 3: West Chester
Street address state: PA
Zip/Postal code: 19383-0001
Country: USA
Mailing address: 253 Sykes Union
Mailing city: West Chester
Mailing state: PA
Mailing zip: 19383-0001
General Phone: (610) 436-2375
General Fax: (610) 436-3280
Advertising Phone: (610) 436-2375
General/National Adv. E-mail: quad@wcupa.edu
Display Adv. E-mail: quadadvertising@wcupa.edu
Editorial e-mail: quadeic@wcupa.edu
Primary Website: www.wcuquad.com
Year Established: 1934
News Services: MCT Campus
Delivery Methods: Racks
Published: Mon
Avg Free Circ: 2500
Classified Equipment»
Personnel: Philip Thompsen (Advisor); Samantha Mineroff (EIC)

WEST MIFFLIN

CMTY. COLLEGE ALLEGHENY COUNTY SOUTH

Street address 1: 1750 Clairton Rd
Street address 2: # RT885
Street address 3: West Mifflin
Street address state: PA
Zip/Postal code: 15122-3029
Country: USA
Mailing address: 1750 Clairton Rd # Rt
Mailing city: West Mifflin
Mailing state: PA
Mailing zip: 15122-3029
General Phone: (412) 469-6352
General Fax: (412) 469-4333
Primary Website: www.ccac.edu
Classified Equipment»
Personnel: Aaron Kindeall (Ed.)

COMMUNITY COLLEGE OF ALLEGHENY:THE FORUM

Street address 1: 1750 Clourton Rd Rt 885
Street address 3: West Mifflin
Street address state: PA
Zip/Postal code: 15122
Country: USA
Mailing address: 1750 Clourton Rd Rt 885
Mailing city: West Mifflin
Mailing state: PA
Mailing zip: 15122
General Phone: 412-469-6352
General Fax: 412-469-4333
Primary Website: http://www.ccac.edu
Classified Equipment»

WILKES BARRE

WILKES UNIV.

Street address 1: 130 S River St, Conyngham Ctr, Office 101
Street address 3: Wilkes Barre
Street address state: PA
Zip/Postal code: 18701
Country: USA
Mailing address: 130 S. River St., Conyngham Ctr., Office 101
Mailing city: Wilkes-Barre
Mailing state: PA
Mailing zip: 18701
General Phone: (570) 408-5903
General Fax: (570) 408-5902
Advertising Phone: (570) 408-2962
General/National Adv. E-mail: wilkesbeacon@wilkes.edu
Primary Website: www.wilkesbeacon.com
Classified Equipment»
Personnel: Andrea Frantz (Advisor); Michele Flannery (Bus./Adv. Mgr.); Nicole Frail (Ed. in Chief)

WILLIAMSPORT

LYCOMING COLLEGE

Street address 1: 700 College Pl
Street address 2: Campus Box 169
Street address 3: Williamsport
Street address state: PA
Zip/Postal code: 17701-5157
Country: USA
Mailing address: 700 College Place
Mailing city: Williamsport
Mailing state: PA
Mailing zip: 17701-5192
General Phone: (570) 321-4315
General/National Adv. E-mail: lycourier@lycoming.edu
Display Adv. E-mail: lycourier@lycoming.edu
Editorial e-mail: lycourier@lycoming.edu
Primary Website: http://lycourier.lycoming.edu
Delivery Methods: Racks
Commercial printers: Y
Published: Other
Published Other: Bi-Wkly on Thursdays
Avg Free Circ: 800
Classified Equipment»
Personnel: Dave Heemer (Advisor); Jordyn Hotchkiss (Editor-in-Chief)

YORK

YORK COLLEGE OF PENNSYLVANIA

Street address 1: 441 Country Club Rd
Street address 3: York
Street address state: PA

Zip/Postal code: 17403-3614
Country: USA
Mailing address: 441 Country Club Rd
Mailing city: York
Mailing state: PA
Mailing zip: 17403-3651
General Phone: (717) 815-1312
General/National Adv. E-mail: spartan@ycp.edu
Primary Website: spartan.ycp.edu
Classified Equipment»
Personnel: Steven Brikowski (Advisor)

RHODE ISLAND

BRISTOL

ROGER WILLIAMS UNIV.

Street address 1: 1 Old Ferry Rd
Street address 3: Bristol
Street address state: RI
Zip/Postal code: 02809-2923
Country: USA
Mailing address: 1 Old Ferry Rd
Mailing city: Bristol
Mailing state: RI
Mailing zip: 02809-2921
General Phone: (401) 254-3229
General Fax: (401) 254-3355
General/National Adv. E-mail: hawksherald@gmail.com
Primary Website: www.hawksherald.com
Classified Equipment»
Personnel: Ben Whitmore (Ed. in Chief); Adrianne Mukiria (Advisor); Adrianne Henderson (Advisor)

KINGSTON

UNIV. OF RHODE ISLAND

Street address 1: 125 Memorial Union, 50 Lower College Rd
Street address 3: Kingston
Street address state: RI
Zip/Postal code: 2881
Country: USA
Mailing address: 125 Memorial Union, 50 Lower College Rd.
Mailing city: Kingston
Mailing state: RI
Mailing zip: 02881
General Phone: (401) 874-2914
General Fax: (401) 874-5607
General/National Adv. E-mail: uricigar@gmail.com
Primary Website: www.ramcigar.com
Classified Equipment»
Personnel: Lindsay Lorenz (Ed. in Chief)

BROWN UNIV./RHODE ISLAND SCHOOL OF DESIGN

Street address 1: PO Box 1930
Street address 3: Providence
Street address state: RI
Country: USA
Mailing address: PO Box 1930
Mailing city: Providence
Mailing state: RI
Mailing zip: 02912-1930
General Phone: (401) 863-2008
General/National Adv. E-mail: independent@brown.edu; theindyads@gmail.com
Primary Website: www.theindy.org
Classified Equipment»
Personnel: Emily Segal (Ed.); Alex Verdolini (Mng. Ed.)

JOHNSON & WALES UNIV.

Street address 1: 8 Abbott Park Pl
Street address 3: Providence
Street address state: RI
Zip/Postal code: 02903-3703
Country: USA
Mailing address: 8 Abbott Park Pl
Mailing city: Providence
Mailing state: RI
Mailing zip: 02903-3775
General Phone: (401) 598-1000
General Fax: (401) 598-1171
Editorail Phone: (401) 598-1489
Editorial Fax: (401) 598-2867
General/National Adv. E-mail: campusherald@jwu.edu
Primary Website: www.jwu.edu
Classified Equipment»
Personnel: Michael Berger (Advisor); Jessica Long (Advisor); Catlin Benoit (Ed. in Chief); Samantha Krivorit (Ed. in Cheif)

PROVIDENCE COLLEGE

Street address 1: 549 River Ave
Street address 3: Providence
Street address state: RI
Zip/Postal code: 02918-7000
Country: USA
Mailing address: 549 River Ave
Mailing city: Providence
Mailing state: RI
Mailing zip: 02918-0001
General Phone: (401) 865-2214
General Fax: (401) 865-1202
General/National Adv. E-mail: cowl@providence.edu
Primary Website: www.providence.edu
Classified Equipment»
Personnel: Richard F. Kless (Advisor)

RHODE ISLAND COLLEGE

Street address 1: Student Union Plz, 600 Mt Pleasant Ave
Street address 3: Providence
Street address state: RI
Zip/Postal code: 2908
Country: USA
Mailing address: Student Union Plz., 600 Mt. Pleasant Ave.
Mailing city: Providence
Mailing state: RI
Mailing zip: 02908-1940
General Phone: (401) 456-8544
General Fax: (401) 456-8792
General/National Adv. E-mail: news@anchorweb.org
Primary Website: www.anchorweb.org
Classified Equipment»
Personnel: Rudy Cheeks (Professional Advisor); Ashley Dalton (Adv. Mgr.); Kameron Stualting (Ed. in Chief)

THE BROWN DAILY HERALD

Street address 1: 195 Angell St
Street address 3: Providence
Street address state: RI
Zip/Postal code: 02906-1207
Country: USA
Mailing address: PO Box 2538
Mailing city: Providence
Mailing state: RI
Mailing zip: 02906-0538
General Phone: (401) 351-3260
General Fax: (401) 351-9297
General/National Adv. E-mail: herald@browndailyherald.com
Display Adv. E-mail: advertising@browndailyherald.com
Primary Website: www.browndailyherald.com
Year Established: 1891
Special Weekly Sections: Post- Magazine
Published: Mon`Tues`Wed`Thur`Fri
Classified Equipment»
Personnel: Lauren Aratani

SMITHFIELD

BRYANT COLLEGE

Street address 1: 1150 Douglas Pike
Street address 2: # 7
Street address 3: Smithfield
Street address state: RI
Zip/Postal code: 02917-1291
Country: USA
Mailing address: 1150 Douglas Pike Ste 1
Mailing city: Smithfield
Mailing state: RI
Mailing zip: 02917-1290
General Phone: (401) 232-6028
General Fax: (401) 232-6710
General/National Adv. E-mail: archway@bryant.edu
Primary Website: www.bryantarchway.com
Classified Equipment»
Personnel: Meagan Sage (Advisor); Tracey Gant (Adv. Mgr.); John Crisafulli (Ed. in Chief)

SOUTH CAROLINA

AIKEN

UNIV. OF SOUTH CAROLINA

Street address 1: 471 University Pkwy
Street address 3: Aiken
Street address state: SC
Zip/Postal code: 29801-6389
Country: USA
Mailing address: 471 University Pkwy
Mailing city: Aiken
Mailing state: SC
Mailing zip: 29801-6399
General Phone: (803) 648-6851
General Fax: (803) 641-3494
Primary Website: www.pacertimes.com
Classified Equipment»
Personnel: Israel Butler (Ed.)

COLLEGE OF CHARLESTON

Street address 1: 66 George St
Street address 3: Charleston
Street address state: SC
Zip/Postal code: 29424-0001
Country: USA
Mailing address: 66 George St
Mailing city: Charleston
Mailing state: SC
Mailing zip: 29424-0001
General Phone: (843) 953-7017
General Fax: (843) 953-7037
General/National Adv. E-mail: mcgeeb@cofc.edu
Primary Website: www.cofc.edu/communication
Classified Equipment»
Personnel: Brian McGee (Chair); Katie Orlando (Ed. in Chief)

MEDICAL UNIV. OF SOUTH CAROLINA

Street address 1: PO Box 12110
Street address 3: Charleston
Street address state: SC
Zip/Postal code: 29422-2110
Country: USA
Mailing address: PO Box 12110
Mailing city: Charleston
Mailing state: SC
Mailing zip: 29422-2110
General Phone: (843) 792-4107
General Fax: (843) 849-0214
General/National Adv. E-mail: catalyst@musc.edu
Primary Website: www.musc.edu/catalyst
Classified Equipment»
Personnel: Kim Draughn (Ed.)

CLEMSON

CLEMSON UNIV.

Street address 1: 315 Hendrix Ctr
Street address 3: Clemson
Street address state: SC
Zip/Postal code: 29634-0001
Country: USA
Mailing address: 315 Hendrix Ctr
Mailing city: Clemson
Mailing state: SC
Mailing zip: 29634-0001
General Phone: (864) 656-2150
General Fax: (864) 656-4772
Primary Website: www.thetigernews.com
Classified Equipment»
Personnel: Patrich Neal (Advisor); Cory Bowers (Bus. Mgr.); Ashley Chris (Ed.)

PRESBYTERIAN COLLEGE

Street address 1: 503 S Broad St
Street address 3: Clinton
Street address state: SC
Zip/Postal code: 29325-2865
Country: USA
Mailing address: 503 S Broad St
Mailing city: Clinton
Mailing state: SC
Mailing zip: 29325-2998
General Phone: (864) 833-8488
General/National Adv. E-mail: pcbluestocking@gmail.com
Year Established: 1927
Published: Mthly
Classified Equipment»
Personnel: Justin Brent (Advisor); Rachel Miles (Co-Editor); Ashleigh Bethea (Co-Editor)

BENEDICT COLLEGE

Street address 1: 1600 Harden St
Street address 3: Columbia
Street address state: SC
Zip/Postal code: 29204-1058
Country: USA
Mailing address: 1600 Harden St
Mailing city: Columbia
Mailing state: SC
Mailing zip: 29204-1086
General Phone: (803) 705-4645
General Fax: (803) 253-5065
Primary Website: www.benedict.edu
Classified Equipment»
Personnel: Carolyn Drakeford (Chair); Momo Rogers (Ed.)

UNIV. OF SOUTH CAROLINA

Street address 1: 1400 Greene St
Street address 3: Columbia
Street address state: SC
Zip/Postal code: 29225-4002
Country: USA
Mailing address: 1400 Greene St
Mailing city: Columbia
Mailing state: SC
Mailing zip: 29225-4002
General Phone: (803) 777-5064
General Fax: (803) 777-6482
Advertising Phone: (803) 777-3888
Editorail Phone: (803) 777-7182
Editorial e-mail: gamecockeditor@sc.edu
Primary Website: www.dailygamecock.com
Classified Equipment»
Personnel: Scott Lindenberg (Dir., Student Media); Erik Collins (Advisor); Amanda Davis (Ed. in Chief); Calli Burnett (Mng. Ed.)

COASTAL CAROLINA UNIV.

Street address 1: PO Box 261954
Street address 3: Conway
Street address state: SC
Zip/Postal code: 29528-6054
Country: USA
Mailing address: PO Box 261954
Mailing city: Conway
Mailing state: SC
Mailing zip: 29528-6054
General Phone: (843) 349-2330
General Fax: (843) 349-2743
General/National Adv. E-mail: chanticleer@coastal.edu
Primary Website: www.coastal.educhanticleer
Classified Equipment»
Personnel: Issac Bailey (Advisor); Kyle Drapeau (Bus. Mgr.); Clarie Arambulla (Ed.)

FRANCIS MARION UNIVERSITY

Street address 1: Rm 201 University Center
Street address 3: Florence
Street address state: SC
Zip/Postal code: 29506
Country: USA
Mailing address: PO Box 100547
Mailing city: Florence
Mailing state: SC

Mailing zip: 29502-0547
General Phone: (843) 661-1350
General Fax: (843) 661-1373
General/National Adv. E-mail: patriotnews@hotmail.com
Display Adv. E-mail: patriotads@hotmail.com
Primary Website: www.patriotnewsonline.com
Delivery Methods: Carrier
Commercial printers: N
Published: Bi-Mthly
Classified Equipment»
Personnel: David Sacash (Faculty Advisor)

BOB JONES UNIVERSITY

Street address 1: 1700 Wade Hampton Blvd
Street address 3: Greenville
Street address state: SC
Zip/Postal code: 29614-1000
Country: USA
Mailing address: 1700 Wade Hampton Blvd
Mailing city: Greenville
Mailing state: SC
Mailing zip: 29614-0001
General Phone: (864) 370-1800
General Fax: (864) 770-1307
Advertising Phone: 864-370-1800
Advertising Fax: 864-770-1307
General/National Adv. E-mail: bsolomon@bju.edu
Editorial e-mail: editor@bju.edu
Primary Website: http://www.collegianonline.com/
Year Established: 1987
Advertising (Open Inch Rate) Weekday/Saturday: Varies
Published: Fri
Classified Equipment»
Personnel: David Lovegrove (Advisor); Betty Solomon (Advisor); Joanne Kappel (Adv. Coord.); Larry Stofer (Campus Media Supervisor)

THE PALADIN

Street address 1: 3300 Poinsett Hwy
Street address 3: Greenville
Street address state: SC
Zip/Postal code: 29613-0002
County: Travelers Rest
Country: USA
Mailing address: PO Box 28584
Mailing city: Greenville
Mailing state: SC
Mailing zip: 29613-0001
General/National Adv. E-mail: contact-databook@thepaladin.news
Primary Website: thepaladin.news
Published: Mon`Tues`Wed`Thur`Fri`Sun`Bi-Mthly
Weekday Frequency: e
Classified Equipment»
Personnel: Tyler Sines (Circ. Mgr.); Evan Bohnenblust (Ed. in Chief); Jessica Lopez (Ed.)

GREENWOOD

LANDER UNIV.

Street address 1: 320 Stanley Ave
Street address 3: Greenwood
Street address state: SC
Zip/Postal code: 29649-2056
Country: USA
Mailing address: 320 Stanley Ave
Mailing city: Greenwood
Mailing state: SC
Mailing zip: 29649-2099
General Phone: (864) 388-8000
General Fax: (864) 388-8890
Primary Website: www.lander.edu
Classified Equipment»
Personnel: Robert Stevenson (Advisor)

HARTSVILLE

COKER COLLEGE

Street address 1: 300 E College Ave
Street address 3: Hartsville
Street address state: SC
Zip/Postal code: 29550-3742
Country: USA
Mailing address: 300 E College Ave
Mailing city: Hartsville
Mailing state: SC
Mailing zip: 29550-3797
General Phone: (843) 383-8000
General Fax: (843) 383-8047
Classified Equipment»
Personnel: Dick Puffer (Advisor); Lance Player (Ed.)

NEWBERRY

NEWBERRY COLLEGE

Street address 1: 2100 College St
Street address 3: Newberry
Street address state: SC
Zip/Postal code: 29108-2126
Country: USA
Mailing address: 2100 College St
Mailing city: Newberry
Mailing state: SC
Mailing zip: 29108-2197
General Phone: (803) 276-5010
General Fax: (803) 321-5269
Primary Website: www.newberry.edu
Classified Equipment»
Personnel: Jodie Peeler (Advisor)

ORANGEBURG

CLAFLIN UNIVERSITY

Street address 1: 400 Magnolia St
Street address 3: Orangeburg
Street address state: SC
Zip/Postal code: 29115-6815
Country: USA
Mailing address: 400 Magnolia Street
Mailing city: Orangeburg
Mailing state: SC
Mailing zip: 29115
Primary Website: claflin.edu/the-panther
Published: Other
Published Other: print once per semester
Classified Equipment»
Personnel: Lee Harter (Advisor)

SOUTH CAROLINA STATE UNIV.

Street address 1: 300 College St NE
Street address 3: Orangeburg
Street address state: SC
Zip/Postal code: 29117-0002
Country: USA
Mailing address: 300 College St NE
Mailing city: Orangeburg
Mailing state: SC
Mailing zip: 29117-0002
General Phone: (803) 536-7237
General Fax: (803) 536-7131
Primary Website: http://www.thescsucollegian.com/
Classified Equipment»
Personnel: Rolondo Davis (Advisor)

ROCK HILL

THE JOHNSONIAN

Street address 1: 1808 Ebenezer Rd Apt B
Street address 2: 1808-B Ebenezer Rd
Street address 3: Rock Hill
Street address state: SC
Zip/Postal code: 29732-1170
Country: USA
Mailing address: 104 Digiorgio Campus Center Winthrop University
Mailing city: Rock Hill
Mailing state: SC
Mailing zip: 29733-0001
General Phone: (803) 323-3419
General Fax: (803) 323-3698
Advertising Phone: 803 984-7748
Advertising Fax: 803 984-7748
Editorail Phone: 803 984-7748
Editorial Fax: 803 984-7748
General/National Adv. E-mail: thejohnsonian@yahoo.com
Editorial e-mail: editors@mytjnow.com
Primary Website: www.mytjnow.com
Classified Equipment»
Personnel: Guy Reel (Faculty Adviser)

SPARTANBURG

CONVERSE COLLEGE

Street address 1: 580 E Main St
Street address 3: Spartanburg
Street address state: SC
Zip/Postal code: 29302-1931
Country: USA
Mailing address: 580 E Main St
Mailing city: Spartanburg
Mailing state: SC
Mailing zip: 29302-0006
General Phone: (864) 596-9000
General/National Adv. E-mail: admissions@converse.edu
Classified Equipment»
Personnel: Whitney Fisher (Advisor.)

UNIV. OF SOUTH CAROLINA

Street address 1: 800 University Way
Street address 2: Clc 112
Street address 3: Spartanburg
Street address state: SC
Zip/Postal code: 29303-4932
Country: USA
Mailing address: 800 University Way Clc 112
Mailing city: Spartanburg
Mailing state: SC
Mailing zip: 29303-4932
General Phone: (864) 503-5138
General Fax: (864) 503-5100
General/National Adv. E-mail: carolinian@uscupstate.edu
Primary Website: www.sc.edu/carolinian/
Classified Equipment»
Personnel: Chioma Ugochukwu (Advisor); India Brown (Ed.)

SOUTH DAKOTA

ABERDEEN

NORTHERN STATE UNIV.

Street address 1: 1200 S Jay St, Student Ctr, Rm 201
Street address 3: Aberdeen
Street address state: SD
Zip/Postal code: 57401
Country: USA
Mailing address: 1200 S. Jay St., Student Ctr., Rm. 201
Mailing city: Aberdeen
Mailing state: SD
Mailing zip: 57401
General Phone: (605) 626-2534
General Fax: (605) 626-2559
General/National Adv. E-mail: stupub@northern.edu
Primary Website: www.nsuexponent.com
Published: Mthly
Classified Equipment»
Personnel: Tracy Rasmussen (Advisor)

DAKOTA STATE UNIV.

Street address 1: 820 N Washington Ave
Street address 3: Madison
Street address state: SD
Zip/Postal code: 57042-1735
Country: USA
Mailing address: 820 N Washington Ave
Mailing city: Madison
Mailing state: SD
Mailing zip: 57042-1799
General Phone: (605) 256-5278
General Fax: (605) 256-5021
General/National Adv. E-mail: times@dsu.edu
Primary Website: www.clubs.dsu.edu/trojantimes
Classified Equipment»
Personnel: Justin Blessinger (Advisor); Jenny Grabinger (Adv. Mgr.); Samantha Moulton (Ed. in Chief)

RAPID CITY

SOUTH DAKOTA SCHOOL OF MINES & TECHNOLOGY

Street address 1: 501 E Saint Joseph St
Street address 3: Rapid City
Street address state: SD
Zip/Postal code: 57701-3901
Country: USA
Mailing address: 501 E Saint Joseph St
Mailing city: Rapid City
Mailing state: SD
Mailing zip: 57701-3995
General/National Adv. E-mail: aurum.sdsmt@gmail.com
Display Adv. E-mail: aurum.sdsmt@gmail.com
Editorial e-mail: aurum.sdsmt@gmail.com
Year Established: 1900
Published: Mthly
Avg Free Circ: 2000
Classified Equipment»
Personnel: Daniel Cerfus (Business Manager); Quinn del Val (Secretary); Robin Jerman (Cuisiner Columnist); Dan Eitreim (EIC)

SIOUX FALLS

AUGUSTANA UNIVERSITY

Street address 1: 2001 S Summit Ave
Street address 3: Sioux Falls
Street address state: SD
Zip/Postal code: 57197-0001
Country: USA
Mailing address: 2001 S Summit Ave
Mailing city: Sioux Falls
Mailing state: SD
Mailing zip: 57197-0002
General Phone: (605) 274-4423
General Fax: (605) 274-5288
Advertising Fax: (605) 274-5288
General/National Adv. E-mail: augustanamirror@gmail.com
Primary Website: www.augiemirror.com
Year Established: 1909
Published: Fri
Avg Free Circ: 1000
Classified Equipment»
Personnel: Jeffrey Miller (Advisor)

UNIV. OF SIOUX FALLS

Street address 1: 1101 W 22nd St
Street address 3: Sioux Falls
Street address state: SD
Zip/Postal code: 57105-1600
Country: USA
Mailing address: 1101 W 22nd St
Mailing city: Sioux Falls
Mailing state: SD
Mailing zip: 57105-1699
General Phone: (605) 331-6776
General Fax: (605) 331-6692
Classified Equipment»
Personnel: Tiffany Leach (Advisor); Janet Davison (Ed.)

SPEARFISH

BLACK HILLS STATE UNIV.

Street address 1: 1200 University St
Street address 3: Spearfish
Street address state: SD
Zip/Postal code: 57799-8840
Country: USA
Mailing address: 1200 University St
Mailing city: Spearfish
Mailing state: SD
Mailing zip: 57799-0002
General Phone: (605) 642-6389
General Fax: (605) 642-6119
General/National Adv. E-mail: jacketjournal@bhsu.edu
Primary Website: www.bhsu.edu/jacketjournal1
Classified Equipment»
Personnel: Mary Caton-Rosser (Advisor); Shelby Cihak (Bus. Mgr.); Kendra Bertsch (Adv. Mgr.)

VERMILLION

UNIV. OF SOUTH DAKOTA

Street address 1: 555 N Dakota St
Street address 3: Vermillion
Street address state: SD
Zip/Postal code: 57069-2300
Country: USA
Mailing address: 555 N Dakota St
Mailing city: Vermillion
Mailing state: SD
Mailing zip: 57069-2300
General Phone: (605) 677-5494
General Fax: (605) 677-5105
General/National Adv. E-mail: volante@usd.edu; volanteonline@gmail.com
Primary Website: www.volanteonline.com
Classified Equipment»

YANKTON

MT. MARTY COLLEGE

Street address 1: 1105 W 8th St
Street address 2: Ste 564
Street address 3: Yankton
Street address state: SD
Zip/Postal code: 57078-3725
Country: USA
Mailing address: 1105 W 8th St Ste 564
Mailing city: Yankton
Mailing state: SD
Mailing zip: 57078-3725
General Phone: (605) 668-1293
General Fax: (605) 668-1508
General/National Adv. E-mail: moderator@mtmc.edu
Primary Website: www.mtmc.edu/student/moderator
Classified Equipment»
Personnel: Jill Paulson (Advisor); Lauren Donlin (Adv. Mgr.); Alicia Pick (Circ. Mgr.)

TENNESSEE

KING COLLEGE

Street address 1: 1350 King College Rd
Street address 3: Bristol
Street address state: TN
Zip/Postal code: 37620-2632
Country: USA
Mailing address: 1350 King College Rd
Mailing city: Bristol
Mailing state: TN
Mailing zip: 37620-2649
General Phone: (423) 652-4829
General Fax: (423) 968-4456
Classified Equipment»
Personnel: Katie Vandebrake (Advisor)

CHATTANOOGA STATE TECH. CMTY. COLLEGE

Street address 1: Paul Starnes Ctr, Rm S-260, 4501 Amnicola Hwy
Street address 3: Chattanooga
Street address state: TN
Country: USA
Mailing address: Paul Starnes Ctr., Rm. S-260, 4501 Amnicola Hwy.
Mailing city: Chattanooga
Mailing state: TN
Mailing zip: 37406
General Phone: (423) 697-2471
General Fax: (423) 697-4758
General/National Adv. E-mail: communicator.editor@gmail.com
Classified Equipment»
Personnel: Betty A. Proctor (Advisor); Keith Burkhalter (Ed.)

UNIV. OF TENNESSEE CHATTANOOGA

Street address 1: 615 McCallie Ave
Street address 3: Chattanooga
Street address state: TN
Zip/Postal code: 37403-2504
Country: USA
Mailing address: 615 McCallie Ave
Mailing city: Chattanooga
Mailing state: TN
Mailing zip: 37403-2504
General Phone: (423) 425-4298
General Fax: (423) 425-8100
Advertising Phone: (423) 425-8101
General/National Adv. E-mail: echo@utcecho.com
Primary Website: www.utcecho.com
Classified Equipment»
Personnel: Holly Cowart (Advisor); Alexa Branblet (Adv. Mgr.); Paige Gabriel (Ed. in Chief); Kate Bissinger (Mng. Ed.); Hayley (Features Ed.); Rachel (News Ed.); Michael (Sports Ed.)

CLEVELAND STATE CMTY. COLLEGE

Street address 1: 3535 Adkisson Dr NW
Street address 3: Cleveland
Street address state: TN
Zip/Postal code: 37312-2813
Country: USA
Mailing address: PO Box 3570
Mailing city: Cleveland
Mailing state: TN
Mailing zip: 37320-3570
General Phone: (423) 472-7141
General Fax: (423) 478-6255
General/National Adv. E-mail: tbartolo@clevelandstatecc.edu
Primary Website: www.clevelandstatecc.edu
Classified Equipment»
Personnel: Tony Bartolo (Adv. Mgr.); Priscilla Simms (Ed.)

LEE UNIV.

Street address 1: 1120 N Ocoee St
Street address 3: Cleveland
Street address state: TN
Zip/Postal code: 37311-4458
Country: USA
Mailing address: 1120 N Ocoee St
Mailing city: Cleveland
Mailing state: TN
Mailing zip: 37311-4475
General Phone: (423) 614-8489
General Fax: (423) 614-8341
General/National Adv. E-mail: news@leeclarion.com
Primary Website: www.leeclarion.com
Classified Equipment»
Personnel: Kevin Trowbridge (Advisor); Michelle Bouman (Ed.)

COOKEVILLE

TENNESSEE TECHNOLOGICAL UNIV.

Street address 1: 1000 N Dixie Ave
Street address 2: Ruc 376
Street address 3: Cookeville
Street address state: TN
Zip/Postal code: 38505-0001
Country: USA
Mailing address: PO Box 5072
Mailing city: Cookeville
Mailing state: TN
Mailing zip: 38505-0001
General Phone: (931) 372-3060
General Fax: (931) 372-6225
Advertising Phone: (931) 372-3031
Advertising Fax: (931) 372-6225
Editorail Phone: (931) 372-3285
Editorial Fax: (931) 372-6225
General/National Adv. E-mail: oracle@tntech.edu
Display Adv. E-mail: ttuoracleads@gmail.com
Editorial e-mail: oracle@tntech.edu
Primary Website: www.tntechoracle.com
Year Established: 1924
Published: Fri
Published Other: Weekly during Fall and Spring semesters
Avg Free Circ: 3000
Classified Equipment»
Personnel: Jon Ezell (Advisor / Assistant Professor)
Parent company (for newspapers): Tennessee Technological University

BRYAN COLLEGE

Street address 1: 721 Bryan Dr
Street address 3: Dayton
Street address state: TN
Zip/Postal code: 37321-6275
Country: USA
Mailing address: Box 7807
Mailing city: Dayton
Mailing state: TN
Mailing zip: 37321
General Phone: (423) 775-7285
General Fax: (423) 775-7330
General/National Adv. E-mail: triangle@bryan.edu; info@bryan.edu
Primary Website: www.bryan.edu/7229; www.bryan.edu
Classified Equipment»
Personnel: John Carpenter (Advisor); Allison McLean (Ed. in Chief)

GALLATIN

VOLUNTEER STATE CMTY. COLLEGE

Street address 1: 1480 Nashville Pike
Street address 3: Gallatin
Street address state: TN
Zip/Postal code: 37066-3148
Country: USA
Mailing address: 1480 Nashville Pike
Mailing city: Gallatin
Mailing state: TN
Mailing zip: 37066-3148
General Phone: (615) 452-8600
General Fax: (615) 230-3481
General/National Adv. E-mail: thesettler@allstate.edu
Primary Website: www.settleronline.com
Classified Equipment»
Personnel: Clay Scott (Advisor); Amy Webb (Ed.)

GREENEVILLE

TUSCULUM COLLEGE

Street address 1: 60 Shiloh Rd
Street address 3: Greeneville
Street address state: TN
Zip/Postal code: 37745-0595
Country: USA
Mailing address: PO Box 5098
Mailing city: Greeneville
Mailing state: TN
Mailing zip: 37743-0001
General Phone: (423) 636-7300
General Fax: (423) 638-7166
Primary Website: www.tusculum.edu
Classified Equipment»
Personnel: Barth Cox (Advisor)

FREED-HARDEMAN UNIV.

Street address 1: 158 E Main St
Street address 3: Henderson
Street address state: TN
Zip/Postal code: 38340-2306
Country: USA
Mailing address: 158 E Main St
Mailing city: Henderson
Mailing state: TN
Mailing zip: 38340-2398
General Fax: (731) 989-6000
General/National Adv. E-mail: belltower@fhu.edu
Primary Website: www.fhu.edu
Classified Equipment»
Personnel: Derrick Spradlin (Advisor); Eddie Eaton (Ed.)

UNION UNIV.

Street address 1: 1050 Union University Dr
Street address 2: Dept Jenningshall
Street address 3: Jackson
Street address state: TN
Zip/Postal code: 38305-3656
Country: USA
Mailing address: 1050 Union University Dr Dept Jenningshall
Mailing city: Jackson
Mailing state: TN
Mailing zip: 38305-3656
General Phone: (731) 668-1818
General Fax: (731) 661-5243
Primary Website: www.cardinalandcream.info
Classified Equipment»
Personnel: Michael Chute (Advisor); Gray Coyner (Adv. Mgr.); Andrea Turner (Ed. in Chief)

CARSON-NEWMAN UNIVERSITY

Street address 1: 1646 Russell Ave
Street address 3: Jefferson City
Street address state: TN
Zip/Postal code: 37760-2204
Country: USA
Mailing address: 1646 Russell Ave
Mailing city: Jefferson City
Mailing state: TN
Mailing zip: 37760
General Phone: (865) 471-3434
General Fax: (865) 471-3416
General/National Adv. E-mail: oandb@cn.edu
Primary Website: www.orangeandblueonline.com; www.cn.edu
Classified Equipment»
Personnel: Glenn Cragwall (Advisor)

JOHNSON CITY

EAST TENNESSEE STATE UNIV.

Street address 1: Culp Ctr, Jl Seehorn Jr Rd
Street address 3: Johnson City
Street address state: TN
Zip/Postal code: 37614
Country: USA
Mailing address: PO Box 70688
Mailing city: Johnson City
Mailing state: TN
Mailing zip: 37614-1709
General Phone: (423) 439-6170
General Fax: (423) 439-8407
Editorail Phone: (423) 439-4677
General/National Adv. E-mail: etnews@etsu.edu
Primary Website: www.easttennessean.com
Classified Equipment»
Personnel: Martha Milner (Advisor); Candy Naff (Office Supvr.)

KNOXVILLE

UT DAILY BEACON (UNIVERSITY OF TENNESSEE)

Street address 1: 11 Communications Bldg
Street address 2: 1345 Circle Park Dr.
Street address 3: Knoxville
Street address state: TN
Zip/Postal code: 37996-0001
Country: USA
Mailing address: 11 Communications Bldg.
Mailing city: Knoxville
Mailing state: TN
Mailing zip: 37996-0314
General Phone: (865) 974-5206
General Fax: (865) 974-5569
Editorail Phone: (865) 974-3226
General/National Adv. E-mail: editorinchief@utdailybeacon.com
Display Adv. E-mail: beaconads@utk.edu
Editorial e-mail: letters@utdailybeacon.com
Primary Website: utdailybeacon.com
Year Established: 1906
Special Editions: Special Editions information available online in Ratecard, Page 8: http://media.utdailybeacon.com/advertising/ratecards/dailybeacon-ad-ratecard-2011-6.pdf For more information, contact Advertising Office: 865-974-5206 Special Editions/Sections: *Welcome Back (August) Contact in June for Section Deadlines in July *Football Preview (First Home Game) Contact in August *Basketball Preview (November) Contact in early November *Student Appreciation Day (February) Contact in early February *Orientation (June/July) Contact in April
Delivery Methods: Mail`Racks
Commercial printers: Y
Advertising (Open Inch Rate) Weekday/Saturday:

Market Information: Rate Card: http://media.utdailybeacon.com/advertising/ratecards/dailybeacon-ad-ratecard-2011-6.pdf
Mechanical available: Rate Card: http://media.utdailybeacon.com/advertising/ratecards/dailybeacon-ad-ratecard-2011-6.pdf
Published: Mon`Thur
Published Other: Special issues (See Rate Card above)
Avg Free Circ: 6000
Classified Equipment»
Note: Call for advertising details
Personnel: Jerry Bush (Dir. of Student Media)

CUMBERLAND UNIV.

Street address 1: 1 Cumberland Sq
Street address 3: Lebanon
Street address state: TN
Zip/Postal code: 37087-3408
Country: USA
Mailing address: 1 Cumberland Sq.
Mailing city: Lebanon
Mailing state: TN
Mailing zip: 37087-3408
General Phone: (615) 444-2562
General Fax: (615) 444-2569
General/National Adv. E-mail: cumberlandchronicle@gmail.com
Primary Website: www.cumberland.edu
Published: Mon`Bi-Mthly
Classified Equipment»
Personnel: Michael Rex (Advisor)

MARTIN

UNIV. OF TENNESSEE MARTIN

Street address 1: 314 Gooch Hall
Street address 3: Martin
Street address state: TN
Zip/Postal code: 38238-0001
Country: USA
Mailing address: 314 Gooch Hall
Mailing city: Martin
Mailing state: TN
Mailing zip: 38238-0001
General Phone: (731) 881-7780
General Fax: (731) 881-7791
General/National Adv. E-mail: pacer@ut.utm.edu
Primary Website: www.utmpacer.com
Classified Equipment»
Personnel: Tomi McCutchen Parrish (Advisor); Josh Lemons (Ed.); Spencer Taylor (Mgr./News Ed.)

MARYVILLE COLLEGE

Street address 1: 502 E Lamar Alexander Pkwy
Street address 3: Maryville
Street address state: TN
Zip/Postal code: 37804-5907
Country: USA
Mailing address: 502 E Lamar Alexander Pkwy
Mailing city: Maryville
Mailing state: TN
Mailing zip: 37804-5919
General Phone: (865) 981-8241
General/National Adv. E-mail: highland.echo@gmail.com
Primary Website: echo.maryvillecollege.edu
Classified Equipment»
Personnel: Kim Trevathan (Advisor)

LEMOYNE-OWEN COLLEGE

Street address 1: 807 Walker Ave
Street address 3: Memphis
Street address state: TN
Zip/Postal code: 38126-6510
Country: USA
Mailing address: 807 Walker Ave
Mailing city: Memphis
Mailing state: TN
Mailing zip: 38126-6595
General Phone: (901) 435-1309
General Fax: (901) 435-1349
Editorail Phone: (901) 435-1318
General/National Adv. E-mail: magican@loc.edu
Primary Website: www.locmagiciononline.com
Classified Equipment»
Personnel: Lydia Lay (Instructor)

RHODES COLLEGE

Street address 1: 2000 N Parkway
Street address 3: Memphis
Street address state: TN
Zip/Postal code: 38112-1624
Country: USA
Mailing address: PO Box 3010
Mailing city: Memphis
Mailing state: TN
Mailing zip: 38173-0010
General Phone: (901) 843-3885
General Fax: (901) 843-3576
General/National Adv. E-mail: Souwester souwester@rhodes.edu
Primary Website: www.thesouwester.org
Classified Equipment»
Personnel: John Blaisdell

SOUTHWEST TENNESSEE CMTY. COLLEGE

Street address 1: 5983 Macon Cv
Street address 3: Memphis
Street address state: TN
Zip/Postal code: 38134-7642
Country: USA
Mailing address: 5983 Macon Cv
Mailing city: Memphis
Mailing state: TN
Mailing zip: 38134-7693
General Phone: (901) 333-4196
General Fax: (901) 333-4995
General/National Adv. E-mail: pworthy@southwest.tn.edu
Display Adv. E-mail: cherron@southwest.tn.edu
Primary Website: southwest.tn.edu/clubs
Year Established: 2000
Advertising (Open Inch Rate) Weekday/Saturday: I will have to email this information
Classified Equipment»
Note: We have not selected an Editor for 2013-2014 for the Southwest Source. We will by August 15, 2013
Personnel: Phoenix Worthy (Advisor); Connie Herron (Coorindator)

UNIV. OF MEMPHIS

Street address 1: 113 Meeman Journalism Bldg
Street address 3: Memphis
Street address state: TN
Zip/Postal code: 38152-3290
Country: USA
Mailing address: 113 Meeman Journalism Bldg
Mailing city: Memphis
Mailing state: TN
Mailing zip: 38152-3290
General Phone: (901) 678-5474
General Fax: (901) 678-0882
Display Adv. E-mail: rlwillis@memphis.edu
Primary Website: www.dailyhelmsman.com
Delivery Methods: Racks
Commercial printers: Y
Advertising (Open Inch Rate) Weekday/Saturday: $10 per col. inch
Mechanical available: Mechanical dimensions contained in 2-page Rates & Data information sheet available at www.dailyhelmsman.com, by navigating Print Advertising Information.
Published: Tues`Wed`Thur`Fri
Avg Free Circ: 6500
Classified Equipment»
Personnel: Bob Willis (Bus. Mgr.)

MILLIGAN COLLEGE

MILLIGAN COLLEGE

Street address 1: 1 Blowers Blvd
Street address 3: Milligan College
Street address state: TN
Zip/Postal code: 37682
Country: USA
Mailing address: PO Box 500
Mailing city: Milligan College
Mailing state: TN
Mailing zip: 37682-0500
General Phone: (423) 461-8995
General Fax: (423) 461-8965
General/National Adv. E-mail: stampede@milligan.edu
Primary Website: www.milliganstampede.com
Year Established: 1866
Classified Equipment»
Personnel: Jim Dahlman (Advisor); Kalee Nagel (Ed.)

WALTERS STATE CMTY. COLLEGE

Street address 1: 500 S Davy Crockett Pkwy
Street address 3: Morristown
Street address state: TN
Zip/Postal code: 37813-1908
Country: USA
Mailing address: 500 S Davy Crockett Pkwy
Mailing city: Morristown
Mailing state: TN
Mailing zip: 37813-6899
General Phone: (423) 585-6816
Classified Equipment»
Personnel: Dianna Pearson (Contact)

MURFREESBORO

MIDDLE TENNESSEE STATE UNIV.

Street address 1: 1301 E Main St
Street address 3: Murfreesboro
Street address state: TN
Zip/Postal code: 37132-0002
Country: USA
Mailing address: 1301 East Main Street, Box 36
Mailing city: Murfreesboro
Mailing state: TN
Mailing zip: 37132-0001
General Phone: (615) 904-8357
General Fax: (615) 494-7648
Editorail Phone: 6156924488
General/National Adv. E-mail: editor@mtsusidelines.com
Display Adv. E-mail: editor@mtsusidelines.com
Editorial e-mail: editor@mtsusidelines.com
Primary Website: www.mtsusidelines.com
Year Established: 1925
Published: Mthly
Avg Free Circ: 4000
Classified Equipment»
Note:
Personnel: Meagan White (Editor-in-chief); Dylan Aycock (Managing Editor); Sarah Taylor (News Editor); Rhiannon Gilbert (Lifestyles Editor); Ethan Clark (Assistant Lifestyles Editor); Michael Ward (Sports Editor); Connor Ulrey (Assistant Sports Editor); Grant Massey (Multimedia Editor); Darian Lindsay (Chief Videographer); Austin Lewis (Photography Editor); Anna Claire Farmer (Design Editor); Justin Morales (Design Editor); Savannah Hazlewood (Assistant News Editor)

BELMONT UNIV.

Street address 1: 1900 Belmont Blvd
Street address 3: Nashville
Street address state: TN
Zip/Postal code: 37212-3758
Country: USA
Mailing address: 1900 Belmont Blvd
Mailing city: Nashville
Mailing state: TN
Mailing zip: 37212-3757
General Phone: (615) 460-6000
General Fax: (615) 460-5532
General/National Adv. E-mail: vision@mail.belmont.edu
Primary Website: www.belmontvision.com; www.belmont.edu
Classified Equipment»
Personnel: Linda Quigley (Advisor); Thom Storey (Chair); Karen Bennett (Adv. Mgr.); Bethany Brinton; Lance Conzett (Ed. in Chief)

FISK UNIV.

Street address 1: Humanities Div, 1000 17th Ave N
Street address 3: Nashville
Street address state: TN
Zip/Postal code: 37208
Country: USA
Mailing address: Humanities Div., 1000 17th Ave. N.
Mailing city: Nashville
Mailing state: TN
Mailing zip: 37208-3045
General Phone: (615) 329-8500
General Fax: (615) 329-8714
Primary Website: www.fisk.edu
Classified Equipment»
Personnel: Karen Taylor (Ed.); Keen West (Ed.)

LIPSCOMB UNIV.

Street address 1: 3901 Granny White Pike
Street address 2: # 4126
Street address 3: Nashville
Street address state: TN
Zip/Postal code: 37204-3903
Country: USA
Mailing address: 1 University Park Dr
Mailing city: Nashville
Mailing state: TN
Mailing zip: 37204-3956
General Phone: (615) 966-6604
General Fax: (615) 966-6605
General/National Adv. E-mail: babbler@lipscomb.edu
Display Adv. E-mail: babbleradvertising@lipscomb.edu
Primary Website: babbler.lipscomb.edu
Classified Equipment»
Personnel: Jimmy McCollum (Advisor); Michael Gilbert (Adv. Mgr.); Kaitie McDermott (Ed. in Chief)

VANDERBILT UNIV.

Street address 1: 2301 Vanderbilt Pl
Street address 2: # 351504
Street address 3: Nashville
Street address state: TN
Zip/Postal code: 37235-0002
Country: USA
Mailing address: 2301 Vanderbilt Place Vu Sta B351504
Mailing city: Nashville
Mailing state: TN
Mailing zip: 37235-0001
General Phone: (615) 322-4705
General Fax: (615) 343-4969
General/National Adv. E-mail: advertising@vanderbilthustler.com
Editorial e-mail: editor@vanderbilthustler.com
Primary Website: www.insidevandy.com
Classified Equipment»
Personnel: Chris Carroll (Advisor); George Fischer (Dir. Mktg.); Carolyn Fischer (Adv. Mgr.); Hannah Twillman (Ed.)

SEWANEE

UNIV. OF THE SOUTH

Street address 1: 735 University Ave
Street address 3: Sewanee
Street address state: TN
Zip/Postal code: 37383-2000
Country: USA
Mailing address: 735 University Ave
Mailing city: Sewanee
Mailing state: TN
Mailing zip: 37383-1000
General Phone: (931) 598-1204
General/National Adv. E-mail: spurple@sewanee.edu
Primary Website: www.sewaneepurple.com
Classified Equipment»
Personnel: Virginia Craighill (Advisor)

TRUE NORTH CUSTOM PUBLISHING

Street address state: TN
Country: USA
Mailing address: 5600 Brainerd Rd Ste 1
Mailing city: Chattanooga
Mailing state: TN
Mailing zip: 37411-5373
General Phone: 423.266.3234
Primary Website: http://www.truenorthcustom.com
Classified Equipment»
Personnel: Emily Young (Ed.); Tim Lale (Advisor); Katie Hammond (Managing Ed.); Alison Quiring (News Ed.); Stephanie (Opinion Ed.)

AUSTIN PEAY STATE UNIV.

Street address 1: 601 College St
Street address state: TN
Country: USA
Mailing address: PO Box 4634

Mailing city: Clarksville
Mailing state: TN
Mailing zip: 37044-0001
General Phone: (931) 221-7376
General Fax: (931) 221-7377
Editorail Phone: (931) 221-7374
General/National Adv. E-mail: theallstate@apsu.edu
Display Adv. E-mail: allstateads@apsu.edu
Primary Website: www.theallstate.org; www.apsu.edu
Classified Equipment»
Personnel: Tabitha Gillaland (Advisor); Nicole June (Adv. Mgr.); Patrick Armstrong (Ed. in Chief)

TEXAS

ABILENE CHRISTIAN UNIV.

Street address 1: PO Box 27892
Street address 3: Abilene
Street address state: TX
Country: USA
Mailing address: PO Box 27892
Mailing city: Abilene
Mailing state: TX
Mailing zip: 79699-0001
General Fax: (325) 674-2463
Advertising Fax: (325) 674-2139
General/National Adv. E-mail: christi.stark@acu.edu
Primary Website: www.acuoptimist.com
Classified Equipment»
Personnel: Colter Hettich (Ed.)

HARDIN-SIMMONS UNIV.

Street address 1: 2200 Hickory St
Street address 3: Abilene
Street address state: TX
Zip/Postal code: 79601-2345
Country: USA
Mailing address: 2200 Hickory St
Mailing city: Abilene
Mailing state: TX
Mailing zip: 79601-2345
General Phone: (325) 670-1438
General Fax: (325) 677-8351
General/National Adv. E-mail: brand@hsutx.edu
Display Adv. E-mail: brandadv@hsutx.edu
Primary Website: www.hsutx.edu
Classified Equipment»
Personnel: Adriel Wong (Ed. in. Chief)

MCMURRY UNIV.

Street address 1: PO Box 277
Street address 3: Abilene
Street address state: TX
Zip/Postal code: 79604-0277
Country: USA
Mailing address: Box 277, McMurry Sta.
Mailing city: Abilene
Mailing state: TX
Mailing zip: 79697
General Phone: (325) 793-3800
General Fax: (325) 793-4679
Classified Equipment»

ALPINE

SUL ROSS STATE UNIV.

Street address 1: PO Box C-112
Street address 3: Alpine
Street address state: TX
Zip/Postal code: 79832-0001
Country: USA
Mailing address: PO Box C112
Mailing city: Alpine
Mailing state: TX
Mailing zip: 79832-0001
General Phone: (432) 837-8011
General Fax: (432) 837-8664
General/National Adv. E-mail: skyline@sulross.edu
Primary Website: ^www.sulross.edu
Classified Equipment»
Personnel: Cheryl Zinsmeyer (Student Publications Advisor)

AMARILLO

AMARILLO COLLEGE

Street address 1: 2201 S Washington St
Street address 3: Amarillo
Street address state: TX
Zip/Postal code: 79109-2411
Country: USA
Mailing address: PO Box 447
Mailing city: Amarillo
Mailing state: TX
Mailing zip: 79178-0001
General Phone: (806) 371-5283
General Fax: (806) 371-5398
General/National Adv. E-mail: therangereditor@gmail.com
Display Adv. E-mail: jigibson@actx.edu
Editorial e-mail: therangereditor@gmail.com
Primary Website: www.acranger.com
Year Established: 1930
Delivery Methods: Racks
Commercial printers: N
Advertising (Open Inch Rate) Weekday/Saturday: SAU
Published: Thur
Published Other: biweekly
Avg Free Circ: 2500
Classified Equipment»
Personnel: Jill Gibson (Student Media Adviser Matney Mass Media Program Coord); Maddisun Fowler (Student Media Coord)
Parent company (for newspapers): Amarillo College

UNIVERSITY OF TEXAS AT ARLINGTON

Street address 1: University Ctr, Lower Level, 300 W 1st St
Street address 2: B100
Street address 3: Arlington
Street address state: TX
Zip/Postal code: 76019-0001
Country: USA
Mailing address: P.O. Box 19038
Mailing city: Arlington
Mailing state: TX
Mailing zip: 76019-0001
General Phone: (817) 272-3188
General Fax: (817) 272-5009
Editorail Phone: (817) 272-3205
General/National Adv. E-mail: editor.shorthorn@uta.edu
Display Adv. E-mail: ads.shorthorn@uta.edu
Editorial e-mail: editor.shorthorn@uta.edu; calendar.shorthorn@uta.edu
Primary Website: www.theshorthorn.com
Year Established: 1919
Delivery Methods: Racks
Advertising (Open Inch Rate) Weekday/Saturday: http://www.theshorthorn.com/site/advertise.html
Published: Wed
Published Other: Daily online
Classified Equipment»
Note: Daily e-newsletter subscription available; creative agency started 2016.
Personnel: Brian Schopf (Office Mgr.); Tammy Skrehart (Adv. Mgr./Asst. Dir.); Adam Drew (Production Mgr.); Beth Francesco (Dir. of Student Pubs.); Laurie Fox (Newsroom advisor); Lori Doskocil (Bus Mgr)
Parent company (for newspapers): University of Texas at Arlington

TRINITY VALLEY CMTY. COLLEGE

Street address 1: 100 Cardinal St
Street address 3: Athens
Street address state: TX
Zip/Postal code: 75751-3243
Country: USA
Mailing address: 100 Cardinal St
Mailing city: Athens
Mailing state: TX
Mailing zip: 75751-3243
General Phone: (903) 675-6302
General Fax: (903) 675-6316
General/National Adv. E-mail: journalstaff@tvcc.edu
Primary Website: www.tvccnewsjournal.com
Year Established: 1972
Classified Equipment»
Personnel: Danny Teague (Advisor); Judy Greenlee (Asst. Advisor); Melisa Boon (Ed.); Deidre Jones (Media Instructor/Adviser)

HUSTON TILLOTSON COLLEGE

Street address 1: 900 Chicon St
Street address 3: Austin
Street address state: TX
Zip/Postal code: 78702-2753
Country: USA
Mailing address: 900 Chicon St
Mailing city: Austin
Mailing state: TX
Mailing zip: 78702-9997
General Phone: (512) 505-3000
Classified Equipment»

ST. EDWARDS UNIV.

Street address 1: 3001 S Congress Ave
Street address 2: Campus Mailox #964
Street address 3: Austin
Street address state: TX
Zip/Postal code: 78704-6425
Country: USA
Mailing address: PO Box 1033
Mailing city: Austin
Mailing state: TX
Mailing zip: 78767-1033
General Phone: (512) 448-8426
General Fax: (512) 428-1084
General/National Adv. E-mail: hilltopviewsonline@gmail.com
Display Adv. E-mail: hilltopviewsads@gmail.com
Editorial e-mail: hilltopviewseditors@gmail.com
Primary Website: hilltopviewsonline.com
Published: Wed
Classified Equipment»
Personnel: Andrea Guzman (Editor-In-Chief); Gabrielle Wilkosz (Editor-In-Chief); Amanda Gonzalez (Managing Editor)

TEXAS STUDENT MEDIA

Street address 1: 2500 Whitis Ave
Street address 3: Austin
Street address state: TX
Zip/Postal code: 78712-1502
Country: USA
Mailing address: PO Box D
Mailing city: Austin
Mailing state: TX
Mailing zip: 78713-8904
General Phone: (512) 471-4591
General Fax: (512) 471-2952
Advertising Phone: (512) 471-1865
Editorail Phone: (512) 232-2207
Primary Website: www.dailytexanonline.com
Year Established: 1900
Delivery Methods: Racks
Commercial printers: N
Published: Mon`Tues`Wed`Thur`Fri
Avg Free Circ: 13000
Classified Equipment»
Personnel: Doug Warren (Advisor)

UNIV. OF TEXAS COLLEGE OF BUS.

Street address 1: Cba 3.328 A
Street address 3: Austin
Street address state: TX
Zip/Postal code: 78712
Country: USA
Mailing address: CBA 3.328 A
Mailing city: Austin
Mailing state: TX
Mailing zip: 78712
General Phone: (512) 708-9357
Classified Equipment»
Personnel: Sunio Varghese (Ed.)

UNIV. OF TEXAS COLLEGE OF ENGINEERING

Street address 1: 301 E Dean Keeton St
Street address 3: Austin
Street address state: TX
Zip/Postal code: 78712-1476
Country: USA
Mailing address: 301 E. Dean Keeton St. C2100
Mailing city: Austin
Mailing state: TX
Mailing zip: 78712-2100
General Phone: (512) 471-3003
General Fax: (512) 471-4304
General/National Adv. E-mail: vector.ut@gmail.com
Primary Website: www.engr.utexas.edu
Classified Equipment»
Personnel: An Nguyen (Ed.)

BEAUMONT

LAMAR UNIV.

Street address 1: 200 Setzer Student Ctr
Street address 3: Beaumont
Street address state: TX
Zip/Postal code: 77710
Country: USA
Mailing address: PO Box 10055
Mailing city: Beaumont
Mailing state: TX
Mailing zip: 77710-0055
General Phone: (409) 880-8102
General Fax: (409) 880-8735
General/National Adv. E-mail: advertising@lamaruniversitypress.com
Primary Website: www.lamaruniversitypress.com
Published: Thur
Published Other: end of semester special editions, seasonal editions
Classified Equipment»
Personnel: Andy Coughlan (Advisor); Linda Barrett (Adv. Mgr.)

BELTON

UNIV. OF MARY HARDIN-BAYLOR

Street address 1: 900 College St
Street address 2: # 8012
Street address 3: Belton
Street address state: TX
Zip/Postal code: 76513-2578
Country: USA
Mailing address: 900 College St # 8012
Mailing city: Belton
Mailing state: TX
Mailing zip: 76513-2578
General Phone: (254) 295-4598
Primary Website: thebells.umhb.edu
Classified Equipment»
Personnel: Crystal Donahue (Ed.)

UNIVERSITY OF TEXAS AT BROWNSVILLE

Street address 1: 1 W University Blvd
Street address 2: Student Union 1.16
Street address 3: Brownsville
Street address state: TX
Zip/Postal code: 78520-4933
Country: USA
Mailing address: 1 West University Boulevard
Mailing city: Brownsville
Mailing state: TX
Mailing zip: 78520-4956
General Phone: (956) 882-5143
General Fax: (956) 882-5176
General/National Adv. E-mail: collegian@utb.edu
Display Adv. E-mail: collegian.advertising@utb.edu
Editorial e-mail: collegian@utb.edu
Primary Website: utbcollegian.com
Advertising (Open Inch Rate) Weekday/Saturday: Full-page ($400); half-page ($200); quarter-page ($105); eighth-page ($75); color (any size, $50 extra)
Published: Mon
Avg Free Circ: 4000
Classified Equipment»
Personnel: Azenett Cornejo (Advisor); Cleiri Quezada (Editor)

CANYON

WEST TEXAS A&M UNIV.

Street address 1: PO Box 60747
Street address 3: Canyon
Street address state: TX

Zip/Postal code: 79016-0001
Country: USA
Mailing address: PO Box 60747
Mailing city: Canyon
Mailing state: TX
Mailing zip: 79016-0001
General Phone: (806) 651-2410
General Fax: (806) 651-2818
Advertising Phone: (806) 651-2413
General/National Adv. E-mail: bleschper@mail.wtamu.edu; theprairiemail@yahoo.com
Primary Website: www.theprairieonline.com; www.theprairienews.com
Classified Equipment»
Personnel: Christaan Eayrs (Advisor); Joe Dowd (Bus. Mgr.); Kayla Goodman (Ed.)

CARTHAGE

PANOLA COLLEGE

Street address 1: 1109 W Panola St
Street address 3: Carthage
Street address state: TX
Zip/Postal code: 75633-2341
Country: USA
Mailing address: 1109 W Panola St
Mailing city: Carthage
Mailing state: TX
Mailing zip: 75633-2397
General Phone: (903) 693-2079
General Fax: (903) 693-5588
Primary Website: www.panola.edu
Classified Equipment»
Personnel: Teresa Beasley (Advisor)

COLLEGE STATION

TEXAS A&M UNIV.

Street address 1: the Grove Bldg 8901, 215 Limar St
Street address 3: College Station
Street address state: TX
Zip/Postal code: 77843-0001
Country: USA
Mailing address: the Grove Bldg 8901, 215 Limar St
Mailing city: College Station
Mailing state: TX
Mailing zip: 77843-0001
General Phone: (979) 845-3313
General Fax: (979) 845-2647
Advertising Phone: (979) 845-0569
Advertising Fax: (979) 845-2678
Editorail Phone: (979) 845-3315
General/National Adv. E-mail: editor@thebatt.com
Display Adv. E-mail: battads@thebatt.com
Primary Website: www.thebatt.com
Classified Equipment»
Personnel: Cheri Shipman (News Advisor); Amanda Casanova (Ed. in Chief)

TEXAS A&M UNIVERSITY

Street address 1: 107 Scoates Hall
Street address 3: College Station
Street address state: TX
Zip/Postal code: 77843-0001
Country: USA
Mailing address: 107 Scoates Hall
Mailing city: College Station
Mailing state: TX
Mailing zip: 77843-0001
General Phone: (979) 862-3003
General Fax: (979) 845-6296
General/National Adv. E-mail: dj-king@tamu.edu
Classified Equipment»
Personnel: Deborah Dunsford (Program Coord.)

TEXAS A&M UNIVERSITY

Street address 1: 4234 Tamu
Street address 3: College Station
Street address state: TX
Zip/Postal code: 77843-0001
Country: USA
Mailing address: 4234 Tamu
Mailing city: College Station
Mailing state: TX
Mailing zip: 77843-0001
General Phone: (979) 458-1802
General Fax: (979) 845-6594
General/National Adv. E-mail: r-sumpter@tamu.edu; journminor@tamu.edu
Classified Equipment»
Personnel: Randall S. Sumpter (Dir., Journ. Studies/ Assoc. Prof., Commun.); Roberto Farias (Program Asst.); Edward L. Walraven (Sr. Lectr.); Dale A. Rice (Lectr.)

THE BATTALION

Street address 1: Grove 215 Lamar St Bldg 8901
Street address 3: College Station
Street address state: TX
Zip/Postal code: 77843-0001
County: Brazos
Country: USA
Mailing address: 1111 Tamu
Mailing city: College Station
Mailing state: TX
Mailing zip: 77843-0001
General Phone: 979-845-3313
General Fax: 979-845-2647
General/National Adv. E-mail: editor@thebatt.com
Primary Website: http://thebatt.com/
Year Established: 1893
Advertising (Open Inch Rate) Weekday/Saturday: Open inch rate $14.00 (Local)
Published: Mon`Tues`Wed`Thur`Fri
Weekday Frequency: m
Classified Equipment»

COMMERCE

TEXAS A&M UNIV. COMMERCE

Street address 1: PO Box 4104
Street address 3: Commerce
Street address state: TX
Zip/Postal code: 75429-4104
Country: USA
Mailing address: PO Box 4104
Mailing city: Commerce
Mailing state: TX
Mailing zip: 75429-4104
General Phone: (903) 886-5985
General Fax: (903) 468-3128
Advertising Phone: (903) 886-5231
General/National Adv. E-mail: theeasttexan@gmail.com
Primary Website: www.theeasttexan.com
Year Established: 1915
Advertising (Open Inch Rate) Weekday/Saturday: $5 per col inca
Published: Bi-Mthly
Avg Free Circ: 1000
Classified Equipment»
Note: www.issuu.com/tamuc.easttexan tamuceasttexan.com
Personnel: Fred Stewart (Fac. Advisor)

DEL MAR COLLEGE FOGHORN

Street address 1: 101 Baldwin Blvd
Street address 2: # HC210
Street address 3: Corpus Christi
Street address state: TX
Zip/Postal code: 78404-3805
Country: USA
Mailing address: 101 Baldwin Blvd # HC210
Mailing city: Corpus Christi
Mailing state: TX
Mailing zip: 78404-3805
General Phone: 361/698-1390
General Fax: (361/698-2153
Advertising Phone: 361/698-1246
Advertising Fax: 361/698-2153
Editorail Phone: 361/698-1390
Editorial Fax: 361/698-2153
General/National Adv. E-mail: editor@delmar.edu
Display Adv. E-mail: rmullenburg@delmar.edu
Editorial e-mail: editor@delmar.edu
Primary Website: www.foghornnews.com
Year Established: 1935
Delivery Methods: Newsstand`Racks
Commercial printers: Y
Advertising (Open Inch Rate) Weekday/Saturday: $4.50 col inch
Mechanical specifications: Broadsheet - 11.625 in. (6 col) X 20.5 in Column widths 1 col - 1.833 2 col - 3.792 3 col - 5.75 4 col - 7.708 5 col - 9.667 6 col - 11.625
Published: Tues`Bi-Mthly
Published Other: Tuesday every two weeks; no issues in summer
Avg Free Circ: 2500
Classified Equipment»
Personnel: Robert Muilenburg (Advisor); Donna Strong (Adv. Mgr.)

TEXAS A&M UNIV. CORPUS CHRISTI

Street address 1: 6300 Ocean Dr
Street address 3: Corpus Christi
Street address state: TX
Zip/Postal code: 78412-5503
Country: USA
Mailing address: 6300 Ocean Dr
Mailing city: Corpus Christi
Mailing state: TX
Mailing zip: 78412-5599
General Phone: (361) 825-7024
General Fax: (361) 825-3931
Display Adv. E-mail: islandwaves.ads@tamucc.edu
Editorial e-mail: editor-in-chief.islandwaves@tamucc.edu
Primary Website: islandwaves.tamucc.edu; www.tamucc.edu
Classified Equipment»
Personnel: Rob Boscamp (Advisor); Brittnye Screws (Adv. Mgr.)

PAUL QUINN COLLEGE

Street address 1: 3837 Simpson Stuart Rd
Street address 3: Dallas
Street address state: TX
Zip/Postal code: 75241-4331
Country: USA
Mailing address: 3837 Simpson Stuart Rd
Mailing city: Dallas
Mailing state: TX
Mailing zip: 75241-4398
General Phone: (214) 302-3600
Classified Equipment»

RICHLAND COLLEGE

Street address 1: 12800 Abrams Rd
Street address 3: Dallas
Street address state: TX
Zip/Postal code: 75243-2104
Country: USA
Mailing address: 12800 Abrams Rd.
Mailing city: Dallas
Mailing state: TX
Mailing zip: 75243-2199
General Phone: (972) 238-6079
General Fax: (972) 238-6037
Advertising Phone: (972) 238-6068
Display Adv. E-mail: advertise@dcccd.edu
Primary Website: www.richlandchronicle.com
Delivery Methods: Racks
Commercial printers: Y
Advertising (Open Inch Rate) Weekday/Saturday: Yes
Published: Tues
Published Other: Weekly on Tuesday
Avg Free Circ: 3000
Classified Equipment»

SOUTHERN METHODIST UNIV.

Street address 1: 3140 Dyer St
Street address 2: Ste 315
Street address 3: Dallas
Street address state: TX
Zip/Postal code: 75205-1977
Country: USA
Mailing address: 3140 Dyer St Ste 315
Mailing city: Dallas
Mailing state: TX
Mailing zip: 75205-1977
General Phone: (214) 768-4555
General Fax: (214) 768-4573
Advertising Phone: (214) 768-4111
Advertising Fax: (214) 768-4573
Editorail Phone: (214) 768-4111
Display Adv. E-mail: dcads@smu.edu
Primary Website: www.smudailycampus.com
Year Established: 1915
News Services: AP, MCT
Delivery Methods: Mail`Racks
Commercial printers: N
Published: Thur
Avg Free Circ: 3000
Classified Equipment»
Personnel: Jay Miller (Exec. Dir./Editorial Advisor); Dyann Slosar (Assoc. Dir.); Candace Barnhill (Int. Exec. Dir.)
Parent company (for newspapers): Student Media Company, Inc

DENTON

TEXAS WOMAN'S UNIV.

Street address 1: PO Box 425828
Street address 3: Denton
Street address state: TX
Zip/Postal code: 76204-5828
Country: USA
Mailing address: PO Box 425828
Mailing city: Denton
Mailing state: TX
Mailing zip: 76204-5828
General Phone: (940) 898-2191
General Fax: (940) 898-2188
Advertising Phone: (940) 898-2183
General/National Adv. E-mail: twu_lasso@yahoo.com
Primary Website: www.twu.edu/lasso
Classified Equipment»
Personnel: Alejandro Barrientos (Bus. Mgr.); Luis Rendon (Ed. in Chief); Rhonda Ross (Advisor)

UNIV. OF NORTH TEXAS

Street address 1: 225 S Ave B, Gab Room 117
Street address 3: Denton
Street address state: TX
Zip/Postal code: 76201
Country: USA
Mailing address: 225 S Ave B, GAB Room 117
Mailing city: Denton
Mailing state: TX
Mailing zip: 76201
General Phone: (940) 565-2851
General Fax: (940) 565-3573
Advertising Phone: (940) 565-3989
Editorail Phone: (940) 565-2353
General/National Adv. E-mail: editor@ntdaily.com
Primary Website: www.ntdaily.com
Classified Equipment»
Personnel: Allie Durham (Adv. Mgr.); Kerry Solan (Ed. in Chief); Courtney Roberts (Mng. Ed.)

EDINBURG

UNIV. OF TEXAS PAN AMERICAN

Street address 1: 1201 W University Dr
Street address 3: Edinburg
Street address state: TX
Zip/Postal code: 78539-2909
Country: USA
Mailing address: 1201 W. University Dr.
Mailing city: Edinburg
Mailing state: TX
Mailing zip: 78539
General Phone: (956) 381-2541
General Fax: (956) 316-7122
General/National Adv. E-mail: spubs@utpa.edu
Primary Website: www.panamericanonline.com
Classified Equipment»
Personnel: Gregory M. Selber (Advisor); Mariel Cantu (Adv. Mgr.); Brian Silva (Ed. in chief)

EL PASO CMTY. COLLEGE

Street address 1: PO Box 20500
Street address 3: El Paso
Street address state: TX
Zip/Postal code: 79998-0500
Country: USA
Mailing address: PO Box 20500
Mailing city: El Paso
Mailing state: TX
Mailing zip: 79998-0500
General Phone: (915) 831-2500
General Fax: (915) 831-2155

General/National Adv. E-mail: tejanotribune@eppcc.edu
Classified Equipment»
Personnel: Steve Escajeda (Contact); Joe Old (Advisor)

UNIV. OF TEXAS EL PASO

Street address 1: 105 Union East
Street address 2: 500 W. University Ave.
Street address 3: El Paso
Street address state: TX
Zip/Postal code: 79968-0001
Country: USA
Mailing address: 105 Union East
Mailing city: El Paso
Mailing state: TX
Mailing zip: 79968-0622
General Phone: (915) 747-5161
General Fax: (915) 747-8031
Advertising Phone: (915) 747-7434
Editorail Phone: (915) 747-7446
General/National Adv. E-mail: studentpublications@utep.edu
Display Adv. E-mail: prospectorads@utep.edu
Editorial e-mail: theprospector1@gmail.com
Primary Website: www.theprospectordaily.com
Year Established: 1914
Published: Tues
Published Other: www.theprospectordaily.com
Avg Paid Circ: 0
Avg Free Circ: 5000
Classified Equipment»
Personnel: Kathleen Flores (Dir); Veronica Gonzalez (Asst. Adv. Dir.)

FARMERS BRANCH

BROOKHAVEN COLLEGE

Street address 1: 3939 Valley View Ln
Street address 3: Farmers Branch
Street address state: TX
Zip/Postal code: 75244-4906
Country: USA
Mailing address: 3939 Valley View Ln
Mailing city: Farmers Branch
Mailing state: TX
Mailing zip: 75244-4997
General Phone: (972) 860-4700
General Fax: (972) 860-4142
General/National Adv. E-mail: bhc2110@dcccd.edu
Primary Website: www.brookhavencourier.com; www.brookhavencollege.edu
Classified Equipment»
Personnel: Wendy Moore (Advisor); Daniel Rodrigue (Advisor)

TEXAS CHRISTIAN UNIVERSITY

Street address 1: 2805 S University Dr
Street address 2: Moudy South Rm. 215
Street address 3: Fort Worth
Street address state: TX
Zip/Postal code: 76129-0001
Country: USA
Mailing address: TCU Box 298050
Mailing city: Fort Worth
Mailing state: TX
Mailing zip: 76129-0001
General Phone: (817) 257-7428
General Fax: (817) 257-7133
Advertising Phone: (817) 257-7426
Advertising Fax: 8172577133
Editorail Phone: 8172573600
Editorial Fax: 8172577133
General/National Adv. E-mail: 360@tcu360.com
Display Adv. E-mail: ads@tcu360.com
Editorial e-mail: 360@tcu360.com
Primary Website: www.tcu360.com
Year Established: 1902
Published: Thur
Published Other: IMAGE Magazine
Avg Paid Circ: 0
Avg Free Circ: 2000
Classified Equipment»
Note: TCU360.com has a mobile website that works on all mobile and tablet platforms but does not have native apps for any of the above platforms.
Personnel: Leah Griffin (Manager of Student Media Sales and Marketing); Jean Marie Brown (Assistant Professor of Professional Practice)

THE RAMBLER

Street address 1: 1201 Wesleyan St
Street address 3: Fort Worth
Street address state: TX
Zip/Postal code: 76105-1536
Country: USA
Mailing address: 1201 Wesleyan St
Mailing city: Fort Worth
Mailing state: TX
Mailing zip: 76105-1536
General Phone: (817) 531-7552
General Fax: (817) 531-4878
Advertising Phone: (817) 531-6526
Advertising Fax: 817-531-4878
Editorail Phone: 817-531-7552
Editorial Fax: 817-531-4878
General/National Adv. E-mail: twurambler@yahoo.com
Display Adv. E-mail: rambleradvertising@yahoo.com
Editorial e-mail: twurambler@yahoo.com
Primary Website: www.therambler.org
Year Established: 1917
Commercial printers: Y
Advertising (Open Inch Rate) Weekday/Saturday: $6.95 per column inch for national
Published Other: online only
Avg Free Circ: 800
Classified Equipment»
Personnel: Jenny Dean (Adviser); Kelli Lamers (Advisor); Ashely Oldham (Adv. Mgr.); Ngozi Akinro; Tiara Nugent (Ed. in Chief); Martin Garcia (News Ed.); Kay Colley (Student Media Director)

GALVESTON

TEXAS A&M UNIV. GALVESTON

Street address 1: PO Box 1675
Street address 3: Galveston
Street address state: TX
Zip/Postal code: 77553-1675
Country: USA
Mailing address: PO Box 1675
Mailing city: Galveston
Mailing state: TX
Mailing zip: 77553-1675
General Phone: (409) 740-4420
General Fax: (409) 740-4775
General/National Adv. E-mail: nautilus@tamug.edu
Primary Website: www.tamug.edu/stuact/Nautilusmain.htm
Classified Equipment»
Personnel: Kayce Peirce (Ed. in Chief)

HOUSTON BAPTIST UNIV.

Street address 1: 7502 Fondren Rd
Street address 3: Houston
Street address state: TX
Zip/Postal code: 77074-3200
Country: USA
Mailing address: 7502 Fondren Rd
Mailing city: Houston
Mailing state: TX
Mailing zip: 77074-3298
General Phone: (281) 649-3670
General Fax: (281) 649-3246
Advertising Phone: (281) 649-3668
Editorail Phone: (281) 649-3670
General/National Adv. E-mail: thecollegian@hbucollegian.com
Display Adv. E-mail: ads@hbucollegian.com
Primary Website: www.hbucollegian.com
Year Established: 1963
Published: Bi-Mthly
Classified Equipment»
Personnel: Jeffrey Wilkinson (Faculty Adviser); Katie Brown (Editor in Chief); Tabatha Trapp (Advertising Manager)

RICE UNIV.

Street address 1: 6100 Main St
Street address 2: Fl 2MS-524
Street address 3: Houston
Street address state: TX
Zip/Postal code: 77005-1827
Country: USA
Mailing address: 6100 Main St., MS-524
Mailing city: Houston
Mailing state: TX
Mailing zip: 77251-1892
General Phone: (713) 348-4801
General/National Adv. E-mail: thresher@rice.edu
Primary Website: www.ricethresher.org
Classified Equipment»
Personnel: Kelley Callaway (Advisor)

TEXAS SOUTHERN UNIV.

Street address 1: 3100 Cleburne Ave, Student Ctr
Street address 3: Houston
Street address state: TX
Zip/Postal code: 77004
Country: USA
Mailing address: 3100 Cleburne Ave., Student Ctr.
Mailing city: Houston
Mailing state: TX
Mailing zip: 77004-4501
General Phone: (713) 313-1976
General Fax: (713) 313-4453
Primary Website: www.tsu.edu
Classified Equipment»
Personnel: Alice Rogers (Advisor)

UNIV. OF HOUSTON

Street address 1: Rm 7, Uc Satellite, Student Publications
Street address 3: Houston
Street address state: TX
Zip/Postal code: 77204-0001
Country: USA
Mailing address: 7 Uc Satellite Student Publications
Mailing city: Houston
Mailing state: TX
Mailing zip: 77204-0001
General Phone: (713) 743-5350
General Fax: (713) 743-5384
Editorail Phone: (713) 743-5360
General/National Adv. E-mail: news@thedailycougar.com
Display Adv. E-mail: ads@thedailycougar.com
Primary Website: www.thedailycougar.com
Classified Equipment»
Personnel: Ronnie Turner (Ed. in Chief); Matthew Keever (Managing Ed.); Hiba Adi (News Ed.); Patricia Estrada (News Ed.); Alan (Opinion Ed.)

UNIV. OF HOUSTON CLEAR LAKE

Street address 1: 2700 Bay Area Blvd
Street address 3: Houston
Street address state: TX
Zip/Postal code: 77058-1002
Country: USA
Mailing address: 2700 Bay Area Blvd
Mailing city: Houston
Mailing state: TX
Mailing zip: 77058-1002
General Phone: (281) 283-2569
General Fax: (281) 283-2569
Advertising Phone: (281) 283-3975
Editorail Phone: (281) 283-2570
General/National Adv. E-mail: thesignal@uhcl.edu
Primary Website: uhclthesignal.com/wordpress; prtl.uhcl.edu/thesignal
Classified Equipment»
Personnel: Taleen Washington (Advisor); Lindsay Humphrey (Adv. Mgr./Prodn. Asst.); Matt Griesmyer (Ed.)

UNIV. OF HOUSTON DOWNTOWN

Street address 1: 1 Main St
Street address 2: S-260
Street address 3: Houston
Street address state: TX
Zip/Postal code: 77002-1014
Country: USA
Mailing address: 1 Main St
Mailing city: Houston
Mailing state: TX
Mailing zip: 77002-1014
General Phone: (713) 221-8569
General Fax: (713) 221-8119
Advertising Phone: (832) 533-7659
Editorail Phone: (832) 495-5381
General/National Adv. E-mail: datelinedowntownhtx@gmail.com
Display Adv. E-mail: editor@dateline-downtown.com
Editorial e-mail: editor@dateline-downtown.com
Primary Website: 2103 Hickory Trail Place
Year Established: 1973
Delivery Methods: Newsstand`Racks
Commercial printers: Y
Advertising (Open Inch Rate) Weekday/Saturday: Ad Space Available
Published: Mon
Published Other: bi-weekly
Classified Equipment»
Note: Multi-Platform Advertising Available (social media, podcast, print)
Personnel: Joe Sample (Associate Prof.)

UNIV. OF ST. THOMAS

Street address 1: 3800 Montrose Blvd
Street address 3: Houston
Street address state: TX
Zip/Postal code: 77006-4626
Country: USA
Mailing address: 3800 Montrose Blvd
Mailing city: Houston
Mailing state: TX
Mailing zip: 77006-4626
General Phone: (713) 525-3579
General Fax: (713) 525-2159
Classified Equipment»
Personnel: Michelle Gautreau (Ed.)

SAM HOUSTON STATE UNIVERSITY

Street address 1: 1804 Ave J
Street address 3: Huntsville
Street address state: TX
Zip/Postal code: 77341-0001
Country: USA
Mailing address: PO Box 2207SHSU
Mailing city: Huntsville
Mailing state: TX
Mailing zip: 77341-0001
General Phone: (936) 294-1341
General Fax: (936) 294-1888
Classified Equipment»
Personnel: Janet A. Bridges (Chair/Prof.); Michael L. Blackman (Philip J. Warner Chair in Journ.); Mickey Herskowitz (Philip J. Warner Chair in Journ.); Tony R. DeMars (Assoc. Prof.); Anthony Friedmann (Assoc. Prof.); Hugh S. Fullerton (Assoc. Prof.); Christopher White (Assoc. Prof.); Rene Qun Chen (Asst. Prof.); Wanda Reyes Velazquez (Asst. Prof.); Ruth M. Pate (Instr.); Richard O. Kosuowei (Lectr.); Mel Strait (Lectr.); Patsy K. Ziegler (Lectr.)

SAM HOUSTON STATE UNIVERSITY

Street address 1: 1804 Ave J, Dan Rather Communications Bldg, Ste 210
Street address 3: Huntsville
Street address state: TX
Zip/Postal code: 77341-0001
Country: USA
Mailing address: PO Box 2178
Mailing city: Huntsville
Mailing state: TX
Mailing zip: 77341-0001
General Phone: (936) 294-1505
General Fax: (936) 294-1888
Advertising Phone: (936) 294-1500
Advertising Fax: (936) 294-1888
Editorail Phone: (936) 294-1505
Editorial Fax: (936) 294-1888
General/National Adv. E-mail: pcm009@shsu.edu
Display Adv. E-mail: advertise@houstonianonline.com
Editorial e-mail: eic@houstonianonline.com
Primary Website: www.houstonianonline.com
Year Established: 1913
Advertising (Open Inch Rate) Weekday/Saturday: see rate card
Published: Wed
Published Other: Orientation Edition, Student Guide
Avg Free Circ: 2500
Classified Equipment»
Personnel: Paty Mason (Business Manager); Dr. Marcus Funk (Faculty Advisor); Carlos Medina (Advertising Manager)

HURST

TARRANT COUNTY COLLEGE

Street address 1: 828 W Harwood Rd
Street address 2: Cab 1124A
Street address 3: Hurst
Street address state: TX
Zip/Postal code: 76054-3219
Country: USA
Mailing address: 828 W Harwood Rd Cab 1124A
Mailing city: Hurst
Mailing state: TX
Mailing zip: 76054-3219
General Phone: (817) 515-6391
General Fax: (817) 515-6767
Editorail Phone: (817) 515-6392
Editorial e-mail: tcceditor@lycos.com
Primary Website: www.tccd.net/collegian
Classified Equipment»
Personnel: Eddye Gallagher (Dir.); Chris Webb (Ed. in Chief)

NORTH LAKE COLLEGE

Street address 1: 5001 N MacArthur Blvd
Street address 2: Rm A-234
Street address 3: Irving
Street address state: TX
Zip/Postal code: 75038-3804
Country: USA
Mailing address: 5001 N MacArthur Blvd Rm A-234
Mailing city: Irving
Mailing state: TX
Mailing zip: 75038-3804
General Phone: (972) 273-3057
General Fax: (972) 273-3441
Advertising Phone: 972-273-3498
General/National Adv. E-mail: nnr7420@dcccd.edu
Primary Website: www.newsregisteronline.com
Published: Mthly
Classified Equipment»
Personnel: Kathleen Stockmier (Advisor); Grant V. Ziegler (Editor-in-Chief); Joanna Mikolajczak (Photography Editor)

UNIV. OF DALLAS

Street address 1: 1845 E Northgate Dr
Street address 2: # 732
Street address 3: Irving
Street address state: TX
Zip/Postal code: 75062-4736
Country: USA
Mailing address: 1845 E Northgate Dr # 732
Mailing city: Irving
Mailing state: TX
Mailing zip: 75062-4736
General Phone: (972) 721-4070
General Fax: (972) 721-4136
Advertising Phone: (972) 721-5142
Editorail Phone: 972-721-5089
General/National Adv. E-mail: udnews1@yahoo.com
Primary Website: www.udallasnews.com
Year Established: 1993
News Services: none
Delivery Methods: Mail`Racks
Classified Equipment»
Personnel: Raymond Wilkerson (Fac. Adviser)

KEENE

SOUTHWESTERN ADVENTIST UNIV.

Street address 1: 100 W Hillcrest St
Street address 3: Keene
Street address state: TX
Zip/Postal code: 76059-1922
Country: USA
Mailing address: 100 W Hillcrest St
Mailing city: Keene
Mailing state: TX
Mailing zip: 76059-1922
General Phone: (817) 645-3921
General Fax: (817) 202-6790
General/National Adv. E-mail: southwesterner@swau.edu
Primary Website: southwesterner.swau.edu
Year Established: 1958
Classified Equipment»
Personnel: Glen Robinson (Ed.); Julena Allen (Associate Editor); Sierra Hernandez

KILGORE

KILGORE COLLEGE

Street address 1: 1100 Broadway Blvd
Street address 3: Kilgore
Street address state: TX
Zip/Postal code: 75662-3204
Country: USA
Mailing address: 1100 Broadway Blvd
Mailing city: Kilgore
Mailing state: TX
Mailing zip: 75662-3299
General Phone: (903) 983-8194
General Fax: (903) 983-8193
General/National Adv. E-mail: kc_flare@yahoo.com
Primary Website: www.theflareonline.com
Classified Equipment»
Personnel: Betty Craddock (Advisor); christian Keit (Ed. in Chief)

KILLEEN

CENTRAL TEXAS COLLEGE

Street address 1: 6200 W Central Texas Expy
Street address 3: Killeen
Street address state: TX
Zip/Postal code: 76549-1272
Country: USA
Mailing address: 6200 W Central Texas Expy
Mailing city: Killeen
Mailing state: TX
Mailing zip: 76549-1272
General Phone: (254) 526-1755
General Fax: (254) 526-1126
Classified Equipment»

KINGSVILLE

TEXAS A&M UNIV. KINGSVILLE

Street address 1: 700 N University Blvd
Street address 3: Kingsville
Street address state: TX
Zip/Postal code: 78363-8202
Country: USA
Mailing address: MSC 123
Mailing state: TX
Mailing zip: 78363
General Phone: (361) 593-2111
General Fax: (361) 593-4046
General/National Adv. E-mail: thesouthtexan@yahoo.com
Primary Website: www.tamek.edu/southtexan
Classified Equipment»
Personnel: Manuel Flores (Advisor); Jaime Gonzalez (Mng. Ed.); Amanda Marcum (Ed. in Chief)

LEVELLAND

SOUTH PLAINS COLLEGE

Street address 1: 1401 College Ave
Street address 3: Levelland
Street address state: TX
Zip/Postal code: 79336-6503
Country: USA
Mailing address: PO Box 46
Mailing city: Levelland
Mailing state: TX
Mailing zip: 79336-0046
General Phone: (806) 894-9611
General Fax: (806) 894-5274
General/National Adv. E-mail: ppress@southplainscollege.edu
Primary Website: http://www.southplainscollege.edu/ppress/News.html
Published Other: Bi-weekly
Classified Equipment»
Personnel: Charles Ehrenfeld (Advisor); Jayme Wheeler

LONGVIEW

LETOURNEAU UNIV.

Street address 1: 2100 S Mobberly Ave
Street address 3: Longview
Street address state: TX
Zip/Postal code: 75602-3564
Country: USA
Mailing address: PO Box 7001
Mailing city: Longview
Mailing state: TX
Mailing zip: 75607-7001
General Phone: (800) 759-8811
General Fax: (903) 236-3129
Classified Equipment»

TEXAS TECH UNIVERSITY

Street address 1: 3003 15th St
Street address 2: Media & Comm. Bldg., Room 180
Street address 3: Lubbock
Street address state: TX
Zip/Postal code: 79409-9816
Country: USA
Mailing address: Box 43081
Mailing city: Lubbock
Mailing state: TX
Mailing zip: 79409-3081
General Phone: (806) 742-3388
General Fax: (806) 742-2434
General/National Adv. E-mail: dailytoreador@ttu.edu
Display Adv. E-mail: dawn.zuerker@ttu.edu
Editorial e-mail: editor@dailytoreador.com
Primary Website: www.dailytoreador.com
Year Established: 1925
Delivery Methods: Mail`Carrier`Racks
Commercial printers: Y
Published: Mon`Thur
Published Other: Summer semesters: once per week
Classified Equipment»
Personnel: Susan Peterson (Student Media Dir.); Dawn Zuerker (Asst. Dir./Adv. Mgr.); Sheri Lewis (Asst. Dir./Editorial/Broadcasting Advisor); Andrea Watson (Asst Dir/Media Advisor); Kristi Deitiker; Amie Ward

LUFKIN

ANGELINA COLLEGE

Street address 1: 3500 S 1st St
Street address 3: Lufkin
Street address state: TX
Zip/Postal code: 75901-7328
Country: USA
Mailing address: PO Box 1768
Mailing city: Lufkin
Mailing state: TX
Mailing zip: 75902-1768
General Phone: (936) 633-5288
General/National Adv. E-mail: lstapleton@angelina.edu
Year Established: 1968
Delivery Methods: Mail`Racks
Commercial printers: N
Published: Bi-Mthly
Avg Free Circ: 1500
Classified Equipment»
Personnel: Libby Stapleton (Advisor)

WILEY COLLEGE

Street address 1: 711 Wiley Ave
Street address 3: Marshall
Street address state: TX
Zip/Postal code: 75670-5151
Country: USA
Mailing address: 711 Wiley Ave
Mailing city: Marshall
Mailing state: TX
Mailing zip: 75670-5151
General Phone: (903) 923-2400
Classified Equipment»

MESQUITE

EASTFIELD COLLEGE

Street address 1: 3737 Motley Dr
Street address 3: Mesquite
Street address state: TX
Zip/Postal code: 75150-2033
Country: USA
Mailing address: 3737 Motley Dr
Mailing city: Mesquite
Mailing state: TX
Mailing zip: 75150-2099
General Phone: (972) 860-7130
General Fax: (972) 860-7040
General/National Adv. E-mail: etc4640@dcccd.edu
Primary Website: www.eastfieldnews.com
Year Established: 1970
Classified Equipment»
Personnel: Sabine Winter (Faculty)

MIDLAND

MIDLAND COLLEGE

Street address 1: 3600 N Garfield St
Street address 3: Midland
Street address state: TX
Zip/Postal code: 79705-6329
Country: USA
Mailing address: 3600 N Garfield St
Mailing city: Midland
Mailing state: TX
Mailing zip: 79705-6397
General Phone: (432) 685-4768
General Fax: (432) 685-4769
General/National Adv. E-mail: studentpublications@midland.edu
Primary Website: www.midland.edu; www.midlandcollegepress.com
Classified Equipment»
Personnel: Karen Lenier (Instructor)

NORTHEAST TEXAS CMTY. COLLEGE

Street address 1: PO Box 1307
Street address 3: Mount Pleasant
Street address state: TX
Zip/Postal code: 75456-9991
Country: USA
Mailing address: PO Box 1307
Mailing city: Mount Pleasant
Mailing state: TX
Mailing zip: 75456-9991
General Phone: (903) 434-8232
General Fax: (903) 572-6712
General/National Adv. E-mail: eagle@ntcc.edu
Primary Website: www.ntcc.edu
Classified Equipment»
Personnel: Mandy Smith (Advisor); Daniel Lockler (Mng. Ed.)

NACOGDOCHES

STEPHEN F. AUSTIN UNIV.

Street address 1: 1936 North St, Baker Center Rm 2.308
Street address 3: Nacogdoches
Street address state: TX
Zip/Postal code: 75962-0001
Country: USA
Mailing address: PO Box 13049, Sfa Station
Mailing city: Nacogdoches
Mailing state: TX
Mailing zip: 75962-0001
General Phone: (936) 468-4703
General Fax: (936) 468-1016
General/National Adv. E-mail: pinelog@sfasu.edu
Primary Website: www.thepinelog.com
Year Established: 1924
Classified Equipment»
Personnel: Pat Spence (Dir.); Mark Rhoudes (Editor in Cheif)

ODESSA

UNIV. OF TEXAS PERMIAN BASIN

Street address 1: 4901 E University Blvd
Street address 2: Rm MB
Street address 3: Odessa
Street address state: TX
Zip/Postal code: 79762-8122
Country: USA
Mailing address: 4901 E University Blvd Rm MB2215A

Mailing city: Odessa
Mailing state: TX
Mailing zip: 79762-8122
General Phone: (432) 552-2659
General Fax: (432) 552-3654
General/National Adv. E-mail: mesajournal@utpb.edu
Primary Website: mesajournalnews.com
Year Established: 1975
Published: Mon`Tues`Wed`Thur`Sat
Avg Free Circ: 6000
Classified Equipment»
Personnel: myra Salcedo (Advisor)

PARIS

PARIS JUNIOR COLLEGE

Street address 1: 2400 Clarksville St
Street address 3: Paris
Street address state: TX
Zip/Postal code: 75460-6258
Country: USA
Mailing address: 2400 Clarksville St
Mailing city: Paris
Mailing state: TX
Mailing zip: 75460-6298
General Phone: (903) 785-7661
General Fax: (903) 782-0370
Primary Website: www.parisjc.edu
Classified Equipment»
Personnel: Sharon Dennehy (Advisor)

SAN JACINTO COLLEGE

Street address 1: 8060 Spencer Hwy
Street address 3: Pasadena
Street address state: TX
Zip/Postal code: 77505-5903
Country: USA
Mailing address: 8060 Spencer Hwy
Mailing city: Pasadena
Mailing state: TX
Mailing zip: 77505-5998
General Phone: (281) 478-2752
General Fax: (281) 478-2703
General/National Adv. E-mail: rsaldivar88@yahoo.com
Primary Website: www.sanjacintotimes.com
Classified Equipment»
Personnel: Fred F. Faour (Advisor)

PLAINVIEW

TRAILBLAZER

Street address 1: 1900 W 7th St
Street address 2: # 1271
Street address 3: Plainview
Street address state: TX
Zip/Postal code: 79072-6900
County: Hale
Country: USA
Mailing address: 1900 W 7th St # 1271
Mailing city: Plainview
Mailing state: TX
Mailing zip: 79072-6900
General Phone: (806) 291-1088
General/National Adv. E-mail: trailblazer@wbu.edu
Primary Website: www.wbu.edu/trailblazer
Mthly Avg Views: 550
Year Established: 1950
Area Served - City: Plainview, TX Wichita Falls, TX San Antonio, TX Lubbock, TX Amarillo, TX Albuquerque, NM Honolulu, HI Anchorage. AK Fairbanks, AK Sierra Vista, AZ Phoenix, AZ
Commercial printers: N
Published: Sun
Published Other: Weekly
Weekday Frequency: All day
Avg Free Circ: 4000
Audit By: Sworn/Estimate/Non-Audited
Classified Equipment»
Personnel: Steven Long (Advisor)
Parent company (for newspapers): Wayland Baptist University

PRAIRIE VIEW

PRAIRIE VIEW A&M UNIV.

Street address 1: PO Box 519
Street address 3: Prairie View
Street address state: TX
Zip/Postal code: 77446-0519
Country: USA
Mailing address: PO Box 519
Mailing city: Prairie View
Mailing state: TX
Mailing zip: 77446-0519
General Phone: (936) 261-1353
General Fax: (936) 261-1365
General/National Adv. E-mail: panther@pvamu.edu
Primary Website: www.pvpanther.com
Classified Equipment»
Personnel: Lewis Smith (Advisor); Whitney Harris (Ed. in chief)

RICHARDSON

UNIV. OF TEXAS DALLAS

Street address 1: PO Box 830688
Street address 3: Richardson
Street address state: TX
Zip/Postal code: 75083-0688
Country: USA
Mailing address: PO Box 830688
Mailing city: Richardson
Mailing state: TX
Mailing zip: 75083-0688
General Phone: (972) 883-2286
General Fax: (972) 883-2772
Editorail Phone: (972) 883-2210
General/National Adv. E-mail: mercury@utdallas.edu
Display Adv. E-mail: ads@mercury.utdallas.edu
Primary Website: www.utdmercury.com
Year Established: 1980
Classified Equipment»
Personnel: James Wooley (Adv. Mgr.); Lauren Buell (Ed.)

SAN ANGELO

ANGELO STATE UNIV.

Street address 1: 2601 W Avenue N
Street address 3: San Angelo
Street address state: TX
Zip/Postal code: 76909-2601
Country: USA
Mailing address: PO Box 10895
Mailing city: San Angelo
Mailing state: TX
Mailing zip: 76909-0001
General Phone: (325) 942-2040
General/National Adv. E-mail: rampage@angelo.edu
Primary Website: www.asurampage.com
Classified Equipment»
Personnel: Leah Cooper (Ed. in Chief)

THE RAM PAGE - ANGELO STATE UNIVERSITY

Street address 1: 2601 W Avenue N
Street address 3: San Angelo
Street address state: TX
Zip/Postal code: 76909-2601
County: Tom Green
Country: USA
Mailing address: PO Box 10895
Mailing city: San Angelo
Mailing state: TX
Mailing zip: 76909-0001
General Phone: (325) 942-2323
General/National Adv. E-mail: rampage@angelo.edu
Primary Website: www.asurampage.com
Mthly Avg Views: 2000
Mthly Avg Unique Visitors: 800
Year Established: 1936
Published: Other
Published Other: Online
Classified Equipment»

Personnel: Jack C. Eli (Prof./Head); Eliada Gamreklidze (Adviser)

OUR LADY OF THE LAKE UNIV.

Street address 1: 411 SW 24th St
Street address 2: Ste 105
Street address 3: San Antonio
Street address state: TX
Zip/Postal code: 78207-4617
Country: USA
Mailing address: 411 SW 24th St Ste 105
Mailing city: San Antonio
Mailing state: TX
Mailing zip: 78207-4617
General Phone: (210) 434-6711
General Fax: (210) 436-0824
General/National Adv. E-mail: lakefront@lake.ollusa.edu; lakefrontads@lake.ollusa.edu
Primary Website: lakefront.ollusa.edu
Classified Equipment»
Personnel: Kay O'Donnell (Advisor); Tessa Benavides (Ed.)

PALO ALTO COLLEGE

Street address 1: 1400 W Villaret Blvd
Street address 3: San Antonio
Street address state: TX
Zip/Postal code: 78224-2417
Country: USA
Mailing address: 1400 W Villaret Blvd
Mailing city: San Antonio
Mailing state: TX
Mailing zip: 78224-2499
General Phone: (210) 486-3880
General Fax: (210) 486-9271
Editorail Phone: 210-486-3237
General/National Adv. E-mail: pac-info@alamo.edu
Primary Website: alamo.edu/pac
Year Established: 1983
Special Editions: Student newsletter published 2x per semester.
Published: Bi-Mthly
Classified Equipment»

SAN ANTONIO COLLEGE

Street address 1: 1300 San Pedro Ave
Street address 3: San Antonio
Street address state: TX
Zip/Postal code: 78212-4201
Country: USA
Mailing address: 1300 San Pedro Ave
Mailing city: San Antonio
Mailing state: TX
Mailing zip: 78212-4299
General Phone: (210) 486-1765
General Fax: (210) 486-9239
Advertising Phone: (210) 486-1786
Advertising Fax: (210) 486-9239
Editorail Phone: (210) 486-1773
Editorial Fax: (210) 486-9292
General/National Adv. E-mail: sac-ranger@alamo.edu
Primary Website: www.theranger.org
Year Established: 1926
Special Editions: Winter edition produced in November for distribution at beginning of Spring Semester Summer edition produced in May for distribution during Summer and before Fall Semester
Delivery Methods: Racks
Commercial printers: Y
Classified Equipment»
Personnel: Marianne Odom (Advisor)

ST. MARY'S UNIV. OF SAN ANTONIO

Street address 1: 1 Camino Santa Maria St
Street address 2: University Center Room 258
Street address 3: San Antonio
Street address state: TX
Zip/Postal code: 78228-5433
Country: USA
Mailing address: 1 Camino Santa Maria
Mailing city: San Antonio
Mailing state: TX
Mailing zip: 78228
General Phone: (210) 436-3401
General Fax: (210) 431-4307
General/National Adv. E-mail: rattlernews@stmarytx.edu
Primary Website: http://www.stmurattlernews.com/home/
Classified Equipment»
Personnel: Patrica R. Garcia (Advisor); Leo Reyes (Adv. Mgr.); Sarah Mills (Ed.)

TRINITY UNIV.

Street address 1: 1 Trinity Pl
Street address 3: San Antonio
Street address state: TX
Zip/Postal code: 78212-4674
Country: USA
Mailing address: 1 Trinity Pl
Mailing city: San Antonio
Mailing state: TX
Mailing zip: 78212-7201
General Phone: (210) 999-8555
General Fax: (210) 999-7034
General/National Adv. E-mail: trinitonian-adv@trinity.edu
Primary Website: www.trinitonian.com
Classified Equipment»
Personnel: Kathryn Martin (Advisor); Jordan Krueger (Ed.)

UNIV. OF TEXAS

Street address 1: 14545 Roadrunner Way
Street address 3: San Antonio
Street address state: TX
Zip/Postal code: 78249-1515
Country: USA
Mailing address: 14545 Roadrunner Way
Mailing city: San Antonio
Mailing state: TX
Mailing zip: 78249-1515
General Phone: (210) 690-9301
General Fax: (210) 690-3423
General/National Adv. E-mail: paisanoeditor@sbcglobal.net
Primary Website: www.Paisano-online.com
Classified Equipment»
Personnel: Rachel Hill (Ed.)

UNIVERSITY OF THE INCARNATE WORD

Street address 1: 4301 Broadway, Cpo 494
Street address 3: San Antonio
Street address state: TX
Zip/Postal code: 78209
Country: USA
Mailing address: 4301 Broadway, CPO 494
Mailing city: San Antonio
Mailing state: TX
Mailing zip: 78209-6318
General Phone: (210) 829-3964
General Fax: (210) 283-5005
Advertising Phone: (210) 829-6069
Advertising Fax: (210) 283-5005
Editorail Phone: (210) 829-6069
Editorial Fax: (210) 283-5005
General/National Adv. E-mail: mercer@uiwtx.edu
Display Adv. E-mail: mercer@uiwtx.edu
Editorial e-mail: mercer@uiwtx.edu
Primary Website: www.uiw.edu/logos
Year Established: 1935
Published: Mthly
Classified Equipment»
Note: Interactive website is http://www.uiwlogos.org
Personnel: Michael L. Mercer (Advisor)

TEXAS STATE UNIV.

Street address 1: 601 University Dr Bldg Trinity
Street address 2: 203 Pleasant Street
Street address 3: San Marcos
Street address state: TX
Zip/Postal code: 78666-4684
Country: USA
Mailing address: 601 University Dr Bldg Trinity
Mailing city: San Marcos
Mailing state: TX
Mailing zip: 78666-4684
General Phone: (512) 245-3487
General Fax: (512) 245-3708
Advertising Phone: (512 245-2261
Advertising Fax: (512) 245-3708
General/National Adv. E-mail: stareditor@txstate.edu
Display Adv. E-mail: starad1@txstate.edu
Editorial e-mail: stareditor@txstate.edu

Primary Website: www.universitystar.com
Year Established: 1911
News Services: Tribune
Delivery Methods: Newsstand`Racks
Commercial printers: Y
Advertising (Open Inch Rate) Weekday/Saturday: Check Rate Sheet Online
Published: Mon`Wed`Thur
Classified Equipment»
Personnel: Bob Bajackson (Advisor)

SEGUIN

TEXAS LUTHERAN UNIV.

Street address 1: 1000 W Court St
Street address 3: Seguin
Street address state: TX
Zip/Postal code: 78155-5978
Country: USA
Mailing address: 1000 W Court St
Mailing city: Seguin
Mailing state: TX
Mailing zip: 78155-9996
General Phone: (830) 372-8073
General Fax: (830) 372-8074
General/National Adv. E-mail: lonestarlutheran@tlu.edu
Primary Website: www.lslonline.net
Classified Equipment»
Personnel: Robin Bisha (Advisor); Steven S. Vrooman (Chair); Kristi Quiros (Pub.); Emmalee Drummond (Ed. in Chief); Naomi Urquiza (Mng. Ed.)

SHERMAN

AUSTIN COLLEGE

Street address 1: 900 N Grand Ave
Street address 2: Ste 6J
Street address 3: Sherman
Street address state: TX
Zip/Postal code: 75090-4440
Country: USA
Mailing address: 900 N Grand Ave Ste 6J
Mailing city: Sherman
Mailing state: TX
Mailing zip: 75090-4400
General Phone: (903) 813-2296
General Fax: (903) 813-2339
General/National Adv. E-mail: observer@austincollege.edu
Classified Equipment»
Personnel: Felecia Garvin (Advisor); Lauren Chiodo (Ed. in Chief)

STEPHENVILLE

TARLETON STATE UNIVERSITY

Street address 1: 201 St Felix
Street address 3: Stephenville
Street address state: TX
Zip/Postal code: 76401
Country: USA
Mailing address: Box T-0440
Mailing city: Stephenville
Mailing state: TX
Mailing zip: 76402
General Phone: (254) 968-9056
General Fax: (254) 968-9709
Advertising Phone: (254) 968-9057
Advertising Fax: (254) 968-9709
Editorail Phone: (254) 968-9058
Editorial Fax: (254) 968-9709
General/National Adv. E-mail: jtac@tarleton.edu
Display Adv. E-mail: jtac_ads@tarleton.edu
Editorial e-mail: jtac@tarleton.edu
Primary Website: www.jtacnews.com
Year Established: 1919
Published: Wed
Avg Free Circ: 1000
Classified Equipment»
Personnel: Caleb Chapman (Dir.)

TEXARKANA

TEXARKANA COLLEGE

Street address 1: 2500 N Robison Rd
Street address 3: Texarkana
Street address state: TX
Zip/Postal code: 75599-0002
Country: USA
Mailing address: 2500 N Robison Rd
Mailing city: Texarkana
Mailing state: TX
Mailing zip: 75599-0001
General Phone: (903) 838-4541
General Fax: (903) 832-5030
Editorail Phone: (903) 838-4541
Primary Website: www.tc.cc.tx.us; www.texarkanacollege.edu
Classified Equipment»
Personnel: Jean Cotten (Advisor); Caitlin Williams (Ed.)

TYLER JUNIOR COLLEGE

Street address 1: 1400 E Devine St
Street address 2: # 204
Street address 3: Tyler
Street address state: TX
Zip/Postal code: 75701-2207
Country: USA
Mailing address: 1400 E Devine St # 204
Mailing city: Tyler
Mailing state: TX
Mailing zip: 75701-2207
General Phone: (903) 510-2335
General Fax: (903) 510-3246
Primary Website: www.tjcnewspaper.com
Classified Equipment»
Personnel: Laura Krantz (Advisor)

UNIV. OF TEXAS AT TYLER

Street address 1: 3900 University Blvd
Street address 3: Tyler
Street address state: TX
Zip/Postal code: 75799-6600
Country: USA
Mailing address: 3900 University Blvd
Mailing city: Tyler
Mailing state: TX
Mailing zip: 75799-0001
General Phone: (903) 565-7131
Advertising Phone: (903) 566-5536
Editorail Phone: (903) 566-7131
Display Adv. E-mail: ads@patriottalon.com
Editorial e-mail: editor@patriottalon.com
Primary Website: www.patriottalon.com
Year Established: 1976
Published: Bi-Mthly
Avg Free Circ: 2000
Classified Equipment»
Personnel: Lorri Allen (Adviser); Nathan Wright (Editor in Chief)

UVALDE

SOUTHWEST TEXAS JUNIOR COLLEGE

Street address 1: 2401 Garner Field Rd
Street address 3: Uvalde
Street address state: TX
Zip/Postal code: 78801-6221
Country: USA
Mailing address: 2401 Garner Field Rd
Mailing city: Uvalde
Mailing state: TX
Mailing zip: 78801-6221
General Phone: (830) 591-7350
General Fax: (830) 591-4185
Primary Website: www.swtjc.net
Classified Equipment»
Personnel: Terrie Wilson (Advisor/Journalism Instructor)

WACO

BAYLOR UNIVERSITY

Street address 1: 1 Bear Pl
Street address 2: Unit 97330
Street address 3: Waco
Street address state: TX
Zip/Postal code: 76798-7330
Country: USA
Mailing address: 1 Bear Pl Unit 97330
Mailing city: Waco
Mailing state: TX
Mailing zip: 76798-7330
General Phone: (254) 710-3407
General Fax: (254) 710-1714
Advertising Phone: (254) 710-3407
Advertising Fax: (254) 710-1714
Editorial Fax: (254) 710-1714
General/National Adv. E-mail: lariat@baylor.edu
Display Adv. E-mail: Lariat_Ads@baylor.edu
Editorial e-mail: Lariat-Letters@baylor.edu
Primary Website: www.baylorlariat.com
Year Established: 1900
Commercial printers: N
Advertising (Open Inch Rate) Weekday/Saturday: (254) 710-3407
Published: Tues`Wed`Thur`Fri
Avg Free Circ: 4000
Classified Equipment»
Personnel: Paul Carr (Dir., Mktg. Information); Jamile Yglecias (Advertising Sales and Marketing Manager); Julie Freeman (Asst. Media Adviser)
Parent company (for newspapers): Baylor University

MCLENNAN CMTY. COLLEGE

Street address 1: 1400 College Dr
Street address 3: Waco
Street address state: TX
Zip/Postal code: 76708-1402
Country: USA
Mailing address: 1400 College Dr
Mailing city: Waco
Mailing state: TX
Mailing zip: 76708-1499
General Phone: (254) 299-8524
General Fax: (254) 299-8568
Classified Equipment»

WICHITA FALLS

MIDWESTERN STATE UNIVERSITY

Street address 1: 3410 Taft Blvd
Street address 3: Wichita Falls
Street address state: TX
Zip/Postal code: 76308-2036
Country: USA
Mailing address: 3410 Taft Blvd
Mailing city: Wichita Falls
Mailing state: TX
Mailing zip: 76307-0014
General Phone: (940) 397-4704
Advertising Phone: (940) 397-4704
Editorail Phone: (940) 397-4704
General/National Adv. E-mail: wichitan@msutexas.edu
Display Adv. E-mail: wichitan@msutexas.edu
Editorial e-mail: wichitan@msutexas.edu
Primary Website: http://thewichitan.com/
Year Established: 1935
Published: Wed
Avg Free Circ: 1000
Classified Equipment»
Personnel: Bradley Wilson (Adviser)

UTAH

CEDAR CITY

SOUTHERN UTAH UNIV.

Street address 1: 351 W University Blvd
Street address 2: University Journal
Street address 3: Cedar City
Street address state: UT
Zip/Postal code: 84720-2415
Country: USA
Mailing address: 351 W University Blvd
Mailing city: Cedar City
Mailing state: UT
Mailing zip: 84720-2415
General Phone: (435) 865-8226
Advertising Phone: 435-704-4733
Editorail Phone: 435-865-8226
General/National Adv. E-mail: journal@suu.edu
Display Adv. E-mail: Gholdston@suuews.com
Editorial e-mail: journal@suu.edu
Primary Website: www.suunews.com
Year Established: 1937
News Services: TMS
Special Editions: Graduation Edition
Delivery Methods: Newsstand`Racks
Commercial printers: Y
Advertising (Open Inch Rate) Weekday/Saturday: $4 Open; $3 Contract
Published: Mon`Thur
Avg Free Circ: 2000
Classified Equipment»
Personnel: John Gholdston (Advisor)
Parent company (for newspapers): Southern Utah University

EPHRAIM

SNOW COLLEGE

Street address 1: 150 College Ave
Street address 3: Ephraim
Street address state: UT
Zip/Postal code: 84627-1550
Country: USA
Mailing address: 150 College Ave
Mailing city: Ephraim
Mailing state: UT
Mailing zip: 84627-1299
General Phone: (435) 283-7385
General/National Adv. E-mail: snowdrift@snow.edu
Primary Website: www.snow.edu/snowdrift
Classified Equipment»
Personnel: Greg Dart (Advisor); Justin Albee (Bus. Mgr.); Kelly Peterson (Ed. in Chief)

LOGAN

UTAH STATE UNIV.

Street address 1: Taggart Ctr 105
Street address 3: Logan
Street address state: UT
Zip/Postal code: 84322-0001
Country: USA
Mailing address: PO Box 1249
Mailing city: Logan
Mailing state: UT
Mailing zip: 84322-0001
General Phone: (435) 797-6397
General Fax: (435) 797-1760
General/National Adv. E-mail: statesmanoffice@aggiemail.com
Primary Website: www.utahstatesman.com
Year Established: 1902
Classified Equipment»
Personnel: Jay Wamsley (Advisor)

WEBER STATE UNIVERSITY

Street address 1: 3910 W Campus Dr
Street address 2: Dept 2110
Street address 3: Ogden
Street address state: UT
Zip/Postal code: 84408-2110
Country: USA
Mailing address: 3910 West Campus Drive Dept 2110
Mailing city: Ogden
Mailing state: UT
Mailing zip: 84408-2110
General Phone: (801) 626-7526
General Fax: (801) 626-7401
Advertising Phone: (801) 626-6359
Advertising Fax: (801) 626-7401
Editorail Phone: (801) 626-7121
Editorial Fax: (801) 626-7401
General/National Adv. E-mail: thesignpost@weber.edu
Display Adv. E-mail: Kcsanders@weber.edu
Editorial e-mail: Kcsanders@weber.edu
Primary Website: MyWeberMedia.com
Year Established: 1937
Advertising (Open Inch Rate) Weekday/Saturday: http://signpost.mywebermedia.com/advertising-information/

Published: Mon`Thur
Published Other: 8 issues (once a week) during the summer semester
Avg Free Circ: 2000
Classified Equipment»
Note: signpost.mywebermedia.com MyWeberMedia app on iTunes and Android
Personnel: KC Sanders (Advt Mgr); Georgia Edwards (Office Mgr); Jean Norman (Signpost Adviser)
Parent company (for newspapers): Weber State University

OREM

UTAH VALLEY UNIVERSITY

Street address 1: 800 W University Pkwy
Street address 3: Orem
Street address state: UT
Zip/Postal code: 84058-6703
Country: USA
Mailing address: 800 W University Pkwy # Mt
Mailing city: Orem
Mailing state: UT
Mailing zip: 84058-6703
General Phone: (801) 863-8688
General Fax: (801) 863-8601
Display Adv. E-mail: robbina@uvu.edu
Primary Website: www.uvureview.com
Delivery Methods: Newsstand
Advertising (Open Inch Rate) Weekday/Saturday: www.uvureview.com
Published: Mon
Classified Equipment»
Personnel: Robbin Anthony (Bus. Mgr.); Brent Sumner (Advisor)

PRICE

UTAH STATE UNIVERSITY EASTERN

Street address 1: 451 N 400 E St
Street address 3: Price
Street address state: UT
Zip/Postal code: 84501
County: Carbon
Country: USA
Mailing address: 451 N. 400 E. St.
Mailing city: Price
Mailing state: UT
Mailing zip: 84501-3315
General Phone: (435) 613-5123
Advertising Phone: (435) 613-5213
General/National Adv. E-mail: Susan.polster@usu.edu
Primary Website: Usueagle.com
Mthly Avg Views: 900
Mthly Avg Unique Visitors: 600
Year Established: 1937
Advertising (Open Inch Rate) Weekday/Saturday: $6.00 column inch
Published: Thur`Other
Avg Free Circ: 1000
Classified Equipment»
Personnel: Susan Polster (Adviser)

PROVO

BRIGHAM YOUNG UNIVERSITY

Street address 1: 152 Brmb
Street address 3: Provo
Street address state: UT
Zip/Postal code: 84602-3701
Country: USA
Mailing address: 152 BRMB
Mailing city: Provo
Mailing state: UT
Mailing zip: 84602-3701
General Phone: (801) 422-2957
General/National Adv. E-mail: dureceptionist@gmail.com
Display Adv. E-mail: ellen_hernandez@byu.edu
Editorial e-mail: universe.ideas@gmail.com
Primary Website: universe.byu.edu
Published: Tues
Classified Equipment»
Personnel: Steve Fidel (Director)

SAINT GEORGE

DIXIE STATE COLLEGE

Street address 1: 225 S 700 E
Street address 3: Saint George
Street address state: UT
Zip/Postal code: 84770-3875
Country: USA
Mailing address: 225 S. 700 E. JEN
Mailing city: Saint George
Mailing state: UT
Mailing zip: 84770
General Phone: (435) 652-7818
General Fax: (435) 656-4019
Advertising Phone: (435) 652-7818
Advertising Fax: (435) 656-4019
General/National Adv. E-mail: dixiesun@dixie.edu
Display Adv. E-mail: dixiesunads@dixie.edu
Editorial e-mail: dixiesun@dixie.edu
Primary Website: www.dixiesunlink.com
News Services: MCT
Delivery Methods: Newsstand`Racks
Commercial printers: Y
Classified Equipment»
Personnel: Rhiannon Bent (Advisor); Taylor Forbes (Adv. Mgr.); Rachel Tanner (Ed. in Chief)

UNIV. OF UTAH

Street address 1: 200 Central Campus Dr
Street address 2: Rm 234
Street address 3: Salt Lake City
Street address state: UT
Zip/Postal code: 84112-9110
Country: USA
Mailing address: 200 Central Campus Dr Rm 234
Mailing city: Salt Lake City
Mailing state: UT
Mailing zip: 84112-9110
General Phone: (801) 581-2788
General Fax: (801) 581-6882
Editorial e-mail: news@chronicle.utah.edu; press@chronicle.utah.edu
Primary Website: www.dailyutahchronicle.com
Classified Equipment»
Personnel: Rachel Hanson (Chief Ed.); Michael Mcfall (Ed.)

WESTMINSTER COLLEGE

Street address 1: 1840 S 1300 E
Street address 3: Salt Lake City
Street address state: UT
Zip/Postal code: 84105-3617
Country: USA
Mailing address: 1840 S 1300 E
Mailing city: Salt Lake City
Mailing state: UT
Mailing zip: 84105-3697
General Phone: (801) 832-2320
General Fax: (801) 466-6916
General/National Adv. E-mail: forum@wesminstercollege.edu
Editorial e-mail: forumeditor@westminstercollege.edu
Primary Website: www.forumfortnightly.com
Classified Equipment»
Personnel: Ann Green (Bus. Mgr.); Fred Fogo (Advisor); Kimberly Zarkin (Advisor)

VIRGINIA

MARYMOUNT UNIV.

Street address 1: 2807 N Glebe Rd
Street address 3: Arlington
Street address state: VA
Zip/Postal code: 22207-4224
Country: USA
Mailing address: 2807 N Glebe Rd
Mailing city: Arlington
Mailing state: VA
Mailing zip: 22207-4299
General Phone: (703) 522-5600
General Fax: (703) 284-3817
General/National Adv. E-mail: banner@marymount.edu
Primary Website: www.marymount.edu
Classified Equipment»
Personnel: Paul Byers (Mass Commun. Coord.); Vincent Stovall (Dir., Student Activities); Ralph Frasca (Mass Commun. Coord.)

RANDOLPH-MACON COLLEGE

Street address 1: 204 Henry St
Street address 3: Ashland
Street address state: VA
Zip/Postal code: 23005-1634
Country: USA
Mailing address: PO Box 5005
Mailing city: Ashland
Mailing state: VA
Mailing zip: 23005-5505
General Phone: (804) 752-7200
General Fax: (804) 752-3748
General/National Adv. E-mail: yellowjacket@rmc.edu
Primary Website: www.rmc.edu
Classified Equipment»
Personnel: Robert Thomas (Bus. Mgr.); Derek Gayle (News Ed.); Lara O'Brien (Sports Ed.)

BLACKSBURG

VIRGINIA POLYTECHNIC INSTITUTE

Street address 1: 365 Squires Student Ctr
Street address 3: Blacksburg
Street address state: VA
Zip/Postal code: 24061-1000
Country: USA
Mailing address: 365 Squires Student Ctr
Mailing city: Blacksburg
Mailing state: VA
Mailing zip: 24061-1000
General Phone: (540) 231-9870
General Fax: (540) 231-9151
Advertising Phone: (540) 961-9860
Display Adv. E-mail: advertising@collegemedia.com
Editorial e-mail: campuseditor@collegiatetimes.com; editor@collegiatetimes.com
Primary Website: www.collegiatetimes.com
Year Established: 1903
Published: Tues`Fri
Classified Equipment»
Personnel: Kiley Thompson (General Manager)
Parent company (for newspapers): Educational Media Company at Virginia Tech

BLUEFIELD

BLUEFIELD COLLEGE

Street address 1: 3000 College Dr
Street address 3: Bluefield
Street address state: VA
Zip/Postal code: 24605-1737
Country: USA
Mailing address: 3000 College Dr
Mailing city: Bluefield
Mailing state: VA
Mailing zip: 24605-1799
General Phone: (276) 326-3682
General Fax: (276) 326-4288
Primary Website: www.bluefield.edu
Classified Equipment»
Personnel: Mimi Merritt (Advisor)

BRIDGEWATER COLLEGE

Street address 1: 101 N 3rd St
Street address 3: Bridgewater
Street address state: VA
Zip/Postal code: 22812-1714
Country: USA
Mailing address: PO Box 193
Mailing city: Bridgewater
Mailing state: VA
Mailing zip: 22812-0193
General Phone: (540) 828-5329
General Fax: (540) 828-5479
Advertising Phone: (540) 828-5329
Editorail Phone: (540) 828-5329
General/National Adv. E-mail: veritas@bridgewater.edu
Display Adv. E-mail: veritas@bridgewater.edu
Editorial e-mail: veritas@bridgewater.edu
Primary Website: http://veritas.bridgewater.edu/
Special Editions: yes
Delivery Methods: Carrier`Racks
Commercial printers: N
Advertising (Open Inch Rate) Weekday/Saturday: contact
Published: Wed
Avg Free Circ: 1700
Classified Equipment»
Personnel: Bernardo Motta (Assistant Professor of Communication Studies)

CHARLOTTESVILLE

COLGATE DARDEN GRAD. SCHOOL OF BUS.

Street address 1: 100 Darden Blvd
Street address 3: Charlottesville
Street address state: VA
Zip/Postal code: 22903-1760
Country: USA
Mailing address: 100 Darden Blvd
Mailing city: Charlottesville
Mailing state: VA
Mailing zip: 22903-1760
General Phone: (434) 982-2395
General/National Adv. E-mail: ccchronicle@darden.virginia.edu
Primary Website: coldcallchronicle.com
Classified Equipment»
Personnel: Sarah Yoder (Pub.); Laura Dart (Adv. Mgr.); Tyler Lifton (Ed.)

UNIV. OF VIRGINIA

Street address 1: PO Box 400703
Street address 3: Charlottesville
Street address state: VA
Zip/Postal code: 22904-4703
Country: USA
Mailing address: PO Box 400703
Mailing city: Charlottesville
Mailing state: VA
Mailing zip: 22904-4703
General Fax: (434) 924-7290
General/National Adv. E-mail: editor@cavalierdaily.com
Primary Website: www.cavalierdaily.com
Year Established: 1890
Published: Mon`Thur
Avg Free Circ: 10000
Classified Equipment»
Personnel: Karoline Komolafe (Editor-in-chief)

UNIV. OF VIRGINIA SCHOOL OF LAW

Street address 1: 580 Massie Rd
Street address 3: Charlottesville
Street address state: VA
Zip/Postal code: 22903-1738
Country: USA
Mailing address: 580 Massie Rd
Mailing city: Charlottesville
Mailing state: VA
Mailing zip: 22903-1789
General Phone: (434) 924-3070
General Fax: (434) 924-7536
General/National Adv. E-mail: editor@lawweekly.org
Primary Website: www.lawweekly.org
Year Established: 1948
Published: Wed
Classified Equipment»
Personnel: Jenna Goldman (Editor-in-Chief)

EMORY

EMORY & HENRY COLLEGE

Street address 1: PO Box 947
Street address 3: Emory
Street address state: VA
Zip/Postal code: 24327-0947
Country: USA
Mailing address: PO Box 947
Mailing city: Emory
Mailing state: VA
Mailing zip: 24327-0947
General Phone: (276) 944-6870
Advertising Phone: (276) 944-6934

General/National Adv. E-mail: ehcwhitetopper@ehc.edu
Classified Equipment»
Personnel: Kathy Borterfield (Advisor)

FAIRFAX

GEORGE MASON UNIVERSITY

Street address 1: 4400 University Dr
Street address 2: MS 2C5
Street address 3: Fairfax
Street address state: VA
Zip/Postal code: 22030-4422
Country: USA
Mailing address: 4400 University Dr MS 2C5
Mailing city: Fairfax
Mailing state: VA
Mailing zip: 22030-4444
General Phone: (703) 993-2947
General Fax: (703) 993-2948
Advertising Phone: (703) 993-2942
Editorail Phone: (703) 993-2944
General/National Adv. E-mail: cwilso12@gmu.edu
Primary Website: gmufourthestate.com
Published: Mon
Avg Free Circ: 6000
Classified Equipment»
Personnel: Kathryn Mangus (Advisor)

FARMVILLE

LONGWOOD COLLEGE

Street address 1: PO Box 2901
Street address 3: Farmville
Street address state: VA
Zip/Postal code: 23909-0001
Country: USA
Mailing address: PO Box 2901
Mailing city: Farmville
Mailing state: VA
Mailing zip: 23909-0001
General Phone: (434) 395-2120
General Fax: (434) 395-2237
General/National Adv. E-mail: rotunda@longwood.edu
Classified Equipment»
Personnel: Ramesh Rao (Advisor); Emily Grove (Ed. in Chief); Benjamin Byrnes (Mng. Ed.)

FERRUM

FERRUM COLLEGE

Street address 1: PO Box 1000
Street address 3: Ferrum
Street address state: VA
Zip/Postal code: 24088-9001
Country: USA
Mailing address: PO Box 1000
Mailing city: Ferrum
Mailing state: VA
Mailing zip: 24088-9001
General Phone: (540) 365-4334
General Fax: (540) 365-4203
Primary Website: www.ferrum.edu/ironblade
Classified Equipment»
Personnel: Dr. Lana Whited (Advisor)

FREDERICKSBURG

UNIVERSITY OF MARY WASHINGTON

Street address 1: 1301 College Ave
Street address 3: Fredericksburg
Street address state: VA
Zip/Postal code: 22401-5300
Country: USA
Mailing address: 1301 College Ave
Mailing city: Fredericksburg
Mailing state: VA
Mailing zip: 22401-5300
General Phone: (540) 654-1536
Display Adv. E-mail: blueandgray.eic@gmail.com
Primary Website: blueandgraypress.com

Delivery Methods: Carrier
Commercial printers: Y
Classified Equipment»
Personnel: Michael McCarthy (Advisor)

HAMPDEN SYDNEY

HAMPDEN-SYDNEY COLLEGE

Street address 1: 1 College Rd
Street address 3: Hampden Sydney
Street address state: VA
Zip/Postal code: 23943
Country: USA
Mailing address: PO Box 127
Mailing city: Hampden Sydney
Mailing state: VA
Mailing zip: 23943-0127
General Phone: (434) 223-6000
General Fax: (434) 223-6345
General/National Adv. E-mail: newspaper@hsc.edu
Year Established: 1920
Published: Bi-Mthly
Classified Equipment»
Personnel: Max Dash (Editor-in-Chief)

HARRISONBURG

JAMES MADISON UNIVERSITY

Street address 1: 1598 S Main St
Street address 3: Harrisonburg
Street address state: VA
Zip/Postal code: 22807-1025
Country: USA
Mailing address: 1598 South Main Street
Mailing city: Harrisonburg
Mailing state: VA
Mailing zip: 22807
General Phone: (540) 568-6127
General Fax: (540) 568-6736
Advertising Phone: (540) 568-6127
Editorail Phone: (540) 568-6127
General/National Adv. E-mail: breezeeditor@gmail.com
Display Adv. E-mail: thebreezeads@gmail.com
Editorial e-mail: breezeeditor@gmail.com
Primary Website: www.breezejmu.org
Year Established: 1922
Syndicated Publications: Port & Main
Delivery Methods: Racks
Commercial printers: N
Published: Thur
Avg Paid Circ: 0
Avg Free Circ: 5000
Classified Equipment»
Personnel: Brad Jenkins (General Manager); Blake Shepherd (Advertising and Marketing Coordinator)

VIRGINIA MILITARY INSTITUTE

Street address 1: PO Box 7
Street address 3: Lexington
Street address state: VA
Zip/Postal code: 24450-0007
Country: USA
Mailing address: PO Box 7
Mailing city: Lexington
Mailing state: VA
Mailing zip: 24450-0007
General Phone: (540) 464-7326
General Fax: (540) 463-5679
General/National Adv. E-mail: vmicadet@vmi.edu
Primary Website: www.vmicadetpublication.com
Classified Equipment»
Personnel: Captain Christopher Perry (Advisor); Nick Weishar (Ed. in Chief)

WASHINGTON AND LEE UNIV.

Street address 1: 204 W Washington St
Street address 3: Lexington
Street address state: VA
Zip/Postal code: 24450-2116
Country: USA
Mailing address: 204 West Washington Street
Mailing city: Lexington
Mailing state: VA
Mailing zip: 24450

General Phone: (540) 458-4060
General Fax: (540) 458-4059
General/National Adv. E-mail: phi-business@wlu.edu; phi@wlu.edu
Classified Equipment»
Personnel: David Seifert (Bus. Mgr.)

LYNCHBURG

LIBERTY UNIV.

Street address 1: 1971 University Blvd
Street address 3: Lynchburg
Street address state: VA
Zip/Postal code: 24515-0002
Country: USA
Mailing address: 1971 University Blvd
Mailing city: Lynchburg
Mailing state: VA
Mailing zip: 24515-0002
General Phone: (434) 582-2128
General Fax: (434) 582-2420
Editorail Phone: (434) 582-2128
General/National Adv. E-mail: advertising@liberty.edu
Primary Website: www.liberty.edu/champion
Year Established: 1971
Classified Equipment»
Personnel: William Gribbin (Dean, School of Commun.); Debra Huff (Advisor); Cecil V. Kramer (Jr. Assoc. Dean); Benjamin Lesley (Adv. Dir.); William Mullen (Chrmn.); Amanda Sullivan (Ed. in Chief)

LYNCHBURG COLLEGE

Street address 1: 1501 Lakeside Dr
Street address 3: Lynchburg
Street address state: VA
Zip/Postal code: 24501-3113
Country: USA
Mailing address: 1501 Lakeside Dr
Mailing city: Lynchburg
Mailing state: VA
Mailing zip: 24501-3113
General Phone: (434) 544-8301
General Fax: (804) 544-8661
General/National Adv. E-mail: critograph@lynchburg.edu
Display Adv. E-mail: critograph@lynchburg.edu
Editorial e-mail: critograph@lynchburg.edu
Primary Website: www.critograph.com
Published: Tues
Classified Equipment»
Personnel: Rachad Davis (Editor-in-Chief); Heywood Greenberg (Dena/Prof., Journ.); Wayne Garret (Copy Desk Chief)

RANDOLPH-MACON WOMAN'S COLLEGE

Street address 1: 2500 Rivermont Ave
Street address 3: Lynchburg
Street address state: VA
Zip/Postal code: 24503-1555
Country: USA
Mailing address: 2500 Rivermont Ave
Mailing city: Lynchburg
Mailing state: VA
Mailing zip: 24503-1526
General Phone: (434) 947-8000
General Fax: (434) 947-8298
Primary Website: www.randolphcollege.edu
Classified Equipment»
Personnel: Dawn Linsner (Ed.)

NEWPORT NEWS

CHRISTOPHER NEWPORT UNIV.

Street address 1: 1 University Pl
Street address 3: Newport News
Street address state: VA
Zip/Postal code: 23606-2949
Country: USA
Mailing address: 1 University Pl
Mailing city: Newport News
Mailing state: VA
Mailing zip: 23606-2949
General Phone: (757) 594-7196

General/National Adv. E-mail: desk@thecaptainslog.org
Primary Website: www.thecaptainslog.org
Published: Wed
Classified Equipment»
Personnel: Terry Lee (Faculty Advisor); Ben Leistensnider (Ed. in Chief); Nicole Emmelhainz (Faculty advisor)

NORFOLK STATE UNIVERSITY

Street address 1: 700 Park Ave
Street address 2: Student Activities
Street address 3: Norfolk
Street address state: VA
Zip/Postal code: 23504-8050
Country: USA
Mailing address: 700 Park Ave.
Mailing city: Norfolk
Mailing state: VA
Mailing zip: 23504-8090
General Phone: (757) 823-8200
Advertising Phone: (757) 823-8200
Editorail Phone: (757) 823-8200
General/National Adv. E-mail: spartanecho@nsu.edu
Display Adv. E-mail: spartanecho@nsu.edu
Editorial e-mail: spartanecho@nsu.edu
Primary Website: www.spartanecho.org
Year Established: 1952
Commercial printers: Y
Published: Bi-Mthly
Avg Free Circ: 1000
Classified Equipment»
Personnel: Tarrye Venable (Student Activities Director)
Parent company (for newspapers): Norfolk State University

OLD DOMINION UNIVERSITY

Street address 1: 1051 Webb Center
Street address 3: Norfolk
Street address state: VA
Zip/Postal code: 23529-0001
Country: USA
Mailing address: 1051 Webb Center
Mailing city: Norfolk
Mailing state: VA
Mailing zip: 23529
General Phone: (757) 683-3452
Advertising Phone: (757) 683-4773
General/National Adv. E-mail: editorinchief@maceandcrown.com
Display Adv. E-mail: advertising@maceandcrown.com
Editorial e-mail: editorinchief@maceandcrown.com
Primary Website: http://www.maceandcrown.com
Year Established: 1930
Delivery Methods: Newsstand
Published: Wed
Classified Equipment»
Personnel: Adam Flores (Editor-in-Chief); Kavita Butani (Advertising & Business Manager)

PETERSBURG

VIRGINIA STATE UNIV.

Street address 1: 402 Foster Hall, Box 9063
Street address 3: Petersburg
Street address state: VA
Zip/Postal code: 23806-0001
Country: USA
Mailing address: 402 Foster Hall # 9063
Mailing city: Petersburg
Mailing state: VA
Mailing zip: 23806-0001
General Phone: (804) 524-5991
General Fax: (804) 524-5406
Classified Equipment»
Personnel: Howard Hall (Advisor); Thysha Shabazz (Ed.)

RADFORD

RADFORD UNIV.

Street address 1: PO Box 6985
Street address 3: Radford
Street address state: VA
Zip/Postal code: 24142-6985
Country: USA
Mailing address: PO Box 6985

Mailing city: Radford
Mailing state: VA
Mailing zip: 24142-6985
General Phone: (540) 831-5474
General Fax: (540) 831-6725
Advertising Fax: (540) 831-6051
General/National Adv. E-mail: tartan@radford.edu
Primary Website: www.thetartan.com
Classified Equipment»
Personnel: Matt Labelle (Ed. in chief); Justin Ward (Mng. Ed.); Colin Daileda (News Ed.)

RICHLANDS

SOUTHWEST VIRGINIA CMTY. COLLEGE

Street address 1: PO Box Svcc
Street address 3: Richlands
Street address state: VA
Zip/Postal code: 24641
Country: USA
Mailing address: PO Box SVCC
Mailing city: Richlands
Mailing state: VA
Mailing zip: 24641
General Phone: (276) 964-2555
General/National Adv. E-mail: pat.bussard@sw.edu
Classified Equipment»
Personnel: Pat Bussard (Advisor)

UNIV. OF RICHMOND

Street address 1: 40 W Hampton Way, North Ct, Rm B1
Street address 3: Richmond
Street address state: VA
Zip/Postal code: 23173-0001
Country: USA
Mailing address: 40 W Hampton Way North Ct Rm B1
Mailing city: Richmond
Mailing state: VA
Mailing zip: 23173-0001
General Phone: (804) 289-8483
General Fax: (804) 287-6092
Editorial e-mail: collegianstories@gmail.com
Primary Website: www.thecollegianur.com
Year Established: 1914
Published: Mon`Tues`Wed`Thur`Fri`Sat`Sun
Classified Equipment»
Personnel: Claire Comey (Editor in Chief); Liza David (Managing Editor)

VIRGINIA COMMONWEALTH UNIV.

Street address 1: 817 W Broad St
Street address 3: Richmond
Street address state: VA
Zip/Postal code: 23284-9104
Country: USA
Mailing address: PO Box 842010
Mailing city: Richmond
Mailing state: VA
Mailing zip: 23284-2010
General Phone: (804) 828-1058
General Fax: (804) 828-9201
Editorial e-mail: editor@commonwealthtimes.com
Primary Website: www.commonwealthtimes.com
Classified Equipment»
Personnel: Greg Weatherford (Student Media Dir.); Lauren Geerdes (Bus. Mgr.)

VIRGINIA UNION UNIV.

Street address 1: 1500 N Lombardy St
Street address 3: Richmond
Street address state: VA
Zip/Postal code: 23220-1711
Country: USA
Mailing address: 1500 N Lombardy St
Mailing city: Richmond
Mailing state: VA
Mailing zip: 23220-1784
General Phone: (804) 257-5655
General Fax: (804) 257-5818
Classified Equipment»
Personnel: Gloria D. Brogdon (Dept. Chair); Peter S. Tahsoh (Advisor)

ROANOKE

HOLLINS UNIV.

Street address 1: PO Box 9707
Street address 3: Roanoke
Street address state: VA
Zip/Postal code: 24020-1707
Country: USA
Mailing address: PO Box 9707
Mailing city: Roanoke
Mailing state: VA
Mailing zip: 24020-1707
General Phone: (540) 362-6000
General Fax: (540) 362-6642
General/National Adv. E-mail: hollinscolumns@hollins.edu
Primary Website: www.columns.proboards.com
Classified Equipment»
Personnel: Emileigh Clare (Ed. in Chief); Julie Abernethy (Ed.); KaRenda J. LaPrade (Copy Ed.)

ROANOKE COLLEGE

Street address 1: 221 College Ln
Street address 2: Ofc Studentactivities
Street address 3: Salem
Street address state: VA
Zip/Postal code: 24153-3747
Country: USA
Mailing address: 221 College Ln Ofc Studentactivities
Mailing city: Salem
Mailing state: VA
Mailing zip: 24153-3794
General Phone: (540) 375-2327
General Fax: (540) 378-5129
General/National Adv. E-mail: bracketyack@roanoke.edu
Primary Website: www.roanoke.edu
Classified Equipment»
Personnel: Daniel Sarabia (Ed.)

STAUNTON

MARY BALDWIN COLLEGE

Street address 1: PO Box 1500
Street address 3: Staunton
Street address state: VA
Zip/Postal code: 24402-1500
Country: USA
Mailing address: PO Box 1500
Mailing city: Staunton
Mailing state: VA
Mailing zip: 24402-1500
General Phone: (540) 887-7112
General Fax: (540) 887-7231
General/National Adv. E-mail: campuscomments@mbc.edu
Classified Equipment»
Personnel: Bruce Dorries (Advisor); Dawn Medley (Advisor); Hannah Barrow (Ed. in Chief)

SWEET BRIAR

SWEET BRIAR COLLEGE

Street address 1: PO Box H
Street address 3: Sweet Briar
Street address state: VA
Zip/Postal code: 24595-1058
Country: USA
Mailing address: PO Box 1058
Mailing city: Sweet Briar
Mailing state: VA
Mailing zip: 24595-1058
General Phone: (434) 381-6100
General Fax: (434) 381-6132
General/National Adv. E-mail: sbvoice@sbc.edu
Primary Website: www.voice.sbc.edu
Classified Equipment»
Personnel: Katy Johnstone (Ed. in chief); Carinna Finn (Mng. Ed.)

COLLEGE OF WILLIAM AND MARY

Street address 1: Campus Ctr, Jamestown Rd
Street address 3: Williamsburg
Street address state: VA
Zip/Postal code: 23187
Country: USA
Mailing address: PO Box 8795
Mailing city: Williamsburg
Mailing state: VA
Mailing zip: 23187-8795
General/National Adv. E-mail: flathat.editor@gmail.com
Display Adv. E-mail: flathatads@gmail.com
Editorial e-mail: fhnews@gmail.com
Primary Website: www.flathatnews.com
Year Established: 1911
Advertising (Open Inch Rate) Weekday/Saturday: Web and Print
Published: Tues
Classified Equipment»
Note: Student newspaper
Personnel: Trici Fredrick (Advisor); Tucker Higgins (Editor-in-chief)

WISE

UNIV. OF VIRGINIA

Street address 1: 1 College Ave
Street address 3: Wise
Street address state: VA
Zip/Postal code: 24293-4400
Country: USA
Mailing address: PO Box 3043
Mailing city: Wise
Mailing state: VA
Mailing zip: 24293-3043
General Fax: (276) 328-0212
General/National Adv. E-mail: info@uvawise.edu
Primary Website: www.wise.virginia.edu
Classified Equipment»
Personnel: Michael McGill (Adv. Mgr.)

VERMONT

BENNINGTON

BENNINGTON COLLEGE

Street address 1: 1 College Dr
Street address 3: Bennington
Street address state: VT
Zip/Postal code: 05201-6003
Country: USA
Mailing address: 1 College Dr
Mailing city: Bennington
Mailing state: VT
Mailing zip: 05201-6004
General Phone: (802) 442-5401
General Fax: (802) 442-6164
Classified Equipment»
Personnel: Veronica Jorgensen (Asst.Dean of Student)

SOUTHERN VERMONT COLLEGE

Street address 1: 982 Mansion Dr
Street address 3: Bennington
Street address state: VT
Zip/Postal code: 05201-9269
Country: USA
Mailing address: 982 Mansion Dr
Mailing city: Bennington
Mailing state: VT
Mailing zip: 05201-6002
General Phone: (802) 447-6347
General Fax: (802) 447-4695
General/National Adv. E-mail: mountainpress@svc.edu
Classified Equipment»
Personnel: Peter Seward (Advisor)

BURLINGTON

UNIVERSITY OF VERMONT

Street address 1: Uvm Student Life
Street address 2: 590 Main St. #310
Street address 3: Burlington
Street address state: VT
Zip/Postal code: 05405-0001
Country: USA
Mailing address: UVM Student Life
Mailing city: Burlington
Mailing state: VT
Mailing zip: 05405
General Phone: (802) 656-4412
General Fax: (802) 656-8482
General/National Adv. E-mail: crevans@uvm.edu
Display Adv. E-mail: crevans@uvm.edu
Editorial e-mail: crevans@uvm.edu
Primary Website: https://vtcynic.com/
Year Established: 1883
Published: Wed
Avg Free Circ: 5000
Classified Equipment»
Personnel: Chris Evans (Adv.)

COLCHESTER

ST. MICHAEL'S COLLEGE

Street address 1: 1 Winooski Park
Street address 3: Colchester
Street address state: VT
Zip/Postal code: 05439-1000
Country: USA
Mailing address: 1 Winooski Park
Mailing city: Colchester
Mailing state: VT
Mailing zip: 05439-1000
General Phone: (802) 654-2421
Advertising Phone: (802) 654-2560
General/National Adv. E-mail: defender@smcvt.edu
Classified Equipment»
Personnel: Paul Beique; Andrew Dennett (Ed.)

JOHNSON

JOHNSON STATE COLLEGE

Street address 1: 337 College Hl
Street address 3: Johnson
Street address state: VT
Zip/Postal code: 05656-9741
Country: USA
Mailing address: 337 College Hl
Mailing city: Johnson
Mailing state: VT
Mailing zip: 05656-9898
General Phone: (802) 635-1357
Primary Website: www.jsc.edu
Classified Equipment»
Personnel: Nathan Burgess (Ed.)

LYNDONVILLE

THE CRITIC

Street address 1: 1001 College Rd
Street address 3: Lyndonville
Street address state: VT
Zip/Postal code: 5851
County: Caledonia
Country: USA
Mailing address: PO Box 919
Mailing city: Lyndonville
Mailing state: VT
Mailing zip: 05851-0919
General Phone: (802) 626-6353
General/National Adv. E-mail: thecritic@northernvermont.edu
Primary Website: https://www.nvulyndoncritic.com/
Year Established: 1965
Classified Equipment»
Personnel: Bryanna Smith (Editor-in-Chief for 2018-2019 Academic Year.); Alexandra Huff (Editor-in-Chief)

MIDDLEBURY

MIDDLEBURY COLLEGE

Street address 1: PO Box 30
Street address 3: Middlebury
Street address state: VT
Zip/Postal code: 05753-0030
Country: USA
Mailing address: PO Box 30

Mailing city: Middlebury
Mailing state: VT
Mailing zip: 05753-0030
General Phone: (802) 443-4827
General Fax: (802) 443-2068
General/National Adv. E-mail: campus@middlebury.edu
Primary Website: www.middleburycampus.com
Classified Equipment»
Personnel: Zachary Karst (Bus. Mgr.); Brian Fung (Ed. in Chief); Tess Russell (Mng. Ed.)

NORWICH UNIV.

Street address 1: Communications Ctr
Street address 3: Northfield
Street address state: VT
Zip/Postal code: 5663
Country: USA
Mailing address: 158 Harmon Dr
Mailing city: Northfield
Mailing state: VT
Mailing zip: 05663-1097
General Phone: (802) 485-2763
General Fax: (802) 485-2580
General/National Adv. E-mail: syoungwo@norwich.edu
Delivery Methods: Racks
Commercial printers: N
Classified Equipment»
Personnel: Susan Youngwood (Advisor)

SOUTH ROYALTON

VERMONT LAW SCHOOL

Street address 1: PO Box 96
Street address 3: South Royalton
Street address state: VT
Zip/Postal code: 05068-0096
Country: USA
Mailing address: PO Box 96
Mailing city: South Royalton
Mailing state: VT
Mailing zip: 05068-0096
General Phone: (802) 831-1299
General Fax: (802) 763-7159
General/National Adv. E-mail: forum@vermontlaw.edu
Primary Website: www.vermontlaw.edu/students/x8685.xml
Classified Equipment»
Personnel: Sean Williams (Adv. Mgr.); Kevin Schrems (Ed. in Chief)

WASHINGTON

GRAYS HARBOR COLLEGE

Street address 1: 1620 Edward P Smith Dr
Street address 3: Aberdeen
Street address state: WA
Zip/Postal code: 98520-7500
Country: USA
Mailing address: 1620 Edward P Smith Dr
Mailing city: Aberdeen
Mailing state: WA
Mailing zip: 98520-7599
General Phone: (360) 532-9020
General Fax: (360) 538-4299
Primary Website: www.ghc.ctc.edu
Classified Equipment»

GREEN RIVER COMMUNITY COLLEGE

Street address 1: 12401 SE 320th St
Street address 3: Auburn
Street address state: WA
Zip/Postal code: 98092-3622
Country: USA
Mailing address: 12401 SE 320th St
Mailing city: Auburn
Mailing state: WA
Mailing zip: 98092-3699
General Phone: (253) 833-9111 x2375
General Fax: (253) 288-3457
Advertising Phone: (253) 833-9111 x2376
Editorail Phone: (253) 833-9111 x2375
General/National Adv. E-mail: thecurrent@greenriver.edu
Primary Website: http://www.thecurrentonline.net
Delivery Methods: Racks
Published Other: Every two weeks (approximately), excluding summer
Avg Free Circ: 1200
Classified Equipment»
Personnel: Brian Schraum (Adviser)

BELLEVUE CMTY. COLLEGE

Street address 1: 3000 Landerholm Cir SE
Street address 3: Bellevue
Street address state: WA
Zip/Postal code: 98007-6406
Country: USA
Mailing address: 3000 Landerholm Cir SE
Mailing city: Bellevue
Mailing state: WA
Mailing zip: 98007-6484
General Phone: (425) 564-2434
General Fax: (425) 564-4152
General/National Adv. E-mail: ataylor@bellevuecollege.edu
Display Adv. E-mail: advertising@thejibsheet.com
Primary Website: www.thejibsheet.com
Classified Equipment»
Personnel: Katherine Oleson (Pub.); Janelle Gardener (Advisor); Anne Taylor (Adv. Mgr.)

BELLINGHAM

WESTERN WASHINGTON UNIV.

Street address 1: 516 High St
Street address 2: # CF230
Street address 3: Bellingham
Street address state: WA
Zip/Postal code: 98225-5946
Country: USA
Mailing address: 516 High St # CF230
Mailing city: Bellingham
Mailing state: WA
Mailing zip: 98225-5946
General Phone: (360) 650-3160
General Fax: (360) 650-7775
Advertising Phone: (360) 650-3160
General/National Adv. E-mail: editor@westernfrontonline.net; thewesternfronteditor@yahoo.com
Primary Website: www.westernfrontonline.net
Year Established: 1899
Delivery Methods: Racks
Commercial printers: N
Classified Equipment»
Personnel: Carolyn Nielsen (Advisor); Aletha Macomber (Bus. Mgr.); Michele Anderson (Advertising Mgr.); Nicholas Johnson (Ed. in Chief); Katie (Managing Ed.); Alex (Online Ed.)

WHATCOM CMTY. COLLEGE

Street address 1: Syre Student Ctr Rm 202 237 W Kellogg Rd
Street address 3: Bellingham
Street address state: WA
Zip/Postal code: 98226
Country: USA
Mailing address: Syre Student Ctr. Rm. 202 237 W. Kellogg Rd.
Mailing city: Bellingham
Mailing state: WA
Mailing zip: 98226
General Phone: (360) 383-3101
General Fax: (360) 676-2171
General/National Adv. E-mail: horizonads@hotmail.com; admanager@whatcomhorizon.com
Editorial e-mail: editor@whatcomhorizon.com
Primary Website: www.whatcomhorizon.com
Year Established: 1972
Published: Bi-Mthly
Avg Free Circ: 1000
Classified Equipment»
Personnel: Toby Sonneman (Faculty Advisor)

BREMERTON

OLYMPIC COLLEGE

Street address 1: 1600 Chester Ave
Street address 3: Bremerton
Street address state: WA
Zip/Postal code: 98337-1600
Country: USA
Mailing address: 1600 Chester Ave
Mailing city: Bremerton
Mailing state: WA
Mailing zip: 98337-1699
General Phone: (360) 792-6050
General Fax: (360) 475-7684
General/National Adv. E-mail: olyeditor@olympic.edu
Primary Website: www.ocolympian.com
Classified Equipment»
Personnel: Michael Prince (Advisor); Jon Miller (Ed.); Josh Nothnagle (Mng. Ed.)

CHENEY

THE EASTERNER

Street address 1: 102 Isle Hall
Street address 3: Cheney
Street address state: WA
Zip/Postal code: 99004-2417
Country: USA
Mailing address: 102 Isle Hall
Mailing city: Cheney
Mailing state: WA
Mailing zip: 99004-2417
General Phone: (509) 359-6737
Advertising Phone: (509) 359-7010
Display Adv. E-mail: advertising@ewu.edu
Editorial e-mail: easterner.editor@ewu.edu
Primary Website: www.easterneronline.com
Year Established: 1916
Delivery Methods: Carrier`Racks
Commercial printers: Y
Published: Wed
Avg Free Circ: 2500
Classified Equipment»
Personnel: Contact Us (Contact Us); Carleigh Hill (Dir.)
Parent company (for newspapers): Eastern Washington University

COLLEGE PLACE

WALLA WALLA COLLEGE

Street address 1: 204 S College Ave
Street address 3: College Place
Street address state: WA
Zip/Postal code: 99324-1139
Country: USA
Mailing address: 204 S College Ave
Mailing city: College Place
Mailing state: WA
Mailing zip: 99324-1198
General Phone: (509) 527-2971
General Fax: (509) 527-2674
General/National Adv. E-mail: comm@wwc.edu
Classified Equipment»
Personnel: Ross Brown (Ed.); Pamela Harris (Chair)

HIGHLINE COLLEGE

Street address 1: 2400 S 240th St
Street address 3: Des Moines
Street address state: WA
Zip/Postal code: 98198-2714
Country: USA
Mailing address: PO Box 98000
Mailing city: Des Moines
Mailing state: WA
Mailing zip: 98198-9800
General Phone: (206) 592-3291
General Fax: (206) 870-3771
Advertising Phone: (206) 592-3292
Editorail Phone: (206) 592-3317
General/National Adv. E-mail: tword@highline.edu; thunderword@highline.edu
Display Adv. E-mail: thunderword@highline.edu
Primary Website: https://thunderword.highline.edu/
Year Established: 1961
Delivery Methods: Carrier
Commercial printers: N
Advertising (Open Inch Rate) Weekday/Saturday: $5 column inch
Mechanical available: 10x16 full page
Published: Thur
Avg Free Circ: 2000
Classified Equipment»
Personnel: T.M. Sell (Advisor)

ELLENSBURG

CENTRAL WASHINGTON UNIV.

Street address 1: 400 E University Way
Street address 2: Mail Stop 7435, Bouillon 222
Street address 3: Ellensburg
Street address state: WA
Zip/Postal code: 98926-7502
Country: USA
Mailing address: 400 E University Way Rm 222
Mailing city: Ellensburg
Mailing state: WA
Mailing zip: 98926-7502
General Phone: (509) 963-1026
General Fax: (509) 963-1027
Advertising Phone: 509-963-1095
Advertising Fax: 509-963-1027
Editorail Phone: (509) 963-1073
Editorial Fax: Free
General/National Adv. E-mail: cwuobserver@gmail.com
Display Adv. E-mail: gaskillk@cwu.edu
Editorial e-mail: cwuobserver@gmail.com
Primary Website: www.cwuobserver.com
Special Editions: Orientation/Back to School
Delivery Methods: Newsstand`Racks
Commercial printers: N
Advertising (Open Inch Rate) Weekday/Saturday: http://cwuobserver.com/advertising
Published: Thur
Avg Free Circ: 6000
Classified Equipment»

EVERETT

EVERETT COMMUNITY COLLEGE

Street address 1: 2000 Tower St
Street address 2: Whitehorse Hall 265-268
Street address 3: Everett
Street address state: WA
Zip/Postal code: 98201-1352
Country: USA
Mailing address: 2000 Tower St.
Mailing city: Everett
Mailing state: WA
Mailing zip: 98201-1390
General Phone: (425) 388-9522
General/National Adv. E-mail: clipper@everettcc.edu
Primary Website: www.everettclipper.com
Year Established: 1943
Special Weekly Sections: Arts and Entertainment
Delivery Methods: Mail`Racks
Commercial printers: Y
Published: Other
Published Other: Every three weeks
Avg Paid Circ: 0
Avg Free Circ: 2500
Classified Equipment»
Personnel: T. Andrew Wahl (Adviser); Terresa King (Business & Circulation Director); Nataya Foss (Editor-in-chief)

PIERCE COLLEGE

Street address 1: 9401 Farwest Dr SW
Street address 3: Lakewood
Street address state: WA
Zip/Postal code: 98498-1919
Country: USA
Mailing address: 9401 Farwest Dr SW
Mailing city: Lakewood
Mailing state: WA
Mailing zip: 98498-1999
General Phone: (253) 964-6604
General Fax: (253) 964-6764
General/National Adv. E-mail: pioneer@pierce.ctc.edu
Primary Website: http://www.piercecollege.edu/
Classified Equipment»
Personnel: Michael Parks (Advisor); Blake York (Ed. in chief)

LOWER COLUMBIA COLLEGE

Street address 1: 1600 Maple St

Street address 3: Longview
Street address state: WA
Zip/Postal code: 98632-3907
Country: USA
Mailing address: PO Box 3010
Mailing city: Longview
Mailing state: WA
Mailing zip: 98632-0310
General Phone: (360) 442-2311
General Fax: (360) 442-2120
Primary Website: www.lowercolumbia.edu
Classified Equipment»
Personnel: Jill Homme (Ed.)

EDMONDS CMTY. COLLEGE

Street address 1: 20000 68th Ave W
Street address 3: Lynnwood
Street address state: WA
Zip/Postal code: 98036-5912
Country: USA
Mailing address: 20000 68th Ave W
Mailing city: Lynnwood
Mailing state: WA
Mailing zip: 98036-5999
General Phone: (425) 640-1315
General/National Adv. E-mail: revedic@edcc.edu
Primary Website: thetritonreview.com
Published: Other
Published Other: Twice per quarter during the academic year.
Classified Equipment»
Personnel: Rob Harrill (Advisor); Madeleine Jenness (Editor in Chief)

SKAGIT VALLEY CMTY. COLLEGE

Street address 1: 2405 E College Way
Street address 3: Mount Vernon
Street address state: WA
Zip/Postal code: 98273-5821
Country: USA
Mailing address: 2405 E College Way
Mailing city: Mount Vernon
Mailing state: WA
Mailing zip: 98273-5899
General Phone: (360) 416-7710
General Fax: (360) 416-7822
General/National Adv. E-mail: cardinal.news@skagit.edu
Classified Equipment»
Personnel: Beverly Saxon (Advisor)

OLYMPIA

THE EVERGREEN STATE COLLEGE

Street address 1: 2700 Evergreen Pkwy
Street address 2: Cab 316
Street address 3: Olympia
Street address state: WA
Zip/Postal code: 98505-0001
Country: USA
Mailing address: 2700 Evergreen Pkwy Cab 316
Mailing city: Olympia
Mailing state: WA
Mailing zip: 98505-0005
General Phone: (360) 867-6213
General Fax: (360) 867-6685
General/National Adv. E-mail: cpj@evergreen.edu
Primary Website: cpj.evergreen.edu
Classified Equipment»
Personnel: Dianne Conrad (Advisor); Madeline Berman (Mng. Ed.); Jason Slotkin (Ed. in Chief)

PULLMAN

WASHINGTON STATE UNIVERSITY, DAILY EVERGREEN

Street address 1: 455 NE Veterans Way
Street address 3: Pullman
Street address state: WA
Zip/Postal code: 99164-0001
Country: USA
Mailing address: PO Box 642510
Mailing city: Pullman
Mailing state: WA
Mailing zip: 99164-2510
General Phone: (509) 335-4573
General Fax: (509) 335-7401
Advertising Phone: (509) 335-1572
Editorail Phone: (509) 335-3194
Display Adv. E-mail: advertise@dailyevergreen.com
Editorial e-mail: news@dailyevergreen.com
Primary Website: www.dailyevergreen.com
Year Established: 1895
Delivery Methods: Carrier`Racks
Commercial printers: N
Advertising (Open Inch Rate) Weekday/Saturday: 12.00/inch
Published: Mon`Tues`Wed`Thur`Fri
Avg Free Circ: 5945
Classified Equipment»
Personnel: Tracy Milano (Program Coord.); Richard Miller (Dir of Student Media); K. Denise Boyd (Fiscal Officer); Jacob Jones (Content Adviser)

SEATTLE CENTRAL CMTY. COLLEGE

Street address 1: 1701 Broadway
Street address 2: # BE1145
Street address 3: Seattle
Street address state: WA
Zip/Postal code: 98122-2413
Country: USA
Mailing address: 1701 Broadway # BE1145
Mailing city: Seattle
Mailing state: WA
Mailing zip: 98122-2413
General Phone: (206) 587-6959
General Fax: (206) 903-3235
General/National Adv. E-mail: editor@thecitycollegian.com
Classified Equipment»
Personnel: Rachel Swedish (Ed. in Chief)

SEATTLE PACIFIC UNIV.

Street address 1: 3307 3rd Ave W
Street address 3: Seattle
Street address state: WA
Zip/Postal code: 98119-1940
Country: USA
Mailing address: 3307 3rd Ave W
Mailing city: Seattle
Mailing state: WA
Mailing zip: 98119-1997
General Phone: (206) 281-2913
General Fax: (206) 378-5003
General/National Adv. E-mail: falcon-ads@spu.edu
Editorial e-mail: falcon-online@spu.edu; falcon-news@spu.edu; falcon-sports@spu.edu; falcon-features@spu.edu; falcon-opinions@spu.edu
Primary Website: www.thefalcononline.com
Classified Equipment»
Personnel: Katie-Joy Blanksma (Ed. in Chief); Haley Libak (Layout Ed.); Madeline Tremain (Layout Ed.)

SEATTLE UNIVERSITY

Street address 1: 901 12th Ave
Street address 3: Seattle
Street address state: WA
Zip/Postal code: 98122-4411
Country: USA
Mailing address: PO Box 222000
Mailing city: Seattle
Mailing state: WA
Mailing zip: 98122-1090
General Phone: (206) 296-6470
General Fax: (206) 296-2163
Advertising Phone: (206) 296-6474
Editorial e-mail: editor@su-spectator.com; support@collegepublisher.com
Primary Website: www.seattlespectator.com
Year Established: 1933
Published: Wed
Classified Equipment»
Personnel: Sonora Jha (Advisor)

SOUTH SEATTLE CMTY. COLLEGE

Street address 1: 6000 16th Ave SW
Street address 2: Jmb 135
Street address 3: Seattle
Street address state: WA
Zip/Postal code: 98106-1401
Country: USA
Mailing address: 6000 16th Ave SW Jmb 135
Mailing city: Seattle
Mailing state: WA
Mailing zip: 98106-1401
General Phone: (206) 764-5335
General Fax: (206) 764-7936
Advertising Phone: (206) 764-5335
Editorail Phone: (206) 764-5333
General/National Adv. E-mail: sentinelads@sccd.ctc.edu
Editorial e-mail: sentineleditor@sccd.ctc.edu
Primary Website: sites.southseattle.edu/thesentinel
Classified Equipment»
Personnel: Betsy Berger (Advisor)

UNIV. OF WASHINGTON

Street address 1: 144 Communications Bldg
Street address 2: Box 353720
Street address 3: Seattle
Street address state: WA
Zip/Postal code: 98195-0001
Country: USA
Mailing address: 132 Communications
Mailing city: Seattle
Mailing state: WA
Mailing zip: 98195-0001
General Phone: (206) 543-2336
General Fax: (206) 543-2345
Advertising Phone: (206) 543-2335
Editorail Phone: 206-543-2700
Display Adv. E-mail: ads@dailyuw.com
Editorial e-mail: editor@dailyuw.com
Primary Website: www.dailyuw.com
Year Established: 1891
Published: Mon`Tues`Wed`Thur`Fri
Avg Free Circ: 7500
Classified Equipment»
Personnel: Diana Kramer (Dir., Student Publications); Andreas Redd (Editor-in-Chief)

SHORELINE

SHORELINE CMTY. COLLEGE

Street address 1: 16101 Greenwood Ave N
Street address 2: Rm 9101
Street address 3: Shoreline
Street address state: WA
Zip/Postal code: 98133-5667
Country: USA
Mailing address: 16101 Greenwood Ave N Rm 9101
Mailing city: Shoreline
Mailing state: WA
Mailing zip: 98133-5667
General Phone: (206) 546-4730
General Fax: (206) 546-5869
General/National Adv. E-mail: webbtide@yahoo.com
Primary Website: www.shoreline.edu/ebbtide/
Classified Equipment»
Personnel: Patti Jones (Advisor); Amelia Rivera (Ed. in Chief); Daniel Demay (Copy Ed.); Sean Sherman (Photo Ed.)

SPOKANE

GONZAGA UNIVERSITY

Street address 1: 502 E Boone Ave
Street address 3: Spokane
Street address state: WA
Zip/Postal code: 99258-1774
Country: USA
Mailing address: Msc # 2477
Mailing city: Spokane
Mailing state: WA
Mailing zip: 99258-0001
General Phone: (509) 313-6826
General Fax: (509) 313-5848
Advertising Phone: (509) 313-6839
Advertising Fax: (509) 313-5848
Editorail Phone: (509) 313-6826
Editorial Fax: (509) 313-5848
General/National Adv. E-mail: bulletin@zagmail.gonzaga.edu
Display Adv. E-mail: adoffice@gonzaga.edu
Editorial e-mail: bulletin@zagmail.gonzaga.edu
Primary Website: www.gonzagabulletin.com
Advertising (Open Inch Rate) Weekday/Saturday: $11.00 pci national, $10.00 pci local
Published: Thur
Avg Paid Circ: 0
Avg Free Circ: 3000
Classified Equipment»
Personnel: Tom Miller (Advisor); Susan English (Adviser); John Kafentzis (Adviser); Joanne Shiosaki (Student Publications Manager); Chris Wheatley (Student Publications Assistant Manager)

SPOKANE CMTY. COLLEGE

Street address 1: 1810 N Greene St
Street address 3: Spokane
Street address state: WA
Zip/Postal code: 99217-5320
Country: USA
Mailing address: 1810 N Greene St
Mailing city: Spokane
Mailing state: WA
Mailing zip: 99217-5399
General Phone: (509) 533-7000
General Fax: (509) 533-8163
General/National Adv. E-mail: reporter@scc.spokane.edu
Classified Equipment»
Personnel: Rob Vogel (Advisor); Danie Elle (Ed.)

SPOKANE FALLS CMTY. COLLEGE

Street address 1: 3410 W Fort George Wright Dr
Street address 2: MS 3180
Street address 3: Spokane
Street address state: WA
Zip/Postal code: 99224-5204
Country: USA
Mailing address: 3410 W Fort George Wright Dr MS 3180
Mailing city: Spokane
Mailing state: WA
Mailing zip: 99224-5204
General Phone: (509) 533-3246
General Fax: (509) 533-3856
General/National Adv. E-mail: communicator@spokanefalls.edu
Primary Website: www.spokanefalls.edu/communicator
Classified Equipment»
Personnel: Jason Nix (Advisor); Sarah Radmer (Mng. Ed.); Madison Mccord (Ed.); Wendy Gaskill (Ed.)

WHITWORTH UNIVERSITY

Street address 1: 300 W Hawthorne Rd
Street address 3: Spokane
Street address state: WA
Zip/Postal code: 99251-2515
Country: USA
Mailing address: 300 W Hawthorne Rd
Mailing city: Spokane
Mailing state: WA
Mailing zip: 99251-2515
General Phone: (509) 777-3248
General Fax: (509) 777-3710
Editorial Fax: Free
Editorial e-mail: editor@whitworthian.com
Primary Website: www.thewhitworthian.com
Year Established: 1905
Published: Wed
Classified Equipment»
Personnel: Jim McPherson (Advisor); Rebekah Bresee (Editor-in-Chief)

TACOMA

PACIFIC LUTHERAN UNIV.

Street address 1: the Mooring Mast Pacific Lutheran University 1010 122nd Street
Street address 3: Tacoma
Street address state: WA
Zip/Postal code: 98447-0001
Country: USA
Mailing address: the Mooring Mast Pacific Lutheran University 1010 122nd Street S
Mailing city: Tacoma
Mailing state: WA
Mailing zip: 98447-0001
General Phone: (253) 535-7492
General Fax: (253) 536-5067
Advertising Phone: (425) 622-2693
General/National Adv. E-mail: mast@plu.edu
Display Adv. E-mail: mastads@plu.edu
Primary Website: www.plu.edu/~mast

Year Established: 1924
Delivery Methods: Racks
Commercial printers: Y
Published: Fri
Avg Free Circ: 3500
Classified Equipment»
Personnel: Winston Alder (Business and Ads Manager); Jessica Trondsen (Editor-in-Chief)

TACOMA CMTY. COLLEGE

Street address 1: 6501 S 19th St
Street address 2: Bldg 216
Street address 3: Tacoma
Street address state: WA
Zip/Postal code: 98466-6139
Country: USA
Mailing address: 6501 S 19th St Bldg 216
Mailing city: Tacoma
Mailing state: WA
Mailing zip: 98466-6139
General Phone: (253) 566-6045
General Fax: (253) 566-5384
Primary Website: www.tacomachallenge.com
Classified Equipment»
Personnel: Serrell Collins (Advisor); Kathy Tavia (Ed.)

THE UNIVERSITY OF WASHINGTON TACOMA LEDGER STUDENT NEWSPAPER

Street address 1: 1900 Commerce St
Street address 2: Mat 151
Street address 3: Tacoma
Street address state: WA
Zip/Postal code: 98402-3112
Country: USA
Mailing address: 1900 Commerce St Mat 151
Mailing city: Tacoma
Mailing state: WA
Mailing zip: 98402-3112
General Phone: (253) 692-4428
General Fax: (253) 692-5602
Advertising Phone: (253) 692-4529
General/National Adv. E-mail: ledger@uw.edu
Display Adv. E-mail: ledger@u.washington.edu
Editorial e-mail: ledger@u.washington.edu
Primary Website: www.thetacomaledger.com
Delivery Methods: Racks
Published: Mon
Classified Equipment»
Personnel: Daniel Nash (Publications Manager); Kelsie Abram (Editor-in-Chief)

UNIV. OF PUGET SOUND

Street address 1: 1500 N Warner St
Street address 2: Stop 1095
Street address 3: Tacoma
Street address state: WA
Zip/Postal code: 98416-1095
Country: USA
Mailing address: 1500 N Warner St Stop 1095
Mailing city: Tacoma
Mailing state: WA
Mailing zip: 98416-1095
General Phone: (253) 879-3100
General Fax: (253) 879-3645
General/National Adv. E-mail: trail@pugetsound.edu
Primary Website: www.pugetsound.edu
Classified Equipment»
Personnel: Anna Marie Ausnes (Contact)

TUMWATER

SOUTH PUGET SOUND CMTY. COLLEGE

Street address 1: 2011 Mottman Rd SW
Street address 3: Tumwater
Street address state: WA
Zip/Postal code: 98512-6218
Country: USA
Mailing address: 2011 Mottman Rd SW
Mailing city: Tumwater
Mailing state: WA
Mailing zip: 98512-6218
General Phone: (360) 754-7711
General Fax: (360) 596-5708
General/National Adv. E-mail: soundsnewspaper@spscc.ctc.edu
Primary Website: www.spscc.ctc.edu
Classified Equipment»
Personnel: Steve Valandra (Advisor); Erin Landgraf (Ed. in Chief)

VANCOUVER

CLARK COLLEGE

Street address 1: 1933 Fort Vancouver Way
Street address 3: Vancouver
Street address state: WA
Zip/Postal code: 98663-3529
Country: USA
Mailing address: 1933 Fort Vancouver Way # 124
Mailing city: Vancouver
Mailing state: WA
Mailing zip: 98663-3598
General Phone: (360) 992-2159
General Fax: (360) 992-2879
Primary Website: clarkindependent.wordpress.com
Classified Equipment»
Personnel: Audrey McDougal (Ed. in Chief); Nick Jensen (Mng. Ed.); Daniel Hampton (News Ed.)

YAKIMA

YAKIMA VALLEY CMTY. COLLEGE

Street address 1: PO Box 22520
Street address 3: Yakima
Street address state: WA
Zip/Postal code: 98907-2520
Country: USA
Mailing address: PO Box 22520
Mailing city: Yakima
Mailing state: WA
Mailing zip: 98907-2520
General Phone: (509) 574-4600
General Fax: (509) 574-6860
Advertising Phone: 509-574-6870
Advertising Fax: 509-574-6870
Display Adv. E-mail: nhopkins@yvcc.edu
Primary Website: www.yvcc.edu
Year Established: 1928
Classified Equipment»
Personnel: Niki Hopkins (Ed.)

WISCONSIN

APPLETON

LAWRENCE UNIVERSITY

Street address 1: 711 E Boldt Way
Street address 2: Spc 51
Street address 3: Appleton
Street address state: WI
Zip/Postal code: 54911-5699
Country: USA
Mailing address: 711 E Boldt Way Spc 51
Mailing city: Appleton
Mailing state: WI
Mailing zip: 54911-5699
General Phone: (920) 832-6768
General Fax: (920) 832-7031
General/National Adv. E-mail: lawrentian@lawrence.edu
Primary Website: www.lawrentian.com
Year Established: 1884
Published: Fri
Avg Paid Circ: 250
Avg Free Circ: 1000
Classified Equipment»
Personnel: Emily Zawacki (Editor-in-Chief); Nathan Lawrence (Copy Chief)

BELOIT

BELOIT COLLEGE

Street address 1: 700 College St
Street address 3: Beloit
Street address state: WI
Zip/Postal code: 53511-5509
Country: USA
Mailing address: 700 College St
Mailing city: Beloit
Mailing state: WI
Mailing zip: 53511-5595
General Phone: (608) 363-2000
General Fax: (608) 363-2718
General/National Adv. E-mail: admiss@beloit.edu
Primary Website: www.beloit.edu
Delivery Methods: Newsstand
Commercial printers: N
Classified Equipment»
Personnel: India John (Co Editor-in-Chief); Steven Jackson (Co Editor-in-Chief)

DE PERE

ST. NORBERT COLLEGE

Street address 1: 100 Grant St
Street address 2: Ste 320
Street address 3: De Pere
Street address state: WI
Zip/Postal code: 54115-2002
Country: USA
Mailing address: 100 Grant St Ste 320
Mailing city: De Pere
Mailing state: WI
Mailing zip: 54115-2002
General Phone: (920) 403-3268
General Fax: (920) 403-4092
General/National Adv. E-mail: times@snc.edu
Classified Equipment»
Personnel: John Pennington (Advisor); Samantha Christian (Ed. in Chief)

EAU CLAIRE

UNIV. OF WISCONSIN EAU CLAIRE

Street address 1: 105 Garfield Ave
Street address 3: Eau Claire
Street address state: WI
Zip/Postal code: 54701-4811
Country: USA
Mailing address: 104B Hibbard Hall, 105 Garfield Ave
Mailing city: Eau Claire
Mailing state: WI
Mailing zip: 54701
General Phone: (715) 836-5618
General Fax: (715) 836-3829
Advertising Phone: (715) 836-4366
Editorail Phone: (715) 836-4416
General/National Adv. E-mail: spectator@uwec.edu
Primary Website: www.spectatornews.com
Classified Equipment»
Personnel: John Cayer (Adv. Mgr.); Scott Hansen (Ed. in Cheif); Breann Schossow (Mng. Ed.); Frank Pellegrino (News Ed.)

FENNIMORE

SOUTHWEST WISCONSIN TECH. COLLEGE

Street address 1: 1800 Bronson Blvd
Street address 3: Fennimore
Street address state: WI
Zip/Postal code: 53809-9778
Country: USA
Mailing address: 1800 Bronson Blvd
Mailing city: Fennimore
Mailing state: WI
Mailing zip: 53809-9778
General Phone: (608) 822-3262
General Fax: (608) 822-6019
General/National Adv. E-mail: jcullen@swtc.edu
Primary Website: www.swtc.edu
Classified Equipment»
Personnel: Jackie Cullen (Advisor)

FOND DU LAC

MARIAN UNIVERSITY

Street address 1: 45 S National Ave
Street address 3: Fond Du Lac
Street address state: WI
Zip/Postal code: 54935-4621
Country: USA
Mailing address: 45 S National Ave
Mailing city: Fond Du Lac
Mailing state: WI
Mailing zip: 54935-4621
General Phone: (920) 923-8776
General Fax: (920) 923-8158
Primary Website: www.marianuniversitysabre.com
Classified Equipment»
Personnel: Vicky Hildebrandt (Advisor); Katie Leist (Ed.)

UNIV. OF WISCONSIN GREEN BAY

Street address 1: 2420 Nicolet Dr
Street address 3: Green Bay
Street address state: WI
Zip/Postal code: 54311-7003
Country: USA
Mailing address: 2420 Nicolet Dr
Mailing city: Green Bay
Mailing state: WI
Mailing zip: 54311-7003
General Phone: (920) 465-2719
General Fax: (920) 465-2895
Advertising Phone: (920) 465-2719
Advertising Fax: (920) 465-2895
Editorail Phone: (920) 465-2719
Editorial Fax: (920) 465-2895
General/National Adv. E-mail: 4e@uwgb.edu
Display Adv. E-mail: 4e@uwgb.edu
Editorial e-mail: 4e@uwgb.edu
Primary Website: www.fourthestatenewspaper.com
Advertising (Open Inch Rate) Weekday/Saturday: Available to business and on campus companies - various sizes available
Published: Thur
Avg Free Circ: 6600
Classified Equipment»
Personnel: Victoria Goff (Advisor); Nicole Angelucci (Adv. Mgr.); Maureen Malone (Ed. in chief)

JANESVILLE

BLACKHAWK TECHNICAL COLLEGE

Street address 1: 6004 Prairie Rd
Street address 3: Janesville
Street address state: WI
Country: USA
Mailing address: PO Box 5009
Mailing city: Janesville
Mailing state: WI
Mailing zip: 53547-5009
General Phone: (608) 757-7702
General Fax: (608) 743-4407
Classified Equipment»
Personnel: Amber Feibel (Advisor)

KENOSHA

CARTHAGE COLLEGE

Street address 1: 2001 Alford Park Dr
Street address 3: Kenosha
Street address state: WI
Zip/Postal code: 53140-1929
Country: USA
Mailing address: 2001 Alford Park Dr
Mailing city: Kenosha
Mailing state: WI
Mailing zip: 53140-1994
General Phone: (262) 551-5800
General Fax: (262) 551-6629
Primary Website: current.carthage.edu
Classified Equipment»

Personnel: Meg Durbin (Ed. in Chief); Carmelo Chimera (Mng. Ed.); Lauren Hansen (Bus. Mng.)

UNIV. OF WISCONSIN PARKSIDE

Street address 1: 900 Wood Rd
Street address 3: Kenosha
Street address state: WI
Zip/Postal code: 53144-1133
Country: USA
Mailing address: PO Box 2000
Mailing city: Kenosha
Mailing state: WI
Mailing zip: 53141-2000
General Phone: (262) 595-2287
General Fax: (262) 595-2295
General/National Adv. E-mail: rangernews@uwp.edu
Display Adv. E-mail: advertising@therangernews.com
Primary Website: www.therangernews.com
Classified Equipment»
Personnel: Jo Kirst (Ed.)

UNIV. OF WISCONSIN LA CROSSE

Street address 1: 1725 State St
Street address 3: La Crosse
Street address state: WI
Zip/Postal code: 54601-3742
Country: USA
Mailing address: 1725 State St
Mailing city: La Crosse
Mailing state: WI
Mailing zip: 54601-3788
General Phone: (608) 785-8378
General Fax: (608) 785-6575
General/National Adv. E-mail: racquet@uwlax.edu
Primary Website: www.theracquet.net
Classified Equipment»
Personnel: Chris Rochester (Ed in Chief); Mary Beth Valhalla (Advisor)

VITERBO COLLEGE

Street address 1: 900 Viterbo Dr
Street address 3: La Crosse
Street address state: WI
Zip/Postal code: 54601-8804
Country: USA
Mailing address: 900 Viterbo Dr
Mailing city: La Crosse
Mailing state: WI
Mailing zip: 54601-8804
General Phone: (608) 796-3046
General Fax: (608) 796-3050
Advertising Phone: (608) 796-3041
General/National Adv. E-mail: communication@viterbo.edu
Primary Website: www.viterbolumen.com
Classified Equipment»
Personnel: Pat Kerrigan (Vice Pres., Commun.); Jessica Weber (Ed.)

MADISON AREA TECHNICAL COLLEGE

Street address 1: 3550 Anderson St
Street address 3: Madison
Street address state: WI
Zip/Postal code: 53704-2520
Country: USA
Mailing address: 1701 Wright St
Mailing city: Madison
Mailing state: WI
Mailing zip: 53704-2599
General Phone: (608) 243-4809
General Fax: (608) 246-6488
General/National Adv. E-mail: clarioned@matcmadison.edu
Primary Website: www.matc-clarion.com
Classified Equipment»
Personnel: Doug Kirchberg (Advisor); Vishmaa Ramsaroop Briggs (Ed.)

UNIVERSITY OF WISCONSIN MADISON

Street address 1: 152 W Johnson St
Street address 2: Ste 202
Street address 3: Madison
Street address state: WI
Zip/Postal code: 53703-2296
Country: USA
Mailing address: 152 West Johnson Street
Mailing city: Madison
Mailing state: WI
Mailing zip: 53703-2017
General Phone: (608) 257-4712
General Fax: (608) 258-3029
Advertising Phone: (608) 257-4712
Editorail Phone: (608) 257-4712
General/National Adv. E-mail: publisher@badgerherald.com
Display Adv. E-mail: addirector@badgerherald.com
Editorial e-mail: editor@badgerherald.com
Primary Website: www.badgerherald.com
Year Established: 1969
Published: Tues
Classified Equipment»
Personnel: Alice Vagun (Editor-in-Chief)

WISCONSIN ENGINEER MAGAZINE

Street address 1: Room M1066, Engineering Centers Bldg
Street address 3: Madison
Street address state: WI
Zip/Postal code: 53706
Country: USA
Mailing address: 1550 Engineering Dr.
Mailing city: Madison
Mailing state: WI
Mailing zip: 53706
General Phone: (608) 262-3494
General Fax: (608) 262-3494
General/National Adv. E-mail: wiscengr@cae.wisc.edu
Primary Website: www.wisconsinengineer.com
Year Established: 1912
Special Editions: Published 4x a year
Commercial printers: N
Classified Equipment»
Personnel: Steven Zwickel (Advisor)

MANITOWOC

UNIV. OF WISCONSIN CENTER

Street address 1: 705 Viebahn St
Street address 3: Manitowoc
Street address state: WI
Zip/Postal code: 54220-6601
Country: USA
Mailing address: 705 Viebahn St
Mailing city: Manitowoc
Mailing state: WI
Mailing zip: 54220-6601
General Phone: (920) 683-4731
General Fax: (920) 683-4776
Classified Equipment»
Personnel: Larry Desch (Advisor)

MARSHFIELD

UNIV. OF WISCONSIN MARSHFIELD

Street address 1: 2000 W 5th St
Street address 3: Marshfield
Street address state: WI
Zip/Postal code: 54449-3310
Country: USA
Mailing city: Marshfield
Mailing state: WI
Mailing zip: 54449
General Phone: (715) 389-6545
General Fax: (715) 389-6517
General/National Adv. E-mail: msfur@uwc.edu
Editorial e-mail: insight@uwc.edu
Primary Website: www.marshfield.uwc.edu
Classified Equipment»
Personnel: Stacey Oelrich (Contact)

MENASHA

UNIVERSITY OF WISCONSIN, FOX VALLEY

Street address 1: 1478 Midway Rd
Street address 3: Menasha
Street address state: WI
Zip/Postal code: 54952-1224
Country: USA
Mailing address: 1478 Midway Rd
Mailing city: Menasha
Mailing state: WI
Mailing zip: 54952-1224
General Phone: (920) 832-2810
General Fax: (920) 832-2674
General/National Adv. E-mail: foxjournal@uwc.edu
Primary Website: www.uwfox.uwc.edu/foxjournal
Classified Equipment»
Personnel: Paula Lovell (Advisor)

MENOMONIE

UNIVERSITY OF WISCONSIN-STOUT

Street address 1: 712 Broadway St S
Street address 2: Memorial Student Center
Street address 3: Menomonie
Street address state: WI
Zip/Postal code: 54751-2458
Country: USA
Mailing address: 712 Broadway St S
Mailing city: Menomonie
Mailing state: WI
Mailing zip: 54751
General Phone: (715) 232-1141
General/National Adv. E-mail: stoutonia@uwstout.edu
Display Adv. E-mail: stoutoniaads@uwstout.edu
Editorial e-mail: stoutonia@uwstout.edu
Primary Website: www.stoutonia.com
Year Established: 1915
Published Other: Every two weeks (7 issues per semester). Not published during the summer.
Avg Free Circ: 2700
Classified Equipment»
Personnel: Kate Edenborg (Advisor); Shaun Dudek

MEQUON

CONCORDIA UNIV. OF WISCONSIN

Street address 1: 12800 N Lake Shore Dr
Street address 3: Mequon
Street address state: WI
Zip/Postal code: 53097-2418
Country: USA
Mailing address: 12800 N Lake Shore Dr
Mailing city: Mequon
Mailing state: WI
Mailing zip: 53097-2402
General Phone: (262) 243-5700
General Fax: (262) 243-4351
Classified Equipment»
Personnel: Sarah Holtan (Faculty Advisor); Alax Tomter (Exec. Ed.)

CARDINAL STRITCH UNIV.

Street address 1: 6801 N Yates Rd
Street address 3: Milwaukee
Street address state: WI
Zip/Postal code: 53217-3945
Country: USA
Mailing address: 6801 N Yates Rd
Mailing city: Milwaukee
Mailing state: WI
Mailing zip: 53217-3985
General Phone: (414) 410-4173
General Fax: (414) 410-4111
Classified Equipment»
Personnel: Mary Carson (Advisor)

MARQUETTE UNIV.

Street address 1: 1131 W Wisconsin Ave
Street address 3: Milwaukee
Street address state: WI
Zip/Postal code: 53233-2313
Country: USA
Mailing address: 1131 W Wisconsin Ave
Mailing city: Milwaukee
Mailing state: WI
Mailing zip: 53233-2313
General Phone: (414) 288-1739
General Fax: (414) 288-5896
General/National Adv. E-mail: student.media@mu.edu; viewpoints@marquettetribune.org
Primary Website: marquettetribune.org
Classified Equipment»
Personnel: Kim Zawada (Advisor); Lauren Frey (Adv. Dir.); Jim McLaughlin (Ed. in Chief)

MILWAUKEE AREA TECH. COLLEGE

Street address 1: 700 W State St
Street address 2: Rm S220
Street address 3: Milwaukee
Street address state: WI
Zip/Postal code: 53233-1419
Country: USA
Mailing address: 700 W State St Rm S220
Mailing city: Milwaukee
Mailing state: WI
Mailing zip: 53233-1419
General Phone: (414) 297-6250
General Fax: (414) 297-7925
General/National Adv. E-mail: matctimes@gmail.com
Primary Website: www.matctimes.com
Year Established: 1959
Delivery Methods: Newsstand
Commercial printers: N
Published Other: bi-weekly
Avg Free Circ: 2500
Classified Equipment»
Personnel: Bob Hanson (Faculty Adviser)

MILWAUKEE SCHOOL OF ENGINEERING

Street address 1: 1025 N Milwaukee St
Street address 3: Milwaukee
Street address state: WI
Zip/Postal code: 53202
Country: USA
Mailing address: 1025 N. Milwaukee St.
Mailing city: Milwaukee
Mailing state: WI
Mailing zip: 53202-3109
General Phone: (414) 277-7255
General Fax: (414) 277-7248
Classified Equipment»
Personnel: Nicholas Petrovits (Ed.)

MOUNT MARY COLLEGE

Street address 1: 2900 N Menomonee River Pkwy
Street address 3: Milwaukee
Street address state: WI
Zip/Postal code: 53222-4545
Country: USA
Mailing address: 2900 N Menomonee River Pkwy
Mailing city: Milwaukee
Mailing state: WI
Mailing zip: 53222-4597
General Phone: (414) 258-4810
General Fax: (414) 443-3602
Primary Website: www.mtmary.edu
Classified Equipment»
Personnel: Heather Schroeder (Advisor); Laura Otto (Ed. in Chief); Elaina Meier (Ed.)

UNIV. OF WISCONSIN MILWAUKEE

Street address 1: 2200 E Kenwood Blvd
Street address 2: Ste EG80
Street address 3: Milwaukee
Street address state: WI
Zip/Postal code: 53211-3361
Country: USA
Mailing address: PO Box 413
Mailing city: Milwaukee
Mailing state: WI
Mailing zip: 53201-0413
General Phone: (414) 229-4578
General Fax: (414) 229-4579
Advertising Phone: (414) 229-5969
General/National Adv. E-mail: post@uwm.edu; post@uwmpost.com
Primary Website: www.uwmpost.com
Classified Equipment»
Personnel: Simon Bouwman (Bus. Mgr.); Kurt Raether (Adv. Mgr.); Kevin Lessmiller (Ed. in Chief)

OSHKOSH

UNIV. OF WISCONSIN OSHKOSH

Street address 1: 800 Algoma Blvd
Street address 3: Oshkosh

Street address state: WI
Zip/Postal code: 54901-3551
Country: USA
Mailing address: 800 Algoma Blvd
Mailing city: Oshkosh
Mailing state: WI
Mailing zip: 54901-8651
General Phone: (920) 424-3048
General Fax: (920) 424-0866
Primary Website: www.advancetitan.com
Published: Thur
Classified Equipment»
Personnel: Vince Filak (Advisor)

PLATTEVILLE

UNIV. OF WISCONSIN PLATTEVILLE

Street address 1: 1 University Plz
Street address 2: 618 Pioneer Tower
Street address 3: Platteville
Street address state: WI
Zip/Postal code: 53818-3001
Country: USA
Mailing address: 1 University Plz Stop 1
Mailing city: Platteville
Mailing state: WI
Mailing zip: 53818-3001
General Phone: (608) 342-1471
General Fax: (608) 342-1671
General/National Adv. E-mail: exponent@uwplatt.edu
Primary Website: www.uwpexponent.org
Year Established: 1889
Delivery Methods: Mail`Newsstand`Carrier
Published: Thur
Avg Free Circ: 3600
Classified Equipment»
Personnel: Becky Troy (Administrative assistant); Arthur Ranney (Advisor)

RIPON

RIPON COLLEGE

Street address 1: 300 W Seward St
Street address 3: Ripon
Street address state: WI
Zip/Postal code: 54971-1477
Country: USA
Mailing address: PO Box 248
Mailing city: Ripon
Mailing state: WI
Mailing zip: 54971-0248
General Phone: (920) 748-8126
General Fax: (920) 748-9262
Primary Website: www.riponcollegedays.com
Classified Equipment»
Personnel: Jonathan Bailey (Ed. in Chief); John Bailey (Asst. Ed.)

RIVER FALLS

UNIVERSITY OF WISCONSIN-RIVER FALLS

Street address 1: 410 S 3rd St
Street address 2: 310 North Hall
Street address 3: River Falls
Street address state: WI
Zip/Postal code: 54022-5010
County: Pierce
Country: USA
Mailing address: 410 S. Third St.
Mailing city: River Falls
Mailing state: WI
Mailing zip: 54022
General Phone: (715) 425-3169
General Fax: (715) 425-0658
General/National Adv. E-mail: journalism@uwrf.edu
Display Adv. E-mail: advertising@uwrfvoice.com
Editorial e-mail: editor@uwrfvoice.com
Primary Website: uwrfvoice.com
Year Established: 1916
Delivery Methods: Racks
Published: Fri
Avg Free Circ: 1000
Classified Equipment»
Personnel: Andris Straumanis (Advisor); Sandra Ellis (Chair)

SHEBOYGAN

LAKELAND COLLEGE

Street address 1: PO Box 359
Street address 3: Sheboygan
Street address state: WI
Zip/Postal code: 53082-0359
Country: USA
Mailing address: PO Box 359
Mailing city: Sheboygan
Mailing state: WI
Mailing zip: 53082-0359
General Phone: (920) 565-1316
General Fax: (920) 565-1344
General/National Adv. E-mail: mirror@lakeland.edu
Primary Website: www.lakelandmirror.com
Classified Equipment»
Personnel: Becky Meyer (Author); Ashley Paulson (Adv. Mgr.)

UNIV. OF WISCONSIN SHEBOYGAN

Street address 1: 1 University Dr
Street address 3: Sheboygan
Street address state: WI
Zip/Postal code: 53081-4760
Country: USA
Mailing address: 1 University Dr
Mailing city: Sheboygan
Mailing state: WI
Mailing zip: 53081-4789
General Phone: (920) 459-6600
General Fax: (920) 459-6602
General/National Adv. E-mail: shbinfo@uwc.edu
Editorial e-mail: shbvoice@uwc.edu
Primary Website: www.sheboygan.uwc.edu
Classified Equipment»

STEVENS POINT

UNIV. OF WISCONSIN STEVENS POINT

Street address 1: 1101 Reserve St
Street address 2: # 104
Street address 3: Stevens Point
Street address state: WI
Zip/Postal code: 54481-3868
Country: USA
Mailing address: 1101 Reserve Street 104 CAC
Mailing city: Stevens Point
Mailing state: WI
Mailing zip: 54481-3897
General Phone: (715) 346-3707
General Fax: (715) 346-4712
General/National Adv. E-mail: pointer@uwsp.edu
Primary Website: http://pointer.uwsp.edu
Classified Equipment»
Personnel: Liz Fakazis (Advisor); Steve Roeland (Ed. in Chief)

UNIV. OF WISCONSIN SUPERIOR

Street address 1: 1600 Catlin Ave
Street address 3: Superior
Street address state: WI
Zip/Postal code: 54880-2953
Country: USA
Mailing address: 1600 Catlin Ave
Mailing city: Superior
Mailing state: WI
Mailing zip: 54880-2954
General Phone: (715) 394-8438
General Fax: (715) 394-8454
General/National Adv. E-mail: stinger@uwsuper.edu
Primary Website: www.uwsuper-stinger.com
Classified Equipment»
Personnel: Joel Anderson (Advisor)

WAUKESHA

THE NEW PERSPECTIVE

Street address 1: 100 N East Ave
Street address 3: Waukesha
Street address state: WI
Zip/Postal code: 53186-3103
Country: USA
Mailing address: 1111 Sentry Dr
Mailing city: Waukesha
Mailing state: WI
Mailing zip: 53186-5965
General Phone: (262) 524-7351
General/National Adv. E-mail: perspect@carrollu.edu
Display Adv. E-mail: npadvertising@gmail.com
Editorial e-mail: persepct@carrollu.edu
Primary Website: www.thedigitalnp.com
Year Established: 1874
Special Editions: Welcome Week
Delivery Methods: Racks
Commercial printers: Y
Classified Equipment»

WAUSAU

UNIV. OF WISCONSIN CENTER MARATHON

Street address 1: 518 S 7th Ave
Street address 3: Wausau
Street address state: WI
Zip/Postal code: 54401-5362
Country: USA
Mailing address: 518 S 7th Ave
Mailing city: Wausau
Mailing state: WI
Mailing zip: 54401-5362
General Phone: (715) 261-6264
General Fax: (715) 261-6333
General/National Adv. E-mail: theforumuwmc@gmail.com
Primary Website: www.uwmcforum.com
Classified Equipment»
Personnel: Mark Parman (Advisor); Haley Zblewski (Ed. in Chief)

WHITEWATER

UNIV. OF WISCONSIN WHITEWATER

Street address 1: 800 W Main St
Street address 2: 66 University Ctr.
Street address 3: Whitewater
Street address state: WI
Zip/Postal code: 53190-1705
Country: USA
Mailing address: 66 University Ctr.
Mailing city: Whitewater
Mailing state: WI
Mailing zip: 53190
General Phone: (262) 472-5100
General Fax: (262) 472-5101
Display Adv. E-mail: rpads@uww.edu
Editorial e-mail: rp@uww.edu
Primary Website: www.royalpurplenews.com
Year Established: 1901
Delivery Methods: Racks
Classified Equipment»
Personnel: Sam Martino (Advisor); Kyle Geissler (Adviser)

WEST VIRGINIA

CONCORD COLLEGE

Street address 1: PO Box 1000
Street address 3: Athens
Street address state: WV
Zip/Postal code: 24712-1000
Country: USA
Mailing address: PO Box 1000
Mailing city: Athens
Mailing state: WV
Mailing zip: 24712-1000
General Phone: (304) 384-5364
General/National Adv. E-mail: concordian@concord.edu
Primary Website: www.cunewspaper.com
Classified Equipment»
Personnel: Lindsey Mullins (Advisor); Wendy Holdren (Ed. in Chief)

BETHANY COLLEGE

Street address 1: 31 E Campus Dr
Street address 3: Bethany
Street address state: WV
Zip/Postal code: 26032-3002
Country: USA
Mailing address: 31 E Campus Dr
Mailing city: Bethany
Mailing state: WV
Mailing zip: 26032-3002
General Phone: (304) 829-7951
General Fax: (304) 829-7950
General/National Adv. E-mail: tower@bethanywv.edu
Primary Website: www2.bethanywv.edu/tower
Classified Equipment»
Personnel: Mike King (Advisor)

UNIV. OF CHARLESTON

Street address 1: 2300 Maccorkle Ave SE
Street address 3: Charleston
Street address state: WV
Zip/Postal code: 25304-1045
Country: USA
Mailing address: 2300 Maccorkle Ave SE
Mailing city: Charleston
Mailing state: WV
Mailing zip: 25304-1099
General Phone: (304) 357-4716
General Fax: (304) 357-4988
Classified Equipment»
Personnel: Andy Spradling (Advisor); Ginny Bennett Helmick (Ed.)

GLENVILLE

GLENVILLE STATE COLLEGE

Street address 1: 200 High St
Street address 3: Glenville
Street address state: WV
Zip/Postal code: 26351-1200
Country: USA
General Phone: (304) 462-4133
General Fax: (304) 462-4407
General/National Adv. E-mail: news.paper@glenville.edu
Primary Website: www.glenville.edu/life/phoenix.php
Published: Thur
Published Other: Print edition twice a semester
Classified Equipment»
Personnel: Marjorie Stewart (Assistant Professor of English)

MARSHALL UNIVERSITY

Street address 1: 109 Communications Bldg
Street address 2: 1 John Marshall Dr.
Street address 3: Huntington
Street address state: WV
Zip/Postal code: 25755-0001
Country: USA
Mailing address: 109 Communications Building
Mailing city: Huntington
Mailing state: WV
Mailing zip: 25755-0001
General Phone: (304) 696-6696
General Fax: (304) 696-2732
Advertising Phone: (304) 526-2836
Editorial Phone: (304) 696-6696
Editorial Fax: (304) 696-2732
General/National Adv. E-mail: parthenon@marshall.edu
Display Adv. E-mail: parthenon@marshall.edu
Editorial e-mail: parthenon@marshall.edu
Primary Website: www.marshallparthenon.com
Year Established: 1898
Delivery Methods: Racks
Commercial printers: N
Published: Tues`Fri
Published Other: Print Tuesday and Friday, online 24-7.
Avg Free Circ: 6000
Classified Equipment»
Personnel: Sandy York (Adviser)

INSTITUTE

WEST VIRGINIA STATE UNIV.

Street address 1: 214 Wilson Student Union
Street address 3: Institute
Street address state: WV
Zip/Postal code: 25112
Country: USA
Mailing address: 214 Wilson Student Union
Mailing city: Institute
Mailing state: WV
Mailing zip: 25112-1000
General Phone: (304) 766-3212
General Fax: (304) 766-3309
Primary Website: www.wvstateu.edu/~yellowjacket
Classified Equipment»
Personnel: Robin Broughton (Advisor); Mary Casto (Ed. in Chief); Patrick Felton (Ed. in Chief)

WEST VIRGINIA UNIV. INST. OF TECHNOLOGY

Street address 1: PO Box 1
Street address 3: Montgomery
Street address state: WV
Zip/Postal code: 25136-0001
Country: USA
Mailing address: PO Box 1
Mailing city: Montgomery
Mailing state: WV
Mailing zip: 25136-0001
General Phone: (304) 442-3180
General Fax: (304) 442-3838
General/National Adv. E-mail: collegianwv@hotmail.com
Primary Website: collegian.wvutech.edu
Classified Equipment»
Personnel: Jim Kerrigan (Advisor); Emily Wilkinson (Ed.)

MORGANTOWN

WEST VIRGINIA UNIV.

Street address 1: 284 Prospect St
Street address 3: Morgantown
Street address state: WV
Zip/Postal code: 26505-5021
Country: USA
Mailing address: PO Box 6427
Mailing city: Morgantown
Mailing state: WV
Mailing zip: 26506-6427
General Phone: (304) 293-2540
General Fax: (304) 293-6857
Editorail Phone: (304) 293-5092
General/National Adv. E-mail: da-mail@mail.wvu.edu
Primary Website: www.da.wvu.edu
Classified Equipment»
Personnel: Alan R. Waters (Advisor)

PARKERSBURG

WEST VIRGINIA UNIV. PARKERSBURG

Street address 1: 300 Campus Dr
Street address 3: Parkersburg
Street address state: WV
Zip/Postal code: 26104-8647
Country: USA
Mailing address: 300 Campus Dr
Mailing city: Parkersburg
Mailing state: WV
Mailing zip: 26104-8647
General Phone: (304) 424-8247
General Fax: (304) 424-8315
Advertising Phone: (304) 424-8247
Editorail Phone: (304) 424-8247
General/National Adv. E-mail: chronicle@wvup.edu
Display Adv. E-mail: chronicle@wvup.edu
Editorial e-mail: chronicle@wvup.edu
Primary Website: http://issuu.com/wvuparkersburgchronicle
Year Established: 1969
Advertising (Open Inch Rate) Weekday/Saturday: $4 per column inch
Published: Thur
Avg Free Circ: 3500
Classified Equipment»
Personnel: Torie Jackson (Advisor)

PHILIPPI

ALDERSON-BROADDUS COLLEGE

Street address 1: 101 College Hill Dr
Street address 3: Philippi
Street address state: WV
Zip/Postal code: 26416-4600
Country: USA
Mailing address: 101 College Hill Dr
Mailing city: Philippi
Mailing state: WV
Mailing zip: 26416
General Phone: (304) 457-6357
General Fax: (304) 457-6239
Primary Website: www.ab.edu/performing_arts/battler_columns
Classified Equipment»
Personnel: Jim Wilkie (Advisor); Melissa Riffle (Asst. Ed.)

SALEM INTERNATIONAL UNIV.

Street address 1: 223 W Main St
Street address 3: Salem
Street address state: WV
Zip/Postal code: 26426-1227
Country: USA
Mailing address: 223 W Main St
Mailing city: Salem
Mailing state: WV
Mailing zip: 26426-1227
General Phone: (304) 326-1538
General Fax: (304) 782-1592
Classified Equipment»
Personnel: Nicole Michaelas (Advisor)

SHEPHERDSTOWN

SHEPHERD UNIVERSITY

Street address 1: PO Box 3210
Street address 3: Shepherdstown
Street address state: WV
Zip/Postal code: 25443-3210
Country: USA
Mailing address: PO Box 3210
Mailing city: Shepherdstown
Mailing state: WV
Mailing zip: 25443-3210
General Phone: (304) 876-5100
General Fax: (304) 876-5100
Advertising Phone: (304) 876-5687
Editorail Phone: (304) 876-5377
General/National Adv. E-mail: pickweb@shepherd.edu
Primary Website: www.picketonline.com
Classified Equipment»
Personnel: Jim Lewin (Advisor); Jeb Inge (Ed. in Chief)

OHIO VALLEY UNIVERSITY

Street address 1: 1 Campus View Dr
Street address 3: Vienna
Street address state: WV
Zip/Postal code: 26105-8000
Country: USA
Mailing address: 1 Campus View Dr
Mailing city: Vienna
Mailing state: WV
Mailing zip: 26105-8000
General Phone: (304) 865-6151
Primary Website: www.ovu.edu/site.cfm/newspaper.cfm
Classified Equipment»
Personnel: Philip Sturm (Advisor)

WEST LIBERTY

WEST LIBERTY UNIVERSITY

Street address 1: 208 Faculty Drive
Street address 2: Cub 153
Street address 3: West Liberty
Street address state: WV
Zip/Postal code: 26074
Country: USA
Mailing address: 208 Faculty Drive
Mailing city: West Liberty
Mailing state: WV
Mailing zip: 26074
General Phone: (304) 336-8873
General Fax: (304) 336-8323
Editorail Phone: (304) 336-8213
General/National Adv. E-mail: wltrumpet@wlsc.edu
Primary Website: westlibertylive.com/thetrumpet
Year Established: 1922
Published: Wed
Avg Free Circ: 1500
Classified Equipment»
Personnel: Tammie Beagle (Advisor)

WHEELING

WHEELING JESUIT UNIV.

Street address 1: 316 Washington Ave
Street address 3: Wheeling
Street address state: WV
Zip/Postal code: 26003-6243
Country: USA
Mailing address: 316 Washington Ave
Mailing city: Wheeling
Mailing state: WV
Mailing zip: 26003-6295
General Phone: (304) 243-2250
Editorial e-mail: news@wju.edu
Primary Website: www.wju.edu/cardinal
Classified Equipment»
Personnel: Becky Forney (Advisor)

CASPER

CASPER COLLEGE

Street address 1: 125 College Dr
Street address 2: # CE-109
Street address 3: Casper
Street address state: WY
Zip/Postal code: 82601-4612
Country: USA
Mailing address: 125 College Dr # CE-109
Mailing city: Casper
Mailing state: WY
Mailing zip: 82601-4699
General Phone: (307) 268-2100
General Fax: (307) 268-2203
Classified Equipment»
Personnel: Pete Vanhouten (Advisor); Derek Schroder (Ed.)

LARAMIE COUNTY CMTY. COLLEGE

Street address 1: 1400 E College Dr
Street address 3: Cheyenne
Street address state: WY
Zip/Postal code: 82007-3204
Country: USA
Mailing address: 1400 E. College Dr.
Mailing city: Cheyenne
Mailing state: WY
Mailing zip: 82007-3204
General Phone: (307) 778-1304
General/National Adv. E-mail: wingspan@lccc.wy.edu
Year Established: 1976
Published: Mthly
Avg Free Circ: 1000
Classified Equipment»
Personnel: J.L. O'Brien (Advisor); Jake Sherlock (Adviser)

LARAMIE

UNIV. OF WYOMING

Street address 1: 1000 E University Ave
Street address 2: Dept 3625
Street address 3: Laramie
Street address state: WY
Zip/Postal code: 82071-2000
Country: USA
Mailing address: 1000 E University Ave Dept 3625
Mailing city: Laramie
Mailing state: WY
Mailing zip: 82071-2000
General Phone: (307) 766-6190
General Fax: (307) 766-4027
Advertising Phone: (307) 766-6336
General/National Adv. E-mail: bi@uwyo.edu
Editorial e-mail: letters@brandingirononline.info
Primary Website: www.brandingirononline.info
Classified Equipment»
Personnel: Carry Berry-Smith (Advisor); Sasha Fahrenkops (Ed. in Chief)

POWELL

NORTHWEST COLLEGE

Street address 1: 231 W 6th St
Street address 3: Powell
Street address state: WY
Zip/Postal code: 82435-1898
Country: USA
Mailing address: 231 W 6th St Bldg 3
Mailing city: Powell
Mailing state: WY
Mailing zip: 82435-1898
General Phone: (307) 754-6438
General Fax: (307) 754-6700
Primary Website: www.northwesttrail.org
Classified Equipment»
Personnel: Rob Breeding (Advisor); Kayla Dumas (Ed.)

COLLEGE AND UNIVERSITY DEPARTMENTS OF JOURNALISM IN THE U.S.

ALASKA

UNIVERSITY OF ALASKA ANCHORAGE

Street address 1: 3211 Providence Dr.
Street address 3: Anchorage
Street address state: AK
Zip/Postal code: 99508
Mailing address: 3211 Providence Dr
Mailing city: Anchorage
Mailing state: AK
Mailing zip: 99508-4645
General Phone: (907) 786-4180
General Fax: (907) 786-4190
General/National Adv. E-mail: journalism@jpc.alaska.edu
Primary Website: www.jpc.uaa.alaska.edu
Classified Equipment»
Personnel: Fred Pearce (Chair)

UNIVERSITY OF ALASKA AT FAIRBANKS

Street address 1: PO Box 756120
Street address 3: Fairbanks
Street address state: AK
Zip/Postal code: 99775
Mailing address: PO Box 756120
Mailing city: Fairbanks
Mailing state: AK
Mailing zip: 99775-61
General Phone: (907) 474-7761
General Fax: (907) 474-6326
General/National Adv. E-mail: fyjnb@uaf.edu
Classified Equipment»
Personnel: Charles Mason (Chair)

ALABAMA

AUBURN UNIVERSITY

Street address 1: 217 Tichenor Hall
Street address 3: Auburn
Street address state: AL
Zip/Postal code: 36849-5211
Mailing address: 217 Tichenor Hall
Mailing city: Auburn
Mailing state: AL
Mailing zip: 36849-0001
General Phone: (334) 844-2727
General Fax: (334) 844-4573
Primary Website: media.cla.auburn.edu/cmjn
Classified Equipment»
Personnel: Mary Helen Brown (Chair/Assoc. Prof.); Susan Brinson (Prof.); George Plasketes (Prof.); Ed Williams (Prof.); J. Emmett Winn (Prof.); Brigitta Brunner (Assoc. Prof.); Nan Fairley (Assoc. Prof.); Margaret Fitch-Hauser (Assoc. Prof.); SeiHill Kim (Assoc. Prof.); Judy Sheppard (Assoc. Prof.); David Sutton (Assoc. Prof.); Debra Worthington (Assoc. Prof.); Robert Agne (Asst. Prof.); Jennifer Wood Adams (Asst. Prof.); John Carvalho (Asst. Prof.); Kristen Hoerl (Asst. Prof.); Hollie Lavenstein (Asst. Prof.); Chris Walker (Asst. Prof.); Kevin Smith (Asst. Prof.); Norman Youngblood (Asst. Prof.)

SAMFORD UNIVERSITY

Street address 1: Dept. of Journalism & Mass Communication
Street address 3: Birmingham
Street address state: AL
Zip/Postal code: 35229
Mailing address: Dept of Journalism & Mass Communication
Mailing city: Birmingham
Mailing state: AL
Mailing zip: 35229-0001
General Phone: (205) 726-2465
General Fax: (205) 726-2586
General/National Adv. E-mail: rnankney@samford.edu
Classified Equipment»
Personnel: Bernie Ankney (Chair)

JACKSONVILLE STATE UNIVERSITY

Street address 1: 700 Pelham Rd. N.
Street address 3: Jacksonville
Street address state: AL
Zip/Postal code: 36265-1602
Mailing address: 700 Pelham Rd N
Mailing city: Jacksonville
Mailing state: AL
Mailing zip: 36265-1623
General Phone: (256) 782-5300
General Fax: (256) 782-8175
General/National Adv. E-mail: kharbor@jsu.edu
Primary Website: www.jsu.edu/depart/edprof/comm
Classified Equipment»
Personnel: Kingsley O. Harbor (Chair/Prof.); Augustine Ihator (Prof.); Jerry Chandler (Asst. Prof./Internship Coord.); Jeffrey Hedrick (Asst. Prof.); Mike Stedham (Part-time Fac./Mgr., Stud. Media); Pamela Hill (Adj. Fac.); Laura Tutor (Adj. Fac.); Mickey Shadrix (Adj. Fac.); William Meehan

SPRING HILL COLLEGE

Street address 1: 4000 Dauphin St
Street address 3: Mobile
Street address state: AL
Zip/Postal code: 36608-1780
County: Mobile
Country: USA
Mailing address: 4000 Dauphin St
Mailing city: Mobile
Mailing state: AL
Mailing zip: 36608-1791
General Phone: (251) 380-3850
General Fax: (251) 460-2185
General/National Adv. E-mail: shcmedia@shc.edu; sbabington@shc.edu
Display Adv. E-mail: hillian@stumail.shc.edu
Editorial e-mail: hillian@stumail.shc.edu
Primary Website: http://newswire.shc.edu/
Delivery Methods: Racks
Commercial printers: Y
Published: Thur
Classified Equipment»
Personnel: Stuart Babington (Advisor); J.L. Stevens II (Integrated Multimedia Center (IMC) Operations Mgr and Student Media adviser)

UNIVERSITY OF SOUTH ALABAMA

Street address 1: 1000 University Commons
Street address 3: Mobile
Street address state: AL
Zip/Postal code: 36688
Mailing address: 1000 University Commons
Mailing city: Mobile
Mailing state: AL
Mailing zip: 36688
General Phone: (251) 380-2800
General Fax: (251) 380-2850
General/National Adv. E-mail: glwilson@usouthal.edu
Classified Equipment»
Personnel: Gerald L. Wilson (Prof./Chair); Donald K. Wright (Prof.); James L. Aucoin (Assoc. Prof.); Steven C. Rockwell (Assoc. Prof.); Richard Ward (Assoc. Prof.); James F. Carstens (Asst. Prof.); Melva Kearney (Asst. Prof.); Patricia Mark (Asst. Prof.); Jeanne McPherson (Asst. Prof.); James M. Rosene (Asst. Prof.); Genevieve Dardeau (Instr.); April Dupree Taylor (Instr.); Heather Terry (Instr.); Jerold Aust (Lectr.); Carolyn Combs (Lectr.); Dre Comiskey (Lectr.); Jill Haynes (Lectr.); Kelly Kendall (Lectr.); Maureen Maclay (Lectr.); Jennifer Penry (Lectr.)

ALABAMA STATE UNIV.

Street address 1: 915 S Jackson St
Street address 3: Montgomery
Street address state: AL
Zip/Postal code: 36104-5716
Country: USA
Mailing address: PO Box 271
Mailing city: Montgomery
Mailing state: AL
Mailing zip: 36101-0271
General Phone: (334) 229-4419
General Fax: (334) 229-4934
General/National Adv. E-mail: ayoleke@aol.com
Primary Website: www.thehornettribune.com
Classified Equipment»
Personnel: David Okeowo (Prof./Chair); Bryan Weaver (Exec. Ed.); E.K. Daufin (Prof.); Julian K. Johnson (Mng. Ed.); Tracy Banks (Assoc. Prof./Dir., Forensics); James B. Lucy (News Ed.); Elizabeth Fitts (Assoc. Prof.); Richard Emmanuel (Asst. Prof.); James Adams (Instr.); Coke Ellington (Instr.); Valerie Heard (Instr.); Jonathan Himsel (Instr.); John Moore (Instr.); Walter Murphy (Instr.); Larry Owens (Instr.)

TROY STATE UNIVERSITY

Street address 1: 101 Wallace Hall
Street address 3: Troy
Street address state: AL
Zip/Postal code: 36082
Mailing address: 101 Wallace Hall
Mailing city: Troy
Mailing state: AL
Mailing zip: 36082-0001
General Phone: (334) 670-3289
General Fax: (334) 670-3707
General/National Adv. E-mail: info@jschool.troyst.edu
Classified Equipment»
Personnel: Steven Padgett (Dir.)

UNIVERSITY OF ALABAMA

Street address 1: 490 Phifer Hall Ste. 490
Street address 2: Corner Colonial Dr., Univ. Blvd.
Street address 3: Tuscaloosa
Street address state: AL
Zip/Postal code: 35487-0172
Mailing address: PO Box 870172
Mailing city: Tuscaloosa
Mailing state: AL
Mailing zip: 35487-0172
General Phone: (205) 348-5520
General Fax: (205) 348-3836
General/National Adv. E-mail: chammond@ua.edu
Classified Equipment»
Personnel: Loy Singleton (Dean); Elizabeth Aversa (Prof./Dir., School of Library & Information Studies); Bruce Berger (Prof./Chair, Adv./PR); Rick Bragg (Prof.); Jennings Bryant (Prof./Reagan Chair, Assoc. Dean, Grad. Studies); Jeremy Butler (Prof.); Matthew Bunker (Phifer Prof.); Karen J. Cartee (Prof.); Gary Copeland (Prof./Chair, Telecommunication/Film); Margaret Dalton (Bristol-EBSCO Prof.); William Evans (Prof./Dir., Institute for Comm. & Information Research); William Gonzenbach (Prof.); Tom Harris (Prof.); Marsha Houston (Prof.); Steven Miller (Prof.); Yorgo Pasadeos (Prof.); Joseph Phelps (Prof./Phifer Prof.); David Sloan (Prof.); Beth Bennett (Assoc. Prof./Chair, Commun. Studies); Kimberly Bissell (Assoc. Prof.)

ARKANSAS

HENDERSON STATE UNIVERSITY

Street address 1: 1100 Henderson St.
Street address 3: Arkadelphia
Street address state: AR
Zip/Postal code: 71999-0001
Mailing address: 1100 Henderson St
Mailing city: Arkadelphia
Mailing state: AR
Mailing zip: 71999-0001
General Phone: (870) 230-5182
General Fax: (870) 230-5144
General/National Adv. E-mail: taylorm@hsu.edu
Classified Equipment»
Personnel: Michael Miller (Chair); Michael Ray Taylor (Dir., Print Journalism)

UNIVERSITY OF CENTRAL ARKANSAS

Street address 1: Dept. of Speech, Theatre & Mass Commun.
Street address 3: Conway
Street address state: AR
Zip/Postal code: 72035
Mailing address: Dept of Speech Theatre & Mass Commun
Mailing city: Conway
Mailing state: AR
Mailing zip: 72035-0001
General Phone: (501) 450-3162
General Fax: (501) 450-3296
General/National Adv. E-mail: bobw@mail.uca.edu
Classified Equipment»
Personnel: Bob Willenbrink (Chair)

UNIVERSITY OF ARKANSAS

Street address 1: 116 Kimpel Hall
Street address 3: Fayetteville
Street address state: AR
Zip/Postal code: 72701
Mailing address: 116 Kimpel Hall
Mailing city: Fayetteville
Mailing state: AR
Mailing zip: 72701
General Phone: (479) 575-3601
General Fax: (479) 575-4314
General/National Adv. E-mail: pwatkins@uark.edu
Primary Website: www.uark.edu/depts/jourinfo/public_html/
Classified Equipment»
Personnel: Patsy Watkins (Chair/Assoc. Prof.); Dale Carpenter (Prof.); Larry Foley (Prof.); Hoyt Purvis (Prof.); Jan LeBlanc Wicks (Prof.); Gerald Jordan (Assoc. Prof.); Phyllis Miller (Assoc. Prof.); Louise Montgomery (Assoc. Prof.); Rick Stockdell (Assoc. Prof.); Ignatius Fosu (Asst. Prof.); Eric Gorder (Instr.); Kim Martin (Instr.); Katherine Shurlds (Instr.); Roy Reed (Prof. Emer.)

JONESBORO

ARKANSAS STATE UNIVERSITY

Street address 1: 114 Cooley Dr., Rm. 331
Street address 3: Jonesboro
Street address state: AR
Zip/Postal code: 72401
Mailing address: PO Box 540
Mailing city: State University
Mailing state: AR
Mailing zip: 72467-0540
General Phone: (870) 972-2468
General Fax: (870) 972-3856
Primary Website: comm.astate.edu
Classified Equipment»
Personnel: Russell E. Shain (Dean/Prof.); Osabuohien Amienyi (Chair, RTV/Prof.); Tom Baglan (Chair, Commun. Studies/Prof.); Gilbert L. Fowler (Prof.); Mary Jackson-Pitts (Prof.); Lillie Fears (Assoc. Prof.); Joel T. Gambill (Assoc. Prof./Chair, Journ.); Jack Zibluk (Assoc. Prof.); Carey Byars (Asst. Prof.); Holly Byars (Asst. Prof.); Linda Clark (Asst. Prof.); Sandra Combs (Asst. Prof.); Robert Franklin (Asst. Prof.); Myleea Hill (Asst. Prof.); Matt Ramsey (Asst. Prof.); Mathew Thatcher (Asst. Prof.); Marcilene Thompson-Hayes (Asst. Prof.); Lily Zeng (Asst. Prof.); Alex Brown (Instr.); Michael B. Doyle (Instr.)

UNIVERSITY OF ARKANSAS AT LITTLE ROCK

Street address 1: 2801 S. University
Street address 3: Little Rock
Street address state: AR
Zip/Postal code: 72204

Mailing address: 2801 S University Ave
Mailing city: Little Rock
Mailing state: AR
Mailing zip: 72204-1000
General Phone: (501) 569-3250
General Fax: (501) 569-8371
Primary Website: www.ualr.edu
Classified Equipment»
Personnel: Jamie Byrne (Dir./Assoc. Prof.); David M. Guerra (Prof.); Bruce L. Plopper (Prof.); Jeanne Rollberg (Assoc. Prof.); Gregory Stefaniak (Assoc. Prof.); Tim Edwards (Asst. Prof.); Mark Giese (Asst. Prof.); Carlton Rhodes (Asst. Prof.); Kristie A. Swain (Asst. Prof.); David Weekley (Instr.); Ron Breeding (Part-time Lectr.); Frank Fellone (Part-time Lectr.); Ben Fry (Part-time Lectr.); John Paul Jones (Part-time Lectr.); Dixie Martin (Part-time Lectr.); Robert Pest (Part-time Lectr.); J.J. Thompson (Part-time Lectr.); Wally Tucker (Part-time Lectr.); Theresa Wallent (Part-time Lectr.); Edward Jay Friedlander (Fac. Emer.)

ARKANSAS TECH UNIVERSITY

Street address 1: T-1, 1209 N. Fargo Ave.
Street address 3: Russellville
Street address state: AR
Zip/Postal code: 72801
Mailing address: T-1, 1209 N. Fargo Ave.
Mailing city: Russellville
Mailing state: AR
Mailing zip: 72801
General Phone: (479) 964-0890
General Fax: (479) 964-0899
General/National Adv. E-mail: dvocate@atu.edu
Classified Equipment»
Personnel: Donna R. Vocate (Head/Prof.); Seok Kang (Assoc. Prof.); Hanna Norton (Assoc. Prof.); Warren Byrd (Asst. Prof.); Anthony Caton (Asst. Prof.); Tommy Mumert (Asst. Prof.); Russ Hancock (Instr.)

HARDING UNIVERSITY

Street address 1: Reynolds Center, 501 S. Burks Blvd.
Street address 3: Searcy
Street address state: AR
Zip/Postal code: 72143
Mailing address: PO Box 10765
Mailing city: Searcy
Mailing state: AR
Mailing zip: 72149-0001
General Phone: (501) 279-4445
General Fax: (501) 279-4605
General/National Adv. E-mail: communication@harding.edu
Classified Equipment»
Personnel: Michael L. James (Dean/Prof.); Jack R. Shock (Prof.); Steven Frye (Prof.); Kelly Elander (Assoc. Prof.); Dutch Hoggatt (Assoc. Prof.); Jim Miller (Asst. Prof.); Steve Shaner (Asst. Prof.); Jeremy Beauchamp (Instr.); Bob Ritchie (Instr.); Mark Prior (Adj.)

JOHN BROWN UNIV.

Street address 1: 2000 W University St
Street address 3: Siloam Springs
Street address state: AR
Zip/Postal code: 72761-2112
Country: USA
Mailing address: 2000 W University St
Mailing city: Siloam Springs
Mailing state: AR
Mailing zip: 72761-2121
General Phone: (479) 524-7255
General Fax: (479) 524-7394
General/National Adv. E-mail: advocate@jbu.edu
Primary Website: advoacte.jbu.edu
Classified Equipment»
Personnel: Candy Gregor (Assistant Professor of Communication Faculty adviser for the Threefold Advocate); KJ Roh (Executive Editor of the Threefold Advocate)

ARIZONA

NORTHERN ARIZONA UNIVERSITY

Street address 1: PO Box 5619
Street address 3: Flagstaff
Street address state: AZ
Zip/Postal code: 86011-5619
Mailing address: PO Box 5619
Mailing city: Flagstaff
Mailing state: AZ
Mailing zip: 86011-0164
General Phone: (928) 523-2232
General Fax: (928) 523-1505
General/National Adv. E-mail: school.communication@nau.edu
Primary Website: www.comm.nau.edu
Classified Equipment»
Personnel: Tom Knights (Dir.)

ARIZONA STATE UNIVERSITY

Street address 1: 555 N. Central Ave.
Street address 3: Tempe
Street address state: AZ
Zip/Postal code: 85004-1248
Mailing address: 555 N Central Ave
Mailing city: Phoenix
Mailing state: AZ
Mailing zip: 85004-1247
General Phone: (602) 496-3867
General Fax: (602) 496-7041
General/National Adv. E-mail: cronkiteinfol@asu.edu
Classified Equipment»
Personnel: Christopher Callahan (Dean); John E. Craft (Prof.); Stephen K. Doig (Prof./Knight Chair in Journ.); Donald G. Godfrey (Prof.); Bruce D. Merrill (Prof./Dir., Media Research Program); Edward J. Sylvester (Prof.); George Watson (Prof.); Mike Pignataro (Assoc. Prof.); Marianne Barrett (Assoc. Prof.); Sharon Bramlett-Solomon (Class Manager); Mary-Lou Galician (Assoc. Prof.); Fran Matera (Assoc. Prof.); Joseph A. Russomanno (Assoc. Prof./Dir., Grad. Studies); Dennis Russell (Assoc. Prof.); Dina Gavrilos (Asst. Prof.); Carol Schwalbe (Asst. Prof.); William Silcock (Asst. Prof.); Xu Wu (Asst. Prof.); Bruce D. Itule (Clinical Prof.); Frederic A. Leigh (Clinical Prof./Assoc. Dir.)

UNIVERSITY OF ARIZONA

Street address 1: 845 N. Park Ave.
Street address 3: Tucson
Street address state: AZ
Zip/Postal code: 85721-0158
Mailing address: 845 N Park Ave
Mailing city: Tucson
Mailing state: AZ
Mailing zip: 85719-4871
General Phone: (520) 621-7556
General Fax: (520) 621-7557
General/National Adv. E-mail: journal@email.arizona.edu
Primary Website: www.journalism.arizona.edu
Classified Equipment»
Personnel: Jacqueline E. Sharkey (Head/Soldwedel Family Prof./Prof.); Terry Wimmer (Prof.); Bruce Itule (Prof.); Shahira Fahmy (Assoc. Prof.); William F. Greer (Assoc. Prof. Emer.); Alan Weisman (Assoc. Prof.); Maggy Zanger (Assoc. Prof.); David Cuillier (Asst. Prof.); Celeste Gonz[illegible]lez de Bustamante (Asst. Prof.); Kevin R. Kemper (Asst. Prof.); Susan Knight (Asst. Prof.); Linda Lumsden (Asst. Prof.); Jeannine Relly (Asst. Prof.); Jay Rochlin (Asst. Prof.); Kim Newton (Asst. Prof.); Steve Auslander (Instr.); Rhonda Bodfield Bloom (Instr.); Mark Evans (Instr.); Tom Beal (Instr.); Cathalena Burch (Instr.)

CALIFORNIA

PACIFIC UNION COLLEGE

Street address 1: Communication Dept.
Street address 3: Angwin
Street address state: CA
Zip/Postal code: 94508
Mailing address: Communication Dept.
Mailing city: Angwin
Mailing state: CA
Mailing zip: 94508
General Phone: (707) 965-6437
General Fax: (707) 965-6624
Primary Website: www.puc.edu/Departments/Communication
Classified Equipment»
Personnel: Jennifer Wareham Best (Chair)

HUMBOLDT STATE UNIVERSITY

Street address 1: 1 Harpst St.
Street address 3: Arcata
Street address state: CA
Zip/Postal code: 95521
Mailing address: 1 Harpst St
Mailing city: Arcata
Mailing state: CA
Mailing zip: 95521-8299
General Phone: (707) 826-4775
General Fax: (707) 826-4770
General/National Adv. E-mail: mcmaster@humboldt.edu
Classified Equipment»
Personnel: Mark Larson (Chair/Prof.); Craig Klein (Prof.); George Estrada (Assoc. Prof.); Marcy Burstiner (Asst. Prof.); Vicky Sama (Asst. Prof.)

MENLO COLLEGE

Street address 1: 1000 El Camino Real
Street address 3: Atherton
Street address state: CA
Zip/Postal code: 94027-4300
County: San Mateo County
Country: USA
Mailing address: 1000 El Camino Real
Mailing city: Atherton
Mailing state: CA
Mailing zip: 94027-4301
General Phone: (650) 543-3786
General/National Adv. E-mail: pr@menlo.edu
Primary Website: www.menlo.edu
Classified Equipment»
Personnel: Priscila de Souza (Dean of Enrollment Management)

UNIVERSITY OF CALIFORNIA AT BERKELEY

Street address 1: North Gate Hall, UC
Street address 3: Berkeley
Street address state: CA
Zip/Postal code: 94720
Mailing address: N Gate Hall Uc
Mailing city: Berkeley
Mailing state: CA
Mailing zip: 94720-0001
General Phone: (510) 642-3383
General Fax: (501) 643-9136
Classified Equipment»

CALIFORNIA STATE UNIVERSITY, DOMINGUEZ HILLS

Street address 1: 1000 E. Victoria
Street address 3: Carson
Street address state: CA
Zip/Postal code: 90747
Mailing address: 1000 E Victoria
Mailing city: Carson
Mailing state: CA
Mailing zip: 90747-0001
General Phone: (310) 243-3313
General Fax: (310) 243-3779
General/National Adv. E-mail: ewhetmore@csudh.edu
Classified Equipment»
Personnel: Edward Whetmore (Chair)

CALIFORNIA STATE UNIVERSITY, CHICO

Street address 1: Tehama Hall
Street address 3: Chico
Street address state: CA
Zip/Postal code: 95929-0145
Mailing address: Tehama Hall
Mailing city: Chico
Mailing state: CA
Mailing zip: 95929-0001
General Phone: (530) 898-4015
General Fax: (530) 898-4345
Classified Equipment»
Personnel: Phyllis Fernlund (Dean)

CALIFORNIA STATE UNIVERSITY, FRESNO

Street address 1: 225 E. San Ramon Ave., M/S MF 10
Street address 3: Fresno
Street address state: CA
Zip/Postal code: 93740-8029
Mailing address: 225 E San Ramon Ave MS MF10
Mailing city: Fresno
Mailing state: CA
Mailing zip: 93740-0001
General Phone: (559) 278-2087
General Fax: (559) 278-4995
General/National Adv. E-mail: sallyan@csufresno.edu
Classified Equipment»
Personnel: Donald M. Priest (Chair); Rich Marshall (General Manager)

CALIFORNIA STATE UNIVERSITY, FULLERTON

Street address 1: PO Box 6846
Street address 3: Fullerton
Street address state: CA
Zip/Postal code: 92834-6846
Mailing address: PO Box 6846
Mailing city: Fullerton
Mailing state: CA
Mailing zip: 92834-6846
General Phone: (714) 278-3517
General Fax: (714) 278-2209
Primary Website: communications.fullerton.edu
Classified Equipment»
Personnel: Anthony R. Fellow (Chair/Prof.); Jeff Brody (Prof.); David DeVries (Prof./Coord., Photocommunications); Cynthia King (Prof.); Paul Lester (Prof.); Coral Ohl (Prof.); Rick Pullen (Prof./Dean); Anthony Rimmer (Prof.); Shay Sayre (Prof./Early Ret. Prog.); Edgar Trotter (Prof.); Diane Witmer (Prof./Vice Chair, Grad. Coord.); Fred Zandpour (Prof./Assoc. Dean); Olan Farnall (Assoc. Prof.); Carolyn Johnson (Assoc. Prof./Early Ret. Prog.); Kuen-Hee Ju-Pak (Assoc. Prof./Coord., Advertising); Dean Kazoleas (Assoc. Prof.); Nancy Snow (Assoc. Prof.); Andi Stein (Assoc. Prof./Coord., Journalism); Carol Ames (Asst. Prof.); Assaf Avni (Asst. Prof.)

CALIFORNIA STATE UNIVERSITY, HAYWARD

Street address 1: 25800 Carlos Bee Blvd.
Street address 3: Hayward
Street address state: CA
Zip/Postal code: 94542
Mailing address: 25800 Carlos Bee Blvd
Mailing city: Hayward
Mailing state: CA
Mailing zip: 94542-3000
General Phone: (510) 885-3292
General Fax: (510) 885-4099
General/National Adv. E-mail: jhammerb@csuhayward.edu
Classified Equipment»
Personnel: John Hammerback (Interim Chair)

BIOLA UNIVERSITY

Street address 1: 13800 Biola Ave
Street address 3: La Mirada
Street address state: CA
Zip/Postal code: 90639-0002
Country: USA
Mailing address: 13800 Biola Ave
Mailing city: La Mirada
Mailing state: CA
Mailing zip: 90639-0001
General Phone: (562) 906-4569
General Fax: (562) 906-4515
Advertising Phone: (562) 587-7339
General/National Adv. E-mail: lily.park@biola.edu
Display Adv. E-mail: chimes.advertising@biola.edu
Primary Website: chimes.biola.edu
Published: Thur
Classified Equipment»
Personnel: Michael A. Longinow (Chair/Prof.); Sarah Sjoberg (Advertising Manager); J. Douglas Tarpley

(Prof.); Michael Bower (Assoc. Prof.); Tamara Welter (Asst. Prof.); James Hirsen (Instr.); Chi-Chung Keung (Instr.); Mark Landsbaum (Instr.); Greg Schneider (Instr.); Melissa Nunnally (Instr.)

CALIFORNIA STATE UNIVERSITY, LONG BEACH

Street address 1: 1250 Bellflower Blvd.
Street address 3: Long Beach
Street address state: CA
Zip/Postal code: 90840-4601
Mailing address: 1250 Bellflower Blvd
Mailing city: Long Beach
Mailing state: CA
Mailing zip: 90840-0004
General Phone: (562) 985-4981
General Fax: (562) 985-5300
Classified Equipment»
Personnel: Raul Reis (Interim Chair/Assoc. Prof.); William Babcock (Prof.); William Mulligan (Prof.); Emma Phillingane (Prof.); Christopher Burnett (Asst. Prof.); Jennifer Fleming (Asst. Prof.); Heloiza Herscovitz (Asst. Prof.); Christopher Karadjov (Asst. Prof.); Carla Yarbrough (Asst. Prof.); Judith Frutig (Lectr.); Barbara Kingsley (Lectr.); Amara Aguilar (Part-time Fac.); Lee Brown (Part-time Fac.); John Canalis (Part-time Fac.); Henrietta Charles (Part-time Fac.); Monica Edwards (Part-time Fac.); David Ferrell (Part-time Fac.); Daniel Garvey (Part-time Fac.); Greg Hardesty (Part-time Fac.); Cees Kendall (Part-time Fac.)

CALIFORNIA STATE UNIVERSITY, LOS ANGELES

Street address 1: Music 104, 5151 State University Dr.
Street address 3: Los Angeles
Street address state: CA
Zip/Postal code: 90032
Mailing address: 5151 State University Dr Music 104
Mailing city: Los Angeles
Mailing state: CA
Mailing zip: 90032-4226
General Phone: (323) 343-4200
General Fax: (323) 343-6467
Classified Equipment»
Newspaper (for newspapers group): California State Univ., Los Angeles

UNIVERSITY OF SOUTHERN CALIFORNIA

Street address 1: 3502 Watt Way, ASC 325
Street address 3: Los Angeles
Street address state: CA
Zip/Postal code: 90089-0281
Mailing address: 3502 Watts Way Asc 325
Mailing city: Los Angeles
Mailing state: CA
Mailing zip: 90089-0054
General Phone: (213) 740-3914
General Fax: (213) 740-8624
General/National Adv. E-mail: ascquery@usc.edu
Primary Website: www.annenberg.usc.edu
Classified Equipment»
Personnel: Geneva Overholser (Dir./Annenberg Family Chair in Commun. Leadership/Univ. Prof.); Jay T. Harris (Wallis Annenberg Chair in Journalism and Democracy/Prof.); Diane Winston (Knight Chair in Media and Religion/Assoc. Prof.); Geoffrey Cowan (Prof./Dean, Annenberg School for Communication); K.C. Cole (Prof.); Ed Cray (Prof.); Felix Gutierrez (Prof.); Bryce Nelson (Prof.); Michael Parks (Prof.); Joe Saltzman (Prof.); Philip Seib (Prof.); Roberto Suro (Prof.); Patricia Dean (Prof., Professional Practice/ Assoc. Dir.); Gerald Swerling (Prof., Professional Practice); William Cells (Assoc. Prof.); Jonathan Kotler (Assoc. Prof.); Josh Kun (Assoc. Prof.); Judy Muller (Assoc. Prof.); Larry Pryor (Assoc. Prof.); Sandy Tolan (Assoc. Prof.)

PEPPERDINE UNIVERSITY

Street address 1: Communication Div.
Street address 3: Malibu
Street address state: CA
Zip/Postal code: 90263
Mailing address: Communication Div.
Mailing city: Malibu
Mailing state: CA
Mailing zip: 90263
General Phone: (310) 456-4211
General Fax: (310) 456-3083
General/National Adv. E-mail: robert.chandler@pepperdine.edu
Classified Equipment»
Personnel: Robert C. Chandler (Chair)

SAINT MARY'S COLLEGE OF CALIFORNIA

Street address 1: Dept. of Communications
Street address 3: Moraga
Street address state: CA
Zip/Postal code: 94575
Mailing address: Dept. of Communications
Mailing city: Moraga
Mailing state: CA
Mailing zip: 94575
General Phone: (510) 631-4000
General Fax: (510) 631-0938
Classified Equipment»
Personnel: Michael A. Russo (Chair)

CALIFORNIA STATE UNIVERSITY, NORTHRIDGE

Street address 1: 18111 Nordhoff St
Street address 3: Northridge
Street address state: CA
Zip/Postal code: 91330-0001
Country: USA
Mailing address: 18111 Nordhoff St
Mailing city: Northridge
Mailing state: CA
Mailing zip: 91330-8200
General Phone: (818) 677-3135
General Fax: (818) 677-3438
Advertising Phone: 818-677-2998
Editorail Phone: (818) 677-2915
Display Adv. E-mail: ads@sundial.csun.edu
Editorial e-mail: editor@csun.edu
Primary Website: www.csun.edu
Year Established: 1957
Delivery Methods: Racks
Published: Mon`Tues`Wed`Thur
Avg Free Circ: 6000
Classified Equipment»
Personnel: Kent Kirkton (Chair/Prof.); Melissa Lalum (Pub.); Susan Henry (Prof.); Jody Holcomb (Gen. Mgr.); Maureen Rubin (Prof.); Rick Marks (Assoc. Prof.); Loren Townsley (Editor); Jose Luis Benavides (Asst. Prof.); David Blumenkrantz (Asst. Prof.); Linda Bowen (Asst. Prof.); Jim Hill (Asst. Prof.); Melissa Wall (Asst. Prof.); Lori Baker-Schena (Lectr.); Jerry Jacobs (Prof. Emer.); DeWayne Johnson (Prof. Emer.); Lawrence Schneider (Prof. Emer.); Joe Giampietro (Part-time Fac.); Henrietta Charles (Part-time Fac.); Jeffrey Duclos (Part-time Fac.); Barbara Eisenstock (Part-time Fac.); Mariel Garza (Part-time Fac.); Keith Goldstein (Part-time Fac.); Lincoln Harrison (Part-time Fac.)

CALIFORNIA STATE POLYTECHNIC UNIVERSITY, POMONA

Street address 1: 3801 W. Temple Ave.
Street address 3: Pomona
Street address state: CA
Zip/Postal code: 91768-4007
Mailing address: 3801 W Temple Ave
Mailing city: Pomona
Mailing state: CA
Mailing zip: 91768-2557
General Phone: (909) 869-3520
General Fax: (909) 869-4823
General/National Adv. E-mail: rakallan@csupomona.edu
Classified Equipment»
Personnel: Richard A. Kallan (Chair); Debra Shea

CALIFORNIA STATE UNIVERSITY, SACRAMENTO

Street address 1: 6000 J St.
Street address 3: Sacramento
Street address state: CA
Zip/Postal code: 95819-6070
Mailing address: 6000 J St
Mailing city: Sacramento
Mailing state: CA
Mailing zip: 95819-6000
General Phone: (916) 278-5340
General/National Adv. E-mail: valsmith@saclink.csus.edu
Classified Equipment»
Personnel: Val Smith (Chair)

POINT LOMA NAZARENE UNIV.

Street address 1: 3900 Lomaland Dr
Street address 3: San Diego
Street address state: CA
Zip/Postal code: 92106-2810
Country: USA
Mailing address: 3900 Lomaland Dr
Mailing city: San Diego
Mailing state: CA
Mailing zip: 92106-2899
General Phone: (619) 849-2444
General Fax: (619) 849-7009
General/National Adv. E-mail: news@pointweekly.com; sports@pointweekly.com; advertising@pointweekly.com
Primary Website: www.pointweekly.com
Classified Equipment»
Personnel: Stephanie Gant (Adv. Mgr.); Dean Nelson (Journalism Dir.); Coco Jones (Ed. in Chief); Nathan Scharn (Features Ed.)

SAN DIEGO STATE UNIVERSITY

Street address 1: 5500 Campanile Dr.
Street address 3: San Diego
Street address state: CA
Zip/Postal code: 92182-4561
Mailing address: 5500 Campanile Dr
Mailing city: San Diego
Mailing state: CA
Mailing zip: 92182-0003
General Phone: (619) 594-5450
General Fax: (619) 594-6246
General/National Adv. E-mail: jmsdesk@mail.sdsu.edu
Classified Equipment»
Personnel: Diane Borden (Dir./Prof.); Joel Davis (Prof.); David Dozier (Prof.); Bill Eadie (Prof.); Barbara Mueller (Prof.); Tim Wulfemeyer (Prof.); Bey-Ling Sha (Assoc. Prof.); Mei Zhong (Assoc. Prof.); Noah Arceneaux (Asst. Prof.); Amy Schmitz Weiss (Asst. Prof.); Valerie Barker (Lectr.); Lora Cicalo (Man. Ed.); Rebecca Coates Nee (Lectr.); David Coddon (Lectr.); John Eger (Lectr./ Van Deerlin Prof. of Commun. & Pub. Policy); David Feldman (Lectr.); Chad Harris (Lectr.); Martin Kruming (Lectr.); Lanie Lockwood (Lectr.); Jim McBride (Lectr.)

SAN FRANCISCO STATE UNIVERSITY

Street address 1: 1600 Holloway Ave
Street address 3: San Francisco
Street address state: CA
Zip/Postal code: 94132-1722
Country: USA
Mailing address: 1600 Holloway Ave # 4200
Mailing city: San Francisco
Mailing state: CA
Mailing zip: 94132-1740
General Phone: (415) 338-1689
General Fax: (415) 338-2084
General/National Adv. E-mail: jour@sfsu.edu
Primary Website: www.journalism.sfsu.edu
Year Established: 1934
Classified Equipment»
Personnel: Venise Wagner (Dept. Chair/Assoc. Prof.); Jon Funabiki (Assoc. Dept. Chair/Prof.); Dottie Katzeff (Adv. Mgr.); John Burks (Prof.); Barbara Landes (Prodn. Mgr.); Nathan Codd (Ed. in Chief); Yvonne Daley (Prof.); Kenneth Kobre (Prof.); Erna R. Smith (Prof.); Rachele Kanigel (Assoc. Prof.); Austin Long-Scott (Assoc. Prof.); Cristina Azocar (Asst. Prof./Dir., Ctr. for Integration/Improvement of Journalism); Yumi Wilson (Asst. Prof.); John T. Johnson (Prof. Emer.); B.H. Liebes (Prof. Emer.); Betty Medsger (Prof. Emer.); Leonard Sellers (Prof. Emer.); Jerrold Werthimer (Prof. Emer.); Harriet Chiang (Lectr.); Roland DeWolk (Lectr.); Jesse Garnier (Lectr.); David Greene (Lectr.); Sibylla Herbrich (Lectr.)

UNIVERSITY OF SAN FRANCISCO

Street address 1: 2130 Fulton St.
Street address 3: San Francisco
Street address state: CA
Zip/Postal code: 94117-1080
Mailing address: 2130 Fulton St
Mailing city: San Francisco
Mailing state: CA
Mailing zip: 94117-1050
General Phone: (415) 422-6680
General Fax: (415) 422-5680
General/National Adv. E-mail: goodwina@usfca.edu
Classified Equipment»
Personnel: Andrew Goodwin (Chair)

SAN JOSE STATE UNIVERSITY

Street address 1: One Washington Sq.
Street address 3: San Jose
Street address state: CA
Zip/Postal code: 95192-0055
Mailing address: 1 Washington Sq
Mailing city: San Jose
Mailing state: CA
Mailing zip: 95192-0001
General Phone: (408) 924-3240
General Fax: (408) 924-3229
General/National Adv. E-mail: jmcinfo@casa.sjsu.edu
Primary Website: www.jmcweb.sjsu.edu
Classified Equipment»
Personnel: William Briggs (Dir./Prof.); Cecelia Baldwin (Prof.); Harvey Gotliffe (Prof.); Clyde Lawrence (Prof.); Diana Stover (Prof.); William Tillinghast (Prof./Coord., Grad. Studies); Dennis Wilcox (Prof.); Richard Craig (Assoc. Prof.); Scott Fosdick (Assoc. Prof.); Tim Hendrick (Assoc. Prof.); Kathleen Martinelli (Assoc. Prof.); Robert Rucker (Assoc. Prof.); Lilly Buchwitz (Asst. Prof.); Michael Cheers (Asst. Prof.); George Coakley (Lectr.); Chris DiSalvo (Lectr.); Stephen Eckstone (Lectr.); Mack Lundstrom (Lectr.); Cynthia McCune (Lectr.); Dona Nichols (Lectr.)

CALIFORNIA POLYTECHNIC STATE UNIVERSTIY

Street address 1: Journalism Dept.
Street address 3: San Luis Obispo
Street address state: CA
Zip/Postal code: 93407
Mailing address: Journalism Dept.
Mailing city: San Luis Obispo
Mailing state: CA
Mailing zip: 93407
General Phone: (805) 756-2508
General Fax: (805) 756-5744
General/National Adv. E-mail: gmramos@calpoly.edu
Classified Equipment»
Personnel: George Ramos (Chair/Prof.); Nishan Havandjian (Prof.); Patrick Munroe (Prof.); Teresa Allen (Prof.); John Soares (Prof.); Douglas J. Swanson (Assoc. Prof.); Brady Teufel (Full-time Lectr.)

SANTA CLARA UNIVERSITY

Street address 1: 500 El Camino Real, Arts and Sciences Bldg., #229
Street address 3: Santa Clara
Street address state: CA
Zip/Postal code: 95053
Mailing address: 500 El Camino Real Arts & Sciences Bldg # 229
Mailing city: Santa Clara
Mailing state: CA
Mailing zip: 95053-0001
General Phone: (408) 554-5498
General Fax: (408) 554-4913
Editorial e-mail: slee@scu.edu
Classified Equipment»
Personnel: Stephen Lee (Head)

STANFORD UNIVERSITY

Street address 1: McClatchy Hall
Street address 3: Stanford
Street address state: CA
Zip/Postal code: 94305-2050
Mailing address: McClatchy Hall
Mailing city: Stanford
Mailing state: CA
Mailing zip: 94305-2050
General Phone: (650) 723-1941
General Fax: (650) 725-2472
General/National Adv. E-mail: comm-inforequest@lists.stanford.edu
Primary Website: communication.stanford.edu
Classified Equipment»
Personnel: James Fishkin (Chair/Prof.); Theodore L. Glasser (Prof.); Shanto Iyengar (Chandler Prof.); Jon Krosnick (Frederic O. Glover Prof.); Clifford I. Nass (Prof.); Byron Reeves (Edwards Prof.); Jeremy Bailenson (Asst. Prof.); Fred Turner (Asst. Prof.); Joel Brinkley (Vstg. Prof.); Glenn Frankel (Vstg. Prof.); Ann Grimes (Vstg. Prof.); Beth Noveck (Vstg. Prof.); Robert

Luskin (Vstg. Prof.); John Markoff (Lectr.); Howard Rheingold (Lectr.); James Wheaton (Lectr.); Gregg Zachary (Lectr.); Jan Krawitz (Courtesy Appointments); Lawrence Lessig (Courtesy Appointments); Walter Powell (Courtesy Appointments)

UNIVERSITY OF THE PACIFIC

Street address 1: 3601 Pacific Ave.
Street address 3: Stockton
Street address state: CA
Zip/Postal code: 95211
Mailing address: 3601 Pacific Ave
Mailing city: Stockton
Mailing state: CA
Mailing zip: 95211-0197
General Phone: (209) 946-2505
General Fax: (209) 946-2694
General/National Adv. E-mail: qdong@uop.edu
Classified Equipment»
Personnel: Qingwen Dong (Chair)

CALIFORNIA LUTHERAN UNIVERSITY

Street address 1: 60 W Olsen Rd
Street address 3: Thousand Oaks
Street address state: CA
Zip/Postal code: 91360-2700
Country: USA
Mailing address: 60 W Olsen Rd # 4200
Mailing city: Thousand Oaks
Mailing state: CA
Mailing zip: 91360-2787
General Phone: (805) 493-3366
General Fax: (805) 493-3479
Advertising Phone: (805) 493-3327
General/National Adv. E-mail: kelley@robles.callutheran.edu
Editorial e-mail: echo@clunet.edu
Classified Equipment»
Personnel: Colleen Cason (Advisor); Sharon Docter (Chair); Jonathan Culmer (Bus. Mgr.); Margaret Nolan (Ed. in Chief)

COLORADO

BOULDER

UNIVERSITY OF COLORADO

Street address 1: Armory Bldg. 116, 1151 University Ave. 478 UCB
Street address 3: Boulder
Street address state: CO
Zip/Postal code: 80309-0478
Mailing address: Armory Bldg. 116, 1151 University Ave. 478 UCB
Mailing city: Boulder
Mailing state: CO
Mailing zip: 80309-0478
General Phone: (303) 492-5007
General Fax: (303) 492-0969
General/National Adv. E-mail: sjmcdean@colorado.edu
Classified Equipment»
Personnel: Paul S. Voakes (Prof./Dean); Andrew Calabrese (Prof./Assoc. Dean/Dir. Graduate Studies); Stewart M. Hoover (Prof./Dir., Ctr. for Media, Religion/Culture); Bella Mody (Prof./James E. de Castro Chair in Global Media Studies); Marguerite J. Moritz (Prof./UNESCO Chair in Int'l Journalism Educ.); Michael Tracey (Prof.); Robert Trager (Prof.); Len Ackland (Assoc. Prof./Co-Dir., Ctr. for Environmental Journalism); Shu-Ling Berggreen (Assoc. Prof./Head, Media Studies seq.); Michael McDevitt (Assoc. Prof.); Polly McLean (Assoc. Prof.); Janice Peck (Assoc. Prof.); Brett Robbs (Assoc. Prof.); David Slayden (Assoc. Prof./Head, Adv. Seq.); Jan Whitt (Assoc. Prof.); Tom Yulsman (Assoc. Prof./Co-Dir., Ctr. for Environmental Journalism/Head, News-Editorial seq.); Deserai Crow (Asst. Prof./Assoc. Dir., Ctr. for Environmental Journalism); Nabil Echchaibi (Asst. Prof.); Kendra Gale (Asst. Prof.); Lee Hood (Asst. Prof.)

METROPOLITAN STATE COLLEGE OF DENVER

Street address 1: PO Box 173362
Street address 3: Denver
Street address state: CO
Zip/Postal code: 80217-3362
Mailing address: PO Box 173362
Mailing city: Denver
Mailing state: CO
Mailing zip: 80217-3362
General Phone: (303) 556-3485
General Fax: (301) 556-3013
General/National Adv. E-mail: hurleyd@mscd.edu
Classified Equipment»
Personnel: Deborah C. Hurley (Chair)

UNIVERSITY OF DENVER

Street address 1: 2490 S. Gaylord St.
Street address 3: Denver
Street address state: CO
Zip/Postal code: 80208
Mailing address: 2490 S Gaylord St
Mailing city: Denver
Mailing state: CO
Mailing zip: 80210-5266
General Phone: (303) 871-3976
General Fax: (303) 871-4949
General/National Adv. E-mail: mcom@du.edu
Primary Website: www.du.edu/mcom
Classified Equipment»
Personnel: Diane Waldman (Assoc. Prof./Chair); Renee Botta (Assoc. Prof./Dir., Mass Commun. Grad. Studies); Rodney Buxton (Assoc. Prof./Dir., Communication Undergrad. Studies); Lynn Clark (Assoc. Prof./Dir., Estlow Int'l. Ctr. Journalism/New Media); Tony Gault (Assoc. Prof.); Trace Reddell (Assoc. Prof./Dir., Digital Media Studies Grad. prog.); Margie Thompson (Assoc. Prof./Dir., Int'l & Intercultural Communication Grad. prog.); Christof Demont-Heinrich (Asst. Prof.); Catherine A. Grieve (Asst. Prof./Dir., Internships); Nadia Kaneva (Asst. Prof.); Sheila Schroeder (Asst. Prof.); Derigan Silver (Asst. Prof.); Bill Depper (Lectr.); Elizabeth Henry (Lectr.); Ania Savage (Lectr./Fac. Advisor to the Clarion); Steve Scully (Lectr.); Noel Jordan (Prof. Emer.); Harold Mendelsohn (Prof. Emer.)

COLORADO STATE UNIVERSITY

Street address 1: C-225 Clark Bldg. 1785 Campus Delivery
Street address 2: Colorado State University
Street address 3: Fort Collins
Street address state: CO
Zip/Postal code: 80523
Mailing address: C225 Clark
Mailing city: Fort Collins
Mailing state: CO
Mailing zip: 80523-0001
General Phone: (970) 491-6310
General Fax: (970) 491-2908
General/National Adv. E-mail: gluft@lamar.colostate.edu
Primary Website: www.colostate.edu/depts/tj
Classified Equipment»
Personnel: Gregory Luft (Prof./Chair); Kirk Hallahan (Prof.); Marilee Long (Prof.); Garrett O'Keefe (Prof.); Donna Rouner (Prof.); Donald Zimmerman (Prof./Dir., Center for Writing and Communication Technology); Cindy Christen (Assoc. Prof.); Kris Kodrich (Assoc. Prof.); James Landers (Assoc. Prof.); Patrick Plaisance (Assoc. Prof.); Peter Seel (Assoc. Prof./Adv., Information Science and Technology prog.); Jamie Switzer (Assoc. Prof.); Craig Trumbo (Assoc. Prof./Grad. Program Coord.); Joseph Champ (Asst. Prof.); Jangyul Kim (Asst. Prof.); Minjeong Kim (Asst. Prof.); Rosa Martey (Asst. Prof.); Jonna Pearson (Asst. Prof.); Jeff Browne (Instr.); Chryss Cada (Instr.)

MESA STATE COLLEGE

Street address 1: PO Box 2647
Street address 3: Grand Junction
Street address state: CO
Zip/Postal code: 81502
Mailing address: PO Box 2647
Mailing city: Grand Junction
Mailing state: CO
Mailing zip: 81502-2647
General Phone: (970) 248-1287
General Fax: (970) 248-1199
General/National Adv. E-mail: bevers@mesastate.edu
Primary Website: www.mesastate.edu/masscomm
Classified Equipment»
Personnel: Byron Evers (Dir.)

UNIVERSITY OF NORTHERN COLORADO

Street address 1: Dept. of Journalism
Street address 3: Greeley
Street address state: CO
Zip/Postal code: 80639
Mailing address: Dept of Journalism
Mailing city: Greeley
Mailing state: CO
Mailing zip: 80639-0001
General Phone: (970) 351-2726
General Fax: (970) 351-2983
Classified Equipment»
Personnel: Charles Ingold (Prof./Chair); Alice Klement (Endowed Prof.); Wayne Melanson (Assoc. Prof.); Lynn Klyde-Silverstein (Asst. Prof.); Lee Anne Peck (Asst. Prof.)

COLORADO STATE UNIVERSITY, PUEBLO

Street address 1: 2200 Bonforte Blvd., AM-117
Street address 3: Pueblo
Street address state: CO
Zip/Postal code: 81001-4901
Mailing address: 2200 Bonforte Blvd # AM-117
Mailing city: Pueblo
Mailing state: CO
Mailing zip: 81001-4901
General Phone: (719) 549-2835
General Fax: (719) 549-2120
General/National Adv. E-mail: jen.mullen@colostate-pueblo.edu
Primary Website: http://chass.colostate-pueblo.edu/mccnm/
Classified Equipment»
Personnel: Jennifer Mullen (Chair)

CONNECTICUT

UNIVERSITY OF BRIDGEPORT

Street address 1: Dept. of Mass Commun.
Street address 3: Bridgeport
Street address state: CT
Zip/Postal code: 6601
Mailing address: Dept. of Mass Commun.
Mailing city: Bridgeport
Mailing state: CT
Mailing zip: 6601
General Phone: (203) 576-4705
General/National Adv. E-mail: carvethr@csusys.ctstateu.edu
Classified Equipment»
Personnel: Rod Carveth (Chair)

FAIRFIELD UNIVERSITY

Street address 1: English Dept., N. Benson Rd.
Street address 3: Fairfield
Street address state: CT
Zip/Postal code: 6824
Mailing address: English Dept., N. Benson Rd.
Mailing city: Fairfield
Mailing state: CT
Mailing zip: 6824
General Phone: (203) 254-4000
General Fax: (203) 254-4131
General/National Adv. E-mail: jsimon@mail.fairfield.edu
Classified Equipment»
Personnel: James Simon (Chair/Fac.); Jack Cavanaugh (Fac.); Marcy Mangels (Fac.); Jean Santopatre (Fac.); Fran Silverman (Fac.)

QUINNIPIAC UNIVERSITY

Street address 1: 275 Mount Carmel Ave
Street address 3: Hamden
Street address state: CT
Zip/Postal code: 06518-1905
Country: USA
Mailing address: 275 Mount Carmel Ave
Mailing city: Hamden
Mailing state: CT
Mailing zip: 06518-1908
General Phone: 8608301017
General/National Adv. E-mail: editor@quchronicle.com
Primary Website: www.quinnipiac.edu; quchronicle.com
Classified Equipment»
Personnel: David Friedlander (Editor-in-Chief)

CENTRAL CONNECTICUT STATE UNIV.

Street address 1: 1615 Stanley St
Street address 3: New Britain
Street address state: CT
Zip/Postal code: 06050-2439
Country: USA
Mailing address: 1615 Stanley St
Mailing city: New Britain
Mailing state: CT
Mailing zip: 06050-2439
General Phone: (860) 832-3744
General Fax: (860) 832-3747
General/National Adv. E-mail: ccsurecorder@gmail.com; ccsurecorder.ads@gmail.com
Primary Website: www.centralrecorder.com
Classified Equipment»
Personnel: Vivian B. Martin (Coord.); Melissa Traynor (Ed. in Chief); Michael Walsh (Mng. Ed.); Christopher Boulay (Sports Ed.); Christina LoBello (Opinion Ed.); Kelsey (Adv. Mgr.)

SOUTHERN CONNECTICUT STATE UNIVERSITY

Street address 1: 501 Crescent St. Morrill 202
Street address 3: New Haven
Street address state: CT
Zip/Postal code: 6515
Mailing address: 501 Crescent St Morrill 202
Mailing city: New Haven
Mailing state: CT
Mailing zip: 06515-1330
General Phone: (203) 392-5800
General Fax: (203) 392-5809
General/National Adv. E-mail: harrisf1@southernct.edu
Classified Equipment»
Personnel: Frank Harris (Chair)

UNIVERSITY OF CONNECTICUT

Street address 1: Journalism Dept., 337 Mansfield Rd.
Street address 3: Storrs
Street address state: CT
Zip/Postal code: 06269-1129
Mailing address: 337 Mansfield Rd
Mailing city: Storrs
Mailing state: CT
Mailing zip: 06269-9015
General Phone: (860) 486-4222
General Fax: (860) 486-3294
General/National Adv. E-mail: jouadm01@unconnvm.uconn.edu
Primary Website: www.journalism.uconn.edu
Classified Equipment»
Personnel: Maureen Croteau (Prof./Head); Wayne Worcester (Prof.); Marcel Dufresne (Assoc. Prof.); Timothy Kenny (Assoc. Prof.); Robert Wyss (Asst. Prof.); Claire Bessette (Lectr.); Bob Hamilton (Lectr.); Douglas Hardy (Lectr.); Terese Karmel (Lectr.); Jonathan Lender (Lectr.); Gail MacDonald (Lectr.); Jon Sandberg (Lectr.); Julie Sprengelmeyer (Lectr.); Greg Stone (Lectr.)

UNIVERSITY OF HARTFORD

Street address 1: 200 Bloomfield Ave.
Street address 3: West Hartford
Street address state: CT
Zip/Postal code: 06117-1599
Mailing address: 200 Bloomfield Ave
Mailing city: West Hartford
Mailing state: CT
Mailing zip: 06117-1599
General Phone: (860) 768-4633
General Fax: (860) 768-4096
General/National Adv. E-mail: kelly@hartford.edu
Classified Equipment»
Personnel: Lynne Kelly (Dir.)

DISTRICT OF

COLUMBIA

AMERICAN UNIVERSITY

Street address 1: 4400 Massachusetts Ave. NW
Street address 3: Washington
Street address state: DC
Zip/Postal code: 20016
Mailing address: 4400 Massachusetts Ave NW
Mailing city: Washington
Mailing state: DC
Mailing zip: 20016-8200
General Phone: (202) 885-2060
General Fax: (202) 885-2099
Primary Website: www.soc.american.edu
Classified Equipment»
Personnel: Larry Kirkman (Prof./Dean); Patricia Aufderheide (Prof.); Kathryn Montgomery (Prof.); Jack Orwant (Prof.); Chris Simpson (Prof.); Rodger Streitmatter (Prof.); Randall Blair (Assoc. Prof.); W. Joseph Campbell (Assoc. Prof.); Wendell Cochran (Assoc. Prof.); Barbara Diggs-Brown (Assoc. Prof.); John Doolittle (Assoc. Prof.); John Douglass (Assoc. Prof.); Charlene Gilbert (Assoc. Prof.); Jane Hall (Assoc. Prof.); Jill Olmsted (Assoc. Prof.); Rick Rockwell (Assoc. Prof.); Richard Stack (Assoc. Prof.); Leonard Steinhorn (Assoc. Prof.); Wendy Swallow (Assoc. Prof.); John Watson (Assoc. Prof.)

CATHOLIC UNIVERSITY SCHOOL OF LAW

Street address 1: Institute for Communications Law Studies
Street address 3: Washington
Street address state: DC
Zip/Postal code: 20064
Mailing address: Institute for Communications Law Studies
Mailing city: Washington
Mailing state: DC
Mailing zip: 20064-0001
General Phone: (202) 319-6295
General Fax: (202) 319-4459
Classified Equipment»
Personnel: Marin Scordato (Dir.)

GEORGE WASHINGTON UNIVERSITY

Street address 1: 805 21st St. NW, Ste. 400
Street address 3: Washington
Street address state: DC
Zip/Postal code: 20052
Mailing address: 805 21st St NW Ste 400
Mailing city: Washington
Mailing state: DC
Mailing zip: 20052-0029
General Phone: (202) 994-6227
General Fax: (202) 994-5806
General/National Adv. E-mail: smpa@gwu.edu
Primary Website: www.gwu.edu/~smpa
Classified Equipment»

HOWARD UNIVERSITY

Street address 1: 525 Bryant St. NW
Street address 3: Washington
Street address state: DC
Zip/Postal code: 20059
Mailing address: 525 Bryant St NW
Mailing city: Washington
Mailing state: DC
Mailing zip: 20059-1005
General Phone: (202) 806-7690
General Fax: (202) 232-8305
Primary Website: www.soc.howard.edu
Classified Equipment»
Personnel: Jannette L. Dates (Grad. Prof./Dean); Noma Anderson (Prof. (LWOP)); Anju Chaudhary (Prof.); Abraham Ford (Prof.); Haile Gerima (Prof.); Barbara Hines (Prof.); Lawrence Kaggwa (Prof.); Judi Moore Latta (Prof.); Abbas Malek (Prof.); Robert L. Nwanko (Prof.); Joan C. Payne (Prof.); Ronald C. Pearlman (Prof.); William H. Starosta (Grad. Prof.); Orlando L. Taylor (Grad. Prof. (LWOP)/Vice Provost); Clint C. Wilson (Prof.); Richard Wright (Prof.); S. Torriano Berry (Assoc. Prof.); Debra A. Busacco (Assoc. Prof.); Alonzo Crawford (Assoc. Prof.); Melbourne S. Cummings (Assoc. Prof.)

DELAWARE

UNIVERSITY OF DELAWARE

Street address 1: Journalism Program
Street address 3: Newark
Street address state: DE
Zip/Postal code: 19716
Mailing address: Journalism Program
Mailing city: Newark
Mailing state: DE
Mailing zip: 19716
General Phone: (302) 451-2361
Classified Equipment»

FLORIDA

UNIVERSITY OF MIAMI

Street address 1: 5202 University Dr.
Street address 3: Coral Gables
Street address state: FL
Zip/Postal code: 33124
Mailing address: 5202 University Dr.
Mailing city: Coral Gables
Mailing state: FL
Mailing zip: 33124
General Phone: (305) 284-2265
General Fax: (305) 284-3648
General/National Adv. E-mail: sgrogg@miami.edu
Classified Equipment»
Personnel: Sam L. Grogg (Dean); Stanley Harrison (Prof.); Anthony Allegro (Prof.); Stephen Bowles (Prof.); Bruce Garrison (Prof.); Paul Lazarus (Prof.); Edward Pfister (Prof.); William Rothman (Prof.); Michael Salwen (Prof.); Mitchell Shapiro (Prof.); Don Stacks (Prof./Prog. Dir., PR); Thomas Steinfatt (Prof.); Grace Barnes (Assoc. Prof.); Marie-Helene Bourgoignie-Robert (Assoc. Prof./Prog. Dir., Vis Comm.); Sanjeev Chatterjee (Assoc. Prof./Vice Dean); Paul Driscoll (Assoc. Prof./Prog. Dir., Broadcast); Michel Dupagne (Assoc. Prof.); Leonardo Ferreira (Assoc. Prof.); Lisa Gottlieb (Assoc. Prof.); Robert Hosmon (Assoc. Prof./Vice Dean, External Affairs/Advancement)
Newspaper (for newspapers group): Univ. of Miami, Coral Gables

KAPLAN UNIVERSITY

Street address 1: 6301 Kaplan University Ave.
Street address 3: Fort Lauderdale
Street address state: FL
Zip/Postal code: 33309
Mailing address: 6301 Kaplan University Ave
Mailing city: Fort Lauderdale
Mailing state: FL
Mailing zip: 33309-1905
General Phone: (954) 515-4015
General Fax: (888) 887-6494
General/National Adv. E-mail: Cstevenson@kaplan.edu
Primary Website: www.kaplan.edu
Classified Equipment»
Personnel: Carolyn N. Stephenson (Academic. Prog. Dir.)

UNIVERSITY OF FLORIDA

Street address 1: 2096 Weimer
Street address 3: Gainesville
Street address state: FL
Zip/Postal code: 32611-8400
Mailing address: PO Box 118400
Mailing city: Gainesville
Mailing state: FL
Mailing zip: 32611-8400
General Phone: (352) 392-0466
General Fax: (352) 392-3919
Primary Website: www.jou.ufl.edu
Classified Equipment»
Personnel: John Wright (Dean/Prof.); Laurence B. Alexander (Prof./Interim Assoc. Dean, UF Grad. School/UF Research Foundation Prof.); Bill F. Chamberlin (Prof./Joseph L. Brechner Eminent Scholar/Dir., Marion Brechner Citizen Access Proj.); Sylvia Chan-Olmsted (Prof./Assoc. Dean, Research/AI and Effie Flanagan Prof. in Journalism & Communications); Sandra Dickson (Prof./Co-Dir., Documentary Institute); Julie Dodd (Prof.); Mary Ann Ferguson (Prof.); Linda Childers Hon (Prof./Sr. Assoc. Dean/AI and Effie Flanagan Prof. in Journalism and Communications); Terry Hynes (Dean Emerita/Prof.); Lynda Lee Kaid (Prof.); John Kaplan (Prof./UF Res. Foundation Prof.); Kathleen Kelly (Prof.); Melinda (Mindy) McAdams (Prof./Knight Chair in Journalism Technologies and the Democratic Process); William McKeen (Prof./Chair, Dept. of Journalism); Jon D. Morris (Prof.); David Ostroff (Prof./Chair, Dept. of Telecommunication); Churchill Roberts (Prof./Co-Dir., Documentary Institute); Jon A. Roosenraad (Prof./Asst. Dean, Student Servs.); John C. Sutherland (Prof./Chair, Dept. of Adv.); Debbie Treise (Prof./Assoc. Dean, Grad. Studies/Research/AI and Effie Flanagan Prof. in Journalism & Communication)

EDWARD WATERS COLLEGE

Street address 1: Mass Communications Program
Street address 3: Jacksonville
Street address state: FL
Zip/Postal code: 32218
Mailing address: Mass Communications Program
Mailing city: Jacksonville
Mailing state: FL
Mailing zip: 32218
General Phone: (904) 366-2502
Classified Equipment»
Personnel: Emmanuel C. Alozie (Coord.)

JACKSONVILLE UNIVERSITY

Street address 1: Dept. of Mass Communication Studies
Street address 3: Jacksonville
Street address state: FL
Zip/Postal code: 32211
Mailing address: Dept. of Mass Communication Studies
Mailing city: Jacksonville
Mailing state: FL
Mailing zip: 32211
General Phone: (904) 744-3950
Classified Equipment»
Personnel: Dennis Stouse (Dir.)

UNIVERSITY OF NORTH FLORIDA

Street address 1: 4567 St. Johns Bluff Rd. S.
Street address 3: Jacksonville
Street address state: FL
Zip/Postal code: 32224-2645
Mailing address: 1 U N F Dr
Mailing city: Jacksonville
Mailing state: FL
Mailing zip: 32224-7699
General Phone: (904) 620-2651
General Fax: (904) 620-2652
General/National Adv. E-mail: opatters@unf.edu
Primary Website: www.unf.edu/coas/cva
Classified Equipment»
Personnel: Oscar Patterson (Chair)

FLORIDA SOUTHERN COLLEGE

Street address 1: 111 Lake Hollingsworth Dr
Street address 3: Lakeland
Street address state: FL
Zip/Postal code: 33801-5607
Country: USA
Mailing address: 111 Lake Hollingsworth Dr
Mailing city: Lakeland
Mailing state: FL
Mailing zip: 33801-5698
General Phone: (863) 680-4155
General Fax: (863) 680-6244
Display Adv. E-mail: mtrice@flsouthern.edu
Editorial e-mail: fscsouthern@gmail.com
Primary Website: www.fscsouthern.com
Published: Fri`Other
Published Other: every other week
Avg Free Circ: 1200
Classified Equipment»
Personnel: Michael Trice (Advisor)

NORTH MIAMI

FLORIDA INTERNATIONAL UNIVERSITY

Street address 1: Biscayne Bay Campus, 3000 NE 151st St.
Street address 3: North Miami
Street address state: FL
Zip/Postal code: 33181
County: Miami-Dade
Mailing address: 3000 NE 151st St
Mailing city: North Miami
Mailing state: FL
Mailing zip: 33181-3000
General Phone: (305) 919-5625
General Fax: (305) 919-5203
General/National Adv. E-mail: kopenhav@fiu.edu
Primary Website: http://jmc.fiu.edu
Classified Equipment»
Personnel: Frederick Blevens (Prof.); Margo Berman (Assoc. Prof.); Mario Diament (Assoc. Prof.); Teresa Ponte (Assoc. Prof./Interim Chair, Dept. of Journ./Broadcasting); Neil Reisner (Assoc. Prof.); Allan Richards (Assoc. Prof./Interim Assoc. Dean); Lorna Veraldi (Assoc. Prof.); Mercedes Vigon (Assoc. Prof.); Lynn Farber (Asst. Prof.); Lilliam Martinez-Bustos (Asst. Prof./Coord., Spanish-language Journ. Master's Prog.); Elizabeth Marsh (Asst. Prof.); Michael Scott Sheerin (Asst. Prof.); Lillian Lodge Kopenhaver; David Park; Moses Shumow; Juliet Pinto; Ted Gutsche; Kathy Fitspatrick; Kurt Wise; Yu Liu; Weirui Wang; Maria Elena Villar; Sigal Segev

UNIVERSITY OF CENTRAL FLORIDA

Street address 1: 4000 Central Florida Blvd.
Street address 3: Orlando
Street address state: FL
Zip/Postal code: 32816-1344
Mailing address: PO Box 161344
Mailing city: Orlando
Mailing state: FL
Mailing zip: 32816-1344
General Phone: (407) 823-2681
General Fax: (407) 823-6360
Primary Website: communication.cos.ucf.edu
Classified Equipment»
Personnel: Mary Alice Shaver (Prof.); Robert Davis (Prof./Head, Adv./PR); Fred Fedler (Prof./Head, Journalism); Burt Pryor (Prof./Grad. Dir.); Ron Smith (Prof.); George Bagley (Assoc. Prof./Head, Radio/TV); Jeff Butler (Assoc. Prof./Head, I/O); Denise DeLorme (Assoc. Prof.); W. Joe Hall (Assoc. Prof.); Jose Maunez (Assoc. Prof.); Maria Cristina Santana (Assoc. Prof.); Kimiko Akita (Asst. Prof.); Tim Brown (Asst. Prof.); Steve Collins (Asst. Prof.); Gene Costain (Asst. Prof.); Sally Hastings (Asst. Prof.); Jim Katt (Asst. Prof.); Rick Kenney (Asst. Prof.); Sam Lawrence (Asst. Prof.); John Malala (Asst. Prof.)

UNIVERSITY OF WEST FLORIDA

Street address 1: 11000 University Pkwy., Bldg. 36
Street address 3: Pensacola
Street address state: FL
Zip/Postal code: 32514
Mailing address: 11000 University Pkwy Bldg 36
Mailing city: Pensacola
Mailing state: FL
Mailing zip: 32514-5750
General Phone: (850) 474-2874
General Fax: (850) 474-3153
General/National Adv. E-mail: bswain@uwf.edu
Classified Equipment»
Personnel: Bruce Swain (Chair)

FLAGLER COLLEGE

Street address 1: Communication Dept., 74 King St.
Street address 3: Saint Augustine
Street address state: FL
Zip/Postal code: 32085-1027
Mailing address: 74 King St
Mailing city: Saint Augustine
Mailing state: FL
Mailing zip: 32084-4342
General Phone: (904) 819-6247
General Fax: (904) 826-3471
General/National Adv. E-mail: halcombt@flagler.edu
Classified Equipment»
Personnel: Tracy Halcomb (Chair/Assoc. Prof.); Jim Gilmore (Assoc. Prof.); James Pickett (Asst. Prof.); Nadia Reardon (Asst. Prof.); Helena Sarkio (Asst. Prof.); Rosemary Tutt (Asst. Prof.); Rob Armstrong (Instr.); Dan McCook (Instr.); Victor Ostrowidzki (Instr.); Barry Sand (Instr.)

UNIVERSITY OF SOUTH FLORIDA ST. PETERSBURG

Street address 1: 140 7th Ave. S, FCT 204

Street address 3: Saint Petersburg
Street address state: FL
Zip/Postal code: 33701-5016
Mailing address: 140 7th Ave S Fct 204
Mailing city: Saint Petersburg
Mailing state: FL
Mailing zip: 33701-5016
General Phone: (727) 873-4850
General Fax: (727) 873-4034
Classified Equipment»
Personnel: Robert Dardenne (Dir./Assoc. Prof.); Deni Elliott (Prof./Grad. Dir.); G. Michael Killenberg (Prof.); Tony Silvia (Prof.); Mark J. Walters (Assoc. Prof.); Xiaopeng (Paul) Wang (Asst. Prof.); Cheryl Koski (Adj. Fac.); Beth Reynolds (Adj. Fac.); Andrew Skerritt (Adj. Fac.); Deborah Wolfe (Adj. Fac.)

FLORIDA A&M UNIVERSITY

Street address 1: 510 Orr Dr., Ste. 4003, School of Journalism & Graphic Communication Bldg.
Street address 3: Tallahassee
Street address state: FL
Zip/Postal code: 32307-4800
Mailing address: 510 Orr Dr Ste 4003
Mailing city: Tallahassee
Mailing state: FL
Mailing zip: 32307-0001
General Phone: (850) 599-3379
General Fax: (850) 561-2399
General/National Adv. E-mail: james.hawkins@famu.edu
Classified Equipment»
Personnel: James E. Hawkins (Dean); Michael E. Abrams (Prof./Dir., Grad. Studies); F. Todd Bertolaet (Prof.); Dorothy Bland (Prof./Dir., Div. of Journalism); Vincent Blyden (Prof.); LaRae Donnellan (Prof.); Gerald O. Grow (Prof.); Arvid Mukes (Prof./Assoc. Dean./Dir., Div. of Graphic Communication); Joe Ritchie (Prof./Knight Chair); Kay Wilder (Prof.); Gale Workman (Prof.); Bettye Grable (Assoc. Prof.); Joseph Ippolito (Assoc. Prof.); Kenneth Jones (Assoc. Prof.); Yanela Gordon (Asst. Prof./Vstg. Dir., Career Devel. Servs.); M. Diane Hall (Asst. Prof./Dir., H.S./Community College Rel.); Gina Kinchlow (Asst. Prof.); Andrew Skerritt (Asst. Prof.); Valerie White (Asst. Prof.); Ernest Jones (Instr./Mgr., FAMU-TV 20)

UNIVERSITY OF SOUTH FLORIDA

Street address 1: 4202 E. Fowler Ave., CIS 1040
Street address 3: Tampa
Street address state: FL
Zip/Postal code: 33620-7800
Mailing address: 4202 E Fowler Ave Cis 1040
Mailing city: Tampa
Mailing state: FL
Mailing zip: 33620-9951
General Phone: (813) 974-2591
General Fax: (813) 974-2592
General/National Adv. E-mail: mcom@cas.usf.edu
Classified Equipment»
Personnel: Edward Jay Friedlander (Prof./Dir.); Dan Bagley (Assoc. Prof.); Kim Golombisky (Assoc. Prof.); Kenneth Killebrew (Assoc. Prof./Grad. Dir.); Larry Leslie (Assoc. Prof.); Scott Liu (Assoc. Prof./Head, Adv. seq./Zimmerman Adv. Prog. Prof.); Randy Miller (Assoc. Prof./Head, Journalism seq.); Kelli Burns (Asst. Prof.); Roxanne Watson (Asst. Prof.); Kelly Page Werder (Asst. Prof./Head, PR seq.); Rick Wilber (Asst. Prof.); Bob Batchelor (Instr.); Marie Curkan-Flanagan (Instr./Head, Tele. seq.); Rebecca Hagen (Instr.); Charles O'Brien (Instr.); Kristin Arnold Ruyle (Instr.); Liisa Hyvarinen Temple (Vstg. Instr.); Kalah Mueller (Advisor); Denise Nicholas (Advisor); Neil Vicino (Adj. Fac.)

GEORGIA

UNIVERSITY OF GEORGIA

Street address 1: 120 Hooper St.
Street address 3: Athens
Street address state: GA
Zip/Postal code: 30602-3018
Mailing address: 120 Hooper St
Mailing city: Athens
Mailing state: GA
Mailing zip: 30602-5042
General Phone: (706) 542-1704
General Fax: (706) 542-2183
Primary Website: www.grady.uga.edu
Classified Equipment»
Personnel: E. Culpepper Clark (Dean/ Prof.); Alison Alexander (Prof./Sr. Assoc. Dean); Lee Becker (Prof./Dir., Cox Ctr.); Joseph R. Domnick (Prof./Interim Head, Telecomm. Dept.); Conrad C. Fink (Prof./Dir., Cox Inst.); Vicki S. Freimuth (Prof./Dir., Ctr. Health & Risk Commun.); John F. Greenman (Carter Prof.); Karen W. King (Prof./Head, Adv./PR Dept.); Bruce Klopfenstein (Prof.); Dean M. Krugman (Prof.); Jeffrey K. Springston (Prof./Assoc. Dean); Ruth Ann Lariscy (Prof.); William Lee (Prof.); Kent Middleton (Prof./Head, Journalism Dept.); Horace Newcomb (Prof./Peabody Awards Dir.); John Soloski (Prof.); Spencer F. Tinkham (Prof.); Leonard N. Reid (Prof.); Scott Shamp (Prof.); Patricia Thomas (Prof./Knight Chair)

CLARK ATLANTA UNIVERSITY

Street address 1: 223 James P. Brawley Dr., SW
Street address 3: Atlanta
Street address state: GA
Zip/Postal code: 30314
Mailing address: 223 James P Brawley Dr SW
Mailing city: Atlanta
Mailing state: GA
Mailing zip: 30314-4385
General Phone: (440) 880-8304
General/National Adv. E-mail: olafjames@earthlink.net
Classified Equipment»
Personnel: James McJunkins (Chair)

GEORGIA STATE UNIVERSITY

Street address 1: 1027 One Park Pl. S
Street address 3: Atlanta
Street address state: GA
Zip/Postal code: 30303
Mailing address: 1027 One Park Pl. S
Mailing city: Atlanta
Mailing state: GA
Mailing zip: 30303
General Phone: (404) 651-3200
General Fax: (404) 651-1409
General/National Adv. E-mail: jouckw@langate.gsu.edu
Classified Equipment»
Personnel: Carol Winkler (Chair)

BRENAU UNIVERSITY

Street address 1: One Centennial Cir.
Street address 3: Gainesville
Street address state: GA
Zip/Postal code: 30501
Mailing address: 1 Centennial Cir
Mailing city: Gainesville
Mailing state: GA
Mailing zip: 30501-3697
General Phone: (770) 538-4743
General Fax: (770) 538-4558
General/National Adv. E-mail: sblakley@lib.brenau.edu
Classified Equipment»
Personnel: Stewart Blakley (Chair)

KENNESAW STATE UNIVERSITY

Street address 1: 1000 Chastain Rd., Box 2207
Street address 3: Kennesaw
Street address state: GA
Zip/Postal code: 30144
Mailing address: 1000 Chastain Rd NW # 2207
Mailing city: Kennesaw
Mailing state: GA
Mailing zip: 30144-5591
General Phone: (770) 423-6298
General Fax: (770) 423-6740
General/National Adv. E-mail: bwassmut@kennesaw.edu
Classified Equipment»
Personnel: Birgit Wassmuth (Chair/Prof.); Deanna Womack (Prof.); Chuck Aust (Prof.); Charles Mayo (Assoc. Prof.); Leonard Witt (Assoc. Prof./Eminent Scholar/Robert D. Fowler Distinguished Chair); Audrey Allison (Asst. Prof.); Philip Aust (Asst. Prof.); Joshua Azriel (Asst. Prof.); Barbara Gainey (Asst. Prof.); May Gao (Asst. Prof.); Amber Hutchins (Asst. Prof.); Heeman Kim (Asst. Prof.); Georgios Triantis (Asst. Prof.); Emily Holler (Instr.); Jan Phillips (Instr.); Stephen J. McNeill (Lectr.); Jeffrey Anderson (Prof. Emer.)

MERCER UNIVERSITY AT MACON

Street address 1: 1400 Coleman Ave.
Street address 3: Macon
Street address state: GA
Zip/Postal code: 31207-0001
Mailing address: 1400 Coleman Ave
Mailing city: Macon
Mailing state: GA
Mailing zip: 31207-0003
General Phone: (912) 752-2979
General/National Adv. E-mail: jottshall_cm@mercer.edu
Classified Equipment»
Personnel: Cynthia Gottshall (Broadcast/Film)

GEORGIA COLLEGE & STATE UNIVERSITY

Street address 1: Campus Box 32
Street address 3: Milledgeville
Street address state: GA
Zip/Postal code: 31061
Mailing address: Campus Box 32
Mailing city: Milledgeville
Mailing state: GA
Mailing zip: 31061
General Phone: (478) 445-8260
General Fax: (478) 445-2364
General/National Adv. E-mail: maryjean.land@gcsu.edu
Classified Equipment»
Personnel: Mary Jean Land (Chair/Prof.); Ginger Carter Miller (Prof.); Macon McGinley (Asst. Prof.); Stephen Price (Asst. Prof.); Angela Criscoe (Instr.); Pate McMichael (Instr.); Hope Buchanan (Advisor)

BERRY COLLEGE

Street address 1: 2277 Martha Berry Hwy.
Street address 3: Mount Berry
Street address state: GA
Zip/Postal code: 30149-0299
Mailing address: PO Box 490299
Mailing city: Mount Berry
Mailing state: GA
Mailing zip: 30149-0299
General Phone: (706) 233-4089
General Fax: (706) 802-6738
General/National Adv. E-mail: bfrank@berry.edu
Classified Equipment»
Personnel: Robert L. Frank (Chair)

GEORGIA SOUTHERN UNIVERSITY

Street address 1: Dept. of Communication Arts
Street address 3: Statesboro
Street address state: GA
Zip/Postal code: 30460
Mailing address: Dept of Communication Arts
Mailing city: Statesboro
Mailing state: GA
Mailing zip: 30460-0001
General Phone: (912) 681-5138
General Fax: (912) 681-0822
General/National Adv. E-mail: hfulmer@gasou.edu
Classified Equipment»
Personnel: Ernest T. Wyatt (Program Head)

TOCCOA FALLS COLLEGE

Street address 1: School of Communication
Street address 3: Toccoa Falls
Street address state: GA
Zip/Postal code: 30598
Mailing address: School of Communication
Mailing city: Toccoa Falls
Mailing state: GA
Mailing zip: 30598
General Phone: (706) 886-7299
General Fax: (706) 886-6412
General/National Adv. E-mail: comm@tfc.edu
Classified Equipment»
Personnel: Jerry Fliger (Dir.)

VALDOSTA STATE UNIVERSITY

Street address 1: 1500 N. Patterson, Dept. Of Communication Arts
Street address 3: Valdosta
Street address state: GA
Zip/Postal code: 31698-0001
Mailing address: 1500 N Patterson Dept of
Mailing city: Valdosta
Mailing state: GA
Mailing zip: 31698-0001
General Phone: (229) 333-5820
General Fax: (229) 293-6182
General/National Adv. E-mail: ccates@valdosta.edu
Classified Equipment»
Personnel: Carl Cates (Head)

HAWAII

CHAMINADE, UNIVERSITY OF HONOLULU

Street address 1: Dept. of Communication
Street address 3: Honolulu
Street address state: HI
Zip/Postal code: 96816-1578
Mailing address: Dept. of Communication
Mailing city: Honolulu
Mailing state: HI
Mailing zip: 96816-1578
General Phone: (808) 735-4711
General Fax: (808) 739-8328
General/National Adv. E-mail: cbieberl@chaminade.edu
Classified Equipment»
Personnel: Clifford Bieberly (Dir.)

HAWAII PACIFIC UNIVERSITY

Street address 1: 1136 Union Mall
Street address 2: Suite 208
Street address 3: Honolulu
Street address state: HI
Zip/Postal code: 96813
Mailing address: 1136 Union Mall
Mailing city: Honolulu
Mailing state: HI
Mailing zip: 96813
General Phone: (808) 544-0825
General Fax: (808) 544-0835
General/National Adv. E-mail: editor@kalamalama.com
Primary Website: http://hpulamalama.com/wp/
Classified Equipment»
Personnel: Steven Combs (Dean/Prof.); John Hart (Prof.); John Barnum (Assoc. Prof.); Peter Britos (Assoc. Prof.); James Whitfield (Assoc. Prof.); Brian Cannon (Asst. Prof.); Matt George (Asst. Prof.); Serena Hashimoto (Asst. Prof.); Lowell Douglas Ing (Asst. Prof.); Anne Kennedy (Asst. Prof.); Laurence LeDoux (Asst. Prof.); Penny Smith (Asst. Prof.); Yanjun Zhao (Asst. Prof.); Dale Burke (Instr.); Katherine Clark (Instr.); Thomas Dowd (Instr.); Rose Helens-Hart (Instr.); Marianne Luken (Instr.); Malia Smith (Instr.); Lewis Trusty (Instr.)

UNIVERSITY OF HAWAII AT MANOA

Street address 1: 2550 Campus Rd.
Street address 3: Honolulu
Street address state: HI
Zip/Postal code: 96822
Mailing address: 2550 Campus Rd
Mailing city: Honolulu
Mailing state: HI
Mailing zip: 96822-2250
General Phone: (808) 956-8881
General Fax: (808) 956-5396
General/National Adv. E-mail: jour@hawaii.edu
Classified Equipment»
Personnel: Gerald Kato (Chair/Assoc. Prof.); Thomas J. Brislin (Prof.); Beverly Deepe Keever (Prof.); Ann Auman (Assoc. Prof.); Jonathan Lillie (Asst. Prof.)

IOWA

IOWA STATE UNIVERSITY OF SCIENCE AND TECHNOLOGY

Street address 1: 101 Hamilton Hall
Street address 3: Ames
Street address state: IA
Zip/Postal code: 50011-1180
Mailing address: 101 Hamilton Hall
Mailing city: Ames
Mailing state: IA
Mailing zip: 50011-1180
General Phone: (515) 294-4342
General Fax: (515) 294-5108
General/National Adv. E-mail: greenlee@iastate.edu
Classified Equipment»
Personnel: Michael Bugeja (Dir.); Eric Abbott (Prof.); Thomas Beell (Prof.); Jane W. Peterson (Prof.); Kim Smith (Prof.); Lulu Rodriguez (Prof.); Joel Geske (Assoc. Prof.); Barbara Mack (Assoc. Prof.); Marcia Prior-Miller (Assoc. Prof.); Jeff Blevins (Asst. Prof.); David Bulla (Asst. Prof.); Dennis Chamberlin (Asst. Prof.); Michael Dahlstrom (Asst. Prof.); Daniela Dimitrova (Asst. Prof.); Jacob Groshek (Asst. Prof.); Chad Harms (Asst. Prof.); Suman Lee (Asst. Prof.); Jay Newell (Asst. Prof.); Sela Sar (Asst. Prof.); Erin Wilgenbusch (Sr. Lectr.)

UNIVERSITY OF NORTHERN IOWA

Street address 1: Communications Studies Dept., 326 Lang
Street address 3: Cedar Falls
Street address state: IA
Zip/Postal code: 50614-01397
Mailing address: Communications Studies Dept 326
Mailing city: Cedar Falls
Mailing state: IA
Mailing zip: 50614-0001
General Phone: (319) 273-2217
General Fax: (319) 273-7356
General/National Adv. E-mail: john.fritch@uni.edu
Classified Equipment»
Personnel: John Fritch (Dept. Chair)

DRAKE UNIVERSITY

Street address 1: 2507 University Ave.
Street address 3: Des Moines
Street address state: IA
Zip/Postal code: 50311
Mailing address: 2507 University Ave
Mailing city: Des Moines
Mailing state: IA
Mailing zip: 50311-4505
General Phone: (515) 271-2838
General Fax: (515) 271-2798
General/National Adv. E-mail: charles.edwards@drake.edu
Primary Website: www.drake.edu/journalism
Classified Equipment»
Personnel: Charles Edwards (Dean); Todd Evans (Prof.); John Lytle (Prof.); Patricia Prijatel (Prof./Assoc. Dean); Janet Hill Keefer (Assoc. Prof.); Ronda Menke (Assoc. Prof.); Lee Jolliffe (Assoc. Prof.); Gary Wade (Assoc. Prof.); David Wright (Assoc. Prof./Asst. Dean); Koji Fuse (Asst. Prof.); Dorothy Pisarski (Asst. Prof.); Angela Renkoski (Asst. Prof.); Kathleen Richardson (Asst. Prof.); Jill Van Wyke (Asst. Prof.); William F. Francois (Prof. Emer.); Barry M. Foskit (Prof. Emer.); Henry Milam (Prof. Emer.); Joe R. Patrick (Prof. Emer.); Herbert Strentz (Prof. Emer.); Louis J. Wolter (Prof. Emer.)

GRAND VIEW COLLEGE

Street address 1: 1331 Grandview Ave.
Street address 3: Des Moines
Street address state: IA
Zip/Postal code: 50316
Mailing address: 1331 Grandview Ave
Mailing city: Des Moines
Mailing state: IA
Mailing zip: 50316-1453
General Phone: (515) 263-2931
General Fax: (515) 263-2990
General/National Adv. E-mail: wschaefer@gvc.edu
Primary Website: www.gvc.edu/academics/comm
Classified Equipment»
Personnel: William Schaefer (Chair)

CLARKE UNIVERSITY

Street address 1: 1550 Clarke Dr
Street address 3: Dubuque
Street address state: IA
Zip/Postal code: 52001-3117
Country: USA
Mailing address: 1550 Clarke Dr
Mailing city: Dubuque
Mailing state: IA
Mailing zip: 52001-3198
General Phone: (563) 588-6335
General Fax: (563) 588-6789
General/National Adv. E-mail: abdul.sinno@clarke.edu
Primary Website: clarke.edu
Classified Equipment»
Personnel: Diana Russo (Advisor); Abdul Karim Sinno (Chair); Sarah Bradford (Ed.); David Deifell, Ph.D. (Assoc. Prof. Comm.)

UNIVERSITY OF IOWA

Street address 1: 100 Adler Journalism Bldg., Rm. E305
Street address 3: Iowa City
Street address state: IA
Zip/Postal code: 52242-2004
Mailing address: 100 Adler Journalism Bldg Rm E305
Mailing city: Iowa City
Mailing state: IA
Mailing zip: 52242-2004
General Phone: (319) 335-3486
General Fax: (319) 335-3502
General/National Adv. E-mail: journalism-admin@uiowa.edu
Primary Website: www.uiowa.edu/jmc
Classified Equipment»
Personnel: Marc Armstrong (Interim Dir.); Kay Amert (Prof.); Dan Berkowitz (Prof.); Stephen Bloom (Prof.); Pamela J. Creedon (Prof./Dir.); Judy Polumbaum (Prof.); Carolyn Stewart Dyer (Prof.); Julie Andsager (Assoc. Prof.); Stephen Berry (Assoc. Prof.); Venise Berry (Assoc. Prof.); Meenakshi Gigi Durham (Assoc. Prof./Coord., Iowa Ctr. for Commun. Study/Advisor, Journal of Communication Inquiry); Lyombe(Leo) Eko (Assoc. Prof.); John Kimmich Javier (Assoc. Prof.); Donald McLeese (Assoc. Prof.); Jane Singer (Assoc. Prof.); John Bennett (Asst. Prof.); Stacey Cone (Asst. Prof.); Frank Durham (Asst. Prof.); Sujatha Sosale (Asst. Prof.); Ann Haugland (George H. Gallup Lectr.)

IDAHO

BOISE STATE UNIV.

Street address 1: 1910 University Dr
Street address 3: Boise
Street address state: ID
Zip/Postal code: 83725-0001
Country: USA
Mailing address: 1910 University Dr
Mailing city: Boise
Mailing state: ID
Mailing zip: 83725-0002
General Phone: (208) 426-6300
General Fax: (208) 426-3884
General/National Adv. E-mail: mcox@boisestate.edu
Primary Website: www.arbiteronline.com
Classified Equipment»
Personnel: Brad Arendt (Gen. Mgr.); V. Marvin Cox (Chrmn.); Steve Lyons (Advisor); Dwight Murphy (Avd. Mgr.); Shannon Morgan (Ed. in Chief)

UNIVERSITY OF IDAHO

Street address 1: PO Box 443178
Street address 3: Moscow
Street address state: ID
Zip/Postal code: 84844-3178
Mailing address: PO Box 443178
Mailing city: Moscow
Mailing state: ID
Mailing zip: 83844-3178
General Phone: (208) 885-6458
General Fax: (208) 885-6450
General/National Adv. E-mail: jamm@uidaho.edu
Classified Equipment»
Personnel: Kenton Bird (Dir./Assoc. Prof.); Sandra Haarsager (Prof.); Mark Secrist (Assoc. Prof.); Patricia Hart (Asst. Prof.); Rebecca Tallent (Asst. Prof.); H. James Clark (Lectr.); Sue Hinz (Lectr.); Denise Bennett (Fac.); Glenn Mosley (Fac.); Vicki Rishling (Fac.); Bert Cross (Prof. Emer.); Peter Haggart (Prof. Emer.); Tom Jenness (Prof. Emer.); Paul Miles (Prof. Emer.); Jane Pritchett (Prof. Emer.)

IDAHO STATE UNIVERSITY

Street address 1: Campus Box 8009
Street address 3: Pocatello
Street address state: ID
Zip/Postal code: 83709
Mailing address: Campus Box 8009
Mailing city: Pocatello
Mailing state: ID
Mailing zip: 83709
General Phone: (208) 282-2247
General Fax: (208) 282-2258
General/National Adv. E-mail: bgchief@isu.edu
Primary Website: isubengal.com
Classified Equipment»

ILLINOIS

GATEWAY JOURNALISM REVIEW

Street address 1: Mailcode 6601
Street address 2: 1100 Lincoln Drive
Street address 3: Carbondale
Street address state: IL
Zip/Postal code: 62901
Country: USA
Mailing address:
Mailing city:
Mailing state: MO
Mailing zip:
General Phone: (618) 536-6631
General Fax: (618) 453-5200
Advertising Phone: 314-322-0396
Editorail Phone: 3140322-0396
General/National Adv. E-mail: gatewayjr@siu.edu
Editorial e-mail: wfreivogel@gmail.com
Primary Website: www.gatewayjr.org
Mthly Avg Views: 7818
Mthly Avg Unique Visitors: 5964
Year Established: 1970
Special Editions: June 2022 - The Road to Jan. 6 Ran through Missouri Dec. 2021 - Legal Roadblocks to Police Accountability Dec. 2020 - GJR at 50 - Legacy, Challenge and Vision - From the St. Louis Journalism Review to GJR June 2020 - The 1857 Project Dec. 2016 - The Bill of Rights at 225 August 2016 - Ferguson: America's Arab Spring
Area Served - City: Midwest, with emphasis on Mo. and Ill
Published: Thur
Avg Paid Circ: 270
Avg Free Circ: 30
Classified Equipment»
Industry: Consulting Services: Editorial
Personnel: Bill Freivogel (Pub.); Jackie Spinner (Ed.)

SOUTHERN ILLINOIS UNIVERSITY CARBONDALE

Street address 1: 1100 Lincoln Dr.
Street address 3: Carbondale
Street address state: IL
Zip/Postal code: 62901-6606
Mailing address: 1100 Lincoln Dr
Mailing city: Carbondale
Mailing state: IL
Mailing zip: 62901-4306
General Phone: (618) 453-4308
General Fax: (618) 453-7714
General/National Adv. E-mail: mcma@siu.edu
Classified Equipment»
Personnel: Gary P. Kolb (Prof./Dean); William Babcock (Prof.); John Downing (Prof./Dir. Global media Research Ctr.); John Hochheimer (Prof.); Phylis Johnson (Interim Chair, Radio- Television/Prof.); Dennis T. Lowry (Prof.); Eileen Meehan (Prof.); Lilly A. Boruszkowski (Assoc. Prof.); Lisa Brooten (Assoc. Prof.); Susan Felleman (Assoc. Prof.); William Freivogel (Assoc. Prof./Dir., Journ.); Katherine Frith (Assoc. Prof.); Walter B. Jaehnig (Assoc. Prof.); Jyotsna Kapur (Assoc. Prof.); Fern Logan (Assoc. Prof.); Daniel Overturf (Assoc. Prof.); Jake Podber (Assoc. Prof.); Jyotika Ramaprasad (Assoc. Prof.); Jan Peterson Roddy (Assoc. Prof./Interim Dir., Grad. Studies); R. William Rowley (Assoc. Prof.)

EASTERN ILLINOIS UNIVERSITY

Street address 1: 600 Lincoln Ave., 2521 Buzzard Hall
Street address 3: Charleston
Street address state: IL
Zip/Postal code: 61920-3099
Mailing address: 600 Lincoln Ave # 2521
Mailing city: Charleston
Mailing state: IL
Mailing zip: 61920-3099
General Phone: (217) 581-6003
General Fax: (217) 581-7188
General/National Adv. E-mail: journal@eiu.edu
Classified Equipment»
Personnel: James Tidwell (Chair/Prof.); Brian Poulter (Prof.); L.R. Hyder (Prof.); John Ryan (Prof./Dir., Stud. Pubs.); Joe Gisondi (Assoc. Prof./Advisor, Minority Newspaper); Terry Johnson (Assoc. Prof./Advisor, PRSSA); Sally Turner (Assoc. Prof./Advisor, Yearbook); Janice Collins (Asst. Prof./Advisor, Broadcast); Eunseong Kim (Asst. Prof.); Lola McElwee (Asst. Prof./Advisor, Newspaper); Bryan Murley (Asst. Prof./Advisor, Online); Wanda Brandon (Instr.); Dan Hagen (Instr.); John Johnson (Instr.); Doug Lawhead (Instr.); Elizabeth Viall (Instr.)

COLUMBIA COLLEGE CHICAGO

Street address 1: 600 S. Michigan Ave.
Street address 3: Chicago
Street address state: IL
Zip/Postal code: 60605-1996
Mailing address: 600 S Michigan Ave Fl 5
Mailing city: Chicago
Mailing state: IL
Mailing zip: 60605-1997
General Phone: (312) 369-7687
General Fax: (312) 369-8059
General/National Adv. E-mail: brice@colum.edu
Classified Equipment»
Personnel: Barry Rice (Acting Chair)

DEPAUL UNIVERSITY

Street address 1: 2320 N. Kenmore Ave.
Street address 3: Chicago
Street address state: IL
Zip/Postal code: 60614
Mailing address: 2320 N Kenmore Ave
Mailing city: Chicago
Mailing state: IL
Mailing zip: 60614-3210
General Phone: (773) 325-7585
General Fax: (773) 325-7584
General/National Adv. E-mail: bspeciche@depaul.edu
Classified Equipment»
Personnel: Barbara L. Speicher (Chair)

LOYOLA UNIVERSITY OF CHICAGO

Street address 1: Lake Shore Campus, Loyola Hall, 1110 W. Loyola Ave.
Street address 3: Chicago
Street address state: IL
Zip/Postal code: 60626
Mailing address: Lake Shore Campus, Loyola Hall, 1110 W. Loyola Ave.
Mailing city: Chicago
Mailing state: IL
Mailing zip: 60626
General Phone: (773) 508-3730
General Fax: (773) 508-8821
General/National Adv. E-mail: cmun@luc.edu
Classified Equipment»
Personnel: Bren A.O. Murphy (Chair)

ROOSEVELT UNIVERSITY

Street address 1: 18 S. Michigan Ave.
Street address 3: Chicago
Street address state: IL
Zip/Postal code: 60605
Mailing address: 430 S Michigan Ave
Mailing city: Chicago
Mailing state: IL
Mailing zip: 60605-1394
General Phone: (312) 281-3337

General Fax: (312) 281-3231
General/National Adv. E-mail: comm@roosevelt.edu
Classified Equipment»
Personnel: Linda Jones (Chair)

UNIVERSITY OF ILLINOIS-CHICAGO

Street address 1: 1007 W. Harrison St., MC132
Street address 3: Chicago
Street address state: IL
Zip/Postal code: 60607-7137
Mailing address: 1140 Behavioral Sciences Bldg.,
Mailing city: Chicago
Mailing state: IL
Mailing zip: 60607-7137
General Phone: (312) 996-3187
General Fax: (312) 413-2125
General/National Adv. E-mail: comm@uic.edu
Classified Equipment»
Personnel: Zizi Papacharissi (Head)

DEKALB

NORTHERN ILLINOIS UNIVERSITY

Street address 1: Dept. of Communication
Street address 3: DeKalb
Street address state: IL
Zip/Postal code: 60115
Mailing address: Dept. of Communication
Mailing city: Dekalb
Mailing state: IL
Mailing zip: 60115
General Phone: (815) 753-1563
General Fax: (815) 753-7109
General/National Adv. E-mail: jchown@niu.edu
Primary Website: www.niu.edu/comm
Classified Equipment»
Personnel: Jeff Chown (Acting Chair); Orayb Najjar (Assoc. Prof.); Craig Seymour (Assoc. Prof.); Bill Cassidy (Asst. Prof./Journ. Area Coord.); Sabryna Cornish (Asst. Prof.); Induk Kim (Asst. Prof.); Thomas Oates (Asst. Prof.); Jason Akst (Instr.); Allen May (Supportive Professional Staff/Gen. Mgr., Broadcast News); Alex Wiertelak (Supportive Professional Staff/News Dir.)

SOUTHERN ILLINOIS UNIVERSITY EDWARDSVILLE

Street address 1: Dept. of Mass Communications
Street address 3: Edwardsville
Street address state: IL
Zip/Postal code: 62026-1775
Mailing address: Dept of Mass Communications
Mailing city: Edwardsville
Mailing state: IL
Mailing zip: 62026-0001
General Phone: (618) 650-2230
General Fax: (618) 650-3716
General/National Adv. E-mail: rdonald@siue.edu
Primary Website: www.siue.edu/MASSCOMM
Classified Equipment»
Personnel: Patrick Murphy (Assoc. Prof./Chair); Ralph R. Donald (Prof.); Riley Maynard (Prof.); Gary Hicks (Assoc. Prof./Dir., Grad. Studies); Bala Baptiste (Asst. Prof.); Judy Landers (Asst. Prof.); Elza Ibroscheva (Instr.); Michael Montgomery (Instr.); Zixue Tai (Instr.); Kimberly Wilmot Voss (Instr.); John A. Regnell (Prof. Emer.); John R. Rider (Prof. Emer.); Jack Shaheen (Prof. Emer.); William G. Ward (Prof. Emer.); Nora Baker (Assoc. Prof. Emer.); Barbara Regnell (Assoc. Prof. Emer.)

NORTHWESTERN UNIVERSITY

Street address 1: 1845 Sheridan Rd
Street address 3: Evanston
Street address state: IL
Zip/Postal code: 60208-0815
Country: USA
Mailing address: 1845 Sheridan Rd
Mailing city: Evanston
Mailing state: IL
Mailing zip: 60208-0815
General Phone: (847) 467-1882
General Fax: (847) 491-5565
Classified Equipment»
Personnel: John Lavine (Dean); David Abrahamson (Prof.); Martin Block (Prof.); Jack Doppelt (Prof.); Loren Ghiglione (Prof.); Alec Klein (Prof.); Donna Leff (Prof.); Frank Mulhern (Prof.); Jon Petrovich (Prof.); David Protess (Prof.); Don Schultz (Prof.); Ellen Shearer (Prof.); Clarke Caywood (Assoc. Prof.); Mary Coffman (Assoc. Prof.); Tom Collinger (Assoc. Prof.); Doug Foster (Assoc. Prof.); Jeremy Gilbert (Assoc. Prof.); Rich Gordon (Assoc. Prof.); John Greening (Assoc. Prof.); Ava Greenwell (Assoc. Prof.)

ILLINOIS COLLEGE

Street address 1: 1101 West College Ave.
Street address 3: Jacksonville
Street address state: IL
Zip/Postal code: 62650
Mailing address: 1101 W College Ave
Mailing city: Jacksonville
Mailing state: IL
Mailing zip: 62650-2299
General Phone: (217) 245-3000
Classified Equipment»
Personnel: Jim Kerbaugh (Chair, English); Peter Verkruyse (Chair, Communications/Theatre)

UNIVERSITY OF ST. FRANCIS

Street address 1: 500 Wilcox St.
Street address 3: Joliet
Street address state: IL
Zip/Postal code: 60435
Mailing address: 500 Wilcox St
Mailing city: Joliet
Mailing state: IL
Mailing zip: 60435-6188
General Phone: (815) 740-5064
General Fax: (815) 740-4285
General/National Adv. E-mail: trosner@stfrancis.edu
Classified Equipment»
Personnel: Terre Layng Rosner (Chair)

WESTERN ILLINOIS UNIVERSITY

Street address 1: 1 University Cir.
Street address 3: Macomb
Street address state: IL
Zip/Postal code: 61455
Mailing address: 1 University Cir
Mailing city: Macomb
Mailing state: IL
Mailing zip: 61455-1390
General Phone: (309) 298-1948
General/National Adv. E-mail: y-tang@wiu.edu
Primary Website: http://www.wiu.edu/cofac/bcj/
Classified Equipment»
Personnel: Yong Tang (Asst Prof Dir of Journalism); Teresa Simmons (Assoc. Prof./Advisor, WAF)

ILLINOIS STATE UNIVERSITY

Street address 1: Campus Box 4480
Street address 3: Normal
Street address state: IL
Zip/Postal code: 61790-4480
Mailing address: Campus # 4480
Mailing city: Normal
Mailing state: IL
Mailing zip: 61790-0001
General Phone: (309) 438-3671
General Fax: (309) 438-3048
General/National Adv. E-mail: communication@ilstu.edu
Classified Equipment»
Personnel: Larry W. Long (Exec. Dir.)

BRADLEY UNIVERSITY

Street address 1: Dept. of Communication
Street address 3: Peoria
Street address state: IL
Zip/Postal code: 61625
Mailing address: Dept of Communication
Mailing city: Peoria
Mailing state: IL
Mailing zip: 61625-0001
General Phone: (309) 677-2354
General Fax: (309) 677-3446
General/National Adv. E-mail: pfg@bradley.edu
Classified Equipment»
Personnel: Paul Gullifor (Chair/Prof.); Bob Jacobs (Prof.); Ali Zohoori (Prof.); Olatunji Dare (Assoc. Prof.); Chris Kasch (Assoc. Prof.); Ron Koperski (Assoc. Prof.); Ed Lamoureux (Assoc. Prof.); Gregory Pitts (Assoc. Prof.); Stephen Banning (Asst. Prof.); Maha Bashri (Asst. Prof.); Elena Gabor (Asst. Prof.); Sara Netzley (Asst. Prof.); Margaret Young (Asst. Prof.); Laura Garfinkel (Lectr.); B.J. Lawrence (Lectr.); Linda Strasma (Lectr.); Jan Frazier (Instr.); Tyler Billman (Instr./Asst. Dir., Forensics); Dan Smith (Dir., Forensics); E. Neal Claussen (Prof. Emer.)

AUGUSTANA COLLEGE

Street address 1: 639 38th St
Street address 3: Rock Island
Street address state: IL
Zip/Postal code: 61201-2210
Country: USA
Mailing address: 639 38th St
Mailing city: Rock Island
Mailing state: IL
Mailing zip: 61201-2296
General Phone: (309) 794-3460
General Fax: (309) 794-3460
Advertising Phone: (309) 794-7484
Editorail Phone: (309) 794-7485
General/National Adv. E-mail: observer@augustana.edu
Primary Website: www.augustana.edu
Classified Equipment»
Personnel: Carolyn Yaschur (Advisor); David Schwartz (Advisor)

GOVERNORS STATE UNIV.

Street address 1: 1 University Pkwy
Street address 2: E2543
Street address 3: University Park
Street address state: IL
Zip/Postal code: 60484-3165
Country: USA
Mailing address: 1 University Pkwy.
Mailing city: University Park
Mailing state: IL
Mailing zip: 60484-3165
General Phone: (708) 534-4517
General Fax: (708) 534-7895
General/National Adv. E-mail: phoenix@govst.edu
Primary Website: www.gsuphoenix.com
Published: Wed
Published Other: First and third Wednesdays
Classified Equipment»
Personnel: Debbie James (Faculty Advisor); Michael Purdy (Emeritus Professor)

URBANA

UNIVERSITY OF ILLINOIS

Street address 1: 810 S. Wright St., 119 Gregory Hall/MC-462
Street address 3: Urbana
Street address state: IL
Zip/Postal code: 61801
Mailing address: 810 S Wright St Gregory HALL/MC-462
Mailing city: Urbana
Mailing state: IL
Mailing zip: 61801-3644
General Phone: (217) 333-2350
General Fax: (217) 333-9882
General/National Adv. E-mail: ccomm@uiuc.edu
Primary Website: www.comm.uiuc.edu
Classified Equipment»
Personnel: Ronald E. Yates (Sleeman Prof./Dean); William F. Brewer (Prof.); Angharad N. Valdivia (Prof.); Clifford G. Christians (Prof./Dir., Institute for Comm. Research/Sandage); C.L. Cole (Prof.); Leon D. Dash (Prof./Swanlund Chair); Matthew C. Ehrlich (Prof.); Norman K. Denzin (Prof./College Scholar); Brant Houston (Knight Chair Prof.); Walter G. Harrington (Prof./Head, Journ.); Steve J. Helle (Prof.); Louis W. Liebovich (Prof.); John C. Nerone (Prof./Dir., Grad. Studies, Inst. of Comm. Research/College Scholar); Kent A. Ono (Prof.); Jan Slater (Prof./Head, Adv.); Amy J. Aidman (Assoc. Dean, Research/Assoc. Prof.); Christopher D. Benson (Assoc. Prof.); Nancy J. Benson (Assoc. Prof.); William E. Berry (Assoc. Prof.); Jay M. Rosenstein (Assoc. Prof.)

INDIANA

ANDERSON UNIVERSITY

Street address 1: 1100 E. Fifth St.
Street address 3: Anderson
Street address state: IN
Zip/Postal code: 46012
Mailing address: 1100 E 5th St
Mailing city: Anderson
Mailing state: IN
Mailing zip: 46012-3495
General Phone: (765) 641-4340
Classified Equipment»
Personnel: Donald G. Boggs (Chair)

INDIANA UNIVERSITY

Street address 1: Bloomington Campus
Street address 2: Ernie Pyle Hall, Rm. 200, 940 E. Seventh St.
Street address 3: Bloomington
Street address state: IN
Zip/Postal code: 47405
Mailing address: Bloomington Campus
Mailing city: Bloomington
Mailing state: IN
Mailing zip: 47405
General Phone: (812) 855-9247
General Fax: (812) 855-0901
Primary Website: journalism.iupui.edu
Classified Equipment»
Personnel: Bradley Hamm (Dean/Prof.); John E. Dvorak (Prof.); Shannon Martin (Prof.); David P. Nord (Prof.); David H. Weaver (Prof./Roy W. Howard Research Prof.); David E. Boeyink (Assoc. Prof.); Bonnie J. Brownlee (Assoc. Prof./Assoc. Dean, Undergrad. Studies); Claude H. Cookman (Assoc. Prof.); Jon P. Dilts (Assoc. Prof.); Michael R. Evans (Assoc. Prof.); Tony Fargo (Assoc. Prof.); Owen V. Johnson (Assoc. Prof.); Jim Kelly (Assoc. Prof.); Radhika Parameswaran (Assoc. Prof.); Steven L. Raymer (Assoc. Prof.); Amy L. Reynolds (Assoc. Prof./Assoc. Dean, Grad. Studies); S. Holly Stocking (Assoc. Prof.); Mike Conway (Asst. Prof.); Lessa Hatley Major (Asst. Prof.); Emily Metzgar (Asst. Prof.)

UNIVERSITY OF EVANSVILLE

Street address 1: 1800 Lincoln Ave.
Street address 3: Evansville
Street address state: IN
Zip/Postal code: 47722
Mailing address: 1800 Lincoln Ave
Mailing city: Evansville
Mailing state: IN
Mailing zip: 47714-1506
General Phone: (812) 488-2341
General Fax: (812) 488-2717
General/National Adv. E-mail: dt4@evansville.edu
Primary Website: www.evansville.edu
Classified Equipment»
Personnel: Mark L. Shifflet (Prof./Chair); Hope Bock (Prof.); Michael J. Stankey (Prof.); T. Dean Thomlison (Prof.); Lori Smith (Instr.)

UNIVERSITY OF SOUTHERN INDIANA

Street address 1: 8600 University Blvd.
Street address 3: Evansville
Street address state: IN
Zip/Postal code: 47712-3596
Mailing address: 8600 University Blvd
Mailing city: Evansville
Mailing state: IN
Mailing zip: 47712-3590
General Phone: (812) 461-5220
General Fax: (812) 465-7152
General/National Adv. E-mail: wrinks@usi.edu
Primary Website: www.usi.edu/libarts/comm
Classified Equipment»
Personnel: J. Wayne Rinks (Chair/Assoc. Prof.); Karen H. Bonnell (Prof.); Gael L. Cooper (Prof.); Leigh Anne Howard (Assoc. Prof.); Chad R. Tew (Assoc. Prof.); David N. Black (Asst. Prof.); Wesley T. Durham (Asst. Prof.); Yoon-Joo Lee (Asst. Prof.); John K. Saliba (Asst. Prof.); Robert E. West (Asst. Prof.); Karen S. Braselton (Instr.); Erin Gibson (Instr.); Robert W. Jeffers (Instr.);

John M. Morris (Instr.); Mary B. Reese (Instr.); Seymour Brodsky (Prof. Emer.); Dal M. Herring (Prof. Emer.); Helen R. Sands (Prof. Emer.); Mary A. Schroeder (Prof. Emer.); Kenneth G. Vance (Prof. Emer.)

FRANKLIN COLLEGE

Street address 1: 501 E. Monroe St.
Street address 3: Franklin
Street address state: IN
Zip/Postal code: 46131
Mailing address: 101 Branigin Blvd
Mailing city: Franklin
Mailing state: IN
Mailing zip: 46131-2598
General Phone: (317) 738-8200
General Fax: (317) 738-8234
General/National Adv. E-mail: bbridges@franklincollege.edu
Primary Website: psj.franklincollege.edu
Classified Equipment»
Personnel: Ray Begovich (Dir.)

GOSHEN COLLEGE

Street address 1: Dept. of Communication
Street address 2: 1700 South Main St.
Street address 3: Goshen
Street address state: IN
Zip/Postal code: 46526-4798
Mailing address: Dept. of Communication
Mailing city: Goshen
Mailing state: IN
Mailing zip: 46526-4798
General Phone: (574) 535-7450
General Fax: (574) 535-7660
General/National Adv. E-mail: dstoltzfus@goshen.edu
Primary Website: www.goshen.edu
Classified Equipment»
Personnel: Duane Stoltzfus (Prof.)

DEPAUW UNIVERSITY

Street address 1: 609 S. Locust Street
Street address 3: Greencastle
Street address state: IN
Zip/Postal code: 46135-00037
Mailing address: PO Box 37
Mailing city: Greencastle
Mailing state: IN
Mailing zip: 46135-0037
General Phone: (765) 658-4495
General Fax: (765) 658-4499
General/National Adv. E-mail: jeffmccall@depauw.edu
Classified Equipment»
Personnel: Jeffrey M. McCall (Professor of media studies)

BUTLER UNIV.

Street address 1: 4600 Sunset Ave
Street address 3: Indianapolis
Street address state: IN
Zip/Postal code: 46208-3443
Country: USA
Mailing address: 4600 Sunset Ave # 112
Mailing city: Indianapolis
Mailing state: IN
Mailing zip: 46208-3487
General Phone: (317) 940-9358
General Fax: (317) 940-9713
General/National Adv. E-mail: mweiteka@butler.edu
Display Adv. E-mail: advertising@butler.edu
Primary Website: dawgnet.butler.edu
Classified Equipment»
Personnel: Kwadwo Anokwa (Dir.); Charles St. Cyr (Advisor); Lauren Fisher (Adv. Mgr); Meg Shaw (Ed.)

INDIANA UNIVERSITY

Street address 1: Indianapolis Campus
Street address 2: 535 W. Michigan St.
Street address 3: Indianapolis
Street address state: IN
Zip/Postal code: 46202
Mailing address: Indianapolis Campus
Mailing city: Indianapolis
Mailing state: IN
Mailing zip: 46202
General Phone: (317) 278-5320
General Fax: (317) 278-5321
General/National Adv. E-mail: dperkins@foi.iupui.edu
Primary Website: www.journalism.iupui.edu
Classified Equipment»
Personnel: James W. Brown (Prof./Exec. Assoc. Dean); Jonas Bjork (Prof.); Sherry Ricchiardi (Prof.); Pamela Laucella (Asst. Prof.); Robert Dittmer (Lectr.); Maggie Balough Hillery (Adj. Prof./Pub., The Sagamore); Patrick McKeand (Adj. Prof./Pub. Emer., The Sagamore); Shirley Quate (Prof. Emer.)

UNIVERSITY OF INDIANAPOLIS

Street address 1: 1400 E. Hanna Ave.
Street address 3: Indianapolis
Street address state: IN
Zip/Postal code: 46227
Mailing address: 1400 E Hanna Ave
Mailing city: Indianapolis
Mailing state: IN
Mailing zip: 46227-3697
General Phone: (317) 788-3280
General Fax: (317) 788-3490
General/National Adv. E-mail: catchings@uindy.edu
Primary Website: www.communication.uindy.edu
Classified Equipment»
Personnel: Billy Catchings (Chair)

INDIANA WESLEYAN UNIVERSITY

Street address 1: 4201 S Washington St
Street address 3: Marion
Street address state: IN
Zip/Postal code: 46953-4974
Country: USA
Mailing address: 4201 S Washington St
Mailing city: Marion
Mailing state: IN
Mailing zip: 46953-4974
General Phone: (765) 677-1818
General Fax: (765) 677-1755
General/National Adv. E-mail: amy.smelser@indwes.edu
Primary Website: https://www.indwes.edu/undergraduate/majors/division-of-communication-and-theatre/
Classified Equipment»
Personnel: Amy Smelser (Ed.); Amy Smelser (Instructor)

BALL STATE UNIVERSITY

Street address 1: Art and Journalism Bldg. 300
Street address 3: Muncie
Street address state: IN
Zip/Postal code: 47306
Mailing address: Art & Journalism Bldg # 300
Mailing city: Muncie
Mailing state: IN
Mailing zip: 47306-0001
General Phone: (765) 285-6000
General Fax: (765) 285-6002
General/National Adv. E-mail: bsujourn@bsu.edu
Primary Website: www.bsu.edu/journalism
Classified Equipment»
Personnel: Roger Lavery (Prof./Dean); Marilyn Weaver (Prof./Chair); Mark Masse (Prof.); David Sumner (Prof./Coord., Mag.); Robert Gustafson (Assoc. Prof.); Alfredo Marin-Carle (Assoc. Prof.); Robert Pritchard (Assoc. Prof./Coord., PR); Jennifer George-Palilonis (Asst. Prof./Coord., Journ. Graphics); Michael Hanley (Asst. Prof./Coord. Advertising); Kenneth Heinen (Asst. Prof.); Tendayi Kumbula (Asst. Prof.); Becky McDonald (Asst. Prof.); Thomas Price (Asst. Prof./Coord., Photojournalism); Mary Spillman (Asst. Prof./Coord., News-Editorial); Dustin Supa (Asst. Prof.); Daniel Waechter (Asst. Prof./Asst. Chair/Curricular Advising/Grad. Advisor); Pamela Farmen (Instr.); Brian Hayes (Instr./Coord. Secondary Education); Sy Jenkins (Instr./Mng. Ed., NewsLink); David Kitchell (Instr.); Pam Gard

UNIVERSITY OF NOTRE DAME

Street address 1: Dept. of American Studies
Street address 3: Notre Dame
Street address state: IN
Zip/Postal code: 46556
Mailing address: Dept. of American Studies
Mailing city: Notre Dame
Mailing state: IN
Mailing zip: 46556
General Phone: (219) 631-7316
General Fax: (219) 631-4268
General/National Adv. E-mail: al.astudiel.l@nd.edu
Classified Equipment»
Personnel: Robert Schmuhl (Dir., John W. Gallivan Program in Journalism, Ethics & Democracy)

SAINT MARY-OF-THE-WOODS

SAINT MARY-OF-THE-WOODS COLLEGE

Street address 1: Hulman Hall, Rm. 011
Street address 3: Saint Mary-of-the-Woods
Street address state: IN
Zip/Postal code: 47876
Mailing address: Hulman Hall, Rm. 011
Mailing city: Saint Mary-Of-The-Woods
Mailing state: IN
Mailing zip: 47876
General Phone: (812) 535-5132
General Fax: (812) 535-5228
General/National Adv. E-mail: nmayfield@smwc.edu
Classified Equipment»
Personnel: Nancy Pieters Mayfield (Chair)

INDIANA STATE UNIVERSITY

Street address 1: Dept. of Communication
Street address 3: Terre Haute
Street address state: IN
Zip/Postal code: 47809
Mailing address: Dept of Communication
Mailing city: Terre Haute
Mailing state: IN
Mailing zip: 47809-0001
General Phone: (812) 237-3221
General Fax: (812) 237-3217
General/National Adv. E-mail: mbuchholz@isugw.indstate.edu
Classified Equipment»
Personnel: Paul D. Hightower (Prof.); Michael O. Buchholz (Assoc. Prof.)

TAYLOR UNIVERSITY

Street address 1: 236 West Reade Avenue
Street address 3: Upland
Street address state: IN
Zip/Postal code: 46989-1001
County: Grant
Country: USA
Mailing address: 236 West Reade Avenue
Mailing city: Upland
Mailing state: IN
Mailing zip: 46989-1001
General Phone: (765) 998-5590
General/National Adv. E-mail: dnhensley@taylor.edu
Primary Website: www.taylor.edu
Classified Equipment»
Personnel: Dennis E. Hensley (Director, Professional Writing major); Linda Taylor (Instructor in Professional Writing)

VALPARAISO UNIVERSITY

Street address 1: 1809 Chapel Dr
Street address 3: Valparaiso
Street address state: IN
Zip/Postal code: 46383-4517
Country: USA
Mailing address: 1809 Chapel Dr
Mailing city: Valparaiso
Mailing state: IN
Mailing zip: 46383-4517
General Phone: (219) 464-5271
General Fax: (219) 464-6742
General/National Adv. E-mail: douglas.kocher@valpo.edu
Primary Website: www.valpo.edu/torch
Classified Equipment»
Personnel: Douglas J. Kocher (Chair); Jason Paupore (Advisor); Andy Simmons (Bus.Mgr.); Luis Fifuentes (Adv.Mgr.); Kathryn Kattalia (Ed. in chief)

JOURNALISM PROGRAM, VINCENNES UNIVERSITY

Street address 1: 1002 N 1st St
Street address 3: Vincennes
Street address state: IN
Zip/Postal code: 47591-1504
Country: USA
Mailing address: 1002 N 1st St
Mailing city: Vincennes
Mailing state: IN
Mailing zip: 47591-1500
General Phone: (812) 888-4551
General Fax: (812) 888-5531
General/National Adv. E-mail: trailblazer@vinu.edu
Primary Website: www.vutrailblazernews.com
Year Established: 1923
Published: Other
Classified Equipment»
Personnel: Emily Taylor (Journalism Asst. Professor, Department Chair of Media Production)

PURDUE UNIVERSITY/BRIAN LAMB SCHOOL OF COMMUNICATION

Street address 1: 100 N. University St.
Street address 3: West Lafayette
Street address state: IN
Zip/Postal code: 47907-2098
County: Tippecanoe
Country: USA
Mailing address: BRNG 2114
Mailing city: West Lafayette
Mailing state: IN
Mailing zip: 47907-2098
General Phone: (765) 494-3429
General Fax: (765) 496-1394
Primary Website: www.cla.purdue.edu/communication
Classified Equipment»

CALUMET COLLEGE OF ST. JOSEPH

Street address 1: 2400 New York Ave
Street address 3: Whiting
Street address state: IN
Zip/Postal code: 46394-2146
Country: USA
Mailing address: 2400 New York Ave
Mailing city: Whiting
Mailing state: IN
Mailing zip: 46394-2195
General Phone: (219) 473-4322
General Fax: (219) 473-4219
Primary Website: www.ccsj.edu
Published: Mthly
Classified Equipment»
Personnel: Mark Cassello (Director of English & Media Communications); Dawn Muhammad (PD); Daren Jasieniecki (Mktg. Mgr.)

KANSAS

BAKER UNIVERSITY

Street address 1: PO Box 65
Street address 3: Baldwin City
Street address state: KS
Zip/Postal code: 66006-0065
Country: USA
Mailing address: PO Box 65
Mailing city: Baldwin City
Mailing state: KS
Mailing zip: 66006-0065
General Phone: (913) 594-6451
General Fax: (913) 594-3570
General/National Adv. E-mail: bayha@harvey.bakeru.edu
Primary Website: www.thebakerorange.com
Classified Equipment»
Personnel: Gwyn Mellinger (Advisor); Ann Rosenthal (Chair); Dave Bostwick (Advisor); Chris Smith (Ed.)

FORT HAYS STATE UNIVERSITY

Street address 1: 600 Park St.
Street address 3: Hays
Street address state: KS
Zip/Postal code: 67601
County: Ellis
Country: U.S.A.
Mailing address: 600 Park St.
Mailing city: Hays
Mailing state: KS
Mailing zip: 67601-4099
General Phone: (785) 628-4018

General Fax: (785) 628-4075
General/National Adv. E-mail: ihunting@fhsu.edu
Primary Website: www.fhsu.edu
Classified Equipment»
Personnel: Linn Ann Huntington (Dir.); Qing Jiang Yao (Dr.); Hsin-Yen Yang (Dr.)

UNIVERSITY OF KANSAS

Street address 1: 1435 Jayhawk Blvd., 200 Stauffer-Flint Hall
Street address 3: Lawrence
Street address state: KS
Zip/Postal code: 66045-7575
Mailing address: 1435 Jayhawk Blvd # 200
Mailing city: Lawrence
Mailing state: KS
Mailing zip: 66045-7594
General Phone: (785) 864-4755
General Fax: (785) 864-4396
General/National Adv. E-mail: jschool@ku.edu
Primary Website: www.journalism.ku.edu
Classified Equipment»
Personnel: Ann M. Brill (Assoc. Prof./Dean); Pam Fine (Prof./Knight Chair on the News, Leadership/ Community); Ted Frederickson (Prof.); James K. Gentry (Prof.); David D. Perlmutter (Prof.); Susanne Shaw (Prof./Accrediting Coun.); Robert Basow (Assoc. Prof.); Timothy Bengtson (Assoc. Prof./Chair, Strategic Commun.); John Broholm (Assoc. Prof.); David Guth (Assoc. Prof./Assoc. Dean); Carol Holstead (Assoc. Prof.); Linda Lee (Assoc. Prof.); Tien-Tsung Lee (Assoc. Prof.); Charles Marsh (Assoc. Prof.); Max Utsler (Assoc. Prof.); Tom Volek (Assoc. Prof./Interim Dir., Grad. Program); Mike Williams (Assoc. Prof./ Chair, News Information); Barbara Barnett (Asst. Prof.); Mugur V. Geana (Asst. Prof.); Crystal Lumpkins (Asst. Prof.)

KANSAS STATE UNIVERSITY

Street address 1: 105 Kedzie Hall
Street address 3: Manhattan
Street address state: KS
Zip/Postal code: 66506-1501
Mailing address: 105 Kedzie Hall
Mailing city: Manhattan
Mailing state: KS
Mailing zip: 66506-1500
General Phone: (785) 532-6890
General Fax: (785) 532-5484
General/National Adv. E-mail: journalism@ksu.edu
Primary Website: jmc.ksu.edu
Classified Equipment»
Personnel: Angela Powers (Prof./Dir.); William J. Adams (Prof.); Todd Simon (Prof./Head, PR seq.); Soontae An (Assoc. Prof.); Louise Benjamin (Assoc. Prof./ Ross Beach Chair); Bonnie Bressers (Assoc. Prof./ Head, Journalism Digital Media Sequence); Joye Gordon (Assoc. Prof.); Thomas Gould (Assoc. Prof.); Hyun-Seung Jin (Assoc. Prof./Assoc. Dir., Research/ Grad. Studies); R. Charles Pearce (Assoc. Prof./Head, Adv. Seq.); J. Steven Smethers (Assoc. Prof./Assoc. Dir., Undergrad. Studies); Kimetris Baltrip (Asst. Prof.); Fred Brock (Asst. Prof./R.M. Seaton Professinal Chair); Gloria Freeland (Asst. Prof.); Ginger Loggins (Asst. Prof.); Sam Mwangi (Asst. Prof.); Nancy Muturi (Asst. Prof.); Linda Puntney (Asst. Prof./Dir., Student Publications Inc./Exec. Dir., Journalism Educ. Assn.); Seong-Hun Yun (Asst. Prof.); Stacy Neumann (Instr.)

PITTSBURG STATE UNIVERSITY

Street address 1: 1701 S. Broadway, 417 Grubbs Hall
Street address 3: Pittsburg
Street address state: KS
Zip/Postal code: 66762
Mailing address: 1701 S Broadway St
Mailing city: Pittsburg
Mailing state: KS
Mailing zip: 66762-7500
General Phone: (620) 235-4716
General Fax: (620) 235-4686
General/National Adv. E-mail: jscott@pittstate.edu
Classified Equipment»
Personnel: Peter K. Hamilton (Chair)

WASHBURN UNIVERSITY

Street address 1: 316 Henderson Learning Resources Ctr.
Street address 2: 1700 SW College Ave.
Street address 3: Topeka
Street address state: KS
Zip/Postal code: 66621
Mailing address: 316 Henderson Learning Resources Ctr.
Mailing city: Topeka
Mailing state: KS
Mailing zip: 66621
General Phone: (785) 670-1836
General Fax: (785) 670-1234
General/National Adv. E-mail: massmedia@washburn.edu
Primary Website: www.morforu.wikidot.com
Classified Equipment»
Personnel: Dr. Barbara DeSanto (Chair/Fellow PRSA/ Prof.); Frank Chorba (Prof.); Charles Cranston (Prof.); Kathy Menzie (Asst. Prof.); Maria Raicheva-Stover (Asst. Prof.); Regina Cassell (Lectr.)

WICHITA STATE UNIVERSITY

Street address 1: Elliott School of Communication
Street address 3: Wichita
Street address state: KS
Zip/Postal code: 67260-0031
Mailing address: Elliott School of Communication
Mailing city: Wichita
Mailing state: KS
Mailing zip: 67260-0001
General Phone: (316) 978-3185
General Fax: (316) 978-3006
General/National Adv. E-mail: susan.huxman@wichita.edu
Classified Equipment»
Personnel: Susan Huxman (Assoc. Prof./Dir.); Philip Gaunt (Prof.); Sharon Iorio (Prof.); Vernon Keel (Prof.); Les Anderson (Assoc. Prof.); Rick Armstrong (Assoc. Prof.); Dan Close (Assoc. Prof.); Patricia Dooley (Assoc. Prof.); Kevin Hager (Assoc. Prof.); Keith Williamson (Assoc. Prof.); Michael Boyle (Asst. Prof.); Jeff Jarman (Asst. Prof.); Amy Lauters (Asst. Prof.); Greg Stene (Asst. Prof.); Mike Wood (Asst. Prof.); Nancy Fisher (Instr.); Kevin Keplar (Instr.); Connie Morris (Instr.); Randy Brown (Sr. Fellow); Al Higdon (Professional-in-Residence)

KENTUCKY

WESTERN KENTUCKY UNIVERSITY

Street address 1: 1660 Normal St
Street address 2: Western Kentucky University
Street address 3: Bowling Green
Street address state: KY
Zip/Postal code: 42101-3536
Country: USA
Mailing address: 1906 College Heights Blvd # 11084
Mailing city: Bowling Green
Mailing state: KY
Mailing zip: 42101-1084
General Phone: (270) 745-2653
Advertising Phone: (270) 745-2653
Editorail Phone: (270) 745-2653
General/National Adv. E-mail: carrie.pratt@wku.edu
Display Adv. E-mail: william.hoagland@wku.edu
Editorial e-mail: herald.editor@wku.edu
Primary Website: www.wkuherald.com
Year Established: 1925
Advertising (Open Inch Rate) Weekday/Saturday: Call for information
Published: Tues`Thur
Published Other: Topper Extra sports section published on home football days
Avg Free Circ: 7000
Classified Equipment»
Personnel: Sherry West (Operations Mgr); Carrie Pratt (Herald Adviser, Multiplatform News Adviser); Tracy Newton (Office Associate); Will Hoagland (Advt Adviser and Sales Mgr); Chuck Clark (Dir of Student Publications); Sam Oldenburg (Talisman adviser)
Parent company (for newspapers): WKU Student Publications

HIGHLAND HEIGHTS

NORTHERN KENTUCKY UNIVERSITY

Street address 1: 134 Landrum Academic Center, Nunn Dr.
Street address 3: Highland Heights
Street address state: KY
Zip/Postal code: 41099
Mailing address: 134 Landrum Academic Center Nunn Dr
Mailing city: Newport
Mailing state: KY
Mailing zip: 41099-0001
General Phone: (859) 572-5435
General Fax: (859) 572-6187
General/National Adv. E-mail: ragsdale@nku.edu
Classified Equipment»
Personnel: Gaut Ragsdale (Chair)

UNIVERSITY OF KENTUCKY

Street address 1: 107 Grehan Bldg.
Street address 3: Lexington
Street address state: KY
Zip/Postal code: 40506-0042
Mailing address: 107 Grehan
Mailing city: Lexington
Mailing state: KY
Mailing zip: 40506-0001
General Phone: (859) 257-1730
General Fax: (859) 323-3168
General/National Adv. E-mail: amy.jarvis@uky.edu
Classified Equipment»
Personnel: Beth E. Barnes (Prof./Dir.); Richard Labunski (Prof.); Thomas Lindlof (Prof.); Chike Anyaegbunam (Assoc. Prof.); Dennis Altman (Assoc. Prof.); Jim Hertog (Assoc. Prof.); Elizabeth Scoobie Ryan (Assoc. Prof.); Leland Buck Ryan (Assoc. Prof.); Scott Whitlow (Assoc. Prof.); Deborah Chung (Asst. Prof.); John Clark (Asst. Prof.); Mel Coffee (Asst. Prof.); Al Cross (Asst. Prof.); Alyssa Eckman (Asst. Prof.); Michael Farrell (Asst. Prof.); Phillip Hutchison (Asst. Prof.); Bobi Ivanov (Asst. Prof.); Yung Soo Kim (Asst. Prof.); Zixue Tai (Asst. Prof.); Kathleen Kakie Urch (Asst. Prof.)

UNIVERSITY OF LOUISVILLE

Street address 1: Dept. of Communication
Street address 2: 310 Strickler Hall
Street address 3: Louisville
Street address state: KY
Zip/Postal code: 40292
Mailing address: Dept. of Communication
Mailing city: Louisville
Mailing state: KY
Mailing zip: 40292-0001
General Phone: (502) 852-6976
General Fax: (502) 852-8166
General/National Adv. E-mail: al@Louisville.edu
Primary Website: comm.louisville.edu
Classified Equipment»
Personnel: Al Futrell (Chair)

MOREHEAD STATE UNIVERSITY

Street address 1: BR 115-A, Dept. of Communication & Theatre
Street address 3: Morehead
Street address state: KY
Zip/Postal code: 40351
Mailing address: BR 115-A, Dept. of Communication & Theatre
Mailing city: Morehead
Mailing state: KY
Mailing zip: 40351
General Phone: (606) 783-5312
General Fax: (606) 783-2457
General/National Adv. E-mail: j.atkins@moreheadstate.edu
Primary Website: www.trailblazeronline.net
Classified Equipment»
Personnel: Robert Willenbrink (Chair); Joan Atkins (Journalism Coord.)

MURRAY STATE UNIVERSITY

Street address 1: 114 Wilson Hall
Street address 3: Murray
Street address state: KY
Zip/Postal code: 42071-3311
Mailing address: 114 Wilson Hall
Mailing city: Murray
Mailing state: KY
Mailing zip: 42071-3311
General Phone: (809) 762-2387
General Fax: (270) 809-2390
General/National Adv. E-mail: journalism@murraystate.edu
Primary Website: www.themurraystatenews.com
Classified Equipment»
Personnel: Allen White (Prof./Interim Chair); John Dillon (Prof.); Roger Haney (Prof.); Bob Lochte (Prof./Grad. Coord.); Jeanne S. Scafella (Prof.); Ann Landini (Assoc. Prof.); Debbie Owens (Assoc. Prof.); Celia Wall (Assoc. Prof.); Bob Valentine (Sr. Lectr.); Gill Welsch (Sr. Lectr.); Joe Hedges (Lectr.); Jeremy McKeel (Lectr.); Robin B. Orvino-Proulx (Lectr.); Darryl Armstrong (Adj.); Janett Blythe (Adj.); Victoria Daughrity (Adj.); Kate Lochte (Adj.); Jeff Prater (Adj.); Ann Thrower (Adj.); Mark Welch (Adj.)

EASTERN KENTUCKY UNIVERSITY

Street address 1: Combs Building, Room 326
Street address 3: Richmond
Street address state: KY
Zip/Postal code: 40475-3102
Mailing address: Combs Building, Room 326
Mailing city: Richmond
Mailing state: KY
Mailing zip: 40475-3102
General Phone: (859) 622-1881
General Fax: (859) 622-2354
General/National Adv. E-mail: reggie.beehner@eku.edu
Primary Website: http://www.easternprogress.com/
Classified Equipment»
Personnel: Reggie Beehner (Adviser, Eastern Progress)

ASBURY COLLEGE

Street address 1: 1 Macklem Dr
Street address 3: Wilmore
Street address state: KY
Zip/Postal code: 40390-1152
Country: USA
Mailing address: 1 Macklem Dr
Mailing city: Wilmore
Mailing state: KY
Mailing zip: 40390-1198
General Phone: (859) 858-3511
General Fax: (859) 858-3921
General/National Adv. E-mail: mlonginow@asbury.edu
Primary Website: collegian.asbury.edu
Classified Equipment»
Personnel: Deanna Morono (Exec. Ed.); James R. Owens (Chair); Kayla Dubois (Mng. Ed.); Zack Klemme (News Ed.); Morgan Schutters (Web Design)

LOUISIANA

LOUISIANA STATE UNIVERSITY

Street address 1: 211 Journalism Bldg.
Street address 3: Baton Rouge
Street address state: LA
Zip/Postal code: 70803-7202
Mailing address: 211 Journalism
Mailing city: Baton Rouge
Mailing state: LA
Mailing zip: 70803-0001
General Phone: (225) 578-2336
General Fax: (225) 578-2125
Primary Website: www.manship.lsu.edu
Classified Equipment»
Personnel: John M. Hamilton (Prof./Dean); Timothy Cook (Prof.); Louis A. Day (Prof.); Ronald G. Garay (Prof.); Robert K. Goidel (Prof.); Ralph Izard (Prof.); Laura Lindsay (Prof.); Richard A. Nelson (Prof.); Jinx Broussard (Assoc. Prof.); Margaret H. DeFleur (Assoc. Prof./Assoc. Dean); David D. Kurpius (Assoc. Prof./ Assoc. Dean); Eileen Meehan (Assoc. Prof.); Anne Osborne (Assoc. Prof./Assoc. Dean); Jay L. Perkins (Assoc. Prof.); Judith Sylvester (Assoc. Prof.); Denis Wu (Assoc. Prof.); Lori Boyer (Asst. Prof.); Ketan Chitnis (Asst. Prof.); Emily Erickson (Asst. Prof.); Craig Freeman (Asst. Prof.)

SOUTHERN UNIVERSITY AND A&M COLLEGE

Street address 1: 220 Stewart Hall
Street address 3: Baton Rouge
Street address state: LA
Zip/Postal code: 70813
Mailing address: 220 Stewart Hall
Mailing city: Baton Rouge
Mailing state: LA
Mailing zip: 70813-0001

General Phone: (225) 771-5790
General Fax: (225) 771-4943
General/National Adv. E-mail: mahmoud_braima@cxs.subr.edu
Classified Equipment»
Personnel: Mahmoud Braima (Head)

GRAMBLING STATE UNIVERSITY

Street address 1: PO Box 45
Street address 3: Grambling
Street address state: LA
Zip/Postal code: 71245
Mailing address: PO Box 45
Mailing city: Grambling
Mailing state: LA
Mailing zip: 71245-0045
General Phone: (318) 274-2403
General Fax: (318) 274-3194
General/National Adv. E-mail: edum@gram.edu
Classified Equipment»
Personnel: Martin O. Edu (Acting Head)

SOUTHEASTERN LOUISIANA UNIVERSITY

Street address 1: 344 D. Vickers Hall, Sycamore St., SLU 10451
Street address 3: Hammond
Street address state: LA
Zip/Postal code: 70402
Mailing address: 344 D Vickers Hall, Sycamore St, Slu 10451
Mailing city: Hammond
Mailing state: LA
Mailing zip: 70402-0001
General Phone: (504) 549-2105
General Fax: (504) 549-5014
General/National Adv. E-mail: fcom1157@selu.edu
Classified Equipment»
Personnel: Karen Fontenot (Head/Assoc. Prof.); Joe Mirando (Prof.); William Parrill (Prof.); T. Win Welford (Prof.); Jack Wellman (Prof.); Lynn Wellmann (Assoc. Prof.); Frances Brandau-Brown (Asst. Prof.); Joe Burns (Asst. Prof.); Mike Applin (Instr.); Terri Miller-Drufner (Instr.)

CYPRESS LAKE WIRE

Street address 1: 326 General Mouton Ave
Street address 3: Lafayette
Street address state: LA
Zip/Postal code: 70503
County: Lafayette
Country: United States
Mailing address: 326 General Mouton Ave
Mailing city: Lafayette
Mailing state: LA
General Phone: 3374825221
General Fax: 3374825221
Year Established: 2018
Own Printing Facility: N
Commercial printers: N
Published: Mon`Tues`Wed`Thur`Fri`Other
Weekday Frequency: All day
Audit By: Sworn/Estimate/Non-Audited
Audit Date: 8/14/2019
Classified Equipment»
Personnel: Stephenson Waters

UNIVERSITY OF LOUISIANA AT LAFAYETTE

Street address 1: Rm. 107, Burke-Hawthorne Hall, Hebrard Blvd.
Street address 3: Lafayette
Street address state: LA
Zip/Postal code: 70503
Mailing address: PO Box 43650
Mailing city: Lafayette
Mailing state: LA
Mailing zip: 70504-0001
General Phone: (337) 482-6103
General Fax: (337) 482-6104
Primary Website: comm.louisiana.edu
Classified Equipment»
Personnel: Bette J. Kauffman (Dept. Head/Assoc. Prof.); Jeffrey M. Gibson (Assoc. Prof.); Tae-hyun Kim (Asst. Prof.); Robert E. Lewis (Asst. Prof.); Joel R. Willer (Asst. Prof.); Jarrett Reeves (Instr.); Mark Simmons (Part-time Adj. Fac)

MCNEESE STATE UNIVERSITY

Street address 1: PO Box 90335
Street address 3: Lake Charles
Street address state: LA
Zip/Postal code: 70609
Mailing address: PO Box 90335
Mailing city: Lake Charles
Mailing state: LA
Mailing zip: 70609-0001
General Phone: (337) 475-5290
General Fax: (337) 475-5291
General/National Adv. E-mail: hover@mcneese.edu
Classified Equipment»
Personnel: Henry Overduin (Head/Prof.); Leonard Barchak (Prof.); Carrie Chrisco (Assoc. Prof.); Larry Vinson (Assoc. Prof., Speech Prog.); Patrick Roddy (Asst. Prof.); Tracy Standley (Asst. Prof.); Davey Stephens (Asst. Prof., Speech Prog.); Robert Markstrom (Instr., Speech Prog.); Amy Veuleman (Instr., Speech Prog.); Jim Beam (Editor Emer., American Press/Journalist-in-Residence)

UNIVERSITY OF LOUISIANA AT MONROE

Street address 1: Dept. of Communication
Street address 3: Monroe
Street address state: LA
Zip/Postal code: 71209-0322
Mailing address: Dept of Communication
Mailing city: Monroe
Mailing state: LA
Mailing zip: 71209-0001
General Phone: (318) 342-1406
General Fax: (318) 342-1422
General/National Adv. E-mail: kauffman@ulm.edu
Classified Equipment»
Personnel: Bette J. Kauffman (Dept. Head/Assoc. Prof.); Jeffrey M. Gibson (Assoc. Prof.); Tae-hyun Kim (Asst. Prof.); Robert E. Lewis (Asst. Prof.); Joel R. Willer (Asst. Prof.); Jarrett Reeves (Instr.); Mark Simmons (Part-time Adj. Fac.)

NORTHWESTERN STATE UNIVERSITY OF LOUISIANA

Street address 1: 103 John S. Kyser Hall
Street address 3: Natchitoches
Street address state: LA
Zip/Postal code: 71497
Mailing address: PO Box 5273
Mailing city: Natchitoches
Mailing state: LA
Mailing zip: 71497-0001
General Phone: (318) 357-4425
General Fax: (318) 357-4434
General/National Adv. E-mail: journalism@nsula.edu
Primary Website: www.liberalarts.nsula.edu/journalism
Classified Equipment»
Personnel: Paula F. Furr (Dept. Head/Assoc. Prof.); Hesham Mesbah (Prof.); Mary Brocato (Assoc. Prof.); William Broussard (Asst. Prof.); Jung Lim (Asst. Prof.); Jerry Pierce (Asst. Prof.); Jarrett Reeves (Asst. Prof.); David Antilley (Dir./Producer NSU 22); Raymond Strother (Wise Endowed Chair); Thomas Whitehead (Prof. Emer.); Michael Lofton (Broadcast Technician); Marie Hall (Admin. Asst.)

LOYOLA UNIVERSITY NEW ORLEANS

Street address 1: 6363 St. Charles Ave., Box 201
Street address 3: New Orleans
Street address state: LA
Zip/Postal code: 70118
Mailing address: 6363 Saint Charles Ave # 201
Mailing city: New Orleans
Mailing state: LA
Mailing zip: 70118-6143
General Phone: (504) 865-3430
General Fax: (504) 865-2333
General/National Adv. E-mail: cfbolner@loyno.edu
Primary Website: www.loyno.edu/communications
Classified Equipment»
Personnel: Teri K. Henley (Chair/Assoc. Prof.); A.L. Lorenz (Prof.); S.L. Alexander (Assoc. Prof.); William M. Hammel (Assoc. Prof.); David M. Myers (Assoc. Prof./Dir., Grad. Prog.); Leslie G. Parr (Assoc. Prof.); J. Cathy Rogers (Assoc. Prof.); Debra A. Woodfork (Asst. Prof.); Lisa C. Martin (Instr.); Trish O'Kane (Instr.); Robert A. Thomas (Loyola University Chair for Environmental Communications)

UNIVERSITY OF NEW ORLEANS

Street address 1: 127 Liberal Arts Bldg.
Street address 3: New Orleans
Street address state: LA
Zip/Postal code: 70148
Mailing address: 127 Liberal Arts
Mailing city: New Orleans
Mailing state: LA
Mailing zip: 70148-0001
General Phone: (504) 286-6273
General Fax: (504) 286-6378 (student newspaper)
General/National Adv. E-mail: english@uno.edu
Classified Equipment»
Personnel: Peter Schock (Chair)

XAVIER UNIVERSITY OF LOUISIANA

Street address 1: 909 S. Jefferson Davis Pkwy.
Street address 3: New Orleans
Street address state: LA
Zip/Postal code: 70125
Mailing address: 1 Drexel Dr # 93
Mailing city: New Orleans
Mailing state: LA
Mailing zip: 70125-1056
General Phone: (504) 520-5092
General Fax: (504) 520-7919
General/National Adv. E-mail: jmelcher@xula.edu
Classified Equipment»
Personnel: Joe Melcher (PD)

RUSTON

LOUISIANA TECH UNIVERSITY

Street address 1: 152 Keeny
Street address 3: Ruston
Street address state: LA
Zip/Postal code: 71272-0045
Mailing address: PO Box 10258
Mailing city: Ruston
Mailing state: LA
Mailing zip: 71272-0001
General Phone: (318) 257-4427
General Fax: (318) 257-4558
General/National Adv. E-mail: blick@latech.edu
Primary Website: eb.journ.latech.edu
Classified Equipment»
Personnel: Thomas Edward Blick (Head)

LOUISIANA STATE UNIVERSITY IN SHREVEPORT

Street address 1: Branson Hall, Rm. 330
Street address 3: Shreveport
Street address state: LA
Zip/Postal code: 71115
Mailing address: Branson Hall, Rm. 330
Mailing city: Shreveport
Mailing state: LA
Mailing zip: 71115
General Phone: (318) 797-5375
General Fax: (318) 797-5132
General/National Adv. E-mail: jnolan@lsus.edu
Classified Equipment»
Personnel: Jack Nolan (Chair)

NICHOLLS STATE UNIVERSITY

Street address 1: PO Box 2031
Street address 3: Thibodaux
Street address state: LA
Zip/Postal code: 70310
Mailing address: PO Box 2031
Mailing city: Thibodaux
Mailing state: LA
Mailing zip: 70310-0001
General Phone: (985) 448-4586
General Fax: (985) 448-4577
General/National Adv. E-mail: james.stewart@nicholls.edu
Primary Website: www.nicholls.edu/maco
Classified Equipment»
Personnel: James L. Stewart (Head/Assoc. Prof.); Lloyd Chiasson (Prof.); Rickey Duet (Assoc. Prof.); Andy Simoncelli (Asst. Prof.); Lance Arnold (Instr.); Nicky Boudreaux (Instr.); Felicia Harry (Instr.); Alfred Delahaye (Prof. Emer.)

MASSACHUSETTS

HAMPSHIRE COLLEGE

Street address 1: School of Communications & Cognitive Science
Street address 3: Amherst
Street address state: MA
Zip/Postal code: 1002
Mailing address: School of Communications & Cognitive Science
Mailing city: Amherst
Mailing state: MA
Mailing zip: 1002
General Phone: (413) 549-4600
Classified Equipment»
Personnel: Richard Muller (Dean)

UNIVERSITY OF MASSACHUSETTS

Street address 1: 108 Bartlett Hall
Street address 3: Amherst
Street address state: MA
Zip/Postal code: 01003-0520
Mailing address: 108 Bartlett Hall
Mailing city: Amherst
Mailing state: MA
Mailing zip: 01003-0520
General Phone: (413) 545-1376
General Fax: (413) 545-3880
General/National Adv. E-mail: klist@journ.umass.edu
Classified Equipment»
Personnel: Karen List (Dir.)

BOSTON UNIVERSITY

Street address 1: 640 Commonwealth Ave.
Street address 3: Boston
Street address state: MA
Zip/Postal code: 2215
Mailing address: 640 Commonwealth Ave
Mailing city: Boston
Mailing state: MA
Mailing zip: 02215-2422
General Phone: (617) 353-3450
General Fax: (617) 353-3405
General/National Adv. E-mail: com@bu.edu
Classified Equipment»
Personnel: Thomas E. Fiedler (Dean)

EMERSON COLLEGE

Street address 1: 120 Boylston St.
Street address 3: Boston
Street address state: MA
Zip/Postal code: 2116
Mailing address: 120 Boylston St Ste 414
Mailing city: Boston
Mailing state: MA
Mailing zip: 02116-4624
General Phone: (617) 824-8354
General Fax: (617) 824-8569
Classified Equipment»
Personnel: Stuart J. Sigman (Dean)

NORTHEASTERN UNIVERSITY

Street address 1: 360 Huntington Ave.
Street address 2: 102 Lake Hall
Street address 3: Boston
Street address state: MA
Zip/Postal code: 02115-5000
Mailing address: 360 Huntington Ave # 315
Mailing city: Boston
Mailing state: MA
Mailing zip: 02115-5000
General Phone: (617) 373-3236
General Fax: (617) 373-8773
General/National Adv. E-mail: s.burgard@neu.edu
Classified Equipment»
Personnel: Stephen Burgard (Dir./Assoc. Prof); Nicholas Daniloff (Prof.); Belle Adler (Assoc. Prof.); Charles Fountain (Assoc. Prof.); William Kirtz (Assoc. Prof.);

Laurel Leff (Assoc. Prof.); James Ross (Assoc. Prof.); Alan Schroeder (Assoc. Prof.); Elizabeth Matson (Asst. Prof); Kellianne Murphy (Asst. Prof./Coord., Cooperative Educ. Placement); Carlene Hempel (Lectr.); Gladys McKie (Lectr.); Lincoln McKie (Lectr.); Daniel Kennedy (Vstg. Prof.); David Abel (Part-time Fac.); Dana Barbuto (Part-time Fac.); Michael Blanding (Part-time Fac.); James Chiavelli (Part-time Fac.); Allan Coukell (Part-time Fac.); Paul Della Valle (Part-time Fac.); Jonathan Kauffman (Dir.)

SIMMONS COLLEGE

Street address 1: Dept. of Communications
Street address 3: Boston
Street address state: MA
Zip/Postal code: 2115
Mailing address: Dept. of Communications
Mailing city: Boston
Mailing state: MA
Mailing zip: 2115
General Phone: (617) 521-2838
General Fax: (617) 521-3199
General/National Adv. E-mail: jcorcoran@bmsvax.simmons.edu
Classified Equipment»

SUFFOLK UNIVERSITY

Street address 1: 41 Temple St.
Street address 3: Boston
Street address state: MA
Zip/Postal code: 2114
Mailing address: 41 Temple St
Mailing city: Boston
Mailing state: MA
Mailing zip: 02114-4280
General Phone: (617) 573-8236
General Fax: (617) 742-6982
General/National Adv. E-mail: rrosenth@suffolk.edu
Classified Equipment»
Personnel: Dr. Robert Rosenthal (Chair)

STONEHILL COLLEGE

Street address 1: 320 Washington St.
Street address 3: Easton
Street address state: MA
Zip/Postal code: 2537
Mailing address: 320 Washington St.
Mailing city: Easton
Mailing state: MA
Mailing zip: 2537
General Phone: (508) 565-1116
General Fax: (508) 565-1565
General/National Adv. E-mail: dwomack@stonehill.edu
Classified Equipment»
Personnel: Israel Khyri Abraham (Chair)

MARYLAND

GOUCHER COLLEGE

Street address 1: 1021 Dulaney Valley Rd.
Street address 3: Baltimore
Street address state: MD
Zip/Postal code: 21204
Mailing address: 1021 Dulaney Valley Rd
Mailing city: Baltimore
Mailing state: MD
Mailing zip: 21204-2780
General Phone: (410) 337-6200
General Fax: (410) 337-6085
General/National Adv. E-mail: communications@goucher.edu
Classified Equipment»
Personnel: Patsy Sims (Dir.)

LOYOLA COLLEGE

Street address 1: 4501 N. Charles St.
Street address 3: Baltimore
Street address state: MD
Zip/Postal code: 21210-2601
Mailing address: 4501 N Charles St
Mailing city: Baltimore
Mailing state: MD
Mailing zip: 21210-2694
General Phone: (410) 617-2528
General Fax: (410) 617-2198
General/National Adv. E-mail: eking@loyola.edu
Classified Equipment»
Personnel: Russell Cook (Chair); Andrew Ciofalo (Journ.); Neil Alperstein (Adv./PR); Elliot King (Journ./PR); Michael Braden (TV-Radio); Diana Samet (Graphics)

BOWIE STATE UNIVERSITY

Street address 1: 14000 Jericho Park Rd.,
Street address 3: Bowie
Street address state: MD
Zip/Postal code: 20715-9465
Mailing address: 14000 Jericho Park Rd
Mailing city: Bowie
Mailing state: MD
Mailing zip: 20715-9465
General Phone: (301) 860-3700
General Fax: (301) 860-3728
General/National Adv. E-mail: conwumechili@bowiestate.edu
Classified Equipment»
Personnel: Dr. Chuka Onwumechili (Chair)

UNIVERSITY OF MARYLAND

Street address 1: 1117 Journalism Bldg.
Street address 3: College Park
Street address state: MD
Zip/Postal code: 20742
Mailing address: 1117 Journalism Bldg
Mailing city: College Park
Mailing state: MD
Mailing zip: 20742-0001
General Phone: (301) 405-2383 (Dean's Office)
General Fax: (301) 314-9166
Classified Equipment»
Personnel: Lee Thornton (Interim Dean/Prof./Richard Eaton Chair in Broadcast); Olive Reid (Assoc. Dean/Dir., Undergrad. Studies); Steve Crane (Acting Assoc. Dean); Marchelle Payne-Gassaway (Asst. Dean); Frank Quine (Asst. Dean); Linda Ringer (Asst. Dean/Dir., Bus. Administration); Sheila Young (Asst. Dean); David Broder (Prof.); Reese Cleghorn (Prof.); Jon Franklin (Prof./Merrill Chair in Journalism); Haynes Johnson (Prof./Knight Chair in Journalism); Eugene L. Roberts (Prof.); Linda Steiner (Prof.); Carl Sessions Stepp (Prof.); Ira Chinoy (Assoc. Prof.); Christopher Hanson (Assoc. Prof.); John Newhagen (Assoc. Prof.); Susan Moeller (Assoc. Prof.); Eric Zanot (Assoc. Prof.); Ron Yaros (Asst. Prof.)

UNIVERSITY OF MARYLAND

Street address 1: 2130A Skinner Hall
Street address 3: College Park
Street address state: MD
Zip/Postal code: 20742-7635
Mailing address: 2130A Skinner Hall
Mailing city: College Park
Mailing state: MD
Mailing zip: 20742-0001
General Phone: (301) 405-8077
General Fax: (301) 314-9471
Classified Equipment»
Personnel: Elizabeth Toth (Chair/Prof., Pub. Rel./Feminist Scholarship); Edward L. Fink (Prof., Commun./Research Methods/Cognition/Persuasion); Robert N. Gaines (Prof., History of Rhetoric/Textual Criticism); James F. Klumpp (Prof., Contemporary Rhetorical Theory & Criticism/Social Change); Shawn J. Parry-Giles (Prof./Dir., Grad. Studies/Political Commun./Rhetorical, Feminist & Media Criticism); Andrew D. Wolvin (Prof., Listening/Commun. Mgmt./Commun. Educ.); Linda Aldoory (Assoc. Prof., Pub. Rel./Health Commun./Feminist Scholarship); Deborah A. Cai (Assoc. Prof., Intercultural Commun./Persuasion, Negotiation & Conflict); Dale Hample (Assoc. Prof., Argumentation/Interpersonal Commun.); Monique Mitchell Turner (Assoc. Prof., Social Influence/Persuasion/Compliance Gaining); Trevor Parry-Giles (Assoc. Prof., Rhetoric & Political Culture/Legal Commun.); Mari Boor Tonn (Assoc. Prof., Feminist & Rhetorical Criticism/Political Commun./Pub. Address); Kathleen E. Kendall (Research Prof., Political Campaign Commun.); Sahar Mohamed Khamis (Asst. Prof., Middle Eastern Media/Pub. Rel.); Meina Liu (Asst. Prof., Intercultural Commun./Organizational Commun., Negotiation & Conflict); Kristy Maddux (Asst. Prof., Rhetoric/Religion/Feminist Theory); Xiaoli Nan (Asst. Prof., Persuasion & Social Influence/Health Commun.); Nneka Ifeoma Ofulue (Asst. Prof., Feminist & Rhetorical Criticism/Religious Commun.); Torsten Reimer (Asst. Prof., Persuasion/Social Influence); Brecken Chinn Swartz (Vstg. Asst. Prof., Commun. Theory/Mass Media)

HOOD COLLEGE

Street address 1: 401 Rosemont Ave
Street address 3: Frederick
Street address state: MD
Zip/Postal code: 21701-8524
Country: USA
Mailing address: 401 Rosemont Ave
Mailing city: Frederick
Mailing state: MD
Mailing zip: 21701-8575
General Phone: (301) 696-3641
General Fax: (301) 696-3578
General/National Adv. E-mail: weinberg@hood.edu
Classified Equipment»
Personnel: Rita Davis (Ed.); Al Weinberg (Dir./Prof. of Journalism)

FT. GEORGE G. MEADE

DEFENSE INFORMATION SCHOOL

Street address 1: 6500 Mapes Rd.
Street address 3: Ft. George G. Meade
Street address state: MD
Zip/Postal code: 20755-5620
Mailing address: 6500 Mapes Rd
Mailing city: Fort George G Meade
Mailing state: MD
Mailing zip: 20755-7082
General Phone: (301) 677-2173
General/National Adv. E-mail: webmeisters@dinfos.osd.mil
Primary Website: www.dinfos.osd.mil
Classified Equipment»
Personnel: Lt. Col. R. Steven Murray (Chief, Pub. Affairs Dept.)

TOWSON UNIVERSITY

Street address 1: 8000 York Rd.
Street address 3: Towson
Street address state: MD
Zip/Postal code: 21252
Mailing address: 8000 York Rd
Mailing city: Towson
Mailing state: MD
Mailing zip: 21252-0002
General Phone: (410) 704-3431
General Fax: (410) 704-3656
General/National Adv. E-mail: cflippen@towson.edu
Classified Equipment»
Personnel: Charles Flippen (Chair)

MAINE

UNIVERSITY OF MAINE

Street address 1: Dept. of Communication & Journalism
Street address 3: Orono
Street address state: ME
Zip/Postal code: 04469-5724
Mailing address: Dept of Communication & Journalism
Mailing city: Orono
Mailing state: ME
Mailing zip: 04469-0001
General Phone: (207) 581-1283
General Fax: (207) 581-1286
General/National Adv. E-mail: john@maine.edu
Classified Equipment»
Personnel: John C. Sherblom (Chair/Prof.); Kristin M. Langellier (Prof.); Paul Grosswiler (Assoc. Prof.); Kathryn Olmstead (Assoc. Prof.); Eric E. Peterson (Assoc. Prof.); Claire F. Sullivan (Assoc. Prof.); Lyombe Eko (Asst. Prof.); Shannon Martin (Asst. Prof.); Michael McCauley (Asst. Prof.); Nathan Stormer (Asst. Prof.); Natalia Tolstikova (Asst. Prof.); Katherine Heidinger (Instr.); Ann James Joles (Instr.); Margaret Nagle (Instr.); Marie Tessier (Instr.); Arthur Guesman (Prof. Emer.); Alan Miller (Prof. Emer.)

MICHIGAN

GRAND VALLEY STATE UNIVERSITY

Street address 1: 1 Campus Dr.
Street address 3: Allendale
Street address state: MI
Zip/Postal code: 49401-9401
Mailing address: 1 Campus Dr
Mailing city: Allendale
Mailing state: MI
Mailing zip: 49401-9403
General Phone: (616) 331-3668
General Fax: (616) 331-2700
General/National Adv. E-mail: barkod@gvsu.edu
Primary Website: www.gvsu.edu
Classified Equipment»
Personnel: Alex Nesterenko (Dir.)

ALMA COLLEGE

Street address 1: 614 W Superior St
Street address 3: Alma
Street address state: MI
Zip/Postal code: 48801-1504
Country: USA
Mailing address: 614 W Superior St
Mailing city: Alma
Mailing state: MI
Mailing zip: 48801-1599
General Phone: (989) 463-7161
General Fax: (989) 463-7161
General/National Adv. E-mail: almanian@alma.edu; almanianopinion@yahoo.com; almanian@hotmail.com
Display Adv. E-mail: almanianadvert@yahoo.com
Primary Website: students.alma.edu/organizations/almanian
Classified Equipment»
Personnel: Robert Vivian (Advisor); Brendan Guilford (Ed. in Chief); Olga Wrobel (News Ed.)

UNIVERSITY OF MICHIGAN

Street address 1: Dept. of Communication Studies
Street address 3: Ann Arbor
Street address state: MI
Zip/Postal code: 48109-1285
Mailing address: Dept. of Communication Studies
Mailing city: Ann Arbor
Mailing state: MI
Mailing zip: 48109-1285
General Phone: (734) 764-0420
General Fax: (734) 764-3288
General/National Adv. E-mail: comm.studies.dept@umich.edu
Classified Equipment»
Personnel: Michael Traugott (Chair); Susan Douglas (Dir., Interdepartmental PhD Prog.)

UNIVERSITY OF DETROIT MERCY

Street address 1: 4001 W. McNichols
Street address 3: Detroit
Street address state: MI
Zip/Postal code: 48219-0900
Mailing address: PO Box 19900
Mailing city: Detroit
Mailing state: MI
Mailing zip: 48219-0900
General Phone: (313) 993-1698
General Fax: (313) 993-1166
General/National Adv. E-mail: boizbj@udmercy.edu
Classified Equipment»
Personnel: Barbara J. Bolz (Chair)

WAYNE STATE UNIVERSITY

Street address 1: Dept. of Communication
Street address 3: Detroit
Street address state: MI
Zip/Postal code: 48201
Mailing address: Dept. of Communication
Mailing city: Detroit
Mailing state: MI
Mailing zip: 48201
General Phone: (313) 577-2627
General Fax: (313) 577-6300
General/National Adv. E-mail: aa5200@wayne.edu
Classified Equipment»

Personnel: Benjamin Burns (Dir.)

MICHIGAN STATE UNIVERSITY

Street address 1: College of Communication Arts & Sciences
Street address 3: East Lansing
Street address state: MI
Zip/Postal code: 48824-1212
Mailing address: College of Communication Arts & Sciences
Mailing city: East Lansing
Mailing state: MI
Mailing zip: 48824-1212
General Phone: (517) 355-3410
General Fax: (517) 432-1244
Primary Website: www.cas.msu.edu
Classified Equipment»
Personnel: Jane Briggs-Bunting (Prof./Dir., School of Journalism); Charles T. Salmon (Prof./Dean Brandt Chair, PR); Charles K. Atkin (Prof./Chair, Dept. of Commun.); Johannes M. Bauer (Prof./Co-Dir., Quello Ctr.); Frank Biocca (Prof./Dir., MIND Lab); Howard S. Bossen (Prof.); Franklin Boster (Prof.); Mary Bresnahan (Prof.); Sue Carter (Prof.); Richard Cole (Prof./Chair, Dept. of Adv., PR and Retailing); Lucinda D. Davenport (Prof./Dir., Media/Information Studies Doctoral Prog.); Jim Detjen (Prof./Dir., Knight Ctr.); William A. Donohue (Prof.); Frederick G. Fico (Prof.); Linda Good (Prof.); Carrie J. Heeter (Prof.); Patricia Huddleston (Prof.); Stephen R. Lacy (Prof.); Robert J. Larose (Prof.); Tim Levine (Prof.)

CALVIN COLLEGE

Street address 1: 3201 Burton SE
Street address 3: Grand Rapids
Street address state: MI
Zip/Postal code: 49546
Mailing address: 3201 Burton St SE
Mailing city: Grand Rapids
Mailing state: MI
Mailing zip: 49546-4388
General Phone: (616) 526-6283
General Fax: (616) 526-6601
General/National Adv. E-mail: bytw@calvin.edu
Classified Equipment»
Personnel: Randall Bytwerk (Chair, Dept. of Commun. Arts & Sciences); Don Hettinga (Prof., Dept. of English)

WESTERN MICHIGAN UNIVERSITY

Street address 1: 1903 W. Michigan St.
Street address 3: Kalamazoo
Street address state: MI
Zip/Postal code: 49008-3805
Mailing address: 1903 W Michigan Ave
Mailing city: Kalamazoo
Mailing state: MI
Mailing zip: 49008-5200
General Phone: (269) 387-3148
General Fax: (269) 387-3990
General/National Adv. E-mail: richard.junger@wmich.edu
Classified Equipment»
Personnel: Dr. Richard Junger (Prog. Dir.)

MADONNA UNIVERSITY

Street address 1: 36600 Schoolcraft
Street address 3: Livonia
Street address state: MI
Zip/Postal code: 48150
Mailing address: 36600 Schoolcraft Rd
Mailing city: Livonia
Mailing state: MI
Mailing zip: 48150-1176
General Phone: (734) 432-5559
General Fax: (734) 432-5393
General/National Adv. E-mail: nhaidane@madonna.edu
Primary Website: www.madonna.edu
Classified Equipment»
Personnel: Neal Haldane (Dir.)

CENTRAL MICHIGAN UNIVERSITY

Street address 1: 454 Moore Hall
Street address 3: Mount Pleasant
Street address state: MI
Zip/Postal code: 48859
Mailing address: 454 Moore Hall
Mailing city: Mount Pleasant
Mailing state: MI
Mailing zip: 48859-0001
General Phone: (989) 774-3196
General Fax: (989) 774-7114
General/National Adv. E-mail: jrndept@cmich.edu
Classified Equipment»
Personnel: Maria B. Marron (Chair/Prof.); John Hartman (Prof.); Dennis Jeffers (Prof.); John Palen (Prof.); Alice Tait (Prof.); Jiafei Yin (Prof.); Carole Eberly (Assoc. Prof.); Elliott Parker (Assoc. Prof.); Jim Wojcik (Full-time Assoc. Prof.); Tim Boudreau (Asst. Prof.); Yun Jung Choi (Asst. Prof.); Jong Hyuk Lee (Asst. Prof.); David London (Asst. Prof.); Ken McDonald (Full-time Asst. Prof.); Kent Miller (Full-time Asst. Prof.); Ed Hutchison (Part-time Asst. Prof.); Ron Marmarelli (Part-time Asst. Prof.); Tereza Dean (Instr.); Steve Jessmore (Instr.); Dawn Paine (Instr.); Cynthia Gall (Editor & Publisher)

OAKLAND UNIVERSITY

Street address 1: Journalism Program
Street address 3: Rochester
Street address state: MI
Zip/Postal code: 48309-4401
Mailing address: Journalism Program
Mailing city: Rochester
Mailing state: MI
Mailing zip: 48309-4401
General Phone: (248) 370-4121
General Fax: (248) 370-4208
General/National Adv. E-mail: shreve@oakland.edu
Primary Website: www.oakland.edu/rcj/jrn
Classified Equipment»
Personnel: Holly Shreve-Gilbert (Co-Dir.)

EASTERN MICHIGAN UNIVERSITY

Street address 1: 612 Pray Harrold
Street address 3: Ypsilanti
Street address state: MI
Zip/Postal code: 48197-4210
Mailing address: 612 Pray Harrold
Mailing city: Ypsilanti
Mailing state: MI
Mailing zip: 48197-4210
General Phone: (734) 487-4220
General Fax: (734) 483-9744
General/National Adv. E-mail: carol.schlagheck@emich.edu
Classified Equipment»
Personnel: Laura George (Head); Carol Schlagheck (Journ. Program Coord.)

MINNESOTA

BEMIDJI STATE UNIVERSITY

Street address 1: 1500 Birchmont Dr., NE
Street address 3: Bemidji
Street address state: MN
Zip/Postal code: 56601-2699
Mailing address: 1500 Birchmont Dr NE
Mailing city: Bemidji
Mailing state: MN
Mailing zip: 56601-2699
General Phone: (218) 755-3358
General Fax: (218) 755-4369
General/National Adv. E-mail: LMengelkock@bemidjistate.edu
Classified Equipment»
Personnel: Louise Mengelkoch (Chair)

MINNESOTA STATE UNIVERSITY MANKATO

Street address 1: 136 Nelson Hall
Street address 3: Mankato
Street address state: MN
Zip/Postal code: 56001
Mailing address: 136 Nelson Hall
Mailing city: Mankato
Mailing state: MN
Mailing zip: 56001-6045
General Phone: (507) 389-6417
General Fax: (507) 389-5525
General/National Adv. E-mail: mass-communications@msus.edu
Classified Equipment»
Personnel: Charles Lewis (Chair/Prof.); Marshel Rossow (Prof.); Ellen M. Mrja (Assoc. Prof.); Jane McConnell (Assoc. Prof.); John Gaterud (Asst. Prof.); Scott Roemhildt (Adj. Fac.); Shelly Schultz (Adj. Fac.); Pete Steiner (Adj. Fac.); John Cross (Adj. Fac.); Dale Ericson (Adj. Fac.); Carlienne Frisch (Adj. Fac.); Rachael Hanel (Adj. Fac.); Bob McConnell (Adj. Fac.); Joe Tougas (Adj. Fac.); Tim Krohn (Adj. Fac.); Michael Larson (Adj. Fac.); Gladys B. Olson (Prof. Emer.)

UNIVERSITY OF MINNESOTA

Street address 1: 111 Murphy Hall, 206 Church St. SE
Street address 3: Minneapolis
Street address state: MN
Zip/Postal code: 55455-0418
Mailing address: 206 Church St SE
Mailing city: Minneapolis
Mailing state: MN
Mailing zip: 55455-0488
General Phone: (612) 625-1338
General Fax: (612) 626-8251
General/National Adv. E-mail: sjmc@umn.edu
Classified Equipment»
Personnel: Albert R. Tims (Dir./Assoc. Prof.); Tsan-Kuo Chang (Prof.); John Eighmey (Prof./Mithun Land Grant Chair in Adv.); Ronald Faber (Prof.); Kathleen Hansen (Prof./Dir., Minnesota Journalism Ctr.); Jane Kirtley (Silha Prof./Dir., Silha Ctr.); Dan Sullivan (Prof./Cowles Chair); Daniel B. Wackman (Prof./Dir., Undergrad. Studies); Kenneth Doyle (Assoc. Prof.); Chris Ison (Assoc. Prof.); Mark Pedelty (Assoc. Prof.); Dona Schwartz (Assoc. Prof.); Gary Schwitzer (Assoc. Prof.); Brian Southwell (Assoc. Prof./Dir., Grad. Studies); Catherine Squires (Assoc. Prof./John and Elizabeth Bates Cowles Prof., Journ., Diversity and Equality); Miranda Brady (Asst. Prof.); Giovanna Dell'Orto (Asst. Prof.); Jisu Huh (Asst. Prof.); Kathy Roberts Forde (Asst. Prof.); Amy Sanders (Asst. Prof.)

MINNESOTA STATE UNIVERSITY, MOOREHEAD

Street address 1: Mass Communications Dept.
Street address 3: Moorhead
Street address state: MN
Zip/Postal code: 56563
Mailing address: Mass Communications Dept.
Mailing city: Moorhead
Mailing state: MN
Mailing zip: 56563
General Phone: (218) 477-2855
General Fax: (218) 477-4333
General/National Adv. E-mail: strandm@mnstate.edu
Classified Equipment»
Personnel: Mark Strand (Chair/Prof.); C.T. Hanson (Prof.); Martin Grindeland (Prof.); Wayne Gudmundson (Prof.); Shelton Gunaratne (Prof.); William B. Hall (Assoc. Prof.); Dan Johnson (Assoc. Prof.); Camilla Wilson (Assoc. Prof.); Jody Mattern (Asst. Prof.); Aaron Quanbeck (Asst. Prof.); Reggie Radnieck (Asst. Prof.); Mark Anthony (Instr.); David Arntson (Instr.); Marv Bossart (Instr.); David Christy (Instr.); Liz Conmy (Instr.); Nancy Edmonds Hanson (Instr.); David Howland (Instr.); Jason Hummel (Instr.); Kerstin Kealy (Instr.)

ST. CLOUD STATE UNIVERSITY

Street address 1: 720 4th Ave. S
Street address 3: Saint Cloud
Street address state: MN
Zip/Postal code: 56301-4498
Mailing address: 720 4th Ave S
Mailing city: Saint Cloud
Mailing state: MN
Mailing zip: 56301-4498
General Phone: (320) 308-3293
General Fax: (320) 654-5337
General/National Adv. E-mail: comm@stcloudstate.edu
Primary Website: www.stcloudstate.edu/comm/index.html
Classified Equipment»
Personnel: Roya Akhavan-Majid (Chair/Prof.); Niaz Ahmed (Prof./Grad. Prog. Dir.); Marjorie Fish (Prof.); Mark Mills (Prof.); Peter Przytula (Prof.); Michael Vadnie (Prof./Coord., News Editorial); Lisa Heinrich (Assoc. Prof.); Gregory Martin (Assoc. Prof./Coord., Broadcast); Gretchen Tiberghien (Assoc. Prof./Coord., PR); Marie Dick (Asst. Prof.); Mark Eden (Asst. Prof.); Bill Huntzicker (Asst. Prof.); Ilia Rodriguez (Asst. Prof.); Roger Rudolph (Asst. Prof./Coord., Adv.); Hon. Bernard Bolan (Adj. Prof.); Michael Larson (Adj. Prof.); Mike Knaak (Adj. Prof.); Paul Middlestaedt (Adj. Prof.); Michael Porter (Adj. Prof.); E. Scott Bryce (Prof. Emer.)

UNIVERSITY OF ST. THOMAS

Street address 1: Dept. of Journalism & Mass Communication
Street address 3: Saint Paul
Street address state: MN
Zip/Postal code: 55105
Mailing address: Dept. of Journalism & Mass Communication
Mailing city: Saint Paul
Mailing state: MN
Mailing zip: 55105
General Phone: (612) 962-5250
General Fax: (612) 962-6360
General/National Adv. E-mail: kebunton@stthomas.edu
Classified Equipment»
Personnel: Kris Bunton (Chair/Prof.); Thomas B. Connery (Prof.); John Cragan (Prof.); Robert L. Craig (Prof.); Mark Neuzil (Prof.); Kevin Sauter (Prof.); Bernard Armada (Assoc. Prof.); Carol Bruess (Assoc. Prof.); Mike O'Donnell (Assoc. Prof.); Debra Petersen (Assoc. Prof.); Tim Scully (Assoc. Prof.); Betsy Anderson (Asst. Prof.); Craig Bryan (Asst. Prof.); Dina Gavrilos (Asst. Prof.); Stephanie Gelarneault (Asst. Prof.); John Purdy (Asst. Prof.); Ellen Riordan (Asst. Prof.); Wendy Wyatt (Asst. Prof.); Mark Anfinson (Part-time Instr.); Bruce Benidt (Part-time Instr.)

ST. MARY'S UNIVERSITY OF MINNESOTA

Street address 1: 700 Terrace Heights
Street address 3: Winona
Street address state: MN
Zip/Postal code: 55987
Mailing address: 700 Terrace Hts
Mailing city: Winona
Mailing state: MN
Mailing zip: 55987-1399
General Phone: (507) 457-1502
General Fax: (507) 457-1633
General/National Adv. E-mail: dbeckman@smumn.edu
Classified Equipment»
Personnel: Dean Beckman (Coord.)

WINONA STATE UNIVERSITY

Street address 1: Dept. of Mass Communication
Street address 3: Winona
Street address state: MN
Zip/Postal code: 55987
Mailing address: Dept. of Mass Communication
Mailing city: Winona
Mailing state: MN
Mailing zip: 55987
General Phone: (507) 457-5474
General Fax: (507) 457-5155
General/National Adv. E-mail: mscmdept@winona.edu
Classified Equipment»
Personnel: Cindy Killion (Chair)

MISSOURI

CULVER-STOCKTON COLLEGE

Street address 1: 1 College Hl
Street address 3: Canton
Street address state: MO
Zip/Postal code: 63435-1257
Country: USA
Mailing address: 1 College Hl
Mailing city: Canton
Mailing state: MO
Mailing zip: 63435-1299
General Phone: (573) 231-6371
General Fax: (573) 231-6611
General/National Adv. E-mail: swiegenstein@culver.edu
Primary Website: www.culver.edu
Year Established: 1853
Classified Equipment»

Personnel: Fred Berger (Asst. Prof Comm.); Tyler Tomlinson (Lecturer in Comm.)

SOUTHEAST MISSOURI STATE UNIVERSITY

Street address 1: Dept. of Mass Communication
Street address 3: Cape Girardeau
Street address state: MO
Zip/Postal code: 63701-2750
Mailing address: Dept. of Mass Communication
Mailing city: Cape Girardeau
Mailing state: MO
Mailing zip: 63701-2750
General Phone: (573) 651-2241
General Fax: (573) 651-5967
General/National Adv. E-mail: masscomm@semo.edu
Classified Equipment»
Personnel: Tamara Baldwin (Prof.); James Dufek (Prof.); Susan Gonders (Prof.); Bruce Mims (Prof.); Mike Weatherson (Prof.); Larry Underberg (Assoc. Prof.); Glen Williams (Assoc. Prof.); Karie Hollerbach (Asst. Prof.); Fred Jones (Asst. Prof.); Don Jung (Asst. Prof.); Roy Keller (Asst. Prof.); Karen Kight (Instr.); Cindie Jeter-Yanow (Instr.); Roger Stout (Instr.); Jennifer Summary (Instr.); Roseanna Whitlow (Instr.); Tamara Zellers-Buck (Instr.); Brooke Clubbs (Adj. Fac.); Kara Cracraft (Adj. Fac.); Ellen Dillon (Adj. Fac.)

STEPHENS COLLEGE

Street address 1: 1200 E. Broadway
Street address 3: Columbia
Street address state: MO
Zip/Postal code: 65215
Mailing address: 1200 E Broadway
Mailing city: Columbia
Mailing state: MO
Mailing zip: 65215-0001
General Phone: (573) 876-7133
General Fax: (314) 876-7248
General/National Adv. E-mail: johnb@stephens.edu
Classified Equipment»
Personnel: John S. Blakemore (Chair)

UNIVERSITY OF MISSOURI

Street address 1: School of Journalism
Street address 3: Columbia
Street address state: MO
Zip/Postal code: 65211
Mailing address: School of Journalism
Mailing city: Columbia
Mailing state: MO
Mailing zip: 65211-0001
General Phone: (573) 882-6686
General Fax: (573) 884-8989
Classified Equipment»
Personnel: Dean Mills (Dean/Prof.); Jacqui Banaszynski (Prof./Knight Chair in Editing); Judy Bolch (Prof./Harte Chair in Innovation); Brian Brooks (Prof./Assoc. Dean, Undergrad. Studies and Admin.); Glen Cameron (Prof./ Maxine Wilson Gregory Chair in Journ. Research); Brant Houston (Prof.); Stuart Loory (Prof.); Daryl Moen (Prof.); Geneva Overholser (Prof.); Byron Scott (Prof.); Zoe Smith (Prof.); Martha Steffens (Prof.); James Sterling (Prof.); Esther Thorson (Prof./Assoc. Dean, Grad. Studies/Research); Wayne Wanta (Prof.); Steve Weinberg (Prof.); Lee Wilkins (Prof.); Betty Winfield (Prof.); Clyde Bentley (Assoc. Prof.); Mary Kay Blakely (Assoc. Prof.)
Newspaper (for newspapers group): Columbia Missourian, Columbia

LINCOLN UNIVERSITY

Street address 1: Dept. of Humanities
Street address 2: MSC03 2240
Street address 3: Jefferson City
Street address state: MO
Zip/Postal code: 65102
Mailing address: Dept. of Humanities
Mailing city: Jefferson City
Mailing state: MO
Mailing zip: 65102
General Phone: (573) 681-5280
General Fax: (573) 681-5438
General/National Adv. E-mail: govangd@lincolnu.edu
Classified Equipment»
Personnel: Don Govang (Dept. Head/Assoc. Prof.); Ted Jacobs (Asst. Prof.); Art Fulcher (Asst. Prof.); Leslie Cross (Part-time Fac.); Tom Cwynar (Part-time Fac.)

MISSOURI SOUTHERN UNIVERSITY

Street address 1: 3950 Newman Rd
Street address 3: Joplin
Street address state: MO
Zip/Postal code: 64801-1512
Country: USA
Mailing address: 3950 Newman Rd
Mailing city: Joplin
Mailing state: MO
Mailing zip: 64801-1595
General Phone: (417) 625-9823
General Fax: (417) 625-9585
General/National Adv. E-mail: chart@mssu.edu
Primary Website: www.thechartonline.com
Year Established: 1939
Classified Equipment»
Personnel: J.R. Moorman (Head); Chad Stebbins (Advisor); T.R. Hanrahan (Publications Mgr.); Alexandra Nicolas (Ed. in Chief)

UNIVERSITY OF MISSOURI-KANSAS CITY

Street address 1: 202 Haag Hall, 5120 Rockhill Rd.
Street address 3: Kansas City
Street address state: MO
Zip/Postal code: 64110
Mailing address: 5120 Rockhill Rd
Mailing city: Kansas City
Mailing state: MO
Mailing zip: 64110-2446
General Phone: (816) 235-1337
General Fax: (816) 235-5539
General/National Adv. E-mail: com-s@umkc.edu
Classified Equipment»
Personnel: Carol Koehler (Chair/Assoc. Prof.); Michael R. Neer (Prof.); Robert Unger (Prof.); G.Thomas Poe (Assoc. Prof.); Peter Morello (Assoc. Prof.); Greg Gutenko (Assoc. Prof.); Caitlin Horsmon (Asst. Prof.); Michael McDonald (Asst. Prof.); Angela Elam (Instr., Radio); Linda H. Kurz (Instr.); Judith K. McCoromick (Instr.); Gaylord Marr (Prof. Emer.); Gregory D. Black (Prof. Emer.); Joan E. Aitken (Prof. Emer.); Larry G. Ehrlich (Prof. Emer.); Robin League (Prof. Emer.)

TRUMAN STATE UNIVERSITY

Street address 1: Communication Dept.
Street address 3: Kirksville
Street address state: MO
Zip/Postal code: 63501
Mailing address: Communication Dept.
Mailing city: Kirksville
Mailing state: MO
Mailing zip: 63501
General Phone: (660) 785-4481
General Fax: (660) 785-7486
General/National Adv. E-mail: heinz@truman.edu
Classified Equipment»
Personnel: Heinz D. Woehlk (Contact)

NORTHWEST MISSOURI STATE UNIVERSITY

Street address 1: 800 University Dr., Wells Hall #237
Street address 3: Maryville
Street address state: MO
Zip/Postal code: 64468-6001
Mailing address: 800 University Dr., Wells Hall #237
Mailing city: Maryville
Mailing state: MO
Mailing zip: 64468-6001
General Phone: (660) 562-1361
General Fax: (660) 562-1947
General/National Adv. E-mail: jerryd@mail.nwmissouri.edu
Classified Equipment»
Personnel: Jerry Donnelly (Chair)

POINT LOOKOUT

COLLEGE OF THE OZARKS

Street address 1: Dept. of Mass Communication
Street address 3: Point Lookout
Street address state: MO
Zip/Postal code: 65726
Mailing address: Dept. of Mass Communication
Mailing city: Point Lookout
Mailing state: MO
Mailing zip: 65726
General Phone: (417) 690-3458
General/National Adv. E-mail: schroeder@cofo.edu
Classified Equipment»
Personnel: Jared Schroeder (Contact)

SAINT CHARLES

LINDENWOOD UNIVERSITY

Street address 1: 209 S. Kingshighway St.
Street address 3: Saint Charles
Street address state: MO
Zip/Postal code: 63301
Mailing address: 209 S Kingshighway St
Mailing city: Saint Charles
Mailing state: MO
Mailing zip: 63301-1695
General Phone: (314) 949-4835
General Fax: (314) 949-4910
General/National Adv. E-mail: jwilson@lindenwood.edu
Classified Equipment»
Personnel: Jim Wilson (Dean)

MISSOURI WESTERN STATE COLLEGE

Street address 1: SS/C 208
Street address 3: Saint Joseph
Street address state: MO
Zip/Postal code: 64507
Mailing address: SS/C 208
Mailing city: Saint Joseph
Mailing state: MO
Mailing zip: 64507
General Phone: (816) 271-4310
General Fax: (816) 271-4543
General/National Adv. E-mail: klr9015@griffon.mwsc.edu
Classified Equipment»
Personnel: Ken Rosenauer (Chair)

MARYVILLE UNIVERSITY

Street address 1: 13550 Conway Rd.
Street address 3: Saint Louis
Street address state: MO
Zip/Postal code: 63141
Mailing address: 650 Maryville University Dr
Mailing city: Saint Louis
Mailing state: MO
Mailing zip: 63141-5849
General Phone: (314) 529-9473
General Fax: (314) 542-9085
General/National Adv. E-mail: gboy@maryville.edu
Classified Equipment»
Personnel: Gerald Boyer (PhD)

SAINT LOUIS UNIVERSITY

Street address 1: 3733 W. Pine Blvd.
Street address 2: Xavier Hall 300
Street address 3: Saint Louis
Street address state: MO
Zip/Postal code: 63108
Mailing address: 3733 W Pine Blvd
Mailing city: Saint Louis
Mailing state: MO
Mailing zip: 63108
General Phone: (314) 977-3191
General Fax: (314) 977-3195
General/National Adv. E-mail: commdept@slu.edu
Classified Equipment»
Personnel: Kathleen Farrell (Chair/Prof.); Rob Anderson (Prof.); Richard Burgin (Prof./Ed., Boulevard Magazine); Avis Meyer (Prof./Dir., Political Journ.); William Tyler (Prof.); Liese Hutchison (Assoc. Prof.); Robert Krizek (Assoc. Prof.); Karla Scott (Assoc. Prof.); Paaige Turner (Assoc. Prof.); Angela Beattie (Asst. Prof.); Matt Carlson (Asst. Prof.); Dan Kozlowski (Asst. Prof.); Jennifer Ohs (Asst. Prof.); Elizabeth Richard (Asst. Prof.); Gary Seibert (Asst. Prof.); Robert Stahl (Asst. Prof.); April Trees (Asst. Prof.)

UNIVERSITY OF MISSOURI-ST. LOUIS

Street address 1: 1 University Blvd., 235 GSB
Street address 3: Saint Louis
Street address state: MO
Zip/Postal code: 63121
Mailing address: 1 University Blvd # 235
Mailing city: Saint Louis
Mailing state: MO
Mailing zip: 63121-4400
General Phone: (314) 516-5496
General Fax: (314) 516-5816
General/National Adv. E-mail: murraymd@umsl.edu
Classified Equipment»
Personnel: Michael D. Murray (UM Board of Curators' Distinguished Prof.)

WEBSTER UNIV.

Street address 1: 470 E Lockwood Ave
Street address 3: Saint Louis
Street address state: MO
Zip/Postal code: 63119-3141
Country: USA
Mailing address: 470 E Lockwood Ave
Mailing city: Saint Louis
Mailing state: MO
Mailing zip: 63119-3194
General Phone: (314) 961-2660
General Fax: (314) 968-7059
Editorail Phone: (314) 968-7088
General/National Adv. E-mail: wujournal@gmail.com
Editorial e-mail: editor@webujournal.com
Primary Website: www.webujournal.com
Published: Wed
Classified Equipment»
Personnel: Don Corrigan (Journ. Seq.); Kelly Kendall (Ed. in Chief)

EVANGEL UNIVERSITY

Street address 1: 1111 N Glenstone Ave
Street address 3: Springfield
Street address state: MO
Zip/Postal code: 65802-2125
Country: USA
Mailing address: 1111 N. Glenstone Ave.
Mailing city: Springfield
Mailing state: MO
Mailing zip: 65802-2125
General Phone: (417) 865-2815
Advertising Phone: (417) 865-2815, ext. 8636
Editorail Phone: (417) 865-2815, ext. 8634
General/National Adv. E-mail: evangellance@gmail.com
Editorial e-mail: evangellance@gmail.com
Primary Website: http://www.evangellance.com
Year Established: 1955
Delivery Methods: Racks
Commercial printers: Y
Published: Fri`Bi-Mthly
Avg Free Circ: 1500
Classified Equipment»
Personnel: Melinda Booze (Advisor)

MISSOURI STATE UNIVERSITY

Street address 1: 901 S. National Ave.
Street address 3: Springfield
Street address state: MO
Zip/Postal code: 65804
Mailing address: 901 S National Ave
Mailing city: Springfield
Mailing state: MO
Mailing zip: 65897-0001
General Phone: (417) 836-5218
General Fax: (417) 836-4637
General/National Adv. E-mail: mjf@missouristate.edu
Classified Equipment»
Personnel: Karen Buzzard (Head/Prof.); Arlen Diamond (Prof.); Thomas Dickson (Prof.); Mark Paxton (Prof.); Joel Persky (Prof.); Mark Biggs (Assoc. Prof.); Jaime Bihlmeyer (Assoc. Prof.); Weiyan Wang (Assoc. Prof.);

Timothy White (Assoc. Prof.); Andrew Cline (Asst. Prof.); Deborah Larson (Asst. Prof.); Mary Jane Pardue (Asst. Prof.); Cheryl Hellmann (Instr.); Jack Dimond (Lectr.)

UNIVERSITY OF CENTRAL MISSOURI

Street address 1: Dept. of Communication
Street address 3: Warrensburg
Street address state: MO
Zip/Postal code: 64093
Mailing address: Dept. of Communication
Mailing city: Warrensburg
Mailing state: MO
Mailing zip: 64093
General Phone: (660) 543-4840
General Fax: (660) 543-8006
General/National Adv. E-mail: fair@umco.edu
Classified Equipment»
Personnel: Charles Fair (Chair)

MISSISSIPPI

ALCORN STATE UNIVERSITY

Street address 1: 1000 ASU Dr., #269
Street address 3: Alcorn State
Street address state: MS
Zip/Postal code: 39096-7500
Mailing address: 1000 Alcorn Dr # 269
Mailing city: Lorman
Mailing state: MS
Mailing zip: 39096-7510
General Phone: (601) 877-6613
General Fax: (601) 877-2213
Classified Equipment»
Personnel: Sherlynn Byrd (Chair); Shafiquir Rahman (Prof./Title III Activity Dir./Gen. Mgr., ASU Cable-TV/WPRL-FM); Duanne Byrge (Asst. Prof.); Terrence Nimor (Instr./Newsletter Advisor); Robert Waller (Instr./Video Supvr./Internship Coord.); Angela Boykin (Instr./News Dir., WPRL-FM)

MISSISSIPPI UNIVERSITY FOR WOMEN

Street address 1: 1100 College Street, MUW - 1619
Street address 3: Columbus
Street address state: MS
Zip/Postal code: 39701-5800
Mailing address: 1100 College St Unit W1
Mailing city: Columbus
Mailing state: MS
Mailing zip: 39701-5802
General Phone: (662) 329-7354
General Fax: (662) 329-7250
General/National Adv. E-mail: mhatton@muw.edu
Classified Equipment»
Personnel: Martin L. Hatton (Chair/Assoc. Prof., Commun.)

UNIVERSITY OF SOUTHERM MISSISSIPPI

Street address 1: Box 5121
Street address 3: Hattiesburg
Street address state: MS
Zip/Postal code: 39406-5121
Mailing address: PO Box 5121
Mailing city: Hattiesburg
Mailing state: MS
Mailing zip: 39406-0001
General Phone: (601) 266-4258
General Fax: (601) 266-6473
General/National Adv. E-mail: journalism@usm.edu
Primary Website: www.usm.edu/mcj
Classified Equipment»
Personnel: Christopher P. Campbell (Dir./Prof. School of Mass Commun. and Journ.); David R. Davies (Prof.); S.M. Mazharul Haque (Prof.); S. Dixon McDowell (Prof.); Phillip Gentile (Asst. Prof.); Cheryl Jenkins (Asst. Prof.); Keith F. Johnson (Asst. Prof.); Kim LeDuff (Asst. Prof.); Mary Lou Sheffer (Asst. Prof.); Jae-Hwa Shin (Asst. Prof.); Fei Xue (Asst. Prof.); Stephen Coleman (Professor of Practice); Gina Gayle (Professor of Practice); Joey Goodsell (Professor of Practice); Maggie Williams (Instr./Publication Mgr.); Ed Wheeler (Prof. Emer.); Gene Wiggins (Prof. Emer.); Clarence Williams (Photojournalist-in-Residence)

DEPARTMENT OF MASS COMMUNICATIONS, RUST COLLEGE

Street address 1: 150 Rust Avenue
Street address 3: Holly Springs
Street address state: MS
Zip/Postal code: 38635
County: Marshall County
Mailing address: 150 Rust Avenue
Mailing city: Holly Springs
Mailing state: MS
Mailing zip: 38635-2328
General Phone: (662) 252-8000
General Fax: (662) 252-8869
General/National Adv. E-mail: dmoyo@rustcollege.edu
Classified Equipment»
Personnel: Debayo R. Moyo (Department Chair)

MISSISSIPPI VALLEY STATE UNIV.

Street address 1: 14000 Highway 82 W
Street address 3: Itta Bena
Street address state: MS
Zip/Postal code: 38941-1400
County: Leflore
Country: USA
Mailing address: 14000 Highway 82 W
Mailing city: Itta Bena
Mailing state: MS
Mailing zip: 38941-1401
General Phone: (662) 254-3458
General Fax: (622) 254-6704
Advertising Phone: (662) 254-3458
Advertising Fax: (662) 254-3458
Editorail Phone: (662) 254-3458
General/National Adv. E-mail: deltadevilsgazettefacad@gmail.com
Display Adv. E-mail: ehmcclary@mvsu.edu
Editorial e-mail: deltadevilsgazettefacad@gmail.com
Primary Website: deltadevilsgazette.com
Advertising (Open Inch Rate) Weekday/Saturday: $100.00 full page & 150.00 back or behind cover,FP
Published Other: three per semester
Avg Free Circ: 2000
Classified Equipment»
Personnel: Esin C. Turk (Asst. Prof.); Samuel Osunde (Asst. Prof./Dir., Forensics); Carolyn Gordon; Zainul Abedin (Mr.)

JACKSON STATE UNIVERSITY

Street address 1: 1230 Raymond Rd.
Street address 3: Jackson
Street address state: MS
Zip/Postal code: 39217-0990
Mailing address: PO Box 18590
Mailing city: Jackson
Mailing state: MS
Mailing zip: 39217-0001
General Phone: (601) 979-2151
General Fax: (601) 979-5800
General/National Adv. E-mail: dwight.e.brooks@jsums.edu
Primary Website: www.jsums.edu/jsumasscom/
Classified Equipment»
Personnel: Dwight Brooks (Chair/Prof.); Olorundare E. Aworuwa (Assoc. Prof.); Joseph Clive Enos (Assoc. Prof.); Li-Jing Chang (Asst. Prof.); Andrea Dilworth (Asst. Prof./Coord., Adv.); Ayana Haaruun (Asst. Prof.); Teresa Taylor (Asst. Prof.); Sunny Smith (Instr./Dir., Programs); Gail H. M. Brown (Adj. Instr.); Riva Brown (Adj. Instr.); Elaina Jackson (Adj. Instr.); Dathan Thigpen (Adj. Instr.); Aly Ash (Admin. Asst.); Regina Clay (Sec.)

MISSISSIPPI STATE UNIVERSITY

Street address 1: 130 McComas Hall
Street address 3: Mississippi State
Street address state: MS
Zip/Postal code: 39762
Mailing address: PO Box Pf
Mailing city: Mississippi State
Mailing state: MS
Mailing zip: 39762-6006
General Phone: (662) 325-3320
General Fax: (662) 325-3210
General/National Adv. E-mail: jforde@comm.msstate.edu
Primary Website: www.comm.msstate.edu
Classified Equipment»
Personnel: John Forde (Assoc. Prof./Head)

TOUGALOO COLLEGE

Street address 1: 500 W County Line Rd
Street address 3: Tougaloo
Street address state: MS
Zip/Postal code: 39174-9700
Country: USA
Mailing address: 500 W County Line Rd
Mailing city: Tougaloo
Mailing state: MS
Mailing zip: 39174-9700
General Phone: (601) 977-6159
General Fax: (601) 977-6160
General/National Adv. E-mail: cwhite@tougaloo.edu
Classified Equipment»
Personnel: Teressa Fulgham (Mng. Ed.); Colleen White (Dir. Journ. Program)

UNIVERSITY

UNIVERSITY OF MISSISSIPPI

Street address 1: 331 Farley Hall
Street address 3: University
Street address state: MS
Zip/Postal code: 38677-1848
Mailing address: PO Box 1848
Mailing city: University
Mailing state: MS
Mailing zip: 38677-1848
General Phone: (662) 915-7146
General Fax: (662) 915-7765
General/National Adv. E-mail: jebaker@olemiss.edu
Primary Website: www.olemiss.edu/depts/Journalism
Classified Equipment»
Personnel: Samir A. Husni (Prof./Hederman Lectr.); Jeanni Atkins (Assoc. Prof.); Joe Atkins (Assoc. Prof./Head, Print seq.); Carmen Manning-Miller (Assoc. Prof./Grad. Coord.); Burnis Morris (Assoc. Prof./Talbert Lectr.); Ken Boutwell (Asst. Prof.); Ralph Braseth (Asst. Prof./Student Media Dir.); Flora Caldwell (Asst. Prof.); D. Michael Cheers (Asst. Prof.); Charles Raiteri (Asst. Prof.); Brad Schultz (Asst. Prof./Head, Broadcast seq.); Melanie Stone (Asst. Prof.); Kathleen Woodruff Wickham (Asst. Prof.); Robin Street (Instr./Dir., MS Scholastic Press); Jack Bass (Prof. Emer.); Jere Hoar (Prof. Emer.)

MONTANA

THE UNIVERSITY OF MONTANA

Street address 1: 32 Campus Dr.
Street address 3: Missoula
Street address state: MT
Zip/Postal code: 59812-0648
Mailing address: 32 Campus Dr
Mailing city: Missoula
Mailing state: MT
Mailing zip: 59812-0004
General Phone: (406) 243-4001
General/National Adv. E-mail: peggy.kuhr@umontana.edu
Primary Website: www.umt.edu/journalism
Classified Equipment»
Personnel: Peggy Kuhr (Dean); Carol Van Valkenburg (Prof.); Dennis Swibold (Prof.); Clem Work (Prof.); Ray Ekness (Assoc. Prof.); Keith Graham (Assoc. Prof.); Denise Dowling (Assoc. Prof.); Ray Fanning (Asst. Prof.); Jeremy Lurgio (Asst. Prof.); Nadia White (Asst. Prof.); Nathaniel Blumberg (Prof. Emer.); Charles Hood (Prof. Emer.); Greg MacDonald (Prof. Emer.); Robert McGiffert (Prof. Emer.); Bill Knowles (Prof. Emer.); Jerry E. Brown (Prof. Emer.); Sharon Barrett (Prof. Emer.); Printer Bowler (Adj. Instr.); Gus Chambers (Adj. Instr.); Jeff Hull (Adj. Instr.)

NORTH CAROLINA

UNIVERSITY OF NORTH CAROLINA-ASHEVILLE

Street address 1: 1 University Heights, CPO 2120
Street address 3: Asheville
Street address state: NC
Zip/Postal code: 28804
Mailing address: 1 University Hts Cpo 2120
Mailing city: Asheville
Mailing state: NC
Mailing zip: 28804-3251
General Phone: (828) 232-5027
General Fax: (828) 232-2421
General/National Adv. E-mail: west@unca.edu
Classified Equipment»
Personnel: Mark D. West (Chair)

APPALACHIAN STATE UNIVERSITY

Street address 1: PO Box 32039
Street address 3: Boone
Street address state: NC
Zip/Postal code: 28608
Mailing address: PO Box 32039
Mailing city: Boone
Mailing state: NC
Mailing zip: 28608-2039
General Phone: (828) 262-2405
General Fax: (828) 262-2543
General/National Adv. E-mail: townsws@appstate.edu
Classified Equipment»
Personnel: Stuart Towns (Chair)

CAMPBELL UNIVERSITY

Street address 1: 180 Main St.
Street address 3: Buies Creek
Street address state: NC
Zip/Postal code: 27506
Mailing address: 180 Main St.
Mailing city: Buies Creek
Mailing state: NC
Mailing zip: 27506
General Phone: (910) 893-1520
General Fax: (910) 893-1924
General/National Adv. E-mail: smithm@campbell.edu
Classified Equipment»
Personnel: Michael R. Smith (Chair); Archie K. Davis (Fellow Chair)

UNIVERSITY OF NORTH CAROLINA

Street address 1: School of Journalism & Mass Communication, Campus Box 3365
Street address 2: UNC-CH, 117 Carroll Hall
Street address 3: Chapel Hill
Street address state: NC
Zip/Postal code: 27514
Mailing address: School of Journalism & Mass Communication, Campus Box 3365
Mailing city: Chapel Hill
Mailing state: NC
Mailing zip: 27599-3365
General Phone: (919) 962-1204
General Fax: (919) 962-0620
General/National Adv. E-mail: jean_folkerts@unc.edu
Primary Website: www.jomc.unc.edu
Classified Equipment»
Personnel: Jean Folkerts (Dean/Alumni Distinguished Prof.); Penelope Muse Abernathy (Prof./Knight Chair in Journ. and Digital Media Economics); Jane Delano Brown (Prof./James L. Knight); Richard R. Cole (Dean Emer./John Thomas Kerr Distinguished Prof.); Anne Johnston (Prof./Assoc. Dean for Grad. Studies); Thomas R. Linden (Glaxo Wellcome Distinguished Prof. of Medical Journalism); Daniel Riffe (Prof./Richard Cole Eminent Prof.); Donald L. Shaw (Kenan Prof.); Richard Simpson (Prof.); Dulcie Straughan (Prof./Sr. Assoc. Dean); John Sweeney (Distinguished Prof. in Sports Commun.); Charles A. Tuggle (Prof.); Ruth Walden (James Howard & Hallie McLean Parker Distinguished Prof.); Jan Yopp (Walter Spearman

Prof.); Xinshu Zhao (Prof.); Deb Aikat (Assoc. Prof.); Lois Boynton (Assoc. Prof.); George W. Cloud (Assoc. Prof.); Pat Davison (Assoc. Prof.); Frank Fee (Assoc. Prof.)

JOHNSON C. SMITH UNIVERSITY

Street address 1: 100 Beatties Ford Rd.
Street address 3: Charlotte
Street address state: NC
Zip/Postal code: 28216
Mailing address: 100 Beatties Ford Rd
Mailing city: Charlotte
Mailing state: NC
Mailing zip: 28216-5398
General Phone: (704) 378-1096
General Fax: (704) 378-3539
General/National Adv. E-mail: klharris@jcsu.edu
Classified Equipment»
Personnel: Kandace L. Harris (Interim Dept. Chair)

NORTH CAROLINA CENTRAL UNIV.

Street address 1: 1801 Fayetteville St
Street address 3: Durham
Street address state: NC
Zip/Postal code: 27707-3129
Country: USA
Mailing address: 1801 Fayetteville St
Mailing city: Durham
Mailing state: NC
Mailing zip: 27707-3129
General Phone: (919) 530-7116
General Fax: (919) 530-7991
General/National Adv. E-mail: campusecho@nccu.edu
Primary Website: www.campusecho.com
Classified Equipment»
Personnel: Dr. Bruce DePyssler (Advisor); Thomas Evans (Associate Professor); Carlton Koonce (Ed. in Chief)

ELON UNIVERSITY

Street address 1: McEwen Communications Bldg., Campus Box 2850
Street address 3: Elon
Street address state: NC
Zip/Postal code: 27244
Mailing address: McEwen Communications Bldg., Campus Box 2850
Mailing city: Elon
Mailing state: NC
Mailing zip: 27244
General Phone: (336) 278-5724
General Fax: (336) 278-5734
General/National Adv. E-mail: communications@elon.edu
Primary Website: www.elon.edu/communications
Classified Equipment»
Personnel: Paul Parsons (Dean/Prof.); David Copeland (Prof./Fletcher Chair/Grad. Dir.); Janna Anderson (Assoc. Prof.); Brooke Barnett (Assoc. Prof.); Constance Book (Assoc. Dean/Assoc. Prof.); Vic Costello (Assoc. Prof.); Michael Frontani (Assoc. Prof.); Jessica Gisclair (Assoc. Prof.); Don Grady (Assoc. Prof./Dept. Chair); Anthony Hatcher (Assoc. Prof.); Byung Lee (Assoc. Prof.); Harlen Makemson (Assoc. Prof.); Tom Nelson (Assoc. Prof.); George Padgett (Assoc. Prof.); Michael Skube (Assoc. Prof./Pulitzer Prize winner); Frances Ward-Johnson (Assoc. Prof.); Lee Bush (Asst. Prof.); Ken Calhoun (Asst. Prof.); Ocek Eke (Asst. Prof.); Amanda Gallagher (Asst. Prof.)

NORTH CAROLINA A&T STATE UNIVERSITY

Street address 1: 1601 E. Market St., A322 New General Classroom Bldg.
Street address 3: Greensboro
Street address state: NC
Zip/Postal code: 27411
Mailing address: 1601 E Market St
Mailing city: Greensboro
Mailing state: NC
Mailing zip: 27411-0001
General Phone: (336) 334-7900
General Fax: (336) 334-7770
Classified Equipment»
Personnel: Humphrey A. Regis (Chair); Kevin Keenan (Prof.); Tamrat Mereba (Prof.); Linda Florence Callahan (Assoc. Prof.); Rita Lauria (Assoc. Prof.); Teresa Jo Styles (Assoc. Prof.); Nagatha Tonkins (Asst. Prof.); Anthony Welborne (Asst. Prof.); Sheila Whitley (Asst. Prof.); Gail Wiggins (Asst. Prof.); Kimberly Moore (Adj. Asst. Prof.); Emily Burch-Harris (Instr.); Bruce Clark (Instr.); Allen Johnson (Instr.); Jacqueline Jones (Instr.); Alexis Nyandwi (Instr.); Willis Smith (Instr.); Brian Tomlin (Instr.); Mary Vanderlinden (Instr.); Frances Ward Johnson (Instr.)

EAST CAROLINA UNIVERSITY

Street address 1: 102 Joyner E.
Street address 3: Greenville
Street address state: NC
Zip/Postal code: 27858-4353
Mailing address: 102 Joyner E.
Mailing city: Greenville
Mailing state: NC
Mailing zip: 27858-4353
General Phone: (252) 328-4227
General Fax: (252) 328-1509
General/National Adv. E-mail: keyesa@mail.ecu.edu
Classified Equipment»
Personnel: Tim Hudson (Dir.)

LENOIR-RHYNE COLLEGE

Street address 1: School of Communication and Literature
Street address 3: Hickory
Street address state: NC
Zip/Postal code: 28603
Mailing address: School of Communication and Literature
Mailing city: Hickory
Mailing state: NC
Mailing zip: 28603
General Phone: (828) 328-7164
General Fax: (828) 328-7163
General/National Adv. E-mail: Richter@lrc.edu
Classified Equipment»
Personnel: William Richter (Chair)

HIGH POINT UNIV.

Street address 1: 1 University Pkwy
Street address 3: High Point
Street address state: NC
Zip/Postal code: 27268-0002
Country: USA
Mailing address: 833 Montlieu Ave
Mailing city: High Point
Mailing state: NC
Mailing zip: 27262-4260
General Phone: (800) 345-6993
General Fax: (336) 841-4513
General/National Adv. E-mail: news@highpoint.edu
Primary Website: www.highpoint.edu
Classified Equipment»
Personnel: Bobby Hayes (Advisor); Wilfrid Tremblay (Dir./Prof.); Kate Fowkes (Prof.); Judy Isaksen (Assoc. Prof.); John Luecke (Assoc. Prof.); Nahed Eltantawy (Asst. Prof.); Jim Goodman (Asst. Prof.); Brad Lambert (Asst. Prof.); Jim Trammell (Asst. Prof.); Gerald Voorhees (Asst. Prof.); Kristina Bell (Lectr.); Don Moore (Opns. Mgr.); Martin Yount (Video Producer); Michelle Devlin (Admin. Asst.)

UNIVERSITY OF NORTH CAROLINA AT PEMBROKE

Street address 1: Box 1510
Street address 3: Pembroke
Street address state: NC
Zip/Postal code: 28372-1510
Mailing address: PO Box 1510
Mailing city: Pembroke
Mailing state: NC
Mailing zip: 28372-1510
General Phone: (910) 522-5723
General Fax: (910) 522-5795
General/National Adv. E-mail: masscomm@uncp.edu
Classified Equipment»
Personnel: Jamie Litty (Chair)

WINGATE UNIVERSITY

Street address 1: Communication Studies
Street address 3: Wingate
Street address state: NC
Zip/Postal code: 28174
Mailing address: Communication Studies
Mailing city: Wingate
Mailing state: NC
Mailing zip: 28174
General Phone: (704) 233-8188
General Fax: (704) 233-8192
General/National Adv. E-mail: coon@wingate.edu
Classified Equipment»
Personnel: Jim Coon (Chair)

WINSTON-SALEM

WINSTON-SALEM STATE UNIVERSITY

Street address 1: 601 Martin Luther King Jr. Dr., 314 Hall-Patterson Bldg.
Street address 3: Winston-Salem
Street address state: NC
Zip/Postal code: 27110
Mailing address: 601 Martin Luther King Jr Dr
Mailing city: Winston Salem
Mailing state: NC
Mailing zip: 27110-0001
General Phone: (336) 750-2320
General Fax: (336) 750-2100
General/National Adv. E-mail: jeterph@wssu.edu
Classified Equipment»
Personnel: Phillip Jeter (Chair/Prof.); Lorna D. Cobb (Prof.); Brian C. Blount (Assoc. Prof.); Marilyn Roseboro (Assoc. Prof.); Abhijit Sen (Assoc. Prof.); Laine Goldman (Asst. Prof.); Doug C. Osman (Asst. Prof.); Valerie S. Saddler (Asst. Prof.); Elvin Jenkins (Instr.); Marcia Bonner (Staff); Ben Donnelly (Staff); Jerome Hancock (Staff); Monica Melton (Staff); Hollie Stevenson-Parrish (Staff); Darlene Vinson (Staff); Harvest R. Williams (Staff); Larry Bell (Part-time Staff); Grady Crosby (Part-time Staff); Nicole Ferguson (Part-time Staff); Bonnie Weymouth (Part-time Staff)

NORTH DAKOTA

NORTH DAKOTA STATE UNIVERSITY

Street address 1: Box 5075, Minard 321
Street address 3: Fargo
Street address state: ND
Zip/Postal code: 58105-5075
Mailing address: Box 5075, Minard 321
Mailing city: Fargo
Mailing state: ND
Mailing zip: 58105-5075
General Phone: (701) 231-7705
General Fax: (701) 231-7784
General/National Adv. E-mail: paul.nelson.1@ndsu.edu
Classified Equipment»
Personnel: Paul E. Nelson (Prof./Head)

UNIVERSITY OF NORTH DAKOTA

Street address 1: PO Box 7169
Street address 3: Grand Forks
Street address state: ND
Zip/Postal code: 58202
Mailing address: PO Box 7169
Mailing city: Grand Forks
Mailing state: ND
Mailing zip: 58202
General Phone: (701) 777-2159
General Fax: (701) 777-3090
General/National Adv. E-mail: scomm@und.nodak.edu
Classified Equipment»
Personnel: Stephen Rendahl (Dir.); Richard Fiordo (Prof.); James Hikins (Prof.); Lana Rakow (Prof.); Lucy Ganje (Assoc. Prof.); Victoria Holden (Assoc. Prof.); Michael Nitz (Assoc. Prof.); Richard Shafer (Assoc. Prof.); Mary Haslerud Opp (Instr.); Raymond Fischer (Prof. Emer.)

NEBRASKA

HASTINGS COLLEGE

Street address 1: 710 N. Turner
Street address 3: Hastings
Street address state: NE
Zip/Postal code: 68901
Mailing address: 710 N Turner Ave
Mailing city: Hastings
Mailing state: NE
Mailing zip: 68901-7696
General Phone: (402) 461-7460
General Fax: (402) 461-7442
Classified Equipment»
Personnel: Jack Kramer (Chair)

UNIVERSITY OF NEBRASKA-KEARNEY

Street address 1: Mitchell Ctr. 146
Street address 3: Kearney
Street address state: NE
Zip/Postal code: 68849
Mailing address: 146 Mitchell Ctr
Mailing city: Kearney
Mailing state: NE
Mailing zip: 68849-0001
General Phone: (308) 865-8249
General Fax: (308) 865-1537
General/National Adv. E-mail: lawsong@unk.edu
Classified Equipment»
Personnel: George Lawson (Chair)

UNIVERSITY OF NEBRASKA-LINCOLN

Street address 1: 200 Centennial Mall N., 147 Andersen Hall
Street address 3: Lincoln
Street address state: NE
Zip/Postal code: 68588-0443
Mailing address: 200 Centennial Mall N # 147
Mailing city: Lincoln
Mailing state: NE
Mailing zip: 68508-1618
General Phone: (402) 472-3041
General Fax: (402) 472-8597
General/National Adv. E-mail: wnorton1@unl.edu
Classified Equipment»
Personnel: Will Norton (Dean/Prof.); Charlyne Berens (Prof.); Laurie Thomas Lee (Prof.); Nancy Mitchell (Prof.); Jan Poley (Prof.); James Randall (Prof.); Jerry Renaud (Prof.); Linda Shipley (Prof./Assoc. Dean); Joe Starita (Prof.); Larry Walklin (Prof.); John Wunder (Prof.); Tim Anderson (Assoc. Prof.); John Bender (Assoc. Prof.); Susan Burzynski Bullard (Assoc. Prof.); Carla Kimbrough (Assoc. Prof.); Frauke Hachtmann (Assoc. Prof.); Barney McCoy (Assoc. Prof.); Mary Kay Quinlan (Assoc. Prof.); Bruce Thorson (Assoc. Prof.); Ruth Brown (Vstg. Assoc. Prof.)

CREIGHTON UNIV.

Street address 1: 2500 California Plz
Street address 3: Omaha
Street address state: NE
Zip/Postal code: 68178-0133
Country: USA
Mailing address: 2500 California Plz
Mailing city: Omaha
Mailing state: NE
Mailing zip: 68178-0002
General Phone: (402) 280-4058
General Fax: (402) 280-1494
General/National Adv. E-mail: emw@creighton.edu
Primary Website: www.creightonian.com
Classified Equipment»
Personnel: Melissa Hillebrand (Ed.); Eileen M. Wirth (Chair/Prof.); Father Don Doll (Prof./Charles and Mary Heider Endowed Jesuit Chair); Kelly Fitzgerald (Asst. Ed.); Timothy S. Guthrie (Assoc. Prof.); Jeffrey Maciejewski (Assoc. Prof.); Carol Zuegner (Assoc. Prof.); Kristoffer Boyle (Asst. Prof.); Joel Davies (Asst. Prof.); Charles Heider (Asst. Prof.); Mary Heider (Asst. Prof.); Andrew Hughes (Lectr.); Kathleen Hughes (Lectr.); Richard Janda (Lectr.); Kathryn Larson (Lectr.); Brian Norton (Lectr.); Wendy Wiseman (Lectr.); Angela Zegers (Lectr.)

UNIVERSITY OF NEBRASKA AT OMAHA

Street address 1: Arts & Sciences Hall 108, 6001 Dodge St.
Street address 3: Omaha
Street address state: NE
Zip/Postal code: 68182-0012
Mailing address: 6001 Dodge St Unit 108
Mailing city: Omaha
Mailing state: NE
Mailing zip: 68182-1107

General Phone: (402) 554-2600
General Fax: (204) 554-3836
General/National Adv. E-mail: jlipschultz@mail.unomaha.edu
Classified Equipment»
Personnel: Gail F. Baker (Dean/Prof.); Jeremy Harris Lipschultz (Dir./Prof.); Shereen Bingham (Prof./Asst. Dir.); Barbara Pickering (Grad. Chair/Assoc. Prof.); Robert Carlson (Prof.); Karen Dwyer (Reilly Prof./Basic Course Dir.); Michael Hilt (Prof./Asst. Dean); Terry Hynes (Prof./Sr. Vice Chancellor); Bruce Johansen (Prof./Kayser Prof.); Marshall Prisbell (Prof.); Michael Sherer (Prof.); Deborah Smith-Howell (Prof./Grad. Dean/Assoc. Vice Chancellor); Chris Allen (Assoc. Prof.); Teresa Lamsam (Assoc. Prof.); David Ogden (Assoc. Prof.); Hugh Reilly (Assoc. Prof./Internship Coord.); Randall Rose (Assoc. Prof.); Sherrie Wilson (Assoc. Prof./Media Writing Coord.); Ana Cruz (Asst. Prof.); Robert Franklin (Asst. Prof./GM, UNO TV & KVNO-FM)

NEW HAMPSHIRE

UNIVERSITY OF NEW HAMPSHIRE

Street address 1: 104 Hamilton Smith Hall
Street address 3: Durham
Street address state: NH
Zip/Postal code: 3824
Country: USA
Mailing address: 104 Hamilton Smith Hall
Mailing city: Durham
Mailing state: NH
Mailing zip: 3824
General Phone: (603) 862-0251
General Fax: (603) 862-3563
General/National Adv. E-mail: lcm@cisunix.unh.edu
Classified Equipment»
Personnel: Lisa Miller (Dir.)
Newspaper (for newspapers group): The New Hampshire, Durham

KEENE STATE COLLEGE OF THE UNIVERSITY SYSTEM OF NEW HAMPSHIRE

Street address 1: 229 Main St.
Street address 3: Keene
Street address state: NH
Zip/Postal code: 03435-1402
Mailing address: 229 Main St
Mailing city: Keene
Mailing state: NH
Mailing zip: 03435-0001
General Phone: (603) 358-2724
General Fax: (603) 358-2138
Classified Equipment»
Personnel: Rose Kundanis (Prof.); David Payson (Assoc. Prof.); Marianne Salcetti (Asst. Prof.); Mark Timney (Asst. Prof.); Craig Brandon (Staff.)

SOUTHERN NEW HAMPSHIRE UNIVERSITY

Street address 1: 2500 N. River Rd.
Street address 2: 3100 Cleburne St.
Street address 3: Manchester
Street address state: NH
Zip/Postal code: 03106-1045
Mailing address: 2500 N River Rd
Mailing city: Manchester
Mailing state: NH
Mailing zip: 03106-1045
General Phone: (603) 668-2211
General Fax: (603) 645-9779
General/National Adv. E-mail: a.kubilius@snhu.edu
Classified Equipment»
Personnel: Ausra Kubilius (Chair)

NEW JERSEY

ROWAN UNIV.

Street address 1: 201 Mullica Hill Rd
Street address 3: Glassboro
Street address state: NJ
Zip/Postal code: 08028-1700
Country: USA
Mailing address: 201 Mullica Hill Rd
Mailing city: Glassboro
Mailing state: NJ
Mailing zip: 08028-1702
General Phone: (856) 256-4713
General Fax: (856) 256-4929
General/National Adv. E-mail: communication@rowan.edu
Primary Website: www.thewhitonline.com
Classified Equipment»
Personnel: Don Bagin (Prof.); Kathryn Quigley (Advisor); R. Michael Donovan (Prof.); Anthony Fulginiti (Prof.); Richard Grupenhoff (Prof.); Kenneth Kaleta (Prof.); Janice Rowan (Prof.); Edward Streb (Prof.); Julia Chang (Assoc. Prof.); Cynthia Corison (Assoc. Prof.); Edgar Eckhardt (Assoc. Prof.); Suzanne Fitzgerald (Assoc. Prof.); Carl Hausman (Assoc. Prof.); Martin Itzkowitz (Assoc. Prof.); Frances Johnson (Assoc. Prof.); Diane Penrod (Assoc. Prof.); Donald Stoll (Assoc. Prof.); Sanford Tweedie (Assoc. Prof.); Kenneth Albone (Asst. Prof.); Lorin Arnold (Asst. Prof.)

RIDER UNIVERSITY

Street address 1: Dept. of Communications
Street address 3: Lawrenceville
Street address state: NJ
Zip/Postal code: 8648
Mailing address: Dept. of Communications
Mailing city: Lawrenceville
Mailing state: NJ
Mailing zip: 8648
General Phone: (609) 896-5089
General Fax: (609) 895-5772
General/National Adv. E-mail: schwartzh@enigma.rider.edu
Classified Equipment»
Personnel: Howard Schwartz (Chair)

RUTGERS UNIVERSITY

Street address 1: 4 Huntington St.
Street address 3: New Brunswick
Street address state: NJ
Zip/Postal code: 8903
Mailing address: 4 Huntington St
Mailing city: New Brunswick
Mailing state: NJ
Mailing zip: 08901-1071
General Phone: (732) 932-7500
General Fax: (732) 932-1523
General/National Adv. E-mail: jpavlik@rutgers.edu
Classified Equipment»
Personnel: John Pavlik (Chair/Prof.); Robert Kubey (Prof.); Linda Steiner (Prof.); Montague Kern (Assoc. Prof.); William Solomon (Assoc. Prof.); Barbara Straus Reed (Assoc. Prof.); Jack Bratich (Asst. Prof.); David Greenberg (Asst. Prof.); Susan Keith (Asst. Prof.); Deepa Kumar (Asst. Prof.); Regina Marchi (Asst. Prof.); Steven Miller (Instr.); Jerome Aumente (Prof. Emer.); Roger Cohen (Prof. Emer.); Thomas B. Hartmann (Prof. Emer.); Richard Heffner (University Prof.); Guy Baehr (Adj. Fac.); Tom Cafferty (Adj. Fac.); Nat Clymer (Adj. Fac.); Benjamin Davis (Adj. Fac.)

RUTGERS UNIVERSITY-NEWARK

Street address 1: Hill Hall Room 501
Street address 3: Newark
Street address state: NJ
Zip/Postal code: 7102
Mailing address: Hill Hall Room 501
Mailing city: Newark
Mailing state: NJ
Mailing zip: 7102
General Phone: (973) 353-5279
General Fax: (973) 353-1450
General/National Adv. E-mail: engnwk@andromeda.Rutgers.edu
Classified Equipment»
Personnel: Virginia Tiger (Chair.)

SETON HALL UNIVERSITY

Street address 1: 400 S. Orange Ave.
Street address 3: South Orange
Street address state: NJ
Zip/Postal code: 7079
Mailing address: 400 S Orange Ave
Mailing city: South Orange
Mailing state: NJ
Mailing zip: 07079-2697
General Phone: (973) 761-9474
General/National Adv. E-mail: readerpe@shu.edu
Classified Equipment»
Personnel: Peter Reader (Chair.)

FAIRLEIGH DICKINSON UNIVERSITY

Street address 1: School of Commun. Arts
Street address 3: Teaneck
Street address state: NJ
Zip/Postal code: 7666
Mailing address: School of Commun. Arts
Mailing city: Teaneck
Mailing state: NJ
Mailing zip: 7666
General Phone: (201) 692-2415
General Fax: (201) 692-2081
Classified Equipment»
Personnel: Bernard F. Dick (Dir.)

WILLIAM PATERSON UNIVERSITY

Street address 1: Hobart Hall, 300 Pompton Rd.
Street address 3: Wayne
Street address state: NJ
Zip/Postal code: 7470
Mailing address: 300 Pompton Rd
Mailing city: Wayne
Mailing state: NJ
Mailing zip: 07470-2152
General Phone: (973) 720-2150
General Fax: (973) 720-2483
General/National Adv. E-mail: leej67@upunj.edu
Classified Equipment»
Personnel: Joann Lee (Chair.)

NEW MEXICO

UNIVERSITY OF NEW MEXICO

Street address 1: Dept. of Communication & Journalism
Street address 3: Albuquerque
Street address state: NM
Zip/Postal code: 87131-0001
Mailing address: Dept of Communication & Journalism
Mailing city: Albuquerque
Mailing state: NM
Mailing zip: 87131-0001
General Phone: (505) 277-5305
General Fax: (505) 277-4206
General/National Adv. E-mail: cjdept@unm.edu
Classified Equipment»
Personnel: John Oetzel (Chair)

NEW MEXICO STATE UNIVERSITY

Street address 1: Dept. 3J, Box 30001
Street address 3: Las Cruces
Street address state: NM
Zip/Postal code: 88003-8001
Mailing address: Dept. 3J, Box 30001
Mailing city: Las Cruces
Mailing state: NM
Mailing zip: 88003-8001
General Phone: (505) 646-1034
General Fax: (505) 646-1255
General/National Adv. E-mail: nanhowel@nmsu.edu
Classified Equipment»
Personnel: Anne Hubbell (Interim Head); J. Sean McCleneghan (Prof.); Hwiman Chung (Assoc. Prof.); Bruce Berman (Asst. Prof.); Mary Lamonica (Asst. Prof.); Roger Mellen (Asst. Prof.); Frank Thayer (Asst. Prof.); Pam Porter (College Fac.); Ralph Escandon (Instr.); Colin Gromatazky (Instr.); Carrie Hamblen (Instr.); J.D. Jarvis (Instr.); Bob Nosbisch (Instr.); Michael Olson (Instr.); Hugo Perez (Instr.); Ronald Salak (Instr.); Charles Scholz (Instr.); Ricardo Trujillo (Instr.); Krista West (Instr.); Gary Worth (Instr.)

NEW MEXICO HIGHLANDS UNIVERSITY

Street address 1: Dept. of English, Speech & Journalism
Street address 2: Box 9000
Street address 3: Las Vegas
Street address state: NM
Zip/Postal code: 87701
Mailing address: Dept. of English, Speech & Journalism
Mailing city: Las Vegas
Mailing state: NM
Mailing zip: 87701
General Phone: (505) 425-7511
General Fax: (505) 454-3389
General/National Adv. E-mail: linderpeter@nmhu.edu
Classified Equipment»
Personnel: Peter Linder (Chair)

EASTERN NEW MEXICO UNIVERSITY

Street address 1: Dept. of Communicative Arts & Sciences
Street address 3: Portales
Street address state: NM
Zip/Postal code: 88130
Mailing address: Dept. of Communicative Arts & Sciences
Mailing city: Portales
Mailing state: NM
Mailing zip: 88130
General Phone: (505) 562-2130
General Fax: (505) 562-2847
General/National Adv. E-mail: janet.roehl@enmu.edu
Primary Website: www.unm.ed/~cjdept
Classified Equipment»

NEVADA

UNIVERSITY OF NEVADA, LAS VEGAS

Street address 1: 4505 S Maryland Pkwy
Street address 2: # 2011
Street address 3: Las Vegas
Street address state: NV
Zip/Postal code: 89154-9900
Country: USA
Mailing address: 4505 S Maryland Pkwy
Mailing city: Las Vegas
Mailing state: NV
Mailing zip: 89154-9900
General Phone: (702) 895-2028
General Fax: (702) 895-1515
Editorial Fax: Free
General/National Adv. E-mail: chief.freepress@univ.edu
Display Adv. E-mail: marketing.freepress@unlv.edu
Editorial e-mail: managing.freepress@unlv.edu
Primary Website: www.unlvfreepress.com
Year Established: 1955
Advertising (Open Inch Rate) Weekday/Saturday: http://www.unlvfreepress.com/advertise-with-us/
Published: Mon
Avg Paid Circ: 0
Avg Free Circ: 3800
Classified Equipment»
Personnel: Rick Velotta (Adviser); Bianca Cseke (Editor-in-Chief); Blaze Lovell (Managing Editor); Nicole Gallego (Director of Marketing & Sales)

UNIVERSITY OF NEVADA-RENO

Street address 1: Mail Stop 310
Street address 3: Reno
Street address state: NV
Zip/Postal code: 89557-0310
Mailing address: Mail Stop 310
Mailing city: Reno
Mailing state: NV
Mailing zip: 89557-0001
General Phone: (775) 784-6531
General Fax: (775) 784-6656
General/National Adv. E-mail: journalism@nevada.edu
Primary Website: journalism.unr.edu
Classified Equipment»
Personnel: Jerry Ceppos (Dean); Larry Dailey (Prof./Endowed Chair); Ed Lenert (Prof./Endowed Chair); Jake Highton (Prof.); Saundra Keyes (Prof.); Warren Lerude (Prof.); Bourne Morris (Prof.); Howard Goldbaum (Assoc. Prof.); Donica Mensing (Assoc. Prof./Grad. Studies Dir.); David Ryfe (Assoc. Prof.); Bob Felten (Asst. Prof.); Todd Felts (Asst. Prof.); Deidre Pike (Lectr.); Theodore Conover (Prof. Emer.); James Ellis (Prof. Emer.); Joseph Howland (Prof. Emer.); Kristin Burgarello (Adm. Fac.); Paul Mitchell (Adm. Fac/Dir., Devel./Coord., Recruiting/Retention)

NEW YORK

STATE UNIVERSITY OF NEW YORK AT ALBANY

Street address 1: 1400 Washington Ave.
Street address 3: Albany
Street address state: NY
Zip/Postal code: 12222
Mailing address: 1400 Washington Ave
Mailing city: Albany
Mailing state: NY
Mailing zip: 12222-1000
General Phone: (518) 442-4884
General/National Adv. E-mail: nroberts@albany.edu
Primary Website: www.albany.edu/journalism
Classified Equipment»
Personnel: Nancy L. Roberts (Prof./Dir., Journ. Prog.)

FORDHAM UNIVERSITY

Street address 1: Rose Hill Campus
Street address 3: Bronx
Street address state: NY
Zip/Postal code: 10458
Mailing address: Rose Hill Campus
Mailing city: Bronx
Mailing state: NY
Mailing zip: 10458
General Phone: (718) 817-4863
General Fax: (718) 817-4868
General/National Adv. E-mail: paullevinson1@cs.com
Classified Equipment»
Personnel: Paul Levinson (Chair)

LONG ISLAND UNIVERSITY - THE BROOKLYN CAMPUS

Street address 1: 1 University Plz.
Street address 3: Brooklyn
Street address state: NY
Zip/Postal code: 11201-5372
Mailing address: 1 University Plz
Mailing city: Brooklyn
Mailing state: NY
Mailing zip: 11201-5372
General Phone: (718) 488-1534 Kalman Siegel Newslab
General Fax: (718) 246-6365
General/National Adv. E-mail: ralph.engelman@liu.edu
Classified Equipment»
Personnel: Ralph Engelman (Dept. Chair)

BUFFALO STATE COLLEGE

Street address 1: 1300 Elmwood Ave., Bishop 210
Street address 3: Buffalo
Street address state: NY
Zip/Postal code: 14222
Mailing address: 1300 Elmwood Ave Bishop 210
Mailing city: Buffalo
Mailing state: NY
Mailing zip: 14222-1095
General Phone: (716) 878-6008
General Fax: (716) 878-4697
General/National Adv. E-mail: smithrd@buffalostate.edu
Primary Website: www.buffalostate.edu/communication
Classified Equipment»
Personnel: Ronald D. Smith (Chair)

CANISIUS COLLEGE

Street address 1: 2001 Main St
Street address 3: Buffalo
Street address state: NY
Zip/Postal code: 14208-1035
Country: USA
Mailing address: 2001 Main St
Mailing city: Buffalo
Mailing state: NY
Mailing zip: 14208-1098
General Phone: (716) 888-2115
General Fax: (716) 888-3118
General/National Adv. E-mail: irwin@canisius.edu
Classified Equipment»
Personnel: Barbara Irwin (Professor of Communications); Eric Koehler (Ed.); Jennifer Gorczynski (Ed.); Marisa Loffredo (News Ed.)

HOFSTRA UNIVERSITY

Street address 1: 111 Hofstra University
Street address 3: Hempstead
Street address state: NY
Zip/Postal code: 11549-1000
Mailing address: 111 Hofstra University
Mailing city: Hempstead
Mailing state: NY
Mailing zip: 11549-1110
General Phone: (516) 463-4873
General Fax: (516) 463-4866
General/National Adv. E-mail: jrnbmk@hofstra.edu
Classified Equipment»
Personnel: Barbara Kelly (Chair)

CORNELL UNIVERSITY

Street address 1: 337 Kennedy Hall
Street address 3: Ithaca
Street address state: NY
Zip/Postal code: 14853-4203
Mailing address: 337 Kennedy Hall
Mailing city: Ithaca
Mailing state: NY
Mailing zip: 14853-4203
General Phone: (607) 255-2601
General Fax: (607) 254-1322
General/National Adv. E-mail: dyd1@cornell.edu
Classified Equipment»
Personnel: Geraldine K. Gay (Chair)

ITHACA COLLEGE

Street address 1: Roy H. Park School of Communications
Street address 3: Ithaca
Street address state: NY
Zip/Postal code: 14850
Mailing address: Roy H. Park School of Communications
Mailing city: Ithaca
Mailing state: NY
Mailing zip: 14850
General Phone: (607) 274-1021
General Fax: (607) 274-1108
Primary Website: www.ithaca.edu
Classified Equipment»
Personnel: Diane Lynch (Dean/Prof.); Jo Ann Caplin (Prof./Park Distinguished Chair); Christopher Harper (Prof./Park Distinguished Chair); Diane Gayeski (Prof.); Sandra Herndon (Prof./Grad. Prog. Chair); Steven Skopik (Prof.); Wenmouth Williams (Prof.); Patricia Zimmermann (Prof.); Ben Crane (Assoc. Prof.); Raymond Gozzi (Assoc. Prof.); John Hochheimer (Assoc. Prof.); Janice Levy (Assoc. Prof./Cinema & Photography Chair); Gina Marchetti (Assoc. Prof.); Sharon Mazzarella (Assoc. Prof./Television/Radio Chair); Barbara Morgenstern (Assoc. Prof.); Megan Roberts (Assoc. Prof.); John Rosenbaum (Assoc. Prof.); Gordon Rowland (Assoc. Prof./Organizational Communication, Learning, and Design Chair); Steven Seidman (Assoc. Prof.); Madelyn Williams (Assoc. Prof.)

SUNY COLLEGE AT NEW PALTZ

Street address 1: Coykendall Science Bldg.
Street address 3: New Paltz
Street address state: NY
Zip/Postal code: 12561
Mailing address: Coykendall Science Bldg.
Mailing city: New Paltz
Mailing state: NY
Mailing zip: 12561
General Phone: (845) 257-3450
General Fax: (845) 257-3461
General/National Adv. E-mail: commedia@newpaltz.edu
Classified Equipment»
Personnel: Pat Sullivan (Chair)

IONA COLLEGE

Street address 1: 715 North Ave.
Street address 3: New Rochelle
Street address state: NY
Zip/Postal code: 10801-1890
Mailing address: 715 North Ave
Mailing city: New Rochelle
Mailing state: NY
Mailing zip: 10801-1890
General Phone: (914) 633-2230
General Fax: (914) 637-2797
General/National Adv. E-mail: masscom@iona.edu
Classified Equipment»
Personnel: Orly Schachar (Chair/Asst. Prof./Undergrad. Coord.); John Darretta (Prof.); George Thottam (Prof.); Nancy-Jo Johnson (Assoc. Prof.); Mike McDermott (Asst. Prof.); Ann Rodriguez (Asst. Prof.); Ray Smith (Asst. Prof.); Susan Vaughn (Asst. Prof.); Virginia Hill (Instr.); Natalie Ryder (Instr.); Ivette Allen (Adj. Fac.); Tom Callahan (Adj. Fac.); Bill Corbett (Adj. Fac.); Nancy Cutler (Adj. Fac.); Jim Eggensperger (Adj. Fac.); Minaz Fazal (Adj. Fac.); Marybeth Kissane (Adj. Fac.); Woody Klein (Adj. Fac.); Nancy Kriz (Adj. Fac.); Drew Kulakovich (Adj. Fac.)

COLUMBIA UNIVERSITY

Street address 1: 2950 Broadway, Mail Code 3800
Street address 3: New York
Street address state: NY
Zip/Postal code: 10027
Mailing address: 2950 Broadway, Mail Code 3800
Mailing city: New York
Mailing state: NY
Mailing zip: 10027
General Phone: (212) 854-8608
General Fax: (212) 854-2352
General/National Adv. E-mail: admissions@journalism.columbia.edu
Primary Website: www.journalism.columbia.edu
Classified Equipment»
Personnel: Helen Benedict (Prof.); Ann Cooper (Prof.); Sheila Coronel (Prof.); Tom Edsall (Prof.); Samuel G. Freedman (Prof.); Todd Gitlin (Prof.); Ari Goldman (Prof.); David Klatell (Prof.); Nicholas Lemann (Prof.); Sylvia Nasar (Prof.); Stephen Isaacs (Prof.); Michael Janeway (Prof./Dir., Nat'l Arts Journalism Prog.); Victor Navasky (Prof.); Michael Schudson (Prof.); James B. Stewart (Prof.); Michael Shapiro (Prof.); Alexander Stille (Prof.); Richard Wald (Prof.); Jonathan Weiner (Prof.); John Dinges (Assoc. Prof.)

CUNY GRADUATE SCHOOL OF JOURNALISM

Street address 1: 230 W. 41st St., 4th Fl.
Street address 3: New York
Street address state: NY
Zip/Postal code: 10036
Mailing address: 230 W 41st St Fl 4
Mailing city: New York
Mailing state: NY
Mailing zip: 10036-7207
General Phone: (646) 758-7800
General Fax: (646) 758-7809
Primary Website: journalism.cuny.edu
Classified Equipment»
Personnel: Stephen Shepard (Dean)

NEW YORK UNIVERSITY

Street address 1: 10 Washington Pl., 5th Fl.
Street address 3: New York
Street address state: NY
Zip/Postal code: 10003
Mailing address: 10 Washington Pl Fl 5
Mailing city: New York
Mailing state: NY
Mailing zip: 10003-6604
General Phone: (212) 998-7980
General Fax: (212) 995-4148
Primary Website: www.nyu.edu/gsas/dept/journal
Classified Equipment»
Personnel: Jay Rosen (Chair)

THE EMPIRE STATE TRIBUNE

Street address 1: 56 Broadway
Street address 2: Fl 5
Street address 3: New York
Street address state: NY
Zip/Postal code: 10004-1613
County: New York
Country: USA
General Phone: 212-659-0742
Advertising Phone: 212-659-0742
Editorial Phone: 212-659-0742
General/National Adv. E-mail: estribune@tkc.edu
Display Adv. E-mail: estribune@tkc.edu
Classified Adv. E-mail: estribune@tkc.edu
Editorial e-mail: estribune@tkc.edu
Primary Website: www.empirestatetribune.com
Mthly Avg Views: 8856
Mthly Avg Unique Visitors: 4124
Year Established: 2005
Delivery Methods: Racks
Area Served - City: 10004
Own Printing Facility: Y
Commercial printers: N
Published: Mon
Weekday Frequency: m
Avg Free Circ: 100
Audit By: Sworn/Estimate/Non-Audited
Audit Date: 2/16/2018
Classified Equipment»
Product or Service: Editorial
Personnel: Clemente Lisi (Assistant Affiliate Professor of Journalism)

NIAGARA UNIVERSITY

Street address 1: 338 Dunleavy Hall
Street address 3: Niagara University
Street address state: NY
Zip/Postal code: 14109
Mailing address: 338 Dunleavy Hall
Mailing city: Niagara University
Mailing state: NY
Mailing zip: 14109
General Phone: (716) 286-8460
General/National Adv. E-mail: barner@niagara.edu
Primary Website: www.niagara.edu/communication
Classified Equipment»
Personnel: Mark R. Barner (Chair/Assoc. Prof.); Brian M. Murphy (Assoc. Prof.); Randy Nichols (Asst. Prof.); Mary Sterpka-King (Asst. Prof.)

PACE UNIVERSITY (PLEASANTVILLE)

Street address 1: 861 Bedford Rd.
Street address 3: Pleasantville
Street address state: NY
Zip/Postal code: 10570
Mailing address: 861 Bedford Rd
Mailing city: Pleasantville
Mailing state: NY
Mailing zip: 10570-2799
General Phone: (914) 773-3790
General/National Adv. E-mail: rklaeger@pace.edu
Classified Equipment»
Personnel: Robert Klaeger (Chair)

MARIST COLLEGE

Street address 1: 3399 North Rd.
Street address 3: Poughkeepsie
Street address state: NY
Zip/Postal code: 12601
Mailing address: 3399 North Rd
Mailing city: Poughkeepsie
Mailing state: NY
Mailing zip: 12601-1387
General Phone: (845) 575-3650
General Fax: (845) 575-3645
General/National Adv. E-mail: subir.sengupta@marist.edu
Classified Equipment»
Personnel: John Ritschdorff (Dean/Prof.); James Fahey (Assoc. Prof.); Laura Linder (Assoc. Prof.); Subir Sengupta (Assoc. Prof./Asst. Dean); Mark Van Dyke (Assoc. Prof.); Paula Willoquet (Assoc. Prof.); Missy Alexander (Asst. Prof.); Cochece Davis (Asst. Prof.); Sue Lawrence (Asst. Prof.); James Maritato (Asst. Prof.); Carol Pauli (Asst. Prof.); Joe Ross (Asst. Prof.); Shannon Roper (Asst. Prof.); Keith Strudler (Asst. Prof.); Jeff Bass (Instr.); Marcia Christ (Instr.); Dennis Conway (Instr.); Keith Hamel (Instr.); Brett Phares (Instr.); Gerald McNulty (Dir., Internship Prog.)

ROCHESTER INSTITUTE OF TECHNOLOGY

Street address 1: 92 Lomb Memorial Dr.
Street address 3: Rochester
Street address state: NY
Zip/Postal code: 14623-5604
Mailing address: 92 Lomb Memorial Dr
Mailing city: Rochester
Mailing state: NY
Mailing zip: 14623-5604

General Phone: (585) 475-6649
General Fax: (585) 475-7732
General/National Adv. E-mail: cmvgpt@rit.edu
Classified Equipment»
Personnel: Bruce Austin (Chair)

ST. JOHN FISHER COLLEGE

Street address 1: 3690 East Ave
Street address 3: Rochester
Street address state: NY
Zip/Postal code: 14618-3537
Country: USA
Mailing address: 3690 East Ave
Mailing city: Rochester
Mailing state: NY
Mailing zip: 14618-3537
General Phone: (585) 385-8360
General Fax: (585) 385-7311
Advertising Phone: (585) 385-7393
General/National Adv. E-mail: cardinalcourier@sjfc.edu
Display Adv. E-mail: mvilla@sjfc.edu
Editorial e-mail: eem00114@sjfc.edu
Primary Website: www.cardinalcourieronline.com
Year Established: 2002
Published: Bi-Mthly
Classified Equipment»
Personnel: Lauren Vicker (Chair/Prof.); Marie Villa (Media Adviser)

ST. BONAVENTURE UNIVERSITY

Street address 1: 3261 W. State Rd.
Street address 3: Saint Bonaventure
Street address state: NY
Zip/Postal code: 14778-2289
Mailing address: PO Box J
Mailing city: Saint Bonaventure
Mailing state: NY
Mailing zip: 14778-2289
General Phone: (716) 375-2520
General Fax: (716) 375-2588
General/National Adv. E-mail: jmc@sbu.edu
Classified Equipment»
Personnel: Lee Coppola (Dean); John Hanchette (Assoc. Prof.); Christopher Mackowski (Assoc. Prof.); Denny Wilkins (Assoc. Prof./Coord., Print); Pauline Hoffmann (Asst. Prof.); Carole McNall (Asst. Prof.); Bro. Basil Valente (Asst. Prof./Coord., PR/Adv.); Patrick Vecchio (Lectr.); Paul Wieland (Lectr./Coord., Broadcast); Breea Willingham (Vstg. Prof.); Mary Beth Garvin (Broadcast Journalism Lab Supvr.); Kathleen Mason (Dir., IMC Grad. Prog.); John Bartimole (Adj. Fac.); Robert Carr (Adj. Fac.); John Eberth (Adj. Fac.); James Eckstrom (Adj. Fac.); Jean Trevarton Ehman (Adj. Fac.); Donald Gilliland (Adj. Fac.); Darrell Gronemeier (Adj. Fac./PhotoJournalism); Kelly Hendrix (Adj. Fac.)

STONY BROOK UNIVERSITY

Street address 1: SUNY 3384 Melville Library N4004
Street address 3: Stony Brook
Street address state: NY
Zip/Postal code: 11790-3384
Mailing address: SUNY 3384 Melville Library N4004
Mailing city: Stony Brook
Mailing state: NY
Mailing zip: 11790-3384
General Phone: (631) 632-7403
General Fax: (631) 632-7550
General/National Adv. E-mail: journalism@stonybrook.edu
Classified Equipment»
Personnel: Howard Schneider (Dean)

SYRACUSE UNIVERSITY

Street address 1: 215 University Pl.
Street address 3: Syracuse
Street address state: NY
Zip/Postal code: 13244-2100
Mailing address: 215 University Pl
Mailing city: Syracuse
Mailing state: NY
Mailing zip: 13244-0001
General Phone: (315) 443-2301
General Fax: (315) 443-3946
General/National Adv. E-mail: newhouse@syr.edu
Classified Equipment»
Personnel: Lorraine Branham (Dean); Stanley R. Alten (Prof.); Richard L. Breyer (Prof.); George A. Comstock (Prof.); Elizabeth L. Flocke (Prof.); William A. Glavin (Prof.); Charlotte Grimes (Prof.); Sharon R. Hollenback (Prof.); John P. Jones (Prof.); Lawrence Mason (Prof.); Peter K. Moller (Prof.); David M. Rubin (Prof.); Maria P. Russell (Prof.); Nancy W. Sharp (Prof.); Pamela J. Shoemaker (Prof.); Robert J. Thompson (Prof.); Jay B. Wright (Prof.); Hubert Brown (Assoc. Prof.); Melissa Chessher (Assoc. Prof.); Fiona Chew (Assoc. Prof.)

UTICA COLLEGE OF SYRACUSE UNIVERSITY

Street address 1: 1600 Burrstone Rd.
Street address 3: Utica
Street address state: NY
Zip/Postal code: 13502
Mailing address: 1600 Burrstone Rd
Mailing city: Utica
Mailing state: NY
Mailing zip: 13502-4892
General Phone: (315) 792-3241
General Fax: (315) 792-3173
General/National Adv. E-mail: cfriend@utica.edu
Classified Equipment»
Personnel: Cecilia Friend (Dir./Prof.)

OHIO

UNIVERSITY OF AKRON

Street address 1: School of Communication
Street address 3: Akron
Street address state: OH
Zip/Postal code: 44325-1003
Mailing address: School of Communication
Mailing city: Akron
Mailing state: OH
Mailing zip: 44325-0001
General Phone: (330) 972-7600
General Fax: (330) 972-8045
General/National Adv. E-mail: dbturner@uakron.edu
Primary Website: www.uakron.edu/schlcomm
Classified Equipment»
Personnel: Dudley B. Turner (Dir.)

OHIO UNIVERSITY

Street address 1: Scripps Hall 105, Court St. & Park Pl.
Street address 3: Athens
Street address state: OH
Zip/Postal code: 45701
Mailing address: Scripps Hall 105, Court St. & Park Pl.
Mailing city: Athens
Mailing state: OH
Mailing zip: 45701
General Phone: (740) 593-2590
General Fax: (740) 593-2592
General/National Adv. E-mail: info@scrippsjschool.org
Primary Website: scrippsjschool.org
Classified Equipment»
Personnel: Thomas Hodson (Dir./Assoc. Prof.); Joseph Bernt (Prof./Assoc. Dir., Grad. Studies/Research); Anne Cooper-Chen (Prof.); Marilyn Greenwald (Prof.); Robert Stewart (Prof./Assoc. Dir.); Patrick Washburn (Prof.); Patricia Westfall (Prof.); Bojinka Bishop (Assoc. Prof.); Hong Cheng (Assoc. Prof.); Bernhard Debatin (Assoc. Prof./Dir. Studies, Honors Tutorial College); Sandra Haggerty (Assoc. Prof.); Ronald Pittman (Assoc. Prof.); Mary Rogus (Assoc. Prof.); Patricia Cambridge (Asst. Prof.); Aimee Edmondson (Asst. Prof.); Cary Frith (Asst. Prof.); Ellen Gerl (Asst. Prof.); Michelle Honald (Asst. Prof.); Yusuf Kalyango (Asst. Prof./Dir., Inst. for Int'l Journalism); Bill Reader (Asst. Prof.)

BOWLING GREEN STATE UNIVERSITY

Street address 1: 302 West Hall
Street address 3: Bowling Green
Street address state: OH
Zip/Postal code: 43403
Mailing address: 302 W Hall
Mailing city: Bowling Green
Mailing state: OH
Mailing zip: 43403-0001
General Phone: (419) 372-8349
General Fax: (419) 372-0202
General/National Adv. E-mail: rfirsdo@bgnet.bgsu.edu
Primary Website: www.bgsu.edu/departments/journalism
Classified Equipment»
Personnel: Terry Rentner (Chair/Assoc. Prof.); J. Oliver Boyd-Barrett (Prof.); Nancy Brendlinger (Assoc. Prof.); Catherine Cassara (Assoc. Prof.); James Foust (Assoc. Prof.); Melissa Spirek (Assoc. Prof.); Katherine Bradshaw (Asst. Prof.); Victoria Smith Ekstrand (Asst. Prof.); Efrem Graham (Instr.); Julie Hagenbuch (Instr.); Kelly Taylor (Instr.); James Bissland (Prof. Emer.); Joseph Delporto (Prof. Emer.); Harold Fisher (Prof. Emer.); James Gordon (Prof. Emer.); F. Dennis Hale (Prof. Emer.); John Huffman (Prof. Emer.); Laurence Jankowski (Prof. Emer.); Raymond Laakaniemi (Prof. Emer.)

UNIVERSITY OF CINCINNATI

Street address 1: Div. of Electronic Media
Street address 3: Cincinnati
Street address state: OH
Zip/Postal code: 45221-0003
Mailing address: Divide of Electronic Media
Mailing city: Cincinnati
Mailing state: OH
Mailing zip: 45221-0001
General Phone: (513) 556-9488
General Fax: (513) 556-0202
General/National Adv. E-mail: wolframk@uc.edu
Classified Equipment»
Personnel: Manfred K. Wolfram (Chair); Marjorie Fox (Journalism Coord.)

XAVIER UNIVERSITY

Street address 1: 3800 Victory Pkwy.
Street address 3: Cincinnati
Street address state: OH
Zip/Postal code: 45207-5171
Mailing address: 3800 Victory Pkwy Unit 1
Mailing city: Cincinnati
Mailing state: OH
Mailing zip: 45207-1092
General Phone: (513) 745-3087
General Fax: (513) 745-3705
General/National Adv. E-mail: desilva@Xavier.edu
Classified Equipment»
Personnel: Indra De Silva (Chair)

CLEVELAND STATE UNIVERSITY

Street address 1: 2121 Euclid Ave.
Street address 3: Cleveland
Street address state: OH
Zip/Postal code: 44115-2214
Mailing address: 2121 Euclid Ave
Mailing city: Cleveland
Mailing state: OH
Mailing zip: 44115-2226
General Phone: (216) 687-4630
General Fax: (216) 687-5435
General/National Adv. E-mail: j.lee@csuohio.edu
Primary Website: www.csuohio.edu/com
Classified Equipment»
Personnel: Richard Perloff (School Dir.); Jae-won Lee (Div. Dir.)

OHIO STATE UNIVERSITY

Street address 1: 3016 Derby Hall, 154 N. Oval Mall
Street address 3: Columbus
Street address state: OH
Zip/Postal code: 43210-1339
Mailing address: 154 N Oval Mall
Mailing city: Columbus
Mailing state: OH
Mailing zip: 43210-1330
General Phone: (614) 292-3400
General Fax: (614) 292-2055
General/National Adv. E-mail: glynn.14@osu.edu
Classified Equipment»
Personnel: Carroll J. Glynn (Dir./Prof.); Donald Cegala (Prof.); Brenda Dervin (Prof.); Daniel McDonald (Prof.); Michael Slater (Prof.); Stephen Acker (Assoc. Prof.); Prabu David (Assoc. Prof.); John Dimmick (Assoc. Prof.); William Eveland (Assoc. Prof.); Lance Holbert (Assoc. Prof.); Susan Kline (Assoc. Prof.); Gerald Kosicki (Assoc. Prof.); Emily Moyer-Gus￿￿￿,£ (Assoc. Prof.); Amy Nathanson (Assoc. Prof.); Felecia Ross (Assoc. Prof.); Thomas Schwartz (Assoc. Prof.); Laura Stafford (Assoc. Prof.); Sharon West (Assoc. Prof.); Osei Appiah (Asst. Prof.); Kelly Garrett (Assoc. Prof.)

UNIVERSITY OF DAYTON

Street address 1: 300 College Park
Street address 3: Dayton
Street address state: OH
Zip/Postal code: 45469-1410
Mailing address: 300 College Park
Mailing city: Dayton
Mailing state: OH
Mailing zip: 45469-0002
General Phone: (917) 229-2028
General Fax: (937) 000-0000
General/National Adv. E-mail: Donald.yoder@notes.udayton.edu
Classified Equipment»
Personnel: Donald D. Yoder (Chair)

WRIGHT STATE UNIVERSITY

Street address 1: Dept. of Communication
Street address 3: Dayton
Street address state: OH
Zip/Postal code: 45435
Mailing address: Dept of Communication
Mailing city: Dayton
Mailing state: OH
Mailing zip: 45435-0001
General Phone: (937) 775-2145
General Fax: (973) 775-2146
General/National Adv. E-mail: james.sayer@wright.edu
Classified Equipment»
Personnel: James Sayer (Chair); Melanie Reach

OHIO WESLEYAN UNIVERSITY

Street address 1: Dept. of Journalism
Street address 3: Delaware
Street address state: OH
Zip/Postal code: 43015
Mailing address: Dept. of Journalism
Mailing city: Delaware
Mailing state: OH
Mailing zip: 43015
General Phone: (740) 368-3650
General Fax: (740) 368-3649
General/National Adv. E-mail: tregan@cc.owu.edu
Classified Equipment»
Personnel: Trace Regan (Chair/Prof.); Paul Kostyu (Assoc. Prof.); Richard McClure (Lectr.); Jim Underwood (Lectr.); Afi-Odelia Scruggs (Vstg. Asst. Prof.)

UNIVERSITY OF FINDLAY

Street address 1: 1000 N. Main St.
Street address 3: Findlay
Street address state: OH
Zip/Postal code: 45840
Mailing address: 1000 N Main St
Mailing city: Findlay
Mailing state: OH
Mailing zip: 45840-3653
General Phone: (419) 434-4445
General Fax: (419) 434-4616
General/National Adv. E-mail: stevens@findlay.edu
Primary Website: www.findlay.edu/academics/info/colleges.htm
Classified Equipment»
Personnel: Dennis Stevens (Dir.)

MARIETTA COLLEGE

Street address 1: 215 5th St
Street address 3: Marietta
Street address state: OH
Zip/Postal code: 45750-4033
Country: USA
Mailing address: 215 5th St Dept 32
Mailing city: Marietta
Mailing state: OH
Mailing zip: 45750-4071
General Phone: (740) 376-4848
General Fax: (740) 376-4807
General/National Adv. E-mail: mac@Marietta.edu
Primary Website: www.marcolian.com/
Classified Equipment»

Personnel: Jack L. Hillwig (Chair)

FRANCISCAN UNIVERSITY OF STEUBENVILLE

Street address 1: G-8 Egan Hall, 1235 University Blvd.
Street address 3: Steubenville
Street address state: OH
Zip/Postal code: 43952
Mailing address: 1235 University Blvd
Mailing city: Steubenville
Mailing state: OH
Mailing zip: 43952-1796
General Phone: (740) 283-3771
General Fax: (740) 283-6452
General/National Adv. E-mail: wlewis@franciscan.edu
Classified Equipment»
Personnel: Wayne Lewis (Chair)

UNIVERSITY OF TOLEDO

Street address 1: 2801 W. Bancroft St., University Hall, Rm. 4600
Street address 3: Toledo
Street address state: OH
Zip/Postal code: 43606-3390
Mailing address: 2801 W Bancroft St Rm 4600
Mailing city: Toledo
Mailing state: OH
Mailing zip: 43606-3390
General Phone: (419) 530-2005
General Fax: (419) 530-4771
General/National Adv. E-mail: jbenjam@utnet.utoledo.edu
Classified Equipment»
Personnel: Jim Benjamin (Chair)

JOHN CARROLL UNIVERSITY

Street address 1: 1 John Carroll Blvd
Street address 3: University Heights
Street address state: OH
Zip/Postal code: 44118-4538
Country: USA
Mailing address: 1 John Carroll Blvd
Mailing city: Cleveland
Mailing state: OH
Mailing zip: 44118-4582
General Phone: (216) 397-1711
General Fax: (216) 397-1729
Advertising Phone: (216) 397-4398
Editorail Phone: (216) 397-1711
General/National Adv. E-mail: jcunews@gmail.com
Display Adv. E-mail: jcunews@gmail.com
Editorial e-mail: jcunews@gmail.com
Primary Website: www.jcunews.com
Year Established: 1925
Published: Thur
Avg Free Circ: 1600
Classified Equipment»
Personnel: Mary Ann Flannery (Chair/Assoc. Prof.); Robert T. Noll (Advisor); Jacqueline J. Schmidt (Prof.); Katie Sheridan (Ed. in Chief); Bob Seeholzer (Mng. Ed.); Alan Stephenson (Prof.); Mary Beadle (Assoc. Prof.); Tim Ertle (Sports Ed.); Margaret Algren (Asst. Prof.); Richard Hendrickson (Asst. Prof.); Robert Prisco (Asst. Prof.); Bob Noll (Instr.); David Reese (Instr.); Fred Buchstein (Part-time Instr.); Mark Eden (Part-time Instr.); Bill Nichols (Part-time Instr.)

OTTERBEIN COLLEGE

Street address 1: 1 Otterbein College
Street address 3: Westerville
Street address state: OH
Zip/Postal code: 43081
Mailing address: 1 S Grove St
Mailing city: Westerville
Mailing state: OH
Mailing zip: 43081-2004
General Phone: (614) 823-3380
General Fax: (614) 823-3367
General/National Adv. E-mail: dwootton@otterbein.edu
Classified Equipment»
Personnel: Susan Millsap (Chair)

YOUNGSTOWN STATE UNIVERSITY

Street address 1: 1 University Plz.
Street address 3: Youngstown
Street address state: OH
Zip/Postal code: 44555-3415
Mailing address: 1 University Plz
Mailing city: Youngstown
Mailing state: OH
Mailing zip: 44555-0002
General Phone: (330) 941-1467
General/National Adv. E-mail: journalism@cc.ysu.edu
Classified Equipment»
Personnel: Alyssa Lenhoff (Dir., Journalism); Gary Salvner (Chair, English)

OKLAHOMA

EAST CENTRAL UNIVERSITY (OKLAHOMA)

Street address 1: 1100 E. 14th St.
Street address 3: Ada
Street address state: OK
Zip/Postal code: 74820-6999
Mailing address: 1100 E 14th St
Mailing city: Ada
Mailing state: OK
Mailing zip: 74820-6999
General Phone: (580) 559-5485
General Fax: (580) 332-1623
General/National Adv. E-mail: bgrnst@ecok.edu
Classified Equipment»
Personnel: Robert Greenstreet (Chair)

SOUTHERN NAZARENE UNIV.

Street address 1: 6729 NW 39th Expy
Street address 3: Bethany
Street address state: OK
Zip/Postal code: 73008-2605
Country: USA
Mailing address: 6729 NW 39th Expy
Mailing city: Bethany
Mailing state: OK
Mailing zip: 73008-2694
General Phone: (405) 491-6382
General Fax: (405) 491-6378
General/National Adv. E-mail: echo@snu.edu
Display Adv. E-mail: grwillia@mail.snu.edu
Editorial e-mail: kirarobe@mail.snu.edu
Primary Website: echo.snu.edu
Published: Fri
Classified Equipment»
Personnel: Pam Broyles (Speech Commun. Dept.); Marcia Feisal (Yearbook); Jim Wilcox (Newspaper); Andrew Baker (Graphic Design); Les Dart (Broadcasting)

OKLAHOMA CHRISTIAN UNIVERSITY

Street address 1: 2501 E. Memorial Rd.
Street address 3: Edmond
Street address state: OK
Zip/Postal code: 73103
Mailing address: 2501 E Memorial Rd
Mailing city: Edmond
Mailing state: OK
Mailing zip: 73013-5599
General Phone: (405) 425-5521
General Fax: (405) 425-5614
General/National Adv. E-mail: philip.patterson@oc.edu
Classified Equipment»
Personnel: Larry Jurney (Chair)

UNIVERSITY OF CENTRAL OKLAHOMA

Street address 1: Mass Communication Dept.
Street address 3: Edmond
Street address state: OK
Zip/Postal code: 73034
Mailing address: Mass Communication Dept.
Mailing city: Edmond
Mailing state: OK
Mailing zip: 73034
General Phone: (405) 974-5303
General Fax: (405) 974-5125
General/National Adv. E-mail: tclark@ucok.edu
Classified Equipment»
Personnel: Terry M. Clark (Chair)

UNIVERSITY OF OKLAHOMA

Street address 1: 395 W. Lindsey St.
Street address 3: Norman
Street address state: OK
Zip/Postal code: 73019-4021
Mailing address: 395 W Lindsey St
Mailing city: Norman
Mailing state: OK
Mailing zip: 73019-4201
General Phone: (405) 325-2721
General Fax: (405) 325-7565
General/National Adv. E-mail: jfoote@ou.edu
Primary Website: jmc.ou.edu
Classified Equipment»
Personnel: Joe Foote (Dean/Prof.); Jim Avery (Prof.); Fred Beard (Prof.); Deborah Chester (Prof.); J. Madison Davis (Prof.); Peter Gross (Prof.); Linda P. Morton (Prof.); Charles C. Self (Prof.); Meta Carstarphen (Assoc. Prof.); David Craig (Assoc. Prof.); Peter Gade (Assoc. Prof.); Timothy Hudson (Assoc. Prof.); Misha Nedeljkovich (Assoc. Prof.); Ralph Beliveau (Asst. Prof.); Matthew Cecil (Asst. Prof.); Robert Kerr (Asst. Prof.); Ken McMillen (Asst. Prof.); Jennifer Tiernan (Asst. Prof.); Katerina Tsetura (Asst. Prof.); Christa Ward (Asst. Prof.)

OKLAHOMA BAPTIST UNIVERSITY

Street address 1: 500 W. University, Box 61308
Street address 3: Shawnee
Street address state: OK
Zip/Postal code: 74804
Mailing address: 500 W University St # 61308
Mailing city: Shawnee
Mailing state: OK
Mailing zip: 74804-2522
General Phone: (405) 878-2236
General Fax: (405) 878-8701
General/National Adv. E-mail: roger.hadley@okbu.edu
Primary Website: www.okbu.edu/jour_pr.htm
Classified Equipment»
Personnel: Roger Hadley (Chair)

OKLAHOMA STATE UNIVERSITY

Street address 1: 206 Paul Miller Bldg.
Street address 3: Stillwater
Street address state: OK
Zip/Postal code: 74078-0195
Mailing address: 206 Paul Miller
Mailing city: Stillwater
Mailing state: OK
Mailing zip: 74078-4052
General Phone: (405) 744-6354
General Fax: (405) 744-7104
General/National Adv. E-mail: melissa.powers@okstate.edu
Classified Equipment»
Personnel: Derina Holtzhausen (Dir.); Brooks Garner (Assoc. Prof.); Jack Hodgson (Assoc. Prof.); Stan Ketterer (Assoc. Prof.); Tom Weir (Assoc. Prof.); Jami Fullerton (Assoc. Prof.); Lori McKinnon (Assoc. Prof.); Joey Senat (Assoc. Prof.); Mike Sowell (Assoc. Prof.); Bobbi K. Hooper (Asst. Prof.); Roy Kelsey (Asst. Prof.); Marc Krein (Asst. Prof.); Sheree Martin (Asst. Prof.); John McGuire (Asst. Prof.); Ray Murray (Asst. Prof.); Ken Graham (Vstg. Asst. Prof.); Bill Handy (Vstg. Asst. Prof.); Harry Hix (Vstg. Asst. Prof.); Scott Lambert (Vstg. Asst. Prof.); Gina Noble (Vstg. Asst. Prof.)

TAHLEQUAH

NORTHEASTERN STATE UNIVERSITY (OKLAHOMA)

Street address 1: Dept. of Mass Communications
Street address 3: Tahlequah
Street address state: OK
Zip/Postal code: 74464
Mailing address: Dept. of Mass Communications
Mailing city: Tahlequah
Mailing state: OK
Mailing zip: 74464
General Phone: (918) 456-5511
General/National Adv. E-mail: osborne@cherokee@nsuok.ed
Classified Equipment»
Personnel: Rodney Osborne (Chair)

UNIVERSITY OF TULSA

Street address 1: 600 S. College
Street address 3: Tulsa
Street address state: OK
Zip/Postal code: 74104
Mailing address: 800 Tucker Dr
Mailing city: Tulsa
Mailing state: OK
Mailing zip: 74104-9700
General Phone: (918) 631-3805
General Fax: (918) 631-3809
General/National Adv. E-mail: john-coward@utulsa.edu
Classified Equipment»
Personnel: John Coward (Chair)

OKLAHOMA CITY UNIVERSITY

Street address state: OK
Mailing address: 2501 N Blackwelder Ave
Mailing city: Oklahoma City
Mailing state: OK
Mailing zip: 73106-1493
General/National Adv. E-mail: kharmon@okcu.edu
Classified Equipment»
Personnel: Karlie Harmon (Chair)
Newspaper (for newspapers group): The Campus / MediaOCU, Oklahoma City

OREGON

SOUTHERN OREGON UNIVERSITY

Street address 1: 1250 Siskiyou Blvd.
Street address 3: Ashland
Street address state: OR
Zip/Postal code: 97520
Mailing address: 1250 Siskiyou Blvd
Mailing city: Ashland
Mailing state: OR
Mailing zip: 97520-5001
General Phone: (541) 552-6424
General Fax: (541) 552-8446
General/National Adv. E-mail: pittman@sou.edu
Classified Equipment»
Personnel: Garth Pittman (Chair)

UNIVERSITY OF OREGON

Street address 1: 1222 E. 13th Ave. #300
Street address 2: University of Oregon
Street address 3: Eugene
Street address state: OR
Zip/Postal code: 97403
Mailing address: 1222 E. 13th Ave. #300
Mailing city: Eugene
Mailing state: OR
Mailing zip: 97403
General Phone: (541) 346-5511
General/National Adv. E-mail: letters@dailyemerald.com
Primary Website: http://www.dailyemerald.com/
Classified Equipment»
Personnel: Timothy W. Gleason (Dean); Thomas H. Bivins (Prof.); Patricia A. Curtin (Prof.); Charles F. Frazer (Prof.); Lauren Kessler (Prof.); Duncan L. McDonald (Prof.); Deborah K. Morrison (Prof.); Julianne H. Newton (Prof./Assoc. Dean, Undergrad. Studies); Jon Palfreman (Prof.); Alan G. Stavitsky (Prof./Sr. Assoc. Dean/Dir., Turnbull Ctr.); H. Leslie Steeves (Prof./Assoc. Dean, Grad. Studies/Research); James Upshaw (Prof.); Janet Wasko (Prof.); Kyu Ho Youm (Prof.); Carol Ann Bassett (Assoc. Prof.); Carl R. Bybee (Assoc. Prof.); Scott R. Maier (Assoc. Prof.); Ann K. Maxwell (Assoc. Prof.); Debra Merskin (Assoc. Prof.); Daniel Miller (Assoc. Prof.)

LINFIELD COLLEGE

Street address 1: 900 SE Baker St.
Street address 3: McMinnville
Street address state: OR
Zip/Postal code: 97128-6894
Mailing address: 900 SE Baker St # A482
Mailing city: McMinnville
Mailing state: OR

Mailing zip: 97128-6894
General Phone: (503) 883-2291
General Fax: (503) 883-2360
General/National Adv. E-mail: bthomps@linfield.edu
Classified Equipment»
Personnel: Brad Thompson (Chair)

UNIVERSITY OF PORTLAND

Street address 1: 5000 N. Willamette Blvd.
Street address 3: Portland
Street address state: OR
Zip/Postal code: 97203-5798
Mailing address: 5000 N Willamette Blvd
Mailing city: Portland
Mailing state: OR
Mailing zip: 97203-5798
General Phone: (503) 283-7229
General Fax: (503) 283-7399
General/National Adv. E-mail: gayle@uofport.edu
Classified Equipment»
Personnel: Barbara Mae Gayle (Chair)

PENNSYLVANIA

THE PENNSYLVANIA STATE UNIVERSITY, ALTOONA COLLEGE

Street address 1: 3000 Ivyside Park
Street address 3: Altoona
Street address state: PA
Zip/Postal code: 16601
Mailing address: 3000 Ivyside Park Ste 1
Mailing city: Altoona
Mailing state: PA
Mailing zip: 16601-3777
General Phone: (814) 949-5769
General Fax: (814) 949-5774
Classified Equipment»
Personnel: Bob Trumpbour (Coord.)

LEHIGH UNIV.

Street address 1: 33 Coppee Dr
Street address 3: Bethlehem
Street address state: PA
Zip/Postal code: 18015-3165
Country: USA
Mailing address: 33 Coppee Dr
Mailing city: Bethlehem
Mailing state: PA
Mailing zip: 18015-3165
General Phone: (610) 758-4454
General Fax: (610) 758-6198
General/National Adv. E-mail: bw@lehigh.edu
Primary Website: www.thebrownandwhite.com
Classified Equipment»
Personnel: Wally Trimble (Head); Julie Stewart (Ed. in Chief); Jack Lule (Ed. in Chief)

BLOOMSBURG UNIVERSITY - THE VOICE

Street address 1: Dept. of Mass Communications
Street address 3: Bloomsburg
Street address state: PA
Zip/Postal code: 17815
Mailing address: Dept. of Mass Communications
Mailing city: Bloomsburg
Mailing state: PA
Mailing zip: 17815
General Phone: (717) 389-4633
General Fax: (570) 389-3983
General/National Adv. E-mail: voiceeditor@huskies.bloomu.edu
Classified Equipment»
Personnel: Dana Ulloth (Chair)

URSINUS COLLEGE

Street address 1: Dept. of Media & Communication Studies
Street address 3: Collegeville
Street address state: PA
Zip/Postal code: 19426-1000
Mailing address: Dept. of Media & Communication Studies
Mailing city: Collegeville
Mailing state: PA
Mailing zip: 19426-1000
General Phone: (610) 409-3603
General Fax: (610) 409-3733
General/National Adv. E-mail: jmiller@ursinus.edu
Classified Equipment»
Personnel: Jay K. Miller (Chair)

ELIZABETHTOWN COLLEGE

Street address 1: Dept. of Communications
Street address 3: Elizabethtown
Street address state: PA
Zip/Postal code: 17022
Mailing address: Dept. of Communications
Mailing city: Elizabethtown
Mailing state: PA
Mailing zip: 17022
General Phone: (717) 361-1262
General Fax: (717) 361-1180
General/National Adv. E-mail: GILLISTL@etown.edu
Classified Equipment»
Personnel: Tamara L. Gillis (Chair/Assoc. Prof.); Robert C. Moore (Prof.); Hans-Erik Wennberg (Assoc. Prof.); Randy K. Yoder (Assoc. Prof./Dir., Broadcasting); David Donovan (Instr.); Kirsten Johnson (Lectr./Dir., Stud. Pubs.); John Feeser (Adj. Instr.); William M. Sloane (Adj. Instr.); Stephen Trapnell (Adj. Instr)

INDIANA UNIVERSITY OF PENNSYLVANIA

Street address 1: Dept. of Journalism
Street address 3: Indiana
Street address state: PA
Zip/Postal code: 15705
Mailing address: Dept of Journalism
Mailing city: Indiana
Mailing state: PA
Mailing zip: 15705-0001
General Phone: (412) 357-4411
General Fax: (412) 357-7845
General/National Adv. E-mail: jn-dept@grove.iup.edu
Classified Equipment»
Personnel: Stanford G. Mukasa (Chair); David Loomis

LINCOLN UNIVERSITY OF THE COMMONWEALTH OF PENNSYLVANIA

Street address 1: 1570 Baltimore Pike
Street address 3: Lincoln University
Street address state: PA
Zip/Postal code: 19352
Mailing address: PO Box 179
Mailing city: Lincoln University
Mailing state: PA
Mailing zip: 19352-0999
General Phone: (484) 365-8145
General Fax: (484) 365-8156
Primary Website: www.thelincolnianonline.com
Classified Equipment»
Personnel: Serajul Bhuiyan (Prof./Dir.)

LOCK HAVEN UNIVERSITY

Street address 1: Dept. of Communication Media
Street address 3: Lock Haven
Street address state: PA
Zip/Postal code: 17745-2390
Mailing address: Dept. of Communication Media
Mailing city: Lock Haven
Mailing state: PA
Mailing zip: 17745-2390
General Phone: (570) 484-2376
General Fax: (570) 484-2436
General/National Adv. E-mail: kkline@lhup.edu
Classified Equipment»
Personnel: Karen E. Kline (Chair)

MILLERSVILLE UNIVERSITY

Street address 1: PO Box 1002
Street address 3: Millersville
Street address state: PA
Zip/Postal code: 17551-0302
Mailing address: PO Box 1002
Mailing city: Millersville
Mailing state: PA
Mailing zip: 17551-0302
General Phone: (717) 872-3233
General Fax: (717) 871-2051
General/National Adv. E-mail: bill.dorman@millersville.edu
Classified Equipment»
Personnel: Bill Dorman (Chair)

LA SALLE UNIVERSITY

Street address 1: 1900 W. Olney Ave.
Street address 3: Philadelphia
Street address state: PA
Zip/Postal code: 19141-1199
Mailing address: 1900 W Olney Ave
Mailing city: Philadelphia
Mailing state: PA
Mailing zip: 19141-1199
General Phone: (215) 951-1844
General Fax: (215) 951-5043
General/National Adv. E-mail: texter@lasalle.edu
Primary Website: www.lasalle.edu/academ/commun/home.htm
Classified Equipment»
Personnel: Lynne Texter (Chair)

SAINT JOSEPH'S UNIVERSITY

Street address 1: 5600 City Ave.
Street address 3: Philadelphia
Street address state: PA
Zip/Postal code: 19131-1395
Mailing address: 5600 City Ave
Mailing city: Philadelphia
Mailing state: PA
Mailing zip: 19131-1376
General Phone: (610) 660-1884
General Fax: (610) 660-3235
General/National Adv. E-mail: jparker@sju.edu
Classified Equipment»
Personnel: Jo Alyson Parker (Chair)

TEMPLE UNIVERSITY

Street address 1: 2020 N. 13th St.
Street address 3: Philadelphia
Street address state: PA
Zip/Postal code: 19122-6080
Mailing address: 2020 N 13th St
Mailing city: Philadelphia
Mailing state: PA
Mailing zip: 19122-6015
General Phone: (215) 204-7433
General Fax: (215) 204-1974
General/National Adv. E-mail: news@temple-news.com
Primary Website: www.temple.edu/journalism
Classified Equipment»
Personnel: Andrew Mendelson (Chair/Assoc. Prof.); Thomas Eveslage (Prof.); Edward Trayes (Prof./Dir., MJ Prog./Dir., Photojournalism seq.); Christopher Harper (Assoc. Prof.); Carolyn Kitch (Assoc. Prof.); Karen M. Turner (Assoc. Prof./Dir., Broadcast Journ. seq.); Linn Washington (Assoc. Prof./Dir., News-Ed. seq.); Fabienne Darling-Wolf (Assoc. Prof.); Shenid Bhayroo (Asst. Prof.); Susan Jacobson (Asst. Prof.); George Miller (Asst. Prof.); Maida Odom (Asst. Prof./Internship Dir.); Larry Stains (Asst. Prof./Dir., Mag. seq.); Francesca Viola (Asst. Prof.)

UNIVERSITY OF PENNSYLVANIA

Street address 1: Annenberg School for Communication
Street address 3: Philadelphia
Street address state: PA
Zip/Postal code: 19104-6220
Mailing address: Annenberg School for Communication
Mailing city: Philadelphia
Mailing state: PA
Mailing zip: 19104-6220
General Phone: (215) 898-7041
General Fax: (215) 898-2024
General/National Adv. E-mail: admin@pobox.asc.upenn.edu
Classified Equipment»

DUQUESNE UNIVERSITY

Street address 1: 600 Forbes Ave.
Street address 3: Pittsburgh
Street address state: PA
Zip/Postal code: 15282
Mailing address: 600 Forbes Ave
Mailing city: Pittsburgh
Mailing state: PA
Mailing zip: 15282-0001
General Phone: (412) 396-6460
General Fax: (412) 396-4792
General/National Adv. E-mail: arnett@duq.edu
Classified Equipment»
Personnel: Ronald C. Arnett (Chair/Prof.); Patricia Arneson (Assoc. Prof.); Robert V. Bellamy (Assoc. Prof.); D. Clark Edwards (Assoc. Prof.); Janie M.H. Fritz (Assoc. Prof.); Margaret Patterson (Assoc. Prof.); Richard H. Thames (Assoc. Prof.); Francis Thornton (Assoc. Prof.); Calvin Troup (Assoc. Prof.); Michael J. Dillon (Asst. Prof.); Roy Joseph (Asst. Prof.); Kathleen Roberts (Asst. Prof.); Joseph Sora (Asst. Prof.); S. Alyssa Groom (Instr.); Eva Robotti (Prof. Emer.)

POINT PARK UNIVERSITY

Street address 1: Dept. of Journalism & Mass Communication
Street address 3: Pittsburgh
Street address state: PA
Zip/Postal code: 15222-1984
Mailing address: Dept. of Journalism & Mass Communication
Mailing city: Pittsburgh
Mailing state: PA
Mailing zip: 15222-1984
General Phone: (412) 392-4730
General Fax: (412) 392-3917
General/National Adv. E-mail: hfallon@pointpark.edu
Primary Website: www.pointpark.edu
Classified Equipment»
Personnel: Helen Fallon (Chair/Prof.); Dane S. Claussen (Prof./Dir., Grad. Prog.); David J. Fabilli (Prof.); Robert O'Gara (Prof.); William R. Moushey (Assoc. Prof.); Heather Starr Fiedler (Asst. Prof.); Jan Getz (Asst. Prof./Broadcaster-in-Residence); Steven M. Hallock (Asst. Prof.); Anthony Moretti (Asst. Prof.); Christopher Rolinson (Asst. Prof.); Johan Yssel (Vstg. Prof.)

UNIVERSITY OF PITTSBURGH

Street address 1: 526 Cathedral of Learning
Street address 3: Pittsburgh
Street address state: PA
Zip/Postal code: 15260
Mailing address: 526 Cathedral of Learning
Mailing city: Pittsburgh
Mailing state: PA
Mailing zip: 15260
General Phone: (412) 624-6536
General Fax: (412) 624-6639
General/National Adv. E-mail: patsy1@pitt.edu
Classified Equipment»
Personnel: Patsy Sims (Coord.)

CABRINI UNIVERSITY LOQUITUR

Street address 1: 610 King of Prussia Rd
Street address 3: Radnor
Street address state: PA
Zip/Postal code: 19087-3623
Country: USA
Mailing address: 610 King of Prussia Rd
Mailing city: Radnor
Mailing state: PA
Mailing zip: 19087-3698
General Phone: (610) 902-8360
General Fax: (610) 902-8285
General/National Adv. E-mail: loquitur@cabrini.edu
Display Adv. E-mail: loquitur@cabrini.edu
Editorial e-mail: loquitur@cabrini.edu
Primary Website: www.theloquitur.com
Year Established: 1959
News Services: MCT
Delivery Methods: Racks
Commercial printers: Y
Published: Thur`Bi-Mthly
Avg Free Circ: 1400
Classified Equipment»
Personnel: Jerome Zurek (Chair); Angelina Miller (EIC)

SUSQUEHANNA UNIVERSITY

Street address 1: 514 University Ave.
Street address 3: Selinsgrove
Street address state: PA
Zip/Postal code: 17870-1164
Mailing address: 514 University Ave
Mailing city: Selinsgrove
Mailing state: PA
Mailing zip: 17870-1164
General Phone: (570) 372-4355

General Fax: (570) 372-2757
General/National Adv. E-mail: augustin@susqu.edu
Classified Equipment»
Personnel: Larry D. Augustine (Chair)

SHIPPENSBURG UNIVERSITY/ COMMUNICATION/JOURNALISM DEPARTMENT

Street address 1: 1871 Old Main Dr.
Street address 3: Shippensburg
Street address state: PA
Zip/Postal code: 17257
County: Cumberland
Country: United States
Mailing address: 1871 Old Main Drive
Mailing city: Shippensburg
Mailing state: PA
Mailing zip: 17257-2299
General Phone: (717) 477-1521
General Fax: (717) 477-4013
General/National Adv. E-mail: commjour@ship.edu
Primary Website: webspace.ship.edu/commjour
Classified Equipment»
Personnel: Carrie Sipes (Chair/Prof./public relations); Michael W. Drager (Assoc. Prof./print& online media); Carrie Sipes (Asst. Prof./public relations); Stephanie Anderson Witmer (Asst. Prof./print & online media); Kyle Heim (Asst. Prof./print & online media); James Lohrey (Assit. Prof./electronic media)

THE PENNSYLVANIA STATE UNIVERSITY

Street address 1: 201 Carnegie Bldg.
Street address 3: University Park
Street address state: PA
Zip/Postal code: 16802
Mailing address: 201 Carnegie Bldg
Mailing city: University Park
Mailing state: PA
Mailing zip: 16802-5101
General Phone: (814) 863-1484
General Fax: (814) 863-8044
Primary Website: www.psu.edu/dept/comm
Classified Equipment»
Personnel: Douglas Anderson (Dean/Prof./Co-Dir., Sports Journ. Ctr.); Tony Barbieri (Foster Prof., Writing/Editing); Clay Calvert (Curley Prof. First Amendment Studies/Co-Dir., PA First Amendment Ctr.); Jeremy Cohen (Prof./Assoc. Vice Pres./Sr. Assoc. Dean, Undergrad. Educ.); John J. Curley (Prof./ Distinguished Professional-in-Residence/Co-Dir., Sports Journ. Ctr.); Robert M. Frieden (Prof./Pioneers Chair, Telecommunications); Malcolm Moran (Prof./ Knight Chair in Sports Journalism and Society and dir., Curley Sports Journalism Ctr.); John S. Nichols (Prof./Assoc. Dean, Grad. Studies/Research/Dir., Page Ctr. for Integrity in Public Com.); Mary Beth Oliver (Prof./Co-Dir., Media Effects Lab); Robert D. Richards (Distinguished Prof./Dir., Washington Prog./Co-Dir., PA First Amendment Ctr.); S. Shyam Sundar (Prof./Co-Dir., Media Effects Lab); Richard D. Taylor (Prof./Palmer Chair, Telecommunications & Law/Co-Dir., Institute for Information Policy); Robert A. Baukus (Assoc. Prof./ Dept. Head, Adv./PR); Ronald V. Bettig (Assoc. Prof.); Barbara O. Bird (Assoc. Prof./Dir., Int'l Programs); Lyn E. Elliot (Assoc. Prof.); Russell Frank (Assoc. Prof.); Jeanne L. Hall (Assoc. Prof.); Martin E. Halstuk (Assoc. Prof.); Marie C. Hardin (Assoc. Prof./Dir., Editing Excellence Ctr./Assoc. Dir., Sports Journ. Ctr.)

LYCOMING COLLEGE

Street address 1: 700 College Pl.
Street address 3: Williamsport
Street address state: PA
Zip/Postal code: 17701
Mailing address: 700 College Pl
Mailing city: Williamsport
Mailing state: PA
Mailing zip: 17701-5192
General Phone: (570) 321-4297
General Fax: (570) 321-4389
General/National Adv. E-mail: wild@lycoming.edu
Classified Equipment»
Personnel: Fredric M. Wild (Chair)

YORK COLLEGE OF PENNSYLVANIA

Street address 1: MAC Ctr., Country Club Rd.
Street address 3: York
Street address state: PA
Zip/Postal code: 17405-7199
Mailing address: MAC Ctr., Country Club Rd.
Mailing city: York
Mailing state: PA
Mailing zip: 17405-7199
General Phone: (717) 815-1354
General Fax: (717) 849-1602
General/National Adv. E-mail: bfurio@ycp.edu
Classified Equipment»
Personnel: Brian Furio (Chair)

PUERTO RICO

SAN JUAN

UNIVERSITY OF PUERTO RICO

Street address 1: PO Box 21880, UPR Sta.
Street address 3: San Juan
Street address state: PR
Zip/Postal code: 931
Mailing address: PO Box 21880
Mailing city: San Juan
Mailing state: PR
Mailing zip: 00931-1880
General Phone: (787) 764-0000
General Fax: (787) 763-5390
Primary Website: copu.upr.clu.edu
Classified Equipment»
Personnel: Eliseo Colon Zayas (Dir.)

UNIVERSITY OF THE SACRED HEART

Street address 1: PO Box 12383
Street address 3: San Juan
Street address state: PR
Zip/Postal code: 00914-0383
Mailing address: PO Box 12383
Mailing city: San Juan
Mailing state: PR
Mailing zip: 00914-8505
General Phone: (787) 728-1515
General Fax: (787) 268-8874
General/National Adv. E-mail: cgarcia@sagrado.edu
Primary Website: www.sagrado.edu
Classified Equipment»
Personnel: Carmen Sara Garcia (Dir.)

RHODE ISLAND

UNIVERSITY OF RHODE ISLAND

Street address 1: Dept. of Journalism
Street address 3: Kingston
Street address state: RI
Zip/Postal code: 2881
Mailing address: Dept. of Journalism
Mailing city: Kingston
Mailing state: RI
Mailing zip: 2881
General Phone: (401) 874-2195
General Fax: (401) 874-4450
General/National Adv. E-mail: lllevin@uri.edu
Primary Website: www.uri.edu/artsci/Jor
Classified Equipment»
Personnel: Linda Lotridge Levin (Chair)

SOUTH CAROLINA

UNIVERSITY OF SOUTH CAROLINA, AIKEN

Street address 1: 471 University Pkwy.
Street address 3: Aiken
Street address state: SC
Zip/Postal code: 29801
Mailing address: 471 University Pkwy
Mailing city: Aiken
Mailing state: SC
Mailing zip: 29801-6399
General Phone: (803) 641-3481
General Fax: (803) 641-3461
General/National Adv. E-mail: williamh@usca.edu
Classified Equipment»
Personnel: William Harpine (Chair)

COLLEGE OF CHARLESTON

Street address 1: 66 George St
Street address 3: Charleston
Street address state: SC
Zip/Postal code: 29424-0001
Country: USA
Mailing address: 66 George St
Mailing city: Charleston
Mailing state: SC
Mailing zip: 29424-0001
General Phone: (843) 953-7017
General Fax: (843) 953-7037
General/National Adv. E-mail: mcgeeb@cofc.edu
Primary Website: www.cofc.edu/communication
Classified Equipment»
Personnel: Brian McGee (Chair); Katie Orlando (Ed. in Chief)

BENEDICT COLLEGE

Street address 1: 1600 Harden St
Street address 3: Columbia
Street address state: SC
Zip/Postal code: 29204-1058
Country: USA
Mailing address: 1600 Harden St
Mailing city: Columbia
Mailing state: SC
Mailing zip: 29204-1086
General Phone: (803) 705-4645
General Fax: (803) 253-5065
Primary Website: www.benedict.edu
Classified Equipment»
Personnel: Carolyn Drakeford (Chair); Momo Rogers (Ed.)

UNIVERSITY OF SOUTH CAROLINA

Street address 1: School of Journalism and Mass Communications
Street address 3: Columbia
Street address state: SC
Zip/Postal code: 29208
Mailing address: School of Journalism and Mass Communications
Mailing city: Columbia
Mailing state: SC
Mailing zip: 29208-0001
General Phone: (803) 777-3244
General Fax: (803) 777-4103
Primary Website: www.jour.sc.edu
Classified Equipment»
Personnel: Carol J. Pardun (Dir./Prof.); Charles Bierbauer (Prof./Dean, College of Mass Commun. and Information Studies); Shirley Staples Carter (Prof.); Lowndes F. Stephens (Prof.); Kenneth Campbell (Assoc. Prof./Chair, Print and Broadcast Journ. Seq.); Erik L. Collins (Assoc. Prof./Assoc. Dir., Grad. Studies); Bonnie L. Drewniany (Assoc. Prof.); Sonya F. Duhe (Assoc. Prof.); Augie Grant (Assoc. Prof.); Cecile S. Holmes (Assoc. Prof.); Keith Kenney (Assoc. Prof./ Int'l Studies Coord.); Bruce E. Konkle (Assoc. Prof.); Vance L. Kornegay (Assoc. Prof./Chair, Vis. Comm. seq.); Richard Moore (Assoc. Prof.); Ran Wei (Assoc. Prof./Chair, Adv./PR Seq.); Thomas Weir (Assoc. Prof.); Ernest L. Wiggins (Assoc. Prof.); Glenda Alvarado (Asst. Prof.); John Besley (Asst. Prof.); Tom Klipstine (Asst. Prof.)

FRANCIS MARION UNIVERSITY

Street address 1: PO Box 100547
Street address 3: Florence
Street address state: SC
Zip/Postal code: 29501-0547
Mailing address: PO Box 100547
Mailing city: Florence
Mailing state: SC
Mailing zip: 29502-0547
General Phone: (843) 661-1605
General Fax: (843) 661-1547
General/National Adv. E-mail: dstewart@fmarion.edu
Classified Equipment»
Personnel: Don Stewart (Chair)

CLAFLIN UNIVERSITY

Street address 1: 400 Magnolia St.
Street address 3: Orangeburg
Street address state: SC
Zip/Postal code: 29115-4498
Mailing address: 400 Magnolia St
Mailing city: Orangeburg
Mailing state: SC
Mailing zip: 29115-6815
General Phone: (803) 535-5769
General/National Adv. E-mail: cgooch@claflin.edu
Classified Equipment»
Personnel: Cheryl R. Gooch (Chair/Prof.); Lynette Lashley (Prof.); Preston Blakely (Asst. Prof.); Julian Williams (Asst. Prof.); Gary Dawkins (Instr.); Lee Harter (Journalist-in-Residence); Ameen Hall (Prodn. Specialist); Michael Fiarwell (Video Studio Dir.)

WINTHROP UNIVERSITY

Street address 1: Dept. of Mass Communication
Street address 3: Rock Hill
Street address state: SC
Zip/Postal code: 29733-0001
Mailing address: Dept of Mass Communication
Mailing city: Rock Hill
Mailing state: SC
Mailing zip: 29733-0001
General Phone: (803) 323-2121
General Fax: (803) 323-2464
General/National Adv. E-mail: clickw@winthrop.edu
Classified Equipment»
Personnel: J. William Click (Chair/Prof.); William A. Fisher (Part-time Prof.); Haney Howell (Assoc. Prof.); Marilyn S. Sarow (Assoc. Prof.); Lawrence C. Timbs (Assoc. Prof.); Padmini Patwardhan (Asst. Prof.); Guy Reel (Asst. Prof.); Mark Nortz (Instr.); Bonnye Stuart (Part-time Instr.)

UNIVERSITY OF SOUTH CAROLINA UPSTATE

Street address 1: 800 University Way
Street address 3: Spartanburg
Street address state: SC
Zip/Postal code: 29303
Mailing address: 800 University Way
Mailing city: Spartanburg
Mailing state: SC
Mailing zip: 29303-4932
General Phone: (864) 503-5844
General Fax: (864) 503-5814
General/National Adv. E-mail: cugochukwu@uscupstate.edu
Classified Equipment»
Personnel: Rachelle Prioleau (Chair)

SOUTH DAKOTA

BROOKINGS

SOUTH DAKOTA STATE UNIVERSITY

Street address 1: Rotunda Ln.
Street address 3: Brookings
Street address state: SD
Zip/Postal code: 57007-0596
Mailing address: Rotunda Ln
Mailing city: Brookings
Mailing state: SD
Mailing zip: 57007-0001
General Phone: (605) 688-4171
General Fax: (605) 688-5034
General/National Adv. E-mail: mary.arnold@sdstate.edu
Classified Equipment»
Personnel: Mary Peterson Arnold (Head); John E. Getz (Prof.); Lyle D. Olson (Prof.); Mary Arnold (Prof.); Doris J. Giago (Assoc. Prof.); Dennis Hinde (Assoc. Prof.); Roxanne Neuberger Lucchesi (Assoc. Prof.); James

L. Paulson (Assoc. Prof.); Matthew Cecil (Asst. Prof.); Frank A. Klock (Instr.); Jennifer Tiernan (Part-time Instr.); Richard W. Lee (Prof. Emer.); Mary J. Perpich (Prof. Emer.)

BLACK HILLS STATE UNIVERSITY

Street address 1: College of Arts & Sciences
Street address 2: 1200 University St., Unit 9003
Street address 3: Spearfish
Street address state: SD
Zip/Postal code: 57799-9003
Mailing address: College of Arts & Sciences
Mailing city: Spearfish
Mailing state: SD
Mailing zip: 57799-0001
General Phone: (605) 642-6420
General Fax: (605) 642-6762
General/National Adv. E-mail: marycatonrosser@bhsu.edu
Classified Equipment»
Personnel: Mary Caton-Rosser (Asst. Prof., Mass Commun.)

UNIVERSITY OF SOUTH DAKOTA

Street address 1: 414 E. Clark St.
Street address 3: Vermillion
Street address state: SD
Zip/Postal code: 57069
Mailing address: 414 E Clark St
Mailing city: Vermillion
Mailing state: SD
Mailing zip: 57069-2390
General Phone: (605) 677-5477
General Fax: (605) 677-4250
General/National Adv. E-mail: troberts@usd.edu
Primary Website: www.usd.edu/cfa/MassComm/mcom.html
Classified Equipment»
Personnel: Terry Robertson (Chair)

MOUNT MARTY COLLEGE

Street address 1: Journalism/Public Relations Program
Street address 3: Yankton
Street address state: SD
Zip/Postal code: 57078
Mailing address: Journalism/Public Relations Program
Mailing city: Yankton
Mailing state: SD
Mailing zip: 57078
General Phone: (605) 668-1506
Classified Equipment»
Personnel: Jerry W. Wilson (Dir.)

TENNESSEE

UNIVERSITY OF TENNESSEE AT CHATTANOOGA

Street address 1: Communication Dept.
Street address 3: Chattanooga
Street address state: TN
Zip/Postal code: 37403-2598
Mailing address: Communication Dept.
Mailing city: Chattanooga
Mailing state: TN
Mailing zip: 37403-2598
General Phone: (423) 425-4400
General Fax: (423) 425-4695
Classified Equipment»
Personnel: Betsy B. Alderman (Interim Head/Assoc. Prof./Luther Masingill Prof.); David B. Sachsman (Prof./West Chair of Excellence in Commun.); S. Kittrell Rushing (Head/Frank McDonald Prof.); Rebekah Bromley (Assoc. Prof.); ELizabeth Gailey (Assoc. Prof.); Charlene Simmons (Asst. Prof.); Felicia McGhee-Hilt (Lectr.); John McCormack (Part-time Instr./Dir., WUTC/Jazz 88); Chris Willis (Part-time Instr.); Deborah Luhrs (Part-time Instr.); Peter K. Pringle (Prof. Emer.)

CLARKSVILLE

AUSTIN PEAY STATE UNIVERSITY

Street address 1: Dept. of Communication & Theatre
Street address 3: Clarksville
Street address state: TN
Zip/Postal code: 37044
Mailing address: Dept of Communication & Theatre
Mailing city: Clarksville
Mailing state: TN
Mailing zip: 37044-0001
General Phone: (931) 221-7378
General Fax: (931) 221-7265
General/National Adv. E-mail: gotcherm@apsu.edu
Classified Equipment»
Personnel: Mike Gotcher (Chair)

TENNESSEE TECHNOLOGICAL UNIVERSITY

Street address 1: Journalism Dept.
Street address 2: 1 William L. Jones Dr.
Street address 3: Cookeville
Street address state: TN
Zip/Postal code: 38505-0001
Mailing address: Journalism
Mailing city: Cookeville
Mailing state: TN
Mailing zip: 38505-0001
General Phone: (931) 372-3060
General Fax: (931) 372-6225
General/National Adv. E-mail: ehutch@tntech.edu
Classified Equipment»
Personnel: Earl R. Hutchison (Dir.)
Newspaper (for newspapers group): Tennessee Technological Univ., Cookeville

EAST TENNESSEE STATE UNIVERSITY

Street address 1: PO Box 70667
Street address 3: Johnson City
Street address state: TN
Zip/Postal code: 37614
Mailing address: PO Box 70667
Mailing city: Johnson City
Mailing state: TN
Mailing zip: 37614-1701
General Phone: (423) 439-4491
General Fax: (423) 439-7540
General/National Adv. E-mail: Robertsc@etsu.edu
Classified Equipment»
Personnel: Charles Roberts (Chair)

THE UNIVERSITY OF TENNESSEE

Street address 1: 1345 Circle Park Dr., 302 Communications-UEB
Street address 3: Knoxville
Street address state: TN
Zip/Postal code: 37996-0332
Mailing address: 1345 Circle Park Dr
Mailing city: Knoxville
Mailing state: TN
Mailing zip: 37996-0001
General Phone: (865) 974-3031
General Fax: (865) 974-3896
General/National Adv. E-mail: cci@utk.edu
Primary Website: cci.utk.edu
Classified Equipment»
Personnel: Michael Wirth (Dean/Prof.); Paul G. Ashdown (Prof.); Benjamin J. Bates (Prof.); Dorothy A. Bowles (Prof.); Charles E. Caudill (Prof.); John E. Haley (Prof.); Roxanne Hovland (Prof.); Mariea G. Hoy (Prof.); Mark E. Littmann (Prof./Chair, Excellence-Journ.); Barbara A. Moore (Prof.); Margaret A. Morrison (Prof.); Norman R. Swan (Prof./Dir., Internationalization/Outreach); Ronald Taylor (Prof./Dir., School of Adv. & PR); Dwight L. Teeter (Prof.); Lisa T. Fall (Assoc. Prof.); Daniel J. Foley (Assoc. Prof.); Mark D. Harmon (Assoc. Prof.); Robert B. Heller (Assoc. Prof.); Barbara K. Kaye (Assoc. Prof.); Catherine A. Luther (Assoc. Prof.)

UNIVERSITY OF TENNESSEE AT MARTIN

Street address 1: Dept. of Communications
Street address 2: 305 Gooch Hall
Street address 3: Martin
Street address state: TN
Zip/Postal code: 38238
Mailing address: Dept of Communications
Mailing city: Martin
Mailing state: TN
Mailing zip: 38238-0001
General Phone: (731) 881-7546
General Fax: (731) 881-7550
General/National Adv. E-mail: Rnanney@utm.edu
Classified Equipment»
Personnel: Robert Nanney (Chair)

CHRISTIAN BROTHERS UNIVERSITY

Street address 1: Dept. of Communication and Performing Arts
Street address 3: Memphis
Street address state: TN
Zip/Postal code: 38104
Mailing address: Dept. of Communication and Performing Arts
Mailing city: Memphis
Mailing state: TN
Mailing zip: 38104
General Phone: (901) 722-0386
General Fax: (901) 722-0494
Classified Equipment»
Personnel: Joseph Ajami (Head)

UNIVERSITY OF MEMPHIS

Street address 1: Journalism Dept.
Street address 3: Memphis
Street address state: TN
Zip/Postal code: 38152
Mailing address: Journalism
Mailing city: Memphis
Mailing state: TN
Mailing zip: 38152-0001
General Phone: (901) 678-2401
General Fax: (901) 678-4287
General/National Adv. E-mail: jredmond@memphis.edu
Classified Equipment»
Personnel: David Arant (Chair/Prof.); E.W. Bill Brody (Prof.); Rick Fischer (Prof./Grad. Coord./Head, PR); Elinor Grusin (Prof.); Dan Lattimore (Prof.); Jim Redmond (Prof.); Ronald Spielberger (Assoc. Prof.); Art Terry (Assoc. Prof.); Sandra Utt (Assoc. Prof./Asst. Chair); Joe Hayden (Asst. Prof.); Cynthia Hopson (Asst. Prof.); Candy Justice (Asst. Prof.); Lurene Kelley (Asst. Prof.); Jin Yang (Asst. Prof.); Norm Hays (Instr.); Olivia Miller (Instr.); Robert Willis (Instr.); John DeMott (Prof. Emer.); John Lee (Prof. Emer.); Herbert Williams (Prof. Emer.)

MILLIGAN COLLEGE

Street address 1: PO Box 500
Street address 3: Milligan College
Street address state: TN
Zip/Postal code: 37682
Mailing address: PO Box 500
Mailing city: Milligan College
Mailing state: TN
Mailing zip: 37682-0500
General Phone: (423) 461-8994
General Fax: (423) 461-8965
General/National Adv. E-mail: sjdahlman@milligan.edu
Primary Website: www.milligan.edu
Classified Equipment»
Personnel: Simon J. Dahlman (Chair)

MIDDLE TENNESSEE STATE UNIVERSITY

Street address 1: MTSU Box 51
Street address 3: Murfreesboro
Street address state: TN
Zip/Postal code: 37132
Mailing address: PO Box 51
Mailing city: Murfreesboro
Mailing state: TN
Mailing zip: 37132-0001
General Phone: (615) 898-2813
General Fax: (615) 898-5682
General/National Adv. E-mail: lmccann@mtsu.edu
Classified Equipment»
Personnel: Roy L. Moore (Dean/Prof.); John Omachonu (Assoc. Dean/Prof.); Steven.J Barnes (Dir., Devel.); Sarah Jackson (Academic Advisor.); Hattie Traylor (Academic Advisor.); Edd Applegate (Prof.); David P. Badger (Prof.); Richard Barnet (Prof.); Marc Barr (Prof.); John Bodle (Prof.); Larry Burriss (Prof.); Cosette Collier (Prof.); David Eason (Prof.); Paul Fischer (Prof.); Christopher R. Harris (Prof.); Christian Haseleu (Prof./Chair, Dept. of Recording Industry); John Hill (Prof.); Thomas Hutchison (Prof.); Tom Jimison (Prof.); Edward M. Kimbrell (Prof.)

BELMONT UNIV.

Street address 1: 1900 Belmont Blvd
Street address 3: Nashville
Street address state: TN
Zip/Postal code: 37212-3758
Country: USA
Mailing address: 1900 Belmont Blvd
Mailing city: Nashville
Mailing state: TN
Mailing zip: 37212-3757
General Phone: (615) 460-6000
General Fax: (615) 460-5532
General/National Adv. E-mail: vision@mail.belmont.edu
Primary Website: www.belmontvision.com; www.belmont.edu
Classified Equipment»
Personnel: Linda Quigley (Advisor); Thom Storey (Chair); Karen Bennett (Adv. Mgr.); Bethany Brinton; Lance Conzett (Ed. in Chief)

LIPSCOMB UNIVERSITY

Street address 1: Dept. of Communication
Street address 3: Nashville
Street address state: TN
Zip/Postal code: 37204-3951
Mailing address: Dept. of Communication
Mailing city: Nashville
Mailing state: TN
Mailing zip: 37204-3951
General Phone: (615) 279-6072
General Fax: (615) 269-1834
Classified Equipment»
Personnel: James F. McCollum (Chair/Assoc. Prof.)

TEXAS

ABILENE CHRISTIAN UNIVERSITY

Street address 1: Journalism & Mass Communication Dept.
Street address 3: Abilene
Street address state: TX
Zip/Postal code: 79699
Mailing address: Journalism & Mass Communication Dept
Mailing city: Abilene
Mailing state: TX
Mailing zip: 79699-0001
General Phone: (325) 674-2296
General Fax: (325) 674-2139
General/National Adv. E-mail: cheryl.bacon@jmc.acu.edu
Classified Equipment»
Personnel: Cheryl M. Bacon (Chair/Prof.); Larry Bradshaw (Prof./Dir., Electronic Media); Merlin Mann (Assoc. Prof./Dir., Journ.); Dave Hogan (Instr.); J.R. Kessler (Instr.); Susan Lewis (Instr.); Cade White (Instr./Dir., Photojourn.); Charles H. Marler (Prof. Emer.)

HARDIN-SIMMONS UNIVERSITY

Street address 1: Dept. of Communication
Street address 3: Abilene
Street address state: TX
Zip/Postal code: 79698
Mailing address: Dept of Communication
Mailing city: Abilene
Mailing state: TX
Mailing zip: 79698-0001
General Phone: (915) 670-1414
General Fax: (915) 670-1409
General/National Adv. E-mail: dbaergen.comm@hsutx.edu
Primary Website: www.hsutx.edu/academics/LiberalArts/communication
Classified Equipment»

Personnel: Darrel Baergen (Chair)

UNIVERSITY OF TEXAS AT ARLINGTON

Street address 1: 700 W. Greek Row Dr.
Street address 3: Arlington
Street address state: TX
Zip/Postal code: 76019
Mailing address: 700 W. Greek Row Dr.
Mailing city: Arlington
Mailing state: TX
Mailing zip: 76019
General Phone: (817) 272-2163
General Fax: (817) 272-2732
General/National Adv. E-mail: commdept@uta.edu
Classified Equipment»
Personnel: Charla Markham Shaw (Chair/Assoc. Prof.); Earl R. Andresen (Prof.); Thomas Christie (Assoc. Prof.); Tom Ingram (Assoc. Prof.); Camille Broadway (Asst. Prof.); Karishma Chatterjee (Asst. Prof.); Andrew Clark (Asst. Prof.); Glenn Hubbard (Asst. Prof.); Chyng-Yang Jang (Asst. Prof.); Sasha Grant (Asst. Prof.); Eronini Megwa (Asst. Prof.); Ivana Segvic Boudreaux (Asst. Prof.); Chunke Su (Asst. Prof.); Shelley Wigley (Asst. Prof.); Rudy Bechtel (Specialist)
Newspaper (for newspapers group): University of Texas at Arlington, Arlington

UNIVERSITY OF TEXAS AT AUSTIN

Street address 1: School of Journalism
Street address 3: Austin
Street address state: TX
Zip/Postal code: 78712
Mailing address: School of Journalism
Mailing city: Austin
Mailing state: TX
Mailing zip: 78712
General Phone: (512) 471-1845
General Fax: (512) 471-7979
General/National Adv. E-mail: jou@journalism.utexas.edu
Classified Equipment»
Personnel: Tracy Dahlby (Dir.); Rosental Alves (Prof.); Lorraine Branham (Prof.); Dennis Darling (Prof.); Maxwell E. McCombs (Prof.); Marvin Olasky (Prof.); Stephen D. Reese (Prof.); Russell G. Todd (Prof.); Gene Burd (Assoc. Prof.); Renita Coleman (Assoc. Prof.); Mercedes L. De Uriarte (Assoc. Prof.); Don Heider (Assoc. Prof./Grad. Advisor); Robert Jensen (Assoc. Prof.); Dominic Lasorsa (Assoc. Prof.); Paula Poindexter (Assoc. Prof.); Maggie Rivas-Rodriguez (Assoc. Prof.); George Sylvie (Assoc. Prof.); Donna DeCesare (Asst. Prof.); Dustin Harp (Asst. Prof.); Mark Tremayne (Asst. Prof.)

LAMAR UNIVERSITY-BEAUMONT

Street address 1: Box 10050
Street address 3: Beaumont
Street address state: TX
Zip/Postal code: 77710
Mailing address: PO Box 10050
Mailing city: Beaumont
Mailing state: TX
Mailing zip: 77710-0050
General Phone: (409) 880-8153
General Fax: (409) 880-8760
General/National Adv. E-mail: commdept@hal.lamar.edu
Classified Equipment»
Personnel: Patrick Harrigan (Chair)

UNIVERSITY OF TEXAS AT BROWNSVILLE

Street address 1: Gorgas Hall, 80 Fort Brown
Street address 3: Brownsville
Street address state: TX
Zip/Postal code: 78520-4993
Mailing address: 80 Fort Brown St
Mailing city: Brownsville
Mailing state: TX
Mailing zip: 78520-4956
General Phone: (956) 882-8851
General Fax: (956) 882-7064
General/National Adv. E-mail: john.a.cook@utb.edu
Classified Equipment»
Personnel: John Cook (Program Coord.)

WEST TEXAS A&M UNIVERSITY

Street address 1: Dept. of Art, Communication and Theatre
Street address 3: Canyon
Street address state: TX
Zip/Postal code: 79016
Mailing address: Dept of Art Communication & Theatre
Mailing city: Canyon
Mailing state: TX
Mailing zip: 79016-0001
General Phone: (806) 651-2411
General Fax: (806) 651-2818
General/National Adv. E-mail: dwohlfarth@mail.wtamu.edu
Classified Equipment»

TEXAS A&M UNIVERSITY

Street address 1: 107 Scoates Hall
Street address 3: College Station
Street address state: TX
Zip/Postal code: 77843-0001
Country: USA
Mailing address: 107 Scoates Hall
Mailing city: College Station
Mailing state: TX
Mailing zip: 77843-0001
General Phone: (979) 862-3003
General Fax: (979) 845-6296
General/National Adv. E-mail: dj-king@tamu.edu
Classified Equipment»
Personnel: Deborah Dunsford (Program Coord.)

TEXAS A&M UNIVERSITY

Street address 1: 4234 Tamu
Street address 3: College Station
Street address state: TX
Zip/Postal code: 77843-0001
Country: USA
Mailing address: 4234 Tamu
Mailing city: College Station
Mailing state: TX
Mailing zip: 77843-0001
General Phone: (979) 458-1802
General Fax: (979) 845-6594
General/National Adv. E-mail: r-sumpter@tamu.edu; jourminor@tamu.edu
Classified Equipment»
Personnel: Randall S. Sumpter (Dir., Journ. Studies/Assoc. Prof., Commun.); Roberto Farias (Program Asst.); Edward L. Walraven (Sr. Lectr.); Dale A. Rice (Lectr.)

TEXAS A&M UNIVERSITY-COMMERCE

Street address 1: 2600 Neal St.
Street address 3: Commerce
Street address state: TX
Zip/Postal code: 75429-3011
Mailing address: 2600 W Neal St
Mailing city: Commerce
Mailing state: TX
Mailing zip: 75428-4311
General Phone: (903) 886-5229
General Fax: (903) 468-3250
Primary Website: www.tamu-commerce.edu
Classified Equipment»
Personnel: John Hanners (Head/Prof.); Lamar W. Bridges (Prof.); Robert Sanders (Prof.); Gary Burton (Assoc. Prof.); John Mark Dempsey (Assoc. Prof.); John Bellotti (Asst. Prof.); Carrie Lee Klypchak (Asst. prof.); Michael G. Knight (Asst. Prof.); James T. Anderson (Instr.); Fred Stewart (Instr./Publications Advisor); Georgia Anne Bomar (Prof. Emer.); Anthony J. Buckley (Prof. Emer.); Otha C. Spencer (Prof. Emer.)

SOUTHERN METHODIST UNIVERSITY

Street address 1: 3300 Dyer St., Umphrey Lee Ctr., Rm. 280
Street address 3: Dallas
Street address state: TX
Zip/Postal code: 75205
Mailing address: 3300 Dyer St., Umphrey Lee Ctr., Rm. 280
Mailing city: Dallas
Mailing state: TX
Mailing zip: 75205
General Phone: (214) 768-2775
General Fax: (214) 768-3307
General/National Adv. E-mail: stratton@mail.sum.edu
Classified Equipment»
Personnel: Judy Stratton (Administrator)

UNIVERSITY OF NORTH TEXAS

Street address 1: PO Box 311460
Street address 3: Denton
Street address state: TX
Zip/Postal code: 76203-1460
Mailing address: PO Box 311460
Mailing city: Denton
Mailing state: TX
Mailing zip: 76203-1460
General Phone: (940) 565-2205
General Fax: (940) 565-2370
General/National Adv. E-mail: zavoina@unt.edu
Classified Equipment»
Personnel: Susan Zavoina (Chair/Assoc. Prof./Coord., Photo seq.); Richard Wells (Prof./Coord., Photo seq.); Roy K. Busby (Prof.); Jim Albright (Assoc. Prof.); Sheri Broyles (Assoc. Prof./Coord., Adv. seq.); Mitchell Land (Assoc. Prof./Dir., Grad. Prog.); Daechun An (Asst. Prof.); Tracy Everbach (Asst. Prof./NT Daily Advisor); Eric Gormly (Asst. Prof./Coord., Broadcast-News seq.); Jacque Lambiase (Asst. Prof.); James Mueller (Asst. Prof./Coord., News-Editorial seq.); Jim Rogers (Prof. Emer.); Reg Westmoreland (Prof. Emer.)

UNIVERSITY OF TEXAS-PAN AMERICAN

Street address 1: 1201 University Dr.
Street address 3: Edinburg
Street address state: TX
Zip/Postal code: 78541
Mailing address: 1201 University Dr.
Mailing city: Edinburg
Mailing state: TX
Mailing zip: 78541
General Phone: (956) 381-3583
General Fax: (956) 381-2685
General/National Adv. E-mail: ghanem@panam.edu
Classified Equipment»
Personnel: Salma Ghanem (Chair)

UNIVERSITY OF TEXAS AT EL PASO

Street address 1: 500 W. University Ave.
Street address 3: El Paso
Street address state: TX
Zip/Postal code: 79968-0550
Mailing address: 500 W University Ave
Mailing city: El Paso
Mailing state: TX
Mailing zip: 79968-8900
General Phone: (915) 747-6285
General Fax: (915) 747-5236
General/National Adv. E-mail: com@utep.edu
Primary Website: www.utep.edu/com/
Classified Equipment»
Personnel: Patricia Witherspoon (Chair/Dir., Sam Donaldson Ctr. for Commun. Studies); Zita Arocha (Assoc. Dir., Sam Donaldson Ctr. for Commun. Studies)

TEXAS CHRISTIAN UNIVERSITY

Street address 1: Dept. of Journalism
Street address 3: Fort Worth
Street address state: TX
Zip/Postal code: 76129
Mailing address: Dept of Journalism
Mailing city: Fort Worth
Mailing state: TX
Mailing zip: 76129-0001
General Phone: (817) 257-7425
General Fax: (817) 257-7322
General/National Adv. E-mail: journalism@tcu.edu
Classified Equipment»
Personnel: Tommy G. Thomason (Dir./Prof.); Douglas Ann Newsom (Prof./Grad. Advisor, Ad/PR); Suzanne Huffman (Prof./Grad. Advisor, News, Chair, Div., Journalism); William T. Slater (Prof.); Amiso George (Assoc. Prof.); Julie O'Neil (Assoc. Prof./Chair, Div., Ad/PR); Maggie Thomas (Assoc. Prof.); John Tisdale (Assoc. Prof.); Stacy Landreth-Grau (Asst. Prof.); Daxton Stewart (Asst. Prof.); Larry Lauer (Asst. Prof.); Janice Wood (Asst. Prof.); Steve Levering (Instr.); Geoff Campell (Adj. Fac.); Dave Ferman (Adj. Fac.); Claudia Butts (Adj. Fac.); Linda Campbell (Adj. Fac.); Carmen Goldthwaite (Adj. Fac.); Kent Chapline (Adj. Fac.); Mark Horvit (Adj. Fac.); John Lumpkin

TEXAS WESLEYAN UNIVERSITY

Street address 1: Dept. of Mass Communication
Street address 2: 1201 Wesleyan St.
Street address 3: Fort Worth
Street address state: TX
Zip/Postal code: 76105
Mailing address: Dept. of Mass Communication
Mailing city: Fort Worth
Mailing state: TX
Mailing zip: 76105
General Phone: (817) 531-4927
General Fax: (817) 531-6585
General/National Adv. E-mail: msewell@txwes.edu
Classified Equipment»
Personnel: Michael Sewell (Chair)

HOUSTON BAPTIST UNIVERSITY

Street address 1: Dept. of Communications
Street address 3: Houston
Street address state: TX
Zip/Postal code: 77074-3298
Mailing address: Dept. of Communications
Mailing city: Houston
Mailing state: TX
Mailing zip: 77074-3298
General Phone: (281) 649-3520
General Fax: (281) 649-3246
General/National Adv. E-mail: srsnyder@hbu.edu
Classified Equipment»
Personnel: Steven R. Snyder (Chair/Assoc. Prof./Photography); James S. Taylor (Prof.); Alice Rowlands (Assoc. Prof./Advisor, Collegian); Laura B. Ashley (Asst. Prof./PR); Clay Porter (Instr./Program Mgr., Instructional TV); Isaac Simpson (Instr./Opns. Mgr., Instructional TV); Vivian Camacho (Adj. Prof.); Don Kobos (Adj. Prof.)

TEXAS SOUTHERN UNIVERSITY

Street address 1: Dept. of Communications
Street address 3: Houston
Street address state: TX
Zip/Postal code: 77004
Mailing address: Dept. of Communications
Mailing city: Houston
Mailing state: TX
Mailing zip: 77004
General Phone: (713) 313-7214
General Fax: (713) 313-7529
General/National Adv. E-mail: moore_sw@tsu.edu
Classified Equipment»
Personnel: Shirley Moore (Chair)

UNIVERSITY OF HOUSTON

Street address 1: 4800 Calhoun Rd.
Street address 3: Houston
Street address state: TX
Zip/Postal code: 77204-3002
Mailing address: 4800 Calhoun Rd # 9
Mailing city: Houston
Mailing state: TX
Mailing zip: 77004-2693
General Phone: (713) 743-2873
General Fax: (713) 743-2876
General/National Adv. E-mail: bolson@uh.edu
Classified Equipment»
Personnel: Beth Olson (Dir./Assoc. Prof.); William Douglas (Prof.); William Hawes (Prof.); Garth Jowett (Prof.); Mike Ryan (Prof.); Martha Haun (Assoc. Prof.); Jaesub Lee (Assoc. Prof.); Jim Query (Assoc. Prof.); Fred Schiff (Assoc. Prof.); Michael Berryhill (Asst. Prof.); Lan Ni (Asst. Prof.); Damion Waymer (Asst. Prof.); David McHam (Clinical Prof.); Deborah Bridges (Clinical Asst. Prof.); Suzanne Buck (Clinical Asst. Prof.); Craig Crowe (Clinical Asst. Prof.); Julie Fix (Clinical Asst. Prof.); Keith Houk (Clinical Asst. Prof.); Randy Polk (Clinical Asst. Prof.)

SAM HOUSTON STATE UNIVERSITY

Street address 1: 1804 Ave J
Street address 3: Huntsville
Street address state: TX
Zip/Postal code: 77341-0001
Country: USA

Mailing address: PO Box 2207SHSU
Mailing city: Huntsville
Mailing state: TX
Mailing zip: 77341-0001
General Phone: (936) 294-1341
General Fax: (936) 294-1888
Classified Equipment»
Personnel: Janet A. Bridges (Chair/Prof.); Michael L. Blackman (Philip J. Warner Chair in Journ.); Mickey Herskowitz (Philip J. Warner Chair in Journ.); Tony R. DeMars (Assoc. Prof.); Anthony Friedmann (Assoc. Prof.); Hugh S. Fullerton (Assoc. Prof.); Christopher White (Assoc. Prof.); Rene Qun Chen (Asst. Prof.); Wanda Reyes Velazquez (Asst. Prof.); Ruth M. Pate (Instr.); Richard O. Kosuowei (Lectr.); Mel Strait (Lectr.); Patsy K. Ziegler (Lectr.)

TEXAS A&M UNIVERSITY-KINGSVILLE

Street address 1: 700 University Blvd., MSC 178
Street address 3: Kingsville
Street address state: TX
Zip/Postal code: 78363
Mailing address: 700 University Blvd Stop 178
Mailing city: Kingsville
Mailing state: TX
Mailing zip: 78363-8302
General Phone: (361) 593-3401
General Fax: (361) 593-3402
General/National Adv. E-mail: william.alnor@tamuk.edu
Classified Equipment»
Personnel: William M. Alnor (Journalism Dir.)

TEXAS TECH UNIVERSITY

Street address 1: University & Broadway
Street address 3: Lubbock
Street address state: TX
Zip/Postal code: 79409-3082
Mailing address: PO Box 43082
Mailing city: Lubbock
Mailing state: TX
Mailing zip: 79409-3082
General Phone: (806) 742-3385
General Fax: (806) 742-1085
Primary Website: www.depts.ttu.edu/masscom
Classified Equipment»
Personnel: Jerry C. Hudson (Dean/Prof.); Dennis A. Harp (Prof./Associate Dean of Faculty); Tom Johnson (Prof./Marshall and Sharleen Formby Regents Prof.); Don Jugenheimer (Prof./Chair, Dept. of Advertising); Michael Parkinson (Prof./Associate Dean for graduate studies); Randy Reddick (Prof./Morris Professor and chair, Dept. of Journalism); Karl Wolfshohl (Prof./Hutcheson Professional); Coy Callison (Assoc. Prof./Chair, Dept. of Public Relations); Todd Chambers (Assoc. Prof./Chair, Dept. Electronic Media); William F. Dean (Assoc. Prof./Associate dean of students); Jimmie Reeves (Assoc. Prof.); Roger C. Saathoff (Assoc. Prof.); Elizabeth Watts (Assoc. Prof.); Kent Wilkinson (Assoc. Prof./Regents professor of Hispanic and International Communication); Shannon Bichard (Asst. Prof.); Lori Boyer (Asst. Prof.); Samuel Bradley (Asst. Prof.); Glenn Cummins (Asst. Prof.); Maria Fontenot (Asst. Prof.); Mandy Gallagher (Asst. Prof.)

STEPHEN F. AUSTIN STATE UNIVERSITY

Street address 1: Dept. of Communication
Street address 3: Nacogdoches
Street address state: TX
Zip/Postal code: 75962
Mailing address: Dept of Communication
Mailing city: Nacogdoches
Mailing state: TX
Mailing zip: 75962-0001
General Phone: (936) 468-4001
General Fax: (936) 468-1331
General/National Adv. E-mail: wmouton@sfasu.edu
Classified Equipment»
Personnel: Wanda Mouton (Interim Chair)

UNIVERSITY OF TEXAS OF THE PERMIAN BASIN

Street address 1: Faculty of Communication
Street address 2: 4901 E. University
Street address 3: Odessa
Street address state: TX
Zip/Postal code: 79762
Mailing address: Faculty of Communication
Mailing city: Odessa
Mailing state: TX
Mailing zip: 79762
General Phone: (432) 552-2323
General Fax: (432) 552-2374
General/National Adv. E-mail: mcgavin_l@utpb.edu
Classified Equipment»
Personnel: Jon Paulson (Area Coord.)

PRAIRIE VIEW A&M UNIVERSITY

Street address 1: PO Box 0156
Street address 3: Prairie View
Street address state: TX
Zip/Postal code: 77446-0156
Mailing address: PO Box 156
Mailing city: Prairie View
Mailing state: TX
Mailing zip: 77446-0156
General Phone: (409) 857-4511
General Fax: (409) 857-2309
General/National Adv. E-mail: dejun_liu@pvamu.edu
Classified Equipment»
Personnel: Dejun Liu (Head)

TRINITY UNIVERSITY

Street address 1: Dept. of Communication
Street address 3: San Antonio
Street address state: TX
Zip/Postal code: 78212-7200
Mailing address: Dept. of Communication
Mailing city: San Antonio
Mailing state: TX
Mailing zip: 78212-7200
General Phone: (210) 999-8113
General Fax: (210) 999-8355
General/National Adv. E-mail: wchrist@trinity.edu
Classified Equipment»
Personnel: William G. Christ (Chair/Prof.); Sammye L. Johnson (Prof.); Robert Huesca (Prof.); Jennifer Henderson (Assoc. Prof.); Aaron Delwiche (Asst. Prof.); Patrick Keating (Asst. Prof.); James Bynum (Instr./Opns. Mgr., Comm. Ctr.); Matt Fleeger (Instr./Opns. Mgr.); Dianah McGreehan (Instr./Dir., Underwriting); Kate Rawley (Instr./Dir., Devl.); Aaron Prado (Instr./Dir., Music/Chief Announcer); Alfredo Cruz (Instr./Sta. Mgr.)

TEXAS STATE UNIVERSITY-SAN MARCOS

Street address 1: 601 University Dr.
Street address 3: San Marcos
Street address state: TX
Zip/Postal code: 78666-4616
Mailing address: 601 University Dr
Mailing city: San Marcos
Mailing state: TX
Mailing zip: 78666-4684
General Phone: (512) 245-2656
General Fax: (512) 245-7649
General/National Adv. E-mail: bergen@txstate.edu
Primary Website: www.masscomm.txstate.edu
Classified Equipment»
Personnel: Lori Bergen (Prof./Dir.); Tom Grimes (Prof.); Kate Pierce (Prof./Coord., Gen. Mass Comm.); Sandhya Rao (Prof./Assoc. Dir., Grad. Studies); Bruce Smith (Prof.); Federico Subervi (Prof.); Tim England (Assoc. Profs./Coord., Electronic Media); Laurie Fluker (Assoc. Prof./Assoc. dean); Judy Oskam (Assoc. Prof./Assoc. Dir. RRHEC); Frank Walsh (Assoc. Prof./Coord., PR); Susan Weill (Assoc. Prof.); Gilbert Martinez (Asst. Prof.); Alexander Muk (Asst. Prof.(Spring 2008)); Ray Niekamp (Asst. Prof.); Cindy Royal (Asst. Prof.); Bob Bajackson (Lectr./Dir., Student Pubs); Larry Carlson (Lectr.); Cunhyeong Ci (Lectr.); Kym Fox (Lectr./Coord., Print); Jody Gibson (Lectr./Coord., Ad)

TEXAS LUTHERAN UNIV.

Street address 1: 1000 W Court St
Street address 3: Seguin
Street address state: TX
Zip/Postal code: 78155-5978
Country: USA
Mailing address: 1000 W Court St
Mailing city: Seguin
Mailing state: TX
Mailing zip: 78155-9996
General Phone: (830) 372-8073
General Fax: (830) 372-8074
General/National Adv. E-mail: lonestarlutheran@tlu.edu
Primary Website: www.lsionline.net
Classified Equipment»
Personnel: Robin Bisha (Advisor); Steven S. Vrooman (Chair); Kristi Quiros (Pub.); Emmalee Drummond (Ed. in Chief); Naomi Urquiza (Mng. Ed.)

TEXAS A&M UNIVERSITY-TEXARKANA

Street address 1: 2600 N. Robison Rd.
Street address 3: Texarkana
Street address state: TX
Zip/Postal code: 75505-5518
Mailing address: 7101 University Ave
Mailing city: Texarkana
Mailing state: TX
Mailing zip: 75503-0597
General Phone: (903) 223-3169
General Fax: (903) 223-3120
Classified Equipment»

BAYLOR UNIVERSITY

Street address 1: 1 Bear Pl
Street address 2: Unit 97330
Street address 3: Waco
Street address state: TX
Zip/Postal code: 76798-7330
Country: USA
Mailing address: 1 Bear Pl Unit 97330
Mailing city: Waco
Mailing state: TX
Mailing zip: 76798-7330
General Phone: (254) 710-3407
General Fax: (254) 710-1714
Advertising Phone: (254) 710-3407
Advertising Fax: (254) 710-1714
Editorial Fax: (254) 710-1714
General/National Adv. E-mail: lariat@baylor.edu
Display Adv. E-mail: Lariat_Ads@baylor.edu
Editorial e-mail: Lariat-Letters@baylor.edu
Primary Website: www.baylorlariat.com
Year Established: 1900
Commercial printers: N
Advertising (Open inch Rate) Weekday/Saturday: (254) 710-3407
Published: Tues`Wed`Thur`Fri
Avg Free Circ: 4000
Classified Equipment»
Personnel: Paul Carr (Dir., Mktg. Information); Jamile Yglecias (Advertising Sales and Marketing Manager); Julie Freeman (Asst. Media Adviser)
Parent company (for newspapers): Baylor University

BAYLOR UNIVERSITY

Street address 1: Dept. of Journalism
Street address 2: 1 Bear Plaza #97330
Street address 3: Waco
Street address state: TX
Zip/Postal code: 76798-7353
Mailing address: Dept. of Journalism
Mailing city: Waco
Mailing state: TX
Mailing zip: 76798-7353
General Phone: (254) 710-3261
General Fax: (254) 710-3363
Primary Website: www.baylorlariat.com
Classified Equipment»
Personnel: Clark Baker (Chair/Assoc. Prof.); Mike Blackman (Prof.); Sara Stone (Prof.); Robert Darden (Assoc. Prof.); Douglas Ferdon (Assoc. Prof.); Mia Moody (Asst. Prof.); Sharon Bracken (Instr.); Cassy Burleson (Instr.); Allin Means (Instr.); Brad Owens (Instr.); Maxey Parrish (Instr.); Carol Perry (Instr.); Amanda Sturgill (Instr.); Kevin Tankersley (Instr.)

MIDWESTERN STATE UNIVERSITY

Street address 1: B110 Fain Fine Arts Ctr.
Street address 3: Wichita Falls
Street address state: TX
Zip/Postal code: 76308
Mailing address: B110 Fain Fine Arts Ctr.
Mailing city: Wichita Falls
Mailing state: TX
Mailing zip: 76308
General Phone: (940) 397-4391
General Fax: (940) 397-4909
General/National Adv. E-mail: jim.sernoe@mwsu.edu
Classified Equipment»
Personnel: Jim Sernoe (Chair/Assoc. Prof.); Jim Gorham (Asst. Prof./Advisor, Campus Watch); Sandra Grant (Asst. Prof.); Liz Minden (Asst. Prof.); Randy Pruitt (Asst. Prof./Advisor, The Wichitan); Judy Braddy (Adj. Fac.); Kory Dorman (Adj. Fac.); Roma Prassel (Adj. Fac.); Donnie Kirk (Adj. Fac.); Pam Morgan (Adj. Fac.); June Kable (Prof. Emer.); Dencil R. Taylor (Assoc. Prof. Emer.)

UTAH

SOUTHERN UTAH UNIVERSITY

Street address 1: 351 W. University Blvd., Centrum 213
Street address 3: Cedar City
Street address state: UT
Zip/Postal code: 84720
Mailing address: 351 W Center St Centrum 213
Mailing city: Cedar City
Mailing state: UT
Mailing zip: 84720-2470
General Phone: (435) 586-7861
General Fax: (435) 865-8352
General/National Adv. E-mail: smith_jo@suu.edu
Classified Equipment»
Personnel: Jon Smith (Chair)

UTAH STATE UNIVERSITY

Street address 1: Dept. of Journalism & Communication
Street address 3: Logan
Street address state: UT
Zip/Postal code: 84322-4605
Mailing address: Dept of Journalism & Communication
Mailing city: Logan
Mailing state: UT
Mailing zip: 84322-0001
General Phone: (435) 797-3292
General Fax: (435) 797-3973
General/National Adv. E-mail: jcom@aggiemail.usu.edu; mike.sweeney@usu.edu
Primary Website: www.usu.edu/journalism; www.hardnewscafe.usu.edu
Classified Equipment»
Personnel: Edward C. Pease (Prof./Grad. Coord.); Cathy Ferrand Bullock (Assoc. Prof.); Penny Byrne (Assoc. Prof.); Brenda Cooper (Assoc. Prof.); Nancy M. Williams (Asst. Prof.); Dean Byrne (Lectr.); R. Troy Oldham (Lectr.); Preston Parker (Lectr.); Ron Boam (Adj. Instr.); Cami Boehme (Adj. Instr.); Jane Koerner (Adj. Instr.); Shane Krebs (Adj. Instr.); Tim Vitale (Adj. Instr.); Jay Wamsley (Adj. Instr.); Friend Weller (Adj. Instr.)

WEBER STATE UNIVERSITY

Street address 1: Dept. of Communication
Street address 3: Ogden
Street address state: UT
Zip/Postal code: 84408-1605
Mailing address: Dept of Communication
Mailing city: Ogden
Mailing state: UT
Mailing zip: 84408-0001
General Phone: (801) 626-6426
General Fax: (801) 626-7975
General/National Adv. E-mail: jjosephson@weber.edu
Classified Equipment»
Personnel: Randolph J. Scott (Chair)

BRIGHAM YOUNG UNIVERSITY

Street address 1: 360 BRMB
Street address 3: Provo
Street address state: UT
Zip/Postal code: 84602
Mailing address: 360 BRMB
Mailing city: Provo
Mailing state: UT
Mailing zip: 84602
General Phone: (801) 422-2997
General Fax: (801) 422-0160
General/National Adv. E-mail: comms_secretary@byu.edu
Classified Equipment»
Personnel: Bradley Rawlins (Chair); Edward E. Adams (Prof.); R. John Hughes (Prof.); Steven R. Thomsen (Prof.); Laurie J. Wilson (Prof.); Sherry L. Baker (Assoc. Prof.); Mark A. Callister (Assoc. Prof.); Larrie

E. Gale (Assoc. Prof.); Douglas R. McKinlay (Assoc. Prof.); Russell H. Mouritsen (Assoc. Prof.); Allen W. Palmer (Assoc. Prof.); Kenneth D. Plowman (Assoc. Prof.); Kevin L. Stoker (Assoc. Prof./Assoc. Chair, Grad. Studies); Robert I. Wakefield (Assoc. Prof.); Joel Campbell (Asst. Prof.); Edward L. Carter (Asst. Prof.); Dale Cressman (Asst. Prof.); Christopher Cutri (Asst. Prof.); L. Kevin Kelly (Asst. Prof.); Quint B. Randle (Asst. Prof.)

UNIVERSITY OF UTAH

Street address 1: 255 S. Central Campus Dr., Rm. 2400
Street address 3: Salt Lake City
Street address state: UT
Zip/Postal code: 84112-0491
Mailing address: 255 Central Campus Dr Rm 2400
Mailing city: Salt Lake City
Mailing state: UT
Mailing zip: 84112-0491
General Phone: (801) 581-6888
General Fax: (801) 585-6255
General/National Adv. E-mail: duignan@admin.comm.utah.edu
Classified Equipment»
Personnel: Ann Darling (Chair)

VIRGINIA

GEORGETOWN UNIVERSITY

Street address 1: 3101 Wilson Blvd., Ste. 200
Street address 3: Arlington
Street address state: VA
Zip/Postal code: 22201
Mailing address: 3101 Wilson Blvd Ste 200
Mailing city: Arlington
Mailing state: VA
Mailing zip: 22201-4447
General Phone: (202) 687-7000
General Fax: (703) 812-9324
Classified Equipment»
Personnel: Denise Li (Assoc. Dean)

MARYMOUNT UNIV.

Street address 1: 2807 N Glebe Rd
Street address 3: Arlington
Street address state: VA
Zip/Postal code: 22207-4224
Country: USA
Mailing address: 2807 N Glebe Rd
Mailing city: Arlington
Mailing state: VA
Mailing zip: 22207-4299
General Phone: (703) 522-5600
General Fax: (703) 284-3817
General/National Adv. E-mail: banner@marymount.edu
Primary Website: www.marymount.edu
Classified Equipment»
Personnel: Paul Byers (Mass Commun. Coord.); Vincent Stovall (Dir., Student Activities); Ralph Frasca (Mass Commun. Coord.)

VIRGINIA POLYTECHNIC INSTITUTE AND STATE UNIVERSITY

Street address 1: Dept. of Communication
Street address 2: 121 Shanks Hall
Street address 3: Blacksburg
Street address state: VA
Zip/Postal code: 24061-0311
Mailing address: Dept of Communication
Mailing city: Blacksburg
Mailing state: VA
Mailing zip: 24061-0001
General Phone: (540) 231-7136
General Fax: (540) 231-9817
General/National Adv. E-mail: rhollowa@vt.edu
Primary Website: www.comm.vt.edu
Classified Equipment»
Personnel: Rachel L. Holloway (Head)

EMORY AND HENRY COLLEGE

Street address 1: PO Box 947, Garnand Dr.
Street address 3: Emory
Street address state: VA
Zip/Postal code: 24327
Mailing address: PO Box 947
Mailing city: Emory
Mailing state: VA
Mailing zip: 24327-0947
General Phone: (276) 944-6822
General Fax: (276) 944-6934
General/National Adv. E-mail: tkeller@ehc.edu
Classified Equipment»
Personnel: Teresa Keller (Chair)

HAMPTON

HAMPTON UNIVERSITY

Street address 1: 546 E. Queen St.
Street address 3: Hampton
Street address state: VA
Zip/Postal code: 23668
Mailing address: 100 E Queen St
Mailing city: Hampton
Mailing state: VA
Mailing zip: 23668-0108
General Phone: (757) 727-5405
General Fax: (757) 728-6011
Classified Equipment»
Personnel: Tony Brown (Dean)

JAMES MADISON UNIVERSITY

Street address 1: MSC # 2104
Street address 3: Harrisonburg
Street address state: VA
Zip/Postal code: 22807
Mailing address: Msc # 2104
Mailing city: Harrisonburg
Mailing state: VA
Mailing zip: 22807-0001
General Phone: (540) 568-7007
General Fax: (540) 568-7026
General/National Adv. E-mail: anderssd@jmu.edu
Primary Website: smad.jmu.edu
Classified Equipment»
Personnel: Steve Anderson (Dir./Prof.); Dietrich Maune (Asst. Dir./Prof.); Dona Gilliam (Prof.); Rustin Greene (Prof.); George Johnson (Prof.); Marilou Johnson (Prof.); Alex Leidholdt (Prof.); Roger Soenksen (Prof.); Charles Turner (Prof.); John Woody (Prof.); John Guiniven (Assoc. Prof.); Joe Hinshaw (Assoc. Prof.); Tom McHardy (Assoc. Prof.); Tom O'Connor (Assoc. Prof.); Kevin Reynolds (Assoc. Prof.); Dave Wendelken (Assoc. Prof.); Mike Grundmann (Asst. Prof.); Kathy Hughes (Asst. Prof.); Nancy Nusser (Asst. Prof.)

WASHINGTON AND LEE UNIVERSITY

Street address 1: Dept. of Journalism & Mass Commun.
Street address 3: Lexington
Street address state: VA
Zip/Postal code: 24450
Mailing address: Dept. of Journalism & Mass Commun.
Mailing city: Lexington
Mailing state: VA
Mailing zip: 24450
General Phone: (540) 458-8432
General Fax: (540) 458-8845
General/National Adv. E-mail: journalism@wlu.edu
Classified Equipment»
Personnel: Brian E. Richardson (Head/Prof.); Robert J. deMaria (Prof.); Pamela K. Luecke (Prof.); Hampden H. Smith (Prof.); Edward Wasserman (Prof.); Claudette Guzan Artwick (Assoc. Prof.); Adedayo Abah (Asst. Prof.); Doug Cumming (Asst. Prof.); Louis W. Hodges (Prof. Emer.); John K. Jennings (Prof. Emer.)

LIBERTY UNIV.

Street address 1: 1971 University Blvd
Street address 3: Lynchburg
Street address state: VA
Zip/Postal code: 24515-0002
Country: USA
Mailing address: 1971 University Blvd
Mailing city: Lynchburg
Mailing state: VA
Mailing zip: 24515-0002
General Phone: (434) 582-2128
General Fax: (434) 582-2420
Editorail Phone: (434) 582-2128
General/National Adv. E-mail: advertising@liberty.edu
Primary Website: www.liberty.edu/champion
Year Established: 1971
Classified Equipment»
Personnel: William Gribbin (Dean, School of Commun.); Debra Huff (Advisor); Cecil V. Kramer (Jr. Assoc. Dean); Benjamin Lesley (Adv. Dir.); William Mullen (Chrmn.); Amanda Sullivan (Ed. in Chief)

LYNCHBURG COLLEGE

Street address 1: 1501 Lakeside Dr
Street address 3: Lynchburg
Street address state: VA
Zip/Postal code: 24501-3113
Country: USA
Mailing address: 1501 Lakeside Dr
Mailing city: Lynchburg
Mailing state: VA
Mailing zip: 24501-3113
General Phone: (434) 544-8301
General Fax: (804) 544-8661
General/National Adv. E-mail: critograph@lynchburg.edu
Display Adv. E-mail: critograph@lynchburg.edu
Editorial e-mail: critograph@lynchburg.edu
Primary Website: www.critograph.com
Published: Tues
Classified Equipment»
Personnel: Rachad Davis (Editor-in-Chief); Heywood Greenberg (Dena/Prof., Journ.); Wayne Garret (Copy Desk Chief)

NORFOLK STATE UNIVERSITY

Street address 1: 700 Park Ave.
Street address 3: Norfolk
Street address state: VA
Zip/Postal code: 23504
Mailing address: 700 Park Ave PH 340
Mailing city: Norfolk
Mailing state: VA
Mailing zip: 23504-8090
General Phone: (757) 823-8331
General Fax: (757) 823-9119
General/National Adv. E-mail: wgbrockington@nsu.edu
Classified Equipment»
Personnel: Wanda Brockington (Chair/Assoc. Prof.); Stan Tickton (Prof./Grad. Coord.); Paula Briggs (Assoc. Prof.); Cathy Jackson (Asst. Prof.); Marcia Taylor (Asst. Prof.); Steve Opfer (Instr.); Battinto Batts (Adj. Fac.); Carl Daniels (Adj. Fac.); Jen'Nein T. Ferrell (Adj. Fac.); Kimberly Payne (Adj. Fac.); Marquita Smith (Adj. Fac.); Spartan Echo

RADFORD UNIVERSITY

Street address 1: 200 Jefferson St.
Street address 2: Campus PO Box 6932
Street address 3: Radford
Street address state: VA
Zip/Postal code: 24142
Mailing address: Dept. of Communication
Mailing city: Radford
Mailing state: VA
Mailing zip: 24142
General Phone: (540) 831-5282
General Fax: (540) 831-5883
Classified Equipment»
Personnel: Lynn Zoch (Dir.)

UNIVERSITY OF RICHMOND

Street address 1: Journalism Dept.
Street address 3: Richmond
Street address state: VA
Zip/Postal code: 23173
Mailing address: Journalism
Mailing city: Richmond
Mailing state: VA
Mailing zip: 23173-0001
General Phone: (804) 289-8323
General Fax: (804) 287-6052
General/National Adv. E-mail: snash@richmond.edu
Classified Equipment»
Personnel: Steve Nash (Journ. Chair)

VIRGINIA COMMONWEALTH UNIVERSITY

Street address 1: 901 W. Main St.
Street address 3: Richmond
Street address state: VA
Zip/Postal code: 23284-2034
Mailing address: PO Box 842034
Mailing city: Richmond
Mailing state: VA
Mailing zip: 23284-2034
General Phone: (804) 828-2660
General Fax: (804) 828-9175
Primary Website: www.has.vcu.edu/mac
Classified Equipment»
Personnel: Judy VanSlyke Turk (Dir./Prof.); June Nicholson (Assoc. Prof./Assoc. Dir.); Michael Hughes (Asst. Dir., Devel.); Carol Mawyer (Asst. Dir., Student Services/Scholastic Journ.); Thomas Donohue (Prof.); Tim Bajkiewicz (Assoc. Prof.); Bonnie Newman Davis (Assoc. Prof.); Ernest F. Martin (Assoc. prof.); Jeff South (Assoc. Prof.); Clarence Thomas (Assoc. Prof.); Debora Wenger (Assoc. Prof.); Pieter Blikslager (Asst. Prof.); Bridget Camden (Asst. Prof.); Soo Yeon Hong (Asst. Prof.); Yan Jin (Asst. Prof.); Suzanne Lysak (Asst. Prof.); Marcus Messner (Asst. Prof.); William Oglesby (Asst. Prof.); Scott Sherman (Asst. Prof.); Will Sims (Asst. Prof.)

VIRGINIA UNION UNIV.

Street address 1: 1500 N Lombardy St
Street address 3: Richmond
Street address state: VA
Zip/Postal code: 23220-1711
Country: USA
Mailing address: 1500 N Lombardy St
Mailing city: Richmond
Mailing state: VA
Mailing zip: 23220-1784
General Phone: (804) 257-5655
General Fax: (804) 257-5818
Classified Equipment»
Personnel: Gloria D. Brogdon (Dept. Chair); Peter S. Tahsoh (Advisor)

MARY BALDWIN COLLEGE

Street address 1: Communication Dept.
Street address 3: Staunton
Street address state: VA
Zip/Postal code: 24401
Mailing address: Communication Dept.
Mailing city: Staunton
Mailing state: VA
Mailing zip: 24401
General Phone: (504) 887-7112
General Fax: (540) 887-7040
General/National Adv. E-mail: bdorries@mbc.edu
Classified Equipment»
Personnel: Bruce Dorries (Chair)

VIRGINIA BEACH

REGENT UNIVERSITY

Street address 1: 1000 Regent University Dr.
Street address 3: Virginia Beach
Street address state: VA
Zip/Postal code: 23464-9800
Mailing address: 1000 Regent University Dr
Mailing city: Virginia Beach
Mailing state: VA
Mailing zip: 23464-9800
General Phone: (757) 226-4237
General Fax: (757) 226-4275
Classified Equipment»
Personnel: Mark Menga (Chair)

VERMONT

ST. MICHAEL'S COLLEGE

Street address 1: Winooski Park
Street address 3: Colchester
Street address state: VT
Zip/Postal code: 5439
Mailing address: Winooski Park
Mailing city: Colchester
Mailing state: VT
Mailing zip: 05439-0001
General Phone: (802) 654-2257
General Fax: (802) 654-2560
General/National Adv. E-mail: ksultze@smcvt.edu

Primary Website: academics.smcvt.edu/journalism
Classified Equipment»
Personnel: Kimberly Sultze (Chair/Assoc. Prof.); David T.Z. Mindich (Prof.); Jon Hyde (Assoc. Prof.); Traci Griffith (Asst. Prof.); Jerry Swope (Asst. Prof.); Donna Atwater (Instr.); Paul Beique (Instr.); Bob Davis (Instr.); Mike Donoghue (Instr.); Kevin Kelley (Instr.); Kerry Litchfield (Instr.); Nick Monsarrat (Instr.); Marybeth Christie Redmond (Instr.); Matt Powers (Instr.); Shay Totten (Instr.); Sarah Tuff (Instr.); Gifford Hart (Assoc. Prof. Emer.)

WASHINGTON

WESTERN WASHINGTON UNIVERSITY

Street address 1: 516 High St., CF 251
Street address 3: Bellingham
Street address state: WA
Zip/Postal code: 98225-9161
Mailing address: 516 High St # CF251
Mailing city: Bellingham
Mailing state: WA
Mailing zip: 98225-5950
General Phone: (360) 650-3252
General Fax: (360) 650-2848
General/National Adv. E-mail: marissa.doiron@wwu.edu
Primary Website: www.ac.wwu.edu/~journal
Classified Equipment»
Personnel: Shearlean Duke (Chair/Assoc. Prof.); Carolyn Dale (Assoc. Prof.); Brad Howard (Assoc. Prof.); Tim Pilgrim (Assoc. Prof.); John Harris (Asst. Prof.); Jennifer Keller (Asst. Prof.); Peggy Watt (Asst. Prof.); Stephen Howie (Lectr.); Carolyn Nielsen-Thompson (Lectr.)

WALLA WALLA COLLEGE

Street address 1: 204 S College Ave
Street address 3: College Place
Street address state: WA
Zip/Postal code: 99324-1139
Country: USA
Mailing address: 204 S College Ave
Mailing city: College Place
Mailing state: WA
Mailing zip: 99324-1198
General Phone: (509) 527-2971
General Fax: (509) 527-2674
General/National Adv. E-mail: comm@wwc.edu
Classified Equipment»
Personnel: Ross Brown (Ed.); Pamela Harris (Chair)

CENTRAL WASHINGTON UNIVERSITY

Street address 1: Dept. of Communication
Street address 3: Ellensburg
Street address state: WA
Zip/Postal code: 98926
Mailing address: Dept. of Communication
Mailing city: Ellensburg
Mailing state: WA
Mailing zip: 98926
General Phone: (509) 963-1066
General Fax: (509) 963-1060
Primary Website: www.cwu.edu/~comm
Classified Equipment»
Personnel: Corwin King (Chair); P A Mauton Hartwig

WASHINGTON STATE UNIVERSITY

Street address 1: Edward R. Murrow School of Communication
Street address 3: Pullman
Street address state: WA
Zip/Postal code: 99164-2520
Mailing address: Edward R Murrow School of Communication
Mailing city: Pullman
Mailing state: WA
Mailing zip: 99164-0001
General Phone: (509) 335-1556
General Fax: (509) 335-1555
General/National Adv. E-mail: communication@wsu.edu
Primary Website: communication.wsu.edu
Classified Equipment»
Personnel: Erica Austin (Interim Dir./Prof.); E. Lincoln James (Prof.); Glenn Johnson (Prof./Cable 8 News Exec. Producer); Bruce Pinkleton (Prof./Head, PR seq.); Joey Reagan (Prof.); Patricia Sias (Prof.); Alexis S. Tan (Prof.); Rick Busselle (Assoc. Prof.); David Demers (Assoc. Prof.); Jolanta Drzewiecka (Assoc. Prof./Head, Comm. Studies seq.); John Irby (Assoc. Prof./Assoc. Dir., Undergrad. Studies); Betsy Krueger (Assoc. Prof.); Michael Salvador (Assoc. Prof./Assoc. Dir., Opns. and Budget); Susan Ross (Assoc. Prof./Exec. Dir., Northwest Access); Elizabeth Blanks Hindman (Assoc. Prof./Head, Journ. seq.); Douglas Blanks Hindman (Asst. Prof.); Stacey Hust (Asst. Prof.); Moon Lee (Asst. Prof.); Todd Norton (Asst. Prof.); Marvin Marcelo (Asst. Prof./Dir., Murrow Symposium/Cable 8 Productions)

SEATTLE UNIVERSITY

Street address 1: 900 Broadway
Street address 3: Seattle
Street address state: WA
Zip/Postal code: 98122
Mailing address: 901 12th Ave
Mailing city: Seattle
Mailing state: WA
Mailing zip: 98122-4411
General Phone: (206) 296-5340
General Fax: (206) 296-5409
General/National Adv. E-mail: damhsoir@seattleu.edu
Classified Equipment»
Personnel: Gary Atkins (Chair)

UNIVERSITY OF WASHINGTON

Street address 1: Box 353740, 102 Communications
Street address 3: Seattle
Street address state: WA
Zip/Postal code: 98195-3740
Mailing address: PO Box 353740
Mailing city: Seattle
Mailing state: WA
Mailing zip: 98195-3740
General Phone: (206) 543-2660
General Fax: (206) 616-3762
General/National Adv. E-mail: kolsen@u.washington.edu
Classified Equipment»
Personnel: Gerald J. Baldasty (Chair)

EASTERN WASHINGTON UNIVERSITY

Street address 1: 705 W. 1st Ave.
Street address 3: Spokane
Street address state: WA
Zip/Postal code: 98201-3900
Mailing address: 705 W 1st Ave
Mailing city: Spokane
Mailing state: WA
Mailing zip: 99201-3909
General Phone: (509) 623-4347
General Fax: (509) 623-4238
General/National Adv. E-mail: steve.blewett@mailserver.ewu.edu
Classified Equipment»
Personnel: Steve Blewett (Dir./Prof.)
Newspaper (for newspapers group): The Easterner, Cheney

GONZAGA UNIVERSITY

Street address 1: Dept. of Communication Arts
Street address 3: Spokane
Street address state: WA
Zip/Postal code: 99258
Mailing address: Dept of Communication Arts
Mailing city: Spokane
Mailing state: WA
Mailing zip: 99258-0001
General Phone: (509) 328-4220
Classified Equipment»
Personnel: Michael Kirkhorn (Dir.)

WHITWORTH UNIVERSITY

Street address 1: Dept. of Communication Studies
Street address 3: Spokane
Street address state: WA
Zip/Postal code: 99251
Mailing address: Dept of Communication Studies
Mailing city: Spokane
Mailing state: WA
Mailing zip: 99251-0001
General Phone: (509) 777-4739
General Fax: (509) 777-4512
General/National Adv. E-mail: gwhitehouse@whitworth.edu
Classified Equipment»
Personnel: Virginia Whitehouse (Chair)

PACIFIC LUTHERAN UNIVERSITY

Street address 1: Dept. of Communication & Theatre
Street address 3: Tacoma
Street address state: WA
Zip/Postal code: 98447
Mailing address: Dept of Communication & Theatre
Mailing city: Tacoma
Mailing state: WA
Mailing zip: 98447-0001
General Phone: (206) 535-7762
General Fax: (206) 536-5063
Classified Equipment»
Personnel: Michael Bartanen (Chair); Clifford Rowe (Area Head)

WISCONSIN

UNIVERSITY OF WISCONSIN-EAU CLAIRE

Street address 1: Dept. of Communication & Journalism
Street address 3: Eau Claire
Street address state: WI
Zip/Postal code: 54702
Mailing address: Dept. of Communication & Journalism
Mailing city: Eau Claire
Mailing state: WI
Mailing zip: 54702
General Phone: (715) 836-2528
General Fax: (715) 836-3820
General/National Adv. E-mail: bakerda@uwec.edu
Classified Equipment»
Personnel: David Baker (Interim Chair); Terry L. Chmielewski (Prof.); Judy Sims (Prof.); W. Robert Sampson (Prof.); Edward Frederick (Assoc. Prof.); Jan Larson (Assoc. Prof.); Arlyn Anderson (Asst. Prof.); Martha Fay (Asst. Prof.); Ellen Mahaffy (Asst. Prof.); Michael Dorsher (Asst. Prof.); Jeanie Geurink (Asst. Prof.); Won Yong Jang (Asst. Prof.); Jack Kapfer (Asst. Prof.); Nichole Schultz (Asst. Prof.); Karen Morris (Sr. Lectr./Dir., Forensics); Kelly Jo Wright (Sr. Lectr.); Rachel Woodward (Part-time Fac.); Elizabeth Danko Chmielewski (Part-time Fac.); Mary Beth Doud (Part-time Fac.); Janet Driever (Part-time Fac.)

UNIVERSITY OF WISCONSIN-LA CROSSE

Street address 1: 346 Center for the Arts
Street address 3: La Crosse
Street address state: WI
Zip/Postal code: 54601
Mailing address: 346 Center for the Arts
Mailing city: La Crosse
Mailing state: WI
Mailing zip: 54601
General Phone: (608) 785-8519
General Fax: (608) 785-6719
General/National Adv. E-mail: rodrick.rich@uwlax.edu
Primary Website: perth.uwlax.edu/commstudies
Classified Equipment»
Personnel: Richard Rodrick (Chair)

UNIVERSITY OF WISCONSIN-MADISON

Street address 1: 821 University Ave.
Street address 3: Madison
Street address state: WI
Zip/Postal code: 53706-1497
Mailing address: 821 University Ave
Mailing city: Madison
Mailing state: WI
Mailing zip: 53706-1412
General Phone: (608) 262-3691
General Fax: (608) 262-1361
Primary Website: www.journalism.wisc.edu
Classified Equipment»
Personnel: James L. Baughman (Dir./Prof.); Deborah L. Blum (Prof.); Robert E. Drechsel (Prof./Chair, Frank Thayer Ctr.); Sharon Dunwoody (Evjue-Bascom Prof.); Jo Ellen Fair (Prof.); Lew Friedland (Prof.); Douglas M. McLeod (Prof.); Jack W. Mitchell (Prof.); Dhavan Shah (Maier-Bascom Prof.); Hemant Shah (Prof.); Stephen L. Vaughn (Prof.); Stephen J. A. Ward (James E. Burgess Prof.); Gregory J. Downey (Assoc. Prof.); Dominique Brossard (Asst. Prof.); Kathleen B. Culver (Instructional Staff); Pat Hastings (Instructional Staff); Debora Pierce (Instructional Staff); Steve Walters (Instructional Staff); Raymond Anderson (Prof. Emer.); William B. Blankenburg (Prof. Emer.)

UNIVERSITY OF WISCONSIN-MADISON

Street address 1: 440 Henry Mall
Street address 3: Madison
Street address state: WI
Zip/Postal code: 53706-1563
Mailing address: 440 Henry Mall
Mailing city: Madison
Mailing state: WI
Mailing zip: 53706-1535
General Phone: (608) 262-1464
General Fax: (608) 265-3042
General/National Adv. E-mail: lifescicomm@cals.wisc.edu
Primary Website: www.wisc.edu/lsc
Classified Equipment»
Personnel: Jacqueline C. Bush Hitchon (Chair/Prof.); Marion R. Brown (Prof.); Albert C. Gunther (Prof.); Alan B. Knox (Prof.); Larry R. Meiller (Prof.); Garrett J. O'Keefe (Prof.); Suzanne Pingree (Prof.); Shiela I. Reaves (Assoc. Prof.); Robin Shepard (Assoc. Prof.); Calvin D. Brutus (Asst. Prof.); Patricia A. Loew (Asst. Prof.); Jacob G. Stockinger (Adj. Assoc. Prof.); Michael J. Flaherty (Lectr.); B. Wolfgang Hoffmann (Lectr.); Brian D. Howell (Lectr.); Susan Lampert-Smith (Lectr.); William Ronald Seely (Lectr.); Mary Ellen Spoerke (Lectr.); Fritz A. Albert (Prof. Emer.); Margaret Andreasen (Prof. Emer.)

MARQUETTE UNIVERSITY

Street address 1: 1131 W. Wisconsin Ave.
Street address 3: Milwaukee
Street address state: WI
Zip/Postal code: 53223-2313
Mailing address: 1131 W Wisconsin Ave
Mailing city: Milwaukee
Mailing state: WI
Mailing zip: 53233-2313
General Phone: (414) 288-7133
General Fax: (414) 288-5227
General/National Adv. E-mail: coc@marquette.edu
Classified Equipment»
Personnel: Lynn H. Turner (Interim Dean/William R. Burleigh and E.W. Scripps Prof.); Claire Badaracco (Prof.); Bonnie S. Brennen (Prof./Nieman Prof., Journ.); Robert J. Griffin (Prof.); Lawrence C. Soley (Prof./Gretchen and Cyril Colnik Chair); Daradirek Ekachai (Assoc. Prof.); John A. Grams (Assoc. Prof.); Michael Havice (Assoc. Prof./Chair, Broadcast/Electronic Commun.); James V. Pokrywczynski (Assoc. Prof.); James F. Scotton (Assoc. Prof.); Karen L. Slattery (Assoc. Prof.); William J. Thorn (Assoc. Prof./Chair, Journ.); Joyce M. Wolburg (Assoc. Prof./Chair, Adv./PR); Ana C. Garner (Assoc. Prof.); Kati Tusinski Berg (Asst. Prof.); Sumana Chattopadhyay (Asst. Prof.); Richard Leonard (Asst. Prof./Nieman Prof. Emer.); Erik F. Ugland (Asst. Prof.); Jean M. Grow (Asst. Prof.); Linda Menck (Professional-in-Residence)

UNIVERSITY OF WISCONSIN-MILWAUKEE / DEPARTMENT OF JOURNALISM, ADVERTISING, AND MEDIA STUDIES (JAMS)

Street address 1: 3210 N Maryland Ave
Street address 2: Bolton Hall, 510B
Street address 3: Milwaukee
Street address state: WI
Zip/Postal code: 53211-3164
County: Milwaukee
Country: USA
Mailing address: PO Box 413
Mailing city: Milwaukee
Mailing state: WI
Mailing zip: 53201-0413
General Phone: (414) 229-4436
General Fax: (414) 229-2411
General/National Adv. E-mail: jams-email@uwm.edu

Primary Website: jams.uwm.edu
Classified Equipment»
Personnel: David Allen (Professor and Director of Graduate Studies); Xiaoxia Cao (Assistant Professor); Jane Hampden Daley (Senior Lecturer); Jackie Leonard-Tackett (Lecturer); Elana Levine (Associate Professor); Jessica McBride (Senior Lecturer); Michael Newman (Associate Professor and Department Chair); Richard Popp (Associate Professor and Director of Undergraduate Studies); David Pritchard (Professor); Joette Rockow (Senior Lecturer); Jeffery Smith (Professor); Marc Tasman (Senior Lecturer); Eric Lohman (Lecturer); Rachael Jurek (Lecturer); Jessie Garcia Marble (Associate Lecturer); Anna Kupiecki (Academic Department Associate); Jeff Loomis (Digital Media Specialist)

UNIVERSITY OF WISCONSIN-OSHKOSH

Street address 1: 800 Algoma Blvd.
Street address 3: Oshkosh
Street address state: WI
Zip/Postal code: 54901-8696
Mailing address: 800 Algoma Blvd
Mailing city: Oshkosh
Mailing state: WI
Mailing zip: 54901-8651
General Phone: (414) 424-1042
General Fax: (414) 424-7146
General/National Adv. E-mail: journalism@uwosh.edu
Primary Website: www.uwosh.edu/journalism
Classified Equipment»
Personnel: Mike Cowling (Chair/Prof.); Julie K. Henderson (Prof.); Timothy R. Gleason (Assoc. Prof.); Miles B. Maguire (Assoc. Prof.); Elizabeth Crisp Crawford (Asst. Prof.)

UNIVERSITY OF WISCONSIN-RIVER FALLS

Street address 1: 410 S 3rd St
Street address 2: 310 North Hall
Street address 3: River Falls
Street address state: WI
Zip/Postal code: 54022-5010
County: Pierce
Country: USA
Mailing address: 410 S. Third St.
Mailing city: River Falls
Mailing state: WI
Mailing zip: 54022
General Phone: (715) 425-3169
General Fax: (715) 425-0658
General/National Adv. E-mail: journalism@uwrf.edu
Display Adv. E-mail: advertising@uwrfvoice.com
Editorial e-mail: editor@uwrfvoice.com
Primary Website: uwrfvoice.com
Year Established: 1916
Delivery Methods: Racks
Published: Fri
Avg Free Circ: 1000
Classified Equipment»
Personnel: Andris Straumanis (Advisor); Sandra Ellis (Chair)

UNIVERSITY OF WISCONSIN-STEVENS POINT

Street address 1: Div. of Communication
Street address 3: Stevens Point
Street address state: WI
Zip/Postal code: 54481
Mailing address: Div. of Communication
Mailing city: Stevens Point
Mailing state: WI
Mailing zip: 54481
General Phone: (715) 346-3409
General Fax: (715) 346-4769
Classified Equipment»
Personnel: Richard Ilkka (Assoc. Dean/Head)

UNIVERSITY OF WISCONSIN-WHITEWATER

Street address 1: 800 W. Main St.
Street address 3: Whitewater
Street address state: WI
Zip/Postal code: 53190
Mailing address: 800 W Main St
Mailing city: Whitewater
Mailing state: WI
Mailing zip: 53190-1790
General Phone: (262) 472-1034
General Fax: (262) 472-1419
General/National Adv. E-mail: voglbaus@uww.edu
Classified Equipment»
Personnel: Sally Vogl-Bauer (Contact)

WEST VIRGINIA

BETHANY COLLEGE

Street address 1: Morlan Hall
Street address 3: Bethany
Street address state: WV
Zip/Postal code: 26032
Mailing address: Morlan Hall
Mailing city: Bethany
Mailing state: WV
Mailing zip: 26032
General Phone: (304) 829-7716
General Fax: (304) 829-7161
General/National Adv. E-mail: psutherl@bethanywv.edu
Classified Equipment»
Personnel: Patrick J. Sutherland (Chair/Assoc. Prof.); Michael King (Vstg. Prof./Dir., Stud. Pubs. Ctr.); Steve Cohen (Asst. Prof.); Jay Libby (Asst. Prof.); Keri Brown (Adj. Prof.); Jim Forbes (Adj. Prof.)

MARSHALL UNIVERSITY

Street address 1: 1 John Marshall Dr.
Street address 3: Huntington
Street address state: WV
Zip/Postal code: 25755-2622
Mailing address: 1 John Marshall Dr
Mailing city: Huntington
Mailing state: WV
Mailing zip: 25755-0003
General Phone: (304) 696-2360
General Fax: (304) 696-2732
General/National Adv. E-mail: sojmc@marshall.edu
Classified Equipment»
Personnel: Corley F. Dennison (Dean/Prof.); Charles G. Bailey (Prof.); Burnis Morris (Prof.); Janet L. Dooley (Assoc. Prof.); Rebecca J. Johnson (Assoc. Prof.); Marc Seamon (Assoc. Prof.); Allyson B. Goodman (Asst. Prof.); Dan W. Hollis (Asst. Prof.); Marilyn H. McClure (Asst. Prof.); Maryl Neff (Asst. Prof.); Joan E. Price (Asst. Prof.); Ruth Sullivan (Asst. Prof.); Sean Stewart (Instr.); Bill Bissett (Part-time Instr.); Sandy Savage (Part-time Instr.)

WEST VIRGINIA UNIVERSITY

Street address 1: 1511 University Ave.
Street address 3: Morgantown
Street address state: WV
Zip/Postal code: 26506-6010
Mailing address: PO Box 6010
Mailing city: Morgantown
Mailing state: WV
Mailing zip: 26506-6010
General Phone: (304) 293-3505
General Fax: (304) 293-3072
General/National Adv. E-mail: pireed@mail.wvu.edu
Primary Website: journalism.wvu.edu
Classified Equipment»
Personnel: Maryanne Reed (Dean/Prof.); John Temple (Associate Professor); Joel Beeson (Assoc. Prof.); Diana Knott Martinelli (Assoc. Dean/Assoc. Prof./Widmeyer Comm. Professorship in PR); Robert Britten (Asst. Prof.); Rita Colistra (Asst. Prof.); Sang (Sammy) Lee (Associate Professor); Stephen Urbanski (Director of Graduate Studies/Associate Professor); Cathy Mezera (Teaching Assistant Professor); Paul A. Atkins (Prof. Emer.); John H. Boyer (Prof. Emer.); Charles F. Cremer (Prof. Emer.); Robert M. Ours (Prof. Emer.); Guy H. Stewart (Prof. Emer./Dean Emer.); Hongmin Ahn (Assistant Professor); Alison Bass (Assistant Professor); Dana Coester (Assistant Professor); Emily Corio (Teaching Assistant Professor); Gina Martino Dahlia (Teaching Associate Professor); Jim Ebel (Harrison/Omnicom Chair, Visiting Assistant Professor); April Johnston (Teaching Assistant Professor); Mary Kay McFarland (Lecturer); Chad Mezera (Director of Online Programs); Elizabeth Oppe (Teaching Assistant Professor); Lois Raimondo (Shott Chair in Journalism, Asst. Prof.); Tom Stewart (Teaching Assistant Professor); Oliver Street (Assistant Dean, Student Services); Ivan Pinnell (Assoc. Prof.); Sara Magee (Asst. Prof.); Bonnie Stewart (Asst. Prof.); George Esper (Ogden Newspapers Vstg. Prof.); Richard Bebout (Lectr.); Jaine Boyles (Lectr.)

WYOMING

UNIVERSITY OF WYOMING

Street address 1: Dept. of Communication & Journalism
Street address 3: Laramie
Street address state: WY
Zip/Postal code: 82071-3904
Mailing address: Dept. of Communication & Journalism
Mailing city: Laramie
Mailing state: WY
Mailing zip: 82071-3904
General Phone: (307) 766-6277
General Fax: (307) 766-3812
General/National Adv. E-mail: klsmith@uwyo.edu
Primary Website: www.uwyo.edu/comm/index.htm
Classified Equipment»
Personnel: Ken Smith (Chair)

SENIOR PUBLICATION

ALASKA

ANCHORAGE

SENIOR VOICE

Street address 1: 3340 Arctic Blvd
Street address 2: Ste 106
Street address city: Anchorage
State: AK
Zip/Postal code: 99503-4550
County: Anchorage
Country: USA
Mailing address: 3340 Artic Blvd.
Mailing city: Anchorage
Mailing state: AK
Mailing zip: 99503
General Phone: (907) 276-1059
General Fax: (907) 278-6724
Advertising Phone: (907) 276-1059
Advertising Fax: (907) 278-6724
Editorial Phone: (907) 276-1059
Editorial Fax: (907) 278-6724
General/National Adv. E-mail: info@seniorvoicealaska.com
Display Adv. E-mail: execdiropag@gci.net
Editorial e-mail: seniorvoice@gci.net
Primary Website: www.seniorvoicealaska.com
Year Established: 1969
State: Arizona

ARIZONA

TEMPE

LOVIN' LIFE

Street address 1: 1900 W Broadway Road
Street address 2:
Street address city: Tempe
State: AZ
Zip/Postal code: 85282
County: Maricopa
Country: USA
Mailing address:
Mailing city:
Mailing state: AZ
Mailing zip:
General Phone:
General Fax: (480) 348-2109
Advertising Phone: (480) 898-5612
Editorial Phone: (480) 898-5612
General/National Adv. E-mail: christina@timeslocalmedia.com
Display Adv. E-mail: gordon@timeslocalmedia.com
Editorial e-mail: christina@timeslocalmedia.com
Primary Website: www.lovinlifeafter50.com
Year Established: 1979

LOVIN' LIFE AFTER 50

Street address 1: 1620 W. Fountainhead Parkway
Street address 2: Ste. 219
Street address city: Tempe
State: AZ
Zip/Postal code: 85282
County: Maricopa
Country: USA
Mailing address: 1620 W. Fountainhead Parkway, Ste. 219
Mailing city: Tempe
Mailing state: AZ
Mailing zip: 85282
General Phone: (480) 898-5612
General Fax: (480) 898-5606
General/National Adv. E-mail: info@lovinlife.com
Display Adv. E-mail: mhiatt@timespublications.com
Editorial e-mail: ndandrea@timespublications.com
Primary Website: lovinlife.com
Year Established: 1979
State: California

CALIFORNIA

SAN LUIS OBISPO

JOURNAL PLUS MAGAZINE

Street address 1: 654 Osos St
Street address city: San Luis Obispo
State: CA
Zip/Postal code: 93401-2713
County: San Luis Obispo
Country: USA
Mailing address: 654 Osos St
Mailing city: San Luis Obispo
Mailing state: CA
Mailing zip: 93401-2713
General Phone: (805) 546-0609
General Fax: (805) 546-8827
General/National Adv. E-mail: slojournal@fix.net
Primary Website: www.slojournal.com
State: Colorado

COLORADO

SENIOR VOICE

Street address 1: 1471 Front Nine Dr
Street address city: Fort Collins
State: CO
Zip/Postal code: 80525-9459
County: Larimer
Country: USA
Mailing address: 1471 Front Nine Dr
Mailing city: Fort Collins
Mailing state: CO
Mailing zip: 80525-9459
General Phone: (970) 223-9271
General Fax: (970) 223-9271
General/National Adv. E-mail: thevoice@frii.com
Primary Website: www.theseniorvoice.net
Year Established: 1980

GRAND JUNCTION

BEACON SENIOR NEWS

Street address 1: 524 30 Rd
Street address 2: Ste 4
Street address city: Grand Junction
State: CO
Zip/Postal code: 81504-4437
County: Mesa
Country: USA
Mailing address: PO Box 3895
Mailing city: Grand Junction
Mailing state: CO
Mailing zip: 81502-3895
General Phone: (970) 243-8829
General Fax: (800) 536-7516
Advertising Phone: (970) 243-8829
Advertising Fax: (800) 536-7516
Editorial Phone: (970) 243-8829
Editorial Fax: (800) 536-7516
General/National Adv. E-mail: brianmoffett123@gmail.com
Display Adv. E-mail: kevin@beaconseniornews.com
Classified Adv. e-mail: stacey@beaconseniornews.com
Editorial e-mail: cloie@beaconseniornews.com
Primary Website: www.beaconseniornews.com
Mthly Avg Views: 55000
Mthly Avg Unique Visitors: 10625
Year Established: 1987

MANITOU SPRINGS

LIFE AFTER 50

Street address 1: 329 Manitou Ave
Street address 2: Ste 103
Street address city: Manitou Springs
State: CO
Zip/Postal code: 80829-2590
County: El Paso
Country: USA
Mailing address: 329 Manitou Ave Ste 103
Mailing city: Manitou Springs
Mailing state: CO
Mailing zip: 80829-2590
General Phone: (719) 685-9690
General Fax: (719) 685-9705
General/National Adv. E-mail: dennis@pikespeakpublishing.com
Display Adv. E-mail: sales@pikespeakpublishing.com
Primary Website: www.pikespeakpublishing.com
State: Florida

FLORIDA

BOCA RATON

BOOMER TIMES AND SENIOR LIFE

Street address 1: 1515 N Federal Hwy
Street address 2: Ste 300
Street address city: Boca Raton
State: FL
Zip/Postal code: 33432-1994
County: Palm Beach
Country: USA
Mailing address: 1515 N Federal Hwy Ste 300
Mailing city: Boca Raton
Mailing state: FL
Mailing zip: 33432-1994
General Phone: (561) 736-8925
General Fax: (561) 369-1476
General/National Adv. E-mail: srlife@gate.net
Primary Website: www.babyboomers-seniors.com
Year Established: 1990
State: Georgia

GEORGIA

WARNER ROBINS

SENIOR NEWS

Street address 1: 115 Bigham Dr
Street address city: Warner Robins
State: GA
Zip/Postal code: 31088-3749
County: Houston
Country: USA
Mailing address: PO Box 8389
Mailing city: Warner Robins
Mailing state: GA
Mailing zip: 31095-8389
General Phone: (478) 929-3636
General Fax: (478) 929-4258
General/National Adv. E-mail: seniornewsga@aol.com
Display Adv. E-mail: seniornewsga@cox.net
Editorial e-mail: seniornewsga@cox.net
Primary Website: www.seniornewsgeorgia.com
Year Established: 1987
State: Iowa

IOWA

ASBURY

VERMONT MATURITY MAGAZINE

Street address 1: 6170 FOREST HILLS DR
Street address city: ASBURY
State: IA
Zip/Postal code: 52002-9349
County: Dubuque
Country: USA
Mailing address: 6170 FOREST HILLS DR
Mailing city: ASBURY
Mailing state: IA
Mailing zip: 52002-9349
General Phone: 5635577571
General Fax: 5635577641
Advertising Phone: 5635577571
Advertising Fax: 5635577641
Editorial Phone: 5635577571
Editorial Fax: 5635577641
General/National Adv. E-mail: VermontMaturityMagazine@gmail.com
Display Adv. E-mail: Robin@VermontMaturity.com
Classified Adv. e-mail: Robin@VermontMaturity.com
Editorial e-mail: Robin@VermontMaturity.com
Primary Website: www.vermontmaturity.com
Mthly Avg Views: 4214
Mthly Avg Unique Visitors: 3532
Year Established: 1993
State: Idaho

IDAHO

EAGLE

IDAHO SENIOR NEWS

Street address 1: 233 W State St
Street address 2: Ste E
Street address city: Eagle
State: ID
Zip/Postal code: 83616-4982
County: Ada
Country: USA
Mailing address: PO Box 937
Mailing city: Eagle
Mailing state: ID
Mailing zip: 83616-0937
General Phone: (208) 336-6707
General Fax: (208) 336-6752
Advertising Phone: (800) 657-6470
General/National Adv. E-mail: editor@idahoseniornews.com
Display Adv. E-mail: advertising@idahoseniornews.som
Editorial e-mail: editor@idahoseniornews.com
Primary Website: www.idahoseniornews.com
Year Established: 1978
State: Illinois

ILLINOIS

DUNDEE

DENBAR PUBLISHING, INC

Street address 1: PO Box 478
Street address city: Dundee
State: IL
Zip/Postal code: 60118-0478
County: Kane
Country: USA
Mailing address: PO Box 478
Mailing city: Dundee
Mailing state: IL
Mailing zip: 60118-0478
General Phone: (847) 931-0234
General Fax: (847) 697-6817
Advertising Phone: (847) 567-0234
Editorial Phone: (630) 531-1670
General/National Adv. E-mail: sn50andbetter@yahoo.com; info@sn50andbetter.com
Display Adv. E-mail: chisrnews@aol.com
Editorial e-mail: chgoseniornews@yahoo.com
Primary Website: www.sn50andbetter.com
Year Established: 1986
State: Kansas

KANSAS

OLATHE

THE BEST TIMES

Street address 1: 111 S Cherry St
Street address 2: Ste 3300
Street address city: Olathe
State: KS
Zip/Postal code: 66061-3487
County: Johnson
Country: USA
Mailing address: 111 South Cherry Street, Suite 3300
Mailing city: Olathe
Mailing state: KS
Mailing zip: 66061-7056
General Phone: (913) 715-8930
General Fax: (913) 715-0440
Advertising Phone: (913) 715-8920
Advertising Fax: (913) 715-0440
Editorial Phone: (913) 715-0736
Editorial Fax: (913) 715-0440
General/National Adv. E-mail: gerald.hay@jocogov.org
Display Adv. E-mail: cherell.bilquist@jocogov.org
Editorial e-mail: gerald.hay@jocogov.org
Primary Website: www.jocogov.org/thebesttimes
Year Established: 1982

WICHITA

THE ACTIVE AGE

Street address 1: 125 S West St
Street address 2: Ste 105
Street address city: Wichita
State: KS
Zip/Postal code: 67213-2114
County: Sedgwick
Country: USA
Mailing address: 125 S West St Ste 105
Mailing city: Wichita
Mailing state: KS
Mailing zip: 67213-2114
General Phone: (316) 942-5385
General Fax: (316) 946-9180
General/National Adv. E-mail: editor@theactiveage.com
Display Adv. E-mail: teresa@theactiveage.com
Editorial e-mail: fran@theactiveage.com
Primary Website: www.theactiveage.com
Year Established: 1979
State: Louisiana

LOUISIANA

SHREVEPORT

THE BEST OF TIMES

Street address 1: PO Box 19510
Street address city: Shreveport
State: LA
Zip/Postal code: 71149-0510
County: Caddo
Country: USA
Mailing address: PO Box 19510
Mailing city: Shreveport
Mailing state: LA
Mailing zip: 71149-0510
General Phone: (318) 636-5510
General/National Adv. E-mail: gary.calligas@gmail.com
Display Adv. E-mail: gary.calligas@gmail.com
Editorial e-mail: gary.calligas@gmail.com
Primary Website: www.thebestoftimesnews.com
Year Established: 1993
State: Massachusetts

MASSACHUSETTS

EAST LONGMEADOW

PRIME TIMES

Street address 1: 280 N Main St
Street address city: East Longmeadow
State: MA
Zip/Postal code: 01028-1868
County: Hampden
Country: USA
Mailing address: 280 N Main St
Mailing city: East Longmeadow
Mailing state: MA
Mailing zip: 01028-1868
General Phone: (413) 525-6661
General Fax: (413) 525-5882
General/National Adv. E-mail: news@thereminder.com
Primary Website: www.thereminder.com

FIFTY PLUS ADVOCATE

Street address 1: 131 Lincoln St
Street address city: Worcester
State: MA
Zip/Postal code: 01605-2408
County: Worcester
Country: USA
Mailing address: 131 Lincoln St
Mailing city: Worcester
Mailing state: MA
Mailing zip: 01605-2408
General Phone: (508) 752-2512
General Fax: (508) 752-9057
Advertising Phone: (508) 752-2512 x128
Display Adv. E-mail: rcapellari@fiftyplusadvocate.com
Primary Website: www.fiftyplusadvocate.com
Year Established: 1975
State: Maryland

MARYLAND

KENSINGTON

THE BEACON

Street address 1: 3720 Farragut Ave
Street address 2: Ste 105
Street address city: Kensington
State: MD
Zip/Postal code: 20895-2110
County: Montgomery
Country: USA
Mailing address: PO Box 2227
Mailing city: Silver Spring
Mailing state: MD
Mailing zip: 20915-2227
General Phone: (301) 949-9766
General Fax: (301) 949-8966
Advertising Phone: 301-949-9766
Advertising Fax: (301) 949-8966
Editorial Phone: (301) 949-9766
Editorial Fax: 301-949-8966
General/National Adv. E-mail: info@thebeaconnewspapers.com
Display Adv. E-mail: alan@thebeaconnewspapers.com
Editorial e-mail: barbara@thebeaconnewspapers.com
Primary Website: www.thebeaconnewspapers.com
Year Established: 1989
State: Michigan

MICHIGAN

ALLEGAN

SENIOR TIMES

Street address 1: 595 Jenner Dr
Street address city: Allegan
State: MI
Zip/Postal code: 49010-1516
County: Allegan
Country: USA
Mailing address: 595 Jenner Dr
Mailing city: Allegan
Mailing state: MI
Mailing zip: 49010-1516
General Phone: (269) 673-1720
General Fax: (269) 673-4761
General/National Adv. E-mail: debra.sloan@flashespublishers.com
Display Adv. E-mail: debra.sloan@flashespublishers.com
Primary Website: flashpublishers.com

BATTLE CREEK

SENIOR TIMES SOUTH CENTRAL MICHIGAN

Street address 1: 4642 Capital Ave SW
Street address city: Battle Creek
State: MI
Zip/Postal code: 49015-9305
County: Calhoun
Country: USA
Mailing address: 4642 Capital Ave SW
Mailing city: Battle Creek
Mailing state: MI
Mailing zip: 49015-9305
General Phone: (269) 979-1411
General Fax: (269) 979-3474
Advertising Phone: (269) 979-1479 x106
Editorial Phone: (269) 979-1412 x102
General/National Adv. E-mail: sherii@wwthayne.com
Display Adv. E-mail: sheriis@wwthayne.com
Editorial e-mail: sheriis@wwthayne.com
Primary Website: www.scenepub.com/seniortimes
Year Established: 1971

HOLLAND

WEST MICHIGAN SENIOR TIMES

Street address 1: 54 W 8th St
Street address city: Holland
State: MI
Zip/Postal code: 49423-3104
County: Ottawa
Country: USA
Mailing address: 54 W 8th St
Mailing city: Holland
Mailing state: MI
Mailing zip: 49423-3104
General Phone:
General Fax:
Advertising Phone: (269) 673-1701
Editorial Phone: (269) 673-1720
Display Adv. E-mail: tiffany.andrus@flashespublishers.com
Editorial e-mail: debra.sloan@flashespublishers.com
Primary Website: flashespublishers.com
Year Established: 1984
State: Minnesota

MINNESOTA

GOOD AGE

Street address 1: 1115 Hennepin Ave
Street address city: Minneapolis
State: MN
Zip/Postal code: 55403-1705
County: Hennepin
Country: USA
Mailing address: 1115 Hennepin Ave
Mailing city: Minneapolis
Mailing state: MN
Mailing zip: 55403-1705
General Phone: (612) 825-9205
General Fax: (612) 825-0929
Primary Website: www.mngoodage.com
Year Established: 1981
State: New Jersey

NEW JERSEY

NEPTUNE

SENIOR SCOOP

Street address 1: 3600 Highway 66
Street address city: Neptune
State: NJ
Zip/Postal code: 7754
County: Monmouth
Country: USA
Mailing address: PO Box 1550
Mailing city: Neptune
Mailing state: NJ
Mailing zip: 07754
General Phone: 732-922-6000
General Fax: (732) 557-5659
General/National Adv. E-mail: senscoop@app.com
Primary Website: www.app.com

PITMAN

THE GOLDEN TIMES

Street address 1: PO Box 134
Street address city: Pitman
State: NJ
Zip/Postal code: 08071-0134
County: Gloucester
Country: USA
Mailing address: PO Box 134
Mailing city: Pitman
Mailing state: NJ
Mailing zip: 08071-0134
General Phone: (856) 582-3940
General Fax: (801) 720-9176
Primary Website: www.thegoldentimes.com
State: New Mexico

NEW MEXICO

PRIME TIME

Street address 1: 6300 Montano Rd NW
Street address 2: Ste G3
Street address city: Albuquerque
State: NM
Zip/Postal code: 87120-1826
County: Bernalillo

Country: USA
Mailing address: PO Box 67560
Mailing city: Albuquerque
Mailing state: NM
Mailing zip: 87193
General Phone: (505) 888-0470
General/National Adv. E-mail: primetime@swcp.com
Editorial e-mail: primeedit@swcp.com
Primary Website: www.ptpubco.com
Year Established: 1991
State: New York

NEW YORK

BELLPORT

50+ LIFESTYLES

Street address 1: 146 S Country Rd
Street address 2: Ste 4
Street address city: Bellport
State: NY
Zip/Postal code: 11713-2530
County: Suffolk
Country: USA
Mailing address: 146 S Country Rd Ste 4
Mailing city: Bellport
Mailing state: NY
Mailing zip: 11713-2530
General Phone: (631) 286-0058
General Fax: (631) 286-6866
Advertising Phone: (877) 677-6397
General/National Adv. E-mail: tim@50plusny.com
Editorial e-mail: editor@50plusny.com
Primary Website: www.50plusny.com
Year Established: 1975

FOREVER YOUNG

Street address 1: 1738 Elmwood Ave
Street address 2: Ste 103
Street address city: Buffalo
State: NY
Zip/Postal code: 14207-2465
County: Erie
Country: USA
Mailing address: 1738 Elmwood Ave Suite 103
Mailing city: Buffalo
Mailing state: NY
Mailing zip: 14207-2465
General Phone: (716) 783-9119
General Fax: (716) 783-9983
General/National Adv. E-mail: calarlev@aol.com; circulation@buffalospree.com
Primary Website: www.foreveryoungwny.com
Year Established: 1988

WSN2DAY.COM

Street address 1: 629 Fifth Ave
Street address 2: Ste 213
Street address city: Pelham
State: NY
Zip/Postal code: 10803-3708
County: Westchester
Country: USA
Mailing address: 629 Fifth Ave Ste 213
Mailing city: Pelham
Mailing state: NY
Mailing zip: 10803-3708
General Phone: (914) 738-7869
General Fax: (914) 738-7876
General/National Adv. E-mail: shorelineproduction@gmail.com
Display Adv. E-mail: hp@shorelinepub.com
Editorial e-mail: hp@shorelinepub.com
Primary Website: www.shorelinepub.com
Year Established: 1992
State: Ohio

OHIO

NEW ALBANY

SENIOR TIMES

Street address 1: PO Box 623
Street address city: New Albany
State: OH
Zip/Postal code: 43054-0623
County: Franklin
Country: USA
Mailing address: PO Box 623
Mailing city: New Albany
Mailing state: OH
Mailing zip: 43054
General Phone: 6143372058
General Fax: (614) 337-2059
General/National Adv. E-mail: publisher@insight.rr.com
Display Adv. E-mail: publisher@insight.rr.com
Editorial e-mail: seniortimes@insight.rr.com
Primary Website: www.seniortimescolumbus.com
Year Established: 1983
State: Pennsylvania

PENNSYLVANIA

NEW HOPE

ICON MAGAZINE

Street address 1: PO Box 120
Street address city: New Hope
State: PA
Zip/Postal code: 18938-0120
County: Bucks
Country: USA
Mailing address: PO Box 120
Mailing city: New Hope
Mailing state: PA
Mailing zip: 18938-0120
General Phone: (215) 862-9558
General Fax: (215) 862-9845
General/National Adv. E-mail: trobba@comcast.net
Primary Website: www.icondv.com

MILESTONES

Street address 1: 642 N Broad St
Street address city: Philadelphia
State: PA
Zip/Postal code: 19130-3424
County: Philadelphia
Country: USA
Mailing address: 642 N Broad St
Mailing city: Philadelphia
Mailing state: PA
Mailing zip: 19130-3424
General Phone: (215) 765-9000
General Fax: (215) 765-9066
Advertising Phone: (215) 765-9000 ext. 5051
Editorial Phone: (215) 765-9000 ext 5081
General/National Adv. E-mail: MilestonesNews@pcaCares.org
Display Adv. E-mail: MilestonesNews@pcaCares.org
Editorial e-mail: MilestonesNews@pcaCares.org
Primary Website: www.pcaCares.org/milestones
Year Established: 1987
State: Tennessee

TENNESSEE

GRMANTOWN

THE BEST TIMES

Street address 1: 4646 Poplar Avenue3107 E. Corporate Edge Dr.
Street address 2: Ste 2
Street address city: Grmantown
State: TN
Zip/Postal code: 38138
County: Shelby
Country: USA
Mailing address: 3107 E. Corporate Edge Dri. #2
Mailing city: Germantown
Mailing state: TN
Mailing zip: 38138
General Phone: (901) 458-2911
General Fax: na
Advertising Phone: (901) 505-0945
Editorial Phone: (901) 505-0940
General/National Adv. E-mail: admin@thebesttimes.com
Display Adv. E-mail: jgrubbs@thebesttimes.com
Editorial e-mail: tjordan@thebesttimes.com
Primary Website: thebesttimes.com
Year Established: 1982

MATURE LIFESTYLES OF TENNESSEE

Street address 1: PO Box 857
Street address city: Lebanon
State: TN
Zip/Postal code: 37088-0857
County: Wilson
Country: USA
Mailing address: PO Box 857
Mailing city: Lebanon
Mailing state: TN
Mailing zip: 37088
General Phone: (615) 444-6008
General Fax: (615) 444-6818
Advertising Phone: (615) 444-6008
Editorial Phone: (615) 444-6008
General/National Adv. E-mail: bharville@mainstreetmediatn.com
Display Adv. E-mail: dgould@mainstreetmediatn.com
Editorial e-mail: bharville@mainstreetmediatn.com

FORWARD FOCUS

Street address 1: 174 Rains Ave
Street address city: Nashville
State: TN
Zip/Postal code: 37203-5319
County: Davidson
Country: USA
Mailing address: 174 Rains Ave
Mailing city: Nashville
Mailing state: TN
Mailing zip: 37203-5319
General Phone: (615) 743-3400
General Fax: (615) 743-3480
General/National Adv. E-mail: info@fiftyforward.org
Primary Website: www.fiftyforward.org
Year Established: 1956
State: Texas

TEXAS

LETTERS FROM NORTH AMERICA

Street address 1: 2002 N Greens Blvd
Street address city: Richmond
State: TX
Zip/Postal code: 77406-6673
County: FORT BEND
Country: USA
Mailing address: 2002 N. Greens Blvd
Mailing city: Richmond
Mailing state: TX
Mailing zip: 77406
General Phone: (512) 653-8545
General Fax: 832-201-9818
General/National Adv. E-mail: pperry@pearyperry.com
Primary Website: www.pearyperry.com
Mthly Avg Views: 5000
Mthly Avg Unique Visitors: 1000
Year Established: 1993

WACO

SENIORIFIC NEWS

Street address 1: PO Box 23307
Street address city: Waco
State: TX
Zip/Postal code: 76702-3307
County: McLennan
Country: USA
Mailing address: PO Box 23307
Mailing city: Waco
Mailing state: TX
Mailing zip: 76702-3307
General Phone: (800) 736-7350
General Fax: (877) 736-7350
Advertising Phone: (800) 736-7350
General/National Adv. E-mail: ads@seniorific.com
Display Adv. E-mail: Ads@Seniorific.com
Editorial e-mail: editor@Seniorific.com
Primary Website: seniorific.com
Year Established: 1988
State: Virginia

VIRGINIA

FIFTY PLUS

Street address 1: 1506 Staples Mill Rd
Street address 2: Ste 102
Street address city: Richmond
State: VA
Zip/Postal code: 23230-3631
County: Richmond City
Country: USA
Mailing address: 8010 Ridge Rd Ste F
Mailing city: Henrico
Mailing state: VA
Mailing zip: 23229-7288
General Phone: (804) 673-5203
General Fax: (804) 673-5308
Editorial Phone: (804) 673-4966
General/National Adv. E-mail: mail@richmondpublishing.com
Primary Website: www.fiftyplusrichmond.com
State: Washington

WASHINGTON

GAUGER MEDIA SERVICE, INC.

Street address 1: 1034 Bradford Street
Street address 2: P.O. Box 627
Street address city: Raymond
State: WA
Zip/Postal code: 98577
County: Pacific
Country: USA
Mailing address: P.O. Box 627
Mailing city: Raymond
Mailing state: WA
Mailing zip: 98577
General Phone: (360) 942-3560
General/National Adv. E-mail: dave@gaugermedia.com
Primary Website: www.gaugermedia.com
Year Established: 1987

TACOMA

SENIOR SCENE

Street address 1: 223 N Yakima Ave
Street address city: Tacoma
State: WA
Zip/Postal code: 98403-2230
County: Pierce
Country: USA
Mailing address: 223 N Yakima Ave
Mailing city: Tacoma
Mailing state: WA
Mailing zip: 98403-2230

General Phone: (253) 722-5687
General Fax: (253) 597-6456
Advertising Phone: (253) 722-5687
Advertising Fax: (253) 597-6456
General/National Adv. E-mail: seniormedia@lcsnw.org
Editorial e-mail: bdicskon@lcsnw.org
Primary Website: www.seniorscene.org
Year Established: 1975

VANCOUVER

SENIOR MESSENGER

Street address 1: 400 E Evergreen Blvd
Street address 2: Ste 111
Street address city: Vancouver
State: WA
Zip/Postal code: 98660-3263
County: Clark
Country: USA
Mailing address: 400 E Evergreen Blvd Ste 111
Mailing city: Vancouver
Mailing state: WA
Mailing zip: 98660-3263
General Phone: (360) 750-9900
General Fax: (360) 750-9907
General/National Adv. E-mail: circulation@seniormessenger.org
Display Adv. E-mail: ads@seniormessenger.org
Editorial e-mail: news@seniormessenger.org
Primary Website: www.vanmessenger.org
State: Wisconsin

WISCONSIN

FOND DU LAC

MATURITY TIMES

Street address 1: PO Box 1955
Street address city: Fond Du Lac
State: WI
Zip/Postal code: 54936-1955
County: Fond Du Lac
Country: USA
Mailing address: PO Box 1955
Mailing city: Fond Du Lac
Mailing state: WI
Mailing zip: 54936-1955
General Phone: (920) 922-8640
General Fax: (920) 922-0125
Display Adv. E-mail: classified@actionadvertiser.com
Editorial e-mail: scottw@actionprinting.com
Primary Website: www.actiononline.net
Year Established: 1987

VERONA

JOURNEY OF AGING

Street address 1: PO Box 930156
Street address city: Verona
State: WI
Zip/Postal code: 53593-0156
County: Dane
Country: USA
General Phone: (608) 274-5200
General Fax: (608) 848-5474
General/National Adv. E-mail: mary@ogarapub.com
Display Adv. E-mail: mary@ogarapub.com
Editorial e-mail: mary@ogarapub.com
Primary Website: www.JourneyofAging.com
Year Established: 1994
State: California

ONLINE ONLY

ARIZONA

TUCSONSENTINEL.COM

Street address 1: 1960 N. Painted Hills
Street address city: Tuscon
Street address state: AZ
Zip/Postal code: 85745
County: Pima
Country: USA
General Phone: (520) 302-5989
General/National Adv. E-mail: ads@tucsonsentinel.com
Editorial e-mail: news@tucsonsentinel.com
Primary Website: tucsonsentinel.com
Year Established: 2009
Areas Served - City/County or Portion Thereof, or Zip codes: Online Only
Parent company (for newspapers): Dylan Smith (Pub./Ed.); Maria Coxon-Smith (News/Engagement Ed.)

ARKANSAS

THE FAYETTEVILLE FLYER

Street address 1: 205 N College Ave
Street address city: Fayetteville
Street address state: AR
Zip/Postal code: 72701-4238
County: Washington
Country: USA
General Phone: (479) 966-4860
Advertising Phone: (479) 387-1002
General/National Adv. E-mail: contact@fayettevilleflyer.com
Primary Website: www.fayettevilleflyer.com
Mthly Avg Views: 200000
Parent company (for newspapers): Dustin Bartholomew (Co-Owner); Todd Gill (Co-Owner)
Newspapers (for newspaper groups): Wonderstate Media, LLC

CALIFORNIA

CALIFORNIA COURIER

Street address 1: PO Box 5390
Street address city: Glendale
Street address state: CA
Zip/Postal code: 91221-5390
County: Los Angeles
Country: USA
Mailing address: PO Box 5390
Mailing city: Glendale
Mailing state: CA
Mailing zip: 91207
Year Established: 1958
Areas Served - City/County or Portion Thereof, or Zip codes: Online daily
Avg Paid Circ: 0
Avg Free Circ: 12000
Audit By: Sworn/Estimate/Non-Audited
Audit Date: 12.[illegible]
Parent company (for newspapers): Harut Sassounian (Pub.)

CAMPUS NEWS

Street address 1: 15930 Harvest Moon Street
Street address city: La Puente
Street address state: CA

SACRAMENTO NEWS & REVIEW

Street address 1: PO Box 13370
Street address city: Sacramento
Street address state: CA
Zip/Postal code: 95813
County: Sacramento
Country: USA
Mailing address: PO Box 13370
Mailing city: Sacramento
Mailing state: CA
Mailing zip: 95813
General Phone: (916) 498-1234
Advertising Phone: (916) 498-1234
Editorial Phone: (916) 498-1234
Display Adv. E-mail: snradinfo@newsreview.com
Editorial e-mail: sactonewstips@newsreview.com
Primary Website: https://sacramento.newsreview.com/
Mthly Avg Views: 134000
Mthly Avg Unique Visitors: 43000
Year Established: 1989
Areas Served - City/County or Portion Thereof, or Zip codes: Online only
Audit By: CVC
Audit Date: 30.06.2018
Parent company (for newspapers): Jeff von Kaenel (President); Greg Erwin (Dist. Dir); Deborah Redmond (COO); Michael Gelbman (Sales Mgr.); Chris Terrazas (Design Mgr.)
Newspapers (for newspaper groups): Chico Community Publishing, Inc.

SACRAMENTO PRESS

Street address 1: PO Box 7981
Street address city: Citrus Heights
Street address state: CA
Zip/Postal code: 95621
County: CA
Country: USA
Mailing address: PO Box 7981
Mailing city: Citrus Heights
Mailing state: CA
Mailing zip: 95621
General Phone: (916) 572-7609
General/National Adv. E-mail: advertising@sacramentopress.com
Editorial e-mail: newstip@sacramentopress.com
Primary Website: sacramentopress.com
Year Established: 2008
Areas Served - City/County or Portion Thereof, or Zip codes: Online Only
Parent company (for newspapers): Bethany Harris (Editor); Cesar Alexander (Editorial Assistant)

SOUTH COAST EDITOR

Street address 1: 5319 University Drive
Street address 2: Suite 227
Street address city: Irvine
Street address state: CA
Zip/Postal code: 92612
County: Orange
Country: USA
General Phone: (949) 287-8330
General/National Adv. E-mail: editor@southcoasteditorcom
Primary Website: www.southcoasteditor.com
Areas Served - City/County or Portion Thereof, or Zip codes: Online Only
Parent company (for newspapers): Saboohi Currim (Ed.)

THE BERKELEY DAILY PLANET

Street address 1: 3023 Shattuck Ave
Street address city: Berkeley
Street address state: CA
Zip/Postal code: 94705
County: Alameda
Country: USA
Mailing address: PO Box 5534
Mailing city: Berkeley
Mailing state: CA
Mailing zip: 94705-0534
Editorial e-mail: news@berkeleydailyplanet.com
Primary Website: berkeleydailyplanet.com
Areas Served - City/County or Portion Thereof, or Zip codes: Online Only
Parent company (for newspapers): Mike O'Malley (Pub.); Becky O'Malley (Ed.)

THE UKIAH DAILY JOURNAL

Street address 1: 415 Talmage Rd Suite A
Street address city: Ukiah
Street address state: CA
Zip/Postal code: 95482-4912
County: Mendocino
Country: USA
Mailing address: 415 Talmage Rd Suite A
Mailing city: UKIAH
Mailing state: CA
Mailing zip: 95482-4912
General Phone: (707) 468-3500
Advertising Phone: (707) 468-3500
Editorial Phone: (707) 468-3500
General/National Adv. E-mail: udjemily@ukiahdj.com
Display Adv. E-mail: udjemily@ukiahdj.com
Classified Adv. e-mail: advertising@record-bee.com
Editorial e-mail: udj@ukiahdj.com
Primary Website: www.ukiahdailyjournal.com
Mthly Avg Views: 600000
Mthly Avg Unique Visitors: 90000
Year Established: 1860
Delivery Methods: Home & Garden (Apr); Redwood Empire Fair Official Program (Aug); Christmas Songbook (Dec); Auto Show (Feb); Ukiah Lifestyles/Almanac (Jul); Summer Fun Coupon Book (Jun); Holy Week Directory (Mar); Mother's Day Dining/Gift Guide (May); Homemakers School (O
Avg Paid Circ: 5070
Audit By: AAM
Audit Date: 30.09.2014
Parent company (for newspapers): Kevin McConnell (Pub.); Jody Martinez (Asst. Ed.); K.C. Meadows (Online Ed.); Sarah McGrath (General Manager/Advertising Manager); Brittany Dashiell (Webpage Ed.); Gail McAlister (Lake Mendo Group Dig. Dir.)
Newspapers (for newspaper groups): Digital First Media; MediaNews Group

THEWEEKLYDRIVER.COM

Street address 1: 122 43rd St
Street address city: Sacramento
Street address state: CA
Zip/Postal code: 95819-2102
County: Sacramento
Country: USA
Mailing address: 122 43rd Street
Mailing city: Sacramento
Mailing state: CA
Mailing zip: 95819
General Phone: (916) 508-5122
Advertising Phone: C
Editorial Phone: C
General/National Adv. E-mail: james@jamesraia.com
Display Adv. E-mail: james@jamesraia.com
Classified Adv. e-mail: james@jamesraia.com
Editorial e-mail: james@jamesraia.com
Primary Website: www.theweeklydriver.com
Mthly Avg Views: 10000
Mthly Avg Unique Visitors: 710000
Year Established: 2004
Areas Served - City/County or Portion Thereof, or Zip codes: daily
Personnel: The Weekly Driver is an automotive column featuring new and vintage car reviews and automotive news, www.theweeklydriver.com. It appears on Sunday in two newspapers in the Bay Area News Group as well as monthly in Gulfshore Business, a monthly business magazine in Naples, Florida.
Parent company (for newspapers): James Raia (Self-Syndicator)

COLORADO

BERTHOUD RECORDER ONLINE

Street address 1: 398 Wildbriar Lane
Street address city: Loveland
Street address state: CO
Zip/Postal code: 80537
County: Larimer
Country: USA
Mailing address: 398 Wildbriar Lane
Mailing city: Loveland
Mailing state: CO
Mailing zip: 80537
General Phone: (970) 532-3715
Advertising Phone: (970) 235-3715
Editorial Phone: (970) 532-3715
General/National Adv. E-mail: editor@berthoudrecorder.com
Display Adv. E-mail: editor@berthoudrecorder.com
Editorial e-mail: editor@berthoudrecorder.com
Primary Website: www.berthoudrecorder.com
Mthly Avg Views: 2000
Areas Served - City/County or Portion Thereof, or Zip codes: Online Only
Parent company (for newspapers): Gary Wamsley (Pub/Ed/Rep/Photo)

CONNECTICUT

THE CONNECTICUT MIRROR

Street address 1: 36 Russ Street
Street address city: Hartford
Street address state: CT
Zip/Postal code: 06106
County: Hartford
Country: USA
Mailing address: 36 Russ Street
Mailing city: Hartford
Mailing state: CT
Mailing zip: 06106
General Phone: (860) 218-6380
Advertising Phone: (860) 218-6380
Editorial Phone: 860-218-6380
General/National Adv. E-mail: bputterman@ctmirror.org
Display Adv. E-mail: bputterman@ctmirror.org
Editorial e-mail: ehamilton@ctmirror.org
Primary Website: www.ctmirror.org
Mthly Avg Views: 500000
Mthly Avg Unique Visitors: 190000
Parent company (for newspapers): Mark Pazniokas (Capital Bur. Chief); Bruce Putterman (CEO / Publisher); Elizabeth Hamilton (Executive Editor)
Newspapers (for newspaper groups): The Connecticut News Project, Inc.

THE NEW HAVEN INDEPENDENT

Street address 1: 51 Elm St.
Street address 2: Suite 307
Street address city: New Haven
Street address state: CT
Zip/Postal code: 06510
County: New Haven
Editorial e-mail: editor@newhavenindependent.org
Primary Website: newhavenindependent.org
Areas Served - City/County or Portion Thereof, or Zip codes: Online Only
Parent company (for newspapers): Paul Bass (Ed.); Melissa Bailey (Managing Editor)

FLORIDA

FLORIDA KEYS KEYNOTER

Street address 1: 3015 Overseas Hwy
Street address city: Marathon
Street address state: FL
Zip/Postal code: 33050-2236
County: Monroe
Country: USA
Mailing address: PO BOX 500158
Mailing city: MARATHON
Mailing state: FL
Mailing zip: 33050-0158
General Phone: (305) 376-4636
General/National Adv. E-mail: jpulis@flkeysnews.com
Display Adv. E-mail: jpulis@flkeysnews.com
Editorial e-mail: dgoodhue@flkeysnews.com
Primary Website: flkeysnews.com
Mthly Avg Views: 550000
Mthly Avg Unique Visitors: 175000
Year Established: 1953
Avg Paid Circ: 9400
Avg Free Circ: 1250
Audit By: Sworn/Estimate/Non-Audited
Audit Date: 16.09.2017
Parent company (for newspapers): David Goodhue (Ed./ Reporter); Glenn Brandt (Adv. Consult.); Omar Mercado (Local Adv. Mgr.); Gwen Filosa (Reporter)
Newspapers (for newspaper groups): The McClatchy Company

MUCKRAKER

Street address 1: 333 SE 2nd Ave
Street address 2: Suite 2000
Street address city: Miami
Street address state: FL
Zip/Postal code: 33131
County: Miami-Dade
Country: United States
General Phone: 786 795 0755
General/National Adv. E-mail: support@muckraker.com
Display Adv. E-mail: support@muckraker.com
Classified Adv. e-mail: support@muckraker.com
Editorial e-mail: support@muckraker.com
Primary Website: muckraker.com
Mthly Avg Views: 30000
Mthly Avg Unique Visitors: 20000
Year Established: 2022
News Services: Investigative Reporting, Multimedia Content, International News, Event Coverage
Audit By: Sworn/Estimate/Non-Audited
Parent company (for newspapers): Anthony Rubin (Founder, CEO)
Newspapers (for newspaper groups): Muckraker Media LLC

ILLINOIS

HEARTLAND NEWSFEED

Street address 1: 800 Capps Ave.
Street address city: Nokomis
Street address state: IL
Zip/Postal code: 62075
County: Montgomery
Country: USA
General Phone: 2175694230
Advertising Phone: 2175659709
Editorial Phone: 2177185281
General/National Adv. E-mail: jake.leonard@heartlandnewsfeed.com
Display Adv. E-mail: ads@heartlandnewsfeed.com
Classified Adv. e-mail: ads@heartlandnewsfeed.com
Editorial e-mail: jake.leonard@heartlandnewsfeed.com
Primary Website: https://www.heartlandnewsfeed.com
Mthly Avg Views: 225000
Mthly Avg Unique Visitors: 135000
Parent company (for newspapers): Jake Leonard (Editor-in-Chief)
Newspapers (for newspaper groups): Heartland Media Group of Central Illinois, LLC

PEOPLE'S WORLD

Street address 1: 3339 S Halsted St
Street address city: Chicago
Street address state: IL
Zip/Postal code: 60608-6882
County: Cook
Country: USA
Mailing address: 3339 S Halsted St
Mailing city: Chicago
Mailing state: IL
Mailing zip: 60608-6882
General Phone: (773) 446-9920
General Fax: (773) 446-9928
General/National Adv. E-mail: contact@peoplesworld.org
Primary Website: www.peoplesworld.org
Areas Served - City/County or Portion Thereof, or Zip codes: Online Only
Avg Paid Circ: 20000
Avg Free Circ: 1700
Audit By: Sworn/Estimate/Non-Audited
Audit Date: 08.11.2007
Parent company (for newspapers): John Wojcik (Ed.-in-Chief); Mariya Strauss (Mng. Ed.)

THE ONION

Street address 1: 212 W Superior St.
Street address 2: Suite 200
Street address city: Chicago
Street address state: IL
Zip/Postal code: 60654-3562
County: Cook
Country: USA
General Phone: (312) 751-0503
General Fax: (312) 751-4137
General/National Adv. E-mail: advertising@theonion.com
Primary Website: theonion.com
Areas Served - City/County or Portion Thereof, or Zip codes: Online Only
Avg Free Circ: 33785
Audit By: Sworn/Estimate/Non-Audited
Audit Date: 30.03.2010
Parent company (for newspapers): Joe Randazzo

INDIANA

THE JOURNAL GAZETTE

Street address 1: 600 W. Main Street, .O. Box 100
Street address city: FORT WAYNE
Street address state: IN
Zip/Postal code: 46802
County: Allen
Country: USA
Mailing address: 600 W Main St
Mailing city: Fort Wayne
Mailing state: IN
Mailing zip: 46802
General Phone: (260) 461-8679
Advertising Phone: (260) 461-8671
Editorial Phone: (260) 461-8377
Editorial Fax: (260) 461-8648
General/National Adv. E-mail: advertising@fwn.fortwayne.com
Display Adv. E-mail: advertising@fwn.fortwayne.com
Classified Adv. e-mail: classifieds@fwn.fortwayne.com
Editorial e-mail: jgnews@jg.net
Primary Website: www.journalgazette.net
Year Established: 1863
News Services: AP, Tribune News Services
Avg Paid Circ: 19854
Audit By: AAM
Audit Date: 31.03.2024
Personnel: For detailed production and mechanical information, see Fort Wayne Newspapers Inc. listing.
Parent company (for newspapers): Julie Inskeep (Pres./Pub.); Jim Chapman (Metro editor); Jim Touvell (Editor); Tom Pellegrene Jr. (Web/Social Media Editor); Sherry Skufca (Publisher); Terri Richardson (Features Ed.); Julie Inskeep (President, Journal Gazette Co.); Mark Jaworski (Sports editor); Lisa Green (Managing editor); Fred McKissack (Editorial page editor); Jeff ` Merritt (News desk editor); Devan Filchak (Metro editor); Corey McMaken (Features/ Engagement editor)
Newspapers (for newspaper groups): Ogden Newspapers Inc.; The Journal Gazette Co.; Fort Wayne Newspapers

IOWA

THEPERRYNEWS.COM

Street address 1: P.O. Box 382
Street address city: Perry
Street address state: IA
Zip/Postal code: 50220
County: Dallas
General/National Adv. E-mail: theperrynews@gmail.com
Display Adv. E-mail: theperrynews@gmail.com
Classified Adv. e-mail: theperrynews@gmail.com
Editorial e-mail: theperrynews@gmail.com
Primary Website: theperrynews.com
Mthly Avg Views: 200000
Mthly Avg Unique Visitors: 66000
Parent company (for newspapers): James Caufield (Editor and publisher)

KANSAS

MANHATTAN FREE PRESS

Street address 1: 313 Spruce
Street address city: Wamego
Street address state: KS
Zip/Postal code: 66547
County: Pottawatomie
Country: USA
Mailing state: KS
General Phone: (785) 556-1694
Advertising Phone: (785) 556-1694
General/National Adv. E-mail: freepress@kansas.net
Primary Website: manhattanfreepress.com
Year Established: 1991
Audit By: Sworn/Estimate/Non-Audited
Audit Date: 10.06.2019
Parent company (for newspapers): Jon Brake (Co-Pub); Linda Brake (Co-Pub)

KENTUCKY

BEECH TREE NEWS

Street address 1: PO Box 140
Street address city: Aberdeen
Street address state: KY
Zip/Postal code: 42201-0140
County: Butler
Country: USA
General Phone: (270) 526-9527
General Fax: (270) 526-2178
General/National Adv. E-mail: diane@beechtreenews.com
Primary Website: www.beechtreenews.com
Year Established: 2009
Areas Served - City/County or Portion Thereof, or Zip codes: Online Only
Parent company (for newspapers): Diane Dyer; John Embry

LEVISA LAZER

Street address 1: 1328 Gene Wilson Blvd
Street address city: Louisa
Street address state: KY
Zip/Postal code: 41230-9681
County: Lawrence
Primary Website: www.thelevisalazer.com
Year Established: 2008
Areas Served - City/County or Portion Thereof, or Zip codes: Online Only
Parent company (for newspapers): Mark Grayson (Ed.)

THE LOGAN JOURNAL

Street address 1: 2575 Bowling Green Rd
Street address city: Russellville
Street address state: KY
Zip/Postal code: 42276-9617
County: Logan
Country: USA
General Phone: (270) 772-1544
General/National Adv. E-mail: jimturner@loganjournal.com
Primary Website: www.loganjournal.com
Areas Served - City/County or Portion Thereof, or Zip codes: Online Only
Parent company (for newspapers): Jim Turner

MAINE

THE ORIGINAL IRREGULAR

Street address 1: PO Box 616
Street address city: Kingfield
Street address state: ME
Zip/Postal code: 04947
County: Franklin
Country: USA
Mailing address: PO BOX 616
Mailing city: KINGFIELD
Mailing state: ME
Mailing zip: 04947
General Phone: (207) 265-2773
General Fax: none
Advertising Phone: (207) 265-2773
Advertising Fax: none
Editorial Phone: (207) 265-2773
Editorial Fax: none
General/National Adv. E-mail: info@theirregular.com
Display Adv. E-mail: advertising@theirregular.com
Classified Adv. e-mail: classifieds@theirregular.com
Editorial e-mail: editor@theirregular.com
Primary Website: www.theirregular.com
Year Established: 1968
Avg Paid Circ: 1000
Avg Free Circ: 0
Audit By: Sworn/Estimate/Non-Audited
Audit Date: 10.06.2019
Parent company (for newspapers): Heidi Murphy (Publisher/Owner); Robert J. Gray (Ed.); Melanie Meldrum (Ad. Director)

MARYLAND

BALTIMORE POST-EXAMINER

Street address 1: PO Box 2094
Street address city: Columbia
Street address state: MD
Zip/Postal code: 21045-2094
County: Howard
Country: USA
General Phone: (443) 745-4363
General/National Adv. E-mail: BaltimorePostExaminer@gmail.com
Primary Website: baltimorepostexaminer.com
Mthly Avg Unique Visitors: 100000
Year Established: 2012
Areas Served - City/County or Portion Thereof, or Zip codes: Online Only
Personnel: Sister site is Los Angeles Post-Examiner
Parent company (for newspapers): Timothy Maier (Pub)

CURRENT

Street address 1: 6930 Carroll Avenue
Street address 2: Suite 625
Street address city: Takoma Park
Street address state: MD
Zip/Postal code: 20912
County: Montgomery
Country: USA
Mailing address: 6930 Carroll Avenue, Suite 625
Mailing city: Takoma Park

Mailing state: MD
Mailing zip: 20912
General Phone: (301) 270-7240
General Fax: (301) 270-7241
Advertising Phone: (301) 270-7240
Editorial Phone: (301) 270-7240
General/National Adv. E-mail: advertising@current.org
Display Adv. E-mail: publicmediajobs@current.org
Editorial e-mail: news@current.org
Primary Website: current.org
Mthly Avg Views: 115835
Mthly Avg Unique Visitors: 53235
Year Established: 1980
Areas Served - City/County or Portion Thereof, or Zip codes: Print edition of curated content and special coverage published 8 times per year
Personnel: Current started as a biweekly print trade newspaper in 1980. In 2019, we will publish all 8 print editions plus two digital only editions through ISSUU.
Parent company (for newspapers): Julie Drizin (Exec. Dir.); Karen Everhart (Mng. Ed.); Mike Janssen (Dig. Ed.); Dru Sefton (Sr. Ed.); Tyler Falk (Asst. Ed.); Laura Rogers (Business Manager)

MICHIGAN

LATINO PRESS

Street address 1: 6301 Michigan Ave
Street address city: Detroit
Street address state: MI
Zip/Postal code: 48210-2954
County: Wayne
Country: USA
Mailing address: 6301 Michigan Ave
Mailing city: Detroit
Mailing state: MI
Mailing zip: 48210-2954
General Phone: (313) 361-3000
General Fax: (313) 361-3001
Advertising Phone: (313) 361-3000
Editorial Phone: (313) 361-3002
General/National Adv. E-mail: clau@latinodetroit.com
Display Adv. E-mail: marketing@latinodetroit.com
Classified Adv. e-mail: clau@latinodetroit.com
Editorial e-mail: editorial@latinodetroit.com
Primary Website: www.latinodetroit.com
Mthly Avg Views: 16000
Mthly Avg Unique Visitors: 19000
Year Established: 1993
Delivery Methods:
Avg Paid Circ: 2500
Avg Free Circ: 15000
Audit By: Sworn/Estimate/Non-Audited
Audit Date: 12.07.2019
Parent company (for newspapers): Elias M. Gutierrez (President)

THE ECHO, THE UNIVERSITY OF OLIVET

Street address 1: 320 S Main St
Street address city: Olivet
Street address state: MI
Zip/Postal code: 49076-9406
County: Eaton
Country: USA
Mailing address: 320 S. Main St.
Mailing city: Olivet
Mailing state: MI
Mailing zip: 49076-9456
General Phone: (269) 749-7622
General/National Adv. E-mail: echo@uolivet.edu
Display Adv. E-mail: echo@uolivet.edu
Editorial e-mail: echo@uolivet.edu
Primary Website: www.ocecho.com
Year Established: 1888
Areas Served - City/County or Portion Thereof, or Zip codes: Online
Parent company (for newspapers): Joanne Williams (Advisor); Brian Freiberger (Editor); Bray Wright (Editor); Josh Edwards (Editor)

MINNESOTA

MINNPOST

Street address 1: 900 6th Avenue SE, Suite 220
Street address city: Minneapolis
Street address state: MN
Zip/Postal code: 55414
County: Hennepin
Country: USA
General Phone: (612) 455-6950
General Fax: (612) 455-6960
Advertising Phone: (612) 455-6953
General/National Adv. E-mail: info@minnpost.com
Primary Website: minnpost.com
Mthly Avg Views: 1000000
Mthly Avg Unique Visitors: 450000
Year Established: 2007
Areas Served - City/County or Portion Thereof, or Zip codes: Online Only
Personnel: MinnPost is a 501(c)3 nonprofit corporation.
Parent company (for newspapers): Andrew Wallmeyer (Publisher & CEO); Corey Anderson (Web Editor); Sally Waterman (Ad. Director); Andrew Putz (Editor)

MISSOURI

PARENT TO PARENT

Street address 1: 2464 Taylor Rd
Street address 2: Ste 131
Street address city: Wildwood
Street address state: MO
Zip/Postal code: 63040-1222
County: St. Louis
Country: USA
Mailing address: 2464 Taylor Rd Ste 131
Mailing city: Wildwood
Mailing state: MO
Mailing zip: 63040-1222
General Phone: (636) 458 8800
General Fax: (636) 458-7688
General/National Adv. E-mail: editor@parenttoparent.com
Editorial e-mail: emparenttoparent@gmail.com
Primary Website: www.parenttoparent.com
Year Established: 1996
Areas Served - City/County or Portion Thereof, or Zip codes: Online and St. Louis Post-Dispatch online
Personnel: Self syndicated
Parent company (for newspapers): Jodie Lynn (Owner); Kyle Johnson (Personal Assistant Assistant Editor)

MONTANA

NEW WEST

Street address 1: 415 N Higgins Ave
Street address 2: Suite 103
Street address city: Missoula
Street address state: MT
Zip/Postal code: 59802
County: Missoula
Country: USA
General Phone: (877) 343-5207
General/National Adv. E-mail: advertise@newwest.net
Editorial e-mail: info@newwest.net

NEBRASKA

THE CATHOLIC VOICE

Street address 1: 2222 N. 111th St.
Street address city: Omaha
Street address state: NE
Zip/Postal code: 68164
County: Douglas
Country: USA
Mailing address: 2222 N. 111th St.
Mailing city: Omaha
Mailing state: NE
Mailing zip: 68164
Audit Date: 19.10.2017
Parent company (for newspapers): Most Rev. George J. Lucas (Pub.); Randy Grosse (Adv. Mgr.); Mike May (Editor)

NEW HAMPSHIRE

AMHERST CITIZEN

Street address 1: 16 Pine Acres Rd
Street address city: Amherst
Street address state: NH
Zip/Postal code: 03031-2710
County: Hillsborough
Country: USA
Mailing state: NH
General Phone: 6036205835
General Fax: 6036205835
Advertising Phone: 6036205835
Advertising Fax: None
Editorial Phone: 6036205835
Editorial Fax: None
General/National Adv. E-mail: jaswales@mac.com
Display Adv. E-mail: jaswales@mac.com
Classified Adv. e-mail: None
Editorial e-mail: jaswales@mac.com
Primary Website: amherstcitizen.net
Year Established: 1992
Areas Served - City/County or Portion Thereof, or Zip codes: Suspended TFN @6-15-23
Audit Date: 10.06.2019
Personnel: Suspended TFN @6-15-23 in favor of new site launched 9-16-23. Want info? email: publisher@amherstcitizen.com
Parent company (for newspapers): Cliff Ann Wales (Pub./Ed.); James Wales (Adv. Dir.)
Newspapers (for newspaper groups): None

NEW JERSEY

ATLANTIC HIGHLANDS HERALD

Street address 1: 25 Second Avenue
Street address city: Atlantic Highlands
Street address state: NJ
Zip/Postal code: 07716
County: Monmouth
General/National Adv. E-mail: allan@ahherald.com
Primary Website: ahherald.com
Mthly Avg Views: 30000
Mthly Avg Unique Visitors: 15000
Year Established: 1999
Areas Served - City/County or Portion Thereof, or Zip codes: Online Only
Personnel: We exclude many foreign visitors and bots.
Parent company (for newspapers): Allan Dean (Pub. & Ed.)

THEMONMOUTHJOURNAL.COM

Street address 1: 421 Higgins Avenue
Street address 2: No. 300
Street address city: Brielle
Street address state: NJ
Zip/Postal code: 08730
County: Monmouth
Country: USA
General Phone: (732) 747-7007
Advertising Phone: 7327477007
Editorial Phone: 7327477007
General/National Adv. E-mail: info@themonmouthjournal.com
Display Adv. E-mail: sales@themonmouthjournal.com
Editorial e-mail: news@themonmouthjournal.com
Primary Website: themonmouthjournal.com
Mthly Avg Views: 200000
Mthly Avg Unique Visitors: 75000
Year Established: 2004
Audit By: Sworn/Estimate/Non-Audited
Audit Date: 10.10.2023
Parent company (for newspapers): Susan Paviluk (Gen. Mgr.); Ryan Walker (Sales Associate); Douglas Paviluk (Editor & Publisher); Lori Schwartz (Sales Associate); Paul Gundlach (Photographer); Ryan Walker (Sales Associate); Douglas Paviluk (Publisher); Lori Schwartz (Sales Associate); Paul Gundlach (Photographer); Gary Chapman (Ed.)
Newspapers (for newspaper groups): Monmouth News Media, LLC; Monmouth News Media, LLC

VAILSBURG LEADER

Street address 1: 1291 Stuyvesant Ave
Street address city: Union
Street address state: NJ
Zip/Postal code: 07083-3823
County: Union
Country: USA
Mailing address: PO Box 3639
Mailing city: Union
Mailing state: NJ
Mailing zip: 07083-1596
General Phone: (908) 686-7700
General Fax: (908) 686-4169
General/National Adv. E-mail: ads@thelocalsource.com
Display Adv. E-mail: class@thelocalsource.com
Editorial e-mail: editorial@thelocalsource.com
Primary Website: www.essexnewsdaily.com
Year Established: 1949
Avg Paid Circ: 41
Audit By: CAC
Audit Date: 30.09.2008
Personnel: E-Edition Only
Parent company (for newspapers): David Worrall (Pub.); Raymond Worrall (Gen. Mgr.); Peter Worrall (Adv. Mgr.); Nancy Worrall
Newspapers (for newspaper groups): Worrall Community Newspapers, Inc.

NEW YORK

GARY JAMES PRESENTS

Street address 1: 111 Shearin Ave
Street address city: East Syracuse
Street address state: NY
Zip/Postal code: 13057-1847
County: Onondaga
Country: USA
Mailing address: 111 Shearin Ave.
Mailing city: East Syracuse
Mailing state: NY
General/National Adv. E-mail: garyjames111@hotmail.com
Editorial e-mail: jim@jamespollock.com
Primary Website: www.classicbands.com
Mthly Avg Views: 250000
Mthly Avg Unique Visitors: 350000
Personnel: I am a Celebrity Interviewer for 2 websites: www.classicbands.com Click: Rock And Roll Interviews And: www.famousinterview.com Click: Interviews
Parent company (for newspapers): Gary James (Feature Interviewer/ Investigative Journalist)
Newspapers (for newspaper groups): Classicbands.com; Classicbands.com

GOTHAM GAZETTE

Street address 1: 299 Broadway
Street address 2: Suite 700
Street address city: New York
Street address state: NY
Zip/Postal code: 10007
County: Manhattan
Country: USA
General Phone: (212) 227-0342
General Fax: (212) 227-0345
General/National Adv. E-mail: advertise@gothamgazette.com
Editorial e-mail: info@gothamgazette.com
Primary Website: gothamgazette.com
Year Established: 1999
Areas Served - City/County or Portion Thereof, or Zip codes: Online Only
Parent company (for newspapers): Ben Max (Exec. Ed.)

Newspapers (for newspaper groups): Citizens Union Foundation

THE BATAVIAN

Street address 1: 200 E. Main St.
Street address 2: Suite 5
Street address city: Batavia
Street address state: NY
Zip/Postal code: 14020
County: NY
Country: USA
Mailing address: 200 E. Main St. #5
Mailing city: Batavia
Mailing state: NY
Mailing zip: 14020
General Phone: (585) 250-4118
General/National Adv. E-mail: lisa@thebatavian.com
Display Adv. E-mail: lisa@thebatavian.com
Editorial e-mail: billie@thebatavian.com
Primary Website: thebatavian.com
Mthly Avg Views: 1500000
Mthly Avg Unique Visitors: 120000
Year Established: 2008
Areas Served - City/County or Portion Thereof, or Zip codes: Online Only
Parent company (for newspapers): Howard Owens (Pub); Billie Owens (Ed.); Lisa Ace (Sales/Mktg. Coord.)

THE FISCAL TIMES

Street address 1: 712 5th Ave
Street address 2: Fl 17
Street address city: New York
Street address state: NY
Zip/Postal code: 10019-4108
County: Manhattan
Country: USA
General Phone: (212) 313-9680
General Fax: (877) 291-7606
General/National Adv. E-mail: info@thefiscaltimes.com
Primary Website: www.thefiscaltimes.com
Areas Served - City/County or Portion Thereof, or Zip codes: Online Only
Parent company (for newspapers): Jacqueline Leo (Ed.-in-Chief); Jeff Czaplicki (Acct. Mgr.)

THE HUFFINGTON POST

Street address 1: 770 Broadway
Street address city: New York
Street address state: NY
Zip/Postal code: 10012
County: Manhattan
Country: USA
General Phone: (212) 652-6400
General/National Adv. E-mail: blogteam@huffingtonpost.com
Primary Website: huffingtonpost.com
Areas Served - City/County or Portion Thereof, or Zip codes: Online Only
Parent company (for newspapers): Karen Mahabir (Managing Editor); Arianna Huffington (Pres.); Lydia polgreen (Ed.-in-Chief)

THE NEW YORK SUN

Street address 1: 105 Chambers St.
Street address 2: 2nd Floor
Street address city: New York
Street address state: NY
Zip/Postal code: 10007-3516
County: Manhattan
Country: USA
Mailing address: 105 Chambers St Fl 2
Mailing city: New York
Mailing state: NY
Mailing zip: 10007-3516
General Phone: (212) 406-2000
General Fax: (212) 571-9836
Advertising Phone: (212) 901-2700
General/National Adv. E-mail: inquiries@nysun.com
Display Adv. E-mail: advertising@nysun.com; classified@nysun.com
Editorial e-mail: editor@nysun.com
Primary Website: www.nysun.com
News Services: AP, Bloomberg, Jerusalem Post, Chicago Sun-Times, Daily Telegraph.
Areas Served - City/County or Portion Thereof, or Zip codes: Online Only
Avg Paid Circ: 45763
Audit Date: 30.09.2004
Parent company (for newspapers): John Garrett (Dir., Classified); Linda Seto (Circ. Dir.); Seth Lipsky (Ed.); Ira Stoll (Mng. Ed.); Dave Propson (Art Ed.); Richard Thomson (Bus. Ed.); Emily Gitter (Features Ed.); Michael Woodsworth (Sports Ed.)

THE PELHAMS-PLUS

Street address 1: P.O. Box 8605
Street address city: Pelham
Street address state: NY
Zip/Postal code: 10803
County: Westchester
Country: USA
General Phone: (914) 738-8717
General/National Adv. E-mail: maggieklein@pelhamweekly.com
Primary Website: www.pelhamwplus.com
Year Established: 1992
Areas Served - City/County or Portion Thereof, or Zip codes: Online Only
Avg Paid Circ: 2200
Avg Free Circ: 40
Audit By: Sworn/Estimate/Non-Audited
Audit Date: 16.07.2013
Parent company (for newspapers): Margaret A. Klein (Ed.)
Newspapers (for newspaper groups): Klein Information Resources, Inc.

NORTH CAROLINA

CREATIVE LOAFING CHARLOTTE

Street address 1: 1000 NC Music Factory Blvd
Street address 2: Apt C2
Street address city: Charlotte
Street address state: NC
Zip/Postal code: 28206-6010
County: Mecklenburg
Country: USA
Mailing address: 1000 NC MUSIC FACTORY BLVD APT C2
Mailing city: CHARLOTTE
Mailing state: NC
Mailing zip: 28206-6010
General Phone: (704) 522-8334
General Fax: (704) 522-8088
General/National Adv. E-mail: Publisher@yesweekly.com
Primary Website: http://clclt.com/
Year Established: 1987
Avg Free Circ: 40000
Audit By: Sworn/Estimate/Non-Audited
Audit Date: 18.12.2017
Newspapers (for newspaper groups): Womack Newspapers, inc

OHIO

THE TIMES BULLETIN

Street address 1: 1167 Westwood Drive
Street address 2: Suite 101
Street address city: Van Wert
Street address state: OH
Zip/Postal code: 45891
County: Van Wert
Country: USA
Mailing address: P.O. Box 271
Mailing city: Van Wert
Mailing state: OH
Mailing zip: 45891-0271
General Phone: (419) 238-2285
General Fax: (419) 238-0447
Advertising Phone: (419) 238-2285
Advertising Fax: (419) 238-0447
Editorial Phone: (419) 238-2285
Editorial Fax: (419) 238-0447
General/National Adv. E-mail: info@timesbulletin.com
Display Adv. E-mail: nswaney@timesbulletin.com
Classified Adv. e-mail: nswaney@timesbulletin.com
Editorial e-mail: editor@timesbulletin.com
Primary Website: www.timesbulletin.com
Mthly Avg Views: 362782
Mthly Avg Unique Visitors: 78299
Year Established: 1844
Delivery Methods: Spring Sports Magazine (Apr); Fall Sports Magazine (Aug); Christmas Greetings (Dec); Progress (Jan); Weddings II (Jun); Agriculture Almanac (Mar); Graduation (May); Holiday Traditions (Nov); Weddings III (Oct); PrimeTime (Quarterly); Home Improvement (Sep
Avg Paid Circ: 2050
Audit By: Sworn/Estimate/Non-Audited
Audit Date: 06.10.2021
Parent company (for newspapers): Ray Geary (COO); Kirsten Barnhart (News Ed.); Nikki Swaney (Advertising Representative); Chris Howell (Sports Editor); Mike Marchek (Cir. Mgr.); Robin Pennell (Editor); Karrie Macke (Graphics)
Newspapers (for newspaper groups): Delphos Herald, Inc.

PENNSYLVANIA

GANT DAILY

Street address 1: 219 S 2nd St
Street address city: Clearfield
Street address state: PA
Zip/Postal code: 16830-2205
County: Clearfield
Country: USA
Mailing address: PO Box 746
Mailing city: Clearfield
Mailing state: PA
Mailing zip: 16830-0746
General Phone: (814) 765-5256
General Fax: (814) 765-5631
General/National Adv. E-mail: dkilmer@gantdaily.com
Display Adv. E-mail: sales@gantdaily.com
Editorial e-mail: jshirey@gantdaily.com
Primary Website: www.gantdaily.com
Mthly Avg Unique Visitors: 300000
Year Established: 2006
Areas Served - City/County or Portion Thereof, or Zip codes: Online Only
Parent company (for newspapers): Christene Dahlem (Pres.); Jessica Shirey (Ed.); Ray Serafini (Adv./Digital Media Sales); Morgan Dubensky (Bus. Dev't. Mgr.)
Newspapers (for newspaper groups): Gant Media LLC

LINGLESTOWN GAZETTE

Street address 1: 6204 Elmer Ave.
Street address city: Linglestown
Street address state: PA
Zip/Postal code: 17112
County: Dauphin
Country: USA
General Phone: (717) 512-0722
General/National Adv. E-mail: linglestowngazette@gmail.com
Primary Website: linglestowngazette.com
Mthly Avg Views: 300
Mthly Avg Unique Visitors: 2000
Areas Served - City/County or Portion Thereof, or Zip codes: Online Only
Parent company (for newspapers): Bill Bostic (Ed./Pub.)

PHILADELPHIA JEWISH VOICE

Street address 1: 327 Pembroke Road
Street address city: Bala Cynwyd
Street address state: PA
Zip/Postal code: 19004
County: Montgomery
Country: USA
General Phone: (610) 649-1454
General Fax: (610) 649-0255
Advertising Phone: (215) 849-2312
Editorial Phone: (610) 649-0998
General/National Adv. E-mail: ads@pjvoice.org
Display Adv. E-mail: ads@pjvoice.org
Editorial e-mail: editor@pjvoice.com
Primary Website: pjvoice.org
Mthly Avg Views: 10000
Mthly Avg Unique Visitors: 9000
Year Established: 2005
Areas Served - City/County or Portion Thereof, or Zip codes: Online Only
Parent company (for newspapers): Daniel Loeb (Pub); Ronit Tretman (Food Editor); Bonnie Squires (President); Ken Myers (VP)

PHILLYVOICE.COM

Street address 1: 1430 Walnut St
Street address city: Philadelphia
Street address state: PA
Zip/Postal code: 19102
County: Philadelphia
Country: USA
General Phone: (26) 519-4500
General/National Adv. E-mail: Sales@PhillyVoice.com
Primary Website: PhillyVoice.com
Areas Served - City/County or Portion Thereof, or Zip codes: Online Only
Parent company (for newspapers): Lexie Norcross (Exec. Dir); Matt Romanoski (Exe. Ed.); Bob McGovern (Exec. Ed.); Hal Donnelly (VP of Sales/Mktg.)
Newspapers (for newspaper groups): WWB Holdings, LLC

RHODE ISLAND

RHODY BEAT

Street address 1: 1944 Warwick Avenue
Street address city: Warwick
Street address state: RI
Zip/Postal code: 02889
County: Kent
Country: USA
Mailing address: 1944 Warwick Avenue
Mailing city: Warwick
Mailing state: RI
Mailing zip: 02889
General Phone: (401) 732-3100
General Fax: (401) 732-3110
General/National Adv. E-mail: suzannew@rhodybeat.com
Display Adv. E-mail: sueh@rhodybeat.com
Primary Website: rhodybeat.com
Areas Served - City/County or Portion Thereof, or Zip codes: Online Only
Parent company (for newspapers): Richard G. Fleischer (Gen. Mgr.); John Howell (Pub./Beacon Ed.)
Newspapers (for newspaper groups): Beacon Communications, Inc

TENNESSEE

CHATTANOOGAN.COM

Street address 1: 100 Cherokee Boulevard
Street address 2: #109
Street address city: Chattanooga
Street address state: TN
Zip/Postal code: 37405
County: Hamilton
Country: USA
Mailing address: PO Box 2331
Mailing city: Chattanooga
Mailing state: TN
Mailing zip: 37409-0331
General Phone: (423) 266-2325
General/National Adv. E-mail: news@chattanoogan.com
Primary Website: www.chattanoogan.com
Areas Served - City/County or Portion Thereof, or Zip codes: Online Only
Parent company (for newspapers): John Wilson (Pub.)

TEXAS

COASTAL BEND LEGAL & BUSINESS NEWS

Street address 1: 526 Mediterranean Drive
Street address city: Corpus Christi
Street address state: TX

Zip/Postal code: 78418-3967
County: Nueces
Country: USA
Mailing address: PO Box 270607
Mailing city: Corpus Christi
Mailing state: TX
Mailing zip: 78427-0607
General Phone: 361-937-4907
General Fax: 361-937-1849
General/National Adv. E-mail: info@cbinews.com
Display Adv. E-mail: info@cbinews.com
Classified Adv. e-mail: info@cbinews.com
Editorial e-mail: cbinews@cbinews.com
Primary Website: www.cbinews.com
Parent company (for newspapers): Kim Gutierrez (Pub./Ed./Adv. Dir.)

DAILYTRIB.COM

Street address 1: 1007 AVENUE K
Street address city: MARBLE FALLS
Street address state: TX
Zip/Postal code: 78654-5039
County: Burnet
Country: USA
Mailing address: PO BOX 10
Mailing city: MARBLE FALLS
Mailing state: TX
Mailing zip: 78654-0010
General Phone: (830) 693-7152
General Fax: (830) 693-3085
General/National Adv. E-mail: advertising@thepicayune.com
Display Adv. E-mail: advertising@thepicayune.com
Classified Adv. e-mail: advertising@thepicayune.com
Editorial e-mail: editor@thepicayune.com
Primary Website: www.dailytrib.com
Mthly Avg Views: 89000
Mthly Avg Unique Visitors: 21500
Year Established: 1991
Avg Free Circ: 26000
Audit By: Sworn/Estimate/Non-Audited
Audit Date: 01.10.2016
Parent company (for newspapers): Mandy Wyatt (Associate Publisher); Amber Weems (Pres./Pub./Adv. Sales)
Newspapers (for newspaper groups): Victory Publishing Co., Ltd.

THE PAPER

Street address 1: 23503 Briarcreek Blvd.
Street address city: Spring
Street address state: TX
Zip/Postal code: 77373
County: Harris
Country: USA
Mailing address: 23503 Briarcreek Blvd.
Mailing city: Spring
Mailing state: TX
Mailing zip: 77373
General Phone: (832) 296-6887
Advertising Phone: (832) 296-6887
Editorial Phone: 8322966887
General/National Adv. E-mail: bobgunner@gmail.com
Display Adv. E-mail: bobgunner@gmail.com
Editorial e-mail: bobgunner@gmail.com
Primary Website: thepapermagazine.com
Year Established: 2008
Areas Served - City/County or Portion Thereof, or Zip codes: Online Only Daily
Parent company (for newspapers): Bob Gunner (Pub./Ed.)

THE TEXAS TRIBUNE

Street address 1: 823 Congress Ave.
Street address 2: Suite 1400
Street address city: Austin
Street address state: TX
Zip/Postal code: 78701
County: Travis
Country: USA
General Phone: (512) 716-8600
General Fax: (512) 716-8601
Advertising Phone: (512) 716-8634
General/National Adv. E-mail: ahinkle@texastribune.org
Primary Website: texastribune.org
Mthly Avg Views: 3632933
Mthly Avg Unique Visitors: 617068
Areas Served - City/County or Portion Thereof, or Zip codes: Online Only
Parent company (for newspapers): Emily Ramshaw (Ed.-in-Chief); Ross Ramsey (Exec. Editor); Maggie Gilburg (Development Director); April Hinkle (CRO & Advertising)

VIRGINIA

FAUQUIER NOW

Street address 1: 50 Culpeper St
Street address 2: Suite 3
Street address city: Warrenton
Street address state: VA
Zip/Postal code: 20188
County: Fauquier
Country: USA
Mailing address: PO BOX 3090
Mailing city: Warrenton
Mailing state: VA
Mailing zip: 20188
Areas Served - City/County or Portion Thereof, or Zip codes: Online Only
Parent company (for newspapers): Ellen Emerson (Pub.); Lawrence Emerson (Ed.)

LIFESITENEWS.COM, INC

Street address 1: 4 Family Life Lane
Street address city: Front Royal
Street address state: VA
Zip/Postal code: 22630
County: Warren
Country: USA
Mailing state: VA
General Phone: (888) 678-6008
General Fax: (540) 635-4374
Advertising Phone: (888) 678-6008 ext 928
General/National Adv. E-mail: cmaagad@lifesitenews.com
Display Adv. E-mail: cmaagad@lifesitenews.com
Classified Adv. e-mail: cmaagad@lifesitenews.com
Editorial e-mail: editor@lifesitenews.com
Primary Website: www.lifesitenews.com
Mthly Avg Views: 4000000
Mthly Avg Unique Visitors: 2200000
Year Established: 1997
Areas Served - City/County or Portion Thereof, or Zip codes: Online Only
Parent company (for newspapers): Clare Maagad (Adv. Mgr.); Patrick Craine (Editor / Journalist); John Jalsevac (Managing Ed.); John-Henry Westen (Ed. & Chief); Steve Jalsevac (Managing Director); Lisa Bourne (Journalist / Photographer); Claire Chretien (Journalist); Doug Bean (Journalist); Doug Mainwaring (Journalist); Diane Montagna (Rome Correspondent); Lianne Laurence (Journalist); Diane Montagna (Rome Correspondent); Martin Barillas (Journalist); Calvin Freiberger (Journalist); Rebecca Fidero (Business Manager)

WASHINGTON

CROSSCUT

Street address 1: 401 Mercer St
Street address city: Seattle
Street address state: WA
Zip/Postal code: 98109
County: King
Country: USA
General Phone: (206) 382-6137
General Fax: (206) 443-6691
General/National Adv. E-mail: advertising@crosscut.com
Primary Website: www.crosscut.com
Areas Served - City/County or Portion Thereof, or Zip codes: Online Only
Parent company (for newspapers): Greg Hascom (Ed.-in-Chief); Tamara Power-Drutis (Exec. Dir.); Jonah Fruchter (Acc. Mgr.); Joe Copeland (Ed.)

GAUGER MEDIA SERVICE, INC.

Street address 1: 1034 Bradford Street
Street address 2: P.O. Box 627
Street address city: Raymond
Street address state: WA
Zip/Postal code: 98577
County: Pacific
Country: USA
Mailing city: Raymond
Mailing state: WA
Parent company (for newspapers): Dave Gauger (Now Retired)

SEATTLE POST-INTELLIGENCER

Street address 1: 2901 3rd Ave
Street address 2: Suite 120
Street address city: Seattle
Street address state: WA
Zip/Postal code: 98121
County: King
Country: USA
General Phone: (206) 448-8030
General Fax: (206) 515-5577
Advertising Phone: (206) 448-8036
Advertising Fax: (206) 493-0993
Editorial Phone: (206) 464-2496
Editorial Fax: (206) 382-6760
General/National Adv. E-mail: advertising@seattlepi.com
Editorial e-mail: citydesk@seattlepi.com
Primary Website: WWW.seattlepi.com
Year Established: 2009
News Services: AP, WP, Bloomberg, MCT-LAT
Delivery Methods: Outdoor living (Feb); Opening Day Boating (Apr); Seattle Home Show (Feb); Careers (Jan); High Tech Employment (Jul); Health & Fitness (Jun); High Tech Employment (Mar); Spring Home and Garden (May); Restaurant Guide (Nov);Summer Guide (May); Spring Home Design (May); Architecture (Sep); Fall Arts Guide (Sep); Travel (Oct); Fall Home Design (Oct); Wine (Nov); Holiday Cuisine (Nov); Arts (Dec)
Areas Served - City/County or Portion Thereof, or Zip codes: Online Only
Avg Paid Circ: 221665
Audit By: AAM
Audit Date: 30.09.2012
Parent company (for newspapers): Ryan Blethen (Assoc. Pub./ Editorial Ed.); Suki Dardarian (Mng. Ed.); Sarah Rupp (Exec. Prod.); Denise Clifton (Dir. of Visuals); Leon Espinoza (Exec. News Ed.); Michael Shepard (Sr. VP, Bus. Ops.); Buster Brown (Sr. VP, Finance); Jill Mackie (VP, Public Affairs); Eileen Takeuchi (VP/CFO); Chris Biencourt (Dir., Labor Rel./Safety); Anna Bertrand (Mktg. Dir., New Media); Dominic Gates (Aerospace/Boeing Reporter)
Newspapers (for newspaper groups): Metro Newspaper Advertising Services, Inc.-OOB

THE STRANGER

Street address 1: 800 Maynard Ave. South
Street address 2: Ste 200
Street address city: Seattle
Street address state: WA
Zip/Postal code: 98134
County: King
Country: USA
Mailing address: 800 Maynard Ave. South, Suite 200
Mailing city: Seattle
Mailing state: WA
Mailing zip: 98134
General Phone: (206) 323-7101
Advertising Phone: (206) 323-7101
Advertising Fax: (206) 325-4865
Editorial Phone: (206) 323-7101
Editorial Fax: (206) 323-7203
General/National Adv. E-mail: press@thestranger.com
Display Adv. E-mail: adinfo@thestranger.com
Editorial e-mail: editor@thestranger.com
Primary Website: www.thestranger.com
Mthly Avg Views: 1553148
Mthly Avg Unique Visitors: 492116
Year Established: 1991
Areas Served - City/County or Portion Thereof, or Zip codes: Daily, Monday-Friday, online only
Audit Date: 30.[illegible]
Personnel: The Stranger stopped publishing a print edition in March 2020 when the coronavirus hit and went online only.
Parent company (for newspapers): Tim Keck (Publisher); Laurie Saito (Publisher); Chase Burns (Editor); Ben Demar (Senior Account Rep); Christopher Frizzelle (Mng. Ed.); Dan Savage (Ed.); Katie Phoenix (Senior Account Rep); Rob Crocker (President); Erica Tarrant (Prodn. Mgr.)
Newspapers (for newspaper groups): Index Newspapers LLC

WEST VIRGINIA

HUNTINGTONNEWS.NET

Street address 1: 528 Ridgewood Rd
Street address city: Huntington
Street address state: WV
Zip/Postal code: 25701-4852
County: Cabell
Country: USA
General Phone: (304) 654-0087
Advertising Phone: (304) 840-1555
Editorial Phone: (304) 544-8160
General/National Adv. E-mail: hnn.ads@gmail.com
Editorial e-mail: trutherford@huntingtonnews.net
Primary Website: www.huntingtonnews.net
Year Established: 2000
Areas Served - City/County or Portion Thereof, or Zip codes: Online Only
Parent company (for newspapers): Matt Pinson (Pub./Owner); Tony Rutherford (Ed.); Dale Anderson II (Adv. Dir.)

WISCONSIN

MYSHEBOYGAN.COM

Street address 1: P.O. Box 33
Street address city: Kohler
Street address state: WI
Zip/Postal code: 53044
County: Sheboygan
Country: USA
General Phone: (920) 917-6311
General/National Adv. E-mail: ads@mysheboygan.com
Editorial e-mail: news@mysheboygan.com
Primary Website: mysheboygan.com
Mthly Avg Views: 100000
Year Established: 2012
Areas Served - City/County or Portion Thereof, or Zip codes: Online Only
Parent company (for newspapers): Jane Van Treeck (News Dir.)

Section III

Services & Organizations in the U.S. and Canada

ADVERTISING/CIRCULATION AND NEWSPAPER PROMOTION SERVICES

FLORIDA

WELLINGTON

WINGO, LLC

Street address 1: 12161 Ken Adams Way
Street address 2: Ste 110J
Street address 3: Wellington
Street address state: FL
Zip/Postal code: 33414-3194
County: Palm Beach
Country: USA
Mailing address: 12161 Ken Adams Way Suite 110J
Mailing city: Wellington
Mailing state: FL
Mailing zip: 33414
General Phone: (561) 379-2635
General/National Adv. E-mail: sat@amerimarketing.com
Display Adv. E-mail: info@amerimarketing.com
Primary Website: www.wingopromo.com; www.amerimarketing.com
Year Established: 1980
Own Printing Facility: N
Commercial printers: Y

NEW MEXICO

SANTA FE

LYON ENTERPRISES

Street address 1: 4305 Cloud Dance
Street address 3: Santa Fe
Street address state: NM
Zip/Postal code: 87507-2591
County: Santa Fe
Country: USA
Mailing address: 4305 Cloud Dance
Mailing city: Santa Fe
Mailing state: NM
Mailing zip: 87507
General Phone: (800) 243-1144
General Fax: (505) 471-1665
General/National Adv. E-mail: ray@lyonenterprises.com
Primary Website: www.lyonenterprises.com
Year Established: 1992
Industry: Circulation Equipment & Supplies; Tubes, Racks (Includes Racks: Motor Route Tubes); Carrier Bags; Point of Purchase; Imprinted Merchandise
Personnel: Ray Lyon (Pres.)

ALTERNATIVE DELIVERY SERVICE

ARIZONA

TUCSON

TUCSON NEWSPAPERS/TMC

Street address 1: 4850 S Park Ave
Street address 3: Tucson
Street address state: AZ
Zip/Postal code: 85714-1637
County: Pima
Country: USA
Mailing address: 4850 S Park Ave
Mailing city: Tucson
Mailing state: AZ
Mailing zip: 85714-1637
General Phone: (520) 573-4167
General Fax: (520) 807-8418
General/National Adv. E-mail: adserv@azstarnet.com
Primary Website: www.azstarnet.com
Personnel: Circ. Dept. (Circ.); Adv. Dept. (Adv.)

CALIFORNIA

HERMOSA BEACH

EASY READER

Street address 1: PO Box 427
Street address 2: 832 Hermosa Ave
Street address 3: Hermosa Beach
Street address state: CA
Zip/Postal code: 90254-0427
County: Los Angeles
Country: USA
Mailing address: PO Box 427
Mailing city: Hermosa Beach
Mailing state: CA
Mailing zip: 90254-0427
General Phone: (310) 372-4611
General Fax: (424) 212-6708
General/National Adv. E-mail: easyreader@easyreader.info
Display Adv. E-mail: classifiedads@easyreader.info; displayads@easyreader.info
Editorial e-mail: news@easyreader.info
Primary Website: http://www.easyreadernews.com/
Year Established: 1970
Delivery Methods: Mail`Newsstand`Carrier`Racks
Area Served - City: 90254, 90266, 90277, 90288, 90245. 90272, 90274
Advertising (Open Inch Rate) Weekday/Saturday: Open inch rate $20.00
Mechanical specifications: Type page 10 1/2 x 11 1/2; E - 4 cols, 2 1/4, 1/6 between; A - 4 cols, 2 1/4, 1/6 between; C - 7 cols, 1 1/4, 1/6 between.
Published: Thur
Avg Paid Circ: 27684
Audit By: AAM
Audit Date: 3/31/2015
Note: Easy Reader is the largest circulation, weekly newspaper serving the South Bay area of Los Angeles.
Personnel: Kevin Cody (Adv. Mgr.); Amy Berg (Dispaly Sales); Erin McCoy (Display Sales); Tami Quattrone (Classifieds); Bondo Wyszpolski (Arts/Entertainment Ed.); Mark McDermott (News Ed.); Graciela Huerta (Prodn. Dir.); Richard Budman
Parent company (for newspapers): C-VILLE Holdings LLC

SACRAMENTO

ADCO MARKETING

Street address 1: 5580 Power Inn Rd
Street address 3: Sacramento
Street address state: CA
Zip/Postal code: 95820-6748
County: Sacramento
Country: USA
Mailing address: 5580 Power Inn Rd
Mailing city: Sacramento
Mailing state: CA
Mailing zip: 95820-6748
General Phone: (916) 388-1101
General Fax: (916) 388-1040
Personnel: Dick Avery (Pres.)

BEE NICHE PRODUCTS

Street address 1: 2100 Q St
Street address 3: Sacramento
Street address state: CA
Zip/Postal code: 95816-6816
County: Sacramento
Country: USA
Mailing address: PO Box 15779
Mailing city: Sacramento
Mailing state: CA
Mailing zip: 95852-0779
General Phone: (916) 321-1000
General Fax: (916) 326-5578
General/National Adv. E-mail: jpaquette@sacbee.com
Primary Website: www.sacbee.com
Year Established: 1983
Personnel: Linda Brooks (Vice-President, Human Resources)
Parent company (for newspapers): The McClatchy Company

SAN JOSE

A & A DISTRIBUTION, INC.

Street address 1: 1780 Rogers Ave
Street address 3: San Jose
Street address state: CA
Zip/Postal code: 95112-1109
County: Santa Clara
Country: USA
Mailing address: PO Box 26991
Mailing city: San Jose
Mailing state: CA
Mailing zip: 95159-6991
General Phone: (408) 436-2300
General Fax: (408) 436-0844
General/National Adv. E-mail: maustinjr2@gmail.com
Primary Website: www.aa-distribution.net
Year Established: 1970
Personnel: Manuel Austin (Pres.)

SANTA ANA

SPECIALIZED MARKETING SERVICES

Street address 1: 3421 W Segerstrom Ave
Street address 3: Santa Ana
Street address state: CA
Zip/Postal code: 92704-6404
County: Orange
Country: USA
Mailing address: 3421 W Segerstrom Ave
Mailing city: Santa Ana
Mailing state: CA
Mailing zip: 92704-6404
General Phone: (949) 553-0890
General Fax: (949) 553-0891
Primary Website: www.teamsms.com
Year Established: 1988

VICTORVILLE

DAILY PRESS

Street address 1: 13891 Park Ave
Street address 3: Victorville
Street address state: CA
Zip/Postal code: 92392-2435
County: San Bernardino
Country: USA
Mailing address: 13891 Park Ave
Mailing city: Victorville
Mailing state: CA
Mailing zip: 92392-2435
General Phone: (760) 241-7744
General Fax: (760) 241-7145
Advertising Phone: (760) 951-6288
Advertising Fax: (760) 241-7145
Editorail Phone: (760) 951-6270
Editorial Fax: (760) 241-7145
General/National Adv. E-mail: rlipscomb@vvdailypress.com
Display Adv. E-mail: acallahan@vvdailypress.com
Classified Adv. E-mail: acallahan@vvdailypress.com
Editorial e-mail: DKeck@vvdailypress.com
Primary Website: www.vvdailypress.com
Year Established: 1937
Advertising (Open Inch Rate) Weekday/Saturday: Open inch rate $40
Published: Mon`Tues`Wed`Thur`Fri`Sat`Sun
Weekday Frequency: m
Saturday Frequency: m
Avg Paid Circ: 8877
Avg Free Circ: 437
Sat. Circulation Paid: 8877
Sat. Circulation Free: 437
Sun. Circulation Paid: 10443
Sun. Circulation Free: 312
Audit By: AAM
Audit Date: 12/31/2018
Personnel: Steve Hunt (Pub.); Mario Mejia (Circ. Mgr.); Steve Nakutin (Interim Advertising Mgr.); Jason Vrtis (Ed.)
Parent company (for newspapers): CherryRoad Media

COLORADO

DENVER

ROAD RUNNER COURIER

Street address 1: 1760 Ulster St
Street address 3: Denver
Street address state: CO
Zip/Postal code: 80220-2053
County: Denver
Country: USA
Mailing address: 1760 Ulster St
Mailing city: Denver
Mailing state: CO

Mailing zip: 80220-2053
General Phone: (833) 303-7874
Primary Website: rrcourier.com
Year Established: 1970
Personnel: Arnold Rundiks (Pres.)

ENGLEWOOD

YANKEE PEDDLER POSTAL SERVICE

Street address 1: 3375 S Bannock St
Street address 3: Englewood
Street address state: CO
Zip/Postal code: 80110-2404
County: Arapahoe
Country: USA
Mailing address: PO Box 1851
Mailing city: Englewood
Mailing state: CO
Mailing zip: 80150-1851
General Phone: (303) 761-4200
General Fax: (303) 761-4291
General/National Adv. E-mail: addenver@aol.com
Primary Website: http://www.yankeepeddlerpostal.com/
Personnel: John Minger (Treasurer)

CONNECTICUT

BRIDGEPORT

CONNECTICUT POST

Street address 1: 410 State St
Street address 3: Bridgeport
Street address state: CT
Zip/Postal code: 06604-4501
County: Fairfield
Country: USA
Mailing address: 301 Merritt 7 - Suite 1
Mailing city: Norwalk
Mailing state: CT
Mailing zip: 06851-1075
General Phone: (203) 842-2500
General Fax: (203) 738-1230
General/National Adv. E-mail: circulation@ctpost.com
Primary Website: www.connpost.com
Personnel: John Alcott (Mng. Ed.); Ralph Hohman (Asst. Mng. Ed.); Randi Weiner (Asst. Mng. Ed.)

GEORGIA

ATLANTA

ATLANTA JOURNAL-CONSTITUTION

Street address 1: 223 Perimeter Center Pkwy NE
Street address 3: Atlanta
Street address state: GA
Zip/Postal code: 30346-1301
County: Dekalb
Country: USA
Mailing address: 223 PERIMETER CENTER PKWY NE
Mailing city: ATLANTA
Mailing state: GA
Mailing zip: 30346-1301
General Phone: (404) 526-7003
General Fax: (404) 526-5746
Advertising Phone: (404) 577-5775
Editorail Phone: (404) 526-2161
Editorial Fax: (404) 526-5746
General/National Adv. E-mail: allen.dunstan@coxinc.com
Display Adv. E-mail: eric.myers@ajc.com
Classified Adv. E-mail: ajcclass@ajc.com
Editorial e-mail: newstips@ajc.com
Primary Website: www.ajc.com
Mthly Avg Unique Visitors: 4808000
Year Established: 1868
News Services: Cox News Service, AP, DJ, LAT-WP, NYT, MCT, CNS, CQ, NNS, PNS, SHNS, TMS.
Special Editions: Breast Cancer Education (Annually); Golf/Masters (Apr); Back to School (Aug); Holiday Gift Guides (Dec); Brides (Feb); Safety Vehicles (Jan); Peachtree Road Race (Jul); Executive Homes (Jun); Braves Baseball Preview (Mar); Fun in the Sun (May); Pulse (Mon
Special Weekly Sections: Food & Drink (Thur); Go Guide, Cars (Fri); AJC Cars (Sat); Homefinder, Business, Jobs (Sun)
Syndicated Publications: Color Comics (S).
Delivery Methods: Mail`Newsstand`Carrier`Racks
Area Served - City: 30002 30004 30005 30008 30009 30011 30012 30013 30014 30016 30017 30018 30019 30021 30022 30024 30025 30028 30030 30032 30033 30034 30035 30038 30039 30040 30041 30043 30044 30045 30046 30047 30052 30054 30055 30056 30058 30060 30062 30064 30066 30067 30068 30071 30075 30076 30078 30079 30080 30082 30083 30084 30087 30088 30092 30093 30094 30096 30097 30101 30102 30103 30104 30105 30106 30107 30108 30110 30113 30114 30115 30116 30117 30120 30121 30122 30124 30125 30126 30127 30132 30134 30135 30137 30141 30143 30144 30145 30147 30152 30153 30157 30161 30165 30168 30170 30171 30172 30173 30176 30178 30179 30180 30183 30184 30185 30187 30188 30189 30204 30213 30214 30215 30220 30223 30228 30229 30233 30236 30238 30248 30250 30252 30253 30259 30260 30263 30265 30268 30269 30272 30273 30274 30276 30277 30281 30288 30290 30291 30294 30295 30296 30297 30303 30305 30306 30307 30308 30309 30310 30311 30312 30313 30314 30315 30316 30317 30318 30319 30320 30322 30324 30326 30327 30328 30329 30331 30334 30336 30337 30338 30339 30340 30341 30342 30344 30345 30346 30349 30350 30354 30360 30361 30363 30501 30504 30506 30507 30510 30517 30518 30519 30523 30525 30527 30528 30529 30533 30534 30542 30548 30549 30554 30564 30566 30577 30601 30605 30606 30607 30620 30621 30622 30642 30655 30656 30666 30677 30680 30683 30701 30733 31024 31029 31030 31061 31088 31201
Own Printing Facility: Y
Commercial printers: N
Advertising (Open Inch Rate) Weekday/Saturday: Open inch rate $566.00 (Mon-Wed); $585.00 (Thur-Sat)
Advertising (Open inch rate) Sunday: Open inch rate $755.00
Market Information: ADS; Split run; TMC; Zoned editions.
Mechanical available: Offset; Black and 3 ROP colors; insert accepted - zoned areas; page cutoffs - 21 1/4.
Mechanical specifications: Type page 12 5/8 x 21 1/4; E - 6 cols, 1 13/16, 1/8 between; A - 6 cols, 1 13/16, 1/8 between; C - 10 cols, 1 1/16, 1/8 between.
Published: Mon`Tues`Wed`Thur`Fri`Sat`Sun
Weekday Frequency: m
Saturday Frequency: m
Avg Paid Circ: 139864
Sat. Circulation Paid: 127777
Sun. Circulation Paid: 207476
Audit By: AAM
Audit Date: 6/30/2018
Pressroom Equipment: Lines -- 4-TKS/(20 half decks; 4 satellites) (Gwinnett); 2-TKS/7000CD tower units (Gwinnett); 4-TKS/(20 half decks; 4 satellites) (Fulton); Folders -- 8-TKS/(Fulton), 8-TKS/(Gwinnett); Reels & Stands -- 40, 40.;
Mailroom Eqipment: Counter Stackers -- 13-SH/257 (Fulton), 16-QWI/300-350 (Gwinnett); Inserters & Stuffers -- 1-NP/1472, 3-QWI/201, 4-QWI/200 (Reach), 2-GMA/SLS 2000 30:2 (Gwinnett), 1-GMA/SLS 2000 36:2 (Gwinnett), 1-QWI/400 (Reach); Tying Machines -- 11-Si/Fulton, 14;
Buisness Equipment: IBM/9672 RC4
Buisness Software: CA, Global
Classified Equipment: Hardware -- 145-IBM/3192, 2-Ad Star;
Classified Software: In-house.
Display Equipment: Hardware -- IBM 9672; Other Hardware -- IBM/7060H75
Display Software: Ad Make-up Applications -- NW/Admarc, NW/Discuss; Layout Software -- DTI/Speed Planner.
Editorial Equipment: Hardware -- 620-APP/Mac, 175-APP/Mac Powerbook/18-Sun/Server, 2-Dell/Gu55 Server; Printers -- HP, Xante, Canon
Editorial Software: DTI.
Production Equipment: Hardware -- 4-KFM/Bender single width, 2-Cx/Bidco, Glunz & Jensen/K2; Cameras -- 4-C/Spartan; Scanners -- 1-Howtek, 2-ECR/1800, 2-ECR/Autokon 1000, 2-Pixel Craft (tab size), 1-Scitex/Smartscan, 1-Tecsa/TS2470, 1-Tecsa/TS2570
Production Software: DTI.
Personnel: Amy Chown (VP, Marketing); Laura Inman (Dir., Mktg. Devel.); Chris Hood (Mktg. Mgr., Classified/Territory); Amy Glennon (Pub.); Kevin Riley (Ed.); Eric Myers (VP, Adv. Sales); Allen Dunstan (Sr. Dir., Nat'l Accts.); Brian Cooper (Sr. VP, Finance & Business Op.); Mark Medici (Sr. VP, Audience & Group Lead for CMG Newspapers); Joe McKinnon (VP, Fulfillment)
Parent company (for newspapers): Cox Media Group
footnotes: General/National Adv. E-mail: SRDS (11/5/2014); Display Adv. E-mail: SRDS (11/5/2014); Special Weekly Sections: SRDS (11/5/2014); Advertising (Open Inch Rate) Weekday/Saturday: SRDS (11/5/2014); Advertising (Open inch rate) Sunday: SRDS (11/5/2014)

IOWA

CEDAR RAPIDS

THE GAZETTE COMPANY

Street address 1: 501 2nd Ave SE
Street address 3: Cedar Rapids
Street address state: IA
Zip/Postal code: 52401-1303
County: Linn
Country: USA
Mailing address: 501 2nd Ave SE
Mailing city: Cedar Rapids
Mailing state: IA
Mailing zip: 52401-1303
General Phone: (319) 398-8422
General Fax: (319) 368-8505
General/National Adv. E-mail: customercare@thegazettecompany.com
Primary Website: www.thegazettecompany.com
Year Established: 1981
Product or Service: Multimedia/Interactive Products`Publisher/Media
Personnel: Joe Hadky (Chrmn.); Chuck Peters (President and CEO); Chris Edwards (VP Sales & Marketing)
Newspaper (for newspapers group): The Gazette, Cedar Rapids; The Fairfield Ledger, Fairfield

THE PENNY SAVER

Street address 1: 100 E Cumberland St
Street address 3: Cedar Rapids
Street address state: IA
Zip/Postal code: 52401
County: Linn
Country: USA
Mailing address: 500 3rd Ave SE
Mailing city: Cedar Rapids
Mailing state: IA
Mailing zip: 52401-1608
General Phone: (319) 398-8222
General Fax: (319) 398-5846
Primary Website: pennysaverguide.com
Personnel: Ron Bode (Adv. Dir.)

ILLINOIS

ANTIOCH

ADS DELIVERY, INC.

Street address 1: 236 W Il Route 173
Street address 3: Antioch
Street address state: IL
Zip/Postal code: 60002-1834
County: Lake
Country: USA
Mailing address: 236 W Il Route 173
Mailing city: Antioch
Mailing state: IL
Mailing zip: 60002-1834
General Phone: (847) 395-7500
General Fax: (847) 395-2814
General/National Adv. E-mail: advertising@advertisernetwork.com
Primary Website: www.advertisernetwork.com
Year Established: 1976
Personnel: Kris Shepard (Administrative Dir.)

KENTUCKY

LEXINGTON

COMMUNITY DELIVERY SERVICE

Street address 1: 1010 E New Circle Rd
Street address 3: Lexington
Street address state: KY
Zip/Postal code: 40505-4117
County: Fayette
Country: USA
Mailing address: 1010 E New Circle Rd
Mailing city: Lexington
Mailing state: KY
Mailing zip: 40505-4117
General Phone: (859) 231-3382
General Fax: (859) 231-3450
Year Established: 1989

LOUISIANA

ALEXANDRIA

ALEXANDRIA DAILY TOWN TALK

Street address 1: 1201 3rd St
Street address 3: Alexandria
Street address state: LA
Zip/Postal code: 71301-8246
County: Rapides
Country: USA
Mailing address: PO Box 7558
Mailing city: Alexandria
Mailing state: LA
Mailing zip: 71306-0558
General Phone: (318) 487-6409
General Fax: (318) 487-2952
Primary Website: www.thetowntalk.com
Year Established: 1883
Personnel: Melissa Gregory (Breaking News Reporter); Melinda Martinez (Photo.); Jeff Mathews (Storyteller); Patrick Denofrio (Reg. Sales Dir.); Jim Smilie (News Dir.)

BATON ROUGE

THE ADVOCATE NEWSPAPER

Street address 1: 7290 Bluebonnet Blvd
Street address 3: Baton Rouge
Street address state: LA
Zip/Postal code: 70810-1611
County: East Baton Rouge
Country: USA
Mailing address: PO Box 588
Mailing city: Baton Rouge
Mailing state: LA
Mailing zip: 70821-0588
General Phone: (225) 383-1111
General Fax: (225) 388-0348
General/National Adv. E-mail: lruth@theadvocate.com
Primary Website: www.theadvocate.com
Year Established: 1992
Published: Mon`Tues`Wed`Thur`Fri`Sat`Sun
Avg Paid Circ: 43475
Avg Free Circ: 44244
Audit By: AAM
Audit Date: 3/31/2019
Personnel: Larry Ruth (Mgr., Customer Sales); Paul Fugarino (Distr. Mgr.)

BOGALUSA

ROBERSON ADVERTISING SERVICE, INC.

Street address 1: 315 Industrial Parkway Drive
Street address 3: Bogalusa
Street address state: LA
Zip/Postal code: 70427-4493
County: Jefferson
Country: USA
Mailing address: 315 Industrial Parkway Drive
Mailing city: Bogalusa
Mailing state: LA
Mailing zip: 70427-4493
General Phone: (985) 520-6059
General/National Adv. E-mail: justin.schuver@bogalusadailynews.com
Primary Website: www.robersonadvertising.com
Year Established: 1939
Personnel: Michael Roberson (Pres.); Joe Chambers (Ed.)

MASSACHUSETTS

HYDE PARK

CARRIGAN ADVERTISING CARRIERS, INC.

Street address 1: 40 Walnut St
Street address 3: Hyde Park
Street address state: MA
Zip/Postal code: 02136-2732
County: Suffolk
Country: USA
Mailing address: 40 Walnut St
Mailing city: Hyde Park
Mailing state: MA
Mailing zip: 02136-2790
General Phone: (617) 361-1950
General Fax: (617) 361-1995
Year Established: 1932
Personnel: James Carrigan (Pres.)

MICHIGAN

ALLEGAN

MIDWEST INDEPENDENT POSTAL

Street address 1: 595 Jenner Dr
Street address 3: Allegan
Street address state: MI
Zip/Postal code: 49010-1516
County: Allegan
Country: USA
Mailing address: 595 Jenner Dr
Mailing city: Allegan
Mailing state: MI
Mailing zip: 49010-1516
General Phone: (269) 673-2141
General Fax: (269) 673-6768
General/National Adv. E-mail: gerald.raab@flashespublishers.com
Primary Website: www.flashespublishers.com
Year Established: 1988
Personnel: Gerald Raab (Prodn. Mgr.)

DETROIT

STANLEY ADVERTISING & DISTRIBUTING CO.

Street address 1: 1947 W Fort St
Street address 3: Detroit
Street address state: MI
Zip/Postal code: 48216-1817
County: Wayne
Country: USA
Mailing address: 1947 W Fort St
Mailing city: Detroit
Mailing state: MI
Mailing zip: 48216-1817
General Phone: (313) 961-7177
General Fax: (734) 525-2340
General/National Adv. E-mail: stanleysadvertising@gmail.com
Primary Website: www.stanleysadvertising.com
Year Established: 1964
Personnel: Stanley Wojtalik (Pres.)

LIVONIA

VALASSIS

Street address 1: 19975 Victor Pkwy
Street address 3: Livonia
Street address state: MI
Zip/Postal code: 48152-7001
County: Wayne
Country: USA
General Phone: (734) 591-3000
Primary Website: www.valassis.com
Year Established: 1970
Personnel: Rob Mason (Pres. & CEO); Larry Berg (VP of ROP Sales); Ron Goolsby (Chief Operating Officer); Brian Husselbee (President and CEO, NCH Marketing Services, Inc.); Donna Schelby; Jeff Price (FSI Project Mgr.); Dave Safford (Sales Exec.); Laura Narbut (Senior Buyer); Bridget Rabel (Senior Buyer); Ruth Williams (Senior Buyer); Tracie Pollet (Senior Client Marketing Mgr.); Janene Graham (Senior Newspaper Specialist); Greg Bogich (Senior VP of Digital Media); Barry Haselden (VP Media Services); Tim Garvey (VP, Integrated Media Sales); Debbie Gauthier; Lisa Kershaw (Client Liason Manager); Lesa Kirkman (Sales Director); Kathy Trumbo (Manager, Media Services)

MINNESOTA

MINNEAPOLIS

CITY PAGES

Street address 1: 800 N 1st St
Street address 2: Ste 300
Street address 3: Minneapolis
Street address state: MN
Zip/Postal code: 55401-1387
County: Hennepin
Country: USA
Mailing address: 401 N 3rd St Ste 550
Mailing city: Minneapolis
Mailing state: MN
Mailing zip: 55401-5050
General Phone: (612) 372-3700
General Fax: (612) 372-3737
General/National Adv. E-mail: adinfo@citypages.com
Primary Website: www.citypages.com
Advertising (Open Inch Rate) Weekday/Saturday: Open inch rate $61.00
Mechanical specifications: Type page 4 x 12.375; E - 4 cols, 2 2/5, 1/6 between; A - 6 cols, 1 9/16, 1/6 between; C - 8 cols, 1 3/16, 1/6 between.
Published: Wed
Avg Free Circ: 112025
Audit By: Sworn/Estimate/Non-Audited
Audit Date: 43806
Personnel: Tom Imberston (Circ. Mgr.); Kevin Hoffman (Ed. in Chief); Matt Smith (Mng. Ed.); Doug Snow (Prodn. Mgr.); Mary Erickson (Editor)

MISSOURI

SAINT LOUIS

THE RIVERFRONT TIMES

Street address 1: 308 N 21st St
Street address 3: Saint Louis
Street address state: MO
Zip/Postal code: 63103-1642
County: Saint Louis City
Country: USA
Mailing address: 308 N. 21st Street Suite 300
Mailing city: Saint Louis
Mailing state: MO
Mailing zip: 63103
General Phone: (314) 754-5966
General Fax: (314) 754-5955
Advertising Phone: (314) 754-5932
Advertising Fax: (314) 754-6449
Editorial Phone: (314) 754-6404
Editorial Fax: (314) 754-6416
General/National Adv. E-mail: Letters@riverfronttimes.com
Display Adv. E-mail: colin.bell@riverfronttimes.com
Editorial e-mail: tips@riverfronttimes.com
Primary Website: www.riverfronttimes.com
Year Established: 1977
Delivery Methods: Mail`Racks
Area Served - City: 63101, 63102, 63103, 63104, 63105, 63106, 63107, 63108, 63109, 63110, 63111, 63112, 63113, 63114, 63115, 63116, 63118, 63120
Advertising (Open Inch Rate) Weekday/Saturday: Open inch rate $57.62
Mechanical specifications: Type page 9.72 x 10.75
Published: Wed
Avg Paid Circ: 297
Avg Free Circ: 55000
Audit By: Sworn/Estimate/Non-Audited
Audit Date: 43806
Personnel: Kevin Powers (Circ. Mgr.); Sarah Fenske (Editor in Chief); Chris Keating (Publisher)
Parent company (for newspapers): Euclid Media Group

NEBRASKA

OMAHA

R-J DELIVERY SYSTEMS, INC.

Street address 1: 4535 Leavenworth Street
Street address 2: Ste. 9
Street address 3: Omaha
Street address state: NE
Zip/Postal code: 68106
County: Washington
Country: USA
Mailing address: 4535 Leavenworth Street, Ste. 9
Mailing city: Omaha
Mailing state: NE
Mailing zip: 68106
General Phone: (402) 345-2778
General/National Adv. E-mail: paul@rjdeliveryomaha.com
Primary Website: www.rjdeliveryomaha.com
Year Established: 1978
Personnel: Paul Green (Sales Rep.)

NEW HAMPSHIRE

NASHUA

THE TELEGRAPH

Street address 1: 110 Main St., Suite 1
Street address 3: Nashua
Street address state: NH
Zip/Postal code: 3060
County: Hillsborough
Country: USA
Mailing address: 110 Main St., Suite 1
Mailing city: Nashua
Mailing state: NH
Mailing zip: 3060
General Phone: (603) 594-1200
General Fax: (603) 882-5138
General/National Adv. E-mail: news@nashuatelegraph.com
Primary Website: www.nashuatelegraph.com
Year Established: 1832
Personnel: Heather Henline (Pub.); Matt Burdette (Ed-in-Cheif); Shawn Paulus (Circ. Dir.); Lynda Vallatini (Ad Director)

NEW JERSEY

ELMWOOD PARK

CBA INDUSTRIES

Street address 1: 669 river dr
Street address 3: elmwood park
Street address state: NJ
Zip/Postal code: 7407
General Phone: 2015054175
Advertising Phone: 9177963544
General/National Adv. E-mail: jpolizano@cbaol.com
Year Established: 1975
Published: Thur
Avg Paid Circ: 1000000
Avg Free Circ: 1000000
Audit By: AAM
Audit Date: 20-Mar
Personnel: Harold Matzner (Chrmn.); Barry Schiro (Pres.); Tom Castello (Market Mapping Specialist); Eva Kohn (Adv. Dir.); Nikki Schultz (Midwest Regional Sales Representative); Nick Passariello (Senior VP, Marketing); John Durante (Senior VP, Sales); Tim Brahney (VP, Sales)

NEPTUNE

ADDRESSES UNLIMITED

Street address 1: 3600 Hwy 66
Street address 3: Neptune
Street address state: NJ
Zip/Postal code: 7754
County: Monmouth
Country: USA
Mailing address: PO Box 1550
Mailing city: Neptune
Mailing state: NJ
Mailing zip: 07754-1550
General Phone: (732) 922-6000
General Fax: (732) 643-3719
General/National Adv. E-mail: editors@app.com
Primary Website: www.app.com
Year Established: 1991
Personnel: Sam Sicliano (Vice Pres.)

NEW YORK

ALBANY

DISTRIBUTION UNLIMITED, INC.

Street address 1: Po Box 98
Street address 2: Guilderland Center
Street address 3: Albany
Street address state: NY
Zip/Postal code: 12085
County: Clark
Country: USA
Mailing address: Po Box 98, Guilderland Center
Mailing city: Albany
Mailing state: NY
Mailing zip: 12085
General Phone: 518-355-3112
General Fax: 518-355-3636
General/National Adv. E-mail: dahl@galesi.com
Primary Website: www.distributionunlimited.com
Year Established: 1969
Personnel: David Ahl (Sales Rep.); Steven Ribet (Sales Rep)

CHEEKTOWAGA

METRO GROUP, INC.

Street address 1: 75 Boxwood Ln
Street address 3: Cheektowaga
Street address state: NY
Zip/Postal code: 14227-2707
County: Erie
Country: USA
Mailing address: PO Box 790
Mailing city: Cheektowaga
Mailing state: NY
Mailing zip: 14225-0790
General Phone: (716) 668-5223
General Fax: (716) 668-4526
General/National Adv. E-mail: edit@metrowny.com
Primary Website: www.metrowny.com
Year Established: 1968
Personnel: Lorne Marshall (Ed.)
Newspaper (for newspapers group): Alden Metro Source, Buffalo; Amherst / Getzville Smart Shopper, Buffalo; Amherst / Tonawanda Metro Source (OOB), Buffalo; Clarence Metro Source, Buffalo; Depew Metro Source, Buffalo; Eggertsville / Snyder Smart Shopper, Buffalo; Gowanda News, Buffalo; Kenmore / Tonawanda Source, Buffalo; Lancaster Source, Buffalo; Lockport Retailer, Buffalo; North Buffalo Smart Shopper, Buffalo; North Cheektowaga Source, Buffalo; North Tonawanda Source, Buffalo; South Buffalo Metro Source, Buffalo; South Cheektowaga Source, Buffalo; Springville Journal, Buffalo; The Sun and Erie County Independent, Hamburg; Williamsville Smart Shopper, Buffalo

FARMINGDALE

PUBLISHERS CIRCULATION FULFILLMENT INC.

Street address 1: 303 Smith St
Street address 2: Ste 1
Street address 3: Farmingdale
Street address state: NY
Zip/Postal code: 11735-1110
County: Suffolk
Country: USA
Mailing address: 303 Smith Street, Suite One
Mailing city: Farmingdale
Mailing state: NY
Mailing zip: 11735
General Phone: (631) 2703133
General/National Adv. E-mail: sales@pcfcorp.com
Primary Website: www.pcfcorp.com
Industry: Newspaper Distribution Technology Services
Personnel: Jerry Giordana (Pres./CEO); Tom Dressler (VP of Growth and Development); James Cunningham

OHIO

ATHENS

MESSENGER CONSUMER SERVICES

Street address 1: 9300 Johnson Hollow Rd
Street address 3: Athens
Street address state: OH
Zip/Postal code: 45701-9028
County: Athens
Country: USA
Mailing address: PO Box 4210
Mailing city: Athens
Mailing state: OH
Mailing zip: 45701-4210
General Phone: (740) 592-6612
General Fax: (740) 592-4647
General/National Adv. E-mail: sbossart@athensmessenger.com
Primary Website: www.athensmessenger.com
Year Established: 1992
Personnel: Sherrie Bossart (Adv. Mgr.); Monica Nieporte (Pub.)

CINCINNATI

THE CINCINNATI ENQUIRER

Street address 1: 312 Elm St
Street address 3: Cincinnati
Street address state: OH
Zip/Postal code: 45202-2739
County: Hamilton
Country: USA
General Phone: (513) 721-2700
Advertising Phone: (513) 768-8404
Advertising Fax: (513) 242-4366
Editorail Phone: (513) 768-8600
Editorial Fax: (513) 768-8340
General/National Adv. E-mail: abaston@enquirer.com
Display Adv. E-mail: abaston@enquirer.com
Classified Adv. E-mail: abaston@enquirer.com
Editorial e-mail: ltrujillo@cincinnati.com
Primary Website: www.cincinnati.com; www.enquirermedia.com
Mthly Avg Views: 5200000
Mthly Avg Unique Visitors: 3300000
Year Established: 1841
News Services: AP, NYT, MCT, GNS.
Special Editions: Summer Vacations-Travel (Apr); Tennis Championships (Aug); Holiday Home Gift Guides (Dec); National Cruise Month Celebration (Feb); Warm Weather Travel Destinations (Jan); Regional Adventures (Jul); Homearama (Jun); Family Vacations (May); Holiday Gift Gu
Special Weekly Sections: Weather, Sports (Daily); Business, Sunday Forum, Good News, (Sun); Food, Classifieds (Wed); Healthy Living, Hometown (Thur); Weekend, Business (Fri); Home, Style, Hometown (Sat)
Syndicated Publications: USA WEEKEND Magazine (S).
Advertising (Open Inch Rate) Weekday/Saturday: Awareness C $817.00; Awareness D $1633.00; 1/12 Pg V $3,901.00
Advertising (Open inch rate) Sunday: Awareness C $851.00; Awareness D $1703.00; 1/12 Pg V $4,068.00
Market Information: Split run; Zoned editions.
Mechanical available: Offset; Black and 3 ROP colors; insert accepted - based on sample submitted; page cutoffs - 22 3/4.
Mechanical specifications: Type page 11 5/8 x 21 1/2; E - 7 cols, 1 1/2, 1/8 between; A - 6 cols, 1 13/16, 1/8 between; C - 10 cols, 1 3/32, 1/8 between.
Published: Mon`Tues`Wed`Thur`Fri`Sat`Sun
Weekday Frequency: m
Saturday Frequency: m
Avg Paid Circ: 84723
Sat. Circulation Paid: 84430
Sun. Circulation Paid: 133477
Audit By: AAM
Audit Date: 3/31/2018
Pressroom Equipment: Lines -- 10-G/Metro (6 half decks) 1978; 10-G/Metro (6 half decks) 1978; 10-G/Metro (6 half decks) 1980; 10-G/Metro (6 half decks) 1988; Folders -- 4-G/double.;
Mailroom Eqipment: Counter Stackers -- 4-QWI/200, 5-QWI/400; Inserters & Stuffers -- 1-HI/1472, 1-HI/1372, AM Graphics/NP 630, 1/Magnapack; Tying Machines -- 8-/Dynaric; Address Machine -- 1-/Ch, X;
Buisness Equipment: IBM/AS-400 520, PC Micro, HP/9000
Buisness Software: Genesys
Classified Equipment: Hardware -- SII/Server Net; SII/Coyote QB, SII/Coyote 22, SII/Coyote 3; Printers -- Centronics/351, Dataproducts/LZR-2600, Tetromix/Phaser 780, HP/8500, HP/4050;
Classified Software: SII/Sys 55, C Text/ALPS Classified Pagination.
Display Equipment: Hardware -- 16-APP/Mac 7500, 1-APP/Mac WGS 80, 1763-350; Printers -- APP/Mac LaserWriter NTX, Textronix/Phaser 780 I, GEI Color Proofer;
Display Software: Ad Make-up Applications -- APP/Mac Appleshare 4.0, First class/BBS software; Layout Software -- Multi-Ad/Creator II.
Editorial Equipment: Hardware -- Tandem/CLX/SII/Coyote QB, SII/Dakota, APP/Mac, SII/CAT-ST, SII/Coyote 22, SII/Coyote 3; Printers -- Centronics/351, Dataproducts/LZR 2600, APP/Mac LaserWriter NTX, Xante/8200, Textronix/Phaser 300 I
Editorial Software: SII/Sys 55, SII/Sys 7
Production Equipment: Hardware -- Nova Publishing/Faxaction, 2-AU/APS 6108, 2-AU/APS 3850, 1-HQ-110PM; Cameras -- 2-C/Newspager; Scanners -- 1-ECR/Autokon 1000, Tecsa/3050.
Personnel: Michael McCarter (Interim Editor); Denette Pfaffenberger (Group Dir/Home Delivery); Kate McGinty (Dir of News Content); Joe Powell (Dir. of Print Prod); Chris Strong (VP of Sales); Peter Bhatia (Ed. & VP of Audience Engagement); Jeff Lawson (Market Sales & Distribution Director); Libby Korosec (Client Strategy Director); John Berry (Major Sales & Marketing Manager)
Parent company (for newspapers): Gannett
footnotes: General/National Adv. E-mail: SRDS (10/23/2014); Display Adv. E-mail: SRDS (10/23/2014)

COLUMBUS

THE COLUMBUS DISPATCH

Street address 1: 62 E. Broad St.
Street address 3: Columbus
Street address state: OH
Zip/Postal code: 43215
County: Delaware
Country: USA
Mailing address: 62 E. Broad St.
Mailing city: Columbus
Mailing state: OH
Mailing zip: 43215
General Phone: (877) 734-7728
General/National Adv. E-mail: mcampbell@dispatch.com
Primary Website: www.dispatch.com
Personnel: Bradley Harmon (Pub.); Allan Miller (Ed.)

DAYTON

DAYTON CITY PAPER

Street address 1: 126 N Main St
Street address 2: Ste 240
Street address 3: Dayton
Street address state: OH
Zip/Postal code: 45402-1766
County: Montgomery
Country: USA
Mailing address: PO Box 10065
Mailing city: Dayton
Mailing state: OH
Mailing zip: 45402
General Phone: (937) 222-8855
Advertising Phone: (937) 222-8855 x 603
Editorail Phone: (937) 222-8855 x 604
General/National Adv. E-mail: contactus@daytoncitypaper.com
Display Adv. E-mail: advertising@daytoncitypaper.com
Editorial e-mail: editor@daytoncitypaper.com
Primary Website: www.daytoncitypaper.com
Year Established: 2003
Delivery Methods: Carrier`Racks
Area Served - City: Entire metro Dayton Ohio region
Published: Tues
Avg Free Circ: 20120
Audit By: Sworn/Estimate/Non-Audited
Audit Date: 43806
Personnel: Paul Noah (CEO, Dayton City Media); Wanda Esken (Publisher)
Parent company (for newspapers): Dayton City Media

MOUNT VERNON

MARKETING INFORMATION DISTRIBUTION SERVICE

Street address 1: 18 E Vine St
Street address 3: Mount Vernon
Street address state: OH
Zip/Postal code: 43050-3226
County: Knox
Country: USA
Mailing address: PO Box 791
Mailing city: Mount Vernon
Mailing state: OH
Mailing zip: 43050-0791
General Phone: (740) 397-5333
General Fax: (740) 397-1321
General/National Adv. E-mail: csplain@mountvernonnews.com
Primary Website: www.mountvernonnews.com
Year Established: 1983
Personnel: Kay H. Culbertson (Pub.); Michael P. McNichols (MIDS Mgr.)

OKLAHOMA

OKLAHOMA CITY

OKLAHOMA GAZETTE

Street address 1: 3701 N Shartel Ave
Street address 3: Oklahoma City
Street address state: OK
Zip/Postal code: 73118-7102
County: Oklahoma
Country: USA
Mailing address: 3701 N Shartel Ave
Mailing city: Oklahoma City
Mailing state: OK
Mailing zip: 73118
General Phone: (405 605-6789
General Fax: (405) 528-4600
Display Adv. E-mail: advertising@tierramediagroup.com
Primary Website: www.okgazette.com
Year Established: 1979
Delivery Methods: Racks
Advertising (Open Inch Rate) Weekday/Saturday: Open inch rate $58
Mechanical specifications: Type page 10.25 x 12.25 Advertising - 4 columns, 2.2" wide with 1/8" between Classifeds - 6 columns, 1.5" wide with 1/16" between
Published: Wed
Avg Paid Circ: 0
Avg Free Circ: 36082
Audit By: VAC
Audit Date: 12/31/2016
Personnel: Peter Brzycki (Publisher)

ONTARIO

HAWKESBURY

CIE D'EDITION ANDRE PAQUETTE, INC.

Street address 1: 1100 Aberdeen C.P.
Street address 3: Hawkesbury
Street address state: ON
Zip/Postal code: K6A 1K7
Country: Canada
Mailing address: P.O. Box 1000
Mailing city: Hawkesbury
Mailing state: ON
Mailing zip: K6A 1K7
General Phone: (613) 632-4155
General Fax: (613) 632-6383
General/National Adv. E-mail: francois.legault@eap.on.ca
Primary Website: editionap.ca
Year Established: 1947
Personnel: Bertrand Castonguay (Pres.); Francois Legault (Mng. Ed.)
Newspaper (for newspapers group): L'argenteuil, Lachute; Le Carillon, Hawkesbury; Tribune Express, Hawkesbury; Vision; Le Reflet/News

PENNSYLVANIA

ALLENTOWN

DIRECT MARKETING DISTRIBUTION

Street address 1: 101 N 6th St
Street address 3: Allentown
Street address state: PA
Zip/Postal code: 18101-1403
County: Lehigh
Country: USA
Mailing address: PO Box 1260
Mailing city: Allentown
Mailing state: PA

Mailing zip: 18105-1260
General Phone: 610-841-2301
General Fax: 610-841-2306
Primary Website: www.mcall.com
Year Established: 1988
Personnel: Todd Wendling (Sales Manager); James Feher (Vice Pres.)

KAPP ADVERTISING SERVICE, INC

Street address state: PA
Country: USA
Mailing address: PO Box 840
Mailing city: Lebanon
Mailing state: PA
Mailing zip: 17042-0840
General/National Adv. E-mail: sales@themerchandiser.com
Primary Website: www.themerchandiser.com
Year Established: 1950
Personnel: Valerie Stokes (Gen. Mgr.); Joanne Walkinshaw (Circ. Mgr.); Randy Miller (General Sales Manager)
Newspaper (for newspapers group): The Merchandiser, Lebanon

TENNESSEE

MEMPHIS

THE DAILY NEWS

Street address 1: 193 Jefferson Ave
Street address 3: Memphis
Street address state: TN
Zip/Postal code: 38103-2322
County: Shelby
Country: USA
Mailing address: 193 JEFFERSON AVE
Mailing city: MEMPHIS
Mailing state: TN
Mailing zip: 38103-2339
General Phone: (901) 523-1561
General Fax: (901) 526-5813
Advertising Phone: (901) 528-5283
Advertising Fax: (901) 526-5813
Editorail Phone: (901) 523-8501
Editorial Fax: (901) 526-5813
General/National Adv. E-mail: jjenkins@memphisdailynews.com
Display Adv. E-mail: jjenkins@memphisdailynews.com
Classified Adv. E-mail: jjenkins@memphisdailynews.com
Editorial e-mail: releases@memphisdailynews.com
Primary Website: www.memphisdailynews.com
Mthly Avg Views: 300000
Mthly Avg Unique Visitors: 100000
Year Established: 1886
News Services: CNS
Delivery Methods: Mail
Area Served - City: Madison, Tipton, Fayette, Shelby
Advertising (Open Inch Rate) Weekday/Saturday: Open inch rate $13.50 (legal)
Online Advertising Rates - CPM (cost per thousand) by Size: Leaderboard (728x90): $550/month; Side Position (250x250): $400/month
Published: Mon`Tues`Wed`Thur`Fri
Weekday Frequency: m
Avg Paid Circ: 1000
Avg Free Circ: 2000
Audit By: Sworn/Estimate/Non-Audited
Audit Date: 43806
Personnel: Don Fancher (Public Notices); Janice Jenkins (Adv. Dir.); Terry Hollahan (Associate Publisher/ Exec. Ed.)
Parent company (for newspapers): The Daily News Publishing Co.

TEXAS

DALLAS

WILLOW BEND COMMUNICATIONS, INC.

Street address 1: 18333 Preston Rd
Street address 2: 250
Street address 3: Dallas
Street address state: TX
Zip/Postal code: 75252-5466
County: Collin
Country: USA
Mailing address: PO Box 797485
Mailing city: Dallas
Mailing state: TX
Mailing zip: 75379-7485
General Phone: (972) 553-3600
General Fax: (972) 732-8807
General/National Adv. E-mail: info@willowbend.com; support@willowbend.com
Primary Website: www.willowbend.com
Year Established: 1988
Personnel: Steve Thompson (Pres); Layton Kolb (Cust Sup Mgr); Diane Thompson (CFO); Steven Lerch (Chief Software Engineer); Jim Schell (VP Bus Development)

FORT WORTH

FORT WORTH WEEKLY

Street address 1: 3311 Hamilton Ave
Street address 3: Fort Worth
Street address state: TX
Zip/Postal code: 76107-1877
County: Tarrant
Country: USA
Mailing address: 3311 Hamilton Ave
Mailing city: Fort Worth
Mailing state: TX
Mailing zip: 76107-1877
General Phone: (817) 321-9700
General Fax: (817) 321-9733
Advertising Phone: (817) 321-9700
Advertising Fax: (817) 321-9733
Editorail Phone: (817) 321-9700
Editorial Fax: (817) 321-9575
General/National Adv. E-mail: Michael.Newquist@fwweekly.com
Display Adv. E-mail: Brian.Martin@fwweekly.com
Editorial e-mail: Gayle.Reaves@fwweekly.com
Primary Website: www.fwweekly.com
Year Established: 1994
Delivery Methods: Mail`Racks
Area Served - City: Tarrant County
Advertising (Open Inch Rate) Weekday/Saturday: Open inch rate $18.25
Published: Wed
Avg Free Circ: 23064
Audit By: VAC
Audit Date: 5/31/2017
Personnel: Gayle Reaves (Ed.); Michael Newquist (Adv. Dir.); Brian Martin (Classified Adv. Dir.); Eric Griffey

SAN ANTONIO

HARTE-HANKS

Street address 1: 9601 McAllister Freeway
Street address 2: Ste. 610
Street address 3: San Antonio
Street address state: TX
Zip/Postal code: 78216
Country: USA
Mailing address: 9601 McAllister Freeway, Ste. 610
Mailing city: San Antonio
Mailing state: TX
Mailing zip: 78216
General Phone: 210-829-9000
Primary Website: www.hartehanks.com
Year Established: 1978
Personnel: Tom Ugast (Gen. Mgr.)

SAN ANTONIO CURRENT

Street address 1: 915 Dallas St
Street address 3: San Antonio
Street address state: TX
Zip/Postal code: 78215-1433
County: Bexar
Country: USA
Mailing address: 915 Dallas St
Mailing city: San Antonio
Mailing state: TX
Mailing zip: 78215-1433
General Phone: (210) 227-0044
General Fax: (210) 227-7755
Primary Website: www.sacurrent.com
Year Established: 1986
Delivery Methods: Newsstand
Advertising (Open Inch Rate) Weekday/Saturday: Open inch rate $9.25
Mechanical specifications: Type page 10 x 12 1/2; E - 4 cols, 2 1/4, 1/20 between; A - 4 cols, 2 1/4, 1/20 between; C - 8 cols, 1 1/5, 1/20 between.
Published: Wed
Avg Free Circ: 19378
Audit By: VAC
Audit Date: 9/30/2015
Personnel: Michael Wagner (Publisher); Greg Harman (Advertising Director)

UTAH

WEST VALLEY CITY

MEDIA ONE OF UTAH

Street address 1: 4770 S 5600 W
Street address 3: West Valley City
Street address state: UT
Zip/Postal code: 84118-7400
County: Salt Lake
Country: USA
Mailing address: PO Box 704005
Mailing city: West Valley City
Mailing state: UT
Mailing zip: 84118-7400
General Phone: (801) 204-6151
General Fax: 801-204-6399
Primary Website: www.mediaoneutah.com
Year Established: 2006
Personnel: Hal Mortensen (Vice President Circulation Operations)

VIRGINIA

NEWPORT NEWS

DAILY PRESS PORCH PLUS

Street address 1: 7505 Warwick Blvd
Street address 3: Newport News
Street address state: VA
Zip/Postal code: 23607-1517
County: Newport News City
Country: USA
Mailing address: PO Box 746
Mailing city: Newport News
Mailing state: VA
Mailing zip: 23607-0746
General Phone: (757) 247-4600
General Fax: (757) 245-7113
Primary Website: www.dailypress.com
Year Established: 1990
Personnel: Timothy Ryan (Pres./CEO/Pub.)

RICHMOND

RICHMOND DELIVERY SERVICE

Street address 1: 7500 Ranco Rd
Street address 3: Richmond
Street address state: VA
Zip/Postal code: 23228-3750
County: Henrico
Country: USA
Mailing address: PO Box 85333
Mailing city: Richmond
Mailing state: VA
Mailing zip: 23293-5333
General Phone: (804) 775-2723
General Fax: (804) 775-2801
General/National Adv. E-mail: rneely@timesdispatch.com
Primary Website: www.timesdispatch.com
Year Established: 1992
Personnel: Richard Neeley (Sales Mgr.); Tom Smith (Metro Home Delivery Mgr.); Raymond Bruett (Circ. Dir.)

STERLING

DHL SMART & GLOBAL MAIL

Street address 1: 21240 Ridgetop Cir
Street address 2: Ste 160
Street address 3: Sterling
Street address state: VA
Zip/Postal code: 20166-6560
County: Loudoun
Country: USA
Mailing address: 21240 Ridgetop Cir Ste 160
Mailing city: Sterling
Mailing state: VA
Mailing zip: 20166-6560
General Phone: (703) 463-2200
General Fax: (800) 455-6615
Primary Website: www.globalmail.com

VIRGINIA BEACH

HOME EXPRESS

Street address 1: 5457 Greenwich Rd
Street address 3: Virginia Beach
Street address state: VA
Zip/Postal code: 23462-6539
County: Virginia Beach City
Country: USA
Mailing address: 5457 Greenwich Rd
Mailing city: Virginia Beach
Mailing state: VA
Mailing zip: 23462-6539
General Phone: (757) 446-2890
General Fax: (757) 499-1966
Year Established: 1984

WASHINGTON

SPOKANE

NEW MEDIA VENTURE

Street address 1: 999 W Riverside Ave
Street address 3: Spokane
Street address state: WA
Zip/Postal code: 99201-1005
County: Spokane
Country: USA
Mailing address: 999 W Riverside Ave
Mailing city: Spokane
Mailing state: WA
Mailing zip: 99201-1006
Personnel: Shaun Higgins (CEO)

VANCOUVER

THE COLUMBIAN ALTERNATE DELIVERY SERVICE

Street address 1: 701 W 8th St
Street address 3: Vancouver
Street address state: WA

Zip/Postal code: 98660-3008
County: Clark
Country: USA
Mailing address: PO Box 180
Mailing city: Vancouver
Mailing state: WA
Mailing zip: 98666-0180
General Phone: (360) 694-3391
General Fax: (360) 735-4605
Primary Website: www.columbian.com
Year Established: 1890
Personnel: Marc Dailey (Circ. Dir.); Rachel Rose (Circ. Mgr., Promo./Sales)

WISCONSIN

GREEN BAY

GREEN BAY COMMUNITY NEWS (EAST/WEST)

Street address 1: 133 S Monroe Ave
Street address 3: Green Bay
Street address state: WI
Zip/Postal code: 54301-4056
County: Brown
Country: USA
Mailing address: PO Box 2467
Mailing city: Green Bay
Mailing state: WI
Mailing zip: 54306-2467
General Phone: (920) 432-2941
General Fax: (920) 432-8581
General/National Adv. E-mail: chronicle@itol.com
Primary Website: www.greenbaynewschronicle.com
Year Established: 1972
Personnel: Al Rasmussen (Vice Pres.); Keith Davis (Circ. Mgr.)

MILWAUKEE

JOURNAL/SENTINEL, INC.

Street address 1: 333 W State St
Street address 3: Milwaukee
Street address state: WI
Zip/Postal code: 53203-1305
County: Milwaukee
Country: USA
Mailing address: PO Box 661
Mailing city: Milwaukee
Mailing state: WI
Mailing zip: 53201-0661
General Phone: (414) 224-2000
General Fax: (414) 224-2485
Primary Website: www.jsonline.com
Year Established: 1882
Personnel: George Stanley (Vice Pres., Ed.); John Diedrich (Investigative Reporter/Assistant Editor); Bob Dohr (Ed.); Chuck Melvin (Asst. Mng. Ed.)

PLATTEVILLE

WOODWARD PRINTING SERVICES

Street address 1: 11 Means Dr
Street address 3: Platteville
Street address state: WI
Zip/Postal code: 53818-3829
County: Grant
Country: USA
Mailing address: PO Box 514
Mailing city: Platteville
Mailing state: WI
Mailing zip: 53818-0514
General Phone: (608) 348-2817
General Fax: (608) 348-2816
General/National Adv. E-mail: woodwardprint@wcinet.com
Primary Website: http://www.woodwardprinting.com/
Year Established: 1994
Personnel: Marty Tloessl (Gen. Mgr.)

ASSOCIATIONS, CLUBS AND PRESS CLUBS - CITY, STATE AND REGIONAL

ALABAMA

BIRMINGHAM

ALABAMA PRESS ASSOCIATION

Street address 1: 3324 Independence Dr
Street address 2: Ste 200
Street address 3: Birmingham
Street address state: AL
Zip/Postal code: 35209-5602
Country: USA
Mailing address: 3324 Independence Dr Ste 200
Mailing city: Birmingham
Mailing state: AL
Mailing zip: 35209-5602
General Phone: (205) 871-7737
General Fax: (205) 871-7740
General/National Adv. E-mail: felicia@alabamapress.org
Primary Website: www.alabamapress.org
Year Established: 1871
Note: Elections held in Feb
Personnel: Felicia Mason (Exec. Dir.); Brad English (Adv. Mgr.); Leigh Tortorici (Senior Marketing Rep.); Amy Metzler (Sales/Mktg Exec); Chris McDaniel (Member Services/Network Coordinator)

ARIZONA

PHOENIX

ARIZONA NEWSPAPERS ASSOCIATION

Street address 1: 1001 N Central Ave
Street address 2: Ste 670
Street address 3: Phoenix
Street address state: AZ
Zip/Postal code: 85004-1947
County: Maricopa
Country: USA
General Phone: (602) 261-7655
General Fax: (602) 261-7525
Advertising Phone: (602) 261-7655 x112
General/National Adv. E-mail: p.casey@ananews.com
Display Adv. E-mail: p.casey@ananews.com
Primary Website: www.ananews.com
Year Established: 1929
Note: Elections held in Sept. Statewide and national one order/one bill advertising placement service
Personnel: Paula Casey (Exec. Dir.); Julie O'Keefe (Communications Manager); Cindy London (Ad Placement Manager)

CALIFORNIA

CALIFORNIA NEWS PUBLISHERS ASSOCIATION

Street address 1: 2701 K St
Street address 3: Sacramento
Street address state: CA
Zip/Postal code: 95816-5131
County: Sacramento
Country: USA
Mailing address: 2701 K St.
Mailing city: Sacramento
Mailing state: CA
Mailing zip: 95816-5131
General Phone: (916) 288-6000
General Fax: (916) 288-6002
Primary Website: www.cnpa.com
Year Established: 1889
Personnel: Charles Champion (President & CEO); Cecelia Drake (Director of Advertising); Joe Wirt (Director of Affiliate Relations); Paulette Brown-Hinds (VP, Sec/Trea); Cecelia Drake (Director of Advertising); Thomas Newton (Exec. Dir.); Brittney Barsotti (General Counsel); Jim Ewert (Gen. Counsel); Ashley Bryant (Director of Finance); Tiffany Chiang (Marketing Analyst); Jennifer Davee (Accounting Specialist); Simon Birch (Dir. of Membership); Renee Smith (Director of Meetings)

CONNECTICUT

HARTFORD

CONNECTICUT DAILY NEWSPAPERS ASSOCIATION

Street address 1: 330 Main St
Street address 2: Fl 3
Street address 3: Hartford
Street address state: CT
Zip/Postal code: 06106-1851
Country: USA
Mailing address: 330 Main St Fl 3
Mailing city: Hartford
Mailing state: CT
Mailing zip: 06106-1851
General Phone: (860) 716-4461
General Fax: (860) 541-6484
Primary Website: www.ctdailynews.com
Year Established: 1904
Note: Elections held in April/May
Personnel: Chris VanDeHoef (Executive Director)

HAWAII

HONOLULU

HAWAII PUBLISHERS ASSOCIATION

Street address 1: 500 Ala Moana Blvd
Street address 2: Ste 7-500
Street address 3: Honolulu
Street address state: HI
Zip/Postal code: 96813-4930
Country: USA
Mailing address: 500 Ala Moana Blvd Ste 7500
Mailing city: Honolulu
Mailing state: HI
Mailing zip: 96813-4930
General Phone: (808) 738-4992
General Fax: (808) 664-8892
General/National Adv. E-mail: info@hawaiipublishersassociation.com
Primary Website: www.hawaiipublishersassociation.com
Personnel: Rick Asbach (Executive Director)

IOWA

DES MOINES

IOWA NEWSPAPER ASSOCIATION, INC.

Street address 1: 319 E 5th St
Street address 2: Fl 2
Street address 3: Des Moines
Street address state: IA
Zip/Postal code: 50309-1927
Country: USA
Mailing address: 319 E 5th St Fl 2nd
Mailing city: Des Moines
Mailing state: IA
Mailing zip: 50309-1931
General Phone: (515) 244-2145
General Fax: (515) 244-4855
General/National Adv. E-mail: ina@inanews.com
Primary Website: www.inanews.com
Year Established: 1931
Note: Elections held in May
Personnel: Susan Patterson Plank (Exec. Dir.); Brent Steemken (Business Mgr.); Jodi Hulbert (Comm. Dir.); Geof Fischer (Dev. Dir); Samantha Fett (Inside Sales Mgr.); Heidi Geisler (Media Dir.); Jana Shepherd (Program Dir.); Susan James (Tech. & Digital Dev. Mgr.); Ryan Harvey (Pres.); Kaitlyn Van Patten (Sales & Mktg. Assist.)

ILLINOIS

SPRINGFIELD

ILLINOIS PRESS ASSOCIATION

Street address 1: 900 Community Dr
Street address 3: Springfield
Street address state: IL

Zip/Postal code: 62703-5180
County: Sangamon
Country: USA
General Phone: (217) 241-1300
General Fax: (217) 241-1301
Advertising Phone: (217) 241-1700
Advertising Fax: (217) 241-1701
General/National Adv. E-mail: ipa@illinoispress.org
Primary Website: www.illinoispress.org
Year Established: 1865
Note: The Illinois Press Advertising Service can place any newspaper product available in Illinois and has several well-established, low-cost networks.
Personnel: Sam Fisher (Pres./CEO); Tracy Spoonmore (CFO); Jeff Holman (Advertising Director); Cindy Bedolli (Administrative Assistant & Member Relations); Ron Kline (Tech & Online Coord.); Melissa Calloway (Dig. Adv. Mgr.); Cindy Bedolli (Admin Assist & Member Rel.)

INDIANA

INDIANAPOLIS

HOOSIER STATE PRESS ASSOCIATION

Street address 1: 41 E Washington St
Street address 2: Ste 101
Street address 3: Indianapolis
Street address state: IN
Zip/Postal code: 46204-3560
County: Marion
Country: USA
General Phone: (317) 803-4772
General Fax: (317) 624-4428
Display Adv. E-mail: map@hspa.com
Primary Website: www.hspa.com
Year Established: 1933
Note: Represents daily and weekly newspapers in Indiana
Personnel: Stephen Key (Exec. Dir./Gen. Counsel); Pamela Lego (Adv. Dir.); Milissa Tuley (Communications Specialist); Karen Braeckel (HSPA Foundation Dir.); Yvonne Yeadon (Office Mgr.); Shawn Goldsby (Adv. Coord.)

KANSAS

TOPEKA

KANSAS PRESS ASSOCIATION

Street address 1: 5423 SW 7th St
Street address 3: Topeka
Street address state: KS
Zip/Postal code: 66606-2330
County: Shawnee
Country: USA
Mailing address: 5423 SW 7th St.
Mailing city: Topeka
Mailing state: KS
Mailing zip: 66606
General Phone: (785) 271-5304
General Fax: (785) 271-7341
General/National Adv. E-mail: info@kspress.com
Display Adv. E-mail: KSAds@kspress.com
Editorial e-mail: info@kspress.com
Primary Website: www.kspress.com
Year Established: 1863
Note: Represents 28 daily and 185 weekly newspapers in Kansas
Personnel: Emily Bradbury (Director of Member Services); Lori Jackson (Admin. Assist./Adv.); Doug Anstaett (Exec. Dir.); Amber Jackson (Adv. Dir.); Judy Beach (Accountant)
Newspaper (for newspapers group): The Oakley Graphic, Oakley; The Iola Register, Iola; The Leader & Times, Liberal; Kansas City Kansan (OOB), Olathe; Coffeyville Journal, Coffeyville; The Manhattan Mercury, Manhattan; Winfield Daily Courier, Winfield; The Arkansas City Traveler, Arkansas City; The Emporia Gazette, Emporia

LOUISIANA

LOUISIANA PRESS ASSOCIATION

Street address 1: 404 Europe St
Street address 3: Baton Rouge
Street address state: LA
Zip/Postal code: 70802-6403
County: East Baton Rouge
Country: USA
General Phone: (225) 344-9309
General Fax: (225) 344-9344
Advertising Phone: (225) 344-9309 x 111
Advertising Fax: (225) 336-9921
Editorial Fax: (225) 346-5060
General/National Adv. E-mail: pam@lapress.com
Display Adv. E-mail: erin@LaPress.com
Primary Website: www.lapress.com
Year Established: 1880
Personnel: Mike Rood (Communications Dir.); Pamela Mitchell (Exec. Dir.); Mitchell-Ann Droge (Dir. of Ops.); Erin Palmintier (Adv. Dir.)

MICHIGAN

LANSING

MICHIGAN PRESS ASSOCIATION

Street address 1: 827 N Washington Ave
Street address 3: Lansing
Street address state: MI
Zip/Postal code: 48906-5135
County: USA
Country: USA
Mailing address: 827 N Washington Ave
Mailing city: Lansing
Mailing state: MI
Mailing zip: 48906-5199
General Phone: (517) 372-2424
General Fax: (517) 372-2429
General/National Adv. E-mail: mpa@michiganpress.org
Primary Website: www.michiganpress.org
Year Established: 1868
Note: Elections held in Jan
Personnel: Roselle Lucus (Growth & Operations Manager); Lisa McGraw (Public Affairs Manager); Sean Wickham (Design & Communications Specialist); Janet Mendler (Mgr.); James Tarrant (Exec. Dir.); Paul Biondi (Adv. Dir.)
Newspaper (for newspapers group): MNI, Lansing

MINNESOTA

MINNESOTA NEWSPAPER ASSOCIATION

Street address 1: 12 S 6th St
Street address 2: Ste 1120
Street address 3: Minneapolis
Street address state: MN
Zip/Postal code: 55402-1501
Country: USA
Mailing address: 10 S 5th St Ste 1105
Mailing city: Minneapolis
Mailing state: MN
Mailing zip: 55402-1036
General Phone: (612) 332-8844
General Fax: (612) 342-2958
General/National Adv. E-mail: info@mna.org
Display Adv. E-mail: advertising@mna.org
Primary Website: www.mna.org
Year Established: 1867
Note: Convention, trade show and elections in January.
Personnel: Lisa Hills (Executive Director); Dan Lind (Managing Director); Barbara Trebisovsky (Asst. Exec. Dir.); Phil Morin (Advertising Account Manager)

NORTH DAKOTA

BISMARCK

NORTH DAKOTA NEWSPAPER ASSOCIATION

Street address 1: 1435 Interstate Loop
Street address 3: Bismarck
Street address state: ND
Zip/Postal code: 58503-0567
County: Burleigh
Country: USA
Mailing address: 1435 Interstate Loop
Mailing city: Bismarck
Mailing state: ND
Mailing zip: 58503-0567
General Phone: (701) 223-6397
General Fax: (701) 223-8185
General/National Adv. E-mail: info@ndna.com
Primary Website: www.ndna.com
Year Established: 1885
Note: Represents daily and weekly newspapers in North Dakota
Personnel: Kelli Richey (Mktg. Dir.); Steve Andrist (Exec. Dir.); Mike Casey (Adv. Dir.); Colleen Park (Adv./Public Notice Coord.); Shari Peterson (Office Coord./Adv. Assist.); Paul Erdelt (NDNA President)

NEW MEXICO

ALBUQUERQUE

NEW MEXICO PRESS ASSOCIATION

Street address 1: 700 Silver Ave SW
Street address 3: Albuquerque
Street address state: NM
Zip/Postal code: 87102-3019
County: Bernalillo
Country: USA
Mailing address: PO Box 95198
Mailing city: Albuquerque
Mailing state: NM
Mailing zip: 87199-5198
General Phone: (505) 275-1241
General Fax: (505) 275-1449
Advertising Phone: (505) 275-1377
General/National Adv. E-mail: info@nmpress.org
Display Adv. E-mail: Ads@NMPress.org
Primary Website: www.nmpress.org
Note: Elections held in Oct
Personnel: Holly Aguilar (Office Mgr.)
Newspaper (for newspapers group): Hobbs News-Sun, Hobbs; Roswell Daily Record, Roswell; Las Vegas Optic, LAS VEGAS; Lincoln County News, Chandler; Union County Leader, Clayton; Cibola Beacon, Grants; Santa Rosa News (OOB), Santa Rosa; Sierra County Sentinel, Truth Or Consequences; The Rio Rancho Observer, Rio Rancho; The Ruidoso News, Ruidoso; The Raton Range (OOB), Raton; Silver City Daily Press & Independent, Silver City

NEW YORK

NEW YORK

NEW YORK PRESS PHOTOGRAPHERS ASSOCIATION, INC.

Street address 1: PO Box 3346
Street address 3: New York
Street address state: NY
Zip/Postal code: 10008-3346
Country: USA
Mailing address: Box 3346 Church Street Station
Mailing city: New York
Mailing state: NY
Mailing zip: 10008-3346
General Phone: (212) 889-6633
General/National Adv. E-mail: office@nyppa.org
Primary Website: www.nyppa.org
Year Established: 1915
Note: Elections held every other year
Personnel: Ray Stubblebine (Trustee); Marc Hermann (Secretary - Historian); Bruce Cotler (President); Todd Maisel (Vice President)

OKLAHOMA

OKLAHOMA PRESS ASSOCIATION

Street address 1: 3601 N Lincoln Blvd
Street address 3: Oklahoma City
Street address state: OK
Zip/Postal code: 73105-5411
Country: USA
Mailing address: 3601 N Lincoln Blvd
Mailing city: Oklahoma City
Mailing state: OK
Mailing zip: 73105-5499
General Phone: (405) 499-0020
General Fax: (405) 499-0048
Advertising Phone: (405) 499-0022
General/National Adv. E-mail: swilkerson@okpress.com
Display Adv. E-mail: lcobb@okpress.com
Primary Website: www.okpress.com
Year Established: 1906
Note: Elections held in June
Personnel: Mark Thomas (Exec. VP); Scott Wilkerson (Office Mgr.); Landon Cobb (Sales Dir.); Lisa Sutliff (Mbr. Serv. Dir.); Jennifer Gilliland (Creat. Serv. Dir.); Keith Burgin (Dig. Clip Serv. Mgr.); Cindy Shea (Adv. Mgr.)

PENNSYLVANIA

HARRISBURG

MANSI MEDIA

Street address 1: 3899 N Front St
Street address 3: Harrisburg
Street address state: PA
Zip/Postal code: 17110-1583
County: Dauphin
Country: USA
General Phone: (717) 703-3030
General Fax: (717) 703-3033
General/National Adv. E-mail: sales@mansimedia.com
Primary Website: www.mansimedia.com
Note: Represents daily and weekly newspapers and their digital products anywhere in the U.S. and beyond.
Personnel: Lisa Knight (VP/Adv.); Chris Kazlauskas; Wes Snider (Dir. Client Solutions); Ronaldo Davis (Sr. Media Buyer); Matthew Caylor (Dir., Interactive Media); Lindsey Artz (Account Manager); Shannon Mohar (Account Manager); Brian Hitchings (Director, Client Solutions)

RHODE ISLAND

PROVIDENCE

RHODE ISLAND PRESS ASSOCIATION

Street address 1: 282 Doyle ave
Street address 3: Providence
Street address state: RI
Zip/Postal code: 2906
County: Providence
Country: USA
Mailing address: 282 Doyle Avenue

Mailing city: Providence
Mailing state: RI
Mailing zip: 2906
General Phone: (401) 874-4287
General Fax: (401) 874-4450
General/National Adv. E-mail: llevin@uri.edu
Primary Website: www.ripress.org
Year Established: 1886
Note: Elections held in Jan
Personnel: Linda Levin (Secretary); Fran Ostendorf (Treasurer)

SOUTH DAKOTA

BROOKINGS

SOUTH DAKOTA NEWSPAPER ASSOCIATION

Street address 1: 1125 32nd Ave
Street address 3: Brookings
Street address state: SD
Zip/Postal code: 57006-4707
County: Brookings
Country: USA
Mailing address: 1125 32nd Ave
Mailing city: Brookings
Mailing state: SD
Mailing zip: 57006-4707
General Phone: (605) 692-4300
General/National Adv. E-mail: sdna@sdna.com
Primary Website: www.sdna.com
Year Established: 1882
Note: Elections held in May
Personnel: David Bordewyk (Exec. Dir.); John Brooks (Advertising Sales Director); Nicole Herrig (Business Manager); Sandy DeBeer (Advertising Placement Coordinator)

WISCONSIN

MADISON

WISCONSIN NEWSPAPER ASSOCIATION

Street address 1: 34 Schroeder Ct
Street address 2: Ste 220
Street address 3: Madison
Street address state: WI
Zip/Postal code: 53711-2528
County: Dane
Country: USA
General Phone: (608) 283-7620
General Fax: (608) 283-7631
General/National Adv. E-mail: wna@wnanews.com
Primary Website: www.wnanews.com
Year Established: 1853
Note: Represents 34 daily and over 225 weekly and specialty newspapers
Personnel: Beth Bennett (Exec. Dir.); Denise Guttery (Media Services Dir.); James Debilzen (Communications Dir.); Julia Hunter (Member Services Dir.)

CANADIAN NEWSPAPER SERVICES

ALBERTA

EDMONTON

ALBERTA WEEKLY NEWSPAPERS ASSOCIATION

Street address 1: 3228 Parsons Rd
Street address 3: Edmonton
Street address state: AB
Zip/Postal code: T6N 1M2
Country: Canada
Mailing address: 3228 Parsons Rd
Mailing city: Edmonton
Mailing state: AB
Mailing zip: T6N 1M2
General Phone: (780) 434-8746
General Fax: (780) 438-8356
General/National Adv. E-mail: info@awna.com
Primary Website: www.awna.com
Personnel: Dennis Merrell (Exec. Dir.)

BRITISH COLUMBIA

BRITISH COLUMBIA/YUKON COMMUNITY NEWSPAPERS ASSOCIATION

Street address 1: #9 West Broadway
Street address 3: Vancouver
Street address state: BC
Zip/Postal code: V5Y 1P1
Country: Canada
Mailing address: #9 West Broadway
Mailing city: Vancouver
Mailing state: BC
Mailing zip: V5Y 1P1
General Phone: (604) 669-9222
General/National Adv. E-mail: info@bccommunitynews.com
Primary Website: www.bccommunitynews.com
Note: Elections held in May
Personnel: George Affleck (Gen. Mgr.)

ORGANIZATION OF NEWS OMBUDSMEN

Street address 1: 6336 Hawthorn Lane
Street address 3: Vancouver
Street address state: BC
Zip/Postal code: V6T 2J6
County: British Columbia
Country: Canada
Mailing address: 6336 Hawthorn Lane
Mailing city: Vancouver
Mailing state: BC
Mailing zip: V6T 2J6
General Phone: (604) 353-6228
General/National Adv. E-mail: klapointe@newsombudsmen.org
Display Adv. E-mail: kirklapointe@gmail.com
Primary Website: www.newsombudsmen.org
Year Established: 1980
Personnel: Kirk LaPointe (Executive Director)

ILLINOIS

KANKAKEE

HUBERGROUP USA, INC.

Street address 1: 2850 Festival Drive
Street address 3: Kankakee
Street address state: IL
Zip/Postal code: 60901
County: Kankakee
Country: USA
Mailing address: 2850 Festival Drive
Mailing city: Kankakee
Mailing state: IL
Mailing zip: 60901
General Phone: (815) 929-9293
General Fax: (815) 929-0412
General/National Adv. E-mail: info.us@hubergroup.com
Primary Website: www.cpima.org
Year Established: 1934
Note: Elections held in Aug. for a two year term
Personnel: Dorothea Nace (Exec. Dir./Sec./Treasurer); Neil Marshall (Pres.); Vivy da Costa (Vice Pres.)

MANITOBA

WINNIPEG

MANITOBA COMMUNITY NEWSPAPER ASSOCIATION

Street address 1: 943 McPhillips Street
Street address 3: Winnipeg
Street address state: MB
Zip/Postal code: R2X 2J9
Country: Canada
Mailing address: 943 McPhillips Street
Mailing city: Winnipeg
Mailing state: MB
Mailing zip: R2X 2J9
General Phone: (204) 947-1691
General Fax: (204) 947-1919
Primary Website: www.mcna.com
Note: Elections held at annual April convention

NOVA SCOTIA

HALIFAX

ATLANTIC COMMUNITY NEWSPAPERS ASSOCIATION

Street address 1: 7075 Bayers Rd., Ste. 216
Street address 3: Halifax
Street address state: NS
Zip/Postal code: B3L 2C2
Country: Canada
Mailing address: 7075 Bayers Rd., Ste. 216
Mailing city: Halifax
Mailing state: NS
Mailing zip: B3L 2C2
General Phone: (902) 832-4480
General Fax: (902) 832-4484
General/National Adv. E-mail: info@newspapersatlantic.ca
Primary Website: www.acna.com
Personnel: Mike Kierstead (Exec. Dir.)

NEW YORK

FOREIGN PRESS ASSOCIATION

Street address 1: 1501 Broadway
Street address 2: 12th Floor
Street address 3: New York
Street address state: NY
Zip/Postal code: 10036
County: New York
Country: USA
Mailing address: 1501 Broadway, 12th Floor
Mailing city: New York
Mailing state: NY
Mailing zip: 10036
General Phone: (212) 370-1054
General/National Adv. E-mail: fpa@foreignpressassociation.org
Primary Website: www.foreignpressassociation.org
Year Established: 1918
Note: Elections held in Dec
Personnel: ⊠⊠‹David P. Michaels (President); Ian Williams (Vice President); Jeffery P. Laner (Treasurer⊠⊠‹⊠⊠‹)

ONTARIO

BURLINGTON

ONTARIO COMMUNITY NEWSPAPERS ASSOCIATION

Street address 1: 3228 South Service Rd. Ste 116
Street address 3: Burlington
Street address state: ON
Zip/Postal code: L7N 3H8
Country: Canada
Mailing address: 3228 South Service Rd. Ste 116
Mailing city: Burlington
Mailing state: ON
Mailing zip: L7N 3H8
General Phone: (905) 639-8720
General Fax: (905) 639-6962
General/National Adv. E-mail: info@ocna.org
Primary Website: www.ocna.org
Year Established: 1950
Personnel: Anne Lannan (Executive Director)
Newspaper (for newspapers group): Member Services Coordinator, Toronto

General Fax: (800) 990-4329
General/National Adv. E-mail: service@napsnet.com; info@napsnet.com
Primary Website: www.napsnet.com
Year Established: 1958
Personnel: Dorothy York (Pres.); Gary Lipton (Vice Pres., Media Rel.); Candace Leiberman (Ed. in Chief); Yauling Wagner (Serv. Mgr.)

SYNDICATED AD FEATURES, INC.

Street address 1: 1600 Providence Hwy
Street address city: Walpole
Street address state: MA
Zip/Postal code: 02081-4408
County: Norfolk
Country: USA
Mailing state: MA
Mailing zip: 02081
General Phone: 508-668-2150
General Fax: (508) 668-2168
General/National Adv. E-mail: info@synadinc.com
Primary Website: www.synadinc.com
Year Established: 1967
Personnel: David G. Margolis (Pres.); Bill Blumsack (Vice Pres./Eastern Regl. Sales Dir.); Susan Gundersen (Office Mgr.); Tim Wydro (Mid-Atlantic Regl. Sales Mgr.); Jodi Rutkowski (Controller)

THOUGHT EQUITY MANAGEMENT, INC.

Street address 1: 1530 16th St
Street address 2: Fl 6
Street address city: Denver
Street address state: CO
Zip/Postal code: 80202-1447
County: Denver
Country: USA
Mailing address: 1530 16th St Ste 600
Mailing city: Denver
Mailing state: CO
Mailing zip: 80202-1447
General Phone: (720) 382-2869
General Fax: (720) 382-2719
General/National Adv. E-mail: sales@thoughtequity.com
Primary Website: www.thoughtequity.com
Year Established: 2003
Personnel: Kevin Schaff (Founder/CEO); Mark Lemmons (CTO); Mike Emerson (Vice Pres., Mktg.); Frank Cardello (Vice Pres., Bus. Devel.)

CLIPPING BUREAUS

ARKANSAS

LITTLE ROCK

ARKANSAS NEWSPAPER CLIPPING SERVICE

Street address 1: 411 S Victory St
Street address 2: Ste 201
Street address 3: Little Rock
Street address state: AR
Zip/Postal code: 72201-2935
County: Pulaski
Country: USA
Mailing address: 411 S Victory St Ste 201
Mailing city: Little Rock
Mailing state: AR
Mailing zip: 72201-2935
General Phone: (573) 474-1000
General Fax: (573) 474-1001
General/National Adv. E-mail: sfrieling@newsgroup.com
Primary Website: www.newzgroup.com
Year Established: 1995
Personnel: Shirley Anderson (Mgr.)

CALIFORNIA

LOS ANGELES

ALLEN'S PRESS CLIPPING BUREAU

Street address 1: 215 W 6th St
Street address 2: Apt 1100
Street address 3: Los Angeles
Street address state: CA
Zip/Postal code: 90014-1931
County: Los Angeles
Country: USA
Mailing address: 215 W 6th St Apt 1100
Mailing city: Los Angeles
Mailing state: CA
Mailing zip: 90014-1931
General Phone: (213) 628-4214
General Fax: (213) 627-0889
General/National Adv. E-mail: la@allenspcb.com
Primary Website: www.allenspress.4t.com
Personnel: Linda Wiser (Office Mgr)

SAN FRANCISCO

ALLEN'S PRESS CLIPPING BUREAU

Street address 1: 657 Mission St
Street address 2: Ste 602
Street address 3: San Francisco
Street address state: CA
Zip/Postal code: 94105-4120
County: San Francisco
Country: USA
Mailing address: 657 Mission St Ste 602
Mailing city: San Francisco
Mailing state: CA
Mailing zip: 94105-4197
General Phone: (415) 392-2353
General Fax: (415) 362-6208
Primary Website: www.allenspress.4t.com
Personnel: John N. McCombs (Gen. Mgr.)

COLORADO

COLORADO PRESS CLIPPING SERVICE

Street address 1: 1120 N Lincoln St
Street address 2: Ste 912
Street address 3: Denver
Street address state: CO
Zip/Postal code: 80203-2138
County: Denver
Country: USA
Mailing address: 1120 Lincoln St., Ste 912
Mailing city: Denver
Mailing state: CO
Mailing zip: 80203
General Phone: (303) 571-5117
General Fax: (303) 571-1803
General/National Adv. E-mail: coloradopress@colopress.net
Primary Website: www.coloradopressassociation.com
Personnel: Jerry Raehal (CEO)

ENG

LONDON

INTERNATIONAL PRESS CUTTING BUREAU

Street address 1: 224/236 Walworth Rd.
Street address 3: London
Street address state: ENG
Zip/Postal code: SE17 1JE
Country: UK
Mailing address: 224/236 Walworth Rd.
Mailing city: London
Mailing state: ENG
Mailing zip: SE17 1JE
General Phone: 77082113
General Fax: 77014489
General/National Adv. E-mail: info@ipcb.co.uk
Primary Website: www.ipcb.co.uk
Personnel: Robert Podro (Sr. Partner/Gen. Mgr.)

IOWA

IOWA PRESS CLIPPING BUREAU

Street address 1: 319 E. 5th St., Ste. 6
Street address 2: Ste 6
Street address 3: Des Moines
Street address state: IA
Zip/Postal code: 50309
County: Polk
Country: USA
Mailing address: PO Box 873
Mailing city: Columbia
Mailing state: MO
Mailing zip: 65205
General Phone: (573) 474-1000
General/National Adv. E-mail: service@newzgroup.com
Primary Website: www.newzgroup.com/
Year Established: 1996
Personnel: Sarah Frieling (Director of Customer Service)
Parent company (for newspapers): Newz Group

ILLINOIS

CHICAGO

CISION

Street address 1: 130 E Randolph St, 7th Floor
Street address 3: Chicago
Street address state: IL
Zip/Postal code: 60601
Country: USA
Mailing address: 130 E Randolph St, 7th Floor
Mailing city: Chicago
Mailing state: IL
Mailing zip: 60601
General Phone: 866-639-5087
General/National Adv. E-mail: CisionPR@cision.com
Primary Website: www.cision.com
Year Established: 1867
Personnel: Kevin Akeroyd (CEO); Jack Pearlstein (Exec. VP And CFO); Whitney Benner (Chief HR Officer)

CISION US, INC.

Street address 1: 332 S Michigan Ave
Street address 3: Chicago
Street address state: IL
Zip/Postal code: 60604-4434
County: Cook
Country: USA
Mailing address: 332 S Michigan Ave Ste 900
Mailing city: Chicago
Mailing state: IL
Mailing zip: 60604-4393
General Phone: (866) 639-5087
General Fax: (312) 922-3127
General/National Adv. E-mail: info.us@cision.com
Primary Website: www.cision.com
Personnel: Michael Renderman (Vice Pres., Bus. Devel.); Diana Eagen (Exec.Dir.)

ILLINOIS PRESS CLIPPING BUREAU

Street address 1: 900 Community Dr
Street address 3: Springfield
Street address state: IL
Zip/Postal code: 62703-5180
County: Sangamon
Country: USA
Mailing address: 900 Community Dr
Mailing city: Springfield
Mailing state: IL
Mailing zip: 62703-5180
General Phone: (217) 241-1300
General Fax: (217) 241-1301
General/National Adv. E-mail: rkline@illinoispress.org
Primary Website: www.IllinoisPress.org
Personnel: Sam Fisher (Executive Director)

KANSAS

KANSAS PRESS CLIPPING SERVICE

Street address 1: 5423 SW 7th St
Street address 3: Topeka
Street address state: KS
Zip/Postal code: 66606-2330
County: Shawnee
Country: USA
Mailing address: PO Box 873
Mailing city: Columbia
Mailing state: MO
Mailing zip: 65205
General Phone: (573) 474-1000
General/National Adv. E-mail: service@newzgroup.com
Primary Website: www.newzgroup.com
Year Established: 2005
Personnel: Sarah Frieling (Director of Customer Service)
Parent company (for newspapers): Newz Group

MISSOURI

COLUMBIA

KENTUCKY PRESS CLIPPING SERVICE - NEWZ GROUP

Street address 1: 409 W. Vandiver, Bldg #3, Ste. 100
Street address 2: Bldg 3 # STE 100
Street address 3: Columbia
Street address state: MO
Zip/Postal code: 65202

County: Boone
Country: USA
Mailing address: PO Box 873
Mailing city: Columbia
Mailing state: MO
Mailing zip: 65205-0873
General Phone: (573) 474-1000
General Fax: (573) 474-1001
General/National Adv. E-mail: info@newzgroup.com
Primary Website: www.newzgroup.com
Year Established: 1995
Parent company (for newspapers): Geotel

MISSOURI PRESS CLIPPING BUREAU - NEWZ GROUP

Street address 1: 409 W. Vandiver, Bldg #3, Ste. 100
Street address 2: Bldg 3 # STE 100
Street address 3: Columbia
Street address state: MO
Zip/Postal code: 65202
County: Boone
Country: USA
Mailing address: PO Box 873
Mailing city: Columbia
Mailing state: MO
Mailing zip: 65205-0873
General Phone: (573) 474-1000
General Fax: (573) 474-1001
General/National Adv. E-mail: info@newzgroup.com
Primary Website: www.newzgroup.com
Year Established: 1995
Personnel: Brad Buchanan (President/CEO); Lee Brooks (Mgr.)
Parent company (for newspapers): Geotel

NEW MEXICO PRESS CLIPPING BUREAU - NEWZ GROUP

Street address 1: 409 W. Vandiver, Bldg #3, Ste. 100
Street address 2: Bldg 3 # STE 100
Street address 3: Columbia
Street address state: MO
Zip/Postal code: 65202
County: Boone
Country: USA
Mailing address: PO Box 873
Mailing city: Columbia
Mailing state: MO
Mailing zip: 65205-0873
General Phone: (573) 474-1000
General Fax: (573) 474-1001
General/National Adv. E-mail: info@newzgroup.com
Primary Website: www.newzgroup.com
Year Established: 1995
Parent company (for newspapers): Geotel

NEWZ GROUP

Street address 1: 409 Vandiver Dr
Street address 2: Bldg 3
Street address 3: Columbia
Street address state: MO
Zip/Postal code: 65202-3754
County: Boone
Country: USA
Mailing address: PO Box 873
Mailing city: Columbia
Mailing state: MO
Mailing zip: 65205-0873
General Phone: (573) 474-1000
General Fax: (573) 474-1001
General/National Adv. E-mail: info@newzgroup.com
Primary Website: www.newzgroup.com
Year Established: 1991
Personnel: Brad Buchanan (Pres.); Scott Buchanan (Vice Pres.); Ian Buchanan (Vice President)

WEST VIRGINIA PRESS CLIPPING BUREAU - NEWZ GROUP

Street address 1: 409 W. Vandiver, Bldg #3, Ste. 100
Street address 2: Bldg 3 # STE 100
Street address 3: Columbia
Street address state: MO
Zip/Postal code: 65202
County: Boone
Country: USA
Mailing address: PO Box 873
Mailing city: Columbia
Mailing state: MO
Mailing zip: 65205-0873
General Phone: (573) 474-1000
General Fax: (573) 474-1001
General/National Adv. E-mail: info@newzgroup.com
Primary Website: www.newzgroup.com
Year Established: 1995
Parent company (for newspapers): Geotel

WYOMING NEWSPAPER CLIPPING SERVICE

Street address 1: 409 Vandiver Dr
Street address 2: Bldg 3 # STE 100
Street address 3: Columbia
Street address state: MO
Zip/Postal code: 65202-3754
County: Boone
Country: USA
Mailing address: PO Box 873
Mailing city: Columbia
Mailing state: MO
Mailing zip: 65205-0873
General Phone: (573) 474-1000
General Fax: (573) 474-1001
General/National Adv. E-mail: info@newzgroup.com
Primary Website: www.newzgroup.com
Year Established: 1995
Parent company (for newspapers): Geotel

NEW JERSEY

FLORHAM PARK

BURRELLES

Street address 1: 30 B Vreeland Road
Street address 2: # B
Street address 3: Florham Park
Street address state: NJ
Zip/Postal code: 7932
County: Morris
Country: USA
Mailing address: PO Box 674
Mailing city: Florham Park
Mailing state: NJ
Mailing zip: 7932
General Phone: (973) 992-6600
General Fax: (973) 992-7675
General/National Adv. E-mail: inquiry@burrellesluce.com
Primary Website: www.burrellesluce.com
Year Established: 1888
Personnel: Robert C. Waggoner (Chrmn./ CEO); John P. French (Pres./COO); Rick Melchers (VP, Director of National Sales); Steven Townsley (Director of Publisher Services); Daniel Schaible (Senior VP, Content Management); Michael Lillis (Content Acquisition Specialist)
Newspaper (for newspapers group): New England Newsclip Agency, Inc., Florham Park

NEW ENGLAND NEWSCLIP AGENCY, INC.

Street address 1: 30 Vreeland Rd
Street address 2: # B
Street address 3: Florham Park
Street address state: NJ
Zip/Postal code: 07932-1901
County: Morris
Country: USA
Mailing address: PO Box 674
Mailing city: Florham Park
Mailing state: NJ
Mailing zip: 07932-0674
General Phone: (800) 631-1160
General Fax: (973) 992-7675
General/National Adv. E-mail: mmckenna@burrellesluce.com
Primary Website: www.burrellesluce.com
Personnel: Michael McKenna (National Sales Manager)
Parent company (for newspapers): Burrelles

OREGON

PORTLAND

ALLEN'S PRESS CLIPPING BUREAU

Street address 1: 621 SW Alder St
Street address 2: Ste 540
Street address 3: Portland
Street address state: OR
Zip/Postal code: 97205-3620
County: Multnomah
Country: USA
Mailing address: 621 SW Alder St Ste 540
Mailing city: Portland
Mailing state: OR
Mailing zip: 97205-3691
General Phone: (503) 223-7824
General Fax: (503) 223-3819
General/National Adv. E-mail: portland@allenspcb.com
Primary Website: www.allenspress.4t.com
Personnel: Whit Draper (Office Mgr.)

SOUTH CAROLINA

SOUTH CAROLINA PRESS CLIPPING BUREAU

Street address 1: 106 Outlet Pointe Blvd
Street address 3: Columbia
Street address state: SC
Zip/Postal code: 29210-5669
County: Lexington
Country: USA
Mailing address: PO Box 873
Mailing city: Columbia
Mailing state: MO
Mailing zip: 65205
General Phone: (573) 474-1000
General/National Adv. E-mail: service@newzgroup.com
Primary Website: www.newzgroup.com
Year Established: 1999
Personnel: Sarah Frieling (Director of Customer Service)
Parent company (for newspapers): Newz Group

SOUTH DAKOTA

SOUTH DAKOTA NEWSPAPER ASSOCIATION

Street address 1: 1125 32nd Ave
Street address 3: Brookings
Street address state: SD
Zip/Postal code: 57006-4707
County: Brookings
Country: USA
Mailing address: 1125 32nd Ave
Mailing city: Brookings
Mailing state: SD
Mailing zip: 57006-4707
General Phone: (605) 692-4300
General/National Adv. E-mail: sdna@sdna.com
Primary Website: www.sdna.com
Year Established: 1882
Note: Elections held in May
Personnel: David Bordewyk (Exec. Dir.); John Brooks (Advertising Sales Director); Nicole Herrig (Business Manager); Sandy DeBeer (Advertising Placement Coordinator)

TENNESSEE

KNOXVILLE

TENNESSEE PRESS ASSOCIATION

Street address 1: 412 N. Cedar Bluff Road
Street address 2: Suite 403
Street address 3: Knoxville
Street address state: TN
Zip/Postal code: 37923
County: Knox
Country: USA
Mailing address: 412 N. Cedar Bluff Road
Mailing city: Knoxville
Mailing state: TN
Mailing zip: 37923
General Phone: 865-584-5761
General Fax: 865-558-8687
General/National Adv. E-mail: info@tnpress.com
Primary Website: www.tnpress.com
Year Established: 1947
Note: Elections held in June
Personnel: Carol Daniels (Exec. V. P.); Shelley Davis (Sales and Marketing); Robyn Gentile (Member Services Manager); Earl Goodman (Senior Media Buyer); Becky Moats (Networks Coordinator); Jason Davidson (National Sales Rep.)

VIRGINIA

ASHLAND

VIRGINIA CLIPPING SERVICE

Street address 1: 10195 Maple Leaf Ct
Street address 3: Ashland
Street address state: VA
Zip/Postal code: 23005-8136
County: Hanover
Country: USA
Mailing address: 10195 Maple Leaf Ct
Mailing city: Ashland
Mailing state: VA
Mailing zip: 23005-8136
General Phone: (804) 550-5114
General Fax: (804) 550-5116
General/National Adv. E-mail: virginiaclipping@burrellesluce.com
Primary Website: www.vaclippingservice.com
Personnel: Duska Adams (Client Servs. Mgr.)

WASHINGTON

SEATTLE

ALLEN'S PRESS CLIPPING BUREAU

Street address 1: 1218 3rd Ave
Street address 2: Ste 1010
Street address 3: Seattle
Street address state: WA
Zip/Postal code: 98101-3290
County: King
Country: USA
Mailing address: 1218 3rd Ave # 1010
Mailing city: Seattle
Mailing state: WA
Mailing zip: 98101-3097
General Phone: (206) 622-8312
General Fax: (206) 622-5748
General/National Adv. E-mail: seattle@allenspcb.com
Primary Website: www.allenspress.4t.com
Year Established: 1888

Personnel: Grace Chrystie (Regional Manager)

ROMEIKE LTD.

Street address 1: Romeike House, 290-296 Green Lanes, Palmers Green
Street address 3: London
Zip/Postal code: N13 5TP
Country: UK
Mailing address: Romeike House, 290-296 Green Lanes
Mailing city: London
Mailing zip: N13 5TP
General Phone: 8820155
General Fax: 8826716
Primary Website: www.romeike.com
Personnel: Giselle Bodie (Mng. Dir.); Michael Higgins (Mng. Dir.)

DAILY NATIONAL NEWSPAPER REPRESENTATIVE

AD REPS

Street address 1: 51 Church St
Street address city: Boston
Street address state: MA
Zip/Postal code: 02116-5417
County: Suffolk
Country: USA
Mailing address: 51 Church St
Mailing city: Boston
Mailing state: MA
Mailing zip: 02116-5417
General Phone: (617) 542-6913
General Fax: (617) 542-7227
General/National Adv. E-mail: adreps1@yahoo.com
Personnel: Steve Ganak (Pres.)

ADVANTAGE NEWSPAPER CONSULTANTS

Street address 1: 2850 Village Dr
Street address 2: Ste 102
Street address city: Fayetteville
Street address state: NC
Zip/Postal code: 28304-3864
County: Cumberland
Country: USA
Mailing address: 2850 Village Dr
Mailing city: Fayetteville
Mailing state: NC
Mailing zip: 28304
General Phone: (910) 323-0349
General Fax: (910) 323-9280
General/National Adv. E-mail: info@newspaperconsultants.com
Primary Website: newspaperconsultants.com
Year Established: 1996
Note: Advantage Newspaper Consultants (ANC) is recognized as the leader in TV Magazine advertising sales in the United States. ANC works with both independent publishers and major newspaper chains to increase their core product ad revenue using innovative campaigns and creative, seasoned sales professionals that produce quantifiable results. Our sales managerâ€™s work with newspaper management to set goals and create an incentive plan which accelerates a TV Magazine sales campaign targeted towards finding key hidden revenue in their market in two weeks or less. Using the same proven formula of enthusiastic joint sales calls and dedicated management support that has lead to thousands of successful TV magazine sales campaigns, ANC also offers a cross-platform advertising sales program - Total Market Reach (TMR) - which includes print, mobile and digital ad combo sales.
Personnel: Timothy O. Dellinger (President); Susan M. Jolley (General Mgr.); Marie Smith (Exec. Dir. of Sales)

ADVERTISING MEDIA PLUS, INC.

Street address 1: 5397 Twin Knolls Rd
Street address 2: Ste 17
Street address city: Columbia
Street address state: MD
Zip/Postal code: 21045-3256
County: Howard
Country: USA
Mailing address: PO Box 1529
Mailing city: Ellicott City
Mailing state: MD
Mailing zip: 21041-1529
General Phone: (410) 740-5009
General Fax: (410) 740-5888
General/National Adv. E-mail: info@ampsinc.net
Primary Website: www.ampsinc.net
Year Established: 2001
Personnel: Daniel Medinger (Owner and President)
Parent company (for newspapers): Medinger Media LLC

AMERICAN NEWSPAPER REPRESENTATIVES, INC.

Street address 1: 2075 W Big Beaver Rd
Street address 2: Ste 310
Street address city: Troy
Street address state: MI
Zip/Postal code: 48084-3439
County: Oakland
Country: USA
Mailing address: 2075 W Big Beaver Rd Ste 310
Mailing city: Troy
Mailing state: MI
Mailing zip: 48084-3439
General Phone: (248) 643-9910
General Fax: (248) 643-9914
General/National Adv. E-mail: accountsales@gotoanr.com
Primary Website: www.gotoanr.com
Year Established: 1943
Note: ANR represents over 9,000 daily and weekly community newspapers nationwide
Personnel: Melanie Cox (Sales Mgr.); John Jepsen (Pres.); Robert Sontag (Exec. Vice Pres./COO)

CALIFORNIA NEWSPAPER SERVICE BUREAU (CNSB)

Street address 1: 915 E 1st St
Street address city: Los Angeles
Street address state: CA
Zip/Postal code: 90012-4050
County: Los Angeles
Country: USA
Mailing address: 915 E 1st St
Mailing city: Los Angeles
Mailing state: CA
Mailing zip: 90012-4000
General Phone: (213) 229-5500
General Fax: (213) 229-5481
General/National Adv. E-mail: bulksales@dailyjournal.com
Primary Website: www.legaladstore.com
Year Established: 1888
Note: The Daily Journal Corporation is a publisher of legal and business publications, including the Los Angeles and San Francisco Daily Journals, distributed in major California cities. Additionally, its in-house clearinghouse service provides ad placement services to government agencies, attorney's and other advertisers for legally mandated and outreach advertising including class action notices in any daily, community and/or ethnic publication and/or websites.
Personnel: Noemi Mendoza (Bulk Sale of Business Assets)

CAMPUS MEDIA GROUP

Street address 1: 7760 France Ave S
Street address 2: Ste 800
Street address city: Bloomington
Street address state: MN
Zip/Postal code: 55435-5929
County: Hennepin
Country: USA
Mailing address: 7760 France Ave South, Suite 800
Mailing city: Bloomington
Mailing state: MN
Mailing zip: 55435
General Phone: (952) 854-3100
General/National Adv. E-mail: sales@campusmediagroup.com
Primary Website: www.campusmediagroup.com
Year Established: 2002
Note: College marketing agency.
Personnel: Jason Bakker (COO); Tom Borgerding (Pres./CEO)

CENTRO INC.

Street address 1: 11 E Madison St
Street address 2: 6th Fl.
Street address city: Chicago
Street address state: IL
Zip/Postal code: 60602-4574
County: Cook
Country: USA
Mailing address: 11 E. Madison St.
Mailing city: Chicago
Mailing state: IL
Mailing zip: 60602
General Phone: (312) 423-1565
General/National Adv. E-mail: socialmedia@centro.net
Primary Website: www.centro.net
Year Established: 2001
Personnel: Katie Risch (EVP, Customer Experience); John Hyland (VP, Pub. Solutions)

C-VILLE HOLDINGS LLC

Street address 1: 308 E Main St
Street address city: Charlottesville
Street address state: VA
Zip/Postal code: 22902-5234
County: Charlottesville City
Country: USA
Mailing address: P.O. Box 119
Mailing city: Charlottesville
Mailing state: VA
Mailing zip: 22902
General Phone: 434/817-2749
General Fax: 434/817-2758
General/National Adv. E-mail: aimee@c-ville.com
Primary Website: www.c-ville.com
Year Established: 1995
Personnel: Jessica Luck (Ed)
Newspapers (for newspaper groups): North Coast Journal, Eureka; Santa Cruz Good Times, Santa Cruz; C-ville Weekly, Charlottesville; Boise Weekly, Boise; Boston Phoenix, Boston; Las Vegas Mercury, Las Vegas; Desert Post Weekly, Palm Springs; Santa Barbara Independent, Santa Barbara; Pacific Sun, San Rafael; Providence Phoenix, Providence; Times Of Acadiana, Lafayette; Urban Tulsa Weekly (OOB), Tulsa; Reno News & Review, Reno; City Link (OOB), Tamarac; Metroland, Albany; San Francisco Bay Guardian (OOB), San Francisco; Palo Alto Weekly, Palo Alto; Nashville Scene, Nashville; The Independent Weekly, Durham; Las Vegas Weekly, Henderson; Hartford Courant-OOB, Hartford; Philadelphia City Paper (OOB), Philadelphia; Style Weekly, Richmond; Illinois Times, Springfield; Easy Reader, Hermosa Beach; Flagpole Magazine, Athens; THE MIRROR

HARTE-HANKS COMMUNICATIONS, INC.

Street address 1: 9601 McAllister Fwy
Street address 2: Ste 610
Street address city: San Antonio
Street address state: TX
Zip/Postal code: 78216-4632
County: Bexar
Country: USA
Mailing address: 9601 McAllister Fwy Ste 610
Mailing city: San Antonio
Mailing state: TX
Mailing zip: 78216-4632
General Phone: (210) 829-9000
General Fax: (210) 829-9101
General/National Adv. E-mail: media@hartehanks.com
Primary Website: www.hartehanks.com
Note: Represents shopper publications
Personnel: Jon Biro (CFO)

INNOTEK CORPORATION

Street address 1: 9140 Zachary Ln N
Street address city: Maple Grove
Street address state: MN
Zip/Postal code: 55369-4003
County: Hennepin
Country: USA
Mailing address: 9140 Zachary Ln N
Mailing city: Maple Grove
Mailing state: MN
Mailing zip: 55369-4003
General Phone: (763) 488 9902
General Fax: (763)488 9904
General/National Adv. E-mail: sales@innotek-ep.com
Primary Website: www.innotek-ep.com
Year Established: 1960
Personnel: Dennis Burns (CEO Chairman); David Kalina (Vice Pres., Finance); Tom Wiese (Vice President of Sales & Engineering)

INTERSECT MEDIA SOLUTIONS

Street address 1: 1025 Greenwood Blvd.
Street address 2: Suite 191
Street address city: Lake Mary
Street address state: FL
Zip/Postal code: 32746-5410
County: Seminole
Country: USA
Mailing address: 1025 Greenwood Blvd., Suite 191
Mailing city: Lake Mary
Mailing state: FL
Mailing zip: 32746-5410
General Phone: (866) 404-5913
General/National Adv. E-mail: info@mediagenius.com
Primary Website: www.intersectmediasolutions.com
Year Established: 1959
Personnel: Dean Ridings (Pres./CEO); Mark Burger (VP, Finance & CFO); Carolyn Nolte (VP, Strategy); Jessica Pitts (VP, Operations)
Parent company (for newspapers): Florida Press Association

JOSEPH JACOBS ORGANIZATION

Street address 1: 349 W 87th St
Street address 2: Ste 1
Street address city: New York
Street address state: NY
Zip/Postal code: 10024-2662
County: New York
Country: USA
Mailing address: 349 W 87th St Ste 1
Mailing city: New York

Mailing state: NY
Mailing zip: 10024-2662
General Phone: (212) 787-9400
General Fax: (212) 787-8080
General/National Adv. E-mail: erosenfeld@josephjacobs.org
Primary Website: www.josephjacobs.org
Year Established: 1919
Note: Represents Jewish publications
Personnel: David Koch (Pres.)
Newspapers (for newspaper groups): Algemeiner Journal, Brooklyn; Jewish Exponent, Philadelphia; Newton TAB, Needham; Canadian Jewish News, Concord; THE OBSERVER, Karachi; The Forward, New York; Aufbau (OOB), New York; Las Vegas Israelite, Las Vegas; Jewish Review, Portland; Texas Jewish Post, Dallas; Ohio Jewish Chronicle, Columbus; The Jewish State (OOB), Highland Park; Berkshire Jewish Voice, Pittsfield ; Buffalo Jewish Review, Buffalo; Jewish Community News, Los Gatos; Jewish Post of New York (OOB), New York; Jewish Standard, Teaneck; The Speaker-OOB, Highland Park; Jewish Times, Pleasantville; Jewish Voice, Cherry Hill; Rockland Jewish Reporter, West Nyack; Jewish Week, New York; The Jewish Reporter, Framingham; The Jewish Civic Press, New Orleans; Washington Jewish Week, Rockville; Jewish Journal, Valley Stream; Der Yid, Brooklyn; Jewish Reporter, Las Vegas; Connecticut Jewish Ledger, West Hartford; Jewish Press, Omaha; Charlotte Jewish News, Charlotte; Intermountain Jewish News, Denver; Manhattan Jewish Sentinel, Far Rockaway; Stark Jewish News, Canton; The American Israelite, Cincinnati; The Detroit Jewish News, Southfield; Jewish News, Metairie

LATINO 247 MEDIA GROUP

Street address 1: 3445 Catalina Dr
Street address city: Carlsbad
Street address state: CA
Zip/Postal code: 92010-2856
County: San Diego
Country: USA
Mailing address: 3445 Catalina Dr.
Mailing city: Carlsbad
Mailing state: CA
Mailing zip: 92010-2856
General Phone: (760) 579-1696
General Fax: (760) 434-7476
General/National Adv. E-mail: kirk@whisler.com
Primary Website: www.latinos247.com
Year Established: 1996
Personnel: Kirk Whisler (Pres.); Ana PatiÃ±o (General Manager); Ericka Benitez (Accounting Manager)

MCNAUGHTON NEWSPAPERS

Street address 1: 424 E State Pkwy
Street address 2: Ste 228
Street address city: Schaumburg
Street address state: IL
Zip/Postal code: 60173-6406
County: Cook
Country: USA
Mailing address: 424 E State Pkwy Ste 228
Mailing city: Schaumburg
Mailing state: IL
Mailing zip: 60173-6408
General Phone: (847) 490-6000
General Fax: (847) 843-9058
General/National Adv. E-mail: rickb@usspi.com
Primary Website: www.usspi.com
Note: Designs cost effective print and digital solutions for national/regional/local advertisers.
Personnel: Rick Baranski (Vice President Media Relations); Philip Miller (CEO); Barbara Ancona (Vice President Sales); Michelle Hammons (Executive Vice President)
Newspapers (for newspaper groups): Benicia Herald, Benicia; Cherokee Tribune, Canton; Monitor, Fraser; The Journal Register, Palmer; Castroville News Bulletin, Castroville; The Noblesville Ledger, Fishers; Tonawanda News (OOB), North Tonawanda; The Edmond Sun, Edmond; Valley News Dispatch, Tarentum; Manassas Journal Messenger (OOB), Manassas; The Davis Enterprise, DAVIS; Rushville Republican, Rushville; DAILY NEWS, Saint Croix; La Opinion, Ica

MEDIASPACE SOLUTIONS

Street address 1: 5600 Rowland Rd
Street address 2: Suite 170
Street address city: Minnetonka
Street address state: MN
Zip/Postal code: 55343
County: Hennepin
Country: USA
Mailing address: 5600 Rowland Rd, Suite 170
Mailing city: Minnetonka
Mailing state: MN
Mailing zip: 55343
General Phone: (612) 253-3900
General Fax: (612) 454-2848
General/National Adv. E-mail: bstcyr@mediaspace.com
Primary Website: www.mediaspacesolutions.com
Year Established: 1999
Personnel: Randy Grunow (Chief Operating Officer); Brian St. Cyr (VP of Business Development & Marketing); Tony Buesing (Dir., Account Development); Brian Kieser (Sr. Med. Supervisor); Colin May (Director of Media Development); Carol Wagner (Buying Manager); Jason Armstrong (Buying Supervisor); Tom Johnson (Director Media Planning)

METRO SUBURBIA, INC./NEWHOUSE NEWSPAPERS

Street address 1: 711 3rd Ave
Street address 2: Fl 6
Street address city: New York
Street address state: NY
Zip/Postal code: 10017-4029
County: New York
Country: USA
Mailing address: 711 3rd Ave Rm 1500
Mailing city: New York
Mailing state: NY
Mailing zip: 10017-9201
General Phone: (212) 697-8020
General Fax: (212) 972-3146
General/National Adv. E-mail: johnt@metrosuburbia.com
Primary Website: www.metrosuburbia.com
Personnel: Kevin Drolet (Adv. Sales Mgr.); John Tingwall (Adv. Sales Mgr.); Chad Johnson (Adv. Sales Mgr.); Robert N. Schoenbacher (Pres.); John A. Colombo (New York Sales Mgr.); Jon Gold (Adv. Sales Mgr.); Brenda Goodwin-Garcia (Adv. Sales Mgr.)
Newspapers (for newspaper groups): Shawano Leader, Shawano

METROLAND MEDIA GROUP LTD.

Street address 1: 3715 Laird Road
Street address 2: Unit 6
Street address city: Mississauga
Street address state: ON
Zip/Postal code: L5L 0A3
Country: Canada
Mailing address: 3715 Laird Road, Unit 6
Mailing city: Mississauga
Mailing state: ON
Mailing zip: L5L 0A3
General Phone: (866) 838-8960
General Fax: (905) 279-5103
General/National Adv. E-mail: result@metroland.com
Primary Website: www.metroland.com
Personnel: Ian Oliver (Pres.); Kathie Bride (Vice Pres.); Tim Whittaker (Sr. Vice Pres.); Ian McLeod (Sr. Vice Pres.); Ian Proudfoot (Vice Pres.); Brenda Biller (Vice Pres., HR); Joe Anderson (Vice Pres.); Bruce Danford (Vice Pres.); Ron Lenyk (Vice Pres.); Ken Nugent (Vice Pres.); Carol Peddie (Vice Pres.); Gordon Paolucci; Kukle Terry (Vice President); Lois Tuffin (Ed-In-Chief); John Willems; Scott Miller Cressman; Tracy Magee-Graham; Haggert Peter (Editor-In-Chief); Terry Kukle (VP, Business Development & Acquisitions)
Newspapers (for newspaper groups): The Wasaga Sun, Wasaga Beach; Banner Post, Grimshaw; Belleville News, Belleville; Fort Erie Post, Thorold; Independent & Free Press, Georgetown; Ajax-pickering News Advertiser, Oshawa; The Alliston Herald, Alliston; Almaguin News, Burks Falls; Ancaster News, Stoney Creek; Arnprior Chronicle-Guide, Arnprior; Arthur Enterprise News, Mount Forest; The Aurora Banner, Aurora; The Barrie Advance, Barrie; Beach-Riverdale Mirror, Toronto; Belleville News Emc, Belleville; Bloor West Villager, Toronto; Bracebridge Examiner, Bracebridge; Bradford & West Gwillimbury Topic, Newmarket; Brampton Guardian, Mississauga; Brant News, Brantford; The Brighton Independent, Brighton; Brock Citizen, Cannington; The Burlington Post, Burlington; Caledon Enterprise, Bolton; Cambridge Times, Cambridge; The Carleton Place-almonte Canadian Gazette Emc, Smith Falls; City Centre Mirror, Toronto; Clarington This Week, Oshawa; Dundas Star News, Stoney Creek; Express, Meaford; The East York Mirror, Willowdale; The Elmira Independent, Elmira; The Erin Advocate, Erin; Etobicoke Guardian, Etobicoke; Times Advocate, Exeter; The Fergus-elora News Express, Fergus; The Flamborough Review, Waterdown; The Frontenac Gazette, Kingston; The Georgina Advocate, Keswick; Glanbrook Gazette, Caledonia; The Gravenhurst Banner, Gravenhurst; The Grimsby Lincoln News, Grimsby; The Guelph Mercury Tribune, Guelph; Guelph Tribune, Guelph; Hamilton Mountain News, Stoney Creek; The Hamilton Spectator, Hamilton; Huntsville Forester, Huntsville; Innisfil Journal, Barrie; Kanata Kourier-standard Emc, Ottawa; Kawartha Lakes This Week, Lindsay; Kemptville Advance Emc, Smiths Falls; Kingston Heritage Emc, Kingston; Kitchener Post, Kitchener; The Listowel Banner, Listowel; Manotick News Emc, Ottawa; Markham Economist & Sun, Markham; The Mirror, Midland; The Milton Canadian Champion, Milton; Minto Express, Palmerston; Mississauga News, Mississauga; The Mount Forest Confederate, Mount Forest; The Muskokan, Bracebridge; Nepean-barrhaven News Emc, Ottawa; New Hamburg Independent, New Hamburg; The Newmarket Era-banner, Newmarket; North York Mirror, Toronto; Northumberland News, Cobourg; Niagara This Week, Thorold; Oakville Beaver, Oakville; The Orangeville Banner, Orangeville; Orillia Today, Orillia; Orleans News Emc, Ottawa; Oshawa-whitby This Week, Oshawa; Ottawa East Emc, Ottawa; Ottawa South Emc, Ottawa; Ottawa West Emc, Ottawa; The Parkdale Villager, Toronto; Parry Sound Beacon Star, Parry Sound; Parry Sound North Star, Parry Sound; The Perth Courier Emc, Smith Falls; Peterborough This Week, Peterborough; The Port Perry Star, Port Perry; Quinte West Emc, Belleville; The Renfrew Mercury Emc, Renfrew; The Richmond Hill Liberal, Markham; The Grand River Sachem, Caledonia; The Scarborough Mirror, Toronto; Smiths Falls Record News Emc, Smiths Falls; South Asian Focus, Brampton; St. Lawrence News, Brockville; St. Mary's Journal Argus, St Marys; St. Thomas/elgin Weekly News, Saint Thomas; The Stayner Sun, Wasaga Beach; The Stittsville News, Ottawa; Stoney Creek News, Stoney Creek; Stratford Gazette, Stratford; Collingwood Connection, Collingwood; Uxbridge Times-journal, Uxbridge; Vaughan Citizen, Vaughan; Walkerton Herald-times, Walkerton; Waterloo Chronicle, Waterloo; The Record, Kitchener; West Carleton Review, Arnprior; The Wingham Advance-times, Wingham; The York Guardian, Toronto

MOTIVATE, INC.

Street address 1: 4141 Jutland Dr Ste 300
Street address 2: Suite 300
Street address city: San Diego
Street address state: CA
Zip/Postal code: 92117-3658
County: San Diego
Country: USA
Mailing address: 4141 Jutland Dr
Mailing city: San Diego
Mailing state: CA
Mailing zip: 92117
General Phone: (866) 664-4432
General/National Adv. E-mail: marcia@MotivateROI.com
Primary Website: www.motivateROI.com
Year Established: 1977
Note: Motivate, Inc. represents the following target markets: Multicultural (Hispanic, African American, Asian); Youth, LGBTQ, Senior, Military.
Personnel: Marcia A. Hansen (Prtnr.); Trevor Hansen (CEO)

NEWBASE

Street address 1: 468 Queen Str. E
Street address 2: Suite 500
Street address city: Toronto
Street address state: ON
Zip/Postal code: M5A 1T7
Country: USA
Mailing address: 468 Queen Str. E, Suite 500
Mailing city: Toronto
Mailing state: ON
Mailing zip: M5A 1T7
General Phone: (416) 363 1388
General Fax: (416) 363 2889
Primary Website: www.thenewbase.com
Personnel: Lesley Conway (Pres.); Doug St. John (Digital Director)

NEWBASE

Street address 1: 468 Queen Str. E
Street address 2: Suite 500
Street address city: Toronto
Street address state: ON
Zip/Postal code: M5A 1T7
Country: Canada
Mailing address: 468 Queen Str. E, Suite 500
Mailing city: Toronto
Mailing state: ON
Mailing zip: M5A 1T7
General Phone: (416) 363 1388
General Fax: (416) 363 2889
Primary Website: http://www.thenewbase.com
Personnel: Lesley Conway (Pres.); Doug St. John (Digital Director, Americas); Cyndy Fleming (Account Dir.); Sheila Cohen (Programmatic Manager)

NEWSPAPER NATIONAL NETWORK

Street address 1: 41899 Waterfall Rd
Street address city: Northville
Street address state: MI
Zip/Postal code: 48168-3267
County: Wayne
Country: USA
Mailing address: 41899 Waterfall Rd
Mailing city: Northville
Mailing state: MI
Mailing zip: 48168-3267
General Phone: (248) 680-4676
General Fax: (248) 680-4667
Personnel: Larry Doyle (Sales Exec.)

REFUEL AGENCY, INC

Street address 1: 1350 Broadway
Street address 2: Suite 830
Street address city: New York
Street address state: NY
Zip/Postal code: 10018
County: New York
Country: USA
Mailing address: 1350 Broadway, Suite 830
Mailing city: New York
Mailing state: NY
Mailing zip: 10018
General Phone: (866) 360-9688
General/National Adv. E-mail: info@refuelagency.com
Primary Website: www.refuelagency.com
Year Established: 1968
Note: Refuel Agency, Inc specializes in the military, college, Hispanic, African-American, ethnic and senior markets.
Personnel: Derik S. White (President/CEO); David Silver (Chief Revenue Officer); Chris Cassino (COO)

RIVENDELL MEDIA, INC.

Street address 1: 1248 US Highway 22
Street address city: Mountainside
Street address state: NJ
Zip/Postal code: 07092-2692
County: Union
Country: USA
Mailing address: 1248 US Highway 22 Ste 2
Mailing city: Mountainside
Mailing state: NJ
Mailing zip: 07092-2692
General Phone: (908) 232-2021 EXT 200
General Fax: (908) 232-0521
General/National Adv. E-mail: info@rivendellmedia.com; sales@rivendellmedia.com
Primary Website: www.rivendellmedia.com
Year Established: 1979
Note: Represents LGBT publications and digital properties.
Personnel: Todd Evans (Pres.)

RUXTON GROUP/VMG ADVERTISING

Street address 1: 1201 E Jefferson St
Street address city: Phoenix
Street address state: AZ
Zip/Postal code: 85034-2300
County: Maricopa
Country: USA
Mailing address: 1201 E. Jefferson Street

Mailing city: Phoenix
Mailing state: AZ
Mailing zip: 85034
General Phone: 1800-278-9866
General Fax: 602.238-4805
General/National Adv. E-mail: ads@voicemediagroup.com
Primary Website: www.vmgadvertising.com
Year Established: 1983
Personnel: Joe Larkin (SVP Sale & Operations); Susan Belair (SVP Sales); Veronica Villela (Business Manager)
Parent company (for newspapers): Voice Media Group

SHELBY PUBLISHING CO. INC.

Street address 1: 517 Green St NW
Street address city: Gainesville
Street address state: GA
Zip/Postal code: 30501-3313
County: Hall
Country: USA
General Phone: (770) 534-8380
General Fax: (678) 343-2197
Primary Website: www.theshelbyreport.com
Year Established: 1967
Personnel: Geoffrey Welch (VP/Sales Mgr. Midwest); C. Ronald Johnston

TOWMAR REPRESENTACIONES S.A.

Street address 1: Presa Endho # 11
Street address 2: Col. Irrigacion, M.H.
Street address city: Mexico City
Street address state: FL
Zip/Postal code: 11500
County: Distrito Federal
Country: Mexico
Mailing address: Presa Endho # 11
Mailing city: Mexico City
Mailing zip: 11500
General Phone: (55) 5395-5888
General Fax: (55) 5395-4985
General/National Adv. E-mail: INFO@towmar.net
Primary Website: www.towmar.net
Year Established: 1967
Note: New address
Personnel: Juan Martinez Dugay (Pres.); Juan Martinez Dugay (Pres.); Cesar Quijas (VP, Sales)

TRIBUNE MEDIA NETWORK

Street address 1: 202 W 1st St
Street address city: Los Angeles
Street address state: CA
Zip/Postal code: 90012-4299
County: Los Angeles
Country: USA
Mailing address: 202 W 1st St
Mailing city: Los Angeles
Mailing state: CA
Mailing zip: 90012-4299
General Phone: (213) 237-2135
General Fax: (213) 237-2007
Personnel: Peter Liguori (Pres./CEO); Richard Jones (Dir., Western Reg.)

TRIBUNE MEDIA NETWORK

Street address 1: 100 Bush St
Street address 2: Ste 925
Street address city: San Francisco
Street address state: CA
Zip/Postal code: 94104-3920
County: San Francisco
Country: USA
Mailing address: 100 Bush St Ste 925
Mailing city: San Francisco
Mailing state: CA
Mailing zip: 94104-3920
General Phone: (415) 693-5600
General Fax: (415) 391-4992
Primary Website: www.tribunemediagroup.com
Personnel: Neal Zimmerman (Mgr.)

TRIBUNE MEDIA NETWORK

Street address 1: 12900 Preston Rd
Street address 2: Ste 615
Street address city: Dallas
Street address state: TX
Zip/Postal code: 75230-1322
County: Dallas
Country: USA
Mailing address: 12900 Preston Rd Ste 615
Mailing city: Dallas
Mailing state: TX
Mailing zip: 75230-1322
General Phone: (972) 789-6920
General Fax: (972) 239-2737
Primary Website: www.tribunemediagroup.com
Personnel: Grant Moise (Southwestern Regl. Sales Dir.)

VOICE MEDIA GROUP

Street address 1: 969 N Broadway
Street address city: Denver
Street address state: CO
Zip/Postal code: 80203-2705
County: Denver
Country: USA
Mailing address: 969 Broadway
Mailing city: Denver
Mailing state: CO
Mailing zip: 80203-2705
General Phone: (602) 271-0040
General/National Adv. E-mail: joe.larkin@voicemediagroup.com
Primary Website: www.voicemediagroup.com
Note: Newspaper represents for 50 alternative newsweeklies
Personnel: Joe Larkin (Sr. Vice Pres. Sales); Susan Belair (Vice Pres., Sales)
Newspapers (for newspaper groups): Dallas Observer, Dallas; Denver Westword, Denver

WIDE AREA CLASSIFIED

Street address 1: 113 N Minnesota St
Street address city: New Ulm
Street address state: MN
Zip/Postal code: 56073-1729
County: Brown
Country: USA
Mailing address: PO Box 9
Mailing city: New Ulm
Mailing state: MN
Mailing zip: 56073-0009
General Phone: 800-324-8236
General Fax: 866-822-5487
General/National Adv. E-mail: info@wideareaclassifieds.com
Primary Website: www.wideareaclassifieds.com
Year Established: 1986
Note: Represents shopper publications in 50 states
Personnel: Shannon Reinhart (Exec. Dir.)

ELECTRONIC CLIPPING BUREAUS

IOWA

IOWA PRESS CLIPPING BUREAU

Street address 1: 319 E. 5th St., Ste. 6
Street address 2: Ste 6
Street address 3: Des Moines
Street address state: IA
Zip/Postal code: 50309
County: Polk
Country: USA
Mailing address: PO Box 873
Mailing city: Columbia
Mailing state: MO
Mailing zip: 65205
General Phone: (573) 474-1000
General/National Adv. E-mail: service@newzgroup.com
Primary Website: www.newzgroup.com/
Year Established: 1996
Personnel: Sarah Frieling (Director of Customer Service)
Parent company (for newspapers): Newz Group

MICHIGAN

ANN ARBOR

PROQUEST DIALOG

Street address 1: 789 E Eisenhower Pkwy
Street address 3: Ann Arbor
Street address state: MI
Zip/Postal code: 48108-3218
County: Washtenaw
Country: USA
Mailing state: MI
General/National Adv. E-mail: customer@dialog.com
Primary Website: proquest.com/go/pqd
Product or Service: Consultants`Other Services`Research

MISSOURI

KENTUCKY PRESS CLIPPING SERVICE - NEWZ GROUP

Street address 1: 409 W. Vandiver, Bldg #3, Ste. 100
Street address 2: Bldg 3 # STE 100
Street address 3: Columbia
Street address state: MO
Zip/Postal code: 65202
County: Boone
Country: USA
Mailing address: PO Box 873
Mailing city: Columbia
Mailing state: MO
Mailing zip: 65205-0873
General Phone: (573) 474-1000
General Fax: (573) 474-1001
General/National Adv. E-mail: info@newzgroup.com
Primary Website: www.newzgroup.com
Year Established: 1995
Parent company (for newspapers): Geotel

MISSOURI PRESS CLIPPING BUREAU - NEWZ GROUP

Street address 1: 409 W. Vandiver, Bldg #3, Ste. 100
Street address 2: Bldg 3 # STE 100
Street address 3: Columbia
Street address state: MO
Zip/Postal code: 65202
County: Boone
Country: USA
Mailing address: PO Box 873
Mailing city: Columbia
Mailing state: MO
Mailing zip: 65205-0873
General Phone: (573) 474-1000
General Fax: (573) 474-1001
General/National Adv. E-mail: info@newzgroup.com
Primary Website: www.newzgroup.com
Year Established: 1995
Personnel: Brad Buchanan (President/CEO); Lee Brooks (Mgr.)
Parent company (for newspapers): Geotel

NEW MEXICO PRESS CLIPPING BUREAU - NEWZ GROUP

Street address 1: 409 W. Vandiver, Bldg #3, Ste. 100
Street address 2: Bldg 3 # STE 100
Street address 3: Columbia
Street address state: MO
Zip/Postal code: 65202
County: Boone
Country: USA
Mailing address: PO Box 873
Mailing city: Columbia
Mailing state: MO
Mailing zip: 65205-0873
General Phone: (573) 474-1000
General Fax: (573) 474-1001
General/National Adv. E-mail: info@newzgroup.com
Primary Website: www.newzgroup.com
Year Established: 1995
Parent company (for newspapers): Geotel

WEST VIRGINIA PRESS CLIPPING BUREAU - NEWZ GROUP

Street address 1: 409 W. Vandiver, Bldg #3, Ste. 100
Street address 2: Bldg 3 # STE 100
Street address 3: Columbia
Street address state: MO
Zip/Postal code: 65202
County: Boone
Country: USA
Mailing address: PO Box 873
Mailing city: Columbia
Mailing state: MO
Mailing zip: 65205-0873
General Phone: (573) 474-1000
General Fax: (573) 474-1001
General/National Adv. E-mail: info@newzgroup.com
Primary Website: www.newzgroup.com
Year Established: 1995
Parent company (for newspapers): Geotel

NEW JERSEY

BURRELLES

Street address 1: 30 B Vreeland Road
Street address 2: # B
Street address 3: Florham Park
Street address state: NJ
Zip/Postal code: 7932
County: Morris
Country: USA
Mailing address: PO Box 674
Mailing city: Florham Park
Mailing state: NJ
Mailing zip: 07932
General Phone: (973) 992-6600
General Fax: (973) 992-7675
General/National Adv. E-mail: inquiry@burrellesluce.com
Primary Website: www.burrellesluce.com
Year Established: 1888
Personnel: Robert C. Waggoner (Chrmn./ CEO); John P. French (Pres./COO); Rick Melchers (VP, Director of National Sales); Steven Townsley (Director of Publisher Services); Daniel Schaible (Senior VP, Content Management); Michael Lillis (Content Acquisition Specalist)

Newspaper (for newspapers group): New England Newsclip Agency, Inc., Florham Park

NEW YORK

ASSOCIATED PRESS INFORMATION SERVICES

Street address 1: 450 W 33rd St
Street address 3: New York
Street address state: NY
Zip/Postal code: 10001-2603
County: New York
Country: USA
Mailing address: 450 W 33rd St Fl 15
Mailing city: New York
Mailing state: NY
Mailing zip: 10001-2647
General Phone: (212) 621-1500
General Fax: (212) 621-7520
General/National Adv. E-mail: info@ap.org
Primary Website: www.ap.org
Product or Service: Publisher/Media
Personnel: Ted Mendelsohn (Dir. Sales)

SOUTH DAKOTA

SOUTH DAKOTA NEWSPAPER ASSOCIATION

Street address 1: 1125 32nd Ave
Street address 3: Brookings
Street address state: SD
Zip/Postal code: 57006-4707
County: Brookings
Country: USA
Mailing address: 1125 32nd Ave
Mailing city: Brookings
Mailing state: SD
Mailing zip: 57006-4707
General Phone: (605) 692-4300
General/National Adv. E-mail: sdna@sdna.com
Primary Website: www.sdna.com
Year Established: 1882
Note: Elections held in May
Personnel: David Bordewyk (Exec. Dir.); John Brooks (Advertising Sales Director); Nicole Herrig (Business Manager); Sandy DeBeer (Advertising Placement Coordinator)

VIRGINIA

ARLINGTON

YELLOWBRIX

Street address 1: 200 North Glebe Road, Ste. 1025
Street address 2: Ste 1025
Street address 3: Arlington
Street address state: VA
Zip/Postal code: 22203
Country: USA
Mailing address: PO Box 1509
Mailing city: Centreville
Mailing state: VA
Mailing zip: 20122-8509
General Phone: (703) 548-3300
General Fax: (703) 548-9151
General/National Adv. E-mail: info@yellowbrix.com
Primary Website: www.yellowbrix.com
Personnel: Jeffrey P. Massa (Founder/Pres./CEO); Tom Hargis (Adv. Mgr.)

EQUIPMENT, SUPPLY AND SERVICE COMPANY

AAA PRESS INTERNATIONAL

Street address 1: 3160 N Kennicott Ave
Street address city: Arlington Heights
Street address state: IL
Zip/Postal code: 60004-1426
Country: USA
Mailing address: 3160 N Kennicott Ave
Mailing city: Arlington Heights
Mailing state: IL
Mailing zip: 60004-1426
General Phone: (847) 818-1100
General Fax: (800) 678-7983
General/National Adv. E-mail: info@aaapress.com
Primary Website: www.aaapress.com
Industry: Cameras & Accessories; Circulation Equipment & Supplies; Equipment Dealers (New); Equipment Dealers (Used); Imagesetters; Plate Mounting & Register Systems; Press Accessories, Parts & Supplies; Presses: Flexographic; Proofing Systems; Rewinders
Personnel: Jack Ludwig (Pres.); Mark Hahn (Vice Pres., Sales/Mktg.)

A-AMERICAN MACHINE & ASSEMBLY (PRESS PARTS DIV.)

Street address 1: 2620 Auburn St
Street address city: Rockford
Street address state: IL
Zip/Postal code: 61101-4222
County: Winnebago
Country: USA
Mailing address: 2620 Auburn St
Mailing city: Rockford
Mailing state: IL
Mailing zip: 61101-4222
General Phone: (815) 965-0884
General Fax: (815) 965-1049
General/National Adv. E-mail: sales@a-americanpressparts.com
Primary Website: www.a-americanpressparts.com
Mthly Avg Unique Visitors: 1986
Industry: Complete line of repair / replacement parts for printing presses, folders and RTP's Large inventories of mechanical consumable parts including, Knives, Slitters, Knife Box Components, Nip (Gain) Rings, Folding Blades, spindles, gears and much, much more. Also stocking many pneumatic and electrical components. In house manufacturing allows for shortened lead time and the quality you expect.
Personnel: Mark Keller (Pres.); Tom Sweeney (Vice Pres., Opns.)

ABB INC.

Street address 1: 9011 Bretshire Dr
Street address city: Dallas
Street address state: TX
Zip/Postal code: 75228-5105
Country: USA
Mailing address: 9011 Bretshire Dr
Mailing city: Dallas
Mailing state: TX
Mailing zip: 75228-5105
General Phone: (214) 328-1202
Primary Website: www.abb/printing.com
Industry: Drives & Controls; Press Control Systems; Plate workflow, System Integration Services;
Personnel: Jeff Gelfand (Nat'l Sales/Mktg. Dir.)

ABB LTD.

Street address 1: Affolternstr. 44, PO Box 8131
Street address city: Zurich
Zip/Postal code: CH-8050
Country: Switzerland
Mailing address: Affolternstr. 44, PO Box 8131
Mailing city: Zurich
Mailing zip: CH-8050
General Phone: 41 43 317-7111
General Fax: 41 43 317-4420
General/National Adv. E-mail: engage.abb@ch.abb.com
Primary Website: www.abb.com
Personnel: Joseph Hogan (CEO); Michel Demare (CFO)

ABB, INC. (PRINTING SYSTEMS)

Street address 1: 16250 W Glendale Dr
Street address city: New Berlin
Street address state: WI
Zip/Postal code: 53151-2840
Country: USA
Mailing address: 16250 W Glendale Dr
Mailing city: New Berlin
Mailing state: WI
Mailing zip: 53151-2858
General Phone: (262) 785-3206
General Fax: (262) 785-6295
Primary Website: www.abb.com/printing
Industry: Drives & Controls; Press Control Systems; System Integration Services
Personnel: Rick Hepperla (Vice Pres.-Paper Drives Systems/Printing); Jeffrey Gelfand (Nat'l Sales/Mktg. Dir.-Printing Systems); Hans Wirth (Mgr.-Sales Applications/Printing Drives Systems)

ACCRAPLY, INC.

Street address 1: 3580 Holly Ln N
Street address city: Minneapolis
Street address state: MN
Zip/Postal code: 55447-1366
Country: USA
Mailing address: 3580 Holly Ln N Ste 60
Mailing city: Plymouth
Mailing state: MN
Mailing zip: 55447-1367
General Phone: (763) 557-1313
General Fax: (763) 519-9656
Primary Website: www.accraply.com
Industry: Label Printing Machines
Personnel: Dave Hansen (Vice Pres., Sales)

ACCUFAST PACKAGE PRINTING SYSTEMS

Street address 1: 120 Defreest Dr
Street address city: Troy
Street address state: NY
Zip/Postal code: 12180-7608
Country: USA
Mailing address: 125 Wolf Rd Ste 318
Mailing city: Albany
Mailing state: NY
Mailing zip: 12205-1221
General Phone: (518) 283-0988
General Fax: (518) 283-0977
General/National Adv. E-mail: sales@accufastpps.com
Primary Website: www.accufastpps.com
Industry: Label Printing Machines; Mailroom Systems & Equipment;
Personnel: Ken St. John (Pres.); Meg Flanigan (Mgr.)

ACER AMERICA

Street address 1: 333 W San Carlos St
Street address 2: Ste 1500
Street address city: San Jose
Street address state: CA
Zip/Postal code: 95110-2738
Country: USA
Mailing address: 333 W San Carlos St Ste 1500
Mailing city: San Jose
Mailing state: CA
Mailing zip: 95110-2738
General Phone: (408) 533-7700
General Fax: (408) 533-4555
Primary Website: www.acer.com
Mthly Avg Unique Visitors: 1976
Industry: Computers: Laptop & Portable
Personnel: George Huang (Chairman); Jason Chen (Chairman and CEO)

ACUTECH LLC

Street address 1: 3702 W Sample St
Street address 2: Unit 1128
Street address city: South Bend
Street address state: IN
Zip/Postal code: 46619-2947
Country: USA
Mailing address: PO Box 543
Mailing city: Granger
Mailing state: IN
Mailing zip: 46530
General Phone: (574) 262-8228
Primary Website: www.acu-tech.net
Mthly Avg Unique Visitors: 2004
Industry: Plate Cylinder Lock Ups Web Register Systems Used Plate Benders Legacy Press and Pre Press equipment Repair and Services Used Presses Used Auxiliary Equipment Installation
Note: Plate Cylinder Lock Ups Web Register Systems Used Plate Benders Legacy Press and Pre Press equipment Repair and Services Used Presses Used Auxiliary Equipment Installation
Personnel: Joe Bella (Managing Director)

AD-A-NOTE

Street address 1: 1000 Rockpointe Blvd
Street address city: Pittsburgh
Street address state: PA
Zip/Postal code: 15084
County: Allegheny
Country: USA
Mailing address: 1000 RockPointe Blvd
Mailing city: Pittsburgh
Mailing state: PA
Mailing zip: 15084-2806
General Phone: (724) 889-7707
General/National Adv. E-mail: Bruce@ad-a-note.com
Display Adv. E-mail: Bruce@ad-a-note.com
Primary Website: www.ad-a-note.com
Mthly Avg Unique Visitors: 2009
Industry: Sticky Notes

Note: Front page sticky note advertising application equipment and printed note system. FREE AD-A-NOTE EQUIPMENT FOR QUALIFIED NEWSPAPERS!
Personnel: Bruce Barna (Executive Vice President)

ADHESIVES RESEARCH, INC.

Street address 1: 400 Seaks Run Rd
Street address city: Glen Rock
Street address state: PA
Zip/Postal code: 17327-9500
Country: USA
Mailing address: PO Box 100
Mailing city: Glen Rock
Mailing state: PA
Mailing zip: 17327-0100
General Phone: (717) 235-7979
General Fax: (717) 235-8320
Primary Website: www.adhesivesresearch.com
Mthly Avg Unique Visitors: 1961
Industry: Adhesives
Personnel: George Cramer (Vice Pres., Commercial Devel.)

ADI/PDM TRADE GROUP

Street address 1: 1509 Bethel Dr
Street address city: High Point
Street address state: NC
Zip/Postal code: 27260-8348
Country: USA
Mailing address: PO Box 220
Mailing city: Sylvania
Mailing state: GA
Mailing zip: 30467-0220
General Phone: (912) 564-2400
General Fax: (912) 564-2402
General/National Adv. E-mail: jlmcd1492@aol.com
Primary Website: www.arcdoyle.com
Mthly Avg Unique Visitors: 1983
Industry: Computers: Storage Devices; Counting, Stacking, Bundling Machines; Feeding, Folding, Delivery Equipment; Folding Machines; Material Handling Equipment: Automatic Guided Vehicles; Material Handling Equipment: Palletizing Machines; Material Handling Equipment: Pallets & Palletizers; Presses: Flexographic; Solvent Recovery Systems
Personnel: Jim McDonald (Pres.)

ADOBE SYSTEMS, INC.

Street address 1: 345 Park Ave
Street address city: San Jose
Street address state: CA
Zip/Postal code: 95110-2704
County: Santa Clara
Country: USA
Mailing address: 345 Park Ave
Mailing city: San Jose
Mailing state: CA
Mailing zip: 95110-2704
General Phone: (408) 536-6000
General Fax: (408) 537-6000
Primary Website: www.adobe.com
Product or Service: Hardware/Software Supplier
Personnel: Ann Lewnes (Sr. Vice Pres., Global Mktg.); Jennifer Reynolds (Dir., Worldwide Adv.)

ADVANCE SYSTEMS, INC.

Street address 1: PO Box 9428
Street address city: Green Bay
Street address state: WI
Zip/Postal code: 54308-9428
Country: USA
Mailing address: PO Box 9428
Mailing city: Green Bay
Mailing state: WI
Mailing zip: 54308-9428
General Phone: (920) 468-5477
General Fax: (920) 468-0931
General/National Adv. E-mail: asi_sales@advancesystems.com
Primary Website: www.advancesystems.com
Mthly Avg Unique Visitors: 1987
Industry: Dryers: Film and Papers; Drying Systems
Personnel: Mike Conway (Pres.); Chelly Pierquet (Office Mgr.); Mike Sellers (Sales/Mktg. Mgr.)

ADVANCED INTERACTIVE MEDIA GROUP, LLC

Street address 1: 402 Spring Valley Rd
Street address city: Altamonte Springs
Street address state: FL
Zip/Postal code: 32714-5845
County: Seminole
Country: USA
Mailing address: 402 Spring Valley Rd
Mailing city: Altamonte Springs
Mailing state: FL
Mailing zip: 32714
General Phone: (407) 788-2780
General/National Adv. E-mail: pzollman@aimgroup.com
Primary Website: www.aimgroup.com
Mthly Avg Unique Visitors: 1997
Industry: Consulting Services Industry Trade Publication Conferences --- Automotive advertising, recruitment advertising and technology
Product or Service: Consultants`Publisher/Media
Note: The AIM Group is a global team of consulting experts in classified advertising, marketplaces and interactive media. We help publishers grow their businesses through strategic and tactical support. We publish AIM Group Marketplaces Report, the international business intelligence service that is often called "the bible of the classified advertising and marketplace industry." We work with news media publishers, dot-coms, print classified publishers, yellow page publishers, broadcasters and technology vendors worldwide to help develop, launch and grow revenue-generating services. We are first and foremost ''consultants who publish,'' not ''publishers who do a little consulting on the side.'' Most of our consulting work is performed on a proprietary basis, so our clients often see only a small fraction of our work-product. We offer solutions for companies planning their strategies, increasing revenue, market share, and in developing products and packing strategies to grow their business. We help build interactive products and services; we don't just talk about them based on flimsy research. We support investors and analysts trying to determine the health of a company, or to find companies ripe for investment or acquisition. Our team includes long-time senior executives, so we work with senior executives to help them understand where their interactive-media and classified services need to evolve. We've been sales reps and sales managers, so we can help sales teams grow and develop traditional and interactive media services. Our writer / analysts get to the heart of the matter, and understand the business inside and out. We work with clients globally. Our worldwide team of almost 40 people follows the evolution in interactive media and classified advertising more closely than anyone else.
Personnel: Peter M. Zollman (Founding Principal); Jim Townsend (Editorial Director); Katja Riefler (Europe Director); Rob Paterson (Principal, director of consulting); Diana Bogdan; Jonathan Turpin (Senior principal)

ADVANCED TECHNICAL SOLUTIONS, INC.

Street address 1: 36 Nason St
Street address city: Maynard
Street address state: MA
Zip/Postal code: 01754-2502
Country: USA
Mailing address: PO Box 386
Mailing city: Maynard
Mailing state: MA
Mailing zip: 01754-0386
General Phone: (978) 849-0533
General Fax: (978) 849-0544
General/National Adv. E-mail: support@atsusa.com
Display Adv. E-mail: sales@atsusa.com
Primary Website: www.atsusa.com
Mthly Avg Unique Visitors: 1987
Industry: Computers: Hardware & Software Integrators; Input & Editing Systems; Publishing Systems; Software: Advertising (Includes Display; Classified); Software: Circulation; Software: Editorial; Software: Press/Post Press
Personnel: Bill Page (Exec. Vice Pres.)

ADVANTEX MARKETING INTERNATIONAL, INC.

Street address 1: 600 Alden Rd
Street address 2: Suite 606
Street address city: Markham
Street address state: ON
Zip/Postal code: L3R 0E7
Country: Canada
Mailing address: 600 Alden Road, Suite 606
Mailing city: Markham
Mailing state: ON
Mailing zip: L3R 0E7
General Phone: (416) 481-5657
General Fax: (416) 481-5692
General/National Adv. E-mail: info@advantex.com
Primary Website: www.advantex.com
Mthly Avg Unique Visitors: 1983
Industry: Consulting Services: Circulation; Consulting Services: Marketing; Promotion Services
Personnel: Kelly Ambrose (Pres.)

ADVERTISING CHECKING BUREAU, INC.

Street address 1: 675 3rd Ave
Street address 2: Fl 29
Street address city: New York
Street address state: NY
Zip/Postal code: 10017-5704
Country: USA
Mailing address: 675 Third Ave. Suite 2905
Mailing city: New York
Mailing state: NY
Mailing zip: 10017
General Phone: (212) 684-3377
General Fax: (212) 684-3381
General/National Adv. E-mail: sales@acbcoop.com
Primary Website: www.acbcoop.com
Mthly Avg Unique Visitors: 1917
Industry: Library Retrieval Systems; Market Research; Research Studies;Co-op advertising management
Personnel: Brian T. McShane (Pres./CEO); John Portelli (VP., Nat'l Sales)

AEC, INC.

Street address 1: 1100 E Woodfield Rd
Street address 2: Ste 588
Street address city: Schaumburg
Street address state: IL
Zip/Postal code: 60173-5135
Country: USA
Mailing address: 1100 E Woodfield Rd Ste 550
Mailing city: Schaumburg
Mailing state: IL
Mailing zip: 60173-5135
General Phone: (847) 273-7700
General Fax: (847) 273-7804
General/National Adv. E-mail: dazzarello@corpemail.com
Primary Website: www.aecinternet.com
Mthly Avg Unique Visitors: 1964
Industry: Architects/Engineers (Includes Design/ Construction Firms); Press Accessories, Parts & Supplies
Personnel: Tom Breslin (Pres.)

AECOM

Street address 1: 303 E Wacker Dr
Street address 2: Ste 1400
Street address city: Chicago
Street address state: IL
Zip/Postal code: 60601-5214
Country: USA
Mailing address: 303 E Wacker Dr Ste 1400
Mailing city: Chicago
Mailing state: IL
Mailing zip: 60601-5214
General Phone: (312) 373-7700
General Fax: (312) 373-7710
Primary Website: www.aecom.com
Mthly Avg Unique Visitors: 1989
Industry: Architects/Engineers (Includes Design/ Construction Firms); Consulting Services: Equipment; Consulting Services: Production;
Personnel: Betty Hendricks (Office Mgr.)

AG INDUSTRIES, INC.

Street address 1: 1 American Rd
Street address city: Cleveland
Street address state: OH
Zip/Postal code: 44144-2301
Country: USA
Mailing address: 1 American Rd
Mailing city: Cleveland
Mailing state: OH
Mailing zip: 44144-2398
General Phone: (216) 252-6737
General Fax: (216) 252-6773
Primary Website: www.agifixtures.com
Mthly Avg Unique Visitors: 1960
Industry: Newspaper Dispensers (Mechanical/ Electronic)
Personnel: Sandy Saunders (Mktg./Adv. Coord.)

AGFA GRAPHICS

Street address 1: 611 River Drive
Street address 2: Center 3
Street address city: Elmwood Park
Street address state: NJ
Zip/Postal code: 07407
Country: USA
Mailing address: 611 River Drive, Center 3
Mailing city: Elmwood Park
Mailing state: NJ
Mailing zip: 07407
General Phone: (201) 440-2500
Primary Website: www.agfagraphics.com
Mthly Avg Unique Visitors: 1867
Industry: Commercial Printing; Sign & Display; Newspapers; Packaging & Labels; Industrial Printing; Security Printing;
Personnel: Julien De Wilde (Chairman); Christian Reinaudo (CEO); Deborah Hutcheson (Director Marketing); Lois Catala

AIRLOC LLC

Street address 1: 5 Fisher St
Street address city: Franklin
Street address state: MA
Zip/Postal code: 02038-2114
County: Norfolk
Country: USA
Mailing address: PO Box 260
Mailing city: Franklin
Mailing state: MA
Mailing zip: 02038-0260
General Phone: (508) 528-0022
General Fax: (508) 528-7555
General/National Adv. E-mail: info@airloc.com
Display Adv. E-mail: info@airloc.com
Primary Website: www.airloc.com
Mthly Avg Unique Visitors: 1954
Industry: Vibration Isolation & Machine Leveling Mounts
Personnel: Philip Littlewood (Engineering Mgr.)

AIRSYSTEMS, INC.

Street address 1: 940 Remillard Ct.
Street address city: San Jose
Street address state: CA
Zip/Postal code: 95122
Country: USA
Mailing address: 940 Remillard Ct.
Mailing city: San Jose
Mailing state: CA
Mailing zip: 95122
General Phone: (408) 280-1666
General Fax: (408) 280-1020
General/National Adv. E-mail: emcor_info@emcorgroup.com
Primary Website: www.airsystemsinc.com
Mthly Avg Unique Visitors: 1982
Industry: Inks; Controllers: Press
Personnel: Art Williams (Pres.)

A-KORN ROLLER, INC.

Street address 1: 3545 S Morgan St
Street address city: Chicago
Street address state: IL
Zip/Postal code: 60609-1525
Country: USA
Mailing address: 3545 S Morgan St

Mailing city: Chicago
Mailing state: IL
Mailing zip: 60609-1590
General Phone: (773) 254-5700
General Fax: (773) 650-7355
General/National Adv. E-mail: a-kornroller@a-kornroller.com
Primary Website: www.a-kornroller.com
Mthly Avg Unique Visitors: 1970
Industry: Roll Cleaning Equipment; Roll Coverings; Roller Grinders; Roller Grinding Services; Rollers; Rollers: Dampening;
Personnel: Michael Koren (Pres.)

ALAR ENGINEERING CORPORATION

Street address 1: 9651 196th St
Street address city: Mokena
Street address state: IL
Zip/Postal code: 60448-9305
Country: USA
Mailing address: 9651 196th St
Mailing city: Mokena
Mailing state: IL
Mailing zip: 60448-9305
General Phone: (708) 479-6100
General/National Adv. E-mail: info@alarcorp.com
Primary Website: www.alarcorp.com
Mthly Avg Unique Visitors: 1970
Industry: Waste Water Treatment Systems
Personnel: Paula Jackfert (President); Vickey Gorski (Vice Pres., Int'l Sales); Steve Gorski (Sales Mgr.)

ALCATEL-LUCENT

Street address 1: 600 Mountain Ave
Street address 2: # 700
Street address city: New Providence
Street address state: NJ
Zip/Postal code: 07974-2008
Country: USA
Mailing address: 600 Mountain Ave # 2F-147
Mailing city: New Providence
Mailing state: NJ
Mailing zip: 07974-2008
General Phone: (908) 582-3000
General Fax: (908) 582-2576
General/National Adv. E-mail: execoffice@alcatel-lucent.com
Primary Website: www.alcatel-lucent.com
Personnel: Ben Verwaayen (CEO); Jeong H. Kim (Pres., Bell Labs)

ALFA CTP SYSTEMS INC.

Street address 1: 229 Billerica Road
Street address 2: Ste 4
Street address city: Chelmsford
Street address state: MA
Zip/Postal code: 01824
Country: USA
Mailing state: MA
General Phone: (603) 689-1101
General/National Adv. E-mail: info@alfactp.com
Primary Website: www.alfactp.com
Mthly Avg Unique Visitors: 2007
Industry: Imagesetters; Plates: Offset (Computer to Plate); Proofing Systems; Software: Pagination/Layout; Typesetters: Laser;
Personnel: Tony Ford (President); Keith Roeske (VP Operations); Paul Norton

ALFAQUEST TECHNOLOGIES

Street address 1: 1150 Rose Rd
Street address city: Lake Zurich
Street address state: IL
Zip/Postal code: 60047-1567
Country: USA
Mailing address: 1150 Rose Rd
Mailing city: Lake Zurich
Mailing state: IL
Mailing zip: 60047-1567
General Phone: (847) 427-8800
General Fax: (847) 427-8860
General/National Adv. E-mail: keith.roeske@alfactp.com
Primary Website: www.alfactp.com
Mthly Avg Unique Visitors: 1982
Industry: Computers: Hardware & Software Integrators; Imagesetters; Interfaces; Laser Printers; Multiplexers/Routers; Output Management and Preflight Software; Photo Archiving; Platemakers: Laser; Raster Image Processors;
Note: Developers and Manufacturers of Newspaper production workflow and CTP.
Personnel: Keith Roeske (Vice President Of Operations)

ALL SYSTEMS GO

Street address 1: 2 Cedar St
Street address city: Woburn
Street address state: MA
Zip/Postal code: 01801-7248
Country: USA
Mailing address: 2 Cedar St Ste 1
Mailing city: Woburn
Mailing state: MA
Mailing zip: 01801-6352
General Phone: (781) 932-6700
General Fax: (781) 932-6711
General/National Adv. E-mail: info@allsysgo.com
Primary Website: www.allsysgo.com
Mthly Avg Unique Visitors: 1993
Industry: Computers: Hardware & Software Integrators; Computers: Laptop & Portable; Computers: Storage Devices; Consulting Services: Advertising; Consulting Services: Circulation; Consulting Services: Computer; Consulting Services: Equipment; Consulting Services: Marketing; Imagesetters; Software: Design/Graphics
Personnel: Richard Pape (Pres.)

ALLIANCE RUBBER CO.

Street address 1: 210 Carpenter Dam Rd
Street address city: Hot Springs
Street address state: AR
Zip/Postal code: 71901-8219
Country: USA
Mailing address: PO Box 20950
Mailing city: Hot Springs
Mailing state: AR
Mailing zip: 71903-0950
General Phone: (501) 262-2700
General Fax: (501) 262-3948
General/National Adv. E-mail: sales@alliance-rubber.com
Primary Website: www.rubberband.com
Mthly Avg Unique Visitors: 1923
Industry: Rubber Band Manufacturer
Personnel: Joan Dennis (Director Sales & Marketing); Sheryl Koller

AMERGRAPH CORPORATION

Street address 1: 520 Lafayette Rd
Street address city: Sparta
Street address state: NJ
Zip/Postal code: 07871-3447
Country: USA
Mailing address: 520 Lafayette Rd
Mailing city: Sparta
Mailing state: NJ
Mailing zip: 07871-3447
General Phone: (973) 383-8700
General Fax: (973) 383-9225
General/National Adv. E-mail: sales@amergraph.com
Primary Website: www.amergraph.com
Mthly Avg Unique Visitors: 1975
Industry: Exposure Lamps; Film & Paper: Film Processing Machines; Ink Bleeding Equipment; Ink Pumping Systems; Offset Plate-Making Service & Equipment; Plate Exposure Units; Plate Processors; Platemakers: Offset (Computer to Plate); Processors: Film & Paper; Vacuum Frames
Personnel: Robert Lesko (Pres.)

AMERICAN CONSULTING SERVICES

Street address 1: 440 NE 4th Ave
Street address city: Camas
Street address state: WA
Zip/Postal code: 98607-2173
Country: USA
Mailing address: 440 NE 4th Ave
Mailing city: Camas
Mailing state: WA
Mailing zip: 98607-2173
General Phone: (800) 597-9798
General Fax: (360) 833-4620
General/National Adv. E-mail: info@toma.com
Primary Website: www.toma.com
Mthly Avg Unique Visitors: 1985
Industry: Consulting Services: Advertising
Personnel: Mark Rood (Pres.); Kate Rood (Office Manager); Shirley Jones (Research Manager)

AMERICAN FIDELITY ASSURANCE CO.

Street address 1: 2000 N Classen Blvd
Street address city: Oklahoma City
Street address state: OK
Zip/Postal code: 73106-6016
Country: USA
Mailing address: PO Box 25523
Mailing city: Oklahoma City
Mailing state: OK
Mailing zip: 73125-0523
General Phone: (405) 523-2000
Primary Website: www.americanfidelity.com
Mthly Avg Unique Visitors: 1960
Industry: Insurance
Personnel: William B. Cameron (CEO and Chairman); Dave Carpenter (President and COO); Jeanette Rice (AVP of Communications)

AMERICAN GRAPHIC ARTS, INC.

Street address 1: 150 Broadway
Street address city: Elizabeth
Street address state: NJ
Zip/Postal code: 07206-1856
Country: USA
Mailing address: PO Box 240
Mailing city: Elizabeth
Mailing state: NJ
Mailing zip: 07206-0240
General Phone: (908) 351-6906
General Fax: (908) 351-7156
Primary Website: www.agamachinery.com
Mthly Avg Unique Visitors: 1927
Industry: Equipment Dealers (Used); Gluing Systems
Personnel: John Jacobson (Pres.)

AMERICAN INTERNATIONAL COMMUNICATIONS, INC.

Street address 1: 101425 Overseas Hwy
Street address 2: 922
Street address city: Key Largo
Street address state: FL
Zip/Postal code: 33037-4505
County: Monroe
Country: USA
Mailing address: 101425 Overseas Hwy #922
Mailing city: Key Largo
Mailing state: FL
Mailing zip: 33037-4505
General Phone: (305) 453-5456
General Fax: (305) 453-5455
General/National Adv. E-mail: pkaic@aol.com
Display Adv. E-mail: pkaic@aol.com
Mthly Avg Unique Visitors: 1985
Industry: Telephone Automated Inbound Programs, Product information, Answering Services, Voice & video Conferencing, Voice Mail, Games, Horoscope, Health info; Voice Over IP; System Programming; Internet; Web site building; Consulting Services; 30 years in business.
Note: Connections World Wide
Personnel: Paul Keever (Pres./CEO)

AMERICAN NEWSPAPER REPRESENTATIVES

Street address 1: 2075 W Big Beaver Rd
Street address 2: Ste 310
Street address city: Troy
Street address state: MI
Zip/Postal code: 48084-3439
Country: USA
Mailing address: 2075 W Big Beaver Rd Ste 310
Mailing city: Troy
Mailing state: MI
Mailing zip: 48084-3439
General Phone: (248) 643-9910
General Fax: (248) 643-9914
General/National Adv. E-mail: accountsales@gotoanr.com
Primary Website: www.anrinc.net
Mthly Avg Unique Visitors: 1943
Industry: Consulting Services: Advertising
Personnel: John Jepsen (Pres.); Robert Sontag (Exec. Vice Pres./COO); Melanie Cox (Regl. Sales Mgr., Minneapolis); Hilary Howe

AMERICAN OPINION RESEARCH

Street address 1: 279 Wall St
Street address city: Princeton
Street address state: NJ
Zip/Postal code: 08540-1519
Country: USA
Mailing address: 279 Wall St., Research Pk.
Mailing city: Princeton
Mailing state: NJ
Mailing zip: 8540
General Phone: (609) 683-4035
General Fax: (609) 683-8398
General/National Adv. E-mail: acasale@imsworld.com
Primary Website: www.imsworld.com
Industry: Consulting Services: Advertising; Consulting Services: Circulation; Consulting Services: Editorial; Consulting Services: Marketing
Personnel: Tony Casale (Chrmn./CEO); Lois Kaufman (Pres.)

AMERICAN ROLLER CO.

Street address 1: 1440 13th Ave
Street address city: Union Grove
Street address state: WI
Zip/Postal code: 53182-1515
County: Racine
Country: USA
Mailing address: 1440 13th Ave.
Mailing city: Union Grove
Mailing state: WI
Mailing zip: 53182
General Phone: (262) 878-2445
General Fax: (262) 878-2241
Primary Website: www.americanroller.com
Mthly Avg Unique Visitors: 1938
Industry: Roll Coverings; Rollers; Rollers: Dampening;

AMERICAN ULTRAVIOLET CO., INC.

Street address 1: 212 S Mount Zion Rd
Street address city: Lebanon
Street address state: IN
Zip/Postal code: 46052-9479
Country: USA
Mailing address: 212 S Mount Zion Rd
Mailing city: Lebanon
Mailing state: IN
Mailing zip: 46052-9479
General Phone: (765) 483-9514
General Fax: (765) 483-9525
Primary Website: www.auvco.com
Industry: Press Accessories, Parts & Supplies
Personnel: David Snyder (Sales Rep.)

ANOCOIL CORPORATION

Street address 1: 60 E Main St
Street address city: Vernon Rockville
Street address state: CT
Zip/Postal code: 06066-3245
Country: USA
Mailing address: PO Box 1318
Mailing city: Vernon Rockville
Mailing state: CT
Mailing zip: 06066-1318
General Phone: (860) 871-1200
General Fax: (860) 872-0534
Primary Website: www.anocoil.com
Mthly Avg Unique Visitors: 1958
Industry: Chemicals: Plate Processing; Plates: Offset (Computer to Plate); Plates: Offset (Conventional)
Personnel: H.A. Fromson (CEO); David Bujese (Pres.); Timothy A. Fromson (Vice Pres., Anocoil); Bud Knorr (Vice President- Sales)

ANYGRAAF USA

Street address 1: 10451 Mill Run Cir
Street address 2: Ste 400
Street address city: Owings Mills
Street address state: MD
Zip/Postal code: 21117-5594
Country: USA
Mailing address: 10451 Mill Run Cir Ste 400
Mailing city: Owings Mills
Mailing state: MD

Mailing zip: 21117-5594
General Phone: (240) 379-6620
General/National Adv. E-mail: anyinc@anygraaf.com
Primary Website: www.anygraaf.com
Industry: Proofing Systems
Personnel: Andy Hunn (Managing Dir.); Bill Ryker (SALES DIR.)

APLUSA BELL FALLA

Street address 1: 199 West Hillcrest Drive
Street address city: Thousand Oaks
Street address state: CA
Zip/Postal code: 91320
Country: USA
Mailing address: 199 West Hillcrest Drive
Mailing city: Thousand Oaks
Mailing state: CA
Mailing zip: 91320
General Phone: (203) 520 9491
Mthly Avg Unique Visitors: 1978
Industry: Market Research; Research Studies;
Personnel: Steve Bell (Senior Partner); Juan Falla (Senior Partner)

APPLE, INC.

Street address 1: 1 Infinite Loop
Street address city: Cupertino
Street address state: CA
Zip/Postal code: 95014-2083
County: Santa Clara
Country: USA
Mailing address: 1 Infinite Loop
Mailing city: Cupertino
Mailing state: CA
Mailing zip: 95014-2084
General Phone: (408) 996â€"1010
General Fax: (408) 996-0275
General/National Adv. E-mail: media.help@apple.com
Primary Website: www.apple.com
Mthly Avg Unique Visitors: 1976
Industry: Consumer Electronics; Computer Software; Online Services;
Product or Service: Hardware/Software Supplier
Personnel: Timothy Cook (CEO); Philip W. Schiller (Sr. V. P. Worldwide Marketing); Jonathan Ive (Chief Design Officer); Craig Federighi (Senior Vice President, Software Engineering)

APPLIED INDUSTRIAL MACHINERY

Street address 1: 1930 SE 29th St
Street address city: Oklahoma City
Street address state: OK
Zip/Postal code: 73129-7626
Country: USA
Mailing address: 1930 SE 29th St
Mailing city: Oklahoma City
Mailing state: OK
Mailing zip: 73129-7626
General Phone: (405) 672-2222
General Fax: (405) 672-2272
Mthly Avg Unique Visitors: 1981
Industry: Equipment Dealers (New); Feeding, Folding, Delivery Equipment; Folding Machines; In-Line Trimming Systems; Three Knife Trimmer; Web Press - Special Equipment
Personnel: Robert Gilson (Pres.)

ARC INTERNATIONAL

Street address 1: 10955 Withers Cove Park Dr
Street address city: Charlotte
Street address state: NC
Zip/Postal code: 28278-0020
Country: USA
Mailing address: 10955 Withers Cove Park Dr
Mailing city: Charlotte
Mailing state: NC
Mailing zip: 28278-0020
General Phone: (704) 588-1809
General Fax: (704) 588-9921
Primary Website: www.arcinternational.com
Mthly Avg Unique Visitors: 1984
Industry: Cleaners & Solvents; Platemakers: Flexographic (Computer to Plate); Platemakers: Laser; Roll Coverings; Rollers

Personnel: Mike Foran (Pres.); Steven Wilkinson (Gen. Mgr.); Steve Woodard (Vice Pres., Cor. Sales)

ARCO ENGINEERING, INC. (NEWSPAPER DIV.)

Street address 1: 3317 Gilmore Industrial Blvd
Street address city: Louisville
Street address state: KY
Zip/Postal code: 40213-2174
Country: USA
Mailing address: 3317 Gilmore Industrial Blvd
Mailing city: Louisville
Mailing state: KY
Mailing zip: 40213-2174
General Phone: (502) 966-3134
General Fax: (502) 966-3135
General/National Adv. E-mail: sales@arcoengineering.com
Primary Website: www.arcoengineering.com
Mthly Avg Unique Visitors: 1954
Industry: Belts, Belting, V-Belts; Equipment Dealers (New); Equipment Dealers (Used); Gauges, Measuring; Noise Control; Pasters; Reels & Tensions; Reels (Inlcudes Paper Reels); Scanners: Color B & W, Plates, Web; Tension & Web Controls
Personnel: James Gunn (Pres.)

ARPAC GROUP

Street address 1: 9511 River St
Street address city: Schiller Park
Street address state: IL
Zip/Postal code: 60176-1019
Country: USA
Mailing address: 9511 River St
Mailing city: Schiller Park
Mailing state: IL
Mailing zip: 60176-1019
General Phone: (847) 678-9034
General Fax: (847) 671-7006
General/National Adv. E-mail: info@arpacgroup.com
Primary Website: www.arpacgroup.com
Mthly Avg Unique Visitors: 1971
Industry: Bundling and Tying Machines; Conveyors; Shrink Wrapping Equipment
Personnel: Michael Levy (Pres.)

ARROW PRINTING CO.

Street address 1: 115 W Woodland Ave
Street address city: Salina
Street address state: KS
Zip/Postal code: 67401-2935
Country: USA
Mailing address: PO Box 2898
Mailing city: Salina
Mailing state: KS
Mailing zip: 67402-2898
General Phone: (785) 825-8124
General Fax: (785) 825-0784
General/National Adv. E-mail: arrow@arrowprintco.com
Primary Website: www.arrowprintco.com
Mthly Avg Unique Visitors: 1946
Industry: Consulting Services: Advertising; Offset Camera, Darkroom Equipment; Offset Plate Files; Photo Proofing Systems; Platemakers: Offset (Conventional); Plates: Offset (Conventional); Prepress Color Proofing Systems; Presses: Offset; Processors: Film & Paper; Scanners: Color B & W, Plates, Web
Personnel: Kent Fellers (Pres.); Dennis Suelter (Adv. Mgr.)

ARTBEATSEXPRESS

Street address 1: 1405 N Myrtle Rd
Street address city: Myrtle Creek
Street address state: OR
Zip/Postal code: 97457-9615
Country: USA
Mailing address: PO Box 709
Mailing city: Myrtle Creek
Mailing state: OR
Mailing zip: 97457-0110
General Phone: (541)863-4429
General Fax: (541)863-4547
General/National Adv. E-mail: info@artbeats.com
Primary Website: www.artbeatsEXPRESS.com
Mthly Avg Unique Visitors: 1989
Industry: Royalty Free Stock Media

Personnel: Phil Bates (Pres.); Laura Hollifield (COO); Julie Hill (Adv./Mktg. Mgr.); Peggy Nichols (Global Dist. Mgr.); Bob Hayes (Dir., Tech.)

ASHWORTH BROTHERS, INC.

Street address 1: 450 Armour Dl
Street address city: Winchester
Street address state: VA
Zip/Postal code: 22601-3459
Country: USA
Mailing address: 450 Armour Dl
Mailing city: Winchester
Mailing state: VA
Mailing zip: 22601-3459
General Phone: (540) 662-3494
General Fax: (540) 662-3150
Primary Website: www.ashworth.com
Industry: Belts, Belting, V-Belts; Conveyors;
Personnel: Joe Lackner (Vice Pres. Mktg); Tim Jones (Mktg. Mgr.)

ATEX

Street address 1: 87 Castle Street
Street address city: Reading
Zip/Postal code: RG1 7SN
Country: United Kingdom
Mailing address: 87 Castle Street
Mailing city: Reading
Mailing zip: RG1 7SN
General Phone: 118 958 7537
General Fax: 118 958 7537
General/National Adv. E-mail: info@atex.com
Primary Website: www.atex.com
Mthly Avg Unique Visitors: 1973
Industry: Software: Advertising (Includes Display; Classified); Software: Asset Management; Software: Circulation; Software: Editorial; Software: Pagination/Layout;
Product or Service: Hardware/Software Supplier
Personnel: Peter Marsh (Sr. Vice Pres./Chief Integration Officer); Malcolm McGrory (Sr. Vice Pres., Sales Americas)

ATEX NORTH AMERICA

Street address 1: 410 N Wickham Rd
Street address city: Melbourne
Street address state: FL
Zip/Postal code: 32935-8648
Country: USA
Mailing address: 410 N Wickham Rd
Mailing city: Melbourne
Mailing state: FL
Mailing zip: 32935-8648
General Phone: (321) 254-5559
General Fax: (321) 254-4392
General/National Adv. E-mail: adbase.support-services.us@atex.com
Primary Website: www.atex.com
Mthly Avg Unique Visitors: 1996
Industry: Consulting Services: Advertising; Software: Advertising (Includes Display; Classified); Software: Business (Includes Administration/Accounting);
Personnel: Scott Roessler (CEO of North America); Lars Jiborn (Vice Pres., Product Mgmt.); Steve Roessler (Vice Pres., Mktg.)

ATEX NORTH AMERICA

Street address 1: 5405 Cypress Center Dr
Street address 2: Ste 200
Street address city: Tampa
Street address state: FL
Zip/Postal code: 33609-1025
Country: USA
Mailing address: 6767 N Wickham Rd Ste 111
Mailing city: Melbourne
Mailing state: FL
Mailing zip: 32940-2024
General Phone: (813) 739-1700
General Fax: (813) 739-1710
General/National Adv. E-mail: info@atex.com
Primary Website: www.atex.com
Mthly Avg Unique Visitors: 2001
Industry: Software: Advertising (Includes Display; Classified); Software: Business (Includes Administration/Accounting); Software: Circulation; Software: Editorial; Software: Pagination/Layout;

Personnel: John Hawkins (CEO); Scott Rossler (CEO, Atex North America); Malcom McGregory (Sales Mgr.)

ATLAS SPECIALTY LIGHTING

Street address 1: 7304 N Florida Ave
Street address city: Tampa
Street address state: FL
Zip/Postal code: 33604-4838
Country: USA
Mailing address: 7304 N Florida Ave
Mailing city: Tampa
Mailing state: FL
Mailing zip: 33604-4889
General Phone: (813) 238-6481
General Fax: (813) 238-6656
Primary Website: www.asltg2.com
Industry: Lighting Equipment
Personnel: Ralph Felten (Mgr.)

AUTOLOGIC INFORMATION INTERNATIONAL

Street address 1: 1050 Rancho Conejo Blvd
Street address city: Thousand Oaks
Street address state: CA
Zip/Postal code: 91320-1717
Country: USA
Mailing address: 1050 Rancho Conejo Blvd
Mailing city: Thousand Oaks
Mailing state: CA
Mailing zip: 91320-1717
General Phone: (805) 498-9611
General Fax: (805) 499-1167
General/National Adv. E-mail: abrunner@autologic.com
Primary Website: www.autologic.com
Mthly Avg Unique Visitors: 1964
Industry: Archiving Systems; Computers: Hardware & Software Integrators; Facsimilie/Fax Transmission Systems; Multiplexers/Routers; Platemakers: Direct; Platemakers: Flexographic (Computer to Plate); Publishing Systems; Scanners: Color B & W, Plates, Web; Software: Advertising (Includes Display; Classified); Software: Electronic Data Interchange; Typesetters: Laser
Personnel: Al Brunner (Pres.); Ratan Bhaunani (Vice Pres., Software Engineering); Doug Arlt (Vice Pres., Mfg.); Jack Embree (Dir., Americas Opns.); Tom LeJeune (Mktg. Mgr.)

AUTOMATED MAILING SYSTEMS CORP.

Street address 1: 10730 Spangler Rd
Street address city: Dallas
Street address state: TX
Zip/Postal code: 75220-7102
Country: USA
Mailing address: PO Box 541326
Mailing city: Dallas
Mailing state: TX
Mailing zip: 75354-1326
General Phone: (972) 869-2844
General Fax: (972) 869-2735
General/National Adv. E-mail: amsco@amscodallas.com
Primary Website: www.amscodallas.com
Mthly Avg Unique Visitors: 1946
Industry: Addressing Machines; Bundling and Tying Machines; Inserting Equipment (Includes Stuffing Machines); Mailroom Systems & Equipment; Strapping Machines
Personnel: Scott Helsley (Vice Pres.); Thomas Helsley (Mktg. Mgr)

AWS, A THERMAL CARE DIVISION

Street address 1: 5680 W Jarvis Ave
Street address city: Niles
Street address state: IL
Zip/Postal code: 60714-4016
County: Cook
Country: USA
Mailing address: 5680 W. Jarvis Ave.
Mailing city: Niles
Mailing state: IL
Mailing zip: 60714
General Phone: (630) 595-3651
General Fax: (630) 595-5433
General/National Adv. E-mail: info@thermalcare.com
Display Adv. E-mail: aguidarelli@thermalcare.com

Primary Website: www.thermalcare.com
Industry: Circulation Equipment & Supplies; Ink Fountains & Accessories; Ink Pumping Systems; Press Accessories, Parts & Supplies
Personnel: Audrey Guidarelli (Mktg. Servs. Mgr.)

AXIS INSURANCE

Street address 1: 1201 Walnut St
Street address 2: Ste 1800
Street address city: Kansas City
Street address state: MO
Zip/Postal code: 64106-2247
Country: USA
Mailing address: 1201 Walnut St Ste 1800
Mailing city: Kansas City
Mailing state: MO
Mailing zip: 64106-2247
General Phone: (816) 471-6118
General Fax: (816) 471-6119
Primary Website: www.axiscapital.com/insurance
Mthly Avg Unique Visitors: 1979
Industry: Insurance
Personnel: Peter Wilson (CEO); Eric Gesick (Chief Underwriting Officer); Noreen McMullan (Chief Human Resource Officer)

B & L MACHINE & DESIGN

Street address 1: 1 Legend Park
Street address city: Effingham
Street address state: IL
Zip/Postal code: 62401-9442
Country: USA
Mailing address: PO Box 743
Mailing city: Effingham
Mailing state: IL
Mailing zip: 62401-0743
General Phone: (217) 342-3918
General Fax: (217) 342-2081
General/National Adv. E-mail: info@blmachinedesign.com
Primary Website: www.blmachinedesign.com
Mthly Avg Unique Visitors: 1981
Industry: Presses: Offset; Training: Press Operation & Maintenance
Personnel: Larry Hines (Pres.); Lara Westjohn (Mktg. Mgr.); Jim Strange (Prodn. Mgr., Mfg.)

B E & K BUILDING GROUP

Street address 1: 201 East McBee Avenue, Suite 400
Street address city: Greenville
Street address state: SC
Zip/Postal code: 29601
Country: USA
Mailing address: 201 East McBee Avenue, Suite 400
Mailing city: Greenville
Mailing state: SC
Mailing zip: 29601
General Phone: (864) 250-5000
General Fax: (864) 250-5099
Primary Website: www.bekbg.com
Mthly Avg Unique Visitors: 1972
Industry: Architects/Engineers (includes Design/ Construction Firms)
Note: RESEARCH TRIANGLE PARK 100 Capitola Drive, Suite 301 Durham, North Carolina 27713 Phone: 919. 781. 0054 Fax: 919. 326. 2999 Business Development: Courtney Skunda 919.326.2947 Frank Holley 919.326.2948 CHARLOTTE 1031 South Caldwell Street, Suite 100 Charlotte, North Carolina 28203 Phone: 704. 412. 9300 Fax: 704. 659. 4161 Business Development: Jeff Thompson 704.351.0007 CHICAGO 205 West Wacker Drive, Suite 615 Chicago, Illinois 60606 Phone: 312. 638. 5680 Fax: 864. 250. 5099 Business Development: Hope Alexander 312.543.8094 HOUSTON 4545 Post Oak Place, Suite 110 Houston, Texas 77027 Phone: 281. 245. 3940 Fax: 713. 583. 7903 Business Development: Steve Olson 972.532.2420 DALLAS 13727 Noel Road, Tower II, Suite 200 Dallas, Texas 75240 Phone: 972. 532. 2420 Fax: 864. 250. 5099 Business Development: Steve Olson 972.532.2420
Personnel: Tim Parker (Business Development); Grant McCullagh (Chairman); Mac Carpenter (Vice President HR)

B.H. BUNN CO.

Street address 1: 2730 Drane Field Rd
Street address city: Lakeland
Street address state: FL
Zip/Postal code: 33811-1325
Country: USA
Mailing address: 2730 Drane Field Rd
Mailing city: Lakeland
Mailing state: FL
Mailing zip: 33811-1325
General Phone: (863) 647-1555
General Fax: (863) 686-2866
General/National Adv. E-mail: info@bunntyco.com
Primary Website: www.bunntyco.com
Mthly Avg Unique Visitors: 1907
Industry: Bundling and Tying Machines; Strapping Machines;
Note: BUNN Tying Machines Since 1907! The longest running product for bundling products using environment friendly materials. Getting pressured to reduce or eliminate plastic packaging? BUNN newly developed Machine Grade 100% Cotton twine to meet the new standards for bundling newspapers! Call Bunn Today, 800-222-BUNN! BUNN was Green when Green was Just a Color!
Personnel: John R. Bunn (Pres.)

BADGER FIRE PROTECTION

Street address 1: 944 Glenwood Station Ln
Street address 2: Ste 303
Street address city: Charlottesville
Street address state: VA
Zip/Postal code: 22901-1480
Country: USA
Mailing address: 944 Glenwood Station Ln Ste 303
Mailing city: Charlottesville
Mailing state: VA
Mailing zip: 22901-1480
General Phone: (800) 446-3857
General Fax: (800) 248-7809
General/National Adv. E-mail: vmodic@badgerfire.com
Primary Website: www.badgerfire.com
Mthly Avg Unique Visitors: 1960
Industry: Fire Protection
Personnel: Alan Owens (Sales/Mktg. Dir.)

BALDOR ELECTRIC CO.

Street address 1: 5711 Rs Boreham Jr St
Street address city: Fort Smith
Street address state: AR
Zip/Postal code: 72901-8301
Country: USA
Mailing address: PO Box 2400
Mailing city: Fort Smith
Mailing state: AR
Mailing zip: 72902-2400
General Phone: (479) 646-4711
General Fax: (479) 648-5752
Primary Website: www.baldor.com
Mthly Avg Unique Visitors: 1920
Industry: Drives & ControlsMotors
Personnel: Peter Voser (Chrmn.); Ulrich Spiesshofer (CEO)

BALDWIN AMERICAS

Street address 1: 3350 W Salt Creek Ln
Street address 2: Ste 110
Street address city: Arlington Heights
Street address state: IL
Zip/Postal code: 60005-1089
Country: USA
Mailing address: 3350 West Salt Creek
Mailing city: Arlington Heights
Mailing state: IL
Mailing zip: 60005
General Phone: 913-888-9800
General/National Adv. E-mail: csrteam@baldwintech.com
Primary Website: www.baldwintech.com/home
Mthly Avg Unique Visitors: 1918
Industry: Sales, Service, and Parts; Sheetfed and Web, Blanket Cleaner/Washer (Automatic); UV/IR/ LED Drying Systems; Web Printing Controls (WPC) systems; Press Accessories, Parts & Supplies, Cleaning Cloth;
Personnel: Denise Jabotte (Sales Contact)

BALDWIN TECHNOLOGY COMPANY, INC.

Street address 1: 3041 Woodcreek Dr
Street address 2: Ste 102
Street address city: Downers Grove
Street address state: IL
Zip/Postal code: 60515-5418
Country: USA
Mailing address: 3041 Woodcreek Dr Ste 102
Mailing city: Downers Grove
Mailing state: IL
Mailing zip: 60515-5418
General Phone: 630-595-3651
General Fax: 630-595-5433
General/National Adv. E-mail: info@baldwintech.com
Primary Website: www.baldwintech.com
Industry: UV & LED Curing and IR Drying Systems; Automatic Blanket Cleaners; Circulation Equipment & Supplies; Dampening Systems; Environmental Control Systems; Fluid Management Systems: Pressroom; Ink Controls, Computerized; Press Accessories, Parts & Supplies; Recirculators; Solvent Recovery Systems; Powder Applicators; Gluing Systems; Anti-Offset Powder; Blanket Cleaning Cloth Consumables; UV Lamps
Note: Baldwin Technology Company, Inc. is a leading international supplier of process automation equipment and related consumables for the graphic arts industry. Newspaper, sheetfed, commercial web, flexographic and digital pressrooms are enhanced and transformed with Baldwin's extensive product lines and systems. Baldwin's cutting edge systems include UV and LED curing, IR drying, spray dampening, blanket, plate and web cleaning, fluid management, ink control, web press protection, and press consumables. New product development and marketing are key initiatives for Baldwin as response to constantly changing market demands is critical in a rapidly evolving marketplace.
Personnel: Donald Gustafson (Vice President, Baldwin Americas Sales & Marketing)

BALEMASTER

Street address 1: 980 Crown Ct
Street address city: Crown Point
Street address state: IN
Zip/Postal code: 46307-2732
Country: USA
Mailing address: 980 Crown Ct
Mailing city: Crown Point
Mailing state: IN
Mailing zip: 46307-2732
General Phone: (219) 663-4525
General Fax: (219) 663-4591
General/National Adv. E-mail: sales@balemaster.com
Primary Website: www.balemaster.com
Mthly Avg Unique Visitors: 1949
Industry: Baling Machines
Personnel: Mike Connell (Sales Mgr.)

BARRY FRENCH

Street address 1: 3 Ashlawn Rd
Street address city: Assonet
Street address state: MA
Zip/Postal code: 02702-1105
Country: USA
Mailing address: 3 Ashlawn Rd
Mailing city: Assonet
Mailing state: MA
Mailing zip: 02702-1105
General Phone: (508) 644-5772
General/National Adv. E-mail: barryfrench@yahoo.com
Mthly Avg Unique Visitors: 1986
Industry: Brokers & Appraisers; Consulting Services: Financial;
Note: Brokerage, consulting & appraisals"
Personnel: Barry French (Owner)

BASF CORPORATION

Street address 1: 100 Park Ave
Street address city: Florham Park
Street address state: NJ
Zip/Postal code: 07932-1049
County: Morris
Country: USA
Mailing address: 100 Park Ave
Mailing city: Florham Park
Mailing state: NJ
Mailing zip: 07932-1089
General Phone: (973) 245-6000
General/National Adv. E-mail: Procurement-Resource-Center@basf.com
Primary Website: www.basf.us
Mthly Avg Unique Visitors: 1865
Industry: Chemicals; Plastics; Catalysts; Coatings; Crop Technology; Crude Oil & Natural Gas Exploration and Production;
Personnel: Wayne T. Smith (Chairman and CEO); Andre Becker (CFO)

BATON LOCK & HARDWARE CO., INC.

Street address 1: 11521 Salinaz Ave
Street address city: Garden Grove
Street address state: CA
Zip/Postal code: 92843-3702
Country: USA
Mailing address: 11521 Salinaz Ave
Mailing city: Garden Grove
Mailing state: CA
Mailing zip: 92843-3702
General Phone: (714) 590-6969
General Fax: (714) 590-6960
General/National Adv. E-mail: info@batonlockusa.com
Primary Website: www.batonlockusa.com
Industry: Calibration Software/Hardware
Personnel: Hwei Ying Chen (Pres.)

BAUMER ELECTRIC LTD.

Street address 1: 122 Spring Street
Street address 2: Unit C-6
Street address city: Southington
Street address state: CT
Zip/Postal code: 06489-1534
Country: USA
Mailing address: 122 Spring Street, Unit C-6
Mailing city: Southington
Mailing state: CT
Mailing zip: 06489-1534
General Phone: (800) 937 9336
General/National Adv. E-mail: sales.us@baumer.com
Primary Website: www.baumer.com
Mthly Avg Unique Visitors: 1952
Industry: Controls: Photo Electric; Newspaper Couter; Totalizing Systems; Web Break Detector
Personnel: Jeremy Jones (Pdct. Mgr.); Kristian Santamaria (Mrkt.)

BAUMFOLDER CORP.

Street address 1: 1660 Campbell Rd
Street address city: Sidney
Street address state: OH
Zip/Postal code: 45365-2480
County: Shelby
Country: USA
Mailing address: 1660 Campbell Rd
Mailing city: Sidney
Mailing state: OH
Mailing zip: 45365-2480
General Phone: (937) 492-1281
General Fax: (937) 492-7280
General/National Adv. E-mail: baumfolder@baumfolder.com
Primary Website: www.baumfolder.com
Mthly Avg Unique Visitors: 1917
Industry: Belts, Belting, V-Belts; Collating Equipment; Counting, Stacking, Bundling Machines; Cutters & TrimmersCutters & Trimmers; Delivery Equipment; Feeding, Folding, Delivery Equipment; Folding Machines; Inserting Equipment (Includes Stuffing Machines); Pumps (Air, Ink, Vacuum)
Personnel: Janice A. Benanzer (Pres.); Mark Pellman (Dir., Sales/Mktg.)

BAUMUELLER-NUERMONT CORP.

Street address 1: 1555 Oakbrook Dr. Ste. 120
Street address city: Norcross
Street address state: GA
Zip/Postal code: 30093
Country: USA
Mailing address: 1555 Oakbrook Dr. Ste. 120
Mailing city: Norcross
Mailing state: GA
Mailing zip: 30093
General Phone: (678) 291-0535
General Fax: (678) 291-0537
General/National Adv. E-mail: info@baumuller.com
Primary Website: www.bnc-america.com
Industry: Motors
Note: Chicago Office: Baumueller-Nuermont Corp. 1858 S. Elmhurst Road Mount Prospect, IL 60056 T: (847) 439-5363 F: (847) 890-6632 Mexico Location:

Baumueller-Nuermont S.A. de C.V. Carretera Estatal 431 km 2+200, Lote 95 MÃ³dulo 11 Parque Industrial TecnolÃ³gico InnovaciÃ³n El MarquÃ©s, QuerÃ©taro, Mexico 76246. T: +52 (442) 221 6670 Canada Location: Baumueller Canada 6581 Kitimat Road Unit 8 Mississauga, ON. L5N3T5 T: (905) 228-1095 F: (905) 247-0609

BECKART ENVIRONMENTAL, INC.

Street address 1: 6900 46th St
Street address city: Kenosha
Street address state: WI
Zip/Postal code: 53144-1749
Country: USA
Mailing address: 6900 46th St
Mailing city: Kenosha
Mailing state: WI
Mailing zip: 53144-1779
General Phone: (262) 656-7680
General Fax: (262) 656-7699
General/National Adv. E-mail: information@beckart.com
Primary Website: www.beckart.com
Mthly Avg Unique Visitors: 1978
Industry: Wastewater Treatment
Personnel: Thomas M. Fedrigon (Pres.); Dan Fedrigon (Mgr., Mktg./Sales)

BELL & HOWELL SCANNERS

Street address 1: 3791 South Alston Ave
Street address city: Durham
Street address state: NC
Zip/Postal code: 27713
Country: USA
Mailing address: 3791 South Alston Ave
Mailing city: Durham
Mailing state: NC
Mailing zip: 27713
General Phone: 800-961-7282
General/National Adv. E-mail: info@bhemail.com
Primary Website: www.bellhowell.net
Mthly Avg Unique Visitors: 1907
Industry: Mailroom Systems & Equipment; Publishing Systems
Personnel: Ramesh Ratan (Vice-Chairman); Larry Blue (Pres.); Arthur Bergens (CFO)

BELLATRIX SYSTEMS, INC.

Street address 1: 1015 SW Emkay Dive
Street address city: Bend
Street address state: OR
Zip/Postal code: 97702
Country: USA
Mailing address: 1015 SW Emkay Dr
Mailing city: Bend
Mailing state: OR
Mailing zip: 97702-1010
General Phone: (541) 382-2208
General Fax: (541) 385-3277
General/National Adv. E-mail: frontoffice@bellatrix.net
Primary Website: www.bellatrix.com
Mthly Avg Unique Visitors: 1987
Industry: Circulation Equipment & Supplies; Electronic Coin Totalizers for Newspaper Vending machines, Credit Card Systems for newspaper vending machines
Personnel: Steve Morris (President and CEO); William Raven (Sr. Vice Pres., Sales/Mktg.)

BELT CORPORATION OF AMERICA

Street address 1: 253 Castleberry Industrial Dr
Street address city: Cumming
Street address state: GA
Zip/Postal code: 30040-9051
Country: USA
Mailing address: 253 Castleberry Industrial Dr
Mailing city: Cumming
Mailing state: GA
Mailing zip: 30040-9051
General Phone: (800) 235-0947
General Fax: (770) 887-4138
General/National Adv. E-mail: sales@beltcorp.com
Primary Website: www.beltcorp.com
Mthly Avg Unique Visitors: 1985
Industry: Belts, Belting, V-Belts
Personnel: William C. Levensailor (Pres.); Rich Blais (Sales Mgr.); Mike Bridges (Inside Sales Supvr.)

BELTING INDUSTRIES CO., INC.

Street address 1: 20 Boright Ave
Street address city: Kenilworth
Street address state: NJ
Zip/Postal code: 07033-1015
Country: USA
Mailing address: PO Box 310
Mailing city: Kenilworth
Mailing state: NJ
Mailing zip: 07033-0310
General Phone: (908) 272-8591
General Fax: (908) 272-3825
General/National Adv. E-mail: info@beltingindustries.com
Primary Website: www.beltingindustries.com
Mthly Avg Unique Visitors: 1958
Industry: Belts, Belting, V-Belts
Personnel: Webb A. Cooper (Chrmn.); Scott Cooper (Pres.); Gene Hobson (COO); Paul West (Controller); Jeff Smith (Sales Mgr.)

BENDER MACHINE, INC.

Street address 1: 2150 E 37th St
Street address city: Vernon
Street address state: CA
Zip/Postal code: 90058-1417
Country: USA
Mailing address: 2150 E 37th St
Mailing city: Vernon
Mailing state: CA
Mailing zip: 90058-1491
General Phone: (323) 232-1790
General Fax: (323) 232-6456
General/National Adv. E-mail: info@bendermachine.com
Primary Website: www.bendermachine.com
Mthly Avg Unique Visitors: 1946
Industry: Newsprint; Newsprint Handeling Equipment; Roller Grinders; Roller Grinding Services;
Personnel: Bruce Perry (Mktg. Mgr.); Doug Martin (Acct. Mgr.)

BERTING COMMUNICATIONS

Street address 1: 6330 Woburn Dr
Street address city: Indianapolis
Street address state: IN
Zip/Postal code: 46250-2710
County: Marion
Country: USA
Mailing address: 6330 Woburn Dr
Mailing city: Indianapolis
Mailing state: IN
Mailing zip: 46250
General Phone: (317) 849-5408
General Fax: (317) 849-5408
General/National Adv. E-mail: bob@bobberting.com
Display Adv. E-mail: bob@bobberting.com
Primary Website: 6330 Woburn Drive
Mthly Avg Unique Visitors: 1990
Industry: Publisher Consultant Services:Merchant Advertising Seminars; Marketing; Training: Sales & Marketing--webinars,tele-seminars
Personnel: Bob Berting (Pres.); Barbara Berting (Vice Pres.); Dan Cooper (Graphic Artist)

BETA SCREEN CORP.

Street address 1: 707 Commercial Ave
Street address city: Carlstadt
Street address state: NJ
Zip/Postal code: 07072-2602
Country: USA
Mailing address: 707 Commercial Ave
Mailing city: Carlstadt
Mailing state: NJ
Mailing zip: 07072-2602
General Phone: (201) 939-2400
General Fax: (201) 939-7656
General/National Adv. E-mail: info@betascreen.com
Primary Website: www.betascreen.com
Mthly Avg Unique Visitors: 1958
Industry: Calibration Software/Hardware; Color Proofing; Color Viewing Equipment; Dark Room Equipment; Densitometers; Gauges, Measuring; Layout Tables, Light Tables & Workstations; Optical Products; Static Eliminators; Tables (Dot, Etch, Opaquing, Register, Retouching, Stripping)
Personnel: Arnold Serchuk (Pres.); Larry Goldberg (Contact)

BISHAMON INDUSTRIES CORP.

Street address 1: 5651 E Francis St
Street address city: Ontario
Street address state: CA
Zip/Postal code: 91761-3601
Country: USA
Mailing address: 5651 E Francis St
Mailing city: Ontario
Mailing state: CA
Mailing zip: 91761-3601
General Phone: (909) 390-0055
General Fax: (909) 390-0060
General/National Adv. E-mail: info@bishamon.com
Primary Website: www.bishamon.com
Mthly Avg Unique Visitors: 1949
Industry: Mailroom Systems & Equipment; Material Handling Equipment: Vehicle Loading; Newsprint Handeling Equipment; Paper Handeling Equipment;
Personnel: Wataru Sugiura (Pres.); Bob Clark (Vice Pres., Sales/Mktg.)

BLOWER APPLICATION CO., INC.

Street address 1: N1114 W19125 Clinton Dr
Street address city: Germantown
Street address state: WI
Zip/Postal code: 53022
Country: USA
Mailing address: PO Box 279
Mailing city: Germantown
Mailing state: WI
Mailing zip: 53022-0279
General Phone: (800) 959-0880
General Fax: (262) 255-3446
General/National Adv. E-mail: info@bloapco.com
Primary Website: www.bloapco.com
Mthly Avg Unique Visitors: 1933
Industry: Cutters & Trimmers; In-Line Trimming Systems; Paper Shredders; System Installations;
Personnel: John Stanislowski (Pres.); Michael J. Young (CEO); Ric Johnson (Mgr., Sales)

BOB RAY & ASSOCIATES, INC.

Street address 1: 3575 Morreim Dr
Street address city: Belvidere
Street address state: IL
Zip/Postal code: 61008-6307
Country: USA
Mailing address: 3575 Morreim Dr
Mailing city: Belvidere
Mailing state: IL
Mailing zip: 61008-6307
General Phone: (815) 547-9393
General Fax: (815) 547-5572
General/National Adv. E-mail: chuck@bobray.com
Primary Website: www.bobray.com
Mthly Avg Unique Visitors: 1988
Personnel: Chuck Britton (Pres.); Nolen G. Lee (Vice Pres., Admin.); John R. Steker (Vice Pres., Sales); John F. Nicoll (Technical Sales Mgr.)

BOB WEBER, INC.

Street address 1: 23850 Commerce Park Rd
Street address city: Cleveland
Street address state: OH
Zip/Postal code: 44122
County: Cuyahoga
Country: USA
Mailing address: 23850 Commerce Park Rd.
Mailing city: Cleveland
Mailing state: OH
Mailing zip: 44122
General Phone: (800) 399-4294
General Fax: (800) 837-8973
General/National Adv. E-mail: info@bob-weber.com
Display Adv. E-mail: leslie@bob-weber.com
Primary Website: www.bob-weber.com
Mthly Avg Unique Visitors: 1982
Industry: Equipment Dealers (New) - BWI Series CTP; Printing Consumables - Plates and Chemistry; Used PrePress Equipment; Platesetters; CTP; Computer-to-plate; Plate Processors; Raster Image Processors; Workflow RIPS; Xitron RIPs, Plate Readers
Note: Equipment Dealer selling new and reconditioned computer-to-plate machines (CTP), along with Paragon Plates and Chemistries - for the newspaper industry. Individual components sold as well as complete systems. We sell new RIP solutions such as the Xitron Navigator GPS, Elite and Sierra RIPs. All equipment is warranted and supported by the BWI network of service people. Sales and service.
Personnel: Leslie DiVincenzo (Director of Marketing); Steve Fondriest (Senior Technician); Bill Weber (Business Development Director)

BODINE ELECTRIC

Street address 1: 2500 W Bradley Pl
Street address city: Chicago
Street address state: IL
Zip/Postal code: 60618-4716
Country: USA
Mailing address: 201 Northfield Rd
Mailing city: Northfield
Mailing state: IL
Mailing zip: 60093-3311
General Phone: (773) 478-3515
General Fax: (773) 478-3232
Primary Website: www.bodine-electric.com
Mthly Avg Unique Visitors: 1905
Industry: Motors
Personnel: John Bodine (Pres.)

BOSCH REXROTH

Street address 1: 5150 Prairie Stone Pkwy
Street address city: Hoffman Estates
Street address state: IL
Zip/Postal code: 60192-3707
Country: USA
Mailing address: 5150 Prairie Stone Pkwy
Mailing city: Hoffman Estates
Mailing state: IL
Mailing zip: 60192-3707
General Phone: (847) 645-3600
General Fax: (847) 645-6201
Primary Website: www.boschrexroth-us.com
Industry: Press Control Systems
Personnel: Berend Bracht (Pres./CEO)

BOTTCHER AMERICA CORP.

Street address 1: 4600 Mercedes Dr
Street address city: Belcamp
Street address state: MD
Zip/Postal code: 21017-1223
Country: USA
Mailing address: 4600 Mercedes Dr
Mailing city: Belcamp
Mailing state: MD
Mailing zip: 21017-1225
General Phone: (800) 637-8120
General Fax: (410) 273-7174
General/National Adv. E-mail: support@boettcher-systems.com
Primary Website: www.bottcher.com
Industry: Rollers
Personnel: Jeff Hoover

BRADY & PAUL COMMUNICATIONS

Street address 1: 7 Orange St
Street address city: Newburyport
Street address state: MA
Zip/Postal code: 01950-2805
Country: USA
Mailing address: 7 Orange St
Mailing city: Newburyport
Mailing state: MA
Mailing zip: 01950-2805
General Phone: (978) 463-2255
General/National Adv. E-mail: bradybrady@aol.com; contact@johnbrady.info
Primary Website: www.bradyandpaul.com; www.johnbrady.info
Mthly Avg Unique Visitors: 1984
Industry: Art & Layout Equipment and Services; Consulting Services: Editorial;
Personnel: John Brady (Pres.); Greg Paul (Designer)

BRAINWORKS SOFTWARE

Street address 1: 100 South Main Street
Street address city: Sayville
Street address state: NY
Zip/Postal code: 11782
Mailing address: 100 South Main Street
Mailing city: Sayville
Mailing state: NY

Mailing zip: 11782
General Phone: (631) 563-5000
General Fax: (631) 563-6320
General/National Adv. E-mail: info@brainworks.com
Display Adv. E-mail: sales@brainworks.com
Primary Website: www.brainworks.com
Mthly Avg Unique Visitors: 1996
Industry: Software: Asset Management; Software: Workflow Management/Tracking; Training: Design & Layout; Training: Keyboard Operation; Training: Pre Press;
Note: We design, develop and deploy advertising solutions to the newspaper industry. With over 350 customers, we make your current and future workflows more efficient.
Personnel: Rick Sanders (President and CEO)

BRAINWORKS SOFTWARE DEVELOPMENT CORP.

Street address 1: 100 S Main St
Street address city: Sayville
Street address state: NY
Zip/Postal code: 11782-3100
Country: USA
Mailing address: 100 S Main St Ste 102
Mailing city: Sayville
Mailing state: NY
Mailing zip: 11782-3148
General Phone: (631) 563-5000
General Fax: (631) 563-6320
General/National Adv. E-mail: info@brainworks.com
Primary Website: www.brainworks.com
Mthly Avg Unique Visitors: 1988
Industry: Pagination Systems; Software: Advertising (Includes Display; Classified, Preprints and Digital); Software: Business (Includes Administration/ Accounting); Software: Design/Graphics; Software: Pagination/Layout; System Integration Services; Software: Circulation Software; Digital Subscriptions, CRM; Digital Advertising; Software: Customer Relationship Management (CRM); iPad Application
Note: Brainworks is the leading provider of Advertising, CRM, Circulation, Production and Web solutions for the Newspaper Media industry.
Personnel: John Barry (President); Rick Sanders (Director of Sales); Frank Collinsworth (Business Development Manager); Matt Griffith (Business Development Manager)

BROCK SOLUTIONS U.S. INC.

Street address 1: 8080 Tristar Dr
Street address 2: Ste 126
Street address city: Irving
Street address state: TX
Zip/Postal code: 75063-2823
Country: USA
Mailing address: 8080 Tristar Dr Ste 126
Mailing city: Irving
Mailing state: TX
Mailing zip: 75063-2823
General Phone: (972) 373-2500
General Fax: (972) 444-0352
General/National Adv. E-mail: info@brocksolutions.com ; hr@brocksolutions.com
Primary Website: www.brocksolutions.com
Mthly Avg Unique Visitors: 1929
Industry: Addressing Machines; Consulting Services: Production;
Personnel: Bill Mctuire (Project Mgr.)

BRODIE SYSTEM, INC.

Street address 1: 1539 W Elizabeth Ave
Street address city: Linden
Street address state: NJ
Zip/Postal code: 07036-6322
County: Union
Country: USA
Mailing address: 1539 W. Elizabeth Ave.
Mailing city: Linden
Mailing state: NJ
Mailing zip: 07036
General Phone: (908) 862-8620
General Fax: (908) 862-8632
General/National Adv. E-mail: customerservice@brodiesystem.com
Primary Website: www.brodiesystem.com
Mthly Avg Unique Visitors: 1929
Industry: Cylinder Repair; Ink Fountains & Accessories; Press Accessories, Parts & Supplies; Roller Grinding Services; Rollers; Rollers: Dampening;
Personnel: Thomas W. Nielsen (Pres.); Nicholas Lloyd (Eng.); John Farrell (Prodn. Mgr., Opns.)

BROWN MANNSCHRECK BUSINESS SYSTEM

Street address 1: 5901 NE Woodbine Rd
Street address city: Saint Joseph
Street address state: MO
Zip/Postal code: 64505-9353
Country: USA
Mailing address: 5901 NE Woodbine Rd
Mailing city: Saint Joseph
Mailing state: MO
Mailing zip: 64505-9353
General Phone: 816-387-8180
General Fax: 816-364-7925
General/National Adv. E-mail: customerservice@browncompanies.net
Primary Website: www.browncompanies.net/
Mthly Avg Unique Visitors: 1867
Industry: Sales and design Office Furniture
Personnel: Steven Pitluck (CEO); Craig Greer (Vice Pres.); Cathie Wayman (Vice Pres., Sales)

BROWN'S WEB PRESS SERVICE & MACHINE SHOP

Street address 1: 21386 Hwy Ff
Street address city: Mexico
Street address state: MO
Zip/Postal code: 65265
Country: USA
Mailing address: PO Box 326
Mailing city: Mexico
Mailing state: MO
Mailing zip: 65265-0326
General Phone: (573) 581-6275
General Fax: (573) 581-7278
General/National Adv. E-mail: lgbrown59@gmail.com
Mthly Avg Unique Visitors: 1983
Industry: Cylinder Repair; Drives & Controls; Equipment Dealers (Used); Erectors & Riggers; Press Rebuilding; Press Repairs; Presses: Offset; Roller Grinding Services;
Note: Machine Shop , Printing Press Sales and Servive "
Personnel: L.G. Brown (Pres.); Gena Brown (Vice President)

BST PRO MARK

Street address 1: 650 W Grand Ave
Street address 2: Ste 301
Street address city: Elmhurst
Street address state: IL
Zip/Postal code: 60126-1026
Country: USA
Mailing address: 650 W Grand Ave Ste 301
Mailing city: Elmhurst
Mailing state: IL
Mailing zip: 60126-1026
General Phone: (630) 833-9900
General Fax: (630) 833-9909
General/National Adv. E-mail: sales@bstpromark.com
Primary Website: www.bstpromark.com
Mthly Avg Unique Visitors: 1987
Industry: Color Management Software; Color Registration; Color Viewing Equipment; Press Accessories, Parts & Supplies; Produciton Control Systems; Web Cleaners; Web Guides
Personnel: John Thome (Vice Pres., Mktg.)

BUFFALO TECHNOLOGY INC.

Street address 1: 11100 Metric Blvd
Street address 2: Ste 750
Street address city: Austin
Street address state: TX
Zip/Postal code: 78758-4072
Country: USA
Mailing address: 11100 Metric Blvd Ste 750
Mailing city: Austin
Mailing state: TX
Mailing zip: 78758-4072
General Phone: (512) 349-1580
General Fax: (512) 339-7272
General/National Adv. E-mail: sales@buffalotech.com
Primary Website: www.buffalotech.com
Mthly Avg Unique Visitors: 1986
Industry: Computers: Hardware & Software Integrators; Computers: Local Area Network (LANS); Computers: Storage Devices;
Personnel: Jay Pechek (PR)

BUHRS BV

Street address 1: Vredeweg 7
Street address 2: 1505 HH Zaandam
Zip/Postal code: 1505
Country: Netherlands
Mailing address: Vredeweg 7, 1505 HH Zaandam
Mailing zip: 1505
General Phone: +31 (0)75 7990600
General Fax: +31 (0)75 7990610
General/National Adv. E-mail: info@buhrs.com
Primary Website: www.buhrs.com
Mthly Avg Unique Visitors: 1908
Industry: Automatic Plastic Bagging Equipment; Feeding, Folding, Delivery Equipment; Folding Machines; Inserting Equipment (Includes Stuffing Machines); Mailroom Systems & Equipment; Newspaper Couter; Software: Press/Post Press;
Personnel: Dick Verheij (Managing Director); Koos Buis (Sales Support); Ton Warger (Service Manager); Arjan de Vries (Manager Engineering)

BULBTRONICS

Street address 1: 45 Banfi Plz
Street address city: Farmingdale
Street address state: NY
Zip/Postal code: 11753
Country: USA
Mailing address: 45 Banfi Plz N
Mailing city: Farmingdale
Mailing state: NY
Mailing zip: 11735-1539
General Phone: (631) 249-2272
General Fax: (631) 249-6066
General/National Adv. E-mail: bulbs@bulbtronics.com
Primary Website: www.bulbtronics.com
Mthly Avg Unique Visitors: 1976
Industry: Lighting Equipment
Personnel: Lee Vestrich (Vice Pres., Sales); Beckie Mullin (Mgr., Mktg.)

BURGESS INDUSTRIES, INC.

Street address 1: 7500 Boone Ave N
Street address 2: Ste 111
Street address city: Brooklyn Park
Street address state: MN
Zip/Postal code: 55428-1026
Country: USA
Mailing address: 7500 Boone Ave N Ste 111
Mailing city: Brooklyn Park
Mailing state: MN
Mailing zip: 55428-1026
General Phone: (763) 553-7800
General Fax: (763) 553-9289
General/National Adv. E-mail: djburgess@burgessind.com
Primary Website: www.burgessind.com
Mthly Avg Unique Visitors: 1977
Industry: Color Proofing; Color Registration; Controls: Exposure; Controls: Register; Light Integrators; Plate Bending Systems; Plate Mounting & Register Systems; Proofing Systems; Static Eliminators; Vacuum Frames
Personnel: Dennis Burgess (Pres./CEO); Joe Stein (Nat'l Pdct. Mgr.); Richard Fream (Nat'l Sales Dir.)

BURNISHINE PRODUCTS

Street address 1: 25392 W Park Ct
Street address city: Lake Villa
Street address state: IL
Zip/Postal code: 60046-9710
Country: USA
Mailing address: 25392 W Park Ct
Mailing city: Lake Villa
Mailing state: IL
Mailing zip: 60046-9710
General Phone: 847-356-0222
General Fax: 847-306-3550
General/National Adv. E-mail: rgiza@burnishine.com
Primary Website: www.burnishine.com
Mthly Avg Unique Visitors: 1887
Industry: Offset Fountain Solutions; Plate Cleaners; Miscellaneous Pressroom Chemicals
Personnel: Patty Vick (Graphic Arts Customer Service); Roger Giza (President)

BURT TECHNOLOGIES, INC.

Street address 1: 32156 Castle Ct
Street address 2: Ste 206
Street address city: Evergreen
Street address state: CO
Zip/Postal code: 80439-9500
Country: USA
Mailing address: 32156 Castle Ct Ste 206
Mailing city: Evergreen
Mailing state: CO
Mailing zip: 80439-9500
General Phone: (303) 674-3232
General Fax: (303) 670-0978
General/National Adv. E-mail: info@burtmountain.com; sales@burtmountain.com; support@burtmountain.com
Primary Website: www.burtmountain.com
Mthly Avg Unique Visitors: 1985
Industry: Computers: Hardware & Software Integrators; Inserting Equipment (Includes Stuffing Machines); Interfaces; Mailroom Systems & Equipment; Software: Press/Post Press; Training: Post Press
Personnel: Jim Burt (Founder/Pres.); Rich Burt (CEO); Billy Calva (Burt Response Center Manager)

BUSCH, INC.

Street address 1: 516 Viking Dr
Street address city: Virginia Beach
Street address state: VA
Zip/Postal code: 23452-7316
Country: USA
Mailing address: 516 Viking Dr
Mailing city: Virginia Beach
Mailing state: VA
Mailing zip: 23452-7316
General Phone: (757) 463-7800
General Fax: (757) 463-7407
General/National Adv. E-mail: marketing@buschusa.com
Primary Website: www.buschpump.com
Mthly Avg Unique Visitors: 1975
Industry: Pumps (Air, Ink, Vacuum)
Personnel: Charles Kane (Pres.); Linda Katz (Mktg. Specialist)

BUTLER AUTOMATIC

Street address 1: 41 Leona Dr
Street address city: Middleboro
Street address state: MA
Zip/Postal code: 02346-1404
Country: USA
Mailing address: 41 Leona Dr
Mailing city: Middleboro
Mailing state: MA
Mailing zip: 02346-1404
General Phone: (508) 923-0544
General Fax: (508) 923-0886
General/National Adv. E-mail: butler@butlerautomatic.com
Primary Website: www.butlerautomatic.com
Mthly Avg Unique Visitors: 1956
Industry: Conveyors; Counting, Stacking, Bundling Machines; Cutters & Trimmers; Flying Pasters; Material Handling Equipment: Palletizing Machines; Pasters; Roll Handeling Equipment; Splicers, Automatic; Tension & Web Controls;
Personnel: John Clifford (Vice Pres., Engineering)

BW PAPERSYSTEMS

Street address 1: 1300 N. Airport Road
Street address city: Phillips
Street address state: WI
Zip/Postal code: 54555
Country: USA
Mailing address: 1300 N. Airport Road
Mailing city: Phillips
Mailing state: WI
Mailing zip: 54555
General Phone: (715) 339-2191
General Fax: (715) 339â€4469
General/National Adv. E-mail: sales@bwpapersystems.com
Display Adv. E-mail: sales@bwpapersystems.com
Primary Website: www.bwpapersystems.com
Mthly Avg Unique Visitors: 1982
Industry: Conversion Equipment; Conveyors; Cutters & Trimmers; Photostat: Paper; Reels & Tensions; Reels (Inlcudes Paper Reels); Roll Handeling Equipment; Splicers, Automatic; Tension & Web Controls; Web Guides;

Personnel: Neal McConnellogue (Pres.)

CACHET FINE ART PHOTOGRAPHIC PAPER

Street address 1: 11661 Martens River Cir
Street address 2: Ste D
Street address city: Fountain Valley
Street address state: CA
Zip/Postal code: 92708-4212
Country: USA
Mailing address: 11661 Martens River Cir Ste D
Mailing city: Fountain Valley
Mailing state: CA
Mailing zip: 92708-4212
General Phone: (714) 432-6331
General Fax: (714) 432-7102
General/National Adv. E-mail: onecachet@aol.com
Primary Website: www.onecachet.com
Mthly Avg Unique Visitors: 1979
Industry: Chemicals: Photographic; Dark Room Equipment; Film & Paper: Filters (Photographic);
Personnel: Ike Royer (Pres.)

CANNON EQUIPMENT

Street address 1: 15100 Business Pkwy
Street address city: Rosemount
Street address state: MN
Zip/Postal code: 55068-1793
Country: USA
Mailing address: 324 Washington St W
Mailing city: Cannon Falls
Mailing state: MN
Mailing zip: 55009-1142
General Phone: (800) 533-2071
General Fax: (651) 322-1583
General/National Adv. E-mail: info@cannonequipment.com
Primary Website: www.cannonequipment.com
Mthly Avg Unique Visitors: 1973
Industry: Cart Distribution Systems; Circulation Equipment & Supplies; Conveyors; Mailroom Systems & Equipment;
Personnel: Chuck Gruber (Pres.); Pat Geraghty (Nat'l Sales Mgr./Newspaper Handling Systems)

CANON USA, INC.

Street address 1: 1 Dakota Dr
Street address city: New Hyde Park
Street address state: NY
Zip/Postal code: 11042-1135
Country: USA
Mailing address: 1 Canon Park
Mailing city: Melville
Mailing state: NY
Mailing zip: 11747-3036
General Phone: (632) 330-5000
General/National Adv. E-mail: mediacontact@cusa.canon.com
Display Adv. E-mail: pr@cusa.canon.com
Primary Website: www.usa.canon.com
Mthly Avg Unique Visitors: 1937
Personnel: Yoroku Adachi (Pres./CEO, Canon U.S.A., Inc.); Seymour Liebman (Exec. Vice Pres./Gen. Counsel Admin./Reg'l Opns.); Tod D. Pike (Sr. Vice Pres./Gen Mgr., Sales Mktg./Admin.); Rick Booth (Adv. Dir., Cameras/Camcorders, Dir., Mktg. Serv./Adv.)

CAPCO MACHINERY SYSTEMS, INC.

Street address 1: 307 Eastpark Dr
Street address city: Roanoke
Street address state: VA
Zip/Postal code: 24019-8227
Country: USA
Mailing address: PO Box 11945
Mailing city: Roanoke
Mailing state: VA
Mailing zip: 24022-1945
General Phone: (540) 977-0404
General Fax: (540) 977-2781
Primary Website: www.capcomachinery.com
Mthly Avg Unique Visitors: 1940
Industry: Roller Grinders
Personnel: Edward E. West (Pres.); Amy S. West (Vice Pres., Finance)

CAPITA TECHNOLOGIES

Street address 1: 17600 Gillette Ave
Street address city: Irvine
Street address state: CA
Zip/Postal code: 92614-5715
Country: USA
Mailing address: 17600 Gillette Ave
Mailing city: Irvine
Mailing state: CA
Mailing zip: 92614-5715
General Phone: (949) 260-3000
General Fax: (949) 851-9875
General/National Adv. E-mail: sales@capita.com
Primary Website: www.capita.com
Industry: Software: Pagination/Layout; System Integration Services;
Personnel: Charles Granville (CEO); Imelda Ford (Exec. Vice Pres., Techn./Opns.)

CAPROCK DEVELOPMENTS, INC.

Street address 1: 475 Speedwell Ave
Street address 2: PO Box 95
Street address city: Morris Plains
Street address state: NJ
Zip/Postal code: 07950-2149
Country: USA
Mailing address: PO Box 95
Mailing city: Morris Plains
Mailing state: NJ
Mailing zip: 07950-0095
General Phone: (973) 267-9292
General Fax: (973) 292-0614
General/National Adv. E-mail: info@caprockdev.com
Primary Website: www.caprockdev.com
Mthly Avg Unique Visitors: 1953
Industry: Densitometers; Exposure Lamps; Gauges, Measuring; Lighting Equipment; Offset Blanket Thickness Gauge; Optical Products; Paper Testing Instruments; Testing Instruments;
Personnel: Alan Schwartz (President)

CARIWEB PRODUCTS

Street address 1: PO Box 1349
Street address city: Harlingen
Street address state: TX
Zip/Postal code: 78551-1349
Country: USA
Mailing address: PO Box 1349
Mailing city: Harlingen
Mailing state: TX
Mailing zip: 78551-1349
General Phone: (956) 423-5766
General Fax: (956) 748-3417
General/National Adv. E-mail: cariwebproducts@aol.com
Mthly Avg Unique Visitors: 1978
Industry: Tape Splicing Equipment
Personnel: Jose Henderson (Pres.)

CARLSON DESIGN CONSTRUCT

Street address 1: 34 Executive Park
Street address 2: Ste 250
Street address city: Irvine
Street address state: CA
Zip/Postal code: 92614-4707
Country: USA
Mailing address: 34 Executive Park Ste 250
Mailing city: Irvine
Mailing state: CA
Mailing zip: 92614-4707
General Phone: (949) 251-0455
General Fax: (949) 251-0465
General/National Adv. E-mail: carlson@carlson-dc.com
Primary Website: www.carlson-dc.com
Mthly Avg Unique Visitors: 1945
Industry: Architects/Engineers (Includes Design/Construction Firms)
Personnel: Tom Ryan (Vice Pres., Mktg)

CASCADE CORP.

Street address 1: 2201 NE 201st Ave
Street address city: Fairview
Street address state: OR
Zip/Postal code: 97024-9718
Country: USA
Mailing address: PO Box 20187
Mailing city: Portland
Mailing state: OR
Mailing zip: 97294-0187
General Phone: (503) 669-6300
General Fax: (800) 693-3768
General/National Adv. E-mail: sales@cascorp.com
Primary Website: www.cascorp.com
Mthly Avg Unique Visitors: 1943
Industry: Material Handling Equipment: Truck Loaders; Paper Handeling Equipment;
Personnel: Pete Drake (Sr. V. P.); Keith Miller (Dir. of Sales); Jim Farance (Corporate Manager)

CATALYST PAPER (USA), INC.

Street address 1: 2200 6th Ave
Street address 2: Ste 800
Street address city: Seattle
Street address state: WA
Zip/Postal code: 98121-1827
Country: USA
Mailing address: 2200 6th Avenue, Suite 800
Mailing city: Seattle
Mailing state: WA
Mailing zip: 98121-2312
General Phone: (206) 838-2070
General Fax: (206) 838-2071
Primary Website: www.catalystpaper.com
Mthly Avg Unique Visitors: 1993
Industry: Newsprint; Paper: Coated Groundwood Offset; Paper: Groundwood Specialties; Paper: Specialty Printing Paper;
Personnel: James Hardt (Sales Director); Peter Hart (VP Sales & Marketing); Mark Petersen (VP International Sales)

CATALYST PAPER CORP.

Street address 1: 3600 Lysander Ln. 2nd Fl.
Street address city: Richmond
Street address state: BC
Zip/Postal code: V7B 1C3
Country: Canada
Mailing address: 3600 Lysander Ln., 2nd Fl.
Mailing city: Richmond
Mailing state: BC
Mailing zip: V7B 1C3
General Phone: (604) 247-4400
General Fax: (604) 247-0512
General/National Adv. E-mail: contactus@catalystpaper.com
Primary Website: www.catalystpaper.com
Mthly Avg Unique Visitors: 1950
Industry: Manufacturing
Note: Pulp and paper manufacturing
Personnel: Jim Bayles (Vice-President and General Manager Newsprint and International)

CCI EUROPE, INC.-GEORGIA BRANCH

Street address 1: 3550 George Busbee Pkwy NW
Street address 2: Ste 300
Street address city: Kennesaw
Street address state: GA
Zip/Postal code: 30144-5433
Country: USA
Mailing address: 600 Townpark Ln NW Ste 350
Mailing city: Kennesaw
Mailing state: GA
Mailing zip: 30144-3758
General Phone: (770) 420-1100
General Fax: (770) 420-5588
General/National Adv. E-mail: info@ccieurope.com
Primary Website: www.ccieurope.com
Mthly Avg Unique Visitors: 1979
Industry: Content Management Systems
Personnel: Dan Korsgaard (CEO); Tor Lillegraven (Business Development Director); Thea Schmidt Borgholm (Vice President of Digital Services)

CELEBRO

Street address 1: 312 Elm St
Street address 2: Fl 20
Street address city: Cincinnati
Street address state: OH
Zip/Postal code: 45202-2739
County: Hamilton
Country: USA
Mailing address: 151 W 4th St Ste 201
Mailing city: Cincinnati
Mailing state: OH
Mailing zip: 45202-2746
General Phone: (513) 665-3777
General Fax: (513) 768-8958
General/National Adv. E-mail: info@celebro.com
Primary Website: www.gmti.com
Mthly Avg Unique Visitors: 1994
Industry: Computers: Hardware & Software Integrators; Electronic Ad Delivery; Software: Advertising (Includes Display; Classified); Software: Electronic Data Interchange
Product or Service: Hardware/Software Supplier
Personnel: Steve Fuschetti (Pres./CEO); Tom Foster (Vice Pres., Celebro Opns.); Michael Hibert (Dir., Implementation Servs.)

CENTRAL GRAPHICS

Street address 1: 1302 Enterprise Dr
Street address city: Romeoville
Street address state: IL
Zip/Postal code: 60446-1016
Country: USA
Mailing address: 1302 Enterprise Dr
Mailing city: Romeoville
Mailing state: IL
Mailing zip: 60446-1016
General Phone: (630) 759-1696
General Fax: (630) 759-1792
General/National Adv. E-mail: cgi@cgipressparts.com
Primary Website: www.cgipressparts.com/
Mthly Avg Unique Visitors: 1984
Industry: Belts, Belting, V-Belts; Copper Plating Drums; Cylinder Repair; Equipment Dealers (Used); Folder Knives; Pin Register Systems; Press Accessories, Parts & Supplies; Presses: Offset; Roller Grinding Services; Rollers: Dampening;
Personnel: Jim Crivellone (Pres.); Pat Murphy (Sales/Opns. Mgr.)

CH2MHILL LOCKWOOD GREENE

Street address 1: 9191 S Jamaica St
Street address city: Englewood
Street address state: CO
Zip/Postal code: 80112-5946
Country: USA
Mailing address: 9191 S Jamaica St
Mailing city: Englewood
Mailing state: CO
Mailing zip: 80112-5946
General Phone: (720) 286-2000
General/National Adv. E-mail: Lorrie.Crum@jacobs.com
Primary Website: www.ch2m.com
Mthly Avg Unique Visitors: 1832
Industry: Architects/Engineers (Includes Design/Construction Firms); Material Handling Equipment: Automatic Guided Vehicles;
Personnel: Lorrie Crum (Global Media Relations)

CHANNELNET

Street address 1: 3 Harbor Dr
Street address 2: Ste 206
Street address city: Sausalito
Street address state: CA
Zip/Postal code: 94965-1491
County: Marin
Country: USA
Mailing address: 3 Harbor Dr Ste 206
Mailing city: Sausalito
Mailing state: CA
Mailing zip: 94965-1491
General Phone: (415) 332-4704
General Fax: (415) 332-1635
General/National Adv. E-mail: info@channelnet.com
Primary Website: www.softad.com; www.channelnet.com
Industry: Consulting Services: Advertising; Software: Advertising (Includes Display; Classified);
Product or Service: Consultants'Hardware/Software Supplier
Personnel: Paula George Tompkins (Founder/CEO); Kevin Kelly (CFO); Mike Behr (Sr. Dir., Professional Servs.)

CHAPEL HILL MANUFACTURING CO.

Street address 1: 1807 Walnut Ave
Street address city: Oreland
Street address state: PA
Zip/Postal code: 19075-1528
Country: USA
Mailing address: PO Box 208
Mailing city: Oreland

Mailing state: PA
Mailing zip: 19075-0208
General Phone: (215) 884-3614
General Fax: (215) 884-3617
General/National Adv. E-mail: sales@chapelhillmfg.com
Primary Website: www.chapelhillmfg.com
Mthly Avg Unique Visitors: 1962
Industry: Dampening Systems
Personnel: John Seeburger (Pres./Vice Pres., Mktg.); J. Robert Seeburger (Vice Pres., Sales)

CHUCK BLEVINS & ASSOC.

Street address 1: 8396 Northhampton Ct
Street address city: Naples
Street address state: FL
Zip/Postal code: 34120-1687
County: Collier
Country: USA
Mailing address: 8396 Northhampton Ct
Mailing city: Naple
Mailing state: FL
Mailing zip: 34120
General Phone: (239) 595-3840
General/National Adv. E-mail: chuckblevins@aol.com
Primary Website: www.chuckblevins.com
Mthly Avg Unique Visitors: 1989
Industry: Consulting Services: Equipment; Consulting Services: Ergonomics; Consulting Services: Production; Mailroom Systems & Equipment; Press Systems and equipment

CHURCH RICKARDS, WHITLOCK & CO., INC.

Street address 1: 10001 W Roosevelt Rd
Street address city: Westchester
Street address state: IL
Zip/Postal code: 60154-2664
Country: USA
Mailing address: 10001 W Roosevelt Rd
Mailing city: Westchester
Mailing state: IL
Mailing zip: 60154-2664
General Phone: (708) 345-7500
General Fax: (708) 345-1166
General/National Adv. E-mail: crwfred@aol.com
Mthly Avg Unique Visitors: 1945
Industry: Consulting Services: Circulation; Consulting Services: Human Resources; Insurance;
Personnel: Fred C. Hohnke (Pres.); Daniel Demjanik (Regl. Mgr.); Tim Solt (Reg. Mgr.)

CIRCULATION DEVELOPMENT, INC.

Street address 1: PO Box 6
Street address city: Wentzville
Street address state: MO
Zip/Postal code: 63385-0006
Country: USA
Mailing address: PO Box 6
Mailing city: Wentzville
Mailing state: MO
Mailing zip: 63385-0006
General Phone: (800) 247-2338
General Fax: (800) 400-4453
General/National Adv. E-mail: increase@circulation.net
Primary Website: www.circulation.net
Mthly Avg Unique Visitors: 1986
Industry: Consulting Services: Circulation; Consulting Services: Marketing;
Note: newspaper circulation telemarketing
Personnel: Bill Wesa (Chrmn.); Jim Oden (Pres.); Rob Oden (Vice Pres.); Carmen Salvati (Mktg. Dir.); David Wesa (Dir., Info. Servs.)

CIRCULATION SOLUTIONS, INC.

Street address 1: 633 Lee Road 51
Street address city: Auburn
Street address state: AL
Zip/Postal code: 36832-8318
Country: USA
Mailing address: PO Box 1575
Mailing city: Auburn
Mailing state: AL
Mailing zip: 36831-1575
General Phone: (334) 826-6847
General/National Adv. E-mail: van@circulationsolutions.com
Mthly Avg Unique Visitors: 1985
Industry: Circulation Equipment & Supplies; Consulting Services: Circulation; Newspaper Marketing;
Note: Marketing Company Dedicated to Newspaper Subscription Sales
Personnel: Van Dozier (Pres.); Wyndol Smith (Sec.)

CLARK MATERIAL HANDLING CO.

Street address 1: 700 Enterprise Dr
Street address city: Lexington
Street address state: KY
Zip/Postal code: 40510-1028
Country: USA
Mailing address: 700 Enterprise Dr
Mailing city: Lexington
Mailing state: KY
Mailing zip: 40510-1028
General Phone: (859) 422-6400
General Fax: (859) 422-7408
Primary Website: www.clarkmhc.com
Mthly Avg Unique Visitors: 1917
Industry: Equipment Dealers (New); Equipment Dealers (Used); Lift Trucks; Material Handling Equipment: Palletizing Machines; Material Handling Equipment: Pallets & Palletizers; Material Handling Equipment: Truck Loaders; Material Handling Equipment: Vehicle Loading;
Personnel: Dennis Lawrence (Pres.); Sherry Myers (Dir., HR)

CLIPPER BELT LACER CO.

Street address 1: 2525 Wisconsin Ave
Street address city: Downers Grove
Street address state: IL
Zip/Postal code: 60515-4241
Country: USA
Mailing address: 2525 Wisconsin Ave
Mailing city: Downers Grove
Mailing state: IL
Mailing zip: 60515-4241
General Phone: 800-323-3444
General Fax: 630-971-1180
General/National Adv. E-mail: info@flexco.com
Primary Website: www.flexco.com
Mthly Avg Unique Visitors: 1908
Industry: Belts, Belting, V-Belts; Cutting Tools;
Personnel: Nancy Ayres (Gen. Mgr.); Bro Ballentine (Treasurer); Dick Reynolds (Sales Mgr.); John H. Meulenberg (Mktg. Mgr.); Beth Miller (Pdct. Mgr.)

CNI CORP.

Street address 1: 394 Elm St
Street address city: Milford
Street address state: NH
Zip/Postal code: 03055-4305
Country: USA
Mailing address: 468 Route 13 S Ste A
Mailing city: Milford
Mailing state: NH
Mailing zip: 03055-3488
General Phone: (603) 673-6600
General/National Adv. E-mail: info@breezeadops.com
Primary Website: www.breezeadworkflow.com
Mthly Avg Unique Visitors: 1988
Industry: Consulting Services: Production; Data Communication; Input & Editing Systems; Optical Character Recognition (OCR); Pagination Systems; Prepress Color Proofing Systems; Publishing Systems; Training: Keyboard Operation; Typesetters: Laser; Word Processing System;
Note: CNI Corporation is a software development company with over 20 years of publishing industry experience specializing in workflow automation. Our solutions have 3 key components; AdDesk the advertisers' facing web portal, Breeze, the sales reps' component and Breeze Creative Suite, the production/creative component. Breeze is a browser-based solution that allows reps to work remotely with tablets and smart phones and manage their accounts more efficiently. The time saved through our centralized automation tools provide sales reps more selling time which results in increased sales totals overall. CNI continues to provide innovation with an online credit card payment solution, Google DFP integration, E-signature capture and electronic insertion order management. Our software solutions streamline and simplify the advertising and production workflows. Through automation and elimination of duplicated manual tasks, CNI provides significant business benefits for media companies.
Personnel: Jon Dickinson (Pres.); Chris Prinos (EVP Business Dev.)

COAST GRAPHIC SUPPLY

Street address 1: 1363 Donlon St
Street address 2: Ste 16
Street address city: Ventura
Street address state: CA
Zip/Postal code: 93003-5638
Country: USA
Mailing address: 1112 Casitas ct.
Mailing city: Ventura
Mailing state: CA
Mailing zip: 93004
General Phone: (805) 642-5585
General/National Adv. E-mail: coastgraphic@earthlink.net
Primary Website: www.coastgraphicsupply.com
Mthly Avg Unique Visitors: 1978
Industry: Digital printing & proofing: Supplies & equipment Ink & Bulk Ink Systems Sublimation Ink Paper & Blanks Chemicals: Plate Processing; Chemicals: Pressroom; Composing Room Equipment & Supplies; Densitometers; Film & Paper: Contact; Film & Paper: Phototypesetting;
Note: Digital Ptng Supplies & Equip Pre & Press
Personnel: James Cagnina (Pres.)

COLD JET, INC.

Street address 1: 455 Wards Corner Rd
Street address city: Loveland
Street address state: OH
Zip/Postal code: 45140-9062
Country: USA
Mailing address: 455 Wards Corner Rd Ste 100
Mailing city: Loveland
Mailing state: OH
Mailing zip: 45140-9033
General Phone: (513) 831-3211
General/National Adv. E-mail: info@coldjet.com
Primary Website: www.coldjet.com; www.dryiceblasting.com
Industry: Cleaners & Solvents
Personnel: Gene Cooke (Pres./CEO)

COLORVISION, INC.

Street address 1: 5 Princess Rd
Street address city: Lawrenceville
Street address state: NJ
Zip/Postal code: 08648-2301
Country: USA
Mailing address: 5 Princess Rd
Mailing city: Lawrenceville
Mailing state: NJ
Mailing zip: 08648-2301
General Phone: (609) 895-7430
General Fax: (609) 895-8110
General/National Adv. E-mail: info@colovision.com
Primary Website: www.datacolor.com
Mthly Avg Unique Visitors: 2000
Industry: Software: Electronic Data Interchange
Personnel: Brian Levey (Vice Pres. Mktg./Sales)

COLTER PETERSON

Street address 1: 414 E 16th St
Street address city: Paterson
Street address state: NJ
Zip/Postal code: 07514-2638
Country: USA
Mailing address: 414 E 16th St
Mailing city: Paterson
Mailing state: NJ
Mailing zip: 07514-2638
General Phone: (515) 276-4528
General Fax: (515) 276-8324
General/National Adv. E-mail: sales@colterpeterson.com
Primary Website: www.colterpeterson.com
Mthly Avg Unique Visitors: 1932
Industry: Paper Cutters, Material Handling, Perfect Binders and & Three Knife Trimmers
Personnel: Vince Payne (Vice President)

COMMODITY RESOURCE & ENVIRONMENT

Street address 1: 116 E Prospect Ave
Street address city: Burbank
Street address state: CA
Zip/Postal code: 91502-2035
Country: USA
Mailing address: 116 E Prospect Ave
Mailing city: Burbank
Mailing state: CA
Mailing zip: 91502-2035
General Phone: (818) 843-2811
General Fax: (818) 843-2862
General/National Adv. E-mail: info@creweb.com
Primary Website: www.creweb.com
Mthly Avg Unique Visitors: 1980
Industry: Hazardous Waste Disposal Services; Silver Recovery
Personnel: Larry Dewitt (Pres.)

COMMUNICATIONS MANAGEMENT SERVICE, INC.

Street address 1: 30 Nutmeg Dr
Street address city: Trumbull
Street address state: CT
Zip/Postal code: 06611-5453
Country: USA
Mailing address: 30 Nutmeg Dr
Mailing city: Trumbull
Mailing state: CT
Mailing zip: 06611-5453
General Phone: (203) 377-3000
General Fax: (203) 377-2632
General/National Adv. E-mail: dan@bargainnews.com
Primary Website: www.bargainnews.com
Mthly Avg Unique Visitors: 1971
Industry: Consulting Services: Circulation; Consulting Services: Marketing; Newspaper Marketing;
Personnel: John F. Roy (Pres.); Daniel F. Rindos (Vice Pres.); Daniel Firoa (New Media Sales Dir.)

COMPUTER TALK TECHNOLOGY, INC.

Street address 1: 150 Commerce Valley Drive West
Street address 2: Suite 800
Street address city: Markham
Street address state: ON
Zip/Postal code: L3T 7Z3
Country: Canada
Mailing address: 150 Commerce Valley Drive West, Suite 800
Mailing city: Markham
Mailing state: ON
Mailing zip: L3T 7Z3
General Phone: (905) 882-5000
General Fax: (905) 882-5501
Primary Website: www.computer-talk.com
Mthly Avg Unique Visitors: 1987
Industry: Software: Electronic Data Interchange; System Integration Services;
Product or Service: Hardware/Software Supplier
Personnel: Mandle Cheung (Pres./CEO); Donald Mcdonald (V. P.)

COMPUTER TREE PROFESSIONAL TRAINING

Street address 1: 121 Peddycord Park Dr
Street address city: Kernersville
Street address state: NC
Zip/Postal code: 27284-0030
County: Forsyth
Country: USA
Mailing address: 121 Peddycord Park Dr.
Mailing city: Kernersville
Mailing state: NC
Mailing zip: 27284
General Phone: (336) 768-9820
General/National Adv. E-mail: sales@computertree.com
Display Adv. E-mail: bobyoungjr@computertree.com
Editorial e-mail: bobyoungjr@computertree.com
Primary Website: www.computertree.com
Mthly Avg Unique Visitors: 1982
Industry: As an Apple Authorized Training Center (AATC), ComputerTree Professional Training provides skills training, certification training, and testing at our own facilities in North Carolina and Georgia or on-site anywhere.
Note: http://www.computertree.com/aboutus.html

Personnel: Bob Young (Pres.); Joe Young (Vice President)

COMTEL INSTRUMENTS CO.

Street address 1: 37000 Plymouth Rd
Street address city: Livonia
Street address state: MI
Zip/Postal code: 48150-1132
Country: USA
Mailing address: 37000 Plymouth Rd
Mailing city: Livonia
Mailing state: MI
Mailing zip: 48150-1132
General Phone: (800) 335-2505
General Fax: (734) 542-1353
General/National Adv. E-mail: comtelcorp@comtel.com
Primary Website: www.comtel.com
Industry: Software: Electronic Data Interchange
Personnel: Gregg Montgomery (Sales Engineer-Kentucky); Eric Hubbard (Sales Engineer- OH, PA, W. VA); Brian Carr (Sales Engineer-Michigan); Jim Bull (Sales Engineer-IN, SW MI, W. KY); Dr. Barbara J. Boroughf PhD. (Government Contract Officer-North America); Lynne Williams (Administrative Assistant); Paul Williams (Inside Sales); Jenny Seaks (Accounting Mgr., Inside Sales); Jenny Boroughf (Controller)

CONDAIR LTD.

Street address 1: 835 Commerce Park Drive
Street address city: Ogdensburg
Street address state: NY
Zip/Postal code: 13669
Country: USA
Mailing address: 835 Commerce Park Drive
Mailing city: Ogdensburg
Mailing state: NY
Mailing zip: 13669
General Phone: 1.866.667.8321
General/National Adv. E-mail: na.info@condair.com
Primary Website: www.humidity.com
Mthly Avg Unique Visitors: 1974
Industry: Humidifiers
Personnel: Urs Schenk (Pres.); Gary Berlin (Vice Pres., Sales); Mike Hurley (Vice Pres., Mktg.); Naomi Cassidy (Mktg. Coord.)

CONLEY PUBLISHING SYSTEMS

Street address 1: 555 Beichl Ave
Street address city: Beaver Dam
Street address state: WI
Zip/Postal code: 53916-3110
Country: USA
Mailing address: PO Box 478
Mailing city: Beaver Dam
Mailing state: WI
Mailing zip: 53916-0478
General Phone: (920) 887-3731
General Fax: (920) 887-0439
General/National Adv. E-mail: concept@conleynet.com
Primary Website: www.conleynet.com
Mthly Avg Unique Visitors: 1984
Industry: Input & Editing Systems; Pagination Systems; Phototypesetting Fonts; Publishing Systems; Software: Advertising (Includes Display; Classified); Software: Design/Graphics; Software: Editorial; Software: Pagination/Layout; Typesetting Programs;
Personnel: James E. Conley (Pres.)

CONSOLIDATED STORAGE COS.

Street address 1: 225 Main St
Street address city: Tatamy
Street address state: PA
Zip/Postal code: 18085-7059
County: Northampton
Country: USA
Mailing address: 225 Main St
Mailing city: Tatamy
Mailing state: PA
Mailing zip: 18085-7059
General Phone: (610) 253.2775
General Fax: (610) 675.2869
General/National Adv. E-mail: sales@equipto.com
Display Adv. E-mail: sales@equipto.com
Primary Website: www.equipto.com
Mthly Avg Unique Visitors: 1907
Industry: Material handling and storage equipment including modular drawer cabinets, other storage cabinets, shelving , shelving with drawers, bulk storage racks, workcenters and work benches, mezzanine and deckover units, stairways, carts and small parts storage units, pallet rack, mobile aisle systems
Note: Manufacturer of Material Handling and Storage Systems for Industiral, Comercial and Distribution Applications
Personnel: Collin Straus (Vice President of Sales and Installations)

CONTINENTAL PRODUCTS

Street address 1: 2000 W Boulevard St
Street address city: Mexico
Street address state: MO
Zip/Postal code: 65265-1209
Country: USA
Mailing address: PO Box 760
Mailing city: Mexico
Mailing state: MO
Mailing zip: 65265-0760
General Phone: (800) 325-0216
General/National Adv. E-mail: mail@continentalproducts.com
Primary Website: www.continentalproducts.com
Mthly Avg Unique Visitors: 1927
Industry: Circulation Equipment & Supplies; Newspaper Bags; Tubes, Racks (Includes Racks: Motor Route Tubes);
Personnel: Thad Fisher (Vice Pres., Sales/Mktg.); Loyd Smith (Cust. Serv. Supervisor)

CONTROL ENGINEERING CO.

Street address 1: 2306 Newport Blvd
Street address city: Costa Mesa
Street address state: CA
Zip/Postal code: 92627-1548
Country: USA
Mailing address: 2306 Newport Blvd
Mailing city: Costa Mesa
Mailing state: CA
Mailing zip: 92627-1548
General Phone: (949) 722-7821
General/National Adv. E-mail: ccarrillo@controlengineering.com
Primary Website: www.controlengineering.com
Industry: Cabinets; Conveyors; Material Handling Equipment: Automatic Guided Vehicles; Material Handling Equipment: Truck Loaders; Newsprint Handeling Equipment; Paper Handeling Equipment;
Personnel: Carlos Carrillo (Engineering Mgr.)

CRAFTSMEN MACHINERY CO., INC.

Street address 1: 1257 Worcester Rd
Street address 2: Unit 167
Street address city: Framingham
Street address state: MA
Zip/Postal code: 01701-5217
County: Middlesex
Country: USA
Mailing address: PO Box 2006
Mailing city: Framingham
Mailing state: MA
Mailing zip: 01703-2006
General Phone: (508) 376-2001
General Fax: (508) 376-2003
General/National Adv. E-mail: sales@craftsmenmachinery.com
Primary Website: www.craftsmenmachinery.com
Mthly Avg Unique Visitors: 1925
Industry: Corner Rounders; Drilling Equipment; Densitometers; Folders, Creasers, Gauges, Measuring; Presses: Offset;
Personnel: Sherwin Marks (Pres./Chief Exec. Officer)

CREATIVE CIRCLE MEDIA SOLUTIONS

Street address 1: 618 Main Street, apartment 3213
Street address city: Coventry
Street address state: RI
Zip/Postal code: 02816
County: Providence
Country: USA
Mailing address: 618 Main Street, apartment 3213
Mailing city: Coventry
Mailing state: RI
Mailing zip: 02816
General Phone: (401) 4551555
General/National Adv. E-mail: teresemihacin18@gmail.com
Display Adv. E-mail: teresemihacin18@gmail.com
Classified Adv. e-mail: teresemihacin18@gmail.com
Editorial e-mail: teresemihacin18@gmail.com
Primary Website: www.creativecirclemedia.com
Mthly Avg Unique Visitors: 1984
Industry: Software: web CMS, advertising, native content; Consulting; Outsourcing; Training; Web and print redesigns; print editorial production platform.
Product or Service: Advertising/Marketing Agency`Circulation`Consultants`Editorial`Graphic/Design Firm`Hardware/Software Supplier`Marketing`Multimedia/Interactive Products`Other Services`Online Service Provider and Internet Hosts
Note: Full service, custom software provider with a dynamic web site CMS, user-contributed content, classifieds, hosting, pay wall, branded content, circulation and print editorial production solutions. We also provide strategic consulting, newsroom training, ad design training, new revenue ideas, webmaster services and high-end print production outsourcing services. Our Premium Pages are an excellent digital features content service. We also have led more than 750 redesigns of print newspapers and magazines and continue to help publishers redefine their print products.
Personnel: Bill Ostendorf (Pres. & founder); Lynn Rognsvoog (Design director); Tim Benson (Chief Developer); Scott Kingsley (COO); Darryl Greenlee (Developer); Sean Finch (VP/Sales); Greg Boras (National Sales Manager); Scott Kingley (COO); Lisa Newby; Terese Mihalcin

CREATIVE HOUSE PRINT MEDIA CONSULTANTS

Street address 1: 227 9th St
Street address city: Sheldon
Street address state: IA
Zip/Postal code: 51201-1419
Country: USA
Mailing address: PO Box 160
Mailing city: Sheldon
Mailing state: IA
Mailing zip: 51201-0160
General Phone: (712) 324-5347
General Fax: (712) 324-2345
General/National Adv. E-mail: pww@iowainformation.com
Mthly Avg Unique Visitors: 1962
Industry: Consulting Services: Advertising; Circulation; Design; Promotion Ideas; Advertising Design
Note: Author of month GET REAL column to press associations, free PAPER MONEY column to publishers and monthly column in Publisher's Auxiliary. Conference and publisher seminars
Personnel: Peter W. Wagner (Pres.); Jeff Wagner (Sec./Treasurer)

CREO

Street address 1: 140 Kendrick Street
Street address city: Needham
Street address state: MA
Zip/Postal code: 02494
Country: USA
Mailing address: 140 Kendrick Street
Mailing city: Needham
Mailing state: MA
Mailing zip: 02494
General Phone: (781) 370-5000
General Fax: (781) 370-6000
Primary Website: www.ptc.com/en/products/cad
Mthly Avg Unique Visitors: 1985
Industry: Color Proofing; Color Seperation Scanners; Computers: Hardware & Software Integrators;
Personnel: James E. Heppelmann (Pres., CEO); Andrew Miller (Exec VP, CFO); Barry F. Cohen (Exec V.P., Chief Strategy Officer); Kathleen Mitford (Executive V. P., Products)

CRYOGENESIS (A DIV. OF WM & C SERVICES, INC.)

Street address 1: 2140 Scranton Rd
Street address city: Cleveland
Street address state: OH
Zip/Postal code: 44113-3544
Country: USA
Mailing address: 2140 Scranton Rd
Mailing city: Cleveland
Mailing state: OH
Mailing zip: 44113-3544
General Phone: (216) 696-8797
General Fax: (216) 696-8794
General/National Adv. E-mail: cryogen@cryogenesis-usa.com
Primary Website: www.cryogenesis-usa.com
Industry: Cleaners & Solvents; Roll Cleaning Equipment;
Personnel: James Becker (Pres.); John R. Whalen (Vice Pres., Sales)

CYGNET STORAGE SOLUTIONS, INC.

Street address 1: 1880 Santa Barbara Ave
Street address 2: Ste 220
Street address city: San Luis Obispo
Street address state: CA
Zip/Postal code: 93401-4482
Country: USA
Mailing address: 1880 Santa Barbara Ave Ste 220
Mailing city: San Luis Obispo
Mailing state: CA
Mailing zip: 93401-4482
General Phone: 805-781-3580
General Fax: 805-781-3583
General/National Adv. E-mail: waynea@cygnet.com
Industry: Archiving Systems; Disk Drive Sales/Repair; Files, Storage; Library Retrieval Systems; Software: Asset Management; Storage Retrieval Systems;
Personnel: Wayne Augsburger (Vice Pres., Mktg.)

D & R ENGINEERING

Street address 1: 12629 Prairie Ave
Street address city: Hawthorne
Street address state: CA
Zip/Postal code: 90250-4611
Country: USA
Mailing address: 12629 Prairie Ave
Mailing city: Hawthorne
Mailing state: CA
Mailing zip: 90250-4611
General Phone: (310) 676-4896
General Fax: (310) 676-3420
Mthly Avg Unique Visitors: 1976
Industry: Counting, Stacking, Bundling Machines; Gluing Systems; Web Cleaners; Web Offset Remoisturizers; Web Press - Special Equipment;
Personnel: Daws Waffer (Owner)

DAC SYSTEMS

Street address 1: 4 Armstrong Park Rd, Bldg II
Street address city: Shelton
Street address state: CT
Zip/Postal code: 6484
Country: USA
Mailing address: 4 Armstrong Park Rd., Bldg II
Mailing city: Shelton
Mailing state: CT
Mailing zip: 6484
General Phone: (203) 924-7000
General Fax: (203) 944-1618
General/National Adv. E-mail: sales@dacsystems.com
Primary Website: www.dacsystems.com
Mthly Avg Unique Visitors: 1988
Industry: Audiotex Systems & Software; Facsimilie/Fax Transmission Systems; Integrated Fax Servers; Optical Character Recognition (OCR); Speech Recognition; Telecommunications;
Personnel: Mark Nickson (Pres.)

DAIGE PRODUCTS, INC.

Street address 1: 1 Albertson Ave
Street address 2: Ste 5
Street address city: Albertson
Street address state: NY
Zip/Postal code: 11507-1444
Country: USA
Mailing address: 1 Albertson Ave Ste 5
Mailing city: Albertson
Mailing state: NY
Mailing zip: 11507-1444
General Phone: (800) 645-3323
General/National Adv. E-mail: info@daige.com
Primary Website: www.daige.com
Mthly Avg Unique Visitors: 1965
Industry: Adhesive Wax Coaters; Adhesives;
Personnel: Ike Harris (Pres.)

DAN-BAR, INC.

Street address 1: 2502 Jmt Industrial Dr
Street address 2: Unit 104

Street address city: Apopka
Street address state: FL
Zip/Postal code: 32703-2138
Country: USA
Mailing address: 2502 JMT Industrial Dr. Suite 104
Mailing city: Apopka
Mailing state: FL
Mailing zip: 32703-6542
General Phone: (407) 292-0600
General Fax: (407) 292-0602
General/National Adv. E-mail: dcmdanbar@aol.com; contact@danbarinc.com
Primary Website: www.danbarinc.com
Mthly Avg Unique Visitors: 1998
Industry: Automatic Plastic Bagging Equipment; Baling Machines; Collating Equipment; System Installations;
Personnel: Dan Baratta (Pres.)

DANFOSS GRAHAM

Street address 1: 8800 W Bradley Rd
Street address city: Milwaukee
Street address state: WI
Zip/Postal code: 53224-2820
Country: USA
Mailing address: 8800 W Bradley Rd
Mailing city: Milwaukee
Mailing state: WI
Mailing zip: 53224-2820
General Phone: (414) 355-8800
General Fax: (414) 355-6117
Primary Website: www.danfoss.com
Mthly Avg Unique Visitors: 1936
Industry: Drives & Controls; Motors;
Personnel: Niels B. Christiansen (Pres./CEO)

DARIO DESIGNS, INC.

Street address 1: 318 Main St
Street address 2: Ste 120
Street address city: Northborough
Street address state: MA
Zip/Postal code: 01532-3611
County: Worcester
Country: USA
Mailing address: 318 Main St. Ste 120
Mailing city: Northborough
Mailing state: MA
Mailing zip: 01532
General Phone: (508) 877-4444
General Fax: (508) 877-4474
General/National Adv. E-mail: dario@dariodesigns.com
Primary Website: www.dariodesigns.com
Mthly Avg Unique Visitors: 1994
Industry: Architects/Engineers (Includes Design/ Construction Firms)
Note: www.dariodesigns.com
Personnel: Dario Dimare (Pres.); David Ehrhardt (VP)

DATAFEST TECHNOLOGIES, INC.

Street address 1: 5961 S Redwood Rd
Street address city: Salt Lake City
Street address state: UT
Zip/Postal code: 84123-5261
Country: USA
Mailing address: 5961 S Redwood Rd
Mailing city: Salt Lake City
Mailing state: UT
Mailing zip: 84123-5261
General Phone: (801) 261-4608
General/National Adv. E-mail: sales@datafest.com
Primary Website: www.datafest.com
Mthly Avg Unique Visitors: 1986
Industry: Software: Advertising (Includes Display; Classified); Software: Business (Includes Administration/Accounting);
Note: Datafest's AdSystem is an industry-leading ad management / CRM package designed for magazines and newspapers.
Personnel: Scott A. Clawson (Pres.)

DAY-GLO COLOR CORP.

Street address 1: 4515 Saint Clair Ave
Street address city: Cleveland
Street address state: OH
Zip/Postal code: 44103-1203
Country: USA
Mailing address: 4515 Saint Clair Ave
Mailing city: Cleveland
Mailing state: OH
Mailing zip: 44103-1268
General Phone: (216) 391-7070
General Fax: (216) 391-7751
General/National Adv. E-mail: dayglo@dayglo.com
Primary Website: www.dayglo.com
Mthly Avg Unique Visitors: 1946
Industry: Inks
Personnel: Mark Wright (Vice Pres., Sales)

DEAN MACHINERY INTERNATIONAL, INC.

Street address 1: 6855 Shiloh Rd E
Street address city: Alpharetta
Street address state: GA
Zip/Postal code: 30005-8372
Country: USA
Mailing address: 6855 Shiloh Rd E
Mailing city: Alpharetta
Mailing state: GA
Mailing zip: 30005-8372
General Phone: (678) 947-8550
General Fax: (678) 947-8554
General/National Adv. E-mail: sales@deanmachinery.com
Primary Website: www.deanmachinery.com
Mthly Avg Unique Visitors: 1991
Industry: Adhesive Wax Coaters; Brokers & Appraisers; Equipment Dealers (Used); Label Printing Machines; Presses: Flexographic; Presses: Offset; Presses: Rotogravure;
Personnel: Walter Dean (Pres.)

DECISIONMARK CORP.

Street address 1: 818 Dows Rd
Street address city: Cedar Rapids
Street address state: IA
Zip/Postal code: 52403-7000
Country: USA
Mailing address: 818 Dows Rd Ste 100
Mailing city: Cedar Rapids
Mailing state: IA
Mailing zip: 52403-7000
General Phone: (319) 365-5597
General Fax: (319) 365-5694
General/National Adv. E-mail: sales@decisionmark.com
Primary Website: www.decisionmark.com
Mthly Avg Unique Visitors: 1993
Industry: Software: Advertising (Includes Display; Classified); Software: Circulation; Software: Editorial;
Personnel: Jack Perry (Pres./CEO); Mick Rinehart (Vice Pres., Pdct. Devel.); Herb Skoog (Vice Pres., Opns.)

DEMATICS

Street address 1: 507 Plymouth Ave NE
Street address city: Grand Rapids
Street address state: MI
Zip/Postal code: 49505-6029
Country: USA
Mailing address: 507 Plymouth Ave NE
Mailing city: Grand Rapids
Mailing state: MI
Mailing zip: 49505-6029
General Phone: (877) 725-7500
General Fax: (616) 913-7701
General/National Adv. E-mail: usinfo@dematic.com
Primary Website: www.dematic.us
Mthly Avg Unique Visitors: 1939
Industry: Conveyors; Material Handling Equipment: Automatic Guided Vehicles; Material Handling Equipment: Truck Loaders;
Personnel: John Baysore (Pres.); S. Buccella (Vice Pres., Field Sales); R. Klaasen (Mgr., Purchasing)

DENEX, INC.

Street address 1: 135 W Illinois Ave
Street address city: Southern Pines
Street address state: NC
Zip/Postal code: 28387-5808
Country: USA
Mailing address: 135 W Illinois Ave
Mailing city: Southern Pines
Mailing state: NC
Mailing zip: 28387-5808
General Phone: (910) 692-5463
General Fax: (910) 222-3100
General/National Adv. E-mail: gcarroll@denexinc.com
Primary Website: www.denex.se; www.denex.com
Mthly Avg Unique Visitors: 1992
Industry: Laser Printers
Personnel: Gary J. Carroll (Pres.)

DENNIS STORCH CO.

Street address 1: 175 W 72nd St
Street address 2: Apt 8G
Street address city: New York
Street address state: NY
Zip/Postal code: 10023-3208
Country: USA
Mailing address: 175 W 72nd St Apt 8G
Mailing city: New York
Mailing state: NY
Mailing zip: 10023-3208
General Phone: (212) 877-2622
General/National Adv. E-mail: dstorch@aol.com
Primary Website: www.dennis-storch.com
Mthly Avg Unique Visitors: 1979
Industry: Printing Equipment Dealer. Used Presses and Offset Presses.
Personnel: Dennis Storch (President)

DESCARTES SYSTEMS GROUP

Street address 1: 120 Randall Dr
Street address city: Waterloo
Street address state: ON
Zip/Postal code: N2V 1C6
Country: Canada
Mailing address: 120 Randall Dr.
Mailing city: Waterloo
Mailing state: ON
Mailing zip: N2V 1C6
General Phone: (519) 746-8110
General Fax: (519) 747-0082
General/National Adv. E-mail: info@descartes.com
Primary Website: www.descartes.com
Mthly Avg Unique Visitors: 1985
Industry: Computers: Hardware & Software Integrators
Personnel: Arthur Mesher (CEO); Stephanie Ratza (CFO); Chris Jones (Exec. Vice Pres., Solutions/Servs.); Scott J. Pagan (Exec. Vice Pres., Cor. Devel./Gen. Counsel); Edward J. Ryan (Exec. Vice Pres., Global Field Opns.); Raimond Diederik (Exec. Vice Pres., Information Servs.)

DESIGN SCIENCE, INC.

Street address 1: 140 Pine Ave
Street address 2: Fl 4
Street address city: Long Beach
Street address state: CA
Zip/Postal code: 90802-9440
Country: USA
Mailing address: 140 Pine Ave Fl 4
Mailing city: Long Beach
Mailing state: CA
Mailing zip: 90802-9440
General Phone: (562) 432-2920
General Fax: (562) 432-2857
General/National Adv. E-mail: sales@dessci.com
Primary Website: www.dessci.com
Industry: Input & Editing Systems; Type, Fonts;
Personnel: Paul Topping (Pres.)

DESKNET, INC.

Street address 1: 30 Montgomery St.
Street address 2: Suite 650
Street address city: Jersey City
Street address state: NJ
Zip/Postal code: 07302
Country: USA
Mailing address: 30 Montgomery St., Suite 650
Mailing city: Jersey City
Mailing state: NJ
Mailing zip: 07302
General Phone: (201) 946-7080
Primary Website: www.desknetinc.com
Mthly Avg Unique Visitors: 1992
Industry: Software: Asset Management; Software: Design/Graphics; Software: Editorial; Software: Electronic Data Interchange; Software: Pagination/ Layout; Software: Workflow Management/Tracking; System Integration Services;
Personnel: Mike Fitzsimons (CEO)

DEVLIN ELECTRONICS LTD.

Street address 1: Unit A1, Davy Close
Street address 2: Hampshire
Street address city: Basingstoke
Zip/Postal code: RG22 6PW
Country: England
Mailing address: Unit A1, Davy Close, Hampshire
Mailing city: Basingstoke
Mailing zip: RG22 6PW
General Phone: +44 1256 467 367
General Fax: +44 1256 840 048
General/National Adv. E-mail: sales@devlin.co.uk
Primary Website: www.devlin.co.uk
Industry: Composing Room Equipment & Supplies; Interfaces;
Personnel: Martin Baker (Mng. Dir.)

DIENAMIC MICROPRINT

Street address 1: 71 King St
Street address 2: Suite 3024
Street address city: St Catharines
Street address state: ON
Zip/Postal code: L2R 3H6
Country: Canada
Mailing address: 71 King St., Ste.3024
Mailing city: Saint Catharine's
Mailing state: ON
Mailing zip: L2R 3H7
General Phone: (905) 688-5593
General Fax: (905) 688-6132
General/National Adv. E-mail: microprint@vaxxine.com
Primary Website: www.dienamicmis.com
Mthly Avg Unique Visitors: 1986
Industry: Mailroom Systems & Equipment
Personnel: Mark Porter (Pres.); Lori Walsh (Vice Pres.- Finance)

DIRECT REPRODUCTION CORP.

Street address 1: 34 S Macquesten Pkwy
Street address city: Mount Vernon
Street address state: NY
Zip/Postal code: 10550-1704
Country: USA
Mailing address: 34 S Macquesten Pkwy
Mailing city: Mount Vernon
Mailing state: NY
Mailing zip: 10550-1704
General Phone: (914) 665-6515
General Fax: (914) 665-6518
General/National Adv. E-mail: Technical@LRADX.com
Primary Website: www.lradx.com/site/
Mthly Avg Unique Visitors: 1941
Industry: Color Proofing; Color Registration; Masking Materials; Offset Negative Masking Paper; Prepress Color Proofing Systems;
Personnel: Ronald L. Russo (Pres.)

DIRKS, VAN ESSEN, MURRAY & APRIL

Street address 1: 119 E Marcy St
Street address 2: Ste 100
Street address city: Santa Fe
Street address state: NM
Zip/Postal code: 87501-2092
County: Santa Fe
Country: USA
Mailing address: 119 E Marcy St Ste 100
Mailing city: Santa Fe
Mailing state: NM
Mailing zip: 87501-2092
General Phone: (505) 820-2700
General Fax: (505) 820-2900
Primary Website: www.dirksvanessen.com
Mthly Avg Unique Visitors: 1980
Industry: Brokers & Appraisers; Consulting Services: Financial;
Personnel: Owen D. Van Essen (Pres.); Philip W. Murray (Exec. Vice Pres.); Sara April (Vice Pres.); Holly Myers (Analyst)

DOMINO NORTH AMERICA

Street address 1: 1290 Lakeside Dr
Street address city: Gurnee
Street address state: IL
Zip/Postal code: 60031-2400
Country: USA
Mailing address: 1290 Lakeside Dr
Mailing city: Gurnee
Mailing state: IL
Mailing zip: 60031-2499

General Phone: (800) 444-4512
General Fax: (847) 244-1421
General/National Adv. E-mail: solutions@domino-na.com
Primary Website: www.domino-printing.com/en-us/home.aspx
Mthly Avg Unique Visitors: 1987
Industry: Addressing Machines; Label Printing Machines; Laser Printers; Numbering Machines

DOMTAR, INC.

Street address 1: 395 de Maisonneuve Blvd W
Street address city: Montreal
Street address state: QC
Zip/Postal code: H3A 1L6
Country: Canada
Mailing address: 395 de Maisonneuve Blvd. W.
Mailing city: Montreal
Mailing state: QC
Mailing zip: H3A 1L6
General Phone: (514) 848-5400
General Fax: (514) 848-6878
Primary Website: www.domtar.com
Mthly Avg Unique Visitors: 1929
Industry: Paper: Specialty Printing Paper
Personnel: Brian Levitt (Chrmn.); Raymond Royer (Pres./CEO)

DOUTHITT CORP.

Street address 1: 245 Adair St
Street address city: Detroit
Street address state: MI
Zip/Postal code: 48207-4214
Country: USA
Mailing address: 245 Adair St
Mailing city: Detroit
Mailing state: MI
Mailing zip: 48207-4287
General Phone: (313) 259-1565
General Fax: (313) 259-6806
General/National Adv. E-mail: em@douthittcorp.com
Primary Website: www.douthittcorp.com
Mthly Avg Unique Visitors: 1919
Industry: Controls: Exposure; Exposure Lamps; Layout Tables, Light Tables & Workstations; Light Integrators; Offset Plate-Making Service & Equipment; Pin Register Systems; Plate Exposure Units; Platemakers: Flexographic (Traditional); Platemakers: Offset (Computer to Plate); Vacuum Frames;
Personnel: Mark W. Diehl (Int'l Sales)

DRAKE COMMUNICATIONS, INC.

Street address 1: 202 W McCart St
Street address 2: Ste 200
Street address city: Krum
Street address state: TX
Zip/Postal code: 76249-5580
County: USA
Country: USA
Mailing address: 202 W McCart St. Ste 200
Mailing city: Krum
Mailing state: TX
Mailing zip: 76249-5580
General Phone: (214) 206-3333
Mthly Avg Unique Visitors: 1979
Industry: Elections Interactive Voice Response (IVR) Information systems
Personnel: Cecil Drake (Pres.); L.G. Drake (Vice Pres.)

DUNHILL INTERNATIONAL LIST CO., INC.

Street address 1: 6400 Congress Ave
Street address 2: Ste 1750
Street address city: Boca Raton
Street address state: FL
Zip/Postal code: 33487-2898
Country: USA
Mailing address: 6400 Congress Ave Ste 1750
Mailing city: Boca Raton
Mailing state: FL
Mailing zip: 33487-2898
General Phone: (561) 998-7800
General Fax: (561) 998-7880
General/National Adv. E-mail: dunhill@dunhillintl.com
Display Adv. E-mail: marketing@dunhillintl.com
Primary Website: www.dunhills.com
Mthly Avg Unique Visitors: 1938
Industry: Mailing List Compiler Mailing List Broker Email List Broker
Personnel: Robert Dunhill (Pres.); Candy Dunhill (Vice Pres.); Cindy Dunhill (Vice Pres.)

DUNNING PHOTO EQUIPMENT, INC.

Street address 1: 605 W Needles Ave
Street address city: Bixby
Street address state: OK
Zip/Postal code: 74008-4131
Country: USA
Mailing address: 605 W Needles Ave
Mailing city: Bixby
Mailing state: OK
Mailing zip: 74008-4131
General Phone: (918) 366-4917
General Fax: (918) 366-4918
General/National Adv. E-mail: ernie@dunningphoto.com
Primary Website: www.dunningphoto.com
Mthly Avg Unique Visitors: 1955
Industry: Dark Room Equipment; Processors: Film & Paper;
Personnel: Ernie Dunning (Pres.)

DYC SUPPLY CO.

Street address 1: 5740 Bayside Rd
Street address city: Virginia Beach
Street address state: VA
Zip/Postal code: 23455-3004
Country: USA
Mailing address: 5740 Bayside Rd
Mailing city: Virginia Beach
Mailing state: VA
Mailing zip: 23455-3004
General Phone: (800) 446-8240
General Fax: (757) 486-5689
General/National Adv. E-mail: kevink@d-y-c.com
Display Adv. E-mail: kevink@d-y-c.com
Primary Website: www.dyc.com
Industry: Blankets; Offset Blankets, Blanket Wash;
Personnel: Joseph Martinez (Pres.); Marc Banks (Asst. Mktg. Mgr.)

DYNARIC, INC.

Street address 1: 5740 Bayside Rd
Street address city: Virginia Beach
Street address state: VA
Zip/Postal code: 23455-3004
County: Princess Anne
Country: USA
Mailing address: 5740 Bayside Rd
Mailing city: Virginia Beach
Mailing state: VA
Mailing zip: 23455-3004
General Phone: (800) 526-0827
General Fax: (757) 363-8016
General/National Adv. E-mail: gd@dynaric.com
Primary Website: www.dynaric.com
Mthly Avg Unique Visitors: 1973
Industry: PLASTIC STRAPPING AND STRAPPING EQUIPMENT
Personnel: Joseph Martinez (Pres.); Marc Banks (Asst. Mktg. Mgr.)

E.I. DU PONT DE NEMOURS & CO.

Street address 1: 1007 Market St
Street address city: Wilmington
Street address state: DE
Zip/Postal code: 19898-1100
Country: USA
Mailing address: 1007 Market St
Mailing city: Wilmington
Mailing state: DE
Mailing zip: 19898-1100
General Phone: (302) 774-1000
General Fax: (302) 355-4013
General/National Adv. E-mail: contact@dupont.com
Primary Website: www2.dupont.com
Industry: Color Analyzers; Color Proofing; Color Registration; Color Seperation Scanners; Color Viewing Equipment; Controls: Register; Phototypesetting Interface Equipment; Prepress Color Proofing Systems; Press Control Systems;
Personnel: Ellen J. Kullman (Chrmn./Pres./CEO); Jeffrey L. Keefer (Exec., Vice Pres./CFO); Thomas M. Connelly (Exec. Vice Pres./Chief Innovation Officer); Richard R. Goodmanson (Exec. Vice Pres./COO); W. Donald Johnson (Exec. Vice Pres./Human Resources); Diane H. Gulyas (Grp. Vice Pres., Chief Mktg./Sales Officer); Barry J. Niziolek (Vice Pres./Controller); Harry Parker (Vice Pres., DuPont Sales Effectiveness); Susan M. Stalnecker (Vice Pres./Treasurer); Cynthia C. Green (Vice Pres./CMO/Chief Sales Officer)

EAM-MOSCA CORP.

Street address 1: 675 Jaycee Dr
Street address city: Hazle Township
Street address state: PA
Zip/Postal code: 18202-1155
County: Luzerne
Country: USA
Mailing address: 675 Jaycee Dr., Valmont Industrial Pk.
Mailing city: Hazle Township
Mailing state: PA
Mailing zip: 18202-1155
General Phone: (570) 459-3426
General Fax: (570) 455-2442
General/National Adv. E-mail: info@eammosca.com
Primary Website: www.eammosca.com
Mthly Avg Unique Visitors: 1982
Industry: Bundling and Tying Machines; Strapping Machines;
Personnel: Pam Kuzmak (Sales Admin.); Edward Martin (VP, Sales); Dan Dreher (Pres.)

EARMARK

Street address 1: 1125 Dixwell Ave
Street address city: Hamden
Street address state: CT
Zip/Postal code: 06514-4735
Country: USA
Mailing address: 1125 Dixwell Ave
Mailing city: Hamden
Mailing state: CT
Mailing zip: 06514-4788
General Phone: (203) 777-2130
General Fax: (203) 777-2886
General/National Adv. E-mail: staff@earmark.com
Primary Website: www.earmark.com
Mthly Avg Unique Visitors: 1973
Industry: Wireless Radio Communication Headsets
Note: â€¢ EARMARK has manufactured durable wireless communication systems for over 30 years to support professionals operating in high noise environments. EARMARK is renowned for its rugged, reliable, yet easy to use products. Our commitment to understanding the challenges facing production teams have allowed us to develop products that have the range, flexibility and performance needed to increase efficiency and safety on the job.

EASTMAN KODAK CO.

Street address 1: 343 State St
Street address city: Rochester
Street address state: NY
Zip/Postal code: 14650-0001
Country: USA
Mailing address: 343 State St
Mailing city: Rochester
Mailing state: NY
Mailing zip: 14650-0002
General Phone: (800) 698-3324
General Fax: (585) 724-1089
Primary Website: www.kodak.com
Mthly Avg Unique Visitors: 1888
Industry: Cameras & Accessories; Film & Paper: Contact; Film & Paper: Filters (Photographic); Film & Paper: Phototypesetting; Microfilming; Offset Plate-Making Service & Equipment; Photo Proofing Papers; Plate Processors; Plates: Offset (Conventional); Processors: Film & Paper;
Personnel: Jeffrey J. Clarke (CEO); David Bullwinkle (Pres./COO); Christopher Payne (Vice Pres.)

ECLIPSE SERVICES (DIV. OF QUADRIVIUM, INC.)

Street address 1: 7721 Beech Ln
Street address city: Wyndmoor
Street address state: PA
Zip/Postal code: 19038-7615
County: Montgomery
Country: USA
Mailing address: 7721 Beech Lane
Mailing city: Wyndmoor
Mailing state: PA
Mailing zip: 19038-7615
General Phone: 484-462-4300
General Fax: 207-373-0723
General/National Adv. E-mail: sales@eclipseservices.com
Display Adv. E-mail: sales@eclipseservices.com
Primary Website: www.eclipseservices.com
Mthly Avg Unique Visitors: 1984
Industry: Software: Advertising (Includes Display; Classified, Online); Software: Business (Includes Administration/Accounting). New: Available on iPhone, iPad for sales reps.
Note: Business software for print and online publications.
Personnel: Jeanette MacNeille (President)

ECRM

Street address 1: 554 Clark Rd
Street address city: Tewksbury
Street address state: MA
Zip/Postal code: 01876-1631
Country: USA
Mailing address: 554 Clark Rd
Mailing city: Tewksbury
Mailing state: MA
Mailing zip: 01876-1631
General Phone: (978) 851-0207
General Fax: (978) 851-7016
General/National Adv. E-mail: sales@ecrm.com
Primary Website: www.ecrm.com
Mthly Avg Unique Visitors: 1968
Industry: Imagesetters; Platemakers: Offset (Computer to Plate); Prepress Color Proofing Systems; Processors: Film & Paper; Proofing Systems;
Personnel: Richard Black (President&CEO)

ED BARON & ASSOCIATES, INC.

Street address 1: PO Box 3203
Street address city: Oakton
Street address state: VA
Zip/Postal code: 22124-9203
Country: USA
Mailing address: PO Box 3203
Mailing city: Oakton
Mailing state: VA
Mailing zip: 22124-9203
General Phone: (703) 620-1725
General Fax: (703) 620-9037
General/National Adv. E-mail: edbaron@edbaron.com
Primary Website: www.edbaron.com
Mthly Avg Unique Visitors: 1995
Industry: Consulting Services: Advertising; Consulting Services: Circulation; Consulting Services: Financial; Consulting Services: Marketing; Training: Sales & Marketing
Personnel: Ed Baron (Pres.)

EDGIL ASSOCIATES, INC.

Street address 1: 222 Rosewood Dr
Street address 2: Ste 210
Street address city: Danvers
Street address state: MA
Zip/Postal code: 01923-4520
County: Essex
Country: USA
Mailing address: 222 Rosewood Dr Ste 210
Mailing city: Danvers
Mailing state: MA
Mailing zip: 01923-4520
General Phone: (800) 457-9932
General Fax: (978) 667-6050
General/National Adv. E-mail: sales@edgil.com
Primary Website: www.edgil.com
Industry: Payment Processing
Product or Service: Hardware/Software Supplier
Personnel: Sean Callahan (Dir., Sales)

EDITOR & PUBLISHER MAGAZINE

Street address 1: 18475 Bandilier Cir
Street address city: Fountain Valley
Street address state: CA
Zip/Postal code: 92708-7000
Country: USA
Mailing address: 18475 Bandilier Circle
Mailing city: Fountain Valley
Mailing state: CA
Mailing zip: 92708
General Phone: 949-660-6150
General Fax: 949-660-6172

General/National Adv. E-mail: circulation@editorandpublisher.com
Display Adv. E-mail: cat@editorandpublisher.com
Primary Website: www.editorandpublisher.com
Mthly Avg Unique Visitors: 1884
Industry: Trade Publications
Personnel: Duncan McIntosh (Pres./ Pub.); Jeff Fleming (V.P./ Editor-in-Chief); Nu Yang (Mng. Ed.); Wendy MacDonald (Sales/Mktg. Consult.); Evelyn Mateos (Asst. Ed.)
Parent company (for newspapers): Duncan McIntosh Co., Inc.

EDIWISE

Street address 1: 690 Dorval Drive
Street address 2: Suite 425
Street address city: Oakville
Street address state: ON
Zip/Postal code: L6K 3X9
Country: Canada
General Phone: (905) 820-3084
General Fax: (905) 820-1498
General/National Adv. E-mail: info@ediwise.com
Display Adv. E-mail: sales@ediwise.com
Primary Website: www.ediwise.com
Mthly Avg Unique Visitors: 1986
Industry: Computers: Hardware & Software Integrators; Newsprint; Newsprint Handeling Equipment; Paper Handeling Equipment; Software: Asset Management; Software: Business (Includes Administration/ Accounting); Software: Electronic Data Interchange
Note: We provide paper inventory management system We also provide EDI services
Personnel: Eric Wee; David Maggs (General Manager)
Parent company (for newspapers): MAJIQ, Inc

EGENOLF MACHINE, INC. (EGENOLF CONTRACTING & RIGGING)

Street address 1: 350 Wisconsin St
Street address city: Indianapolis
Street address state: IN
Zip/Postal code: 46225-1536
Country: USA
Mailing address: 350 Wisconsin St
Mailing city: Indianapolis
Mailing state: IN
Mailing zip: 46225-1536
General Phone: (317) 637-9891
General Fax: (317) 631-8153
General/National Adv. E-mail: egenolfma@gmail.com
Mthly Avg Unique Visitors: 1927
Industry: Press Rebuilding; Press Repairs;
Personnel: James Egenolf (Pres.)

ELAPLAN BUCHHOLZ GMBH & CO.

Street address 1: D-24217
Street address city: Schonberg
Country: Germany
Mailing address: D-24217
Mailing city: Schonberg
General Phone: +49 4344 309 158
General Fax: +49 4344 309 172
General/National Adv. E-mail: info@uniton.de
Primary Website: www.elaplan.de
Industry: Facsimilie/Fax Transmission Systems; Press Control Systems;
Personnel: Hans-Herbert Buchholz (Mng. Dir.)

ELCORSY TECHNOLOGY, INC.

Street address 1: 4405 Poirier Blvd
Street address city: Saint-Laurent
Street address state: QC
Zip/Postal code: H4R 2A4
Country: Canada
Mailing address: 4405 Poirier Blvd.
Mailing city: Saint Laurent
Mailing state: QC
Mailing zip: H4R 2A4
General Phone: (888) 352-6779
General Fax: (514) 337-0042
General/National Adv. E-mail: marketing@elcorsy.com
Primary Website: www.elcorsy.com
Mthly Avg Unique Visitors: 1981
Industry: Inks; Presses: DiLitho;
Personnel: Pierre Castegnier (Vice Pres., Mktg.); Robert Jollet (Sales Rep.)

ELECTRONIC SYSTEMS ENGINEERING CO.

Street address 1: 1 E Eseco Rd
Street address city: Cushing
Street address state: OK
Zip/Postal code: 74023-5531
Country: USA
Mailing address: 1 E Eseco Rd
Mailing city: Cushing
Mailing state: OK
Mailing zip: 74023-5531
General Phone: (918) 225-1266
General Fax: (918) 225-1284
General/National Adv. E-mail: wallace@eseco-speedmaster.com
Primary Website: www.eseco-speedmaster.com
Mthly Avg Unique Visitors: 1956
Industry: Color Analyzers; Dark Room Equipment; Densitometers; Enlargers (Photographic); Film & Paper: Film Processing Machines;
Personnel: Ed Handlin (CFO); Wallace Hallman (Pres.)

ELECTRONIC TELE-COMMUNICATIONS, INC.

Street address 1: 1915 Mac Arthur Rd
Street address city: Waukesha
Street address state: WI
Zip/Postal code: 53188-5702
County: Waukesha
Country: USA
Mailing address: 1915 Mac Arthur Rd
Mailing city: Waukesha
Mailing state: WI
Mailing zip: 53188-5702
General Phone: (262) 542-5600
General Fax: (262) 542-1524
General/National Adv. E-mail: etc_mkt@etcia.com
Primary Website: www.etcia.com
Mthly Avg Unique Visitors: 1980
Industry: Telecommunications
Product or Service: Telecommunications/Service Bureaus
Personnel: Dean W. Danner (Pres./CEO); Joseph A. Voight (Vice Pres., Sales)

EMT INTERNATIONAL, INC.

Street address 1: 780 Centerline Drive
Street address city: Hobart
Street address state: WI
Zip/Postal code: 54155
Country: USA
Mailing address: 780 Centerline Drive
Mailing city: Hobart
Mailing state: WI
Mailing zip: 54155
General Phone: (920) 468-5475
General Fax: (920) 468-7991
General/National Adv. E-mail: info@emtinternational.com
Primary Website: www.emtinternational.com
Mthly Avg Unique Visitors: 1990
Industry: Slitting systems; Printing machinery; Equipment and Consumables for Web Processing Applications; Air-Actuated Lug, Leaf, and Multi-Bladder Shafts and Chucks; and Pneumatic-Mechanical Chucks and Mechanical Shafts;
Personnel: Bron Tamulion (Engineering Manager); Chad Winkka (Production Manager); Carl Castelic (Director of Finance and Cost Accounting); Jim Driscoll (VP)

ENGINEERING PRODUCTS CO., INC.

Street address 1: 3278 Pleasant Hill Rd
Street address city: Genoa
Street address state: IL
Zip/Postal code: 60135
Country: USA
Mailing address: 3278 Pleasant Hill Rd
Mailing city: Genoa
Mailing state: IL
Mailing zip: 60135
General Phone: (815) 784-4020
General Fax: (815) 784-4020
Primary Website: www.engineeringproductco.com
Mthly Avg Unique Visitors: 1963
Industry: Conveyors
Personnel: Jamie Courtney (Owner)

EPUBLISH4ME

Street address 1: 1375 Gateway Blvd
Street address city: Boynton Beach
Street address state: FL
Zip/Postal code: 33426-8304
County: Palm Beach
Country: USA
Mailing address: 1375 Gateway Blvd
Mailing city: Boynton Beach
Mailing state: FL
Mailing zip: 33426-8304
General Phone: (561) 370-3336
General/National Adv. E-mail: sales@epublish4me.com
Primary Website: www.epublish4me.com
Industry: Advertising
Product or Service: Advertising/Marketing Agency`Graphic/Design Firm`Multimedia/Interactive Products`Online Service Provider and Internet Hosts`Publisher/Media
Note: Digitize your pubs at http://www.epublish4me.com/?r=403. It automatically posts them on TitleStand where you can sell them by getting local and worldwide distribution (see http://titlestand.com/t). Your PDFs are converted into digital 3-D page flipping revenue generator books, newspapers or magazines with video, audio, hyperlinks and extensive tracking where they can be read on Tablet, PC, Mac, iPad, iPhone, iTouch, iOS, Android and Kindle Fire. Kind regards, Nick.Koriakin@ePublish4me.com 561-370-3336
Personnel: Nicholas Koriakin (Senior Account Executive)

ERGOTRON, INC.

Street address 1: 1181 Trapp Rd
Street address city: Saint Paul
Street address state: MN
Zip/Postal code: 55121-1325
Country: USA
Mailing address: 1181 Trapp Rd Ste 100
Mailing city: Saint Paul
Mailing state: MN
Mailing zip: 55121-1266
General Phone: (651) 681-7600
General Fax: (651) 681-7715
General/National Adv. E-mail: sales@ergotron.com
Primary Website: www.ergotron.com
Mthly Avg Unique Visitors: 1982
Industry: Cabinets; Computers: Local Area Network (LANS); Computers: Storage Devices; Consulting Services: Ergonomics;
Personnel: Pete Segar (Pres.)

ERNEST SCHAEFER, INC.

Street address 1: 731 Lehigh Ave
Street address city: Union
Street address state: NJ
Zip/Postal code: 07083-7626
Country: USA
Mailing address: 731 Lehigh Ave
Mailing city: Union
Mailing state: NJ
Mailing zip: 07083-7626
General Phone: (908) 964-1280
General Fax: (908) 964-6787
General/National Adv. E-mail: eschaefe@aol.com
Primary Website: www.ernestschaeferinc.com
Mthly Avg Unique Visitors: 1922
Industry: Type, Fonts, Letters, Cover Board, Book Glue.
Note: Hot Stamping Type & Bookbinding Supplies
Personnel: Ernest Schaefer (Pres.)

ESKO-GRAPHICS

Street address 1: 721 Crossroads Ct
Street address city: Vandalia
Street address state: OH
Zip/Postal code: 45377-9676
Country: USA
Mailing address: 8535 Gander Creek Dr
Mailing city: Miamisburg
Mailing state: OH
Mailing zip: 45342-5436
General Phone: (937) 454-1721
General Fax: (937) 454-1522
Primary Website: www.esko.com
Mthly Avg Unique Visitors: 1989
Industry: Software: Design/Graphics
Personnel: Tony Wiley (Division Mgr., Printers Systems); Carrie Woryk (Mktg. Commun. Mgr.)

ESSEX PRODUCTS GROUP

Street address 1: 30 Industrial Park Rd
Street address city: Centerbrook
Street address state: CT
Zip/Postal code: 06409-1019
Country: USA
Mailing address: 30 Industrial Park Rd
Mailing city: Centerbrook
Mailing state: CT
Mailing zip: 06409-1019
General Phone: (800) 394-7130
General Fax: (860) 767-9137
General/National Adv. E-mail: sales@epg-inc.com
Primary Website: www.epg-inc.com
Mthly Avg Unique Visitors: 1951
Industry: Ink Controls, Computerized
Personnel: Peter Griffin (Pres.); Matt Strand (Operations Mgr.)

EURO-KNIVES USA

Street address 1: 11516 W 90th St
Street address city: Overland Park
Street address state: KS
Zip/Postal code: 66214-1710
County: Johnson
Country: USA
Mailing address: 11516 W 90th St
Mailing city: Overland Park
Mailing state: KS
Mailing zip: 66214-1710
General Phone: (913) 648-7860
General Fax: (913) 859-0334
General/National Adv. E-mail: al@euro-knivesusa.com; rob@euro-knivesusa.com
Primary Website: www.euro-knivesusa.com/index.php
Mthly Avg Unique Visitors: 1984
Industry: Cut-off knives, slitters, Tucker's, grippers, pin screws, cutting sticks, cheekwoods
Personnel: Al Elton (Owner); Rob Elton (Sales Mgr.)

EWERT AMERICA ELECTRONICS LTD.

Street address 1: 869 Pickens Industrial Dr
Street address 2: Ste 12
Street address city: Marietta
Street address state: GA
Zip/Postal code: 30062-3164
Country: USA
Mailing address: 869 Pickens Industrial Dr Ste 12
Mailing city: Marietta
Mailing state: GA
Mailing zip: 30062-3164
General Phone: 678-996-2411
General Fax: 770-421-0731
General/National Adv. E-mail: ceickhoff@eaeusa.com
Primary Website: www.eaeusa.com
Mthly Avg Unique Visitors: 1962
Industry: Computers: Hardware & Software Integrators; Drives & Controls; Press Control Systems; Software: Workflow Management/Tracking; Closed loop ink density controls System Installations; System Integration Services; Training: Press Operation & Maintenance;
Personnel: Chris Eickhoff (CM, COO)

EXTRATEC CORP.

Street address 1: 5930 Muncaster Mill Rd
Street address city: Rockville
Street address state: MD
Zip/Postal code: 20855-1734
Country: USA
Mailing address: 5930 Muncaster Mill Rd
Mailing city: Rockville
Mailing state: MD
Mailing zip: 20855-1734
General Phone: (301) 924-5150
General Fax: (301) 924-5151
General/National Adv. E-mail: sales@extratek.com
Mthly Avg Unique Visitors: 1979
Industry: Environmental Control Systems
Personnel: Regis E. Finn (Pres.)

FAKE BRAINS, INC.

Street address 1: 791 Southpark Dr Ste 300

Street address 2: Fake Brains Software
Street address city: Littleton
Street address state: CO
Zip/Postal code: 80120-6401
County: Douglas
Country: USA
Mailing address: 791 Southpark Dr Ste 300
Mailing city: Littleton
Mailing state: CO
Mailing zip: 80120-6401
General Phone: (303) 791-3301
General Fax: (303) 470-5218
General/National Adv. E-mail: sales@fakebrains.com
Primary Website: www.fakebrains.com
Mthly Avg Unique Visitors: 1991
Industry: Software: Advertising (Includes Display; Classified, Digital Media); Software: Business (Includes Administration/Accounting); Software: CRM (Customer Relations); Software: Cloud; Software: OnPremise
Personnel: Pat Pfeifer (President); Lisa Pfeifer (VP/ Sales Dir.)

FANUC ROBOTICS AMERICA, INC.

Street address 1: 3900 W Hamlin Rd
Street address city: Rochester Hills
Street address state: MI
Zip/Postal code: 48309-3253
Country: USA
Mailing address: 3900 W Hamlin Rd
Mailing city: Rochester Hills
Mailing state: MI
Mailing zip: 48309-3253
General Phone: 888-326-8287
General Fax: 847-898-5001
General/National Adv. E-mail: marketing@fanucrobotics.com
Primary Website: www.fanucrobotics.com
Mthly Avg Unique Visitors: 1982
Industry: Conveyors; Material Handling Equipment: Palletizing Machines; Newsprint Handeling Equipment; Paper Handeling Equipment; Roll Handeling Equipment;
Personnel: Cathy Powell (Sr. Mktg. Analyst)

FCI DIGITAL

Street address 1: 2032 S Alex Rd
Street address 2: Ste A
Street address city: West Carrollton
Street address state: OH
Zip/Postal code: 45449-4023
Country: USA
Mailing address: 2032 S Alex Rd Ste A
Mailing city: West Carrollton
Mailing state: OH
Mailing zip: 45449-4023
General Phone: (937) 859-9701
General Fax: (937) 859-9709
General/National Adv. E-mail: service@fcidigital.com
Primary Website: www.fcidigital.com
Mthly Avg Unique Visitors: 1989
Industry: Color Proofing; Color Seperation Scanners; Color Seperations, Positives; Prepress Color Proofing Systems
Personnel: George Dick (CEO)

FELINS, INC.

Street address 1: 8306 W Parkland Ct
Street address city: Milwaukee
Street address state: WI
Zip/Postal code: 53223-3832
Country: USA
Mailing address: 8306 W Parkland Ct
Mailing city: Milwaukee
Mailing state: WI
Mailing zip: 53223-3832
General Phone: (800) 843-5667
General Fax: (414) 355-7759
General/National Adv. E-mail: sales@felins.com
Primary Website: www.felins.com
Mthly Avg Unique Visitors: 1921
Industry: Bundling and Tying Machines; Mailroom Systems & Equipment; Strapping Machines;

FIBERWEB

Street address 1: 842 SE Main St
Street address city: Simpsonville
Street address state: SC
Zip/Postal code: 29681-7118
Country: USA
Mailing address: 842 SE Main St
Mailing city: Simpsonville
Mailing state: SC
Mailing zip: 29681-7118
General Phone: (864) 963-2106
General/National Adv. E-mail: sdavis@fiberweb.com
Primary Website: www.fiberwebgraphics.com
Industry: Cleaners & Solvents; Plate Cleaners; Press Accessories, Parts & Supplies;
Personnel: Shawn Davis (Area Mgr.)

FIFE CORPORATION

Street address 1: 222 W Memorial Rd
Street address city: Oklahoma City
Street address state: OK
Zip/Postal code: 73114-2300
Country: USA
Mailing address: PO Box 26508
Mailing city: Oklahoma City
Mailing state: OK
Mailing zip: 73126-0508
General Phone: (405) 755-1600
General Fax: (405) 755-8425
General/National Adv. E-mail: fife@fife.com
Primary Website: www.fife.com
Industry: Visual Display Terminals; Web Break Detector; Web Guides; Web Press - Special Equipment;
Personnel: Marcel Hage (Mgr.)

FKI LOGISTEX

Street address 1: 9301 Olive Blvd
Street address city: Saint Louis
Street address state: MO
Zip/Postal code: 63132-3207
Country: USA
Mailing address: 9301 Olive Blvd
Mailing city: Saint Louis
Mailing state: MO
Mailing zip: 63132-3207
General Phone: (314) 993-4700
General Fax: (314) 995-2400
Primary Website: www.fkilogistex.com
Industry: Material Handling Equipment: Palletizing Machines; Remanufactures Equipment

FLEMING ENTERPRISES

Street address 1: 928 S Blue Mound Rd
Street address city: Fort Worth
Street address state: TX
Zip/Postal code: 76131-1402
Country: USA
Mailing address: 928 S Blue Mound Rd
Mailing city: Fort Worth
Mailing state: TX
Mailing zip: 76131-1402
General Phone: (817) 232-9575
General Fax: (817) 847-6705
Primary Website: www.flemingenterprises.net
Mthly Avg Unique Visitors: 1982
Industry: Drives & Controls; Drying Systems; Equipment Dealers (Used); Erectors & Riggers; Feeder Press; Feeding, Folding, Delivery Equipment; Produciton Control Systems; Roll Handeling Equipment; Roller Grinders; Tension & Web Controls;
Note: We specialize in (but not limited to) web offset services
Personnel: Jeff M. Fleming (Owner); Patrick Fleming (Office Manager)

FLEXOGRAPHIC TECHNICAL ASSOCIATION

Street address 1: 3920 Veterans Memorial Hwy
Street address 2: Ste 9
Street address city: Bohemia
Street address state: NY
Zip/Postal code: 11716-1074
County: Suffolk
Country: USA
Mailing address: 3920 Veterans Memorial Hwy Ste 9
Mailing city: Bohemia
Mailing state: NY
Mailing zip: 11716-1074
General Phone: (631) 737-6020
General Fax: (631) 737-6813
General/National Adv. E-mail: membership@flexography.org
Primary Website: www.flexography.org
Mthly Avg Unique Visitors: 1958
Industry: Trade Publications; Training: Post Press; Training: Pre Press; Training: Press Operation & Maintenance;
Note: Technical association for the flexographic printing industry
Personnel: Mark Cisternino (Pres.); Robert Moran (Pub., FLEXO Mag.); Jay Kaible (Membership & Buss. Dev. Dir.); Joe Tuccitto (Education Director); Eileen Cosma (Marketing Manager)

FLINT GROUP

Street address 1: 14909 N Beck Rd
Street address city: Plymouth
Street address state: MI
Zip/Postal code: 48170-2411
Country: USA
Mailing address: 14909 N Beck Rd
Mailing city: Plymouth
Mailing state: MI
Mailing zip: 48170-2411
General Phone: (734) 781-4600
General Fax: (734) 781-4699
General/National Adv. E-mail: info@na.flintgrp.com
Primary Website: www.flintgrp.com
Mthly Avg Unique Visitors: 1920
Industry: Ink Pumping Systems; Ink Storage Tanks; Inks;
Personnel: Bill Miller (Pres., North Amer.); Mike Green (Vice Pres./Gen. Mgr., News Ink/Pub. Div.); Norm Harbin (Vice Pres., Bus./Technical Devel.)

FLINT GROUP.

Street address 1: 14909 N Beck Rd
Street address city: Plymouth
Street address state: MI
Zip/Postal code: 48170-2411
County: Wayne
Country: USA
Mailing address: 14909 North Beck
Mailing city: Plymouth
Mailing state: MI
Mailing zip: 48170
General Phone: (734) 781-4600
General Fax: (734) 781-4699
General/National Adv. E-mail: info@flintgrp.com
Primary Website: www.flintgrp.com
Industry: Printing inks (including coldset UV; black and color; and soy-based options); Offset fabric and Metalback Blankets; Blanket Mounting and Bars; Pressroom Chemicals including Washes Fountain Solutions, Cleaners and more; Pressroom Supplies; Digital inks; and more.
Note: The only company to develop and manufacture inks, chemistry and blankets, making printers' jobs easier and pressroom performance stronger.

FLYNN BURNER CORP.

Street address 1: 425 5th Ave
Street address city: New Rochelle
Street address state: NY
Zip/Postal code: 10801-2203
Country: USA
Mailing address: PO Box 431
Mailing city: New Rochelle
Mailing state: NY
Mailing zip: 10802-0431
General Phone: (914) 636-1320
General Fax: (914) 636-3751
Primary Website: www.flynnburner.com
Mthly Avg Unique Visitors: 1942
Industry: Web Press - Special Equipment
Personnel: Julian Modzeleski (Pres.); Dom Medina (Vice Pres.)

FORREST CONSULTING

Street address 1: 725 Kenilworth Ave
Street address city: Glen Ellyn
Street address state: IL
Zip/Postal code: 60137-3805
Country: USA
Mailing address: 725 Kenilworth Ave
Mailing city: Glen Ellyn
Mailing state: IL
Mailing zip: 60137-3805
General Phone: (630) 730-9619
General/National Adv. E-mail: fasttrackhelp@strategicbusinessleader.com
Primary Website: www.strategicbusinessleader.com
Mthly Avg Unique Visitors: 1988
Industry: Consulting Services: Advertising; Consulting Services: Circulation; Consulting Services: Financial; Consulting Services: Marketing;
Personnel: Lee Crumbaugh (Pres.)

FORTEC, INC.

Street address 1: 3831 W Wells St
Street address city: Milwaukee
Street address state: WI
Zip/Postal code: 53208-3167
Country: USA
Mailing address: 613 N 36th St
Mailing city: Milwaukee
Mailing state: WI
Mailing zip: 53208-3826
General Phone: (414) 344-1900
General Fax: (414) 935-3309
General/National Adv. E-mail: email@fortec.com
Primary Website: www.fortec.com
Mthly Avg Unique Visitors: 1979
Industry: Newspaper Dispensers (Mechanical/ Electronic); Tubes, Racks (Includes Racks: Motor Route Tubes);
Personnel: Jack Olson (Pres.)

FOSTER MFG. CO.

Street address 1: 204B Progress Dr
Street address city: Montgomeryville
Street address state: PA
Zip/Postal code: 18936-9616
Country: USA
Mailing address: 204B Progress Dr
Mailing city: Montgomeryville
Mailing state: PA
Mailing zip: 18936-9616
General Phone: 267-413-6220
General Fax: 267-413-6227
General/National Adv. E-mail: information@fostermfg.com
Primary Website: www.fostermfg.com
Mthly Avg Unique Visitors: 1947
Industry: Archiving Systems; Art & Layout Equipment and Services; Cabinets; Color Viewing Equipment; Composing Room Equipment & Supplies; Cutters & Trimmers; Cutting Tools; Dark Room Equipment; Files, Storage; Layout Tables, Light Tables & Workstations; Offset Plate Files; Photo Archiving; Plastic Folders; Prepress Color Proofing Systems; Proofing Systems; Storage Retrieval Systems; Tables (Dot, Etch, Opaquing, Register, Retouching, Stripping)
Personnel: Ted Borowsky (Pres.)

FOX BAY INDUSTRIES, INC.

Street address 1: 4150 B Pl NW
Street address 2: Ste 101
Street address city: Auburn
Street address state: WA
Zip/Postal code: 98001-2449
Country: USA
Mailing address: 4150 B Pl NW Ste 101
Mailing city: Auburn
Mailing state: WA
Mailing zip: 98001-2449
General Phone: (253) 941-9155
General Fax: (253) 941-9197
General/National Adv. E-mail: info@foxbay.com; sales@foxbay.com
Primary Website: www.foxbay.com
Mthly Avg Unique Visitors: 1989
Industry: Consulting Services: Ergonomics
Personnel: Ladele Walker (Pres.); Wayne Walker (Sales Mgr.)

FRANK N MAGID ASSOCIATES

Street address 1: 1 Research Ctr
Street address city: Marion
Street address state: IA
Zip/Postal code: 52302-5868
County: Linn
Country: USA
Mailing address: 1 Research Ctr
Mailing city: Marion
Mailing state: IL
Mailing zip: 52302-5868
General Phone: 847-9220418
General Fax: (319) 377-5861
General/National Adv. E-mail: Bhague@magid.com
Primary Website: www.magid.com

Mthly Avg Unique Visitors: 1957
Product or Service: Consultants`Research
Personnel: Bill Hague (Exec. Vice Pres.); Bill Day

FRANKLIN WIRE WORKS, INC.

Street address 1: 910 E Lincoln Ave
Street address city: Belvidere
Street address state: IL
Zip/Postal code: 61008-2928
Country: USA
Mailing address: 910 E Lincoln Ave
Mailing city: Belvidere
Mailing state: IL
Mailing zip: 61008-2928
General Phone: (815) 544-6676
General Fax: (815) 547-5356
Primary Website: www.franklindisplay.com
Mthly Avg Unique Visitors: 1978
Industry: Circulation Equipment & Supplies
Personnel: Dick Boyett (Sales Mgr.)

FRY COMMUNICATIONS, INC.

Street address 1: 800 W Church Rd
Street address city: Mechanicsburg
Street address state: PA
Zip/Postal code: 17055-3179
County: Cumberland
Country: USA
Mailing address: 800 W. Church Rd.
Mailing city: Mechanicsburg
Mailing state: PA
Mailing zip: 17055
General Phone: (800) 334-1429
General/National Adv. E-mail: info@frycomm.com
Primary Website: www.frycomm.com
Mthly Avg Unique Visitors: 1934
Industry: Publishing Systems; Trade Publications; Commercial Printer
Note: Fry Communications is a privately held commercial printer with almost 90 years experience printing and distributing everything from newspapers to high end magazines and catalogs. We also help with progressive digital device delivery and custom web publishing.
Personnel: Henry Fry (Chairman of the Board); Mike Lukas (CEO); Kevin Quinn (VP Sales); Cheri Stryker (VP of Sales); Mike Weber (VP Manufacturing)

FUJI PHOTO FILM USA/GRAPHIC SYSTEMS DIV.

Street address 1: 850 Central Ave
Street address city: Hanover Park
Street address state: IL
Zip/Postal code: 60133-5422
Country: USA
Mailing address: 850 Central Ave
Mailing city: Hanover Park
Mailing state: IL
Mailing zip: 60133-5422
General Phone: (630) 259-7200
General Fax: (630) 259-7078
General/National Adv. E-mail: contact@fujifilmgs.com
Primary Website: www.fujifilm.com
Mthly Avg Unique Visitors: 1934
Industry: Chemicals: Plate Processing; Color Proofing; Film & Paper: Contact; Film & Paper: Duplicating; Film & Paper: Filters (Photographic); Imagesetters; Plates: Offset (Computer to Plate); Proofing Systems; Plates: Offset (Conventional); Scanners: Color B & W, Plates, Web;
Personnel: Tim Combs (Pres., Industrial Imaging Markets Grp.); Bill Diminno (Sr. Vice Pres./Gen. Mgr., PhotoImaging Grp.)

FUJIFILM GRAPHIC SYSTEMS USA, INC.

Street address 1: 2507 W Erie Dr
Street address 2: Ste 103
Street address city: Tempe
Street address state: AZ
Zip/Postal code: 85282-3117
Country: USA
Mailing address: 2507 W Erie Dr Ste 103
Mailing city: Tempe
Mailing state: AZ
Mailing zip: 85282-3117
General Phone: (800) 279-1673
General Fax: (602) 437-8483
Primary Website: www.fujifilmusa.com/products/graphic_arts_printing/index.html
Industry: Blankets; Chemicals: Pressroom; Color Management Software; Imagesetters; Inks; Offset Chemicals & Supplies; Platemakers: Flexographic (Computer to Plate); Plates: Offset (Conventional); Proofing Systems; Software: Press/Post Press;
Personnel: Richard Pyane (Reg'l Sales Mgr.)

FUJIFILM GRAPHIC SYSTEMS USA, INC.

Street address 1: 6200 Phyllis Drive
Street address city: Cypress
Street address state: CA
Zip/Postal code: 90630
Country: USA
Mailing address: 6200 Phyllis Drive
Mailing city: Cypress
Mailing state: CA
Mailing zip: 90630
General Phone: (714) 933-3300
General Fax: (714) 899-4707
Primary Website: www.fujifilmusa.com/products/graphic_arts_printing/index.html
Industry: Blankets; Chemicals: Pressroom; Color Management Software; Imagesetters; Inks; Offset Chemicals & Supplies; Platemakers: Flexographic (Computer to Plate); Plates: Offset (Conventional); Proofing Systems; Software: Press/Post Press;
Personnel: Jeffrey Buchman (Reg'l Sales Mgr.)

FUJIFILM GRAPHIC SYSTEMS USA, INC.

Street address 1: 30962 San Benito St
Street address city: Hayward
Street address state: CA
Zip/Postal code: 94544-7935
Country: USA
Mailing address: 30962 San Benito St
Mailing city: Hayward
Mailing state: CA
Mailing zip: 94544-7935
General Phone: (800) 734.8745
General Fax: (510) 266.0707
Primary Website: www.fujifilmusa.com/products/graphic_arts_printing/index.html
Industry: Blankets; Chemicals: Pressroom; Color Management Software; Imagesetters; Inks; Offset Chemicals & Supplies; Platemakers: Flexographic (Computer to Plate); Plates: Offset (Conventional); Proofing Systems; Software: Press/Post Press;
Personnel: Richard Cay (Reg'l Sales Mgr.)

FUJIFILM GRAPHIC SYSTEMS USA, INC.

Street address 1: 850 Central Ave
Street address city: Hanover Park
Street address state: IL
Zip/Postal code: 60133-5422
Country: USA
Mailing address: 850 Central Ave
Mailing city: Hanover Park
Mailing state: IL
Mailing zip: 60133-5422
General Phone: (630) 259-7200
General Fax: (630) 259-7078
Primary Website: www.fujifilmusa.com/products/graphic_arts_printing/index.html
Industry: Blankets; Chemicals: Pressroom; Color Management Software; Imagesetters; Inks; Offset Chemicals & Supplies; Platemakers: Flexographic (Computer to Plate); Plates: Offset (Conventional); Proofing Systems; Software: Press/Post Press;
Personnel: John Briar (Reg'l Sales Mgr.)

FUJIFILM GRAPHIC SYSTEMS USA, INC.

Street address 1: 6810 Deerpath Road
Street address 2: Suite 405
Street address city: Elkridge
Street address state: MD
Zip/Postal code: 21075
Country: USA
Mailing address: 6810 Deerpath Road, Suite 405
Mailing city: Elkridge
Mailing state: MD
Mailing zip: 21075
General Phone: (301) 317-7480
General Fax: (301) 317-7480
Primary Website: www.fujifilmusa.com/products/graphic_arts_printing/index.html
Industry: Blankets; Chemicals: Pressroom; Color Management Software; Imagesetters; Inks; Offset Chemicals & Supplies; Platemakers: Flexographic (Computer to Plate); Plates: Offset (Conventional); Proofing Systems; Software: Press/Post Press;
Personnel: Tony Aquino (Reg'l Sales Mgr.)

FUJIFILM GRAPHIC SYSTEMS USA, INC.

Street address 1: 4001 Lakebreeze Avenue N.
Street address 2: Ste 400
Street address city: Brooklyn Center
Street address state: MN
Zip/Postal code: 554429-3844
Country: USA
Mailing address: 4001 Lakebreeze Avenue N., Ste 400
Mailing city: Brooklyn Center
Mailing state: MN
Mailing zip: 554429-3844
General Phone: (651) 855-6000
General Fax: (651) 855-6025
Primary Website: www.fujifilmusa.com/products/graphic_arts_printing/index.html
Industry: Blankets; Chemicals: Pressroom; Color Management Software; Imagesetters; Inks; Offset Chemicals & Supplies; Platemakers: Flexographic (Computer to Plate); Plates: Offset (Conventional); Proofing Systems; Software: Press/Post Press;
Personnel: Jamie Walsh (Reg'l Sales Mgr.)

FUJIFILM GRAPHIC SYSTEMS USA, INC.

Street address 1: 1100 King Georges Post Road
Street address city: Edison
Street address state: NJ
Zip/Postal code: 08837
Country: USA
Mailing address: 1100 King Georges Post Road
Mailing city: Edison
Mailing state: NJ
Mailing zip: 08837
General Phone: (732) 857-3280
General Fax: (732) 857-3470
Primary Website: www.fujifilmusa.com/products/graphic_arts_printing/index.html
Industry: Blankets; Chemicals: Pressroom; Color Management Software; Imagesetters; Inks; Offset Chemicals & Supplies; Platemakers: Flexographic (Computer to Plate); Plates: Offset (Conventional); Proofing Systems; Software: Press/Post Press;
Personnel: Michael Sharpe (Regional Sales Manager)

FUJIFILM GRAPHIC SYSTEMS USA, INC.

Street address 1: 1650 Magnolia Dr
Street address city: Cincinnati
Street address state: OH
Zip/Postal code: 45215-1976
Country: USA
Mailing address: 1650 Magnolia Dr
Mailing city: Cincinnati
Mailing state: OH
Mailing zip: 45215-1976
General Phone: (800) 582-7406
General Fax: (513) 563-0377
Primary Website: www.fujifilmusa.com/products/graphic_arts_printing/index.html
Industry: Blankets; Chemicals: Pressroom; Color Management Software; Imagesetters; Inks; Offset Chemicals & Supplies; Platemakers: Flexographic (Computer to Plate); Plates: Offset (Conventional); Proofing Systems; Software: Press/Post Press;
Personnel: Kurt Paskert (Reg'l Sales Mgr.)

FUJIFILM GRAPHIC SYSTEMS USA, INC.

Street address 1: 3926 Willow Lake Blvd
Street address city: Memphis
Street address state: TN
Zip/Postal code: 38118-7040
Country: USA
Mailing address: 3926 Willow Lake Blvd
Mailing city: Memphis
Mailing state: TN
Mailing zip: 38118-7040
General Phone: (800) 365-2457
General Fax: (901) 795-1251
Primary Website: www.fujifilmusa.com/products/graphic_arts_printing/index.html
Industry: Blankets; Chemicals: Pressroom; Color Management Software; Imagesetters; Inks; Offset Chemicals & Supplies; Platemakers: Flexographic (Computer to Plate); Plates: Offset (Conventional); Proofing Systems; Software: Press/Post Press;
Personnel: Tommy Aquino (Reg'l Sales Mgr.)

FUJIFILM GRAPHIC SYSTEMS USA, INC.

Street address 1: 330 Westway Pl
Street address 2: Ste 446
Street address city: Arlington
Street address state: TX
Zip/Postal code: 76018-1025
Country: USA
Mailing address: 330 Westway Pl Ste 446
Mailing city: Arlington
Mailing state: TX
Mailing zip: 76018-1025
General Phone: (800) 404.3228
General Fax: (817) 467-7351
Primary Website: www.fujifilmusa.com/products/graphic_arts_printing/index.html
Industry: Blankets; Chemicals: Pressroom; Color Management Software; Imagesetters; Inks; Offset Chemicals & Supplies; Platemakers: Flexographic (Computer to Plate); Plates: Offset (Conventional); Proofing Systems; Software: Press/Post Press;
Personnel: Bob O'Shea (Reg'l Sales Mgr.)

FUJIFILM GRAPHIC SYSTEMS USA, INC.

Street address 1: 1795 Fremont Drive
Street address city: Salt Lake City
Street address state: UT
Zip/Postal code: 84104
Mailing address: 1795 Fremont Drive
Mailing city: Salt Lake City
Mailing state: UT
Mailing zip: 84104
General Phone: (801) 975-1234
General Fax: (801) 972-3981
Industry: Blankets; Chemicals: Pressroom; Color Management Software; Imagesetters; Inks; Offset Chemicals & Supplies; Platemakers: Flexographic (Computer to Plate); Plates: Offset (Conventional); Proofing Systems; Software: Press/Post Press;
Personnel: Matt Miller (Regional Sales Manager)

FUJIFILM GRAPHIC SYSTEMS USA, INC.

Street address 1: 5103 "D" Street NW
Street address 2: Suite 102
Street address city: Auburn
Street address state: WA
Zip/Postal code: 98001
Mailing address: 5103 "D" Street NW, Suite 102
Mailing city: Auburn
Mailing state: WA
Mailing zip: 98001
General Phone: (800) 628-0317
General Fax: (253) 852-4701
Primary Website: www.fujifilmusa.com/products/graphic_arts_printing/index.html
Industry: Blankets; Chemicals: Pressroom; Color Management Software; Imagesetters; Inks; Offset Chemicals & Supplies; Platemakers: Flexographic (Computer to Plate); Plates: Offset (Conventional); Proofing Systems; Software: Press/Post Press;
Personnel: Jeffrey Buchman (Reg'l Sales Mgr.)

FUJIFILM HUNT CHEMICALS U.S.A., INC.

Street address 1: 40 Boroline Rd
Street address city: Allendale
Street address state: NJ
Zip/Postal code: 07401-1616
Country: USA
Mailing address: 40 Boroline Rd
Mailing city: Allendale
Mailing state: NJ
Mailing zip: 07401-1616
General Phone: (201) 236-8633
General Fax: (201) 995-2299

Primary Website: www.fujihuntusa.com
Mthly Avg Unique Visitors: 1989
Industry: Chemicals: Photographic; Chemicals: Pressroom;
Personnel: Scott Clouston (Vice Pres.); Albert Adrts (Pres.)

FUJIFILM NORTH AMERICA CORPORATION

Street address 1: 850 Central Ave
Street address city: Hanover Park
Street address state: IL
Zip/Postal code: 60133-5422
County: DuPage
Country: USA
Mailing address: 850 Central Ave.
Mailing city: Hanover Park
Mailing state: IN
Mailing zip: 60133
General Phone: (866) 378-1429
General Fax: (765) 482-0288
Primary Website: www.fujifilmus.com
Industry: Plates Chemistry Films Pressroom products CTP equipment Processors Workflow Proofing supplies Safety equipment Service Color management
Personnel: Lane Palmer (VP, Corp. Accounts & Newspapers); Lorna Borghese (Newspaper Acct. Mgr., SE Region); Bob Veyera (Newspaper Acct. Mgr., NW Reg.); Michael Mossman (Newspaper Support Specialist); Brian Moser (Newspaper Acct. Mgr., SW Reg.); J. Faulkner (Newspaper Acct. Mgr., NE Reg.)

FULCO, INC.

Street address 1: 30 Broad St
Street address city: Denville
Street address state: NJ
Zip/Postal code: 07834-1236
County: Morris
Country: USA
Mailing address: 30 Broad St.
Mailing city: Denville
Mailing state: NJ
Mailing zip: 07834
General Phone: (973) 627-2427
General Fax: 973-627-5872
General/National Adv. E-mail: support@fulcoinc.com
Primary Website: www.fulcoinc.com
Mthly Avg Unique Visitors: 1981
Industry: Subscription Fulfillment
Note: Subscription Fulfillment Company
Personnel: Jim Duffy (Owner/Pres.); Dave Ross (Client Services Director)

G&K-VIJUK INTERNATIONAL

Street address 1: 715 N Church Rd
Street address city: Elmhurst
Street address state: IL
Zip/Postal code: 60126-1415
County: DuPage
Country: USA
Mailing address: 715 N Church Rd
Mailing city: Elmhurst
Mailing state: IL
Mailing zip: 60126-1415
General Phone: (630) 530-2203
General Fax: (630) 530-2245
General/National Adv. E-mail: info@guk-vijuk.com
Primary Website: www.guk-vijuk.com
Mthly Avg Unique Visitors: 1967
Industry: Folding Machines
Personnel: Rick Jasnica (Op. Mgr.); Kevin Boivin (Sales Mgr.)
Parent company (for newspapers): GUK group in Germany

G.T. SPECIALTIES

Street address 1: 2901A Edith Blvd NE
Street address city: Albuquerque
Street address state: NM
Zip/Postal code: 87107-1517
County: Bernalillo
Country: USA
Mailing address: PO Box 6383
Mailing city: Albuquerque
Mailing state: NM
Mailing zip: 87197-6383
General Phone: (505) 343-0600
General Fax: (505) 343-0606
General/National Adv. E-mail: Sales@gt-specialties.com
Primary Website: www.gt-specialties.com
Mthly Avg Unique Visitors: 1980
Industry: Offset Press, New made in USA grippers, Recondition grippers with a Diamond Coating
Personnel: Louis Nunez (Owner)

GAMMERLER (US) CORP.

Street address 1: 431 Lakeview Ct
Street address 2: Ste B
Street address city: Mt Prospect
Street address state: IL
Zip/Postal code: 60056-6048
County: USA
Country: Canada
Mailing address: 431 Lakeview Ct Ste B
Mailing city: Mt Prospect
Mailing state: IL
Mailing zip: 60103
General Phone: 224 361-8300
General Fax: (224) 361-8301
General/National Adv. E-mail: joe.jastrzebski@gammerler.com
Primary Website: www.gammerler.com
Mthly Avg Unique Visitors: 1985
Industry: Conveyors; Counting, Stacking, Bundling Machines; Cutters & Trimmers; Feeding, Folding, Delivery Equipment; Gluing Systems; In-Line Trimming Systems; Mailroom Systems & Equipment; Material Handling Equipment: Palletizing Machines; Material Handling Equipment: Pallets & Palletizers;
Personnel: Joe Jastrzebski (Managing Director)

GAMMERLER AG

Street address 1: Lietenstr. 26
Street address city: Geretsried-Gelting
Zip/Postal code: D-82538
Country: Germany
Mailing address: Lietenstr. 26
Mailing city: Geretsried-Gelting
Mailing zip: D-82538
General Phone: +49 8171 404-326
General Fax: +49 8171 404-244
General/National Adv. E-mail: dietrich.lauber@gammerler.de
Primary Website: www.gammerler.com
Personnel: Dietrich Lauber (Sales Mgr.)

GANNETT MEDIA TECHNOLOGIES INTERNATIONAL (GMTI)

Street address 1: 312 Elm St
Street address 2: Fl 20
Street address city: Cincinnati
Street address state: OH
Zip/Postal code: 45202-2739
County: Hamilton
Country: USA
Mailing address: 312 Elm St Ste 2G
Mailing city: Cincinnati
Mailing state: OH
Mailing zip: 45202-2763
General Phone: (513) 665-3777
General Fax: (513) 768-8958
General/National Adv. E-mail: gmti-info@gmti.gannett.com
Primary Website: www.gmti.com
Mthly Avg Unique Visitors: 1994
Industry: Archiving Systems; Computers: Hardware & Software Integrators; Library Retrieval Systems; Marketing Database Design and Implementation; Photo Archiving; Software: Advertising (Includes Display; Classified); Storage Retrieval Systems;
Product or Service: Multimedia/Interactive Products
Personnel: Steve Fuschetti (Pres./CEO)

GE INSTRUMENT CONTROL SYSTEMS, INC.

Street address 1: PO Box 7126
Street address city: Pensacola
Street address state: FL
Zip/Postal code: 32503
Country: USA
Mailing address: PO Box 7126
Mailing city: Pensacola
Mailing state: FL
Mailing zip: 32534-0126
General Phone: 800-433-2682
General Fax: 780-420-2010
General/National Adv. E-mail: customercare.ip@ge.com
Primary Website: www.geautomation.com
Industry: Architects/Engineers (Includes Design/Construction Firms); Controls: Exposure; Controls: Photo Electric; Controls: Register;
Personnel: Sharon Stall (Sales)

GENERAL BINDING CORP.

Street address 1: 4 Corporate Dr
Street address city: Lake Zurich
Street address state: IL
Zip/Postal code: 60047-8924
Country: USA
Mailing address: 4 Corporate Dr
Mailing city: Lake Zurich
Mailing state: IL
Mailing zip: 60047-8924
General Phone: (800) 723-4000
General Fax: (800) 914-8178
General/National Adv. E-mail: info@acco.com
Primary Website: www.gbcconnect.com
Mthly Avg Unique Visitors: 1947
Industry: Paper Shredders

GENERAL DATACOMM, LLC

Street address 1: 353 Christian Street
Street address city: Oxford
Street address state: CT
Zip/Postal code: 06478
Country: USA
Mailing address: 353 Christian Street
Mailing city: Oxford
Mailing state: CT
Mailing zip: 06478
General Phone: (203) 729-0271
General Fax: (203) 266-2133
Primary Website: www.gdc.com
Mthly Avg Unique Visitors: 1969
Industry: Computers: Hardware & Software Integrators; Telecommunications;
Personnel: Mike Conway (Pres. & CEO); Mark Johns (COO); Joe Autem (CFO)

GEORGIA-PACIFIC CORP.

Street address 1: 133 Peachtree St NE
Street address city: Atlanta
Street address state: GA
Zip/Postal code: 30303-1804
Country: USA
Mailing address: 133 Peachtree St NE Ste 3700
Mailing city: Atlanta
Mailing state: GA
Mailing zip: 30303-1862
General Phone: (404) 652-4000
General Fax: (404) 230-1674
General/National Adv. E-mail: gpfinance@gapac.com
Primary Website: www.gp.com
Mthly Avg Unique Visitors: 1927
Industry: Photostat; Paper
Personnel: Dave Robertson (Chrmn.); Jim Hannan (Pres./CEO); Simon H. Davies (Pres., Recycled Fibers); John P. O'Donnell (Pres., N. American Retail Bus.); Richard G. Urschel (Pres., Chemicals); Sean R. Fallmann (Pres., Dixie); Kathleen A. Walters (Exec. Vice Pres., Global Consumer Pdcts.); Ronald L. Paul (Exec. Vice Pres., Wood Pdcts.); Sheila M. Weidman (Sr. Vice Pres., Commun. government and Pub. Aff.); Rob Lorys (Vice Pres., Mktg. Commun.); Chris Beyer (Dir., Mktg. Servs.); Gino Biondi (Brand Mktg. Dir., Brawny); H. James Dallas (Vice Pres., Information Resources/CIO)

GILBANE BUILDING CO.

Street address 1: 7 Jackson Walkway
Street address city: Providence
Street address state: RI
Zip/Postal code: 02903-3638
Country: USA
Mailing address: 7 Jackson Walkway
Mailing city: Providence
Mailing state: RI
Mailing zip: 02903-3694
General Phone: (401) 456-5800
General Fax: (401) 456-5930
Primary Website: www.gilbaneco.com
Mthly Avg Unique Visitors: 1873
Industry: Architects/Engineers (Includes Design/Construction Firms)
Personnel: Paul J. Choquette (Chrmn./CEO); Thomas F. Gilbane (Pres./COO); William Gilbane (Exec. Vice Pres.); Alfred K. Potter (Sr. Vice Pres.-Mktg./Sales); Walter Mckelvey (Sr. Vice Pres./Mgr.-Central Reg.); Wandell Holmes (Sr. Vice Pres./Mgr., Southwest); Bruce Hoffman (Sr. Vice Pres./Mgr., Mid Atlantic); George Cavallo (Sr. Vice Pres./Mgr.-North East Reg.)

GLOBAL TURNKEY SYSTEMS, INC.

Street address 1: 2001 US Highway 46
Street address 2: Ste 203
Street address city: Parsippany
Street address state: NJ
Zip/Postal code: 07054-1315
Country: USA
Mailing address: 2001 US Highway 46 Ste 203
Mailing city: Parsippany
Mailing state: NJ
Mailing zip: 07054-1315
General Phone: (973) 331-1010
General Fax: (973) 331-0042
General/National Adv. E-mail: sales@gtsystems.com
Primary Website: www.gtsystems.com
Mthly Avg Unique Visitors: 1969
Industry: Computers: Hardware & Software Integrators; Computers: Local Area Network (LANS); Consulting Services: Circulation; Consulting Services: Computer; Software: Circulation; Software: Electronic Data Interchange; Subscription Fulfillment Software; System Installations; System Integration Services;
Personnel: Al Altesiane (Pres./CEO)

GLOBIX CORP.

Street address 1: 95 Christopher Columbus Dr
Street address 2: Fl 16
Street address city: Jersey City
Street address state: NJ
Zip/Postal code: 07302-2927
Country: USA
Mailing address: 95 Christopher Columbus Dr Fl 16
Mailing city: Jersey City
Mailing state: NJ
Mailing zip: 07302-2927
General Phone: (212) 334-8500
General Fax: (212) 625-8650
General/National Adv. E-mail: support@qualitytech.com
Primary Website: www.qualitytech.com
Mthly Avg Unique Visitors: 1989
Industry: Computers: Hardware & Software Integrators; Computers: Laptop & Portable; Computers: Local Area Network (LANS); Computers: Storage Devices;
Personnel: Kurt Van Wagenen (Pres./CEO/COO); Shelagh Montgomery (Gen. Mgr.)

GLUNZ & JENSEN, INC.

Street address 1: 500 Commerce Dr
Street address city: Quakertown
Street address state: PA
Zip/Postal code: 18951-3730
County: Bucks
Country: USA
Mailing address: 500 Commerce Drive
Mailing city: Quakertown
Mailing state: PA
Mailing zip: 18951
General Phone: (267) 405-4000
General Fax: (267) 227-3615
General/National Adv. E-mail: gj-americas@glunz-jensen.com
Display Adv. E-mail: gj-americas.com
Primary Website: www.glunz-jensen.com
Mthly Avg Unique Visitors: 1973
Industry: Offset Platemaking: processors for thermal, UV and violet plates Offset Plate; plate stackers and conveyors Flexo Platemaking: exposure units, processors, dryers, light finishers, automated plate making plate mounting, sleeve trimming and plate cleaning equipment CtP: inkjet computer to plate system
Personnel: Michael Bugge' (VP Sales)

GMTI (DIGITAL COLLECTIONS)

Street address 1: 312 Elm St
Street address 2: Fl 20
Street address city: Cincinnati
Street address state: OH
Zip/Postal code: 45202-2739
County: Hamilton

Country: USA
Mailing address: 312 Elm St Fl 20
Mailing city: Cincinnati
Mailing state: OH
Mailing zip: 45202-2739
General Phone: (513) 665-3777
General Fax: (513) 768-8958
General/National Adv. E-mail: contentfeedback@gannett.com
Primary Website: www.gannett.com
Mthly Avg Unique Visitors: 1995
Industry: Digital Asset Management Systems: Full service contractor; Hardware & Software Integrators; Content Aggregation and Distribution; Semantic Engine Services; Archive Content Management software.
Product or Service: Consultants`Hardware/Software Supplier`Online Service Provider and Internet Hosts
Personnel: Steve Fuschetti (Pres./CEO); Bill Mahlock (Vice Pres., Installations/Support); Michael Tucker (Dir., Sales & Marketing)

GO PLASTICS/STREETSMART LLC

Street address 1: 120 Wes Walker Memorial Drive
Street address city: Canton
Street address state: GA
Zip/Postal code: 30107
Country: USA
Mailing state: GA
General Phone: 866-366-6166 x 6
General/National Adv. E-mail: brianb@goplastics.com
Primary Website: www.goplastics.com
Mthly Avg Unique Visitors: 1987
Industry: Circulation Equipment & Supplies; Newspaper Dispensers (Mechanical/Electronic);
Note: Manufacturer of newspaper boxes and display racks.
Personnel: Brian Bauman (Dir.-Sales/Mktg.); Michelle Gollob (Adv. Customer Info Serv.)

GOLD COUNTY ADVISORS, INC.

Street address 1: 604 Sutter St
Street address 2: Ste 394
Street address city: Folsom
Street address state: CA
Zip/Postal code: 95630-2698
County: Sacramento
Country: USA
Mailing address: 604 Sutter St Ste 394
Mailing city: Folsom
Mailing state: CA
Mailing zip: 95630-2698
General Phone: (916) 673-9778
General Fax: (888) 933-0807
General/National Adv. E-mail: jeff@goldcountryadvisors.com
Primary Website: www.goldcountryadvisors.com
Mthly Avg Unique Visitors: 2003
Industry: Brokers & Appraisers, Merger & Acquisition Advisors for the newspaper business.
Personnel: Jeffrey Potts (Principal)

GOSS INTERNATIONAL CORPORATION

Street address 1: 121 Technology Dr
Street address city: Durham
Street address state: NH
Zip/Postal code: 03824-4721
Country: USA
Mailing address: 121 Technology Dr
Mailing city: Durham
Mailing state: NH
Mailing zip: 03824-4716
General Phone: 603-749-6600
General Fax: 603-750-6860
General/National Adv. E-mail: info@gossinternational.com
Primary Website: www.gossinternational.com
Mthly Avg Unique Visitors: 1885
Industry: Press Accessories, Parts & Supplies; Press Rebuilding; Press Repairs; Presses: Offset;
Personnel: Ed Padilla (Chrmn.); Jochen Meissner (CEO); Joseph Gaynor (CFO); Richard Schultz (Sr. Vice Pres., Global Sales); Cecilia Chou (Mktg. Mgr.); Greg Norris

GRAFIKAMERICA

Street address 1: 1285 W King St
Street address city: York
Street address state: PA
Zip/Postal code: 17404-3409
Country: USA
Mailing address: 1285 W King St
Mailing city: York
Mailing state: PA
Mailing zip: 17404-3409
General Phone: (717) 843-3183
General Fax: (717) 845-8828
General/National Adv. E-mail: sales@grafikam.com
Mthly Avg Unique Visitors: 1993
Industry: Color Registration; Controls: Register; Ink Controls, Computerized; Tension & Web Controls; Web Offset Remoisturizers;
Personnel: Ward Walsh (Pres.)

GRAPHIC ARTS BLUE BOOK ONLINE

Street address 1: 2000 Clearwater Dr
Street address city: Oak Brook
Street address state: IL
Zip/Postal code: 60523-8809
Country: USA
Mailing address: 2000 Clearwater Dr
Mailing city: Oak Brook
Mailing state: IL
Mailing zip: 60523-8809
General Phone: 800/323-4958, x8333
General Fax: 678/680-1667
General/National Adv. E-mail: info@gabb.com
Primary Website: www.gabb.com
Mthly Avg Unique Visitors: 1929
Industry: Trade Publications
Personnel: Mary Miller (Global Marketing Director)

GRAPHIC MACHINE SALES, INC.

Street address 1: 8917 Hickory Ln
Street address city: Wonder Lake
Street address state: IL
Zip/Postal code: 60097-9179
County: McHenry
Country: USA
Mailing address: 8917 Hickory Ln
Mailing city: Wonder Lake
Mailing state: IL
Mailing zip: 60097-9179
General Phone: (815) 382-1914
General/National Adv. E-mail: graphic@stans.net
Primary Website: www.graphicmachinesales.com
Mthly Avg Unique Visitors: 1986
Industry: Used web presses and auxiliaries
Note: Markets used and reconditioned web presses and auxiliary equipment worldwide
Personnel: James Anzelmo (Pres.)

GRAPHIC ROLL COVERINGS

Street address 1: 300B Newkirk Road
Street address city: Richmond Hill
Street address state: ON
Zip/Postal code: L4C 3G7
County: Ontario
Country: Canada
Mailing address: 300-B, Newkirk Road
Mailing city: Richmond Hill
Mailing state: ON
Mailing zip: L4C 3G7
General Phone: (905) 475-2357
General Fax: (905) 475-3421
General/National Adv. E-mail: info@graphicroller.com
Primary Website: www.graphicroller.com
Mthly Avg Unique Visitors: 1972
Industry: Ink Rollers; Rollers; Dampening; Rollers; UV; Nylon Roller Coating; Chrome Roller Coating; Split Nip Folder Rolls; Infeed Nip Rolls; Grater Wrap-Roller Covering; Ink Fountains & Accessories; Press Accessories, Parts & Supplies; Roller Grinding Services;
Personnel: Brian Venis (Pres.)

GRAPHIC SYSTEMS SERVICES

Street address 1: 400 South Pioneer Blvd.
Street address city: Springboro
Street address state: OH
Zip/Postal code: 45066
Country: USA
Mailing address: 400 South Pioneer Blvd.
Mailing city: Springboro
Mailing state: OH
Mailing zip: 45066
General Phone: (937) 746-0708
General Fax: (937) 746-0783
General/National Adv. E-mail: john.sillies@gsspress.com
Primary Website: www.gsspress.com
Mthly Avg Unique Visitors: 1954
Industry: Printing Presses & Color Inkjet Web Presses
Personnel: John Sillies (Support); Mark Pellman (Engineering & Product Development); Lynn Dahm; Mike Deno (Service Support)

GRAPHIC TECHNOLOGY, INC. (GTI)

Street address 1: 211 Dupont Ave
Street address city: Newburgh
Street address state: NY
Zip/Postal code: 12550-4019
Country: USA
Mailing address: PO Box 3138
Mailing city: Newburgh
Mailing state: NY
Mailing zip: 12550-0651
General Phone: (845) 562-7066
General Fax: (845) 562-2543
General/National Adv. E-mail: sales@gtilite.com
Primary Website: www.gtilite.com
Mthly Avg Unique Visitors: 1975
Industry: Art & Layout Equipment and Services; Color Viewing Equipment; Layout Tables, Light Tables & Workstations; Lighting Equipment; Press Accessories, Parts & Supplies;
Personnel: Frederic McCurdy (Pres.); Robert McCurdy (Vice Pres., Sales/Mktg.); Linda Sutherland (Sales/Mktg Coord.)

GRAPHICS MICROSYSTEMS, INC.

Street address 1: 1655 Science Pl
Street address city: Rockwall
Street address state: TX
Zip/Postal code: 75032-6202
Country: USA
Mailing address: 1655 Science Pl
Mailing city: Rockwall
Mailing state: TX
Mailing zip: 75032-6202
General Phone: (972) 290-3120
General Fax: (972) 722-1128
General/National Adv. E-mail: avt@avt-inc.com
Primary Website: www.avt-inc.com
Mthly Avg Unique Visitors: 1983
Industry: Color Registration; Controls: Register; Densitometers; Ink Controls, Computerized; Press Control Systems;
Personnel: Bill Fleck (Southern Regional Sales Mgr.)

GREAT SOUTHERN CORP. (SIRCO DIV.)

Street address 1: PO Box 18710
Street address city: Memphis
Street address state: TN
Zip/Postal code: 38181-0710
Country: USA
Mailing address: PO Box 18710
Mailing city: Memphis
Mailing state: TN
Mailing zip: 38181-0710
General Phone: (901) 365-1611
General Fax: (901) 365-4498
General/National Adv. E-mail: sales@gsmemphis.com
Primary Website: www.gsmemphis.com
Mthly Avg Unique Visitors: 1961
Industry: Circulation Equipment & Supplies; Newspaper Bags;
Personnel: Scott Vaught (Pres.)

GRIMES, MCGOVERN & ASSOCIATES

Street address 1: 10 W 15th St
Street address 2: Ste 903
Street address city: New York
Street address state: NY
Zip/Postal code: 10011-6823
County: New York
Country: USA
Mailing address: 10 West 15th Street
Mailing city: New York City
Mailing state: NY
Mailing zip: 10011
General Phone: (917) 881-6563
General/National Adv. E-mail: lgrimes@mediamergers.com
Primary Website: www.mediamergers.com
Mthly Avg Unique Visitors: 1959
Industry: Brokers & Appraisers; Consulting Services: Advertising; Consulting Services: Financial; Consulting Services: Human Resources; Consulting Services: Marketing;
Note: Over 1,600 newspapers sold. Thousands Appraised. Regional Offices nationwide.
Personnel: Julie Bergman (V.P., Head of Newspaper Division); John Szefc (Senior Associate-Northeast/New England); David Slavin (Senior Associate- Southeast/South); John McGovern (Owner, CEO); Lewis Floyd (Senior Associate-Southern States); Gary Borders (Sr. Assoc.-SW/Plains); Gord Carley (Sr. Assoc.-CANADA-Mag. & Newspapers); Joe Bella (Sr. Advisor-Newspapers); Ken Amundson (Sr. Assoc.-Western/Mtn. States); Ken Blum (Senior Associate-Sales Nationwide)

GSP, INC.

Street address 1: 78 Airport Rd
Street address city: Westerly
Street address state: RI
Zip/Postal code: 02891-3402
Country: USA
Mailing address: PO Box 2358
Mailing city: Westerly
Mailing state: RI
Mailing zip: 02891-0922
General Phone: (401) 348-0210
General Fax: (401) 348-0689
General/National Adv. E-mail: gspmystic@gsptoday.com
Primary Website: www.gsptoday.com
Mthly Avg Unique Visitors: 1987
Industry: Presses: Offset; Web Press - Special Equipment; Labeling Equipment
Personnel: Jens E. Ljungberg (Pres.); Maurice Blanchet (Vice Pres.); Mary Ponte (Controller)

H & M PASTER SALES & SERVICE, INC.

Street address 1: 21828 87th Ave SE
Street address city: North Chesterfield
Street address state: VA
Zip/Postal code: 23236
Country: USA
Mailing address: 21828 87th Ave SE
Mailing city: North Chesterfield
Mailing state: VA
Mailing zip: 23236
General Phone: 804-276-4668
Primary Website: www.hmrva.com
Mthly Avg Unique Visitors: 1991
Industry: Adhesives; Gluing Systems; Pasters; Web Press - Special Equipment;

H.R. SLATER CO., INC.

Street address 1: 2050 W 18th St
Street address city: Chicago
Street address state: IL
Zip/Postal code: 60608-1816
Country: USA
Mailing address: 2050 W 18th St
Mailing city: Chicago
Mailing state: IL
Mailing zip: 60608-1816
General Phone: (312) 666-1855
General Fax: (312) 666-1856
General/National Adv. E-mail: hrslatercompany@aol.com
Mthly Avg Unique Visitors: 1965
Industry: Delivery Equipment; Gauges, Measuring; Mailroom Systems & Equipment; Newsprint Handeling Equipment; Paper Handeling Equipment;
Personnel: Robert Kurzka (Pres.); William C. St. Hilaire (Office Mgr.)

HADRONICS

Street address 1: 4570 Steel Pl
Street address city: Cincinnati
Street address state: OH
Zip/Postal code: 45209-1133
County: Hamilton
Country: USA
Mailing address: 4570 Steel Pl.
Mailing city: Cincinnati

Mailing state: OH
Mailing zip: 45209
General Phone: (513) 321-9350
General Fax: (513) 321-9377
General/National Adv. E-mail: sales@hadronics.com
Primary Website: www.hadronics.com
Mthly Avg Unique Visitors: 1969
Industry: Copper Plating Drums; Cylinder Repair; Dampening Systems; Ink Fountains & Accessories; Roller Grinding Services; Rollers; Rollers: Dampening;
Personnel: Jeff McCarty (VP., Sales)

HALL CONTRACTING SERVICES, INC.

Street address 1: 33530 Pin Oak Pkwy.
Street address city: Avon Lake
Street address state: OH
Zip/Postal code: 44012
County: Lorain
Country: Avon Lake
Mailing address: 33530 Pin Oak Pkwy.
Mailing city: Avon Lake
Mailing state: OH
Mailing zip: 44012
General Phone: (440) 930-0050
General Fax: (440) 930-0025
General/National Adv. E-mail: hcs@hallcontractingservices.com
Primary Website: www.hallcontractingservices.com
Mthly Avg Unique Visitors: 1956
Industry: New Press controls;Equipment Dealer (Used); Erectors & Riggers; Press Engineers; Press Rebuilding; Press Repairs; Remanufactures Equipment; Web Width Change mods;
Personnel: Robert Bowers (CEO); Tom Julius (Vice President of Operations); Larry Wojcik (Director of Sales)

HAMILTON CIRCULATION SUPPLIES CO.

Street address 1: 3068 Hickory Rd.
Street address city: Homewood
Street address state: IL
Zip/Postal code: 60430
County: Cook
Country: USA
Mailing state: IL
General Phone: (708)829-3377
General/National Adv. E-mail: jbeaudry@hamiltoncirculation.com
Mthly Avg Unique Visitors: 1965
Industry: Adhesives; Circulation Equipment & Supplies; Delivery Equipment; Material Handling Equipment: Pallets & Palletizers; Newspaper Bags; Newspaper Dispensers (Mechanical/Electronic); Newspaper Marketing; Rack Display Cards; Software: Circulation; Tubes, Racks (Includes Racks: Motor Route Tubes); Strapping and Twine. Rubber Bands
Note: Main Products: Rubber Bands, Plastic Bags, Motor Route Tubes & Posts, Hot Dots, Single Copy & POP items. Plus Mailroom Supplies."
Personnel: Joseph M. Beaudry (Pres.); Thomas P. Hamilton (Vice Pres.); Susan Beaudry (Vice Pres.); Carrie Dolan (Administration)

HARLAND SIMON

Street address 1: 210 W 22nd St
Street address 2: Ste 138
Street address city: Oak Brook
Street address state: IL
Zip/Postal code: 60523-4061
Country: USA
Mailing address: 210 W 22nd St Ste 138
Mailing city: Oak Brook
Mailing state: IL
Mailing zip: 60523-4061
General Phone: (630) 572-7650
General Fax: (630) 572-7653
General/National Adv. E-mail: sales@harlandsimon.com
Primary Website: www.harlandsimon.com
Industry: Color Proofing; Drives & Controls; Ink Controls, Computerized; Mailroom Systems & Equipment; Inserting Equipment (Includes Stuffing Machines); Press Control Systems; Press Data Accumulators; Produciton Control Systems; Software: Pagination/Layout; Software: Press/Post Press; Software: Workflow Management/Tracking;
Personnel: John Staiano (Managing Director - Americas)

HARPER CORPORATION OF AMERICA

Street address 1: 11625 Steele Creek Rd
Street address city: Charlotte
Street address state: NC
Zip/Postal code: 28273-3731
Country: USA
Mailing address: PO Box 38490
Mailing city: Charlotte
Mailing state: NC
Mailing zip: 28278-1008
General Phone: 800-438-3111
General Fax: (704) 588-3819
General/National Adv. E-mail: customer@harperimage.com
Display Adv. E-mail: customer@harperimage.com
Primary Website: www.harperimage.com
Mthly Avg Unique Visitors: 1971
Industry: Anilox manufacturer
Personnel: Margaret Harper Kluttz (President); Lee Kluttz (VP of Operations); Alan Rogers (VP of Sales)

HARRIS CORP.

Street address 1: 1025 W Nasa Blvd
Street address city: Melbourne
Street address state: FL
Zip/Postal code: 32919-0002
Country: USA
Mailing address: 1025 W Nasa Blvd # A11-0
Mailing city: Melbourne
Mailing state: FL
Mailing zip: 32919-0001
General Phone: (321) 727-9100
Primary Website: www.harris.com
Mthly Avg Unique Visitors: 1895
Industry: Business Computers; Data Communication; Facsimilie/Fax Transmission Systems; Pagination Systems; Input & Editing Systems; Press Control Systems; Publishing Systems; Visual Display Terminals;
Personnel: Howard L. Lance (Pres./CEO/Chrmn.); Robert K. Henry (COO); Gary L. McArthur (Sr. Vice Pres./CFO); Pamela Padgett (Vice Pres., Investor Rel.); Charles J. Greene (Treasurer)

HART INDUSTRIES

Street address 1: 43 Doran St
Street address city: East Haven
Street address state: CT
Zip/Postal code: 06512-2212
Country: USA
Mailing address: 43 Doran St
Mailing city: East Haven
Mailing state: CT
Mailing zip: 06512-2212
General Phone: (203) 469-6344
General Fax: (203) 469-6592
General/National Adv. E-mail: steve@hartindus.com
Primary Website: www.hartindus.com
Mthly Avg Unique Visitors: 1984
Industry: Dark Room Equipment; Environmental Control Systems; Silver Recovery; Wastewater Treatment;
Personnel: Steve Mancuso (Pres.)

HEAT AND CONTROL, INC.

Street address 1: 21121 Cabot Blvd
Street address city: Hayward
Street address state: CA
Zip/Postal code: 94545-1132
Country: USA
Mailing address: 21121 Cabot Blvd
Mailing city: Hayward
Mailing state: CA
Mailing zip: 94545-1177
General Phone: 800-227-5980
General Fax: (510) 259-0600
General/National Adv. E-mail: info@heatandcontrol.com
Primary Website: www.heatandcontrol.com
Mthly Avg Unique Visitors: 1950
Industry: Counting, Stacking, Bundling Machines
Personnel: Andy Caridis (Chrmn./CEO); Tony Caridis (Pres.); Audrey Waidelich (Dir., Mktg.)

HEIDELBERG USA

Street address 1: 1000 Gutenberg Dr NW
Street address city: Kennesaw
Street address state: GA
Zip/Postal code: 30144-7028
County: Cobb
Country: USA
Mailing address: 1000 Gutenberg Dr
Mailing city: Kennesaw
Mailing state: GA
Mailing zip: 30144
General Phone: (800) 437-7388
General/National Adv. E-mail: info@heidelberg.com
Primary Website: www.heidelberg.com/us
Mthly Avg Unique Visitors: 1895
Industry: Manufacturing
Personnel: Felix Mueller (President, Heidelberg Americas)

HEIDELBERG USA, INC.

Street address 1: 1000 Gutenberg Dr NW
Street address city: Kennesaw
Street address state: GA
Zip/Postal code: 30144-7028
Country: USA
Mailing address: 1000 Gutenberg Dr NW
Mailing city: Kennesaw
Mailing state: GA
Mailing zip: 30144-7028
General Phone: (888) 472-9655
General/National Adv. E-mail: info@heidelberg.com
Primary Website: www.us.heidelberg.com
Mthly Avg Unique Visitors: 1850
Industry: Sheetfed offset presses; digital production presses; wide format inkjet; prepress software and CtP output systems; inkjet proofing systems; color managment; business and production managment software; cutters, stitchers, folders, binders, and other postpress package producing systems; all consumables including plates, inks, coating solutions, blanket washes, and much more.
Personnel: Susan Nofi (Sr. Vice Pres., HR/Gen. Counsel); Thomas Topp (Sr. Vice Pres., Finance); Harald Weimer (President); Andrew Rae (Sr. V.P. Equipment Marketing); Ulrich Koehler (Sr. V.P. Service)

HERCO GRAPHIC PRODUCTS

Street address 1: PO Box 369
Street address city: Wauconda
Street address state: IL
Zip/Postal code: 60084-0369
Country: USA
Mailing address: PO Box 369
Mailing city: Wauconda
Mailing state: IL
Mailing zip: 60084-0369
General Phone: (800) 235-5541
General Fax: (815) 578-9593
General/National Adv. E-mail: hercographics@aol.com
Primary Website: www.hercographics.com
Mthly Avg Unique Visitors: 1979
Industry: Roll Coverings; Rollers;
Personnel: Christine Polanzi (Dir. Sales)

HERMAN H. STICHT CO., INC.

Street address 1: 45 Main St
Street address 2: Ste 701
Street address city: Brooklyn
Street address state: NY
Zip/Postal code: 11201-1075
Country: USA
Mailing address: 45 Main St Ste 401
Mailing city: Brooklyn
Mailing state: NY
Mailing zip: 11201-1084
General Phone: (718) 852-7602
General Fax: (718) 852-7915
General/National Adv. E-mail: stichtco@aol.com
Primary Website: www.stichtco.com
Mthly Avg Unique Visitors: 1917
Industry: Static Eliminators
Personnel: Paul H. Plotkin (Pres.)

HEXAGON METROLOGY, INC.

Street address 1: 250 Circuit Dr
Street address city: North Kingstown
Street address state: RI
Zip/Postal code: 02852-7441
Country: USA
Mailing address: 250 Circuit Dr
Mailing city: North Kingstown
Mailing state: RI
Mailing zip: 02852-7441
General Phone: (401) 886-2000
General Fax: (401) 886-2727
Primary Website: www.hexagonmetrology.com
Mthly Avg Unique Visitors: 1833
Industry: Gauges, Measuring
Personnel: William Fetter (Adv. Mgr.)

HFW INDUSTRIES

Street address 1: 196 Philadelphia St
Street address city: Buffalo
Street address state: NY
Zip/Postal code: 14207-1734
Country: USA
Mailing address: PO Box 8
Mailing city: Buffalo
Mailing state: NY
Mailing zip: 14207-0008
General Phone: (716) 875-3380
General Fax: (716) 875-3385
Primary Website: www.hfwindustries.com
Mthly Avg Unique Visitors: 1940
Industry: Cylinder reconditioning
Personnel: John Watson (Pres.); Ron Jurewicz (Manufacturing Manager)

HONEYWELL, INC.

Street address 1: 101 Columbia Rd
Street address city: Morristown
Street address state: NJ
Zip/Postal code: 07960-4640
Country: USA
Mailing address: 101 Columbia Rd
Mailing city: Morristown
Mailing state: NJ
Mailing zip: 07960-4658
General Phone: (973) 455-2000
General Fax: (973) 455-4002
General/National Adv. E-mail: lois.sills@honeywell.com
Primary Website: www.honeywell.com
Industry: Fire Protection; Humidifiers; Press Control Systems;
Personnel: Dave Cote (CEO)

HORIZONS, INC.

Street address 1: 18531 S Miles Rd
Street address city: Cleveland
Street address state: OH
Zip/Postal code: 44128-4237
Country: USA
Mailing address: 18531 S Miles Rd
Mailing city: Cleveland
Mailing state: OH
Mailing zip: 44128-4237
General Phone: 1.800.482.7758
General/National Adv. E-mail: info@horizonsisg.com
Primary Website: www.horizonsisg.com
Mthly Avg Unique Visitors: 1960
Industry: Adhesives; Chemicals: Photographic; Input & Editing Systems; Label Printing Machines;
Personnel: Herb Wainer (Pres.); Wayne Duignan (Vice Pres., Mktg.)

HOWTEK

Street address 1: 98 Spit Brook Rd
Street address 2: Ste 100
Street address city: Nashua
Street address state: NH
Zip/Postal code: 03062-5737
Country: USA
Mailing address: 98 Spit Brook Rd Ste 100
Mailing city: Nashua
Mailing state: NH
Mailing zip: 03062-5737
General Phone: 866-280-2239
General Fax: 937-431-1465
General/National Adv. E-mail: sales@icadmed.com
Primary Website: www.icadmed.com
Mthly Avg Unique Visitors: 1984
Industry: Color Seperation Scanners

Personnel: Ken Ferry (Pres.)

HP INC.

Street address 1: 1501 Page Mill Road
Street address city: Palo Alto
Street address state: CA
Zip/Postal code: 94304-1112
Country: USA
Mailing address: 1501 Page Mill Road
Mailing city: Palo Alto
Mailing state: CA
Mailing zip: 94304-1112
General Phone: (650) 857-1501
General/National Adv. E-mail: hp-leads@hp.com
Primary Website: www8.hp.com
Mthly Avg Unique Visitors: 1939
Industry: Personal computers; Printers; 3D Printers; Inks; Scanners; Copiers; Displays;
Personnel: Dion Weisler (Pres./CEO); Steve Fieler (CFO); Alex Cho (Pres., Personal Systems); Enrique Lores (Pres., Imaging & Printing); Christoph Schell (Pres., 3D Printing & Digital Manufacturing); Tracy Keogh (CHRO); Vikrant Batra (Chief Marketing Officer)

HUDSON-SHARP

Street address 1: 975 Lombardi Ave
Street address city: Green Bay
Street address state: WI
Zip/Postal code: 54304-3735
Country: USA
Mailing address: 975 Lombardi Ave
Mailing city: Green Bay
Mailing state: WI
Mailing zip: 54304-3735
General Phone: (920) 494-4571
General/National Adv. E-mail: sales@hudsonsharp.com
Primary Website: www.hudsonsharp.com
Mthly Avg Unique Visitors: 1978
Industry: Automatic Plastic Bagging Equipment
Personnel: Rod Drummond (CEO)

IAC ACOUSTICS

Street address 1: 401 Airport Rd
Street address city: North Aurora
Street address state: IL
Zip/Postal code: 60542-1818
Country: USA
Mailing address: 401 Airport Rd
Mailing city: North Aurora
Mailing state: IL
Mailing zip: 60542-1818
General Phone: (800) 954-1998
General Fax: (630) 966-9710
General/National Adv. E-mail: sales@industrialnoisecontrol.com
Primary Website: www.industrialnoisecontrol.com
Mthly Avg Unique Visitors: 1971
Industry: Architects/Engineers (Includes Design/Construction Firms); Noise Control;
Personnel: Dana Cullum (Pres.)

ICANON ASSOCIATES, INC.

Street address 1: 2321 N Penn Rd
Street address 2: Suite C
Street address city: Hatfield
Street address state: PA
Zip/Postal code: 19440-1972
Country: USA
Mailing address: 2321 N Penn Rd Ste C
Mailing city: Hatfield
Mailing state: PA
Mailing zip: 19440-1972
General Phone: (800) 544-4450
General/National Adv. E-mail: sales@icanon.com
Primary Website: www.newzware.com
Mthly Avg Unique Visitors: 1990
Industry: Computers: Hardware & Software Integrator; Consulting Services: Computer; Consulting Services: Financial; Software: Advertising (Includes Display; Classified); Software: Business (Includes Administration/Accounting); Software: Circulation; Software: Editorial; Software: Pagination/Layout;
Personnel: Joe Lewinski (Pres.); Gary Markle (Dir., Mktg.); Mike Hanson (Engineering)

IDEAFISHER SYSTEMS, INC.

Street address 1: 5640 SE Riverside Way
Street address city: Vancouver
Street address state: WA
Zip/Postal code: 98661-7175
County: Clark
Country: USA
Mailing address: 5640 SE Riverside Way
Mailing city: Vancouver
Mailing state: WA
Mailing zip: 98661-7175
General Phone: 360-450-6888
General/National Adv. E-mail: info@ideafisher.com
Primary Website: www.ideafisher.com
Mthly Avg Unique Visitors: 1988
Industry: Software: Advertising (Includes Display; Classified)
Personnel: Marsh Fisher (CEO); Mark Effinger (CEO)

IGS KNIVES, INC.

Street address 1: 760 W Wallick Ln
Street address city: Red Lion
Street address state: PA
Zip/Postal code: 17356-8859
Country: USA
Mailing address: 760 W Wallick Ln
Mailing city: Red Lion
Mailing state: PA
Mailing zip: 17356-8859
General Phone: (888) 295-3747
General Fax: (717) 244-6529
General/National Adv. E-mail: info@igsknives.com
Primary Website: www.igsknives.com
Mthly Avg Unique Visitors: 1992
Industry: Web Press - Special Equipment
Personnel: Katie Howard (Corporate Sec)

IKS KLINGELNBERG GMBH

Street address 1: In der Fleute 18
Street address 2: 42897 Remscheid
Country: Germany
Mailing address: In der Fleute 18
Mailing city: 42897 Remscheid
General Phone: 2191 969-0
General Fax: 2191 969-111
General/National Adv. E-mail: info@interknife.com
Display Adv. E-mail: jraida@interknife.com
Primary Website: www.interknife.com
Mthly Avg Unique Visitors: 1863
Personnel: Thomas Meyer (Pres./CEO)

ILLINOIS TOOL WORKS INC.

Street address 1: 155 Harlem Avenue
Street address city: Glenview
Street address state: IL
Zip/Postal code: 60025
Country: USA
Mailing address: 155 Harlem Avenue
Mailing city: Glenview
Mailing state: IL
Mailing zip: 60025
General Phone: (224) 661-8870
Primary Website: www.itw.com
Mthly Avg Unique Visitors: 1912
Industry: Strapping Machines
Personnel: E. Scott Santi (Chairman & CEO); Michael M. Larsen (Vice Pres. & CFO); Norman D. Finch Jr. (Senior Vice President, General Counsel & Secretary)

I-MANY, INC.

Street address 1: 1735 Market St
Street address city: Philadelphia
Street address state: PA
Zip/Postal code: 19103-7501
Country: USA
Mailing address: 1735 Market St Ste 3700
Mailing city: Philadelphia
Mailing state: PA
Mailing zip: 19103-7527
General Phone: (800) 832-0228
General/National Adv. E-mail: info@imany.com
Primary Website: www.imany.com
Industry: Consulting Services: Financial
Personnel: John A. Rade (Pres./CEO)

IMAPRO CORP.

Street address 1: 85 Pond St
Street address city: Rockcliffe
Street address state: ON
Zip/Postal code: K1L 8J1
Country: Canada
Mailing address: 400 St. Laurent Blvd
Mailing city: Ottawa
Mailing state: ON
Mailing zip: K1G 6C4
General Phone: (613) 738-3000
General Fax: (613) 738-5038
General/National Adv. E-mail: sales@imapro.com
Primary Website: www.imapro.com
Mthly Avg Unique Visitors: 1976
Industry: Computers: Hardware & Software Integrators; Computers: Local Area Network (LANS); Disk Drive Sales/Repair; Dryers: Film and Papers; Software: Pagination/Layout;
Personnel: Fred Andreone (Pres.)

IMC AMERICA

Street address 1: 1285 W King St
Street address city: York
Street address state: PA
Zip/Postal code: 17404-3409
Country: USA
Mailing address: PO Box 2771
Mailing city: York
Mailing state: PA
Mailing zip: 17405-2771
General Phone: (717) 845-4807
General Fax: (717) 845-8828
General/National Adv. E-mail: sales@imcamerica.com
Primary Website: www.imcamerica.com
Mthly Avg Unique Visitors: 1983
Industry: Newsprint Handeling Equipment; Paper Handeling Equipment; Roll Handeling Equipment;
Personnel: Ward Walsh (Pres.); Ric Mayle (Vice Pres., Sales./Mktg.)

IMC AMERICA

Street address 1: 1285 W King St
Street address city: York
Street address state: PA
Zip/Postal code: 17404-3409
Country: USA
Mailing address: 1285 W King St
Mailing city: York
Mailing state: PA
Mailing zip: 17404-3409
General Phone: (717) 845-4807
General Fax: (717) 845-8828
General/National Adv. E-mail: imcsales@imcamerica.com
Primary Website: www.imcamerica.com
Mthly Avg Unique Visitors: 1981
Industry: Blanket Cleaner/Washer (Automatic); Conveyors; Counting, Stacking, Bundling Machines; Cutters & Trimmers; In-Line Trimming Systems; Material Handling Equipment: Automatic Guided Vehicles; Material Handling Equipment: Palletizing Machines; Paper Handling Equipment; Roll Handling Equipment;
Personnel: Ward Walsh (Pres.); Ric Mayle (Vice Pres., Mktg./Sales)

IMPACT RACKS, INC.

Street address 1: 12 Wheatland Dr
Street address city: Mechanicsburg
Street address state: PA
Zip/Postal code: 17050-1600
County: Cumberland
Country: USA
Mailing address: 12 Wheatland Dr.
Mailing city: Mechanicsburg
Mailing state: PA
Mailing zip: 17050
General Phone: (717) 200-1213
General/National Adv. E-mail: impactracks@aol.com
Display Adv. E-mail: impactracks@aol.com
Mthly Avg Unique Visitors: 1995
Industry: Circulation Equipment & Supplies; Newspaper Dispensers (Mechanical/Electronic); Remanufactures Equipment; Strapping Machines; Tubes, Racks (Includes Racks: Motor Route Tubes);
Personnel: John Knowles (Pres.); Stefan Knowles (VP)

IMSI

Street address 1: 25 Leveroni Ct
Street address city: Novato
Street address state: CA
Zip/Postal code: 94949-5726
Country: USA
Mailing address: 25 Leveroni Ct Ste B
Mailing city: Novato
Mailing state: CA
Mailing zip: 94949-5726
General Phone: 415-483-8000
General Fax: 415-884-9023
General/National Adv. E-mail: sales@imsisoft.com
Primary Website: www.imsidesign.com
Mthly Avg Unique Visitors: 1985
Industry: Software: Design/Graphics; Software: Electronic Data Interchange; Software: Pagination/Layout;
Personnel: Royal Farros (Chrmn./CEO); Robert Mayer (COO)

INDUSTRIAL ACOUSTICS CO.

Street address 1: 1160 Commerce Ave
Street address city: Bronx
Street address state: NY
Zip/Postal code: 10462-5537
Country: USA
Mailing address: 1160 Commerce Ave
Mailing city: Bronx
Mailing state: NY
Mailing zip: 10462-5537
General Phone: (718) 931-8000
General Fax: (718) 863-1138
General/National Adv. E-mail: newyork@iac-acoustics.com
Primary Website: www.industrialacoustics.com
Mthly Avg Unique Visitors: 1949
Industry: Environmental Control Systems
Personnel: Kenneth Delasho (Pres.)

INFORMATICA DALAI SA DE CV

Street address 1: Prolongacion A. Reyes 4508, Col. Villa del Rio
Street address city: Monterrey
County: Nuevo Leon
Country: Mexico
Mailing address: Prolongacion A. Reyes 4508, Col. Villa del Rio
Mailing city: Monterrey
Mailing zip: 64850
General Phone: +52 81 365-4077
General Fax: +52 81 365-5990
Primary Website: www.dalai.com
Mthly Avg Unique Visitors: 1990
Industry: Pagination Systems; Software: Advertising (Includes Display; Classified); Software: Asset Management; Software: Editorial;
Personnel: Gerardo Trevino (Devel. Mgr.); Juan Lauro Aguirre (Mng. Dir.); David Valdez (Adv. Mgr.)

INGERSOLL-RAND-ARO FLUID PRODUCT DIV.

Street address 1: 1 Aro Ctr
Street address city: Bryan
Street address state: OH
Zip/Postal code: 43506-1100
Country: USA
Mailing address: PO Box 151
Mailing city: Bryan
Mailing state: OH
Mailing zip: 43506-0151
General Phone: (419) 636-4242
General Fax: (419) 633-1674
General/National Adv. E-mail: arowebleads@irco.com
Primary Website: www.ingersollrandproducts.com
Mthly Avg Unique Visitors: 1930
Industry: Ink Bleeding Equipment; Ink Pumping Systems; Pumps (Air, Ink, Vacuum);
Personnel: Herbert L. Henkel (Chrmn./Pres.)

INNOTEK CORPORATION

Street address 1: 9140 Zachary Ln N
Street address city: Maple Grove
Street address state: MN
Zip/Postal code: 55369-4003
County: Hennepin
Country: USA
Mailing address: 9140 Zachary Ln N
Mailing city: Maple Grove
Mailing state: MN
Mailing zip: 55369-4003
General Phone: (763) 488 9902
General Fax: (763)488 9904

General/National Adv. E-mail: sales@innotek-ep.com
Display Adv. E-mail: www.innotek-ep.com
Primary Website: www.innotek-ep.com
Mthly Avg Unique Visitors: 1960
Industry: Hydraulic & Pneumatic components and systems. Electronic systems / UL panel shop. Power Units / Test cells. contract manufacturing / machine shop/ hydraulic service and repair. Hydraulic hose assemblies.
Personnel: Dennis Burns (CEO Chairman); David Kalina (Vice Pres., Finance); Tom Wiese (Vice President of Sales & Engineering)

INNOVATIVE SYSTEMS DESIGN, INC.

Street address 1: 222 Brunswick Blvd
Street address city: Pointe-Claire
Street address state: QC
Zip/Postal code: H9R 1A6
Country: Canada
Mailing address: 222 Brunswick Blvd.
Mailing city: Pointe-Claire
Mailing state: QC
Mailing zip: H9R 1A6
General Phone: (514) 459-0200
General Fax: (514) 459-0300
General/National Adv. E-mail: sales@isd.ca
Display Adv. E-mail: sales@isd.ca
Primary Website: www.isd.ca
Mthly Avg Unique Visitors: 1983
Industry: Telecommunications
Product or Service: Telecommunications/Service Bureaus
Personnel: Jeff Tierney (Pres.); Rob Dumas (Director of Sales and Marketing); Monica Steibelt (Sales Coord.)

INSERT EAST, INC.

Street address 1: 7045 Central Hwy
Street address city: Pennsauken
Street address state: NJ
Zip/Postal code: 08109-4312
Country: USA
Mailing address: 7045 Central Hwy
Mailing city: Pennsauken
Mailing state: NJ
Mailing zip: 08109-4312
General Phone: (856) 663-8181
General Fax: (856) 663-3288
Primary Website: www.insertseast.com
Mthly Avg Unique Visitors: 1996
Industry: Circulation Equipment & Supplies
Personnel: Gino Maiale (Owner); Nick Maiale (Pres.); Frank Oliveti (Plant Mgr.)

INSURANCE SPECIALTIES SERVICES, INC.

Street address 1: 946 Town Ctr
Street address city: New Britain
Street address state: PA
Zip/Postal code: 18901-5182
Country: USA
Mailing address: 946 Town Ctr
Mailing city: New Britain
Mailing state: PA
Mailing zip: 18901-5182
General Phone: 800-533-4579
General Fax: 215-918-0507
General/National Adv. E-mail: info@issisvs.com
Primary Website: www.issisvs.com
Mthly Avg Unique Visitors: 1987
Industry: Insurance
Note: An Insurance Brokerage Firm Specializing In Liability Insurance Coverage For All Types of Media
Personnel: Kenneth P. Smith (Pres.); Kathy Liney (Sales)

INTERACTIVE DATA REAL-TIME SERVICES, INC.

Street address 1: 32 Crosby Dr
Street address city: Bedford
Street address state: MA
Zip/Postal code: 01730-1448
Country: USA
Mailing address: 32 Crosby Dr
Mailing city: Bedford
Mailing state: MA
Mailing zip: 01730-1448
General Phone: 781-687-8500
General Fax: 781-687-8005
General/National Adv. E-mail: sales.us@interactivedata.com
Primary Website: www.interactivedata-rts.com
Industry: Consulting Services: Financial
Personnel: Mark Hopsworth (Pres.); Azriane Carnan (Mktg. Mgr.)

INTERCONTINENTAL ENGINEERING CO.

Street address 1: 25944 Northline Rd
Street address city: Taylor
Street address state: MI
Zip/Postal code: 48180-4413
Country: USA
Mailing address: 25944 Northline Rd
Mailing city: Taylor
Mailing state: MI
Mailing zip: 48180-4413
General Phone: (734) 946-9931
General Fax: (734) 946-9992
Industry: Presses: Offset
Personnel: Michael Schwartz (Pres.); Somendra Khosla (Dir.)

INTERLINK

Street address 1: 9046 US Highway 31
Street address 2: Ste 7
Street address city: Berrien Springs
Street address state: MI
Zip/Postal code: 49103-1698
County: Berrien
Country: USA
Mailing address: PO Box 207
Mailing city: Berrien Springs
Mailing state: MI
Mailing zip: 49103-0207
General Phone: (269) 473-3103
General Fax: (206) 984-2240
General/National Adv. E-mail: info@ilsw.com
Display Adv. E-mail: sales@ilsw.com
Primary Website: www.ilsw.com
Mthly Avg Unique Visitors: 1980
Industry: Software: Circulation Management. Software: Advertising Billing (Includes Display; Classified)
Note: Circulation-management software provider for community newspapers.
Personnel: William E. Garber (Founder); Bradley Hill (President)

INTERNATIONAL IMAGING MATERIALS, INC.

Street address 1: 310 Commerce Drive
Street address city: Amherst
Street address state: NY
Zip/Postal code: 14228
Country: USA
Mailing address: 310 Commerce Drive
Mailing city: Amherst
Mailing state: NY
Mailing zip: 14228
General Phone: (716) 691-6333
General Fax: (888) 329-0260
General/National Adv. E-mail: salesinfo@iimak.com
Primary Website: www.iimak.com
Mthly Avg Unique Visitors: 1983
Industry: Inks
Personnel: Douglas C. Wagner (Pres./CEO); Joseph G. Perna (CFO); Susan Stamp (Sr. VP, HR and Admin.); Jose Morlin (VP, Sales and Marketing)

INTERNATIONAL TRADEMARK ASSOCIATION

Street address 1: 655 3rd Ave
Street address 2: Fl 10
Street address city: New York
Street address state: NY
Zip/Postal code: 10017-5646
Country: USA
Mailing address: 655 3rd Ave Fl 10
Mailing city: New York
Mailing state: NY
Mailing zip: 10017-5646
General Phone: (212) 642-1700
General Fax: (212) 768-7796
General/National Adv. E-mail: info@inta.org
Primary Website: www.inta.org
Mthly Avg Unique Visitors: 1878
Personnel: Alan Drewsen (Exec. Dir.); Devin Toporek

INTERSTATE DISTRIBUTOR CO.

Street address 1: 11707 21st Avenue Ct S
Street address city: Tacoma
Street address state: WA
Zip/Postal code: 98444-1236
Country: USA
Mailing address: 11707 21st Avenue Ct S
Mailing city: Tacoma
Mailing state: WA
Mailing zip: 98444-1236
General Phone: (253) 537-9455
General/National Adv. E-mail: web_info@intd.com
Primary Website: www.intd.com
Mthly Avg Unique Visitors: 1933
Personnel: George Payne (President & CEO); Gary McLean (Pres.); Dolores Fitzerald (Sec.); Peter M. Carlander (Sr. Vice Pres., Sales/Mktg.)

INTRALOX, LLC

Street address 1: 301 Plantation Rd
Street address city: Harahan
Street address state: LA
Zip/Postal code: 70123-5326
Country: USA
Mailing address: 301 Plantation Rd
Mailing city: Harahan
Mailing state: LA
Mailing zip: 70123-5326
General Phone: (504) 733-0463
General Fax: (504) 734-0063
Primary Website: www.intralox.com
Mthly Avg Unique Visitors: 1971
Industry: Conveyors
Personnel: Edel Blanks (Sales Mgr.)

INX INTERNATIONAL INK CO.

Street address 1: 150 N Martingale Rd
Street address 2: Ste 700
Street address city: Schaumburg
Street address state: IL
Zip/Postal code: 60173-2009
Country: USA
Mailing address: 150 N Martingale Rd Ste 700
Mailing city: Schaumburg
Mailing state: IL
Mailing zip: 60173-2009
General Phone: (630) 682-1800
General Fax: (847) 969-9758
General/National Adv. E-mail: general@inxinternational.com; info@inxintl.com
Primary Website: www.inxinternational.com
Mthly Avg Unique Visitors: 1990
Industry: Chemicals: Pressroom; Cleaners & Solvents; Consulting Services: Marketing; Ink Bleeding Equipment; Ink Fountains & Accessories; Ink Pumping Systems; Ink Storage Tanks; Inks;
Personnel: M. Matsuzawa (Chrmn.); Richard Clendenning (Pres./CEO); Joe Cichon (Sr. Vice Pres., Product/Mfg. Technology); John Carlson (Sr. Vice Pres.-Gen. Affairs/Admin.); Charles Weinholzer (Sr. Vice Pres.-Liquid Div.); Kenneth O'Callaghan (Sr. Vice Pres.-Metal Div.); George Polasik (Sr. Vice Pres.-Offset Div./COO); Betty Leavitt (Dir., PR)

IPC

Street address 1: 136 Bucks and Doe Lane
Street address city: La follette,
Street address state: TN
Zip/Postal code: 37766
County: Campbell
Country: USA
Mailing address: 136 Bucks and Doe Lane
Mailing city: La Follette
Mailing state: TN
Mailing zip: 37766
General Phone: 423-352-6078
General/National Adv. E-mail: charlie@ipcpoly.com
Primary Website: www.ipcpoly.com
Mthly Avg Unique Visitors: 1995
Industry: Newspaper Poly Bags, RACKS & Supplies, Single Copy Items, PROMOTIONAL ITEMS, Twine, Rubber Bands, Business Cards
Note: GREAT PROMOTIONAL items and TUMBLERS FOR FUNDRAISING AND GIFTS, give aways
Personnel: Charlie Hencye (Pres.); Cheryl Hencye (Asst. Mgr.)

ITW HOBART BROTHERS CO.

Street address 1: 400 Trade Sq E
Street address city: Troy
Street address state: OH
Zip/Postal code: 45373-2463
Country: USA
Mailing address: 400 Trade Sq E
Mailing city: Troy
Mailing state: OH
Mailing zip: 45373-2463
General Phone: (937) 332-4000
General Fax: (937) 332-5224
Primary Website: www.hobartbrothers.com
Mthly Avg Unique Visitors: 1917
Industry: Motors
Personnel: Dean Phillips (Welding Equip. Mgr.); Debbie Doench (Adv./Commun. Mgr.)

J. THOMAS MCHUGH CO., INC.

Street address 1: 12931 Ford Dr
Street address city: Fishers
Street address state: IN
Zip/Postal code: 46038-2899
Country: USA
Mailing address: 12931 Ford Dr
Mailing city: Fishers
Mailing state: IN
Mailing zip: 46038-2899
General Phone: (317) 577-2121
General Fax: (317) 577-2125
General/National Adv. E-mail: tbryant@jtmchugh.com
Primary Website: www.jtmchugh.com
Mthly Avg Unique Visitors: 1933
Industry: Blanket Mounting and Bars; Blankets; Offset Blanket Thickness Gauge; Offset Blankets, Blanket Wash;
Personnel: Thomas J. Bryant (Owner/CEO)

JARDIS INDUSTRIES INC.

Street address 1: 1201 Ardmore Ave
Street address city: Itasca
Street address state: IL
Zip/Postal code: 60143-1187
Country: USA
Mailing address: 1201 Ardmore Ave
Mailing city: Itasca
Mailing state: IL
Mailing zip: 60143-1187
General Phone: (630) 860-5959
General Fax: (630) 860-6515
General/National Adv. E-mail: info@jardis.com
Display Adv. E-mail: sales@jardis.com
Primary Website: www.jardis.com
Mthly Avg Unique Visitors: 1986
Industry: Architects/Engineers (Includes Design/Construction Firms); Consulting Services: Equipment; Ink Pumping Systems; Pasters; Press Accessories, Parts & Supplies; Pumps (Air, Ink, Vacuum); Remanufactures Equipment; Splicers, Automatic; Tension & Web Controls; Web Press - Special Equipment;
Personnel: Allan Jardis (Pres.); Gary Klawinski (Mgr.)

JARDIS INDUSTRIES, INC.

Street address 1: 1201 Ardmore Ave
Street address city: Itasca
Street address state: IL
Zip/Postal code: 60143-1187
Country: USA
Mailing address: 1201 Ardmore Ave
Mailing city: Itasca
Mailing state: IL
Mailing zip: 60143-1187
General Phone: (630) 860-5959
General Fax: (630) 860-6515
General/National Adv. E-mail: info@jardis.com
Primary Website: www.jardis.com
Mthly Avg Unique Visitors: 1986
Industry: Film and Papers; Drying Systems; Festoon Splicers; Flying Pasters; Constant tension Infeeds; Web guides;Plow folders; Angle Bar arrangemdnts ; Custom designed web handling Equipment;Offset and Flexographic printing press for newspaper, commercial , book and packaging applications

Personnel: Alan W. Jardis (Pres.); Adam Jardis (Gen. Mgr.)

JBT CORPORATION (FORMERLY FMC TECHNOLOGIES)

Street address 1: 400 Highpoint Dr
Street address city: Chalfont
Street address state: PA
Zip/Postal code: 18914-3924
Country: USA
Mailing address: 400 Highpoint Dr
Mailing city: Chalfont
Mailing state: PA
Mailing zip: 18914-3924
General Phone: (215) 822-4600
General Fax: (215) 822-4553
General/National Adv. E-mail: sgv.sales@jbtc.com
Primary Website: www.jbtc-agv.com
Mthly Avg Unique Visitors: 1920
Industry: Material Handling Equipment: Automatic Guided Vehicles; Newsprint Handling Equipment; Paper Handling Equipment; Roll Handling Equipment; Roll Preparation Equipment; Software: Workflow Management/Tracking; System Integration Services;
Personnel: Mark Longacre (Mktg. Mgr.)

JERVIS B. WEBB CO.

Street address 1: 34375 W 12 Mile Rd
Street address city: Farmington Hills
Street address state: MI
Zip/Postal code: 48331-3375
Country: USA
Mailing address: 34375 W 12 Mile Rd
Mailing city: Farmington Hills
Mailing state: MI
Mailing zip: 48331-5624
General Phone: (248) 553-1000
General/National Adv. E-mail: info@jerviswebb.com
Primary Website: www.daifukuna.com
Mthly Avg Unique Visitors: 1919
Industry: Computers: Hardware & Software Integrators; Consulting Services: Equipment; Conveyors; Mailroom Systems & Equipment; Material Handling Equipment: Automatic Guided Vehicles; Material Handling Equipment: Vehicle Loading; Newsprint Handeling Equipment; Paper Handeling Equipment; Roll Handeling Equipment; Storage Retrieval Systems;
Personnel: John S. Doychich (Sr. Vice Pres./CFO); Aki Nishimura (Daifuku North America Holding Company President and CEO)

JOHN JULIANO COMPUTER SERVICES CO.

Street address 1: 2152 Willivee Pl
Street address city: Decatur
Street address state: GA
Zip/Postal code: 30033-4114
County: DeKalb
Country: USA
Mailing address: 2152 Willive Pl.
Mailing city: Decatur
Mailing state: GA
Mailing zip: 30033
General Phone: (404) 327-6010
General Fax: (815) 301-8581
General/National Adv. E-mail: info@jjcs.com
Primary Website: www.jjcs.com
Mthly Avg Unique Visitors: 1982
Industry: Consulting Services: Computer; Consulting Services: Marketing;
Personnel: John Juliano (Pres.); L. Carol Christopher (Principal Analyst)

JOHNSTONE ENGINEERING & MACHINE CO.

Street address 1: PO Box 66
Street address city: Parkesburg
Street address state: PA
Zip/Postal code: 19365-0066
Country: USA
Mailing address: PO Box 66
Mailing city: Parkesburg
Mailing state: PA
Mailing zip: 19365-0066
General Phone: 610-593-6350
General Fax: 610-593-2172
General/National Adv. E-mail: jemco2@comcast.net
Mthly Avg Unique Visitors: 1940
Industry: Reels & Tensions; Reels (Inlcudes Paper Reels); Rewinders; Roll Handeling Equipment;
Personnel: Raymond E. Sullivan (Sales Mgr.); Bill Haag (President)

JUPITER IMAGES CORP.

Street address 1: 6000 N Forest Park Dr
Street address city: Peoria
Street address state: IL
Zip/Postal code: 61614-3556
County: Peoria
Country: USA
Mailing address: 6000 N Forest Park Dr
Mailing city: Peoria
Mailing state: IL
Mailing zip: 61614-3556
General Phone: (309) 688-8800
General Fax: (309) 688-3075
General/National Adv. E-mail: sales@jupiterimages.com
Primary Website: www.jupiterimages.com
Mthly Avg Unique Visitors: 1964
Industry: Software: Design/Graphics; Trade Publications;
Product or Service: Hardware/Software Supplier
Note: All-purpose art and idea service.
Personnel: Mark Nickerson (Vice Pres., Opns.)

JUST NORMLICHT, INC.

Street address 1: 2000 Cabot Blvd W
Street address 2: Ste 120
Street address city: Langhorne
Street address state: PA
Zip/Postal code: 19047-2408
Country: USA
Mailing address: 2000 Cabot Blvd W Ste 120
Mailing city: Langhorne
Mailing state: PA
Mailing zip: 19047-2408
General Phone: (267) 852-2200
General Fax: (267) 852-2207
General/National Adv. E-mail: sales@justnormlicht.com
Primary Website: www.justnormlicht.com
Mthly Avg Unique Visitors: 1985
Industry: Color Proofing; Color Viewing Equipment;
Personnel: Eric Dalton (Vice President)

K & M NEWSPAPER SERVICES, INC.

Street address 1: 45 Gilbert St Ext
Street address city: Monroe
Street address state: NY
Zip/Postal code: 10950-2815
Country: USA
Mailing address: 45 Gilbert St Ext
Mailing city: Monroe
Mailing state: NY
Mailing zip: 10950-2815
General Phone: (845) 782-3817
General Fax: (845) 783-2972
General/National Adv. E-mail: info@kmnewspaper.com
Primary Website: www.kmnewspaper.com
Industry: Belts, Belting, V-Belts; Controls: Photo Electric; Conveyors; Mailroom Systems & Equipment; Motors; Remanufactures Equipment;
Personnel: Mark Jacobs (Pres.); Micki Jacobs (Controller); Karla Hahan (Office Mgr.); Rick Walter (Vice Pres., Sales)

KAIM & ASSOCIATES INTERNATIONAL MARKETING, INC.

Street address 1: 102 Industrial Park Rd
Street address city: Lodi
Street address state: WI
Zip/Postal code: 53555-1374
Country: USA
Mailing address: 102 Industrial Park Rd
Mailing city: Lodi
Mailing state: WI
Mailing zip: 53555-1374
General Phone: (608) 592-7404
General Fax: (608) 592-7404
Mthly Avg Unique Visitors: 1988
Industry: Color Registration; Controls: Register; Paper Shredders; Pasters; Reels & Tensions; Roll Cleaning Equipment; Rollers; Tension & Web Controls; Web Break Detector; Web Cleaners;
Personnel: Wayne Kaim (Pres.)

KAMEN & CO. GROUP SERVICES

Street address 1: 626 Rxr Plz
Street address city: Uniondale
Street address state: NY
Zip/Postal code: 11556-0626
County: Nassau
Country: USA
Mailing address: 626 RXR Plz
Mailing city: Uniondale
Mailing state: NY
Mailing zip: 11556-0626
General Phone: (516) 379-2797
General Fax: (516) 379-3812
General/National Adv. E-mail: info@kamengroup.com
Primary Website: www.kamengroup.com
Mthly Avg Unique Visitors: 1981
Industry: Architects/Engineers (Includes Design/Construction Firms); Brokers & Appraisers; Circulation Equipment & Supplies; Consulting Services: Advertising; Consulting Services: Circulation; Consulting Services: Financial; Consulting Services: Human Resources; Consulting Services: Marketing; Training: Sales & Marketing; Tubes, Racks (Includes Racks: Motor Route Tubes);
Note: Media Appraisers, Accountants, Advisors & Brokers
Personnel: Kevin Brian Kamen (Pres./CEO); Celeste Myers (Vice Pres.)

KANALY TRUST CO.

Street address 1: 5555 San Felipe St
Street address 2: Ste 200
Street address city: Houston
Street address state: TX
Zip/Postal code: 77056-2760
Country: USA
Mailing address: 5555 San Felipe St Ste 200
Mailing city: Houston
Mailing state: TX
Mailing zip: 77056-2760
General Phone: (713)561-9300
General Fax: (713) 877-8744
General/National Adv. E-mail: kanaly@kanaly.com
Primary Website: www.kanaly.com
Industry: Consulting Services: Financial
Personnel: Drew Kanaly (Chairman/CEO)

KANSA TECHNOLOGY, LLC

Street address 1: 3700 Oakes Dr
Street address city: Emporia
Street address state: KS
Zip/Postal code: 66801-5132
County: Lyon
Country: USA
Mailing address: 3700 Oakes Dr
Mailing city: Emporia
Mailing state: KS
Mailing zip: 66801-5136
General Phone: (620) 343-6700
General Fax: (620) 343-2108
General/National Adv. E-mail: marketing@kansa.com
Primary Website: www.kansa.com
Mthly Avg Unique Visitors: 1977
Industry: Addressing Machines; Collating Equipment; Conveyors; Counting, Stacking, Bundling Machines; Feeding, Folding, Delivery Equipment; Folding Machines; Infeed Stackers; Inserting Equipment (Includes Stuffing Machines); Mailroom Systems & Equipment; Remanufactures Equipment;
Personnel: Jerry Waddell (CEO); Lonnie Worthington (Chief Operating Officer); Megan Kropff

KASPAR MANUFACTURING

Street address 1: 959 State Hwy 95 N
Street address city: Shiner
Street address state: TX
Zip/Postal code: 77984
Country: USA
Mailing address: 959 State Hwy 95 N
Mailing city: Shiner
Mailing state: TX
Mailing zip: 77984
General Phone: (361) 594.3327
General Fax: (361) 594.3311
General/National Adv. E-mail: info@kasparmfg.com
Primary Website: www.kasparmfg.com
Mthly Avg Unique Visitors: 1898
Industry: Circulation Equipment & Supplies; Cleaners & Solvents; Newspaper Dispensers (Mechanical/Electronic); Software: Circulation;
Personnel: Stephen Bindus (Director of Operations); Lori Hamilton (Director of Business & Brand Development); Ronnie Kresta (Supervisor of Quality Assurance); Dan Jalufka (Wire Forming Supervisor)

KBA NORTH AMERICA, INC. (KOENIG & BAUER AG)

Street address 1: 2555 Regent Blvd
Street address city: Dallas
Street address state: TX
Zip/Postal code: 75261
Country: USA
Mailing address: 2555 Regent Blvd
Mailing city: Dallas
Mailing state: TX
Mailing zip: 75261
General Phone: 469-532-8040
General Fax: 469-532-8190
General/National Adv. E-mail: na-marketing@kba,com
Primary Website: www.kba.com
Mthly Avg Unique Visitors: 1814
Industry: Flexogrpahic Press Conversion; Flying Pasters; Pasters; Presses: Flexographic; Presses: Offset; Reels & Tensions; Reels (Inlcudes Paper Reels); Tension & Web Controls;
Personnel: Mark Hischar (Pres./CEO); Eric Frank (Vice Pres., Mktg.); Ulrich Wicke (Vice-President of Sales & Service); Pernice Samuel (Executive Sales); Bruce Richardson (National Sales Manager); Schenker Winfried (Sales Director Web Presses); Denise Prewitt (Digital Sales and Marketing Specialist); Alex Stepanian (Regional Sales Dir.)

KEENE TECHNOLOGY, INC. (KTI)

Street address 1: 14357 Commercial Pkwy
Street address city: South Beloit
Street address state: IL
Zip/Postal code: 61080-2621
Country: USA
Mailing address: 14357 Commercial Pkwy
Mailing city: South Beloit
Mailing state: IL
Mailing zip: 61080-2621
General Phone: (815) 624-8989
General Fax: (815) 624-4223
General/National Adv. E-mail: info@keenetech.com
Primary Website: www.keenetech.com
Mthly Avg Unique Visitors: 1985
Industry: Rewinders; Splicers, Automatic;
Personnel: Kery Wallace (Office Mgr.)

KEISTER WILLIAMS NEWSPAPER SERVICES, INC.

Street address 1: 1807 Emmet St N
Street address 2: Ste 6B
Street address city: Charlottesville
Street address state: VA
Zip/Postal code: 22901-3616
Country: USA
Mailing address: PO Box 8187
Mailing city: Charlottesville
Mailing state: VA
Mailing zip: 22906-8187
General Phone: (434) 293-4709
General Fax: (434) 293-4884
General/National Adv. E-mail: ky@kwnews.com
Primary Website: www.kwnews.com
Mthly Avg Unique Visitors: 1973
Industry: Consulting Services: Advertising; Consulting Services: Marketing;
Personnel: Walton C. (Ky) Lindsay (Pres./Treasurer); Meta L. Nay (Vice Pres., Mktg.); Carol Lindsay (Admin.); Walton Lindsay (Pres.)

KEPES, INC.

Street address 1: 9016 58th Pl
Street address city: Kenosha
Street address state: WI
Zip/Postal code: 53144-7818
Country: USA
Mailing address: 9016 58th Pl Ste 600
Mailing city: Kenosha
Mailing state: WI
Mailing zip: 53144-7819
General Phone: (262) 652-7889

General Fax: (262) 652-7787
General/National Adv. E-mail: inquire@kepes.com
Primary Website: www.kepes.com
Industry: Equipment Dealers (Used); Feeding, Folding, Delivery Equipment; Gluing Systems; Remanufactures Equipment; Roll Handeling Equipment; Rollers;
Personnel: Wayne Pagel (Pres./Sales Mgr.); John Slanchik (Mktg. Mgr.)

KIDDE FIRE SYSTEMS

Street address 1: 400 Main Street
Street address city: Ashland
Street address state: MA
Zip/Postal code: 01721
Country: USA
Mailing address: 400 Main Street
Mailing city: Ashland
Mailing state: MA
Mailing zip: 01721
General Phone: (508) 881-2000
General Fax: (708) 748-2847
Primary Website: www.kidde-fenwal.com/Public/Kidde
Mthly Avg Unique Visitors: 1917
Industry: Architects/Engineers (Includes Design/ Construction Firms); Fire Protection; System Installations; System Integration Services; Telecommunications;
Personnel: Kelly Sanderson (West Coast Sales Director); Greg Lindsey (Northwest Sales); Ron Parker (Southwest Sales)

KIDDER, INC.

Street address 1: 270 Main St
Street address city: Agawam
Street address state: MA
Zip/Postal code: 01001-1838
Country: USA
Mailing address: 270 Main St
Mailing city: Agawam
Mailing state: MA
Mailing zip: 01001-1838
General Phone: (413) 786-8692
General Fax: (413) 786-8785
General/National Adv. E-mail: kidderpress@worldnet.att.net
Mthly Avg Unique Visitors: 1876
Industry: Dryers: Film and Papers; Ink Fountains & Accessories; Presses: Flexographic; Rewinders;
Personnel: Charles Rae (Pres.); Thomas K. Trant (CFO); John Rico (Vice Pres.-HR); Harris Barnard (Vice Pres.-Engineering); Cheryl N. Smith (Mktg. Mgr.)

KIMOTO TECH

Street address 1: 1701 Howard St
Street address 2: Ste G
Street address city: Elk Grove Village
Street address state: IL
Zip/Postal code: 60007-2479
Country: USA
Mailing address: 1701 Howard St Ste G
Mailing city: Elk Grove Village
Mailing state: IL
Mailing zip: 60007-2479
General Phone: (847) 640-8022
General Fax: (847) 640-7942
General/National Adv. E-mail: info@kimototech.com
Primary Website: www.kimototech.com
Mthly Avg Unique Visitors: 1980
Industry: Film & Paper: Filters (Photographic); Film & Paper: Phototypesetting;
Personnel: Alex Jasinowski (Sales Supvr.); Serina Vartanian (Kimosetter Support)

KINETIC CORPORATION

Street address 1: 200 Distillery Cmns
Street address 2: Ste 200
Street address city: Louisville
Street address state: KY
Zip/Postal code: 40206-1987
County: Jefferson
Country: USA
Mailing address: 200 Distillery Commons Ste 200
Mailing city: Louisville
Mailing state: KY
Mailing zip: 40206-1987
General Phone: (502) 719-9500
General Fax: (502) 719-9569
General/National Adv. E-mail: info@theTechnologyAgency.com
Primary Website: www.theTechnologyAgency.com
Mthly Avg Unique Visitors: 1979
Industry: Consulting Services: Production; Photo Archiving; Preprint Service & Production; Software: Asset Management; Software: Design/Graphics; Software: Pagination/Layout; Software: Workflow Management/Tracking;
Product or Service: Graphic/Design Firm
Personnel: G. Raymond Schuhmann (Pres.); Cindi Ramm (Chief Brand Strategist)

KIRK-RUDY, INC.

Street address 1: 125 Lorraine Pkwy
Street address city: Woodstock
Street address state: GA
Zip/Postal code: 30188-2487
Country: USA
Mailing address: 125 Lorraine Pkwy
Mailing city: Woodstock
Mailing state: GA
Mailing zip: 30188-2487
General Phone: (770) 427-4203
General Fax: (770) 427-4036
Primary Website: www.kirkrudy.com
Mthly Avg Unique Visitors: 1967
Industry: Addressing Machines; Inserting Equipment (Includes Stuffing Machines); Mailroom Systems & Equipment;
Personnel: Rick Marshal (Pres.)

K-JACK ENGINEERING CO., INC.

Street address 1: 1522 W 134th St
Street address city: Gardena
Street address state: CA
Zip/Postal code: 90249-2216
Country: USA
Mailing address: PO Box 2320
Mailing city: Gardena
Mailing state: CA
Mailing zip: 90247-0320
General Phone: (310) 327-8389
General Fax: (310) 769-6997
General/National Adv. E-mail: info@kjack.com
Primary Website: www.kjack.com
Mthly Avg Unique Visitors: 1963
Industry: Cart Distribution Systems; Circulation Equipment & Supplies; Delivery Equipment; Newspaper Dispensers (Mechanical/Electronic); Software: Circulation; Tubes, Racks (Includes Racks: Motor Route Tubes);
Personnel: Jack S. Chalabian (Pres.); Jacqueline Chalabian-Jernigan (Vice Pres.); Steven H. Chalabian (Vice Pres., Sales); Steve Ruitenschild (Engineer)

KODAK GCG

Street address 1: 401 Merritt 7
Street address city: Norwalk
Street address state: CT
Zip/Postal code: 06851-1000
Country: USA
Mailing address: 401 Merritt 7 Ste 22
Mailing city: Norwalk
Mailing state: CT
Mailing zip: 06851-1068
General Phone: (203) 845-7115
General Fax: (203) 845-7173
Primary Website: www.kodak.com
Mthly Avg Unique Visitors: 1935
Industry: Chemicals: Photographic; Chemicals: Plate Processing; Color Management Software; Color Proofing; Film & Paper: Contact; Film & Paper: Duplicating; Film & Paper: Filters (Photographic); Offset Plate-Making Service & Equipment; Plates: Offset (Computer to Plate); Plates: Offset (Conventional);
Personnel: Andrew Copley (Sr. Cor. Vice Pres.)

KOENIG & BAUER AKTIENGESELLSCHAFT (KBA)

Street address 1: Friedrich-Koenig-Str. 4
Street address city: Wuerzburg
Zip/Postal code: D 97080
Country: Germany
Mailing address: Postfach 6060
Mailing city: Wuerzburg
Mailing zip: D 97010
General Phone: +49 931 909 4336
General Fax: +49 931 909 6015
General/National Adv. E-mail: kba-wuerzburg@kba-print.de
Primary Website: www.kba-print.de
Mthly Avg Unique Visitors: 1817
Industry: Flexogrpahic Press Conversion; Flying Pasters; Press Control Systems; Presses: Flexographic; Presses: Offset; Presses: Rotogravure; Reels & Tensions; Roll Handeling Equipment; Roll Preparation Equipment; Web Press - Special Equipment;
Personnel: Helge Hansen (Pres.); Klaus Schmidt (Dir., Mktg.)

KOLBUS AMERICA, INC.

Street address 1: 812 Huron Rd E
Street address 2: Ste 750
Street address city: Cleveland
Street address state: OH
Zip/Postal code: 44115-1126
Country: USA
Mailing address: 812 Huron Rd E Ste 750
Mailing city: Cleveland
Mailing state: OH
Mailing zip: 44115-1126
General Phone: (216) 931-4940
General Fax: (216) 931-5101
General/National Adv. E-mail: robert.shafer@kolbus.com
Primary Website: www.kolbus.com
Mthly Avg Unique Visitors: 1960
Industry: Counting, Stacking, Bundling Machines; Cutters & Trimmers; Material Handling Equipment: Palletizing Machines;
Personnel: Ruth Wilson (Office Mgr.); Robert Shafer (Pres./Dir., Sales/Distr. Americas)

KOMORI AMERICA CORP.

Street address 1: 5520 Meadowbrook Industrial Ct
Street address city: Rolling Meadows
Street address state: IL
Zip/Postal code: 60008-3800
Country: USA
Mailing address: 5520 Meadowbrook Industrial Ct
Mailing city: Rolling Meadows
Mailing state: IL
Mailing zip: 60008-3898
General Phone: 847-806-9000
General/National Adv. E-mail: contact@komori-america.us
Primary Website: www.komori-america.us
Mthly Avg Unique Visitors: 1983
Industry: Presses: Offset; Proofing Systems;
Personnel: Kosh Miyao (Pres./COO, Komori America Cor.); Angelo Possemato (Director of National Accounts); Susan Baines (Director of Marketing); Clark Scherer (District Sales Manager)

KONICA MINOLTA BUSINESS SOLUTIONS USA INC.

Street address 1: 100 Williams Dr
Street address city: Ramsey
Street address state: NJ
Zip/Postal code: 07446-2907
County: Bergen
Country: USA
Mailing address: 100 Williams Dr
Mailing city: Ramsey
Mailing state: NJ
Mailing zip: 07446-2907
General Phone: (201) 825-4000
General/National Adv. E-mail: PR@kmbs.konicaminolta.us
Primary Website: 100 Williams Drive
Mthly Avg Unique Visitors: 1899
Industry: IT Services and Solutions and Technology
Personnel: Rick Taylor (Pres., CEO); Sam Errigo (Exec. VP, Sales and Business Development); Kay Du Fernandez (Senior VP, Marketing)

KUBRA

Street address 1: 5050 Tomken Rd
Street address city: Mississauga
Street address state: ON
Zip/Postal code: L4W 5B1
Country: Canada
Mailing address: 5050 Tomken Rd.
Mailing city: Mississauga
Mailing state: ON
Mailing zip: L4W 5B1
General Phone: (905) 624-2220
General Fax: (905) 624-2886
Primary Website: www.kubra.com
Personnel: Rick Watkin (Pres./CEO); Robert Iantorno (Vice Pres., Opns.); Rick Huff (Vice Pres., Sales/Mktg.); Mark Visic (Sr. Vice Pres., Bus. Devel.)

KYE SYSTEMS CORP

Street address 1: 12675 Colony Ct
Street address city: Chino
Street address state: CA
Zip/Postal code: 91710-2975
Country: USA
Mailing address: 12675 Colony Ct
Mailing city: Chino
Mailing state: CA
Mailing zip: 91710-2975
General Phone: 909) 628-8836
General/National Adv. E-mail: webmaster@geniusnet.com.tw
Primary Website: www.geniusnet.com
Mthly Avg Unique Visitors: 1986
Industry: PC products, mobile phone and Tablet PC, including mice, keyboards, graphics tablets, touch pen, power banks, webcams, speakers, headphones, microphones, sleeves, backpacks, and professional gaming gear, digital cameras, camcorders, vehicle recorders, and projectors.
Personnel: Geoffrey Lin (Pres.); Ken Chao

LASER PRODUCTS TECHNOLOGIES

Street address 1: 3936 Circle Dr
Street address city: Holmen
Street address state: WI
Zip/Postal code: 54636-9187
Country: USA
Mailing address: 3936 Circle Dr
Mailing city: Holmen
Mailing state: WI
Mailing zip: 54636-9187
General Phone: 800-999-9749
General/National Adv. E-mail: info@lptnow.com
Primary Website: www.lptnow.com
Industry: Laser Printers
Personnel: Michael Marty (Pres.); Bob King (Vice Pres.)

LATIN AMERICAN DIV./FLINT INK

Street address 1: 9100 S Dadeland Blvd
Street address 2: Ste 1800
Street address city: Miami
Street address state: FL
Zip/Postal code: 33156-7817
Country: USA
Mailing address: 9100 S Dadeland Blvd Ste 1800
Mailing city: Miami
Mailing state: FL
Mailing zip: 33156-7817
General Phone: (305) 670-0066
General Fax: (305) 670-0060
Primary Website: www.flintink.com
Mthly Avg Unique Visitors: 1983
Industry: Blankets; Chemicals: Plate Processing; Chemicals: Pressroom; Chemicals: Roller Cleaning; Ink Pumping Systems; Ink Recovery Systems; Inks; Plates: Offset (Conventional); Presses: Offset;
Personnel: Jerko E. Rendic (Pres.); Claudia Anderson (Bus. Mgr.); Paul Chmielewicz (Regl. Sales Mgr., Brazil); Fernando Tavara (Regl. Sales Mgr., South America); Nestor Porto (Regl. Sales Mgr., Central America/Caribbean); Al Miller (Technical Serv. Mgr.)

LAUTERBACH GROUP

Street address 1: W222 N5710 Miller Way
Street address city: Sussex
Street address state: WI
Zip/Postal code: 53089
Country: USA
Mailing address: W222 N5710 Miller Way
Mailing city: Sussex
Mailing state: WI
Mailing zip: 53089
General Phone: (262) 820-8130
General Fax: (262) 820-1806
General/National Adv. E-mail: info@lauterbachgroup.com
Primary Website: www.masclabels.com
Mthly Avg Unique Visitors: 1970
Industry: Label Printing Machines

Personnel: Shane Lauterbach (Chief Executive Officer, President and Director); Rebecca Kerschinske (Vice President of Sales); Derek Wilcox (Director of Marketing)

LAZER-FARE MEDIA SERVICES

Street address 1: PO Box 48114 RPO Lakewood
Street address city: Winnipeg
Street address state: MB
Zip/Postal code: R2J 4A3
Country: Canada
Mailing address: PO Box 48114 RPO Lakewood
Mailing city: Winnipeg
Mailing state: MB
Mailing zip: R2J 4A3
General Phone: (204) 452-5023
General Fax: (204) 272-3499
General/National Adv. E-mail: sales@lazerfare.com
Primary Website: www.lazerfare.com
Mthly Avg Unique Visitors: 1985
Industry: Archiving Systems; Consulting Services: Advertising; Consulting Services: Computer; Consulting Services: Editorial; Content and Digital Asset Management systems
Product or Service: Consultants`Hardware/Software Supplier
Personnel: Kelly Armstrong (Pres.)

LEARNING TREE INTERNATIONAL

Street address 1: 400 Continental Blvd
Street address 2: Ste 150
Street address city: El Segundo
Street address state: CA
Zip/Postal code: 90245-5059
Country: USA
Mailing address: 400 Continental Blvd Ste 150
Mailing city: El Segundo
Mailing state: CA
Mailing zip: 90245-5059
General Phone: (310) 417-9700
General Fax: (310) 410-2952
General/National Adv. E-mail: uscourses@learningtree.com
Primary Website: www.learningtree.com
Mthly Avg Unique Visitors: 1974
Industry: Training: Keyboard Operation
Personnel: David Collins (Chrmn.); Nicholas Schacht (Pres./CEO)

LEXISNEXIS

Street address 1: 555 W 5th St
Street address 2: Ste 4500
Street address city: Los Angeles
Street address state: CA
Zip/Postal code: 90013-3003
County: Los Angeles
Country: USA
Mailing address: 555 W 5th St Ste 4500
Mailing city: Los Angeles
Mailing state: CA
Mailing zip: 90013-3003
General Phone: (213) 627-1130
General/National Adv. E-mail: lexisnexiscommunities@lexisnexis.com
Primary Website: www.lexisnexis.com
Product or Service: Consultants
Personnel: Andrew Prozes (CEO, Lexis-Nexis Grp.); Kurt Sanford (Pres./CEO, Cor. & Fed. Mkts.); Michael Walsh (Pres./CEO, U.S. Legal Mkts.); James M. Peck (CEO, Risk Mgmt.); Richard Sobelsohn

LINCOLN INDUSTRIAL

Street address 1: 5148 N. Hanley Road
Street address city: Saint Louis
Street address state: MO
Zip/Postal code: 63134
Country: USA
Mailing address: 5148 N. Hanley Road
Mailing city: Saint Louis
Mailing state: MO
Mailing zip: 63134
General Phone: (314) 679-4200
General Fax: (314) 679-4359
Primary Website: www.lincolnindustrial.com
Mthly Avg Unique Visitors: 1910
Industry: Lubricants; Pumps (Air, Ink, Vacuum);
Personnel: Bart Aitken (Pres.)

LINDE LIFT TRUCK CORP.

Street address 1: 2450 W 5th North St
Street address city: Summerville
Street address state: SC
Zip/Postal code: 29483-9621
Country: USA
Mailing address: 2450 W 5th North St
Mailing city: Summerville
Mailing state: SC
Mailing zip: 29483-9621
General Phone: (843) 875-8000
General Fax: (843) 875-8362
Display Adv. E-mail: trucksales@lmh-na.com; trucksales@lindelifttruck.com
Primary Website: www.linde-mh.com
Mthly Avg Unique Visitors: 1853
Industry: Material Handling Equipment: Automatic Guided Vehicles; Material Handling Equipment: Truck Loaders; Material Handling Equipment: Vehicle Loading;
Personnel: Andreas Krinninger (CEO); Christophe Lautray (Chief Sales Officer)

LISSOM CORP. INC.

Street address 1: Pondfield Rd W
Street address city: Bronxville
Street address state: NY
Zip/Postal code: 10708
Country: USA
Mailing address: PO Box 441
Mailing city: Bronxville
Mailing state: NY
Mailing zip: 10708
General Phone: (914) 761-6360
General/National Adv. E-mail: hank@weboffsetpress.com
Primary Website: www.weboffsetpress.com
Mthly Avg Unique Visitors: 1981
Industry: Presses: Web Offset
Note: Web Offset Presses & Auxiliary Equipment
Personnel: Hank Damhuis

LITCO INTERNATIONAL, INC.

Street address 1: 1 Litco Dr
Street address city: Vienna
Street address state: OH
Zip/Postal code: 44473-9600
County: Trumbull
Country: USA
Mailing address: PO Box 150
Mailing city: Vienna
Mailing state: OH
Mailing zip: 44473
General Phone: 330-539-5433
General Fax: (330) 539-5388
General/National Adv. E-mail: info@litco.com
Display Adv. E-mail: info@litco.com
Primary Website: www.litco.com/molded-wood-pallets
Mthly Avg Unique Visitors: 1962
Industry: Material Handling Equipment: Pallets & Palletizers
Note: Litco offers Engineered Molded Wood Pallets. Pallets are clean and dry at 8% MC at the time of manufacture. Certified sustainable and USDA BioPreferred, Meets all export requirements of IPPC-ISPM15.
Personnel: Gary L. Trebilcock (President); Lionel F. Trebilcock (CEO); Gary A. Sharon (Executive Vice President)

LITHCO INC.

Street address 1: 9449 Jefferson Blvd
Street address city: Culver City
Street address state: CA
Zip/Postal code: 90232-2915
Country: USA
Mailing address: 9449 Jefferson Blvd
Mailing city: Culver City
Mailing state: CA
Mailing zip: 90232-2913
General Phone: (310) 559-7770
General/National Adv. E-mail: lithco@lithcoinc.com
Primary Website: www.lithcoinc.com
Mthly Avg Unique Visitors: 1946
Industry: Gauges, Measuring; Layout Tables, Light Tables & Workstations; Optical Products; Prepress Color Proofing Systems; Rules;
Personnel: Gerald Gaebel (Pres.); Sheila Martin (Office Mgr.); Jeff Simon (President)

LITHO RESEARCH, INC.

Street address 1: 1621 W Carroll Ave
Street address city: Chicago
Street address state: IL
Zip/Postal code: 60612-2501
Country: USA
Mailing address: 1621 W Carroll Ave
Mailing city: Chicago
Mailing state: IL
Mailing zip: 60612-2501
General Phone: (312) 738-0292
General Fax: (312) 738-2386
Mthly Avg Unique Visitors: 1985
Industry: Environmental Control Systems; Offset Blankets, Blanket Wash; Offset Chemicals & Supplies; Plate Cleaners; Roll Cleaning Equipment; Static Eliminators;
Personnel: Michael T. Miske (Pres.)

LOGETRONICS CORP.

Street address 1: 6521 Arlington Blvd
Street address 2: Ste 210
Street address city: Falls Church
Street address state: VA
Zip/Postal code: 22042-3009
Country: USA
Mailing address: 6521 Arlington Blvd Ste 210
Mailing city: Falls Church
Mailing state: VA
Mailing zip: 22042-3009
General Phone: (703) 536-9841
General Fax: (703) 912-7745
General/National Adv. E-mail: loge@starpower.net
Mthly Avg Unique Visitors: 1955
Industry: Film & Paper: Film Processing Machines; Film & Paper: Film Roll Dispensers; Plate Coating Machines; Plate Exposure Units; Plate Processors; Plate Scanning Systems; Processors: Diffusion Transfer; Processors: Film & Paper; Remanufactures Equipment;
Personnel: Raymond Luca (Pres.)

LONZA GROUP LTD.

Street address 1: 90 Boroline Road
Street address city: Allendale
Street address state: NJ
Zip/Postal code: 07401
Country: USA
Mailing address: 90 Boroline Road
Mailing city: Allendale
Mailing state: NJ
Mailing zip: 07401
General Phone: (201) 316-9200
General Fax: (201) 785-9973
General/National Adv. E-mail: allendale@lonza.com
Primary Website: www.lonza.com
Mthly Avg Unique Visitors: 1986
Industry: Acid Dispensing Systems; Chemicals: Plate Processing; Chemicals: Pressroom;
Personnel: Albert M. Baehny (Chairman); Richard Ridinger (CEO)

LORENTZEN & WETTRE

Street address 1: 305 Gregson Drive
Street address city: Cary
Street address state: NC
Zip/Postal code: 27511
Country: USA
Mailing address: 305 Gregson Drive
Mailing city: Cary
Mailing state: NC
Mailing zip: 27511
General Phone: 919 653 0840
General/National Adv. E-mail: contact.center@us.abb.com
Primary Website: www.lorentzen-wettre.com
Mthly Avg Unique Visitors: 1980
Industry: Consulting Services: Production; Maintenance, Plant & Equipment; Paper Testing Instruments;
Personnel: Phillip Westmoreland (Pres.)

LOUISIANA SHERIFF'S ASSOCIATION

Street address 1: 1175 Nicholson Drive
Street address city: Baton Rouge
Street address state: LA
Zip/Postal code: 70802
Country: USA
Mailing address: 1175 Nicholson Drive
Mailing city: Baton Rouge
Mailing state: LA
Mailing zip: 70802
General Phone: (225) 343-8402
General Fax: (225) 336-0343
Primary Website: www.lsa.org
Mthly Avg Unique Visitors: 1945
Industry: Art & Layout Equipment and Services; Consulting Services; Advertising; Editorial; Software: Design/Graphics; Software: Editorial: mobile
Product or Service: Consultants`Editorial`Graphic/Design Firm`Marketing`Other Services`Trade Association
Personnel: Michael Ranatza (Executive Director); Cynthia Butler (Office Manager); Lauren Labbe' Meher (Dir. of Comm. and Pub. Affairs); Darlene Petty (Accounting)

LYNNE MEENA CO.

Street address 1: 130 Saint Matthews Ave Ste 302
Street address 2: Advertising Federation
Street address city: Louisville
Street address state: KY
Zip/Postal code: 40207-3142
County: Jefferson
Country: USA
Mailing address: 130 St. Matthews Avenue, Suite 303
Mailing city: Louisville
Mailing state: KY
Mailing zip: 40207
General Phone: (800) 818-1181
Display Adv. E-mail: lynnemeena@aol.com
Mthly Avg Unique Visitors: 1992
Industry: Advertising headlines. Rewrite your advertising headlines for more effective results.
Note: Former Creative VP of Newspaper Association of America,

LYON ENTERPRISES

Street address 1: 4305 Cloud Dance
Street address city: Santa Fe
Street address state: NM
Zip/Postal code: 87507-2591
County: Santa Fe
Country: USA
Mailing address: 4305 Cloud Dance
Mailing city: Santa Fe
Mailing state: NM
Mailing zip: 87507
General Phone: (800) 243-1144
General Fax: (505) 471-1665
General/National Adv. E-mail: ray@lyonenterprises.com
Primary Website: www.lyonenterprises.com
Mthly Avg Unique Visitors: 1992
Industry: Circulation Equipment & Supplies; Tubes, Racks (Includes Racks: Motor Route Tubes); Carrier Bags; Point of Purchase; Imprinted Merchandise
Personnel: Ray Lyon (Pres.)

M.W. BURKE & ASSOCIATES, INC.

Street address 1: 185 Front St
Street address 2: Ste 207
Street address city: Danville
Street address state: CA
Zip/Postal code: 94526-3340
Country: USA
Mailing address: 185 Front St Ste 207
Mailing city: Danville
Mailing state: CA
Mailing zip: 94526-3340
General Phone: (925) 838-9070
General Fax: (925) 838-4695
General/National Adv. E-mail: mwburke@aol.com
Mthly Avg Unique Visitors: 1976
Industry: Consulting Services: Advertising; Consulting Services: Circulation; Consulting Services: Production; Prepress Color Proofing Systems;
Personnel: M.W. (Maury) Burke (Pres./Chrmn.)

MAC DERMID AUTOTYPE INC.

Street address 1: 245 Freight Street
Street address city: Waterbury
Street address state: CT

Zip/Postal code: 06702
Country: USA
Mailing address: 245 Freight Street
Mailing city: Waterbury
Mailing state: CT
Mailing zip: 06702
General Phone: (800) 323-0632
General Fax: (800) 933-2345
General/National Adv. E-mail: autotypeusinfo@macdermid.com
Primary Website: www.autotype.macdermid.com
Mthly Avg Unique Visitors: 1981
Industry: Chemicals: Photographic; Masking Materials; Plates: Offset (Computer to Plate)
Personnel: Terry Watson (Lead Operator)

MACDERMID GRAPHICS SOLUTIONS

Street address 1: 5210 Phillip Lee Dr SW
Street address city: Atlanta
Street address state: GA
Zip/Postal code: 30336-2217
Country: USA
Mailing address: 245 Freight St
Mailing city: Atlanta
Mailing state: GA
Mailing zip: 30336
General Phone: (404) 696-4565
General Fax: (404) 699-3354
General/National Adv. E-mail: mpsproductinfo@macdermid.com
Primary Website: www.macdermid.com/companies/macdermid-graphics-solutions
Mthly Avg Unique Visitors: 1922
Industry: Blanket Mounting and Bars; Blankets; Platemakers: Direct; Platemakers: Flexographic (Computer to Plate); Platemakers: Flexographic (Traditional); Platemakers: Letterpress; Plates: Flexographic (Conventional); Plates: Letterpress; Plates: Offset (Computer to Plate);
Personnel: Scot Benson (Pres.); Steve Racca (V. P. and Gen. Mgr.)

MACDONALD MEDIA

Street address 1: 141 West 36th Street
Street address 2: 16th floor
Street address city: New York
Street address state: NY
Zip/Postal code: 10018
Country: USA
Mailing address: 141 West 36th Street, 16th floor
Mailing city: New York
Mailing state: NY
Mailing zip: 10018
General Phone: (212) 578-8735
General/National Adv. E-mail: Hello@macdonaldmedia.com
Primary Website: www.macdonaldmedia.com
Industry: Art & Layout Equipment and Services; Consulting Services: Advertising; Software: Design/Graphics; Trade Publications;
Personnel: Andrea MacDonald (Pres./CEO)

MAH MACHINE CO., INC.

Street address 1: 3301 S Central Ave
Street address city: Cicero
Street address state: IL
Zip/Postal code: 60804-3941
Country: USA
Mailing address: 3301 S Central Ave
Mailing city: Cicero
Mailing state: IL
Mailing zip: 60804-3986
General Phone: (708) 656-1826
General Fax: (708) 656-4152
General/National Adv. E-mail: info@mahmachine.com
Primary Website: www.mahmachine.com
Mthly Avg Unique Visitors: 1977
Industry: Cylinder Repair; Equipment Dealers (New); Equipment Dealers (Used); Feeding, Folding, Delivery Equipment; Presses: Offset; Roller Grinding Services; Rollers; Rollers: Dampening;
Personnel: Martin Hozjan (Pres.)

MALOW CORP.

Street address 1: 1835 S Nordic Rd
Street address city: Mt Prospect
Street address state: IL
Zip/Postal code: 60056-5715
Country: USA
Mailing address: 1835 S Nordic Rd
Mailing city: Mt Prospect
Mailing state: IL
Mailing zip: 60056-5715
General Phone: (847) 956-0200
General Fax: (847) 956-0935
Primary Website: www.malow.com
Mthly Avg Unique Visitors: 1947
Industry: Automatic Plastic Bagging Equipment; Bundling and Tying Machines; Strapping Machines;
Personnel: Terry Luzader (Sales Mgr.)

MANAGING EDITOR, INC.

Street address 1: 610 York Rd
Street address 2: Ste 400
Street address city: Jenkintown
Street address state: PA
Zip/Postal code: 19046-2866
Country: USA
Mailing address: 610 York Rd., Ste. 400
Mailing city: Jenkintown
Mailing state: PA
Mailing zip: 19046
General Phone: (215) 886-5662
General Fax: (215) 886-5681
General/National Adv. E-mail: info@maned.com
Primary Website: www.maned.com
Mthly Avg Unique Visitors: 1989
Industry: Pagination Systems; Preprint Service & Production; Software: Advertising (Includes Display; Classified); Software: Editorial; Software: Pagination/Layout; Software: Workflow Management/Tracking; Digital Publishing;
Personnel: Mark Leister (Managing Director); Mark Wasserman (Head of Global Sales and Marketing)

MANASSY SALES INC.

Street address 1: 6861 Yellowstone Blvd
Street address city: Forest Hills
Street address state: NY
Zip/Postal code: 11375-9403
Country: USA
Mailing address: 6861 Yellowstone Blvd Ste 106
Mailing city: Forest Hills
Mailing state: NY
Mailing zip: 11375-9404
General Phone: (718) 544-4739
General Fax: (347) 642 8060
General/National Adv. E-mail: manassyparts@yahoo.com
Mthly Avg Unique Visitors: 1961
Industry: Press Accessories, Parts & Supplies; Rollers;
Note: Replacement Parts for Newspaper folders Primarily gain rings for TKS & Man Rolland
Personnel: Joel Marcus (Pres.)

MANROLAND WEB SYSTEMS INC.

Street address 1: 2150 Western Ct
Street address 2: Ste 420
Street address city: Lisle
Street address state: IL
Zip/Postal code: 60532-1973
Country: USA
Mailing address: 2150 Western Ct Ste 420
Mailing city: Lisle
Mailing state: IL
Mailing zip: 60532-1973
General Phone: (630) 920-5850
General Fax: (630) 920-5851
Display Adv. E-mail: denise.lease@manroland-web.com
Primary Website: www.manroland-web.com
Mthly Avg Unique Visitors: 2012
Industry: Material Handling Equipment: Automatic Guided Vehicles; Newsprint Handling Equipment; Press Accessories, Parts & Supplies; Press Control Systems; Presses: Flexographic; Presses: Offset; Reels (Includes Paper Reels); Roll Cleaning Equipment; Ink Jet & Digital Press Equipment; Folding & Finishing Equipment
Note: Leading with the broadest and freshest product portfolio in web offset printing, manroland web systems Inc., based in Augsburg, Germany, and operating in North America out of Westmont, Illinois, Toronto, Ontario, and Ansonia, Connecticut, is part of the Lubeck, Germany-based Possehl Group, as their 10th business division. Their clear strategy Â£ stability, investment security, groundbreaking technology, and a strong service offerings Â£ gives the principles that guide manroland web systems. Web offset presses from Augsburg provide tailor-made solutions for newspaper, publishing, and commercial printing. A worldwide sales and service network also markets ancillary printing equipment and pressroom products as well as software products and workflow management systems. The companyÂ£s partnership with OcÂ£ Printing Systems features the first innovations in industrial digital four-color printing, including graphics networking and finishing equipment, developed by manroland web systems.
Personnel: Denise Lease (Marketing Manager); Greg Blue (CEO); Ron Sams (VP of Sales)

MARATEK ENVIRONMENTAL TECHNOLOGIES, INC.

Street address 1: 60 Healey Rd
Street address 2: Unit 8-10
Street address city: Bolton
Street address state: ON
Zip/Postal code: L7E 5A6
Country: Canada
Mailing address: 60 Healey Rd., Unit 8-10
Mailing city: Bolton
Mailing state: ON
Mailing zip: L7E 5A5
General Phone: (905) 857-2738
General/National Adv. E-mail: sales@maratek.com
Display Adv. E-mail: sales@maratek.com
Primary Website: www.maratek.com
Mthly Avg Unique Visitors: 1968
Industry: Environmental Control Systems; Equipment Dealers (New); Fluid Handeling: Pressroom; Ink Recovery Systems; Silver Recovery; Wastewater Treatment; Solvent Recovery Systems;
Personnel: Colin Darcel (Owner/Pres.)

MARKEM-IMAJE

Street address 1: 100 Chastain Center Blvd NW
Street address 2: Ste 165
Street address city: Kennesaw
Street address state: GA
Zip/Postal code: 30144-5561
Country: USA
Mailing address: 100 Chastain Center Blvd NW Ste 165
Mailing city: Kennesaw
Mailing state: GA
Mailing zip: 30144-5561
General Phone: (770) 421-7700
General Fax: (770) 421-7702
Primary Website: www.markem-imaje.com
Mthly Avg Unique Visitors: 1987
Industry: Addressing Machines; Inks; Label Printing Machines; Mailroom Systems & Equipment;
Personnel: Omar Kerbage (President); Jacques Desroches (Gen. Mgr.); Alisha Howard (Mgr., Mktg.)

MARKETING PLUS, INC.

Street address 1: 135 Green St
Street address city: Woodbridge
Street address state: NJ
Zip/Postal code: 07095-2961
Country: USA
Mailing address: 135 Green St
Mailing city: Woodbridge
Mailing state: NJ
Mailing zip: 07095-2961
General Phone: (732) 694-1020
General/National Adv. E-mail: mpi@marketingplusinc.com
Primary Website: www.marketingplusinc.com
Industry: Consulting Services: Marketing; Market Research;
Personnel: Monty Cerasani (Pres./CEO); Susan Taylor (Gen. Mgr.); John Saparito (Office Mgr.); Karen Marov (HR Mgr.); John Lederer (Vice Pres., Bus. Devel.); Phil Lyman (IT Mgr.)

MARKETING STRATEGIES INCORPORATED

Street address 1: 4603 OLEANDER DRIVE, SUITE 4
Street address city: Myrtle Beach
Street address state: SC
Zip/Postal code: 29577
Country: USA
Mailing address: 4603 OLEANDER DRIVE, SUITE 4
Mailing city: Myrtle Beach
Mailing state: SC
Mailing zip: 29577
General Phone: (843)692-9662
General Fax: (843) 692-0558
General/National Adv. E-mail: info@marketingstrategiesinc.com
Primary Website: www.marketingstrategies.org
Mthly Avg Unique Visitors: 1980
Industry: Consulting Services: Advertising; Consulting Services: Marketing;
Personnel: Denise Blackburn-Gay (Pres., CEO); Samantha Bower (Mktg. Dir.); Lauren Davis (Graphic Designer); Pablo Marin (Creative Dir.)

MARKZWARE SOFTWARE, INC.

Street address 1: 1805 E Dyer Rd
Street address 2: Ste 101
Street address city: Santa Ana
Street address state: CA
Zip/Postal code: 92705-5742
Country: USA
Mailing address: 1805 E Dyer Rd Ste 101
Mailing city: Santa Ana
Mailing state: CA
Mailing zip: 92705-5742
General Phone: (949) 756-5100
General/National Adv. E-mail: info@markzware.com
Primary Website: www.markzware.com
Mthly Avg Unique Visitors: 1985
Industry: Software: Editorial; Software: Electronic Data Interchange;
Personnel: Patrick Marchese (Pres./CEO); Mary Gay Marchese (Public Relations); Patty Talley

MARTIN AUTOMATIC, INC.

Street address 1: 1661 Northrock Ct
Street address city: Rockford
Street address state: IL
Zip/Postal code: 61103-1202
Country: USA
Mailing address: 1661 Northrock Ct
Mailing city: Rockford
Mailing state: IL
Mailing zip: 61103-1296
General Phone: (815) 654-4800
General Fax: (815) 654-4810
General/National Adv. E-mail: info@martinauto.com
Primary Website: www.martinauto.com
Mthly Avg Unique Visitors: 1968
Industry: Conversion Equipment; Flying Pasters; Newsprint Handeling Equipment; Pasters; Press Accessories, Parts & Supplies; Rewinders; Web Guides;
Personnel: David A. Wright (Vice Pres., Sales); Bob Sanderson (Contract Admin.); Tim Delhotal (Contract Admin.); Tim Ward (Mktg. Mgr.)

MARTIN YALE, INC.

Street address 1: 251 Wedcor Ave
Street address city: Wabash
Street address state: IN
Zip/Postal code: 46992-4201
Country: USA
Mailing address: 251 Wedcor Ave
Mailing city: Wabash
Mailing state: IN
Mailing zip: 46992-4201
General Phone: (260) 563-0641
General Fax: (260) 563-4575
General/National Adv. E-mail: info@martinyale.com
Primary Website: www.martinyale.com
Mthly Avg Unique Visitors: 1934
Industry: Cutters & Trimmers; Folding Machines; Label Printing Machines; Paper Handeling Equipment; Paper Shredders;
Personnel: Greg German (Pres.)

MASTER FLO TECHNOLOGY

Street address 1: 1233 Tessier St
Street address city: Hawkesbury
Street address state: ON
Zip/Postal code: K6A 3R1
Country: Canada
Mailing address: 1233 Tessier St.
Mailing city: Hawkesbury
Mailing state: ON
Mailing zip: K6A 3R1
General Phone: (613) 636-0539
General Fax: (613) 636-0762
General/National Adv. E-mail: info@mflo.com
Primary Website: www.mflo.com

Mthly Avg Unique Visitors: 1984
Industry: Circulation Equipment & Supplies; Dampening Systems; Delivery Equipment; Feeding, Folding, Delivery Equipment; Ink Fountains & Accessories; Inserting Equipment (Includes Stuffing Machines); Material Handling Equipment: Pallets & Palletizers; Offset Fountain Controls; Press Accessories, Parts & Supplies; Recirculators;
Personnel: Edward Desaulniers (President); Tim Duffy (Vice Pres., Opns)

MASTHEAD INTERNATIONAL, INC.

Street address 1: 3602 S 16th St
Street address city: Phoenix
Street address state: AZ
Zip/Postal code: 85040-1311
Country: USA
Mailing address: 3602 S 16th St
Mailing city: Phoenix
Mailing state: AZ
Mailing zip: 85040-1311
General Phone: 602-276-5373
General Fax: 602-276-8116
General/National Adv. E-mail: steve.stone@masthead.net
Primary Website: www.masthead.net
Mthly Avg Unique Visitors: 1971
Industry: Controllers: Press; Drives & Controls; Erectors & Riggers; Pasters; Press Parts; Press Rebuilding; Press Repairs; Presses: Flexographic; Presses: Letterpress; Presses: Offset; Tension & Web Controls; Training: Press Operation & Maintenance; Web Width Changer;
Personnel: Steve Stone (Branch Mgr.); Kent Kraft (Bus. Devel. Mgr.)

MASTHEAD INTERNATIONAL, INC.

Street address 1: 700 Quantum Rd NE
Street address city: Rio Rancho
Street address state: NM
Zip/Postal code: 87124-4500
Country: USA
Mailing address: 700 Quantum Rd NE
Mailing city: Rio Rancho
Mailing state: NM
Mailing zip: 87124-4500
General Phone: 505-890-7103
General Fax: 505-890-7104
General/National Adv. E-mail: info@masthead.net
Primary Website: www.masthead.net
Personnel: Joel Birket (Proj. Mgr./Estimator)

MATTHEWS INTERNATIONAL CORP.

Street address 1: 6515 Penn Ave
Street address city: Pittsburgh
Street address state: PA
Zip/Postal code: 15206-4407
Country: USA
Mailing address: 6515 Penn Ave
Mailing city: Pittsburgh
Mailing state: PA
Mailing zip: 15206-4482
General Phone: (412) 665-2550
General Fax: (412) 365-2055
General/National Adv. E-mail: info@matw.com
Primary Website: www.matthewsmarking.com; www.matw.com
Mthly Avg Unique Visitors: 1850
Industry: Laser Printers
Personnel: Joseph C. Bartolacci (Pres./CEO)

MAXCESS

Street address 1: 222 W Memorial Rd
Street address city: Oklahoma City
Street address state: OK
Zip/Postal code: 73114-2300
Country: USA
Mailing address: PO Box 26508
Mailing city: Oklahoma City
Mailing state: OK
Mailing zip: 73126-0508
General Phone: (405) 755-1600
General Fax: (405) 755-8425
General/National Adv. E-mail: sales@maxcessintl.com
Primary Website: www.maxcessintl.com
Industry: Chemicals: Chuck (Paper Roll); Cutters & Trimmers; Cutting Tools; Drives & Controls; Reels & Tensions; Tension & Web Controls; Visual Display Terminals; Web Break Detector; Web Guides; Web Press - Special Equipment;
Personnel: Greg Jehlik (CEO, Pres.); Doug Knudtson (COO, VP); Robert Sweet (CFO); Andy Wissenback (Sales Rep); Pat Johnson (Sales Rep)

MAXX MATERIAL HANDLING LLC

Street address 1: 315 E St
Street address city: Hampton
Street address state: VA
Zip/Postal code: 23661-1209
Country: USA
Mailing address: 315 E St
Mailing city: Hampton
Mailing state: VA
Mailing zip: 23661-1209
General Phone: (757) 825-8100
General Fax: (757) 825-8800
General/National Adv. E-mail: mhogan@maxxmh.com
Primary Website: www.maxxmh.com
Industry: Material Handling Equipment: Truck Loaders; Material Handling Equipment: Vehicle Loading;
Personnel: Randy Gilliland (Pres.); Mark Hogan (Vice Pres.)

MBM CORP.

Street address 1: 3134 Industry Dr
Street address city: North Charleston
Street address state: SC
Zip/Postal code: 29418-8450
Country: USA
Mailing address: PO Box 40249
Mailing city: North Charleston
Mailing state: SC
Mailing zip: 29423-0249
General Phone: (843) 552-2700
General Fax: (843) 552-2974
Display Adv. E-mail: mikev@mbmcorp.com
Primary Website: www.mbmcorp.com
Mthly Avg Unique Visitors: 1936
Industry: Cutters & Trimmers; Cutting Tools; Feeding, Folding, Delivery Equipment; Folding Machines; In-Line Trimming Systems;
Personnel: Ned Ginsburg (Pres. and CFO); Michael Venittelli (Senior VP of Sales and Marketing); Wanda Ford (VP of National Sales); Lisa Hutchinson (Product Manager); Jeffery Chase (Service Manager); Sandra Robinson (Parts Representative)

MCCAIN BINDERY SYSTEMS

Street address 1: 14545 W Edison Dr
Street address city: New Lenox
Street address state: IL
Zip/Postal code: 60451-3672
Country: USA
Mailing address: 14545 W Edison Dr
Mailing city: New Lenox
Mailing state: IL
Mailing zip: 60451-3672
General Phone: 800-225-9363
General Fax: 815-462-1471
General/National Adv. E-mail: mccainbind@earthlink.net
Primary Website: www.mccainbindery.com
Mthly Avg Unique Visitors: 1926
Industry: Saddle Stitching, Side Sewers, Sheeters, Inserting Equipment (Includes Stuffing Machines); Bindery and Mailroom Systems & Equipment;
Personnel: Nancy Jones (Pres.); Bill Whitehead (Sales Manager); Chester Zurek (National Service/ Product Manager); Dennis Keem (Vice Pres./Gen. Mgr.)

MCCAIN PRINTING CO.

Street address 1: 525 Wilson St
Street address city: Danville
Street address state: VA
Zip/Postal code: 24541-1437
Country: USA
Mailing address: 525 Wilson St
Mailing city: Danville
Mailing state: VA
Mailing zip: 24541-1490
General Phone: (434) 792-1331
General Fax: (434) 793-5473
General/National Adv. E-mail: efsounders@mccainprint.com
Primary Website: www.mccainprint.com
Personnel: Eugene Sounders (Owner)

MCCRRORY PUBLISHING

Street address 1: 2530 Deerwood Dr.
Street address city: Fort Wayne
Street address state: IN
Zip/Postal code: 46825
Country: USA
Mailing address: 2530 Deerwood Dr.
Mailing city: Fort Wayne
Mailing state: IN
Mailing zip: 46825
General Phone: (260) 485-1812
General/National Adv. E-mail: info@mccpub.com
Primary Website: www.mccpub.com
Mthly Avg Unique Visitors: 2001
Industry: Computers: Hardware & Software Integrators; Consulting Services: Computer; Consulting Services: Editorial; Software: Advertising (Includes Display; Classified); Software: Editorial; Software: Electronic Data Interchange; Software: Pagination/Layout; System Integration Services;
Note: Digital Graphics and Printing

MCGRANN PAPER CORP.

Street address 1: 2101 Westinghouse Blvd
Street address city: Charlotte
Street address state: NC
Zip/Postal code: 28273-6310
Country: USA
Mailing address: 2101 Westinghouse Blvd # A
Mailing city: Charlotte
Mailing state: NC
Mailing zip: 28273-6310
General Phone: (704) 583-2101
General Fax: (704) 369-2229
Primary Website: www.mcgrann.com
Mthly Avg Unique Visitors: 1996
Industry: Newsprint; Paper: Coated Groundwood Offset; Paper: Groundwood Specialties; Paper: Specialty Printing Paper;
Personnel: Karl McGrann (Owner/Pres.); Bob Marko (Sales Rep.); Kirk Castle (Sr. VP, Sales)

MCGRANN PAPER CORPORATION

Street address 1: 10865 Jersey Blvd
Street address city: Rancho Cucamonga
Street address state: CA
Zip/Postal code: 91730-5113
County: Riverside
Country: USA
Mailing address: 2101 Westinghouse Blvd
Mailing city: Charlotte
Mailing state: NC
Mailing zip: 28273-6310
General Phone: 909-595-2727
General Fax: 704-369-2227
Primary Website: www.mcgrann.com
Mthly Avg Unique Visitors: 1974
Industry: Paper - Marchant - Converter- Distributor
Personnel: Anthony V. Nanna (Partner)

MCI

Street address 1: 22001 Loudoun County Pkwy
Street address city: Ashburn
Street address state: VA
Zip/Postal code: 20147-6105
County: Loudoun
Country: USA
Mailing address: 22001 Loudoun County Pkwy
Mailing city: Ashburn
Mailing state: VA
Mailing zip: 20147-6122
General Phone: (703) 206-5600
General Fax: (703) 206-5601
General/National Adv. E-mail: info@mci.com
Primary Website: www.mci.com
Mthly Avg Unique Visitors: 1968
Industry: Data Communication
Product or Service: Online Service Provider and Internet Hosts`Telecommunications/Service Bureaus
Personnel: Ivan Siedenberg (Chrmn./CEO); Fred Briggs (Pres., Opns./Tech.); Robert Blakely (Exec. Vice Pres./CFO); Daniel Casaccia (Exec. Vice Pres., HR); Jonathan Crane (Exec. Vice Pres., Strategy/Cor. Devel.); Grace Chentent (Sr. Vice Pres., Commun.); Nancy B. Gofus (Sr. Vice Pres., Mktg./CMO); Shane King

MEDIA AMERICA BROKERS

Street address 1: 1130 Piedmont Ave NE
Street address 2: Apt 912
Street address city: Atlanta
Street address state: GA
Zip/Postal code: 30309-3783
County: Fulton
Country: USA
Mailing address: 1130 Piedmont Ave NE Ste. 912
Mailing city: Atlanta
Mailing state: GA
Mailing zip: 30309-3783
General Phone: (404) 875-8787
General/National Adv. E-mail: lonwwilliams@aol.com
Mthly Avg Unique Visitors: 1989
Industry: Brokers & Appraisers
Personnel: Lon W Williams (Owner)

MEDIA CYBERNETICS LP

Street address 1: 401 N Washington St
Street address 2: Ste 350
Street address city: Rockville
Street address state: MD
Zip/Postal code: 20850-0707
Country: USA
Mailing address: 401 N Washington St Ste 350
Mailing city: Rockville
Mailing state: MD
Mailing zip: 20850-0707
General Phone: (301) 495-3305
General Fax: 240-328-6193
General/National Adv. E-mail: info@mediacy.com
Primary Website: www.mediacy.com
Mthly Avg Unique Visitors: 1981
Industry: Optical Character Recognition (OCR)
Personnel: Doug Paxson (Pres.)

MEDIA DATA TECHNOLOGY, INC. (MDTI)

Street address 1: 20 Roundelay Rd
Street address city: South Hadley
Street address state: MA
Zip/Postal code: 01075-1614
Country: USA
Mailing address: 20 Roundelay Rd
Mailing city: South Hadley
Mailing state: MA
Mailing zip: 01075-1614
General Phone: (413) 534-3307
General/National Adv. E-mail: jpeters@mediadatatech.com
Industry: Software: Advertising (Includes Display; Classified)
Personnel: John Peters (Pres.)

MEDIA MONITORS, INC.

Street address 1: 445 Hamilton Ave
Street address 2: Fl 7
Street address city: White Plains
Street address state: NY
Zip/Postal code: 10601-1807
Country: USA
Mailing address: 445 Hamilton Ave Ste 700
Mailing city: White Plains
Mailing state: NY
Mailing zip: 10601-1828
General Phone: (914) 428-5971
General Fax: (914) 259-4541
General/National Adv. E-mail: jselig@mediamonitors.com
Primary Website: www.mediamonitors.com
Mthly Avg Unique Visitors: 1982
Industry: Consulting Services: Advertising
Personnel: Philippe Generali (Pres.); John L. Selig (Sales Executive); Cheryl Lohr (National Account Manager); Frank Cammarata (VP, Sales)

MEENA COPY & LAYOUT

Street address 1: 130 Saint Matthews Ave
Street address city: Louisville
Street address state: KY
Zip/Postal code: 40207-3148

Country: USA
Mailing address: 130 Saint Matthews Ave
Mailing city: Louisville
Mailing state: KY
Mailing zip: 40207-3105
General Phone: (800) 818-1181
General Fax: (800) 818-8329
General/National Adv. E-mail: lynnemeena@aol.com
Mthly Avg Unique Visitors: 1990
Industry: Consulting Services: Advertising: How to make a good ad better. Advertising; Design & Layout;
Personnel: Lynne Meena (Pres.)

MEGASYS INTERNATIONAL, INC.

Street address 1: 45 Industrial Park Rd W
Street address 2: Ste H
Street address city: Tolland
Street address state: CT
Zip/Postal code: 06084-2839
Country: USA
Mailing address: 45 Industrial Park Rd W Ste H
Mailing city: Tolland
Mailing state: CT
Mailing zip: 06084-2839
General Phone: (860) 871-8713
General Fax: (860) 871-8710
General/National Adv. E-mail: megasysint@aol.com
Primary Website: megasysinternational.com
Mthly Avg Unique Visitors: 1990
Industry: Bundling and Tying Machines; Composing Room Equipment & Supplies; Equipment Dealers (New); Equipment Dealers (Used); Folding Machines; Label Printing Machines; Paper Shredders; Photostat: Machines;
Note: HP Designjet and Wide Format Equipment Sales, Service and Supplies"
Personnel: Fred McNutt (Pres.)

MEGTEC SYSTEMS

Street address 1: 830 Prosper St
Street address city: De Pere
Street address state: WI
Zip/Postal code: 54115-3104
Country: USA
Mailing address: PO Box 5030
Mailing city: De Pere
Mailing state: WI
Mailing zip: 54115-5030
General Phone: (920) 337-1410
General Fax: (920) 558-5535
General/National Adv. E-mail: info@megtec.com
Primary Website: www.megtec.com
Mthly Avg Unique Visitors: 1969
Industry: Dryers: Film and Papers; Drying Systems; Environmental Control Systems; Flying Pasters; Roll Handeling Equipment;
Personnel: Mary Van Vonderen (Mktg. Mgr.)

MERCER, LLC

Street address 1: 70 Linden Oaks
Street address 2: Ste 310
Street address city: Rochester
Street address state: NY
Zip/Postal code: 14625-2804
Country: USA
Mailing address: 70 Linden Oaks
Mailing city: Rochester
Mailing state: NY
Mailing zip: 14625-2804
General Phone: (585) 389-8700
General Fax: (585) 389-8801
Primary Website: www.mercer.com
Mthly Avg Unique Visitors: 1937
Industry: Human Resources Consulting;
Personnel: Micaela McPadden (Press Contact); Julio Portalatin (Pres. & CEO); RenÃ© Beaudoin (COO); Jackie Marks (CFO)

MERLINONE, INC.

Street address 1: 50 Braintree Hill Office Park
Street address city: Braintree
Street address state: MA
Zip/Postal code: 02184
County: Norfolk
Country: USA
Mailing state: MA
General Phone: (617) 328-6645
General Fax: (617) 328-9845
General/National Adv. E-mail: info@merlinone.com
Primary Website: www.merlinone.com
Mthly Avg Unique Visitors: 1988
Industry: publishing, print, online, broadcast media, marketing departments across all industries-Picture Desks, Assignment systems, Archiving and Digital Asset Management systems for all your data types including audio, video, PDF's, electronic tearsheets
Personnel: David M. Tenenbaum (Pres./CEO); Rande Simpson (Merlin Sales Manager); Jeff Seidensticker (VP of IT & Managed Services); David Breslauer (Inside sales rep)

MERRIMAC SOFTWARE ASSOCIATES

Street address 1: 9 Mason Hill Rd
Street address city: South Tamworth
Street address state: NH
Zip/Postal code: 3883
County: Carroll
Country: USA
Mailing address: PO Box 28
Mailing city: South Tamworth
Mailing state: NH
Mailing zip: 03883-0028
General Phone: 603-323-5077
General Fax: (603) 218-2140
General/National Adv. E-mail: sales@merrsoft.com
Display Adv. E-mail: tvachon@merrsoft.com
Editorial e-mail: tvachon@merrsoft.com
Primary Website: www.merrsoft.com
Mthly Avg Unique Visitors: 1987
Industry: Publishing Software: Advertising (includes Display and Classified); Pagination/Layout; Circulation and Distribution; Commercial Sales; Management (includes Administration and Accounting);
Note: Merrimac Software Associates
Personnel: Tom Vachon (Owner); Sabrina Fobes (Support Manager); Jim Loughner (Programmer)

MESA CORP.

Street address 1: 4546 S 86th St
Street address 2: Ste B
Street address city: Lincoln
Street address state: NE
Zip/Postal code: 68526-9252
Country: USA
Mailing address: 4546 S 86th St Ste B
Mailing city: Lincoln
Mailing state: NE
Mailing zip: 68526-9252
General Phone: (402) 489-9303
General Fax: (402) 489-7524
General/National Adv. E-mail: info@mesacorp.com; sales@mesacorp.com
Primary Website: www.mesacorp.com
Industry: Storage Retrieval Systems
Personnel: Thomas Manning (Vice Pres.-Sales/Mktg.)

METAFIX, INC.

Street address 1: 1925 46e Ave
Street address city: Lachine
Street address state: QC
Zip/Postal code: H8T 2P1
Country: Canada
Mailing address: 1925 46th Ave.
Mailing city: Montreal
Mailing state: QC
Mailing zip: H8T 2P1
General Phone: (514) 633-8663
General Fax: (514) 633-1678
General/National Adv. E-mail: sales@metafix.com
Primary Website: www.metafix.com
Mthly Avg Unique Visitors: 1988
Industry: Environmental Control Systems; Silver Recovery;

METALS RECOVERY SERVICE

Street address 1: 1660 Georgesville Rd
Street address city: Columbus
Street address state: OH
Zip/Postal code: 43228-3613
County: Franklin
Country: USA
Mailing address: 1660 Georgesville Rd.
Mailing city: Columbus
Mailing state: OH
Mailing zip: 43228
General Phone: (614) 870-9444
General Fax: (614) 878-6000
General/National Adv. E-mail: sales@msitarget.com
Display Adv. E-mail: sales@msitarget.com
Primary Website: www.msitarget.com
Mthly Avg Unique Visitors: 2001
Industry: Silver Recovery
Personnel: Steven P. Dahms (Vice Pres.)

METRO EDITORIAL SERVICES

Street address 1: 519 8th Ave
Street address 2: Fl 18
Street address city: New York
Street address state: NY
Zip/Postal code: 10018-4577
County: New York
Country: USA
Mailing address: 519 8th Ave Fl 18
Mailing city: New York
Mailing state: NY
Mailing zip: 10018-4577
General Phone: (212) 947-5100
General Fax: (212) 714-9139
General/National Adv. E-mail: mes@metro-email.com
Primary Website: www.mcg.metrocreativeconnection.com
Mthly Avg Unique Visitors: 1910
Industry: Art & Layout Equipment and Services; Consulting Services: Advertising; Consulting Services: Editorial; Software: Design/Graphics; Software: Editorial;
Note: Metro is a leading provider of advertising, creative and editorial resources designed to help media companies make money with their print, online, and mobile products. We provide ready-to-use images, ads, stock-quality photos, logos/trademarks, auto photos, marketing/sales materials, copyright-free features, print templated sections, online e-Sections, and groundbreaking digital ad development tools, plus custom image, ad design and editorial services.
Personnel: Robert Zimmerman (Publisher); Debra Weiss (Exec. Vice Pres./Mktg. Dir.); Lauren Lekoski (Mktg. Mgr.); Jo Ann Shapiro (VP, Sales); Lou Ann Sornson (Regional Sales Mgr.); Tina Dentner (Regional Sales Mgr.); Cathy Agee (Regional Sales Mgr.); Gwen Tomaselli (Regional Sales Mgr.); Jennifer Steiner (Regional Sales Mgr.); Joann Johnson

METROLAND PRINTING/ PUBLISHING & DISTRIBUTING LTD.

Street address 1: 3125 Wolfedale Rd
Street address city: Mississauga
Street address state: ON
Zip/Postal code: L5C 1V8
Country: Canada
Mailing address: 3125 Wolfedale Rd.
Mailing city: Mississauga
Mailing state: ON
Mailing zip: L5C 1W1
General Phone: 905-281-5656
General Fax: 905-279-5103
Primary Website: www.metroland.com
Mthly Avg Unique Visitors: 1981
Industry: Presses: Offset; Publishing Systems;
Personnel: Brenda Biller (Vice Pres., HR)

MICRO SYSTEMS SPECIALISTS, INC. (MSSI)

Street address 1: 3272 Franklin Ave
Street address city: Millbrook
Street address state: NY
Zip/Postal code: 12545-5975
County: Dutchess
Country: USA
Mailing address: PO Box 347
Mailing city: Millbrook
Mailing state: NY
Mailing zip: 12545-0347
General Phone: (845) 677-6150
General Fax: (845) 677-6620
General/National Adv. E-mail: mssisoftware@cs.com
Mthly Avg Unique Visitors: 1988
Industry: Software: Advertising Billing; Software: Business (includes Administration/Accounting); Software: Circulation
Note: Newspaper Business, Advertising & Circulation Software
Personnel: Dawn Blackburn (Pres.)

MICROFILM PRODUCTS CO.

Street address 1: 157 Avalon Gardens Dr
Street address city: Nanuet
Street address state: NY
Zip/Postal code: 10954-7417
Country: USA
Mailing address: 266 Germonds Rd
Mailing city: West Nyack
Mailing state: NY
Mailing zip: 10994-1320
General Phone: (845) 371-3700
General Fax: (845) 371-3780
General/National Adv. E-mail: info@microfilmproducts.com
Primary Website: www.microfilmproducts.com
Industry: Addressing Machines; Bundling and Tying Machines; Equipment Dealers (New); Equipment Dealers (Used); Folding Machines;
Personnel: Gary Moelis (Pres.)

MICROTEK

Street address 1: No.6 Industry East Road 3
Street address 2: Science-based Industrial Park
Street address city: Hsinchu
Zip/Postal code: 30075
Country: Taiwan
Mailing address: No.6 Industry East Road 3, Science-based Industrial Park
Mailing city: Hsinchu
Mailing zip: 30075
General Phone: +886-3-577-2155 Ext.551
General Fax: +886-3-577-2598 Ext.551
General/National Adv. E-mail: sales@microtek.com
Primary Website: www.microtek.com
Mthly Avg Unique Visitors: 1980
Industry: Color Seperation Scanners; Scanners: Color B & W, Plates, Web;
Personnel: Jerry Su (Sales OEM projects); Jerry Tsai (Sales (USA))

MID-AMERICA GRAPHICS, INC.

Street address 1: 1501 W Vine St
Street address city: Harrisonville
Street address state: MO
Zip/Postal code: 64701-4017
Country: USA
Mailing address: PO Box 466
Mailing city: Harrisonville
Mailing state: MO
Mailing zip: 64701-0466
General Phone: (816) 887-2414
General Fax: (816) 887-2762
General/National Adv. E-mail: sales@midamericagraphics.com
Primary Website: www.midamericagraphics.com
Mthly Avg Unique Visitors: 1983
Industry: Conveyors; In-Line Trimming Systems; Infeed Stackers; Inserting Equipment (Includes Stuffing Machines); Newsprint Handeling Equipment;
Personnel: Charles George (Pres.); William David George (Exec. Vice Pres.); Dan George (Gen. Mgr.); Terri Widdle (Sec.)

MIDLANTIC EQUIPMENT CO., INC.

Street address 1: 567 Wyckoff Ave
Street address city: Wyckoff
Street address state: NJ
Zip/Postal code: 07481-1336
Country: USA
Mailing address: 567 Wyckoff Ave
Mailing city: Wyckoff
Mailing state: NJ
Mailing zip: 07481-1336
General Phone: (201) 891-1448
General Fax: (201) 891-2664
General/National Adv. E-mail: midequip@yahoo.com
Primary Website: www.agfa-imagesetters.com
Mthly Avg Unique Visitors: 1985
Industry: Imagesetters
Personnel: Arlene Vanderweert (Mktg. Mgr.)

MIDSYSTEMS TECHNOLOGY LTD.

Street address 1: One Kingdom Street
Street address city: London
Zip/Postal code: W8 5SF

Country: United Kingdom
Mailing address: One Kingdom Street
Mailing city: London
Mailing zip: W8 5SF
General Phone: (0)20 3320 5000
General Fax: (0)20 3320 1771
General/National Adv. E-mail: sales@midsys.co.uk
Primary Website: www.misys.co.uk
Industry: Produciton Control Systems
Personnel: John Sussens (Mng. Dir.)

MIDWEST PUBLISHERS SUPPLY CO.

Street address 1: 4640 N Olcott Ave
Street address city: Harwood Heights
Street address state: IL
Zip/Postal code: 60706-4604
Country: USA
Mailing address: 4640 N. Olcott Ave.
Mailing city: Harwood Heights
Mailing state: IL
Mailing zip: 60706
General Phone: (708) 867-4646
General Fax: (708) 867-6954
General/National Adv. E-mail: info@mps-co.com
Mthly Avg Unique Visitors: 1947
Industry: Art & Layout Equipment and Services; Blankets; Blue Line Grids; Chemicals: Pressroom; Composing Room Equipment & Supplies; Lift Trucks; Mailroom Systems & Equipment; Offset Chemicals & Supplies; Press Accessories, Parts & Supplies;
Personnel: James Rezabek (Pres.)

MILES 33

Street address 1: 40 Richards Ave
Street address 2: Pendegast Street, 5170
Street address city: Norwalk
Street address state: CT
Zip/Postal code: 06854-2319
County: Fairfield
Country: USA
Mailing address: 40 Richards Ave Ste 29
Mailing city: Norwalk
Mailing state: CA
Mailing zip: 06854-2322
General Phone: (203) 838-2333
General Fax: (203) 838-4473
General/National Adv. E-mail: info@miles33.com
Display Adv. E-mail: albert_debruijn@yahoo.com
Primary Website: www.miles33.com
Mthly Avg Unique Visitors: 1976
Industry: Computers: Hardware & Software Integrators; Consulting Services: Advertising; Consulting Services: Editorial; Software: Advertising (Includes Display; Classified; Digital and Print); Software: Digital Asset Management; Software: Content Management Systems for newsroom and Web; Software: Pagination/Layout; Software: Ad Tracking; Software: Self Service Advertising; Software: Digital Video Ad Production; Software: Ipad and Android Apps; Software: Business Analytics/Datamining
Product or Service: Hardware/Software Supplier`Multimedia/Interactive Products
Personnel: Chris Habasinski (Pres.); Albert De Bruijn (VP Marketing and Western USA Sales); Edward Hubbard (VP, Business Development)

MINNESOTA OPINION RESEARCH, INC. (MORI)

Street address 1: 8500 Normandale Lake Blvd
Street address 2: Ste 630
Street address city: Minneapolis
Street address state: MN
Zip/Postal code: 55437-3809
Country: USA
Mailing address: 8500 Normandale Lake Blvd Ste 630
Mailing city: Minneapolis
Mailing state: MN
Mailing zip: 55437-3809
General Phone: (952) 835-3050
General Fax: (952) 835-3385
General/National Adv. E-mail: minneapolis@magid.com
Primary Website: www.moriresearch.com
Mthly Avg Unique Visitors: 1982
Industry: Consulting Services: Advertising; Consulting Services: Circulation; Consulting Services: Editorial; Consulting Services: Marketing; Market Research; Newspaper Marketing; Research Studies;
Personnel: Ron Mulder (Pres.); Brent Stahl (Vice Pres., Research)

MIRACHEM CORP.

Street address 1: PO Box 14059
Street address city: Phoenix
Street address state: AZ
Zip/Postal code: 85063-4059
Country: USA
Mailing address: PO Box 14059
Mailing city: Phoenix
Mailing state: AZ
Mailing zip: 85063-4059
General Phone: 808-847-3527
General Fax: (602) 353-1411
General/National Adv. E-mail: cservice@mirachem.com
Primary Website: www.mirachem.com
Mthly Avg Unique Visitors: 1978
Industry: Chemicals: Pressroom; Chemicals: Roller Cleaning; Cleaners & Solvents;
Personnel: Pat Doughty (COO); Bob Boyle (Sales Mgr.)

MIRACLE INDUSTRIES, INC.

Street address 1: 118 Colebrook River Rd
Street address city: Winsted
Street address state: CT
Zip/Postal code: 06098-2241
Country: USA
Mailing address: 118 Colebrook River Rd Ste 1
Mailing city: Winsted
Mailing state: CT
Mailing zip: 06098-2241
General Phone: (203) 723-0928
General Fax: (203) 723-0394
Industry: Motors; Press Accessories, Parts & Supplies; Press Control Systems; Press Engineers; Presses: Offset; Roller Grinding Services; Web Break Detector; Web Press - Special Equipment;
Personnel: John Chabot (Pres.); Phyllis Fennlly (Vice Pres., Sales/Mktg.)

MIRACOM COMPUTER CORP.

Street address 1: PO Box 44
Street address city: Eastchester
Street address state: NY
Zip/Postal code: 10709-0044
County: Westchester
Country: USA
Mailing address: PO Box 44
Mailing city: Eastchester
Mailing state: NY
Mailing zip: 10709
General Phone: (888) 309-0639
General/National Adv. E-mail: info@miracomcomputer.com
Primary Website: www.miracomcomputer.com
Mthly Avg Unique Visitors: 1995
Industry: Inserter Control Systems Production Control Systems Planning Systems Inventory Systems Inkjet Labeling Systems
Note: Miracom is the Newspaper Post-Press control and software leader. Producers of MiraSert for inserter control, MiraLabel for in-line address labeling, MiraPkg for planning and inventory, and other software systems for managing your production facility from start to finish.
Personnel: Judah Holstein (CEO); Bill Harley (Vice President); Tom Whelan (Director, Customer Service); Ralph Valero (Field Application Engineer); Michael Dodds (Project Engineer); Alex Gray (Application Developer); Amy Arkawy (Inside Sales); Tina Dalton (Finance Representative)

MITCHELL'S

Street address 1: PO Box 2431
Street address city: New York
Street address state: NY
Zip/Postal code: 11106
Country: USA
Mailing address: PO Box 2431
Mailing city: New York
Mailing state: NY
Mailing zip: 10116-2431
General Phone: 800-662-2275
General Fax: (212) 594-7254
General/National Adv. E-mail: papers@mitchellsny.com
Primary Website: www.mitchellsny.com
Mthly Avg Unique Visitors: 1946
Industry: Delivery Equipment
Personnel: Mitchell Newman (Owner); Roy Newman (Owner)

MOBILE COMPUTING CORPORATION USA

Street address 1: 2600 Skymark Ave
Street address 2: Bldg # 8 Suite 202
Street address city: Mississauga
Street address state: ON
Zip/Postal code: L4W 5B2
Country: Canada
Mailing address: 2600 Skymark Ave, Bldg # 8 Suite 202
Mailing city: Mississauga
Mailing state: ON
Mailing zip: L4W 5B2
General Phone: (800) 392-8651
General Fax: (905) 676-9191
General/National Adv. E-mail: MCCMarketing@mobilecom.com
Primary Website: www.mobilecom.com
Mthly Avg Unique Visitors: 1977
Industry: Business Computers; Computers: Hardware & Software Integrators; Consulting Services: Circulation; Consulting Services: Computer; Software: Circulation;
Personnel: Les Feasey (Sales Rep.)

MO-MONEY ASSOCIATES, INC.

Street address 1: 3838 N Palafox St
Street address city: Pensacola
Street address state: FL
Zip/Postal code: 32505-5239
Country: USA
Mailing address: 3838 N Palafox St
Mailing city: Pensacola
Mailing state: FL
Mailing zip: 32505-5222
General Phone: (850) 432-6301
General Fax: (850) 434-5645
General/National Adv. E-mail: momoney@momoney.com
Primary Website: www.momoney.com
Mthly Avg Unique Visitors: 1979
Personnel: Cliff Mowe (Pres.); Tom McVoy (Mktg. Mgr.)

MONACO SYSTEMS, INC.

Street address 1: 100 Burtt Rd
Street address 2: Ste 203
Street address city: Andover
Street address state: MA
Zip/Postal code: 01810-5920
Country: USA
Mailing address: 100 Burtt Rd Ste 203
Mailing city: Andover
Mailing state: MA
Mailing zip: 01810-5920
General Phone: (978) 749-9944
General Fax: (978) 749-9977
General/National Adv. E-mail: corporateemail@xrite.com
Primary Website: www.monacosys.com
Mthly Avg Unique Visitors: 1993
Industry: Color Management Software; Software: Workflow Management/Tracking;
Personnel: Bonnie Fladung (Dir.-Mktg.)

MOTTERSTITCH COMPANY, INC.

Street address 1: 220 Richmond Townhouse Rd
Street address city: Carolina
Street address state: RI
Zip/Postal code: 02812-1106
Country: USA
Mailing address: P.O. Box 97
Mailing city: Carolina
Mailing state: RI
Mailing zip: 02812
General Phone: (401)364-6061
General Fax: (401)364-6063
General/National Adv. E-mail: tom@motterstitch.com
Display Adv. E-mail: tom@motterstitch.com
Primary Website: www.motterstitch.com
Mthly Avg Unique Visitors: 1985
Industry: In-Line Stapling/Stitching Machine for Newspaper and Commercial Press, Stitching Wire Sales
Note: Custom In-Line High Speed Stapling/Stitching machines for Newspaper and Commercial Press and Wire Sales
Personnel: Thomas Northup (President); Linda Northup (Office Admin.); David Mr. Gilman (Chief Engineer); Adam Mr. Northup (Office Assist.); Cheryl Mrs. Bernat (Secretary); David Northup (Sales VP); Roland Reuterfors (Consultant); Bengt Magnusson (Consultant Engineer)

MSP COMMUNICATIONS

Street address 1: 220 S 6th St
Street address 2: Ste 500
Street address city: Minneapolis
Street address state: MN
Zip/Postal code: 55402-4501
Country: USA
Mailing address: 220 S 6th St Ste 500
Mailing city: Minneapolis
Mailing state: MN
Mailing zip: 55402-4507
General Phone: (612) 339-7571
General Fax: (612) 339-5806
General/National Adv. E-mail: edit@mspmag.com
Primary Website: www.mspmag.com
Mthly Avg Unique Visitors: 1982
Industry: Trade Publications
Personnel: Gary Johnson (Pres.); Brian Anderson (Ed. in Chief)

MULLER MARTINI CORP.

Street address 1: 456 Wheeler Rd
Street address city: Hauppauge
Street address state: NY
Zip/Postal code: 11788-4343
Country: USA
Mailing address: 456 Wheeler Rd
Mailing city: Hauppauge
Mailing state: NY
Mailing zip: 11788-4343
General Phone: (631) 582-4343
General Fax: (631) 582-1961
General/National Adv. E-mail: info@mullermartiniusa.com
Display Adv. E-mail: q@qgroupltd.com
Primary Website: www.mullermartiniusa.com
Mthly Avg Unique Visitors: 1946
Industry: Bundling and Tying Machines; Counting, Stacking, Bundling Machines; Cutters & Trimmers; Inserting Equipment (Includes Stuffing Machines); Mailroom Systems & Equipment; Material Handling Equipment: Palletizing Machines; Newsprint Handeling Equipment; Paper Handeling Equipment; Shrink Wrapping Equipment; Storage Retrieval Systems;
Personnel: Weiner Naegeli (Vice-President); Anthony Quaranta; Herbert Carrington

N/S CORPORATION

Street address 1: 235 W Florence Ave
Street address city: Inglewood
Street address state: CA
Zip/Postal code: 90301-1212
Country: USA
Mailing address: 235 W Florence Ave
Mailing city: Inglewood
Mailing state: CA
Mailing zip: 90301-1293
General Phone: (800) 782-1582
General/National Adv. E-mail: info@nswash.com
Primary Website: www.nswash.com
Mthly Avg Unique Visitors: 1961
Industry: Conveyors; Drying Systems; Environmental Control Systems;
Personnel: Thomas Ennis (CEO); Thomas G. Ennis (Pres.); Gary Avrech (Mktg. Mgr.)

NAMA GRAPHICS E, LLC

Street address 1: 15751 Annico Dr
Street address city: Homer Glen
Street address state: IL
Zip/Postal code: 60491-8449
Country: USA
Mailing address: 15751 Annico Dr Ste 2
Mailing city: Homer Glen
Mailing state: IL
Mailing zip: 60491-4739
General Phone: (630) 668-6262
General Fax: (262) 966-3852
General/National Adv. E-mail: rsnama@wi.rr.com

Primary Website: www.namagraphicse.com
Mthly Avg Unique Visitors: 1991
Industry: Environmental Control Systems; Flying Pasters; Ink Fountains & Accessories; Rollers: Dampening;
Personnel: John Griffin (Owner); Rick Smith (Owner)

NATIONAL MEDIA ASSOCIATES

Street address 1: PO Box 2001
Street address city: Branson
Street address state: MO
Zip/Postal code: 65615-2001
County: Taney
Country: USA
Mailing address: PO Box 2001
Mailing city: Branson
Mailing state: MO
Mailing zip: 65615-2001
General Phone: (417) 338-6397
General Fax: (417) 338-6510
General/National Adv. E-mail: Brokered1@gmail.com
Primary Website: www.nationalmediasales.com
Mthly Avg Unique Visitors: 1997
Industry: Brokers & Appraisers; Consulting Services: Financial;
Personnel: Edward M. Anderson (Owner)

NATIONAL MEDIA ASSOCIATES

Street address 1: 1412 Kerr Research Dr
Street address city: Ada
Street address state: OK
Zip/Postal code: 74820
County: Pontifical
Country: USA
Mailing address: PO Box 849
Mailing city: Ada
Mailing state: OK
Mailing zip: 74821-0849
General Phone: (580) 421-9600
General Fax: (580) 421-9960
General/National Adv. E-mail: bolitho@bolitho.com
Primary Website: www.nationalmediasales.com
Mthly Avg Unique Visitors: 1966
Industry: Brokers & Appraisers; Consulting Services: Financial;
Personnel: Thomas C. Bolitho (Broker)

NATIONAL NEWSPAPER ASSOCIATION PUBLISHERS' AUXILIARY

Street address 1: 900 Community Dr
Street address city: Springfield
Street address state: IL
Zip/Postal code: 62703-5180
Country: USA
Mailing address: 900 Community Drive
Mailing city: Springfield
Mailing state: IL
Mailing zip: 62703
General Phone: (217) 241-1400
General/National Adv. E-mail: pubaux@nna.org
Display Adv. E-mail: wendy@nna.org
Primary Website: www.nnaweb.org
Mthly Avg Unique Visitors: 1865
Industry: Trade Publications
Personnel: Stan Schwartz (Comm. Dir.); Lynne Lance (Chief Operating Officer); Sam Fisher (Publisher)

NB FINISHING, INC.

Street address 1: 1075 Morse Ave
Street address city: Schaumburg
Street address state: IL
Zip/Postal code: 60193-4503
Country: USA
Mailing address: 1075 Morse Ave
Mailing city: Schaumburg
Mailing state: IL
Mailing zip: 60193-4503
General Phone: (847) 895-0900
General Fax: (847) 895-0999
General/National Adv. E-mail: info@nbfinishing.com
Primary Website: www.nbfinishing.com
Mthly Avg Unique Visitors: 1983
Industry: Plate Processors; Roller Grinding Services;
Personnel: Bruce Nichols (Pres.); Dave Nichols (Mgr., Opns.)

NEASI-WEBER INTERNATIONAL

Street address 1: 25115 Avenue Stanford
Street address 2: Ste A300
Street address city: Valencia
Street address state: CA
Zip/Postal code: 91355-1290
Country: USA
Mailing address: 25115 Avenue Stanford Ste 300
Mailing city: Valencia
Mailing state: CA
Mailing zip: 91355-4806
General Phone: (818) 895-6900
General Fax: (818) 830-0889
General/National Adv. E-mail: info@nwintl.com
Primary Website: www.nwintl.com
Mthly Avg Unique Visitors: 1977
Industry: Mailroom Systems & Equipment; Software: Advertising (Includes Display; Classified); Software: Circulation;
Personnel: Jim S. Weber (Pres.); Dennis J. Neasi (CEO)

NELA

Street address 1: 610 Whitetail Blvd
Street address city: River Falls
Street address state: WI
Zip/Postal code: 54022-5209
Country: USA
Mailing address: 610 Whitetail Blvd
Mailing city: River Falls
Mailing state: WI
Mailing zip: 54022-5209
General Phone: (715) 425-1900
General Fax: (751) 425-1901
General/National Adv. E-mail: info@nela-usa.com
Primary Website: www.nela-usa.com
Mthly Avg Unique Visitors: 2000
Industry: Color Registration; Controls: Register; Offset Plate-Making Service & Equipment; Pin Register Systems; Plate Bending Systems; Plate Mounting & Register Systems; Press Accessories, Parts & Supplies; Punching Equipment; Web Press - Special Equipment;
Personnel: David Klein (Pres.); Bob Deis (Mgr., Engineering); Taag Erickson (Pdct. Mgr., Web & Sheetfed); Jurgen Gruber (Sales Dir.); Katharina Gruber (Mktg. Mgr.)

NESBITT PUBLISHING LTD.

Street address 1: 353 Station Road
Street address city: Shoal Lake
Street address state: MB
Zip/Postal code: R0J 1Z0
Country: Canada
Mailing address: PO Box 160
Mailing city: Shoal Lake
Mailing state: MB
Mailing zip: R0J 1Z0
General Phone: 204-759-2644
General Fax: 204-759-2521
General/National Adv. E-mail: smpnews@mymts.net
Display Adv. E-mail: smpdisplay@mymts.net
Editorial e-mail: smpnews@mts.net
Mthly Avg Unique Visitors: 2007
Industry: South Mountain Press community newspaper
Product or Service: Publisher/Media
Personnel: Ryan Nesbitt (Publisher); Marcie Harrison (Editor); Connie Kay (Advertising); Ryan Nesbitt (Publisher)
Parent company (for newspapers): ()

NET-LINX AG

Street address 1: Kathe-Kollwitz-Ufer 76-79
Street address city: Dresden
Country: Germany
Mailing address: Kathe-Kollwitz-Ufer 76-79
Mailing city: Dresden
Mailing zip: 01309
General Phone: +49 351 3187 5888
General Fax: +49 351 3187 5550
General/National Adv. E-mail: nxinfo@net-linx.com
Primary Website: www.net-linx.com
Personnel: Holm Hallbauer (Pres.)

NETWORK NEWSPAPER ADVERTISING, INC.

Street address 1: 23811 Chagrin Blvd
Street address 2: Ste LL25
Street address city: Cleveland
Street address state: OH
Zip/Postal code: 44122-5525
Country: USA
Mailing address: 23811 Chagrin Blvd Ste LL25
Mailing city: Cleveland
Mailing state: OH
Mailing zip: 44122-5525
General Phone: (216) 595-3990
General Fax: (216) 595-3992
General/National Adv. E-mail: cccamh@aol.com
Mthly Avg Unique Visitors: 1907
Industry: Consulting Services: Advertising
Personnel: Charles Hickman (Pres.)

NEWMAN INTERNATIONAL, LLC

Street address 1: 4121 W 83rd St
Street address 2: Ste 155
Street address city: Prairie Village
Street address state: KS
Zip/Postal code: 66208-5323
Country: USA
Mailing address: 5405 W 97th Cir
Mailing city: Overland Park
Mailing state: KS
Mailing zip: 66207-3271
General Phone: (913) 648-2000
General Fax: (913) 648-7750
General/National Adv. E-mail: j.newman@att.net
Primary Website: www.timsonsusedprintingpresses.com
Mthly Avg Unique Visitors: 1977
Industry: Presses: Offset; Web Press - Special Equipment;
Personnel: John T. Newman (Pres.); Mary C. Newman (Vice Pres.)

NEWSCOLOR, LLC

Street address 1: PO Box 802
Street address city: Silverton
Street address state: OR
Zip/Postal code: 97381-0802
Country: USA
Mailing address: PO Box 802
Mailing city: Silverton
Mailing state: OR
Mailing zip: 97381-0802
General Phone: (503) 873-2414
General/National Adv. E-mail: sales@newscolor.com
Primary Website: www.newscolor.com
Mthly Avg Unique Visitors: 2004
Industry: Color Proofing
Note: NEWSCOLOR proofing software (formerly SeeColor) is the standard for inkjet newsprint proofing, used by customers including USA TODAY, The Washington Post, Houston Chronicle, Investors Business Daily, Dallas Morning News, & Seattle Times.
Personnel: Ron LaForge (Mng. Dir.); Karen Barr (Sales Dir.)

NEWSCURRENTS

Street address 1: 2320 Pleasant View Rd
Street address city: Middleton
Street address state: WI
Zip/Postal code: 53562-5521
Country: USA
Mailing address: PO Box 52
Mailing city: Madison
Mailing state: WI
Mailing zip: 53701-0052
General Phone: 608 836-6660
General Fax: 608 836-6684
General/National Adv. E-mail: csis@newscurrents.com
Primary Website: www.newscurrents.com
Mthly Avg Unique Visitors: 1983
Industry: NIE Print & Website Weekly Content
Personnel: Matt Cibula (Marketing Mgr.)

NEWSCYCLE SOLUTIONS

Street address 1: 7900 International Dr
Street address 2: Ste 800
Street address city: Bloomington
Street address state: MN
Zip/Postal code: 55425-1581
County: Hennepin
Country: USA
Mailing address: 7900 International Drive Suite 800
Mailing city: Bloomington
Mailing state: MN
Mailing zip: 55425
General Phone: 651-639-0662
General/National Adv. E-mail: info@newscycle.com
Primary Website: www.newscycle.com
Industry: Software: Advertising (Includes Display; Classified); Software: Circulation; Software: Design/Graphics; Software: Editorial; Software: Pagination/Layout;
Product or Service:
Circulation`Consultants`Editorial`Hardware/Software Supplier`Multimedia/Interactive Products`Online Service Provider and Internet Hosts`Publisher/Media
Note: Newscycle Solutions, which was formed by the combination of DTI, SAXOTECH, Atex AdBase and MediaSpan, delivers the most complete range of software solutions for the global news media industry, including news content management, advertising, circulation, audience, and analytics. Newscycle is a trusted technology partner serving more than 1,200 media companies with 8,000 properties across more than 30 countries on six continents. The company is headquartered in Bloomington, MN and has U.S. offices in Florida, Michigan and Utah; with international offices in Australia, Canada, Denmark, Germany, Malaysia, Norway, Sweden, and the United Kingdom. For more information, go to: http://www.newscycle.com.
Personnel: Paul Mrozinski (Sales Director); John Pukas (VP., Business Relations); Steve Moon (Rgl. Sales Dir.); Marc Thompson (Rgl. Sales Dir.); Lisa Speth (Marketing Communications Mgr.); Bryan Hooley (Asia-Pacific Bus. Mgr.); Ken Freedman (Vice President of Market Development); Pete Marsh (Vice President of Marketing); Julie Maas (Sales Director); Chris McKee (Sales Director); Mike McLaughlin (Sales Director); Geoff Kehrer (Sales Engineer); Robert Bohlin (Executive Sales Director, EMEA)

NEWSCYCLE SOLUTIONS

Street address 1: 7900 International Drive
Street address 2: Suite 800
Street address city: Bloomington
Street address state: MN
Zip/Postal code: 55425-1581
Country: USA
Mailing address: 7900 International Dr Ste 800
Mailing city: Minneapolis
Mailing state: MN
Mailing zip: 55425-1581
General Phone: (651) 639-0662
General Fax: (651) 639-0306
General/National Adv. E-mail: info@newscycle.com
Primary Website: www.newscycle.com
Mthly Avg Unique Visitors: 2013
Industry: Software: Advertising (Includes Display; Classified); Software: Business (Includes Administration/Accounting); Software: Circulation;
Personnel: Scott Roessler (CEO); Dan Paulus (Chief Revenue Officer); Jeff Neunsinger (CFO); Bill Mercer (Executive VP of Services and Support); Patrick Glennon (Executive VP Subscriber Platform)

NEWSENGIN, INC.

Street address 1: 15560 Golden Ridge Ct
Street address city: Chesterfield
Street address state: MO
Zip/Postal code: 63017-5124
Country: USA
Mailing address: 15560 Golden Ridge Ct
Mailing city: Chesterfield
Mailing state: MO
Mailing zip: 63017-5124
General Phone: (636) 537-8548
General Fax: (636) 532-9408
Primary Website: www.newsengin.com
Industry: Archiving Systems; News Wire Capture Systems; Software: Editorial; Software: Pagination/Layout;

Personnel: Jim Mosley (CEO); George Landau (Pres.); Virgil Tipton (CTO)

NEWSTECH CO. (DIV. OF ROVINTER, INC.)

Street address 1: 675 NW 97th St
Street address city: Miami
Street address state: FL
Zip/Postal code: 33150-1652
Country: USA
Mailing address: 675 NW 97th St
Mailing city: Miami
Mailing state: FL
Mailing zip: 33150-1652
General Phone: (305) 757-5577
General Fax: (305) 757-2255
General/National Adv. E-mail: e-mail@newstech.com
Primary Website: www.newstech.com
Mthly Avg Unique Visitors: 1979
Industry: Blankets; Film & Paper: Phototypesetting; Inks; Offset Chemicals & Supplies; Plate Mounting & Register Systems; Plate Processors; Plates: Offset (Computer to Plate); Plates: Offset (Conventional); Press Parts; Rollers;
Personnel: Oscar Rovito (Pres.); Diego A. Rovito (Vice Pres.)

NEXSTAR-TRIBUNE MEDIA

Street address 1: 545 E. John Carpenter Freeway
Street address 2: Suite 700
Street address city: Irving
Street address state: TX
Zip/Postal code: 75062
Country: USA
Mailing address: 545 E. John Carpenter Freeway
Mailing city: Irving
Mailing state: TX
Mailing zip: 75062
General Phone: (972) 373-8800
General Fax: (972) 373-8888
Primary Website: www.nexstar.tv
Mthly Avg Unique Visitors: 1965
Industry: Software: Pagination/Layout; Training: Design & Layout;
Note: As one of the nationâ€™s largest independent broadcasters, Tribune Media combines distinctive content with nationwide broadcast distribution and cutting-edge digital properties. WGN America, the companyâ€™s widely distributed general entertainment cable channel, is home to a number of high quality exclusives and original series. In every aspect of the company, whether in producing critical local news, riveting programming, or premier sporting events, Tribune Media engages and connects viewers with must-have content across every distribution platform.
Personnel: Perry A. Sook (Chairman, Pres. and CEO); Thomas E. Carter (CFO)

NIKON, INC.

Street address 1: 1300 Walt Whitman Rd
Street address city: Melville
Street address state: NY
Zip/Postal code: 11747-3001
Country: USA
Mailing address: 1300 Walt Whitman Rd Fl 2
Mailing city: Melville
Mailing state: NY
Mailing zip: 11747-3064
General Phone: (631) 547-4200
General Fax: (631) 547-0299
Primary Website: www.nikonusa.com
Industry: Consumer Electronics
Personnel: Nobuyoshi Gokyu (Pres./CEO); David Lee (Sr. Vice Pres.); Steve Heiner (Gen. Mgr., Mktg. Pro Pdcts./ Digital SLR Systems/Speedlights); William Giordano (Nat'l Mktg. Mgr., Nikon USA); Kristina Kurtzke (Communications Coordinator)

NISUS SOFTWARE, INC.

Street address 1: 107 S Cedros Ave
Street address city: Solana Beach
Street address state: CA
Zip/Postal code: 92075-1994
Country: USA
Mailing address: PO Box 1302
Mailing city: Solana Beach
Mailing state: CA
Mailing zip: 92075-7302
General Phone: (858) 481-1477
General Fax: (858) 764-0573
General/National Adv. E-mail: info@nisus.com
Primary Website: www.nisus.com
Mthly Avg Unique Visitors: 1984
Industry: Word Processing System

NOBLE SYSTEM CORPORATION

Street address 1: 1200 Ashwood Pkwy
Street address 2: Ste 300
Street address city: Atlanta
Street address state: GA
Zip/Postal code: 30338-4747
Country: USA
Mailing address: 1200 Ashwood Pkwy Ste 300
Mailing city: Atlanta
Mailing state: GA
Mailing zip: 30338-4747
General Phone: (404) 851 1331
General Fax: (404) 851 1421
General/National Adv. E-mail: info@noblesystems.com
Primary Website: www.noblesystems.com
Mthly Avg Unique Visitors: 1985
Industry: Omnichannel Contact Management Call Center Software Telecommunications
Personnel: Jim Noble Jr (Pres./CEO); Rita Dearing (COO); Jay S. Mayne (CFO); Mark M. Moore (CTO); Christopher Saulkner (Vice Pres., Sales/Mktg.)

NORMAN X GUTTMAN, INC.

Street address 1: 135 Green St
Street address city: Woodbridge
Street address state: NJ
Zip/Postal code: 07095-2961
Country: USA
Mailing address: 135 Green St
Mailing city: Woodbridge
Mailing state: NJ
Mailing zip: 07095-2961
General Phone: (732) 636-8671
General Fax: (732) 636-8673
Primary Website: www.advertoon.com
Mthly Avg Unique Visitors: 1975
Industry: Inks; Roll Converters; Roller Grinding Services; Rollers; Rollers: Dampening; Tension & Web Controls;
Personnel: Daniel Guttman (Pres.)

NORTH ATLANTIC PUBLISHING SYSTEMS, INC.

Street address 1: 66 Commonwealth Ave
Street address city: Concord
Street address state: MA
Zip/Postal code: 01742-2974
Country: USA
Mailing address: 66 Commonwealth Ave
Mailing city: Concord
Mailing state: MA
Mailing zip: 01742-2974
General Phone: (978) 371-8989
General Fax: (978) 371-5678
General/National Adv. E-mail: naps@napsys.com; xthelp@napsys.com
Primary Website: www.napsys.com
Mthly Avg Unique Visitors: 1989
Industry: Consulting Services: Editorial; Software: Asset Management; Software: Editorial; Software: Pagination/Layout; Software: Workflow Management/ Tracking;
Personnel: Andrew W. Koppel (Retail Sales Mgr.)

NORTH SHORE CONSULTANTS, INC.

Street address 1: 4910 N Monitor Ave
Street address city: Chicago
Street address state: IL
Zip/Postal code: 60630-2025
Country: USA
Mailing address: 613 Thorndale Ave
Mailing city: Elk Grove Village
Mailing state: IL
Mailing zip: 60007-4334
General Phone: (773) 286-7245
General Fax: (773) 286-1974
General/National Adv. E-mail: nsc@enescee.com
Primary Website: www.enescee.com
Industry: Adhesives; Flying Pasters; Splicers, Automatic; Tape Splicing Equipment;
Personnel: Audrey Mysliwiec (Pres.); Dennis B. Wojtecki (Mgr.)

NORTHEAST INDUSTRIES, INC.

Street address 1: 2965 Tolemac Way
Street address city: Prescott
Street address state: AZ
Zip/Postal code: 86305-2179
Country: USA
Mailing address: 2965 Tolemac Way
Mailing city: Prescott
Mailing state: AZ
Mailing zip: 86305-2179
General Phone: 800-821-6257
General Fax: (928) 443-0851
General/National Adv. E-mail: sam@neiinc.com
Primary Website: www.neiinc.com
Mthly Avg Unique Visitors: 1978
Industry: Consulting Services: Equipment; Presses: DiLitho; Presses: Flexographic; Presses: Letterpress; Presses: Offset;
Personnel: Sam W. Boyles (Pres.)

NORTHERN GRAPHIC SUPPLY

Street address 1: 64 Hardy Dr
Street address city: Sparks
Street address state: NV
Zip/Postal code: 89431-6307
Country: USA
Mailing address: 64 Hardy Dr
Mailing city: Sparks
Mailing state: NV
Mailing zip: 89431-6307
General Phone: (775) 359-6466
General Fax: (775) 359-6966
General/National Adv. E-mail: 4ngs@sbcglobal.net
Mthly Avg Unique Visitors: 1965
Industry: Newspaper Marketing
Personnel: Barbara Gouldstone (Pres.)

NORWOOD PAPER

Street address 1: 7001 W 60th St
Street address city: Chicago
Street address state: IL
Zip/Postal code: 60638-3101
Country: USA
Mailing address: 7001 W 60th St
Mailing city: Chicago
Mailing state: IL
Mailing zip: 60638-3101
General Phone: (773) 788-1508
General Fax: (773) 788-1528
General/National Adv. E-mail: sales@norwoodpaper.com
Primary Website: www.norwoodpaper.com
Mthly Avg Unique Visitors: 1972
Industry: Newsprint; Paper: Coated Groundwood Offset; Paper: Groundwood Specialties; Paper: Specialty Printing Paper; Rewinders;
Personnel: Laura Martin (President); Robert Zeman (Vice President); Kathleen Zemen (COO)

NOTEADS.COM, INC./POST-IT NOTE ADVERTISING

Street address 1: 6906 Martin Way E
Street address city: Olympia
Street address state: WA
Zip/Postal code: 98516-5567
Country: USA
Mailing address: 6906 Martin Way E
Mailing city: Olympia
Mailing state: WA
Mailing zip: 98516-5567
General Phone: 800-309-7502
General Fax: (800) 309-7503
General/National Adv. E-mail: john@noteads.com
Primary Website: www.noteads.com
Mthly Avg Unique Visitors: 1997
Industry: Consulting Services: Advertising
Note: Hand and Machine Applied Front Page Sticky Note Ads
Personnel: John Grantham (President); Kristin Gustin (Sales)

NOVATECH, INC.

Street address 1: 4106 Charlotte Ave
Street address city: Nashville
Street address state: TN
Zip/Postal code: 37209
Country: USA
Mailing address: 4106 Charlotte Ave
Mailing city: Nashville
Mailing state: TN
Mailing zip: 37209
General Phone: (615) 577-7677
General/National Adv. E-mail: novatechusa@novatech.net
Primary Website: www.novatech.net
Mthly Avg Unique Visitors: 1987
Industry: Facsimilie/Fax Transmission Systems; Laser Printers;
Personnel: Darren Metz (CEO); Joe White (Pres.); Jeff Hoctor (CPA, CFO); Jason Levkulich (Dir. of Marketing); John Sutton (Dir. of Sales)

NOVUS IMAGING, INC.

Street address 1: 440 Medinah Rd.
Street address city: Roselle
Street address state: IL
Zip/Postal code: 60172
Country: USA
Mailing address: 440 Medinah Rd.
Mailing city: Roselle
Mailing state: IL
Mailing zip: 60172
General Phone: 630-858-6101
General/National Adv. E-mail: info@mrprint.com
Primary Website: www.mrprint.com
Mthly Avg Unique Visitors: 1948
Industry: Cameras & Accessories; Color Printing Frames; Controls: Exposure; Dark Room Equipment; Diffusion Transfer Processors; Offset Plate-Making Service & Equipment; Plate Exposure Units; Platemakers: Offset (Conventional); Processors: Diffusion Transfer; Proofing Systems;

NRD LLC

Street address 1: 2937 Alt Blvd
Street address city: Grand Island
Street address state: NY
Zip/Postal code: 14072-1285
County: Erie
Country: USA
Mailing address: PO Box 310
Mailing city: Grand Island
Mailing state: NY
Mailing zip: 14072-0310
General Phone: (716) 773-7634
General Fax: (716) 773-7744
General/National Adv. E-mail: sales@nrdinc.com
Primary Website: www.nrdinc.com
Mthly Avg Unique Visitors: 1970
Industry: Static Eliminators
Personnel: John Glynn (Director of Sales and Marketing)

NSA MEDIA

Street address 1: 3025 Highland Pkwy,
Street address 2: Suite 700
Street address city: Downers Grove
Street address state: IL
Zip/Postal code: 60515
County: Dupage
Country: USA
Mailing address: 3025 Highland Pkwy Ste 700
Mailing city: Downers Grove
Mailing state: IL
Mailing zip: 60515-5553
General Phone: (630) 729-7500
General/National Adv. E-mail: info@nsamedia.com
Primary Website: www.nsamedia.com
Mthly Avg Unique Visitors: 1991
Industry: Consulting Services: Advertising
Personnel: Randy Novak (VP, Bus. Dev.)

NUANCE COMMUNICATIONS INC.

Street address 1: 1 Wayside Rd
Street address city: Burlington
Street address state: MA
Zip/Postal code: 01803-4609
Country: USA
Mailing address: 1 Wayside Rd
Mailing city: Burlington
Mailing state: MA
Mailing zip: 01803-4609
General Phone: (781) 565-5000

General Fax: (781) 565-5001
General/National Adv. E-mail: info@dragonsys.com
Primary Website: www.nuance.com
Mthly Avg Unique Visitors: 1982
Industry: Speech Recognition
Personnel: Renee Blodgett (Mgr., Cor. Commun.); Paul Ricci (Chrmn./CEO); Thomas Beaudoin (Exec. Vice Pres./CFO); Richard Palmer (Sr. Vice Pres., Cor. Devel.); Robert Weideman (Sr. Vice Pres., Mktg.); Rick Broyles (Vice Pres., Opns.); Steve Chambers (Sr. Vice Pres., Worldwide Sales); Dawn Howarth (Vice Pres., HR)

NUS CONSULTING GROUP

Street address 1: 1 Maynard Dr
Street address city: Park Ridge
Street address state: NJ
Zip/Postal code: 07656-1878
Country: USA
Mailing address: PO Box 712
Mailing city: Park Ridge
Mailing state: NJ
Mailing zip: 07656-0712
General Phone: (201) 391-4300
General Fax: (201) 391-8158
General/National Adv. E-mail: contact@nusconsulting.com
Primary Website: www.nusconsulting.com
Mthly Avg Unique Visitors: 1933
Industry: Telecommunications
Personnel: Gary Soultanian (Co-Pres.); Richard Soultanian (Co-Pres.)

OLEC

Street address 1: 1850 E Saint Andrew Pl
Street address city: Santa Ana
Street address state: CA
Zip/Postal code: 92705-5043
Country: USA
Mailing address: 1850 E Saint Andrew Pl
Mailing city: Santa Ana
Mailing state: CA
Mailing zip: 92705-5043
General Phone: (714) 881-2000
General Fax: (714) 881-2001
General/National Adv. E-mail: sales@olec.com
Primary Website: www.olec.com
Industry: Produciton Control Systems
Personnel: Don Ohlig (Mng. Dir.); Al Mora (Sales Mgr.); Gordon Quinn (Vice Pres.,Electronics Sales)

OLYMPUS AMERICA, INC.

Street address 1: 3500 Corporate Pkwy
Street address city: Center Valley
Street address state: PA
Zip/Postal code: 18034-8229
Country: USA
Mailing address: 3500 Corporate Pkwy
Mailing city: Center Valley
Mailing state: PA
Mailing zip: 18034-8229
General Phone: (888) 553-4448
General Fax: (484) 896-7115
Primary Website: www.olympusamerica.com
Mthly Avg Unique Visitors: 1977
Industry: Cameras & Audio; Medical & Surgical Components; Industrial Microscopes; Aerospace; Automotive; Oil & Gas;
Personnel: Michael C. Woodford (CEO & Pres.); Karl Watanabe (Pres. & CFO); Stephanie Sherry (Executive Director)

ONE CORP.

Street address 1: 455 E Paces Ferry Rd NE
Street address 2: Ste 350
Street address city: Atlanta
Street address state: GA
Zip/Postal code: 30305-3315
Country: USA
Mailing address: 455 E Paces Ferry Rd NE Ste 350
Mailing city: Atlanta
Mailing state: GA
Mailing zip: 30305-3315
General Phone: (404) 842-0111
General Fax: (404) 848-0525
General/National Adv. E-mail: dboles@onecorp.com
Primary Website: www.onecorp.com; www.webpresses.com
Mthly Avg Unique Visitors: 1971
Industry: Equipment Dealers (New); Equipment Dealers (Used); Web Offset Presses; Flying Pasters; Presses: Offset; Remanufactures Equipment; Splicers, Automatic;
Personnel: Durelle Boles (Pres.); Jennifer Boles (CFO)

OUTSOURCING USA

Street address 1: 1200 Twin Stacks Dr
Street address city: Dallas
Street address state: PA
Zip/Postal code: 18612-8507
County: Luzerne
Country: USA
Mailing address: 1200 Twin Stacks Dr
Mailing city: Dallas
Mailing state: PA
Mailing zip: 18612
General Phone: (570) 674-5600
General/National Adv. E-mail: info@outsourcingusa.net
Primary Website: www.outsourcingusa.net
Mthly Avg Unique Visitors: 2009
Industry: Pre-press ad production services for both print and web
Personnel: Lynn Banta (CEO); Maureen Missal (VP Business Development); Tony Banta (VP of Information Systems)

OVERLAND STORAGE, INC.

Street address 1: 9112 Spectrum Center Blvd
Street address city: San Diego
Street address state: CA
Zip/Postal code: 92123-1439
Country: USA
Mailing address: 9112 Spectrum Center Blvd
Mailing city: San Diego
Mailing state: CA
Mailing zip: 92123-1599
General Phone: (858) 571-5555
General Fax: (858) 571-3664
General/National Adv. E-mail: sales@overlandstorage.com
Primary Website: www.overlandstorage.com
Mthly Avg Unique Visitors: 1980
Industry: Computers: Storage Devices
Personnel: Eric Kelly (Pres); Veritta Wells (Vice Pres., HR); Mike Gawarecki (Vice Pres., Opns.); Ravi Pendekanti (Vice Pres., Sales)

PACESETTER GRAPHIC SERVICE CORP.

Street address 1: 2672 Hickory Grove Rd NW
Street address city: Acworth
Street address state: GA
Zip/Postal code: 30101-3643
Country: USA
Mailing address: 2672 Hickory Grove Rd NW
Mailing city: Acworth
Mailing state: GA
Mailing zip: 30101-3643
General Phone: (800) 241-7970
General Fax: 770-974-2980
Primary Website: www.pacesetterusa.com
Mthly Avg Unique Visitors: 1977
Industry: Blankets; Rollers; Rollers: Dampening;
Personnel: Robert Allen (Pres.); Jeri Hammond (Exec. Vice Pres.)

PAGE

Street address 1: 700 American Ave
Street address 2: Ste 101
Street address city: King Of Prussia
Street address state: PA
Zip/Postal code: 19406-4031
Country: USA
Mailing address: 700 American Ave Ste 101
Mailing city: King Of Prussia
Mailing state: PA
Mailing zip: 19406-4031
General Phone: (610) 592-0646
General Fax: (610) 592-0647
Primary Website: www.pagecooperative.com
Mthly Avg Unique Visitors: 1984
Industry: Composing Room Equipment & Supplies; Inks; Newsprint; Paper: Groundwood Specialties; Plates: Offset (Conventional);
Personnel: John Snyder (CEO); Evelyn Jayne (Office Mgr.)

PALOS SOFTWARE

Street address 1: 520 Kearny Villa Way, Ste 108
Street address city: San Diego
Street address state: CA
Zip/Postal code: 92123
Country: USA
Mailing address: 520 Kearny Villa Way, Ste. 108
Mailing city: San Diego
Mailing state: CA
Mailing zip: 92123-1869
General Phone: (858) 836-4400
General/National Adv. E-mail: marketing@palos.com
Primary Website: www.palos.com
Mthly Avg Unique Visitors: 1988
Industry: Software: Pagination/Layout
Personnel: David Altomare (Pres.)

PAMARCO GLOBAL GRAPHICS

Street address 1: 150 Marr Ave NW
Street address city: Marietta
Street address state: GA
Zip/Postal code: 30060-1050
Country: USA
Mailing address: 150 Marr Ave NW
Mailing city: Marietta
Mailing state: GA
Mailing zip: 30060-1050
General Phone: (770) 795-8556
General Fax: (770) 795-8943
General/National Adv. E-mail: info@pamarcoglobal.com
Primary Website: www.pamarcoglobal.com
Mthly Avg Unique Visitors: 1970
Industry: Press Accessories, Parts & Supplies; Presses: Offset; Rollers; Rollers: Dampening;
Personnel: James Miller (Vice Pres., Mfg.); Greg Anderson (Vice Pres., Sales/Mktg.)

PAMARCO GLOBAL GRAPHICS

Street address 1: 235 E 11th Ave
Street address city: Roselle
Street address state: NJ
Zip/Postal code: 07203-2015
Country: USA
Mailing address: 235 E 11th Ave
Mailing city: Roselle
Mailing state: NJ
Mailing zip: 07203-2015
General Phone: (908) 241-1200
General Fax: (908) 241-4009
Display Adv. E-mail: sales@pamarcoinc.com
Primary Website: www.pamarcoglobal.com
Mthly Avg Unique Visitors: 1944
Industry: Rollers
Personnel: Terry Ford (Pres./CEO)

PAN AMERICAN PAPERS, INC.

Street address 1: 5101 NW 37th Ave
Street address city: Miami
Street address state: FL
Zip/Postal code: 33142-3232
Country: USA
Mailing address: 5101 NW 37th Ave
Mailing city: Miami
Mailing state: FL
Mailing zip: 33142-3232
General Phone: (305) 635-2534
General Fax: (305) 635-2538
Primary Website: www.panampap.com
Mthly Avg Unique Visitors: 1967
Industry: Newsprint; Paper: Specialty Printing Paper;
Personnel: Jesus A. Roca (Sr. Vice Pres.)

PANTONE, INC.

Street address 1: 590 Commerce Blvd
Street address city: Carlstadt
Street address state: NJ
Zip/Postal code: 07072-3013
Country: USA
Mailing address: 590 Commerce Blvd
Mailing city: Carlstadt
Mailing state: NJ
Mailing zip: 07072-3098
General Phone: (201) 935-5500
General Fax: (201) 935-3338
General/National Adv. E-mail: support@pantone.com
Primary Website: www.pantone.com
Mthly Avg Unique Visitors: 1962
Industry: Color Management Software; Software: Design/Graphics;
Personnel: Ron Potesky (Pres.)

PARAGON TECHNOLOGIES INC.

Street address 1: 600 Kuebler Rd
Street address city: Easton
Street address state: PA
Zip/Postal code: 18040-9201
Country: USA
Mailing address: 101 Larry Holmes Dr Ste 500
Mailing city: Easton
Mailing state: PA
Mailing zip: 18042-7723
General Phone: (610) 252-7321
General Fax: (610) 252-3102
General/National Adv. E-mail: info@sihs.com; sales@sihs.com
Primary Website: www.sihs.com
Mthly Avg Unique Visitors: 1958
Industry: Conveyors; Mailroom Systems & Equipment; Material Handling Equipment: Automatic Guided Vehicles;
Personnel: Theodore W. Myers (Chrmn.)

PARSONS CORPORATION

Street address 1: 100 W Walnut St
Street address city: Pasadena
Street address state: CA
Zip/Postal code: 91124-0001
Country: USA
Mailing address: 100 W Walnut St
Mailing city: Pasadena
Mailing state: CA
Mailing zip: 91124-0001
General Phone: (626) 440-2000
General Fax: (626) 440-2630
Primary Website: www.parsons.com
Mthly Avg Unique Visitors: 1944
Industry: Engineering, construction, technical, and professional services
Personnel: Charles Harrington (Chairman and CEO); Erin Kuhlman (Corporate Vice President, Marketing & Communications)

PASSUR AEROSPACE, INC.

Street address 1: 1 Landmark Sq
Street address 2: Ste 1900
Street address city: Stamford
Street address state: CT
Zip/Postal code: 06901-2671
Country: USA
Mailing address: 1 Landmark Sq Ste 1900
Mailing city: Stamford
Mailing state: CT
Mailing zip: 06901-2671
General Phone: (888) 340-3712
General/National Adv. E-mail: sales@passur.com
Primary Website: www.passur.com
Mthly Avg Unique Visitors: 1974
Industry: Data Communication; Input & Editing Systems;
Personnel: Ron Dunsky (Media); G.S. Beckwith Gilbert (Chairman); James T. Barry (Pres. & CEO); Tim Campbell (COO); Louis J. Petrucelly (Sr. V. P. & CFO)

PASTE-UP SUPPLY

Street address 1: 10930 1/2 Grand Ave
Street address city: Temple City
Street address state: CA
Zip/Postal code: 91780-3551
Country: USA
Mailing address: 10930 1/2 Grand Ave
Mailing city: Temple City
Mailing state: CA
Mailing zip: 91780-3551
General Phone: (626) 448-4543
Mthly Avg Unique Visitors: 1965
Industry: Adhesive Wax Coaters
Personnel: Pat Treanor (Owner)

PC INDUSTRIES

Street address 1: 176 Ambrogio Dr
Street address city: Gurnee

Street address state: IL
Zip/Postal code: 60031-3373
County: Lake
Country: USA
Mailing address: 176 Ambrogio Dr.
Mailing city: Gurnee
Mailing state: IL
Mailing zip: 60031
General Phone: (847) 336-3300
General Fax: (847) 336-3232
General/National Adv. E-mail: sales@pcindustries.com
Primary Website: www.pcindustries.com
Mthly Avg Unique Visitors: 1975
Industry: Cameras & Accessories; Color Registration; Controls: Register; Optical Character Recognition (OCR); Press Control Systems; Proofing Systems;
Personnel: John Woolley (Pres./Sales Mgr.)

PDI PLASTICS

Street address 1: 5037 Pine Creek Dr
Street address city: Westerville
Street address state: OH
Zip/Postal code: 43081-4849
Country: USA
Mailing address: 5037 Pine Creek Dr
Mailing city: Westerville
Mailing state: OH
Mailing zip: 43081-4849
General Phone: (800)634-0017
General Fax: (614) 890-0467
General/National Adv. E-mail: sales@pdisaneck.com
Primary Website: www.newsbags.com
Mthly Avg Unique Visitors: 1984
Industry: Circulation Equipment & Supplies
Personnel: Frank Cannon (Pres.); Todd Wilson (Exec. VP)

PENCO PRODUCTS

Street address 1: 1820 Stonehenge Dr
Street address city: Greenville
Street address state: NC
Zip/Postal code: 27858-5965
Country: USA
Mailing address: 1820 Stonehenge Drive
Mailing city: Greenville
Mailing state: PA
Mailing zip: 27585
General Phone: 800-562-1000
General/National Adv. E-mail: general@pencoproducts.com
Primary Website: www.pencoproducts.com
Mthly Avg Unique Visitors: 1869
Industry: Cabinets; Storage Retrieval Systems;
Personnel: Greg Grogan (Pres.); Philip H. Krugler (Mktg. Mgr.)

PERFORMANCE CONTRACTING GROUP

Street address 1: 16400 College Blvd
Street address city: Lenexa
Street address state: KS
Zip/Postal code: 66219-1389
Country: USA
Mailing address: 16400 College Blvd
Mailing city: Lenexa
Mailing state: KS
Mailing zip: 66219-1389
General Phone: 1-800-255-6886
General/National Adv. E-mail: info@pcg.com
Primary Website: www.pcg.com

PERMA-FIX ENVIRONMENTAL SERVICES

Street address 1: 8302 Dunwoody Pl
Street address 2: Ste 250
Street address city: Atlanta
Street address state: GA
Zip/Postal code: 30350-3390
Country: USA
Mailing address: 8302 Dunwoody Pl Ste 250
Mailing city: Atlanta
Mailing state: GA
Mailing zip: 30350-3390
General Phone: (770) 587-9898
General Fax: (770) 587-9937
General/National Adv. E-mail: corporate@perma-fix.com
Primary Website: www.perma-fix.com
Mthly Avg Unique Visitors: 1989
Industry: Environmental Control Systems
Personnel: Lou Centofanti (Pres./CEO); Pam Ittah (Mgr.)

PERRETTA GRAPHICS CORP.

Street address 1: 46 Violet Ave
Street address city: Poughkeepsie
Street address state: NY
Zip/Postal code: 12601-1521
Country: USA
Mailing address: 46 Violet Ave
Mailing city: Poughkeepsie
Mailing state: NY
Mailing zip: 12601-1521
General Phone: (845) 473-0550
General Fax: (845) 454-7507
General/National Adv. E-mail: mailbox@perretta.com; service@perretta.com
Primary Website: www.perretta.com
Mthly Avg Unique Visitors: 1981
Industry: Controls: Register; Ink Controls, Computerized; Keyless Inking Conversion & Add-ons; Web Press - Special Equipment;
Personnel: Christopher Perretta (Pres.); Bruce Quilliam (Bus. Mgr., Int'l Sales); Bruce L. Quilliam (Vice Pres., Sales/Mktg.); Jean Laird (Sales Mgr.); Paul Jorde (Serv. Mgr.); Jordan Terziyski (Asst. Serv. Mgr.)

PETCO ROLLER CO.

Street address 1: 28041 N Bradley Rd
Street address city: Lake Forest
Street address state: IL
Zip/Postal code: 60045-1163
Country: USA
Mailing address: 28041 N Bradley Rd
Mailing city: Lake Forest
Mailing state: IL
Mailing zip: 60045-1163
General Phone: (847) 362-1820
General Fax: (847) 362-1833
General/National Adv. E-mail: mail@petcorolls.com
Primary Website: www.petcorolls.com
Mthly Avg Unique Visitors: 1964
Industry: Roll Coverings; Rollers; Rollers: Dampening;
Personnel: Dale Glen (Sales Mgr.)

PHELPS, CUTLER & ASSOCIATES

Street address 1: 35 Barnard St
Street address 2: Ste 300
Street address city: Savannah
Street address state: GA
Zip/Postal code: 31401-2515
County: Chatham
Country: USA
Mailing address: 35 Barnard St Ste 300
Mailing city: Savannah
Mailing state: GA
Mailing zip: 31401
General Phone: (912) 388-4692
General Fax: (678) 826-4708
General/National Adv. E-mail: phelpscutler@aol.com
Display Adv. E-mail: sales@coastalempirenews.com
Primary Website: www.phelpscutler.com
Mthly Avg Unique Visitors: 1991
Industry: M&A Broker; Expert Witness on Valuation; General Operational Consulting: Print and Digital Revenue Strategies; Niche (print and digital websites) specialist; Circulation Consulting Services: Editorial; Consulting Services: Financial; Consulting Services: Human Resources; Consulting Services: Marketing;
Note: PC&A is a diverse media consulting and Mergers & Acquisition firm. Proven core competencies in new revenue strategies for print and digital. Turnaround specialist. Recent clients include some of the largest media companies in the U.S. Qualified Expert Witness in Valuation. Owner of Coastal Empire News, Savannah, GA. with eight online-only news and content sites. www.CoastalEmpireNews.com.
Personnel: Louise Phelps (Managing Partner)

PHOTO SYSTEMS, INC.

Street address 1: 7200 Huron River Dr
Street address city: Dexter
Street address state: MI
Zip/Postal code: 48130-1099
Country: USA
Mailing address: 7200 Huron River Dr
Mailing city: Dexter
Mailing state: MI
Mailing zip: 48130-1099
General Phone: (734) 424-9625
General/National Adv. E-mail: lori@photosys.com
Primary Website: www.photosys.com
Mthly Avg Unique Visitors: 1968
Industry: Chemicals: Photographic; Chemicals: Plate Processing; Chemicals: Pressroom; Chemicals: Roller Cleaning; Film & Paper: Film Processing Machines;
Personnel: Alan Fischer (Pres.)

PITMAN PHOTO SUPPLY

Street address 1: 13911 S Dixie Hwy
Street address city: Miami
Street address state: FL
Zip/Postal code: 33176-7234
Country: USA
Mailing address: 13911 S Dixie Hwy
Mailing city: Miami
Mailing state: FL
Mailing zip: 33176-7234
General Phone: 800-252-3008
General/National Adv. E-mail: pitmanphoto@att.net
Primary Website: www.pitmanphotosupply.com
Mthly Avg Unique Visitors: 1928
Industry: Cameras & Accessories; Chemicals: Photographic; Dark Room Equipment; Dryers: Film and Papers; Enlargers (Photographic); Film & Paper: Film Roll Dispensers; Film & Paper: Filters (Photographic); Fixing & Stop Baths; Lenses (Camera); Photography: Digital/Electronic Cameras;
Personnel: Michael Werner (Pres.); Lowell H. Elsea (Sales Mgr.)

PLUMTREE CO.

Street address 1: PO Box 14216
Street address city: Savannah
Street address state: GA
Zip/Postal code: 31416-1216
Country: USA
Mailing address: PO Box 14216
Mailing city: Savannah
Mailing state: GA
Mailing zip: 31416-1216
General Phone: (912) 354-5155
General Fax: (912) 354-1375
General/National Adv. E-mail: email@plumtreecompany.com
Primary Website: www.plumtreecompany.com
Mthly Avg Unique Visitors: 1985
Industry: Consulting Services: Production; Mailroom Systems & Equipment; Newspaper Couter; Newspaper Marketing; Newsprint Handeling Equipment; Promotion Services; Software: Press/Post Press; Software: Workflow Management/Tracking; Totalizing Systems;
Personnel: Tim Cooper (Pres.); Julian Cooper (Vice Pres., Sales)

POLAROID HOLDING CO.

Street address 1: 300 Baker Ave
Street address city: Concord
Street address state: MA
Zip/Postal code: 01742-2131
Country: USA
Mailing address: 300 Baker Ave Ste 330
Mailing city: Concord
Mailing state: MA
Mailing zip: 01742-2131
General Phone: (781) 386-2000
General Fax: (781) 386-6243
General/National Adv. E-mail: marketing@polaroid.com
Primary Website: www.polaroid.com
Personnel: Mary L. Jeffries (CEO); Jim Koestler (Vice Pres., Product Mgmt.); Jon Pollock (Vice Pres./Gen. Mgr., Digital Imaging); Cheryl Mau (Vice Pres., Mktg.); Lorrie Parent (Media Rel.)

POLKADOTS SOFTWARE INC.

Street address 1: 216-2555 Av Dollard
Street address city: Lasalle
Street address state: QC
Zip/Postal code: H8N 3A9
Country: Canada
Mailing state: QC
General Phone: (514) 595-6866
General/National Adv. E-mail: info@polkadots.ca
Display Adv. E-mail: sales@polkadots.ca
Primary Website: www.polkadots.ca
Mthly Avg Unique Visitors: 1998
Industry: Newspaper prepress automation, page pairing, ink optimizing, RIP, web growth compensation, internet proofing, internet job definition
Note: PrePress Software
Personnel: Gilles Duhamel (Pres.); Sylvain Audet (VP)

PORTAGE NEWSPAPER SUPPLY CO.

Street address 1: 655 Winding Brook Dr
Street address 2: Ste 205
Street address city: Glastonbury
Street address state: CT
Zip/Postal code: 06033-4364
Country: USA
Mailing address: 655 Winding Brook Dr Ste 205
Mailing city: Glastonbury
Mailing state: CT
Mailing zip: 06033-4364
General Phone: (877) 659-8318
General Fax: (877) 806-6397
General/National Adv. E-mail: info@portagegraphic.com
Primary Website: www.portagenotebooks.com
Mthly Avg Unique Visitors: 1955
Industry: Cutters & Trimmers
Personnel: Robert Belter (Pres.)

POYRY MANAGEMENT CONSULTING (USA) INC.

Street address 1: 52 Vanderbilt Ave
Street address 2: Rm 1405
Street address city: New York
Street address state: NY
Zip/Postal code: 10017-0080
Country: USA
Mailing address: 52 Vanderbilt Ave Rm 1405
Mailing city: New York
Mailing state: NY
Mailing zip: 10017-0080
General Phone: (646) 651-1547
General Fax: (212) 661-3830
Primary Website: www.poyry.us
Industry: Consulting Services: Management Consulting; Market Research; Market Strategy; paper; media
Personnel: Soile Kilpi (Director)

PPI MEDIA GMBH

Street address 1: Hindenburgstrasse 49
Street address city: Hamburg
Zip/Postal code: D-22297
Country: Germany
Mailing address: Hindenburgstrasse 49
Mailing city: Hamburg
Mailing zip: D-22297
General Phone: +49 40 227433-60
General Fax: +49 40 227433-666
General/National Adv. E-mail: ppimedia.de
Display Adv. E-mail: info@ppimedia.de
Primary Website: www.ppimedia.de
Mthly Avg Unique Visitors: 1984
Industry: Mailroom Systems & Equipment; Output Management and Preflight Software; Pagination Systems; Produciton Control Systems; Software: Advertising (includes Display; Classified); Software: Pagination/Layout; Software: Workflow Management/ Tracking; System Integration Services;
Personnel: Hauke Berndt (COO); Jan Kasten (CTO); Thomas Reinacher (CEO ppi Media US Inc.); Annika Schulz (Marketing Manager); Heiko Bichel (PR Manager); Jan Kasten (Managing Director (R&D) I CTO); Sven ClauÃŸen (IT Infrastructure Manager); Manuel Scheyda (SVP Business Innovation); Cindy Eggers (Senior Product Designer); Steffen Landsberg (VP Sales (Europe)); Claus Harders (Head of Key Account Mgmt)

PRAXAIR, INC.

Street address 1: 10 Riverview Dr.
Street address city: Danbury
Street address state: CT
Zip/Postal code: 06810
Country: USA
Mailing address: 10 Riverview Dr.
Mailing city: Danbury
Mailing state: CT
Mailing zip: 06810
General Phone: (800) 772-9247
General Fax: (800) 772-9985
General/National Adv. E-mail: info@praxair.com
Primary Website: www.praxair.com

Mthly Avg Unique Visitors: 1992
Industry: Rollers
Personnel: Stephen F. Angel (Chrmn./Pres./CEO); Matthew J. White (Sr. V. P. & CFO); Eduardo Menezes (Exec. Vice Pres.); Kelcey E. Hoyt (V. P. & Controller); Lisa A. Esneault (Vice Pres., Global Commun./Pub. Rel.)

PRESS-ENTERPRISE, INC. (COLOR GRAPHICS DEPT.)

Street address 1: 3185 Lackawanna Ave
Street address city: Bloomsburg
Street address state: PA
Zip/Postal code: 17815-3329
Country: USA
Mailing address: 3185 Lackawanna Ave
Mailing city: Bloomsburg
Mailing state: PA
Mailing zip: 17815-3398
General Phone: (570) 784-2121
General Fax: (570) 784-9226
Primary Website: www.pressenterpriseonline.com
Mthly Avg Unique Visitors: 1902
Industry: Color Proofing; Color Seperations, Positives; Electronic Pre-Scan Systems; Input & Editing Systems;
Personnel: Bill Bason (Prodn. Mgr., Color Graphics)

PRESSLINE SERVICES, INC.

Street address 1: 731 Prairie Dupont Dr
Street address city: Dupo
Street address state: IL
Zip/Postal code: 62239-1819
Country: USA
Mailing address: 731 Prairie Dupont Dr
Mailing city: Dupo
Mailing state: IL
Mailing zip: 62239
General Phone: (314) 682-3800
General Fax: (314) 487-3150
Primary Website: www.pressline.info; www.presslineservices.com
Mthly Avg Unique Visitors: 1995
Industry: Consulting Services: Equipment; Cylinder Repair; Press Rebuilding; Press Repairs; Web Width Changer;
Personnel: Jim Gore (Pres.)

PRESSROOM CLEANERS, INC.

Street address 1: 5709 S 60th St
Street address 2: Ste 100B
Street address city: Omaha
Street address state: NE
Zip/Postal code: 68117-2204
County: Douglas
Country: USA
Mailing address: 5709 SOUTH 60TH STREET, SUITE 100B
Mailing city: OMAHA
Mailing state: NE
Mailing zip: 68117-2204
General Phone: (402) 597-3199
General Fax: (402) 597-8765
General/National Adv. E-mail: theresa@pressroomcleaners.com
Primary Website: www.pressroomcleaners.com
Mthly Avg Unique Visitors: 1956
Industry: Industrial Cleaning Services
Personnel: Theresa Frangoulis (Pres.); Angie Clarke (Office Mgr.)

PRESSTEK, INC.

Street address 1: 18081 Chesterfield Airport Road
Street address city: Chesterfield
Street address state: MO
Zip/Postal code: 63005
Country: USA
Mailing address: 18081 Chesterfield Airport Road
Mailing city: Chesterfield
Mailing state: MO
Mailing zip: 63005
General Phone: (800) 225-4835
Primary Website: www.presstek.com
Mthly Avg Unique Visitors: 1987
Industry: Presstek DI Digital Offset Presses; ABDick Conventional Offset Presses Platemakers: Offset (Computer to Plate); Plates: Offset (Computer to Plate); Press Accessories, Parts & Supplies; Press Repairs; Presses: Offset; Processors: Film & Paper; Proofing Systems; Punching Equipment; Post Press
Personnel: Eric Vandenberg (Equipment Sales); Chris Yanko (Digital Sales Director); Steve Schulte (Vice President Sales & Marketing); Mike Russell (International Sales Director)

PRESTELIGENCE

Street address 1: 8328 Cleveland Ave NW
Street address city: North Canton
Street address state: OH
Zip/Postal code: 44720-4820
Country: USA
Mailing address: 8328 Cleveland Ave NW
Mailing city: North Canton
Mailing state: OH
Mailing zip: 44720-4820
General Phone: (330) 305-6960
General Fax: (330) 497-5562
General/National Adv. E-mail: info@presteligence.com
Primary Website: www.presteligence.com
Mthly Avg Unique Visitors: 1990
Industry: Calibration Software/Hardware; Color Proofing; Multiplexers/Routers; Ink Controls, Computerized; Output Management and Preflight Software; Prepress Color Proofing Systems; Software: Advertising (Includes Display; Classified); Software: Press/Post Press; Software: Workflow Management/Tracking; System Integration Services; eTearsheets & eInvoices, e-Editions, Mobile Apps, High School Sports Platform and Web CMS
Note: With more than 1500 installations, Presteligence offers a suite of solutions including online ad proofing, e-tearsheets & invoice delivery + payment, color calibrated hard and soft proofing systems, prepress production workflow, ink optimization, print production consolidation projects, web cms, digital replicas, high school sports management platform, and mobile apps. These cost-effective and time efficient solutions, combined with the responsive support team make Presteligence a best-in-class partner for media companies.
Personnel: Bob Behringer (Pres. & CEO); Melissa McBride (Controller); Denise Franken (Dir. of Mktg.); Randy Plant (VP, Ops.); Jeff Bernhardt (Major Accnt. Mgr.)

PRIM HALL ENTERPRISES, INC.

Street address 1: 11 Spellman Rd
Street address city: Plattsburgh
Street address state: NY
Zip/Postal code: 12901-5326
Country: USA
Mailing address: 11 Spellman Rd
Mailing city: Plattsburgh
Mailing state: NY
Mailing zip: 12901-5326
General Phone: (518) 561-7408
General Fax: (518) 563-1472
General/National Adv. E-mail: sales@primhall.com; primhall@primhall.com
Primary Website: www.primhall.com
Mthly Avg Unique Visitors: 1988
Industry: Collating Equipment; Conveyors; Mailroom Systems & Equipment; Paper Handeling Equipment; Three Knife Trimmer;
Personnel: John E. Prim (Pres.); David E. Hall (Vice Pres.); Matt Demers (Mktg. Coord.)

PRINTERS HOUSE AMERICAS LLC

Street address 1: 10, Scindia House, Connaught Place
Street address city: New Delhi
Country: India
Mailing address: 10, Scindia House, Connaught Place
Mailing city: New Delhi
General Phone: 91-11-23313071
General Fax: 91-11-23356637
General/National Adv. E-mail: tphindia@bol.net.in
Primary Website: www.phaorient.com
Note: Printers House Americas, LLC is the distributor of Orient Web Presses. Orient models are single width presses with production"

PRINTERS' SERVICE/PRISCO/ PRISCODIGITAL

Street address 1: 26 Blanchard St
Street address city: Newark
Street address state: NJ
Zip/Postal code: 07105-4702
County: Essex
Country: USA
Mailing address: 26 Blanchard St.
Mailing city: Newark
Mailing state: NJ
Mailing zip: 07105-4784
General Phone: (973) 589-7800
General Fax: (973) 589-3225
General/National Adv. E-mail: inquiries@prisco.com
Primary Website: www.prisco.com
Mthly Avg Unique Visitors: 1903
Industry: Chemicals: Pressroom; Circulation Equipment & Supplies; Cleaners & Solvents; Lubricants; Offset Blankets, Blanket Wash; Offset Chemicals & Supplies; Offset Fountain Solutions; Plate Cleaners; Press Accessories, Parts & Supplies; Solvent Recovery Systems; Wide Format Inkjet systems, Wide Format Inkjet supplies, Automated Cutting Systems, Software
Personnel: Richard B. Liroff (Chrmn.); Bruce Liroff (Pres.); Russ Mantione (CFO); David Gerson (Vice Pres., Research/Technology); Eric A. Gutwillig (Vice Pres., Mktg.); Steve Zunde (President, PriscoDigital LLC); Joe Schleck (Vice Pres., Prodn./Mfg.); Michael White (Senior VP)

PRINTING PRESS SERVICES, INC.

Street address 1: Sellers St. Works
Street address city: Preston Lancs
Zip/Postal code: PR1 5EU
Country: United Kingdom
Mailing address: Sellers St. Works
Mailing city: Preston Lancs
Mailing zip: PR1 5EU
General Phone: +44 1772 797 050
General Fax: +44 1772 705 761
General/National Adv. E-mail: stephenm@ppsi.co.uk
Primary Website: www.ppsi.co.uk
Mthly Avg Unique Visitors: 1976
Industry: Conversion Equipment; Drives & Controls; Equipment Dealers (New); Equipment Dealers (Used); Erectors & Riggers; Ink Controls, Computerized; Ink Fountains & Accessories; Presses: Offset; Splicers, Automatic;
Personnel: Joe McManamon (Pres.); Stephen McManamon (Mng. Dir.-Press Division); David McManamon (Mng. Dir.-Inking Systems Division); Marilyn Lloyd (Office Mgr.)

PRINTING TECHNOLOGIES, INC.

Street address 1: 6266 Morenci Trail
Street address city: Indianapolis
Street address state: IN
Zip/Postal code: 46268
Country: USA
Mailing address: 6266 Morenci Trail
Mailing city: Indianapolis
Mailing state: IN
Mailing zip: 46268
General Phone: (800) 428-3786
General/National Adv. E-mail: info@ptionaroll.com
Primary Website: www.ptionaroll.com
Mthly Avg Unique Visitors: 1994
Industry: Cylinder Repair; Equipment Dealers (Used); Folder Knives; Ink Fountains & Accessories; Press Accessories, Parts & Supplies; Press Rebuilding; Press Repairs; Presses: Offset; Rollers; Rollers: Dampening;
Personnel: Walt Alfred (Pres.)

PRINTMARK

Street address 1: 432 Johnson Rd
Street address city: East Montpelier
Street address state: VT
Zip/Postal code: 05651-4250
Country: USA
Mailing address: 432 Johnson Rd
Mailing city: East Montpelier
Mailing state: VT
Mailing zip: 05651-4250
General Phone: (802) 229-9743
General/National Adv. E-mail: alex@printmark.net
Primary Website: www.printmark.net
Mthly Avg Unique Visitors: 1983
Industry: Consulting Services: Computer; Consulting Services: Editorial; Consulting Services: Production;
Note: Consultants to publishers on manufacturing, distribution, and technology."
Personnel: Alex Brown (Dir., Prodn.)

PRINTRONIX, INC.

Street address 1: 6440 Oak Canyon Dr. Ste. 200
Street address city: Irvine
Street address state: CA
Zip/Postal code: 92618
Country: USA
Mailing address: 6440 Oak Canyon Dr. Ste. 200
Mailing city: Irvine
Mailing state: CA
Mailing zip: 92618
General Phone: (714) 368-2300
General Fax: (714) 368-2600
Primary Website: www.printronix.com
Mthly Avg Unique Visitors: 1974
Industry: Computers: Hardware & Software Integrators
Personnel: Werner Heid (CEO); Mark Tobin (CFO); Ron Gillies (V. Pres. of Sales and Marketing)

PRINTSOFT AMERICAS, INC.

Street address 1: 70 West Madison St Three First National Plaza
Street address 2: Suite 1400
Street address city: Chicago
Street address state: IL
Zip/Postal code: 60602
Country: USA
Mailing address: 70 West Madison St. Three First National Plaza Suite 1400
Mailing city: Chicago
Mailing state: IL
Mailing zip: 60602
General Phone: (630) 625-5400
General Fax: (630) 625-5401
General/National Adv. E-mail: sales@printsoftamericas.com
Primary Website: www.printsoft.com
Mthly Avg Unique Visitors: 1995
Industry: Laser Printers; Software: Circulation;
Personnel: Daniel Sheedy (Nat'l Sales Mgr.)

PRINTWARE

Street address 1: 2935 Waters Rd
Street address 2: Ste 160
Street address city: Saint Paul
Street address state: MN
Zip/Postal code: 55121-1688
Country: USA
Mailing address: 2935 Waters Rd Ste 160
Mailing city: Saint Paul
Mailing state: MN
Mailing zip: 55121-1688
General Phone: (651) 456-1400
General Fax: (651) 454-3684
General/National Adv. E-mail: sales@printwarellc.com
Primary Website: www.printwarellc.com
Mthly Avg Unique Visitors: 1985
Industry: Offset Plate-Making Service & Equipment; Plate Processors; Platemakers: Offset (Conventional); Plates: Offset (Conventional);
Personnel: Stan Goldberg (Pres.); Tim Murphy (Vice Pres.-Sales/Mktg.)

PROIMAGE AMERICA, INC.

Street address 1: 103 Carnegie Ctr
Street address 2: Ste 300
Street address city: Princeton
Street address state: NJ
Zip/Postal code: 08540-6235
Country: USA
Mailing address: 103 Carnegie Ctr Ste 300
Mailing city: Princeton
Mailing state: NJ
Mailing zip: 08540-6235
General Phone: (609) 587-5222
General/National Adv. E-mail: sales.us@new-proimage.com
Display Adv. E-mail: sales.us@new-proimage.com
Primary Website: www.new-proimage.com
Mthly Avg Unique Visitors: 1995
Industry: Calibration Software/Hardware; Color Management; Consulting Services: Production; Software: Electronic Data Interchange; Software: Pagination/Layout; Software: Workflow Management/ Tracking, Ripping, Imposition; Training: Automated Pre Press workflow; Ink Optimization; Press Registration; Content Management Systems; Tablet & Mobile Solutions

Note: ProImage America, Inc. is a solutions provider specializing in cloud based and local automated workflow solutions, production tracking systems and is dedicated to newspaper, commercial and magazine workflow systems. Our NewsWayX workflow features a single, integrated user interface that keeps all users informed about editions and their status. It provides the latest workflow tools and offers faster turnaround and increased productivity for cost savings in the production process. Because it is based on HTML5, NewsWayX can be fully accessed from any computer platform that supports a browser. With its new easy-to-use interface, the production staff does not require lengthy training sessions in order to learn the software. It is ideal for centralized workflows. Our Cloud workflow includes hosting on redundant AWS Regions, 24x7 support, and Major version software upgrades so publishers no longer have to budget for hardware and software future upgrades. In many cases the cloud annual fees are less than ongoing support and hardware maintenance costs. ProImage also offers cloud based Ink Optimization for reducing color ink costs and a Color Management solution for automatically toning and color correcting images.
Personnel: John J. Ialacci (President/CEO); Mike Monter (Vice President, Operations); Rick Shafranek (Vice President, Sales and Marketing)

PROQUEST LLC

Street address 1: 789 E Eisenhower Pkwy
Street address city: Ann Arbor
Street address state: MI
Zip/Postal code: 48108-3218
Country: USA
Mailing address: PO Box 1346
Mailing city: Ann Arbor
Mailing state: MI
Mailing zip: 48106-1346
General Phone: (734) 761-4700
General/National Adv. E-mail: info@proquest.com
Primary Website: www.proquest.com
Industry: Archiving Systems
Personnel: Marty Kahn (CEO); Simon Beale (Sr. Vice Pres., Global Sales); Lynda James-Gilboe (Sr. Vice Pres., Mktg.); Chris Cowan

PSC FLO-TURN, INC.

Street address 1: 1050 Commerce Ave
Street address city: Union
Street address state: NJ
Zip/Postal code: 07083-5087
Country: USA
Mailing address: 1050 Commerce Ave Ste 1
Mailing city: Union
Mailing state: NJ
Mailing zip: 07083-5080
General Phone: (908) 687-3225
General Fax: (908) 687-1715
General/National Adv. E-mail: sales@flow-turn.com
Primary Website: www.flow-turn.com
Mthly Avg Unique Visitors: 1981
Industry: Conveyors
Personnel: Rod Chrysler (Pres.)

PUBLICATION DESIGN, INC.

Street address 1: 6449 Meadowview Ter S
Street address city: Zionsville
Street address state: PA
Zip/Postal code: 18092-2091
Country: USA
Mailing address: 6449 Meadowview Ter S
Mailing city: Zionsville
Mailing state: PA
Mailing zip: 18092-2091
General Phone: (610) 928-1111
General Fax: (610) 928-1110
General/National Adv. E-mail: ayers@publicationdesign.com
Primary Website: www.publicationdesign.com
Mthly Avg Unique Visitors: 1987
Industry: Publication Design & Layout Services
Personnel: Robert Ayers (Pres., V.P., Sec. Tres.)

PUBLICATION DESIGN, INC.

Street address 1: 6449 Meadowview Ter S
Street address city: Zionsville
Street address state: PA
Zip/Postal code: 18092-2091
Country: USA
Mailing address: 6449 Meadowview Ter S
Mailing city: Zionsville
Mailing state: PA
Mailing zip: 18092-2091
General Phone: (610) 928-1111
General/National Adv. E-mail: ayers@publicationdesign.com
Primary Website: www.publicationdesign.com
Mthly Avg Unique Visitors: 1987
Industry: Media Kit Design Support; Newsletter Design; Etc.;
Personnel: Robert Ayers (Owner)

PUBLISHERS CIRCULATION FULFILLMENT INC.

Street address 1: 303 Smith St
Street address 2: Ste 1
Street address city: Farmingdale
Street address state: NY
Zip/Postal code: 11735-1110
County: Suffolk
Country: USA
Mailing address: 303 Smith Street, Suite One
Mailing city: Farmingdale
Mailing state: NY
Mailing zip: 11735
General Phone: (631) 2703133
General/National Adv. E-mail: sales@pcfcorp.com
Primary Website: www.pcfcorp.com
Industry: Newspaper Distribution Technology Services
Personnel: Jerry Giordana (Pres./CEO); Tom Dressler (VP of Growth and Development); James Cunningham

PULSE RESEARCH, INC.

Street address 1: PO Box 2884
Street address city: Portland
Street address state: OR
Zip/Postal code: 97208-2884
Country: USA
Mailing address: PO Box 2884
Mailing city: Portland
Mailing state: OR
Mailing zip: 97208-2884
General Phone: (503) 626-5224
General Fax: (503) 277-2184
General/National Adv. E-mail: info@pulsesearch.com; support@pulseresearch.com
Primary Website: www.pulseresearch.com
Mthly Avg Unique Visitors: 1985
Industry: Consulting Services: Advertising; Consulting Services: Circulation; Consulting Services: Marketing;
Personnel: John W. Marling (PRESIDENT); John Bertoglio (CIO); Denice Nichols (Vice Pres., Sales); Andrew Dove (Vice Pres.); Brian Knapp (Vice Pres.)

QUAD GRAPHICS

Street address 1: N61 W23044 Harry's Way
Street address city: Sussex
Street address state: WI
Zip/Postal code: 53089
Country: USA
Mailing address: N61 W23044 Harry's Way
Mailing city: Sussex
Mailing state: WI
Mailing zip: 53089
General Phone: (888) 782.3226
General/National Adv. E-mail: info@qg.com
Primary Website: www.qg.com
Industry: Software: Advertising (Includes Display; Classified)
Personnel: Joel Quadracci (Pres., CEO); Bill Blackmer (Global Procurement); Chris Grond (Paper Serv.)

QUAD TECH

Street address 1: N64W23110 Main St
Street address city: Sussex
Street address state: WI
Zip/Postal code: 53089-3230
Country: USA
Mailing address: N64W23110 Main St
Mailing city: Sussex
Mailing state: WI
Mailing zip: 53089-5301
General Phone: (414) 566-7500
General Fax: (414) 566-9670
General/National Adv. E-mail: info@qtiworld.com
Primary Website: www.quadtechworld.com
Mthly Avg Unique Visitors: 1979
Industry: Color Registration; Controls: Register; Ink Controls, Computerized; Press Control Systems; Web Break Detector;
Personnel: Karl Fritchen (Pres.); Randy Freeman (Vice Pres.,Sales)

QUADTECH

Street address 1: N64W23110 Main St
Street address city: Sussex
Street address state: WI
Zip/Postal code: 53089-3230
Country: USA
Mailing address: N64W23110 Main St
Mailing city: Sussex
Mailing state: WI
Mailing zip: 53089-3230
General Phone: (414) 566-7500
General Fax: (414) 566-9670
General/National Adv. E-mail: sales@quadtechworld.com
Primary Website: www.quadtechworld.com
Mthly Avg Unique Visitors: 1979
Industry: Color Registration; Controls: Register; Ink Controls, Computerized; Press Control Systems; Web Break Detector;
Personnel: Karl Fritchen (Pres.); Randy Freeman (Vice Pres., Bus. Devel.); Vince Balistrieri (Dir., Engineering/Gen. Mgr.,Commercial/Newspaper); Greg Kallman (Regional Sales Manager)

QUARK, INC.

Street address 1: 1225 17th St
Street address 2: Ste 1200
Street address city: Denver
Street address state: CO
Zip/Postal code: 80202-5503
Country: USA
Mailing address: 1225 17th St Ste 1200
Mailing city: Denver
Mailing state: CO
Mailing zip: 80202-5503
General Phone: (303) 894-8888
General Fax: (303) 894-3399
General/National Adv. E-mail: quarkxpress@quark.com
Primary Website: www.quark.com
Mthly Avg Unique Visitors: 1981
Industry: Software: Asset Management; Software: Design/Graphics; Software: Editorial; Software: Pagination/Layout;
Personnel: Kamar Aulakh (Pres./CEO)

QUEBECOR WORLD

Street address 1: 612 Rue Saint-Jacques
Street address city: Montreal
Street address state: QC
Zip/Postal code: H3C 4M8
Country: Canada
Mailing address: 612 Rue Saint-Jacques
Mailing city: MontrÃ©al
Mailing state: QC
Mailing zip: H3C 4M8
General Phone: (514) 380-1999
Primary Website: www.quebecor.com
Mthly Avg Unique Visitors: 1990
Industry: Consulting Services: Production; Input & Editing Systems; Preprint Service & Production; Presses: Rotogravure;
Personnel: Charles Cavell (Pres./CEO); Brian Freschi (Exec. Vice Pres., Sales); Jeremy Roberts (Dir. Cor. Commun.)

QUICKSET USA INC

Street address 1: PO Box 542707
Street address city: Lake Worth
Street address state: FL
Zip/Postal code: 33454
County: Palm Beach
Country: USA
Mailing address: PO Box 542707
Mailing city: Lake Worth
Mailing state: FL
Mailing zip: 33454
General Phone: (206) 849-7770
General/National Adv. E-mail: info@quicksetcorporation.com
Display Adv. E-mail: steve@quicksetcorporation.com
Primary Website: www.quicksetcorporation.com
Mthly Avg Unique Visitors: 1981
Industry: Ink Pre-setting Systems
Note: QuickSet has installed its proprietary ink presetting system on hundreds of press lines and has over 250,000 retrofit levers installed worldwide. We boast the most accurate ink presets in the world due to our singular breakthrough technology that has never been duplicated: It that allows us to completely fingerprint/map each ink-key on any press and then duplicate ink density for any level of image coverage.
Personnel: Steve Surbrook (President)

QUICKWIRE LABS

Street address 1: 300 Carlton St.
Street address city: Winnipeg
Street address state: MB
Zip/Postal code: R3B 2K6
Country: Canada
Mailing address: 300 Carlton St.
Mailing city: Winnipeg
Mailing state: MB
Mailing zip: R3B 2K6
General Phone: (905) 785-0748
General Fax: (204) 926-4686
General/National Adv. E-mail: bmiller@quickwire.com
Primary Website: www.quickwire.com
Mthly Avg Unique Visitors: 1993
Industry: Software: Advertising (Includes Display; Classified); Software: Editorial; Software: Pagination/Layout;
Personnel: Bill Miller (Gen. Mgr.); Paul Medland (Quicktrac Developer); Richard Bliss (Integrator)

QUIPP SYSTEM, INC.

Street address 1: 5881 NW 151 St
Street address 2: Suite 102
Street address city: Miami Lakes
Street address state: FL
Zip/Postal code: 33014
Country: USA
Mailing address: 5881 NW 151 St, Suite 102
Mailing city: Miami Lakes
Mailing state: FL
Mailing zip: 33014
General Phone: (800) 258-1390
General Fax: (305) 623-0980
Display Adv. E-mail: sales@quipp.com
Editorial e-mail: news@quipp.com
Primary Website: www.quipp.com
Mthly Avg Unique Visitors: 1983
Industry: Conveyors; Material Handling Equipment: Pallets & Palletizers; Material Handling Equipment: Truck Loaders; Software: Press/Post Press; System Installations; System Integration Services; Training: Post Press;
Personnel: Angel Arrabal (Vice Pres., Sales.); Leticia Gostisa (Mktg. Mgr.); David Switalski (Vice Pres., Opns.)

R.B. INTERMARK, INC.

Street address 1: 15 Kirkland Blvd
Street address 2: Suite 108
Street address city: Kirkland
Street address state: QC
Zip/Postal code: H9J 1N2
Country: Canada
Mailing address: 15 Kirkland Blvd., Ste. 108
Mailing city: Kirkland
Mailing state: QC
Mailing zip: H9J 1N2
General Phone: (514) 695-7172
General Fax: (514) 695-2108
General/National Adv. E-mail: social@theloop.ca
Mthly Avg Unique Visitors: 1996
Industry: Silver Recovery; Solvent Recovery Systems; Wastewater Treatment; Water Management Systems;
Personnel: Rene J. Brimo (Pres.)

R.R. DONNELLEY & SONS CO.

Street address 1: 35 West Wacker Drive
Street address 2: Suite 1
Street address city: Chicago
Street address state: IL
Zip/Postal code: 60601
Country: USA
Mailing address: 35 West Wacker Drive, Suite 1
Mailing city: Chicago
Mailing state: IL
Mailing zip: 60606-4300
General Phone: 312-326-8000

General Fax: 312-326-8001
General/National Adv. E-mail: info@rrd.com
Primary Website: www.rrdonnelley.com
Mthly Avg Unique Visitors: 1985
Industry: Marketing & Business Communications; Commercial Printing & Related Services;
Personnel: Daniel L. Knotts (CEO); Ken Oâ€™Brien (Executive Vice President, Chief Information Officer); John Pecaric (President, Business Services); Terry D. Peterson (Exec. V. Pres., CFO); Sheila Rutt (Exec. V. Pres., C.H.R.O.); Doug Ryan (Pres., Marketing Solutions)

RANDOM ACCESS

Street address 1: 62 Birdsall St
Street address city: Greene
Street address state: NY
Zip/Postal code: 13778-1049
Country: USA
Mailing address: 62 Birdsall St
Mailing city: Greene
Mailing state: NY
Mailing zip: 13778-1049
General Phone: (607) 656-7584
General/National Adv. E-mail: marsland@aol.com
Mthly Avg Unique Visitors: 1986
Industry: Consulting Services: Computer; System Integration Services;
Personnel: William Marsland (Pres.)

RANGER DATA TECHNOLOGIES INC.

Street address 1: 360 E Maple Rd
Street address 2: Ste X
Street address city: Troy
Street address state: MI
Zip/Postal code: 48083-2707
County: Oakland
Country: USA
Mailing address: 360 E Maple Rd Ste X
Mailing city: Troy
Mailing state: MI
Mailing zip: 48083-2707
General Phone: (248) 336-7300
General Fax: (248) 336-8775
General/National Adv. E-mail: info@rangerdata.com
Primary Website: www.rangerdata.com
Mthly Avg Unique Visitors: 2001
Industry: Software: Advertising (Includes Display; Classified)
Product or Service: Hardware/Software Supplier
Personnel: George Willard (Sr. VP of Operations); Grace Shields (Director of Marketing & Customer Service); Dolores Gauthier (National Dir. of Sales & Marketing)

RAYONIER ADVANCED MATERIALS

Street address 1: 1301 Riverplace Blvd.
Street address 2: Suite 2300
Street address city: Jacksonville
Street address state: FL
Zip/Postal code: 32207
Country: Canada
Mailing address: 1301 Riverplace Blvd.
Mailing city: Jacksonville
Mailing state: FL
Mailing zip: 32207
General Phone: (904) 357-4600
Primary Website: www.rayonieram.com
Mthly Avg Unique Visitors: 1926
Industry: Newsprint
Personnel: Paul G. Boynton (Chairman, Pres. and CEO); Chris Black (Senior VP); James L. Posze (Senior Vice President HR); Frank A. Ruperto (CFO and Senior VP)

REED BRENNAN MEDIA ASSOCIATES, INC.

Street address 1: 628 Virginia Dr
Street address city: Orlando
Street address state: FL
Zip/Postal code: 32803-1858
County: USA
Country: USA
Mailing address: 628 Virginia Dr
Mailing city: Orlando
Mailing state: FL
Mailing zip: 32803-1858
General Phone: (407) 894-7300
General Fax: (407) 894-7900
General/National Adv. E-mail: rbma@rbma.com
Primary Website: www.rbma.com
Mthly Avg Unique Visitors: 1993
Industry: Input & Editing Systems; Pagination Systems;
Personnel: Jeff Talbert (VP); Timothy Brennan (Mgr., Mktg.); David Cohea (King Features Weekly Service)

REEVES BROTHERS, INC.

Street address 1: 790 Reeves St
Street address city: Spartanburg
Street address state: SC
Zip/Postal code: 29301-5078
Country: USA
Mailing address: PO Box 1531
Mailing city: Spartanburg
Mailing state: SC
Mailing zip: 29304-1531
General Phone: (864) 576-1210
General Fax: (864) 595-2270
Primary Website: www.trelleborg.com
Industry: Blanket Mounting and Bars; Blankets;
Personnel: Keith Dye (CEO)

REPUBLIC ROLLER CORP.

Street address 1: 1233 Millard St
Street address city: Three Rivers
Street address state: MI
Zip/Postal code: 49093
Country: USA
Mailing address: PO Box 330
Mailing city: Three Rivers
Mailing state: MI
Mailing zip: 49093-0330
General Phone: (800) 765-5377
General Fax: (269) 273-7655
General/National Adv. E-mail: bestroll@aol.com
Primary Website: www.republicroller.com
Mthly Avg Unique Visitors: 1981
Industry: Roll Coverings; Roller Grinding Services; Rollers; Rollers: Dampening;
Personnel: G.L. Umphrey (Pres.); Bill Gross (Sales Mgr.)

RESEARCH USA, INC.

Street address 1: 180 N Wacker Dr
Street address 2: Ste 202
Street address city: Chicago
Street address state: IL
Zip/Postal code: 60606-1600
County: Cook
Country: USA
Mailing address: 180 N Wacker Dr Ste 202
Mailing city: Chicago
Mailing state: IL
Mailing zip: 60606-1600
General Phone: (800) 863-4800
General Fax: (312) 658-0085
General/National Adv. E-mail: info@researchusainc.com; hr@researchusainc.com
Primary Website: www.researchusainc.com
Mthly Avg Unique Visitors: 1972
Industry: Market Research

RESOLUTE FOREST PRODUCTS

Street address 1: 111 Duke St
Street address 2: Suite 5000
Street address city: Montreal
Street address state: QC
Zip/Postal code: H3C 2M1
Country: Canada
Mailing address: 111 Duke Street, Suite 5000
Mailing city: MontrÃ©al
Mailing state: QC
Mailing zip: H3C 2M1
General Phone: (514) 875-2160
General Fax: (423) 336-7950
General/National Adv. E-mail: info@resolutefp.com
Primary Website: www.resolutefp.com
Mthly Avg Unique Visitors: 1954
Industry: Pulp & Paper
Personnel: Devon Mike (VP, Sales-Southern Market); Garry Grissom (Rgl. Mgr.)

RFC WIRE FORMS

Street address 1: 525 Brooks St
Street address city: Ontario
Street address state: CA
Zip/Postal code: 91762-3702
Country: USA
Mailing address: 525 Brooks St
Mailing city: Ontario
Mailing state: CA
Mailing zip: 91762-3702
General Phone: (909) 984-5500
General Fax: (909) 984-2322
General/National Adv. E-mail: rfccompany@aol.com
Primary Website: www.rfcwireforms.com
Mthly Avg Unique Visitors: 1946
Industry: Rack Display Cards
Personnel: Don Kemby (Pres.); Greg Lunsmann (Gen. Mgr.)

RICHMOND/GRAPHIC PRODUCTS, INC.

Street address 1: 20 Industrial Dr
Street address city: Smithfield
Street address state: RI
Zip/Postal code: 02917-1502
Country: USA
Mailing address: 20 Industrial Dr
Mailing city: Smithfield
Mailing state: RI
Mailing zip: 02917-1502
General Phone: (401) 233-2700
General Fax: (401) 233-0179
General/National Adv. E-mail: info@richmond-graphic.com
Primary Website: www.richmond-graphic.com
Mthly Avg Unique Visitors: 1984
Industry: Art & Layout Equipment and Services; Exposure Lamps; Film & Paper: Film Processing Machines; Layout Tables, Light Tables & Workstations; Offset Plate-Making Service & Equipment; Plate Processors; Processors: Diffusion Transfer; Processors: Film & Paper; Tables (Dot, Etch, Opaquing, Register, Retouching, Stripping); Vacuum Frames;
Personnel: Hugh C. Neville (CEO); P.J. Griffee (Controller); Frank Ragazzo (Vice Pres., Sales/Mktg.)

RICKENBACHER MEDIA

Street address 1: 6731 Desco Dr
Street address city: Dallas
Street address state: TX
Zip/Postal code: 75225-2704
County: Dallas
Country: USA
Mailing address: 6731 Desco Dr
Mailing city: Dallas
Mailing state: TX
Mailing zip: 75225-2704
General Phone: (214) 384 2779
General/National Adv. E-mail: rmedia@msn.com
Primary Website: www.rickenbachermedia.com
Mthly Avg Unique Visitors: 1985
Industry: Brokers & Appraisers
Personnel: Ted Rickenbacher (Pres./Exec. Dir.); Jim Afinowich (Western States Dir.)

RICOH CORP.

Street address 1: 70 Valley Stream Parkway
Street address city: Malvern
Street address state: PA
Zip/Postal code: 19355
Country: USA
Mailing address: 5 Dedrick Pl
Mailing city: West Caldwell
Mailing state: NJ
Mailing zip: 07006-6398
General Phone: (973) 882-2000
General Fax: (973) 808-7555
Primary Website: www.ricoh-usa.com
Mthly Avg Unique Visitors: 1936
Industry: Digital Copiers; Facsimiles; Multi-functional Systems; Scanners; Printers; Digital Cameras; Projectors;
Personnel: Joji Tokunaga (President and CEO); Jeff Paterra (Executive Vice President); Peter H. Stuart (Executive Vice President, Office Solutions Business Group); Donna Venable (Exec. V. Pres., HR & Dep. Gen. Mgr.); Dennis Dispenziere (Sr. V. P. & CFO of Ricoh Americas); Glenn Laverty (Sr. V.P., Marketing, Shared Services)

ROBERTSON EQUIPMENTS

Street address 1: 1301 S Maiden Ln
Street address city: Joplin
Street address state: MO
Zip/Postal code: 64801-3844
Country: USA
Mailing address: 1301 S Maiden Ln
Mailing city: Joplin
Mailing state: MO
Mailing zip: 64801-3844
General Phone: (800) 288-1929
General Fax: (417) 781-3704
General/National Adv. E-mail: sales@robertsonpress.com
Primary Website: www.robertsonpress.com
Mthly Avg Unique Visitors: 1991
Industry: Consulting Services: Computer; System Integration Services; Conveyors; Material Handling Equipment: Automatic Guided Vehicles; Material Handling Equipment: Truck Loaders;
Personnel: Bob Robertson (Owner); Charles J. Robertson (Pres.); Jason Bard (Dir., Mktg.); Dave Reddick (Parts Mgr.)

ROBERTSON PRESS MACHINERY CO., INC.

Street address 1: 1301 S Maiden Ln
Street address city: Joplin
Street address state: MO
Zip/Postal code: 64801-3844
Country: USA
Mailing address: 1301 S Maiden Ln
Mailing city: Joplin
Mailing state: MO
Mailing zip: 64801-3844
General Phone: (417) 673-1929
General Fax: (417) 781-3704
General/National Adv. E-mail: sales@robertsonpress.com
Primary Website: www.robertsonpress.com
Mthly Avg Unique Visitors: 1991
Industry: Color Registration; Dampening Systems; Equipment Dealers (New); Equipment Dealers (Used); Press Accessories, Parts & Supplies; Press Rebuilding; Presses: Offset; Remanufactures Equipment; Tension & Web Controls; Web Press - Special Equipment;
Personnel: Charles Robertson (Pres.)

ROCHESTER INSTITUTE OF TECHNOLOGY

Street address 1: 69 Lomb Memorial Dr
Street address city: Rochester
Street address state: NY
Zip/Postal code: 14623-5602
Country: USA
Mailing address: 69 Lomb Memorial Dr
Mailing city: Rochester
Mailing state: NY
Mailing zip: 14623-5602
General Phone: (585) 475-2728
General Fax: (585) 475-7029
General/National Adv. E-mail: spmofc@rit.edu
Primary Website: www.rit.edu
Mthly Avg Unique Visitors: 1829
Industry: Abrasives; Cameras & Accessories; Consulting Services: Computer; Consulting Services: Equipment; Consulting Services: Production;
Personnel: Patricia Sores (Admin. Chair)

ROCKWELL AUTOMATION

Street address 1: 1201 S 2nd St
Street address city: Milwaukee
Street address state: WI
Zip/Postal code: 53204-2410
Country: USA
Mailing address: PO Box 760
Mailing city: Milwaukee
Mailing state: WI
Mailing zip: 53201-0760
General Phone: (262) 512-8200
General Fax: (262) 512-8579
Primary Website: www.rockwellautomation.com
Industry: Controllers: Press; Drives & Controls; Press Control Systems;
Personnel: Michael Faase (Mktg. Commun. Specialist)

ROCONEX CORP.

Street address 1: 20 Marybill Dr S
Street address city: Troy
Street address state: OH
Zip/Postal code: 45373-1034
Country: USA
Mailing address: 20 Marybill Dr S

Mailing city: Troy
Mailing state: OH
Mailing zip: 45373-1034
General Phone: (937) 339-2616
General Fax: (937) 339-1470
General/National Adv. E-mail: info@roconex.com
Primary Website: www.roconex.com
Mthly Avg Unique Visitors: 1954
Industry: Art & Layout Equipment and Services; Cabinets; Files, Storage; Layout Tables, Light Tables & Workstations; Offset Plate Holders; Plate Exposure Units; Platemakers: Offset (Conventional); Storage Retrieval Systems; Tables (Dot, Etch, Opaquing, Register, Retouching, Stripping);
Personnel: Tyrone Spear (Pres.)

ROGGEN MANAGEMENT CONSULTANTS, INC.

Street address 1: 223 Egremont Plain Rd
Street address 2: # 603
Street address city: North Egremont
Street address state: MA
Zip/Postal code: 01230-2284
County: Berkshire
Country: USA
Mailing address: 223 Egremont Plain Rd #603
Mailing city: North Egremont
Mailing state: MA
Mailing zip: 01230
General Phone: (413) 528-2300
General Fax: (413) 528-2300
General/National Adv. E-mail: mark.roggen@roggenconsultants.com; mnroggen@aol.com
Primary Website: www.roggenconsultants.com
Mthly Avg Unique Visitors: 1975
Industry: Newspaper Distribution & Logistics Consultant
Note: Operations & Distribution Consultant
Personnel: Mark N. Roggen (Pres.)

ROLLEM CORP. OF AMERICA

Street address 1: 43 Polk Ave
Street address city: Hempstead
Street address state: NY
Zip/Postal code: 11550-5434
Country: USA
Mailing address: 95 Hoffman Ln Ste T
Mailing city: Islandia
Mailing state: NY
Mailing zip: 11749-5020
General Phone: (516) 485-6655
General Fax: (516) 485-5936
General/National Adv. E-mail: info@rollemusa.com
Primary Website: www.rollemusa.com
Mthly Avg Unique Visitors: 1963
Industry: Numbering Machines
Personnel: Richard Nigro (Vice Pres., Sales)

ROOSEVELT PAPER

Street address 1: 1 Roosevelt Dr
Street address city: Mount Laurel
Street address state: NJ
Zip/Postal code: 08054-6307
Country: USA
Mailing address: 1 Roosevelt Dr
Mailing city: Mount Laurel
Mailing state: NJ
Mailing zip: 08054-6312
General Phone: (856) 303-4100
General Fax: (856) 642-1949
Primary Website: www.rooseveltpaper.com
Mthly Avg Unique Visitors: 1932
Industry: Newsprint; Paper: Coated Groundwood Offset; Paper: Specialty Printing Paper;
Personnel: David Kosloff (President); Ted Kosloff (CEO); Lynn Perce (Mktg. Dir.)

ROSBACK CO.

Street address 1: 125 Hawthorne Ave
Street address city: Saint Joseph
Street address state: MI
Zip/Postal code: 49085-2636
Country: USA
Mailing address: 125 Hawthorne Ave
Mailing city: Saint Joseph
Mailing state: MI
Mailing zip: 49085-2636
General Phone: (269) 983-2582
General Fax: (269) 983-2516
General/National Adv. E-mail: Sales@RosbackCompany.com
Display Adv. E-mail: Sales@RosbackCompany.com
Primary Website: www.rosbackcompany.com
Mthly Avg Unique Visitors: 1881
Industry: Adhesives; Collating Equipment; Equipment Dealers (New); Folding Machines;
Personnel: Larry R. Bowman (Pres.); Ron F. Bowman (Vice Pres., Sales/Mktg.)

ROTADYNE

Street address 1: 15151 Prater Dr
Street address 2: Ste L
Street address city: Covington
Street address state: GA
Zip/Postal code: 30014-4961
Country: USA
Mailing address: 15151 Prater Dr Ste L
Mailing city: Covington
Mailing state: GA
Mailing zip: 30014-4961
General Phone: (630) 769-9700
General Fax: (770) 787-4589
Primary Website: www.rotadyne.com
Mthly Avg Unique Visitors: 1917
Industry: Blanket Mounting and Bars
Personnel: Rita Harper (Mgr., Customer Serv.)

ROTADYNE CORP.

Street address 1: 8140 Cass Ave
Street address city: Darien
Street address state: IL
Zip/Postal code: 60561-5013
Country: USA
Mailing address: 8140 S Cass Ave
Mailing city: Darien
Mailing state: IL
Mailing zip: 60561-5013
General Phone: (630) 769-9700
General Fax: (630) 769-9255
General/National Adv. E-mail: rotadynecorp@rotadyne.com
Primary Website: www.rotadyne.com
Mthly Avg Unique Visitors: 1982
Industry: Blankets; Roll Coverings; Rollers; Rollers: Dampening;
Personnel: John A. Costello (Vice Pres., OEM Sales); John Kaminski (Vice Pres. Industrial Sales); John Breau (Vice Pres. Graphic Sales)

ROTOFLEX MARK ANDY CANADA, INC.

Street address 1: 420 Ambassador Dr.
Street address city: Mississauga
Street address state: ON
Zip/Postal code: L5T 2J3
Country: Canada
Mailing address: 420 Ambassador Dr.
Mailing city: Mississauga
Mailing state: ON
Mailing zip: L5T 2R5
General Phone: (905) 670-8700
General Fax: (905) 670-3402
General/National Adv. E-mail: sales@rotoflex.com
Primary Website: www.rotoflex.com
Mthly Avg Unique Visitors: 1974
Industry: Conversion Equipment; Dies (Perforating and Slitting); Rewinders;
Personnel: Rod Allen (Vice Pres., Finance); Brian Nicoll (Dir., Mfg.); Val Rimas (Gen. Mgr./Vice Pres., Sales/Mktg.)

ROWLETT ADVERTISING SERVICE, INC.

Street address 1: 2003 Crencor Dr
Street address city: Goodlettsville
Street address state: TN
Zip/Postal code: 37072-4314
County: Sumner
Country: USA
Mailing address: PO Box 50
Mailing city: Goodlettsville
Mailing state: TN
Mailing zip: 37070-0050
General Phone: (615) 859-6609
General Fax: (615) 851-7187
General/National Adv. E-mail: rowlettadvertising@att.net
Display Adv. E-mail: ras@rowlettadv.com
Primary Website: www.rowlettadv.com
Mthly Avg Unique Visitors: 1978
Industry: Church Page Advertising Sales
Personnel: Richard Rowlett (Pres.); Mary Belcher (Sec./Treasurer)

ROYAL CONSUMER INFORMATION PRODUCTS, INC.

Street address 1: 2 Riverview Dr
Street address 2: Ste 3
Street address city: Somerset
Street address state: NJ
Zip/Postal code: 08873-1150
Country: USA
Mailing address: 2 Riverview Dr Ste 1
Mailing city: Somerset
Mailing state: NJ
Mailing zip: 08873-1150
General Phone: (732) 627-9977
General Fax: (800) 232-9769
General/National Adv. E-mail: info@royalsupplies.com
Primary Website: www.royal.com
Industry: Facsimilie/Fax Transmission Systems; Laser Printers;
Personnel: Salomon Suwalsky (Pres.); Terry Setar (Vice Pres., Sales (Royal)); Wendy Donnelly (Mgr., Sales/Supplies)

RYDER SYSTEM, INC.

Street address 1: 11690 NW 105th St
Street address city: Medley
Street address state: FL
Zip/Postal code: 33178-1103
Country: USA
Mailing address: 11690 NW 105th St
Mailing city: Medley
Mailing state: FL
Mailing zip: 33178-1103
General Phone: (305) 500-3726
General Fax: (305) 500-4339
Primary Website: www.ryder.com
Mthly Avg Unique Visitors: 1933
Industry: Lift Trucks
Personnel: Robert E. Sanchez (Chrmn./CEO); Dennis C. Cooke (Pres. Global Fleet Management Solutions); Art A. Garcia (Executive VP and CFO); Todd Skiles (SVP, Global Supply Chain Solutions Sales)

SAKURAI USA

Street address 1: 1700 Basswood Rd
Street address city: Schaumburg
Street address state: IL
Zip/Postal code: 60173-5318
Country: USA
Mailing address: 1700 Basswood Rd
Mailing city: Schaumburg
Mailing state: IL
Mailing zip: 60173-5318
General Phone: (847) 490-9400
General Fax: (847) 490-4200
General/National Adv. E-mail: sales@sakurai.com; info@sakurai.com; inquiry@sakurai.com
Primary Website: www.sakurai.com
Mthly Avg Unique Visitors: 1928
Industry: Presses: Offset
Personnel: Don Bence (Vice Pres., Sales)

SALES TRAINING CONSULTANTS, INC.

Street address 1: 5550 Glades Rd
Street address 2: Ste 515
Street address city: Boca Raton
Street address state: FL
Zip/Postal code: 33431-7205
Country: USA
Mailing address: 5550 Glades Rd Ste 515
Mailing city: Boca Raton
Mailing state: FL
Mailing zip: 33431
General Phone: (561) 482-8801
General/National Adv. E-mail: akemper@salestrainingconsultants.com
Primary Website: www.newspapertraining.com
Mthly Avg Unique Visitors: 1983
Industry: Training: Sales, Leadership, Subscription Retention (Stopbusters), Customer Service
Note: Newspaper Training Experts Since 1983
Personnel: Alice Kemper (Pres.); Diane Rossi (Consultant/Trainer); Denise Zagnoli (Consultant/Trainer); Margo Berman (Consultant/Trainer); Ed Baron (Consultant/Trainer); Anne Stein (Consultant/Trainer)

SALESFUEL, INC.

Street address 1: 600 N Cleveland Ave
Street address 2: Ste 260
Street address city: Westerville
Street address state: OH
Zip/Postal code: 43082-7265
Country: USA
Mailing address: 600 N Cleveland Ave Ste 260
Mailing city: Westerville
Mailing state: OH
Mailing zip: 43082-7265
General Phone: (614) 794-0500
General Fax: (614) 961-3268
General/National Adv. E-mail: info@salesdevelopment.com
Primary Website: www.salesfuel.com
Mthly Avg Unique Visitors: 1989
Industry: Consulting Services: Advertising; Consulting Services: Computer; Consulting Services: Marketing; Facsimilie/Fax Transmission Systems; Integrated Fax Servers; Market Research; Marketing Database Design and Implementation; Software: Advertising (Includes Display; Classified); Trade Publications;
Personnel: Audrey Strong (VP of Communications); C. Lee Smith (President/CEO)

SAMUEL PACKAGING SYSTEMS GROUP

Street address 1: 1401 Davey Road
Street address city: Woodridge
Street address state: IL
Zip/Postal code: 60517
Country: USA
Mailing address: 1401 Davey Road
Mailing city: Woodridge
Mailing state: IL
Mailing zip: 60517
General Phone: (630) 783-8900
General/National Adv. E-mail: packaging@samuel.com
Primary Website: www.samuelpsg.com
Mthly Avg Unique Visitors: 1855
Industry: Strapping Machines
Personnel: Dean Campbell (Director Sales and Marketing, Admin); Morris Gant (Service Manager)

SAMUEL STRAPPING SYSTEM

Street address 1: 1401 Davey Rd
Street address 2: Ste 300
Street address city: Woodridge
Street address state: IL
Zip/Postal code: 60517-4963
Country: USA
Mailing address: 1401 Davey Rd Ste 300
Mailing city: Woodridge
Mailing state: IL
Mailing zip: 60517-4991
General Phone: (800) 667-1264
General Fax: (630) 783-8901
General/National Adv. E-mail: info@samuelsystem.com
Primary Website: www.samuelsystems.com
Mthly Avg Unique Visitors: 1857
Industry: Bundling and Tying Machines; Strapping Machines;

SAMUEL, SON & CO.

Street address 1: 735 Oval Crt
Street address city: Burlington
Street address state: ON
Zip/Postal code: L7L 6A9
County: Burlington
Country: Canada
Mailing address: 735 Oval Ct.
Mailing city: Burlington
Mailing state: ON
Mailing zip: L7L 6A9
General Phone: (905) 279-9580
General Fax: (905) 639-2290
General/National Adv. E-mail: packaging@samuel.com
Display Adv. E-mail: packaging@samuel.com
Primary Website: www.goval.com
Mthly Avg Unique Visitors: 1855

Industry: Baling Machines; Bundling and Tying Machines; Conveyors; Counting, Stacking, Bundling Machines; Flooring; Mailroom Systems & Equipment; Roll Handeling Equipment; Strapping Machines;
Personnel: Kevin McEldowney (U.S. Manager of Inside Sales and Administration)

SAP AMERICA, INC.

Street address 1: 18101 Von Karman Ave
Street address 2: Ste 900
Street address city: Irvine
Street address state: CA
Zip/Postal code: 92612-0151
County: Orange
Country: USA
Mailing address: 18101 Von Karman Ave Ste 900
Mailing city: Irvine
Mailing state: CA
Mailing zip: 92612-0151
General Phone: (949) 622-2200
General/National Adv. E-mail: press@sap.com
Primary Website: www.sap.com
Industry: Software: Advertising (Includes Display; Classified); Software: Circulation;
Product or Service: Hardware/Software Supplier
Personnel: Mark White (CFO); Costanza Tedesco (Vice Pres., Global Adv./Branding); Brian Ellefritz (Sr. Dir., Social Media Mktg.)

SAPPI FINE PAPER NORTH AMERICA

Street address 1: 255 State St
Street address 2: Fl 4
Street address city: Boston
Street address state: MA
Zip/Postal code: 02109-2618
Country: USA
Mailing address: 255 State St Fl 4
Mailing city: Boston
Mailing state: MA
Mailing zip: 02109-2618
General Phone: (617) 423-7300
General Fax: (617) 423-5494
General/National Adv. E-mail: info@sappi.com
Primary Website: www.sappi.com
Industry: Paper: Coated Groundwood Offset; Paper: Groundwood Specialties; Paper: Specialty Printing Paper; Photostat: Paper;
Personnel: Mark Gardner (Pres./CEO); Annette Luchene (Vice Pres., Finance/CFO); Bob Forsberg (Vice Pres., Sales)

SAXMAYER CORP.

Street address 1: 318 W Adrian St
Street address city: Blissfield
Street address state: MI
Zip/Postal code: 49228-1205
Country: USA
Mailing address: PO Box 10
Mailing city: Blissfield
Mailing state: MI
Mailing zip: 49228-0010
General Phone: (517) 486-2164
General Fax: (517) 486-2055
General/National Adv. E-mail: info@saxmayercorp.com
Primary Website: www.erichbaumeister.com
Mthly Avg Unique Visitors: 1912
Industry: Newsprint Handeling Equipment; Strapping Machines;
Personnel: Michael Vennekotter (Pres., Mktg./Sales); James Fischer (Vice Pres., Engineering/Mfg.); Jeremy Sell (Process Supvr., Information Technology)

SAXOTECH

Street address 1: 360 Route 101
Street address 2: Ste 1302C
Street address city: Bedford
Street address state: NH
Zip/Postal code: 03110-5030
Country: USA
Mailing address: 302 Knights Run Ave Ste 1150
Mailing city: Tampa
Mailing state: FL
Mailing zip: 33602-5974
General Phone: (603) 472-5825
General Fax: (603) 472-3082
General/National Adv. E-mail: ussales@saxotech.com
Primary Website: www.ckp.com; www.saxotech.com
Industry: Pagination Systems; Software: Advertising (Includes Display; Classified); Software: Editorial; Software: Pagination/Layout;
Personnel: Pat Stewart (Pres.); Dick Mooney (Mng. Partner/CFO); James Mooney (Vice Pres., Opns.); Jeff Rapson (Dir., Sales)

SAXOTECH, INC.

Street address 1: 302 Knights Run Ave Ste 1150
Street address 2: Suite 1150
Street address city: Tampa
Street address state: FL
Zip/Postal code: 33602-5974
Country: USA
Mailing address: 302 Knights Run Ave Ste 1150
Mailing city: Tampa
Mailing state: FL
Mailing zip: 33602-5974
General Phone: (813) 221-1600
General Fax: (813) 221-1604
General/National Adv. E-mail: info@saxotechonline.com
Display Adv. E-mail: info@saxotechonline.com
Editorial e-mail: communications@saxotech.com
Primary Website: www.saxotechonline.com
Mthly Avg Unique Visitors: 1991
Industry: Archiving Systems; News Wire Capture Systems; Pagination Systems; Photo Archiving; Publishing Systems; Software: Asset Management; Software: Editorial; Software: Pagination/Layout; Software: Workflow Management/Tracking;
Personnel: Anders Christiansen (CEO); Bill Gilmour (Exec. V. P. & CFO); Jesper Frank (Sr. V. P.); Ed Ross (V. P. Sales); Mette Kvistgaard (Director of Global HR)

SCA PROMOTIONS, INC.

Street address 1: 3030 Lbj Fwy
Street address 2: Ste 300
Street address city: Dallas
Street address state: TX
Zip/Postal code: 75234-2753
Country: USA
Mailing address: 3030 Lbj Fwy Ste 300
Mailing city: Dallas
Mailing state: TX
Mailing zip: 75234-2753
General Phone: (214) 860-3700
General Fax: (214) 860-3480
General/National Adv. E-mail: info@scapromo.com
Primary Website: www.scapromotions.com
Mthly Avg Unique Visitors: 1986
Industry: Insurance; Newspaper Marketing; Promotion Services;
Personnel: Robert D. Hamman (Pres.); Shiela Bryan (Vice Pres., Sales)

SCARBOROUGH RESEARCH

Street address 1: 85 Broad St
Street address city: New York
Street address state: NY
Zip/Postal code: 10004
Country: USA
Mailing address: 85 Broad St
Mailing city: New York
Mailing state: NY
Mailing zip: 10004
General Phone: (800) 864-1224
General/National Adv. E-mail: corporatepressinquiries@nielsen.com
Primary Website: www.nielsen.com/us/en/solutions/capabilities/scarborough-local.html
Mthly Avg Unique Visitors: 1974
Industry: Consulting Services: Advertising; Consulting Services: Marketing; Market Research; Newspaper Marketing; Research Studies; Software: Advertising (Includes Display; Classified); Training: Keyboard Operation;
Personnel: David Kenny (CEO); Dave Anderson (CFO); Nancy Phillips (Chief Human Resources Officer); Eric Dale (Chief Legal Officer); John Burbank (Corporate Development & Strategy)

SCHAEFER MACHINE CO., INC.

Street address 1: 200 Commercial Dr
Street address city: Deep River
Street address state: CT
Zip/Postal code: 06417-1682
Country: USA
Mailing address: 200 Commercial Dr
Mailing city: Deep River
Mailing state: CT
Mailing zip: 06417-1682
General Phone: (860) 526-4000
General Fax: (860) 526-4654
General/National Adv. E-mail: schaefer01@snet.net
Primary Website: www.schaeferco.com
Mthly Avg Unique Visitors: 1945
Industry: Adhesives; Gluing Systems;
Personnel: Bob Gammons (Pres.); Virginia Gammons (Vice Pres.)

SCHAWK

Street address 1: 225 W Superior St
Street address city: Chicago
Street address state: IL
Zip/Postal code: 60654-3507
Country: USA
Mailing address: 1 N Dearborn St Ste 700
Mailing city: Chicago
Mailing state: IL
Mailing zip: 60602-4340
General Phone: (312) 943-0400
General Fax: (312) 943-2450
Primary Website: www.schawk.com
Industry: Color Management Software; Library Retrieval Systems; Preprint Service & Production; Storage Retrieval Systems;
Personnel: Jamie Mandarion (Sales Mgr.)

SCHERMERHORN BROS. CO.

Street address 1: 340 Eisenhower Ln N
Street address city: Lombard
Street address state: IL
Zip/Postal code: 60148-5405
Country: USA
Mailing address: 340 Eisenhower Ln N
Mailing city: Lombard
Mailing state: IL
Mailing zip: 60148-5470
General Phone: (630) 627-9860
General Fax: (630) 627-1178
Primary Website: www.schermerhornbrosco.com
Mthly Avg Unique Visitors: 1893
Industry: Circulation Equipment & Supplies
Note: Circulation Supplies
Personnel: Dennis Jenkins (Sales Contact)

SCHLENK-BOTH INDUSTRIES

Street address 1: 40 Nickerson Rd
Street address city: Ashland
Street address state: MA
Zip/Postal code: 01721-1912
Country: USA
Mailing address: 40 Nickerson Rd
Mailing city: Ashland
Mailing state: MA
Mailing zip: 01721-1912
General Phone: (508) 881-4100
General Fax: (508) 881-1278
General/National Adv. E-mail: customerservice@schlenkusa.com
Primary Website: www.schlenk.com/about-us/global/usa-global/
Industry: Inks
Personnel: Carl-Joachim von Schlenk-Barnsdorf (CEO); Alois Seidl (Pres.)

SCHUR INTERNATIONAL A/S

Street address 1: DK-8700 Horsens
Street address city: Dk-8700 Horsens
Country: Denmark
Mailing address: J.W. Schurs Vej 1
Mailing city: Dk-8700 Horsens
General Phone: +45 7627 2727
General Fax: +45 7627 2700
General/National Adv. E-mail: sin@schur.com
Primary Website: www.schur.com
Personnel: Hans Schur (Owner)

SCHUR PACKAGING SYSTEMS, INC.

Street address 1: 3200 Lionshead Ave
Street address 2: Suite 110
Street address city: Carlsbad
Street address state: CA
Zip/Postal code: 92010
Country: USA
Mailing address: 3200 Lionshead Ave, Suite 110
Mailing city: Carlsbad
Mailing state: CA
Mailing zip: 92010
General Phone: (760) 421-6404
General/National Adv. E-mail: schurstarusa@schur.com
Primary Website: www.schur.com
Mthly Avg Unique Visitors: 2003
Industry: Mailroom Systems & Equipment;
Personnel: Magnus Wall (Parts/Serv. Dir.); Dan Kemper (President); Gert Jensen (Technical Sales Dir.)

SCREEN (USA)

Street address 1: 5110 Tollview Dr
Street address city: Rolling Meadows
Street address state: IL
Zip/Postal code: 60008-3715
Country: USA
Mailing address: 5110 Tollview Dr
Mailing city: Rolling Meadows
Mailing state: IL
Mailing zip: 60008-3715
General Phone: (847) 870-7400
General Fax: (847) 870-0149
General/National Adv. E-mail: rsiwicki@screenusa.com
Primary Website: www.screenusa.com
Mthly Avg Unique Visitors: 1943
Industry: Color Proofing; Color Seperation Scanners; Imagesetters; Proofing Systems; Raster Image Processors; Software: Pagination/Layout; Tables (Dot, Etch, Opaquing, Register, Retouching, Stripping);
Personnel: Mike Fox (Pres); Robert Bernstein (CFO); Richard Siwicki (Application Support Mgr.); Edvardo Navarro (Opns. Mgr.)

SEMLER INDUSTRIES, INC. (PRESSROOM FLUIDS EQUIPMENT DIV.)

Street address 1: 3800 Carnation St
Street address city: Franklin Park
Street address state: IL
Zip/Postal code: 60131-1202
Country: USA
Mailing address: 3800 Carnation St
Mailing city: Franklin Park
Mailing state: IL
Mailing zip: 60131-1202
General Phone: (847) 671-5650
General Fax: (847) 671-7686
General/National Adv. E-mail: semler@semlerindustries.com
Primary Website: www.semlerindustries.com
Mthly Avg Unique Visitors: 1905
Industry: Circulation Equipment & Supplies; Fluid Handeling: Pressroom; Ink Recovery Systems; Ink Storage Tanks; Wastewater Treatment;
Personnel: Loren H. Semler (Pres.); William E. Schulz (Dir. Sales)

SHOOM, INC.

Street address 1: 6345 Balbow Blvd, Ste 247
Street address city: Incino
Street address state: CA
Zip/Postal code: 91316
Country: USA
Mailing address: 6345 Balboa Blvd Ste 247
Mailing city: Encino
Mailing state: CA
Mailing zip: 91316-1580
General Phone: (408) 702-2167
General Fax: (408) 824-1543
Primary Website: www.inpixon.com/solutions/shoom/
Industry: Software: Electronic Data Interchange
Personnel: Nadir Ali (Chairman & CEO); Soumya Das (COO)

SHREVE SYSTEMS

Street address 1: 1200 Marshall St
Street address city: Shreveport
Street address state: LA
Zip/Postal code: 71101-3936
Country: USA
Mailing address: 3080 Knolin Dr Ste 2
Mailing city: Bossier City
Mailing state: LA
Mailing zip: 71112-2465

General Phone: (318) 424-9791
General Fax: (318) 424-9771
General/National Adv. E-mail: ssystems@bellsouth.net
Primary Website: www.shrevesystems.com
Mthly Avg Unique Visitors: 1981
Industry: Computers: Hardware & Software Integrators
Personnel: Rich Harold (Pres.)

SHUTTLEWORTH, LLC

Street address 1: 10 Commercial Rd
Street address city: Huntington
Street address state: IN
Zip/Postal code: 46750-8805
Country: USA
Mailing address: 10 Commercial Rd
Mailing city: Huntington
Mailing state: IN
Mailing zip: 46750-9044
General Phone: (260) 356-8500
General Fax: (260) 359-7810
General/National Adv. E-mail: inc@shuttleworth.com
Primary Website: www.shuttleworth.com
Mthly Avg Unique Visitors: 1962
Industry: Conveyors; Masking Materials; Paper Handeling Equipment; Roll Handeling Equipment;

SIEBERT, INC.

Street address 1: 8134 47th St
Street address city: Lyons
Street address state: IL
Zip/Postal code: 60534-1836
Country: USA
Mailing address: 8134 47th St
Mailing city: Lyons
Mailing state: IL
Mailing zip: 60534-1836
General Phone: (708) 442-2010
General Fax: (708) 447-9353
General/National Adv. E-mail: customerservice@siebertinc.com
Primary Website: www.siebertinc.com
Mthly Avg Unique Visitors: 1969
Industry: Chemicals: Roller Cleaning; Cleaners & Solvents;
Personnel: J.P. Mulcahy (Pres.)

SIEMENS COMMUNICATIONS GROUP

Street address 1: 300 New Jersey Avenue
Street address 2: Suite 1000
Street address city: Washington
Street address state: DC
Zip/Postal code: 20001
Country: USA
Mailing address: 300 New Jersey Avenue, Suite 1000
Mailing city: Washington
Mailing state: DC
Mailing zip: 20001
General Phone: (800) 743-6367
General Fax: (678) 297-8316
General/National Adv. E-mail: email.us@siemens.com
Primary Website: www.siemens.com
Industry: Telecommunications
Personnel: Lisa Davis (Chairman); Barbara Humpton (CEO); Heribert Stumpf (CFO)

SIIX USA CORP.

Street address 1: 651 Bonnie Ln
Street address city: Elk Grove Village
Street address state: IL
Zip/Postal code: 60007-1911
Country: USA
Mailing address: 651 Bonnie Ln
Mailing city: Elk Grove Village
Mailing state: IL
Mailing zip: 60007-1911
General Phone: (847) 593-3211
General Fax: (847) 364-5290
General/National Adv. E-mail: bpusczan@siix-usa.com
Primary Website: www.siix.co.jp
Mthly Avg Unique Visitors: 1972
Industry: Scanners: Color B & W, Plates, Web
Personnel: Steve Swanson (Mgr., Sales/Engineering)

SIMCO INDUSTRIAL STATIC CONTROL PRODUCTS

Street address 1: 2257 N Penn Rd
Street address city: Hatfield
Street address state: PA
Zip/Postal code: 19440-1906
Country: USA
Mailing address: 2257 N Penn Rd
Mailing city: Hatfield
Mailing state: PA
Mailing zip: 19440-1998
General Phone: (215) 822-6401
General/National Adv. E-mail: customerservice@simco-ion.com
Primary Website: www.simco-ion.com
Mthly Avg Unique Visitors: 1936
Industry: Inserting Equipment (Includes Stuffing Machines); Paper Cleaners; Press Accessories, Parts & Supplies; Static Eliminators; Testing Instruments;
Personnel: Ed Huber (Customer Serv. Mgr.); Brian Mininger (Technical Rep.)

SIMON MILLER SALES CO.

Street address 1: 1218 Chestnut St
Street address city: Philadelphia
Street address state: PA
Zip/Postal code: 19107-4848
Country: USA
Mailing address: 3409 W Chester Pike Ste 204
Mailing city: Newtown Square
Mailing state: PA
Mailing zip: 19073-4290
General Phone: (215) 923-3600
General Fax: (215) 923-1173
General/National Adv. E-mail: info@simonmiller.com
Primary Website: www.simonmiller.com
Mthly Avg Unique Visitors: 1920
Industry: Newspaper Couter; Newspaper Marketing; Newsprint; Paper: Coated Groundwood Offset; Paper: Groundwood Specialties; Paper: Specialty Printing Paper; Roll Converters;
Personnel: Joseph Levit (Pres.); Henri C. Levit (COO); David Donde (Vice Pres., Mktg.)

SITMA USA, INC.

Street address 1: 45 Empire Dr
Street address city: Saint Paul
Street address state: MN
Zip/Postal code: 55103-1856
Country: USA
Mailing address: 45 Empire Dr
Mailing city: Saint Paul
Mailing state: MN
Mailing zip: 55103-1856
General Phone: (651) 222-2324
General Fax: (651) 222-4652
General/National Adv. E-mail: sitma@sitma.com
Primary Website: www.sitma.com
Mthly Avg Unique Visitors: 1980
Industry: Automatic Plastic Bagging Equipment; Collating Equipment; Conveyors; Counting, Stacking, Bundling Machines; Feeding, Folding, Delivery Equipment; Folding Machines; Inserting Equipment (Includes Stuffing Machines); Mailroom Systems & Equipment; Remanufactures Equipment; Shrink Wrapping Equipment;
Personnel: Ann Butzer (Mktg. Mgr.)

SKO BRENNER AMERICAN

Street address 1: 841 Merrick Rd
Street address 2: # CS9320
Street address city: Baldwin
Street address state: NY
Zip/Postal code: 11510-3331
Country: USA
Mailing address: 841 Merrick Rd # CS9320
Mailing city: Baldwin
Mailing state: NY
Mailing zip: 11510-3331
General Phone: (516) 771-4400
General Fax: (516) 771-7810
General/National Adv. E-mail: stu@skobrenner.com
Primary Website: www.skobrenner.com
Mthly Avg Unique Visitors: 1939
Industry: Credit & Collections
Personnel: Stuart Brenner (CEO); Jon R. Lunn (COO); Jim Graziano (Sr. Vice Pres.)

SMARTFOCUS INC.

Street address 1: 13810 SE Eastgate Way
Street address 2: Suite 550
Street address city: Bellevue
Street address state: WA
Zip/Postal code: 98005
Country: USA
Mailing address: 13810 SE Eastgate Way, Suite 550
Mailing city: Bellevue
Mailing state: WA
Mailing zip: 98005
General Phone: (425) 460-1000
Primary Website: www.smartfocus.com
Mthly Avg Unique Visitors: 1998
Industry: Consulting Services: Advertising; Consulting Services: Circulation; Consulting Services: Computer; Consulting Services: Marketing; Marketing Database Design and Implementation; Software: Circulation; Training: Sales & Marketing
Product or Service: Online Service Provider and Internet Hosts
Personnel: Chris Allan (CEO); Jamie Gunn (COO)

SMITH PRESSROOM PRODUCTS, INC.

Street address 1: 9215 Bond St
Street address city: Overland Park
Street address state: KS
Zip/Postal code: 66214-1728
County: Johnson
Country: USA
Mailing address: 9215 Bond St.
Mailing city: Overland Park
Mailing state: KS
Mailing zip: 66214
General Phone: (913) 888-0695
General Fax: (913) 888-0699
General/National Adv. E-mail: info@smithpressroomproducts.com
Primary Website: www.smithpressroomproducts.com
Mthly Avg Unique Visitors: 1968
Industry: Blanket Cleaner/Washer (Automatic); Dampening Systems; Offset Fountain Controls; Offset Fountain Solutions; Pumps (Air, Ink, Vacuum); Recirculators; Solvent Recovery Systems; Wastewater Treatment; Water Management Systems; Web Offset Remoisturizers;
Personnel: Dennis Schupp (Pres.); Ross Hart (VP)

SNAP-ON BUSINESS SOLUTIONS

Street address 1: 3900 Kinross Lakes Pkwy
Street address city: Richfield
Street address state: OH
Zip/Postal code: 44286-9381
Country: USA
Mailing address: 4025 Kinross Lakes Pkwy
Mailing city: Richfield
Mailing state: OH
Mailing zip: 44286-9371
General Phone: (330) 659-1600
General Fax: (330) 659-1601
General/National Adv. E-mail: info@snaponbusinesssolutions.com
Primary Website: www.snaponbusinesssolutions.com
Industry: Computers: Storage Devices; Developing and Processing
Personnel: Mary Beth Siddons (Pres.)

SOFTWARE BUSINESS SYSTEMS

Street address 1: 7401 Metro Blvd
Street address 2: Ste 550
Street address city: Edina
Street address state: MN
Zip/Postal code: 55435
Country: USA
Mailing address: 7401 Metro Blvd Ste 550
Mailing city: Edina
Mailing state: MN
Mailing zip: 55435
General Phone: (952) 835-0100
General/National Adv. E-mail: marketing@sbsweb.com
Primary Website: www.sbsweb.com
Mthly Avg Unique Visitors: 1980
Industry: Software: Business (Includes Administration/Accounting); Payroll/HR; Procurement; System Installations; System Integration Services;
Personnel: Curtis Cerf (Pres.); Katherine Gladney (Office Manager)

SOFTWARE CONSULTING SERVICES, LLC

Street address 1: 630 Municipal Dr
Street address 2: Ste 420
Street address city: Nazareth
Street address state: PA
Zip/Postal code: 18064-8990
County: Northampton
Country: USA
Mailing address: 630 Municipal Dr Ste 420
Mailing city: Nazareth
Mailing state: PA
Mailing zip: 18064-8990
General Phone: (610) 746-7700
General Fax: (610) 746-7900
General/National Adv. E-mail: sales@newspapersystems.com
Primary Website: www.newspapersystems.com
Mthly Avg Unique Visitors: 1975
Industry: Software: Advertising (Includes Display; Classified); Page Design (dummying); Editorial; Digital Asset Management; Ad Tracking; Managed Services
Personnel: Richard J. Cichelli (Pres.); Curtis Jackson (Vice Pres., Opns.); Martha J. Cichelli (Mktg. Dir.)

SOLAR SYSTEMS

Street address 1: 605 Hawaii Ave.
Street address city: Torrance
Street address state: CA
Zip/Postal code: 90503
Country: USA
Mailing address: 605 Hawaii Ave.
Mailing city: Torrance
Mailing state: CA
Mailing zip: 90503
General Phone: (425) 270-6100
General Fax: (425) 270-6150
Primary Website: www.solarsystems.com
Mthly Avg Unique Visitors: 1990
Industry: Computers: Hardware & Software Integrators; Remanufactures Equipment; Storage Retrieval Systems;
Personnel: Jean McCall (CFO)

SOLNA WEB USA, INC.

Street address 1: 14500 W 105th St
Street address city: Lenexa
Street address state: KS
Zip/Postal code: 66215-2014
Country: USA
Mailing address: PO Box 15066
Mailing city: Lenexa
Mailing state: KS
Mailing zip: 66285-5066
General Phone: (913) 492-9925
General Fax: (913) 492-0170
General/National Adv. E-mail: rkerns@solnaweb.com
Primary Website: www.solnaweb.com
Mthly Avg Unique Visitors: 1992
Industry: Presses: Offset
Personnel: Richard Kerns (Pres.)

SONOCO PRODUCTS CO.

Street address 1: 1 N 2nd St
Street address city: Hartsville
Street address state: SC
Zip/Postal code: 29550-3300
Country: USA
Mailing address: PO Box 160
Mailing city: Hartsville
Mailing state: SC
Mailing zip: 29551-0160
General Phone: (843) 383-7000
General Fax: (843) 383-7008
Primary Website: www.sonoco.com
Mthly Avg Unique Visitors: 1899
Industry: Newspaper Bags; Recycling Newsprint; Tubes, Racks (Includes Racks: Motor Route Tubes);
Personnel: Harris Deloach (Pres.); Don Gore (Division Vice Pres., Sales)

SOUTH BEND LATHE CORP.

Street address 1: 1735 N Bendix Dr
Street address city: South Bend

Street address state: IN
Zip/Postal code: 46628-1601
Country: USA
Mailing address: 1735 N Bendix Dr
Mailing city: South Bend
Mailing state: IN
Mailing zip: 46628-1601
General Phone: (574) 289-7771
General Fax: (574) 236-1210
General/National Adv. E-mail: sales@southbendlathe.com
Primary Website: www.southbendlathe.com
Mthly Avg Unique Visitors: 1906
Industry: Roller Grinders
Personnel: Carmine Martino (Pres.); Joseph Mittiga (Vice Pres.)

SOUTHERN LITHOPLATE, INC.

Street address 1: 105 Jeffrey Way
Street address city: Youngsville
Street address state: NC
Zip/Postal code: 27596-9759
County: Franklin
Country: USA
Mailing address: PO Box 9400
Mailing city: Wake Forest
Mailing state: NC
Mailing zip: 27588-6400
General Phone: (800) 638-7990
General Fax: (919) 556-1977
General/National Adv. E-mail: info@slp.com
Primary Website: www.slp.com
Mthly Avg Unique Visitors: 1934
Industry: Chemicals: Plate Processing; Chemicals: Pressroom; Film & Paper: Film Processing Machines; Film & Paper: Filters (Photographic); Offset Chemicals & Supplies; Offset Film; Offset Fountain Solutions; Plate Processors; Plates: Offset (Computer to Plate); Plates: Offset (Conventional);
Personnel: Edward A. Casson (Chrmn./CEO); Steve Mattingly (Sr. VP); Ted McGrew (VP Sales); Gary Blakeley (Dir. Global Technical Solutions)

SPARTANICS

Street address 1: 3605 Edison Pl
Street address city: Rolling Meadows
Street address state: IL
Zip/Postal code: 60008-1012
Country: USA
Mailing address: 3605 Edison Pl
Mailing city: Rolling Meadows
Mailing state: IL
Mailing zip: 60008-1077
General Phone: (847) 394-5700
General Fax: (847) 394-0409
General/National Adv. E-mail: sales@spartanico.com
Primary Website: www.spartanics.com
Mthly Avg Unique Visitors: 1963
Industry: Laser Cutting Machines, Die Cutting Machines, Screen Printing Lanes, Plastic Card Counting, Plastic Card Inspection, Registration Shears
Personnel: Mike Bacon (VP., Sales/Mktg.)

SPECTRA LOGIC

Street address 1: 1700 55th St
Street address city: Boulder
Street address state: CO
Zip/Postal code: 80301-2974
Country: USA
Mailing address: 6285 Lookout Rd # 100
Mailing city: Boulder
Mailing state: CO
Mailing zip: 80301-3318
General Phone: (303) 449-6400
General Fax: (303) 939-8844
General/National Adv. E-mail: sales@spectralogic.com
Primary Website: www.spectralogic.com
Mthly Avg Unique Visitors: 1979
Industry: Computers: Hardware & Software Integrators; Library Retrieval Systems;
Personnel: Molly Rector (Dir., Cor. Mktg.)

SPECTRUM HUMAN RESOURCE SYSTEMS CORP.

Street address 1: 707 17th St
Street address 2: Ste 3800
Street address city: Denver
Street address state: CO
Zip/Postal code: 80202-3438
Country: USA
Mailing address: 999 18th St Ste 200
Mailing city: Denver
Mailing state: CO
Mailing zip: 80202-2424
General Phone: (303) 592-3200
General Fax: (303) 595-9970
General/National Adv. E-mail: info@spectrumhr.com
Primary Website: www.spectrumhr.com
Mthly Avg Unique Visitors: 1984
Industry: Software: Asset Management; Software: Business (Includes Administration/Accounting);
Personnel: Sybil Romley (Pres.); Matthew Keitlen (Exec. Vice Pres.)

SRDS, A KANTAR MEDIA COMPANY

Street address 1: 1700 E Higgins Rd
Street address 2: Fl 5
Street address city: Des Plaines
Street address state: IL
Zip/Postal code: 60018-5621
Country: USA
Mailing address: 1700 E Higgins Rd Ste 500
Mailing city: Des Plaines
Mailing state: IL
Mailing zip: 60018-5610
General Phone: (847) 375-5000
General Fax: (847) 375-5001
General/National Adv. E-mail: contact@srds.com
Primary Website: www.srds.com
Mthly Avg Unique Visitors: 1919
Industry: Trade Publications
Note: Media buyers today develop integrated plans from a media landscape that is more complex than ever. They use the SRDS multimedia planning platform daily to navigate that landscape and effectively identify their best options from 125,000+ media brands.
Personnel: Kevin McNally (CFO); Stephen Davis (President); Valerie LaMorte (Vice Pres., HR); Trish DeLaurier (VP, Information Sales & Client Service); Gayle Paprocki (Vice Pres., Pdct. Opns.); Dave Kostolansky (Vice Pres., Mktg./Bus. Devel.); Lindsay Morrison (VP Marketing Communications); Ronald Speechley (Publisher); June Levy (Director, Data Services); John Cronan (Sales Director, Southwest Region)

STANFORD PRODUCTS

Street address 1: 1139 S Broadway Ave
Street address city: Salem
Street address state: IL
Zip/Postal code: 62881-2404
Country: USA
Mailing address: 1139 S Broadway Ave
Mailing city: Salem
Mailing state: IL
Mailing zip: 62881-2404
General Phone: (618) 548-2600
General Fax: (618) 548-6782
Primary Website: www.stanfordproductsllc.com
Mthly Avg Unique Visitors: 1940
Industry: Rewinders
Personnel: Deann Sager (Customer Serv. Mgr.); Tim Andrews (Sales Mgr.); Larry Boyles (Sales Mgr.)

STEEL CITY CORP.

Street address 1: 1000 Hedstrom Dr
Street address city: Ashland
Street address state: OH
Zip/Postal code: 44805-3587
County: Ashland
Country: USA
Mailing address: 1000 Hedstrom Dr
Mailing city: Ashland
Mailing state: OH
Mailing zip: 44805
General Phone: (800) 321-0350
General Fax: (330) 797-2947
General/National Adv. E-mail: jsmith@scity.com
Display Adv. E-mail: jsmith@scity.com
Primary Website: 1000 Hedstrom Drive
Mthly Avg Unique Visitors: 1939
Industry: In addition to offering traditional circulation and distribution supplies (Home Delivery/Single Copy), Steel City Corp. now offers a digital in-store display; providing publishers an opportunity to increase circulation and advertising revenue .The company also provides circulation marketing ideas via their Gaining Readers and Subscribers Program (G.R.A.S.P).
Note: Circulation Supplies: Home Delivery/Distribution/ Single Copy
Personnel: Jim Smith (National Sales Mgr.); Deb Walker (Customer Service); Heather Beasley (Operations Manager)

STERLING PACKAGING SYSTEMS

Street address 1: 6275 Heisley Rd
Street address city: Mentor
Street address state: OH
Zip/Postal code: 44060-1858
Country: USA
Mailing address: 6275 Heisley Rd
Mailing city: Mentor
Mailing state: OH
Mailing zip: 44060-1858
General Phone: (440) 358-7060
General Fax: (440) 358-7061
Primary Website: www.polychem.com
Mthly Avg Unique Visitors: 1992
Industry: Bundling and Tying Machines; Consulting Services: Equipment; Conveyors; Mailroom Systems & Equipment; Remanufactures Equipment;
Personnel: Mihia Cojocaru (Gen. Mgr.)

STERLING TYPE FOUNDRY

Street address 1: 7830 Ridgeland Dr
Street address city: Indianapolis
Street address state: IN
Zip/Postal code: 46250-2269
Country: USA
Mailing address: PO Box 50234
Mailing city: Indianapolis
Mailing state: IN
Mailing zip: 46250-0234
General Phone: (317) 849-5665
General Fax: (317) 849-1616
Primary Website: www.sterlingtype.com
Mthly Avg Unique Visitors: 1922
Industry: Platemakers: Letterpress; Presses: Letterpress; Type, Fonts;
Personnel: David C. Churchman (Works Mgr.)

STEWART GLAPAT CORP.

Street address 1: 1639 Moxahala Ave
Street address city: Zanesville
Street address state: OH
Zip/Postal code: 43701-5950
County: Muskingum
Country: USA
Mailing address: PO Box 3030
Mailing city: Zanesville
Mailing state: OH
Mailing zip: 43702-3030
General Phone: (740) 452-3601
General Fax: (740) 452-9140
General/National Adv. E-mail: sglapat@adjustoveyor.com
Primary Website: www.adjustoveyor.com
Mthly Avg Unique Visitors: 1939
Industry: Material Handling Equipment: Telescopic Conveyors, Truck Loaders & Unloaders
Personnel: Charles T. Stewart (C.E.O and Chairman); David T. Stewart (Sales Manager); Amy Stewart (Executive Vice President); William T. Stewart (President & C.O.O); Mike Hinton (Director of Engineering); Russ Lindamood (Production Manager); Jerry Funk (Purchasing Manager); Ron Bachelor (Spare Parts Sales Mgr.)

STM NETWORKS

Street address 1: 2 Faraday
Street address city: Irvine
Street address state: CA
Zip/Postal code: 92618-2737
Country: USA
Mailing address: 2 Faraday
Mailing city: Irvine
Mailing state: CA
Mailing zip: 92618-2737
General Phone: (949) 753-7864
General Fax: (949) 273-6020
General/National Adv. E-mail: info@stmi.com
Primary Website: www.stmi.com
Mthly Avg Unique Visitors: 1982
Industry: Facsimile/Fax Transmission Systems; Interfaces;
Personnel: Emil Youssefzadeh (Chrmn.); Faramarz Youssefzadeh (COB); Umar Javed (Vice Pres., Sales); Rick Forberg (Vice Pres., Mktg.)

STOCK, FUND, OR ETF

Street address 1: PO Box 488
Street address 2: 122 Mill Pond Lane,
Street address city: Water Mill
Street address state: NY
Zip/Postal code: 11976-0488
County: New York
Country: USA
Mailing address: 122 Mill Pond Lane, PO Box 488
Mailing city: Water Mill
Mailing state: NY
Mailing zip: 11976
General Phone: (631) 204-9100
General Fax: (631) 204-0002
General/National Adv. E-mail: stevea@hamptons.com
Display Adv. E-mail: stevea@hamptons.com
Primary Website: www.VATinfo.org
Mthly Avg Unique Visitors: 1990
Industry: Process Color Reference Guides
Note: 4-color printing guides; 4-color system in Adobe, Corel, Quark
Personnel: Steve Abramson (Pres.); Jane E. Nichols (Vice Pres.); Joan Dalessandro (Office Mgr.)

STORAENSO

Street address 1: 6 Landmark Sq
Street address 2: Fl 4
Street address city: Stamford
Street address state: CT
Zip/Postal code: 06901-2704
Country: USA
Mailing address: 201 Broad St
Mailing city: Stamford
Mailing state: CT
Mailing zip: 06901-2004
General Phone: (203) 359-5707
General Fax: (203) 359-5858
Primary Website: www.storaenso.com
Mthly Avg Unique Visitors: 1996
Industry: Paper: Coated Groundwood Offset
Personnel: Paul Lukaszewski (Mgr., Mktg.)

SUN CHEMICAL CORPORATION

Street address 1: 35 Waterview Boulevard
Street address city: Parsippany
Street address state: NJ
Zip/Postal code: 07054-1285
Country: USA
Mailing address: 35 Waterview Boulevard
Mailing city: Parsippany
Mailing state: NJ
Mailing zip: 07054-1285
General Phone: (973) 404-6000
General Fax: (973) 404-6001
Primary Website: www.sunchemical.com
Mthly Avg Unique Visitors: 1945
Industry: Blankets; Chemicals: Plate Processing; Chemicals: Pressroom; Circulation Equipment & Supplies; Cleaners & Solvents; Offset Blanket Thickness Gauge; Offset Blankets, Blanket Wash; Offset Chemicals & Supplies; Offset Fountain Solutions;
Personnel: Rudi Lenz (Pres. & CEO); Kevin Michaelson (VP & CFO); Felipe Mellado (Chief Marketing Officer and Board Member)

SUNSHINE PAPER CO.

Street address 1: 12601 E 33rd Ave
Street address 2: Ste 109
Street address city: Aurora
Street address state: CO
Zip/Postal code: 80011-1839
Country: USA
Mailing address: 12601 E 33rd Ave Ste 109
Mailing city: Aurora
Mailing state: CO
Mailing zip: 80011-1839
General Phone: (303) 341-2990
General Fax: (303) 341-2995
General/National Adv. E-mail: mgallagher@sunshinepaper.com
Primary Website: www.sunshinepaper.com
Mthly Avg Unique Visitors: 1983

Industry: Calibrated Under-Packing made from Fiber Based, Synthetic, Compressible and Hybrid materials, ParaTex compressible under lay, Plate and Blanket Under-Packing, Offset Blanket Thickness Gauge; Offset Supplies; Ink Jet Papers and Substrates,
Personnel: Michael S. Gallagher (Vice Pres., Sales/Mktg.); Geri Hancock (Adv. Customer Info Serv.)

SUPERIOR HANDLING EQUIPMENT, INC.

Street address 1: 8 Aviator Way
Street address city: Ormond Beach
Street address state: FL
Zip/Postal code: 32174-2983
County: Volusia
Country: USA
Mailing address: 8 Aviator Way
Mailing city: Ormond Beach
Mailing state: FL
Mailing zip: 32174-2983
General Phone: (386) 677-0004
General/National Adv. E-mail: info@superiorlifts.com
Primary Website: www.superiorlifts.com
Mthly Avg Unique Visitors: 1977
Industry: Material Handling Equipment: Truck Loaders; Material Handling Equipment: Vehicle Loading; Paper Handeling Equipment;
Personnel: Mike Vollmar (CEO); Beth Vollmar (Pres.); Gary Clark (Operations Dir.); Carle Davis (Sales Dir.)

SUPERIOR LITHOPLATE OF INDIANA, INC.

Street address 1: Strawberry Rd
Street address city: Rockville
Street address state: IN
Zip/Postal code: 47872
Country: USA
Mailing address: PO Box 192
Mailing city: Rockville
Mailing state: IN
Mailing zip: 47872-0192
General Phone: (765) 569-2094
General Fax: (765) 569-2096
Primary Website: www.superiorlithoplate.com
Mthly Avg Unique Visitors: 1984
Industry: Chemicals: Plate Processing; Chemicals: Pressroom; Offset Chemicals & Supplies; Plate Cleaners; Platemakers: Offset (Conventional);
Personnel: Robert T. Blane (Pres.); Steven C. Blane (Vice Pres.); Miriam Blane (Office Mgr.); Thomas J. Casson (Nat'l Sales Mgr.)

SUPPORT PRODUCTS, INC.

Street address 1: 309 Professional Park Ave
Street address city: Effingham
Street address state: IL
Zip/Postal code: 62401-2940
Country: USA
Mailing address: PO Box 1185
Mailing city: Effingham
Mailing state: IL
Mailing zip: 62401-1185
General Phone: (217) 536-6171
General Fax: (217) 536-6828
General/National Adv. E-mail: supprot@supportproducts.com; custserv@supportproducts.com; sales@supportproducts.com
Primary Website: www.supportproducts.com
Mthly Avg Unique Visitors: 1984
Industry: Adhesives; Chemicals: Roller Cleaning; Composing Room Equipment & Supplies; Ink Fountains & Accessories; Layout Tables, Light Tables & Workstations; Masking Materials; Offset Blanket Thickness Gauge; Plate Cleaners; Rules; Static Eliminators;
Personnel: Jim Calhoon (CEO); Rob Bradshaw (Dir., Sales)

SUPPORT SYSTEMS INTERNATIONAL CORP.

Street address 1: 136 S 2nd St
Street address 2: Fiber Optic Cable Shop
Street address city: Richmond
Street address state: CA
Zip/Postal code: 94804-2110
County: Contra Costa
Country: USA
Mailing address: 136 S 2nd St
Mailing city: Richmond
Mailing state: CA
Mailing zip: 94804-2110
General Phone: (510) 234-9090
General Fax: (510) 233-8888
General/National Adv. E-mail: sales@FiberMailbox.com
Primary Website: www.FiberOpticCableShop.com
Mthly Avg Unique Visitors: 1976
Industry: fiber optic cable assembly manufacturing; fiber optic related products.
Personnel: Ben Parsons (Pres.)

SYNTELLECT, INC.

Street address 1: 2095 W Pinnacle Peak Rd
Street address 2: Ste 110
Street address city: Phoenix
Street address state: AZ
Zip/Postal code: 85027-1262
County: Maricopa
Country: USA
Mailing address: 2095 W Pinnacle Peak Rd Ste 110
Mailing city: Phoenix
Mailing state: AZ
Mailing zip: 85027-1262
General Phone: (602) 789-2800
General Fax: (602) 789-2768
General/National Adv. E-mail: info.ie@enghouse.com
Primary Website: www.syntellect.com
Mthly Avg Unique Visitors: 1984
Industry: Computers: Hardware & Software Integrators; Computers: Local Area Network (LANS); Consulting Services: Advertising; Consulting Services: Circulation; Consulting Services: Equipment; Consulting Services: Marketing; Speech Recognition; Subscription Fulfillment Software; System Integration Services; Telecommunications;
Product or Service: Telecommunications/Service Bureaus
Personnel: Steve Dodenhoff (Pres.); Peter Pamplin (CFO); Keith Gyssler (Vice Pres., Sales Americas); Tricia Lester (Vice Pres., Pdct. Mktg.); Jackie Dasta (Contact)

SYSTEMS TECHNOLOGY, INC.

Street address 1: 1351 Riverview Dr
Street address city: San Bernardino
Street address state: CA
Zip/Postal code: 92408-2945
County: San Bernardino
Country: USA
Mailing address: 1351 E. Riverview Dr.
Mailing city: San Bernardino
Mailing state: CA
Mailing zip: 92408
General Phone: (909) 799-9950
General Fax: (909) 796-8297
General/National Adv. E-mail: info@systems-technology-inc.com
Primary Website: www.systems-technology-inc.com
Mthly Avg Unique Visitors: 2000
Industry: Bundling and Tying Machines; Counting, Stacking, Compensating Stackers, Count-O-Veyors, Bundling Machines; Cutters & Trimmers; In-Line Trimming Systems; Material Handling Equipment: Palletizing Machines; Strapping Machines; Conveyors
Personnel: John St. John (Pres.); Brad Siegel (Sales Dir.)

TALLY GENICOM

Street address 1: 15345 Barranca Parkway
Street address city: Irvine
Street address state: CA
Zip/Postal code: 92618
Country: USA
Mailing address: 15345 Barranca Parkway
Mailing city: Irvine
Mailing state: CA
Mailing zip: 92618
General Phone: (714) 368-2300
Primary Website: www.tallygenicom.com
Industry: Laser Printers
Personnel: Randy Eisenbach (CEO)

TALX CORP.

Street address 1: 11432 Lackland Rd
Street address city: Saint Louis
Street address state: MO
Zip/Postal code: 63146-3516
County: Saint Louis
Country: USA
Mailing address: 11432 Lackland Rd
Mailing city: Saint Louis
Mailing state: MO
Mailing zip: 63146-3516
General Phone: (314) 214-7000
General Fax: (314) 214-7588
General/National Adv. E-mail: moreinfo@talx.com
Primary Website: www.talx.com
Mthly Avg Unique Visitors: 1973
Industry: Speech Recognition
Product or Service: Telecommunications/Service Bureaus
Personnel: William Canfield (CEO); Michael Smith (Vice Pres., Market Devel.)

TAPCLICKS

Street address 1: 3101 Tisch Way
Street address 2: Ste 1002
Street address city: San Jose
Street address state: CA
Zip/Postal code: 95128
County: California
Country: USA
Mailing address: 3101 Tisch Way, Suite 1002
Mailing city: San Jose
Mailing state: CA
Mailing zip: 95128-2533
General Phone: 408-725-2942
General/National Adv. E-mail: sales@tapclicks.com
Display Adv. E-mail: marketing@tapclicks.com
Primary Website: www.tapclicks.com
Mthly Avg Unique Visitors: 2009
Industry: Marketing Technology Big Data Marketing Analytics

TECH-ENERGY CO.

Street address 1: 1111 Schneider
Street address city: Cibolo
Street address state: TX
Zip/Postal code: 78108-3101
Country: USA
Mailing address: 1111 Schneider
Mailing city: Cibolo
Mailing state: TX
Mailing zip: 78108-3101
General Phone: (210) 658-0614
General Fax: (210) 658-0653
General/National Adv. E-mail: techenergy@techenergy.com
Primary Website: www.techenergy.com
Mthly Avg Unique Visitors: 1977
Industry: Blanket Mounting and Bars; Blankets; Ink Fountains & Accessories; Press Accessories, Parts & Supplies; Press Engineers; Press Rebuilding; Press Repairs; Presses: Letterpress; Presses: Offset; Rollers;
Personnel: John E. Pickard (Pres.); Beth Benke (Vice Pres.); Phyllis Pickard (Sec.); Teresa Moeller (Treasurer); Louis Benke (Serv. Mgr.); Rachel Bell (Int'l Sales Mgr.); David N. Moeller (Nat'l Sales Mgr.)

TECHNIDYNE CORP.

Street address 1: 100 Quality Ave
Street address city: New Albany
Street address state: IN
Zip/Postal code: 47150-2272
Country: USA
Mailing address: 100 Quality Ave
Mailing city: New Albany
Mailing state: IN
Mailing zip: 47150-7222
General Phone: (812) 948-2884
General Fax: (812) 945-6847
General/National Adv. E-mail: spectrum@technidyne.com
Primary Website: www.technidyne.com
Mthly Avg Unique Visitors: 1974
Industry: Color Analyzers; Color Management Software; Equipment Dealers (New); Equipment Dealers (Used); Paper Testing Instruments;
Personnel: M. Todd Popson (Pres./CEO); Paul M. Crawford (Bus. Dir.); Thomas Crawford (Vice Pres., Sales/Mktg.); Patrick Robertson (Mgr., Technical Servs.)

TECHNOLOGY INTEGRATORS

Street address 1: 2 Legend Park
Street address city: Effingham
Street address state: IL
Zip/Postal code: 62401-9442
Country: USA
Mailing address: PO Box 334
Mailing city: Effingham
Mailing state: IL
Mailing zip: 62401-0334
General Phone: 217-342-3981
General Fax: 217-3421286
Primary Website: www.technologyintegrators.net; www.airstamping.com
Mthly Avg Unique Visitors: 1992
Industry: Press Accessories, Parts & Supplies; Vacuum Frames;
Personnel: Gene Williams (Sales Engineer); Troy Ramey (Sales Engineer); Kim Schmidt (Acct. Exec.)

TECHNOTRANS AMERICA, INC.

Street address 1: 1441 E Business Center Dr
Street address city: Mount Prospect
Street address state: IL
Zip/Postal code: 60056-2182
County: Cook
Country: USA
Mailing address: 1050 E Business Center Dr
Mailing city: Mount Prospect
Mailing state: IL
Mailing zip: 60056-2180
General Phone: (847) 227-9200
General Fax: (847) 227-9400
General/National Adv. E-mail: ttasales@technotrans.com; info@technotrans.com
Primary Website: www.technotrans.com
Mthly Avg Unique Visitors: 1967
Industry: Blanket Cleaner/Washer (Automatic); Dampening Systems; Dies (Perforating and Slitting); Water Management Systems; Web Offset Remoisturizers;
Personnel: Thomas Carbery (Vice Pres.); Victoria Moore (Sales Admin.)

TEK-TOOLS, INC.

Street address 1: 4040 McEwen Rd
Street address 2: Ste 240
Street address city: Dallas
Street address state: TX
Zip/Postal code: 75244-5032
Country: USA
Mailing address: 4040 McEwen Rd Ste 240
Mailing city: Dallas
Mailing state: TX
Mailing zip: 75244-5032
General Phone: (972) 980-2890
General Fax: (972) 866-0714
General/National Adv. E-mail: contact@tek-tools.com
Primary Website: www.tek-tools.com
Mthly Avg Unique Visitors: 1993
Industry: Software: Advertising (Includes Display; Classified); Software: Editorial; Software: Electronic Data Interchange; Software: Workflow Management/Tracking;
Personnel: Ken Barth (Pres./CEO); Cindy Whitley (Dir., Sales); Stephen Harding (Dir., Mktg.)

TEL-AIRE PUBLICATIONS, INC.

Street address 1: 3105 E John Carpenter Fwy
Street address city: Irving
Street address state: TX
Zip/Postal code: 75062-4933
Country: USA
Mailing address: 3105 E John Carpenter Fwy
Mailing city: Irving
Mailing state: TX
Mailing zip: 75062-4933
General Phone: (972) 438-4111
General Fax: (972) 579-7483
General/National Adv. E-mail: sales@tel-aire.com
Primary Website: www.tel-aire.com
Mthly Avg Unique Visitors: 1969
Industry: Trade Publications
Note: WE NO LONGER SELL FEATURES.
Personnel: David McGee (Pres.)

TELESONIC PACKAGING CORP., AMES ENGINEERING DIV.

Street address 1: 805 E 13th St
Street address city: Wilmington
Street address state: DE

Zip/Postal code: 19802-5000
Country: USA
Mailing address: 805 E 13th St
Mailing city: Wilmington
Mailing state: DE
Mailing zip: 19802-5000
General Phone: (302) 658-6945
General Fax: (302) 658-6946
General/National Adv. E-mail: telesonics@aol.com
Primary Website: www.telesoniconline.com
Mthly Avg Unique Visitors: 1958
Industry: Automatic Plastic Bagging Equipment; Shrink Wrapping Equipment; Packaging machinery
Personnel: Bernard Katz (Pres.)

TELETYPE CO.

Street address 1: 20 Park Plz
Street address city: Boston
Street address state: MA
Zip/Postal code: 02116-4303
Country: USA
Mailing address: 20 Park Plz
Mailing city: Boston
Mailing state: MA
Mailing zip: 02116-4303
General Phone: (617) 542-6220
General Fax: (617) 542-6289
General/National Adv. E-mail: info@teletype.com
Primary Website: www.teletype.com
Mthly Avg Unique Visitors: 1981
Industry: Publishing Systems
Personnel: Marlene Winer (Mktg. Mgr.); Edward Freeman (Mktg. Mgr.)

TENSOR INTERNATIONAL LLC

Street address 1: 10330 Argonne Woods Dr
Street address 2: Ste 300
Street address city: Woodridge
Street address state: IL
Zip/Postal code: 60517-5088
Country: USA
Mailing address: 10330 Argonne Woods Dr Ste 300
Mailing city: Woodridge
Mailing state: IL
Mailing zip: 60517-5088
General Phone: (630) 739-9600
General Fax: (630) 739-9339
General/National Adv. E-mail: info@ustensor.com
Primary Website: www.ustensor.com
Industry: Presses: Offset
Personnel: Michael Pavone (COO); Scott Ahlberg (Director of Eng.); John Bonk (VP of Projects & Service Operations); Christopher Dalu (V.P. Production & Purchasing); Rick R. (Accounting)

TERA DIGITAL PUBLISHING

Street address 1: 40 Richards Ave
Street address 2: Ste 29
Street address city: Norwalk
Street address state: CT
Zip/Postal code: 06854-2322
Country: USA
Mailing address: 40 Richards Ave Ste 29
Mailing city: Norwalk
Mailing state: CT
Mailing zip: 06854-2322
General Phone: (203) 838-2333
General Fax: (203) 838-4473
General/National Adv. E-mail: info@miles33.com
Primary Website: www.teradp.com
Industry: Consulting Services: Editorial; Software: Editorial Content Management Systems; Software: Web Publishing; Software: Digital Asset Management/ Archiving
Personnel: Don Sullivan (Sr. VP Sales); Albert De Bruijn (VP Marketing and Sales for Western USA)

TEUFELBERGER GMBH

Street address 1: Vogelweiderstrasse 50
Street address city: Wels
Zip/Postal code: 4600
Country: Austria
Mailing address: Vogelweiderstrasse 50
Mailing city: Wels
Mailing zip: 4600
General Phone: 43 7242 4130
General Fax: 43 7242 413100
General/National Adv. E-mail: fibersplastics@teufelberger.com; mailbox@teufelberger.com
Primary Website: www.teufelberger.com
Mthly Avg Unique Visitors: 1890
Industry: Bundling and Tying Machines; Counting, Stacking, Bundling Machines; Strapping Machines;
Personnel: Teufel Berger (Owner); Harald Katzinger (Mgr., Mktg./Sales Agriculture)

THE AUSTIN COMPANY

Street address 1: 6095 Parkland Blvd
Street address city: Cleveland
Street address state: OH
Zip/Postal code: 44124-6139
Country: USA
Mailing address: 6095 Parkland Blvd Ste 100
Mailing city: Cleveland
Mailing state: OH
Mailing zip: 44124-6140
General Phone: (440) 544-2600
General Fax: (440) 544-2690
General/National Adv. E-mail: austin.info@theaustin.com; ne@theaustin.com
Primary Website: www.theaustin.com
Mthly Avg Unique Visitors: 1878
Industry: Architects/Engineers (Includes Design/ Construction Firms); Consulting Services: Equipment; Consulting Services: Financial; Consulting Services: Marketing; Consulting Services: Production; Mailroom Systems & Equipment; Maintenance, Plant & Equipment; Newsprint Handeling Equipment; Roll Handeling Equipment; System Integration Services
Note: The Austin Company's Newspaper Group offers in-house business, process and facility consulting, architectural, engineering, construction services that address the unique requirements of the printing and publishing industry. Our mission is to assist Newspa"
Personnel: Curt Miller (Gen. Mgr.); Duane Lofdahl (Vice Pres., Planning/Design); Michael G. Pierce (Sr. Vice Pres., Sales/Mktg. Gen. Mgr.); Michael Craft (Sr. Newspaper Consultant)

THE CANNON GROUP, INC.

Street address 1: 5037 Pine Creek Dr
Street address city: Westerville
Street address state: OH
Zip/Postal code: 43081-4849
Country: USA
Mailing address: 5037 Pine Creek Dr
Mailing city: Westerville
Mailing state: OH
Mailing zip: 43081-4849
General Phone: (614) 890-0343
General Fax: (614) 890-0467
General/National Adv. E-mail: sales@pdisaneck.com
Primary Website: www.newsbags.com
Industry: Circulation Supplies and Equipment
Personnel: Frank Cannon (Pres.)

THE DOW CHEMICAL CO.

Street address 1: 2030 Dow Ctr
Street address city: Midland
Street address state: MI
Zip/Postal code: 48674-1500
Country: USA
Mailing address: 2030 Dow Ctr
Mailing city: Midland
Mailing state: MI
Mailing zip: 48674-2030
General Phone: (989) 636-1000
General Fax: (989) 636-3518
General/National Adv. E-mail: dowmedia.relations@dow.com
Primary Website: www.dow.com
Industry: Adhesives; Cleaners & Solvents;
Personnel: Andrew Liveris (Chrmn./Pres./CEO); Matt Davis (Vice Pres., Global Pub. Aff.); Fernando Ruiz (Vice Pres./Treasurer)

THE GAZETTE COMPANY

Street address 1: 501 2nd Ave SE
Street address city: Cedar Rapids
Street address state: IA
Zip/Postal code: 52401-1303
County: Linn
Country: USA
Mailing address: 501 2nd Ave SE
Mailing city: Cedar Rapids
Mailing state: IA
Mailing zip: 52401-1303
General Phone: (319) 398-8422
General Fax: (319) 368-8505
General/National Adv. E-mail: customercare@thegazettecompany.com
Primary Website: www.thegazettecompany.com
Mthly Avg Unique Visitors: 1981
Product or Service: Multimedia/Interactive Products`Publisher/Media
Personnel: Joe Hadky (Chrmn.); Chuck Peters (President and CEO); Chris Edwards (VP Sales & Marketing)

THE HASKELL CO.

Street address 1: 111 Riverside Ave
Street address city: Jacksonville
Street address state: FL
Zip/Postal code: 32202-4905
Country: USA
Mailing address: PO Box 44100
Mailing city: Jacksonville
Mailing state: FL
Mailing zip: 32231-4100
General Phone: (904) 791-4500
General Fax: (904) 791-4699
Primary Website: www.thehaskellco.com
Mthly Avg Unique Visitors: 1965
Industry: Architects/Engineers (Includes Design/ Construction Firms); Consulting Services: Equipment;
Personnel: Steve Halverson (Pres.); Sara Guthrie (Resource Center Administrator)

THE JOSS GROUP

Street address 1: 1528 Meadoview Dr
Street address city: Pottstown
Street address state: PA
Zip/Postal code: 19464
Country: USA
Mailing state: PA
General Phone: (610) 427-1512
General/National Adv. E-mail: contact@thejossgroup.com
Editorial e-mail: mollyjoss@thejossgroup.com
Primary Website: www.thejossgroup.com
Mthly Avg Unique Visitors: 1971
Industry: Trade Publications
Note: The first rule of any technology used in business is automation applied to an efficient operation will magnify the efficiency. The second is automation applied to an inefficient operation will magnify the inefficiency. Bill Gates said that, and we agree but from what we have seen there is a ten-fold increase in magnification of all inefficiencies!
Personnel: Molly Joss (Publisher, Editor, Owner)

THE KEENAN GROUP, INC.

Street address 1: 155 Keenan Ct
Street address city: Pleasant View
Street address state: TN
Zip/Postal code: 37146-3706
County: CHEATHAM
Country: USA
Mailing address: PO Box 458
Mailing city: Pleasant View
Mailing state: TN
Mailing zip: 37146-0458
General Phone: (615) 746-2443
General Fax: (615) 746-2270
General/National Adv. E-mail: info@keenangroup.com
Display Adv. E-mail: debbiekeenan@earthlink.net
Primary Website: www.keenangroup.com
Mthly Avg Unique Visitors: 1984
Industry: Consulting Services: Advertising; Consulting Services: Circulation; Consulting Services: Equipment; Consulting Services: Marketing; Consulting Services: Production; Newspaper Bags; Newspaper Dispensers (Mechanical/Electronic); Newspaper Marketing;
Personnel: Robert P. Keenan (Pres.); Debra B. Keenan (Vice Pres., Sales/Mktg.)

THE NEWARK GROUP

Street address 1: 312 E Ellawood Ave
Street address city: Cedartown
Street address state: GA
Zip/Postal code: 30125-3902
Country: USA
Mailing address: 312 E Ellawood Ave
Mailing city: Cedartown
Mailing state: GA
Mailing zip: 30125-3902
General Phone: (770) 748-3715
General Fax: (770) 748-7414
Industry: Newsprint Handeling Equipment
Personnel: Mickey Thompson (Vice Pres.); Randy Tillery (Sales Mgr.)

THE SIEBOLD COMPANY, INC. (TSC)

Street address 1: 808 S 26th Street
Street address city: Harrisburg
Street address state: PA
Zip/Postal code: 66061-6859
County: Dauphin
Country: USA
Mailing address: 4201 NW 124TH Avenue
Mailing city: Coral Springs
Mailing state: FL
Mailing zip: 33065
General/National Adv. E-mail: Sales@siebold.com
Display Adv. E-mail: Sales@siebold.com
Primary Website: www.sieboldgraphicarts.com
Mthly Avg Unique Visitors: 1989
Industry: Single and Double-Width Press Parts; Service; Web Offset Press Equipment Brokers & Appraisers; Consulting Services: Equipment; Equipment Dealers (New); Equipment Dealers (Used); Press Rebuilding; Press Reconditioning; Press Repairs; Presses: Offset.
Note: TSC has completed over 5,000 successful equipment installation projects since 1989 throughout North America and the English-speaking Caribbean Islands, and specializes in the Graphic Arts and Material Handling industries. TSC is the parent company of: DR Press Equipment, Inc. (Single & Double-Width Press Parts); DGM; and Smith Pressroom Products. TSC also offers press equipment brokering services and is the exclusive distributor for GWS Printing Systems. For additional TSC information, please visit our website: www.sieboldgraphicarts.com or call 800-452-9481.
Personnel: Bruce Barna (VP Sales & Marketing)

THE SLATONITE

Street address 1: 139 S 9th St
Street address city: Slaton
Street address state: TX
Zip/Postal code: 79364-4121
County: Lubbock
Country: USA
Mailing address: PO Box 667
Mailing city: Slaton
Mailing state: TX
Mailing zip: 79364-0667
General Phone: 806-828-6201
General Fax: 806-828-6202
General/National Adv. E-mail: slatonite@sbcglobal.net
Display Adv. E-mail: detta@slatonitenews.com
Primary Website: www.slatonitenews.com
Mthly Avg Unique Visitors: 1911
Industry: newspaper, advertising
Personnel: Ken Richardson (Ed./Pub.); James Villanueva (Managing Editor); D'Etta Brown (Production Editor / advertising director); Malva Richardson (Business Manager); Gloria Olivares (Copy Editor)

THE SOFTWARE CONSTRUCTION CO. (SCC)

Street address 1: 3810 Hamby Rd
Street address city: Alpharetta
Street address state: GA
Zip/Postal code: 30004-3953
Country: USA
Mailing address: 3810 Hamby Rd
Mailing city: Alpharetta
Mailing state: GA
Mailing zip: 30004-3953
General Phone: (770) 751-8500
General/National Adv. E-mail: sales@sccmediaserver.com
Primary Website: www.sccmediaserver.com
Mthly Avg Unique Visitors: 1995
Industry: Software: Digital Asset Management; Software: Multimedia Photo Story Archiving; Software: News Budgeting; Software: Workflow Management; Software: Assignment Tracking; Software: Syndicated Data Delivery
Personnel: Rick Marucci (CEO); Lee Funnell (Vice Pres.)

THE WELLMARK COMPANY

Street address 1: 1903 SE 29th St
Street address city: Oklahoma City

Street address state: OK
Zip/Postal code: 73129-7625
Country: USA
Mailing address: 1903 SE 29th St
Mailing city: Oklahoma City
Mailing state: OK
Mailing zip: 73129-7625
General Phone: (405) 672-6660
General Fax: (405) 672-6661
General/National Adv. E-mail: twc@wellmarkco.com
Primary Website: www.wellmarkco.com
Mthly Avg Unique Visitors: 1963
Industry: Gauges, Measuring; Ink Storage Tanks;
Personnel: Dick Pfieffer (Pres.); Steve Lawson (VP Sales/Mktg.)

THOUGHT EQUITY MANAGEMENT, INC.

Street address 1: 1530 16th St
Street address 2: Fl 6
Street address city: Denver
Street address state: CO
Zip/Postal code: 80202-1447
County: Denver
Country: USA
Mailing address: 1530 16th St Ste 600
Mailing city: Denver
Mailing state: CO
Mailing zip: 80202-1447
General Phone: (720) 382-2869
General Fax: (720) 382-2719
General/National Adv. E-mail: sales@thoughtequity.com
Primary Website: www.thoughtequity.com
Mthly Avg Unique Visitors: 2003
Industry: Electronic Ad Delivery
Note: Thought Equity Libraries: Supplier of motion content to newspaper, cable and broadcast companies. Thousands of affordable, top-quality ads and commercials are searchable and accessible online."
Personnel: Kevin Schaff (Founder/CEO); Mark Lemmons (CTO); Mike Emerson (Vice Pres., Mktg.); Frank Cardello (Vice Pres., Bus. Devel.)

TILT-LOCK

Street address 1: 12070 43rd St NE
Street address city: Saint Michael
Street address state: MN
Zip/Postal code: 55376-8427
Country: USA
Mailing address: 12070 43rd St NE
Mailing city: Saint Michael
Mailing state: MN
Mailing zip: 55376-8427
General Phone: (800) 999-8458
General Fax: (763) 497-7046
General/National Adv. E-mail: sales@tiltlock.com
Primary Website: www.tiltlock.com
Mthly Avg Unique Visitors: 1963
Industry: Chemicals: Chuck (Paper Roll); Roll Handeling Equipment;
Personnel: Jerry Morton (Sales Mgr.)

TKM UNITED STATES, INC.

Street address 1: 1845 Airport Exchange Blvd
Street address 2: Ste 150
Street address city: Erlanger
Street address state: KY
Zip/Postal code: 41018-3503
County: Kenton
Country: USA
Mailing address: PO Box 75015
Mailing city: Cincinnati
Mailing state: OH
Mailing zip: 45275-0015
General Phone: (859) 689-7094
General Fax: (859) 689-7565
General/National Adv. E-mail: sales@tkmus.com
Primary Website: www.tkmus.com
Mthly Avg Unique Visitors: 2002
Industry: Cutters & Trimmers
Personnel: Michael Clark (Market Mgr.)

TKS (USA), INC.

Street address 1: 101 E Park Blvd
Street address 2: Ste 600
Street address city: Plano
Street address state: TX
Zip/Postal code: 75074-8818
Country: USA
Mailing address: 3001 E Plano Pkwy Ste 200
Mailing city: Plano
Mailing state: TX
Mailing zip: 75074-7480
General Phone: (972) 983 0600
General Fax: (972) 870-5857
General/National Adv. E-mail: sales@tkspress.com
Primary Website: www.tksusa.com
Mthly Avg Unique Visitors: 1980
Industry: Presses: Offset and digital ink jet and gripper conveyor
Personnel: Mike Shafer (Vice President of Sales and Marketing)

TKS LTD.

Street address 1: 26-24 Shiba 5-Chome Minato-Ku
Street address city: Tokyo
Zip/Postal code: 108-8375
Country: Japan
Mailing address: 26-24 Shiba 5-Chome Minato-Ku
Mailing city: Tokyo
Mailing zip: 108-8375
General Phone: +81 3 3451-8141
General Fax: +81 3 3451-7425
General/National Adv. E-mail: sales@tkspress.com
Display Adv. E-mail: sales@tkspress.com
Primary Website: www.tks-net.co.jp
Mthly Avg Unique Visitors: 1874
Industry: Newspaper Web Offset Presses & Digital Presses; Automated and Manpower Saving Equipment for Newspaper Presses; Commercial Web Offset Presses; Automated and Manpower Saving Equipment for Commercial Presses;
Personnel: Noriyuki Shiba (Pres.); Osamu Kurata (Sales Chief Officer)

TNS GLOBAL

Street address 1: 11 Madison Ave
Street address 2: Ste 1201
Street address city: New York
Street address state: NY
Zip/Postal code: 10010-3624
County: New York
Country: USA
Mailing address: 11 Madison Ave Ste 1201
Mailing city: New York
Mailing state: NY
Mailing zip: 10010-3624
General Phone: (212) 991-6000
General/National Adv. E-mail: enquiries@tnsglobal.com
Primary Website: www.tnsglobal.com
Mthly Avg Unique Visitors: 1946
Industry: Consulting Services: Advertising; Consulting Services: Marketing; Market Research;
Product or Service: Advertising/Marketing Agency
Personnel: Leendert De Voogd (Sales Rep.); Mark Francas (Sales Rep.)

TOBIAS ASSOCIATES, INC.

Street address 1: 50 Industrial Dr
Street address city: Ivyland
Street address state: PA
Zip/Postal code: 18974-1433
Country: USA
Mailing address: PO Box 2699
Mailing city: Ivyland
Mailing state: PA
Mailing zip: 18974-0347
General Phone: (800) 877-3367
General Fax: (215) 322-1504
General/National Adv. E-mail: sales@tobiasinc.com
Primary Website: www.densitometer.com
Mthly Avg Unique Visitors: 1960
Industry: Calibration Software/Hardware; Color Analyzers; Dark Room Equipment; Densitometers; Electronic Pre-Scan Systems; Press Accessories, Parts & Supplies; Testing Instruments;
Personnel: Eric M. Tobias (Vice Pres.); William D. Bender (Sales Mgr.)

TOLERANS AB SWEDEN

Street address 1: Vindkraftsvagen 6
Street address 2: Vindkraftsvagen 6
Street address city: Stockholm
Zip/Postal code: 135 70
Country: Sweden
Mailing address: P.O Box 669
Mailing city: Tyreso
Mailing zip: 135 26
General Phone: +46 8 4487030
General Fax: +46 8 4487040
General/National Adv. E-mail: info@tolerans.com
Primary Website: www.tolerans.com
Industry: Printing
Personnel: Jan Melin (CEO)

TOWER PRODUCTS, INC.

Street address 1: 2703 Freemansburg Ave
Street address city: Easton
Street address state: PA
Zip/Postal code: 18045-6090
County: Northampton
Country: USA
Mailing address: PO Box 3070
Mailing city: Palmer
Mailing state: PA
Mailing zip: 18043-3070
General Phone: (610) 253-6206
General Fax: (610) 258-9695
General/National Adv. E-mail: info@towerproducts.com
Primary Website: www.towerproducts.com
Mthly Avg Unique Visitors: 1964
Industry: Chemicals: Pressroom; Chemicals: Roller Cleaning; Cleaners & Solvents; Fountain Solutions, Low VOC Cleaners
Note: Tower Products is a manufacturer of pressroom chemical products including fountain solutions, low voc washes and specialty chemicals."
Personnel: Richard Principato (Pres./CEO)

TRANSPORTATION CONSULTANTS, INC.

Street address 1: 8302 Dunwoody Pl
Street address 2: Ste 352
Street address city: Atlanta
Street address state: GA
Zip/Postal code: 30350-3351
County: Fulton
Country: USA
Mailing address: 8302 Dunwoody Pl Ste 352
Mailing city: Atlanta
Mailing state: GA
Mailing zip: 30350-3351
General Phone: (404) 250-0100
General Fax: (404) 250-0253
General/National Adv. E-mail: tci@transpconsult.com
Primary Website: www.transpconsult.com
Mthly Avg Unique Visitors: 1981
Industry: Consulting Services: Fleet Operations
Personnel: Paul Gold (Pres.)

TRAUNER CONSULTING SERVICES, INC.

Street address 1: 1617 John F Kennedy Blvd
Street address 2: Ste 600
Street address city: Philadelphia
Street address state: PA
Zip/Postal code: 19103-1807
Country: USA
Mailing address: 1617 John F Kennedy Blvd Frnt
Mailing city: Philadelphia
Mailing state: PA
Mailing zip: 19103-1856
General Phone: (215) 814-6400
General Fax: (215) 814-6440
General/National Adv. E-mail: philadelphia@traunerconsulting.com
Primary Website: www.traunerconsulting.com
Mthly Avg Unique Visitors: 1988
Industry: Architects/Engineers (Includes Design/Construction Firms); Training: Keyboard Operation;
Personnel: Russ Thomas (Mgr., New Bus.)

TSA

Street address 1: 2050 W Sam Houston Pkwy N
Street address city: Houston
Street address state: TX
Zip/Postal code: 77043-2422
Country: USA
Mailing address: 2050 W Sam Houston Pkwy N
Mailing city: Houston
Mailing state: TX
Mailing zip: 77043-2422
General Phone: (713) 935-1500
General Fax: (713) 935-1555
General/National Adv. E-mail: info@tsa.com
Primary Website: www.tsa.com
Mthly Avg Unique Visitors: 1985
Industry: Computers: Hardware & Software Integrators; Equipment Dealers (New); Equipment Dealers (Used);
Personnel: William C. Smith (Pres.); Steven Perry (Sales Mgr.); Rick Valanta (Servs. Devel. Mgr.)

U.S. PETROLON INDUSTRIAL

Street address 1: 11442 Queens Dr
Street address city: Omaha
Street address state: NE
Zip/Postal code: 68164-2229
Country: USA
Mailing address: 11442 Queens Dr
Mailing city: Omaha
Mailing state: NE
Mailing zip: 68164-2229
General Phone: (402) 727-1577
General Fax: (402) 445-8608
General/National Adv. E-mail: al@uspetrolon.com
Primary Website: www.uspetrolon.com
Mthly Avg Unique Visitors: 1979
Industry: Fluid Handeling: Pressroom
Personnel: Al Harrell (Regl. Distributor)

UMAX TECHNOLOGIES, INC.

Street address 1: 10460 Brockwood Rd
Street address city: Dallas
Street address state: TX
Zip/Postal code: 75238-1640
Country: USA
Mailing address: 10460 Brockwood Rd
Mailing city: Dallas
Mailing state: TX
Mailing zip: 75238-1640
General Phone: (214) 342-9799
General Fax: (214) 342-9046
General/National Adv. E-mail: sales@umax.com
Primary Website: www.umax.com
Industry: Color Seperation Scanners; Scanners: Color B & W, Plates, Web;
Personnel: Tenny Sin (Vice Pres., Mktg.); Linn Lin (Sr. Line Mgr.)

UNICOM, INC.

Street address 1: 5450 A St
Street address city: Anchorage
Street address state: AK
Zip/Postal code: 99518-1278
Country: USA
Mailing address: PO Box 92730
Mailing city: Anchorage
Mailing state: AK
Mailing zip: 99509-2730
General Phone: (907) 561-1674
General Fax: (907) 563-3185
General/National Adv. E-mail: unicom@unicom-alaska.com
Primary Website: www.unicom-alaska.com
Mthly Avg Unique Visitors: 1977
Industry: Telecommunications
Personnel: Rob Taylor (Vice Pres./Gen. Mgr.)

UNIQUE PHOTO

Street address 1: 123 US Highway 46
Street address city: Fairfield
Street address state: NJ
Zip/Postal code: 07004-3225
Country: USA
Mailing address: 123 US Highway 46
Mailing city: Fairfield
Mailing state: NJ
Mailing zip: 07004-3225
General Phone: (973) 377-5555
General Fax: (973) 377-8800
Primary Website: www.uniquephoto.com
Mthly Avg Unique Visitors: 1947
Industry: Cameras & Accessories; Chemicals: Photographic; Cutters & Trimmers; Dark Room Equipment; Developing and Processing; Film & Paper: Film Roll Dispensers; Film & Paper: Filters (Photographic); Lenses (Camera); Photography: Digital/Electronic Cameras; Photostat: Chemicals;

Personnel: Matthew Sweetwood (COO); Jonathon Sweetwood (CFO)

UNISYS CORP.

Street address 1: 801 Lakeview Drive
Street address 2: Ste 100
Street address city: Blue Bell
Street address state: PA
Zip/Postal code: 19422
County: Montgomery
Country: USA
Mailing address: 801 Lakeview Drive, Ste 100
Mailing city: Blue Bell
Mailing state: PA
Mailing zip: 19422
General Phone: (215) 274-2742
Primary Website: www.unisys.com
Mthly Avg Unique Visitors: 1986
Industry: Archiving Systems; Computers: Hardware & Software Integrators; Electronic Ad Delivery; Software: Advertising (Includes Display; Classified); Software: Business (Includes Administration/Accounting); Software: Editorial; Software: Pagination/Layout; Software: Workflow Management/Tracking; System Integration Services;
Product or Service: Hardware/Software Supplier
Personnel: Maria Allen (Vice Pres. and Global Head of Financial Services); Lakshmi Ashok (CTO); Mark Cohn (CTO)

UNITED PAPER MILLS KYMMENE, INC.

Street address 1: 1270 Avenue of the Americas
Street address 2: Ste 203
Street address city: New York
Street address state: NY
Zip/Postal code: 10020-1700
Country: USA
Mailing address: 1270 Avenue of the Americas Ste 203
Mailing city: New York
Mailing state: NY
Mailing zip: 10020-1700
General Phone: (212) 218-8232
General Fax: (212) 218-8240
Primary Website: www.upm.com
Mthly Avg Unique Visitors: 1930
Industry: Newsprint
Personnel: Tapio Korpeinen (Pres.); Jyrki Salo (Exec. Vice Pres./CFO)

UNITED STATES POSTAL SERVICE

Street address 1: 475 Lenfant Plz SW
Street address city: Washington
Street address state: DC
Zip/Postal code: 20260-0004
Country: USA
Mailing address: 475 Lenfant Plz SW
Mailing city: Washington
Mailing state: DC
Mailing zip: 20260-0004
General Phone: (202) 268-2500
General Fax: (202) 268-5211
Primary Website: www.usps.gov; www.usps.com; www.usps.com/mailingonline
Industry: Mailroom Systems & Equipment
Personnel: Megan Brennan (CEO & Postmaster General); Guy Cottrell (Chief Postal Inspector); Janice Walker (Corporate Communications VP); Ronald Stroman (Deputy Postmaster Gen. & Chief Govt. Relations Officer); David Williams (COO and Exec. VP); Kristin Seaver (Chief Information Officer & Exec. VP); Joseph Corbett (CFO & Exec. VP); Jeffrey Williamson (CHRO and Exec. VP); Jacqueline Krage Strako (Chief Customer & Marketing Officer and Exec. VP); Thomas Marshall (General Counsel and Exec. VP); Kevin McAdams (Delivery Operations VP)

USSPI MEDIA

Street address 1: 424 E State Pkwy
Street address 2: Ste 228
Street address city: Schaumburg
Street address state: IL
Zip/Postal code: 60173-6406
County: Cook
Country: USA
Mailing address: 424 E. State Pkwy., Ste. 228
Mailing city: Schaumburg
Mailing state: IL
Mailing zip: 60173
General Phone: (847) 490-6000
General Fax: (847) 843-9058
General/National Adv. E-mail: info@usspi.com
Display Adv. E-mail: sales@ usspi.com
Primary Website: www.usspi.com
Mthly Avg Unique Visitors: 1989
Industry: Newspaper, email, digital solutions.
Personnel: Phil Miller (CEO); Rick Baranski (VP Media Relations); Michelle Hammons (Executive VP); Barbara Ancona (VP Sales)

UTILIMASTER

Street address 1: 100 State Road 19 N
Street address city: Wakarusa
Street address state: IN
Zip/Postal code: 46573-9312
Country: USA
Mailing address: 603 Earthway Blvd
Mailing city: Bristol
Mailing state: IN
Mailing zip: 46507-9182
General Phone: (574) 862-4561
General Fax: (574) 862-4517
General/National Adv. E-mail: info@utilimaster.com
Primary Website: www.utilimaster.com
Mthly Avg Unique Visitors: 1973
Industry: Delivery Equipment
Personnel: John Marshall (Sr. Vice Pres., Sales/Mktg.)

UV PROCESS SUPPLY, INC.

Street address 1: 1229 W Cortland St
Street address city: Chicago
Street address state: IL
Zip/Postal code: 60614-4805
County: Cook
Country: USA
Mailing address: 1229 W Cortland St
Mailing city: Chicago
Mailing state: IL
Mailing zip: 60614-4805
General Phone: (773) 248-0099
General Fax: (773) 880-6647
General/National Adv. E-mail: info@uvps.com
Display Adv. E-mail: sbsiegel@gmail.com
Primary Website: www.uvprocess.com
Mthly Avg Unique Visitors: 1979
Industry: Color Analyzers; Drying Systems; Ink Bleeding Equipment; Ink Fountains & Accessories; Ink Pumping Systems; Ink Storage Tanks; Lubricants; Offset Chemicals & Supplies; Pumps (Air, Ink, Vacuum); Static Eliminators;
Personnel: Stephen Siegel (Pres.)

UVP, LLC

Street address 1: 2066 W 11th St
Street address city: Upland
Street address state: CA
Zip/Postal code: 91786-3509
Country: USA
Mailing address: 2066 W 11th St
Mailing city: Upland
Mailing state: CA
Mailing zip: 91786-3509
General Phone: (909) 946-3197
General Fax: (909) 946-3597
General/National Adv. E-mail: uvp@uvp.com
Primary Website: www.uvp.com
Mthly Avg Unique Visitors: 1932
Industry: Exposure Lamps; Inks;
Personnel: Leighton Smith (Pres.); Alex Waluszko (Vice Pres., Mktg./Sales); Kathy Buckman (Commun. Mktg. Serv.)

VAN SON HOLLAND INK CORP. OF AMERICA

Street address 1: 185 Oval Dr
Street address city: Islandia
Street address state: NY
Zip/Postal code: 11749-1402
Country: USA
Mailing address: 185 Oval Dr
Mailing city: Islandia
Mailing state: NY
Mailing zip: 11749-1402
General Phone: (800) 645-4182
General Fax: (800) 442-8744
General/National Adv. E-mail: info@vansonink.com
Primary Website: www.vansonink.com
Industry: Inks
Personnel: Joseph Bendowski (Pres.)

VEGRA USA

Street address 1: 1621 W Carroll Ave
Street address city: Chicago
Street address state: IL
Zip/Postal code: 60612-2501
Country: USA
Mailing address: 1621 W Carroll Ave
Mailing city: Chicago
Mailing state: IL
Mailing zip: 60612-2501
General Phone: (312) 733-3400
General Fax: (312) 738-2386
General/National Adv. E-mail: info@vegra.de
Primary Website: www.vegra.de
Mthly Avg Unique Visitors: 1997
Industry: Chemicals: Pressroom; Core Strippers & Seperators; Dies (Perforating and Slitting); Offset Blankets, Blanket Wash; Offset Chemicals & Supplies; Offset Fountain Solutions; Static Eliminators;
Personnel: Michael Miske (Vice Pres., Sales)

VER-A-FAST

Street address 1: 20545 Center Ridge Rd
Street address 2: Ste 300
Street address city: Rocky River
Street address state: OH
Zip/Postal code: 44116-3423
County: Cuyahoga
Country: USA
Mailing address: 20545 Center Ridge Rd Ste 300
Mailing city: Rocky River
Mailing state: OH
Mailing zip: 44116-3423
General Phone: (440) 331-0250
General/National Adv. E-mail: info@verafast.com
Primary Website: www.verafast.com
Mthly Avg Unique Visitors: 1976
Industry: Consulting Services: Circulation; Market Research; Research Studies; Telecommunications; Complete Data Services; Sunday Select; Complete Telemarketing Services Outbound
Personnel: Robert Bensman (President); Steve Lucek (CEO); Cathy Soprano (Exec. Vice Pres.); James Tanner (Mktg./Research Specialist)

VERITIV CORPORATION

Street address 1: 400 Northpark Town Center, 1000 Abernathy Road
Street address 2: Suite 1700
Street address city: Atlanta
Street address state: GA
Zip/Postal code: 30328
Country: USA
Mailing address: 400 Northpark Town Center, 1000 Abernathy Road NE, Building 400, Suite 1700
Mailing city: Atlanta
Mailing state: GA
Mailing zip: 30328
General Phone: (770) 391-8200
Primary Website: www.veritivcorp.com
Mthly Avg Unique Visitors: 2014
Industry: Cutters & Trimmers; Paper Handeling Equipment; Presses: Offset;
Personnel: Mary A. Laschinger (Chairman & CEO); Stephen J. Smith (Sr. V. P. & CFO); John Biscanti (V. P. of Publishing & Print Management); Thomas S. Lazzaro (Sr. V. P. Field Sales & Operations)

VERSAR INC.

Street address 1: 6850 Versar Ctr
Street address 2: Suite 201
Street address city: Springfield
Street address state: VA
Zip/Postal code: 22151-4175
Country: USA
Mailing address: 6850 Versar Ctr, Suite 201
Mailing city: Springfield
Mailing state: VA
Mailing zip: 22151-4196
General Phone: 703-750-3000
General Fax: 703-642-6825
Primary Website: www.versar.com
Mthly Avg Unique Visitors: 1988
Industry: Architects/Engineers (Includes Design/ Construction Firms); System Installations;
Personnel: Dwane Stone (CEO); Christine Tarrago (CFO); Nayna Diehl (V.P. Corporate Counsel & Director for Contracts); Alessandria Albers (V. P. of H.R.); Travis C. Cooper (Corporate Vice President Engineering & Construction Management)

VIDAR SYSTEMS CORP.

Street address 1: 365 Herndon Pkwy
Street address city: Herndon
Street address state: VA
Zip/Postal code: 20170-5613
Country: USA
Mailing address: 365 Herndon Pkwy Ste 105
Mailing city: Herndon
Mailing state: VA
Mailing zip: 20170-6236
General Phone: (703) 471-7070
General Fax: (703) 471-1165
General/National Adv. E-mail: order@3dsystems.com
Primary Website: www.vidar.com
Mthly Avg Unique Visitors: 1984
Industry: Scanners: Color B & W, Plates, Web
Personnel: Greg Elfering (V. P.); Joe Barden (Global Sales Mgr.); Bob May (Global Customer Support)

VIDEOJET TECHNOLOGIES INC.

Street address 1: 1500 N Mittel Blvd
Street address city: Wood Dale
Street address state: IL
Zip/Postal code: 60191-1072
County: DuPage
Country: USA
Mailing address: 1500 Mittel Blvd.
Mailing city: Wood Dale
Mailing state: IL
Mailing zip: 60191
General Phone: (630) 860-7300
General Fax: (630) 582-1343
General/National Adv. E-mail: info@videojet.com
Primary Website: www.videojet.com
Mthly Avg Unique Visitors: 1980
Industry: Addressing Machines; Inks; Label Printing Machines; Mailroom Systems & Equipment;

VISION DATA EQUIPMENT CORP.

Street address 1: 1377 3rd St
Street address city: Rensselaer
Street address state: NY
Zip/Postal code: 12144-1815
Country: USA
Mailing address: 1377 3rd St
Mailing city: Rensselaer
Mailing state: NY
Mailing zip: 12144-1899
General Phone: (518) 434-2193
General Fax: (518) 434-3457
General/National Adv. E-mail: sales@vdata.com
Primary Website: www.vdata.com
Mthly Avg Unique Visitors: 1973
Industry: Print & Digital Media Software: Total Advertising & sales management for print & web pubs. (Includes CRM, Sales, A/R/Accounting, VisionWeb customer ad entry); Software: Total Circulation Management for print & web pubs; Software: Electronic Data Interchange; Software: Pagination/Layout; Software: Ad tracking, production management; Software: Remote Workflow Management.
Personnel: Dempsey Tom (President); Timothy Donnelly (Sales Mgr); Amy Weaver (Southwest U.S. Sales manager)

WALTERRY INSURANCE BROKERS

Street address 1: 7411 Old Branch Ave
Street address city: Clinton
Street address state: MD
Zip/Postal code: 20735-1323
Country: USA
Mailing address: 7411 Old Branch Ave
Mailing city: Clinton
Mailing state: MD
Mailing zip: 20735-1323
General Phone: (301) 868-7200
General Fax: (301) 868-2611
General/National Adv. E-mail: insurance@walterry.com
Primary Website: www.walterry.com
Mthly Avg Unique Visitors: 1968
Industry: Insurance

Personnel: Walter J. Coady (Dir., Mktg.)

WEATHERLINE, INC.

Street address 1: 12119 St Charles Rock Rd
Street address city: Saint Louis
Street address state: MO
Zip/Postal code: 63103
Country: USA
Mailing address: 12119 St. Charles Rock Rd.
Mailing city: Saint Louis
Mailing state: MO
Mailing zip: 63044
General Phone: (314) 291-1000
General Fax: (314) 291-3226
General/National Adv. E-mail: info@weatherline.com
Primary Website: www.weatherline.com
Mthly Avg Unique Visitors: 1968
Industry: Consulting Services: Advertising; Consulting Services: Marketing; Promotion Services;
Personnel: Richard H. Friedman (Pres.); Michelle Parent (Exec. Vice Pres.); Nancy J. Friedman (Sr. Vice Pres.); Martha Murphy (Sr. Vice Pres.); Stephen L. Smith (Sr. Vice Pres.)

WEB PRINTING CONTROLS, A BALDWIN COMPANY

Street address 1: 3350 W Salt Creek Ln
Street address 2: Ste 110
Street address city: Arlington Heights
Street address state: IL
Zip/Postal code: 60005-1089
Country: USA
Mailing address: 3350 West Salt Creek Ln., Ste 110
Mailing city: Arlington Heights
Mailing state: IL
Mailing zip: 60005
General Phone: 847-477-6323
General/National Adv. E-mail: mark.krueger@Baldwintech.com
Display Adv. E-mail: mark.krueger@Baldwintech.com
Primary Website: www.wpcteam.com
Mthly Avg Unique Visitors: 1971
Industry: Controls: Color Register; Color Density: Cut-off, Press controls, ribbon controls: Web Break Detector systems: Web Guides
Personnel: Herman Gnuechtel (Product Line Leader WPC); Mark Krueger (Director Of Sales; WPC)

WEBER SYSTEMS, INC.

Street address 1: 23850 Commerce Park Rd, Ste 108
Street address city: Beachwood
Street address state: OH
Zip/Postal code: 44122-5829
Country: USA
Mailing address: 23850 Commerce Park Rd., Ste. 108
Mailing city: Beachwood
Mailing state: OH
Mailing zip: 44122-5829
General Phone: (432) 687-5445
General Fax: (432) 687-5445
Primary Website: www.jeffweber.net
Mthly Avg Unique Visitors: 1981
Industry: Prepress Color Proofing Systems; Storage Retrieval Systems; Computers: Hardware & Software Integrators; Equipment Dealers (New); Equipment Dealers (Used); Software: Pagination/Layout;
Personnel: Jeff Weber (Pres.)

WEBPRESS, LLC

Street address 1: 701 E D St
Street address city: Tacoma
Street address state: WA
Zip/Postal code: 98421-1811
Country: USA
Mailing address: PO Box 2274
Mailing city: Tacoma
Mailing state: WA
Mailing zip: 98401-2274
General Phone: 253-620-4747
General Fax: 253-722-0378
General/National Adv. E-mail: info@webpressllc.com
Primary Website: www.webpressllc.com
Mthly Avg Unique Visitors: 1965
Industry: Folding Machines; Presses: Offset; Remanufactures Equipment; Roll Handeling Equipment; Web Press - Special Equipment;
Note: WebPress LLC is the proud manufacturer of the Quad-Stack 4 over 4 color printing unit and the UPM perfector system. Units combine with WPC folders to make an efficient, cost saving press line with low waste, tight registration, and single level operation."
Personnel: Rick Guinn (Operations Manager); Brian Haun (President); Brian Hilsendager (Customer Service/Parts); Jim Merek (Sales)

WESCO GRAPHICS

Street address 1: 410 E Grant Line Rd
Street address 2: Ste B
Street address city: Tracy
Street address state: CA
Zip/Postal code: 95376-2838
Country: USA
Mailing address: 410 E Grant Line Rd Ste B
Mailing city: Tracy
Mailing state: CA
Mailing zip: 95376-2838
General Phone: (209) 832-1000
General Fax: (209) 832-7800
General/National Adv. E-mail: jim@wescographics.com
Primary Website: www.wescographics.com
Mthly Avg Unique Visitors: 1977
Industry: Consulting Services: Equipment; Equipment Dealers (Used); Erectors & Riggers; Inserting Equipment (Includes Stuffing Machines); Press Rebuilding; Press Repairs; Presses: Offset; Reels & Tensions; Roll Handeling Equipment; Web Press - Special Equipment;
Personnel: Jim Estes (Pres.); Betty Estes (Vice Pres.)

WEST COAST COMPUTER SYSTEMS

Street address 1: 2010 N Wilson Way
Street address city: Stockton
Street address state: CA
Zip/Postal code: 95205-3126
Country: USA
Mailing address: 2010 N Wilson Way
Mailing city: Stockton
Mailing state: CA
Mailing zip: 95205-3126
General Phone: (209) 948-5499
General/National Adv. E-mail: sales@wccsys.com
Primary Website: www.wccsys.com
Mthly Avg Unique Visitors: 1976
Industry: Ink Storage Tanks; Lubricants; Offset Chemicals & Supplies; Pumps (Air, Ink, Vacuum); Static Eliminators; Consulting Services: Marketing; Market Research;
Personnel: Ed Kobrin (Sales/Mktg. Mgr.); Simon Young (Application Software Mgr.); Jim Ponder (System Software Mgr.)

WESTERN PRINTING MACHINERY

Street address 1: 9228 Ivanhoe St
Street address city: Schiller Park
Street address state: IL
Zip/Postal code: 60176-2305
Country: USA
Mailing address: 9228 Ivanhoe St
Mailing city: Schiller Park
Mailing state: IL
Mailing zip: 60176-2348
General Phone: (847) 678-1740
General Fax: (847) 678-6176
General/National Adv. E-mail: info@wpm.com
Primary Website: www.wpm.com
Mthly Avg Unique Visitors: 1933
Industry: Counting, Stacking, Bundling Machines; Cutters & Trimmers; Dies (Perforating and Slitting); Web Press - Special Equipment;

WESTERN QUARTZ PRODUCTS, INC.

Street address 1: 2432 Spring St
Street address city: Paso Robles
Street address state: CA
Zip/Postal code: 93446-1226
County: San Luis Obispo
Country: USA
Mailing address: 2432 Spring St
Mailing city: Paso Robles
Mailing state: CA
Mailing zip: 93446-1296
General Phone: (805) 238-3524
General Fax: (805) 238-6811
General/National Adv. E-mail: info@westernquartz.com
Primary Website: www.westernquartz.com
Mthly Avg Unique Visitors: 1931
Industry: UV Exposure Lamps
Personnel: Jon Dallons (President/CEO); Katy Wetterstrand (Director/CFO)

WESTERN ROLLER CORP.

Street address 1: 63393 Nels Anderson Rd
Street address city: Bend
Street address state: OR
Zip/Postal code: 97701-5743
Country: USA
Mailing address: 63393 Nels Anderson Rd
Mailing city: Bend
Mailing state: OR
Mailing zip: 97701-5743
General Phone: (541) 382-5643
General Fax: (541) 382-0159
Primary Website: www.westernroller.com
Mthly Avg Unique Visitors: 1972
Industry: Delivery Equipment; Mailroom Systems & Equipment; Web Press - Special Equipment;
Personnel: Doug Collver (Owner)

WHITE BIRCH PAPER

Street address 1: 80 Field Point Rd
Street address city: Greenwich
Street address state: CT
Zip/Postal code: 06830-6416
Country: USA
Mailing address: 80 Field Point Rd Ste 1
Mailing city: Greenwich
Mailing state: CT
Mailing zip: 06830-6416
General Phone: (203) 661-3344
General Fax: (203) 661-3349
Primary Website: www.whitebirchpaper.com
Mthly Avg Unique Visitors: 1941
Industry: Newsprint; Paper: Groundwood Specialties;
Note: Mfg. of Pulpa paper.. Newsprint, specialties & directory. "
Personnel: Peter M. Brant (Chrmn./CEO); Edward D. Sherrick (Sr. Vice Pres./CFO); Christopher M. Brant (President & COO); Russel Lowder (Sr. Vice Pres., Sales)

WHITING TECHNOLOGIES

Street address 1: PO 222
Street address city: La Grange
Street address state: IL
Zip/Postal code: 60525
Country: USA
Mailing state: IL
General Phone: (630) 850-9680
General/National Adv. E-mail: fred@whitingtech.com
Primary Website: www.whitingtech.com
Industry: Press Equipment
Note: Press Design, Custom Engineering Products, Engineering Analysis"
Personnel: Fred Whiting (Pres.)

WHITNEY WORLDWIDE, INC.

Street address 1: 553 Hayward Ave N
Street address 2: Ste 250
Street address city: Saint Paul
Street address state: MN
Zip/Postal code: 55128-9006
Country: USA
Mailing address: 553 Hayward Ave N Ste 250
Mailing city: Saint Paul
Mailing state: MN
Mailing zip: 55128-9006
General Phone: (800) 597-0227
General Fax: (651) 748-4000
General/National Adv. E-mail: whitney@whitneyworld.com
Primary Website: www.whitneyworld.com
Mthly Avg Unique Visitors: 1983
Industry: Consulting Services: Circulation; Consulting Services: Marketing; Mailing List Compiler; Market Research; Newspaper Marketing;
Personnel: Les Layton (CEO)

WHITWORTH KNIFE COMPANY

Street address 1: 825 Delta Ave
Street address 2: Ste C
Street address city: Cincinnati
Street address state: OH
Zip/Postal code: 45226-1220
Country: USA
Mailing address: 508 Missouri Ave
Mailing city: Cincinnati
Mailing state: OH
Mailing zip: 45226-1121
General Phone: (513) 321-9177
General Fax: (513) 321-9938
General/National Adv. E-mail: sales@whitworthknifecompany.com
Primary Website: www.whitworthknifecompany.com
Mthly Avg Unique Visitors: 1995
Industry: Consulting Services: Production; Core Cutters, Restorers, Rounders; Core Strippers & Seperators; Cutters & Trimmers; Cutting Tools; Dies (Perforating and Slitting); Folder Knives; In-Line Trimming Systems; Ink Fountains & Accessories; Roller Grinders;
Personnel: Ray Whitworth (Owner)

WIFAG

Street address 1: 26, route de la GlÃ¢ne,
Street address city: Fribourg
Street address state: NJ
Zip/Postal code: 1701
Country: Switzerland
Mailing address: 26, route de la GlÃ¢ne
Mailing city: Fribourg
Mailing zip: 1701
General Phone: +41 26 426 11 11
General Fax: +41 26 426 11 12
General/National Adv. E-mail: info@wifag-polytype.com
Primary Website: www.wifag-polytype.com
Mthly Avg Unique Visitors: 1904
Industry: Printing Presses: Offset & Digital, New & Preowned, Automation & Press Controls, Upgrades, Rertrofits and Service
Personnel: Noel McEvoy (Director of Sales & Marketing)

WILLIAM DUNKERLEY PUBLISHING CONSULTANT

Street address 1: 275 Batterson Dr
Street address city: New Britain
Street address state: CT
Zip/Postal code: 06053-1005
County: Hartford
Country: USA
Mailing address: 275 Batterson Dr.
Mailing city: New Britain
Mailing state: CT
Mailing zip: 06053
General Phone: (860) 827-8896
General Fax: (508) 507-3021
General/National Adv. E-mail: wdpc@publishinghelp.com
Primary Website: www.publishinghelp.com
Mthly Avg Unique Visitors: 1981
Industry: Consulting Services: Business Analysis; Consulting Services: Advertising; Consulting Services: Editorial; Consulting Services: Financial; Consulting Services: Marketing; Market Research
Personnel: William Dunkerley (Principal)

WILSON GREGORY AGENCY, INC.

Street address 1: 2309 Market St
Street address city: Camp Hill
Street address state: PA
Zip/Postal code: 17011-4627
Country: USA
Mailing address: PO Box 8
Mailing city: Camp Hill
Mailing state: PA
Mailing zip: 17001-0008
General Phone: (717) 730-9777
General Fax: (717) 730-9328
General/National Adv. E-mail: info@wilsongregory.com
Primary Website: www.wilsongregory.com
Mthly Avg Unique Visitors: 1923
Industry: Consulting Services: Circulation; Insurance;

Personnel: Ted Gregory (Chrmn./CEO); Richard Hively (Pres.); Todd Gregory (Vice Pres.); Mark Gregory (Vice Pres., Opns.)

WINDMOELLER AND HOELSCHER CORP.

Street address 1: 23 New England Way
Street address city: Lincoln
Street address state: RI
Zip/Postal code: 02865-4252
Country: USA
Mailing address: 23 New England Way
Mailing city: Lincoln
Mailing state: RI
Mailing zip: 02865-4200
General Phone: (401) 333-2770
General Fax: (401) 333-6491
General/National Adv. E-mail: info@whcorp.com
Primary Website: www.whcorp.com
Mthly Avg Unique Visitors: 1977
Industry: Presses: Flexographic; Presses: Rotogravure;
Personnel: Andrew Wheeler (President); Klaus Kleeman (Vice President of Sales); Buch Javeed (Sr. VP)

WINTON ENGINEERING CO.

Street address 1: 2303 W 18th St
Street address city: Chicago
Street address state: IL
Zip/Postal code: 60608-1808
Country: USA
Mailing address: 2303 W 18th St
Mailing city: Chicago
Mailing state: IL
Mailing zip: 60608-1808
General Phone: (312) 733-5200
General Fax: (312) 733-0446
General/National Adv. E-mail: d.allison@w-rindustries.com
Primary Website: ^www.w-rindustries.com
Mthly Avg Unique Visitors: 1896
Industry: Chemicals: Pressroom; Chemicals: Roller Cleaning; Cleaners & Solvents; Offset Chemicals & Supplies; Press Accessories, Parts & Supplies;
Personnel: David Allison (Vice Pres.)

WOLK ADVERTISING, INC. (RETAIL CARPET AD SERVICE)

Street address 1: 920 E Lincoln St
Street address city: Birmingham
Street address state: MI
Zip/Postal code: 48009-3608
Country: USA
Mailing address: 920 E Lincoln St
Mailing city: Birmingham
Mailing state: MI
Mailing zip: 48009-3608
General Phone: (248) 540-5980
General/National Adv. E-mail: wolkadv@earthlink.net
Primary Website: www.flooringads.com
Mthly Avg Unique Visitors: 1954
Industry: Art & Layout Equipment and Services; Consulting Services: Advertising; Training: Design & Layout;
Personnel: Erv Wolk (Pres.)

WPC MACHINERY CORP.

Street address 1: 1600 Downs Dr
Street address 2: Ste 4
Street address city: West Chicago
Street address state: IL
Zip/Postal code: 60185-1888
Country: USA
Mailing address: 23872 N Kelsey Rd
Mailing city: Lake Barrington
Mailing state: IL
Mailing zip: 60010-1563
General Phone: (630) 231-7721
General Fax: (630) 231-7827
Mthly Avg Unique Visitors: 1989
Industry: Consulting Services: Production; Cylinder Repair; Drives & Controls; Erectors & Riggers; Ink Fountains & Accessories; Paper Handeling Equipment; Press Rebuilding; Press Repairs; Rollers;
Personnel: Mark Krueger (Prodn. Mgr., Press Servs.)

WRANGLER TECH, LLC

Street address 1: 9000 67th St
Street address city: Hodgkins
Street address state: IL
Zip/Postal code: 60525-7606
Country: USA
Mailing address: 9000 67th St
Mailing city: Hodgkins
Mailing state: IL
Mailing zip: 60525-7606
General Phone: (312) 301-7254
Primary Website: www.wranglertech.net
Mthly Avg Unique Visitors: 2016
Industry: IT; Telecomm; Data Center; Security;
Personnel: Susie Cassidy (Sales); Danene McMahon (Co-Owner/Manager)

WRH GLOBAL AMERICAS

Street address 1: 24 Worlds Fair Dr
Street address 2: Ste G
Street address city: Somerset
Street address state: NJ
Zip/Postal code: 08873-1349
County: USA
Country: USA
Mailing address: 24 World's Fair Dr. Unit G
Mailing city: Somerset
Mailing state: NJ
Mailing zip: 08873
General Phone: (856) 842-0600
General Fax: (732) 356-1637
General/National Adv. E-mail: info@wrh-global-americas.com
Primary Website: www.wrh-global-americas.com
Mthly Avg Unique Visitors: 1969
Industry: Provider of Ferag Systems, Service and Spare Parts
Personnel: Barry Evans (VP); Rene Luchsinger (CEO)

WRUBEL COMMUNICATIONS

Street address 1: 12-32 River Rd
Street address city: Fair Lawn
Street address state: NJ
Zip/Postal code: 07410-1802
Country: USA
Mailing address: 12-32 River Rd
Mailing city: Fair Lawn
Mailing state: NJ
Mailing zip: 07410-1802
General Phone: (201) 796-3331
General Fax: (201) 796-5083
General/National Adv. E-mail: Chasnews@aol.com
Mthly Avg Unique Visitors: 1988
Industry: Consulting Services: Advertising; Consulting Services: Circulation; Consulting Services: Editorial; Consulting Services: Financial; Consulting Services: Marketing;
Personnel: Charles Wrubel (Pres.)

XERIUM TECHNOLOGIES INC.

Street address 1: 14101 Capital Blvd
Street address city: Youngsville
Street address state: NC
Zip/Postal code: 27596-0166
Country: USA
Mailing address: 14101 Capital Blvd
Mailing city: Youngsville
Mailing state: NC
Mailing zip: 27596
General Phone: 919-556-7235
General Fax: 919-556-1063
Mthly Avg Unique Visitors: 1886
Industry: Roll Coverings; Roller Grinding Services; Rollers;
Personnel: Kevin Frank (Vice Pres., Sales)

XEROX (CORP. HEADQUARTERS)

Street address 1: 800 Long Ridge Rd
Street address city: Stamford
Street address state: CT
Zip/Postal code: 06902-1227
Country: USA
Mailing address: PO Box 1600
Mailing city: Stamford
Mailing state: CT
Mailing zip: 06904-1600
General Phone: (800) ASK-XEROX (275-9376)
Mthly Avg Unique Visitors: 1906
Industry: Scanners: Color B & W, Plates, Web
Personnel: Paul Allaire (Chrmn. of the Bd./Chrmn.-Exec. Committee); Anne Mulcahy (Pres./CEO)

XEROX CORP.

Street address 1: 201 Merritt 7
Street address city: Norwalk
Street address state: CT
Zip/Postal code: 06851-1056
County: Fairfield
Country: USA
Mailing address: 201 Merritt 7
Mailing city: Norwalk
Mailing state: CT
Mailing zip: 06851-1056
General Phone: (203) 968-3000
Primary Website: www.xerox.com
Mthly Avg Unique Visitors: 1906
Industry: Xerox provides business process services, printing equipment, hardware and software technology for managing information -- from data to documents. Learn more at www.xerox.com.
Note: Xerox Corporation provides business process and document management solutions worldwide. Its Services segment offers business process outsourcing services, such as customer care, transaction processing, finance and accounting, human resources, communication and marketing, and consulting and analytics services, as well as services in the areas of healthcare, transportation, financial services, retail, and telecommunications areas. This segment also provides document outsourcing services comprising managed print services, including workflow automation and centralized print services. The companyÂ's Document Technology segment offers desktop monochrome and color printers, multifunction printers, copiers, digital printing presses, and light production devices; and production printing and publishing systems for the graphic communications marketplace and large enterprises. Its Other segment sells paper, wide-format systems, global imaging systems network integration solutions, and electronic presentation systems. The company sells its products and services directly to its customers; and through its sales force, as well as through a network of independent agents, dealers, value-added resellers, systems integrators, and the Web. Xerox Corporation was founded in 1906 and is headquartered in Norwalk, Connecticut.
Personnel: Keith Cozza (Chairman); John Visentin (Vice Chairman & CEO); Steve Bandrowczak (Exec. V. P. & Pres. & COO); William F. Osbourn (Exec. V. Pres. & CFO); Farooq Muzaffar (Sr. V. P. & Chief Strategy and Marketing Officer)

XEROX CORP.

Street address 1: 6336 Austin Center Blvd, Ste.300
Street address city: Austin
Street address state: TX
Zip/Postal code: 78712
Country: USA
Mailing address: 6336 Austin Center Blvd., Ste.300
Mailing city: Austin
Mailing state: TX
Mailing zip: 78729
General Phone: (512) 343-5600
General Fax: (512) 343-5635
General/National Adv. E-mail: marketing@omnifax.xerox.com
Primary Website: www.omnifax.com
Mthly Avg Unique Visitors: 1993
Industry: Facsimilie/Fax Transmission Systems
Personnel: Erin Hunt (Mgr.)

XITRON

Street address 1: 4750 Venture Drive
Street address 2: Suite 200A
Street address city: Ann Arbor
Street address state: MI
Zip/Postal code: 48108
Country: USA
Mailing address: 4750 Venture Drive, Suite 200A
Mailing city: Ann Arbor
Mailing state: MI
Mailing zip: 48108
General Phone: (734) 913-8080
General Fax: (734) 913-8088
General/National Adv. E-mail: xitronsales@xitron.com
Display Adv. E-mail: xitronsales@xitron.com
Primary Website: www.xitron.com
Mthly Avg Unique Visitors: 1977
Industry: CtP RIPs and Workflows, High-Speed Digital and Inkjet RIPs and workflows, Ink Key Presetting software, Ctp Interfaces, CtP TIFF Catchers, Prepress Software Development
Personnel: Bret Farrah (Executive Vice President); Jennifer Graustein (Marketing Coordinator)

X-RITE INC.

Street address 1: 4300 44th St SE
Street address city: Grand Rapids
Street address state: MI
Zip/Postal code: 49512-4009
Country: USA
Mailing address: 4300 44th St SE
Mailing city: Grand Rapids
Mailing state: MI
Mailing zip: 49512-4009
General Phone: (616) 803-2100
General Fax: (888) 826-3061
General/National Adv. E-mail: info@xrite.com; investor@xrite.com; customerservice@xrite.com
Primary Website: www.xrite.com
Mthly Avg Unique Visitors: 1958
Industry: Color Analyzers; Color Proofing; Color Viewing Equipment; Densitometers; Ink Controls, Computerized; Lighting Equipment; Photo Proofing Systems; Proofing Systems; Testing Instruments;
Personnel: Thomas J. Vacchiano (Pres./CEO/COO); Mary E Chowning (CFO); Raj Shah (Exec. Vice Pres./CFO); Francis Lamy (CTO)

XYONICZ

Street address 1: 6754 Martin St
Street address city: Rome
Street address state: NY
Zip/Postal code: 13440-7119
Country: USA
Mailing address: 6754 Martin St
Mailing city: Rome
Mailing state: NY
Mailing zip: 13440-7119
General Phone: (315) 334-4214
General Fax: (315) 336-3177
Mthly Avg Unique Visitors: 1994
Industry: Equipment Dealers (New); Feeding, Folding, Delivery Equipment; Mailroom Systems & Equipment; Material Handling Equipment: Truck Loaders; Newsprint Handeling Equipment;
Personnel: Ed Zionc (Pres./Mgr., Mktg.)

YALE MATERIALS HANDLING CORP.

Street address 1: 1400 Sullivan Dr
Street address city: Greenville
Street address state: NC
Zip/Postal code: 27834-9007
Country: USA
Mailing address: 1400 Sullivan Dr
Mailing city: Greenville
Mailing state: NC
Mailing zip: 27834-9007
General Phone: (800) 233-9253
General Fax: (252) 931-7873
General/National Adv. E-mail: ayinfo@yale.com
Primary Website: www.yale.com
Mthly Avg Unique Visitors: 1920
Industry: Lift Trucks
Personnel: Don Chance (Pres.); Tina Goodwin (Dir., Financial Servs.); Jay Costello (Vice Pres., Aftermarket Sales); Walt Nawicki (Dir., Dealer Devel.)

INTERACTIVE PRODUCTS AND SERVICES COMPANIES

ALABAMA

DTN/THE PROGRESSIVE FARMER

Street address 1: 2204 Lakeshore Dr
Street address 2: Ste 415
Street address 3: Birmingham
Street address state: AL
Zip/Postal code: 35209-8856
County: Jefferson
Country: USA
Mailing address: PO Box 62400
Mailing city: Tampa
Mailing state: FL
Mailing zip: 33662-2400
General Phone: (800) 292-2340
General/National Adv. E-mail: onlinehelp@dtn.com
Primary Website: www.dtn.com
Product or Service: Online Service Provider and Internet Hosts`Publisher/Media
Personnel: Gregg Hillyer (Ed.-in-Chief)

HUNTSVILLE

ADTRAN

Street address 1: 901 Explorer Blvd NW
Street address 3: Huntsville
Street address state: AL
Zip/Postal code: 35806-2807
County: Madison
Country: USA
Mailing address: 901 Explorer Blvd NW
Mailing city: Huntsville
Mailing state: AL
Mailing zip: 35806-2807
General Phone: (800) 923-8726
General/National Adv. E-mail: info@adtran.com
Primary Website: www.adtran.com
Product or Service: Hardware/Software Supplier
Personnel: Tammie Dodson (PR Dir.)

MAGNACOM, INC.

Street address 1: 615 Discovery Dr NW
Street address 2: Ste B
Street address 3: Huntsville
Street address state: AL
Zip/Postal code: 35806-2801
County: Madison
Country: USA
Mailing address: 310 Voyager Way NW
Mailing city: Huntsville
Mailing state: AL
Mailing zip: 35806-3200
General Phone: (256) 327-8900
General Fax: (256) 327-8998
General/National Adv. E-mail: info@magnacom-inc.com
Primary Website: www.magnacom-inc.com
Product or Service: Telecommunications/Service Bureaus
Personnel: John Trainor (Pres.)

VESTAVIA HILLS

INFOMEDIA, INC.

Street address 1: 2081 Columbiana Rd
Street address 3: Vestavia Hills
Street address state: AL
Zip/Postal code: 35216-2139
County: Jefferson
Country: USA
Mailing address: 2081 Columbiana Rd
Mailing city: Birmingham
Mailing state: AL
Mailing zip: 35216-2139
General Phone: (205) 823-4440
General/National Adv. E-mail: jason@infomedia.com
Primary Website: www.infomedia.com
Product or Service: Advertising/Marketing Agency`Consultants`Graphic/Design Firm`Marketing`Online Service Provider and Internet Hosts`Publisher/Media`Web Site Auditor
Personnel: Jason Lovoy (President)

ARKANSAS

ROGERS

DIGICONNECT

Street address 1: 8004 Cedar Dr
Street address 3: Rogers
Street address state: AR
Zip/Postal code: 72756-7729
County: Benton
Country: USA
Mailing address: 8004 Cedar Dr
Mailing city: Rogers
Mailing state: AR
Mailing zip: 72756
General Phone: (877) 235-7714
General Fax: (479) 595-8748
General/National Adv. E-mail: info@digiconow.com
Primary Website: www.digiconow.com
Product or Service: Telecommunications/Service Bureaus
Personnel: Kim Gustafson (CEO)

ARIZONA

ARIZONA REPUBLIC DIGITAL MEDIA

Street address 1: 200 E Van Buren St
Street address 3: Phoenix
Street address state: AZ
Zip/Postal code: 85004-2238
County: Maricopa
Country: USA
Mailing address: PO Box 1950
Mailing city: Phoenix
Mailing state: AZ
Mailing zip: 85001-1950
General Phone: (602) 444-8000
General Fax: (602) 444-8044
Primary Website: www.azcentral.com
Product or Service: Publisher/Media
Personnel: Nicole Carroll (VP News Executive Editor)

ASPECT COMMUNICATIONS

Street address 1: 2325 East Camelback Road
Street address 2: Suite 700
Street address 3: Phoenix
Street address state: AZ
Zip/Postal code: 85016
Country: USA
Mailing address: 2325 East Camelback Road, Suite 700
Mailing city: Phoenix
Mailing state: CA
Mailing zip: 85016
General Phone: (978) 250 7900
General Fax: (602) 954 2294
General/National Adv. E-mail: contact@aspect.com
Primary Website: www.aspect.com
Year Established: 1985
Product or Service: Hardware/Software Supplier
Personnel: Patrick Dennis (Pres./CEO); Chris DeBiase (CFO); Michael Harris (Chief Marketing Officer)

STONEMAN LAW OFFICES LTD.

Street address 1: 3724 N 3rd St
Street address 2: Ste 200
Street address 3: Phoenix
Street address state: AZ
Zip/Postal code: 85012-2035
County: Maricopa
Country: USA
Mailing address: PO Box 40070
Mailing city: Phoenix
Mailing state: AZ
Mailing zip: 85067-0070
General Phone: (602) 263-9200
General Fax: (602) 277-4883
General/National Adv. E-mail: request@patentdoc.com
Primary Website: www.patentdoc.com
Year Established: 1994
Product or Service: Consultants
Personnel: Marty Stoneman (Registered Patent Attorney); Eric Fish (Registered Patent Attorney)

SYNTELLECT, INC.

Street address 1: 2095 W Pinnacle Peak Rd
Street address 2: Ste 110
Street address 3: Phoenix
Street address state: AZ
Zip/Postal code: 85027-1262
County: Maricopa
Country: USA
Mailing address: 2095 W Pinnacle Peak Rd Ste 110
Mailing city: Phoenix
Mailing state: AZ
Mailing zip: 85027-1262
General Phone: (602) 789-2800
General Fax: (602) 789-2768
General/National Adv. E-mail: info.ie@enghouse.com
Primary Website: www.syntellect.com
Year Established: 1984
Industry: Computers: Hardware & Software Integrators; Computers: Local Area Network (LANS); Consulting Services: Advertising; Consulting Services: Circulation; Consulting Services: Equipment; Consulting Services: Marketing; Speech Recognition; Subscription Fulfillment Software; System Integration Services; Telecommunications;
Product or Service: Telecommunications/Service Bureaus
Personnel: Steve Dodenhoff (Pres.); Peter Pamplin (CFO); Keith Gyssler (Vice Pres., Sales Americas); Tricia Lester (Vice Pres., Pdct. Mktg.); Jackie Dasta (Contact)

VERTICAL COMMUNICATIONS, INC.

Street address 1: 4717 E Hilton Ave
Street address 2: Ste 400
Street address 3: Phoenix
Street address state: AZ
Zip/Postal code: 85034-6414
County: Maricopa
Country: USA
Mailing address: 4717 E Hilton Ave Ste 400
Mailing city: Phoenix
Mailing state: AZ
Mailing zip: 85034-6414
General Phone: (480) 374-8900
General Fax: (480) 998-2469
General/National Adv. E-mail: info@vertical.com
Primary Website: www.vertical.com
Product or Service: Hardware/Software Supplier
Personnel: William Tauscher (CEO); Dick Anderson (Exec. Vice Pres./Gen. Mgr.); Ken Clinebell (CFO); Scott Pickett (CTO); Peter H. Bailey (Sr. Vice Pres., Bus. Dev.); Chris Brookins (Sr. Vice Pres., Dev.); Jim Scanlon (Vice Pres., Sales); Ben Alves (Vice Pres., Sales-Distributed Enterprise Solutions); Mel Passarelli (Vice Pres., International Sales)

SCOTTSDALE

INTACTIX

Street address 1: 15059 N Scottsdale Rd
Street address 2: Ste 400
Street address 3: Scottsdale
Street address state: AZ
Zip/Postal code: 85254-2666
Country: USA
Mailing address: 15059 N Scottsdale Rd
Mailing city: Scottsdale
Mailing state: AZ
Mailing zip: 85254-2666
General Phone: (888) 441-1532
General/National Adv. E-mail: support.jda.com
Primary Website: www.jda.com
Product or Service: Hardware/Software Supplier
Personnel: Girish Rishi (CEO)

JDA SOFTWARE GROUP, INC.

Street address 1: 14400 N 87th St
Street address 3: Scottsdale
Street address state: AZ
Zip/Postal code: 85260-3649
County: Maricopa
Country: USA
Mailing address: 14400 N 87th St
Mailing city: Scottsdale
Mailing state: AZ
Mailing zip: 85260-3657
General Phone: (480) 308-3000
General Fax: (480) 308-3001
General/National Adv. E-mail: info@jda.com
Primary Website: www.jda.com
Product or Service: Hardware/Software Supplier
Personnel: Hamish Brewer (CEO)

MULTI-MEDIA COMMUNICATIONS

Street address 1: 8160 E Butherus Dr
Street address 2: Ste 10
Street address 3: Scottsdale
Street address state: AZ
Zip/Postal code: 85260-2523
County: Maricopa
Country: USA
Mailing address: PO Box 27740
Mailing city: Las Vegas
Mailing state: NV
Mailing zip: 89126-7740
General Phone: (508) 653-3392
General Fax: (508) 651-9970
General/National Adv. E-mail: info@mmcom.com
Primary Website: www.mmcom.com
Year Established: 1974
Product or Service: Multimedia/Interactive Products
Personnel: Don Baine (Pres.)

CALIFORNIA

ALAMEDA

ELFWORKS 3D CONSTRUCTION CO.

Street address 1: 1421 Page St
Street address 3: Alameda
Street address state: CA
Zip/Postal code: 94501-3822
County: Alameda
Country: USA
Mailing address: 1421 Page St
Mailing city: Alameda
Mailing state: CA
Mailing zip: 94501-3822
General Phone: (510) 769-9391
General/National Adv. E-mail: first_contact@elfworks.com
Primary Website: www.elfworks.com
Product or Service: Graphic/Design Firm
Personnel: Erik Flom (Owner)

ANAHEIM

NEW HORIZONS COMPUTER LEARNING CENTER

Street address 1: 1900 S State College Blvd
Street address 2: Ste 450
Street address 3: Anaheim
Street address state: CA
Zip/Postal code: 92806-6163
County: Orange
Country: USA
Mailing address: 1900 S State College Blvd Ste 450
Mailing city: Anaheim
Mailing state: CA
Mailing zip: 92806-6163
General Phone: (714) 940-8000
General/National Adv. E-mail: info.corp@newhorizons.com
Primary Website: www.newhorizons.com
Product or Service: Multimedia/Interactive Products
Personnel: Mark Miller (CEO); Heidi Rose (Sr. Vice Pres., Mktg.); Mark Tucker (Vice. Pres., Mktg.)

BERKELEY

AARON MARCUS AND ASSOCIATES.

Street address 1: 1196 Euclid Ave
Street address 3: Berkeley
Street address state: CA
Zip/Postal code: 94708-1640
County: Alameda
Country: USA
Mailing address: 1196 Euclid Avenue
Mailing city: Berkeley
Mailing state: CA
Mailing zip: 94708-1640
General Phone: (510)599-3195
General/National Adv. E-mail: aaron.marcus@bamanda.com
Primary Website: www.bamanda.com
Product or Service: CD-ROM Designer/Manufacturer`Consultants`Graphic/Design Firm`POP/Kiosk Designer`Research
Note: Available to author research and other publications, to be interviewed, or to give lectures/workshops
Personnel: Aaron Marcus (Principal)

ADVANCED PUBLISHING TECHNOLOGY

Street address 1: 123 S Victory Blvd
Street address 3: Burbank
Street address state: CA
Zip/Postal code: 91502-2347
County: Los Angeles
Country: USA
Mailing address: 123 S Victory Blvd
Mailing city: Burbank
Mailing state: CA
Mailing zip: 91502-2347
General Phone: (818) 557-3035
General Fax: (818) 557-1281
General/National Adv. E-mail: aptsales@advpubtech.com
Primary Website: www.advpubtech.com
Product or Service: Circulation`Editorial`Hardware/Software Supplier`Online Service Provider and Internet Hosts
Personnel: David Kraai (Pres.); Ken Barber (COO); Diane Duren (Online Product Mgr.); Shellie Sommerson (Adv. Prod. Mgr); Sid Kendrick (Cir. Prod. Mgr.); Joe Kennedy (Ed. Prod. Mgr.)

CAMERON PARK

CBS MAXPREPS, INC.

Street address 1: 4080 Plaza Goldorado Cir
Street address 2: Ste A
Street address 3: Cameron Park
Street address state: CA
Zip/Postal code: 95682-7455
County: El Dorado
Country: USA
Mailing address: 4080 Plaza Goldorado Cir Ste A
Mailing city: Cameron Park
Mailing state: CA
Mailing zip: 95682-7455
General Phone: (800) 329-7324
General Fax: (530) 672-8559
General/National Adv. E-mail: sales@maxpreps.com
Primary Website: www.maxpreps.com
Product or Service: Multimedia/Interactive Products`Publisher/Media
Personnel: Andy Beal (Pres.)

ANIMATED SOFTWARE CO.

Street address 1: PO Box 1936
Street address 3: Carlsbad
Street address state: CA
Zip/Postal code: 92018-1936
County: San Diego
Country: USA
Mailing address: PO Box 1936
Mailing city: Carlsbad
Mailing state: CA
Mailing zip: 92018-1936
General Phone: (760) 720-7261
General/National Adv. E-mail: rhoffman@animatedsoftware.com
Primary Website: www.animatedsoftware.com
Product or Service: Multimedia/Interactive Products
Personnel: Ace Hoffman (Owner/Chief Programmer)

CSTV ONLINE, INC.

Street address 1: 2035 Corte Del Nogal
Street address 2: Ste 250
Street address 3: Carlsbad
Street address state: CA
Zip/Postal code: 92011-1465
County: San Diego
Country: USA
Mailing address: 2035 Corte Del Nogal Ste 250
Mailing city: Carlsbad
Mailing state: CA
Mailing zip: 92011-1465
General Phone: (760) 431-8221
General Fax: (760) 431-8108
General/National Adv. E-mail: customersupport@cstv.com
Primary Website: www.cstv.com
Product or Service: Multimedia/Interactive Products
Personnel: Tim Rivere (Vice Pres., Sales); George Scott (Dir., Finance); Tom Keyes (Exec. Producer)

VERVE MOBILE

Street address 1: 5973 Avenida Encinas
Street address 2: Ste 101
Street address 3: Carlsbad
Street address state: CA
Zip/Postal code: 92008-4477
County: San Diego
Country: USA
Mailing address: 5973 Avenida Encinas Ste 101
Mailing city: Carlsbad
Mailing state: CA
Mailing zip: 92008-4477
General Phone: (760) 479-0055
General Fax: (760) 479-0056
General/National Adv. E-mail: hello@verve.com
Editorial e-mail: verve@digcommunications.com
Primary Website: www.verve.com
Product or Service: Advertising/Marketing Agency`Multimedia/Interactive Products
Personnel: Tom Kenney (CEO); Erin Madorsky (Chief Revenue Officer); Julie Bernard (Chief Marketing Officer); Brian Crook (CTO)

APPLE, INC.

Street address 1: 1 Infinite Loop
Street address 3: Cupertino
Street address state: CA
Zip/Postal code: 95014-2083
County: Santa Clara
Country: USA
Mailing address: 1 Infinite Loop
Mailing city: Cupertino
Mailing state: CA
Mailing zip: 95014-2084
General Phone: (408) 996⊠⊠"1010
General Fax: (408) 996-0275
General/National Adv. E-mail: media.help@apple.com
Primary Website: www.apple.com
Year Established: 1976
Industry: Consumer Electronics; Computer Software; Online Services;
Product or Service: Hardware/Software Supplier
Personnel: Timothy Cook (CEO); Philip W. Schiller (Sr. V. P. Worldwide Marketing); Jonathan Ive (Chief Design Officer); Craig Federighi (Senior Vice President, Software Engineering)

EMERALD HILLS

OMIX, INC.

Street address 1: 102 Vaquero Way
Street address 3: Emerald Hills
Street address state: CA
Zip/Postal code: 94062-3152
County: San Mateo
Country: USA
Mailing address: 102 Vaquero Way
Mailing city: Emerald Hills
Mailing state: CA
Mailing zip: 94062-3152
General Phone: (650) 568-9800
General Fax: (650) 368-6973
General/National Adv. E-mail: information@omix.com
Primary Website: www.omix.com
Product or Service: Online Service Provider and Internet Hosts
Personnel: Terry Lillie (Pres./CTO); Kyle Hurlbut (Vice Pres.); Sandy Lillie (Gen. Mgr.); Jim Chabrier (Dir., Bus. Devel.); Maxine Lym (Dir., Mktg.); Jim Rodgers (Creative Dir.); Gail Price (Dir., Finance/Opns.)

EMERYVILLE

GRACENOTE

Street address 1: 2000 Powell Street
Street address 2: Suite 1500
Street address 3: Emeryville
Street address state: CA
Zip/Postal code: 94608
County: Warren
Country: USA
Mailing address: 2000 Powell Street, Suite 1500
Mailing city: Emeryville
Mailing state: CA
Mailing zip: 94608
General Phone: (510) 428-7200
General/National Adv. E-mail: support@gracenote.com
Primary Website: www.gracenote.com
Product or Service: Multimedia/Interactive Products
Personnel: Karthik Rao (Pres.); Amilcar Perez (Chief Revenue Officer); Shannon Buggy (Senior Vice President, Human Resources)

FREMONT

PARTSRIVER, INC.

Street address 1: 3155 Kearney St
Street address 2: Ste 210
Street address 3: Fremont
Street address state: CA
Zip/Postal code: 94538-2268
County: Alameda
Country: USA
Mailing address: 3155 Kearney St Ste 210
Mailing city: Fremont
Mailing state: CA
Mailing zip: 94538-2268
General Phone: (510) 360-5361
General Fax: (510) 413-0079
General/National Adv. E-mail: support@partsriver.com
Primary Website: www.partsriver.com
Year Established: 1997
Product or Service: Hardware/Software Supplier
Personnel: Horacio Woolcott (CEO); Steve De Laet (Chief Devel. Officer); Rishi Agarwal (CTO); Sherry Arnold (Vice Pres., Servs./Content Mgmt.)

HOLLYWOOD

LAURA SMITH ILLUSTRATION

Street address 1: 6545 Cahuenga Ter
Street address 3: Hollywood
Street address state: CA
Zip/Postal code: 90068-2744
County: Los Angeles
Country: USA
Mailing address: 6545 Cahuenga Ter
Mailing city: Hollywood
Mailing state: CA
Mailing zip: 90068-2744
General Phone: (323) 467-1700
General Fax: (323) 467-1700
General/National Adv. E-mail: Laura@LauraSmithArt.com
Primary Website: www.laurasmithart.com
Product or Service: Editorial`Graphic/Design Firm`Marketing

EDITOR & PUBLISHER INTERACTIVE

Street address 1: 17782 Cowan
Street address 2: Ste C
Street address 3: Irvine
Street address state: CA
Zip/Postal code: 92614-6042
County: Orange
Country: USA
Mailing address: 17782 Cowan Ste C
Mailing city: Irvine
Mailing state: CA
Mailing zip: 92614-6042
General Phone: (949) 660-6150
General Fax: (949) 660-6172
Primary Website: www.editorandpublisher.com
Year Established: 1884
Product or Service: Publisher/Media

SAP AMERICA, INC.

Street address 1: 18101 Von Karman Ave
Street address 2: Ste 900
Street address 3: Irvine
Street address state: CA
Zip/Postal code: 92612-0151
County: Orange
Country: USA
Mailing address: 18101 Von Karman Ave Ste 900
Mailing city: Irvine
Mailing state: CA
Mailing zip: 92612-0151
General Phone: (949) 622-2200
General/National Adv. E-mail: press@sap.com
Primary Website: www.sap.com
Industry: Software: Advertising (Includes Display; Classified); Software: Circulation;
Product or Service: Hardware/Software Supplier
Personnel: Mark White (CFO); Costanza Tedesco (Vice Pres., Global Adv./Branding); Brian Ellefritz (Sr. Dir., Social Media Mktg.)

KENTFIELD

UPSHAW & ASSOCIATES

Street address 1: 14 Altamira Ave
Street address 3: Kentfield
Street address state: CA
Zip/Postal code: 94904-1407
County: Marin
Country: USA
Mailing address: 99 Via La Paz
Mailing city: Greenbrae
Mailing state: CA
Mailing zip: 94904-1239
General Phone: (415) 785-8735
General Fax: (415) 507-9194
General/National Adv. E-mail: upshaw@upshawmarketing.com
Primary Website: www.upshawmarketing.com
Product or Service: Consultants
Personnel: Lynn B. Upshaw (Principal)

LAGUNA NIGUEL

GRIFFIN CHASE OLIVER, INC.

Street address 1: 25262 Monte Verde Dr
Street address 3: Laguna Niguel
Street address state: CA
Zip/Postal code: 92677-1535
County: Orange
Country: USA

Mailing address: 25262 Monte Verde Dr
Mailing city: Laguna Niguel
Mailing state: CA
Mailing zip: 92677-1535
General Phone: (949) 495-1144
General Fax: (815) 366-3885
General/National Adv. E-mail: sales@GriffinChaseOliver.com
Primary Website: www.griffinchaseoliver.com
Product or Service: POP/Kiosk Designer
Personnel: Jim Redfield (CEO)

DESIGNORY.COM

Street address 1: 211 E Ocean Blvd
Street address 2: Ste 100
Street address 3: Long Beach
Street address state: CA
Zip/Postal code: 90802-4850
County: Los Angeles
Country: USA
Mailing address: 211 E Ocean Blvd
Mailing city: Long Beach
Mailing state: CA
Mailing zip: 90802-4809
General Phone: (562) 624-0200
Primary Website: www.designory.com
Year Established: 1995
Product or Service: Advertising/Marketing Agency

B/HI

Street address 1: 11500 W Olympic Blvd
Street address 2: Ste 399
Street address 3: Los Angeles
Street address state: CA
Zip/Postal code: 90064-1530
County: Los Angeles
Country: USA
Mailing address: 11500 W Olympic Blvd Ste 399
Mailing city: Los Angeles
Mailing state: CA
Mailing zip: 90064-1530
General Phone: (310) 473-4147
General Fax: (310) 478-4727
General/National Adv. E-mail: info@bhimpact.com
Primary Website: www.bhimpact.com
Product or Service: Advertising/Marketing Agency
Personnel: Dean Bender (Partner); Shawna Lynch (Sr. Vice Pres.); Jerry Griffin (Managing Partner)

EUR/ELECTRONIC URBAN REPORT

Street address 1: PO Box 412081
Street address 3: Los Angeles
Street address state: CA
Zip/Postal code: 90041-9081
County: Los Angeles
Country: USA
Mailing address: PO Box 412081
Mailing city: Los Angeles
Mailing state: CA
Mailing zip: 90041-9081
General Phone: (323) 254-9599
General Fax: (323)-421-9383
General/National Adv. E-mail: editorial@eurweb.com
Primary Website: www.eurweb.com
Product or Service: Publisher/Media
Personnel: Lee Bailey (Pub.)

L@IT2'D (LATITUDE)

Street address 1: 714 N Laurel Ave
Street address 3: Los Angeles
Street address state: CA
Zip/Postal code: 90046-7008
County: Los Angeles
Country: USA
Mailing address: 714 N Laurel Ave
Mailing city: Los Angeles
Mailing state: CA
Mailing zip: 90046-7008
General Phone: (323) 852-1425
General Fax: (323) 856-0704
General/National Adv. E-mail: info@lati2d.com
Primary Website: www.lati2d.com
Year Established: 1993
Product or Service: Graphic/Design Firm
Personnel: Water Kerner (CCO)

LEXISNEXIS

Street address 1: 555 W 5th St
Street address 2: Ste 4500
Street address 3: Los Angeles
Street address state: CA
Zip/Postal code: 90013-3003
County: Los Angeles
Country: USA
Mailing address: 555 W 5th St Ste 4500
Mailing city: Los Angeles
Mailing state: CA
Mailing zip: 90013-3003
General Phone: (213) 627-1130
General/National Adv. E-mail: lexisnexiscommunities@lexisnexis.com
Primary Website: www.lexisnexis.com
Product or Service: Consultants
Personnel: Andrew Prozes (CEO, Lexis-Nexis Grp.); Kurt Sanford (Pres./CEO, Cor. & Fed. Mkts.); Michael Walsh (Pres./CEO, U.S. Legal Mkts.); James M. Peck (CEO, Risk Mgmt.); Richard Sobelsohn

LIEBERMAN RESEARCH WORLDWIDE

Street address 1: 1900 Avenue of the Stars
Street address 2: Ste 1600
Street address 3: Los Angeles
Street address state: CA
Zip/Postal code: 90067-4412
County: Los Angeles
Country: USA
Mailing address: 1900 Avenue of the Stars Ste 1600
Mailing city: Los Angeles
Mailing state: CA
Mailing zip: 90067-4483
General Phone: (310) 553-0550
General Fax: (310) 553-4607
General/National Adv. E-mail: info@lrwonline.com
Primary Website: www.lrwonline.com
Year Established: 1973
Product or Service: Advertising/Marketing Agency
Personnel: Dave Sackman (Chairman and CEO)

NEW MEDIA HOLLYWOOD

Street address 1: 6150 Santa Monica Blvd
Street address 3: Los Angeles
Street address state: CA
Zip/Postal code: 90038-1712
County: Los Angeles
Country: USA
Mailing address: 6150 Santa Monica Blvd
Mailing city: Los Angeles
Mailing state: CA
Mailing zip: 90038-1712
General Phone: (323) 957-5000
General Fax: (323) 957-8500
General/National Adv. E-mail: info@nmh.com
Primary Website: www.nmh.com
Product or Service: Multimedia/Interactive Products
Personnel: Chris Speer (Pres.)

NEWSCOM

Street address 1: 145 S Spring St
Street address 2: Fl 10
Street address 3: Los Angeles
Street address state: CA
Zip/Postal code: 90012-4053
County: Los Angeles
Country: USA
Mailing address: 145 S Spring St Fl 10
Mailing city: Los Angeles
Mailing state: CA
Mailing zip: 90012-3601
General Phone: (213) 237-4643
General Fax: (213) 237-7914
General/National Adv. E-mail: sales@newscom.com
Primary Website: www.newscom.com
Product or Service: Telecommunications/Service Bureaus
Personnel: Jay Brodsky (Gen Mgr.); Melanie Rockwell (IP Rel. Dir.); Dan Royal (Dir., Opns.); Diana Backlund (Dir., Sales/Mktg.)

NEXTCOM

Street address 1: 5933 W Century Blvd
Street address 2: Ste 410
Street address 3: Los Angeles
Street address state: CA
Zip/Postal code: 90045-5471
County: Los Angeles
Country: USA
Mailing address: 5757 W Century Blvd Ste 675
Mailing city: Los Angeles
Mailing state: CA
Mailing zip: 90045-6435
General Phone: (310) 360-1000
General Fax: (310) 360-5000
General/National Adv. E-mail: customercare@nextcom.net
Primary Website: www.nextcom.net
Product or Service: Telecommunications/Service Bureaus
Personnel: David Hajian (Opns. Mgr.)

THE PRESENTATION PROFESSOR

Street address 1: 2276 S Beverly Glen Blvd
Street address 2: Unit 108
Street address 3: Los Angeles
Street address state: CA
Zip/Postal code: 90064-2440
County: Los Angeles
Country: USA
Mailing address: 2276 S Beverly Glen Blvd Unit 108
Mailing city: Los Angeles
Mailing state: CA
Mailing zip: 90064-2440
General Phone: (310) 286-0969
General Fax: (310) 286-0970
General/National Adv. E-mail: tom@professorpowerpoint.com
Primary Website: www.professorppt.com
Product or Service: Multimedia/Interactive Products
Personnel: Tom Bunzel (Pres.)

MANHATTAN BEACH

ADSTREAM AMERICA

Street address 1: 1240 Rosecrans Avenue
Street address 2: Suite 120
Street address 3: Manhattan Beach
Street address state: CA
Zip/Postal code: 90266
County: New York
Country: USA
Mailing address: 1240 Rosecrans Avenue, Suite 120
Mailing city: Manhattan Beach
Mailing state: CA
Mailing zip: 90266
General Phone: (818) 860-0420
General/National Adv. E-mail: hello@adstream.com
Primary Website: www.adstream.com
Product or Service: Hardware/Software Supplier
Personnel: Bruce Akhurst (Executive Chairman); Daniel Mark (CEO)

MILPITAS

SILICON GRAPHICS, INC.

Street address 1: 900 N McCarthy Blvd
Street address 3: Milpitas
Street address state: CA
Zip/Postal code: 95035-5128
County: Santa Clara
Country: USA
Mailing address: 900 N McCarthy Blvd
Mailing city: Milpitas
Mailing state: CA
Mailing zip: 95035-5128
General Phone: (669) 900-8000
General/National Adv. E-mail: support@sgi.com
Primary Website: www.sgi.com
Product or Service: Hardware/Software Supplier
Personnel: Mark Barrenechea (Pres./CEO); Tony Carrozza (Sr. Vice Pres., Worldwide Sales/Mktg.); Jim Wheat (Sr. Vice Pres./CFO); George Skaff (Vice Pres./CMO)

SS8 NETWORKS

Street address 1: 750 Tasman Dr
Street address 3: Milpitas
Street address state: CA
Zip/Postal code: 95035-7456
County: Santa Clara
Country: USA
Mailing address: 750 Tasman Dr
Mailing city: Milpitas
Mailing state: CA
Mailing zip: 95035-7456
General Phone: (408) 944-0250
General Fax: (408) 428-3732
General/National Adv. E-mail: info@ss8.com
Primary Website: www.ss8.com
Product or Service: Telecommunications/Service Bureaus
Personnel: Dennis Haar (CEO); Kam Wong (CFO); Dr. Cemal Dikmen (CTO); Faizel Lakhani (President & COO); Tony Thompason (VP of Marketing)

MONROVIA

MCMONIGLE & ASSOCIATES

Street address 1: 818 E Foothill Blvd
Street address 3: Monrovia
Street address state: CA
Zip/Postal code: 91016-2408
County: Los Angeles
Country: USA
Mailing address: 818 E Foothill Blvd
Mailing city: Monrovia
Mailing state: CA
Mailing zip: 91016-2408
General Phone: (626) 303-1090
General Fax: (626) 303-5431
General/National Adv. E-mail: jamie@mcmonigle.com
Primary Website: www.mcmonigle.com
Year Established: 1987
Product or Service: Advertising/Marketing Agency

MONTEREY

COMMUNICATION DESIGN

Street address 1: 24 Caribou Ct
Street address 3: Monterey
Street address state: CA
Zip/Postal code: 93940-6303
County: Monterey
Country: USA
Mailing address: 24 Caribou Court
Mailing city: Monterey
Mailing state: CA
Mailing zip: 93940
General Phone: (831) 373-3925
General/National Adv. E-mail: www.ittelson.com
Product or Service: Multimedia/Interactive Products
Personnel: John C. Ittelson (Prof); Bobbi Kamil (Project Mgr.); Brendan Ittelson (Webmaster)

MOUNTAIN VIEW

SYMANTEC CORP.

Street address 1: 350 Ellis St
Street address 3: Mountain View
Street address state: CA
Zip/Postal code: 94043-2202
County: Santa Clara
Country: USA
Mailing address: 350 Ellis St
Mailing city: Mountain View
Mailing state: CA
Mailing zip: 94043-2202
General Phone: (650) 527-8000
General/National Adv. E-mail: info@symantec.com
Primary Website: www.symantec.com
Product or Service: Online Service Provider and Internet Hosts
Personnel: Steve Bennett (Pres./CEO)

NEWBURY PARK

CAPTURED DIGITAL, INC.

Street address 1: 2520 Turquoise Cir
Street address 2: Ste B
Street address 3: Newbury Park

Street address state: CA
Zip/Postal code: 91320-1218
County: Ventura
Country: USA
Mailing address: 2520 Turquoise Cir Ste B
Mailing city: Newbury Park
Mailing state: CA
Mailing zip: 91320-1218
General Phone: (805) 499-7333
General Fax: (805) 499-4590
General/National Adv. E-mail: jobs@captureddigital.com
Primary Website: www.capturedimages.com
Product or Service: Telecommunications/Service Bureaus
Personnel: John Chater

OCEANSIDE

BRANFMAN LAW GROUP, P.C.

Street address 1: 708 Civic Center Dr
Street address 3: Oceanside
Street address state: CA
Zip/Postal code: 92054-2504
County: San Diego
Country: USA
Mailing address: 708 Civic Center Dr
Mailing city: Oceanside
Mailing state: CA
Mailing zip: 92054-2504
General Phone: (760) 637-2400
General Fax: (760) 687-7421
General/National Adv. E-mail: info@branfman.com
Primary Website: www.branfman.com
Product or Service: Consultants
Personnel: David Branfman (Owner); Mark Reichenthal (Assoc.)

REDDING

NORTH VALLEY DIVER PUBLICATIONS

Street address 1: 585 Royal Oaks Dr
Street address 3: Redding
Street address state: CA
Zip/Postal code: 96001-0133
County: Shasta
Country: USA
Mailing address: PO Box 991413
Mailing city: Redding
Mailing state: CA
Mailing zip: 96099-1413
General Phone: (530) 246-2009
General/National Adv. E-mail: nvdp@c-zone.net
Primary Website: www.northvalleydiver.com
Year Established: 1982
Own Printing Facility: Y
Commercial printers: N
Product or Service: Publisher/Media
Personnel: Dan Bailey (CEO)

REDWOOD CITY

BROADVISION

Street address 1: 1700 Seaport Blvd
Street address 2: Ste 210
Street address 3: Redwood City
Street address state: CA
Zip/Postal code: 94063-5579
County: San Mateo
Country: USA
Mailing address: 1700 Seaport Blvd Ste 210
Mailing city: Redwood City
Mailing state: CA
Mailing zip: 94063-5579
General Phone: (650) 295-0716
General Fax: (650) 364-3425
General/National Adv. E-mail: info@broadvision.com
Primary Website: www.broadvision.com
Product or Service: Hardware/Software Supplier
Personnel: Jean Mc Corthy (Dir.)

ORACLE & SUN MICROSYSTEMS, INC.

Street address 1: 500 Oracle Pkwy
Street address 3: Redwood City
Street address state: CA
Zip/Postal code: 94065-1677
County: San Mateo
Country: USA
Mailing address: 500 Oracle Pkwy
Mailing city: Redwood City
Mailing state: CA
Mailing zip: 94065-1677
General Phone: (650) 506-7000
General Fax: (408) 276-3804
General/National Adv. E-mail: oraclesales_us@oracle.com
Primary Website: www.oracle.com/us/sun
Product or Service: Hardware/Software Supplier
Personnel: Scott G. McNealy (Chrmn.); Jonathan I. Schwartz (Pres./CEO); Michael Lehman (Exec. Vice Pres., Cor. Resources/CFO); Kalyani Chatterjee (Chief Acctg. Officer); Lawrence Hambly (Pres., Enterprise Servs.); Don Grantham (Exec. Vice Pres., Sun Servs.); Crawford Beveridge (Exec. Vice Pres., People/Places/Chief HR Officer); Greg Papadopoulos (Exec. Vice Pres./CTO, SunLabs); Richard Green (Exec. Vice Pres., Sun Software); Tom Herbst (Sr. Brand Strategist, Java); Rhodes Klement (Sr. Dir., Brand Experience, Java); Ingrid Van der Hoogen (Sr. Vice Pres., Brand/Global Commun./Integrated Mktg.); Scott Kraft (Vice Pres., Client Brand Mktg./Adv.)

STATE NET

Street address 1: 2101 K St
Street address 3: Sacramento
Street address state: CA
Zip/Postal code: 95816-4920
County: Sacramento
Country: USA
Mailing address: 2101 K St
Mailing city: Sacramento
Mailing state: CA
Mailing zip: 95816-4920
General Phone: (916) 444-0840
General Fax: (916) 446-5369
General/National Adv. E-mail: info@statenet.com
Primary Website: www.statenet.com
Product or Service: Online Service Provider and Internet Hosts
Personnel: Laurie Stinson (Pres.); Jud Clark (Pres.)

SAN CARLOS

RG CREATIONS, INC.

Street address 1: 9638 Industrial Rd
Street address 3: San Carlos
Street address state: CA
Zip/Postal code: 94070-
County: San Mateo
Country: USA
Mailing address: 9638 Industrial Rd
Mailing city: San Carlos
Mailing state: CA
Mailing zip: 94070
General Phone: (650) 596-0123
General Fax: (650) 596-8590
General/National Adv. E-mail: bob@rgcreations.com
Primary Website: www.rgcreations.com
Product or Service: Graphic/Design Firm
Personnel: Robert G. Fuller (Owner)

CLARITAS

Street address 1: 9444 Waples St
Street address 2: Ste 280
Street address 3: San Diego
Street address state: CA
Zip/Postal code: 92121-2985
County: San Diego
Country: USA
Mailing address: 9444 Waples Street
Mailing city: San Diego
Mailing state: CA
Mailing zip: 92121
General Phone: (800) 234-5973
General Fax: (858) 500-5800
General/National Adv. E-mail: Marketing@Claritas.com
Primary Website: www.claritas.com
Product or Service: Consultants`Research
Personnel: Dave Miller (Sr. VP)

DESIGN MEDIA, INC.

Street address 1: 650 Alabama St
Street address 3: San Francisco
Street address state: CA
Zip/Postal code: 94110-2039
County: San Francisco
Country: USA
Mailing address: 650 Alabama St Ste 203
Mailing city: San Francisco
Mailing state: CA
Mailing zip: 94110-2038
General Phone: (415) 641-4848
General Fax: (415) 641-5245
General/National Adv. E-mail: info@designmedia.com
Primary Website: www.designmedia.com
Year Established: 1978
Product or Service: Multimedia/Interactive Products
Personnel: Pamela May (Pres./CEO); Marlita Kahn (Sr. Project Mgr.); Barbara Berry (Sr. Project Mgr.); Wallace Murray (Project Mgr.); Alison DeGrassi (Project Mgr.); Cori Freeland (Office Mgr.); Rylan North (Sr. Web Developer)

LUMINARE

Street address 1: 65 Norfolk St
Street address 2: Unit 4
Street address 3: San Francisco
Street address state: CA
Zip/Postal code: 94103-4357
County: San Francisco
Country: USA
Mailing address: 65 Norfolk St Unit 4
Mailing city: San Francisco
Mailing state: CA
Mailing zip: 94103-4357
General Phone: (415) 661-1436
General/National Adv. E-mail: info@luminare.com
Primary Website: www.luminare.com
Year Established: 1986
Product or Service: CD-ROM Designer/Manufacturer
Personnel: Caitlin Curtin (Pres.)

PC WORLD

Street address 1: 501 2nd St
Street address 2: Ste 600
Street address 3: San Francisco
Street address state: CA
Zip/Postal code: 94107-4133
County: San Francisco
Country: USA
Mailing address: 501 2nd St Ste 600
Mailing city: San Francisco
Mailing state: CA
Mailing zip: 94107-1496
General Phone: (415) 243-0500
General Fax: (415) 442-1891
General/National Adv. E-mail: webmaster@pcworld.com
Primary Website: www.pcworld.com
Product or Service: Publisher/Media
Personnel: Michael Carrol (Assoc. Pub., PC World.com); Brian Bulzer (Mgr., Online Ad Opns.); David Lake (Mgr. Bus Devl)

SPOTMAGIC, INC.

Street address 1: 1700 California St
Street address 2: Ste 430
Street address 3: San Francisco
Street address state: CA
Zip/Postal code: 94109-0429
County: San Francisco
Country: USA
Mailing address: 1700 California St Ste 430
Mailing city: San Francisco
Mailing state: CA
Mailing zip: 94109-0429
General Phone: (415) 692-0117
General/National Adv. E-mail: info@spotmagic.com
Primary Website: www.spotmagic.com
Product or Service: Multimedia/Interactive Products
Personnel: John Armstrong (Founder, Affiliate Rel.); Robin Solis (Founder, Pub. Rel.)

ADOBE SYSTEMS, INC.

Street address 1: 345 Park Ave
Street address 3: San Jose
Street address state: CA
Zip/Postal code: 95110-2704
County: Santa Clara
Country: USA
Mailing address: 345 Park Ave
Mailing city: San Jose
Mailing state: CA
Mailing zip: 95110-2704
General Phone: (408) 536-6000
General Fax: (408) 537-6000
Primary Website: www.adobe.com
Product or Service: Hardware/Software Supplier
Personnel: Ann Lewnes (Sr. Vice Pres., Global Mktg.); Jennifer Reynolds (Dir., Worldwide Adv.)

LUMINA NETWORKS

Street address 1: 2077 Gateway Pl
Street address 2: Ste 500
Street address 3: San Jose
Street address state: CA
Zip/Postal code: 95110-1085
County: Santa Clara
Country: USA
Mailing address: 2077 Gateway Pl
Mailing city: San Jose
Mailing state: CA
Mailing zip: 95110-1085
General Phone: (669) 231-3838
Primary Website: www.luminanetworks.com
Year Established: 1995
Product or Service: Hardware/Software Supplier
Personnel: Andrew Coward (CEO); Nitin Serro (COO); Kevin Woods (V. P. Marketing)

MERCURY CENTER

Street address 1: 750 Ridder Park Dr
Street address 3: San Jose
Street address state: CA
Zip/Postal code: 95131-2432
County: Santa Clara
Country: USA
Mailing address: 750 Ridder Park Dr
Mailing city: San Jose
Mailing state: CA
Mailing zip: 95190-0001
General Phone: (408) 920-5000
General Fax: (408) 288-8060
General/National Adv. E-mail: tmooreland@sjmercury.com
Primary Website: www.mercurycenter.com
Product or Service: Online Service Provider and Internet Hosts
Personnel: Tom Mooreland (Dir., Mercury Center)

METRO NEWSPAPER

Street address 1: 550 S 1st St
Street address 3: San Jose
Street address state: CA
Zip/Postal code: 95113-2806
County: Santa Clara
Country: USA
Mailing address: 550 S 1st St
Mailing city: San Jose
Mailing state: CA
Mailing zip: 95113-2806
General Phone: (408) 298-8000
General Fax: (408) 279-5813
General/National Adv. E-mail: press@metronews.com
Primary Website: www.metroactive.com; www.metronews.com
Product or Service: Online Service Provider and Internet Hosts
Personnel: Dan Pulcrano (Pres.)

POLYCOM, INC.

Street address 1: 6001 America Center Dr.
Street address 3: San Jose
Street address state: CA
Zip/Postal code: 95002
Country: USA
Mailing address: 6001 America Center Dr.

Mailing city: San Jose
Mailing state: CA
Mailing zip: 95002
General Phone: (408) 58-66000
Primary Website: www.polycom.com
Product or Service: Telecommunications/Service Bureaus
Personnel: Joe Burton (Pres./CEO)

THE STEPHENZ GROUP

Street address 1: 75 E Santa Clara St
Street address 2: Ste 900
Street address 3: San Jose
Street address state: CA
Zip/Postal code: 95113-1842
County: Santa Clara
Country: USA
Mailing address: 75 E Santa Clara St Ste 900
Mailing city: San Jose
Mailing state: CA
Mailing zip: 95113-1842
General Phone: (408) 286-9899
General Fax: (408) 286-9866
General/National Adv. E-mail: info@stephenz.com
Primary Website: www.stephenz.com
Product or Service: Advertising/Marketing Agency
Personnel: Barbara Zenz (Pres./CEO); Stephanie Paulson (Vice Pres., Creative Servs.)

SAN LEANDRO

DIRECT IMAGES INTERACTIVE, INC.

Street address 1: 1933 Davis St
Street address 2: Ste 314
Street address 3: San Leandro
Street address state: CA
Zip/Postal code: 94577-1259
County: Alameda
Country: USA
Mailing address: 1933 Davis St Ste 314
Mailing city: San Leandro
Mailing state: CA
Mailing zip: 94577-1259
General Phone: (510) 613-8299
General/National Adv. E-mail: info@directimages.com
Primary Website: www.directimages.com
Product or Service: Multimedia/Interactive Products
Personnel: Bill Knowland (Producer/Dir.); Beverly Knowland (Art Dir.)

INFORMATION PRESENTATION TECH.

Street address 1: 825 Buckley Rd
Street address 2: Ste 200
Street address 3: San Luis Obispo
Street address state: CA
Zip/Postal code: 93401-8193
County: San Luis Obispo
Country: USA
Mailing address: 4072 Campbellsville Pike
Mailing city: Columbia
Mailing state: TN
Mailing zip: 38401-8632
General Phone: (805) 541-3000
General Fax: (805) 541-3037
General/National Adv. E-mail: info@iptech.com
Primary Website: www.iptech.com
Product or Service: Multimedia/Interactive Products
Personnel: Olivia Favela (Vice Pres., Sales/Mktg.)

RED HILL STUDIOS

Street address 1: 1017 E St
Street address 2: Ste C
Street address 3: San Rafael
Street address state: CA
Zip/Postal code: 94901-2845
County: Marin
Country: USA
Mailing address: 10 Elm Ct
Mailing city: San Anselmo
Mailing state: CA
Mailing zip: 94960-2211
General Phone: (415) 457-0440
General Fax: (415) 457-0450
General/National Adv. E-mail: info@redhillstudios.com
Primary Website: www.redhillstudios.com
Product or Service: Graphic/Design Firm`Multimedia/Interactive Products`POP/Kiosk Designer
Personnel: Robert Hone (Creative Dir./Founder); Adrienne Macbeth (Dir. Business Development)

MUSE PRESENTATION TECHNOLOGIES

Street address 1: 3510 S Susan St
Street address 3: Santa Ana
Street address state: CA
Zip/Postal code: 92704-6938
County: Orange
Country: USA
Mailing address: 3510 S Susan St
Mailing city: Santa Ana
Mailing state: CA
Mailing zip: 92704-6938
General Phone: (800) 950-4955
General Fax: (714) 850-1018
General/National Adv. E-mail: jimmuse@museprestech.com
Primary Website: www.museprestech.com
Product or Service: Other Services`POP/Kiosk Designer
Personnel: Joyce Logan (Pres.); Jim Muse (CEO); Wil Bigelow (Gen. Mgr.)

SANTA BARBARA

MAPS.COM

Street address 1: 120 Cremona Dr
Street address 2: Ste 260
Street address 3: Santa Barbara
Street address state: CA
Zip/Postal code: 93117-5564
County: Santa Barbara
Country: USA
Mailing address: 120 Cremona Dr
Mailing city: Santa Barbara
Mailing state: CA
Mailing zip: 93117-5564
General Phone: (805) 685-3100
General Fax: (805) 685-3330
General/National Adv. E-mail: info@maps.com
Primary Website: www.maps.com
Year Established: 1991
Product or Service: Online Service Provider and Internet Hosts
Personnel: John Serpa (Pres.); Robert H. Temkin (Founder/Chrmn./CEO); Charles Regan (Exec. Vice Pres.); Anne Messner (Vice Pres., Finance/Admin.); Bruce Kurtz (Dir., Mktg.); Bill Spicer (Dir., Online Commerce); Ed Easton (Dir., Mapping Servs.); Mitch McCoy (Dir., Tech./Project Devel.); Erik Davis (Dir., Education Mktg.)

SANTA CLARA

CD TECHNOLOGY

Street address 1: 1112 Walsh Ave
Street address 3: Santa Clara
Street address state: CA
Zip/Postal code: 95050-2646
County: Santa Clara
Country: USA
Mailing address: 1112 Walsh Ave
Mailing city: Santa Clara
Mailing state: CA
Mailing zip: 95050-2646
General Phone: (408) 982-0990
General Fax: (408) 982-0991
Primary Website: www.cdtechnology.com
Product or Service: CD-ROM Designer/Manufacturer
Personnel: William W. Liu (Pres.)

SANTA MONICA

FLI, INCORPORATED

Street address 1: 400 Palisades Ave
Street address 3: Santa Monica
Street address state: CA
Zip/Postal code: 90402-2720
County: Los Angeles
Country: USA
Mailing address: 400 Palisades Ave
Mailing city: Santa Monica
Mailing state: CA
Mailing zip: 90402-2720
General Phone: (310) 451-3307
General Fax: (310) 451-4207
General/National Adv. E-mail: jcwills@fliinc.com
Primary Website: www.fliinc.com
Year Established: 1980
Product or Service: Consultants
Personnel: John Wills (President/CEO); Jane Wills (Vice President)

MEDIA DESIGN GROUP

Street address 1: 3250 Ocean Park Blvd
Street address 2: Ste 200
Street address 3: Santa Monica
Street address state: CA
Zip/Postal code: 90405-3250
County: Los Angeles
Country: USA
Mailing address: 3250 Ocean Park Blvd Ste 200
Mailing city: Santa Monica
Mailing state: CA
Mailing zip: 90405-3250
General Phone: (310) 584-9200
General Fax: (310) 584-9725
General/National Adv. E-mail: info@mediadesigngroup.com
Primary Website: www.mediadesigngroup.com
Product or Service: CD-ROM Designer/Manufacturer
Personnel: John D. Slack (CEO)

MOTION CITY FILMS

Street address 1: 1424 4th St
Street address 2: Ste 604
Street address 3: Santa Monica
Street address state: CA
Zip/Postal code: 90401-3447
County: Los Angeles
Country: USA
Mailing address: 1424 4th St Ste 604
Mailing city: Santa Monica
Mailing state: CA
Mailing zip: 90401-3447
General Phone: (310) 434-1272
General/National Adv. E-mail: editor@motioncity.com
Primary Website: www.motioncity.com
Product or Service: Multimedia/Interactive Products
Personnel: G. Michael Witt (Producing Dir.); Marty Blasick (Composer/Audio Engineer)

CHANNELNET

Street address 1: 3 Harbor Dr
Street address 2: Ste 206
Street address 3: Sausalito
Street address state: CA
Zip/Postal code: 94965-1491
County: Marin
Country: USA
Mailing address: 3 Harbor Dr Ste 206
Mailing city: Sausalito
Mailing state: CA
Mailing zip: 94965-1491
General Phone: (415) 332-4704
General Fax: (415) 332-1635
General/National Adv. E-mail: info@channelnet.com
Primary Website: www.softad.com; www.channelnet.com
Industry: Consulting Services: Advertising; Software: Advertising (Includes Display; Classified);
Product or Service: Consultants`Hardware/Software Supplier
Personnel: Paula George Tompkins (Founder/CEO); Kevin Kelly (CFO); Mike Behr (Sr. Dir., Professional Servs.)

SCOTTS VALLEY

TAM COMMUNICATIONS

Street address 1: 5610 Scotts Valley Dr
Street address 2: Ste 552B
Street address 3: Scotts Valley
Street address state: CA
Zip/Postal code: 95066-3473
County: Santa Cruz
Country: USA
Mailing address: 5610 Scotts Valley Dr Ste 552B
Mailing city: Scotts Valley
Mailing state: CA
Mailing zip: 95066-3476
General Phone: (831) 439-1500
General Fax: (831) 439-0298
General/National Adv. E-mail: susan@tamcom.com
Primary Website: www.tamcom.com
Year Established: 1979
Product or Service: Advertising/Marketing Agency
Personnel: Susan O'Connor Fraser (Pres./CEO)

PTI MARKETING TECHNOLOGIES, INC.

Street address 1: 201 Lomas Santa Fe Dr
Street address 2: Ste 300
Street address 3: Solana Beach
Street address state: CA
Zip/Postal code: 92075-1288
County: San Diego
Country: USA
Mailing address: 201 Lomas Santa Fe Dr Ste 300
Mailing city: Solana Beach
Mailing state: CA
Mailing zip: 92075-1288
General Phone: (858) 847-6600
General Fax: (858) 793-4120
General/National Adv. E-mail: inquiries@pti.com
Primary Website: www.pti.com
Product or Service: Advertising/Marketing Agency
Personnel: Coleman Kane (Pres./CEO); Jim Van Natter (Sales Vice Pres.)

SUNNYVALE

MULTIMEDIA RESOURCE GROUP

Street address 1: 505 W Olive Ave
Street address 2: Ste 312
Street address 3: Sunnyvale
Street address state: CA
Zip/Postal code: 94086-7604
County: Santa Clara
Country: USA
Mailing address: 598 Margaret St
Mailing city: San Jose
Mailing state: CA
Mailing zip: 95112-2303
General Phone: (408) 315-8720
Year Established: 1993
Product or Service: Consultants
Personnel: Ken Durso (Owner)

FLIP YOUR LID

Street address 1: 1288 Paseo Rancho Serrano
Street address 2: Ste 200
Street address 3: Thousand Oaks
Street address state: CA
Zip/Postal code: 91356-6082
County: Los Angeles
Country: USA
Mailing address: 1288 Paseo Rancho Serrano
Mailing city: Thousand Oaks
Mailing state: CA
Mailing zip: 91362
General Phone: (818) 307-4165
General/National Adv. E-mail: jay@flipyourlid.com
Primary Website: www.flipyourlid.com
Product or Service: Graphic/Design Firm`Multimedia/Interactive Products
Note: Design, character design. Flash, 3d, and logo graphic design and traditional animation.
Personnel: Jay Jacoby (CEO)

TUSTIN

MEDIA ENTERPRISES

Street address 1: 360 E 1st St
Street address 2: # 605
Street address 3: Tustin
Street address state: CA
Zip/Postal code: 92780-3211
County: Orange
Country: USA
Mailing address: 360 E. 1st Street
Mailing city: Tustin
Mailing state: CA
Mailing zip: 92806

General Phone: (714) 778-5336
General/National Adv. E-mail: john@media-enterprises.com
Primary Website: www.media-enterprises.com
Year Established: 1970
Product or Service: Advertising/Marketing Agency`Consultants`Editorial`Graphic/Design Firm`Marketing`Multimedia/Interactive Products`Research`Trade Association
Personnel: John Lemieux Rose (Principal)

WALNUT CREEK

MARCOLE ENTERPRISES, INC.

Street address 1: 2920 Camino Diablo
Street address 2: Ste 200
Street address 3: Walnut Creek
Street address state: CA
Zip/Postal code: 94597-3966
County: Contra Costa
Country: USA
Mailing address: 2920 Camino Diablo Ste 200
Mailing city: Walnut Creek
Mailing state: CA
Mailing zip: 94597-3966
General Phone: (888) 885-3939
General/National Adv. E-mail: salesteam@marcole.com
Primary Website: www.marcole.com
Year Established: 1991
Product or Service: Hardware/Software Supplier`Multimedia/Interactive Products`Online Service Provider and Internet Hosts`POP/Kiosk Designer
Personnel: David Pava (Vice Pres., Sales & Marketing)

WEST HOLLYWOOD

CITYSEARCH.COM

Street address 1: 8833 W Sunset Blvd
Street address 3: West Hollywood
Street address state: CA
Zip/Postal code: 90069-2110
County: Los Angeles
Country: USA
Mailing address: 8833 W Sunset Blvd
Mailing city: West Hollywood
Mailing state: CA
Mailing zip: 90069-2110
General Phone: (310) 360-4500
General/National Adv. E-mail: customerservice@citygrid.com
Primary Website: www.citysearch.com
Product or Service: Multimedia/Interactive Products
Personnel: Jay Herratti (CEO)

WESTLAKE VILLAGE

ILIO ENTERTAINMENT

Street address 1: 5356 Sterling Center Dr
Street address 3: Westlake Village
Street address state: CA
Zip/Postal code: 91361-4612
County: Los Angeles
Country: USA
Mailing address: 5356 Sterling Center Dr
Mailing city: Westlake Village
Mailing state: CA
Mailing zip: 91361-4612
General Phone: (818) 707-7222
General Fax: (818) 707-8552
General/National Adv. E-mail: info@ilio.com
Primary Website: www.ilio.com
Product or Service: Hardware/Software Supplier
Personnel: Shelly Williams (Co-Owner); Mark Hiskey (Co-Owner)

MACTECH MAGAZINE

Street address 1: PO Box 5200
Street address 3: Westlake Village
Street address state: CA
Zip/Postal code: 91359-5200
County: Ventura
Country: USA
Mailing address: PO Box 5200
Mailing city: Westlake Village
Mailing state: CA
Mailing zip: 91359-5200
General Phone: (805) 494-9797
General Fax: (805) 494-9798
General/National Adv. E-mail: press_releases@mactech.com
Primary Website: www.mactech.com
Product or Service: Publisher/Media
Personnel: Neil Ticktin (Pub.); Dave Mark (Ed. in Chief); Michael R. Harvey (Reviews/KoolTools Ed.)

WOODLAND HILLS

FILM ARTISTS ASSOCIATES

Street address 1: 21044 Ventura Blvd
Street address 2: Ste 215
Street address 3: Woodland Hills
Street address state: CA
Zip/Postal code: 91364-6501
County: Los Angeles
Country: USA
Mailing address: 21044 Ventura Blvd Ste 215
Mailing city: Woodland Hills
Mailing state: CA
Mailing zip: 91364-6501
General Phone: (818) 883-5008
General Fax: (818) 386-9363
Product or Service: Advertising/Marketing Agency
Personnel: Chris Dennis (Contact)

NETWORK TELEPHONE SERVICES

Street address 1: 21135 Erwin St
Street address 3: Woodland Hills
Street address state: CA
Zip/Postal code: 91367-3713
County: Los Angeles
Country: USA
Mailing address: 21135 Erwin St
Mailing city: Woodland Hills
Mailing state: CA
Mailing zip: 91367-3713
General Phone: (818) 992-4300
General Fax: (818) 992-8415
General/National Adv. E-mail: sales@nts.net
Primary Website: www.nts.net
Product or Service: Telecommunications/Service Bureaus
Personnel: Gary Passon (Pres.)

COLORADO

BROOMFIELD

ESOFT

Street address 1: 295 Interlocken Blvd
Street address 2: Ste 500
Street address 3: Broomfield
Street address state: CO
Zip/Postal code: 80021-8002
County: Broomfield
Country: USA
Mailing address: 1490 W 121st Ave Ste 205
Mailing city: Denver
Mailing state: CO
Mailing zip: 80234-3497
General Phone: (866) 233-2296
General/National Adv. E-mail: info@esoft.com
Primary Website: www.esoft.com
Product or Service: Hardware/Software Supplier
Personnel: Jeff Finn (CEO/Pres.); Patrick Walsh (CTO); Tim Olson (Dir., Finance); Jason Rollings (Vice Pres., Opns.)

COLORADO SPRINGS

ORIGIN COMMUNICATIONS, INC.

Street address 1: 4140 Regency Dr
Street address 3: Colorado Springs
Street address state: CO
Zip/Postal code: 80906-7200
County: El Paso
Country: USA
Mailing address: 4140 Regency Dr
Mailing city: Colorado Springs
Mailing state: CO
Mailing zip: 80906-7200
General Phone: (719) 785-9900
General Fax: (719) 314-0168
General/National Adv. E-mail: info@origincom.com
Primary Website: www.origincom.com
Year Established: 1986
Product or Service: Advertising/Marketing Agency`Consultants`Graphic/Design Firm
Personnel: Randel Castleberry (President); Jil Goebel (Acct. Servs./Media Dir.)

XTIVIA

Street address 1: 304 S 8th St
Street address 2: Ste 201
Street address 3: Colorado Springs
Street address state: CO
Zip/Postal code: 80905-1825
County: El Paso
Country: USA
Mailing address: 304 S 8th St Ste 201
Mailing city: Colorado Springs
Mailing state: CO
Mailing zip: 80905-1825
General Phone: (888) 685-3101 ext. 2
General Fax: (719) 685-3400
General/National Adv. E-mail: nir.gryn@xtivia.com
Primary Website: www.xtivia.com
Product or Service: Consultants
Personnel: Nir Gryn (CEO)

LIQUID LUCK PRODUCTIONS

Street address 1: 1221 Auraria Pkwy
Street address 3: Denver
Street address state: CO
Zip/Postal code: 80204-1836
County: Denver
Country: USA
Mailing address: 1221 Auraria Pkwy
Mailing city: Denver
Mailing state: CO
Mailing zip: 80204-1836
General Phone: (303) 518-8909
General/National Adv. E-mail: info@LiquidLuckProductions.com
Primary Website: www.liquidluckproductions.com
Year Established: 2002
Product or Service: Multimedia/Interactive Products
Personnel: Lena Telep (Marketing Manager)

PROLINE DIGITAL

Street address 1: PO Box 27682
Street address 3: Denver
Street address state: CO
Zip/Postal code: 80227-0682
County: Denver
Country: USA
Mailing address: PO Box 27682
Mailing city: Denver
Mailing state: CO
Mailing zip: 80227-0682
General Phone: (303) 761-3999
General Fax: (303) 761-1818
General/National Adv. E-mail: info@prolinedigital.com
Primary Website: www.prolinedigital.com
Product or Service: CD-ROM Designer/Manufacturer
Personnel: Tony Marcon (Pres.)

DOVE CREEK

COMPETENCE SOFTWARE

Street address 1: PO Box 353
Street address 3: Dove Creek
Street address state: CO
Zip/Postal code: 81324-0353
County: Dolores
Country: USA
Mailing address: PO Box 353
Mailing city: Dove Creek
Mailing state: CO
Mailing zip: 81324-0353
General Phone: (727) 459-0531
Primary Website: www.competencesoftware.net
Year Established: 1992
Product or Service: Multimedia/Interactive Products
Personnel: Larry Byrnes (Founder); Mary Lou Dewyngaert (Vice Pres., Devel.); Shannon Byrnes (Vice Pres., Mkt. Devel.); Jessica Byrnes (Asst. to CEO)

LAKEWOOD

CUSTOMER COMMUNICATIONS GROUP

Street address 1: 165 S Union Blvd
Street address 2: Ste 260
Street address 3: Lakewood
Street address state: CO
Zip/Postal code: 80228-2241
County: Jefferson
Country: USA
Mailing address: 165 S Union Blvd Ste 260
Mailing city: Lakewood
Mailing state: CO
Mailing zip: 80228-2241
General Phone: (303) 986-3000
General Fax: (303) 989-4805
General/National Adv. E-mail: info@customer.com
Primary Website: www.customer.com
Product or Service: Advertising/Marketing Agency
Personnel: Sandra Gudat (Pres.)

KIOSK INFORMATION SYSTEMS

Street address 1: 346 S Arthur Ave
Street address 3: Louisville
Street address state: CO
Zip/Postal code: 80027-3010
County: Boulder
Country: USA
Mailing address: 346 S Arthur Ave
Mailing city: Louisville
Mailing state: CO
Mailing zip: 80027-3010
General Phone: (303) 466-5471
General Fax: (303) 466-6730
General/National Adv. E-mail: sales@kiosk.com
Primary Website: www.kiosk.com
Product or Service: POP/Kiosk Designer
Personnel: Rick Malone (Pres.); Tom Weaver (Vice Pres., Sales/Mktg.)

CONNECTICUT

AL BREDENBERG CREATIVE SERVICES

Street address 1: 71 Franklin St
Street address 3: Danbury
Street address state: CT
Zip/Postal code: 06810-5483
County: Fairfield
Country: USA
Mailing address: 71 Franklin St
Mailing city: Danbury
Mailing state: CT
Mailing zip: 06810-5483
General Phone: (203) 791-8204
General/National Adv. E-mail: ab@copywriter.com
Primary Website: www.copywriter.com
Product or Service: Advertising/Marketing Agency
Personnel: Al Bredenberg (Contact)

GCN PUBLISHING

Street address 1: 194 Main St
Street address 2: Ste 2NW
Street address 3: Norwalk
Street address state: CT
Zip/Postal code: 06851-3502
County: Fairfield
Country: USA
Mailing address: 194 Main St Ste 2NW
Mailing city: Norwalk
Mailing state: CT
Mailing zip: 06851-3502
General Phone: (203) 665-6211

General Fax: (203) 665-6212
General/National Adv. E-mail: info@one-count.com
Primary Website: www.one-count.com
Product or Service: Multimedia/Interactive Products
Personnel: Joanne Persico (President/Co-founder); Sean Fulton (Vice President of Technology/Co-founder)

MILES 33

Street address 1: 40 Richards Ave
Street address 2: Pendegast Street, 5170
Street address 3: Norwalk
Street address state: CT
Zip/Postal code: 06854-2319
County: Fairfield
Country: USA
Mailing address: 40 Richards Ave Ste 29
Mailing city: Norwalk
Mailing state: CA
Mailing zip: 06854-2322
General Phone: (203) 838-2333
General Fax: (203) 838-4473
Advertising Phone: (916) 225-0939
General/National Adv. E-mail: info@miles33.com
Display Adv. E-mail: albert_debruijn@yahoo.com
Primary Website: www.miles33.com
Year Established: 1976
Industry: Computers: Hardware & Software Integrators; Consulting Services: Advertising; Consulting Services: Editorial; Software: Advertising (Includes Display; Classified; Digital and Print); Software: Digital Asset Management; Software: Content Management Systems for newsroom and Web; Software: Pagination/Layout; Software: Ad Tracking; Software: Self Service Advertising; Software: Digital Video Ad Production; Software: Ipad and Android Apps; Software: Business Analytics/Datamining
Product or Service: Hardware/Software Supplier`Multimedia/Interactive Products
Personnel: Chris Habasinski (Pres.); Albert De Bruijn (VP Marketing and Western USA Sales); Edward Hubbard (VP, Business Development)

DAC SYSTEMS

Street address 1: 4 Armstrong Park Rd
Street address 3: Shelton
Street address state: CT
Zip/Postal code: 6484-
County: Fairfield
Country: USA
Mailing address: 4 Armstrong Park Rd.
Mailing city: Shelton
Mailing state: CT
Mailing zip: 6484
General Phone: (203) 924-7000
General Fax: (203) 944-1618
General/National Adv. E-mail: sales@dacsystems.com
Primary Website: www.dacsystems.com
Year Established: 1988
Product or Service: Telecommunications/Service Bureaus
Personnel: Mark Nickson (Pres.)

SIMBA INFORMATION

Street address 1: 60 Long Ridge Rd
Street address 2: Ste 300
Street address 3: Stamford
Street address state: CT
Zip/Postal code: 06902-1841
County: Fairfield
Country: USA
Mailing address: 1266 E Main St Ste 700R
Mailing city: Stamford
Mailing state: CT
Mailing zip: 06902-3507
General Phone: (203) 325-8193
General Fax: (203) 325-8975
General/National Adv. E-mail: customerservice@simbainformation.com
Primary Website: www.simbainformation.com
Year Established: 1989
Product or Service: Publisher/Media
Personnel: Linda Kopp (Pub.); David Goddard (Sr. Ed.); Michael Norris (Sr. Ed.); Dan Strempel (Sr. Ed.); Kathy Mickey (Mng. Ed.); Karen Meaney (Ed.)

STRATFORD

ULTITECH, INC.

Street address 1: 0 Foot of Broad St
Street address 2: Ste 202
Street address 3: Stratford
Street address state: CT
Zip/Postal code: 06615-9201
County: Fairfield
Country: USA
Mailing address: 0 Foot of Broad St Ste 202
Mailing city: Stratford
Mailing state: CT
Mailing zip: 06615-9201
General Phone: (203) 375-7300
General Fax: (203) 375-6699
General/National Adv. E-mail: ultitech@meds.com
Editorial e-mail: editor@meds.com
Primary Website: www.meds.com
Product or Service: Multimedia/Interactive Products
Personnel: William J. Comcowich (Pres.); Laura McClatchie (Mgr., Opns.)

MEDIABIDS, INC.

Street address 1: 448 Main St
Street address 3: Winsted
Street address state: CT
Zip/Postal code: 06098-1528
County: Litchfield
Country: USA
Mailing address: 448 Main St
Mailing city: Winsted
Mailing state: CT
Mailing zip: 06098-1528
General Phone: (860) 379-9602
General Fax: (860) 379-9617
General/National Adv. E-mail: info@mediabids.com
Primary Website: www.mediabids.com
Product or Service: Advertising/Marketing Agency`Multimedia/Interactive Products
Note: MediaBids connects publications with thousands of advertisers nationwide. Additionally, MediaBids offers a unique performance-based print advertising program that provides publications with high-quality ads from national advertisers and a way to monetize unused inventory.
Personnel: Jedd Gould (President); June Peterson (Director, Media Relations)

DISTRICT OF COLUMBIA

APCO WORLDWIDE

Street address 1: 700 12th St NW
Street address 2: Ste 800
Street address 3: Washington
Street address state: DC
Zip/Postal code: 20005-3949
County: District Of Columbia
Country: USA
Mailing address: 700 12th St NW Ste 800
Mailing city: Washington
Mailing state: DC
Mailing zip: 20005-3949
General Phone: (202) 778-1000
General Fax: (202) 466-6002
General/National Adv. E-mail: information@apcoworldwide.com
Primary Website: www.apcoworldwide.com
Year Established: 1984
Product or Service: Advertising/Marketing Agency`Consultants

COGENT COMMUNICATIONS, INC.

Street address 1: 1015 31st St NW
Street address 3: Washington
Street address state: DC
Zip/Postal code: 20007-4406
County: District Of Columbia
Country: USA
Mailing address: 1015 31st St NW
Mailing city: Washington
Mailing state: DC
Mailing zip: 20007-4406
General Phone: (202) 295-4200
General Fax: (202) 338-8798
General/National Adv. E-mail: info@cogentco.com
Primary Website: www.cogentco.com
Year Established: 1989
Product or Service: Online Service Provider and Internet Hosts
Personnel: Dave Schaeffer (Founder/CEO); Reed Harrison (Pres./COO); Tad Weed (CFO)

FISCALNOTE

Street address 1: 1201 Pennsylvania Ave NW
Street address 2: 6th Floor
Street address 3: Washington
Street address state: DC
Zip/Postal code: 20004
County: District Of Columbia
Country: USA
Mailing address: 1201 Pennsylvania Ave NW
Mailing city: Washington
Mailing state: DC
Mailing zip: 20004
General Phone: (202) 793-5300
Advertising Phone: 202-650-6823
Advertising Fax: 202-650-6743
Editorail Phone: 202-650-6548
Editorial Fax: 202-650-6750
General/National Adv. E-mail: contact@fiscalnote.com
Display Adv. E-mail: advertise@cqrollcall.com
Primary Website: www.fiscalnote.com
Year Established: 1945
Product or Service: Publisher/Media
Personnel: Tim Hwang (CEO); Richard Kim (CFO); Mike Stubbs (Vice President, Operations)

FISHER PHOTOGRAPHY

Street address 1: 2234 Cathedral Ave NW
Street address 3: Washington
Street address state: DC
Zip/Postal code: 20008-1504
County: District Of Columbia
Country: USA
Mailing address: 2234 Cathedral Ave NW
Mailing city: Washington
Mailing state: DC
Mailing zip: 20008-1504
General Phone: (202) 232-3781
General/National Adv. E-mail: info@fisherphoto.com
Primary Website: www.fisherphoto.com
Product or Service: Graphic/Design Firm
Personnel: Patricia Fisher (Owner); Wayne W. Fisher (Contact)

SOFTWARE & INFORMATION INDUSTRY ASSOCIATION

Street address 1: 1090 Vermont Ave NW
Street address 2: Fl 6
Street address 3: Washington
Street address state: DC
Zip/Postal code: 20005-4930
County: District Of Columbia
Country: USA
Mailing address: 1090 Vermont Ave NW Fl 6
Mailing city: Washington
Mailing state: DC
Mailing zip: 20005-4930
General Phone: (202) 289-7442
General Fax: (202) 289-7097
General/National Adv. E-mail: piracy@siia.net
Primary Website: www.siia.net
Product or Service: Trade Association
Personnel: Ken Wasch (Pres.)

TELECOMPUTE CORP.

Street address 1: 4919 Upton St NW
Street address 3: Washington
Street address state: DC
Zip/Postal code: 20016-2349
County: District Of Columbia
Country: USA
Mailing address: 4919 Upton St NW
Mailing city: Washington
Mailing state: DC
Mailing zip: 20016-2349
General Phone: (202) 789-7860
General Fax: (800) 533-2329
General/National Adv. E-mail: warren@telecompute.com
Primary Website: www.telecompute.com
Product or Service: Telecommunications/Service Bureaus
Personnel: Warren Miller (Pres.)

WIRELESS COMMUNICATIONS ASSOCIATION INTERNATIONAL

Street address 1: 1333 H St NW
Street address 2: Ste 700
Street address 3: Washington
Street address state: DC
Zip/Postal code: 20005-4707
County: District Of Columbia
Country: USA
Mailing address: 1333 H St NW Ste 700W
Mailing city: Washington
Mailing state: DC
Mailing zip: 20005-4754
General Phone: (202) 452-7823
Primary Website: www.wcai.com
Year Established: 1988
Product or Service: Trade Association
Personnel: Fred Cambell (Pres.)

DELAWARE

OCEAN VIEW

SUSSEX COUNTY ONLINE

Street address 1: PO Box 874
Street address 3: Ocean View
Street address state: DE
Zip/Postal code: 19970-0874
County: Sussex
Country: USA
Mailing address: PO Box 874
Mailing city: Ocean View
Mailing state: DE
Mailing zip: 19970-0874
General Phone: (302) 537-4198
General/National Adv. E-mail: emagill@scdel.net
Primary Website: www.sussexcountyonline.com
Product or Service: Consultants
Personnel: Eric Magill (Owner/Pub.); Kerin Magill (Content Ed.)

ENG

BATH

M2 COMMUNICATIONS LTD.

Street address 1: PO Box 4030
Street address 3: Bath
Street address state: ENG
Zip/Postal code: BA1 0EE
Country: United Kingdom
Mailing address: PO Box 4030
Mailing city: Bath
Mailing state: ENG
Mailing zip: BA1 0EE
General Phone: 7047 0200
General Fax: 7057 0200
General/National Adv. E-mail: info@m2.com
Primary Website: www.m2.com
Product or Service: Publisher/Media
Personnel: Jamie Ayres (Ed. in Cheif)

FLORIDA

ADVANCED INTERACTIVE MEDIA GROUP, LLC

Street address 1: 402 Spring Valley Rd

Street address 3: Altamonte Springs
Street address state: FL
Zip/Postal code: 32714-5845
County: Seminole
Country: USA
Mailing address: 402 Spring Valley Rd
Mailing city: Altamonte Springs
Mailing state: FL
Mailing zip: 32714
General Phone: (407) 788-2780
General/National Adv. E-mail: pzollman@aimgroup.com
Primary Website: www.aimgroup.com
Year Established: 1997
Area Served - City: Global business intelligence
Industry: Consulting Services Industry Trade Publication Conferences --- Automotive advertising, recruitment advertising and technology
Product or Service: Consultants`Publisher/Media
Note: The AIM Group is a global team of consulting experts in classified advertising, marketplaces and interactive media. We help publishers grow their businesses through strategic and tactical support. We publish AIM Group Marketplaces Report, the international business intelligence service that is often called "the bible of the classified advertising and marketplace industry." We work with news media publishers, dot-coms, print classified publishers, yellow page publishers, broadcasters and technology vendors worldwide to help develop, launch and grow revenue-generating services. We are first and foremost "consultants who publish," not "publishers who do a little consulting on the side." Most of our consulting work is performed on a proprietary basis, so our clients often see only a small fraction of our work-product. We offer solutions for companies planning their strategies, increasing revenue, market share, and in developing products and packing strategies to grow their business. We help build interactive products and services; we don't just talk about them based on flimsy research. We support investors and analysts trying to determine the health of a company, or to find companies ripe for investment or acquisition. Our team includes long-time senior executives, so we work with senior executives to help them understand where their interactive-media and classified services need to evolve. We've been sales reps and sales managers, so we can help sales teams grow and develop traditional and interactive media services. Our writer / analysts get to the heart of the matter, and understand the business inside and out. We work with clients globally. Our worldwide team of almost 40 people follows the evolution in interactive media and classified advertising more closely than anyone else.
Personnel: Peter M. Zollman (Founding Principal); Jim Townsend (Editorial Director); Katja Riefler (Europe Director); Rob Paterson (Principal, director of consulting); Diana Bogdan; Jonathan Turpin (Senior principal)

DANIEL LAMPERT COMMUNICATIONS CORP.

Street address 1: PO Box 151719
Street address 3: Altamonte Springs
Street address state: FL
Zip/Postal code: 32715-1719
County: Seminole
Country: USA
Mailing address: PO Box 151719
Mailing city: Altamonte Springs
Mailing state: FL
Mailing zip: 32715-1719
General Phone: (407) 327-7000
General Fax: (407) 695-9014
General/National Adv. E-mail: service@dlc2.com
Primary Website: www.dlc2.com
Product or Service: Multimedia/Interactive Products`Online Service Provider and Internet Hosts
Personnel: Dan Lampert (Pres.)

INTERACTIVE PUBLISHING CORP.

Street address 1: 7639 Edarwood Cir
Street address 3: Boca Raton
Street address state: FL
Zip/Postal code: 33434-
County: Palm Beach
Country: USA
Mailing address: 7639 Cedarwood Cir
Mailing city: Boca Raton
Mailing state: FL
Mailing zip: 33434-4248
General Phone: (561) 483-7734
General/National Adv. E-mail: vicmilt@victormilt.com
Primary Website: www.victormilt.com
Product or Service: CD-ROM Designer/Manufacturer
Personnel: Kim Milt (CEO); Victor Milt (Creative Dir.); Martin Ross (Exec. Producer)

EPUBLISH4ME

Street address 1: 1375 Gateway Blvd
Street address 3: Boynton Beach
Street address state: FL
Zip/Postal code: 33426-8304
County: Palm Beach
Country: USA
Mailing address: 1375 Gateway Blvd
Mailing city: Boynton Beach
Mailing state: FL
Mailing zip: 33426-8304
General Phone: (561) 370-3336
General/National Adv. E-mail: sales@epublish4me.com
Primary Website: www.epublish4me.com
Area Served - City: Worldwide
Own Printing Facility: Y
Industry: Advertising
Product or Service: Advertising/Marketing Agency`Graphic/Design Firm`Multimedia/Interactive Products`Online Service Provider and Internet Hosts`Publisher/Media
Note: Digitize your pubs at http://www.epublish4me.com/?r=403. It automatically posts them on TitleStand where you can sell them by getting local and worldwide distribution (see http://titlestand.com/t). Your PDFs are converted into digital 3-D page flipping revenue generator books, newspapers or magazines with video, audio, hyperlinks and extensive tracking where they can be read on Tablet, PC, Mac, iPad, iPhone, iTouch, iOS, Android and Kindle Fire. Kind regards, Nick.Koriakin@ePublish4me.com 561-370-3336
Personnel: Nicholas Koriakin (Senior Account Executive)

HOMESTEAD

SANTRONICS SOFTWARE

Street address 1: 15600 SW 288th St
Street address 2: Ste 306
Street address 3: Homestead
Street address state: FL
Zip/Postal code: 33033-1200
County: Miami-Dade
Country: USA
Mailing address: 15600 SW 288th St Ste 306
Mailing city: Homestead
Mailing state: FL
Mailing zip: 33033-1200
General Phone: (305) 248-3204
General Fax: (305) 248-0394
Advertising Phone: (800) 845-6944
General/National Adv. E-mail: sales@santronics.com
Primary Website: www.santronics.com
Product or Service: Hardware/Software Supplier
Personnel: Hector Santos (Pres.); Andrea Santos (Dir., Mktg.)

LONGWOOD

INETUSA

Street address 1: PO Box 917208
Street address 3: Longwood
Street address state: FL
Zip/Postal code: 32791-7208
County: Seminole
Country: USA
Mailing address: 3935 Fenner Rd
Mailing city: Cocoa
Mailing state: FL
Mailing zip: 32926-4205
General Phone: (321) 733-5391
General Fax: (321) 723-4552
General/National Adv. E-mail: info@inetusa.com
Primary Website: www.inetusa.com
Product or Service: Multimedia/Interactive Products`Online Service Provider and Internet Hosts
Personnel: Tim Yandell (Pres.)

EMPHASYS SOFTWARE

Street address 1: 9675 NW 117 Avenue
Street address 2: Suite 305
Street address 3: Miami
Street address state: FL
Zip/Postal code: 33178
County: San Diego
Country: USA
Mailing address: 9675 NW 117 Avenue, Suite 305
Mailing city: Miami
Mailing state: FL
Mailing zip: 33178
General Phone: (800) 968-6884
General/National Adv. E-mail: info@emphasys-software.com
Primary Website: www.emphasys-software.com
Product or Service: Hardware/Software Supplier
Personnel: Mike Byrne (CEO)

SOLO PHOTOGRAPHY, INC.

Street address 1: 3503 NW 15th St
Street address 3: Miami
Street address state: FL
Zip/Postal code: 33125-1715
County: Miami-Dade
Country: USA
Mailing address: 3503 NW 15th St
Mailing city: Miami
Mailing state: FL
Mailing zip: 33125-1715
General Phone: (305) 634-8820
General Fax: (305) 635-9367
General/National Adv. E-mail: rp@solo-photography.com
Primary Website: www.solo-photography.com
Year Established: 1989
Commercial printers: N
Product or Service: Graphic/Design Firm`Publisher/Media
Personnel: Raul Pedroso (Pres.)

SAINT PETERSBURG

KOBIE MARKETING, INC.

Street address 1: 100 2nd Ave S
Street address 2: Ste 1000
Street address 3: Saint Petersburg
Street address state: FL
Zip/Postal code: 33701-4360
County: Pinellas
Country: USA
Mailing address: 100 2nd Ave S Ste 1000
Mailing city: Saint Petersburg
Mailing state: FL
Mailing zip: 33701-6307
General Phone: (727) 822-5353
General Fax: (727) 822-5265
General/National Adv. E-mail: info@kobie.com
Primary Website: www.kobie.com
Product or Service: Advertising/Marketing Agency
Personnel: Don Hughes (CIO); Robert Gilley (Project Mgr.)

SANIBEL

SAME PAGE.COM

Street address 1: PO Box 325
Street address 3: Sanibel
Street address state: FL
Zip/Postal code: 33957-0325
County: Lee
Country: USA
Mailing address: PO Box 325
Mailing city: Sanibel
Mailing state: FL
Mailing zip: 33957-0325
General Phone: (239) 395-7655
General Fax: (239) 395-6745
General/National Adv. E-mail: press@same-page.com
Primary Website: www.same-page.com
Product or Service: Graphic/Design Firm
Personnel: Bruce Collen (Pres.)

THE VILLAGES

ISRAEL FAXX

Street address 1: 611 Saint Andrews Blvd
Street address 3: The Villages
Street address state: FL
Zip/Postal code: 32159-2280
County: Lake
Country: USA
Mailing address: 611 Saint Andrews Blvd
Mailing city: The Villages
Mailing state: FL
Mailing zip: 32159-2280
General Phone: (352) 750-9420
General/National Adv. E-mail: dcanaan@israelfaxx.com
Primary Website: www.israelfaxx.com
Year Established: 1991
Product or Service: CD-ROM Designer/Manufacturer`Publisher/Media
Personnel: Don Canaan (Contact)

GEORGIA

CONVERGENT MEDIA SYSTEMS

Street address 1: 190 Bluegrass Valley Pkwy
Street address 3: Alpharetta
Street address state: GA
Zip/Postal code: 30005-2204
County: Forsyth
Country: USA
Mailing address: 190 Bluegrass Valley Pkwy
Mailing city: Alpharetta
Mailing state: GA
Mailing zip: 30005-2204
General Phone: (770) 369-9000
General Fax: (770) 369-9100
General/National Adv. E-mail: convergent@convergent.com
Primary Website: www.convergent.com
Product or Service: Multimedia/Interactive Products
Personnel: Bryan Allen (CEO); Rick Hutcheson (Vice Pres., Mktg.)

EASE CT SOLUTIONS

Street address 1: 5995 Windward Pkwy
Street address 3: Alpharetta
Street address state: GA
Zip/Postal code: 30005-4184
County: Fulton
Country: USA
Mailing address: 5995 Windward Pkwy
Mailing city: Alpharetta
Mailing state: GA
Mailing zip: 30005-4184
General Phone: (404) 338-2241
General Fax: (404) 338-6101
Product or Service: Hardware/Software Supplier

PREMIERE GLOBAL SERVICES, INC.

Street address 1: 2300 Lakeview Parkway
Street address 2: Suite 300
Street address 3: Alpharetta
Street address state: GA
Zip/Postal code: 30009
County: Jefferson
Country: USA
Mailing address: 2300 Lakeview Parkway, Suite 300
Mailing city: Alpharetta
Mailing state: GA
Mailing zip: 30009
General Phone: (866) 962-8400
Primary Website: www.pgi.com
Product or Service: Multimedia/Interactive Products
Personnel: Don Joos (CEO); Patrick Harper (CTO); Kevin McAdams (CFO); Mark Roberts (Chief Marketing Officer)

PREMIERE GLOBAL SERVICES, INC.

Street address 1: 3280 Peachtree Rd NE
Street address 2: Ste 1000
Street address 3: Atlanta
Street address state: GA

Zip/Postal code: 30305-2451
County: Fulton
Country: USA
Mailing address: 3280 Peachtree Rd NE Ste 1000
Mailing city: Atlanta
Mailing state: GA
Mailing zip: 30305-2451
General Phone: (404) 262-8400
General/National Adv. E-mail: auinfo@pgi.com
Primary Website: www.premiereglobal.com
Product or Service: Telecommunications/Service Bureaus
Personnel: Boland T. Jones (Chrmn./CEO); Theodore P. Schrafft (Pres.); Michael E. Havener (CFO)

REECE & ASSOCIATES

Street address 1: 4200 Northside Pkwy NW
Street address 2: Bldg 7
Street address 3: Atlanta
Street address state: GA
Zip/Postal code: 30327-3007
County: Fulton
Country: USA
Mailing address: 4200 Northside Pkwy NW Bldg 7
Mailing city: Atlanta
Mailing state: GA
Mailing zip: 30327-3007
General Phone: (404) 586-2100
General Fax: (404) 586-2150
General/National Adv. E-mail: info@reeceassociates.com
Primary Website: www.reeceassociates.com
Product or Service: Multimedia/Interactive Products
Personnel: Gary Reece (Owner); Lynda Reece (Owner)

BROOKHAVEN

WE GET AROUND NETWORK

Street address 1: 3527 Knollhaven Dr NE
Street address 3: Brookhaven
Street address state: GA
Zip/Postal code: 30319-1908
County: Dekalb
Country: USA
Mailing address: 3527 Knollhaven Dr NE
Mailing city: Brookhaven
Mailing state: GA
Mailing zip: 30319-1908
General Phone: (404) 303-7311
General Fax: (404) 252-0697
Advertising Phone: (404) 303-7311
Advertising Fax: (404) 252-0697
Editorail Phone: (404) 303-7311
Editorial Fax: (404) 252-0697
General/National Adv. E-mail: DanSmigrod@WeGetAroundNetwork.com
Display Adv. E-mail: DanSmigrod@WeGetAroundNetwork.com
Classified Adv. E-mail: DanSmigrod@WeGetAroundNetwork.com
Editorial e-mail: DanSmigrod@WeGetAroundNetwork.com
Primary Website: https://www.wegetaroundnetwork.com/
Mthly Avg Views: 57000
Mthly Avg Unique Visitors: 21000
Year Established: 2014
Published: Mon`Tues`Wed`Thur`Fri`Sat`Sun`Mthly`Other
Published Other: 44766
Product or Service: Telecommunications/Service Bureaus
Note: DanSmigrod@WeGetAroundNetwork.com Sister Podcast: WGAN-TV Podcast https://podcast.wgan-tv.com/
Personnel: Dan Smigrod (Founder and Managing Editor)

DULUTH

MOVIUS INTERACTIVE CORPORATION

Street address 1: 11360 Lakefield Dr
Street address 3: Duluth
Street address state: GA
Zip/Postal code: 30097-1569
County: Fulton
Country: USA
Mailing address: 11360 Lakefield Dr
Mailing city: Duluth
Mailing state: GA
Mailing zip: 30097-1569
General Phone: (770) 283-1000
General Fax: (770) 497-3990
Primary Website: www.moviuscorp.com
Product or Service: Telecommunications/Service Bureaus
Personnel: Oscar Rodriguez (CEO)

PAGE INTERNATIONAL

Street address 1: 21 Chatham Center S Dr
Street address 3: Savannah
Street address state: GA
Zip/Postal code: 31405-
County: Chatham
Country: USA
Mailing address: 21 Chatham Center S Dr
Mailing city: Savannah
Mailing state: GA
Mailing zip: 31405
General Phone: (912) 964-7243
General Fax: (912) 965-1225
General/National Adv. E-mail: info@pageint.com
Primary Website: www.page-int.com
Product or Service: Multimedia/Interactive Products
Personnel: Michael Clark (Pres.); Terence Bower (Vice Pres.); Susan Vander Masp (Gen. Mgr.)

SMYRNA

BLUECIELO ECM SOLUTIONS

Street address 1: 2400 Lake Park Dr SE
Street address 2: Ste 450
Street address 3: Smyrna
Street address state: GA
Zip/Postal code: 30080-7644
County: Cobb
Country: USA
Mailing address: 2400 Lake Park Dr SE Ste 450
Mailing city: Smyrna
Mailing state: GA
Mailing zip: 30080-7644
General Phone: (404) 634-3302
General Fax: (404) 633-4604
General/National Adv. E-mail: info@bluecieloecm.com
Primary Website: www.bluecieloecm.com
Product or Service: Hardware/Software Supplier
Personnel: Karen Rhymer (Contact)
Newspaper (for newspapers group): Monticello Shopper, Monticello

TUCKER

EMERGENCE LABS, INC.

Street address 1: 5150 N Royal Atlanta Dr
Street address 3: Tucker
Street address state: GA
Zip/Postal code: 30084-3047
County: Dekalb
Country: USA
Mailing address: 5150 N Royal Atlanta Dr
Mailing city: Tucker
Mailing state: GA
Mailing zip: 30084-3047
General Phone: (770) 908-5650
General Fax: (770) 908-5673
Primary Website: www.emergencelabs.com
Year Established: 1973
Product or Service: Advertising/Marketing Agency

ZANE PUBLISHING, INC.

Street address 1: PO Box 1697
Street address 3: Woodstock
Street address state: GA
Zip/Postal code: 30188-1366
County: Cherokee
Country: USA
Mailing address: PO Box 1697
Mailing city: Woodstock
Mailing state: GA
Mailing zip: 30188-1366
General Phone: (650) 488 8204
Primary Website: www.zane.com
Product or Service: CD-ROM Designer/Manufacturer
Personnel: Nicholas Tee (CEO)

IOWA

THE GAZETTE COMPANY

Street address 1: 501 2nd Ave SE
Street address 3: Cedar Rapids
Street address state: IA
Zip/Postal code: 52401-1303
County: Linn
Country: USA
Mailing address: 501 2nd Ave SE
Mailing city: Cedar Rapids
Mailing state: IA
Mailing zip: 52401-1303
General Phone: (319) 398-8422
General Fax: (319) 368-8505
General/National Adv. E-mail: customercare@thegazettecompany.com
Primary Website: www.thegazettecompany.com
Year Established: 1981
Product or Service: Multimedia/Interactive Products`Publisher/Media
Personnel: Joe Hadky (Chrmn.); Chuck Peters (President and CEO); Chris Edwards (VP Sales & Marketing)
Newspaper (for newspapers group): The Gazette, Cedar Rapids; The Fairfield Ledger, Fairfield

APPLIED ART & TECHNOLOGY

Street address 1: 2430 106th St
Street address 3: Des Moines
Street address state: IA
Zip/Postal code: 50322-3763
County: Polk
Country: USA
Mailing address: 2430 106th St
Mailing city: Des Moines
Mailing state: IA
Mailing zip: 50322-3763
General Phone: (515) 331-7400
General Fax: (515) 331-7401
General/National Adv. E-mail: mail@appliedart.com; info@appliedart.com
Primary Website: www.appliedart.com
Product or Service: Multimedia/Interactive Products
Personnel: Jeanie Jorgensen (Media Mgr.)

DUBUQUE

WOODWARD COMMUNICATIONS, INC.

Street address 1: 801 Bluff St
Street address 3: Dubuque
Street address state: IA
Zip/Postal code: 52001-4661
County: Dubuque
Country: USA
Mailing address: P.O. Box 688
Mailing city: Dubuque
Mailing state: IA
Mailing zip: 52004-0688
General Phone: (563) 588-5685
General/National Adv. E-mail: tom.woodward@wcinet.com
Primary Website: www.wcinet.com
Product or Service: Advertising/Marketing Agency`Editorial`Marketing`Multimedia/Interactive Products`Online Service Provider and Internet Hosts`Publisher/Media`Research
Note: WCI is a diversified, employee-owned company, composed of community media, agency and targeted business trade services. The corporation has seven operating divisions: TH Media, Woodward Community Media, Woodward Radio Group, Woodward Printing Services, Two Rivers Marketing, ON Communication, and WoodwardBizMedia.
Personnel: Tom Woodward (CEO/Pres.)
Newspaper (for newspapers group): Stoughton Courier Hub, Stoughton; Great Dane Shopping News, Verona; Oregon Observer, Oregon; Cascade Pioneer, Cascade; Dyersville Commercial, Dyersville; Grant, Iowa, Lafayette Shopping News, Platteville; Telegraph Herald, Dubuque; The Verona Press, Verona; Eastern Iowa Shopping News, Dyersville; Richland Center Shopping News, Richland Center; Wisconsin-Iowa Shopping News, Prairie Du Chien; Unified Newspaper Group, Verona; Manchester Press; Fitchburg Star; Mount Vernon-Lisbon Sun; Solon Economist; West Liberty Index; West Branch Times; North Liberty Leader; Marion Times; Linn News-Letter

FRANK N MAGID ASSOCIATES

Street address 1: 1 Research Ctr
Street address 3: Marion
Street address state: IA
Zip/Postal code: 52302-5868
County: Linn
Country: USA
Mailing address: 1 Research Ctr
Mailing city: Marion
Mailing state: IL
Mailing zip: 52302-5868
General Phone: 847-9220418
General Fax: (319) 377-5861
General/National Adv. E-mail: Bhague@magid.com
Primary Website: www.magid.com
Year Established: 1957
Product or Service: Consultants`Research
Personnel: Bill Hague (Exec. Vice Pres.); Bill Day

ILLINOIS

ALLIANCE FOR AUDITED MEDIA

Street address 1: 48 W Seegers Rd
Street address 3: Arlington Heights
Street address state: IL
Zip/Postal code: 60005-3900
County: Cook
Country: USA
Mailing address: 48 W Seegers Rd
Mailing city: Arlington Heights
Mailing state: IL
Mailing zip: 60005-3900
General Phone: (224) 366-6939
General Fax: (224) 366-6949
Primary Website: www.auditedmedia.com/services/digital-services.aspx
Product or Service: Consultants`Trade Association`Web Site Auditor
Personnel: Steve Guenther (VP, Digital Auditing Services); Tom Drouillard (CEO, President and Managing Director)

COMMUNITECH SERVICES INC.

Street address 1: 2340 S Arlington Heights Rd
Street address 2: Ste 360
Street address 3: Arlington Heights
Street address state: IL
Zip/Postal code: 60005-4517
County: Cook
Country: USA
Mailing address: 2340 S Arlington Heights Rd Ste 360
Mailing city: Arlington Heights
Mailing state: IL
Mailing zip: 60005-4517
General Phone: (847) 981-1200
General Fax: (847) 981-9085
General/National Adv. E-mail: info@communitechservices.com
Primary Website: www.communitechservices.com
Product or Service: Telecommunications/Service Bureaus
Personnel: Barb Gendes Shact (Vice Pres.)

BUFFALO GROVE

TECH IMAGE LTD.

Street address 1: 1130 W Lake Cook Rd
Street address 2: Ste 250
Street address 3: Buffalo Grove
Street address state: IL
Zip/Postal code: 60089-1994
County: Lake
Country: USA
Mailing address: 1130 W Lake Cook Rd Ste 250
Mailing city: Buffalo Grove
Mailing state: IL
Mailing zip: 60089-1994
General Phone: (847) 279-0022

General Fax: (847) 279-8922
General/National Adv. E-mail: pr@techimage.com
Primary Website: www.techimage.com
Year Established: 1993
Product or Service: Marketing
Personnel: Dan O'Brien (Blog Ed.); Tom McFeeley (Blog Ed.)

BURR RIDGE

TOM O'TOOLE COMMUNICATION, INC.

Street address 1: 115 79th St
Street address 3: Burr Ridge
Street address state: IL
Zip/Postal code: 60527-5954
County: Dupage
Country: USA
Mailing address: 115 79th St
Mailing city: Burr Ridge
Mailing state: IL
Mailing zip: 60527-5954
General Phone: (630) 789-8666
General/National Adv. E-mail: tom@tomotoole.com
Primary Website: www.tomotoole.com
Product or Service: Advertising/Marketing Agency
Personnel: Tom O'Toole (Pres.)

CHAMPAIGN

DREAMSCAPE DESIGN, INC.

Street address 1: 10 Henson Pl
Street address 2: Ste A
Street address 3: Champaign
Street address state: IL
Zip/Postal code: 61820-7836
County: Champaign
Country: USA
Mailing address: 10 Henson Pl Ste A
Mailing city: Champaign
Mailing state: IL
Mailing zip: 61820-7836
General Phone: (217) 359-8484
General Fax: (217) 239-5858
General/National Adv. E-mail: info@dreamscapedesign.com
Primary Website: www.dreamscapedesign.com
Year Established: 1981
Product or Service: Advertising/Marketing Agency`CD-ROM Designer/Manufacturer`Consultants`Graphic/Design Firm`Multimedia/Interactive Products`POP/Kiosk Designer`Web Site Auditor
Personnel: Amy Moushon (Bus. Devel. Mgr.)

AMASIS

Street address 1: 1538 W Cullerton St
Street address 3: Chicago
Street address state: IL
Zip/Postal code: 60608-2918
County: Cook
Country: USA
Mailing address: 1538 W Cullerton St
Mailing city: Chicago
Mailing state: IL
Mailing zip: 60608-2918
General Phone: (312) 850-9459
General Fax: (312) 850-9459
General/National Adv. E-mail: amasis@amasis.com
Primary Website: www.amasis.com
Product or Service: Graphic/Design Firm
Personnel: Tamara Manning (Head Designer)

ANSWERS MEDIA INC.

Street address 1: 30 N Racine Ave
Street address 2: Ste 300
Street address 3: Chicago
Street address state: IL
Zip/Postal code: 60607-2184
County: Cook
Country: USA
Mailing address: 30 N Racine Ave Ste 300
Mailing city: Chicago
Mailing state: IL
Mailing zip: 60607-2184
General Phone: (312) 421-0113
General Fax: (312) 421-1457
General/National Adv. E-mail: info@answersmediainc.com
Primary Website: www.answersmediainc.com
Product or Service: Multimedia/Interactive Products
Personnel: Jeff Bohnson (Pres.)

ATOMIC IMAGING, INC.

Street address 1: 1501 N Magnolia Ave
Street address 3: Chicago
Street address state: IL
Zip/Postal code: 60642-2427
County: Cook
Country: USA
Mailing address: 1501 N Magnolia Ave
Mailing city: Chicago
Mailing state: IL
Mailing zip: 60642-2427
General Phone: (312) 649-1800
General Fax: (312) 642-7441
General/National Adv. E-mail: info@atomicimaging.com
Primary Website: www.atomicimaging.com
Year Established: 1985
Product or Service: Graphic/Design Firm
Personnel: Ari Golan (Pres.); Nick Brown (Commun. Consultant); Algar Dombrouskis (Producer); Jim Abreu (Interactive Design)

DESIGNORY.COM

Street address 1: 200 E Randolph St
Street address 2: Ste 3620
Street address 3: Chicago
Street address state: IL
Zip/Postal code: 60601-6512
County: Cook
Country: USA
Mailing address: 200 E Randolph St
Mailing city: Chicago
Mailing state: IL
Mailing zip: 60601-6436
General Phone: (312) 729-4500
Primary Website: www.designory.com
Year Established: 1994
Product or Service: Advertising/Marketing Agency

MOTOROLA MOBILITY, LLC.

Street address 1: 500 W Monroe Street
Street address 2: Ste 4400
Street address 3: Chicago
Street address state: IL
Zip/Postal code: 60661-3781
Country: USA
Mailing address: 500 W Monroe Street, Ste 4400
Mailing city: Chicago
Mailing state: IL
Mailing zip: 60661-3781
General Phone: (847) 523-5000
General Fax: (847) 523-8770
Primary Website: httwww.motorola.com
Product or Service: Telecommunications/Service Bureaus
Personnel: Sergio Buniac (Pres.); Grant Hoffman (Vice Pres. Bus. Op.); Terry Vega (Vice Pres. & Gen. Mgr.); Sanjay Vanjani (CFO)

SOURCELINK

Street address 1: 500 Park Blvd
Street address 2: Ste 1245
Street address 3: Itasca
Street address state: IL
Zip/Postal code: 60143-2610
County: Dupage
Country: USA
Mailing address: 500 Park Blvd Ste 1245
Mailing city: Itasca
Mailing state: IL
Mailing zip: 60143-2610
General Phone: (310) 208-2024
General Fax: (310) 208-5681
General/National Adv. E-mail: info@sourcelink.com
Primary Website: www.sourcelink.com
Product or Service: Advertising/Marketing Agency
Personnel: Don Landrum (CEO); Don Lewis (CFO); Brent Tartar (Exec. V.P.); Keith Chadwell (COO)

LOVES PARK

UNIVERSAL TECHNICAL SYSTEMS, INC.

Street address 1: 4053 N Perryville Rd
Street address 2: Ste 700
Street address 3: Loves Park
Street address state: IL
Zip/Postal code: 61111-8653
County: Winnebago
Country: USA
Mailing address: 4053 N Perryville Rd
Mailing city: Loves Park
Mailing state: IL
Mailing zip: 61111-8653
General Phone: (815) 963-2220
General Fax: (815) 963-8884
General/National Adv. E-mail: support@uts.com
Primary Website: www.uts.com
Product or Service: Hardware/Software Supplier
Personnel: Sharad Marathe (Pres. & CEO)

MCHENRY

CORPORATE DISK COMPANY

Street address 1: 4610 Prime Pkwy
Street address 3: McHenry
Street address state: IL
Zip/Postal code: 60050-7005
County: McHenry
Country: USA
Mailing address: 4610 Prime Pkwy
Mailing city: McHenry
Mailing state: IL
Mailing zip: 60050-7005
General Phone: (815) 331-6000
General Fax: (815) 331-6030
General/National Adv. E-mail: info@disk.com
Primary Website: www.disk.com
Product or Service: CD-ROM Designer/Manufacturer
Note: Specializing in CD and DVD Manufacturing along with all the related printing, packaging, technical, and fulfillment services. Providing complete start to finish solutions.
Personnel: William Mahoney (Pres.)

MOLINE

SILVER OAKS COMMUNICATIONS

Street address 1: 824 17th St
Street address 3: Moline
Street address state: IL
Zip/Postal code: 61265-2126
County: Rock Island
Country: USA
Mailing address: PO Box 1224
Mailing city: Moline
Mailing state: IL
Mailing zip: 61266-1224
General Phone: (309) 797-9898
General Fax: (309) 797-9653
General/National Adv. E-mail: info@silveroaks.com
Primary Website: www.silveroaks.com
Product or Service: CD-ROM Designer/Manufacturer
Personnel: Charles Dostale (System Mgr.)

TOWNNEWS.COM

Street address 1: 1510 47th Ave
Street address 3: Moline
Street address state: IL
Zip/Postal code: 61265-7021
County: Rock Island
Country: USA
Mailing address: 1510 47th Ave
Mailing city: Moline
Mailing state: IL
Mailing zip: 61265
General Phone: (800) 293-9576
General Fax: (309) 743-0830
General/National Adv. E-mail: info@townnews.com
Primary Website: www.townnews.com
Product or Service: Editorial`Graphic/Design Firm`Hardware/Software Supplier`Multimedia/Interactive Products`Other Services`Online Service Provider and Internet Hosts`Web Site Auditor
Note: No. 1 provider of Content Management Systems to U.S. daily newspapers, according to Reynolds Journalism Institute.
Personnel: Marc Wilson (Exec Chairman); Brad Ward (CEO); Carol Grubbe (Rgl. Sales Mgr.); Teri Sutton (Tech. Sales Rep.); Roger Lee (Reg. Sales Mgr.); Theresa Nelson (Dir./Buss. Dev.); Marc Filby (Sr. Tech. Sales Rep.); Loren Widrick (Reg. Sales Mgr.); Christine Masters (Dir./Product Mgmt.); Aaron Gillette (Dir. Mktg.); David Sutton (Reg. Sales Mgr.); John Montgomery (Regional Sales Manager)

NORTHBROOK

STATS, LLC.

Street address 1: 2775 Shermer Rd
Street address 3: Northbrook
Street address state: IL
Zip/Postal code: 60062-7700
County: Cook
Country: USA
Mailing address: 2775 Shermer Rd Stop 2
Mailing city: Northbrook
Mailing state: IL
Mailing zip: 60062-7700
General Phone: (847) 583-2100
General Fax: (847) 583-2600
General/National Adv. E-mail: sales@stats.com
Primary Website: www.stats.com
Product or Service: Multimedia/Interactive Products
Personnel: Jim Morganthaler (Gen. Mgr.)

OAK PARK

HUTCHINSON ASSOCIATES, INC.

Street address 1: 822 Linden Ave
Street address 2: Ste 200
Street address 3: Oak Park
Street address state: IL
Zip/Postal code: 60302-1562
County: Cook
Country: USA
Mailing address: 822 Linden Ave Ste 200
Mailing city: Oak Park
Mailing state: IL
Mailing zip: 60302-1562
General Phone: (312) 455-9191
General/National Adv. E-mail: hutch@thisishutchinson.com
Primary Website: www.thisishutchinson.com
Year Established: 1986
Product or Service: Advertising/Marketing Agency`Consultants`Graphic/Design Firm`Marketing`Other Services`Web Site Auditor
Personnel: Jerry Hutchinson (Pres.); Doug White (Prod.)

ORLAND PARK

MPI MEDIA GROUP

Street address 1: 16101 108th Ave
Street address 3: Orland Park
Street address state: IL
Zip/Postal code: 60467-5305
County: Cook
Country: USA
Mailing address: 16101 108th Ave
Mailing city: Orland Park
Mailing state: IL
Mailing zip: 60467-5305
General Phone: (708) 460-0555
General Fax: (708) 873-3177
General/National Adv. E-mail: info@mpimedia.com
Primary Website: www.mpimedia.com
Product or Service: Publisher/Media
Personnel: Nicola Goelzhaeufer (Contact)

WPA FILM LIBRARY

Street address 1: 16101 108th Ave
Street address 3: Orland Park
Street address state: IL
Zip/Postal code: 60467-5305
County: Cook
Country: USA
Mailing address: 16101 108th Ave
Mailing city: Orland Park

Mailing state: IL
Mailing zip: 60467-5305
General Phone: (708) 460-0555
General Fax: (708) 460 0187
General/National Adv. E-mail: sales@wpafilmlibrary.com
Primary Website: www.wpafilmlibrary.com
Product or Service: Publisher/Media
Personnel: Diane Paradiso (Dir., Sales)

JUPITER IMAGES CORP.

Street address 1: 6000 N Forest Park Dr
Street address 3: Peoria
Street address state: IL
Zip/Postal code: 61614-3556
County: Peoria
Country: USA
Mailing address: 6000 N Forest Park Dr
Mailing city: Peoria
Mailing state: IL
Mailing zip: 61614-3556
General Phone: (309) 688-8800
General Fax: (309) 688-3075
General/National Adv. E-mail: sales@jupiterimages.com
Primary Website: www.jupiterimages.com
Year Established: 1964
Industry: Software: Design/Graphics; Trade Publications;
Product or Service: Hardware/Software Supplier
Note: All-purpose art and idea service.
Personnel: Mark Nickerson (Vice Pres., Opns.)

COPIA INTERNATIONAL LTD.

Street address 1: 52 Salt Creek Rd
Street address 3: Roselle
Street address state: IL
Zip/Postal code: 60172-1420
County: Dupage
Country: USA
Mailing address: 52 Salt Creek Road
Mailing city: Roselle
Mailing state: IL
Mailing zip: 60172
General Phone: (630) 388-6900
General Fax: (630) 778-8848
Advertising Phone: 800-689-8898
Editorail Phone: 800-516-5189
General/National Adv. E-mail: sales@copia.com
Display Adv. E-mail: sales@copia.com
Editorial e-mail: dorothy@copia.com
Primary Website: www.copia.com
Year Established: 1987
Delivery Methods: Mail
Area Served - City: All
Own Printing Facility: N
Commercial printers: Y
Product or Service: Hardware/Software Supplier`Other Services
Personnel: Steve Hersee (Pres.); Dorothy Gaden-Flanagan (Vice Pres., Mktg.); Terry Flanagan (VP, Eng.)

MOTOROLA SOLUTIONS, INC.

Street address 1: 1303 E Algonquin Rd
Street address 3: Schaumburg
Street address state: IL
Zip/Postal code: 60196-4041
County: Cook
Country: USA
Mailing address: 1303 E Algonquin Rd
Mailing city: Schaumburg
Mailing state: IL
Mailing zip: 60196-1079
General Phone: (847) 576-5000
General Fax: (561) 739-2341
General/National Adv. E-mail: Training.NA@motorolasolutions.com
Primary Website: www.motorolasolutions.com
Product or Service: Telecommunications/Service Bureaus
Personnel: Gregory Brown (Pres./CEO); David Dorman (Lead Independent Dir. of the Board)

SKOKIE

DUNN SOLUTIONS GROUP

Street address 1: 5550 Touhy Ave
Street address 3: Skokie
Street address state: IL
Zip/Postal code: 60077-3253
County: Cook
Country: USA
Mailing address: 5550 Touhy Ave Ste 400A
Mailing city: Skokie
Mailing state: IL
Mailing zip: 60077-3254
General Phone: (847) 673-0900
General Fax: (847) 673-0904
Primary Website: www.dunnsolutions.com
Product or Service: Multimedia/Interactive Products
Personnel: David Skwarczek (Pres.)

INDIANA

TELSPAN, INC.

Street address 1: 101 W Washington St Ste 1200E
Street address 2: Pnc Center
Street address 3: Indianapolis
Street address state: IN
Zip/Postal code: 46204-3409
County: Marion
Country: USA
Mailing address: 101 W Washington St. Ste 1200E
Mailing city: Indianapolis
Mailing state: IN
Mailing zip: 46204
General Phone: (317) 631-6565
General Fax: (317) 687-1747
General/National Adv. E-mail: info@telspan.com
Primary Website: www.telspan.com
Year Established: 1989
Product or Service: Telecommunications/Service Bureaus
Personnel: J. Bruce Laughrey (Chrmn.); Patrick Martin (COO)

BKR STUDIO, INC.

Street address 1: 110 East Madison Street
Street address 3: South Bend
Street address state: IN
Zip/Postal code: 46601
County: St Joseph
Country: USA
Mailing address: 110 East Madison Street
Mailing city: South Bend
Mailing state: IN
Mailing zip: 46601
General Phone: (574) 245-9576
General Fax: (574) 245-9577
General/National Adv. E-mail: info@bkrstudio.com
Primary Website: www.bkrstudio.com
Product or Service: Multimedia/Interactive Products
Personnel: Brian Rideout (Pres.); Tina Merrill (Studio Mgr.)

KANSAS

MISSION

FAMILY FEATURES EDITORIAL SYNDICATE, INC.

Street address 1: 5825 Dearborn St
Street address 3: Mission
Street address state: KS
Zip/Postal code: 66202-2745
County: Johnson
Country: USA
Mailing address: 5825 Dearborn St
Mailing city: Mission
Mailing state: KS
Mailing zip: 66202-2745
General Phone: (913) 563-4752
General Fax: (913) 789-9228
General/National Adv. E-mail: clong@familyfeatures.com
Primary Website: www.familyfeatures.com
Year Established: 1974
Product or Service: Multimedia/Interactive Products
Personnel: Dianne Hogerty (Owner); Clarke Smith (President); Cindy Long (Media Relations Manager)

SPRINT CORP.

Street address 1: 6480 Sprint Pkwy
Street address 2: Bldg 13
Street address 3: Overland Park
Street address state: KS
Zip/Postal code: 66251-6100
County: Johnson
Country: USA
Mailing address: 6480 Sprint Pkwy, Bldg 13
Mailing city: Overland Park
Mailing state: KS
Mailing zip: 66251-6100
General Phone: (913) 315-8081
General/National Adv. E-mail: boardinquiries@sprint.com
Primary Website: www.sprint.com
Product or Service: Telecommunications/Service Bureaus
Personnel: Marcelo Claure (Exec. Chrmn.); Michel Combes (Pres./CEO); N安stor Cano (COO); Andrew Davies (CFO); John Saw (CTO); Brandon Draper (Chief Commercial Officer); Jan Geldmacher (Pres. - Sprint Business); Deeanne King (Chief Human Resources Officer); Christina Sternberg (Chief Administrative Officer); Marci Carris (Senior Vice Pres. - Customer Care); Jim Curran (Senior Vice Pres. - Marketing, Acquisition, and Base Management)

KENTUCKY

C-T INNOVATIONS

Street address 1: 11509 Commonwealth Dr
Street address 3: Louisville
Street address state: KY
Zip/Postal code: 40299-2379
County: Jefferson
Country: USA
Mailing address: 11509 Commonwealth Dr Ste 101
Mailing city: Louisville
Mailing state: KY
Mailing zip: 40299-2379
General Phone: (502) 814-5100
General Fax: (502) 814-5110
Primary Website: www.ct-innovations.com
Product or Service: Telecommunications/Service Bureaus
Personnel: Robert Flynn (Pres.)

KINETIC CORPORATION

Street address 1: 200 Distillery Cmns
Street address 2: Ste 200
Street address 3: Louisville
Street address state: KY
Zip/Postal code: 40206-1987
County: Jefferson
Country: USA
Mailing address: 200 Distillery Commons Ste 200
Mailing city: Louisville
Mailing state: KY
Mailing zip: 40206-1987
General Phone: (502) 719-9500
General Fax: (502) 719-9569
General/National Adv. E-mail: info@theTechnologyAgency.com
Primary Website: www.theTechnologyAgency.com
Year Established: 1979
Industry: Consulting Services: Production; Photo Archiving; Preprint Service & Production; Software: Asset Management; Software: Design/Graphics; Software: Pagination/Layout; Software: Workflow Management/Tracking;
Product or Service: Graphic/Design Firm
Personnel: G. Raymond Schuhmann (Pres.); Cindi Ramm (Chief Brand Strategist)

LOUISIANA

LOUISIANA SHERIFF'S ASSOCIATION

Street address 1: 1175 Nicholson Drive
Street address 3: Baton Rouge
Street address state: LA
Zip/Postal code: 70802
Country: USA
Mailing address: 1175 Nicholson Drive
Mailing city: Baton Rouge
Mailing state: LA
Mailing zip: 70802
General Phone: (225) 343-8402
General Fax: (225) 336-0343
Primary Website: www.lsa.org
Year Established: 1945
Industry: Art & Layout Equipment and Services; Consulting Services; Advertising; Editorial; Software: Design/Graphics; Software: Editorial: mobile
Product or Service: Consultants`Editorial`Graphic/Design Firm`Marketing`Other Services`Trade Association
Personnel: Michael Ranatza (Executive Director); Cynthia Butler (Office Manager); Lauren Labbe' Meher (Dir. of Comm. and Pub. Affairs); Darlene Petty (Accounting)

MASSACHUSETTS

ASHBURNHAM

PRECISION ARTS ADVERTISING, INC.

Street address 1: 57 Fitchburg Rd
Street address 3: Ashburnham
Street address state: MA
Zip/Postal code: 01430-1409
County: Worcester
Country: USA
Mailing address: 57 Fitchburg Rd
Mailing city: Ashburnham
Mailing state: MA
Mailing zip: 01430-1409
General Phone: (978) 827-4552
General/National Adv. E-mail: sales@precisionarts.com
Primary Website: www.precisionarts.com
Year Established: 1985
Product or Service: Advertising/Marketing Agency

RISI, INC.

Street address 1: 4 Alfred Cir
Street address 3: Bedford
Street address state: MA
Zip/Postal code: 01730-2340
County: Middlesex
Country: USA
Mailing address: 4 Alfred Cir
Mailing city: Bedford
Mailing state: MA
Mailing zip: 01730-2340
General Phone: (781) 734-8900
General Fax: (781) 271-0337
General/National Adv. E-mail: info@risi.com
Primary Website: www.risiinfo.com
Product or Service: Publisher/Media
Personnel: Mike Cossey (CEO)

COLLEGE PUBLISHER, INC.

Street address 1: 31 Saint James Ave
Street address 2: Ste 920
Street address 3: Boston
Street address state: MA
Zip/Postal code: 02116-4155
County: Suffolk
Country: USA
Mailing address: 31 Saint James Ave Ste 920
Mailing city: Boston
Mailing state: MA
Mailing zip: 02116-4155

General Phone: (888) 735-5578
General/National Adv. E-mail: support@collegemedianetwork.com
Primary Website: www.collegepublisher.com
Year Established: 1999
Product or Service: Hardware/Software Supplier
Personnel: Chris Gillon (Contact)

Y2M: YOUTH MEDIA & MARKETING NETWORKS

Street address 1: 31 Saint James Ave
Street address 2: Ste 920
Street address 3: Boston
Street address state: MA
Zip/Postal code: 02116-4155
County: Suffolk
Country: USA
Mailing address: 31 Saint James Ave Ste 920
Mailing city: Boston
Mailing state: MA
Mailing zip: 02116-4155
General Phone: (888) 738-5578
General/National Adv. E-mail: support@collegemedianetwork.com
Primary Website: www.y2m.com
Product or Service: Advertising/Marketing Agency
Personnel: Dina Witter Pradel (Vice Pres./Gen.Mgr.); Tom Peterson (Dir., Strategic Devel./Opns.); Sara Steele-Rogers (Gen. Mgr.)

NUANCE COMMUNICATIONS, INC.

Street address 1: 1 Wayside Rd
Street address 3: Burlington
Street address state: MA
Zip/Postal code: 01803-4609
County: Middlesex
Country: USA
Mailing address: 1 Wayside Rd
Mailing city: Burlington
Mailing state: MA
Mailing zip: 01803-4609
General Phone: (781) 565-5000
General Fax: (781) 565-5001
General/National Adv. E-mail: kevin.faulkner@nuance.com
Primary Website: www.nuance.com
Year Established: 1923
Product or Service: Multimedia/Interactive Products
Personnel: Robert Schwager (Pres.); Tim Ledwick (CFO); Ed Rucinski (Sr. Vice Pres./Gen. Mgr., Int'l/Commun. Recording Systems); Bob Attanasio (Sr. Vice Pres./Gen. Mgr., Integrated Voice Systems); Donald Fallati (Sr. Vice Pres., Mktg./Strategic Planning); Joe Delaney (Sr. Vice Pres., Worldwide Servs.); Jim Davis (Sr. Vice Pres., Mfg./Logistics)

EDGIL ASSOCIATES, INC.

Street address 1: 222 Rosewood Dr
Street address 2: Ste 210
Street address 3: Danvers
Street address state: MA
Zip/Postal code: 01923-4520
County: Essex
Country: USA
Mailing address: 222 Rosewood Dr Ste 210
Mailing city: Danvers
Mailing state: MA
Mailing zip: 01923-4520
General Phone: (800) 457-9932
General Fax: (978) 667-6050
General/National Adv. E-mail: sales@edgil.com
Primary Website: www.edgil.com
Industry: Payment Processing
Product or Service: Hardware/Software Supplier
Personnel: Sean Callahan (Dir., Sales)

DEVENS

NORTHROP GRUMMAN'S AOA XINETICS (AOX)

Street address 1: 115 Jackson Road
Street address 3: Devens
Street address state: MA
Zip/Postal code: 01432
Country: USA
Mailing address: 115 Jackson Road
Mailing city: Devens
Mailing state: MA
Mailing zip: 01432
General Phone: (978) 757-9600
General Fax: (978) 772-6720
General/National Adv. E-mail: AOXinfo@ngc.com
Primary Website: www.northropgrumman.com/BusinessVentures/AOAXinetics/Pages/default.aspx
Product or Service: Hardware/Software Supplier
Personnel: Kathy J. Warden (Pres. & CEO)

PROCESS SOFTWARE

Street address 1: 959 Concord St
Street address 3: Framingham
Street address state: MA
Zip/Postal code: 01701-4682
County: Middlesex
Country: USA
Mailing address: 959 Concord St Ste 120
Mailing city: Framingham
Mailing state: MA
Mailing zip: 01701-4682
General Phone: (508) 879-6994
General Fax: (508) 879-0042
General/National Adv. E-mail: info@process.com; careers@process.com; international@process.com
Display Adv. E-mail: sales@process.com
Primary Website: www.process.com
Product or Service: Hardware/Software Supplier
Personnel: Mick McCarthy (Vice Pres., Sales)

INFORONICS, INC.

Street address 1: 25 Porter Rd
Street address 3: Littleton
Street address state: MA
Zip/Postal code: 01460-1434
County: Middlesex
Country: USA
Mailing address: 25 Porter Rd Ste 4
Mailing city: Littleton
Mailing state: MA
Mailing zip: 01460-1434
General Phone: (978) 698-7400
General Fax: (978) 698-7500
Advertising Phone: (978) 698-6593
Primary Website: www.inforonics.com
Product or Service: Multimedia/Interactive Products
Personnel: Bruce Mills (Pres.); Andy Kramer (Vice Pres., Sales); Tom Pellegriti (Vice Pres., Opns.)

MELROSE

BKJ PRODUCTIONS

Street address 1: 99 Washington St
Street address 3: Melrose
Street address state: MA
Zip/Postal code: 02176-6024
County: Middlesex
Country: USA
Mailing address: 99 Washington St Ste 21A
Mailing city: Melrose
Mailing state: MA
Mailing zip: 02176-6026
General Phone: (781) 662-8800
General/National Adv. E-mail: info@bkjproductions.com
Primary Website: www.bkjproductions.com
Product or Service: Multimedia/Interactive Products
Personnel: Brian K. Johnson (Pres.)

METHUEN

3M TOUCH SYSTEMS, INC.

Street address 1: 501 Griffin Brook Dr
Street address 3: Methuen
Street address state: MA
Zip/Postal code: 01844
County: Essex
Country: USA
Mailing address: 501 Griffin Brook Dr
Mailing city: Methuen
Mailing state: MA
Mailing zip: 01844
General Phone: (978) 659-9000
Primary Website: www.3mtouch.com
Product or Service: Hardware/Software Supplier
Personnel: Chris Tsourides (Bus. Unit Mgr.)

NEWTON

CYWAYS, INC.

Street address 1: 19 Westchester Rd
Street address 3: Newton
Street address state: MA
Zip/Postal code: 02458-2519
County: Middlesex
Country: USA
Mailing address: 19 Westchester Rd
Mailing city: Newton
Mailing state: MA
Mailing zip: 02458-2519
General Phone: (617) 965-9465
General Fax: (617) 796-8997
General/National Adv. E-mail: support@cyways.com
Product or Service: Online Service Provider and Internet Hosts
Personnel: Peter H. Lemieux (Pres.)

PEMBROKE

MRW COMMUNICATIONS, LLC.

Street address 1: 6 Barker Square Dr
Street address 3: Pembroke
Street address state: MA
Zip/Postal code: 02359-2225
County: Plymouth
Country: USA
Mailing address: 6 Barker Square Dr
Mailing city: Pembroke
Mailing state: MA
Mailing zip: 02359-2225
General Phone: (781) 924-5282
General Fax: (781) 926-0371
General/National Adv. E-mail: jim@mrwinc.com
Primary Website: www.mrwinc.com
Year Established: 1983
Product or Service: Hardware/Software Supplier
Personnel: Jim Watts (Account Services Dir.); Tom Matzell (Creative Dir., Copy); Kristen Balunas (Creative Dir., Art)

SHARON

THE TUCKER GROUP

Street address 1: 19 Edgewood Rd
Street address 3: Sharon
Street address state: MA
Zip/Postal code: 02067-1938
County: Norfolk
Country: USA
Mailing address: 19 Edgewood Rd
Mailing city: Sharon
Mailing state: MA
Mailing zip: 02067-1938
General Phone: (781) 784-0932
General/National Adv. E-mail: mtucker@tuckergroup.com
Product or Service: Advertising/Marketing Agency
Personnel: Michael Tucker (Owner)

WAKEFIELD

EPSILON

Street address 1: 601 Edgewater Dr
Street address 3: Wakefield
Street address state: MA
Zip/Postal code: 01880-6237
County: Middlesex
Country: USA
Mailing address: 601 Edgewater Dr Ste 250
Mailing city: Wakefield
Mailing state: MA
Mailing zip: 01880-6238
General Phone: (781) 685-6000
General Fax: (781) 685-0830
Primary Website: www.epsilon.com
Year Established: 1969
Product or Service: Advertising/Marketing Agency

WALTHAM

CGI GROUP, INC.

Street address 1: 460 Totten Pond Rd
Street address 2: Ste 530
Street address 3: Waltham
Street address state: MA
Zip/Postal code: 02451-1944
County: Middlesex
Country: USA
Mailing address: 460 Totten Pond Rd Ste 530
Mailing city: Waltham
Mailing state: MA
Mailing zip: 02451-1944
General Phone: (781) 810-4022
General Fax: (781) 890-4361
General/National Adv. E-mail: web@cgi.com
Primary Website: www.cgi.com
Product or Service: Consultants
Personnel: Jennifer Peters (Global Mktg. Mgr.)

MANITOBA

LAZER-FARE MEDIA SERVICES

Street address 1: PO Box 48114 RPO Lakewood
Street address 3: Winnipeg
Street address state: MB
Zip/Postal code: R2J 4A3
Country: Canada
Mailing address: PO Box 48114 RPO Lakewood
Mailing city: Winnipeg
Mailing state: MB
Mailing zip: R2J 4A3
General Phone: (204) 452-5023
General Fax: (204) 272-3499
General/National Adv. E-mail: sales@lazerfare.com
Primary Website: www.lazerfare.com
Year Established: 1985
Industry: Archiving Systems; Consulting Services: Advertising; Consulting Services: Computer; Consulting Services: Editorial; Content and Digital Asset Management systems
Product or Service: Consultants`Hardware/Software Supplier
Personnel: Kelly Armstrong (Pres.)

MARYLAND

ANNAPOLIS

SPAR ASSOCIATES, INC.

Street address 1: 927 West St
Street address 3: Annapolis
Street address state: MD
Zip/Postal code: 21401-3653
County: Anne Arundel
Country: USA
Mailing address: 927 West St Ste 101
Mailing city: Annapolis
Mailing state: MD
Mailing zip: 21401-3646
General Phone: (410) 263-8593
General Fax: (410) 267-0503
General/National Adv. E-mail: info@sparusa.com
Primary Website: www.sparusa.com
Year Established: 1972
Own Printing Facility: Y
Product or Service: Consultants`Hardware/Software Supplier
Personnel: Laurent C. Deschamps (Pres.); Charles Greenwell (Vice Pres., Opns.)

BETHESDA

ARLEN COMMUNICATIONS LLC

Street address 1: 6407 Landon Ln
Street address 3: Bethesda
Street address state: MD

Zip/Postal code: 20817-5603
County: Montgomery
Country: USA
Mailing address: 6407 Landon Lane
Mailing city: Bethesda
Mailing state: MD
Mailing zip: 20817
General Phone: (301) 229 2199
General/National Adv. E-mail: garlen@arlencom.com
Primary Website: www.arlencom.com
Year Established: 1980
Product or Service: Consultants
Personnel: Gary Arlen (Pres.)

L-SOFT INTERNATIONAL, INC.

Street address 1: 7550 Wisconsin Ave # 400
Street address 3: Bethesda
Street address state: MD
Zip/Postal code: 20814-3573
Country: USA
Mailing address: 7550 Wisconsin Ave # 400
Mailing city: Bethesda
Mailing state: MD
Mailing zip: 20814-3573
General Phone: (301) 731-0440
General Fax: (301) 731-6302
General/National Adv. E-mail: sales@lsoft.com
Display Adv. E-mail: sales@lsoft.com
Primary Website: www.lsoft.com
Product or Service: Hardware/Software Supplier
Personnel: Eric Thomas (CEO); Outi Tuomaala (Vice Pres., Marketing)

GAITHERSBURG

MICROLOG CORP.

Street address 1: 401 Professional Dr
Street address 2: Ste 125
Street address 3: Gaithersburg
Street address state: MD
Zip/Postal code: 20879-3468
County: Montgomery
Country: USA
Mailing address: 401 Professional Dr Ste 125
Mailing city: Gaithersburg
Mailing state: MD
Mailing zip: 20879-3468
General Phone: (301) 540-5500
General Fax: (301) 330-2450
General/National Adv. E-mail: sales@mlog.com
Primary Website: www.mlog.com
Product or Service: Hardware/Software Supplier
Personnel: W. Joseph Brookman (Pres./CEO/Dir.); John C. Mears (CTO); Steve Feldman (Exec. Vice Pres., Worldwide Sales)

HAGERSTOWN

CONSERVIT, INC.

Street address 1: 18656 Leslie Dr
Street address 3: Hagerstown
Street address state: MD
Zip/Postal code: 21740
County: Lake
Country: USA
Mailing address: P.O. Box 1517
Mailing city: Hagerstown
Mailing state: MD
Mailing zip: 21741-1517
General Phone: (301) 791-0100
General Fax: (301) 739-8548
General/National Adv. E-mail: sales@conservit.com
Primary Website: www.conservit.net
Product or Service: Telecommunications/Service Bureaus
Personnel: Peter F. Theis (Pres.)

LAUREL

NETVILLAGE.COM, LLC.

Street address 1: 342 Main St
Street address 3: Laurel
Street address state: MD
Zip/Postal code: 20707-7100
County: Prince Georges
Country: USA
Mailing address: PO Box 1241
Mailing city: Laurel
Mailing state: MD
Mailing zip: 20725-1241
General Phone: (301) 498-7797
General Fax: (301) 498-8110
General/National Adv. E-mail: info@netvillage.com
Display Adv. E-mail: sales@gcomm.com
Primary Website: www.netvillage.com
Product or Service: Hardware/Software Supplier`Online Service Provider and Internet Hosts
Personnel: Harold Van Arnem (CEO); Nathan Hammond (Pres./COO); Stephen Bathurst (CTO); Tony Burgess (Controller)

CABLEFAX DAILY LLC

Street address 1: 4 Choke Cherry Rd
Street address 2: Fl 2
Street address 3: Rockville
Street address state: MD
Zip/Postal code: 20850-4024
County: Montgomery
Country: USA
Mailing address: 4 Choke Cherry Rd Fl 2
Mailing city: Rockville
Mailing state: MD
Mailing zip: 20850-4024
General Phone: (301) 354-2000
General Fax: (301) 738-8453
General/National Adv. E-mail: sarenstein@accessintel.com
Primary Website: www.cablefax.com
Product or Service: Online Service Provider and Internet Hosts
Personnel: Seth Arenstein (Editorial Dir.)

MICRO FOCUS

Street address 1: One Irvington Center
Street address 2: 700 King Farm Boulevard, Suite 400
Street address 3: Rockville
Street address state: MD
Zip/Postal code: 20850-5736
Country: USA
Mailing address: One Irvington Center
Mailing city: Rockville
Mailing state: MD
Mailing zip: 20850-5736
General Phone: (301) 838-5000
General Fax: (301) 838-5025
Primary Website: www.microfocus.com
Product or Service: Multimedia/Interactive Products
Personnel: Kevin Loosemore (Exec. Chrmn.); Stephen Murdoch (CEO)

WALDORF

APDI-APPLICATION PROGRAMMING & DEVELOPMENT, INC.

Street address 1: 1282 Smallwood Dr W
Street address 2: Ste 276
Street address 3: Waldorf
Street address state: MD
Zip/Postal code: 20603-4732
County: Charles
Country: USA
Mailing address: 1282 Smallwood Dr W Ste 276
Mailing city: Waldorf
Mailing state: MD
Mailing zip: 20603-4732
General Phone: (301) 893-9115
General Fax: (301) 645-5035
General/National Adv. E-mail: mburnett@apdi.net
Primary Website: www.apdi.net
Product or Service: Online Service Provider and Internet Hosts
Personnel: Mark Burnett (Pres./CEO)

AUTOMATED GRAPHIC SYSTEMS

Street address 1: 4590 Graphics Dr
Street address 3: White Plains
Street address state: MD
Zip/Postal code: 20695-3122
County: Charles
Country: USA
Mailing address: 4590 Graphics Dr
Mailing city: White Plains
Mailing state: MD
Mailing zip: 20695-3122
General Phone: (301) 843-1800
General Fax: (301) 843-6339
General/National Adv. E-mail: mike.donohue@rrd.com
Primary Website: www.ags.com
Product or Service: CD-ROM Designer/Manufacturer
Personnel: Mike Donohue (Pres.); Mike Akers (Sr. Acct. Exec.)

MICHIGAN

PROQUEST DIALOG

Street address 1: 789 E Eisenhower Pkwy
Street address 3: Ann Arbor
Street address state: MI
Zip/Postal code: 48108-3218
County: Washtenaw
Country: USA
Mailing state: MI
General/National Adv. E-mail: customer@dialog.com
Primary Website: proquest.com/go/pqd
Product or Service: Consultants`Other Services`Research

ADITYA BIRLA MINACS

Street address 1: 34115 W 12 Mile Rd
Street address 3: Farmington Hills
Street address state: MI
Zip/Postal code: 48331-3368
County: Oakland
Country: USA
Mailing address: 34115 W 12 Mile Rd
Mailing city: Farmington Hills
Mailing state: MI
Mailing zip: 48331-3368
General Phone: (248) 553-8355
General/National Adv. E-mail: info@minacs.adityabirla.com
Primary Website: www.minacs.adityabirla.com
Product or Service: Telecommunications/Service Bureaus
Personnel: Anil Bhalia (COO); Deepak Patel (CEO)

MORPACE INTERNATIONAL

Street address 1: 31700 Middlebelt Rd
Street address 2: Ste 200
Street address 3: Farmington Hills
Street address state: MI
Zip/Postal code: 48334-2375
County: Oakland
Country: USA
Mailing address: 31700 Middlebelt Rd Ste 200
Mailing city: Farmington Hills
Mailing state: MI
Mailing zip: 48334-2375
General Phone: (248) 737-5300
General Fax: (248) 737-5326
General/National Adv. E-mail: information@morpace.com
Primary Website: www.morpace.com
Product or Service: Consultants
Personnel: Jack McDonald (Pres.); Francis Ward (CEO)

NOVI

DENSO TEN AMERICA LIMITED

Street address 1: 30155 Hudson Dr.
Street address 3: Novi
Street address state: MI
Zip/Postal code: 48377
Country: USA
Mailing address: 30155 Hudson Dr.
Mailing city: Novi
Mailing state: MI
Mailing zip: 48377
General Phone: (734) 414-6620
General Fax: (734) 414-6660
General/National Adv. E-mail: info@lao.ten.fujitsu.com
Primary Website: www.denso-ten.com
Product or Service: Multimedia/Interactive Products
Personnel: Satoshi Iwata (President and Representative Director)

CIBER, INC.

Street address 1: 3270 West Big Beaver Road
Street address 3: Troy
Street address state: MI
Zip/Postal code: 48084
Country: USA
Mailing address: 3270 West Big Beaver Road
Mailing city: Troy
Mailing state: MI
Mailing zip: 48084
General Phone: (303) 220-0100
Primary Website: www.ciber.com
Product or Service: Consultants
Personnel: Madhava Reddy (Pres./CEO); Vicki Hickman (Sr. Vice Pres., Reg. Sales)

RANGER DATA TECHNOLOGIES INC.

Street address 1: 360 E Maple Rd
Street address 2: Ste X
Street address 3: Troy
Street address state: MI
Zip/Postal code: 48083-2707
County: Oakland
Country: USA
Mailing address: 360 E Maple Rd Ste X
Mailing city: Troy
Mailing state: MI
Mailing zip: 48083-2707
General Phone: (248) 336-7300
General Fax: (248) 336-8775
General/National Adv. E-mail: info@rangerdata.com
Primary Website: www.rangerdata.com
Year Established: 2001
Industry: Software: Advertising (Includes Display; Classified)
Product or Service: Hardware/Software Supplier
Personnel: George Willard (Sr. VP of Operations); Grace Shields (Director of Marketing & Customer Service); Dolores Gauthier (National Dir. of Sales & Marketing)

MINNESOTA

CONVERGEONE

Street address 1: 10900 Nesbitt Avenue South
Street address 3: Bloomington
Street address state: MN
Zip/Postal code: 55437
County: Hennepin
Country: USA
Mailing address: 10900 Nesbitt Avenue South
Mailing city: Bloomington
Mailing state: MN
Mailing zip: 55437
General Phone: (888) 321-6227
General/National Adv. E-mail: Econtactus@convergeone.com
Primary Website: www.convergeone.com
Product or Service: Telecommunications/Service Bureaus
Personnel: John A. Mckenna (Chairman & CEO); Jeffrey E. Nachbor (CFO); Scott Clark (Vice Pres., Mrkt.)

NEWSCYCLE SOLUTIONS

Street address 1: 7900 International Dr
Street address 2: Ste 800
Street address 3: Bloomington
Street address state: MN
Zip/Postal code: 55425-1581
County: Hennepin
Country: USA
Mailing address: 7900 International Drive Suite 800
Mailing city: Bloomington
Mailing state: MN
Mailing zip: 55425
General Phone: 651-639-0662
General/National Adv. E-mail: info@newscycle.com
Primary Website: www.newscycle.com
Industry: Software: Advertising (Includes Display; Classified); Software: Circulation; Software: Design/Graphics; Software: Editorial; Software: Pagination/Layout;

Product or Service: Circulation`Consultants`Editorial`Hardware/Software Supplier`Multimedia/Interactive Products`Online Service Provider and Internet Hosts`Publisher/Media
Note: Newscycle Solutions, which was formed by the combination of DTI, SAXOTECH, Atex AdBase and MediaSpan, delivers the most complete range of software solutions for the global news media industry, including news content management, advertising, circulation, audience, and analytics. Newscycle is a trusted technology partner serving more than 1,200 media companies with 8,000 properties across more than 30 countries on six continents. The company is headquartered in Bloomington, MN and has U.S. offices in Florida, Michigan and Utah; with international offices in Australia, Canada, Denmark, Germany, Malaysia, Norway, Sweden, and the United Kingdom. For more information, go to: http://www.newscycle.com.
Personnel: Paul Mrozinski (Sales Director); John Pukas (VP., Business Relations); Steve Moon (Rgl. Sales Dir.); Marc Thompson (Rgl. Sales Dir.); Lisa Speth (Marketing Communications Mgr.); Bryan Hooley (Asia-Pacific Bus. Mgr.); Ken Freedman (Vice President of Market Development); Pete Marsh (Vice President of Marketing); Julie Maas (Sales Director); Chris McKee (Sales Director); Mike McLaughlin (Sales Director); Geoff Kehrer (Sales Engineer); Robert Bohlin (Executive Sales Director, EMEA)

NICOLLET TECHNOLOGIES

Street address 1: 7901 12th Ave S
Street address 3: Bloomington
Street address state: MN
Zip/Postal code: 55425-1017
County: Hennepin
Country: USA
Mailing address: 7901 12th Ave S
Mailing city: Bloomington
Mailing state: MN
Mailing zip: 55425-1017
General Phone: (952) 854-3336
General Fax: (952) 854-5774
General/National Adv. E-mail: info@nicollet.com
Primary Website: www.nicollet.com
Product or Service: Telecommunications/Service Bureaus
Personnel: Marco Scibora (Pres.)

LAKEVILLE

BUZZ360 LLC

Street address 1: 17728 Kingsway Path
Street address 2: # 120
Street address 3: Lakeville
Street address state: MN
Zip/Postal code: 55044-5208
County: Dakota
Country: USA
Mailing address: 17728 Kingsway Path #120
Mailing city: Lakeville
Mailing state: MN
Mailing zip: 55044
General Phone: (612) 567 0396
Advertising Phone: 952-500 9878
General/National Adv. E-mail: info@buzz360.co
Primary Website: www.buzz360.co
Year Established: 2011
Industry: Internet Software
Product or Service: Marketing
Note: A new world of Partner Marketing

INTERALIA COMMUNICATIONS

Street address 1: 701 24th Ave SE
Street address 3: Minneapolis
Street address state: MN
Zip/Postal code: 55414-2691
County: Hennepin
Country: USA
Mailing address: 701 24th Ave SE
Mailing city: Minneapolis
Mailing state: MN
Mailing zip: 55414-2691
General Phone: (952) 942-6088
General Fax: (952) 942-6172
General/National Adv. E-mail: info@interalia.com
Primary Website: www.interalia.com
Product or Service: Telecommunications/Service Bureaus
Personnel: Mary Mcracken (Bus. Admin. Assoc.)

NEW BRIGHTON

RISDALL MARKETING GROUP

Street address 1: 550 Main St
Street address 2: Ste 100
Street address 3: New Brighton
Street address state: MN
Zip/Postal code: 55112-3272
County: Ramsey
Country: USA
Mailing address: 550 Main St Ste 100
Mailing city: New Brighton
Mailing state: MN
Mailing zip: 55112-3272
General Phone: (651) 286-6700
General Fax: (651) 631-2561
General/National Adv. E-mail: info@risdall.com
Primary Website: www.risdall.com
Year Established: 1971
Product or Service: Advertising/Marketing Agency`Graphic/Design Firm`Marketing
Personnel: John Risdall (Chrmn./CEO); Ted Risdall (Chrmn./Pres.); Joel Koenigs (Vice Pres./Dir. Web Dev.)

SOUTH ST PAUL

GOLDEN GATE ENTERPRISES, LLC

Street address 1: 490 Villaume Ave
Street address 3: South St Paul
Street address state: MN
Zip/Postal code: 55075-2443
Country: USA
Mailing address: 490 Villaume Ave
Mailing city: South Saint Paul
Mailing state: MN
Mailing zip: 55075-2443
General Phone: (651) 450-1000
General Fax: (651) 493-0372
General/National Adv. E-mail: info@ggedigital.com
Primary Website: http://www.ggedigital.com
Product or Service: Multimedia/Interactive Products
Personnel: Marco Scibora (Pres./CEO)

MISSOURI

BRIDGETON

TELEPHONE DOCTOR CUSTOMER SERVICE TRAINING

Street address 1: 30 Hollenberg Ct
Street address 3: Bridgeton
Street address state: MO
Zip/Postal code: 63044-2454
County: Saint Louis
Country: USA
Mailing address: 30 Hollenberg Ct
Mailing city: Hazelwood
Mailing state: MO
Mailing zip: 63044-2454
General Phone: (314) 291-1012
General Fax: (314) 291-3710
General/National Adv. E-mail: info@telephonedoctor.com
Primary Website: www.telephonedoctor.com
Product or Service: Online Service Provider and Internet Hosts
Personnel: Nancy Friedman (Pres.); David Friedman (Gen. Mgr./Vice Pres.)

NICHOLSON KOVAC, INC.

Street address 1: 600 Broadway Blvd
Street address 3: Kansas City
Street address state: MO
Zip/Postal code: 64105-1536
County: Jackson
Country: USA
Mailing address: 600 Broadway Blvd Ste 500
Mailing city: Kansas City
Mailing state: MO
Mailing zip: 64105-1543
General Phone: (816) 842-8881
General Fax: (816) 842-6340
General/National Adv. E-mail: nk@nicholsonkovac.com
Primary Website: www.nicholsonkovac.com
Year Established: 1981
Product or Service: Advertising/Marketing Agency

UNITED MEDIA

Street address 1: 1130 Walnut St
Street address 3: Kansas City
Street address state: MO
Zip/Postal code: 64106-2109
County: Jackson
Country: USA
Mailing address: 1130 Walnut St
Mailing city: Kansas City
Mailing state: MO
Mailing zip: 64106-2109
General Phone: (816) 581-7340
General Fax: (816) 581-7346
General/National Adv. E-mail: salesdirector@amuniversal.com
Primary Website: www.universaluclick.com
Product or Service: Publisher/Media
Personnel: Kerry Slagle (Pres.)

RAYTOWN

USA 800, INC.

Street address 1: 9808 E 66th Ter
Street address 3: Raytown
Street address state: MO
Zip/Postal code: 64133-5850
County: Jackson
Country: USA
Mailing address: 9808 E 66th Ter
Mailing city: Raytown
Mailing state: MO
Mailing zip: 64133-5850
General Phone: (816) 358-1303
General Fax: (816) 358-8845
General/National Adv. E-mail: tdavis@usa-800.com
Primary Website: www.usa800.com
Product or Service: Telecommunications/Service Bureaus
Personnel: Tom Davis (Pres./CEO); Dan Quigley (Exec. Vice Pres./CFO); Mike Langel (Vice Pres./Dir., Techn.)

ARCH COMMUNICATIONS, INC.

Street address 1: 1327 Hampton Ave
Street address 3: Saint Louis
Street address state: MO
Zip/Postal code: 63139-3113
County: Saint Louis City
Country: USA
Mailing address: 1327 Hampton Ave
Mailing city: Saint Louis
Mailing state: MO
Mailing zip: 63139-3113
General Phone: (314) 645-8000
General Fax: (314) 645-8100
General/National Adv. E-mail: info@archcom.net
Primary Website: www.archcom.net
Product or Service: Telecommunications/Service Bureaus
Personnel: David Brandstetter (Pres.)

CYBERCON.COM

Street address 1: 210 N Tucker Blvd
Street address 2: Fl 7
Street address 3: Saint Louis
Street address state: MO
Zip/Postal code: 63101-1941
County: Saint Louis City
Country: USA
Mailing address: 210 N Tucker Blvd Fl 7
Mailing city: Saint Louis
Mailing state: MO
Mailing zip: 63101-1978
General Phone: (314) 621-9991
General Fax: (314) 241-1777
General/National Adv. E-mail: staff@cybercon.com
Primary Website: www.cybercon.com
Product or Service: Online Service Provider and Internet Hosts
Personnel: Joshua Chen (Pres.)

TALX CORP.

Street address 1: 11432 Lackland Rd
Street address 3: Saint Louis
Street address state: MO
Zip/Postal code: 63146-3516
County: Saint Louis
Country: USA
Mailing address: 11432 Lackland Rd
Mailing city: Saint Louis
Mailing state: MO
Mailing zip: 63146-3516
General Phone: (314) 214-7000
General Fax: (314) 214-7588
General/National Adv. E-mail: moreinfo@talx.com
Primary Website: www.talx.com
Year Established: 1973
Industry: Speech Recognition
Product or Service: Telecommunications/Service Bureaus
Personnel: William Canfield (CEO); Michael Smith (Vice Pres., Market Devel.)

NORTH CAROLINA

CHAPEL HILL

B-LINKED, INC.

Street address 1: PO Box 3721
Street address 3: Chapel Hill
Street address state: NC
Zip/Postal code: 27515-3721
County: Orange
Country: USA
Mailing address: PO Box 3721
Mailing city: Chapel Hill
Mailing state: NC
Mailing zip: 27515-3721
General Phone: (919) 883-5362
General/National Adv. E-mail: tmelet@b-linked.com
Primary Website: www.adtransit.com
Year Established: 1995
Product or Service: Online Service Provider and Internet Hosts
Personnel: Todd Melet (President); Michael-Anne Ashman (VP of Technology)

DAVIDSON

TRADEWINDS PUBLISHING

Street address 1: 6695 Fox Ridge Cir
Street address 3: Davidson
Street address state: NC
Zip/Postal code: 28036-8090
County: Cabarrus
Country: USA
Mailing address: 6695 Fox Ridge Cir
Mailing city: Davidson
Mailing state: NC
Mailing zip: 28036-8090
General Phone: (704) 896-9978
General Fax: (615) 841-3288
General/National Adv. E-mail: wgray01@wgray.com
Primary Website: www.wgray.com
Year Established: 1958
Delivery Methods: Mail
Own Printing Facility: Y
Commercial printers: N
Product or Service: Publisher/Media
Personnel: Bill Gray (Ed.)

RALEIGH

MCCLATCHY INTERACTIVE

Street address 1: 1100 Situs Ct
Street address 3: Raleigh
Street address state: NC
Zip/Postal code: 27606-5446
County: Wake
Country: USA

Mailing address: 1100 Situs Ct Ste 100
Mailing city: Raleigh
Mailing state: NC
Mailing zip: 27606-4295
General Phone: (919) 861-1200
General Fax: (919) 861-1300
General/National Adv. E-mail: jcalloway@mcclatchyinteractive.com
Primary Website: www.mcclatchyinteractive.com
Product or Service: Publisher/Media
Personnel: Christian A. Hendricks (Vice Pres.); Fraser Van Asch (Exec. Vice Pres./Gen. Mgr.); James Calloway (Vice President Strategic Development); Kathy Lehmen (Product Management Director); Damon Kiesow (Senior Manager Mobile Initiatives)

RESEARCH TRIANGLE PARK

NORTEL NETWORKS, INC.

Street address 1: 4001 Chapel Hill Nelson Hwy
Street address 3: Research Triangle Park
Street address state: NC
Zip/Postal code: 27709-0158
County: Durham
Country: USA
Mailing address: 4001 Chapel Hill Nelson Hwy
Mailing city: Research Triangle Park
Mailing state: NC
Mailing zip: 27709-0019
General Phone: (905) 863-7000
General Fax: (905) 238-7350
General/National Adv. E-mail: NortelMediaRelations@nortel.com
Primary Website: www.nortel.com
Product or Service: Telecommunications/Service Bureaus

NEBRASKA

COMMGRAPHICS INTERACTIVE, INC.

Street address 1: 9259 Pioneer Ct
Street address 3: Lincoln
Street address state: NE
Zip/Postal code: 68520-9307
County: Lancaster
Country: USA
Mailing address: 9259 Pioneer Ct
Mailing city: Lincoln
Mailing state: NE
Mailing zip: 68520-9307
General Phone: (402) 432-1450
General/National Adv. E-mail: nwineman@commgraphics.com
Product or Service: Multimedia/Interactive Products
Personnel: Neil Wineman (New Bus. Dir.)

SANDHILLS PUBLISHING

Street address 1: 120 W. Harvest Dr.
Street address 3: Lincoln
Street address state: NE
Zip/Postal code: 68521-4408
County: Lancaster
Country: USA
Mailing address: PO Box 82545
Mailing city: Lincoln
Mailing state: NE
Mailing zip: 68501-5310
General Phone: (402) 479-2181
General Fax: (402) 479-2195
General/National Adv. E-mail: feedback@sandhills.com
Primary Website: www.sandhills.com
Product or Service: Publisher/Media
Personnel: Thomas J. Peed (Pres.); Mark Peery (Coord./Mgr.)

FIRST DATA VOICE SERVICES

Street address 1: 10910 Mill Valley Rd
Street address 3: Omaha
Street address state: NE
Zip/Postal code: 68154-3930
County: Douglas
Country: USA
Mailing address: 10910 Mill Valley Rd
Mailing city: Omaha
Mailing state: NE
Mailing zip: 68154-3930
General Phone: (402) 777-2100
General Fax: (402) 222-7910
General/National Adv. E-mail: fdvsinfo@firstdata.com
Primary Website: www.callit.com/FDVSSite/contact.aspx
Product or Service: Telecommunications/Service Bureaus
Personnel: James Harvey (Vice Pres., Devel.); Bob Van Stry (Vice Pres., Sales)

WESSAN INTERACTIVE

Street address 1: 15022 Chalco Pointe Cir
Street address 3: Omaha
Street address state: NE
Zip/Postal code: 68138
County: Douglas
Country: USA
Mailing address: 15022 Chalco Pointe Cir
Mailing city: Omaha
Mailing state: NE
Mailing zip: 68138
General Phone: (800) 468-7800 x405
General/National Adv. E-mail: kschaaf@wessan.com
Primary Website: www.wessan.com
Product or Service: Consultants`Multimedia/Interactive Products`Other Services`Online Service Provider and Internet Hosts`Telecommunications/Service Bureaus
Personnel: Kevin Schaaf (VP Sales & Marketing); Mike Kepler (Sales Associate)

WEST INTERACTIVE CORP.

Street address 1: 11650 Miracle Hills Dr
Street address 3: Omaha
Street address state: NE
Zip/Postal code: 68154-4448
County: Douglas
Country: USA
Mailing address: 11650 Miracle Hills Dr
Mailing city: Omaha
Mailing state: NE
Mailing zip: 68154-4448
General Phone: (402) 963-1300
General Fax: (402) 963-1602
General/National Adv. E-mail: sales@west.com
Primary Website: www.westinteractive.com
Product or Service: Multimedia/Interactive Products
Personnel: Nancee Berger (Pres.); Mack McKenzie (Vice Pres., Sales/Mktg.)

NEW HAMPSHIRE

NEWPORT

EN TECHNOLOGY CORP.

Street address 1: 322 N Main St
Street address 3: Newport
Street address state: NH
Zip/Postal code: 03773-1496
County: Sullivan
Country: USA
Mailing address: PO Box 505
Mailing city: Marlow
Mailing state: NH
Mailing zip: 03456-0505
General Phone: (603) 863-8102
General Fax: (603) 863-7316
General/National Adv. E-mail: sales@entechnology.com
Primary Website: www.entechnology.com
Product or Service: Telecommunications/Service Bureaus
Personnel: David Hall (Chrmn. of the Bd.); Patricia Gallup (Pres.); Matt Cookson (Opns. Mgr.)

NEW JERSEY

BERNARDSVILLE

CYBERSMART

Street address 1: 201 Lloyd Rd
Street address 3: Bernardsville
Street address state: NJ
Zip/Postal code: 07924-1711
County: Somerset
Country: USA
Mailing address: 201 Lloyd Rd
Mailing city: Bernardsville
Mailing state: NJ
Mailing zip: 07924-1711
General Phone: (908) 221-1516
General Fax: (908) 221-0617
General/National Adv. E-mail: information@cybersmart.org
Primary Website: www.cybersmart.org
Product or Service: Multimedia/Interactive Products
Personnel: Jim Teicher (Exec. Dir.); Mala Bawer (Exec. Dir.)

BOONTON

INTERACTIVE MEDIA ASSOCIATES

Street address 1: 612 Main St
Street address 3: Boonton
Street address state: NJ
Zip/Postal code: 07005-1761
County: Morris
Country: USA
Mailing address: 612 Main St
Mailing city: Boonton
Mailing state: NJ
Mailing zip: 07005-1761
General Phone: (973) 539-5255
General Fax: (973) 917-4730
Advertising Phone: (973) 539-5255
General/National Adv. E-mail: info@imedianinc.com
Primary Website: www.imediainc.com
Product or Service: Consultants
Personnel: Len Muscarella (Founder); Sally Muscarella (Pres.); Michelle Camaron (Vice Pres./Creative Dir.); Anthony Zarro (Vice Pres., Bus. Devel.); Brian McGovern (Dir., Devel.); Geri Ricciani (Dir., Pjct. Mgmt.)

LOGICAL DESIGN SOLUTIONS, INC.

Street address 1: 200 Park Ave
Street address 2: Ste 210
Street address 3: Florham Park
Street address state: NJ
Zip/Postal code: 07932-1026
County: Morris
Country: USA
Mailing address: 200 Park Ave Ste 210
Mailing city: Florham Park
Mailing state: NJ
Mailing zip: 07932-1026
General Phone: (973) 210-6300
General Fax: (973) 971-0103
General/National Adv. E-mail: info@lds.com
Primary Website: www.lds.com
Product or Service: Multimedia/Interactive Products
Personnel: Mimi Brooks (Pres./CEO); E. Bruce Lovenberg (CFO); Mauricio Barberi (Sr. Vice Pres., Bus. Devel.); Ken Kuhl (Vice Pres., Pjct. Mgmt.); Marty Burns (Vice Pres., Techn.); John Fee (Vice Pres., Sales); Kevin Casey (Vice Pres., Mktg.); Eric Dalessio (Vice Pres., Client Servs.); Gary Sikorski (Vice Pres., Opns.)

HOLDCOM

Street address 1: 955 Lincoln Ave
Street address 3: Glen Rock
Street address state: NJ
Zip/Postal code: 07452-3226
County: Bergen
Country: USA
Mailing address: 955 Lincoln Ave
Mailing city: Glen Rock
Mailing state: NJ
Mailing zip: 07452-3226
General Phone: (201) 444-6488
General Fax: (201) 445-4653
General/National Adv. E-mail: info@holdcom.com
Primary Website: www.holdcom.com
Product or Service: Advertising/Marketing Agency
Personnel: Neil Fishman (Pres.); Harvey Edelman (CEO)

HAMILTON

VOXWARE, INC.

Street address 1: 3705 Quakerbridge Road
Street address 2: Suite 210
Street address 3: Hamilton
Street address state: NJ
Zip/Postal code: 08619
Country: USA
Mailing address: 3705 Quakerbridge Road, Suite 210
Mailing city: Hamilton
Mailing state: NJ
Mailing zip: 08619
General Phone: (609) 570-6800
General/National Adv. E-mail: support@voxware.com
Primary Website: www.voxware.com
Product or Service: Hardware/Software Supplier
Personnel: Charlie Rafferdy (Vice Pres., Sales/Bus. Devel.)

HOPEWELL

DANA COMMUNICATIONS

Street address 1: 2 E Broad St
Street address 3: Hopewell
Street address state: NJ
Zip/Postal code: 08525-1810
County: Mercer
Country: USA
Mailing address: 2 E Broad St
Mailing city: Hopewell
Mailing state: NJ
Mailing zip: 08525-1899
General Phone: (609) 466-9187
General Fax: (609) 466-0285
General/National Adv. E-mail: bprewitt@danacommunications.com
Primary Website: www.danacommunications.com
Product or Service: Advertising/Marketing Agency

DESKNET, INC.

Street address 1: 10 Exchange Pl
Street address 2: Fl 20
Street address 3: Jersey City
Street address state: NJ
Zip/Postal code: 07302-3918
County: Hudson
Country: USA
Mailing address: 10 Exchange Pl Ste 2040
Mailing city: Jersey City
Mailing state: NJ
Mailing zip: 07302-3935
General Phone: (201) 946-7080
General/National Adv. E-mail: sales@desknetinc.com
Primary Website: www.desknetinc.com
Product or Service: Consultants
Personnel: Michael Fitzsimons (Co-CEO)

LIVINGSTON

PROJECTS IN KNOWLEDGE, INC.

Street address 1: 290 W Mt Pleasant Ave
Street address 2: Ste 2350
Street address 3: Livingston
Street address state: NJ
Zip/Postal code: 07039-2763
County: Essex
Country: USA
Mailing address: 290 W Mt Pleasant Ave Ste 2350
Mailing city: Livingston
Mailing state: NJ
Mailing zip: 07039-2763
General Phone: (973) 890-8988
General Fax: (973) 890-8866
General/National Adv. E-mail: rstern@projectsinknowledge.com
Primary Website: www.projectsinknowledge.com

Product or Service: Multimedia/Interactive Products
Personnel: Robert Stern (Pres.); Patricia Peterson (Sr. Vice Pres.); Susan Hostetler (Sr. Vice Pres.); Adrian Holmes (Vice Pres., Design Servs.)

MAYWOOD

KEN PETRETTI PRODUCTIONS, LLC

Street address 1: 33 Parkway
Street address 3: Maywood
Street address state: NJ
Zip/Postal code: 07607-1556
County: Bergen
Country: USA
Mailing address: 33 Parkway
Mailing city: Maywood
Mailing state: NJ
Mailing zip: 07607-1556
General Phone: (201) 368-2296
General Fax: (201) 368-1489
General/National Adv. E-mail: ken@kenpetretti.com
Primary Website: www.kenpetretti.com
Year Established: 1991
Product or Service: Advertising/Marketing Agency`CD-ROM Designer/Manufacturer`Consultants`Graphic/Design Firm`Multimedia/Interactive Products`Online Service Provider and Internet Hosts`POP/Kiosk Designer`Publisher/Media`Web Site Auditor
Personnel: Ken Petretti (Producer)

MONMOUTH JUNCTION

DOW JONES INTERACTIVE PUBLISHING

Street address 1: RR 1 Box 4300
Street address 3: Monmouth Junction
Street address state: NJ
Zip/Postal code: 08852-9801
County: Middlesex
Country: USA
Mailing address: PO Box 300
Mailing city: Princeton
Mailing state: NJ
Mailing zip: 08543-0300
General Phone: (609) 520-4000
General Fax: (609) 520-4662
General/National Adv. E-mail: marianne.krafinski@dowjones.com
Primary Website: www.dowjones.com
Product or Service: Multimedia/Interactive Products
Personnel: Les Hinton (CEO)

ASBURY PARK PRESS

Street address 1: 3600 Hwy 66
Street address 3: Neptune
Street address state: NJ
Zip/Postal code: 7754-
County: Monmouth
Country: USA
Mailing address: PO Box 1550
Mailing city: Neptune
Mailing state: NJ
Mailing zip: 07754-1550
General Phone: (732) 922-6000
Primary Website: www.app.com
Product or Service: Multimedia/Interactive Products`Publisher/Media
Personnel: Paul D'Ambrosio (Executive Editor)
Parent company (for newspapers): Gannett Co Inc.

PARAMUS

JABLONSKI DESIGN, INC.

Street address 1: 8 Daisy Way
Street address 2: Ste B
Street address 3: Paramus
Street address state: NJ
Zip/Postal code: 07652-4305
County: Bergen
Country: USA
Mailing address: 8 Daisy Way Ste B
Mailing city: Paramus
Mailing state: NJ
Mailing zip: 07652-4305
General Phone: (201) 843-0228
General/National Adv. E-mail: info@jablonskidesign.com
Primary Website: www.jablonskidesign.com
Product or Service: Graphic/Design Firm
Personnel: Carl Jablonski (Pres.)

DIALOGIC CORP.

Street address 1: 1515 State Rt 10
Street address 3: Parsippany
Street address state: NJ
Zip/Postal code: 07054-4538
County: Morris
Country: USA
Mailing address: 1515 State Rt 10 Ste 1
Mailing city: Parsippany
Mailing state: NJ
Mailing zip: 07054-4538
General Phone: (973) 967-6000
General Fax: (973) 967-6006
General/National Adv. E-mail: sales@dialogic.com
Primary Website: www.dialogic.com
Product or Service: Telecommunications/Service Bureaus
Personnel: Howard Bubb (Pres./CEO); Athena Mandros (Contact)

PLAINSBORO

CREATIVE DIRECT

Street address 1: 10 Schalks Crossing Rd
Street address 2: Ste 501
Street address 3: Plainsboro
Street address state: NJ
Zip/Postal code: 08536-1612
County: Middlesex
Country: USA
Mailing address: 10 Schalks Crossing Rd Ste 501
Mailing city: Plainsboro
Mailing state: NJ
Mailing zip: 08536-1612
General Phone: (908) 239-8965
Product or Service: Advertising/Marketing Agency

HOTWAX MULTIMEDIA, INC.

Street address 1: 16 Stoney Brook Ct
Street address 3: Ramsey
Street address state: NJ
Zip/Postal code: 07446-1456
County: Bergen
Country: USA
Mailing address: 16 Stoney Brook Ct
Mailing city: Ramsey
Mailing state: NJ
Mailing zip: 07446-1456
General Phone: (201) 818-0001
General/National Adv. E-mail: info@hotwax.com
Primary Website: www.hotwax.com
Year Established: 1988
Own Printing Facility: Y
Product or Service: Multimedia/Interactive Products
Personnel: David R. Huber (Owner)

CASCADE TECHNOLOGIES, INC.

Street address 1: 1075 Eastern Ave
Street address 3: Somerset
Street address state: NJ
Zip/Postal code: 8873-
County: Somerset
Country: USA
Mailing address: 1075 Eastern Ave.
Mailing city: Somerset
Mailing state: NJ
Mailing zip: 08873-2220
General Phone: (732) 560-9908
General Fax: (908) 626-1209
General/National Adv. E-mail: info@cascadetechnologies.com
Primary Website: www.cascadetechnologies.com
Product or Service: Telecommunications/Service Bureaus
Personnel: Vigdis Austad (Pres.); Frank Joicy (Vice Pres.-Technology); Barbara Bishop (Sales); Janice Harrison (Mktg. Assoc.)

TOMS RIVER

SPECIALTY SYSTEMS, INC.

Street address 1: 1451 Route 37 W
Street address 2: Ste 1
Street address 3: Toms River
Street address state: NJ
Zip/Postal code: 08755-4969
County: Ocean
Country: USA
Mailing address: 1451 Route 37 W Ste 1
Mailing city: Toms River
Mailing state: NJ
Mailing zip: 08755-4969
General Phone: (732) 341-1011
General Fax: (732) 341-0655
General/National Adv. E-mail: contact@specialtysystems.com
Primary Website: www.specialtysystems.com
Product or Service: Hardware/Software Supplier
Personnel: Bill Cabey (Vice Pres.)

NEW MEXICO

D & H INFORMATION SERVICES, INC.

Street address 1: 5720 Osuna Rd NE
Street address 3: Albuquerque
Street address state: NM
Zip/Postal code: 87109-2527
County: Bernalillo
Country: USA
Mailing address: 5720 Osuna Rd NE
Mailing city: Albuquerque
Mailing state: NM
Mailing zip: 87109-2527
General Phone: (505) 888-3620
General Fax: (505) 888-3722
General/National Adv. E-mail: dhinfo@dhinfo.com
Primary Website: www.dhinfo.com

NEVADA

CARSON CITY

COBBEY & ASSOCIATES FULL SERVICE MARKETING RESEARCH

Street address 1: PO Box 12
Street address 3: Carson City
Street address state: NV
Zip/Postal code: 89702-0012
County: Carson City
Country: USA
Mailing address: PO Box 12
Mailing city: Carson City
Mailing state: NV
Mailing zip: 89702-0012
General Phone: (877) 433-3242
General Fax: (775) 847-0327
General/National Adv. E-mail: cobbey@cobbey.com
Primary Website: www.cobbey.com
Product or Service: Consultants

RENO

RENO REAL ESTATE CONSULTING GROUP

Street address 1: PO Box 12598
Street address 3: Reno
Street address state: NV
Zip/Postal code: 89510-2598
County: Washoe
Country: USA
Mailing state: NV
Mailing zip: 89521
General Phone: (801) 599-3183
General Fax: (888) 771-7180
General/National Adv. E-mail: info@LivingInReno.com
Primary Website: www.LivingInReno.com
Product or Service: Consultants
Note: Real Estate Investments Residential & Commercial
Personnel: Frank Borghetti (Real Estate Consultant)

NEW YORK

AUDIO SERVICE AMERICA PRODUCTIONS / FREEHOLD DIVISION

Street address 1: 28 Ten Eyck Ave
Street address 3: Albany
Street address state: NY
Zip/Postal code: 12209-1518
County: Albany
Country: USA
Mailing address: 28 Ten Eyck Ave
Mailing city: Albany
Mailing state: NY
Mailing zip: 12209-1518
General Phone: (800) 723-4272
General/National Adv. E-mail: holdit@4asap.com
Primary Website: www.4asap.com
Year Established: 1977
Product or Service: Advertising/Marketing Agency`Consultants`Multimedia/Interactive Products
Note: Production Division: FreeHold Business Marketing Solutions
Personnel: Kevin Childs (Consultant); T. Raymond Gruno (Mktg. Dir.)

MEDIA LOGIC USA, LLC

Street address 1: 59 Wolf Rd
Street address 3: Albany
Street address state: NY
Zip/Postal code: 12205-2612
County: Albany
Country: USA
Mailing address: 59 Wolf Road
Mailing city: Albany
Mailing state: NY
Mailing zip: 12205
General Phone: (518) 456-3015
General Fax: (518) 456-4279
General/National Adv. E-mail: jmcdonald@medialogic.com
Primary Website: www.medialogic.com
Year Established: 1984
Product or Service: Advertising/Marketing Agency`Graphic/Design Firm`Marketing`Multimedia/Interactive Products
Personnel: Jim McDonald (New Business); David Schultz (Press Mgr.)

READMEDIA

Street address 1: 418 Broadway
Street address 3: Albany
Street address state: NY
Zip/Postal code: 12207-2922
County: Albany
Country: USA
Mailing address: PO Box 1262
Mailing city: Albany
Mailing state: NY
Mailing zip: 12201-1262
General Phone: (518) 429-2800
General Fax: (518) 429-2801
General/National Adv. E-mail: customerservice@eisinc.com
Primary Website: www.readmedia.com
Year Established: 1985
Product or Service: Other Services
Personnel: Colin Mathews (CEO/Pres.)

ARMONK

IBM CORP.

Street address 1: 1 New Orchard Rd
Street address 3: Armonk
Street address state: NY
Zip/Postal code: 10504-1722
County: Westchester

Country: USA
Mailing address: 6303 Barfield Rd
Mailing city: Atlanta
Mailing state: GA
Mailing zip: 30328-4233
General Phone: (404) 236-2600
General Fax: (404) 236-2626
Primary Website: www.ibm.com
Year Established: 1888
Product or Service: Hardware/Software Supplier
Personnel: Virginia Rometty (Chrmn./Pres./CEO); Michelle Browdy (Sr. Vice Pres./Legal & Reg. Affairs, & Gen. Counsel); James J. Kavanaugh (Sr. Vice Pres., CFO); Michelle Peluso (Sr. Vice Pres., Chief Marketing Officer); John E. Kelly III (Sr. Vice Pres., Dir. of Research)

BETHPAGE

CABLEVISION SYSTEMS CORPORATION

Street address 1: 1111 Stewart Ave
Street address 3: Bethpage
Street address state: NY
Zip/Postal code: 11714-3533
County: Nassau
Country: USA
Mailing address: 1111 Stewart Ave
Mailing city: Bethpage
Mailing state: NY
Mailing zip: 11714-3581
General Phone: (516) 803-2300
Primary Website: www.cablevision.com
Year Established: 1973
Product or Service: Telecommunications/Service Bureaus
Personnel: Charles F. Dolan (Chairman); James L. Dolan (President and CEO); Hank Ratner (Vice Chairman); David Ellen (Executive Vice President & General Counsel); Gregg Seibert (Vice Chairman & CFO); Tad Smith (President, Local Media); Wilt Hildenbrand (Sr. Advisor, Customer Care, Technology and Networks); Kristin Dolan (President, Optimum Services)

CYBER SALES ONE, INC.

Street address 1: PO Box 84
Street address 3: Bronxville
Street address state: NY
Zip/Postal code: 10708-0084
County: Westchester
Country: USA
Mailing address: PO Box 84
Mailing city: Bronxville
Mailing state: NY
Mailing zip: 10708-0084
General Phone: (917) 250-6074
General/National Adv. E-mail: albertcran@aol.com
Product or Service: Advertising/Marketing Agency
Personnel: Albert H. Crane (Pres./CEO)

AMPLIFY EDUCATION, INC.

Street address 1: 5 Washington St.
Street address 2: #800
Street address 3: Brooklyn
Street address state: NY
Zip/Postal code: 11201
County: Fulton
Country: USA
Mailing address: 5 Washington St., #800
Mailing city: Brooklyn
Mailing state: NY
Mailing zip: 11201
General Phone: (800) 823-1969
General/National Adv. E-mail: help@amplify.com
Primary Website: www.amplify.com
Product or Service: Multimedia/Interactive Products
Personnel: Larry Berger (CEO)

CALVERTON

MICRO PERFECT CORP.

Street address 1: PO Box 285
Street address 3: Calverton
Street address state: NY
Zip/Postal code: 11933-0285
County: Suffolk
Country: USA
Mailing address: PO Box 285
Mailing city: Calverton
Mailing state: NY
Mailing zip: 11933-0285
General Phone: (631) 727-9639
General Fax: (631) 727-9638
General/National Adv. E-mail: info@microperfect.com; perfect@microperfect.com
Primary Website: www.microperfect.com
Year Established: 1985
Product or Service: Hardware/Software Supplier
Personnel: Gregory Fischer (Mgr.)

CARMEL

JUDSON ROSEBUSH CO.

Street address 1: 15 China Circle Ct
Street address 3: Carmel
Street address state: NY
Zip/Postal code: 10512-4452
County: Putnam
Country: USA
Mailing address: 15 China Circle Court
Mailing city: Carmel
Mailing state: NY
Mailing zip: 10512
General Phone: (212) 581-3000
General/National Adv. E-mail: info@rosebush.com
Primary Website: www.rosebush.com
Year Established: 1986
Product or Service: Multimedia/Interactive Products
Personnel: Judson Rosebush (Pres.)

COHOES

INTERACTIVE PICTURES CORPORATION (IPIX)

Street address 1: 48 Western Ave
Street address 3: Cohoes
Street address state: NY
Zip/Postal code: 12047-3903
County: Albany
Country: USA
Mailing address: 48 Western Avenue
Mailing city: Cohoes
Mailing state: NY
Mailing zip: 12047
General Phone: (518) 235-3455
General/National Adv. E-mail: support@ipix.com
Primary Website: https://www.ipix.com
Product or Service: Multimedia/Interactive Products
Personnel: Mary Pam Claiborne (Contact)

GETZVILLE

VOICE TECHNOLOGIES GROUP, INC.

Street address 1: 2350 N Forest Rd
Street address 3: Getzville
Street address state: NY
Zip/Postal code: 14068-1296
County: Erie
Country: USA
Mailing address: 2350 N Forest Rd
Mailing city: Getzville
Mailing state: NY
Mailing zip: 14068-1296
General Phone: (716) 689-6700 ext. 255
General Fax: (716) 689-6800
General/National Adv. E-mail: info@vtg.com
Primary Website: www.vtg.com
Product or Service: Telecommunications/Service Bureaus
Personnel: Joseph Miller (Sales Dir.); Cathryn Apenowich (Mktg. Serv. Mgr.)

GLEN HEAD

FILESTREAM, INC.

Street address 1: PO Box 93
Street address 3: Glen Head
Street address state: NY
Zip/Postal code: 11545-0093
County: Nassau
Country: USA
Mailing address: PO Box 93
Mailing city: Glen Head
Mailing state: NY
Mailing zip: 11545-0093
General Phone: (516) 759-4100
General Fax: (516) 759-3011
General/National Adv. E-mail: info@filestream.com ; support@filestream.com; server@filestream.com; reseller@filestream.com
Display Adv. E-mail: sales@filestream.com
Editorial e-mail: presscontact@filestream.com
Primary Website: www.filestream.com
Product or Service: Hardware/Software Supplier
Personnel: Yao Chu (Chrmn./CEO)

ITHACA

IRON DESIGN

Street address 1: 120 N Aurora St
Street address 2: Ste 5A
Street address 3: Ithaca
Street address state: NY
Zip/Postal code: 14850-4337
County: Tompkins
Country: USA
Mailing address: 120 N Aurora St Ste 5A
Mailing city: Ithaca
Mailing state: NY
Mailing zip: 14850-4337
General Phone: (607) 275-9544
General Fax: (607) 275-0370
General/National Adv. E-mail: todd@irondesign.com
Primary Website: www.irondesign.com
Year Established: 1993
Product or Service: Graphic/Design Firm

LONG ISLAND CITY

COSMOS COMMUNICATIONS, INC.

Street address 1: 1105 44th Dr
Street address 3: Long Island City
Street address state: NY
Zip/Postal code: 11101-5107
County: Queens
Country: USA
Mailing address: 1105 44th Dr
Mailing city: Long Island City
Mailing state: NY
Mailing zip: 11101-7027
General Phone: (718) 482-1800
General Fax: (718) 482-1968
Primary Website: www.cosmoscommunications.com
Product or Service: Graphic/Design Firm
Personnel: Arnold Weiss (Pres.)

MACEDON

WOLFF/SMG

Street address 1: 1641 Commons Pkwy
Street address 3: Macedon
Street address state: NY
Zip/Postal code: 14502-9190
County: Wayne
Country: USA
Mailing address: 1641 Commons Pkwy
Mailing city: Macedon
Mailing state: NY
Mailing zip: 14502-9190
General Phone: (315) 986-1155
General Fax: (315) 986-1157
General/National Adv. E-mail: info@wolff-smg.com
Primary Website: www.wolff-smg.com
Year Established: 1935
Product or Service: Advertising/Marketing Agency`Consultants`Graphic/Design Firm`Multimedia/Interactive Products

MOUNT KISCO

LOGOPREMIUMS.COM

Street address 1: PO Box 295
Street address 3: Mount Kisco
Street address state: NY
Zip/Postal code: 10549-0295
County: Westchester
Country: USA
Mailing address: PO Box 295
Mailing city: Mount Kisco
Mailing state: NY
Mailing zip: 10549-0295
General Phone: (914) 244-0735
General Fax: (914) 244-1995
General/National Adv. E-mail: manager@logopremiums.com
Primary Website: www.logopremiums.com
Year Established: 1989
Product or Service: Advertising/Marketing Agency
Personnel: Jeff Levine (Project Mgr.)

24/7 REAL MEDIA, INC.

Street address 1: 132 W 31st St
Street address 2: Fl 9
Street address 3: New York
Street address state: NY
Zip/Postal code: 10001-3406
County: New York
Country: USA
Mailing address: 132 W 31st St Fl 9
Mailing city: New York
Mailing state: NY
Mailing zip: 10001-3406
General Phone: (212) 231-7100
General Fax: (646) 259-4200
General/National Adv. E-mail: info@xaxis.com
Primary Website: www.247realmedia.com
Year Established: 1995
Product or Service: Advertising/Marketing Agency

ADVANCE LOCAL

Street address 1: 1 World Trade Center
Street address 2: 40th Floor
Street address 3: New York
Street address state: NY
Zip/Postal code: 10007
County: Hudson
Country: USA
Mailing address: 1 World Trade Center
Mailing city: New York
Mailing state: NY
Mailing zip: 10007
General/National Adv. E-mail: advancelocalinfo@advance.net
Primary Website: www.advancelocal.com
Product or Service: Publisher/Media
Personnel: Randy Siegel (CEO); Caroline Harrison (Pres.)

ADVERTISING AGE

Street address 1: 711 3rd Ave
Street address 3: New York
Street address state: NY
Zip/Postal code: 10017-4014
County: New York
Country: USA
Mailing address: 711 3rd Ave Fl 3
Mailing city: New York
Mailing state: NY
Mailing zip: 10017-9214
General Phone: (212) 210-0100
General Fax: (212) 210-0200
General/National Adv. E-mail: editor@adage.com
Display Adv. E-mail: adv@adage.com
Primary Website: www.adage.com
Product or Service: Publisher/Media
Personnel: Allison Price Arden (Pub.)

AMERIKIDS USA

Street address 1: 10 Leonard St
Street address 2: Apt 3SW
Street address 3: New York
Street address state: NY
Zip/Postal code: 10013-2961
County: New York
Country: USA
Mailing address: 10 Leonard St Apt 3SW
Mailing city: New York
Mailing state: NY
Mailing zip: 10013-2961
General Phone: (212) 941-8461

General/National Adv. E-mail: developer@amerikids.com
Editorial e-mail: legal@amerikids.com
Primary Website: www.amerikids.com
Product or Service: Multimedia/Interactive Products
Note: We just launched Green Kids Media's Endanger Games http:// www.amerikids/com
Personnel: Lynn Rogoff (CEO); Mark Tabashnick (Media Producer)

ASSOCIATED PRESS INFORMATION SERVICES

Street address 1: 450 W 33rd St
Street address 3: New York
Street address state: NY
Zip/Postal code: 10001-2603
County: New York
Country: USA
Mailing address: 450 W 33rd St Fl 15
Mailing city: New York
Mailing state: NY
Mailing zip: 10001-2647
General Phone: (212) 621-1500
General Fax: (212) 621-7520
General/National Adv. E-mail: info@ap.org
Primary Website: www.ap.org
Product or Service: Publisher/Media
Personnel: Ted Mendelsohn (Dir. Sales)

BMC GROUP, INC.

Street address 1: 477 Madison Ave
Street address 2: Fl 6
Street address 3: New York
Street address state: NY
Zip/Postal code: 10022-5827
County: New York
Country: USA
Mailing address: 12 W 31st St Fl 2
Mailing city: New York
Mailing state: NY
Mailing zip: 10001-4415
General Phone: (212) 310-5900
General Fax: (212) 644-4552
Primary Website: www.bmcgroup.com
Product or Service: Hardware/Software Supplier
Personnel: Matt Morris (Sales Contact)

BUSINESS WIRE - NEW YORK, NY

Street address 1: 40 E 52nd St
Street address 2: Fl 14
Street address 3: New York
Street address state: NY
Zip/Postal code: 10022-5911
County: New York
Country: USA
Mailing address: 40 E 52nd St Fl 14
Mailing city: New York
Mailing state: NY
Mailing zip: 10022-5911
General Phone: (212) 752-9600
Primary Website: www.businesswire.com
Product or Service: Online Service Provider and Internet Hosts
Personnel: Geff Scott (CEO); Richard DeLeo (COO)

CARL WALTZER DIGITAL SERVICES, INC.

Street address 1: 873 Broadway
Street address 2: Ste 412
Street address 3: New York
Street address state: NY
Zip/Postal code: 10003-1234
County: New York
Country: USA
Mailing address: 873 Broadway Ste 412
Mailing city: New York
Mailing state: NY
Mailing zip: 10003-1234
General Phone: (212) 475-8748
General Fax: (212) 475-9359
General/National Adv. E-mail: wdigital@nyc.rr.com
Primary Website: www.waltzer.com
Product or Service: Telecommunications/Service Bureaus
Personnel: Carl Waltzer (Pres.); Bill Waltzer (Photographer)

COMTEX NEWS NETWORK

Street address 1: 295 Madison Avenue
Street address 2: 12th Floor
Street address 3: New York
Street address state: NY
Zip/Postal code: 10017⊠⊠‹
County: Alexandria City
Country: USA
Mailing address: 295 Madison Avenue, 12th Floor
Mailing city: New York
Mailing state: NY
Mailing zip: 10017⊠⊠‹
General Phone: (703) 797-8135
General Fax: (212) 688-6241
General/National Adv. E-mail: sales@comtex.com
Primary Website: www.comtex.com
Product or Service: Online Service Provider and Internet Hosts
Personnel: Kan Devnani (Pres. & CEO); Chip Brian (Chairman); Robert J. Lynch (Dir.)

DLS DESIGN

Street address 1: 232 Madison Ave
Street address 2: Rm 800
Street address 3: New York
Street address state: NY
Zip/Postal code: 10016-2940
County: New York
Country: USA
Mailing address: 232 Madison Ave Rm 800
Mailing city: New York
Mailing state: NY
Mailing zip: 10016-2901
General Phone: (212) 255-3464
General/National Adv. E-mail: info@dlsdesign.com
Primary Website: www.dlsdesign.com
Product or Service: Graphic/Design Firm
Personnel: David Schiffer (Pres.)

DOUBLECLICK

Street address 1: 111 8th Ave
Street address 2: Fl 10
Street address 3: New York
Street address state: NY
Zip/Postal code: 10011-5210
County: New York
Country: USA
Mailing address: 111 8th Ave Fl 10
Mailing city: New York
Mailing state: NY
Mailing zip: 10011-5210
General Phone: (212) 271-2542
General Fax: (212) 287-1203
General/National Adv. E-mail: publicrelations@doubleclick.net
Primary Website: www.doubleclick.com
Year Established: 1996
Product or Service: Advertising/Marketing Agency

ENIGMA

Street address 1: 245 Fifth Avenue
Street address 2: Floor 17
Street address 3: New York
Street address state: NY
Zip/Postal code: 10016
County: Norfolk
Country: USA
Mailing address: 245 Fifth Avenue, Floor 17
Mailing city: New York
Mailing state: NY
Mailing zip: 10016
General Phone: (800) 510-2856
General/National Adv. E-mail: press@enigma.com
Primary Website: www.enigma.com
Product or Service: Hardware/Software Supplier
Personnel: Hicham Oudghiri (CEO); Craig Danton (Vice Pres., Product)

EPSILON INTERACTIVE

Street address 1: 11 W 19th St
Street address 2: Fl 9
Street address 3: New York
Street address state: NY
Zip/Postal code: 10011-4275
County: New York
Country: USA
Mailing address: 11 W 19th St Fl 9
Mailing city: New York
Mailing state: NY
Mailing zip: 10011-4275
General Phone: (212) 457-7000
General Fax: (212) 457-7040
General/National Adv. E-mail: info@epsilon.com
Primary Website: www.epsilon.com
Year Established: 1997
Product or Service: Advertising/Marketing Agency

FUSEBOX, INC.

Street address 1: 36 W 20th St
Street address 2: Fl 11
Street address 3: New York
Street address state: NY
Zip/Postal code: 10011-4241
County: New York
Country: USA
Mailing address: 36 W 20th St Fl 11
Mailing city: New York
Mailing state: NY
Mailing zip: 10011-4241
General Phone: (212) 929-7644
General Fax: (212) 929-7947
General/National Adv. E-mail: info@fusebox.com
Primary Website: www.fusebox.com
Year Established: 1989
Product or Service: Graphic/Design Firm

G2 DIRECT & DIGITAL

Street address 1: 636 11th Ave
Street address 3: New York
Street address state: NY
Zip/Postal code: 10036-2005
County: New York
Country: USA
Mailing address: 636 11th Ave
Mailing city: New York
Mailing state: NY
Mailing zip: 10036-2005
General Phone: (212) 537-3700
General Fax: (212) 537-3737
General/National Adv. E-mail: steve.harding@geometry.com
Primary Website: www.g2.com
Year Established: 1979
Product or Service: Advertising/Marketing Agency

ICONNICHOLSON

Street address 1: 11 W 19th St
Street address 2: Fl 3
Street address 3: New York
Street address state: NY
Zip/Postal code: 10011-4280
County: New York
Country: USA
Mailing address: 295 Lafayette St
Mailing city: New York
Mailing state: NY
Mailing zip: 10012-2701
General Phone: (212) 274-0470
General Fax: (888) 847-5321
Primary Website: www.iconnicholson.com
Product or Service: Multimedia/Interactive Products
Personnel: Tom Nicholson (CEO)

IMAGE ZONE, INC.

Street address 1: 11 W 69th St
Street address 2: # 10
Street address 3: New York
Street address state: NY
Zip/Postal code: 10023-4720
County: New York
Country: USA
Mailing address: 11 W 69th St # 10
Mailing city: New York
Mailing state: NY
Mailing zip: 10023-4720
General Phone: (212) 924-8804
General/National Adv. E-mail: mail@imagezone.com
Primary Website: www.imagezone.com
Product or Service: Multimedia/Interactive Products
Personnel: Doug Ehrlich (MD); Peter Smallman (Creative Dir.)

INTERACTIVE EDUCATIONAL SYSTEMS DESIGN, INC.

Street address 1: 33 W 87th St
Street address 3: New York
Street address state: NY
Zip/Postal code: 10024-3082
County: New York
Country: USA
Mailing address: 33 W 87th St
Mailing city: New York
Mailing state: NY
Mailing zip: 10024-3082
General Phone: (631) 691-2606
General/National Adv. E-mail: iesdinc@aol.com
Primary Website: www.iesdinc.com
Product or Service: Consultants
Personnel: Ellen Bialo (Pres.); Jay Sivin Kachala (Vice Pres.)

INTERACTIVE INTERNATIONAL, INC.

Street address 1: 290 W End Ave
Street address 3: New York
Street address state: NY
Zip/Postal code: 10023-8106
County: New York
Country: USA
Mailing address: 290 W End Ave
Mailing city: New York
Mailing state: NY
Mailing zip: 10023-8106
General Phone: (212) 580-5015
General Fax: (212) 580-5017
Advertising Phone: 2125805015
Editorail Phone: 2125805015
General/National Adv. E-mail: ivie@erols.com
Display Adv. E-mail: ivie@erols.com
Editorial e-mail: ivie@erols.com
Primary Website: www.erols.com
Year Established: 1987
Area Served - City: 10023-8106
Product or Service: Hardware/Software Supplier
Personnel: George M. Bulow (Pres.)

KING FEATURES SYNDICATE

Street address 1: 300 W 57th St
Street address 2: Fl 41
Street address 3: New York
Street address state: NY
Zip/Postal code: 10019-3741
County: New York
Country: USA
Mailing address: 300 W 57th St
Mailing city: New York
Mailing state: NY
Mailing zip: 10019-5238
General Phone: (212) 969-7550
General Fax: (646) 280-1550
General/National Adv. E-mail: kfs-cartoonists@hearst.com
Primary Website: www.kingfeatures.com
Year Established: 1915
Product or Service: Publisher/Media
Personnel: Keith McCloat (VP., Gen. Mgr.); David Cohea (Gen. Mgr., King Feat. Weekly Service Inside Sales); Claudia Smith (Dir., PR); Jack Walsh (Sr. Sales Consultant/Printing & New England Newspaper Sales); Dennis Danko (Inside Sales Mgr.); Michael Mancino (Sales Mgr., New Media Inside Sales); John Killian (VP, Syndication Sales); Jim Clarke (Editorial Dir., King Feat. Weekly Service); Brendan Burford (Gen. Mgr., Syndication); Randy Noble (SE Sales); Diana Smith (Executive Editor); Evelyn Smith (Senior Comics Editor); Chris Richcreek (Senior Features Editor); Curtis Trammell (Western Region Sales); Robin Graham (International Sales Consultant); Monique Prioleau (Sales Coordinator); C.J. Kettler (President)

MARKE COMMUNICATIONS, INC.

Street address 1: 45 W 45th St
Street address 2: Fl 16
Street address 3: New York
Street address state: NY
Zip/Postal code: 10036-4602
County: New York
Country: USA
Mailing address: 45 W 45th St Fl 16

Mailing city: New York
Mailing state: NY
Mailing zip: 10036-4602
General Phone: (212) 201-0600
General Fax: (212) 213-0785
Primary Website: www.marke.com
Product or Service: Advertising/Marketing Agency

NIELSEN AUDIO

Street address 1: 85 Broad Street
Street address 3: New York
Street address state: NY
Zip/Postal code: 10004
County: New York
Country: USA
Mailing address: 85 Broad Street
Mailing city: New York
Mailing state: NY
Mailing zip: 10004
General Phone: (800) 543-7300
General/National Adv. E-mail: clientsupport@nielsen.com
Primary Website: www.nielsen.com/us/en/solutions/capabilities/audio.html
Product or Service: Telecommunications/Service Bureaus
Personnel: David Kenny (CEO); Dave Anderson (CFO); John Tavolieri (CTO)

NY INFORMATION TECHNOLOGY CENTER

Street address 1: 55 Broad St
Street address 2: Frnt 4
Street address 3: New York
Street address state: NY
Zip/Postal code: 10004-2565
County: New York
Country: USA
Mailing address: 55 Broad St Frnt 4
Mailing city: New York
Mailing state: NY
Mailing zip: 10004-2565
General Phone: (212) 482-0857
General Fax: (212) 482-0815
General/National Adv. E-mail: nyitc@55broadst.com
Primary Website: www.55broadst.com
Product or Service: Multimedia/Interactive Products
Personnel: William C. Rudin (Pres.); John J. Gilbert (COO/Exec. Vice Pres.); Jason Largever (Dir.-Info Serv.)

O & J DESIGN, INC.

Street address 1: 41 W 25th St
Street address 2: Fl 4
Street address 3: New York
Street address state: NY
Zip/Postal code: 10010-2085
County: New York
Country: USA
Mailing address: 41 W 25th St Fl 4
Mailing city: New York
Mailing state: NY
Mailing zip: 10010-2085
General Phone: (212) 242-1080
General Fax: (212) 242-1081
General/National Adv. E-mail: info@oandjdesign.com
Primary Website: www.oandjdesign.com
Year Established: 1984
Product or Service: Multimedia/Interactive Products

PEARSON, INC.

Street address 1: 330 Hudson St
Street address 3: New York
Street address state: NY
Zip/Postal code: 10013-1046
County: New York
Country: USA
Mailing address: 330 Hudson St
Mailing city: New York
Mailing state: NY
Mailing zip: 10013-1014
General Phone: (212) 641-2400
General/National Adv. E-mail: internationaleo@pearson.com
Primary Website: www.pearson.com
Product or Service: Multimedia/Interactive Products
Personnel: Sidney Taurel (Chairman); John Fallon (Chief Exec.); Coram Williams (CFO); Kevin Capitani (Pres.); Albert Hitchcock (CTO)

PENTON MEDIA

Street address 1: 1166 Avenue of the Americas
Street address 2: Fl 10
Street address 3: New York
Street address state: NY
Zip/Postal code: 10036-2750
County: New York
Country: USA
Mailing address: 1166 Avenue of the Americas Fl 10
Mailing city: New York
Mailing state: NY
Mailing zip: 10036-2743
General Phone: (212) 204-4200
General Fax: (212) 206-3622
General/National Adv. E-mail: CorporateCustomerService@penton.com
Primary Website: www.penton.com
Product or Service: Publisher/Media
Personnel: Eliane Kauck (Comm. Mgr.); Bev Walter (Sr. Customer Service Mgr.)

PR & MARKETING NEWS

Street address 1: 110 William St
Street address 2: Fl 11
Street address 3: New York
Street address state: NY
Zip/Postal code: 10038-3901
County: New York
Country: USA
Mailing address: 110 William St Fl 11
Mailing city: New York
Mailing state: NY
Mailing zip: 10038-3901
General Phone: (212) 621-4964
General/National Adv. E-mail: info@wrightsmedia.com
Primary Website: www.prandmarketing.com
Product or Service: Publisher/Media
Personnel: Diane Schwartz (Vice Pres./Pub.)

PR NEWSWIRE

Street address 1: 350 Hudson St
Street address 2: Ste 300
Street address 3: New York
Street address state: NY
Zip/Postal code: 10014-4504
County: New York
Country: USA
Mailing address: 350 Hudson St Ste 300
Mailing city: New York
Mailing state: NY
Mailing zip: 10014-5827
General Phone: 1.888-776-0942
General/National Adv. E-mail: MediaInquiries@prnewswire.com
Primary Website: www.prnewswire.com
Year Established: 1954
Product or Service: Multimedia/Interactive Products
Personnel: Christine Cube (Audience Relations Manager); Dave Haapaoja (SVP, Global Operations); Victoria Harres (VP, Strategic Communications & Content)

PRESS+

Street address 1: 25 W 52nd St
Street address 2: Fl 15
Street address 3: New York
Street address state: NY
Zip/Postal code: 10019-6104
County: New York
Country: USA
Mailing address: 25 W 52nd St Fl 15
Mailing city: New York
Mailing state: NY
Mailing zip: 10019-6104
General Phone: (212) 332-6405
General/National Adv. E-mail: info@mypressplus.com
Primary Website: www.mypressplus.com
Year Established: 2009
Product or Service: Consultants
Personnel: Steven Brill (Co-Founder); Gordon Crovitz (Co-Founder); Matt Skibinski; Leo Hindery (Co-Founder); Cindy Rosenthal (Director of Public Affairs)

RAPP

Street address 1: 437 Madison Ave
Street address 3: New York
Street address state: NY
Zip/Postal code: 10022-7001
County: New York
Country: USA
Mailing address: 437 Madison Ave Bsmt 1
Mailing city: New York
Mailing state: NY
Mailing zip: 10022-7043
General Phone: (212) 817-6800
General Fax: (212) 817-6750
General/National Adv. E-mail: social.rapp@rapp.com
Primary Website: www.rapp.com
Year Established: 1965
Product or Service: Advertising/Marketing Agency

REUTERS MEDIA

Street address 1: 3 Times Sq
Street address 3: New York
Street address state: NY
Zip/Postal code: 10036-6564
County: New York
Country: USA
Mailing address: 3 Times Sq
Mailing city: New York
Mailing state: NY
Mailing zip: 10036-6564
General Phone: (646) 223-4000
General Fax: (646) 223-4393
General/National Adv. E-mail: rosalina.thomas@thomsonreuters.com
Primary Website: www.reuters.com/newsagency
Product or Service: Multimedia/Interactive Products`Publisher/Media
Personnel: Ms. Rosalina Thomas (Vice Pres./Head of Sales - The Americas, Reuters News Agency, Thomson Reuters); Melissa Metzger (Publishing Solutions Specialist); Bipasha Ghosh (Global Director of Marketing)

TNS GLOBAL

Street address 1: 11 Madison Ave
Street address 2: Ste 1201
Street address 3: New York
Street address state: NY
Zip/Postal code: 10010-3624
County: New York
Country: USA
Mailing address: 11 Madison Ave Ste 1201
Mailing city: New York
Mailing state: NY
Mailing zip: 10010-3624
General Phone: (212) 991-6000
General/National Adv. E-mail: enquiries@tnsglobal.com
Primary Website: www.tnsglobal.com
Year Established: 1946
Industry: Consulting Services: Advertising; Consulting Services: Marketing; Market Research;
Product or Service: Advertising/Marketing Agency
Personnel: Leendert De Voogd (Sales Rep.); Mark Francas (Sales Rep.)

TRIBAL DDB

Street address 1: 437 Madison Ave
Street address 2: Fl 8
Street address 3: New York
Street address state: NY
Zip/Postal code: 10022-7046
County: New York
Country: USA
Mailing address: 437 Madison Ave Fl 8
Mailing city: New York
Mailing state: NY
Mailing zip: 10022-7046
General Phone: (212) 515-8321
General Fax: (212) 515-8660
Primary Website: www.tribalddb.com
Year Established: 1998
Product or Service: Advertising/Marketing Agency

TSANG SEYMOUR DESIGN, INC.

Street address 1: 526 W 26th St
Street address 2: Rm 708
Street address 3: New York
Street address state: NY
Zip/Postal code: 10001-5524
County: New York
Country: USA
Mailing address: 526 W 26th St Rm 708
Mailing city: New York
Mailing state: NY
Mailing zip: 10001-5524
General Phone: (212) 352-0063
General/National Adv. E-mail: info@tsangseymour.com
Primary Website: www.tsangseymour.com
Year Established: 1993
Product or Service: Graphic/Design Firm
Personnel: Patrick Seymour (Principal); Catarina Tsang (Principal)

TWO TWELVE

Street address 1: 902 Broadway
Street address 2: Fl 20
Street address 3: New York
Street address state: NY
Zip/Postal code: 10010-6002
County: New York
Country: USA
Mailing address: 902 Broadway Ste 2001
Mailing city: New York
Mailing state: NY
Mailing zip: 10010-6019
General Phone: (212) 254-6670
General Fax: (212) 254-6614
General/National Adv. E-mail: info@twotwelve.com
Primary Website: www.twotwelve.com
Year Established: 1980
Product or Service: Graphic/Design Firm
Personnel: David Gibson (Founder/Principal/Pres.); Ann Harakawa (Principal); Sarah Haun (CMO)

VERIZON COMMUNICATIONS, INC.

Street address 1: 1095 Avenue of the Americas
Street address 3: New York
Street address state: NY
Zip/Postal code: 10036-6797
County: New York
Country: USA
Mailing address: 1095 Avenue of the Americas
Mailing city: New York
Mailing state: NY
Mailing zip: 10036-6797
General Phone: (212) 395-1000
General Fax: (212) 719-3349
Primary Website: www.verizon.com
Product or Service: Telecommunications/Service Bureaus
Personnel: Hans Vestberg (Chrmn./CEO); Ronan Dunne (Vice Chrmn./Pres.); Matthew D. Ellis (CFO); James J. Gerace (Chief Communications Officer); Rose Stuckey Kirk (Chief Corporate Social Responsibility Officer); Kyle Malady (CTO)

VNU EMEDIA

Street address 1: 85 Broad St
Street address 3: New York
Street address state: NY
Zip/Postal code: 10004-2434
County: New York
Country: USA
Mailing address: 85 Broad St
Mailing city: New York
Mailing state: NY
Mailing zip: 10004-2434
General Phone: (646) 654-5550
General Fax: (646) 654-5584
General/National Adv. E-mail: corporatepressinquiries@nielsen.com
Primary Website: www.vnuemedia.com
Product or Service: Publisher/Media

Personnel: Toni Nevitt (Pres., eMedia/Information Mktg.); John Lerner (Vice Pres., eMedia); Christian Evans (Vice Pres., Technology); Eileen Long (Dir., Sales); Jeff Green (Nat'l Sales Dir.); Evan Ambinder (Bus. Devel. Mgr.)

WORLD INTERACTIVE NETWORK

Street address 1: 3960 Broadway
Street address 2: Fl 4
Street address 3: New York
Street address state: NY
Zip/Postal code: 10032-1543
County: New York
Country: USA
Mailing address: 3960 Broadway Fl 4
Mailing city: New York
Mailing state: NY
Mailing zip: 10032-1543
General Phone: (212) 740-4400
General Fax: (212) 795-8553
General/National Adv. E-mail: winnet@panix.com
Primary Website: www.winglobal.com
Product or Service: Multimedia/Interactive Products
Personnel: Claudia Soifer (Vice Pres./Gen. Mgr.); Charles David Padro (Exec. Producer, Multimedia)

NORTH BALDWIN

LIGHT FANTASTIC STUDIOS, INC.

Street address 1: 618 Portland Ave
Street address 3: North Baldwin
Street address state: NY
Zip/Postal code: 11510-2642
County: Nassau
Country: USA
Mailing address: 618 Portland Ave
Mailing city: North Baldwin
Mailing state: NY
Mailing zip: 11510-2642
General Phone: (212) 604-0666
General Fax: (212) 604-0666
General/National Adv. E-mail: info@lightfantasticstudios.com
Primary Website: www.lightfantasticstudios.com
Product or Service: Multimedia/Interactive Products
Personnel: Paul Hollett (Pres./Creative Dir.); Ray Rue (Art Dir.); Ranee Chong (Designer)

OLD CHATHAM

BLASS COMMUNICATIONS

Street address 1: 17 Drowne Rd
Street address 3: Old Chatham
Street address state: NY
Zip/Postal code: 12136-3006
County: Columbia
Country: USA
Mailing address: 17 Drowne Rd
Mailing city: Old Chatham
Mailing state: NY
Mailing zip: 12136-3006
General Phone: (518) 766-2222
General Fax: (518) 766-2445
General/National Adv. E-mail: info@blasscommunications.com
Primary Website: www.blasscommunications.com
Year Established: 1969
Product or Service: Advertising/Marketing Agency

PLAINVIEW

TADIRAN TELECOM, INC.

Street address 1: 265 Executive Dr
Street address 2: Ste 250
Street address 3: Plainview
Street address state: NY
Zip/Postal code: 11803-1743
County: Nassau
Country: USA
Mailing address: 265 Executive Dr Ste 250
Mailing city: Plainview
Mailing state: NY
Mailing zip: 11803-1743
General Phone: (516) 632-7200
General Fax: (516) 632-7210
Primary Website: www.tadirantele.com
Product or Service: Telecommunications/Service Bureaus
Personnel: David Sopko (CEO)

PLEASANTVILLE

THE CREATORS MEDIA GROUP

Street address 1: 2 Jackson St
Street address 3: Pleasantville
Street address state: NY
Zip/Postal code: 10570-3025
County: Westchester
Country: USA
Mailing address: 2 Jackson St
Mailing city: Pleasantville
Mailing state: NY
Mailing zip: 10570-3025
General Phone: (914) 769-0676
General Fax: (914) 769-0763
General/National Adv. E-mail: admin@creatorsmedia.com
Primary Website: www.creatorsmedia.com
Year Established: 1987
Product or Service: Multimedia/Interactive Products
Personnel: Anthony Trama (CEO)

BBS COMPUTING

Street address 1: 3400 W Ridge Rd
Street address 3: Rochester
Street address state: NY
Zip/Postal code: 14626
County: Monroe
Country: USA
Mailing address: 3400 W Ridge Rd
Mailing city: Rochester
Mailing state: NY
Mailing zip: 14626
General Phone: (585) 544-3669
Primary Website: www.bbscomputing.com
Product or Service: Online Service Provider and Internet Hosts
Personnel: Russell Frey (Pres.)

SAG HARBOR

UNET 2 CORPORATION

Street address 1: 84 Mount Misery Dr
Street address 3: Sag Harbor
Street address state: NY
Zip/Postal code: 11963-3922
County: Suffolk
Country: USA
Mailing address: 84 Mount Misery Drive
Mailing city: Sag Harbor
Mailing state: NY
Mailing zip: 11963
General Phone: (631) 725-9513
General Fax: (631) 725-9513
General/National Adv. E-mail: JMonaco@UNET2.net
Primary Website: www.UNET2.net
Year Established: 1992
Product or Service: Editorial`Multimedia/Interactive Products`Online Service Provider and Internet Hosts`Publisher/Media
Personnel: James Monaco (Pres.)

TUCKAHOE

CAMPUS GROUP COMPANIES

Street address 1: 42 Oak Ave
Street address 3: Tuckahoe
Street address state: NY
Zip/Postal code: 10707-4025
County: Westchester
Country: USA
Mailing address: 42 Oak Ave
Mailing city: Tuckahoe
Mailing state: NY
Mailing zip: 10707-4025
General Phone: (914) 395-1010
General/National Adv. E-mail: sales@campusgroup.com
Primary Website: www.campusgroup.com
Product or Service: Telecommunications/Service Bureaus
Personnel: Steve Campus (Owner)

VOLT INFORMATION SCIENCES

Street address 1: 50 Charles Lindbergh Blvd.
Street address 2: Ste. 206
Street address 3: Uniondale
Street address state: NY
Zip/Postal code: 11553
Country: USA
Mailing address: 50 Charles Lindbergh Blvd., Ste. 206
Mailing city: Uniondale
Mailing state: NY
Mailing zip: 11553
General Phone: (212) 704-2400
General Fax: (212) 704-2413
General/National Adv. E-mail: voltinvest@volt.com
Primary Website: www.volt.com
Product or Service: Multimedia/Interactive Products
Personnel: Linda Perneau (Pres. & CEO); Paul Tomkins (Sr. Vice Pres./CFO); Lori Schultz (COO)

BLACK STAR PUBLISHING CO., INC.

Street address 1: 333 Mamaroneck Ave
Street address 2: # 175
Street address 3: White Plains
Street address state: NY
Zip/Postal code: 10605-1440
County: Westchester
Country: USA
Mailing address: 333 Mamaroneck Ave # 175
Mailing city: White Plains
Mailing state: NY
Mailing zip: 10605-1440
General Phone: (212) 679-3288
General/National Adv. E-mail: sales@blackstar.com
Primary Website: www.blackstar.com
Product or Service: Advertising/Marketing Agency
Personnel: Ben Chapnick (Pres.); John P. Chapnick (Vice Pres.)

OHIO

AKRON

HITCHCOCK FLEMING AND ASSOCIATES, INC.

Street address 1: 500 Wolf Ledges Pkwy
Street address 3: Akron
Street address state: OH
Zip/Postal code: 44311-1022
County: Summit
Country: USA
Mailing address: 500 Wolf Ledges Pkwy
Mailing city: Akron
Mailing state: OH
Mailing zip: 44311-1080
General Phone: (330) 376-2111
General Fax: (330) 376-2808
General/National Adv. E-mail: jdeleo@teamhfa.com
Primary Website: www.teamhfa.com
Year Established: 1940
Product or Service: Advertising/Marketing Agency

CELEBRO

Street address 1: 312 Elm St
Street address 2: Fl 20
Street address 3: Cincinnati
Street address state: OH
Zip/Postal code: 45202-2739
County: Hamilton
Country: USA
Mailing address: 151 W 4th St Ste 201
Mailing city: Cincinnati
Mailing state: OH
Mailing zip: 45202-2746
General Phone: (513) 665-3777
General Fax: (513) 768-8958
General/National Adv. E-mail: info@celebro.com
Primary Website: www.gmti.com
Year Established: 1994
Industry: Computers: Hardware & Software Integrators; Electronic Ad Delivery; Software: Advertising (Includes Display; Classified); Software: Electronic Data Interchange
Product or Service: Hardware/Software Supplier
Personnel: Steve Fuschetti (Pres./CEO); Tom Foster (Vice Pres., Celebro Opns.); Michael Hibert (Dir., Implementation Servs.)

CONVERGYS

Street address 1: 201 E 4th St
Street address 3: Cincinnati
Street address state: OH
Zip/Postal code: 45202-4248
County: Hamilton
Country: USA
Mailing address: 201 E 4th St Bsmt
Mailing city: Cincinnati
Mailing state: OH
Mailing zip: 45202-4206
General Phone: (513) 723-7000
General/National Adv. E-mail: marketing@convergys.com
Primary Website: www.convergys.com
Product or Service: Multimedia/Interactive Products
Personnel: Keith Wolters (Sr. Dir., Mktg.)

GANNETT MEDIA TECHNOLOGIES INTERNATIONAL (GMTI)

Street address 1: 312 Elm St
Street address 2: Fl 20
Street address 3: Cincinnati
Street address state: OH
Zip/Postal code: 45202-2739
County: Hamilton
Country: USA
Mailing address: 312 Elm St Ste 2G
Mailing city: Cincinnati
Mailing state: OH
Mailing zip: 45202-2763
General Phone: (513) 665-3777
General Fax: (513) 768-8958
General/National Adv. E-mail: gmti-info@gmti.gannett.com
Primary Website: www.gmti.com
Year Established: 1994
Industry: Archiving Systems; Computers: Hardware & Software Integrators; Library Retrieval Systems; Marketing Database Design and Implementation; Photo Archiving; Software: Advertising (Includes Display; Classified); Storage Retrieval Systems;
Product or Service: Multimedia/Interactive Products
Personnel: Steve Fuschetti (Pres./CEO)

GMTI (DIGITAL COLLECTIONS)

Street address 1: 312 Elm St
Street address 2: Fl 20
Street address 3: Cincinnati
Street address state: OH
Zip/Postal code: 45202-2739
County: Hamilton
Country: USA
Mailing address: 312 Elm St Fl 20
Mailing city: Cincinnati
Mailing state: OH
Mailing zip: 45202-2739
General Phone: (513) 665-3777
General Fax: (513) 768-8958
General/National Adv. E-mail: contentfeedback@gannett.com
Primary Website: www.gannett.com
Year Established: 1995
Industry: Digital Asset Management Systems: Full service contractor; Hardware & Software Integrators; Content Aggregation and Distribution; Semantic Engine Services; Archive Content Management software.
Product or Service: Consultants`Hardware/Software Supplier`Online Service Provider and Internet Hosts
Personnel: Steve Fuschetti (Pres./CEO); Bill Mahlock (Vice Pres., Installations/Support); Michael Tucker (Dir., Sales & Marketing)

THUNDERSTONE SOFTWARE LLC

Street address 1: 815 Superior Ave E
Street address 3: Cleveland
Street address state: OH
Zip/Postal code: 44114-2706

County: Cuyahoga
Country: USA
Mailing address: 815 Superior Ave E
Mailing city: Cleveland
Mailing state: OH
Mailing zip: 44114-2706
General Phone: (216) 820-2200
General Fax: (216) 820-2211
General/National Adv. E-mail: info@thunderstone.com
Primary Website: www.thunderstone.com
Product or Service: Hardware/Software Supplier`Online Service Provider and Internet Hosts
Personnel: Peter Thusat (CMO)

THE NEXT WAVE

Street address 1: 100 Bonner St
Street address 3: Dayton
Street address state: OH
Zip/Postal code: 45410-1306
County: Montgomery
Country: USA
Mailing address: 100 Bonner St
Mailing city: Dayton
Mailing state: OH
Mailing zip: 45410-1306
General Phone: (937) 228-4433
General Fax: (937) 228-4111
General/National Adv. E-mail: surf@thenextwave.biz
Primary Website: www.thenextwave.biz
Year Established: 1988
Product or Service: Advertising/Marketing Agency

ROSSFORD

TYJILL ENTERPRISES, INC.

Street address 1: 1009 E Elm Tree Rd
Street address 3: Rossford
Street address state: OH
Zip/Postal code: 43460-1353
County: Wood
Country: USA
Mailing address: 1009 E Elm Tree Rd
Mailing city: Rossford
Mailing state: OH
Mailing zip: 43460-1353
General Phone: (419) 349-6513
General Fax: (419) 666-4249
General/National Adv. E-mail: jappt@tyjill.com
Primary Website: www.tyjill.com
Year Established: 1994
Product or Service: Multimedia/Interactive Products
Personnel: John J. Appt (Pres.)

OKLAHOMA

TULSA

SMARTMAX SOFTWARE, INC.

Street address 1: 8801 S Yale Ave
Street address 2: Ste 460
Street address 3: Tulsa
Street address state: OK
Zip/Postal code: 74137-3503
County: Tulsa
Country: USA
Mailing address: 8801 S Yale Ave Ste 460
Mailing city: Tulsa
Mailing state: OK
Mailing zip: 74137-3503
General Phone: (918) 388-5900
General/National Adv. E-mail: sales@chatbeacon.io
Primary Website: www.chatbeacon.io
Product or Service: Hardware/Software Supplier
Personnel: Eric Weber (Pres.)

ONTARIO

COMPUTER TALK TECHNOLOGY, INC.

Street address 1: 150 Commerce Valley Drive West
Street address 2: Suite 800
Street address 3: Markham
Street address state: ON
Zip/Postal code: L3T 7Z3
Country: Canada
Mailing address: 150 Commerce Valley Drive West, Suite 800
Mailing city: Markham
Mailing state: ON
Mailing zip: L3T 7Z3
General Phone: (905) 882-5000
General Fax: (905) 882-5501
Primary Website: www.computer-talk.com
Year Established: 1987
Industry: Software: Electronic Data Interchange; System Integration Services;
Product or Service: Hardware/Software Supplier
Personnel: Mandle Cheung (Pres./CEO); Donald Mcdonald (V. P.)

OTTAWA

COREL

Street address 1: 1600 Carling Ave.
Street address 3: Ottawa
Street address state: ON
Zip/Postal code: K1Z 8R7
Country: Canada
Mailing address: 1600 Carling Ave.
Mailing city: Ottawa
Mailing state: ON
Mailing zip: K1Z 8R7
General Phone: (613) 728-8200
General Fax: (613) 728-9790
Primary Website: www.corel.com
Product or Service: Hardware/Software Supplier
Personnel: Patrick Nichols (CEO); Brad Jewett (CFO); Jason Wesbecher (Exec. Vice Pres. of Sales and Marketing)

OPEN TEXT CORP.

Street address 1: 275 Frank Tompa Dr
Street address 3: Waterloo
Street address state: ON
Zip/Postal code: N2L 0A1
Country: Canada
Mailing address: 275 Frank Tompa Dr
Mailing city: Waterloo
Mailing state: ON
Mailing zip: N2L 0A1
General Phone: (519) 888-7111
General Fax: (519) 888-0677
General/National Adv. E-mail: info@opentext.com
Primary Website: www.opentext.com
Product or Service: Hardware/Software Supplier
Personnel: Tom Jenkins (CEO); John Shackleton (CEO)

OREGON

HTS INTERACTIVE HEALTH CARE

Street address 1: 434 NW 6th Ave
Street address 2: Ste 202
Street address 3: Portland
Street address state: OR
Zip/Postal code: 97209-3651
County: Multnomah
Country: USA
Mailing address: 434 NW 6th Ave Ste 202
Mailing city: Portland
Mailing state: OR
Mailing zip: 97209-3651
General Phone: (503) 241-9315
General Fax: (503) 241-8466
General/National Adv. E-mail: sales@interactivehealthinc.com
Primary Website: www.interactivehealthinc.com
Product or Service: Multimedia/Interactive Products
Personnel: Bill Goldberg (Pres & CEO); Christine Solberg (CFO)

INFOCUS CORP.

Street address 1: 13190 SW 68th Pkwy
Street address 2: Ste 200
Street address 3: Portland
Street address state: OR
Zip/Postal code: 97223-8368
County: Washington
Country: USA
Mailing address: 13190 SW 68th Pkwy Ste 200
Mailing city: Portland
Mailing state: OR
Mailing zip: 97223-8368
General Phone: (503) 207-4700
General Fax: (503) 207-4707
Primary Website: www.infocus.com
Product or Service: Hardware/Software Supplier
Personnel: Randy Arnold (Pres.); Loren Shaw (Vice Pres., Marketing); Surendra Arora (Vice Pres., Strategic Relationships & Business Development)

PULSE RESEARCH

Street address 1: 1500 SW 11th Ave
Street address 3: Portland
Street address state: OR
Zip/Postal code: 97201-3532
County: Multnomah
Country: USA
Mailing address: PO Box 2884
Mailing city: Portland
Mailing state: OR
Mailing zip: 97208-2884
General Phone: (503) 626-5224
General/National Adv. E-mail: support@pulseresearch.com
Primary Website: www.pulseresearch.com
Year Established: 1985
Product or Service: Consultants`Multimedia/Interactive Products`Web Site Auditor
Personnel: John Marling (Pres.)

PENNSYLVANIA

BETHLEHEM

ACTIVE DATA EXCHANGE

Street address 1: 190 Brodhead Rd Ste 300
Street address 2: Lehigh Valley Industrial Pk. IV
Street address 3: Bethlehem
Street address state: PA
Zip/Postal code: 18017-8617
County: Northampton
Country: USA
Mailing address: 190 Brodhead Rd Ste 300
Mailing city: Bethlehem
Mailing state: PA
Mailing zip: 18017-8617
General Phone: (610) 997-8100
General Fax: (610) 866-7899
General/National Adv. E-mail: info@activedatax.com
Primary Website: www.activedatax.com
Product or Service: Publisher/Media
Personnel: Susan C. Yee (Pres./CEO); Kendra Hollinger (COO)

PEIRCE-PHELPS, INC.

Street address 1: 516 E. Township Line Rd.
Street address 3: Blue Bell
Street address state: PA
Zip/Postal code: 19422
County: Philadelphia
Country: USA
Mailing address: 516 E. Township Line Rd.
Mailing city: Blue Bell
Mailing state: PA
Mailing zip: 19422
General Phone: (215) 879-7217
General Fax: (215) 879-5427
General/National Adv. E-mail: websupport@peirce.com
Primary Website: www.peirce.com
Product or Service: Hardware/Software Supplier
Personnel: Brian Peirce (Pres.)

UNISYS CORP.

Street address 1: 801 Lakeview Drive
Street address 2: Ste 100
Street address 3: Blue Bell
Street address state: PA
Zip/Postal code: 19422
County: Montgomery
Country: USA
Mailing address: 801 Lakeview Drive, Ste 100
Mailing city: Blue Bell
Mailing state: PA
Mailing zip: 19422
General Phone: (215) 274-2742
Primary Website: www.unisys.com
Year Established: 1986
Industry: Archiving Systems; Computers: Hardware & Software Integrators; Electronic Ad Delivery; Software: Advertising (Includes Display; Classified); Software: Business (Includes Administration/Accounting); Software: Editorial; Software: Pagination/Layout; Software: Workflow Management/Tracking; System Integration Services;
Product or Service: Hardware/Software Supplier
Personnel: Maria Allen (Vice Pres. and Global Head of Financial Services); Lakshmi Ashok (CTO); Mark Cohn (CTO)

ERIE

LARSON TEXTS, INC.

Street address 1: 1762 Norcross Rd
Street address 3: Erie
Street address state: PA
Zip/Postal code: 16510-3838
County: Erie
Country: USA
Mailing address: 1762 Norcross Rd
Mailing city: Erie
Mailing state: PA
Mailing zip: 16510-3838
General Phone: (814) 824-6365
General Fax: (814) 824-6377
General/National Adv. E-mail: eforish@larsontexts.com
Primary Website: www.larsontexts.com
Product or Service: Multimedia/Interactive Products`Publisher/Media

EXTON

MEDIA SUPPLY, INC.

Street address 1: 611 Jeffers Cir
Street address 3: Exton
Street address state: PA
Zip/Postal code: 19341-2525
County: Chester
Country: USA
Mailing address: 611 Jeffers Cir
Mailing city: Exton
Mailing state: PA
Mailing zip: 19341-2525
General Phone: (610) 884-4400
General Fax: (610) 884-4500
General/National Adv. E-mail: info@mediasupply.com
Primary Website: www.mediasupply.com
Product or Service: CD-ROM Designer/Manufacturer
Personnel: Steven P. Derstine (Sales Mgr.)

HORSHAM

CYBERTECH, INC.

Street address 1: 935 Horsham Rd
Street address 3: Horsham
Street address state: PA
Zip/Postal code: 19044-1230
County: Montgomery
Country: USA
Mailing address: 935 Horsham Rd Ste I
Mailing city: Horsham
Mailing state: PA
Mailing zip: 19044-1270
General Phone: (215) 957-6220
General Fax: (215) 674-8515

General/National Adv. E-mail: sales@cbrtech.com
Primary Website: www.cbrtech.com
Product or Service: Hardware/Software Supplier`POP/Kiosk Designer
Personnel: Ronald Schmidt (Pres.); Lloyd Barnett (Sec./Treasurer)

ADVANCED TELECOM SERVICES, INC. (CANADA)

Street address 1: 1150 1st Ave
Street address 2: Ste 105
Street address 3: King Of Prussia
Street address state: PA
Zip/Postal code: 19406-1350
County: Montgomery
Country: USA
Mailing address: 1150 First Ave. Ste. 105
Mailing city: King of Prussia
Mailing state: PA
Mailing zip: 19406
General Phone: (416) 800-2490
General Fax: (610) 964-9117
Advertising Phone: (610) 254-7191
General/National Adv. E-mail: sales@advancedtele.com
Primary Website: www.advancedtele.com
Year Established: 1989
Product or Service: Telecommunications/Service Bureaus
Personnel: Bob Bentz (Dir. of Marketing)

LANCASTER

GODFREY

Street address 1: 40 N Christian St
Street address 3: Lancaster
Street address state: PA
Zip/Postal code: 17602-2828
County: Lancaster
Country: USA
Mailing address: 40 N Christian St
Mailing city: Lancaster
Mailing state: PA
Mailing zip: 17602-2828
General Phone: (717) 393-3831
General Fax: (717) 393-1403
General/National Adv. E-mail: curt@godfrey.com
Primary Website: www.godfrey.com
Year Established: 1947
Product or Service: Advertising/Marketing Agency

SCALA, INC.

Street address 1: 7 Great Valley Parkway
Street address 2: Suite 300
Street address 3: Malvern
Street address state: PA
Zip/Postal code: 19355
County: Chester
Country: USA
Mailing address: 7 Great Valley Parkway, Suite 300
Mailing city: Malvern
Mailing state: PA
Mailing zip: 19355
General Phone: (610) 363-3350
General Fax: (610) 363-4010
General/National Adv. E-mail: team@scala.com
Primary Website: www.scala.com
Product or Service: Hardware/Software Supplier
Personnel: Chris Riegel (Chairman & CEO); Joe Sullivan (COO); Harry Horn (Gen. Mgr.); Manish Kumar (Sr. Vice Pres. & Managing Dir. of Asia Pacific Op.)

SOFTWARE CONSULTING SERVICES, LLC

Street address 1: 630 Municipal Dr
Street address 2: Ste 420
Street address 3: Nazareth
Street address state: PA
Zip/Postal code: 18064-8990
County: Northampton
Country: USA
Mailing address: 630 Municipal Dr Ste 420
Mailing city: Nazareth
Mailing state: PA
Mailing zip: 18064-8990
General Phone: (610) 746-7700
General Fax: (610) 746-7900
General/National Adv. E-mail: sales@newspapersystems.com
Primary Website: www.newspapersystems.com
Year Established: 1975
Product or Service: Hardware/Software Supplier
Note: 800 number goes directly to the sales department
Personnel: Richard Cichelli (Pres.); Susan Fenstermaker (VP of Finance and HR); Kurt M. Jackson (VP and Gen. Man.)

CRAMP + TATE, INC.

Street address 1: 230 S 15th St
Street address 2: Fl 2
Street address 3: Philadelphia
Street address state: PA
Zip/Postal code: 19102-3806
County: Philadelphia
Country: USA
Mailing address: 230 S. 15th St., 2nd Floor
Mailing city: Philadelphia
Mailing state: PA
Mailing zip: 19102-3837
General Phone: (215) 893-0500
General Fax: (215) 893-0543
General/National Adv. E-mail: jeff.cramp@cramp.com
Primary Website: www.cramp.com
Year Established: 1988
Product or Service: Advertising/Marketing Agency

SLINGSHOT TECHNOLOGIES

Street address 1: 1811 Chestnut St
Street address 2: Apt 304
Street address 3: Philadelphia
Street address state: PA
Zip/Postal code: 19103-3706
County: Philadelphia
Country: USA
Mailing address: 1811 Chestnut St Apt 304
Mailing city: Philadelphia
Mailing state: PA
Mailing zip: 19103-3706
General Phone: (800) 405-5755
General Fax: (610) 277-1748
General/National Adv. E-mail: info@slingshot-tech.com
Primary Website: www.slingshot-tech.com
Product or Service: Telecommunications/Service Bureaus
Personnel: Christopher S. Stephano (Pres./CEO)

DIGITAL DESIGN GROUP LIMITED

Street address 1: 955 Milton St
Street address 3: Pittsburgh
Street address state: PA
Zip/Postal code: 15218-1031
County: Allegheny
Country: USA
Mailing address: 955 Milton St
Mailing city: Pittsburgh
Mailing state: PA
Mailing zip: 15218-1031
General Phone: (412) 243-9119
General Fax: (412) 243-2285
General/National Adv. E-mail: rob@ddg-designs.com
Primary Website: www.ddg-designs.com
Year Established: 1993
Product or Service: Multimedia/Interactive Products

PLYMOUTH MEETING

TELEPERFORMANCE INTERACTIVE

Street address 1: 502 W Germantown Pike
Street address 2: Ste 610
Street address 3: Plymouth Meeting
Street address state: PA
Zip/Postal code: 19462-1321
County: Montgomery
Country: USA
Mailing address: 502 W Germantown Pike Ste 610
Mailing city: Plymouth Meeting
Mailing state: PA
Mailing zip: 19462-1321
General Phone: (610) 684-2701
General Fax: (610) 941-9844
General/National Adv. E-mail: mcohen@teleperformance.com
Primary Website: www.teleperformance.com
Product or Service: Telecommunications/Service Bureaus
Personnel: Marc Cohen (Pres.); Jeffrey Cohen (COO); Charles Dowbird (Vice Pres., Sales)

RADNOR

BACKE DIFITAL BRAND MARKETING

Street address 1: 100 W Matsonford Rd
Street address 2: Bldg 101
Street address 3: Radnor
Street address state: PA
Zip/Postal code: 19087-4558
County: Delaware
Country: USA
Mailing address: 100 Matsonford Rd Ste 101
Mailing city: Radnor
Mailing state: PA
Mailing zip: 19087-4566
General Phone: (610) 947-6900
General Fax: (610) 896-9242
General/National Adv. E-mail: info@backemarketing.com
Primary Website: www.backemarketing.com
Year Established: 1995
Product or Service: Advertising/Marketing Agency
Personnel: John E. Backe (Pres./CEO); Malcolm Brown (Sr. Vice Pres.)

STATE COLLEGE

ACCUWEATHER, INC.

Street address 1: 385 Science Park Rd
Street address 3: State College
Street address state: PA
Zip/Postal code: 16803-2215
County: Centre
Country: USA
Mailing address: 385 Science Park Rd.
Mailing city: State College
Mailing state: PA
Mailing zip: 16803
General Phone: (814) 237-0309
General Fax: (814) 235-8609
General/National Adv. E-mail: support@accuweather.com
Primary Website: www.accuweather.com
Product or Service: Multimedia/Interactive Products`Other Services`Online Service Provider and Internet Hosts
Personnel: Dr. Joel N. Myers (Founder & President); Evan Myers (CEO); Steven Smith (Pres., Digital Media); Jonathan Porter (Vice Pres. of Business Services and General Mgr. of Enterprise Solutions); John Dokes (Chief Content Officer); James Candor (Chief Strategy Officer); John Dokes (Chief Marketing Officer)

SUNGARD

Street address 1: 680 E Swedesford Rd
Street address 3: Wayne
Street address state: PA
Zip/Postal code: 19087-1605
County: Chester
Country: USA
Mailing address: 680 E Swedesford Rd
Mailing city: Wayne
Mailing state: PA
Mailing zip: 19087-1605
General Phone: (800) 825-2518
General Fax: (212) 406-2861
General/National Adv. E-mail: getinfo@sungard.com
Display Adv. E-mail: sales@sungard.com
Primary Website: www.sungard.com
Product or Service: Hardware/Software Supplier
Personnel: Nicole Burn (Vice Pres., Mktg.); Cristobal Conde (Pres.)

QUEBEC

INNOVATIVE SYSTEMS DESIGN, INC.

Street address 1: 222 Brunswick Blvd
Street address 3: Pointe-Claire
Street address state: QC
Zip/Postal code: H9R 1A6
Country: Canada
Mailing address: 222 Brunswick Blvd.
Mailing city: Pointe-Claire
Mailing state: QC
Mailing zip: H9R 1A6
General Phone: (514) 459-0200
General Fax: (514) 459-0300
General/National Adv. E-mail: sales@isd.ca
Display Adv. E-mail: sales@isd.ca
Primary Website: www.isd.ca
Year Established: 1983
Industry: Telecommunications
Product or Service: Telecommunications/Service Bureaus
Personnel: Jeff Tierney (Pres.); Rob Dumas (Director of Sales and Marketing); Monica Steibelt (Sales Coord.)

RHODE ISLAND

CREATIVE CIRCLE MEDIA SOLUTIONS

Street address 1: 945 Waterman Ave
Street address 3: East Providence
Street address state: RI
Zip/Postal code: 02914-1342
County: Providence
Country: USA
Mailing address: 945 Waterman Ave.
Mailing city: East Providence
Mailing state: RI
Mailing zip: 02914-1342
General Phone: (401) 272-1122
General/National Adv. E-mail: info@creativecirclemedia.com
Primary Website: www.creativecirclemedia.com
Year Established: 1984
Industry: Software: web CMS, advertising, native content; Consulting; Outsourcing; Training; Web and print redesigns; print editorial production platform.
Product or Service: Advertising/Marketing Agency`Circulation`Consultants`Editorial`Graphic/Design Firm`Hardware/Software Supplier`Marketing`Multimedia/Interactive Products`Other Services`Online Service Provider and Internet Hosts
Note: Full service, custom software provider with a dynamic web site CMS, user-contributed content, classifieds, hosting, pay wall, branded content, circulation and print editorial production solutions. We also provide strategic consulting, newsroom training, ad design training, new revenue ideas and high-end outsourcing services. Our Premium Pages are an excellent digital features content service. We also have led more than 750 redesigns of print newspapers and magazines and continue to help publishers redefine their print products.
Personnel: Bill Ostendorf (Pres. & founder); Lynn Rognsvoog (Design director); Tim Benson (Chief Developer); Scott Kingsley (COO); Darryl Greenlee (Developer); Sean Finch (VP/Sales); Greg Boras (National Sales Manager)
Newspaper (for newspapers group): The Sumter Item, Sumter

JAMESTOWN

ZHIVAGO MANAGEMENT PARTNERS

Street address 1: 381 Seaside Dr
Street address 3: Jamestown
Street address state: RI
Zip/Postal code: 02835-2376
County: Newport
Country: USA
Mailing address: 381 Seaside Dr
Mailing city: Jamestown
Mailing state: RI
Mailing zip: 02835-2376
General Phone: (401) 423-2400
General/National Adv. E-mail: kristin@zhivago.com
Primary Website: www.zhivago.com
Product or Service: Consultants
Personnel: Kristin Zhivago (Pres.)

SOUTH CAROLINA

MOUNT PLEASANT

ASSIGNMENT DESK

Street address 1: 665 Johnnie Dodds Blvd.
Street address 2: Suite 201
Street address 3: Mount Pleasant
Street address state: SC
Zip/Postal code: 29464
County: Cook
Country: USA
Mailing address: 665 Johnnie Dodds Blvd., Suite 201
Mailing city: Mount Pleasant
Mailing state: SC
Mailing zip: 29464
General Phone: (312) 464-8600
General/National Adv. E-mail: cya@assignmentdesk.com
Primary Website: www.assignmentdesk.com
Year Established: 1992
Product or Service: Multimedia/Interactive Products`Telecommunications/Service Bureaus
Personnel: Evelyn Beldam (Bus. Mgr.)

TENNESSEE

DIALOGIC COMMUNICATIONS CORP.

Street address 1: 730 Cool Springs Blvd
Street address 2: Ste 300
Street address 3: Franklin
Street address state: TN
Zip/Postal code: 37067-7290
County: Williamson
Country: USA
Mailing address: 117 Seaboard Ln Ste D100
Mailing city: Franklin
Mailing state: TN
Mailing zip: 37067-2871
General Phone: (615) 790-2882
General Fax: (615) 790-1329
General/National Adv. E-mail: sales@dccusa.com; bcarman@dccusa.com
Primary Website: www.dccusa.com
Product or Service: Telecommunications/Service Bureaus
Personnel: Bill Carman (Sales Rep.)

DESIGNORY.COM

Street address 1: 209 10th Ave S
Street address 2: Ste 409
Street address 3: Nashville
Street address state: TN
Zip/Postal code: 37203-0767
County: Davidson
Country: USA
Mailing address: 209 10th Ave S
Mailing city: Nashville
Mailing state: TN
Mailing zip: 37203-4144
General Phone: (615) 514-7514
Primary Website: www.designory.com
Product or Service: Advertising/Marketing Agency

HEALTHSTREAM

Street address 1: 209 10th Ave S
Street address 2: Ste 450
Street address 3: Nashville
Street address state: TN
Zip/Postal code: 37203-0788
County: Davidson
Country: USA
Mailing address: 209 10th Ave S Ste 450
Mailing city: Nashville
Mailing state: TN
Mailing zip: 37203-0788
General Phone: (615) 301-3100
General Fax: (615) 301-3200
General/National Adv. E-mail: contact@healthstream.com
Primary Website: www.healthstream.com
Year Established: 1990
Product or Service: Multimedia/Interactive Products
Personnel: Robert A. Frist (CEO); Arthur E. Newman (Sr. Vice Pres., Finance)

TEXAS

ADDISON

RIBIT, INC.

Street address 1: 4287 Belt Line Rd
Street address 2: Ste 135
Street address 3: Addison
Street address state: TX
Zip/Postal code: 75001-4510
County: Dallas
Country: USA
Mailing address: 4287 Belt Line Rd Ste 135
Mailing city: Addison
Mailing state: TX
Mailing zip: 75001-4510
General Phone: (972) 239-8866
General Fax: (972) 239-8788
General/National Adv. E-mail: ribit@ribit.com
Primary Website: www.ribit.com
Year Established: 1994
Product or Service: Advertising/Marketing Agency`Marketing`Multimedia/Interactive Products
Personnel: Robin Moss (Pres./Founder); Jason Landry (Creative Dir.); Linda Krauss (Multimedia Developer)

IGNITE OLIVE SOFTWARE SOLUTIONS

Street address 1: 401 Congress Ave.
Street address 2: Suite 2650
Street address 3: Austin
Street address state: TX
Zip/Postal code: 78701
County: Travis
Country: USA
Mailing address: 401 Congress Ave., Suite 2650
Mailing city: Austin
Mailing state: TX
Mailing zip: 78701
General Phone: 855-453-8174
Advertising Phone: 720-747-1220
Editorail Phone: 720-747-1220
General/National Adv. E-mail: success@ignitetech.com
Display Adv. E-mail: info@olivesoftware.com
Classified Adv. E-mail: info@olivesoftware.com
Editorial e-mail: info@olivesoftware.com
Primary Website: www.ignitetech.com
Year Established: 2000
Weekday Frequency: All day
Saturday Frequency: All day
Industry: eEdition Archive Tearsheet eBook eMagazine eDirectory (Yellow pages) Digital Replica Content Reuse
Product or Service: Multimedia/Interactive Products`Online Service Provider and Internet Hosts
Personnel: Davin Cushman (CEO); Eric Vaughan (COO)

NEWSSTAND, INC.

Street address 1: 1835 Kramer Ln
Street address 2: Ste B150
Street address 3: Austin
Street address state: TX
Zip/Postal code: 78758-4230
County: Travis
Country: USA
Mailing address: 1835 Kramer Ln Ste B150
Mailing city: Austin
Mailing state: TX
Mailing zip: 78758-4230
General Phone: (512) 334-5102
General Fax: (512) 334-5199
General/National Adv. E-mail: support@newsstand.com
Primary Website: www.newsstand.com
Product or Service: Telecommunications/Service Bureaus

VOICETEXT COMMUNICATIONS

Street address 1: 211 E 7th St
Street address 2: Ste 1200
Street address 3: Austin
Street address state: TX
Zip/Postal code: 78701-3218
County: Travis
Country: USA
Mailing address: 211 E 7th St Ste 1200
Mailing city: Austin
Mailing state: TX
Mailing zip: 78701-3218
General Phone: (512) 404-2300
General Fax: (512) 479-6464
General/National Adv. E-mail: conference@voicetext.com
Primary Website: www.voicetext.com
Product or Service: Telecommunications/Service Bureaus
Personnel: Eileen Williams (Pres.); Jennifer Mackin (Mgr., Audio Conference)

CARROLLTON

LAUNCH AGENCY

Street address 1: 4100 Midway Rd
Street address 2: Ste 2110
Street address 3: Carrollton
Street address state: TX
Zip/Postal code: 75007-1965
County: Denton
Country: USA
Mailing address: 4100 Midway Rd Ste 2110
Mailing city: Carrollton
Mailing state: TX
Mailing zip: 75007-1965
General Phone: (972) 818-4100
General Fax: (972) 818-4101
General/National Adv. E-mail: mboone@launchagency.com
Primary Website: www.launchagency.com
Year Established: 2000
Product or Service: Advertising/Marketing Agency

VOICE RETRIEVAL & INFORMATION SERVICES, INC.

Street address 1: 3222 Skylane Dr
Street address 2: Ste 100
Street address 3: Carrollton
Street address state: TX
Zip/Postal code: 75006-2522
County: Dallas
Country: USA
Mailing address: 3222 Skylane Dr Ste 100
Mailing city: Carrollton
Mailing state: TX
Mailing zip: 75006-2522
General Phone: (972) 380-8400
General Fax: (972) 380-0118
General/National Adv. E-mail: sales@vri.com
Primary Website: www.vri.com
Product or Service: Telecommunications/Service Bureaus
Personnel: Melissa Guevara (Customer Service Rep.)

AT&T, INC.

Street address 1: 208 S. Akard Street
Street address 2: Suite 2954
Street address 3: Dallas
Street address state: TX
Zip/Postal code: 75202
County: Bexar
Country: USA
Mailing address: 208 S. Akard Street
Mailing city: Dallas
Mailing state: TX
Mailing zip: 75202
General Phone: (210) 821-4105
General Fax: (210) 351-2071
Primary Website: www.att.com
Product or Service: Telecommunications/Service Bureaus
Personnel: Randall L. Stephenson (Chrmn./CEO); Dennis M. Payne (Pres./CEO, AT&T Directory Opns.); Lea Ann Champion (Sr. Exec. Vice Pres./CMO); Cathy Coughlin (SVP/Global Mktg. Officer); Linda Hanacek

CENTURYTEL INTERACTIVE

Street address 1: 8750 N Central Expy
Street address 2: Ste 720
Street address 3: Dallas
Street address state: TX
Zip/Postal code: 75231-6462
County: Dallas
Country: USA
Mailing address: 8750 N Central Expy Ste 720
Mailing city: Dallas
Mailing state: TX
Mailing zip: 75231-6462
General Phone: (214) 360-6280
General Fax: (972) 996-0868
General/National Adv. E-mail: jd@centuryinteractive.com
Primary Website: www.centuryinteractive.com
Year Established: 1989
Product or Service: Telecommunications/Service Bureaus
Personnel: Jack Doege (COO)

DEX MEDIA

Street address 1: 2200 W Airfield Dr
Street address 3: Dallas
Street address state: TX
Zip/Postal code: 75261-4008
County: Dallas
Country: USA
Mailing address: 2200 W. Airfield Dr.
Mailing city: Grapevine
Mailing state: TX
Mailing zip: 75261
General Phone: (919) 297-1600
Primary Website: www.dexmedia.com
Product or Service: Advertising/Marketing Agency`Marketing
Personnel: Richard C. Notebaert (Chrmn./CEO, Qwest); Oren G. Shaffer (Vice Chrmn./CFO); George Burnett (Pres./CEO, Qwest Dex); Robin R. Szeliga (Exec. Vice Pres., Finance); Joan H. Walker (Sr. Vice Pres., Cor. Commun.)

DEX ONE CORP.

Street address 1: 2200 W Airfield Dr
Street address 3: Dallas
Street address state: TX
Zip/Postal code: 75261-4008
County: Dallas
Country: USA
Mailing address: 1001 Winstead Dr
Mailing city: Cary
Mailing state: NC
Mailing zip: 27513-2117
General Phone: (919) 297-1600
General Fax: (919) 297-1285
General/National Adv. E-mail: info@dexone.com
Primary Website: www.dexone.com
Product or Service: Publisher/Media
Personnel: Steven M. Blondy (Exec. Vice Pres./CFO); Maggie LeBeau (Sr. Vice Pres./CMO)

D-SQUARED STUDIOS, INC.

Street address 1: 4312 Elm St
Street address 3: Dallas
Street address state: TX
Zip/Postal code: 75226-1133
County: Dallas
Country: USA
Mailing address: 4312 Elm St
Mailing city: Dallas
Mailing state: TX
Mailing zip: 75226-1133
General Phone: (214) 746-6336
General Fax: (214) 746-6338
General/National Adv. E-mail: doug.davis@d2studios.net
Primary Website: www.d2studios.net
Product or Service: Multimedia/Interactive Products
Personnel: Doug Davis (Pres.)

IMAGEN, INC.

Street address 1: PO Box 814270

Street address 3: Dallas
Street address state: TX
Zip/Postal code: 75381-4270
County: Dallas
Country: USA
Mailing address: PO Box 814270
Mailing city: Dallas
Mailing state: TX
Mailing zip: 75381-4270
General Phone: (214) 232-3385
General Fax: (419) 821-2047
General/National Adv. E-mail: al@imageninc.com
Primary Website: www.imageninc.com
Product or Service: Graphic/Design Firm
Personnel: Al Schmidt (Pres.)

M/C/C

Street address 1: 12377 Merit Dr.
Street address 2: Suite 800
Street address 3: Dallas
Street address state: TX
Zip/Postal code: 75251
County: Dallas
Country: USA
Mailing address: 12377 Merit Dr., Suite 800
Mailing city: Dallas
Mailing state: TX
Mailing zip: 75251
General Phone: (972) 480-8383
General Fax: (972) 669-8447
General/National Adv. E-mail: pam_watkins@mccom.com
Primary Website: www.mccom.com
Year Established: 1986
Product or Service: Advertising/Marketing Agency
Personnel: Mike Crawford (Pres.); Pam Watkins (SVP, Business and Media Strategy); Jim Terry (SVP, Account Service); Shannon Sullivan (Vice President, Account Supervisor); Todd Brashear (Vice President, Creative Director)

SEALANDER & CO.

Street address 1: 611 N Buckner Blvd
Street address 3: Dallas
Street address state: TX
Zip/Postal code: 75218-2708
County: Dallas
Country: USA
Mailing address: 611 N Buckner Blvd
Mailing city: Dallas
Mailing state: TX
Mailing zip: 75218-2708
General Phone: (214) 321-8612
General Fax: (214) 328-0779
General/National Adv. E-mail: john@sealander.com
Primary Website: www.sealander.com
Product or Service: Advertising/Marketing Agency
Personnel: John Sealander (Owner)

AGILITY

Street address 1: 15900 Morales Rd
Street address 3: Houston
Street address state: TX
Zip/Postal code: 77032-2126
County: Harris
Country: USA
Mailing address: 15900 Morales Rd
Mailing city: Houston
Mailing state: TX
Mailing zip: 77032-2126
General Phone: (714) 617-6300
General/National Adv. E-mail: americas@logistics.com
Primary Website: www.agilitylogistics.com
Product or Service: Telecommunications/Service Bureaus
Personnel: Pam Holdrup (Sales)

INTERNATIONAL DEMOGRAPHICS/ THE MEDIA AUDIT

Street address 1: 10333 Richmond Ave
Street address 2: Ste 200
Street address 3: Houston
Street address state: TX
Zip/Postal code: 77042-4142
County: Harris
Country: USA
Mailing address: 10333 Richmond Ave Ste 200
Mailing city: Houston
Mailing state: TX
Mailing zip: 77042-4142
General Phone: (713) 626-0333
General Fax: (713) 626-0418
General/National Adv. E-mail: tma@themediaaudit.com
Primary Website: www.themediaaudit.com
Year Established: 1971
Product or Service: Advertising/Marketing Agency
Personnel: James B. Higginbotham (Chrmn.); Robert A. Jordan (Pres.); J. Phillip Beswick (Exec. Vice Pres., Sales); Michael W. Bustell (Exec. Vice Pres./Sales Mgr.)

AUTHORLINK

Street address 1: 103 Guadalupe Dr
Street address 3: Irving
Street address state: TX
Zip/Postal code: 75039-3334
County: Dallas
Country: USA
Mailing address: 103 Guadalupe Dr
Mailing city: Irving
Mailing state: TX
Mailing zip: 75039-3334
General Phone: (972) 402-0101
General Fax: (866) 381-1587
General/National Adv. E-mail: dbooth@authorlink.com
Primary Website: www.authorlink.com
Product or Service: Multimedia/Interactive Products`Publisher/Media
Note: Authorlink specializes in e-book conversion and distribution. We also provide news and informatin for editors, agents, writers and readers.
Personnel: Doris Booth (Ed. in Chief)

NEC CORPORATION OF AMERICA

Street address 1: 6535 State Highway 161
Street address 3: Irving
Street address state: TX
Zip/Postal code: 75039-2402
County: Dallas
Country: USA
Mailing address: 6535 State Highway 161
Mailing city: Irving
Mailing state: TX
Mailing zip: 75039-2402
General Phone: (800) 240-0632
General Fax: (888) 318-7932
General/National Adv. E-mail: info@neclease.com
Primary Website: www.necunifiedsolutions.com
Product or Service: Telecommunications/Service Bureaus
Personnel: Albert F. Kelly (Gen. Mgr.)

TARGETBASE

Street address 1: 7850 N Belt Line Rd
Street address 3: Irving
Street address state: TX
Zip/Postal code: 75063-6062
County: Dallas
Country: USA
Mailing address: 7850 N Belt Line Rd
Mailing city: Irving
Mailing state: TX
Mailing zip: 75063-6062
General Phone: (972) 506-3400
General Fax: (972) 506-3505
General/National Adv. E-mail: info@targetbase.com
Primary Website: www.targetbase.com
Year Established: 1965
Product or Service: Advertising/Marketing Agency
Personnel: Mark Wright (Pres./CEO); Robin Rettew (Mng. Dir.)

MAGNOLIA

TREEHOUSE ONE INTERACTIVE

Street address 1: 40310 Three Forks Rd
Street address 3: Magnolia
Street address state: TX
Zip/Postal code: 77354-4628
County: Montgomery
Country: USA
Mailing address: 40310 Three Forks Rd
Mailing city: Magnolia
Mailing state: TX
Mailing zip: 77354-4628
General Phone: (512) 682-6943
General Fax: (512) 682-6943
General/National Adv. E-mail: info@treehouse1.com
Primary Website: www.treehouse1.com
Product or Service: Multimedia/Interactive Products
Personnel: Brian K. Hecht (Contact)

VICORP.COM

Street address 1: 101 E Park Blvd
Street address 2: Ste 600-15
Street address 3: Plano
Street address state: TX
Zip/Postal code: 75074-5483
County: Collin
Country: USA
Mailing address: 101 E Park Blvd Ste 600-15
Mailing city: Plano
Mailing state: TX
Mailing zip: 75074-5483
General Phone: (972) 596-2969
General/National Adv. E-mail: sales@vicorp.com; info@vicorp.com
Primary Website: www.vicorp.com
Product or Service: Hardware/Software Supplier
Personnel: Brendan Treacy (CEO); Lee Cottle (COO)

NEWMAN BROTHERS

Street address 1: 112 E Pecan St
Street address 2: Ste 2222
Street address 3: San Antonio
Street address state: TX
Zip/Postal code: 78205-1536
County: Bexar
Country: USA
Mailing address: 112 E Pecan St Ste 2222
Mailing city: San Antonio
Mailing state: TX
Mailing zip: 78205-1536
General Phone: (210) 226-0371
General Fax: (210) 226-6506
Product or Service: Multimedia/Interactive Products
Personnel: John Newman (Owner)

THE WOODLANDS

EPIC SOFTWARE GROUP, INC.

Street address 1: 701 Sawdust Rd
Street address 3: The Woodlands
Street address state: TX
Zip/Postal code: 77380-2943
County: Montgomery
Country: USA
Mailing address: 701 Sawdust Rd
Mailing city: The Woodlands
Mailing state: TX
Mailing zip: 77380-2943
General Phone: (281) 363-3742
General Fax: (281) 419-4509
General/National Adv. E-mail: epic@epicsoftware.com
Primary Website: www.epicsoftware.com
Year Established: 1990
Product or Service: Multimedia/Interactive Products
Personnel: Vic Cherubini (Pres.)

TEXAS

INTERCOM

Street address 1: 3 Grogans Park Dr
Street address 2: Ste 200
Street address 3: The Woodlands
Street address state: TX
Zip/Postal code: 77380-2922
County: Montgomery
Country: USA
Mailing address: 3 Grogans Park Dr Ste 200
Mailing city: The Woodlands
Mailing state: TX
Mailing zip: 77380-2922
General Phone: (800) 298-7070
General Fax: (281) 364-7032
General/National Adv. E-mail: intercom@intercom-interactive.com
Primary Website: www.intercom-interactive.com
Product or Service: Multimedia/Interactive Products
Personnel: Bob Yeager (Pres.); Margo Pearson (Gen. Mgr.)

UTAH

KAYSVILLE

READING HORIZONS

Street address 1: 1194 Flint Meadow Dr
Street address 3: Kaysville
Street address state: UT
Zip/Postal code: 84037-9564
County: Davis
Country: USA
Mailing address: 1194 Flint Meadow
Mailing city: Kaysville
Mailing state: UT
Mailing zip: 84037
General Phone: (801) 295-7054
General Fax: (801) 295-7088
General/National Adv. E-mail: info@readinghorizons.com
Primary Website: www.readinghorizons.com
Year Established: 1984
Product or Service: Publisher/Media
Personnel: Tyson Smith (Pres.)

OREM

VERIO, INC.

Street address 1: 1203 Research Way
Street address 3: Orem
Street address state: UT
Zip/Postal code: 84097-6207
County: Utah
Country: USA
Mailing address: 1203 Research Way
Mailing city: Orem
Mailing state: UT
Mailing zip: 84097-6207
General Phone: (303) 645-1900
General Fax: (303) 708-2490
General/National Adv. E-mail: compliance@verio-inc.com
Primary Website: www.verio.com
Product or Service: Online Service Provider and Internet Hosts
Personnel: Kiyoshi Maeda (Pres.)

ROY

MALL MARKETING MEDIA

Street address 1: 1877 W 4000 S
Street address 3: Roy
Street address state: UT
Zip/Postal code: 84067-3500
County: Weber
Country: USA
Mailing address: 1877 W 4000 S
Mailing city: Roy
Mailing state: UT
Mailing zip: 84067-3500
General Phone: (801) 927-2600
General/National Adv. E-mail: michael@mallmarketingmedia.com
Primary Website: www.thecpsgroup.com
Product or Service: Advertising/Marketing Agency
Personnel: Michael O'Connell (Pres. & CEO); Jazz Mann (Dir., Business Development); Maria Bell (Vice Pres.)

XMISSION

Street address 1: 51 E 400 S
Street address 2: Ste 200
Street address 3: Salt Lake City
Street address state: UT
Zip/Postal code: 84111-2753
County: Salt Lake
Country: USA
Mailing address: 51 E 400 S Ste 200
Mailing city: Salt Lake City

Mailing state: UT
Mailing zip: 84111-2753
General Phone: (801) 539-0852
General Fax: (801) 539-0853
General/National Adv. E-mail: info@xmission.com
Primary Website: www.xmission.com
Product or Service: Online Service Provider and Internet Hosts
Personnel: Howard Gordon (Founder); Peter Ashdown (Pres.); Sue Ashdown (Gen. Mgr.); Bret Jensen (Cor. Sales); Bob Dobbs (Mktg. Mgr.)

VIRGINIA

NEWS MEDIA ALLIANCE

Street address 1: 4401 Wilson Blvd
Street address 2: Ste 900
Street address 3: Arlington
Street address state: VA
Zip/Postal code: 22203-4195
County: Arlington
Country: USA
Mailing address: 4401 Wilson Blvd Ste 900
Mailing city: Arlington
Mailing state: VA
Mailing zip: 22203-4195
General Phone: (571) 366-1000
General Fax: (571) 366-1195
General/National Adv. E-mail: sheila.owens@naa.org
Primary Website: www.naa.org
Year Established: 1979
Product or Service: Publisher/Media
Note: Elections held in April/May
Personnel: David Chavern (Pres. & CEO); Robert Walden (CFO); Sarah Burkman (VP of HRO); Rich Schiekofer (SVP Bus. Dev.); John Murray (VP of Audience Dev.); Lindsey Loving (Comm. Mgr.); Paul Boyle (SVP of Public Policy); Danielle Coffey (VP of Strategic Initiatives and Counsel); Jim Conaghan (VP, Research & Industry Analysis); Kristina Zaumseil (Public Policy Mgr.)

MCI

Street address 1: 22001 Loudoun County Pkwy
Street address 3: Ashburn
Street address state: VA
Zip/Postal code: 20147-6105
County: Loudoun
Country: USA
Mailing address: 22001 Loudoun County Pkwy
Mailing city: Ashburn
Mailing state: VA
Mailing zip: 20147-6122
General Phone: (703) 206-5600
General Fax: (703) 206-5601
General/National Adv. E-mail: info@mci.com
Primary Website: www.mci.com
Year Established: 1968
Industry: Data Communication
Product or Service: Online Service Provider and Internet Hosts`Telecommunications/Service Bureaus
Personnel: Ivan Siedenberg (Chrmn./CEO); Fred Briggs (Pres., Opns./Tech.); Robert Blakely (Exec. Vice Pres./CFO); Daniel Casaccia (Exec. Vice Pres., HR); Jonathan Crane (Exec. Vice Pres., Strategy/Cor. Devel.); Grace Chentent (Sr. Vice Pres., Commun.); Nancy B. Gofus (Sr. Vice Pres., Mktg./CMO); Shane King

CHANTILLY

BIAKELSEY

Street address 1: 15120 Enterprise Ct
Street address 3: Chantilly
Street address state: VA
Zip/Postal code: 20151-1274
County: Fairfax
Country: USA
Mailing address: 15120 Enterprise Ct Ste 100
Mailing city: Chantilly
Mailing state: VA
Mailing zip: 20151-1275
General Phone: (800) 331-5086
General/National Adv. E-mail: info@biakelsey.com
Primary Website: www.kelseygroup.com
Year Established: 1986
Product or Service: Publisher/Media
Personnel: Neal Polachek (CEO)

CHESAPEAKE

NEWTON MEDIA ASSOCIATES, INC.

Street address 1: 824 Greenbrier Pkwy
Street address 2: Ste 200
Street address 3: Chesapeake
Street address state: VA
Zip/Postal code: 23320-3697
County: Chesapeake City
Country: USA
Mailing address: 824 Greenbrier Pkwy Ste 200
Mailing city: Chesapeake
Mailing state: VA
Mailing zip: 23320-3697
General Phone: (757) 547-5400
General Fax: (757) 547-7383
General/National Adv. E-mail: info@newtonmedia.com
Primary Website: www.newtonmedia.com
Year Established: 1995
Product or Service: Advertising/Marketing Agency
Personnel: Steven Newton (Pres.); Janet Burke (Media Dir.); Aimee James (Media Consultant); Aubry Winfrey (Account Executive/ Media Buyer); Steve Warnecke (Director New Business Development)

DULLES

AOL INC.

Street address 1: 22000 Aol Way
Street address 3: Dulles
Street address state: VA
Zip/Postal code: 20166-9302
County: Loudoun
Country: USA
Mailing address: 22000 Aol Way
Mailing city: Dulles
Mailing state: VA
Mailing zip: 20166-9302
General Phone: (703) 265-2100
Primary Website: www.aol.com
Product or Service: Publisher/Media
Personnel: Guru Gowrappan (CEO); Sowmyanarayan Sampath (CFO)

NEWSUSA, INC.

Street address 1: 1069 W Broad St
Street address 2: Ste 205
Street address 3: Falls Church
Street address state: VA
Zip/Postal code: 22046-4610
County: Falls Church City
Country: USA
Mailing address: 1069 W Broad St Ste 205
Mailing city: Falls Church
Mailing state: VA
Mailing zip: 22046
General Phone: (703) 462-2700
Primary Website: www.newsusa.com
Year Established: 1987
Product or Service: Publisher/Media
Personnel: Richard Rothstein (Vice Pres., Sales); Rick Smith (Pub.)

RESTON

FOUR PALMS, INC.

Street address 1: 11260 Roger Bacon Dr
Street address 2: Fl 4
Street address 3: Reston
Street address state: VA
Zip/Postal code: 20190-5227
County: Fairfax
Country: USA
Mailing address: 11260 Roger Bacon Dr Fl 4
Mailing city: Reston
Mailing state: VA
Mailing zip: 20190-5227
General Phone: (703) 834-0200
General Fax: (703) 834-0219
General/National Adv. E-mail: info@fourpalms.com
Primary Website: www.fourpalms.com
Product or Service: Multimedia/Interactive Products
Personnel: Pat Buteux (Pres.)

BIG, (BEATLEY GRAVITT, INC.)

Street address 1: One East Cary Street
Street address 3: Richmond
Street address state: VA
Zip/Postal code: 23219
County: Richmond City
Country: USA
Mailing address: One East Cary Street
Mailing city: Richmond
Mailing state: VA
Mailing zip: 23219
General Phone: (804) 355-9151
General/National Adv. E-mail: hello@bigaddress.com
Primary Website: www.bigaddress.com
Product or Service: Graphic/Design Firm
Personnel: Ed Lacy (Pres./Dir., Mktg.)

PROXIOS

Street address 1: 707 E Main St
Street address 2: Ste 1425
Street address 3: Richmond
Street address state: VA
Zip/Postal code: 23219-2807
County: Richmond City
Country: USA
Mailing address: 707 E Main St Ste 1425
Mailing city: Richmond
Mailing state: VA
Mailing zip: 23219-2807
General Phone: (804) 342-1200
General Fax: (804) 342-1209
General/National Adv. E-mail: sales@proxios.com
Primary Website: www.proxios.com
Product or Service: Multimedia/Interactive Products
Personnel: Frank E. Butler (Pres.)

PYRAMID STUDIOS

Street address 1: 1710 Altamont Ave
Street address 3: Richmond
Street address state: VA
Zip/Postal code: 23230-4504
County: Richmond City
Country: USA
Mailing address: 1710 Altamont Ave
Mailing city: Richmond
Mailing state: VA
Mailing zip: 23230-4504
General Phone: (804) 353-0700
General Fax: (804) 355-5019
General/National Adv. E-mail: dhornstein@pyramidstudios.com
Primary Website: www.pyramidstudios.com
Product or Service: Multimedia/Interactive Products
Personnel: Bruce Hornstein (Pres.)

PAGE COOPERATIVE

Street address 1: 1112 Moorefield Creek Rd SW
Street address 3: Vienna
Street address state: VA
Zip/Postal code: 22180-6245
County: Fairfax
Country: USA
Mailing address: 1112 Moorefield Creek Rd SW
Mailing city: Vienna
Mailing state: VA
Mailing zip: 22180
General Phone: (610) 687-3778
General Fax: (610) 592-0647
General/National Adv. E-mail: info@pagecooperative.com
Primary Website: www.pagecooperative.com
Year Established: 1983
Product or Service: Telecommunications/Service Bureaus
Personnel: John Snyder (CEO); Steve Schroeder (General Manager); Marcy Emory (Accnt. Supervisor); Graff Joan (Director)

V! STUDIOS

Street address 1: 8229 Boone Blvd
Street address 2: Ste 420
Street address 3: Vienna
Street address state: VA
Zip/Postal code: 22182-2651
County: Fairfax
Country: USA
Mailing address: 8229 Boone Blvd Ste 420
Mailing city: Vienna
Mailing state: VA
Mailing zip: 22182-2651
General Phone: (703) 760-0440
General Fax: (703) 760-0417
General/National Adv. E-mail: operations@v-studios.com
Display Adv. E-mail: technical@v-studios.com; marketing@v-studios.com; creative@v-studios.com
Primary Website: www.v-studios.com
Product or Service: Online Service Provider and Internet Hosts
Personnel: Cindy Benesch (Vice Pres.); Troy Benesch (Vice Pres., Promo.); Jim Hatch (Dir., Mktg./Sales)

WASHINGTON

NEWSPHERE

Street address 1: 12412 SE 26th Pl
Street address 3: Bellevue
Street address state: WA
Zip/Postal code: 98005-4157
County: King
Country: USA
Mailing address: 12412 SE 26th Pl
Mailing city: Bellevue
Mailing state: WA
Mailing zip: 98005-4157
General Phone: (425) 957-0219
Primary Website: www.newsphere.org
Product or Service: Publisher/Media
Personnel: Alan Boyle (Ed.)

SMARTFOCUS INC.

Street address 1: 13810 SE Eastgate Way
Street address 2: Suite 550
Street address 3: Bellevue
Street address state: WA
Zip/Postal code: 98005
Country: USA
Mailing address: 13810 SE Eastgate Way, Suite 550
Mailing city: Bellevue
Mailing state: WA
Mailing zip: 98005
General Phone: (425) 460-1000
Primary Website: www.smartfocus.com
Year Established: 1998
Industry: Consulting Services: Advertising; Consulting Services: Circulation; Consulting Services: Computer; Consulting Services: Marketing; Marketing Database Design and Implementation; Software: Circulation; Training: Sales & Marketing
Product or Service: Online Service Provider and Internet Hosts
Personnel: Chris Allan (CEO); Jamie Gunn (COO)

SUMTOTAL SYSTEM INC.

Street address 1: 110 110th Ave NE
Street address 2: Ste 700
Street address 3: Bellevue
Street address state: WA
Zip/Postal code: 98004-5867
County: King
Country: USA
Mailing address: 2850 NW 43rd St Ste 150
Mailing city: Gainesville
Mailing state: FL
Mailing zip: 32606-6966
General Phone: (877) 868-2527 (Technical Support)
General Fax: (425) 455 3071
General/National Adv. E-mail: sales@click2learn.com
Primary Website: www.click2learn.com; www.asymetrix.com
Year Established: 1984
Product or Service: Multimedia/Interactive Products
Personnel: Gary Millrood (Vice Pres., Worldwide Sales/Alliances); Ray Pitts (Vice Pres., Professional Servs.)

WINSTAR/NORTHWEST NEXUS, INC.

Street address 1: 15821 NE 8th St
Street address 2: Ste W200
Street address 3: Bellevue

Street address state: WA
Zip/Postal code: 98008-3957
County: King
Country: USA
Mailing address: 15821 NE 8th St Ste W200
Mailing city: Bellevue
Mailing state: WA
Mailing zip: 98008-3957
General Phone: (206) 415-2500
General Fax: (206) 415-2500
General/National Adv. E-mail: sales@nwnexus.com
Primary Website: www.nwnexus.net
Product or Service: Online Service Provider and Internet Hosts
Personnel: Ed Morin (Pres.); Ralph Sims (Vice Pres.)

MOSES LAKE

COLUMBIA BASIN HERALD/ HAGADONE MEDIA WASHINGTON

Street address 1: 813 West Third Ave
Street address 3: Moses Lake
Street address state: WA
Zip/Postal code: 98837
County: Grant
Country: United States
General Phone: 509-765-4561
General Fax: 509-765-8659
Advertising Phone: 509-765-4561
Advertising Fax: 509-765-8659
Editorall Phone: 509-765-4561
Editorial Fax: 509-765-8659
Display Adv. E-mail: jrountree@columbiabasinherald.com
Classified Adv. E-mail: lherbert@columbiabasinherald.com
Editorial e-mail: editor@columbiabasinherald.com
Primary Website: columbiabasinherald.com
Mthly Avg Views: 285000
Mthly Avg Unique Visitors: 90000
Year Established: 1941
Special Editions: Moses Lake Magazine Grant County Magazine Adams County Magazine Tourism Magazine Year in Review Potato Conference Columbia Basin Resource Guide Moses Lake Map Home Buyers Guide The Strength of the Columbia Basin Grant County Fair Adams County Fair Health & Wellness Puzzle Books
Special Weekly Sections: Home & Garden Local News/ Local Life
Delivery Methods: Mail`Newsstand`Carrier`Racks
Area Served - City: Grant & Adams County
Own Printing Facility: Y
Commercial printers: Y
Advertising (Open Inch Rate) Weekday/Saturday: Open inch rate $17.80
Online Advertising Rates - CPM (cost per thousand) by Size: $7-$10 cpm
Market Information: ADS; TMC.
Mechanical available: Offset; Black and 3 ROP colors; insert accepted - others accepted; page cutoffs - 22 3/4.
Mechanical specifications: Type page 13 x 21 1/2; E - 6 cols, 1 5/6, 1/8 between; A - 6 cols, 1 5/6, 1/8 between; C - 8 cols, 1 1/3, 1/8 between.
Published: Mon`Tues`Wed`Thur`Fri
Avg Paid Circ: 3500
Avg Free Circ: 2000
Audit By: Sworn/Estimate/Non-Audited
Audit Date: 12-Oct
Mailroom Eqipment: Tying Machines -- 1/Bu, 1-/El; Address Machine -- Ch/730S.;
Classified Equipment: Hardware -- Mac/G4; Printers -- HP/4200;
Classified Software: Baseview 2.1.4.
Display Equipment: Hardware -- Mac/G4; Printers -- HP/4200;
Display Software: Ad Make-up Applications -- Baseview 2.1.4; Layout Software -- Adforce.
Editorial Equipment: Hardware -- Mac/G4; Printers -- HP/4200
Editorial Software: Quark 4.0.
Production Equipment: Hardware -- 2-Fr, 1-P, 1-Ma, 1-Fi; Cameras -- 1-K.
Note: Also publish a monthly targeted, direct mail Agricultural Business Journal
Personnel: Denise Lembcke (Bus. Mgr.); Caralyn Bess (Regional Publisher); Joyce McLanahan (Nat'l Adv. Mgr.); Dave Burgess (Managing Editor); Curt Weaver (Prodn. Supt.); Bob Richardson (Advertising Director Columbia Basin Herald/Publisher Basin Business Journal); Dana Moreno (Marketing/ Audience Development Director); Rosalie Black (Sales Manager); Emily Thornton (Assistant Managing Editor); Tom Hinde (Circ. Dir.); Bill Stevenson (Mng. Ed.); Karyll Van Ness (Circulation District Manager); Sheri Jones (HR/Business Manager)
Parent company (for newspapers): Hagadone Corporation; Hagadone Media
footnotes: General/National Adv. E-mail: SRDS (10/30/2014); Classified Adv. e-mail: SRDS (10/30/2014); Special Weekly Sections: SRDS (10/30/2014); Advertising (Open Inch Rate) Weekday/ Saturday: SRDS (10/30/2014)

REDMOND

MICROSOFT CORP.

Street address 1: 1 Microsoft Way
Street address 3: Redmond
Street address state: WA
Zip/Postal code: 98052-8300
County: King
Country: USA
Mailing address: 1 Microsoft Way # 41-375
Mailing city: Redmond
Mailing state: WA
Mailing zip: 98052-8300
General Phone: (425) 882-8080
General Fax: (425) 936-7329
General/National Adv. E-mail: storesoc@microsoft.com
Primary Website: www.microsoft.com
Year Established: 1975
Product or Service: Hardware/Software Supplier
Personnel: John W. Thompson (Chrmn.); Satya Nadella (CEO); Judson Althoff (Exec. Vice Pres.); Chris Capossela (Chief Marketing Officer); Jean-Philippe Courtois (Pres., Global Sales, Marketing and Operations); Amy Hood (Exec. Vice Pres. & CFO); Kevin Scott (CTO and Exec. Vice Pres.)

CHASE BOBKO, INC.

Street address 1: 750 N 34th St
Street address 3: Seattle
Street address state: WA
Zip/Postal code: 98103-8801
County: King
Country: USA
Mailing address: 750 N 34th St
Mailing city: Seattle
Mailing state: WA
Mailing zip: 98103-8801
General Phone: (206) 547-4310
General Fax: (206) 548-0749
General/National Adv. E-mail: information@chasebobko.com
Product or Service: Multimedia/Interactive Products
Personnel: Bob Boiko (Pres.); Jayson Antonoff (CEO); Patricia Chase (Vice Pres.)

ENVISION INTERACTIVE

Street address 1: 901 5th Ave
Street address 2: Ste 3300
Street address 3: Seattle
Street address state: WA
Zip/Postal code: 98164-2024
County: King
Country: USA
Mailing address: 901 5th Ave Ste 3300
Mailing city: Seattle
Mailing state: WA
Mailing zip: 98164-2024
General Phone: (206) 225-0800
General Fax: (206) 225-0801
General/National Adv. E-mail: info@envisioninc.com
Primary Website: www.envisioninc.com
Product or Service: Multimedia/Interactive Products

METHODOLOGIE, INC.

Street address 1: 720 3rd Ave
Street address 2: Ste 800
Street address 3: Seattle
Street address state: WA
Zip/Postal code: 98104-1870
County: King
Country: USA
Mailing address: 720 3rd Ave Ste 800
Mailing city: Seattle
Mailing state: WA
Mailing zip: 98104-1870
General Phone: (206) 623-1044
General Fax: (206) 625-0154
General/National Adv. E-mail: info@methodologie.com
Primary Website: www.methodologie.com
Year Established: 1988
Product or Service: CD-ROM Designer/ Manufacturer`Graphic/Design Firm`Multimedia/ Interactive Products

WISCONSIN

MIDWEST DIGITAL COMMUNICATIONS

Street address 1: 701 Walsh Rd
Street address 3: Madison
Street address state: WI
Zip/Postal code: 53714-1372
County: Dane
Country: USA
Mailing address: PO Box 8431
Mailing city: Madison
Mailing state: WI
Mailing zip: 53708-8431
General Phone: (608) 257-5673
General Fax: (608) 257-5669
General/National Adv. E-mail: info@midwestdigital.com
Primary Website: www.midwestdigital.com
Product or Service: Advertising/Marketing Agency
Personnel: Jay Jurado (CEO)

CATALYST INTERNATIONAL, INC.

Street address 1: 8989 N Deerwood Dr
Street address 3: Milwaukee
Street address state: WI
Zip/Postal code: 53223-2446
County: Milwaukee
Country: USA
Mailing address: 8989 N Deerwood Dr
Mailing city: Milwaukee
Mailing state: WI
Mailing zip: 53223-2446
General Phone: (414) 362-6800
General Fax: (414) 362-6794
General/National Adv. E-mail: info@ctcsoftware.com
Primary Website: www.ctcsoftware.com
Product or Service: Hardware/Software Supplier
Personnel: Mark Shupac (Contact)

ELECTRONIC TELE-COMMUNICATIONS, INC.

Street address 1: 1915 Mac Arthur Rd
Street address 3: Waukesha
Street address state: WI
Zip/Postal code: 53188-5702
County: Waukesha
Country: USA
Mailing address: 1915 Mac Arthur Rd
Mailing city: Waukesha
Mailing state: WI
Mailing zip: 53188-5702
General Phone: (262) 542-5600
General Fax: (262) 542-1524
General/National Adv. E-mail: etc_mkt@etcia.com
Primary Website: www.etcia.com
Year Established: 1980
Industry: Telecommunications
Product or Service: Telecommunications/Service Bureaus
Personnel: Dean W. Danner (Pres./CEO); Joseph A. Voight (Vice Pres., Sales)

NEWS/PICTURE/SYNDICATE SERVICE

ACCURACY IN MEDIA

Street address 1: 4350 E West Hwy
Street address 2: Ste 555
Street address city: Bethesda
Street address state: MD
Zip/Postal code: 20814-4582
Country: USA
Mailing address: 4350 E West Hwy Ste 555
Mailing city: Bethesda
Mailing state: MD
Mailing zip: 20814-4582
General Phone: (202) 364-4401
General Fax: (202) 364-4098
General/National Adv. E-mail: info@aim.org
Primary Website: www.aim.org
Personnel: Donald K. Irvine (Chrmn.); Deborah Lambert (Special Projects Dir.); Roger Aronoff (Exec. Secretary)

ACCUWEATHER, INC.

Street address 1: 385 Science Park Rd
Street address city: State College
Street address state: PA
Zip/Postal code: 16803-2215
County: Centre
Country: USA
Mailing address: 385 Science Park Rd.
Mailing city: State College
Mailing state: PA
Mailing zip: 16803
General Phone: (814) 237-0309
General Fax: (814) 235-8609
General/National Adv. E-mail: support@accuweather.com
Primary Website: www.accuweather.com
Personnel: Dr. Joel N. Myers (Founder & President); Evan Myers (CEO); Steven Smith (Pres., Digital Media); Jonathan Porter (Vice Pres. of Business Services and General Mgr. of Enterprise Solutions); John Dokes (Chief Content Officer); James Candor (Chief Strategy Officer); John Dokes (Chief Marketing Officer)

ADLINK-INTERNATIONAL LTD

Street address 1: Global Advertising Services
Street address 2: 16 Upper Woburn Street
Street address city: London
Zip/Postal code: WC1H 0AF
Country: United Kingdom
Mailing address: 16 Upper Woburn Street

Mailing city: London
Mailing zip: WC1H 0AF
General Phone: 330 606 1438
General Fax: 330 606 1468
General/National Adv. E-mail: info@adlinkinternational.com
Primary Website: www.adlinkinternational.com
Note: Publishers Representatives, Advertising services in Africa, Middle East, Far East, Caribbean, Europe, Press Freedom in Africa, Editorial services, Special Supplements.
Personnel: Shamlal Puri (Mng. Dir.)

ADVERTISING WORKSHOP

Street address 1: University of Oklahoma-Gaylord/Amc, Herbert School of Journalism & Mass Co
Street address 2: 395 W Lindsey St
Street address city: Norman
Street address state: OK
Zip/Postal code: 73019-0001
Country: USA
Mailing city: Norman
Mailing state: OK
Mailing zip: 73019-0001
General Phone: (405) 325-5209
General Fax: (405) 325-7565
General/National Adv. E-mail: javery@ou.edu
Primary Website: www.ou.edu/gaylord
Note: University of Oklahoma-Gaylord/AMC, Herbert School of Journalism & Mass Communication
Personnel: Jim Avery (Self-Syndicator); Kelly Storm (Staff Asst.)

AGENCE FRANCE-PRESSE - WASHINGTON, DC

Street address 1: 1500 K St NW
Street address 2: Ste 600
Street address city: Washington
Street address state: D.C.
Zip/Postal code: 20005-1200
Country: USA
Mailing address: 1500 K St NW Ste 600
Mailing city: Washington
Mailing state: DC
Mailing zip: 20005-1200
General Phone: (202) 289-0700
General Fax: (202) 414-0634
General/National Adv. E-mail: afp-us@afp.com
Primary Website: www.afp.com
Personnel: Gilles Tarot (Mktg & Sales Dir., North America); Sue Lisk (Senior Account Manager)

AGENCIA PRENSA INTERNACIONAL INC.

Street address 1: 112 W 9th St
Street address 2: Ste 518
Street address city: Los Angeles
Street address state: CA
Zip/Postal code: 90015-1529
Country: USA
Mailing address: 112 W 9th Street Suite 518
Mailing city: Los Angeles
Mailing state: CA
Mailing zip: 90015
General Phone: 213-800-9896
General Fax: (213) 388-0563
General/National Adv. E-mail: prensa@agenciapi.com
Primary Website: agenciapi.com
Year Established: 1997
Personnel: Javier Rojas (Media Mgr.); Antonio Nava (Ed.)

AGEVENTURE NEWS SERVICE

Street address 1: 2199 Astor St
Street address 2: Suite 503
Street address city: Orange Park
Street address state: FL
Zip/Postal code: 32073-5619
Country: USA
Mailing address: 2199 Astor Street, Suite 503
Mailing city: Orange Park
Mailing state: FL
Mailing zip: 32073
General Phone: (904) 629-6020
General/National Adv. E-mail: AgeVentureNews@demko.com
Primary Website: www.demko.com
Year Established: 1987
Note: See print and broadcast news placements at: www.demko.com/circulation.html
Personnel: David J. Demko (Editor, Retirement Research Scholar)

ALAN LAVINE, INC.

Street address 1: 10199 Willow Ln
Street address city: Palm Beach Gardens
Street address state: FL
Zip/Postal code: 33410-5141
Country: USA
Mailing address: 10199 Willow Ln
Mailing city: Palm Beach Gardens
Mailing state: FL
Mailing zip: 33410-5141
General Phone: (561) 630-7112
General/National Adv. E-mail: mwliblav@aol.com
Year Established: 1980
Personnel: Alan Lavine (Chrmn./Pres.); Gail Liberman (Mktg. Mgr.)

ALM

Street address 1: 120 Broadway
Street address 2: Fl 5
Street address city: New York
Street address state: NY
Zip/Postal code: 10271-1100
Country: USA
Mailing address: 120 Broadway Fl 5
Mailing city: New York
Mailing state: NY
Mailing zip: 10271-1100
General Phone: (212) 457-9400
Primary Website: www.alm.com
Personnel: William L. Pollak (Pres./CEO); Jack Berkowitz (Sr. Vice Pres.); Ellen Sigel (Vice Pres., Licensing/Bus. Devel.); Aric Press (Editorial Dir.); Jeffrey Litvack (Chief Digital Officer)

ALTERNET

Street address 1: 77 Federal St
Street address city: San Francisco
Street address state: CA
Zip/Postal code: 94107-1414
Country: USA
Mailing address: 1881 Harmon St
Mailing city: Berkeley
Mailing state: CA
Mailing zip: 94703-2415
General Phone: (415) 284-1420
General Fax: (415) 284-1414
General/National Adv. E-mail: info@alternet.org
Primary Website: www.alternet.org
Personnel: Don Hazen (Pub./Exec. Ed.); Leigh Johnson (Bus. Mgr.); Tai Moses (Sr. Ed.); Davina Baum (Mng. Ed.)

AMERICAN CROSSWORD FEDERATION

Street address 1: PO Box 69
Street address city: Massapequa Park
Street address state: NY
Zip/Postal code: 11762-0069
Country: USA
Mailing address: PO Box 69
Mailing city: Massapequa Park
Mailing state: NY
Mailing zip: 11762
General Phone: (561) 989-0550
General/National Adv. E-mail: snpuzz@aol.com
Primary Website: www.stanxwords.com
Personnel: Stanley Newman (Pres./Ed. in Chief); Joseph Vallely (Vice Pres./Sales Dir.)

AMERICAN FEDERATION OF TEACHERS

Street address 1: 555 New Jersey Ave NW
Street address city: Washington
Street address state: D.C.
Zip/Postal code: 20001-2029
Country: USA
Mailing address: 555 New Jersey Ave NW Ste A
Mailing city: Washington
Mailing state: DC
Mailing zip: 20001-2029
General Phone: (202) 879-4400
General Fax: (202) 879-4545
General/National Adv. E-mail: aftpres@aol.com; online@aft.org
Primary Website: www.aft.org
Year Established: 1916
Personnel: Randi Weingarten (Pres.); Antonia Portese (Sec./Treasurer); Lorretta Johnson (Exec. Vice Pres.)

AMPERSAND COMMUNICATIONS

Street address 1: 2311 S Bayshore Dr
Street address city: Miami
Street address state: FL
Zip/Postal code: 33133-4728
Country: USA
Mailing address: 2311 S Bayshore Dr
Mailing city: Miami
Mailing state: FL
Mailing zip: 33133-4728
General Phone: (305) 285-2200
General/National Adv. E-mail: amprsnd@aol.com
Primary Website: www.ampersandcom.com
Year Established: 1980
Personnel: George Leposky (Ed.); Rosalie E. Leposky (Mng. Partner)

ANDREWS MCMEEL SYNDICATION

Street address 1: 1130 Walnut St
Street address city: Kansas City
Street address state: MO
Zip/Postal code: 64106-2109
Country: USA
Mailing address: 1130 Walnut Street
Mailing city: Kansas City
Mailing state: MO
Mailing zip: 64106-2109
General Phone: (816) 581-7500
General/National Adv. E-mail: press@amuniversal.com
Primary Website: http://syndication.andrewsmcmeel.com/
Personnel: John Vivona (Vice Pres. of Sales); Jan Flemington (Office Manager)

ANTIQUE DETECTIVE SYNDICATE

Street address 1: 5808 Royal Club Dr
Street address city: Boynton Beach
Street address state: FL
Zip/Postal code: 33437-4264
Country: USA
Mailing address: 5808 Royal Club Dr
Mailing city: Boynton Beach
Mailing state: FL
Mailing zip: 33437-4264
General Phone: (561) 364-5798
General/National Adv. E-mail: antique2@bellsouth.net
Year Established: 1983
Personnel: Anne Gilbert (Pres./Writer)

ANTIQUES & COLLECTIBLE SELF-SYNDICATED COLUMN

Street address 1: PO Box 597401
Street address city: Chicago
Street address state: IL
Zip/Postal code: 60659-7401
Country: USA
Mailing address: PO Box 597401
Mailing city: Chicago
Mailing state: IL
Mailing zip: 60659-7401
General Phone: (773) 267-9773
General/National Adv. E-mail: thecapecod@aol.com
Primary Website: www.anitagold.com
Personnel: Anita Gold (Author/Creator/Owner)

AP DIGITAL AND COMMERCIAL SERVICES

Street address 1: 450 W 33rd St
Street address city: New York
Street address state: NY
Zip/Postal code: 10001-2603
Country: USA
Mailing address: 450 W 33rd St
Mailing city: New York
Mailing state: NY
Mailing zip: 10001-2603
General Phone: (212) 621-1997
General Fax: (212) 621-1955
Display Adv. E-mail: apimages_us@ap.org
Primary Website: www.apimages.com
Personnel: Ian Cameron (Vice Pres.)

ARRIGONI TRAVEL SYNDICATION

Street address 1: 15 Rock Ridge Rd
Street address city: Fairfax
Street address state: CA
Zip/Postal code: 94930-1413
Country: USA
Mailing address: PO Box 1030
Mailing city: Fairfax
Mailing state: CA
Mailing zip: 94978-1030
General Phone: (415) 456-2697
General Fax: (415) 456-2697
General/National Adv. E-mail: patarrigoni@comcast.net
Primary Website: www.travelpublishers.com
Year Established: 1990
Note: Creeators Syndicate freelancer
Personnel: Patricia Arrigoni (Pres.)

ARTISTMARKET.COM

Street address 1: 35336 Spring Hill Rd
Street address city: Farmington Hills
Street address state: MI
Zip/Postal code: 48331-2044
Country: USA
Mailing address: 35336 Spring Hill Rd
Mailing city: Farmington Hills
Mailing state: MI
Mailing zip: 48331-2044
General Phone: (248) 661-8585
General Fax: (248) 788-1022
General/National Adv. E-mail: info@artistmarket.com
Primary Website: www.artistmarket.com
Year Established: 1996
Personnel: A. David Kahn (CEO/Ed.)

ARTIZANS.COM SYNDICATE

Street address 1: 11136 - 75 A St. NW
Street address city: Edmonton
Street address state: AB
Zip/Postal code: T5B 2C5
Country: Canada
Mailing address: 11136 - 75 A St. NW
Mailing city: Edmonton
Mailing state: AB
Mailing zip: T5B 2C5
General Phone: (780) 471-6112
General Fax: (877) 642-8666
General/National Adv. E-mail: sales@artizans.com; support@artizans.com
Primary Website: www.artizans.com; www.dialanartist.com
Year Established: 1999
Personnel: Malcolm Mayes (Pres.)

ASHLEIGH BRILLIANT

Street address 1: 117 W Valerio St
Street address city: Santa Barbara
Street address state: CA
Zip/Postal code: 93101-2927
Country: USA
Mailing address: 117 W Valerio St
Mailing city: Santa Barbara
Mailing state: CA
Mailing zip: 93101-2927
General Phone: (805) 682-0531
General/National Adv. E-mail: ashleigh@ashleighbrilliant.com
Primary Website: www.ashleighbrilliant.com
Year Established: 1967
Personnel: Ashleigh Brilliant (Pres.); Dorothy Brilliant (Vice Pres.)

ASSOCIATED PRESS

Street address 1: 200 Liberty St.
Street address city: New York
Street address state: NY
Zip/Postal code: 10281
Country: USA
Mailing address: 200 Liberty St.
Mailing city: New York
Mailing state: NY
Mailing zip: 10281
General Phone: (877) 836-9477
General/National Adv. E-mail: info@ap.org

Primary Website: www.ap.org
Note: U.S. States and Territories: ALABAMA Birmingham: (205) 251-4221 Montgomery: (334) 262-5947 ALASKA Anchorage: (907) 272-7549 Juneau: (907) 586-1515 ARIZONA Phoenix: (602) 258-8934 ARKANSAS Little Rock: (501) 225-3668 CALIFORNIA Sacramento: (916) 448-9555 Los Angeles: (213) 626-1200 San Diego: (619) 231-9365 San Francisco: (415) 495-1708 COLORADO Denver: (303) 825-0123 CONNECTICUT Hartford: (860) 246-6876 New Haven: (203) 964-9270 DISTRICT OF COLUMBIA Washington: (202) 641-9000 FLORIDA Cape Canaveral: (212) 621-1699 Orlando: (407) 425-4547 Tallahassee: (850) 224-1211 West Palm Beach: (305) 594-5825 Miami: (305) 594-5825 GEORGIA Atlanta: (404) 653-8460 HAWAII Honolulu: (808) 536-5510 IDAHO Boise: (208) 343-1894 ILLINOIS Springfield: (217) 789-2700 Chicago: (312) 781-0500 INDIANA Indianapolis: (317) 639-5501 IOWA Des Moines: (515) 243-3281 Iowa City: (319) 337-5615 KANSAS Topeka: (785) 234-5654 Wichita: (316) 263-4601 KENTUCKY Frankfort: (502) 227-2410 Louisville: (502) 583-7718 LOUISIANA Baton Rouge: (225) 343-1325 New Orleans: (504) 523-3931 MAINE Augusta: (207) 622-3018 Portland: (207) 772-4157 MARYLAND Baltimore: (410) 837-8315 MASSACHUSETTS Boston: (617) 357-8100 MICHIGAN Lansing: (517) 482-8011 Traverse City: (231) 929-4180 Detroit: (313) 259-0650 MINNESOTA Minneapolis: (612) 332-2727 St. Paul: (651) 222-4821 MISSISSIPPI Jackson: (601) 948-5897 MISSOURI Columbia: (573) 884-9934 Jefferson City: (573) 636-9415 St. Louis: (314) 241-2496 Kansas City: (816) 421 4844 MONTANA Billings: (406) 896-1528 Helena: (406) 442-7440 NEBRASKA Lincoln: (402) 476-2525 Omaha: (402) 391-0031 NEVADA Carson City: (775) 322-3639 Las Vegas: (702) 382-7440 Reno: (775) 322-3639 NEW HAMPSHIRE Concord: (603) 224-3327 NEW JERSEY Newark: (973) 642-0151 Atlantic City: (609) 645-2063 Trenton: (609) 392-3622 NEW MEXICO Albuquerque: (505) 822-9022 NEW YORK New York: (212) 621-1500 Albany: (518) 458-7821 Buffalo: (716) 852-1051 NORTH CAROLINA Charlotte: (704) 334-4624 Raleigh: (919) 510-8937 NORTH DAKOTA Bismarck: (701) 223-8450 Fargo: (701) 235-1908 OHIO Cincinnati: (513) 241-2386 Cleveland: (216) 771-2172 Columbus: (614) 885-2727 Toledo: (419) 255-7113 OKLAHOMA Oklahoma City: (405) 525-2121 Tulsa: (918) 584-4346 OREGON Portland: (503) 228-2169 PENNSYLVANIA Allentown: (610) 207-9297 Harrisburg: (717) 238-9413 Philadelphia: (215) 561-1133 Pittsburgh: (412) 281-3747 State College: (814) 238-3649 PUERTO RICO San Juan: (717) 793-5833 or (305) 594-1845 RHODE ISLAND Providence: (401) 274-2270 SOUTH CAROLINA Charleston: (843) 722-1660 Columbia: (803) 799-5510 SOUTH DAKOTA Pierre: (605) 224-7811 TENNESSEE Memphis: (901) 525-1972 Nashville: (615) 373-9988 TEXAS Austin: (512) 472-4004 Dallas: (972) 991-2100 Fort Worth: (817) 348-0367 Lubbock: (806) 765-0394 San Antonio: (210) 222-2713 Houston: (281) 872-8900 UTAH Salt Lake City: (801) 322-3405 VERMONT Montpelier: (802) 229-0577 VIRGINIA Richmond: (804) 643-6646 McLean: (703) 761-0187 WASHINGTON Olympia: (360) 753-7222 Seattle: (206) 682-1812 Spokane: (800) 300-8340 Yakima: (509) 453-1951 WEST VIRGINIA Charleston: (304) 346-0897 WISCONSIN Milwaukee: (414) 225-3580 Madison: (608) 255-3679 WYOMING Cheyenne: (307) 632-9351
Personnel: Gary Pruitt (Pres./CEO); Jessica Bruce (Sen. V.P./HR); Sally Buzbee (Senior V.P./Exec. Ed.); Ken Dale (Senior V.P./ CFO); Gianluca D'Aniello (Senior V.P./CTO); Dave Gwizdowski (Senior V.P./ Revenue, Americas); Karen Kaiser (Senior V.P./Gen. Counsel, Corp. Sec.); Jim Kennedy (Senior V.P./Strategic Planning); Daisy Veerasingham (Senior V.P. Revenue, Int.'l)

ASSOCIATED PRESS INFORMATION SERVICES

Street address 1: 450 W 33rd St
Street address city: New York
Street address state: NY
Zip/Postal code: 10001-2603
County: New York
Country: USA
Mailing address: 450 W 33rd St Fl 15
Mailing city: New York
Mailing state: NY
Mailing zip: 10001-2647
General Phone: (212) 621-1500
General Fax: (212) 621-7520
General/National Adv. E-mail: info@ap.org
Primary Website: www.ap.org
Personnel: Ted Mendelsohn (Dir. Sales)

ASSOCIATED PRESS MANAGING EDITORS ASSOCIATION

Street address 1: 450 W 33rd St
Street address city: New York
Street address state: NY
Zip/Postal code: 10001-2603
County: New York
Country: USA
Mailing address: 450 W 33rd St
Mailing city: New York
Mailing state: NY
Mailing zip: 10001-2603
General Phone: (212) 621-1838
General Fax: (212) 506-6102
General/National Adv. E-mail: apme@ap.org
Primary Website: www.apme.com
Year Established: 1933
Note: Elections held in Oct
Personnel: Sally Jacobsen (Gen. Mgr.)

ATLANTIC FEATURE SYNDICATE

Street address 1: 16 Slayton Rd
Street address city: Melrose
Street address state: MA
Zip/Postal code: 02176-4222
Country: USA
Mailing address: 16 Slayton Rd
Mailing city: Melrose
Mailing state: MA
Mailing zip: 02176-4222
General Phone: (781) 665-4442
General/National Adv. E-mail: lynn@offthemarkcartoons.com
Primary Website: www.offthemark.com
Year Established: 1987
Personnel: Mark Parisi (Pres.); Lynn Reznick (Mktg. Dir.)

AUTOEDITOR SYNDICATION

Street address 1: 186 Cypress Point Rd
Street address city: Half Moon Bay
Street address state: CA
Zip/Postal code: 94019-2212
Country: USA
Mailing address: 186 CYPRESS POINT ROAD
Mailing city: HALF MOON BAY
Mailing state: CA
Mailing zip: 94019-2212
General Phone: (650) 726-2386
General Fax: (650) 726-2386
General/National Adv. E-mail: brian@autoeditor.com
Primary Website: 186 CYPRESS POINT ROAD
Year Established: 1999
Note: Automotive editorial website
Personnel: Brian Douglas (Ed./Pub.)

AUTOWRITERS ASSOCIATES, INC. (MOTOR MATTERS)

Street address 1: PO Box 3305
Street address city: Wilmington
Street address state: DE
Zip/Postal code: 19804-4305
Country: USA
Mailing address: PO Box 3305
Mailing city: Wilmington
Mailing state: DE
Mailing zip: 19804-4305
General Phone: (302) 998-1650
General/National Adv. E-mail: info@motormatters.biz
Primary Website: www.motormatters.biz
Year Established: 1992
Note: Motor Matters helps publications drive revenue growth across print/digital platforms, and build marketing partnerships with advertisers, the business community, and readers. Revenue-driven content assets to build advertising dollars include high-value article titles and photography: Truck Talk, Get Off the Road, Green Wheeling, New on Wheels, Ask the Auto Doctor, Down the Road, Tech Out My New Car, Automotive Female, Classic Classics, Rolling Homes and 2-Wheeling Today. Motor Matters supports publications in maximizing advertising to in-market new car buyers and recapture buyers in the used-car market with the annual Buyers Guides. Strengths we promise to deliver are are rooted in accuracy, credibility, and clarity in messaging. Plus, we are eagle-eyed editors and fierce under deadlines. (www.motormatters.biz).
Personnel: Connie Keane (Owner); Julianne Crane (Contributor, Rolling Homes); Junior Damato (Contributor, Ask the Auto Doctor); Evelyn Kanter (Contributor, FreeWheeling); Dan Lyons (Contributor, Get Off the Road); Sue Mead (Contributor, Bonus Wheels, New on Wheels); Kate McLeod (Contributor, FreeWheeling); Vern Parker (Contributor, Classic Classics); Tim Spell (Contributor, Truck Talk); Arv Voss (Contributor, 2-Wheeling Today, New On Wheels, Bonus Wheels); Brandy Schaffels (Editor, Contributor, Women Auto Know); Frank Aukofer (Contributor, New On Wheels, Get Off the Road, Bonus Wheels); Steve Wheeler (Contributor, Classic Classics, New on Wheels, Bonus Wheels); Lyndon Conrad Bell (Contributor, New On Wheels, Down the Road, Bonus Wheels); Joe Michaud; Lynn Walford

BANKRATE.COM

Street address 1: 11760 US Highway 1
Street address 2: Ste 200
Street address city: North Palm Beach
Street address state: FL
Zip/Postal code: 33408-3003
Country: USA
Mailing address: 11760 US Highway 1 Ste 200
Mailing city: North Palm Beach
Mailing state: FL
Mailing zip: 33408-3003
General Phone: (561) 630-2400
General Fax: (561) 625-4540
Primary Website: www.bankrate.com
Personnel: Tom Evans (President & CEO (Former)); Donald M. Ross (Sr. Vice Pres./Chief Revenue Officer); Robert J. DeFranco (Sr. Vice Pres., Finance/CFO); Bruce Zanca (Sr. Vice Pres./Chief Mktg./Commun. Officer); Beth Planakis (Mktg. Dir.)

BASIC CHESS FEATURES

Street address 1: 102 Blatchley Rd
Street address city: Windsor
Street address state: NY
Zip/Postal code: 13865-3304
Country: USA
Mailing address: 102 Blatchley Rd
Mailing city: Windsor
Mailing state: NY
Mailing zip: 13865-3304
General Phone: (607) 775-0587
General/National Adv. E-mail: slyman@tds.net
Personnel: Shelby Lyman (Pres.)

BEAVER CREEK FEATURES

Street address 1: 3508 W 151st St
Street address city: Cleveland
Street address state: OH
Zip/Postal code: 44111-2105
Country: USA
Mailing address: 3508 W 151st St
Mailing city: Cleveland
Mailing state: OH
Mailing zip: 44111-2105
General Phone: (216) 251-1389
General/National Adv. E-mail: dnorman@bge.net
Primary Website: www.sites.google.com/site/wallyswoods
Year Established: 1993
Personnel: Dean Norman (Artist/Owner)

BIG RING MEDIA TEAM, INC.

Street address 1: PO Box 231
Street address city: Madison
Street address state: ID
Zip/Postal code: 47250-0231
Country: USA
Mailing address: PO Box 231
Mailing city: Madison
Mailing state: IN
Mailing zip: 47250-0231
General Phone: (812) 265-6313
General Fax: (812) 418-3368
General/National Adv. E-mail: info@bigringwriting.com
Primary Website: www.bigringwriting.com
Year Established: 1999
Personnel: Richard Ries (Dir.); Julie Ries (Admin. Asst.)

BILL'S CARTOON SHOW

Street address 1: 420 Livermore Road
Street address city: Williamsport
Street address state: PA
Zip/Postal code: 17701
Country: USA
General Phone: (570) 494-6789
General/National Adv. E-mail: wildbill@wildbillsartshow.net
Primary Website: www.wildbillsartshow.net
Year Established: 2001
Personnel: Bill Stanford (Cartoonist, Artist, Creator)

BIOFILE

Street address 1: 995 Teaneck Rd
Street address 2: Apt 3N
Street address city: Teaneck
Street address state: NJ
Zip/Postal code: 07666-4543
Country: USA
Mailing address: 995 Teaneck Rd Apt 3N
Mailing city: Teaneck
Mailing state: NJ
Mailing zip: 07666-4543
General Phone: (201) 833-2350
General Fax: (201) 833-2350
General/National Adv. E-mail: mrbiofile@aol.com
Primary Website: www.thebiofile.com
Personnel: Mark (Scoop) Malinowski (Ed.)

BLACK PRESS SERVICE, INC.

Street address 1: 375 5th Ave
Street address city: New York
Street address state: NY
Zip/Postal code: 10016-3323
Country: USA
Mailing address: 375 5th Ave Fl 3
Mailing city: New York
Mailing state: NY
Mailing zip: 10016-3323
General Phone: (212) 686-6850
General Fax: (212) 686-7308
General/National Adv. E-mail: news@blackradionetwork.com
Primary Website: www.blackradionetwork.com
Year Established: 1964
Personnel: Jay R. Levy (Pres.); Peter Knight (Sales Mgr.); Roy Thompson (Ed.); Bill Baldwin (Assoc. Ed.)

BLACK STAR PUBLISHING CO., INC.

Street address 1: 333 Mamaroneck Ave
Street address 2: # 175
Street address city: White Plains
Street address state: NY
Zip/Postal code: 10605-1440
County: Westchester
Country: USA
Mailing address: 333 Mamaroneck Ave # 175
Mailing city: White Plains
Mailing state: NY
Mailing zip: 10605-1440
General Phone: (212) 679-3288
General/National Adv. E-mail: sales@blackstar.com
Primary Website: www.blackstar.com
Personnel: Ben Chapnick (Pres.); John P. Chapnick (Vice Pres.)

BLOOMBERG NEWS

Street address 1: Pierre 3., Ste, 101
Street address city: San Francisco
Street address state: CA
Zip/Postal code: 94111
Country: USA
Mailing address: Pierre 3., Ste., 101
Mailing city: San Francisco
Mailing state: CA
Mailing zip: 94111
Primary Website: https://www.bloomberg.com

BLOOMBERG NEWS

Street address 1: 1399 New York Ave NW
Street address 2: Fl 11
Street address city: Washington
Street address state: D.C.

Zip/Postal code: 20005-4749
Country: USA
Mailing address: 1399 New York Ave NW Fl 11
Mailing city: Washington
Mailing state: DC
Mailing zip: 20005-4749
Primary Website: https://www.bloomberg.com

BLOOMBERG NEWS

Street address 1: 111 S Wacker Dr
Street address 2: Ste 4950
Street address city: Chicago
Street address state: IL
Zip/Postal code: 60606-4418
Country: USA
Mailing address: 111 S Wacker Dr Ste 4950
Mailing city: Chicago
Mailing state: IL
Mailing zip: 60606-4418
Primary Website: https://www.bloomberg.com

BLOOMBERG NEWS

Street address 1: 100 Business Park Dr
Street address city: Skillman
Street address state: NJ
Zip/Postal code: 08558-2601
Country: USA
Mailing address: 100 Business Park Dr
Mailing city: Skillman
Mailing state: NJ
Mailing zip: 08558-2693
Primary Website: https://www.bloomberg.com

BLOOMBERG NEWS

Street address 1: 731 Lexington Ave
Street address city: New York
Street address state: NY
Zip/Postal code: 10022-1331
Country: USA
Mailing address: 731 Lexington Ave Frnt 6
Mailing city: New York
Mailing state: NY
Mailing zip: 10022-1343
Primary Website: https://www.bloomberg.com
Year Established: 1990

BLOOMBERG NEWS

Street address 1: 161 Bay St., Ste. 4300
Street address city: Toronto
Street address state: ON
Zip/Postal code: M5J 2S1
Country: Canada
Mailing address: 161 Bay St., Ste. 4300
Mailing city: Toronto
Mailing state: ON
Mailing zip: M5J 2S1
Primary Website: https://www.bloomberg.com

BLOOMBERG NEWS

Street address 1: Neue Mainzer Strasse 75
Street address city: Frankfurt
Zip/Postal code: 60311
Country: Germany
Mailing address: Neue Mainzer Strasse 75
Mailing city: Frankfurt
Mailing zip: 60311
Primary Website: https://www.bloomberg.com

BLOOMBERG NEWS

Street address 1: 27 Fl., Cheung Kong Ctr., 2 Queens Rd. Central
Street address city: Hong Kong
Country: Hong Kong
Mailing address: 27 Fl., Cheung Kong Ctr., 2 Queens Rd. Central
Mailing city: Hong Kong
Primary Website: https://www.bloomberg.com

BLOOMBERG NEWS

Street address 1: 7 Rue Scribe
Street address city: Paris
Zip/Postal code: 75009
Country: France
Mailing address: 7 Rue Scribe
Mailing city: Paris
Mailing zip: 75009
Primary Website: https://www.bloomberg.com

BLOOMBERG NEWS

Street address 1: Capital Square, 23 Church St., 12th Fl.
Street address city: Singapore
Zip/Postal code: 49481
Country: Singapore
Mailing address: Capital Square, 23 Church St., 12th Fl.
Mailing city: Singapore
Mailing zip: 49481
Primary Website: https://www.bloomberg.com

BLOOMBERG NEWS

Street address 1: 1 Macquarie Pl., Level 36, Gtwy. 36
Street address city: Sydney
Zip/Postal code: 2000
Country: Australia
Mailing address: 1 Macquarie Pl., Level 36, Gtwy. 36
Mailing city: Sydney
Mailing zip: 2000
Primary Website: https://www.bloomberg.com

BLOOMBERG NEWS

Street address 1: Yusen Bldg., 1st Fl., 2-3-2 Marunouchi
Street address city: Tokyo
Zip/Postal code: 100
Country: Japan
Mailing address: Yusen Bldg., 1st Fl., 2-3-2 Marunouchi
Mailing city: Tokyo
Mailing zip: 100
General/National Adv. E-mail: https://www.bloomberg.com

BROADCAST NEWS LIMITED

Street address 1: PO Box 10109, 106th St., Ste. 504
Street address city: Edmonton
Street address state: AB
Zip/Postal code: T5J 3L7
Country: Canada
Mailing address: PO Box 10109, 106th St., Ste. 504
Mailing city: Edmonton
Mailing state: AB
Mailing zip: T5J 3L7
General Phone: (780) 428-6490
General Fax: (780) 428-0663
Personnel: Kathy Bell (Bureau Chief)

BROADCAST NEWS LIMITED

Street address 1: 840 Howe St., Ste. 250
Street address city: Vancouver
Street address state: BC
Zip/Postal code: V6Z 2L2
Country: Canada
Mailing address: 840 Howe St., Ste. 250
Mailing city: Vancouver
Mailing state: BC
Mailing zip: V6Z 2L2
General Phone: (604) 687-1662
General Fax: (604) 687-5040
Personnel: Jill St. Louis (Bureau Chief)

BROADCAST NEWS LIMITED

Street address 1: 386 Broadway Ave., Ste. 101
Street address city: Winnipeg
Street address state: MB
Zip/Postal code: R3C 3R6
Country: Canada
Mailing address: 386 Broadway Ave., Ste. 101
Mailing city: Winnipeg
Mailing state: MB
Mailing zip: R3C 3R6
General Phone: (204) 988-1781
General Fax: (204) 942-4788
Personnel: Steve Lambert (Manitoba Correspondent)

BROADCAST NEWS LIMITED

Street address 1: The Press Gallery, Box 6000, Queen St.
Street address city: Fredericton
Street address state: NB
Zip/Postal code: E3B 5H1
Country: Canada
Mailing address: The Press Gallery, Box 6000, Queen St.
Mailing city: Fredericton
Mailing state: NB
Mailing zip: E3B 5H1
General Phone: (506) 457-0746
General Fax: (506) 457-9708
Personnel: Kevin Bissett (New Brunswick Correspondent)

BROADCAST NEWS LIMITED

Street address 1: 1888 Brunswick St., Ste. 100
Street address city: Halifax
Street address state: NS
Zip/Postal code: B3J 3J8
Country: Canada
Mailing address: 1888 Brunswick St., Ste. 100
Mailing city: Halifax
Mailing state: NS
Mailing zip: B3J 3J8
General Phone: (902) 422-9284
General Fax: (902) 565-7588
Personnel: Dean Beeby (Bureau Chief); Murray Brewster (Legislative Reporter)

BROADCAST NEWS LIMITED

Street address 1: 165 Sparks St., Ste. 800
Street address city: Ottawa
Street address state: ON
Zip/Postal code: K1P 5B9
Country: Canada
Mailing address: P.O. Box 595, Station B
Mailing city: Ottawa
Mailing state: ON
Mailing zip: K1P 5P7
General Phone: (613) 238-4142
General Fax: (613) 232-5163
Primary Website: www.thecanadianpress.com
Personnel: Robert Russo (Bureau Chief)

BROADCAST NEWS LIMITED

Street address 1: 36 King St. E.
Street address city: Toronto
Street address state: ON
Zip/Postal code: M5C 2L9
Country: Canada
Mailing address: 36 King St. E.
Mailing city: Toronto
Mailing state: ON
Mailing zip: M5C 2L9
General Phone: (416) 364-0321
General Fax: (416) 364-8896
Primary Website: www.thecanadianpress.com
Personnel: Ellen Huebert (News Editor); David Ross (CFO); Terry Scott (Gen. Exec./Client Liaison); Charles Messina (Sales/Mktg. Dir.); Sandra Clarke

BROADCAST NEWS LIMITED

Street address 1: 215 St. Jacques W., Ste. 100
Street address city: Montreal
Street address state: QC
Zip/Postal code: H2Y 1M6
Country: Canada
Mailing address: 215 St. Jacques W., Ste. 100
Mailing city: Montreal
Mailing state: QC
Mailing zip: H2Y 1M6
General Phone: (514) 849-8008
General Fax: (514) 282-6915
Personnel: Peter Ray (Quebec Correspondent)

BROADCAST NEWS LIMITED

Street address 1: 1050 rue Des Parlementaires, Bureau 207
Street address city: Quebec City
Street address state: QC
Zip/Postal code: G1R 5A4
Country: Canada
Mailing address: 1050 rue Des Parlementaires, Bureau 207
Mailing city: Quebec City
Mailing state: QC
Mailing zip: G1R 5A4
General Phone: (418) 646-5377
General Fax: (418) 523-9686
Personnel: Martin Ouellett (Correspondent)

BROADCAST NEWS LIMITED

Street address 1: Rm. 335, Press Gallery
Street address city: Regina
Street address state: SK
Zip/Postal code: S4S 0B3
Country: Canada
Mailing address: Rm. 335, Press Gallery
Mailing city: Regina
Mailing state: SK
Mailing zip: S4S 0B3
General Phone: (306) 585-1024
General Fax: (306) 585-1027
Personnel: Jay Branch (Saskatchewan Correspondent)

BUSINESS NEWSFEATURES

Street address 1: 417 Lexington Rd
Street address city: Grosse Pointe Farms
Street address state: MI
Zip/Postal code: 48236-2820
Country: USA
Mailing address: 417 Lexington Rd
Mailing city: Grosse Pointe Farms
Mailing state: MI
Mailing zip: 48236-2820
General Phone: (313) 929 - 0800
General/National Adv. E-mail: cmeyering@ameritech.net
Year Established: 1970
Personnel: Robert H. Meyering (Writer, Computer Columns); Carl E. Meyering (Ed.)

BUSINESS WIRE - BOSTON, MA

Street address 1: 2 Center Plz
Street address 2: Ste 500
Street address city: Boston
Street address state: MA
Zip/Postal code: 02108-1921
Country: USA
Mailing address: 1 Boston Pl Ste 2330
Mailing city: Boston
Mailing state: MA
Mailing zip: 02108-4473
General Phone: (617) 742-2760
General Fax: (617) 742-2782
General/National Adv. E-mail: news@businesswire.com
Primary Website: Business Wire - Boston, MA
Personnel: Cathy Baron Tamraz (Pres./COO)

BUSINESS WIRE - CLEVELAND, OH

Street address 1: 1001 Lakeside Ave E
Street address 2: Ste 1525
Street address city: Cleveland
Street address state: OH
Zip/Postal code: 44114-1193
Country: USA
Mailing address: 1001 Lakeside Ave E Ste 1525
Mailing city: Cleveland
Mailing state: OH
Mailing zip: 44114-1193
General Phone: (800) 769-0220
General Fax: (800) 827-0237
Primary Website: www.businesswire.com
Personnel: Jill Connor (Midwest Reg. Mgr.)

BUSINESS WIRE - DENVER, CO

Street address 1: 1725 Blake St
Street address 2: Ste 100
Street address city: Denver
Street address state: CO
Zip/Postal code: 80202-5917
Country: USA
Mailing address: 1725 Blake St Ste 100
Mailing city: Denver
Mailing state: CO
Mailing zip: 80202-5917
General Phone: (800) 308-0166
General Fax: (303) 830-2442
Primary Website: www.businesswire.com
Personnel: Dylan Frusciano (Vice Pres.)

BUSINESS WIRE - LOS ANGELES, CA

Street address 1: 12100 Wilshire Blvd

Street address 2: Ste 780
Street address city: Los Angeles
Street address state: CA
Zip/Postal code: 90025-1281
Country: USA
Mailing address: 12100 Wilshire Blvd Ste 780
Mailing city: Los Angeles
Mailing state: CA
Mailing zip: 90025-1281
General Phone: (800) 237-8212
General Fax: (310) 820-7363
Primary Website: www.businesswire.com
Personnel: Mike Iannuzzi (Mgr., Southwest Reg.); Tom Becktold (Nat'l Dir., Mktg. Programs)

BUSINESS WIRE - NEW YORK, NY

Street address 1: 40 E 52nd St
Street address 2: Fl 14
Street address city: New York
Street address state: NY
Zip/Postal code: 10022-5911
County: New York
Country: USA
Mailing address: 40 E 52nd St Fl 14
Mailing city: New York
Mailing state: NY
Mailing zip: 10022-5911
General Phone: (212) 752-9600
Primary Website: www.businesswire.com
Personnel: Geff Scott (CEO); Richard DeLeo (COO)

BUSINESS WIRE - SAN FRANCISCO, CA

Street address 1: 44 Montgomery St
Street address 2: Fl 39
Street address city: San Francisco
Street address state: CA
Zip/Postal code: 94104-4602
Country: USA
Mailing address: 44 Montgomery St Fl 39
Mailing city: San Francisco
Mailing state: CA
Mailing zip: 94104-4812
General Phone: (415) 986-4422
General Fax: (415) 788-5335
General/National Adv. E-mail: news@businesswire.com
Primary Website: www.businesswire.com
Year Established: 1961
Personnel: Cathy Baron Tamraz; Gregg Castano (Co-Chief Opns.); news@businesswire.com Neil (Vice Pres., Global Media)

CAGLE CARTOONS, INC.

Street address 1: PO Box 22342
Street address city: Santa Barbara
Street address state: CA
Zip/Postal code: 93121-2342
Country: USA
Mailing address: PO Box 22342
Mailing city: Santa Barbara
Mailing state: CA
Mailing zip: 93121-2342
General Phone: (805) 969-2829
General/National Adv. E-mail: cari@cagle.com
Primary Website: www.caglecartoons.com
Note: Cagle Cartoons, Inc. does not accept unsolicited submissions.
Personnel: Daryl Cagle (Pres./CEO); Cari Dawson Bartley (Exec. Ed./Mktg. Dir.)

CANADIAN ARTISTS SYNDICATE INCORPORATED

Street address 1: 5 Ramsgate Lane, Suite 116
Street address city: Halifax
Street address state: NS
Zip/Postal code: B3P 2S6
Country: Canada
Mailing address: 5 Ramsgate Lane, Suite 116
Mailing city: Halifax
Mailing state: NS
Mailing zip: B3P 2S6
General Phone: (902) 407-3440
General/National Adv. E-mail: rvroom@artistsyndicate.ca
Primary Website: www.artistsyndicate.ca
Personnel: Richard Vroom (President)

CANADIAN PRESS, THE - CALGARY, AB

Street address 1: 131 9 Avenue SW, Suite 310
Street address city: Calgary
Street address state: AB
Zip/Postal code: T2P 1K1
Country: Canada
Mailing address: 131 9 Avenue SW, Suite 310
Mailing city: Calgary
Mailing state: AB
Mailing zip: T2P 1K1
General Phone: (403) 543-7238
General Fax: (403) 262-7520
General/National Adv. E-mail: calgary@thecanadianpress.com
Primary Website: www.thecanadianpress.com
Year Established: 1917
Personnel: Bill Graveland (National Correspondent); Lauren Krugel (National Business Correspondent); Dan Healing (Business reporter)

CANADIAN PRESS, THE - EDMONTON, AB

Street address 1: Cornerpoint, 10109 106th St., Ste. 504
Street address city: Edmonton
Street address state: AB
Zip/Postal code: T5J 3L7
Country: Canada
Mailing address: Cornerpoint, 10109 106th St., Ste. 504
Mailing city: Edmonton
Mailing state: AB
Mailing zip: T5J 3L7
General Phone: (780) 428-6490
General Fax: (780) 428-0663
Primary Website: www.thecanadianpress.com
Personnel: Heather Boyd (Bureau Chief)

CANADIAN PRESS, THE - FREDERICTON, NB

Street address 1: Press Gallery, 96 Saint John St
Street address city: Fredericton
Street address state: NB
Zip/Postal code: E3B 1C5
Country: Canada
Mailing address: PO Box 6000
Mailing city: Fredericton
Mailing state: NB
Mailing zip: E3B 5H1
General Phone: (506) 457-0746
General Fax: (506) 457-9708
Primary Website: www.thecanadianpress.com
Personnel: Kevin Bissett (Correspondent)

CANADIAN PRESS, THE - HALIFAX, NS

Street address 1: 1888 Brunswick St., Ste. 701
Street address city: Halifax
Street address state: NS
Zip/Postal code: B3J 3J8
Country: Canada
Mailing address: PO Box 37, Sta. M
Mailing city: Halifax
Mailing state: NS
Mailing zip: B3J 2L4
General Phone: (902) 422-8496
General Fax: (902) 425-2675
Primary Website: www.thecanadianpress.com
Personnel: Dean Beeby (Bureau Chief)

CANADIAN PRESS, THE - MONTREAL, QC

Street address 1: 215 St. Jacques St., Ste. 100
Street address city: Montreal
Street address state: QC
Zip/Postal code: H2Y 1M6
Country: Canada
Mailing address: 215 St. Jacques St., Ste. 100
Mailing city: Montreal
Mailing state: QC
Mailing zip: H2Y 1M6
General Phone: (514) 849-3212
General Fax: (514) 282-6915
General/National Adv. E-mail: info@thecanadianpress.com
Primary Website: www.thecanadianpress.com
Personnel: Eric Morrison (Pres.); Claude Papineau (Vice Pres.-French Serv.)

CANADIAN PRESS, THE - OTTAWA, ON

Street address 1: 165 Sparks St., Ste. 800
Street address city: Ottawa
Street address state: ON
Zip/Postal code: K1P 5P7
Country: Canada
Mailing address: PO Box 595, Sta. B (Letters)
Mailing city: Ottawa
Mailing state: ON
Mailing zip: K1P 5P7
General Phone: (613) 238-4142
General Fax: (613) 238-4452
General/National Adv. E-mail: ottowa@thecanadianpress.com
Primary Website: www.thecanadianpress.com
Personnel: Robert Russo (Bureau Chief)

CANADIAN PRESS, THE - QUEBEC CITY, QC

Street address 1: 1050 Des Parlementaires, Ste. 2
Street address city: Quebec City
Street address state: QC
Zip/Postal code: G1R 5J1
Country: Canada
Mailing address: 1050 Des Parlementaires, Ste. 2
Mailing city: Quebec City
Mailing state: QC
Mailing zip: G1R 5J1
General Phone: (418) 646-5377
General Fax: (418) 523-9686
General/National Adv. E-mail: info@thecanadianpress.com
Primary Website: www.thecanadianpress.com
Personnel: Jean Roy (Director)

CANADIAN PRESS, THE - REGINA, SK

Street address 1: Legislative Bldg., Press Gallery, Rm. 335
Street address city: Regina
Street address state: SK
Zip/Postal code: S4S 0B3
Country: Canada
Mailing address: Legislative Bldg., Press Gallery, Rm. 335
Mailing city: Regina
Mailing state: SK
Mailing zip: S4S 0B3
General Phone: (306) 585-1024
General Fax: (306) 585-1027
General/National Adv. E-mail: info@thecanadianpress.com
Primary Website: www.thecanadianpress.com
Personnel: Stephanie Graham (Correspondent)

CANADIAN PRESS, THE - SAINT JOHN'S, NL

Street address 1: 139 Water St., Ste. 901
Street address 2: The Fortis Bldg.
Street address city: Saint John's
Street address state: NL
Zip/Postal code: A1C 1B2
Country: Canada
Mailing address: PO Box 5951
Mailing city: Saint John's
Mailing state: NL
Mailing zip: A1C 5X4
General Phone: (709) 576-0687
General Fax: (709) 576-0049
Primary Website: www.thecanadianpress.com
Personnel: Michelle MacAfee (Correspondent)

CANADIAN PRESS, THE - TORONTO, ON

Street address 1: 36 King St. E.
Street address city: Toronto
Street address state: ON
Zip/Postal code: M5C 2L9
County: York
Country: Canada
Mailing address: 36 King St. E.
Mailing city: Toronto
Mailing state: ON
Mailing zip: M5C 2L9
General Phone: (416) 507-2099
General/National Adv. E-mail: support@thecanadianpress.com
Display Adv. E-mail: sales@thecanadianpress.com
Editorial e-mail: editorial@thecanadianpress.com
Primary Website: www.thecanadianpress.com
Note: Elections held in April
Personnel: John Honderich (Chrmn.); Ellen Huebert (News Editor); Keith Leslie (Legislature Correspondent); Eric Morrison (Pres.); David Ross (CFO); Wendy McCann (Chief, Ontario Servs.); Terry Scott (Vice Pres., Broadcasting); Jean Roy (Vice Pres., French Servs.); Paul Woods (Dir., HR); Sharon Hockin (Office Mgr.); Philipe Mercure (Exec. Dir.)

CANADIAN PRESS, THE - VANCOUVER, BC

Street address 1: 840 Howe St., Ste. 250
Street address city: Vancouver
Street address state: BC
Zip/Postal code: V6Z 2L2
Country: Canada
Mailing address: 840 Howe St., Ste. 250
Mailing city: Vancouver
Mailing state: BC
Mailing zip: V6Z 2L2
General Phone: (604) 687-1662
General Fax: (604) 687-5040
Primary Website: www.thecanadianpress.com
Personnel: Wendy Cox (Bureau Chief)

CANADIAN PRESS, THE - VICTORIA, BC

Street address 1: Press Gallery, Rm. 360
Street address city: Victoria
Street address state: BC
Zip/Postal code: V8V 1X4
Country: Canada
Mailing address: Press Gallery
Mailing city: Victoria
Mailing state: BC
Mailing zip: V8V 1X4
General Phone: (250) 384-4912
General Fax: (250) 356-9597
General/National Adv. E-mail: dirk.meissner@thecanadianpress.com
Primary Website: www.thecanadianpress.com
Personnel: Dirk Meissner (Correspondent)

CANADIAN PRESS, THE - WASHINGTON, DC

Street address 1: 1100 13th St NW
Street address city: Washington
Street address state: D.C.
Zip/Postal code: 20005-4051
Country: USA
Mailing address: 1100 13th St NW
Mailing city: Washington
Mailing state: DC
Mailing zip: 20005-4051
General Phone: (202) 638-3367
General Fax: (202) 638-3369
Primary Website: www.thecanadianpress.com
Personnel: Robert Russo (Bureau Chief)

CANADIAN PRESS, THE - WINNIPEG, MB

Street address 1: 386 Broadway Ave., Ste. 101
Street address city: Winnipeg
Street address state: MB
Zip/Postal code: R3C 3R6
Country: Canada
Mailing address: 386 Broadway Ave., Ste. 101
Mailing city: Winnipeg
Mailing state: MB
Mailing zip: R3C 3R6
General Phone: (204) 988-1781
General Fax: (204) 942-4788
General/National Adv. E-mail: info@thecanadianpress.com
Primary Website: www.thecanadianpress.com

Personnel: Steve Lambert (Manitoba Correspondent)

CAPITAL CONNECTIONS

Street address 1: 1698 32nd St NW
Street address city: Washington
Street address state: D.C.
Zip/Postal code: 20007-2969
Country: USA
Mailing address: 304 E 65th St Apt 26C
Mailing city: New York
Mailing state: NY
Mailing zip: 10065-6785
General Phone: (202) 337-2044
General Fax: (202) 338-4750
General/National Adv. E-mail: karen@karenfeld.com
Primary Website: www.karenfeld.com
Year Established: 1985
Personnel: Karen Feld (Owner/Editor)

CAPITOL NEWS SERVICE

Street address 1: 530 Bercut Dr
Street address 2: Ste E
Street address city: Sacramento
Street address state: CA
Zip/Postal code: 95811-0101
Country: USA
Mailing address: 530 Bercut Dr Ste E
Mailing city: Sacramento
Mailing state: CA
Mailing zip: 95811-0101
General Phone: (916) 445-6336
General Fax: (916) 443-5871
General/National Adv. E-mail: editor@senior-spectrum.com
Primary Website: www.senior-spectrum.com
Personnel: Susan Carlson

CAREER SOURCE/COLUMN

Street address 1: PO Box 94
Street address city: Birmingham
Street address state: MI
Zip/Postal code: 48012-0094
Country: USA
Mailing address: PO Box 94
Mailing city: Birmingham
Mailing state: MI
Mailing zip: 48012-0094
General Phone: (248) 647-3662
General/National Adv. E-mail: sgsilver2002@yahoo.com; sheryl.silver@yahoo.com
Personnel: Sheryl Silver (Owner/Author)

CARTOON RESOURCE

Street address 1: 3568 Cascade Rd SE
Street address city: Grand Rapids
Street address state: MI
Zip/Postal code: 49546-2141
Country: USA
Mailing address: 3568 Cascade Rd SE
Mailing city: Grand Rapids
Mailing state: MI
Mailing zip: 49546-2141
General Phone: (616) 551-2238
General/National Adv. E-mail: andrew@cartoonresource.com
Primary Website: www.cartoonresource.com
Note: Cartoon Resource delivers customized editorial art with rapid turn-around.
Personnel: Andrew Grossman (Creative Dir.); Nancy Terrell (Mktg. Dir.)

CARTOONEWS, INC.

Street address 1: 15 Central Park W
Street address city: New York
Street address state: NY
Zip/Postal code: 10023-7708
Country: USA
Mailing address: 15 Central Park W
Mailing city: New York
Mailing state: NY
Mailing zip: 10023-7708
General Phone: (212) 980-0855
General Fax: (212) 980-1664
General/National Adv. E-mail: cartoonews@aol.com; luriestudios@aol.com
Primary Website: www.luriecartoon.com
Personnel: T.R. Fletcher (Pres.); L. Raymond (Vice Pres., Sales); Lisa Duval (Admin. Dir.); John Schmitt (Accountant/CPA)

CARTOONISTS & WRITERS SYNDICATE/CARTOON ARTS INTERNATIONAL - NEW YORK, NY

Street address 1: 67 Riverside Dr
Street address 2: Apt 7A
Street address city: New York
Street address state: NY
Zip/Postal code: 10024-6136
Country: USA
Mailing address: 67 Riverside Dr Apt 7A
Mailing city: New York
Mailing state: NY
Mailing zip: 10024-6136
General Phone: (212) CARTOON (277-8666)
General/National Adv. E-mail: cwss@cartoonweb.com
Primary Website: www.nytsyn.com/cartoons
Personnel: Jerry Robinson (Pres.)

CARTOONISTS & WRITERS SYNDICATE/CARTOON ARTS INTERNATIONAL - RANCHO PALOS VERDES, CA

Street address 1: 28028 Lobrook Dr
Street address city: Rancho Palos Verdes
Street address state: CA
Zip/Postal code: 90275-3132
Country: USA
Mailing address: 28028 Lobrook Dr
Mailing city: Rancho Palos Verdes
Mailing state: CA
Mailing zip: 90275-3132
General Phone: (212) 227-8666
General Fax: (310) 541-9017
General/National Adv. E-mail: cwsmedia@cartoonweb.com
Primary Website: www.nytsyn.com/cartoons
Year Established: 1978
Personnel: Jerry Robinson (Pres.); Jens Robinson (Vice Pres./Ed.); Bojan Jovanovic (Assoc. Ed.)

CATHOLIC NEWS SERVICE

Street address 1: 3211 4th St NE
Street address city: Washington
Street address state: D.C.
Zip/Postal code: 20017-1104
Country: USA
General Phone: (202) 541-3250
General/National Adv. E-mail: cns@catholicnews.com
Primary Website: www.catholicnews.com
Year Established: 1920
Note: Catholic news since 1920.
Personnel: Tony Spence (Director/Editor in Chief); Julie Asher (General News Editor); Edmond Brosnan (Features Editor); Katherine M. Nuss (Library/Information Services/Archives); James Lackey (Web Editor)

CITY NEWS SERVICE, INC. - LOS ANGELES, CA

Street address 1: 11400 W Olympic Blvd
Street address 2: Ste 780
Street address city: Los Angeles
Street address state: CA
Zip/Postal code: 90064-1553
Country: USA
Mailing address: 11400 W Olympic Blvd Ste 780
Mailing city: Los Angeles
Mailing state: CA
Mailing zip: 90064-1553
General Phone: (310) 481-0407
General Fax: (310) 481-0416
General/National Adv. E-mail: citynews@pacbell.net; info@socalnews.com
Primary Website: www.socalnews.com
Year Established: 1928
Personnel: Doug Faigin (Pres.); Lori Streifler (Ed.); Marty Sauerzopf (City Ed.)

CITY NEWS SERVICE, INC. - SAN DIEGO, CA

Street address 1: 202 C St
Street address 2: Rm 13A
Street address city: San Diego
Street address state: CA
Zip/Postal code: 92101-4806
Country: USA
Mailing address: 202 C St Rm 13A
Mailing city: San Diego
Mailing state: CA
Mailing zip: 92101-4806
General Phone: (619) 231-9097
General Fax: (619) 231-9633
General/National Adv. E-mail: fdrim@fdcglobal.net
Personnel: Kelly Wheeler (Bureau Chief); Lori Streifler (Ed.)

CLARIN CONTENIDOS

Street address 1: Tacuari 1840
Street address city: Buenos Aires
Street address state: CA
Zip/Postal code: 1139
Country: Argentina
Mailing address: abeltrame@clarin.com
Mailing city: Buenos Aires
Mailing zip: 1139
General Phone: 4309-7216
General Fax: 4309-7635
General/National Adv. E-mail: contenidos@clarin.com
Primary Website: www.clarin.com
Personnel: Matilde Sanchez (Ed.); Agustin Beltrame (Photo Editor); Hernan DiMenna (Ed.)

CLASSICSTOCK / ROBERTSTOCK

Street address 1: 4203 Locust St
Street address city: Philadelphia
Street address state: PA
Zip/Postal code: 19104-5228
Country: USA
Mailing address: 4203 Locust St
Mailing city: Philadelphia
Mailing state: PA
Mailing zip: 19104-5290
General Phone: (215) 386-6300
General Fax: (215) 386-3521
General/National Adv. E-mail: robertag@classicstock.com
Primary Website: www.classicstock.com
Year Established: 1920
Personnel: H. Armstrong Roberts (Pres., ClassicStock); Roberta Groves (Vice Pres., Creative)

CLEAR CREEK FEATURES

Street address 1: PO Box 3289
Street address city: Grass Valley
Street address state: CA
Zip/Postal code: 95945-3289
Country: USA
Mailing address: PO Box 3289
Mailing city: Grass Valley
Mailing state: CA
Mailing zip: 95945-3289
General Phone: (530) 272-7176
General/National Adv. E-mail: clearcreekrancher@yahoo.com
Personnel: Mike Drummond (Author/Self-Syndicator/Pub.)

COLLINS COMMUNICATIONS

Street address 1: 21-07 Maple Ave
Street address city: Fair Lawn
Street address state: NJ
Zip/Postal code: 07410-1524
Country: USA
Mailing address: 21-07 Maple Ave
Mailing city: Fair Lawn
Mailing state: NJ
Mailing zip: 07410-1524
General Phone: (201) 703-0911
General Fax: (201) 703-0211
General/National Adv. E-mail: stepoutmag@aol.com
Display Adv. E-mail: stepoutmag@aol.com
Editorial e-mail: chaunce100@aol.com
Primary Website: www.so-mag.com
Year Established: 1988
Personnel: Lawrence Collins (Publisher); Dan Lorenzo (Editor)

COMMUNITY FEATURES

Street address 1: 1733 Dawsonville Hwy
Street address city: Gainesville
Street address state: GA
Zip/Postal code: 30501-1531
Country: USA
Mailing address: 1733 Dawsonville Hwy
Mailing city: Gainesville
Mailing state: GA
Mailing zip: 30501-1531
General Phone: (770) 287-3798
General Fax: (770) 287-0112
General/National Adv. E-mail: commfeat@charter.net
Primary Website: www.communityfeatures.com
Year Established: 1909
Note: Community Features sells and maintains church and Bible verse pages, and offers features for religious pages.
Personnel: Christina Smith (Co-Owner); Bill Johnson (Co-Owner)

COMPUTERUSER

Street address 1: 220 S 6th St
Street address 2: Ste 500
Street address city: Minneapolis
Street address state: MN
Zip/Postal code: 55402-4501
Country: USA
Mailing address: 220 S 6th St Ste 500
Mailing city: Minneapolis
Mailing state: MN
Mailing zip: 55402-4501
General Phone: (612) 339-7571
General/National Adv. E-mail: info@computeruser.com
Primary Website: www.computeruser.com
Personnel: Dan Heilman (Ed.); Nathaniel Opperman (Vice Pres., Publishing)

CONSULATE GENERAL OF SWEDEN IN NEW YORK

Street address 1: 885 Second Avenue
Street address 2: 40th Floor
Street address city: New York
Street address state: NY
Zip/Postal code: 10017
Country: USA
Mailing address: 885 Second Avenue, 40th floor
Mailing city: New York
Mailing state: NY
Mailing zip: 10017
General Phone: (212) 583-2560
General Fax: (212) 583-2585
General/National Adv. E-mail: generalkonsulat.new-york@gov.se
Primary Website: www.swedenabroad.se

CONTENT THAT WORKS

Street address 1: 4410 N Ravenswood Ave
Street address 2: Ste 101
Street address city: Chicago
Street address state: IL
Zip/Postal code: 60640-5873
Country: USA
Mailing address: 4410 N Ravenswood Ave Ste 101
Mailing city: Chicago
Mailing state: IL
Mailing zip: 60640-5873
General Phone: (773) 728-8351
General Fax: (773) 728-8326
General/National Adv. E-mail: info@contentthatworks.com
Primary Website: www.contentthatworks.com
Personnel: Paul A. Camp (CEO); Jenn Goebel (COO); Dan Dalton (Vice Pres., Sales); Mary Connors (Editorial Director)

CONTINENTAL FEATURES/ CONTINENTAL NEWS SERVICE

Street address 1: 501 W Broadway
Street address 2: Ste A PMB 265
Street address city: San Diego
Street address state: CA
Zip/Postal code: 92101-3562
Country: USA
Mailing address: 501 W Broadway Ste A PMB 265
Mailing city: San Diego
Mailing state: CA
Mailing zip: 92101-3562
General Phone: (858) 492-8696

General/National Adv. E-mail: continentalnewsservice@yahoo.com
Editorial e-mail: continentalnewstime@lycos.com
Primary Website: www.continentalnewsservice.com
Year Established: 1981
Note: CF/CNS publishes (1) Continental Newstime general-interest newsmagazine as an available newspaper insert, with its individual newspaper features also marketed separately; (2) the children's newspaper, Kids' Newstime approximately 154-158 times a year; (3) a Northern California community newspaper regularly and a San Diego News Edition intermittently; (4) CF/CNS has launched special, periodic, on-line Washington D.C., Chicago, Atlanta, Honolulu, Miami, Anchorage, Minneapolis, Rochester (N.Y.), Houston, Seattle, and Boston News Editions; and (5) CF/CNS now offers a Country Neighbor Edition of Continental Newstime for our rural friends in the West and East.
Personnel: Gary P. Salamone (Ed. in-Chief)

CRAINÂ‚¬Â„¢S DETROIT BUSINESS

Street address 1: 1155 Gratiot Ave
Street address city: Detroit
Street address state: MI
Zip/Postal code: 48207-2732
Country: USA
Mailing address: 1155 Gratiot Ave
Mailing city: Detroit
Mailing state: MI
Mailing zip: 48207-2732
General Phone: (313) 446-6000
General Fax: (313) 446-8030
General/National Adv. E-mail: info@crain.com
Primary Website: www.crain.com
Personnel: Keith Crain (Chairman); KC Crain (President, Chief Operating Officer); Bob Recchia (CFO); Mary Kramer (Vice President, Group Publisher)

CREATIVE CIRCLE MEDIA SOLUTIONS

Street address 1: 618 Main Street, apartment 3213
Street address city: Coventry
Street address state: RI
Zip/Postal code: 02816
County: Providence
Country: USA
Mailing address: 618 Main Street, apartment 3213
Mailing city: Coventry
Mailing state: RI
Mailing zip: 02816
General Phone: (401) 4551555
General/National Adv. E-mail: teresemihacin18@gmail.com
Display Adv. E-mail: teresemihacin18@gmail.com
Classified Adv. e-mail: teresemihacin18@gmail.com
Editorial e-mail: teresemihacin18@gmail.com
Primary Website: www.creativecirclemedia.com
Year Established: 1984
Note: Full service, custom software provider with a dynamic web site CMS, user-contributed content, classifieds, hosting, pay wall, branded content, circulation and print editorial production solutions. We also provide strategic consulting, newsroom training, ad design training, new revenue ideas, webmaster services and high-end print production outsourcing services. Our Premium Pages are an excellent digital features content service. We also have led more than 750 redesigns of print newspapers and magazines and continue to help publishers redefine their print products.
Personnel: Bill Ostendorf (Pres. & founder); Lynn Rognsvoog (Design director); Tim Benson (Chief Developer); Scott Kingsley (COO); Darryl Greenlee (Developer); Sean Finch (VP/Sales); Greg Boras (National Sales Manager); Scott Kingley (COO); Lisa Newby; Terese Mihalcin

CREATIVE CIRCLE MEDIA SYNDICATION

Street address 1: 945 Waterman Ave
Street address city: East Providence
Street address state: RI
Zip/Postal code: 02914-1342
Country: USA
Mailing address: 945 Waterman Ave
Mailing city: East Providence
Mailing state: RI
Mailing zip: 02914-1342
General Phone: (401) 455-1555
General Fax: (401) 272-1150
General/National Adv. E-mail: info@creativecirclemedia.com
Editorial e-mail: scott@creativecirclemedia.com
Primary Website: www.creativecirclemedia.com
Year Established: 2000
Note: We distribute a features wire, call Premium Pages, and a news distribution system to hundreds of local and community newspapers nationwide.
Personnel: Bill Ostendorf (President)

CREATIVE COMIC PRODUCTIONS

Street address 1: 1608 S Dakota Ave
Street address city: Sioux Falls
Street address state: SD
Zip/Postal code: 57105-1819
Country: USA
Mailing address: 1608 S Dakota Ave
Mailing city: Sioux Falls
Mailing state: SD
Mailing zip: 57105-1819
General Phone: (605) 336-9434
General/National Adv. E-mail: smoments7@aol.com
Primary Website: www.creativecomics.net
Personnel: Ken Alvine (Owner/Mgr.)

CREATORS

Street address 1: 737 3rd St
Street address city: Hermosa Beach
Street address state: CA
Zip/Postal code: 90254-4714
Country: USA
Mailing address: 737 3rd St
Mailing city: Hermosa Beach
Mailing state: CA
Mailing zip: 90254-4714
General Phone: (310) 337-7003
General Fax: (310) 337-7625
General/National Adv. E-mail: sales@creators.com; info@creators.com
Primary Website: www.creators.com
Year Established: 1987
Personnel: Rick Newcombe (CEO); Margo Sugrue (National Sales Director); Mary Ann Veldman (Sales Director); Marianne Sugawara (Vice President of Operations); Sheila Telle (Sales Administrator); Jessica Burtch (Editor); Anthony Zurcher (Editor); Anica Wong (Associate, Business Development, Operations & Sales); Brandon Telle (Head of development, programming and technology); David Yontz (Managing Editor); Gunner Coll (Associate, Business Development, Operations & Sales); Mikaela Conley (Editor); Simone Slykhous (Editor); Sarah Follette (Head of accounting); Pete Kaminski (Production; Animator); Katie Ransom (Accounting/finance analyst); Jack Newcombe (President & COO)

CRICKET COMMUNICATIONS, INC.

Street address 1: PO Box 527
Street address city: Ardmore
Street address state: PA
Zip/Postal code: 19003-0527
Country: USA
Mailing address: PO Box 527
Mailing city: Ardmore
Mailing state: PA
Mailing zip: 19003-0527
General Phone: (610) 924-9158
General Fax: (610) 924-9159
General/National Adv. E-mail: crcktinc@aol.com
Year Established: 1976
Personnel: Edwin Marks (Pres./Pub.); Mark E. Battersby (Vice Pres./Ed.); E. Arthur Stern (Mng. Ed.)

CRITICS, INC.

Street address city: Dublin
Street address state: OH
Zip/Postal code: 43017
Country: USA
Mailing city: Dublin
Mailing state: OH
Mailing zip: 43017-3202
General Phone: (614) 408-3865
General/National Adv. E-mail: info@criticsinc.com
Primary Website: www.criticsinc.com
Personnel: Aris T. Christofides (Pub./Ed.); Lori Pearson (Commun. Dir.); Teressa L. Elliott (Contributing Ed.); Wade R. Gossett (Contributing Ed.); Ethan Cuhulinn (Bus. Mgr.)

CURT SCHLEIER REVIEWS

Street address 1: 646 Jones Rd
Street address city: River Vale
Street address state: NJ
Zip/Postal code: 07675-6034
Country: USA
Mailing address: 646 Jones Rd
Mailing city: Rivervale
Mailing state: NJ
Mailing zip: 07675-6034
General Phone: (201) 391-7135
General/National Adv. E-mail: writa1@me.com
Personnel: Curt Schleier (Pres./Ed.)

DAVE GOODWIN & ASSOCIATES

Street address 1: 721 86th St
Street address city: Miami Beach
Street address state: FL
Zip/Postal code: 33141-1115
Country: USA
Mailing address: 721 86th St.
Mailing city: Miami Beach
Mailing state: FL
Mailing zip: 33141
General Phone: (305) 865-0158
General/National Adv. E-mail: davegoodwi@aol.com
Primary Website: www.davegoodwin.weebly.com
Personnel: Dave Goodwin (Author/Owner); Ari Goodwin (Writer)

DEG SYNDICATION

Street address 1: 25 Columbus Cir
Street address 2: # 55E
Street address city: New York
Street address state: NY
Zip/Postal code: 10019-1107
Country: USA
Mailing address: 25 Columbus Cir # 55E
Mailing city: New York
Mailing state: NY
Mailing zip: 10019-1107
General Phone: (212) 2090847
General Fax:
General/National Adv. E-mail: expert@deg.com
Primary Website: www.deg.com
Personnel: Marisa D'Vari (Pres./Writer)

DISABILITY NEWS SERVICE

Street address 1: 13703 Southernwood Ct
Street address city: Chantilly
Street address state: VA
Zip/Postal code: 20151-3345
Country: USA
Mailing address: 13703 Southernwood Ct
Mailing city: Chantilly
Mailing state: VA
Mailing zip: 20151-3345
General Phone: (703) 437-6635

DOING BIZ IN

Street address 1: 1865 River Falls Dr
Street address city: Roswell
Street address state: GA
Zip/Postal code: 30076-5114
Country: USA
Mailing address: 1865 River Falls Dr
Mailing city: Roswell
Mailing state: GA
Mailing zip: 30076-5114
General Phone: (770) 998-9911
General/National Adv. E-mail: info@thewritepublicist.com
Primary Website: www.thewritepublicist.com
Year Established: 2002
Personnel: Regina Lynch-Hudson (Creator/Writer)

DORK STORM PRESS/SHETLAND PRODUCTIONS

Street address 1: PO Box 45063
Street address city: Madison
Street address state: WI
Zip/Postal code: 53744-5063
Country: USA
Mailing address: PO Box 45063
Mailing city: Madison
Mailing state: WI
Mailing zip: 53744-5063
General Phone: (608) 222-5522
General Fax: (608) 222-5585
General/National Adv. E-mail: john@kovalic.com
Primary Website: www.kovalic.com
Personnel: Alexander Schiller (Office Mgr.); Eleanor Williams (Ed.); Alex Aulisi (Business Manager)

DOW JONES NEWSWIRES - BOGOTA, COLOMBIA

Street address 1: Calle 93B No. 13-30 Oficina 301
Street address city: Bogota
Country: Colombia
Mailing address: Calle 93B No. 13-30 Oficina 301
Mailing city: Bogota
General Phone: 481-1785
General Fax: 483-5623
General/National Adv. E-mail: datanewsdj@hotmail.com
Primary Website: www.dowjones.com/djnewswires.asp
Personnel: Richard Sanders (Correspondent); Martha De Rengifo (Sales Exec.)

DOW JONES NEWSWIRES - BRUSSELS, BELGIUM

Street address 1: Blvd. Brand Whitlock 87
Street address city: Brussels
Zip/Postal code: 1200
Country: Belgium
Mailing address: Blvd. Brand Whitlock 87
Mailing city: Brussels
Mailing zip: 1200
General Phone: 285-0130
General Fax: 741 1429
General/National Adv. E-mail: dirk.geeraerts@dowjones.com; vanessa.stolk@dowjones.com
Primary Website: www.dowjones.com/djnewswires.asp
Personnel: Vanessa Stolk (Rep.); Peter Greiff (Correspondent); Dirk Geeraerts (Acct. Mgr.)

DOW JONES NEWSWIRES - BUENOS AIRES, ARGENTINA

Street address 1: Leandro N. Alem 712, Piso 4
Street address city: Buenos Aires
Zip/Postal code: 1001
Country: Argentina
Mailing address: Leandro N. Alem 712, Piso 4
Mailing city: Buenos Aires
Mailing zip: 1001
General Phone: 4314-8788
General Fax: 4311-0083
General/National Adv. E-mail: ana.del-riccio@dowjones.com
Primary Website: www.dowjones.com/djnewswires.asp
Personnel: Michelle Wallin (Correspondent); Ana Del-Riccio (Sales Exec.)

DOW JONES NEWSWIRES - FRANKFURT, GERMANY

Street address 1: Wilhem Leuschner Strasse 78
Street address city: Frankfurt
Zip/Postal code: D-60329
Country: Germany
Mailing address: Wilhem Leuschner Strasse 78
Mailing city: Frankfurt
Mailing zip: D-60329
General Phone: 29 725 200
General Fax: 29 725 222
Primary Website: www.dowjones.com/djnewswires.asp
Personnel: Fridrich Geiger (Ed.)

DOW JONES NEWSWIRES - HONG KONG, HONG KONG

Street address 1: 25F Central Plz., 18 Harbour Rd., Wanchai
Street address city: Hong Kong
Country: Hong Kong
Mailing address: 25F Central Plz., 18 Harbour Rd., Wanchai
Mailing city: Hong Kong
General Phone: 2573 7121

General/National Adv. E-mail: djnews.hk@dowjones.com
Primary Website: www.dowjones.com
Personnel: Jeffrey Ng (Correspondent)

DOW JONES NEWSWIRES - KUALA LUMPUR, MALAYSIA

Street address 1: Ste. 21A-8-2, 8th Floor, Faber Imperial Ct., Jalan Sultan Ismail
Street address city: Kuala Lumpur
Zip/Postal code: 50250
Country: Malaysia
Mailing address: Ste. 21A-8-2, 8th Floor, Faber Imperial Ct., Jalan Sultan Ismail
Mailing city: Kuala Lumpur
Mailing zip: 50250
General Phone: (65) 6415-4200
General Fax: (65) 6225-8959
General/National Adv. E-mail: janet.leau@dowjones.com
Personnel: Matthew Geiger (Correspondent); Janet Leau (Acct. Mgr.)

DOW JONES NEWSWIRES - LONDON, UNITED KINGDOM

Street address 1: Commodity Quay, E. Smithfield
Street address city: London
Zip/Postal code: E1W 1AZ
Country: United Kingdom
Mailing address: Commodity Quay, E. Smithfield
Mailing city: London
Mailing zip: E1W 1AZ
General Phone: 726-7903
General Fax: 726-7855
General/National Adv. E-mail: adam.howes@dowjones.com
Primary Website: www.dowjones.com
Personnel: Adam Howes (Regl. Sales Mgr.)

DOW JONES NEWSWIRES - LONDON, UNITED KINGDOM

Street address 1: 12 Norwich St.
Street address city: London
Zip/Postal code: EC4A 1QN
Country: United Kingdom
Mailing address: 12 Norwich St.
Mailing city: London
Mailing zip: EC4A 1QN
General Phone: 842-9550
General Fax: 842-9551
Personnel: Bhushan Bahree (Correspondent); Sarah Money (Sales Mgr.)

DOW JONES NEWSWIRES - MADRID, SPAIN

Street address 1: Espronceda 32 1st Planta
Street address city: Madrid
Zip/Postal code: 28003
Country: Spain
Mailing address: Espronceda 32 1st Planta
Mailing city: Madrid
Mailing zip: 28003
General Phone: 395-8120
General Fax: 399-1930
Personnel: Santiago Perez (Bureau Chief)

DOW JONES NEWSWIRES - MANILA, PHILIPPINES

Street address 1: 12/F Tower One & Exchange Plaza Ayala Triangle
Street address 2: Ayala Ave, Makati City
Street address city: Manila
Country: Philippines
Mailing address: 12/F Tower One & Exchange Plaza Ayala Triangle, Ayala Ave, Makati City
Mailing city: Manila
General Phone: 574-616
General Fax: 885-0293
General/National Adv. E-mail: Lilian.Karununean@dowjones.com
Primary Website: www.djnewswires.com
Personnel: Lilian Karununean (Correspondent)

DOW JONES NEWSWIRES - MEXICO CITY, MEXICO

Street address 1: Av. Issac Newton No. 286, Piso 9, Col. Chapultepec Morales
Street address city: Mexico City
Zip/Postal code: 11560
Country: Mexico
Mailing address: Av. Issac Newton No. 286, Piso 9, Col. Chapultepec Morales
Mailing city: Mexico City
Mailing zip: 11560
General Phone: (525) 254-5581
General Fax: (525) 254-7510
Personnel: Peter R. Fritsch (Correspondent)

DOW JONES NEWSWIRES - MILANO, ITALY

Street address 1: Via Burigozzo 5
Street address city: Milano
Zip/Postal code: 20122
Country: Italy
Mailing address: Via Burigozzo 5
Mailing city: Milano
Mailing zip: 20122
General Phone: 7601-5386
General Fax: 5821 9752
Personnel: Susan Peiffer (Correspondent)

DOW JONES NEWSWIRES - NEW YORK, NY

Street address 1: 1211 Avenue of the Americas
Street address city: New York
Street address state: NY
Zip/Postal code: 10036-8701
Country: USA
Mailing address: 1211 Avenue of the Americas Lowr C3
Mailing city: New York
Mailing state: NY
Mailing zip: 10036-8711
General Phone: (212) 416-2400
General Fax: (212) 416-2410
General/National Adv. E-mail: spotnews@priority.dowjones.com
Primary Website: www.djnewswires.com
Personnel: Tim Turner (Vice Pres./Gen. Mgr.); James Donoghue (Vice Pres., Sales/Mktg.); Neal Lipschutz (Mng. Ed., Dow Jones Newswire Americas)

DOW JONES NEWSWIRES - NEW YORK, NY

Street address 1: 1155 Avenue of the Americas
Street address 2: Fl 7
Street address city: New York
Street address state: NY
Zip/Postal code: 10036-2758
Country: USA
Mailing address: 1155 Avenue of the Americas Fl 7
Mailing city: New York
Mailing state: NY
Mailing zip: 10036-2711
General Phone: (609) 520-4000
General/National Adv. E-mail: SpotNews@dowjones.com
Primary Website: www.djnewswires.com
Personnel: Gregory White (Correspondent)

DOW JONES NEWSWIRES - PARIS, FRANCE

Street address 1: 6-8 Boulevard Haussmann
Street address city: Paris
Zip/Postal code: 75009
Country: France
Mailing address: 6-8 Boulevard Haussmann
Mailing city: Paris
Mailing zip: 75009
General Phone: 7036 5502
General Fax: 4017-1781
General/National Adv. E-mail: thierry.cadin@dowjones.com
Personnel: Thierry Cadi (Reg'l Sales Mgr.); David Pearson (Correspondent)

DOW JONES NEWSWIRES - SAO PAULO, BRAZIL

Street address 1: Rua Joaquim Floriano 488. 6 andar
Street address city: Sao Paulo
Zip/Postal code: 04534 002
Country: Brazil
Mailing address: Rua Joaquim Floriano 488. 6 andar
Mailing city: Sao Paulo
Mailing zip: 04534 002
General Phone: 256-0520
General Fax: 3044-2813
General/National Adv. E-mail: ana.gresenberg@dowjones.com
Personnel: John Wright (Correspondent); Ana Gresenberg (Sales Exec.)

DOW JONES NEWSWIRES - SINGAPORE, SINGAPORE

Street address 1: 10 Anson Rd., Ste. 32-09/10 Int'l Plz.
Street address city: Singapore
Zip/Postal code: 079903
Country: Singapore
Mailing address: 10 Anson Rd., Ste. 32-09/10 Int'l Plz.
Mailing city: Singapore
Mailing zip: 079903
General Phone: 6415-4200
General Fax: 6225-8959
General/National Adv. E-mail: hweekun.ho@dowjones.com
Personnel: Lim Mui Khi (Correspondent); Hwee-Kun Ho (Regl. Sales Mgr.)

DOW JONES NEWSWIRES - SYDNEY, AUSTRALIA

Street address 1: Level 10 56 Titt St.
Street address city: Sydney
Zip/Postal code: 2000
Country: Australia
Mailing address: Level 10 56 Titt St.
Mailing city: Sydney
Mailing zip: 2000
General Phone: 8272 4600
General Fax: 8272 4601
Primary Website: www.dowjones.com
Personnel: Ian McDonald (Correspondent); Tom Rustowski (Regl. Sales Mgr.)

DOW JONES NEWSWIRES - TOKYO, JAPAN

Street address 1: Marunouchi Mitsui Bldg. 1F, 2-2-2, Marunouchi Chiyoda-ku
Street address city: Tokyo
Zip/Postal code: 100 0004
Country: Japan
Mailing address: Marunouchi Mitsui Bldg. 1F, 2-2-2, Marunouchi Chiyoda-ku
Mailing city: Tokyo
Mailing zip: 100 0004
General Phone: 5220 2730
General Fax: 5220-2746
General/National Adv. E-mail: masashi.takeuchi@dowjones.com
Personnel: Masashi Takeuchi (Sales Mgr.)

DOW JONES NEWSWIRES - WASHINGTON, DC

Street address 1: 1025 Connecticut Ave NW
Street address 2: Ste 800
Street address city: Washington
Street address state: D.C.
Zip/Postal code: 20036-5419
Country: USA
Mailing address: 1025 Connecticut Ave NW Ste 800
Mailing city: Washington
Mailing state: DC
Mailing zip: 20036-5419
General Phone: (202) 862-9272
General Fax: (202) 862-6621
Personnel: Rob Wells (Bureau Chief)

DOW JONES NEWSWIRES - ZURICH, SWITZERLAND

Street address 1: Sihlquai 253, Postfach 1128
Street address city: Zurich
Zip/Postal code: 8031
Country: Switzerland
Mailing address: Sihlquai 253, Postfach 1128
Mailing city: Zurich
Mailing zip: 8031
General Phone: 960 5870
General Fax: 960 5701
General/National Adv. E-mail: sarah.money@dowjones.com; penny.greenwood@awp.ch
Personnel: Penny Greenwood (Sr. Acct. Mgr.)

DOWN TO BUSINESS - COLUMN

Street address 1: 836 Buttonwood Ct
Street address city: Marco Island
Street address state: FL
Zip/Postal code: 34145-2310
County: Collier
Country: USA
Mailing address: 836 Buttonwood Ct.
Mailing city: Marco Island
Mailing state: FL
Mailing zip: 34145
General Phone: 9782702590
General/National Adv. E-mail: andy.singer@singerexecutivedevelopment.com
Display Adv. E-mail: andy.singer@singerexecutivedevelopment.com
Classified Adv. e-mail: andy.singer@singerexecutivedevelopment.com
Editorial e-mail: andy.singer@singerexectuivedevelopment/.com
Primary Website: www.singerexecutivedevelopment.com
Year Established: 2013
Note: Weekly and well liked business column sent out every Tuesday. Discusses any and all aspects of business.

DR. BEE EPSTEIN-SHEPHERD

Street address 1: PO Box 221383
Street address city: Carmel
Street address state: CA
Zip/Postal code: 93922-1383
Country: USA
Mailing address: PO Box 221383
Mailing city: Carmel
Mailing state: CA
Mailing zip: 93922-1383
General Phone: (831) 625-3188
General Fax: (831) 625-0611
General/National Adv. E-mail: drbeemm@aol.com
Primary Website: www.drbee.com
Personnel: Dr. Bee Epstein-Shepherd (Mental Skills Coach/Writer)

DSENTERTAINMENT/NORTH SHORE PUBLISHING

Street address 1: PO Box 318
Street address city: Vermilion
Street address state: OH
Zip/Postal code: 44089-0318
Country: USA
Mailing address: PO Box 318
Mailing city: Vermilion
Mailing state: OH
Mailing zip: 44089-0318
General Phone: (440) 967-0293
General Fax: (440) 967-0293
General/National Adv. E-mail: dave@northshorepublishing.com; dave@thecomedybook.com
Primary Website: www.thecomedybook.com; www.davelaughs.com; www.beatlesincleveland.com; www.northshorepublishing.com
Year Established: 1993
Personnel: Dave Schwensen (Author/Award-Winning Humor Columnist)

DUNKEL SPORTS RESEARCH SERVICE

Street address 1: PO Box 133

Street address city: Mount Vernon
Street address state: VA
Zip/Postal code: 22121-0133
Country: USA
Mailing address: PO Box 133
Mailing city: Mount Vernon
Mailing state: VA
Mailing zip: 22121-0133
General Phone: (202) 253-3899
General/National Adv. E-mail: dunkelratings@msn.com
Primary Website: www.dunkelindex.com
Personnel: Richard H. Dunkel Jr. (Co-Ed./Co-Owner); Bob Dunkel (Co-Ed./Co-Owner)

EARTH TALK: QUESTIONS & ANSWERS ABOUT OUR ENVIRONMENT

Street address 1: 28 Knight St
Street address city: Norwalk
Street address state: CT
Zip/Postal code: 06851-4719
Country: USA
Mailing address: PO Box 5098
Mailing city: Westport
Mailing state: CT
Mailing zip: 06881-5098
General Phone: (203) 854-5559/x106
General Fax: (203) 866-0602
General/National Adv. E-mail: earthtalkcolumn@emagazine.com
Primary Website: www.earthtalk.org
Year Established: 2003
Personnel: Doug Moss (Pub./Exec. Ed.)

ED FISCHER PRODUCTION

Street address 1: 215 Elton Hills Dr NW
Street address 2: Apt 56
Street address city: Rochester
Street address state: MN
Zip/Postal code: 55901-2497
Country: USA
Mailing address: 215 Elton Hills Number 56
Mailing city: Rochester
Mailing state: MN
Mailing zip: 55906-4019
General Phone: (651) 491-3613
General/National Adv. E-mail: ed.fischer.toons@gmail.com
Primary Website: www.edfischer.com
Note: 75 newspapers pay to receive 9 Ed Fischer cartoons a week plus Cartoonstock. Com sells my cartoons world-wide plus selling 500,000 books
Personnel: Ed Fischer (Self-Syndicator plus 3,500 cartoons on a variety of subjects for papers, books, advertising, newsletters,magazines. 28 awards)

EFE NEWS SERVICES - ALGIERS, ALGERIA

Street address 1: 4 Ave. Pasteur, 1st Fl.
Street address city: Algiers
Zip/Postal code: 16000
Country: Algeria
Mailing address: 4 Ave. Pasteur, 1st Fl.
Mailing city: Algiers
Mailing zip: 16000
General Phone: 173 5680
General Fax: 174 0456
General/National Adv. E-mail: javiergarcia@efe.com
Personnel: Javier Garcia (Rep.)

EFE NEWS SERVICES - BEIJING, CHINA

Street address 1: Julong Garden, 7-14 L. Xinzhongjie, 68 Dongcheng
Street address city: Beijing
Zip/Postal code: 100027
Country: China
Mailing address: Julong Garden, 7-14 L. Xinzhongjie, 68 Dongcheng
Mailing city: Beijing
Mailing zip: 100027
General Phone: 6553 1198
General Fax: 6552 7861
Primary Website: www.efe.es
Personnel: Paloma Caballero (Rep.)

EFE NEWS SERVICES - BERLIN, GERMANY

Street address 1: Reinhardtstrasse 58
Street address city: Berlin
Street address state: NY
Zip/Postal code: 10117
Country: Germany
Mailing address: Reinhardtstrasse 58
Mailing city: Berlin
Mailing zip: 10117
General Phone: (206) 039-860
General Fax: (206) 039-840
General/National Adv. E-mail: berlin@efe.com
Personnel: Noelia LÃƒÂ³pez

EFE NEWS SERVICES - BOGOTA, COLOMBIA

Street address 1: Calle 67 No 7-35
Street address city: Bogota
Country: Colombia
Mailing address: Calle 67 No 7-35
Mailing city: Bogota
General Phone: 321 48 55
General Fax: 321 47 51
General/National Adv. E-mail: efecol@efebogota.com.co
Personnel: Esther Rebollo (Rep.)

EFE NEWS SERVICES - BRUSSELS, BELGIUM

Street address 1: Residence Palace, Rue de la Loi, 155
Street address city: Brussels
Zip/Postal code: 1040
Country: Belgium
Mailing address: Residence Palace, Rue de la Loi, 155
Mailing city: Brussels
Mailing zip: 1040
General Phone: 285-4831
General Fax: 230-9319
General/National Adv. E-mail: bruselas@efe.com
Personnel: Jose Manuel Sanz (Rep.)

EFE NEWS SERVICES - BUENOS AIRES, ARGENTINA

Street address 1: Av. Alicia Moreau de Justo 1720
Street address city: Buenos Aires
Zip/Postal code: 1107
Country: Argentina
Mailing address: Av. Alicia Moreau de Justo 1720
Mailing city: Buenos Aires
Mailing zip: 1107
General Phone: 43 11 12 11
General Fax: 43 12 75 18
General/National Adv. E-mail: redaccion@efe.com.ar
Personnel: Mar Marin (Rep.)

EFE NEWS SERVICES - CAIRO, EGYPT

Street address 1: 4 Mohamed Mazhar, 3 - apt. 5. Zamalek
Street address city: Cairo
Country: Egypt
Mailing address: 4 Mohamed Mazhar, 3 - apt. 5. Zamalek
Mailing city: Cairo
General Phone: 738-0792
General Fax: 361-2198
Personnel: Grace Augustine (Rep.)

EFE NEWS SERVICES - GENEVA, SWITZERLAND

Street address 1: Bureau 49, Palas des Nations B, Ave. Paix
Street address city: Geneva
Zip/Postal code: 1211
Country: Switzerland
Mailing address: Bureau 49, Palas des Nations B, Ave. Paix
Mailing city: Geneva
Mailing zip: 1211
General Phone: 7336273
General/National Adv. E-mail: ginebra@efe.com
Primary Website: www.efe.com
Personnel: Celine Aemisegger (Bureau Chief)

EFE NEWS SERVICES - GUATEMALA CITY, GUATEMALA

Street address 1: 8 Ave. 8-56 Zone 1, Edif. 10-24, Segundo Nivel, Oficina 203
Street address city: Guatemala City
Country: Guatemala
Mailing address: 8 Ave. 8-56 Zone 1, Edif. 10-24, Segundo Nivel, Oficina 203
Mailing city: Guatemala City
General Phone: 51 94 84
General Fax: 51 84 59
General/National Adv. E-mail: guatemala@acan-efe.com
Personnel: Carlos Arrazola (Rep.)

EFE NEWS SERVICES - LA PAZ, BOLIVIA

Street address 1: Avda. Sanchez Lima, 2520. Edificio Anibal - MZ 01
Street address city: La Paz
Zip/Postal code: 7403
Country: Bolivia
Mailing address: Avda. Sanchez Lima, 2520. Edificio Anibal - MZ 01
Mailing city: La Paz
Mailing zip: 7403
General Phone: 235-9837
General Fax: 239-1441
General/National Adv. E-mail: efebol@entelnet.bo
Primary Website: www.efe.com
Personnel: Soledad Alvarez (Rep.)

EFE NEWS SERVICES - LIMA, PERU

Street address 1: Mauel Gonzalez Olaechea, 207
Street address city: Lima
Zip/Postal code: 27
Country: Peru
Mailing address: Mauel Gonzalez Olaechea, 207
Mailing city: Lima
Mailing zip: 27
General Phone: 441 24 22
General Fax: 421 13 72
General/National Adv. E-mail: lima@efe.com
Personnel: Javier Otazu (Rep.)

EFE NEWS SERVICES - LISBON, PORTUGAL

Street address 1: Rua Castilho, 13 D, 5A
Street address city: Lisbon
Street address state: DC
Zip/Postal code: 1250 066
Country: Portugal
Mailing address: Rua Castilho, 13 D, 5A
Mailing city: Lisbon
Mailing zip: 1250 066
General Phone: 351 39 30
General Fax: 351 39 38
General/National Adv. E-mail: lisboa@efe.com
Personnel: Emilio Crespo (Rep.)

EFE NEWS SERVICES - LONDON, UNITED KINGDOM

Street address 1: 299 Oxford St. 6th Fl.
Street address city: London
Zip/Postal code: W1C 2DZ
Country: United Kingdom
Mailing address: 299 Oxford St. 6th Fl.
Mailing city: London
Mailing zip: W1C 2DZ
General Phone: 7493 7313
General Fax: 7493-7114
Personnel: Joaquin Rabago (Rep.)

EFE NEWS SERVICES - MANAGUA, NICARAGUA

Street address 1: Garden City S-22
Street address city: Managua
Country: Nicaragua
Mailing address: Garden City S-22
Mailing city: Managua
General Phone: 49 11 66
General Fax: 49 59 28
General/National Adv. E-mail: nicaragua@acan-efe.com
Personnel: Philadelphus Martinez (Rep.)

EFE NEWS SERVICES - MANILA, PHILIPPINES

Street address 1: Unit 1006, 88 Corporate Center, 141 Sedeno corner
Street address city: Manila
Zip/Postal code: 1227
Country: Philippines
Mailing address: Unit 1006, 88 Corporate Center, 141 Sedeno corner
Mailing city: Manila
Mailing zip: 1227
General Phone: 843 1986
General Fax: 843 1973
General/National Adv. E-mail: manila@efe.com
Primary Website: www.efe.es
Personnel: Miguel Frau Rovira (Bureau Chief); Marco Zabaleta (Ed.)

EFE NEWS SERVICES - MEXICO CITY, MEXICO

Street address 1: Lafayette, 69, Colonia Ave.
Street address city: Mexico City
Zip/Postal code: 011590
Country: Mexico
Mailing address: Lafayette, 69, Colonia Ave.
Mailing city: Mexico City
Mailing zip: 011590
General Phone: 5545 8256
General Fax: 5254 1412
Personnel: Alejandro Amezcua (Sales Mgr.); Manuel Fuentes (Rep.)

EFE NEWS SERVICES - MONTEVIDEO, URUGUAY

Street address 1: Wilson Ferreira Aldunate 1294
Street address city: Montevideo
Zip/Postal code: 11100
Country: Uruguay
Mailing address: Wilson Ferreira Aldunate 1294
Mailing city: Montevideo
Mailing zip: 11100
General Phone: 902 03 38
General Fax: 902 67 26
General/National Adv. E-mail: montevideo@efe.com
Personnel: Raul Cortes (Rep.)

EFE NEWS SERVICES - MOSCOW, RUSSIA

Street address 1: Ria Novosti International Press Center, Zubovski blvd. 4
Street address city: Moscow
Zip/Postal code: 119021
Country: Russia
Mailing address: Ria Novosti International Press Center, Zubovski blvd. 4
Mailing city: Moscow
Mailing zip: 119021
General Phone: 637 5137
General Fax: 637 5137
General/National Adv. E-mail: efemos@gmail.com
Personnel: Miguel Bas (Rep.)

EFE NEWS SERVICES - NEW DELHI, INDIA

Street address 1: 48, Hanuman Road. Instituto Cervantes building
Street address 2: Connaught Place
Street address city: New Delhi
Zip/Postal code: 110001
Country: India
Mailing address: 48, Hanuman Road. Instituto Cervantes building. Connaught Palce
Mailing city: New Delhi
Mailing zip: 110001
General Phone: 41501999
General/National Adv. E-mail: india@efe.com
Primary Website: www.efe.com

Personnel: Moncho Torres (Correspondent)

EFE NEWS SERVICES - PANAMA CITY, PANAMA

Street address 1: Avda. Samuel Lewis y Manuel Icaza. Edif. Comosa 22
Street address city: Panama City
Zip/Postal code: 0834 00749
Country: Panama
Mailing address: Avda. Samuel Lewis y Manuel Icaza. Edif. Comosa 22
Mailing city: Panama City
Mailing zip: 0834 00749
General Phone: 23 90 14
General Fax: 64 84 42
General/National Adv. E-mail: panama@acan-efe.com
Personnel: Hernan Martin (Rep.)

EFE NEWS SERVICES - PARIS, FRANCE

Street address 1: 10 rue St. Marc, Buro. 165
Street address city: Paris
Zip/Postal code: 75002
Country: France
Mailing address: 10 rue St. Marc, Buro. 165
Mailing city: Paris
Mailing zip: 75002
General Phone: 44 82 65 40
General Fax: 40 39 91 78
General/National Adv. E-mail: paris@efe.com
Primary Website: www.efe.com
Personnel: Javier Alonso (Rep.)

EFE NEWS SERVICES - QUITO, ECUADOR

Street address 1: Edificio Platinum Oficinas, piso 8 C. Carlos Padilla s/n
Street address city: Quito
Zip/Postal code: 4043
Country: Ecuador
Mailing address: Edificio Platinum Oficinas, piso 8 C. Carlos Padilla s/n
Mailing city: Quito
Mailing zip: 4043
General Phone: 251-9466
General Fax: 225-5769
General/National Adv. E-mail: redacquito@efe.com
Personnel: Enrique Ibanez (Rep.)

EFE NEWS SERVICES - RABAT, MOROCCO

Street address 1: 14, rue de Kairoajne, Apt. 13, 5 ME (Angle rue d'Alger)
Street address city: Rabat
Country: Morocco
Mailing address: 14, rue de Kairoajne, Apt. 13, 5 ME (Angle rue d'Alger)
Mailing city: Rabat
General Phone: 723 218
General Fax: 732 195
General/National Adv. E-mail: efe@menara.ma
Personnel: Javier Otazu (Director); Enrique Rubio (Rep.)

EFE NEWS SERVICES - RIO DE JANEIRO, BRAZIL

Street address 1: Praia de Botafogo, 228 Rm. 605 B
Street address city: Rio de Janeiro
Street address state: AL
Zip/Postal code: 22359-900
Country: Brazil
Mailing address: Praia de Botafogo, 228 Rm. 605 B
Mailing city: Rio de Janeiro
Mailing state: AL
Mailing zip: 22359-900
General Phone: 553-6355
General Fax: 553-8823
General/National Adv. E-mail: rio@efebrasil.com.br
Primary Website: www.efe.com
Personnel: Jaime Ortega (Rep.)

EFE NEWS SERVICES - ROME, ITALY

Street address 1: Via dei Canestrari, 5-2
Street address city: Rome
Zip/Postal code: 00186
Country: Italy
Mailing address: Via dei Canestrari, 5-2
Mailing city: Rome
Mailing zip: 00186
General Phone: 683-4087
General Fax: 687-4918
General/National Adv. E-mail: roma@efe.com
Personnel: Javier Alonso (Director)

EFE NEWS SERVICES - SAN JOSE, COSTA RICA

Street address 1: Avda., 10 Calles 19/21 n. 1912, Apanado 8.4930
Street address city: San Jose
Zip/Postal code: 1000
Country: Costa Rica
Mailing address: Avda., 10 Calles 19/21 n. 1912, Apanado 8.4930
Mailing city: San Jose
Mailing zip: 1000
General Phone: 2222-6785
General Fax: 2233-7681
General/National Adv. E-mail: costarica@acan-efe.com
Display Adv. E-mail: ndelemos@acan-efe.com
Editorial e-mail: ndelemos@acan-efe.com
Primary Website: Curridabat
Year Established: 1976
Personnel: Nancy De Lemos (Director)

EFE NEWS SERVICES - SAN SALVADOR, EL SALVADOR

Street address 1: Condominio Balam Quitze, Local 17. 2. P. General Sta.
Street address city: San Salvador
Country: El Salvador
Mailing address: Condominio Balam Quitze, Local 17. 2. P. General Sta.
Mailing city: San Salvador
General Phone: 263 7063
General Fax: 263 5281
General/National Adv. E-mail: elsalvador@acan-efe.com
Personnel: Laura Barros (Rep.)

EFE NEWS SERVICES - SANTIAGO, CHILE

Street address 1: Almirante Pastene, 333 - office 502
Street address city: Santiago
Country: Chile
Mailing address: Almirante Pastene, 333 - office 502
Mailing city: Santiago
General Phone: 632-4946
General Fax: 519-3912
General/National Adv. E-mail: redaccion@agenciaefe.tie.cl
Personnel: Manuel Fuentes (Rep.)

EFE NEWS SERVICES - SANTURCE, PUERTO RICO

Street address 1: Edificio Cobian's Plz., Of. 214
Street address 2: Av Ponce de 1607
Street address city: San Juan
Street address state: PR
Zip/Postal code: 00909
Country: Puerto Rico
Mailing address: Edificio Cobian's Plz., Of. 214 Av Ponce de LeÃ³n 1607
Mailing city: San Juan
Mailing state: PR
Mailing zip: 00909
General Phone: (787) 721-8821
General/National Adv. E-mail: redacpr@efe.com
Personnel: Cristina Ozaeta (Head of Puerto Ricos Bureau)

EFE NEWS SERVICES - TEGUCIGALPA, HONDURAS

Street address 1: Col. Elvel, Segunda Calle, Apt. 2012
Street address city: Tegucigalpa
Country: Honduras
Mailing address: Col. Elvel, Segunda Calle, Apt. 2012
Mailing city: Tegucigalpa
General Phone: 231 1730
General Fax: 231 1772
General/National Adv. E-mail: honduras@acan-efe.com
Personnel: German Reyes (Rep.)

EFE NEWS SERVICES - VIENNA, AUSTRIA

Street address 1: Rechte Wienzeile 51/16
Street address city: Vienna
Zip/Postal code: 1050
Country: Austria
Mailing address: Rechte Wienzeile 51/16
Mailing city: Vienna
Mailing zip: 1050
General Phone: 368 4174
General Fax: 369 8842
General/National Adv. E-mail: viena@efe.com
Personnel: Ramon Santaularia (Rep.)

EFE NEWS SERVICES - WASHINGTON, D.C

Street address 1: 1252 National Press Building. 529, 14 Street, NW
Street address 2: Washington D.C. 20045Â
Street address city: Washington
Street address state: D.C.
Zip/Postal code: 20045
Country: USA
Mailing address: 1252 National Press Building. 529, 14 street, NW
Mailing city: Washington D.C.
Mailing state: DC
Mailing zip: 20045
General Phone: (202) 745 76 92
General Fax: (202) 393 41 18 / 19
General/National Adv. E-mail: info@efeamerica.com
Primary Website: www.efe.com
Personnel: Manuel Ortega (Business Development Director)

EFE NEWS SERVICES - WASHINGTON, DC

Street address 1: 529 14th St NW
Street address city: Washington
Street address state: D.C.
Zip/Postal code: 20045-1217
Country: USA
Mailing address: 529 14th St NW Ste 1252
Mailing city: Washington
Mailing state: DC
Mailing zip: 20045-2202
General Phone: (202) 745-7692
General Fax: (305) 262-7557
General/National Adv. E-mail: info@efeamerica.com
Display Adv. E-mail: mromero@efeamerica.com
Editorial e-mail: info@efeamerica.com
Primary Website: www.efe.com
Year Established: 1939
Note: EFE is the leading Spanish-language news agency and the fourth largest in the world.
Personnel: Jose Antonio Vera (Pres.); Maria Luisa Azpiazu (Vice Pres.); Rafael Carranza (Sales and Business Dev. Dir.); Mar Gonzalo (Bureau Chief-Miami); Elena Moreno (Bureau Chief- New York); Marcela Romero (Marketing Coordinator)

ELIZABETH S. SMOOTS

Street address 1: 5735 27th Ave NE
Street address city: Seattle
Street address state: WA
Zip/Postal code: 98105-5511
Country: USA
Mailing address: 5735 27th Ave NE
Mailing city: Seattle
Mailing state: WA
Mailing zip: 98105-5511
General/National Adv. E-mail: doctor@practicalprevention.com
Primary Website: www.practicalprevention.com
Year Established: 1996
Personnel: Elizabeth S. Smoots MD (Self-Syndicator)

EUROPA PRESS NEWS SERVICE

Street address 1: Paseo de la Castellana, 210
Street address city: Madrid
Zip/Postal code: 28046
Country: Spain
Mailing address: Paseo de la Castellana, 210
Mailing city: Madrid
Mailing zip: 28046
General Phone: 359-2600
General Fax: 350-3251
General/National Adv. E-mail: noticias@europapress.es
Primary Website: www.europapress.es

EXHIBITOR RELATIONS CO.

Street address 1: 1262 Westwood Blvd
Street address city: Los Angeles
Street address state: CA
Zip/Postal code: 90024-4801
Country: USA
Mailing address: 550 N Larchmont Blvd Ste 102
Mailing city: Los Angeles
Mailing state: CA
Mailing zip: 90004-1318
General Phone: (310) 441-7400
General Fax: (310) 475-0316
General/National Adv. E-mail: info@ercboxoffice.com
Primary Website: www.ercboxoffice.com
Year Established: 1974
Personnel: Robert Bucksbaum (Pres.); Jeff Bock (Box Office Analyst)

FAMILY ALMANAC

Street address 1: 420 Constitution Ave NE
Street address city: Washington
Street address state: D.C.
Zip/Postal code: 20002-5924
Country: USA
Mailing address: 420 Constitution Ave NE
Mailing city: Washington
Mailing state: DC
Mailing zip: 20002-5924
General Phone: (202) 544-5698
General Fax: (202) 544-5699
General/National Adv. E-mail: marguerite.kelly@gmail.com
Primary Website: www.margueritekelly.com
Year Established: 1975
Note: retired free-lance columnist of Family Almanac which ran in the Washington Post for 35 years and was syndicated in other papers for nearly that long.
Personnel: Marguerite Kelly (Columnist of Family Almanac, WA Post and other papers)

FAMILY FEATURES EDITORIAL SYNDICATE, INC.

Street address 1: 5825 Dearborn St
Street address city: Mission
Street address state: KS
Zip/Postal code: 66202-2745
County: Johnson
Country: USA
Mailing address: 5825 Dearborn St
Mailing city: Mission
Mailing state: KS
Mailing zip: 66202-2745
General Phone: (913) 563-4752
General Fax: (913) 789-9228
General/National Adv. E-mail: clong@familyfeatures.com
Primary Website: www.familyfeatures.com
Year Established: 1974
Personnel: Dianne Hogerty (Owner); Clarke Smith (President); Cindy Long (Media Relations Manager)

FASHION SYNDICATE PRESS

Street address 1: PO Box 727
Street address city: Woodstock
Street address state: VT
Zip/Postal code: 05091-0727
Country: USA
Mailing address: PO Box 727
Mailing city: Woodstock
Mailing state: VT
Mailing zip: 05091-0727
General Phone: (917) 749-8421
General Fax: (212) 202-4604
General/National Adv. E-mail: fashionshowroom@yahoo.com
Primary Website: www.fashionsyndicatepress.com
Note: Films, video and photos syndication.

Personnel: Andres Aquino (Owner); Elaine Hallgren (Ed.); Justin Alexander (Prodn. Art Dir.)

FEATURE PHOTO SERVICE, INC.

Street address 1: 450 7th Ave
Street address 2: Ste 1700
Street address city: New York
Street address state: NY
Zip/Postal code: 10123-0096
Country: USA
Mailing address: 450 7th Avenue, Suite 1700
Mailing city: New Yiork
Mailing zip: 10123
General Phone: (212) 944-1060
General Fax: (212) 944-7801
General/National Adv. E-mail: editor@featurephoto.com
Editorial e-mail: editor@featurephoto.com
Primary Website: https://www.featurephoto.com
Year Established: 1984
Note: Photo distribution via: AP, FeaturePhoto.com, NewsCom and 25+ worldwide media partners
Personnel: Oren Hellner (Pres./CEO); Marla Edwards (Office Mgr.)

FEATUREWELL.COM

Street address 1: 238 W 4th St
Street address city: New York
Street address state: NY
Zip/Postal code: 10014-2610
Country: USA
Mailing address: 238 W 4th St
Mailing city: New York
Mailing state: NY
Mailing zip: 10014-2610
General Phone: (212) 924-2283
General/National Adv. E-mail: featurewell@featurewell.com; sales@featurewell.com; contactus@featurewell.com
Primary Website: www.featurewell.com
Year Established: 2000
Personnel: David Wallis (Founder/CEO); Marc Deveaux (CTO)

FINANCIAL TIMES

Street address 1: 1 Southwark Bridge
Street address city: London
Zip/Postal code: SE1 9HL
Country: United Kingdom
Mailing address: 1 Southwark Bridge
Mailing city: London
Mailing zip: SE1 9HL
General Phone: 7775 6248
General Fax: 873-3070
General/National Adv. E-mail: synd.admin@ft.com
Primary Website: www.ft.com
Personnel: Sophie DeBrito (Synd. Mgr.); Richard Pigden (Picture Synd.)

FISCALNOTE

Street address 1: 1201 Pennsylvania Ave NW
Street address 2: 6th Floor
Street address city: Washington
Street address state: DC
Zip/Postal code: 20004
County: District Of Columbia
Country: USA
Mailing address: 1201 Pennsylvania Ave NW
Mailing city: Washington
Mailing state: DC
Mailing zip: 20004
General Phone: (202) 793-5300
General/National Adv. E-mail: contact@fiscalnote.com
Display Adv. E-mail: advertise@cqrollcall.com
Primary Website: www.fiscalnote.com
Year Established: 1945
Personnel: Tim Hwang (CEO); Richard Kim (CFO); Mike Stubbs (Vice President, Operations)

FOCUS ON STYLE

Street address 1: PO Box 532
Street address city: New York
Street address state: NY
Zip/Postal code: 10276-0532
Country: USA
Mailing address: PO Box 1476
Mailing city: New York
Mailing state: NY
Mailing zip: 10276-1476
General Phone: (212) 473-8353
General/National Adv. E-mail: information@focusonstyle.com
Primary Website: www.sharonhaver.com; www.focusonstyle.com
Personnel: Sharon Haver (Syndicated Columnist, Newspaper/Online)

FOOD NUTRITION HEALTH NEWS SERVICE

Street address 1: 1712 Taylor St NW
Street address city: Washington
Street address state: D.C.
Zip/Postal code: 20011-5313
Country: USA
General Phone: (202) 723-2477
General/National Adv. E-mail: goody.solomon@verizon.net
Primary Website: www.fnhnews.com
Year Established: 1990
Personnel: Goody L. Solomon (Owner/Exec. Ed./Author)

FOTOPRESS INDEPENDENT NEWS SERVICE INTERNATIONAL

Street address 1: 266 Charlotte St., Ste. 297
Street address city: Peterborough
Street address state: ON
Zip/Postal code: K9J 2V4
Country: Canada
Mailing address: 266 Charlotte St., Ste. 297
Mailing city: Peterborough
Mailing state: ON
Mailing zip: K9J 2V4
General Phone: (705) 745-5770
General Fax: (705) 745-9459
General/National Adv. E-mail: kubikjohn@fotopressnews.org
Primary Website: www.fotopressnews.org
Year Established: 1982
Personnel: John M. Kubik (Opns. Dir.); Steven Brown (Accts. Administrator); Hugo Fernandez (South America Journalist); Vincent Delgado (Central America Photo Journalist); Elizabeth McKinney Bennett (North America Journalist); Frederick Brown (North America Journalist); Irene Clark (North America Journalist); Jarrett Dubois (North America Journalist); Barbara Jividen (North America Journalist); Jacquelyn Johnson (North America Journalist); Kevin G. Marty (North America Journalist); Lauren McFaul (North America Photographer); Peter Kozak (Australia Artist); Mulenga Chola (Africa Journalist); Luis Managonde (Africa Journalist); Nariz Bhugaloo (Africa Photographer); Gordon Irving (United Kingdom Journalist); Robert O'Connor (United Kingdom Journalist); Edward Neilam (Japan Journalist); Naohiro Kimura (Japan Photo Journalist)

GANNETT NEWS SERVICE - ALBANY, NY

Street address 1: 150 State St
Street address city: Albany
Street address state: NY
Zip/Postal code: 12207-1646
Country: USA
Mailing address: 150 State St
Mailing city: Albany
Mailing state: NY
Mailing zip: 12207-1626
General Phone: (518) 436-9781
General Fax: (518) 436-0130
Personnel: Joe Spector (Bureau Chief); Robert Hauptman (Account Executive); Keith Zurenda (Account Executive); Mary Murcko (President of Sales); Howard Griffin (VP, Gannett National Sales, USCP)

GANNETT NEWS SERVICE - BATON ROUGE, LA

Street address 1: 900 N 3rd St
Street address city: Baton Rouge
Street address state: LA
Zip/Postal code: 70802-5236
Country: USA
Mailing address: 900 N 3rd St
Mailing city: Baton Rouge
Mailing state: LA
Mailing zip: 70802
General Phone: (225) 342-7333
Personnel: Mike Hasten (Bureau Chief)

GANNETT NEWS SERVICE - MCLEAN, VA

Street address 1: 7950 Jones Branch Dr
Street address city: Mc Lean
Street address state: VA
Zip/Postal code: 22108-0003
Country: USA
Mailing address: 7950 Jones Branch Dr
Mailing city: Mc Lean
Mailing state: VA
Mailing zip: 22102-3302
General Phone: (703) 854-6000
General Fax: (703) 854-2152
General/National Adv. E-mail: candrews@gns.gannett.com
Primary Website: www.gannett.com
Personnel: Marie Marino (Office Mgr.); Jeannette Barrett-Stokes (Mng. Ed., Features/Graphics/Photography); Phil Pruitt (Mng. Ed., News); Bev Winston (Copy Desk Chief); Michelle Washington (Asst. Copy Desk Chief); Laura Rehrmann (Regl. Ed.); Val Ellicott (Regl. Ed.); Theresa Harrah (Regl. Ed.); Robert Benincasa (Regl./Database Ed.); Craig Schwed (News/Sports/Technology Ed.); Jeff Franko (Photo Ed.); Linda Dono (Special Projects Ed.); John Yaukey (Nat'l Correspondent, Defense/Security); Chuck Raasch (Nat'l Ed./Correspondent, Politics); Mike Lopresti (Sports Correspondent); Doug Abrahms (Regl. Correspondent, California/Nevada); Faith Bremner (Regl. Correspondent, Colorado/Montana/Idaho); Erin Kelly (Regl. Correspondent, Delaware/Maryland/Vermont); Larry Wheeler (Regl. Correspondent, Florida/Georgia); Maureen Groppe (Regl. Correspondent, Indiana/Illinois)

GEORGE WATERS

Country: USA
Mailing state: CA
General/National Adv. E-mail: george@georgewaters.net
Primary Website: www.georgewaters.net
Personnel: George Waters (Humor Columnist)

GET FIT WITH THE WORLD'S FITTEST MAN

Street address 1: 2707 3rd Ave
Street address city: San Diego
Street address state: CA
Zip/Postal code: 92103-6269
Country: USA
Mailing address: 2707 3rd Ave
Mailing city: San Diego
Mailing state: CA
Mailing zip: 92103-6269
General Phone: (858) 375-6150
General/National Adv. E-mail: info@gutcheckfitness.com
Primary Website: www.gutcheckfitness.com
Personnel: Joe Decker (Pres./Author)

GETTY IMAGES

Street address 1: 605 5th Avenue South
Street address 2: Suite 400
Street address city: Seattle
Street address state: WA
Zip/Postal code: 98104
Country: USA
Mailing address: 605 5th Avenue South, Suite 400
Mailing city: Seattle
Mailing state: WA
Mailing zip: 98104
General Phone: (206) 925-5000
General Fax: (206) 925-562
General/National Adv. E-mail: service.na@gettyimages.com
Primary Website: www.gettyimages.com
Year Established: 1988
Personnel: Craig Peters (CEO); Jonathan D. Klein (Co-Founder & Chairman); Mark H. Getty (Co-Founder and Director)

GLENMOOR ENTERPRISE MEDIA GROUP

Street address 1: 75 N Main St
Street address 2: No 203
Street address city: Willits
Street address state: CA
Zip/Postal code: 95490-3107
Country: USA
Mailing address: 75 N Main St No 203
Mailing city: Willits
Mailing state: CA
Mailing zip: 95490-3107
General Phone: (707) 367-4608
General Fax: (707) 459-6106
General/National Adv. E-mail: glenmoorent@yahoo.com
Year Established: 1986
Personnel: Ron C. Moorhead (Gen. Mgr.)

GLOBAL HORIZONS

Street address 1: 1330 New Hampshire Ave NW
Street address 2: Apt 609
Street address city: Washington
Street address state: D.C.
Zip/Postal code: 20036-6311
Country: USA
Mailing address: 1330 New Hampshire Ave NW Apt 609
Mailing city: Washington
Mailing state: DC
Mailing zip: G20036-6311
General Phone: (202) 363-1270
General/National Adv. E-mail: edflattau@msn.com
Primary Website: www.edflattau.com
Year Established: 1982
Personnel: Edward Flattau (Pres.); Pam Ebert (Ed.)

GLOBAL INFORMATION NETWORK

Street address 1: 220 5th Ave
Street address 2: Fl 8
Street address city: New York
Street address state: NY
Zip/Postal code: 10001-7708
Country: USA
General Phone: (212) 244-3123
General/National Adv. E-mail: ipsgin@igc.org
Year Established: 1981
Personnel: Lisa Vives (Exec. Dir.)

GLOBE PHOTOS, INC.

Street address 1: 24 Edmore Ln S
Street address city: West Islip
Street address state: NY
Zip/Postal code: 11795-4016
Country: USA
Mailing address: 24 Edmore Ln S
Mailing city: West Islip
Mailing state: NY
Mailing zip: 11795-4016
General Phone: (631) 661-3131
General Fax: (631) 321-4063
General/National Adv. E-mail: requests@globephotos.com
Primary Website: www.globephotos.com
Personnel: Mary Beth Whelan (Pres.); Raymond D. Whelan (Vice Pres.)

GLOBE SYNDICATE

Street address 1: 499 Richardson Rd
Street address city: Strasburg
Street address state: VA
Zip/Postal code: 22657-5236
Country: USA
Mailing address: 499 Richardson Rd
Mailing city: Strasburg
Mailing state: VA
Mailing zip: 22657-5236
General Phone: (540) 635-3229
General/National Adv. E-mail: publisher@globesyndicate.com
Primary Website: www.globesyndicate.com
Personnel: Gavin Bourjaily (Ed./Pub.); M.F. Bourjaily, III (Asst. Pub./Assoc. Ed.)

GOLF PUBLISHING SYNDICATE

Street address 1: 2743 Saxon St
Street address city: Allentown
Street address state: PA
Zip/Postal code: 18103-2825
Country: USA
Mailing address: 2743 Saxon St
Mailing city: Allentown

Mailing state: PA
Mailing zip: 18103-2825
General Phone: (610) 437-4982
General/National Adv. E-mail: info@galvgolf.com
Primary Website: www.galvgolf.com
Personnel: Karl D. Gilbert (Pres.)

GOT INFLUENCE? PUBLISHING

Street address 1: 190 Dundee Rd
Street address city: Inverness
Street address state: IL
Zip/Postal code: 60010-5254
Country: USA
Mailing address: 190 Dundee Rd
Mailing city: Inverness
Mailing state: IL
Mailing zip: 60010-5254
General Phone: (847) 359-7860
General/National Adv. E-mail: info@GotInfluenceInc.com
Primary Website: www.GotInfluenceInc.com
Personnel: Dan Seidman (Founder/Self-Syndicator/Columnist)

HEALTHY MINDS

Street address 1: 3709 Crestbrook Rd
Street address city: Mountain Brook
Street address state: AL
Zip/Postal code: 35223-1512
Country: USA
Mailing address: 3709 Crestbrook Rd
Mailing city: Mountain Brk
Mailing state: AL
Mailing zip: 35223-1512
General Phone: (205) 969-2963
General Fax: (205) 969-1972
General/National Adv. E-mail: wfleisig@hotmail.com
Personnel: Dr. Wayne Fleisig (Writer/Self-Syndicator)

HEARST NEWS SERVICE

Street address 1: 700 12th St NW
Street address 2: Ste 1000
Street address city: Washington
Street address state: D.C.
Zip/Postal code: 20005-3994
Country: USA
Mailing address: 700 12th St NW Ste 1000
Mailing city: Washington
Mailing state: DC
Mailing zip: 20005-3994
General Phone: (202) 263-6400
General Fax: (202) 263-6441
General/National Adv. E-mail: chuck@hearstdc.com
Primary Website: www.hearst.com
Personnel: David McCumber (Bureau Chief)

HEART TONES

Street address 1: PO Box 304
Street address 2: P. O. Box 304
Street address city: Lumberton
Street address state: NC
Zip/Postal code: 28359-0304
Country: USA
Mailing address: P. O. Box 304
Mailing city: Lumberton
Mailing state: NC
Mailing zip: 28359
General Phone: (913) 433-3877
General/National Adv. E-mail: info@hearttones.com
Primary Website: www.hearttones.com
Personnel: Gloria Thomas-Anderson (Pres./Founder); Tracee Jackson (Public Relations Director); Tammy Iroku (Webmaster and Graphics Specialist)

HELLENIC NEWS OF AMERICA

Street address 1: P.O. Box 465
Street address city: Concordville
Street address state: PA
Zip/Postal code: 19331-0465
County: Delaware
Country: USA
Mailing address: P.O. BOX 465
Mailing city: Concordville
Mailing state: PA
Mailing zip: 19331-0465
General Phone: 6102024465
General/National Adv. E-mail: info@hellenicnews.com
Display Adv. E-mail: paul@hellenicnews.com
Editorial e-mail: aphrodite@hellenicnews.com
Primary Website: www.hellenicnews.com
Year Established: 1987
Personnel: Paul Kotrotsios (Adv. Mgr.); Linda Kotrotsios (Circ. Mgr.); Aphrodite Kotrotsios (CO-Publisher)

HIGH COUNTRY NEWS

Street address 1: 119 Grand Ave
Street address 2: PO Box 1090
Street address city: Paonia
Street address state: CO
Zip/Postal code: 81428-9905
Country: USA
Mailing address: PO Box 1090
Mailing city: Paonia
Mailing state: CO
Mailing zip: 81428-1090
General Phone: (970) 527-4898
General Fax: (970) 527-4897
General/National Adv. E-mail: hcnsyndicate@hcnsyndicate.org
Primary Website: www.hcn.org
Year Established: 1970
Personnel: Jonathan Thompson (Ed. in Chief); JoeAnn Kalenak (Syndicate Representative); Paul Larmer (Exec. Dir.)

HISPANIC LINK NEWS SERVICE

Street address 1: 1420 N St NW
Street address city: Washington
Street address state: D.C.
Zip/Postal code: 20005-2843
Country: USA
Mailing address: 1420 N St NW Ste 101
Mailing city: Washington
Mailing state: DC
Mailing zip: 20005-2895
General Phone: (202) 234-0280
General Fax: (202) 234-4090
General/National Adv. E-mail: editor@hispaniclink.org
Primary Website: www.hispaniclink.org
Year Established: 1980
Personnel: Carlos Ericksen-Mendoza (Pub.); Patricia Guadalupe (Capitol Hill Ed.)

HOLLISTER KIDS

Street address 1: 763 W Lancaster Ave
Street address 2: Ste 250
Street address city: Bryn Mawr
Street address state: PA
Zip/Postal code: 19010-3401
Country: USA
Mailing address: 763 W Lancaster Ave Ste 250
Mailing city: Bryn Mawr
Mailing state: PA
Mailing zip: 19010-3401
General Phone: (484) 829-0024
General Fax: (484) 829-0027
General/National Adv. E-mail: contactus@hollisterkids.com
Primary Website: www.hollisterkids.com
Personnel: Kim Landry (Pres.); Peter Landry (Vice Pres.); Heidi Karl (Art Dir.)

HOLLYWOOD NEWS SERVICE

Street address 1: 13636 Ventura Blvd
Street address 2: Ste 303
Street address city: Sherman Oaks
Street address state: CA
Zip/Postal code: 91423-3700
Country: USA
Mailing address: Same
General Phone: (818) 986-8168
General Fax: (818) 789-8047
General/National Adv. E-mail: editor@newscalendar.com
Primary Website: www.newscalendar.com
Year Established: 1988
Note: Hollywood News Service is an entertainment wire service and does not accept solicitations for new features.

Personnel: Carolyn Fox (Ed. in Chief); Susan Fox (Mng. Ed.); Fujita Greg; Margaret Miller; John Carlin; John Fox; Sindy Saito (Editor)

HOME IMPROVEMENT TIME, INC.

Street address 1: 7425 Steubenville Pike
Street address city: Oakdale
Street address state: PA
Zip/Postal code: 15071-9311
Country: USA
Mailing address: PO Box 247
Mailing city: Oakdale
Mailing state: PA
Mailing zip: 15071-0247
General Phone: (412) 787-2881
General Fax: (412) 787-3233
General/National Adv. E-mail: info@homeimprovementtime.com
Primary Website: www.homeimprovementtime.com
Personnel: Carole C. Stewart (President); Jeff Stewart (Website Marketing Manager)

HOT TOPICS PUBLICATIONS, INC.

Street address 1: PO Box 183
Street address city: Wyncote
Street address state: PA
Zip/Postal code: 19095-0183
Country: USA
Mailing address: PO Box 183
Mailing city: Wyncote
Mailing state: PA
Mailing zip: 19095-0183
General Phone: (215) 635-1120
General/National Adv. E-mail: nie@hottopicshotserials.com
Primary Website: www.hottopicshotserials.com
Personnel: Deborah Carroll (Pres.); Ned Carroll (Vice Pres.)

HURST SPORTS MEDIA

Street address 1: 2740 N Pine Grove Ave
Street address 2: Apt 4C
Street address city: Chicago
Street address state: IL
Zip/Postal code: 60614-6101
Country: USA
Mailing address: 2740 N Pine Grove Ave Apt 4C
Mailing city: Chicago
Mailing state: IL
Mailing zip: 60614-6101
General Phone: (773) 871-3918
General/National Adv. E-mail: hurstsportsmedia@yahoo.com
Primary Website: www.hurstsportsmedia.blogspot.com
Personnel: Bob Hurst (Owner/Editor/Columnist)

IMORTGAGEGUIDE.COM LLC

Street address 1: PO Box 5795
Street address city: Scottsdale
Street address state: AZ
Zip/Postal code: 85261-5795
Country: USA
Mailing address: PO Box 5795
Mailing city: Scottsdale
Mailing state: AZ
Mailing zip: 85261-5795
General Phone: (480) 905-8000
General Fax: (480) 905-8190
General/National Adv. E-mail: info@imortgageguide.com
Primary Website: www.imortgageguide.com
Year Established: 1982
Note: Revenue-sharing content for real estate/print and online

INDEPENDENCE FEATURE SYNDICATE

Street address 1: 727 E 16th Ave
Street address city: Denver
Street address state: CO
Zip/Postal code: 80203-2048
Country: USA
Mailing address: 727 E 16th Ave
Mailing city: Denver
Mailing state: CO
Mailing zip: 80203-2048
General Phone: (303) 279-6536
General Fax: (303) 279-4176
General/National Adv. E-mail: mike@i2i.org
Primary Website: www.independenceinstitute.org
Year Established: 1985
Personnel: Jon Caldara (Pres.); David Kopel (Research Dir.); Mike Krause (Media/Publications Mgr.)

INMAN NEWS

Street address 1: 4225 Hollis St
Street address city: Emeryville
Street address state: CA
Zip/Postal code: 94608-3507
Country: USA
Mailing address: 4225 Hollis St
Mailing city: Emeryville
Mailing state: CA
Mailing zip: 94608
General Phone: (720)635-9065
General/National Adv. E-mail: amber@inman.com
Primary Website: www.inman.com
Personnel: Andrea Brambila (Assoc. Ed.); Amber Taufen (Ed. In Chief); Caroline Feeney (Assoc. Ed.)

INTERNATIONAL PHOTO NEWS

Street address 1: 2902 29th Way
Street address city: West Palm Beach
Street address state: FL
Zip/Postal code: 33407-6742
Country: USA
Mailing address: 2902 29th Way
Mailing city: West Palm Beach
Mailing state: FL
Mailing zip: 33407-6742
General Phone: (561) 683-9090
General Fax: (561) 683-9090
General/National Adv. E-mail: jay@jaykravetz.com
Primary Website: www.jaykravetz.com
Year Established: 1971
Personnel: Jay N. Kravetz (Ed.); Cheryl Dupree (Ed.)

INTERNATIONAL PUZZLE FEATURES

Street address 1: 4507 Panther Pl
Street address city: Charlotte
Street address state: NC
Zip/Postal code: 28269-3189
Country: USA
Mailing address: 4507 Panther Pl
Mailing city: Charlotte
Mailing state: NC
Mailing zip: 28269-3189
General Phone: (704) 921-1818
General/National Adv. E-mail: publisher@cleverpuzzles.com
Primary Website: www.cleverpuzzles.com
Year Established: 1990
Personnel: Pat Battaglia (Owner)

J FEATURES

Street address 1: 10 Wood Way
Street address city: Cohasset
Street address state: MA
Zip/Postal code: 02025-2127
Country: USA
Mailing address: 10 Wood Way
Mailing city: Cohasset
Mailing state: MA
Mailing zip: 02025-2127
General Phone: (781) 383-6688
General/National Adv. E-mail: jfeatures@aol.com
Personnel: Chuck Jaffe (Columnist)

J.D. CROWE

Street address 1: 212 Fig Ave
Street address city: Fairhope
Street address state: AL
Zip/Postal code: 36532-1415
Country: USA
Mailing address: 212 Fig Avenue
Mailing city: Fairhope
Mailing state: AL
Mailing zip: 36532
General Phone: (251) 219-5676
General Fax: (251) 219-5799
General/National Adv. E-mail: jdcrowe@AL.com
Primary Website: http://connect.al.com/user/jcrowe/posts.html
Note: Artizans.com

Personnel: J.D. Crowe (Statewide Editorial Cartoonist, AL.com & Alabama Media Group)

JACKSON MEDICAL GROUP, INC.

Street address 1: 220 Pacific Oaks Rd.
Street address city: Goleta
Street address state: CA
Zip/Postal code: 93117
Country: USA
Mailing address: 220 Pacific Oaks Rd.
Mailing city: Goleta
Mailing state: CA
Mailing zip: 93117
General Phone: (805) 979-4646
General Fax: (805) 685-2800
Primary Website: www.jacksonmedicalgroup.com
Personnel: Karen M. Engberg, M.D. (Self-Syndicator)

JASON LOVE (HUMOR FEATURES)

Street address 1: 165 N 5th St
Street address 2: Apt 208
Street address city: Port Hueneme
Street address state: CA
Zip/Postal code: 93041-3061
Country: USA
Mailing address: 165 N 5th St Apt 208
Mailing city: Port Hueneme
Mailing state: CA
Mailing zip: 93041-3061
General Phone: (805) 271-9560
General/National Adv. E-mail: mail@jasonlove.com
Primary Website: www.jasonlove.com
Year Established: 1994
Personnel: Jason Love (Sole Proprietor); Yahaira Quintero (Office Mgr.); Philippe Marquis (Agent); Rima Rudner (Writer); Vladimir Stankovski (Illustrator); Jose Angel (Gogue) Rodriguez (Illustrator); Thaum Blumel (Illustrator)

JEWISH TELEGRAPHIC AGENCY, INC.

Street address 1: 24 W 30th St
Street address 2: Fl 4
Street address city: New York
Street address state: NY
Zip/Postal code: 10001-4443
Country: USA
Mailing address: 24 W 30th St Fl 4
Mailing city: New York
Mailing state: NY
Mailing zip: 10001-4443
General Phone: (212) 643-1890
General Fax: (212) 643-8498
General/National Adv. E-mail: newsdesk@jta.org
Primary Website: www.jta.org
Personnel: Andrew Silow-Carrol (Ed.); Marc Brodsky (Copy Ed.); Gabe Friedman (Assoc. Dig. Ed.); Ami Eden (CEO & Exec. Ed.); Deborah Kolben (COO)

JIJI PRESS AMERICA LTD.

Street address 1: 120 W 45th St
Street address 2: Ste 1401
Street address city: New York
Street address state: NY
Zip/Postal code: 10036-4062
Country: USA
Mailing address: 70 E 55th St Ste 4L
Mailing city: New York
Mailing state: NY
Mailing zip: 10022-3395
General Phone: (212) 575-5830
General Fax: (212) 764-3950
General/National Adv. E-mail: edit@jijiusa.com
Primary Website: www.jiji.com
Personnel: Hiroshi Masuda (Pres.)

JOE HARKINS

Street address 1: 2595 John F Kennedy Blvd
Street address city: Jersey City
Street address state: NJ
Zip/Postal code: 07306-6014
Country: USA
Mailing address: 2595 John F Kennedy Blvd
Mailing city: Jersey City
Mailing state: NJ
Mailing zip: 07306-6014
General Phone: (201) 985-2105
General/National Adv. E-mail: joe@travelthenet.com
Primary Website: www.travelthenet.com
Personnel: Joe Harkins (Self-Syndicator)

JONATHON ALSOP (BOSTON WINE SCHOOL)

Street address 1: 1354 Commonwealth Ave
Street address city: Allston
Street address state: MA
Zip/Postal code: 02134-3809
Country: USA
Mailing address: 1354 Commonwealth Ave
Mailing city: Allston
Mailing state: MA
Mailing zip: 02134-3809
General Phone: (617) 784-7150
General Fax: (888) 833-9528
General/National Adv. E-mail: jalsop@BostonWineSchool.com
Primary Website: www.bostonwineschool.com
Year Established: 1988
Personnel: Jonathon Alsop (Wine Writer/Self-Syndicator)

JOURNAL PRESS SYNDICATE

Street address 1: 545 W End Ave
Street address 2: Apt 2C
Street address city: New York
Street address state: NY
Zip/Postal code: 10024-2723
Country: USA
Mailing address: 545 W End Ave Apt 2C
Mailing city: New York
Mailing state: NY
Mailing zip: 10024-2723
General Phone: (212) 580-8559
General/National Adv. E-mail: ijbnyc@aol.com
Year Established: 2000
Personnel: Irwin J. Breslauer (Ed.); John Lynker (Mng. Ed.); Todd Lewis (Automotive Ed.); William Kresse (Comics Ed.)

KEISTER WILLIAMS NEWSPAPER SERVICES, INC.

Street address 1: 1807 Emmet St N
Street address 2: Ste 6B
Street address city: Charlottesville
Street address state: VA
Zip/Postal code: 22901-3616
Country: USA
Mailing address: PO Box 8187
Mailing city: Charlottesville
Mailing state: VA
Mailing zip: 22906-8187
General Phone: (434) 293-4709
General Fax: (434) 293-4884
General/National Adv. E-mail: ky@kwnews.com
Primary Website: www.kwnews.com
Year Established: 1973
Personnel: Walton C. (Ky) Lindsay (Pres./Treasurer); Meta L. Nay (Vice Pres., Mktg.); Carol Lindsay (Admin.); Walton Lindsay (Pres.)

KEYSTONE PICTURES

Street address 1: 408 N El Camino Real
Street address city: San Clemente
Street address state: CA
Zip/Postal code: 92672-4717
Country: USA
Mailing address: 408 N El Camino Real
Mailing city: San Clemente
Mailing state: CA
Mailing zip: 92672-4717
General Phone: (949) 481-3747
General Fax: (949) 481-3941
General/National Adv. E-mail: info@zumapress.com
Primary Website: www.zumapress.com
Personnel: Scott McKiernan (Dir.)

KID SCOOP

Street address 1: PO Box 1802
Street address city: Sonoma
Street address state: CA
Zip/Postal code: 95476-1802
Country: USA
Mailing address: PO Box 1802
Mailing city: Sonoma
Mailing state: CA
Mailing zip: 95476-1802
General Phone: (707) 996-6077
General Fax: (707) 938-8718
General/National Adv. E-mail: thescoop@kidscoop.com
Primary Website: www.kidscoop.com
Year Established: 1991
Personnel: Vicki Whiting (Pres./CEO)

KING & KANGO KOMIX & ILLUSTRATIONS

Street address 1: PO Box 7914
Street address city: Vallejo
Street address state: CA
Zip/Postal code: 94590
Country: USA
Mailing address: PO Box 7914
Mailing city: Vallejo
Mailing state: CA
Mailing zip: 94590-1914
General Phone: (707) 704-2086
General/National Adv. E-mail: Tuckyart@att.net
Primary Website: www.tuckyart.com
Personnel: Tucky McKey (Pub.)

KING FEATURES SYNDICATE

Street address 1: 300 W 57th St
Street address 2: Fl 41
Street address city: New York
Street address state: NY
Zip/Postal code: 10019-3741
County: New York
Country: USA
Mailing address: 300 W 57th St
Mailing city: New York
Mailing state: NY
Mailing zip: 10019-5238
General Phone: (212) 969-7550
General Fax: (646) 280-1550
General/National Adv. E-mail: kfs-cartoonists@hearst.com
Primary Website: www.kingfeatures.com
Year Established: 1915
Personnel: Keith McCloat (VP., Gen. Mgr.); David Cohea (Gen. Mgr., King Feat. Weekly Service Inside Sales); Claudia Smith (Dir., PR); Jack Walsh (Sr. Sales Consultant/Printing & New England Newspaper Sales); Dennis Danko (Inside Sales Mgr.); Michael Mancino (Sales Mgr., New Media Inside Sales); John Killian (VP, Syndication Sales); Jim Clarke (Editorial Dir., King Feat. Weekly Service); Brendan Burford (Gen. Mgr., Syndication); Randy Noble (SE Sales); Diana Smith (Executive Editor); Evelyn Smith (Senior Comics Editor); Chris Richcreek (Senior Features Editor); Curtis Trammell (Western Region Sales); Robin Graham (International Sales Consultant); Monique Prioleau (Sales Coordinator); C.J. Kettler (President)

KYODO NEWS INTERNATIONAL, INC.

Street address 1: 780 3rd Ave
Street address 2: Rm 1103
Street address city: New York
Street address state: NY
Zip/Postal code: 10017-2158
Country: USA
Mailing address: 780 3rd Ave Ste. 1103
Mailing city: New York
Mailing state: NY
Mailing zip: 10017-2024
General Phone: (212) 508-5440
General Fax: (212) 508-5441
General/National Adv. E-mail: kni@kyodonews.com
Primary Website: www.kyodo.co.jp; www.kyodonews.com
Personnel: Toshi Mitsudome (Vice President)

LEVIN REPRESENTS

Street address 1: 2402 4th St
Street address 2: Apt 6
Street address city: Santa Monica
Street address state: CA
Zip/Postal code: 90405-3664
Country: USA
Mailing address: 2402 4th St Apt 6
Mailing city: Santa Monica
Mailing state: CA
Mailing zip: 90405-3664
General Phone: (310) 392-5146
General Fax: (310) 392-3856
General/National Adv. E-mail: deblevin@aol.com
Primary Website: www.callahanonline.com
Personnel: Deborah Levin (Pres.)

LISTENING, INC.

Street address 1: 105 E 3rd St
Street address city: Hobart
Street address state: ID
Zip/Postal code: 46342-4308
Country: USA
Mailing address: PO Box 187
Mailing city: Hobart
Mailing state: IN
Mailing zip: 46342-0187
General Phone: (219) 947-5478
General/National Adv. E-mail: info@familiesbesafe.com
Primary Website: listeninginc.com
Personnel: Patricia Work Bennett (Pres.); Richard Bennett (Vice Pres.)

LITERARY FEATURES SYNDICATE

Street address 1: 92 East St
Street address city: North Grafton
Street address state: MA
Zip/Postal code: 01536-1806
Country: USA
Mailing address: 92 East St
Mailing city: North Grafton
Mailing state: MA
Mailing zip: 01536-1806
General Phone: (508) 839-4404
General/National Adv. E-mail: nick@gentlymad.com
Personnel: Constance V. Basbanes (Pres.); Nicholas A. Basbanes (Mng. Ed./Columnist)

LONA O'CONNOR

Street address 1: 2751 S Dixie Hwy
Street address city: West Palm Beach
Street address state: FL
Zip/Postal code: 33405-1233
Country: USA
Mailing address: 2751 S Dixie Hwy
Mailing city: West Palm Beach
Mailing state: FL
Mailing zip: 33405-1233
General Phone: (561) 820-4100
General/National Adv. E-mail: lona_oconnor@pbpost.com
Primary Website: www.palmbeachpost.com
Personnel: Lona O'Connor (Author, journalist)

MAGNUM PHOTOS, INC.

Street address 1: 12 W 31st St
Street address 2: Fl 11
Street address city: New York
Street address state: NY
Zip/Postal code: 10001-4415
Country: USA
Mailing address: 12 W 31st St Fl 11
Mailing city: New York
Mailing state: NY
Mailing zip: 10001-4415
General Phone: (212) 929-6000
General Fax: (212) 929-9325
General/National Adv. E-mail: photography@magnumphotos.com
Primary Website: www.magnumphotos.com

MALE CALL

Street address 1: 721 Shore Acres Dr
Street address city: Mamaroneck
Street address state: NY
Zip/Postal code: 10543-4214
Country: USA
Mailing address: 721 Shore Acres Dr
Mailing city: Mamaroneck
Mailing state: NY
Mailing zip: 10543-4214
General Phone: (914) 698-0721
General/National Adv. E-mail: lois.fenton@prodigy.net
Note: Columnist/Advice, Men's Business & Social Dress Consultant/Men's Personal Shopper, Blogger

Personnel: Lois Fenton (Columnist/Advice, Men's Business & Social Dress Consultant/Men's Personal Shopper, Blogger)

MARION JOYCE

Street address 1: 52 Sagamore Rd
Street address city: Bronxville
Street address state: NY
Zip/Postal code: 10708-1544
Country: USA
Mailing address: 52 Sagamore Rd
Mailing city: Bronxville
Mailing state: NY
Mailing zip: 10708-1544
General Phone: (914) 961-2020
General Fax: (914) 793-3434
Personnel: Marion Joyce (Pres.)

MARKET NEWS INTERNATIONAL

Street address 1: 40 Fulton St
Street address 2: Fl 5
Street address city: New York
Street address state: NY
Zip/Postal code: 10038-5092
Country: USA
Mailing address: 40 Fulton St Fl 5
Mailing city: New York
Mailing state: NY
Mailing zip: 10038-5065
General Phone: (212) 669-6400
General Fax: (212) 608-3024
General/National Adv. E-mail: tony@marketnews.com
Primary Website: www.marketnews.com
Year Established: 1983
Note: Market News Service has bureaus in New York, Chicago, Washington DC, London, Frankfurt, Berlin, Paris, Brussels, Beijing, Tokyo, Singapore and Sydney.
Personnel: Tony Mace (Mng. Ed.); Denis Gulino (Washington Bureau Chief); Kevin Woodfield (London Bureau Chief/European Ed.); John Carter (managing editor); Clive Tillbrook

MARKS & FREDERICK ASSOC., LLC

Street address 1: 11 Green Hill Rd
Street address city: Kent
Street address state: CT
Zip/Postal code: 06757-1246
Country: USA
Mailing address: 11 Green Hill Rd
Mailing city: Kent
Mailing state: CT
Mailing zip: 06757-1246
General Phone: (860) 927-3948
General Fax: (860) 927-3062
General/National Adv. E-mail: info@mfamedia.com
Primary Website: www.mfamedia.com
Year Established: 1990
Note: Marks & Frederick Associates represents various publishing interests in Europe and Asia.
Personnel: Ted Marks (Pres.)

MATURE LIFE FEATURES

Street address 1: 1505 e Willis Rd
Street address 2: Ste 1404
Street address city: Gilbert
Street address state: AZ
Zip/Postal code: 85297
County: Maricopa
Country: USA
Mailing state: AZ
General Phone: 480 275-4323
General/National Adv. E-mail: cecilscag@gmail.com
Primary Website: www.maturelifefeatures.com
Year Established: 1989
Personnel: Cecil F. Scaglione (Ed. in Chief/Financial Ed.); Beverly Rahn Scaglione (Book Ed.); James B. Gaffney (Nat'l Affairs/Health Ed.); Igor Lobanov (Travel Ed.)

MEADOWLANDS MEDIA GROUP

Street address 1: 20 Nevins St
Street address city: Rutherford
Street address state: NJ
Zip/Postal code: 07070-2819
Country: USA
Mailing address: 20 Nevins St
Mailing city: Rutherford
Mailing state: NJ
Mailing zip: 07070-2819
General Phone: (201) 939-7875
General Fax: (201) 896-8619
General/National Adv. E-mail: salfino@comcast.net
Primary Website: www.rotoaction.com
Year Established: 2004
Personnel: Catherine Salfino (Pres.); Michael Salfino (Columnist); David Ferris (Columnist)

MEDIA GENERAL SYNDICATION SERVICES

Street address 1: 418 N Marshall St
Street address city: Winston Salem
Street address state: NC
Zip/Postal code: 27101-2815
Country: USA
Mailing address: 418 N Marshall St
Mailing city: Winston Salem
Mailing state: NC
Mailing zip: 27101-2815
General Phone: (800) 457-1156
General Fax: (336) 727-7461
General/National Adv. E-mail: jsarver@wsjournal.com
Personnel: Jodi Stephenson Sarver (Rep.)

MEGALO MEDIA

Street address 1: PO Box 1503
Street address city: New York
Street address state: NY
Zip/Postal code: 10021-0042
Country: USA
Mailing address: PO Box 1503
Mailing city: New York
Mailing state: NY
Mailing zip: 10021-0042
General Phone: (212) 861-8048
General/National Adv. E-mail: megalomedia@lawtv.com
Primary Website: www.megalomedia.biz; www.crossword.org
Personnel: J. Baxter Newgate (Pres.); Sandy Applegreen (Ed./Vice Pres.); Paul Merenbloom (Assoc. Ed.); Arthur Wynne (Puzzle Ed.)

METRO EDITORIAL SERVICES

Street address 1: 519 8th Ave
Street address 2: Fl 18
Street address city: New York
Street address state: NY
Zip/Postal code: 10018-4577
County: New York
Country: USA
Mailing address: 519 8th Ave Fl 18
Mailing city: New York
Mailing state: NY
Mailing zip: 10018-4577
General Phone: (212) 947-5100
General Fax: (212) 714-9139
General/National Adv. E-mail: mes@metro-email.com
Primary Website: www.mcg.metrocreativeconnection.com
Year Established: 1910
Note: Metro is a leading provider of advertising, creative and editorial resources designed to help media companies make money with their print, online, and mobile products. We provide ready-to-use images, ads, stock-quality photos, logos/trademarks, auto photos, marketing/sales materials, copyright-free features, print templated sections, online e-Sections, and groundbreaking digital ad development tools, plus custom image, ad design and editorial services.
Personnel: Robert Zimmerman (Publisher); Debra Weiss (Exec. Vice Pres./Mktg. Dir.); Lauren Lekoski (Mktg. Mgr.); Jo Ann Shapiro (VP, Sales); Lou Ann Sornson (Regional Sales Mgr.); Tina Dentner (Regional Sales Mgr.); Cathy Agee (Regional Sales Mgr.); Gwen Tomaselli (Regional Sales Mgr.); Jennifer Steiner (Regional Sales Mgr.); Joann Johnson

MIC INSURANCE SERVICES

Street address 1: 170 Kinnelon Rd
Street address 2: Rm 11
Street address city: Kinnelon
Street address state: NJ
Zip/Postal code: 07405-2324
Country: USA
Mailing address: 170 Kinnelon Rd Rm 11
Mailing city: Kinnelon
Mailing state: NJ
Mailing zip: 07405-2324
General Phone: (973) 492-2828
General Fax: 973-492-9068
Editorial e-mail: irenec@micinsurance.com
Primary Website: www.micinsurance.com
Note: Medical Insurance Claims, Inc. changed name to MIC Insurance Services
Personnel: Irene C. Card (Pres./Author); Betsy Chandler (Sec./Treasurer/Author)

MIDWEST FEATURES SYNDICATE

Street address 1: PO Box 259623
Street address city: Madison
Street address state: WI
Zip/Postal code: 53725-9623
Country: USA
Mailing address: PO Box 259623
Mailing city: Madison
Mailing state: WI
Mailing zip: 53725-9623
General Phone: (608) 274-8925
General/National Adv. E-mail: info@roadstraveled.com
Primary Website: www.roadstraveled.com; www.marybergin.com;
Note: Producing since 2002 weekly travel columns, with art, usually about America's Heartland, especially the Upper Midwest.
Personnel: Mary Bergin (Columnist)

MIKO'S PACIFIC NEWS SERVICE

Street address 1: 33280 E Nimrod St
Street address city: Solon
Street address state: OH
Zip/Postal code: 44139-4433
Country: USA
Mailing address: 33289 East Nimrod St
Mailing city: Solon
Mailing state: OH
Mailing zip: 44139
General Phone: (203) 378 2893
General/National Adv. E-mail: bmiko@pacificdialogue.com
Primary Website: www.pacificdialogue.com
Year Established: 1978
Personnel: Robert J. Miko (Ed.)

MILITARY UPDATE

Street address 1: PO Box 231111
Street address city: Centreville
Street address state: VA
Zip/Postal code: 20120-7111
Country: USA
Mailing address: PO Box 231111
Mailing city: Centreville
Mailing state: VA
Mailing zip: 20120-7111
General Phone: (703) 830-6863
General/National Adv. E-mail: tomphilpott@militaryupdate.com
Primary Website: www.militaryupdate.com
Note: For daily newspapers near military bases across the country, Military Update has for 20 years covered breaking news affecting service members -- active, reserve, retirees and family members.
Personnel: Tom Philpott (Self-Syndicator)

MOTOR NEWS MEDIA CORP.

Street address 1: 3710 SE Capitol Cir
Street address 2: Ste F
Street address city: Grimes
Street address state: IA
Zip/Postal code: 50111-5046
Country: USA
Mailing address: 3710 SE Capitol Cir Ste F
Mailing city: Grimes
Mailing state: IA
Mailing zip: 50111-5046
General Phone: (515) 986-1155
General/National Adv. E-mail: motornewsmedia@live.com
Primary Website: www.motornewsmedia.com
Year Established: 1989
Note: automotive news and photography service.
Personnel: Kenneth J. Chester (Pres./CEO)

MOVE, INC.

Street address 1: 30700 Russell Ranch Rd
Street address city: Westlake Village
Street address state: CA
Zip/Postal code: 91362-9500
Country: USA
Mailing address: 30700 Russell Ranch Rd Ste 100
Mailing city: Westlake Village
Mailing state: CA
Mailing zip: 91362-9501
General Phone: (805) 557-2300
General Fax: (805) 557-2680
General/National Adv. E-mail: corporateinfo@move.com
Primary Website: www.move.com
Year Established: 1946
Personnel: Joe F. Hanauer (Chrmn.); W. Michael Long (CEO)

NATIONAL NEWS BUREAU

Street address 1: PO Box 43039
Street address city: Philadelphia
Street address state: PA
Zip/Postal code: 19129-3039
Country: USA
General Phone: (215) 849-9016
General Fax: 215-754-4488
General/National Adv. E-mail: nnbfeature@aol.com; fashionnnb@aol.com; travelnnb@aol.com; foodandwinennb@aol.com; booksnnb@aol.com
Primary Website: www.nationalnewsbureau.com
Year Established: 1979
Note: We specialize in fashion, food, wine, theater, movie reviews, celebrity interviews, Our "BEST" series from kitchen appliances to household items, travel to exotic, romantic destinations, men and women's apparel.
Personnel: Harry Jay Katz (Pub./Ed. in Chief); Debra Renee Cruz (Fashion/Beauty/Lifestyles Ed.); Andy Edelman (Features Ed.)

NEW ENGLAND NEWS SERVICE, INC.

Street address 1: 66 Alexander Rd
Street address city: Newton
Street address state: MA
Zip/Postal code: 02461-1831
Country: USA
Mailing address: 66 Alexander Rd
Mailing city: Newton
Mailing state: MA
Mailing zip: 02461-1831
General Phone: 617-244-3075
General/National Adv. E-mail: nenewsnow@rcn.com
Primary Website: www.rcn.com
Year Established: 1986
Personnel: Milton J. Gun (Bureau Chief); Lee Ann Jacob (Staff); Eleanor Margolis (Staff); Howard Neal (Staff); Kate Tattlebaum (Staff); Steve Richards (Corresp.)

NEW LIVING SYNDICATE

Street address 1: 99 Waverly Ave
Street address 2: Apt 6D
Street address city: Patchogue
Street address state: NY
Zip/Postal code: 11772-1922
Country: USA
Mailing address: PO Box 1001
Mailing city: Patchogue
Mailing state: NY
Mailing zip: 11772-0800
General Phone: (631) 751-8819
General/National Adv. E-mail: charvey@newliving.com
Primary Website: www.newliving.com
Year Established: 1991
Personnel: Christine Lynn Harvey (Pub./Ed. in Chief)

NEW YORK PRESS PHOTOGRAPHERS ASSOCIATION

Street address 1: 225 W 36th St
Street address 2: Ste 1-P
Street address city: New York
Street address state: NY
Zip/Postal code: 10018-7525
Country: USA
Mailing address: 225 W 36th St Ste 1P
Mailing city: New York
Mailing state: NY
Mailing zip: 10018-7525
General/National Adv. E-mail: office@nyppa.org

Primary Website: www.nyppa.org

NEWS LICENSING

Street address 1: The News Building, 13th Floor,
Street address 2: 1 London Bridge
Street address city: London
Zip/Postal code: SE1 9GF
Country: United Kingdom
Mailing address: The News Building, 13th Floor,
Mailing city: London
Mailing zip: SE1 9GF
General Phone: 711 7888
General Fax: n/a
General/National Adv. E-mail: enquiries@newslicensing.co.uk
Primary Website: www.newslicensing.co.uk
Personnel: Darren Hendry (Licensing Sales Mngr.)

NEWSCOM

Street address 1: 375 S Chipeta Way
Street address 2: Ste B
Street address city: Salt Lake City
Street address state: UT
Zip/Postal code: 84108-1261
Country: USA
Mailing address: 375 S Chipeta Way Ste B
Mailing city: Salt Lake City
Mailing state: UT
Mailing zip: 84108-1261
General Phone: (801) 584-3900
General Fax: (202) 383-6190
General/National Adv. E-mail: sales@newscom.com
Primary Website: www.newscom.com
Year Established: 1985
Personnel: Bill Creighton (Gen. Mgr.); Tom Bannon (Sales Mgr.); Lily Cheung (IP Rel. Mgr.); Ericka Calvert (Mktg. Dir.)

NEWSFINDER

Street address 1: 1700 E Racine Ave
Street address city: Waukesha
Street address state: WI
Zip/Postal code: 53186-6934
Country: USA
Mailing address: 1700 E Racine Ave
Mailing city: Waukesha
Mailing state: WI
Mailing zip: 53186-6934
General Phone: (262) 544-5252
General/National Adv. E-mail: nf-support@newsfinder.com
Primary Website: www.newsfinder.com
Year Established: 1984
Note: Full AP wire of stories and photos for non-daily publications.
Personnel: Sandy Hamm (Gen. Mgr.); Linda Kalinowski (Acct. Mgr.); Colleen Hamm (Account Manager)

NEWSPAPER TOOLBOX

Street address 1: CP 666
Street address city: St-Jean-sur-Richelieu
Street address state: QC
Zip/Postal code: J3B 6Z8
Country: Canada
General Phone: 450-349-0450
General/National Adv. E-mail: marc@textuel.ca
Display Adv. E-mail: production@textuel.ca
Primary Website: newspapertoolbox.com
Year Established: 1990
Personnel: Susie Slifer (Media consultant)

NEWSUSA, INC.

Street address 1: 1104 W Broad St
Street address 2: Ste 1024
Street address city: Falls Church
Street address state: VA
Zip/Postal code: 22046-4610
County: Fairfax
Country: US
Mailing address: 7816 Maple Ridge Road
Mailing city: Bethesda
Mailing state: MD
Mailing zip: 20814
General Phone: (703) 5088700
Primary Website: www.newsusa.com
Year Established: 1987
Personnel: Rick Smith (Founder); Richard Rothstein (Vice Pres., Sales)

NORTH AMERICA SYNDICATE

Street address 1: 300 W 57th St
Street address 2: Fl 41
Street address city: New York
Street address state: NY
Zip/Postal code: 10019-3741
Country: USA
Mailing address: 300 W 57th St Fl 41
Mailing city: New York
Mailing state: NY
Mailing zip: 10019-3741
General Phone: (212) 969-7550
General Fax: (646) 280-1550
General/National Adv. E-mail: kfs-public-relations@hearst.com
Primary Website: www.kingfeatures.com
Note: North America Syndicate is an affiliated company of King Features Syndicate.
Personnel: T.R. Shepard III (Pres.); Keith McCloat (Vice Pres./Gen. Mgr.); John Killian (VP, Syndication Sales); David Cohea (Gen. Mgr., King Feat. Weekly Service); Jack Walsh (Sr. Sales Consultant/Printing & New England Newspaper Sales); Claudia Smith (PR Dir.); Dennis Danko (Inside Sales Mgr.); Michael Mancino (Sales Mgr., New Media Inside Sales Rep); Brendan Burford (Gen. Mgr., Syndication); Jim Clarke (Editorial Dir., King Feat. Weekly Service); Randy Noble (SE Sales); Curtis Trammell (West Coast Sales); Robin Graham (International Sales Consultant); Diana Smith (Executive Editor); Chris Richcreek (Senior Features Editor); Evelyn Smith (Senior Comics Editor'); Monique Prioleau (Sales Coordinator)

NORTH AMERICAN PRECIS SYNDICATE, INC.

Street address 1: 415 Madison Ave
Street address 2: Fl 12
Street address city: New York
Street address state: NY
Zip/Postal code: 10017-7947
County: New York
Country: USA
Mailing address: 415 Madison Ave Fl 12
Mailing city: New York
Mailing state: NY
Mailing zip: 10017-7956
General Phone: (212) 867-9000
General Fax: (800) 990-4329
General/National Adv. E-mail: service@napsnet.com; info@napsnet.com
Primary Website: www.napsnet.com
Year Established: 1958
Personnel: Dorothy York (Pres.); Gary Lipton (Vice Pres., Media Rel.); Candace Leiberman (Ed. in Chief); Yauling Wagner (Serv. Mgr.)

OASIS NEWSFEATURES, INC.

Street address 1: PO Box 2144
Street address city: Middletown
Street address state: OH
Zip/Postal code: 45042
Country: USA
Mailing address: PO Box 2144
Mailing city: Middletown
Mailing state: OH
Mailing zip: 45042
General Phone: (800) 245-7515
General/National Adv. E-mail: kwilliams@oasisnewsfeatures.com
Primary Website: www.oasisnewsfeatures.com
Year Established: 1991
Personnel: Kevin Williams (Exec. Ed.)

ON THE HOUSE SYNDICATION, INC.

Street address 1: 2420 Sand Creek Rd
Street address 2: C-1318
Street address city: Brentwood
Street address state: CA
Zip/Postal code: 94513-2707
Country: USA
Mailing address: 2420 Sand Creek Rd
Mailing city: Brentwood
Mailing state: CA
Mailing zip: 94513-2707
General Phone: (925) 432-7246 x24
General Fax: (925) 420-5690
General/National Adv. E-mail: info@onthehouse.com
Display Adv. E-mail: james@onthehouse.com
Editorial e-mail: morris@onthehouse.com
Primary Website: www.onthehouse.com
Year Established: 1995
Personnel: James Carey (Pres./Co-Host); Morris Carey (Vice Pres./Co-Host); Sylvie Castaniada (Affiliate Rel. Dir.)

PACIFIC NEWS SERVICE

Street address 1: 209 9th St
Street address 2: Ste 200
Street address city: San Francisco
Street address state: CA
Zip/Postal code: 94103-6800
Country: USA
Mailing address: 209 9th St Ste 200
Mailing city: San Francisco
Mailing state: CA
Mailing zip: 94103-6800
General/National Adv. E-mail: eshore@newamericamedia.org
Primary Website: www.newamericamedia.org
Year Established: 1963

PAPPOCOM

Street address 1: 3 Birch Ledge Rd
Street address city: Glen
Street address state: NH
Zip/Postal code: 03838-6453
Country: USA
Mailing address: PO Box 1253
Mailing city: Glen
Mailing state: NH
Mailing zip: 03838-1253
General Phone: (603) 383-6729
General/National Adv. E-mail: info@waynegouldpuzzles.com
Primary Website: www.waynegouldpuzzles.com
Personnel: Wayne Gould (Dir.); Scott Gould (Mgr.)

PARENT TO PARENT

Street address 1: 2464 Taylor Rd
Street address 2: Ste 131
Street address city: Wildwood
Street address state: MO
Zip/Postal code: 63040-1222
County: St. Louis
Country: USA
Mailing address: 2464 Taylor Rd Ste 131
Mailing city: Wildwood
Mailing state: MO
Mailing zip: 63040-1222
General Phone: (636) 458 8800
General Fax: (636) 458-7688
General/National Adv. E-mail: editor@parenttoparent.com
Editorial e-mail: emparenttoparent@gmail.com
Primary Website: www.parenttoparent.com
Year Established: 1996
Note: Self syndicated
Personnel: Jodie Lynn (Owner); Kyle Johnson (Personal Assistant Assistant Editor)

PEDIATRIC POINTS

Street address 1: 5 Chain Bridge Dr
Street address city: Newburyport
Street address state: MA
Zip/Postal code: 01950-1723
Country: USA
Mailing address: 5 Chain Bridge Dr
Mailing city: Newburyport
Mailing state: MA
Mailing zip: 01950-1723
General Phone: (978) 476-9121
General Fax: (978) 521-8372
General/National Adv. E-mail: carolynroybornstein@gmail.com
Primary Website: www.carolynroybornstein.com
Personnel: Carolyn Roy-Bornstein (MD)

PLAIN LABEL PRESS

Street address 1: 1690 Carman Mill Dr
Street address city: Manchester
Street address state: MO
Zip/Postal code: 63021-7107
Country: USA
Mailing address: PO Box 240331
Mailing city: Ballwin
Mailing state: MO
Mailing zip: 63024-0331
General Phone: (636) 207-9880
General Fax: (636) 207-9880
General/National Adv. E-mail: mail@plainlabelpress.com
Primary Website: www.creativeon-line.com/syndicate
Year Established: 1989
Personnel: Ed Chermoore (Vice Pres./Mng. Ed.); Laura Meyer (Submissions Ed.)

PR NEWSWIRE

Street address 1: 350 Hudson St
Street address 2: Ste 300
Street address city: New York
Street address state: NY
Zip/Postal code: 10014-4504
County: New York
Country: USA
Mailing address: 350 Hudson St Ste 300
Mailing city: New York
Mailing state: NY
Mailing zip: 10014-5827
General Phone: 1.888-776-0942
General/National Adv. E-mail: MediaInquiries@prnewswire.com
Primary Website: www.prnewswire.com
Year Established: 1954
Personnel: Christine Cube (Audience Relations Manager); Dave Haapaoja (SVP, Global Operations); Victoria Harres (VP, Strategic Communications & Content)

PRACTICAL ECOMMERCE

Street address 1: 125 S Park St
Street address 2: Ste 430
Street address city: Traverse City
Street address state: MI
Zip/Postal code: 49684-3610
Country: USA
Mailing address: 125 S. Park Street, Suite 430
Mailing city: Traverse City
Mailing state: MI
Mailing zip: 49684
General Phone: (231) 946-0606
General/National Adv. E-mail: kmurdock@practicalecommerce.com
Primary Website: http://www.practicalecommerce.com
Year Established: 1995
Personnel: Kerry Murdock (Pub and Ed); Armando Roggio (Senior Contributing Editor)

PRESS ASSOCIATES, INC.

Street address 1: 2605 P St NW
Street address 2: Ste A
Street address city: Washington
Street address state: D.C.
Zip/Postal code: 20007-5029
Country: USA
Mailing address: 2605 P St NW Ste A
Mailing city: Washington
Mailing state: DC
Mailing zip: 20007-5029
General Phone: (202) 898-4825
General/National Adv. E-mail: press_associates@yahoo.com
Year Established: 1955
Personnel: Mark J. Gruenberg (Ed. in Chief); Janet Brown (Ed.); Dick Belland (Cartoonist); Martha Turner (Accounting)

PROTOTYPE CAREER SERVICES

Street address 1: 626 Armstrong Ave
Street address city: St Paul
Street address state: MN
Zip/Postal code: 55102
Country: USA
Mailing address: 626 Armstrong
Mailing city: St Paul
Mailing state: MN
Mailing zip: 55102
General Phone: (651) 224-2856
General/National Adv. E-mail: getajob@prototypecareerservice.com
Primary Website: www.prototypecareerservice.com
Note: Award-winning 800- word weekly column on careers topics such as job search strategies, salary

negotiations, career transition, business start-up, etc. Special content for millennials, older workers, others. Reliable, clean, engaging content has appeared in 100+ publications since 1995. Weekly rates start at $20 depending on publication size and/or contract. Careers expert, Amy Lindgren also appears frequently on public radio call-in shows.
Personnel: Amy Lindgren (Columnist/Career Expert)

PUNCH IN TRAVEL, FOOD, WINE & ENTERTAINMENT NEWS SYNDICATE

Street address 1: 400 E 59th St
Street address 2: Apt 9F
Street address city: New York
Street address state: NY
Zip/Postal code: 10022-2344
Country: USA
Mailing address: 400 E 59th St Apt 9F
Mailing city: New York
Mailing state: NY
Mailing zip: 10022-2344
General Phone: (212) 755-4363
General/National Adv. E-mail: info@punchin.com
Primary Website: www.punchin.com
Personnel: Nancy Preiser (Pres./Mng. Ed.); Betty Andrews (Contributing Writer); Bob Andrews (Contributing Writer); John Edwards (Contributing Writer); Bette Johns (Contributing Writer); Nina Lindt (Contributing Writer); Tom Weston (Contributing Writer)

Q SYNDICATE

Street address 1: 20222 Farmington Rd
Street address city: Livonia
Street address state: MI
Zip/Postal code: 48152-1412
Country: USA
Mailing address: 20222 Farmington Rd
Mailing city: Livonia
Mailing state: MI
Mailing zip: 48152-1412
General Phone: (734) 293-7200
General Fax: (734) 293-7201
General/National Adv. E-mail: qsyndicate@pridesource.com
Primary Website: www.qsyndicate.com
Note: Q Syndicate provides content and community to the gay and lesbian press.
Personnel: Susan Horowitz (Pres.); Jan Stevenson (CFO); Christopher Azzopardi (Ed.)

RAFFERTY CONSULTING GROUP

Street address 1: 45775 Indian Wells Ln
Street address city: Indian Wells
Street address state: CA
Zip/Postal code: 92210-8835
Country: USA
Mailing address: 20960 Hilliard Blvd
Mailing city: Rocky River
Mailing state: OH
Mailing zip: 44116-3311
General Phone: (760) 776-9606
General Fax: (760) 776-9608
General/National Adv. E-mail: rrafferty@raffertyconsulting.com
Primary Website: www.raffertyconsulting.com
Personnel: Renata J. Rafferty (Pres.)

REEL TO REAL CELEBRITY PROFILES

Street address 1: 8643 N Fielding Rd
Street address city: Milwaukee
Street address state: WI
Zip/Postal code: 53217-2427
Country: USA
Mailing address: 8643 N Fielding Rd
Mailing city: Milwaukee
Mailing state: WI
Mailing zip: 53217-2427
General/National Adv. E-mail: david.fantle@gmail.com
Primary Website: www.reeltoreal.com
Note: We specialize in interviews with stars that have a track record and appeal to 50 plus readers. We do not need to be pitched reality stars or young "flavor of the month" stars who desperately need some press.
Personnel: David Fantle (Creator/Writer); Tom Johnson (Creator/Writer)

RELIGION NEWS SERVICE

Street address 1: 529 14th St NW
Street address 2: Ste 1009
Street address city: Washington
Street address state: D.C.
Zip/Postal code: 20045-2001
Country: USA
Mailing address: 529 14th St NW Ste 1009
Mailing city: Washington
Mailing state: DC
Mailing zip: 20045-2001
General Phone: (202) 463-8777
General Fax: (202) 662-7154
General/National Adv. E-mail: info@religionnews.com
Primary Website: www.religionnews.com
Year Established: 1934
Personnel: David E. Anderson (Senior Editor); Kevin Eckstrom (Editor-in-Chief); Tracy Gordon (Editorial/Publishing Consultant); Adelle Banks (Production Editor); Daniel Burke (Associate Editor); Lauren Markoe (National Correspondent); Claudia M. Sans Werner (Bus./Sales Mgr.); David Shaw (Bus. Coord.)

REUTERS

Street address 1: 311 S Wacker Dr
Street address 2: Ste 1200
Street address city: Chicago
Street address state: IL
Zip/Postal code: 60606-6623
Country: USA
Mailing address: 311 S Wacker Dr Ste 1200
Mailing city: Chicago
Mailing state: IL
Mailing zip: 60606-6623

REUTERS

Street address 1: 3 Times Sq
Street address 2: Fl 17
Street address city: New York
Street address state: NY
Zip/Postal code: 10036-6564
Country: USA
Mailing address: 3 Times Sq Lbby F
Mailing city: New York
Mailing state: NY
Mailing zip: 10036-6567

REUTERS MEDIA

Street address 1: 3 Times Sq
Street address city: New York
Street address state: NY
Zip/Postal code: 10036-6564
County: New York
Country: USA
Mailing address: 3 Times Sq
Mailing city: New York
Mailing state: NY
Mailing zip: 10036-6564
General Phone: (646) 223-4000
General Fax: (646) 223-4393
General/National Adv. E-mail: rosalina.thomas@thomsonreuters.com
Primary Website: www.reuters.com/newsagency
Personnel: Ms. Rosalina Thomas (Vice Pres./Head of Sales - The Americas, Reuters News Agency, Thomson Reuters); Melissa Metzger (Publishing Solutions Specialist); Bipasha Ghosh (Global Director of Marketing)

RICK HOROWITZ

Street address 1: 4014 N Morris Blvd
Street address city: Shorewood
Street address state: WI
Zip/Postal code: 53211-1844
Country: USA
Mailing address: 4014 N Morris Blvd
Mailing city: Shorewood
Mailing state: WI
Mailing zip: 53211-1844
General Phone: (414) 963-9333
General/National Adv. E-mail: rickhoro@execpc.com
Primary Website: www.huffingtonpost.com/rick-horowitz/
Personnel: Rick Horowitz (Self-Syndicator); Charlie White (Webmaster)

RON BERNTHAL

Street address 1: PO Box 259
Street address city: Hurleyville
Street address state: NY
Zip/Postal code: 12747-0259
Country: USA
Mailing address: PO Box 259
Mailing city: Hurleyville
Mailing state: NY
Mailing zip: 12747-0259
General Phone: (845) 292-3071
General Fax: (845) 434-4806
General/National Adv. E-mail: ronbernthal@wjffradio.org
Personnel: Ron Bernthal (Self-Syndicator, Travel/Historic Preservation Audio Programs)

SAM MANTICS ENTERPRISES

Street address 1: 3650 Mockingbird Dr
Street address city: Vero Beach
Street address state: FL
Zip/Postal code: 32963-1514
Country: USA
Mailing address: 3650 Mockingbird Dr
Mailing city: Vero Beach
Mailing state: FL
Mailing zip: 32963-1514
General Phone: (772) 492-9032
General Fax: (772) 492-9032
General/National Adv. E-mail: jancook@myvocabulary.com
Primary Website: www.syndicate.com; myvocabulary.com; www.rootonym.com
Year Established: 1994
Note: We syndicate vocabulary word puzzles, word games and educational activities (K-12+.)
Personnel: Carey Orr Cook (Pres./Cartoon Ed.); Jan Cook (Bus. Devel.); Keith Cook (Sr. Vice Pres., Mktg./Sales); Kylie Cook (Internet/Web Ed.); Brad Cook (Prodn. Mgr., Opns.); Corry Cook (Senior Ed.)

SCHWADRON CARTOON & ILLUSTRATION SERVICE

Street address 1: PO Box 1347
Street address city: Ann Arbor
Street address state: MI
Zip/Postal code: 48106-1347
Country: USA
Mailing address: P.O. Box 1347
Mailing city: Ann Arbor
Mailing state: MI
Mailing zip: 48106
General Phone: (734) 665-8272
General Fax: (734) 665-8272
General/National Adv. E-mail: schwaboo@comcast.net
Primary Website: www.schwadroncartoons.com
Personnel: Harley Schwadron (Ed.); Sally Booth (Sec.)

SCRIPPS HOWARD NEWS SERVICE

Street address 1: 1090 Vermont Ave NW
Street address 2: Ste 1000
Street address city: Washington
Street address state: D.C.
Zip/Postal code: 20005-4965
Country: USA
Mailing address: 1090 Vermont Ave NW Ste 1000
Mailing city: Washington
Mailing state: DC
Mailing zip: 20005-4906
General Phone: (202) 408-1484
General Fax: (202) 408-5950
Primary Website: www.shns.com
Personnel: Peter Copeland (Ed./Gen. Mgr.); David Johnson (Chief Tech. Officer/Webmaster); Lisa Klem Wilson (Sales & Mktg. Contact/Sr. Vice Pres. & Gen. Mgr., United Media); Bob Jones (Desk Ed.); John Lindsay (Sports Ed.)

SCRIPPS-MCCLATCHY WESTERN SERVICES

Street address 1: 1090 Vermont Ave NW
Street address 2: Ste 1000
Street address city: Washington
Street address state: D.C.
Zip/Postal code: 20005-4965
Country: USA
Mailing address: 1090 Vermont Ave NW Ste 1000
Mailing city: Washington
Mailing state: DC
Mailing zip: 20005-4965
General Phone: (202) 408-1484
General Fax: (202) 408-5950

SENIOR WIRE NEWS SERVICE

Street address 1: 2377 Elm St
Street address city: Denver
Street address state: CO
Zip/Postal code: 80207-3206
Country: USA
Mailing address: 2377 Elm St
Mailing city: Denver
Mailing state: CO
Mailing zip: 80207-3206
General Phone: (303) 355-3882
General/National Adv. E-mail: clearmountain@tde.com
Primary Website: www.seniorwire.net
Year Established: 1990
Note: Contact through website or email. Use submission or query and subject of article in subject line for editorial matter. Paste stories into email rather than as an attachment.
Personnel: Allison St. Claire (Pub./Ed.)

SERVICEQUALITY.US

Street address 1: 2401 Stanwell Dr.
Street address 2: Ste 340
Street address city: Concord
Street address state: CA
Zip/Postal code: 94520
Country: USA
Mailing address: 2401 Stanwell Dr., Ste 340
Mailing city: Concord
Mailing state: CA
Mailing zip: 94520
General Phone: (925) 798-0896
General Fax: (925) 215-2320
General/National Adv. E-mail: support@servicequality.us
Primary Website: www.service-quality.com
Year Established: 1990
Personnel: Dr. Jeffrey S. Kasper (Pres.)

SHARPNACK, JOE

Street address 1: PO Box 3325
Street address city: Iowa City
Street address state: IA
Zip/Postal code: 52244-3325
Country: USA
Mailing city: Iowa City
Mailing state: IA
Mailing zip: 52240-5755
General Phone: (319) 512 9705
General/National Adv. E-mail: sharptoons@yahoo.com
Primary Website: www.sharptoons.com
Personnel: Joe Sharpnack (Self-Syndicator)

SIPA NEWS SERVICE

Street address 1: 59 E 54th St
Street address city: New York
Street address state: NY
Zip/Postal code: 10022-4211
Country: USA
Mailing address: 59 E 54th St
Mailing city: New York
Mailing state: NY
Mailing zip: 10022-4211
General Phone: (212) 758-0740
General Fax: (212) 593-5194
General/National Adv. E-mail: info@leadersmag.com
Primary Website: www.leadersmag.com
Personnel: Henry O. Dormann (Chrmn./Ed. in Chief); Darrell Brown (Vice Pres./Exec. Ed.)

SLIGHTLY OFF!

Street address 1: 24730 Illini Dr
Street address city: Plainfield
Street address state: IL
Zip/Postal code: 60544-2435
Country: USA
Mailing address: 24730 Illini Dr
Mailing city: Plainfield

Mailing state: IL
Mailing zip: 60544-2435
General Phone: (815) 954-5817
General/National Adv. E-mail: deb@slightlyoff.com
Primary Website: www.slightlyoff.com
Year Established: 1990
Personnel: Deb DiSandro (Author/Owner)

SMARTYPANTS

Street address 1: 120 E Broadway
Street address city: Cushing
Street address state: OK
Zip/Postal code: 74023
County: Payne
Country: USA
Mailing address: P. O. Box 910
Mailing city: Cushing
Mailing state: OK
Mailing zip: 74023
General Phone: (918) 285-5555
General/National Adv. E-mail: support@smartypantsnews.com
Display Adv. E-mail: support@smartypantsnews.com
Classified Adv. e-mail: support@smartypantsnews.com
Editorial e-mail: support@smartypantsnews.com
Primary Website: www.smartypantsnews.com
Mthly Avg Views: 16000
Mthly Avg Unique Visitors: 1400
Year Established: 2020
Note: Smartypants is a beautifully-designed, weekly, kids activity page, emailed every Sunday for the upcoming week. It is available in 22" and 24" web widths in full page, half page or quarter page formats. Covering a different topic each week, Smartypants is targeted at 3rd - 6th grade students. It is a great way for community newspapers to engage this young audience and their parents. Written by a licensed educator with more than 25 years of classroom experience, Smartypants is utilized by teachers and homeschoolers as an alternative teaching tool. Teaching modules, activities and informative videos related to each week's topic are available on the smartypants website. Cost is $50 a month for a weekly upload.
Personnel: J. D. Meisner (Owner/designer/pants); Sapphire Smith (Bookkeeper)

SOVFOTO/EASTFOTO

Street address 1: 263 W 20th St
Street address 2: Apt 3
Street address city: New York
Street address state: NY
Zip/Postal code: 10011-3542
Country: USA
Mailing address: 263 W 20th St Apt 3
Mailing city: New York
Mailing state: NY
Mailing zip: 10011-3542
General Phone: (212) 727-8170
General Fax: (212) 727-8228
General/National Adv. E-mail: info@sovfoto.com
Primary Website: www.sovfoto.com
Year Established: 1932
Personnel: Vanya Edwards (President)

SPECTRUM FEATURES SYNDICATE

Street address 1: 2351 Wyda Way
Street address 2: Apt 1113
Street address city: Sacramento
Street address state: CA
Zip/Postal code: 95825-1609
Country: USA
Mailing address: 2460 2nd St
Mailing city: Bloomsburg
Mailing state: PA
Mailing zip: 17815-3113
General Phone: (916)417-1688
General/National Adv. E-mail: editor@greeleyandstone.com
Primary Website: www.greeleyandstone.com
Year Established: 1986
Personnel: Walter Brasch (Ed. in Chief); Rose Renn (Exec. Ed.); Matt Gerber (Assoc. Ed.); Mary Jayne Reibsome (Art/Prodn. Dir.); Diana Saavedra (Dir. of Mktg.)

SPRINGER FOREIGN NEWS SERVICE

Street address 1: 500 5th Ave
Street address 2: Ste 2800
Street address city: New York
Street address state: NY
Zip/Postal code: 10110-0002
Country: USA
Mailing address: 500 5th Ave Ste 2800
Mailing city: New York
Mailing state: NY
Mailing zip: 10110-0002
General Phone: (212) 983-1983

STADIUM CIRCLE FEATURES

Street address 1: 82 Nassau St
Street address 2: Ste 521
Street address city: New York
Street address state: NY
Zip/Postal code: 10038-3703
Country: USA
Mailing address: 82 Nassau St., Ste. 521
Mailing city: New York
Mailing state: NY
Mailing zip: 10038
General Phone: (917) 267-2493
General/National Adv. E-mail: info@paperpc.net
Primary Website: www.paperpc.com
Year Established: 1991
Note: Home of The Paper PC blog: www.paperpc.com Twitter: @newyorkbob Pinterest: Top 250 worldwide with 1.2 million followers: www.paperpcpicks.com
Personnel: Robert Anthony (Ed./Columnist)

STARCOTT MEDIA SERVICES, INC.

Street address 1: 6906 Royalgreen Dr
Street address city: Cincinnati
Street address state: OH
Zip/Postal code: 45244-4004
Country: USA
Mailing address: 6906 Royalgreen Dr
Mailing city: Cincinnati
Mailing state: OH
Mailing zip: 45244-4004
General Phone: (513) 231-6034
General/National Adv. E-mail: dulley@dulley.com; contact@dulley.com
Primary Website: www.dulley.com
Personnel: James T. Dulley (Pres.)

STATE NET

Street address 1: 2101 K St
Street address city: Sacramento
Street address state: CA
Zip/Postal code: 95816-4920
County: Sacramento
Country: USA
Mailing address: 2101 K St
Mailing city: Sacramento
Mailing state: CA
Mailing zip: 95816-4920
General Phone: (916) 444-0840
General Fax: (916) 446-5369
General/National Adv. E-mail: info@statenet.com
Primary Website: www.statenet.com
Personnel: Laurie Stinson (Pres.); Jud Clark (Pres.)

STRAIGHT DOPE - WRAPPORTS/ SUN-TIMES MEDIA, INC.

Street address 1: 350 N Orleans St
Street address city: Chicago
Street address state: IL
Zip/Postal code: 60654-1975
Country: USA
Mailing address: 350 N Orleans St
Mailing city: Chicago
Mailing state: IL
Mailing zip: 60654-1975
General/National Adv. E-mail: cecil@straightdope.com
Primary Website: www.straightdope.com
Note: Direct business inquiries to: webmaster@straightdope.com
Personnel: Cecil Adams (Creator/Writer); Ed Zotti (Editor/General Mgr)

SUN FEATURES

Street address 1: 1100 Garden View Rd
Street address 2: Apt 122
Street address city: Encinitas
Street address state: CA
Zip/Postal code: 92024-1360
Country: USA
Mailing address: above
Mailing city: Encinitas
Mailing state: CA
Mailing zip: 92024
General Phone: (760) 652-5302
General/National Adv. E-mail: jlk@sunfeatures.com
Primary Website: www.sunfeatures.com
Year Established: 1973
Personnel: Joyce Lain Kennedy (Pres.); Tim K. Horrell (Vice Pres.)

SYLVIA DI PIETRO

Street address 1: 55 W 14th St
Street address 2: Apt 4H
Street address city: New York
Street address state: NY
Zip/Postal code: 10011-7409
Country: USA
Mailing address: 55 W 14th St Apt 4H
Mailing city: New York
Mailing state: NY
Mailing zip: 10011-7409
General Phone: (212) 242-8800
General Fax: (212) 633-6298
General/National Adv. E-mail: info@sylviadipietro.com
Primary Website: www.sylviadipietro.com
Personnel: Sylvia Di Pietro (Self-Syndicator)

TAIPEI ECONOMIC & CULTURAL OFFICE, PRESS DIVISION - NEW YORK, NY

Street address 1: 1E E 42nd St
Street address 2: Fl 11
Street address city: New York
Street address state: NY
Zip/Postal code: 10017-6904
Country: USA
Mailing address: 1 E 42nd St Fl 11
Mailing city: New York
Mailing state: NY
Mailing zip: 10017-6904
General Phone: (212) 557-5122
General Fax: (212) 557-3043
General/National Adv. E-mail: roctaiwan@taipei.org
Primary Website: www.taiwanembassy.org
Personnel: Ching Yi Ting (Contact)

TAIPEI ECONOMIC & CULTURAL REPRESENTATIVE OFFICE, PRESS DIVISION - WASHINGTON, DC

Street address 1: 4201 Wisconsin Ave NW
Street address city: Washington
Street address state: D.C.
Zip/Postal code: 20016-2146
Country: USA
Mailing address: 4201 Wisconsin Ave. NW
Mailing state: DC
Mailing zip: 20016
General Phone: (202) 895-1800
General Fax: (202) 362-6144
General/National Adv. E-mail: tecroinfodc@tecro.us
Primary Website: http://www.roc-taiwan.org/US
Personnel: Frank Wang (Dir. Press)

TAIPEI ECONOMIC AND CULTURAL OFFICE IN CHICAGO

Street address 1: 55 W Wacker Dr
Street address 2: Ste 1200
Street address city: Chicago
Street address state: IL
Zip/Postal code: 60601-1797
Country: USA
Mailing address: 55 West Wacker Drive, Suite 1200
Mailing city: Chicago
Mailing state: IL
Mailing zip: 60601
General Phone: (312) 616-0100
General Fax: (312) 616-1486
General/National Adv. E-mail: teco@tecochicago.org
Primary Website: www.taiwanembassy.org
Personnel: Justin Lee (Deputy Director)

TELEGRAPH MEDIA GROUP

Street address 1: 111 Buckingham Palace Road
Street address city: London
Zip/Postal code: SW1W 0DT
Country: United Kingdom
Mailing address: 111 Buckingham Palace Rd.
Mailing city: London
Mailing zip: SW1W 0DT
General Phone: 020 7931 1010
General/National Adv. E-mail: syndication@telegraph.co.uk
Primary Website: www.telegraph.co.uk/syndication
Year Established: 1855
Note: Syndication manages all commercial licensing and content partnerships for all print publications and digital platforms for The Telegraph Media Group.
Personnel: Sophie Hanbury (Content Partnerships Director)

THE BOOKWORM SEZ, LLC

Street address 1: 18857 Icestorm Road
Street address city: Sparta
Street address state: WI
Zip/Postal code: 54656
County: Monroe
Country: USA
Mailing address: 18857 Icestorm Road
Mailing city: Sparta
Mailing state: WI
Mailing zip: 54656
General Phone: (608) 782-2665
General Fax: (608)-487-8398
General/National Adv. E-mail: bookwormsez@yahoo.com; bookwormsez@gmail.com
Primary Website: www.bookwormsez.com
Year Established: 2003
Note: Book reviewer; work with more than 140 publications in print and online. Also: writer of humor / fun fact columns. Ask for details.
Personnel: Terri Schlichenmeyer (Book Reviewer)

THE CHRISTIAN SCIENCE MONITOR NEWS SERVICE

Street address 1: 210 Massachusetts Ave
Street address city: Boston
Street address state: MA
Zip/Postal code: 02115-3012
Country: USA
Mailing address: 210 Massachusetts Ave
Mailing city: Boston
Mailing state: MA
Mailing zip: 02115-3195
General Phone: (617) 450-2123
General/National Adv. E-mail: syndication@csmonitor.com
Primary Website: www.csmonitor.com
Personnel: Andy Bickerton

THE CLASSIFIED GUYS

Street address 1: 12 Bates Pl
Street address city: Danbury
Street address state: CT
Zip/Postal code: 06810-6803
Country: USA
Mailing address: 12 Bates Pl
Mailing city: Danbury
Mailing state: CT
Mailing zip: 06810-6803
General Phone: (203) 798-0462
General/National Adv. E-mail: comments@classifiedguys.com
Primary Website: www.classifiedguys.com
Personnel: Duane Holze (Co-Pres.); Todd Holze (Co-Pres.)

THE FUNNY PAGES

Street address 1: 4185 Bonway Dr
Street address city: Pensacola
Street address state: FL
Zip/Postal code: 32504-7701
Country: USA
Mailing address: 4185 Bonway Dr
Mailing city: Pensacola
Mailing state: FL
Mailing zip: 32504-7701
General Phone: (850) 484-8622
General Fax: (850) 484-8622
General/National Adv. E-mail: thejoker@thefunnypages.com
Primary Website: www.thefunnypages.com
Year Established: 1997

Personnel: Phillip A. Ryder (Creator)

THE GELMAN FEATURE SYNDICATE

Street address 1: PO Box 399
Street address city: Roscoe
Street address state: NY
Zip/Postal code: 12776-0399
Country: USA
Mailing address: PO Box 399
Mailing city: Roscoe
Mailing state: NY
Mailing zip: 12776-0399
General Phone: (607) 498-4700
Personnel: Bernard Gelman (Owner/Ed.)

THE JERUSALEM POST FOREIGN SERVICE

Street address 1: The Jerusalem Post Bldg.
Street address city: Jerusalem
Zip/Postal code: 91000
Country: Israel
Mailing address: PO Box 81
Mailing city: Jerusalem
Mailing zip: 91000
General Phone: 5315666
General Fax: 5389527
General/National Adv. E-mail: ads@jpost.co.il
Primary Website: www.jpost.com
Personnel: Steve Linde (Editor in Chief); David Brinn (Managing Ed.)

THE NAME GAME INTERNATIONAL, INC.

Street address 1: 401 SW 54th Ave
Street address city: Plantation
Street address state: FL
Zip/Postal code: 33317-3628
Country: USA
Mailing address: 401 SW 54th Ave
Mailing city: Plantation
Mailing state: FL
Mailing zip: 33317-3628
General Phone: (954) 321-0032
General Fax: (954) 321-8617
General/National Adv. E-mail: namegameco@aol.com
Year Established: 1976
Personnel: Melodye Hecht Icart (Pres.); Mitchell J. Free (Vice Pres., Sales/Dev.)

THE NEW YORK TIMES NEWS SERVICE & SYNDICATE

Street address 1: 620 8th Ave
Street address city: New York
Street address state: NY
Zip/Postal code: 10018-1618
Country: USA
Mailing address: 620 8th Ave
Mailing city: New York
Mailing state: NY
Mailing zip: 10018
General Phone: 212-556-1927
General/National Adv. E-mail: nytsyn-sales@nytimes.com
Primary Website: www.nytsyn.com
Personnel: Andrea Mariano (Mkt Mgr.); Aidan McNulty (Regional Director, US & Canada); Christopher Lalime (Regional Director, Latin America, Mexico & the Caribbean); Patti Sonntag (Managing Editor, Syndicate); Whye-Ko Tan (Regional Director, Asia Pacific); Michael Greenspon (General Manager, News Services & Print Innovation); Nancy Lee (Vice President and Executive Editor, News Service & Syndicate); Alice Ting (Vice President, Licensing & Syndication); Cass Adamson (Regional Director, Europe, Middle East & Africa); Anita Patil (Editorial Director, News Service & Syndicate); Sergio Florez (Managing Editor, Images); Ray Krueger (Managing Editor, News Service)

THE NEWS ITEM

Street address 1: 707 N Rock St
Street address city: Shamokin
Street address state: PA
Zip/Postal code: 17872-4930
Country: USA
Mailing address: 707 N Rock St
Mailing city: Shamokin
Mailing state: PA
Mailing zip: 17872-4956
General Phone: (570) 644-6397
General Fax: (570) 648-7581
General/National Adv. E-mail: publisher@newsitem.com
Primary Website: www.newsitem.com
Year Established: 1987
Personnel: Andy Hentzelman (Ed.); Greg Zyla (Pub.)

THE NYT NEWS SERVICE/ SYNDICATE - PHOTOS & GRAPHICS

Street address 1: 620 8th Ave
Street address 2: Fl 9
Street address city: New York
Street address state: NY
Zip/Postal code: 10018-1618
Country: USA
Mailing address: 620 8th Ave
Mailing city: New York
Mailing state: NY
Mailing zip: 10018-1618
General Phone: (212) 556-4204
General Fax: (212) 556-3535
Primary Website: www.nytsyn.com
Personnel: Sergio Florez (Managing Editor/Images)

THE ROMANTIC SYNDICATED COLUMN

Street address 1: PO Box 1567
Street address city: Cary
Street address state: NC
Zip/Postal code: 27512-1567
Country: USA
Mailing address: PO Box 1567
Mailing city: Cary
Mailing state: NC
Mailing zip: 27512-1567
General Phone: (919) 701-9818
General/National Adv. E-mail: column@theromantic.com
Primary Website: www.theromantic.com
Personnel: Michael Webb (Writer)

THE SCIENCE ADVICE GODDESS-AMY ALKON

Street address 1: 171 Pier Ave
Street address 2: Ste 280
Street address city: Santa Monica
Street address state: CA
Zip/Postal code: 90405-5311
Country: USA
Mailing address: 171 Pier Ave Ste 280
Mailing city: Santa Monica
Mailing state: CA
Mailing zip: 90405-5311
General/National Adv. E-mail: adviceamy@aol.com
Primary Website: http://www.advicegoddess.com
Note: Award-winning science-based nationally-syndicated advice columnist. Author of science-based books including "Good Manners For Nice People Who Sometimes Say F*ck" (St. Martin's Press, 2014). Next book, "Unf*ckology," "science-help" on how to live with guts and confidence (Jan 2018). Weekly science podcast featuring the luminaries of behavioral science talking about their books. Speaking engagements through Macmillan.
Personnel: Amy Alkon (Syndicated science-based advice columnist on love, dating, sex, relationships. Science-based manners expert. Upcoming book, "Unf*ckology" - a "science-help" book on how to transform to live with guts and confidence. @amyalkon on Twitter.); Lucy Furry (Vice Pres., Syndication)

THE WALL STREET JOURNAL SUNDAY

Street address 1: 1211 Avenue of the Americas
Street address city: New York
Street address state: NY
Zip/Postal code: 10036-8701
Country: USA
Mailing address: 1211 Avenue of the Americas Lowr C3
Mailing city: New York
Mailing state: NY
Mailing zip: 10036-0003
General Phone: (212) 597-5733
General Fax: (212) 597-5633
General/National Adv. E-mail: wsj.ltrs@wsj.com
Primary Website: www.wsj.com
Personnel: Paul Bell (Vice Pres., Partner Businesses); Steven Townsley (Dir., Sales); David Crook (Ed.)

THE WASHINGTON POST NEWS SERIVICE & SYNDICATE

Street address 1: 1301 K St NW
Street address city: Washington
Street address state: DC
Zip/Postal code: 20071-0004
Country: USA
Mailing address: 1301 K Street, NW
Mailing city: Washington
Mailing state: DC
Mailing zip: 20071
General Phone: (202) 334-5375
General Fax: (202) 334-5669
General/National Adv. E-mail: syndication@washpost.com
Primary Website: https://syndication.washingtonpost.com/
Year Established: 1973
Personnel: Karen H. Greene (Ops. Mgr.); Maria Gatti (Dir., Sales & Mktg.); Amy Lago (Comics Ed.); Richard Aldacushion (CEO/General Manager); Rob Cleland (Sr. Systems Admin.); Sophie Yarborough (Mgr., Editorial Prod.); Gabriella Ferrufino (Marketing Rep.); Josh Alvarez (Manager/Editorial Production); Jim Toler (Marketing Rep.); Claudia Mendez (Customer Service Coordinator)

THE WEATHER UNDERGROUND, INC.

Street address 1: 185 Berry St
Street address 2: Ste 5501
Street address city: San Francisco
Street address state: CA
Zip/Postal code: 94107-1761
Country: USA
Mailing address: 185 Berry St Ste 5501
Mailing city: San Francisco
Mailing state: CA
Mailing zip: 94107-1761
General Phone: (415) 983-2602
General Fax: (415) 543-5044
General/National Adv. E-mail: chuck@wunderground.com
Primary Website: www.wunderground.com
Personnel: Alan Steremberg (Pres.); Brian Read (Office Mgr.); Andria Stark (Vice Pres. Sales/Mktg.)

THE WILD SIDE

Street address 1: 2222 Fish Ridge Rd
Street address city: Cameron
Street address state: WV
Zip/Postal code: 26033-1367
Country: USA
Mailing address: 2222 Fish Ridge Rd
Mailing city: Cameron
Mailing state: WV
Mailing zip: 26033-1367
General Phone: (304) 686-2630
General/National Adv. E-mail: sshalaway@aol.com
Primary Website: http://scottshalaway.googlepages.com/
Note: Provide a 700-word weekly column about nature, wild birds, and conservation to newspapers
Personnel: Scott Shalaway (Nature Writer, Wildlife Biologist)

THE WITZZLE CO.

Street address 1: PO Box 866933
Street address city: Plano
Street address state: TX
Zip/Postal code: 75086-6933
Country: USA
Mailing address: PO Box 866933
Mailing city: Plano
Mailing state: TX
Mailing zip: 75086-6933
General Phone: (972) 398-3897
General Fax: (972) 398-8154
General/National Adv. E-mail: care@kaidy.com
Primary Website: www.mathfun.com
Personnel: Louis Y. Sher (Owner/Pres.)

THINK GLINK INC.

Street address 1: 395 Dundee Road
Street address city: Glencoe
Street address state: IL
Zip/Postal code: 60022-1585
County: Cook
Country: USA
Mailing address: 395 Dundee Road
Mailing city: Glencoe
Mailing state: IL
Mailing zip: 60022
General Phone: 847-242-0550
General/National Adv. E-mail: ilyce@ThinkGlink.com
Primary Website: www.thinkglink.com; www.lawproblems.com; www.expertrealestatetips.net
Mthly Avg Views: 30000
Mthly Avg Unique Visitors: 25000
Year Established: 1988
Note: We offer a twice weekly written column, called "Real Estate Matters." There is a monthly newsletter called "Love, Money, and Real Estate." We also are launching a podcast in 2023. Samples are available. See ThinkGlink.com. If you are looking to design a deep, content-rich online real estate section, we can help with that, too. Contact Ilyce Glink (ilyce@thinkglink.com) for details. In addition, we write a weekly newsletter about employee financial wellness, providing insights and looking at new research. If you have a news section on business news or for employers, this would be perfect.
Personnel: Ilyce R. Glink (Publisher); Samuel J. Tamkin (Ed.)

THIS MODERN WORLD

Street address 1: PO Box 150673
Street address city: Brooklyn
Street address state: NY
Zip/Postal code: 11215-0673
Country: USA
Mailing address: PO Box 150673
Mailing city: Brooklyn
Mailing state: NY
Mailing zip: 11215-0673
General Phone: (718) 768-2522
General/National Adv. E-mail: tom.tomorrow@gmail.com
Primary Website: www.thismodernworld.com
Note: Please do not send submissions for syndication.
Personnel: Dan Perkins (Creator)

THIS SIDE OF 60

Street address 1: PO Box 332
Street address city: North Newton
Street address state: KS
Zip/Postal code: 67117-0332
Country: USA
Mailing address: PO Box 332
Mailing city: North Newton
Mailing state: KS
Mailing zip: 67117-0332
General Phone: (316) 283-5231
General/National Adv. E-mail: vsnider@southwind.net
Primary Website: www.thisside60.com
Note: Motivational column about empowerment in mature years
Personnel: Snider Vada

TMS SPECIALTY PRODUCTS

Street address 1: 435 N Michigan Ave
Street address 2: Ste 1400
Street address city: Chicago
Street address state: IL
Zip/Postal code: 60611-7551
County: Cook
Country: USA
Mailing address: 435 N Michigan Ave Ste 1400
Mailing city: Chicago
Mailing state: IL
Mailing zip: 60611-7551
General Phone: (800) 637-4082
General Fax: (312) 527-8256
General/National Adv. E-mail: ctrammell@tribune.com
Primary Website: www.tmsspecialtyproducts.com
Note: TMS Specialty Products provides articles and images suitable for use in advertorial sections, niche publications and other targeted media, as well as custom ordered content, including local and paginated products.

Personnel: Marco Buscaglia (Gen. Mgr.); Curtis Trammell (Sales manager); Mary Elson (Mng. Ed.); Todd Rector (Art Dir.)

TORSTAR SYNDICATION SERVICES

Street address 1: One Yonge St.
Street address city: Toronto
Street address state: ON
Zip/Postal code: M5E 1E6
Country: Canada
Mailing address: One Yonge St.
Mailing city: Toronto
Mailing state: ON
Mailing zip: M5E 1E6
General Phone: (416) 869-4994 (Sales)
General Fax: (416) 869-4587
General/National Adv. E-mail: syndicate@torstar.com
Primary Website: www.torstarsyndicate.com; www.tsscontent.ca;www.getstock.com
Personnel: Robin Graham (Managing Director); Ted Cowan (Sales Representative Torstar Syndication Services GetStock.com); Evi Docherty (Account Information); Joanne MacDonald (Sales Asst.); Julie Murtha (Associate Director, Business Development)

TRADE NEWS SERVICE (FATS AND OILS)

Street address 1: 3701 State Route 21
Street address city: Canandaigua
Street address state: NY
Zip/Postal code: 14424-9020
Country: USA
Mailing address: 3701 State Route 21
Mailing city: Canandaigua
Mailing state: NY
Mailing zip: 14424-9020
General Phone: (585) 396-0027
General/National Adv. E-mail: tns@rochester.rr.com
Primary Website: www.fats-and-oils.com
Year Established: 1914
Note: Serving the fats and oils industry exclusively, since 1914.
Personnel: Dennis C Maxfield (Sr. Ed.)

TRAVELIN' LIGHT

Street address 1: 4001 W Kings Row St
Street address city: Muncie
Street address state: ID
Zip/Postal code: 47304-2431
Country: USA
Mailing address: 4001 W Kings Row St
Mailing city: Muncie
Mailing state: IN
Mailing zip: 47304-2431
General Phone: (937) 423-3517
General/National Adv. E-mail: kelsey@travelin-light.com
Primary Website: www.travelin-light.com
Personnel: Kelsey Timmerman (Writer/Photographer); Geoff Hassing (Cartoonist)

TRIBUNE CONTENT AGENCY

Street address 1: 560 West Grand Avenue
Street address city: Chicgao
Street address state: IL
Zip/Postal code: 60654
Country: United States of America
Note: https://tribunecontentagency.com
Newspapers (for newspaper groups): 1918

TRIBUNE MEDIA SERVICES ENTERTAINMENT PRODUCTS

Street address 1: 40 Media Dr
Street address city: Queensbury
Street address state: NY
Zip/Postal code: 12804-4086
Country: USA
Mailing address: 40 Media Dr
Mailing city: Queensbury
Mailing state: NY
Mailing zip: 12804-4086
General Phone: (800) 833-9581
General Fax: (518) 792-4414
General/National Adv. E-mail: cyung@tribune.com
Primary Website: www.tribunemediaentertainment.com
Personnel: Cameron Yung (Exec. Dir., Newspapers); Kathleen Tolstrup (Gen. Mgr., Sales/Mktg.); Ken Hyatt (Account Executive)

TRIBUNE NEWS SERVICE

Street address 1: 560 West Grand Avenue
Street address city: Chicago
Street address state: IL
Zip/Postal code: 60654
Country: USA
Mailing state: IL
General Phone: 800-346-8798
General/National Adv. E-mail: tcasales@tribpub.com
Primary Website: tribunecontentagency.com
Year Established: 1973
Personnel: Rick DeChantal (Sales Dir.); Wayne Lown (Gen. Mgr.); Zach Finken (Assoc. Ed.)

TV TIMES/NEW ENGLAND MOTORSPORTS SYNDICATION

Street address 1: 1324 Belmont St
Street address 2: Ste 102
Street address city: Brockton
Street address state: MA
Zip/Postal code: 02301-4435
Country: USA
Mailing address: 1324 Belmont St Unit 2
Mailing city: Brockton
Mailing state: MA
Mailing zip: 02301-4435
General Phone: (781) 784-7857
General Fax: (781) 784-7857
General/National Adv. E-mail: lmodestino@hotmail.com
Primary Website: www.enterprisenews.com/tracktalk
Year Established: 1988
Note: My webpage changed for 2012 and beyond
Personnel: Lou Modestino (Author)

U-BILD NEWSPAPER FEATURES

Street address 1: 821 S Tremont St
Street address 2: Ste B
Street address city: Oceanside
Street address state: CA
Zip/Postal code: 92054-4158
Country: USA
Mailing address: 821 S Tremont St Ste B
Mailing city: Oceanside
Mailing state: CA
Mailing zip: 92054-4158
General Phone: (800) 828-2453
General Fax: (760) 754-2356
General/National Adv. E-mail: ktaylor@u-bild.com
Primary Website: www.u-bild.com
Year Established: 1948
Personnel: Kevin Taylor (Pres.); Jeffrey Reeves (Features Ed.)

UNITED FEATURE SYNDICATE (DIV. OF UNITED MEDIA)

Street address 1: 200 Madison Ave
Street address city: New York
Street address state: NY
Zip/Postal code: 10016-3903
Country: USA
Mailing address: 200 Madison Ave Fl 4
Mailing city: New York
Mailing state: NY
Mailing zip: 10016-3905
General Phone: (800) 221-4816
General Fax: (212) 293-8600
Primary Website: www.unitedfeatures.com; www.comics.com
Year Established: 1902
Personnel: Douglas R. Stern (Pres./CEO); Lisa Klem Wilson (Sr. Vice Pres./Gen. Mgr.); Mary Anne Grimes (Exec. Dir., Pub. Rel.); Suma CM (Exec. Ed.); Carmen Puello (Sales/Admin. Mgr.); Colette Cogley (Regl. Sales Mgr.); Ron O'Neal (Regl. Sales Mgr.); Jim Toler (Regl. Sales Mgr.); Dawn Gregory (Customer Serv. Rep); Emily Stephens (Sales Mgr., Int'l/E-rights); Reprint Rights Coord. (Reprint Rights Sales); Vincent Marciano

UNITED MEDIA/EW SCRIPPS

Street address 1: 312 Walnut St
Street address 2: Ste 2800
Street address city: Cincinnati
Street address state: OH
Zip/Postal code: 45202-4019
Country: USA
Mailing address: 312 Walnut St
Mailing city: Cincinnati
Mailing state: OH
Mailing zip: 45202-4024
General Phone: (513) 977-3000
General Fax: (513) 977-3024
Primary Website: www.scripps.com
Year Established: 1902
Note: United Media's operations were outsourced to Universal Uclick in Kansas City, Mo., June 1, 2011. Please direct all inquiries to Universal Uclick.
Personnel: Vincent Marciano (General Manager, United Media); Donald Murray (Senior Analyst/ Systems Engineer)

UNITED PRESS INTERNATIONAL

Street address 1: 1200 N Federal Hwy
Street address 2: Ste 200
Street address city: Boca Raton
Street address state: FL
Zip/Postal code: 33432-2813
Country: USA
Mailing address: 1200 N. Federal Hwy., Suite 200
Mailing city: Boca Raton
Mailing state: FL
Mailing zip: 33432
General Phone: 202-898-8000
General/National Adv. E-mail: media@upi.com
Primary Website: www.upi.com
Year Established: 1907
Note: United Press International is a leading provider of news, photos and information to millions of readers around the globe via UPI.com and its licensing services. With a history of reliable reporting dating back to 1907, today's UPI is a credible source for the most important stories of the day, continually updated - a one-stop site for U.S. and world news, as well as entertainment, trends, science, health and stunning photography. UPI also provides insightful reports on key topics of geopolitical importance, including energy and security. UPI is based in Washington, D.C., and Boca Raton, Fla.
Personnel: Nicholas Chiaia (President); Charlene Pacenti (Chief Content Officer); Franco Fernandez (Business Manager)

UNIVERSAL UCLICK INTERNATIONAL DIVISON

Street address 1: 1130 Walnut St
Street address city: Kansas City
Street address state: MO
Zip/Postal code: 64106-2109
Country: USA
Mailing address: 1130 Walnut St
Mailing city: Kansas City
Mailing state: MO
Mailing zip: 64106-2109
General Phone: (816) 581-7500
General/National Adv. E-mail: sales@amuniversal.com
Primary Website: www.amuniversal.com
Personnel: Kerry Slagle (Pres.); Milka Pratt (Mng. Dir., Latin America)

VOTERAMA IN CONGRESS - THOMAS VOTING REPORTS

Street address 1: PO Box 363
Street address city: Washington
Street address state: D.C.
Zip/Postal code: 22747-0363
Country: USA
Mailing address: PO Box 363
Mailing city: Washington
Mailing state: VA
Mailing zip: 22747-0363
General Phone: (202) 332-0857
General/National Adv. E-mail: info@voterama.info
Primary Website: www.voterama.info
Note: Covers House and Senate legislative actions and members' voting records and campaign-finance data for U.S. news media -- a finished editorial product transmitted daily and weekly in text, graphic and online formats.
Personnel: Mr. Richard G. Thomas (Pub./Ed.)

W.D. FARMER RESIDENCE DESIGNER, INC.

Street address 1: 5238 Rocky Hill Dr SW
Street address city: Lilburn
Street address state: GA
Zip/Postal code: 30047-6631
Country: USA
Mailing address: PO Box 450025
Mailing city: Atlanta
Mailing state: GA
Mailing zip: 31145-0025
General Phone: (770) 934-7380
General Fax: (770) 934-1700
General/National Adv. E-mail: wdfarmer@wdfarmerplans.com; vstarkey@wdfarmerplans.com
Primary Website: www.wdfarmer.com; www.wdfarmerplans.com/featurehomes; www.wdfplans.com
Year Established: 1961
Personnel: W.D. Farmer (Designer); Vickie Starkey (Pres.)

WAGNER INTERNATIONAL PHOTOS, INC.

Street address 1: 62 W 45th St
Street address 2: Fl 6
Street address city: New York
Street address state: NY
Zip/Postal code: 10036-4208
Country: USA
Mailing address: 62 W 45th St Fl 6
Mailing city: New York
Mailing state: NY
Mailing zip: 10036-4208
General Phone: (212) 827-0500
General Fax: (212) 944-9536
General/National Adv. E-mail: larry@nycphoto.com; info@nycphoto.com
Primary Website: www.nycphoto.com
Personnel: Larry Lettera (Adv. Mgr.); Jeff Connell (Chief Photographer)

WARWICK VALLEY DISPATCH

Street address 1: 2 Oakland Ave
Street address city: Warwick
Street address state: NY
Zip/Postal code: 10990-1530
County: Orange
Country: USA
Mailing address: PO BOX 594
Mailing city: WARWICK
Mailing state: NY
Mailing zip: 10990-0594
General Phone: (845) 986-2216
General Fax: (845) 987-1180
General/National Adv. E-mail: ads@wvdispatch.com
Display Adv. E-mail: ads@wvdispatch.com
Classified Adv. e-mail: ads@wvdispatch.com
Editorial e-mail: editor@wvdispatch.com
Primary Website: wvdispatch.com
Year Established: 1885
Personnel: F. Eugene Wright (Publisher/Owner); Lon Tytell (Adv. Mgr.); Marion Maroski (Mng. Ed.); David DeWitt (Prodn. Mgr.); Eleanor Horoshun; Evelyn Card; Eric Meyer; Margaret Bezares; Myrek Zastavnyi; Mary Klym; Sue Mykytsei; Jennifer O'Connor (Ed.)

WASHINGTON MONTHLY

Street address 1: 1200 18th St NW
Street address 2: Ste 330
Street address city: Washington
Street address state: DC
Zip/Postal code: 20036-2556
Country: USA
Mailing address: 1200 18th St NW Ste 330
Mailing city: Washington
Mailing state: DC
Mailing zip: 20036-2556
General Phone: (202) 955-9010
General/National Adv. E-mail: business@WashingtonMonthly.com
Editorial e-mail: editors@washingtonmonthly.com
Primary Website: www.washingtonmonthly.com
Year Established: 1969

Personnel: Claire Iseli (VP Cir.); Paul Glastris (Ed. in Chief); Alice Gallin-Dwyer (Deputy Director); Diane Straus Tucker (Publisher); Carl Iseli (VP, Operations & Marketing); Charles Peters (Founding Ed.); Ambi Ambachew (Adv. Mgr.)

WASHINGTON POST NEWS SERVICE WITH BLOOMBERG NEWS

Street address 1: 1301 K St NW
Street address city: Washington
Street address state: D.C.
Zip/Postal code: 20071-0004
Country: USA
Mailing address: 1301 K Street NW
Mailing city: Washington
Mailing state: DC
Mailing zip: 20071-0002
General Phone: (800) 879-9794 ext. 1
General/National Adv. E-mail: syndication@washpost.com
Primary Website: syndication.washingtonpost.com
Personnel: Brian Patten (Sales Mgr./North America); Maria Gatti (Dir., Int. Sales & Marketing); Jim Toler (Marketing Representative/Northeast & South); Robert Cleland (Senior Systems Administrator); Gabriella Ferrufino (Marketing Representative/Midwest & West); Richard Aldacushion (General Manager/Editorial Director); Sally Ragsdale (Marketing Representative/Midwest)

WATAUGA CONSULTING, INC.

Street address 1: 192 Abbey Rd
Street address city: Boone
Street address state: NC
Zip/Postal code: 28607-8606
Country: USA
Mailing address: 192 Abbey Rd
Mailing city: Boone
Mailing state: NC
Mailing zip: 28607-8606
General Phone: (828) 773-3481
General/National Adv. E-mail: info@supin.com
Primary Website: www.supin.com
Year Established: 1994
Note: Helping you make changes that matter.
Personnel: Jeanne Supin

WAUBAY CLIPPER

Street address 1: 122 N Main St
Street address city: Waubay
Street address state: SD
Zip/Postal code: 57273
County: Day
Country: USA
Mailing address: PO BOX 47
Mailing city: WAUBAY
Mailing state: SD
Mailing zip: 57273-0047
General Phone: (605) 947-4501
General Fax: (605) 947-4501
General/National Adv. E-mail: linda@waubayclipper.com
Display Adv. E-mail: linda@waubayclipper.com
Editorial e-mail: linda@waubayclipper.com
Primary Website: waubayclipper.blogspot.com
Year Established: 1890
Personnel: Linda M. Walters (Pub./Ed./Adv. Dir.)

WEATHER UNDERGROUND, INC., THE

Street address 1: 185 Berry St
Street address 2: Ste 5501
Street address city: San Francisco
Street address state: CA
Zip/Postal code: 94107-1761
Country: USA
Mailing address: 550 Kearny St Ste 600
Mailing city: San Francisco
Mailing state: CA
Mailing zip: 94108-2599
General Phone: (415) 983-2602
General Fax: (415) 543-5044
General/National Adv. E-mail: press@wunderground.com
Display Adv. E-mail: chuck@wunderground.com
Primary Website: www.wunderground.com
Personnel: Andria Stark (Press & Media)

WERNER RENBERG

Street address 1: PO Box 496
Street address city: Chappaqua
Street address state: NY
Zip/Postal code: 10514-0496
Country: USA
Mailing address: PO Box 496
Mailing city: Chappaqua
Mailing state: NY
Mailing zip: 10514-0496
General Phone: (914) 241-2038
General Fax: (914) 242-0470
General/National Adv. E-mail: werren@att.net
Year Established: 1991
Personnel: Werner Renberg (Self-Syndicator)

WHITEGATE FEATURES SYNDICATE

Street address 1: 71 Faunce Dr
Street address 2: Ste 1
Street address city: Providence
Street address state: RI
Zip/Postal code: 02906-4805
Country: USA
Mailing address: 71 Faunce Dr Ste 1
Mailing city: Providence
Mailing state: RI
Mailing zip: 02906-4805
General Phone: (401) 274-2149
General/National Adv. E-mail: webmaster@whitegatefeatures.com; staff@whitegatefeatures.com
Primary Website: www.whitegatefeatures.com
Year Established: 1985
Personnel: Ed Isaac (Pres./CEO); Steve Corey (Vice Pres./Gen. Mgr.); Mari Howard (Office Mgr.); Eve Green (Talent Dir./Special Projects Mgr.)

WIECK

Street address 1: 1651 N Collins Blvd
Street address 2: Ste 100
Street address city: Richardson
Street address state: TX
Zip/Postal code: 75080-3604
Country: USA
Mailing address: 1651 N. Collins Blvd., Suite 100
Mailing city: Richardson
Mailing state: TX
Mailing zip: 75080
General Phone: (972) 392-0888
General Fax: (972) 934-8848
General/National Adv. E-mail: info@wieck.com
Primary Website: www.wieck.com
Year Established: 1991
Personnel: James Wieck (Chrmn.); Tim Roberts (Pres.); Marc Newman (Sr. VP)

WINGO, LLC

Street address 1: 12161 Ken Adams Way
Street address 2: Ste 110J
Street address city: Wellington
Street address state: FL
Zip/Postal code: 33414-3194
County: Palm Beach
Country: USA
Mailing address: 12161 Ken Adams Way Suite 110J
Mailing city: Wellngton
Mailing state: FL
Mailing zip: 33414
General Phone: (561) 379-2635
General/National Adv. E-mail: sat@amerimarketing.com
Display Adv. E-mail: info@amerimarketing.com
Primary Website: www.wingopromo.com; www.amerimarketing.com
Year Established: 1980
Personnel: Scott Thompson (Pres.)

WIRELESS FLASH NEWS, INC.

Street address 1: PO Box 633030
Street address city: San Diego
Street address state: CA
Zip/Postal code: 92163-3030
Country: USA
Mailing address: PO Box 633030
Mailing city: San Diego
Mailing state: CA
Mailing zip: 92163-3030
General Phone: (619) 220-7191
General Fax: (619) 220-8590
General/National Adv. E-mail: newsdesk2@flashnews.com
Primary Website: www.flashnews.com
Year Established: 1980
Personnel: Patrick Glynn (Mng. Ed.); Monica Garske (Sr. Ed.); David Louie (Sales/Mktg. Mgr.)

WOMBANIA

Street address 1: 249 Kensington Ave. N.
Street address city: Hamilton
Street address state: ON
Zip/Postal code: L8L 7N8
Country: Canada
Mailing address: 249 Kensington Ave. N.
Mailing city: Hamilton
Mailing state: ON
Mailing zip: L8L 7N8
General Phone: (905) 544-6174
General/National Adv. E-mail: wombania@wombania.com
Editorial e-mail: pdm@wombania.com
Primary Website: www.wombania.com; www.comics.wombania.com
Year Established: 1999
Note: Color and B&W weekly comic strip since 2003
Personnel: Peter Marinacci (Owner/Cartoonist); R.L.B. Hartmann (Ed.)

WORLD FEATURES SYNDICATE

Street address 1: 5842 Sagebrush Rd
Street address city: La Jolla
Street address state: CA
Zip/Postal code: 92037-7037
Country: USA
Mailing address: 5842 Sagebrush Rd
Mailing city: La Jolla
Mailing state: CA
Mailing zip: 92037-7037
General Phone: (858) 456-6215
General/National Adv. E-mail: info@worldfeaturessyndicate.com
Primary Website: www.worldfeaturessyndicate.com
Year Established: 1981
Personnel: Tom Robbins (Sales Dir.); Ronald A. Sataloff (Ed.); Karl A. Van Asselt (Sr. Assoc. Ed./Columnist); Ernie A. Gomez (Assoc. Ed.)

WORLD IMAGES NEWS SERVICE

Street address 1: 14745 Green Park Way
Street address city: Centreville
Street address state: VA
Zip/Postal code: 20120-3126
Country: USA
Mailing address: 14745 Green Park Way
Mailing city: Centreville
Mailing state: VA
Mailing zip: 20120
General Phone: (703) 380-2808
General/National Adv. E-mail: jack@winsphoto.com
Editorial e-mail: newseditor@winsphoto.com
Primary Website: http://www.winsphoto.com
Year Established: 1989
Note: International photo agency
Personnel: Jack Sykes (CEO/Chief Photographer)

WORLDWATCH/FOREIGN AFFAIRS SYNDICATE

Street address 1: 14421 Charter Rd
Street address 2: Apt 5C
Street address city: Jamaica
Street address state: NY
Zip/Postal code: 11435-1292
Country: USA
Mailing address: 14421 Charter Rd Apt 5C
Mailing city: Jamaica
Mailing state: NY
Mailing zip: 11435-1292
General Phone: (718) 591-7246
General/National Adv. E-mail: jjmcolumn@earthlink.net
Personnel: John J. Metzler (Editor)

YELLOWBRIX

Street address 1: 200 North Glebe Road, Ste. 1025
Street address 2: Ste 1025
Street address city: Arlington
Street address state: VA
Zip/Postal code: 22203
Country: USA
Mailing address: PO Box 1509
Mailing city: Centreville
Mailing state: VA
Mailing zip: 20122-8509
General Phone: (703) 548-3300
General Fax: (703) 548-9151
General/National Adv. E-mail: info@yellowbrix.com
Primary Website: www.yellowbrix.com
Personnel: Jeffrey P. Massa (Founder/Pres./CEO); Tom Hargis (Adv. Mgr.)

ZUMA PRESS, INC.

Street address 1: 408 N El Camino Real
Street address city: San Clemente
Street address state: CA
Zip/Postal code: 92672-4717
Country: USA
Mailing address: 408 N El Camino Real
Mailing city: San Clemente
Mailing state: CA
Mailing zip: 92672
General/National Adv. E-mail: zinfo@zumapress.com
Primary Website: 408 N El Camino Real
Personnel: Scott McKiernan (CEO/Founder); Ruaridh Stewart (News Dir./Picture Desk Mgr.); Patrick Johnson (CTO); Julie Mason (CFO)

NEWSPAPER COMICS SECTION GROUPS AND NETWORKS

GOCOMICS

Street address 1: 1130 Walnut St.
Street address city: Kansas City
Street address state: MO
Postal code: 64109-2109
Country: USA
Mailing address 1: 1130 Walnut St.
Mailing city: Kansas City
Mailing state: MO
Mailing zip: 64106-2109
Office phone: 844-426-1256
General e-mail: ComicArtPrints@AMUniversal.com
Web address: GoComics.com
Affiliated Newspapers:
Employee Associations: Go Comics; Go Comics Art
Main (survey) contact: Go Comics
Newspaper Comics Section Groups and Networks

KING FEATURES SYNDCATE

Street address 1: 300 West 57th Street
Street address city: New York
Street address state: NY
Postal code: 10019-5238
Country: USA
Mailing address 1: 300 West 57th Street
Mailing city: New York
Mailing state: NY
Mailing zip: 10019-5238
Office phone: 212-969-7550
Office fax: 646-280-1550
Web address: kingfeatures.com
Affiliated Newspapers:
Employee Associations: CJ Kettler; Keith McCloat (VP, GM)
Main (survey) contact: Keith McCloat
Newspaper Comics Section Groups and Networks

SMARTYPANTS

Street address 1: 120 E Broadway
Street address city: Cushing
Street address state: OK
Postal code: 74023
County: Payne
Country: USA
Mailing address 1: P. O. Box 910
Mailing city: Cushing
Mailing state: OK
Mailing zip: 74023
Office phone: (918) 285-5555
General e-mail: support@smartypantsnews.com
Web address: www.smartypantsnews.com
Year established: 2020
Affiliated Newspapers:
Weekly Paper Frequency: Sun
Note: Smartypants is a beautifully-designed, weekly, kids activity page, emailed every Sunday for the upcoming week. It is available in 22" and 24" web widths in full page, half page or quarter page formats. Covering a different topic each week, Smartypants is targeted at 3rd - 6th grade students. It is a great way for community newspapers to engage this young audience and their parents. Written by a licensed educator with more than 25 years of classroom experience, Smartypants is utilized by teachers and homeschoolers as an alternative teaching tool. Teaching modules, activities and informative videos related to each week's topic are available on the smartypants website. Cost is $50 a month for a weekly upload.
Employee Associations: J. D. Meisner (Owner/designer/pants); Sapphire Smith (Bookkeeper)
Main (survey) contact: James Meisner
Newspaper Comics Section Groups and Networks

THE DAILY CARTOONIST

Web address: dailycartoonist.com
Affiliated Newspapers:
Employee Associations: D.D. Degg (Ed.); John Glynn (Ed.)
Parent company: Andrews McMeel Universal
Main (survey) contact: D.D. Degg; John Glynn

NEWSPAPER DISTRIBUTED MAGAZINE AND TMC PUBLICATION

AMERICAN PROFILE - CHICAGO, IL

Street address 1: 500 N Michigan Ave
Street address 2: Ste 910
Street address city: Chicago
Street address state: IL
Zip/Postal code: 60611-3741
County: Cook
Country: USA
Mailing address: 500 N Michigan Ave Ste 910
Mailing city: Chicago
Mailing state: IL
Mailing zip: 60611-3741
General Phone: (312) 948-0333
General Fax: (312) 948-0555
Primary Website: www.americanprofile.com
Personnel: Nanci Davidson (Executive Director, Integrated Media)

AMERICAN PROFILE - FRANKLIN, TN

Street address 1: 341 Cool Springs Blvd
Street address 2: Ste 400
Street address city: Franklin
Street address state: TN
Zip/Postal code: 37067-7224
County: Williamson
Country: USA
Mailing address: 131 3rd Ave N Ste 200
Mailing city: Franklin
Mailing state: TN
Mailing zip: 37064-2510
General Phone: (615) 468-6021
Primary Website: www.americanpub.com
Personnel: Frank Zier (Nashville/West Coast Assoc. Pub.)

AMERICAN PROFILE - LOS ANGELES, CA

Street address 1: 6255 W Sunset Blvd
Street address 2: Ste 705
Street address city: Los Angeles
Street address state: CA
Zip/Postal code: 90028-7408
County: Los Angeles
Country: USA
Mailing address: 6255 W Sunset Blvd Ste 705
Mailing city: Los Angeles
Mailing state: CA
Mailing zip: 90028-7408
General Phone: (323) 467-5906
General Fax: (323) 467-7180
Primary Website: www.americanprofile.com
Personnel: Debbie Siegel (Adv Sales Rep.)

AMERICAN PROFILE - NEW YORK, NY

Street address 1: 60 E 42nd St
Street address 2: Ste 1111
Street address city: New York
Street address state: NY
Zip/Postal code: 10165-1111
County: New York
Country: USA
Mailing address: 60 E 42nd St Ste 1111
Mailing city: New York
Mailing state: NY
Mailing zip: 10165-1111
General Phone: (212) 478-1900
General Fax: (646) 865-1921
Primary Website: www.americanprofile.com
Personnel: Amy Chernoff (Sr. Vice Pres./Grp. Pub.); Shannon Hay (Adv. Dir.); Linda Rich (Assoc. Ed., Direct Response)

AMERICAN PROFILE - NORTHVILLE, MI

Street address 1: 22185 Heatheridge Ln
Street address city: Northville
Street address state: MI
Zip/Postal code: 48167-9300
County: Oakland
Country: USA
Mailing address: 22185 Heatheridge Ln
Mailing city: Northville
Mailing state: MI
Mailing zip: 48167-9300
General Phone: (248) 991-1810
Primary Website: www.americanprofile.com
Personnel: Jim Main (Auto Adv. Mgr.)

ASSOCIATION OF ALTERNATIVE NEWSMEDIA

Street address 1: 1156 15th St NW
Street address 2: Ste 1005
Street address city: Washington
Street address state: DC
Zip/Postal code: 20005-1722
County: District Of Columbia
Country: USA
Mailing address: 1156 15th St NW Ste 1005
Mailing city: Washington
Mailing state: DC
Mailing zip: 20005-1722
General Phone: 289-8484
General Fax: (202) 289-2004
General/National Adv. E-mail: web@aan.org
Display Adv. E-mail: jason@aan.org
Primary Website: www.altweeklies.com
Year Established: 1978
Note: Annual convention held in summer.
Personnel: Debra Silvestrin (Dir. of Meetings); Jason Zaragoza (Int. Exec. Dir.)

GAUGER MEDIA SERVICE, INC.

Street address 1: 1034 Bradford Street
Street address 2: P.O. Box 627
Street address city: Raymond
Street address state: WA
Zip/Postal code: 98577
County: Pacific
Country: USA
Mailing city: Raymond
Mailing state: WA
Mailing zip: 98577
General Phone: (360) 942-2661
General/National Adv. E-mail: dave@gaugermedia.com
Personnel: Dave Gauger (Now Retired)

LETTERS FROM NORTH AMERICA

Street address 1: 2002 N Greens Blvd
Street address city: Richmond
Street address state: TX
Zip/Postal code: 77406-6673
County: FORT BEND
Country: USA
Mailing address: 2002 N. Greens Blvd
Mailing city: Richmond
Mailing state: TX
Mailing zip: 77406
General Phone: (512) 653-8545
General Fax: 832-201-9818
General/National Adv. E-mail: pperry@pearyperry.com
Primary Website: www.pearyperry.com
Year Established: 1993
Note: Political column- 'A Nation of Fools' General commentary on life (satire) - 'Letters From North America' Trivia column- 'Ponder Points'
Personnel: Peary Perry (Self-Synd/Columnist)

MALVERN DAILY TMC

Street address 1: 219 Locust St
Street address city: Malvern
Street address state: AR
Zip/Postal code: 72104-3721
County: Hot Spring
Country: USA
Mailing address: PO Box 70
Mailing city: Malvern
Mailing state: AR
Mailing zip: 72104-0070
General Phone: (501) 337-7523
General Fax: (501) 337-1226
General/National Adv. E-mail: mdrecord@sbcglobal.net
Display Adv. E-mail: mdradvertising@ sbcglobal.met
Editorial e-mail: mdrecord@sbcglobal.net
Primary Website: www.malvern-online.com
Year Established: 1914
Personnel: Kim Taber (Bus. Mgr.); Richard Folds (Adv. Dir.); Kathi Ledbetter (Circ. Mgr.); Mark Bivens (News Ed.); James Liegh (Online Ed.); LaJuan Monney (Sports Ed.); Jessica Mathis (Composing Mgr.)

MARTINEZ NEWS-GAZETTE

Street address 1: 802 Alhambra Ave
Street address city: Martinez
Street address state: CA
Zip/Postal code: 94553-1604
County: Contra Costa
Country: USA
Mailing state: CA
Mailing zip: 94513
General Phone: (408) 603-5640
General Fax: (925) 228-1536
General/National Adv. E-mail: rickj64@gmail.com
Editorial e-mail: editor@martinezgazette.com
Year Established: 1858

MOLINE/ROCK ISLAND/QUAD CITY METRO UNIT

Street address 1: 1720 5th Ave
Street address city: Moline
Street address state: IL
Zip/Postal code: 61265-7907
County: Rock Island
Country: USA
General Phone: (309) 764-4344

General/National Adv. E-mail: advertising@qconline.com
Primary Website: www.qconline.com
Personnel: Val Yazbec (CRO); Jerry Taylor (Ed.); Kelly Johannes (Adv. Dir.)

NEW HAMPSHIRE UNION LEADER

Street address 1: 100 William Loeb Drive
Street address city: Manchester
Street address state: NH
Zip/Postal code: 03109
Country: USA
Note: 36859

PARADE

Street address 1: 60 E 42nd St
Street address 2: Ste 820
Street address city: New York
Street address state: NY
Zip/Postal code: 10165-0820
County: New York
Country: USA
Mailing address: 60 East 42nd Street, suite 820
Mailing city: New York
Mailing state: NY
Mailing zip: 10165
General Phone: (212) 478-1910
General/National Adv. E-mail: sales@amgparade.com
Primary Website: www.parade.com
Year Established: 1941
Personnel: David Barber (Sr. Vice Pres., Newspaper Rel.)

PARADE PUBLICATIONS, INC. - BLOOMFIELD HILLS, MI

Street address 1: 100 W Long Lake Rd
Street address city: Bloomfield Hills
Street address state: MI
Zip/Postal code: 48304-2773
County: Oakland
Country: USA
Mailing address: 22824 Canterbury St
Mailing city: Saint Clair Shores
Mailing state: MI
Mailing zip: 48080-1920
General Phone: (248) 540-9820
General Fax: (248) 540-9891
General/National Adv. E-mail: det_sales@parade.com
Primary Website: www.parade.com
Personnel: Mike DeBartolo (Vice Pres., Adv.)

PARADE PUBLICATIONS, INC. - CHICAGO, IL

Street address 1: 500 N Michigan Ave
Street address 2: Ste 910
Street address city: Chicago
Street address state: IL
Zip/Postal code: 60611-3741
County: Cook
Country: USA
Mailing address: 401 N Michigan Ave Ste 2900
Mailing city: Chicago
Mailing state: IL
Mailing zip: 60611-5517
General Phone: (312) 661-1620
General Fax: (312) 661-0776
General/National Adv. E-mail: chi_sales@parade.com
Primary Website: www.parade.com
Personnel: Eric Karaffa (Vice Pres./Mid-Western Mgr.)

PARADE PUBLICATIONS, INC. - LOS ANGELES, CA

Street address 1: 6300 Wilshire Blvd
Street address city: Los Angeles
Street address state: CA
Zip/Postal code: 90048-5204
County: Los Angeles
Country: USA
Mailing address: 6300 Wilshire Blvd Fl 10
Mailing city: Los Angeles
Mailing state: CA
Mailing zip: 90048-5204
General Phone: (323) 965-3649
General Fax: (323) 965-4971
Primary Website: www.parade.com
Personnel: Greg Hancock (Acct. Dir.)

PARADE PUBLICATIONS, INC. - SAN FRANCISCO, CA

Street address 1: 50 Francisco St
Street address 2: Ste 400
Street address city: San Francisco
Street address state: CA
Zip/Postal code: 94133-2114
County: San Francisco
Country: USA
Mailing address: 50 Francisco St Ste 400
Mailing city: San Francisco
Mailing state: CA
Mailing zip: 94133-2114
General Phone: (415) 955-8222
General Fax: (415) 397-0562
General/National Adv. E-mail: sf_sales@parade.com
Primary Website: www.parade.com
Personnel: Bill Murray (Adv. Contact)

RELISH - CHICAGO, IL

Street address 1: 500 N Michigan Ave
Street address 2: Ste 910
Street address city: Chicago
Street address state: IL
Zip/Postal code: 60611-3741
County: Cook
Country: USA
Mailing address: 500 N Michigan Ave Ste 910
Mailing city: Chicago
Mailing state: IL
Mailing zip: 60611-3741
General Phone: (312) 948-0333
General Fax: (312) 948-0555
Primary Website: www.pubgroup.com
Personnel: Andrea Blank (Adv. Coord.)

RELISH - FRANKLIN, TN

Street address 1: 341 Cool Springs Blvd
Street address 2: Ste 400
Street address city: Franklin
Street address state: TN
Zip/Postal code: 37067-7224
County: Williamson
Country: USA
Mailing address: 131 3rd Ave N Ste 200
Mailing city: Franklin
Mailing state: TN
Mailing zip: 37064-2510
General Phone: (615) 468-6000
General Fax: (615) 468-6100
Primary Website: www.pubgroup.com
Personnel: Frank Zier (Nashville/West Coast Assoc. Pub.)

RELISH - LOS ANGELES, CA

Street address 1: 300 Corporate Pointe
Street address 2: Ste 340
Street address city: Culver City
Street address state: CA
Zip/Postal code: 90230-8713
County: Los Angeles
Country: USA
Mailing address: 300 Corporate Pointe Ste 340
Mailing city: Culver City
Mailing state: CA
Mailing zip: 90230-7614
General Phone: (310) 216-7270
General Fax: (310) 216-7212
Primary Website: www.relishmag.com
Personnel: Jamie Relis (Acct. Mgr.)

RELISH - NEW YORK, NY

Street address 1: 60 E 42nd St
Street address 2: Ste 1115
Street address city: New York
Street address state: NY
Zip/Postal code: 10165-1115
County: New York
Country: USA
Mailing address: 60 E 42nd St Ste 1115
Mailing city: New York
Mailing state: NY
Mailing zip: 10165-1115
General Phone: (212) 478-1900
General Fax: (646) 865-1921
Primary Website: www.relishmag.com
Personnel: Amy Chernoff (Sr. Vice Pres./Grp. Pub.); Shannon Hay (Adv. Dir.); Linda Rich (Assoc. Ed., Direct Response)

SPOTLIGHT

Street address 1: 250 Yonge St
Street address city: Winston Salem
Street address state: NC
Zip/Postal code: 27101
County: Forsyth
Country: USA
Mailing address: PO Box 3159
Mailing city: Winston Salem
Mailing state: NC
Mailing zip: 27102-3159
General Phone: (800) 457-1156
General Fax: (336) 727-7461
Primary Website: www.starwatch.com
Personnel: Alan Cronk (Bus. Mgr.); Jody Stephenson Sarver (Sales Agent)

STAR WATCH

Street address 1: 418 N Marshall St
Street address city: Winston Salem
Street address state: NC
Zip/Postal code: 27101-2815
County: Forsyth
Country: USA
Mailing address: PO Box 3159
Mailing city: Winston Salem
Mailing state: NC
Mailing zip: 27102-3159
General Phone: (336) 727-7406
General Fax: (800) 430-0532
Primary Website: www.starwatch.com
Personnel: Jody Stephenson Sarver (Sales Agent); Alan Cronk (Exec. Ed.)

THE SALINE COURIER

Street address 1: 321 N Market St
Street address city: Benton
Street address state: AR
Zip/Postal code: 72015-3734
County: Saline
Country: USA
Mailing address: PO Box 207
Mailing city: Benton
Mailing state: AR
Mailing zip: 72018-0207
General Phone: (501) 315-8228
General Fax: (501) 315-1230
General/National Adv. E-mail: news@bentoncourier.com
Display Adv. E-mail: sales@bentoncourier.com
Editorial e-mail: news@bentoncourier.com; subscription@bentoncourier.com
Primary Website: www.bentoncourier.com
Year Established: 1876
Personnel: Terri Leifeste (Vice President/Group Publisher Santa Maria California News Media, Inc.); Rhonda Overbey (Regional Publisher and Advertising Director); Vicki Dorsch (Bus. Mgr.); Sarah Perry (Editor); Lynda Hollenback (Assoc. Ed.); Patricia Stuckey (Prodn. Mgr.); David Wills (Addvertising Director); Megan Reynolds (Editor)

TMS SPECIALTY PRODUCTS

Street address 1: 435 N Michigan Ave
Street address 2: Ste 1400
Street address city: Chicago
Street address state: IL
Zip/Postal code: 60611-7551
County: Cook
Country: USA
Mailing address: 435 N Michigan Ave Ste 1400
Mailing city: Chicago
Mailing state: IL
Mailing zip: 60611-7551
General Phone: (800) 637-4082
General Fax: (312) 527-8256
General/National Adv. E-mail: ctrammell@tribune.com
Primary Website: www.tmsspecialtyproducts.com
Note: TMS Specialty Products provides articles and images suitable for use in advertorial sections, niche publications and other targeted media, as well as custom ordered content, including local and paginated products.
Personnel: Marco Buscaglia (Gen. Mgr.); Curtis Trammell (Sales manager); Mary Elson (Mng. Ed.); Todd Rector (Art Dir.)

TRIBUNE MEDIA SERVICES TV LOG - CHICAGO, IL

Street address 1: 435 N Michigan Ave
Street address 2: Ste 1300
Street address city: Chicago
Street address state: IL
Zip/Postal code: 60611-4037
County: Cook
Country: USA
Mailing address: 435 N Michigan Ave Ste 1300
Mailing city: Chicago
Mailing state: IL
Mailing zip: 60611-4037
General Phone: (312) 222-3394
Primary Website: www.tribunemediaservices.com
Personnel: David D.

TRIBUNE MEDIA SERVICES TV LOG - LOS ANGELES, CA

Street address 1: 5800 W Sunset Blvd
Street address city: Los Angeles
Street address state: CA
Zip/Postal code: 90028-6607
County: Los Angeles
Country: USA
Mailing address: 5800 W Sunset Blvd
Mailing city: Los Angeles
Mailing state: CA
Mailing zip: 90028-6607
General Phone: (310) 581-5011
General Fax: (310) 581-8025
Primary Website: www.tribunemediaservices.com

TRIBUNE MEDIA SERVICES TV LOG - QUEENSBURY, NY

Street address 1: 40 Media Dr
Street address city: Queensbury
Street address state: NY
Zip/Postal code: 12804-4086
County: Warren
Country: USA
Mailing address: 40 Media Dr
Mailing city: Queensbury
Mailing state: NY
Mailing zip: 12804-4086
General Phone: (518) 792-9914
General Fax: (212) 210-2863
Primary Website: www.tribunemediaservices.com

TVTIMES

Street address 1: 250 Yonge St.
Street address city: Toronto
Street address state: ON
Zip/Postal code: M5B 2L7
County: York
Country: Canada
Mailing address: 250 Yonge St.
Mailing city: Toronto
Mailing state: ON
Mailing zip: M5B 2L7
General Phone: (416) 593-6556
General Fax: (416) 593-7329
General/National Adv. E-mail: tvtimes3@canwest.com
Primary Website: www.canwest.com
Personnel: Quin Millar (Dir., Newspaper Sales)

VERMONT NEWS AND MEDIA

Street address 1: 70 Landmark Hill drive
Street address city: Brattleboro
Street address state: VT
Zip/Postal code: 05301
County: Windham
Mailing state: MA
General Phone: 802-254-2311
General/National Adv. E-mail: publisher@reformer.com
Year Established: 2020

NEWSPAPER TRADE UNION

DISTRICT OF COLUMBIA

COMMUNICATIONS WORKERS OF AMERICA

Street address 1: 501 3rd St NW
Street address 3: Washington
Street address state: DC
Zip/Postal code: 20001-2760
County: District Of Columbia
Country: USA
Mailing address: 501 3rd St NW
Mailing city: Washington
Mailing state: DC
Mailing zip: 20001-2760
General Phone: (202) 434-1100
General Fax: (202) 434-1279
Primary Website: www.cwa-union.org
Personnel: Larry Cohen (Pres.); Jeffrey Rechenbach (Sec./Treasure)

GRAPHIC COMMUNICATIONS INTERNATIONAL

Street address 1: 1900 L St NW
Street address 3: Washington
Street address state: DC
Zip/Postal code: 20036-5002
County: District Of Columbia
Country: USA
Mailing address: 1900 L St NW Fl 8
Mailing city: Washington
Mailing state: DC
Mailing zip: 20036-5007
General Phone: (202) 721-0537
General Fax: (202) 721-0641
General/National Adv. E-mail: webmessenger@gciu.org
Primary Website: gtedeschi@gciu.org
Personnel: George Tedeschi (Pres.); Robert Lacey (Vice Pres.); Richard Whitworth (Executive Assistant to the President)

INTERNATIONAL UNION OF OPERATING ENGINEERS

Street address 1: 1125 17th St NW
Street address 3: Washington
Street address state: DC
Zip/Postal code: 20036-4709
County: District Of Columbia
Country: USA
Mailing address: 1125 17th St NW
Mailing city: Washington
Mailing state: DC
Mailing zip: 20036-4709
General Phone: (202) 429-9100
General Fax: (202) 778-2688
Primary Website: www.iuoe.org
Personnel: Vincent J. Giblin (Gen. Pres.); Christopher Hanley (Gen. Sec./Treasurer)

SERVICE EMPLOYEES INTERNATIONAL UNION, CLC

Street address 1: 1800 Massachusetts Ave NW
Street address 3: Washington
Street address state: DC
Zip/Postal code: 20036-1806
County: District Of Columbia
Country: USA
Mailing address: 1800 Massachusetts Ave NW
Mailing city: Washington
Mailing state: DC
Mailing zip: 20036-1806
General Phone: (202) 730-7000
General Fax: (202) 429-5660
Primary Website: www.seiu.org
Personnel: Andrew L. Stern (Int'l Pres.); Anna Burger (Sec./Treasurer); Mary Kay Henry (Int'l Exec. Vice Pres.); Gerald Hudson (Int'l Vice Pres.); Eliseo Medina (Int'l Exec. Vice Pres.); Tom Woodruff (Int'l Exec. Vice Pres.)

THE LABORERS' INTERNATIONAL UNION OF NORTH AMERICA

Street address 1: 905 16th St NW
Street address 3: Washington
Street address state: DC
Zip/Postal code: 20006-1703
County: District Of Columbia
Country: USA
Mailing address: 905 16th St NW
Mailing city: Washington
Mailing state: DC
Mailing zip: 20006-1703
General Phone: (202) 737-8320
General Fax: (202) 737-2754
General/National Adv. E-mail: communications@liuna.org
Primary Website: www.liuna.org
Year Established: 1903
Personnel: Greg Davis (Director)

THE NEWSGUILD-CWA

Street address 1: 501 3rd St NW
Street address 2: Fl 6
Street address 3: Washington
Street address state: DC
Zip/Postal code: 20001-2797
County: District Of Columbia
Country: USA
Mailing address: 501 3rd St NW, Fl 6
Mailing city: Washington
Mailing state: DC
Mailing zip: 20001-2797
General Phone: (202) 434-7177
General Fax: (202) 434-1472
General/National Adv. E-mail: guild@cwa-union.org
Primary Website: www.newsguild.org
Year Established: 1933
Personnel: Bernard Lunzer (President); Martha Waggoner (International Chairperson); Marian Needham (Exec. VP)

NEWSPAPERS REPRESENTATIVE - FOREIGN

CALIFORNIA

ADMAX INTERNATIONAL MEDIA

Street address 1: 7326 McLaren Ave
Street address 3: West Hills
Street address state: CA
Zip/Postal code: 91307-2123
County: Los Angeles
Country: USA
Mailing address: 7326 McLaren Ave
Mailing city: West Hills
Mailing state: CA
Mailing zip: 91307-2123
General Phone: (818) 715-9931
General Fax: (253) 648-4574
General/National Adv. E-mail: admax@sbcglobal.net
Primary Website: www.admaxinternational.com
Year Established: 1992
Personnel: Maria de los Angeles (Pres.); Edward G. Wilson (Pres.); Maria Teresa Perez (Media Dir.); Brad Brigg (Acct. Exec.); Simon English (Acct. Exec.); Larry Redd (Acct. Exec.); Julio Vender (Acct. Exec.)

CONNECTICUT

LEE & STEEL LLC

Street address 1: 25 Burroughs Rd
Street address 3: Easton
Street address state: CT
Zip/Postal code: 06612-1409
County: Fairfield
Country: USA
Mailing address: PO Box 2007
Mailing city: Darien
Mailing state: CT
Mailing zip: 06820-0007
General Phone: (203) 445-8900
General Fax: (203) 445-1885
General/National Adv. E-mail: michael.lee@leeandsteel.com
Year Established: 1991
Personnel: Michael Lee (CEO)

SOUTHPORT

ADMARKET INTERNATIONAL (DIV. OF MARCOM INTERNATIONAL, INC.)

Street address 1: 105 Woodrow Ave
Street address 3: Southport
Street address state: CT
Zip/Postal code: 06890-1121
County: Fairfield
Country: USA
Mailing address: 105 Woodrow Ave
Mailing city: Southport
Mailing state: CT
Mailing zip: 06890-1121
General Phone: (203) 319-1000
General Fax: (203) 319-1004
Year Established: 1986
Note: AdMarket International plans and places advertising in 15,000 media newspapers in over 200 countries worldwide
Personnel: Nabil E. Fares (Pres./CEO); Kristina Kalman (Acct. Exec.)
Newspaper (for newspapers group): CHINA DAILY, Kaohsiung; EL FINANCIERO, Toluca, Mexico; KOREA ECONOMIC DAILY, Seoul; KOREA HERALD, Seoul; OBSERVER, Manila; STAR, Athens, Central Greece; EL MERCURIO, Manta, Manabi; TIMES OF INDIA, Hong Kong; Korea Times, Los Angeles; GAZETA MERCANTIL, Sao Paulo; HURRIYET

FLORIDA

CHARNEY/PALACIOS & CO.

Street address 1: 5201 Blue Lagoon Dr
Street address 2: Ste 200
Street address 3: Miami
Street address state: FL
Zip/Postal code: 33126-2065
County: Miami-Dade
Country: USA
Mailing address: 5201 Blue Lagoon Dr Ste 200
Mailing city: Miami
Mailing state: FL
Mailing zip: 33126-2065
General Phone: (786) 388-6340
General Fax: (786) 388-9113
General/National Adv. E-mail: miami@publicitas.com
Primary Website: www.publicitas.com
Note: Charney/Palacios is a subsidiary of Publicitas
Personnel: Grace Palacios (CEO); Maria Jose Torres (Sales Mktg. Mgr.)
Newspaper (for newspapers group): EL DIARIO, Maturin, Monagas; EL DIARIO DE HOY, San Salvador; El Nacional, Dolores, Provincia de Buenos Aires; La Prensa, Lima; GUARDIAN, Karachi; The San Juan Star (OOB), San Juan; LA ESTRELLA DE PANAMA, Panama City; LE MATIN, Port-Au-Prince; Nuevo Dia, Apatzingan, Michoacan; PRENSA LIBRE, Tepic, Nayarit; EXPRESS, Tepic, Nayarit; NOVEDADES DE YUCATAN, Merida, Yucatan

MULTIMEDIA, INC.

Street address 1: 7061 Grand National Dr
Street address 2: Ste 127
Street address 3: Orlando
Street address state: FL
Zip/Postal code: 32819-8992
County: Orange
Country: USA
Mailing address: 7061 Grand National Dr Ste 127
Mailing city: Orlando
Mailing state: FL
Mailing zip: 32819-8992
General Phone: (407) 903-5000
General Fax: (407) 363-9809
General/National Adv. E-mail: info@multimediausa.com
Primary Website: www.multimediausa.com
Personnel: Fernando Mariano (Pres.)
Newspaper (for newspapers group): EXTRA, Guayaquil, Guayas; O Globo, Rio De Janeiro

NORTH CAROLINA

FAYETTEVILLE

ADVANTAGE NEWSPAPER CONSULTANTS

Street address 1: 2850 Village Dr
Street address 2: Ste 102
Street address 3: Fayetteville
Street address state: NC
Zip/Postal code: 28304-3864
County: Cumberland
Country: USA
Mailing address: 2850 Village Dr
Mailing city: Fayetteville
Mailing state: NC
Mailing zip: 28304
General Phone: (910) 323-0349
General Fax: (910) 323-9280
General/National Adv. E-mail: info@newspaperconsultants.com
Primary Website: newspaperconsultants.com
Year Established: 1996
Published: Other
Audit By: Sworn/Estimate/Non-Audited
Audit Date: 43744
Note: Advantage Newspaper Consultants (ANC) is recognized as the leader in TV Magazine advertising sales in the United States. ANC works with both independent publishers and major newspaper chains to increase their core product ad revenue using innovative campaigns and creative, seasoned sales professionals that produce quantifiable results. Our sales managerâ€™s work with newspaper management to set goals and create an incentive plan which accelerates a TV Magazine sales campaign targeted towards finding key hidden revenue in their market in two weeks or less. Using the same proven formula of enthusiastic joint sales calls and dedicated management support that has lead to thousands of successful TV magazine sales campaigns, ANC also offers a cross-platform advertising sales program - Total Market Reach (TMR) - which includes print, mobile and digital ad combo sales.
Personnel: Timothy O. Dellinger (President); Susan M. Jolley (General Mgr.); Marie Smith (Exec. Dir. of Sales)

NEW YORK

DICOMM MEDIA

Street address 1: 350 5th Ave
Street address 2: Fl 59
Street address 3: New York
Street address state: NY
Zip/Postal code: 10118-5999
County: New York
Country: USA
Mailing address: 350 Fifth Ave. 59th Floor
Mailing city: New York
Mailing state: NY
Mailing zip: 10118
General Phone: (646) 536-7206
General Fax: (973) 335-1038
General/National Adv. E-mail: info@dicommintl.com
Primary Website: www.dicommintl.com
Year Established: 1995
Note: A unique media sales firm which represents numerous different Canadian media companies and publishers. We also work with many clients on assisting with their planning and buying efforts in Canada across all media types including print, digital/mobile, broadcast, radio, out of home and any other medium available.
Personnel: Thibaud Wallaert (Gen. Mgr.)

DOW JONES INTERNATIONAL MARKETING SERVICES

Street address 1: 1211 Avenue of the Americas
Street address 3: New York
Street address state: NY
Zip/Postal code: 10036
County: New York
Country: USA
Mailing address: 1211 Avenue of the Americas
Mailing city: New York
Mailing state: NY
Mailing zip: 10036
General Phone: (800) 369-0166
General/National Adv. E-mail: service@dowjones.com
Primary Website: www.dowjones.com
Year Established: 1882
Personnel: William Lewis (CEO); Almar Latour (Pub, Exec. V. P.); Christina Tassell (CFO); Matthew Murray (Editor in Chief)
Newspaper (for newspapers group): STRAITS TIMES, Singapore

MARSTON WEBB INTERNATIONAL

Street address 1: 60 Madison Ave
Street address 2: Ste 1212
Street address 3: New York
Street address state: NY
Zip/Postal code: 10010-1636
County: New York
Country: USA
Mailing address: 270 Madison Ave Rm 1203
Mailing city: New York
Mailing state: NY
Mailing zip: 10016-0601
General Phone: (212) 684-6601
General Fax: (212) 725-4709
General/National Adv. E-mail: marwebint@cs.com
Primary Website: www.marstonwebb.com
Year Established: 1981
Note: MWI also represents South African and Middle Eastern papers
Personnel: Victor Webb (Pres.); Madlene Olson (Vice Pres.)
Newspaper (for newspapers group): YOMIURI SHIMBUN, Hong Kong

OKLAHOMA

LAWTON

LAWTON MEDIA INC.

Street address 1: 102 SW 3rd St
Street address 3: Lawton
Street address state: OK
Zip/Postal code: 73501-4031
County: Comanche
Country: USA
Mailing address: P.O. Box 2069
Mailing city: Lawton
Mailing state: OK
Mailing zip: 73502
General Phone: (580) 353-0620
General Fax: (580) 585-5140
General/National Adv. E-mail: srobertson@swoknews.com
Primary Website: www.swoknews.com
Year Established: 1901
Personnel: David Hale (Pres.)

ONTARIO

MEMBER SERVICES COORDINATOR

Street address 1: 37 Front St E
Street address 2: Suite 200
Street address 3: Toronto
Street address state: ON
Zip/Postal code: M5E 1B3
County: York
Country: Canada
Mailing address: 37 Front Street E
Mailing city: Toronto
Mailing state: ON
Mailing zip: M5E 1B3
General Phone: (416) 923-7724
General/National Adv. E-mail: adreach@ocna.org
Primary Website: www.adreach.ca
Personnel: Kelly Gorven (Member Services Coordinator); Caroline Medwell (Executive Director)
Parent company (for newspapers): Ontario Community Newspapers Association

NEWBASE

Street address 1: 468 Queen Str. E
Street address 2: Suite 500
Street address 3: Toronto
Street address state: ON
Zip/Postal code: M5A 1T7
Country: USA
Mailing address: 468 Queen Str. E, Suite 500
Mailing city: Toronto
Mailing state: ON
Mailing zip: M5A 1T7
General Phone: (416) 363 1388
General Fax: (416) 363 2889
Primary Website: www.thenewbase.com
Personnel: Lesley Conway (Pres.); Doug St. John (Digital Director)

NEWSPAPERS REPRESENTATIVE - NATIONAL

ARIZONA

RUXTON GROUP/VMG ADVERTISING

Street address 1: 1201 E Jefferson St
Street address 3: Phoenix
Street address state: AZ
Zip/Postal code: 85034-2300
County: Maricopa
Country: USA
Mailing address: 1201 E. Jefferson Street
Mailing city: Phoenix
Mailing state: AZ
Mailing zip: 85034
General Phone: 1800-278-9866
General Fax: 602.238-4805
General/National Adv. E-mail: ads@voicemediagroup.com
Primary Website: www.vmgadvertising.com
Year Established: 1983
Personnel: Joe Larkin (SVP Sale & Operations); Susan Belair (SVP Sales); Veronica Villela (Business Manager)
Parent company (for newspapers): Voice Media Group

CALIFORNIA

LATINO 247 MEDIA GROUP

Street address 1: 3445 Catalina Dr
Street address 3: Carlsbad
Street address state: CA
Zip/Postal code: 92010-2856
County: San Diego
Country: USA
Mailing address: 3445 Catalina Dr.
Mailing city: Carlsbad
Mailing state: CA
Mailing zip: 92010-2856
General Phone: (760) 579-1696
General Fax: (760) 434-7476
General/National Adv. E-mail: kirk@whisler.com
Primary Website: www.latinos247.com
Year Established: 1996
Personnel: Kirk Whisler (Pres.); Ana Pati±o (General Manager); Ericka Benitez (Accounting Manager)

CALIFORNIA NEWSPAPER SERVICE BUREAU (CNSB)

Street address 1: 915 E 1st St
Street address 3: Los Angeles
Street address state: CA
Zip/Postal code: 90012-4050
County: Los Angeles
Country: USA
Mailing address: 915 E 1st St
Mailing city: Los Angeles
Mailing state: CA
Mailing zip: 90012-4000
General Phone: (213) 229-5500
General Fax: (213) 229-5481
General/National Adv. E-mail: bulksales@dailyjournal.com
Primary Website: www.legaladstore.com
Year Established: 1888
Note: The Daily Journal Corporation is a publisher of legal and business publications, including the Los Angeles and San Francisco Daily Journals, distributed in major California cities. Additionally, its in-house clearinghouse service provides ad placement services to government agencies, attorney's and other advertisers for legally mandated and outreach advertising including class action notices in any daily, community and/or ethnic publication and/or websites.
Personnel: Noemi Mendoza (Bulk Sale of Business Assets)

TRIBUNE MEDIA NETWORK

Street address 1: 202 W 1st St
Street address 3: Los Angeles
Street address state: CA
Zip/Postal code: 90012-4299
County: Los Angeles
Country: USA
Mailing address: 202 W 1st St
Mailing city: Los Angeles
Mailing state: CA
Mailing zip: 90012-4299
General Phone: (213) 237-2135
General Fax: (213) 237-2007
Personnel: Peter Liguori (Pres./CEO); Richard Jones (Dir., Western Reg.)

MOTIVATE, INC.

Street address 1: 4141 Jutland Dr Ste 300
Street address 2: Suite 300
Street address 3: San Diego
Street address state: CA
Zip/Postal code: 92117-3658
County: San Diego
Country: USA
Mailing address: 4141 Jutland Dr
Mailing city: San Diego
Mailing state: CA
Mailing zip: 92117
General Phone: (866) 664-4432
General/National Adv. E-mail: marcia@MotivateROI.com

Primary Website: www.motivateROI.com
Year Established: 1977
Note: Motivate, Inc. represents the following target markets: Multicultural (Hispanic, African American, Asian); Youth, LGBTQ, Senior, Military.
Personnel: Marcia A. Hansen (Prtnr.); Trevor Hansen (CEO)

TRIBUNE MEDIA NETWORK

Street address 1: 100 Bush St
Street address 2: Ste 925
Street address 3: San Francisco
Street address state: CA
Zip/Postal code: 94104-3920
County: San Francisco
Country: USA
Mailing address: 100 Bush St Ste 925
Mailing city: San Francisco
Mailing state: CA
Mailing zip: 94104-3920
General Phone: (415) 693-5600
General Fax: (415) 391-4992
Primary Website: www.tribunemediagroup.com
Personnel: Neal Zimmerman (Mgr.)

COLORADO

VOICE MEDIA GROUP

Street address 1: 969 N Broadway
Street address 3: Denver
Street address state: CO
Zip/Postal code: 80203-2705
County: Denver
Country: USA
Mailing address: 969 Broadway
Mailing city: Denver
Mailing state: CO
Mailing zip: 80203-2705
General Phone: (602) 271-0040
General/National Adv. E-mail: joe.larkin@voicemediagroup.com
Primary Website: www.voicemediagroup.com
Note: Newspaper represents for 50 alternative newsweeklies
Personnel: Joe Larkin (Sr. Vice Pres. Sales); Susan Belair (Vice Pres., Sales)
Newspaper (for newspapers group): Dallas Observer, Dallas; Denver Westword, Denver

FLORIDA

INTERSECT MEDIA SOLUTIONS

Street address 1: 1025 Greenwood Blvd.
Street address 2: Suite 191
Street address 3: Lake Mary
Street address state: FL
Zip/Postal code: 32746-5410
County: Seminole
Country: USA
Mailing address: 1025 Greenwood Blvd., Suite 191
Mailing city: Lake Mary
Mailing state: FL
Mailing zip: 32746-5410
General Phone: (866) 404-5913
General/National Adv. E-mail: info@mediagenius.com
Primary Website: www.intersectmediasolutions.com
Year Established: 1959
Personnel: Dean Ridings (Pres./CEO); Mark Burger (VP, Finance & CFO); Carolyn Nolte (VP, Strategy); Jessica Pitts (VP, Operations)
Parent company (for newspapers): Florida Press Association

TOWMAR REPRESENTACIONES S.A.

Street address 1: Presa Endho # 11
Street address 2: Col. Irrigacion, M.H.
Street address 3: Mexico City
Street address state: FL
Zip/Postal code: 11500
County: Distrito Federal
Country: Mexico
Mailing address: Presa Endho # 11
Mailing city: Mexico City
Mailing zip: 11500
General Phone: (55) 5395-5888
General Fax: (55) 5395-4985
General/National Adv. E-mail: INFO@towmar.net
Primary Website: www.towmar.net
Year Established: 1967
Note: New address
Personnel: Juan Martinez Dugay (Pres.); Juan Martinez Dugay (Pres.); Cesar Quijas (VP, Sales)

GEORGIA

SHELBY PUBLISHING CO. INC.

Street address 1: 517 Green St NW
Street address 3: Gainesville
Street address state: GA
Zip/Postal code: 30501-3313
County: Hall
Country: USA
General Phone: (770) 534-8380
General Fax: (678) 343-2197
Primary Website: www.theshelbyreport.com
Year Established: 1967
Personnel: Geoffrey Welch (VP/Sales Mgr. Midwest); C. Ronald Johnston

ILLINOIS

CENTRO INC.

Street address 1: 11 E Madison St
Street address 2: 6th Fl.
Street address 3: Chicago
Street address state: IL
Zip/Postal code: 60602-4574
County: Cook
Country: USA
Mailing address: 11 E. Madison St.
Mailing city: Chicago
Mailing state: IL
Mailing zip: 60602
General Phone: (312) 423-1565
General/National Adv. E-mail: socialmedia@centro.net
Primary Website: www.centro.net
Year Established: 2001
Personnel: Katie Risch (EVP, Customer Experience); John Hyland (VP, Pub. Solutions)

MCNAUGHTON NEWSPAPERS

Street address 1: 424 E State Pkwy
Street address 2: Ste 228
Street address 3: Schaumburg
Street address state: IL
Zip/Postal code: 60173-6406
County: Cook
Country: USA
Mailing address: 424 E State Pkwy Ste 228
Mailing city: Schaumburg
Mailing state: IL
Mailing zip: 60173-6408
General Phone: (847) 490-6000
General Fax: (847) 843-9058
General/National Adv. E-mail: rickb@usspi.com
Primary Website: www.usspi.com
Note: Designs cost effective print and digital solutions for national/regional/local advertisers.
Personnel: Rick Baranski (Vice President Media Relations); Philip Miller (CEO); Barbara Ancona (Vice President Sales); Michelle Hammons (Executive Vice President)
Newspaper (for newspapers group): Benicia Herald, Benicia; Cherokee Tribune, Canton; Monitor, Fraser; The Journal Register, Palmer; Castroville News Bulletin, Castroville; The Noblesville Ledger, Fishers; Tonawanda News (OOB), North Tonawanda; The Edmond Sun, Edmond; Valley News Dispatch, Tarentum; Manassas Journal Messenger (OOB), Manassas; The Davis Enterprise, DAVIS; Rushville Republican, Rushville; DAILY NEWS, Saint Croix; La Opinion, Ica

MASSACHUSETTS

AD REPS

Street address 1: 51 Church St
Street address 3: Boston
Street address state: MA
Zip/Postal code: 02116-5417
County: Suffolk
Country: USA
Mailing address: 51 Church St
Mailing city: Boston
Mailing state: MA
Mailing zip: 02116-5417
General Phone: (617) 542-6913
General Fax: (617) 542-7227
General/National Adv. E-mail: adreps1@yahoo.com
Personnel: Steve Ganak (Pres.)

MARYLAND

ADVERTISING MEDIA PLUS, INC.

Street address 1: 5397 Twin Knolls Rd
Street address 2: Ste 17
Street address 3: Columbia
Street address state: MD
Zip/Postal code: 21045-3256
County: Howard
Country: USA
Mailing address: PO Box 1529
Mailing city: Ellicott City
Mailing state: MD
Mailing zip: 21041-1529
General Phone: (410) 740-5009
General Fax: (410) 740-5888
General/National Adv. E-mail: info@ampsinc.net
Primary Website: www.ampsinc.net
Year Established: 2001
Personnel: Daniel Medinger (Owner and President)
Parent company (for newspapers): Medinger Media LLC

MICHIGAN

NEWSPAPER NATIONAL NETWORK

Street address 1: 41899 Waterfall Rd
Street address 3: Northville
Street address state: MI
Zip/Postal code: 48168-3267
County: Wayne
Country: USA
Mailing address: 41899 Waterfall Rd
Mailing city: Northville
Mailing state: MI
Mailing zip: 48168-3267
General Phone: (248) 680-4676
General Fax: (248) 680-4667
Personnel: Larry Doyle (Sales Exec.)

AMERICAN NEWSPAPER REPRESENTATIVES, INC.

Street address 1: 2075 W Big Beaver Rd
Street address 2: Ste 310
Street address 3: Troy
Street address state: MI
Zip/Postal code: 48084-3439
County: Oakland
Country: USA
Mailing address: 2075 W Big Beaver Rd Ste 310
Mailing city: Troy
Mailing state: MI
Mailing zip: 48084-3439
General Phone: (248) 643-9910
General Fax: (248) 643-9914
General/National Adv. E-mail: accountsales@gotoanr.com
Primary Website: www.gotoanr.com
Year Established: 1943
Note: ANR represents over 9,000 daily and weekly community newspapers nationwide
Personnel: Melanie Cox (Sales Mgr.); John Jepsen (Pres.); Robert Sontag (Exec. Vice Pres./COO)

MINNESOTA

CAMPUS MEDIA GROUP

Street address 1: 7760 France Ave S
Street address 2: Ste 800
Street address 3: Bloomington
Street address state: MN
Zip/Postal code: 55435-5929
County: Hennepin
Country: USA
Mailing address: 7760 France Ave South, Suite 800
Mailing city: Bloomington
Mailing state: MN
Mailing zip: 55435
General Phone: (952) 854-3100
General/National Adv. E-mail: sales@campusmediagroup.com
Primary Website: www.campusmediagroup.com
Year Established: 2002
Note: College marketing agency.
Personnel: Jason Bakker (COO); Tom Borgerding (Pres./CEO)

MINNETONKA

MEDIASPACE SOLUTIONS

Street address 1: 5600 Rowland Rd
Street address 2: Suite 170
Street address 3: Minnetonka
Street address state: MN
Zip/Postal code: 55343
County: Hennepin
Country: USA
Mailing address: 5600 Rowland Rd, Suite 170
Mailing city: Minnetonka
Mailing state: MN
Mailing zip: 55343
General Phone: (612) 253-3900
General Fax: (612) 454-2848
General/National Adv. E-mail: bstcyr@mediaspace.com
Primary Website: www.mediaspacesolutions.com
Year Established: 1999
Personnel: Randy Grunow (Chief Operating Officer); Brian St. Cyr (VP of Business Development & Marketing); Tony Buesing (Dir., Account Development); Brian Kieser (Sr. Med. Supervisor); Colin May (Director of Media Development); Carol Wagner (Buying Manager); Jason Armstrong (Buying Supervisor); Tom Johnson (Director Media Planning)

NEW ULM

WIDE AREA CLASSIFIED

Street address 1: 113 N Minnesota St
Street address 3: New Ulm
Street address state: MN
Zip/Postal code: 56073-1729
County: Brown
Country: USA
Mailing address: PO Box 9
Mailing city: New Ulm
Mailing state: MN
Mailing zip: 56073-0009
General Phone: 800-324-8236
General Fax: 866-822-5487
General/National Adv. E-mail: info@wideareaclassifieds.com
Primary Website: www.wideareaclassifieds.com
Year Established: 1986
Note: Represents shopper publications in 50 states
Personnel: Shannon Reinhart (Exec. Dir.)

NORTH CAROLINA

ADVANTAGE NEWSPAPER CONSULTANTS

Street address 1: 2850 Village Dr
Street address 2: Ste 102
Street address 3: Fayetteville
Street address state: NC
Zip/Postal code: 28304-3864
County: Cumberland
Country: USA
Mailing address: 2850 Village Dr
Mailing city: Fayetteville
Mailing state: NC
Mailing zip: 28304
General Phone: (910) 323-0349
General Fax: (910) 323-9280
General/National Adv. E-mail: info@newspaperconsultants.com
Primary Website: newspaperconsultants.com
Year Established: 1996
Published: Other
Audit By: Sworn/Estimate/Non-Audited
Audit Date: 43744
Note: Advantage Newspaper Consultants (ANC) is recognized as the leader in TV Magazine advertising sales in the United States. ANC works with both independent publishers and major newspaper chains to increase their core product ad revenue using innovative campaigns and creative, seasoned sales professionals that produce quantifiable results. Our sales managerâ€™s work with newspaper management to set goals and create an incentive plan which accelerates a TV Magazine sales campaign targeted towards finding key hidden revenue in their market in two weeks or less. Using the same proven formula of enthusiastic joint sales calls and dedicated management support that has lead to thousands of successful TV magazine sales campaigns, ANC also offers a cross-platform advertising sales program - Total Market Reach (TMR) - which includes print, mobile and digital ad combo sales.
Personnel: Timothy O. Dellinger (President); Susan M. Jolley (General Mgr.); Marie Smith (Exec. Dir. of Sales)

NEW JERSEY

MOUNTAINSIDE

RIVENDELL MEDIA, INC.

Street address 1: 1248 US Highway 22
Street address 3: Mountainside
Street address state: NJ
Zip/Postal code: 07092-2692
County: Union
Country: USA
Mailing address: 1248 US Highway 22 Ste 2
Mailing city: Mountainside
Mailing state: NJ
Mailing zip: 07092-2692
General Phone: (908) 232-2021 EXT 200
General Fax: (908) 232-0521
General/National Adv. E-mail: info@rivendellmedia.com; sales@rivendellmedia.com
Primary Website: www.rivendellmedia.com
Year Established: 1979
Note: Represents LGBT publications and digital properties.
Personnel: Todd Evans (Pres.)

NEW YORK

JOSEPH JACOBS ORGANIZATION

Street address 1: 349 W 87th St
Street address 2: Ste 1
Street address 3: New York
Street address state: NY
Zip/Postal code: 10024-2662
County: New York
Country: USA
Mailing address: 349 W 87th St Ste 1
Mailing city: New York
Mailing state: NY
Mailing zip: 10024-2662
General Phone: (212) 787-9400
General Fax: (212) 787-8080
General/National Adv. E-mail: erosenfeld@josephjacobs.org
Primary Website: www.josephjacobs.org
Year Established: 1919
Note: Represents Jewish publications
Personnel: David Koch (Pres.)
Newspaper (for newspapers group): Algemeiner Journal, Brooklyn; Jewish Exponent, Philadelphia; Newton TAB, Needham; Canadian Jewish News, Concord; THE OBSERVER, Karachi; The Forward, New York; Aufbau (OOB), New York; Las Vegas Israelite, Las Vegas; Jewish Review, Portland; Texas Jewish Post, Dallas; Ohio Jewish Chronicle, Columbus; The Jewish State (OOB), Highland Park; Berkshire Jewish Voice, Pittsfield ; Buffalo Jewish Review, Buffalo; Jewish Community News, Los Gatos; Jewish Post of New York (OOB), New York; Jewish Standard, Teaneck; The Speaker-OOB, Highland Park; Jewish Times, Pleasantville; Jewish Voice, Cherry Hill; Rockland Jewish Reporter, West Nyack; Jewish Week, New York; The Jewish Reporter, Framingham; The Jewish Civic Press, New Orleans; Washington Jewish Week, Rockville; Jewish Journal, Valley Stream; Der Yid, Brooklyn; Jewish Reporter, Las Vegas; Connecticut Jewish Ledger, West Hartford; Jewish Press, Omaha; Charlotte Jewish News, Charlotte; Intermountain Jewish News, Denver; Manhattan Jewish Sentinel, Far Rockaway; Stark Jewish News, Canton; The American Israelite, Cincinnati; The Detroit Jewish News, Southfield; Jewish News, Metairie

METRO SUBURBIA, INC./NEWHOUSE NEWSPAPERS

Street address 1: 711 3rd Ave
Street address 2: Fl 6
Street address 3: New York
Street address state: NY
Zip/Postal code: 10017-4029
County: New York
Country: USA
Mailing address: 711 3rd Ave Rm 1500
Mailing city: New York
Mailing state: NY
Mailing zip: 10017-9201
General Phone: (212) 697-8020
General Fax: (212) 972-3146
General/National Adv. E-mail: johnt@metrosuburbia.com
Primary Website: www.metrosuburbia.com
Personnel: Kevin Drolet (Adv. Sales Mgr.); John Tingwall (Adv. Sales Mgr.); Chad Johnson (Adv. Sales Mgr.); Robert N. Schoenbacher (Pres.); John A. Colombo (New York Sales Mgr.); Jon Gold (Adv. Sales Mgr.); Brenda Goodwin-Garcia (Adv. Sales Mgr.)
Newspaper (for newspapers group): Shawano Leader, Shawano

REFUEL AGENCY, INC

Street address 1: 1350 Broadway
Street address 2: Suite 830
Street address 3: New York
Street address state: NY
Zip/Postal code: 10018
County: New York
Country: USA
Mailing address: 1350 Broadway, Suite 830
Mailing city: New York
Mailing state: NY
Mailing zip: 10018
General Phone: (866) 360-9688
General/National Adv. E-mail: info@refuelagency.com
Primary Website: www.refuelagency.com
Year Established: 1968
Note: Refuel Agency, Inc specializes in the military, college, Hispanic, African-American, ethnic and senior markets.
Personnel: Derik S. White (President/CEO); David Silver (Chief Revenue Officer); Chris Cassino (COO)

ONTARIO

METROLAND MEDIA GROUP LTD.

Street address 1: 3715 Laird Road
Street address 2: Unit 6
Street address 3: Mississauga
Street address state: ON
Zip/Postal code: L5L 0A3
Country: Canada
Mailing address: 3715 Laird Road, Unit 6
Mailing city: Mississauga
Mailing state: ON
Mailing zip: L5L 0A3
General Phone: (866) 838-8960
General Fax: (905) 279-5103
General/National Adv. E-mail: result@metroland.com
Primary Website: www.metroland.com
Personnel: Ian Oliver (Pres.); Kathie Bride (Vice Pres.); Tim Whittaker (Sr. Vice Pres.); Ian McLeod (Sr. Vice Pres.); Ian Proudfoot (Vice Pres.); Brenda Biller (Vice Pres., HR); Joe Anderson (Vice Pres.); Bruce Danford (Vice Pres.); Ron Lenyk (Vice Pres.); Ken Nugent (Vice Pres.); Carol Peddie (Vice Pres.); Gordon Paolucci; Kukle Terry (Vice President); Lois Tuffin (Ed-In-Chief); John Willems; Scott Miller Cressman; Tracy Magee-Graham; Haggert Peter (Editor-in-Chief); Terry Kukle (VP, Business Development & Acquisitions)
Newspaper (for newspapers group): The Wasaga Sun, Wasaga Beach; Banner Post, Grimshaw; Belleville News, Belleville; Fort Erie Post, Thorold; Independent & Free Press, Georgetown; Ajax-pickering News Advertiser, Oshawa; The Alliston Herald, Alliston; Almaguin News, Burks Falls; Ancaster News, Stoney Creek; Arnprior Chronicle-Guide, Arnprior; Arthur Enterprise News, Mount Forest; The Aurora Banner, Aurora; The Barrie Advance, Barrie; Beach-Riverdale Mirror, Toronto; Belleville News Emc, Belleville; Bloor West Villager, Toronto; Bracebridge Examiner, Bracebridge; Bradford & West Gwillimbury Topic, Newmarket; Brampton Guardian, Mississauga; Brant News, Brantford; The Brighton Independent, Brighton; Brock Citizen, Cannington; The Burlington Post, Burlington; Caledon Enterprise, Bolton; Cambridge Times, Cambridge; The Carleton Place-almonte Canadian Gazette Emc, Smith Falls; City Centre Mirror, Toronto; Clarington This Week, Oshawa; Dundas Star News, Stoney Creek; Express, Meaford; The East York Mirror, Willowdale; The Elmira Independent, Elmira; The Erin Advocate, Erin; Etobicoke Guardian, Etobicoke; Times Advocate, Exeter; The Fergus-elora News Express, Fergus; The Flamborough Review, Waterdown; The Frontenac Gazette, Kingston; The Georgina Advocate, Keswick; Glanbrook Gazette, Caledonia; The Gravenhurst Banner, Gravenhurst; The Grimsby Lincoln News, Grimsby; The Guelph Mercury Tribune, Guelph; Guelph Tribune, Guelph; Hamilton Mountain News, Stoney Creek; The Hamilton Spectator, Hamilton; Huntsville Forester, Huntsville; Innisfil Journal, Barrie; Kanata Kourier-standard Emc, Ottawa; Kawartha Lakes This Week, Lindsay; Kemptville Advance Emc, Smiths Falls; Kingston Heritage Emc, Kingston; Kitchener Post, Kitchener; The Listowel Banner, Listowel; Manotick News Emc, Ottawa; Markham Economist & Sun, Markham; The Mirror, Midland; The Milton Canadian Champion, Milton; Minto Express, Palmerston; Mississauga News, Mississauga; The Mount Forest Confederate, Mount Forest; The Muskokan, Bracebridge; Nepean-barrhaven News Emc, Ottawa; New Hamburg Independent, New Hamburg; The Newmarket Era-banner, Newmarket; North York Mirror, Toronto; Northumberland News, Cobourg; Niagara This Week, Thorold; Oakville Beaver, Oakville; The Orangeville Banner, Orangeville; Orillia Today, Orillia; Orleans News Emc, Ottawa; Oshawa-whitby This Week, Oshawa; Ottawa East Emc, Ottawa; Ottawa South Emc, Ottawa; Ottawa West Emc, Ottawa; The Parkdale Villager, Toronto; Parry Sound Beacon Star, Parry Sound; Parry Sound North Star, Parry Sound; The Perth Courier Emc, Smith Falls; Peterborough This Week, Peterborough; The Port Perry Star, Port Perry; Quinte West Emc, Belleville; The Renfrew Mercury Emc, Renfrew; The Richmond Hill Liberal, Markham; The Grand River Sachem, Caledonia; The Scarborough Mirror, Toronto; Smiths Falls Record News Emc, Smiths Falls; South Asian Focus, Brampton; St. Lawrence News, Brockville; St. Mary's Journal Argus, St Marys; St. Thomas/elgin Weekly News, Saint Thomas; The Stayner Sun, Wasaga Beach; The Stittsville News, Ottawa; Stoney Creek News, Stoney Creek; Stratford Gazette, Stratford; Collingwood Connection, Collingwood; Uxbridge Times-journal, Uxbridge; Vaughan Citizen, Vaughan; Walkerton Herald-times, Walkerton; Waterloo Chronicle, Waterloo; The Record, Kitchener; West Carleton Review, Arnprior; The Wingham Advance-times, Wingham; The York Guardian, Toronto

NEWBASE

Street address 1: 468 Queen Str. E
Street address 2: Suite 500
Street address 3: Toronto
Street address state: ON
Zip/Postal code: M5A 1T7
Country: USA
Mailing address: 468 Queen Str. E, Suite 500
Mailing city: Toronto
Mailing state: ON
Mailing zip: M5A 1T7
General Phone: (416) 363 1388
General Fax: (416) 363 2889
Primary Website: www.thenewbase.com
Personnel: Lesley Conway (Pres.); Doug St. John (Digital Director)

NEWBASE

Street address 1: 468 Queen Str. E
Street address 2: Suite 500
Street address 3: Toronto
Street address state: ON
Zip/Postal code: M5A 1T7
Country: Canada
Mailing address: 468 Queen Str. E, Suite 500
Mailing city: Toronto
Mailing state: ON
Mailing zip: M5A 1T7
General Phone: (416) 363 1388
General Fax: (416) 363 2889
Primary Website: http://www.thenewbase.com
Personnel: Lesley Conway (Pres.); Doug St. John (Digital Director, Americas); Cyndy Fleming (Account Dir.); Sheila Cohen (Programmatic Manager)

TEXAS

TRIBUNE MEDIA NETWORK

Street address 1: 12900 Preston Rd
Street address 2: Ste 615
Street address 3: Dallas
Street address state: TX
Zip/Postal code: 75230-1322
County: Dallas
Country: USA
Mailing address: 12900 Preston Rd Ste 615
Mailing city: Dallas
Mailing state: TX
Mailing zip: 75230-1322
General Phone: (972) 789-6920
General Fax: (972) 239-2737
Primary Website: www.tribunemediagroup.com
Personnel: Grant Moise (Southwestern Regl. Sales Dir.)

HARTE-HANKS COMMUNICATIONS, INC.

Street address 1: 9601 McAllister Fwy
Street address 2: Ste 610
Street address 3: San Antonio
Street address state: TX
Zip/Postal code: 78216-4632
County: Bexar
Country: USA
Mailing address: 9601 McAllister Fwy Ste 610
Mailing city: San Antonio
Mailing state: TX
Mailing zip: 78216-4632
General Phone: (210) 829-9000
General Fax: (210) 829-9101
General/National Adv. E-mail: media@hartehanks.com
Primary Website: www.hartehanks.com
Note: Represents shopper publications
Personnel: Jon Biro (CFO)

VIRGINIA

C-VILLE HOLDINGS LLC

Street address 1: 308 E Main St
Street address 3: Charlottesville
Street address state: VA
Zip/Postal code: 22902-5234
County: Charlottesville City
Country: USA
Mailing address: P.O. Box 119
Mailing city: Charlottesville
Mailing state: VA
Mailing zip: 22902
General Phone: 434/817-2749
General Fax: 434/817-2758
General/National Adv. E-mail: aimee@c-ville.com
Primary Website: www.c-ville.com
Year Established: 1995
Personnel: Jessica Luck (Ed)
Newspaper (for newspapers group): North Coast Journal, Eureka; Santa Cruz Good Times, Santa Cruz; C-ville Weekly, Charlottesville; Boise Weekly, Boise; Boston Phoenix, Boston; Las Vegas Mercury, Las Vegas; Desert Post Weekly, Palm Springs; Santa Barbara Independent, Santa Barbara; Pacific Sun, San Rafael; Providence Phoenix, Providence; Times Of Acadiana, Lafayette; Urban Tulsa Weekly (OOB), Tulsa; Reno News & Review, Reno; City Link (OOB), Tamarac; Metroland, Albany; San Francisco Bay Guardian (OOB), San Francisco; Palo Alto Weekly, Palo Alto; Nashville Scene, Nashville; The Independent Weekly, Durham; Las Vegas Weekly, Henderson; Hartford Courant-OOB, Hartford; Philadelphia City Paper (OOB), Philadelphia; Style Weekly, Richmond; Illinois Times, Springfield; Easy Reader, Hermosa Beach; Flagpole Magazine, Athens; THE MIRROR

NEWSPAPERS REPRESENTATIVE - STATE

ALABAMA

ALABAMA NEWSPAPER ADVERTISING SERVICE, INC.

Street address 1: 3324 Independence Dr
Street address 2: Ste 200
Street address 3: Birmingham
Street address state: AL
Zip/Postal code: 35209-5602
County: Jefferson
Country: USA
Mailing address: 3324 Independence Dr Ste 200
Mailing city: Birmingham
Mailing state: AL
Mailing zip: 35209-5602
General Phone: (205) 871-7737
General Fax: (205) 871-7740
General/National Adv. E-mail: mail@alabamapress.org
Primary Website: www.alabamapress.org
Personnel: Felicia Mason (Exec. Dir.); Brad English (Adv. Mgr.)

ARKANSAS

ARKANSAS PRESS SERVICES

Street address 1: 411 S Victory St
Street address 3: Little Rock
Street address state: AR
Zip/Postal code: 72201-2933
County: Pulaski
Country: USA
Mailing address: 411 S Victory St Ste 100
Mailing city: Little Rock
Mailing state: AR
Mailing zip: 72201-2934
General Phone: (501) 374-1500
General Fax: (501) 374-7509
General/National Adv. E-mail: info@arkansaspress.org
Primary Website: www.arkansaspress.org
Year Established: 1873
Note: Represents daily and weekly newspapers in Arkansas
Personnel: Tom Larimer (Exec. Dir.); Ashley Wimberley (Adv. & Mktg. Dir.)

ARIZONA

ANA ADVERTISING SERVICES, INC. (ARIZONA NEWSPAPER ASSOCIATION)

Street address 1: 1001 N Central Ave
Street address 2: Ste 670
Street address 3: Phoenix
Street address state: AZ
Zip/Postal code: 85004-1947
County: Maricopa
Country: USA
General Phone: (602) 261-7655
General Fax: (602) 261-7525
General/National Adv. E-mail: office@ananews.com
Primary Website: www.ananews.com
Year Established: 1931
Note: Represents daily and weekly newspapers in Arizona
Personnel: Paula Casey (Exec. Dir.); Cindy London (Media Buyer); Julie O'Keefe (Communications Manager)
Parent company (for newspapers): Arizona Newspapers Association
Newspaper (for newspapers group): Inside Tucson Business, Tucson; Ajo Copper News, Ajo; Surprise Independent, Sun City; The Winslow Mail, Winslow; Eloy Enterprise, Florence; The Bisbee Observer, Bisbee; San Manuel Miner, Kearny; Williams-Grand Canyon News, Williams; Chandler/Sun Lakes Independent, Chandler; Prescott Valley Tribune, Chino Valley; NEW KABUL TIMES, Kabul; Tombstone Tumbleweed, Tombstone

CALIFORNIA

CNPA ADVERTISING SERVICES

Street address 1: 2000 O St
Street address 2: Ste 120
Street address 3: Sacramento
Street address state: CA
Zip/Postal code: 95811-5299
County: Sacramento
Country: USA
Mailing address: 2000 O St Ste 120
Mailing city: Sacramento
Mailing state: CA
Mailing zip: 95811-5299
General Phone: (916) 288-6000
General Fax: (916) 288-6003
General/National Adv. E-mail: bryan@cnpa.com
Primary Website: www.cnpa.com
Personnel: Jack Bates (Exec. Dir.); Sharla Trillo (Dir.); Patrice Bayard-Miller (Client Rel./Sales Mgr.)

COLORADO

SYNC2 MEDIA

Street address 1: 1120 N Lincoln St
Street address 2: Ste 912
Street address 3: Denver
Street address state: CO
Zip/Postal code: 80203-2138
County: Denver
Country: USA
General Phone: (303) 571-5117
General Fax: (303) 571-1803
General/National Adv. E-mail: info@sync2media.com
Primary Website: www.sync2media.com
Note: Represents daily and weekly newspapers in Colorado
Personnel: Jerry Raehal (CEO); Judy Queich (Account Executive); Peyton Jacobson (Account Executive)
Parent company (for newspapers): Colorado Press Association

FLORIDA

BELLEVIEW

COMMUNITY PAPERS OF FLORIDA

Street address 1: 12601 SE 53rd Terrace Rd
Street address 3: Belleview
Street address state: FL
Zip/Postal code: 34420-5106
County: Marion
Country: USA
Mailing address: PO Box 1149
Mailing city: Summerfield
Mailing state: FL
Mailing zip: 34492-1149
General Phone: (352) 237-3409
General Fax: (352) 347-3384
General/National Adv. E-mail: djneuharth@aol.com
Primary Website: www.communitypapersofflorida.com
Year Established: 1960
Note: Classified advertising in 82 community news and shopper publications in Florida.
Personnel: Dave Neuharth (Exec. Dir.); Barbara Holmes (Admin. Asst.)

INTERSECT MEDIA SOLUTIONS

Street address 1: 1025 Greenwood Blvd.
Street address 2: Suite 191
Street address 3: Lake Mary
Street address state: FL
Zip/Postal code: 32746-5410
County: Seminole
Country: USA
Mailing address: 1025 Greenwood Blvd., Suite 191
Mailing city: Lake Mary
Mailing state: FL
Mailing zip: 32746-5410
General Phone: (866) 404-5913
General/National Adv. E-mail: info@mediagenius.com
Primary Website: www.intersectmediasolutions.com
Year Established: 1959
Personnel: Dean Ridings (Pres./CEO); Mark Burger (VP, Finance & CFO); Carolyn Nolte (VP, Strategy); Jessica Pitts (VP, Operations)
Parent company (for newspapers): Florida Press Association

TALLAHASSEE

FLORIDA PRESS SERVICE, INC.

Street address 1: 336 E College Ave
Street address 2: Ste 203
Street address 3: Tallahassee
Street address state: FL
Zip/Postal code: 32301-1559
County: Leon
Country: USA
Mailing address: 336 E College Ave Ste 203
Mailing city: Tallahassee
Mailing state: FL
Mailing zip: 32301-1559
General Phone: (850) 222-5790
General Fax: (850) 222-4498
General/National Adv. E-mail: fps-info@flpress.com
Primary Website: www.flpress.com
Note: Represents 42 daily and 135 weekly newspapers in Florida
Personnel: Dean Riddings (Pres./CEO)

GEORGIA

GEORGIA NEWSPAPER SERVICE, INC.

Street address 1: 3066 Mercer University Dr
Street address 2: Ste 200
Street address 3: Atlanta
Street address state: GA
Zip/Postal code: 30341-4137
County: Dekalb
Country: USA
Mailing address: 3066 Mercer University Dr Ste 200
Mailing city: Atlanta
Mailing state: GA
Mailing zip: 30341-4137
General Phone: (770) 454-6776
General Fax: (770) 454-6778
General/National Adv. E-mail: mail@gapress.org
Primary Website: www.gapress.org
Note: Represents daily and weekly newspapers in Georgia
Personnel: Robin Rhodes (Exec. Dir.)

IOWA

CUSTOMIZED NEWSPAPER ADVERTISING (IOWA)

Street address 1: 319 E 5th St
Street address 3: Des Moines
Street address state: IA
Zip/Postal code: 50309-1927
County: Polk
Country: USA
Mailing address: 319 E 5th St
Mailing city: Des Moines
Mailing state: IA
Mailing zip: 50309-1927
General Phone: (515) 244-2145
General Fax: (515) 244-4855
Primary Website: www.cnaads.com; www.inanews.com
Note: Represents 302 daily and weekly newspapers in Iowa and can place advertising in any newspaper in the country.

Personnel: Chris Mudge (Exec. Dir.); Bryan Rohe (Acct. Exec.); Ron Bode (Sales Dir.); Bruce Adams (Sales Rep.)

MIDWEST FREE COMMUNITY PAPERS

Street address 1: PO Box 1350
Street address 3: Iowa City
Street address state: IA
Zip/Postal code: 52244-1350
County: Johnson
Country: USA
Mailing address: PO Box 1350
Mailing city: Iowa City
Mailing state: IA
Mailing zip: 52244-1350
General Phone: (319) 341-4352
General Fax: (319) 341-4358
General/National Adv. E-mail: mfcp@mchsi.com
Primary Website: www.mfcp.org
Year Established: 1955
Note: Classified advertising for 124 publications
Personnel: Jori Hendon (Office Mgr.)

KENTUCKY

FRANKFORT

KENTUCKY PRESS SERVICE, INC.

Street address 1: 101 Consumer Ln
Street address 3: Frankfort
Street address state: KY
Zip/Postal code: 40601-8489
County: Franklin
Country: USA
Mailing address: 101 Consumer Ln
Mailing city: Frankfort
Mailing state: KY
Mailing zip: 40601-8489
General Phone: (502) 223-8821
General Fax: (502) 875-2624
General/National Adv. E-mail: dthompson@kypress.com
Primary Website: www.kypress.com
Year Established: 1959
Note: Represents daily and weekly newspapers in Kentucky
Personnel: David Thompson (Exec. Dir.); Bonnie Howard (Controller)

LOUISIANA

LOUISIANA PRESS ASSOCIATION

Street address 1: 404 Europe St
Street address 3: Baton Rouge
Street address state: LA
Zip/Postal code: 70802-6403
County: East Baton Rouge
Country: USA
General Phone: (225) 344-9309
General Fax: (225) 344-9344
Advertising Phone: (225) 344-9309 x 111
Advertising Fax: (225) 336-9921
Editorial Fax: (225) 346-5060
General/National Adv. E-mail: pam@lapress.com
Display Adv. E-mail: erin@LaPress.com
Primary Website: www.lapress.com
Year Established: 1880
Personnel: Mike Rood (Communications Dir.); Pamela Mitchell (Exec. Dir.); Mitchell-Ann Droge (Dir. of Ops.); Erin Palmintier (Adv. Dir.)

MASSACHUSETTS

NENPA AD NETWORK (NEW ENGLAND NEWSPAPER AND PRESS ASSOCIATION)

Street address 1: 1 Arrow Dr
Street address 2: Ste 6
Street address 3: Woburn
Street address state: MA
Zip/Postal code: 01801-2039
County: Middlesex
Country: USA
Mailing address: 1 Arrow Drive, Suite 6
Mailing city: Woburn
Mailing state: MA
Mailing zip: 1801
General Phone: (781) 281-2053
General Fax: (339) 999-2174
General/National Adv. E-mail: info@nenpa.com
Primary Website: www.nenpa.com
Year Established: 1930
Note: Represents daily, weekly and specialty newspapers in the six New England states
Personnel: Linda Conway (Executive Director)

MICHIGAN

EAST LANSING

COMMUNITY PAPERS OF MICHIGAN, INC.

Street address 1: 5000 Northwind Dr
Street address 2: Ste 240
Street address 3: East Lansing
Street address state: MI
Zip/Postal code: 48823-5032
County: Ingham
Country: USA
Mailing address: 5000 Northwind Dr Ste 240
Mailing city: East Lansing
Mailing state: MI
Mailing zip: 48823-5032
General Phone: (800) 783-0267
General Fax: (517) 333-3322
General/National Adv. E-mail: jackguza@cpapersmi.com
Primary Website: www.communitypapersofmichigan.com
Note: Display advertising for 90 publications in Michigan that in cooperation with Community Papers of Michigan reaches more than 2.5 million Michigan households. Classifed advertising reaches 1.7 million Michigan households
Personnel: Terry Roby (Pres.); Jack Guza (Exec.Dir.); Stacy Kotecki (Office Mgr.)

MNI

Street address 1: 827 N Washington Ave
Street address 3: Lansing
Street address state: MI
Zip/Postal code: 48906-5135
County: Ingham
Country: USA
Mailing address: 827 N Washington Ave
Mailing city: Lansing
Mailing state: MI
Mailing zip: 48906-5135
General Phone: (517) 372-2424
General Fax: (517) 372-2429
General/National Adv. E-mail: mpa@michiganpress.org
Primary Website: www.michiganpress.org
Year Established: 1868
Note: Represents print and digital media in Michigan
Personnel: Lisa McGraw (Public Affairs Manager); James Tarrant (Executive Director); Mike MacLaren (Executive Director); Rose Lucas (Growth & Operations Manager)
Parent company (for newspapers): Michigan Press Association

MISSOURI

MISSOURI PRESS SERVICE, INC.

Street address 1: 802 Locust St
Street address 3: Columbia
Street address state: MO
Zip/Postal code: 65201-4888
County: Boone
Country: USA
Mailing address: 802 Locust St
Mailing city: Columbia
Mailing state: MO
Mailing zip: 65201-7799
General Phone: (573) 449-4167
General Fax: (573) 874-5894
General/National Adv. E-mail: mmaassen@socket.net
Display Adv. E-mail: mopressads@socket.net
Editorial e-mail: mbarba@mopress.com
Primary Website: www.mopress.com
Year Established: 1867
Industry: Newspapers. Consulting Services: Advertising; Consulting Services: Editorial;
Note: Represents daily and weekly newspapers in Missouri
Personnel: Mark Maassen (Exec. Dir.)
Parent company (for newspapers): Missouri Press Association

MISSISSIPPI

JACKSON

MISSISSIPPI PRESS SERVICES, INC.

Street address 1: 371 Edgewood Terrace Dr
Street address 3: Jackson
Street address state: MS
Zip/Postal code: 39206-6217
County: Hinds
Country: USA
Mailing address: 371 Edgewood Terrace Dr.
Mailing city: Jackson
Mailing state: MS
Mailing zip: 39206-6217
General Phone: (601) 981-3060
General Fax: (601) 981-3676
General/National Adv. E-mail: admin@mspress.org
Primary Website: www.mspress.org
Year Established: 1866
Note: Represents daily and weekly newspapers in Mississippi
Personnel: Layne Bruce (Exec. Dir.); Monica Gilmer (Member Services Manager); Sue Hicks (Business Development Manager); Andrea Ross (Media Director)

MONTANA

MONTANA NEWSPAPER ADVERTISING SERVICE, INC.

Street address 1: 825 Great Northern Blvd
Street address 2: Ste 202
Street address 3: Helena
Street address state: MT
Zip/Postal code: 59601-3340
County: Lewis And Clark
Country: USA
Mailing address: 825 Great Northern Blvd Ste 202
Mailing city: Helena
Mailing state: MT
Mailing zip: 59601-3358
General Phone: (406) 443-2850
General Fax: (406) 443-2860
General/National Adv. E-mail: randy@mtnewspapers.com
Primary Website: www.mtnewspapers.com
Year Established: 1955
Note: Represents daily and weekly newspapers in Montana.
Personnel: Randy Schmoldt (Accounting Specialist)
Newspaper (for newspapers group): Cascade Courier, Cascade; Lewistown News-Argus, Lewistown; The Whitefish Pilot, Whitefish; The Terry Tribune, Terry; Seeley Swan Pathfinder, Seeley Lake; Whitehall Ledger, Whitehall; The Shelby Promoter, Shelby; Three Forks Herald, Three Forks; The Philipsburg Mail, Philipsburg; Jordan Tribune (OOB), Jordan; Glendive Ranger-Review, Glendive; The Circle Banner, Circle; The Ekalaka Eagle, Ekalaka; Townsend Star (OOB), Townsend; Livingston Enterprise, Livingston

NORTH CAROLINA

NORTH CAROLINA PRESS SERVICE, INC.

Street address 1: 5171 Glenwood Ave
Street address 2: Ste 364
Street address 3: Raleigh
Street address state: NC
Zip/Postal code: 27612-3266
County: Wake
Country: USA
Mailing address: 5171 Glenwood Ave Ste 364
Mailing city: Raleigh
Mailing state: NC
Mailing zip: 27612-3266
General Phone: (919) 787-7443
General Fax: (919) 787-5302
Primary Website: www.ncpress.com
Year Established: 1985
Note: Represents all daily and weekly newspapers in North Carolina
Personnel: Beth Grace (Exec. Dir.); Laura Nakoneczny (Member Services Director); Mark Holmes (Director of Sales)
Newspaper (for newspapers group): Sanford Herald, Sanford; The Eden Daily News, Reidsville

NORTH DAKOTA

NORTH DAKOTA NEWSPAPER ASSOCIATION

Street address 1: 1435 Interstate Loop
Street address 3: Bismarck
Street address state: ND
Zip/Postal code: 58503-0567
County: Burleigh
Country: USA
Mailing address: 1435 Interstate Loop
Mailing city: Bismarck
Mailing state: ND
Mailing zip: 58503-0567
General Phone: (701) 223-6397
General Fax: (701) 223-8185
General/National Adv. E-mail: info@ndna.com
Primary Website: www.ndna.com
Year Established: 1885
Note: Represents daily and weekly newspapers in North Dakota
Personnel: Kelli Richey (Mktg. Dir.); Steve Andrist (Exec. Dir.); Mike Casey (Adv. Dir.); Colleen Park (Adv./Public Notice Coord.); Shari Peterson (Office Coord./Adv. Assist.); Paul Erdelt (NDNA President)

NEBRASKA

NEBRASKA PRESS ADVERTISING SERVICE

Street address 1: 845 S St
Street address 3: Lincoln
Street address state: NE
Zip/Postal code: 68508-1226
County: Lancaster
Country: USA
General Phone: (402) 476-2851
General Fax: (402) 476-2942
General/National Adv. E-mail: nebpress@nebpress.com

Primary Website: www.nebpress.com
Year Established: 1879
Personnel: Rob James (Adv. Sales Dir.); Allen Beermann (Exec. Dir., Nebraska Press Assoc.)

NEW HAMPSHIRE

NEW HAMPSHIRE UNION LEADER

Street address 1: 100 William Loeb Drive
Street address 3: Manchester
Street address state: NH
Zip/Postal code: 3109
Country: USA
Delivery Methods: Mail`Newsstand`Carrier`Racks
Own Printing Facility: N
Commercial printers: N
Advertising (Open inch Rate) Weekday/Saturday: $36.70
Advertising (Open inch rate) Sunday: $38.95
Market Information: TMC; Zoned editions.
Mechanical available: Offset; Black and 3 ROP colors; inserts accepted - samples, post-its; page cutoffs - 22.
Mechanical specifications: Type page 10 1/4 x 21 1/4; E - 6 cols, 1 5/6, 1/8 between; A - 6 cols, 1 5/6, 1/8 between; C - 9 cols, 1 3/16, 1/8 between.
Published: Mon`Tues`Wed`Thur`Fri`Sun
Published Other: Sat e-edition only
Weekday Frequency: m
Saturday Frequency: m
Sat. Circulation Paid: 17143
Sun. Circulation Paid: 36859
Pressroom Equipment: Printing is outsourced
Mailroom Eqipment: Mailroom operation outsourced
Buisness Software: AltiPro
Classified Equipment: Hardware -- Dell/PowerEdge 4600, 20-Dell/Optiplex GX605;
Classified Software: SCS/AdMAX-ClassPag
Display Equipment: Hardware -- Dell/PG 266-GXA;
Display Software: Ad Make-up Applications -- SCS/AdBoss, AdMAX; Layout Software -- SCS/Layout-8000
Editorial Equipment: Hardware -- 52-HP & Dell desktops
Editorial Software: DTI-Saxotech
Circulation Software: DTI
Personnel: Dirk F. Ruemenapp (Exec. Vice Pres.); Joyce M. Levesque (VP Finance); Brendan McQuaid (President); Robin Wilson (Adv. Servs. Mgr.); Lucien G. Trahan (Circ. Dir., Opns.); Mike Cote (Deputy Mng. Ed., Bus.); Grant Boss (Editorial Page Ed.); Joseph McQuaid (Publisher); Trent Spiner (Exec. Ed.); Shannon Sullivan (Community Relations Mgr.); James Normandin (Chief Operating Officer); Andrew Loranger (IT Manager); Sherry Wood (Night Editor); Matt Sartwell (Managing Editor)
Parent company (for newspapers): Union Leader Corporation; Nackey Loeb School of Journalism

NEW JERSEY

EWING

NEW JERSEY NEWSMEDIA NETWORK (NJNN)

Street address 1: 810 Bear Tavern Rd
Street address 2: Ste 307
Street address 3: Ewing
Street address state: NJ
Zip/Postal code: 08628-1022
County: Mercer
Country: USA
Mailing address: 810 Bear Tavern Rd Ste 307
Mailing city: Ewing
Mailing state: NJ
Mailing zip: 08628-1022
General Phone: (609) 406-0600
General Fax: (609) 406-0399
General/National Adv. E-mail: njnn@njpa.org
Primary Website: www.njpa.org/njnn
Year Established: 1991
Note: Media planning and placement service for print and digital campaigns. Specializing in daily, weekly, ethnic and specialty pubs reaching New Jersey.
Personnel: Amy Lear (Adv. Dir.); George White (NJPA Exec Dir); Diane Trent (NJNN Networks Mgr)
Parent company (for newspapers): New Jersey Press Association

NEW MEXICO

NEW MEXICO PRESS ASSOCIATION

Street address 1: 700 Silver Ave SW
Street address 3: Albuquerque
Street address state: NM
Zip/Postal code: 87102-3019
County: Bernalillo
Country: USA
Mailing address: PO Box 95198
Mailing city: Albuquerque
Mailing state: NM
Mailing zip: 87199-5198
General Phone: (505) 275-1241
General Fax: (505) 275-1449
Advertising Phone: (505) 275-1377
General/National Adv. E-mail: info@nmpress.org
Display Adv. E-mail: Ads@NMPress.org
Primary Website: www.nmpress.org
Note: Elections held in Oct
Personnel: Holly Aguilar (Office Mgr.)
Newspaper (for newspapers group): Hobbs News-Sun, Hobbs; Roswell Daily Record, Roswell; Las Vegas Optic, LAS VEGAS; Lincoln County News, Chandler; Union County Leader, Clayton; Cibola Beacon, Grants; Santa Rosa News (OOB), Santa Rosa; Sierra County Sentinel, Truth Or Consequences; The Rio Rancho Observer, Rio Rancho; The Ruidoso News, Ruidoso; The Raton Range (OOB), Raton; Silver City Daily Press & Independent, Silver City

NEW YORK

NEW YORK NEWS PUBLISHERS ASSOCIATION

Street address 1: 252 Hudson Ave
Street address 3: Albany
Street address state: NY
Zip/Postal code: 12210-1802
County: Albany
Country: USA
General Phone: (518) 449-1667
General Fax: (518) 449-1667
Primary Website: www.nynpa.com
Year Established: 1927
Personnel: Diane Kennedy (Pres.); Mary H. Miller (Education Services Dir.); Don Ferlazzo (Dir. of Adv. & Event Mgmt.)

NEW YORK PRESS SERVICE

Street address 1: 1681 Western Ave
Street address 3: Albany
Street address state: NY
Zip/Postal code: 12203-4305
County: Albany
Country: USA
Mailing address: 1681 Western Ave
Mailing city: Albany
Mailing state: NY
Mailing zip: 12203-4340
General Phone: (518) 464-6483
General Fax: (518) 464-6489
General/National Adv. E-mail: nypa@nynewspapers.com
Primary Website: www.nynewspapers.com
Year Established: 1853
Note: Represents weekly newspapers in New York
Personnel: Phil Anthony (Adv. Rep., Classified Sales); Jill Van Dusen (Mktg. Dir.)

SYRACUSE

ADNETWORKNY

Street address 1: 109 Twin Oaks Dr
Street address 2: Ste D
Street address 3: Syracuse
Street address state: NY
Zip/Postal code: 13206-1204
County: Onondaga
Country: USA
Mailing address: 109 Twin Oaks Dr
Mailing city: Syracuse
Mailing state: NY
Mailing zip: 13206
General Phone: (315) 472-6007
General Fax: (877) 790-1976
General/National Adv. E-mail: ads@fcpny.com
Primary Website: www.fcpny.com
Year Established: 1950
Note: Classified and display advertising
Personnel: Dan Holmes (Exec. Dir.); Tom Cuskey (Sales & Training Director)
Parent company (for newspapers): Free Community Papers of NY

OHIO

OHIO NEWSPAPER SERVICES, INC.

Street address 1: 1335 Dublin Rd
Street address 2: Ste 216B
Street address 3: Columbus
Street address state: OH
Zip/Postal code: 43215-1000
County: Franklin
Country: USA
Mailing address: 1335 Dublin Rd Ste 216B
Mailing city: Columbus
Mailing state: OH
Mailing zip: 43215-1000
General Phone: (614) 486-6677
General Fax: (614) 486-4940
Primary Website: www.ohionews.org; www.adohio.net
Year Established: 1933
Note: Represents all 81 daily and 154 weekly Ohio newspaper and affiliated websites.
Personnel: Dennis Hetzel (Executive Director Ohio Newspaper Association); Walt Dozier (Acting Director of Advertising); Sue Bazzoli (Manager, Administrative Services); Jason Sanford (Manager of Communications & Content); Ann Riggs (Receptionist and Secretary); Patricia Conkle (Advertising Coordinator); Kathy McCutcheon (Network Account Executive); Casey Null (Advertising Account Executive)
Newspaper (for newspapers group): Mount Vernon News, Mount Vernon

OHIAD

Street address 1: PO Box 69
Street address 3: Covington
Street address state: OH
Zip/Postal code: 45318-0069
County: Miami
Country: USA
Mailing address: PO Box 69
Mailing city: Covington
Mailing state: OH
Mailing zip: 45318-0069
General Phone: (937) 473-2028
General Fax: (937) 473-2500
General/National Adv. E-mail: dselanders@woh.rr.com
Primary Website: www.arenspub.com
Note: Classified advertising for 16 publications. In cooperation with Community Papers of Ohio.
Personnel: Gary Godfrey (Secretary/Treasurer)

OKLAHOMA

OKLAHOMA PRESS SERVICE

Street address 1: 3601 N Lincoln Blvd
Street address 3: Oklahoma City
Street address state: OK
Zip/Postal code: 73105-5411
County: Oklahoma
Country: USA
Mailing address: 3601 N Lincoln Blvd
Mailing city: Oklahoma City
Mailing state: OK
Mailing zip: 73105-5499
General Phone: (405) 524-4421
General Fax: (405) 499-0048
General/National Adv. E-mail: sysop@okpress.com
Primary Website: www.okpress.com
Note: Represents daily and weekly newspapers in Oklahoma
Personnel: Mark Thomas (Exec. Vice Pres.)

ONTARIO

RESEAU SELECT/SELECT NETWORK

Street address 1: 25 Sheppard Ave W
Street address 2: Suite 500
Street address 3: Toronto
Street address state: ON
Zip/Postal code: M2N 6S7
County: York
Country: Canada
Mailing address: 25 Sheppard Ave. West Suite 500
Mailing city: Toronto
Mailing state: ON
Mailing zip: M2N 6S7
General Phone: (416) 733-7600
General Fax: (416) 726-8519
General/National Adv. E-mail: inforeseauselect@tc.tc
Primary Website: www.reseauselect.com
Newspaper (for newspapers group): Brossard Eclair, Longueuil; L'Information Regionale, Chateauguay; L'oeil Regional, Beloeil; L'oie Blanche, Montmagny; First Informer, Grosse Ile; Les Actualites, Asbestos; L'echo De La Tuque, La Tuque; La Voix De L'est Plus, Granby; Le Radar, Cap-aux-Meules; L'echo De Frontenac, Lac Megantic; Charlesbourg Express, Quebec; Le Placoteux, Saint Pascal

PENNSYLVANIA

MACNET

Street address 1: PO Box 408
Street address 3: Hamburg
Street address state: PA
Zip/Postal code: 19526-0408
County: Berks
Country: USA
Mailing address: PO Box 408
Mailing city: Hamburg
Mailing state: PA
Mailing zip: 19526-0408
General Phone: (800) 450-7227
General Fax: (610) 743-8500
General/National Adv. E-mail: info@macpa.net
Primary Website: www.macpa.net; www.macnetonline.com
Note: Classified advertising for 360 publications in PA, OH, NY, NJ, DE, MD, WV, VA, Washington DC.
Personnel: Alyse Mitten (Exec. Dir.)

MANSI MEDIA

Street address 1: 3899 N Front St
Street address 3: Harrisburg
Street address state: PA
Zip/Postal code: 17110-1583
County: Dauphin
Country: USA
General Phone: (717) 703-3030
General Fax: (717) 703-3033
General/National Adv. E-mail: sales@mansimedia.com
Primary Website: www.mansimedia.com
Note: Represents daily and weekly newspapers and their digital products anywhere in the U.S. and beyond.
Personnel: Lisa Knight (VP/Adv.); Chris Kazlauskas; Wes Snider (Dir. Client Solutions); Ronaldo Davis

(Sr. Media Buyer); Matthew Caylor (Dir., Interactive Media); Lindsey Artz (Account Manager); Shannon Mohar (Account Manager); Brian Hitchings (Director, Client Solutions)

PENNSYLVANIA

HITCHINGS & CO.

Street address 1: 580 W Germantown Pike
Street address 2: Ste 108
Street address 3: Plymouth Meeting
Street address state: PA
Zip/Postal code: 19462-1370
County: Montgomery
Country: USA
Mailing address: Plymouth Plz., 580 W. Germantown Pk., Ste. 108
Mailing city: Plymouth Meeting
Mailing state: PA
Mailing zip: 19462
General Phone: (610) 941-3555
General Fax: (610) 941-1289
General/National Adv. E-mail: brian@phillyareapapers.com
Primary Website: www.phillyareapapers.com
Personnel: Brian Hitchings (Pres.); Donna DeFrangesco (Acct. Supvr.)

QUEBEC

RESEAU SELECT/SELECT NETWORK

Street address 1: 8000 Av Blaise-Pascal
Street address 3: Montreal
Street address state: QC
Zip/Postal code: H1E 2S7
County: Quebec
Country: Canada
Mailing address: 8000 Ave. Blaise-Pascal
Mailing city: Montreal
Mailing state: QC
Mailing zip: H1E 2S7
General Phone: (514) 643-2300
General Fax: (514) 866-3030
General/National Adv. E-mail: inforeseauselect@tc.tc
Primary Website: www.reseauselect.com
Year Established: 1976
Note: Represents more than 148 weekly French-language newspapers in Quebec, Ontario, Manitoba and New Brunswick
Newspaper (for newspapers group): L'ACTION, Tunis; L'argenteuil, Lachute; Le Pharillon, Gaspe; La Parole, Drummondville; Le Progres De Coaticook, Coaticook; Journal De Chambly, Chambly; L'EXPRESS, Neuchatel; THE NATION, Islamabad; LA GAZETTE, Douala; THE MONITOR, Kampala

SOUTH CAROLINA

SOUTH CAROLINA PRESS SERVICES, INC.

Street address 1: 106 Outlet Pointe Blvd
Street address 3: Columbia
Street address state: SC
Zip/Postal code: 29210-5669
County: Lexington
Country: USA
Mailing address: PO Box 11429
Mailing city: Columbia
Mailing state: SC
Mailing zip: 29211-1429
General Phone: (803) 750-9561
General Fax: (803) 551-0903
General/National Adv. E-mail: rsavely@scpress.org
Primary Website: http://www.scnewspapernetwork.com/
Year Established: 1985
Note: Represents all South Carolina newspapers in placement of classified and display advertising
Personnel: Randall Savely (Director of Opertions)
Parent company (for newspapers): S.C. Press Association

TENNESSEE

SOUTHEASTERN ADVERTISING PUBLISHERS ASSOCIATION

Street address 1: 104 Westland Dr
Street address 3: Columbia
Street address state: TN
Zip/Postal code: 38401-6522
County: Maury
Country: USA
Mailing address: 104 Westland Dr
Mailing city: Columbia
Mailing state: TN
Mailing zip: 38401-6522
General Phone: (931) 223-5708
General Fax: (888) 450-8329
General/National Adv. E-mail: info@sapatoday.com
Primary Website: www.sapatoday.com
Year Established: 1979
Note: Classified advertising for 75 publications in 10 Southeastern states. Display Network also available.
Personnel: Douglas Fry (Exec. Dir.)

TEXAS

ALLEN

TEXCAP

Street address 1: 1226 Newberry Dr
Street address 3: Allen
Street address state: TX
Zip/Postal code: 75013-3669
County: Collin
Country: USA
Mailing address: 570 Dula St
Mailing city: Alvin
Mailing state: TX
Mailing zip: 77511-2942
General Phone: (972) 741-6258
General Fax: (866) 822-4920
General/National Adv. E-mail: jack@tcnatoday.com
Primary Website: www.tcnatoday.com
Year Established: 1964
Note: Classified advertising for 109 publications. In cooperation with Texas Community Newspapers Assoc
Personnel: Dick Colvin (Exec. Dir.)

WASHINGTON

ALLIED DAILY NEWSPAPERS OF WASHINGTON

Street address 1: 1110 Capitol Way S
Street address 3: Olympia
Street address state: WA
Zip/Postal code: 98501-2251
County: Thurston
Country: USA
Mailing address: 1110 Capitol Way S
Mailing city: Olympia
Mailing state: WA
Mailing zip: 98501-2251
General Phone: (360) 943-9960
General Fax: (360) 943-9962
General/National Adv. E-mail: anewspaper@aol.com
Personnel: Rowland Thompson (Exec. Dir.)

PACIFIC NORTHWEST ASSOCIATION OF WANT AD NEWSPAPERS (PNAWAN) & WESTERN REGIONAL ADVERTISING PROGRAM (WRAP)

Street address 1: 304 W 3rd Ave
Street address 2: C/O Exchange Publishing
Street address 3: Spokane
Street address state: WA
Zip/Postal code: 99201-4314
County: Spokane
Country: USA
Mailing address: PO Box 427
Mailing city: Spokane
Mailing state: WA
Mailing zip: 99210
General Phone: (509) 922-3456
General Fax: (509) 455-7940
Advertising Phone: 509-922-3456
Advertising Fax: 509-455-7940
General/National Adv. E-mail: Ads@PNAWAN.org
Display Adv. E-mail: Kylah@ExchangePublishing.com
Primary Website: www.RegionalAds.org
Year Established: 1977
Note: We are audited and verified by the Circulation Verification Council annually. PNAWAN headquarters are located at the offices of hosting member publication, Exchange Publishing, in Spokane, WA.
Personnel: Kylah Strohte (Executive Director of the Pacific Northwest Association of Want Ad Newspapers (PNAWAN) & Western Regional Advertising Program (WRAP)); PNAWAN Office
Parent company (for newspapers): Exchange Publishing, LLC

WISCONSIN

FOND DU LAC

PUBLISHERS DEVELOPMENT SERVICE

Street address 1: PO Box 1256
Street address 3: Fond Du Lac
Street address state: WI
Zip/Postal code: 54936-1256
County: Fond Du Lac
Country: USA
Mailing address: PO Box 1256
Mailing city: Fond Du Lac
Mailing state: WI
Mailing zip: 54936-1256
General Phone: (920) 922-4864
General Fax: (920) 922-0861
General/National Adv. E-mail: janelle@pdsadnet.com
Primary Website: www.pdsadnet.com
Year Established: 1978
Note: Display advertising for 122 publications. In cooperation with Wisconsin Free Community Papers
Personnel: Janelle Anderson (CEO); Jeanne Schmal (Gen. Mgr.); Kathy Braun (Classified Sales Mgr.)

LENA

GREAT NORTHERN CONNECTION

Street address 1: 8703 Midway Rd
Street address 3: Lena
Street address state: WI
Zip/Postal code: 54139-9769
County: Oconto
Country: USA
Mailing address: 8703 Midway Rd
Mailing city: Lena
Mailing state: WI
Mailing zip: 54139-9769
General Phone: (920) 829-5145
General/National Adv. E-mail: classifieds@greatnorthernconn.com
Primary Website: www.greatnorthernconn.com
Year Established: 1985
Note: Represents 35 publications in northeastern Wisconsin and upper peninsula Michigan
Personnel: Char Meier (Adv. Contact)

WISCONSIN NEWSPAPER ASSOCIATION

Street address 1: 34 Schroeder Ct
Street address 2: Ste 220
Street address 3: Madison
Street address state: WI
Zip/Postal code: 53711-2528
County: Dane
Country: USA
General Phone: (608) 283-7620
General Fax: (608) 283-7631
General/National Adv. E-mail: wna@wnanews.com
Primary Website: www.wnanews.com
Year Established: 1853
Note: Represents 34 daily and over 225 weekly and specialty newspapers
Personnel: Beth Bennett (Exec. Dir.); Denise Guttery (Media Services Dir.); James Debilzen (Communications Dir.); Julia Hunter (Member Services Dir.)

PROFESSIONAL, BUSINESS AND SPECIAL SERVICES

ARKANSAS

THE DAILY RECORD

Street address 1: 300 S Izard St
Street address 3: Little Rock
Street address state: AR
Zip/Postal code: 72201-2114
County: Pulaski
Country: USA
Mailing address: PO Box 3595
Mailing city: Little Rock
Mailing state: AR
Mailing zip: 72203-3595
General Phone: (501) 374-5103
General Fax: (501) 372-3048
General/National Adv. E-mail: bobby@dailydata.com
Display Adv. E-mail: jedwards@dailydata.com
Editorial e-mail: editor@dailydata.com
Primary Website: www.dailyrecord.us
Year Established: 1925
News Services: NNS, TMS, DRNW, INS
Advertising (Open Inch Rate) Weekday/Saturday: Column Inch Rate - $20.00
Avg Paid Circ: 3210
Avg Free Circ: 25
Audit Date: 40643
Personnel: Bill F. Rector (Pub.); Jay Edwards (Adv./Mktg. Dir.); Bobby Burton (Gen. Mgr.); Robin Hill (Comptroller)

ARIZONA

THE RECORD REPORTER

Street address 1: 2025 N 3rd St
Street address 2: Ste 155
Street address 3: Phoenix
Street address state: AZ
Zip/Postal code: 85004-1425
County: Maricopa
Country: USA
General Phone: (602) 417-9900
General Fax: (602) 417-9910
General/National Adv. E-mail: Diane_Heuel@dailyjournal.com
Display Adv. E-mail: record_reporter@dailyjournal.com
Editorial e-mail: diane_heuel@dailyjournal.com
Primary Website: www.recordreporter.com
Year Established: 1914
Area Served - City: 85005
Published: Mon`Wed`Fri
Personnel: Diane Heuel (Pub.); Christopher Gilfillan (Ed.)
Parent company (for newspapers): DAILY JOURNAL CORPORATION

THE DAILY TERRITORIAL

Street address 1: 7225 N. Mona Lisa Rd.
Street address 2: #125
Street address 3: Tucson
Street address state: AZ
Zip/Postal code: 85741
County: Pima
Country: USA
Mailing address: 7225 N. Mona Lisa Rd., #125
Mailing city: Tucson
Mailing state: AZ
Mailing zip: 85741
General Phone: (520) 797-4384
General Fax: (520) 575-8891
Advertising Phone: (520) 294-1200
Editorail Phone: (520) 294-1200
General/National Adv. E-mail: tucsoneditor@tucsonlocalmedia.com
Display Adv. E-mail: classifieds@tucsonlocalmedia.com
Classified Adv. E-mail: jahearn@azbiz.com
Editorial e-mail: tucsoneditor@tucsonlocalmedia.com
Primary Website: www.azbiz.com
Year Established: 1966
News Services: American Newspaper Representatives Inc..
Area Served - City: 856-857
Advertising (Open Inch Rate) Weekday/Saturday: Open inch rate $5.45
Mechanical available: Offset; Black and 3 ROP colors; insert accepted; page cutoffs - 22 3/4.
Mechanical specifications: Type page 10 1/4 x 13; E - 4 cols, 2 3/8, 1/8 between; A - 4 cols, 2 3/8, 1/8 between; C - 6 cols, 1 1/2, 3/16 between.
Published: Mon`Tues`Wed`Thur`Fri
Weekday Frequency: m
Avg Paid Circ: 753
Audit By: Sworn/Estimate/Non-Audited
Audit Date: 43806
Pressroom Equipment: Lines -- 6-HI/V-15A; Atlas/Web Leader 2000;
Mailroom Eqipment: Counter Stackers -- BG/Count-O-Veyor; Tying Machines -- 2-Ace/Tyer; Address Machine -- 1-Ch/612.;
Buisness Equipment: NCR/LAN Sys
Classified Equipment: Hardware -- Mk/3000, 1-PC.;
Display Equipment: Hardware -- APP/Mac; Printers -- APP/Mac LaserWriter II, HP/Laserwriter 4MV (11x17);
Display Software: Ad Make-up Applications -- Aldus/PageMaker, Aldus/Freehand; Layout Software -- Mk.
Editorial Equipment: Hardware -- 1-Mk/3000, 10-PC/Mk.
Production Equipment: Hardware -- Microtek/Scanmaker Plus, HP/Laserwriter 4MV (11x17), Pre Press/Panther Plus 46; Cameras -- 1-SCREEN/Companica-6500D, 1-AG/20 x 24; Scanners -- Umax/Powerlook II
Production Software: Adobe/PageMaker 6.5.
Personnel: Jason Joseph (Pres./Pub.); Laura Horvath (Circulation Manager & Special Events Manager); Meredith Hansen (Sales Admin); Jim Nintzel (News Editor); Logan Burtch-Buus (Ed.); Casey Anderson (Art Dir./Associate Pub.); Pamela Laramie (Bookkeeping)
Parent company (for newspapers): Wick Communications

CALIFORNIA

DAILY COMMERCE

Street address 1: 915 E 1st St
Street address 3: Los Angeles
Street address state: CA
Zip/Postal code: 90012-4050
County: Los Angeles
Country: USA
Mailing address: PO Box 54026
Mailing city: Los Angeles
Mailing state: CA
Mailing zip: 90054-0026
General Phone: (213) 229-5300
General Fax: (213) 229 5481
Advertising Phone: (213) 229-5511
Advertising Fax: (213) 229 5481
Editorail Phone: (213) 229-5558
Editorial Fax: (213) 229-5462
General/National Adv. E-mail: audreymiller@dailyjournal.com
Primary Website: www.dailyjournal.com
Year Established: 1888
News Services: AP, LAT-WP, NYT.
Special Editions: Special Focus (Monthly).
Syndicated Publications: Real Estate in Review (Monthly).
Advertising (Open Inch Rate) Weekday/Saturday: Open inch rate $12.00
Mechanical available: Offset; Black and 4 ROP colors; insert accepted; page cutoffs - 11.
Mechanical specifications: Type page 10 x 13 1/2; E - 4 cols, 2, 1/4 between; A - 4 cols, 2 3/8, 1/2 between; C - 3 cols, 3, 1/2 between.
Published: Mon`Tues`Wed`Thur`Fri
Weekday Frequency: e
Avg Paid Circ: 1254
Audit Date: 43806
Classified Equipment: Hardware -- AT.;
Editorial Equipment: Hardware -- AT, IBM/486, Viewsonic/20 inch monitor; Printers -- HP/LaserJet
Editorial Software: APT/ACT, Microsoft 2.1, QPS 3.1.
Production Equipment: Hardware -- 3-COM/8600.
Personnel: Gerald L. Salzman (Pub.); Audrey Miller (Adv. Rep.); Ray Chagolla (Circ. Mgr.); Lisa Churchill (Ed.); Ky Tu (Mgmt. Info Servs. Mgr.); Manuel Azuiler (Prodn. Mgr.)

DAILY VARIETY

Street address 1: 5900 Wilshire Blvd
Street address 2: Ste 3100
Street address 3: Los Angeles
Street address state: CA
Zip/Postal code: 90036-5030
County: Los Angeles
Country: USA
Mailing address: 5900 Wilshire Blvd Ste 3100
Mailing city: Los Angeles
Mailing state: CA
Mailing zip: 90036-5805
General Phone: (323) 617-9100
Advertising Phone: (323) 857-6600
Advertising Fax: (323) 932-0393
Editorail Phone: (323) 965-4476
Display Adv. E-mail: advertising@variety.com
Primary Website: www.variety.com
News Services: DJ, AP
Advertising (Open Inch Rate) Weekday/Saturday: Open inch rate $216.00
Audit Date: 43806
Personnel: Charles C. Koones (Grp. Vice Pres./Pub.); Madelyn Hammond (CMO, Variety Entertainment Grp.); Peter Bart; Craig Hitchcock (Adv. Dir., West Coast Sales); Dan Hart; Christopher Wessel (Circ. Dir.); Joseph Brescia (Circ. Mgr.); Timothy M. Gray (Grp. Ed.); Leo Wolinsky (Ed.); Ted Johnson (Mng. Ed.); Phil Gallo (Assoc. Ed.); Stuart Levine (Assoc. Ed., Special Reports); Kirstin Wilder (Asst. Mng. Ed.); Cynthia Littleton (Deputy News Ed.); Lindsay Chaney (Sr. Ed.); Patricia Saperstein (Sr. Ed.); Steve Chagollan (Sr. Ed., Special Reports); Sharon Swart (Sr. Ed., Special Reports); Michael Schneider

INVESTOR'S BUSINESS DAILY

Street address 1: 12655 Beatrice St
Street address 3: Los Angeles
Street address state: CA
Zip/Postal code: 90066-7300
County: Los Angeles
Country: USA
Mailing address: 12655 Beatrice St
Mailing city: Los Angeles
Mailing state: CA
Mailing zip: 90066-7303
General Phone: (310) 448-6700
General Fax: (310) 577-7301
Advertising Phone: (310) 448-6700
Advertising Fax: (310) 577-7301
Editorail Phone: (310) 448-6373
Editorial Fax: (310) 577-7350
Editorial e-mail: IBDnews@investors.com
Primary Website: www.investors.com
Year Established: 1984
News Services: AP
Delivery Methods: Mail`Newsstand`Carrier`Racks
Area Served - City: all
Market Information: Split run.
Mechanical available: Web Offset; Black and 3 ROP colors; insert accepted; page cutoffs - 22.
Mechanical specifications: Type page 11 5/8 x 20 3/4; E - 6 cols, 1 7/8, 1/8 between; A - 6 cols, 1 7/8, 1/8 between; C - 8 cols, 1 2/3, 1/16 between.
Published: Mon`Tues`Wed`Thur`Fri
Weekday Frequency: m
Avg Paid Circ: 113547
Avg Free Circ: 5572
Audit By: AAM
Audit Date: 12/31/2015
Pressroom Equipment: Lines -- 13-G/Urbanite single width 1992, 13-RKW/U5055 single width 1992, 3-RKW/U5055 single width 1994; Press Drive -- 2-Fin/SPC 3000 1992, 1-Fin/SPC 3000 1994; Folders -- 1-RKW/U5055; Pasters --3-Jardis/FP4540 1994, 10-Jardis/FP4540.
Mailroom Eqipment: Counter Stackers -- Id/NS660, Id/2100; Tying Machines -- OVL/JP80, OVL/Constellation K-101, OVL/Constellation 415, 2-OVL/JB40; Address Machine -- KAN/500 BL2, Barstrom, Scitex/Ink Jet 5000.;
Buisness Equipment: Bs/A9
Classified Equipment: Hardware -- PC;
Classified Software: Admax, Classpag 8.0.
Display Equipment: Hardware -- HAS, APP/Mac, PC; Printers -- HP/5SI, Linotype-Hell/Linotronic 500, XIT;
Display Software: Ad Make-up Applications -- Adobe/PageMaker, Admax 6.5, QPS/QuarkXPress 3.32, HAS/Tops 5 2.4, Adobe/Illustrator 6.0, SCS; Layout Software -- HAS, APP/Mac, Layout/8000.
Editorial Equipment: Hardware -- APP/Mac, HP/5SI; Printers -- Printronix/P 600, HP/LaserJet 4, HP/LaserJet 5
Editorial Software: HAS/Tops 5 2.4.
Production Equipment: Hardware -- W, III/3750, SCREEN/Photace DS C 260D; Cameras -- SCREEN/Photace DS C 260D; Scanners -- CD, ECR/Autokon, 2-III/3750
Production Software: HAS/Tops 5 2.4.
Personnel: Margo Schuster (Vice Pres., Customer Rel.); Kathy Murray (Director, Advertising Operations); Janice Janendo (Adv. Mgr., Opns. (E. Coast)); Chris Gessel (Exec. Ed.); Susan Warfel (Mng. Ed.); Mike Krey (Technology Bureau Chief, Silicon Valley); Terry Jones (Assoc. Ed.); Mary Ann Edwards (Graphic Arts Ed.); Ken Hoover (New America Ed.); Doug Rogers (Mutual Funds/Personal Finance Ed.); Ed Carson (To The Point Ed.); Mark Sharar (Prodn. Ed.); Ralph Perrini (Vice Pres., Mktg.); Harlan Ratzky (Vice Pres., Internet Mktg.); Doug Fuller (Circ. Vice Pres.); Wesley F. Mann (Ed.); Bucky Fox (Leaders Ed.); Ken Popovich (To The Point Ed.); Terri Chiodo (Vice Pres./Nat'l Adv. Dir.); Ken Brown (Asst. Ed.)

METROPOLITAN NEWS-ENTERPRISE

Street address 1: 210 S Spring St
Street address 3: Los Angeles
Street address state: CA
Zip/Postal code: 90012-3710
County: Los Angeles
Country: USA
Mailing address: 210 S Spring St
Mailing city: Los Angeles
Mailing state: CA
Mailing zip: 90012-3710
General Phone: (213) 346-0033
General Fax: (213) 687-3886
General/National Adv. E-mail: news@metnews.com
Primary Website: www.metnews.com
Year Established: 90012
News Services: AP
Advertising (Open Inch Rate) Weekday/Saturday: Open inch rate $6.00
Personnel: Jo-Ann W. Grace (Co-Pub.); Rodger M. Grace (Co-Pub.); S. John Babigan (Gen. Mgr.); Vahn C. Babigan (Asst. Mgr.)

THE HOLLYWOOD REPORTER

Street address 1: 5700 Wilshire Blvd
Street address 2: Ste 500
Street address 3: Los Angeles
Street address state: CA
Zip/Postal code: 90036-3767
County: Los Angeles
Country: USA
Mailing address: 5700 Wilshire Blvd, Suite 500
Mailing city: Los Angeles
Mailing state: CA
Mailing zip: 90036-3767
General Phone: (323) 525-2000
Advertising Phone: (323) 525-2013
Advertising Fax: (323) 525-2372
Editorail Phone: (323) 525-2130
Editorial Fax: (323) 525-2377
General/National Adv. E-mail: subscriptions@thr.com
Editorial e-mail: thrnews@thr.com

Primary Website: www.hollywoodreporter.com
Year Established: 1930
News Services: AP
Advertising (Open Inch Rate) Weekday/Saturday: Open inch rate $100.00(fri)(classified)
Personnel: Eric Mika; Rose Einstein (Vice Pres./Assoc. Pub., Sales/Mktg.); Katie Fillingame (Audience Mktg. Dir.); Elizabeth Guider (Ed.); David Morgan; Mike Barnes (Mng. Ed.); Scott McKenzie (Vice Pres., Digital Content); Gregg Kilday (Film Ed.); Steve Brennan; Erik Pedersen (News Ed); .Nellie Andreeva

THE LOS ANGELES DAILY JOURNAL

Street address 1: 915 E 1st St
Street address 3: Los Angeles
Street address state: CA
Zip/Postal code: 90012-4050
County: Los Angeles
Country: USA
Mailing address: 915 E 1st St
Mailing city: Los Angeles
Mailing state: CA
Mailing zip: 90012-4042
General Phone: (213) 229-5300
General Fax: (213) 229-5481
Editorial Fax: (213) 229-5462
Primary Website: www.dailyjournal.com
News Services: AP, NYT, CNS, McClatchy
Advertising (Open Inch Rate) Weekday/Saturday: Open inch rate $69.16 (page)
Personnel: Charles T. Munger (Chrmn. of the Bd.); J.P. Guerin (Vice Chrmn. of the Bd.); Gerald Salzman (Pub.); Audrey Miller (Adv. Dir.); Ramond Chagolla; Martin Berg (Ed.)

WOMEN'S WEAR DAILY

Street address 1: 11175 Santa Monica Blvd
Street address 3: Los Angeles
Street address state: CA
Zip/Postal code: 90025
County: New York
Country: USA
Mailing address: 11175 Santa Monica Blvd
Mailing city: Los Angeles
Mailing state: CA
Mailing zip: 90025
General Phone: (310) 484-2536
Primary Website: www.wwd.com
Year Established: 1910
Advertising (Open Inch Rate) Weekday/Saturday: Open inch rate $322.00
Avg Paid Circ: 56562
Audit Date: 9/30/2011
Personnel: Patrick McCarthy (Chrmn./Editorial Dir.); Gina Sanders (Pres./CEO, Fairchild Fashion Grp.); Robert Sauerberg; Christine Guilfoyle (Pub.); Dale Reich; Ed Nardoza (Ed. in Chief); Richard Rosen (Mng. Ed.); Dianne Pogoda (Mng. Ed., Special Reports); Cristina Mojca (Prodn. Mgr., Distr.)

DODGE CONSTRUCTION NEWS GREENSHEET

Street address 1: 1333 S Mayflower Ave
Street address 2: Fl 3
Street address 3: Monrovia
Street address state: CA
Zip/Postal code: 91016-4066
County: Los Angeles
Country: USA
Mailing address: 1333 S Mayflower Ave Fl 3
Mailing city: Monrovia
Mailing state: CA
Mailing zip: 91016-4066
General Phone: (626) 932-6161
General Fax: (626) 932-6163
Editorail Phone: (626) 932-6175
Editorial Fax: (626) 932-6163
Primary Website: www.construction.com
Year Established: 91016
Advertising (Open Inch Rate) Weekday/Saturday: Open inch rate $36.90 (display); $25.00 (classified)
Personnel: James McGraw (Pub.)

OAKLAND

THE INTER-CITY EXPRESS

Street address 1: 1109 Oak St
Street address 3: Oakland
Street address state: CA
Zip/Postal code: 94607-4904
County: Alameda
Country: USA
Mailing address: 1109 Oak St Ste 103
Mailing city: Oakland
Mailing state: CA
Mailing zip: 94607-4917
General Phone: (510) 272-4747
General Fax: (510) 465-1576
Primary Website: www.intercityexpress.news/home.cfm
Personnel: Neil Fields (Pub.); Dan Gougherty (Adv. Dir.); Tonya Peacock (Adv. Mgr., Legal); Tom Barkley (Ed.); Ronald McNees

THE DAILY RECORDER

Street address 1: 901 H St
Street address 2: Ste 312
Street address 3: Sacramento
Street address state: CA
Zip/Postal code: 95814-1808
County: Sacramento
Country: USA
Mailing address: PO Box 1048
Mailing city: Sacramento
Mailing state: CA
Mailing zip: 95812-1048
General Phone: (916) 444-2355
General Fax: (916) 444-0636
Advertising Phone: (800) 652-1700
General/National Adv. E-mail: daily_recorder@dailyjournal.com
Editorial e-mail: jt_long@dailyjournal.com
Primary Website: www.dailyjournal.com
Year Established: 1901
News Services: AP, dj
Advertising (Open Inch Rate) Weekday/Saturday: Open inch rate $26.00
Personnel: Jerry Salzman (Pres./Pub.); Raymond Chagolla (Cor. Office Dir.); Dorothy Salzman (Personnel Dir.); Michael Gottlieb (Ed.); Tom Barragan; Houay Keobouth (Prodn. Designer)

THE DAILY TRANSCRIPT

Street address 1: 2131 3rd Ave
Street address 3: San Diego
Street address state: CA
Zip/Postal code: 92101-2021
County: San Diego
Country: USA
Mailing address: PO Box 85469
Mailing city: San Diego
Mailing state: CA
Mailing zip: 92186-5469
General Phone: (619) 232-4381
General Fax: (619) 239-5716
Advertising Phone: (619) 232-4381
Advertising Fax: (619) 239-4312
Editorail Phone: (619) 232-4381
Editorial Fax: (619) 236-8126
General/National Adv. E-mail: editor@sddt.com
Display Adv. E-mail: sales@sddt.com
Classified Adv. E-mail: contact@sddt.com
Editorial e-mail: editor@sddt.com
Primary Website: www.sddt.com
Year Established: 1886
News Services: AP, Bloomberg.
Special Editions: Soaring Dimensions (Aug); San Diego Sourcebook (Dec); Commercial Real Estate Report (Jan); Health Care (Jun); San Diego Business Resource Guide (May); Inside Biotech (Oct); Architecture & Design (Sept).
Special Weekly Sections: Weekend Watch (Fri); Business Matters (Mon); High Performance (Thur); Tech Talk (Tues); Law Briefs (Wed).
Syndicated Publications: Monday Memo (Mon); The Lenders (Thur).
Delivery Methods: Mail`Carrier`Racks
Area Served - City: San Diego & Riverside Counties
Advertising (Open Inch Rate) Weekday/Saturday: Open inch rate $100.00
Market Information: ADS.
Mechanical available: Offset; Black and 3 ROP colors; insert accepted; page cutoffs - 21 1/2.
Mechanical specifications: Type page 13 x 21 1/2; E - 6 cols, 2 1/16, 1/8 between; A - 6 cols, 2 1/16, 1/8 between; C - 8 cols, 1 1/2, 1/8 between.
Published: Mon`Tues`Wed`Thur`Fri
Weekday Frequency: m
Avg Paid Circ: 6404
Audit Date: 43806
Pressroom Equipment: Lines -- 5-KP/News King; Ryobi/2800 CD 11X17; Folders -- 1-KP/2:1.;
Mailroom Eqipment: Counter Stackers -- 1-BG/Count-O-Veyor 105; Inserters & Stuffers -- MM/327 4 Station; Tying Machines -- MLN/Spirit Model 257; Address Machine -- KR.;
Buisness Equipment: HP/3000 Micro XE
Buisness Software: CJ
Classified Equipment: Hardware -- APP/Mac;
Classified Software: Baseview.
Display Equipment: Hardware -- 3-APP/Mac IIcx, APP/Mac Radius Monitor; Printers -- APP/Mac LaserWriter II NTX;
Display Software: Layout Software -- HP/3000.
Editorial Equipment: Hardware -- APP/Mac
Editorial Software: Mircosoft/Word.
Production Equipment: Hardware -- Nu/Carbon; Cameras -- R, LE/48D 24 x 48
Production Software: QPS/QuarkXPress.
Personnel: Robert Loomis (Pub./CEO); Patricia Techaira (Mgr., HR); Christine Tran (Dir., Mktg.); Shelley Barry (Circ. Mgr.); Andrea Lane (Adv. Dir., Classified); Joe Guerin (Ed. in Chief); Shelly Barry (Circ. Mgr.); Joseph Schmitt; Joseph Guerin (Ed.); George Chamberlin (Exec. Ed.); Richard Spaulding (Real Estate Ed.); Joey Schmitt (Dir., Info Systems); Steve Lovelace (Prodn. Mgr.); Cathy Krueger

SAN FRANCISCO DAILY JOURNAL

Street address 1: 44 Montgomery St
Street address 2: Ste 500
Street address 3: San Francisco
Street address state: CA
Zip/Postal code: 94104-4607
County: San Francisco
Country: USA
Mailing address: 44 Montgomery St Ste 500
Mailing city: San Francisco
Mailing state: CA
Mailing zip: 94104-4607
General Phone: (415) 296-2400
General Fax: (415) 296-2440
Primary Website: www.dailyjournal.com
News Services: AP
Advertising (Open Inch Rate) Weekday/Saturday: Open inch rate $754.00 (quarter page)
Personnel: David Houston (Ed.); Craig Anderson (Ed.)

THE RECORDER

Street address 1: 1035 Market St
Street address 2: Ste 500
Street address 3: San Francisco
Street address state: CA
Zip/Postal code: 94103-1650
County: San Francisco
Country: USA
Mailing address: 1035 Market St Ste 500
Mailing city: San Francisco
Mailing state: CA
Mailing zip: 94103-1650
General Phone: (415) 749-5400
General Fax: (415) 749-5449
Advertising Phone: (415) 749-5444
Advertising Fax: (415) 749-5566
Editorial Fax: (415) 749-5549
General/National Adv. E-mail: recorder_editor@alm.com
Primary Website: www.therecorder.com
Year Established: 1877
News Services: AP
Advertising (Open Inch Rate) Weekday/Saturday: Open inch rate $3,200.00 (Full Page Display)
Personnel: Chris Braun (Pub.); Janice Tang (Controller); Patrick Vigil (Adv. Mgr., Classified); Jim Tamietti (Adv. Mgr., Display); Robert Salapuddin; Heather Ragsdale (Adv. Coord., Display); John Cosmides (Mktg. Dir.); Ed Vergara (Circ. Mgr.); Scott Graham; George Forcier (Mng. Ed.); Tess Herrmann (Prodn. Mgr./Art Dir.)

SAN FERNANDO VALLEY BUSINESS JOURNAL

Street address 1: 21550 Oxnard St
Street address 2: Ste 540
Street address 3: Woodland Hills
Street address state: CA
Zip/Postal code: 91367
County: Los Angeles
Country: USA
Mailing address: 21550 Oxnard St
Mailing city: Woodland Hills
Mailing state: CA
Mailing zip: 91367
General Phone: 818-676-1750
General Fax: 818-676-1747
General/National Adv. E-mail: circulation@labusinessjournal.com
Display Adv. E-mail: dglezerman@sfvbj.com
Editorial e-mail: ccrumpley@sfvbj.com
Primary Website: sfvbj.com
Year Established: 2001
Avg Paid Circ: 2673
Avg Free Circ: 2060
Audit Date: 12/16/2018
Personnel: Charles Crumpley (Pub.); Diane Glezerman (Adv.); Sarah Ewald (Circ.)

COLORADO

THE DAILY JOURNAL

Street address 1: 1114 W 7th Ave
Street address 2: Ste 100
Street address 3: Denver
Street address state: CO
Zip/Postal code: 80204-4455
County: Denver
Country: USA
Mailing address: 1114 W 7th Ave Ste 100
Mailing city: Denver
Mailing state: CO
Mailing zip: 80204-4455
General Phone: (303) 756-9995
General Fax: (303) 756-4465
Advertising Phone: (303) 584-6737
Advertising Fax: (303) 584-6717
Editorail Phone: (303) 584-6724
Editorial Fax: (303) 756-4465
Primary Website: www.colorado.construction.com
Year Established: 1897
Advertising (Open Inch Rate) Weekday/Saturday: Open inch rate $25.20
Personnel: Open inch rate $25.20 John; John Rhoades (Adv. Dir.); Michael Branigan (Adv. Mgr.); Melissa Leslie (Ed.); Mark Shaw

DISTRICT OF COLUMBIA

ROLLCALL

Street address 1: 1201 Pennsylvania Ave, NW
Street address 2: Suite 600
Street address 3: Washington
Street address state: DC
Zip/Postal code: 20004
County: District Of Columbia
Country: USA
Mailing address: 1201 Pennsylvania Ave, NW, Suite 600
Mailing city: Washington
Mailing state: DC
Mailing zip: 20004
General Phone: (202) 650-6500
General Fax: (202) 824-0902
General/National Adv. E-mail: customerservice@cqrollcall.com
Display Adv. E-mail: advertisedept@cqrollcall.com
Editorial e-mail: tips@rollcall.com
Primary Website: www.rollcall.com
Year Established: 1945
Personnel: Laurie Battaglia (Pub.)

FLORIDA

ADVANCED INTERACTIVE MEDIA GROUP, LLC

Street address 1: 402 Spring Valley Rd
Street address 3: Altamonte Springs
Street address state: FL

Zip/Postal code: 32714-5845
County: Seminole
Country: USA
Mailing address: 402 Spring Valley Rd
Mailing city: Altamonte Springs
Mailing state: FL
Mailing zip: 32714
General Phone: (407) 788-2780
General/National Adv. E-mail: pzollman@aimgroup.com
Primary Website: www.aimgroup.com
Year Established: 1997
Area Served - City: Global business intelligence
Industry: Consulting Services Industry Trade Publication Conferences --- Automotive advertising, recruitment advertising and technology
Product or Service: Consultants`Publisher/Media
Note: The AIM Group is a global team of consulting experts in classified advertising, marketplaces and interactive media. We help publishers grow their businesses through strategic and tactical support. We publish AIM Group Marketplaces Report, the international business intelligence service that is often called "the bible of the classified advertising and marketplace industry." We work with news media publishers, dot-coms, print classified publishers, yellow page publishers, broadcasters and technology vendors worldwide to help develop, launch and grow revenue-generating services. We are first and foremost "consultants who publish," not "publishers who do a little consulting on the side." Most of our consulting work is performed on a proprietary basis, so our clients often see only a small fraction of our work-product. We offer solutions for companies planning their strategies, increasing revenue, market share, and in developing products and packing strategies to grow their business. We help build interactive products and services; we don't just talk about them based on flimsy research. We support investors and analysts trying to determine the health of a company, or to find companies ripe for investment or acquisition. Our team includes long-time senior executives, so we work with senior executives to help them understand where their interactive-media and classified services need to evolve. We've been sales reps and sales managers, so we can help sales teams grow and develop traditional and interactive media services. Our writer / analysts get to the heart of the matter, and understand the business inside and out. We work with clients globally. Our worldwide team of almost 40 people follows the evolution in interactive media and classified advertising more closely than anyone else.
Personnel: Peter M. Zollman (Founding Principal); Jim Townsend (Editorial Director); Katja Riefler (Europe Director); Rob Paterson (Principal, director of consulting); Diana Bogdan; Jonathan Turpin (Senior principal)

MIAMI DAILY BUSINESS REVIEW

Street address 1: 1 SE 3rd Ave
Street address 2: Ste 900
Street address 3: Miami
Street address state: FL
Zip/Postal code: 33131-1706
County: Miami-Dade
Country: USA
Mailing address: PO Box 10589
Mailing city: Miami
Mailing state: FL
Mailing zip: 33101-0589
General Phone: (305) 377-3721
General Fax: (305) 374-8474
Advertising Phone: (305) 347-6623
Advertising Fax: (305) 347-6644
Editorail Phone: (305) 347-6694
Editorial Fax: (305) 347-6626
General/National Adv. E-mail: DailyBusinessReview@alm.com
Display Adv. E-mail: ccurbelo@alm.com
Editorial e-mail: dlyons@alm.com
Primary Website: www.dailybusinessreview.com
Year Established: 1926
News Services: AP, Bloomberg, Florida News Service
Advertising (Open Inch Rate) Weekday/Saturday: Varies: http://www.dailybusinessreview.com/advertising.jsp
Advertising (Open inch rate) Sunday: N/A
Market Information: Miami-Dade, law and commercial real estate
Note: See Daily Business Review editions in Broward and Palm Beach, FL.
Personnel: Chris Mobley (Group Publisher, FL/GA/TX); Jeff Fried (Associate Publisher/Chief Financial Officer); Carlos Curbelo (Director of Advertising); David Lyons (Editor-in-Chief); Jay Rees (Business Editor); Catherine Wilson (Law Editor); John Michael Rindo (Director of Creative Services); Guillermo Garcia (Director of Operations & MIS); John Hernandez (Web Adminstrator); Sookie Williams (Vice President/Miami-Dade Legal & Court Relations)
Parent company (for newspapers): ALM Media

PALM BEACH DAILY BUSINESS REVIEW

Street address 1: 1 SE 3rd Ave
Street address 2: Ste 900
Street address 3: Miami
Street address state: FL
Zip/Postal code: 33131-1706
County: Miami-Dade
Country: USA
Mailing address: 1 SE 3rd Ave
Mailing city: Miami
Mailing state: FL
Mailing zip: 33131-1700
General Phone: (305) 377-3721
General Fax: (561) 820-2077
Advertising Phone: (305) 347-6623
Advertising Fax: (305) 347-6644
Editorail Phone: (305) 347-6694
Editorial Fax: (305) 347-6626
General/National Adv. E-mail: DailyBusinessReview@alm.com
Display Adv. E-mail: ccurbelo@alm.com
Editorial e-mail: dlyons@alm.com
Primary Website: www.dailybusinessreview.com
Year Established: 1979
News Services: AP, Bloomberg, Florida News Service
Advertising (Open Inch Rate) Weekday/Saturday: http://www.dailybusinessreview.com/advertising.jsp
Advertising (Open inch rate) Sunday: N/A
Market Information: Palm Beach County, law and commercial real estate
Note: See Daily Business Reviews editions in Broward and Miami, FL.
Personnel: Chris Mobley (Group Publisher, FL/GA/TX); Jeff Fried (Associate Publisher/Chief Financial Officer); David Lyons (Editor-in-Chief); Deborah Mullin (Vice President/Broward & Palm Beach Legals); Carlos Curbelo (Director of Advertising); Annette Martinez (Group Subscriptions Manager); John Hernandez (Web Administrator); Jay Rees (Business Editor); Cathy Wilson (Law Editor); Stephanie Hemmerich (Director of Client Development); Adam Kaplan (Audience Development Manager)
Parent company (for newspapers): ALM Media

OPS PREMEDIA

Street address 1: 6465 33rd Ave. N
Street address 3: Saint Petersburg
Street address state: FL
Zip/Postal code: 33710
County: Pinellas
Country: USA
General Phone: 727-510-5269
General Fax: 727-381-5061
General/National Adv. E-mail: greg@ops-projects.com
Primary Website: www.opspremedia.com
Year Established: 2008
Area Served - City: State of Florida
Published Other: We produce weeklies and monthlies
Note: We are a source for ad design, production and pagination for a umber of publications

GEORGIA

DAILY REPORT

Street address 1: 190 Pryor St SW
Street address 3: Atlanta
Street address state: GA
Zip/Postal code: 30303-3607
County: Fulton
Country: USA
Mailing address: 190 Pryor St SW
Mailing city: Atlanta
Mailing state: GA
Mailing zip: 30303-3607
General Phone: (404) 521-1227
General Fax: (404) 523-5924
General/National Adv. E-mail: fcdr@amlaw.com
Primary Website: www.dailyreportonline.com
Year Established: 1890
Advertising (Open Inch Rate) Weekday/Saturday: Open inch rate $1,800.00 (page)
Personnel: Sarah Wagner (Office Mgr.); Mischelle Grant (Adv. Dir.); Ed Bean (Assoc. Pub.); Jonathan Ringel (Mng. Ed.); Jason Bennitt (Art. Dir.); Wayne Curtis (Pub.)

FULTON COUNTY DAILY REPORT

Street address 1: 190 Pryor St SW
Street address 3: Atlanta
Street address state: GA
Zip/Postal code: 30303-3607
County: Fulton
Country: USA
Mailing address: 190 PRYOR ST SW
Mailing city: ATLANTA
Mailing state: GA
Mailing zip: 30303-3685
General Phone: (404) 521-1227
Advertising Phone: (404) 419-2870
Advertising Fax: (404) 419 - 2819
General/National Adv. E-mail: lsimcoe@alm.com
Primary Website: www.dailyreportonline.com
Delivery Methods: Mail`Newsstand`Carrier`Racks
Own Printing Facility: N
Commercial printers: Y
Published: Mon`Tues`Wed`Thur`Fri`Sat`Sun
Weekday Frequency: m
Saturday Frequency: m
Avg Paid Circ: 2805
Avg Free Circ: 225
Sat. Circulation Paid: 3095
Sat. Circulation Free: 225
Sun. Circulation Paid: 3095
Sun. Circulation Free: 225
Audit By: VAC
Audit Date: 12/31/2016
Personnel: Ed Bean (Editor); Wayne Curtis (Group Publisher); Scott Pitman (Systems Director); George Haj (Regional Editor-in-Chief); Jonathan Ringel (Mng. Ed.)
Parent company (for newspapers): ALM

ILLINOIS

CHICAGO DAILY LAW BULLETIN

Street address 1: 415 N State St
Street address 3: Chicago
Street address state: IL
Zip/Postal code: 60654-4607
County: Cook
Country: USA
Mailing address: 415 N State St
Mailing city: Chicago
Mailing state: IL
Mailing zip: 60654-4674
General Phone: (312) 644-7800
General Fax: (312) 644-4255
General/National Adv. E-mail: displayads@lbpc.com
Primary Website: www.lawbulletin.com
News Services: AP, NYT
Advertising (Open Inch Rate) Weekday/Saturday: Open inch rate $26.40 (Classified), $2,588.00 (Full Page Display)
Personnel: Brewster Macfarland (Pres./CEO); Neil Breen (Exec. Vice Pres.); James Banich; Bernie Judge (Consultant); Mark Menzies (Adv. Sr. Dir., Sales/Mktg.); Stephen Brown (Mng. Ed.); Fred Faulkner; Adam Music; Patrick Milhizer; Sandy Macfarland (Chmn.)

DODGE CONSTRUCTION NEWS CHICAGO

Street address 1: 130 E Randolph St
Street address 2: Fl 14
Street address 3: Chicago
Street address state: IL
Zip/Postal code: 60601-6207
County: Cook
Country: USA
Mailing address: 130 E Randolph St Fl 14
Mailing city: Chicago
Mailing state: IL
Mailing zip: 60601-6207
General Phone: (312) 233-7499
General Fax: (312) 233-7486
Primary Website: www.mediacourier.net
Year Established: 1946
Advertising (Open Inch Rate) Weekday/Saturday: Open inch rate $34.00
Personnel: Craig Barner (Ed.)

INDIANA

COURT & COMMERCIAL RECORD

Street address 1: 41 E Washington St
Street address 2: Ste 200
Street address 3: Indianapolis
Street address state: IN
Zip/Postal code: 46204-3517
County: Marion
Country: USA
Mailing address: 41 E Washington St Ste 200
Mailing city: Indianapolis
Mailing state: IN
Mailing zip: 46204-3517
General Phone: (317) 363-5408
Advertising Fax: (317) 263-5259
General/National Adv. E-mail: judy.smith@ibj.com
Display Adv. E-mail: karuta@ibj.com
Primary Website: www.courtcommercialrecord.com
Year Established: 1895
Advertising (Open Inch Rate) Weekday/Saturday: Notice of Administration: $82.00, Adoptions: $132.00, Car Sales: $44.00, Determine Heirship: $132.00, Dissolution of Corporation: $52.00, Foundation Report: $72.00, Guardianship Notice: $132.00, Final Account or Intermediate Account: $68.00, Name Change: $132.00, Summons Notice of Suit: $132.00
Published: Mon`Wed`Fri
Personnel: Kelly Lucas (Ed./Pub.); Judy Smith (Adv. Mgr.); Bill Wright (Circulation Manager)
Parent company (for newspapers): IBJ Media Corporation

KENTUCKY

THE DAILY RECORD

Street address 1: 436 S 7th St
Street address 2: Ste 300
Street address 3: Louisville
Street address state: KY
Zip/Postal code: 40203-1980
County: Jefferson
Country: USA
Mailing address: PO Box 1062
Mailing city: Louisville
Mailing state: KY
Mailing zip: 40201-1062
General Phone: (502) 583-4471
General Fax: (502) 585-5453
General/National Adv. E-mail: janicep@nacms-c.com
Year Established: 40201
News Services: National Association of Credit Management
Advertising (Open Inch Rate) Weekday/Saturday: Open inch rate $1.20 (legal line)
Personnel: Connie J. Cheak (Pub.); Janice Prichard (Mng. Ed.)

LOUISIANA

GREATER BATON ROUGE BUSINESS REPORT

Street address 1: 9029 Jefferson Hwy
Street address 2: Ste 300
Street address 3: Baton Rouge
Street address state: LA
Zip/Postal code: 70809-2417
County: East Baton Rouge
Country: USA
Mailing address: 9029 Jefferson Hwy

Mailing city: Baton Rouge
Mailing state: LA
Mailing zip: 70809-2417
General Phone: (225) 928-1700
General Fax: (225) 928-5019
Editorial e-mail: editor@businessreport.com
Primary Website: businessreport.com
Year Established: 1982
Delivery Methods: Mail`Newsstand
Area Served - City: 9 parish region
Published: Tues
Published Other: Bi-weekly
Avg Paid Circ: 1585
Avg Free Circ: 8640
Audit By: Sworn/Estimate/Non-Audited
Audit Date: 43112
Personnel: Benjamin Gallagher; Rolfe McCollister (Ed.); Kerrie Richmond (Adv.)

LOUISIANA MEDICAL NEWS

Street address 1: 600 Guilbeau Rd
Street address 2: Ste A
Street address 3: Lafayette
Street address state: LA
Zip/Postal code: 70506-8405
County: Lafayette
Country: USA
Mailing address: PO Box 60010
Mailing city: Lafayette
Mailing state: LA
Mailing zip: 70596-0010
General Phone: (337) 235-5455
General Fax: (337) 232-2959
Display Adv. E-mail: brandycav@gmail.com
Editorial e-mail: editor@medicalnewsinc.com
Primary Website: www.louisianamedicalnews.com

METAIRIE

DAILY JOURNAL OF COMMERCE

Street address 1: 3445 N Causeway Blvd
Street address 2: Ste 901
Street address 3: Metairie
Street address state: LA
Zip/Postal code: 70002-3768
County: Jefferson
Country: USA
Mailing address: 3445 N. Causeway Blvd. Suite 901
Mailing city: Metairie
Mailing state: LA
Mailing zip: 70002
General Phone: (504) 834-9292
General Fax: (504) 832-3534
General/National Adv. E-mail: mail@nopg.com
Display Adv. E-mail: anne.lovas@nopg.com
Editorial e-mail: greg.larose@nopg.com
Primary Website: www.djcgulfcoast.com
Year Established: 1922
Advertising (Open Inch Rate) Weekday/Saturday: Email or call for rates
Personnel: Anne Lovas (Gen. Mgr.); Greg Larose (Managing Editor); Lisa Blossman (Pub); Rebecca Naquin (Asst. Data Ed.); Mark Singletary (Pub.)

MARYLAND

THE DAILY RECORD

Street address 1: 11 E Saratoga St
Street address 3: Baltimore
Street address state: MD
Zip/Postal code: 21202-2115
County: Baltimore City
Country: USA
Mailing address: 11 E SARATOGA ST STE 1
Mailing city: BALTIMORE
Mailing state: MD
Mailing zip: 21202-2199
General Phone: (443) 524-8100
General Fax: (410) 752-2894
Advertising Phone: (443) 524-8100
Advertising Fax: (410) 752-2894
Editorail Phone: (443) 524-8150
Editorial Fax: (410) 752-2894
General/National Adv. E-mail: suzanne.huettner@thedailyrecord.com
Display Adv. E-mail: advertising@thedailyrecord.com
Classified Adv. E-mail: justin.carson@thedailyrecord.com
Editorial e-mail: tbaden@thedailyrecord.com
Primary Website: www.thedailyrecord.com
Year Established: 1888
Area Served - City: 21202-2115
Advertising (Open Inch Rate) Weekday/Saturday: Open inch rate $510.00/Day
Online Advertising Rates - CPM (cost per thousand) by Size: 3:1 Rectangle $355.00/month; Medium Rectangle $430.00/month; Leaderboard $850.00/month
Published: Mon`Tues`Wed`Thur`Fri
Weekday Frequency: m
Avg Paid Circ: 2572
Avg Free Circ: 384
Audit By: CVC
Audit Date: 43806
Personnel: Suzanne Fischer-Huettner (Publisher); Maria Kelly (Comptroller); Tracy Bumba (Audience Dev. Dir.); Shelby Carter (Admin. Asst.); Thomas Baden Jr. (Ed.); Jason Whong (Digital Ed.); Danny Jacobs (Legal Ed.); Maximilian Franz (Sr. Photographer); Jessica Gregg (Special Products Ed.); Darice Miller (Acc. Mgr.); Terri Thompson (Acc. Mgr.); Haley Poling (Mktg. and Event Coord.)
Parent company (for newspapers): The Dolan Company; Gannett

THE DELMARVA FARMER

Street address 1: 7913 Industrial Park Rd
Street address 3: Easton
Street address state: MD
Zip/Postal code: 21601-8603
County: Talbot
Country: USA
Mailing address: 7913 Industrial Park Rd
Mailing city: Easton
Mailing state: MD
Mailing zip: 21601-8603
General Phone: 410-822-3965
General Fax: 410-822-5068
General/National Adv. E-mail: editorial@americanfarm.com
Primary Website: www.americanfarm.com
Year Established: 1978
Personnel: Ralph Hostetter (Pub.)

MICHIGAN

DETROIT LEGAL NEWS

Street address 1: 1409 Allen Dr
Street address 2: Ste B
Street address 3: Troy
Street address state: MI
Zip/Postal code: 48083-4003
County: Oakland
Country: USA
Mailing address: 1409 Allen Dr Ste B
Mailing city: Troy
Mailing state: MI
Mailing zip: 48083-4003
General Phone: (248) 577-6100
General Fax: (248) 577-6111
Advertising Phone: (248) 577-6100
Advertising Fax: (248) 577-6111
Editorail Phone: (248) 577-6100
Editorial Fax: (248) 967-5532
General/National Adv. E-mail: editor@legalnews.com
Display Adv. E-mail: paul@legalnews.com
Editorial e-mail: editor@legalnews.com
Primary Website: www.legalnews.com
News Services: AP
Advertising (Open Inch Rate) Weekday/Saturday: Open inch rate $23.00
Personnel: Ban Ibrahim (Pub.); Brad Thompson (Pres.); Tom Kirvan (Editor-In-Chief); Mary Steinmetz (Circ. Mgr.); Suzanne Ketner (Classified Ads)

MINNESOTA

FINANCE AND COMMERCE

Street address 1: 222 South Ninth Street
Street address 2: Suite 900, Campbell Mithun Tower
Street address 3: Minneapolis
Street address state: MN
Zip/Postal code: 55402
County: Hennepin
Country: USA
Mailing address: 222 South Ninth Street, Suite 900, Campbell Mithun Tower
Mailing city: Minneapolis
Mailing state: MN
Mailing zip: 55402
General Phone: (612) 333-4244
General Fax: (612) 333-3243
Advertising Phone: (612) 584-1534
Editorail Phone: (612) 584-1556
General/National Adv. E-mail: service@bridgetowermedia.com
Primary Website: www.finance-commerce.com
Year Established: 1887
News Services: AP
Advertising (Open Inch Rate) Weekday/Saturday: Open inch rate $12.00
Personnel: Bill Gaier (Pres./Pub.); Kelsey Broadwell (Event Mgr.); Joel Schettler (Ed.); Disa Ehrler (Circulation/Audience Development Mgr.)

SAINT PAUL LEGAL LEDGER

Street address 1: 332 Minnesota St
Street address 2: Ste E1432
Street address 3: Saint Paul
Street address state: MN
Zip/Postal code: 55101-1309
County: Ramsey
Country: USA
Mailing address: 332 Minnesota St Ste E1432
Mailing city: Saint Paul
Mailing state: MN
Mailing zip: 55101-1309
General Phone: (612) 333-4244
General Fax: (651) 222-2640
Editorail Phone: (651) 602-0575
General/National Adv. E-mail: steve.jahn@finance-commerce.com
Primary Website: www.legal-ledger.com
Year Established: 55101-1163
News Services: AP
Advertising (Open Inch Rate) Weekday/Saturday: Open inch rate $12.00 (legal)
Personnel: Patrick Boulay (Pres./Pub.); Barbara Jones (Ed.); Jeff Sjerven (Associate Ed.); Disa Ehrler (Circulation/Audience Development Mgr.)

MISSOURI

ST. JOSEPH DAILY COURIER

Street address 1: 1020 S 10th St
Street address 3: Saint Joseph
Street address state: MO
Zip/Postal code: 64503-2407
County: Buchanan
Country: USA
Mailing address: 1020 S 10th St
Mailing city: Saint Joseph
Mailing state: MO
Mailing zip: 64503-2407
General Phone: (816) 279-3441
General Fax: (816) 279-2091
General/National Adv. E-mail: sjdailycourier@sbcglobal.net
Personnel: Bill Cunningham (Pres./Pub.)

MISSOURI LAWYERS MEDIA

Street address 1: 319 N 4th St Fl 5
Street address 2: 5th Floor
Street address 3: Saint Louis
Street address state: MO
Zip/Postal code: 63102-1907
County: Saint Louis City
Country: USA
Mailing address: 319 N 4th St Fl 5
Mailing city: Saint Louis
Mailing state: MO
Mailing zip: 63102-1907
General Phone: (314) 421-1880
General Fax: (314) 621-1913
Advertising Phone: (314) 558-3260
Advertising Fax: (314) 421-7080
Editorail Phone: (314) 558-3220
Editorial Fax: (314) 621-1913
General/National Adv. E-mail: service@bridgetowermedia.com
Classified Adv. E-mail: lisa.elbe@molawyersmedia.com
Primary Website: www.molawyersmedia.com
Year Established: 1890
Delivery Methods: Mail`Newsstand`Racks
Area Served - City: St. Louis County
Own Printing Facility: Y
Commercial printers: Y
Advertising (Open Inch Rate) Weekday/Saturday: Full Page $2,360.00
Published: Mon`Tues`Wed`Thur`Fri
Weekday Frequency: e
Avg Paid Circ: 4500
Avg Free Circ: 10820
Audit By: Sworn/Estimate/Non-Audited
Audit Date: 43806
Personnel: John Reno (Prod. Mgr.); Liz Irwin (Pub.); Johnny Aguirre (Adv. Dir.)
Parent company (for newspapers): CherryRoad Media

ST. LOUIS DAILY RECORD

Street address 1: 319 N 4th St
Street address 2: Fl 5
Street address 3: Saint Louis
Street address state: MO
Zip/Postal code: 63102-1907
County: Saint Louis City
Country: USA
Mailing address: PO Box 88910
Mailing city: Saint Louis
Mailing state: MO
Mailing zip: 63188-1910
General Phone: (314) 421-1880
General Fax: (314) 421-0436
Advertising Phone: (314) 421-1880
Advertising Fax: (314) 421-7080
Editorail Phone: (314) 421-1880
Editorial Fax: (314) 421-0436
General/National Adv. E-mail: editcopy@thedailyrecord.com
Display Adv. E-mail: johnny.aguirre@molawyersmedia.com
Editorial e-mail: fred.ehrlich@molawyersmedia.com
Primary Website: www.molawyers.com
News Services: RN
Advertising (Open Inch Rate) Weekday/Saturday: Open inch rate $6.56
Personnel: Amanda Passmore (Bus. Mgr.); John M. Reno (Prodn. Mgr.)
Parent company (for newspapers): CherryRoad Media

THE ST. LOUIS COUNTIAN

Street address 1: 319 N 4th St
Street address 3: Saint Louis
Street address state: MO
Zip/Postal code: 63102-1910
County: Saint Louis City
Country: USA
Mailing address: 319 N 4th St
Mailing city: Saint Louis
Mailing state: MO
Mailing zip: 63102-1906
General Phone: (314) 421-1880
General Fax: (314) 421-0436
Advertising Phone: (314) 421-1880
Advertising Fax: (314) 421-0436
Editorail Phone: (314) 421-1880
Editorial Fax: (314) 421-0436
Display Adv. E-mail: carol.prycma@thedailyrecord.com
Editorial e-mail: willc@thedailyrecord.com
Primary Website: www.thedailyrecord.com
News Services: RN
Advertising (Open Inch Rate) Weekday/Saturday: Open inch rate $6.56

Personnel: Richard Gard (Pub.); Amanda Passmore (Bus. Mgr.); Amy Burdge (Adv. Dir.); Stacey Fish (Circ. Mgr.); William B. Connaghan; John M. Reno (Prodn. Mgr.)

THE DAILY EVENTS

Street address 1: 310 W Walnut St
Street address 3: Springfield
Street address state: MO
Zip/Postal code: 65806-2118
County: Greene
Country: USA
Mailing address: PO Box 1
Mailing city: Springfield
Mailing state: MO
Mailing zip: 65801-0001
General Phone: (417) 866-1401
General Fax: (417) 866-1491
General/National Adv. E-mail: info@dailyevents.com
Primary Website: www.thedailyevents.com
Year Established: 1881
News Services: American Court & Commercial Newspapers
Personnel: Wendy Greyowl (Editor); Susan Barnes (Associate Editor); Andrea Donohue (Court Reporter); Jasmin Adams (Circulation Manager); Lindsey Wheeler (Court Reporter); Jeff Schrag (Publisher)

NORTH DAKOTA

GRAND FORKS

AGWEEK

Street address 1: 375 2nd Ave N
Street address 3: Grand Forks
Street address state: ND
Zip/Postal code: 58203-3707
County: Grand Forks
Country: USA
Mailing address: 375 2nd Ave North
Mailing city: Grand Forks
Mailing state: ND
Mailing zip: 58201
General Phone: (800) 477-6572 ext. 1236
Primary Website: www.agweek.com
Published: Tues`Wed`Thur`Fri`Sat`Sun
Personnel: Lisa Gibson (Ed.); Kirsten Stromsodt (Director); Bianca Bina (Managing Ed.)
Parent company (for newspapers): Forum Communications Co.

NEBRASKA

DAILY RECORD

Street address 1: 3323 Leavenworth St
Street address 3: Omaha
Street address state: NE
Zip/Postal code: 68105-1915
County: Douglas
Country: USA
Mailing address: 3323 Leavenworth St
Mailing city: Omaha
Mailing state: NE
Mailing zip: 68105-1900
General Phone: (402) 345-1303
General Fax: (402) 345-2351
General/National Adv. E-mail: ihenningsen@omahadailyrecord.com
Display Adv. E-mail: diane@omahadailyrecord.com
Editorial e-mail: lorraine@omahadailyrecord.com
Primary Website: www.omahadailyrecord.com
Year Established: 1886
News Services: Associated Press, Creators Syndicate, U.S. News Syndicate
Advertising (Open Inch Rate) Weekday/Saturday: Open inch rate $7.25
Note: Bona fide paid circulation in Douglas County in excess of 300 copies, printed in Omaha, NE
Personnel: Lynda K. Henningsen (Publisher); Lorraine Boyd (Editor); Brian Henningsen (Production); Diane Bilek (Advertising (Classified, Display, Website)); Mary Mosher (Legal Editor/Legal Notices); Judy Boyd (Legal Notice)

NEW JERSEY

BAYVILLE

URNER BARRY'S PRICE-CURRENT

Street address 1: 182 Queens Blvd
Street address 3: Bayville
Street address state: NJ
Zip/Postal code: 08721-2741
County: Ocean
Country: USA
Mailing address: PO Box 389
Mailing city: Toms River
Mailing state: NJ
Mailing zip: 08754-0389
General Phone: (732) 240-5330
General Fax: (732) 341-0891
General/National Adv. E-mail: help@urnerbarry.com
Primary Website: www.urnerbarry.com
Advertising (Open Inch Rate) Weekday/Saturday: Open inch rate $17.00
Personnel: Paul B. Brown (Pres.)

NEW YORK

BROOKLYN DAILY EAGLE & DAILY BULLETIN

Street address 1: 16 Court St
Street address 2: Ste 1208
Street address 3: Brooklyn
Street address state: NY
Zip/Postal code: 11241-1012
County: Kings
Country: USA
Mailing address: 16 Court St Ste 1208
Mailing city: Brooklyn
Mailing state: NY
Mailing zip: 11241-1012
General Phone: (718) 858-2300
General Fax: (718) 858-8281
General/National Adv. E-mail: publisher@brooklyneagle.net
Primary Website: www.brooklyneagle.net
Advertising (Open Inch Rate) Weekday/Saturday: Open inch rate $24.00
Personnel: J.D. Hasty (Pub.); Patricia Higgins (Adv. Mgr.); Daniel Doctorow (Adv. Mgr., Legal); Ted Cutler (Adv. Mgr., Special Projects); Sam Howe; Ron Geberer (Mng. Ed.)

AMERICAN BANKER

Street address 1: 1 State St
Street address 2: Fl 27
Street address 3: New York
Street address state: NY
Zip/Postal code: 10004-1561
County: New York
Country: USA
Mailing address: 1 State St Fl 26
Mailing city: New York
Mailing state: NY
Mailing zip: 10004-1483
General Phone: (212) 803-8200
General Fax: (212) 843-9600
Advertising Phone: (212) 803-8691
Editorial Phone: (212) 803-8399
General/National Adv. E-mail: Liesbeth.Severiens@sourcemedia.com
Display Adv. E-mail: Liesbeth.Severiens@sourcemedia.com
Classified Adv. E-mail: joanne.kao@sourcemedia.com
Editorial e-mail: Dean.Anason@sourcemedia.com
Primary Website: www.americanbanker.com
Mthly Avg Views: 1236866
Mthly Avg Unique Visitors: 427786
Year Established: 1835
News Services: AP, RN, UPI
Advertising (Open Inch Rate) Weekday/Saturday: $6,280 (1/2P); $3,735 (1/4P); $3,370 (1/8P)
Published: Mon`Tues`Wed`Thur`Fri
Weekday Frequency: m
Avg Paid Circ: 2373
Audit By: AAM
Audit Date: 9/30/2014
Personnel: James Malkin (CEO); John DelMauro (SVP, Conferences); Neil Weinberg (Ed. in Chief); Marc Hochstein (Ed.-in-chief); Dean Anason (Managing Ed.); Daniel Wolfe (Contributing Editor); Rob Blackwell (Washington Bureau Chief, Regulation & Reform); Joe Adler (Deputy Bureau Chief, Regulation & Reform); Paul Davis (Editor, Comm. Banking); Robert Barba (Deputy Editor, Merger & Acquisitions); Penny Crosman (Ed., Technology); Sarah Todd (Deputy Editor, Bankthink); Alan Kline (Ed., News); Neil Cassidy (Co-Chief, Copy Desk); Mark Sanborne (Co-Chief, Copy Desk); Michael Chu (Senior Art Director); Christopher Wood (Ed., American Banker Online); Brian Lewis (Asst. Ed., American Banker Online); Yong Lim (Asst. Ed., American Banker Online); Zanub Saeed (Managing Ed., American Banker Online); Gary Siegel (Asst. Ed., American Banker Online); Liesbeth Severiens (Adv., Northeast); David Cleworth (Adv., Southeast); Jeff Dembski (Adv., Midwest); Sara Culley (Adv., West); JoAnne Kao (Assoc. Dir. of Classified Sales); Jeannie Nguyen (Mktg. Dir.); Ashley Tavoularis (Mktg. Cord.); Michael Candemeres (Dist. Mgr.); Joylyn Yaw (Reprints, Circ/Cust. Service); Douglas Manoni (CEO, SourceMedia); Rebecca Knoop (CFO, SourceMedia); Minna Rhee (Chief Mktg. & Digital Officer); David Longobardi (EVP & CCO); Karl Elken (EVP & Managing Dir., Banking & Capital Markets); Adam Reinebach (EVP & Managing Dir, Professional Services Group); Ying Wong (SVP, Human Resources/Office Management)
footnotes: General/National Adv. E-mail: SRDS (10/23/2014); Display Adv. E-mail: SRDS (10/23/2014); Classified Adv. e-mail: SRDS (10/23/2014); Editorial e-mail: SRDS (10/23/2014)

AMERICAN METAL MARKET

Street address 1: 225 Park Ave S
Street address 2: Fl 6
Street address 3: New York
Street address state: NY
Zip/Postal code: 10003-1604
County: New York
Country: USA
Mailing address: 225 Park Ave S Fl 6
Mailing city: New York
Mailing state: NY
Mailing zip: 10003-1604
General Phone: (212) 213-6202
General Fax: (212) 213-1804
Advertising Phone: (646) 274-6213
Advertising Fax: (412) 471-7203
Editorial Phone: (212) 213-6202
Editorial Fax: (212) 213-6202
General/National Adv. E-mail: ammnews@amm.com
Display Adv. E-mail: kross@amm.com
Editorial e-mail: jisenberg@amm.com
Primary Website: www.amm.com
Year Established: 1882
News Services: RN, AP, PRN, Bridge News, Business Wire.
Advertising (Open Inch Rate) Weekday/Saturday: Open inch rate $36.48 (page)
Personnel: Raju Daswani; Derek Lundquist (Pricing Dir.); Jo Isenberg-O'loughlin (Mng. Ed.); David Brooks (Sen. Vice Pres./Ed in Chief); Michael Greenlund

DAILY RACING FORM

Street address 1: 708 3rd Ave
Street address 2: Fl 12
Street address 3: New York
Street address state: NY
Zip/Postal code: 10017-4129
County: New York
Country: USA
Mailing address: 708 3rd Ave Fl 12
Mailing city: New York
Mailing state: NY
Mailing zip: 10017-4129
General Phone: (212) 366-7600
Advertising Phone: (212) 366-7607
Editorial Fax: (212) 366-7718
General/National Adv. E-mail: Daily Racing Form publishes several editions nationwide.
Display Adv. E-mail: advert@drf.com
Editorial e-mail: editor@drf.com
Primary Website: www.drf.com
News Services: RN, UPI
Advertising (Open Inch Rate) Weekday/Saturday: Open inch rate $21.75 (national)
Note: Daily Racing Form publishes several editions nationwide.
Personnel: Jim Kostas (Pres./Gen. Mgr.); Steven Crist (Pub.); Jim Hajney (Dir., HR); Jeffery Burch; Joel Brady (Circ. Mgr.); Rich Rosenbush (Ed. in Chief); Irwin Cohen

NEW YORK LAW JOURNAL

Street address 1: 150 East 42nd Street
Street address 2: Mezzanine Level
Street address 3: New York
Street address state: NY
Zip/Postal code: 10017
County: New York
Country: USA
Mailing address: 150 East 42nd Street, Mezzanine Level
Mailing city: New York
Mailing state: NY
Mailing zip: 10017
General Phone: (720) 895-4985
General/National Adv. E-mail: customercare@alm.com
Primary Website: www.nylj.com
Year Established: 10271
News Services: AP
Advertising (Open Inch Rate) Weekday/Saturday: Open inch rate $99.40
Personnel: William L. Pollak (Pres./CEO); Eric Lundberg (CFO); George Dillehay (Pub.); Steve Lincoln (Adv. Vice Pres., Nat'l); Martha Sturgeon; Michael Bennett (Circ. Mktg. Mgr.); Rex Bossert (Ed. in Chief)

THE BOND BUYER

Street address 1: 1 State St
Street address 3: New York
Street address state: NY
Zip/Postal code: 10004-1561
County: New York
Country: USA
Mailing address: 1 State St Fl 26
Mailing city: New York
Mailing state: NY
Mailing zip: 10004-1483
General Phone: (212) 803-8200
General Fax: (212) 803-1592
Advertising Phone: (212) 843-9617
Advertising Fax: (212) 843-9617
Editorial Fax: (212) 843-9614
General/National Adv. E-mail: michael.stanton@sourcemedia.com
Primary Website: www.bondbuyer.com
Advertising (Open Inch Rate) Weekday/Saturday: Open inch rate $168.00
Personnel: Jim Malkin (CEO); Michael Stanton (Pub.); Bill Baneky (Adv. Dir., Legal); Amy Resnick (Ed. in Chief)

THE DAILY DEAL

Street address 1: 14 Wall St
Street address 2: Fl 15
Street address 3: New York
Street address state: NY
Zip/Postal code: 10005-2139
County: New York
Country: USA
Mailing address: 14 Wall St Fl 15
Mailing city: New York
Mailing state: NY
Mailing zip: 10005-2139
General Phone: (212) 313-9200
General Fax: (212) 545-8442
Advertising Phone: (212) 313-9264
Editorial Fax: (212) 313-9293
General/National Adv. E-mail: advertising@thedeal.com
Editorial e-mail: epaisley@thedeal.com; rteitelman@thedeal.com
Primary Website: www.thedeal.com
Personnel: Kevin Worth (Pres./Pub.); Robert Clark (COO); Kurt Streams (CFO); Mike Danforth (Adv. Sr. Mgr.); Tom Spanos; Martha Brown (Dir., Cor. Commun.); Jeff Hartford (Circ. Vice Pres.); Carol Harms (Circ. Sr. Mgr.); Robert Teitelman (Ed. in Chief); Yvette Kantrow (Exec. Ed.); Josh Karlen (Asst. Mng. Ed.); Frances A.

McMorris (Asst. Mng. Ed.); Richard Morgan (Asst. Mng. Ed.); John E. Morris (Asst. Mng. Ed.); Alain Sherter (Asst. Mng. Ed.); Robert Walzer (Asst. Mng. Ed.); Lawrence R Gendron (Art/Design Dir.); Anthony Baido (Statistics Ed.); Adam S. Feinberg (Dir., Info Techology); Thomas Groppe

THE DAILY RECORD

Street address 1: 16 W Main St
Street address 3: Rochester
Street address state: NY
Zip/Postal code: 14614-1602
County: Monroe
Country: USA
Mailing address: PO Box 30006
Mailing city: Rochester
Mailing state: NY
Mailing zip: 14603-3006
General Phone: (585) 232-6920
General Fax: (585) 232-2740
General/National Adv. E-mail: kevin.momot@nydailyrecord.com
Primary Website: www.nydailyrecord.com
Year Established: 14603-3006
News Services: American Court & Commercial Newspapers, National Newspaper Association
Advertising (Open Inch Rate) Weekday/Saturday: Open inch rate $.90 (agency line), $.75 (retail line)
Personnel: James P. Dolan (Chrmn./CEO); Kevin Momot (Vice Pres./Pub.); Scott Pollei (CFO); Tara Buck

OHIO

AKRON LEGAL NEWS

Street address 1: 60 S Summit St
Street address 3: Akron
Street address state: OH
Zip/Postal code: 44308-1719
County: Summit
Country: USA
Mailing address: 60 S Summit St
Mailing city: Akron
Mailing state: OH
Mailing zip: 44308-1775
General Phone: (330) 376-0917
General Fax: (330) 376-7001
Advertising Phone: (330) 376-0917
General/National Adv. E-mail: aln97@apk.net
Primary Website: www.akronlegalnews.com
News Services: AP
Advertising (Open Inch Rate) Weekday/Saturday: Open inch rate $11.00
Personnel: John L. (Pres./Pub.); Robert Heffern (Vice Pres./Gen. Mgr.); Susan Maybury (Ed.); Jason Crosten (Gen. Mngr.)

CINCINNATI COURT INDEX

Street address 1: 119 W Central Pkwy
Street address 2: Fl 2
Street address 3: Cincinnati
Street address state: OH
Zip/Postal code: 45202-1075
County: Hamilton
Country: USA
Mailing address: 119 W Central Pkwy Fl 2
Mailing city: Cincinnati
Mailing state: OH
Mailing zip: 45202-1075
General Phone: (513) 241-1450
General Fax: (513) 684-7821
General/National Adv. E-mail: support@courtindex.com
Primary Website: www.courtindex.com
News Services: AP
Advertising (Open Inch Rate) Weekday/Saturday: Open inch rate $9.00
Personnel: Mark Veatty (Ed.)

THE DAILY LEGAL NEWS AND CLEVELAND RECORDER

Street address 1: 2935 Prospect Ave E
Street address 3: Cleveland
Street address state: OH
Zip/Postal code: 44115-2607
County: Cuyahoga
Country: USA
Mailing address: 2935 Prospect Ave E
Mailing city: Cleveland
Mailing state: OH
Mailing zip: 44115-2688
General Phone: (216) 696-3322
General Fax: (216) 696-6329
General/National Adv. E-mail: dln@dln.com
Display Adv. E-mail: ads@dln.com
Editorial e-mail: editor@dln.com
Primary Website: www.dln.com
Year Established: 1885
News Services: AP, National Newspaper Association, Ohio Newspaper Association
Advertising (Open Inch Rate) Weekday/Saturday: Open inch rate $16.00
Personnel: John D. Karlovec (Sec./Gen. Counsel); Frederick Davis (Controller); Richard Karlovec; Jeffrey B. Karlovec (Mng. Ed.); Lisa Cech (editor@dln.com); Terry Machovina (Prodn. Mgr.); Kurt Gutwein

THE DAILY REPORTER

Street address 1: 580 S High St
Street address 2: Ste 316
Street address 3: Columbus
Street address state: OH
Zip/Postal code: 43215-5659
County: Franklin
Country: USA
Mailing address: 580 S High St Ste 316
Mailing city: Columbus
Mailing state: OH
Mailing zip: 43215-5659
General Phone: (614) 224-4835
General Fax: (614) 224-8649
General/National Adv. E-mail: editor@sourcenews.com
Editorial e-mail: editor@thedailyreporteronline.com
Primary Website: www.thedailyreporteronline.com
Year Established: 1896
News Services: AP
Advertising (Open Inch Rate) Weekday/Saturday: Open inch rate $3,880.00 (Page)
Personnel: Ed Frederickson (Pres.); Dan Shillingburg (Vice Pres./Pub.); Jeff Zeigler (Adv. Mgr., Sales); Cindy Ludlow (Editor); Chris Bailey (Assoc. Ed.)

DAILY COURT REPORTER

Street address 1: 120 W 2nd St
Street address 2: Ste 418
Street address 3: Dayton
Street address state: OH
Zip/Postal code: 45402-1602
County: Montgomery
Country: USA
Mailing address: 120 W 2nd St Ste 418
Mailing city: Dayton
Mailing state: OH
Mailing zip: 45402-1602
General Phone: (419) 470-8602
General Fax: (937) 341-5020
General/National Adv. E-mail: info@thedailycourt.com
Primary Website: www.dailycourt.com
News Services: American Court & Commercial Newspapers
Advertising (Open Inch Rate) Weekday/Saturday: Open inch rate $12.00
Audit Date: 43806
Personnel: Jeffrey Foster (Pres./Pub.); Virginia Steitz (Editorial Mgr.)

TOLEDO

TOLEDO LEGAL NEWS

Street address 1: 247 Gradolph St
Street address 3: Toledo
Street address state: OH
Zip/Postal code: 43612-1421
County: Lucas
Country: USA
Mailing address: PO Box 6816
Mailing city: Toledo
Mailing state: OH
Mailing zip: 43612-0816
General Phone: (419) 470-8600
General Fax: (419) 470-8602
General/National Adv. E-mail: tlnmain@bex.net
Primary Website: www.toledolegalnews.com
Year Established: 1894
Advertising (Open Inch Rate) Weekday/Saturday: Open inch rate $12.00
Audit Date: 43806
Personnel: Jim Schubargo (V.P. Finance)

YOUNGSTOWN

DAILY LEGAL NEWS

Street address 1: 100 E Federal St
Street address 2: Ste 126
Street address 3: Youngstown
Street address state: OH
Zip/Postal code: 44503-1834
County: Mahoning
Country: USA
Mailing address: 100 E Federal St Ste 126
Mailing city: Youngstown
Mailing state: OH
Mailing zip: 44503-1834
General Phone: (330) 747-7777
General Fax: (330) 747-3977
General/National Adv. E-mail: john@akronlegalnews.com
Primary Website: www.dlnnews.com
Advertising (Open Inch Rate) Weekday/Saturday: Open inch rate $5.00
Personnel: Robert G. Heffern (Vice President/Publisher); Kimberly L. Durgala (General Manager)

OKLAHOMA

ENID

GARFIELD COUNTY LEGAL NEWS

Street address 1: 302 E Maine Ave
Street address 3: Enid
Street address state: OK
Zip/Postal code: 73701-5746
County: Garfield
Country: USA
Mailing address: 302 E Maine Ave
Mailing city: Enid
Mailing state: OK
Mailing zip: 73701-5746
General Phone: (580) 234-4739
General Fax: (580) 237-3237
Advertising Phone: (580) 234-4739
Advertising Fax: (580) 237-3237
Editorail Phone: (580) 234-4739
Editorial Fax: (580) 237-3237
General/National Adv. E-mail: info@garfieldcountylegalnews.com
Editorial e-mail: publisher@garfieldcountylegalnews.com
Primary Website: www.garfieldcountylegalnews.com
Year Established: 1913
Area Served - City: Garfield County (OK)
Advertising (Open Inch Rate) Weekday/Saturday: $50.00 ($0.15 per word) (Notice to Creditors)
Published: Mon`Tues`Wed`Thur`Fri
Weekday Frequency: m

THE JOURNAL RECORD

Street address 1: 101 N Robinson Ave
Street address 2: Ste 101
Street address 3: Oklahoma City
Street address state: OK
Zip/Postal code: 73102-5500
County: Oklahoma
Country: USA
Mailing address: PO Box 26370
Mailing city: Oklahoma City
Mailing state: OK
Mailing zip: 73126-0370
General Phone: (405) 235-3100
General Fax: (405) 278-6907
Advertising Phone: (405) 278-2830
Editorail Phone: (405) 278-2850
Editorial Fax: (405) 278-2890
Editorial e-mail: news@journalrecord.com
Primary Website: www.journalrecord.com
Year Established: 1903
News Services: AP
Advertising (Open Inch Rate) Weekday/Saturday: Open inch rate $18.62
Market Information: Daily, statewide business paper
Avg Paid Circ: 2800
Avg Free Circ: 69
Audit Date: 12/31/2012
Personnel: Russell Ray (Ed.); Terri VanHooser (Director of Operations); Sarah Barrow (Advertising Director); Shaun Witt (Audience Development Manager)
Parent company (for newspapers): CherryRoad Media

ONTARIO

DAILY COMMERCIAL NEWS AND CONSTRUCTION RECORD

Street address 1: 500 Hood Rd., 4th Fl.
Street address 3: Markham
Street address state: ON
Zip/Postal code: L3R 9Z3
Country: Canada
Mailing address: 500 Hood Rd., 4th Fl.
Mailing city: Markham
Mailing state: ON
Mailing zip: L3R 9Z3
General Phone: (905) 752-9292
General Fax: (905) 752-5450
General/National Adv. E-mail: bev.akerfeldt@cmdg.com
Display Adv. E-mail: cindy.littler@cmdg.com
Editorial e-mail: john.leckie@cmdg.com
Primary Website: www.dcnonl.com
Advertising (Open Inch Rate) Weekday/Saturday: Open inch rate $63.00 (Canadian)
Personnel: Andrew Cook (Vice Pres./Pub.); Rod Oyco (Circ. Mgr.); Tarin Elbert (Ed.); Todd McGill; Elena Langlois (Adv. Sales Mgr.-Display)

OREGON

DAILY JOURNAL OF COMMERCE

Street address 1: 921 SW Washington St
Street address 2: Ste 210
Street address 3: Portland
Street address state: OR
Zip/Postal code: 97205-2810
County: Multnomah
Country: USA
Mailing address: 921 SW Washington St Ste 210
Mailing city: Portland
Mailing state: OR
Mailing zip: 97205-2810
General Phone: (503) 226-1311
General Fax: (503) 226-1315
Advertising Phone: (503) 226-1311
Advertising Fax: (503) 802-7219
Editorial Fax: (503) 802-7239
General/National Adv. E-mail: newsroom@djcoregon.com
Display Adv. E-mail: rynni.henderson@djcoregon.com
Editorial e-mail: stephanie.basalyga@djcoregon.com
Primary Website: www.djcoregon.com
Year Established: 1872
News Services: AP, RN, TMS
Advertising (Open Inch Rate) Weekday/Saturday: Open inch rate $25.00
Personnel: Stephanie Basalyga (Ed.); Rynni Henderson (Publisher/Vice President)
Parent company (for newspapers): The Dolan Company

PENNSYLVANIA

THE LEGAL INTELLIGENCER

Street address 1: 1617 John F Kennedy Blvd
Street address 2: Ste 1750
Street address 3: Philadelphia
Street address state: PA

Zip/Postal code: 19103-1854
County: Philadelphia
Country: USA
Mailing address: 1617 John F Kennedy Blvd Ste 1750
Mailing city: Philadelphia
Mailing state: PA
Mailing zip: 19103-1854
General Phone: (215) 557-2300
General Fax: (215) 557-2301
Advertising Phone: (215) 557-2359
Advertising Fax: (215) 557-2301
Editorail Phone: (215) 557-2489
Editorial Fax: (215) 557-2301
General/National Adv. E-mail: HGREZLAK@ALM.COM
Display Adv. E-mail: dchalphin@alm.com
Editorial e-mail: hgrezlak@alm.com
Primary Website: www.thelegalintelligencer.com
Mthly Avg Views: 168000
Mthly Avg Unique Visitors: 48029
Year Established: 1843
News Services: AP
Published: Mon`Tues`Wed`Thur`Fri
Note: See media kit for market information.
Personnel: Hal Cohen (Publisher); Donald Chalphin (Associate Publisher)
Parent company (for newspapers): ALM Media

PITTSBURGH LEGAL JOURNAL

Street address 1: 436 7th Ave
Street address 3: Pittsburgh
Street address state: PA
Zip/Postal code: 15219-1826
County: Allegheny
Country: USA
Mailing address: 436 7th Ave Ste 4
Mailing city: Pittsburgh
Mailing state: PA
Mailing zip: 15219-1827
General Phone: (412) 402-6623
General Fax: (412) 320-7965
General/National Adv. E-mail: JPULICE@SCBA.ORG
Primary Website: www.pittsburghlegaljournal.com
Year Established: 1853
Advertising (Open Inch Rate) Weekday/Saturday: Open inch rate $8.75
Published: Mon`Tues`Wed`Thur`Fri
Weekday Frequency: m
Personnel: David Blaner (Exec. Dir.)
Parent company (for newspapers): Pennsylvania NewsMedia Association

RHODE ISLAND

CREATIVE CIRCLE MEDIA SOLUTIONS

Street address 1: 945 Waterman Ave
Street address 3: East Providence
Street address state: RI
Zip/Postal code: 02914-1342
County: Providence
Country: USA
Mailing address: 945 Waterman Ave.
Mailing city: East Providence
Mailing state: RI
Mailing zip: 02914-1342
General Phone: (401) 272-1122
General/National Adv. E-mail: info@creativecirclemedia.com
Primary Website: www.creativecirclemedia.com
Year Established: 1984
Industry: Software: web CMS, advertising, native content; Consulting; Outsourcing; Training; Web and print redesigns; print editorial production platform.
Product or Service: Advertising/Marketing Agency`Circulation`Consultants`Editorial`Graphic/Design Firm`Hardware/Software Supplier`Marketing`Multimedia/Interactive Products`Other Services`Online Service Provider and Internet Hosts
Note: Full service, custom software provider with a dynamic web site CMS, user-contributed content, classifieds, hosting, pay wall, branded content, circulation and print editorial production solutions. We also provide strategic consulting, newsroom training, ad design training, new revenue ideas and high-end outsourcing services. Our Premium Pages are an excellent digital features content service. We also have led more than 750 redesigns of print newspapers and magazines and continue to help publishers redefine their print products.
Personnel: Bill Ostendorf (Pres. & founder); Lynn Rognsvoog (Design director); Tim Benson (Chief Developer); Scott Kingsley (COO); Darryl Greenlee (Developer); Sean Finch (VP/Sales); Greg Boras (National Sales Manager)
Newspaper (for newspapers group): The Sumter Item, Sumter

TENNESSEE

THE DAILY NEWS

Street address 1: 193 Jefferson Ave
Street address 3: Memphis
Street address state: TN
Zip/Postal code: 38103-2322
County: Shelby
Country: USA
Mailing address: 193 JEFFERSON AVE
Mailing city: MEMPHIS
Mailing state: TN
Mailing zip: 38103-2339
General Phone: (901) 523-1561
General Fax: (901) 526-5813
Advertising Phone: (901) 528-5283
Advertising Fax: (901) 526-5813
Editorail Phone: (901) 523-8501
Editorial Fax: (901) 526-5813
General/National Adv. E-mail: jjenkins@memphisdailynews.com
Display Adv. E-mail: jjenkins@memphisdailynews.com
Classified Adv. E-mail: jjenkins@memphisdailynews.com
Editorial e-mail: releases@memphisdailynews.com
Primary Website: www.memphisdailynews.com
Mthly Avg Views: 300000
Mthly Avg Unique Visitors: 100000
Year Established: 1886
News Services: CNS
Delivery Methods: Mail
Area Served - City: Madison, Tipton, Fayette, Shelby
Advertising (Open Inch Rate) Weekday/Saturday: Open inch rate $13.50 (legal)
Online Advertising Rates - CPM (cost per thousand) by Size: Leaderboard (728x90): $550/month; Side Position (250x250): $400/month
Published: Mon`Tues`Wed`Thur`Fri
Weekday Frequency: m
Avg Paid Circ: 1000
Avg Free Circ: 2000
Audit By: Sworn/Estimate/Non-Audited
Audit Date: 43806
Personnel: Don Fancher (Public Notices); Janice Jenkins (Adv. Dir.); Terry Hollahan (Associate Publisher/ Exec. Ed.)
Parent company (for newspapers): The Daily News Publishing Co.

TEXAS

DAILY COMMERCIAL RECORD

Street address 1: 706 Main St
Street address 2: Bsmt
Street address 3: Dallas
Street address state: TX
Zip/Postal code: 75202-3620
County: Dallas
Country: USA
Mailing address: 706 Main St Bsmt
Mailing city: Dallas
Mailing state: TX
Mailing zip: 75202-3699
General Phone: (214) 741-6366
General Fax: (214) 741-6373
General/National Adv. E-mail: dcr@dailycommercialrecord.com
Primary Website: www.dailycommercialrecord.com
Advertising (Open Inch Rate) Weekday/Saturday: Open inch rate $14.76
Personnel: E. Nuel Cates Jr. (Pub.); Emily Cates (Ed.)

COMMERCIAL RECORDER

Street address 1: 3032 S Jones St
Street address 3: Fort Worth
Street address state: TX
Zip/Postal code: 76104-6747
County: Tarrant
Country: USA
Mailing address: PO Box 11038
Mailing city: Fort Worth
Mailing state: TX
Mailing zip: 76134
General Phone: (817) 255-0779
General Fax: (817) 926-5377
Advertising Phone: (817) 255-0779
Editorail Phone: (817) 255-0779
General/National Adv. E-mail: johnybska@gmail.com
Display Adv. E-mail: johnybska@gmail.com
Editorial e-mail: johnybska@gmail.com
Primary Website: www.commercialrecorder.com
Year Established: 1903
Advertising (Open Inch Rate) Weekday/Saturday: Open inch rate $9.00
Personnel: Janet R. Ratcliff (Publisher); John Bondurant (Editor n Chief Assoc. Publisher)

DAILY COURT REVIEW

Street address 1: 8 Greenway Plz
Street address 2: Ste 101
Street address 3: Houston
Street address state: TX
Zip/Postal code: 77046-0830
County: Harris
Country: USA
Mailing address: PO Box 1889
Mailing city: Houston
Mailing state: TX
Mailing zip: 77251-1889
General Phone: (713) 869-5434
General Fax: (713) 869-8887
Editorail Phone: (713) 869-5434
Editorial e-mail: editor@dailycourtreview.com
Primary Website: www.dailycourtreview.com
Year Established: 1889
News Services: RN, National Newspaper Association, Texas Press Association
Advertising (Open Inch Rate) Weekday/Saturday: Open inch rate $16.80
Personnel: Tom Morin (Pub.); Michael Clements (Editor)

THE DAILY COMMERCIAL RECORDER

Street address 1: 301 Avenue E
Street address 3: San Antonio
Street address state: TX
Zip/Postal code: 78205-2006
County: Bexar
Country: USA
Mailing address: P.O. Box 2171
Mailing city: San Antonio
Mailing state: TX
Mailing zip: 78297
General Phone: (210) 250-2438
General Fax: (210) 250-2360
General/National Adv. E-mail: dcr@primetimenewspapers.com
Primary Website: www.primetimenewspapers.com
News Services: ACCN, Creator Syndicates, LAT-WP, National American Press Syndicate, NYT.
Advertising (Open Inch Rate) Weekday/Saturday: Open inch rate $25.00
Personnel: Mickey Urias (General Sales Manager); Cindy Castillo (Legal Coordinator)
Parent company (for newspapers): Hearst Communications, Inc.

WASHINGTON

GAUGER MEDIA SERVICE, INC.

Street address 1: 1034 Bradford Street
Street address 2: P.O. Box 627
Street address 3: Raymond
Street address state: WA
Zip/Postal code: 98577
County: Pacific
Country: USA
Mailing address: P.O. Box 627
Mailing city: Raymond
Mailing state: WA
Mailing zip: 98577
General Phone: (360) 942-3560
General/National Adv. E-mail: dave@gaugermedia.com
Primary Website: www.gaugermedia.com
Year Established: 1987
Personnel: Dave Gauger (Pres/Broker)

TACOMA DAILY INDEX

Street address 1: 402 Tacoma Ave S
Street address 2: Ste 200
Street address 3: Tacoma
Street address state: WA
Zip/Postal code: 98402-5400
County: Pierce
Country: USA
Mailing address: 402 Tacoma Ave S Ste 200
Mailing city: Tacoma
Mailing state: WA
Mailing zip: 98402-5400
General Phone: (253) 627-4853
General Fax: (253) 627-2253
Advertising Phone: (253) 627-4853
Advertising Fax: (253) 627-2253
Editorail Phone: (253) 627-4853
Editorial Fax: (253) 627-2253
General/National Adv. E-mail: legals@tacomadailyindex.com
Display Adv. E-mail: publisher@tacomadailyindex.com
Editorial e-mail: editor@tacomadailyindex.com
Primary Website: www.tacomadailyindex.com
Year Established: 1890
News Services: American Court & Commercial Printing
Advertising (Open Inch Rate) Weekday/Saturday: Open inch rate $9.65
Personnel: Ken Spurrell (Pub.); Matthews Todd
Parent company (for newspapers): Black Press Group Ltd.

DAILY SHIPPING NEWS

Street address 1: 13715 SE Eastridge Dr
Street address 2: Apt 12
Street address 3: Vancouver
Street address state: WA
Zip/Postal code: 98683-4717
County: Clark
Country: USA
Mailing address: 4106 SE Llewellyn St
Mailing city: Portland
Mailing state: OR
Mailing zip: 97222-5870
General Phone: (360) 254-5504
General Fax: (360) 254-7145
General/National Adv. E-mail: dsnews@europa.com
Primary Website: www.wwshipper.com
Year Established: 98607
Advertising (Open Inch Rate) Weekday/Saturday: Open inch rate $10.00
Personnel: Jim Egger (Pub.)

WISCONSIN

THE DAILY REPORTER

Street address 1: 225 E Michigan St
Street address 2: Ste 300
Street address 3: Milwaukee
Street address state: WI
Zip/Postal code: 53202-4900
County: Milwaukee
Country: USA
Mailing address: 225 E. Michigan St.
Mailing city: Milwaukee
Mailing state: WI
Mailing zip: 53202
General Phone: (414) 276-0273
General Fax: (414) 276-4416
Editorail Phone: (414) 225-1807
General/National Adv. E-mail: news@dailyreporter.com
Display Adv. E-mail: squinn@dailyreporter.com
Editorial e-mail: dshaw@dailyreporter.com

Primary Website: www.dailyreporter.com
Year Established: 1897
News Services: AP
Avg Paid Circ: 3105
Personnel: Joe Yovino (Associate Publisher/Editor); Susan Quinn (Advertising Director); Dan Shaw (Managing Editor)
Parent company (for newspapers): BridgeTower Media

WYOMING

CHEYENNE

WYOMING BUSINESS REPORT

Street address 1: 702 W Lincolnway
Street address 3: Cheyenne
Street address state: WY
Zip/Postal code: 82001-4359
County: Laramie
Country: USA
General Phone: (307) 633-3193
General Fax: (307) 633-3191
Display Adv. E-mail: bnelson@wyomingbusinessreport.com
Primary Website: www.wyomingbusinessreport.com
Published: Wed
Personnel: Belinda Nelson (Pub. Dir of Sals); Dionne Roccaforte (Controller)
Parent company (for newspapers): Adams Publishing Group, LLC

U.S. STATE NEWSPAPER ASSOCIATIONS

ALABAMA

ALABAMA PRESS ASSOCIATION

Street address 1: 3324 Independence Dr
Street address 2: Ste 200
Street address 3: Birmingham
Street address state: AL
Zip/Postal code: 35209-5602
Country: USA
Mailing address: 3324 Independence Dr Ste 200
Mailing city: Birmingham
Mailing state: AL
Mailing zip: 35209-5602
General Phone: (205) 871-7737
General Fax: (205) 871-7740
General/National Adv. E-mail: felicia@alabamapress.org
Primary Website: www.alabamapress.org
Year Established: 1871
Note: Elections held in Feb
Personnel: Felicia Mason (Exec. Dir.); Brad English (Adv. Mgr.); Leigh Tortorici (Senior Marketing Rep.); Amy Metzler (Sales/Mktg Exec); Chris McDaniel (Member Services/Network Coordinator)

ARIZONA

ARIZONA NEWSPAPERS ASSOCIATION

Street address 1: 1001 N Central Ave
Street address 2: Ste 670
Street address 3: Phoenix
Street address state: AZ
Zip/Postal code: 85004-1947
County: Maricopa
Country: USA
General Phone: (602) 261-7655
General Fax: (602) 261-7525
Advertising Phone: (602) 261-7655 x112
General/National Adv. E-mail: p.casey@ananews.com
Display Adv. E-mail: p.casey@ananews.com
Primary Website: www.ananews.com
Year Established: 1929
Note: Elections held in Sept. Statewide and national one order/one bill advertising placement service
Personnel: Paula Casey (Exec. Dir.); Julie O'Keefe (Communications Manager); Cindy London (Ad Placement Manager)

CALIFORNIA

CALIFORNIA NEWS PUBLISHERS ASSOCIATION

Street address 1: 2701 K St
Street address 3: Sacramento
Street address state: CA
Zip/Postal code: 95816-5131
County: Sacramento
Country: USA
Mailing address: 2701 K St.
Mailing city: Sacramento
Mailing state: CA
Mailing zip: 95816-5131
General Phone: (916) 288-6000
General Fax: (916) 288-6002
Primary Website: www.cnpa.com
Year Established: 1889
Personnel: Charles Champion (President & CEO); Cecelia Drake (Director of Advertising); Joe Wirt (Director of Affiliate Relations); Paulette Brown-Hinds (VP, Sec/Trea); Cecelia Drake (Director of Advertising); Thomas Newton (Exec. Dir.); Brittney Barsotti (General Counsel); Jim Ewert (Gen. Counsel); Ashley Bryant (Director of Finance); Tiffany Chiang (Marketing Analyst); Jennifer Davee (Accounting Specialist); Simon Birch (Dir. of Membership); Renee Smith (Director of Meetings)

CONNECTICUT

CONNECTICUT DAILY NEWSPAPERS ASSOCIATION

Street address 1: 330 Main St
Street address 2: Fl 3
Street address 3: Hartford
Street address state: CT
Zip/Postal code: 06106-1851
Country: USA
Mailing address: 330 Main St Fl 3
Mailing city: Hartford
Mailing state: CT
Mailing zip: 06106-1851
General Phone: (860) 716-4461
General Fax: (860) 541-6484
Primary Website: www.ctdailynews.com
Year Established: 1904
Note: Elections held in April/May
Personnel: Chris VanDeHoef (Executive Director)

HAWAII

HAWAII PUBLISHERS ASSOCIATION

Street address 1: 500 Ala Moana Blvd
Street address 2: Ste 7-500
Street address 3: Honolulu
Street address state: HI
Zip/Postal code: 96813-4930
Country: USA
Mailing address: 500 Ala Moana Blvd Ste 7500
Mailing city: Honolulu
Mailing state: HI
Mailing zip: 96813-4930
General Phone: (808) 738-4992
General Fax: (808) 664-8892
General/National Adv. E-mail: info@hawaiipublishersassociation.com
Primary Website: www.hawaiipublishersassociation.com
Personnel: Rick Asbach (Executive Director)

IOWA

IOWA NEWSPAPER ASSOCIATION, INC.

Street address 1: 319 E 5th St
Street address 2: Fl 2
Street address 3: Des Moines
Street address state: IA
Zip/Postal code: 50309-1927
Country: USA
Mailing address: 319 E 5th St Fl 2nd
Mailing city: Des Moines
Mailing state: IA
Mailing zip: 50309-1931
General Phone: (515) 244-2145
General Fax: (515) 244-4855
General/National Adv. E-mail: ina@inanews.com
Primary Website: www.inanews.com
Year Established: 1931
Note: Elections held in May
Personnel: Susan Patterson Plank (Exec. Dir.); Brent Steemken (Business Mgr.); Jodi Hulbert (Comm. Dir.); Geof Fischer (Dev. Dir); Samantha Fett (Inside Sales Mgr.); Heidi Geisler (Media Dir.); Jana Shepherd (Program Dir.); Susan James (Tech. & Digital Dev. Mgr.); Ryan Harvey (Pres.); Kaitlyn Van Patten (Sales & Mktg. Assist.)

ILLINOIS

ILLINOIS PRESS ASSOCIATION

Street address 1: 900 Community Dr
Street address 3: Springfield
Street address state: IL
Zip/Postal code: 62703-5180
County: Sangamon
Country: USA
General Phone: (217) 241-1300
General Fax: (217) 241-1301
Advertising Phone: (217) 241-1700
Advertising Fax: (217) 241-1701
General/National Adv. E-mail: ipa@illinoispress.org
Primary Website: www.illinoispress.org
Year Established: 1865
Note: The Illinois Press Advertising Service can place any newspaper product available in Illinois and has several well-established, low-cost networks.
Personnel: Sam Fisher (Pres./CEO); Tracy Spoonmore (CFO); Jeff Holman (Advertising Director); Cindy Bedolli (Administrative Assistant & Member Relations); Ron Kline (Tech & Online Coord.); Melissa Calloway (Dig. Adv. Mgr.); Cindy Bedolli (Admin Assist & Member Rel.)

INDIANA

HOOSIER STATE PRESS ASSOCIATION

Street address 1: 41 E Washington St
Street address 2: Ste 101
Street address 3: Indianapolis
Street address state: IN
Zip/Postal code: 46204-3560
County: Marion
Country: USA
General Phone: (317) 803-4772
General Fax: (317) 624-4428
Display Adv. E-mail: map@hspa.com
Primary Website: www.hspa.com
Year Established: 1933
Note: Represents daily and weekly newspapers in Indiana
Personnel: Stephen Key (Exec. Dir./Gen. Counsel); Pamela Lego (Adv. Dir.); Milissa Tuley (Communications Specialist); Karen Braeckel (HSPA Foundation Dir.); Yvonne Yeadon (Office Mgr.); Shawn Goldsby (Adv. Coord.)

KANSAS

KANSAS PRESS ASSOCIATION

Street address 1: 5423 SW 7th St
Street address 3: Topeka
Street address state: KS
Zip/Postal code: 66606-2330
County: Shawnee
Country: USA
Mailing address: 5423 SW 7th St.
Mailing city: Topeka
Mailing state: KS
Mailing zip: 66606
General Phone: (785) 271-5304
General Fax: (785) 271-7341
General/National Adv. E-mail: info@kspress.com
Display Adv. E-mail: KSAds@kspress.com
Editorial e-mail: info@kspress.com
Primary Website: www.kspress.com
Year Established: 1863
Note: Represents 28 daily and 185 weekly newspapers in Kansas
Personnel: Emily Bradbury (Director of Member Services); Lori Jackson (Admin. Assist./Adv.); Doug Anstaett (Exec. Dir.); Amber Jackson (Adv. Dir.); Judy Beach (Accountant)
Newspaper (for newspapers group): The Oakley Graphic, Oakley; The Iola Register, Iola; The Leader & Times, Liberal; Kansas City Kansan (OOB), Olathe; Coffeyville Journal, Coffeyville; The Manhattan Mercury, Manhattan; Winfield Daily Courier, Winfield; The Arkansas City Traveler, Arkansas City; The Emporia Gazette, Emporia

LOUISIANA

LOUISIANA PRESS ASSOCIATION

Street address 1: 404 Europe St
Street address 3: Baton Rouge
Street address state: LA
Zip/Postal code: 70802-6403
County: East Baton Rouge
Country: USA
General Phone: (225) 344-9309
General Fax: (225) 344-9344
Advertising Phone: (225) 344-9309 x 111
Advertising Fax: (225) 336-9921
Editorial Fax: (225) 346-5060
General/National Adv. E-mail: pam@lapress.com
Display Adv. E-mail: erin@LaPress.com
Primary Website: www.lapress.com
Year Established: 1880
Personnel: Mike Rood (Communications Dir.); Pamela Mitchell (Exec. Dir.); Mitchell-Ann Droge (Dir. of Ops.); Erin Palmintier (Adv. Dir.)

MICHIGAN

MICHIGAN PRESS ASSOCIATION

Street address 1: 827 N Washington Ave
Street address 3: Lansing
Street address state: MI
Zip/Postal code: 48906-5135
County: USA
Country: USA
Mailing address: 827 N Washington Ave
Mailing city: Lansing
Mailing state: MI
Mailing zip: 48906-5199
General Phone: (517) 372-2424
General Fax: (517) 372-2429
General/National Adv. E-mail: mpa@michiganpress.org
Primary Website: www.michiganpress.org
Year Established: 1868
Note: Elections held in Jan
Personnel: Roselie Lucus (Growth & Operations Manager); Lisa McGraw (Public Affairs Manager); Sean Wickham (Design & Communications Specialist); Janet Mendler (Mgr.); James Tarrant (Exec. Dir.); Paul Biondi (Adv. Dir.)
Newspaper (for newspapers group): MNI, Lansing

MINNESOTA

MINNESOTA NEWSPAPER ASSOCIATION

Street address 1: 12 S 6th St
Street address 2: Ste 1120
Street address 3: Minneapolis
Street address state: MN
Zip/Postal code: 55402-1501
Country: USA
Mailing address: 10 S 5th St Ste 1105
Mailing city: Minneapolis
Mailing state: MN
Mailing zip: 55402-1036
General Phone: (612) 332-8844
General Fax: (612) 342-2958
General/National Adv. E-mail: info@mna.org
Display Adv. E-mail: advertising@mna.org
Primary Website: www.mna.org
Year Established: 1867
Note: Convention, trade show and elections in January.
Personnel: Lisa Hills (Executive Director); Dan Lind (Managing Director); Barbara Trebisovsky (Asst. Exec. Dir.); Phil Morin (Advertising Account Manager)

NORTH DAKOTA

NORTH DAKOTA NEWSPAPER ASSOCIATION

Street address 1: 1435 Interstate Loop
Street address 3: Bismarck
Street address state: ND
Zip/Postal code: 58503-0567
County: Burleigh
Country: USA
Mailing address: 1435 Interstate Loop
Mailing city: Bismarck
Mailing state: ND
Mailing zip: 58503-0567
General Phone: (701) 223-6397
General Fax: (701) 223-8185
General/National Adv. E-mail: info@ndna.com
Primary Website: www.ndna.com
Year Established: 1885
Note: Represents daily and weekly newspapers in North Dakota
Personnel: Kelli Richey (Mktg. Dir.); Steve Andrist (Exec. Dir.); Mike Casey (Adv. Dir.); Colleen Park (Adv./Public Notice Coord.); Shari Peterson (Office Coord./Adv. Assist.); Paul Erdelt (NDNA President)

NEW MEXICO

NEW MEXICO PRESS ASSOCIATION

Street address 1: 700 Silver Ave SW
Street address 3: Albuquerque
Street address state: NM
Zip/Postal code: 87102-3019
County: Bernalillo
Country: USA
Mailing address: PO Box 95198
Mailing city: Albuquerque
Mailing state: NM
Mailing zip: 87199-5198
General Phone: (505) 275-1241
General Fax: (505) 275-1449
Advertising Phone: (505) 275-1377
General/National Adv. E-mail: info@nmpress.org
Display Adv. E-mail: Ads@NMPress.org
Primary Website: www.nmpress.org
Note: Elections held in Oct
Personnel: Holly Aguilar (Office Mgr.)
Newspaper (for newspapers group): Hobbs News-Sun, Hobbs; Roswell Daily Record, Roswell; Las Vegas Optic, LAS VEGAS; Lincoln County News, Chandler; Union County Leader, Clayton; Cibola Beacon, Grants; Santa Rosa News (OOB), Santa Rosa; Sierra County Sentinel, Truth Or Consequences; The Rio Rancho Observer, Rio Rancho; The Ruidoso News, Ruidoso; The Raton Range (OOB), Raton; Silver City Daily Press & Independent, Silver City

NEW YORK

NEW YORK PRESS PHOTOGRAPHERS ASSOCIATION, INC.

Street address 1: PO Box 3346
Street address 3: New York
Street address state: NY
Zip/Postal code: 10008-3346
Country: USA
Mailing address: Box 3346 Church Street Station
Mailing city: New York
Mailing state: NY
Mailing zip: 10008-3346
General Phone: (212) 889-6633
General/National Adv. E-mail: office@nyppa.org
Primary Website: www.nyppa.org
Year Established: 1915
Note: Elections held every other year
Personnel: Ray Stubblebine (Trustee); Marc Hermann (Secretary - Historian); Bruce Cotler (President); Todd Maisel (Vice President)

OKLAHOMA

OKLAHOMA PRESS ASSOCIATION

Street address 1: 3601 N Lincoln Blvd
Street address 3: Oklahoma City
Street address state: OK
Zip/Postal code: 73105-5411
Country: USA
Mailing address: 3601 N Lincoln Blvd
Mailing city: Oklahoma City
Mailing state: OK
Mailing zip: 73105-5499
General Phone: (405) 499-0020
General Fax: (405) 499-0048
Advertising Phone: (405) 499-0022
General/National Adv. E-mail: swilkerson@okpress.com
Display Adv. E-mail: lcobb@okpress.com
Primary Website: www.okpress.com
Year Established: 1906
Note: Elections held in June
Personnel: Mark Thomas (Exec. VP); Scott Wilkerson (Office Mgr.); Landon Cobb (Sales Dir.); Lisa Sutliff (Mbr. Serv. Dir.); Jennifer Gilliland (Creat. Serv. Dir.); Keith Burgin (Dig. Clip Serv. Mgr.); Cindy Shea (Adv. Mgr.)

PENNSYLVANIA

MANSI MEDIA

Street address 1: 3899 N Front St
Street address 3: Harrisburg
Street address state: PA
Zip/Postal code: 17110-1583
County: Dauphin
Country: USA
General Phone: (717) 703-3030
General Fax: (717) 703-3033
General/National Adv. E-mail: sales@mansimedia.com
Primary Website: www.mansimedia.com
Note: Represents daily and weekly newspapers and their digital products anywhere in the U.S. and beyond.
Personnel: Lisa Knight (VP/Adv.); Chris Kazlauskas; Wes Snider (Dir. Client Solutions); Ronaldo Davis (Sr. Media Buyer); Matthew Caylor (Dir., Interactive Media); Lindsey Artz (Account Manager); Shannon Mohar (Account Manager); Brian Hitchings (Director, Client Solutions)

RHODE ISLAND

RHODE ISLAND PRESS ASSOCIATION

Street address 1: 282 Doyle ave
Street address 3: Providence
Street address state: RI
Zip/Postal code: 02906
County: Providence
Country: USA
Mailing address: 282 Doyle Avenue
Mailing city: Providence
Mailing state: RI
Mailing zip: 02906
General Phone: (401) 874-4287
General Fax: (401) 874-4450
General/National Adv. E-mail: llevin@uri.edu
Primary Website: www.ripress.org
Year Established: 1886
Note: Elections held in Jan
Personnel: Linda Levin (Secretary); Fran Ostendorf (Treasurer)

SOUTH DAKOTA

SOUTH DAKOTA NEWSPAPER ASSOCIATION

Street address 1: 1125 32nd Ave
Street address 3: Brookings
Street address state: SD
Zip/Postal code: 57006-4707
County: Brookings
Country: USA
Mailing address: 1125 32nd Ave
Mailing city: Brookings
Mailing state: SD
Mailing zip: 57006-4707
General Phone: (605) 692-4300
General/National Adv. E-mail: sdna@sdna.com
Primary Website: www.sdna.com
Year Established: 1882
Note: Elections held in May
Personnel: David Bordewyk (Exec. Dir.); John Brooks (Advertising Sales Director); Nicole Herrig (Business Manager); Sandy DeBeer (Advertising Placement Coordinator)

WISCONSIN

WISCONSIN NEWSPAPER ASSOCIATION

Street address 1: 34 Schroeder Ct
Street address 2: Ste 220
Street address 3: Madison
Street address state: WI
Zip/Postal code: 53711-2528
County: Dane
Country: USA
General Phone: (608) 283-7620
General Fax: (608) 283-7631
General/National Adv. E-mail: wna@wnanews.com
Primary Website: www.wnanews.com
Year Established: 1853
Note: Represents 34 daily and over 225 weekly and specialty newspapers
Personnel: Beth Bennett (Exec. Dir.); Denise Guttery (Media Services Dir.); James Debilzen (Communications Dir.); Julia Hunter (Member Services Dir.)

WEEKLY STATE NEWSPAPER REPRESENTATIVE

ALABAMA NEWSPAPER ADVERTISING SERVICE, INC.

Street address 1: 3324 Independence Dr
Street address 2: Ste 200
Street address city: Birmingham
Street address state: AL
Zip/Postal code: 35209-5602
County: Jefferson
Country: USA
Mailing address: 3324 Independence Dr Ste 200
Mailing city: Birmingham
Mailing state: AL
Mailing zip: 35209-5602
General Phone: (205) 871-7737
General Fax: (205) 871-7740
General/National Adv. E-mail: mail@alabamapress.org
Primary Website: www.alabamapress.org

ANA ADVERTISING SERVICES, INC. (ARIZONA NEWSPAPER ASSOCIATION)

Street address 1: 1001 N Central Ave
Street address 2: Ste 670
Street address city: Phoenix
Street address state: AZ
Zip/Postal code: 85004-1947
County: Maricopa
Country: USA
General Phone: (602) 261-7655
General Fax: (602) 261-7525
General/National Adv. E-mail: office@ananews.com
Primary Website: www.ananews.com
Year Established: 1931

ARKANSAS BUSINESS

Street address 1: 114 Scott St
Street address city: Little Rock
Street address state: AR
Zip/Postal code: 72201-1514
County: Pulaski
Country: USA
Mailing address: PO Box 3686
Mailing city: Little Rock
Mailing state: AR
Mailing zip: 72203-3686
General Phone: (501) 372-1443
General Fax: (501) 375-7933
Display Adv. E-mail: bonnie@abpg.com
Editorial e-mail: mbettis@abpg.com
Primary Website: www.arkansasbusiness.com
Year Established: 1984
Avg Paid Circ: 7500

ARKANSAS PRESS SERVICES

Street address 1: 411 S Victory St
Street address city: Little Rock
Street address state: AR
Zip/Postal code: 72201-2933
County: Pulaski
Country: USA
Mailing address: 411 S Victory St Ste 100
Mailing city: Little Rock
Mailing state: AR
Mailing zip: 72201-2934
General Phone: (501) 374-1500
General Fax: (501) 374-7509
General/National Adv. E-mail: info@arkansaspress.org
Primary Website: www.arkansaspress.org
Year Established: 1873

CNPA ADVERTISING SERVICES

Street address 1: 2000 O St
Street address 2: Ste 120
Street address city: Sacramento
Street address state: CA
Zip/Postal code: 95811-5299
County: Sacramento
Country: USA
Mailing address: 2000 O St Ste 120
Mailing city: Sacramento
Mailing state: CA
Mailing zip: 95811-5299
General Phone: (916) 288-6000
General Fax: (916) 288-6003
General/National Adv. E-mail: bryan@cnpa.com
Primary Website: www.cnpa.com

COMMUNITY PAPERS ADVERTISING NETWORK

Street address 1: 750 W. Genesee St.
Street address city: Syracuse
Street address state: NY
Zip/Postal code: 13204
Mailing address: PO Box 11279
Mailing city: Syracuse
Mailing state: NY
Mailing zip: 13218
General Phone: (315) 472-6007
General Fax: (315) 472-5919
General/National Adv. E-mail: ads@fcpny.com
Primary Website: www.fcpny.org

COMMUNITY PAPERS OF FLORIDA

Street address 1: 12601 SE 53rd Terrace Rd
Street address city: Belleview
Street address state: FL
Zip/Postal code: 34420-5106
County: Marion
Country: USA
Mailing address: PO Box 1149
Mailing city: Summerfield
Mailing state: FL
Mailing zip: 34492-1149
General Phone: (352) 237-3409
General Fax: (352) 347-3384
General/National Adv. E-mail: djneuharth@aol.com
Primary Website: www.communitypapersofflorida.com
Year Established: 1960

COMMUNITY PAPERS OF MICHIGAN, INC.

Street address 1: 5000 Northwind Dr
Street address 2: Ste 240
Street address city: East Lansing
Street address state: MI
Zip/Postal code: 48823-5032
County: Ingham
Country: USA
Mailing address: 5000 Northwind Dr Ste 240
Mailing city: East Lansing
Mailing state: MI
Mailing zip: 48823-5032
General Phone: (800) 783-0267
General Fax: (517) 333-3322
General/National Adv. E-mail: jackguza@cpapersmi.com
Primary Website: www.communitypapersofmichigan.com

CUSTOMIZED NEWSPAPER ADVERTISING (IOWA)

Street address 1: 319 E 5th St
Street address city: Des Moines
Street address state: IA
Zip/Postal code: 50309-1927
County: Polk
Country: USA
Mailing address: 319 E 5th St
Mailing city: Des Moines
Mailing state: IA
Mailing zip: 50309-1927
General Phone: (515) 244-2145
General Fax: (515) 244-4855
Primary Website: www.cnaads.com; www.inanews.com

FLORIDA PRESS SERVICE, INC.

Street address 1: 336 E College Ave
Street address 2: Ste 203
Street address city: Tallahassee
Street address state: FL
Zip/Postal code: 32301-1559
County: Leon
Country: USA
Mailing address: 336 E College Ave Ste 203
Mailing city: Tallahassee
Mailing state: FL
Mailing zip: 32301-1559
General Phone: (850) 222-5790
General Fax: (850) 222-4498
General/National Adv. E-mail: fps-info@flpress.com
Primary Website: www.flpress.com

GEORGIA NEWSPAPER SERVICE, INC.

Street address 1: 3066 Mercer University Dr
Street address 2: Ste 200
Street address city: Atlanta
Street address state: GA
Zip/Postal code: 30341-4137
County: Dekalb
Country: USA
Mailing address: 3066 Mercer University Dr Ste 200
Mailing city: Atlanta
Mailing state: GA
Mailing zip: 30341-4137
General Phone: (770) 454-6776
General Fax: (770) 454-6778
General/National Adv. E-mail: mail@gapress.org
Primary Website: www.gapress.org

GRANT COUNTY HERALD

Street address 1: 35 Central Ave N
Street address city: Elbow Lake
Street address state: MN
Zip/Postal code: 56531-4123
County: Grant
Country: USA
Mailing address: PO BOX 2019
Mailing city: ELBOW LAKE
Mailing state: MN
Mailing zip: 56531-2019
General Phone: (218) 685-5326
General Fax: (218) 685-5327
Advertising Phone: (218) 685-5326
Advertising Fax: (218) 685-5327
Editorial Phone: (218) 685-5326
Editorial Fax: (218) 685-5327
General/National Adv. E-mail: gcanne@runestone.net
Display Adv. E-mail: gcanne@runestone.net
Classified Adv. e-mail: gcanne@runestone.net
Editorial e-mail: gcnews@runestone.net
Primary Website: www.grantherald.com
Year Established: 1879
Avg Paid Circ: 1900
Avg Free Circ: 35

GREAT NORTHERN CONNECTION

Street address 1: 8703 Midway Rd
Street address city: Lena
Street address state: WI
Zip/Postal code: 54139-9769
County: Oconto
Country: USA
Mailing address: 8703 Midway Rd
Mailing city: Lena
Mailing state: WI
Mailing zip: 54139-9769
General Phone: (920) 829-5145
General/National Adv. E-mail: classifieds@greatnorthernconn.com
Primary Website: www.greatnorthernconn.com
Year Established: 1985

HAWAII PUBLISHERS ASSOCIATION

Street address 1: 500 Ala Moana Blvd
Street address 2: Ste 7-500
Street address city: Honolulu
Street address state: HI
Zip/Postal code: 96813-4930
Country: USA
Mailing address: 500 Ala Moana Blvd Ste 7500
Mailing city: Honolulu
Mailing state: HI
Mailing zip: 96813-4930
General Phone: (808) 738-4992
General Fax: (808) 664-8892
General/National Adv. E-mail: info@hawaiipublishersassociation.com
Primary Website: www.hawaiipublishersassociation.com

HITCHINGS & CO.

Street address 1: 580 W Germantown Pike
Street address 2: Ste 108
Street address city: Plymouth Meeting
Street address state: PA
Zip/Postal code: 19462-1370
County: Montgomery
Country: USA
Mailing address: Plymouth Plz., 580 W. Germantown Pk., Ste. 108
Mailing city: Plymouth Meeting
Mailing state: PA
Mailing zip: 19462
General Phone: (610) 941-3555
General Fax: (610) 941-1289
General/National Adv. E-mail: brian@phillyareapapers.com
Primary Website: www.phillyareapapers.com

KENTUCKY PRESS SERVICE, INC.

Street address 1: 101 Consumer Ln
Street address city: Frankfort
Street address state: KY
Zip/Postal code: 40601-8489
County: Franklin
Country: USA
Mailing address: 101 Consumer Ln
Mailing city: Frankfort
Mailing state: KY
Mailing zip: 40601-8489
General Phone: (502) 223-8821
General Fax: (502) 875-2624
General/National Adv. E-mail: dthompson@kypress.com
Display Adv. E-mail: rmccarty@kypress.com, hwillard@kypress.com
Classified Adv. e-mail: rmccarty@kypress.com, hwillard@kypress.com
Primary Website: www.kypress.com
Year Established: 1959

LATINO PRESS

Street address 1: 6301 Michigan Ave
Street address city: Detroit
Street address state: MI
Zip/Postal code: 48210-2954
County: Wayne
Country: USA
Mailing address: 6301 Michigan Ave
Mailing city: Detroit
Mailing state: MI
Mailing zip: 48210-2954
General Phone: (313) 361-3000
General Fax: (313) 361-3001
Advertising Phone: (313) 361-3000
Editorial Phone: (313) 361-3002
General/National Adv. E-mail: clau@latinodetroit.com
Display Adv. E-mail: marketing@latinodetroit.com
Classified Adv. e-mail: clau@latinodetroit.com
Editorial e-mail: editorial@latinodetroit.com
Primary Website: www.latinodetroit.com
Mthly Avg Views: 16000
Mthly Avg Unique Visitors: 19000
Year Established: 1993
Avg Paid Circ: 2500
Avg Free Circ: 15000

LONG ISLAND ADVANCE

Street address 1: 20 Medford Ave
Street address 2: Ste 112
Street address city: Patchogue

Street address state: NY
Zip/Postal code: 11772-1220
County: Suffolk
Country: USA
Mailing address: PO BOX 780
Mailing city: PATCHOGUE
Mailing state: NY
Mailing zip: 11772-0780
General Phone: (631) 475-1000
General Fax: (631) 475-1565
Advertising Phone: (631) 475-1000 x28
Editorial Phone: (631) 475-1000 x21
General/National Adv. E-mail: ttlia@optonline.net
Display Adv. E-mail: ttlia@optonline.net
Classified Adv. e-mail: classifieds@longislandadvance.net
Editorial e-mail: advletters@optonline.net
Primary Website: longislandadvance.net
Mthly Avg Views: 80000
Mthly Avg Unique Visitors: 12000
Year Established: 1871
Avg Paid Circ: 5000

LOUISIANA PRESS ASSOCIATION

Street address 1: 404 Europe St
Street address city: Baton Rouge
Street address state: LA
Zip/Postal code: 70802-6403
County: East Baton Rouge
Country: USA
General Phone: (225) 344-9309
General Fax: (225) 344-9344
Advertising Phone: (225) 344-9309 x 111
Advertising Fax: (225) 336-9921
Editorial Fax: (225) 346-5060
General/National Adv. E-mail: pam@lapress.com
Display Adv. E-mail: erin@LaPress.com
Primary Website: www.lapress.com
Year Established: 1880

MACNET

Street address 1: 150 Valley Rd.
Street address city: Bernville
Zip/Postal code: 19506
Mailing address: PO Box 408
Mailing city: Hamburg
Mailing state: PA
Mailing zip: 19526-0408
General Phone: (800) 450-7227
General Fax: (610) 743-8500
General/National Adv. E-mail: info@macpa.net
Primary Website: www.macpa.net; www.macnetonline.com

MANSI MEDIA

Street address 1: 3899 N Front St
Street address city: Harrisburg
Street address state: PA
Zip/Postal code: 17110-1583
County: Dauphin
Country: USA
General Phone: (717) 703-3030
General Fax: (717) 703-3033
General/National Adv. E-mail: sales@mansimedia.com
Primary Website: www.mansimedia.com

MIDWEST FREE COMMUNITY PAPERS

Street address 1: PO Box 1350
Street address city: Iowa City
Street address state: IA
Zip/Postal code: 52244-1350
County: Johnson
Country: USA
Mailing address: PO Box 1350
Mailing city: Iowa City
Mailing state: IA
Mailing zip: 52244-1350
General Phone: (319) 341-4352
General Fax: (319) 341-4358
General/National Adv. E-mail: mfcp@mchsi.com
Primary Website: www.mfcp.org
Year Established: 1955

MISSISSIPPI PRESS SERVICES, INC.

Street address 1: 371 Edgewood Terrace Dr
Street address city: Jackson
Street address state: MS
Zip/Postal code: 39206-6217
County: Hinds
Country: USA
Mailing address: 371 Edgewood Terrace Dr.
Mailing city: Jackson
Mailing state: MS
Mailing zip: 39206-6217
General Phone: (601) 981-3060
General Fax: (601) 981-3676
Advertising Phone: (601) 981-3060 ext 2
General/National Adv. E-mail: admin@mspress.org
Primary Website: www.mspress.org
Year Established: 1978

MISSOURI PRESS SERVICE, INC.

Street address 1: 802 Locust St
Street address city: Columbia
Street address state: MO
Zip/Postal code: 65201-4888
County: Boone
Country: USA
Mailing address: 802 Locust St
Mailing city: Columbia
Mailing state: MO
Mailing zip: 65201-7799
General Phone: (573) 449-4167
General Fax: (573) 874-5894
General/National Adv. E-mail: mmaassen@socket.net
Display Adv. E-mail: mopressads@socket.net
Editorial e-mail: mbarba@mopress.com
Primary Website: www.mopress.com
Year Established: 1867

MNI

Street address 1: 827 N Washington Ave
Street address city: Lansing
Street address state: MI
Zip/Postal code: 48906-5135
County: Ingham
Country: USA
Mailing address: 827 N Washington Ave
Mailing city: Lansing
Mailing state: MI
Mailing zip: 48906-5135
General Phone: (517) 372-2424
General Fax: (517) 372-2429
General/National Adv. E-mail: mpa@michiganpress.org
Primary Website: www.michiganpress.org
Year Established: 1868

MONTANA NEWSPAPER ADVERTISING SERVICE, INC.

Street address 1: 825 Great Northern Blvd
Street address 2: Ste 202
Street address city: Helena
Street address state: MT
Zip/Postal code: 59601-3340
County: Lewis And Clark
Country: USA
Mailing address: 825 Great Northern Blvd Ste 202
Mailing city: Helena
Mailing state: MT
Mailing zip: 59601-3358
General Phone: (406) 443-2850
General Fax: (406) 443-2860
General/National Adv. E-mail: randy@mtnewspapers.com
Primary Website: www.mtnewspapers.com
Year Established: 1955

NEBRASKA PRESS ADVERTISING SERVICE

Street address 1: 845 S St
Street address city: Lincoln
Street address state: NE
Zip/Postal code: 68508-1226
County: Lancaster
Country: USA
General Phone: (402) 476-2851
General Fax: (402) 476-2942
General/National Adv. E-mail: nebpress@nebpress.com
Primary Website: www.nebpress.com
Year Established: 1879

NENPA AD NETWORK (NEW ENGLAND NEWSPAPER AND PRESS ASSOCIATION)

Street address 1: 1 Arrow Dr
Street address 2: Ste 6
Street address city: Woburn
Street address state: MA
Zip/Postal code: 01801-2039
County: Middlesex
Country: USA
Mailing address: 1 Arrow Drive, Suite 6
Mailing city: Woburn
Mailing state: MA
Mailing zip: 01801
General Phone: (781) 281-2053
General Fax: (339) 999-2174
General/National Adv. E-mail: info@nenpa.com
Primary Website: www.nenpa.com
Year Established: 1930

NEW JERSEY NEWSMEDIA NETWORK (NJNN)

Street address 1: 810 Bear Tavern Rd
Street address 2: Ste 307
Street address city: Ewing
Street address state: NJ
Zip/Postal code: 08628-1022
County: Mercer
Country: USA
Mailing address: 810 Bear Tavern Rd Ste 307
Mailing city: Ewing
Mailing state: NJ
Mailing zip: 08628-1022
General Phone: (609) 406-0600
General Fax: (609) 406-0399
General/National Adv. E-mail: njnn@njpa.org
Primary Website: www.njpa.org/njnn
Year Established: 1991

NEW MEXICO PRESS ASSOCIATION

Street address 1: 700 Silver Ave SW
Street address city: Albuquerque
Street address state: NM
Zip/Postal code: 87102-3019
County: Bernalillo
Country: USA
Mailing address: PO Box 95198
Mailing city: Albuquerque
Mailing state: NM
Mailing zip: 87199-5198
General Phone: (505) 275-1241
General Fax: (505) 275-1449
Advertising Phone: (505) 275-1377
General/National Adv. E-mail: info@nmpress.org
Display Adv. E-mail: Ads@NMPress.org
Primary Website: www.nmpress.org

NEW YORK NEWS PUBLISHERS ASSOCIATION

Street address 1: 252 Hudson Ave
Street address city: Albany
Street address state: NY
Zip/Postal code: 12210-1802
County: Albany
Country: USA
General Phone: (518) 449-1667
General Fax: (518) 449-1667
Primary Website: www.nynpa.com
Year Established: 1927

NEW YORK PRESS SERVICE

Street address 1: 1681 Western Ave
Street address city: Albany
Street address state: NY
Zip/Postal code: 12203-4305
County: Albany
Country: USA
Mailing address: 1681 Western Ave
Mailing city: Albany
Mailing state: NY
Mailing zip: 12203-4340
General Phone: (518) 464-6483
General Fax: (518) 464-6489
General/National Adv. E-mail: nypa@nynewspapers.com
Primary Website: www.nynewspapers.com
Year Established: 1853

NORTH CAROLINA PRESS SERVICE, INC.

Street address 1: 5171 Glenwood Ave
Street address 2: Ste 364
Street address city: Raleigh
Street address state: NC
Zip/Postal code: 27612-3266
County: Wake
Country: USA
Mailing address: 5171 Glenwood Ave Ste 364
Mailing city: Raleigh
Mailing state: NC
Mailing zip: 27612-3266
General Phone: (919) 787-7443
General Fax: (919) 787-5302
Primary Website: www.ncpress.com
Year Established: 1985

NORTH DAKOTA NEWSPAPER ASSOCIATION

Street address 1: 1435 Interstate Loop
Street address city: Bismarck
Street address state: ND
Zip/Postal code: 58503-0567
County: Burleigh
Country: USA
Mailing address: 1435 Interstate Loop
Mailing city: Bismarck
Mailing state: ND
Mailing zip: 58503-0567
General Phone: (701) 223-6397
General Fax: (701) 223-8185
General/National Adv. E-mail: info@ndna.com
Primary Website: www.ndna.com
Year Established: 1885

OHIAD

Street address 1: 395 S. High St.
Street address city: Covington
Street address state: OH
Zip/Postal code: 45318
Mailing address: PO Box 69
Mailing city: Covington
Mailing state: OH
Mailing zip: 45318
General Phone: (937) 473-2028
General Fax: (937) 473-2500
General/National Adv. E-mail: production@woh.rr.com
Primary Website: www.arenspub.com

OHIO NEWSPAPER SERVICES, INC.

Street address 1: 1335 Dublin Rd
Street address 2: Ste 216B
Street address city: Columbus
Street address state: OH
Zip/Postal code: 43215-1000
County: Franklin
Country: USA
Mailing address: 1335 Dublin Rd Ste 216B
Mailing city: Columbus
Mailing state: OH
Mailing zip: 43215-1000
General Phone: (614) 486-6677
General Fax: (614) 486-4940
Primary Website: www.ohionews.org; www.adohio.net
Year Established: 1933

OKLAHOMA PRESS SERVICE

Street address 1: 3601 N Lincoln Blvd
Street address city: Oklahoma City
Street address state: OK
Zip/Postal code: 73105-5411
County: Oklahoma
Country: USA
Mailing address: 3601 N Lincoln Blvd
Mailing city: Oklahoma City
Mailing state: OK
Mailing zip: 73105-5499
General Phone: (405) 524-4421
General Fax: (405) 499-0048
General/National Adv. E-mail: sysop@okpress.com

Primary Website: www.okpress.com

OSHKOSH HERALD

Street address 1: 36 Broad St
Street address 2: Suite 300
Street address city: Oshkosh
Street address state: WI
Zip/Postal code: 54901
County: Winnebago
Country: USA
Mailing city: Oshkosh
Mailing state: WI
Mailing zip: 54901
General Phone: 9203854512
General/National Adv. E-mail: advertise@oshkoshherald.com
Display Adv. E-mail: advertise@oshkoshherald.com
Classified Adv. e-mail: Classifieds@OshkoshHerald.com
Editorial e-mail: submit@oshkoshherald.com
Primary Website: oshkoshherald.com
Mthly Avg Views: 7000
Mthly Avg Unique Visitors: 3000
Year Established: 2017
Avg Paid Circ: 625
Avg Free Circ: 31115

PACIFIC NORTHWEST ASSOCIATION OF WANT-AD NEWSPAPERS

Street address 1: 626 Thain Rd.
Street address city: Lewiston
Street address state: ID
Zip/Postal code: 83501-0682
Mailing address: PO Box 682
Mailing city: Lewiston
Mailing state: ID
Mailing zip: 83501-0682
General Phone: (208) 746-0483
General Fax: (208) 746-8507
Display Adv. E-mail: ads@moneysav.com
Primary Website: www.pnawan.org
Year Established: 1977

PUBLISHERS DEVELOPMENT SERVICE

Street address 1: 101 S. Main St.
Street address city: Fond du Lac
Street address state: WI
Zip/Postal code: 54935
Mailing address: PO Box 1256
Mailing city: Fond du Lac
Mailing state: WI
Mailing zip: 54936-1256
General Phone: (920) 922-4864
General Fax: (920) 922-0861
General/National Adv. E-mail: janelle@pdsadnet.com
Primary Website: www.pdsadnet.com
Year Established: 1978

RESEAU SELECT/SELECT NETWORK

Street address 1: 25 Sheppard Ave W
Street address 2: Suite 500
Street address city: Toronto
Street address state: ON
Zip/Postal code: M2N 6S7
County: York
Country: Canada
Mailing address: 25 Sheppard Ave. West Suite 500
Mailing city: Toronto
Mailing state: ON
Mailing zip: M2N 6S7
General Phone: (416) 733-7600
General Fax: (416) 726-8519
General/National Adv. E-mail: inforeseauselect@tc.tc
Primary Website: www.reseauselect.com

RESEAU SELECT/SELECT NETWORK

Street address 1: 8000 Av Blaise-Pascal
Street address city: Montreal
Street address state: QC
Zip/Postal code: H1E 2S7
County: Quebec
Country: Canada
Mailing address: 8000 Ave. Blaise-Pascal
Mailing city: Montreal
Mailing state: QC
Mailing zip: H1E 2S7
General Phone: (514) 643-2300
General Fax: (514) 866-3030
General/National Adv. E-mail: inforeseauselect@tc.tc
Primary Website: www.reseauselect.com
Year Established: 1976

SOUTH CAROLINA PRESS SERVICES, INC.

Street address 1: 106 Outlet Point Blvd.
Street address city: Columbia
Street address state: SC
Zip/Postal code: 29210
Mailing address: PO Box 11429
Mailing city: Columbia
Mailing state: SC
Mailing zip: 29211-1429
General Phone: (803) 750-9561
General Fax: (803) 551-0903
General/National Adv. E-mail: scpress@scpress.org
Primary Website: www.scpress.org
Year Established: 1985

SOUTHEASTERN ADVERTISING PUBLISHERS ASSOCIATION

Street address 1: 104 Westland Dr
Street address city: Columbia
Street address state: TN
Zip/Postal code: 38401-6522
County: Maury
Country: USA
Mailing address: 104 Westland Dr
Mailing city: Columbia
Mailing state: TN
Mailing zip: 38401-6522
General Phone: (931) 223-5708
General Fax: (888) 450-8329
General/National Adv. E-mail: info@sapatoday.com
Primary Website: www.sapatoday.com
Year Established: 1979

SYNC2 MEDIA

Street address 1: 1120 N Lincoln St
Street address 2: Ste 912
Street address city: Denver
Street address state: CO
Zip/Postal code: 80203-2138
County: Denver
Country: USA
General Phone: (303) 571-5117
General Fax: (303) 571-1803
General/National Adv. E-mail: info@sync2media.com
Primary Website: www.sync2media.com

TEXCAP

Street address 1: 1226 Newberry Dr
Street address city: Allen
Street address state: TX
Zip/Postal code: 75013-3669
County: Collin
Country: USA
Mailing address: 570 Dula St
Mailing city: Alvin
Mailing state: TX
Mailing zip: 77511-2942
General Phone: (972) 741-6258
General Fax: (866) 822-4920
General/National Adv. E-mail: jack@tcnatoday.com
Primary Website: www.tcnatoday.com
Year Established: 1964

THE BILTMORE BEACON

Street address 1: 220 N. Main St.
Street address city: Waynesille
Street address state: NC
Zip/Postal code: 28786
County: Buncombe
Country: U.S.
General Phone: 8284520661
Advertising Phone: 8284520661
General/National Adv. E-mail: sdufour@themountaineer.com
Display Adv. E-mail: sdufour@themountaineer.com
Primary Website: themountaineer.com
Mthly Avg Views: 450000
Year Established: 1995
Avg Free Circ: 5000

THE SKAGWAY NEWS

Street address 1: 208b Broadway Street
Street address city: Skagway
Street address state: AK
Zip/Postal code: 99840
County: Municipality of Skagway
Country: United States
Mailing address: PO Box 244
Mailing city: Skagway
Mailing state: AK
Mailing zip: 99840
General Phone: 907-983-2354
Advertising Phone: 907-983-2354
Editorial Phone: 907-983-2354
General/National Adv. E-mail: editor@skagwaynews.com
Display Adv. E-mail: sales@skagwaynews.com
Classified Adv. e-mail: sales@skagwaynews.com
Editorial e-mail: editor@skagwaynews.com
Primary Website: www.skagwaynews.com
Year Established: 1978 (1898)
Avg Paid Circ: 300

TIMES COMMUNITY NEWSPAPERS

Street address 1: 500 Stony Brook Ct
Street address 2: Suite 2
Street address city: Newburgh
Street address state: NY
Zip/Postal code: 12550
County: Orange
Country: USA
General Phone: 8455610170
General Fax: 8455613967
General/National Adv. E-mail: editor@tcnewspapers.com
Display Adv. E-mail: advertising@tcnewspapers.com
Classified Adv. e-mail: classifieds@tcnewspapers.com
Editorial e-mail: editor@tcnewspapers.com
Primary Website: www.timeshudsonvalley.com

VILLE PLATTE (LA.) GAZETTE

Street address 1: 425 Court Street
Street address city: Ville Platte
Street address state: LA
Zip/Postal code: 70586
County: Evangeline
Country: United States
General Phone: 337-363-3939
General Fax: 337-363-2841
Advertising Phone: 337-363-3939
Advertising Fax: 337-363-2841
Editorial Phone: 337-363-3939
Editorial Fax: 337-363-2841
General/National Adv. E-mail: editor@evangelinetoday.com
Display Adv. E-mail: kathy.gazette@yahoo.com
Classified Adv. e-mail: kathy.gazette@yahoo.com
Editorial e-mail: editor@evangelinetoday.com
Primary Website: evangelinetoday.com
Mthly Avg Views: 30000
Mthly Avg Unique Visitors: 15000
Year Established: 1914
Avg Paid Circ: 1500
Avg Free Circ: 6400

WAUBAY CLIPPER

Street address 1: 122 N Main St
Street address city: Waubay
Street address state: SD
Zip/Postal code: 57273
County: Day
Country: USA
Mailing address: PO BOX 47
Mailing city: WAUBAY
Mailing state: SD
Mailing zip: 57273-0047
General Phone: (605) 947-4501
General Fax: (605) 947-4501
Advertising Phone: (605) 947-4501
Advertising Fax: (605) 947-4501
Editorial Phone: (605) 947-4501
Editorial Fax: (605) 947-4501
General/National Adv. E-mail: linda@waubayclipper.com
Display Adv. E-mail: linda@waubayclipper.com
Editorial e-mail: linda@waubayclipper.com
Primary Website: waubayclipper.blogspot.com
Year Established: 1890
Avg Paid Circ: 500
Avg Free Circ: 7

WISCONSIN NEWSPAPER ASSOCIATION

Street address 1: 34 Schroeder Ct
Street address 2: Ste 220
Street address city: Madison
Street address state: WI
Zip/Postal code: 53711-2528
County: Dane
Country: USA
General Phone: (608) 283-7620
General Fax: (608) 283-7631
General/National Adv. E-mail: wna@wnanews.com
Primary Website: www.wnanews.com
Year Established: 1853

WEEKLY CITY/STATE/REGIONAL ASSOCIATION, CLUB OR PRESS CLUB

ADVERTISING CLUB OF GREATER NEW YORK

Street address 1: 989 Avenue of the Americas
Street address 2: 7th floor
Street address city: New York
Street address state: NY
Zip/Postal code: 10018
Country: USA
Mailing address: 989 Avenue of the Americas Fl 7
Mailing city: New York
Mailing state: NY
Mailing zip: 10018-0872
General Phone: (212) 533-8080
General Fax: (212) 533-1929
General/National Adv. E-mail: memberships@theadvertisingclub.org
Primary Website: www.theadvertisingclub.org

ALABAMA BAPTIST

Street address 1: 3310 INDEPENDENCE DR
Street address city: BIRMINGHAM
Street address state: AL
Zip/Postal code: 35209-5602
Country: USA
General Phone: (205) 870-4720
General Fax: (205) 870-8957
General/National Adv. E-mail: news@thealabamabaptist.org
Display Adv. E-mail: bgilmore@thealabamabaptist.org
Primary Website: www.thealabamabaptist.org
Year Established: 1843

ALABAMA PRESS ASSOCIATION

Street address 1: 3324 Independence Dr
Street address 2: Ste 200
Street address city: Birmingham
Street address state: AL
Zip/Postal code: 35209-5602
Country: USA
Mailing address: 3324 Independence Dr Ste 200
Mailing city: Birmingham
Mailing state: AL
Mailing zip: 35209-5602
General Phone: (205) 871-7737
General Fax: (205) 871-7740
General/National Adv. E-mail: felicia@alabamapress.org
Primary Website: www.alabamapress.org
Year Established: 1871

ALBERTA WEEKLY NEWSPAPERS ASSOCIATION

Street address 1: 3228 Parsons Rd
Street address city: Edmonton
Street address state: AB
Zip/Postal code: T6N 1M2
Country: Canada
Mailing address: 3228 Parsons Rd
Mailing city: Edmonton
Mailing state: AB
Mailing zip: T6N 1M2
General Phone: (780) 434-8746
General Fax: (780) 438-8356
General/National Adv. E-mail: info@awna.com
Primary Website: www.awna.com

ALLIED DAILY NEWSPAPERS OF WASHINGTON

Street address 1: 1110 Capitol Way S
Street address city: Olympia
Street address state: WA
Zip/Postal code: 98501-2251
County: Thurston
Country: USA
Mailing address: 1110 Capitol Way S
Mailing city: Olympia
Mailing state: WA
Mailing zip: 98501-2251
General Phone: (360) 943-9960
General Fax: (360) 943-9962
General/National Adv. E-mail: anewspaper@aol.com

ARIZONA ASSOCIATED PRESS MANAGING EDITORS ASSOCIATION

Street address 1: 1850 N. Central Ave., Ste. 640
Street address city: Phoenix
Street address state: AZ
Zip/Postal code: 85004
Country: USA
Mailing address: 1850 N Central Ave Ste 640
Mailing city: Phoenix
Mailing state: AZ
Mailing zip: 85004-4573
General Phone: (602) 258-8934
General Fax: (602) 254-9573
General/National Adv. E-mail: aparizona@ap.org
Primary Website: www.ap.org/arizona

ARKANSAS PRESS WOMEN ASSOCIATION, INC.

Street address 1: 1301 Golden Pond Rd
Street address city: Little Rock
Street address state: AR
Zip/Postal code: 72223-9549
Country: USA
Mailing address: 1301 Golden Pond Rd
Mailing city: Little Rock
Mailing state: AR
Mailing zip: 72223-9549
General Phone: 501-671-2126
General Fax: 501-671-2121
General/National Adv. E-mail: arkpresswomen@yahoo.com
Primary Website: arkpresswomen.wordpress.com
Year Established: 1949

ASSOCIATED PRESS/CALIFORNIA-NEVADA NEWS EXECUTIVES

Street address 1: 221 S. Figueroa St., Ste. 300
Street address city: Los Angeles
Street address state: CA
Zip/Postal code: 90012
Country: USA
Mailing address: 221 S Figueroa St Ste 300
Mailing city: Los Angeles
Mailing state: CA
Mailing zip: 90012-2553
General Phone: (213) 626-5833
General/National Adv. E-mail: losangeles@ap.org
Primary Website: www.ap.org/losangeles
Year Established: 1848

ASSOCIATED PRESS/OKLAHOMA NEWS EXECUTIVES

Street address 1: 525 Central Park Dr., Ste. 202
Street address city: Oklahoma City
Street address state: OK
Zip/Postal code: 73105
Country: USA
Mailing address: 525 Central Park Dr Ste 202
Mailing city: Oklahoma City
Mailing state: OK
Mailing zip: 73105-1799
General Phone: (405) 525-2121
General Fax: (405) 524-7465
General/National Adv. E-mail: apoklahoma@ap.org
Primary Website: www.ap.org/oklahoma

ATLANTIC COMMUNITY NEWSPAPERS ASSOCIATION

Street address 1: 7075 Bayers Rd., Ste. 216
Street address city: Halifax
Street address state: NS
Zip/Postal code: B3L 2C2
Country: Canada
Mailing address: 7075 Bayers Rd., Ste. 216
Mailing city: Halifax
Mailing state: NS
Mailing zip: B3L 2C2
General Phone: (902) 832-4480
General Fax: (902) 832-4484
General/National Adv. E-mail: info@newspapersatlantic.ca
Primary Website: www.acna.com

BRITISH COLUMBIA/YUKON COMMUNITY NEWSPAPERS ASSOCIATION

Street address 1: #9 West Broadway
Street address city: Vancouver
Street address state: BC
Zip/Postal code: V5Y 1P1
Country: Canada
Mailing address: #9 West Broadway
Mailing city: Vancouver
Mailing state: BC
Mailing zip: V5Y 1P1
General Phone: (604) 669-9222
General/National Adv. E-mail: info@bccommunitynews.com
Primary Website: www.bccommunitynews.com

CAL WESTERN CIRCULATION MANAGERS ASSOCIATION

Street address 1: 8345 Singh Ct.
Street address city: Hemet
Street address state: CA
Zip/Postal code: 92545-9388
Mailing address: 8345 Singh Ct
Mailing city: Hemet
Mailing state: CA
Mailing zip: 92545-9388
General Phone: (951) 492-9330
General Fax: (951) 926-6361
General/National Adv. E-mail: director@cwcma.com
Primary Website: www.cwcma.com
Year Established: 1919

CALIFORNIA NEWS PUBLISHERS ASSOCIATION

Street address 1: 1517 H St. #407
Street address city: Sacramento
Street address state: CA
Zip/Postal code: 95814
County: Sacramento
Country: USA
Mailing address: 1517 H St. #407
Mailing city: Sacramento
Mailing state: CA
Mailing zip: 95814
General Phone: (916) 288-6000
General Fax: (916) 288-6002
Primary Website: www.cnpa.com
Year Established: 1889

CALIFORNIA PRESS ASSOCIATION

Street address 1: Cal. Newspr. Publs. Assoc., 2000 O St., Suite 120
Street address city: Sacramento
Street address state: CA
Zip/Postal code: 95811
Country: USA
Mailing address: 2000 O St Ste 120
Mailing city: Sacramento
Mailing state: CA
Mailing zip: 95811-5299
General Phone: (916) 288-6000
Primary Website: www.cnpa.com
Year Established: 1878

CAPE GAZETTE

Street address 1: 17585 Nassau Commons Blvd.
Street address city: Lewes
Street address state: DE
Zip/Postal code: 19958
County: Sussex County
Country: United States
Mailing address: P.O. Box 213
Mailing city: Lewes
Mailing state: DE
Mailing zip: 19958
General Phone: 302-645-7700
General Fax: 302-644-1664
General/National Adv. E-mail: info@capegazette.com
Display Adv. E-mail: adsales@capegazette.com
Classified Adv. e-mail: adsales@capegazette.com
Editorial e-mail: newsroom@capegazette.com
Primary Website: Capegazette.com
Year Established: 1993

CAPITOL PRESS ASSOCIATION

Street address 1: PO Box 191
Street address city: Raleigh
Street address state: NC
Zip/Postal code: 27602
Country: USA
Mailing address: PO Box 191
Mailing city: Raleigh
Mailing state: NC
Mailing zip: 27602-9150
General Phone: (919) 836-2858
General/National Adv. E-mail: smooneyh@ncinsider.com
Primary Website: www.ncinsider.com

CCNMA: LATINO JOURNALISTS OF CALIFORNIA

Street address 1: ASU Walter Cronkite School of Journalism
Street address 2: 725 Arizona Ave. Ste. 404
Street address city: Santa Monica
Street address state: CA
Zip/Postal code: 90401-1723
County: Los Angeles
Country: USA
Mailing address: ASU Walter Cronkite School of Journalism
Mailing city: Santa Monica
Mailing state: CA
Mailing zip: 90401-1723
General Phone: (424) 229-9482
General Fax: (424) 238-0271
General/National Adv. E-mail: ccnmainfo@ccnma.org
Primary Website: www.ccnma.org
Year Established: 1972

CENTRAL STATES CIRCULATION MANAGERS ASSOCIATION

Street address 1: 130 S. 5th St.
Street address city: Quincy
Street address state: IL
Zip/Postal code: 62301
Country: USA
Mailing address: Central States Circulation Managers Association
Mailing city: Munster
Mailing state: IL
Mailing zip: 46321
General Phone: (217) 221-3327
General/National Adv. E-mail: rrobertson@whig.com
Display Adv. E-mail: rrobertson@whig.com
Editorial e-mail: rrobertson@whig.com
Primary Website: 130 S. 5th St.
Year Established: 1935

COLORADO ASSOCIATED PRESS EDITORS AND REPORTERS

Street address 1: 1444 Wazee St., Ste. 130
Street address city: Denver
Street address state: CO
Zip/Postal code: 80202-1395
Country: USA
Mailing address: 1444 Wazee St Ste 130
Mailing city: Denver
Mailing state: CO
Mailing zip: 80202-1326
General Phone: (303) 825-0123
General Fax: (303) 892-5927
General/National Adv. E-mail: apdenver@ap.org

Primary Website: www.ap.org/colorado

COMMUNITY PAPERS OF INDIANA

Street address 1: PO Box 1004
Street address city: Crown Point
Street address state: IN
Zip/Postal code: 46308
Country: USA
Mailing address: PO Box 1004
Mailing city: Crown Point
Mailing state: IN
Mailing zip: 46308-1004
General Phone: (219) 689-6262
General Fax: (219) 374-7558

COMMUNITY PAPERS OF MICHIGAN

Street address 1: 5000 Northwind Dr., Ste. 240
Street address city: East Lansing
Street address state: MI
Zip/Postal code: 48823
County: Ingham
Country: USA
Mailing address: 5000 Northwind Dr Ste 240
Mailing city: East Lansing
Mailing state: MI
Mailing zip: 48823-5032
General Phone: (517) 333-3355
General Fax: (517) 333-3322
General/National Adv. E-mail: jackguza@cpapersmi.com;sikotecki@cpapersmi.com
Primary Website: www.communitypapersofmichigan.com
Year Established: 1969

CONNECTICUT ASSOCIATED PRESS MANAGING EDITORS ASSOCIATION

Street address 1: 10 Columbus Blvd.
Street address city: Hartford
Street address state: CT
Zip/Postal code: 06106
Country: USA
Mailing address: 10 Columbus Blvd
Mailing city: Hartford
Mailing state: CT
Mailing zip: 06106-1976
General Phone: (860) 246-6876
General Fax: (860) 727-4003
General/National Adv. E-mail: aphartford@ap.org
Primary Website: www.ap.org

CONNECTICUT DAILY NEWSPAPERS ASSOCIATION

Street address 1: 330 Main St
Street address 2: Fl 3
Street address city: Hartford
Street address state: CT
Zip/Postal code: 06106-1851
Country: USA
Mailing address: 330 Main St Fl 3
Mailing city: Hartford
Mailing state: CT
Mailing zip: 06106-1851
General Phone: (860) 716-4461
General Fax: (860) 541-6484
Primary Website: www.ctdailynews.com
Year Established: 1904

CONSEIL DE PRESSE DU QUEBEC

Street address 1: 1000, rue Fullum, Ste. A.208
Street address city: Montreal
Street address state: QC
Zip/Postal code: H2K 3L7
Country: Canada
Mailing address: 1000, rue Fullum, Ste. A.208
Mailing city: Montreal
Mailing state: QC
Mailing zip: H2K 3L7
General Phone: (514) 529-2818
General Fax: (514) 873-4434
General/National Adv. E-mail: info@conseildepresse.qc.ca
Primary Website: www.conseildepresse.qc.ca

Year Established: 1973

FLORIDA NEWSPAPER ADVERTISING & MARKETING EXECUTIVES

Street address 1: 610 Crescent Executive Court
Street address 2: Suite 112
Street address city: Lake Mary
Street address state: FL
Zip/Postal code: 32746
County: Seminole
Country: USA
Mailing address: 610 Crescent Executive Court
Mailing city: Lake Mary
Mailing state: FL
Mailing zip: 32746
General Phone: (321) 283-5273
General/National Adv. E-mail: hello@fname.org
Primary Website: www.fname.org
Year Established: 1929

FLORIDA SOCIETY OF NEWSPAPER EDITORS

Street address 1: 336 E. College Ave. Suite 203
Street address city: Tallahassee
Street address state: FL
Zip/Postal code: 32301
Country: USA
Mailing address: 336 E College Ave Ste 203
Mailing city: Tallahassee
Mailing state: FL
Mailing zip: 32301-1559
General Phone: (850) 222-5790
General Fax: 850-224-6012
General/National Adv. E-mail: fpa-info@flpress.com
Primary Website: www.fsne.org

FREE COMMUNITY PAPERS OF NEW ENGLAND

Street address 1: 700 Main St.
Street address city: Willimantic
Street address state: CT
Zip/Postal code: 6226
Mailing address: 403 Us Route 302
Mailing city: Barre
Mailing state: VT
Mailing zip: 05641-2272
General Phone: (860) 423-6398
General Fax: (860) 423-6391
General/National Adv. E-mail: bne@fcpne.com
Primary Website: www.communitypapersne.com

FREE COMMUNITY PAPERS OF NEW YORK

Street address 1: 750 W. Genesee St.
Street address city: Syracuse
Street address state: NY
Zip/Postal code: 13204
Country: USA
Mailing address: PO Box 11279
Mailing city: Syracuse
Mailing state: NY
Mailing zip: 13218-1279
General Phone: (315) 472-6007
General Fax: (315) 472-5919
General/National Adv. E-mail: ads@fcpny.com
Primary Website: www.fcpny.org

FREE LANCE JOURNALIST/ BLOGGER

Street address 1: 121 South Street
Street address 2: 121 South Street
Street address city: Churubusco
Street address state: IN
Zip/Postal code: 46723
County: Whitley
Country: USA
Mailing address: 121 South Street
Mailing city: Churubusco
Mailing state: IN
Mailing zip: 46801-0088
General Phone: (260) 241-7737
General/National Adv. E-mail: vsade8@gmail.com

Display Adv. E-mail: vsade8@gmail.com

FREEDOM OF INFORMATION FOUNDATION OF TEXAS

Street address 1: 3001 N Lamar Blvd., Ste. 302
Street address city: Austin
Street address state: TX
Zip/Postal code: 78705
Country: USA
Mailing address: 3001 N Lamar Blvd Ste 302
Mailing city: Austin
Mailing state: TX
Mailing zip: 78705-2024
General Phone: (512) 377 1575
General Fax: (512) 377 1578
General/National Adv. E-mail: kelley.shannon@foift.org
Primary Website: www.foift.org
Year Established: 1978

GATEWAY JOURNALISM REVIEW

Street address 1: Mailcode 6601
Street address 2: 1100 Lincoln Drive
Street address city: Carbondale
Street address state: IL
Zip/Postal code: 62901
County: Jackson
Country: USA
Mailing address:
Mailing city:
Mailing state: MO
Mailing zip:
General Phone: (618) 536-6631
General Fax: (618) 453-5200
General/National Adv. E-mail: gatewayjr@siu.edu
Editorial e-mail: wfreivogel@gmail.com
Primary Website: www.gatewayjr.org
Year Established: 1970

GREAT LAKES/MIDSTATES NEWSPAPER CONFERENCE, INC.

Street address 1: 1335 Dublin Rd., Suite 216-B
Street address city: Colombus
Street address state: OH
Zip/Postal code: 43215
Country: USA
Mailing address: 1335 Dublin Rd Ste 216B
Mailing city: Columbus
Mailing state: OH
Mailing zip: 43215-1000
General Phone: (614) 486-6677
General Fax: (614) 486-4940
General/National Adv. E-mail: glmsconf@comcast.net
Primary Website: www.ohionews.org
Year Established: 1945

HEAVENER LEDGER

Street address 1: 704 West 5th Street
Street address city: Heavener
Street address state: OK
Zip/Postal code: 74937
County: LeFlore
Country: United States
Mailing address: Box 38
Mailing city: Heavener
Mailing state: OK
Mailing zip: 74937
General Phone: 9186532425
General Fax: 9186537305
General/National Adv. E-mail: craig@heavenerledger.com
Primary Website: www.heavenerledger.com
Year Established: 1904

HOLLYWOOD FOREIGN PRESS ASSOCIATION

Street address 1: 646 N. Robertson Blvd.
Street address city: West Hollywood
Street address state: CA
Zip/Postal code: 90069-5078
Country: USA
Mailing address: 646 N Robertson Blvd
Mailing city: West Hollywood
Mailing state: CA
Mailing zip: 90069-5022
General Phone: (310) 657-1731
General Fax: (310) 657-5576

General/National Adv. E-mail: info@hfpa.org
Primary Website: www.hfpa.org
Year Established: 1943

HOOSIER STATE PRESS ASSOCIATION

Street address 1: 41 E Washington St
Street address 2: Ste 101
Street address city: Indianapolis
Street address state: IN
Zip/Postal code: 46204-3560
County: Marion
Country: USA
General Phone: (317) 803-4772
General Fax: (317) 624-4428
Display Adv. E-mail: map@hspa.com
Primary Website: www.hspa.com
Year Established: 1933

IDAHO PRESS CLUB

Street address 1: PO Box 2221
Street address city: Boise
Street address state: ID
Zip/Postal code: 83701-2221
Country: USA
Mailing address: PO Box 2221
Mailing city: Boise
Mailing state: ID
Mailing zip: 83701-2221
General Phone: (208) 389-2879
General/National Adv. E-mail: email@idahopressclub.org
Primary Website: www.idahopressclub.org

ILLINOIS ASSOCIATED PRESS MANAGING EDITORS

Street address 1: 10 S. Wacker Drive
Street address 2: Suite 2500
Street address city: Chicago
Street address state: IL
Zip/Postal code: 60606
Country: USA
Mailing address: 10 S Wacker Dr
Mailing city: Chicago
Mailing state: IL
Mailing zip: 60606-7453
General Phone: (312) 781-0500
General/National Adv. E-mail: chifax@ap.org
Primary Website: www.ap.org

ILLINOIS PRESS ASSOCIATION

Street address 1: 900 Community Dr
Street address city: Springfield
Street address state: IL
Zip/Postal code: 62703-5180
County: Sangamon
Country: USA
General Phone: (217) 241-1300
General Fax: (217) 241-1301
General/National Adv. E-mail: ipa@illinoispress.org
Primary Website: www.illinoispress.org
Year Established: 1865

ILLINOIS WOMAN'S PRESS ASSOCIATION, INC.

Street address 1: PO Box 180150
Street address city: Chicago
Street address state: IL
Zip/Postal code: 60618-9997
County: Cook
Country: USA
Mailing address: PO Box 180150
Mailing city: Chicago
Mailing state: IL
Mailing zip: 60618-9997
General Phone: (708) 296-8669
General/National Adv. E-mail: iwpa@gmail.com
Display Adv. E-mail: iwpa1885@gmail.com
Editorial e-mail: iwpa1885@gmail.com
Primary Website: www.iwpa.org
Year Established: 1885

INDEPENDENT FREE PAPERS OF AMERICA

Street address 1: 107 Hemlock Dr

Street address city: Rio Grande
Street address state: NJ
Zip/Postal code: 08242-1731
County: Cape May
Country: USA
Mailing address: 107 Hemlock Dr
Mailing city: Rio Grande
Mailing state: NJ
Mailing zip: 08242-1731
General Phone: (609) 408-8000
General Fax: (609) 889-0141
Primary Website: www.ifpa.com

INDIANA ASSOCIATED PRESS MANAGING EDITORS

Street address 1: 251 N. Illinois St., Ste. 1600
Street address city: Indianapolis
Street address state: IN
Zip/Postal code: 46204
Country: USA
Mailing address: 251 N Illinois St Ste 1600
Mailing city: Indianapolis
Mailing state: IN
Mailing zip: 46204-4309
General Phone: (317) 639-5501
General/National Adv. E-mail: indy@ap.org

INDIANAPOLIS PRESS CLUB FOUNDATION

Street address 1: PO Box 40923
Street address city: Indianapolis
Street address state: IN
Zip/Postal code: 46240
Country: USA
Mailing address: PO Box 40923
Mailing city: Indianapolis
Mailing state: IN
Mailing zip: 46240-0923
General Phone: (317) 701-1130
General/National Adv. E-mail: jlabalme@indypress@att.net
Primary Website: www.indypressfoundation.org

INLAND PRESS ASSOCIATION

Street address 1: 701 Lee St., Ste. 925
Street address city: Des Plaines
Street address state: IL
Zip/Postal code: 60016
County: Cook
Country: USA
Mailing address: 701 Lee Street, Suite 925
Mailing city: Des Plaines
Mailing state: IL
Mailing zip: 60016
General Phone: (847) 795-0380
General Fax: (847) 795-0385
General/National Adv. E-mail: inland@inlandpress.org
Primary Website: www.inlandpress.org
Year Established: 1885

KANSAS ASSOCIATED PRESS MANAGING EDITORS ASSOCIATION

Street address 1: Associated Press, 215 W. Pershing St., Ste. 221
Street address city: Kansas City
Street address state: MO
Zip/Postal code: 64108
Country: USA
Mailing address: 215 W Pershing Rd Ste 221
Mailing city: Kansas City
Mailing state: MO
Mailing zip: 64108-4300
General Phone: (816) 421-4844
General Fax: (816) 421-3590
General/National Adv. E-mail: apkansascity@ap.org
Primary Website: www.ap.org/kansas

KANSAS ASSOCIATED PRESS PUBLISHERS AND EDITORS

Street address 1: Associated Press, 215 W. Pershing, Ste. 221
Street address city: Kansas City
Street address state: MO
Zip/Postal code: 64108
Country: USA
Mailing address: 215 W Pershing Rd Ste 221
Mailing city: Kansas City
Mailing state: MO
Mailing zip: 64108-4300
General Phone: (816) 421-4844
General Fax: (816) 421-3590

KANSAS PRESS ASSOCIATION

Street address 1: 5423 SW 7th St
Street address city: Topeka
Street address state: KS
Zip/Postal code: 66606-2330
County: Shawnee
Country: USA
Mailing address: 5423 SW 7th St.
Mailing city: Topeka
Mailing state: KS
Mailing zip: 66606
General Phone: (785) 271-5304
General Fax: (785) 271-7341
General/National Adv. E-mail: info@kspress.com
Display Adv. E-mail: KSAds@kspress.com
Editorial e-mail: info@kspress.com
Primary Website: www.kspress.com
Year Established: 1863

KANSAS PROFESSIONAL COMMUNICATORS

Street address 1: 2369 Road J5
Street address city: Americus
Street address state: KS
Zip/Postal code: 66835
Country: USA
Mailing address: 2369 Road J5
Mailing city: Americus
Mailing state: KS
Mailing zip: 66835-9540
General Phone: 620-227-1807
General Fax: 620 227-1806
General/National Adv. E-mail: kansasprocom@gmail.com
Display Adv. E-mail: jlatzke@hpj.com
Editorial e-mail: jlatzke@hpj.com
Primary Website: www.kansasprofessionalcommunicators.org
Year Established: 1941

KENTUCKY ASSOCIATED PRESS EDITORS ASSOCIATION

Street address 1: 525 W. Broadway
Street address city: Louisville
Street address state: KY
Zip/Postal code: 40202
Country: USA
Mailing address: 525 W Broadway
Mailing city: Louisville
Mailing state: KY
Mailing zip: 40202-2206
General Phone: (502) 583-7718
General Fax: (502) 589-4831
General/National Adv. E-mail: ayeomans@ap.org
Primary Website: www.ap.org/kentucky

LEGISLATIVE CORRESPONDENTS ASSOCIATION OF NYS

Street address 1: 25 Eagle St.
Street address 2: NYS Capitol
Street address city: Albany
Street address state: NY
Zip/Postal code: 12224
County: Albany
Country: USA
Mailing address: PO Box 7269
Mailing city: Albany
Mailing state: NY
Mailing zip: 12224-0269
General Phone: (518) 455-2388
Primary Website: www.lcapressroom.com
Year Established: 1885

LOCAL MEDIA ASSOCIATION

Street address 1: PO Box 450
Street address city: Lake City
Street address state: MI
Zip/Postal code: 49651-0450
County: Missaukee
Country: USA
Mailing address: P.O. Box 450
Mailing city: Lake City
Mailing state: MI
Mailing zip: 49651-0450
General Phone: (888) 486-2466
General Fax: (888) 317-0856
General/National Adv. E-mail: hq@localmedia.org
Primary Website: www.localmedia.org
Year Established: 1971

LOS ANGELES PRESS CLUB

Street address 1: 4773 Hollywood Blvd.
Street address city: Los Angeles
Street address state: CA
Zip/Postal code: 90027
Country: USA
Mailing address: 4773 Hollywood Blvd
Mailing city: Los Angeles
Mailing state: CA
Mailing zip: 90027-5333
General Phone: (323) 669-8081
General Fax: (323) 669-8069
General/National Adv. E-mail: info@lapressclub.org
Primary Website: www.lapressclub.org
Year Established: 1913

LOUISIANA PRESS WOMEN, INC.

Street address 1: The Advocate, 7290 Blue Bonnet Rd.
Street address city: Baton Rouge
Street address state: LA
Zip/Postal code: 70810
Country: USA
Mailing address: PO Box 588
Mailing city: Baton Rouge
Mailing state: LA
Mailing zip: 70821-0588
General Phone: (225) 383-1111
General Fax: (225) 388-0323
General/National Adv. E-mail: mshuler@theadvocate.com
Primary Website: www.theadvocate.com

LOUISIANA-MISSISSIPPI ASSOCIATED PRESS MANAGING EDITORS ASSOCIATION

Street address 1: 125 south congress st. suite 1330
Street address city: Jackson
Street address state: MS
Zip/Postal code: 39201
Country: USA
Mailing address: 125 S Congress St Ste 1330
Mailing city: Jackson
Mailing state: MS
Mailing zip: 39201-3310
General Phone: 601-948-5897
General Fax: 601-948-7975
General/National Adv. E-mail: jkme@ap.org
Primary Website: www.ap.org

M. ROBERTS MEDIA

Street address 1: 320 E. Methvin St.
Street address city: Longview
Street address state: TX
Zip/Postal code: 75601
Country: USA
Mailing address: 320 E. Methvin St.
Mailing city: Longview
Mailing state: TX
Mailing zip: 75601
General Phone: (903) 757-3311
Primary Website: www.mrobertsmedia.com
Year Established: 1942

MAINE DAILY NEWSPAPER PUBLISHERS ASSOCIATION

Street address 1: 104 Park St.
Street address city: Lewiston
Street address state: ME
Zip/Postal code: 4240
Mailing address: PO Box 4400
Mailing city: Lewiston
Mailing state: ME
Mailing zip: 04243-4400
General Phone: (207) 784-5411
General/National Adv. E-mail: scostello@sunjournal.com
Primary Website: www.sunjournal.com

MANITOBA COMMUNITY NEWSPAPER ASSOCIATION

Street address 1: 943 McPhillips Street
Street address city: Winnipeg
Street address state: MB
Zip/Postal code: R2X 2J9
Country: Canada
Mailing address: 943 McPhillips Street
Mailing city: Winnipeg
Mailing state: MB
Mailing zip: R2X 2J9
General Phone: (204) 947-1691
General Fax: (204) 947-1919
Primary Website: www.mcna.com

MARYLAND-DELAWARE-DC PRESS ASSOCIATION

Street address 1: 60 West St.
Street address 2: Ste. 107
Street address city: Annapolis
Street address state: MD
Zip/Postal code: 21401-2479
County: Anne Arundel
Country: USA
Mailing address: 60 West St.
Mailing city: Annapolis
Mailing state: MD
Mailing zip: 21401-2479
General Phone: (855) 721-6332
General Fax: (855) 721-6332
General/National Adv. E-mail: rsnyder@mddc.com
Display Adv. E-mail: wsmith@mddcpress.com
Editorial e-mail: rsnyder@mddcpress.com
Primary Website: www.mddcpress.com
Year Established: 1908

MASSACHUSETTS NEWSPAPER PUBLISHERS ASSOCIATION

Street address 1: 16 Mckays Dr.
Street address city: 16 Mckays Dr.
Street address state: MA
Zip/Postal code: 1966
Mailing address: 16 McKays Dr
Mailing city: Rockport
Mailing state: MA
Mailing zip: 01966-1404
General Phone: (978) 546-3400
General Fax: (978) 418-9161
General/National Adv. E-mail: info@masspublishers.org
Primary Website: www.masspublishers.org

METROPOLITAN NEW YORK FOOTBALL WRITERS ASSOCIATION

Street address 1: American Football Networks, Inc.
Street address 2: P.O. Box 477
Street address city: Roseland
Street address state: NJ
Zip/Postal code: 07068-0477
County: Essex
Country: USA
Mailing address: PO Box 477
Mailing city: Roseland
Mailing state: NJ
Mailing zip: 07068-0477
General Phone: (973) 364-0605
General Fax: (973) 364-0425
General/National Adv. E-mail: americanfootballnetworks@gmail.com
Primary Website: www.mnyfwa.com
Year Established: 1935

MICHIGAN ASSOCIATED PRESS EDITORIAL ASSOCIATION

Street address 1: 300 River Pl., Ste. 2400
Street address city: Detroit
Street address state: MI
Zip/Postal code: 48207
Country: USA
Mailing address: 300 River Place Dr Ste 2400
Mailing city: Detroit
Mailing state: MI
Mailing zip: 48207-4260
General Phone: (313) 259-0650

General Fax: (313) 259-4966
General/National Adv. E-mail: apmichigan@ap.org
Primary Website: www.ap.org

MID-ATLANTIC CIRCULATION MANAGERS ASSOCIATION

Street address 1: Daily Herald, PO Box 520
Street address city: Roanoke Rapids
Street address state: NC
Zip/Postal code: 27870-0520
Country: USA
Mailing address: PO Box 520
Mailing city: Roanoke Rapids
Mailing state: NC
Mailing zip: 27870-0520
General Phone: (252) 537-2505
General Fax: (252) 537-1887
Primary Website: www.midatlanticcma.org

MID-ATLANTIC COMMUNITY PAPERS ASSOCIATION

Street address 1: 16515 Pottsville Pike
Street address 2: Suite C
Street address city: Hamburg
Street address state: PA
Zip/Postal code: 19526
County: Berks
Country: USA
Mailing address: PO Box 408
Mailing city: Hamburg
Mailing state: PA
Mailing zip: 19526-0408
General Phone: 484-709-6564
General/National Adv. E-mail: info@macpa.net
Display Adv. E-mail: info@macnetonline.com
Primary Website: www.macpa.net
Year Established: 1955

MID-ATLANTIC NEWSPAPER ADVERTISING & MARKETING EXECUTIVES

Street address 1: 359-C Wando Place Drive
Street address city: Mt. Pleasant
Street address state: SC
Zip/Postal code: 29464
Country: USA
Mailing address: 359 Wando Place Dr Ste C
Mailing city: Mt Pleasant
Mailing state: SC
Mailing zip: 29464-7926
General Phone: (509)540-1534
General/National Adv. E-mail: edwardrbryant@yahoo.com
Primary Website: www.midatlanticname.com

MIDWEST FREE COMMUNITY PAPERS

Street address 1: PO Box 1350
Street address city: Iowa City
Street address state: IA
Zip/Postal code: 52244-1350
Mailing address: PO Box 1350
Mailing city: Iowa City
Mailing state: IA
Mailing zip: 52244-1350
General Phone: (319) 341-4352
General Fax: (319) 341-4358
General/National Adv. E-mail: mfcp@mchsi.com
Primary Website: www.mypaper.com

MIDWEST TRAVEL WRITERS ASSOCIATION

Street address 1: 902 S. Randall Road, Suite C311
Street address city: St. Charles
Street address state: IL
Zip/Postal code: 60174
Country: USA
Mailing address: 902 S Randall Rd Ste C311
Mailing city: Saint Charles
Mailing state: IL
Mailing zip: 60174-1554
General Phone: 888-551-8184
General/National Adv. E-mail: sylvia@forbesfreelance.com
Primary Website: www.mtwa.org
Year Established: 1951

MINNESOTA ASSOCIATED PRESS ASSOCIATION

Street address 1: 425 Portland Ave
Street address 2: Third Floor
Street address city: Minneapolis
Street address state: MN
Zip/Postal code: 55488
County: Hennepin
Country: USA
General Phone: (612) 332-2727
General Fax: (612) 342-5299
General/National Adv. E-mail: apminneapolis@ap.org
Primary Website: www.ap.org

MINNESOTA FREE PAPER ASSOCIATION

Street address 1: 21998 Hwy. 27
Street address city: Little Falls
Street address state: MN
Zip/Postal code: 56345
Country: USA
Mailing address: 21998 Highway 27
Mailing city: Little Falls
Mailing state: MN
Mailing zip: 56345-6279
General Phone: 320-630-5312
General Fax: (320) 632-2348
General/National Adv. E-mail: terry@littlefalls.net
Primary Website: www.mfpa.com

MINNESOTA NEWSPAPER ASSOCIATION

Street address 1: 10 South 5th St.
Street address 2: Ste 110
Street address city: Minneapolis
Street address state: MN
Zip/Postal code: 55402-1501
County: Hennepin
Country: USA
Mailing address: 10 S 5th St Ste 1105
Mailing city: Minneapolis
Mailing state: MN
Mailing zip: 55402-1036
General Phone: (612) 332-8844
General Fax: (612) 342-2958
General/National Adv. E-mail: Member@mna.org
Display Adv. E-mail: advertising@mna.org
Primary Website: www.mna.org
Year Established: 1867

MISSOURI ASSOCIATED PRESS MANAGING EDITORS

Street address 1: Associated Press, 215 W. Pershing, Ste. 221
Street address city: Kansas City
Street address state: MO
Zip/Postal code: 64108
Country: USA
Mailing address: 215 W Pershing Rd Ste 221
Mailing city: Kansas City
Mailing state: MO
Mailing zip: 64108-4300
General Phone: (816) 421-4844
General Fax: (816) 421-3590
General/National Adv. E-mail: apkansascity@ap.org
Primary Website: www.ap.org

MISSOURI PRESS WOMEN

Street address 1: 528 Pamela Ln.
Street address city: Kirkwood
Street address state: MO
Zip/Postal code: 63122-1138
County: St. Louis
Country: USA
Mailing address: 528 Pamela Ln
Mailing city: Kirkwood
Mailing state: MO
Mailing zip: 63122-1138
General/National Adv. E-mail: MPCNFPW@gmail.com
Primary Website: www.mpc-nfpw.org
Year Established: 1937

MONTANA ASSOCIATED PRESS ASSOCIATION

Street address 1: 321 Fuller Ave. #2
Street address city: Helena
Street address state: MT
Zip/Postal code: 59601
Country: USA
Mailing address: 825 Great Northern Blvd Ste 203
Mailing city: Helena
Mailing state: MT
Mailing zip: 59601-3340
General Phone: (406) 442-7440
General Fax: (406) 442-5162
General/National Adv. E-mail: apmontana@ap.org
Primary Website: www.ap.org/montana

NASJA EAST

Street address 1: 22 Cavalier Way
Street address city: Latham
Street address state: NY
Zip/Postal code: 12110
Country: USA
Mailing address: 22 Cavalier Way
Mailing city: Latham
Mailing state: NY
Mailing zip: 12110
General Phone: 518 339-5334
General/National Adv. E-mail: nasjaeast@nasja.org
Display Adv. E-mail: nasjaeast@nasja.org
Editorial e-mail: nasjaeast@nasja.org
Primary Website: http://www.nasja.org/east/index.cfm
Year Established: 1963

NEBRASKA ASSOCIATED PRESS ASSOCIATION

Street address 1: 845 â€œSâ€ Street
Street address city: Lincoln
Street address state: NE
Zip/Postal code: 68508
Country: USA
Mailing address: 845 ?Ç£S?Ç¥ Street
Mailing city: Lincoln
Mailing state: NE
Mailing zip: 68508
General Phone: (402)476-2851
General Fax: (402)476-2942
General/National Adv. E-mail: nebpress@nebpress.com
Primary Website: www.ap.org/nebraska

NENPA AD NETWORK (NEW ENGLAND NEWSPAPER AND PRESS ASSOCIATION)

Street address 1: 1 Arrow Dr
Street address 2: Ste 6
Street address city: Woburn
Street address state: MA
Zip/Postal code: 01801-2039
County: Middlesex
Country: USA
Mailing address: 1 Arrow Drive, Suite 6
Mailing city: Woburn
Mailing state: MA
Mailing zip: 01801
General Phone: (781) 281-2053
General Fax: (339) 999-2174
General/National Adv. E-mail: info@nenpa.com
Primary Website: www.nenpa.com
Year Established: 1930

NEW ENGLAND ASSOCIATED PRESS NEWS EXECUTIVES ASSOCIATION

Street address 1: Associated Press, 184 High St.
Street address city: Boston
Street address state: MA
Zip/Postal code: 2110
Mailing address: High St Associated Press 184
Mailing city: Boston
Mailing state: MA
Mailing zip: 02110-3089
General Phone: (617) 357-8100
General Fax: (617) 338-8125
General/National Adv. E-mail: apboston@ap.org
Primary Website: www.ap.org/boston

NEW ENGLAND ASSOCIATION OF CIRCULATION EXECUTIVES

Street address 1: 4 Trotting Rd.
Street address city: Chelmsford
Street address state: MA
Zip/Postal code: 1824
Country: USA
Mailing address: 4 Trotting Rd
Mailing city: Chelmsford
Mailing state: MA
Mailing zip: 01824-1928
General Phone: (978) 256-0691
General Fax: (978) 256-4873
General/National Adv. E-mail: neace@neace.com
Primary Website: www.neace.com

NEW ENGLAND NEWSPAPER & PRESS ASSOCIATION

Street address 1: 1 Arrow Drive, Suite 6
Street address city: Woburn
Street address state: MA
Zip/Postal code: 01801
Country: USA
Mailing address: 1 Arrow Drive, Suite 6
Mailing city: Woburn
Mailing state: MA
Mailing zip: 01801
General Phone: (781) 281-2053
General Fax: (339) 999-2174
General/National Adv. E-mail: info@nenpa.com
Primary Website: www.nenpa.com
Year Established: 1930

NEW ENGLAND NEWSPAPER ADVERTISING EXECUTIVES ASSOCIATION

Street address 1: 370 Common St.
Street address city: Dedham
Street address state: MA
Zip/Postal code: 2026
Mailing address: 370 Common St
Mailing city: Dedham
Mailing state: MA
Mailing zip: 02026-4097
General Phone: (781) 320-8050
General Fax: (781) 320-8055
Primary Website: www.nenpa.com

NEW ENGLAND NEWSPAPER ASSOCIATION, INC.

Street address 1: 70 Washington St., Ste. 214
Street address city: Salem
Street address state: MA
Zip/Postal code: 1970
Mailing address: 370 Common St
Mailing city: Dedham
Mailing state: MA
Mailing zip: 02026-4097
General Phone: (978) 744-8940
General Fax: (978) 744-0333
General/National Adv. E-mail: mlp@nenews.org
Primary Website: www.nenews.org

NEW ENGLAND SOCIETY OF NEWSPAPER EDITORS

Street address 1: 370 Common Street, 3rd Floor Ste 319
Street address 2: Barletta Hall
Street address city: Dedham
Street address state: MA
Zip/Postal code: 02026
Country: USA
Mailing address: 370 Common St
Mailing city: Dedham
Mailing state: MA
Mailing zip: 02026-4097
General Phone: 781-320-8050
General Fax: 781-320-8055
General/National Adv. E-mail: info@nenpa.com

Primary Website: www.nesne.org

NEW JERSEY ASSOCIATED PRESS MANAGING EDITORS ASSOCIATION

Street address 1: 50 W. State St., Ste. 1114
Street address city: Trenton
Street address state: NJ
Zip/Postal code: 8608
Country: USA
Mailing address: 50 W State St Ste 1114
Mailing city: Trenton
Mailing state: NJ
Mailing zip: 08608-1220
General Phone: (609) 392-3622
General Fax: (609) 392-3525
General/National Adv. E-mail: aptrenton@ap.org
Primary Website: www.ap.org/nj

NEW JERSEY LEGISLATIVE CORRESPONDENTS CLUB

Street address 1: Hackensack Record
Street address city: Trenton
Street address state: NJ
Zip/Postal code: 8625
Country: USA
Mailing address: PO Box 21
Mailing city: Trenton
Mailing state: NJ
Mailing zip: 08625-0021
General Phone: (609) 292-5159
General Fax: (609) 984-1888

NEW MEXICO PRESS WOMEN

Street address 1: 256 DP Rd.
Street address city: Los Alamos
Street address state: NM
Zip/Postal code: 87544
Country: USA
Mailing address: 256 Dp Rd
Mailing city: Los Alamos
Mailing state: NM
Mailing zip: 87544-3233
General Phone: (505) 662-4185
General Fax: (505) 827-6496
General/National Adv. E-mail: lanews@lamonitor.com
Primary Website: www.newmexicopresswomen.org

NEW ORLEANS PRESS CLUB

Street address 1: 846 Howard Avenue
Street address city: New Orleans
Street address state: LA
Zip/Postal code: 70113
Country: USA
Mailing address: 846 Howard Ave
Mailing city: New Orleans
Mailing state: LA
Mailing zip: 70113-1134
General Phone: 504-259-4687
General/National Adv. E-mail: info@pressclubneworleans.org
Primary Website: www.pressclubneworleans.org

NEW YORK FINANCIAL WRITERS ASSOCIATION, INC.

Street address 1: PO Box 338
Street address city: Ridgewood
Street address state: NJ
Zip/Postal code: 07451-0338
Country: USA
Mailing address: PO Box 338
Mailing city: Ridgewood
Mailing state: NJ
Mailing zip: 07451-0338
General Phone: (201) 612-0100
General Fax: (201) 612-9915
General/National Adv. E-mail: nyfwa@aol.com
Primary Website: www.nyfwa.org
Year Established: 1938

NEW YORK NEWS PUBLISHERS ASSOCIATION

Street address 1: 252 Hudson Ave
Street address city: Albany
Street address state: NY
Zip/Postal code: 12210
Country: USA
Mailing address: 252 Hudson Ave
Mailing city: Albany
Mailing state: NY
Mailing zip: 12210-1802
General Phone: (518) 449-1667
Primary Website: www.nynpa.com
Year Established: 1927

NEW YORK PRESS PHOTOGRAPHERS ASSOCIATION, INC.

Street address 1: PO Box 3346
Street address city: New York
Street address state: NY
Zip/Postal code: 10008-3346
Country: USA
Mailing address: Box 3346 Church Street Station
Mailing city: New York
Mailing state: NY
Mailing zip: 10008-3346
General Phone: (212) 889-6633
General/National Adv. E-mail: office@nyppa.org
Primary Website: www.nyppa.org
Year Established: 1915

NEW YORK SOCIETY OF NEWSPAPER EDITORS

Street address 1: 222 Waverly Avenue
Street address city: Syracuse
Street address state: NY
Zip/Postal code: 13244
County: Onondaga
Country: USA
Mailing address: 222 Waverly Ave
Mailing city: Syracuse
Mailing state: NY
Mailing zip: 13210-2412
General Phone: (315) 443-2305
General Fax: (315) 443-3946
Primary Website: https://library.syr.edu/about/

NEW YORK STATE ASSOCIATED PRESS ASSOCIATION

Street address 1: 450 W. 33rd St.
Street address city: Albany
Street address state: NY
Zip/Postal code: 10001
Country: USA
Mailing address: 450 W 33rd St
Mailing city: New York
Mailing state: NY
Mailing zip: 10001-2603
General Phone: 212-621-1670
General Fax: 212-621-1679
General/National Adv. E-mail: info@ap.org
Primary Website: www.ap.org
Year Established: 1848

NEW YORK STATE CIRCULATION MANAGERS ASSOCIATION

Street address 1: 85 Civic Center Plz.
Street address city: Poughkeepsie
Street address state: NY
Zip/Postal code: 12601
Country: USA
Mailing address: 85 Civic Center Plz
Mailing city: Poughkeepsie
Mailing state: NY
Mailing zip: 12601-2498
General Phone: (845) 437-4738
General Fax: (845) 437-4902
General/National Adv. E-mail: farrellb@poughkee.gannett.com
Primary Website: www.poughkeepsiejournal.com

NEWS MEDIA ALLIANCE

Street address 1: 4401 Wilson Blvd
Street address 2: Ste 900
Street address city: Arlington
Street address state: VA
Zip/Postal code: 22203-4195
County: Arlington
Country: USA
Mailing address: 4401 Wilson Blvd Ste 900
Mailing city: Arlington
Mailing state: VA
Mailing zip: 22203-4195
General Phone: (571) 366-1000
General Fax: (571) 366-1195
General/National Adv. E-mail: sheila.owens@naa.org
Primary Website: www.naa.org
Year Established: 1979

NORTH CAROLINA PRESS CLUB

Street address 1: 200 Countryside Rd
Street address city: Harmony
Street address state: NC
Zip/Postal code: 28634-9420
County: Iredell
Country: USA
Mailing address: 200 Countryside Rd
Mailing city: Harmony
Mailing state: NC
Mailing zip: 28634-9420
General Phone: (704)546-7900
General/National Adv. E-mail: suzyb3@gmail.com
Primary Website: www.nfpw.org

NORTH DAKOTA ASSOCIATED PRESS

Street address 1: PO Box 1018
Street address city: Bismarck
Street address state: ND
Zip/Postal code: 58502-5646
Country: USA
Mailing address: PO Box 1018
Mailing city: Bismarck
Mailing state: ND
Mailing zip: 58502-1018
General Phone: (701) 223-8450
General Fax: (701) 224-0158
General/National Adv. E-mail: apbismarck@ap.org

NORTHERN ILLINOIS NEWSPAPER ASSOCIATION

Street address 1: Campus Life Building, Suite 130
Street address city: DeKalb
Street address state: IL
Zip/Postal code: 60115
Country: USA
Mailing address: Campus Life Building, Suite 130
Mailing city: Dekalb
Mailing state: IL
Mailing zip: 60115
General Phone: (815) 753-4239
General Fax: (815) 753-0708
Primary Website: www.ninaonline.org
Year Established: 1961

NORTHERN STATES CIRCULATION MANAGERS ASSOCIATION

Street address 1: PO Box 220
Street address city: Grand Rapids
Street address state: MN
Zip/Postal code: 55744
Country: USA
Mailing address: PO Box 220
Mailing city: Grand Rapids
Mailing state: MN
Mailing zip: 55744-0220
General Phone: (218) 326-6623
General Fax: (218) 326-6627
General/National Adv. E-mail: ron.oleheiser@grandrapidsmn.com
Primary Website: www.grandrapidsmn.com

NORTHWEST INTERNATIONAL CIRCULATION EXECUTIVES

Street address 1: PO Box 778
Street address city: La Conner
Street address state: WA
Zip/Postal code: 98257
Country: USA
Mailing address: PO Box 778
Mailing city: La Conner
Mailing state: WA
Mailing zip: 98257-0778
General Phone: (360) 466-2006
General Fax: (360) 466-2006
General/National Adv. E-mail: nice@galaxynet.com
Primary Website: www.nicex.org

OHIO CIRCULATION MANAGERS ASSOCIATION

Street address 1: 1335 Dublin Rd., Suite 216-B
Street address city: Columbus
Street address state: OH
Zip/Postal code: 43215
Country: USA
Mailing address: 1335 Dublin Rd Ste 216B
Mailing city: Columbus
Mailing state: OH
Mailing zip: 43215-1000
General Phone: (614) 486-6677
General Fax: (614) 486-4940
General/National Adv. E-mail: bbarker@plaind.com
Primary Website: www.ohiocirculation.com

OHIO NEWSPAPER ADVERTISING EXECUTIVES

Street address 1: 1335 Dublin Rd. S., Ste. 216-B
Street address city: Columbus
Street address state: OH
Zip/Postal code: 43215
Country: USA
Mailing address: 1335 Dublin Rd Ste 216B
Mailing city: Columbus
Mailing state: OH
Mailing zip: 43215-1000
General Phone: (614) 486-6677
General Fax: (614) 486-6373
General/National Adv. E-mail: mhenry@adohio.net
Primary Website: www.adohio.net

OKLAHOMA PRESS ASSOCIATION

Street address 1: 3601 N Lincoln Blvd
Street address city: Oklahoma City
Street address state: OK
Zip/Postal code: 73105-5411
Country: USA
Mailing address: 3601 N Lincoln Blvd
Mailing city: Oklahoma City
Mailing state: OK
Mailing zip: 73105-5499
General Phone: (405) 499-0020
General Fax: (405) 499-0048
General/National Adv. E-mail: swilkerson@okpress.com
Display Adv. E-mail: lcobb@okpress.com
Primary Website: www.okpress.com
Year Established: 1906

ONTARIO COMMUNITY NEWSPAPERS ASSOCIATION

Street address 1: 3228 South Service Rd. Ste 116
Street address city: Burlington
Street address state: ON
Zip/Postal code: L7N 3H8
Country: Canada
Mailing address: 3228 South Service Rd. Ste 116
Mailing city: Burlington
Mailing state: ON
Mailing zip: L7N 3H8
General Phone: (905) 639-8720
General Fax: (905) 639-6962
General/National Adv. E-mail: info@ocna.org
Primary Website: www.ocna.org
Year Established: 1950

ORANGE COUNTY PRESS CLUB

Street address 1: 1835 Newport Blvd., #A-109-538
Street address city: Costa Mesa
Street address state: CA
Zip/Postal code: 92627
Country: USA
Mailing address: 1835 Newport Blvd # A-109-538
Mailing city: Costa Mesa
Mailing state: CA
Mailing zip: 92627-5031
General Phone: (714) 564-1052
General Fax: (714) 564-1047
General/National Adv. E-mail: OCPressClub@orangecountypressclub.com

Primary Website: www.ocpressclub.org

OVERSEAS PRESS CLUB OF PUERTO RICO (ESTABLISHED 1968)

Street address 1: 1399 Ave. Ana G. M?ndez
Street address city: San Juan
Street address state: PR
Zip/Postal code: 00928-1345
Country: Puerto Rico
Mailing address: P.O Box 12326, Loiza St. Station, Santurce
Mailing city: San Juan
Mailing state: PR
Mailing zip: 00914-0326
General Phone: (787) 525-8901
General Fax: N/A
General/National Adv. E-mail: opcpr@yahoo.com
Display Adv. E-mail: opcpr@yahoo.com
Editorial e-mail: opcpr@yahoo.com
Primary Website: www.opcpr.wordpress.com
Year Established: 1968

PACIFIC NORTHWEST ASSOCIATION OF WANT AD NEWSPAPERS (PNAWAN) & WESTERN REGIONAL ADVERTISING PROGRAM (WRAP)

Street address 1: 304 W 3rd Ave
Street address 2: C/O Exchange Publishing
Street address city: Spokane
Street address state: WA
Zip/Postal code: 99201-4314
County: Spokane
Country: USA
Mailing address: PO Box 427
Mailing city: Spokane
Mailing state: WA
Mailing zip: 99210
General Phone: (509) 922-3456
General Fax: (509) 455-7940
General/National Adv. E-mail: Ads@PNAWAN.org
Display Adv. E-mail: Kylah@ExchangePublishing.com
Primary Website: www.RegionalAds.org
Year Established: 1977

PACIFIC NORTHWEST NEWSPAPER ASSOCIATION

Street address 1: 708 Tenth St.
Street address city: Sacramento
Street address state: CA
Zip/Postal code: 95814
Country: USA
Mailing address: 708 10th St
Mailing city: Sacramento
Mailing state: CA
Mailing zip: 95814-1803
General Phone: (888) 344-7662
General Fax: (916) 288-6002
General/National Adv. E-mail: tom@cnpa.com
Primary Website: www.pnna.com

PENNSYLVANIA NEWSPAPER ASSOCIATION

Street address 1: 3899 N. Front St.
Street address city: Harrisburg
Street address state: PA
Zip/Postal code: 17110
Mailing address: 3899 N Front St
Mailing city: Harrisburg
Mailing state: PA
Mailing zip: 17110-1583
General Phone: (717) 703-3000
General Fax: (717) 703-3001
Primary Website: www.pa-newspaper.org

PENNSYLVANIA SOCIETY OF NEWS EDITORS

Street address 1: 3899 N. Front St.
Street address city: Harrisburg
Street address state: PA
Zip/Postal code: 17110
Country: USA
Mailing address: 3899 N Front St
Mailing city: Harrisburg
Mailing state: PA
Mailing zip: 17110-1583
General Phone: (717) 703-3000
General Fax: (717) 703-3001
General/National Adv. E-mail: teresas@pa-news.org
Primary Website: www.panewsmedia.org

PENNSYLVANIA WOMEN'S PRESS ASSOCIATION

Street address 1: 511 Lenox St.
Street address city: Stroudsburg
Street address state: PA
Zip/Postal code: 18360
Country: USA
Mailing address: 511 Lenox St
Mailing city: Stroudsburg
Mailing state: PA
Mailing zip: 18360-1516
General Phone: (717) 295-7869
General/National Adv. E-mail: pwpa@lancasteronline.com
Primary Website: www.pwpa.us

QUEBEC COMMUNITY NEWSPAPERS ASSOCIATION

Street address 1: 400 Grand Blvd., Ste. 5
Street address city: Ile Perrot
Street address state: QC
Zip/Postal code: J7V 4X2
Country: Canada
Mailing address: 400 Grand Blvd., Ste. 5
Mailing city: Ile Perrot
Mailing state: QC
Mailing zip: J7V 4X2
General Phone: (514) 453-6300
General Fax: (514) 453-6330
General/National Adv. E-mail: info@qcna.qc.ca
Primary Website: www.qcna.org

QUICKNEWS

Street address 1: 2608 Lakewood Road
Street address 2: St. 3
Street address city: Point Pleasant
Street address state: NJ
Zip/Postal code: 08742
County: Ocean
Country: USA
General Phone: 201-914-0495
General Fax: 570-226-8696
General/National Adv. E-mail: protella@njba.com
Primary Website: www.njba.com
Year Established: 1946

RHODE ISLAND PRESS ASSOCIATION

Street address 1: 282 Doyle ave
Street address city: Providence
Street address state: RI
Zip/Postal code: 02906
County: Providence
Country: USA
Mailing address: 282 Doyle Avenue
Mailing city: Providence
Mailing state: RI
Mailing zip: 02906
General Phone: (401) 874-4287
General Fax: (401) 874-4450
General/National Adv. E-mail: lilevin@uri.edu
Primary Website: www.ripress.org
Year Established: 1886

SASKATCHEWAN WEEKLY NEWSPAPERS ASSOCIATION

Street address 1: 14-401 45th St. W.
Street address city: Saskatoon
Street address state: SK
Zip/Postal code: S7L 5Z9
Country: Canada
Mailing address: 14-401 45th St. W.
Mailing city: Saskatoon
Mailing state: SK
Mailing zip: S7L 5Z9
General Phone: (306) 382-9683
General Fax: (306) 382-9421
General/National Adv. E-mail: swna@swna.com
Primary Website: www.swna.com

SOUTH CAROLINA ASSOCIATED PRESS

Street address 1: 1401 Shop Road, Suite B
Street address city: Columbia
Street address state: SC
Zip/Postal code: 29201
Country: USA
Mailing address: 1401 Shop Rd Ste B
Mailing city: Columbia
Mailing state: SC
Mailing zip: 29201-4843
General Phone: (803) 799-5510
General Fax: (803) 252-2913
General/National Adv. E-mail: apcolumbia@ap.org

SOUTHEASTERN ADVERTISING PUBLISHERS ASSOCIATION

Street address 1: 104 Westland Dr
Street address city: Columbia
Street address state: TN
Zip/Postal code: 38401-6522
County: Maury
Country: USA
Mailing address: 104 Westland Dr
Mailing city: Columbia
Mailing state: TN
Mailing zip: 38401-6522
General Phone: (931) 223-5708
General Fax: (888) 450-8329
General/National Adv. E-mail: info@sapatoday.com
Primary Website: www.sapatoday.com
Year Established: 1979

SOUTHERN CIRCULATION MANAGERS ASSOCIATION

Street address 1: P.O. Box 1163
Street address city: Kingsport
Street address state: TN
Zip/Postal code: 37662
County: Mobile County
Country: USA
Mailing address: PO Box 1163
Mailing city: Kingsport
Mailing state: TN
Mailing zip: 37662-1163
General/National Adv. E-mail: info@scmaonline.net
Primary Website: www.southerncma.com

SOUTHERN CLASSIFIED ADVERTISING MANAGERS ASSOCIATION

Street address 1: PO Box 531335
Street address city: Mountain Brook
Street address state: AL
Zip/Postal code: 35253-1335
Mailing address: PO Box 531335
Mailing city: Mountain Brook
Mailing state: AL
Mailing zip: 35253-1335
General Phone: (205) 823-3448
General Fax: (205) 951-5446
General/National Adv. E-mail: hrushing@usit.net
Primary Website: www.scama.com

SOUTHERN NEWSPAPER PUBLISHERS ASSOCIATION

Street address 1: 3680 N. Peachtree Rd., Ste. 300
Street address city: Atlanta
Street address state: GA
Zip/Postal code: 30341
Country: USA
Mailing address: 3680 N Peachtree Rd Ste 300
Mailing city: Atlanta
Mailing state: GA
Mailing zip: 30341-2346
General Phone: (404) 256-0444
General Fax: (404) 252-9135
General/National Adv. E-mail: edward@snpa.org
Primary Website: www.snpa.org
Year Established: 1903

SOUTHWEST CLASSIFIED ADVERTISING MANAGERS ASSOCIATION

Street address 1: Dallas Morning News
Street address 2: 508 Young St.
Street address city: Dallas
Street address state: TX
Zip/Postal code: 75265-5237
Country: USA
Mailing address: Dallas Morning News
Mailing city: Dallas
Mailing state: TX
Mailing zip: 75265-5237
General Phone: 214-977-8222
General/National Adv. E-mail: jmckeon@dallasnews.com
Primary Website: www.dallasnews.com
Year Established: 1885

SPALDING ENTERPRISE

Street address 1: 140 S Cedar St
Street address city: Spalding
Street address state: NE
Zip/Postal code: 68665
County: Greeley
Country: USA
Mailing address: PO BOX D
Mailing city: SPALDING
Mailing state: NE
Mailing zip: 68665-0110
General Phone: (308) 497-2153
General Fax: (308) 497-2153
General/National Adv. E-mail: spalding2002@hotmail.com
Year Established: 1900

STATE HISTORICAL SOCIETY OF WISCONSIN

Street address 1: 816 State St.
Street address city: Madison
Street address state: WI
Zip/Postal code: 53706-1482
County: Dane
Country: USA
Mailing address: 816 State St
Mailing city: Madison
Mailing state: WI
Mailing zip: 53706-1482
General Phone: (608) 264-6534
General Fax: (608) 264-6520
Primary Website: www.wisconsinhistory.org

TENNESSEE PRESS ASSOCIATION

Street address 1: 412 N. Cedar Bluff Road
Street address 2: Suite 403
Street address city: Knoxville
Street address state: TN
Zip/Postal code: 37923
County: Knox
Country: USA
Mailing address: 412 N. Cedar Bluff Road
Mailing city: Knoxville
Mailing state: TN
Mailing zip: 37923
General Phone: 865-584-5761
General Fax: 865-558-8687
General/National Adv. E-mail: info@tnpress.com
Primary Website: www.tnpress.com
Year Established: 1947

TEXAS ASSOCIATED PRESS MANAGING EDITORS

Street address 1: The Dallas Morning News, 508 Young St.
Street address city: Dallas
Street address state: TX
Zip/Postal code: 75202
Country: USA
Mailing address: 508 Young St
Mailing city: Dallas
Mailing state: TX
Mailing zip: 75202-4808
General Phone: (214) 977-8222

Primary Website: www.txapme.org

TEXAS CIRCULATION MANAGEMENT ASSOCIATION

Street address 1: c/o PO Box 9577
Street address city: The Woodlands
Street address state: TX
Zip/Postal code: 77387
Country: USA
Mailing address: c/o TCMA, PO Box 9577
Mailing city: The Woodlands
Mailing state: TX
Mailing zip: 77387
General/National Adv. E-mail: tcma@texascma.org
Primary Website: www.texascma.org
Year Established: 1913

THE AD CLUB

Street address 1: 9 Hamilton Pl.
Street address city: Boston
Street address state: MA
Zip/Postal code: 02108-3210
Country: USA
Mailing address: 9 Hamilton Pl Ste 200
Mailing city: Boston
Mailing state: MA
Mailing zip: 02108-4715
General Phone: (617) 262-1100
General Fax: (617) 456-1772
General/National Adv. E-mail: newsfeed@adclub.org
Primary Website: www.adclub.org
Year Established: 1904

THE AD CLUB

Street address 1: 38 Newbury St. 5th Fl.
Street address city: Boston
Street address state: MA
Zip/Postal code: 2116
Mailing address: 38 Newbury St Fl 5
Mailing city: Boston
Mailing state: MA
Mailing zip: 02116-3210
General Phone: (617) 262-1100
General Fax: (617) 262-0739
Primary Website: www.adclub.org

THE BILTMORE BEACON

Street address 1: 220 N. Main St.
Street address city: Waynesille
Street address state: NC
Zip/Postal code: 28786
County: Buncombe
Country: U.S.
General Phone: 8284520661
General/National Adv. E-mail: sdufour@themountaineer.com
Display Adv. E-mail: sdufour@themountaineer.com
Primary Website: themountaineer.com
Year Established: 1995

THE FALMOUTH ENTERPRISE

Street address 1: 50 Depot Ave
Street address city: Falmouth
Street address state: MA
Zip/Postal code: 02540-2302
County: Barnstable
Country: USA
General Phone: (508) 548-4700
General Fax: (508) 540-8407
General/National Adv. E-mail: ptheall@capenews.net
Display Adv. E-mail: ads@capenews.net
Editorial e-mail: bennett@capenews.net
Primary Website: capenews.net
Year Established: 1895

THE LAUREL OUTLOOK

Street address 1: 415 E. Main St.
Street address city: Laurel
Street address state: MT
Zip/Postal code: 59044
County: Yellowstone
Country: USA
Mailing address: P.O. Box 278
Mailing city: Laurel
Mailing state: MT
Mailing zip: 59044
General Phone: (406) 628-4412
General/National Adv. E-mail: news@laureloutlook.com
Classified Adv. e-mail: classifieds@laureloutlook.com
Editorial e-mail: news@laureloutlook.com
Primary Website: www.laureloutlook.com
Year Established: 1908

THE PRESS CLUB OF CLEVELAND

Street address 1: 28022 Osborn Road
Street address city: Cleveland
Street address state: OH
Zip/Postal code: 44140
County: Cuyahoga
Country: USA
Mailing address: 28022 Osborn Rd
Mailing city: Cleveland
Mailing state: OH
Mailing zip: 44140-2011
General Phone: 440-899-1222
General/National Adv. E-mail: pressclubcleveland@oh.rr.com
Display Adv. E-mail: same
Editorial e-mail: same
Primary Website: pressclubcleveland.com
Year Established: 1887

TIMES COMMUNITY NEWSPAPERS

Street address 1: 500 Stony Brook Ct
Street address 2: Suite 2
Street address city: Newburgh
Street address state: NY
Zip/Postal code: 12550
County: Orange
Country: USA
General Phone: 8455610170
General Fax: 8455613967
General/National Adv. E-mail: editor@tcnewspapers.com
Display Adv. E-mail: advertising@tcnewspapers.com
Classified Adv. e-mail: classifieds@tcnewspapers.com
Editorial e-mail: editor@tcnewspapers.com
Primary Website: www.timeshudsonvalley.com

TOMPKINS WEEKLY

Street address 1: 3100 N. Triphammer Road
Street address 2: Suite 100
Street address city: Lansing
Street address state: NY
Zip/Postal code: 14882
County: Tompkins
Country: USA
General Phone: 607-533-0057
General/National Adv. E-mail: info@VizellaMedia.com
Display Adv. E-mail: ToddM@VizellaMedia.com
Classified Adv. e-mail: TinaM@VizellaMedia.com
Editorial e-mail: editorial@VizellaMedia.com
Primary Website: www.TompkinsWeekly.com
Year Established: 2006

TRAILL COUNTY TRIBUNE

Street address 1: 12 3rd St SE
Street address city: Mayville
Street address state: ND
Zip/Postal code: 58257-1414
County: Traill
Country: USA
Mailing address: PO BOX 567
Mailing city: MAYVILLE
Mailing state: ND
Mailing zip: 58257-0567
General Phone: (701) 788-3281
General/National Adv. E-mail: news@tctribune.net
Editorial e-mail: news@tctribune.net

UNIVERSITY PRESS OF KENTUCKY

Street address 1: 663 S. Limestone St.
Street address city: Lexington
Street address state: KY
Zip/Postal code: 40508-4008
Country: USA
Mailing address: 663 S Limestone
Mailing city: Lexington
Mailing state: KY
Mailing zip: 40508-4008
General Phone: (859) 257-8419
General Fax: (859) 323-1873
General/National Adv. E-mail: smwrin2@uky.edu
Primary Website: www.kentuckypress.com

UTAH-IDAHO-SPOKANE ASSOCIATED PRESS ASSOCIATION

Street address 1: 30 E. 100 South St., Ste. 200
Street address city: Salt Lake City
Street address state: UT
Zip/Postal code: 84111
Country: USA
Mailing address: 30 E. 100 South St., Ste. 200
Mailing city: Salt Lake City
Mailing state: UT
Mailing zip: 84111
General Phone: (801) 322-3405
General Fax: (801) 322-0051
General/National Adv. E-mail: apsaltlake@ap.org

VALLEY PRESS CLUB, INC.

Street address 1: PO Box 5475
Street address city: Springfield
Street address state: MA
Zip/Postal code: 01101-5475
County: USA
Country: USA
Mailing address: PO Box 5475
Mailing city: Springfield
Mailing state: MA
Mailing zip: 01101-5475
General Phone: (413) 682-0007
General/National Adv. E-mail: info@valleypressclub.com
Primary Website: www.valleypressclub.com

WASHINGTON ASSOCIATED PRESS NEWSPAPER EXECUTIVES ASSOCIATION

Street address 1: 3131 Elliott Ave., Ste. 750
Street address city: Seattle
Street address state: WA
Zip/Postal code: 98121
Country: USA
Mailing address: 3131 Elliott Ave Ste 750
Mailing city: Seattle
Mailing state: WA
Mailing zip: 98121-1095
General Phone: (206) 682-1812
General Fax: (206) 621-1948
General/National Adv. E-mail: apseattle@ap.org
Primary Website: www.ap.org

WASHINGTON PRESS ASSOCIATION

Street address 1: c/o 15642 129th Court SE
Street address city: Renton
Street address state: WA
Zip/Postal code: 98058
Country: USA
Mailing address: c/o 15642 129th Court SE
Mailing city: Renton
Mailing state: WA
Mailing zip: 98058
Primary Website: www.washingtonpressassociation.com
Year Established: 1946

WAUBAY CLIPPER

Street address 1: 122 N Main St
Street address city: Waubay
Street address state: SD
Zip/Postal code: 57273
County: Day
Country: USA
Mailing address: PO BOX 47
Mailing city: WAUBAY
Mailing state: SD
Mailing zip: 57273-0047
General Phone: (605) 947-4501
General Fax: (605) 947-4501
General/National Adv. E-mail: linda@waubayclipper.com
Display Adv. E-mail: linda@waubayclipper.com
Editorial e-mail: linda@waubayclipper.com
Primary Website: waubayclipper.blogspot.com
Year Established: 1890

WEST TEXAS PRESS ASSOCIATION

Street address 1: 706 SW 10th St.
Street address city: Perryton
Street address state: TX
Zip/Postal code: 79070
Country: USA
Mailing address: 706 SW 10th Ave
Mailing city: Perryton
Mailing state: TX
Mailing zip: 79070-3802
General Phone: (806) 435-3631
General Fax: (806) 435-2420
General/National Adv. E-mail: secretary@wtpa.org
Primary Website: www.wtpa.org

WHITE HOUSE CORRESPONDENTS' ASSOCIATION

Street address 1: 600 New Hampshire Ave., Ste. 800
Street address city: Washington
Street address state: DC
Zip/Postal code: 20037
Country: USA
Mailing address: 600 New Hampshire Ave NW Ste 610
Mailing city: Washington
Mailing state: DC
Mailing zip: 20037
General Phone: 202-499-4187
General/National Adv. E-mail: director@whca.press
Primary Website: www.whca.press
Year Established: 1914

WHITE HOUSE NEWS PHOTOGRAPHERS ASSOCIATION, INC.

Street address 1: PO Box 7119
Street address city: Washington
Street address state: DC
Zip/Postal code: 20044-7119
Country: USA
Mailing address: PO Box 7119
Mailing city: Washington
Mailing state: DC
Mailing zip: 20044-7119
General Phone: (202) 785-5230
General/National Adv. E-mail: info@whnpa.org
Primary Website: www.whnpa.org
Year Established: 1921

WISCONSIN ASSOCIATED PRESS ASSOCIATION

Street address 1: 111 E. Wisconsin Ave., Ste.1925
Street address city: Milwaukee
Street address state: WI
Zip/Postal code: 53202
Country: USA
Mailing address: 111 E Wisconsin Ave Ste 1925
Mailing city: Milwaukee
Mailing state: WI
Mailing zip: 53202-4825
General Phone: (414) 225-3580
General/National Adv. E-mail: apmlw@ap.org
Primary Website: www.ap.org

WISCONSIN FREE COMMUNITY PAPERS

Street address 1: 101 S. Main St.
Street address city: Fond Du Lac
Street address state: WI
Zip/Postal code: 54935
Country: USA
Mailing address: 101 S Main St
Mailing city: Fond Du Lac
Mailing state: WI
Mailing zip: 54935-4228
General Phone: 800-727-8745
General Fax: 920-922-0861
General/National Adv. E-mail: wcp@wisad.com
Primary Website: wisad.com

WYOMING ASSOCIATED PRESS

Street address 1: 320 W. 25th St., Ste. 310
Street address city: Cheyenne
Street address state: WY

Zip/Postal code: 82001
Country: USA
Mailing address: 2121 Evans Ave
Mailing city: Cheyenne
Mailing state: WY
Mailing zip: 82001-3733
General Phone: (307) 632-9351
General Fax: (307) 637-8538
Primary Website: www.ap.org

DAILY STATE NEWSPAPER REPRESENTATIVE

ADNETWORKNY

Street address 1: 109 Twin Oaks Dr
Street address 2: Ste D
Street address city: Syracuse
Street address state: NY
Zip/Postal code: 13206-1204
County: Onondaga
Country: USA
Mailing address: 109 Twin Oaks Dr
Mailing city: Syracuse
Mailing state: NY
Mailing zip: 13206
General Phone: (315) 472-6007
General Fax: (877) 790-1976
General/National Adv. E-mail: ads@fcpny.com
Primary Website: www.fcpny.com
Year Established: 1950

ALABAMA NEWSPAPER ADVERTISING SERVICE, INC.

Street address 1: 3324 Independence Dr
Street address 2: Ste 200
Street address city: Birmingham
Street address state: AL
Zip/Postal code: 35209-5602
County: Jefferson
Country: USA
Mailing address: 3324 Independence Dr Ste 200
Mailing city: Birmingham
Mailing state: AL
Mailing zip: 35209-5602
General Phone: (205) 871-7737
General Fax: (205) 871-7740
General/National Adv. E-mail: mail@alabamapress.org
Primary Website: www.alabamapress.org

ALLIED DAILY NEWSPAPERS OF WASHINGTON

Street address 1: 1110 Capitol Way S
Street address city: Olympia
Street address state: WA
Zip/Postal code: 98501-2251
County: Thurston
Country: USA
Mailing address: 1110 Capitol Way S
Mailing city: Olympia
Mailing state: WA
Mailing zip: 98501-2251
General Phone: (360) 943-9960
General Fax: (360) 943-9962
General/National Adv. E-mail: anewspaper@aol.com

ANA ADVERTISING SERVICES, INC. (ARIZONA NEWSPAPER ASSOCIATION)

Street address 1: 1001 N Central Ave
Street address 2: Ste 670
Street address city: Phoenix
Street address state: AZ
Zip/Postal code: 85004-1947
County: Maricopa
Country: USA
General Phone: (602) 261-7655
General Fax: (602) 261-7525
General/National Adv. E-mail: office@ananews.com
Primary Website: www.ananews.com
Year Established: 1931

ARKANSAS PRESS SERVICES

Street address 1: 411 S Victory St
Street address city: Little Rock
Street address state: AR
Zip/Postal code: 72201-2933
County: Pulaski
Country: USA
Mailing address: 411 S Victory St Ste 100
Mailing city: Little Rock
Mailing state: AR
Mailing zip: 72201-2934
General Phone: (501) 374-1500
General Fax: (501) 374-7509
General/National Adv. E-mail: info@arkansaspress.org
Primary Website: www.arkansaspress.org
Year Established: 1873

CNPA ADVERTISING SERVICES

Street address 1: 2000 O St
Street address 2: Ste 120
Street address city: Sacramento
Street address state: CA
Zip/Postal code: 95811-5299
County: Sacramento
Country: USA
Mailing address: 2000 O St Ste 120
Mailing city: Sacramento
Mailing state: CA
Mailing zip: 95811-5299
General Phone: (916) 288-6000
General Fax: (916) 288-6003
General/National Adv. E-mail: bryan@cnpa.com
Primary Website: www.cnpa.com

COMMUNITY PAPERS OF FLORIDA

Street address 1: 12601 SE 53rd Terrace Rd
Street address city: Belleview
Street address state: FL
Zip/Postal code: 34420-5106
County: Marion
Country: USA
Mailing address: PO Box 1149
Mailing city: Summerfield
Mailing state: FL
Mailing zip: 34492-1149
General Phone: (352) 237-3409
General Fax: (352) 347-3384
General/National Adv. E-mail: djneuharth@aol.com
Primary Website: www.communitypapersofflorida.com
Year Established: 1960

COMMUNITY PAPERS OF MICHIGAN, INC.

Street address 1: 5000 Northwind Dr
Street address 2: Ste 240
Street address city: East Lansing
Street address state: MI
Zip/Postal code: 48823-5032
County: Ingham
Country: USA
Mailing address: 5000 Northwind Dr Ste 240
Mailing city: East Lansing
Mailing state: MI
Mailing zip: 48823-5032
General Phone: (800) 783-0267
General Fax: (517) 333-3322
General/National Adv. E-mail: jackguza@cpapersmi.com
Primary Website: www.communitypapersofmichigan.com

CUSTOMIZED NEWSPAPER ADVERTISING (IOWA)

Street address 1: 319 E 5th St
Street address city: Des Moines
Street address state: IA
Zip/Postal code: 50309-1927
County: Polk
Country: USA
Mailing address: 319 E 5th St
Mailing city: Des Moines
Mailing state: IA
Mailing zip: 50309-1927
General Phone: (515) 244-2145
General Fax: (515) 244-4855
Primary Website: www.cnaads.com; www.inanews.com

FLORIDA PRESS SERVICE, INC.

Street address 1: 336 E College Ave
Street address 2: Ste 203
Street address city: Tallahassee
Street address state: FL
Zip/Postal code: 32301-1559
County: Leon
Country: USA
Mailing address: 336 E College Ave Ste 203
Mailing city: Tallahassee
Mailing state: FL
Mailing zip: 32301-1559
General Phone: (850) 222-5790
General Fax: (850) 222-4498
General/National Adv. E-mail: fps-info@flpress.com
Primary Website: www.flpress.com

GEORGIA NEWSPAPER SERVICE, INC.

Street address 1: 3066 Mercer University Dr
Street address 2: Ste 200
Street address city: Atlanta
Street address state: GA
Zip/Postal code: 30341-4137
County: Dekalb
Country: USA
Mailing address: 3066 Mercer University Dr Ste 200
Mailing city: Atlanta
Mailing state: GA
Mailing zip: 30341-4137
General Phone: (770) 454-6776
General Fax: (770) 454-6778
General/National Adv. E-mail: mail@gapress.org
Primary Website: www.gapress.org

GREAT NORTHERN CONNECTION

Street address 1: 8703 Midway Rd
Street address city: Lena
Street address state: WI
Zip/Postal code: 54139-9769
County: Oconto
Country: USA
Mailing address: 8703 Midway Rd
Mailing city: Lena
Mailing state: WI
Mailing zip: 54139-9769
General Phone: (920) 829-5145
General/National Adv. E-mail: classifieds@greatnorthernconn.com
Primary Website: www.greatnorthernconn.com
Year Established: 1985

HITCHINGS & CO.

Street address 1: 580 W Germantown Pike
Street address 2: Ste 108
Street address city: Plymouth Meeting
Street address state: PA
Zip/Postal code: 19462-1370
County: Montgomery
Country: USA
Mailing address: Plymouth Plz., 580 W. Germantown Pk., Ste. 108
Mailing city: Plymouth Meeting
Mailing state: PA
Mailing zip: 19462
General Phone: (610) 941-3555
General Fax: (610) 941-1289
General/National Adv. E-mail: brian@phillyareapapers.com
Primary Website: www.phillyareapapers.com

INTERSECT MEDIA SOLUTIONS

Street address 1: 1025 Greenwood Blvd.
Street address 2: Suite 191
Street address city: Lake Mary
Street address state: FL
Zip/Postal code: 32746-5410
County: Seminole
Country: USA
Mailing address: 1025 Greenwood Blvd., Suite 191
Mailing city: Lake Mary
Mailing state: FL
Mailing zip: 32746-5410
General Phone: (866) 404-5913
General/National Adv. E-mail: info@mediagenius.com
Primary Website: www.intersectmediasolutions.com
Year Established: 1959

KENTUCKY PRESS SERVICE, INC.

Street address 1: 101 Consumer Ln
Street address city: Frankfort
Street address state: KY
Zip/Postal code: 40601-8489
County: Franklin
Country: USA
Mailing address: 101 Consumer Ln
Mailing city: Frankfort
Mailing state: KY
Mailing zip: 40601-8489
General Phone: (502) 223-8821
General Fax: (502) 875-2624
General/National Adv. E-mail: dthompson@kypress.com
Display Adv. E-mail: rmccarty@kypress.com, hwillard@kypress.com
Classified Adv. e-mail: rmccarty@kypress.com, hwillard@kypress.com
Primary Website: www.kypress.com
Year Established: 1959

LOUISIANA PRESS ASSOCIATION

Street address 1: 404 Europe St
Street address city: Baton Rouge
Street address state: LA
Zip/Postal code: 70802-6403
County: East Baton Rouge
Country: USA
General Phone: (225) 344-9309
General Fax: (225) 344-9344
General/National Adv. E-mail: pam@lapress.com
Display Adv. E-mail: erin@LaPress.com
Primary Website: www.lapress.com
Year Established: 1880

MACNET

Street address 1: PO Box 408
Street address city: Hamburg
Street address state: PA
Zip/Postal code: 19526-0408
County: Berks
Country: USA
Mailing address: PO Box 408
Mailing city: Hamburg
Mailing state: PA
Mailing zip: 19526-0408
General Phone: (800) 450-7227
General Fax: (610) 743-8500

General/National Adv. E-mail: info@macpa.net
Primary Website: www.macpa.net; www.macnetonline.com

MANSI MEDIA

Street address 1: 3899 N Front St
Street address city: Harrisburg
Street address state: PA
Zip/Postal code: 17110-1583
County: Dauphin
Country: USA
General Phone: (717) 703-3030
General Fax: (717) 703-3033
General/National Adv. E-mail: sales@mansimedia.com
Primary Website: www.mansimedia.com

MIDWEST FREE COMMUNITY PAPERS

Street address 1: PO Box 1350
Street address city: Iowa City
Street address state: IA
Zip/Postal code: 52244-1350
County: Johnson
Country: USA
Mailing address: PO Box 1350
Mailing city: Iowa City
Mailing state: IA
Mailing zip: 52244-1350
General Phone: (319) 341-4352
General Fax: (319) 341-4358
General/National Adv. E-mail: mfcp@mchsi.com
Primary Website: www.mfcp.org
Year Established: 1955

MISSISSIPPI PRESS SERVICES, INC.

Street address 1: 371 Edgewood Terrace Dr
Street address city: Jackson
Street address state: MS
Zip/Postal code: 39206-6217
County: Hinds
Country: USA
Mailing address: 371 Edgewood Terrace Dr.
Mailing city: Jackson
Mailing state: MS
Mailing zip: 39206-6217
General Phone: (601) 981-3060
General Fax: (601) 981-3676
General/National Adv. E-mail: admin@mspress.org
Primary Website: www.mspress.org
Year Established: 1978

MISSOURI PRESS SERVICE, INC.

Street address 1: 802 Locust St
Street address city: Columbia
Street address state: MO
Zip/Postal code: 65201-4888
County: Boone
Country: USA
Mailing address: 802 Locust St
Mailing city: Columbia
Mailing state: MO
Mailing zip: 65201-7799
General Phone: (573) 449-4167
General Fax: (573) 874-5894
General/National Adv. E-mail: mmaassen@socket.net
Display Adv. E-mail: mopressads@socket.net
Editorial e-mail: mbarba@mopress.com
Primary Website: www.mopress.com
Year Established: 1867

MNI

Street address 1: 827 N Washington Ave
Street address city: Lansing
Street address state: MI
Zip/Postal code: 48906-5135
County: Ingham
Country: USA
Mailing address: 827 N Washington Ave
Mailing city: Lansing
Mailing state: MI
Mailing zip: 48906-5135
General Phone: (517) 372-2424
General Fax: (517) 372-2429
General/National Adv. E-mail: mpa@michiganpress.org
Primary Website: www.michiganpress.org
Year Established: 1868

MONTANA NEWSPAPER ADVERTISING SERVICE, INC.

Street address 1: 825 Great Northern Blvd
Street address 2: Ste 202
Street address city: Helena
Street address state: MT
Zip/Postal code: 59601-3340
County: Lewis And Clark
Country: USA
Mailing address: 825 Great Northern Blvd Ste 202
Mailing city: Helena
Mailing state: MT
Mailing zip: 59601-3358
General Phone: (406) 443-2850
General Fax: (406) 443-2860
General/National Adv. E-mail: randy@mtnewspapers.com
Primary Website: www.mtnewspapers.com
Year Established: 1955

NEBRASKA PRESS ADVERTISING SERVICE

Street address 1: 845 S St
Street address city: Lincoln
Street address state: NE
Zip/Postal code: 68508-1226
County: Lancaster
Country: USA
General Phone: (402) 476-2851
General Fax: (402) 476-2942
General/National Adv. E-mail: nebpress@nebpress.com
Primary Website: www.nebpress.com
Year Established: 1879

NENPA AD NETWORK (NEW ENGLAND NEWSPAPER AND PRESS ASSOCIATION)

Street address 1: 1 Arrow Dr
Street address 2: Ste 6
Street address city: Woburn
Street address state: MA
Zip/Postal code: 01801-2039
County: Middlesex
Country: USA
Mailing address: 1 Arrow Drive, Suite 6
Mailing city: Woburn
Mailing state: MA
Mailing zip: 01801
General Phone: (781) 281-2053
General Fax: (339) 999-2174
General/National Adv. E-mail: info@nenpa.com
Primary Website: www.nenpa.com
Year Established: 1930

NEW HAMPSHIRE UNION LEADER

Street address 1: 100 William Loeb Drive
Street address city: Manchester
Street address state: NH
Zip/Postal code: 03109
Country: USA

NEW JERSEY NEWSMEDIA NETWORK (NJNN)

Street address 1: 810 Bear Tavern Rd
Street address 2: Ste 307
Street address city: Ewing
Street address state: NJ
Zip/Postal code: 08628-1022
County: Mercer
Country: USA
Mailing address: 810 Bear Tavern Rd Ste 307
Mailing city: Ewing
Mailing state: NJ
Mailing zip: 08628-1022
General Phone: (609) 406-0600
General Fax: (609) 406-0399
General/National Adv. E-mail: njnn@njpa.org
Primary Website: www.njpa.org/njnn
Year Established: 1991

NEW MEXICO PRESS ASSOCIATION

Street address 1: 700 Silver Ave SW
Street address city: Albuquerque
Street address state: NM
Zip/Postal code: 87102-3019
County: Bernalillo
Country: USA
Mailing address: PO Box 95198
Mailing city: Albuquerque
Mailing state: NM
Mailing zip: 87199-5198
General Phone: (505) 275-1241
General Fax: (505) 275-1449
General/National Adv. E-mail: info@nmpress.org
Display Adv. E-mail: Ads@NMPress.org
Primary Website: www.nmpress.org

NEW YORK NEWS PUBLISHERS ASSOCIATION

Street address 1: 252 Hudson Ave
Street address city: Albany
Street address state: NY
Zip/Postal code: 12210-1802
County: Albany
Country: USA
General Phone: (518) 449-1667
General Fax: (518) 449-1667
Primary Website: www.nynpa.com
Year Established: 1927

NEW YORK PRESS SERVICE

Street address 1: 1681 Western Ave
Street address city: Albany
Street address state: NY
Zip/Postal code: 12203-4305
County: Albany
Country: USA
Mailing address: 1681 Western Ave
Mailing city: Albany
Mailing state: NY
Mailing zip: 12203-4340
General Phone: (518) 464-6483
General Fax: (518) 464-6489
General/National Adv. E-mail: nypa@nynewspapers.com
Primary Website: www.nynewspapers.com
Year Established: 1853

NORTH CAROLINA PRESS SERVICE, INC.

Street address 1: 5171 Glenwood Ave
Street address 2: Ste 364
Street address city: Raleigh
Street address state: NC
Zip/Postal code: 27612-3266
County: Wake
Country: USA
Mailing address: 5171 Glenwood Ave Ste 364
Mailing city: Raleigh
Mailing state: NC
Mailing zip: 27612-3266
General Phone: (919) 787-7443
General Fax: (919) 787-5302
Primary Website: www.ncpress.com
Year Established: 1985

NORTH DAKOTA NEWSPAPER ASSOCIATION

Street address 1: 1435 Interstate Loop
Street address city: Bismarck
Street address state: ND
Zip/Postal code: 58503-0567
County: Burleigh
Country: USA
Mailing address: 1435 Interstate Loop
Mailing city: Bismarck
Mailing state: ND
Mailing zip: 58503-0567
General Phone: (701) 223-6397
General Fax: (701) 223-8185
General/National Adv. E-mail: info@ndna.com
Primary Website: www.ndna.com
Year Established: 1885

OHIAD

Street address 1: PO Box 69
Street address city: Covington
Street address state: OH
Zip/Postal code: 45318-0069
County: Miami
Country: USA
Mailing address: PO Box 69
Mailing city: Covington
Mailing state: OH
Mailing zip: 45318-0069
General Phone: (937) 473-2028
General Fax: (937) 473-2500
General/National Adv. E-mail: dselanders@woh.rr.com
Primary Website: www.arenspub.com

OHIO NEWSPAPER SERVICES, INC.

Street address 1: 1335 Dublin Rd
Street address 2: Ste 216B
Street address city: Columbus
Street address state: OH
Zip/Postal code: 43215-1000
County: Franklin
Country: USA
Mailing address: 1335 Dublin Rd Ste 216B
Mailing city: Columbus
Mailing state: OH
Mailing zip: 43215-1000
General Phone: (614) 486-6677
General Fax: (614) 486-4940
Primary Website: www.ohionews.org; www.adohio.net
Year Established: 1933

OKLAHOMA PRESS SERVICE

Street address 1: 3601 N Lincoln Blvd
Street address city: Oklahoma City
Street address state: OK
Zip/Postal code: 73105-5411
County: Oklahoma
Country: USA
Mailing address: 3601 N Lincoln Blvd
Mailing city: Oklahoma City
Mailing state: OK
Mailing zip: 73105-5499
General Phone: (405) 524-4421
General Fax: (405) 499-0048
General/National Adv. E-mail: sysop@okpress.com
Primary Website: www.okpress.com

PACIFIC NORTHWEST ASSOCIATION OF WANT AD NEWSPAPERS (PNAWAN) & WESTERN REGIONAL ADVERTISING PROGRAM (WRAP)

Street address 1: 304 W 3rd Ave
Street address 2: C/O Exchange Publishing
Street address city: Spokane
Street address state: WA
Zip/Postal code: 99201-4314
County: Spokane
Country: USA
Mailing address: PO Box 427
Mailing city: Spokane
Mailing state: WA
Mailing zip: 99210
General Phone: (509) 922-3456
General Fax: (509) 455-7940
General/National Adv. E-mail: Ads@PNAWAN.org
Display Adv. E-mail: Kylah@ExchangePublishing.com
Primary Website: www.RegionalAds.org
Year Established: 1977

PUBLISHERS DEVELOPMENT SERVICE

Street address 1: PO Box 1256
Street address city: Fond Du Lac
Street address state: WI
Zip/Postal code: 54936-1256
County: Fond Du Lac
Country: USA
Mailing address: PO Box 1256
Mailing city: Fond Du Lac
Mailing state: WI
Mailing zip: 54936-1256
General Phone: (920) 922-4864
General Fax: (920) 922-0861
General/National Adv. E-mail: janelle@pdsadnet.com
Primary Website: www.pdsadnet.com

Year Established: 1978

RESEAU SELECT/SELECT NETWORK

Street address 1: 25 Sheppard Ave W
Street address 2: Suite 500
Street address city: Toronto
Street address state: ON
Zip/Postal code: M2N 6S7
County: York
Country: Canada
Mailing address: 25 Sheppard Ave. West Suite 500
Mailing city: Toronto
Mailing state: ON
Mailing zip: M2N 6S7
General Phone: (416) 733-7600
General Fax: (416) 726-8519
General/National Adv. E-mail: inforeseauselect@tc.tc
Primary Website: www.reseauselect.com

RESEAU SELECT/SELECT NETWORK

Street address 1: 8000 Av Blaise-Pascal
Street address city: Montreal
Street address state: QC
Zip/Postal code: H1E 2S7
County: Quebec
Country: Canada
Mailing address: 8000 Ave. Blaise-Pascal
Mailing city: Montreal
Mailing state: QC
Mailing zip: H1E 2S7
General Phone: (514) 643-2300
General Fax: (514) 866-3030
General/National Adv. E-mail: inforeseauselect@tc.tc
Primary Website: www.reseauselect.com
Year Established: 1976

SOUTH CAROLINA PRESS SERVICES, INC.

Street address 1: 106 Outlet Pointe Blvd
Street address city: Columbia
Street address state: SC
Zip/Postal code: 29210-5669
County: Lexington
Country: USA
Mailing address: PO Box 11429
Mailing city: Columbia
Mailing state: SC
Mailing zip: 29211-1429
General Phone: (803) 750-9561
General Fax: (803) 551-0903
General/National Adv. E-mail: rsavely@scpress.org
Primary Website: http://www.scnewspapernetwork.com/
Year Established: 1985

SOUTHEASTERN ADVERTISING PUBLISHERS ASSOCIATION

Street address 1: 104 Westland Dr
Street address city: Columbia
Street address state: TN
Zip/Postal code: 38401-6522
County: Maury
Country: USA
Mailing address: 104 Westland Dr
Mailing city: Columbia
Mailing state: TN
Mailing zip: 38401-6522
General Phone: (931) 223-5708
General Fax: (888) 450-8329
General/National Adv. E-mail: info@sapatoday.com
Primary Website: www.sapatoday.com
Year Established: 1979

SYNC2 MEDIA

Street address 1: 1120 N Lincoln St
Street address 2: Ste 912
Street address city: Denver
Street address state: CO
Zip/Postal code: 80203-2138
County: Denver
Country: USA
General Phone: (303) 571-5117
General Fax: (303) 571-1803
General/National Adv. E-mail: info@sync2media.com
Primary Website: www.sync2media.com

TEXCAP

Street address 1: 1226 Newberry Dr
Street address city: Allen
Street address state: TX
Zip/Postal code: 75013-3669
County: Collin
Country: USA
Mailing address: 570 Dula St
Mailing city: Alvin
Mailing state: TX
Mailing zip: 77511-2942
General Phone: (972) 741-6258
General Fax: (866) 822-4920
General/National Adv. E-mail: jack@tcnatoday.com
Primary Website: www.tcnatoday.com
Year Established: 1964

WISCONSIN NEWSPAPER ASSOCIATION

Street address 1: 34 Schroeder Ct
Street address 2: Ste 220
Street address city: Madison
Street address state: WI
Zip/Postal code: 53711-2528
County: Dane
Country: USA
General Phone: (608) 283-7620
General Fax: (608) 283-7631
General/National Adv. E-mail: wna@wnanews.com
Primary Website: www.wnanews.com
Year Established: 1853

WEEKLY NATIONAL/INTERNATIONAL ASSOCIATION, CLUB OR PRESS CLUB

AAF COLLEGE CHAPTERS

Street address 1: 1101 Vermont Ave NW
Street address 2: Ste 500
Street address city: Washington
Street address state: DC
Zip/Postal code: 20005-3521
County: District Of Columbia
Country: USA
Mailing address: 1101 Vermont Ave NW Ste 500
Mailing city: Washington
Mailing state: DC
Mailing zip: 20005-3521
General Phone: (202) 898-0089
General Fax: (202) 898-0159
General/National Adv. E-mail: education@aaf.org
Primary Website: www.aaf.org

ACCREDITING COUNCIL ON EDUCATION IN JOURNALISM AND MASS COMMUNICATIONS

Street address 1: University of Kansas
Street address 2: 1435 Jayhawk Blvd.
Street address city: Lawrence
Street address state: KS
Zip/Postal code: 66045-0001
County: Douglas
Country: USA
Mailing address: Stauffer-Flint Hall
Mailing city: Lawrence
Mailing state: KS
Mailing zip: 66045-7575
General Phone: (785) 864-3973
General Fax: (785)864-5225
General/National Adv. E-mail: sshaw@ku.edu
Primary Website: www.acejmc.org
Year Established: 1947

ADVERTISING MEDIA CREDIT EXECUTIVES ASSOCIATION INTERNATIONAL

Street address 1: PO Box 43514
Street address city: Louisville
Street address state: KY
Zip/Postal code: 40253-0514
County: Jefferson
Country: USA
Mailing address: PO Box 40253
Mailing city: Louisville
Mailing state: KY
Mailing zip: 40253
Primary Website: www.amcea.org
Year Established: 1953

AIGA, THE PROFESSIONAL ASSOCIATION FOR DESIGN

Street address 1: 233 Broadway
Street address 2: Suite 1740
Street address city: New York
Street address state: NY
Zip/Postal code: 10279-1803
County: New York
Country: USA
Mailing address: 233 Broadway
Mailing city: New York
Mailing state: NY
Mailing zip: 10279-1803
General Phone: (212) 807-1990
Primary Website: www.aiga.org
Year Established: 1914

ALLIANCE FOR AUDITED MEDIA (AAM)

Street address 1: 1600 McConnor Parkway
Street address 2: Suite 200-217
Street address city: Schaumburg
Street address state: IL
Zip/Postal code: 60173
Country: USA
Mailing state: IL
General Phone: (224) 366-6939
General Fax: (224) 366-6949
Primary Website: www.auditedmedia.com
Year Established: 1914

AMERICAN ADVERTISING FEDERATION

Street address 1: 1101 Vermont Ave NW
Street address 2: Ste 500
Street address city: Washington
Street address state: DC
Zip/Postal code: 20005-3521
County: District Of Columbia
Country: USA
Mailing address: 1101 Vermont Ave NW Ste 500
Mailing city: Washington
Mailing state: DC
Mailing zip: 20005-6306
General Phone: (202) 898-0089
General Fax: (202) 898-0159
General/National Adv. E-mail: aaf@aaf.org
Primary Website: www.aaf.org
Year Established: 1905

AMERICAN ASSOCIATION OF INDEPENDENT NEWS DISTRIBUTORS

Street address 1: PO Box 70244
Street address city: Washington
Street address state: DC
Zip/Postal code: 20024-0244
County: District Of Columbia
Country: USA
Mailing address: PO Box 70244
Mailing city: Washington
Mailing state: DC
Mailing zip: 20024-0244
General Phone: (202)678-8350
General Fax: (202)889-9209
General/National Adv. E-mail: cnnorthrop@southwestdistribution.com
Primary Website: www.aaind.org

AMERICAN BUSINESS MEDIA

Street address 1: 201 E 42nd St Fl 7
Street address 2: Suite 2200
Street address city: New York
Street address state: NY
Zip/Postal code: 10017-5704
County: New York
Country: USA
Mailing address: 201 E 42nd St Rm 2200
Mailing city: New York
Mailing state: NY
Mailing zip: 10017-5714
General Phone: (212) 661-6360
General Fax: (212) 370-0736
General/National Adv. E-mail: info@abmmail.com
Primary Website: www.abmassociation.com
Year Established: 1906

AMERICAN BUSINESS MEDIA AGRICULTURAL COUNCIL

Street address 1: 201 E 42nd St
Street address 2: Rm 2200
Street address city: New York
Street address state: NY
Zip/Postal code: 10017-5714
County: New York
Country: USA
Mailing address: 201 E 42nd St Rm 2200
Mailing city: New York
Mailing state: NY
Mailing zip: 10017-5714
General Phone: (212) 661-6360
General Fax: (212) 370-0736
General/National Adv. E-mail: info@abmmail.com
Primary Website: www.americanbusinessmedia.com

AMERICAN FOREST & PAPER ASSOCIATION, INC.

Street address 1: 1101 K Street, NW
Street address 2: Suite 700
Street address city: Washington
Street address state: DC
Zip/Postal code: 20005
County: District Of Columbia
Country: USA
Mailing address: 1101 K Street, NW, Suite 700
Mailing city: Washington

Mailing state: DC
Mailing zip: 20005
General Phone: (202) 463-2700
General/National Adv. E-mail: info@afandpa.org
Primary Website: www.afandpa.org

AMERICAN JEWISH PRESS ASSOCIATION

Street address 1: C/O Kca Association Management
Street address 2: 107 S. Southgate Dr.
Street address city: Washington
Street address state: DC
Zip/Postal code: 20036
County: District Of Columbia
Country: USA
Mailing address: c/o KCA Association Management
Mailing city: Chandler
Mailing state: AZ
Mailing zip: 85226-3222
General Phone: 480-403-4602
General Fax: 480-893-7775
General/National Adv. E-mail: info@aipa.org
Primary Website: www.ajpa.org

AMERICAN MARKETING ASSOCIATION

Street address 1: 311 S Wacker Dr
Street address 2: Ste 5800
Street address city: Chicago
Street address state: IL
Zip/Postal code: 60606-6629
County: Cook
Country: USA
Mailing address: 311 S Wacker Dr Ste 5800
Mailing city: Chicago
Mailing state: IL
Mailing zip: 60606-6629
General Phone: (312) 542-9000
General Fax: (312) 542-9001
General/National Adv. E-mail: info@ama.org
Primary Website: www.marketingpower.com
Year Established: 1937

AMERICAN NEWS WOMEN'S CLUB, INC.

Street address 1: 1607 22nd St NW
Street address city: Washington
Street address state: DC
Zip/Postal code: 20008-1921
County: District Of Columbia
Country: USA
Mailing address: 1607 22nd St NW
Mailing city: Washington
Mailing state: DC
Mailing zip: 20008-1921
General Phone: (202) 332-6770
General Fax: (202) 265-6092
General/National Adv. E-mail: anwclub@comcast.net
Primary Website: www.anwc.org
Year Established: 1932

AMERICAN PRESS INSTITUTE

Street address 1: 4401 N. Fairfax Drive
Street address 2: Suite 300
Street address city: Arlington
Street address state: VA
Zip/Postal code: 22203
County: Arlington
Country: USA
Mailing address: 4401 N. Fairfax Drive
Mailing city: Arlington
Mailing state: VA
Mailing zip: 22203
General Phone: (571) 366-1200
General/National Adv. E-mail: hello@pressinstitute.org
Primary Website: www.americanpressinstitute.org
Year Established: 1946

AMERICAN SOCIETY OF JOURNALISTS AND AUTHORS

Street address 1: 1501 Broadway
Street address 2: Ste 302
Street address city: New York
Street address state: NY
Zip/Postal code: 10036-5501
County: New York
Country: USA
Mailing address: 1501 Broadway Ste 403
Mailing city: New York
Mailing state: NY
Mailing zip: 10036-5507
General Phone: (212) 997-0947
General Fax: (212) 937-2315
General/National Adv. E-mail: staff@asja.org
Primary Website: www.asja.org
Year Established: 1948

AMERICAN SOCIETY OF NEWS EDITORS

Street address 1: 209 Reynolds Journalism Institute
Street address 2: Missouri School of Journalism
Street address city: Columbia
Street address state: MO
Zip/Postal code: 65211-0001
County: Boone
Country: USA
Mailing address: 209 Reynolds Journalism Institute
Mailing city: Columbia
Mailing state: MO
Mailing zip: 65211-0001
General Phone: (573)884-2405
General Fax: (573)884-3824
General/National Adv. E-mail: asne@asne.org
Primary Website: www.asne.org
Year Established: 1922

ANA BUSINESS MARKETING

Street address 1: 708 Third Avenue
Street address 2: 33rd Floor
Street address city: New York
Street address state: NY
Zip/Postal code: 10017
County: Manhattan
Country: USA
Mailing address: 708 Third Avenue, 33rd Floor
Mailing city: New York
Mailing state: NY
Mailing zip: 10017
General Phone: (212) 697-5950
General Fax: (212) 687-7310
General/National Adv. E-mail: info@ana.net
Primary Website: www.marketing.org

ANGLO-AMERICAN PRESS ASSOCIATION OF PARIS

Street address 1: 67 Rue Halle
Street address city: Paris
Zip/Postal code: 75014
Country: France
Mailing address: 67 Rue Halle
Mailing city: Paris
Mailing zip: 75014
General Phone: 4545 7400
General/National Adv. E-mail: axelkrause@wanadoo.fr
Primary Website: www.aapafrance.com
Year Established: 1907

ARIZONA NEWSPAPERS ASSOCIATION

Street address 1: 1001 N Central Ave
Street address 2: Ste 670
Street address city: Phoenix
Street address state: AZ
Zip/Postal code: 85004-1947
County: Maricopa
Country: USA
General Phone: (602) 261-7655
General Fax: (602) 261-7525
General/National Adv. E-mail: p.casey@ananews.com
Primary Website: www.ananews.com
Year Established: 1929

ASIAN AMERICAN JOURNALISTS ASSOCIATION

Street address 1: 5 3rd St
Street address 2: Ste 1108
Street address city: San Francisco
Street address state: CA
Zip/Postal code: 94103-3212
County: San Francisco
Country: USA
Mailing address: 5 3rd St Ste 1108
Mailing city: San Francisco
Mailing state: CA
Mailing zip: 94103-3212
General Phone: (415) 346-2051
General Fax: (415) 346-6343
General/National Adv. E-mail: national@aaja.org
Primary Website: www.aaja.org
Year Established: 1981

ASSOCIATED PRESS MANAGING EDITORS ASSOCIATION

Street address 1: 450 W 33rd St
Street address city: New York
Street address state: NY
Zip/Postal code: 10001-2603
County: New York
Country: USA
Mailing address: 450 W 33rd St
Mailing city: New York
Mailing state: NY
Mailing zip: 10001-2603
General Phone: (212) 621-1838
General Fax: (212) 506-6102
General/National Adv. E-mail: apme@ap.org
Primary Website: www.apme.com
Year Established: 1933

ASSOCIATION FOR EDUCATION IN JOURNALISM AND MASS COMMUNICATION

Street address 1: 234 Outlet Pointe Blvd
Street address 2: Ste A
Street address city: Columbia
Street address state: SC
Zip/Postal code: 29210-5667
County: Lexington
Country: USA
Mailing address: 234 Outlet Pointe Blvd Ste A
Mailing city: Columbia
Mailing state: SC
Mailing zip: 29210-5667
General Phone: (803) 798-0271
General Fax: (803) 772-3509
General/National Adv. E-mail: aejmchq@aol.com
Primary Website: www.aejmc.org
Year Established: 1912

ASSOCIATION FOR WOMEN IN COMMUNICATIONS

Street address 1: 3337 Duke St
Street address city: Alexandria
Street address state: VA
Zip/Postal code: 22314-5219
County: Alexandria City
Country: USA
Mailing address: 3337 Duke St
Mailing city: Alexandria
Mailing state: VA
Mailing zip: 22314-5219
General Phone: (703) 370-7436
General Fax: (703) 342-4311
General/National Adv. E-mail: info@womcom.org
Primary Website: www.womcom.org
Year Established: 1909

ASSOCIATION OF ALTERNATE POSTAL SYSTEMS

Street address 1: 1725 Oaks Way
Street address city: Oklahoma City
Street address state: OK
Zip/Postal code: 73131-1220
County: Oklahoma
Country: USA
Mailing address: 1725 Oaks Way
Mailing city: Oklahoma City
Mailing state: OK
Mailing zip: 73131-1220
General Phone: (405) 478-0006
General/National Adv. E-mail: aaps@cox.net
Primary Website: www.aapsinc.org

ASSOCIATION OF ALTERNATIVE NEWSMEDIA

Street address 1: 1156 15th St NW
Street address 2: Ste 1005
Street address city: Washington
Street address state: DC
Zip/Postal code: 20005-1722
County: District Of Columbia
Country: USA
Mailing address: 1156 15th St NW Ste 1005
Mailing city: Washington
Mailing state: DC
Mailing zip: 20005-1722
General Phone: 289-8484
General Fax: (202) 289-2004
General/National Adv. E-mail: web@aan.org
Primary Website: www.altweeklies.com
Year Established: 1978

ASSOCIATION OF AMERICAN EDITORIAL CARTOONISTS

Street address 1: 3899 N Front St
Street address city: Harrisburg
Street address state: PA
Zip/Postal code: 17110-1583
County: Dauphin
Country: USA
Mailing address: 3899 N Front St
Mailing city: Harrisburg
Mailing state: PA
Mailing zip: 17110-1583
General Phone: (717) 703-3003
General Fax: (717) 703-3008
General/National Adv. E-mail: info@pa-news.org; aaec@pa-news.org
Primary Website: www.editorialcartoonists.com

ASSOCIATION OF CANADIAN ADVERTISERS

Street address 1: 95 St Clair Ave. W., Ste. 1103
Street address city: Toronto
Street address state: ON
Zip/Postal code: M4V 1N6
Country: Canada
Mailing address: 95 St Clair Ave. W., Ste. 1103
Mailing city: Toronto
Mailing state: ON
Mailing zip: M4V 1N6
General Phone: (416) 964-3805
General Fax: (416) 964-0771
Primary Website: www.acaweb.ca
Year Established: 1914

ASSOCIATION OF FOOD JOURNALISTS, INC.

Street address 1: 7 Avenida Vista Grande
Street address 2: Ste B7 # 467
Street address city: Santa Fe
Street address state: NM
Zip/Postal code: 87508-9207
County: Santa Fe
Country: USA
Mailing address: 7 Avenida Vista Grande
Mailing city: Santa Fe
Mailing state: NM
Mailing zip: 87508-9198
General Phone: 505-466-4742
General/National Adv. E-mail: caroldemasters@yahoo.com
Primary Website: www.afjonline.com
Year Established: 1974

ASSOCIATION OF NATIONAL ADVERTISERS, INC.

Street address 1: 2020 K St NW
Street address 2: Ste 660
Street address city: Washington
Street address state: DC
Zip/Postal code: 20006-1900
County: District Of Columbia
Country: USA
Mailing address: 2020 K St NW
Mailing city: Washington
Mailing state: DC
Mailing zip: 20006-1806
General Phone: (202) 296-1883
General Fax: (202) 296-1430

Primary Website: www.ana.net

ASSOCIATION OF NATIONAL ADVERTISERS, INC.

Street address 1: 708 3rd Ave
Street address 2: 33rd Flr.
Street address city: New York
Street address state: NY
Zip/Postal code: 10017-4201
County: New York
Country: USA
Mailing address: 708 3rd Ave
Mailing city: New York
Mailing state: NY
Mailing zip: 10017-4201
General Phone: (212) 697-5950
General Fax: (212) 687-7310
Primary Website: www.ana.net

ASSOCIATION OF OPINION JOURNALISTS (FORMERLY THE NATIONAL CONFERENCE OF EDITORIAL WRITERS)

Street address 1: 801 3rd St S
Street address city: Saint Petersburg
Street address state: FL
Zip/Postal code: 33701-4920
County: Pinellas
Country: USA
Mailing address: 3899 N Front St
Mailing city: Harrisburg
Mailing state: PA
Mailing zip: 33701
General Phone: 727-821-9494
General/National Adv. E-mail: david.haynes@jrn.com
Primary Website: aoj.wildapricot.org
Year Established: 1947

ASSOCIATION OF SCHOOLS OF JOURNALISM AND MASS COMMUNICATION

Street address 1: 234 Outlet Pointe Blvd
Street address 2: Ste A
Street address city: Columbia
Street address state: SC
Zip/Postal code: 29210-5667
County: Lexington
Country: USA
Mailing address: 234 Outlet Pointe Blvd Ste A
Mailing city: Columbia
Mailing state: SC
Mailing zip: 29210-5667
General Phone: (803) 798-0271
General Fax: (803) 772-3509
General/National Adv. E-mail: aejmchq@aol.com
Primary Website: www.asjmc.org
Year Established: 1912

BASEBALL WRITERS ASSOCIATION OF AMERICA

Street address 1: PO Box 610611
Street address city: Bayside
Street address state: NY
Zip/Postal code: 11361-0611
County: Queens
Country: USA
Mailing address: PO Box 610611
Mailing city: Bayside
Mailing state: NY
Mailing zip: 11361-0611
General Phone: (718) 767-2582
General Fax: (718) 767-2583
General/National Adv. E-mail: bbwaa@aol.com
Primary Website: http://bbwaa.com
Year Established: 1908

BPA WORLDWIDE

Street address 1: 100 Beard Sawmill Rd
Street address 2: Fl 6
Street address city: Shelton
Street address state: CT
Zip/Postal code: 06484-6156
County: Fairfield
Country: USA
Mailing address: 100 Beard Sawmill Rd Fl 6
Mailing city: Shelton
Mailing state: CT
Mailing zip: 06484-6151
General Phone: (203) 447-2800
General Fax: (203) 447-2900
Primary Website: www.bpaww.com
Year Established: 1931

CANADIAN BUSINESS PRESS

Street address 1: 2100 Banbury Cresent
Street address city: Oakville
Street address state: ON
Zip/Postal code: L6H 5P6
Country: Canada
Mailing address: 2100 Banbury Crescent
Mailing city: Oakville
Mailing state: ON
Mailing zip: L6H 5P6
General Phone: 905-844-6822
General/National Adv. E-mail: torrance@cbp.ca
Primary Website: www.cbp.ca

CANADIAN CIRCULATIONS AUDIT BOARD (CCAB, INC.)

Street address 1: 1 Concorde Gate Suite 800
Street address 2: SUITE 800
Street address city: Toronto
Street address state: ON
Zip/Postal code: M3C 3N6
County: Ontario
Country: Canada
Mailing address: 1 Concorde Gate Ste. 800
Mailing city: Toronto
Mailing state: ON
Mailing zip: M3C 3N6
General Phone: (416) 487-2418
General Fax: (416) 487-6405
General/National Adv. E-mail: info@bpaww.com
Primary Website: www.bpaww.com
Year Established: 1937

CANADIAN NEWS MEDIA ASSOCITION

Street address 1: 37 Front Street East Suite 200
Street address city: Toronto
Street address state: ON
Zip/Postal code: M5E 1B3
Country: Canada
Mailing address: 37 Front Street East, Suite 200
Mailing city: Toronto
Mailing state: ON
Mailing zip: M5E 1B3
General Phone: (416) 923-3567
General Fax: (416) 923-7206
General/National Adv. E-mail: info@newsmediacanada.ca
Primary Website: https://nmc-mic.ca
Year Established: 2017

CANADIAN PRESS, THE - TORONTO, ON

Street address 1: 36 King St. E.
Street address city: Toronto
Street address state: ON
Zip/Postal code: M5C 2L9
County: York
Country: Canada
Mailing address: 36 King St. E.
Mailing city: Toronto
Mailing state: ON
Mailing zip: M5C 2L9
General Phone: (416) 507-2099
General/National Adv. E-mail: support@thecanadianpress.com
Primary Website: www.thecanadianpress.com

CATHOLIC PRESS ASSOCIATION

Street address 1: 205 W Monroe St
Street address 2: Ste 470
Street address city: Chicago
Street address state: IL
Zip/Postal code: 60606-5011
County: Cook
Country: USA
Mailing address: 205 W Monroe St Ste 470
Mailing city: Chicago
Mailing state: IL
Mailing zip: 60606-5011
General Phone: (312) 380-6789
General Fax: (312) 361-0256
General/National Adv. E-mail: cathjourn@catholicpress.org
Primary Website: www.catholicpress.org

COLLEGE MEDIA ASSOCIATION

Street address 1: 355 Lexington Ave
Street address 2: Fl 15
Street address city: New York
Street address state: NY
Zip/Postal code: 10017-6603
County: New York
Country: USA
Mailing address: 355 Lexington Avenue, 15
Mailing city: New York
Mailing state: NY
Mailing zip: 10017
General Phone: 212-297-2195
General/National Adv. E-mail: info@collegemedia.org
Primary Website: www.collegemedia.org
Year Established: 1954

COUNCIL FOR ADVANCEMENT AND SUPPORT OF EDUCATION

Street address 1: 1307 New York Ave NW
Street address 2: Ste 1000
Street address city: Washington
Street address state: DC
Zip/Postal code: 20005-4726
County: District Of Columbia
Country: USA
Mailing address: 1307 New York Ave NW Ste 1000
Mailing city: Washington
Mailing state: DC
Mailing zip: 20005-4726
General Phone: (202) 328-2273
General Fax: (202) 387-4973
General/National Adv. E-mail: memberservicecenter@case.org
Primary Website: www.case.org

COUNCIL FOR THE ADVANCEMENT OF SCIENCE WRITING, INC.

Street address 1: PO Box 17337
Street address city: SEATTLE
Street address state: WA
Zip/Postal code: 98127
County: King
Country: USA
Mailing address: PO Box 17337
Mailing city: SEATTLE
Mailing state: WA
Mailing zip: 98127
General Phone: (206) 880-0177
General/National Adv. E-mail: info@casw.org
Primary Website: www.casw.org
Year Established: 1959

DIGITAL CONTENT NEXT

Street address 1: 1350 Broadway
Street address 2: Rm 606
Street address city: New York
Street address state: NY
Zip/Postal code: 10018-7205
County: New York
Country: USA
Mailing address: 1350 Broadway Rm 606
Mailing city: New York
Mailing state: NY
Mailing zip: 10018-7205
General Phone: (646) 473-1000
General Fax: (646) 473-0200
General/National Adv. E-mail: info@online-publishers.org
Primary Website: www.online-publishers.org
Year Established: 2001

DOG WRITERS' ASSOCIATION OF AMERICA

Street address 1: 173 Union Rd
Street address city: Coatesville
Street address state: PA
Zip/Postal code: 19320-1326
County: Chester
Country: USA
Mailing address: 173 Union Rd
Mailing city: Coatesville
Mailing state: PA
Mailing zip: 19320-1326
General Phone: (610) 384-2436
General Fax: (610) 384-2471
General/National Adv. E-mail: dwaa@dwaa.org
Primary Website: www.dwaa.org
Year Established: 1935

EUROPEAN NEWSPAPER PUBLISHERS' ASSOCIATION

Street address 1: Square du Bastion 1A, Bte 3
Street address city: 1050 Bruxelles
Country: Belgium
Mailing address: Square du Bastion 1A, Bte 3
Mailing city: 1050 Bruxelles
General Phone: 551 0190
General Fax: 551 0199
General/National Adv. E-mail: enpa@enpa.be
Primary Website: www.enpa.be

FOREIGN PRESS ASSOCIATION

Street address 1: 1501 Broadway
Street address 2: 12th Floor
Street address city: New York
Street address state: NY
Zip/Postal code: 10036
County: New York
Country: USA
Mailing address: 1501 Broadway, 12th Floor
Mailing city: New York
Mailing state: NY
Mailing zip: 10036
General Phone: (212) 370-1054
General/National Adv. E-mail: fpa@foreignpressassociation.org
Primary Website: www.foreignpressassociation.org
Year Established: 1918

FREEDOM FORUM

Street address 1: 555 Pennsylvania Ave NW
Street address city: Washington
Street address state: DC
Zip/Postal code: 20001-2114
County: District Of Columbia
Country: USA
Mailing address: 555 Pennsylvania Ave NW
Mailing city: Washington
Mailing state: DC
Mailing zip: 20001-2114
General Phone: (202) 292-6100
General/National Adv. E-mail: firstamendmentcenter@newseum.org
Primary Website: www.freedomforuminstitute.org

GRAPHIC COMMUNICATIONS CONFERENCE/INTERNATIONAL BROTHERHOOD OF TEAMSTERS

Street address 1: 25 Louisiana Ave NW
Street address city: Washington
Street address state: DC
Zip/Postal code: 20001-2130
County: District Of Columbia
Country: USA
Mailing address: 25 Louisiana Ave NW
Mailing city: Washington
Mailing state: DC
Mailing zip: 20001-2130
General Phone: (202) 508-6800
General Fax: (202) 508-6661
Primary Website: www.gciu.org

GRAPHIC COMMUNICATIONS COUNCIL

Street address 1: 1899 Preston White Dr
Street address city: Reston
Street address state: VA
Zip/Postal code: 20191-5458
County: Fairfax
Country: USA
Mailing address: 1899 Preston White Dr
Mailing city: Reston
Mailing state: VA

Mailing zip: 20191-5435
General Phone: (703) 264-7200
General Fax: (703) 620-0994
General/National Adv. E-mail: npes@npes.org
Primary Website: www.npes.org
Year Established: 1950

GRAVURE ASSOCIATION OF AMERICA

Street address 1: 8281 Pine Lake Rd
Street address city: Denver
Street address state: NC
Zip/Postal code: 28037-8812
County: Lincoln
Country: USA
Mailing address: 8281 Pine Lake Rd
Mailing city: Denver
Mailing state: NC
Mailing zip: 28037-8812
General Phone: (201) 523-6042
General Fax: (201) 523-6048
General/National Adv. E-mail: gaa@gaa.org
Primary Website: www.gaa.org

HEBDOS QUEBEC

Street address 1: 2550 Daniel-Johnson,
Street address 2: Bureau 345
Street address city: Laval
Street address state: QC
Zip/Postal code: H7T 2L1
County: QC
Country: Canada
Mailing address: 2550 Daniel-Johnson
Mailing city: Laval
Mailing state: QC
Mailing zip: H7T 2L1
General Phone: (514) 861-2088
General Fax: (514) 861-1966
General/National Adv. E-mail: communications@hebdos.com
Primary Website: hebdos.com
Year Established: 1932

HUBERGROUP USA, INC.

Street address 1: 2850 Festival Drive
Street address city: Kankakee
Street address state: IL
Zip/Postal code: 60901
County: Kankakee
Country: USA
Mailing address: 2850 Festival Drive
Mailing city: Kankakee
Mailing state: IL
Mailing zip: 60901
General Phone: (815) 929-9293
General Fax: (815) 929-0412
General/National Adv. E-mail: info.us@hubergroup.com
Primary Website: www.cpima.org
Year Established: 1934

IDEALLIANCE

Street address 1: 1600 Duke St
Street address 2: Ste 420
Street address city: Alexandria
Street address state: VA
Zip/Postal code: 22314-3421
County: Alexandria City
Country: USA
Mailing address: 1600 Duke St Ste 420
Mailing city: Alexandria
Mailing state: VA
Mailing zip: 22314-3421
General Phone: (703)837-1070
General/National Adv. E-mail: http://idealliance.org
Primary Website: www.ipa.org

INDEPENDENT FREE PAPERS OF AMERICA

Street address 1: 107 Hemlock Dr
Street address city: Rio Grande
Street address state: NJ
Zip/Postal code: 08242-1731
County: Cape May
Country: USA
Mailing address: 107 Hemlock Dr
Mailing city: Rio Grande
Mailing state: NJ
Mailing zip: 08242-1731
General Phone: (609) 408-8000
General Fax: (609) 889-0141
Primary Website: www.ifpa.com

INTER AMERICAN PRESS ASSOCIATION

Street address 1: 1801 SW 3rd Ave
Street address 2: Fl 7
Street address city: Miami
Street address state: FL
Zip/Postal code: 33129-1500
County: Miami-Dade
Country: USA
Mailing address: 1801 SW 3rd Ave Fl 7
Mailing city: Miami
Mailing state: FL
Mailing zip: 33129-1487
General Phone: (305) 634-2465
General Fax: (305)635-2272
General/National Adv. E-mail: info@sipiapa.org
Primary Website: www.sipiapa.org

INTERMARKET AGENCY NETWORK

Street address 1: 5307 S 92nd St
Street address city: Hales Corners
Street address state: WI
Zip/Postal code: 53130-1681
County: Milwaukee
Country: USA
Mailing address: 5307 S 92nd St
Mailing city: Hales Corners
Mailing state: WI
Mailing zip: 53130-1677
General Phone: (414) 425-8800
General Fax: (414) 425-0021
Primary Website: www.intermarketnetwork.com

INTERNATIONAL ADVERTISING ASSOCIATION, INC.

Street address 1: 747 3rd Ave
Street address 2: Fl 2
Street address city: New York
Street address state: NY
Zip/Postal code: 10017-2878
County: New York
Country: USA
Mailing address: 747 3rd Ave Rm 200
Mailing city: New York
Mailing state: NY
Mailing zip: 10017-2878
General Phone: 646-722-2612
General Fax: 646 722 2501
General/National Adv. E-mail: iaa@iaaglobal.org; membership@iaaglobal.org
Primary Website: www.iaaglobal.org
Year Established: 1938

INTERNATIONAL ASSOCIATION OF BUSINESS COMMUNICATORS (IABC)

Street address 1: 601 Montgomery St
Street address 2: Ste 1900
Street address city: San Francisco
Street address state: CA
Zip/Postal code: 94111-2690
County: San Francisco
Country: USA
Mailing address: 601 Montgomery St Ste 1900
Mailing city: San Francisco
Mailing state: CA
Mailing zip: 94111-2623
General Phone: (415) 544-4700
General Fax: (415) 544-4747
General/National Adv. E-mail: service_centre@iabc.com
Primary Website: www.iabc.com

INTERNATIONAL ASSOCIATION OF SPORTS NEWSPAPERS (IASN)

Street address 1: 7 rue Geoffroy Saint Hilaire
Street address city: Paris
Zip/Postal code: 75005
Country: France
Mailing address: 7 rue Geoffroy Saint Hilaire
Mailing city: Paris
Mailing zip: 75005
General Phone: 47 42 85 29
General Fax: 47 42 49 48
General/National Adv. E-mail: rcuccoli@press-iasn.org
Primary Website: www.press-iasn.org
Year Established: 2008

INTERNATIONAL CENTER FOR JOURNALISTS

Street address 1: 1616 H St NW
Street address 2: Fl 3
Street address city: Washington
Street address state: DC
Zip/Postal code: 20006-4903
County: District Of Columbia
Country: USA
Mailing address: 1616 H St NW Fl 3
Mailing city: Washington
Mailing state: DC
Mailing zip: 20006-4903
General Phone: (202) 737-3700
General Fax: (202) 737-0530
General/National Adv. E-mail: editor@icfj.org
Primary Website: www.icfj.org
Year Established: 1984

INTERNATIONAL LABOR COMMUNICATIONS ASSOCIATION AFL/CIO/CLC

Street address 1: 815 16th St NW
Street address city: Washington
Street address state: DC
Zip/Postal code: 20006-4101
County: District Of Columbia
Country: USA
Mailing address: 815 16th St NW
Mailing city: Washington
Mailing state: DC
Mailing zip: 20006-4101
General Phone: (202) 637-5068
General Fax: (202) 637-5069
General/National Adv. E-mail: info@ilcaonline.org
Primary Website: www.ilcaonline.org
Year Established: 1995

INTERNATIONAL NEWS MEDIA ASSOCIATION (INMA)

Street address 1: PO Box 740186
Street address city: Dallas
Street address state: TX
Zip/Postal code: 75374-0186
County: Dallas
Country: USA
Mailing address: PO Box 740186
Mailing city: Dallas
Mailing state: TX
Mailing zip: 75374-0186
General Phone: (214) 373-9111
General Fax: (214) 373-9112
General/National Adv. E-mail: inma@inma.org
Primary Website: www.inma.org

INTERNATIONAL PRESS CLUB OF CHICAGO (IPCC)

Street address 1: PO Box 2498
Street address city: Chicago
Street address state: IL
Zip/Postal code: 60690-2498
County: Cook
Country: USA
Mailing address: PO Box 2498
Mailing city: Chicago
Mailing state: IL
Mailing zip: 60690-2498
General Phone: 312-834-7228
General/National Adv. E-mail: info@ipcc.org
Primary Website: www.internationalpressclubofchicago.org
Year Established: 1992

INTERNATIONAL PRESS INSTITUTE

Street address 1: Spiegelgasse 2
Street address city: Vienna
Zip/Postal code: A-1010
Country: Austria
Mailing address: Spiegelgasse 2
Mailing city: Vienna
Mailing zip: A-1010
General Phone: 512 9011
General Fax: 512 9014
General/National Adv. E-mail: ipi@freemedia.at
Primary Website: www.freemedia.at

INTERNATIONAL SOCIETY OF WEEKLY NEWSPAPER EDITORS

Street address 1: 3950 Newman Rd
Street address city: Joplin
Street address state: MO
Zip/Postal code: 64801-1512
County: Jasper
Country: USA
Mailing address: 3950 Newman Rd
Mailing city: Joplin
Mailing state: MO
Mailing zip: 64801-1512
General Phone: (417) 625-9736
General Fax: (417) 659-4445
General/National Adv. E-mail: stebbins-c@mssu.edu
Primary Website: www.iswne.org
Year Established: 1955

INVESTIGATIVE REPORTERS AND EDITORS (IRE)

Street address 1: 141 Neff Annex
Street address city: Columbia
Street address state: MO
Zip/Postal code: 65211-0001
County: Boone
Country: USA
Mailing address: 141 Neff Anx
Mailing city: Columbia
Mailing state: MO
Mailing zip: 65211-0001
General Phone: (573) 882-2042
General Fax: (573) 882-5431
General/National Adv. E-mail: info@ire.org
Primary Website: www.ire.org
Year Established: 1975

KAPPA ALPHA MU HONORARY SOCIETY IN PHOTO JOURNALISM

Street address 1: 316F Lee Hills Hall
Street address city: Columbia
Street address state: MO
Zip/Postal code: 65211-1370
County: Boone
Country: USA
Mailing address: 316F Lee Hills Hall
Mailing city: Columbia
Mailing state: MO
Mailing zip: 65211-1370
General Phone: 573-882-4821
General Fax: 573-884-5400
General/National Adv. E-mail: kratzerb@missouri.edu
Primary Website: www.photojournalism.missouri.edu

KAPPA TAU ALPHA NATIONAL HONOR SOCIETY FOR JOURNALISM & MASS COMMUNICATION

Street address 1: University of Missouri
Street address 2: 76 Gannett Hall
Street address city: Columbia
Street address state: MO
Zip/Postal code: 65211-1200
County: Boone
Country: USA
Mailing address: University of Missouri
Mailing city: Columbia
Mailing state: MO
Mailing zip: 65211-1200
General Phone: (573) 882-7685
General/National Adv. E-mail: umcjourkta@missouri.edu
Primary Website: www.kappataualpha.org
Year Established: 1910

LEAGUE OF ADVERTISING AGENCIES, INC.

Street address 1: 65 Reade St
Street address 2: Apt 3A
Street address city: New York

Street address state: NY
Zip/Postal code: 10007-1841
County: New York
Country: USA
Mailing address: 65 Reade St Apt 3A
Mailing city: New York
Mailing state: NY
Mailing zip: 10007-1841
General Phone: (212) 528-0364
General Fax: (212) 766-1181
Primary Website: www.adagencies.org

LOCAL MEDIA ASSOCIATION

Street address 1: PO Box 450
Street address city: Lake City
Street address state: MI
Zip/Postal code: 49651-0450
County: Missaukee
Country: USA
Mailing address: P.O. Box 450
Mailing city: Lake City
Mailing state: MI
Mailing zip: 49651-0450
General Phone: (888) 486-2466
General Fax: (888) 317-0856
General/National Adv. E-mail: hq@localmedia.org
Primary Website: www.localmedia.org
Year Established: 1971

MARKETING ADVERTISING GLOBAL NETWORK

Street address 1: 1017 Perry Hwy
Street address 2: Ste 5
Street address city: Pittsburgh
Street address state: PA
Zip/Postal code: 15237-2173
County: Allegheny
Country: USA
Mailing address: 1017 Perry Hwy Ste 5
Mailing city: Pittsburgh
Mailing state: PA
Mailing zip: 15237-2173
General Phone: (412) 366-6850
General Fax: (412) 366-6840
General/National Adv. E-mail: cheri@magnetglobal.org
Primary Website: www.magnetglobal.org
Year Established: 1944

MEDIA FINANCIAL MANAGEMENT ASSOCIATION

Street address 1: 550 W Frontage Rd
Street address 2: Ste 3600
Street address city: Northfield
Street address state: IL
Zip/Postal code: 60093-1243
County: Cook
Country: USA
Mailing address: 550 W Frontage Rd Ste 3600
Mailing city: Northfield
Mailing state: IL
Mailing zip: 60093-1243
General Phone: 847-716-7000
General Fax: 847-716-7004
General/National Adv. E-mail: info@mediafinance.org
Primary Website: www.mediafinance.org
Year Established: 1961

MEDIA HUMAN RESOURCES ASSOCIATION

Street address 1: 1800 Duke St
Street address city: Alexandria
Street address state: VA
Zip/Postal code: 22314-3494
County: Alexandria City
Country: USA
Mailing address: 1800 Duke St
Mailing city: Alexandria
Mailing state: VA
Mailing zip: 22314-3494
General Phone: (800) 283-7476
General Fax: (703) 535-6490
General/National Adv. E-mail: shrm@shrm.org
Primary Website: www.shrm.org

NATIONAL ASSOCIATION FOR PRINTING LEADERSHIP

Street address 1: 75 W. Century Rd., Ste. 100
Street address city: Paramus
Street address state: NJ
Zip/Postal code: 7652
Mailing address: 75 W Century Rd Ste 100
Mailing city: Paramus
Mailing state: NJ
Mailing zip: 07652-1461
General Phone: (201) 634-9600
General Fax: (201) 634-0324
General/National Adv. E-mail: info@napl.org
Primary Website: www.napl.org

NATIONAL ASSOCIATION OF BLACK JOURNALISTS

Street address 1: 1100 Knight Hall
Street address 2: Suite 3100
Street address city: College Park
Street address state: MD
Zip/Postal code: 20742-0001
County: Prince Georges
Country: USA
Mailing address: 1100 Knight Hall
Mailing city: College Park
Mailing state: MD
Mailing zip: 20742-0001
General Phone: (301) 405-0248
General Fax: (301) 314-1714
General/National Adv. E-mail: nabj@nabj.org
Primary Website: www.nabj.org

NATIONAL ASSOCIATION OF BROADCASTERS

Street address 1: 1771 N St NW
Street address city: Washington
Street address state: DC
Zip/Postal code: 20036-2800
County: District Of Columbia
Country: USA
Mailing address: 1771 N St NW
Mailing city: Washington
Mailing state: DC
Mailing zip: 20036-2800
General Phone: (202) 429-5300
General Fax: (202) 429-4199
General/National Adv. E-mail: nab@nab.org
Primary Website: www.nab.org

NATIONAL ASSOCIATION OF CREDIT MANAGEMENT

Street address 1: 8840 Columbia 100 Pkwy
Street address city: Columbia
Street address state: MD
Zip/Postal code: 21045-2100
County: Howard
Country: USA
Mailing address: 8840 Columbia 100 Pkwy
Mailing city: Columbia
Mailing state: MD
Mailing zip: 21045-2100
General Phone: (410) 740-5560
General Fax: (410) 740-5574
General/National Adv. E-mail: info@nacm.org
Primary Website: www.nacm.org

NATIONAL ASSOCIATION OF HISPANIC JOURNALISTS

Street address 1: 1050 Connecticut Ave NW
Street address 2: Fl 10
Street address city: Washington
Street address state: DC
Zip/Postal code: 20036-5334
County: District Of Columbia
Country: USA
Mailing address: 1050 Connecticut Ave NW Fl 10
Mailing city: Washington
Mailing state: DC
Mailing zip: 20036-5334
General Phone: (202) 662-7145
General Fax: (202) 662-7144
General/National Adv. E-mail: nahj@nahj.org
Primary Website: www.nahj.org

NATIONAL ASSOCIATION OF HISPANIC PUBLICATIONS

Street address 1: 529 14th St NW
Street address 2: Ste 1126
Street address city: Washington
Street address state: DC
Zip/Postal code: 20045-2120
County: District Of Columbia
Country: USA
Mailing address: 529 14th St NW Ste 923
Mailing city: Washington
Mailing state: DC
Mailing zip: 20045-1930
General Phone: (202) 662-7250
General/National Adv. E-mail: directory@nahp.org
Primary Website: www.nahp.org

NATIONAL ASSOCIATION OF REAL ESTATE EDITORS (NAREE)

Street address 1: 1003 NW 6th Ter
Street address city: Boca Raton
Street address state: FL
Zip/Postal code: 33486-3455
County: Palm Beach
Country: USA
Mailing address: 1003 NW 6th Ter
Mailing city: Boca Raton
Mailing state: FL
Mailing zip: 33486-3455
General Phone: (561) 391-3599
General Fax: (561) 391-0099
General/National Adv. E-mail: madkimba@aol.com
Primary Website: www.naree.org
Year Established: 1929

NATIONAL ASSOCIATION OF REAL ESTATE PUBLISHERS

Street address 1: PO Box 5292
Street address city: Florence
Street address state: SC
Zip/Postal code: 29502-5292
County: Florence
Country: USA
General/National Adv. E-mail: narep2014@gmail.com
Primary Website: www.narep.org

NATIONAL ASSOCIATION OF SCIENCE WRITERS

Street address 1: PO Box 7905
Street address city: Berkeley
Street address state: CA
Zip/Postal code: 94707-0905
County: Alameda
Country: USA
Mailing address: PO Box 7905
Mailing city: Berkeley
Mailing state: CA
Mailing zip: 94707-0905
General Phone: 510-647-9500
General/National Adv. E-mail: director@nasw.org
Primary Website: www.nasw.org
Year Established: 1934

NATIONAL CARTOONISTS SOCIETY

Street address 1: 341 N Maitland Ave
Street address 2: Ste 130
Street address city: Maitland
Street address state: FL
Zip/Postal code: 32751-4761
County: Orange
Country: USA
Mailing address: 341 N Maitland Ave Ste 260
Mailing city: Maitland
Mailing state: FL
Mailing zip: 32751-4782
General Phone: (407) 647-8839
General Fax: (407) 629-2502
General/National Adv. E-mail: crowsegal@crowsegal.com
Primary Website: www.reuben.org
Year Established: 1946

NATIONAL FEDERATION OF PRESS WOMEN

Street address 1: 200 Little Falls St
Street address 2: Ste 405
Street address city: Falls Church
Street address state: VA
Zip/Postal code: 22046-4302
County: Falls Church City
Country: USA
Mailing address: PO Box 5556
Mailing city: Arlington
Mailing state: VA
Mailing zip: 22205-0056
General Phone: 800-780-2715
General Fax: (703) 237-9808
General/National Adv. E-mail: presswomen@aol.com
Primary Website: www.nfpw.org
Year Established: 1937

NATIONAL LESBIAN AND GAY JOURNALISTS ASSOCIATION

Street address 1: 2120 L St NW
Street address 2: Ste 850
Street address city: Washington
Street address state: DC
Zip/Postal code: 20037-1550
County: District Of Columbia
Country: USA
Mailing address: 2120 L St NW Ste 850
Mailing city: Washington
Mailing state: DC
Mailing zip: 20037-1550
General Phone: (202) 588-9888
General Fax: (202) 588-1818
General/National Adv. E-mail: info@nlgja.org
Primary Website: www.nlgja.org
Year Established: 1990

NATIONAL NEWSPAPER ASSOCIATION

Street address 1: 900 Community Drive
Street address city: Springfield
Street address state: IL
Zip/Postal code: 62703
County: Sangamon
Country: USA
Mailing address: 900 Community Drive
Mailing city: Springfield
Mailing state: IL
Mailing zip: 62703
General Phone: (217)241-1400
General Fax: (217) 241-1301
General/National Adv. E-mail: lynne@nna.org
Primary Website: www.nna.org
Year Established: 1835

NATIONAL NEWSPAPER PUBLISHERS ASSOCIATION BLACK PRESS OF AMERICA

Street address 1: 1816 12th St NW
Street address city: Washington
Street address state: DC
Zip/Postal code: 20009-4422
County: District Of Columbia
Country: USA
Mailing address: 1816 12th St NW
Mailing city: Washington
Mailing state: DC
Mailing zip: 20009-4422
General Phone: 202-588-8764
General Fax: 202-588-8960
General/National Adv. E-mail: nnpadc@nnpa.org
Primary Website: www.nnpa.org
Year Established: 1939

NATIONAL PAPER TRADE ASSOCIATION, INC.

Street address 1: 330 N Wabash Ave
Street address 2: Ste 2000
Street address city: Chicago
Street address state: IL
Zip/Postal code: 60611-7621
County: Cook
Country: USA

Mailing zip: 63043-5000
General Phone: (314) 298-2681
General/National Adv. E-mail: hbalzer@aol.com
Primary Website: www.pfwa.org
Year Established: 1966

PROMOTION MARKETING ASSOCIATION, INC.

Street address 1: 650 1st Ave
Street address 2: Ste 2-SW
Street address city: New York
Street address state: NY
Zip/Postal code: 10016-3240
County: New York
Country: USA
Mailing address: 650 1st Ave Fl 2
Mailing city: New York
Mailing state: NY
Mailing zip: 10016-3207
General Phone: (212) 420-1100
General Fax: (212) 533-7622
General/National Adv. E-mail: pma@pmalink.org
Primary Website: www.pmalink.org
Year Established: 1911

PROMOTIONAL PRODUCTS ASSOCIATION INTERNATIONAL

Street address 1: 3125 Skyway Cir N
Street address city: Irving
Street address state: TX
Zip/Postal code: 75038-3526
County: Dallas
Country: USA
Mailing address: 3125 Skyway Cir N
Mailing city: Irving
Mailing state: TX
Mailing zip: 75038-3539
General Phone: 972-252-0404
General Fax: (972) 258-3004
General/National Adv. E-mail: pr@ppai.org
Primary Website: www.ppai.org
Year Established: 1903

PUBLIC RELATIONS SOCIETY OF AMERICA, INC.

Street address 1: 33 Maiden Ln
Street address 2: Fl 11
Street address city: New York
Street address state: NY
Zip/Postal code: 10038-5149
County: New York
Country: USA
Mailing address: 33 Maiden Ln Fl 11
Mailing city: New York
Mailing state: NY
Mailing zip: 10038-5150
General Phone: (212) 460-1400
General Fax: (212) 995-0757
General/National Adv. E-mail: hq@prsa.org
Primary Website: www.prsa.org
Year Established: 1948

QUILL AND SCROLL SOCIETY

Street address 1: 100 Adler Journalism Bldg Ste W111
Street address 2: Univ. of Iowa School of Journalism and Mass Comm.
Street address city: Iowa City
Street address state: IA
Zip/Postal code: 52242-2004
County: Johnson
Country: USA
General Phone: (319) 335-3457
General Fax: (319) 335-3989
General/National Adv. E-mail: quill-scroll@uiowa.edu
Primary Website: www.uiowa.edu
Year Established: 1926

RADIO TELEVISION DIGITAL NEWS ASSOCIATION

Street address 1: 529 14th St NW
Street address 2: Ste 1240
Street address city: Washington
Street address state: DC
Zip/Postal code: 20045-2520
County: District Of Columbia
Country: USA
Mailing address: 529 14th Street, NW Ste 1240
Mailing city: Washington
Mailing state: DC
Mailing zip: 20045
General Phone: (770) 622-7011
General Fax: (202) 223-4007
General/National Adv. E-mail: mikec@rtdna.org
Primary Website: www.rtdna.org
Year Established: 1945

REGIONAL REPORTERS ASSOCIATION

Street address 1: 1575 Eye St NW Suite 350
Street address city: Washington
Street address state: DC
Zip/Postal code: 20008
County: District Of Columbia
Country: USA
Mailing address: 1575 I St NW Ste 350
Mailing city: Washington
Mailing state: DC
Mailing zip: 20005-1114
General Phone: (202) 408-2705
General/National Adv. E-mail: president@rra.org
Primary Website: www.rra.org

RELIGION NEWS ASSOCIATION

Street address 1: University of Missouri
Street address 2: 30 Neff Annex
Street address city: Columbia
Street address state: MO
Zip/Postal code: 65211-0001
County: Boone
Country: USA
Mailing address: 30 Neff Annex
Mailing city: Columbia
Mailing state: MO
Mailing zip: 65211-0001
General Phone: (740)263-7875
General/National Adv. E-mail: McCallen@RNA.org
Display Adv. E-mail: wendy@rrna.org
Primary Website: www.RNA.org
Year Established: 1949

REPORTERS COMMITTEE FOR FREEDOM OF THE PRESS

Street address 1: 1101 Wilson Blvd
Street address 2: Ste 1100
Street address city: Arlington
Street address state: VA
Zip/Postal code: 22209-2275
County: Arlington
Country: USA
Mailing address: 1101 Wilson Blvd Ste 1100
Mailing city: Arlington
Mailing state: VA
Mailing zip: 22209-2275
General Phone: (703) 807-2100
General Fax: (703) 807-2109
General/National Adv. E-mail: rcfp@rcfp.org
Primary Website: www.rcfp.org
Year Established: 1970

RTDNA - CANADA (RADIO TELEVISION DIGITAL NEWS ASSOCIATION)

Street address 1: 2800 - 14th Ave.
Street address 2: Ste. 210
Street address city: Markham
Street address state: ON
Zip/Postal code: L3R 0E4
Country: Canada
General Phone: (416) 756 2213
General Fax: (416) 491-1670
General/National Adv. E-mail: sherry@associationconcepts.ca; info@rtdnacanada.com
Primary Website: www.rtdnacanada.com
Year Established: 1962

SALES AND MARKETING EXECUTIVES INTERNATIONAL

Street address 1: PO Box 1390
Street address city: Sumas
Street address state: WA
Zip/Postal code: 98295-1390
County: Whatcom
Country: USA
Mailing address: PO Box 1390
Mailing city: Sumas
Mailing state: WA
Mailing zip: 98295-1390
General Phone: (312) 893-0751
General Fax: (604) 855-0165
General/National Adv. E-mail: willis.turner@smei.org
Display Adv. E-mail: marketing.times@smei.org
Editorial e-mail: marketing.times@smei.org
Primary Website: www.smei.org
Year Established: 1935

SOCIETY FOR FEATURES JOURNALISM

Street address 1: 1100 Knight Hall
Street address city: College Park
Street address state: MD
Zip/Postal code: 20742-0001
County: Prince Georges
Country: USA
Mailing address: 1100 Knight Hall
Mailing city: College Park
Mailing state: MD
Mailing zip: 20742-0001
General Phone: (301) 314-2631
General Fax: (301) 314-9166
General/National Adv. E-mail: aasfe@jmail.umd.edu
Primary Website: www.aasfe.org
Year Established: 19473

SOCIETY FOR NEWS DESIGN, INC.

Street address 1: 424 E Central Blvd
Street address 2: Ste 406
Street address city: Orlando
Street address state: FL
Zip/Postal code: 32801-1923
County: Orange
Country: USA
Mailing address: 424 E Central Blvd Ste 406
Mailing city: Orlando
Mailing state: FL
Mailing zip: 32801-1923
General Phone: (407) 420-7748
General Fax: (407) 420-7697
General/National Adv. E-mail: snd@snd.org
Primary Website: www.snd.org
Year Established: 1979

SOCIETY OF AMERICAN BUSINESS EDITORS AND WRITERS, INC.

Street address 1: 555 N Central Ave
Street address 2: Ste 302
Street address city: Phoenix
Street address state: AZ
Zip/Postal code: 85004-1248
County: Maricopa
Country: USA
General Phone: (602) 496-7862
General Fax: (602) 496-7041
General/National Adv. E-mail: sabew@sabew.org
Primary Website: www.sabew.org
Year Established: 1964

SOCIETY OF AMERICAN TRAVEL WRITERS, INC.

Street address 1: 7044 S 13th St
Street address city: Oak Creek
Street address state: WI
Zip/Postal code: 53154-1429
County: Milwaukee
Country: USA
Mailing address: 11950 W Lake Park Dr Ste 320
Mailing city: Milwaukee
Mailing state: WI
Mailing zip: 53224-3049
General Phone: (414) 908-4949
General Fax: (414) 768-8001
General/National Adv. E-mail: satw@satw.org
Primary Website: www.satw.org

SOCIETY OF ENVIRONMENTAL JOURNALISTS (SEJ)

Street address 1: PO Box 2492
Street address 2: Suite 301
Street address city: Jenkintown
Street address state: PA
Zip/Postal code: 19046-8492
County: Montgomery
Country: USA
Mailing address: PO Box 2492
Mailing city: Jenkintown
Mailing state: PA
Mailing zip: 19046-8492
General Phone: (215) 884-8174
General Fax: (215) 884-8175
General/National Adv. E-mail: sej@sej.org
Primary Website: www.sej.org
Year Established: 1990

SOCIETY OF PROFESSIONAL JOURNALISTS

Street address 1: 3909 N Meridian St
Street address 2: Ste 200
Street address city: Indianapolis
Street address state: IN
Zip/Postal code: 46208-4011
County: Marion
Country: USA
Mailing address: 3909 N Meridian St
Mailing city: Indianapolis
Mailing state: IN
Mailing zip: 46208-4011
General Phone: (317) 927-8000
General Fax: (317) 920-4789
General/National Adv. E-mail: spj@spj.org
Primary Website: www.spj.org
Year Established: 1909

SOCIETY OF THE SILURIANS

Street address 1: PO Box 1195
Street address 2: Madison Square Station
Street address city: New York
Street address state: NY
Zip/Postal code: 10159-1195
County: New York
Country: USA
Mailing address: PO Box 1195
Mailing city: New York
Mailing state: NY
Mailing zip: 10159-1195
General Phone: (212) 532-0887
General/National Adv. E-mail: silurians@aol.org
Primary Website: www.silurians.org
Year Established: 1924

SPECIAL LIBRARIES ASSOCIATION, NEWS DIVISION

Street address 1: 331 S Patrick St
Street address city: Alexandria
Street address state: VA
Zip/Postal code: 22314-3501
County: Alexandria City
Country: USA
Mailing address: 331 S Patrick St
Mailing city: Alexandria
Mailing state: VA
Mailing zip: 22314-3501
General Phone: (703) 647-4900
General Fax: (703) 647-4901
General/National Adv. E-mail: sla@sla.org
Primary Website: www.sla.org

TECHNICAL ASSOCIATION OF THE GRAPHIC ARTS

Street address 1: 200 Deer Run Rd
Street address city: Sewickley
Street address state: PA
Zip/Postal code: 15143-2324
County: Allegheny
Country: USA
Mailing address: 200 Deer Run Rd
Mailing city: Sewickley
Mailing state: PA
Mailing zip: 15143-2324
General Phone: (412) 259-1706
General Fax: (412) 741-2311
General/National Adv. E-mail: taga@printing.org
Primary Website: www.taga.org

Year Established: 1948

THE 4 A'S

Street address 1: 1065 Avenue of the Americas
Street address 2: Fl 16
Street address city: New York
Street address state: NY
Zip/Postal code: 10018-0174
County: New York
Country: USA
Mailing address: 1065 Avenue of the Americas Fl 16
Mailing city: New York
Mailing state: NY
Mailing zip: 10018-0174
General Phone: (212) 682-2500
General Fax: (212) 682-8391
General/National Adv. E-mail: info@aaaa.com
Primary Website: www.aaaa.org
Year Established: 1917

THE ADVERTISING COUNCIL, INC.

Street address 1: 815 2nd Ave
Street address 2: Fl 9
Street address city: New York
Street address state: NY
Zip/Postal code: 10017-4500
County: New York
Country: USA
Mailing address: 815 2nd Ave Fl 9
Mailing city: New York
Mailing state: NY
Mailing zip: 10017-4500
General Phone: (212) 922-1500
General Fax: (212) 922-1676
General/National Adv. E-mail: info@adcouncil.org
Primary Website: www.adcouncil.org
Year Established: 1942

THE ADVERTISING RESEARCH FOUNDATION (ARF)

Street address 1: 432 Park Ave S
Street address 2: Fl 6
Street address city: New York
Street address state: NY
Zip/Postal code: 10016-8013
County: New York
Country: USA
Mailing address: 432 Park Ave S Fl 6
Mailing city: New York
Mailing state: NY
Mailing zip: 10016-8013
General Phone: (212) 751-5656
General Fax: (212) 689-1859
General/National Adv. E-mail: help@thearf.org
Primary Website: www.thearf.org
Year Established: 1936

THE DIRECT MARKETING ASSOCIATION, INC.

Street address 1: 1120 Avenue of the Americas
Street address city: New York
Street address state: NY
Zip/Postal code: 10036-6700
County: New York
Country: USA
Mailing address: 1120 Avenue of the Americas Fl 14
Mailing city: New York
Mailing state: NY
Mailing zip: 10036-6713
General Phone: (212) 768-7277
General Fax: (212) 302-6714
Primary Website: www.the-dma.org
Year Established: 1917

THE NATIONAL SOCIETY OF NEWSPAPER COLUMNISTS, INC.

Street address 1: 205 Gun Hill St
Street address city: Milton
Street address state: MA
Zip/Postal code: 02186-4026
County: Norfolk
Country: USA
Mailing address: 205 Gun Hill Street
Mailing city: Milton
Mailing state: CA
Mailing zip: 02186
General Phone: 617 322-1420
General/National Adv. E-mail: director@columnists.com
Primary Website: www.columnists.com
Year Established: 1972

THE NEWSGUILD-CWA

Street address 1: 501 3rd St NW
Street address 2: Fl 6
Street address city: Washington
Street address state: DC
Zip/Postal code: 20001-2797
County: District Of Columbia
Country: USA
Mailing address: 501 3rd St NW, Fl 6
Mailing city: Washington
Mailing state: DC
Mailing zip: 20001-2797
General Phone: (202) 434-7177
General Fax: (202) 434-1472
General/National Adv. E-mail: guild@cwa-union.org
Primary Website: www.newsguild.org
Year Established: 1933

TRANS-CANADA ADVERTISING AGENCY NETWORK

Street address 1: 25 Sheppard Ave. West, Suite 300
Street address city: Toronto
Street address state: ON
Zip/Postal code: M2N 6S6
Country: Canada
Mailing address: 25 Sheppard Ave. West, Suite 300
Mailing city: Toronto
Mailing state: ON
Mailing zip: M2N 6S6
General Phone: 416-221-8883
General/National Adv. E-mail: bill@waginc.ca
Primary Website: www.tcaan.ca
Year Established: 1963

UNITED NATIONS CORRESPONDENTS ASSOCIATION

Street address 1: United Nations, Room S-308
Street address city: New York
Street address state: NY
Zip/Postal code: 10017
County: New York
Country: USA
Mailing address: United Nations, Rm. S-308
Mailing city: New York
Mailing state: NY
Mailing zip: 10017
General Phone: (212) 963-7137
General/National Adv. E-mail: contactus@unca.com
Primary Website: www.unca.com

WORLD ASSOCIATION OF NEWSPAPERS AND NEWS PUBLISHERS (WAN-IFRA)

Street address 1: Rotfeder-Ring 11
Street address city: Frankfurt
Zip/Postal code: 60327
Country: Germany
Mailing address: Rotfeder-Ring 11
Mailing city: Frankfurt
Mailing zip: 60327
General Phone: 240063-0
General Fax: 240063-300
General/National Adv. E-mail: info@wan-ifra.org
Primary Website: www.wan-ifra.org

WORLD ASSOCIATION OF NEWSPAPERS AND NEWS PUBLISHERS (WAN-IFRA)

Street address 1: Rotfeder-Ring 11
Street address city: Frankfurt am Main
Zip/Postal code: 60327
Country: Germany
Mailing address: Rotfeder-Ring 11
Mailing city: Frankfurt am Main
Mailing zip: 60327
General Phone: 240063-0
General Fax: 240063-300
General/National Adv. E-mail: info@wan-ifra.org
Display Adv. E-mail: maria.belem@wan-ifra.org
Primary Website: www.wan-ifra.org
Year Established: WAN: 1948 / IFRA: 1961 / WAN-IFRA: 2009

WORLD PRESS INSTITUTE

Street address 1: 3415 University Ave W
Street address city: Saint Paul
Street address state: MN
Zip/Postal code: 55114-1019
County: Ramsey
Country: USA
Mailing address: 3415 University Ave W
Mailing city: Saint Paul
Mailing state: MN
Mailing zip: 55114-1019
General Phone: 612-205-7582
General/National Adv. E-mail: info@worldpressinstitute.org
Primary Website: www.worldpressinstitute.org
Year Established: 1961